# WHO WAS WHO

## VOL. VIII

### 1981–1990

# WHO'S WHO

*An annual biographical dictionary
first published in 1849*

## WHO WAS WHO

*Published by*
A & C BLACK

# WHO WAS WHO

## 1981–1990

### A COMPANION TO
### WHO'S WHO

**CONTAINING THE BIOGRAPHIES
OF THOSE WHO DIED DURING
THE DECADE 1981–1990**

WEST DUNBARTONSHIRE LIBRARIES

### A & C BLACK
### LONDON

FIRST PUBLISHED 1991
BY A & C BLACK (PUBLISHERS) LIMITED
35 BEDFORD ROW LONDON WC1R 4JH

COPYRIGHT © 1991 A & C BLACK (PUBLISHERS) LTD

ISBN 0–7136–3336–0

TITLE

WEST
DUNBARTONSHIRE
LIBRARIES

PRICE
£60·00

SUPPLIER
Cawder

LOCATION
Main

CLASS
920·02

INVOICE DATE
21·5·01

ACCESSION NUMBER
C 01 037551 2

All rights reserved. No part of this
publication may be reproduced, stored in a
retrieval system, or transmitted, in any
form or by any means, electronic, mechanical,
photocopying, recording or otherwise,
without the prior permission of A & C
Black (Publishers) Ltd.

The publishers make no representation, express
or implied, with regard to the accuracy of the
information contained in this book and
cannot accept any legal responsibility for
any errors or omissions that may take place.

Typeset by Clowes Computer Composition, printed and bound in Great Britain by William Clowes Ltd,
Beccles and London

# PREFACE

This, the eighth volume of biographies removed from *Who's Who* on account of death, contains the entries of those who died between 1981 and 1990. Those whose deaths were not notified until after this volume went to press are listed as Addenda at the beginning of the biographical section.

The entries are as they last appeared in *Who's Who*, with the date of death added and in some cases further information, such as posthumous publications. It has not always been possible to ascertain the exact date of death, and the editors will welcome such information for inclusion in the next edition of this volume.

The *Cumulated Index to Who Was Who 1897–1980*, first published in conjunction with *Who Was Who* Volume VII, has been extended to include information arising from research on recently revised earlier volumes of *Who Was Who* as well as the names which now appear in Volume VIII. It is hoped that *Who Was Who 1981–1990* and *A Cumulated Index 1897–1990* will prove as great a resource to scholars and as interesting to general readers as the previous seven volumes.

ADAM AND CHARLES BLACK

# ERRATUM

## BRUCE LOCKHART, John Macgregor, CB, CMG, OBE

The publishers regret that the entry
under this name was wrongly transferred
to WHO WAS WHO volume VIII whilst
the biographee was still living.

# CONTENTS

# ABBREVIATIONS USED IN THIS BOOK

Some of the designatory letters in this list are used merely for economy of space and do not necessarily imply any professional or other qualification.

## A

| | |
|---|---|
| **AA** | Anti-Aircraft; Automobile Association; Architectural Association; Augustinians of the Assumption |
| **AAA** | Amateur Athletic Association; American Accounting Association |
| **AAAL** | American Academy of Arts and Letters (*now see* AAIL) |
| **AA&QMG** | Assistant Adjutant and Quartermaster-General |
| **AAAS** | American Association for the Advancement of Science |
| **AAC** | Army Air Corps |
| **AACCA** | Associate, Association of Certified and Corporate Accountants (*now see* ACCA) |
| **AACE** | Association for Adult and Continuing Education |
| **AAF** | Auxiliary Air Force (*now see* RAuxAF) |
| **AAFCE** | Allied Air Forces in Central Europe |
| **AAG** | Assistant Adjutant-General |
| **AAI** | Associate, Chartered Auctioneers' and Estate Agents' Institute (*now* (after amalgamation) *see* ARICS) |
| **AAIL** | American Academy and Institute of Arts and Letters |
| **AAM** | Association of Assistant Mistresses in Secondary Schools |
| **AAMC** | Australian Army Medical Corps (*now see* RAAMC) |
| **A&AEE** | Aeroplane and Armament Experimental Establishment |
| **AASA** | Associate, Australian Society of Accountants |
| **AASC** | Australian Army Service Corps |
| **AAUQ** | Associate in Accountancy, University of Queensland |
| **AB** | Bachelor of Arts (US); able-bodied seaman; airborne |
| **ABA** | Amateur Boxing Association; Antiquarian Booksellers' Association; American Bar Association |
| **ABC** | Australian Broadcasting Commission; American Broadcasting Companies |
| **ABCA** | Army Bureau of Current Affairs |
| **ABCC** | Association of British Chambers of Commerce |
| **ABCFM** | American Board of Commissioners for Foreign Missions |
| **ABIA** | Associate, Bankers' Institute of Australasia |
| **ABINZ** | Associate, Bankers' Institute of New Zealand |
| **ABNM** | American Board of Nuclear Medicine |
| **ABP** | Associated British Ports |
| **Abp** | Archbishop |
| **ABPsS** | Associate, British Psychological Society (*now see* AFBPsS) |
| **ABRC** | Advisory Board for the Research Councils |
| **ABS** | Associate, Building Societies' Institute (*now see* ACBSI) |
| **ABSI** | Associate, Boot and Shoe Institution |
| **ABSM** | Associate, Birmingham and Midland Institute School of Music |
| **ABTA** | Association of British Travel Agents |
| **ABTAPL** | Association of British Theological and Philosophical Libraries |
| **AC** | Companion, Order of Australia; *Ante Christum* (before Christ) |
| **ACA** | Associate, Institute of Chartered Accountants |
| **Acad.** | Academy |
| **ACARD** | Advisory Council for Applied Research and Development |
| **ACAS** | Advisory, Conciliation and Arbitration Service; Assistant Chief of the Air Staff |
| **ACBSI** | Associate, Chartered Building Societies Institute |
| **ACC** | Association of County Councils; Anglican Consultative Council |
| **ACCA** | Associate, Association of Certified Accountants |
| **ACCM** | Advisory Council for the Church's Ministry |
| **ACCS** | Associate, Corporation of Secretaries (formerly of Certified Secretaries) |
| **ACDP** | Australian Committee of Directors and Principals |
| **ACDS** | Assistant Chief of Defence Staff |
| **ACE** | Association of Consulting Engineers; Member, Association of Conference Executives |
| **ACF** | Army Cadet Force |
| **ACFA** | Army Cadet Force Association |
| **ACFAS** | Association Canadienne-Française pour l'avancement des sciences |
| **ACFHE** | Association of Colleges for Further and Higher Education |
| **ACG** | Assistant Chaplain-General |
| **ACGI** | Associate, City and Guilds of London Institute |
| **ACGS** | Assistant Chief of the General Staff |
| **ACIArb** | Associate, Chartered Institute of Arbitrators |
| **ACIB** | Associate, Chartered Institute of Bankers |

| | |
|---|---|
| **ACII** | Associate, Chartered Insurance Institute |
| **ACIS** | Associate, Institute of Chartered Secretaries and Administrators (*formerly* Chartered Institute of Secretaries) |
| **ACIT** | Associate, Chartered Institute of Transport |
| **ACLS** | American Council of Learned Societies |
| **ACM** | Association of Computing Machinery |
| **ACMA** | Associate, Institute of Cost and Management Accountants |
| **ACNS** | Assistant Chief of Naval Staff |
| **ACommA** | Associate, Society of Commercial Accountants (*now see* ASCA) |
| **ACORD** | Advisory Committee on Research and Development |
| **ACOS** | Assistant Chief of Staff |
| **ACOST** | Advisory Council on Science and Technology |
| **ACP** | Association of Clinical Pathologists; Associate, College of Preceptors; African/Caribbean/Pacific |
| **ACPO** | Association of Chief Police Officers |
| **ACRE** | Action with Rural Communities in England |
| **ACS** | American Chemical Society; Additional Curates Society |
| **ACSEA** | Allied Command South East Asia |
| **ACSM** | Associate, Camborne School of Mines |
| **ACT** | Australian Capital Territory; Australian College of Theology; Associate, College of Technology; Association of Corporate Treasurers |
| **ACTT** | Association of Cinematograph, Television and Allied Technicians |
| **ACTU** | Australian Council of Trade Unions |
| **ACU** | Association of Commonwealth Universities |
| **ACWA** | Associate, Institute of Cost and Works Accountants (*now see* ACMA) |
| **AD** | Dame of the Order of Australia; *Anno Domini*; Air Defence |
| **aD** | ausser Dienst |
| **ADAS** | Agricultural Development and Advisory Service |
| **ADB** | Asian Development Bank; Associate of the Drama Board (Education) |
| **ADB/F** | African Development Bank/Fund |
| **ADC** | Aide-de-camp |
| **ADCM** | Archbishop of Canterbury's Diploma in Church Music |
| **AD Corps** | Army Dental Corps (*now* RADC) |
| **ADC(P)** | Personal Aide-de-camp to HM The Queen |
| **ADEME** | Assistant Director Electrical and Mechanical Engineering |
| **Ad eund** | *Ad eundem gradum*; and *see under* aeg |
| **ADFManc** | Art and Design Fellow, Manchester |
| **ADFW** | Assistant Director of Fortifications and Works |
| **ADGB** | Air Defence of Great Britain |
| **ADGMS** | Assistant Director-General of Medical Services |
| **ADH** | Assistant Director of Hygiene |
| **Adjt** | Adjutant |
| **ADJAG** | Assistant Deputy Judge Advocate General |
| **ADK** | Order of Ahli Darjah Kinabalu |
| **Adm.** | Admiral |
| **ADMS** | Assistant Director of Medical Services |
| **ADOS** | Assistant Director of Ordnance Services |
| **ADP** | Automatic Data Processing |
| **ADPA** | Associate Diploma of Public Administration |
| **ADS&T** | Assistant Director of Supplies and Transport |
| **Adv.** | Advisory; Advocate |
| **ADVS** | Assistant Director of Veterinary Services |
| **ADWE&M** | Assistant Director of Works, Electrical and Mechanical |
| **AE** | Air Efficiency Award |
| **AEA** | Atomic Energy Authority; Air Efficiency Award (*now see* AE) |
| **AEAF** | Allied Expeditionary Air Force |
| **AEC** | Agriculture Executive Council; Army Educational Corps (*now see* RAEC); Atomic Energy Commission |
| **AECMA** | Association Européenne des Constructeurs de Matériel Aérospatial |
| **AEF** | Amalgamated Union of Engineering and Foundry Workers (*now see* AEU); American Expeditionary Forces |
| **aeg** | *ad eundem gradum* (to the same degree—of the admission of a graduate of one university to the same degree at another without examination) |
| **AEGIS** | Aid for the Elderly in Government Institutions |
| **AEI** | Associated Electrical Industries |

9

| | |
|---|---|
| AEM | Air Efficiency Medal |
| AER | Army Emergency Reserve |
| AERE | Atomic Energy Research Establishment (Harwell) |
| Æt., Ætat. | Ætatis (aged) |
| AEU | Amalgamated Engineering Union |
| AFA | Amateur Football Alliance |
| AFAIAA | Associate Fellow, American Institute of Aeronautics and Astronautics |
| AFBPsS | Associate Fellow, British Psychological Society |
| AFC | Air Force Cross; Association Football Club |
| AFCAI | Associate Fellow, Canadian Aeronautical Institute |
| AFCEA | Armed Forces Communications and Electronics Association |
| AFCENT | Allied Forces in Central Europe |
| AFD | Doctor of Fine Arts (US) |
| AFDS | Air Fighting Development Squadron |
| AFHQ | Allied Force Headquarters |
| AFI | American Film Institute |
| AFIA | Associate, Federal Institute of Accountants (Australia) |
| AFIAP | Artiste, Fédération Internationale de l'Art Photographique |
| AFIAS | Associate Fellow, Institute of Aeronautical Sciences (US) (now see AFAIAA) |
| AFICD | Associate Fellow, Institute of Civil Defence |
| AFIMA | Associate Fellow, Institute of Mathematics and its Applications |
| AFM | Air Force Medal |
| AFOM | Associate, Faculty of Occupational Medicine |
| AFRAeS | Associate Fellow, Royal Aeronautical Society (now see MRAeS) |
| AFRC | Agricultural and Food Research Council |
| AFV | Armoured Fighting Vehicles |
| AG | Attorney-General |
| AGAC | American Guild of Authors and Composers |
| AGARD | Advisory Group for Aerospace Research and Development |
| AGH | Australian General Hospital |
| AGI | Artistes Graphiques Internationaux; Associate, Institute of Certificated Grocers |
| AGR | Advanced Gas-cooled Reactor |
| AGRA | Army Group Royal Artillery; Association of Genealogists and Record Agents |
| AGSM | Associate, Guildhall School of Music and Drama; Australian Graduate School of Management |
| AHA | Area Health Authority; American Hospitals Association; Associate, Institute of Health Service Administrators (now see AHSM) |
| AHA(T) | Area Health Authority (Teaching) |
| AHQ | Army Headquarters |
| AHSM | Associate, Institute of Health Services Management |
| AH-WC | Associate, Heriot-Watt College, Edinburgh |
| ai | ad interim |
| AIA | Associate, Institute of Actuaries; American Institute of Architects; Association of International Artists |
| AIAA | American Institute of Aeronautics and Astronautics |
| AIAgrE | Associate, Institution of Agricultural Engineers |
| AIAL | Associate Member, International Institute of Arts and Letters |
| AIArb | Associate, Institute of Arbitrators (now see ACIArb) |
| AIAS | Associate Surveyor Member, Incorporated Association of Architects and Surveyors |
| AIB | Associate, Institute of Bankers (now see ACIB) |
| AIBD | Associate, Institute of British Decorators |
| AIBP | Associate, Institute of British Photographers |
| AIBScot | Associate, Institute of Bankers in Scotland |
| AIC | Agricultural Improvement Council; Associate of the Institute of Chemistry (later ARIC, MRIC; now see MRSC) |
| AICA | Associate Member, Commonwealth Institute of Accountants; Association Internationale des Critiques d'Art |
| AICC | All-India Congress Committee |
| AICE | Associate, Institution of Civil Engineers |
| AICPA | American Institute of Certified Public Accountants |
| AICS | Associate, Institute of Chartered Shipbrokers |
| AICTA | Associate, Imperial College of Tropical Agriculture |
| AIE | Associate, Institute of Education |
| AIEE | Associate, Institution of Electrical Engineers |
| AIF | Australian Imperial Forces |
| AIG | Adjutant-Inspector-General |
| AIIA | Associate, Insurance Institute of America; Associate, Indian Institute of Architects |
| AIInfSc | Associate, Institute of Information Scientists |
| AIL | Associate, Institute of Linguists |
| AILA | Associate, Institute of Landscape Architects (now see ALI) |
| AILocoE | Associate, Institution of Locomotive Engineers |
| AIM | Associate, Institution of Metallurgists (now see MIM); Australian Institute of Management |
| AIMarE | Associate, Institute of Marine Engineers |
| AIME | American Institute of Mechanical Engineers |
| AIMSW | Associate, Institute of Medical Social Workers |
| AInstM | Associate Member, Institute of Marketing |
| AInstP | Associate, Institute of Physics |
| AInstPI | Associate, Institute of Patentees and Inventors |
| AIP | Association of Independent Producers |
| AIPR | Associate, Institute of Public Relations |
| AIProdE | Associate, Institution of Production Engineers |
| AIQS | Associate Member, Institute of Quantity Surveyors |
| AIRTE | Associate, Institute of Road Transport Engineers |
| AIRTO | Association of Independent Research and Technology Organizations |
| AIS | Associate, Institute of Statisticians (now see MIS) |
| AISA | Associate, Incorporated Secretaries' Association |
| AIStructE | Associate, Institution of Structural Engineers |
| AITI | Associate, Institute of Translators and Interpreters |
| AITP | Associate, Institute of Town Planners, India |
| AJAG | Assistant Judge Advocate General |
| AJEX | Association of Jewish Ex-Service Men and Women |
| AK | Knight, Order of Australia |
| AKC | Associate, King's College London |
| ALA | Associate, Library Association |
| Ala | Alabama (US) |
| ALAA | Associate, Library Association of Australia |
| ALAM | Associate, London Academy of Music and Dramatic Art |
| ALCD | Associate, London College of Divinity |
| ALCM | Associate, London College of Music |
| ALCS | Authors Lending and Copyright Society |
| ALFSEA | Allied Land Forces South-East Asia |
| ALI | Argyll Light Infantry; Associate, Landscape Institute |
| ALICE | Autistic and Language Impaired Children's Education |
| ALLC | Association for Literary and Linguistic Computing |
| ALP | Australian Labor Party |
| ALPSP | Association of Learned and Professional Society Publishers |
| ALS | Associate, Linnean Society |
| Alta | Alberta |
| ALVA | Association of Leading Visitor Attractions |
| AM | Albert Medal; Member, Order of Australia; Master of Arts (US); Alpes Maritimes |
| AMA | Association of Metropolitan Authorities; Assistant Masters Association; Associate, Museums Association; Australian Medical Association |
| AMARC | Associated Marine and Related Charities |
| Amb. | Ambulance; Ambassador |
| AMBIM | Associate Member, British Institute of Management (now see MBIM) |
| AMBritIRE | Associate Member, British Institution of Radio Engineers (now see AMIERE) |
| AMC | Association of Municipal Corporations |
| AMCT | Associate, Manchester College of Technology |
| AME | Association of Municipal Engineers |
| AMEME | Association of Mining Electrical and Mechanical Engineers |
| AMet | Associate of Metallurgy |
| AMF | Australian Military Forces |
| AMGOT | Allied Military Government of Occupied Territory |
| AMIAE | Associate Member, Institution of Automobile Engineers |
| AMIAgrE | Associate Member, Institution of Agricultural Engineers |
| AMIBF | Associate Member, Institute of British Foundrymen |
| AMICE | Associate Member, Institution of Civil Engineers (now see MICE) |
| AMIChemE | Associate Member, Institution of Chemical Engineers |
| AMIE(Aust) | Associate Member, Institution of Engineers, Australia |
| AMIED | Associate Member, Institution of Engineering Designers |
| AMIEE | Associate Member, Institution of Electrical Engineers (now see MIEE) |
| AMIE(Ind) | Associate Member, Institution of Engineers, India |
| AMIERE | Associate Member, Institution of Electronic and Radio Engineers |
| AMIH | Associate Member, Institute of Housing |
| AMIMechE | Associate Member, Institution of Mechanical Engineers (now see MIMechE) |
| AMIMinE | Associate Member, Institution of Mining Engineers |
| AMIMM | Associate Member, Institution of Mining and Metallurgy |
| AMInstBE | Associate Member, Institution of British Engineers |
| AMInstCE | Associate Member, Institution of Civil Engineers (now see MICE) |
| AmInstEE | American Institute of Electrical Engineers |
| AMInstR | Associate Member, Institute of Refrigeration |
| AMInstT | Associate Member, Institute of Transport (now see ACIT) |
| AMInstTA | Associate Member, Institute of Traffic Adminstration |
| AMINucE | Associate Member, Institution of Nuclear Engineers |
| AMIRSE | Associate Member, Institute of Railway Signalling Engineers |
| AMIStructE | Associate Member, Institution of Structural Engineers |
| AMN | Ahli Mangku Negara (Malaysia) |
| AMP | Advanced Management Program |
| AMRINA | Associate Member, Royal Institution of Naval Architects |
| AMS | Assistant Military Secretary; Army Medical Services |
| AMTE | Admiralty Marine Technology Establishment |
| AMTRI | Advanced Manufacturing Technology Research Institute |
| ANA | Associate National Academician (America) |
| ANAF | Arab Non-Arab Friendship |
| Anat. | Anatomy; Anatomical |
| ANC | African National Congress |
| ANECInst | Associate, NE Coast Institution of Engineers and Shipbuilders |
| ANGAU | Australian New Guinea Administrative Unit |
| Anon. | Anonymously |
| ANU | Australian National University |

**ANZAAS** Australian and New Zealand Association for the Advancement of Science
**Anzac** Australian and New Zealand Army Corps
**AO** Officer, Order of Australia; Air Officer
**AOA** Air Officer in charge of Administration
**AOC** Air Officer Commanding
**AOC-in-C** Air Officer Commanding-in-Chief
**AOD** Army Ordnance Department
**AOER** Army Officers Emergency Reserve
**APA** American Psychiatric Association
**APACS** Association of Payment and Clearing Systems
**APCK** Association for Promoting Christian Knowledge, Church of Ireland
**APD** Army Pay Department
**APEX** Association of Professional, Executive, Clerical and Computer Staff
**APHA** American Public Health Association
**APIS** Army Photographic Intelligence Service
**APM** Assistant Provost Marshal
**APMI** Associate, Pensions Management Institute
**APR** Accredited Public Relations Practitioner
**APS** Aborigines Protection Society; American Physics Society
**APsSI** Associate, Psychological Society of Ireland
**APSW** Association of Psychiatric Social Workers
**APT&C** Administrative, Professional, Technical and Clerical
**APTC** Army Physical Training Corps
**AQ** Administration and Quartering
**AQMG** Assistant Quartermaster-General
**AR** Associated Rediffusion (Television)
**ARA** Associate, Royal Academy
**ARACI** Associate, Royal Australian Chemical Institute
**ARAD** Associate, Royal Academy of Dancing
**ARAeS** Associate, Royal Aeronautical Society
**ARAM** Associate, Royal Academy of Music
**ARAS** Associate, Royal Astronomical Society
**ARBA** Associate, Royal Society of British Artists
**ARBC** Associate, Royal British Colonial Society of Artists
**ARBS** Associate, Royal Society of British Sculptors
**ARC** Architects' Registration Council; Agricultural Research Council (*now see* AFRC); Aeronautical Research Council
**ARCA** Associate, Royal College of Art; Associate, Royal Canadian Academy
**ARCamA** Associate, Royal Cambrian Academy of Art
**ARCE** Academical Rank of Civil Engineer
**ARCIC** Anglican-Roman Catholic International Commission
**ARCM** Associate, Royal College of Music
**ARCO** Associate, Royal College of Organists
**ARCO(CHM)** Associate, Royal College of Organists with Diploma in Choir Training
**ARCPsych** Associate Member, Royal College of Psychiatrists
**ARCS** Associate, Royal College of Science
**ARCST** Associate, Royal College of Science and Technology (Glasgow)
**ARCUK** Architects' Registration Council of the United Kingdom
**ARCVS** Associate, Royal College of Veterinary Surgeons
**ARE** Associate, Royal Society of Painter-Etchers and Engravers; Arab Republic of Egypt; Admiralty Research Establishment
**ARELS** Association of Recognised English Language Schools
**ARIAS** Associate, Royal Incorporation of Architects in Scotland
**ARIBA** Associate, Royal Institute of British Architects (*now see* RIBA)
**ARIC** Associate, Royal Institute of Chemistry (later MRIC; *now see* MRSC)
**ARICS** Professional Associate, Royal Institution of Chartered Surveyors
**ARINA** Associate, Royal Institution of Naval Architects
**Ark** Arkansas (US)
**ARLT** Association for the Reform of Latin Teaching
**ARMS** Associate, Royal Society of Miniature Painters
**ARP** Air Raid Precautions
**ARPS** Associate, Royal Photographic Society
**ARR** Association of Radiation Research
**ARRC** Associate, Royal Red Cross
**ARSA** Associate, Royal Scottish Academy
**ARSCM** Associate, Royal School of Church Music
**ARSM** Associate, Royal School of Mines
**ARTC** Associate, Royal Technical College (Glasgow) (*now see* ARCST)
**ARVIA** Associate, Royal Victoria Institute of Architects
**ARWA** Associate, Royal West of England Academy
**ARWS** Associate, Royal Society of Painters in Water-Colours
**AS** Anglo-Saxon
**ASA** Associate Member, Society of Actuaries; Associate of Society of Actuaries (US); Australian Society of Accountants; Army Sailing Asssociation
**ASAA** Associate, Society of Incorporated Accountants and Auditors
**ASAI** Associate, Society of Architectural Illustrators
**ASAM** Associate, Society of Art Masters
**AS&TS of SA** Associated Scientific and Technical Societies of South Africa
**ASBAH** Association for Spina Bifida and Hydrocephalus

**ASC** Administrative Staff College, Henley
**ASCA** Associate, Society of Company and Commercial Accountants
**ASCAB** Armed Services Consultant Approval Board
**ASCAP** American Society of Composers, Authors and Publishers
**ASCE** American Society of Civil Engineers
**AScW** Association of Scientific Workers (*now see* ASTMS)
**ASD** Armament Supply Department
**ASE** Amalgamated Society of Engineers (*now see* AUEW)
**ASEAN** Association of South East Asian Nations
**ASH** Action on Smoking and Health
**ASIAD** Associate, Society of Industrial Artists and Designers
**ASIA(Ed)** Associate, Society of Industrial Artists (Education)
**ASLE** American Society of Lubrication Engineers
**ASLEF** Associated Society of Locomotive Engineers and Firemen
**ASLIB or Aslib** Association for Information Management (*formerly* Association of Special Libraries and Information Bureaux)
**ASM** Association of Senior Members
**ASME** American Society of Mechanical Engineers; Association for the Study of Medical Education
**ASO** Air Staff Officer
**ASSC** Accounting Standards Steering Committee
**ASSET** Association of Supervisory Staffs, Executives and Technicians (*now see* ASTMS)
**AssocISI** Associate, Iron and Steel Institute
**AssocMCT** Associateship of Manchester College of Technology
**AssocMIAeE** Associate Member, Institution of Aeronautical Engineers
**AssocRINA** Associate, Royal Institution of Naval Architects
**AssocSc** Associate in Science
**Asst** Assistant
**ASTC** Administrative Service Training Course
**ASTMS** Association of Scientific, Technical and Managerial Staffs (now part of MSF)
**ASVU** Army Security Vetting Unit
**ASWDU** Air Sea Warfare Development Unit
**ASWE** Admiralty Surface Weapons Establishment
**ATA** Air Transport Auxiliary
**ATAE** Association of Tutors in Adult Education
**ATAF** Allied Tactical Air Force
**ATC** Air Training Corps; Art Teacher's Certificate
**ATCDE** Association of Teachers in Colleges and Departments of Education (*now see* NATFHE)
**ATCL** Associate, Trinity College of Music, London
**ATD** Art Teacher's Diploma
**ATI** Associate, Textile Institute
**ATII** Associate Member, Institute of Taxation
**ato** Ammunition Technical Officer
**ATPL (A) or (H)** Airline Transport Pilot's Licence (Aeroplanes), or (Helicopters)
**ATS** Auxiliary Territorial Service (*now see* WRAC)
**ATTI** Association of Teachers in Technical Institutions (*now see* NATFHE)
**ATV** Associated TeleVision
**AUA** American Urological Association
**AUCAS** Association of University Clinical Academic Staff
**AUEW** Amalgamated Union of Engineering Workers (*now see* AEU)
**AUS** Army of the United States
**AUT** Association of University Teachers
**AVCC** Australian Vice-Chancellors' Committee
**AVCM** Associate, Victoria College of Music
**AVD** Army Veterinary Department
**AVLA** Audio Visual Language Association
**AVR** Army Volunteer Reserve
**AWA** Anglian Water Authority
**AWO** Association of Water Officers
**AWRE** Atomic Weapons Research Establishment
**aws** Graduate of Air Warfare Course

# B

**b** born; brother
**BA** Bachelor of Arts
**BAA** British Airports Authority
**BAAB** British Amateur Athletic Board
**BAAL** British Association for Applied Linguistics
**BAAS** British Association for the Advancement of Science
**BAB** British Airways Board
**BAC** British Aircraft Corporation
**BACM** British Association of Colliery Management
**BACUP** British Association of Cancer United Patients
**BAe** British Aerospace
**BAED** Bachelor of Arts in Enviromental Design
**B&FBS** British and Foreign Bible Society
**BAFO** British Air Forces of Occupation
**BAFPA** British Association of Fitness Promotion Agencies
**BAFTA** British Academy of Film and Television Arts
**BAG** Business Art Galleries
**BAgrSc** Bachelor of Agricultural Science

| | | | |
|---|---|---|---|
| **BAI** | *Baccalarius in Arte Ingeniaria* (Bachelor of Engineering) | **BJ** | Bachelor of Journalism |
| **BAIE** | British Association of Industrial Editors | **BJSM** | British Joint Services Mission |
| **BALPA** | British Air Line Pilots' Association | **BKSTS** | British Kinematograph, Sound and Television Society |
| **BAO** | Bachelor of Art of Obstetrics | **BL** | Bachelor of Law |
| **BAOMS** | British Association of Oral and Maxillo-Facial Surgeons | **BLA** | British Liberation Army |
| **BAOR** | British Army of the Rhine (formerly *on* the Rhine) | **BLE** | Brotherhood of Locomotive Engineers; Bachelor of Land Economy |
| **BAOS** | British Association of Oral Surgeons (*now see* BAOMS) | | |
| **BAppSc(MT)** | Bachelor of Applied Science (Medical Technology) | **BLESMA** | British Limbless Ex-Servicemen's Association |
| **BARB** | Broadcasters' Audience Research Board | **BLitt** | Bachelor of Letters |
| **BARC** | British Automobile Racing Club | **BM** | British Museum; Bachelor of Medicine; Brigade Major; British Monomark |
| **Bart** | Baronet | | |
| **BAS** | Bachelor in Agricultural Science | **BMA** | British Medical Association |
| **BASc** | Bachelor of Applied Science | **BMedSci** | Bachelor of Medical Science |
| **BASCA** | British Academy of Songwriters, Composers and Authors | **BMEO** | British Middle East Office |
| **BASEEFA** | British Approvals Service for Electrical Equipment in Flammable Atmospheres | **BMet** | Bachelor of Metallurgy |
| | | **BMEWS** | Ballistic Missile Early Warning System |
| **BASW** | British Association of Social Workers | **BMH** | British Military Hospital |
| **Batt.** | Battery | **BMJ** | British Medical Journal |
| **BBA** | British Bankers' Association; Bachelor of Business Administration | **BMM** | British Military Mission |
| | | **BMRA** | Brigade Major Royal Artillery |
| **BB&CIRly** | Bombay, Baroda and Central India Railway | **Bn** | Battalion |
| **BBB of C** | British Boxing Board of Control | **BNAF** | British North Africa Force |
| **BBC** | British Broadcasting Corporation | **BNC** | Brasenose College |
| **BBM** | Bintang Bakti Masharakat (Public Service Star) (Singapore) | **BNEC** | British National Export Council |
| | | **BNFL** | British Nuclear Fuels Ltd |
| **BBS** | Bachelor of Business Studies | **BNOC** | British National Oil Corporation; British National Opera Company |
| **BC** | Before Christ; British Columbia; Borough Council | | |
| **BCC** | British Council of Churches | **BNSC** | British National Space Centre |
| **BCE** | Bachelor of Civil Engineering | **BNSc** | Bachelor of Nursing Science |
| **BCh or** | | **BOAC** | British Overseas Airways Corporation |
| **BChir** | Bachelor of Surgery | **BomCS** | Bombay Civil Service |
| **BCL** | Bachelor of Civil Law | **BomSC** | Bombay Staff Corps |
| **BCMF** | British Ceramic Manufacturers' Federation | **BoT** | Board of Trade |
| **BCMS** | Bible Churchmen's Missionary Society | **Bot.** | Botany; Botanical |
| **BCOF** | British Commonwealth Occupation Force | **BOTB** | British Overseas Trade Board |
| **BCom or BComm** | Bachelor of Commerce | **Bp** | Bishop |
| **BComSc** | Bachelor of Commercial Science | **BPA** | British Paediatric Association |
| **BCS** | Bengal Civil Service; British Computer Society | **BPG** | Broadcasting Press Guild |
| **BCSA** | British Constructional Steelwork Association | **BPharm** | Bachelor of Pharmacy |
| **BCURA** | British Coal Utilization Research Association | **BPIF** | British Printing Industries Federation |
| **BCYC** | British Corinthian Yacht Club | **BPMF** | British Postgraduate Medical Federation |
| **BD** | Bachelor of Divinity | **BPsS** | British Psychological Society |
| **Bd** | Board | **BR** | British Rail |
| **BDA** | British Dental Association | **Br.** | Branch |
| **Bde** | Brigade | **BRA** | Brigadier Royal Artillery; British Rheumatism & Arthritis Association |
| **BDS** | Bachelor of Dental Surgery | | |
| **BDSc** | Bachelor of Dental Science | **BRB** | British Railways Board |
| **BE** | Bachelor of Engineering; British Element | **BRCS** | British Red Cross Society |
| **BEA** | British East Africa; British European Airways; British Epilepsy Association | **BRE** | Building Research Establishment |
| | | **Brig.** | Brigadier |
| **BEAMA** | Federation of British Electrotechnical and Allied Manufacturers' Associations (formerly British Electrical and Allied Manufacturers' Association) | **BritIRE** | British Institution of Radio Engineers (*now see* IERE) |
| | | **BRNC** | Britannia Royal Naval College |
| | | **BRS** | British Road Services |
| **BE&A** | Bachelor of Engineering and Architecture (Malta) | **BS** | Bachelor of Surgery; Bachelor of Science; British Standard |
| **BEAS** | British Educational Administration Society | **BSA** | Bachelor of Scientific Agriculture; Birmingham Small Arms; Building Societies' Association |
| **BEC** | Business Education Council (*now see* BTEC) | | |
| **BEc** | Bachelor of Economics | | |
| **BEd** | Bachelor of Education | **BSAA** | British South American Airways |
| **Beds** | Bedfordshire | **BSAP** | British South Africa Police |
| **BEE** | Bachelor of Electrical Engineering | **BSC** | British Steel Corporation; Bengal Staff Corps |
| **BEF** | British Expeditionary Force; British Equestrian Federation | **BSc** | Bachelor of Science |
| **BEM** | British Empire Medal | **BScA** | Bachelor of Science in Agriculture |
| **BEMAS** | British Education Management and Administration Society | **BSc(Dent)** | Bachelor of Science in Dentistry |
| **BEME** | Brigade Electrical and Mechanical Engineer | **BScSoc** | Bachelor of Social Sciences |
| **BEO** | Base Engineer Officer | **BSE** | Bachelor of Science in Engineering (US) |
| **Berks** | Berkshire | **BSES** | British Schools Exploring Society |
| **BESO** | British Executive Service Overseas | **BSF** | British Salonica Force |
| **BFI** | British Film Institute | **BSFA** | British Science Fiction Association |
| **BFMIRA** | British Food Manufacturing Industries Research Association | **BSI** | British Standards Institution |
| **BFPO** | British Forces Post Office | **BSIA** | British Security Industry Association |
| **BFSS** | British Field Sports Society | **BSJA** | British Show Jumping Association |
| **BGS** | Brigadier General Staff | **BSME** | Bachelor of Science in Mechanical Engineering |
| **Bhd** | Berhad | **BSN** | Bachelor of Science in Nursing |
| **BHRA** | British Hydromechanics Research Association | **BSNS** | Bachelor of Naval Science |
| **BHRCA** | British Hotels, Restaurants and Caterers' Association | **BSocSc** | Bachelor of Social Science |
| **BHS** | British Horse Society | **BSRA** | British Ship Research Association |
| **BIBA** | British Insurance Brokers' Association | **BSS** | Bachelor of Science (Social Science) |
| **BIBRA** | British Industrial Biological Research Association | **BST** | Bachelor of Sacred Theology |
| **BICC** | British Insulated Callender's Cables | **BT** | Bachelor of Teaching; British Telecommunications |
| **BICERA** | British Internal Combustion Engine Research Association (*now see* BICERI) | **Bt** | Baronet; Brevet |
| | | **BTA** | British Tourist Authority (*formerly* British Travel Association) |
| **BICERI** | British Internal Combustion Engine Research Institute | | |
| **BICSc** | British Institute of Cleaning Science | **BTC** | British Transport Commission |
| **BIEC** | British Invisible Exports Council | **BTCV** | British Trust for Conservation Volunteers |
| **BIEE** | British Institute of Energy Economics | **BTDB** | British Transport Docks Board (*now see* ABP) |
| **BIF** | British Industries Fair | **BTEC** | Business and Technician Education Council |
| **BIFU** | Banking Insurance and Finance Union | **BTh** | Bachelor of Theology |
| **BIM** | British Institute of Management | **BTP** | Bachelor of Town Planning |
| **BIR** | British Institute of Radiology | **Btss** | Baroness |
| **BIS** | Bank for International Settlements | **BUAS** | British Universities Association of Slavists |
| **BISF** | British Iron and Steel Federation | **BUPA** | British United Provident Association |
| **BISFA** | British Industrial and Scientific Film Association | **BV** | Besloten Vennootschap |
| **BISPA** | British Independent Steel Producers' Association | **BVA** | British Veterinary Association |
| **BISRA** | British Iron and Steel Research Association | **BVM** | Blessed Virgin Mary |

BVMS    Bachelor of Veterinary Medicine and Surgery
**Bucks**    Buckinghamshire
BVetMed    Bachelor of Veterinary Medicine
BWI    British West Indies
BWM    British War Medal

# C

(C)    Conservative; 100
c    child; cousin; *circa* (about)
CA    Central America; County Alderman; Chartered Accountant (Scotland and Canada)
CAA    Civil Aviation Authority
CAABU    Council for the Advancement of Arab and British Understanding
CAAV    Central Association of Agricultural Valuers; *also* Member of the Association
CAB    Citizens' Advice Bureau; Commonwealth Agricultural Bureau
CACTM    Central Advisory Council of Training for the Ministry (*now see* ACCM)
CAER    Conservative Action for Electoral Reform
CALE    Canadian Army Liaison Executive
CAM    Communications, Advertising and Marketing
**Cambs**    Cambridgeshire
CAMC    Canadian Army Medical Corps
CAMRA    Campaign for Real Ale
CAMS    Certificate of Advanced Musical Study
CAMW    Central Association for Mental Welfare
**Cantab**    *Cantabrigiensis* (of Cambridge)
**Cantuar**    *Cantuariensis* (of Canterbury)
CARD    Campaign against Racial Discrimination
CARE    Cottage and Rural Enterprises
CARICOM    Caribbean Community
CARIFTA    Caribbean Free Trade Area (*now see* CARICOM)
CAS    Chief of the Air Staff
CASI    Canadian Aeronautics and Space Institute
CAT    College of Advanced Technology
**Cav.**    Cavalry
CAWU    Clerical and Administrative Workers' Union (*now see* APEX)
CB    Companion, Order of the Bath; County Borough
CBC    County Borough Council
CBCO    Central Board for Conscientious Objectors
CBE    Commander, Order of the British Empire
CBI    Confederation of British Industry
CBIM    Companion, British Institute of Management
CBiol    Chartered Biologist
CBNS    Commander British Navy Staff
CBS    Columbia Broadcasting System
CBSA    Clay Bird Shooting Association
CBSI    Chartered Building Societies Institute
CC    Companion, Order of Canada; City Council; County Council; Cricket Club; Cycling Club; County Court
CCAB    Consultative Committee of Accountancy Bodies
CCAHC    Central Council for Agricultural and Horticultural Co-operation
CCBE    Commission Consultative des Barreaux de la Communauté Européenne
CCC    Corpus Christi College; Central Criminal Court; County Cricket Club
CCE    Chartered Civil Engineer
CCF    Combined Cadet Force
CCFM    Combined Cadet Forces Medal
CCG    Control Commission Germany
CCH    Cacique's Crown of Honour, Order of Service of Guyana
CChem    Chartered Chemist
CCHMS    Central Committee for Hospital Medical Services
CCIA    Commission of Churches on International Affairs
CCJ    Council of Christians and Jews
CCPR    Central Council of Physical Recreation
CCRA    Commander Corps of Royal Artillery
CCRE    Commander Corps of Royal Engineers
CCREME    Commander Corps of Royal Electrical and Mechanical Engineers
CCRSigs    Commander Corps of Royal Signals
CCS    Casualty Clearing Station; Ceylon Civil Service
CCSU    Council of Civil Service Unions
CCTA    Commission de Coopération Technique pour l'Afrique
CCTS    Combat Crew Training Squadron
CD    Canadian Forces Decoration; Commander, Order of Distinction (Jamaica); Civil Defence
CDEE    Chemical Defence Experimental Establishment
CDipAF    Certified Diploma in Accounting and Finance
Cdo    Commando
CDRA    Committee of Directors of Research Associations
Cdre    Commodore
CDS    Chief of the Defence Staff
CDU    Christlich-Demokratische Union
CE    Civil Engineer

CEA    Central Electricity Authority
CECD    Confédération Européenne du Commerce de Détail
CEDEP    Centre Européen d'Éducation Permanente
CEE    Communauté Economique Européenne
CEED    Centre for Economic and Environmental Development
CEF    Canadian Expeditionary Force
CEFIC    Conseil Européen des Fédérations de l'Industrie Chimique
CEGB    Central Electricity Generating Board
CEI    Council of Engineering Institutions
CEIR    Corporation for Economic and Industrial Research
CEM    Council of European Municipalities (*now see* CEMR)
CEMA    Council for the Encouragement of Music and the Arts
CEMR    Council of European Municipalities and Regions
CEMS    Church of England Men's Society
CEN    Comité Européen de Normalisation
CENELEC    European Committee for Electrotechnical Standardization
CEng    Chartered Engineer
Cento    Central Treaty Organisation
CEPT    Conférence Européenne des Postes et des Télécommunications
CERL    Central Electricity Research Laboratories
CERN    Organisation (*formerly* Centre) Européenne pour la Recherche Nucléaire
CERT    Charities Effectiveness Review Trust
Cert Ed    Certificate of Education
CertITP    Certificate of International Teachers' Program (Harvard)
CEST    Centre for Exploitation of Science and Technology
CET    Council for Educational Technology
CETS    Church of England Temperance Society
CF    Chaplain to the Forces
CFA    Canadian Field Artillery
CFE    Central Fighter Establishment
CFM    Cadet Forces Medal
CFR    Commander, Order of the Federal Republic of Nigeria
CFS    Central Flying School
CGA    Community of the Glorious Ascension; Country Gentlemen's Association
CGH    Order of the Golden Heart of Kenya (1st class)
CGIA    Insignia Award of City and Guilds of London Institute
CGLI    City and Guilds of London Institute
CGM    Conspicuous Gallantry Medal
CGRM    Commandant-General Royal Marines
CGS    Chief of the General Staff
CH    Companion of Honour
Chanc.    Chancellor; Chancery
Chap.    Chaplain
ChapStJ    Chaplain, Order of St John of Jerusalem (*now see* ChStJ)
CHAR    Campaign for the Homeless and Rootless
CHB    Companion of Honour of Barbados
ChB    Bachelor of Surgery
CHC    Community Health Council
Ch.Ch.    Christ Church
Ch.Coll.    Christ's College
CHE    Campaign for Homosexual Equality
ChLJ    Chaplain, Order of St Lazarus of Jerusalem
CHM    Chevalier of Honour and Merit (Haiti)
(CHM)    *See under* ARCO(CHM), FRCO(CHM)
ChM    Master of Surgery
Chm.    Chairman or Chairwoman
CHSC    Central Health Services Council
ChStJ    Chaplain, Most Venerable Order of the Hospital of St John of Jerusalem
CI    Imperial Order of the Crown of India; Channel Islands
CIA    Chemical Industries Association; Central Intelligence Agency
CIAD    Central Institute of Art and Design
CIAgrE    Companion, Institution of Agricultural Engineers
CIAL    Corresponding Member of the International Institute of Arts and Letters
CIArb    Chartered Institute of Arbitrators
CIB    Chartered Institute of Bankers
CIBS    Chartered Institution of Building Services (*now see* CIBSE)
CIBSE    Chartered Institution of Building Services Engineers
CIC    Chemical Institute of Canada
CICHE    Committee for International Co-operation in Higher Education
CICI    Confederation of Information Communication Industries
CID    Criminal Investigation Department
CIDEC    Conseil International pour le Développement du Cuivre
CIE    Companion, Order of the Indian Empire; Confédération Internationale des Etudiants
CIEx    Companion, Institute of Export
CIFRS    Comité International de la Rayonne et des Fibres Synthétiques
CIGasE    Companion, Institution of Gas Engineers
CIGRE    Conférence Internationale des Grands Réseaux Electriques
CIGS    Chief of the Imperial General Staff (*now see* CGS)
CIIA    Canadian Institute of International Affairs
CIM    China Inland Mission
CIMA    Chartered Institute of Management Accountants
CIMarE    Companion, Institute of Marine Engineers
CIMEMME    Companion, Institution of Mining Electrical and Mining Mechanical Engineers

| | |
|---|---|
| CIMGTechE | Companion, Institution of Mechanical and General Technician Engineers |
| C-in-C | Commander-in-Chief |
| CINCHAN | Allied Commander-in-Chief Channel |
| CIOB | Chartered Institute of Building |
| CIPFA | Chartered Institute of Public Finance and Accountancy |
| CIPL | Comité International Permanent des Linguistes |
| CIPM | Companion, Institute of Personnel Management |
| CIR | Commission on Industrial Relations |
| CIRIA | Construction Industry Research and Information Association |
| CIRP | Collège Internationale pour Recherche et Production |
| CIS | Institute of Chartered Secretaries and Administrators (*formerly* Chartered Institute of Secretaries); Command Control Communications and Information Systems |
| CISAC | Confédération Internationale des Sociétés d'Auteurs et Compositeurs; Centre for International Security and Arms Control |
| CIT | Chartered Institute of Transport; California Institute of Technology |
| CIU | Club and Institute Union |
| CIV | City Imperial Volunteers |
| CJ | Chief Justice |
| CJM | Congregation of Jesus and Mary (Eudist Fathers) |
| CL | Commander, Order of Leopold |
| cl | *cum laude* |
| Cl. | Class |
| CLA | Country Landowners' Association |
| CLit | Companion of Literature (Royal Society of Literature Award) |
| CLJ | Commander, Order of St Lazarus of Jerusalem |
| CLP | Constituency Labour Party |
| CLRAE | Conference of Local and Regional Authorities of Europe |
| CM | Member, Order of Canada; Congregation of the Mission (Vincentians); Master in Surgery; Certificated Master; Canadian Militia |
| CMA | Canadian Medical Association; Cost and Management Accountant (NZ) |
| CMAC | Catholic Marriage Advisory Council |
| CMB | Central Midwives' Board |
| CMF | Commonwealth Military Forces; Central Mediterranean Force |
| CMG | Companion, Order of St Michael and St George |
| CMLJ | Commander of Merit, Order of St Lazarus of Jerusalem |
| CMM | Commander, Order of Military Merit (Canada) |
| CMO | Chief Medical Officer |
| CMP | Corps of Military Police (*now see* CRMP) |
| CMS | Church Missionary Society; Certificate in Management Studies |
| CMT | Chaconia Medal of Trinidad |
| CNAA | Council for National Academic Awards |
| CND | Campaign for Nuclear Disarmament |
| CNI | Companion, Nautical Institute |
| CNR | Canadian National Railways |
| CNRS | Centre National de la Recherche Scientifique |
| CO | Commanding Officer; Commonwealth Office (after Aug. 1966) (*now see* FCO); Colonial Office (before Aug. 1966); Conscientious Objector |
| Co. | County; Company |
| C of E | Church of England |
| C of S | Chief of Staff; Church of Scotland |
| Coal.L or Co.L | Coalition Liberal |
| Coal.U or Co.U | Coalition Unionist |
| COHSE | Confederation of Health Service Employees |
| COI | Central Office of Information |
| CoID | Council of Industrial Design (*now* Design Council) |
| Col | Colonel |
| Coll. | College; Collegiate |
| Colo | Colorado (US) |
| Col.-Sergt | Colour-Sergeant |
| Com | Communist |
| Comd | Command |
| Comdg | Commanding |
| Comdr | Commander |
| Comdt | Commandant |
| COMEC | Council of the Military Education Committees of the Universities of the UK |
| COMET | Committee for Middle East Trade |
| Commn | Commission |
| Commnd | Commissioned |
| CompAMEME | Companion, Association of Mining Electrical and Mechanical Engineers |
| CompICE | Companion, Institution of Civil Engineers |
| CompIEE | Companion, Institution of Electrical Engineers |
| CompIERE | Companion, Institution of Electronic and Radio Engineers |
| CompIGasE | Companion, Institution of Gas Engineers |
| CompIMechE | Companion, Institution of Mechanical Engineers |
| CompIWES | Companion, Institution of Water Engineers and Scientists |
| CompTI | Companion of the Textile Institute |
| Comr | Commissioner |
| Comy-Gen. | Commissary-General |
| CON | Commander, Order of the Niger |
| Conn | Connecticut (US) |
| Const. | Constitutional |
| Co-op. | Co-operative |
| COPA | Comité des Organisations Professionels Agricoles de la CEE |
| COPEC | Conference of Politics, Economics and Christianity |
| Corp. | Corporation; Corporal |
| Corresp. Mem. | Corresponding Member |
| COS | Chief of Staff; Charity Organization Society |
| COSA | Colliery Officials and Staffs Association |
| CoSIRA | Council for Small Industries in Rural Areas |
| COSLA | Convention of Scottish Local Authorities |
| COSPAR | Committee on Space Research |
| COSSAC | Chief of Staff to Supreme Allied Commander |
| COTC | Canadian Officers' Training Corps |
| CP | Central Provinces; Cape Province |
| CPA | Commonwealth Parliamentary Association; Chartered Patent Agent; Certified Public Accountant (Canada) (*now see* CA) |
| CPAG | Child Poverty Action Group |
| CPAS | Church Pastoral Aid Society |
| CPC | Conservative Political Centre |
| CPhys | Chartered Physicist |
| CPL | Chief Personnel and Logistics |
| CPM | Colonial Police Medal |
| CPR | Canadian Pacific Railway |
| CPRE | Council for the Protection of Rural England |
| CPSA | Civil and Public Services Association |
| CPSU | Communist Party of the Soviet Union |
| CPsychol | Chartered Psychologist |
| CPU | Commonwealth Press Union |
| CQSW | Certificate of Qualification in Social Work |
| CR | Community of the Resurrection |
| cr | created or creation |
| CRA | Commander, Royal Artillery |
| CRAC | Careers Research and Advisory Centre |
| CRAeS | Companion, Royal Aeronautical Society |
| CRASC | Commander, Royal Army Service Corps |
| CRC | Cancer Research Campaign; Community Relations Council |
| CRCP(C) | Certificant, Royal College of Physicians of Canada |
| CRE | Commander, Royal Engineers; Commission for Racial Equality; Commercial Relations and Exports |
| Cres. | Crescent |
| CRMP | Corps of Royal Military Police |
| CRNCM | Companion, Royal Northern College of Music |
| CRO | Commonwealth Relations Office (before Aug. 1966; *now see* FCO) |
| CS | Civil Service; Clerk to the Signet |
| CSA | Confederate States of America |
| CSB | Bachelor of Christian Science |
| CSC | Conspicuous Service Cross; Congregation of the Holy Cross |
| CSCA | Civil Service Clerical Association (*now see* CPSA) |
| CSCE | Conference on Security and Co-operation in Europe |
| CSD | Civil Service Department; Co-operative Secretaries Diploma; Chartered Society of Designers |
| CSEU | Confederation of Shipbuilding and Engineering Unions |
| CSG | Companion, Order of the Star of Ghana; Company of the Servants of God |
| CSI | Companion, Order of the Star of India |
| CSIR | Commonwealth Council for Scientific and Industrial Research (*now see* CSIRO) |
| CSIRO | Commonwealth Scientific and Industrial Research Organization (Australia) |
| CSO | Chief Scientific Officer; Chief Signal Officer; Chief Staff Officer |
| CSP | Chartered Society of Physiotherapists; Civil Service of Pakistan |
| CSS | Companion, Star of Sarawak; Council for Science and Society |
| CSSB | Civil Service Selection Board |
| CSSp | Holy Ghost Father |
| CSSR | Congregation of the Most Holy Redeemer (Redemptorist Order) |
| CSTI | Council of Science and Technology Institutes |
| CStJ | Commander, Most Venerable Order of the Hospital of St John of Jerusalem |
| CSU | Christlich-Soziale Union in Bayern |
| CSV | Community Service Volunteers |
| CTA | Chaplain Territorial Army |
| CTB | College of Teachers of the Blind |
| CTC | Cyclists' Touring Club; Commando Training Centre |
| CText | Chartered Textile Technologist |
| CTR(Harwell) | Controlled Thermonuclear Research |
| CU | Cambridge University |
| CUAC | Cambridge University Athletic Club |
| CUAFC | Cambridge University Association Football Club |
| CUBC | Cambridge University Boat Club |
| CUCC | Cambridge University Cricket Club |
| CUF | Common University Fund |
| CUHC | Cambridge University Hockey Club |
| CUMS | Cambridge University Musical Society |
| CUNY | City University of New York |

CUP        Cambridge University Press
CURUFC     Cambridge University Rugby Union Football Club
CV         Cross of Valour (Canada)
CVCP       Committee of Vice-Chancellors and Principals of the
           Universities of the United Kingdom
CVO        Commander, Royal Victorian Order
CVS        Council of Voluntary Service
CVSNA      Council of Voluntary Service National Association
CWA        Crime Writers Association
CWGC       Commonwealth War Graves Commission
CWS        Co-operative Wholesale Society

# D

D          Duke
d          died; daughter
DA         Dame of St Andrew, Order of Barbados; Diploma in
           Anaesthesia; Diploma in Art
DAA&QMG    Deputy Assistant Adjutant and Quartermaster-General
DAAG       Deputy Assistant Adjutant-General
DA&QMG     Deputy Adjutant and Quartermaster-General
DAC        Development Assistance Committee
DACG       Deputy Assistant Chaplain-General
DAD        Deputy Assistant Director
DAdmin     Doctor of Administration
DADMS      Deputy Assistant Director of Medical Services
DADOS      Deputy Assistant Director of Ordnance Services
DADQ       Deputy Assistant Director of Quartering
DADST      Deputy Assistant Director of Supplies and Transport
DAG        Deputy Adjutant-General
DAgr       Doctor of Agriculture
DAMS       Deputy Assistant Military Secretary
D&AD       Designers and Art Directors Association
DAppSc     Doctor of Applied Science
DAQMG      Deputy Assistant Quartermaster-General
DArt       Doctor of Art
DASc       Doctor in Agricultural Sciences
DATA       Draughtsmen's and Allied Technicians' Association (later
           AUEW(TASS))
DATEC      Art and Design Committee, Technician Education Council
DBA        Doctor of Business Administration
DBE        Dame Commander, Order of the British Empire
DC         District Council; District of Columbia (US)
DCAe       Diploma of College of Aeronautics
DCAS       Deputy Chief of the Air Staff
DCB        Dame Commander, Order of the Bath
DCC        Diploma of Chelsea College
DCG        Deputy Chaplain-General
DCGRM      Department of the Commandant General Royal Marines
DCGS       Deputy Chief of the General Staff
DCh        Doctor of Surgery
DCH        Diploma in Child Health
DCIGS      Deputy Chief of the Imperial General Staff (now see
           DCGS)
DCL        Doctor of Civil Law
DCLI       Duke of Cornwall's Light Infantry
DCLJ       Dame Commander, Order of St Lazarus of Jerusalem
DCM        Distinguished Conduct Medal
DCMG       Dame Commander, Order of St Michael and St George
DCMHE      Diploma of Contents and Methods in Health Education
DCnL       Doctor of Canon Law
DCO        Duke of Cambridge's Own
DComm      Doctor of Commerce
DCP        Diploma in Clinical Pathology; Diploma in Conservation of
           Paintings
DCS        Deputy Chief of Staff; Doctor of Commercial Sciences
DCSO       Deputy Chief Scientific Officer
DCT        Doctor of Christian Theology
DCVO       Dame Commander, Royal Victorian Order
DD         Doctor of Divinity
DDGAMS     Deputy Director General, Army Medical Services
DDL        Deputy Director of Labour
DDME       Deputy Director of Mechanical Engineering
DDMI       Deputy Director of Military Intelligence
DDMO       Deputy Director of Military Operations
DDMS       Deputy Director of Medical Services
DDMT       Deputy Director of Military Training
DDNI       Deputy Director of Naval Intelligence
DDO        Diploma in Dental Orthopaedics
DDPH       Diploma in Dental Public Health
DDPR       Deputy Director of Public Relations
DDPS       Deputy Director of Personal Services
DDR        Deutsche Demokratische Republik
DDRA       Deputy Director Royal Artillery
DDS        Doctor of Dental Surgery; Director of Dental Services
DDSc       Doctor of Dental Science
DDSD       Deputy Director Staff Duties
DDSM       Defense Distinguished Service Medal
DDST       Deputy Director of Supplies and Transport
DDWE&M     Deputy Director of Works, Electrical and Mechanical

DE         Doctor of Engineering
DEA        Department of Economic Affairs
decd       deceased
DEconSc    Doctor of Economic Science
DEd        Doctor of Education
Del        Delaware (US)
Deleg.     Delegate
DEME       Directorate of Electrical and Mechanical Engineering
DEMS       Defensively Equipped Merchant Ships
(DemU)     Democratic Unionist
DEng       Doctor of Engineering
DenM       Docteur en Médicine
DEOVR      Duke of Edinburgh's Own Volunteer Rifles
DEP        Department of Employment and Productivity; European
           Progressive Democrats
Dep.       Deputy
DES        Department of Education and Science
DèsL       Docteur ès lettres
DèsS or DèsSc   Docteur ès sciences
DesRCA     Designer of the Royal College of Art
DFA        Doctor of Fine Arts
DFC        Distinguished Flying Cross
DFH        Diploma of Faraday House
DFLS       Day Fighter Leaders' School
DFM        Distinguished Flying Medal
DG         Director General; Dragoon Guards
DGAA       Distressed Gentlefolks Aid Association
DGAMS      Director-General Army Medical Services
DGEME      Director General Electrical and Mechanical Engineering
DGLP(A)    Director General Logistic Policy (Army)
DGMS       Director-General of Medical Services
DGMT       Director-General of Military Training
DGMW       Director-General of Military Works
DGNPS      Director-General of Naval Personal Services
DGP        Director-General of Personnel
DGPS       Director-General of Personal Services
DGS        Diploma in Graduate Studies
DGStJ      Dame of Grace, Order of St John of Jerusalem (now see
           DStJ)
DGU        Doctor of Griffith University
DH         Doctor of Humanities
DHA        District Health Authority
Dhc        Doctor honoris causa
DHEW       Department of Health Education and Welfare (US)
DHL        Doctor of Humane Letters; Doctor of Hebrew Literature
DHM        Dean Hole Medal
DHMSA      Diploma in the History of Medicine (Society of
           Apothecaries)
DHQ        District Headquarters
DHSS       Department of Health and Social Security (now see DoH
           and DSS)
DHumLit    Doctor of Humane Letters
DIAS       Dublin Institute of Advanced Sciences
DIC        Diploma of the Imperial College
DICTA      Diploma of Imperial College of Tropical Agriculture
DIG        Deputy Inspector-General
DIH        Diploma in Industrial Health
DIMP       Darjah Indera Mahkota Pahang
Dio.       Diocese
DipAD      Diploma in Art and Design
DipAe      Diploma in Aeronautics
DipASE     Diploma in Advanced Study of Education, College of
           Preceptors
DipAvMed   Diploma of Aviation Medicine, Royal College of
           Physicians
DipBA      Diploma in Business Administration
DipBS      Diploma in Fine Art, Byam Shaw School
DipCAM     Diploma in Communications, Advertising and Marketing
           of CAM Foundation
DipCC      Diploma of the Central College
DipCD      Diploma in Civic Design
DipCE      Diploma in Civil Engineering
DipEcon    Diploma in Economics
DipEd      Diploma in Education
DipEl      Diploma in Electronics
DipESL     Diploma in English as a Second Language
DipEth     Diploma in Ethnology
DipFD      Diploma in Funeral Directing
DipFE      Diploma in Further Education
DipGSM     Diploma in Music, Guildhall School of Music and Drama
DipHA      Diploma in Hospital Administration
DipHum     Diploma in Humanities
DipLA      Diploma in Landscape Architecture
DipLib     Diploma of Librarianship
DipM       Diploma in Marketing
DipN       Diploma in Nursing
DipNEC     Diploma of Northampton Engineering College (now City
           University)
DipPA      Diploma of Practitioners in Advertising (now see DipCAM)
DipREM     Diploma in Rural Estate Management
DipSoc     Diploma in Sociology
DipTA      Diploma in Tropical Agriculture
DipT&CP    Diploma in Town and Country Planning

| | |
|---|---|
| DipTh | Diploma in Theology |
| DipTP | Diploma in Town Planning |
| DipTPT | Diploma in Theory and Practice of Teaching |
| DistTP | Distinction in Town Planning |
| Div. | Division; Divorced |
| DJAG | Deputy Judge Advocate General |
| DJPD | Dato Jasa Purba Di-Raja Negeri Sembilan (Malaysia) |
| DJStJ | Dame of Justice, Order of St John of Jerusalem (*now see* DStJ) |
| DJur | *Doctor Juris* |
| DK | Most Esteemed Family Order (Brunei) |
| DL | Deputy Lieutenant |
| DLC | Diploma Loughborough College |
| DLES | Doctor of Letters in Economic Studies |
| DLI | Durham Light Infantry |
| DLit or DLitt | Doctor of Literature; Doctor of Letters |
| DLittS | Doctor of Sacred Letters |
| DLJ | Dame of Grace, Order of St Lazarus of Jerusalem |
| DLO | Diploma in Laryngology and Otology |
| DM | Doctor of Medicine |
| DMA | Diploma in Municipal Administration |
| DMD | Doctor of Medical Dentistry (Australia) |
| DME | Director of Mechanical Engineering |
| DMet | Doctor of Metallurgy |
| DMI | Director of Military Intelligence |
| DMin | Doctor of Ministry |
| DMJ | Diploma in Medical Jurisprudence |
| DMJ(Path) | Diploma in Medical Jurisprudence (Pathology) |
| DMLJ | Dame of Merit, Order of St Lazarus of Jerusalem |
| DMO | Director of Military Operations |
| DMR | Diploma in Medical Radiology |
| DMRD | Diploma in Medical Radiological Diagnosis |
| DMRE | Diploma in Medical Radiology and Electrology |
| DMRT | Diploma in Medical Radio-Therapy |
| DMS | Director of Medical Services; Decoration for Meritorious Service (South Africa); Diploma in Management Studies |
| DMSSB | Direct Mail Services Standards Board |
| DMT | Director of Military Training |
| DMus | Doctor of Music |
| DN | Diploma in Nursing |
| DNB | Dictionary of National Biography |
| DNE | Director of Naval Equipment |
| DNI | Director of Naval Intelligence |
| DO | Diploma in Ophthalmology |
| DOAE | Defence Operational Analysis Establishment |
| DObstRCOG | Diploma of Royal College of Obstetricians and Gynaecologists |
| DOC | District Officer Commanding |
| DocEng | Doctor of Engineering |
| DoE | Department of the Environment |
| DoH | Department of Health |
| DoI | Department of Industry |
| DOL | Doctor of Oriental Learning |
| Dom. | *Dominus* |
| DOMS | Diploma in Ophthalmic Medicine and Surgery |
| DOR | Director of Operational Requirements |
| DOS | Director of Ordnance Services; Doctor of Ocular Science |
| Dow. | Dowager |
| DP | Data Processing |
| DPA | Diploma in Public Administration; Discharged Prisoners' Aid |
| DPD | Diploma in Public Dentistry |
| DPEc | Doctor of Political Economy |
| DPed | Doctor of Pedagogy |
| DPH | Diploma in Public Health |
| DPh or DPhil | Doctor of Philosophy |
| DPhysMed | Diploma in Physical Medicine |
| DPLG | Diplômé par le Gouvernement |
| DPM | Diploma in Psychological Medicine |
| DPMS | Dato Paduka Mahkota Selangor (Malaysia) |
| DPP | Director of Public Prosecutions |
| DPR | Director of Public Relations |
| DPS | Director of Postal Services; Director of Personal Services; Doctor of Public Service |
| DQMG | Deputy Quartermaster-General |
| Dr | Doctor |
| DRAC | Director Royal Armoured Corps |
| DRC | Diploma of Royal College of Science and Technology, Glasgow |
| DRD | Diploma in Restorative Dentistry |
| Dr ing | Doctor of Engineering |
| Dr jur | Doctor of Laws |
| DrŒcPol | *Doctor Œconomiæ Politicæ* |
| Dr rer. nat. | Doctor of Natural Science |
| DRS | Diploma in Religious Studies |
| DRSAMD | Diploma of the Royal Scottish Academy of Music and Drama |
| DS | Directing Staff; Doctor of Science |
| DSA | Diploma in Social Administration |
| DSAC | Defence Scientific Advisory Council |
| DSAO | Diplomatic Service Adinistration Office |
| DSC | Distinguished Service Cross |

| | |
|---|---|
| DSc | Doctor of Science |
| DScA | Docteur en sciences agricoles |
| DSCHE | Diploma of the Scottish Council for Health Education |
| DScMil | Doctor of Military Science |
| DSD | Director Staff Duties |
| DSIR | Department of Scientific and Industrial Research (later SRC; *now see* SERC) |
| DSL | Doctor of Sacred Letters |
| DSLJ | Dato Seri Laila Jasa Brunei |
| DSM | Distinguished Service Medal |
| DSNB | Dato Setia Negara Brunei |
| DSNS | Dato Setia Negeri Sembilan (Malaysia) |
| DSO | Companion of the Distinguished Service Order |
| DSocSc | Doctor of Social Science |
| DSP | Director of Selection of Personnel; Docteur en sciences politiques (Montreal) |
| dsp | *decessit sine prole* (died without issue) |
| DSS | Department of Social Security; Doctor of Sacred Scripture |
| Dss | Deaconess |
| DSSc | Doctor of Social Science |
| DST | Director of Supplies and Transport |
| DStJ | Dame of Grace, Most Venerable Order of the Hospital of St John of Jerusalem; Dame of Justice, Most Venerable Order of the Hospital of St John of Jerusalem |
| DTA | Diploma in Tropical Agriculture |
| DTD | Dekoratie voor Trouwe Dienst (Decoration for Devoted Service) |
| DTech | Doctor of Technology |
| DTH | Diploma in Tropical Hygiene |
| DTheol | Doctor of Theology |
| DThPT | Diploma in Theory and Practice of Teaching |
| DTI | Department of Trade and Industry |
| DTM&H | Diploma in Tropical Medicine and Hygiene |
| DU | Doctor of the University |
| Dunelm | *Dunelmensis* (of Durham) |
| DUniv | Doctor of the University |
| DUP | Docteur de l'Université de Paris |
| (DUP) | Democratic Unionist Party |
| DVA | Diploma of Veterinary Anaesthesia |
| DVH | Diploma in Veterinary Hygiene |
| DVLC | Driver and Vehicle Licensing Centre |
| DVM | Doctor of Veterinary Medicine |
| DVMS | Doctor of Veterinary Medicine and Surgery |
| DVR | Diploma in Veterinary Radiology |
| DVSc | Doctor of Veterinary Science |
| DVSM | Diploma in Veterinary State Medicine |

# E

| | |
|---|---|
| E | East; Earl; England |
| e | eldest |
| EAA | Edinburgh Architectural Association |
| EAHY | European Architectural Heritage Year |
| EAP | East Africa Protectorate |
| EAW | Electrical Association for Women |
| EBC | English Benedictine Congregation |
| Ebor | *Eboracensis* (of York) |
| EBU | European Broadcasting Union |
| EC | Etoile du Courage (Canada); European Commission; Emergency Commission |
| ECA | Economic Co-operation Administration; Economic Commission for Africa |
| ECAFE | Economic Commission for Asia and the Far East (*now see* ESCAP) |
| ECE | Economic Commission for Europe |
| ECGD | Export Credits Guarantee Department |
| ECLA | Economic Commission for Latin America |
| ECOVAST | European Council for the Village and Small Town |
| ECSC | European Coal and Steel Community |
| ECU | English Church Union |
| ED | Efficiency Decoration; Doctor of Engineering (US); European Democrat |
| ed | edited |
| EdB | Bachelor of Education |
| EDC | Economic Development Committee |
| EdD | Doctor of Education |
| EDF | European Development Fund |
| EDG | European Democratic Group |
| Edin. | Edinburgh |
| Edn | Edition |
| EDP | Executive Development Programme |
| Educ | Educated |
| Educn | Education |
| EEC | European Economic Community; Commission of the European Communities |
| EEF | Engineering Employers' Federation; Egyptian Expeditionary Force |
| EETPU | Electrical Electronic Telecommunication & Plumbing Union |
| EETS | Early English Text Society |

| | |
|---|---|
| **EFCE** | European Federation of Chemical Engineering |
| **EFTA** | European Free Trade Association |
| **eh** | ehrenhalber (honorary) |
| **EI** | East Indian; East Indies |
| **EIA** | Engineering Industries Association |
| **EIB** | European Investment Bank |
| **EICS** | East India Company's Service |
| **E-in-C** | Engineer-in-Chief |
| **EIS** | Educational Institute of Scotland |
| **EISCAT** | European Incoherent Scatter Association |
| **EIU** | Economist Intelligence Unit |
| **ELBS** | English Language Book Society |
| **ELSE** | European Life Science Editors |
| **ELT** | English Language Teaching |
| **EM** | Edward Medal; Earl Marshal |
| **EMBL** | European Molecular Biology Laboratory |
| **EMBO** | European Molecular Biology Organisation |
| **EMP** | Electro Magnetic Pulse |
| **EMS** | Emergency Medical Service |
| **Enc.Brit.** | Encyclopaedia Britannica |
| **Eng.** | England |
| **Engr** | Engineer |
| **ENO** | English National Opera |
| **ENSA** | Entertainments National Service Association |
| **ENT** | Ear Nose and Throat |
| **EOPH** | Examined Officer of Public Health |
| **EORTC** | European Organisation for Research on Treatment of Cancer |
| **EPP** | European People's Party |
| **er** | elder |
| **ER** | Eastern Region (BR) |
| **ERA** | Electrical Research Association |
| **ERC** | Electronics Research Council |
| **ERD** | Emergency Reserve Decoration (Army) |
| **ESA** | European Space Agency |
| **ESCAP** | Economic and Social Commission for Asia and the Pacific |
| **ESL** | English as a Second Language |
| **ESNS** | Educational Sub-Normal Serious |
| **ESRC** | Economic and Social Research Council; Electricity Supply Research Council |
| **ESRO** | European Space Research Organization (*now see* ESA) |
| **ESU** | English-Speaking Union |
| **ETH** | Eidgenössische Technische Hochschule |
| **ETUC** | European Trade Union Confederation |
| **EUDISED** | European Documentation and Information Service for Education |
| **Euratom** | European Atomic Energy Community |
| **Eur Ing** | European Engineer |
| **EUROM** | European Federation for Optics and Precision Mechanics |
| **EUW** | European Union of Women |
| **eV** | eingetragener Verein |
| **Ext** | Extinct |

# F

| | |
|---|---|
| **FA** | Football Association |
| **FAA** | Fellow, Australian Academy of Science; Fleet Air Arm |
| **FAAAS** | Fellow, American Association for the Advancement of Science |
| **FAAO** | Fellow, American Academy of Optometry |
| **FAAP** | Fellow, American Academy of Pediatrics |
| **FAARM** | Fellow, American Academy of Reproductive Medicine |
| **FAAV** | Fellow, Central Association of Agricultural Valuers |
| **FAAVCT** | Fellow, American Academy of Veterinary and Comparative Toxicology |
| **FACC** | Fellow, American College of Cardiology |
| **FACCA** | Fellow, Association of Certified and Corporate Accountants (*now see* FCCA) |
| **FACCP** | Fellow, American College of Chest Physicians |
| **FACD** | Fellow, American College of Dentistry |
| **FACDS** | Fellow, Australian College of Dental Surgeons (*now see* FRACDS) |
| **FACE** | Fellow, Australian College of Education |
| **FACerS** | Fellow, American Ceramic Society |
| **FACI** | Fellow, Australian Chemical Institute (*now see* FRACI) |
| **FACMA** | Fellow, Australian College of Medical Administrators (*now see* FRACMA) |
| **FACOG** | Fellow, American College of Obstetricians and Gynæcologists |
| **FACOM** | Fellow, Australian College of Occupational Medicine |
| **FACP** | Fellow, American College of Physicians |
| **FACR** | Fellow, American College of Radiology |
| **FACRM** | Fellow, Australian College of Rehabilitation Medicine |
| **FACS** | Fellow, American College of Surgeons |
| **FACVT** | Fellow, American College of Veterinary Toxicology (*now see* FAAVCT) |
| **FAeSI** | Fellow, Aeronautical Society of India |
| **FAGO** | Fellowship in Australia in Obstetrics and Gynaecology |
| **FAGS** | Fellow, American Geographical Society |
| **FAHA** | Fellow, Australian Academy of the Humanities |

| | |
|---|---|
| **FAI** | Fellow, Chartered Auctioneers' and Estate Agents' Institute (*now (after amalgamation) see* FRICS); Fédération Aéronautique Internationale |
| **FAIA** | Fellow, American Institute of Architects |
| **FAIAA** | Fellow, American Institute of Aeronautics and Astronautics |
| **FAIAS** | Fellow, Australian Institute of Agricultural Science |
| **FAIB** | Fellow, Australian Institute of Bankers |
| **FAIBiol** | Fellow, Australian Institute of Biology |
| **FAIE** | Fellow, Australian Institute of Energy |
| **FAIEx** | Fellow, Australian Institute of Export |
| **FAIFST** | Fellow, Australian Institute of Food Science and Technology |
| **FAII** | Fellow, Australian Insurance Institute |
| **FAIM** | Fellow, Australian Institute of Management |
| **FAIP** | Fellow, Australian Institute of Physics |
| **FAMA** | Fellow, Australian Medical Association |
| **FAMI** | Fellow, Australian Marketing Institute |
| **FAmNucSoc** | Fellow, American Nuclear Society |
| **FAMS** | Fellow, Ancient Monuments Society |
| **F and GP** | Finance and General Purposes |
| **FANY** | First Aid Nursing Yeomanry |
| **FANZCP** | Fellow, Australian and New Zealand College of Psychiatrists (*now see* FRANZCP) |
| **FAO** | Food and Agriculture Organization of the United Nations |
| **FAPA** | Fellow, American Psychiatric Association |
| **FAPHA** | Fellow, American Public Health Association |
| **FAPI** | Fellow, Australian Planning Institute (*now see* FRAPI) |
| **FAPS** | Fellow, American Phytopathological Society |
| **FArborA** | Fellow, Arboricultural Association |
| **FARE** | Federation of Alcoholic Rehabilitation Establishments |
| **FARELF** | Far East Land Forces |
| **FAS** | Fellow, Antiquarian Society; Fellow, Nigerian Academy of Science |
| **FASA** | Fellow, Australian Society of Accountants |
| **FASc** | Fellow, Indian Academy of Sciences |
| **FASCE** | Fellow, American Society of Civil Engineers |
| **FASI** | Fellow, Architects' and Surveyors' Institute |
| **FASSA** | Fellow, Academy of the Social Sciences in Australia |
| **FAusIMM** | Fellow, Australasian Institute of Mining and Metallurgy |
| **FAustCOG** | Fellow, Australian College of Obstetricians and Gynæcologists (*now see* FRACOG) |
| **FBA** | Fellow, British Academy; Federation of British Artists |
| **FBCO** | Fellow, British College of Ophthalmic Opticians (Optometrists) |
| **FBCS** | Fellow, British Computer Society |
| **FBEC(S)** | Fellow, Business Education Council (Scotland) |
| **FBHI** | Fellow, British Horological Institute |
| **FBHS** | Fellow, British Horse Society |
| **FBI** | Federation of British Industries (*now see* CBI); Federal Bureau of Investigation |
| **FBIA** | Fellow, Bankers' Institute of Australasia (*now see* FAIB) |
| **FBIBA** | Fellow, British Insurance Brokers' Association |
| **FBID** | Fellow, British Institute of Interior Design |
| **FBIM** | Fellow, British Institute of Management |
| **FBINZ** | Fellow, Bankers' Institute of New Zealand |
| **FBIPP** | Fellow, British Institute of Professional Photography |
| **FBIRA** | Fellow, British Institute of Regulatory Affairs |
| **FBIS** | Fellow, British Interplanetary Society |
| **FBKS** | Fellow, British Kinematograph Society (*now see* FBKSTS) |
| **FBKSTS** | Fellow, British Kinematograph, Sound and Television Society |
| **FBOA** | Fellow, British Optical Association |
| **FBOU** | Fellow, British Ornithologists' Union |
| **FBPICS** | Fellow, British Production and Inventory Control Society |
| **FBritIRE** | Fellow, British Institution of Radio Engineers (*now see* FIERE) |
| **FBPsS** | Fellow, British Psychological Society |
| **FBS** | Fellow, Building Societies Institute (*now see* FCBSI) |
| **FBSI** | Fellow, Boot and Shoe Institution (*now see* FCFI) |
| **FBSM** | Fellow, Birmingham School of Music |
| **FC** | Football Club |
| **FCA** | Fellow, Institute of Chartered Accountants; Fellow, Institute of Chartered Accountants in Australia; Fellow, New Zealand Society of Accountants; Federation of Canadian Artists |
| **FCAI** | Fellow, New Zealand Institute of Cost Accountants; Fellow, Canadian Aeronautical Institute (*now see* FCASI) |
| **FCAM** | Fellow, CAM Foundation |
| **FCAnaes** | Fellow, College of Anaesthetists |
| **FCASI** | Fellow, Canadian Aeronautics and Space Institute |
| **FCBSI** | Fellow, Chartered Building Societies Institute |
| **FCCA** | Fellow, Association of Certified Accountants |
| **FCCEA** | Fellow, Commonwealth Council for Educational Administration |
| **FCCS** | Fellow, Corporation of Secretaries (*formerly* of Certified Secretaries) |
| **FCCT** | Fellow, Canadian College of Teachers |
| **FCEC** | Federation of Civil Engineering Contractors |
| **FCFI** | Fellow, Clothing and Footwear Institute |
| **FCGI** | Fellow, City and Guilds of London Institute |
| **FCGP** | Fellow, College of General Practitioners (*now see* FRCGP) |
| **FCH** | Fellow, Coopers Hill College |

FChS        Fellow, Society of Chiropodists
FCI         Fellow, Institute of Commerce
FCIA        Fellow, Corporation of Insurance Agents
FCIArb      Fellow, Chartered Institute of Arbitrators
FCIB        Fellow, Corporation of Insurance Brokers; Fellow,
            Chartered Institute of Bankers
FCIBS       Fellow, Chartered Institution of Building Services (now see
            FCIBSE)
FCIBSE      Fellow, Chartered Institution of Building Services Engineers
FCIC        Fellow, Chemical Institute of Canada (formerly Canadian
            Institute of Chemistry)
FCII        Fellow, Chartered Insurance Institute
FCILA       Fellow, Chartered Institute of Loss Adjusters
FCIM        Fellow, Chartered Institute of Marketing
FCIOB       Fellow, Chartered Institute of Building
FCIPA       Fellow, Chartered Institute of Patent Agents (now see CPA)
FCIS        Fellow, Institute of Chartered Secretaries and
            Administrators (formerly Chartered Institute of
            Secretaries)
FCISA       Fellow, Chartered Institute of Secretaries and
            Administrators (Australia)
FCIT        Fellow, Chartered Institute of Transport
FCM         Faculty of Community Medicine
FCMA        Fellow, Institute of Cost and Management Accountants
FCMSA       Fellow, College of Medicine of South Africa
FCNA        Fellow, College of Nursing, Australia
FCO         Foreign and Commonwealth Office (departments merged
            Oct. 1968)
FCOG(SA)    Fellow, South African College of Obstetrics and
            Gynæcology
FCollH      Fellow, College of Handicraft
FCollP      Fellow, College of Preceptors
FCommA      Fellow, Society of Commercial Accountants (now see
            FSCA)
FCOphth     Fellow, College of Ophthalmologists
FCP         Fellow, College of Preceptors
FCPath      Fellow, College of Pathologists (now see FRCPath)
FCPS        Fellow, College of Physicians and Surgeons
FCP(SoAf)   Fellow, College of Physicians, South Africa
FCPSO(SoAf) Fellow, College of Physicians and Surgeons and
            Obstetricians, South Africa
FCRA        Fellow, College of Radiologists of Australia (now see
            FRACR)
FCS         Federation of Conservative Students
FCS or FChemSoc  Fellow, Chemical Society (now absorbed into
            Royal Society of Chemistry)
FCSD        Fellow, Chartered Society of Designers
FCSP        Fellow, Chartered Society of Physiotherapy
FCSSA or FCS(SoAf)  Fellow, College of Surgeons, South Africa
FCSSL       Fellow, College of Surgeons of Sri Lanka
FCST        Fellow, College of Speech Therapists
FCT         Federal Capital Territory (now see ACT); Fellow,
            Association of Corporate Treasurers
FCTB        Fellow, College of Teachers of the Blind
FCU         Fighter Control Unit
FCWA        Fellow, Institute of Cost and Works Accountants (now see
            FCMA)
FDF         Food and Drink Federation
FDI         Fédération Dentaire Internationale
FDP         Freie Demokratische Partei
FDS         Fellow in Dental Surgery
FDSRCPSGlas  Fellow in Dental Surgery, Royal College of
            Physicians and Surgeons of Glasgow
FDSRCS or FDS RCS  Fellow in Dental Surgery, Royal College of
            Surgeons of England
FDSRCSE     Fellow in Dental Surgery, Royal College of Surgeons of
            Edinburgh
FE          Far East
FEAF        Far East Air Force
FEANI       Fédération Européenne d'Associations Nationales
            d'Ingénieurs
FEBS        Federation of European Biochemical Societies
FECI        Fellow, Institute of Employment Consultants
FEE         Fédération des Expertes Comptables Européens
FEF         Far East Fleet
FEI         Fédération Equestre Internationale
FEIDCT      Fellow, Educational Institute of Design Craft and
            Technology
FEIS        Fellow, Educational Institute of Scotland
FEng        Fellow, Fellowship of Engineering
FES         Fellow, Entomological Society; Fellow, Ethnological
            Society
FF          Fianna Fáil; Field Force
FFA         Fellow, Faculty of Actuaries (in Scotland); Fellow, Institute
            of Financial Accountants
FFARACS     Fellow, Faculty of Anaesthetists, Royal Australian
            College of Surgeons
FFARCS      Fellow, Faculty of Anaesthetists, Royal College of
            Surgeons of England
FFARCSI     Fellow, Faculty of Anaesthetists, Royal College of
            Surgeons in Ireland
FFAS        Fellow, Faculty of Architects and Surveyors, London (now
            see FASI)

FFA(SA)     Fellow, Faculty of Anaesthetists (South Africa)
FFB         Fellow, Faculty of Building
FFCM        Fellow, Faculty of Community Medicine (now see FFPHM)
FFCMI       Fellow, Faculty of Community Medicine of Ireland
FFDRCSI     Fellow, Faculty of Dentistry, Royal College of Surgeons in
            Ireland
FFF         Free French Forces
FFHC        Freedom from Hunger Campaign
FFHom       Fellow, Faculty of Homœopathy
FFI         French Forces of the Interior; Finance for Industry
FFOM        Fellow, Faculty of Occupational Medicine
FFOMI       Fellow, Faculty of Occupational Medicine of Ireland
FFPath, RCPI  Fellow, Faculty of Pathologists of the Royal College of
            Physicians of Ireland
FFPHM       Fellow, Faculty of Public Health Medicine
FFPM        Fellow, Faculty of Pharmaceutical Medicine
FFPS        Fauna and Flora Preservation Society
FFR         Fellow, Faculty of Radiologists (now see FRCR)
FG          Fine Gael
FGA         Fellow, Gemmological Association
FGCM        Fellow, Guild of Church Musicians
FGDS        Fédération de la Gauche Démocratique et Socialiste
FGGE        Fellow, Guild of Glass Engineers
FGI         Fellow, Institute of Certificated Grocers
FGS         Fellow, Geological Society
FGSM        Fellow, Guildhall School of Music and Drama
FGSM(MT)    Fellow, Guildhall School of Music and Drama (Music
            Therapy)
FHA         Fellow, Institute of Health Service Administrators (formerly
            Hospital Administrators; now see FHSM)
FHAS        Fellow, Highland and Agricultural Society of Scotland
FHCIMA      Fellow, Hotel Catering and Institutional Management
            Association
FHFS        Fellow, Human Factors Society
FHKIE       Fellow, Hong Kong Institution of Engineers
FHMAAAS     Foreign Honorary Member, American Academy of Arts
            and Sciences
FHS         Fellow, Heraldry Society; Forces Help Society and Lord
            Roberts Workshops
FHSM        Fellow, Institute of Health Services Management
FH-WC       Fellow, Heriot-Watt College (now University), Edinburgh
FIA         Fellow, Institute of Actuaries
FIAA        Fellow, Institute of Actuaries of Australia
FIAAS       Fellow, Institute of Australian Agricultural Science
FIAA&S      Fellow, Incorporated Association of Architects and
            Surveyors
FIAgrE      Fellow, Institution of Agricultural Engineers
FIAI        Fellow, Institute of Industrial and Commercial Accountants
FIAL        Fellow, International Institute of Arts and Letters
FIAM        Fellow, Institute of Administrative Management; Fellow,
            International Academy of Management
FIAP        Fellow, Institution of Analysts and Programmers
FIArb       Fellow, Institute of Arbitrators (now see FCIArb)
FIArbA      Fellow, Institute of Arbitrators of Australia
FIAS        Fellow, Institute of Aeronautical Sciences (US) (now see
            FAIAA)
FIASc       Fellow, Indian Academy of Sciences
FIAWS       Fellow, International Academy of Wood Sciences
FIB         Fellow, Institute of Bankers (now see FCIB)
FIBA        Fellow, Institute of Business Administration, Australia
FIBD        Fellow, Institute of British Decorators
FIBiol      Fellow, Institute of Biology
FIBiotech   Fellow, Institute for Biotechnical Studies
FIBP        Fellow, Institute of British Photographers
FIBScot     Fellow, Institute of Bankers in Scotland
FIC         Fellow, Institute of Chemistry (now see FRIC, FRSC);
            Fellow, Imperial College, London
FICA        Fellow, Commonwealth Institute of Accountants; Fellow,
            Institute of Chartered Accountants in England and Wales
            (now see FCA)
FICAI       Fellow, Institute of Chartered Accountants in Ireland
FICD        Fellow, Institute of Civil Defence; Fellow, Indian College of
            Dentists
FICE        Fellow, Institution of Civil Engineers
FICeram     Fellow, Institute of Ceramics
FICFM       Fellow, Institute of Charity Fundraising Managers
FICFor      Fellow, Institute of Chartered Foresters
FIChemE     Fellow, Institution of Chemical Engineers
FICI        Fellow, Institute of Chemistry of Ireland; Fellow,
            International Colonial Institute
FICM        Fellow, Institute of Credit Management
FICMA       Fellow, Institute of Cost and Management Accountants
FICorrST    Fellow, Institution of Corrosion Science and Technology
FICS        Fellow, Institute of Chartered Shipbrokers; Fellow,
            International College of Surgeons
FICT        Fellow, Institute of Concrete Technologists
FICW        Fellow, Institute of Clerks of Works of Great Britain
FIDA        Fellow, Institute of Directors, Australia
FIDCA       Fellow, Industrial Design Council of Australia
FIDE        Fédération Internationale des Echecs; Fellow, Institute of
            Design Engineers
FIE(Aust)   Fellow, Institution of Engineers, Australia
FIEC        Fellow, Institute of Employment Consultants

| | |
|---|---|
| **FIED** | Fellow, Institution of Engineering Designers |
| **FIEE** | Fellow, Institution of Electrical Engineers |
| **FIEEE** | Fellow, Institute of Electrical and Electronics Engineers (NY) |
| **FIEHK** | Fellow, Institution of Engineering, Hong Kong |
| **FIElecIE** | Fellow, Institution of Electronic Incorporated Engineers |
| **FIEI** | Fellow, Institution of Engineering Inspection (*now see* FIQA); Fellow, Institution of Engineers of Ireland |
| **FIEJ** | Fédération Internationale des Editeurs de Journaux et Publications |
| **FIERE** | Fellow, Institution of Electronic and Radio Engineers (*now see* FIEE) |
| **FIES** | Fellow, Illuminating Engineering Society (later FIllumES; *now see* FCIBSE) |
| **FIET** | Fédération Internationale des Employés, Techniciens et Cadres |
| **FIEx** | Fellow, Institute of Export |
| **FIExpE** | Fellow, Institute of Explosives Engineers |
| **FIFA** | Fédération Internationale de Football Association |
| **FIFF** | Fellow, Institute of Freight Forwarders |
| **FIFireE** | Fellow, Institution of Fire Engineers |
| **FIFM** | Fellow, Institute of Fisheries Management |
| **FIFor** | Fellow, Institute of Foresters (*now see* FICFor) |
| **FIFST** | Fellow, Institute of Food Science and Technology |
| **FIGasE** | Fellow, Institution of Gas Engineers |
| **FIGCM** | Fellow, Incorporated Guild of Church Musicians |
| **FIGD** | Fellow, Institute of Grocery Distribution |
| **FIGO** | International Federation of Gynaecology and Obstetrics |
| **FIH** | Fellow, Institute of Housing; Fellow, Institute of the Horse |
| **FIHE** | Fellow, Institute of Health Education |
| **FIHM** | Fellow, Institute of Housing Managers (*now see* FIH) |
| **FIHort** | Fellow, Institute of Horticulture |
| **FIHospE** | Fellow, Institute of Hospital Engineering |
| **FIHT** | Fellow, Institution of Highways and Transportation |
| **FIHVE** | Fellow, Institution of Heating & Ventilating Engineers (later FCIBS and MCIBS; *now see* FCIBSE) |
| **FIIA** | Fellow, Institute of Industrial Administration (*now see* CBIM and FBIM); Fellow, Institute of Internal Auditors |
| **FIIC** | Fellow, International Institute for Conservation of Historic and Artistic Works |
| **FIIM** | Fellow, Institution of Industrial Managers |
| **FIInfSc** | Fellow, Institute of Information Scientists |
| **FIInst** | Fellow, Imperial Institute |
| **FIIP** | Fellow, Institute of Incorporated Photographers (*now see* FBIPP) |
| **FIIPE** | Fellow, Indian Institution of Production Engineers |
| **FIL** | Fellow, Institute of Linguists |
| **FILA** | Fellow, Institute of Landscape Architects (*now see* FLI) |
| **FILDM** | Fellow, Institute of Logistics and Distribution Management |
| **FilDr** | Doctor of Philosophy |
| **Fil.Hed.** | Filosofie Hedersdoktor |
| **FILLM** | Fédération Internationale des Langues et Littératures Modernes |
| **FIllumES** | Fellow, Illuminating Engineering Society (*now see* FCIBSE) |
| **FIM** | Fellow, Institute of Metals (*formerly* Institution of Metallurgists) |
| **FIMA** | Fellow, Institute of Mathematics and its Applications |
| **FIMarE** | Fellow, Institute of Marine Engineers |
| **FIMBRA** | Financial Intermediaries, Managers and Brokers Regulatory Association |
| **FIMC** | Fellow, Institute of Management Consultants |
| **FIMCB** | Fellow, International Management Centre from Buckingham |
| **FIMechE** | Fellow, Institution of Mechanical Engineers |
| **FIMFT** | Fellow, Institute of Maxillo-facial Technology |
| **FIMGTechE** | Fellow, Institution of Mechanical and General Technician Engineers |
| **FIMH** | Fellow, Institute of Materials Handling; Fellow, Institute of Military History |
| **FIMI** | Fellow, Institute of the Motor Industry |
| **FIMinE** | Fellow, Institution of Mining Engineers |
| **FIMIT** | Fellow, Institute of Musical Instrument Technology |
| **FIMLS** | Fellow, Institute of Medical Laboratory Sciences |
| **FIMLT** | Fellow, Institute of Medical Laboratory Technology (*now see* FIMLS) |
| **FIMM** | Fellow, Institution of Mining and Metallurgy |
| **FIMMA** | Fellow, Institute of Metals and Materials Australasia |
| **FIMS** | Fellow, Institute of Mathematical Statistics |
| **FIMT** | Fellow, Institute of the Motor Trade (*now see* FIMI) |
| **FIMTA** | Fellow, Institute of Municipal Treasurers and Accountants (*now see* IPFA) |
| **FIMunE** | Fellow, Institution of Municipal Engineers (now amalgamated with Institution of Civil Engineers) |
| **FIN** | Fellow, Institute of Navigation (*now see* FRIN) |
| **FINA** | Fédération Internationale de Natation Amateur |
| **FInstAM** | Fellow, Institute of Administrative Management |
| **FInstB** | Fellow, Institution of Buyers |
| **FInstBiol** | Fellow, Institute of Biology (*now see* FIBiol) |
| **FInstD** | Fellow, Institute of Directors |
| **FInstE** | Fellow, Institute of Energy |
| **FInstF** | Fellow, Institute of Fuel (*now see* FInstE) |
| **FInstFF** | Fellow, Institute of Freight Forwarders Ltd |
| **FInstHE** | Fellow, Institution of Highways Engineers (*now see* FIHT) |
| **FInstLEx** | Fellow, Institute of Legal Executives |
| **FInstM** | Fellow, Institute of Meat; Fellow, Institute of Marketing (*now see* FCIM) |
| **FInstMC** | Fellow, Institute of Measurement and Control |
| **FInstMSM** | Fellow, Institute of Marketing and Sales Management (later FInstM; *now see* FCIM) |
| **FInstMet** | Fellow, Institute of Metals (later part of Metals Society; *now see* FIM) |
| **FInstP** | Fellow, Institute of Physics |
| **FInstPet** | Fellow, Institute of Petroleum |
| **FInstPI** | Fellow, Institute of Patentees and Inventors |
| **FInstPS** | Fellow, Institute of Purchasing and Supply |
| **FInstSM** | Fellow, Institute of Sales Management (*now see* FInstSMM) |
| **FInstSMM** | Fellow, Institute of Sales and Marketing Management |
| **FInstW** | Fellow, Institute of Welding (*now see* FWeldI) |
| **FINucE** | Fellow, Institution of Nuclear Engineers |
| **FIOA** | Fellow, Institute of Acoustics |
| **FIOB** | Fellow, Institute of Building (*now see* FCIOB) |
| **FIOM** | Fellow, Institute of Office Management (*now see* FIAM) |
| **FIOP** | Fellow, Institute of Printing |
| **FIP** | Fellow, Australian Institute of Petroleum |
| **FIPA** | Fellow, Institute of Practitioners in Advertising |
| **FIPDM** | Fellow, Institute of Physical Distribution Management (*now see* FILDM) |
| **FIPENZ** | Fellow, Institution of Professional Engineers, New Zealand |
| **FIPG** | Fellow, Institute of Professional Goldsmiths |
| **FIPHE** | Fellow, Institution of Public Health Engineers (*now see* FIWEM) |
| **FIPlantE** | Fellow, Institution of Plant Engineers (*now see* FIIM) |
| **FIPM** | Fellow, Institute of Personnel Management |
| **FIPR** | Fellow, Institute of Public Relations |
| **FIProdE** | Fellow, Institution of Production Engineers |
| **FIQ** | Fellow, Institute of Quarrying |
| **FIQA** | Fellow, Institute of Quality Assurance |
| **FIQS** | Fellow, Institute of Quantity Surveyors |
| **FIRA** | Furniture Industry Research Association |
| **FIRA(Ind)** | Fellow, Institute of Railway Auditors and Accountants (India) |
| **FIRE(Aust)** | Fellow, Institution of Radio Engineers (Australia) (*now see* FIREE(Aust) |
| **FIREE(Aust)** | Fellow, Institution of Radio and Electronics Engineers (Australia) |
| **FIRI** | Fellow, Institution of the Rubber Industry (*now see* FPRI) |
| **FIRSE** | Fellow, Institute of Railway Signalling Engineers |
| **FIRTE** | Fellow, Institute of Road Transport Engineers |
| **FIS** | Fellow, Institute of Statisticians |
| **FISA** | Fellow, Incorporated Secretaries' Association; Fédération Internationale des Sociétés d'Aviron |
| **FISE** | Fellow, Institution of Sales Engineers; Fellow, Institution of Sanitary Engineers |
| **FISITA** | Fédération Internationale des Sociétés d'Ingénieurs des Techniques de l'Automobile |
| **FISP** | Fédération Internationale des Sociétés de Philosophie |
| **FIST** | Fellow, Institute of Science Technology |
| **FISTC** | Fellow, Institute of Scientific and Technical Communicators |
| **FISTD** | Fellow, Imperial Society of Teachers of Dancing |
| **FIStructE** | Fellow, Institution of Structural Engineers |
| **FISW** | Fellow, Institute of Social Work |
| **FITD** | Fellow, Institute of Training and Development |
| **FITE** | Fellow, Institution of Electrical and Electronics Technician Engineers |
| **FIW** | Fellow, Welding Institute (*now see* FWeldI) |
| **FIWE** | Fellow, Institution of Water Engineers (later FIWES; *now see* FIWEM) |
| **FIWEM** | Fellow, Institution of Water and Environmental Management |
| **FIWES** | Fellow, Institution of Water Engineers and Scientists (*now see* FIWEM) |
| **FIWM** | Fellow, Institution of Works Managers (*now see* FIIM) |
| **FIWPC** | Fellow, Institution of Water Pollution Control (*now see* FIWEM) |
| **FIWSc** | Fellow, Institute of Wood Science |
| **FIWSP** | Fellow, Institute of Work Study Practitioners (*now see* FMS) |
| **FJI** | Fellow, Institute of Journalists |
| **FJIE** | Fellow, Junior Institution of Engineers (*now see* CIMGTechE) |
| **FKC** | Fellow, King's College London |
| **FKCHMS** | Fellow, King's College Hospital Medical School |
| **FLA** | Fellow, Library Association |
| **Fla** | Florida (US) |
| **FLAI** | Fellow, Library Association of Ireland |
| **FLAS** | Fellow, Chartered Land Agents' Society (*now (after amalgamation) see* FRICS) |
| **FLCM** | Fellow, London College of Music |
| **FLHS** | Fellow, London Historical Society |
| **FLI** | Fellow, Landscape Institute |
| **FLIA** | Fellow, Life Insurance Association |
| **FLS** | Fellow, Linnean Society |
| **Flt** | Flight |
| **FM** | Field-Marshal |
| **FMA** | Fellow, Museums Association |

FMANZ      Fellow, Medical Association of New Zealand
FMES       Fellow, Minerals Engineering Society
FMF        Fiji Military Forces
FMS        Federated Malay States; Fellow, Medical Society; Fellow,
           Institute of Management Services
FMSA       Fellow, Mineralogical Society of America
FNA        Fellow, Indian National Science Academy
FNAEA      Fellow, National Association of Estate Agents
FNCO       Fleet Naval Constructor Officer
FNECInst   Fellow, North East Coast Institution of Engineers and
           Shipbuilders
FNI        Fellow, Nautical Institute; Fellow, National Institute of
           Sciences in India (now see FNA)
FNIA       Fellow, Nigerian Institute of Architects
FNZEI      Fellow, New Zealand Educational Institute
FNZIA      Fellow, New Zealand Institute of Architects
FNZIAS     Fellow, New Zealand Institute of Agricultural Science
FNZIC      Fellow, New Zealand Institute of Chemistry
FNZIE      Fellow, New Zealand Institution of Engineers
FNZIM      Fellow, New Zealand Institute of Management
FNZPsS     Fellow, New Zealand Psychological Society
FO         Foreign Office (now see FCO); Field Officer; Flying Officer
FODA       Fellow, Overseas Doctors' Association
FOIC       Flag Officer in charge
FOMI       Faculty of Occupational Medicine of Ireland
FONA       Flag Officer, Naval Aviation
FONAC      Flag Officer Naval Air Command
FOR        Fellowship of Operational Research
For.       Foreign
FOREST     Freedom Organisation for the Right to Enjoy Smoking
           Tobacco
FOX        Futures and Options Exchange
FPA        Family Planning Association
FPC        Family Practitioner Committee
FPEA       Fellow, Physical Education Association
FPhS       Fellow, Philosophical Society of England
FPI        Fellow, Plastics Institute (now see FPRI)
FPIA       Fellow, Plastics Institute of Australia
FPMI       Fellow, Pensions Management Institute
FPRI       Fellow, Plastics and Rubber Institute
FPS        Fellow, Pharmaceutical Society (now see FRPharmS);
           Fauna Preservation Society (now see FFPS)
FPhysS     Fellow, Physical Society
f r        fuori ruole
FRACDS     Fellow, Royal Australian College of Dental Surgeons
FRACGP     Fellow, Royal Australian College of General Practitioners
FRACI      Fellow, Royal Australian Chemical Institute
FRACMA     Fellow, Royal Australian College of Medical
           Administrators
FRACO      Fellow, Royal Australian College of Ophthalmologists
FRACOG     Fellow, Royal Australian College of Obstetricians and
           Gynaecologists
FRACP      Fellow, Royal Australasian College of Physicians
FRACR      Fellow, Royal Australasian College of Radiologists
FRACS      Fellow, Royal Australasian College of Surgeons
FRAD       Fellow, Royal Academy of Dancing
FRAeS      Fellow, Royal Aeronautical Society
FRAgS      Fellow, Royal Agricultural Societies (ie of England,
           Scotland and Wales)
FRAHS      Fellow, Royal Australian Historical Society
FRAI       Fellow, Royal Anthropological Institute
FRAIA      Fellow, Royal Australian Institute of Architects
FRAIB      Fellow, Royal Australian Institute of Building
FRAIC      Fellow, Royal Architectural Institute of Canada
FRAIPA     Fellow, Royal Australian Institute of Public Administration
FRAM       Fellow, Royal Academy of Music
FRAME      Fund for the Replacement of Animals in Medical
           Experiments
FRANZCP    Fellow, Royal Australian and New Zealand College of
           Psychiatrists
FRAPI      Fellow, Royal Australian Planning Institute
FRAS       Fellow, Royal Astronomical Society; Fellow, Royal Asiatic
           Society
FRASB      Fellow, Royal Asiatic Society of Bengal
FRASE      Fellow, Royal Agricultural Society of England
FRBS       Fellow, Royal Society of British Sculptors; Fellow, Royal
           Botanic Society
FRCCO      Fellow, Royal Canadian College of Organists
FRCD(Can.) Fellow, Royal College of Dentists of Canada
FRCGP      Fellow, Royal College of General Practitioners
FRCM       Fellow, Royal College of Music
FRCN       Fellow, Royal College of Nursing
FRCO       Fellow, Royal College of Organists
FRCO(CHM)  Fellow, Royal College of Organists with Diploma in
           Choir Training
FRCOG      Fellow, Royal College of Obstetricians and
           Gynaecologists
FRCP       Fellow, Royal College of Physicians, London
FRCPA      Fellow, Royal College of Pathologists of Australasia
FRCP&S (Canada)   Fellow, Royal College of Physicians and
           Surgeons of Canada
FRCPath    Fellow, Royal College of Pathologists
FRCP(C)    Fellow, Royal College of Physicians of Canada

FRCPE or FRCPEd    Fellow, Royal College of Physicians, Edinburgh
FRCPGlas   Fellow, Royal College of Physicians and Surgeons of
           Glasgow
FRCPI      Fellow, Royal College of Physicians of Ireland
FRCPS(Hon.)   Hon. Fellow, Royal College of Physicians and
           Surgeons of Glasgow
FRCPsych   Fellow, Royal College of Psychiatrists
FRCR       Fellow, Royal College of Radiologists
FRCS       Fellow, Royal College of Surgeons of England
FRCSCan    Fellow, Royal College of Surgeons of Canada
FRCSE or FRCSEd    Fellow, Royal College of Surgeons of
           Edinburgh
FRCSGlas   Fellow, Royal College of Physicians and Surgeons of
           Glasgow
FRCSI      Fellow, Royal College of Surgeons in Ireland
FRCSoc     Fellow, Royal Commonwealth Society
FRCUS      Fellow, Royal College of University Surgeons (Denmark)
FRCVS      Fellow, Royal College of Veterinary Surgeons
FREconS    Fellow, Royal Economic Society
FREI       Fellow, Real Estate Institute (Australia)
FRES       Fellow, Royal Entomological Society of London
FRFPSG     Fellow, Royal Faculty of Physicians and Surgeons,
           Glasgow (now see FRCPGlas)
FRG        Federal Republic of Germany
FRGS       Fellow, Royal Geographical Society
FRGSA      Fellow, Royal Geographical Society of Australasia
FRHistS    Fellow, Royal Historical Society
FRHS       Fellow, Royal Horticultural Society
FRHSV      Fellow, Royal Historical Society of Victoria
FRIAS      Fellow, Royal Incorporation of Architects of Scotland;
           Royal Institute for the Advancement of Science
FRIBA      Fellow, Royal Institute of British Architects (and see RIBA)
FRIC       Fellow, Royal Institute of Chemistry (now see FRSC)
FRICS      Fellow, Royal Institution of Chartered Surveyors
FRIH       Fellow, Royal Institute of Horticulture (NZ)
FRIN       Fellow, Royal Institute of Navigation
FRINA      Fellow, Royal Institution of Naval Architects
FRIPA      Fellow, Royal Institute of Public Administration (the
           Institute no longer has Fellows)
FRIPHH     Fellow, Royal Institute of Public Health and Hygiene
FRMCM      Fellow, Royal Manchester College of Music
FRMedSoc   Fellow, Royal Medical Society
FRMetS     Fellow, Royal Meteorological Society
FRMIA      Fellow, Retail Management Institute of Australia
FRMS       Fellow, Royal Microscopical Society
FRNCM      Fellow, Royal Northern College of Music
FRNS       Fellow, Royal Numismatic Society
FRPharmS   Fellow, Royal Pharmaceutical Society
FRPS       Fellow, Royal Photographic Society
FRPSL      Fellow, Royal Philatelic Society, London
FRS        Fellow, Royal Society
FRSA       Fellow, Royal Society of Arts
FRSAI      Fellow, Royal Society of Antiquaries of Ireland
FRSAMD     Fellow, Royal Scottish Academy of Music and Drama
FRSanI     Fellow, Royal Sanitary Institute (now see FRSH)
FRSC       Fellow, Royal Society of Canada; Fellow, Royal Society of
           Chemistry
FRS(Can)   Fellow, Royal Society of Canada (used when a person is
           also a Fellow of the Royal Society of Chemistry)
FRSCM      Fellow, Royal School of Church Music
FRSC (UK)   Fellow, Royal Society of Chemistry (used when a
           person is also a Fellow of the Royal Society of Canada)
FRSE       Fellow, Royal Society of Edinburgh
FRSGS      Fellow, Royal Scottish Geographical Society
FRSH       Fellow, Royal Society for the Promotion of Health
FRSL       Fellow, Royal Society of Literature
FRSM or FRSocMed    Fellow, Royal Society of Medicine
FRSNZ      Fellow, Royal Society of New Zealand
FRSSAf     Fellow, Royal Society of South Africa
FRST       Fellow, Royal Society of Teachers
FRSTM&H    Fellow, Royal Society of Tropical Medicine and Hygiene
FRTPI      Fellow, Royal Town Planning Institute
FRTS       Fellow, Royal Television Society
FRVA       Fellow, Rating and Valuation Association (now see IRRV)
FRVC       Fellow, Royal Veterinary College
FRVIA      Fellow, Royal Victorian Institute of Architects
FRZSScot   Fellow, Royal Zoological Society of Scotland
FS         Field Security
fs         Graduate, Royal Air Force Staff College
FSA        Fellow, Society of Antiquaries
FSAA       Fellow, Society of Incorporated Accountants and Auditors
FSAE       Fellow, Society of Automotive Engineers; Fellow, Society
           of Art Education
FSAI       Fellow, Society of Architectural Illustrators
FSAIEE     Fellow, South African Institute of Electrical Engineers
FSAM       Fellow, Society of Art Masters
FSArc      Fellow, Society of Architects (merged with the RIBA 1952)
FSAScot    Fellow, Society of Antiquaries of Scotland
FSASM      Fellow, South Australian School of Mines
FSBI       Fellow, Savings Banks Institute
fsc        Foreign Staff College
FSCA       Fellow, Society of Company and Commercial Accountants
FScotvec   Fellow, Scottish Vocational Educational Council

| | |
|---|---|
| FSDC | Fellow, Society of Dyers and Colourists |
| FSE | Fellow, Society of Engineers |
| FSG | Fellow, Society of Genealogists |
| FSGT | Fellow, Society of Glass Technology |
| FSI | Fellow, Chartered Surveyors' Institution (*now see* FRICS) |
| FSIAD | Fellow, Society of Industrial Artists and Designers (*now see* FCSD) |
| FSLAET | Fellow, Society of Licensed Aircraft Engineers and Technologists |
| FSLCOG | Fellow, Sri Lankan College of Obstetrics and Gynaecology |
| FSLTC | Fellow, Society of Leather Technologists and Chemists |
| FSMA | Fellow, Incorporated Sales Managers' Association (later FInstMSM; *now see* FInstM) |
| FSMC | Freeman of the Spectacle-Makers' Company |
| FSME | Fellow, Society of Manufacturing Engineers |
| FSRHE | Fellow, Society for Research into Higher Education |
| FSRP | Fellow, Society for Radiological Protection |
| FSS | Fellow, Royal Statistical Society |
| FSTD | Fellow, Society of Typographic Designers |
| FSVA | Fellow, Incorporated Society of Valuers and Auctioneers |
| FT | Financial Times |
| FTAT | Furniture, Timber and Allied Trades Union |
| FTC | Flying Training Command; Full Technological Certificate, City and Guilds of London Institute |
| FTCD | Fellow, Trinity College, Dublin |
| FTCL | Fellow, Trinity College of Music, London |
| FTI | Fellow, Textile Institute |
| FTII | Fellow, Institute of Taxation |
| FTP | Fellow, Thames Polytechnic |
| FTS | Fellow, Australian Academy of Technological Sciences and Engineering; Flying Training School; Fellow, Tourism Society |
| FUCUA | Federation of University Conservative and Unionist Associations (*now see* FCS) |
| FUMIST | Fellow, University of Manchester Institute of Science and Technology |
| FVRDE | Fighting Vehicles Reearch and Development Establshment |
| FWA | Fellow, World Academy of Arts and Sciences |
| FWACP | Fellow, West African College of Physicians |
| FWeldI | Fellow, Welding Institute |
| FWSOM | Fellow, Institute of Practitioners in Work Study, Organisation and Method (*now see* FMS) |
| FZS | Fellow, Zoological Society |
| FZSScot | Fellow, Zoological Society of Scotland (*now see* FRZSScot) |

# G

| | |
|---|---|
| GA | Geologists' Association; Gaelic Athletic (Club) |
| Ga | Georgia (US) |
| GAI | Guild of Architectural Ironmongers |
| GAP | Gap Activity Projects |
| GAPAN | Guild of Air Pilots and Air Navigators |
| GATT | General Agreement on Tariffs and Trade |
| GB | Great Britain |
| GBA | Governing Bodies Association |
| GBE | Knight or Dame Grand Cross, Order of the British Empire |
| GBGSA | Governing Bodies of Girls' Schools Association (*formerly* Association of Governing Bodies of Girls' Public Schools) |
| GBSM | Graduate of Birmingham and Midland Institute School of Music |
| GC | George Cross |
| GCB | Knight or Dame Grand Cross, Order of the Bath |
| GCBS | General Council of British Shipping |
| GCFR | Grand Commander, Order of the Federal Republic of Nigeria |
| GCH | Knight Grand Cross, Hanoverian Order |
| GCHQ | Government Communications Headquarters |
| GCIE | Knight Grand Commander, Order of the Indian Empire |
| GCLJ | Grand Cross, St Lazarus of Jerusalem |
| GCLM | Grand Commander, Order of the Legion of Merit of Rhodesia |
| GCM | Gold Crown of Merit (Barbados) |
| GCMG | Knight or Dame Grand Cross, Order of St Michael and St George |
| GCON | Grand Cross, Order of the Niger |
| GCSE | General Certificate of Secondary Education |
| GCSG | Knight Grand Cross, Order of St Gregory the Great |
| GCSI | Knight Grand Commander, Order of the Star of India |
| GCSJ | Knight Grand Cross of Justice, Order of St John of Jerusalem (Knights Hospitaller) |
| GCSL | Grand Cross, Order of St Lucia |
| GCStJ | Bailiff or Dame Grand Cross, Most Venerable Order of the Hospital of St John of Jerusalem |
| GCVO | Knight or Dame Grand Cross, Royal Victorian Order |
| g d | grand-daughter |
| GDBA | Guide Dogs for the Blind Association |
| GDC | General Dental Council |
| Gdns | Gardens |
| GDR | German Democratic Republic |

| | |
|---|---|
| Gen. | General |
| Ges. | Gesellschaft |
| GFD | Geophysical Fluid Dynamics |
| GFS | Girls' Friendly Society |
| g g d | great-grand-daughter |
| g g s | great-grandson |
| GGSM | Graduate in Music, Guildhall School of Music and Drama |
| GHQ | General Headquarters |
| Gib. | Gibraltar . |
| GIMechE | Graduate Institution of Mechanical Engineers |
| GL | Grand Lodge |
| GLAA | Greater London Arts Association (*now see* GLAB) |
| GLAB | Greater London Arts Board |
| GLC | Greater London Council |
| Glos | Gloucestershire |
| GM | George Medal; Grand Medal (Ghana) |
| GMB | (Union for) General, Municipal, Boilermakers |
| GMBATU | General, Municipal, Boilermakers and Allied Trades Union (*now see* GMB) |
| GmbH | Gesellschaft mit beschränkter Haftung |
| GMC | General Medical Council; Guild of Memorial Craftsmen |
| GMIE | Grand Master, Order of the Indian Empire |
| GMSI | Grand Master, Order of the Star of India |
| GMWU | General and Municipal Workers' Union (later GMBATU; *now see* GMB) |
| GNC | General Nursing Council |
| GOC | General Officer Commanding |
| GOC-in-C | General Officer Commanding-in-Chief |
| GOE | General Ordination Examination |
| Gov. | Governor |
| Govt | Government |
| GP | General Practitioner; Grand Prix |
| GPDST | Girls' Public Day School Trust |
| GPO | General Post Office |
| GQG | Grand Quartier Général |
| Gr. | Greek |
| GRSM | Graduate of the Royal Schools of Music |
| GS | General Staff; Grammar School |
| g s | grandson |
| GSA | Girls' Schools Association |
| GSM | General Service Medal; (Member of) Guildhall School of Music and Drama |
| GSMD | Guildhall School of Music and Drama |
| GSO | General Staff Officer |
| GTCL | Graduate, Trinity College of Music |
| GTS | General Theological Seminary (New York) |
| GUI | Golfing Union of Ireland |
| GWR | Great Western Railway |

# H

| | |
|---|---|
| HA | Historical Association; Health Authority |
| HAA | Heavy Anti-Aircraft |
| HAC | Honourable Artillery Company |
| Hants | Hampshire |
| HARCVS | Honorary Associate, Royal College of Veterinary Surgeons |
| Harv. | Harvard |
| HBM | His (or Her) Britannic Majesty (Majesty's); Humming Bird Gold Medal (Trinidad) |
| hc | *honoris causa* |
| HCEG | Honourable Company of Edinburgh Golfers |
| HCF | Honorary Chaplain to the Forces |
| HCIMA | Hotel, Catering and Institutional Management Association |
| HCSC | Higher Command and Staff Course |
| HDA | Hawkesbury Diploma in Agriculture (Australia) |
| HDD | Higher Dental Diploma |
| HDipEd | Higher Diploma in Education |
| HE | His (or Her) Excellency; His Eminence |
| HEC | Ecole des Hautes Etudes Commerciales; Higher Education Corporation |
| HEH | His (or Her) Exalted Highness |
| HEIC | Honourable East India Company |
| HEICS | Honourable East India Company's Service |
| Heir-pres. | Heir-presumptive |
| Herts | Hertfordshire |
| HFARA | Honorary Foreign Associate of the Royal Academy |
| HFRA | Honorary Foreign Member of the Royal Academy |
| HG | Home Guard |
| HGTAC | Home Grown Timber Advisory Committee |
| HH | His (or Her) Highness; His Holiness; Member, Hesketh Hubbard Art Society |
| HHA | Historic Houses Association |
| HHD | Doctor of Humanities (US) |
| HIH | His (or Her) Imperial Highness |
| HIM | His (or Her) Imperial Majesty |
| HJ | Hilal-e-Jurat (Pakistan) |
| HKIA | Hong Kong Institute of Architects |
| HKIPM | Hong Kong Institute of Personnel Management |
| HLD | Doctor of Humane Letters |
| HLI | Highland Light Infantry |

| | |
|---|---|
| HM | His (or Her) Majesty, or Majesty's |
| HMA | Head Masters' Association |
| HMAS | His (or Her) Majesty's Australian Ship |
| HMC | Headmasters' Conference; Hospital Management Committee |
| HMCIC | His (or Her) Majesty's Chief Inspector of Constabulary |
| HMCS | His (or Her) Majesty's Canadian Ship |
| HMHS | His (or Her) Majesty's Hospital Ship |
| HMI | His (or Her) Majesty's Inspector |
| HMIED | Honorary Member, Institute of Engineering Designers |
| HMOCS | His (or Her) Majesty's Overseas Civil Service |
| HMS | His (or Her) Majesty's Ship |
| HMSO | His (or Her) Majesty's Stationery Office |
| HNC | Higher National Certificate |
| HND | Higher National Diploma |
| H of C | House of Commons |
| H of L | House of Lords |
| Hon. | Honourable; Honorary |
| HPk | Hilal-e-Pakistan |
| HQ | Headquarters |
| HQA | Hilal-i-Quaid-i-Azam (Pakistan) |
| (HR) | Home Rule |
| HRCA | Honorary Royal Cambrian Academician |
| HRGI | Honorary Member, The Royal Glasgow Institute of the Fine Arts |
| HRH | His (or Her) Royal Highness |
| HRHA | Honorary Member, Royal Hibernian Academy |
| HRI | Honorary Member, Royal Institute of Painters in Water Colours |
| HROI | Honorary Member, Royal Institute of Oil Painters |
| HRSA | Honorary Member, Royal Scottish Academy |
| HRSW | Honorary Member, Royal Scottish Water Colour Society |
| HSC | Health and Safety Commission |
| HSE | Health and Safety Executive |
| HSH | His (or Her) Serene Highness |
| Hum. | Humanity, Humanities (Classics) |
| Hunts | Huntingdonshire |
| HVCert | Health Visitor's Certificate |
| Hy | Heavy |

# I

| | |
|---|---|
| I | Island; Ireland |
| Ia | Iowa (US) |
| IA | Indian Army |
| IAAF | International Amateur Athletic Federation |
| IAC | Indian Armoured Corps; Institute of Amateur Cinematographers |
| IACP | International Association of Chiefs of Police |
| IADR | International Association for Dental Research |
| IAEA | International Atomic Energy Agency |
| IAF | Indian Air Force; Indian Auxiliary Force |
| IAHM | Incorporated Association of Headmasters |
| IAM | Institute of Advanced Motorists; Institute of Aviation Medicine |
| IAMC | Indian Army Medical Corps |
| IAMTACT | Institute of Advanced Machine Tool and Control Technology |
| IAO | Incorporated Association of Organists |
| IAOC | Indian Army Ordnance Corps |
| IAPS | Incorporated Association of Preparatory Schools |
| IAPSO | International Association for the Physical Sciences of the Oceans |
| IARO | Indian Army Reserve of Officers |
| IAS | Indian Administrative Service; Institute of Advanced Studies |
| IASS | International Association for Scandinavian Studies |
| IATA | International Air Transport Association |
| IATUL | International Association of Technological University Libraries |
| IAU | International Astronomical Union |
| IAWPRC | International Association on Water Pollution Research and Control |
| ib. or ibid. | ibidem (in the same place) |
| IBA | Independent Broadcasting Authority; International Bar Association |
| IBG | Institute of British Geographers |
| IBRD | International Bank for Reconstruction and Development (World Bank) |
| IBRO | International Bank Research Organisation; International Brain Research Organisation |
| IBTE | Institution of British Telecommunications Engineers |
| i/c | in charge; in command |
| ICA | Institute of Contemporary Arts; Institute of Chartered Accountants in England and Wales |
| ICAA | Invalid Children's Aid Association |
| ICAI | Institute of Chartered Accountants in Ireland |
| ICAO | International Civil Aviation Organization |
| ICBP | International Council for Bird Preservation |
| ICBS | Irish Christian Brothers' School |

| | |
|---|---|
| ICC | International Chamber of Commerce |
| ICCROM | International Centre for Conservation at Rome |
| ICD | *Iuris Canonici Doctor;* Independence Commemorative Decoration (Rhodesia) |
| ICE | Institution of Civil Engineers |
| ICED | International Council for Educational Development |
| ICEF | International Federation of Chemical, Energy and General Workers' Unions |
| Icel. | Icelandic |
| ICES | International Council for the Exploration of the Sea |
| ICF | International Federation of Chemical and General Workers' Unions (*now see* ICEF) |
| ICFC | Industrial and Commercial Finance Corporation (later part of Investors in Industry) |
| ICFTU | International Confederation of Free Trade Unions |
| ICHCA | International Cargo Handling Co-ordination Association |
| IChemE | Institution of Chemical Engineers |
| ICI | Imperial Chemical Industries |
| ICL | International Computers Ltd |
| ICM | International Confederation of Midwives |
| ICMA | Institute of Cost and Management Accountants (*now see* CIMA) |
| ICME | International Commission for Mathematical Education |
| ICOM | International Council of Museums |
| ICOMOS | International Council of Monuments and Sites |
| ICorrST | Institution of Corrosion Science and Technology |
| ICPO | International Criminal Police Organization (Interpol) |
| ICRC | International Committee of the Red Cross |
| ICRF | Imperial Cancer Research Fund |
| ICS | Indian Civil Service |
| ICSA | Institute of Chartered Secretaries and Administrators |
| ICSID | International Council of Societies of Industrial Design; International Centre for Settlement of Investment Disputes |
| ICSS | International Committee for the Sociology of Sport |
| ICSU | International Council of Scientific Unions |
| ICT | International Computers and Tabulators Ltd (*now see* ICL) |
| Id | Idaho (US) |
| ID | Independence Decoration (Rhodesia) |
| IDA | International Development Association |
| IDB | Internal Drainage Board |
| IDC | Imperial Defence College (*now see* RCDS); Inter-Diocesan Certificate |
| idc | completed a course at, or served for a year on the Staff of, the Imperial Defence College (*now see* rcds) |
| IDRC | International Development Research Centre |
| IDS | Institute of Development Studies; Industry Department for Scotland |
| IEA | Institute of Economic Affairs |
| IEC | International Electrotechnical Commission |
| IEE | Institution of Electrical Engineers |
| IEEE | Institute of Electrical and Electronics Engineers (NY) |
| IEEIE | Institution of Electrical and Electronics Incorporated Engineers |
| IEETE | Institution of Electrical and Electronics Technician Engineers (*now see* IEEIE) |
| IEI | Institution of Engineers of Ireland |
| IEME | Inspectorate of Electrical and Mechanical Engineering |
| IEng | Incorporated Engineer |
| IERE | Institution of Electronic and Radio Engineers |
| IES | Indian Educational Service; Institution of Engineers and Shipbuilders in Scotland |
| IExpE | Institute of Explosives Engineers |
| IFAC | International Federation of Automatic Control |
| IFAD | International Fund for Agricultural Development (UNO) |
| IFAW | International Fund for Animal Welfare |
| IFC | International Finance Corporation |
| IFIAS | International Federation of Institutes of Advanced Study |
| IFIP | International Federation for Information Processing |
| IFL | International Friendship League |
| IFLA | International Federation of Library Associations |
| IFORS | International Federation of Operational Research Societies |
| IFPI | International Federation of the Phonographic Industry |
| IFS | Irish Free State; Indian Forest Service |
| IG | Instructor in Gunnery |
| IGasE | Institution of Gas Engineers |
| IGPP | Institute of Geophysics and Planetary Physics |
| IGS | Independent Grammar School |
| IGU | International Geographical Union; International Gas Union |
| IHA | Institute of Health Service Administrators |
| IHospE | Institute of Hospital Engineering |
| IHVE | Institution of Heating and Ventilating Engineers (*now see* CIBS) |
| IIM | Institution of Industrial Managers |
| IIMT | International Institute for the Management of Technology |
| IInfSc | Institute of Information Scientists |
| IIS | International Institute of Sociology |
| IISS | International Institute of Strategic Studies |
| IIT | Indian Institute of Technology |
| ILA | International Law Association |
| ILEA | Inner London Education Authority |
| ILEC | Inner London Education Committee |

| | |
|---|---|
| Ill | Illinois (US) |
| ILO | International Labour Office; International Labour Organisation |
| ILP | Independent Labour Party |
| ILR | Independent Local Radio; International Labour Review |
| IM | Individual Merit |
| IMA | International Music Association; Institute of Mathematics and its Applications |
| IMCB | International Management Centre from Buckingham |
| IMCO | Inter-Governmental Maritime Consultative Organization (*now see* IMO) |
| IMEA | Incorporated Municipal Electrical Association |
| IMechE | Institution of Mechanical Engineers |
| IMEDE | Institut pour l'Etude des Méthodes de Direction de l'Entreprise |
| IMF | International Monetary Fund |
| IMGTechE | Institution of Mechanical and General Technician Engineers |
| IMinE | Institution of Mining Engineers |
| IMM | Institution of Mining and Metallurgy |
| IMMLEP | Immunology of Leprosy |
| IMMTS | Indian Mercantile Marine Training Ship |
| IMO | International Maritime Organization |
| Imp. | Imperial |
| IMRO | Investment Management Regulatory Organisation |
| IMS | Indian Medical Service; Institute of Management Services; International Military Staff |
| IMTA | Institute of Municipal Treasurers and Accountants (*now see* CIPFA) |
| IMU | International Mathematical Union |
| IMunE | Institution of Municipal Engineers (now amalgamated with Institution of Civil Engineers) |
| IN | Indian Navy |
| Inc. | Incorporated |
| INCA | International Newspaper Colour Association |
| Incog. | Incognito |
| Ind. | Independent; Indiana (US) |
| Inf. | Infantry |
| INSA | Indian National Science Academy |
| INSEA | International Society for Education through Art |
| INSEAD or Insead | Institut Européen d'Administration des Affaires |
| Insp. | Inspector |
| Inst. | Institute |
| InstBE | Institution of British Engineers |
| Instn | Institution |
| InstSMM | Institute of Sales and Marketing Management |
| InstT | Institute of Transport |
| INTELSAT | International Telecommunications Satellite Organisation |
| IOB | Institute of Building (*now see* CIOB) |
| IOC | International Olympic Committee |
| IOCD | International Organisation for Chemical Science in Development |
| IODE | Imperial Order of the Daughters of the Empire |
| I of M | Isle of Man |
| IOGT | International Order of Good Templars |
| IOM | Isle of Man; Indian Order of Merit |
| IOOF | Independent Order of Odd-fellows |
| IOP | Institute of Painters in Oil Colours |
| IoW | Isle of Wight |
| IPA | International Publishers' Association |
| IPCS | Institution of Professional Civil Servants |
| IPFA | Member or Associate, Chartered Institute of Public Finance and Accountancy |
| IPHE | Institution of Public Health Engineers (*now see* IWEM) |
| IPI | International Press Institute; Institute of Patentees and Inventors |
| IPlantE | Institution of Plant Engineers (*now see* IIM) |
| IPM | Institute of Personnel Management |
| IPPA | Independent Programme Producers' Association |
| IPPF | International Planned Parenthood Federation |
| IPPS | Institute of Physics and The Physical Society |
| IProdE | Institution of Production Engineers |
| IPS | Indian Police Service; Indian Political Service; Institute of Purchasing and Supply |
| IPU | Inter-Parliamentary Union |
| IRA | Irish Republican Army |
| IRAD | Institute for Research on Animal Diseases |
| IRC | Industrial Reorganization Corporation; Interdisciplinary Research Centre |
| IRCAM | Institute for Research and Co-ordination in Acoustics and Music |
| IRCert | Industrial Relations Certificate |
| IREE(Aust) | Institution of Radio and Electronics Engineers (Australia) |
| IRI | Institution of the Rubber Industry (*now see* PRI) |
| IRO | International Refugee Organization |
| IRPA | International Radiation Protection Association |
| IRRV | (Fellow/Member of) Institute of Revenues, Rating and Valuation |
| IRTE | Institute of Road Transport Engineers |
| IS | International Society of Sculptors, Painters and Gravers |
| Is | Island(s) |
| ISBA | Incorporated Society of British Advertisers |

| | |
|---|---|
| ISC | Imperial Service College, Haileybury; Indian Staff Corps |
| ISCM | International Society for Contemporary Music |
| ISCO | Independent Schools Careers Organisation |
| ISE | Indian Service of Engineers |
| ISI | International Statistical Institute |
| ISIS | Independent Schools Information Service |
| ISJC | Independent Schools Joint Council |
| ISM | Incorporated Society of Musicians |
| ISME | International Society for Musical Education |
| ISMRC | Inter-Services Metallurgical Research Council |
| ISO | Imperial Service Order; International Organization for Standardization |
| ISSTIP | International Society for Study of Tension in Performance |
| ISTC | Iron and Steel Trades Confederation; Institute of Scientific and Technical Communicators |
| ISTD | Imperial Society of Teachers of Dancing |
| IStructE | Institution of Structural Engineers |
| IT | Information Technology; Indian Territory (US) |
| ITA | Independent Television Authority (*now see* IBA) |
| Ital. or It. | Italian |
| ITB | Industry Training Board |
| ITC | International Trade Centre; Independent Television Commission |
| ITCA | Independent Television Companies Association Ltd (*now* Independent Television Association) |
| ITDG | Intermediate Technology Development Group |
| ITEME | Institution of Technician Engineers in Mechanical Engineering |
| ITF | International Transport Workers' Federation |
| ITN | Independent Television News |
| ITO | International Trade Organization |
| ITU | International Telecommunication Union |
| ITV | Independent Television |
| IUA | International Union of Architects |
| IUB | International Union of Biochemistry |
| IUC | Inter-University Council for Higher Education Overseas (*now see* IUPC) |
| IUCN | International Union for the Conservation of Nature and Natural Resources |
| IUCW | International Union for Child Welfare |
| IUGS | International Union of Geological Sciences |
| IUHPS | International Union of the History and Philosophy of Science |
| IULA | International Union of Local Authorities |
| IUP | Association of Independent Unionist Peers |
| IUPAC | International Union of Pure and Applied Chemistry |
| IUPAP | International Union of Pure and Applied Physics |
| IUPC | Inter-University and Polytechnic Council for Higher Education Overseas |
| IUPS | International Union of Physiological Sciences |
| IUTAM | International Union of Theoretical and Applied Mechanics |
| IVF | In-vitro Fertilisation |
| IVS | International Voluntary Service |
| IWA | Inland Waterways Association |
| IWEM | Institution of Water and Environmental Management |
| IWES | Institution of Water Engineers and Scientists (*now see* IWEM) |
| IWGC | Imperial War Graves Commission (*now see* CWGC) |
| IWM | Institution of Works Managers (*now see* IIM) |
| IWPC | Institute of Water Pollution Control (*now see* IWEM) |
| IWSOM | Institute of Practitioners in Work Study Organisation and Methods (*now see* IMS) |
| IWSP | Institute of Work Study Practitioners (*now see* IMS) |
| IY | Imperial Yeomanry |
| IYRU | International Yacht Racing Union |
| IZ | I Zingari |

# J

| | |
|---|---|
| JA | Judge Advocate |
| JACT | Joint Association of Classical Teachers |
| JAG | Judge Advocate General |
| Jas | James |
| JCB | *Juris Canonici* (or *Civilis*) *Baccalaureus* (Bachelor of Canon (or Civil) Law) |
| JCS | Journal of the Chemical Society |
| JCD | *Juris Canonici* (or *Civilis*) *Doctor* (Doctor of Canon (or Civil) Law) |
| JCI | Junior Chamber International |
| JCL | *Juris Canonici* (or *Civilis*) *Licentiatus* (Licentiate in Canon (or Civil) Law) |
| JCO | Joint Consultative Organisation (of AFRC, MAFF, and Department of Agriculture and Fisheries for Scotland) |
| JD | Doctor of Jurisprudence |
| JDipMA | Joint Diploma in Management Accounting Services |
| JG | Junior Grade |
| JInstE | Junior Institution of Engineers (*now see* IMGTechE) |
| jl(s) | journal(s) |
| JMB | Joint Matriculation Board |
| JMN | Johan Mangku Negara (Malaysia) |
| Joh. or Jno. | John |

| | |
|---|---|
| **JP** | Justice of the Peace |
| **Jr** | Junior |
| **jsc** | qualified at a Junior Staff Course, or the equivalent, 1942–46 |
| **JSD** | Doctor of Juristic Science |
| **JSDC** | Joint Service Defence College |
| **jsdc** | completed a course at Joint Service Defence College |
| **JSLS** | Joint Services Liaison Staff |
| **JSM** | Johan Setia Mahkota (Malaysia) |
| **JSPS** | Japan Society for the Promotion of Science |
| **JSSC** | Joint Services Staff College |
| **jssc** | completed a course at Joint Services Staff College |
| **jt, jtly** | joint, jointly |
| **JUD** | *Juris Utriusque Doctor*, Doctor of Both Laws (Canon and Civil) |
| **Jun.** | Junior |
| **Jun.Opt.** | Junior Optime |
| **JWS** or **jws** | Joint Warfare Staff |

# K

| | |
|---|---|
| **KA** | Knight of St Andrew, Order of Barbados |
| **Kans** | Kansas (US) |
| **KAR** | King's African Rifles |
| **KBE** | Knight Commander, Order of the British Empire |
| **KC** | King's Counsel |
| **KCB** | Knight Commander, Order of the Bath |
| **KCC** | Commander of Order of Crown, Belgium and Congo Free State |
| **KCH** | King's College Hospital; Knight Commander, Hanoverian Order |
| **KCHS** | Knight Commander, Order of the Holy Sepulchre |
| **KCIE** | Knight Commander, Order of the Indian Empire |
| **KCL** | King's College London |
| **KCLJ** | Knight Commander, Order of St Lazarus of Jerusalem |
| **KCMG** | Knight Commander, Order of St Michael and St George |
| **KCSA** | Knight Commander, Military Order of the Collar of St Agatha of Paterna |
| **KCSG** | Knight Commander, Order of St Gregory the Great |
| **KCSI** | Knight Commander, Order of the Star of India |
| **KCSJ** | Knight Commander, Order of St John of Jerusalem (Knights Hospitaller) |
| **KCSS** | Knight Commander, Order of St Silvester |
| **KCVO** | Knight Commander, Royal Victorian Order |
| **KCVSA** | King's Commendation for Valuable Services in the Air |
| **KDG** | King's Dragoon Guards |
| **KEH** | King Edward's Horse |
| **KEO** | King Edward's Own |
| **KG** | Knight, Order of the Garter |
| **KGStJ** | Knight of Grace, Order of St John of Jerusalem (*now see* KStJ) |
| **KH** | Knight, Hanoverian Order |
| **KHC** | Hon. Chaplain to the King |
| **KHDS** | Hon. Dental Surgeon to the King |
| **KHNS** | Hon. Nursing Sister to the King |
| **KHP** | Hon. Physician to the King |
| **KHS** | Hon. Surgeon to the King; Knight, Order of the Holy Sepulchre |
| **K-i-H** | Kaisar-i-Hind |
| **KJStJ** | Knight of Justice, Order of St John of Jerusalem (*now see* KStJ) |
| **KLJ** | Knight, Order of St Lazarus of Jerusalem |
| **KM** | Knight of Malta |
| **KORR** | King's Own Royal Regiment |
| **KOSB** | King's Own Scottish Borderers |
| **KOYLI** | King's Own Yorkshire Light Infantry |
| **KP** | Knight, Order of St Patrick |
| **KPM** | King's Police Medal |
| **KRRC** | King's Royal Rifle Corps |
| **KS** | King's Scholar |
| **KSC** | Knight of St Columba |
| **KSG** | Knight, Order of St Gregory the Great |
| **KSJ** | Knight, Order of St John of Jerusalem (Knights Hospitaller) |
| **KSLI** | King's Shropshire Light Infantry |
| **KSS** | Knight, Order of St Silvester |
| **KStJ** | Knight, Most Venerable Order of the Hospital of St John of Jerusalem |
| **KStJ(A)** | Associate Knight of Justice, Most Venerable Order of the Hospital of St John of Jerusalem |
| **KT** | Knight, Order of the Thistle |
| **Kt** | Knight |
| **Ky** | Kentucky (US) |

# L

| | |
|---|---|
| **(L)** | Liberal |
| **LA** | Los Angeles; Library Association; Literate in Arts; Liverpool Academy |
| **La** | Louisiana (US) |
| **LAA** | Light Anti-Aircraft |
| **(Lab)** | Labour |
| **LAC** | London Athletic Club |
| **LACSAB** | Local Authorities Conditions of Service Advisory Board |
| **LAMDA** | London Academy of Music and Dramatic Art |
| **LAMSAC** | Local Authorities' Management Services and Computer Committee |
| **LAMTPI** | Legal Associate Member, Town Planning Institute (*now see* LMRTPI) |
| **L-Corp.** or **Lance-Corp.** | Lance-Corporal |
| **Lancs** | Lancashire |
| **LARSP** | Language Assessment, Remediation and Screening Procedure |
| **Lautro** | Life Assurance and Unit Trust Regulatory Organisation |
| **LBC** | London Broadcasting Company |
| **LC** | Cross of Leo |
| **LCAD** | London Certificate in Art and Design (University of London) |
| **LCC** | London County Council (later GLC) |
| **LCh** | Licentiate in Surgery |
| **LCJ** | Lord Chief Justice |
| **LCL** | Licentiate of Canon Law |
| **LCP** | Licentiate, College of Preceptors |
| **LCSP** | London and Counties Society of Physiologists |
| **LCST** | Licentiate, College of Speech Therapists |
| **LD** | Liberal and Democratic; Licentiate in Divinity |
| **LDDC** | London Docklands Development Corporation |
| **LDiv** | Licentiate in Divinity |
| **LDS** | Licentiate in Dental Surgery |
| **LDV** | Local Defence Volunteers |
| **LEA** | Local Education Authority |
| **LEPRA** | British Leprosy Relief Association |
| **LèsL** | Licencié ès lettres |
| **LG** | Lady Companion, Order of the Garter |
| **LGSM** | Licentiate, Guildhall School of Music and Drama |
| **LGTB** | Local Government Training Board |
| **LH** | Light Horse |
| **LHD** | *Literarum Humaniorum Doctor* (Doctor of Literature) |
| **LHSM** | Licentiate, Institute of Health Services Management |
| **LI** | Light Infantry; Long Island |
| **LIBA** | Lloyd's Insurance Brokers' Association |
| **Lib Dem** | Liberal Democrat |
| **LIBER** | Ligue des Bibliothèques Européennes de Recherche |
| **LicMed** | Licentiate in Medicine |
| **Lieut** | Lieutenant |
| **LIFFE** | London International Financial Futures Exchange |
| **Lincs** | Lincolnshire |
| **LIOB** | Licentiate, Institute of Building |
| **Lit.** | Literature; Literary |
| **LitD** | Doctor of Literature; Doctor of Letters |
| **Lit.Hum.** | *Literae Humaniores* (Classics) |
| **LittD** | Doctor of Literature; Doctor of Letters |
| **LJ** | Lord Justice |
| **LLA** | Lady Literate in Arts |
| **LLB** | Bachelor of Laws |
| **LLCM** | Licentiate, London College of Music |
| **LLD** | Doctor of Laws |
| **LLL** | Licentiate in Laws |
| **LLM** | Master of Laws |
| **LM** | Licentiate in Midwifery |
| **LMBC** | Lady Margaret Boat Club |
| **LMC** | Local Medical Committee |
| **LMCC** | Licentiate, Medical Council of Canada |
| **LMed** | Licentiate in Medicine |
| **LMH** | Lady Margaret Hall, Oxford |
| **LMR** | London Midland Region (BR) |
| **LMS** | London, Midland and Scottish Railway; London Missionary Society |
| **LMSSA** | Licentiate in Medicine and Surgery, Society of Apothecaries |
| **LMRTPI** | Legal Member, Royal Town Planning Institute |
| **(LNat)** | Liberal National |
| **LNER** | London and North Eastern Railway |
| **LOB** | Location of Offices Bureau |
| **L of C** | Library of Congress; Lines of Communication |
| **LP** | Limited Partnership |
| **LPH** | Licentiate in Philosophy |
| **LPO** | London Philharmonic Orchestra |
| **LPTB** | London Passenger Transport Board (later LTE; *now see* LRT) |
| **LRAD** | Licentiate, Royal Academy of Dancing |
| **LRAM** | Licentiate, Royal Academy of Music |
| **LRCP** | Licentiate, Royal College of Physicians, London |
| **LRCPE** | Licentiate, Royal College of Physicians, Edinburgh |
| **LRCPI** | Licentiate, Royal College of Physicians of Ireland |
| **LRCPSGlas** | Licentiate, Royal College of Physicians and Surgeons of Glasgow |
| **LRCS** | Licentiate, Royal College of Surgeons of England |
| **LRCSE** | Licentiate, Royal College of Surgeons, Edinburgh |
| **LRCSI** | Licentiate, Royal College of Surgeons in Ireland |
| **LRFPS(G)** | Licentiate, Royal Faculty of Physicians and Surgeons, Glasgow (*now see* LRCPSGlas) |
| **LRIBA** | Licentiate, Royal Institute of British Architects (*now see* RIBA) |

| | |
|---|---|
| LRPS | Licentiate, Royal Photographic Society |
| LRT | London Regional Transport |
| LSA | Licentiate, Society of Apothecaries; Licence in Agricultural Sciences |
| LSE | London School of Economics and Political Science |
| LSHTM | London School of Hygiene and Tropical Medicine |
| LSO | London Symphony Orchestra |
| Lt | Lieutenant; Light |
| LT | London Transport (now see LRT); Licentiate in Teaching |
| LTA | Lawn Tennis Association |
| LTB | London Transport Board (later LTE; now see LRT) |
| LTCL | Licentiate of Trinity College of Music, London |
| Lt-Col | Lieutenant-Colonel |
| LTE | London Transport Executive (now see LRT) |
| Lt-Gen. | Lieutenant-General |
| LTh | Licentiate in Theology |
| (LU) | Liberal Unionist |
| LUOTC | London University Officers' Training Corps |
| LVO | Lieutenant, Royal Victorian Order (formerly MVO (Fourth Class)) |
| LWT | London Weekend Television |
| LXX | Septuagint |

# M

| | |
|---|---|
| M | Marquess; Member; Monsieur |
| m | married |
| MA | Master of Arts; Military Assistant |
| MAA | Manufacturers' Agents Association of Great Britain |
| MAAF | Mediterranean Allied Air Forces |
| MAAT | Member, Association of Accounting Technicians |
| MACE | Member, Australian College of Education; Member, Association of Conference Executives |
| MACI | Member, American Concrete Institute |
| MACM | Member, Association of Computing Machines |
| MACS | Member, American Chemical Society |
| MADO | Member, Association of Dispensing Opticians |
| MAEE | Marine Aircraft Experimental Establishment |
| MAF | Ministry of Agriculture and Fisheries |
| MAFF | Ministry of Agriculture, Fisheries and Food |
| MAI | Magister in Arte Ingeniaria (Master of Engineering) |
| MAIAA | Member, American Institute of Aeronautics and Astronautics |
| MAICE | Member, American Institute of Consulting Engineers |
| MAIChE | Member, American Institute of Chemical Engineers |
| Maj.-Gen. | Major-General |
| Man | Manitoba (Canada) |
| MAO | Master of Obstetric Art |
| MAOT | Member, Association of Occupational Therapists |
| MAOU | Member, American Ornithologists' Union |
| MAP | Ministry of Aircraft Production |
| MAPsS | Member, Australian Psychological Society |
| MARAC | Member, Australasian Register of Agricultural Consultants |
| MArch | Master of Architecture |
| Marq. | Marquess |
| MASAE | Member, American Society of Agricultural Engineers |
| MASC | Member, Australian Society of Calligraphers |
| MASCE | Member, American Society of Civil Engineers |
| MASME | Member, American Society of Mechanical Engineers |
| Mass | Massachusetts (US) |
| MATh | Master of Arts in Theology |
| Math. | Mathematics; Mathematical |
| MATSA | Managerial Administrative Technical Staff Association |
| MAusIMM | Member, Australasian Institute of Mining and Metallurgy |
| MB | Medal of Bravery (Canada); Bachelor of Medicine |
| MBA | Master of Business Administration |
| MBASW | Member, British Association of Social Workers |
| MBC | Metropolitan/Municipal Borough Council |
| MBCS | Member, British Computer Society |
| MBE | Member, Order of the British Empire |
| MBFR | Mutual and Balanced Force Reductions (negotiations) |
| MBHI | Member, British Horological Institute |
| MBIFD | Member, British Institute of Funeral Directors |
| MBIM | Member, British Institute of Management (now see FBIM) |
| MBKS | Member, British Kinematograph Society (now see MBKSTS) |
| MBKSTS | Member, British Kinematograph, Sound and Television Society |
| MBOU | Member, British Ornithologists' Union |
| MBPICS | Member, British Production and Inventory Control Society |
| MBPS | Member, British Computer Society |
| MBritRE | Member, British Institution of Radio Engineers (later MIERE; now see MIEE) |
| MBS | Member, Building Societies Institute (now see MCBSI) |
| MBSc | Master of Business Science |
| MC | Military Cross; Missionaries of Charity |
| MCAM | Member, CAM Foundation |
| MCB | Master in Clinical Biochemistry |
| MCBSI | Member, Chartered Building Societies Institute |

| | |
|---|---|
| MCC | Marylebone Cricket Club; Metropolitan County Council |
| MCCD RCS | Member in Clinical Community Dentistry, Royal College of Surgeons |
| MCD | Master of Civic Design |
| MCE | Master of Civil Engineering |
| MCFP | Member, College of Family Physicians (Canada) |
| MCh or MChir | Master in Surgery |
| MChE | Master of Chemical Engineering |
| MChemA | Master in Chemical Analysis |
| MChOrth | Master of Orthopaedic Surgery |
| MCIBS | Member, Chartered Institution of Building Services (now see MCIBSE) |
| MCIBSE | Member, Chartered Institution of Building Services Engineers |
| MCIM | Member, Chartered Institute of Marketing |
| MCIOB | Member, Chartered Institute of Building |
| M.CIRP | Member, International Institution for Production Engineering Research |
| MCIS | Member, Institute of Chartered Secretaries and Administrators |
| MCIT | Member, Chartered Institute of Transport |
| MCL | Master in Civil Law |
| MCMES | Member, Civil and Mechanical Engineers' Society |
| MCom | Master of Commerce |
| MConsE | Member, Association of Consulting Engineers |
| MCOphth | Member, College of Ophthalmologists |
| MCP | Member of Colonial Parliament; Master of City Planning (US) |
| MCPA | Member, College of Pathologists of Australia (now see MRCPA) |
| MCPath | Member, College of Pathologists (now see MRCPath) |
| MCPP | Member, College of Pharmacy Practice |
| MCPS | Member, College of Physicians and Surgeons |
| MCS | Madras Civil Service; Malayan Civil Service |
| MCSEE | Member, Canadian Society of Electrical Engineers |
| MCSP | Member, Chartered Society of Physiotherapy |
| MCST | Member, College of Speech Therapists |
| MCT | Member, Association of Corporate Treasurers |
| MD | Doctor of Medicine; Military District |
| Md | Maryland (US) |
| MDC | Metropolitan District Council |
| MDes | Master of Design |
| MDS | Master of Dental Surgery |
| MDSc | Master of Dental Science |
| Me | Maine (US) |
| ME | Mining Engineer; Middle East; Master of Engineering |
| MEAF | Middle East Air Force |
| MEC | Member of Executive Council; Middle East Command |
| MEc | Master of Economics |
| MECAS | Middle East Centre for Arab Studies |
| Mech. | Mechanics; Mechanical |
| MECI | Member, Institute of Employment Consultants |
| Med. | Medical |
| MEd | Master of Education |
| MEF | Middle East Force |
| MEIC | Member, Engineering Institute of Canada |
| MELF | Middle East Land Forces |
| Mencap | Royal Society for Mentally Handicapped Children and Adults |
| MEng | Master of Engineering |
| MEO | Marine Engineering Officer |
| MEP | Member of the European Parliament |
| MetR | Metropolitan Railway |
| MetSoc | Metals Society (formed by amalgamation of Institute of Metals and Iron and Steel Institute; now merged with Institution of Metallurgists to form Institute of Metals) |
| MEXE | Military Engineering Experimental Establishment |
| MF | Master of Forestry |
| MFA | Master of Fine Arts |
| MFC | Mastership in Food Control |
| MFCM | Member, Faculty of Community Medicine |
| MFGB | Miners' Federation of Great Britain (now see NUM) |
| MFH | Master of Foxhounds |
| MFHom | Member, Faculty of Homœopathy |
| MFOM | Member, Faculty of Occupational Medicine |
| MGA | Major-General in charge of Administration |
| MGC | Machine Gun Corps |
| MGDS RCS | Member in General Dental Surgery, Royal College of Surgeons |
| MGGS | Major-General, General Staff |
| MGI | Member, Institute of Certificated Grocers |
| MGO | Master General of the Ordnance; Master of Gynaecology and Obstetrics |
| Mgr | Monsignor |
| MHA | Member of House of Assembly |
| MHCIMA | Member, Hotel Catering and Institutional Management Association |
| MHK | Member of the House of Keys |
| MHR | Member of the House of Representatives |
| MHRA | Modern Humanities Research Association |
| MHRF | Mental Health Research Fund |
| MI | Military Intelligence |
| MIAeE | Member, Institute of Aeronautical Engineers |
| MIAgrE | Member, Institution of Agricultural Engineers |

MIAM        Member, Institute of Administrative Management
MIAS        Member, Institute of Aeronautical Science (US) (now see MAIAA)
MIBF        Member, Institute of British Foundrymen
MIBritE     Member, Institution of British Engineers
MIB(Scot)   Member, Institute of Bankers in Scotland
MICE        Member, Institution of Civil Engineers
MICEI       Member, Institution of Civil Engineers of Ireland
MICFor      Member, Institute of Chartered Foresters
Mich        Michigan (US)
MIChemE     Member, Institution of Chemical Engineers
MICorrST    Member, Institution of Corrosion Science and Technology
MICS        Member, Institute of Chartered Shipbrokers
MIDPM       Member, Institute of Data Processing Management
MIE(Aust)   Member, Institution of Engineers, Australia
MIED        Member, Institution of Engineering Designers
MIEE        Member, Institution of Electrical Engineers
MIEEE       Member, Institute of Electrical and Electronics Engineers (NY)
MIEI        Member, Institution of Engineering Inspection
MIE(Ind)    Member, Institution of Engineers, India
MIERE       Member, Institution of Electronic and Radio Engineers (now see MIEE)
MIES        Member, Institution of Engineers and Shipbuilders, Scotland
MIEx        Member, Institute of Export
MIExpE      Member, Institute of Explosives Engineers
MIFA        Member, Institute of Field Archaeologists
MIFF        Member, Institute of Freight Forwarders
MIFireE     Member, Institution of Fire Engineers
MIFor       Member, Institute of Foresters (now see MICFor)
MIGasE      Member, Institution of Gas Engineers
MIGeol      Member, Institution of Geologists
MIH         Member, Institute of Housing
MIHM        Member, Institute of Housing Managers (now see MIH)
MIHort      Member, Institute of Horticulture
MIHT        Member, Institution of Highways and Transportation
MIHVE       Member, Institution of Heating and Ventilating Engineers (now see MCIBS)
MIIA        Member, Institute of Industrial Administration (now see FBIM)
MIIM        Member, Institution of Industrial Managers
MIInfSc     Member, Institute of Information Sciences
MIL         Member, Institute of Linguists
Mil.        Military
MILGA       Member, Institute of Local Government Administrators
MILocoE     Member, Institution of Locomotive Engineers
MIM         Member, Institute of Metals (formerly Institution of Metallurgists)
MIMarE      Member, Institute of Marine Engineers
MIMC        Member, Institute of Management Consultants
MIMechE     Member, Institution of Mechanical Engineers
MIMGTechE   Member, Institution of Mechanical and General Technician Engineers
MIMI        Member, Institute of the Motor Industry
MIMinE      Member, Institution of Mining Engineers
MIMM        Member, Institution of Mining and Metallurgy
MIMunE      Member, Institution of Municipal Engineers (now amalgamated with Institution of Civil Engineers)
Min.        Ministry
MIN         Member, Institute of Navigation (now see MRIN)
Minn        Minnesota (US)
MInstAM     Member, Institution of Administrative Management
MInstBE     Member, Institution of British Engineers
MInstCE     Member, Institution of Civil Engineers (now see FICE)
MInstD      Member, Institute of Directors
MInstE      Member, Institute of Energy
MInstEnvSci Member, Institute of Environmental Sciences
MInstF      Member, Institute of Fuel (now see MInstE)
MInstHE     Member, Institution of Highway Engineers (now see MIHT)
MInstM      Member, Institute of Marketing (now see MCIM)
MInstMC     Member, Institute of Measurement and Control
MInstME     Member, Institution of Mining Engineers
MInstMet    Member, Institute of Metals (later part of Metals Society, now see MIM)
MInstP      Member, Institute of Physics
MInstPet    Member, Institute of Petroleum
MInstPI     Member, Institute of Patentees and Inventors
MInstPkg    Member, Institute of Packaging
MInstPS     Member, Institute of Purchasing and Supply
MInstR      Member, Institute of Refrigeration
MInstRA     Member, Institute of Registered Architects
MInstT      Member, Institute of Transport
MInstTM     Member, Institute of Travel Managers in Industry and Commerce
MInstW      Member, Institute of Welding (now see MWeldI)
MInstWM     Member, Institute of Wastes Management
MINucE      Member, Institution of Nuclear Engineers
MIOB        Member, Institute of Building (now see MCIOB)
MIOM        Member, Institute of Office Management (now see MIAM)
MIOSH       Member, Institution of Occupational Safety and Health
MIPA        Member, Institute of Practitioners in Advertising

MIPlantE    Member, Institution of Plant Engineers (now see MIIM)
MIPM        Member, Institute of Personnel Management
MIPR        Member, Institute of Public Relations
MIProdE     Member, Institution of Production Engineers
MIQ         Member, Institute of Quarrying
MIRE        Member, Institution of Radio Engineers (now see MIERE)
MIREE(Aust) Member, Institution of Radio and Electronics Engineers (Australia)
MIRT        Member, Institute of Reprographic Technicians
MIRTE       Member, Institute of Road Transport Engineers
MIS         Member, Institute of Statisticians
MISI        Member, Iron and Steel Institute (later part of Metals Society)
MIS(India)  Member, Institution of Surveyors of India
Miss        Mississippi (US)
MIStructE   Member, Institution of Structural Engineers
MIT         Massachusetts Institute of Technology
MITA        Member, Industrial Transport Association
MITD        Member, Institute of Training and Development
MITE        Member, Institution of Electrical and Electronics Technician Engineers
MITT        Member, Institute of Travel and Tourism
MIWE        Member, Institution of Water Engineers (later MIWES; now see MIWEM)
MIWEM       Member, Institution of Water and Environmental Management
MIWES       Member, Institution of Water Engineers and Scientists (now see MIWEM)
MIWM        Member, Institution of Works Managers (now see MIIM)
MIWPC       Member, Institute of Water Pollution Control (now see MIWEM)
MIWSP       Member, Institute of Work Study Practitioners (now see MMS)
MJI         Member, Institute of Journalists
MJIE        Member, Junior Institution of Engineers (now see MIGTechE)
MJS         Member, Japan Society
MJur        Magister Juris
ML          Licentiate in Medicine; Master of Laws
MLA         Member of Legislative Assembly; Modern Language Association; Master in Landscape Architecture
MLC         Member of Legislative Council
MLCOM       Member, London College of Osteopathic Medicine
MLitt       Master of Letters
Mlle        Mademoiselle (Miss)
MLM         Member, Order of the Legion of Merit (Rhodesia)
MLO         Military Liaison Officer
MLR         Modern Language Review
MM          Military Medal
MMA         Metropolitan Museum of Art
MMB         Milk Marketing Board
MME         Master of Mining Engineering
Mme         Madame
MMechE      Master of Mechanical Engineering
MMet        Master of Metallurgy
MMGI        Member, Mining, Geological and Metallurgical Institute of India
MMin        Master of Ministry
MMM         Member, Order of Military Merit (Canada)
MMS         Member, Institute of Management Services
MMSA        Master of Midwifery, Society of Apothecaries
MN          Merchant Navy
MNAS        Member, National Academy of Sciences (US)
MNECInst    Member, North East Coast Institution of Engineers and Shipbuilders
MNI         Member, Nautical Institute
MNSE        Member, Nigerian Society of Engineers
MO          Medical Officer; Military Operations
Mo          Missouri (US)
MoD         Ministry of Defence
Mods        Moderations (Oxford)
MOF         Ministry of Food
MOH         Medical Officer(s) of Health
MOI         Ministry of Information
MOMI        Museum of the Moving Image
Mon         Monmouthshire
Mont        Montana (US); Montgomeryshire
MOP         Ministry of Power
MoS         Ministry of Supply
Most Rev.   Most Reverend
MoT         Ministry of Transport
MP          Member of Parliament
MPA         Master of Public Administration; Member, Parliamentary Assembly, Northern Ireland
MPBW        Ministry of Public Building and Works
MPH         Master of Public Health
MPIA        Master of Public and International Affairs
MPO         Management and Personnel Office
MPP         Member, Provincial Parliament
MPRISA      Member, Public Relations Institute of South Africa
MPS         Member, Pharmaceutical Society (now see MRPharmS)
MR          Master of the Rolls; Municipal Reform
MRAC        Member, Royal Agricultural College

MRACP    Member, Royal Australasian College of Physicians
MRACS    Member, Royal Australasian College of Surgeons
MRAeS    Member, Royal Aeronautical Society
MRAIC    Member, Royal Architectural Institute of Canada
MRAS    Member, Royal Asiatic Society
MRC    Medical Research Council
MRCA    Multi-Role Combat Aircraft
MRCGP    Member, Royal College of General Practitioners
MRC-LMB    Medical Research Council Laboratory of Molecular Biology
MRCOG    Member, Royal College of Obstetricians and Gynaecologists
MRCP    Member, Royal College of Physicians, London
MRCPA    Member, Royal College of Pathologists of Australia
MRCPE    Member, Royal College of Physicians, Edinburgh
MRCPGlas    Member, Royal College of Physicians and Surgeons of Glasgow
MRCPI    Member, Royal College of Physicians of Ireland
MRCPsych    Member, Royal College of Psychiatrists
MRCS    Member, Royal College of Surgeons of England
MRCSE    Member, Royal College of Surgeons of Edinburgh
MRCSI    Member, Royal College of Surgeons in Ireland
MRCVS    Member, Royal College of Veterinary Surgeons
MRE    Master of Religious Education
MRES or MREmpS    Member, Royal Empire Society
MRI    Member, Royal Institution
MRIA    Member, Royal Irish Academy
MRIAI    Member, Royal Institute of the Architects of Ireland
MRIC    Member, Royal Institute of Chemistry (*now see* MRSC)
MRIN    Member, Royal Institute of Navigation
MRINA    Member, Royal Institution of Naval Architects
MRPharmS    Member, Royal Pharmaceutical Society
MRSanI    Member, Royal Sanitary Institute (*now see* MRSH)
MRSC    Member, Royal Society of Chemistry
MRSH    Member, Royal Society for the Promotion of Health
MRSL    Member, Order of the Republic of Sierra Leone
MRSM or MRSocMed    Member, Royal Society of Medicine
MRST    Member, Royal Society of Teachers
MRTPI    Member, Royal Town Planning Institute
MRUSI    Member, Royal United Service Institution
MRVA    Member, Rating and Valuation Association
MS    Master of Surgery; Master of Science (US)
MS, MSS    Manuscript, Manuscripts
MSA    Master of Science, Agriculture (US); Mineralogical Society of America
MSAE    Member, Society of Automotive Engineers (US)
MSAICE    Member, South African Institution of Civil Engineers
MSAInstMM    Member, South African Institute of Mining and Metallurgy
MS&R    Merchant Shipbuilding and Repairs
MSAutE    Member, Society of Automobile Engineers
MSC    Manpower Services Commission; Missionaries of the Sacred Heart; Madras Staff Corps
MSc    Master of Science
MScD    Master of Dental Science
MSD    Meritorious Service Decoration (Fiji)
MSE    Master of Science in Engineering (US)
MSF    (Union for) Manufacturing, Science, Finance
MSH    Master of Stag Hounds
MSIAD    Member, Society of Industrial Artists and Designers
MSINZ    Member, Surveyors' Institute of New Zealand
MSIT    Member, Society of Instrument Technology (*now see* MInstMC)
MSM    Meritorious Service Medal; Madras Sappers and Miners
MSN    Master of Science in Nursing
MSocIS    Member, Société des Ingénieurs et Scientifiques de France
MSocSc    Master of Social Sciences
MSR    Member, Society of Radiographers
MSTD    Member, Society of Typographic Designers
Mt    Mount, Mountain
MT    Mechanical Transport
MTA    Music Trades Association
MTAI    Member, Institute of Travel Agents
MTB    Motor Torpedo Boat
MTCA    Ministry of Transport and Civil Aviation
MTD    Midwife Teachers' Diploma
MTEFL    Master in the Teaching of English as a Foreign or Second Language
MTh    Master of Theology
MTIRA    Machine Tool Industry Research Association (*now see* AMTRI)
MTPI    Member, Town Planning Institute (*now see* MRTPI)
MTS    Master of Theological Studies
MUniv    Master of the University
MusB    Bachelor of Music
MusD    Doctor of Music
MusM    Master of Music
MV    Merchant Vessel, Motor Vessel (naval)
MVEE    Military Vehicles and Engineering Establishment
MVO    Member, Royal Victorian Order
MVSc    Master of Veterinary Science
MW    Master of Wine
MWA    Mystery Writers of America

MWeldI    Member, Welding Institute
MWSOM    Member, Institute of Practitioners in Work Study Organisation and Methods (*now see* MMS)

# N

(N)    Nationalist; Navigating Duties
N    North
n    nephew
NA    National Academician (America)
NAACP    National Association for the Advancement of Colored People
NAAFI    Navy, Army and Air Force Institutes
NAAS    National Agricultural Advisory Service
NAB    National Advisory Body for Public Sector Higher Education
NABC    National Association of Boys' Clubs
NAC    National Agriculture Centre
NACCB    National Accreditation Council for Certification Bodies
NACRO    National Association for the Care and Resettlement of Offenders
NADFAS    National Association of Decorative and Fine Arts Societies
NAE    National Academy of Engineering
NAEW    Nato Airborn Early Warning
NAHA    National Association of Health Authorities (*now see* NAHAT)
NAHAT    National Association of Health Authorities and Trusts
NALGO or Nalgo    National and Local Government Officers' Association
NAMAS    National Measurement and Accreditation Service
NAMCW    National Association for Maternal and Child Welfare
NAMH    MIND (National Association for Mental Health)
NAMMA    NATO MRCA Management Agency
NAPT    National Association for the Prevention of Tuberculosis
NASA    National Aeronautics and Space Administration (US)
NASDIM    National Association of Security Dealers and Investment Managers (*now see* FIMBRA) National Association of Schoolmasters/Union of Women Teachers
NATCS    National Air Traffic Control Services (*now see* NATS)
NATFHE    National Association of Teachers in Further and Higher Education (combining ATCDE and ATTI)
NATLAS    National Testing Laboratory Accreditation Scheme
NATO    North Atlantic Treaty Organisation
NATS    National Air Traffic Services
Nat. Sci.    Natural Sciences
NATSOPA    National Society of Operative Printers, Graphical and Media Personnel (*formerly* of Operative Printers and Assistants)
NAYC    Youth Clubs UK (*formerly* National Association of Youth Clubs)
NB    New Brunswick
NBA    North British Academy
NBC    National Book Council (later NBL); National Broadcasting Company (US)
NBL    National Book League
NBPI    National Board for Prices and Incomes
NC    National Certificate; North Carolina (US)
NCA    National Certificate of Agriculture
NCARB    National Council of Architectural Registration Boards
NCB    National Coal Board
NCC    National Computing Centre; Nature Conservancy Council
NCCI    National Committee for Commonwealth Immigrants
NCCL    National Council for Civil Liberties
NCDAD    National Council for Diplomas in Art and Design
NCET    National Council for Educational Technology
NCLC    National Council of Labour Colleges
NCSE    National Council for Special Education
NCTA    National Community Television Association (US)
NCU    National Cyclists' Union
NCVCCO    National Council of Voluntary Child Care Organisations
NCVO    National Council for Voluntary Organisations
NCVQ    National Council for Vocational Qualifications
NDA    National Diploma in Agriculture
NDak    North Dakota (US)
ndc    National Defence College
NDD    National Diploma in Dairying; National Diploma in Design
NDH    National Diploma in Horticulture
NDIC    National Defence Industries Council
NDTA    National Defense Transportation Association (US)
NE    North-east
NEAC    New English Art Club
NEAF    Near East Air Force
NEARELF    Near East Land Forces
NEB    National Enterprise Board
Neb    Nebraska (US)
NEBSS    National Examinations Board for Supervisory Studies
NEC    National Executive Committee
NECCTA    National Educational Closed Circuit Television Association
NECInst    North East Coast Institution of Engineers and Shipbuilders

NEDC    National Economic Development Council; North East Development Council
NEDO    National Economic Development Office
NEH    National Endowment for the Humanities
NEL    National Engineering Laboratory
NERC    Natural Environment Research Council
Nev    Nevada (US)
New M    New Mexico (US)
NFC    National Freight Consortium (*formerly* Corporation, then Company)
NFER    National Foundation for Educational Research
NFMS    National Federation of Music Societies
NFS    National Fire Service
NFT    National Film Theatre
NFU    National Farmers' Union
NFWI    National Federation of Women's Institutes
NGO    Non-Governmental Organisation(s)
NGTE    National Gas Turbine Establishment
NH    New Hampshire (US)
NHBC    National House-Building Council
NHS    National Health Service
NI    Northern Ireland; Native Infantry
NIAB    National Institute of Agricultural Botany
NIACRO    Northern Ireland Association for the Care and Resettlement of Offenders
NIAE    National Institute of Agricultural Engineering
NIAID    National Institute of Allergy and Infectious Diseases
NICEC    National Institute for Careers Education and Counselling
NICG    Nationalised Industries Chairmen's Group
NICS    Northern Ireland Civil Service
NID    Naval Intelligence Division; National Institute for the Deaf; Northern Ireland District; National Institute of Design (India)
NIESR    National Institute of Economic and Social Research
NIH    National Institutes of Health (US)
NIHCA    Northern Ireland Hotels and Caterers Association
NII    Nuclear Installations Inspectorate
NILP    Northern Ireland Labour Party
NISTRO    Northern Ireland Science and Technology Regional Organisation
NJ    New Jersey (US)
NL    National Liberal; No Liability
NLCS    North London Collegiate School
NLF    National Liberal Federation
NLYL    National League of Young Liberals
NMR    Nuclear Magnetic Resonance
NNMA    Nigerian National Merit Award
NNOM    Nigerian National Order of Merit
Northants    Northamptonshire
NOTB    National Ophthalmic Treatment Board
Notts    Nottinghamshire
NP    Notary Public
NPA    Newspaper Publishers' Association
NPFA    National Playing Fields Association
NPk    Nishan-e-Pakistan
NPL    National Physical Laboratory
NRA    National Rifle Association; National Recovery Administration (US)
NRAO    National Radio Astronomy Observatory
NRCC    National Research Council of Canada
NRD    National Registered Designer
NRDC    National Research Development Corporation
NRPB    National Radiological Protection Board
NRR    Northern Rhodesia Regiment
NS    Nova Scotia; New Style in the Calendar (in Great Britain since 1752); National Society; National Service
ns    Graduate of Royal Naval Staff College, Greenwich
NSA    National Skating Association
NSAIV    Distinguished Order of Shaheed Ali (Maldives)
NSF    National Science Foundation (US)
NSM    Non-Stipendiary Minister
NSMHC    National Society for Mentally Handicapped Children (*now see* Mencap, RSMHCA)
NSPCC    National Society for Prevention of Cruelty to Children
NSRA    National Small-bore Rifle Association
N/SSF    Novice, Society of St Francis
NSTC    Nova Scotia Technical College
NSW    New South Wales
NT    New Testament; Northern Territory (Australia); National Theatre; National Trust
NT&SA    National Trust & Savings Association
NTDA    National Trade Development Association
NUAAW    National Union of Agricultural and Allied Workers
NUBE    National Union of Bank Employees (*now see* BIFU)
NUFLAT    National Union of Footwear Leather and Allied Trades
NUGMW    National Union of General and Municipal Workers (*now see* GMBATU)
NUHKW    National Union of Hosiery and Knitwear Workers
NUI    National University of Ireland
NUJ    National Union of Journalists
NUJMB    Northern Universities Joint Matriculation Board
NUM    National Union of Mineworkers

NUMAST    National Union of Marine, Aviation and Shipping Transport Officers
NUPE    National Union of Public Employees
NUR    National Union of Railwaymen
NUT    National Union of Teachers
NUTG    National Union of Townswomen's Guilds
NUTN    National Union of Trained Nurses
NUU    New University of Ulster
NW    North-west
NWFP    North-West Frontier Province
NWP    North-Western Province
NWT    North-Western Territories
NY    New York
NYC    New York City
NYO    National Youth Orchestra
NZ    New Zealand
NZEF    New Zealand Expeditionary Force
NZIA    New Zealand Institute of Architects

# O

O    Ohio (US)
o    only
OA    Officier d'Académie
O & E    Operations and Engineers (US)
O & M    organisation and method
O & O    Oriental and Occidental Steamship Co.
OAS    Organisation of American States; On Active Service
OAU    Organisation for African Unity
OB    Order of Barbados
ob    *obiit* (died)
OBE    Officer, Order of the British Empire
OBI    Order of British India
OC    Officer, Order of Canada (equivalent to former award SM)
o c    only child
OC or o/c    Officer Commanding
OCA    Old Comrades Association
OCDS or **ocds Can**    Overseas College of Defence Studies (Canada)
OCF    Officiating Chaplain to the Forces
OCSS    Oxford and Cambridge Shakespeare Society
OCTU    Officer Cadet Training Unit
OCU    Operational Conversion Unit
OD    Officer, Order of Distinction (Jamaica)
ODA    Overseas Development Administration
ODI    Overseas Development Institute
ODM    Ministry of Overseas Development
ODSM    Order of Diplomatic Service Merit (Lesotho)
OE    Order of Excellence (Guyana)
OEA    Overseas Education Association
OECD    Organization for Economic Co-operation and Development
OED    Oxford English Dictionary
OEEC    Organization for European Economic Co-operation (*now see* OECD)
OF    Order of the Founder, Salvation Army
OFEMA    Office Française d'Exportation de Matériel Aéronautique
OFM    Order of Friars Minor (Franciscans)
OFMCap    Order of Friars Minor Capuchin (Franciscans)
OFMConv    Order of Friars Minor Conventual (Franciscans)
OFR    Order of the Federal Republic of Nigeria
OFS    Orange Free State
OFT    Office of Fair Trading
Oftel    Office of Telecommunications
OGS    Oratory of the Good Shepherd
OHMS    On His (or Her) Majesty's Service
O i/c    Officer in charge
OJ    Order of Jamaica
OL    Officer, Order of Leopold; Order of the Leopard (Lesotho)
OLM    Officer, Legion of Merit (Rhodesia)
OM    Order of Merit
OMCS    Office of the Minister for the Civil Service
OMI    Oblate of Mary Immaculate
OMM    Officer, Order of Military Merit (Canada)
ON    Order of the Nation (Jamaica)
OND    Ordinary National Diploma
Ont    Ontario
ONZ    Order of New Zealand
OON    Officer, Order of the Niger
OP    *Ordinis Praedicatorum* (of the Order of Preachers (Dominican)); Observation Post
OPCON    Operational Control
OPCS    Office of Population Censuses and Surveys
OQ    Officer, National Order of Quebec
OR    Order of Rorima (Guyana); Operational Research
ORC    Orange River Colony
Ore    Oregon (US)
ORGALIME    Organisme de Liaison des Industries Métalliques Européennes
ORL    Otorhinolaryngology
ORS    Operational Research Society
ORSL    Order of the Republic of Sierra Leone

| | |
|---|---|
| ORT | Organization for Rehabilitation by Training |
| ORTF | Office de la Radiodiffusion et Télévision Française |
| o s | only son |
| OSA | Order of St Augustine (Augustinian); Ontario Society of Artists |
| OSB | Order of St Benedict (Benedictine) |
| osc | Graduate of Overseas Staff College |
| OSFC | Franciscan (Capuchin) Order |
| O/Sig | Ordinary Signalman |
| OSNC | Orient Steam Navigation Co. |
| o s p | *obiit sine prole* (died without issue) |
| OSRD | Office of Scientific Research and Development |
| OSS | Office of Strategic Services |
| OStJ | Officer, Most Venerable Order of the Hospital of St John of Jerusalem |
| OSUK | Ophthalmological Society of the United Kingdom |
| OT | Old Testament |
| OTC | Officers' Training Corps |
| OTL | Officer, Order of Toussaint L'Ouverture (Haiti) |
| OTU | Operational Training Unit |
| OTWSA | Ou-Testamentiese Werkgemeenskap in Suider-Afrika |
| OU | Oxford University; Open University |
| OUAC | Oxford University Athletic Club |
| OUAFC | Oxford University Association Football Club |
| OUBC | Oxford University Boat Club |
| OUCC | Oxford University Cricket Club |
| OUDS | Oxford University Dramatic Society |
| OUP | Oxford University Press; Official Unionist Party |
| OURC | Oxford University Rifle Club |
| OURFC | Oxford University Rugby Football Club |
| OURT | Order of the United Republic of Tanzania |
| Oxon | Oxfordshire; *Oxoniensis* (of Oxford) |

# P

| | |
|---|---|
| PA | Pakistan Army; Personal Assistant |
| Pa | Pennsylvania (US) |
| PAA | President, Australian Academy of Science |
| pac | passed the final examination of the Advanced Class, The Military College of Science |
| PACE | Protestant and Catholic Encounter |
| PAg | Professional Agronomist |
| P&O | Peninsular and Oriental Steamship Co. |
| P&OSNCo. | Peninsular and Oriental Steam Navigation Co. |
| PAO | Prince Albert's Own |
| PASI | Professional Associate, Chartered Surveyors' Institution (*now see* ARICS) |
| PBS | Public Broadcasting Service |
| PC | Privy Counsellor; Police Constable; Perpetual Curate; Peace Commissioner (Ireland); Progressive Conservative (Canada) |
| pc | *per centum* (in the hundred) |
| PCC | Parochial Church Council |
| PCE | Postgraduate Certificate of Education |
| PCFC | Polytechnics and Colleges Funding Council |
| PCMO | Principal Colonial Medical Officer |
| PdD | Doctor of Pedagogy (US) |
| PDG | Président Directeur Général |
| PDR | People's Democratic Republic |
| PDRA | post doctoral research assistant |
| PDSA | People's Dispensary for Sick Animals |
| PDTC | Professional Dancer's Training Course Diploma |
| PE | Procurement Executive |
| PEI | Prince Edward Island |
| PEN | Poets, Playwrights, Editors, Essayists, Novelists (Club) |
| PEng | Registered Professional Engineer (Canada); Member, Society of Professional Engineers |
| Penn | Pennsylvania |
| PEP | Political and Economic Planning (*now see* PSI) |
| PER | Professional and Executive Recruitment |
| PEST | Pressure for Economic and Social Toryism |
| PETRAS | Polytechnic Educational Technology Resources Advisory Service |
| PF | Procurator-Fiscal |
| PFA | Professional Footballers' Association |
| pfc | Graduate of RAF Flying College |
| PFE | Program for Executives |
| PGA | Professional Golfers' Association |
| PGCE | Post Graduate Certificate of Education |
| PH | Presidential Order of Honour (Botswana) |
| PHAB | Physically Handicapped & Able-bodied |
| PhB | Bachelor of Philosophy |
| PhC | Pharmaceutical Chemist |
| PhD | Doctor of Philosophy |
| Phil. | Philology, Philological; Philosophy, Philosophical |
| PhL | Licentiate of Philosophy |
| PHLS | Public Health Laboratory Service |
| PhM | Master of Philosophy (USA) |
| PhmB | Bachelor of Pharmacy |
| Phys. | Physical |

| | |
|---|---|
| PIARC | Permanent International Association of Road Congresses |
| PIB | Prices and Incomes Board (later NBPI) |
| PICAO | Provisional International Civil Aviation Organization (*now* ICAO) |
| pinx. | *pinxit* (he painted it) |
| PIRA | Paper Industries Research Association |
| PITCOM | Parliamentary Information Technology Committee |
| PJG | Pingat Jasa Gemilang (Singapore) |
| PJK | Pingkat Jasa Kebaktian (Malaysia) |
| Pl. | Place; Plural |
| PLA | Port of London Authority |
| PLC or plc | public limited company |
| Plen. | Plenipotentiary |
| PLI | President, Landscape Institute |
| PLP | Parliamentary Labour Party |
| PMA | Personal Military Assistant |
| PMC | Personnel Management Centre |
| PMD | Program for Management Development |
| PMG | Postmaster-General |
| PMN | Panglima Mangku Negara (Malaysia) |
| PMO | Principal Medical Officer |
| PMRAFNS | Princess Mary's Royal Air Force Nursing Service |
| PMS | Presidential Order of Meritorious Service (Botswana); President, Miniature Society |
| PNBS | Panglima Negara Bintang Sarawak |
| PNEU | Parents' National Educational Union |
| PNG | Papua New Guinea |
| PNP | People's National Party |
| PO | Post Office |
| POB | Presidential Order of Botswana |
| POMEF | Political Office Middle East Force |
| Pop. | Population |
| POUNC | Post Office Users' National Council |
| POW | Prisoner of War; Prince of Wales's |
| PP | Parish Priest; Past President |
| pp | pages |
| PPA | Periodical Publishers Association |
| PPCLI | Princess Patricia's Canadian Light Infantry |
| PPE | Philosophy, Politics and Economics |
| PPInstHE | Past President, Institution of Highway Engineers |
| PPIStructE | Past President, Institution of Structural Engineers |
| PPITB | Printing and Publishing Industry Training Board |
| PPP | Private Patients Plan |
| PPRA | Past President, Royal Academy |
| PPRBA | Past President, Royal Society of British Artists |
| PPRBS | Past President, Royal Society of British Sculptors |
| PPRE | Past President, Royal Society of Painter-Etchers and Engravers |
| PPROI | Past President, Royal Institute of Oil Painters |
| PPRTPI | Past President, Royal Town Planning Institute |
| PPS | Parliamentary Private Secretary |
| PPSIAD | Past President, Society of Industrial Artists and Designers |
| PQ | Province of Quebec |
| PR | Public Relations |
| PRA | President, Royal Academy |
| PRBS | President, Royal Society of British Sculptors |
| PRCS | President, Royal College of Surgeons |
| PRE | President, Royal Society of Painter-Etchers and Engravers |
| Preb. | Prebendary |
| PrEng. | Professional Engineer |
| Pres. | President |
| PRHA | President, Royal Hibernian Academy |
| PRI | President, Royal Institute of Painters in Water Colours; Plastics and Rubber Institute |
| PRIA | President, Royal Irish Academy |
| PRIAS | President, Royal Incorporation of Architects in Scotland |
| Prin. | Principal |
| PRISA | Public Relations Institute of South Africa |
| PRO | Public Relations Officer; Public Records Office |
| Proc. | Proctor; Proceedings |
| Prof. | Professor; Professional |
| PROI | President, Royal Institute of Oil Painters |
| PRONED | Promotion of Non-Executive Directors |
| PRORM | Pay and Records Office, Royal Marines |
| Pro tem. | *Pro tempore* (for the time being) |
| Prov. | Provost; Provincial |
| Prox. | *Proximo* (next) |
| Prox.acc. | *Proxime accessit* (next in order of merit to the winner) |
| PRS | President, Royal Society; Performing Right Society Ltd |
| PRSA | President, Royal Scottish Academy |
| PRSE | President, Royal Society of Edinburgh |
| PRSH | President, Royal Society for the Promotion of Health |
| PRSW | President, Royal Scottish Water Colour Society |
| PRUAA | President, Royal Ulster Academy of Arts |
| PRWA | President, Royal West of England Academy |
| PRWS | President, Royal Society of Painters in Water Colours |
| PS | Pastel Society; Paddle Steamer |
| ps | passed School of Instruction (of Officers) |
| PSA | Property Services Agency; Petty Sessions Area |
| psa | Graduate of RAF Staff College |
| psc | Graduate of Staff College († indicates Graduate of Senior Wing Staff College) |
| PSD | Petty Sessional Division |

| | |
|---|---|
| PSGB | Pharmaceutical Society of Great Britain (now see RPSGB) |
| PSI | Policy Studies Institute |
| PSIAD | President, Society of Industrial Artists and Designers |
| PSM | Panglima Setia Mahkota (Malaysia) |
| psm | Certificate of Royal Military School of Music |
| PSMA | President, Society of Marine Artists |
| PSNC | Pacific Steam Navigation Co. |
| PSO | Principal Scientific Officer; Personal Staff Officer |
| PSOE | Partido Socialista Obrero Español |
| PSSC | Personal Social Services Council |
| PTA | Passenger Transport Authority; Parent-Teacher Association |
| PTE | Passenger Transport Executive |
| Pte | Private |
| ptsc | passed Technical Staff College |
| Pty | Proprietary |
| PUP | People's United Party |
| PVSM | Param Vishishc Seva Medal (India) |
| PWD | Public Works Department |
| PWE | Political Welfare Executive |
| PWO | Prince of Wales's Own |
| PWR | Pressurized Water Reactor |

# Q

| | |
|---|---|
| Q | Queen |
| QAIMNS | Queen Alexandra's Imperial Military Nursing Service |
| QALAS | Qualified Associate, Chartered Land Agents' Society (now (after amalgamation) see ARICS) |
| QARANC | Queen Alexandra's Royal Army Nursing Corps |
| QARNNS | Queen Alexandra's Royal Naval Nursing Service |
| QBD | Queen's Bench Division |
| QC | Queen's Counsel |
| QCVSA | Queen's Commendation for Valuable Service in the Air |
| QEH | Queen Elizabeth Hall |
| QEO | Queen Elizabeth's Own |
| QFSM | Queen's Fire Service Medal for Distinguished Service |
| QGM | Queen's Gallantry Medal |
| QHC | Queen's Honorary Chaplain |
| QHDS | Queen's Honorary Dental Surgeon |
| QHNS | Queen's Honorary Nursing Sister |
| QHP | Queen's Honorary Physician |
| QHS | Queen's Honorary Surgeon |
| Qld | Queensland |
| Qly | Quarterly |
| QMAAC | Queen Mary's Army Auxiliary Corps |
| QMC | Queen Mary College, London (now see QMW) |
| QMG | Quartermaster-General |
| QMW | Queen Mary and Westfield College, London |
| QO | Qualified Officer |
| QOOH | Queen's Own Oxfordshire Hussars |
| Q(ops) | Quartering (operations) |
| QPM | Queen's Police Medal |
| Qr | Quarter |
| QRIH | Queen's Royal Irish Hussars |
| QRV | Qualified Valuer, Real Estate Institute of New South Wales |
| QS | Quarter Sessions |
| qs | RAF graduates of the Military or Naval Staff College |
| QSM | Queen's Service Medal (NZ) |
| QSO | Queen's Service Order (NZ) |
| QUB | Queen's University, Belfast |
| qv | quod vide (which see) |

# R

| | |
|---|---|
| (R) | Reserve |
| RA | Royal Academician; Royal Artillery |
| RAA | Regional Arts Association |
| RAAF | Royal Australian Air Force |
| RAAMC | Royal Australian Army Medical Corps |
| RABI | Royal Agricultural Benevolent Institution |
| RAC | Royal Automobile Club; Royal Agricultural College; Royal Armoured Corps |
| RACGP | Royal Australian College of General Practitioners |
| RAChD | Royal Army Chaplains' Department |
| RACI | Royal Australian Chemical Institute |
| RACO | Royal Australian College of Ophthalmologists |
| RACOG | Royal Australian College of Obstetricians and Gynaecologists |
| RACP | Royal Australasian College of Physicians |
| RACS | Royal Australasian College of Surgeons; Royal Arsenal Co-operative Society |
| RADA | Royal Academy of Dramatic Art |
| RADAR | Royal Association for Disability and Rehabilitation |
| RADC | Royal Army Dental Corps |
| RADIUS | Religious Drama Society of Great Britain |
| RAE | Royal Australian Engineers; Royal Aerospace Establishment (formerly Royal Aircraft Establishment) |

| | |
|---|---|
| RAEC | Royal Army Educational Corps |
| RAeS | Royal Aeronautical Society |
| RAF | Royal Air Force |
| RAFA | Royal Air Force Association |
| RAFO | Reserve of Air Force Officers (now see RAFRO) |
| RAFRO | Royal Air Force Reserve of Officers |
| RAFVR | Royal Air Force Volunteer Reserve |
| RAI | Royal Anthropological Institute; Radio Audizioni Italiane |
| RAIA | Royal Australian Institute of Architects |
| RAIC | Royal Architectural Institute of Canada |
| RAM | (Member of) Royal Academy of Music |
| RAMC | Royal Army Medical Corps |
| RAN | Royal Australian Navy |
| R&D | Research and Development |
| RANR | Royal Australian Naval Reserve |
| RANVR | Royal Australian Naval Volunteer Reserve |
| RAOC | Royal Army Ordnance Corps |
| RAPC | Royal Army Pay Corps |
| RARDE | Royal Armament Research and Development Establishment |
| RARO | Regular Army Reserve of Officers |
| RAS | Royal Astronomical Society; Royal Asiatic Society |
| RASC | Royal Army Service Corps (now see RCT) |
| RASE | Royal Agricultural Society of England |
| RAuxAF | Royal Auxiliary Air Force |
| RAVC | Royal Army Veterinary Corps |
| RB | Rifle Brigade |
| RBA | Member, Royal Society of British Artists |
| RBC | Royal British Colonial Society of Artists |
| RBK&C | Royal Borough of Kensington and Chelsea |
| RBS | Royal Society of British Sculptors |
| RBSA | (Member of) Royal Birmingham Society of Artists |
| RBY | Royal Bucks Yeomanry |
| RC | Roman Catholic |
| RCA | Member, Royal Canadian Academy of Arts; Royal College of Art; (Member of) Royal Cambrian Academy |
| RCAC | Royal Canadian Armoured Corps |
| RCAF | Royal Canadian Air Force |
| RCamA | Member, Royal Cambrian Academy |
| RCAS | Royal Central Asian Society (now see RSAA) |
| RCDS | Royal College of Defence Studies |
| rcds | completed a course at, or served for a year on the Staff of, the Royal College of Defence Studies |
| RCGP | Royal College of General Practitioners |
| RCHA | Royal Canadian Horse Artillery |
| RCHM | Royal Commission on Historical Monuments |
| RCM | (Member of) Royal College of Music |
| RCN | Royal Canadian Navy; Royal College of Nursing |
| RCNC | Royal Corps of Naval Constructors |
| RCNR | Royal Canadian Naval Reserve |
| RCNVR | Royal Canadian Naval Volunteer Reserve |
| RCO | Royal College of Organists |
| RCOG | Royal College of Obstetricians and Gynaecologists |
| RCP | Royal College of Physicians, London |
| RCPath | Royal College of Pathologists |
| RCPE or RCPEd | Royal College of Physicians, Edinburgh |
| RCPI | Royal College of Physicians of Ireland |
| RCPSG | Royal College of Physicians and Surgeons of Glasgow |
| RCPsych | Royal College of Psychiatrists |
| RCR | Royal College of Radiologists |
| RCS | Royal College of Surgeons of England; Royal Corps of Signals; Royal College of Science |
| RCSE or RCSEd | Royal College of Surgeons of Edinburgh |
| RCSI | Royal College of Surgeons in Ireland |
| RCT | Royal Corps of Transport |
| RCVS | Royal College of Veterinary Surgeons |
| RD | Rural Dean; Royal Naval and Royal Marine Forces Reserve Decoration |
| Rd | Road |
| RDA | Royal Defence Academy |
| RDC | Rural District Council |
| RDF | Royal Dublin Fusiliers |
| RDI | Royal Designer for Industry (Royal Society of Arts) |
| RDS | Royal Dublin Society |
| RE | Royal Engineers; Fellow, Royal Society of Painter-Etchers and Engravers; Religious Education |
| REACH | Retired Executives Action Clearing House |
| react | Research Education and Aid for Children with potentially Terminal illness |
| Rear-Adm. | Rear-Admiral |
| REconS | Royal Economic Society |
| Regt | Regiment |
| REME | Royal Electrical and Mechanical Engineers |
| REngDes | Registered Engineering Designer |
| REPC | Regional Economic Planning Council |
| RERO | Royal Engineers Reserve of Officers |
| RES | Royal Empire Society (now Royal Commonwealth Society) |
| Res. | Resigned; Reserve; Resident; Research |
| RETI | Association of Traditional Industrial Regions |
| Rev. | Reverend; Review |
| RFA | Royal Field Artillery |
| RFC | Royal Flying Corps (now RAF); Rugby Football Club |
| RFH | Royal Festival Hall |

| | |
|---|---|
| **RFN** | Registered Fever Nurse |
| **RFPS(G)** | Royal Faculty of Physicians and Surgeons, Glasgow (*now see* RCPGlas) |
| **RFR** | Rassemblement des Français pour la République |
| **RFU** | Rugby Football Union |
| **RGA** | Royal Garrison Artillery |
| **RGI** | Royal Glasgow Institute of the Fine Arts |
| **RGJ** | Royal Green Jackets |
| **RGN** | Registered General Nurse |
| **RGS** | Royal Geographical Society |
| **RGSA** | Royal Geographical Society of Australasia |
| **RHA** | Royal Hibernian Academy; Royal Horse Artillery; Regional Health Authority |
| **RHAS** | Royal Highland and Agricultural Society of Scotland |
| **RHB** | Regional Hospital Board |
| **RHBNC** | Royal Holloway and Bedford New College, London |
| **RHC** | Royal Holloway College, London (*now see* RHBNC) |
| **RHF** | Royal Highland Fusiliers |
| **RHG** | Royal Horse Guards |
| **RHistS** | Royal Historical Society |
| **RHR** | Royal Highland Regiment |
| **RHS** | Royal Horticultural Society; Royal Humane Society |
| **RI** | Member, Royal Institute of Painters in Water Colours; Rhode Island |
| **RIA** | Royal Irish Academy |
| **RIAI** | Royal Institute of the Architects of Ireland |
| **RIAM** | Royal Irish Academy of Music |
| **RIAS** | Royal Incorporation of Architects in Scotland |
| **RIASC** | Royal Indian Army Service Corps |
| **RIBA** | (Member of) Royal Institute of British Architects |
| **RIBI** | Rotary International in Great Britain and Ireland |
| **RIC** | Royal Irish Constabulary; Royal Institute of Chemistry (*now see* RSC) |
| **RICS** | Royal Institution of Chartered Surveyors |
| **RIE** | Royal Indian Engineering (College) |
| **RIF** | Royal Inniskilling Fusiliers |
| **RIIA** | Royal Institute of International Affairs |
| **RIM** | Royal Indian Marines |
| **RIN** | Royal Indian Navy |
| **RINA** | Royal Institution of Naval Architects |
| **RINVR** | Royal Indian Naval Volunteer Reserve |
| **RIPA** | Royal Institute of Public Administration |
| **RIPH&H** | Royal Institute of Public Health and Hygiene |
| **RIrF** | Royal Irish Fusiliers |
| **RLSS** | Royal Life Saving Society |
| **RM** | Royal Marines; Resident Magistrate; Registered Midwife |
| **RMA** | Royal Marine Artillery; Royal Military Academy Sandhurst (*now incorporating* Royal Military Academy, Woolwich) |
| **RMB** | Rural Mail Base |
| **RMC** | Royal Military College Sandhurst (*now see* RMA) |
| **RMCM** | (Member of) Royal Manchester College of Music |
| **RMCS** | Royal Military College of Science |
| **RMedSoc** | Royal Medical Society, Edinburgh |
| **RMetS** | Royal Meterological Society |
| **RMFVR** | Royal Marine Forces Volunteer Reserve |
| **RMIT** | Royal Melbourne Institute of Technology |
| **RMLI** | Royal Marine Light Infantry |
| **RMN** | Registered Mental Nurse |
| **RMO** | Resident Medical Officer(s) |
| **RMP** | Royal Military Police |
| **RMPA** | Royal Medico-Psychological Association |
| **RMS** | Royal Microscopical Society; Royal Mail Steamer; Royal Society of Miniature Painters |
| **RN** | Royal Navy; Royal Naval |
| **RNAS** | Royal Naval Air Service |
| **RNAY** | Royal Naval Aircraft Yard |
| **RNC** | Royal Naval College |
| **RNCM** | (Member of) Royal Northern College of Music |
| **RNEC** | Royal Naval Engineering College |
| **RNIB** | Royal National Institute for the Blind |
| **RNID** | Royal National Institute for the Deaf |
| **RNLI** | Royal National Life-boat Institution |
| **RNLO** | Royal Naval Liaison Officer |
| **RNR** | Royal Naval Reserve |
| **RNS** | Royal Numismatic Society |
| **RNSA** | Royal Naval Sailing Association |
| **RNSC** | Royal Naval Staff College |
| **RNT** | Registered Nurse Tutor |
| **RNTNEH** | Royal National Throat, Nose and Ear Hospital |
| **RNUR** | Régie Nationale des Usines Renault |
| **RNVR** | Royal Naval Volunteer Reserve |
| **RNVSR** | Royal Naval Volunteer Supplementary Reserve |
| **RNXS** | Royal Naval Auxiliary Service |
| **RNZAC** | Royal New Zealand Armoured Corps |
| **RNZAF** | Royal New Zealand Air Force |
| **RNZIR** | Royal New Zealand Infantry Regiment |
| **RNZN** | Royal New Zealand Navy |
| **RNZNVR** | Royal New Zealand Naval Volunteer Reserve |
| **ROC** | Royal Observer Corps |
| **ROF** | Royal Ordnance Factories |
| **R of O** | Reserve of Officers |
| **ROI** | Member, Royal Institute of Oil Painters |
| **RoSPA** | Royal Society for the Prevention of Accidents |
| **(Rot.)** | Rotunda Hospital, Dublin (after degree) |
| **RP** | Member, Royal Society of Portrait Painters |
| **RPC** | Royal Pioneer Corps |
| **RPMS** | Royal Postgraduate Medical School |
| **RPO** | Royal Philharmonic Orchestra |
| **RPR** | Rassemblement pour la République |
| **RPS** | Royal Photographic Society |
| **RPSGB** | Royal Pharmaceutical Society of Great Britain |
| **RRC** | Royal Red Cross |
| **RRE** | Royal Radar Establishment (*now see* RSRE) |
| **RRF** | Royal Regiment of Fusiliers |
| **RRS** | Royal Research Ship |
| **RSA** | Royal Scottish Academician; Royal Society of Arts; Republic of South Africa |
| **RSAA** | Royal Society for Asian Affairs |
| **RSAD** | Royal Surgical Aid Society |
| **RSAF** | Royal Small Arms Factory |
| **RSAI** | Royal Society of Antiquaries of Ireland |
| **RSAMD** | Royal Scottish Academy of Music and Drama |
| **RSanI** | Royal Sanitary Institute (*now see* RSH) |
| **RSC** | Royal Society of Canada; Royal Society of Chemistry; Royal Shakespeare Company |
| **RSCM** | Royal School of Church Music |
| **RSCN** | Registered Sick Children's Nurse |
| **RSE** | Royal Society of Edinburgh |
| **RSF** | Royal Scots Fusiliers |
| **RSFSR** | Russian Socialist Federated Soviet Republic |
| **RSGS** | Royal Scottish Geographical Society |
| **RSH** | Royal Society for the Promotion of Health |
| **RSL** | Royal Society of Literature; Returned Services League of Australia |
| **RSM** | Royal School of Mines |
| **RSM** or **RSocMed** | Royal Society of Medicine |
| **RSMA** | Royal Society of Marine Artists |
| **RSME** | Royal School of Military Engineering |
| **RSMHCA** | Royal Society for Mentally Handicapped Children and Adults (*see* Mencap) |
| **RSNC** | Royal Society for Nature Conservation |
| **RSO** | Rural Sub-Office; Railway Sub-Office; Resident Surgical Officer |
| **RSPB** | Royal Society for Protection of Birds |
| **RSPCA** | Royal Society for Prevention of Cruelty to Animals |
| **RSRE** | Royal Signals and Radar Establishment |
| **RSSAILA** | Returned Sailors, Soldiers and Airmen's Imperial League of Australia (*now see* RSL) |
| **RSSPCC** | Royal Scottish Society for Prevention of Cruelty to Children |
| **RSTM&H** | Royal Society of Tropical Medicine and Hygiene |
| **RSUA** | Royal Society of Ulster Architects |
| **RSV** | Revised Standard Version |
| **RSW** | Member, Royal Scottish Society of Painters in Water Colours |
| **RTE** | Radio Telefis Eireann |
| **Rt Hon.** | Right Honourable |
| **RTL** | Radio-Télévision Luxembourg |
| **RTO** | Railway Transport Officer |
| **RTPI** | Royal Town Planning Institute |
| **RTR** | Royal Tank Regiment |
| **Rt Rev.** | Right Reverend |
| **RTS** | Religious Tract Society; Royal Toxophilite Society; Royal Television Society |
| **RTYC** | Royal Thames Yacht Club |
| **RU** | Rugby Union |
| **RUC** | Royal Ulster Constabulary |
| **RUI** | Royal University of Ireland |
| **RUKBA** | Royal United Kingdom Beneficent Association |
| **RUR** | Royal Ulster Regiment |
| **RURAL** | Society for the Responsible Use of Resources in Agriculture & on the Land |
| **RUSI** | Royal United Services Institute for Defence Studies (*formerly* Royal United Service Institution) |
| **RVC** | Royal Veterinary College |
| **RWA** or **RWEA** | Member, Royal West of England Academy |
| **RWAFF** | Royal West African Frontier Force |
| **RWF** | Royal Welch Fusiliers |
| **RWS** | (Member of) Royal Society of Painters in Water Colours |
| **RYA** | Royal Yachting Association |
| **RYS** | Royal Yacht Squadron |
| **RZSScot** | Royal Zoological Society of Scotland |

# S

| | |
|---|---|
| **(S)** | (in Navy) Paymaster; Scotland |
| **S** | Succeeded; South; Saint |
| **s** | son |
| **SA** | South Australia; South Africa; Société Anonyme |
| **SAAF** | South African Air Force |
| **SABC** | South African Broadcasting Corporation |
| **SAC** | Scientific Advisory Committee |
| **sac** | qualified at small arms technical long course |
| **SACEUR** | Supreme Allied Commander Europe |

SACLANT    Supreme Allied Commander Atlantic
SACSEA    Supreme Allied Command, SE Asia
SA de CV    sociedad anónima de capital variable
SADF    Sudanese Auxiliary Defence Force
SADG    Société des Architectes Diplômés par le Gouvernement
SAE    Society of Automobile Engineers (US)
SAMC    South African Medical Corps
SARL    Société à Responsabilité Limitée
Sarum    Salisbury
SAS    Special Air Service
Sask    Saskatchewan
SASO    Senior Air Staff Officer
SAT    Senior Member, Association of Accounting Technicians
SATRO    Science and Technology Regional Organisation
SB    Bachelor of Science (US)
SBAA    Sovereign Base Areas Administration
SBAC    Society of British Aerospace Companies (formerly Society of British Aircraft Constructors)
SBS    Special Boat Service
SBStJ    Serving Brother, Most Venerable Order of the Hospital of St John of Jerusalem
SC    Star of Courage (Canada); Senior Counsel (Eire, Guyana, South Africa); South Carolina (US)
sc    student at the Staff College
SCAO    Senior Civil Affairs Officer
SCAPA    Society for Checking the Abuses of Public Advertising
SCAR    Scientific Committee for Antarctic Research
ScD    Doctor of Science
SCDC    Schools Curriculum Development Committee
SCF    Senior Chaplain to the Forces; Save the Children Fund
Sch.    School
SCI    Society of Chemical Industry
SCL    Student in Civil Law
SCM    State Certified Midwife; Student Christian Movement
SCONUL    Standing Conference of National and University Libraries
Scot.    Scotland
ScotBIC    Scottish Business in the Community
SCOTVEC    Scottish Vocational Education Council
SD    Staff Duties
SDA    Social Democratic Alliance; Scottish Diploma in Agriculture; Scottish Development Agency
SDak    South Dakota (US)
SDB    Salesian of Don Bosco
SDF    Sudan Defence Force; Social Democratic Federation
SDI    Strategic Defence Initiative
SDLP    Social Democratic and Labour Party
SDP    Social Democratic Party
SE    South-east
SEAC    South-East Asia Command
SEALF    South-East Asia Land Forces
SEATO    South-East Asia Treaty Organization
SEC    Security Exchange Commission
Sec.    Secretary
SEE    Society of Environmental Engineers
SEN    State Enrolled Nurse
SEPM    Society of Economic Palaeontologists and Mineralogists
SERC    Science and Engineering Research Council
SERT    Society of Electronic and Radio Technicians
SESO    Senior Equipment Staff Officer
SFInstE    Senior Fellow, Institute of Energy
SFInstF    Senior Fellow, Institute of Fuel (now see SFInstE)
SFTA    Society of Film and Television Arts (now see BAFTA)
SFTCD    Senior Fellow, Trinity College Dublin
SG    Solicitor-General
SGA    Member, Society of Graphic Art
SGBI    Schoolmistresses' and Governesses' Benevolent Institution
Sgt    Sergeant
SHA    Secondary Heads Association; Special Health Authority
SHAC    London Housing Aid Centre
SHAEF    Supreme Headquarters, Allied Expeditionary Force
SH&MA    Scottish Horse and Motormen's Association
SHAPE    Supreme Headquarters, Allied Powers, Europe
SHHD    Scottish Home and Health Department
SIAD    Society of Industrial Artists and Designers (now see CSD)
SIAM    Society of Industrial and Applied Mathematics (US)
SIB    Shipbuilding Industry Board; Securities and Investments Board
SICOT    Société Internationale de Chirurgie Orthopédique et de Traumatologie
SID    Society for International Development
SIESO    Society of Industrial and Emergency Services Officers
SIMA    Scientific Instrument Manufacturers' Association of Great Britain
SIME    Security Intelligence Middle East
SIMG    Societas Internationalis Medicinae Generalis
SinDrs    Doctor of Chinese
SITA    Société Internationale de Télécommunications Aéronautiques
SITPRO    Simpler Trade Procedures Board (formerly Simplification of International Trade Procedures)
SJ    Society of Jesus (Jesuits)
SJAB    St John Ambulance Brigade
SJD    Doctor of Juristic Science
SL    Serjeant-at-Law

SLA    Special Libraries Association
SLAC    Stanford Linear Accelerator Centre
SLAET    Society of Licensed Aircraft Engineers and Technologists
SLAS    Society for Latin-American Studies
SLD    Social and Liberal Democrats
SLP    Scottish Labour Party
SM    Medal of Service (Canada) (now see OC); Master of Science; Officer qualified for Submarine Duties
SMA    Society of Marine Artists (now see RSMA)
SMB    Setia Mahkota Brunei
SME    School of Military Engineering (now see RSME)
SMHO    Sovereign Military Hospitaller Order (Malta)
SMIEEE    Senior Member, Institute of Electrical and Electronics Engineers (New York)
SMIRE    Senior Member, Institute of Radio Engineers (New York)
SMMT    Society of Motor Manufacturers and Traders Ltd
SMN    Seri Maharaja Mangku Negara (Malaysia)
SMO    Senior Medical Officer; Sovereign Military Order
SMP    Senior Managers' Program
SMPTE    Society of Motion Picture and Television Engineers (US)
SMRTB    Ship and Marine Requirements Technology Board
SNAME    Society of Naval Architects and Marine Engineers (US)
SNCF    Société Nationale des Chemins de Fer Français
SND    Sisters of Notre Dame
SNP    Scottish National Party
SNTS    Society for New Testament Studies
SO    Staff Officer; Scientific Officer
SOAS    School of Oriental and African Studies
Soc.    Society
Soc & Lib Dem    Social and Liberal Democrats (now see Lib Dem)
SocCE(France)    Société des Ingénieurs Civils de France
SODEPAX    Committee on Society, Development and Peace
SOE    Special Operations Executive
SOGAT    Society of Graphical and Allied Trades
SOLACE or Solace    Society of Local Authority Chief Executives
SOM    Society of Occupational Medicine
SOSc    Society of Ordained Scientists
SOTS    Society for Old Testament Study
sowc    Senior Officers' War Course
sp    sine prole (without issue)
SP    Self-Propelled (Anti-Tank Regiment)
SpA    Società per Azioni
SPAB    Society for the Protection of Ancient Buildings
SPCA    Society for the Prevention of Cruelty to Animals
SPCK    Society for Promoting Christian Knowledge
SPCM    Darjah Seri Paduka Cura Si Manja Kini (Malaysia)
SPD    Salisbury Plain District
SPDK    Seri Panglima Darjal Kinabalu
SPG    Society for the Propagation of the Gospel (now see USPG)
SPk    Sitara-e-Pakistan
SPMB    Seri Paduka Makhota Brunei
SPMO    Senior Principal Medical Officer
SPNC    Society for the Promotion of Nature Conservation (now see RSNC)
SPNM    Society for the Promotion of New Music
SPR    Society for Psychical Research
SPRC    Society for Prevention and Relief of Cancer
sprl    société de personnes à responsabilité limitée
SPSO    Senior Principal Scientific Officer
SPTL    Society of Public Teachers of Law
SPUC    Society for the Protection of the Unborn Child
Sq.    Square
sq    staff qualified
SQA    Sitara-i-Quaid-i-Azam (Pakistan)
Sqdn or Sqn    Squadron
SR    Special Reserve; Southern Railway; Southern Region (BR)
SRC    Science Research Council (now see SERC); Students' Representative Council
SRHE    Society for Research into Higher Education
SRIS    Science Reference Information Service
SRN    State Registered Nurse
SRNA    Shipbuilders and Repairers National Association
SRO    Supplementary Reserve of Officers
SRP    State Registered Physiotherapist
SRY    Sherwood Rangers Yeomanry
SS    Saints; Straits Settlements; Steamship
SSA    Society of Scottish Artists
SSAC    Social Security Advisory Committee
SSAFA or SS&AFA    Soldiers', Sailors', and Airmen's Families Association
SSBN    Nuclear Submarine, Ballistic
SSC    Solicitor before Supreme Court (Scotland); Sculptors Society of Canada; Societas Sanctae Crucis (Society of the Holy Cross); Short Service Commission
SSEB    South of Scotland Electricity Board
SSEES    School of Slavonic and East European Studies
SSF    Society of St Francis
SSJE    Society of St John the Evangelist
SSM    Society of the Sacred Mission; Seri Setia Mahkota (Malaysia)
SSO    Senior Supply Officer; Senior Scientific Officer
SSRC    Social Science Research Council (now see ESRC)

| | |
|---|---|
| SSStJ | Serving Sister, Most Venerable Order of the Hospital of St John of Jerusalem |
| STA | Sail Training Association |
| St | Street; Saint |
| STB | *Sacrae Theologiae Baccalaureus* (Bachelor of Sacred Theology) |
| STC | Senior Training Corps |
| STD | *Sacrae Theologiae Doctor* (Doctor of Sacred Theology) |
| STh | Scholar in Theology |
| Stip. | Stipend; Stipendiary |
| STL | *Sacrae Theologiae Lector* (Reader or a Professor of Sacred Theology) |
| STM | *Sacrae Theologiae Magister* (Master of Sacred Theology) |
| STP | *Sacrae Theologiae Professor* (Professor of Divinity, old form of DD) |
| STRIVE | Society for Preservation of Rural Industries and Village Enterprises |
| STSO | Senior Technical Staff Officer |
| STV | Scottish Television |
| SUNY | State University of New York |
| Supp. Res. | Supplementary Reserve (of Officers) |
| Supt | Superintendent |
| Surg. | Surgeon |
| Surv. | Surviving |
| SW | South-west |
| SWET | Society of West End Theatre |
| SWIA | Society of Wildlife Artists |
| SWPA | South West Pacific Area |
| SWRB | Sadler's Wells Royal Ballet |
| Syd. | Sydney |

# T

| | |
|---|---|
| T | Telephone; Territorial |
| TA | Telegraphic Address; Territorial Army |
| TAA | Territorial Army Association |
| TA&VRA | Territorial Auxiliary and Volunteer Reserve Association |
| TAF | Tactical Air Force |
| T&AFA | Territorial and Auxiliary Forces Association |
| T&AVR | Territorial and Army Volunteer Reserve |
| TANS | Territorial Army Nursing Service |
| TANU | Tanganyika African National Union |
| TARO | Territorial Army Reserve of Officers |
| TAS | Torpedo and Anti Submarine Course |
| TASS | Technical, Administrative and Supervisory Section of AUEW (now part of MSF) |
| TAVRA | Territorial Auxiliary and Volunteer Reserve Association |
| TC | Order of the Trinity Cross (Trinidad and Tobago) |
| TCCB | Test and County Cricket Board |
| TCD | Trinity College, Dublin (University of Dublin, Trinity College) |
| TCF | Temporary Chaplain to the Forces |
| TCPA | Town and Country Planning Association |
| TD | Territorial Efficiency Decoration; Efficiency Decoration (T&AVR) (since April 1967); Teachta Dala (Member of the Dáil, Eire) |
| TDD | Tubercular Diseases Diploma |
| TEAC | Technical Educational Advisory Council |
| TEC | Technician Education Council (now see BTEC); Training and Enterprise Council |
| Tech(CEI) | Technician |
| TEFL | Teaching English as a Foreign Language |
| TEM | Territorial Efficiency Medal |
| TEMA | Telecommunication Engineering and Manufacturing Association |
| Temp. | Temperature; Temporary |
| TEng(CEI) | Technician Engineer (now see IEng) |
| Tenn | Tennessee (US) |
| TeolD | Doctor of Theology |
| TES | Times Educational Supplement |
| TET | Teacher of Electrotherapy |
| Tex | Texas (US) |
| TF | Territorial Force |
| TFR | Territorial Force Reserve |
| TGEW | Timber Growers England and Wales Ltd |
| TGO | Timber Growers' Organisation (now see TGEW) |
| TGWU | Transport and General Workers' Union |
| ThD | Doctor of Theology |
| THED | Transvaal Higher Education Diploma |
| THELEP | Therapy of Leprosy |
| THES | Times Higher Education Supplement |
| ThL | Theological Licentiate |
| ThSchol | Scholar in Theology |
| TIMS | The Institute of Management Sciences |
| TLS | Times Literary Supplement |
| TMMG | Teacher of Massage and Medical Gymnastics |
| TNC | Theatres National Committee |
| TOSD | Tertiary Order of St Dominic |
| TP | Transvaal Province |
| TPI | Town Planning Institute (now see RTPI) |

| | |
|---|---|
| Trans. | Translation; Translated |
| Transf. | Transferred |
| TRC | Thames Rowing Club |
| TRE | Telecommunications Research Establishment (now see RRE) |
| TRH | Their Royal Highnesses |
| TRIC | Televison and Radio Industries Club |
| Trin. | Trinity |
| TRRL | Transport and Road Research Laboratory |
| TS | Training Ship |
| TSB | Trustee Savings Bank |
| tsc | passed a Territorial Army Course in Staff Duties |
| TSD | Tertiary of St Dominic |
| TSSA | Transport Salaried Staffs' Association |
| TUC | Trades Union Congress |
| TULV | Trade Unions for a Labour Victory |
| TUS | Trade Union Side |
| TV | Television |
| TVEI | Technical and Vocational Education Initiative |
| TWA | Thames Water Authority |
| TYC | Thames Yacht Club (now see RTYC) |

# U

| | |
|---|---|
| (U) | Unionist |
| u | uncle |
| UAE | United Arab Emirates |
| UAR | United Arab Republic |
| UAU | Universities Athletic Union |
| UBC | University of British Columbia |
| UBI | Understanding British Industry |
| UC | University College |
| UCCA | Universities Central Council on Admissions |
| UCET | Universities Council for Education of Teachers |
| UCH | University College Hospital (London) |
| UCL | University College London |
| UCLA | University of California at Los Angeles |
| UCMSM | University College and Middlesex School of Medicine |
| UCNS | Universities' Council for Non-academic Staff |
| UCNW | University College of North Wales |
| UCRN | University College of Rhodesia and Nyasaland |
| UCS | University College School |
| UCSD | University of California at San Diego |
| UCW | University College of Wales; Union of Communication Workers |
| UDC | Urban District Council; Urban Development Corporation |
| UDF | Union Defence Force; Union démocratique française |
| UDR | Ulster Defence Regiment; Union des Démocrates pour la Vème République (now see RFR) |
| UDSR | Union Démocratique et Socialiste de la Résistance |
| UEA | University of East Anglia |
| UED | University Education Diploma |
| UEFA | Union of European Football Associations |
| UF | United Free Church |
| UFAW | Universities Federation of Animal Welfare |
| UFC | Universities' Funding Council |
| UGC | University Grants Committee (now see UFC) |
| UIAA | Union Internationale des Associations d'Alpinisme |
| UICC | Union Internationale contre le Cancer |
| UIE | Union Internationale des Etudiants |
| UISPP | Union Internationale des Sciences Préhistoriques et Protohistoriques |
| UJD | *Utriusque Juris Doctor* (Doctor of both Laws, Doctor of Canon and Civil Law) |
| UK | United Kingdom |
| UKAC | United Kingdom Automation Council |
| UKAEA | United Kingdom Atomic Energy Authority |
| UKCC | United Kingdom Central Council for Nursing, Midwifery and Health Visiting |
| UKCIS | United Kingdom Chemical Information Service |
| UKIAS | United Kingdom Immigrants' Advisory Service |
| UKISC | United Kingdom Industrial Space Committee |
| UKLF | United Kingdom Land Forces |
| UKMF(L) | United Kingdom Military Forces (Land) |
| UKMIS | United Kingdom Mission |
| UKOOA | United Kingdom Offshore Operators Association |
| UKPIA | United Kingdom Petroleum Industry Association Ltd |
| UKSLS | United Kingdom Services Liaison Staff |
| ULCI | Union of Lancashire and Cheshire Institutes |
| UMDS | United Medical and Dental Schools |
| UMIST | University of Manchester Institute of Science and Technology |
| UN | United Nations |
| UNA | United Nations Association |
| UNCAST | United Nations Conference on the Applications of Science and Technology |
| UNCIO | United Nations Conference on International Organisation |
| UNCITRAL | United Nations Commission on International Trade Law |
| UNCSTD | United Nations Conference on Science and Technology for Development |

UNCTAD or **Unctad**   United Nations Commission for Trade and Development
UNDP   United Nations Development Programme
UNDRO   United Nations Disaster Relief Organisation
UNECA   United Nations Economic Commission for Asia
UNEP   United Nations Environment Programme
UNESCO or **Unesco**   United Nations Educational, Scientific and Cultural Organisation
UNFAO   United Nations Food and Agriculture Organisation
UNFICYP   United Nations Force in Cyprus
UNHCR   United Nations High Commissioner for Refugees
UNICE   Union des Industries de la Communauté Européenne
UNICEF or **Unicef**   United Nations Children's Fund (*formerly* United Nations International Children's Emergency Fund)
UNIDO   United Nations Industrial Development Organisation
UNIDROIT   Institut International pour l'Unification du Droit Privé
UNIFIL   United Nations Interim Force in Lebanon
UNIPEDE   Union Internationale des Producteurs et Distributeurs d'Energie Electrique
UNISIST   Universal System for Information in Science and Technology
UNITAR   United Nations Institute of Training and Research
Univ.   University
UNO   United Nations Organization
UNRRA   United Nations Relief and Rehabilitation Administration
UNRWA   United Nations Relief and Works Agency
UNSCOB   United Nations Special Commission on the Balkans
UP   United Provinces; Uttar Pradesh; United Presbyterian
UPGC   University and Polytechnic Grants Committee
UPNI   Unionist Party of Northern Ireland
UPU   Universal Postal Union
(UPUP)   Ulster Popular Unionist Party
URC   United Reformed Church
URSI   Union Radio-Scientifique Internationale
US   United States
USA   United States of America
USAAF   United States Army Air Force
USAF   United States Air Force
USAID   United States Agency for International Development
USAR   United States Army Reserve
USC   University of Southern California
USDAW   Union of Shop Distributive and Allied Workers
USM   Unlisted Securities Market
USMA   United States Military Academy
USN   United States Navy
USNR   United States Naval Reserve
USPG   United Society for the Propagation of the Gospel
USPHS   United States Public Health Service
USR   Universities' Statistical Record
USS   United States Ship
USSR   Union of Soviet Socialist Republics
USVI   United States Virgin Islands
UTC   University Training Corps
(UU)   Ulster Unionist
(UUUC)   United Ulster Unionist Coalition
(UUUP)   United Ulster Unionist Party
UWIST   University of Wales Institute of Science and Technology
UWT   Union of Women Teachers

# V

V   Five (Roman numerals); Version; Vicar; Viscount; Vice
v   *versus* (against)
v or **vid.**   *vide* (see)
Va   Virginia (US)
VAD   Voluntary Aid Detachment
V&A   Victoria and Albert
VAT   Value Added Tax
VC   Victoria Cross
VCAS   Vice-Chief of the Air Staff
VCDS   Vice-Chief of the Defence Staff
VCGS   Vice-Chief of the General Staff
VCNS   Vice-Chief of Naval Staff
VD   Royal Naval Volunteer Reserve Officers' Decoration (*now* VRD); Volunteer Officers' Decoration; Victorian Decoration
VDC   Volunteer Defence Corps
Ven.   Venerable
Vet.   Veterinary
VG   Vicar-General
VHS   Hon. Surgeon to Viceroy of India
VIC   Victoria Institute of Colleges
Vice-Adm.   Vice-Admiral
Visc.   Viscount
VM   Victory Medal
VMH   Victoria Medal of Honour (Royal Horticultural Society)
Vol.   Volume; Volunteers
VP   Vice-President

VPP   Volunteer Political Party
VPRP   Vice-President, Royal Society of Portrait Painters
VQMG   Vice-Quartermaster-General
VR   *Victoria Regina* (Queen Victoria); Volunteer Reserve
VRD   Royal Naval Volunteer Reserve Officers' Decoration
VSO   Voluntary Service Overseas
Vt   Vermont (US)
(VUP)   Vanguard Unionist Party

# W

W   West
WA   Western Australia
WAAF   Women's Auxiliary Air Force (*now see* WRAF)
**Wash**   Washington State (US)
WCC   World Council of Churches
W/Cdr   Wing Commander
WEA   Workers' Educational Association; Royal West of England Academy
WES/PNEU   Worldwide Education Service of Parents' National Educational Union
WEU   Western European Union
WFSW   World Federation of Scientific Workers
WFTU   World Federation of Trade Unions
WhF   Whitworth Fellow
WHO   World Health Organization
WhSch   Whitworth Scholar
WI   West Indies; Women's Institute
Wilts   Wiltshire
WIPO   World Intellectual Property Organization
Wis   Wisconsin (US)
Wits   Witwatersrand
WJEC   Welsh Joint Education Committee
WLA   Women's Land Army
WLF   Women's Liberal Federation
Wm   William
WMO   World Meteorological Organization
WNO   Welsh National Opera
WO   War Office; Warrant Officer
Worcs   Worcestershire
WOSB   War Office Selection Board
WR   West Riding; Western Region (BR)
WRAC   Women's Royal Army Corps
WRAF   Women's Royal Air Force
WRNS   Women's Royal Naval Service
WRVS   Women's Royal Voluntary Service
WS   Writer to the Signet
WSPU   Women's Social and Political Union
WUS   World University Service
WVa   West Virginia (US)
WVS   Women's Voluntary Services (*now see* WRVS)
WWF   World Wide Fund for Nature (*formerly* World Wildlife Fund)
Wyo   Wyoming (US)

# X

X   Ten (Roman numerals)
XO   Executive Officer

# Y

y   youngest
YC   Young Conservative
YCNAC   Young Conservatives National Advisory Committee
Yeo.   Yeomanry
YES   Youth Enterprise Scheme
YHA   Youth Hostels Association
YMCA   Young Men's Christian Association
Yorks   Yorkshire
YPTES   Young People's Trust for Endangered Species
yr   younger
yrs   years
YTS   Youth Training Scheme
YVFF   Young Volunteer Force Foundation
YWCA   Young Women's Christian Association

# Z

ZANU   Zimbabwe African National Union
ZAPU   Zimbabwe African People's Union

# ADDENDA

The following biographies are of those whose deaths occurred between 1981 and 1990, but were not reported until after the main part of this volume had gone to press.

**BALLANTYNE, Colin Sandergrove,** CMG 1971; photographer and director; Chairman, Performing Arts Collection of South Australia, since 1980; *b* 12 July 1908; *s* of James Fergusson Ballantyne, Adelaide; *m* 1934, Gwenneth Martha Osborne Richmond; one *s* two *d*. *Educ:* Adelaide High School. Directed: cycle Shakespeare plays, 1948–52; 100 contemporary plays, 1948–78; five major productions Adelaide Festival of Arts, 1960–68. Dir, Sheridan Theatre, 1962–72. Chm. Bd of Governors, State Theatre Co., 1972–78; Pres., Arts Council of Australia (SA), 1974–77 (Federal Dir, 1966–74). Hon. FIAP 1971. *Publications:* (plays) Harvest, 1936; The Ice-Cream Cart, 1962; Between Gunshots, 1964; also Pacific Rape, unpublished. *Address:* 77 Kingston Terrace, North Adelaide, SA 5006, Australia. *T:* Adelaide 267 1138. *Died* 1988.

**DAVIES, George Francis,** CMG 1962; Chairman, Davies Brothers Ltd, since 1954; *b* 26 Jan. 1911; *yr s* of late C. B. Davies, CBE, MIEA, and late Ruby A. Davies; *m* 1935, Margaret Ingles; one *s* three *d*. *Educ:* Clemes Coll., Hobart, Tasmania. Director: Commercial Broadcasters Pty Ltd (Chm., 1950–); Australian Newsprint Mills Ltd, 1954–; Tasmanian Fibre Containers Pty Ltd (Chm., 1975–); Packaging Investments Pty Ltd (Chm., 1965–); Perpetual Trustees and Natural Executors Ltd, 1968–. *Recreations:* golf, fishing, racing. *Address:* 5/46 Marieville Esplanade, Sandy Bay, Tasmania 7005, Australia. *T:* 34.6411. *Clubs:* Tasmanian, Athenæum (Hobart). *Died* 29 *Aug.* 1987.

**DRIDAN, Julian Randal,** CMG 1955; retired; Chairman, Electricity Trust of South Australia, 1970–78 (Member, 1953–78); *b* 24 Nov. 1901; *s* of Sydney John Dridan and Eliza Gundry Dridan; *m* 1925, Ivy Viola Orr; two *d*. *Educ:* South Australian Sch. of Mines; University of Adelaide (BE). Entered service with Govt of S Australia, 1923; construction of locks and weirs on River Murray, 1923–34; District Engineer, 1934–44; Deputy Engineer-in-Chief, 1946; Engineer-in-Chief, 1949; Dir and Engineer-in-Chief, 1960–66. Mem. River Murray Commission, 1947–66. Coronation Medal, 1953; Jubilee Medal, 1978. *Recreations:* bowls, fishing. *Address:* 555 Fullarton Road, Mitcham, South Australia 6032. *Club:* Rotary (Adelaide).

**FRASER, Sir Douglas (Were),** Kt 1966; ISO 1962; Fellow, Royal Institute of Public Administration (Queensland); Honorary Fellow: Queensland Conservatorium of Music; Institute of Ambulance Officers (Australia); *b* 24 Oct. 1899; *s* of late Robert John Fraser and late Edith Harriet (*née* Shepherd); *m* 1927, Violet Pryke (*d* 1968); three *s*. *Educ:* State High Sch., Gympie, Qld. Entered Qld State Public Service, 1916; Public Service Board and Public Service Comr's Dept; Sec. to Public Service Comr, 1939; Sen. Public Service Inspector, 1947; Dep. Public Service Comr, 1952; Public Service Comr, 1956; retired 1965; War-time Asst Dir of Civil Defence, Sec., Public Safety Adv. Cttee. Mem. Senate, Univ. of Queensland, 1956–74; Chm. Council, Qld Conservatorium of Music, 1971–79; Pres., Qld Ambulance Transport Brigade Council, 1967–80. *Recreations:* gardening, fishing, music, reading. *Address:* 76 Prince Edward Parade, Redcliffe, Qld 4020, Australia. *T:* 203 4393. *Died* 2 *Jan.* 1988.

**KEMSLEY, Col Sir Alfred Newcombe,** KBE 1980 (CBE 1960); CMG 1973; MSM 1916; ED 1947; FIA; business consultant; *b* Prospect, SA, 29 March 1896; *s* of Alfred Kemsley; *m* 1st, 1921, Glydus Logg (decd); one *s* (killed, RAAF, 1941); 2nd, 1925, Jean Oldfield (decd); one *s* one *d*; 3rd, 1972, Anne Copsey. *Educ:* Adelaide Business Training Academy. Lands Dept, Adelaide, 1911–15; served War, AIF, 1915–18 (Private to Staff Captain; MSM); BHP Co., 1920–23; Sec., Melbourne Metrop. Town Planning Commn, 1923–29; Sec., Liquor Trades Defence Union, 1930–34; Gen. Manager, 3UZ Melbourne, 1934–44; Vice-Pres., Aust. Fedn of Commercial

Broadcasting Stations, 1935–36, Trustee, 1938–40; War of 1939–45 (Captain to Colonel): DADOS, 4th Div.; Dir of Organisation and Recruiting, Army HQ, 1941–43; Business Adviser and Army Rep., Bd of Administration, 1943–46; Mem., Mil. Bd, 1946; R of O. Dir, United Services Publicity, later USP Needham Pty Ltd, 1945–65 (Chm., 1960–64), Consultant Dir, 1965–. Director: Fire Fighting Equipment Pty Ltd, 1959–62; Ponsford Newman and Benson, 1964–69; Aust. Inhibitor Paper Pty Ltd, 1965–73; Consultant, TraveLodge Aust. Ltd, 1966–75. Member: Town and Country Planning Bd, 1945–68 (Mem. Aust. Planning Inst.; Sir James Barnett Meml Medal for Town Planning, 1964); Council, Melb. Chamber of Commerce, 1947–76; Inst. of Public Affairs, 1950–69; Aust. Inst. of Management, 1956–64; Aust. Nat. Travel Assoc., 1956–68 (Dep. Chm., 1967–68); Inst. of Directors, 1958–. Trustee, Melb. Nat. War Meml, 1938– (Chm., 1978); Founder Mem., Bd of Governors, Corps of Commissionaires, 1946– (Vice-Chm., 1964); Founder Mem., Field Marshal Sir Thomas Blamey Meml Cttee, 1954– (Chm., 1978); Member: War Nurses Meml Cttee, 1945–; Discharged Servicemen's Employment Bd, 1969–74; Fourth University Cttee, 1970–71; Dep. Chm., Lt-Gen. Sir Edmund Herring Meml Cttee, 1982–. *Address:* 41 Bay Street, Brighton, Victoria 3186, Australia. *Clubs:* Melbourne Legacy (Founder Mem., 1923; Pres., 1932); Australian (Melbourne); Melbourne Cricket. *Died* 24 *Feb.* 1987.

**MATHIAS, Winifred Rachel,** CBE 1974; Lord Mayor of City of Cardiff, May 1972–May 1973; Member, Local Government Boundary Commission for Wales, 1974–79; *b* 11 Feb. 1902; *d* of Charles and Selina Vodden; *m* 1923, William John Mathias (*d* 1949). *Educ:* Howard Gardens High Sch. Sec., ship-owning co., 1919–23. Member, Cardiff City Council, 1954–74; Alderman, 1967–74; formerly Mem., Estates, Public Works, Civic Buildings and Children's Cttees; Deputy Chairman: Health Cttee, 1961–64, 1967–74; Welfare Cttee, 1961–64 (Mem., 1954–70; Chm., 1967–70); Mem., Educn Cttee, 1956–74; Chairman: Social Services, 1970–74; all Primary Schs, 1965–70; Primary Schs Gp 3, 1970–74. Governor, Coll. of Food Technology and Commerce, 1957– (Dep. Chm., 1960–63, Chm., 1963–74). Life Mem., Blind Council (rep. of City Council); Mem., Management Cttee, "The Rest", Porthcawl, 1954–; Past Mem., Whitchurch Hosp. Gp; Founder Mem., Danybryn Cheshire Home, 1961– (Pres., 1986); Mem., Cardiff Council for the Elderly (Cartref Cttee). *Recreations:* reading, music, needlework, travel. *Address:* 19 Timbers Square, Cardiff CF2 3SH. *T:* Cardiff (0222) 483853. *Club:* Roath Conservative (Life Vice-Pres.) (Cardiff). *Died* 24 *Sept.* 1988.

**RANCHHODLAL, Sir Chinubhai Madhowlal,** 2nd Bt, *cr* 1913; *b* 18 April 1906; *s* of 1st Bt and Sulochana, *d* of Chunilal Khushalrai; *S* father, 1916; *m* 1924, Tanumati (*d* 1970), *d* of late Jhaverilal Bulakhiram Mehta of Ahmedabad; three *s*. Father was only member of Hindu community to receive a baronetcy. *Heir: s* Udayan Chinubhai [*b* 25 July 1929; *m* 1953, Muneera Khodadad Fozdar; one *s* three *d*. Arjuna Award, 1972]. *Address:* Shantikunj, PO Shahibaug, Ahmedabad, India. *T:* 26953. *Club:* Willingdon (Bombay). *Died* 28 *Aug.* 1990.

**TOOTH, Hon. Sir (Seymour) Douglas,** Kt 1975; retired from Government of Queensland; *b* 28 Jan. 1904; *s* of Percy Nash Tooth and Laura Tooth; *m* 1937, Eileen Mary O'Connor; one *d*. *Educ:* Univ. of Queensland (Teacher's Trng). Cl. 1 Teacher's Certif. Certificated Teacher, Qld Dept of Educn, 1922. Entered Qld Parlt as MP: Kelvin Grove, 1957; Ashgrove, 1960–74; apptd Minister for Health in Govt of Qld, 1964; retd from Parlt and Cabinet, 1974. Chairman: Duke of Edinburgh Award Cttee, Qld, 1977–; Brisbane Forest Park Adv. Bd. *Died* 3 *July* 1982.

# A

**AARON, Richard Ithamar**, MA, DPhil; FBA 1955; Professor of Philosophy, University College of Wales, Aberystwyth, 1932–69; *b* 6 Nov. 1901; *s* of William and Margaret Aaron, Ynystawe, Swansea; *m* Rhiannon, *d* of Dr M. J. Morgan, Aberystwyth; two *s* three *d*. *Educ:* Ystalyfera Grammar School; Cardiff University College; Oriel College, Oxford. Fellow, Univ. of Wales, 1923; Lectr at Swansea, 1926; Chm., Central Adv. Coun. for Educn (Wales), 1946–52; Mem., Coun. for Wales, 1956–63 (Chm., 1960–63); Chm. Library Advisory Council (Wales), 1965–72; Mem. Gen. Advisory Council, BBC, 1962–73, and TV Research Council, 1963–69; Mem. Council, National Library of Wales, 1953–73; Vice-Chm., Coleg Harlech Residential Coll.; Chm., Pembroke and Cardigan Agricultural Wages Cttee, 1962–73. Vis. Prof. in Philosophy, Yale Univ., US, 1952–53 (Fell. of Pierson Coll.). Pres., Mind Assoc., 1955–56; Pres., Aristotelian Society, London, 1957–58. Hon. DLitt Wales, 1973. *Publications:* The Nature of Knowing, 1930; Hanes Athroniaeth, 1932; An Early Draft of Locke's Essay (with Jocelyn Gibb), 1936; John Locke, 1937, 3rd rev. edn 1971 (trans. Chinese, 1986); The Limitations of Locke's Rationalism, in Seventeenth Century Studies, 1938; Our Knowledge of Universals, Annual Philosophical Lecture to British Academy, 1945; The Theory of Universals, 1952, 2nd rev. edn 1967; The True and the Valid, Friends of Dr Williams's Library Lecture, 1954; Knowing and the Function of Reason, 1971; Editor, Efrydiau Athronyddol, 1938–68; contributor to Mind, Proc. Arist. Soc., Philosophy, Mod. Lang. Rev., Llenor, etc. *Address:* 22 North Parade, Aberystwyth, Dyfed SY23 2NF. *T:* 3535. *Died 29 March 1987.*

**AARONS, Sir Daniel (Sidney)**, Kt 1970; OBE 1966; MC 1917 and Bar, 1918; retired; *b* 1 Aug. 1885; *s* of Solomon Aarons and Hannah Hart; *m* 1925, Jessie Chaddock Stronach; no *c*. *Educ:* North Broken Hill Public School. Joined Vacuum Oil Co. Australia in West Australia, 1903; enlisted AIF, 1915, 16th Infantry Battalion; returned 1920 and joined Head Office of Company, Melbourne; transf. to Sydney as Gen. Man. NSW, 1935; retd 1947. Foundn Mem., Liberal Party of Australia, 1945; subseq. Chm. of Finance Cttee; Treas. 1969. Past Pres., Legacy Club of Sydney; Mem. Federal Council, Legacy Clubs of Australia; Past Pres., Civic Reform Assoc. (local govt). *Recreations:* lawn bowls; formerly rowing (Mem. King's Cup 8-oared Crew WA 1912), lacrosse (Player Man., WA Interstate Lacrosse Team, 1912) and golf. *Address:* Australian Club, 165 Macquarie Street, Sydney, NSW 2000, Australia. *T:* 221 1533. *Club:* Australian (Sydney). *Died 23 June 1983.*

**ABBOT, Dermot Charles Hyatt**, CB 1959; Assistant Under-Secretary of State, Department of Health and Social Security, 1968–69 (Under-Secretary, Ministry of Pensions and National Insurance, 1955–66, Ministry of Social Security, 1966–68); retired 1969; *b* 8 Sept. 1908; *e s* of late Reginald Arthur Brame Abbot and late Sarah Ethel Abbot; *m* 1947, Elsie Myrtle Arnott (Dame Elsie Abbot, DBE) (*d* 1983). *Educ:* High School, Newcastle-under-Lyme; High School, Southend-on-Sea; University College, London. Post Office, 1929–40 and 1945–49; transferred to Ministry of Pensions and National Insurance, 1949. *Died 5 July 1990.*

**ABBOT, Dame Elsie (Myrtle)**, DBE 1966 (CBE 1957); Third Secretary, HM Treasury, 1958–67; *b* 3 Sept. 1907; *d* of Leonard and Frances Tostevin, Streatham, London; *m* 1st, 1938, E. A. Arnott, *s* of R. E. Arnott, Pontypridd; one *s* one *d*; 2nd, 1947, D. C. H. Abbot, CB. *Educ:* Clapham County Secondary School; St Hugh's College, Oxford. 1st Class Hons Modern History, 1929; 1st Class Hons Philosophy, Politics and Economics, 1930. Entered Administrative Class of Home Civil Service, 1930; Post Office, 1930–47; transferred to HM Treasury, 1947. *Address:* 4 Constable Close, NW11. *T:* 01–455 9413. *Died 26 May 1983.*

**ABBOTT, Arthur William**, CMG 1956; CBE 1949; FRHistS; *b* 5 Feb. 1893; *s* of late William Henry Abbott, Southampton, sometime President, Hampshire Law Society; *m* 1926, Kathleen, *d* of Richard Way; one *s*. *Educ:* Blundell's School, Tiverton. Entered Crown Agents' Office, 1912; served European War, 1914–18, Hampshire Regt, North Russia, 1917–19; Secretary, East African Currency Board, 1930–38; Head of Department, 1938; Establishment Officer, 1948; Secretary to the Crown Agents (for oversea governments and administrations), 1954–58. *Publications:* History of the Crown Agents (printed for private circulation, 1960); review and magazine articles. *Address:* Frithys Orchard, West Clandon, Surrey. *T:* Guildford 222565. *Died 8 Oct. 1986.*

**ABBOTT, Hon. Douglas Charles**, PC (Can.) 1945; QC 1939; BCL (McGill); Hon. LLD, Hon. DCL; Justice of the Supreme Court, Canada, 1954–73; *b* Lennoxville, PQ, 29 May 1899; *s* of Lewis Duff Abbott and Mary Jane Pearce; *m* 1st, 1925, Mary Winifred Chisholm (*d* 1980); two *s* one *d*; 2nd, 1981, Elizabeth Peters. *Educ:* Bishop's College; McGill University; Dijon University, France. Elected to House of Commons, 1940; re-elected, 1945, 1949 and 1953. Minister of National Defence for Naval Services, April 1945; Minister of National Defence (Army), Aug. 1945; Min. of Finance, Canada, 1946–54. Practised law in Montreal with firm of Robertson, Abbott, Brierley and O'Connor. Chancellor, Bishop's Univ., 1958–68. *Recreations:* fishing, curling, golf. *Address:* 45 Lakeway Drive, Ottawa K1L 5A9, Canada. *TA:* Ottawa Canada. *T:* 746–6271. *Clubs:* University, Royal Montreal Curling (Montreal); Rideau (Ottawa). *Died 17 March 1987.*

**ABBOTT, Rev. Eric Symes**, KCVO 1966; DD (Lambeth); MA Cantab and Oxon (by incorporation); Dean of Westminster, 1959–74; *b* 26 May 1906; *s* of William Henry and Mary Abbott, Nottingham. *Educ:* Nottingham High School; Jesus College, Cambridge. Curate, St John's, Smith Square, Westminster, 1930–32; Chaplain, King's College, London, 1932–36; Chaplain to Lincoln's Inn, 1935–36; Warden of the Scholae Cancellarii, Lincoln, 1936–45; Canon and Prebendary of Lincoln Cathedral, 1940–60; Dean of King's College, London, 1945–55; Warden of Keble College, Oxford, 1956–60; Chaplain to King George VI, 1948–52, and to the Queen, 1952–59; an Extra Chaplain to the Queen, 1974–. Chaplain and Sub-Prelate, Order of St John of Jerusalem, 1969–. Freeman, City of Westminster, 1973. FKC, London, 1946; Hon. Fellow: Keble Coll., Oxford, 1960; Jesus Coll., Cambridge, 1966. Hon. DD London, 1966. *Address:* Redcot, Three Gates Lane, Haslemere, Surrey. *Club:* Athenæum. *Died 6 June 1983.*

**ABBOTT, Sir Myles (John)**, Kt 1964; Chief Justice of Bermuda, 1961–71; *b* 27 Feb. 1906; *s* of Edmund Rushworth Abbott, 13 Victoria Street, London, Solicitor; *m* 1st, 1932, Grace Ada Jeffery; one *d*; 2nd, 1960, Dorothy Anne Campbell, *widow* of Robert Currie Campbell. *Educ:* King's Sch., Canterbury. Admitted Solicitor, 1929; Partner, Chas Rogers Sons & Abbott, 1930. 2nd Lieut 9th Middlesex Regt. (TA), 1933. Selected for appointment to Colonial Legal Service, 1935; Lieut 9th Middx Regt and transferred to TARO, 1936; Asst Crown Solicitor, Hong Kong, 1936; called to the Bar, 1940; Official Receiver and Registrar of Trade Marks, Hong Kong, 1941. Served War of 1939–45 (prisoner); released, 1945. President, High Court of Ethiopia, Oct. 1946–Oct. 1949; Puisne Judge, Nigeria, 1950–55; Judge of High Court of Lagos, 1955–57; Federal Justice of Federal Supreme Court of Nigeria, 1957–61. *Publications:* (ed) West African Court of Appeal Reports, 1946–49; (ed) Federal Supreme Court Reports, Nigeria, Vol. 4, 1959, 1960. *Address:* 36 Mizzen-Top, Warwick 7–20, Bermuda. *T:* Bermuda 22658. *Club:* Naval and Military. *Died 12 Jan. 1984.*

**ABDUL RAHMAN PUTRA, Tunku (Prince),** CH 1961; Hon. AC 1987; Order of the National Crown, Malaysia; Kedah Order of Merit; Secretary General, Islamic Conference of Foreign Ministers, 1969–73; Prime Minister of Malaysia, 1963–70; Chairman, Star Publications, Penang; *b* 8 Feb. 1903; *s* of Abdul Halim Shah, 24th Sultan of Kedah; *m* 3rd, 1939, Puan Sharifah Rodziah binti Syed Alwi Barakbah; one *s* one *d* (both by 1st wife); one *s* three *d* (all adopted). *Educ:* Alor Star; Bangkok; St Catharine's Coll., Cambridge (Research Fellow, 1980); Inner Temple, London (Hon. Master, 1971). Joined Kedah State Civil Service, 1931, District Officer. During the occupation, when the Japanese returned Kedah to Siam, he served as Supt of Educn and Dir of Passive Defence until the reoccupation, Sept. 1945; opposed British Govt fusion of States and Colonies to form the Malayan Union and took a leading part in formation of United Malays National Organisation (UMNO); when the Malayan Union gave way to the Federation of Malaya in 1949, he became Chairman of UMNO in Kedah; after being called to Bar (Inner Temple), he returned to Kedah and was seconded to Federal Legal Dept as a Dep. Public Prosecutor, 1949; President of UMNO, 1951; resigned from CS and a year later was apptd an unofficial Mem. Federal Executive and Legislative Councils; leader of the Alliance Party (UMNO, Malayan Chinese Association, Malayan Indian Congress), 1954; Mem., Federal Legislative Council, 1955–73; became Chief Minister and Minister of Home Affairs; in reshuffle of 1956 also took portfolio of Minister for Internal Defence and Security; was also Chm. Emergency Ops Council which decides on policy in fighting Malayan Communist Party; headed Alliance deleg. to London to negotiate Independence for the Federation, Dec. 1955; after Independence on 31 Aug. 1957, became Prime Minister and Minister of External Affairs and continued to be Chm. Emergency Ops Council; resigned as Prime Minister in Feb. 1959 to prepare for general elections in Aug.; became Prime Minister for second time, Aug. 1959, and in Sept. initiated Min. of Rural Development; became also Minister of Ext. Affairs, Nov. 1960, and Minister of Information and Broadcasting, June 1961; Prime Minister, Federation of Malaya, until it became Malaysia, 1963; became Prime Minister for third time, April 1964, following Gen. Elections in States of Malaya, also Minister of External Affairs and Minister of Culture, Youth and Sports. Attended Prime Ministers' Conferences in London, May 1960 and March 1961; Head of mission to London to discuss and agree in principle proposed formation of Federation of Malaysia, Nov. 1961; Head of second mission to London on formation of Malaysia, July 1962; attended Prime Ministers' Confs, London, 1965, 1966. Apptd Chancellor, Univ. Malaya, 1962. Pres., Football Assoc. of Malaya; Pres., Asian Football Confedn; Vice-Pres. (for life), Royal Commonwealth Society. Dr of Law, Univ. of Malaya; Hon. LLD: Araneta Univ., 1958; Cambridge Univ., 1960; Univ. of Sydney, 1960; Univ. of Saigon, 1961; Aligarh Muslim Univ., 1962; Univ. Sains, Malaysia, 1975; Hon. DLitt, Seoul National Univ., 1965; Hon. DCL Oxford, 1970. Holds various foreign orders. *Publications:* Mahsuri (imaginary play of Malaya; performed on stage in North Malaya throughout 1941; filmed in Malaya, 1958); Raja Bersiong (filmed 1966); May 13—Before and After, 1969; Looking Back, 1977; Viewpoints, 1978; As a Matter of Interest, 1981; Lest We Forget, 1983; Something to Remember, 1983; The Road to Independence, 1984; Political Awakening, 1986; *relevant publications:* Prince and Premier (Biography) by Harry Miller, 1959; Pictorial Biography of Tunku Abdul Rahman Putra by Tan Sri Dato Dr Mubin Sheppard, Vol. 1 (1903–1957), 1984, Vol. 2 (1957–1987), 1987. *Recreations:* golf, football, tennis, walking, swimming, racing, motor-boating, photography (both cine and still); collector of ancient weapons, particularly the Malay kris. *Address:* 1 Jalan Tunku, 50480 Kuala Lumpur, Malaysia; 16 Jalan Tunku Abdul Rahman, 10350 Pulau Pinang, Malaysia.
*Died 6 Dec. 1990.*

**ABELSMITH, Vice-Adm. Sir (Edward Michael) Conolly,** GCVO 1958 (KCVO 1954; CVO 1946); CB 1951; JP; RN retd; Extra Equerry to the Queen since 1952; *b* 3 Dec. 1899; 2nd *s* of Eustace Abel Smith, Longhills, Lincoln, and Ailleen Geta, *d* of Col. John A. Conolly, VC, Coldstream Guards; *m* 1932, Lady Mary Elizabeth Carnegie, *d* of 10th Earl of Southesk; one *s* one *d*. *Educ:* Royal Naval Colleges, Osborne and Dartmouth. Mid. HMS Princess Royal, 1915; Qualified Pilot, 1924; Comdr 1933; Naval Equerry to the King, 1939; Capt. 1940; HMS Biter, 1942; Naval Attaché, British Embassy, Washington, DC, 1944–46; HMS Triumph, 1947; Naval ADC to the King, 1949; Rear-Adm. 1949; Vice-Controller (Air), Chief of Naval Air Equipment and Chief Naval Representative, Min. of Supply, 1950; Vice-Adm. 1952; Flag Officer, Royal Yachts, 1953–58. JP 1958. HM Lieutenant for Selkirk, 1958–74. Grand Cross of St Olav, 1955. *Recreations:* hunting, shooting. *Address:* Ashiestiel, Galashiels TD1 3LJ. *T:* Clovenfords 214. *Clubs:* Naval and Military, Buck's. *Died 3 Dec. 1985.*

**ABELL, Sir George (Edmond Brackenbury),** KCIE 1947 (CIE 1946); OBE 1943; Hon. LLD (Aberdeen), 1947; First Civil Service Commissioner, 1964–67; *b* 22 June 1904; *s* of late G. F. Abell, JP,

Foxcote Manor, Andoversford, Glos; *m* 1928, Susan Norman-Butler; two *s* one *d*. *Educ:* Marlborough; Corpus Christi Coll., Oxford (Hon. Fellow, 1971). Joined Indian Civil Service, 1928; Private Sec. to the Viceroy, 1945–47. Advisor, 1948–52, Director, 1952–64, Bank of England; Dir, Portals Hldgs, 1968–76. Rhodes Trustee, 1949–74 (Chm., 1969–74). Pres. Council, Reading Univ., 1969–74; Mem. Council, 1955–77, Chm., 1974–77, Marlborough Coll. *Address:* Whittonditch House, Ramsbury, Wilts. *T:* Marlborough 20449. *Club:* Oriental. *Died 11 Jan. 1989.*

**ABERCROMBIE, Nigel James;** free-lance writer; *b* 5 Aug. 1908; 2nd *s* of late Lieutenant-Colonel A. W. Abercrombie; *m* 1931, Elisabeth Brownlees; one *s* one *d*. *Educ:* Haileybury; Oriel College, Oxford. BA 1929; DPhil 1933; MA 1934. Lecturer in French, Magdalen College, Oxford, 1931–36; Paget Toynbee Prize, 1934; Professor of French and Head of Mod. Lang. Dept, University College, Exeter, 1936–40. Entered Secretary's Department, Admiralty, 1940; Asst Sec., 1942; Under-Secretary, 1956; Cabinet Office, 1962–63; Sec.-Gen., 1963–68, Chief Regional Advr, 1968–73, Arts Council of Great Britain. Editor, Dublin Review, 1953–55. *Publications:* The Origins of Jansenism, 1936; St Augustine and French Classical Thought, 1938, repr. 1972; editions of Le Misanthrope and Tartuffe, 1938; Life and Work of Edmund Bishop, 1959; The Arts in the South-East, 1974; Artists and Their Public, 1975; Cultural Policy in the United Kingdom, 1982; contrib. to: Times Anthology of Detective Stories, 1972; New Stories I, 1976; The State and the Arts, 1980; Studies in Sussex Church History, 1981; Challoner and his Church, 1981; articles and reviews in theological, historical and literary periodicals. *Recreations:* The 3 R's. *Address:* 32 Springett Avenue, Ringmer, Lewes, E Sussex BN8 5HE. *T:* Ringmer 813029. *Died 17 Feb. 1986.*

**ABERDEEN AND TEMAIR, 5th Marquess of,** *cr* 1916; **Archibald Victor Dudley Gordon;** Bt of Nova Scotia, 1642; Earl of Aberdeen, Viscount Formartine, Lord Haddo, Methlic, Tarves and Kellie, 1682, Peerage of Scotland; Viscount Gordon, 1814, and Earl of Haddo, 1916, Peerage of UK; writer and broadcaster; *b* 9 July 1913; 2nd *s* of 3rd Marquis of Aberdeen and Temair, DSO, and Cécile Elizabeth (*d* 1948), *d* of George Drummond, Swaylands, Penshurst, Kent; *S* brother, 1974; unmarried. *Educ:* Harrow. An assistant secretary, Council for the Protection of Rural England, 1936–40; joined BBC Monitoring Service, April 1940; BBC Talks Dept (Radio), 1946–72; Producer of The Week in Westminster, and of party political and election broadcasts (radio), 1946–66; Editor, Radio Documentaries and Talks, 1967–72. Independent. *Publications:* (as Archie Gordon): Towers, 1979; A Wild Flight of Gordons, 1985. *Heir-pres.:* b Lord Alastair Ninian John Gordon [*b* 20 July 1920; *m* 1950, Anne, *d* of late Lt-Col Gerald Barry, MC; one *s* two *d*]. *Address:* Haughley Grange, Stowmarket, Suffolk IP14 3QT. *T:* Stowmarket 673245. *Died 7 Sept. 1984.*

**ABERDEEN, David du Rieu,** FRIBA, MRTPI; Architect (Private Practice); *b* 13 Aug. 1913; *s* of David Aberdeen and Lilian du Rieu; *m* 1940, Phyllis Irene Westbrook (*née* Buller), widow; two step *c*. *Educ:* privately; Sch. of Architecture, London Univ. (BA Hons, Arch.). RIBA Donaldson Medallist, 1934; RIBA Alfred Bossom Research Fell., 1946–47. Works include: Brabazon Hangars, Filton, for Bristol Aeroplane Co.; TUC Headquarters, London, won in open architectural competition, 1948 (RIBA London Architecture Bronze Medal, 1958); 13–storey point block flats, New Southgate; housing for Basildon and Harlow New Towns. Architect for: new headquarters in City for Swiss Bank Corp.; redevelopment of Paddington Gen. Hosp.; New Gen. Market Hall, Shrewsbury; Swiss Centre, cultural and trade Headquarters, Leicester Square; First National City Bank of NY, London Office. Lectr, Atelier of Advanced Design, Sch. of Architecture, London Univ., 1947–53. *Publications:* contrib. to architectural press. *Address:* 20 Green Moor Link, N21. *Died 15 Jan. 1987.*

**ABRAHALL, Rt. Rev. Anthony Leigh Egerton H.;** see Hoskyns-Abrahall.

**ABRAHAM, Gerald Ernest Heal,** CBE 1974; MA; FBA 1972; FTCL; President, Royal Musical Association, 1970–74; *b* 9 March 1904; *s* of Ernest and Dorothy Mary Abraham; *m* 1936, Isobel Patsie Robinson; one *d*. Asst Editor, Radio Times, 1935–39; Dep. Editor, The Listener, 1939–42; Director of Gramophone Dept, BBC, 1942–47; James and Constance Alsop Prof. of Music, Liverpool Univ., 1947–62; BBC Asst Controller of Music, 1962–67; Music Critic, The Daily Telegraph, 1967–68; Ernest Bloch Prof. of Music, Univ. of Calif (Berkeley), 1968–69. Chairman, Music Section of the Critics' Circle, 1944–46. Editor, Monthly Musical Record, 1945–60; Editor, Music of the Masters (series of books); General Editor: The History of Music in Sound (gramophone records and handbooks); New Oxford History of Music; Chm., Early English Church Music Cttee, 1970–80; Mem. Editorial Cttee, Musica Britannica. President, International Society for Music Education, 1958–61; Dep. Chm. Haydn Institute (Cologne), 1961–68; Mem. Directorium, Internat. Musicological Soc., 1967–77; Corr. Mem., Amer.

Musicological Soc., 1980; Governor, Dolmetsch Foundn, 1970–73. Hon. RAM 1970. Hon. DMus: Dunelm, 1961; Liverpool, 1978; Southampton, 1979; Hon. Dr of Fine Arts, California (Berkeley), 1969. *Publications:* This Modern Stuff, 1933; Nietzsche, 1933; Studies in Russian Music, 1935; Tolstoy, 1935; Masters of Russian Music (with M. D. Calvocoressi), 1936; Dostoevsky, 1936; A Hundred Years of Music, 1938; On Russian Music, 1939; Chopin's Musical Style, 1939; Beethoven's Second-Period Quartets, 1942; Eight Soviet Composers, 1943; Tchaikovsky, 1944; Rimsky-Korsakov, 1945; Design in Music, 1949; Slavonic and Romantic Music, 1968; The Tradition of Western Music, 1974; The Concise Oxford History of Music, 1979; Essays on Russian and East European Music, 1984; (ed) New Oxford History of Music: (with Dom Anselm Hughes) Vol. III (Ars Nova and the Renaissance), 1960; Vol. IV (The Age of Humanism), 1968; Vol. VIII (The Age of Beethoven), 1982; Vol. VI (Concert Music: 1630–1750), 1985. *Recreations:* walking, languages, military history. *Address:* The Old School House, Ebernoe, near Petworth, West Sussex. *T:* North Chapel 325. *Died 18 March 1988.*

**ABRAHAM, Louis Arnold,** CB 1956; CBE 1950; *b* 26 Nov. 1893; *y s* of late William Abraham, MP for West Limerick, 1885–92, North East Cork, 1893–1910, Dublin (Harbour), 1910–15; *m* 1921, Irene (*d* 1974), *yr d* of late Frederick George Kerin, Ennis, County Clare. *Educ:* Owen's School, London; Peterhouse, Cambridge (Exhibr) (1st cl. Hist. Tripos, pt 2, 1920). Pres., Cambridge Union, 1920. Asst Clerk, House of Commons, 1920; called to the Bar (certif. of honour), 1928; Pres., Hardwicke Soc., 1928; Senior Clerk, House of Commons, 1932; Clerk of Private Bills, 1945–52; Examr of Petitions for Private Bills and Taxing Officer, 1946–52; Principal Clerk of Committees, 1952–58. *Publications:* (with S. C. Hawtrey) A Parliamentary Dictionary, 1956; Defamation as Contempt of Parliament, in, Wicked, Wicked Libels, 1972; (ed) Palgrave's Chairman's Handbook, 1964. *Address:* 13 Lushington Road, Eastbourne, East Sussex BN21 4LG. *T:* Eastbourne 32223. *Died 31 Jan. 1983.*

**ABRAHAM, Robert John Elliot;** Counsellor, Budget and Infrastructure, UK Delegation to NATO, Brussels, since 1983; *b* 13 Sept. 1927; *s* of Robert John Elliott and Ivy Doreen Abraham; *m* 1971, Lorraine (*née* Langley). *Educ:* Plymouth College; Brasenose College, Oxford. BA (Greats). Admiralty, 1952; Private Sec. to Parly Sec., 1955, to Perm. Sec., 1956; Resident Clerk: Admiralty, 1955–64; Ministry of Defence, 1964–68; Head of Naval Personnel I, MoD, 1968–73; Head of Defence Secretariat 6, 1973–77; RCDS 1977; Head of Defence Secretariat 16, 1978–83. *Recreations:* walking, gardening, good fare, music, serendipity. *Address:* c/o Foreign and Commonwealth Office, SW1. *Died 26 Nov. 1985.*

**ABRAHAMS, Sir Charles (Myer),** KCVO 1970; Deputy Chairman and Joint Managing Director, Aquascutum and associated companies, 1949–82, then President; *b* 25 April 1914; *s* of late Isidor and Eva Abrahams; *m* 1940, Luisa (*née* Kramer); two *d. Educ:* Westminster School. Hon. President, Friends of the Duke of Edinburgh's Award Scheme, 1975–; Vice-President: Nightingale House, Home for Aged Jews, 1971–; British Paraplegic Sports Soc., 1976–80. Freeman, City of London, 1981. Served War of 1939–45 in Italy, Flt-Lt RAFVR. OStJ 1977. *Recreations:* golf and sculpture. *Address:* 59 Cranbourne Gardens, NW11. *Clubs:* Coombe Hill Golf (Surrey); Sunningdale Golf (Berks). *Died 11 June 1985.*

**ABRAHAMS, Doris Caroline;** see Brahms, Caryl.

**ACKERMAN, Myron,** CBE 1972 (Hon.); Chairman, Tuscan Clothing Co. Ltd; Director: Atlas Avenue Ltd; d'Avenza spa, Carrara, Italy; *b* 21 Sept. 1913; *s* of late Simon Ackerman and late May Krones Ackerman; *m* 1954, Marjorie Molyneux Jacob; no *c. Educ:* Yale Univ. Hon. Freeman, Borough of Crewe, 1973. *Address:* Steward's Cottage, Combermere, near Whitchurch, Salop SY13 4AJ. *T:* Burleydam 665. *Clubs:* American; Yale (New York). *Died 24 May 1985.*

**ACKROYD, Dame (Dorothy) Elizabeth,** DBE 1970; MA, BLitt (Oxon); Chairman, Patients Association, since 1978; *b* 13 Aug. 1910; *d* of late Major Charles Harris Ackroyd, MC. *Educ:* privately; St Hugh's Coll., Oxford. Civil servant, 1940–70 (Under-Sec., 1952); Commonwealth Fund Fellow, 1949–50; Dir of Steel and Power Div., Economic Commn for Europe, 1950–51; UK Delegn to High Authority of ECSC, 1952–55; Dir, Consumer Council, 1963–71. Chairman: Bloodstock and Racehorse Industries Confedn Ltd, 1977–78; Cinematograph Films Council, 1981–85 (Mem., 1970–85); SE Electricity Consultative Council, 1972–84; Indep. Mem., Council for the Securities Industry, 1978–83; Member: Exec. Cttee, Consumers' Assoc., 1986– (Vice-Pres., 1970–86); PO Users' Nat. Council, 1970–84; Seeboard, 1972–84; Bedford Coll. Council, 1970–85; Royal Holloway and Bedford New Coll. Council, 1985–; Horserace Totalisator Bd, 1975–84; Waltham Forest Community Health Council, 1974–; Council, RSA, 1975–81; Exec. Cttee, Nat. Council for Voluntary Organisations, 1980–; Exec. Cttee,

Pedestrians' Assoc. for Road Safety; Governor, Birkbeck Coll., 1973–; Vice-Chm., London Voluntary Service Council, 1977–; Pres., Patients Assoc., 1971–78. *Address:* 73 St James's Street, SW1A 1PH. *T:* 01-493 6686. *Club:* Jockey. *Died 28 June 1987.*

**ACLAND, Sir Antony Guy,** 5th Bt *cr* 1890; *b* 17 Aug. 1916; *s* of Captain Sir Hubert Guy Dyke Acland, 4th Bt, DSO, RN, and Lalage Mary Kathleen (*d* 1961), *e d* of Captain John Edward Acland; *S father,* 1978; *m* 1st, 1939, Avriel Ann Wingfield-Stratford (*d* 1943); one *d*; 2nd, 1944, Margaret Joan Rooke; one *s* one *d. Educ:* Winchester; RMA, Woolwich. Served RA, 1937–58: War of 1939–45, France, 1939–40; specialised in Anti-Aircraft; Instructor, Fire Control; Instructor in Gunnery, Military Coll. of Science, 1948–49; retired as Major, 1958. Joined Saunders-Roe on Rocket Development and Trials, 1958; projects included Black Knight and Black Arrow research rockets; retired, 1967. *Heir:* s Major Christopher Guy Dyke Acland, RA [*b* 24 March 1946; *m* 1971, Christine Mary Carden, *y d* of Dr J. W. B. Waring; two *s*]. *Died 14 Dec. 1983.*

**ACLAND, Sir (Hugh) John (Dyke),** KBE 1968; a Member, 1947–72, Chairman, 1960–72, New Zealand Wool Board; Vice-Chairman, International Wool Secretariat, to 1972; *b* 18 Jan. 1904; *es* of Sir Hugh Acland, CMG, CBE, FRCS, and Lady Acland; *m* 1935, Katherine Wilder Ormond; three *s* three *d. Educ:* Christ's College, Christchurch, NZ. MHR, NZ, 1942–47. JP S Canterbury. *Address:* Mount Peel, Peel Forest, South Canterbury, New Zealand. *Died 26 Jan. 1981.*

**ACLAND, Sir Richard Thomas Dyke,** 15th Bt, *cr* 1644; *b* 26 Nov. 1906; *e s* of Rt Hon. Sir Francis Acland, 14th Bt, MP; *S father,* 1939; *m* 1936, Anne Stella Alford; three *s* (and one *s* decd). *Educ:* Rugby; Balliol Coll., Oxford. MP (L) Barnstaple Div. Devon, 1935–45; contested: Torquay Div., 1929; Barnstaple, 1931; Putney, 1945; MP (Lab) Gravesend Division of Kent, 1947–55. Sen. Lectr, St Luke's College of Educn, Exeter, 1959–74. Second Church Estates Commissioner, 1950–51. *Publications:* Unser Kampf, 1940; The Forward March, 1941; What It Will Be Like, 1942; How It Can Be Done, 1943; Public Speaking, 1946; Nothing Left to Believe?, 1949; Why So Angry?, 1958; Waging Peace, 1958; We Teach Them Wrong: religion and the young, 1963; (with others) Sexual Morality: three views, 1965; Curriculum or Life, 1966; Moves to the Integrated Curriculum, 1967; The Next Step, 1974; Hungry Sheep, 1988. *Heir:* s John Dyke Acland [*b* 13 May 1939; *m* 1961, Virginia, *d* of Roland Forge; two *s* one *d*]. *Address:* College, Broadclyst, Exeter EX5 3HX. *T:* Exeter (0392) 61452. *Died 24 Nov. 1990.*

**à COURT;** see Holmes à Court.

**ACTON,** 3rd Baron, *cr* 1869, of Aldenham, Salop; **John Emerich Henry Lyon-Dalberg-Acton;** Bt 1643; CMG 1963; MBE 1945; TD 1949; Hereditary Duke of Dalberg; Patrician of Naples; Major RA, TA; Director, Canadian Overseas Packaging Industries, since 1983; Trustee, Cold Comfort Farm Society, since 1967; *b* 15 Dec. 1907; *e s* of 2nd Baron Acton, KCVO, and Dorothy (*d* 1923), *d* of late T. H. Lyon, Appleton Hall, Cheshire; *S father,* 1924; *m* 1931, Daphne Strutt, *o d* of 4th Baron Rayleigh, FRS, and late Mary Hilda, 2nd *d* of 4th Earl of Leitrim; five *s* five *d. Educ:* Downside; RMC Sandhurst; Trinity Coll., Cambridge. Served War of 1939–45, Italy; Major, Shropshire Yeo. (MBE). Partner, Barham & Brooks, Mem. Birmingham Stock Exchange, 1936–47; emigrated S Rhodesia, 1947; Dir, Amal. Packaging Industries Ltd, 1950–67; Chm. and Man. Dir, API (Rhodesia) Ltd, Central Africa Paper Sacks Ltd, 1951–67; Director: Canadian Overseas Packaging Industries Ltd, 1962–65; Monterrey Packaging (Zambia) Ltd, 1964–67; Rhodesian Bd Standard Bank Ltd, 1958–67; Discount Co. of Rhodesia Ltd, 1960–67; East African Packaging, Jamaica Packaging Ltd, Caribbean Packaging Ltd, to 1965; Old Mutual Fire and General Insurance (Rhodesia) Ltd, to 1967; Chairman: Colcom Ltd, 1959–67; Rhodesian Insurances Ltd, Wright Dean (Rhodesia) Ltd, to 1967. Pres., Rhodesian Royal Agricl Show Soc., 1960–64; qualified Judge of Jersey cattle and pigs; Chairman: Gwebi Agricl Coll., 1958–62; Chibero Agricl Coll., 1960–65 (resigned on illegal declaration of independence); Mem. African Farm Develt Cttee, 1964–67; Chm., BRCS Rhodesia Council Br., 1962–68 (Life Mem. BRCS, 1966); Founding Chm., National (non-racial) Club, Salisbury, 1962; served SR Legal Aid and Welfare Cttee (detainees), 1965–67. Patron, Rhodesian Coll. of Music, to 1967. Chm., Mashonaland Owners and Trainers Assoc., 1956–57; Steward, Mashonaland Turf Club, 1957–67. Emigrated to Swaziland, 1967. Chairman: NEOPAC (Swaziland) Ltd, 1968–70; Swaziland Bd, Standard Bank Ltd, 1968–70; Dir, Swaziland Building Soc., 1968–70. Dir, Swaziland Br., BRCS, 1967–70; Founding Chm., Tattersalls Swaziland, 1969. Retired to Majorca, 1971. *Recreations:* music, bridge, roulette. *Heir:* s Hon. Richard Gerald Lyon-Dalberg-Acton [*b* 30 July 1941; *m* 1st, 1965, Hilary Juliet Sarah Cookson (*d* 1973); one *s*; 2nd, 1974, Judith (writer) (marr. diss. 1987), *d* of Hon. Sir Garfield Todd; 3rd, 1988, Patricia, *o d* of late M. Morey Nassif, and

of Mrs Nassif, Iowa, USA. *Educ:* St George's Coll., Salisbury, Rhodesia; Trinity Coll., Oxford (BA Hist. 1963). Called to Bar, Inner Temple, 1976. Dir, Coutts & Co., 1970–74]. *Address:* Hotel Maricel, 07015 Palma de Mallorca, Mallorca. *Clubs:* Royal Commonwealth Society; British American (Palma).
*Died* 23 *Jan.* 1989.

**ACUTT, Sir Keith (Courtney),** KBE 1962 (CBE 1957); Director: Anglo American Corporation, since 1953 (joined company, 1928; Deputy Chairman, 1957–82); De Beers Consolidated Mines, since 1958; several other mining and finance companies; *b* 6 Oct. 1909; *s* of late Guy Courtney Acutt. *Educ:* in South Africa. Served War of 1939–45 (despatches, 1944). *Address:* 44 Main Street, Johannesburg, South Africa. *T:* 638–9111. *Died* 21 *July* 1986.

**ADAIR, Maj.-Gen. Sir Allan (Henry Shafto),** 6th Bt, *cr* 1838; GCVO 1974 (KCVO 1967; CVO 1957); CB 1945; DSO 1940; MC 1918, and Bar 1919; DL; JP; Lieutenant of HM Bodyguard of the Yeomen of the Guard, 1951–67; *b* 3 Nov. 1897; *o s* of Sir R. Shafto Adair, 5th Bt and Mary (*d* 1950), *d* of Henry Anstey Bosanquet; *S* father, 1949; *m* Enid (*d* 1984), *d* of late Hon. Mrs Dudley Ward; three *d* (one *s* killed in action, 1943). *Educ:* Harrow. Grenadier Guards, 1916–41; commanded 3rd Battalion, 1940; Comdr 30 Guards Brigade, 1941; Comdr 6 Guards Brigade, 1942; Comdr Guards Armoured Division 1942–45; retired pay, 1947. Colonel of the Grenadier Guards, 1961–74. DL for Co. Antrim; JP for Suffolk. Governor of Harrow School, 1947–52. Dep. Grand Master, United Grand Lodge of Freemasons, 1969–76. *Address:* 55 Green Street, W1. *T:* 01–629 3860; Denton Lodge, Harleston, Norfolk. *Clubs:* Turf, Cavalry and Guards. *Died* 4 *Aug.* 1988 (*ext*).

**ADAIR, Arthur Robin,** CVO 1961; MBE 1947; HM Diplomatic Service, retired Aug. 1972; State and Ministerial Visit Escorting Officer, Government Hospitality Fund, 1973–75; retired 1975; *b* 10 Feb. 1913; *s* of late Francis Robin Adair and Ethel Anne Adair, Grove House, Youghal, Eire; *m* 1952, Diana Theodora Synnott; one *s*. *Educ:* abroad; Emmanuel College, Cambridge. Indian Civil Service, 1937–47 (incl. 3 yrs in Army in charge of recruitment for Bihar Prov.); Dist Magistrate and Dep. Comr, 1944–47; Treasury, July 1947; transferred to CRO, Oct. 1947; First Secretary: Dacca, 1947–50; Colombo, 1952–56; British Dep. High Comr in: Dacca, 1960–64; Cyprus, 1964–68; British High Comr in Brunei, 1968–Jan. 1972. *Recreation:* flying as private pilot. *Address:* Grove House, Youghal, Co. Cork, Eire. *T:* Youghal 2930. *Club:* Naval and Military. *Died* 26 *Dec.* 1981.

**ADAM, Hon. Sir Alexander Duncan Grant** (known as Hon. Sir Alistair Adam), Kt 1970; MA, LLM; Judge, Supreme Court of Victoria, 1957–74; *b* Greenock, Scotland, 30 Nov. 1902; *s* of late Rev. Prof. Adam and of Mrs D. S. Adam; *m* 1930, Nora Laver; one *s* two *d*. *Educ:* Scotch Coll., Melbourne; Melbourne Univ. Associate to Mr Justice Starke, 1927–28; Victorian Bar, 1928–57; Independent Lecturer in Real Property, Melbourne Univ., 1932–51; Defence Dept, 1942–45; QC 1950; Member Council: Melbourne Univ., 1957–69; Nat. Museum of Victoria, 1962–74. *Publications:* contributor to learned jls. *Recreation:* bowls. *Address:* 39 Walsh Street, Balwyn, Vic 3103, Australia. *T:* 801524. *Clubs:* Australian (Melbourne); Deepdene Bowling. *Died* 20 *Sept.* 1986.

**ADAM, Colin Gurdon Forbes,** CSI 1924; *b* 18 Dec. 1889; *y s* of Sir Frank Forbes Adam, 1st Bt; *m* 1920, Hon. Irene Constance Lawley, *o c* of 3rd Baron Wenlock; two *s* one *d* (and one *s* decd). *Educ:* Eton; King's Coll., Cambridge (BA). Entered Indian Civil Service, 1912; Asst Collector and Magistrate, Poona, 1913–15; Under-Sec. to Government of Bombay, 1919; Private Sec. to Governor of Bombay, 1920; Dep. Sec. to Govt, 1925; retired, 1927; District Comr for Special Area of Durham and Tyneside, 1934–39; Chairman, Yorkshire Conservative Newspaper Co., 1960–65. Served Indian Army Reserve of Officers, 1915–18; Indian Expeditionary Force, Mesopotamia and Palestine, 1916–18. DL Kingston upon Hull, 1958–66. *Publication:* Life of Lord Lloyd, 1948. *Address:* The Grange, Elvington, York YO4 5AD. *T:* Elvington 493.
*Died* 12 *Nov.* 1982.

**ADAM, Randle R.;** *see* Reid-Adam.

**ADAM, General Sir Ronald Forbes,** 2nd Bt, *cr* 1917; GCB 1946 (KCB 1941; CB 1939); DSO 1918; OBE 1919; late RA; Hon. LLD (Aberdeen); Hon. Fellow, Worcester College, Oxford; President, United Nations Association; *b* 30 Oct. 1885; *e s* of Sir Frank Forbes Adam, 1st Bt, and Rose Frances (*d* 1944), *d* of C. G. Kemball, late Judge, High Court, Bombay; *S* father, 1926; *m* 1915, Anna Dorothy (*d* 1972), *d* of late F. I. Pitman; three *d*. *Educ:* Eton; RMA, Woolwich. Served Great War (France and Flanders, Italy), 1914–18 (despatches, DSO, OBE); GSO1, Staff College, Camberley, 1932–35; GSO1, War Office, 1935–36; Deputy Director of Military Operations, War Office, 1936; Commander Royal Artillery, 1st Division, 1936–37; Commandant of Staff College, Camberley, 1937; Deputy Chief of Imperial General Staff, 1938–39; Commanding 3rd Army Corps, 1939–40; General Officer Commanding-in-Chief,

Northern Command, 1940–41; Adjutant-General to the Forces, 1941–46; General, 1942; retired pay, 1946. Col Comdt of RA and of Army Educational Corps, 1940–50; Col Comdt Royal Army Dental Corps, 1945–51 (Representative, 1950). President: MCC, 1946–47; Library Assoc., 1949; Nat. Inst. of Adult Education, 1949–64; Chairman: Linoleum Working Party, 1946; Nat. Inst. Industrial Psychology, 1947–52; Council, Inst. of Education, London Univ., 1948–67; Mem., Miners Welfare Commn, 1946–52; Chm. and Dir-Gen., British Council, 1946–54; Executive Board UNESCO, 1950–54, Chm., 1952–54; Principal, Working Men's Coll., 1956–61. *Heir: n* Christopher Eric Forbes Adam [*b* 12 Feb 1920; *m* 1957, Patricia Ann Wreford, *y d* of late John Neville Wreford Brown]. *Address:* Carylls Lea, Faygate, Sussex RH12 4SJ. *Clubs:* Athenæum, Naval and Military. *Died* 26 *Dec.* 1982.

**ADAMS, Air Vice-Marshal Alexander Annan,** CB 1957; DFC 1944; *b* 14 Nov. 1908; *s* of Capt. Norman Anderson Adams, Durham; *m* 1933, Eileen Mary O'Neill; one *s* (one *d* decd). *Educ:* Beechmont, Sevenoaks; Bellerive, Switzerland; Austria. Commnd RAF, 1930; 54 Fighter Sqdn, 1931–32; 604 Aux. Sqdn, Hendon, 1933–35; CFS, 1935; Asst Air Attaché, Berlin, Brussels, The Hague, Berne, 1938–40; Ops, Air Min., 1940; British Embassy, Washington, 1941–42; in comd 49 (Lancaster) Sqdn, 1943–44; RAF Staff Coll., 1945; Head of RAF Intelligence, Germany, 1946–48; in comd RAF Binbrook, 1948–50; NATO Standing Gp, Washington, DC, 1951–53; idc, 1954; Air Attaché, Bonn, 1955; Min. of Defence, 1956; Chief of Staff, Far East Air Force, 1957–59. Hawker Siddeley Aviation, 1961–66. Dir, Mental Health Trust and Res. Fund, later Mental Health Foundn, 1970–77. Comdr Order of Orange Nassau, 1950. *Recreation:* painting. *Address:* c/o Lloyds Bank, Beaminster, Dorset DT8 3AT. *Club:* Royal Air Force.
*Died* 1 *March* 1990.

**ADAMS, Allender Steele, (Allen);** JP; MP (Lab) Paisley North, since 1983 (Paisley, 1979–83); computer analyst; *b* 16 Feb. 1946; *m* 1968, Kathleen; one *s* two *d*. *Educ:* Camphill High Sch., Paisley; Reid-Kerr Technical Coll., Paisley. Chief Magistrate, Paisley Borough, 1974–79; Mem., Strathclyde Regl Council, 1974–79; Vice Chm., Strathclyde Social Services Council, 1974–79. Labour Irish Whip; Member: Scottish Exec. Cttee, Labour Party; Exec. Cttee, Scottish PLP. *Recreations:* boating, gardening. *Address:* House of Commons, SW1A 0AA; Oaklands, Hunterhill Road, Paisley.
*Died* 5 *Sept.* 1990.

**ADAMS, Prof. Colin Wallace Maitland,** MD, DSc; FRCP, FRCPath; Sir William Dunn Professor of Pathology, 1965–88, and Chairman, 1984–87, Division of Histopathology, Guy's Campus, United Medical and Dental Schools of Guy's and St Thomas's Hospitals, University of London; *b* 17 Feb. 1928; *s* of Sidney Ewart Adams and Gladys Alethea Fletcher Adams; *m* 1953, Anne Brownhill; one *s*. *Educ:* Oundle School; Christ's College, Cambridge. Sir Lionel Whitby Medal, Cambridge Univ., 1959–60; MD Cantab, 1960; DSc London, 1967. FRCP 1977; FRCPath 1975. Visiting Scientist, National Institutes of Health, Bethesda, USA, 1960–61. Hon. Prof. in Neuropathology, Runwell Hosp., Wickford, Essex. *Publications:* Neurohistochemistry, 1965; Vascular Histochemistry, 1967; Research on Multiple Sclerosis, 1972; (jtly) Multiple Sclerosis, Pathology, Diagnosis and Treatment, 1983; Colour Atlas of Multiple Sclerosis, 1989; papers on arterial diseases, neuropathology and microscopical chemistry in medical and biological journals. *Address:* The Priory, Braxted Road, Tiptree, Essex. *T:* Tiptree 818446.
*Died* 30 *Jan.* 1990.

**ADAMS, Air Commodore Cyril Douglas,** CB 1948; OBE 1942; retired; *b* 18 Sept. 1897; British; *m* 1927, D. M. Le Brocq (*d* 1957), Highfield, Jersey; one *s* one *d*; *m* 1959, Joan (marr. diss.), *d* of late Comdr W. G. A. Ramsay-Fairfax; *m* 1968, Mrs K. E. Webster, NZ. *Educ:* Parkstone Grammar School. Served European War in Army, 1915–18, Egypt, Palestine; Commissioned RFC, 1918; Flying Instructor, 1918–25; Staff Duties, Iraq Command, 1925–27; Staff and Flying Duties, Halton Comd, 1928–35; CO 15 Sqdn, 1936–38; HQ Bomber Comd, 1938; CO 38 Sqdn, 1938–39; Sen. Officer i/c Administration, No 3 Group, 1939–40; Station Comdr, Kemble, Oakington, Abingdon, 1940–44; Base Comdr, Marston Moor and North Luffenham, 1944–45; India Command, AOA, AHQ, 1945–46; Base Comdr, Bombay, 1946; AOC No 2 Indian Group, 1946–47 (despatches 6 times, OBE (immediate award for gallantry)); Air Officer Commanding No 85 Group, BAFO, 1948–49, retired, 1949. *Recreations:* represented: RAF (Rugby, cricket, athletics); Hampshire (Rugby); Dorset and minor counties (cricket); keen golfer. *Address:* 6 Solent Pines, Whitby Road, Milford-on-Sea, Lymington, Hants. *T:* Milford-on-Sea 43754.
*Died* 19 *Aug.* 1988.

**ADAMS, Prof. James Whyte Leitch;** Professor of Education, University of Dundee (formerly Queen's College), 1955–80, now Emeritus; *b* 7 Nov. 1909; *o s* of Charles and Helen Adams, Stirling; *m* 1939, Isobel Margaret, ARIBA, *d* of Robert Gordon, Fraserburgh; one *s* two *d*. *Educ:* Arbroath High School; St Andrews University;

Oxford University. Harkness Scholar, St Andrews, 1928; Guthrie Scholar, 1931; 1st cl. hons Classics, 1932; Marshall Prizeman, Miller Prizeman, Lewis Campbell Medallist, etc; Waugh Scholar, Exeter Coll., Oxford, 1932; 1st cl. Classical Mods, 1934; 1st cl. Lit. Hum., 1936; Craven Fellowship, 1936; Dipl. in Educn, St Andrews Univ., 1937. Teacher of Classics, Golspie Senior Secondary Sch., 1937–39; Educn Officer (Scotland), BBC, 1939–47; RAF Education Service, 1942–45; HM Inspector of Schools, 1947–50; Lecturer in Humanity, Aberdeen University, 1950–55. *Publications:* various contributions, especially on Renaissance Latin Poetry. *Recreations:* golf and "brither" Scots. *Address:* Red Cottage, 80 Forthill Road, Broughty Ferry, Dundee. *T:* Dundee 78138.      *Died 9 May 1983.*

**ADAMS, Sir John (Bertram),** Kt 1981; CMG 1962; FRS 1963; Engineer, European Organisation for Nuclear Research (CERN); *b* 24 May 1920; *s* of John A. Adams and Emily Searles; *m* 1943, Renie Warburton; one *s* two *d. Educ:* Eltham College; Res. Lab., Siemens. Telecommunications Res. Estabt, Swanage and Malvern, 1940–45; Atomic Energy Research Establishment, Harwell, 1945–53; European Organisation for Nuclear Research (CERN), Geneva, 1953, Dir of Proton Synchrotron Division, 1954–60; Director-Gen., CERN, 1960–61; Director, Culham Laboratory, AEA, Oxford, 1960–67; Controller, Min. of Technology, 1965–66; Member: Council for Scientific Policy, 1965–68; Board, UKAEA, 1966–69; Adv. Council on Technology, 1966–69; Dir-Gen., 300 GeV Accelerator Project, CERN, 1969–75; Executive Dir-Gen., CERN, 1976–80. Fellow, Wolfson College, Oxford, 1966 (MA), Emeritus Fellow 1981. Guthrie Lecturer, Phys. Soc., 1965. DSc *hc:* Univ. of Geneva, 1960; Birmingham Univ., 1961; Univ. of Surrey, 1966; Univ. of Strathclyde, 1978; Univ. of Milan, 1980. Röntgen Prize, Univ. of Giessen, 1960; Duddell Medal, Physical Soc., 1961; Leverhulme Medal, Royal Soc., 1972; Faraday Medal, IEE, 1977; Royal Medal, Royal Soc., 1977. *Publications:* contributions to Nature, Nuovo Cimento, etc. *Recreations:* swimming, ski-ing. *Address:* (home) Champ Rosset, 1297 Founex VD, Switzerland; (office) European Organisation for Nuclear Research (CERN), 1211 Geneva 23, Switzerland.      *Died 4 March 1984.*

**ADAMS, Prof. J(ohn) Frank,** MA, ScD; FRS 1964; Lowndean Professor of Astronomy and Geometry, Cambridge University, since 1970; Fellow of Trinity College, Cambridge; *b* 5 Nov. 1930; *m* 1953, Grace Rhoda, BA, BD, AAPSW, MBASW; one *s* three *d. Educ:* Bedford School; Trinity College, Cambridge; The Institute for Advanced Study, Princeton. Junior Lecturer, Oxford, 1955–56; Research Fellow, Trinity College, Cambridge, 1955–58; Commonwealth Fund Fellow, 1957–58; Assistant Lecturer, Cambridge, and Director of Studies in Mathematics, Trinity Hall, Cambridge, 1958–61; Reader, Manchester, 1962–64; Fielden Prof. of Pure Mathematics, Manchester Univ., 1964–71. For. Associate, Nat. Acad. of Scis, USA, 1985; Mem., Royal Danish Acad. of Scis, 1988. Hon. ScD Heidelberg, 1986. Sylvester Medal, Royal Society, 1982. *Publications:* Stable Homotopy Theory, 1964; Lectures on Lie Groups, 1969; Algebraic Topology, 1972; Stable Homotopy and Generalised Homology, 1974; Infinite Loop Spaces, 1978; papers in mathematical jls. *Recreations:* walking, climbing, enamel. *Address:* 7 Westmeare, Hemingford Grey, Huntingdon PE18 9BZ.      *Died 7 Jan. 1989.*

**ADAMS, Rt. Hon. John Michael Geoffrey Manningham,** PC 1977; QC 1979; MP Barbados Labour Party, since 1966; Prime Minister of Barbados, since 1976; *b* 24 Sept. 1931; *s* of late Sir Grantley Adams, CMG, QC, and Grace Adams; *m* 1962, Genevieve, *d* of Philip Turner, CBE; two *s. Educ:* Harrison Coll., Barbados; Magdalen Coll., Oxford (MA, PPE; Hon. Fellow, 1982). Barrister-at-Law, Gray's Inn. Producer, BBC London, 1958–62; Polit. Party Sec., Barbados Labour Party, 1965–69; Leader of Opposition, 1971–76. Mem., Scotia No 340 SC (Roll of the Grand Lodge of Scotland) (Past Master, etc), and of other Masonic Lodges. *Recreations:* gardening, philately; watching, reading and writing about cricket. *Address:* (home) 14 Walkers Terrace, Gun Hill, St George, Barbados; (office) Prime Minister's Office, Bridgetown, Barbados. *Clubs:* Reform; Union (Bridgetown).      *Died 11 March 1985.*

**ADAMS, (John) Roland,** QC 1949; *b* 24 July 1900; *s* of late Alfred Courthope Adams and Sabina Newberry; *m* 1st, 1924, Ruth (marr. diss. 1946), *d* of late David Schlivek, merchant, Woonsocket, RI; no *c*; 2nd, 1944, Violet, *d* of late Sir Francis Hanson, London; no *c. Educ:* Charterhouse; New College, Oxford. Hon. Exhibitioner of New College, 1919; BA 1922; MA 1926. Barrister, Inner Temple, 1925; Master of the Bench, Inner Temple, 1957. Essex County Council, 1930–39; Vice-Chm., Essex Rivers Catchment Bd, 1935–39. Major, The Essex Regt, 1939–45; GSO3, War Office, 1939–40; DAAG, War Office, 1940–42; specially employed, 1942–45. Member, panel of Lloyd's arbitrators in salvage cases, 1950; appeal arbitrator, 1974; a Dep. Chm., Essex QS, 1950–56, Chairman, 1956–71. *Recreation:* staying at home. *Address:* Little Gubbions, Gubbions Hall Farm, Great Leighs, Chelmsford, Essex. *T:* Great Leighs 248.      *Died 22 April 1983.*

**ADAMS, Mary Grace Agnes, (Mrs Vyvyan Adams),** OBE 1953; *b* Hermitage, Berks, 10 March 1898; *o d* of late Catherine Elizabeth Mary and Edward Bloxham Campin; *m* 1925, S. Vyvyan T. Adams (*d* 1951), sometime MP for W Leeds; one *d. Educ:* Godolphin Sch.; University Coll., Cardiff (1st class Hons BSc; Hon. Fellow 1983); Newnham Coll., Cambridge. 1851 Res. Scholar and Bathurst Student, Univ. of Cambridge, 1921–25; Lectr and Tutor under Cambridge Extra-Mural Board and Board of Civil Service Studies, and broadcaster, 1925–30; joined staff of BBC, 1930; Producer, BBC TV, 1936–39; Dir, Home Intelligence, Min. of Information, 1939–41; N Amer. Broadcasting, 1942–45; Head of Talks and Current Affairs, 1945–54; Asst to Controller of Television Programmes, BBC, 1954–58, retired. Member, ITA, 1965–70; Dep. Chm., Consumers' Assoc., 1958–70. Chm., Telephone Users Assoc. Vice-Chairman: Nat. Council for the Unmarried Mother and her Child; Soc. for Anglo–Chinese Understanding. Member: Women's Group on Public Welfare; Council, Nat. Assoc. for Mental Health; Design Panel, British Railways Board; BMA Planning Unit. Trustee: Res. Inst. for Consumer Affairs; Galton Foundn; Anglo–Chinese Educational Inst. *Publications:* Six Talks on Heredity, 1929; papers on genetical cytology; (ed) various symposia. *Recreation:* children. *Address:* 10 Regent's Park Road, NW1. *T:* 01–485 8324.      *Died 15 May 1984.*

**ADAMS, Sir Maurice (Edward),** KBE 1958 (OBE 1943); Life FICE; consultant, since 1971; *b* 20 Aug. 1901; *s* of Herbert William and Minnie Adams; *m* 1st, 1924, Hilda May Williams (*d* 1980); one *s* one *d*; 2nd, 1980, Esther Marie Ottilie Overdyck. *Educ:* Bristol. Served European War, Midshipman, RNR. Entered Admty as Asst Civil Engr, 1927; HM Dockyards: Devonport, 1927–30; Malta, 1930–33; Portsmouth, 1933–35; Civil Engr: Trincomalee, 1935–37; Aden, 1937–38; Portsmouth, 1938–39; Superintending CE, Lower grade, 1939, Higher grade, 1940; served War of 1939–45: Admty, 1939–41; Singapore, from 1941 to evacuation; Simonstown, 1942–43; Asst CE-in-Chief, 1943; Eastern Theatre, 1943–45; Admty, 1945–46; Dep. CE-in-Chief, 1946; resigned to take up appt with Balfour Beatty & Co. Ltd, Public Works Contractors, 1949; re-entered Admty service, 1954; Civil Engr-in-Chief, Admty, 1954–59. Mem. Council, Instn of Civil Engrs, 1955. *Recreation:* writing. *Address:* 32 Cavendish Avenue, Ealing, W13. *Club:* Caledonian.      *Died 23 Jan. 1982.*

**ADAMS, Robert;** sculptor and designer; works in wood, stone, bronze, steel; *b* 5 Oct. 1917; *s* of Arthur Adams; *m* 1951, Patricia Devine; one *d. Educ:* Northampton School of Art. Instructor, Central School of Arts and Crafts, London, 1949–60. One man exhibitions: Gimpel Fils, London, 1947–; Galerie Jeanne Bucher, Paris, 1949; Passedoit Gall., New York, 1950; Victor Waddington Gall., Dublin, 1955; Douglas Coll., NJ, USA, 1955; Galerie Parnass, Wuppertal, Germany, 1957; Nebelung Galerie, Düsseldorf, 1957; Galerie Vertiko, Bonn, 1957; Museum am Ostwall, Dortmund, 1957; Bertha Schaefer Gall., New York, 1963; Northampton, Sheffield, Newcastle and London, 1971 Gimpel-Hanover Gall., Zurich, 1980; Lister Gall., Perth, WA, 1981; Gimpel & Weitenhofer, 1981. International Biennales: São Paulo, Brazil, 1950–57; Antwerp, 1951–53; Venice, 1952; Holland Park, London, 1954–57; Battersea Park, 1961; Venice, 1962; 7th Tokyo, 1963; work in: British Sculpture in the 'Sixties' exhibn, Tate Gall., 1965; Internat. Sculpture, Sonsbeek, 1966; Fest. of London, 1968; Open Air Sculpture, Edinburgh, 1970. Various Arts Council and British Council travelling exhibns in Europe, USA and Japan. Works in permanent collections: Arts Council; British Council; Tate Gallery; Museums of Modern Art: New York, Rome and Turin; New York Public Library; São Paulo Museum; Univ. of Michigan, Ann Arbor; and many private collections. Commissions include sculptures for: Kings Heath Sch., Northampton; Sconce Hills Secondary Sch., Newark; The State Theatre, Gelsenkirchen; LCC Comprehensive Sch., Eltham; Hull City Centre; P & O Liner Canberra; Sekers Showroom, London; BP Building, Moorgate; London Airport; Maths Building, UCL; Kings Well, NW3; Fire Services Trng Coll., Glos; Williams & Glyn's Bank, London. *Address:* Rangers Hall, Great Maplestead, Halstead, Essex. *T:* Hedingham 60142.      *Died 5 April 1984.*

**ADAMS, Roland;** *see* Adams, J. R.

**ADAMS, Sherman;** Chairman and Chief Executive Officer, Loon Mountain Corporation, since 1980 (President, 1966–80); *b* 8 Jan. 1899; *s* of Clyde H. Adams and Winnie Marion (*née* Sherman); *m* 1923, Rachel Leona White; one *s* three *d. Educ:* Dartmouth College (Montgomery Fellow, 1980). Graduated, 1920; Manager, timberland and lumber operations, The Parker-Young Co., Lincoln, NH, 1928–45. Mem., New Hampshire House of Representatives, 1941–44; Chm. Cttee on Labor, 1941–42; Speaker of House, 1943–44; mem. 79th Congress, 2nd New Hampshire Dist; Gov. of New Hampshire, 1949–53; Chief of White House Staff, Asst to President of US, 1953–58, resigned. Chairman: Conf. of New England Govs, 1951–52; Mt Washington Commn, 1969–. Director (life), Northeastern Lumber Mfrs Assoc., New England Council. Served with US Marine Corps, 1918. First Robert Frost Award,

Plymouth State Coll., 1970. Holds several hon. degrees. *Publications:* First Hand Report, 1961 (Gt Brit. 1962); articles in Life, American Forests, Appalachia, 1958–70. *Recreations:* golf, fishing, ski-ing. *Address:* Pollard Road, Lincoln, New Hampshire 03251, USA.
*Died 27 Oct.* 1986.

**ADAMSON, Very Rev. Alexander Campbell;** Dean of Aberdeen and Orkney, since 1978; Rector of St Thomas Aboyne with St Kentigern, Ballater, with pastoral care of St Margaret's, Braemar, since 1979; *b* 21 June 1921; *s* of David Watson Adamson and Margaret Kinnaird Rae Adamson; *m* 1959, Betty Reeves (*d* 1980); one *s* one *d. Educ:* Petershill Public School, Glasgow; Albert Secondary School, Glasgow; Lichfield Theological Coll., Staffs. Served RAF, 1941–46. Employed Glasgow Welfare Dept, 1946–48; Executive Officer, Nat. Assistance Bd, 1948–57; professional footballer, 1948–51; worked on Philmont Ranch, New Mexico, 1954. Deacon, Wakefield, Yorks, 1959; priest, Pontefract, Yorks, 1960; Curate, Pontefract Parish Church, 1959–62; Vicar of Honley with Brockholes, 1962–69; Royal Army Chaplaincy Dept, 1962–68; Rector of St John the Evangelist, Aberdeen, 1969–79. Canon, St Andrew's Cathedral, Aberdeen, 1973; Synod Clerk of Aberdeen and Orkney, 1976. Actors' Union Chaplain, His Majesty's Theatre, 1969–; Grampian Area Scout Chaplain, 1972–; Member: Religious Adv. Cttee, Scouts, Scotland, 1972–; Adv. Cttee, Royal Mission to Deep Sea Fishermen, 1973–; Adv. Cttee, Prince's Trust, 1975–; Religious Adv. Cttee, Grampian TV, 1978–. *Recreations:* theatre, Scout movement, sport, and the three R's: reading, 'riting and reconciliation. *Address:* Glenmoriston, 7 Invercauld Road, Ballater, Aberdeenshire. *T:* Ballater 55726.                 *Died 3 Sept.* 1983.

**ADAMSON, Estelle Inez Ommanney,** OBE 1962; Director of Nursing, St Thomas' Hospital, London, 1965–70, retired; *b* 21 May 1910; *d* of late R. O. Adamson, MA, MD, and late Evelyn Mary Ommanney. *Educ:* Benenden School, Cranbrook, Kent. Nurse training, St Thomas' Hosp., 1932–35; Sister, etc, St Thomas' Hosp., 1936–43; Asst Matron, King Edward VII Sanatorium, Midhurst, Sussex, 1943–45; Secretary, Nursing Recruitment Service, Nuffield Provincial Hospitals Trust, Scotland, 1946–51; Matron, Western General Hosp., Edinburgh, 1951–65. *Address:* Thames Bank Nursing Home, Thames Road, Goring-on-Thames, Reading, Berks RG8 9AJ.                                        *Died 25 March* 1990.

**ADCOCK, Sir Robert (Henry),** Kt 1950; CBE 1941; retired as Clerk of County Council, Lancashire (1944–60), also as Clerk of the Peace for Lancashire and Clerk of the Lancashire Lieutenancy; *b* 27 Sept. 1899; *s* of late Henry Adcock, Polesworth, Warwicks; *m* Mary, *d* of late R. K. Wadsworth, Handforth Hall, Cheshire; one *s* one *d* (and one *d* decd). *Educ:* Atherstone, Warwicks. Asst Solicitor, Manchester, 1923; Asst Solicitor and Asst Clerk of the Peace, Notts CC, 1926; Senior Asst Solicitor, Manchester, 1929; Deputy Town Clerk, Manchester, 1931; Town Clerk, Manchester, 1938. DL Lancs, 1950–74. *Recreation:* golf. *Address:* South Devon Hotel, Marychurch, Torquay, Devon TQ1 4LP. *T:* Torquay (0803) 22775.
*Died 16 Oct.* 1990.

**ADDINGTON, 5th Baron** *cr* 1887; **James Hubbard;** *b* 3 Nov. 1930; *s* of John Francis Hubbard, OBE (*g s* of 1st Baron) (*d* 1953) and of Betty Riversdale, *d* of late Horace West; *S* kinsman, 1971; *m* 1961, Alexandra Patricia, *yr d* of late Norman Ford Millar; two *s* two *d. Educ:* Eastbourne College; Chadacre Agricultural Institute. Served British S Africa Police, S Rhodesia, 1955–58. *Heir: s* Hon. Dominic Bryce Hubbard, *b* 24 Aug. 1963.              *Died 26 June* 1982.

**ADDIS, Sir John (Mansfield),** KCMG 1973 (CMG 1959); HM Diplomatic Service, retired; Supernumerary Fellow, Wolfson College, Oxford, since 1982 (Senior Research Fellow in Contemporary Chinese Studies, 1975–82); *b* 11 June 1914; 5th *s* and 12th *c* of late Sir Charles and Lady Addis. *Educ:* Rugby School; Christ Church, Oxford. 3rd Sec., Foreign Office, 1938; with Allied Force HQ (Mediterranean), 1942–44; Junior Private Sec. to Prime Minister (Mr Attlee), 1945–47; 1st Sec., Nanking, 1947–50, Peking, 1950; Counsellor, Peking, 1954–57; Counsellor in the Foreign Office, 1957–60; Ambassador to Laos, 1960–62; Fellow at Harvard Centre for Internat. Affairs, 1962–63; Ambassador to the Philippines, 1963–70; Senior Civilian Instructor, IDC, later Royal Coll. of Defence Studies, 1970–71; Ambassador to China, 1972–74 (Chargé d'Affaires, Jan.–March 1972). Member: Expert Adv. Council, Percival David Foundn of Chinese Art, 1977–; Adv. Council, V&A Museum, 1977–79; a Trustee, British Museum, 1977–; Pres., Oriental Ceramic Soc., 1974–77. *Publications:* Chinese Ceramics from Datable Tombs, 1978; Chinese Porcelain from the Addis Collection, 1979. *Address:* Woodside, Frant, Tunbridge Wells TN3 9HW. *T:* Frant 202; Wolfson College, Oxford. *T:* Oxford 55605; 7D Pont Street, SW1X 9EJ. *T:* 01–235 7784. *Club:* Boodle's.
*Died 31 July* 1983.

**ADDISON, Air Vice-Marshal Edward Barker,** CB 1945; CBE 1942 (OBE 1938); MA; CEng, FIEE; RAF, retired; *b* 4 Oct. 1898; *m* 1926, Marie-Blanche Marguerite Rosain; one *s* one *d. Educ:* Sidney Sussex Coll., Cambridge. Served European War, 1915–18, RFC and

RAF; Cambridge Univ., 1918–21; BA (Cantab), 1921; MA (Cantab), 1926; Ingénieur Diplomé de l'Ecole Supérieure d'Electricité, Paris, 1927; re-commissioned RAF, 1921; retd from RAF, 1955; Dir and Div. Manager, Redifon Ltd, 1956–63, retd; Director, Intercontinental Technical Services Ltd, 1964–75, retd; Consultant to Vocational Guidance Assoc., 1966–72. AMIEE 1933; MIEE 1941; FIEE 1966. Commander of US Legion of Merit, 1947. *Address:* 7 Hall Place Drive, Weybridge, Surrey. *T:* Weybridge 47450.                                             *Died 4 July* 1987.

**ADDLESHAW, Very Rev. George William Outram;** Dean of Chester, 1963–77; *b* 1 Dec. 1906; *s* of late Canon Stanley Addleshaw and Mrs Rose Elgood Addleshaw. *Educ:* Bromsgrove School; Trinity College, Oxford; Cuddesdon College, Oxford. 2nd cl. hons Modern History, 1928; BA 1929; MA 1932; BD 1935; FSA 1945; FRHistS 1949. Curate of Christ Church, Highfield, Southampton, 1930–36; Curate of Basingstoke, 1936–39; Vice-Principal and Fellow of St Chad's College, Durham, 1939–46; Treasurer and Canon Residentiary of York Minster, and Prebendary of Tockerington in York Minster, 1946–63. Examining Chaplain to Archbishop of York, 1942–63; Hon. Secretary, Archbishops' Canon Law Commn 1943–47; Lecturer, Leeds Parish Church, 1947–54; Proctor in Convocation of York, 1945–75; a Deputy Prolocutor, Lower House of Convocation of York, 1957–66; Prolocutor, Lower House of Convocation of York, 1966–75. Hon. Treas., York Minster Appeal, 1950–63. Select Preacher: Univ. of Oxford, 1954–56; Univ. of Cambridge, 1955–; Examining Chaplain to Bp of Chester, 1955–; Chaplain to the Queen, 1957–63; Hon. Chaplain, Cheshire Regt, 1969–77. *Publications:* Jocism, 1939; Dogma and Youth Work, 1941; The High Church Tradition, 1941; Divine Humanity and the Young Worker, 1942; (with Frederick Etchells) The Architectural Setting of Anglican Worship, 1948; The Beginnings of the Parochial System, 1953; The Parochial System from Charlemagne to Urban II, 1954; Rectors, Vicars and Patrons, 1956; The Early Parochial System and the Divine Office, 1957; The Pastoral Structure of the Celtic Church in Northern Britain, 1973; contrib. to: The History of Christian Thought, 1937; The Priest as Student, 1939; The Mission of the Anglican Communion, 1948; Architectural History, 1967. *Recreations:* travel, ecclesiology. *Address:* Flat 3, The New Manor House, 37 Station Road, Thames Ditton, Surrey. *T:* 01–398 7650. *Clubs:* Athenæum; Yorkshire (York).              *Died 14 June* 1982.

**ADDLESHAW, His Honour John Lawrence;** a Circuit Judge (formerly County Court Judge), 1960–75; *b* 30 Oct. 1902; *s* of Harold Pope Addleshaw, Solicitor and Mary Gertrude (*née* Shore), Manchester; unmarried. *Educ:* Shrewsbury School; University College, Oxford (BA). Called to the Bar, Inner Temple, 1925. Auxiliary Air Force, 1939–45. *Recreations:* golf, walking. *Address:* 3 College House, Southdowns Road, Bowdon, Altrincham, Cheshire WA14 3DZ. *T:* 061–928 2139. *Club:* St James's (Manchester).
*Died 13 Feb.* 1989.

**ADEANE, Baron** *cr* 1972 (Life Peer), of Stamfordham; **Michael Edward Adeane,** PC 1953; GCB 1968 (KCB 1955; CB 1947); GCVO 1962 (KCVO 1951; MVO 1946); Royal Victorian Chain, 1972; MA; FSA; Extra Equerry to the Queen, since 1972; Chairman, Royal Commission on Historical Monuments, since 1972; Member, British Library Board, since 1972; *b* 30 Sept. 1910; *s* of late Capt. H. R. A. Adeane, Coldstream Guards (killed in action, 1914), and Hon. Victoria Eugenie Bigge (*d* 1969); *m* 1939, Helen Chetwynd-Stapylton; one *s* (one *d* decd). *Educ:* Eton; Magdalene Coll., Cambridge (1st Cl. Hons Historical Tripos Part II); Hon. Fellow 1971. 2nd Lieut Coldstream Guards, 1931; ADC to Governor-General of Canada, 1934–36; Major, 1941; Lieut-Col, 1942. Served War of 1939–45: with 2nd Bn Coldstream Guards, 1940–42; on Joint Staff Mission, Washington, 1942–43; 5th Bn Coldstream Guards, 1943–45; in NW Europe from 1944 (wounded, despatches). Page of honour to King George V; Equerry and Asst Private Sec. to King George VI, 1937–52, to the Queen, 1952–53; Private Sec. to the Queen and Keeper of HM's Archives, 1953–72. Lieut-Col (R of O) 1954. Director: Phoenix Assurance Co. Ltd, 1972–80; Banque Belge Ltd, 1972–80; Royal Bank of Canada, 1972–80; The Diners Club Ltd, 1976–82. Governor, Wellington College, 1960–81. *Recreations:* shooting and fishing. *Address:* 22 Chelsea Square, SW3 6LF. *T:* 01–352 3080; Mosshead Cottage, Kildrummy, Alford, Aberdeenshire. *T:* Kildrummy 260. *Clubs:* Brooks's, Beefsteak, Pratt's.                                             *Died 30 April* 1984.

**ADEY, (Arthur) Victor;** Director: Ampex Corporation (USA), 1973–85; Motability and Motability Finance Ltd, 1978–85; *b* 2 May 1912; *s* of Arthur Frederick and Pollie Adey; *m* 1936, Kathleen Mary Lewis; one *s* one *d. Educ:* Wolverhampton Secondary Sch. Articled clerk, Crombie, Lacon & Stevens, 1928; Office Manager and Accountant, Attwoods Factors Ltd, 1933; Branch Man., Mercantile Union Guarantee Corp., 1937; Man. Dir, Mercantile Credit Co. of Ireland Ltd, 1949; Mercantile Credit Co. Ltd: Dir, Bd of Management, 1955; Director, 1957–; Man. Dir, 1964; Dep. Chm. and Man. Dir, 1973; Chm. and Man. Dir, 1975–77; Chm., 1977–80; Dir, Barclays Bank UK Management Ltd, 1975–79. *Recreations:*

shooting, fishing. *Address:* Rosemount, Burtons Lane, Chalfont St Giles, Bucks HP8 4BN. *T:* Little Chalfont (02404) 2160.
*Died 25 Aug.* 1990.

**ADLER, Lawrence James,** AO 1988; Chairman, FAI Insurances Group, since 1968; *b* 2 Nov. 1931; *s* of late Bela Adler and of Antonia Adler (*née* Vorosvary); *m* 1956, Ethel Kaminer; one *s* two *d*. *Educ:* Budapest Jewish High School (Matriculation). Chairman: Fire & All Risks Insurance Co., 1968–; Cumberland Credit Corp., 1987–. *Address:* 12th Floor, 185 Macquarie Street, Sydney, NSW 2000, Australia. *T:* (office) (02) 221.1155.
*Died 13 Dec.* 1988.

**ADORIAN, Paul;** consulting engineer; *b* 29 Nov. 1905; *s* of Dr Emil Adorian; *m* 1932, Lilian A. Griffiths; two *s* one *d*. *Educ:* City and Guilds (Eng) Coll., London. Joined Rediffusion as development engineer, 1932; retd 1970, as Man. Dir; Dep. Chm., Wembley Stadium 1960–70; Dir, British Electric Traction, 1960–70; Dir and advisor, Resource Sciences Corp., Tulsa, Oklahoma and subs. co. Williams Bros Engineering Ltd, 1970–80. Member, Bd of Governors, British Film Inst., 1964–72. Past Pres., IERE. FCGI. *Publications:* several technical papers and lectures on electronics in general, flight simulation and distribution of broadcast sound and television programmes in particular. *Recreations:* lawn tennis (umpired Drobny-Patty match, also Drobny-Rosewall final, at Wimbledon), industrial archæology. *Address:* The Mill House, Gibbons Mill, near Billingshurst, West Sussex. *T:* Rudgwick 2477. *Club:* Athenæum.
*Died 17 May* 1983.

**AGHNIDES, Thanassis;** Chairman, Advisory Committee on Administrative and Budgetary Questions of UNO, 1946–64; *b* Nigdé, Asia Minor, 1889; *s* of Prodromos and Anastasia Aghnides. *Educ:* Superior National Greek Coll., Phanar, Istanbul; Anatolia Coll. (Asia Minor); Univ. of Istanbul; University of Paris. Directed Greek Press Bureau at Greek Legation, London, 1918–19; worked for League of Nations, 1919–42; Dir of Disarmament Section, 1930, and Under Secretary-General of the League, 1939; Secretary of Disarmament Conference, 1932–34; Secretary-General Montreux Conference concerning the Straits, May 1936; Secretary-General Conference for the suppression of Egyptian Capitulations, 1937; Secretary-General Nyon Conference for the suppression of piracy in the Mediterranean, 1937; Permanent Under-Secretary for Foreign Affairs in Greek Cabinet, 1942–43; Greek Ambassador to the Court of St James's, 1942–47; Greek Delegate to San Francisco Conference on International Organisation, 1945; Chief Delegate for Greece on Preparatory Commission of UNO; Chm. 6th Committee, on organisation of UNO Secretariat, Dec. 1945; Delegate to the 1st Assembly of UNO; Rapporteur of its 5th Cttee (on organisation), Jan. 1946; rep. Greece on Security Council when it dealt with question of presence of British troops in Greece, 1–6 Feb. 1946; Chairman Greek Deleg. to Gen. Assembly of UNO, Oct.–Dec. 1946; Chm. Cttee on Admin of UNESCO, Feb.–April 1948. Member Curatorium Acad. of Internat. Law of The Hague, 1948–68. *Recreation:* music. *Address:* 3 Avenue Bertrand, Geneva, Switzerland. *T:* 463602. *Club:* Brooks's.  *Died 12 May* 1984.

**AGLEN, Anthony John,** CB 1957; FRSE; Her Majesty's Government special representative on international fisheries questions, 1972–81; *b* 30 May 1911; 2nd *s* of late Sir Francis A. Aglen, GCMG, KBE, Alyth, Perthshire; *m* 1946, Audrey Louise Murray, *o d* of late Andrew E. Murray, WS, Edinburgh; one *s* one *d*. *Educ:* Marlborough; Trinity Coll., Cambridge (Scholar). First Class Mathematical Tripos, Part I, 1931, and Part II 1933, BA 1933. Entered Civil Service (Scottish Office), 1934; Private Secretary to successive Secretaries of State for Scotland, 1939–41; Assistant Secretary, Scottish Home Dept, 1942; Under-Sec., 1953; Dep. Sec., 1956–60; Jt Dep. Sec., Dept of Agric. and Fisheries for Scotland, 1960–71, also Fisheries Sec. for Scotland, 1946–71. President, North East Atlantic Fisheries Commission, 1963–66. *Recreation:* gardening. *Address:* Birkhill, Earlston, Berwickshire. *T:* Earlston 307. *Club:* New (Edinburgh).  *Died 25 April* 1984.

**AGNEW, Sir Garrick;** *see* Agnew, Sir R. D. G.

**AGNEW, Sir Geoffrey (William Gerald),** Kt 1973; Chairman, Thos Agnew & Sons, Ltd (Fine Art Dealers), 1965–82; *b* 11 July 1908; *er s* of late Charles Gerald Agnew and Olive Mary (*née* Danks); *m* 1934, Hon. Doreen Maud Jessel, *y d* of 1st Baron Jessel, CB, CMG; two *s* one *d*. *Educ:* Eton (Oppidan Scholar, 1923; Hon. Fellow, 1976); Trinity College, Cambridge (BA 1930; MA 1971); Munich. Joined Thos Agnew & Sons (Fine Art Dealers), 1931, a Managing Director, 1937–. Assistant master (History), Eton College, 1939–45. Chairman, Evelyn (Agnew) Nursing Home, Cambridge, 1955–81, Pres., 1981–. A Permanent Steward, 1955– and a Vice-Pres., 1968–, Artists' General Benevolent Institution; President, Fine Art Provident Institution, 1969–45; Chairman: St George's Arts Trust, King's Lynn, 1966–73; Society of London Art Dealers, 1970–74; Friends of the Courtauld Institute, 1970–; Vice-Pres., Guildhall of St George, King's Lynn, 1975–. *Publications:* Agnew's 1817–1967, 1967; various broadcasts on art published in the Listener.

*Recreations:* works of art, travel, gardening. *Address:* Flat 3, 6 Onslow Square, SW7. *T:* 01–589 8536; Egmere Farm House, Walsingham, Norfolk. *T:* Walsingham 247. *Clubs:* Brooks's, Garrick.  *Died 22 Nov.* 1986.

**AGNEW, Commander Sir Peter (Garnett),** 1st Bt *cr* 1957; *b* 9 July 1900; *s* of late C. L. Agnew; *m* 1st, 1928, Enid Frances (*d* 1982), *d* of late Henry Boan, Perth, Western Australia, and *widow* of Lt Col O. Marescaux; one *s*; 2nd, 1984, Mrs Julie Marie Watson. *Educ:* Repton. Entered Royal Navy, 1918; ADC to Governor of Jamaica, 1927–28; retired, 1931; returned to service at sea, Aug. 1939 (despatches). MP (C) Camborne Div. of Cornwall, 1931–50; PPS to Rt Hon. Walter Runciman, President of Board of Trade, 1935–37, and to Rt Hon. Sir Philip Sassoon, First Commissioner of Works, 1937–39; an Assistant Government Whip, May-July, 1945; a Conservative Whip, Aug. 1945–Feb. 1950; contested (C) Falmouth and Camborne Div., Feb. 1950; MP (C) South Worcs, 1955–66. Member of House of Laity, Church Assembly, 1935–65; a Church Comr for England, 1948–68; Trustee, Historic Churches Preservation Trust, 1968–. Chm., Iran Society, 1966–73; Internat. Pres., European Centre of Documentation and Information, 1974–76. Order of Homayoun (Iran), 1973; Kt Grand Cross, Order of Civil Merit (Spain), 1977. *Recreation:* travelling. *Heir:* *s* Quentin Charles Agnew-Somerville [*b* 8 March 1929; *m* 1963, Hon. April, *y d* of 15th Baron Strange; one *s* two *d*. *Educ:* RNC Dartmouth]. *Address:* Grove House, Grove Mount, Ramsey, Isle of Man. *Clubs:* Carlton, Buck's.  *Died 26 Aug.* 1990.

**AGNEW, Sir (Robert David) Garrick,** Kt 1983; CBE 1978; Director, Australian Bank Ltd (Founding Chairman, 1981–85); *b* 21 Sept. 1930; *s* of late R. Agnew; *m* 1959, Fay (*d* 1981), *d* of Colin Ferguson; two *s* one *d* (and one *d* decd). *Educ:* Perth Modern Sch.; Univ. of WA; Ohio State Univ. (BS); Harvard Business Sch. Chm., Agnew Clough; Dir, Qantas Airways; former Dir, Australian Industry Develt Corp. *Recreation:* swimming (rep. Australia, Olympic Games, 1948, 1952 and Commonwealth Games, 1950). *Address:* 16 Victoria Avenue, Claremont, WA 6010, Australia. *Club:* Weld (Perth).  *Died 3 Aug.* 1987.

**AICKIN, Hon. Sir Keith Arthur,** KBE 1976; Hon. Mr Justice Aickin; Justice of High Court of Australia, since 1976; *b* Melbourne, 1 Feb. 1916; *s* of J. L. Aickin, Belfast, Ireland; *m* 1952, Elizabeth May, *d* of S. W. Gullett; one *s* one *d*. *Educ:* Church of England Grammar Sch., Melbourne; Univ. of Melbourne (LLM). Associate to Justice Dixon, High Court of Aust., 1939–41; Third Sec., Aust. Legation, Washington, DC, 1942–44; Legal Adviser, European Regional Office, UNRRA, 1944–48; in Legal Dept, UN, NY, 1948; Melbourne Bar, 1949–76. QC Vic 1957, Tas. 1959, NSW 1967. Mem., Interim Council, La Trobe Univ., 1966, Council, 1967–73. Director: Mayne Nickless Ltd, 1958–76; P & O Aust Ltd, 1969–76; Comalco Ltd, 1970–76; BHP Co. Ltd, 1971–76. *Address:* High Court of Australia, Canberra, ACT, Australia; 41 Marne Street, South Yarra, Vic 3141, Australia. *Clubs:* Melbourne, Australian (Melbourne); Frankston Golf.  *Died 18 June* 1982.

**AIERS, David Pascoe,** CMG 1971; HM Diplomatic Service, retired; High Commissioner in Malta, 1979–82; *b* 19 Sept. 1922; *s* of late George Aiers and Sarah Adshead; *m* 1948, Pauleen Victoria Brittain-Jones; one *s* one *d*. *Educ:* Stationers' Company's Sch.; Trinity Coll., Oxford. Royal Artillery, 1942–46; Third Sec., Warsaw, 1946–48; FO, 1948; Second Sec., Copenhagen, 1951–53, Buenos Aires, 1953–55; FO, 1955; First Sec. (Commercial), Manila, 1958–62; First Sec. and Head of Chancery, Ankara, 1962–65; Counsellor and Head of Chancery, Political Adviser's Office, Singapore, 1965–68; Head of SW Pacific Dept, FCO, 1968–71; Minister, Canberra, 1971–75; High Comr to Sri Lanka, and Ambassador to the Republic of Maldives, 1976–79. *Address:* c/o Barclays Bank Ltd, 230 Kentish Town Road, NW5. *Clubs:* Royal Automobile, Royal Commonwealth Society.
*Died 15 July* 1983.

**AIKEN, Frank;** Member, Dáil Eirann for County Louth, 1923–73; Tánaiste (Deputy Prime Minister) in the Government of Ireland, 1965–69; *b* Camlough, Co. Armagh, 13 Feb. 1898; *y s* of James Aiken and Mary McGeeny; *m* 1934, Maud Davin; two *s* one *d*. *Educ:* Christian Brothers' Secondary Schools, Newry. Joined Irish Volunteers, 1913; Captain, Camlough Co., IRA, 1918; Comdt, Camlough Bn, IRA, 1919; Vice-Brig., Newry Bde, IRA, 1920; Comdt, 4th Northern Div., IRA, 1921; Chief of Staff, IRA, 1923. Secretary, Camlough Br., Gaelic League, 1914; Secretary, Sinn Fein Organisation, S Armagh, 1917. Military Service Medal (with Bar). Local and CCs, 1920. Minister for: Defence, Ireland, 1932–39; Lands and Fisheries, June–Nov. 1936; Co-ordination of Defensive Measures, 1939–45; Finance, 1945–48; External Affairs, 1951–54 and 1957–69; Agriculture, March–May 1957. Leader, Irish Delegn to Council of Europe, 1969. Hon. LLD: NUI; St John's Univ., Jamaica, New York; Dublin Univ. Military Service Medal with Bar. Grand Cross: Pian Order; Order of Merit of Federal Republic

of Germany; Belgian Order of Crown. Grand Officer with plaque, Order of St Charles. *Address:* Dúngaoithe, Sandyford, Co. Dublin.
*Died* 18 *May* 1983.

**AILWYN,** 4th Baron *cr* 1921; **Carol Arthur Fellowes,** TD 1946; *b* 23 Nov. 1896; 4th *s* of 1st Baron Ailwyn, PC, KCVO, KBE, 2nd *s* of 1st Baron de Ramsey, and Hon. Agatha Eleanor Augusta Jolliffe, *d* of 2nd Baron Hylton; *S* brother, 1976; *m* 1936, Caroline (Cudemore) (*d* 1985), *d* of late Maynard Cowan, Victoria, BC; one adopted step *d. Educ:* Royal Naval Colls, Osborne and Dartmouth. Lieut, 3rd and 2nd Norfolk Regt., 1916–19; served in Mesopotamia, 1917–19. Subsequently fruit farmer; Agent to Earl of Strafford, 1930–52. Formed 334 (Barnet) AA Company, RE (T), 1937; served War as Major RA (T) comdg 334 Co. and on staff of Anti-Aircraft Command, 1939–44. Asst Sec., RASE, 1952–59; Sec., Norfolk Club, Norwich, 1964–69; Trustee, Lord Wandsworth Coll., 1955–72; Governor, Felixstowe Coll., 1960–74 (Chm., 1966–72). Late JP Herts and Middlesex. *Heir:* none. *Address:* Hethersett Hall, Norwich NR9 3AP. *T:* Norwich 812335. *Club:* (Hon. Member) Norfolk (Norwich).                    *Died* 27 *Sept.* 1988 (*ext*).

**AINLEY, Eric Stephen;** Under-Secretary, Department of the Environment (formerly Ministry of Transport), 1968–75; *b* 15 Sept. 1918; *s* of late Captain Eric E. Ainley and Dorothy Ainley (*née* Sharp); *m* 1946, Pamela, *d* of late Mr and Mrs Philip G. Meadows; two *s. Educ:* Giggleswick Sch.; Trinity Coll., Cambridge (BA, Classics and English; MA); Open Univ., 1977–83 (BA 1981; BA Hons Ist Cl. Maths, 1983). Served War of 1939–45: RA, RIASC, and Civil Affairs (Malaya), 1940–46. Asst Principal, Min. of Civil Aviation, 1948; Principal, 1950; Civil Air Adviser and Attaché, Singapore and Far East, 1955–58; Asst Sec., Min. of Transport, 1960; seconded as the Traffic Manager, GLC, 1965–67. *Publications:* Mathematical Puzzles, 1978; Coarse Mathematics, 1986; puzzles and verses in New Scientist, M500, Vox Latina. *Recreations:* mathematics, golf. *Address:* 8 Poynder Place, Hilmarton, near Calne, Wilts. *T:* Hilmarton 650. *Club:* N Wilts Golf.
*Died* 26 *March* 1986.

**AINSWORTH, Sir John (Francis),** 3rd Bt *cr* 1916; Inspector, Irish Manuscripts Commission, since 1943; *b* 4 Jan. 1912; *s* of Sir Thomas Ainsworth, 2nd Bt, and Lady Edina Dorothy Hope (*d* 1964), *d* of 4th Marquess Conyngham; *S* father, 1971; *m* 1st, 1938, Josephine (marr. diss. 1946), *e d* of Comdr W. R. Bernard, RN; 2nd, 1946, Anita M. A., *e d* of H. A. Lett, Ballynadara, Enniscorthy, Co. Wexford; no *c. Educ:* Eton (Newcastle Medallist); Trinity College, Cambridge (Sen. Scholar, BA 1933, MA 1937). Hon. General Editor, British Record Society, 1937–40; External Lecturer in Mediaeval History, University College, Cork, 1966–69; Tutor, Archives Dept, University College, Dublin, 1969–. District Commissioner, Kildare Branch, Irish Pony Club, 1960–62; Chairman, Dublin SPCA, 1965–66 and 1976– (Vice-Chm. 1964–65 and 1967–76); 1st Whipper-in, Curragh Beagles, 1964–. *Publications:* Editor or Joint Editor: Records of the Carpenters' Company, 1936; Prerogative Court of Canterbury Wills, 1671–75, 1942; The Inchiquin MSS, 1960; Analecta Hibernica nos 20 and 25, 1958 and 1967. *Recreations:* hunting and horse trials (both at ground level). *Heir:* half-*b* Thomas David Ainsworth [*b* 22 Aug. 1926; *m* 1957, Sarah Mary, *d* of late Lt-Col H. C. Walford; two *s* two *d*]. *Address:* Carraphuca, Shankill, Co. Dublin. *T:* Dublin 854721.
*Died* 30 *April* 1981.

**AIRD, Ronald,** MC 1942; TD; Secretary Marylebone Cricket Club, 1952–62, retired; *b* 4 May 1902; 2nd *s* of late Malcolm R. Aird; *m* 1925, Viola Mary (*d* 1965), 2nd *d* of late Sir Godfrey Baring, Bt; one *d. Educ:* Eton; Clare College, Cambridge. Stock Exchange, 1924–26; Assistant Secretary, MCC, 1926–52; President: MCC, 1968–69; Hampshire CCC, 1971–83. *Recreations:* cricket, rackets, real tennis, golf, National Hunt racing. *Address:* West Down House, Yapton, West Sussex. *T:* Yapton 551140. *Clubs:* Oriental, MCC.
*Died* 16 *Aug.* 1986.

**AIREY, Lt-Gen. Sir Terence (Sydney),** KCMG 1951; CB 1944; CBE 1943 (OBE 1941); psc; retired; *b* 9 July 1900; *s* of late Sydney Airey, Orchard Cottage, Holbrook, Suffolk; *m* 1934, Constance Hedley (marr. diss. 1947); one *s; m* 1947, Bridget Georgiana, *d* of late Col the Hon. Thomas Vesey. 2nd Lieutenant Durham Light Infantry, 1919; Eastern Arab Corps and HQ Sudan Defence Force, 1929–36; Capt. 1933; Major 1938; Temp. Lieut-Col 1940; War Subst. Lieut-Col; Col 1945; Temp. Maj.-Gen. 1944; Brig. Sept. 1945; Maj.-Gen. 1947; Lieut-Gen. 1952. Served War of 1939–45 (despatches, OBE, CBE, CB): Acting Deputy Supreme Allied Commander, Italy, 1946; Allied Commander and Military Gov., British-US Zone of Free Territory, Trieste, 1947–51; Assistant Chief of Staff, Supreme HQ, Allied Powers, Europe, 1951–52; Commdr, British Forces, Hong-Kong, 1952–54; representative Col Light Inf. Bde, 1954–55; retd 1954. Col The Durham Light Infantry, 1952–56. Commander, Order of Merit (US); Officer, Légion d'Honneur, and Croix de Guerre (France). *Address:* Fritton Old Rectory, Fritton, near Norwich, Norfolk. *T:* Hempnall 214.                    *Died* 26 *March* 1983.

**AITKEN, Sir Arthur Percival Hay, (Sir Peter Aitken),** Kt 1968; *b* 2 Oct. 1905; *e s* of late Canon R. A. Aitken, Great Yarmouth; *m* 1937, Ursula Wales, *d* of Herbert Wales, MA, MB; one *s* one *d. Educ:* Norwich Gram. Sch.; Trinity Coll., Oxford. Formerly: Man. Dir Textile Machinery Makers Ltd, 1949, Chm. 1960; Dep. Chm., Stone-Platt Industries Ltd (retd 1975); Director: Norwich General Trust (Chm.); Norwich Union Insurance Group; Norwich Union Life Insurance Soc.; Norwich Union Fire Insurance Soc.; Maritime Insurance Co. Chm., BNEC's Australia Cttee, 1966–69; Bd Mem., Commonwealth Develt Corp., 1960–69. *Recreations:* golf, fishing. *Address:* The Lodge, Alde House Drive, Aldeburgh, Suffolk IP15 5EE. *T:* Aldeburgh 3450. *Clubs:* Royal Thames Yacht; Aldeburgh Golf, Aldeburgh Yacht.                    *Died* 25 *May* 1984.

**AITKEN, Ian Hugh,** CBE 1964; *b* 4 Dec. 1919; *y s* of late James Maven Aitken and Anne Stevenson Aitken (*née* Lowe); *m* 1944, Sheila Agnes Hamilton, *d* of late F. A. Green, Arusha, Tanzania; one *s* one *d. Educ:* Greenock High Sch. Served War in 51st (Highland) Div. and 11th (E African) Div., in France, Belgium, Western Desert and E Africa, 1939–44. HMOCS, Kenya, 1944, Tanganyika, 1944–47, Kenya, 1947; Dep. Principal Immigration Officer, 1952; Principal Immigration Officer and Passport Control Officer, Colony and Protectorate of Kenya, 1960; retired after acting as Adviser on Immigration and related matters to independent Kenya Govt, 1964. Gen. Management, British Uralite Gp, 1964–70; Admin. Sec., Royal Soc. of Medicine, 1971–74; Dep. Sec., ICE, 1974–84 (Actg Sec., Sept. 1981–May 1982); Dir-Gen., Internat. Fedn of Municipal Engrs, 1984–85; Dir, Professional Engineers Insurance Bureau Ltd, 1976–85; Dep. Man. Dir, Thomas Telford Ltd, 1983–85. *Recreations:* most games, music. *Address:* 22 Pitfield Drive, Meopham, Kent. *T:* Meopham 812350. *Clubs:* MCC; Nairobi (Kenya).                    *Died* 12 *June* 1986.

**AITKEN, Janet Kerr,** CBE 1950; MD London; FRCP; retired; late Consulting Physician: Elizabeth Garrett Anderson Hospital; Princess Louise Kensington Hospital for Children; Mothers' (Salvation Army) Hospital; *b* Buenos Aires, 1886; Scottish parents. *Educ:* St Leonard's School, St Andrews; London School of Medicine for Women (Royal Free Hospital). LRCP, MRCS and MB, BS, London 1922; MD London 1924; MRCP 1926; FRCP 1943. Vice-Dean, London Royal Free Hospital School of Medicine for Women, 1930–34; President, Medical Women's Federation, 1942–44; late Pres., Med. Women's Internat. Assoc.; late Councillor Royal College of Physicians; late Council Mem. BMA; late Member: Central Health Services Council; General Medical Council. *Publications:* papers in medical journals. *Recreation:* music; LRAM (piano), Gold Medallist (singing). *Address:* 70 Viceroy Court, Prince Albert Road, Regent's Park, NW8. *T:* 01-722 3833.
*Died* 21 *April* 1982.

**AITKEN, Sir (John William) Max,** 2nd Bt, *cr* 1916; DSO 1942; DFC 1940; President, Express (formerly Beaverbrook) Newspapers Ltd, since 1977 (Chairman, 1968–77); former Director, Trafalgar House Ltd; Associated Television Ltd; *b* Montreal, 15 February 1910; *e s* of 1st Baron Beaverbrook (Bt 1916), PC, ED, CD; *S* father, 1964; disclaimed the barony, 11 June 1964; *m* 1st, 1939, Cynthia Monteith (who obtained a divorce, 1950); 2nd, 1946, Mrs Jane Lindsay (who obtained a divorce, 1950); two *d;* 3rd, 1951, Violet, *d* of Sir Humphrey de Trafford, 4th Bt, MC; one *s* one *d. Educ:* Westminster; Pembroke Coll., Cambridge. Joined RAuxAF, 1935. Served War of 1939–45, RAF (despatches, DSO, DFC, Czech War Cross); day fighter pilot during Battle of Britain; comd night fighter squadron, 1941–42; Group Capt. comdg Strike Mosquito Wing, Norwegian waters, 1943. MP (C) Holborn, 1945–50. President, Newspaper Press Fund, 1965–. Chancellor, Univ. of New Brunswick, Fredericton, NB, 1966–81. Hon. LLD, New Brunswick, 1966. *Recreations:* Cambridge Assoc. Football Blue, 1930, 1931; golf, sailing. *Heir:* s Hon. (*as heir to disclaimed barony*) Maxwell William Humphrey Aitken [*b* 29 Dec. 1951; *m* 1974, Susan Angela More O'Ferrall; two *s* one *d*]. *Address:* 46 Chelsea Square, SW3. *T:* 01-351 0116. *Clubs:* White's, Buck's, Royal Yacht Squadron.
*Died* 30 *April* 1985.

**AITKEN, Sir Peter;** *see* Aitken, Sir A. P. H.

**AITKEN, Air Vice-Marshal (Robert) Stanley,** CB 1945; CBE 1942 (OBE 1938); MC 1917; AFC 1918; retired; *b* 4 April 1896; *s* of late Robert Aitken, Newcastle, and late Emma Louise Townsend, Manchester; *m* 1st, 1925, Jeanie Allison (*d* 1963), *o d* of late Rev. David Tweedie, Stitchill, Roxburghshire; one *s* (and one *s* decd); 2nd, 1964, Laura Barler (*d* 1976), widow of Arthur Sewall. *Educ:* Highgate; Wiesbaden. Enlisted 15th London Regt, 1914; commnd 1/1st (Essex) RGA, 1915; seconded RFC, July 1916; served France with 41, 52 and 7 Sqdns; Flying Instructor, 1918–21; Comd 41(F) and 25(F) Sqdns, 1928–30; British Air Attaché, China, 1938–40; Air Staff signals duties, Air Ministry, and CSO, varying periods, Air Defence of GB and Fighter Comd, 1940–42; AOC 60 (Radar) Group, 1942–43; ASO in C, HQ, MAAF, 1944–45; retired 1946. Legion of Merit (USA). *Address:* Rose Cottage, Shalfleet, Isle of

Wight PO30 4ND. *T:* Calbourne 337. *Club:* Royal Solent Yacht.
*Died* 21 *Jan.* 1982.

**AITKEN, Rt. Rev. William Aubrey;** Bishop Suffragan of Lynn, since 1973; also Archdeacon of Lynn, 1973–80; *b* 2 Aug. 1911; *s* of late Canon R. A. Aitken, Great Yarmouth; *m* 1937, Margaret Cunningham; three *s* two *d. Educ:* Norwich Grammar Sch.; Trinity Coll. Oxford (MA Mod. Hist., 2nd cl. Hons). Curate of: Tynemouth, 1934–37; Kingston, Jamaica, 1937–40; Rector of Kessingland, 1940–43; Vicar of: Sprowston, 1943–53; St Margaret's, King's Lynn, 1953–61; Archdeacon of Norwich, 1961–73. Proctor in Convocation, 1944–74; Hon. Canon of Norwich, 1958. *Recreations:* football, cricket, sailing. *Address:* Bishop's House, Ranworth, Norwich. *T:* South Walsham 348. *Died* 1 *June* 1985.

**ALAM, Hon. Anthony Alexander;** Member of Legislative Council, 1925–59, and 1963–73; Director: Alam Homes Pty Ltd; Alam Stores Pty Ltd; Mala Homes Pty Ltd; Latec Ltd; *b* Wallsend, NSW, 23 Jan. 1898; parents born Republic Lebanon; *m* 1924, Therese, *d* of S. Anthony; no *c. Educ:* De La Salle College, Armidale, NSW. King George V Silver Jubilee Medal; Merit of Lebanon; Commander Nichan Iftikar; King George VI Coronation Medal; Commander Toile Noir; Chevalier, Legion of Honour; Commander Order Cedars (Liban); Queen Elizabeth Coronation Medal; Grand Cross; Order of Torsani; Order of St Mark; Grand Officer, Order of Phoenix, Greece. *Recreations:* bowls, billiards, tennis, motoring, horse-racing. *Address:* 69 Bradleys Head Road, Mosman, NSW 2088, Australia. *Club:* Commercial Travellers' (Sydney).
*Died* 9 *Aug.* 1983.

**ALBERY, Sir Donald (Arthur Rolleston),** Kt 1977; Former Chairman and Managing Director, The Wyndham Theatres Ltd, Donmar Productions Ltd and associated companies and Piccadilly Theatre Ltd; Director, Anglia Television Ltd, 1958–78; Chairman, Theatres' National Committee, 1974–78; *b* London, 19 June 1914; *s* of late Sir Bronson Albery and Una Gwen, *d* of T. W. Rolleston; *g s* of James Albery, dramatist and Mary Moore (Lady Wyndham), actress; *m* 1935, Rubina McGilchrist (decd); one *s*; *m* 1946, Heather Boys (marr. diss. 1974); two *s* one *d*; *m* 1978, Nobuko Uenishi. *Educ:* Alpine Coll., Switzerland. Gen. Man., Sadler's Wells Ballet (now Royal Ballet at Covent Garden), 1941–45; formerly Dir-Gen., London's Festival Ballet; Jt Patron with Dame Ninette de Valois of the Royal Ballet Benevolent Fund. Has presented or jtly presented plays: The Living Room, 1953; Birthday Honours, 1953; I Am a Camera, The Living Room (NY, with Gilbert Miller), 1954; The Remarkable Mr Pennypacker, Lucky Strike, Waiting for Godot, 1955; The Waltz of the Toreadors, Gigi, Grab Me a Gondola, 1956; Zuleika, Tea and Sympathy, Dinner With the Family, Paddle Your Own Canoe, 1957; The Potting Shed, George Dillon, Irma La Douce (NY, 1960), 1958; The Rose Tattoo, A Taste of Honey (NY, 1960), The Hostage (NY, 1960), The Complaisant Lover, One to Another, The Ring of Truth, The World of Suzie Wong, Make Me an Offer, 1959; Fings Ain't Wot They Used T' Be, A Passage to India, Call It Love, The Art of Living, Oliver! (NY, 1963; tour, 1965), The Tinker, 1960; The Miracle Worker, Breakfast for One, Sparrers Can't Sing, Beyond the Fringe (NY, 1962), Celebration, Bonne Soupe, 1961; Not to Worry, Blitz!, Semi-Detached, Fiorello!, 1962; Licence to Murder, The Perils of Scobie Prilt (tour), A Severed Head (NY, 1964), The Time of the Barracudas (US), 1963; The Fourth of June, The Poker Session, Who's Afraid of Virginia Woolf?, A Little Winter Love (tour), Entertaining Mr Sloane (NY, 1965), Instant Marriage, Carving a Statue, The Diplomatic Baggage, Portrait of a Queen, Jorrocks, The Prime of Miss Jean Brodie, 1966; Mrs Wilson's Diary, Spring and Port Wine, The Restoration of Arnold Middleton, 1967; The Italian Girl, Man of La Mancha, 1968; Conduct Unbecoming (NY, 1970; Australia, 1971), 1969; It's a Two Foot Six Inches Above the Ground World, Mandrake, Poor Horace, 1970; Popkiss, 1972; Very Good Eddie, The Thoughts of Chairman Alf, 1976. *Address:* 31 Avenue Princesse Grace, Monte Carlo, Monaco. *T:* 507082. *Club:* Garrick.
*Died* 14 *Sept.* 1988.

**ALBRECHT, Ralph Gerhart;** American lawyer, barrister and international legal consultant; *b* Jersey City, NJ, 11 Aug. 1896; *s* of J. Robert Albrecht and Gertrude A. F. Richter; *m* 1936, Aillinn, *d* of late William Elderkin Leffingwell, Watkins Glen, NY; one *s. Educ:* Pennsylvania Univ. (AB); Harvard Univ. (JD). Admitted to Bar of NY, 1924, US Supreme Court, 1927; senior partner, Peaslee, Albrecht & McMahon, 1931–61, counsel to firm, 1961; gen. practice, specializing in foreign causes and internat. law. Special Dep. Attorney-Gen. of New York, 1926; Special Asst to US Attorney-Gen., 1945; Mem. US War Crimes Commn and leading trial counsel in Prosecution of Major Nazi War Criminals, before Internat. Mil. Tribunal, Nuremberg, 1945–46, prosecuted Hermann Goering; counsel to German steel, coal and chem. industries in decartelization procs before Allied High Commn for Germany, 1950–53. Mem. Republican County Cttee, NY Co., 1933–35; Harvard Univ. Overseers' Visiting Cttee to Faculty of Germanic Langs and Lits, 1949–63. Apprentice Seaman, USN Res. Force, 1918; served with

Sqdn A (101st Cavalry, NY Nat. Guard), 1924–30; Comdr USNR, on active duty, 1941–45; Naval Observer, American Embassy, London, 1942 (letter of commendation from Chief of Naval Ops); Asst Dir OSS (War Crimes), 1945. Member: NY City Bar Assoc.; Amer. Bar Assoc.; Amer. Soc. of Internat. Law (Donor of Manley O. Hudson Gold Medal Award; Chm., Medal Cttee, 1958–78); Internat. Bar Assoc.; International Law Assoc.; World Peace Through Law Center (Cttee on Conciliation and Mediation of Disputes). Fellow: Nat. Audubon Society; Massachusetts Audubon Soc.; Amer. Geog. Soc., etc. Delegate, First Internat. Congress Comparative Law, The Hague, 1932. Republican; Mason. *Publications:* (with Prof. Walter B. Pitkin) Studies for Vocational Guidance of Recent School and College Graduates; contrib. Peter Markham's (pseud.) America Next, 1940. *Address:* 520 East 86th Street, New York, NY 10028, USA. *Clubs:* University, Harvard, Pilgrims of the US, Squadron A (all in NY).
*Died* 27 *Sept.* 1985.

**ALDENHAM, 5th Baron** *cr* 1896, **and HUNSDON OF HUNSDON, 3rd Baron** *cr* 1923; **Antony Durant Gibbs;** *b* 18 May 1922; *s* of 4th Baron and Beatrix Elinor (*d* 1978), *d* of Herbert Paul; *S* father, 1969; *m* 1947, Mary Elizabeth, *o d* of late Walter Parkyns Tyser; two *s* one *d* (and one *s* decd). *Educ:* Eton; Christ Church, Oxford. RNVR, 1940–46. Antony Gibbs & Sons, Ltd, 1947 (Chile, 1948–51); Dir, 1954; Dir, Antony Gibbs Holdings Ltd, 1972–80. Master, Merchant Taylors' Co., 1977. *Recreations:* shooting, fishing, sailing. *Heir:* s Hon. Vicary Tyser Gibbs [*b* 9 June 1948; *m* 1980, Josephine Nicola, *er d* of John Fell, Lower Bourne, Farnham, Surrey; one *d*]. *Address:* Rimpton Manor, Yeovil, Somerset BA22 8AE. *Clubs:* Pratt's; MCC. *Died* 25 *Jan.* 1986.

**ALDERSON, Dr Michael Rowland;** Cancer Research Campaign Senior Research Fellow, since 1987; *b* 8 June 1931; *s* of Christopher Rowland and Phyllis Maud Alderson; *m* 1956, Dorothy Carter; two *d. Educ:* Epsom Coll.; Guy's Hospital. MD; FFCM; FRCR; DPH etc. Prof. of Medical Information Science, Southampton Univ., 1970–75; Prof. of Epidemiology, Inst. of Cancer Research, 1975–81; Chief Med. Statistician, OPCS, 1981–87. *Publications:* Central Government Routine Health Statistics, 1974; An Introduction to Epidemiology, 1976, 2nd edn 1983; Health Surveys and Related Studies, 1979; International Mortality Statistics, 1981; Prevention of Cancer, 1982; Occupational Cancer, 1985; Mortality, Morbidity and Health Statistics, 1988. *Recreation:* sailing. *Address:* 8 Westgate Street, Southampton SO1 0AY. *T:* Southampton 631804. *Club:* Little Ship. *Died* 1 *July* 1988.

**ALDINGTON, John Norman,** BSc, PhD; FRSC; FInstP; CEng; FIEE; Chairman, Royal Worcester Ltd, 1974–75 (Director, 1968–75); *b* 2 March 1905; *s* of Allen Aldington, Preston, Lancashire; *m* 1930, Edna, *d* of late John James Entwisle; one *s. Educ:* Balshaws Grammar Sch., Leyland; Harris Inst., Preston. Joined Siemens Electric Lamps and Supplies Ltd, 1923; Head of Laboratories, 1935; Dir of Research, 1948; Dir of the firm, 1948; Dir Alfred Graham & Co. Ltd, 1950; Man. Dir of Siemens Bros & Co. Ltd, 1955; former Man. Dir and Vice-Chm., AEI Ltd; former Director: LEW Ltd; Sub. Cables Ltd; Welwyn Electric Co. Ltd; Worcester Industrial Ceramics Ltd; Worcester Royal Porcelain Co. Ltd. Fellow and Past Pres., Illuminating Engrg Soc.; Mem. Amer. Illum. Engrg Soc., 1950; Chm. of Light Sources Secretariat, Internat. Commn on Illumination, 1945–54; Mem. various BSI Cttees. Part-time Lectr Harris Inst., Preston, 1928–38; Gov., Preston Grammar Sch., 1950–55; JP Duchy of Lancaster, 1953–55. MRI 1958. Leon Gaster Meml Award, IES, 1945 and 1947; Crompton Award, IEE, 1949; Gold Medal, IES, 1970. *Publications:* The High Current Density Mercury Vapour Arc, 1944 (thesis, London Univ. Library); numerous papers, particularly on light sources and kindred devices, and on high current discharges and xenon gas arc. *Recreations:* gardening and golf. *Address:* The Turn, Townside, Haddenham, Bucks HP17 8BG. *T:* Haddenham 291145. *Club:* Athenæum.
*Died* 3 *June* 1987.

**ALDOUS, Guy Travers,** QC 1956; *b* 30 Aug. 1906; *s* of H. G. Aldous, Gedding Hall, Suffolk; *m* 1932, Elizabeth Angela Paul; four *s* one *d. Educ:* Harrow; Trinity College, Cambridge. Retired Bar, 1967. Director, Showerings Ltd, 1968–. MFH Suffolk, 1958–60, Essex and Suffolk, 1967–76. *Recreation:* hunting. *Address:* 5 King's Bench Walk, Temple, EC4; Freston House, near Ipswich, Suffolk IP9 1AF. *T:* Woolverstone 243. *Died* 4 *Aug.* 1981.

**ALDRIDGE, John Arthur Malcolm,** RA 1963 (ARA 1954); painter; Assistant at The Slade School of Fine Art, 1949–67, Lecturer (part-time), 1967–70; *b* 26 July 1905; *s* of Major John Bartelott Aldridge, DSO, RHA, and Margaret Jessica (*née* Goddard); *m* 1st, 1940, Cecilia Lucie Leeds Brown (*née* Saunders) (marr. diss. 1970); no *c*; 2nd, 1970, Margareta Anna Maria Cameron (*née* Bajardi) (*d* 1983). *Educ:* Uppingham Sch.; Corpus Christi Coll., Oxford (MA). London, 1928–33; Essex, 1933–. Served, 1941–45, Army (N Africa and Italy, 1943–45). Member of 7 and 5 Soc.; exhibitions at Leicester Galleries, 1933, 1936, 1940, 1947; exhibited Royal Acad., 1948–.

Pictures acquired by: Nat. Portrait Gallery; Royal Acad. of Arts, Tate Gallery, Min. of Works, Italian Min. of Education, Aberdeen, Leeds, Manchester, Newport, Northampton, British Council, Contemporary Art Society. *Publications:* Illustrations: The Life of the Dead (text by Laura Riding), 1933; Adam was a Ploughman (text by C. Henry Warren), 1948. *Recreation:* gardening. *Address:* The Place House, Great Bardfield, Essex. *T:* Great Dunmow 810275. *Died 3 May* 1983.

**ALEC-SMITH, Col Rupert Alexander,** TD 1950; FSA; Lord-Lieutenant of Humberside, 1980–83; *b* 5 Sept. 1913; *o s* of late Alexander Alec-Smith, OBE, Wawne Lodge, Hull, and Lucy Adelaide, *e d* of Joseph Henry Horsley, Cottingham; *m* 1952, Suzette Genevieve, *e d* of James Watson, Holyrood House, Hedon, Yorks; one *d. Educ:* Malvern. Entered Horsley, Smith & Co. Ltd, timber importers, 1932, Dir 1945–78. Served War of 1939–45: temp. Lt-Col Green Howards (TA); Hon. Col 20th (N and E Ridings) Bn Mobile Defence Corps, 1956–59; Mem. E Riding TA Assoc., 1947–68 (Vice-Chm., 1961–65); Mem. Yorks TA & VRA, 1968–74; Vice-Pres., Yorks and Humberside TA & VRA, 1980–; Pres., Regtl Council Yorks Volunteers, 1982–83. Hon. Brother, Kingston upon Hull, Trinity House, 1950; Patronage Trustee, living of Holy Trinity, Kingston upon Hull, 1963; Patron, Kingston upon Hull Conservative Fedn, 1970–75; Georgian Soc. for E Yorks: Founder, 1937; Hon. Sec., 1937–74; Pres., 1975; Mem. Exec. Cttee, Georgian Group, 1953; Mem. Yorks Regional Cttee, National Trust, 1969. Pres., Hull and E Riding Inst. for the Blind, 1980. Kingston upon Hull: Mem. City Council, 1947–74 (leader Conservative Gp, 1955–70); Sheriff, 1949–50; Alderman, 1968–74 (Hon. Alderman, 1978–); Lord Mayor, 1970–71; Hon. Freeman, 1973; JP 1950; DL, ER Yorks and City and County of Kingston upon Hull, 1958; JP and DL Humberside, 1974, High Sheriff 1975, Vice Lord-Lieutenant, 1975–80. FSA 1975; Hon. RIBA (Yorks Region), 1983. Hon. DLitt Hull, 1979. KStJ 1980. *Publications:* A Catalogue Raisonné of the Corporation Plate and Insignia of the City and County of Kingston upon Hull, 1973. *Recreation:* looking at buildings. *Address:* Winestead, Hull HU12 0NN. *T:* Patrington 30297.
*Died 23 Dec.* 1983.

**ALEIXANDRE, Vicente Pio Marcelino Cirilo;** Spanish writer; *b* Seville, 26 April 1898; *s* of Cirilo Aleixandre Ballester and Elvira Merlo García de Pruneda. *Educ:* Univ. of Madrid (Law degree; diploma in Business Admin.). Associate Prof., Central Sch. of Commerce, Madrid, 1919–21; worked for Ferrocarriles Andaluces, 1921–25. Teacher of Business Terminology, Residencia de Estudiantes, 1921; contrib., La Semana Financiera. Member: Royal Spanish Acad.; Hispanic Soc. of America; Monde Latin Acad., Paris; Corresponding Member: Arts Acad., Malaga; Scis and Arts Acad., Puerto Rico; Hispano-American Acad., Bogotá. Hon. Fellow, Profs of Spanish Assoc., USA. Nat. Prize for Literature, 1933; Spanish Critics Prize, 1962, 1974; Nobel Prize for Literature, 1977. Grand Cross of Order of Carlos III, 1977. *Publications:* Ambito, 1928; Espadas como Labios, 1932; Pasión de la Tierra, 1935; La Destrucción o el Amor, 1935; Sombra del Paraíso, 1944; Mundo a Solas, 1950; Vida del Poeta: el amor y la poesía, 1950; Poemas Paradisíacos, 1952; Nacimiento Ultimo, 1953; Historia del Corazón, 1954; Algunos Carácteres de la Nueva Poesía Española, 1955; Ocho Poemas de Aleixandre, 1955; Mis Poemas Mejores, 1957; Los Encuentros, 1958; Poemas Amorosos, 1960; Poesías Completas, 1960; Picasso, 1961; Antigua Casa Madrileña, 1961; En Un Vasto Dominio, 1962; María la Gorda, Retratos con Nombre, 1965; Presencias, 1965; Dos Vidas, 1967; Obras Completas, 1968; Poemas de la Consumación, 1968; Antología del Mar y la Noche, 1971; Poesía Superrealista, 1971; Sonido de la Guerra, 1971; Diálogos del Conocimiento, 1974; Antología Total, 1976. *Address:* Vicente Aleixandre 3, Madrid 3, Spain.
*Died 14 Dec.* 1984.

**ALEXANDER, Sir Darnley (Arthur Raymond),** Kt 1974; CBE 1963; CFR 1979; GCON 1983; Chairman, Nigerian Law Reform Commission, since 1979; *b* Castries, St Lucia, 28 Jan. 1920; *e s* of late Pamphile Joseph Alexander, MBE, and late Lucy Alexander; *m* 1943, Mildred Margaret King (*d* 1980); one *s* one *d. Educ:* St Mary's Coll., St Lucia; University Coll., London (LLB). Called to Bar, Middle Temple, 1942. Served in: legal service, Jamaica, WI, and Turks and Caicos Is, 1944–57; legal service, Western Nigeria, 1957–63; Solicitor-Gen. QC 1961; Judge, High Court of Lagos (later Lagos State), 1964–69; Chief Justice: South Eastern State of Nigeria, 1969–75; Fed. Repub. of Nigeria, 1975–79. Chairman: Nigerian Council of Legal Educn, 1975–76; Kiribati Constitutional Commn re status of Banabans, 1985. Life Mem., Nigerian Body of Benchers, 1971 (Chm., 1977–78); Member: Nigerian Soc. of Internat. Law, 1968–; Nigerian Inst. of Internat. Affairs, 1979–. Patron, Nigerian-West Indian Assoc., 1979–. *Publications:* Report of Inquiry into Owegbe Cult, 1966; Report of Inquiry into Examination Leakages, 1969. *Recreations:* cricket, football, table-tennis, swimming, reading. *Address:* (office) Nigerian Law Reform Commission, Secretariat Complex, Ikoyi, PO Box 60008, Lagos,

Nigeria; (home) 18 Osborne Road, Ikoyi, Lagos, Nigeria. *T:* 681080. *Died 10 Feb.* 1989.

**ALEXANDER, Sir Desmond William Lionel C.;** *see* Cable-Alexander.

**ALEXANDER, Sir Douglas (Hamilton),** 2nd Bt, *cr* 1921; *b* 6 June 1900; *e s* of Sir Douglas Alexander, 1st Bt, and Helen Hamilton (*d* 1923), *d* of George Hamilton Gillespie, Hamilton; *S* father, 1949. *Educ:* Appleby College; Phillips Exeter Academy; Princeton University. BA 1921. The Singer Manufacturing Company, 1922; Secretary of the Company, 1946; later retired. *Heir: nephew* Prof. Douglas Alexander [*b* 9 Sept. 1936; *m* 1958, Marylon Scatterday; two *s*]. *Address:* 118 Palmers Hill Road, Stamford, Conn 06902, USA. *Died 18 Dec.* 1983.

**ALEXANDER, Duncan Hubert David,** CBE 1980 (OBE 1959); TD; DL; MA; Consultant, Stephenson & Alexander, Chartered Surveyors, Chartered Auctioneers and Estate Agents, Cardiff, retired 1985; *b* 15 June 1911; *e c* of late Hubert G. and Edith Alexander; *m* 1937, Dorothy Evelyn, 3rd *d* of late Edmund L. Hann; three *d. Educ:* Sherborne School, Dorset; Trinity College, Cambridge (MA). Family business of Stephenson & Alexander, 1933– (except War Service, RA, 1939–45; served as G2 RA Combined Ops, then Germany). Mem., 1960–80, Dep. Chm., 1973–80, Cwmbran New Town Corporation. National Pres. of Chartered Auctioneers' and Estate Agents' Institute, 1964–65; Member, Housing Corporation, 1964–74. Indep. Mem., Lord Nugent's MoD Lands Rev. Cttee, 1971–73. Hon. Col, Glamorgan Army Cadet Force, 1975–82. DL 1958, High Sheriff 1960, Glamorgan. *Recreations:* golf, gardening. *Address:* Star House, Capel Llanilterne, Glamorgan. *T:* Pentyrch 890332; (business) 5 High Street, Cardiff. *T:* Cardiff 40244. *Clubs:* MCC; Cardiff and County (Cardiff) (Trustee); Royal Porthcawl Golf.
*Died 18 Dec.* 1985.

**ALEXANDER, Freda Mary, (Mrs Arthur Alexander);** *see* Swain, F. M.

**ALEXANDER, Henry Joachim,** Dr phil, Dr jur Breslau; formerly Member, Conseil Fédéral, Fédération Internationale des Communautés d'Enfants, Trogen, 1960–83 (Secrétaire Général Adjoint, 1960–67; Chairman of UK Section, 1960–70; Vice-Pres., 1967–71); *b* 4 Jan. 1897; *s* of Bruno and Lisbeth Alexander-Katz; *m* 1st, 1925, Hilda (*née* Speyer) (*d* 1974); two *s*; 2nd, 1975, Amalia Cornelia (*née* Amato). *Educ:* Gymnasium Augustum Germany; Univs of Göttingen and Breslau. Member, Berlin Bar, 1925–37. Member, European Service of BBC, 1942–56; Vice-Chm. and Trustee, Assoc. of Broadcasting Staff, 1952–54 (Chm., Foreign Langs Panel, 1952–55). Chm., British Pestalozzi Children's Village Assoc., 1947–57; Chm. Pestalozzi Children's Village Trust, 1957–62 (Exec. Vice-Pres., 1962–63); Mem. Council, Pestalozzi Children's Village Foundation, Trogen, Switzerland, 1954–77; Mem. Exec. Cttee, Lifeline, an Internat. Refugee Organisation, 1965–72; Mem. Residential Care Assoc., 1965–, and Chm. of its Internat. Cttee, 1965–70. Hon. Mem., Mark Twain Soc., USA, 1977–. *Publication:* International Trade Mark Law, 1935. *Recreations:* music, hill walking. *Address:* Hildings, Pett, Hastings, East Sussex TN35 4JG. *T:* Pett 3055; Villa Hélios, Avenue des Amandiers, CH-1820 Montreux, Switzerland. *T:* Montreux 021. 631771.
*Died 13 June* 1988.

**ALEXANDER, Nell Haigh;** President of Baptist Union, Great Britain and Ireland (first woman so appointed), 1978–79; *b* 24 Feb. 1915; *d* of William Henry and Grace Caroline Fowler; *m* 1938, Arthur Alexander; one *s. Educ:* Higher Grade (Central) Girls' Sch., Cambridge. Nat. Chm., Women's Work, Baptist Union, 1971–76; Representative for Europe, Baptist World Alliance (Women's Dept). *Recreations:* classical music, reading, theatre, church drama, poetry. *Address:* 86 Thornton Road, Cambridge. *T:* Cambridge 276368. *Died 29 May* 1986.

**ALEXANDER-SINCLAIR, John Alexis Clifford Cerda,** SMOM, FRSA, RMS; Founder and Chairman, Human Rights Trust, 1969; Vice-Chairman: British Institute of Human Rights, since 1971; Anti-Slavery Society, since 1951 (Committee Member, since 1965); Chairman: British League for Animal Rights; Art Registration Committee, since 1969; *b* 22 Feb. 1906; *s* of Col C. H. Alexander, Jacob's Horse, and Donna Lyta Alexander dei Marchesi della Cerda; *m* 1st, 1927, Baroness von Gottberg (decd); one *d*; 2nd, 1933, Stella Tucker; one *s* one *d*; 3rd, 1950, Simonee de Rougemont (*née* Vion); 4th, 1965, Maureen Dover (*née* Wood); one step *s. Educ:* Charterhouse; Goettingen and Munich Univs. Entered HM Foreign Service, 1928; served in China as Vice-Consul and Consul; despatches (Admiralty) 1938; Founder and Mem., Chinese Industrial Co-operatives, 1940–41; Liaison Free French Headquarters, Far East, 1941 (POW Shanghai, 1942); served in Washington as 1st Sec. of Embassy, 1943; seconded to UNRRA, London and Paris, 1944 (Mem., Cabinet Particulier, French Minister Henri Frenay, Refugees, Deportees, and PoWs, Paris); CCG as Controller (Col) Economic Plans, 1945; 1st Sec. UK

Delegation, UN Econ. and Social Council, NY, 1946, 1947, 1948; Vice-Chm. UNICEF, 1946, 1947; Sec. Gen. UK Delegation Geneva Red Cross Conf., 1949; served UN, NY, 1950; Dir UN Office of High Comr for refugees, Geneva, 1951–52; transf. UN High Comr for Refugees Rep. (local rank Minister), Rome, 1953–55; European Dir (Paris), International Rescue Cttee, NY, 1957–58; UN Tech. Assistance Adviser to Min. of Finance, Govt of Thailand, Jan.-Feb. 1959, to Nat. Iranian Oil Co., Tehran, Iran, 1959–60; Head of Oil Industry Labour Re-deployment Unit, 1960; Manpower Expert, FAO (UN Special Fund) in the Rif, Morocco, 1961–62. Founder Mem., Hansard Soc. for Parliamentary Govt, 1944; Executive Sec. Liberal International, London, 1963–64; Hon. Campaign Dir, UK Cttee for Human Rights Year, UN, 1967, 1968, 1969; Member: Cttee, Internat. Social Service, 1972; Cttee, League Against Cruel Sports, 1974–81; World Orgn for Animal Rights, Brussels, 1987–; Dir, Animal Welfare Year, 1976; Vice Pres., Internat. League for Animal Rights, Paris, 1986; Vice-Pres., British Assoc. of Former UN Civil Servants, 1978–81. Exec. Chm., British Visual Artists Rights Soc., 1981–82; UK Consultant, Société de la Propriété Artistique Dessins et Modèles, 1981–83; Mem. Council, Design and Artists Copyright Soc., 1984–. Knight of Magistral Grace, British Assoc. of SMO Malta, 1957. Distinguished Service Award (Internat. Rescue Cttee), 1959. Life Member, Fellow 1965, Royal Soc. of Arts; Mem., Royal Soc. of Miniature Painters, Sculptors and Gravers, 1971–86; Hon. Mem. Exec. Cttee, UK Section, Association Internationale des Arts Plastiques et Graphiques, 1977–82. *Address:* 5 Aysgarth Road, Dulwich Village, SE21 7JR. *T:* 01–733 1666; The Clink, Goodings, Woodlands St Mary, Newbury RG16 7BD. *T:* Great Shefford 450. *Club:* Athenæum.                                              *Died* 27 *Oct.* 1988.

**ALGAR, Claudius Randleson,** JP; barrister-at-law; *b* 18 May 1900; *s* of Claudius G. Algar; *m* 1930, Constance, *d* of Edgar Tucker, Carmarthen; one *s*. *Educ:* Highgate School. Barrister-at-law, Inner Temple, 1925. Dep. Chm., Wilts QS, 1945–71. Member of the Corporation of London, 1930–48. JP Wiltshire, 1941. *Address:* Rye Hill, Longbridge Deverill, Warminster, Wilts. *T:* Maiden Bradley 316.                                              *Died* 27 *Aug.* 1988.

**ALKER, Thomas,** CBE 1958; LLM Liverpool (Hon.); Town Clerk of Liverpool and Legal and Parliamentary Officer to the Mersey Tunnel Joint Committee, 1947–67, retired; *b* 25 Aug. 1904; *m* 1930, Marion Eckersley Dove; four *d*. *Educ:* Wigan Grammar School; Manchester University. Asst Solicitor, Wigan, 1928–30; Sen. Asst Solicitor and Dep. Town Clerk, Kingston-upon-Hull, 1930–37; Town Clerk and Clerk of the Peace, Oldham, 1937–47. President, Society of Town Clerks, 1954–55. Hon. Solicitor for England, National and Local Government Officers Association, 1957–61. *Recreations:* music, photography. *Address:* 278 Allerton Road, Liverpool L18 6JP. *T:* 051-724 2768. *Club:* National Liberal.            *Died* 21 *Sept.* 1981.

**ALLAN, Commissioner Janet Laurie;** retired 1957; *b* 20 March 1892; *d* of Thomas Alexander Allan, chemist, Strathaven, Scotland. *Educ:* in Scotland. Entered Salvation Army Training Coll., 1911; commissioned as sergeant to the College, 1912; opened Salvation Army work in Castle Douglas, Scotland, 1913; returned to Training College as a Brigade Officer, 1915; Home Officer at Training Coll., 1918; with "Calypso" Party sailed to India (South Travancore, South India), 1921; returned to England, 1929, and appointed to slum and goodwill work in British Isles; returned to India; served in Travancore, Calcutta, and Eastern India; also Madras and Telegu country as Territorial Comdr; Territorial Comdr of Western India, 1951–54; Territorial Comdr of Southern India, 1954–57, Salvation Army. Leader Salvation Army Women's Social Work, Great Britain and Ireland, 1947; Comr, 1951. *Address:* Glebelands, 1 Grove Hill Road, SE5 8DF.                                      *Died* 9 *July* 1985.

**ALLAN, John Arthur Briscoe,** CMG 1965; *b* 30 Nov. 1911; Scottish; *er s* of late Eng. Capt. George Allan, New Malden; *m* 1935, Dorothy Mary; one *d*. *Educ:* Douai School. Served with HM Forces, 1940–48 (despatches); Lt-Col. Joined HMOCS, 1948; retired 1964 as Comr of Prisons, Kenya. Prisons assignments, ODM, FCO; Adviser of Prisons, Kenya, 1964–67; Dir of Prisons, Swaziland, 1968–71; Adviser of Prisons: Mauritius, 1974; Commonwealth Caribbean Dependencies, 1976. *Recreations:* golf, bowls, bridge. *Address:* 24 Cheddington Road, Bournemouth BH9 3NB. *T:* Bournemouth 510526. *Clubs:* Special Forces; Queens Park, West Hants Tennis (Bournemouth).                                      *Died* 30 *Nov.* 1981.

**ALLAN, William Nimmo,** CMG 1948; MC 1917; FICE; engineering consultant; *b* 10 Nov. 1896; *s* of late Rev. W. G. Allan, MA, BD, Callander, Perthshire; *m* 1932, Mary Helen Burnett, *o d* of late Rev. T. Burnett Peter, MA, BD, Callander, Perthshire; two *s*. *Educ:* George Watson's Boys' College, Edinburgh. Served European War, 1914–19, 9th (Ser.) Bn The Gordon Highlanders, Captain (MC). BSc(Eng) Glasgow Univ., 1921. AMICE 1923, MICE 1944, FICE. Engineer with Kassala Cotton Co., Sudan, 1924; Irrigation Dept of Sudan Govt, 1927; Asst Director, 1941; Director, 1944; Irrigation Consultant to Sudan Govt, 1946–69; Consultant to FAO of UNO,

Rome, 1959–67. *Address:* St Petroc's Cottage, Bread Street, Ruscombe, Stroud, Glos GL6 6EQ. *T:* Stroud 3941.
                                                            *Died* 15 *Sept.* 1984.

**ALLCOCK, John Gladding Major,** CB 1964; *b* 20 July 1905; *o s* of Rev. William Gladding Allcock, MA (TCD), and Ada Allcock (*née* Hall); *m* 1936, Eileen, *d* of Dr Ll. A. Baiss, OBE, Swanage, Dorset; one *s* one *d*. *Educ:* St Paul's School; Jesus College, Cambridge. Classical Tripos Cl. II in Pts I and II, BA 1927; MA 1931. Awarded Commonwealth Fund Fellowship, 1939. War Service in Admiralty, 1939–44. Asst Master: Exeter School, 1927–28; Liverpool College, 1928–35; HM Inspector of Schools, 1935–66; Divisional Inspector (NW Div.), 1949; Chief Inspector for Educational Developments, 1959–66, retired. *Recreations:* music, theatre, foreign travel. *Address:* Russet Cottage, Corfe Castle, Dorset. *T:* Corfe Castle 480574.                                          *Died* 14 *Dec.* 1986.

**ALLCROFT, Sir Philip M.;** *see* Magnus-Allcroft, Sir Philip.

**ALLDRITT, Walter,** JP; Regional Secretary, National Union of General and Municipal Workers, in Liverpool, North Wales, and Northern Ireland, 1970–81; *b* 4 July 1918; *s* of late Henry and Bridget Alldritt; *m* 1945, Mary Teresa, *d* of W. H. McGuinness; four *s* one *d*. *Educ:* St Francis de Sales; Liverpool University (WEA). Served with HM Forces, 1939–46. Trade Union Officer. MP (Lab) Scotland Div. of Liverpool, June 1964–Feb. 1971. Member various public bodies. Councillor 1955, JP 1958, Liverpool. *Address:* 104 Longmeadow Road, Knowsley, Prescot, Merseyside L34 0HT. *T:* 051–546 5703.                      *Died* 27 *July* 1990.

**ALLEGRO, John Marco;** author; *b* 17 Feb. 1923; *s* of late John Marco Allegro and Mabel Jessie (*née* Perry); *m* 1948, Joan Ruby Lawrence (marr. diss. 1985); one *s* one *d*. *Educ:* Wallington County Grammar Sch.; Univ. of Manchester. Royal Navy, 1941–46; Manchester Univ. 1947–52; BA 1st cl. Hons Oriental Studies, 1951; MA 1952; Bles Hebrew Prize, 1950; Scarborough Sen. Studentship, 1951–54; Leverhulme Research Award, 1958; Oxford Univ. (Magdalen), research in Hebrew dialects, 1952–53; University of Manchester: Lectureship in Comparative Semitic Philology and in Hebrew, 1954–62; Lectr in Old Testament and Intertestamental Studies, 1962–70. Brit. rep. on Internat. editing team for Dead Sea Scrolls, Jerusalem, 1953–; Adviser to Jordanian Govt on Dead Sea Scrolls, 1961–; Trustee and Hon. Sec. of Dead Sea Scrolls Fund, 1962–70. Organiser and leader of archaeological expedns to Jordan, 1959–. Popular lectr and broadcaster on archaeological subjects. TV films include: Dead Sea Scrolls, BBC, 1957; Search in the Kidron, BBC, 1963; The Mystery of the Dead Sea Scrolls, BBC; Physician, Heal Thyself, CBS, 1987. *Publications:* The Dead Sea Scrolls (Pelican), 1956 (revised edn 1964); The People of the Dead Sea Scrolls, 1958; The Treasure of the Copper Scroll, 1960 (revised edn 1964); Search in the Desert, 1964; The Shapira Affair, 1964; Discoveries in the Judæan Desert, V, 1968; The Sacred Mushroom and the Cross, 1970; The End of a Road, 1970; The Chosen People, 1971; Lost Gods, 1977; The Dead Sea Scrolls and the Christian Myth, 1979; All Manner of Men, 1982; Physician, Heal Thyself..., 1985; articles in learned jls on Semitic philology. *Recreations:* fell walking, sketching. *Address:* 18 Wellbank, Sandbach, Crewe, Cheshire CW11 0EP. *T:* Crewe 761076. *Club:* Explorers' (New York).
                                                            *Died* 17 *Feb* 1988.

**ALLEN OF FALLOWFIELD,** Baron *cr* 1974 (Life Peer), of Fallowfield; **Alfred Walter Henry Allen,** CBE 1967; General Secretary, Union of Shop Distributive & Allied Workers, 1962–79; a Crown Estate Commissioner, 1965–84; *b* Bristol, 7 July 1914; *m* 1940, Ruby Millicent Hounsell; one *s* one *d*. *Educ:* East Bristol Sch. RAF (Sergeant), 1940–45. Apptd Area Organiser, Nat. Union Distributive & Allied Workers, 1946; Nat. Officer, Union of Shop Distributive & Allied Workers, 1951. Member: Gen. Council of TUC, 1962–79 (Chm., 1973–74); Industrial Arbitration Bd, 1973–; Government Cttee of Inquiry into Statutory Smallholdings, 1963; Council of the Manchester Business Sch.; NEDC, 1963–79; CIR, 1969–70; British Airports Authority, 1976–82; Cttee to Review the Functioning of Financial Institutions, 1977–80; Central Lancashire Develt Corp., 1978–; Cttee on Enforcement Powers, Inland Revenue and Customs and Excise Depts, 1980–. Chairman: EDC for Chemical Industry, 1975–81; TUC Economic Cttee, 1975–79 (Mem., 1963–79); Governor: BBC, 1976–82; The Ditchley Foundn. Dir Industrial Training Service, 1974–80. *Recreations:* reading, theatre, gardening, cricket. *Address:* 83 Manley Road, Sale, Cheshire. *T:* 061–973 3058.                          *Died* 14 *Jan.* 1985.

**ALLEN, Hon. Alfred Ernest,** CMG 1973; JP; President, Associated Trustee Savings Banks of New Zealand, 1976–78 (Vice-President, 1974–76); Chairman, Blinded Servicemen's Trust Board, since 1961; *b* Onehunga, NZ, 20 May 1912; 4th *s* of Ernest Richard Allen and Harriet May Allen; *m* 1935, Nancy, 3rd *d* of Frederick Arthur Cutfield and Ethel Cutfield; one *s* three *d*. *Educ:* numerous primary schs; Auckland Grammar School. Farm hand, 1927; farming on own account from 1933. Served War of 1939–45, 24 Bn 2 NZEF, Middle East (Sgt-Major). MP Franklin, NZ, 1957–72; Junior Govt

Whip, 1963–66; Chief Govt Whip, 1966–69; Chm. of Cttees and Deputy Speaker, 1969–71; Speaker, House of Representatives, 1972. A Freemason (Past Master). Mem., Auckland Electric Power Bd, 1948–77 (Chm., 1956, 1957 and 1958). Pres., Bd of Trustees, Auckland Savings Bank, 1973–75 (Vice-Pres., 1972–73). *Recreations:* bowls, horse racing; formerly Rugby football (Country Union Rep.), tennis. *Address:* 32 Carlton Crescent, Maraetai Beach, Auckland, New Zealand. *T:* Beachlands 6595. *Clubs:* Franklin (Pukekohe); Returned Servicemen's (Franklin); (Hon. Mem.) Bellamy's (Wellington).                                *Died* 9 *March* 1987.

**ALLEN, Arthur Cecil;** retired as MP (Lab) Market Bosworth Division of Leicestershire (1945–Sept. 1959) and Opposition Whip (1951); *b* 10 Jan. 1887; *s* of Charles Allen; *m* 1914, Polly Mary Bradshaw; one *s* one *d. Educ:* Elementary School; Ruskin College. Served War of 1914–18. Mem. Exec. Nat. Union of Boot and Shoe Operatives, 1933. Alderman, Northants CC, 1937–49. Parliamentary Private Sec. to Chancellor of Exchequer and to Minister of State for Economic Affairs, 1950–51, to Leader of the Opposition, 1955–59. *Recreation:* reading. *Address:* 5 Rowlett Close, Higham Ferrers, Wellingborough, Northants. *T:* 55777.                *Died* 8 *Oct.* 1981.

**ALLEN, Dr Clabon Walter;** Professor of Astronomy at University College, London University, 1951–72, later Emeritus Professor; *b* 28 Dec. 1904; *s* of J. B. Allen and A. H. Allen; *m* 1937, Rose M. Smellie; five *s. Educ:* Perth High School; University of Western Australia. DSc (WA), 1935. Assistant at Commonwealth Observatory, Canberra, 1926–51. Solar Eclipse Expeditions, 1936, 1940, 1954, 1955 and 1959; Hackett Research Studentship, 1935–37. *Publications:* Astrophysical Quantities, 1955, 3rd rev. edn 1973; Hiking from Early Canberra, 1977; papers in Monthly Notices of Royal Astronomical Soc., Astro-physical Jl, Memoirs of Commonwealth Observatory, etc. *Address:* 3 Norfolk Street, Red Hill, Canberra, ACT 2603, Australia.                *Died* 11 *Dec.* 1987.

**ALLEN, Sir Denis;** *see* Allen, Sir W. D.

**ALLEN, Sir Donald (Richard),** Kt 1954; OBE 1944; MC and Bar 1917; Clerk to Trustees of London Parochial Charities, 1930–65; *b* 31 Aug. 1894; *s* of Thomas Allen and Elizabeth (*née* Willett); *m* 1918, Irene Dora Andrews (*d* 1965); one *s* one *d. Educ:* William Morris School, Walthamstow. Served European War, RFA, 1914–18; Ministry of Health, 1919–25; Clerk, London Parochial Charities, 1930; Barrister-at-Law, Inner Temple, 1928; Mem. Cttee on Charitable Trusts, 1950–52. *Publication:* History of the City Parochial Foundation, 1951. *Address:* Sprigg's Court, Epping, Essex. *Club:* Reform.                                *Died* 24 *Sept.* 1983.

**ALLEN, Rt. Rev. Geoffrey Francis,** DD; *b* 25 August 1902; 2nd *s* of late John Edward Taylor Allen, Holt House, Mobberley, Cheshire, and Mabel Saunders; *m* 1932, Madeline, *d* of Rev. R. J. S. Gill, Tadworth, Surrey. *Educ:* Rugby (Scholar); University College, Oxford (Scholar); Ripon Hall, Oxford (1st Class Philosophy, Politics and Economics, 1924; 2nd Class Theology, 1926). Liverpool Intercollegiate Secretary of the Student Christian Movement, 1926; Curate of St Saviour's, Liverpool, 1927; Chaplain of Ripon Hall, Oxford, 1928; Fellow and Chaplain of Lincoln College, Oxford, 1930–35; Union Theological College, Canton, 1935; Deputy Provost, Birmingham Cathedral, 1941; Sec. National Christian Council of China and Chaplain to British Embassy, Chungking, 1942–44; Archdeacon of Birmingham, 1944–47; Bishop in Egypt, 1947–52; Principal of Ripon Hall, Oxford, 1952–59; Bishop of Derby, 1959–69. *Publications:* Tell John, 1932 (part author); He that Cometh, 1932; Christ the Victorious, 1935; The Courage to be Real, 1938; Law with Liberty, 1942; The Theology of Missions, 1943; contributor, The Churches and Christian Unity (ed. R. J. W. Bevan), 1963. *Recreations:* the company of our friends, our garden. *Address:* The Knowle, Deddington, Oxford OX5 4TB. *T:* Deddington 38225. *Club:* English-Speaking Union.
                                                                                *Died* 8 *Nov.* 1982.

**ALLEN, Prof. George Cyril,** CBE 1958; FBA 1965; MCom, PhD; Emeritus Professor of Political Economy in the University of London; *b* Kenilworth, Warwickshire, 28 June 1900; *s* of late George Henry and Elizabeth Allen; *m* 1929, Eleanora (*d* 1972), *d* of late David Shanks, JP, Moseley, Birmingham. *Educ:* King Henry VIII School, Coventry; University of Birmingham. Lecturer in Economics at the Higher Commercial College, Nagoya, Japan, 1922–25; Research Fellow and Lecturer in the Faculty of Commerce, University College, Hull, 1929–33; Brunner Professor of Economic Science, University of Liverpool, 1933–47; Prof. of Political Economy, Univ. of London, 1947–67; Temp. Asst. Sec., Board of Trade, 1941–44. Member of Central Price Regulation Cttee, 1944–53; Temp. Counsellor, Foreign Office, Oct. 1945–April 1946. President of Economics Section, British Association, 1950; Mem. of Monopolies (and Restrictive Practices) Commn, 1950–62; Vice-Pres., Royal Economic Soc. Hon. Fellow, SOAS, Univ. of London, 1973. Supernumerary Fellow, St Antony's Coll., Oxford, 1980. Japan Foundn Award, 1980. Order of the Rising Sun (Third Class) (Japan). *Publications:* The Industrial Development of Birmingham

and the Black Country 1860–1927, 1929, repr. 1966; British Industries and their Organization, 1933 (rev. edn 1970); Japan: the Hungry Guest, 1938; Japanese Industry: Its Recent Development and Present Condition, 1939; (part-author) The Industrialization of Japan and Manchukuo, 1930–40, 1940; A Short Economic History of Japan, 1946 (rev. edn 1981); (jt) Western Enterprise in Far Eastern Economic Development: China and Japan, 1954; (jt) Western Enterprise in Indonesia and Malaya, 1957; Japan's Economic Expansion, 1965; The Structure of Industry in Britain, 1961 (rev. edn 1970); Japan as a Market and Source of Supply, 1967; Monopoly and Restrictive Practices, 1968; The British Disease, 1976 (rev. edn 1979); How Japan Competes, 1978; British Industry and Economic Policy, 1979; Japan's Economic Policy, 1980. *Recreations:* painting, reading. *Address:* Flat 15, Ritchie Court, 380 Banbury Road, Oxford. *T:* Oxford 50417. *Club:* Reform.
                                                                                *Died* 31 *July* 1982.

**ALLEN, Sir George (Oswald Browning),** Kt 1986; CBE 1962; TD 1945; *b* 31 July 1902; *s* of late Sir Walter M. Allen, KBE. *Educ:* Eton; Trinity College, Cambridge. GSO1, War Office, 1940–45. Member of London Stock Exchange, 1933–72. Cricket: Eton XI, 1919–21; Cambridge Univ., 1922–23; represented England in 25 Test Matches; Captain *v* India, 1936, *v* Australia, 1936–37, *v* West Indies, 1948; Chm. Selection Cttee, 1955–61; Chm. MCC cricket sub cttee, 1956–63; President, MCC, 1963–64; Treasurer, 1964–76; Mem., Cricket Council, 1968–82, resigned; Hon. Vice-Pres., Nat. Cricket Assoc., 1985. Legion of Merit (USA). *Recreations:* cricket, golf. *Address:* 4 Grove End Road, NW8. *T:* 01–286 4601. *Club:* White's.                                        *Died* 29 *Nov.* 1989.

**ALLEN, Godfrey;** *see* Allen, W. G.

**ALLEN, Jack,** DSc, LLD; FICE; FRSE; Professor of Engineering, Aberdeen University, 1946–69; *b* 19 Sept. 1905; *s* of late John and Phoebe Annie Allen, Heywood; *m* 1933, Elizabeth (*d* 1979), *d* of late Samuel and Frances Hall, Heaton Park, Lancs. *Educ:* Elton Council School; Bury Grammar School; Manchester University, BSc (First Class Hons in Engineering) 1926. Vulcan Research Fellow, 1928–29; Asst Lecturer, 1929–35, Lecturer, 1935–43; DSc 1939; Senior Lecturer, 1943–46, Manchester Univ. Engaged on investigations of Severn Barrage Scheme, Liverpool Bay training walls, proposed Humber Bridge, improvement of rivers Mersey, Dee and Parrett, Scapa Flow causeways (all as Asst to Prof. A. H. Gibson); flood relief in river Great Ouse, harbour developments at Dundee and Aberdeen, spillways on hydro-electric schemes, etc. MICE 1946; FRSE 1951 (Vice-Pres., 1964–67). James Forrest Lecturer, Institution of Civil Engineers, 1947. Member: Hydraulics Research Bd (DSIR), 1946–53, 1957–61, 1962–65; Hydraulics Research Station Steering Cttee, 1965–68; Research Advisory Council, British Transport Commn, 1957–64; Academic Advisory Council, Univs of St Andrews and Dundee, 1964–66; Chm., Res. Adv. Gp, British Transport Docks Bd, 1968–81. Hon. LLD Manchester, 1968; Hon. DSc Aberdeen, 1975. *Publications:* Scale Models in Hydraulic Engineering, 1947; many papers in Jl ICE, Phil. Mag., etc. *Address:* 4 Finches Gardens, Lindfield, Sussex RH16 2PA.                                *Died* 1 *Feb.* 1984.

**ALLEN, James Godfrey Colquhoun,** CMG 1956; Secretary, Nigeria Timber Association, 1961–69, retired; re-employed as Head of Social Welfare Services, 1972–76. Adviser Field Administration 1976, and General Director, 1977, Rivers State Rural Development Association, Port Harcourt, Nigeria, retired finally, 1978; *b* 26 May 1904; *s* of Dr. J. D. C. Allen and F. D. L. Allen (*née* Beckett), Bath; *m* 1982, Josephine Patricia Mary George, widow, *d* of Dominic La Posta. *Educ:* Blundell's Sch.; Ecole Supérieure de Commerce, Lausanne; Univ. of Munich. Asst Master, Alleyn Court School, Westcliff-on-Sea, 1926. Cadet, Nigerian Administrative Service, 1926; Asst District Officer and District Officer, 1929–45 (Major, Nigeria Regt, 1942–43); Resident, 1947; Senior Resident, 1953. Anglo-French Cameroons Boundary Commissioner, 1937–39; Nigerian Rep. with Free French, Douala, 1940; Chief Censor and Chief of Military Intelligence, Nigeria, 1940–41; W African Liaison Officer with Free French forces in Equatorial Africa, 1942–43; Political Sec. to Resident Minister, W Africa, 1943; Dep. Commissioner of the Colony, Lagos, 1946–52; Senior Resident, Rivers Province, Nigeria, 1952–56. Director of Administration, Nigerian Broadcasting Corporation, 1957–61. Mem. Bath Preservation Trust. Coronation Medal, 1953. *Publications:* A Native Court Handbook, 1955; The Organisation and Procedure of Local Government Councils, 1956. *Recreations:* golf, music. *Address:* 39 Lyncombe Hill, Bath, Avon BA2 4PQ. *T:* Bath 334826. *Club:* Royal Commonwealth Society.                                *Died* 12 *Nov.* 1982.

**ALLEN, Maurice;** *see* Allen, W. M.

**ALLEN, Sir Milton (Pentonville),** Kt 1972; OBE 1964; Governor, St Kitts/Nevis/Anguilla, 1972–75 (Acting Governor, 1969–Aug. 1972); *b* St Kitts, WI, 22 June 1888; *m* 1937, Annie Matilda (*née* Locker), MBE (*d* 1979); no *c. Educ:* (primary) Palmetto Point, St Kitts; then (for tailoring) studied at David Mitchell designing and cutting

Academy, NY (diploma). Worked at trade of tailor until the Depression, 1929. Nominated Member, 1957, Speaker, 1962, House of Assembly, St Kitts. Patron: St Kitts Cricket Assoc.; St Kitts Net Ball Assoc.; Boy Scouts Assoc. KStJ 1974. *Publication:* Chosen Poems (a collection), (New York) 1945. *Recreations:* reading, music, gardening; interested in Arts Festival of Basseterre (one of his chosen poems set to music for a choir, by Dr Leon Forrester, FRCO). *Address:* The Fortlands, Basseterre, St Kitts, West Indies.
*Died 17 Sept. 1981.*

**ALLEN, Maj.-Gen. Robert Hall,** CB 1942; MC; *b* 11 June 1886; *s* of R. Allen, LLD, Barrister-at-Law; *m* 1916, Margaret Lawrence (*d* 1974), *d* of Maj.-Gen. Sir David Mercer, KCB; one *d*. *Educ:* Charterhouse; RMA, Woolwich; served War of 1914–18, Gallipoli and Egypt (MC; despatches twice); comd 5 AA Div., 1939, 8 AA Div., 1941; retired pay, 1942. *Recreation:* solving simple chess problems. *Address:* The Old Vicarage, St Mary Street, Chippenham, Wilts.
*Died 20 Sept. 1981.*

**ALLEN, Brig. Ronald Lewis,** CBE 1970 (OBE 1956); General Manager, Building Societies' Staff College, Ware, 1971–81; *b* 2 April 1916; *s* of W. J. Allen and M. B. Allen (*née* Lewis); *m* 1st, 1945, Jirina Georgette (*née* Valachova) (marr. diss. 1952); one *d*; 2nd, 1956, Christine Maude (*née* Scott); one *s* one *d*. *Educ:* privately; Univ. of South Wales and Monmouthshire. BSc Hons London 1939. Scientist, Safety in Mines Research Bd; Birmingham Univ., 1939; Imperial Chemical Industries, 1939. War of 1939–45: commissioned, RAOC, 1940; served UK, 1940–42; MEF, 1942–44 (despatches, 1943); CMF, 1944–45. Egypt, 1949–50; USA, 1951–52; Cyprus, 1960–61; BAOR, 1961–62; Principal Ammunition Technical Officer, 1962–66; Comdr Ammunition Organisation and Chief Inspector, Land Service Ammunition, 1966–67; Dep. Comdr, Base Organisation RAOC, and Head of Inventory Systems Develt, 1967–71. Mem., Acceptable Risk Working Party, Council for Sci. and Soc., 1977. Mem., E Herts DC, 1973–83 (Chairman: A & R Cttee; Computer WP; Organisational WP). FRIC 1962 (ARIC 1939); MBIM 1967; Fellow Brit. Computer Soc. 1969. Queen's Commendation for Brave Conduct, 1964. *Recreations:* bridge, music, astrophysics, conservation, computers. *Address:* Yew Tree House, The Hall Close, North Aston, Oxon OX5 4HR.
*Died 19 June 1986.*

**ALLEN, Sir Roy George Douglas,** Kt 1966; CBE 1954 (OBE 1946); MA, DSc (Econ.); FBA 1952; Professor of Statistics, University of London, 1944–73, later Professor Emeritus; Consultant, Royal Commission on Civil Liability, 1974–78; *b* 3 June 1906; *er s* of G. H. Allen, Worcester; *m* 1936; two *s* one *d*. *Educ:* Royal Grammar School, Worcester; Sidney Sussex College, Cambridge (Wrangler, 1927; Hon. Fellow, 1971); DSc (Econ.) London, 1943. Assistant and later Lecturer in Statistics, London School of Economics, 1928–39; Reader in Economic Statistics, Univ. of London, 1939–44; Statistician, HM Treasury, 1939–41; Dir of Records and Statistics, British Supply Council, Washington, 1941–42; British Dir of Research and Statistics, Combined Production and Resources Board, Washington, 1942–45; Statistical Adviser, HM Treasury, 1947–48; Consultant, UN Statistical Office, 1949–50 and 1952. Visiting Professor, Univ. of California, 1958–59. Member: Air Transport Licensing Bd, 1960–72; Civil Aviation Authority, 1972–73; Cttee of Inquiry on Decimal Currency, 1962–63; Chm., Impact of Rates Cttee, 1963–65; Mem. Research Council, DSIR, 1964–65; Mem., SSRC, 1967–70. Hon. Fellow, LSE, 1977. Hon. DSc (Soc. Sci.) Southampton, 1970. Guy Medal (Gold), Royal Statistical Soc., 1979. *Publications:* Family Expenditure (with Sir Arthur Bowley), 1935; Mathematical Analysis for Economists, 1938; Statistics for Economists, 1949; International Trade Statistics (with J. Edward Ely), 1953; Mathematical Economics, 1956; Basic Mathematics, 1962; Macro-economic Theory, 1967; Index Numbers in Theory and Practice, 1975; Introduction to National Accounts Statistics, 1980; articles in economic and statistical journals. *Address:* 11 The Limes, Linden Gardens, W2. *T:* 01–727 9979; Greyfriars (South), South Green, Southwold, Suffolk. *T:* Southwold 723307.
*Died 29 Sept. 1983.*

**ALLEN, W(alter) Godfrey,** MA; FSA, FRIBA; Hon. DLitt (Oxford), 1963; Surveyor of the Fabric of St Paul's Cathedral, 1931–56; Consulting Architect to Southwark Cathedral, 1932–55, to Exeter Cathedral, 1942–52, to Gloucester Cathedral since 1953; architect in private practice; *b* 21 Oct. 1891; *s* of Walter Allen and Frances Baker; *m* 1931, Phyllis Seyler Gill (*d* 1973). *Educ:* Berkhampstead Sch.; Slade Sch.; King's Coll., London. Articled, later Asst to Sir Mervyn Macartney; Sec. to Commn of architects and engrs apptd in 1921 to investigate and report on condition of St Paul's Cathedral, Asst Architect to the Dean and Chapter, 1925–31. Member: Royal Commn on Historical Monuments (Eng.), 1952–60; Exec. Cttee of Wren Soc., 1933–43; Advisory Panel of Specialist Architects, Historic Churches Preservation Trust (London Region); Chairman Church Roofing Committee set up by Central Council for the Care of Churches and Society for the Protection of Ancient Buildings, 1952; Commander of St Paul's Watch, 1939–45; Prime Warden

Goldsmiths' Co., 1951–53; Master of Art Workers' Guild, 1953–54; Hon. Mem., City and Guilds of London Inst. A Governor, Westminster Sch., 1951–70. *Works include:* restoration of St Bride's, Fleet Street; St Giles, Cripplegate; St Mary Abchurch; St Dunstan-in-the-West; St James, Louth; St James's Chapel, Exeter Cathedral; Chapter-House, St Paul's Cathedral; Sheldonian Theatre; Old Ashmolean Building and Radcliffe Camera, Oxford. *Publications:* The Preservation of St Paul's Cathedral, RIBA Jl; A Survey of Views of St Paul's Cathedral; numerous articles. *Recreation:* walking. *Address:* Morden College, Blackheath, SE3 0PW.
*Died 12 June 1986.*

**ALLEN, Sir (William) Denis,** GCMG 1969 (KCMG 1958; CMG 1950); CB 1955; HM Diplomatic Service, retired; *b* 24 Dec. 1910; *s* of John Allen; *m* 1939, Elizabeth Helen (*née* Watkin Williams); one *s*. *Educ:* Wanganui, New Zealand; Cambridge. HM Diplomatic Service, 1934–69; Deputy Commissioner General for South East Asia, 1959–62; Ambassador to Turkey, 1963–67; Dep. Under-Sec., Foreign Office (later FCO), 1967–69. *Address:* Stockland, Honiton, Devon.
*Died 20 May 1987.*

**ALLEN, (William) Maurice;** Executive Director, Bank of England, 1964–70; *b* 16 April 1908; *s* of David Allen. *Educ:* Dulwich College; London School of Economics. Army 1940–45. Asst Dir of Research, International Monetary Fund, 1947–49; Adviser, Bank of England, 1950–64. Fellow of Balliol Coll., Oxford, 1931–48; Visiting Fellow Nuffield Coll., Oxford, 1954–62. Hon. Fellow, LSE, 1963. Governor, LSE, 1951. *Address:* Bank of England, EC2. *Club:* Reform.
*Died 26 May 1988.*

**ALLENBY,** 2nd Viscount, *cr* 1919, of Megiddo and of Felixstowe; **Dudley Jaffray Hynman Allenby;** late 11th Hussars; *b* 8 Jan. 1903; *e s* of late Capt. Frederick Claude Hynman Allenby, CBE, RN, JP; *S* uncle, 1936; *m* 1st, 1930, Mary (marr. diss. 1949), *d* of Edward Champneys, Otterpool Manor, Kent; one *s*; 2nd, 1949, Mrs Daisy Neame, CStJ. *Educ:* Eton; RMC, Sandhurst. Joined 11th Hussars, 1923; served in India, 1923–26; Adjutant, 11th Hussars, 1926–30; Instructor, Royal Military College, Sandhurst, 1930–34; Captain, 1936; served Egypt, 1934–37; Adjutant, Army Fighting Vehicles School, 1937–40; Major, 1938; 2nd in Command Royal Gloucestershire Hussars, 1940–42; Lt-Col 2nd Derbyshire Yeomanry, 1942; retd (Lt-Col) 1946. *Heir:* *s* Lt-Col Hon. Michael Jaffray Hynman Allenby, The Royal Hussars [*b* 20 April 1931; *m* 1965, Sara Margaret Wiggin; one *s*]. *Address:* Parsonage Farm, Westwell, Ashford, Kent. *T:* Ashford 24783. *Club:* Cavalry and Guards.
*Died 17 July 1984.*

**ALLERTON, Reginald John,** CBE 1964; FRICS, FIH; retired 1963; *b* 20 June 1898; 3rd *s* of late Robert Sterry Allerton, Lowestoft, and Mary Maria (*née* Bailey); *m* 1924, Dorothy Rose Saunders; one *s*. *Educ:* Lowestoft Grammar School. Entered Local Government Service, 1915; on Active Service with RNVR, 1917–19. Various urban and borough appointments until 1926; Chief Architectural and Building Asst, Reading Borough Council, 1926–30; Estates Surveyor, City of Norwich, 1930–39; Housing Manager and Sec., City of Bristol, 1939–51; Housing Manager, City of Birmingham, 1951–54; Director of Housing to the London County Council, 1954–63. Pres., Inst. of Housing, 1949–50, 1960–61. Apptd (by Minister of Housing and Local Govt) as Vice-Pres., Surrey and Sussex Rent Assessment Panel, 1965–71. Served on Govt Cttees on Housing and Immigration, and Housing in Greater London (Sir Milner Holland Cttee); Founder Mem., Hanover Housing Assoc. *Publications:* many papers and lectures to professional societies and conferences dealing mainly with municipal housing work. *Recreation:* gardening. *Address:* 10 Mill Mead, Wendover, Bucks HP22 6BY. *T:* Wendover 622691.
*Died 22 March 1990.*

**ALLEYNE, Captain Sir John (Meynell),** 4th Bt *cr* 1769; DSO 1918; DSC; RN retired; *b* 11 Aug. 1889; *s* of Reynold Alleyne, *e s* of 3rd Bt and Susanna, *d* of late John Meynell of Meynell Langley, Derbyshire; *S* grandfather, 1912; *m* 1920, Alice Violet, *d* of late James Campbell, and Mrs Campbell, 12 Cornwall Gardens, SW; one *s* two *d*. Served World War I; was navigator of HMS Vindictive when sunk to block Ostend Harbour, May 1918 (severely wounded); retired list, 1936. Served World War II. *Heir:* *s* Rev. John Olpherts Campbell Alleyne [*b* 18 Jan. 1928; *m* 1968, Honor Irwin; one *s* one *d*]. *Address:* Greenacres, Seamans Lane, Minstead, Lyndhurst, Hants. *T:* Southampton 813235. *Club:* Naval and Military.
*Died 17 Dec. 1983.*

**ALLINSON, Air Vice-Marshal Norman Stuart,** CB 1946; DL: retired; *b* 19 April 1904; *s* of late Rev. H. C. W. Allinson, Hinxhill, Kent; *m* 1928, Florence Muriel Hall (*d* 1975); one *s* ... *d*. *Educ:* Trent Coll.; RAF, Cranwell. Served with No 13 Sqdn, 1924–29; in HMS Hermes, 1930–32; Dept of Air Member of Personnel, 1933–35; RAF Staff Coll., 1936; comd No 269 Sqdn, 1938; HQ Coastal Comd, 1938–39; served War of 1939–45, Armament duties, Air Min. and MAP, 1940–41; HQ Army Co-operation Comd, 1942; served in Middle East, 1943–45, on planning duties, as AOC No 212 Group and Force 438 and as Dep. SASO, HQ Middle East; Dir of Operational Trng, Air Min., 1945–47; Imperial Defence Coll., 1948; AOC Rhodesian Air Trng Group, Bulawayo, S Rhodesia, 1949–51; Director-General of Manning, 1951–52; Director-General of Personnel I, 1953–54; Air Officer i/c Administration, Flying Training Command, 1954–56; retired, 1956. DL Essex, 1964. *Recreation:* sailing. *Address:* Dene House, Layer de la Haye, Colchester, Essex. *Club:* Royal Air Force. *Died* 8 *Oct.* 1984.

**ALLISON, Rt. Rev. Oliver Claude,** CBE 1971; *b* Stafford, 28 May 1908; *s* of Rev. W. S. Allison. *Educ:* Dean Close School, Cheltenham; Queens' College and Ridley Hall, Cambridge. BA 1930; MA 1934. Deacon, 1932; Priest, 1933; Curate of Fulwood, 1932–36; Curate of St John, Boscombe, and Jt Sec. Winchester Dio. Council of Youth, 1936–38; CMS Miss. at Juba, Dio. Sudan, 1938–47; Asst Bp in the Sudan, 1948–53; Bishop in the Sudan, 1953–74. Patron (formerly Travelling Sec.), Sudan Church Assoc. *Publications:* A Pilgrim Church's Progress, 1966; Through Fire and Water, 1976; Travelling Light, 1983. *Address:* 1 Gloucester Avenue, Bexhill-on-Sea, East Sussex TN40 2LA. *Club:* Royal Commonwealth Society.
*Died* 7 *June* 1989.

**ALLISON, Ralph Victor,** CMG 1967; retired industrialist, Australia; *b* 20 Feb. 1900; *s* of late Albert John and Edith Victoria Allison; *m* 1923, Myrtle Ellen Birch; two *d*. *Educ:* public and night schools, Milang, SA. General Store, A. H. Landseer Ltd: Milang, 1916–19; Adelaide, 1919–26; R. J. Finlayson Ltd, Adelaide: Company Sec., 1926–39; Dir, 1939–64; Man. Dir, 1954–64; Chm. Dirs of subsidiaries, 1954–64. Mem. Council: Royal Agric. and Hort. Soc. of SA, 1937–72 (Exec. Mem. 8 yrs, subseq. Hon. Mem.); SA Chamber of Manufactures, later Chamber of Commerce and Industry SA Inc. 1948– (now Hon. Mem.; (also Mem. Exec. Cttee); Pres., 1962, 1963); Mem. SA Dairy Bd, 1957. Pres. Aust. Chamber of Manufactures, 1964; Mem. Aust. Export Develt Council, 1964–68; Director, Australian Export Promotions Ltd and various other Australian cos until 1966. Mem., many Aust. Commonwealth Cttees. *Died* 9 *July* 1987.

**ALLSOPP, Prof. Cecil Benjamin,** MA, PhD, DSc; FInstP; Professor of Physics Applied to Medicine, University of London at Guy's Hospital Medical School, 1953–70, later Emeritus; Consultant Physicist Emeritus to Guy's Hospital; *b* 2 Sept. 1904; *m* 1935, Ivy Kathleen Johns; one *s* one *d*. *Educ:* Emmanuel College, Cambridge; University of Frankfurt-am-Main. MA, Cambridge, 1930; PhD, Cambridge, 1932; DSc, London, 1951. Pres., British Institute of Radiology, 1963–64; Silvanus Thompson Memorial Lectr, 1965. *Publications:* Absorption Spectrophotometry (with F. Twyman, FRS), 1934. Papers in Proc. of the Royal Soc., Jl of the Chemical Soc., Trans of the Faraday Soc., British Journal of Radiology, British Journal of Experimental Pathology, Cancer Research, etc. *Address:* 40 Queen Edith's Way, Cambridge CB1 4PW.
*Died* 16 *Oct.* 1989.

**ALTY, Thomas,** DSc Liverpool; PhD Cantab; DCL Dunelm; LLD Glasgow, Toronto, Rhodes; FInstP; FRSC; FRSE; Deputy Principal, University of Birmingham, 1963–69; Life Governor, University of Birmingham; *b* 30 Sept. 1899; *s* of James Alty, Rufford, Lancashire; *m* 1925, Stella West (*d* 1979), *d* of W. Harris, solicitor, Liverpool; no *c*. *Educ:* Univ. of Liverpool (Oliver Lodge Fellow, 1921); University of Cambridge. Lecturer in Physics, University of Durham, 1924–25; Prof. of Physics, Univ. of Saskatchewan, Canada, 1925–29; Research Physicist, Imperial Chemical Industries, Northwich, Cheshire, 1929–30; Prof. of Physics, Univ. of Saskatchewan, 1930–32; Research Prof. of Physics, Univ. of Saskatchewan, 1932–35; Cargill Prof. of Applied Physics, Univ. of Glasgow, 1935–45; Cargill Prof. of Natural Philosophy, Univ. of Glasgow, 1945–48; Master of Rhodes University Coll., 1948–51; Principal and Vice-Chancellor of Rhodes Univ., Grahamstown, S Africa, 1951–63. Chm. Assoc. of Univs of British Commonwealth, 1958–60. Mem., SA Council for Scientific and Industrial Research, 1956–63. Member, SA National Council for Social Research, 1955–63. *Publications:* scientific papers. *Address:* 105 Fitzroy Avenue, Harborne, Birmingham B17 8RG.
*Died* 2 *May* 1982.

**ALVAREZ, Prof. Luis Walter;** Professor of Physics, University of California, Berkeley, since 1945; *b* 13 June 1911; *s* of late Dr Walter C. Alvarez and Harriet Smyth; *m* 1st, 1936, Geraldine Smithwick; one *s* one *d*; 2nd, 1958, Janet Landis; one *s* one *d*. *Educ:* University of Chicago. SB 1932, PhD 1936. Radiation Lab., Univ. of California, 1936–; MIT Radiation Lab., 1940–43; Metallurgical Lab., Univ. of Chicago, 1943–44; Los Alamos Sci. Lab., 1944–45; Associate Dir, Lawrence Rad. Lab., 1954–59. Pres., Amer. Physical Soc., 1969; Member: Nat. Acad. of Sciences; Nat. Acad. of Engineering; Am. Phil. Soc.; Am. Acad. of Arts and Sciences; Assoc. Mem., Institut d'Egypte. Awarded: Collier Trophy, 1946; John Scott Medal, 1953; US Medal for Merit, 1947; Einstein Medal, 1961; Pioneer Award, AIEEE, 1963; Nat. Medal of Science, 1964; Michelson Award, 1965; Nobel Prize in Physics, 1968. Nat. Inventors' Hall of Fame, 1978. Hon. ScD: Chicago, 1967; Carnegie-Mellon, 1968; Kenyon,

1969; Notre Dame, 1976; Ain Shams Univ., Cairo, 1979; Penn. Coll. of Optometry, 1982. *Publications:* more than 100 contributions to Physics Literature, largely in Nuclear Physics and High Energy Physics; many pubns developing evidence that mass extinctions were caused by impacts of asteroids or comets; 40 US Patents, largely in Electronics and Optics. *Recreations:* flying, golf, music. *Address:* (business) Lawrence Berkeley Laboratory, University of California, 1 Cyclotron Road, Berkeley, Calif 94720, USA. *T:* 415–486 4400; (home) 131 Southampton Avenue, Berkeley, Calif 94707, USA. *T:* 415–525–0590. *Clubs:* Bohemian (San Francisco); Faculty (Berkeley); Miravista Golf (El Cerrito).
*Died* 1 *Sept.* 1988.

**ALVIN, Madame Juliette Louise,** FGSMT; violoncellist and viola da gamba player; registered Music Therapist (USA, Britain); Head of Music Therapy Department, Guildhall School of Music; 2nd *d* of Jeanne and Henri Alvin, Paris; *m* William A. Robson (*d* 1980); two *s* one *d*. *Educ:* Lycée de Versailles; Conservatoire National de Musique, Paris (First prix d'Excellence); later studied with Pablo Casals; has played in principal musical centres of Europe, including London, Paris, Berlin, Vienna, Brussels, Prague, Buda Pesth, Belgrade, Bucarest, The Hague, Warsaw, Stockholm, etc; often with the Philharmonic Orchestra; toured USA frequently, 1932–68. Has broadcast as a soloist in BBC programmes from London and provinces; musical activities during War of 1939–45 included war factory tours and other concerts organised by the Arts Council (CEMA); also recitals in military and Red Cross hospitals and service concerts; more than 200 recitals in aid of War Charities. Recognised as a leading authority on musical education in England through special recitals for school children, and a teacher of internat. reputation. Appointed for winter session, 1950–51, in music dept of North Carolina Univ., USA. Has lectured at numerous universities and colleges in Great Britain, on the Continent, in USA, Canada, S America, and Japan, esp., in recent years, on her experiments in music therapy with handicapped children and mental patients; has televised and made films on her work in music therapy; has given courses in music therapy in Spain, Portugal, Sweden, Belgium, France, USA, Germany, Japan, 1976–. Member American National Assoc. for Music Therapy; Hon. Member: Argentine Assoc. for Music Therapy; German Assoc. for Music Therapy; Spanish Assoc. for Music Therapy; Italian Assoc. for Music Therapy; Canadian Assoc. for Music Therapy; Hon. Adviser, Japanese Soc. for Music Therapy; Founder and Chm., British Society for Music Therapy (formerly Soc. for Music Therapy and Remedial Music), London, 1958–; Founder and Hon. Mem., Assoc. of Professional Music Therapists in GB, 1976; Vice-Pres., Internat. Council for Music Therapy and Social Psychiatry; Head of Music Therapy Dept and Dir, Diploma Course in Music Therapy, Guildhall School of Music and Drama, London. *Publications:* The Logic of Casals' Technique; Introducing music to children; Class Teaching of Instruments; Bach and the 'Cello; Musical Theory and Instrumental Technique, 1953; Casals, a great teacher; A Musical Experiment on Backward Children, 1954; 'Cello Tutor for Beginners, 1955 (2nd volume, 1958); Music for the Handicapped Child, 1965, 2nd edn 1976; Music Therapy, 1966, 2nd edn 1975; Report on a Research Project on Music Therapy, 1970; Music Therapy for the Autistic Child, 1978; contrib. to American Jl of Mental Deficiency, Cerebral Palsy Bulletin, The World of Music, Musik and Medizin, British Jl of Music Therapy and other learned jls. *Recreations:* tennis and swimming. *Address:* 48 Lanchester Road, N6 4TA. *T:* 01-883 1331. *Clubs:* London Violoncello, Hospitality (LSE).
*Died* 30 *Sept.* 1982.

**ALWYN, William,** CBE 1978; composer; Professor of Composition, Royal Academy of Music, 1926–55; *b* Northampton, 1905; *m* 1929, Olive Pull; two *s*. *Educ:* Northampton Sch.; Royal Acad. of Music. FRAM 1936; Collard Fellow, Worshipful Company of Musicians, 1938; Chm. of Composers' Guild of Gt Britain, 1949, 1950 and 1954; Fellow, British Film Acad., 1958. Hon. DMus Leicester, 1982. *Works:* Five Orchestral Preludes (Proms, 1927); Divertimento for Flute (Internat. Contemp. Music Festival, New York, 1940); Concerto Grosso No I (commnd by BBC, 1942); Symphony No I (Cheltenham Festival, 1950, London, 1953); Concerto Grosso No II (LSO and Proms, 1951); Festival March (commnd by Arts Council for Festival of Britain, 1951); Symphonic Prelude, The Magic Island (Hallé Concerts, 1953); Symphony No II (Hallé Concerts, Manchester, 1953, BBC, Festival Hall, 1954); Lyra Angelica, Concerto for Harp Proms, 1954; Autumn Legend, for cor anglais and strings (Cheltenham Festival and Proms, 1955); Symphony No III (commnd by BBC, 1956); Elizabethan Dances (commnd by BBC, Festival Hall, 1957); Symphony No IV (Promenade Concerts, 1959); Overture: Derby Day (commnd by BBC, Proms, 1960); Concerto Grosso No III (commnd by BBC, Proms, 1964); Sinfonietta for Strings (commnd by Cheltenham Festival, 1970); Hydriotaphia, Symphony No V (commnd by Arts Council for Norwich Triennial Festival, 1973); Miss Julie, 2-act opera, 1976; String Quartet no 2 (Aldeburgh Fest., 1976). *Film Music* since 1936 includes: Odd Man Out, The Way Ahead, The

True Glory, World of Plenty, The Magic Box, etc. *Publications: orchestral:* 5 symphonies, 3 concerti grossi, Oboe Concerto, Festival March, The Magic Island, Scottish Dances, Harp Concerto (Lyra Angelica); *chamber music:* Rhapsody for Piano Quartet, String Quartet in D Minor, Sonata alla Toccata for Piano, Divertimento for Solo Flute, Fantasy-Waltzes for Piano, 12 Preludes for Piano; String Trio; Movements for Piano; Sonata for Clarinet and Piano; Mirages for baritone and piano; Naiades for flute and harp; String Quartet No 2 (Spring Waters), 1976; Concerto for Flute and eight wind-instruments, 1980; String Quartet No 3, 1984; *song cycles:* A Leave-Taking, 1979; Invocations, 1979; Seascapes (for soprano, treble recorder and piano), 1980. *Publications:* Ariel to Miranda *in* Adam Internat. Review, 1968; Anthology of 20th Century French Poetry, 1969; Winter in Copenhagen, 1971; Daphne, 1972; The World in my Mind, 1975; The Prayers and Elegies of Francis Jammes (trans. from French), 1979; Winged Chariot, 1982. *Address:* Lark Rise, Blythburgh, Suffolk. *T:* Blythburgh 331. *Clubs:* Savile; Island Sailing (Cowes). *Died* 11 *Sept.* 1985.

**AMALDI, Prof. Edoardo,** PhD; Italian physicist; Professor of Physics, University of Rome, 1937, Emeritus Professor, since 1984; *b* Carpaneto, Piacenza, 5 Sept. 1908; *s* of Ugo Amaldi and Luisa Basini; *m* 1933, Ginestra Giovene; two *s* one *d*. *Educ:* Rome Univ. Dr of Physics, 1929. Sec.-Gen., European Org. for Nuclear Research, 1952–54; Pres., Internat. Union of Pure and Applied Physics, 1957–60; President: Istituto Nazionale di Fisica Nucleare, 1960–65; Council, CERN, 1970–71; Fellow: Acad. Naz. dei Lincei (Pres., 1988); Acad. Naz. dei XL; Foreign member: Royal Soc. of Sciences, Uppsala; Acad. of Sciences, USSR; Amer. Philos. Soc.; Amer. Acad. of Arts and Sciences; Nat. Acad. of Sciences, USA; Royal Acad., Netherlands; Acad. Leopoldina; Royal Instn of GB; Royal Society, London; Royal Acad. Sweden, 1968; Real Acad. Ciencias, Spain. Hon. DSc: Glasgow, 1973; Oxford, 1974. *Publications:* The production and slowing down of neutrons, 1959; (with S. Fulini and G. Furlan) Pion–Electroproduction, 1979; (with G. Pizzella) contrib., Search for Gravitational Waves, in Relativity, Quanta and Cosmology in the Development of the Scientific Thought of A. Einstein, 1979; contributor many papers on atomic, molecular, nuclear physics and gravitational waves to learned jls. *Address:* Dipartimento di Fisica, Città Universitaria, Piazzale Aldo Moro 2, 00185 Rome, Italy; (home) Viale Parioli 50, 00197 Rome. *Died* 5 *Dec.* 1989.

**AMAN,** family name of **Baron Marley.**

**AMBLER, Harry,** OBE 1963; QPM 1955; Chief Constable, City of Bradford Police, 1957–73; *b* 27 June 1908; *m* 1934, Kathleen Freda Muriel Mitchell; one *d*. *Educ:* Hanson Secondary Sch., Bradford; Oulton Sch., Liverpool. Joined City of Bradford Police as a Constable, 1930; Inspector, 1940; Staff Officer to HM Inspector of Constabulary, 1941–43; Superintendent, 1943; Asst and Dep. Chief Constable, 1952; Chief Constable, 1957. Hon. MA Bradford, 1973. Police Long Service and Good Conduct Medal, 1952; Coronation Medal, 1953. *Address:* 854 Leeds Road, Bramhope, near Leeds LS16 9ED. *T:* Leeds 673765. *Died* 31 *May* 1988.

**AMERS, Maj.-Gen. John Henry,** OBE 1941; *b* 8 July 1904; *s* of John Amers; *m* 1st, 1933, Muriel Henrietta Ethel Haeberlin (*d* 1983); one *d*; 2nd, 1984, Mrs Nora Jessie Harding. *Educ:* Christ's Hospital; Royal Military Acad., Woolwich; Cambridge Univ. Commissioned 2nd Lieut into Royal Engineers, 1925. Served War of 1939–45, E Africa, Middle East and Italy. Col 1951; Brig. 1955; Maj.-Gen. 1958. Served HQ, BCOF, Japan, 1947–48; Chief Engineer, Salisbury Plain District, 1951–54; Deputy Director of Works, BAOR, 1955–57; Director of Fortification and Works, 1958–59; retired, 1959. *Address:* c/o Lloyds Bank, Cox's and King's Branch, 6 Pall Mall, SW1Y 5NH. *Died* 21 *May* 1990.

**AMOROSO, Prof. Emmanuel Ciprian,** CBE 1969; TC 1977; FRS 1957; FRCP; FRCS; FRCOG; FRCPath; FInstBiol; DSc(London), PhD, MD, BCh, BAO; Professor Emeritus, Royal Veterinary College, University of London, since 1968; *b* 16 Sept. 1901. *Educ:* University Coll., Dublin (Grad. in Medicine, 1st cl. Hons and 1st place in all examinations in Science and Medicine); Kaiser Wilhelm Inst. für Zellforschung, Berlin; Albert-Ludwigs Univ., Freiburg; University Coll., London. McArdle Medal in Surgery and a travelling fellowship in science at NUI, 1929; then appointed to staff of Royal Veterinary College, 1935; Prof. of Physiology, Univ. of London, 1948–68; Special Prof., Dept of Physiol. and Environmental Studies, Sch. of Agric., Nottingham Univ., 1973–82. Privy Council Rep., Houghton Poultry Res. Station, 1956–63; Vis. Prof. Washington Univ., St Louis, 1958, 1961; Royal Soc. Leverhulme Visiting Professor: Univ. of Chile, 1968–69; Univ. of Nairobi, 1975–76; Vis. Prof., Univ. of Guelph, Ont, 1977, 1978; T. L. Pawlett Scholar, Univ. of Sydney, 1970–71. Treas., Soc. for Endocrinology and Jl endocrinol. Ltd, 1955–60; Chm., 1960–65; Chm., 2nd Internat. Congress of Endocrinology, London, 1964; Trinidad and Tobago Rep., Commonwealth Scientific Cttee, 1968–; Mem., Biol Scis Cttee, IPPF, 1968–; Mem., Scientific Adv. Cttee,

Brit. Egg Mkting Bd, 1963–70. Chm. Council, Jl Reprodn and Fertility Ltd, 1968–76 (Chm., Adv. Cttee, 1969–71; Chm. Exec. Cttee, 1971–76). Lectures: Univ. Voordtrachten, Rijksuniv., Gent, 1953; Goldwin Smith, Cornell, 1954; Holme, UCL, 1956; Keibel, Free Univ., Berlin, 1957; Josiah Macey, Harvard, 1958; Ingleby, Birmingham, 1958; Leo Loeb, Washington Univ., St Louis, 1958; Terry, Washington Univ., St Louis, 1961; Liebig, Univ. of Geissen, 1964; Darwin, Eugenics Soc., 1967; Sir James Mackenzie Oration, Burnley, 1970; J. Y. Simpson Oration, RCOG, 1971; Keith Entwhistle, Univ. of Cambridge, 1972; Woolridge, Brit. Vet. Assoc., 1976; E. H. W. Wilmott, Univ. of Bristol, 1979; William Dick, Edinburgh Univ., 1979; Shear Jones, RCVS, 1979. Hon. ARCVS 1959; Fellow: Royal Veterinary Coll., 1969; UCL, 1970. Hon. ScD NUI, 1963; Hon. DSc: Illinois, 1967; Nottingham, 1970; West Indies, 1971; Guelph, 1976; Hon DVetMed Santiago, 1967; Hon. Member: Soc. for Endocrinology, 1965; Soc. for Study of Fertility, 1965; Phys. Soc., 1976; Anat. Soc., 1976. *Prizes,* NUI: Botany, Zoology, Chemistry, Physics, 1923; Anatomy, Physiology, 1925; Pathology, Pharmacology, Materia Medica and Therapeutics, 1927; Medicine, Surgery and Obstetrics, 1929; Mary Marshall Medalist, Soc. of Fertility, 1972; Ludwig-Schunk Prize, Justus-Liebig Univ., Giessen, 1977; Henry Dale Medal, Soc. for Endocrinol., 1981; Carl G. Hartman Award, Soc. for Study of Reprodn, 1982. *Publications:* The Physiology of the Domestic Fowl, 1965; Protein Utilization by Poultry, 1967; Reproduction in the Female Mammal, 1967; chapter on Placentation in 3rd edn of Marshall's Physiology of Reproduction, 1952; papers in Phil. Trans and Proc. Roy. Soc., Jl of Physiol., Jl of Anat. *Recreations:* travel, languages, Westerns, Association football, cricket. *Address:* Agricultural Research Council Institute of Animal Physiology, Babraham, Cambridge CB2 4AT. *T:* Cambridge 832312; 29 Derwent Close, Cherry Hinton Road, Cambridge CB1 4DY. *T:* Cambridge 47825. *Died* 30 *Oct.* 1982.

**AMORY, 1st Viscount,** *cr* 1960; **Derick Heathcoat Amory,** KG 1968; PC 1953; GCMG 1961; TD; DL; Bt 1874; Lieutenant-Colonel (hon. rank); RA (TA) retired; Chancellor of Exeter University, since 1972; *b* 26 Dec. 1899; *s* of Sir Ian Murray Heathcoat Amory, 2nd Bt, CBE; *S* brother as 4th Bt, 1972. *Educ:* Eton; Christ Church, Oxford (MA). Served war of 1939–45. Governor, Hudson's Bay Co., 1965–70; Dir, Lloyds Bank, 1948–51 and 1964–70; Pres., John Heathcoat & Co., 1973 (Chm., 1966–72); Director, ICI, 1964–70. Member Devon CC, 1932–51; MP (C) Tiverton Div. of Devon, 1945–60; Minister of Pensions, Nov. 1951–Sept. 1953; Minister of State, Board of Trade, 1953–54; Minister of Agriculture and Fisheries, July 1954; Minister of Agriculture and Fisheries, July 1954; Minister of Agricultural and Fisheries and Minister of Food, Oct. 1954; Minister of Agriculture, Fisheries and Food, April 1955–Jan. 1958; Chancellor of the Exchequer, Jan. 1958–July 1960; High Commissioner for the United Kingdom in Canada, 1961–63. Jt Pro-Chancellor, University of Exeter, 1966–72; Chairman: Medical Research Council, 1960–61, and 1965–69; Voluntary Service Overseas, 1964–75; President: Association of County Councils, 1974–79 (County Councils Assoc., 1961–74); London Federation of Boys' Clubs, 1963–; Exeter Cathedral Appeal, 1978–. Prime Warden, Goldsmiths' Co., 1971–72. High Steward Borough of South Molton, 1960–74; DL Devon, 1962. Hon. FRCS 1974. Hon. LLD: Exeter Univ., 1959; McGill Univ., 1961; Hon. DCL, Oxon, 1974. *Heir* (to baronetcy only): *b* William Heathcoat Amory, DSO [*b* 19 Aug. 1901; *m* 1933, Margaret Isabella Dorothy Evelyn, *yr d* of Sir Arthur Havelock James Doyle, 4th Bt; two *s* two *d*]. *Address:* 150 Marsham Court, SW1; The Wooden House, Chevithorne, Tiverton, Devon. *Clubs:* Carlton; Royal Yacht Squadron. *Died* 20 *Jan.* 1981 (*ext*).

**AMORY, Sir William H.;** *see* Heathcoat Amory.

**AMULREE, 2nd Baron,** *cr* 1929; **Basil William Sholto Mackenzie,** KBE 1977; MD; FRCP; Liberal Whip, House of Lords, 1955–77; Chairman, Attendance Allowance Board, 1970–76; *b* 25 July 1900; *o s* of 1st Baron and Lilian (*d* 1916), *e d* of late W. H. Bradbury; *S* father, 1942. *Educ:* Lancing Coll.; Gonville and Caius Coll., Cambridge (MA 1925); Paris; University Coll. Hosp. MRCS, LRCP 1925; MRCP 1928; MD Cantab 1936; FRCP 1946. Asst Pathologist: University Coll. Hosp., 1929–31; Royal Northern Hosp., 1931–36; MO, Min. of Health, 1936–50; Physician, University Coll. Hosp., 1949–66. President: London Co. Div., British Red Cross, 1945–60; Assoc. of Occupational Therapists, 1956–60; Soc. of Chiropodists, 1963; Assoc. of Welfare Officers, 1960–68; British Geriatric Soc., 1949–65. Chm., Invalid Meals for London, 1956–59 (Mem. Inner London Area Adv. Cttee, 1965–75). Chm. Bd of Governors, London Medical Gp, 1968. Vice-Chm., Chadwick Trust, 1955–56. Member: Nat. Radium Commn, 1942–48; (professional) Assoc. of Water Engineers; Royal Inst. of Health. Hon. Mem. Faculty of Radiologists; Hon. FRGCP. Star of Ethiopia (1st class), 1952. *Publications:* Adding Life to Years; Min. of Health Report on Public Health and Medical Subjects, No 89; various articles in periodicals. *Recreation:* walking. *Heir:* none. *Address:* Cranbrook Lodge, Cranbrook, Kent. *Club:* Reform. *Died* 15 *Dec.* 1983 (*ext*).

**AMWELL,** 2nd Baron *cr* 1947, of Islington; **Frederick Norman Montague;** *b* 6 Nov. 1912; *o s* of 1st Baron Amwell, CBE, and Constance (*d* 1964), *d* of James Craig; *S* father, 1966; *m* 1939, Kathleen Elizabeth Fountain; one *s* one *d*. *Educ:* Highbury Grammar School; Northampton Coll. of Technology. Aircraft Design Engineer (Apprenticeship in 1930), now retired. AFRAeS. *Heir: s* Hon. Keith Norman Montague, BSc, CEng, MICE, AMInstHE, FGS [*b* 1 April 1943; *m* 1970, Mary, *d* of Frank Palfreyman, Potters Bar, Herts; two *s*]. *Died* 12 *Oct* 1990.

**ANCASTER,** 3rd Earl of, *cr* 1892; **Gilbert James Heathcote-Drummond-Willoughby,** KCVO 1971; TD; DL; Baron Willoughby de Eresby, 1313; Baron Aveland, 1856; Bt 1733; Lord-Lieutenant of County of Lincoln, 1950–75; *b* 8 Dec. 1907; *s* of 2nd Earl of Ancaster, GCVO, and late Eloise, *e d* of W. L. Breese, New York; *S* father, 1951; *m* 1933, Hon. Nancy Phyllis Louise Astor (*d* 1975), *o d* of 2nd Viscount Astor; one *d* (one *s* decd). *Educ:* Eton; Magdalene Coll., Cambridge (MA). Served War of 1939–45: Leicestershire Yeomanry and Major RA (wounded, despatches). MP (C) Rutland and Stamford, 1933–50; summoned to the Upper House of Parliament as Baron Willoughby de Eresby, 1951; Lord Great Chamberlain of England, 1950–52. Nat. Pres., BLESMA, 1956–83. JP 1937, CC 1950, Alderman, 1954, Kesteven; DL 1947–50, 1977–, Co. Lincoln. KStJ 1957. *Heir:* (to Barony of Willoughby de Eresby): *d* Lady Nancy Jane Marie Heathcote-Drummond-Willoughby, *b* 1 Dec. 1934; (to Baronetcy): Brig. Gilbert Simon Heathcote, CBE, *b* 21 Sept. 1913. *Address:* Grimsthorpe, Bourne, Lincs. *T:* Edenham 222; Drummond Castle, Crieff. *T:* Muthill 321.
*Died* 29 *March* 1983 (*ext*).

**ANDERSON, Lt-Col Charles Groves Wright,** VC 1942; MC; Member House of Representatives, for Hume, New South Wales, 1949–51 and 1955–61; grazier; *b* Capetown, South Africa, 12 Feb. 1897; *s* of A. G. W. Anderson; *m* 1931, Edith M. Tout (*d* 1984); two *s* two *d*. Served European War, 1914–18 (MC), KAR, E Africa. Served War of 1939–45 (VC, POW), 2nd AIF, Malaya. *Recreation:* motoring. *Address:* 119 Mugga Way, Canberra, ACT 2603, Australia.
*Died* 11 *Nov.* 1988.

**ANDERSON, David Fyfe,** MD, ChB, FRCOG, FRCPGlas; Muirhead Professor of Obstetrics and Gynæcology, University of Glasgow, 1946–70, now Emeritus Professor; Obstetric Surgeon, Royal Maternity Hospital, Glasgow; Gynæcological Surgeon, Royal Infirmary, Glasgow; *b* 8 June 1904; *o s* of David Fyfe Anderson and Mary Ann Mackay, Viewfield, Strathaven, Lanarkshire; *m* 1945, Elizabeth Rose, 2nd *d* of W. F. McAusland, Wyndyknowe, Scotstounhill, Glasgow; three *s* one *d*. *Educ:* Strathaven Academy (Dux); High Sch. of Glasgow (Dux, Modern Side); Univ. of Glasgow (Gardiner Bursary); Johns Hopkins Univ. MB, ChB (Commendation), Univ. of Glasgow, 1926; McCunn Research Scholar, 1929–31; MRCOG 1932; FRFPSG 1935; MD (Hons) 1935; FRCOG 1940; Rockefeller Travelling Fellowship 1935–36; FRCPGlas 1964; Fellow of Glasgow Obstetrical and Gynæcological Soc. and of Edinburgh Obstetrical Soc.; formerly Examiner to Central Midwives Board for Scotland; lately Professor of Midwifery and Diseases of Women at Anderson College of Medicine, Glasgow. Fellow, Ancient Monuments Soc. Freeman of City of Glasgow. Member of Incorporations of: Barbers, Bonnetmakers and Dyers, and Tailors (Ex-Deacon). OStJ 1973. *Publications:* medical papers and verse. *Address:* 55 Kingston Road, Bishopton, Renfrewshire PA7 5BA. *T:* Bishopton 862403. *Died* 5 *July* 1988.

**ANDERSON, Prof. David Steel;** Emeritus Professor of Accounting and Business Method, Edinburgh University; *b* 27 Oct. 1902; *s* of David Anderson and Jessie Marian Steel; *m* 1931, Cicely Bouskell Hockin (*d* 1980); one *s*. *Educ:* Viewpark School; George Watson's College, Edinburgh. Mem. Soc. of Accountants in Edinburgh, 1925; private practice as Chartered Accountant, 1927–29; joined firm of Wallace & Somerville, Edinburgh, as partner, 1929; retired partner of Whinney Murray & Co, 1973. External Examiner in Accounting, Faculty of Law, Edinburgh Univ., 1938–41; Mem. Gen. Examining Bd, Chartered Accountants of Scotland, 1939; Mem. Council Soc. of Accountants in Edinburgh, 1942–46; Mem. Advisory Cttee, Gen. Examining Bd, Inst. of Chartered Accountants of Scotland, 1937–57; Mem. Council Inst. of Chartered Accountants of Scotland, 1955–57, Vice-Pres., 1966, President, 1967–68. Hon. MA (Edinburgh Univ.), 1957. *Recreations:* golf, fishing. *Address:* Napier House, 8 Colinton Road, Edinburgh EH10 5DS. *T:* 031–447 3130.
*Died* 11 *Feb.* 1986.

**ANDERSON, Sir David (Stirling),** Kt 1957; PhD, LLD Glasgow and Strathclyde; FRSE; FIMechE; *b* 25 Sept. 1895; *s* of Alexander Anderson and Sarah Stirling; *m* 1st, 1932, Grace Boyd (*d* 1973); 2nd, 1974, Lorna Ticehurst. *Educ:* Royal Technical College, Glasgow (Greenock Research Schol.). Engineering experience with North British Locomotive Company and Fullerton, Hodgart and Barclay; 2nd Lieut RAF 1918; Head of Dept of Mech. Engineering, Derby Tech. Coll., 1924–26, Principal, 1926–30; Principal, Coll. of Technology, Birmingham, 1930–46; Dir, Royal College of Science

and Technology, Glasgow, 1946–59; part-time Mem., S of Scotland Electricity Bd, 1960–67; Mem., Cttee on Higher Education, 1961–63; Chm., Scottish Certificate of Education Examination Bd, 1964–69. Pres. Assoc. of Principals of Technical Institutions, 1937; Chm. of Council, Assoc. of Tech. Instns, 1951; Mem. Council, Inst. Mech. Engrs, 1941–42, 1948–50. Hon. LLD: Glasgow, 1961; Strathclyde, 1965; Hon. DSc Aston, 1966. *Publications:* numerous papers and contributions on technical education. *Recreation:* climbing. *Address:* Braehead, Helensburgh, Dunbartonshire. *T:* 2227. *Clubs:* Royal Automobile; Royal Scottish Automobile, Western (Glasgow); Scottish Mountaineering (Edinburgh).
*Died* 18 *Jan.* 1981.

**ANDERSON, Prof. Edward William,** MD, FRCP; Hon. MSc; Lord Chancellor's Visitor, 1965–73; retired as Professor of Psychiatry, Victoria University of Manchester and Director of Department of Psychiatry, Manchester Royal Infirmary (1949–65), now Professor Emeritus; *b* 8 July 1901; *s* of Edward Ross Anderson and Elizabeth Leith (*née* Dow); *m* 1934, Margaret Mottram Hutton; two *s* one *d*. *Educ:* Daniel Stewart's Coll., Edinburgh; Univs of Edinburgh, London and Frankfurt-on-Main. MD Edinburgh 1927, MB, ChB 1923, FRCP 1946; DPM London 1925; Founder FRCPsych 1972. Junior hosp. appts in medicine and surgery, 1923–24; various mental hosp. appts, 1924–29; Asst MO, The Maudsley Hosp., 1929–35; Med. Dir Cassel Hosp. for Functional Nervous Disorders, 1935–37; Cons. Psychiatrist, Devon CC, 1938–47; Neuropsychiatric Specialist, Royal Navy (Temp. Actg Surg. Comdr, RNVR), 1940–45. Physician, The Maudsley Hospital and Lecturer in Psychiatry, The Institute of Psychiatry, 1947–49. Govt delegate, WHO Conference on health of Seamen, Marseilles, 1959. Rockefeller Fellow in Psychiatry, 1937–38. Visiting Professor, Univs of Witwatersrand and Cape Town, 1964. Examiner in Psychological Medicine, Univ. of London, 1950–58, and in Psychological Medicine (Pt I), Conjoint Examining Bd, England, 1956–60; also (in the Membership) to RCP, 1964–70. Pres. Sect. Psychiatry RSM, 1961–62; Pres. (1964) Sect. Med., Manchester Med. Society. Hon. MSc (Vict.) 1953; Hon. Fellow (Psychiatry), Coll. of Medicine of S Africa, 1964. *Publications:* (jointly with W. H. Trethowan) Psychiatry, 1964, 3rd edn 1973; various articles on psychiatric topics in professional journals. *Address:* Linden Cottage, High Street, Wadhurst, Sussex TN5 6AQ. *Died* 3 *Sept.* 1981.

**ANDERSON, George David,** CMG 1967; HM Diplomatic Service, retired; *b* 11 Sept. 1913; *m* 1950, Audrey Rowena Money; one *d*. *Educ:* King Edward VII Gram. Sch., King's Lynn; Emmanuel Coll., Cambridge. National Association of Boys' Clubs, 1935–37; Macgregor and Co., Rangoon, Burma, 1937–41. Army Service, Burma Rifles, 1941–44; Combined Services Detailed Interrogation Centre (India), 1944–46. Min. of Food, 1946; CRO, 1947. Office of British High Commission in New Delhi and Calcutta, 1947–51; British Embassy, Dublin, 1957–60; Dep. High Comr, Ceylon, 1961–66; Diplomatic Service, 1964; Head of Chancery, British High Commn, Lagos, Nigeria, 1967–69; British High Comr in Botswana, 1969–73. *Recreations:* music, gardening and the enjoyment of retirement. *Address:* c/o Grindlay's Bank Ltd, 13 St James's Square, SW1. *T:* (home) 01–650 4613. *Club:* Royal Commonwealth Society. *Died* 4 *March* 1983.

**ANDERSON, Rev. Hector David,** LVO 1951; MA, BD; Chaplain to the Queen, 1955–76; *b* 16 Aug. 1906; *s* of Rev. David Anderson, LLD, Dublin; *m* 1931, Muriel Louise Peters; one *s*. *Educ:* The Abbey, Tipperary; Trinity Coll., Dublin. Schol. 1928, BA Mods 1929, MA 1932, BD 1949. Curate, Shirley, Croydon, 1930–33; St Michael's, Chester Square, SW1, 1933–39; CF, Sept. 1939–42; Domestic Chaplain to King George VI, 1942–52, to the Queen, 1952–55; Rector: Sandringham, 1942–55; Lutterworth, 1955–61; Swanage, 1961–69. Hon. Canon of Leicester, 1959–61. *Address:* Adare, The Hyde, Langton Matravers, Swanage, Dorset. *T:* Swanage 3206. *Died* 27 *Feb.* 1989.

**ANDERSON, Hugh Fraser,** MA, FRCS; Urological Surgeon, St George's Hospital, London, 1948–76, later Emeritus; Honorary Archivist, St George's Hospital, since 1976; late Surgeon, West Park Hospital, Epsom; *b* 19 April 1910; *s* of late William Thomson Anderson and late Madeline Bertha (*née* Grubb); *m* 1942, Nancy Singleton; one *s* one *d*. *Educ:* King William's Coll., I of M; Gonville and Caius Coll., Cambridge (Open Exhibition, 1929); St George's Hospital (Anne Selina Fernee Exhibition, 1932). MA (Cantab) 1939; MB, BCh (Cantab) 1935; LRCP 1935; FRCS 1940. Allingham Prize in Surgery, St George's Hospital, 1938. Served War of 1939–45 (Major, RAMC) (despatches). Examiner in Surgery: Univ. of London, 1958; Univ. of Basrah, 1973; Univ. of Lagos, 1975–80; Member: Court of Examiners, RCS, 1966; Med. Appeals Tribunal, 1975; Assoc. of Surgeons; British Association of Urological Surgeons; International Soc. of Urology. *Publications:* articles on urological subjects and the infected hand in learned journals and textbooks. *Recreations:* golf, railways, gardening. *Address:* 13 Durrington Park Road, Wimbledon, SW20 8NU. *T:* 01–946 2114. *Clubs:* MCC Ski Club of Great Britain; Walton Heath Golf, St Enodoc Golf (Rock, Cornwall). *Died* 1 *July* 1986.

**ANDERSON, John,** CB 1956; CBE 1950; CEng, FIEE; retired as Chief Scientist, Admiralty Surface Weapons Establishment, Portsmouth, 1961; *b* 29 Aug. 1896; *s* of John Anderson, Beith, Ayrshire; *m* 1928, Isabella Mary Morton Crerar (*d* 1975); no *c*. *Educ:* Spiers Sch., Beith, Ayrshire; Royal Technical Coll., Glasgow (Diploma). Joined RN Scientific Service, 1918; Chief Scientist: HM Underwater Detection Establishment, Portland, 1943–51; Admiralty Signal and Radar Establishment, Portsmouth, 1951. American Medal of Freedom, 1946. *Address:* Blue Hills, Denbigh Road, Haslemere, Surrey. *T:* Haslemere 3575.

*Died 11 Nov. 1984.*

**ANDERSON, General Sir John (D'Arcy),** GBE 1967 (CBE 1945); KCB 1961 (CB 1957); DSO 1940; *b* 23 Sept. 1908; *s* of late Major Reginald D'Arcy Anderson, RGA, and Norah Anderson (*née* Gracey), Ballyhossett, Downpatrick, Co. Down; *m* 1937, Elizabeth, *d* of late Augustus M. Walker. *Educ:* Winchester; New Coll., Oxford (MA). 2nd Lieut 5th Royal Inniskilling Dragoon Guards, 1929; served War of 1939–45, France, Middle East and Italy (wounded, despatches twice); GOC 11th Armoured Div., BAOR, 1955–56. Chief of Staff, Headquarters Northern Army Group and BAOR, 1956–58; Director, RAC, WO, 1958–59; Dir-Gen. of Military Training, 1959–61; DCIGS, 1961–63; Military Sec. to: Sec. of State for War, 1963–64; Min. of Defence, 1964–65. Commandant IDC, 1966–68; Col 5th Royal Inniskilling Dragoon Guards, 1962–67; Col Comdt, RAEC, 1964–70; Col Comdt, UDR, 1969–79 (Rep., 1969–77); Hon. Col: Oxford Univ. OTC, 1961–67; Queen's Univ., Belfast, OTC, 1964–75. ADC General to the Queen, 1966–68. Pro-Chancellor, QUB, 1969–80. Mem., Commonwealth War Graves Commn, 1963–71. Mem., Army Museums Ogilby Trust; Vice-Pres. Sandes Soldiers' and Airmen's Homes; Deputy Pres., ACF Assoc. (NI). DL Co. Down 1969–80, High Sheriff Co. Down 1974. Hon. LLD QUB, 1980. Grand Officer, Order of the Crown (Belgium), 1963. Grand Officer, Order of Leopold (Belgium), 1966. *Recreation:* painting. *Address:* 36 Whitelands House, Cheltenham Terrace, SW3 4QY. *T:* 01–730 1307.

*Died 16 April 1988.*

**ANDERSON, Prof. John Stuart,** MA, PhD, MSc; FRS 1953; Professor of Inorganic Chemistry, Oxford University, 1963–75, now Emeritus; *b* 9 Jan. 1908; *m* 1935, Joan Taylor; one *s* three *d*. Formerly Dep. Chief Scientific Officer, Chemistry Div., Atomic Energy Research Establishment, Harwell, Berks; Prof. of Inorganic and Physical Chemistry and Head of the Dept of Chemistry, Univ. of Melbourne, Australia, 1954–59; Director of the National Chemical Laboratory (Department of Scientific and Industrial Research), Teddington, 1959–63. Pres., Dalton Div. of Chemical Soc., 1974–76. Hon. Fellow, Indian Acad. of Sciences, 1978. Hon. DSc Bath, 1979. Davy Medal, Royal Soc., 1973. *Address:* Research School of Chemistry, Australian National University, PO Box 4, Canberra, ACT 2600, Australia. *Died 25 Dec. 1990.*

**ANDERSON, Hon. Sir Kenneth (McColl),** KBE 1972; Kt 1970; Senator for New South Wales, Australia, 1953–75; Government Leader in the Senate, 1968–72; Commonwealth Minister for Health, 1971–72; *b* 11 Oct. 1909; *m*; one *d*. MLA, NSW, for Ryde, 1950–53; Minister for Customs and Excise, 1964–68 (Actg Minister for Civil Aviation, 1966; Actg PMG, 1967); Minister for Supply, 1968–71. Alderman, Ryde Municipal Council, and Mayor of Ryde, 1949–50; Mem., Cumberland CC, 1949–50. Member: Cttee of Disputed Returns and Qualifications, 1953–62; Standing Cttee on Public Works, 1956–64; Jt Cttee on New and Permanent Parliament House, 1967; Standing Cttee on Standing Orders, 1968–72; Chm., Senate Select Cttee to consider problems of Road Safety, 1960. Served with 2nd AIF, Lieut, 8 Div. Signals, Malaya (PoW). *Recreation:* bowls. *Address:* 80 East Parade, Eastwood, NSW, Australia. *Clubs:* National, Union, Ryde RSL.

*Died 29 March 1985.*

**ANDERSON, Robert Bernerd;** lawyer and statesman, United States; Chairman, Robert B. Anderson & Co. Ltd; *b* Burleson, Texas, 4 June 1910; *s* of Robert Lee Anderson and Elizabeth (*née* Haskew); *m* 1935, Ollie Mae Anderson; two *s*. *Educ:* Weatherford Coll., Texas; Univ. of Texas (LLB). Admitted to Texas Bar, and began law practice, Fort Worth, Texas, 1932; elected to Texas legislature, 1932; Asst Attorney-Gen., Texas, 1932; Prof. of Law, Univ. of Texas, 1933; State Tax Commr, Texas, 1934; Racing Commr, Texas, 1934; Member State Tax Board, 1934; Chm. and Executive Director, Texas Unemployment Commn, 1936; Gen. Counsel for the Waggoner Estate (oil and ranching), 1937–40 (Gen. Man., 1941–53). Secretary of US Navy, 1953–54; Dep. Secretary of Defense, 1954–55; Secretary of the Treasury, 1957–61. *Address:* 535 Fifth Avenue, Suite 1004, New York, NY 10017, USA.

*Died 14 Aug. 1989.*

**ANDERSON, Thomas,** CBE 1972; MD, FRCPE, FRCPGlas, FFCM; Henry Mechan Professor of Public Health, University of Glasgow, 1964–71, retired (Professor of Infectious Diseases, 1959–64); *b* 7 Dec. 1904; *e s* of Thomas Anderson and Mary (*née* Johnstone); *m*

1935, Helen Turner Massey (*d* 1974); one *s* three *d*. *Educ:* The High Sch. of Glasgow; Glasgow Univ. (MB, ChB 1928; MD, Hons and Bellahouston Gold Medal, 1945); MRCPE 1934; FRCPE 1940; FRCPGlas 1947. Dep. Phys., Ruchill Hosp., 1933–41; Phys. Supt, Knightswood Hosp., 1941–47; Sen. Lectr, subseq. Reader, Infectious Diseases, Glasgow Univ., 1947–59. Mem., Industrial Injuries Adv. Council, 1971–77. Formerly Consultant in Infectious Diseases to Western Region of Scotland. Founder, Scottish-Scandinavian Conf. on Infectious Disease. Hon. Member: Soc. for Study of Infectious Disease; Royal Medico-Chirurgical Soc., Glasgow; Swedish Med. Assoc.; Soc. for Social Med.; Section of Epidemiology and Preventive Med., RSM. Pres., Arran Heritage Museum, 1986–. *Publications:* various, on Infectious Diseases, in med. scientific jls. *Recreation:* bowls. *Died 14 March 1990.*

**ANDERTON, Col Geoffrey,** OBE 1944; *b* 23 Jan. 1902; *s* of late Frederic Anderton, Embsay, Yorks, and Jersey, CI; *m* 1930, Edyth Cecile Hastings; two *s* one *d*. *Educ:* Ermysted's Sch., Skipton-in-Craven, Yorks; St Mary's Hospital, Paddington, W2. MRCS, LRCP 1924; MB, BS London 1925; DRCOG 1947. Entered RAMC Jan. 1927; War of 1939–45 (despatches twice: Tunisia, 1943; Italy, 1944); Korean War (despatches, Cross of Honour of Norwegian Red Cross, 1952); retd Dec. 1952. Comdt Star and Garter Home for Disabled Sailors, Soldiers and Airmen, Richmond, Surrey, 1953–67. Officer, Legion of Merit (USA), 1954; OStJ 1960. *Recreation:* sailing. *Address:* Grove Farm House, Grove Lane, Iden, near Rye, Sussex TN31 7 PX. *T:* Iden 275. *Died 13 Aug. 1981.*

**ANDRÉ, Brigadier James Richard Glencoe,** CBE 1950; DSO 1945; retired; *b* 20 Oct. 1899; *s* of Dr J. E. F. André and Mrs D. K. André (*née* Fowler); *m* 1929, Grace Douglas Darbyshire; two *s* one *d* (and one *s* decd). *Educ:* Killcott; RMC, Sandhurst. Commissioned, 1918, Royal Lincolns. Served European War, with Royal Lincolns, France, 1918–19; Ireland, 1919 and 1920; India, 1920–27; UK, 1927–34; seconded for service with Colonial Office, 1934; served with Malay Regt, 1935–42. Commanded 1st Bn The Malay Regt during Malaya Campaign, 1941–42; in battle for Singapore (DSO); despatches, 1946; Commandant (Col), Malay Regt, 1947; despatches, 1949; Brig. (temp.) 1948, (subs.) 1952; retired 1953. *Recreations:* gardening, handicraft. *Address:* Peaked Croft, Sidlesham Common, Chichester, W Sussex. *T:* Sidlesham 260.

*Died 12 Jan. 1981.*

**ANDREW, Rt. Rev. Agnellus Matthew,** OFM; DD; (His Excellency the Right Reverend Agnellus Andrew); Bishop of Numana; Chairman, Communications Committee of the Episcopal Conference of England and Wales, since 1983; *b* 27 May 1908; *s* of Hugh Andrew and Mary Andrew (*née* Burns). *Educ:* Jesuit College, Garnet Hill; London Univ. Entered Franciscan Order, 1925; ordained priest, 1932; parish, missionary and retreat work, Manchester, 1932–55; Asst Chaplain, Manchester Univ., 1939–42. Began broadcasting career, 1942; Roman Catholic Adviser, BBC, 1946; attended BBC Staff College, 1946 and 1956; Assistant to Head of Religious Broadcasting, BBC, Director and Producer, 1955–67; Adviser to IBA, 1968–75; TV Commentator for many Papal and national occasions. President: Internat. Catholic Assoc. for Radio and Television (UNDA), 1968–80 (Life Pres. of Honour); Catholic Media Council, 1979–; Churches' Advisory Cttee for Local Broadcasting; Founder (1955) and Director, Nat. Catholic Radio and TV Centre, Hatch End, 1955–80, subseq. Director Emeritus and Trustee; Exec. Head, Vatican Commn for Communication, 1980–83; Mem. Adv. Bd, Communications Dept, Gregorian Univ., Rome. DD, Gregorian Univ., Rome, 1980. *Publications:* numerous contribs to media and religious jls. *Recreation:* music (founded the Greyfriars Players, choral and orchestral society). *Address:* St Ninian's, Oakleigh Road, Hatch End, Middlesex. *Clubs:* BBC, KSC. *Died 19 Jan. 1987.*

**ANDREW, Rev. Sir (George) Herbert,** KCMG 1963; CB 1956; retired; *b* 19 March 1910; *s* of James Andrew and Harriet Rose, Woodley, Cheshire; *m* 1936, Irene Jones; two *s* two *d*. *Educ:* Godley Sch.; Manchester Grammar Sch.; Corpus Christi Coll., Oxford (MA). Patent Office (Asst Examiner), 1931; Transf. to Board of Trade headquarters, 1938; Asst Sec., 1945; Second Secretary: (General) 1955–60, (Overseas) 1960–63, Bd of Trade; Mem., UK delegn to Common Market Conf., 1961–63; Deputy Secretary, Ministry of Education, during 1963, Permanent Secretary, 1963–64; Permanent Under-Sec. of State for Education and Science, 1964–70. Hon. Fellow, Corpus Christi Coll., Oxford, 1965. *Recreations:* sitting and listening. *Address:* 18 Stangrove Road, Edenbridge, Kent. *T:* Edenbridge 862569. *Died 18 Aug. 1985.*

**ANDREWES, Antony,** MBE 1945; FBA 1957; Wykeham Professor of Ancient History, Oxford, 1953–77; Fellow of New College, Oxford, 1946–77, Hon. Fellow, since 1978; *b* 12 June 1910; *s* of late P. L. Andrewes; *m* 1938, Alison Blakeway (*née* Hope) (*d* 1983); two *d*. *Educ:* Winchester; New College, Oxford. Fellow of Pembroke Coll., Oxford, 1933–46. Intelligence Corps, 1941–45. Comdr of Order of Phœnix, Greece, 1978. *Publications:* (with R. Meiggs) revised edition of Sir George Hill's Sources for Greek History, 1951; The Greek Tyrants, 1955; The Greeks, 1967; (with K. J. Dover) Vol. IV of A. W. Gomme's Historical Commentary on Thucydides, 1970, Vol. V, 1981; articles in Classical Quarterly, etc. *Address:* 13 Manor Place, Oxford OX1 3UW. *T:* Oxford (0865) 248807.

*Died 13 June 1990.*

**ANDREWES, Sir Christopher (Howard),** Kt 1961; FRS 1939; Deputy Director, National Institute for Medical Research, 1952–June 1961 (Member of Scientific Staff from 1927) and in charge of World Influenza Centre (WHO) until June 1961; *b* 7 June 1896; *s* of late Sir Frederick William Andrewes, MD, FRS and Phyllis Mary Hamer; *m* 1927, Kathleen Helen Lamb (*d* 1984); three *s. Educ:* Highgate Sch.; St Bartholomew's Hospital. Surgeon Sub-Lt (RNVR), 1918–19; MRCS, LRCP, 1921, MB BS London (Univ. Gold Medal), 1921, MD London (Univ. Gold Medal), 1922, MRCP, 1923; FRCP, 1935; House Physician and Asst to Medical Unit St Bartholomew's Hospital, 1921–23 and 1925–26; Assistant Resident Physician, Hospital of the Rockefeller Institute, New York City, 1923–25; William Julius Mickle Fellowship, Univ. of London, 1931; Oliver-Sharpey Lectureship, Royal Coll. of Physicians, 1934; Bisset-Hawkins Medal, RCP, 1947; Stewart Prize, BMA, 1952; Robert Koch Gold Medal, 1979; Hon LLD Aberdeen 1963; Hon. MD Lund, 1968. *Publications:* Viruses of Vertebrates, 1964, 4th edn (with H. G. Pereira and P. Wildy) 1978; The Common Cold, 1965; Viruses and Evolution (Huxley lecture), 1966; Natural History of Viruses, 1967; The Lives of Wasps and Bees, 1969; Viruses and Cancer, 1970. *Recreation:* natural history, especially entomology. *Address:* Overchalke, Coombe Bissett, Salisbury, Wilts. *T:* Coombe Bissett 201. *Died 31 Dec. 1988.*

**ANDREWES, Edward David Eden;** Deputy Chairman and Managing Director, Tube Investments Ltd, 1972–75; *b* Portmadoc, 4 Oct. 1909; *s* of Edward and Norah Andrewes; *m* 1935, Katherine Sheila (*d* 1984), *d* of Brig. W. B. G. Barne, CBE, DSO; one *s* two *d. Educ:* Repton Sch.; Oriel Coll., Oxford (BA). Admitted Solicitor, 1935. Joined Tube Investments Ltd, 1935. Former Dir, Maen Offeren Slate Quarry Co. Ltd. Trustee, Cheshire Foundn, 1976–80. Legion of Merit (USA). *Recreations:* gardening, hunting, shooting, fishing. *Address:* Stockton House, Worcester WR6 6UT. *T:* Eardiston (058470) 272. *Club:* Boodle's. *Died 20 Sept. 1990.*

**ANDREWS, (Arthur) John (Francis),** CBE 1970; Chairman, Clark Equipment Ltd, UK, 1962–73; Deputy Chairman, Clark Equipment Co. AG Zürich, 1963–73; Chairman, All Wheel Drive Ltd, 1954–73; *b* 15 May 1906; *s* of Arthur Andrews and Gertrude Ellen Andrews (*née* Francis); *m* 1936, Elsy Maud (*née* Johns); one *d. Educ:* Malvern; Paris. Development Engineer, AC Cars Ltd, 1926; Chief Purchasing Manager, Gardner Diesel Engines, 1935. *Recreations:* sailing, golf. *Address:* 3 Branksome Grange, 1 Lakeside Road, Branksome, Poole, Dorset BH13 6LR. *T:* Poole 761553. *Clubs:* Royal Automobile, Royal Thames Yacht; Royal Motor Yacht (Poole); Berkshire Gold (Ascot); Ferndown Golf (Ferndown); Isle of Purbeck Golf; Parkstone Golf. *Died 1984.*

**ANDREWS, Éamonn,** Hon. CBE 1970; Television Compère; Broadcaster; Writer; *b* 19 Dec. 1922; *s* of William and Margaret Andrews; *m* 1951, Gráinne Bourke; one *s* two *d. Educ:* Irish Christian Brothers, Synge Street, Dublin. Radio Eireann broadcaster (boxing commentaries, general sports commentating, interview programmes, etc.), 1941–50; first broadcast for the BBC, 1950; first appeared on BBC Television, 1951; BBC programmes included: What's My Line?, This Is Your Life, Sports Report, Crackerjack, Playbox; also boxing commentaries, variety, interview and general sports programmes. Chm. Radio Eireann Statutory Authority, charged with establishment of television in Ireland, 1960–66; joined ABC Television, 1964, Thames Television, 1968; ITV programmes include: This Is Your Life, Today, Time for Business, Eamonn Andrews Show, Top of the World, What's My Line. Former All-Ireland Amateur Junior Boxing Champion (Middle Weight). Knight of St Gregory, 1964. *Publications:* The Moon is Black (play), 1941; This Is My Life (autobiog.), 1963; Surprise of Your Life, 1978; articles for magazines and newspapers. *Recreations:* walking and talking. *Address:* Windsor House, Heathfield Gardens, Chiswick, W4 4JT. *Clubs:* Irish, Royal Automobile.

*Died 5 Nov. 1987.*

**ANDREWS, Harry (Fleetwood),** CBE 1966; actor since 1933; *b* 10 Nov. 1911. *Educ:* Tonbridge; Wrekin Coll. With Liverpool Repertory, 1933–35. Played Horatio in Hamlet, New York 1936; John Gielgud's Season, 1937; served War of 1939–45 (despatches); with Old Vic, 1945–49; Bolingbroke, Mirabel, Warwick in St Joan; Shakespeare Memorial Theatre; Wolsey, Macduff Brutus, Bolingbroke in Henry IV Pts I and II, 1949–51; Enobarbus, Buckingham, Kent, 1953; Othello, Claudius, 1956; Menenius in Coriolanus, 1959; Casanova in Camino Real, Phoenix, 1957; Henry VIII, Old Vic, 1958; Allenby in Ross, Haymarket, 1960; Rockhart in The Lizard on the Rock, Phoenix, 1962; Ekhart in Baal, Phoenix, 1963; Crampton in You Never Can Tell, Haymarket, 1966; Lear,

Royal Court, 1971; Ivan in The Family, Haymarket, 1978; Serebryakov in Uncle Vanya, Haymarket, 1982; The General in A Patriot for Me, Haymarket, 1983, Los Angeles, 1984. *Films:* Red Beret, Helen of Troy, Alexander the Great, Hill in Korea, Moby Dick, St Joan, Dreyfus, Ice Cold in Alex, Solomon and Sheba, Question of Larceny, Circle of Deception, The Best of Enemies, The Inspector, Barabbas, Reach for Glory, Nine Hours to Rama, 55 Days at Peking, The Snout, The Best of Everything, The Hill, The Agony and the Ecstasy, The Sands of Kalahari, Modesty Blaise, The Deadly Affair, The Jokers, The Long Duel, A Dandy in Aspic, The Charge of The Light Brigade, The Night They Raided Minsky's, The Southern Star, The Seagull, A Nice Girl Like Me; Too Late The Hero; The Gaunt Woman; Entertaining Mr Sloan; I want what I want; Burke and Hare; Country Dance; Wuthering Heights; Nicholas and Alexandra; The Nightcomers; The Ruling Class; Man of La Mancha; Theatre of Blood; The Mackintosh Man; Man at the Top; Jacob and Esau; The Bluebird; Sky Riders; The Passover Plot; The Prince and the Pauper; Equus; The Four Feathers; Superman—the Movie; The Titanic; The Captain; The Curse of King Tutankhamen (Earl of Carnarvon); Mesmerised. *Television: series:* Edward VII; Clayhanger; 7 Dials Mystery; Tom Carrington in Dynasty; *plays:* Leo Tolstoy; An Affair of Honour; The Garth People; Valley Forge; Two Gentle People, adapted from Graham Greene; A Question of Faith; A Question of Guilt; Constance Kent; Closing Ranks; The Sound Machine; Tales of the Unexpected; A. J. Wentworth, BA; Lent; Inside Story; All Passion Spent; Cause Célèbre; Clowns. *Recreations:* cricket, tennis, sailing, gardening. *Address:* Church Farm Oast, Salehurst, Robertsbridge, E Sussex. *Died 7 March 1989.*

**ANDREWS, Harry Thomson;** Director, Welkom GM Co. (Anglo-American Corp. of South Africa); *b* Capetown, South Africa, 11 Dec. 1897; *s* of late H. Andrews, Capetown; *m* 1926, R. D. Williams, Pretoria; one *d. Educ:* Observatory High Sch., Capetown; Marist Brothers' Coll., Capetown; Univ. of Pretoria. Served European War, 1917–19, in France, South African Signals, RE. Advocate, Supreme Court (Transvaal), 1927; Political Secretary South Africa House, London, 1930–35; Accredited Representative of Union of South Africa to League of Nations, Geneva, 1936–40; Asst Sec. for Defence, Pretoria; Under-Sec. for External Affairs, Pretoria; Head of South Africa Govt Supply Mission to USA, 1942–45; Ambassador of South Africa to USA, 1945–49; Permanent Representative of SA to United Nations, 1945–49; South African Ambassador to France, 1949–57; Minister to Switzerland, 1954–56. Member French-Commonwealth War Graves Commission, 1954–57. Vice-Pres., S Africa Foundn, 1977. *Recreation:* golf. *Address:* 214 Bretton Woods, Killarney, Johannesburg, 2193, S Africa. *Clubs:* Kimberley (Kimberley); Rand, Bryanston Country (Johannesburg); West Province Sports (Cape Town). *Died 29 April 1985.*

**ANDREWS, John;** *see* Andrews, A. J. F.

**ANDREWS, Rt. Hon. Sir John (Lawson Ormrod),** PC (Northern Ireland) 1957; KBE 1974; DL; Senator, 1964–72; Minister and Leader in the Senate, Northern Ireland, 1964–72; *b* 15 July 1903; *o s* of late Right Hon. John Miller Andrews, CH, DL, LLD, MP, Maxwell Court, Comber, Co. Down, and Jessie, *er d* of Joseph Ormrod, Morelands, Heaton, Bolton; *m* 1928, Marjorie Elaine Maynard James (*d* 1980), *d* of Alfred Morgan James, The Fields, Newport, Mon; three *s* one *d. Educ:* Mourne Grange Preparatory Sch., Kilkeel, Co. Down; Shrewsbury. Served apprenticeship to flax spinning trade and joined family firm, John Andrews & Co. Ltd, Comber, 1922; now Chm. and Man. Dir. Northern Ireland Government: MP (U) Mid-Down, 1953–64; Minister of Health and Local Govt, 1957–61; Minister of Commerce, 1961–63; Minister of Finance, 1963–64; Dep. Prime Minister, 1970–72. President, Ulster Unionist Council, 1969–73. DL Co. Down, N Ireland, 1961. *Recreation:* yachting (Commodore Strangford Lough Yacht Club). *Address:* Maxwell Court, Comber, Co. Down. *T:* Comber 872263. *Club:* Royal Ulster Yacht. *Died 12 Jan. 1986.*

**ANDREWS, Air Vice-Marshal John Oliver,** CB 1942; DSO 1917; MC; idc; *b* 20 July 1896; *s* of John Andrews, Waterloo, Lancs; *m* 1923, Bertha, *d* of Wilfred Bisdée, Hambrook, Glos; two *s. Educ:* Royal Scots; seconded RFC, 1914; served France, 1914–18; S Russia, 1919; India, 1920 (MC and bar, Montenegrin Silver Medal for bravery, DSO, despatches thrice); transferred to RAF, 1919; retired, 1945. *Died 29 May 1989.*

**ANDREWS, Rev. Canon (Leonard) Martin,** CVO 1946; MBE; MC 1917; Rector of Stoke Climsland, Cornwall, 1922–68; Chaplain to the Queen, 1952–69 (to King Edward VIII, 1936, and to King George VI, 1936–52); Hon. Canon of Truro since 1932; *b* 24 Sept. 1886. *Educ:* Queens' Coll., Cambridge. BA 1909; MA 1921; Deacon, 1909; Priest, 1910; Rector of Brewarrina, NSW, 1913–14; Vice-Principal Brotherhood of the Good Shepherd, NSW, 1914–15; Temp. CF, 1914–19; Chaplain at Khartoum, 1920–22; Rural Dean of Trigg Major, 1929–32. *Publication:* Canon's Folly, 1974. *Address:*

Climsland, Downderry, Torpoint, Cornwall PL11 3LW.
*Died* 13 Feb. 1989.

**ANDREWS, Stanley George B.;** *see* Burt-Andrews.

**ANDREWS, Winifred Agnes, (Mrs F. S. Andrews),** CBE 1976; Area Nursing Officer, Wolverhampton Area Health Authority, since 1974; *b* 20 Jan. 1918; *d* of Isaac and Winifred Jones; *m* 1961, Frederick S. Andrews. *Educ:* Bargoed Grammar Sch., Bargoed, Glam. SRN, RFN, SCM, HV Cert. Supervisor of Midwives, Birmingham, 1954–72; Dir of Nursing Services, Wolverhampton, 1972–74. Member: W Midlands Regional Health Authority, 1973–; Central Health Services Council, 1974–; Standing Nursing and Midwifery Adv. Cttee, 1974; President: Royal Coll. of Midwives, 1975–81; ICM, 1978–; Sec., British Commonwealth Nurses and Midwives Meml Fund, 1978–. *Recreations:* gardening, music. *Address:* 9 Frankley Avenue, Halesowen, West Midlands B62 0EH. *T:* 021–422 3140. *Died* 12 Feb. 1983.

**ANGUS, Col Edmund Graham,** CBE 1944; MC; TD; DL, JP; Chairman, George Angus & Co. Ltd, Newcastle upon Tyne 1933–64, later President; *b* 9 June 1889; *s* of Col W. M. Angus, CB; *m* 1922, Bridget E. I. Spencer (*d* 1973); one *s* one *d* (and two *s* decd, of whom *e's* was presumed killed in action, Anzio, Italy, 1944). *Educ:* Felsted Sch. Joined George Angus & Co. Ltd, 1906. Commissioned in Volunteer Forces (RA). Served in firm's Boston office, 1910–11, mobilised Aug. 1914; served in France and Flanders with 50th Div. Artillery till Feb. 1919; demobilised with rank of Major; rejoined G. Angus & Co. Ltd, Dir. 1920. Rejoined TA 1920; commanded 74th Northumbrian Field Regt, 1925–32; subst. Col with effect, 1929. FRSA 1974. DL Co. Durham, 1945; JP Northumberland, 1948. KStJ 1966. *Recreation:* horticulture. *Address:* Ravenstone, Corbridge, Northumberland NE45 5RZ. *T:* Corbridge 2122.
*Died* 19 March 1983.

**ANGUS, Brig. (hon.) Tom Hardy,** DSO 1938; psc†; fs; late Indian Army; *b* 22 May 1899; *s* of late J. B. Angus and M. S. D. Hardy; *m* 1954, Lilian Maud, *er d* of late John Emil and Ada Hyort. *Educ:* privately; RMC, Sandhurst. First Commission, 1918; Joined 45th Rattray's Sikhs, now 3rd Bn 11th Sikh Regt (Rattray's Sikhs, 1918; Regimental duty until 1932; Staff Coll., Quetta, 1932–33; RAF Staff Coll., Andover, 1935; Brigade Major, 1st Infantry Brigade, Abbottabad, NWFP, 1936–40; served Waziristan (DSO); Instructor (GSO2) Staff Coll., Quetta, 1940; Brig. Gen. Staff, Ceylon, 1942; Commander 51 Indian Infantry Brigade, 1943–44; DDMT, GHQ, India, 1945; Director of Air, India, 1946–47; retired 1948. *Recreation:* golf. *Address:* c/o Lloyd's Bank Ltd, St Mary Street, Weymouth, Dorset. *Club:* Royal Dorset Yacht (Weymouth).
*Died* 20 Feb. 1984.

**ANNALY, 5th Baron** *cr* 1863; **Luke Robert White;** Director, Greenwell Montagu Stockbrokers, 1986–89 (Partner, W. Greenwell & Co., Members of London Stock Exchange, 1963–86); *b* 15 March 1927; *o s* of 4th Baron Annaly and Lady Annaly (formerly Lady Lavinia Spencer); *S* father, 1970; *m* 1st, 1953, Lady Marye Pepys (marr. diss. 1957; she *d* 1992); one *s*; 2nd, 1960, Jennifer Carey (marr. diss. 1967); two *d*; *m* 1984, Mrs Beverley Healy, *d* of late William Maxwell; one step *d*. *Educ:* Eton. RAF, 1944–48; RAuxAF, 1948–51; Flying Officer (601 Sqdn). Livery, Haberdashers' Company; Freeman of City of London, 1953. *Recreations:* cricket, golf, theatre. *Heir:* *s* Hon. Luke Robert White [*b* 29 June 1954; *m* 1983, Caroline Nina, *yr d* of Col Robert Garnett, Hope Bowdler House, near Church Stretton; two *d*. *Educ:* Eton; RMA Sandhurst. Commnd Royal Hussars, 1974–78, RARO]. *Address:* House of Lords, SW1A 0PW. *Clubs:* Turf, Royal Air Force, MCC; Hawks (Cambridge). *Died* 30 Sept. 1990.

**ANNAMUNTHODO, Sir Harry,** Kt 1967; FRCS, FACS, FRACS; Professor of Surgery, University Kebangsaan, since 1980; *b* 26 April 1920; *s* of George Annamunthodo and Rosaline (*née* Viapree); *m* 1953, Margaret Pullman; one *s* three *d*. *Educ:* Queen's Coll., Guyana; London Hospital Medical Coll. MB, BS London, 1946; DTM&H, 1947; FRCS, 1951; FACS, 1961; FRACS 1982. Lectr in Surg., Univ. of the W Indies, 1955–57; Sen. Lectr in Surg., UWI, 1957–61; Prof. and Head of Dept of Surg., UWI, 1961–80, now Professor Emeritus. Rockefeller Research Fellow, 1959–60; Hunterian Prof., Royal Coll. of Surgeons, 1960. *Publications:* (Co-author) Lymphogranuloma Venereum, 1962; papers on: various cancers and diseases of stomach, rectum, etc in British and American Med. Jls. *Recreation:* horticulture. *Address:* Department of Surgery, University Kebangsaan, PO Box 12418, Jalan Raja Muda, Kuala Lumpur, Malaysia. *Died* 6 Sept. 1986.

**ANNAN, Robert;** President, Consolidated Gold Fields Ltd, 1960–73 (Chairman, 1944–60); director of mining companies; *b* 16 May 1885; *er s* of John and Marion Annan; *m* 1st, 1911, Dely (*d* 1967), *yr d* of Everett Loraine Weston, New York; two *s*; 2nd, 1971, Betty, *yr d* of Richard Abenheim. *Educ:* Uppingham Sch.; Columbia Univ., New York City. Served European War, 1915–18, in France, with Royal Engineers (TF). Institution of Mining and Metallurgy: Mem.

1920; Pres. 1936–37; Hon. Treas., 1946–68; Gold Medallist, 1949; Hon. Fellow, Imperial Coll. of Science and Technology, 1951; Egleston Medal, Columbia Univ., 1957. Mem.: South African Institute of Mining and Metallurgy, 1936; Newcomen Soc. *Recreations:* history and early literature of mining and metallurgy; book collecting. *Address:* 132 Bickenhall Mansions, W1. *T:* 01–935 2065. *Died* 22 Oct. 1981.

**ANNIGONI, Pietro,** RP; Italian painter; artist in oil, tempera, etching and fresco; *b* Milan, 7 June 1910; *s* of Ricciardo Annigoni, engineer; *m* 1st, Anna Maggini (*d* 1969); one *s* one *d*; 2nd, 1976, Rosa Segreto. *Educ:* Accademia delle Belle Arti, Florence. Member of: Accademia di S Luca, Rome; Accademia delle Arti del Disegno, Florence; Academy of Design, New York. Portraits exhibited: (at Nat. Portrait Gallery) The Queen, 1970; (at Royal Academy, London) The Queen (for the Fishmongers' Company), 1955, Dame Margot Fonteyn, 1956 (now at Nat. Portrait Gall.), The Duke of Edinburgh (for the Fishmongers' Company), 1957, Maharanee of Jaipur, 1958. Other works: Portrait of Princess Margaret, 1958; The Immaculate Heart of Mary, 1962; Crucifix, Cathedral of Mirandola, 1983; Crucifix, Basilica del Santo, Padova, 1983; frescoes: The Last Supper, San Michele Arcangelo, Ponte Buggianese, 1974–75; Glory of St Benedict, Montecassino, 1978; Scenes of St Benedict's life, dome of Montecassino Cathedral, 1980–81; The Last Supper, Monastery of St Antony, Padua, 1984; The seven founders climbing the mountain, Montesenario, Florence, 1986; Basilica del Santo, Padova: scenes of St Antony's life, 1981–82; St Antony preaching from the walnut tree, 1985; the Prodigal Son, 1987. Permanent collections showing his works include: Uffizi (Print Room, Selfportraits Collection), Florence; Galleria Arte Moderna, Milan; Modern Art Collection, Vatican, Rome; Frescoes: S Martino, Florence; Madonna del Consiglio, Pistoia; Basilica of S Lorenzo, Florence. Exhibitions include: Wildenstein Gall., London, 1954; Royal Academy, 1956; Wildenstein, NY, 1957; Galleries of Fedn of British Artists, 1961; retrospective exhbn, New York and San Francisco, 1969; Arts Unlimited Gall., London, 1971. Has also exhibited in Rome, Turin, Paris, Florence, Milan, etc. *Publications:* Memoirs, 1956; Spanish Sketchbook, 1957; An Artist's Life (autobiog.), 1977. *Address:* Borgo degli Albizi 8, 50122 Florence, Italy. *Died* 28 Oct. 1988.

**ANOUILH, Jean;** French dramatic author; *b* Bordeaux, 23 June 1910; *s* of François Anouilh and Marie-Magdeleine Soulue; *m* 1953, Nicole Lançon; one *s* two *d*. *Educ:* Collège Chaptal; Univ. of Paris. *Plays include:* L'Ermine, 1934 (prod Nottingham, 1955, as The Ermine); Y'avait un prisonnier, 1935; Le Voyageur sans bagages, 1937; Le Bal des Voleurs, 1938 (prod London, 1952, as Thieves' Carnival); La Sauvage, 1938 (prod London, 1957, as Restless Heart); Cavalcade d'Amour, 1941; Le Rendez-vous de Senlis, 1942: Léocadia, 1942 (prod London, 1954, as Time Remembered); Eurydice, 1942 (prod London as Point of Departure, 1950); Humulus le Muet (in collaboration with Jean Aurenche), 1945; Oreste, 1945; Antigone, 1946 (prod London, 1949); Jézébel, 1946; Roméo et Jeannette, 1946 (prod London, 1949, as Fading Mansion); Médée, 1946; L'Invitation au château, 1948 (prod London, 1950, 1968, as Ring Round the Moon); Ardèle ou la Marguerite, 1949; La Répétition, ou l'amour puni, 1950 (prod Edinburgh Festival 1957, and London, 1961); Colombe, 1950 (prod London, 1951); La Valse des toréadors, 1952 (prod London, 1956); L'Alouette, 1953 (prod London, 1955, as The Lark); Ornifle, 1955; L'Hurluberlu, 1958 (prod Chichester and London, 1966, as The Fighting Cock); La Foire d'Empoigne, 1960; Becket (prod London, 1961); La Grotte, 1961 (prod London, 1965, as The Cavern); Poor Bitos (prod London, 1963–64); Le Boulanger, la Boulangère et le Petit Mitson, 1968; Cher Antoine, 1969; Les Poissons Rouges, 1969; Ne Réveillez Pas, Madame, 1970; Tu étais si gentil quand tu étais petit, 1974; L'arrestation, 1975; Le Scénario, 1976; Chers Zoiseaux, 1976; Vive Henri IV, 1977; La Culotte, 1978; Le Nombril, 1981; Number One (prod London, 1984). *Films include:* Monsieur Vincent (awarded Grand Prix du Cinéma Français); Pattes blanches; Caprice de Caroline, etc. *Address:* c/o Les Editions de la Table Ronde, 40 rue du Bac, 75007 Paris, France.
*Died* 3 Oct. 1987.

**ANSETT, Sir Reginald (Myles),** KBE 1969; Chairman, Ansett Transport Industries Ltd; *b* 13 Feb. 1909; *s* of late Charles John and Mary Ann Ansett; *m* 1944, Joan McAuliffe Adams; three *d*. *Educ:* State Sch. and Swinburne Techn. Coll., Victoria. Founded Ansett Roadways, 1931, and Ansett Airways Ltd, 1936; Managing Dir, Ansett Airways Ltd, 1936, later Ansett Transport Industries Ltd, 1946. Subsidiary cos include: Ansett Transport Industries (Ops) Pty Ltd (operating as Ansett Airlines of Australia, Ansett Airlines of NSW, Ansett Airlines of S Australia, MacRobertson Miller Airline Services, Ansett Freight Express, Aviation Engineering Supplies, N.I.C. Instrument Co.; Ansett-Pioneer, Mildura Bus Lines, Ansett Hotels, Barrier Reef Islands; Ansair; Ansett Motors; Provincial Motors; Ansett General Aviation; Ansett Wridgways; Kalamunda Transport; P. E. Power (Wagga) Transport; Cooper Airmotive); Austarama Television Pty Ltd; Ansett Niugini Enterprises Ltd; Transport Industries Insurance Co. Ltd. Chm., Peninsula Church of England Sch. Council, 1965–74, Mem. Council, 1974–. *Recreations:* horse racing (Chm., Port Phillip Dist Racing Assoc.); game shooting. *Address:* (private) Gunyong Valley, Mount Eliza, Vic 3930, Australia; (business) 489 Swanston Street, Melbourne, Vic. 3000, Australia. *T:* 3453144. *Clubs:* Victoria Racing, Victoria Amateur Turf, Moonee Valley Racing, Mornington Racing (Chm.) (all in Victoria). *Died 23 Dec.* 1981.

**ANSTEY, Edgar (Harold Macfarlane),** OBE 1969; Documentary Film Producer, Lecturer and Critic; *b* 16 Feb. 1907; *s* of Percy Edgar Macfarlane Anstey and Kate Anstey (*née* Clowes); *m* 1949, Daphne Lilly, Canadian film-maker; one *s* one *d*. *Educ:* Watford Grammar Sch. Empire Marketing Board Film Unit, 1931; associated with Grierson group in develt of sociological and scientific documentaries, 1931–; organised Shell Film Unit, 1934; March of Time: London Dir of Productions, later Foreign Editor, NY, 1936–38. Produced wartime films for Ministries and Services, 1940–46. Film planning and prod. for BOAC, for oil industry in Venezuela and for CO in WI, 1946–49; rep. short films on Cinematograph Films Council, 1947–49; org. and acted as producer-in-charge, British Transport Films, 1949–74. Formerly film critic of The Spectator; regular mem., BBC Radio programme The Critics. Chairman: Brit. Film Acad., 1956; and again (with Soc. of Film and Television Arts), 1967; Pres., Internat. Scientific Film Assoc., 1961–63; Mem. Council RCA, 1963–74 (Sen. Fellow, 1970); led British cultural delegns to USSR, 1964, 1966; Pres., British Industrial and Scientific Film Assoc., 1974–81 (Chm., 1969–70); Chm., Children's Film Foundn Production Cttee, 1981–83; Governor, British Film Inst., 1965–75; Adjunct Prof., Temple Univ., 1982–. Hon. Fellow, British Kinematograph Soc., 1974. *Notable films include:* Housing Problems, 1935; Enough to Eat?, 1936; Journey into Spring, 1957 (British Film Acad. and Venice Award); Terminus, 1961 (British Film Acad. and Venice Award); Between the Tides, 1958 (Venice Award); Wild Wings, 1965 (Hollywood Oscar). *Publication:* The Development of Film Technique in Britain (Experiment in the Film), 1948. *Recreations:* formerly football, tennis and walking, now mental exercising with students of communications. *Address:* 6 Hurst Close, Hampstead Garden Suburb, NW11. *T:* 01–455 2385. *Club:* Savile. *Died 26 Sept.* 1987.

**ANSTRUTHER-GOUGH-CALTHORPE, Brigadier Sir Richard (Hamilton),** 2nd Bt *cr* 1929; CBE 1946 (OBE 1940); DL, JP, CA; Croix de Guerre, 1947; Hon. LLD Birmingham 1950; MA (Cantab); *b* 28 March 1908; *o s* of Sir FitzRoy Anstruther-Gough-Calthorpe, 1st Bt; *S* father, 1957; *m* 1939, Nancy Moireach (*d* 1976), *o d* of late Vernon Austen Malcolmson, MA, JP, Aston Bury, Stevenage, Herts; two *s* (and one *s* decd). *Educ:* Harrow; Magdalene Coll., Cambridge (MA). 2nd Lieut Royal Scots Greys, 1930, Captain, 1938. Served War of 1939–45, Norway and Middle East; Dep. Director Military Operations, War Office, 1944–47; retd 1947. Director: Rowton Hotels Ltd, 1958–79; Lloyds Bank Ltd, 1972–78. CC 1949, JP 1950, DL 1955, CA 1956, Chm. CC 1967–74, Hants; Chm., Hants Local Govt Reorganisation Jt Cttee, 1972–73. *Heir: g s* Euan Hamilton Anstruther-Gough-Calthorpe, *b* 22 June 1966. *Clubs:* Royal Yacht Squadron; Warwickshire County Cricket. *Died 7 Feb.* 1985.

**ANSTRUTHER-GRAY,** family name of **Baron Kilmany.**

**ANTHONY, C. L.;** *see* Smith, Dodie.

**ANTROBUS, Maurice Edward,** CMG 1943; OBE 1938; *b* 20 July 1895; *er s* of late Sir Reginald Antrobus and late Dame Edith Antrobus, DBE; *m* 1929, Betty (*d* 1982), *er d* of late Sir Llewelyn Dalton; two *s*. *Educ:* Winchester; Trinity Coll., Cambridge (Exhibitioner). BA 1920; served European War, 1914–19, KRRC (wounded twice); Asst Principal, Colonial Office, 1920; Private Sec. to Governor of Ceylon, 1927–30; Principal Dominions Office, 1930; Political Sec., Office of UK High Comr in Union of S Africa, 1935–39; Asst Sec., Colonial Office, 1939; Principal Sec., Office of UK Representative to Eire, 1939–41; Official Sec., Office of UK High Comr in Commonwealth of Australia, 1941–44; Official Sec., Office of UK High Commissioner in New Zealand, 1944–45; Asst Sec., Commonwealth Relations Office, 1945; retd 1955. *Address:* Yaffles, Ashdown Road, Forest Row, East Sussex RH18 5BN. *T:* Forest Row 2159. *Club:* Royal Ashdown Forest Golf (Forest Row). *Died 23 Sept.* 1985.

**APPLEBY, Maj.-Gen. David Stanley,** CB 1979; MC 1943; TD 1950; Director of Army Legal Services, 1976–78, retired; *b* 4 Dec. 1918; *s* of Stanley Appleby and Mabel Dorothy Mary (*née* Dickson); *m* 1942, Prudence Marianne Chisholm; one *s* one *d* (and one *s* decd). *Educ:* St Peter's School. Barrister, Middle Temple, 1951. Rifleman, London Rifle Bde (TA), 1938; 2nd Lieut, Royal Fusiliers (TA), 1939; Army Legal Services, 1950–; Captain, 1950; Maj.-Gen. 1976. *Recreations:* sailing, military and other history. *Address:* Two Acres, Beechwood Lane, Burley, Ringwood, Hants. *Clubs:* Royal Lymington Yacht; Island Sailing (Cowes). *Died 4 Oct.* 1989.

**ARAGON, Louis;** Chevalier de la Légion d'Honneur, 1981; poet; novelist, essayist; *b* 3 Oct. 1897; *m* 1939, Elsa Triolet (*née* Kagan). *Educ:* Faculty of Medicine, Paris Univ. Served European War, 1914–18, Infantry; War of 1939–45, Tank Div., 1939–40 (prisoner, escaped to unoccupied France); one of leaders of intellectual Resistance. Co-founder, 1919, and leader since 1924 of former Surrealist Movement, now Socialistic Realism Movement; founder, 1935, and Sec. of Internat. Assoc. of Writers for Defence of Culture; founder, 1944, and co-director, Editeurs français réunis; Vice-Pres., Assoc. des Ecrivains Combattants, 1945–60. Editor: Les Lettres Françaises, 1944–; Ce Soir, Paris, 1950; Member: Cttee of Dirs, Europe review; Nat. Cttee of Authors, 1958–; Goncourt Academy, 1967–68. Mem., French Communist Party Central Cttee. *Publications:* poems: Feu de joie, 1920; Le mouvement perpétuel, 1925; La grande gaîté; Persécuté persécuteur; Hourra l'Oural, 1934; Le crève-coeur, 1941; Les yeux d'Elsa, 1942; Brocéliande; Le Musée Grévin; La Diane Française, 1945; Les yeux et la mémoire, 1954; Elsa, 1959; Le fou d'Elsa, 1963; *novels:* Anicet ou le panorama, 1921; Le libertinage; Le paysan de Paris, 1926 (trans. as Paris Peasant, 1971); Les cloches de Bâle, 1933; Les beaux quartiers, 1936 (awarded Prix Renardot); Les voyageurs de l'Impériale, 1942; Aurélien, 1945; La Semaine Sainte, 1958 (trans. as Holy Week, 1961); La mise à mort, 1965; Blanche ou l'oubli, 1967; Henri Matisse, 1972; *history:* Histoire de l'URSS de 1917–60; (with A. Maurois) Histoire parallèle des USA et de l'URSS, 1962; *essays:* La lumière de Stendhal, 1954; Litterature sovietique, 1955; Traité du style; Les aventures de Télémaque; Pour un réalisme socialiste; La culture et les hommes; Chroniques du Bel-Canto; Matisse ou comme il vous plaira; *translations:* La chasse au Snark by Lewis Carroll, 1928; Cinq sonnets de Pétrarque, 1947. *Address:* 56 rue de Varenne, 75007 Paris, France; 78730 Saint-Arnoult-en-Yvelines, France. *Died 24 Dec.* 1982.

**ARBUTHNOT, Sir Hugh Fitz-Gerald,** 7th Bt, *cr* 1823; late Temporary Captain Welsh Guards; *b* 2 Jan. 1922; *s* of Brig.-Gen. Sir Dalrymple Arbuthnot, 5th Bt, CMG, DSO, and Alice Maude (*d* 1969), *d* of Hugh Arbuthnot; *S* brother 1944; *m* 1st, 1949, Elizabeth K. (*d* 1972), *e d* of Sqdn Ldr G. G. A. Williams, Curral Hall, Tenbury Wells; two *s* one *d*; 2nd, 1977, Julia Grace, *d* of Lt-Col F. G. Peake, Hawkslee, St Boswells. *Educ:* Eton. MFH: Ludlow Hounds, 1948–52; Cotswold Hounds, 1952–64; Duke of Buccleuch's Hounds, 1964–76; Jedforest Hounds, 1977–82. *Heir: s* Keith Robert Charles Arbuthnot [*b* 23 Sept. 1951; *m* 1982, Anne, *yr d* of Brig. Peter Moore]. *Address:* Brundeanlaws, Jedburgh, Roxburghshire. *Died 3 July* 1983.

**ARCHER, Sir Archibald,** Kt 1982; CMG 1961; grazier; company director; *b* 10 Jan. 1902; *s* of late Robert Stubbs Archer and Alice Manon Archer, Gracemere Station, Queensland; *m* 1930, Sarah Beatrice Cameron Crombie, *er d* of late Donald Charles Cameron Crombie and Mildred Ida Lloyd Crombie, Greenhills Station, Longreach, Qld; one *s* two *d*. *Educ:* Church of England Grammar Sch., Sydney, NSW, Australia. Land Consultant to Qld Govt, 1961–63. Dep. Chm., Picture Theatre and Films Commn, 1972–76 (Mem., 1957–76); Vice-Pres., Royal National Assoc., 1961–80, Pres., 1980–; President: Australian Agricl Socs, 1975–76; Qld Electoral Commn, 1971–72, 1977–; City of Brisbane, Electoral Wards Commn, 1972. Pres., Royal Geog. Soc. Qld, 1971–72, Fellow, 1972. *Address:* 23 Sefton Avenue, Clayfield, Queensland 4011, Australia. *T:* Brisbane 2623375. *Clubs:* Queensland (Brisbane); Australasian Pioneers (Sydney). *Died 26 Nov.* 1983.

**ARCHER, Maj.-Gen. Gilbert Thomas Lancelot,** CB 1960; FRCPI; retired; *b* 6 April 1903; *s* of Gilbert Archer, Dublin, Ireland, and Kate Archer (*née* Lamb); *m* 1928, Catherine, *d* of Edward O'Malley, Louisburgh, Westport, Co. Mayo, Ireland; two *s* one *d*. *Educ:* St Andrews Coll., Dublin; Dublin Univ. (TCD). MB 1926; Lieut RAMC, 1928; Major, 1937; Deputy Asst Dir of Pathology, China Command, 1937–40; Asst Dir of Pathology, West Africa, 1943–45; Reader in Pathology, Royal Army Medical Coll., 1946–48; Asst Dir of Pathology, Middle East Land Forces, 1949–52; MRCPI, 1953; Officer Commanding David Bruce Laboratories, 1952–53; QHS 1953–61; Dir of Pathology and Consulting Pathologist to the Army, 1953–61; Brig., 1956; Major-General, 1958; FRCPI 1958. *Publications:* Articles on bacteriology, immunity, etc., in Jl of the RAMC, Brit. Med. Jl, etc. *Address:* 7 Nutley Avenue, Ballsbridge, Dublin, Eire. *Died 5 June* 1986.

**ARCHIBALD, James Montgomery,** MBE 1945; JP; Chairman and Managing Director, James Archibald & Associates Ltd, since 1963; film producer, writer and director; *b* 3 April 1920; *s* of Brig. Gordon King Archibald, DSO, and Helen Archibald; *m* 1956, Sheila Elizabeth Maud Stafford; two *s*. *Educ:* Westminster Sch.; Merton Coll., Oxford (MA). Rep. Oxford Univ., Foil and Epée, 1939. Served War, 1939–45: Private 1939, Lt-Col 1944 (mentioned in despatches, 1943). Anglo-Iranian Oil Co., 1946–49; Rank Org., 1950–56; Dir, J. Walter Thompson Ltd, 1956–63; Chm., Academy Sound & Vision Ltd, 1980–82. Gen. Comr of Income Tax, St Martin's in the Fields, 1961; Chm. Comrs of Income Tax, St

Martin's in the Fields and Charing Cross, 1974. Chairman: Nat. Music Council of GB, 1974–80, Vice-Pres., 1980–; Arts Panel, Inst. of Dirs; Member: Exec. Cttee, Assoc. for Business Sponsorship of the Arts; BAFTA; Royal Television Soc.; British Film & TV Producers' Assoc. Governor: BFI, 1976–79; Loughborough Coll. of Art and Design, 1972–80; Trinity Coll. of Music; Yehudi Menuhin's Live Music Now, 1979– (Chm., 1979–80). Member: Ct, Worshipful Co. of Bowyers (Master, 1982–83); Worshipful Co. of Musicians (Pres., Livery Club, 1981–82). JP Inner London, 1967. FRSA, Hon. FTCL. 67 Internat. Awards for films. OStJ 1977. *Address:* 35 Morpeth Mansions, Morpeth Terrace, SW1P 1EU. *T:* 01–828 9691; 1 The Coastguards, Thorpeness, Leiston, Suffolk. *T:* Aldeburgh 2922. *Clubs:* Brooks's, Royal Thames Yacht; Myrmidon (Oxford).
*Died 25 July* 1983.

**ARIAS, Roberto Emilio;** *b* 1918; *s* of Dr Harmodio Arias (President of Panama, 1932–36) and Rosario Guardia de Arias; *m;* one *s* two *d;* *m* 1955, Margot Fonteyn (Dame Margot Fonteyn de Arias, DBE). *Educ:* Peddie Sch., New Jersey, USA; St John's Coll., Cambridge (BA); Sorbonne, Univ. of Paris (Doctorat d'Etat); Columbia Univ. (researched comparative laws of Admiralty). Called to the Bar, Panama, 1939; Fifth Circuit, Court of Appeals, US, 1941; Editor, El Panama-America, 1942–46; Counsellor to Panama Embassy, Chile, 1947; Publisher, La Hora, 1948–68; Delegate to UN Assembly, New York, 1953; Panamanian Ambassador to the Court of St James's, 1955–58, 1960–62; Elected Dep. to the Nat. Assembly of Panama, Oct. 1964–Sept. 1968. Paralyzed from June 1964, as result of gunshot wounds in political assassination attempt. *Address:* PO Box 6–1140, Eldorado, Panama, Republic of Panama.
*Died 22 Nov.* 1989.

**ARKELL, Captain Sir (Thomas) Noël,** Kt 1937; DL; President, J. Arkell and Sons, Ltd, Brewers, Swindon, Wiltshire; Local Director, Royal Insurance Group; *b* 25 Dec. 1893; 2nd *s* of James Arkell, Redlands Court, Highworth, Wilts, and Laura Jane Rixon; *m* 1919, Olive Arscott Quick, Tiverton, Devon; two *s* (and one *s* killed in action) three *d. Educ:* Bradfield Coll. Joined 4th Wiltshire Regt (Territorials) in 1912 as 2nd Lieut; served European War in India, Mesopotamia and Palestine (thrice wounded); invalided with rank of Captain, 1919; Chm., Swindon Conservative Assoc., 1927–47, Pres. 1947–52; Chm. Wessex Provincial Area of Conservative Party, 1933–35; Mem. of National Executive Cttee of Conservative Party, 1933–38. DL 1945, High Sheriff 1953–54, Wilts. *Recreation:* fishing. *Address:* Hillcrest, Highworth, near Swindon, Wilts. *T:* Highworth 762 216.
*Died 22 June* 1981.

**ARMER, Sir (Isaac) Frederick,** KBE 1954; CB 1945; MC 1918; *b* 1891; 2nd *s* of William and Gwenllian Armer; *m* 1925, Elsie Maude Neale; one *s* two *d. Educ:* Welsh University Coll., Cardiff. BSc (Hons). Served European War, 1914–19. Entered Civil Service Sept. 1919 as Assistant Principal; Sec. Royal Commission on London Squares, 1928; Assistant Sec., 1938; Chm. Welsh Board of Health, 1940–44; Under Sec., Min. of Health, 1946, Dep. Sec., 1951–56; Chm., Board of Control, 1952–60. *Address:* Picketston Cottage, Flemingston, Barry, South Glam.
*Died 15 Nov.* 1982.

**ARMITAGE, Sir Arthur (Llewellyn),** Kt 1975; MA, LLB, LLD; Vice-Chancellor, and Professor of Common Law, Victoria University of Manchester, 1970–80, now Professor Emeritus; Chairman, Social Security Advisory Committee, since 1980; *b* 1 Aug. 1916; *s* of Kenyon Armitage and Lucy Amelia Armitage; *m* 1940, Joan Kenyon Marcroft; two *d. Educ:* Oldham Hulme Grammar Sch.; Queens' Coll., Cambridge. Law Tripos 1936; LLB 1937; Commonwealth Fund Fellow, Yale Univ., USA, 1937–39; called to the Bar, 1940, Inner Temple. Served Army, 1940–45, KRRC and 2nd Army, temp. Major. Fellow Queens' Coll., Cambridge, 1945–58; Asst Tutor, 1945; Tutor, 1946; Senior Tutor, 1957; President, 1958–70; Hon. Fellow, 1970. University Lectr in Law, 1947–70; Vice-Chancellor, Univ. of Cambridge, 1965–67, Dep. Vice-Chancellor, 1967–70. Dep. Chm. QS, Co. Huntingdon, 1963–65, Co. Huntingdon and Peterborough, 1965–71. Mem. and Chm., Wages Councils, 1955–70; Chairman: Trustee Savings Bank Arbitration Tribunal, 1964–78; Cttee on Pay of Postmen, 1964; Adv. Cttee on Trng and Supply of Teachers, 1973–79; British Cttee of Award of Commonwealth Fund, 1969–74; NI Cttee on Legal Educn, 1973–74; Cttee of Vice-Chancellors and Principals of Univs of UK, 1974–76; Cttee on Political Activities of Civil Servants, 1976–78; Cttee on Lorries, People and the Environment (Report, 1981); Member: Departmental Cttee on Summary Trial of Minor Offences, 1954–55; Chm.'s Panel Industrial Ct, 1962–74; Agric. Wages Bd for England and Wales, 1967–72 (Chm., 1968–72); Nat. Adv. Council on Training of Magistrates, 1964–70; UGC, 1967–70; Lord Chancellor's Cttee on Legal Educn, 1967–71; UNESCO Adv. Mission for Develt of Univ. of W Indies, 1964; Standing Adv. Cttee on Grants to Students, 1961–65; Council, ACU, 1972–80 (Vice-Chm., 1979–80); Inter-Univ. Council for Higher Educn Overseas, 1972–81 (Dep. Chm., 1978–80); Adv. Council on the Penal System, 1976–78; Council for the Securities Industry, 1980–. Pres., Soc. of Public Teachers of Law, 1967–68; Trustee, Henry Fund, 1961–70;

Mem., Council of Management, Chatsworth House Trust, 1981–; Chm. Governors, Leys Sch., Cambridge, 1971–; Visitor, Leicester Polytechnic, 1980–. Hon. Bencher, Inner Temple. JP City of Cambridge, 1950–70. Hon. LLD: Manchester, 1970; Belfast, 1980; Liverpool, 1981; Birmingham, 1981. Order of Andrés Bello 1st Class (Venezuela), 1968. *Publications:* Case Book on Criminal Law (with J. W. C. Turner), 1952, 1958, 1964; Jt Editor Clerk and Lindsell on Torts, 1954, 1961, 1969, 1975. *Address:* Rowley Lodge, Kermincham, near Holmes Chapel, Cheshire. *Club:* Athenæum.
*Died 1 Feb.* 1984.

**ARMITAGE, Sir Robert (Perceval),** KCMG 1954 (CMG 1951); MBE 1944; MA; *b* 21 Dec. 1906; *s* of late F. Armitage, CIE; *m* 1930, Gwladys Lyona, *d* of late Lt-Col H. M. Meyler, CBE, DSO, MC, Croix de Guerre; two *s. Educ:* Winchester; New Coll. District Officer, Kenya Colony, 1929; Sec. to Mem. for Agriculture and Natural Resources, 1945; Administrative Sec., 1947; Under Sec., Gold Coast, 1948; Financial Sec., 1948; Min. for Finance, Gold Coast, 1951–53; Governor and C-in-C, Cyprus, 1954–55; Governor of Nyasaland, 1956–61, retired. KStJ 1954. *Address:* Amesbury Abbey Nursing Home, Amesbury, Wilts SP4 7EX. *T:* Amesbury (0980) 23635.
*Died 7 June* 1990.

**ARMSTRONG,** 3rd Baron *cr* 1903, of Bamburgh and Cragside; **William Henry Cecil John Robin Watson-Armstrong;** *b* 6 March 1919; *s* of 2nd Baron Armstrong and Winifreda (*d* 1978), *e d* of Cecil Drummond-Wolff; *S* father, 1972; *m* 1947, Baroness Maria-Teresa du Four Chiodelli Manzoni, *o c* of late Mme Paul Ruegger (formerly Countess Isabella Salazar y Munatones); one adopted *s* one adopted *d. Educ:* Eton; Trinity College, Cambridge. An Underwriting Member of Lloyd's. Served War of 1939–45, Captain Scots Guards. *Heir:* none. *Address:* Bamburgh Castle, Northumberland. *Club:* Brooks's.
*Died 1 Oct.* 1987 (*ext*).

**ARMSTRONG, Sir Andrew St Clare,** 5th Bt *cr* 1841; *b* 20 Dec. 1912; *s* of Sir Nesbitt William Armstrong, 4th Bt, and Clarice Amy, *d* of John Carter Hodkinson, Maryborough, Victoria, Australia; *S* father 1953. *Educ:* Waitaki; Wellesley Coll. Served War of 1939–45 with RAE, 2nd AIF. *Heir: cousin* Andrew Clarence Francis Armstrong, CMG.
*Died 27 Jan.* 1987.

**ARMSTRONG, Brig. Charles Douglas,** CBE 1945; DSO 1940; MC 1919; late East Surrey Regiment; *b* 11 June 1897; *s* of late C. F. Armstrong, Kitale, Kenya Colony; *m* 1935, Sylvia Holden Earle Bailey; one *s* three *d. Educ:* Cheltenham Coll.; RMC, Sandhurst. Served European War (wounded twice, MC): France, 1916–18; North Russia, Mesopotamia, 1920–21; NWF India, 1930–31; War of 1939–45 (wounded twice, DSO, Africa Star, CBE): France, 1939–40; N Africa, 1943; Jugoslavia, 1943–44. Retired 1948. *Address:* Rushetts, Old Green Lane, Camberley, Surrey GU15 4LG. *T:* Camberley 21028. *Club:* Special Forces.
*Died 11 Dec.* 1985.

**ARMSTRONG, Christopher Wyborne,** OBE 1943; farming in Kenya since 1959; *b* 9 May 1899; *s* of Rt Hon. H. B. Armstrong, Dean's Hill, Armagh; *m* 1956, Hilde Ingeburg Kolz, Lübeck; one *s* one *d. Educ:* Winchester; Trinity Coll., Cambridge (MA). Lieutenant RFA, BEF, France, 1918; Burmah Oil Co., Burma, 1922–39; Royal Engineers, BEF, France, 1939–40; Burmah Oil Co., Burma, 1940–42; Member, House of Representatives, Burma, 1942; Controller of Petroleum Industry, Burma, 1942; AQMG, MEF, Egypt, 1942–43; GHQ, India, 1944–45; Commissioner, Magwe Division, Burma, 1945–46; farming in Kenya, 1947–54 and 1959–. MP (UU) Co. Armagh, 1954–59. Mem., UK delegn to Council of Europe and WEU, 1957–59. *Address:* Kwetu Farm, Gilgil, Kenya. *Club:* United Oxford & Cambridge University.
*Died 8 July* 1986.

**ARMSTRONG, Rev. Canon Claude Blakeley,** MA, BD; Canon residentiary of Worcester, 1947–70, Canon Emeritus 1970; Vice-Dean and Treasurer, 1965–70; *b* 31 Oct. 1889; *e s* of late Rev. J. B. Armstrong, MA; *m* 1914, Hester (*d* 1968), *d* of late Sir Samuel Dill, LittD; one *d. Educ:* St Stephen's Green School and Trinity Coll., Dublin (First Classical Scholar). Senior Moderator in Classics and Philosophy; Fellowship prizeman; Vice-Chancellor's prizeman and Medallist. Lieut, OTC, 1914–18; Observer Officer, ROC, 1940–45. Deputy for the Professor of Greek, Queen's Univ. Belfast, 1913–14; Headmaster of Cork Grammar Sch., 1914–19; Warden of St Columba's Coll., Rathfarnham, 1920–33; Headmaster of St Andrew's Coll., Grahamstown, SA, 1934–38; Rector of Clannaborough, near Exeter, 1940–43; Rector of Clyst St George, 1943–47; Lectr in Classics, University Coll. of the South-West, Exeter,1940–47. Pres. Irish Schoolmasters Assoc., 1929; Pres. Exeter Clerical Soc., 1942; Vice-Pres. Classical Assoc. (Chm. Council). Examining Chaplain to the Bishop of Worcester, and Director of Training, 1948; Warden, Worcester Ordination Coll., 1952–64; Founder, Worcester Ordination Coll., 1965. Editor, Veritas (for Anglican Assoc.). *Publications:* The Persians of Aeschylus translated into English verse; Outline of Western Philosophy, 1964; Foundations Unshaken, 1966; Creeds and Credibility, 1969;

Autumn Leaves, 3 vols, (light verse), 1979, 1980, 1981; contributor to Reviews and Punch; Editor Sir S. Dill's Roman Society in Gaul in the Merovingian Age. *Address:* 12a College Green, Worcester. *T:* Worcester 25837. *Club:* Kildare Street and University (Dublin).
*Died 18 Oct. 1982.*

**ARMSTRONG, Francis William,** CB 1977; LVO 1953; *b* 11 July 1919; *s* of late W. T. Armstrong, Gravesend, Kent; *m* 1st, 1945, Brenda Gladys de Wardt (*d* 1967); one *d*; 2nd, 1969, Muriel Ernestine Hockaday, MBE. *Educ:* King's Sch., Rochester; Brasenose Coll., Oxford (Open Scholarship in Classics) (MA). Served War of 1939-45: RA (commissioned, 1940); Western Desert, India, Burma. Asst Principal, War Office, 1947; Private Sec. to Permanent Under-Sec., War Office, 1948-50; Principal Private Sec. to Sec. of State for War, 1957-60; Director of Finance, Metropolitan Police, 1968-69; Asst Under-Sec. of State, MoD, 1969-72; Under Sec., Cabinet Office, 1972-74; Dep. Sec., N Ireland Office, 1974-75; Dep. Sec., MoD, 1975-77, retired 1977. Comr, Royal Hospital, Chelsea, 1977-83. *Recreations:* walking, cricket, reading. *Address:* 7 Sandown Lodge, Avenue Road, Epsom, Surrey. *T:* Epsom 40951. *Clubs:* Royal Commonwealth Society; Kent CCC.
*Died 15 Aug. 1988.*

**ARMSTRONG, John Anderson,** CB 1980; OBE 1945; TD 1945; Master of the Court of Protection, 1970-82; *b* 5 May 1910; *s* of W. A. Armstrong; *m* 1938, Barbara, *d* of Rev. W. L. Gantz; two *d* (and one *s* decd). *Educ:* Wellington Coll.; Trinity Coll., Cambridge. BA 1931, MA 1943. Called to Bar, Lincoln's Inn, 1936. City of London Yeomanry, RHA(T), 1931-40. Served War: Lt-Col Comdg 73 Light AA Regt, 1940-45 (Normandy, 1944). Practice at Chancery Bar, 1946-70; Bencher, Lincoln's Inn, 1969. *Recreations:* gardening, walking, fishing, golf. *Address:* Dacre Cottage, Penrith, Cumbria CA11 0HL. *T:* Pooley Bridge (07684) 86224. *Club:* Brooks's.
*Died 3 Oct. 1990.*

**ARMSTRONG, Most Rev. John Ward;** *b* 30 Sept. 1915; *s* of John and Elizabeth Armstrong, Belfast; *m* 1941, Doris Winifred, *d* of William J. Harrison, PC and Florence Harrison, Dublin; two *s* two *d* (and one *d* decd). *Educ:* Belfast Royal Academy; Trinity College, Dublin, BA, Respondent, 1938; Toplady Memorial Prize, Past. Theol Pr. and Abp. King's Prize (2) 1937; Biblical Greek Prize and Downes Prize (1) 1938; 1st Class Hons Hebrew, 1936 and 1937; 1st Class Divinity Testimonium, 1938; BD 1945; MA 1957 (SC). Deacon, then Priest, All Saints, Grangegorman, 1938; Hon. Clerical Vicar, Christ Church Cathedral, 1939; Dean's Vicar, St Patrick's Cathedral, 1944; Prebend. of Tassagard, St Patrick's Cathedral, 1950; Rector of Christ Church, Leeson Park, 1951; Dean of St Patrick's Cathedral, Dublin, 1958-68; Bishop of Cashel and Emly, Waterford and Lismore, 1968-77 (when diocese reorganised), of Cashel, Waterford, Lismore, Ossory, Ferns and Leighlin (known as Bishop of Cashel and Ossory), 1977-80; Archbishop of Armagh and Primate of All Ireland, 1980-86. Wallace Lecturer, TCD, 1954-65; Dean of Residences, University College, Dublin, 1954-63. Vice-Pres. Boys' Brigade, 1963-73. Trustee, Nat. Library of Ireland, 1964-74; Member: British Council of Churches, 1966-80; Anglican Consultative Council, 1971-81. Hon. DD Trinity Coll. Dublin, 1981. *Publication:* contrib. to Church and Eucharist-an Ecumenical Study (ed Rev. M. Hurley, SJ), 1966. *Recreations:* carpentering and bird-watching. *Address:* 53 Greenlawns, Skerries, Co. Dublin. *T:* Dublin 490180. *Clubs:* Friendly Brothers of St Patrick, Hibernian Catch.
*Died 21 July 1987.*

**ARMSTRONG, Rt. Rev. Mervyn,** OBE 1946; Adviser on Industry to the Archbishop of York, and Assistant Bishop of York, 1964-70, retired; *b* 10 Mar. 1906; *o s* of Rev. Evan Armstrong and Sarah Armstrong; *m* 1st, 1933, Charlotte Stewart (*d* 1961), *y d* of Rev. A. Irvine-Robertson, DD, Clackmannan; 2nd, 1963, Mrs Barbara Newborn, *widow* of G. R. Newborn, Epworth. *Educ:* Balliol Coll., Oxford. In business in China, 1928-37; ordained 1938; served War of 1939-45 as Chaplain, RNVR, 1940-43; Adviser on Seamen's Welfare, Min. of War Transport and Dir of Seamen's Welfare, Govt of India, 1944-45; Vicar of Margate, 1946-49; Chaplain to Archbishop of Canterbury, 1949-51; Archdeacon of Stow and Rector of Epworth and of Wroot, 1951-54; Provost of Leicester, 1954-58; Bishop Suffragan of Jarrow, 1958-64. *Address:* Glen Brathay, Skelwith Fold, Ambleside, Cumbria LA22 0HT. *T:* Ambleside 3249.
*Died 2 Oct. 1984.*

**ARMYTAGE, Captain Sir John Lionel,** 8th Bt cr 1738; *b* 23 Nov. 1901; *s* of Brig.-Gen. Sir George (Ayscough) Armytage, 7th Bt, CMG, DSO, and Aimée (*d* 1955), 3rd *d* of Sir Lionel Milborne Swinnerton-Pilkington, 11th Bt; *S* father, 1953; *m* 1st, 1927, Evelyne Mary Jessamine (marr. diss., 1946), *d* of Edward Herbert Fox, Adbury Park, Newbury; one *s* one *d*; 2nd, 1949, Maria Margarete, *o d* of Paul Hugo Tenhaeff, Bruenen, Niederrhein; one *d*. *Educ:* Eton; Royal Military Coll., Sandhurst. Joined King's Royal Rifle Corps, 1921; retired owing to ill-health, 1940. *Heir:* *s* John Martin Armytage, *b* 26 Feb. 1933. *Address:* (seat) Kirklees Park, Brighouse,

West Yorks. *T:* Brighouse 713016. *Clubs:* Naval and Military, Oriental.
*Died 21 June 1983.*

**ARMYTAGE, Rear-Adm. Reginald William,** GC (AM 1928); CBE 1959; retired; *b* 18 May 1903; *s* of Sir George Ayscough Armytage, 7th Bt, CMG, DSO, Kirklees Park, Brighouse; *heir-pres.* to nephew, Sir Martin Armytage, 9th Bt; *m* 1928, Sylvia Beatrice Staveley; three *s*. *Educ:* Osborne and Dartmouth. Entered Royal Navy, 1917. Served in HMS: Royal Oak, 1921; Capetown, 1922-24; Emergency Destroyers, 1925; Warspite, 1926-28 (Albert Medal 1928). Qualified in Gunnery, 1929. Served HMS: Devonshire, 1930-32; Mackay, 1932-34; Frobisher, 1935. Took up Naval Ordnance Design, Experiment and Inspection Duties, 1935; Head of Gun Design and Senior Naval Representative at Armament Design Estab., 1946; Deputy Chief Inspector of Naval Ordnance, 1949; Chief Inspector of Naval Ordnance, 1956; Vice-Pres. (Naval), Ordnance Board, 1959; President of The Ordnance Board, 1961-62. *Address:* The Malt House, Downton, Wilts.
*Died 9 Nov. 1984.*

**ARNEY, Frank Douglas,** CBE 1959; *b* 4 Feb. 1899; *s* of Frank Charles Arney; *m* 1925, Mildred, *d* of W. J. Dallin; three *s*. *Educ:* Grammar Sch., Bristol. Formerly: General Manager, Port of Bristol Authority, for 16 years until retd Oct. 1961; Part-time Chm. British Waterways Board, Dec. 1962-June 1963; Mem., National Ports Council, 1963-71. *Recreations:* fly fishing, golf. *Address:* Summerhaze, Bosbury Road, Cradley, near Malvern, Worcs WR13 5LT.
*Died 2 May 1983.*

**ARNOLD, Prof. Denis Midgley,** CBE 1983; FBA 1976; Heather Professor of Music, University of Oxford, since 1975; *b* 15 Dec. 1926; *m* 1951, Elsie Millicent Dawrant; two *s*. *Educ:* Sheffield Univ. (MA, BMus). ARCM. Queen's Univ., Belfast: Lectr in Music, Extra-Mural Studies, 1951-60; Reader in Music, 1960-64; Sen. Lectr in Music, Hull Univ., 1964-69; Prof. of Music, Nottingham Univ., 1969-75. Mem. Council, Internat. Musicological Assoc., 1977-. Pres., Royal Musical Assoc., 1978-. Foreign Mem., Accademia dei Lincei, 1976. Hon. RAM; Hon. DMus: Belfast, 1980, Sheffield, 1980; FRCM 1981. Galileo Prize, 1977. Jt Editor, Music and Letters, 1976-80. *Publications:* Monteverdi, 1963; Marenzio, 1965; Monteverdi's Madrigals, 1967; (ed with N. Fortune) Monteverdi Companion, 1969; Beethoven Companion, 1971; Giovanni Gabrieli, 1974; Giovanni Gabrieli and Venetian music of the High Renaissance, 1980; Monteverdi's Church Music, 1982; (ed) The New Oxford Companion to Music, 1983; J. S. Bach, 1984; Gesualdo, 1984; (ed with N. Fortune) The New Monteverdi Companion, 1985; articles in Music and Letters, Musical Qly, Monthly Musical Record, Brass Qly, Musical Times, Galpin Soc. Jl, Rivista Musicale Italiana. *Address:* Faculty of Music, Oxford University, St Aldate's, Oxford, OX1 1DB. *T:* Oxford 247069.
*Died 28 April 1986.*

**ARNOTT, Most Rev. Felix Raymond,** CMG 1981; MA (Oxon); ThD; MACE; *b* Ipswich, Suffolk, 8 March 1911; *s* of late Richard Girling Arnott, Ipswich; *m* 1938, Anne Caroline, *d* of W. A. P. Lane, Kingston Gorse, Sussex; two *s* two *d*. *Educ:* Ipswich Sch.; Keble Coll., Oxford; Cuddesdon Theol Coll. Curate, Elland, Yorks, 1934-38; Exam. Chaplain, Bp of Wakefield, 1936-39; Vice-Prin., Cheshunt, 1938; Warden, St John's Coll., Brisbane, 1939-46; Warden, St Paul's Coll., Univ. of Sydney, 1946-63; Lectr i/c of Ecclesiastical History, Univ. of Sydney, 1951-63; a Co-Adjutor Bishop of Melbourne, 1963-70; Archbishop of Brisbane and Metropolitan of Queensland, 1970-80; Hon. Chaplain in Venice, 1980-85. Member: Monash Univ. Council, 1964-70; Anglican-Roman Catholic Internat. Cttee, 1969-81; Queensland Univ. Senate, 1971-80. Comr, Royal Commn on Human Relations, Australia, 1974-. A Founder of Blake Prize for Religious Art, 1951. *Publications:* The Anglican Via Media in the Seventeenth Century, 1948; contribs to learned jls. *Recreations:* walking, music. *Address:* Los Monteros, Flat 6, 282 Marine Parade, Labrador, Qld 4215, Australia. *Clubs:* Melbourne, Royal Automobile (Victoria); Australian (Sydney); Queensland (Brisbane).
*Died 27 July 1988.*

**ARNOTT, Prof. James Fullarton,** TD and bar 1952; Professor of Drama, Glasgow University, 1973-79, later Emeritus Professor; *b* 29 April 1914; *s* of late Hezekiah Merricks Arnott and Susannah Willock Fullarton; *m* 1945, Martha Lawrence Miller (*née* Grant); one *s*. *Educ:* Ardrossan Acad.; Glasgow Univ. (MA); Merton Coll., Oxford (MLitt); Peterhouse, Cambridge. Asst Lectr in English Lang., University Coll. of Hull, 1938; Glasgow Univ: Asst in Eng. Lit., 1939; Lectr, 1944; Sen. Lectr, 1962; first Head of Drama Dept, 1966; Reader, 1971. Rockefeller Fellow, 1950; Gillespie Vis. Prof., Coll. of Wooster, Ohio, 1959-60; Fellow, Folger Shakespeare Library, 1964; British Acad. Overseas Fellow, 1978; Fellow, Huntington Libr., 1978; Vis. Prof., Arizona State Univ., 1981-82. Chm., Standing Cttee of Univ. Drama Depts, 1976-79; Pres., Internat. Fedn for Theatre Res., 1976-79. Member: Coll. of Drama Cttee, Royal Scottish Acad. of Music, 1949 (Governor, 1965-81); Bd, Glasgow Citizens' Theatre, 1970-76; Bd, Scottish Ballet, 1970-;

Scottish Arts Council, 1972–79 (Chm., Drama Cttee, 1976–79); Council, British Theatre Institute, 1975–80 (Hon. Vice-Chm., 1980–); Bd, Third Eye Centre, 1975–80; Arts Council of GB, 1977–79; UK Nat. Commn for Unesco, 1980–81; Bd, Scottish Theatre Co., 1980– (Chm., 1980–81). Chairman: J. D. Fergusson Art Foundn, 1978–81; British Liaison Cttee of Internat. Theatre Organisations, 1979–; Exec. Cttee, British Centre of Internat. Theatre Inst., 1980–; Bd, Internat. Assoc. of Margaret Morris Movement, 1979–; Trustee, Theatres Trust, 1980–. Editor, Theatre Research International (formerly Theatre Research/Recherches Théâtrales), 1964–81. FRSAMD 1979. *Publications:* English Theatrical Literature 1559–1900 (with J. W. Robinson), 1970; Sale Catalogues of the Libraries of Eminent Persons: actors, 1973. *Recreation:* directing plays. *Address:* 1 Huntly Gardens, Glasgow G12 9AS. *T:* 041–339 8494. *Clubs:* Lansdowne; College (Glasgow).
*Died 22 Nov. 1982.*

**ARNOTT, Sir John (Robert Alexander),** 5th Bt *cr* 1896, of Woodlands, Shandon, Co. Cork; *b* 9 April 1927; *er s* of Sir Robert John Arnott, 4th Bt, and Emita Amelia (*d* 1948), *d* of Francis James, formerly of Royston, Herts; *S* father, 1966; *m* 1974, Ann Margaret, *d* of late T. A. Farrelly, Kilcar, Co. Cavan; two *s*. *Educ:* Harrow. Formerly Lt, Royal Irish Fusiliers. Chm., Phoenix Park Racecourse, Dublin; Member: Irish Racing Board; Irish Turf Club. *Heir: s* Alexander John Maxwell Arnott, *b* 18 Sept. 1975. *Address:* Ashtown House, Castlenock, Co. Dublin, Ireland.
*Died 14 Feb. 1981.*

**ARON, Prof. Raymond Claude Ferdinand;** Officier de la Légion d'Honneur; author; President, comité éditorial, l'Express; Columnist, Figaro, 1947–77; *b* Paris, 14 March 1905; *m* 1933, Suzanne Gauchon; two *d* (and one *d* decd). *Educ:* Ecole Normale Supérieur and Sorbonne, Paris. Lectr, Univ. of Cologne, 1931; French Academic House, Berlin, 1931–33; Lycée du Havre, 1933–34; Centre Documentation sociale ENS, 1934–39; Maître de Conférences, Univ. of Toulouse, 1939; Editor, La France Libre, in London, 1940–44; Columnist, Combat, 1946–47; Professor of Sociology at Sorbonne, 1955–68; Prof. at Ecole Pratique des Hautes Etudes, 1960; Prof. at Coll. de France, 1970–78. Several hon. doctorates from foreign univs, 1958–; For. Hon. Mem., Amer. Acad. of Arts and Sciences, Boston, 1962; Mem., Académie des Sciences Morales et Politiques, Paris, 1963; Mem., Philosophical Soc., Philadelphia, 1967; Corres. Fellow, British Acad., 1970; Hon. Fellow, LSE, 1974; Hon. LittD Cambridge, 1981. Mem., Acad. Royale de Belgique, 1977. Goethe Prize, 1979; Tocqueville Prize, 1979; Aujourd'hui Prize, 1982. *Publications:* Introduction à la philosophie de l'histoire, 1938 (Introduction to the Philosophy of History, 1961); Le grand schisme, 1948; Les guerres en chaîne, 1951 (Century of Total War, 1954); L'Opium des intellectuels, 1955 (Opium of the Intellectuals, 1957); Espoir et paur du siècle, 1957 (Part III trans. as On War: atomic weapons and global diplomacy, 1958); Diversity of Worlds, 1957; La tragédie algérienne, 1957; Immuable et changeante, 1959 (France: steadfast and changing, 1960); La société industrielle et la guerre, 1959; Dimensions de la conscience historique, 1960 (parts trans. in Evidence and Inference, 1959, and The Dawn of Universal History, 1961); France: the new republic, 1960; Imperialism and Colonialism, 1960; Paix et guerre entre les nations, 1962 (Peace and War, 1967); Dix-huit leçons sur la société industrielle, 1963 (Eighteen Lectures on Industrial Society, 1968); Le grand débat, 1963 (The Great Debate: theories of nuclear strategy, 1965); (ed) World Technology and Human Destiny, 1963; La lutte de classes, 1964; Démocratie et totalitarisme, 1965 (Democracy and Totalitarianism, 1968); Trois essais sur la société industrielle, 1966 (The Industrial Society, 1967); Les étapes de la pensée sociologique, 1967 (Main Currents in Sociological Thought: I, Montesquieu, Comte, Marx, Tocqueville, the sociologist and the revolution of 1848, 1965; II, Durkheim, Pareto, Weber, 1968); De Gaulle, Israël et les juifs, 1968 (De Gaulle, Israel and the Jews, 1969); La révolution introuvable, 1968 (The Elusive Revolution: anatomy of a student revolt, 1970); Les désillusions du progrès, 1969 (Progress and Disillusion, 1968); Etudes politiques, 1972; République impériale, 1973 (The Imperial Republic, 1975); Histoire et Dialectique de la Violence, 1973 (History and the Dialectic of Violence, 1975); Penser la Guerre, Clausewitz, vol. I, L'Age européen, vol. II, L'Age planétaire, 1976 (Clausewitz, Philosopher of War, 1983); Plaidoyer pour l'Europe décadente, 1977 (In Defense of Decadent Europe); Le spectateur engagé, 1982; Mémoires, 50 ans de réflexion politique, 1983. *Address:* 87 Boulevard Saint-Michel, 75005 Paris, France.
*Died 17 Oct. 1983.*

**ARRAN, 8th Earl of,** *cr* 1762; **Arthur Kattendyke Strange David Archibald Gore;** Bt 1662; Viscount Sudley, Baron Saunders, 1758; Earl of Arran of the Arran Islands, Co. Galway, 1762; Baron Sudley (UK) 1884; journalist; broadcaster on radio and television; *b* 5 July 1910; *s* of 6th Earl of Arran, KP, PC(Ire.), and Maud, *o d* of Baron Huyssen van Kattendijke; *S* brother, 1958; *m* 1937, Fiona Bryde, *d* of Sir Iain Colquhoun, 7th Bt, of Luss, KT, DSO; one *s* (and one *s* decd). *Educ:* Eton; Balliol Coll., Oxford. Assistant Press Attaché, British Legation, Berne, 1939–40; Attaché, British Embassy, Lisbon, 1941–42; Deputy Dir, Overseas General Div., MOI, 1943–45; Dir

of Secretariat, Central Office of Information, 1945–49. Introduced in House of Lords: Sexual Offences Bill (now Act) (3 times); Badger Protection Bill (now Act). Director, Daily Mail and General Trust Ltd, to 1981. Chm., Children's Country Holidays Fund; Hon. Treasurer of Moorfields Eye Hospital. *Publications:* Lord Arran Writes, 1964; columnist, Evening News; contributions to Encounter, Punch, The Observer, Manchester Guardian, Daily Mail and Evening Standard. *Recreations:* shooting and tennis. *Heir: s* Viscount Sudley. *Address:* Pimlico House, Hemel Hempstead, Herts. *Club:* Beefsteak.
*Died 23 Feb. 1983.*

**ARTHUR, Hon. Sir Basil (Malcolm),** 5th Bt, *cr* 1841; MP (Lab) for Timaru, New Zealand, since 1962; Minister of Transport, and Minister in charge of State Insurance Office, New Zealand, 1972–75; *b* 18 Sept. 1928; *o s* of Sir George Malcolm Arthur, 4th Bt, and Doris Fay, *y d* of Joseph Wooding, JP, Woodland Grange, Woodbury, Geraldine, New Zealand; *S* father 1949; *m* 1950, Elizabeth Rita, *d* of late Alan Wells, Wakefield, Nelson, New Zealand; one *s* two *d*. *Heir: s* Stephen John Arthur [*b* 1 July 1953; *m* Carolyn Margaret Rita, *d* of Burney Lawrence Diamond, Cairns, Queensland; one *s* two *d*]. *Address:* Seadown, No 3 RD, Timaru, New Zealand.
*Died 1 May 1985.*

**ARTHUR, Prof. Donald Ramsay,** MSc, PhD, DSc; Professor and Head of Department of Zoology, King's College, London University, 1963–80, now Emeritus Professor; Director of Studies, School of Human Environmental Studies, 1975–79, and since 1981; FKC 1972; *b* 1 May 1917; *s* of Henry and Rachel Arthur; *m* 1945, Iris Doreen (*née* Gingell); one *d*. *Educ:* Amman Valley Gram. Sch.; UCW, Aberystwyth. School Master, Brockley Co. Sch., London, 1938–39; Scientist, Royal Ordnance Factory, 1939–42; Sen. Entomologist, University Coll. South Wales (working under grant from ARC), 1943–47; Sen. Biology Master, City of Cardiff High Sch., 1947–48; King's Coll., London: Lectr in Zoology, 1948–59; Leverhulme Research Award, 1954–55; Reader in Zoology, 1959–63; Dean, Faculty of Science, 1968–70; Consultant: US Naval Med. Res. Unit, Cairo, 1955–62; Environmental Resources Ltd, 1972; TEST (Transport and Environment Studies), 1970–. Vis. Prof., Univ. of Rhodesia, 1962; Vis. Res. Fellow, Tick Res. Unit, Rhodes Univ., 1972; Mem. Council, Brit. Soc. Parasitol., 1962–64; Chm., Bd of Studies in Zoology, Univ. of London, 1965–67; Mem. Bd of Studies (as other person), 1981–; Vis. Prof., Queen Mary Coll., Univ. of London, 1981–; Pres., London Branch of Assoc. for Science Educn, 1965–66; Member: Exec. Cttee and Finance and Admin. Cttee, Field Studies Council, 1963–72; Council of Environmental Educn, 1968–72; Editorial Bd, Parasitology, 1964–83; Editorial Bd, Internat. Jl of Environmental Sciences, 1970–; Council, John Cass Coll., 1965–69; Delegacy, King's Coll., 1970–76; Finance Cttee, King's Coll., 1970–77; Cleaner Thames Consultative Cttee, 1968–72; Adv. Cttee of Pollution by oil of the sea, 1970–72; Council, Instn of Environmental Sciences, 1970–79. Editor, Biological Science Texts, 1966–82. President: London Old Aberystwythians, 1967–68; London Carms Soc., 1970–71. FIBiol, 1965; FRSA 1981. *Publications:* Ticks: a Monograph of the Ixodoidea, Pt V, 1960; Ticks and Disease, 1962; (ed) Aspects of Disease Transmission by Ticks, 1962; British Ticks, 1963; Ticks of the Genus Ixodes in Africa, 1965; (ed) Looking at Animals Again, 1966; Survival: Man and his Environment, 1969; (ed with J. D. Carthy) Oil Pollution and Littoral Organisms, 1968; Joint Editor, Symposium vol., 2nd Internat. Acarological Congress, 1969; Adv. Editor, Encyclopaedia of Zoology, 1970; chapter (with I. Birtwell) in Aquatic Oligochaeta Biology, 1980; papers in Parasitology, Jl Parasitology, Proc. Zool. Soc., Bulletin Entomological Research, etc. *Recreation:* Rugby football. *Address:* 57 Rushgrove Avenue, NW9. *T:* 01–205 6375.
*Died 8 Oct. 1984.*

**ARTHUR, Sir Geoffrey (George),** KCMG 1971 (CMG 1963); HM Diplomatic Service, retired; Master of Pembroke College, Oxford, since 1975; *b* 19 March 1920; *s* of G. J. Arthur; *m* 1946, Margaret, *d* of late T. A. Woodcock, OBE; no *c*. *Educ:* Ashby de la Zouch Grammar Sch.; Christ Church, Oxford. Served in Army, 1940–45. Joined HM Foreign Service, 1947. Served in: Baghdad, 1948–50; Ankara, 1950–53; Foreign Office, 1953–55; Bonn, 1956–58; Cairo, 1959–63; Counsellor in Foreign Office, 1963–67; Ambassador to Kuwait, 1967–68; Asst Under-Sec. of State, FCO, 1968–70; Political Resident in the Persian Gulf, 1970–72; Visiting FCO Fellow, St Antony's Coll., Oxford, 1972–73; Dep. Under-Sec. of State, FCO, 1973–75. Dir, 1975–79, Special Advr to Bd, 1980–, British Bank of the Middle East. *Address:* Master's Lodgings, Pembroke College, Oxford. *T:* Oxford 243482. *Clubs:* United Oxford & Cambridge University, Beefsteak.
*Died 15 May 1984.*

**ARUNDELL, Dennis Drew,** OBE 1978; (formerly D. D. Arundel); actor, composer, producer, writer for theatre, radio, films and television, since 1926; *b* 22 July 1898; *s* of Arundel Drew Arundel and Rose Lucy Campbell. *Educ:* Tonbridge Sch.; St John's Coll., Cambridge. Lieut, RGA, 1917–19 (gassed, 1918). St John's Coll., 1919–29 (Sizarship, 1917; Strathcona Studentship, 1922); BA (Classics) 1922, MusB 1923, MA 1924. Fellow of St John's Coll.,

Cambridge, 1923–29; Lecturer in Music and English Drama, Deputy Organist St John's, 1924. First appeared on professional stage at Lyric, Hammersmith, 1926; subseq. joined Old Vic Company, playing Trofimov in A Month in the Country, Lucio in Measure for Measure, and has since taken many parts, inc. first Lord Peter Wimsey, Manningham in Gaslight; directed and composed music for plays in West End theatres, films, radio and television. Chief Producer, RCM Opera Sch., 1959–73 (Crees Lectr, RCM, 1970; FRCM 1969); Resident Opera Producer and Coach, Royal Northern Coll. of Music, Manchester, 1974. Chm., Internat. Jury of Singing, Jeunesses Musicales, Belgrade, 1972. As an opera director his work has been especially with Sadler's Wells and the BBC; producer of over 50 operas; translator of some 15 operas; arr. Purcell's Indian Queen for Opera da Camera, 1973; directed both operas and plays in Australia, 1956, 1975 and Finland, 1947, 1952, 1957 (scene from 1952 production of Hamlet inc. in centenary prog. of Helsinki Nat. Theatre, 1973). Lectures: Soc. of Theatre Research, 1971; Mozart's criteria for presentations of Marriage of Figaro, RAM, 1986 (also Master Class, RCM, 1985) and Vrige Univ. and Sweelinck Conservatoire, Amsterdam, 1987. Publications: Henry Purcell, 1927 (in German, 1929); (ed) King Arthur, Purcell Soc. edn, 1928; Dryden and Howard, 1929; The Critic at the Opera, 1957 (repr. NY, with subtitle Contemporary Comments on Opera in London over Three Centuries, 1980); The Story of Sadler's Wells, 1965 (new edn as The Story of Sadler's Wells, 1633–1977, 1978); Introduction to Le Nozze di Figaro and Cosi fan Tutte (Cassell Opera Guides), 1971; (ed) Congreve's Semele, 1925; (trans.) Morax and Honegger's King David, 1929; (trans.) Weinberger's Schwanda the Bagpiper, 1946; (trans.) Claudel's and Honegger's Jeanne d'Arc au Bûcher, 1939; (trans.) Monteverdi's Il Combattimento di Tancredi e Clorinda, 1974; Sibelius's Kullervo, 1974; article on Mozart's criteria for presentations of Marriage of Figaro, Opera, 1984; various musical compositions and musical articles. Recreation: operatic research. Address: 21 Lloyd Square, WC1. T: 01–837 2942. Died 10 Dec. 1988.

**ARUNDELL, Brig. Sir Robert (Duncan Harris),** KCMG 1950 (CMG 1947); OBE 1943; retired as Governor and Commander-in-Chief, Barbados (1953–59) (Acting Governor-General and C-in-C, The West Indies, 1959); Zanzibar Delimitation Commissioner, 1962; b Lifton, Devon, 22 July 1904; s of late C. H. Arundell; m 1929, Joan (d 1984), d of late Capt. J. A. Ingles, RN; one s. Educ: Blundell's Sch.; Brasenose Coll., Oxford. Colonial Administrative Service, Tanganyika Territory, 1927; seconded Colonial Office, 1935–37; Sec. Nyasaland Financial Commission, 1937–38; Tanganyika Territory, 1938–39; Assistant Chief Sec. Uganda, 1939; Army, Civil Affairs, 1941–45; served War of 1939–45 in Middle East and East Africa (despatches, OBE); Chief Civil Affairs Officer MEF (Brig.), 1944–45; British Resident Mem. in Washington of Caribbean Commission, 1946–47; Governor and C-in-C, Windward Islands, 1948–53. KStJ 1952. Address: Wakehill, Ilminster, Somerset TA19 0NR. Club: East India. Died 24 March 1989.

**ARUP, Sir Ove (Nyquist),** Kt 1971; CBE 1953; RA 1986; FEng, FICE, FIStructE, FCSD; MICEI; MSocCE(France); Founder, Ove Arup Partnerships; b Newcastle upon Tyne, 16 April 1895; s of Jens Simon Johannes Arup and Mathilde B. Nyquist; m 1925, Ruth Sœrensen; one s two d. Educ: Preparatory Sch., Hamburg, Germany; Public Sch., Sorl; Univ. of Copenhagen, Denmark. MIngF (Medlem Ingeniłr Forening), Copenhagen. Designer Christiani & Nielsen, GmbH, Hamburg, 1922–23, transf. to London 1923; Designer, 1923–25, Chief Designer, 1925–34, Christiani & Nielsen, Ltd, London; Director and Chief Designer, J. L. Kier & Co., Ltd, London, 1934–38; Consulting Engineer for: schools, flats, air raid shelters, industrial projects, marine work (Air Min.); Director: Arup Designs, Ltd; Arup & Arup, Ltd; Pipes, Ltd, 1938–45; Senior Partner: Ove Arup & Partners, Consulting Engineers, 1949; Arup Associates, 1963. Chm. Soc. of Danish Civil Engineers in Gt Britain and Ireland, 1955–59; Visiting Lectr, Harvard Univ., 1955; Alfred Bossom Lectr, RSA, 1970; Maitland Lecture, IStructE, 1968. RIBA Royal Gold Medal for Architecture for 1966; Gold Medal, IStructE, 1973. Hon. DSc: Durham, 1967; Heriot-Watt, 1976; City Univ., 1979; Hon. ScD East Anglia, 1968; Hon. Dr Tekniske Hojskole, Lyngby, Denmark, 1974. Fellow Amer. Concrete Inst., 1975. Commander (First Class), Order of the Dannebrog, 1975 (Chevalier, 1965). Publications: Design, Cost, Construction and Relative Safety of Trench, Surface, Bomb-proof and other AirRaid Shelters, 1939; papers and articles in various technical jls. Recreations: music and reading. Address: 6 Fitzroy Park, Highgate, N6. T: 01–340 3388. Clubs: Athenæum; Danish. Died 5 Feb. 1988.

**ASHBOURNE,** 3rd Baron, cr 1885; **Edward Russell Gibson,** CB 1950; DSO 1943; Vice-Admiral, retired; b 1 June 1901; s of Hon. Edward Graves Mayne Gibson (3rd s of 1st Baron Ashbourne) and Mary Philips Greg; S uncle, 1942; m 1929, Reta Frances Manning, e d of E. M. Hazeland, Hong Kong; one s one d. Educ: Osborne; Dartmouth; Caius Coll., Cambridge. Entered Osborne, 1915; Midshipman, 1917; served in HMS Superb, Dreadnought, Monarch, in War of 1914–18; Lieut, 1922; specialised in submarines, 1925;

Commander 1934; served on staff of Admiral of the Fleet Sir Dudley Pound in Mediterranean, 1938–39; Capt., 1939; served War of 1939–45 (DSO, Legion of Merit, US); served on staff of Adm. Sir Max Horton, 1940–42; Sicily Assault (DSO), 1943; commanded HMS Ariadne (Legion of Merit, US), 1943–45; commanded 3rd Submarine Flotilla, 1945; served on Naval Staff at Admiralty, 1946–47; commanded HMS Mauritius, 1947–48; Rear-Adm., 1948; Naval Representative on Military Staff Cttee, UN, 1949–50; Flag Officer, Gibraltar, and Admiral Supt, HM Dockyard, Gibraltar, 1950–52; Vice-Adm. 1952; retired list, 1952. JP Co. of Devon, 1955. County Pres., St John Ambulance Brigade for Devon, 1963. OStJ 1964. Heir: s Lieut-Comdr Hon. Edward Barry Greynville Gibson, RN, retired [b 28 Jan. 1933; m 1967, Yvonne Georgina, d of late Major G. W. Ham; three s]. Address: 56 Chiltley Way, Liphook, Hampshire. Club: Army and Navy. Died 3 Sept. 1983.

**ASHBY, Dame Margery (Irene) C.;** see Corbett Ashby.

**ASHCROFT, (Charles) Neil;** Clerk and Chief Executive, Derbyshire County Council, since 1979; b 27 Aug. 1937; s of Charles and Maggie Ashcroft; m 1962, Irene Riding; one s. Educ: Hutton Grammar Sch., near Preston. CIPFA. Lancashire County Council, 1954–58; Wigan County Borough Council, 1958–66; Liverpool City Council, 1966–69; Derbyshire County Council: Chief Accountant, 1969–72; Asst Clerk, 1972–74; Dep. Clerk, 1974–79. Recreations: shooting, motoring, modern history. Address: Lumb Lane, Darley Dale, Matlock, Derbyshire. T: Matlock 732210.
Died 14 April 1984.

**ASHENHEIM, Sir Neville (Noel),** Kt 1963; CBE 1958; Leader of Government Business in the Senate and Minister without Portfolio, Jamaica, 1967–72; b 18 Dec. 1900; s of Lewis Ashenheim and Estelle Lillian de Cordova; m 1926, Leonie Vivienne Delevante; three s. Educ: Jamaica Coll.; Munro Coll.; Wadham Coll., Oxford. BA 1922, MA 1943. Admitted Solicitor of Supreme Court, 1926, and joined father's firm of Milholland, Ashenheim & Stone. HM's Jamaican Ambassador to the USA, 1962–67. Chairman: "The Gleaner" Company, 1946–67 (newspaper in Caribbean founded by his forbears in 1834); Jamaica Industrial Development Corporation, 1952–57; Caribbean Cement Co., 1965–73; Caribbean Steel Co., 1965–73; Wray & Nephew Gp Ltd (formerly Consolidated Internat. Corporation), 1958–73; Standard Life Assurance Co. (Jamaican Branch), 1958–61, 1967–71; Jamaica Housing Develt Co., 1957–62. Director: Lascelles de Merado & Co. Ltd; Henriques Brothers Ltd, 1950–73; West Indies Glass Co. Ltd, 1961–73. Hon. DHL Hebrew Union Coll., 1964. Address: Apartment B5, Roxdene, Pitts Bay Road, Pembroke, Bermuda. Clubs: Jamaica, Liguanea, St Andrew, Kingston Cricket, Jamaica Jockey (all in Jamaica); Royal Bermuda Yacht. Died 1 Sept. 1984.

**ASHERSON, Nehemiah,** MA Cape; MB, BS London; FRCS, LRCP; FZS, etc; Fellow International College of Surgeons; Hon. Fellow Surgical Academy, Madrid; Associate, Royal Institute of Chemistry, 1919; Hon. Cons. Surgeon, The Royal National (Central London) Throat, Nose, and Ear Hospital (late Member of Board of Governors, 1948–49–50–58); late Hon. Secretary to the Medical Council; Lecturer to the Institute of Otology and Laryngology (Member Academic Board); Teacher in Oto-laryngology in the University of London; Consulting Surgeon for Diseases of the Ear, Nose, and Throat to the NE, NW and SE regional hospital boards, including the Queen Elizabeth Hospital for Children; FRSocMed (Hon. Fellow, former Pres., Section of Laryngology; Hon. Fellow, former Member Council, Section History of Medicine; late Member Council Section Otology, and Library Committee); Trustee (Hon. Fellow, former Pres., Hunterian Society); formerly Hon. Treasurer, BMA, St Marylebone Division, and Mem. Ethical Cttee; Hon. Fellow and Librarian, late Councillor, Medical Society of London; b 1897; s of Isaac Asherson; m; one s one d. Educ: South African Coll.; Univ. of Cape Town (Entrance Scholar); University Coll. and Hospital, London; postgraduate study in speciality in London and Vienna. Medallist in Chemistry; exhibitioner at the BA examination; Jamieson Scholar at MA; Alexander Bruce Gold Medallist in Surgery and Liston Gold Medal in Surgical Pathology, University Coll. Hosp.; Geoffrey Duveen Travelling Scholar of the Univ. of London in Oto-rhino Laryngology; late Harker Smith Cancer (radium) Registrar and Casualty Surgical Officer at University Coll. Hosp.; Chief Asst to the Royal Ear Hosp., University Coll. Hosp.; Chief Asst to the Ear, Nose, and Throat Dept of the Bolingbroke Hosp., etc; Late: Ear Consultant to Army Medical Boards; Surgeon Emergency Medical Service, 1939–45; Consulting Surgeon to LCC and to the Charterhouse Rheumatism Clinic. Hunterian Prof., RCS, 1942. Mem. Royal Instn (Visitor, 1969–71). Mem., Apothecaries Soc. Publications: Diagnosis and Treatment of Foreign Bodies in the Upper Food and Respiratory Passages, 1932; Acute Otitis and Mastoiditis in General Practice, 1934; Chronic Ear Discharge (Otorrhœa) and its complications, 1936; Otogenic Cerebellar Abscess, Hunterian Lecture, 1942; Identification by Frontal Sinus Prints, 1965; The Deafness of Beethoven, 1965; Bibliography of G. J. Du Verney's Traité de l'Organe de l'Ouïe, 1683 (first scientific treatise on the ear), 1979; communications in Jl of Laryngology, of the Royal Society of Medicine, in The Lancet and in medical journals on subjects relating to the speciality. *Recreations:* numismatics, book collecting. *Address:* 21 Harley Street, W1. *T:* 01–580 3197.                    *Died* 1 *Nov.* 1989.

**ASHMOLE, Professor Bernard,** CBE 1957; MC 1917; MA, BLitt; Hon. FRIBA; FBA 1938; FKC 1986; Hon. Fellow of Lincoln College, Oxford, 1980; Hon. Fellow, University College, London, 1974; Hon. Fellow, Hertford College, Oxford, 1961; *b* Ilford, 22 June 1894; 2nd *s* of late William Ashmole and Caroline Wharton Tiver; *m* 1920, Dorothy Irene, 2nd *d* of late Everard de Peyer, Newent Court, Glos; one *s* two *d. Educ:* Forest; privately; Hertford Coll., Oxford (Classical Scholar). 11th Royal Fusiliers, 1914–18; Captain (severely wounded, Somme, 1917). Craven Fellow, and Student of the British Schools at Athens and Rome, 1920–22; Asst Curator of Coins, Ashmolean Museum, 1923–25; Director of the British Sch. at Rome, 1925–28; Florence Bursar, RIBA, 1937; Hon. Member of the Archæological Institute of America, 1940; RAF 1940–45, Adjutant of 84 Sqdn in Greece, Iraq, Western Desert, Sumatra and India (despatches twice, Hellenic Flying Cross). Yates Professor of Archæology, University of London, 1929–48; Keeper of Greek and Roman Antiquities, British Museum, 1939–56; Lincoln Professor of Classical Archæology, Univ. of Oxford, 1956–61, and Fellow of Lincoln Coll., Oxford, 1956–80; Geddes-Harrower Professor of Greek Art and Archæology, Univ. of Aberdeen, 1961–63; Visiting Professor in Archæology, Univ. of Yale, 1964. Rhind Lectr, 1952; Myres Memorial Lectr, Oxford, 1961; Norton Lectr, Archæological Inst. of America, 1963; Wrightsman Lectr, New York, 1967. Hon. LLD Aberdeen, 1968. Hon. Fellow, Archaeol Soc. of Athens, 1978. Kenyon Medal, British Acad., 1979; Cassano Medal, Taranto, 1980. *Publications:* Catalogue of Ancient Marbles at Ince Blundell, 1929; Greek Sculpture and Painting (with Beazley), 1932, repr. 1966; The Ancient World (with Groenewegen-Frankfort), 1967; Olympia: sculptures of the temple of Zeus (with Yalouris and Frantz), 1967; Architect and Sculptor in Classical Greece, 1972; articles on Greek sculpture in the Journal of Hellenic Studies and other periodicals. *Address:* 5 Tweed Green, Peebles. *T:* Peebles 21154. *Club:* Athenæum.

*Died* 25 *Feb.* 1988.

**ASHTON OF HYDE,** 2nd Baron *cr* 1911; **Thomas Henry Raymond Ashton,** DL, JP; Major, late 1st Royal Gloucestershire Hussars, RAC, TA; Joint Master, Heythrop, 1934–36, sole Master, 1936–48, Joint Master, 1948–52; *b* 2 Oct. 1901; *s* of 1st Baron and Eva Margaret (*d* 1938) *d* of J. H. James Kingswood, Watford, Herts; *S* father, 1933; *m* 1925, Marjorie Nell, *d* of late Hon. Marshall Brooks; one *s* (two *d* decd). *Educ:* Eton; New Coll., Oxford (MA). DL 1957, JP 1944, Gloucestershire. *Recreations:* hunting, shooting, deerstalking. *Heir: s* Hon. Thomas John Ashton [*b* 19 Nov. 1926; *m* 1957, Pauline Trewlove, *er d* of late Lieut-Col R. H. L. Brackenbury, Yerdley House, Long Compton, Shipston-on-Stour; two *s* two *d*]. *Address:* Broadwell Hill, Moreton-in-Marsh, Glos. *T:* Stow-on-the-Wold 30626. *Club:* Boodle's.                    *Died* 21 *March* 1983.

**ASHTON, Sir (Arthur) Leigh (Bolland),** Kt 1948; Director and Secretary, Victoria and Albert Museum, 1945–55, retired; *b* London, 20 Oct. 1897; *o s* of late A. J. Ashton, KC, Recorder of Manchester; *m* 1952, Mrs Madge Garland (marr. diss. 1962). *Educ:* Horris Hill; Winchester; Balliol Coll., Oxford, BA (war degree). Served European War, Lieut RGA, 1916–19. Victoria and Albert Museum: Asst Keeper (2nd class), Dept of Architecture and Sculpture, 1922–25; Dept of Textiles, 1925–31; Dept of Ceramics, 1931–37; Keeper of Special Collections, 1937, Secretary of the Advisory Council, 1935, and Asst to Dir, 1937; Asst Keeper, 1st class, 1932; Keeper (1st Class) 1938. Mem. Committee, City Companies Exhibition, 1927; Asst Dir International Exhibition of Persian Art, RA, 1931; Executive Committee and arranger of the Exhibition of Chinese Art, RA, 1935–36; Executive Committee, Exhibition of 17th Century Art, RA, 1937; Dir, Exhibition of the Arts of India and Pakistan, RA 1947–48; loaned to Ministry of Information, April 1939; Officer i/c Finance, 1939; Dep.-Dir of Foreign Division, 1940; Director of Neutral Countries Division, 1941; Dir of British Information Office, Istanbul, 1942, and head of Press Office, HM Embassy, Ankara, with rank of Counsellor. Comdr of the Dannebrog. *Publications:* Introduction to the History of Chinese Sculpture, 1922; Samplers, 1927; Memoirs of the Prince de Ligne, 1928; Chinese Art (with Basil Gray), 1935; Chinese Art (with others), 1935; (ed) Commemoration Catalogue of Chinese Exhibition, 1936; (ed) Commemorative Catalogue of the Exhibition of the Arts of India and Pakistan, 1950; numerous articles and lectures on the decorative arts. *Recreations:* music, the theatre, travel, bridge.                    *Died* 12 *March* 1983.

**ASHTON, Ellis,** MBE 1975; variety artiste, stage director and touring manager, since 1947; now theatre historian, lecturer, broadcaster; *b* Whiston, Liverpool, 1 Dec. 1919; *s* of Joseph and Beatrice Ashton; *m* 1957, Margaret Mitchell, speciality dancer; one *s* one *d. Educ:* Holy Trinity, Liverpool; Army Formation Coll. Various positions

before the War; served War, Scots Guards and Personnel Selection Staff, 1939–47. Pres., British Music Hall Soc., 1984– (Chm., 1968–84); Patron, Cinema Theatre Assoc.; Pres., National Assoc. of Theatrical, Television and Kine Employees, 1982. Founder Member: Theatres' Trust; British Theatre Inst. Exec. Member: Actors' Church Union; Entertainment Artistes Benevolent Fund. Member: Theatres Adv. Council; Variety Adv. Cttee; Radio and Television Safeguards Cttee. Life Member: National Trust; Ancient Monuments Soc.; Victorian Soc.; British Archaeol Assoc.; Royal Archaeol Inst.; Picture Palace Preservation Soc. Governor, Ruskin Coll., Oxford; Vice-Pres., Ruskin Fellowship, London. FRSA; FLS, FZS, FRGS. *Publications:* contrib. books on the theatre; contrib. The Stage, and The Call Boy. *Recreation:* preserving the British way of life. *Address:* 1 King Henry Street, N16. *T:* 01–254 4209.

*Died* 31 *Oct.* 1985.

**ASHTON, Sir Frederick (William Mallandaine),** OM 1977; CH 1970; Kt 1962; CBE 1950; Founder-choreographer to the Royal Ballet (Principal Choreographer, 1933–70, and Director, 1963–70); *b* Guayaquil, Ecuador, 17 Sept. 1904; *s* of George Ashton and Georgiana Fulcher. *Educ:* The Dominican Fathers, Lima, Peru; Dover Coll., Dover. With Ballet Rambert, 1926–33, as dancer and choreographer; Ida Rubinstein Company, Paris, 1929–30. Best known ballets: Les Patineurs, Apparitions, Horoscope, Symphonic Variations, Façade, Wedding Bouquet, Scènes de Ballet, Cinderella (first English choreographer to do a 3–act ballet), Illuminations, Sylvia, Romeo and Juliet, Ondine, La Fille Mal Gardée, Les Deux Pigeons, Marguerite and Armand, The Dream, Sinfonietta, Jazz Calendar, Enigma Variations, Walk to the Paradise Garden, Birthday Offering, A Month in the Country, Rhapsody, Varii Capricci, etc. Film: The Tales of Beatrix Potter (choreography, and appeared as Mrs Tiggywinkle), 1971. Served in Royal Air Force during War as Flight Lieut. Queen Elizabeth II Coronation Award, Royal Academy of Dancing, 1959. Freedom of City of London, 1981. Hon. DLitt: Durham, 1962; East Anglia, 1967; Hon. DMus: London, 1970; Hull, 1971; Oxon, 1976. Legion of Honour (France), 1960; Order of Dannebrog (Denmark), 1964. *Relevant publications:* Frederick Ashton: a Choreographer and his Ballets, by Z. Dominic and J. S. Gilbert, 1971; Frederick Ashton and his Ballets, by David Vaughan, 1977. *Recreation:* dancing. *Address:* Royal Opera House, Covent Garden, WC2.                    *Died* 18 *Aug.* 1988.

**ASHTON, Gilbert,** MC 1916; MA Cantab; DL; Headmaster, Abberley Hall (Preparatory School), near Worcester, 1921–61; *b* 27 Sept. 1896; *s* of Hubert Shorrock Ashton and Victoria Alexandrina, *d* of Maj.-Gen. Sir John Inglis, KCB; *m* 1921, Joan Mary, *d* of Rev. H. R. Huband; four *d. Educ:* Winchester Coll.; Trinity Coll., Cambridge. Served European War (wounded, MC): 2nd Lieut RFA, 1915; Instructor Army Signal Sch., 1918. Underwriter, Lloyd's, 1936. Chm. Incorporated Association of Preparatory Schs, 1937 and 1946. Major, Home Guard, 1940–45; Governor, Abberley Hall Sch., 1961-. Pres., Worcs CC 1967–69. JP 1934, DL 1968, Worcs. *Recreations:* formerly cricket (CU Cricket XI, 1919–21, Capt.; CU Assoc. XI, 1919–20, Capt.). *Address:* Abberley Lodge, near Worcester. *T:* Great Witley 305. *Clubs:* United Oxford & Cambridge University, MCC; Worcester Church House (Worcester).                    *Died* 6 *Feb.* 1981.

**ASHTON, Sir Leigh;** *see* Ashton, Sir A. L. B.

**ASHTOWN,** 6th Baron *cr* 1800; **Christopher Oliver Trench;** *b* 23 March 1931; *s* of Algernon Oliver Trench (*d* 1955) (*g g s* of 2nd Baron) and Muriel Dorothy (*d* 1954), *d* of Frank Thorne, Weston-super-Mare; *S* kinsman, 1979. *Recreation:* study of the philosophy of Gurdjeff and Ouspensky. *Heir: cousin* Sir Nigel Clive Cosby Trench, KCMG [*b* 27 Oct. 1916; *m* 1939, Marcelle Catherine Clotterbooke Payton; one *s*].                    *Died* 27 *April* 1990.

**ASHWELL, Major Arthur Lindley,** DSO 1916; OBE 1946; TD 1926; DL; late 8th Battalion Sherwood Foresters; *b* 19 Jan. 1886; *o s* of Arthur Thomas Ashwell, solicitor, Nottingham; *m* 1932, Sylvia Violet (*d* 1980), *widow* of Harold Gallatly, MC, and *d* of Philip Scratchley. *Educ:* Lambrook, Bracknell; Winchester Coll. Served European War, 1915 (wounded thrice, despatches, DSO). DL Notts, 1941. *Address:* Flat 3, 19 The Vale, SW3. *Clubs:* Naval and Military, Royal Automobile.                    *Died* 31 *Dec.* 1986.

**ASKEW, Herbert Royston,** QC 1955; BSc; MICE; *b* 15 March 1891; *e s* of late Leonard Askew; *m* 1st, 1919, Christiana Rachel (decd), *o d* of late C. Wolryche Dixon, Great Roke, Witley, Surrey; one *d* (one *s* killed on active service, 1942; and one *d* decd); 2nd, 1948, Dorothy Beatrice, *o d* of late J. Gale Wilson, Aberdour, Fife. *Educ:* Alleyn's Sch., Dulwich; London Univ. Served European War 1914–18, Capt. Middlesex Regt and Royal Tank Corps. Called to the Bar, Middle Temple, 1926; Master of the Bench, 1963. Mem. Kensington Borough Council, 1931–39. Served War of 1939–45, Lieut-Col, Gen. List (GSO1). *Address:* 24 Palace Court, W2. *T:* 01–727 6033.                    *Died* 18 *Aug.* 1986.

**ASKEY, Arthur Bowden,** CBE 1981 (OBE 1969); theatrical artiste; *b* 6 June 1900; *s* of Samuel Askey, Liverpool, and Betty Askey (*née* Bowden), Knutsford, Cheshire; *m* 1925, Elizabeth May Swash (*d* 1974); one *d*. *Educ:* Liverpool Institute. Liverpool Education Offices, 1916–24; concert parties, pantomimes, broadcasts, London and Provincial Concerts, 1924–38. *Films:* Band Waggon, Charlie's Big-Hearted Aunt, The Ghost Train, I Thank You, Back-Room Boy, King Arthur was a Gentleman, Miss London Ltd, Bees in Paradise, 1939–44; The Love Match; Ramsbottom Rides Again; Make Mine a Million; Friends and Neighbours. *Broadcast Series:* Band Waggon, 1938–39, and 1971; Big's Broadcast, 1940; Big Time, 1942; Forever Arthur, 1945; How Do You Do, 1949; Arthur's Inn, 1952; Hello, Playmates, 1954; Askey Galore, 1957; The Arthur Askey Show, 1958. *Television Series:* Before Your Very Eyes, 1953, 1955, 1956, 1957; Living it up, 1958; Arthur's Treasured Volumes, 1960; The Arthur Askey Show, 1961; Raise Your Glasses, 1962. *London Theatres:* The Boy Who Lost His Temper, Garrick, 1937, Cambridge, 1938; Band Waggon, London Palladium, 1939; Jack and Jill, Palace, 1941, His Majesty's, 1942; The Love Racket, Victoria Palace, Prince's and Adelphi, 1944–45; Follow the Girls, His Majesty's, 1945–47; Cinderella, London Casino, 1948; The Kid from Stratford, Prince's, Winter Garden, 1948–49; Goody Two Shoes, London Casino, 1950; Bet Your Life, London Hippodrome, 1951–52; The Love Match, Palace, 1953–54; Babes in the Wood, Golders Green, 1954; Babes in the Wood, Streatham Hill, 1955; Humpty Dumpty, Golders Green Hippodrome, 1956; Robinson Crusoe, Palladium, 1957; Dick Whittington, Golders Green Hippodrome, 1958; Dick Whittington, Streatham Hill Theatre, 1959–60; Cinderella, Golders Green Hippodrome, 1961–62; *Pantomime:* Robin Hood, Coventry Theatre, 1963–64; Babes in the Wood, Wimbledon, 1966–67; Sleeping Beauty, Wimbledon, 1969–70; Cinderella, Manchester, 1970–71; Cinderella, Nottingham, 1971–72; Cinderella, Birmingham, 1972–73; Babes in the Wood, Richmond, 1973–74; Cinderella, Bournemouth, 1974–75; Babes in the Wood, Bristol, 1975–76; Cinderella, Richmond, 1976–77; Jack and the Beanstalk, Richmond, 1977–78, Birmingham, 1978–79, Richmond, 1979–80; Aladdin, Richmond, 1981–82. London Palladium: Aladdin, 1964–65; Babes in the Wood, 1965–66; Robinson Crusoe, 1967–68; Jack and the Beanstalk, 1968–69. Royal Command Performance (Palladium), 1946, 1948, 1952, 1954, 1955, 1957, 1968, 1972, 1978, 1980; Command Performance (Manchester), 1959. Australian tour, 1949–50; various radio and television broadcasts and provincial variety tours. Summer seasons: Blackpool, Bournemouth, Southsea, Margate, Shanklin, Hastings, Rhyl, Torquay, Eastbourne, etc. Pres., Stage Golfing Soc. Variety Club of GB Special Award, 1978. Jubilee Medal, 1977. *Publication:* Before Your Very Eyes (autobiog.), 1975. *Recreations:* reading, music, watching sport, reminiscing. *Club:* Savage.

*Died 16 Nov. 1982.*

**ASKIN, Hon. Sir Robert William,** GCMG 1975 (KCMG 1972); Premier of New South Wales, 1965–75; retired; *b* 4 April 1909; *s* of William James Askin and Ellen Laura Askin (*née* Halliday); *m* 1937, Mollie Isabelle Underhill; no *c*. *Educ:* Sydney Techn. High Sch.; Central Coaching College. War Service, 1941–45. Mem. NSW Parlt, 1950; Dep. Opposition Leader, 1954; Leader of Opposition, 1959. Hon. DLitt New South Wales, 1966. Order of St Peter and St Paul, Lebanon, 1972; Grand Officer, Order of Cedar of Lebanon, 1972. *Recreations:* gardening, racing. *Address:* 86 Bower Street, Manly, NSW 2095, Australia. *T:* 977–1844. *Club:* University.

*Died 9 Sept. 1981.*

**ASLIN, Elizabeth Mary;** art historian; *b* 23 March 1923; *d* of Charles Herbert Aslin and Ethel Fawcett Aslin. *Educ:* various schools; Slade Sch. of Fine Art, Univ. of London. Res. Asst, Circulation Dept, V & A Museum, 1947; Asst Keeper i/c, Bethnal Green Museum, 1964–68; Asst Dir, V & A Museum, 1968–74; Keeper i/c, Bethnal Green Museum, 1974–81. Member: Victorian Soc.; Decorative Arts Soc. FRSA. *Publications:* Nineteenth Century English Furniture, 1962; The Aesthetic Movement: Prelude to Art Nouveau, 1969; E. W. Godwin, Furniture and Interior Decoration, 1986. *Recreations:* drawing, etching, travel. *Address:* 11 Fulmar Close, Hove, East Sussex BN3 6NW. *T:* Brighton 508467.

*Died 14 April 1989.*

**ASPINALL, William Briant Philip,** OBE 1945; Headmaster, Queen's School, HQ Northern Army Group, Rheindahlen, 1960–72, retired; *b* 1912; *s* of William Pryce Aspinall and Ethel Eleanor (*née* Ravenscroft); *m* 1st, Aileen, *d* of Major R. FitzGerald; one *s*; 2nd, Phyllis, *d* of Leopold Hill. *Educ:* Royal Masonic Sch.; St John's Coll., Cambridge. Served War, GSO1 MI14, 1940–45. Headmaster, Sutton Valence Sch., 1950–53; Windsor Sch., Hamm, BAOR, 1953–58; King Richard Sch., Cyprus, 1959. *Recreations:* cricket, hockey, golf, etc. *Address:* 6 Cramptons, Mill Lane, Sissinghurst, Kent. *Clubs:* MCC; Rye Golf.

*Died 31 Dec. 1988.*

**ASTAIRE, Fred;** actor, motion pictures; *b* 10 May 1899; *s* of F. E. Astaire and Ann Geilus; *m* 1933, Phyllis Livingston Potter (*d* 1954); two *s* one *d*; *m* 1980, Robyn Smith. *Educ:* private. Stage musical comedy-vaudeville until 1933, then motion pictures. First appearance in London, 1923, in Stop Flirting; American and English successes: Lady Be Good, Funny Face, The Band Waggon, Gay Divorce. *Films:* Flying Down to Rio, Top Hat, Roberta, Gay Divorce, Follow the Fleet, Swingtime, Shall We Dance?, Story of Vernon and Irene Castle, Holiday Inn, Ziegfeld Follies, Blue Skies, Easter Parade, The Barkleys of Broadway, Three Little Words, Let's Dance, Daddy Longlegs, Funny Face, Silk Stockings, On the Beach, The Pleasure of His Company, Finian's Rainbow, The Midas Run, A Run on Gold, The Towering Inferno, Un Taxi Mauve, Ghost Story. *Television Shows:* An Evening with Fred Astaire, 1958; Another Evening with Fred Astaire, 1959; Astaire Time, 1960; The Fred Astaire Show, 1968; Family Upside Down, 1978. *Publication:* Autobiography, Steps in Time, 1959. *Recreations:* golf, thoroughbred racing. *Address:* Beverly Hills, California 90210, USA. *Clubs:* Racquet and Tennis, The Brook, Lamb's (New York).

*Died 22 June 1987.*

**ASTBURY, Sir George,** Kt 1966; JP; *b* 10 May 1902; 2nd *s* of Thomas Astbury, Longton, Stoke-on-Trent; *m* 1930, Nellie (decd), 2nd *d* of Albert Bagnall, Sandford Hill, Longton; two *s*. *Educ:* St James's, Longton. Retired as Co-operative Soc. Insurance Agent. Former Mem. Nat. Wages Bd of Co-op. Union. CC 1937, JP 1938, CA 1951, Hon. Alderman 1974, Cheshire. *Address:* West Winds, Strawberry Roundabout, Backford, near Chester.

*Died 20 Dec. 1985.*

**ASTBURY, Norman Frederick,** CBE 1968; MA, ScD Cantab; CEng, FIEE, CPhys, FInstP; Director, British Ceramic Research Association, 1960–73; *b* 1 Dec. 1908; *y c* of William and Clara Astbury, Normacot, Staffs; *m* 1933, Nora Enid (*d* 1979), *yr d* of William and Mary Wilkinson; three *s* one *d*. *Educ:* Longton High Sch.; St John's Coll., Cambridge (Scholar and Prizeman). National Physical Laboratory, 1929–39; HM Anti-Submarine Experimental Establishment, 1939–45; Dir of Research, J. Sankey & Sons Ltd and Guest, Keen & Nettlefold Ltd, 1945–49; Prof. of Applied Physics, NSW Univ. of Technology, 1949–51; Prof. of Physics, Univ. of Khartoum, 1951–56; Royal Aircraft Establishment, 1956–57; Dep. Dir of Research, Brit. Ceram. Research Assoc., 1957–60. Pres., Brit. Ceram. Soc., 1969; Member: Coun. Inst. of Physics and Phys. Soc., 1963–66; Nat. Coun. for Technological Awards, 1958–64; Coun. for Nat. Academic Awards, 1964–66; Inter-services Metallurgical Research Coun., 1962–64; Joint Services Non-metallic Materials Research Board, 1964–69; Chm. Cttee of Directors of Research Assocs, 1964–66; Vice-Pres., Parly and Sci. Cttee, 1965–68; Mem., Construction Res. Adv. Council, DoE (formerly MPBW), 1968–71. Hon. FICeram. FRSA. *Publications:* Industrial Magnetic Testing, 1952; Electrical Applied Physics, 1956; numerous papers in scientific jls. *Recreations:* music, model railways. *Address:* 85 Atlantic Way, Westward Ho!, Devon. *T:* Bideford 75482. *Clubs:* Athenæum; Federation (Stoke-on-Trent).

*Died 28 Oct. 1987.*

**ASTELL HOHLER, Thomas Sidney,** MC 1944; Director, King & Shaxson Plc, since 1946 (Chairman, 1965–84); *b* 1919; *s* of late Lt-Col Arthur Preston Hohler, DSO and late Mrs Stanley Barry, Long Crendon Manor, Bucks; granted name and arms of Astell in lieu of name and arms of Hohler, by Royal Licence, 1978; *m* 1952, Jacqueline, *d* of late Marquis de Jouffroy d'Abbans, Chateau d'Abbans, Doubs, France; one *d*. *Educ:* Eton. 2nd Lieut SRO Grenadier Guards, 1939; Major 1944; served in: France; N Africa, 1942; Italy, 1943–44. Director: Henry Sotheran Ltd; Britannia Internat. High Income Fund Ltd. Chm., London Discount Market Assoc., 1972. Liveryman, Grocers' Co., 1956. *Recreations:* farming, shooting. *Address:* Wolverton Park, Basingstoke, Hants RG26 5RU. *T:* Kingsclere 298200; 9 Kylestrome House, Cundy Street, SW1W 9JT. *T:* 01-730 9595. *Clubs:* Brooks's, City of London.

*Died 29 April 1989.*

**ASTON, Arthur Vincent,** CMG 1950; MC 1917; *b* 5 Nov. 1896; *m* 1922, Rita Bethia Walker Simpson (*d* 1972); two *s*. *Educ:* King's Sch., Chester; Queen's Coll., Oxford. Malayan Civil Service, 1919; ADC to Officer Administering the Govt, 1929; Resident Commissioner, Pahang, 1946, Perak, 1947, Penang, 1948–51; retired, 1951. Served European War, 1914–18 (MC); War of 1939–45 (despatches). *Address:* Croylands, Hindon, Salisbury, Wilts. *T:* Hindon 285.

*Died 25 Aug. 1981.*

**ASTON, Sir Christopher (Southcote),** KCVO 1981; JP; Director, Ready Mixed Concrete Ltd, since 1968; *b* Salisbury, Wilts, 9 Jan. 1920; *s* of late Maj.-Gen. Sir George Aston, KCB, RM, and Lady Aston; *m* 1949, Eileen Fitzgerald McNair; one *s* two *d*. *Educ:* Marlborough Coll.; University Coll., Southampton (BScEng). Served War, RN, 1941–46: taken prisoner in attack on St Nazaire, 1942; Marlag Nord prison camp, Germany, 1942–45. Associated Industrial Consultants Ltd, 1950–64; Man. Dir, Hall & Ham River Ltd, 1967–68; Dep. Chm., 1977–78, Chm., 1978–81, Powell Duffryn Ltd. Director: Rolls-Royce Motors Ltd, 1972–80; Windsor Festival Soc. Ltd, 1976–. Chairman: Windsor Theatre Royal Co. Ltd, 1976–;

Local Authorities' Aircraft Noise Council, 1972–74; Windsor Silver Jubilee Celebrations Cttee, 1976–77; Tree Council, 1977–80; HRH Princess Christian's Nursing Home, Windsor, 1979–; Internat. Year of Disabled People (England), 1981. Founder Chairman: The Queen's Trees Trust, 1977–78; The Prince Philip Trust Fund, 1978–; Disabled Sports Foundn, 1979–. Member: Eton RDC, 1967–74; Bucks CC, 1971–74; Berks CC, 1974–. First Mayor, Royal Bor. of Windsor and Maidenhead, 1974–76. JP Slough, 1972. Order of Dannebrog, Denmark, 1974. *Recreations:* natural history, music, theatre. *Address:* Longfield, 102 Staines Road, Wraysbury, Staines TW19 5AG. *T:* Wraysbury 2470. *Died 25 Jan. 1982.*

**ASTON, Thomas William,** CMG 1969; HM Diplomatic Service; British Consul-General, Los Angeles, since 1974; *b* 14 May 1922; *s* of late Henry Herbert Aston, Birmingham, and of Lilian Perks; *m* 1947, Eve Dunning; one *d. Educ:* Saltley Grammar Sch., Birmingham. Entered Civil Service as Employment Clerk, Ministry of Labour, 1939. Served with RAF, 1941–46: Middle East, Palestine, Persian Gulf, Egypt, South Africa; Navigator, 1942; Flight-Lieut, 1944. Executive Officer (Inspector), Ministry of National Insurance, 1947; Assistant Principal, Commonwealth Relations Office, 1951; Delhi, 1953–54; Principal, 1954; seconded to Joint Intelligence Cttee, 1954–56; First Secretary, South Africa, 1957–60; CO, 1961–63; First Sec., Kenya, 1963–64; Deputy British High Commissioner, Kampala, 1964–65; Dir, Internat. Affairs Div., Commonwealth Secretariat, 1966–69; Inspector, FCO, 1969–72; Sen. British Trade Comr, Hong Kong, 1972–74. Hon. LLD San Diego Nat., 1978. *Recreations:* tennis, cricket, gardening, bird watching. *Address:* c/o Foreign and Commonwealth Office, SW1. *Club:* Royal Commonwealth Society. *Died 24 Jan. 1981.*

**ASTOR OF HEVER,** 2nd Baron *cr* 1956, of Hever Castle; **Gavin Astor;** *b* 1 June 1918; *e s* of 1st Baron Astor of Hever, and Lady Violet Mary Elliot (*d* 1965), *y d* of 4th Earl of Minto, KG, PC, GCSI, GCMG, GCIE, and *widow* of Lord Charles Mercer Nairne, 2nd *s* of 5th Marquess of Lansdowne; *S* father, 1971; *m* 1945, Lady Irene Haig, *d* of late Field Marshal Earl Haig, KT, GCB, OM, GCVO, KCIE; two *s* three *d. Educ:* Eton; New Coll., Oxford. Served with The Life Guards, 1940–46. Director: Alliance Assurance Co., 1954–; C. Townsend Hook Ltd, 1954–65; Reuters Ltd, 1955–61; Electrolux Ltd, 1959–70; Monotype Corp. Ltd, 1952–73; Chm., The Times Publishing Co. Ltd, 1959–66 (Dir, 1952–66); Co-Chief Proprietor of The Times, 1964–66; Pres., Times Newspapers Ltd, 1967–81; Dir, Times Newspapers Holdings Ltd, 1981–. Commonwealth Press Union: Chm. Council, 1959–72; Pres., 1972–81; Hon. Life Mem., 1981; Chairman: 9th Commonwealth Press Conf., India and Pakistan, 1961; 10th Conf., West Indies, 1965; 11th Conf., UK, 1970; 12th Conf., SE Asia, 1974; 13th Conf., Canada, 1978; Exec. Cttee, Pilgrims Soc. of Gt Britain, 1967–77 (Pres., 1977–82); Central Council, Royal Commonwealth Soc., 1972–75. Nat. Vice Pres., Royal British Legion. Master of Guild of St Bride's Ch., Fleet St, 1970–78. Seneschal of Canterbury Cathedral, 1973–82. Mem. Ct of Assts, Goldsmiths' Company, 1973– (Prime Warden, 1981–82). High Sheriff 1955–56, DL 1956–62, Sussex; DL 1966, JP 1973, Lord-Lieutenant and Custos Rotulorum, 1972–82, Kent. FRSA 1965. KStJ 1974. *Heir: s* Hon. John Jacob Astor [*b* 16 June 1946; *m* 1970, Fiona Diana, *d* of Captain R. E. L. Harvey; three *d*]. *Address:* 11 Lyall Street, SW1X 8DH; Tillypronie, Tarland, Aberdeenshire. *T:* Tarland 238. *Club:* White's. *Died 28 June 1984.*

**ASTOR, Hon. John;** *b* 26 Sept. 1923; 3rd *s* of 1st Baron Astor of Hever; *m* 1950, Diana Kathleen Drummond (*d* 1982); two *s* one *d; m* 1982, Penelope Eve Rolt (*née* Bradford). *Educ:* Summerfields, Hastings; Eton Coll. RAFVR, 1942–45. Berkshire County Council, 1953–74; Alderman, 1960; Chairman, Education Cttee, 1961–66. Vice-Chm., South Berkshire Conservative Assoc., 1958 until 1963, when adopted as candidate. MP (C) Newbury, 1964–Feb. 1974. *Recreations:* fishing, shooting. *Address:* Kirby House, Inkpen, Berks. *T:* Inkpen 284. *Club:* Royal Yacht Squadron. *Died 27 Dec. 1987.*

**ATHAIDE, Most Rev. Dominic Romuald,** DD; OFMCap; Archbishop of Agra (RC), since 1956; *b* Bandra, India, 7 Feb. 1909. *Educ:* Holland; France; Pontifical Gregorian Univ., Rome. Priest, 1932. Lectr in Philosophy and Theology, Quilon, India, 1937; Missionary, Aden, 1940; subseq. Dir, St Joseph's High Sch. and Parish Priest, Aden. Mem. Order of Friars Minor (Capuchins). Member: Standing Cttee, Catholic Bishops' Conf. of India; CBCI Commn for Dialogue with other faiths. *Address:* Cathedral House, Wazirpura Road, Agra 282003, UP, India. *T:* 7–24–07. *TA:* Cathedral. *Died 26 June 1982.*

**ATHLONE, Countess of; (HRH Princess Alice Mary Victoria Augusta Pauline; Princess Alice, Countess of Athlone),** VA 1898; GCVO 1948; GBE 1937; *b* 25 Feb. 1883; *d* of HRH Prince Leopold George Duncan Albert, 1st Duke of Albany, KG, PC, KT, GCSI, GCMG (4th *s* of Queen Victoria) and HSH Princess Helene Friederike Auguste, VA, CI, RRC (*d* 1922); *m* 1904, Maj.-Gen. the 1st Earl of Athlone, KG, PC, GCB, GCMG, GCVO, DSO, FRS (*d* 1957), 3rd *s* of HH the 1st Duke of Teck, GCB, and brother of HM Queen Mary; one *d* (two *s* decd). Commandant-in-Chief, Women's Transport Service (FANY). Chairman of Governors, Royal Holloway Coll., 1936–Dec. 1958, resigned; Chancellor, Univ. of West Indies, 1950–71. Hon. DLitt: Eton Univ., 1933; Queen's Univ., Kingston, Ont., 1943; McGill Univ., 1944; Birmingham Univ., 1946; Hon. LLD St Andrews Univ., 1951. Hon. Freeman: Weavers' Co., 1947; Vintners' Co., 1956; Royal Borough of Kensington, 1961. DGStJ. Grand Cross, Legion of Honour, France. *Publication:* For My Grandchildren, 1966, repr. 1979. *Address:* Clock House, Kensington Palace, W8. *Died 3 Jan. 1981.*

**ATKINS, Prof. Sir Hedley (John Barnard),** KBE 1967; DM, MCh, FRCS, FRCP: Emeritus Professor of Surgery, University of London; formerly Director of the Department of Surgery, Guy's Hospital; *b* 30 Dec. 1905; *s* of Col Sir John Atkins, KCMG, KCVO, FRCS; *m* 1933, Gladwys Gwendolen, *e d* of Frank Harding Jones; two *s. Educ:* Rugby; Trinity Coll., Oxford; Guy's Hospital. War of 1939–45 (despatches): Temp. Lieut-Col RAMC, 1941. Surgeon to Guy's Hosp., 1936; Hunterian Professor, RCS, 1936; Examiner in Surgery at: Cambridge Univ., 1947; London Univ., 1948; Durham Univ., 1950; Univ. of The W Indies, 1960; Member: Court of Examiners, RCS, 1950, Council, 1952; Gen. Dental Council, 1954; Gen. Medical Council, 1955; Central Health Services Council, 1956; Dean of the Institute of Basic Med. Sciences, 1957–62; Clinical Research Bd, Med. Research Council, 1959; Pres. Surgical Research Soc., 1960. Visiting Professor: Johns Hopkins Hosp., 1947; UCLA, 1954; Univ. of California, 1956; Univ. of Miami, 1972; Sims Commonwealth Travelling Prof., 1961. Lectures: Syme Oration, Brisbane, 1961; Bradshaw, RCS, 1965; Astor, Middlesex Hosp., 1970; Cavendish, W London Med. Chir. Soc., 1970; Gideon de Laune, Soc. of Apothecaries, 1970; Hunterian Orator, RCS, 1971; Macewen, Glasgow, 1972; First Leah Lederman, RSM, 1973; Purvis Oration, 1975. Mem. Med. Advisory Cttee of British Council, 1962; Chm., MRC working party, on Tristan da Cunha, 1962; Mem. Med. Consultative Cttee of Nuffield Provincial Hosps Trust, 1962; Chm., Med. Res. Council Cttee on Uses of High Oxygen Tension, 1963, and on Gastric Hypothermia, 1963; Mem., Med. Research Council, 1963; Thomas Vicary Lecturer, Royal Coll. of Surgeons, 1964; Examr in Surgery, at Birmingham Univ., 1964; Vice-Chm., Standing Med. Adv. Cttee (of Central Health Services Council), 1964; Chairman: (MRC) Cttee on Endolymphatic Therapy, 1965; Jt Bd, Clinical Nursing Studies, 1969–; Med. Bd, St John, 1969. Chm. Council, Queen Elizabeth Coll., Univ. of London, 1969–. President: Med. Soc. of London, 1972; RSM, 1971–72 (Hon. Fellow, 1974; Pres., Section of Measurement in Medicine, 1965); RCS, 1966–69 (Vice-Pres. 1964–66). Governor, Strangeways Research Laboratory, Cambridge, 1968. Hon. FACS, 1956; Hon. FRACS, 1961; Hon. FCS (So. Af.), 1968; Hon. FRCS Glas., 1971; Hon. FRCP&S (Can.) 1969; Hon. FDSRCS 1972; Hon. Fellow: Trinity Coll., Oxford, 1968; Queen Elizabeth Coll., Univ. of London, 1968; Assoc. of Surgeons of GB and Ireland, 1973; American Surgical Assoc., 1966; New England Surgical Soc. Thomas and Edith Dixon Medal, 1965. Hon. DSc: East Anglia, 1968; Kent, 1971. KStJ 1968. *Publications:* After-Treatment, 1942; (author of Biographical introduction) Hilton's Rest and Pain, 1950; (ed) Tools of Biological Research, 1959; The Surgeon's Craft, 1965; Down, the Home of the Darwins, 1974; Memoirs of a Surgeon, 1977; numerous articles in med. jls. *Recreation:* gardening. *Address:* Down House, Downe, Kent BR6 7JT. *Clubs:* Athenæum; Vincent's (Oxford), Harlequins. *Died 26 Nov. 1983.*

**ATKINS, John Spencer,** DSO 1945; TD; DL; President, Atkins Brothers (Hosiery) Ltd; *b* 28 Oct. 1905; 3rd *s* of late Col E. C. Atkins, CB, DL; *m* 1936, Monica Lucy Standish; one *s* two *d. Educ:* Uppingham Sch. DL Leics 1946. *Address:* White House, Ullesthorpe, Lutterworth, Leics. *T:* Leire 209274. *Club:* Naval and Military. *Died 8 Feb. 1987.*

**ATKINS, Sir William Sydney Albert,** Kt 1976; CBE 1966; FEng, FICE, FIStructE; President: W. S. Atkins Ltd, since 1986; Atkins Holdings Ltd, since 1986; *b* 6 Feb. 1902; 2nd *s* of Robert Edward and Martha Atkins; *m* 1928, Elsie Jessie, *d* of Edward and Hilda Barrow, Hockley, Essex; two *d. Educ:* Coopers' Sch.; University Coll., London (BSc; Fellow, 1955). Chief Engr, Smith Walker Ltd, 1928; Founder and Man. Dir, The London Ferro-Concrete Co. Ltd, 1935–50; Founder and Chm., R. E. Eagan Ltd, 1946–50; Founder and Sen. Partner, W. S. Atkins & Partners, 1938–50; Chairman: W. S. Atkins & Partners, 1950–82; W. S. Atkins Group Ltd and associated cos (incorporating W. S. Atkins & Partners), 1970–84; Founder and Partner, Round Pond Nurseries, 1965–. CIMechE; CInstMC; Hon. FInstW; PEng(Ont); FHS. Hon. Freeman, Borough of Epsom and Ewell. *Publications:* many technical papers. *Recreations:* gardening and horticultural research, swimming. *Address:* Chobham Place, Chobham, near Woking, Surrey GU24 8TN. *T:* Chobham 8867. *Died 15 Aug. 1989.*

**ATKINSON, Brooks;** *see* Atkinson, J. B.

**ATKINSON, Sir (John) Kenneth,** Kt 1953; retired as Chief Valuer, Valuation Office, Board of Inland Revenue (1951–66); *b* 21 May 1905; 2nd *s* of late James Oswald and Jane Atkinson, Liverpool; *m* 1930, Ellen Elsie Godwin Dod (*d* 1975); one *d. Educ:* The Leys, Cambridge. Joined Valuation Office, 1928; Deputy Chief Valuer, 1950. Fellow of the Royal Institution of Chartered Surveyors. *Recreation:* Rugby football. *Address:* 38 Clarence Road South, Weston-super-Mare, Avon BS23 4BW. *T:* Weston-super-Mare 623205. *Died* 12 *May* 1989.

**ATKINSON, (Justin) Brooks;** US journalist and writer; retired as Staff Writer, New York Times; *b* Melrose, Massachusetts, USA, 28 Nov. 1894; *s* of Jonathan H. Atkinson and Garafelia Taylor; *m* 1926, Oriana Torrey MacIlveen; one step *d. Educ:* Harvard Univ. (AB). Reporter, Springfield Daily News, 1917; Teacher of English, Dartmouth Coll., 1917–18; Boston Evening Transcript, Reporter and Asst Drama Critic, 1919–22; New York Times, 1922–65: Editor Book Review, 1922–25; Drama Critic, 1925–42; War Correspondent, China, 1942–44; Correspondent in Russia, 1945–46; Drama Critic, 1946–60; retd, 1965. Pulitzer Prize for Journalism, 1947. Hon. LHD Williams College, Mass, 1941; Hon. LLD: Adelphi Coll., NY; Pace Coll., NY, 1961; Franklin and Marshall Coll., 1962; Brandeis Univ., 1965; Clark Univ., 1966; Washington Coll., 1966; Dartmouth Coll., 1975. *Publications:* Skyline Promenades, 1925; Henry Thoreau, the Cosmic Yankee, 1927; East of the Hudson, 1931; Cingalese Prince, 1935; Broadway Scrapbook, 1948; Once Around the Sun, 1951; Tuesdays and Fridays, 1963; Brief Chronicles, 1966; Broadway, 1970; This Bright Land, 1972; (with Al Hirschfeld) The Lively Years, 1973; (ed) Walden and other writings of Henry David Thoreau, 1937; (ed) Complete Essays and other writings of Ralph Waldo Emerson, 1940; (ed) Sean O'Casey Reader, 1968; Sean O'Casey: From Times Past, (critical essays), 1982. *Address:* 2004 Max Luther Drive, Parkview Village, Huntsville, Ala 35810, USA. *Died* 13 *Jan.* 1984.

**ATKINSON, Sir Kenneth;** *see* Atkinson, Sir J. K.

**ATKINSON, Maj.-Gen. Sir Leonard Henry,** KBE 1966 (OBE 1945); *b* 4 Dec. 1910; *s* of A. H. Atkinson; *m* 1939, Jean Eileen, *d* of C. A. Atchley, OBE; one *s* three *d. Educ:* Wellington Coll., Berks; University Coll., London (Fellow, 1977). BSc (Eng) 1932. Satchwell controls, GEC, 1932–36. Commnd in RAOC, 1936; transf. to REME, 1942; Comdr REME (Lieut-Col) Guards Armd Div. (NW Europe), 1943–45; DDEME (Col) Brit. Airborne Corps, India, 1945; Staff Coll., Quetta, 1945–46; served in Far East, UK and WO, 1946–50; JSSC, 1950–51; GSO1, REME Trg Centre, 1951–53; DDEME (Col) HQ 1st Corps (Germany), 1953–55; DDEME (Brig.). WO, 1956–58; Comdt (Brig.) REME Training Centre and Commander Berkshire Dist, 1958–63; Dir (Maj.-Gen.), Electrical and Mechanical Engineering, Army, 1963–66; Col Comdt, REME, 1967–72. Man. Dir, Harland Simon, 1970–72; Director: Harland Engineering, 1966–69; Simon Equipment, 1966–69; Weir Engineering Industries, 1970–74; United Gas Industries, 1972–76; C. & W. Walker Ltd, 1974–77; Bespoke Securities, 1974–82; Emray, 1978–85; Equity & General, 1985–89. Chairman: Christopher Gold Associates, 1976–87; DTI Cttee on Terotechnology, 1970–75; Council of Engineering Instns, 1974–75 (Vice-Chm., 1973); Technology Transfer Associates Ltd, 1980–89; Berks Central Training Ltd (YTS), 1984–88; Vice Chm., Southern Regional Council for Further Educn, 1978–85. Member: Court of Bradford Univ., 1968–76; Court of Cranfield Inst. of Technology, 1975–77; Governor, Reading Coll. of Technology, 1968–85. FIMechE; FIEE; FIGasE; FIERE (past Pres.); FIMI; FRPSL; FRSA; Hon. MIPlantE. Liveryman, 1966–, Master, 1987–88, Turners' Co. *Address:* Fair Oak, Ashford Hill, Newbury RG15 8BJ. *T:* Tadley (0734) 814845. *Club:* Naval and Military.

*Died* 17 *May* 1990.

**ATTENBOROUGH, James,** CMG 1915; TD; Colonel (retired) TF; solicitor; *b* 7 Aug. 1884; *e s* of Stanley J. Attenborough, 30 Clarges Street, Piccadilly; *m* 1915, Phyllis, *d* of late Edwin J. Layton. *Educ:* Rugby. Served European War, 1914–18 (CMG) and War of 1939–45; commanded 9th Batt. Royal Fusiliers (TF) and Halton Camp RAF. *Recreations:* shooting and golf. *Address:* The Old Rectory, Great Mongeham, near Deal, Kent. *Clubs:* East India, Devonshire, Sports and Public Schools; Royal St George's (Sandwich). *Died* 4 *Aug.* 1984.

**AUBREY, Henry M. W.;** *see* Windsor-Aubrey.

**AUCHINLECK, Field-Marshal Sir Claude John Eyre,** GCB 1945 (CB 1934); GCIE 1940; CSI 1936; DSO 1917; OBE 1919; Hon. LLD Aberdeen, 1948; Hon. LLD St Andrews, 1948; Hon. LLD Manchester, 1970; *b* 21 June 1884; *s* of late Col John Claude Auchinleck, RA; *m* 1921, Jessie (from whom he obtained a divorce, 1946), *d* of late Alexander Stewart, of Innerhadden, Kinloch-Rannoch, Perthshire. *Educ:* Wellington Coll.; RMC Sandhurst. 2nd Lieut, Indian Army Unattached List, 1903; joined 62nd Punjabis 1904; served Egypt, 1914–15; Aden, 1915; Mesopotamia, 1916–19; Kurdistan, 1919 (despatches, DSO, Croix de Guerre,

OBE, Brevet Lieut-Col); operations against Upper Mohmands, 1933 (despatches, CB); Mohmand Operations, 1935 (despatches, CSI); Imperial Defence Coll., 1927; commanded 1st Batt. 1st Punjab Regt, 1929–30; Instructor Staff Coll., Quetta, 1930–33; Comdr Peshawar Brigade, India, 1933–36; Dep. Chief of General Staff Army Headquarters, India, 1936–38; Comdr Meerut District, India, 1938; Mem., Expert Cttee on the Defence of India, 1938; GOC-in-C, Northern Norway, 1940; GOC-in-C, Southern Command, 1940; C-in-C in India, 1941 and 1943–47; C-in-C Middle East, 1941–42; ADC Gen. to the King, 1941–46; War Mem. of the Viceroy's Executive Council, 1943–46; Field-Marshal, 1946; Supreme Comdr in India and Pakistan, 1947, under Joint Defence Council; Col of 1st Punjab Regt; Col of the Indian Grenadiers, 1939–47, of the Royal Inniskilling Fusiliers, 1941–47; a Governor of Wellington Coll., 1946–59; Pres., London Federation of Boys' Clubs, 1949–55; Pres. National Small-bore Rifle Association, 1956; a Vice-Pres. Forces Help Soc. and Lord Roberts Workshops; Chm., Armed Forces Art Soc., 1950–67. Virtuti Militari (Poland), 1942; War Cross (Czecho-Slovakia), 1944; Order of Chief Comdr, Legion of Merit (USA), 1945; Order of the Star of Nepal, 1st Class, 1945; Grand Cross of Order of St Olaf (Norway), 1947; 1st Class Order of Cloud and Banner (China), 1947; Grand Officer Legion of Honour; Croix-de-Guerre (France), 1918, 1949. *Recreations:* walking, fishing, sketching. *Address:* Villa Rikichou, rue Hafid Ibrahim, Marrakech, Morocco; c/o Grindlays Bank, 13 St James's Square, SW1. *Clubs:* East India, Devonshire, Sports and Public Schools, Naval and Military, Cavalry, Army and Navy, Norwegian; Karachi Yacht.

*Died* 23 *March* 1981.

**AUCHMUTY, Prof. James Johnston,** CBE 1971; Vice-Chancellor and Principal, University of Newcastle, New South Wales, 1965–74; Professor of History, 1955–74, now Emeritus Professor; *b* Portadown, N Ireland, 29 Nov. 1909; *s* of Canon J. W. Auchmuty, MA; *m* 1934, Margaret (BA (Vassar), Phi Beta Kappa (Mem., Churchill Fellowship Trust Cttee, NSW, 1965–80, Nat. Cttee, 1980–; Pres., Aust. Fedn of Univ. Women, 1974–77), *d* of R. F. Walters, Detroit, USA; one *s* one *d* (and one *s* decd). *Educ:* Armagh Royal Sch.; Trinity Coll., Dublin (Scholar). First Cl. Moderator and Gold Medallist in Hist. and Polit. Science, 1931 (Gold Medallist in Hist., 1930, and Auditor, 1931–32, of College Hist. Soc.); MA 1934, PhD 1935. Lectr in Sch. of Educn, Dublin Univ., 1936–46; Head of Dept of Mod. Hist., Farouk Univ., Alexandria, 1946–52; joined Univ. of NSW, 1952; Dean of Faculty of Humanities and Social Sciences, 1956–59 and Mem. Council, 1959–61; Head of Dept of Arts at Newcastle Univ. Coll., 1954; Warden of the College, 1960–64. Vis. Prof. of Modern Commonwealth Hist., Leeds Univ., 1976–77; Hon. Vis. Fellow, Humanities Res. Centre, ANU, 1975–76. First Chm. of Irish Cttee of Historical Sciences, 1938–44; Mem., Internat. Commn on the Teaching of History, 1938. Chm., Aust. Humanities Research Council, 1962–65; Chm., Aust. Nat. Commn for UNESCO, 1973–76 (Mem., 1962–80); Chm., Aust. Nat. Inquiry into Teacher Educn, 1978–80; Member: Aust. Delegn to 4th Commonwealth Educn Conf., Lagos, 1968; 5th Conf., Canberra, 1971; Aust. Educl Mission to S Pacific, 1970; Chm., Aust. Commonwealth Adv. Cttee on the Teaching of Asian Languages and Cultures, 1969. Chm., Aust. Vice-Chancellors' Cttee, 1969–71; Mem. Council, Assoc. of Commonwealth Univs, 1967–74. FRHistS 1938; MRIA 1941; Foundn Fellow, Aust. Acad. of the Humanities, 1970. Hon. DLitt: Sydney, 1974; Newcastle, NSW, 1974; Hon. LLD Dublin, 1974. Silver Jubilee Medal, 1977. *Publications:* US Government and Latin American Independence 1810–1830, 1937; Irish Education: a historical survey, 1937; Sir Thomas Wyse, 1791–1862, 1939; The Teaching of History, 1940; Lecky, 1946; (ed) The Voyage of Governor Phillip to Botany Bay, 1970; contrib. to: The Australian Dictionary of Biography; The New History of Australia; many papers in historical and other jls. *Recreations:* golf, swimming. *Address:* 9 Glynn Street, Hughes, ACT 2605, Australia. *T:* 815410. *Clubs:* Athenæum; Pioneers (Sydney); Newcastle (NSW); Commonwealth (Canberra).

*Died* 16 *Oct.* 1981.

**AURIC, Georges;** Grand Cross, Legion of Honour, 1981; Commander, Order of Academic Palms; French composer; General Administrator, Paris Opéra and Opéra Comique, 1962–68; *b* Lodève, 15 Feb. 1899; *m* 1930, Nora Vilter. *Educ:* Paris Conservatoire; Schola Cantorum, Paris. Co-founder Les Six movement, 1916. Mem. Acad. des Beaux-Arts, 1962–. Pres., CISAC, 1968–70. *Publications include:* Trois Interludes; Chandelles Romaines; Trio pour Hautbois; *ballet music:* Le Peintre et son Modèle, 1949; Phèdre, 1950; Chemin de Lumière, 1952; Coup de Feu, 1952; Tricolore, 1978; *opera:* Sous le Masque; *music for films:* Le Sang d'un Poète; A Nous la Liberté; Entrée des Artistes; L'Eternel Retour; La Belle et la Bête; La Symphonie Pastorale; Torrents; Ruy Blas; L'Aigle à Deux Têtes; Les Parents Terribles; Maya; Orphée: Caroline Chérie; La P . . . Respectueuse; La Fête à Henriette, etc. *Address:* 36 avenue Matignon, 75008 Paris, France.

*Died* 24 *July* 1983.

**AUSTIN, Sir John (Byron Fraser),** 3rd Bt, *cr* 1894; *b* 14 July 1897; *s* of Sir William Austin, 2nd Bt, and Violet Irene (*d* 1962), *d* of Alex.

Fraser, Westerfield House, near Ipswich; *S* father, 1940; *m* 1st, 1953, Sheila McNaught (marr. diss., 1958); 2nd, 1960, Rhoda Noreen Rose, *widow of* Col C. V. D. Rose. *Educ:* Downside; Royal Military Coll., Sandhurst. Late Lieut 7th Hussars; Major Indian Army; retired, 1935; served with Somaliland Camel Corps and King's African Rifles, Tanganyika; European War, 1915–18, as Flight-Comdr RFC and RAF; served War of 1939–45, Lieut-Col Comdg Bn (despatches). Director: St Anthonys Properties Ltd; Austin Properties Ltd. *Heir: b* William Ronald Austin [*b* 20 July 1900; *m* 1st, 1926, Dorothy Mary (*d* 1957), *d* of late L. A. Bidwell, FRCS; two *s*; 2nd, 1958, Mary Helen Farrell]. *Address:* Pax, St George's Lane, Hurstpierpoint, Sussex. *Club:* Royal Air Force.
*Died 23 Sept.* 1981.

**AUSTIN, Dame (Mary) Valerie (Hall),** DBE 1979 (OBE 1952); JP; *b* London, 29 July 1900; *d* of Admiral Percival Henry Hall Thompson, CB, CMG, RN, and Helen Sydney Hall Thompson (*née* Deacon); *m* 1925, Ronald Albert Austin, MC; one *s. Educ:* Marsden College, New Zealand. Travelled with father, etc, to Australia, New Zealand, Malta, England; married Australia; lived on land at Eilyer, Mortlake, Vic. Vice Pres., Liberal Party, Victoria, 1947–76; Hon. Life Member: Red Cross, Australia, 1979 (Mem., 1936–); Victoria League; Victorian Family Council. Coronation Medal, 1953. *Address:* 255 Domain Road, South Yarra, Victoria 3141, Australia. *Clubs:* Alexandra (Melbourne); Barwon Heads Golf.
*Died 10 Sept.* 1986.

**AUSTIN, Richard,** FRCM; Professor, 1946–76, Director of Opera, 1955–76, Royal College of Music; *b* 26 Dec. 1903; *s* of Frederic and Amy Austin; *m* 1935, Leily, *y d* of Col Wilfred Howell, CBE, DSO. *Educ:* Gresham's Sch., Holt; RCM; Munich. Conductor, Carl Rosa Opera Co., 1929; Musical Dir of the Bournemouth Corporation, 1934–40; Music Advisor Northern Command, 1941–45; Music Dir, New Era Concert Soc., 1947–57. Guest Conductor: Sadler's Wells, London and provincial orchestras, Holland, Belgium, Germany, Spain, Sweden, Switzerland, Finland, Yugoslavia, Czechoslovakia, Cuba, Mexico, South Africa, South America and USA. *Recreations:* squash, tennis. *Address:* Stubbles, Ashampstead, Berks. *T:* Compton 565. *Club:* Savage. *Died* 1 *April* 1989.

**AUSTIN, Sumner Francis,** MA Oxon; Hon. FGSM; late Technical Director, Sadler's Wells Opera, London; late Captain Intelligence Corps; *b* Anerley, Kent, 24 Sept. 1888; *s* of late Ware Plumtre Austin, ICS, and Frances Laura Greenaway; *m* 1921, Dorothy Stirling (*née* Blackwell) (*d* 1979). *Educ:* Bexhill; Magdalen Coll. Sch.; St John's Coll., Oxford. Studied for Indian Forest Service; studied singing and music, Dresden, Germany, 1910–14; first engagement, Royal Theatre, Potsdam; interned Prisoner of War, Ruhleben, 1914–18; Carl Rosa Opera Co., 1919; Surrey Theatre, 1920; Old Vic and later Sadler's Wells, 1919–; recitals in Holland, Berlin, London, and provinces, BBC, and various Choral Societies; Scarborough Open Air Production, 1935; Covent Garden, 1952, 1955, etc; numerous productions. *Publications:* translations from the Italian, French and German. *Address:* Clarendon Cottage, 43 Park Town, Oxford OX2 6SL. *Died* 9 *July* 1981.

**AUSTIN, Thomas Aitken,** CMG 1949; LRCP, LRCS, LM (Ireland); DTM&H (Liverpool); DPH (Dublin); late Public Health Officer for East and Central Africa, UN World Health Organisation; *b* 1895. *Educ:* Derry Church Sch.; Royal Coll. of Surgeons, Dublin. Storey Memorial Gold Medal (Anatomy), De Renzy Centenary Prize, 1st place 1st class honours DPH, Royal Coll. of Surgeons, Dublin. Served War of 1939–45, 1939–40; Major. Appointed Zanzibar Protectorate, 1924; Nyasa, 1930; SMO, Tanganyika Territory, 1939; DMS: Nyasa, 1943; Uganda, 1946; PMO, Colonial Office, 1949. *Address:* 38 Sycamore Road, Mount Merrion, Blackrock, Co. Dublin. *Died* 12 *April* 1982.

**AUSTIN, Dame Valerie;** *see* Austin, Dame M. V. H.

**AUSTIN, Sir William (Ronald),** 4th Bt *cr* 1894; *b* 20 July 1900; *s* of Sir William Michael Byron Austin, 2nd Bt, and Violet Irene (*d* 1962), *d* of Alexander Fraser, Westerfield House, near Ipswich; *S* brother, 1981; *m* 1st, 1926, Dorothy Mary (*d* 1957), *d* of late L. A. Bidwell, FRCS; two *s*; 2nd, 1958, Mary Helen Farrell. *Heir: s* Michael Trescawen Austin [*b* 27 Aug. 1927; *m* 1951, Bridget Dorothea Patricia, *d* of late Francis Farrell; three *d*]. *Address:* Creagan, Appin, Argyll. *T:* Appin 213. *Died* 16 *March* 1989.

**AUSWILD, Sir James (Frederick John),** Kt 1974; CBE 1970; FCA, FAIM; Chartered Accountant and Company Director, Australia; Commissioner of Rural Bank of New South Wales (now State Bank of New South Wales), 1961–81; *b* Canbelego, 12 April 1908; *s* of late James Auswild, Temora, and Janet Caroline Auswild (*née* Starr); *m* 1933, Kathleen, *d* of late M. Conway, Lake Cargelligo; two *d. Educ:* Temora High Sch. Principal of James F. J. Auswild & Co., Business Consultants and Chartered Accountants, 1930–. Supervisor, Rural Reconstr. Bd, 1932–39. Mem., Advanced Educn Bd, NSW, 1969–74. Past Dir: Skandia Aust. Insurance Ltd, 1966–74; Glass Togheners Pty Ltd, 1967–70. Governing Dir,

Auswild Org., embracing 130 associated cos; Chairman, Austwide Corp. Pty Ltd and many private cos; Jt Chm. and Managing Dir, Preston Motors Holdings Ltd and Subsidiary Cos. Director: Boyded Pty Ltd; C. V. Holland Pty Ltd; Finance & Guarantee Co. Ltd; Rossfield House Pty Ltd; Auswild Securities Pty Ltd; Embassy Motel, Statesman Hotel Pty Ltd, Canberra; ACT Motors Pty Ltd; Holden Dealers, Canberra; Ambassador Hotel, Canberra; Cooma-Monaro Express Pty Ltd; Canberra Publishing & Printing Co. Pty Ltd; J. F. J. Auswild (Holdings) Pty Ltd; Auswild Properties Pty Ltd; Denman Estate Wines Pty Ltd; Fellow of Local Govt Auditors' Assoc. (FLGA), Aust. *Recreation:* yachting. *Address:* 609 New South Head Road, Rose Bay, Sydney, NSW 2029, Australia. *T:* 36.1711. *Clubs:* American National, Tattersall's, RMYC, CYC, AJC, STC (Sydney); Athenaeum (Melbourne).
*Died 28 May* 1985.

**AVERILL, Leslie Cecil Lloyd,** CMG 1961; MC 1918; MD; FRCSE; FRCOG; Specialist in Obstetrics and Gynaecology, Christchurch, NZ, 1934–68; Chairman, North Canterbury Hospital Board, NZ, 1956–74; *b* 25 March 1897; 2nd *s* of late Most Rev. A. W. Averill, CMG, DD (Oxon) (Archbp of NZ, 1925–40); *m* 1925, Isabel Mary Wilkie Roberton, *o d* of Ernest Roberton, MD, Auckland; two *s* two *d. Educ:* Christ's Coll., Christchurch, NZ; Univ. of Edinburgh (medical). War Service with NZ Rifle Brigade: Lieut, France (MC), 1917–19. General medical practice, Christchurch, NZ, 1925–34. Pres. BMA (NZ), 1951–52; Chm. NZ Regional Council, Royal Coll. of Obstetricians and Gynaecologists, 1951–55. Chm., Christchurch Clinical Sch. Council, 1972–74. Pres., NZ Rifle Brigade Assoc., 1972–79. Citoyen d'Honneur, Le Quesnoy, France, 1968 (Bronze medal), 1975 (Silver medal), 1977 (Gold medal); Chevalier de la Légion d'Honneur, 1973. *Publications:* History of St George's Hospital, Christchurch, 1978; articles in medical journals. *Recreations:* golf, horticulture. *Address:* 41 Wairarapa Terrace, Christchurch 1, New Zealand. *T:* 557751. *Club:* Christchurch (NZ). *Died* 4 *June* 1981.

**AVERY, David Robert,** OBE 1976; HM Diplomatic Service, retired; *b* 20 Oct. 1921; *o s* of late Percival John Avery and of Mary Woodcock Avery; *m* 1948, Vera Andrews; one *s* one *d. Educ:* Plympton Grammar Sch., Devonport; Dockyard Technical Coll. Admiralty service in Sierra Leone, India and Ceylon, 1939–59. Lieut RNVR, 1943. Commonwealth Relations Office, 1960; First Secretary, Lagos, Nigeria, 1963–65; Consul, Basra, Iraq, 1966; FCO, 1967–71; First Sec., Nairobi, Kenya, 1972–76; FCO, 1976; Counsellor and Head of Claims Dept, FCO, 1978–80. *Recreations:* gardening, shooting. *Address:* Little Acre, 1 Woodland Way, Kingsgate, Broadstairs, Kent CT10 3QD. *T:* Thanet 602400. *Club:* Nairobi (Kenya). *Died 20 June* 1983.

**AVES, Dame Geraldine (Maitland),** DBE 1977 (CBE 1963; OBE 1946); *b* 22 Aug. 1898; *er d* of Ernest Aves, MA, FSS, and Eva Mary (*née* Maitland). *Educ:* Frognal Sch., Hampstead; Newnham Coll., Cambridge (MA; Hon. Fellow, 1981). Education Dept, LCC: Sch. Care Organiser, 1924–38; assisting planning and develt of war-time evacuation services, 1938–41; Ministry of Health, Chief Welfare Officer and Head of Welfare Divn, 1941–63. Seconded: to UNRRA as Chief Child Care Consultant (Europe), 1945–46; to Home Office, to initiate child care training, 1947–48; various assignments to UN Headqrs, in field of family and child welfare and to direct UN Seminars for European Region, 1949–69. Governor, Nat. Inst. for Social Work Training, 1961–71; Mem. Council for Training in Social Work, 1962–72; Associate Fellow, Newnham Coll., 1962–65 and 1966–69. Chairman: Adv. Council of Nat. Corp. for the Care of Old People, 1965–72; Cttee of Enquiry into Voluntary Workers in the Social Services, 1966–69 (Report: The Voluntary Worker in the Social Services, 1969); N Islington Welfare Centre, 1977–81 (Vice-Pres., 1981-). Pres., Newnham College Roll, 1969–72. Mem., London Diocesan Synod and Bishop's Council, 1971–79; Vice-Chm., London Diocesan Bd for Social Responsibility, 1979–86; Founder Mem., Governing Body, The Volunteer Centre, 1973– (Vice-Pres., 1977-); Chairman: Working Party that produced PIVOT (People Involved in Volunteer Organisation and Tasks), published 1976; Bd of Dirs, The Harington Scheme (horticultural trng centre for mentally handicapped young people), 1980–85 (Vice-Pres., 1986-; Chm., Prep. Cttee, 1977); President: Highgate Cemetery Trust, 1981– (Chm., 1977–81); N London Hospice Gp, 1984-; has served on several local environmental and parochial organisations. *Recreation:* birdwatching. *Address:* 24 North Grove, Highgate Village, N6 4SL. *T:* 01–340 1685.
*Died 23 June* 1986.

**AVGHERINOS, George,** QC 1982; *b* Poti, Georgia, Caucasus, 6 Jan. 1906; *s* of Homer and Eftichia Avgherinos; *m* 1944, Beatrice Eleanor, *d* of Oscar and Mabel Siewert; one *s. Educ:* St Paul's School; Brasenose Coll., Oxford. MA, BCL. Served RAF, 1941–46, Administration. Harmsworth Scholarship, Middle Temple, 1929; called to the Bar, Middle Temple, 1932; Barstow Scholarship, 1932; Bencher, Middle Temple, 1964. *Publications:* (ed jtly) Landlord and Tenant Act 1927, 3rd edn 1949; (jtly) Leasehold Property

(Temporary Provisions) Act 1951, 1951; (jtly) Housing Repairs and Rents Act 1954, 1954; (ed jtly) Rent and Mortgage Interest Restrictions, 23rd edn, 1956. *Recreations:* music, braille. *Address:* Flat 5, 1 Linden Gardens, W2 4HA. *Died* 16 *Sept.* 1989.

**AVON**, 2nd Earl of, *cr* 1961; **Nicholas Eden**, OBE 1970; TD 1965; DL; *b* 3 Oct. 1930; *o* surv. *s* of 1st Earl of Avon, KG, PC, MC, and Beatrice Helen (*d* 1957), *d* of Hon. Sir Gervase Beckett, 1st Bt; *S* father, 1977. *Educ:* Eton. Served with KRRC, 1949-51; ADC to the Governor-Gen. of Canada, 1952-53; served in Queen Victoria's Rifles (TA), 1953-61; on amalgamation, served in Queen's Royal Rifles (TA), 1961-67; 4th (Volunteer) Bn, Royal Green Jackets, 1967-70; Major, 1959; Lt-Col, 1965; Col, TAVR, 1972-75; Hon. Col. ACF, NE Sector Greater London, 1970; Vice-Chm., Greater London TA&VRA, 1976-81. ADC (TA) to the Queen, 1978-82. An Opposition Whip, 1978-79; a Lord in Waiting (Govt Whip), and spokesman for arts, envt and transport, 1980-83; Parliamentary Under-Secretary of State: Dept of Energy, 1983-84; DoE, 1984-85; Parly deleg. to N Atlantic Assembly, 1979-80. Master, Salters' Co., 1979-80. DL Greater London, 1973. *Address:* House of Lords, SW1. *Club:* All England Lawn Tennis. *Died* 17 *Aug.* 1985 (*ext*).

**AYER, Sir Alfred (Jules)**, Kt 1970; FBA 1952; Wykeham Professor of Logic in the University of Oxford, and Fellow of New College, Oxford, 1959-78, Hon. Fellow, 1980; Fellow of Wolfson College, Oxford, 1978-83; *b* 29 Oct. 1910; *s* of late Jules Louis Cyprien Ayer; *m* 1st, 1932, Grace Isabel Renée Lees; one *s* one *d*; 2nd, 1960, Alberta Constance Chapman, (Dee Wells) (marr. diss. 1983); one *s*; 3rd, 1983, Vanessa Mary Addison Lawson (*née* Salmon) (*d* 1985). *Educ:* Eton Coll. (scholar); Christ Church, Oxford (scholar; Hon. Student, 1979). 1st class Lit. Hum. 1932; MA 1936; Lecturer in Philosophy at Christ Church, 1932-35; Research Student, 1935-44; Fellow of Wadham Coll., Oxford, 1944-46, Hon. Fellow, 1957; Dean, 1945-46; Grote Professor of the Philosophy of Mind and Logic, 1946-59, and Dean of the Arts Faculty, UCL, 1950-52, Univ. of London; Hon. Fellow, UCL, 1979. Visiting Prof. at: NY Univ., 1948-49; City Coll., New York, 1961-62; Surrey Univ., 1978-84; Bard Coll., NY, 1986-; Lectures: William James, Harvard, 1970; John Dewey, Columbia, 1970; Gifford, St Andrews, 1972-73; Montgomery Fellow, Dartmouth Coll., 1982-83. Mem., Central Advisory Council for Education, 1963-66; President: Independent (formerly Agnostics) Adoption Soc., 1965-85; Humanist Assoc., 1965-70; Modern Languages Assoc., 1966-67; Internat. Inst. of Philosophy, 1968-71. Chm., Booker Prize Cttee, 1978. Hon. Mem. Amer. Acad. of Arts and Sciences 1963; For. Mem., Royal Danish Acad. of Sciences and Letters, 1976. Dr *hc* Univ. of Brussels, 1962; Hon. DLitt: East Anglia, 1972; London, 1978; Trent, Ontario, 1980; Durham, 1986; Hon. DHL Bard Coll., 1983. Chevalier de la Légion d'Honneur, 1977; Order of Cyril and Methodius, 1st cl. (Bulgaria), 1977. Enlisted in Welsh Guards, 1940; commissioned, 1940; Capt. 1943. Attaché at HM Embassy, Paris, 1945. *Publications:* Language, Truth and Logic, 1936 (revised edn 1946); The Foundations of Empirical Knowledge, 1940; Thinking and Meaning (Inaugural Lecture), 1947; (ed with Raymond Winch) British Empirical Philosophers, 1952; Philosophical Essays, 1954; The Problem of Knowledge, 1956; (ed) Logical Positivism, 1959; Privacy (British Academy lecture), 1960; Philosophy and Language (Inaugural lecture), 1960; The Concept of a Person and Other Essays, 1963; Man as a Subject for Science (Auguste Comte Lecture), 1964; The Origins of Pragmatism, 1968; (ed) The Humanist Outlook, 1968; Metaphysics and Common Sense, 1969; Russell and

Moore: the analytical heritage, 1971; Probability and Evidence, 1972; Russell, 1972; Bertrand Russell as a Philosopher (British Acad. Lecture), 1973; The Central Questions of Philosophy, 1974; Part of my Life, 1977; Perception and Identity (Festschrift with reply to critics), 1979; Hume, 1980; Philosophy in the Twentieth Century, 1982; More of my Life, 1984; Freedom and Morality and Other Essays, 1984; Wittgenstein, 1985; Voltaire, 1986; Thomas Paine, 1988; articles in philos. and lit. jls; *posthumous publication:* The Meaning of Life and Other Essays, 1990. *Address:* 51 York Street, W1H 1PU. *T:* 01-402 0235; La Migoua, 83330 Le Beausset, Var, France. *T:* 94902433. *Clubs:* Athenæum, Beefsteak, Garrick. *Died* 27 *June* 1989.

**AYERS, Herbert Wilfred**, CB 1951; CBE 1948; retired; Under Secretary for Finance and Accountant-General, Ministry of National Insurance, 1948-53; *b* 22 May 1889; *s* of Joseph Drake Ayers; *m* Ethel M. Pitcher (decd); two *s*. Entered Civil Service, 1905; Ministry of Labour, 1913-44; joined Ministry of National Insurance, Dec. 1944 (Deputy Accountant-General). *Recreation:* philately. *Address:* 3158 Mallbridge Crescent, Malton, Ontario L4T 2C6, Canada. *Died* 27 *June* 1986.

**AYLMER**, 12th Baron *cr* 1718; **Hugh Yates Aylmer**; Bt 1662; retired; *b* 5 Feb. 1907; *s* of Arthur Lovell Aylmer (*d* 1961) and Georgina Henrietta Emmeline (*d* 1936), *d* of Lt-Col J. F. Sweeny; *S* kinsman, 1977; *m* 1939, Althea, *e d* of late Lt-Col John Talbot; one *d*. *Educ:* Minneapolis, Minnesota, USA. General business career; sales, purchasing and management; retired, 1971. *Recreations:* badminton, fishing, hunting and varied outdoor sports. *Heir:* cousin Michael Anthony Aylmer [*b* 27 March 1923; *m* 1950, Countess Maddalena Sofia Maria Gabriella Cecilia Stefania Francesca, *d* of late Count Arbeno Attems di Santa Croce; one *s* one *d*]. *Address:* 601-1159 Beach Drive, Victoria, BC V8S 2N2, Canada. *Died* 6 *Dec.* 1982.

**AYLMER, Sir Fenton Gerald**, 15th Bt, *cr* 1622; *b* 12 March 1901; *s* of Sir Gerald Evans-Freke Aylmer, 14th Bt, and Mabel Howard, *d* of late Hon. J. K. Ward, MLC, Province of Quebec; *S* father, 1939; *m* 1928, Rosalind Boultbee, *d* of J. Percival Bell, Hamilton, Ont; one *s* one *d*. *Educ:* Lower Canada Coll., Montreal; Bishop's Coll. Sch., Lennoxville. *Heir:* *s* Richard John Aylmer [*b* 23 April 1937; *m* 1962, Lise Demers; one *s* one *d*]. *Died* 16 *Oct.* 1987.

**AYNSLEY, George Ayton**, CMG 1956; CBE 1949; *b* 2 May 1896; *e s* of George Morrison Thomas Aynsley and Annie Sarah Jones Aynsley (*née* Ayton); *m* 1920, Margaret Studdy Oliver; one *d*. *Educ:* Rutherford Coll., Newcastle upon Tyne. Colonial Office, 1912-13; Crown Agents for Colonies, 1913-15; joined London Scottish, 1915; served France, Balkans, Egypt and Palestine, 1916-19; Min. of Pensions, 1919-20; Mercantile Marine Dept, Bd of Trade, 1920-23; Customs and Excise, 1923-39; Establishment Officer, Min. of Information, 1939-44; recruited personnel for Allied Commission in Austria, and Control Commission for Germany, 1944-45; administration of Commissions under War Office, 1945, Control Office for Germany and Austria, 1946-47, and Foreign Office, 1947. Head of Personnel Dept, Foreign Office (German Section), 1947-56; Establishment Officer, British Council for Aid to Refugees (Hungarian Dept), 1956-57 (reception and administration of refugees from Hungary). Coronation Medal, 1953. *Recreations:* golf, bowls. *Address:* 9 The Grove, St Margarets, Twickenham, Middlesex. *T:* 01-892 8556. *Died* 14 *Sept.* 1981.

# B

**BABINGTON, Ven. Richard Hamilton;** Archdeacon of Exeter and Canon Residentiary of Exeter Cathedral, 1958–70, Archdeacon Emeritus, 1970; Treasurer of Exeter Cathedral, 1962–70; retired; *b* 30 Nov. 1901; *s* of Very Rev. R. Babington; *m* 1926, Evelyn Ruth Montgomery; two *s* two *d*. *Educ:* Malvern; Keble Coll., Oxford. Curate of Banstead, 1925; Vicar of West End, Southampton, 1929; Vicar of St Mary-le-Tower, Ipswich, 1942; Hon. Canon of St Edmundsbury, 1947. *Recreations:* gardening, trout fishing. *Address:* 2 Beauvale Close, Ottery St Mary, Devon EX11 1AA.
*Died 9 June 1984.*

**BABINGTON SMITH, Michael James,** CBE 1945; Chairman, London Committee of Ottoman Bank, 1975–82; Director of other companies; Brigadier R of O (TA); *b* 20 March 1901; *e s* of Sir Henry Babington Smith, GBE, KCB, CH, and Lady Elisabeth Mary Bruce; *m* 1943, Jean Mary Meade, *yr d* of late Admiral Hon. Sir Herbert Meade-Fetherstonhaugh, GCVO, CB, DSO; one *s* two *d*. *Educ:* Eton; Trinity Coll., Cambridge. Dir of Finance, SHAEF, 1943–45. Dep. Chm., Glyn, Mills & Co., 1947–63; Director: Bank of England, 1949–69; Bank for International Settlements, 1965–74; Compagnie Financière de Suez, 1957–74. Sheriff of London, 1953 and 1962. *Recreation:* sketching. *Address:* Flat 6, 20 Embankment Gardens, SW3 4LW. *T:* 01–352 2854. *Club:* Brooks's.
*Died 26 Oct. 1984.*

**BACK, Ronald Eric George,** CBE 1985; Corporate Director, British Telecom, retired; *b* 20 April 1926; *s* of George Ernest Back and Margery A. (*née* Stupples); *m* 1949, Beryl Gladys Clark. *Educ:* Ashford Grammar School; Northampton Polytechnic. CEng; FIEE; CBIM. Joined Post Office as engineering trainee, 1942; Asst Engineer on plant protection, 1949; Exec. Engineer, civil engineering projects, 1951–60; Sen. Exec. Engineer, microwave link provision, 1960–65; Asst Staff Engineer and Staff Engineer, Satellite Earth Station design and provision, 1965–72; Dep. Dir Engineering, Network Planning, 1972–76; Dir, Service Dept, 1976–79; Sen. Dir, Network, 1979–82; Asst Man. Dir, Nat. Network, 1982–83; Corporate Dir, British Telecom, 1983. FRSA. *Recreations:* breeding and exhibiting Airedale terriers (International Judge). *Address:* High Oaks, Lamberhurst, Kent TN3 8EP. *T:* Lamberhurst 890317. *Clubs:* Reform, Kennel.
*Died 25 June 1989.*

**BACON, Sir Edmund (Castell),** 13th Bt of Redgrave, *cr* 1611, and 14th Bt of Mildenhall, *cr* 1627; KG 1970; KBE 1965 (OBE 1945); TD; JP; Premier Baronet of England; Lord-Lieutenant of Norfolk, 1949–78; Church Commissioner, 1955–63; *b* 18 March 1903; *s* of Sir Nicholas Henry Bacon, 12th and 13th Bt, and Constance Alice, CBE (*d* 1962), *y d* of late A. S. Leslie Melville; *S* father 1947; *m* 1936, Priscilla Dora, *d* of Col Sir Charles Ponsonby, 1st Bt, TD, and of Hon. Winifred Gibbs, *d* of 1st Baron Hunsdon; one *s* four *d*. *Educ:* Eton Coll.; Trinity Coll., Cambridge. Served War of 1939–45, Lieut-Col commanding 55 (Suffolk Yeomanry) Anti-tank Regt RA, 1940–44, Normandy and Belgium 1944 (despatches, OBE). Hon. Col, RA (TA), 1947–67, Chairman: British Sugar Corp., Ltd, 1957–68; Agricultural EDC, 1966–71; Dir, Lloyds Bank, 1949–73. Pro-Chancellor, Univ. of East Anglia, 1964–73. High Steward: of Norwich Cathedral, 1956–79; of Great Yarmouth, 1968–. JP Norfolk. Hon. DCL East Anglia, 1969. *Heir:* *s* Nicholas Hickman Ponsonby Bacon [*b* 17 May 1953; *m* 1981, Susan, *d* of Raymond Dinnis, Edenbridge, Kent. *Educ:* Eton; Dundee Univ. (MA). Barrister-at-Law, Gray's Inn]. *Address:* Raveningham Hall, Norwich. *T:* Raveningham 206; Ash Villa, Morton Terrace, Gainsborough, Lincs. *T:* Gainsborough 2898. *Clubs:* Carlton, Pratt's.
*Died 30 Sept. 1982.*

**BACON, Sir Ranulph Robert Maunsell,** Kt 1966; KPM 1953; Consultant, International Intelligence Inc., USA, 1981–86 (Director, 1970–81); *b* 6 Aug. 1906; *s* of late Arthur Ranulph and Hester Mary (*née* Ayles), Westgate-on-Sea; *m* 1932, Alfreda Violet (*née* Annett) (*d* 1984); one *d* decd. *Educ:* Tonbridge Sch; Queens' Coll., Cambridge (BA). Joined Metropolitan Police, 1928; Metropolitan Police Coll., 1935 (Baton of Honour); seconded to Provost Service, 1940; Capt. 1940, Major 1941, Lieut-Col 1941; all service was in Middle East; Dep. Provost Marshal, Ninth Army, 1942; seconded to Colonial Police Service, 1943; Dep. Inspector-Gen., 1943, Inspector-Gen., 1944–47, Ceylon Police; Chief Constable of Devon, 1947–61; Asst Comr, Met. Police, 1961–66; Dep. Comr New Scotland Yard, 1966. Dir, Securicor Ltd, 1966–81. Mem., Gaming Board, 1968–75. President: Gun Trade Assoc., 1972–77; Shooting Sports Trust, 1972–77. CStJ 1964. *Address:* 3 Royal Court, 8 King's Gardens, Hove, Sussex BN3 2PF. *T:* Brighton 732396. *Club:* United Oxford & Cambridge University.
*Died 30 March 1988.*

**BADDELEY, Hermione;** actress; *b* Broseley, Shropshire, 13 Nov. 1908; *d* of late W. H. Clinton-Baddeley and Louise Bourdin; *m* 1st, 1928, Hon. David Tennant (marr. diss., 1939); one *s* one *d*; 2nd, Captain J. H. Willis, MC. *Educ:* privately. Appeared on London stage in La Boîte à Joujoux, Court Theatre, 1918; Makebelieve,

Lyric, Hammersmith, 1920; West End parts; early success as Florrie Small in The Likes of Her, St Martin's, 1923; Punchbowl revue, Palace, 1924; joined the Co-Optimists, London Pavilion, 1925; continuous appearances in West End theatres in varied plays, including The Greeks had a Word for It; Nine Sharp; Rise Above It; Sky High; Brighton Rock; one and a half years entertaining the troops; A La Carte; Grand National Night; Fallen Angels; Far East and Middle East tour in Cabaret, 1955–56; A Taste of Honey, US tour, 1961–62; The Milk Train Doesn't Stop Here Any More, (New York) 1963; The Killing of Sister George, St Martin's, 1966; The Threepenny Opera, Prince of Wales, 1972. Debut in Commercial Television, 1956; constant appearances in films and TV, 1957–61. *US TV:* Julia (Golden Globe Award, 1976); Mrs Naugutuck in Maude (comedy series) (Emmy nomination, 1976). *Films include:* Caste; Kipps; It Always Rains on Sunday; Brighton Rock; No Room at the Inn; Quartet; Passport to Pimlico; Scrooge; The Belles of St Trinian's; Midnight Lace; Room at the Top (Oscar nomination); Mary Poppins; The Unsinkable Molly Brown; Marriage on the Rocks; Harlow; Do Not Disturb; The Black Windmill. *Recreations:* swimming, reading, entertaining. *Address:* c/o Peter Campbell, Leading Players Management Ltd, 31 Kings Road, SW3. *T:* 01–730 9411.
*Died 19 Aug. 1986.*

**BADEL, Alan;** actor; *b* 11 Sept. 1923; *s* of Auguste Firman Joseph Badel and Elizabeth Olive Durose; *m* Yvonne Owen; one *d*. *Educ:* Burnage High Sch., Manchester; Royal Acad. of Dramatic Art (Bancroft Gold Medallist). First London appearance as Pierrot in L'Enfant Prodigue, Mercury, 1941; Lennox and 1st Murderer in Macbeth, Piccadilly, 1941. Served with 6th Airborne Div., 1942–47 (appearing with Army Play Unit in Egypt, ME, and Germany). Stevie in Peace in Our Time, Lyric, 1947; Sandman in Frenzy, St Martins (and tour), 1948; Stratford-on-Avon, 1950; Claudio in Measure for Measure, Octavius in Julius Caesar, the Fool in King Lear, and others; Stratford Fest. Season, 1951: parts incl.: The Dauphin in Henry V, Ariel in The Tempest, Justice Shallow and Poins in Henry IV Parts I and II; Old Vic Seasons, 1951–53: Quince in A Midsummer Night's Dream, Romeo, François Villon in The Other Heart; Stratford, 1956: Hamlet, Berowne in Love's Labour's Lost, Lucio in Measure for Measure; Tinville in The Public Prosecutor (which he also directed), Arts, 1957; Kreton in Visit to a Small Planet, Alex in The Life of the Party, 1960, Hero in The Rehearsal, Globe, 1961 (first NY appearance in same part, 1963); John Tanner in Man and Superman, New Arts, 1965; Kean, Globe, 1971. Entered management (with Lord Furness), 1957, as Furndel Productions Ltd, and presented: Ulysses Nighttown (played Stephen Dedalus), Arts 1959 (again, in Paris and Holland); The Ark, 1959; Visit to a Small Planet, and others, 1960. *Films include:* Bitter Harvest, Children of the Damned, 1964; Arabesque, 1966; This Sporting Life, 1968; Otley, 1969; Day of the Jackal, Luther, 1975; *television series include:* Pride and Prejudice; The Count of Monte Cristo, 1975; The Woman in White, 1982. *Address:* c/o ICM, 22 Grafton Street, W1.
*Died 19 March 1982.*

**BADER, Group Captain Sir Douglas (Robert Steuart),** Kt 1976; CBE 1956; DSO 1940; DFC 1940; FRAeS; DL; *b* 21 Feb. 1910; *s* of Frederick Roberts Bader and Jessie Scott-Mackenzie; *m* 1st, 1933, Olive Thelma Exley Edwards (*d* 1971); no *c*; 2nd, 1973, Mrs Joan Eileen Murray. *Educ:* St Edward's Sch., Oxford; RAF Coll., Cranwell. Commissioned 1930. Lost both legs in flying accident, Dec. 1931; invalided out of RAF, May 1933; joined Asiatic Petroleum Co. Ltd; re-joined RAF as Flying Officer, Nov. 1939; Flight Lieut April 1940; fought first action during evacuation of BEF from Dunkirk May–June 1940: Squadron Leader, June 1940, commanding first RAF Canadian Fighter Squadron (242); Wing Comdr, March 1941; captured 9 Aug. 1941, after collision with enemy aircraft over Bethune; released 15 April 1945 by American 1st Army from Colditz, near Leipzig (despatches thrice, DSO and Bar, DFC and Bar, Légion d'Honneur, Croix de Guerre); Group Capt. June 1945; retired 1946; rejoined Shell Petroleum Co. (late Asiatic Petroleum Co.); Man. Dir, Shell Aircraft Ltd, 1958–69, retd. Led first post-war Battle of Britain fly-past, 15 Sept. 1945. Mem., Civil Aviation Authority, 1972–78; Chm., Flight Time Limitations Bd, 1974–78. FRAeS 1976. Hon. DSc New Univ. of Ulster, 1976. DL Greater London, 1977. *Publication:* Fight for the Sky: the story of the Spitfire and the Hurricane, 1973; *relevant publication:* biography, Reach for the Sky, by Paul Brickhill. *Recreation:* golf. *Address:* 5 Petersham Mews, Gloucester Road, SW7 5NR. *T:* 01–584 0902. *Clubs:* Buck's, Royal Air Force.
*Died 4 Sept. 1982.*

**BADMIN, Stanley Roy,** RE 1935 (ARE 1931); (Hon. retired 1965); RWS 1939 (ARWS 1932); ARCA 1927; *b* Sydenham, 18 April 1906; 2nd *s* of Charles James and Margaret Badmin, Somersetshire; *m* 1st, 1929; one *s* one *d*; 2nd, 1950, Mrs Rosaline Flew, widow of Dr R. Flew; one *d* one step-*d*. *Educ:* private tutor; Royal College of Art. One man exhibitions: Twenty One Gall., London, 1930; Fine Art Soc., 1933, 1937; MacDonald's Gall., NY, 1936; Leicester Gall., 1955; Worthing Art Gall., 1967; (retrospective), Chris Beetles Gall., London, 1985, 1987; works bought by Liverpool, Manchester,

Huddersfield, Bradford, Birmingham, V & A Museum, Chicago Inst. of Art, South London Galleries, Newport, Ashmolean, Worthing, Boston Museum, London Museum, NY Metropolitan Museum, Derby, etc. *Publications:* Etched Plates; Autolithoed Educational books; Village and Town, Trees in Britain and Farm Crops in Britain; colour prints; illustrations to: British Countryside in Colour; Trees for Town & Country and Famous Trees; Shell Guide to Trees and Shrubs; The Seasons (by Ralph Wightman); Trees of Britain (Sunday Times); Readers' Digest Publications; Royles Publications. *Relevant publication:* S. R. Badmin and the English Landscape, ed Dr C. Beetles, 1985. *Recreations:* painting and gardening. *Address:* Streamfield, Bignor, Pulborough, West Sussex RH20 1PQ. *T:* Sutton (Sussex) 229.

*Died 28 April* 1989.

**BAGGE, Sir John (Alfred Picton),** 6th Bt *cr* 1867; ED; DL; *b* 27 Oct. 1914; *e s* of Sir Picton Bagge, 5th Bt, CMG, and Olive Muriel Mary (*d* 1965), *d* of late Samuel Mendel; *S* father, 1967; *m* 1939, Elizabeth Helena (Lena), *d of* late Daniel James Davies, CBE, Comr for Newfoundland in London; three *s* three *d. Educ:* Eton and abroad. Served Inns of Court Regt, 1936–39; commnd into Cheshire Yeo., 1939; served War of 1939–45, Palestine, Sudan, Liberation Campaign of Ethiopia; Major 1941; GSO 2, Brit. Mil. Mission to Ethiopia, 1941–44; GSO 2, HQ, E Africa Comd Liaison with French, 1944; Mil. Asst to Brit. Comdr Allied Control Commn for Bulgaria, 1944–45; GSO 2, War Office, 1945. KStJ 1975; Chm. Council of St John in Norfolk, 1969–80. Vice-Chm., W Norfolk DC, 1973–76, Chm., 1976–77; High Sheriff of Norfolk, 1977; DL Norfolk, 1978. *Recreations:* shooting, ski-ing and water ski-ing. *Heir: s* (John) Jeremy (Picton) Bagge [*b* 21 June 1945; *m* 1979, Sarah, *d* of late James Armstrong; two *s* one *d.* Chartered Accountant, 1968]. *Address:* Stradsett Hall, Kings Lynn, Norfolk. *T:* Fincham (03664) 215. *Club:* Allsorts (Norfolk).

*Died 17 June* 1990.

**BAGLEY, Desmond (Simon);** professional novelist since 1962; *b* Kendal, 29 Oct. 1923; *s* of John Bagley and Hannah Marie Bagley (*née* Whittle); *m* 1960, Joan Margaret (*née* Brown). *Educ:* spottily, mainly by reading and travel. British Aircraft Industry, 1940–46. Travelled overland to Africa, 1947; worked in: Uganda, 1947, Kenya, 1948; Rhodesia, 1949; S Africa, 1950–64; variety of jobs incl. nightclub photographer, film scenario writer; freelance journalist from 1956, contrib. S African press; travels extensively. Member: Soc. Authors; Crime Writers' Assoc.; Mystery Writers of America; Writers' Guild (US). *Publications:* The Golden Keel, 1963; High Citadel, 1965; Wyatt's Hurricane, 1966; Landslide, 1967; The Vivero Letter, 1968; The Spoilers, 1969; Running Blind, 1970 (adapted as BBC serial, 1979); The Freedom Trap, 1971; The Tightrope Men, 1973; The Snow Tiger, 1975; The Enemy, 1977; Flyaway, 1978; Bahama Crisis, 1980; Windfall, 1982; work trans. into many languages. *Recreations:* sailing, travel, military history, reading, recreational mathematics, computer programming. *Address:* Câtel House, Les Rohais de haut, St Andrew, Guernsey, CI. *T:* Guernsey 56435. *Clubs:* Savage, Detection; United Royal Channel Islands Yacht (Guernsey); Aero (Johannesburg); Antarctic Press (McMurdo Sound). *Died 12 April* 1983.

**BAGNALL, Frank Colin,** CBE 1950; Commercial Director, Imperial Chemical Industries Ltd, 1965–70, also Finance Director, 1967–68; Director, African Explosives and Chemical Industries Ltd, 1965–70; *b* 6 Nov. 1909; *s* of late Francis Edward Bagnall, OBE and Edith Bagnall; *m* 1st, 1933, Ethel Hope Robertson (killed in an air raid, by enemy action, 1941), Blechingley; 2nd, 1941, Rona Rooker Roberts (marr. diss. 1975), Belmont, Mill Hill; one *s* one *d;* 3rd, 1975, Christine Bagnall, Westhill, Ledbury. *Educ:* Repton; Brasenose Coll., Oxford (MA); Dept of Business Administration, London Sch. of Economics. ICI Ltd, 1932–38; Urwick, Orr and Partners, 1938–40. Advr on Organisation, War Office, 1940–42. Farming, 1942–44. Man. Dir, British Nylon Spinners, 1944–64; Non-Exec. Dir, ICI, 1964; Dir, Richard Thomas & Baldwins, 1964–67. Mem., Oxford Univ. Appts Cttee, 1948–69; Governor, Ashridge Coll., 1958–70; Chm. Regular Forces Resettlement Cttee for Wales, 1958–68. Chm. Wales Business Training Cttee, 1946–49; Founder Mem., BIM (Mem. Council, 1949–52); Dir Oxford Univ. Business Summer Sch., 1954; Mem. Govt Cttee of Enquiry into Electricity Supply Industry, 1954–55; Chm. SW Reg. Council, FBI, 1956–57; Mem. Air Transport Licensing Bd, 1960–64; Chm. Man-Made Fibres Producers Cttee, 1961–65; Vice-Pres. British Man-Made Fibres Fedn, 1965–70 (Chm. 1963–65); Pres. Textile Inst., 1964–65. Pres., UC of S Wales and Monmouthshire, 1963–68 (Hon. Fellow and Life Governor). Hon. LLD, Wales, 1969. OStJ. *Address:* Vermont, Budleigh Salterton, Devon. *T:* Budleigh Salterton 3068. *Club:* Boodle's. *Died 7 Jan.* 1989.

**BAGNALL, Rt. Rev. Walter Edward,** DD; *b* 1903. *Educ:* Masonic School, Dublin, Ireland; University of Western Ontario; Huron College, London, Ont. BA, Univ. of Western Ontario, 1927; Licentiate in Theology, Huron Coll., 1927. Deacon, 1927; Priest, 1928; Curate of All Saints, Windsor, Ont, 1927–28; Incumbent of

St Mark's, London, Ont, 1928–30; Rector of St John's, Preston, Ont, Canada, 1930–36; Rural Dean of Waterloo, Ont, 1932–36; Rector of All Saints, Hamilton, Ont, 1936–40; Rector of St George's, St Catharine's, Ont, 1940–47; Canon of Niagara, 1944–47; Dean of Niagara and Rector of Ch. Ch. Cathedral, Hamilton, 1947–49; Bishop of Niagara, 1949–73. Hon. Degrees: DD Univ. of Western Ontario, 1949; DD Trinity Coll., Toronto, 1953; DCL Bishops Univ., Lennoxville, 1956; LLD McMaster Univ., 1959. *Address:* 252 James Street North, Hamilton, Ont, Canada.

*Died 21 Aug.* 1984.

**BAGNOLD, Enid, (Lady Jones),** CBE 1976; writer; *b* 1889; *d* of late Colonel A. H. Bagnold, CB, CMG; *m* 1920, Sir Roderick Jones KBE (*d* 1962), for 25 years Chairman of Reuters; three *s* one *d. Educ:* Prior's Field, Godalming; Paris; Marburg. *Publications: general:* A Diary Without Dates, 1918, repr. 1978; Sailing Ships (poems), 1917; *novels:* The Happy Foreigner, 1920; Serena Blandish (or the Difficulty of Getting Married), 1924; Alice and Thomas and Jane, 1930; National Velvet, 1935 (filmed and TV); The Squire (in US, The Door of Life), 1938; The Loved and Envied, 1951; The Girl's Journey, 1956; Letters to Frank Harris, 1980; *plays:* Lottie Dundass, (perf. Vaudeville, 1943); National Velvet, (perf. Embassy, 1945); Poor Judas, (perf. Arts, 1951; Arts Theatre Prize, with John Whiting, 1951); Gertie, (perf. New York, 1952; perf. London as Little Idiot); The Chalk Garden, 1956 (perf. New York and London, 1956; Award of Merit Medal, Amer. Acad. of Arts and Letters); The Last Joke, (perf. Phoenix, 1960); The Chinese Prime Minister, (perf. New York, 1964, London, 1965); Call me Jacky, (perf. Oxford, 1967); Four Plays, 1970; A Matter of Gravity, NY, 1975 (tour, with Katharine Hepburn, 1976–77); *translation:* Alexander of Asia (from Princess Marthe Bibesco, Alexandre Asiatique), 1955; *autobiography:* Enid Bagnold's Autobiography, 1969. *Recreations:* "as above". *Address:* 17A Hamilton Terrace, NW8 9RE. *T:* 01 286 7479. *Died 31 March* 1981.

**BAGNOLD, Brig. Ralph Alger,** OBE 1941; FRS 1944; Consultant on movement of sediments by wind and water, since 1956; Fellow of Imperial College, University of London, since 1971; *b* 3 April 1896; *s* of late Col A. H. Bagnold, CB, CMG: *m* 1946, Dorothy Alice (*d* 1989), *d* of late A. E. Plank; one *s* one *d. Educ:* Malvern College; Royal Military Academy, Woolwich; Gonville and Caius Coll., Cambridge. Commission RE, 1915; Capt, 1918; transferred Royal Corps of Signals, 1920; Major, 1927; retired, 1935. Served European War, Western Front, 1915–18 (despatches); North-West Frontier of India, 1930 (despatches). Organised and led numerous explorations in Libyan Desert and elsewhere, 1925–32; Founder's Medal of Royal Geographical Soc., 1935. Called up, 1939. Raised and commanded Long Range Desert Group in Middle East, 1940–41 (despatches); Deputy Signal-Officer-in-Chief, Middle East, 1943–44; released from Army Service, 1944. G. K. Warren Prize, US Acad. of Sciences, 1969; Penrose Medal, Geolog. Soc. of America, 1970; Wollaston Medal, Geolog. Soc. of London, 1971; Sorby Medal, Internat. Assoc. of Sedimentologists, 1978. *Publications:* Libyan Sands, 1935, new edn 1987; Physics of Blown Sand and Desert Dunes, 1941; papers, etc, on deserts, hydraulics, beach formation, and random distributions. *Recreations:* exploration, research. *Address:* 7 Manor Way, Blackheath, SE3 9EF. *T:* 081–852 1210. *Died 28 May* 1990.

**BAILEY, Rev. Dr (Derrick) Sherwin;** Non-residentiary Canon of Wells Cathedral and Prebendary of Ashill, since 1975; *b* 30 June 1910; *s* of William Thomas and Ellen Mary Bailey, Alcester, Warwicks; *m* 1st, 1939, Philippa Eleanor (*d* 1964), *d* of Capt. Philip James and Eleanor Frances Vandeleur Green; one *s* two *d;* 2nd, 1966, Morag Stuart Macdonald, MD, DPM, *d* of Lachlan John and Mary Stuart Macdonald. *Educ:* The Grammar Sch., Alcester, Warwks; Lincoln Theological Coll.; Edinburgh Univ. In business, 1928–40; ACII 1934; Linc. Theol Coll., 1940–42; Univ. of Edin., PhD 1947; DLitt, 1962; Fellow of Eugenics Soc., 1957–74. Deacon, 1942; Priest, 1943; Curate, Mablethorpe St Mary and Theddlethorpe St Helen with Theddlethorpe All Saints, 1942–44; Chaplain to Anglican students at Univ. and Colls of Edinburgh, and Curate of St John Evang., Edin., 1944–51; Anglican Lectr in Divinity, Moray House Trg Coll., Edin., 1948–51; Central Lectr, C of E Moral Welfare Counc., 1951–55; Actg Educ. Sec., 1954–55; Study Sec., 1955–59; Permission to officiate in Dio. B'ham, 1951–59; Rector of Lyndon with Manton, Martinsthorpe and Gunthorpe, 1959–62; Canon Residentiary of Wells Cathedral, 1962–74; Chancellor of Wells, and Prebendary of Litton, 1962–69; Precentor of Wells and Prebendary of Whitchurch, 1968–74. Select Preacher, Univ. of Camb., 1963. Examining Chaplain to Bishop of Bath and Wells, 1963–76. *Publications:* Sponsors at Baptism and Confirmation, 1952; Thomas Becon and the Reformation of the Church in England, 1952; The Mystery of Love and Marriage, 1952; Homosexuality and the Western Christian Tradition, 1955; Sexual Offenders and Social Punishment, 1956; The Man-Woman Relation in Christian Thought, 1959; Common Sense about Sexual Ethics, 1962; The Canonical Houses of Wells, 1982; (Joint-Author) Celibacy and Marriage, 1944; (ed) Wells

Cathedral Chapter Act Book 1666–1683, 1973; (ed jtly) Le Neve, Fasti Ecclesiae Anglicanae Dioc. Bath and Wells V, 1979; contributor: They Stand Apart, 1955; The Human Sum 1957; Die Religion in Geschichte und Gegenwart, 1959; Westminster Dictionary of Christian Education, 1961; Dictionary of Christian Ethics, 1967; Sexual Ethics and Christian Responsibility, 1970; Oxford Dictionary of the Christian Church, 1974; Medieval Art and Architecture at Wells and Glastonbury, 1981; also contrib. to: Theology; Journal of Ecclesiastical History; Church Quarterly Review; Scottish Jl of Theol.; London Quarterly and Holborn Review; The Churchman, etc. *Recreations:* chess, stamp collecting, railways. *Address:* 23 Kippax Avenue, Wells, Somerset BA5 2TT. *T:* Wells 75061. *Died 9 Feb. 1984.*

**BAILEY, Sir Donald Coleman,** Kt 1946; OBE 1944; JP; *b* 15 Sept. 1901; *s* of J. H. Bailey, Rotherham, Yorkshire; *m* 1st, Phyllis (*d* 1971), *d* of Charles Frederick Andrew, Wick, Bournemouth; one *s*; 2nd, 1979, Mrs Mildred Stacey. *Educ:* The Leys, Cambridge; Univ. of Sheffield (BEng). Posts: Rowntree & Co. Ltd, York, Efficiency Dept; London Midland & Scottish Rly, Civil Engineers Dept; City Engineer's Dept, Sheffield; Dir, Military Engineering Experimental Estabt; Dean, RMCS, 1962–66. Hon. FIW; FIStructE; MICE; Hon. Member: Instn of Royal Engrs; Inst. of Engrg Designers. Hon. DEng Sheffield, 1946. JP Bournemouth, 1946. Commander of the Order of Orange-Nassau, 1947. *Recreation:* golf. *Address:* 46 The Grove, Christchurch, Dorset BH23 2HB. *T:* Christchurch 486152. *Died 5 May 1985.*

**BAILEY, James Vincent;** Executive Director, Bank of England, 1964–69; *b* 26 July 1908; *s* of R. H. Bailey; *m* 1946, Ida Hope Weigall; no *c. Educ:* Malvern; Pembroke Coll., Oxford. Entered Bank of England, 1928; Deputy Chief Cashier, 1959–62; Chief Accountant, 1962–64. *Address:* Common Barn, Remenham, Henley-on-Thames, Oxon. *T:* Henley 2480. *Died 26 Nov. 1984.*

**BAILEY, Rev. Dr Sherwin;** *see* Bailey, Rev. Dr D. S.

**BAILLIE. Dame Isobel,** DBE 1978 (CBE 1951); Hon. MA (Manchester Univ.), 1950; RCM, RAM; singer; *b* Hawick, Scotland, 1895; *m* 1918, H. L. Wrigley (*d* 1957); one *d. Educ:* Dover Street High Sch. for Girls, Manchester. Appeared at all leading Festivals, including Three Choirs, Edinburgh, London, etc.; only British singer to appear with Toscanini on three occasions. Concerts with Sir Malcolm Sargent, Sir Adrian Boult, Sir Hamilton Harty, Sir Henry Wood, Bruno Walter, De Sabata, etc. Sang at Covent Garden in Orphée, and in Hollywood Bowl. Toured New Zealand twice; concerts in Malaya, 1948, South Africa, 1952, etc. Professor of Singing: Cornell Univ., USA, 1960–61; Royal Coll. of Music, London; Manchester Sch. of Music. Hon. DLitt Salford, 1977. *Address:* Flat 14, Pavilion Lodge, Edgbaston Drive, Old Trafford, Manchester M16 0JN. *T:* 061-860 6458. *Club:* VAD Ladies. *Died 24 Sept. 1983.*

**BAILLIE, John Strachan,** CBE 1965; *b* 1896; *s* of William T. Baillie, Belfast; *m* 1926, Eileen Mary, *d* of Saxon J. Payne. *Educ:* Queen's Univ., Belfast (BComSc). Joined Harland and Wolff, Belfast, 1913, and (apart from service in RN, 1914–18) was with Co. throughout his career; transf. to Co.'s London Office, 1924; Asst Sec., Harland & Wolff, Belfast, 1937; London Manager, 1945; Dir 1947; Dep. Chm. 1958; Chm. 1962–65; Dir, Short Brothers & Harland Ltd, 1948–67; Dep. Chm. Brown Bros & Co. Ltd, 1962–67. Liveryman, Worshipful Co. of Shipwrights. Commander: Order of St Olav (Norway), 1960; Dannebrog (Denmark) 1964. *Address:* Merrydown, 12 Aldersey Road, Guildford, Surrey GU1 2ES. *Died 14 Nov. 1989.*

**BAIN, Cyril William Curtis,** MC; DM Oxford; FRCP; Hon. Consulting Physician, Harrogate General Hospital; Past President BMA; *b* Thornfield, Heaton Mersey, near Manchester, 5 June 1895; *e s* of late William Bain, MD, FRCP, and Ellen, *d* of late John Curtis, Rose Leigh, Heaton Chapel, near Manchester; *m* 1930, Diana Alice, *y d* of late Lt-Col H. R. Pease, and *ggd* of late Joseph Robinson Pease, Hesslewood, near Hull; two *s* one *d* (and one *s* decd). *Educ:* Bilton Grange, near Rugby; Wellington Coll.; Christ Church, Oxford; St Thomas's Hospital, London. Served European War, 1914–18; gazetted to the Duke of Wellington's Regt 29 August 1914; Captain, 1916; Major, 1918; served in Machine Gun Corps (despatches, MC); active service in France and Flanders, 1915–17; retired, 1918; Extra-ordinary member of the Cardiac Society. *Publications:* Recent Advances in Cardiology (with C. F. T. East), 5th edn, 1959; Incomplete Bundle Branch Block; Bilateral Bundle Branch Block; The Oesophageal Lead; Clinical Value of Unipolar Chest and Limb Leads, etc. *Address:* Kirklands Nursing Home, Ursula Square, Selsey, Chichester, W Sussex. *Died 14 Aug. 1987.*

**BAIN, Kenneth Bruce Findlater;** *see* Findlater, Richard.

**BAIRAMIAN, Sir Vahé (Robert),** Kt 1959; *b* 30 Nov. 1900; 2nd *s* of Dr Bairamian, Cyprus; *m* 1934, Eileen Elsie Connelly; one *s. Educ:* English Sch., Nicosia, Cyprus; University Coll., London. Barrister-at-Law, Middle Temple, 1923. Served in the Courts and Land Registry, Cyprus, 1926–44; Legal Asst, Lands and Survey, Nigeria, 1944; Chief Registrar, Supreme Court, Nigeria, 1944; Magistrate, 1946; Puisne Judge, 1949; Senior Puisne Judge, High Court, Northern Region of Nigeria, 1955; Chief Justice, Sierra Leone, 1957–60; Justice, Supreme Court of Nigeria, 1960–68. Fellow UCL, 1963. Jubilee Medal, 1935; Coronation Medal, 1953. *Publications:* Editor, All Nigeria Law Reports of 1963, 1964, 1965 and 1966 (Supreme Court Judgments) (wrote a Synopsis of Criminal Procedure and Evidence in Nigeria based on them, and a Supplement for 1967–76 cases, with notes on interpretation of written law and appeals). *Address:* 36 The Crescent, Sandgate, Folkestone, Kent CT20 3EE. *T:* Folkestone 38240. *Club:* Royal Commonwealth Society. *Died 14 July 1984.*

**BAIRD, Sir Dugald,** Kt 1959; MD, FRCOG, Hon. FRCPGlas, BSc, DPH; Belding Scholar, Association for Aid to Crippled Children, New York, 1966–71; Regius Professor of Midwifery in the University of Aberdeen, 1937–65, retired; formerly Obstetrician-in-Chief, Aberdeen Maternity Hospital and Visiting Gynæcologist, Aberdeen Royal Infirmary and Hon. Director, Obstetric Medicine Research Unit, Medical Research Council; *b* 16 Nov. 1899; *er s* of David Baird, MA, Gourock, Renfrewshire; *m* 1928, May Tennent, CBE (*d* 1983); two *s* two *d. Educ:* Greenock Acad.; University of Glasgow; University of Strasbourg. Formerly with Glasgow Royal Maternity and Women's Hosp., Glasgow Royal Infirmary, and Glasgow Royal Cancer Hosp. Hon. FRCOG, 1986. Freedom of City of Aberdeen, 1966. Hon. LLD: Glasgow, 1959; Aberdeen, 1966; Hon. DSc: Manchester, 1962; Wales, 1966; Hon. DCL, Newcastle; DUniv Stirling, 1974. *Publications:* various papers on obstetrical and gynæcological subjects. *Recreation:* golf. *Address:* Manor House, Boswall Road, Edinburgh.
*Died 7 Nov. 1986.*

**BAIRD, Lady, (May Deans),** CBE 1962; National Governor of the BBC in Scotland, 1966–70; *b* 14 May 1901; *er d* of Matthew Tennent, Newton, Lanarks; *m* 1928, Sir Dugald Baird, MD, FRCOG; two *s* two *d. Educ:* Glasgow High Sch. for Girls; Glasgow Univ. BSc 1922; MB, ChB 1924. Hospital appts until marriage; social and local govt work, 1938–54; Chm. of Public Health Cttee, Aberdeen Town Council; Chm. NE Regional Hosp. Bd (Scotland), 1947–66. Freedom of City of Aberdeen, 1966. Hon. LLD Aberdeen Univ., 1958. *Address:* Manor House, 17 Boswall Road, Edinburgh.
*Died 16 Aug. 1983.*

**BAKER;** *see* Noel-Baker.

**BAKER,** Baron *cr* 1977 (Life Peer), of Windrush, Gloucestershire; **John Fleetwood Baker,** Kt 1961; OBE 1941; MA, ScD Cantab; DSc Wales; FRS 1956; FEng; Hon. LLD Glasgow; Hon. DSc Leeds, Manchester, Edinburgh, Aston, Leicester, Salford, Cranfield, Lancaster, Bristol; Hon. DEng Liverpool; Hon. DS Ghent; Hon. FIMechE; Hon. ARIBA; Hon. FWeldI; Hon. Mem., Inst. of Royal Engineers; FICE; FIStructE; Associate MASCE; Fellow of Clare College, Cambridge, 1943; Director of Research and Development, IDC Group plc; Deputy Chairman, IDC Consultants Ltd; Director, IDC Project Management Consultants Ltd; *b* 19 March 1901; *s* of J. W. Baker, Wallasey, and Emily C. Fleetwood; *m* 1928, Fiona Mary MacAlister (*d* 1979), *d* of late John Walker; two *d. Educ:* Rossall; Clare Coll., Cambridge (Scholar). Technical Asst, Design Dept, Royal Airship Works, 1925; Asst Lecturer, University Coll., Cardiff, 1926; Scientific Asst, Building Research Station, 1928; Technical Officer to Steel Structures Res. Cttee, 1931–36; Prof. of Civil Engineering, Bristol Univ., 1933–43; Prof. of Mechanical Sciences and Head of Dept of Engineering, Cambridge Univ., 1943–68, Prof. Emeritus, 1968. Chm. Council, Sch. of Physical Sciences, Cambridge Univ., 1945–72. Telford Gold Medal, 1932, Telford Premium, 1936 and 1953; Howard Quinquennial Medal and Prize, 1937; Ewing Medal, 1952; Inst. Lecture to Students, 1936–37. Unwin Memorial Lecture, 1961. Mem. of Council 1947–56, 1958–63, 1964–69, Vice-Pres., 1968–70, Inst. of Civil Engrs; Research Medal 1951, Instn Silver Medal 1951, Gold Medal 1953; Mem. of Council, 1936–39, Chm., Western Counties Br., 1935–39, Midland Lecture, 1971, Instn of Structural Engineers; Royal Medal, Royal Soc., 1970; Sir Alfred Herbert Paper, Instn of Production Engrs, 1973. Member: Civil Defence Research Cttee, 1939–1948; Scientific Adv. Com., Min. of Works, 1945–46; Adv. Council to Military Coll. of Science, 1947–52; UGC, 1953–63; Council, British Welding Res. Assoc.; Pres., Welding Inst., 1971–73 (Brooker Medal, 1977); Pres., British Assoc. for the Advancement of Science, 1975–76; Chm., Naval Educn Adv. Cttee, 1958–64; Consultant, Naval Constructional Research Establishment, Rosyth, 1948–63; Director: Technical Development Capital Ltd, 1962–74; John Brown & Co. Ltd, 1963–71; Cambridge Fender & Engineering Co. Ltd, 1964–74. Scientific Adviser, and in charge of Design and Development Section, Ministry of Home Security, ARP Dept, 1939–43; designer of Morrison indoor shelter, 1940. Founder Fellow, Fellowship of Engineering, 1976. Officier du Mérite pour la Recherche et l'Invention, Paris, 1964. *Publications:* Differential

Equations of Engineering Science, 1929; Analysis of Engineering Structures, 1936, 4th edn, 1968; The Steel Skeleton, Vol 1, 1954, Vol. 2, 1956; Plastic Design of Frames, Vol. 1, 1969; Enterprise versus Bureaucracy, 1978; numerous scientific and technical papers on Theory of Structures and Strength of Materials, etc. *Address:* 42 Crossways Gardens, Cambridge CB2 2JT. *T:* Cambridge 840152. *Club:* Athenæum. *Died 9 Sept.* 1985.

**BAKER, Alfreda Helen,** MD; FRCS; Consulting Surgeon: to Elizabeth Garrett Anderson Hospital, 1937–68; to Hounslow Hospital, 1930–68; to Marie Curie Hospital, 1937–68; *b* 2 Oct. 1897; *d* of Alfred Rawlings and Hannah Mary Baker. *Educ:* Queen's Univ., Belfast. MB, BCh, QU Belfast, 1921 (hons); MD 1926 (Commendation); FRCS, Eng. 1927. Demonstrator of Anatomy, QU Belfast, 1922–24; House Surgeon, Royal Cancer Hosp., 1926; Riddel Research Fellow, Royal Free Hosp., 1924–26; Surgical Registrar, Elizabeth Garrett Anderson Hosp., 1930–33; Surgeon, EMS, 1939–45. Fellow Assoc. of Surgeons of Gt Brit. and Ire., 1950. *Publications:* original work published in: British Journal of Surgery; Lancet; British Journal of Obstetrics and Gynæcology, etc. *Recreations:* water colour painting, oil painting, photography, foreign travel. *Address:* Arkesden, Saffron Walden, Essex. *T:* Clavering 370. *Died 1 June* 1984.

**BAKER, Allan;** *see* Baker, J. F. A.

**BAKER, Prof. Arthur Lemprière Lancey,** DSc (Eng), FICE, FIStructE, FACI; Professor of Concrete Structures and Technology, University of London (Imperial College), 1945–73, then Emeritus; *b* 16 Dec. 1905; *s* of late W. L. Baker, Exeter; *m* 1930, Lillian Hollings; two *d*. *Educ:* Queen Elizabeth's Sch., Crediton; University of Manchester. Asst Engineer, Mersey Tunnel, Edmund Nuttall, Sons & Co. Ltd, 1926–28; Dist Engineer, PWD, Nigeria, 1928–30; Asst Engineer, Christiani & Nielsen Ltd, 1930–33; Senior Design Engineer, Reinforcing Steel Co., Johannesburg, 1933–36; Senior Civil Engineer, Trinidad Leaseholds Ltd, 1936–45. Mem., BSI Cttee for the Structural Use of Concrete, 1970–; Hon. ACGI; Hon. DTech Bradford, 1971. *Publications:* Raft Foundations, 1937; Reinforced Concrete, 1949; The Ultimate Load Theory Applied to the Design of Reinforced and Pre-stressed Concrete Frames, 1956; The Inelastic Space Frame, 1967; Limit State Design of Reinforced Concrete, 1970. *Address:* Department of Mechanical Engineering, Imperial College of Science and Technology, SW7 2BU. *T:* 01–589 5111. *Died 20 May* 1986.

**BAKER, Colin Lewis Gilbert,** CBE 1974; FCA; Director of companies; *b* 24 Aug. 1913; *m* 1942, Pauleen Denice Hartley; two *s* two *d*. *Educ:* Queen's Univ., Taunton. Professional accountancy, 1931–39. Served War, Somerset LI, Major, 1939–45. George Angus & Co. Ltd, 1945–73; Director, 1958–63; Dep. Chm., 1963–64; Chm., 1964–73; Exec. Dir, The Dunlop Co. Ltd (later Dunlop Holdings Ltd), 1968–73; Local Dir, Baring Bros & Co. Ltd, 1975–79. Mem., Companies Consultative Gp, DoT, 1972–80. Other interests include: Mem., Northern Regional Bd, Lloyds Bank (Chm., 1979–); Dir, Lloyds Bank UK Management Ltd; Commissaris, Royal Boskalis Westminster NV. Former Member: Northern Economic Planning Council (Chm. 1973–77); Northern Regional Council, CBI (Chm. 1972–73); Newcastle upon Tyne AHA (T), 1975–79. Gen. Comr of Income Tax, 1965–80. *Recreations:* fishing, gardening, going to cottage in Cornwall. *Address:* Lynton, Apperley Road, Stocksfield, Northumberland. *T:* Stocksfield 3454. *Club:* Army and Navy. *Died 25 Nov.* 1982.

**BAKER, Brig. Euston Edward Francis,** CB 1957; CBE 1936; DSO 1919; MC 1917 and Bar 1918; TD; JP; Chairman, Amersham Bench, 1954–69; Hon. Colonel 5th Battalion Middlesex Regiment, 1961–63; Chairman: Middlesex T & AFA, 1951–59; Middlesex County Cadet Committee, 1944–51; National Association of Bolt and Nut Stockholders, 1948–59; *b* 5 April 1895; *s* of H. R. Baker; *m* 1920, Mary Helena, *d* of T. Sampson; two *s* one *d* (and *y s* decd). *Educ:* Sherborne (captain of football and shooting, 1913–14). Winner of Spencer Cup, Bisley, 1914. Gazetted to 5th Middlesex Regt, 15 Aug. 1914; served in France, 1914–19, continuously; commanded 2nd Bn Middlesex Regt 1918–19 (DSO, MC and bar, despatches thrice); commanded 8th Bn Middlesex Regt 1923–30 and 1936–37; Brevet Col, 1927; commanded 7th City of London Regt, 1931–36; Col, 1927; Comdr Infantry Bde, TA, 1939–42; ADC to the King, 1941–51; retd (ill-health), 1945; Hon. Col, 2/8th Batt. Middlesex Regt, 1939–47; Hon. Col 11th Bn Parachute Regt, 1948–56; Hon. Col 8th Bn Middlesex Regt, 1956–61. DL Mddx (later Greater London) 1938–76; JP Bucks 1945. Citoyen d'Honneur of Douai, France, 1947–. *Address:* Stanbridge House, Chesham Road, Amersham, Bucks HP6 5ES. *T:* 6230. *Died 17 Jan.* 1981.

**BAKER, Rt. Hon. Sir George (Gillespie),** PC 1971; Kt 1961; OBE 1945; President of the Family Division (formerly of the Probate, Divorce and Admiralty Division) of the High Court of Justice, 1971–79, a Judge in the Division, 1961–79; *b* 25 April 1910; *s* of late Captain John Kilgour Baker, Stirling; *m* 1935, Jessie McCall

Findlay (*d* 1983); three *s*. *Educ:* Glasgow Academy; Strathallan Sch., Perthshire; Brasenose Coll., Oxford (Hon. Schol.; Sen. Hulme Schol.). Called to the Bar, Middle Temple, 1932 (Harmsworth Schol.); Bencher, 1961; Lent Reader, 1975; Treasurer, 1976. Army, 1939–45; Queen's Own RWK 1939–40; commissioned The Cameronians (Scottish Rifles), 1940; DAAG War Office, 1941–42; AAG Allied Force HQ, 1942–44; Col. 'A' 15 Army Gp, 1945: AAG British War Crimes Executive, Nuremberg, 1945. Contested (C) Southall (Middlesex), 1945. Recorder: of Bridgnorth, 1946–51; of Smethwick, 1951–52; of Wolverhampton, 1952–61. Dep. Chm. QS, Shropshire, 1954–71. QC 1952, Leader of Oxford Circuit, 1954–61; Presiding Judge, Wales and Chester Circuit, 1970–71. Governor, Strathallan Sch., 1947–57, Hon. Governor, 1968–; Governor: Epsom Coll., 1958–72; Wycombe Abbey, 1972–82. Commissioner holding Government enquiry, Feb.–April 1956 into objections to proposed British Egg Marketing Scheme and for Kenya Government into pyrethrum industry, 1960; reviewed (for Sec. of State for NI) and reported on operation of NI Emergency Provisions Act of 1978, 1983–84. Chairman: (First) General Optical Council, 1959–61; Departmental Cttee on Mechanical Recording of Court Proceedings, 1964–70; Statute Law Soc., 1980–. Hon. Mem., Canadian Bar Assoc. Hon. Fellow, Brasenose Coll., Oxford, 1966. Freeman, City of London, 1981. *Recreations:* golf, fishing. *Clubs:* Caledonian; Denham Golf (Captain 1967–68). *Died 13 June* 1984.

**BAKER, Sir Humphrey D. B. S.;** *see* Sherston-Baker.

**BAKER, (John Frederic) Allan,** CB 1957; FEng; Ministry of Transport, retired; *b* 5 Oct. 1903; *s* of late H. J. Baker; *m* 1927, Nancy Elizabeth Wells (*d* 1985); one *d* (and one *s* decd). *Educ:* St Paul's Sch. After Local Authority experience in Middlesex, 1922–, joined Ministry of Transport, 1929, serving in Exeter, Bedford, Nottingham and London; apptd Divisional Road Engineer for Wales and Mon, at Cardiff, 1947, and Dep. Chief Engineer at Headquarters, 1953; Chief Engineer and Dir of Highway Engineering, 1954–65. Member: Road Research Board, 1954–65; London Roads Cttee, 1959; Traffic Signs Cttee, 1963; Cons. Adviser to Automobile Assoc., 1965–69. Past Chm., Road Engrg Industry Cttee of BSI; Vice-Pres., Internat. Exec. Cttee of Permanent Internat. Assoc. of Road Congresses, 1960–72 and Pres. d'Honneur, Brit. Nat. Cttee. Mem. Council, ICE, 1956–61, 1962–67. Founder Fellow, Fellowship of Engineering, 1976; Hon. FIMunE; Hon. FInstHE; Hon. FICE. Viva Shield and Gold Medal, Worshipful Co. of Carmen, (for pioneering the British Motorway system), 1967. *Address:* 36 Imber Close, Ember Lane, Esher, Surrey. *T:* 01–398 3331. *Died 20 July* 1987.

**BAKER, Rt. Rev. John Gilbert Hindley;** Assistant Bishop, Diocese of Guildford, since 1983; Hon. Canon of Guildford Cathedral, since 1984; *b* 10 Oct. 1910; 3rd and *y s* of late Arthur Ernest Baker, MRCS, LRCP, and Agnes Flora Baker (*née* Hindley), Bromley, Kent; *m* 1st, 1941, Martha Levering Sherman (*d* 1976), *d* of late Rev. Arthur Sherman, STD and Mrs Martha Sherman, Wuchang, China and Ohio, USA; two *s* two *d*; 2nd, 1980, Mrs Joan Rogers, *widow* of Rev. Dennis Rogers (Minister of Union Church, Hong Kong, 1965–77). *Educ:* Westminster Sch.; Christ Church, Oxford. Deacon, 1935; Priest, 1936. SCM Sec., London, 1932–34; Dio. of Hong Kong and S China, 1935–51; taught at Lingnan Univ., Canton, 1936–38; in Kunming, Yunnan, 1939–45; St John's Univ., Shanghai, 1947–49; Union Theol. Coll., Lingnan, 1949–51; Rector of Christ Church, Guilford, Conn, 1952–55; Gen. Sec., Church Assembly Overseas Coun., London, 1955–63; Vicar, St Nicholas Cole Abbey, London, 1955–66; Actg Dir, Christian Study Centre, Hong Kong, 1966; Bishop of Hong Kong and Macao, 1966–81. Res. Fellow, Divinity Sch., Yale Univ., 1983. *Publications:* The Changing Scene in China, 1946 (US 1948); The Church on Asian Frontiers, 1963; St Nicholas Cole Abbey: a short history, 1964; (contrib.) All One Body, 1969; (contrib.) Yes to Women Priests, 1978; Bishop Speaking, 1981. *Recreations:* walking, swimming, listening to music. *Address:* Orchard End, Nower Road, Dorking, Surrey RH4 3BY. *Club:* Royal Commonwealth Society. *Died 29 April* 1986.

**BAKER, Dr John Randal,** MA, DPhil, DSc Oxon; FRS 1958; Emeritus Reader in Cytology, Oxford University (Reader, 1955–67); *b* 23 Oct. 1900; *y s* of Rear-Adm. Julian A. Baker, RN; *m* 1st, 1923, Inezita Davis; one *s* one *d*; 2nd, 1939, Mrs Helen Savage. *Educ:* New Coll., Oxford (1st Class in Honour Sch. of Natural Science). Scientific expeditions to New Hebrides, 1922–23, 1927, 1933–34; Joint Editor, Quarterly Journal of Microscopical Science, 1946–64; Professorial Fellow, New Coll., Oxford, 1964–67; Pres. Royal Microscopical Society, 1964–65, Hon. Fellow, 1968. Oliver Bird Medal for researches on chemical contraception, 1958. *Publications:* Sex in Man and Animals, 1926; Man and Animals in the New Hebrides, 1929; Cytological Technique, 1933 (5th edn, 1966); The Chemical Control of Conception, 1935; The Scientific Life, 1942; Science and the Planned State, 1945; Abraham Trembley of Geneva, 1952; Principles of Biological Microtechnique, 1958; Race, 1974 (German edn, Die Rassen der Menschheit, 1976); Julian Huxley: scientist and world citizen, 1978. *Address:* 45 Lakeside, Oxford OX2 8JQ. *Died 8 June* 1984.

**BAKER, Sir Joseph;** see Baker, Sir S. J.

**BAKER, Prof. Peter Frederick,** ScD; FRS 1976; FKC 1985; Halliburton Professor and Head of Department of Physiology, King's College, London, since 1975; *b* 11 March 1939; *s* of F. T. Baker and D. E. Skelton; *m* 1966, Phyllis Light; one *s* three *d*. *Educ:* Lincoln Sch.; Emmanuel Coll., Cambridge (Scholar; BA Natural Sciences Tripos, Cl. 1, 1960; PhD 1964; ScD 1980). FIBiol 1976. Univ. of Cambridge: Demonstrator in Physiol., 1963–66; Lectr in Physiol., 1966–74; Fellow, Emmanuel Coll., Cambridge, 1962–74. Mem., AFRC, 1986–. Mem., Univ. of London Senate, 1982–. Guest Investigator, Rockefeller Univ., NY, 1964. G. L. Brown Lectr, Physiological Soc., 1977. Scientific Medal, Zool Soc. of London, 1975; Wander Prize, Switzerland, 1981. *Publications:* Calcium Movement in Excitable Cells (with H. Reuter), 1975; The Squid Axon, 1984; papers on cell physiol. in Jl of Physiol. and other sci. jls. *Recreation:* natural history. *Address:* Meadow Cottage, Bourn, Cambridge. *T:* Caxton 212.                        *Died 10 March 1987.*

**BAKER, Richard St Barbe,** OBE 1978; FIAL; Forestry Adviser and Silviculturist; Founder of The Men of the Trees, 1922; *b* 9 Oct. 1889; *s* of John R. St Barbe Baker and Charlotte Purrott; *m* 1st, 1946, Doreen Whitworth (from whom he obtained a divorce, 1953), *d* of G. H. W. Long, Strensham, Worcs; one *s* one *d*; 2nd, 1959, Catriona Burnett. *Educ:* Dean Close Sch., Cheltenham; Saskatchewan Univ.; Gonville and Caius Coll., Cambridge. Forestry Diploma, Cantab., 1920; Canada, 1909–13; Expeditionary Force, France, King Edward's Horse, Royal Field Artillery and Remounts, 1914–18; Army Sch. of Education, 1919; Asst Conservator of Forests, Kenya, 1920–23, Nigeria, 1924–29; initiated silvicultural experiments in the mahogany forests: delegate to World Forestry Congress, Rome; forest research Oxford and Continent, 1926; lecture tours 1930, 1931; founded Junior Men of the Trees, 1956; travelled 17,000 miles visiting forests of USA and Canada to prepare forestry plan; conf. with Franklin D. Roosevelt developed into Civilian Conservation Corps Camps; Ottawa Conf. on Empire Forestry, 1932–33; forest survey, S. America, 1936; organised Forestry Summer Sch., Oxford, 1938, and others; lectured to Army and RAF Cadets; supervised forestry training and prepared plan for rehabilitation of returning service men; General Meeting of The Men of the Trees, Chelsea, assumed world leadership in earthwide regeneration, 1947; took New Earth Charter to USA, 1950; convened World Forestry Charter Gatherings, 1945–56; led Sahara Univ. Expedn, surveying 9000 miles of desert and equatorial Africa; revisited NZ for Forest and Soil Conservation, 1954; settled in NZ, 1959; Deleg., 5th World Forestry Congress, Seattle; convened 1st Redwood Reunion, Mill Creek, 1960; for UNA covered 1200 miles on horseback in NZ, giving talks to schools on Trees, 1962–63; convened 1st Sahara Reclamation Conf., Rabat; reported 1964; broadcasts, lectures, NZ Schs, Conservation and Sahara Reclamation, 1965; vis. Australia to check felling and burning high forest, Kenya, Nat. Tree-Planting Week and Reunion of Men of the Trees; deleg., 6th World Forestry Congress, Spain, 1966; fact finding mission for Forestry, NZ and Q'land; rep. NZ, S Island at S Pacific Conf. Sydney, 1967; promoted afforestation, India and Pakistan, and inspected progress, Kuwait, Iran, Lebanon, UAR, Tunisia, and Spain; prepared forestry plans, Jamaica and British Honduras, 1968; conferred FAO, Rome, then visited Tunisian Pre-Sahara with group of scientists; inspected Austrian techniques of dune-stabilisation, Libya; addressed students, Univ. of Vienna, to recruit personnel for Sahara Reclamation Programme, 1969; revisited Silvicultural Experimental Area, Mahogany Forests, Nigeria, expl. S Sahara, Nigerian and Niger frontiers, 1970; conducted seminars on place of trees in farming, Univ. Saskatchewan, 1971; visited UN, NY, re Sahara Reclamation Prog., 1971; completed survey, N Nigeria, route for spiral shelter belt; led delegn, Nairobi, Golden Jubilee Kenya where 500,000 trees planted in 3 days; 7th World Forestry Congress, Argentine, to help launch World Year of the Tree, 1972; Men of the Trees, seminar on Trees and the Environment, 1973; convened 13th World Forestry Charter Gathering, London, 1974; reported on Redwood Park, USA Sub-Cttee on Nat. Parks, 1976; Sen. Adv., UN Conf., Nairobi, 1976; deleg. to 1st Wilderness Conf., S Africa and World Congress, India; Founding Mem., Ecoworld, Victoria, BC; 1st Pres., Internat. Tree Crops Inst., 1977; repr. Sahara countries, World Forestry Congress, Jakarta, 1978; 1st world symposium on Sahara reclamation; inaug. 15 million trees a year planning prog., Nat. Women's Union, Kenya; deleg. Friends of the Trees conf., Bombay, and promoted Chipko, to save Himalayan forests, 1979; founded Children of the Green Earth, Grove of Understanding, to save 12,000 acres of Coast Redwoods, advising Mins of the Environment, Ottawa and Toronto; deleg., conf. on Future, Toronto; opened conf. on Re-afforestation and Unemployment, NSW. Hon. LLD Saskatchewan, 1971. *Publications:* Tree Lovers Calendar, 1929 and following years; Book of the Seasons, 1940; Among the Trees, 2 vols, 1941; Africa Drums, 1942; The Redwoods, 1943; I Planted Trees, 1944; Green Glory: Forests of the World, 1947; New Earth Charter, 1949; Famous Trees, 1953; Sahara

Challenge, 1954; Land of Tané, 1956; Dance of the Trees, 1957; Kamiti: A Forester's Dream, 1958; The Redwoods (Famous Trees of the World, 1), 1959; Horse Sense: Story of My Horses in War and Peace, 1961; Trees of the World, 1962; Trees of the Bible Lands, Famous Trees of New Zealand, True Book of Trees, 1963; Sahara Conquest, 1966; Caravan Story and Country Notes 1969; My Life, My Trees, 1970; Famous Trees of Bible Lands, 1974; The Tree of Life, 1977; Tall Timber, 1978; My Horse—My Kingdom, My Health—My Wealth. Founder Trees and Life, Journal of The Men of the Trees; many articles and pamphlets on forestry. *Recreations:* riding, gardening, music and tree photography. *Address:* Mount Cook Station, Box 3 Tekapo, New Zealand. *T:* Lake Tekapo 842; 21 Royal Avenue, SW3. *T:* 01-730 5583; Applesham, Forest Row, Sussex. *Club:* Naval and Military.                        *Died 9 June 1982.*

**BAKER, Sir Rowland,** Kt 1968; OBE 1946; RCNC; Director, Balrena Group; *b* 3 June 1908; *s* of Isaac and Lizzie Baker; *m* 1931, Frances Cornish; one *s* three *d*; *m* 1972, Barbara Mary Comley. *Educ:* RNC Greenwich. Assistant Constructor, HM Dockyards, 1933–39; Constructor, Admty, 1939–42; Supt of Landing Craft, 1942–46; Naval Constructor-in-Chief, Royal Canadian Navy, 1948–56; Technical Chief Exec., Dreadnought Project, 1958–63; Tech. Dir, Polaris Exec., MoD (Navy), 1963–68, retired. Medal of Freedom with Silver Palm (US), 1946. *Publications:* contribs to jls. *Recreations:* golf, bridge. *Address:* Newfield, Entry Hill, Bath. *T:* Bath 22452.
                                                                                 *Died 25 Nov. 1983.*

**BAKER, Sir (Stanislaus) Joseph,** Kt 1958; CB 1947; retired as Receiver for the Metropolitan Police District and Courts (1952–60); *b* 7 March 1898; *s* of Henry G. Baker, Liverpool; *m* 1920, Eleonora White (*d* 1981); one *d* (and one *d* decd). *Educ:* St Francis Xavier Sch.; Liverpool Univ. BSc 1919, Hons 1920. Served European War, 1914–18, RE 1915–17; Royal Artillery, 1917–18. Local Government Board for Ireland, 1920; Chief Sec.'s Office, Dublin Castle, 1922; Irish Office, 1922; Home Office, 1924; Sec. to Privy Council Cttee on question of contributions to Imperial Funds from the Islands of Jersey, Guernsey and Man, 1925. Asst Under-Sec. of State, Home Office, 1941–52. Chairman: National Police Fund Advisory Council, 1946–52; Police Regional Services Cttee, 1945–48; Police Common Services Cttee, 1948–52; Mem. Board of Governors of Police Coll., 1947–52. Chm., Kenya Police Commission, 1953. *Address:* Camplehaye Hotel, Lamerton, Tavistock, Devon PL19 8QD. *T:* Tavistock 2702.                                          *Died 3 Jan. 1989.*

**BAKER, Rt. Rev. William Scott,** MA; *b* 22 June 1902; *s* of late Rev. Canon William Wing Carew Baker, Vicar of Southill, Beds; unmarried. *Educ:* King's Coll. Choir Sch., Cambridge; Aldenham; King's Coll., Cambridge; Cuddesdon. Deacon, 1925; Priest, 1927; Chaplain of King's Coll., Cambridge, and Asst Curate of St Giles with St Peter's Church, Cambridge, 1925–32; Vicar of St John The Baptist's, Newcastle on Tyne, 1932–43; Examining Chaplain to Bishop of Wakefield, 1928–32; to Bishop of Newcastle, 1941–43; Proctor in Convocation for Diocese of Newcastle, 1943; Bishop of Zanzibar and Dar-es-Salaam, 1943–65, of Zanzibar and Tanga, 1965–68; Lectr, St Katherine's Coll., Liverpool, 1968–75; Asst Bishop, Dio. Liverpool, 1968–87. *Publication:* (contributor) The Parish Communion, 1937. *Address:* 26 Crompton Court, Crompton's Lane, Liverpool L18 3EZ. *T:* 051–722 5035.
                                                                                 *Died 30 Nov. 1990.*

**BAKEWELL, Robert Donald,** CMG 1952; JP; Chm. Australian Woolgrowers' Council, 1949–54 (Member, 1940–); Member Australian Wool Realization Commission, 1945–59; *b* 9 Sept. 1899; *s* of late E. H. Bakewell, Adelaide; *m* 1929, Ydonea, *d* of Hylton Dale, Toorak; one *d*. *Educ:* Kyre Coll. (now Scotch Coll.), Adelaide. Man. Dir, Farnley Grazing Pty. Ltd, 1935–73; Pres., Graziers' Federal Council of Aust., 1948–49 (Mem. 1940–50); Pres., Graziers' Assoc. of Vic., 1943–46 (Mem. Council and Exec., 1937–, Trustee, 1945–80); Mem. Exec. Chamber of Agric. of Vic., 1940–50 (Vice-Pres. 1946–48); Graziers Rep., Primary Producers' Council of Aust., 1947–49; Mem. Wool Industry Conference, 1963–70. *Recreation:* bowls. *Address:* 22 Parkview Parade, Benalla, Vic 3672, Australia. *T:* Benalla 62-3368. *Clubs:* Australian (Melbourne); Adelaide (S Australia); Benalla (Victoria).                          *Died 11 July 1982.*

**BALANCHINE, George Melitonovitch;** choreographer; Artistic Director, 1948–83, Ballet Master Emeritus, since 1983, New York City Ballet Company; *b* St Petersburg (now Leningrad), Russia, 22 Jan. 1904; *s* of Meliton Balanchivadze, composer, and Maria Vassiliev; became a citizen of the US; *m* 1st, Tamara Geva (marr. diss.); 2nd, Vera Zorina; 3rd, Maria Tallchief; 4th, 1952, Tanaquil LeClerq. *Educ:* Imperial Academy of Dance, Imperial Academy of Music, St Petersburg. Left Russia on a European tour with the Soviet State Dancers, 1924, playing in Germany, England and France. Ballet-Master: for Serge Diaghilev, 1925–29; staged dances for Cole Porter production of Wake up and Dream, London, 1929; Maître de Ballet at Royal Theatre, Copenhagen, 1930; with Boris Kochno organized Ballets de Théâtre de Monte Carlo, under patronage of Princess of Monaco, 1932; presented Les Ballets, 1933;

went to US, 1933, and founded School of American Ballet, 1934 (Chm. of Faculty); Artistic Director, Ballet Society, New York, 1946; with Lincoln Kirstein as General Director and himself as Artistic Director the New York City Ballet Company was started, 1948; it has subsequently made many tours in US and abroad. Has composed over 100 ballets and his choreography includes ballets in operas, musical comedies and films. Was guest of Grand Opera, Paris, 1947, and Sadler's Wells, London, 1950. *Publications:* Balanchine's Complete Stories of the Great Ballets, 1954; (with Francis Mason) Festival of Ballet, 1978. *Address:* c/o School of American Ballet, Inc., NY State Theatre, NY 10023, USA.
*Died 30 April 1983.*

**BALDWIN, James (Arthur);** Author; *b* Harlem, New York City, 2 Aug. 1924; *s* of David and Berdis Emma Baldwin. *Educ:* DeWitt Clinton High Sch., New York. Various non-literary jobs, 1942–45. Moved to Paris, 1948; lived in Europe until 1956. Active in civil rights movement in USA. Saxton Fellow, 1945; Rosenwald Fellow, 1948; Guggenheim Fellow, 1954; Nat. Inst. of Arts and Letters Award, and Partisan Review Fellow, 1956. Mem. Nat. Inst. of Arts and Letters, 1964. Martin Luther King Jr Award, City Coll. of Univ. of NY, 1978. DLitt, Univ. of British Columbia, 1963. *Publications: novels:* Go Tell It on the Mountain, 1953; Giovanni's Room, 1956; Another Country, 1962; Going to Meet the Man, 1965; Tell Me How Long the Train's Been Gone, 1968; If Beale Street Could Talk, 1974; Little Man, Little Man (with Yoran Cazac), 1975; The Devil Finds Work, 1976; Just Above my Head, 1979; *essays:* Notes of a Native Son, 1955; Nobody Knows My Name, 1961; The Fire Next Time, 1963; Nothing Personal (with Richard Avedon), 1964; No Name in the Street, 1971; (with Margaret Mead) A Rap on Race, 1971; (with Nikki Giovanni) A Dialogue, 1975; Evidence of Things not Seen, 1985; The Price of the Ticket, 1985; *plays:* The Amen Corner, 1955 (prod Saville, London, 1965); Blues for Mr Charlie, 1964; One Day when I was Lost, 1972; The Woman at the Well, 1972; essays and short stories in many jls and anthologies, 1946–. *Died 1 Dec. 1987.*

**BALERNO,** Baron *cr* 1963, of Currie (Life Peer); **Alick Drummond Buchanan-Smith;** Kt 1956; CBE 1945 (OBE 1939); TD 1938; DL; MA, DSc; MSA Iowa; FRSE; FRSGS; Lecturer in Animal Genetics, University of Edinburgh, 1925–60, retired; *b* 9 Oct. 1898; *s* of late Very Rev. Sir George Adam Smith, DD, LLD, FBA, Principal of Aberdeen Univ., 1909–35 and of late Lilian, *d* of Sir George Buchanan, LLD, FRS; *m* 1926, Mary Kathleen (*d* 1947), *d* of late Captain George Smith of Pittodrie; three *s* one *d* (and one *s* decd). *Educ:* Glasgow Acad., Glenalmond; University of Aberdeen; Iowa State Univ. Lt-Col Comdg 5/7th, 5th and 9th Bns The Gordon Highlanders, TA, 1936–42; Brigadier and Dir Selection of Personnel, War Office, 1942–45; Col Comdg Edinburgh Univ. Contingent, OTC, 1945–53; Chm. Edinburgh, Lothians and Peebles TA & AFA, 1953–57. Pres. Scottish Unionist Assoc., 1955–56; Dep. Chm., Unionist Party in Scotland, 1960–63. Vice-Chm., Pigs Industry Develt Authority, 1957–69; Vice-Pres. Brit. Council of Churches, 1967–71; Pres., Royal Scottish Geographical Soc., 1968–74. Hon. Mem., BVA, 1976. Mem., Edinburgh Univ. Court, 1961–68; Mem., Heriot-Watt Univ. Court, 1966–78 (Chm., 1966–72). Pres. Edinburgh Bn The Boys' Brigade, 1955–68. Hon. Col 5/6th Bn The Gordon Highlanders, 1958–61, of 3rd Bn, 1961. Hon. DSc Heriot-Watt, 1970. Hon. ARCVS, 1971. Iowa State Univ. Distinguished Achievement Citation, 1967. DL, Midlothian, 1975. *Publications:* papers on breeding of farm livestock, in various sci. jls. *Address:* House of Cockburn, Balerno, Midlothian EH14 7JD. *T:* 031-449 3737. *Clubs:* Caledonian; New (Edinburgh).
*Died 28 July 1984.*

**BALFOUR OF INCHRYE,** 1st Baron *cr* 1945, of Shefford; **Harold Harington Balfour,** PC 1941; MC and Bar; *b* 1 Nov. 1897; *s* of Col N. H. Balfour, OBE, Belton, Camberley, Surrey; *m* 1st, 1921, Diana Blanche (marr. diss. 1946; she *d* 1982), *d* of Sir Robert G. Harvey, 2nd Bt; one *s*; 2nd, 1947, Mary Ainslie Profumo, *d* of late Baron Profumo, KC, and of Baroness Profumo; one *d. Educ:* Chilverton Elms, Dover; RN Coll., Osborne. Joined 60th Rifles, 1914; attached RFC 1915; served European War, 1914–18 (MC and bar); RAF 1918–23; journalism and business since 1923; contested (C) Stratford, West Ham, 1924; MP (C) Isle of Thanet, 1929–45; Parly Under-Sec. of State for Air, 1938–44; Minister Resident in West Africa, 1944–45. President, Federation Chambers of Commerce of the British Empire, 1946–49; President, Commonwealth and Empire Industries Association, 1956–60; Part-time Member, Board of BEA, 1955–66; Chairman, BEA Helicopters Ltd, 1964–66. Senior Member, Privy Council. *Publications:* An Airman Marches, 1935; Wings over Westminster, 1973; Folk, Fish and Fun, 1978. *Recreation:* fishing. *Heir: s* Hon. Ian Balfour [*b* 21 Dec. 1924; *m* 1953, Josephine Maria Jane, *d* of late Mr and of the Hon. Mrs Morogh Bernard, Shankill, Co. Dublin; one *d*]. *Address:* End House, St Mary Abbot's Place, W8 6LS. *T:* 01–603 6231. *Club:* Carlton.
*Died 21 Sept. 1988.*

**BALFOUR, David,** CBE 1960; DPhil; FIL; retired diplomat; freelance conference interpreter; *b* London, 20 Jan. 1903; *s* of Reginald

Balfour and Charlotte Warre Cornish; *m* 1948, Louise Fitzherbert; one *d. Educ:* Oratory Sch., Edgbaston; and at Angers, Prague, Salzburg, Rome, Athens. Graduate of Oriental Institute, Rome, and of Athens Univ. (1940); DPhil (Oxon), 1978. On staff of the Institute of English Studies, Athens, 1939–41. Served War of 1939–45 in Army, 1941–43, GSO II, GHQ, Middle East Forces (despatches). Entered HM Foreign Service, 1943, established 1946; served Cairo, Athens, Foreign Office, Tel Aviv (Oriental Sec., 1949–50), Smyrna (Consul-Gen., 1951–55), Genoa (Consul-Gen., 1955–60), and Geneva (Consul-Gen., 1960–63); Interpreter and Translator, FO, 1963–68; retd 1968. Mem., Internat. Assoc. of Conf. Interpreters, 1969. *Recreations:* theology, byzantinology (especially 14th and 15th century). *Publications:* critical editions of unedited works of Symeon of Thessalonica, 1979 and 1981, of Gregory of Sinai, 1982, of Gregory Palamas and of John of Karpathos, 1988; The Palamas/Gregoras Debate of 1355 (16th Internat. Byzantine Congress), 1982. *Address:* The Old Mill, Kingsclere, Hants. *T:* Kingsclere 298610. *Died 11 Oct. 1989.*

**BALFOUR, Sir John,** GCMG 1954 (KCMG 1947; CMG 1941); GBE 1959; *b* 26 May 1894; *s* of Charles Barrington Balfour, CB, Newton Don and Balgonie, and of Lady Nina Balfour; *m* 1933, Frances (CVO 1969; Lady-in-Waiting to HRH Princess Marina, Duchess of Kent, 1961–68), *d* of Prof. Alexander van Millingen, DD. *Educ:* Eton; New Coll., Oxford. Interned in Germany, 1914–18; 3rd Sec. in the Diplomatic Service or Foreign Office, 1919; served in Foreign Office, at HM Legations at Budapest, Sofia and Belgrade, and at HM Embassies at Madrid and Washington; IDC 1937; Minister in Lisbon, 1941–43; in Moscow, 1943–45; in Washington, 1945–48; Ambassador to Argentine Republic, 1948–51; Ambassador to Spain, 1951–54; retired from Foreign Service, 1954. UK Commissioner-Gen. to Brussels International Exhibition of 1958. Chairman: British and French Bank, 1959–69; United Bank for Africa, 1961–69. Officier de la Légion d'Honneur, 1972. *Posthumous publication:* Not too Correct an Aureole: the recollections of a diplomat, 1984. *Address:* 38 Onslow Square, SW7. *T:* 01-584 1970. *Club:* Brooks's. *Died 26 Feb. 1983.*

**BALFOUR-LYNN, Dr Stanley;** Consultant, AMI Inc., Los Angeles, since 1983; Chairman and Chief Executive, AMI (Hospitals) Ltd, 1969–83; *b* 21 June 1922; *s* of John and Yetta; *m* 1952, Valerie Eker (marr. diss. 1985); three *s* one *d*; *m* 1985, Mrs Annette Brown. *Educ:* City of London Sch.; Guy's Hosp., London. MB, BS London; MRCS, LRCP; MRCGP. Prosector and Demonstr of Anatomy, RCS, 1949–51; RMO, Queen Charlotte's Maternity Hosp., 1951–52; Sen. Registrar, Edgware Gen. Hosp. Underwriting Mem. of Lloyd's. Founder, Independent Hosp. Gp; Hon. Exec. Mem., NSPCC. *Publications:* contribs on parthenogenesis, and osteoarthritis and cobra venom to Lancet and THS Health Services Jl. *Recreations:* scuba diving, flying, unsolicited advisor to the NHS. *Address:* 97 Harley Street, W1. *T:* 01–935 9964; Flat 7, 26 Gloucester Square, W2. *T:* 01–724 3979. Hush Heath Manor, Cranbrook, Goudhurst, Kent. *T:* Goudhurst 211312. *Clubs:* MCC, Annabel's, Mark's; David Lloyd Tennis; British Sub Aqua; Kidlington Flying.
*Died 23 Feb. 1986.*

**BALL, Alan Hugh;** Deputy Chairman, Lonrho Ltd, since 1982 and Director of associated companies (Chairman and Joint Managing Director, 1961–72; Executive Deputy Chairman, 1972–78); *b* 8 June 1924; *s* of late Sir George Joseph Ball, KBE and Mary Caroline Ball; *m* 1948, Eleanor Katharine Turner; two *s* one *d. Educ:* Eton. KRRC, 1943–47. Lonrho Ltd and associated cos, 1947–. *Recreations:* fishing, shooting. *Address:* The Old Mill, Ramsbury, Marlborough, Wilts. *T:* Marlborough 20266. *Died 5 Oct. 1987.*

**BALL, Sir George Thomas T.;** *see* Thalben-Ball.

**BALL, Rev. Kenneth Vernon James,** MA; *b* 10 July 1906; *s* of Vernon Arthur and Eveline Ball, Brighton; *m* 1939, Isabella Jane Armstrong, MB, ChB, *d* of Archibald Armstrong, JP, and Eleanor Elsie Armstrong, Strachur, Argyll; one *s* one *d. Educ:* The College, Swindon; Jesus Coll., Oxford; Wycliffe Hall, Oxford. Acting Headmaster, Busoga High Sch., Uganda, 1930–32; Curate, St Paul, Bedminster, 1932–35; Curate, Temple or Holy Cross Church, Bristol, 1935–38; Vicar, St Barnabas, Bristol, 1938–42; Vicar, St Leonard, Redfield, Bristol, 1942–47; Bishop of Liverpool's Special Service Staff, 1947–50; Vicar, St Nicholas, and Chap. St Bartholomew's Hosp., Rochester, 1950–59; Oriel Canon of Rochester Cath., 1955–59; Vicar of Leatherhead, Surrey, 1959–70; Rector of Piddlehinton, Dorset, 1970–72; retd. *Publication:* Spiritual Approach to Marriage Preparation, 1948. *Recreation:* singing. *Address:* Manormead Nursing Home, Tilford Road, Hindhead, Surrey. *T:* Hindhead 4044. *Died 12 Nov. 1986.*

**BALL, Robert Edward,** CB 1977; MBE 1946; Chief Master of the Supreme Court of Judicature (Chancery Division), 1969–79 (Master, 1954–68); *b* 8 March 1911; *s* of James Ball, LLB, Purley, Surrey, and Mabel Louise (*née* Laver); *m* 1935, Edith Margaret Barbara, *d* of late Dr Patrick Edward Campbell; one *s* two *d* (and one *s* decd). *Educ:* Westminster Sch.; Lycée de Vendôme, France; Germany;

London Univ. (LLB). Law Soc.'s Studentship, 1929. Admitted Solicitor, 1933; junior partner, James Ball & Son, 1933–46; served War, 1939–46; commissioned in Queen's Royal Regt, 1940; served KORR and in various staff appts, England, France and India; AA & QMG, Madras; released with rank of Lt-Col, 1946; formed practice of Potts and Ball, Chester and London, with Henry Potts, 1946. Chm., Friends of Friendless Churches, 1988–. Original Mem., British Assoc. for Club of Rome, 1989. Formerly: Hon. Sec., Chester and North Wales Incorp. Law Soc.; Chm. Chester Insurance Tribunal, etc. *Publications:* The Law and the Cloud of Unknowing, 1976; The Crown, The Sages and Supreme Morality, 1983; contrib. to publications of the Inst. of Moralogy, Chiba, Japan. *Recreations:* history, oriental studies, gardening. *Address:* 62 Stanstead Road, Caterham, Surrey. *T:* Caterham 43675. *Club:* Athenæum.
*Died 7 Feb.* 1990.

**BALLANTYNE, Alexander Hanson,** CVO 1957; CBE 1963; HM Diplomatic Service, retired; Consultant, Organisation for Economic Co-operation and Development, 1971–80; *b* 27 Feb. 1911; *s* of late Dr Harold Sherman Ballantyne and Mrs Gladys Pauline Ballantyne; *m* 1944, Hélène Georgette Contoroussi; one *s* one *d. Educ:* Rugby; Christ's Coll., Cambridge. BA (Hons) Cantab. HM Consular Service, 1934. Vice-Consul: Bangkok, 1934–38; Valencia, 1938 and 1939; Tokyo, 1940–42; Antananarivo, 1942–45; Actg Consul-Gen. Antananarivo, 1945 and 1946; Foreign Office, 1946 and 1947; First Sec. (Commercial), Istanbul, 1947–50; Actg Consul-Gen, Istanbul, 1950 and 1951; Foreign Office, 1951 and 1952; First Sec. (Commercial), Bangkok, 1952–55; Counsellor (Commercial) and Consul-General, Copenhagen, 1959–60; Chargé d'Affaires, Ankara, 1962; Counsellor (Commercial), Ankara, 1960–64; Consul-General, Frankfurt-am-Main, 1964–69. Commander of the Dannebrog, 1957. *Publication:* French Clocks the World Over (translation of Tardy's La Pendule Française dans le Monde): vol. I, 1981; vols II and III, 1982; vol. IV, 1983; Montgolfières (Hot-air balloons), 1982 (trans. of Pierre-Louis Clément's Montgolfières). *Recreation:* music. *Address:* 2 Avenue Marie-Christine, 06 Nice, France.
*Died 28 March* 1983.

**BALLANTYNE, Air Vice-Marshal Gordon Arthur,** CBE 1945; DFC 1918; FDSRCS; FDSRCSE; Director of Dental Services, RAF, 1943–54; *b* 12 Feb. 1900; *e s* of late John Alexander and Ida Ballantyne; *m* 1st, 1925, Brenda Muriel, *d* of Rev. Bernard Cuzner; one *d*; 2nd, 1945 Rachel Mary, *er d* of late Francis Reid Brown. *Educ:* King's Coll.; London Hosp. Probationary Flight Officer, Royal Naval Air Service, 1917; Flying Officer RAF 1918. Served in France with No 8 Squadron, RFC (wounded); LDS, RCS 1923; Lieut Army Dental Corps, 1924; Captain, 1927. Transferred to RAF Dental Branch, 1930; Squadron Leader, 1934; Wing Commander, 1937; Acting Group Captain, 1941; Temp. Group Captain, 1942; Group Captain and Acting Air Commodore, 1943; Temp. Air Commodore, 1944; Air Commodore, 1947; Air Vice-Marshal, 1952; Senior Dental Officer, Iraq, 1935; Inspecting Dental Officer, Home Commands, 1938; Training Officer (Dental), 1941; retd 1954; Hon. Dental Surgeon to King George VI, 1945–52. Member Board of Faculty of Dental Surgery of Royal Coll. of Surgeons of England, 1947–53; Hon. member British Dental Association; Hon. Pres. Armed Forces Commn, Federation Dentaire Internationale, 1953; Hon. Dental Surgeon to the Queen, 1952–54. *Publications:* various professional papers. *Recreations:* painting and motoring. *Address:* 3 St Martin's Hill, Canterbury, Kent. *T:* Canterbury 61103.
*Died 7 Nov.* 1981.

**BALLANTYNE, Henry,** CBE 1968; DL, JP; President, Henry Ballantyne & Sons Ltd, since 1981 (Chairman, 1977–81); *b* 27 Nov. 1912; *er s* of late Lieut-Col David Ballantyne, OBE, Barns Kirkton Manor, Peeblesshire; *m* 1938, Barbara Mary, *d* of late C. S. Gavin, Worthing; one *s* three *d. Educ:* Cheltenham Coll.; Pembroke Coll., Cambridge. Entered family business, D. Ballantyne Bros & Co. Ltd, 1937: Dir, 1937; Chm., 1940, also of subsid. cos; merged twelve Border woollen firms to form Scottish Worsteds & Woollens Ltd, 1968, new holding co. Henry Ballantyne & Sons Ltd formed 1977; Dir, Chagford Investment Hldgs Ltd and other cos. Pres., S of Scotland Chamber of Commerce, 1942–44; Pres., Nat. Assoc. of Scottish Woollen Manufrs, 1951–55; Member: BoT Adv. Cttee, 1961–67; Scottish Econ. Planning Cttee, 1965–68; Royal Commn on Local Govt in Scotland, 1967–69; Scottish Constitutional Cttee of Conservative Party, 1969–70; Scottish Woollen Publicity Council (Chm., 1974–80); Scottish Veterans' Garden City Assoc. (Chm., 1974–). Member of the Royal Company of Archers (Queen's Body Guard for Scotland). DL 1953, JP 1943, Peeblesshire. *Recreations:* shooting, yachting, gardening. *Address:* The Kirklands, Innerleithen, Peeblesshire. *T:* Innerleithen 392. *Clubs:* Lansdowne, Royal Ocean Racing; Leander (Henley-on-Thames).
*Died 19 March* 1983.

**BALLARD, Ven. Arthur Henry;** Archdeacon of Manchester and Canon Residentiary of Manchester Cathedral, 1972–80; *b* 9 March 1912; 3rd *s* of Alfred and Lillian Ballard; *m* 1943, Phyllis Marion, *d* of Walter East, Theydon Bois, Essex; two *s. Educ:* privately; St

John's Coll., Univ. of Durham (Van Mildert Scholar). BA (with distinction) 1938; DipTh. 1939; MA 1941. Deacon 1939; Curate of Walthamstow, 1939–43; Rector of Broughton, Manchester, 1943–46; Rector of All Saints, Stand, Manchester, 1946–72. Rural Dean of Radcliffe and Prestwich, 1952–67; Hon. Canon of Manchester, 1958–66; Archdeacon of Rochdale, 1966–72. Mem., Gen. Synod of CofE, 1972–80. *Recreations:* restoration of clocks, antique furniture, paintings. *Address:* 30 Rathen Road, Withington, Manchester M20 9GH. *T:* 061–445 4703. *Club:* Manchester.
*Died 2 Feb.* 1984.

**BALLARD, Geoffrey Horace,** CBE 1978; JP; DL; Managing Director: G. H. Ballard (Farms) Ltd, since 1968; G. H. Ballard (Leasing) Ltd, since 1968; Chairman, MSF Ltd, since 1984; Vice-Chairman, NFU Mutual Insurance Society Ltd, since 1982; *b* 21 May 1927; *s* of Horace and Mary Catherine Ballard; *m* 1st, 1948, Dorothy Sheila Bache (*d* 1979); two *s* one *d*; 2nd, 1983, Anne Ballard. *Educ:* Hanley Castle Grammar Sch. Farming with father at Home Farm, Abberley, 1943; Maesllwch Castle Estates: Cowman, 1947, Bailiff, 1948; in partnership with father and brother at Home Farm, 1950; farming, on own account, at Old Yates Farm, Abberley, 1953; Nuffield Farming Schol. to USA, 1965. Chm., W Midlands Reg. panel for Agric., 1972–80. Chm., Worcestershire County NFU, 1967. JP 1967–; DL Hereford and Worcester, 1987. *Recreations:* sailing, shooting. *Address:* Orchard House, Abberley, Worcester WR6 6AT. *T:* Great Witley (0299) 307. *Clubs:* Farmers'; Dale Sailing (Dyfed); Astley and District Farmers Discussion (Worcs).
*Died 27 May* 1990.

**BALMAIN, Pierre Alexandre;** Officier de la Légion d'Honneur, 1978; Couturier, established in 1945; *b* St-Jean-de-Maurienne (Savoie), 18 May 1914; *s* of Maurice Balmain and Françoise Balmain (*née* Ballinari). *Educ:* Lycée de Chambéry; Ecole des Beaux-Arts, Paris. Dress designer with Molyneux, 1934–39; dress designer with Lelong, 1939–45. Mem., Rotary Club of Paris. Kt Order of Dannebrog (Denmark) 1963. Cavaliere Ufficiale del Merito Italiano, 1966. *Publication:* My Years and Seasons, 1964. *Recreations:* horse-riding, yachting. *Address:* 44 rue François 1er, 75008 Paris, France. *T:* 720.35.34.
*Died 29 June* 1982.

**BALME, Prof. David Mowbray,** CMG 1955; DSO 1943; DFC 1943; MA; Professor of Classics, Queen Mary College, London University, 1964–78, retired; *b* 8 Sept. 1912; *s* of late Harold Balme, OBE, MD, FRCS; *m* 1936, Beatrice Margaret Rice; four *s* one *d. Educ:* Marlborough; Clare Coll., Cambridge. Res. Student, Clare Coll. and Univ. of Halle, Germany, 1934–36; Lecturer, Reading Univ., 1936–37; Research Fellow, Clare Coll., Cambridge, 1937–40; Fellow of Jesus Coll., 1940. Served with No 207 (Bomber) Squadron, 1943; Comd Nos 227 and 49 Squadrons, 1945. Tutor of Jesus Coll., 1945–47; Senior Tutor, 1947–48; University Lecturer in Classics, 1947–48; Principal, University College of Ghana, 1948–57; Reader in Classics, Queen Mary Coll., London, 1957–64. Vis. Prof., Princeton Univ., 1973. Hon. LLD Lincoln, Pa, 1955; Hon. LittD Ghana, 1970. Editor, Phronesis, 1965–70. *Publications:* Aristotle's De Partibus Animalium, I, 1972; articles in classical journals on Greek Philosophy. *Recreations:* music, foxhunting. *Address:* Gumley, near Market Harborough, Leics. *T:* Kibworth 2762.
*Died 23 Feb.* 1989.

**BALOGH, Baron** *cr* 1968 (Life Peer), of Hampstead; **Thomas Balogh,** MA, Dr rer. pol. Budapest; Hon. Dr econ. Budapest, 1979; Dr *hc* econ. York Univ., Toronto, 1980; Fellow Emeritus of Balliol College, Oxford, 1973; *b* Budapest, 2 Nov. 1905; *e s* of Emil Balogh; *m* 1945, Penelope (marr. diss. 1970), widow of Oliver Gatty, sometime Fellow of Balliol; two *s* one *d* one step-*d*; *m* 1970, Catherine Storr; three step-*d. Educ:* The Gymnasium of Budapest Univ.; Univs of Budapest, Berlin, Harvard. Fellow of Hungarian Coll., Berlin, 1927; Rockefeller Fellow, 1928–30; League of Nations, 1931; economist in the City, 1931–39; National Institute of Economic Research, 1938–42; Oxford Univ. Institute of Statistics, 1940–55; Special Lecturer, 1955–60; Fellow of Balliol Coll., Oxford, 1945–73; Reader in Econs, Oxford Univ., 1960–73; Leverhulme Fellow, Oxford, 1973–76; Senior Research Associate, Queen Elizabeth House, Oxford, 1979–. Visiting Prof., Minnesota and Wisconsin, 1951; Delhi and Calcutta, 1955. Consultant: Reserve Bank of Australia, 1942–64; UNRRA Mission to Hungary, 1946; Govt of Malta, 1955–57, of Jamaica, 1956, 1961–62; Food and Agricultural Organisation of UN, 1957–59, 1961–62; UN Economic Commn for Latin America, 1960; Government of India Statistical Inst., 1960, 1971; Greece, 1962; Mauritius, 1962–63; UN Special Fund, 1964, 1970, 1971; OECD, 1964; Turkey, Peru, 1964. Member, Economic and Financial Cttee of the Labour Party, 1943–64, 1971–; Mem. and acting Chm., Minerals Cttee, Min. of Fuel and Power, 1964–68; Economic Advr to Cabinet, 1964–67; Consultant to Prime Minister, 1968; Minister of State, Dept of Energy, 1974–75. Dep. Chm., BNOC, 1976–78, Economic Adviser, 1978–79. Chm., Fabian Soc., 1970. Fellow, New York Univ., 1969; Fellow, W. Wilson Center, Washington, 1976. Hon. Res. Fellow, UCL, 1980–81. Mem., Hungarian Acad. of Science. *Publications:* Hungarian

Reconstruction and the Reparation Question, 1946; Studies in Financial Organisation, 1946; Dollar Crisis, 1949; Planning through the Price Mechanism, 1950; (with D. Seers) The Economic Future of Malta (Valetta), 1955; Planning and Monetary Organisation in Jamaica, 1956; The Economic Problem of Iraq, 1957; The Economic Development of the Mediterranean (as Head of a Research team), 1957; Economic Policy and Price Mechanism, 1961; Development Plans in Africa, 1961; (with M. Bennett) Sugar Industry in Mauritius; Unequal Partners, 2 vols, 1963; Planning for Progress, 1963; Economics of Poverty, 1966; Labour and Inflation, 1970; Fact and Fancy: an essay in monetary reform, 1973; (co-author): Economics of Full Employment, 1945; War Economics, 1947; Foreign Economic Policy for the US; Fabian International and Colonial Essays; The Establishment, 1960; Crisis in the Civil Service, 1968; Keynes College Essays, 1976, 1978, 1980; (co-author) Crisis of Capitalism, 1978; The Irrelevance of Conventional Economics, 1982; papers in Economic Journal, Bulletin of Oxford Institute of Statistics, etc. *Address:* The Cottage, Greenfields, Watlington, Oxon. *T:* Watlington 2735.

*Died 20 Jan. 1985.*

**BANBURY OF SOUTHAM,** 2nd Baron, *cr* 1924, of Southam; **Charles William Banbury;** 2nd Bt, *cr* 1902; DL; late 12th Lancers; *b* 18 May 1915; *s* of Captain Charles William Banbury, *e s* of 1st Baron (killed in action, Sept. 1914), and Josephine, *d* of José Reixach; *S* grandfather, 1936; *m* 1945, Hilda Ruth (marr. diss. 1958), 2nd *d* of late A. H. R. Carr; one *s* two *d. Educ:* Stowe. DL 1965, CC 1967, CA 1967–74, Glos. *Heir: s* Hon. Charles William Banbury, *b* 29 July 1953. *Address:* Stratton Cleeve, Circencester, Glos GL7 2JD. *T:* Cirencester 3464. *Died 29 April 1981.*

**BANERJEE, Rabindra Nath,** CSI 1946; CIE 1938; Chairman, Union Public Service Commission, India, 1949–55, retired; *b* 1 Feb 1895; *s* of late Haradhan Banerjee; *m* Manisha (*d* 1953) *d* of late Lieut-Col Upendra Nath Mukerjee, IMS; one *s* (one *d* decd). *Educ:* Calcutta Univ. (MA 1915); Emmanuel Coll., Cambridge (BA 1918). Entered Indian Civil Service, 1920; Registrar Co-operative Societies and Dir Of Industries, Central Provinces and Berar, 1929–33; Vice-Chm. Provincial Banking Enquiry Cttee, 1929; Sec. to Govt, Central Provinces and Berar, Revenue Dept, 1933; Sec. to Govt, CP and Berar, Local Self-Government Dept, 1936; Mem. CP and Berar Legislative Council, 1929–36; Sec. to the Governor, CP and Berar, 1937; Commissioner, 1941; Commissioner of Food Supply, 1943; Sec. to Govt of India, Commonwealth Relations Dept and Min. of Home Affairs, 1944–48. Mem. Council of State (India), 1944, 1945, 1947; MLA (India), 1946. Mem. of Cttee of Experts of International Labour Organisation, 1956–58. *Address:* 175 Jor Bagh, New Delhi 110003, India. *T:* 611219. *Died 11 Jan. 1985.*

**BANHAM, Prof. (Peter) Reyner;** appointed Sheldon H. Solow Professor of the History of Architecture, Institute of Fine Arts, New York University, 1987; *b* 2 March 1922; *m* 1946, Mary Mullett; one *s* one *d. Educ:* King Edward VI Sch., Norwich; Courtauld Institute of Art, London. BA 1952, PhD 1958. Bristol Aeroplane Co., 1939–45. Editorial Staff, Architectural Review, 1952–64; Sen. Lectr, University Coll., London, 1964, Reader in Architecture, 1967, Prof. of History of Architecture, 1969–76; Chm., Dept of Design Studies, State Univ. of NY at Buffalo, NY, 1976–80; Prof. of Art Hist., Univ. of California at Santa Cruz, 1980–87. Research Fellow, Graham Foundation (Chicago), 1964–66; Bannister Fletcher Vis. Prof., UCL, 1982. Mem., Architect-Selection Panel, J. Paul Getty Trust, 1983–84. Architectural Advr, Brooklyn Mus., 1985–86. Jury Mem., Pirelli-Bicocca redevelt competition, Milan, 1986. Hon. FRIBA, 1983. Hon. DLitt East Anglia, 1986. Prix Jean Tschumi, 1975; AIA Honor Award, 1984. *Publications:* Theory and Design in the First Machine Age, 1960; Guide to Modern Architecture, 1962; The New Brutalism, 1966; Architecture of the Well-tempered Environment, 1969; Los Angeles, 1971; (ed) The Aspen Papers, 1974; The Age of the Masters: a Personal View of Architecture, 1975; Megastructure, 1976; Design by Choice, 1981; Scenes in America Deserta, 1982; A Concrete Atlantis, 1986. *Recreations:* indistinguishable from daily interests in architecture and design.

*Died 18 March 1988.*

**BANKES, Henry John Ralph;** JP; Barrister, Inner Temple, 1925; *b* 14 July 1902; *s* of Walter Ralph Bankes of Corfe Castle and Kingston Lacy, Dorset; *m* 1935, Hilary (*d* 1966), *d* of late Lieut-Col F. Strickland-Constable, Wassand Hall, Yorks; one *s* one *d. Educ:* Eton; Magdalen Coll., Oxford. JP Dorset, 1936; High Sheriff of Dorset, 1939. RNVR, 1939–45. *Address:* Kingston Lacy, Wimborne, Dorset. *Clubs:* Carlton; Royal Dorset Yacht (Weymouth); Royal Motor Yacht (Sandbanks). *Died 19 Aug. 1981.*

**BANKOLE-JONES, Sir Samuel;** *see* Jones.

**BANKS, A(rthur) Leslie,** MA Cantab; MD London; FRCP; DPH; Barrister-at-Law (Lincoln's Inn); Professor of Human Ecology, Cambridge, 1949–71, then Emeritus; Fellow, Gonville and Caius College, since 1951; *b* 12 Jan. 1904; *o s* of late A. C. and E. M. F. Banks; *m* 1933, Eileen Mary (*d* 1967), *d* of Sidney Barrett, Arkley,

Herts; two *s. Educ:* Friern Barnet Gram. Sch.; Middlesex Hospital and Medical Sch. MD 1931; MRCP 1936. Resident hospital appointments, including house-surgeon, resident officer to special depts and acting Registrar, Middlesex Hosp., 1926–28; Locum tenens and asst in general practice, Asst Medical Officer, Gen. Post Office, EC1, 1928–34; Divisional Medical Officer, Public Health Dept, LCC (duties included special public health enquiries and slum clearance), 1934–37; Min. of Health, 1937–49; seconded as Medical Officer of Health to City of Newcastle, 1946. Formerly Principal Medical Officer, Min. of Health. Mem., GMC, 1957–70; WHO: Consultant, 1950–76; Founder Mem. and Vice-Chm., UK Cttee, 1950–67; Mem., Expert Adv Panel on Orgn of Med. Care, Geneva, 1972–76. Member: Hon. Society of Lincoln's Inn; Middlesex Hosp. Club. FRSocMed. First Viscount Bennett Prize, Lincoln's Inn, for essay on Jurisdiction of Judicial Cttee of Privy Council. *Publications:* Social Aspects of Disease, 1953; (ed) Development of Tropical and Sub-tropical Countries, 1954; Health and Hygiene, 1957; (with J. A. Hislop) Art of Administration, 1961; private and official papers on medical and social subjects. *Address:* 4 Heycroft, Eynsham, Oxford. *T:* Oxford 880791.

*Died 14 June 1989.*

**BANKS, Air Cdre Francis Rodwell,** CB 1946; OBE 1919; RAF (retired); *b* 22 March 1898; *s* of late Bernard Rodwell and Frances Emily Banks; *m* 1925, Christine Constance Grant Langlands; two *d. Educ:* Christ's Coll., London, N. Served in two wars, 1914–19 in Navy and 1939–46 in RAF. Between the two wars specialised in the development of aviation engines and their fuels with The Associated Ethyl Co.; responsible in the recent war successively for the production, the research and development of aero engines, including gas turbines, at MAP. Principal Dir of Engine Research and Development, Min. of Supply, 1952–53; Dir, The Bristol Aeroplane Co., 1954–59; Dir, Hawker Siddeley Aviation Ltd, 1954–59, now Engrg Consultant. Pres. RAeS, 1969. CEng; Hon. CGIA; Hon. FRAeS; Hon. FAIAA; FIMechE; FInstPet. *Publications:* I Kept No Diary, memoirs, 1978, 2nd rev. edn 1983; technical papers on aviation engines and their fuels. *Recreation:* golf. *Address:* 5a Albert Court, SW7. *T:* 01–584 2740. *Club:* Royal Air Force.

*Died 12 May 1985.*

**BANKS, James Dallaway,** MA; seconded to Regional and Planning Division, Department of Health and Social Security, 1973–75, retired 1975; *b* 3 Jan. 1917; *s* of late Dr Cyril Banks; *m* 1st, 1942, Winifred Holt (*d* 1982); one *s* one *d* (and one *s* decd); 2nd, 1983, Janette Marian Morgan. *Educ:* Nottingham High Sch.; St John's Coll., Cambridge. BA 1938, MA 1943. Indian Civil Service, 1939–47. Dep. House Governor, King's Coll. Hosp., 1947–53; House Governor: Royal Marsden Hospital 1953–59; The Hospital for Sick Children, Great Ormond Street, 1959–60; Sec. to Bd of Governors, KCH, Denmark Hill, 1960–73. Vis. Fellow, Computer Studies Dept, Univ. of Southampton, 1978–. *Address:* 8 Newenham Road, Lymington, Hants. *T:* Lymington 74999. *Club:* Lymington Town Sailing. *Died 17 Oct. 1985.*

**BANKS, Captain William Eric,** CBE 1943; DSC; RN retired; *b* 17 July 1900; *er s* of late Walter Banks; *m* 1937, Audrey Steel (decd); two *s. Educ:* University Coll. Sch. Joined Navy in 1918; retired list, 1952. *Address:* 2 College Yard, Gloucester. *Club:* Naval and Military. *Died 1 Nov. 1986.*

**BANNER, Sir George Knowles H.;** *see* Harmood-Banner.

**BANNERMAN, Sir (Alexander) Patrick,** 14th Bt *cr* 1682 (NS), of Elsick, Kincardineshire; *b* 5 May 1933; *s* of Lt-Col Sir Donald Arthur Gordon Bannerman, 13th Bt and of Barbara Charlotte, *d* of late Lt-Col Alexander Cameron, OBE; *S* father, 16 Sept. 1989; *m* 1977, Joan Mary, *d* of late John Henry Wilcox. *Educ:* Gordonstoun; RAC, Cirencester. *Heir: b* David Gordon Bannerman, OBE [*b* 18 Aug. 1935; *m* 1960, Mary Prudence, *d* of Rev. Philip Frank Ardagh-Walter; four *d*]. *Died 21 Nov. 1989.*
*This entry did not appear in Who's Who.*

**BANNERMAN, Lt-Col Sir Donald Arthur Gordon,** 13th Bt, *cr* 1682; *b* 2 July 1899; *s* of Lt-Col Sir Arthur D'Arcy Gordon Bannerman, KCVO, CIE, 12th Bt and of late Virginia Emilie Bannerman; *S* father, 1955; *m* 1932, Barbara Charlotte, *d* of late Lieut-Col A. Cameron, OBE, IMS; two *s* twin *d. Educ:* Harrow; Royal Military Coll., Sandhurst; commissioned into Queen's Own Cameron Highlanders, 1918; served in N Russian Campaign, 1919; 1st Class Interpreter (Russian), 1925; served with 1st and 2nd Bns of his Regt in Egypt and India, 1931–34 and 1936–39; served War of 1939–45: with 4th Indian Div. and in MEF, 1940–43; in NW Europe, 1945, attached to US 9th Army, in closing stages of fighting, and then for 3 yrs with Control Commission as Senior Control Officer; retired from Army as Lieut-Col, 1947. On staff of Gordonstoun Sch., 1948–52, of Fettes Coll., 1952–69. *Publications:* Bannerman of Elsick: a short family history, 1975; Random Recollections, 1980. *Recreations:* gardening, walking, reading. *Heir: s* Alexander Patrick Bannerman [*b* 5 May 1933; *m* 1977, Joan Mary Wilcox].

*Died 16 Sept. 1989.*

**BANNERMAN, Sir Patrick;** *see* Bannerman, Sir A. P.

**BANNISTER, Grace,** OBE 1984; JP; Lord Mayor of Belfast, 1981–82; *d* of William H. Collim and Grace (*née* Johnston); *m* 1948, John Bannister; one *d. Educ:* Park Parade Sch. Belfast County Borough Council, later City Council: Councillor, 1965–85; Dep. Lord Mayor, 1975–77; High Sheriff, 1979; Chm., Parks and Cemeteries Cttee, 1969–72 (Dep. Chm., 1966–69, 1972–73); Dep. Chm., Parks and Recreation Cttee, 1973–78; Chm., Parks Cttee, 1978–85; Member: Improvement, Educn, Town Planning and Traffic Special Cttees, 1965–73; Gen. Purposes Cttee, 1969–73; Gen. Purposes and Finance Cttee, 1978–81; Leisure Centres/Services Cttee, 1976–81. Member: Belfast, Holywood and Castlereagh Jt Bd, 1969–73; Belfast Educn and Library Area Board, 1973–81. JP Belfast, 1965. *Recreations:* welfare, community work, knitting, pottery, music, school management committees. *Address:* 34 Grand Parade, Belfast BT5 5HH. *T:* Belfast 57879. *Died 4 Dec.* 1986.

**BANWELL, Sir (George) Harold,** Kt 1955; President, Lincoln Civic Trust; *b* 11 Dec. 1900; *yr s* of late Edward and Marion Banwell, Whitstable, Kent; *m* 1924, Kate Mary, *d* of late Rev. A. B. Bull, Durham; two *s* three *d. Educ:* Tankerton Coll., Kent. Admitted Solicitor, 1922; articled to Town Clerk, Canterbury; Asst Solicitor: West Hartlepool; Cumberland County Council; Sheffield City Council; Dep. Town Clerk, Norwich, 1929–32; Town Clerk, Lincoln, 1932–41; Clerk of the County Council of Lincoln, (Parts of Kesteven), 1941–44; Sec., Association of Municipal Corporations, 1944–Oct. 1962; Chm., Nat. Citizens Advice Bureaux Council, 1961–71; Dep. Chm., Commn for the New Towns, 1964–71. Alderman, Lincoln City Council, 1967–74. Chairman: Cttee on Placing and Management of Contracts for Building and Civil Engineering Work, 1962–64; Congregational Church in England and Wales, 1966–69; Member: Gen. Adv. Council of BBC, 1961–64; Nat. Incomes Commn, 1962–65; Deptl Cttee on the Fire Services, 1967–70; Adv. Council on Commonwealth Immigration, 1962–64; Parly Boundary Commn for England, 1963–74. Hon. LLD Nottingham, 1972. *Address:* 2 Vicars' Court, Lincoln. *T:* Lincoln 28869. *Died 10 April* 1982.

**BANWELL, Godwin Edward,** CBE 1955; MC 1917 and Bar 1918; KPM; Chief Constable of Cheshire 1946–63; *b* 1897; *s* of Edward and Rose Banwell, Polegate, Sussex; *m* 1st, 1924, Kathleen Frances Cole (*d* 1939); 2nd, 1940, Gladys Lilian Banwell; three *s* one *d. Educ:* Merchant Taylors' Sch., London. Leics Regiment, TA, 1916–19; Indian Police, Burma, 1920–38; Regional Officer, Min. of Home Security, 1939–41; Actg Inspector of Constabulary, 1941–42; Chief Constable of East Riding of Yorks, 1942–46. KPM 1931. *Address:* 4 Evenhill Road, Littlebourne, Canterbury, Kent. *Club:* National Liberal. *Died 9 Oct.* 1981.

**BANWELL, Sir Harold;** *see* Banwell, Sir G. H.

**BARBER, Alan Theodore,** MA (Oxon); Headmaster of Ludgrove Preparatory School, Wokingham, Berks, 1937–73, retired; *b* 17 June 1905; *s* of Harold Priestman Barber, Todwick House, Todwick, Yorks; *m* 1937, Dorothy Shaw; one *s* two *d. Educ:* Shrewsbury Sch.; Queen's Coll., Oxford. BA 1929; Triple Blue, captained cricket and football XIs, Oxford; captained Yorks County Cricket XI, 1929 and 1930; played football regularly for Corinthians. Asst master, Ludgrove, 1930. *Recreations:* golf, cricket, Eton Fives. *Address:* The Garden Cottage, Ludgrove, Wokingham, Berks. *T:* Wokingham 782639. *Clubs:* Sports, MCC; Berkshire Golf (Bagshot). *Died 10 March* 1985.

**BARBER, Noël John Lysberg;** author; *b* 9 Sept. 1909; *s* of John Barber, CBE, and Danish-born 'Musse' Barber (*née* Lysberg); *m* 1st, 1938, Helen Whichello, in Singapore; 2nd, 1954, Countess de Feo of Florence; one *s* one *d. Educ:* erratically, briefly, terminated by attack of lockjaw at age of fourteen. After unsuccessful attempts to write books and articles, became professional journalist in the 1930s with Yorkshire Post group, then Daily Express, Manchester; after travelling world by tramp steamer, became editor, Malaya Tribune, Singapore, 1937–38; travels in China, Siberia, Russia, 1938–39; Editor, Overseas Daily Mail, London, 1940. RAF navigator, 1942–45. Légion d'Honneur, 1945. Editor and Man. Dir, Continental Daily Mail, Paris, 1945–53; paintings exhibited at Salon d'Hiver, Paris, 1950–53; Foreign Correspondent, Daily Mail, 1953–65; wounded, Morocco, during French N African war, 1954; wounded, Hungarian Uprising, 1956; first Briton to reach South Pole since Captain Scott, 1957. Organized and appeared in Assignment Unknown, series of TV documentary travelogues, 1959–60; Foreign Manager, then Syndication Manager and Dir, Associated Newspapers Ltd, 1962–73. Ridder of Danneborg, Denmark, 1948. Jordanian Order of Merit, 1961. *Publications:* (after 19 full-length books had been rejected) Newspaper Reporting, 1936; How Strong is America, 1941; The Menace of Japan, 1942; Trans-Siberian, 1943; Prisoner of War, 1944; Fires of Spring, 1952; Strangers in the Sun, 1952; Distant Places, 1956; A Handful of Ashes, 1957; The White Desert, 1958; From the Land of Lost Content, 1960; Life with Titina, 1961; Conversations with Painters,

1964; The Black Hole of Calcutta, 1965; Sinister Twilight, the Fall of Singapore, 1968; The War of the Running Dogs, 1971; Lords of the Golden Horn, 1973; Seven Days of Freedom, 1974; The Week France Fell, 1976; The Natives were Friendly, an autobiography, 1977, revd edn 1985; The Singapore Story, 1979; The Fall of Shanghai, 1979; *juveniles:* Adventures at Both Poles, 1958; Let's Visit the USA, 1960; *novels:* Tanamera, 1981; A Farewell to France, 1983; A Woman of Cairo, 1984; The Other Side of Paradise, 1986; The Weeping and the Laughter, 1988; *in partnership:* Hitler's Last Hope (with Ernest Phillips), 1942; Cities (with Rupert Croft-Cooke), 1946; An Island to Oneself (with Tom Neale), 1966. *Recreations:* writing, music, painting, travel, bridge, watching cricket. *Address:* 4 Grove Court, Drayton Gardens, SW10. *Clubs:* Savage, Savile, International Lawn Tennis of Great Britain. *Died 10 July* 1988.

**BARBER, Samuel;** Composer; *b* West Chester, Pennsylvania, 9 March 1910; *s* of Samuel Leroy Barber and Marguerite McCleod Beatty; unmarried. *Educ:* Curtis Institute of Music, Philadelphia. Compositions performed by all leading American orchestras and by many European orchestras; Conductors include Toscanini, Koussevitzky, Walter, etc. Has conducted own works in Prague, Vienna, London, Three Choirs Festival (Hereford, 1946), etc. Member: AAAL; American Society of Composers, Authors and Publishers (Dir, 1969-). Prix de Rome, 1935; Guggenheim Award, 1945; NY Music Critics Award, 1946; Pulitzer prize for music (opera, Vanessa), 1958, (piano concerto), 1963. Hon. Dr Harvard, 1959. Served AUS, 1943. *Compositions:* First Symphony, 1936; Violin Concerto, 1941; Second Essay, 1942; Capricorn Concerto (flute, oboe, trumpet and strings), 1944; Cello Concerto, 1946; Piano Sonata, 1949; Souvenirs (for piano), 1953; Prayers of Kierkegaard (for chorus, soprano and orch.), 1954; Overture to The School for Scandal, 1932; Music for a Scene from Shelley, 1933; Adagio for Strings, 1936; First Essay for Orchestra, 1942; Medea's Dance of Vengeance (for orch.), 1946; Knoxville: Summer of 1915 (for soprano and orchestra), 1947; Vanessa (opera), 1958; Toccata Festiva (for organ and orch.), 1960; Die Natali (for orch.), 1960; Piano Concerto, 1962; Andromache's Farewell (soprano and orch.), 1963; Antony and Cleopatra (opera), 1966; The Lovers (for baritone, chorus and orch.), 1971; also songs, piano pieces, chamber music, choruses. *Address:* c/o G. Schirmer Inc., 866 Third Avenue, New York, NY 10022, USA. *Died 23 Jan.* 1981.

**BARCLAY, Alexander,** CBE 1957; ARCS, FRSC; Keeper, Department of Chemistry and Photography, Science Museum, S Kensington, 1938–59; retired; *b* 25 July 1896; *o s* of late Alexander Barclay; *m* 1921, Irene Margaret (*d* 1973), *y d* of late Frank Carrington Falkner, Wisbech. *Educ:* Berkhamsted Sch.; Royal College of Science. Served European War with Special Gas Brigade, RE, 1916–17; invalided, 1917; Postal Censorship Research Dept, 1918; entered Science Museum, 1921; Asst Keeper, 1930; Board of Education, 1940 and 1943; Postal Censorship, 1944–45. Hon. Member Royal Photographic Soc.; Mem. of Nat. Film Library Cttee, British Film Institute, 1938–55. *Publications:* Official Handbooks to the Chemistry Collections, Science Museum, 1927–37; various papers in scientific journals. *Address:* Towers End, Walberswick, Southwold, Suffolk. *T:* Southwold 722146. *Died 23 Aug.* 1987.

**BARCLAY, Theodore David;** retired banker; *b* 6 Sept. 1906; *e s* of Rev. Canon David Barclay and Loetitia Caroline Rowley, *d* of late Rt Rev. Rowley Hill, Bishop of Sodor and Man; *m* 1934, Anne Millard, *d* of late T. W. M. Bennett, Hatfield; two *s* one *d. Educ:* Harrow; Trinity Coll., Cambridge. Entered Barclays Bank Ltd, 1927; Local Director at 54 Lombard Street, 1934, Director of the Bank, 1948–77; Dir, Sun Alliance and London Insurance Ltd, 1948–77 (Chm., 1956–68); Dir, British Linen Bank, 1951–70; Dir, The Bank of Scotland, 1970–77. High Sheriff of Suffolk, 1959. *Recreations:* shooting and fishing. *Address:* Desnage Lodge, Higham, Bury St Edmunds. *T:* Newmarket 750254. *Clubs:* Boodle's, Pratt's; New (Edinburgh). *Died 30 Oct.* 1981.

**BARING, Sir Charles Christian,** 2nd Bt, *cr* 1911; JP; *b* 16 Dec. 1898; *s* of Sir Godfrey Baring, 1st Bt, KBE, DL, and Eva Hermione Mackintosh of Mackintosh (*d* 1934); *S* father, 1957; *m* 1948, Jeanette (Jan), (*d* 1985), *d* of Henry Charles Daykin. *Educ:* Eton. Served European War: Lieut Coldstream Guards, 1917–18 (severely wounded); War of 1939–45: Major Coldstream Guards, 1940–45; Political Warfare Executive, 1943–44; Staff, AFHQ, Italy, War Office, 1944–45. Attaché, HM Legation, Warsaw, 1922–23; Cunard White Star Ltd, 1933–36; HM Prison Service, 1936–38; Probation Officer: West London Magistrates' Court, 1938–40; Central Criminal Court, 1945–46; Inspector, Probation Branch Home Office, 1946–49; Colonial Service: Warden of Prisons, Bermuda, 1949–53. Member, Cttee of Management, RNLI (Vice-Pres., 1972). JP Isle of Wight County, 1956; DL Co. Southampton subseq. IoW, 1962–84; Chm. of Justices, IoW Petty Sessional Div., 1962–70. *Recreations:* golf, swimming, walking. *Heir: nephew* John Francis Baring [*b* 21 May 1947; *m* 1971, Elizabeth, *yr d* of Robert D. H.

Pillitz; two s one d]. Address: Springvale Hotel, Seaview, Isle of Wight.
                                                            Died 26 Jan. 1990.

**BARING, Sir Mark,** KCVO 1980 (CVO 1970); JP; General Commissioner for Income Tax, 1966-79; Executive Chairman, 1969-86, Vice President, since 1986, King Edward VII's Hospital for Officers; b 9 June 1916; yr s of late Hon. Windham Baring and Lady Gweneth Cavendish, 3rd d of 8th Earl of Bessborough; m 1949, Victoria Winifred Russell, d of late Col R. E. M. Russell, CVO, CBE, DSO; two d. Educ: Eton Coll.; Trinity Coll., Cambridge. Served War of 1939-45, Grenadier Guards; in Italy and UK; Mil. Liaison Officer HM Embassy, Rome, 1945-46 (Major 1945); retd 1946. Man. Dir, Seccombe Marshall and Campion Ltd, Discount Brokers, 1950-76. JP, Inner Area of London, 1963. Treasurer, Inst. of Urology, 1969-74; Mem. Bd of Governors, St Peter's Hosp., 1970-74; Governor, The Peabody Trust, 1971; Mem. Council, Baring Foundn, 1975-; Chm., Assoc. of Independent Hosps; Pres., St Marylebone Housing Assoc., 1956-77. High Sheriff, Greater London, 1976-77. Recreations: tennis, bridge. Address: 18 Thurloe Square, SW7. T: 01-589 8485. Clubs: Brooks's, White's.
                                                            Died 6 Feb. 1988.

**BARKE, James Allen;** Director: D.B. Holdings, since 1985; David Barke Holdings Ltd, 1988; b 16 April 1903; s of James E. Barke and Emma Livsey; m 1st, 1937, Doris Marian Bayne (d 1952); two s one d; 2nd, 1953, Marguerite Amy Sutcliffe (née Williams) (d 1968); one step d. Educ: Birley Street Central Sch.; Manchester Coll. of Technology. Mather & Platt and general engineering experience, 1922-32; joined Ford Motor Co., 1932; Buyer, Purchase Dept, 1939; Chief Buyer (Tractors), 1947; Manager, Leamington Foundry, 1948; Executive Dir and General Manager, Briggs Motor Bodies Ltd, 1953; Ford Motor Co.: Dir, Product Divs, 1959; Asst Man. Dir, 1961; Man. Dir, 1962; Chief Exec. Officer and Man. Dir, 1963-65; Vice-Chm., 1965-68; Director: De La Rue Company Ltd, 1970-73; Falcon Engineering Co., 1972-87. Recreations: golf, rock climbing, walking, reading. Address: Thurlestone, Mill Green, Ingatestone, Essex. Club: Oriental.                Died 29 Jan. 1990.

**BARKER, Alan;** see Barker, William A.

**BARKER, Lt-Col Arthur James;** writer; retired from Army; b 20 Sept. 1918; o s of late John Robert Barker and Caroline Barker, Hull; m 1st, 1939, Dorothy Jean (marr. diss. 1968), o d of late W. E. Hirst, MBE; one s; 2nd, 1969, Alexandra Franziska, o d of late Eugen Franz Roderbourg, Berlin. Educ: Hymers Coll., Hull; Royal Mil. Coll. of Science. Commissioned E Yorks Regt, 1936; E African campaign with 1st/4th KAR, 1940-41; Ceylon, India, Burma, 1941-46; Staff Coll., Quetta, 1944. Subseq. service as a Staff Officer in Middle East, 1947-48; WO (Techn. intell.), 1950-52; Far East, 1956-58; a Regtl Officer in Malaya, 1952-53; Mem. Directing Staff, RMCS, 1954-56; retd, 1958, and employed until 1968 by UKAEA; NATO Research Fellowship, 1968; Illinois Inst. of Technology, 1971-72. Publications: Principles of Small Arms, 1953; The March on Delhi, 1963; Suez: The Seven Day War, 1964; Eritrea 1941, 1966; The Neglected War, 1967; Townshend of Kut, 1967; The Civilising Mission, 1968; German Infantry Weapons of World War 2, 1969; British and US Infantry Weapons of World War 2, 1969; Pearl Harbour, 1969; The War Against Russia, 1970; The Vainglorious War, 1854-56, 1970; Midway, 1971; The Suicide Weapon, 1971; The Rape of Ethiopia, 1971; Fortune Favours the Brave, 1974; Behind Barbed Wire, 1974; The Red Army Handbook, 1975; Redcoats, 1976; Mortars of the World, 1976; Dunkirk, 1977; Panzers at War, 1978; Afrika Korps, 1978; Arab-Israeli Wars, 1980; Stuka, 1980; Complete Book of Dogs, 1981 (with A. F. Barker); contrib. Warsaw Pact and NATO Infantry and Weapons. Recreation: travel. Address: c/o National Westminster Bank, 60 Market Place, Beverley, North Humberside HU17 8AH; 5 Cherry Street, Newlands, Cape Town, South Africa. Club: Army and Navy.                                    Died 10 June 1981.

**BARKER, Denis William Knighton;** a Managing Director, The British Petroleum Co. Ltd, 1967-72; b 21 Aug. 1908; m 1938, Esmee Doris Marsh; two d. Educ: Holgate Grammar School, Barnsley; Sheffield Univ. (MSc). With the British Petroleum Co. Ltd, 1929-72; President, BP (North America) Ltd, 1959; Asst Gen. Manager, Refineries Dept, 1960; Gen. Manager, Refineries Dept, 1966. Formerly Director: BP Trading Ltd, BP Refineries Ltd, Britannic Estates Ltd, The British Petroleum Co. of Canada Ltd, and others. Recreations: golf, gardening. Address: Stable Cottage, Upper House Lane, Shamley Green, near Guildford, Surrey GU5 OSX. T: Cranleigh 2726.                                Died 3 Sept. 1981.

**BARKER, Dennis Albert;** Justice of Appeal, Hong Kong, 1981-88; b 9 June 1926; s of J. W. and R. E. Barker; m 1st, 1949, Daphne (née Ruffle) (marr. diss. 1984); one s one d (and one d decd); 2nd, 1984, Deirdre (née Rendall-Day). Educ: Nottingham High Sch.; The Queen's Coll. Oxford (Jodrell Schol.). Flying Officer, RAFVR, 1944-47. 1st cl. hons (Jurisprudence), Oxon, 1949; 1st cl. Certif. of Honour and Studentship, Bar Finals, 1950; Harmsworth Law Schol., 1950; Eldon Law Schol., 1950; called to the Bar, Middle Temple,

1950, Bencher, 1975. Mem. Midland Circuit; Dep. Chm., Bucks QS, 1963-71; QC 1968; a Recorder of the Crown Court, 1972-79. Former Mem., Criminal Injuries Compensation Bd. Recreations: golf, flying, music. Address: c/o Supreme Court, Hong Kong. Clubs: Hong Kong, Sheko Country (Hong Kong); Ashridge Golf (Bucks).
                                                            Died 13 Nov. 1989.

**BARKER, Eric Leslie;** author and entertainer; b 20 Feb. 1912; s of Charles and Maude Barker; m 1936, Pearl Hackney; one d. Educ: Whitgift Sch. Character actor Birmingham, Oxford and Croydon Repertory Theatres, 1932-33; Comedian, also sketch and lyric writer, Charlot revues, Windmill, and Prince of Wales Theatre, 1933-38. Author and star of radio series: Howdyfolks, 1939-40; Navy Mixture, 1944-45; Merry-Go-Round, 1945-49; Just Fancy, 1950-62; Passing Parade, 1957; Barker's Folly, 1958; Law and Disorder, 1960. Lieut RNVR, 1940-45. Author and star of television series: Eric Barker Half Hour, 1952-55; Absolutely Barkers, 1963. Films: Brothers-in-Law (British Film Acad. Award); Clean Sweep; Blue Murder at St Trinians; Happy Is The Bride; Carry on, Sergeant; Eye Spy; Bachelor of Hearts; Right, Left and Centre; Carry on, Constable; Dentist in the Chair; Raising the Wind; The Fast Lady; Those Magnificent Men in their Flying Machines; Doctor in Clover; Maroc 7. Publications: short stories, 3 novels, 1931-33; The Watch Hunt, 1931; Day Gone By, 1932; Steady Barker (Autobiog.), 1956; Golden Gimmick, 1958. Recreations: antiques, photography, gardening, history, cricket, swimming. Address: c/o Lloyds Bank, Faversham, Kent.
                                                            Died 1 June 1990.

**BARKER, Gen. Sir Evelyn Hugh,** KCB 1950 (CB 1944); KBE 1945 (CBE 1940); DSO 1918; MC; b 22 May 1894; y s of late Maj.-Gen. Sir George Barker, KCB, and late Hon. Lady Barker; m 1923, Violet Eleanor (d 1983), y d of T. W. Thornton of Brockhall, near Weedon, Northants; one s. Educ: Wellington Coll.; RM Coll., Sandhurst. Joined KRRC, 1913; Capt. 1916; Bt-Maj. 1929; Major 1930; Bt Lt-Col 1934; Lt-Col 1936; Bt-Col 1937; Col 1938; Maj.-Gen., 1941; Lt-Gen., 1944; General, 1948. Served European War, 1914-18, France, Salonica, and South Russia; GSO3, 1917; Bde-Major, 1917; despatches, DSO, MC; GSO3 (War Office), 1919; Brigade-Major 8th Infantry Brigade, 1931-33; commanded 2nd Bn KRRC, 1936-38; commanded 10th Infantry Brigade, 1938-40; commanded 54th Div. 1941-42, and 49th (West Riding) Div. 1943-44; commanded 8 Corps, 1944-April 1946; commanded British Troops in Palestine and Transjordan, 1946; ADC General to the King, 1949-50; GOC-in-C Eastern Command, 1947-50; retd 1950. Col Comdt 2nd Bn KRRC, 1946-56; Hon. Col Loyal Suffolk Hussars (Yeomanry), 1946-50; Hon. Col, Beds Yeo., 1951-60; Hon. Col, Herts and Beds Yeo., 1961-62. DL Beds, 1952-67. Comdr, Legion of Honour; Croix de Guerre (with palm) France; Silver Medal, Italy; O St Stanislas, Russia; Grand Cross of Dannebrog, Denmark. Address: Park House, Bromham, Bedford. T: Oakley 2332.                                        Died 23 Nov. 1983.

**BARKER, Hugh Purslove;** Chairman, 1956-71 and Managing Director, 1945-71, Parkinson Cowan Group; Chairman, Boosey & Hawkes Ltd, 1974-79; Vice-President, British Institute of Management, since 1962 (Chairman, 1960-62); b 11 March 1909; s of Arthur Henry Barker and Florence Barker (née Saich); m 1935, Joye Frances Higgs (decd); two s one d; m Kathleen Mary Miles (decd); m Rosemary Ursula Meyer. Educ: Oundle Sch. Mech. Engr Apprenticeship (concurrently studied Engineering, Accountancy and Law), Waygood-Otis Ltd, 1927-31; private mfg business, 1931-35; Cons. Engr, A. H. Barker & Partners, 1935-39. Dir Mfg Cos. Min. of Aircraft Prodn (Dep. Dir Instrument Prodn), 1940-44. Part-time Mem., British Railways Bd, 1962-67 (British Transport Commn, 1951-62); Chm., EDC for the Rubber Industry, 1968-71. Mem., Royal Commn on Assizes, 1967-70. CEng; FIEE; FIMechE; FInstGasE; FCIBS; FCIT; CBIM. Publications: papers and articles to Technical Institutes and press, on engineering subjects, and to financial and econ. press on management. Recreations: fishing, music. Address: 7 Stopham House, Stopham, Pulborough, W Sussex RH20 1EA. T: Fittleworth 619. Club: Carlton.                                       Died 26 July 1984.

**BARKER, Brig. Lewis Ernest Stephen,** CBE 1943; DSO 1941; MC 1918; b 5 May 1895; s of late Richard Barker, Mulgrave, Vic, Australia; m 1921, Alice Hope McEachern; two s. Educ: Brighton Grammar Sch., Vic.; Royal Military Coll., Duntroon. Permanent Army Officer. European War, 1917-18 (MC). Various staff appointments AMF, 1919-39. Comd 2/1 Australian Fd Regt in first Libyan campaign, 1940-41 (DSO); Dir of Artillery, LHQ Melbourne, 1941-42; CCRA 1 Australian Corps in New Guinea for the operations for the capture of Buna (CBE); subsequently BRA New Guinea up to the capture of Madang, 1944. BRA LHQ Melbourne, July 1945; Commandant, 4th Military District (S Australia), 1946-Dec. 1948; retired. Address: 53 Donaldson Street, Corryong, Vic 3707, Australia.               Died 13 Dec. 1981.

**BARKER, (William) Alan;** Head Master, University College School, Hampstead, 1975-82, retired through ill-health; b 1 Oct. 1923; 2nd *s* of late T. L. Barker, Edinburgh and Beaconsfield and late I. N. Barker, Salisbury, Zimbabwe; *m* 1954, Jean Alys (later Baroness Trumpington); one *s*. *Educ:* Rossall Sch.; Jesus Coll., Cambridge (scholar). Lieut Royal Artillery, 69 (WR) Field Regt, NW Europe; wounded, 1944. 1st cl. Hons Hist. Tripos Pt I, 1946, Pt II, 1947; BA 1946, MA 1948. Part-time Lectr, WEA (Eastern Region), 1946–47; Asst Master, Eton Coll., 1947–53; Commonwealth Fund Fellow, Yale Univ., 1951–52, MA (Yale) 1952. Fellow Queens' Coll., Cambridge, and Dir Studies in History, 1953–55; Asst Master, Eton Coll., 1955–58; Headmaster, The Leys School, 1958–75. Governor, Sandwich County Sec. Sch.; Life Governor, Rossall Sch.; Mem. Eton UDC, 1956–59; Councillor, Cambs and I of Ely, 1959–70, Alderman 1970–74. Select Preacher, Oxford Univ., 1966; Paul M. Angle Meml Lectr, Chicago, 1978. Patron, Sandwich Local History Soc., 1964–. *Publications:* (jt) A General History of England 1688–1950, 2 vols, 1952, 1953; Religion and Politics (1558–1642), 1957; The Civil War in America, 1961, repr. US 1974, UK 1977; (contrib.) The Rebirth of Britain, 1964. *Recreations:* bridge, American history, accumulating books and dust. *Address:* The Royal Star and Garter Home, Richmond Hill, Richmond, Surrey. *Clubs:* Pitt (Cambridge); Elizabethan (Yale); Royal St George's Golf (Sandwich).                              *Died 25 April 1988.*

**BARKLEY, Brenda Edith, (Mrs Harry Barkley);** *see* Ryman, B. E.

**BARLAS, Sir Richard (Douglas),** KCB 1977 (CB 1968); OBE 1943; Clerk of the House of Commons, 1976–79; *b* 19 May 1916; *s* of E. D. M. Barlas and Elena Barlas (*née* Kenyon); *m* 1940, Ann, *d* of Canon R. W. Porter; three *s*. *Educ:* Westminster; Christ Church, Oxford. War Service, 1939–45, RAF. Asst Clerk, House of Commons, 1946; Senior Clerk, 1947. Called to the Bar, Middle Temple, 1949. Fourth Clerk at the Table, House of Commons, 1959; Second Clerk Asst, 1962; Clerk Asst, 1974. *Recreations:* inland waterways, travel, gardening. *Address:* Walnut House, Ticehurst, E Sussex. *Club:* Royal Air Force.                   *Died 10 Nov. 1982.*

**BARLOW, Prof. Harold Everard Monteagle,** BSc (Eng.) London, PhD (Sci.), London; FRS 1961; FEng; FIEEE; FIEE; MIMechE; Emeritus Professor of Electrical Engineering, University College, London (Pender Professor, 1950–67); *b* Highbury, 15 Nov. 1899; *s* of late Leonard Barlow, MIEE, and Katharine Monteagle, Glasgow; *m* 1931, Janet Hastings, *d* of the late Rev. J. Hastings Eastwood, BA; three *s* one *d*. *Educ:* Wallington Grammar School; City & Guilds Engineering College; University College, London. FEng 1976. Sub-Lieut. RNVR 1917–19; Student at University College, London, 1919–23; Practical engineering training with East Surrey Ironworks and Barlow & Young Ltd, 1923–25; Member of Academic Staff, Faculty of Engineering, UCL, 1925–67 (absent from University on War Service, Sept. 1939–Oct. 1945). Joined staff of Telecommunications Research Establishment, Air Ministry, to deal with Radar development, Sept. 1939; Superintendent, Radio Dept, RAE, 1943–45. Fellow of University College, 1946, Prof. of Elec. Engineering, 1945–50; Dean of Engineering Faculty, and Mem. UCL Cttee, 1949, 1961. Mem. of: Radar and Signals Advisory Bd, Min. of Supply, 1947; Scientific Advisory Council, Min. of Supply, 1949; Radio Research Bd, DSIR, 1948 and 1960; London Regional Advisory Council and of Academic Bd for Higher Technological Educn, 1952–67; Academic Council, Univ. of London, 1953–55; BBC Scientific Advisory Committee, 1953–76; Governor, Woolwich Polytechnic, 1948; Dir, Marconi Instruments, 1963. Member of Council of IEE, 1955–58 and 1960–; awarded Kelvin Premium, J. J. Thomson Premium, Oliver Lodge and Fleming Premium of IEE; Faraday Medal, 1967; Mem. Council, IERE, 1973–76. FCGI 1969. Hon. FIERE 1971; Hon. FIEE 1971. For. Mem., Polish Acad. of Science, 1966; Hon. Mem., Japanese Inst. of Electronics and Communications Engineers, 1973; For. Associate, US Nat. Acad. of Engineering, 1979. Chm., British Nat. Cttee for Radio Science, 1968; Mem., Nat. Electronics Council, 1969–. Dellinger Gold Medal, Internat. Radio Union, 1969; Harold Hartley Medal, Inst. of Measurement and Control, 1973; Mervin J. Kelly Award, IEEE, 1975; Microwave Career Award, IEEE, 1985; Royal Medal, Royal Soc., 1988. Hon. DSc Heriot-Watt, 1971; Hon. DEng Sheffield, 1973. *Publications:* Micro-waves and Wave-guides, 1947; (with A. L. Cullen) Micro-Wave Measurements, 1950; (with J. Brown) Radio Surface Waves, 1962; many scientific papers. *Recreations:* sailing, walking, reading. *Address:* 13 Hookfield, Epsom, Surrey. *T:* Epsom 21586; University College, Gower Street, WC1. *T:* 01–387 7050.
                                                        *Died 20 April 1989.*

**BARLOW, Sir John (Denman),** 2nd Bt, *cr* 1907; JP for Cheshire; Consultant, Thomas Barlow and Bro., Manchester and London; Emeritus Director, Manchester Chamber of Commerce; Chairman: various Rubber Plantation Companies; United Kingdom Falkland Islands Committee; *b* 15 June 1898; *er s* of Sir John Barlow, 1st Bt, and Hon. Anna Maria Heywood Denman (*d* 1965), *sister* of 3rd Baron Denman, PC, GCMG, KCVO; *S* father, 1932; *m* 1928, Hon. Diana Helen Kemp, *d* of 1st Baron Rochdale, CB, and *sister* of 1st Viscount Rochdale, OBE, TD; three *s* one *d*. Contested (L) Northwich Division of Cheshire, 1929; MP (Nat Lib) Eddisbury

Division of Cheshire, 1945–50; contested (U and Nat Lib) Walsall Div. of Staffordshire, 1950; MP (C) Middleton and Prestwich Division of Lancashire, 1951–66. Led CPA Mission to Malaya, 1959; led Parly Mission to new Malaysian Parlt, taking gift of Speaker's chair, 1963; Chm., Cons. Trade and Industries Cttee, 1955–60. Vice-Chm., Cotton Bd, 1940; Director: Union Bank of Manchester, 1932–40; Barclays Bank Ltd (Manchester Local Bd), 1940–73; Calico Printers Assoc., 1952–68; The Falklands Islands Co. Mem. Council, RASE, 1942–53. *Recreations:* hunting, polo, shooting. *Heir:* *s* John Kemp Barlow [*b* 22 April 1934; *m* 1962, Susan, *er d* of Col Sir Andrew Horsbrugh-Porter, 3rd Bt, DSO; four *s*]. *Address:* Bradwall Manor, Sandbach, Cheshire. *T:* Sandbach 2036. *Club:* Brooks's.                              *Died 5 Jan. 1986.*

**BARLOW, Thomas Bradwall;** merchant banker; director of rubber, insurance and other public companies; Joint Senior Consultant in Thomas Barlow & Bro. Ltd, London and Manchester; *b* 7 March 1900; 2nd *s* of Sir John Emmott Barlow, 1st Bt; *m* 1943, Elizabeth Margaret (*d* 1988), *d* of Hon. B. G. Sackville-West; one *s* one *d*. Chairman: Br. Assoc. of Straits Merchants, 1937; Rubber Trade Assoc., 1942–43; Rubber Growers' Assoc., 1945–46; British Assoc. of Malaysia, 1965; Highlands & Lowlands Para Rubber Co. Ltd; Chersonese (F.M.S.) Estates Ltd. Farming. *Recreations:* hunting, steeplechasing, and travelling. *Address:* Thornby House, Northampton. *T:* Northampton 740214. *Clubs:* Brooks's, City of London, Hurlingham.                              *Died 27 July 1988.*

**BARNARD, Sir Henry William,** Kt 1944; Judge of High Court of Justice (Probate, Divorce and Admiralty Division), 1944–59; *b* 18 April 1891; *s* of late William Tyndal Barnard, KC. *Educ:* Wellington Coll.; Merton Coll., Oxford. Called to Bar, Gray's Inn, 1913; KC 1939. Bencher Gray's Inn, 1939, Treasurer, 1953. Served European War as a Captain in Royal West Kent Regt (5th Bn). *Address:* Boscobel, Hawshill, Walmer, Kent. *Club:* Royal Cornwall Yacht.
                                                        *Died 20 July 1981.*

**BARNARD, Howard Clive,** MA, BLitt Oxon; MA (Educ), DLit London, FCP, FTCL; Professor of Education, Reading University, 1937–51; Emeritus since 1951; *b* City of London, 7 June 1884; Freeman of the City and Mem. of the Goldsmiths' Co. by patrimony; *s* of late Howard Barnard, journalist; *m* Edith Gwendolen (*d* 1956), *d* of late John Wish, Civil Servant; one *s* one *d*. *Educ:* University Coll. Sch., London; Brasenose Coll., Oxford (Sen. Hulme Scholar); London Sch. of Economics; King's Coll., London (Advanced Student); also studied in France and Germany. Asst Master at Manchester, Ramsgate, and Bradford; Headmaster, Grammar Sch., Gillingham, Kent; Examiner at various times to Univs of Oxford, Cambridge, London, Durham, Birmingham, Liverpool, Manchester, Leeds, Sheffield, Wales, Nottingham and Hull, the Civil Service Commission, the LCC, the Coll. of Preceptors, etc. Hon. DLitt Reading, 1974. *Publications:* The Little Schools of Port-Royal; The Port-Royalists on Education (source-book); The French Tradition in Education; Madame de Maintenon and Saint-Cyr; Fénelon on Education; Girls at School under the Ancien Régime; Education and the French Revolution (also Italian edn); A History of English Education from 1760 (also Hindi edn); Were those the Days?; A Clowder of Cats; An Introduction to Teaching; Principles and Practice of Geography Teaching; Observational Geography and Regional Survey; The Expansion of the Anglo-Saxon Nations (ed); A Handbook of British Educational Terms (with Prof. J. A. Lauwerys); and numerous school books. *Recreations:* walking, organ-playing. *Address:* c/o The School of Education, University of Reading, Whiteknights, Reading, Berks RG6 2AH.
                                                        *Died 12 Sept. 1985.*

**BARNARD, Thomas Theodore,** MC; MA Oxon; PhD Cantab; *b* 31 Aug. 1898; *e s* of late T. H. Barnard, banker, Bedford; *m* 1924, Gillian Sarah (*d* 1961), *d* of late Lieut-Col Hon. A. S. Byng, DSO; one *s* two *d*. *Educ:* Eton; Christ Church, Oxford; King's Coll., Cambridge. Lieut, Coldstream Guards, 1917–19; Prof. of Social Anthropology, and Dir of the Sch. of African Life and Languages, University of Cape Town, 1926–34. Rejoined Coldstream Guards, 1940–45, Captain, Guards Depôt. VMH 1965. *Address:* Furzebrook, Wareham, Dorset. *Club:* Cavalry and Guards.
                                                        *Died 29 Aug. 1983.*

**BARNBY, 2nd Baron,** *cr* 1922; **Francis Vernon Willey;** CMG 1918; CBE 1919; MVO 1918; *b* 1884; *e s* of 1st Baron and Florence (*d* 1933), *d* of Frederick Chinnock, Dinorbin Court, Hants; *S* father, 1929; *m* 1940, Banning Grange, Bryn Mawr, Pennsylvania. *Educ:* Eton; Magdalen Coll., Oxford. Late Brevet Col Comdg Sherwood Rangers, Notts Yeomanry (TF). Hon. Col 1948; mobilised, 1914; served Egypt and Gallipoli, 1915; recalled as Asst Dir of Ordnance Stores; Controller of Wool Supplies under War Dept, June 1916, and organised the purchase and distribution of the British and Colonial Wool Clips on Government and civilian account; MP (Co. U) South Bradford, Dec. 1918–22; MFH Blankney Hunt, Lincolnshire, 1919–33. Past Pres. CBI; Member: Surplus Govt Property Disposals Board, 1918–21; Central Electricity Board,

1927–46; Overseas Settlement Board, 1937–; a former Director: Lloyds Bank Ltd; Commercial Union Assurance Co. Ltd; President: Textile Institute, 1961–62; Aire Wool Co. Ltd; Past Master, Worshipful Company of Woolmen. Hon DTech Bradford, 1968. *Heir:* none. *Address:* Hillthorpe, Ashtead, Surrey; 2 Caxton Street, SW1. *T:* 01-222 3003; 35–37 Grosvenor Square, W1. *T:* 01-499 2112. *Clubs:* Carlton, Cavalry and Guards, Hurlingham.

*Died 30 April 1982 (ext).*

**BARNES, Arthur Chapman,** CMG 1936; BSc (Hons); CChem, FRSC; Sugar Consultant; *b* 1891. *Educ:* Deacon's School, Peterborough; Municipal College of Technology and Victoria Univ., Manchester. AMIChemE, MChemA. Entered Survey Dept, East Africa Protectorate, 1914; agricultural chemist, Nigeria, 1923; Asst Director of Agriculture, Zanzibar, 1927; Director of Agriculture, Fiji, 1929; Director of Agriculture and Island Chemist, Jamaica, 1933; General Manager, West Indies Sugar Co. Ltd, 1938; seconded for duty as Director of Research for The Sugar Manufacturers' Association (of Jamaica), Ltd, 1947; Technical Consultant, S African Cane Growers' Assoc., 1958; retired 1972. *Publications:* Agriculture of the Sugar-Cane, 1953; The Sugar Cane, 1964, 2nd edn, 1974. *Address:* 8 Newlands, Musgrave Road, Durban, Natal, South Africa. *Died 4 July 1985.*

**BARNES, Eric Cecil,** CMG 1954; Colonial Administrative Service; Provincial Commissioner, Nyasaland, 1949–55, retired; *b* 1899; *m* 1950, Isabel Margaret Lesley, MBE, *d* of late Mrs Isabel Wauchope; one *s* one *d*. *Educ:* Bishop Cotton's Sch., Simla; Bedford Sch. and Cadet Coll., Quetta, India. Indian Army, 1917–23; Administrative Service, Nyasaland, 1925. Deputy Provincial Commissioner, 1946. *Address:* 9 Riverdale Close, Fordingbridge, Hants. *T:* Fordingbridge 53860. *Died 4 July 1987.*

**BARNES, Harold William;** Director, Telecommunications Finance, Telecommunications Headquarters, GPO, 1968–72; *b* 7 Nov. 1912; *s* of Edgar and Florence Barnes; *m* 1941, Mary M. Butchart; one *s* one *d*. *Educ:* Chesterfield Grammar Sch. Entered Civil Service as Exec. Officer, 1931. Served HM Forces, RE Postal Services, 1940–46 (final rank, Major). Asst Accountant Gen., GPO, 1952–55; Dep. Dir, Finance and Accounts, GPO, 1955–64; Controller, Post Office Supplies Dept, 1964–68. *Recreations:* golf, choral music, (City of London Choir). *Address:* 3 Little Court, West Wickham, Kent. *T:* 01-777 6785. *Club:* Langley Park Golf (Beckenham).

*Died 13 July 1981.*

**BARNES, Sir Harry (Jefferson),** Kt 1980; CBE 1971; MA; Director (Principal), Glasgow School of Art, 1964–80; *b* 3 April 1915; *yr s* of Prof. Alfred Edward Barnes, FRCP; *m* 1941, Joan Alice Katherine, *d* of Prof. Randolph Schwabe, RWS; two *d* (one *s* decd). *Educ:* Repton Sch.; The Slade Sch., Univ. of London. Diploma of Fine Art (Lond) 1936. Tour of Europe, studying the teaching of Art in Schools, 1937–38; Secondary Sch. teaching (refused for mil. service), 1938–44; joined Staff of Glasgow Sch. of Art, 1944; Dep. Dir and Registrar, 1947–64. Dir, Edinburgh Tapestry Co., Dovecot Studios, 1953–; Founder Mem., Scottish Craft Centre (Chm., 1972–78; Hon. Life Mem., 1978). Member: Senate, Glasgow Univ., 1973–80; CNAA, 1974–81; Scottish Arts Council, 1972–78; Historic Buildings Council for Scotland, 1979–. Hon. MA Glasgow, 1966; Hon. LLD Glasgow, 1980; Hon. FSIAD, 1980. *Recreation:* gardening. *Address:* 11 Whittingehame Drive, Glasgow. *T:* 041-339 1019. *Club:* Glasgow Art. *Died 31 May 1982.*

**BARNES, Sir William Lethbridge G.;** *see* Gorell Barnes.

**BARNES, Prof. Winston Herbert Frederick,** MA (Oxon); Professor Emeritus, Universities of Manchester and Liverpool; *b* 30 May 1909; *er s* of Frederick Charles and Martha Lilley Barnes; *m* 1938, Sarah (*d* 1985), *d* of late Thomas David Davies; two *d*. *Educ:* Manchester Grammar Sch.; Corpus Christi Coll., Oxford (Hugh Oldham Scholar, Haigh Scholar). 1st Cl., Classical Hon. Mods. 1930; 1st Cl., Lit. Hum. 1932; John Locke Scholar in Mental Philosophy, Oxford, 1932; Sen. Demy, Magdalen Coll., Oxford, 1933–34. Asst Lecturer in Philosophy, 1936–39; Lecturer 1939–41, Univ. of Liverpool; served in RAFVR, 1941–42; Temporary Principal, Ministry of Supply, 1942–45; Prof. of Philosophy, Univ. of Durham (Durham Colls) 1945–59; Prof. of Moral Philosophy, Univ. of Edinburgh, 1959–63, Gifford Lectr in Natural Theology, 1968–69, 1969–70; Vice-Chancellor, Univ. of Liverpool, 1963–69; Vis. Prof. of Philosophy, Univ. of Auckland, NZ, 1970; Sir Samuel Hall Prof. of Philosophy, Manchester Univ., 1970–73. Pres., Mind Assoc., 1948. Mem. Planning Bd, Independent Univ., 1970–73; Mem. Council, University Coll. at Buckingham, 1973–78 (Hon. Fellow, 1979–83). Hon. DCL Durham, 1964; Hon. DLitt Buckingham, 1979. *Publications:* The Philosophical Predicament, 1950; contributions to Mind, Philosophy, Aristotelian Society Proceedings. *Recreations:* walking, swimming. *Address:* 7 Great Stuart Street, Edinburgh EH3 7TP. *T:* 031–226 3158.

*Died 15 Sept. 1990.*

**BARNETSON, Maj.-Gen. James Craw,** CB 1965; OBE 1945; Director of Medical Services, BAOR, December 1964–66, retired; *b* 26 July 1907; *s* of Dr R. B. Barnetson; *m* 1935, Sylvia Joan Milner Moore; three *s*. *Educ:* Edinburgh Academy; Edinburgh Univ. (MB, ChB). Staff Coll., Camberley, 1942; ADMS, AFHQ, 1942–43; ADMS, 6th Armd Div., 1943–46, ADMS, Scot. Comd, 1946–47; Asst DGAMS, War Office, 1947–50; Joint Staff Coll., Latimer, 1950; ADMS, 11th Armd Div., 1951; ADMS, Plans, SHAPE, 1951–53; OC Commonwealth Mil. Hosp., Japan, 1953–54; ADMS, GHQ, E Africa, 1954–57; ADMS, 6 Armd Div., 1958–59; Comdt Field Trg Centre, HQ, AER, RAMC, 1959–60; DDMS, Northern Comd, 1960–61; Dep. DGAMS, 1961–64. QHP 1961–66. Col Comdt, RAMC, 1968–72. OStJ 1965. *Recreation:* gardening. *Address:* The Old Cottage, Wardley Green, Milland, West Sussex. *T:* Milland 371. *Died 4 Jan. 1984.*

**BARNETT, Guy;** *see* Barnett, N. G.

**BARNETT, Dame (Mary) Henrietta,** DBE 1958 (CBE 1956; OBE 1950); Director of the Women's Royal Air Force, 1956–60; *b* 16 Feb. 1905; *d* of Col George Henry Barnett, 60th Rifles, Glympton Park, Woodstock, Oxon. *Educ:* Heathfield, Ascot. Joined Women's Auxiliary Air Force in 1939. *Address:* Hoggrove House, Park Street, Woodstock, Oxon. *T:* Woodstock 811502.

*Died 11 Sept. 1985.*

**BARNETT, (Nicolas) Guy;** MP (Lab) Greenwich, since July 1971; *b* 23 Aug. 1928; *s* of late B. G. Barnett; *m* 1967, Daphne Anne, *d* of Geoffrey William Hortin, JP; one *s* one *d*. *Educ:* Highgate; St Edmund Hall, Oxford. Teacher: Queen Elizabeth Gram. Sch., 1953–59; Friends Sch., Kamusinga, Kenya, 1960–61. Famine Relief Sec., Christian Council of Kenya, 1962; on staff VSO, 1966–69; Chief Educn Officer, Commonwealth Inst., 1969–71. Contested (Lab) NR Yorks (Scarborough and Whitby Div.), 1959; MP (Lab) S Dorset Div., Nov. 1962–Sept. 1964; PPS to Minister for Local Govt and Planning, 1974–75; Parly Under-Sec. of State, DoE, 1976–79; junior opposition spokesman: on overseas development, 1980–81; on European and Community affairs, 1981–82; opposition spokesman on overseas development, 1982–83; Jt Sec., Parly Gp on Overseas Develt, 1984–; Member: Parly Select Cttee on Race Relations and Immigration, 1972–74; Public Accts Cttee, 1975; Exec. Cttee, UK Br., CPA, 1982– (Jt Hon. Treas., 1985–). Mem., European Parlt, 1975–76. Parly Adviser, Soc. of Civil Servants, 1973–76. Member: Gen. Adv. Council of BBC, 1973–76; Bd, Christian Aid, 1984–. Chm., UK Chapter, Soc. for Internat. Develt, 1983–. Governor, Inst. of Develt Studies, 1984–; Trustee, Nat. Maritime Museum, 1974–76; Chm. of Trustees, Greenwich Fest., 1984–. *Publication:* By the Lake, 1964. *Recreations:* music, walking. *Address:* 32 Westcombe Park Road, SE3. *Club:* Royal Commonwealth Society. *Died 24 Dec. 1986.*

**BARNETT, Richard David,** CBE 1974; MA, DLitt; FBA 1962; FSA; *b* Acton, 23 Jan. 1909; *o s* of late Lionel David Barnett, CB; *m* 1948, Barbara Joan, *d* of Ralph Pinto; two *s* one *d*. *Educ:* St Paul's Sch., London; Corpus Christi Coll., Cambridge. Student of British Sch. of Archaeology at Athens, 1930–32, Sec., 1933–35; Asst Keeper, Dept of Egyptian and Assyrian Antiquities, British Museum, 1932; Dep. Keeper, 1953; Keeper, Dept of Western Asiatic Antiquities, 1955–74. Vis. Prof., Hebrew Univ., Jerusalem, 1974–75. Pres. Jewish Historical Society of England, 1959–61; Chm., Anglo-Israel Archaeol Soc., 1968–86. Corr. Mem., Greek Archaeological Soc.; Ordinary Fellow, German Archaeological Inst., 1961. Served War of 1939–45; Admiralty 1939–40; Foreign Office, 1940–42; Intelligence Officer, RAF, 1942–46, Egypt, Syria, Libya, Turkey. *Publications:* (ed) Treasures of a London Temple, 1951; (with Sir L. Woolley) British Museum Excavations at Carchemish, Vol. III, 1952; Catalogue of Nimrud Ivories in the British Museum, 1957, 2nd edn 1975; (trans.) The Jewish sect of Qumran and the Essenes (by J. Dupont-Sommer), 1954; Assyrian Palace Reliefs, 1960; (with M. Falkner) The Sculptures of Tiglath-pileser III, 1962, 2nd edn, 1970; Illustrations of Old Testament History, 1966, 2nd edn 1977; (ed) The Sephardi Heritage, 1971; (ed) Catalogue of the Jewish Museum, London, 1974; (with Amleto Lorenzini) Assyrian Sculpture, 1976; The Sculptures of Ashurbanipal, 1976; Ancient Ivories from the Middle East, 1982; articles on archæology and Anglo-Jewish history in various learned jls. *Address:* 14 Eldon Grove, NW3 5PT. *T:* 01–794 2066. *Died 29 July 1986.*

**BARNSLEY, Alan Gabriel;** *see* Fielding, Gabriel.

**BARNSLEY, (William) Edward,** CBE 1945; designer and maker of furniture and building woodwork; Adviser in woodwork design, Loughborough Training College, 1938–65; Consultant in Furniture Design to Rural Industries Bureau, 1945–60; *b* 7 Feb. 1900; *s* of Sidney Howard Barnsley, Sapperton, Cirencester; *m* 1925, Tatiana, *d* of late Dr Harry Kellgren; one *s* one *d*. *Educ:* Bedales. Retrospective exhibition, 60 Years of Designing and Making, at Fine Arts Society Gallery, London, and then at Holburne of Menstrie Museum, Bath, 1982. Work includes Throne and Prie-Dieu for Archbishop, Canterbury Cathedral; practically all work in private or public use; examples in V & A Museum and Melbourne Art Gall., Australia. *Address:* Froxfield, Petersfield, Hants. *T:* Hawkley 233. *Died* 2 *Dec.* 1987.

**BARNWELL, Col Ralph Ernest,** CBE 1943; retired; *b* 20 Jan. 1895; *s* of late E. F. Barnwell, Rugby; *m* 1927, Lilian Katharine Oliphant, *d* of late C. R. Bradburne, Official Solicitor to the Supreme Court of Judicature; one *d* (one *s* decd). *Educ:* Rugby Sch. HAC 1914; 2nd Lieut Royal Warwicks Regt 1914; served in France in European War, 1914–18 (despatches); Capt. 1923; Adjutant, 7th Bn Royal Warwicks Regt, 1924–27; Staff Coll., Camberley, 1928–29; Staff Capt., War Office, 1930–32; GSO Weapon Training, Eastern Command, 1932–34; Bt Major 1935; Major, 1938; DAAG Lahore District, 1937–39; Lieut-Col 1939; DAA and QMG (France), 1939; AQMG 2nd Corps (France), 1940; Asst Adjutant-Gen., War Office, 1940–45; Col (temp.) 1941; retd pay 1945; Commandant, Duke of York's Royal Military Sch., 1945–53. *Recreation:* painting. *Address:* Woodrow House, Fifehead Neville, Sturminster Newton, Dorset. *T:* Hazelbury Bryan 297. *Club:* Army and Navy.
*Died* 26 *Nov.* 1984.

**BARODA, Maharaja of;** *see* Gaekwad, Lt-Col F. P.

**BARON, Colin;** Director General, Research (General) and Assistant Chief Scientific Adviser (Research), Ministry of Defence, 1977–81; *b* 20 May 1921; *s* of John Henry Baron and Dorothy May (*née* Crumpler); *m* 1961, Anita Veronica Hale; one *s* one *d* by former marriage. *Educ:* Carlton Grammar Sch., Bradford; Univ. of Leeds (BSc Hons 1941, MSc 1947). Scientific Civil Service, 1941–81; Royal Radar Estabt, Malvern: radar trials and res., 1941–57; weapon systems assessment, 1957–66; RAE, Farnborough: Head, Weapons Res. Gp, 1966–70; Head, Avionics Dept, 1970–74; Head, Flt Systems Dept, 1974–76; Dir Gen., Weapons Res., MoD, 1976–77; (pt-time) Head, Sen. Appointments Secretariat, MoD, 1981–86. *Publications:* contribs to JI IEE and JI Applied Physics. *Recreations:* gardening, badminton, economics. *Address:* Tanglewood, Vicarage Lane, The Bourne, Farnham, Surrey. *T:* Farnham 721433.
*Died* 7 *Nov.* 1987.

**BARRACLOUGH, Geoffrey;** *b* 10 May 1908; *e s* of late Walter and Edith M. Barraclough. *Educ:* Bootham Sch., York; Oriel Coll., Oxford; Univ. of Munich. Bryce Research Student, 1931; Rome Scholar, British Sch. at Rome, 1931; Fellow of Merton Coll., Oxford, 1934; Fellow and Lectr, St John's Coll., Cambridge, 1936; Univ. Lectr, Cambridge, 1937; Foreign Office, 1940; RAFVR, 1942–45; Prof. of Mediæval History, University of Liverpool, 1945–56. Research Prof. of Internat. History, University of London, 1956–62; Prof. of History, Univ. of California, 1965–68; Springer Prof. of History, Brandeis Univ., 1968–70; Chichele Prof. of Modern History, and Fellow of All Souls Coll., Oxford Univ., 1970–73. Arnold Bernhard Vis. Prof., Williams Coll., Mass, 1982; Eric Voegelin Vis. Prof., Munich Univ., 1983. President: Historical Assoc., 1964–67; Internat. Soc. Sci. Council, Gp of Twenty, 1975–. Hon. Mem., Austrian Inst. Historical Research. *Publications:* Public Notaries and the Papal Curia, 1934; Papal Provisions, 1935; Mediæval Germany, 1938; The Origins of Modern Germany, 1946; Factors in German History, 1946; The Mediæval Empire, 1950; The Earldom and County Palatine of Chester, 1953; History in a Changing World, 1955; Early Cheshire Charters, 1957; (ed) Social Life in Early England, 1960; European Unity in Thought and Action, 1963; An Introduction to Contemporary History, 1964; The Mediæval Papacy, 1968; (ed) Eastern and Western Europe in the Middle Ages, 1970; The Crucible of Europe, 1976; Management in a Changing Economy, 1976; Atlante della Storia 1945–1975, 1977; Main Trends in History, 1979; (ed) Times Atlas of World History, 1978; Turning Points in World History, 1979; From Agadir to Armageddon, 1982; (ed) Times Concise Atlas of World History, 1982; (with R. F. Wall) Survey of International Affairs, 1955–56; Survey of International Affairs, 1956–58; Survey of International Affairs, 1958–60. *Died* 26 *Dec.* 1984.

**BARRACLOUGH, Henry,** CVO 1976 (MVO 1958); *b* 10 Aug. 1894; *s* of late Thomas Barraclough, Shipowner, West Hartlepool; *m* 1922, Ethel Mary, *d* of Wilkinson Dix Sunderland; two *s*. *Educ:* Giggleswick Sch. On leaving school joined staff of Lambert Bros Ltd, Newcastle on Tyne office, 1911. Served European War, 1914–18, Durham LI, retiring as Capt.; served in Mesopotamia and NW Persia, 1916–19. Silver Line Ltd: Treasury Dir, 1940–48; Chm. and Man. Dir, 1948–60. Chairman, Prince of Wales Dry Dock Co., Swansea, Ltd, 1943–65 (Dir of the company, 1931–66); Dir, Dene Shipping Co. Ltd from formation until 1970 (Chm., 1941–66), and of other cos; Mem. of Lloyd's. Chm. London General Shipowners' Soc., 1946–47; Dep. Chm. and Chm. of Sub-Cttees of Classification of Lloyd's Register of Shipping, 1949–50. Chm. Governors, The "Cutty Sark" Soc., from foundation to 1976. Liveryman of Worshipful Company of Shipwrights. *Address:* Cotehow, Martindale, Penrith, Cumbria. *T:* Pooley Bridge 521.
*Died* 10 *Dec.* 1982.

**BARRACLOUGH, Brig. Sir John (Ashworth),** Kt 1962; CMG 1950; DSO 1941; OBE 1941; MC 1918; DL; *b* 4 Aug. 1894; *s* of John and Isobella Barraclough; *m* 1951, Monica (Nick) (*née* Jenvey). Served European War, 1914–19, with KORR, RFC, and Machine Gun Corps; served in Iraq (severely wounded), 1920, Ireland, 1922, Palestine, 1929, Egypt, 1932, and India, 1934; military commander, Hebron District, Palestine, 1939; War of 1939–45, comd 1st Bn King's Own Royal Regt, Syria, Lebanon and at Siege of Tobruk, 1941 (despatches five times, wounded); reg. comdr North Rhine Province, 1945–46; dep. reg. cmdr Land North Rhine-Westphalia, 1946–50. Chm., W Midlands Engineering Employers' Assoc. (formerly Birmingham Assoc.), 1951–67. Member: Nat. Adv. Council for the Employment of the Disabled; Piercy Cttee on the Rehabilitation of the Disabled, 1953–56. KStJ, 1964. DL Warwicks, 1962. Comdr Order of Orange Nassau with Swords (Netherlands). *Address:* 6 Devonshire Mews South, W1. *T:* 01–935 3686.
*Died* 31 *Aug.* 1981.

**BARRÈRE, Prof. Jean-Bertrand Marie;** Croix de Guerre (France), 1940; Légion d'Honneur, 1969; Professor of French Literature, University of Cambridge, 1954–82, later Emeritus Professor; Fellow of St John's College, Cambridge, 1957; *b* Paris, 15 Dec. 1914; *s* of Alexandre Barrère and Marie-Claire Lavigne; *m* 1941, Micheline, *d* of Henri Cousin and Inès Dumontier; three *s* three *d*. *Educ:* Lycées Buffon and Louis-le-Grand; Ecole Normale Supérieure and Sorbonne, Paris. MA; Agrégé des Lettres; Docteur ès Lettres. Served War: Sous-Lieut, 32e Régiment d'Infanterie, 1939–40; 1re Armée Française, 1945; Lieut 1945; Capitaine de réserve, 1954; Capitaine Honoraire, 1967. Teacher of French and Classics, Lycée d'Amiens, 1940–42; Asst Lectr on French Literature, Sorbonne, 1942–46; Lectr on French Literature, Institut Français, London, 1946–49; Lectr on French Literature, Univ. of Lyons, 1949–50; appointed Prof. of French Literature, Univ. of Lyons, 1950; seconded as Prof. of French Literature, Ibrahim Univ., Cairo, 1950–52; Prof. at Lyons, 1952–54. *Publications:* Explications françaises, 1946; La Fantaisie de Victor Hugo, 3 vols, 1949, 1960, 1950, rev. edn 1973; Victor Hugo, l'homme et l'œuvre, 1952, rev. edn 1984; Romain Rolland par lui-même, 1955; Le Regard d'Orphée, 1956; La Cure d'amaigrissement du roman, 1964; Critique de chambre, 1964; Un Carnet des Misérables, 1965; Victor Hugo devant Dieu, 1965; Victor Hugo à l'œuvre, 1966; Romain Rolland, l'âme et l'art, 1966; L'Idée de Goût, 1972; Ma Mère qui boite, 1975; L'Echange poétique, 1977; Claudel, le destin et l'œuvre, 1979; (ed) Victor Hugo Poésies (1830–1840), 2 vols, 1984. *Recreations:* painting, violin. *Address:* Coleby, 31 Storey's Way, Cambridge.
*Died* 16 *Oct.* 1985.

**BARRETT, Anthony Arthur;** Clerk of Standing Committees, House of Commons, since 1982; *b* 28 Dec. 1930; *s* of late Arthur Henry Barrett and of Alice Edith (*née* Haynes); *m* 1st, 1958, Shirley Jane Twining (marr. diss. 1977); one *s* one *d*; 2nd, 1981, Vera Reckinger. *Educ:* Bishop Wordsworth's Sch., Salisbury; Peterhouse, Cambridge (Schol.; 1st Cl. Historical Tripos, Parts 1 and 2, MA 1957). A Clerk in the House of Commons, 1957–; seconded to European Parliament as Head of External Economic Relations Division, 1973–79. *Publications:* articles in books and jls on Parliament. *Recreation:* playing the bassoon. *Address:* 25 Paultons Square, SW3 5AP. *T:* 01–351 4764. *Died* 25 *May* 1986.

**BARRETT, Sir Arthur George,** Kt 1942; *b* Geelong, 7 May 1895; *s* of A. O. and F. M. Barrett, Melbourne; *m* 1st, 1922, Jean Beatrice (*d* 1980), *d* of late E. S. Mair, Melbourne; two *d*; 2nd, 1982, Phyllis Jean Mair. *Educ:* Melbourne Church of England Grammar Sch. Served European War, AIF, 1916–19; Lord Mayor of Adelaide, 1937–41; Alderman, Adelaide City Council, 1941–53; retired. Formerly Wing Comdr Air Training Corps RAAF. Former Chairman: Red Cross Soc., Adelaide; Nat. Heart Foundation, Adelaide. *Address:* 210 Stanley Street, North Adelaide, South Australia 5006, Australia. *T:* 267.1171. *Club:* Adelaide (Adelaide).
*Died* 26 *June* 1984.

**BARRETT, Edwin Cyril Geddes,** CMG 1958; MA; *b* 15 Feb. 1909; *s* of late Lieut-Col C. C. J. Barrett, CSI, CIE, IA, and late Mrs Mabel Ada Barrett (*née* Geddes); *m* 1936, Eleanor Nelson Raymond (*d* 1970); one *s*. *Educ:* Marlborough Coll.; Jesus Coll., Cambridge. Cadet, Malayan Civil Service, 1931; many appts in Malaya and Borneo, 1931–42. Military Service, 1942–45. Resumed duty in Malayan CS, 1946; Chief Registration Officer, Fedn of Malaya, 1949; Pres. Municipal Council, Kuala Lumpur, 1951; Comr for Resettlement of Special Constables in Civil Life, Fedn of Malaya, 1952; Acting British Adviser, Perak, 1953; British Adviser, Kedah, 1953; left Malaya on abolition of appt, 1957; Lectr in Malay, SOAS, Univ. of London, 1957–71. *Recreation:* walking dogs. *Address:* 12 Well Walk, Hampstead, NW3.
*Died* 8 *Feb.* 1986.

**BARRETT, Hugh T.;** *see* Tufnell-Barrett.

**BARRIE, Derek Stiven Maxwelton,** OBE 1969 (MBE 1945); FCIT; *b* 8 Aug. 1907; *s* of John Stiven Carruthers Barrie and Dorothea Barrie; *m* 1936, Kathleen Myrra Collins; one *s* one *d*. *Educ:* Apsley

House, Clifton; Tonbridge Sch. London and provincial journalism (Daily Graphic, Allied Newspapers, etc), reporter and sub-editor, 1924–32; joined LMS Railway, 1932; on return from war service, rejoined LMS, 1946; PRO Railway Exec., 1948; Chief PRO British Transport Commn, 1956; Asst Sec.-Gen., BTC, 1958; Asst Gen. Man., York, 1961; Chm., British Railways (Eastern) Bd, and Gen. Man., British Railways Eastern Region, 1968–70. Mem. Council, Inst. of Transport, 1968. Served with Royal Engineers, 1941–46; Hon. Col 74 Movement Control Regt, RE and RCT, 1961–67; Major, Engr. and Rly Staff Corps (T & AVR), 1967, Lt-Col 1968–73. Bronze Star Medal (US), 1945. OStJ 1968. *Publications:* A Regional History of the Railways of Great Britain, vol. 12, South Wales, 1980; numerous railway historical books and monographs; contribs various transport jls, 1928–. *Recreations:* railways, authorship, country life. *Address:* 1 Norman Close, Castlegate, Pickering, N Yorks YO18 7AZ. *T:* Pickering 73580. *Died 24 June 1989.*

**BARRIE, Sir Walter,** Kt 1958; Chairman of Lloyd's, 1953, 1954, 1957, 1958; Director: Jos. W. Hobbs Ltd; Westminster Bank Ltd, 1958–63; Ulster Bank, 1964–72; *b* 31 May 1901; *y s* of late Right Hon. H. T. Barrie, MP, DL, JP, and late Katie Barrie; *m* 1927, Noele Margaret (*d* 1968), *d* of G. J. Furness, JP; one *s* (and one *s* decd). *Educ:* Coleraine; Merchiston Castle, Edinburgh; Gonville and Caius Coll., Cambridge. Entered Lloyd's, 1926; first served on Cttee of Lloyd's, 1946; Deputy-Chm. of Lloyd's, 1951, 1952. Lloyd's Gold Medal, 1958. Pres., Insurance Inst. of London, 1955–56; Vice-Pres., Chartered Insurance Inst., 1957, 1958, 1959, Dep. Pres. 1961. Pres. 1962–63. *Recreation:* golf. *Address:* Compton Elms, Pinkneys Green, Maidenhead, Berks SL6 6NR. *T:* Maidenhead 27151. *Died 8 Dec. 1988.*

**BARRINGTON,** 11th Viscount *cr* 1720; **Patrick William Daines Barrington;** Baron Barrington, 1720; Baron Shute (UK) 1880 (sits as Baron Shute); *b* 29 Oct. 1908; *s* of Hon. Walter Bernard Louis Barrington (*d* 1959); *S* uncle, 1960. *Educ:* Eton; Magdalen Coll., Oxford (BA). Called to the Bar, Inner Temple, 1933 and Lieut, RA. Formerly Hon. Attaché, HBM's Embassy, Berlin, and sometime in Foreign Office. *Heir:* none. *Died 6 April 1990 (ext).*

**BARRINGTON, Prof. Ernest James William,** FRS 1967; Professor of Zoology, Nottingham University, 1949–74, then Emeritus; *b* 17 Feb. 1909; *o s* of late William Benedict and Harriet Barrington; *m* 1943, Muriel Catherine Anne Clinton; one *s* one *d. Educ:* Christ's Hosp.; Oriel Coll., Oxford (Organ Scholar). ARCO 1926; LRAM 1927; BA (Oxford), 1931; BSc 1934; MA 1936; DSc 1947. Lectr in Zoology, Univ. Coll., Nottingham, 1932, Head of Zoology Dept, 1934, Reader, 1945; Dep. Vice-Chancellor, 1956–59; Public Orator, 1964–70. Rockefeller Foundation Fellow in Comparative Physiology at McGill Univ., 1939, and Harvard Univ., 1940; Buell Gallagher Vis. Prof., City Coll., New York, 1966; Royal Soc. Leverhulme Vis. Prof., Univ. of Buenos Aires, 1970; Vis. Prof., Univ. of São Paulo, 1972. European Editor, General and Comparative Endocrinology, 1960–74. Mem. Council, Royal Society, 1970–72, a Vice-Pres., 1971–72; Pres., Inst. of Biology, 1980–82. Membre d'honneur, European Soc. for Comparative Endocrinology, 1974. Organist and Choirmaster, St Margaret's Church, Alderton, 1983–85. Hon. DSc Nottingham, 1975. Frink Medal, Zool Soc. of London, 1976. *Publications:* Introduction to General and Comparative Endocrinology, 1963, 2nd edn, 1975; Hormones and Evolution, 1964; The Biology of Hemichordata and Protochordata, 1965; Zoological Editor, Contemporary Biology Series, 1966; Invertebrate Structure and Function, 1967, 2nd edn, 1979; The Chemical Basis of Physiological Regulation, 1968; Perspectives in Endocrinology (Jt Editor with C. B. Jørgensen), 1968; (Jt Editor with M. Hamburgh) Hormones in Development, 1972; (ed) Trends in Comparative Endocrinology, 1975; (ed) Hormones and Evolution, vols 1 and 2, 1979; Environmental Biology, 1980; papers on chordate morphology and physiology in various jls. *Recreation:* music. *Address:* Cornerways, 2 St Margaret's Drive, Alderton, Tewkesbury, Glos GL20 8NY. *T:* Alderton 375. *Died 15 Dec. 1985.*

**BARRINGTON, Sir Kenneth (Charles Peto),** Kt 1973; *b* 27 Aug. 1911; *er s* of C. W. Barrington; *m* 1938, Eileen Doris Stone; one *d. Educ:* St Paul's School. FCA. Joined Morgan Grenfell & Co. Ltd, Merchant Bankers, 1929; Naval Service, 1939–46; Chartered Accountant, 1952; Director: Morgan Grenfell & Co. Ltd, 1961–76; Morgan Grenfell Holdings Ltd, 1971–76 (Mem., Internat. Adv. Council, 1980–83); English & New York Trust plc, 1967–84; Ultramar plc, 1970–83. *Died 11 Sept. 1987.*

**BARRITT, Sir David (Thurlow),** Kt 1969; BSc, FEng, FIChemE; Chairman, Cammell Laird, 1971–79; *b* 17 Oct. 1903; *er s* of late David Webster Barritt and Rachel Barritt; *m* 1931, Hilda Marshall Creyke; one *s. Educ:* High Sch., Newcastle-under-Lyme, Staffs; N Staffs Polytechnic. Chairman: Simon Engineering Ltd, 1963–70; Twyfords Holdings Ltd, 1969–71; Davy International, 1970–73. Chm. Govs, The Newcastle-under-Lyme Endowed Schs, Newcastle, Staffs, 1962–72. SFInstE; Vice-Pres., IChemE 1974. MUniv Keele, 1981. *Publications:* papers in technical jls. *Recreations:* golf, music,

gardening, photography. *Address:* 7 Prestbury Court, Castle Rise, Prestbury, Cheshire SK10 4UR. *T:* Prestbury (0625) 829716. *Died 21 Aug. 1990.*

**BARROW, Rt. Hon. Errol Walton,** PC 1969; QC 1979; MP (Democratic Labour Party), Barbados; Prime Minister of Barbados, since 1986; *b* 21 Jan. 1920; *s* of late Reginald Grant Barrow, LTh, DD, and of Ruth Barrow (*née* O'Neal); *m* 1945, Carolyn Plaskett; one *s* one *d. Educ:* Harrison Coll., Barbados; LSE (BSc); Hon. Fellow 1975. Royal Air Force, 1940–47. Barrister, Lincoln's Inn, 1949. Elected House of Assembly, Barbados, 1951; Minister of Finance, 1961–76; Premier, 1961; Prime Minister, 1966–76. Founder Mem., Democratic Labour Party, 1955, Chm. 1958–76. Hon. LLD: McGill, 1966; Sussex. *Publications:* What Canada Can Do for the West Indies, 1964; Democracy and Development, 1979. *Recreations:* sailing, flying, diving, tennis. *Address:* Office of the Prime Minister, Bay Street, Bridgetown, Barbados, W Indies; PO Box 125, Bridgetown, Barbados. *Died 1 June 1987.*

**BARROW, Rev. Canon John Harrison,** MA; Vicar of Stansted Mountfitchet, Essex, 1932–54; Honorary Canon of Chelmsford Cathedral, 1935–75, now Emeritus; *b* 11 Oct. 1881; *s* of James and Elizabeth Agnes Barrow; *m* 1917, Mary Irene Debnam (*d* 1976); one *s. Educ:* Durham Sch.; Pembroke Coll., Oxford. Curate of St Luke, Victoria Docks, E, 1904–10; St Mary's, Chelmsford, 1911–14; Precentor of St Mary's Cathedral, Chelmsford, 1914–17; Rector of St Andrew, Romford, 1917; Curate of Dalton-in-Furness, 1917–19; Sec. of Bishop of Chelmsford's Crusade Fund, 1919–22; Metropolitan Organising Sec. of SPCK, Dioceses Chelmsford, London, St Albans, and Southwark, 1922–32; Surrogate, 1915–75; Proctor in Convocation, Diocese of Chelmsford, 1926–50; Vice-Chm. Council, RSCM, 1945–76. Hon. Chaplain to Bishop of Chelmsford, 1951–61, 1962–70, 1971–75; Chaplain to High Sheriff, 1955–56, 1962–63; Chapter Clerk, 1957–75; Priest-in-charge, Margaret Roding, 1955–56, Roxwell, 1957–59. *Address:* c/o 7 Westfield Avenue, South Croydon, Surrey CR2 9JY. *Died 4 Jan. 1981.*

**BARRY, (Donald Angus) Philip,** CBE 1980 (OBE 1969); HM Chief Inspector of Prisons for Scotland, 1981–85; *b* 16 Sept. 1920; *s* of John and Dorothy Barry; *m* 1942, Margaret Orr; five *s* one *d. Educ:* The Abbey Sch., Fort Augustus. Army Service, 1939–46: Captain Gordon Highlanders, 51st (Highland) Div., N Africa, Sicily. Family Business, 1946–82, Man. Dir, 1964–82. Cruz de Caballero del Orden de Isabel La Católica (Spain), 1980. *Address:* c/o Bank of Scotland, 28 Bernard Street, Edinburgh EH6 6QD. *Club:* University Staff (Edinburgh). *Died 6 May 1987.*

**BARRY, Michael, (James Barry Jackson);** OBE 1956; Principal, London Academy of Music and Dramatic Art, 1973–78, retired; *b* 15 May 1910; *s* of A. G. and Helen Jackson; *m* 1st, 1934, Judith Gick (marr. diss. 1947); one *d*; 2nd, 1948, Rosemary Corbett (*d* 1968); one *d*; 3rd, 1973, Pamela Corbett. Studied farming and horticulture in Glos and Herts. Studied for theatre at RADA (Baliol Holloway Award, Best Diploma Performance, 1930) and subsequently as actor, stage-manager, designer and producer at the Northampton, Birmingham, Hull and Croydon Repertory Theatres before working in London. Appointed BBC television producer, 1938. Served Royal Marine Brigade, Landing-Craft and as AMS, RM Office, 1939–45 (Major); Producer and writer, BBC television drama and documentary, 1946–51 (Programmes included: The Silence of the Sea, I Want to Be a Doctor, Promise of Tomorrow, The Passionate Pilgrim, Shout Aloud Salvation); Head of Drama, BBC Television, 1952–61; Programme Controller, Irish Television, 1961–63; prod The Wars of the Roses (TV), 1966; Prof. of Drama and Dept Head, Stanford Univ., Calif, 1968–72. Literary Adviser, Council of Repertory Theatres, 1964–67; Dir, Manchester Royal Exchange Theatre (formerly 1969 Theatre), 1972–85. Member: Drama Panel, Arts Council, 1955–68; Council, RADA, 1966–69; Nat. Council Drama Training, 1976–78; Governing Body, Wimbledon Sch. of Art, 1976–78. Desmond Davis Award, SFTA, 1961. *Publication:* (selected) The Television Playwright, 1960. *Address:* The Gate House, Marlborough Mews, Marlborough Street, Brighton, East Sussex BN1 2EG. *Died 28 June 1988.*

**BARRY, Norman,** OBE 1978; SRN, RMN, RMPA; Divisional Nursing Officer (Mental Illness), South District, Kensington, Chelsea and Westminster Area Health Authority, 1975–77 retired (based at Banstead Hospital); Chairman, General Nursing Council, 1974–76; *b* 30 July 1916; *s* of Edward and Annie Barry; *m* 1940, Winifred McGowan; two *d. Educ:* Houghton-le-Spring Intermed. Sch. Graylingwell Hosp.: completed Mental Nurse trng, 1939; Staff Nurse, 1939; served RAMC, 1940–47; Staff Nurse, Graylingwell Hosp., 1947–50; qual. SRN, Lambeth Hosp., 1951; Graylingwell Hosp.: Charge Nurse, 1951, Night Supt, 1953; Sen. Asst Chief Male Nurse, Park Prewett Hosp., 1954; Banstead Hosp.: Dep. Chief Male Nurse, 1955, Chief Male Nurse, 1960, Chief Nursing Officer, 1972. Gen. Nursing Council: Mem., 1970– (Mem. Mental Nurses Cttee, Dec. 1960–); Vice-Chm., 1972–74; Mem. DHSS and Nat.

Assoc. for Mental Health gps examining care of patients in mental hosps; Chm., Nat. Assoc. Chief and Prin. Nursing Officers. *Recreation:* reading (lay reader, All Saints Church, Banstead). *Address:* 130 Winkworth Road, Banstead, Surrey SM7 2QT. *T:* Burgh Heath 57376. *Died 19 Jan. 1984.*

**BARRY, Philip;** *see* Barry, D. A. P.

**BARTER, John (Wilfred); JP;** Chartered Secretary; Management and Financial Consultant; Chairman, Ealing and Acton Building Society, since 1975; *b* 6 Oct. 1917; *s* of late W. F. Barter; *m* 1st, 1941, Joan Mackay (*d* 1973); two *s* one *d*; 2nd, 1974, Jessica Crabtree. *Educ:* Royal Pinner Sch. Contested (C) East Ham South, 1951; MP (C) Ealing North, 1955–64; PPS to Minister of Health, 1957; PPS to Parly Sec., Min. of Power, 1958–60. Middlesex County Council: Mem., 1949; Alderman, 1961–65; Leader of Majority Party, 1962–63; Vice-Chm., 1963–64; last Chm., 1964–65. Chm. subseq. Pres., Middlesex County Assoc., 1964–76. JP Greater London, Middlesex, 1974. *Died 17 Dec. 1983.*

**BARTHOLOMEW, John Eric, (Eric Morecambe), OBE** 1976; actor comedian; *b* 14 May 1926; *m* 1952, Joan Dorothy Bartlett; one *s* one *d* (and one adopted *s*). *Educ:* Euston Road Elementary Sch., Morecambe. First double act (with E. Wise), at Empire Theatre, Liverpool, 1941; first broadcast, 1943; BBC television series, 1955; BBC TV and ATV series, 1961–; joined Thames TV, 1978. Best Light Entertainment Award, BAFTA (formerly SFTA), 1963, 1971, 1972, 1973, 1974, 1977. A Vice-Pres., Luton Town Football Club (Dir, 1969–75). Pres., Lord's Taverners', 1977–79. Freeman, City of London, 1976. Hon. DLitt Lancaster, 1977. *Films:* The Intelligence Men, 1964; That Riviera Touch, 1965; The Magnificent Two, 1966. *Publications:* (with E. Wise) Eric and Ernie: an autobiography of Morecambe and Wise, 1973; (with E. Wise) The Best of Morecambe and Wise, ed E. Braben, 1975; (with E. Wise) The Morecambe and Wise Special, 1977; (with E. Wise) Bring me Sunshine, 1978; Mr Lonely (novel), 1981; (with E. Wise) There's No Answer to That, 1981; The Reluctant Vampire (for children), 1982; *posthumous publication:* Stella (novel), 1987. *Recreations:* fishing, bird-watching, photography. *Address:* 235/241 Regent Street, W1A 2JT. *T:* 01–734 8851. *Died 28 May 1984.*

**BARTINGTON, Dennis Walter, CB** 1950; *b* 12 May 1901; *s* of late Walter Bartington; *m* 1934, Margaret Christina Skinner. *Educ:* Dulwich Coll.; Trinity Coll., Cambridge (Sen. Schol., MA). Inland Revenue, 1923; Department of Scientific and Industrial Research, 1925; War Office, 1926–39; Asst Sec., Ministry of Supply, 1939, Principal Asst Sec., 1942; Under-Sec., 1947–59. Min. of Aviation, 1959–61; retired, 1961. *Address:* Coombe Hill Private Nursing Home, 3 Adelaide Road, Surbiton, Surrey KT6 4TA. *T:* 01–399 3388. *Died 18 May 1985.*

**BARTLETT, Lt-Col Sir Basil Hardington, 2nd Bt,** *cr* 1913; MA (Cantab); dramatic author; *b* 15 Sept. 1905; *s* of late Hardington Arthur Bartlett, *e s* of 1st Bt and Irene (*d* 1974), *d* of Prof. Henry Robinson; *m* 1937, Mary (marr. diss. 1960), *o d* of late Sir Ian Malcolm, KCMG; three *d*. *Educ:* Repton; Corpus Christi Coll., Cambridge. Served War of 1939–45 (wounded, despatches); Lt-Col, Intelligence Corps. Drama script supervisor, BBC, Television, 1952–55. *Publications:* My First War, 1940; Next of Kin, 1944. *Plays:* This Seat of Mars, 1938; The Intruder, 1939; The Jersey Lily, produced Gate Theatre, 1940; Less than Kind, 1947; A Fish in the Family, 1947. *Heir: b* Henry David Hardington Bartlett, MBE [*b* 18 March 1912; *m* 1936, Kathlene Rosamond (marr. diss. 1974), *d* of Lt-Col W. H. Stanbury; three *s*; 2nd, 1974, Joyce Lillian Odell (*d* 1982); one adopted *d*; 3rd, 1982, Jeanne Margaret Esther Brewer]. *Clubs:* Garrick, Beefsteak. *Died 2 Jan. 1985.*

**BARTLETT, (Charles) Vernon (Oldfeld), CBE** 1956; author; *b* Westbury, Wilts, 30 April 1894; *s* of late T. O. Bartlett, Swanage; *m* 1st, Marguerite van den Bemden (*d* 1966); two *s*; 2nd, 1969, Eleanor Needham Ritchie. *Educ:* Blundell's, Tiverton. Travelled abroad, 1911–14; European War, 1914–16; joined staff of Daily Mail, 1916; Reuter's Agency, 1917; Paris Peace Conference for Reuter's, and later, for Daily Herald; joined staff of The Times, 1919; special correspondent of that paper in Switzerland, Germany, Poland, 1919–20; Correspondent in Rome, 1921–22; London Director of the League of Nations, 1922–32; broadcast regularly on foreign affairs, 1928–34 and during the war; Staff of News Chronicle, 1934–54; Political Commentator for the Straits Times, Singapore, 1954–61; SE Asia Correspondent for Manchester Guardian (now The Guardian), 1954–61. MP (Ind Prog) Bridgwater Div. of Som, 1938–50; Mem. of UN Advisory Cttee of Information Experts, 1948. *Publications:* some twenty-eight books including: Calf Love, 1929; (with R. C. Sherriff) Journey's End, 1930; Nazi Germany Explained, 1933; This is My Life, 1937; Tomorrow Always Comes, 1943; East of the Iron Curtain, 1950; Struggle for Africa, 1953; And Now, Tomorrow, 1960; Tuscan Retreat, 1964; A Book about Elba, 1965; Introduction to Italy, 1967; The Past of Pastimes, 1969; The Colour of their Skin, 1969; Tuscan Harvest, 1971; Central Italy,

1972; Northern Italy, 1973; I Know What I Liked, 1974. *Recreation:* meeting and making friends. *Address:* Middle Barn, Rimpton, Yeovil, Somerset BA22 8AB. *T:* Marston Magna 850708. *Clubs:* Garrick, Beefsteak. *Died 18 Jan. 1983.*

**BARTLETT, Sir (Henry) David (Hardington), 3rd Bt** *cr* 1913; **MBE** (mil.) 1943; *b* 18 March 1912; *s* of Hardington Arthur Bartlett (*d* 1920) (2nd *s* of 1st Bt) and Irene (*d* 1974), *d* of Prof. Henry Robinson; *S* brother, 1985; *m* 1st, 1936, Kathlene Rosamond Stanbury (marr. diss. 1974); three *s*; 2nd, 1974, Joyce Lillian Odell (*d* 1982); one adopted *d*; 3rd, 1982, Jeanne Margaret Esther Brewer. *Educ:* Stowe; Corpus Christi Coll., Cambridge. Successes in fencing: British Amateur Men's Champion, 1934 and 1935; Mem., British Olympic Team, Berlin, 1936. War service with TA; passed War Gunnery Staff Course; Lt-Col RA, retired rank Hon. Major. *Recreations:* gardening, cooking, playing with soldiers. *Heir: s* John Hardington Bartlett [*b* 15 March 1938; *m* 1971, Elizabeth Joyce, *d* of George Raine; two *s*]. *Address:* Brockley Place, Brockley, Bury St Edmunds, Suffolk IP29 4AG. *T:* Bury St Edmunds 830473. *Died 13 Sept. 1989.*

**BARTLETT, Peter Geoffrey, DipArch, FRIBA, ARIAS, FRSA;** independent consultant architect; founded Bartlett Gray & Partners, Chartered Architects and Quantity Surveyors, Nottingham (Partner, 1951–82, Consultant, 1982–84); *b* Bristol, 15 May 1922; *s* of Percy Bartlett, FRIBA, and Daisy Bartlett (*née* Eungblut); *m* 1944, Joan Trevor Lees; one *s*. *Educ:* Nottingham High Sch.; Nottingham Sch. of Architecture, 1939–40 and 1946–49 (Governor's Prize 1949). LDV, 1939–40. Served War, Pilot, RAF, 1940–46 (Bomber, Middle East and Transport Commands). Lectr, Sch. of Architecture, Nottingham, and Asst Architect, Dudding and Thornely, 1949–51. (With Colin Gray) RIBA Bronze Medal (for Notts, Derbys, Lincs), 1958–61; Civic Trust Awards and Commendations in 1960, 1965, 1968, 1969; Craftmanship Awards in E Midlands, 1967, 1968; Competitions: (Jt winners) Brit. Columbia Lumber Manufrs Assoc. of Canada for Housing of Timber Construction, 1958; Special Collective Insts for the Physically Handicapped, Kuwait, Arabia, 1961; original research into: timber constr. in Canada, 1958; precast concrete constr. in Denmark, 1958; bldgs in hot climates in Kuwait, 1962. Major works: Mary Ward Coll. of Educn, Nottingham, 1965; Collective Inst., Kuwait, 1968; HQ, British Geol Survey, 1978–84; schools in Notts, Derbys, Leics and Lincs; works for MoD, DoE and for industry; housing for local authorities. RIBA Part III Examr, Univ. of Nottingham, 1975–78; Member: Court of Governors, Univ. of Nottingham, 1975–83; Council, RIBA, 1973–76; Press Council, 1973–76; Lower Trent Water Consumers Cttee, 1984–85. Past Pres., Nottingham and Derby Soc. of Architects. Liveryman, Guild of Air Pilots and Air Navigators; Freeman, City of London. Papal Cross (for services to architecture), 1981. Qual. Flying Instr, Gps A and B, until 1972; Mem. Flying Trng Cttee of Brit. Light Aviation Centre, 1966–68; Bd of Trade Examr for Private Pilot's Licence, 1967–69; Hon. Life Mem., Sherwood Flying Club, Nottingham. *Recreations:* inland waterways, gardening. *Address:* Millhall End, by Borgue, Kirkcudbright DG6 4TN. *T:* Kirkcudbright 291. *Died 25 June 1986.*

**BARTLETT, Vernon;** *see* Bartlett, C. V. O.

**BARTON, Arthur Edward Victor, CBE** 1936 (OBE 1933); *b* 26 Aug. 1892; *s* of Arthur Moore Barton and Margaret (*née* Bourke); *m* 1st, 1919, Megan Lewis (*d* 1960), *d* of Anthony Matthews, Liverpool; one *s* one *d*; 2nd, 1962, Aileen, *widow* of Ronald S. Lonergan, Mexico City and London. *Educ:* Manchester Grammar Sch. Imperial Customs and Excise Service, 1912; Asst to Chief of Customs, Kenya and Uganda, 1919; Comptroller Customs and MLC, Br. Guiana, 1924; Collector General and MLC, Jamaica, 1927; Collector of Customs and Excise and MLC, Trinidad and Tobago, 1929; MEC, 1936; Mem. West Indies Cricket Board of Control, 1938–39; Comptroller of Customs and Mem. of Legislative Council, Nigeria, 1939–44; retired from Colonial Service, 1944; Sec. to the West India Cttee, 1949–61. Mem. Council, Football Assoc., 1952–70. *Address:* 64 Seabright, West Parade, Worthing, W Sussex BN11 3QU. *T:* Worthing 33935. *Clubs:* Royal Commonwealth Society; Queen's Park Cricket (Port of Spain); British Caribbean Association. *Died 5 Nov. 1983.*

**BARTON, Sir Charles Newton, Kt** 1974; **OBE; ED; BE;** Hon. FIEAust; FAIM; FTS 1978; Chairman: Port of Brisbane Authority, 1977–79; Queensland Local Government Grants Commission, 1977–79; *b* 5 July 1907; *s* of J. Barton, Maryborough, Qld; *m* 1935, Enid, *d* of W. Wetherell. *Educ:* Maryborough Boys' Grammar Sch.; Queensland Univ. (BE Civil). Consulting Engr, Mackay, 1935–59; Comr of Main Roads, Qld, 1960–68; Co-ordinator-Gen., Qld, 1969–76. Served War, AIF, 1940–41; 2/15th Bn (PW), Europe, 1941–45. CO, 31 Bn, CMF, 1948–52, 42 Bn, 1952–57; Hon. Col, Kennedy Regt, 1958–60; Aust. Cadet Corps, N Comd, 1962–66; Qld Univ. Regt, 1966–73. Peter Nicol Russel Medal, 1978. *Recreations:* gardening, fishing. *Address:* 78 Jilba Street, Indooroopilly, Queensland 4068, Australia. *Clubs:* Queensland,

Johnsonian, United Service, Mackay (all in Qld).
*Died 31 March 1987.*

**BARTON, Sidney James;** Part-time Member, London Transport Executive, 1969–76; Additional Chairman, National Health Service Appeal Tribunals, South West Thames/Wessex Regions, since 1974; *b* 5 March 1909; *s* of James George Barton and Emily Hannah Jury; *m* 1933, Lorna Beatrice Mary Williams; one *s* one *d*. *Educ:* Elliott Sch., Wandsworth. Laboratory Technician, Metropolitan Asylums Board and LCC, 1927–34; appointed a full-time Officer, National Union of Public Employees, 1934, National Officer, 1962–73. Mem. Exec. Cttee, London Labour Party, 1950–78; Vice-Chm., Greater London Regional Council, Labour Party, 1969–74. Former Member: General Council, Nurses and Midwives Council; Ancillary Staffs Council; Professional and Technical Staffs Council for the Health Services; TUC Local Govt and Nurses Advisory Cttees; Chm., London Trades Council, 1970–74 (Vice-Chm., 1952–70); Former Member: Surrey County Council (1945–49); Sutton and Cheam Borough Council (1945–48); Surrey Exec. Council for Health Services (1947–54); Epsom Group Hosp. Management Cttee and Long Grove Hosp. Management Cttee; South West Metropolitan Regional Hosp. Bd Farming Adv. Cttee. JP 1955; Alderman LCC 1953–65 (Chm. Public Control Cttee, 1954–59); Chm., LCC, 1959–60 (Chm., Primary and Secondary Schools Sub-Cttee, 1960–61); Vice-Chm. General Purposes Cttee, 1961–65. Alderman London Borough of Sutton, 1964–68. Chm., Governors, Garratt Green Comprehensive Sch. 1958–67, 1970–78 (Vice-Chm., 1967–70); Governor, Hosp. for Sick Children, Great Ormond Street, 1969–75. Member: Met. Regional Exams Bd for Cert. of Secondary Educn, 1964–72; London and Home Counties Regional Advisory Council for Technological Educn, 1965–73; Heathrow Airport London Consultative Cttee; Exec. Mem., British Pensioners and Trade Unions Action Assoc. (Chm., Sutton & Dist Br.). Order of Homayoun Class III (Iran), 1959; Grand Cross of Order Al Merito (Peru), 1960; Comdr Legion of Honour (France), 1960. *Address:* 14 Chatsworth Road, Cheam, Surrey. *T:* 01–644 9222. *Died 20 Jan. 1986.*

**BASING, 4th Baron** *cr* 1887; **George Lutley Sclater-Booth;** *b* 7 Dec. 1903; *s* of Hon. Charles Lutley Sclater-Booth (*d* 1931) (2nd *s* of 1st Baron) and Ellen Geraldine (*d* 1957), *y d* of George Jones, Mitton Manor, Staffs; *S* cousin, 1969; *m* 1st, 1938, Jeannette (marr. diss. 1944; she *d* 1957), *d* of late N. B. MacKelvie, New York; one *s*; 2nd, 1951, Cynthia (*d* 1982), *widow* of Carl H. Beal, Los Angeles, and *d* of late Charles W. Hardy, Salt Lake City, Utah. *Educ:* Winchester. *Heir: s* Hon. Neil Lutley Sclater-Booth [*b* 16 Jan. 1939; *m* 1967, Patricia Ann, *d* of G. B. Whitfield; two *s*]. *Address:* PO Box 301, Pebble Beach, California, USA. *Died 18 Sept. 1983.*

**BASNETT, Baron** *cr* 1987 (Life Peer); of Leatherhead in the county of Surrey; **David Basnett;** General Secretary: General and Municipal Workers' Union, 1973; General, Municipal, Boilermakers and Allied Trades Union, 1982; retired 1986; *b* 9 Feb. 1924; British; *m* 1956, Kathleen Joan Molyneaux; two *s*. *Educ:* Quarry Bank High School, Liverpool. Served War of 1939–45, RAF. Trade Union Official, 1948; Nat. Industrial Officer, GMWU, 1960–72. Mem. TUC General Council, 1966–86 (Chm., 1977–78): Chairman: Trade Union Adv. Cttee to OECD, 1983–86; TULV, 1979–85. Pres., Unity Trust, 1984–86. Numerous committees of enquiry including: Royal Commission on Penal Reform; Commission on the Constitution, 1969–71; Royal Commn on the Press, 1974–77. Mem., NEDC, 1973–86; Mem., National Enterprise Bd, 1975–79 (and of Organising Cttee, 1975). *Address:* Windrush, St John's Avenue, Leatherhead, Surrey. *T:* Leatherhead 372216.
*Died 25 Jan. 1989.*

**BASSETT SMITH, (Newlands) Guy,** CVO 1977; Consultant, Blundell-Permoglaze Holdings Ltd, since 1981 (Managing Director and Chief Executive, 1969–75, Chairman 1975–81); *b* 14 July 1910; *s* of Guy Burroughs Bassett Smith and Elizabeth Hawkins; *m* 1939, Barbara, *d* of Clement Lionel Tyrer. Joined Dunlop Rubber Co. Ltd, 1927. Served War, Army, 1940–46; passed Staff Coll., Camberley, 1943; Staff appt, 8th Army in Italy, 1944; demobilised 1946, with rank of Lt-Col. Rejoined Dunlop Ltd; General Manager: Dunlop Chem. Products Ltd, 1946–60; Dunlop Footwear Ltd, 1960–69, Dir, 1960–69; Man. Dir, Blundell-Permoglaze Holdings Ltd, 1969; Chairman: Blundell Spence Ltd, Melbourne, Australia, 1969–71; Blundell Eomite Paints Ltd, Bombay, 1971–76; Dir, Federated Paints (South Africa) Ltd, 1970–73. Chm., British Rubber Adhesive Mfrs Assoc., 1958–60; Council Member: Fedn of British Rubber Mfrs, 1951–60; Inst. of British Carriage and Automobile Mfrs, 1958–77 (Fellow, 1958). Mem. Council, Liverpool Sch. of Tropical Med., 1962. Hon. Trustee, Duke of Edinburgh Award Scheme, 1977– (Liaison Officer, 1956–71, Trustee 1971–77); Sec., English Tennis and Racquets Assoc., 1972–76. Freeman, City of London, 1980. *Recreations:* fishing, youth work, local affairs. *Address:* Upper Derculich, by Strathtay, Pitlochry, Perthshire PH9 0LR. *Clubs:* Boodle's, Queen's; New (Edinburgh). *Died 18 May 1984.*

**BASTIN, Brig. David Terence,** CBE 1943 (OBE 1942); TD; DL; Chairman, Surrey County Council, 1975–78 (Vice-Chairman, 1972–75); *b* 20 July 1904; *s* of Edward Matthews Bastin and Alice Marie Bastin; *m* 1938, Margaret Nancy Clark Steven (*d* 1981); two *s*. *Educ:* Sherborne Sch. Commnd TA, 1923; transf. Royal Signals, 1938; served War: ME, N Africa, Palestine, Iraq, Persia, Sicily and Italy; staff of Gen. Alexander, 18 and 15 Army Gps; CSO 1 Tactical Air Force; CSO 2 Tactical Air Force, Normandy and N Europe Campaign; Gen. Montgomery's staff, 21 Army Gp. Surrey County Council, 1961–: Alderman, 1970–74; formerly Chm. Policy Cttee, and Chm. Highways and Bridges Cttee. Former Chairman: Surrey Civil Def. Cttee; Landrake Sch. and Pierrepont Sch. Former Member: SE TA&VRA; Thames Conservancy; Thames Water Authority; Assoc. of County Councils (Vice-Chm., Fire and Emergency Cttee); Council, Surrey Univ. Mem., BAAS 1974–. Governor: Wye Coll., 1964–; East Malling Res. Station, 1964–. Master, Worshipful Co. of Ironmongers, 1967. High Sheriff of Surrey, 1969; DL Surrey, 1968. *Recreations:* hunting, fishing, ski-ing, gardening. *Address:* Crooksbury Cottage, Tilford, Farnham, Surrey. *T:* Runfold 2010. *Club:* Flyfishers'. *Died 23 July 1982.*

**BATCHELOR, Alfred Alexander Meston,** MA; Headmaster, Temple Grove School, Heron's Ghyll, near Uckfield, 1935–57; *b* 8 March 1901; *s* of late Rev. Canon A. W. Batchelor, and late Agnes Lowe; *m* 1949, Thelma Williams (*d* 1973). *Educ:* Temple Grove; Charterhouse (Scholar); Christ Church, Oxford (Holford Exhibitioner). Hon. Mods 1922; Lit. Hum. 1924; Senior Asst Master, The Old Ride, Bournemouth, 1926–30; Joint Headmaster, St Christopher's, near Bath, 1930–35; Private Holiday Tutor to the late Duke of Connaught, 1929–34. *Publications:* Cradle of Empire, 1981; contributor to Country Life, Punch, BBC, The Times, etc. *Recreations:* natural history, music. *Address:* Hundred End, Fairwarp, near Uckfield, East Sussex. *T:* Nutley 2151.
*Died 25 Nov. 1982.*

**BATCHELOR, G(eorge) F(rederick) Grant,** MB, ChB, LRCP, FRCS; retired as consulting surgeon; *b* 6 April 1902; *s* of Robert and Margaret Grant Batchelor; *m* 1944, Helen Elspeth Mackintosh (*d* 1976), *d* of late Lieut-Col C. H. Simpson, Harrogate. *Educ:* Dundee High Sch.; St Andrews Univ. MB, ChB (St Andrews), 1923; MRCS, LRCP, 1925; FRCS, 1926; Asst Surgeon, West London Hospital, 1929; Hounslow Hospital, 1930; Surgeon: Wembley Hospital, 1930; West London Hospital, 1935; EMS, London, 1939–42; Lieut-Col, RAMC, 1942. Consulting Surgeon, Charing Cross Hosp., 1972. *Recreations:* golf; shooting. *Address:* Apartado 45, 8600 Lagos, Algarve, Portugal. *Club:* Constitutional. *Died 22 July 1984.*

**BATCHELOR, John Stanley,** FRCS; Orthopaedic Surgeon, Guy's Hospital, 1946–70, retired; *b* 4 Dec. 1905; *s* of Dr Ferdinand Stanley Batchelor and Florence Batchelor; *m* 1934, Marjorie Blanche Elvina Rudkin; two *s* one *d*. *Educ:* Christ's Coll., Christchurch, NZ; Otago Univ.; Guy's Hospital. MRCS, LRCP 1931; FRCS 1934. Pres., Section of Orthopaedics, RSocMed, 1958–59; British Orthopaedic Assoc.: Hon. Treas. 1960–65; Hon. Sec. 1964; Vice-Pres. 1967–68; Pres. 1970–72. *Publications:* contribs to med. jls. *Recreations:* golf, walking, antiques. *Died 20 Feb. 1987.*

**BATE, Ven. Alban F.,** MA; DCnL; Archdeacon of St John, 1949–63, retired; Rector of St Paul's Church, St John, New Brunswick, 1936–63, retired; *b* 12 May 1893; *s* of Rev. William John Bate and Alice C. McMullen; *m* 1919, Norah F. Warburton (*d* 1985), Charlottetown, PEI; two *s* five *d*. *Educ:* Rothesay Collegiate Sch.; Dalhousie, Superior Sch.; University of King's Coll., Nova Scotia, (made Hon. Fellow 1939), BA, 1914; Divinity Testamur, 1916; MA, 1918; Deacon, 1916; Priest, 1917; Curate of Cathedral, Fredericton, 1916–19; Asst at Parish Church, Fredericton, 1919–20; Rector of Fredericton 1920–36 and Archdeacon of Fredericton, 1932–36; Canon of Christ Church Cathedral, Fredericton, 1946; Chaplain of the Legislature of Province of New Brunswick, 1925–35; Chaplain 7th Machine Gun Bn, 1927–36; Chaplain, St George's Soc., 1939–42; Pres. Rotary Club of Fredericton, 1928–29; Saint John, 1941–42. DCnL (King's Univ. Halifax) 1955. *Recreation:* gardening. *Address:* 351 Charlotte Street West, Saint John, NB E2M 1Y7, Canada. *Clubs:* Rotary, Canadian (St John, NB).
*Died 24 July 1986.*

**BATE, (Isaac) Henry,** OBE 1971; Vice-Chairman of Press Council, 1960–75; founder member, 1953–75; *b* 14 Oct. 1899; *m* 1st, 1926, Annie Stonehewer (marr. diss.); one *s*; 2nd, 1949, May Abbott. Journalist, provincial newspapers in Brecon, Cardiff, Aberystwyth, 1918–22; Evening Chronicle, Manchester, 1922–45 (Industrial Corresp. 1933–45); Daily Telegraph, Fleet Street, 1945–70 (Architectural Reporter 1959–70). National Union of Journalists: Mem. Exec. Council, 1946–76; Nat. Pres., 1952–53; Trustee 1956–76; Appeals Tribunal, 1976–80; Mem. Exec. Cttee, Internat. Fedn of Journalists, 1957–60; Mem. Newspaper Mergers Panel, Monopolies Commn, 1965–73. *Address:* 26 York Court, The Albany, Kingston upon Thames, Surrey. *Club:* Press.
*Died 19 May 1986.*

**BATE, Dame Zara (Kate),** DBE 1968; *b* 10 March 1909; *d* of Sidney Herbert Dickens; *m* 1st, 1935, Captain James Fell (marr. diss.); three *s*; 2nd, 1946, Rt Hon. Harold Edward Holt, PC, CH (*d* 1967), Prime Minister of Australia; 3rd, 1969, Hon. Henry Jefferson Percival Bate, MHR (*d* 1984). *Educ:* Ruyton and Toorak Coll. Director: John Stafford & Co.; Colebrook Estates. Hon. Dr Lit and Hum, Ewha Women's Univ., Seoul, Korea, 1967. Coronation Medal, 1953. *Recreations:* reading, committee work, grandchildren, bridge. *Address:* 58 Monaco Street, Florida Gardens, Gold Coast, Qld, Australia.                                   *Died* 14 *June* 1989.

**BATE-SMITH, Dr Edgar Charles,** CBE 1963; FLS 1959; Hon. FIFST; ScD; Director, Low Temperature Research Station, Cambridge, 1947–65, retired; *b* 24 Aug. 1900; *s* of Albert Edward Smith and Avis Ellen Jenkinson; *m* 1933, Margaret Elizabeth Bate Hardy (*d* 1982); one *s*. *Educ:* Wellingborough Sch.; Manchester Univ.; Gonville and Caius Coll., Cambridge. Mem., Soc. of Chemical Industry Food Group Cttee, 1939–41, 1956–60; (Jubilee Memorial Lectr, 1962–63); formerly Mem. Council, Inst. of Food Science and Technology; Pres., Cambridge Philosophical Soc., 1953–55; Chm., Phytochemical Soc. (formerly Plant Phenolics Group), 1958–60. *Publications:* Food Science (with T. N. Morris), 1952. Papers in scientific jls on post-mortem physiology of muscle, chemistry and taxonomy of plants. *Recreations:* plants and animals; sketching. *Address:* c/o Institute of Animal Physiology, Babraham, Cambridge.                                   *Died* 8 *May* 1989.

**BATEMAN, Sir Charles Harold,** KCMG 1950 (CMG 1937); MC; *b* Portsmouth, 4 Jan. 1892; *s* of late Charles Bateman; *m* 1940, Bridget Mary, *d* of late Michael Kavanagh, Co. Wicklow. *Educ:* London Univ. (BA); Sorbonne, Paris. Served European War, 1914–18, with 2nd London Regt (Royal Fusiliers), Gallipoli and France; Royal Artillery, France and Belgium (MC, twice wounded); entered Diplomatic Service, 1920; Third Sec., Santiago, Chile; Foreign Office, 1924; First Sec., 1929; transferred Bagdad, 1932; Acting Counsellor, 1935; Counsellor, Lisbon, 1937; Minister at Cairo, 1938; transferred Foreign Office, 1940; Minister to Mexico, 1941–44, Ambassador, 1944–47; Asst Under Sec., Foreign Office, 1948–50; British Ambassador to Poland, 1950–52; retired, 1952. *Address:* Amesbury Abbey, Amesbury, Wiltshire.                 *Died* 7 *Nov.* 1986.

**BATES, Sir Darrell;** *see* Bates, Sir J. D.

**BATES, Harry Stuart,** CSI 1947; *b* 16 March 1893; *s* of late Albert Bates, Congleton, Cheshire; *m* 1920, *d* of late William Hammond Walker, Congleton, Cheshire; two *s* one *d*. *Educ:* Denstone; St Catharine's Coll., Cambridge (BA). Served in British and Indian Armies 1914–19. Joined Indian Civil Service, 1920: Collector, Settlement Offr and Manager, Balrampur Estate, 1926–42; Comr, 1942–45; Mem., Bd of Revenue, UP, 1945–47; retired, 1949. Employed Colonial Office, 1948–57. *Address:* Rowhurst Cottage, Milford-on-Sea, Hants. *T:* Milford 2906.

                                        *Died* 1 *Sept.* 1985.

**BATES, Sir (Julian) Darrell,** Kt 1966; CMG 1956; CVO 1954; *b* 10 Nov. 1913; *y s* of late E. Stuart Bates; *m* 1944, Susan Evelyn June Sinclair; two *s* one *d*. *Educ:* Sevenoaks Sch.; Keble Coll., Oxford. Entered Colonial Service, Tanganyika Territory, 1936; served King's African Rifles (despatches), 1940–43; seconded Colonial Office, 1944–46; Officer Administering the Government, Seychelles, 1950–51; Deputy Chief Secretary, Somaliland Protectorate, 1951–53; Colonial Sec., Gibraltar, 1953–64, Permanent Sec., 1964–68. *Publications:* A Fly Switch from the Sultan, 1961; The Shell at My Ear, 1961; The Mango and the Palm, 1962; A Longing for Quails, 1964; Susie, 1964; A Gust of Plumes, 1972; The Companion Guide to Devon and Cornwall, 1976; The Abyssinian Difficulty, 1979; The Fashoda Incident of 1898, 1984. *Address:* 21 Carrallack Terrace, St Just, Penzance, Cornwall.

                                        *Died* 11 *June* 1989.

**BATESON, Air Vice-Marshal Robert Norman,** CB 1964; DSO 1943 and Bar, 1944; DFC 1940; idc; jssc; psa; *b* 10 June 1912; *s* of late George Rowland Bateson; *m* 1st, 1942, Elizabeth Lindsay Davidson (*d* 1975); 2nd, 1976, Margaret Graham Craig. *Educ:* Watford Grammar Sch. Joined RAF 1936. Served War of 1939–45. Asst Chief of Air Staff, Operational Requirements, Air Min., 1959–61; Air Officer Comdg No. 12 Group, Fighter Comd, 1961–62; SASO, Fighter Comd, 1963–67. ADC to the Queen, 1958–60. Air Cdre, 1958; actg Air Vice-Marshal, 1959; Air Vice-Marshal, 1960. Dutch Flight Cross, 1943; Order of Dannebrog, 1944. *Recreations:* squash, tennis, sailing, motor sport. *Address:* Cleave Cottage, Weir Quay, Bere Alston, Yelverton, Devon. *T:* Tavistock 840366. *Clubs:* Royal Air Force; Weir Quay Yacht.                         *Died* 6 *March* 1986.

**BATEY, Charles Edward,** OBE 1943; Hon. MA Oxon, 1941 (by Decree, 1946, Lincoln College); JP; *b* 22 Feb. 1893; *e s* of Edward Batey and Christian Allan Morison; *m* 1922, Ethel May, *d* of George Reed; one *d*. *Educ:* Edinburgh Board Schs; Heriot Watt College (Hon. Fellow 1954). Apprenticed Leith Observer, 1908–15; served European War, 1915–20, RAMC. Hazell, Watson & Viney,

Aylesbury, 1920; Works Manager, Univ. Tutorial Press, 1922–28; Asst Printer, University of Oxford, 1929–46; Printer to the University of Oxford, 1946–58. Mem. Council British Federation of Master Printers, 1944–50, and Mem. of Labour Cttee, 1944–49; Chairman: Jt Industrial Council of Printing and Allied Trades, 1948–49; Apprenticeship Authority, 1946–48; City of Oxford Youth Employment Cttee, 1944–54. Pres., Assoc. of Teachers of Printing and Allied Subjects, 1953–58. Mem. various industrial education cttees. Hon. Mem. City and Guilds of London Institute, 1959; Hon. Fellow, Inst. of Printing, 1961; Hon. City and Guilds Insignia Award, 1965. *Publication:* (with T. W. Chaundy and P. R. Barrett) The Printing of Mathematics, 1954. *Recreations:* calligraphy, gardening. *Address:* Carfax, Up Nately, Basingstoke, Hants. *T:* Hook 2170.                                      *Died* 16 *Oct.* 1981.

**BATHER, Elizabeth Constance,** OBE 1946; retired as Chief Superintendent Metropolitan (Women) Police, (1946–60); *b* 11 Oct. 1904; *d* of late Rev. Arthur George Bather, MA, and Lilian Dundas Firth, Winchester. *Educ:* St Swithuns Sch., Winchester. Mem. Hampshire County Council, 1937–46. Served in WAAF, 1939–45; Group Officer, 1944–45. JP Winchester, 1937–46; Councillor, Hartley Witney and Hart DCs, 1967–76. *Address:* 8 South Ridge, Odiham, Basingstoke RG25 1NG.               *Died* 8 *Jan.* 1988.

**BATHO, Edith Clara,** MA, DLit (London); Principal, Royal Holloway College, University of London, 1945–62, retired; *b* 21 Sept. 1895; 3rd *d* of late William John Batho and Ellen Clara Hooton. *Educ:* Highbury Hill High Sch.; University Coll., London. BA (Hons English), 1915, MA 1920, DLit 1935; war work, 1916–18; on staff of Roedean Sch., 1918–19; Downe House Sch., 1919–21; Quain Student and Asst in English at University Coll., London, 1921; Fellow of University Coll., London, 1934; Reader in English Literature, University Coll., London, 1935–45. Visiting Prof., Univ. of Wisconsin, 1963. An active mem. British Fedn of Univ. Women. Hon. D de l'U Poitiers, 1962. *Publications:* The Ettrick Shepherd, 1927 (reprinted 1969); The Later Wordsworth, 1934 (reprinted, 1964); The Poet and the Past (Warton Lecture of the British Acad.), 1937; The Victorians and After (with Bonamy Dobrée), 1938; Chronicles of Scotland by Hector Boece, tr. Bellenden (ed for STS), Vol. I with R. W. Chambers, 1936, Vol. II with H. W. Husbands, 1941; A Wordsworth Selection, 1962; other articles and reviews. *Recreations:* travelling, languages, needlework. *Clubs:* New Arts Theatre, English-Speaking Union.                 *Died* 21 *Jan.* 1986.

**BATHO, Sir Maurice Benjamin,** 2nd Bt, *cr* 1928; Chairman and Managing Director, Ridgley (Huntingdon) Ltd and associated companies; *b* 14 Jan. 1910; *o surv. s* of Sir Charles Albert Batho, 1st Bt, and Bessie (*d* 1961), 4th *d* of Benjamin Parker, Oulton Broad, Suffolk; *S* father, 1938; *m* 1934, Antoinette, *o d* of Baron d'Udekem d'Acoz, Ghent; two *s* two *d*. *Educ:* Uppingham; Belgium. Served War of 1939–45: Lt-Col, KRRC. Jt Sub-Dir, Syrian Wheat Collection Scheme of Spears Mission, 1943; Adviser on Cereals Collection, Min. of Finance of Imp. Iranian Govt, 1944; Dep. Dir, Rice Procurement, Bengal, 1945; Managing Dir, Reed Paper & Board Sales Ltd, 1959, resigned 1965; formerly Director: Reed Paper & Board (UK) Ltd; London Paper Mills Co. Ltd; Empire Paper Mills Ltd; Reed Board Mills (Colthorp) Ltd; Reed Brookgate Ltd. *Recreation:* golf. *Heir:* *s* Peter Ghislain Batho [*b* 9 Dec. 1939; *m* 1966, Lucille Mary, *d* of Wilfrid F. Williamson; three *s*]. *Address:* Carlton Hall, Saxmundham, Suffolk. *T:* 2505. *Clubs:* Naval and Military, St Stephen's Constitutional.               *Died* 12 *Jan.* 1990.

**BATTEN, Edith Mary,** OBE 1948; Principal, William Temple College, 1950–66; *b* 1905, British. *Educ:* High Sch. for Girls, Southport; Liverpool Univ.; London School of Economics; St Anne's Coll., Oxford. BSc Liverpool; BSc (Econ) London; MA Oxon. Asst Industrial Personnel Officer; Sec. North West Ham Branch, Invalid Children's Aid Association; Sub-Warden, St Helen's Settlement, E15; Warden, Birmingham Settlement, 1933–38; JP City of Birmingham, 1937–38; Organising Sec. British Assoc. of Residential Settlements, 1938–42; Mem. Factory and Welfare Advisory Board to Min. of Labour, 1940–42; Min. of Labour and National Service, 1942–47. Res. Officer, Bd for Social Responsibility of Church Assembly, 1967–70. *Recreations:* reading, listening to music. *Address:* Guillard's Oak House, Midhurst, West Sussex. *Club:* Royal Commonwealth Society.                         *Died* 28 *Jan.* 1985.

**BATTEN, Jean Gardner,** CBE 1936; *b* 1909; *d* of Capt. F. H. Batten, Dental Surg., Auckland, New Zealand. *Educ:* Cleveland House Coll., Auckland, NZ. Gained Private pilot's licence at London Aeroplane Club, 1930; commercial pilot's licence London, 1932; solo flight England-Australia (women's record) May 1934; solo flight Australia-England (first woman to complete return flight), April 1935; solo flight England-Argentina (first woman to make solo flight across South Atlantic Ocean to South America), Nov. 1935; world records established: England-Brazil 61 hrs 15 mins; fastest crossing of South Atlantic Ocean by air 13 hrs 15 mins; solo flight England-New Zealand 11 days 45 mins, Oct. 1936; first direct flight from England to Auckland, NZ; solo record England-Australia 5 days 21

hrs; record flight across Tasman Sea, Australia-New Zealand, 9hrs 29 mins; record solo flight Australia-England, 5 days 18 hrs 15 mins, Oct. 1937. Jean Batten Archive estbd RAF Museum, Hendon, 1972; Museum issued 13,000 Jean Batten Commemorative Covers which were flown over route to New Zealand by British Airways to mark 40th anniversary of first direct flight, 1976; 1981 Airliner of Britannia Airways named 'Jean Batten'. Invited to visit Auckland, NZ by Mus. of Transport and Technology to open new Pavilion, 1977. Officer of the Order of the Southern Cross, Brazil; Chevalier of the Legion of Honour, France; awarded Britannia Trophy, Royal Aero Club, 1935 and 1936; Harmon Trophy awarded by international vote, 1935, 1936 and 1937; Johnston Memorial Air Navigation Trophy, 1935; Challenge Trophy (USA), Women's International Association of Aeronautics, 1934, 1935 and 1936; Segrave Trophy, 1936; Coupe de Sibour, 1937; gold medals: Fédération Aéronautique Internationale; Royal Aero Club, Aero Club de France, Belgian Royal Aero Club, Académie des Sports, Royal Swedish Aero Club, Ligue International des Aviateurs, Aero Club of Argentine, Royal Danish Aeronautical Society, Royal Norwegian Aero Club, Aero Club of Finland. City of Paris Medal, 1971. Liveryman, Guild of Air Pilots and Air Navigators, 1978. Freeman, City of London, 1978. *Publication:* My Life, 1938, repr. as Alone in the Sky, 1979. *Recreations:* walking, swimming, music.
*Died Nov. 1982.*

**BATTLE, Richard John Vulliamy,** MBE 1945; FRCS; Plastic Surgeon, retired 1972; Hon. Consultant in Plastic Surgery: St Thomas' Hospital; Westminster Hospital; Queen Elizabeth Hospital for Children; King Edward VII Hospital for Officers; Consultant in Plastic Surgery to the Army, 1955–71; *b* 21 Jan. 1907; *s* of late William Henry Battle and Anna Marguerite (*née* Vulliamy); *m* 1941, Jessie Margaret King; three *s. Educ:* Gresham's Sch.; Trinity Coll., Cambridge. BA 1928, MA 1935, Cantab; MRCS, LRCP, 1931; FRCS, 1933; MChir (Cantab) 1935. Joined Territorial Army; served War of 1939–45 in RAMC, France, 1939–40, Italy, 1943–46; Comd No 1 Maxillo Facial Unit and 98 General Hospital; Major 1940; Lt-Col 1945. Pres., Brititsh Assoc. of Plastic Surgs, 1952, 1967, Gillies Gold Medal, 1970. *Publications:* Plastic Surgery, 1964; contrib. on plastic surgery to scientific periodicals. *Recreations:* golf, music. *Address:* Benhall Green, Saxmundham, Suffolk. *T:* Saxmundham 2334. *Clubs:* East India, Devonshire, Sports and Public Schools; Woodbridge Golf.
*Died 26 May 1982.*

**BATTYE, Maj.-Gen. (Retd) Stuart Hedley Molesworth,** CB 1960; *b* 21 June 1907; *s* of late Lieut-Col W. R. Battye, DSO, MS, LRCP, Chev. de Legion d'Honneur, CStJ, and late M. St G. Molesworth; *m* 1940, Evelyn Désirée, *d* of late Capt. G. B. Hartford, DSO and bar, RN; one *s* two *d. Educ:* Marlborough Coll.; RMA, Woolwich; Cambridge Univ. (MA). Commissioned 2nd Lieut, RE, 1927; served with Bengal Sappers and Miners, India, 1930–44 (NW Frontier Campaign, 1930–31); Iraq, 1941–42; India, 1942–44; 21 Army Group, BLA, 1945–47; MELF, 1952–55; War Office, 1955; Dir of Movements, the War Office, 1958–61; Dir, Council for Small Industries in Rural Areas (formerly Rural Industries Bureau), 1963–73. FRSA 1963. *Publications:* contrib. to Blackwood's and RE Journal. *Recreations:* fishing, painting. *Club:* Army and Navy.
*Died 17 April 1987.*

**BAUDOUX, Most Rev. Maurice,** STD, PhD, DèsL; *b* Belgium, 1902. *Educ:* Prud'homme convent, Saskatchewan; St Boniface College, Manitoba; St Joseph's Seminary, Alberta; Grand Seminary, Quebec. Priest, 1929; Curate then Pastor, Prud'homme, Sask; Domestic Prelate, 1944; First Bishop of Saint Paul in Alberta, 1948; Coadjutor-Archbishop of Saint Boniface, 1952; Archbishop of St Boniface, 1955–74. *Address:* c/o Archbishop's Residence, 151 Cathedral Avenue, St Boniface, Manitoba R2H 0H6, Canada.
*Died 1 July 1988.*

**BAWDEN, Edward,** CBE 1946; RA 1956 (ARA 1947); RDI 1949; Painter and Designer; Draughtsman; formerly a Tutor in the School of Graphic Design, Royal College of Art; *b* Braintree, Essex, 1903; *m* 1932, Charlotte (*d* 1970), *d* of Robert Epton, Lincoln; one *s* one *d. Educ:* Cambridge Sch. of Art; Royal Coll. of Art. As an Official War Artist he travelled in Middle East, 1940–45; visited Canada during 1949 and 1950 as a guest instructor at Banff Sch. of Fine Arts, Alberta. His work is represented in the Tate Gallery, London, and by water-colour drawings in several London, Dominion and provincial galleries; exhibitions at: Leicester Galleries, 1938, 1949, 1952; Zwemmer Gallery, 1934, 1963; Fine Art Soc., 1968, 1975, 1978, 1979, 1987, 1989; Fitzwilliam Museum, 1978; Imperial War Museum, 1983; V&A, 1988, 1989; retrospective touring exhibn, 1988–89. Printmaker and graphic designer. He has designed and cut blocks for a series of wallpapers printed by Messrs Cole & Son, and has painted mural decorations for the SS Orcades and SS Oronsay, also for Lion and Unicorn Pavilion on South Bank site of Festival of Brtain. Trustee of Tate Gallery, 1951–58. Hon. Dr RCA; DUniv Essex; Hon. RE; *Illustrated books include:* The Histories of Herodotus, Salammbô, Tales of Troy and Greece, The Arabs, Life in an English Village. *Relevant publications:* Edward Bawden, by J.

M. Richards (Penguin Modern Painters); Edward Bawden, by Robert Harling (English Masters of Black and White); Edward Bawden: A Book of Cuts, 1978; Edward Bawden, by Douglas Percy Bliss, 1979. *Address:* 2 Park Lane, Saffron Walden, Essex CB10 1DA.
*Died 21 Nov. 1989.*

**BAX, Rodney Ian Shirley,** QC 1966; **His Honour Judge Bax;** a Circuit Judge, since 1973; *b* 16 Sept. 1920; *s* of late Rudolph Edward Victor Bax, Barrister, and of Shirley Winifred, *d* of Canon G. A. Thompson; *m* 1953, Patricia Anne, *d* of late Martin Stuart Turner, MC; one *s* one *d. Educ:* Bryanston Sch. (Scholar); Royal Coll. of Music (Exhibitioner). Served with Royal Fusiliers and Intelligence Corps, 1940–46 (Major GS). Called to Bar, Gray's Inn, 1947, Bencher, 1972; S Eastern Circuit. A Recorder, 1972–73. Mem., General Council of the Bar, 1961–65. Asst Comr, Boundary Commn for England, 1965–69. Comr, Central Criminal Court, 1971. Chm., Barristers' Benevolent Assoc., 1979– (Dep. Chm., 1974–79). Governor, Ashfold Sch. Trust, Bucks. *Recreations:* music, books. *Address:* 4 Jocelyn Road, Richmond, Surrey. *T:* 01–940 3395; Alderney, Channel Islands.
*Died 1 Nov. 1983.*

**BAXTER, Prof. Alexander Duncan,** CEng; Research Consultant, since 1970; Director, de Havilland Engine Co. Ltd, 1958–63; Chief Executive Rocket Division and Nuclear Power Group, de Havilland Engine Co. Ltd, 1957–63; *b* 17 June 1908; *e s* of Robert Alexander and Mary Violet Baxter; *m* 1933, Florence Kathleen McClean; one *s* two *d. Educ:* Liverpool Institute High Sch.; Liverpool Univ. BEng (1st Cl. Hons MechEng) 1930; MEng 1933. Post-graduate pupil with Daimler Company, 1930–34; commissioned in RAFO, 1930–38; Research Engineer with Instn. of Automobile Engrs, 1934–35; Scientific Officer at RAE, Farnborough, 1935; engaged on aircraft propulsion and gas turbine research until 1947; Supt, Rocket Propulsion, RAE, 1947–50; Prof. of Aircraft Propulsion, Coll. of Aeronautics, Cranfield, 1950–57; Dep. Principal, Cranfield, 1954–57; Sen. Exec., Bristol Siddeley Engines Ltd, 1963–68, Bristol Engine Div. of Rolls Royce Ltd, 1968–70. Mem. Council: InstMechE, 1955–57; RAeS, 1953–70 (Vice-Pres, 1962–66, Pres., 1966–67). Served as member of many educnl bodies, incl.: jt Cttee on Higher Nat. Certificate in Engrg; RAF Educn Adv. Cttee; Aeronautical Board, CNAA; Board of CEI, 1962–69; various Govt advisory cttees. Member of Court: Univ. of Bristol; Cranfield Inst. of Technology. Hon. DSc Cranfield Inst. of Technology, 1980. FIMechE, FRAeS, FInstPet, Fellow, British Interplanetary Soc. *Publications:* Professional Aero Engineer, Novice Civil Servant, 1988; various reports in government R & M series; papers in Proc. Instn Mech. Engineers and RAeS. *Recreations:* do-it-yourself, grandchildren, cine photography. *Address:* Glebe Cottage, Pucklechurch, Avon. *T:* Abson 2204.
*Died 23 March 1988.*

**BAXTER, Prof. James Thomson;** William Dick Professor of Veterinary Medicine, since 1970 and Dean, Faculty of Veterinary Medicine, since 1984, University of Edinburgh; *b* Feb. 1925; *e s* of James T. Baxter and Victoria A. D. Montgomery; *m* 1951, Muriel Elizabeth Knox; two *s* one *d. Educ:* Trinity Academy, Edinburgh; Royal (Dick) Veterinary Coll., Edinburgh. MA(Dub), PhD(Dub); MRCVS; FIBiol; FRSH. Served War, Royal Navy, 1944–46. Gen. veterinary practice, 1950–52; Veterinary Officer, then Veterinary Research Officer, Min. of Agr., N Ireland, 1952–60; Lectr, Loughry Agr. Coll., 1955–60; Asst Lectr in Vet. Sci., Queen's Univ., Belfast, 1958–60; Prof. in Clinical Vet. Practices, Dublin Univ., 1960–70; Dir, Sch. of Veterinary Medicine, Dublin Univ., 1963–70. Vis. Prof., Al-Fateh Univ., Tripoli, Libya, 1984, 1985. Mem. Council: Irish Grassland and Animal Production Assoc., 1961–70 (Pres. 1963–64); RCVS, 1962–70, 1978–82, 1984–; Agricl Inst. (An Foras Taluntais), 1964–70. Mem., Irish Veterinary Council, 1962–70. Fellow, Trinity Coll., Dublin, 1965–70. Editor (with Prof. A. van Miert): Veterinary Science Communications, 1976–80; Veterinary Research Communications, 1980–. *Publications:* articles in vety and other jls. *Address:* 1 Wilton Road, Edinburgh EH16 5NX. *T:* 031–667 3055.
*Died 11 Nov. 1985.*

**BAXTER, Prof. Sir (John) Philip,** KBE 1965 (OBE 1945); CMG 1959; PhD, FAA, FTS; Chairman, Sydney Opera House Trust, 1968–75; *b* 7 May 1905; *s* of John and Mary Netta Baxter; *m* 1931, Lilian May Baxter (*née* Thatcher) (decd); two *s* one *d* (and one *s* decd). *Educ:* University of Birmingham. BSc 1925, PhD 1928. University of Birmingham. Research Dir, ICI General Chemicals Ltd and Dir, Thorium Ltd, until 1949; Prof. Chem. Eng, NSW University of Technology, 1950; Vice-Chancellor, Univ. of NSW, 1953–69. Chm, Australian Atomic Energy Commn, 1957–72. Fellow: Aust. Acad. of Science; Aust. Acad. of Technological Sciences. FRACI; MIE(Aust). Hon. LLD Montreal, 1958; Hon. DSc: Newcastle, Queensland; NSW; Hon. DTech Loughborough, 1969. *Address:* 1 Kelso Street, Enfield, NSW 2136, Australia. *T:* 7474261.

**BAYLISS, Colonel George Sheldon,** CB 1966; OBE 1945; TD 1941; DL; *b* 26 Dec. 1900; *s* of Francis and E. M. Bayliss, Walsall; *m* 1935, Margaret Muriel Williamson (*d* 1962), *widow* of Dr K. B. Williamson, MC, and *d* of J. S. Harker, Penrith; one *s* and one step

s. *Educ:* Shrewsbury Sch. Joined TA, 2nd Lieut, 1921; Major 1926–40; Lieut-Col 1940–45 (despatches 4 times, 1941–45). Hon. Col 473 HAA Regt, 1947–53. DL Co. Stafford, 1953–83; Chm., Staffs T&AFA, 1959–65. Managing Dir, S B & N Ltd, Walsall, 1930–76, retired. Bronze Star (USA). *Address:* 24 West Pasture, Kirbymoorside, York YO6 6BR. *T:* Kirbymoorside 31508.
*Died 13 Feb. 1984.*

**BAYNHAM, Tom**, CBE 1975 (OBE 1964); County Councillor, South Yorkshire CC, 1973–81 (Chairman, 1973, 1974, 1975); *b* 12 Aug. 1904; *s* of James Baynham and Elizabeth Baynham (*née* Heathcote); *m* 1926, Florence May (*née* Jones); one *s* two *d. Educ:* state school. Miner, 1918–69. Adwick Le Street UDC, 1939–74; W Riding CC, 1946–74; W Riding Health Exec. Council, 1948–74. Served on Mental Health Tribunal for approx. nine years to 1974; past Trade Union local official, also Safety Inspector. *Recreations:* reading, gardening. *Address:* 17 Willington Road, Skellow, Doncaster, South Yorkshire DN6 8JE. *T:* Doncaster 722226. *Clubs:* Carcroft Village; Skellow Grange Working Men's; Doncaster Trade Union and Labour; Hooton Pagnell.
*Died 30 Jan 1985.*

**BAZELL, Prof. Charles Ernest**; Professor of General Linguistics, School of Oriental and African Studies, University of London, 1957–77; *b* 7 Dec. 1909; *s* of Charles Thomas Bazell. *Educ:* Berkhamstead Sch.; Wadham Coll., Oxford. Fellow of Magdalen Coll., Oxford, 1934–42; Prof. of English Language and General Linguistics, Univ. of Istanbul, 1942–57. *Publications:* Linguistic Form, 1953; articles and reviews for Archivum Linguisticum, Word, Acta Linguistica, etc. *Address:* c/o Lloyds Bank, 23 Old Woking Road, West Byfleet, Surrey.
*Died 5 April 1984.*

**BAZIN, Germain René Michel**; Officier, Légion d'Honneur; Commandeur des Arts et des Lettres; Conservateur en chef honoraire du Musée du Louvre, since 1971; Professeur honoraire à L'Ecole du Louvre, since 1971; Conservateur de musée Condé, Chantilly, since 1983; Research Professor Emeritus, York University, Toronto; Membre de l'Institut, 1975; *b* Paris, 1901; *s* of Charles Bazin, Industrialist and engineer of Ecole Centrale de Paris, and J. Laurence Mounier-Pouthot; *m* 1947, Countess Heller de Bielotzerkowka. *Educ:* Ste Croix de Neuilly; Ste Croix d'Orléans; Collège de Pontlevoy; Sorbonne. D ès L; Lic. en Droit; Dipl. Ecole du Louvre. Served French Infantry (Capt.), 1939–45. Prof., Univ. Libre de Bruxelles, since 1934; joined staff of Louvre, 1937; Conservateur en chef du Musée du Louvre, 1951–71; Professeur de muséologie, Ecole du Louvre, 1942–71; lecturer and writer; responsible for more than 30 exhibitions of paintings in France and elsewhere; his books are translated into English, German, Spanish, Italian, Japanese, Portuguese, Yugoslav, Hebrew, Swedish, Dutch, Rumanian, Czech, Danish, Chinese. Corresponding Mem. of many Academies. Grand Officier, Ordre Léopold, Belgium; Grand Officier, Couronne, Belgium; Commandeur, Mérite, République d'Italie; Officier: Ordre de Santiago, Portugal; Star of the North, Sweden; Cruzeiro do Sul, Brazil, etc. Dr *hc:* Univ. of Rio de Janiero; Villanova, Pa, Univ. *Publications:* Mont St Michel, 1933; Le Louvre, 1935, rev. edn 1980; Les primitifs français, 1937; La peinture italienne aux XIVe et XVe siècles, 1938; Memling, 1939; De David à Cézanne, 1941; Fra Angelico, 1941; Corot, 1942; Le crépuscule des images, 1946; L'Epoque impressioniste, 1947; Les grands maîtres de la peinture hollandaise, 1950; Histoire générale de l'art, 1951; L'Architecture religieuse baroque au Brésil, 1956–58; Trésors de la peinture au Louvre, 1957; Musée de l'Ermitage: écoles étrangères, 1957; Trésors de l'impressionisme au Louvre, 1958; A gallery of Flowers, 1960; Baroque and Rococo, 1964; Message de l'absolu, 1964; Aleijadinho, 1963; Francesco Messina, 1966; Le Temps des Musées, 1967; La Scultura francese, 1968; Destins du baroque, 1968; La peinture d'avant garde, 1969; Le Monde de la sculpture, 1972 (trans. as Sculpture in the World, 1968); Manet, 1972; Langage des styles, 1976; Les Palais de la Foi, 1980; L'Univers impressioniste, 1981; Les fleurs vues par les peintres, 1984; Histoire de l'Histoire de l'Art, 1986; Paradeiso ou l'art des Jardins, 1988; Géricault, 1988; numerous articles in principal reviews and French periodicals and foreign art journals of Europe and America. *Recreation:* rowing. *Address:* 23 Quai Conti, 75006 Paris, France. *Clubs:* Army and Navy, Carlton, East India, Devonshire, Sports and Public Schools; Cercle de l'Union, Fondateur de la Maison de l'Amérique Latine (Paris).
*Died 3 May 1990.*

**BAZIRE, Rev. Canon Reginald Victor**; Archdeacon and Borough Dean of Wandsworth, 1973–75; an Honorary Canon of Southwark, 1959–67 and since 1975; *b* 30 Jan. 1900; *s* of Alfred Arsène Bazire and Edith Mary (*née* Reynolds); *m* 1927, Eileen Crewsdon Brown (*d* 1988); two *s. Educ:* Christ's Hospital. Missionary, China Inland Mission, 1922–45; Vicar, St Barnabas, Clapham Common, 1949–67; Rural Dean of Battersea, 1953–66; Archdeacon of Southwark, 1967–73. Proctor in convocation: 1959–64, 1970–75. *Address:* 7 Grosvenor Park, Bath BA1 6BL. *T:* Bath (0225) 447418.
*Died 20 Oct. 1990.*

**'BB';** *see* Watkins-Pitchford, D. J.

**BEACHCROFT, Thomas Owen**; Author; Chief Overseas Publicity Officer, BBC, 1941–61; *b* 3 Sept. 1902; *s* of Dr R. O. Beachcroft, Dir of Music at Clifton Coll., and Nina Cooke, Beckley Grove, Oxfordshire; *m* 1926, Marjorie Evelyn Taylor (*d* 1978); one *d. Educ:* Clifton Coll.; Balliol Coll., Oxford. Scholarship, Balliol. Joined BBC 1924; subsequently in Messrs. Unilevers Advertising Service; rejoined BBC 1941. *Publications: fiction:* A Young Man in a Hurry, 1934; You Must Break Out Sometimes, 1936; The Man Who Started Clean, 1937; The Parents Left Alone, 1940; Collected Stories, 1946; Asking for Trouble, 1948; Malice Bites Back, 1948; A Thorn in The Heart, 1952; Goodbye Aunt Hesther, 1955; *non-fiction:* (with Lowes Luard) Just Cats, 1936; Calling All Nations, 1942; British Broadcasting, 1946 (booklets about BBC); The English Short Story, 1964; The Modest Art, 1968; (with W. Emms) Five Hide Village: a history of Datchworth, 1984; contributor of short stories and literary criticism to numerous publications throughout world, and to BBC. Gen. Editor British Council series Writers and their Work, 1949–54. *Recreations:* the arts in general; formerly track and cross-country running (represented Oxford against Cambridge at mile and half-mile). *Club:* United Oxford & Cambridge University.
*Died 11 Dec. 1988.*

**BEADLE, Prof. George Wells**; President Emeritus and Professor of Biology Emeritus, University of Chicago; *b* Wahoo, Nebraska, 22 Oct. 1903; *s* of Chauncey E. Beadle and Hattie Albro; *m* 1st, 1928, Marion Cecile Hill (marr. diss., 1953); one *s*; 2nd, 1953, Muriel McClure Barnett; one step *s. Educ:* Univ. of Nebraska; Cornell Univ. BS 1926, MS 1927, Nebraska; MA Oxford, 1958; PhD Cornell, 1931. Teaching Asst, Cornell, 1926–27; Experimentalist, 1927–31; National Research Fellow, Calif. Institute of Technology, 1931–33; Research Fellow and Instructor, Calif. Institute of Technology, 1933–35; Guest Investigator, Institut de Biologie Physico-Chimique, Paris, 1935; Asst Prof. of Genetics, Harvard Univ., 1936–37; Prof. of Biology, Stanford Univ., 1937–46; Prof. of Biology and Chm. of the Division of Biology, California Institute of Technology, 1946–60, Acting Dean of Faculty, 1960–61; Univ. of Chicago: Pres., 1961–68, Emeritus, 1969. Trustee and Prof. of Biology, 1961–68; William E. Wrather Distinguished Service Prof., 1969–75. Research interests: genetics, cytology and origin of Indian corn (*Zea*); genetics and development of the fruit fly Drosophila; biochemical genetics of the bread mould Neurospora. Hon. Trustee, Univ. of Chicago, 1971–. Hon. DSc: Yale, 1947; Nebraska, 1949; Northwestern, 1952; Rutgers, 1954; Kenyon Coll., 1955; Wesleyan Univ., 1956; Oxford Univ., 1959; Birmingham Univ., 1959; Pomona Coll., 1961; Lake Forest Coll., 1962; Univ. of Rochester, Univ. of Illinois, 1963; Brown Univ., Kansas State Univ., Univ. of Pennsylvania, 1964; Wabash Coll., 1966; Syracuse, 1967; Loyola, 1970; Eureka Coll., 1972; Butler Univ., 1973; Hon. PhD: Gustavus Adolphus Coll.; Indiana State Univ., 1976; Hon. LLD: UCLA, 1962; Univ. of Miami, Brandeis Univ., 1963; Johns Hopkins Univ., Beloit Coll., 1966; Michigan, 1969; Hon. DHL: Jewish Theological Seminary of America, 1966; DePaul Univ., 1969; Univ. of Chicago, 1969; Canisius Coll., 1969; Knox Coll., 1969; Roosevelt Univ., 1971; Carroll Coll., 1971; DPubSer, Ohio Northern Univ., 1970. Pres., Chicago Horticultural Soc., 1968–71; Trustee: Museum of Sci. and Industry, Chicago, 1967–68; Nutrition Foundn, 1969–73. Member: Twelfth Internat. Congress of Genetics (Hon. Pres.), 1968; National Academy of Sciences (Mem. Council, 1969–72); American Philosophical Soc.; Amer. Assoc. of Adv. Sci. (Pres., 1946); Amer. Acad. of Arts and Sciences; Genetics Soc. of America (Pres., 1955); President's Sci. Adv. Cttee, 1960; Genetics Soc. (Gt Britain); Indian Soc. of Genetics and Plant Breeding; Inst. Lombardo di Scienze E Lettre; Sigma Xi. Hon. Member: Japan Acad.; Phi Beta Kappa. Royal Danish Academy of Sciences; Foreign Member: Royal Society 1960; Indian Nat. Science Acad. Lasker Award, American Public Health Association, 1950; Emil Christian Hansen Prize (Denmark), 1953; Albert Einstein Commemorative Award in Science, 1958; Nobel Prize for Medicine (jointly), 1958; National Award, American Cancer Soc., 1959; Kimber Genetics Award, National Academy of Sciences, 1959; Priestley Memorial Award, 1967; Donald Forsha Jones Award, 1972; (with Muriel B. Beadle) Edison Award for Best science book for youth, 1967. George Eastman Visiting Professor, University of Oxford, 1958–59. Trustee Pomona Coll., 1958–61. *Publications:* An Introduction to Genetics (with A. H. Sturtevant), 1939; Genetics and Modern Biology, 1963; The Language of Life (with Muriel Beadle), 1966. Technical articles in Cytology and Genetics. *Address:* 900 East Harrison Avenue, Apt D33, Pomona, Calif 91767, USA.
*Died 9 June 1989.*

**BEALE, Evelyn Martin Lansdowne**, FRS 1979; Scientific Adviser, Scicon Ltd, since 1982; Visiting Professor, Mathematics Department, Imperial College of Science and Technology, since 1967; Director, Beale International Technology Ltd, since 1983; *b* 8 Sept. 1928; *s* of late Evelyn Stewart Lansdowne Beale and of Muriel Rebecca Beale, OBE; *m* 1953, Violette Elizabeth Anne (*née* Lewis); two *s* one *d. Educ:* Winchester Coll.; Trinity Coll., Cambridge (BA, DipMathStat). Member, Mathematics Gp, Admiralty Research

Laboratory, 1950–61; Research Associate, Princeton Univ., 1958; posts in Scicon (originally known as CEIR), 1961–. Hon. Sec., Royal Statistical Soc., 1970–76; Chm., Mathematical Programming Soc., 1974–76. Silver Medal, ORS, 1980. *Publications:* Mathematical Programming in Practice, 1968, repr. 1976; papers in Jl of Royal Stat. Soc., Mathematical Programming, etc. *Address:* Scicon Ltd, Wavendon Tower, Wavendon, Milton Keynes, Bucks MK17 8LX. *T:* Milton Keynes 585858. *Died 23 Dec.* 1985.

**BEALE, Hon. Sir (Oliver) Howard,** KBE 1961; QC; Australian Ambassador to United States, 1957–64; formerly Barrister-at-Law, Member of Commonwealth Parliament and Cabinet Minister; *b* 10 Dec. 1898; *s* of late Rev. Joseph Beale; *m* 1927, Margery Ellen Wood; one *s. Educ:* Sydney High Sch.; University of Sydney. BA 1921; LLB 1925. Called to NSW Bar and High Court of Australia, 1925; served War of 1939–45, RANVR, 1942–45. Elected MHR (L) Parramatta, 1946, re-elected, 1949, 1951, 1954, 1955; Mem. Commonwealth Parly. Public Works Cttee, 1947–49; Austr. Deleg., Internat. Bar Congress at The Hague, 1948; apptd KC 1950. Minister for Information and Minister for Transport (Menzies Govt), 1949–50; Chm., Austr. Transp. Adv. Council, 1949–50; Minister for Supply, 1950–58, including control of guided missiles research and Woomera Rocket Range, and atomic weapons research and Maralinga atomic testing ground; Minister i/c Austr. Aluminium Prod. Commn, 1950–58; Minister i/c Austr. Atomic Energy Commn and Rum Jungle uranium project, 1950–56; Minister for Defence Prod., 1956–58, responsible for govt ordnance ammunition, explosives, chemicals, aircraft and engine factories; Actg Minister: for Immigration, 1951–52, 1953 and 1954; for Nat. Development, 1952–53; for Air, 1952; for Defence, 1957; Mem. Austr. Defence Council, 1950–58; Mem. Cabinet Defence Preparations Cttee and Cabinet Cttee on Uranium and Atomic Energy, 1950–58. Austr. rep., Anzus Council, Washington, 1958, 1959, Canberra, 1962; Leader, Austr. Delegn, Colombo Plan Conf., Seattle, 1958; Dep. Leader, Austr. Delegn to UN, New York, 1959; Dep. Leader, later Leader Austr. Delegn to Antarctic Conf., Washington, 1959; Austr. Deleg. SEATO Conf., Washington, 1959, 1960; Alt. Gov., Internat. Monetary Fund, 1960, 1962, 1963; Leader, Austr. Delegn, World Food Congress, Washington, 1963; State Visitor to Mexico and Chile, 1963; Woodward Lectr, Yale Univ., 1960; Dean of British Commonwealth Diplomatic Corps, Washington, 1961–64; Pres., Arts Council of Australia, 1964–68. Dir of various corporations. Regents' Visiting Prof., Univ. of Calif., 1966; Marquette Univ., Wisconsin, 1967, 1969. Holds Hon. degrees. *Publication:* This Inch of Time: memoirs of politics and diplomacy, 1977. *Address:* 4 Marathon Road, Darling Point, Sydney, NSW 2027, Australia. *Clubs:* Union, Australasian Pioneers' (Sydney). *Died 17 Oct.* 1983.

**BEALE, Percival Spencer;** *b* 14 Sept. 1906; *m* 1938, Rachel M. H. (*née* Wilson); two *s. Educ:* St Paul's Sch. Entered Bank of England Oct. 1924; Chief Cashier, Bank of England, 1949–Jan. 1955; General Manager, Industrial Credit and Investment Corporation of India, 1955–58. Director: Samuel Montagu & Co. Ltd, 1960–65; The British Oxygen Co. Ltd, 1958–69; Carpet Manufacturing Co. Ltd, 1958–69. An Underwriting Mem. of Lloyd's, 1971–75. *Address:* Villa Aurore, Route de Genève, 1299 Commugny, Vaud, Switzerland. *Died 4 Feb.* 1981.

**BEALES, Hugh Lancelot;** Reader in Economic History in University of London, 1931–56; *b* 18 Feb. 1889; 3rd *s* of Rev. W. Beales; *m;* two *s* one *d. Educ:* Kingswood Sch., Bath; University of Manchester. Lecturer in Economic History, University of Sheffield, 1919–26; Lecturer in Economic History, University of London (London Sch. of Economics), 1926–31. Visiting Prof., Columbia Univ., 1954–55, Harvard Univ., 1956, University of Washington, 1959, USA. Editorial Adviser, Penguin and Pelican Books, to 1945; Ed. of Agenda, a journal of reconstruction issued by London Sch. of Economics to 1945; mem. of Editorial Bd of Political Quarterly; Editor, Kingswood Books on Social History. Mem. of CS Arbitration Tribunal, 1955–65. Hon. Fellow, LSE, 1971. Hon. DLitt: Exeter, 1969; Sheffield, 1971; Hon. DrRCA, 1974. *Publications:* Industrial Revolution, 1929; Early English Socialists, 1932; Making of Social Policy (Hobhouse Lecture), 1945, etc. Contributor to Economic History Review and various periodicals. *Address:* 16 Denman Drive, NW11. *T:* 01–455 4091. *Died 19 April* 1988.

**BEAN, Ven. Arthur Selwyn,** MBE 1939; Chaplain to the Queen, 1952–69, Extra Chaplain, since 1969; *b* 23 April 1886; *s* of Charles and Ellen Annie Bean; *m* 1912, Nellie Lingard Hackwood (*d* 1979); two *d* (one *s* decd). *Educ:* Christ's Coll., Christchurch, NZ; Keble Coll., Oxford (MA); University of Manchester (BD). Curate of Rugby, 1910–17; Vicar of Ribby with Wrea, 1917–22; Vicar of Weaste, 1922–27; Vicar of Astley, 1927–34; Archdeacon of Manchester and Canon Residentiary of Manchester Cathedral, 1934–66. Church Comr, 1948–68. Dir, Ecclesiastical Insurance Office Ltd, 1949–66; Chm., CofE Pensions Board, 1959–65. Prolocutor, Lower House, York Convocation, 1955–66. Archdeacon

Emeritus, 1966. *Address:* 2 The Brae, Longdown Road, Lower Bourne, Farnham, Surrey. *T:* Farnham 715348.
*Died 4 July* 1981.

**BEAN, Robert Ernest;** *b* 5 Sept. 1935; *m* 1970, Hilary Wynne-Burch; one *s* one *d. Educ:* Rochester Mathematical Sch.; Medway Coll. of Technol. MIOB; AMBIM. Polytechnic Lectr. Joined Labour Party, 1950. Mem., Chatham Borough Council, 1958–74; formerly Member: Fabian Soc.; Co-operative party. MP (Lab) Rochester and Chatham, Oct. 1974–1979. Contested (Lab): Gillingham, 1970; Thanet East, Feb. 1974; Rochester and Chatham, 1979; Medway, 1983. Mem., Medway Borough Council, 1974–76. *Address:* 22 Horsted Way, Rochester, Kent ME1 2XY. *T:* Medway 42689.
*Died 7 Dec.* 1987.

**BEAN, Thomas Ernest,** CBE 1957; *b* 11 Feb. 1900; *s* of Arthur Charles Bean; *m* 1929, Eleanor Child; one *d.* Asst Circulation Manager, Manchester Guardian, 1928–44; General Manager: Hallé Concerts Soc., Manchester, 1944–51; Royal Festival Hall, London, 1951–65; Sec., London Orchestral Concert Bd, 1965–71. Austrian Order of Merit (Officer's Class), 1959. *Recreation:* gradening. *Address:* 5 Pixholme Court, Dorking, Surrey. *T:* Dorking 2900.
*Died 11 Feb.* 1983.

**BEANEY, Alan;** *b* 3 March 1905; *s* of John Beaney, New Silksworth, Co. Durham; *m* 1926, Mary Elizabeth, *d* of William Wass, New Silksworth, Co. Durham; one *s* two *d. Educ:* Elementary Sch.; NCLC. Mem. Dearne Urban District Council, 1938; County Councillor, WR Yorks, 1949; MP (Lab) Hemsworth Div. WR Yorks, 1959–Feb. 1974. Formerly Mem., Yorks Executive Cttee, National Union of Mineworkers. *Recreations:* hiking, fishing, reading. *Address:* 190 Houghton Road, Thurnscoe, Rotherham, W Yorks. *T:* Rotherham 893304. *Club:* Royal Automobile.
*Died 3 March* 1985.

**BEARD, Paul,** OBE 1952; FRAM; FGSM; Professor of Violin, Guildhall School of Music, retired 1968; *b* 4 Aug. 1901; *m* 1925, Joyce Cass-Smith; one *s* one *d. Educ:* Birmingham Oratory and St Philip's. Began violin playing at 4, being taught by father; first public appearance at 6; studied as Scholarship holder at RAM; appointed ARAM, 1921, and FRAM 1939; Principal 1st Violin of following Orchestras: City of Birmingham and Spa, Scarborough, 1920–32; National of Wales, 1929; London Philharmonic, 1932–36; BBC Symphony Orchestra, 1936–62. *Recreations:* golf, gardening. *Address:* 84 Downs Wood, Epsom Downs, Surrey. *T:* Burgh Heath 50759. *Died 22 April* 1989.

**BEARD, Paul Michael;** a Recorder of Crown Courts since 1972; Chairman, Medical Appeal Tribunal, Nottingham, since 1984; Barrister-at-Law; *b* 21 May 1930; *s* of late Harold Beard, Sheffield; *m* 1959, Rhoda Margaret, *er d* of late James Henry Asquith, Morley, Yorks; one *s* one *d. Educ:* The City Grammar Sch., Sheffield; King's Coll., London. LLB (Hons). Commissioned RASC, 1949; served BAOR (Berlin), 1949–50. Called to Bar, Gray's Inn, 1955; North-Eastern Circuit. Contested (C): Huddersfield East, 1959; Oldham East, 1966; Wigan, Feb. and Oct. 1974; Doncaster, 1979; Chm., Brightside Conservative Assoc., 1961–68. *Recreations:* reading, walking. *Address:* Flowerdale, Church Street, East Markham, near Newark, Notts NG22 0SA. *T:* Tuxford 870074; 42 Bank Street, Sheffield S1 1EE. *T:* Sheffield 751223. *Clubs:* Naval; Sheffield (Sheffield). *Died 26 March* 1989.

**BEARN, Col Frederic Arnot,** CBE 1945; DSO 1917; MC; MB, ChB Manchester; MD Manchester 1920; Dauntesey, Turner, and Bradley Scholar, Platt Scholar, University of Manchester; Hon. Consultant Physician, District Hospital, Buxton, and Devonshire Royal Hospital, Buxton; retired; *b* 1890; *m* Alice (*d* 1968), *d* of James Bell, JP, Colinton, Edinburgh. Late House Physician and Senior House Surg., Manchester Royal Infirmary; served European War, 1914–19 (despatches, DSO, MC); also in Mesopotamia, 1918; and in India, 1919; war of 1939–45, Col AMS (four Bars to DSO, CBE, King Haakon VII Liberty Cross; gazetted Hon. Col, 1945). County Commissioner, SJAB, Derbys; KStJ. *Recreation:* shooting. *Address:* c/o Bank of Scotland, 16 Piccadilly, W1. *Club:* Caledonian.
*Died 22 Sept.* 1981.

**BEARSTED, 3rd Viscount,** *cr* 1925, of Maidstone; **Marcus Richard Samuel,** TD 1945; DL; Baron, *cr* 1921; Bt *cr* 1903; Chairman: 1928 Investment Trust Ltd, 1948–82; Samuel Properties Ltd and subsidiary companies, 1961–82; Hill Samuel & Co. (Jersey) Ltd, 1962–80; Negit SA, Luxembourg, 1966–82; Director: Hill Samuel Group Ltd, 1933–79 (formerly Chairman); Sun Alliance & London Insurance Group, 1949–80; Lloyds Bank Ltd and subsidiary companies, 1963–80; *b* 1 June 1909; *e s* of 2nd Viscount and Dorothea (*d* 1949), *e d* of late E. Montefiore Micholls; *S* father, 1948; *m* 1st, 1947, Elizabeth Heather (marr. diss. 1966), *er d* of G. Firmston-Williams; one *d* (and one *d* decd); 2nd, 1968, Mrs Jean Agnew Somerville (*d* 1978), *d* of R. A. Wallace. *Educ:* Eton; New Coll., Oxford. Served War of 1939–45, Warwicks Yeomanry (Major), Middle East, Italy (wounded). Chm., Warwicks Hunt, 1960–69.

Trustee and Chm. of Whitechapel Art Gallery, 1949–73. Chm., Bearsted Meml Hosp., 1948–; President: Jewish Home and Hosp. at Tottenham, 1948–; St Mary's Hosp. Med. Sch., 1964–80; Dep. Chm., St Mary's Hosp., Paddington, 1958–74; Vice-Chm., Tottenham Gp HMC, 1949–74; Board Member: Eastman Dental Hosp., 1970–75; Kensington, Chelsea and Westminster AHA, 1973–77; St John's Hosp. for Diseases of the Skin, 1975–78. Pres., Nat. Soc. for Epileptics, Chalfont Colony, 1960–; Jt Pres., Barkingside Jewish Youth Centre, 1969–. DL Warwicks, 1950. *Recreation:* tapestry. *Heir: b* Hon. Peter Montefiore Samuel. *Address:* 3 Netherton Grove, SW10 9TQ. *T:* 01–730 2026; Upton House, Banbury, Oxon OX15 6HT. *T:* Edgehill 242. *Club:* White's.
*Died 15 Oct. 1986.*

**BEATON, Arthur Charles,** CMG 1954; Assistant Area General Manager, North Staffs Area, West Midlands Division, National Coal Board, 1955–61; National Coal Board Civil Defence Organiser, 1961, retired 1967; *b* 22 Aug. 1904; *s* of Samuel and Alice Ellen Beaton; *m* 1935, Jessie, *d* of Albert and Sarah Burrow; one *s* one *d*. *Educ:* Leeds Grammar Sch.; Keble Coll., Oxford. BA Litt. Hum. (Oxon), 1927; MA (Oxon), 1935. Sudan Political Service, 1927; District Comr, 1937; Dep. Gov., Equatoria, 1947; Dir, Local Govt Branch, 1950; Dep. Civil Sec., 1952; Actg Civil Sec., 1953; Permanent Under Sec. Ministry of the Interior, Sudan Government, 1954. 4th Class, Order of the Nile, 1941. *Publications:* Handbook, Equatoria Province, 1952. Articles in Sudan Notes and Records on anthropological subjects. *Recreations:* gardening, reading. *Address:* Barr Cottage, Clubhouse Lane, Waltham Chase, Southampton, Hampshire SO3 2NN. *T:* Bishop's Waltham (0489) 894680.
*Died 29 Nov. 1990.*

**BEATON, Surg. Rear-Adm. Douglas Murdo,** CB 1960; OBE 1940; retired as Medical Officer in Charge, RN Hospital, Plymouth, and Command Medical Officer, Plymouth Command (1957–60); *b* 27 May 1901; *s* of late Murdo Duncan Beaton, Kishorn, Ross-shire; *m* 1929, Violet (*d* 1988), 2nd *d* of late David R. Oswald, MD, Kinross, Scotland; one *s* one *d*. *Educ:* Bristol Grammar Sch.; Edinburgh, Royal Colleges LDS 1923; LRCPE, LRCSE, LRFPS (Glas), 1924; Surg. Lieut Royal Navy, 1924; Surg. Comdr, 1936; Surg. Capt., 1948; Surg. Rear-Adm., 1957. Asst to Medical Dir-Gen., 1944–46; Medical Officer in Charge, HMHS Maine, 1947–48; MO i/c RN Sick Quarters, Shotley, 1949–51; Senior Medical Officer, Medical Section, RN Hospital, Plymouth, 1951–54; Asst to Medical Dir-Gen., Admiralty, 1954–57. QHP 1956–60; KStJ 1979. *Recreations:* golf, gardening, sailing. *Address:* Ardarroch, Auchterarder, Perthshire. *T:* Auchterarder 2329. *Died 13 Feb. 1990.*

**BEATON, John Angus,** CB 1975; solicitor; Director, Scottish Courts Administration, 1974–75 (Deputy Director, 1972–74); *b* 24 July 1909; *s* of Murdoch Beaton, TD, ISO, Inverness, and Barbara Mackenzie Beaton (*née* Rose); *m* 1942, Margaret Florence McWilliam; two *s* one *d*. *Educ:* Inverness Royal Acad.; Edinburgh Univ. (BL). Scottish Office: Sen. Legal Asst, 1947; Asst Solicitor, 1960; Deputy Solicitor, 1966–72. Vice-Pres., 1960–63 and Hon. Mem., 1963–, Instn of Professional Civil Servants. *Publications:* Glossary of Scottish Legal Terms, 1980; Scots Law Terms and Expressions, 1982; articles in the Stair Memorial and Green's Encycls of Scots Law and in legal jls. *Recreations:* reading, golf, fishing. *Address:* 2 Dryden Place, Edinburgh EH9 1RP. *T:* 031–667 3198. *Clubs:* Edinburgh University Staff (Edinburgh); Gullane Golf (East Lothian); New Golf (St Andrews).
*Died 30 May 1987.*

**BEATTIE, Colin Panton,** MA, MB, ChB, DPH; FRCPath; Professor of Bacteriology, University of Sheffield, 1946–67; then Emeritus Professor; *b* 11 Sept. 1902; *s* of James Beattie, MA, and Eleanor Anne Beattie; *m* 1937, May Hamilton Christison, BA, PhD; no *c*. *Educ:* Fettes Coll., Edinburgh; University of Edinburgh. House appointments in Royal Infirmary, Edinburgh, and Royal Northern Infirmary, Inverness, 1928–30; Asst in Bacteriology Dept., University of Edinburgh, 1930–32; Rockefeller Travelling Fellow, 1932–33; Lecturer in Bacteriology Dept, University of Edinburgh, 1933–37; Prof. of Bacteriology in The Royal Faculty of Medicine of Iraq and Dir of Govt Bacteriology Laboratory, Baghdad, 1937–46. *Publications:* various papers on bacteriological and parasitological subjects. *Recreation:* gardening. *Address:* 391a Fulwood Road, Sheffield S10 3GE. *T:* Sheffield 302158. *Died 16 July 1987.*

**BEATTIE, Brigadier Joseph Hamilton,** CBE 1945; DSO 1944; *b* 29 Sept. 1903; *s* of late Malcolm Hamilton Beattie and Maria Isabel Beattie; *m* 1938, Margaret Antonia, *er d* of J. R. Makeig-Jones, CBE, Budleigh Salterton, Devon; three *s* (and one *s* decd), three *d*. *Educ:* Rugby; RMA Woolwich, 2nd Lieut RA, 1924; ADC to Viceroy of India, 1933–34; served Mohmand Campaign, NWF, India, 1935; served War of 1939–45; France, Belgium, Holland, Germany and Burma (despatches twice); Lieut-Col 1942, Brig. 1945; retd, 1956. *Recreations:* shooting, fishing. *Address:* San Anard, Zabbar, Malta. *Died 4 Feb. 1985.*

**BEATTIE, Prof. William,** CBE 1963; Librarian, National Library of Scotland, 1953–70; Director, Institute for Advanced Studies in the Humanities, Edinburgh University, 1972–80; *b* 27 Aug. 1903; *s* of William Beattie and Elizabeth Vallance; *m* 1932, Agnes Howie (*d* 1979), *d* of Henry Wood; two *d* (and one *d* decd). *Educ:* Jedburgh Grammar Sch.; George Watson's Coll.; University of Edinburgh. Asst Librarian, University of Edinburgh, 1926–30; Keeper of Printed Books, National Library of Scotland, 1931–53. Visiting Fellow, Folger Library, 1957. Lyell Reader in Bibliography, University of Oxford, 1964–65. David Murray Lectr, Glasgow Univ., 1976. Chm., Standing Conference of National and University Libraries, 1964–67. Vice-Pres., 1963–75, Pres., 1975–77, Bibliographical Soc.; Pres., Scottish Soc. for Northern Studies, 1976–79. Hon. LLD St Andrews, 1957; Hon. LittD, Trinity Coll., Dublin, 1967; Hon. Prof., Univ. of Edinburgh, 1967. St Olav's Medal (Norway), 1977. *Publications:* The Chepman and Myllar Prints, The Taill of Rauf Coilyear (facsimiles, with introductions), 1950, 1966; (with H. W. Meikle) selection of Robert Burns, 1946, rev. edn, 1972; selection of Border Ballads, 1952; articles in Edinburgh Bibliographical Soc. Transactions. *Address:* 7 South Gillsland Road, Edinburgh EH10 5DE.
*Died 28 March 1986.*

**BEATTY, (Alfred) Chester;** Chairman, 1950–78, then President, Selection Trust; *b* 17 Oct. 1907; *o s* of late Sir (Alfred) Chester Beatty and late Grace Madeline, *d* of Alfred Rickard, Denver, USA; *m* 1st, 1933, Pamela (marr. diss. 1936; she *d* 1957), *o d* of Captain George Belas; one *d*; 2nd, 1937, Enid (marr. diss. 1950), *d* of S. H. Groome, Golfe Juan, France; 3rd, 1953, Helen Gertrude, widow of Roger Casalis de Pury. *Educ:* Eton; Trinity Coll., Cambridge. Past-Pres., Overseas Mining Assoc.; Jt Master, Ashford Valley Foxhounds, 1927–31, Master, 1931–53. *Address:* Owley, Wittersham, Kent; 76 Park Street, W1. *Club:* Royal Yacht Squadron.
*Died 6 June 1983.*

**BEAUCHAMP, Sir Douglas Clifford, (Sir Peter Beauchamp),** 2nd Bt, *cr* 1918; *b* 11 March 1903; *s* of Sir Frank Beauchamp, 1st Bt, and Mabel Constance (*d* 1957), *e d* of James Norman Bannon, Kent; *S* father, 1950; *m* 1st, 1926, Nancy (who obtained a divorce, 1933), *o d* of Laurence E. Moss, Sydney, NSW; 2nd, 1933, Pamela Dorothy May Chandor (*d* 1971); 3rd, 1972, M. Elizabeth, widow of J. H. Tilbury. *Educ:* Eton. *Heir:* none. *Address:* The Pebbles, Budleigh Salterton, Devon. *T:* Budleigh Salterton 3197.
*Died 13 June 1983 (ext).*

**BEAUCHAMP, Dr Guy;** Manipulative Surgeon since 1935; Consultant: London Transport Friendly Society; Lloyd Memorial Society; Printers Medical Aid Fund; *b* 30 July 1902; *s* of Thomas and Elizabeth Beauchamp, Dudley, Worcs; *m* 1943, Hon. Susan Silence North, *yr d* of late Hon. Dudley North and *sister* of 13th Baron North; three *d*. *Educ:* Dudley Grammar Sch.; Birmingham Univ. MB, ChB, MRCS, LRCP, FICS, FRSocMed, Mem. Brit. Assoc. of Manip, Med. Hon. Manipulative Surgeon, Charterhouse Clinic, 1938–48; Hon. Physician: War Hosp., 1942–48; British Home and Hosp. for Incurables, 1942–70. Vis. Consultant to the State of Qatar, 1976–. Kt of Grace, SMO Malta, 1964; Gold Medal of Honour, Soc. d'Encouragement au Progrès, Paris, 1974. *Publications:* (jtly, play) Death on the Table, 1938; (jtly) Honourable Jeux des Gentilhommes, 1944; numerous contrib. med. jls and text books. *Recreations:* fishing, swimming, theatre. *Address:* 38 Harley House, Marylebone Road, NW1 5HF. *T:* 01-935 3088; (home) 19 Beaumont Street, W1 1FF. *T:* 01-935 5958. *Club:* Buck's.
*Died 10 Nov. 1981.*

**BEAUCHAMP, Sir Peter;** *see* Beauchamp, Sir D. C.

**BEAUFORT, 10th Duke of,** *cr* 1682; **Henry Hugh Arthur FitzRoy Somerset,** KG 1937; GCVO 1930; Royal Victoria Chain, 1953; PC 1936; JP; Baron Botetourt, 1305, confirmed, 1803; Baron Herbert of Raglan, Chepstow, and Gower, 1506; Earl of Worcester, 1514; Marquess of Worcester, 1642; late Royal Horse Guards; Hon. Colonel: Royal Gloucestershire Hussars, TA, 1925–69, T&AVR, 1969–71; A and C Squadrons, The Wessex Yeomanry, T&AVR, since 1972; *b* 4 April 1900; *o s* of 9th Duke and Louise Emily (*d* 1945), *d* of William H. Harford of Oldown, Almondsbury, Glos, and widow of Baron Carlo de Tuyll; *S* father, 1924; *m* 1923, Lady Mary Cambridge, *er d* of 1st Marquess of Cambridge. *Educ:* Eton; Sandhurst. Master of the Horse, 1936–78. Chancellor, Univ. of Bristol, 1966–70. High Steward: Bristol, 1925–; Gloucester, 1925–; Tewkesbury, 1948–. Lord Lieutenant of Co. of Gloucester and Bristol, 1931–74, Lord-Lieutenant of Gloucestershire, 1974–78. Received Freedom of City of Gloucester 1945. KStJ 1935. *Publications:* Fox Hunting, 1980; Memoirs, 1981. *Heir: cousin* David Robert Somerset. *Address:* Badminton, Glos GL9 1DB. *TA:* Badminton. *Club:* Turf. *Died 5 Feb. 1984.*

**BEAUMAN, Wing Commander Eric Bentley;** Librarian, Royal United Service Institution, 1952–57; *b* 7 Feb. 1891; *yr s* of late Bentley Martin Beauman; *m* 1940, Katharine Burgoyne, MA, *yr d* of late F. W. Jones; one *s*. *Educ:* Malvern Coll.; Geneva Univ.; Royal Aero

Flying Certificate, 1913; served European war, 1914–18: commnd RNAS Aug. 1914; Anti-Submarine patrols, Home and Aegean; Home Defence and flying instruction: comd seaplane stations at Dundee and Newhaven (despatches). Major, RAF 1918; psa 1922–23 (first course of RAF Staff College); psc 1929–30; instructor at RAF Staff Coll., 1932–33; retd, 1938; Air Ministry, 1938–51. War of 1939–45; RAF liaison officer with BBC. Expeditions: Mount Kamet, Himalaya, 1931; Coast Range of British Columbia, 1934 (paper to RGS on Coast Range Crossing); climbed the Matterhorn 5 times. Pres. Alpine Ski Club, 1933–35, Hon. Mem., 1978–; Hon. Librarian, Alpine Club, 1947–58. Vice-Pres. RAF Mountaineering Assoc. 1951–; Chm., Touring and Mountaineering Cttee of Ski Club of Gt Britain, 1952–54. Broadcasts on many occasions. *Publications:* compiled: Winged Words, 1941 (Book Soc. Choice); The Airmen Speak, 1941; (with Cecil Day Lewis) compiled: We Speak from the Air, 1942; Over to You, 1943; chapters in: Living Dangerously, 1936; Travellers' Tales, 1945; The Boys' Country Book, 1955; contributor to: The Second Cuckoo; The Way to Lords; The Times, Guardian, Sunday Times, The Field, The Listener, National Review, The Geographical Magazine, Alpine Jl, RUSI Jl, British Ski Year Book, Dictionary of National Biography, Encyclopædia Britannica. *Recreations:* writing, reading, gardening. *Address:* 59 Chester Row, SW1W 8JL. *T:* 01–730 9038. *Clubs:* Alpine (elected 1920), Royal Air Force. *Died 26 July 1989.*

**BEAUVOIR, Simone (Lucie Ernestine Marie Bertrand) de;** French author; *b* Paris, 9 Jan. 1908; *d* of Georges Bertrand de Beauvoir and Françoise (*née* Brasseur). *Educ:* Institut Catholique; Institut Sainte-Marie; Univ. of Paris. Taught, 1931–43. President, Ligue du Droit des Femmes, 1974–. *Publications:* L'Invitée, 1943 (trans. She Came to Stay, 1949); Le Sang des autres, 1944 (trans. The Blood of Others, 1948); Pyrrhus et Cinéas (essay), 1945; Les Bouches Inutiles (play), 1945; Tous les hommes sont mortels, 1947 (trans. All Men are Mortal, 1955); Pour une morale de l'ambiguïté (essay), 1947; L'Amérique au jour le jour, 1948 (trans. America Day by Day, 1952); L'existentialisme et la sagesse des nations (essay), 1948; Le Deuxième Sexe, 1949: vol. I, Les faits et les mythes; vol. II, L'expérience vécue; Faut-il brûler Sade?, 1951 (trans. Must We Burn Sade?, 1963); Les Mandarins, 1954 (Prix Goncourt, 1954; trans. The Mandarins, 1957); Privilèges (essay), 1955; La longue marche (essay on China), 1957 (trans. The Long March, 1958); Mémoires d'une jeune fille rangée, 1958 (trans. The Memoirs of a Dutiful Daughter, 1959); La force de l'âge, 1960 (trans. The Prime of Life, 1963); Brigitte Bardot, 1960; (with G. Halimi) Djamila Boupacha, 1962; La force des choses, 1963 (trans. Force of Circumstance, 1965); Une mort très douce, 1964 (trans. A Very Easy Death, 1966); Les belles images, 1966; La femme rompue, 1968 (trans. The Woman Destroyed, 1969); L'âge de discrétion, 1968; La vieillesse, 1969 (trans. Old Age, 1972); Tout compte fait, 1972 (trans. All Said and Done, 1974); Quand prime le spirituel, 1979 (When Things of the Spirit Come First, 1982); La Cérémonie des adieux, 1981 (trans. Adieux: a farewell to Sartre, 1984). *Address:* 11 bis rue Schoelcher, 75014 Paris, France.

*Died 14 April 1986.*

**BEAVIS, David,** CBE 1976; retired; Chairman, West Midlands Gas Region (formerly West Midlands Gas Board), 1968–77; Part-time Member, British Gas Corporation, 1973–77; *b* 12 Dec. 1913; *s* of David Beavis; *m* 1946, Vera, *d* of F. C. Todd; one *s* one *d*. *Educ:* Whitehill Secondary Sch.; Royal Technical Coll., Glasgow (now Strathclyde Univ.). Dep. Engineer and Manager, Helensburgh Town Council Gas Dept, 1935–41; Asst Engineer, Camb. Univ. and Town Gas Light Co., 1942–47; Dep. Engineer and Manager, Edin. Corp. Gas Dept, 1947–49; Divisional Gen. Man. Edin. and SE Div., and subseq. Area Manager, Scottish Gas Bd, 1949–64; Mem. Scottish Gas Bd, 1962–64; Dep. Chm., Eastern Gas Bd, 1964–68. President: Scottish Assoc. of Gas Managers, 1960–61; IGasE, 1967. *Publications:* technical papers presented to Engineering Instns. *Recreations:* technological education, golf, sailing. *Address:* 1 Sandal Rise, Solihull, West Midlands. *T:* 021–704 1819. *Died 10 Oct. 1987.*

**BECKETT, John Angus,** CB 1965; CMG 1956; MA; Davy Offshore Modules Ltd, since 1984; Director, Total Oil Marine Ltd, since 1979; *b* 6 July 1909; *s* of late John Beckett, BA; *m* 1935, Una Joan, *yr d* of late George Henry Wright; one *s* two *d*. *Educ:* privately; Sidney Sussex Coll., Cambridge. BA 2nd Cl. Hons (Geog. Tripos); Mem., Cambridge Iceland Expedition, 1932. Schoolmaster, 1933–40; entered Civil Service, 1940; Principal Private Sec. to Minister of Fuel and Power, 1946–47; Asst Sec., Min. of Fuel and Power, 1947–59; Under-Sec., 1959 (Gas Div., 1959–64, Petroleum Div., 1964–72) Min. of Power, Min. of Technology, DTI; retired 1972. Chm., Petroleum Cttee of OEEC, 1948–50, 1955–59, 1965–72; Petroleum Attaché, British Embassy, Washington, 1950–53. Chm., Press Offshore Gp (formerly William Press Production Systems), 1972–83. *Publication:* Iceland Adventure, 1934. *Recreations:* enjoying vintage wines and real ales, following rowing and Rugby football. *Address:* Tyle Cottage, Needlesbank, Godstone, Surrey

RH9 8LN. *T:* Godstone (0883) 842295. *Clubs:* St Stephen's Constitutional; Arctic (Cambridge). *Died 9 June 1990.*

**BECKETT, Noel George Stanley;** HM Diplomatic Service, retired; *b* 3 Dec. 1916; *s* of Captain J. R. Beckett, MC, and Ethel Barker; *m* 1948, Huguette Laure Charlotte Voos (*d* 1982); one *s* two *d*. *Educ:* Peterhouse, Cambridge. MA Hons Cantab 1938, BScEcon Hons London 1961. Mem., Inst. of Linguists. British Embassy, Paris, 1946; UK Commercial Rep., Frankfurt and Cologne, 1949; Lima, 1956; Bonn, 1959; British Embassy, Addis Ababa, 1963 and liaison officer with Econ. Commn for Africa; Sec., European Conf. on Satellite Communications, FO, 1965; British Embassy, Beirut, 1968; Consul-Gen., Casablanca, 1973–76. *Recreations:* painting, art studies, photography, reading, travel. *Address:* The Second House, South Drive, Dorking, Surrey. *T:* Dorking (0306) 882665. *Club:* Commonwealth Trust. *Died 3 Sept. 1990.*

**BECKETT, Richard Henry,** CSI 1934; CIE 1928; *b* 1882; *s* of Richard Beckett; *m* 1928, Doris May (*d* 1974), *d* of W. T. Sutcliffe and widow of Capt. Cedric F. Horsfall. *Educ:* Imperial Coll. of Science. Entered Indian Educational Service, 1906; Principal, Coll. of Science, Nagpur, 1908; Officiating Dir of Public Instruction and Sec. for Education to the Govt of the Central Provinces India, 1924; Dir of Public Instruction, Bombay Presidency, 1930–34. *Recreations:* tennis, golf. *Address:* Western House, Odiham, Hants. *Club:* East India, Devonshire, Sports and Public Schools.

*Died 15 June 1981.*

**BECKETT, Samuel Barclay,** CLit 1984; author and playwright; *b* Dublin, 13 May 1906; *m* 1961, Suzanne Deschevaux-Dumesnil (*d* 1989). *Educ:* Portora Royal School; Trinity Coll., Dublin (MA). Lectr in English, Ecole Normale Supérieure, Paris, 1928–30; Lectr in French, Trinity Coll., Dublin, 1930–32; from 1932 has lived mostly in France, in Paris since 1937. Nobel Prize for Literature, 1969. *Publications: verse:* Whoroscope, 1930; Echo's Bones, 1935; Collected Poems in English and French, 1977; Collected Poems 1930–1978, 1984; *prose:* Collected Shorter Prose 1945–1980, 1984; Stirrings Still, 1989; *novels:* Murphy, 1938; Watt, 1944; Molloy, 1951 (Eng. trans. 1956); Malone meurt, 1952 (Eng. trans. Malone Dies, 1956); L'Innommable, 1953 (Eng. trans. 1960); Comment c'est, 1961 (Eng. trans. 1964); Imagination Dead Imagine, 1966 (trans. from French by author); First Love, 1973; Mercier and Camier, 1974; Company, 1980; Ill Seen Ill Said, 1982; *short stories:* More Pricks than Kicks, 1934; Nouvelles et textes pour rien, 1955; Le Dépeupleur, 1971 (Eng. trans., The Lost Ones, 1972); Four Novellas, 1977; *plays:* En attendant Godot, 1952 (Eng. trans. Waiting for Godot, 1954); Fin de Partie, 1957 (Eng. trans. End Game); Krapp's Last Tape, 1959; La Dernière Bande, 1961; Happy Days, 1961; Play, 1963; Film, 1972; Breath and Other Short Plays, 1972; Not I, 1973; Collected Shorter Plays of Samuel Beckett, 1984; The Complete Dramatic Works, 1986; *radio plays:* All that Fall, 1957; Embers, 1959; Cascando, 1964; *TV plays:* Ghost Trio and . . . But the Clouds . . . , 1977. *Address:* c/o Faber & Faber Ltd, 3 Queen Square, WC1. *Died 22 Dec. 1989.*

**BEDDARD, Dr Frederick Denys,** CB 1974; Deputy Chief Medical Officer, Department of Health and Social Security, 1972–77, retired; *b* 28 Feb. 1917; *s* of late Rev. F. G. Beddard and late Mrs Emily Beddard; *m* 1942, Anne (*née* Porter); two *d*. *Educ:* Haileybury Coll.; St Mary's Hosp. Med. Sch., London Univ. MRCS, LRCP 1939; MB, BS 1940; FRCPE 1972; FFCM 1972. House Phys. and Surg., St Mary's, 1939–41; RAMC, 1941–45 (Lt-Col). St Mary's Hosp. and Brompton Hosp., 1946–49; SE Metrop. Reg. Hosp. Bd, 1950–55; SE Reg. Hosp. Bd (Scotland), 1955–57; NE Reg. Hosp. Bd (Scotland), 1957–68 (seconded to Dept of Health, New Zealand, 1967); Chief Medical Officer, Min. of Health and Social Services, NI, 1968–72. Short-term consultant, WHO, 1978–79 and 1983. Governor, Charlotte Mason Coll. of Educn, Ambleside, 1981–. Chm., Westmorland Geological Soc., 1983–. *Publications:* various contribs to Lancet, etc. *Recreations:* gardening, geology. *Address:* Birk Field, Staveley, Kendal, Cumbria LA8 9QU. *T:* Staveley 821454. *Died 29 Dec. 1985.*

**BEDDINGTON, Nadine Dagmar,** MBE 1982; architect in own practice, since 1967; *b* 27 Aug. 1915; *d* of Frank Maurice Beddington and Mathilde Beddington. *Educ:* New Hall; Regent Polytechnic Sch. of Architecture. FRIBA (ARIBA 1940); FCSD; FRSA. Asst in central and local govt, 1940–45; asst in private practice, 1945–55; Chief Architect to part of British Shoe Corporation, 1957–67; sole principal in private practice, 1968–. Vice-Chm., Architects in Industry Group, 1965–67; Mem., RIBA Council, 1969–72, 1975–79; Vice-Pres., RIBA, 1971–72; Mem., ARCUK, 1969–87; Chm., Camberwell Soc., 1970–77. Silver Jubilee Medal, 1977. *Publications:* Design for Shopping Centres, 1982, 2nd edn 1990; articles on shops, shopping centres, building maintenance, building legislation. *Recreations:* reading, riding, people, music, travel, dogs. *Address:* 17 Champion Grove, SE5 8BN. *Clubs:* Reform; Brixton and District Dog Training (Vice Chm.). *Died 15 April 1990.*

**BEDDOE, Jack Eglinton,** CB 1971; Chief Executive, Severn Trent Water Authority, 1974–77; *b* 6 June 1914; *s* of Percy Beddoe and Mabel Ellen Hook; *m* 1st, 1940, Audrey Alison Emelie (*d* 1954); two *s* one *d*; 2nd, 1957, Edith Rosina Gillanders. *Educ:* Hitchin Grammar Sch.; Magdalene Coll., Cambridge. Entered Ministry of Health, 1936; Principal Private Sec. to Minister of Health, 1948–51; to Minister of Housing and Local Government, 1951–53; Asst Sec., 1953; Under-Sec., Ministry of Housing and Local Government, 1961–65; Asst Under-Sec. of State, Dept of Economic Affairs, 1965–66; Chm., SE Planning Board, during 1966; Under-Sec., Min. of Housing and Local Govt, later DoE, 1966–74. *Address:* 32 Northfield End, Henley, Oxfordshire RG9 2JL.
*Died 15 Dec. 1990.*

**BEDFORD, Leslie Herbert,** CBE 1956 (OBE 1942); retired as Director of Engineering, Guided Weapons Division, British Aircraft Corporation Ltd, 1968; *b* 23 June 1900; *s* of Herbert Bedford; *m* 1928, Lesley Florence Keitley Duff (*d* 1987); three *s*. *Educ:* City and Guilds Engineering Coll., London (BSc); King's Coll., Cambridge (MA). Standard Telephones & Cables Ltd, 1924–31; Dir Research, A. C. Cossor Ltd, 1931–47; Chief TV Engr, Marconi's Wireless Telegraph Co. Ltd, 1947–48. Chief Engineer, GW Div., The English Electric Aviation Ltd, 1948–59; Dir, 1959–60. Mem., Council for Scientific and Industrial Research, 1961–. CEng, FCGI, FIERE, FIEE, FRAeS. Silver Medal (RAeS), 1963; Gold Medal, Société d'Encouragement pour la Recherche et l'Invention, 1967; Faraday Medal, 1968; Achievement Award, Scientific Instrument Makers' Co., 1980. *Publications:* Articles in: Proc. Phys. Soc., Jl BritIRE, Jl RSA, Jl RAeS, Jl IEE, Wireless Engineer, Electronic and Radio Engineer, Electronic Technology. *Recreations:* music, sailing. *Address:* 29 Holly Park, N3 3JB. *Died 21 Dec. 1989.*

**BEDNALL, Maj.-Gen. Sir (Cecil Norbury) Peter,** KBE 1953 (OBE 1941); CB 1949; MC 1917; director of companies; *b* 1895; *s* of late Peter Bednall, Endon, Staffs; *m* 1937, Eileen Margaret, *d* of late Col C. M. Lewin, Cowfold, Sussex; one *s* one *d*. *Educ:* Hanley; privately. Army Officer since 1915; Chartered Accountant since 1920. Commissioned 1915, RFA; served European War, 1916–19, France and Belgium. Palestine, 1936–37; War of 1939–45 in France, Abyssinia, and East Africa. Maj.-Gen., 1948. Paymaster-in-Chief, the War Office, 1948–55. Col Comdt RAPC, 1955–60. *Recreation:* golf. *Address:* Sandapple House, Ruwa, Salisbury, Zimbabwe. *Clubs:* Army and Navy; New, Ruwa Country (Salisbury, Zimbabwe). *Died 28 May 1982.*

**BEECHAM, Sir Adrian (Welles),** 3rd Bt *cr* 1914; *b* 4 Sept. 1904; *er s* of Sir Thomas Beecham, 2nd Bt, CH (Kt 1916) and Utica (*d* 1977), *d* of Dr Charles S. Welles, New York; *S* father, 1961; *m* 1939, Barbara Joyce Cairn; two *s* one *d*. *Educ:* privately. MusBac Durham, 1926. *Publications:* Four Songs, 1950; Little Ballet Suite, 1951; Traditional Irish Tunes, 1953; Three part-songs, 1955; Ruth (sacred cantata), 1957; Sonnet cxlvi (Shakespeare), 1962. *Recreation:* country life. *Heir: er s* John Stratford Roland Beecham, *b* 21 April 1940. *Address:* Compton Scorpion Manor, Shipston-on-Stour, Warwicks. *T:* Shipston 61482. *Club:* Savage. *Died 4 Sept. 1982.*

**BEECHER, Most Rev. Leonard James,** CMG 1961; ARCS, MA, DD; *b* 21 May 1906; *er s* of Robert Paul and Charlotte Beecher; *m* 1930, Gladys Sybil Bazett (*d* 1982), *yr d* of late Canon Harry and Mrs Mary Leakey; two *s* one *d*. *Educ:* St Olave's Grammar Sch., Southwark; Imperial Coll. and London Day Trg Coll., University of London. ARCS 1926; BSc 1927; MA (London) 1937. DD Lambeth, 1962. Asst Master, Alliance High Sch., Kikuyu, Kenya, 1927–30; Missionary, Church Missionary Soc., Diocese of Mombasa, 1930–57; Unofficial Mem. of Legislative Council, Colony of Kenya, representing African interests, 1943–47; MEC of the Colony of Kenya, 1947–52; Asst Bishop of Mombasa, Kenya Colony, 1950–53; Archdeacon and Canon of the Diocese, 1945–53; Bishop of Mombasa, 1953–64; Archbishop of East Africa, 1960–70; Bishop of Nairobi, 1964–70; Archbishop Emeritus, 1970. *Publications:* (with G. S. B. Beecher) A Kikuyu-English Dictionary, 1933; translator of parts of the Kikuyu Old Testament, 1939–49; Editor, Kenya Church Review, 1941–50. *Recreations:* recorded music, bird-watching, photography. *Address:* PO Box 21066, Nairobi, Kenya. *T:* Nairobi 567485. *Died 16 Dec. 1987.*

**BEECHING, Baron,** *cr* 1965 (Life Peer); **Richard Beeching,** PhD; Director, Lloyds Bank Ltd, since 1965; *b* 21 April 1913; *s* of Hubert J. Beeching; *m* 1938, Ella Margaret Tiley. *Educ:* Maidstone Grammar Sch.; Imperial Coll. of Science and Technology, London. ARCS, BSc, 1st Cl. Hons; DIC; PhD London. Fuel Research Station, 1936; Mond Nickel Co. Ltd 1937; Armaments Design Dept, Min. of Supply, 1943; Dep. Chief Engineer of Armaments Design, 1946. Joined Imperial Chemical Industries, 1948, Dir, 1957–61 and 1965, Dep. Chm. 1966–68. Vice-Pres. ICI of Canada Ltd, 1953; Chm., Metals Div., ICI, 1955. Furness Withy & Co. Ltd: Dir, 1972–75; Chm., 1973–75; Chm., Redland Ltd, 1970–77. Member: Special Adv. Gp on BTC, 1960; NEDC, 1962–64; Top Salaries Review Body, 1971–75; Chairman: British Railways Bd,

1963–65; BTC, 1961–63. Chm., Royal Commn on Assizes and QS, 1966. First Pres., Inst. of Work Study Practitioners, 1967–72; Pres., RoSPA, 1968–73. Fellow, Imperial Coll.; CIMechE, FInstP; Hon. LLD London; Hon. DSc NUI. *Publication:* Electron Diffraction, 1936. *Address:* Little Manor, East Grinstead, West Sussex.
*Died 23 March 1985.*

**BEECK, Sir Marcus (Truby),** Kt 1979; farmer and company director; *b* 28 Dec. 1923; 2nd *s* of Gustav Edwin Beeck and Martha Ellen (*née* Keast); *m* 1950, Léonie Pamela Dale Robertson, *y d* of Robert Robertson, retired grazier; one *s* two *d*. *Educ:* State Correspondence Sch., W Australia; Katanning State Sch., W Australia. Served War, RAAF, SW Pacific, 1942–45. Community service in many fields, 1946–, including: Leader, Australian Materials and Equipment Trade Mission to Indonesia, 1974; Chm., Grain Pool of Western Australia, 1975–76; Pres., Royal Agricultural Soc. of Western Australia, 1975–77; Member: Australian Trade Exhibition and Mission to Moscow, 1976; 3-Man Western Australian Agricl Mission to Japan, 1978. Chm., Westralian Farmers Co-operative Ltd, 1983–. Queen's Silver Jubilee Medal, 1977. *Recreations:* flying, rifle shooting, golf, tennis. *Address:* Coyrecup, PO Box 110, Katanning, WA 6317, Australia. *T:* Badgebup 221523 *Clubs:* Weld, West Australian (Perth); Katanning (Katanning).
*Died 3 May 1986.*

**BEER, Mrs Nellie,** OBE 1957; JP; DL; Member of Manchester City Council, 1937–72 (Alderman 1964–72; Lord Mayor of Manchester, 1966); *b* 22 April 1900; *d* of Robert Robinson and Nelly Laurie Robinson (*née* Hewitt); *m* 1927, Robert Beer (*d* 1977); one *d*. *Educ:* Ardwick Higher Grade Sch. Hon. MA Univ. of Manchester, 1978. JP Manchester, 1942; DL Lancs, 1970. *Address:* c/o 7 Norfolk Road, Lytham St Annes, Lancs. *T:* Lytham 733016.
*Died 17 Sept. 1988.*

**BEESLEY, Mrs Alec M.;** *see* Smith, Dodie.

**BEEVOR, John Grosvenor,** OBE 1945; *b* 1 March 1905; *s* of Henry Beevor, Newark-on-Trent, Notts; *m* 1st, 1933, Carinthia Jane (marr. diss., 1956), *d* of Aubrey and Caroline Waterfield, Aulla, Italy; three *s*; 2nd, 1957, Mary Christine Grepe. *Educ:* Winchester; New Coll., Oxford. Solicitor, 1931–33, Slaughter and May, London, EC2. Served HM Army, 1939–45, RA and SOE. Adviser to British Delegation to Marshall Plan Conf., Paris, 1947; Mem. Lord Chancellor's Cttee on Private Internat. Law, 1952–53; Man. Dir, Commonwealth Development Finance Co. Ltd, 1954–56; Vice-Pres., Internat. Finance Corp., Washington, DC, 1956–64. Chairman: Doulton & Co., 1966–75; Tilbury Contracting Group, 1966–76; Lafarge Organisation Ltd, 1966–76; Director: Lafarge SA, 1969–80; Williams & Glyn's Bank Ltd, 1970–75; Glaxo Holdings Ltd, 1965–75. Member Councils: The Officers' Assoc.; Overseas Develt Inst. *Publications:* The Effective Board, a Chairman's View, 1975; SOE, Recollections and Reflections, 1981. *Address:* 161 Fulham Road, Chelsea, SW3 6SN. *T:* 01–581 8386.
*Died 26 Feb. 1987.*

**BEGG, Rt. Rev. Ian Forbes,** MA, DD; Priest-in-charge of St Machar, Bucksburn, Aberdeen, since 1978; *b* 12 Feb. 1910; *e s* of Rev. John Smith Begg and Elizabeth Macintyre; *m* 1949, Lillie Taylor Paterson. *Educ:* Aberdeen Grammar Sch.; Aberdeen Univ.; Westcott House, Cambridge. Deacon 1933; Priest 1934. Curate, St Paul's, Prince's Park, Liverpool, 1933–35; Priest-in-Charge of St Ninian's Episcopal Church, Seaton, Aberdeen, 1935–73; Dean, United Diocese of Aberdeen and Orkney, 1969–73; Bishop of Aberdeen and Orkney, 1973–77; permission to officiate in Diocese, 1978; Canon of St Andrew's Cathedral, Aberdeen, 1965. Chm., Church Guest Houses' Assoc., 1969–. Hon. DD Aberdeen, 1971. *Recreations:* fishing, gardening. *Address:* 430 King Street, Aberdeen. *T:* Aberdeen 632169. *Died 18 Nov. 1989.*

**BEHRMAN, Simon,** FRCP; Hon. Consultant Emeritus in Neurology, Guy's Health District; Consulting Physician, Moorfields, Eye Hospital; formerly Consulting Neurologist: Regional Neurosurgical Centre, Brook Hospital; Lewisham, Dulwich, St Giles', St Francis', St Leonard's, Bromley and Farnborough Hospitals; *b* 14 Dec. 1902; *s* of late Leopold Behrman; *m* 1940, Dorothy, *d* of late Charles Engelbert; two *s* two *d*. *Educ:* University Coll. and St Bartholomew's Hosp., London. BSc (Hons) London. 1925; MRCS Eng. 1928; MRCP London 1932. Member: Assoc. of British Neurologists; Ophthalmological Soc. of UK; Academic Bd of Inst of Ophthalmology, University of London; FRSocMed. House Physician and Registrar, Hosp. for Nervous Diseases, Maida Vale, 1930–33; Registrar: Nat. Hosp., Queen Square, 1934–38; Dept of Nervous Diseases, Guy's Hosp., 1935–45. *Publications:* articles on neurology and neuro-ophthalmology. *Address:* 33 Harley Street, W1. *T:* 01–580 3388; The Dower House, Oxney, St Margaret's-at-Cliffe, Kent. *T:* Dover 852161. *Died 9 Dec. 1988.*

**BELCHEM, Maj.-Gen. Ronald Frederick King, (David),** CB 1946; CBE 1944; DSO 1943; *b* 21 Jan. 1911; *s* of O. K. Belchem and Louise Morris; *m* 1947, Mrs Constance King, 2nd *d* of late John

Hutton (marr. diss. 1954); *m* 1958, Ellen, *d* of late William Cameron, Ross-shire. *Educ:* Guildford; Sandhurst. 2nd Lieut Royal Tank Regt, 1931, Interpreter, Russian, Italian and French. Served Egypt and Palestine, 1936–39 (despatches); War of 1939–45 (despatches seven times); Greece, 1941; Eighth Army, Western Desert (commanded 1st Royal Tank Regiment, 1943); Sicily and Italy, BGS (Ops); North-West Europe (BGS (Ops) 21 Army Group). IDC 1947; Comd 6 Highland Bde BAOR, 1948; Chief of Staff to Field Marshal Viscount Montgomery, 1948–50; retd 1953. Chairman's Staff, Tube Investments Ltd, 1954–59; Chairman's Staff, BSA Group, 1959–61; Managing Dir Metal Components Div. of the BSA Group 1961; Chm. and Man. Dir, GUS Export Corp. Ltd, 1964–70; Dir of Exports, GUS Industrial Div., 1970; Chm., BNEC Hotel and Public Buildings Equipment Group, 1968–69; Director: National Bank Ltd Brunei, 1971–73; Fitch Lovell Ltd, 1973–77; Le Vexin SA France, 1973–79; Consultant, Goodwood Hotels Corp., Singapore, 1973–79. Freeman, City of London, 1956. Mem., Worshipful Co. of Barbers, 1956. Legion of Merit (US), Order of White Lion and MC (Czech), 1946; Order of Orange-Nassau (Dutch), 1947. *Publications:* A Guide to Nuclear Energy, 1957; (as David Belchem): All in the Day's March (memoirs), 1978; Victory in Normandy, 1981. *Recreation:* language study. *Address:* c/o Williams & Glyn's Bank, Holt's Branch, Whitehall, SW1. *Club:* Army and Navy.                                  *Died* 19 *July* 1981.

**BELFRAGE, Leif Axel Lorentz,** GBE (Hon.), 1956; former Swedish Ambassador; *b* 1 Feb. 1910; *s* of J. K. E. Belfrage and G. U. E. Löfgren; *m* 1937, Greta Jering; one *s* three *d*. *Educ:* Stockholm University. Law degree, 1933. Practised law at Stockholm Magistrates Court; joined Min. of Commerce, 1937; Dir, Swedish Clearing Office, 1940; Dir, war-time Swedish Trade Commn, 1943–45; entered Swedish Diplomatic Service, as Head of Section in Commercial Dept, 1945; Commercial Counsellor, Swedish Embassy, Washington, 1946; Head of Commercial Dept, FO, Stockholm, 1949–53; Dep. Under-Sec. of State, FO, 1953; Perm. Under-Sec. of State, FO, 1956; Ambassador to Court of St James's, 1967–72; Ambassador and Head of Swedish Delegn to OECD and UNESCO, 1972–76. Internat. Advr, PKbanken, Stockholm, 1976–. Grand Cross, Order of North Star (Sweden). *Address:* Sturegatan 14, 11436 Stockholm, Sweden.               *Died* 30 *Aug*. 1990.

**BELL, Sir Charles (William),** Kt 1980; CBE 1968; Chairman of Coats Patons Ltd, 1967–75; *b* 4 June 1907; *s* of Herbert James Bell and Bertha Alice Bell (*née* Jones), Pen-y-Ffordd, Flintshire; *m* 1931, Eileen (*d* 1987), *d* of Edwin James Hannaford, Eastham, Cheshire; three *s*. *Educ:* Chester City Grammar Sch.; Selwyn Coll., Cambridge (Open Exhibr). Joined Coats Patons Ltd, 1930; Dir, Central Agency Ltd (subsid. co.), 1934; Dir, J. & P. Coats Ltd (Subsid. Co.), 1947; Man. Dir, J. & P. Coats Ltd, 1961; Dir, Coats Patons Ltd, 1961. Dep. Chm., and Nat. Treasurer, Scottish Conservative and Unionist Party, 1971–81. *Recreations:* shooting, fishing, golf. *Address:* The White Cottage, 19 Lennox Drive East, Helensburgh, Dunbartonshire. *T:* Helensburgh 4973. *Clubs:* Royal and Ancient (St Andrews); Royal Northern Yacht; Helensburgh Golf.
                                                    *Died* 12 *March* 1988.

**BELL, (Edward) Percy,** OBE 1974; Member for Newham South, Greater London Council, 1973–81 (for Newham, 1964–73); *b* 3 April 1902; *m* 1932, Ethel Mary Bell (*d* 1974). *Educ:* Rutherford Coll., Newcastle upon Tyne; King's Coll., London. Teacher in the service of West Ham County Borough, 1922–64; Headmaster, Shipman County Secondary School, West Ham, 1951–64. Chairman: Planning Cttee of GLC, 1973–74; Town Development Cttee, 1974–75; Docklands Jt Cttee, 1974–77. *Recreations:* foreign travel; local and national social history. *Address:* 151c Ham Park Road, E7 9LE. *T:* (private) 081–472 8897.

                                                    *Died* 27 *Feb*. 1987.

**BELL, Geoffrey Foxall,** MC; MA; *b* 16 April 1896; *s* of late F. R. Bell, Burton-on-Trent; *m* 1926, Margaret, *d* of late R. Austin-Carewe, Montreal, Canada; three *s*. *Educ:* Repton; Balliol Coll., Oxford. Served in RFA, 1915–19 (despatches). Asst Master, Upper Canada Coll. and Christ's Hospital; Headmaster, Trent Coll., Derbs, 1927–36; Headmaster, Highgate Sch., 1936–54. Retired from fruit farming, 1972. Oxford Univ. Cricket XI, 1919. *Publications:* Establishing a Fruit Garden, 1963; Seven Old Testament Figures (Bishop of London's Lent Book), 1968. *Address:* Widford Flat, Haslemere, Surrey.                          *Died* 17 *Jan*. 1984.

**BELL, Prof. George Howard,** MD; FRCPGlas 1946; FRSE 1947; Symers Professor of Physiology in the University of Dundee (formerly Queen's College, Dundee), 1947–75, later Emeritus; Dean of The Faculty of Medicine, 1954–56 and 1963; *b* 24 Jan. 1905; *m* 1934, Isabella Margaret Thomson, MB, ChB; two *s*. *Educ:* Ayr Academy; Glasgow Univ. BSc 1929; MB (Hons) 1930; MD (Hons) 1943. House Physician, Royal Hosp. for Sick Children, 1930; Asst Lecturer in Physiology Dept, University of Glasgow, 1931–34; Lecturer in Physiology: Univ. of Bristol, 1934–35; Univ. of Glasgow, 1935–47. Mem. Physiological Soc., 1934–, and Sec., 1949–54; Mem.

Inter-University Council for Higher Education Overseas, 1957–75; Mem. Eastern Regional Hospital Board, 1957–67 (Vice-Chm., 1966–67); Gen. Dental Council Visitor, 1960–62; Comr, Royal University of Malta, 1962–70. Hon. Fellow, Accademia Anatomico-Chirurgica, Perugia, 1959. *Publications:* (with D. Emslie Smith and C. R. Paterson) Textbook of Physiology, 10th edn, 1980; papers in Journal of Physiology, Journal of Endocrinology, Lancet, etc. *Address:* Duntulm, 80 Grove Road, Broughty Ferry, Dundee DD5 1LB. *T:* Dundee 78724.                         *Died* 17 *April* 1986.

**BELL George Trafford,** CMG 1961; OBE 1952; retired; *b* 9 March 1913; 2nd *s* of late George H. Bell and of Veronica Jessie Bell, Alderley Edge, Ches.; *m* 1944, Eileen Patricia, *d* of late A. Geoffrey Southern, Wilmslow, Ches.; two *s* one *d*. *Educ:* Sedbergh; St John's Coll., Cambridge. Apptd Admin. Offr, Tanganyika, 1936; Sen. Admin. Offr, 1954; Provincial Comr, 1958–62. *Recreations:* golf, fishing. *Address:* Dukenfield Grange, Mobberley, Knutsford, Cheshire WA16 7PT.                            *Died* 5 *May* 1984.

**BELL, Harry,** OBE 1945; MA; MEd; Research Fellow, University of St Andrews, since 1972 (Research Scholar, 1967); *b* 11 April 1899; *s* of late John Nicol Bell, Aberdeen, and late Isabella Georgina Reith; *m* 1933, Sophia McDonald, *d* of late Alexander B. Fulton, Kilkerran, Newlands, Glasgow; two *s* one *d*. *Educ:* Robert Gordon's Coll.; Aberdeen Univ. (Kay Prize and Dey Scholarship); Clare Coll., Cambridge (Foundation Scholar); Glasgow Univ. (MEd). Served Army, 1917–19. Asst Master, Glasgow Academy, 1927–33; Rector of Elgin Academy, 1933–36; Rector of Dollar Academy, 1936–60. Scottish Educational Adviser Air Training Corps, 1941–45; Mem. of Scottish Youth Advisory Cttee, 1942–45; Pres. of Scottish Association of Headmasters, 1948. Adviser with UNESCO Delegation, Florence, 1950; Mem. of Advisory Council on Scottish Education, 1957–61. Fellow Internat. Inst. of Arts and Letters, 1960. *Publications:* English for Air Cadets; Stevenson's Travels and Essays; Thirteen Short Stories; Selected English Prose; Approach to English Literature; General Editor of Oxford Comprehension Course; articles on literary, historical and educational subjects. *Recreations:* reading, writing, walking. *Address:* Viewpark, 31 Lawhead Road East, St Andrews, Fife. *T:* St Andrews 72867. *Clubs:* Royal Over-Seas League; Scottish Mountaineering.
                                                    *Died* 5 *June* 1984.

**BELL, Very Rev. John,** MM 1917; Dean Emeritus of Perth, WA; Dean, 1953–59, retired; *b* 11 Nov. 1898; *s* of Thomas and Isabella McCracken Bell; unmarried. *Educ:* Gair Sch., Dumfriesshire; privately; St John's Coll., Perth, WA. Deacon, 1926, Priest, 1928; Curate of Christ Church, Claremont, 1926–29; Rector of S Perth, 1929–32; Priest-in-Charge of Claremont, 1933, Rector, 1933–43; Canon of St George's Cathedral, Perth, 1938–44; Org. Sec. (for NSW) Austr. Bd of Missions, 1943–46; Dean of Armidale, 1946–48; Exam. Chap. to Bp of Armidale, 1946–48; Rector of Oddington with Adlestrop, Dio. Gloucester, 1948–52. *Publications:* This Way Peace, 1939; Many Coloured Glass, 1943; Facing the Week, 1947; For Comfort and Courage, 1958. *Recreation:* travel. *Address:* 22/8 Darley Street, South Perth, Western Australia 6151. *T:* 367–4434. *Club:* Weld (Perth, WA).                       *Died* 31 *Aug*. 1983.

**BELL, John Elliot;** *b* 6 Nov. 1886; *e s* of late David Bell and Elizabeth Elliot; *m* 1924, Olga, *er d* of late Henry Banks and Elizabeth Ritchie, Edinburgh; one *s* one *d*. *Educ:* George Watson's Coll.; Edinburgh Univ. Vice-Consul at Paris, 1911; Boston, USA, 1912; Leopoldville, Belgian Congo, 1913–14; Magallanes, Chile, 1915–19; Santo Domingo, 1920; Consul at Galveston, USA, 1920–23; Portland, Ore., 1923–29; Bahia, Brazil, 1930–32; Basle, 1932–34; Consul Gen. at Cologne, 1934–39; at Zurich, 1939–42; at Strasbourg, 1945–46; retired, 1947. *Recreations:* golf, riding. *Address:* 3175 Point Grey Road, Vancouver 8, BC, Canada. *T:* 731–3490.
                                                    *Died* 7 *Jan*. 1985.

**BELL, Dr John Stewart,** FRS 1972; Physicist, CERN, Geneva, since 1960; *b* 28 July 1928; *s* of John Bell and Annie (*née* Brownlee); *m* 1954, Mary Ross. *Educ:* Ulsterville Public Elementary Sch., Belfast; Fane Street Public Elementary Sch., Belfast; Technical High Sch., Belfast; Queen's Univ., Belfast (BSc); Univ of Birmingham (PhD 1956). Lab. Asst, Physics Dept, QUB, 1944–45; AERE, Malvern and Harwell, 1949–53; Dept of Mathematical Physics, Birmingham Univ., on leave from AERE, 1953–54; AERE, Harwell, 1954–60; CERN, Geneva, 1960– (SLAC, 1963–64, on leave from CERN). Hon. Foreign Mem., Amer. Acad. of Arts and Scis, 1987. Hon.. DSc QUB, 1988; Hon. ScD Trinity Coll. Dublin, 1988. Dirac Medal, Inst. of Physics, 1988. *Publications:* various papers on electromagnetic, nuclear, elementary particle, and quantum theory. *Address:* CERN, 1211 Geneva 23, Switzerland.
                                                    *Died* 1 *Oct*. 1990.

**BELL, Joseph,** CBE 1953; Chief Constable, City of Manchester, 1943–58, retired; *b* 15 July 1899; *s* of late Joseph Bell; *m* 1926, Edith (*d* 1980), *d* of late Matthew Adamson; one *s* (one *d* decd). *Educ:* Alderman Wood Sch., Stanley, Co. Durham. Royal Naval Volunteer Reserve, 1917–19. Newcastle on Tyne City Police, 1919–33; Chief

Constable, Hastings, 1933–41; Asst Chief Constable, Manchester, 1941–43. *Address:* Norwood, 246 Windlehurst Road, Marple, Cheshire.                                      *Died* 10 *Jan.* 1989.

**BELL, Percy;** see Bell, E. P.

**BELL, His Honour P(hilip) Ingress,** TD 1950; QC 1952; a Circuit Judge (formerly Judge of County Courts), 1960–75; *b* 10 Jan. 1900; *s* of Geoffrey Vincent and Mary Ellen Bell; *m* 1933, Agnes Mary Eastwood (*d* 1983); two *s* one *d. Educ:* Stonyhurst, Blackburn; Royal Naval College, Keyham; Queen's Coll., Oxford (BA Jurisprudence, BCL). Called to the Bar, Inner Temple, 1925. Cadet RN, 1918; Midshipman RN, 1918–20. Lieut TA, 1939; JAG Dept, 1941, Temp. Major, 1944. MP (C) Bolton East, 1951–60. *Publication:* Idols and Idylls, 1918. *Recreations:* golf; Capt., Oxford University Boxing Club, 1923. *Address:* Windlesham Manor, Crowborough, Sussex. *Club:* Carlton.                          *Died* 12 *Sept.* 1986.

**BELL, Sir Ronald (McMillan),** Kt 1980; QC 1966; MP (C) Beaconsfield, since 1974 (South Buckinghamshire, 1950–74); *b* 14 April 1914; *yr s* of late John Bell, Cardiff; *m* 1954, Elizabeth Audrey, *e d* of late Kenneth Gossell, MC, Burwash, Sussex; two *s* two *d. Educ:* Cardiff High Sch.; Magdalen Coll., Oxford (Demy). BA 1936; MA 1941; Sec. and Treas., Oxford Union Soc., 1935; Pres., Oxford Univ. Conservative Assoc., 1935. MP (C) for Newport (Monmouth), May–July 1945. Contested Caerphilly Div. of Glamorgan at by-election 1939, Newport, Monmouth, July 1945. Served RNVR, 1939–46. Called to Bar, Gray's Inn, 1938; practises in London and on South-Eastern circuit. Mem. Paddington Borough Council, 1947–49. Mem., Select Cttee on European Legislation, 1974–. Mem. Court, Univ. of Reading, 1975–. *Publication:* Crown Proceedings, 1948. *Address:* 2 Mitre Court Buildings, Temple, EC4. *T:* 01-583 1355; First House, West Witheridge, Knotty Green, Beaconsfield, Bucks. *T:* Beaconsfield 4606.
                                                       *Died* 27 *Feb.* 1982.

**BELL, Rev. Vicars (Walker),** MBE 1964; author; Vicar of Clawton, and Rector of Tetcott with Luffincott, 1966–78; formerly Lecturer; *b* 24 Jan. 1904; *s* of W. A. Bell, Edinburgh; *m* 1926, Dorothy Carley. *Educ:* Radnor Sch., Redhill; Reigate Grammar Sch.; Goldsmiths' Coll., King's Coll., Univ. of London. Asst master at Horley Boys' Council Sch., 1925; Headmaster: Spaldwick Council Sch., 1926; Little Gaddesden C of E Sch., 1929–63. *Publications:* Little Gaddesden: the story of an English parish, 1949; Death Under the Stars, 1949; The Dodo, 1950; Two by Day and One by Night, 1950; Death has Two Doors, 1950; This Way Home, 1951; Death Darkens Council, 1952; On Learning the English Tongue, 1953; Death and the Night Watches, 1954; To Meet Mr Ellis, 1956; Death Walks by the River, 1959; That Night, a play for the Nativity, 1959; Orlando and Rosalind, three tales, 1960; Steep Ways and Narrow, 1963; The Flying Cat, 1964; (ed) Prayers for Every Day, 1965. *Address:* 20B Watts Road, Tavistock, Devon.                        *Died* 21 *April* 1988.

**BELLAIRS, Prof. Angus d'Albini;** Emeritus Professor of Vertebrate Morphology in the University of London, at St Mary's Hospital Medical School, 1982 (Professor, 1970); *b* 11 Jan. 1918; *s* of late Nigel Bellairs and Kathleen Bellairs (*née* Niblett); *m* 1949 (Madeline) Ruth (PhD, Professor of Embryology at UCL), *d* of Trevor Morgan; one *d. Educ:* Stowe Sch.; Queens' Coll., Cambridge (MA); University Coll. Hosp., London. DSc London, MRCS, LRCP. Served War, RAMC, 1942–46; Major, Operational Research, SE Asia, 1944–46. Lectr in Anat. and Dental Anat., London Hosp. Med. Coll., 1946–51; Lectr in Anat., Univ. of Cambridge, 1951–53; St Mary's Hosp. Med. Sch.: Reader in Anatomy, 1953–66, in Embryology, 1966–70. Vis. Prof. of Zoology, Kuwait Univ., 1970. Scientific Fellow and Hon. Cons. Herpetologist, Zoological Soc. of London; Trustee, Hunterian Collection, RCS, 1986–. FLS 1941; FIBiol 1974. *Publications:* Reptiles, 1957 (4th edition with J. Attride, 1975); The World of Reptiles (with Richard Carrington), 1966; The Life of Reptiles, 1969; The Isle of Sea Lizards (novel), 1989; contribs to zoological literature, mainly on reptiles. *Recreations:* natural history (especially reptiles and cats), modern fiction, military history. *Address:* 7 Champion Grove, SE5. *T:* 01-274 1834.                                       *Died* 26 *Sept.* 1990.

**BELLAMY, Albert Alexander, (Alec),** registered architect, 1938; Under-Secretary, Department of the Environment, Housing Directorate C, 1972–74 retired; *b* 19 April 1914; *m* 1941, Renée Florence Burge; three *d. Educ:* Clapham Xaverian Coll.; RIBA. Asst Architect in private practice in City of London 1932–39; LCC: Mem. Abercrombie/Forshaw Team on 'County of London Plan 1943' and until 1946. Architect specialising on housing with MoH and successors, 1946–74 (Dep. Chief Archictect, Min. of Housing and Local Govt, 1964–72). Awarded Commonwealth Fund Fellowship (now Harkness), 1956–57, studying design of housing in USA for 12 months. *Recreation:* watercolour painting. *Address:* 1 Buckingham Place, The Steyne, Bognor Regis PO21 1TU.
                                                       *Died* 17 *Nov.* 1981.

**BELLAMY, Basil Edmund,** CB 1971; Under-Secretary, Department of Trade and Industry (formerly Board of Trade), 1965–74; *b* 9 Feb. 1914; *s* of William Henry and Mary Bellamy; *m* 1943, Sheila Mary Dolan; one *d. Educ:* Whitgift Sch. Joined Board of Trade, 1932; Asst Dir, Min. of War Transport, 1943; Asst Sec., Min. of Transport, 1951; Under-Sec., 1963–65. Joint Services Staff Coll., 1950; Imperial Defence Coll., 1957. *Address:* 52 Denmark Road, Wimbledon, SW19 4PQ.                                         *Died* 17 *Aug.* 1989.

**BELLAMY, Dr Lionel John,** CBE 1970; Visiting Professor, University of East Anglia, since 1976; Director: Explosives Research and Development Establishment, Ministry of Defence, 1964–76; Rocket Propulsion Establishment, 1972–76; *b* 23 Sept. 1916; *m* Jill Stanley, BA; one *s* one *d* (and one *s* decd). *Educ:* Clapham Coll.; London Univ. BSc Lond 1st cl. 1937; PhD Lond 1939. Scientific Civil Service: Chemical Inspectorate, Min. of Supply, 1939–59; Explosives Research and Development Establishment, Min. of Aviation, later Min. of Technology, 1954–, Dir, 1964–. Adrian Visiting Fellow, Dept of Chemistry, Univ. of Leicester, 1967–76; Hon. Prof., Univ. of East Anglia, 1968–. *Publications:* The Infra-Red Spectra of Complex Molecules, 1954 (2nd edn 1958); Advances in IR Group Frequencies, 1968; contribs to Jl Chem. Soc., Spectrochimica Acta, Transactions Faraday Soc., etc. *Recreation:* spectroscopy. *Address:* The Lodge, Powdermill Lane, Waltham Abbey, Essex. *T:* Lea Valley 716597.                    *Died* 9 *May* 1982.

**BELLEW, 6th Baron** *cr* 1848; **Bryan Bertram Bellew,** MC 1916; Bt 1688; *b* 11 June 1890; 2nd *s* of Hon. Richard Eustace Bellew (*d* 1933) (4th *s* of 2nd Baron), and Ada Kate (*d* 1893), *d* of Henry Parry Gilbey; *S* brother, 1975; *m* 1918, Jeanie Ellen Agnes (*d* 1973), *d* of late James Ormsby Jameson; one *s. Educ:* Stubbington; Trinity Hall, Cambridge. Served European War, 1914–19 (MC); Lieut S Irish Horse. *Heir:* *s* Hon. James Bryan Bellew [*b* 5 Jan. 1920; *m* 1942, Mary Elizabeth (*d* 1978), *d* of Rev. Edward Eustace Hill; two *s* one *d*; *m* 1978, Gwendoline, formerly wife of Major P. Hall and *d* of late Charles Redmond Clayton-Daubeny]. *Address:* Barmeath Castle, Togher, Drogheda, Co. Louth, Eire.
                                                       *Died* 7 *Sept.* 1981.

**BELLEW, Sir Arthur (John) G.;** *see* Grattan-Bellew.

**BELOE, Robert,** CBE 1960; Liaison Officer between Anglican Communion and World Council of Churches, 1969–71; *b* 12 May 1905; *s* of late Rev. R. D. Beloe, Headmaster of Bradfield Coll., and of Clarissa, *d* of Rev. Prebendary J. T. Bramston, Winchester Coll.; *m* 1933, Amy, (JP), *d* of Capt. Sir Frank Rose, 2nd Bt (killed in action, 1914) and of late Daphne, Lady Rose; one *s* two *d. Educ:* Winchester; Hertford Coll., Oxford. Asst Master: Bradfield, 1927–28; Eton, 1928–30; Reading elementary sch., 1930–31. Kent Education Office, 1931–34; Asst Education Officer, Surrey, 1934–39; Dep. Education Officer, 1939–40; Chief Education Officer, 1940–59; Sec. to Archbishop of Canterbury, 1959–69. Mem. of various commissions and departmental cttees, including Royal Commission on Marriage and Divorce, 1951–55; Mauritius Electoral Boundary Commission, 1957; Higher Agricultural Education Cttee, 1944–46; Secondary Sch. Examinations Council, 1947–64 (Chm. Cttee on Exams other than GCE, 1958–60, leading to establishment of Cert. of Secondary Educn); Hon. Consultant, CSE Sub-Cttee of Schools Council, 1964–78; Mem., Home Office Central Training Council for Child Care, 1947–53. Hon. Sec. County Education Officers Soc., 1958–59; Governor of Commonwealth Inst., 1949–67. Trustee of Duke of Edinburgh's Award Scheme, 1960–66. Secretary: Monckton Cttee on Admin of Church Comrs, 1963; Archbishop's Advisers on Needs and Resources, 1963–69; General Synod C of E: Mem., 1970–75; Mem., Standing Cttee, 1971–75. Hon DCL Kent, 1979. *Recreations:* gardening, travel. *Address:* The Hill House, Queen's Road, Richmond, Surrey.                          *Died* 26 *April* 1984.

**BEMROSE, Sir Max, (John Maxwell),** Kt 1960; DL; Director, 1938–79, and Chairman, Bemrose Corporation Ltd, 1953–78; now retired; *b* 1 July 1904; *y s* of late Dr Henry Howe Bemrose and late Mrs Bemrose; *m* 1933, Margaret Le Mare; one adopted *s* and one adopted *d. Educ:* Derby Sch.; Brighton Coll.; Clare Coll., Cambridge. MA (Economics). Joined family firm, 1926. Prospective Conservative Candidate for Derby, 1938; fought Gen. Election, 1945; contested Watford Div., 1950; Chm. East Midlands Provincial Area, Conservative & Unionist Assoc., 1957–61; Mem. Exec. and Gen. Purposes Cttee of Conservative Assoc.; Chm. Nat. Union of Conservative & Unionist Associations, 1964–65; Chm., Printing and Publishing Industry Training Bd, 1972–77; Pres., British Fedn of Master Printers, 1967–68, 1971–72. DL Derbyshire, 1967, High Sheriff of Derbyshire, 1969–70. *Recreations:* music, gardening. *Address:* Old Barn House, Nether Lane, Hazelwood, Derbyshire. *T:* Cowers Lane 544. *Clubs:* Carlton, Lansdowne.
                                                       *Died* 13 *July* 1986.

**BENEY, Frederick William,** CBE 1962; QC 1943; *b* 9 March 1884; *s* of late William Augustus Beney, JP, Beckenham, Kent; *m* 1914, Irene Constance, *e d* of Henry Ward-Meyer, Weybridge; two *s. Educ:* Mill Hill Sch.; New Coll., Oxford (MA). Called to Bar, Inner

Temple, 1909, Bencher 1948. Legal Asst, War Office, 1914–20; Recorder of Norwich, 1944–59; Mem., Deptl Cttee on Alternative Remedies, 1944–46; Chm. Deptl Cttee on Nat. Insurance against Industrial Diseases, 1953–54; Commissioner, Central Criminal Court, 1959–64; Commissioner of Assize, SE Circuit, 1959; Western Circuit, 1961; retd from practice, 1961. BBC Broadcasting, 1961–66. Mem. Appeal Tribunal, Assoc. of British Travel Agents. *Publications:* contributions to legal journals. *Address:* Imberley, Coombe Hill Road, East Grinstead, West Sussex RH19 4LY. *T:* East Grinstead 23163. *Died 5 April 1986.*

**BENN, Sir John Andrews,** 3rd Bt *cr* 1914; formerly consultant, Benn Brothers plc and Ernest Benn Ltd; *b* 28 Jan. 1904; *e s* of Sir Ernest Benn, 2nd Bt, CBE and Gwendolen, *d* of F. M. Andrews, Edgbaston; *S* father, 1954; *m* 1929, Hon. Ursula Helen Alers Hankey, *o d* of 1st Baron Hankey, PC, GCB, GCMG, GCVO, FRS; two *s* three *d*. *Educ:* Harrow; Princeton Univ., USA (Class of 1926 Achievement Award 1970); Gonville and Caius Coll., Cambridge. Toured Latin America, founding Industria Britanica to promote British export trade, 1931. Helped to get new industries to Crook, South-West Durham, depressed area, 1936–38. Served War of 1939–45, KOYLI. Contested Bradford N (Nat. C), General Election, 1945. Chm. and Man. Dir, UK Provident Instn, 1949–68; Chairman: Crosby Trust Management Ltd, 1958–61; Cincinnati Milacron Ltd, 1969–76; Founder, 1962, and former Chm., Technical Development Capital Ltd. Chairman: English-Speaking Union of the Commonwealth, 1969–72; Benn Charitable Foundn, 1972–80; Vice-Pres., Book Trade Benevolent Soc., 1974. Associate, Princeton Univ. Press, 1965; Pres., Princeton Club of London, 1969–70. *Publications:* Columbus-Undergraduate, 1928; A Merchant Adventurer in South America, 1931; Tradesman's Entrance, 1935; I Say Rejoice, 1942; Something in the City, 1959. *Recreations:* painting, swimming, reading. *Heir: s* James Jonathan Benn [*b* 27 July 1933; *m* 1960, Jennifer, *e d* of Dr Wilfred Howells; one *s* one *d*. *Educ:* Harrow]. *Address:* High Field, Limpsfield, Surrey.

*Died 19 Dec. 1984.*

**BENNETT, Sir Arnold (Lucas),** Kt 1975; QC (Aust.); Barrister-at-Law of Supreme Courts of Queensland, New South Wales and Victoria and of High Court of Australia, in private practice, since 1932; *b* 12 Nov. 1908; *s* of George Thomas Bennett and Celia Juliana Bennett (*née* Lucas); *m* 1st, 1934, Majorie Ella May Williams (*d* 1942); two *s* two *d*; 2nd, 1944, Nancy Margaret Mellor; one *s* three *d*. *Educ:* Brisbane Grammar Sch.; University of Queensland. Called to Bar, 1932, and except for a period of war service, has practised ever since in Australian Courts and in the Privy Council. Served War, AIF (2 service medals), 1939–45: Captain in Artillery; Captain and Major, Sqdn Ldr 2/5 Aust. Armoured Regt, and as 2 i/c of 2/1 Ind. Light Tank Sqdn, and as 2 i/c and Actg CO, 2/7 Aust. Armoured Regt. KC (Qld), 1947 (automatically became KC in High Court of Aust.), Victoria, 1952, NSW, 1953. Served 2/14 Qld Mounted Inf., 1950–54. Has conducted cases in all jurisdictions and increasingly in sphere of constitutional law. At present (1982–) opinion practice only, but serves in Qld Adv. Cttee on constitutional law and as Mem. Qld Treaties Commn. For over 40 yrs, Member: Barristers' Bd of Qld (Chm. 1957–80); Supreme Court Library Cttee, Qld; Incorp. Council of Law Reporting (Chm. 1957–79); Rotary International (Governor D260, now D960, 1972–73, in Qld's Fiftieth Rotary Year); (Chm.) Constitution and By-Laws Cttee, RI. Coronation Medal, 1953; Silver Jubilee Medal, 1977. *Publications:* Rotary in Queensland—an historical survey, 1980; articles in Australian Law Jl, Sunday Mail, Weekend Australian. *Recreations:* tennis, farming, golf, aviation. *Address:* 20 Markwell Street, Auchenflower, Brisbane, Qld 4066, Australia. *T:* (07) 371 3313; (home) Fairthorpe, 16 Bellevue Terrace, St Lucia, Brisbane, Qld 4067, Australia. *T:* (07) 370 8485. *Club:* Rotary (Pres., 1959–60) (Brisbane). *Died 30 Jan. 1983.*

**BENNETT, Daniel,** JP; Chairman, Greater Manchester Council, 1976–77, retired; *b* 18 Jan. 1900; *s* of Daniel Bennett and Margaret Bennett; *m* 1923, Helen Holt Atherton; two *d*. *Educ:* elementary sch. Elected to Orrell UDC, 1946; served continuously until 1974 (Chm. 3 times); elected to Lancs CC, 1946; elected to Divnl Educn Exec., 1950, Chm., 1969–74; elected to Greater Manchester CC, 1973, now retired. JP Lancs 1952. *Recreation:* bowling. *Address:* 56 Lodge Road, Orrell, Wigan, Lancs. *T:* Up Holland 622894.

*Died 22 Sept. 1985.*

**BENNETT, Air Vice-Marshal Donald Clifford Tyndall,** CB 1944; CBE 1943; DSO 1942; late Royal Air Force; Chairman, Fairthorpe Ltd, and other companies; consultant, director, etc; *b* 14 Sept. 1910; *s* of G. T. Bennett, Brisbane, Queensland; *m* 1935, Elsa Gubler, Zürich; one *s* one *d*. Royal Australian Air Force; Royal Air Force; AOC the Pathfinder Force of RAF Bomber Command, war of 1939–45; resigned commission, 1945; Imperial Airways; Empire and Atlantic Air Route Development; holder of the world's long-distance seaplane record (Dundee, Scotland, to Alexandra Bay, South Africa); a founder as Flying Superintendent of the Atlantic Ferry organisation (later Ferry Command); MP (L) Middlesbrough West,

1945; Managing Director and Chief Exec., British South American Airways, 1945–48. Chairman: Exec. Cttee, UNA of GB and NI, 1946–49; Political Freedom Movement, 1964–; Nat. Council of Anti Common Mkt Organisations, 1973–76; Vice-Chm., British Anti-Common Market Campaign (formerly Safeguard Britain Campaign), 1947–. President: Radar Assoc., 1952–55; Air Crew Assoc., 1984–; Bomber Command Assoc., 1984–; Patron: Pathfinder Assoc., 1947–; British League of Rights, 1970–. FRAeS. Oswald Watt Medallist, 1938, 1946; Johnston Memorial Trophy, 1937–38. Order of Alexander Nevsky, 1944. *Publications:* Complete Air Navigator, 1935, 7th edn 1967; Air Mariner, 1937, 2nd edn 1943; Freedom from War, 1945; Pathfinder, 1958, repr. 1983; Let us try Democracy, 1970. *Recreations:* tennis, ski-ing, car racing, sailing. *Address:* Fairthorpe, Denham, Uxbridge; Monte Carlo; Brisbane. *Club:* Royal Air Force. *Died 15 Sept. 1986.*

**BENNETT, Captain Geoffrey Martin,** DSC 1944; RN retired; *b* 7 June 1909; *s* of late Rear-Adm. Martin Gilbert Bennett and Ella Esme Geraldine Bennett (*née* Hicks); *m* 1932, Rosemary Alys (*née* Béchervaise); two *s*. *Educ:* Royal Naval Coll., Dartmouth, 1923–26; Flag Lieut, Second Cruiser Squadron, Home Fleet, 1938–40; Fleet Signal Officer, S Atlantic, 1940–42; Signal Officer to Adm. Comdg Force H, 1943; Sig. Off. to Flag Officer Levant and E Med., 1943–44; Admlty, 1945–47; HMS Ajax, 1947–48; HMS St Bride's Bay, 1948–49; COHQ, 1949–51; Admiralty, 1951–53; Naval Attaché, Moscow, Warsaw and Helsinki, 1953–55; CSO to CINCHAN, 1956–58; retd 1958. City Marshal. Common Cryer and Serjeant-at-Arms (London), 1958–60. Secretary to Lord Mayor of Westminster, 1960–74; Vis. Lectr on War Studies, Univ. of Frederickton, NB, 1973. Gold Medal and Trench-Gascoigne Prize of RUSI, 1934, 1942 and 1943. FRHistS, 1963. Order of Orange Nassau, 1972. *Publications:* By Human Error, 1961; Coronel and Falklands, 1962; Cowans' War, 1963; Battle of Jutland, 1964; Charlie B: biography of Admiral Lord Beresford, 1968; Naval Battles of First World War, 1968; Nelson the Commander, 1972; Battle of the River Plate, 1972; Loss of the 'Prince of Wales' and 'Repulse', 1973; Naval Battles of World War Two, 1975; Battle of Trafalgar, 1977; *novels:* (under pseudonym "Sea-Lion"): Phantom Fleet, 1946; Sink Me the Ship, 1947; Sea of Troubles, 1947; Cargo for Crooks, 1948; When Danger Threatens, 1949; Invisible Ships, 1950; This Creeping Evil, 1950; Quest of John Clare, 1951; Diamond Rock, 1952; Meet Desmond Drake, 1952; Damn Desmond Drake!, 1953; Desmond Drake Goes West, 1956; Death in Russian Habit, 1958; Operation Fireball, 1959; Down Among the Dead Men, 1961; Death in the Dog Watches, 1962; also books for children; radio scripts, etc. *Address:* Stage Coach Cottage, 57 Broad Street, Ludlow, Shropshire SY8 1NH. *T:* Ludlow 3863. *Died 5 Sept. 1983.*

**BENNETT, Prof. Jack Arthur Walter,** MA, DPhil; FBA 1971; Professor of Medieval and Renaissance English, Cambridge University, 1964–78; Fellow of Magdalene College, Cambridge, since 1964; Keeper of the Old Library, Magdalene College, 1968–78; *b* Auckland, New Zealand, 28 Feb. 1911; *s* of Ernest and Alexandra Bennett; *m* 1st, Edith Bannister (marr. annulled, 1949); 2nd, 1951, Gwyneth Mary Nicholas (*d* 1980); two *s*. *Educ:* Mt Albert Grammar Sch.; Auckland Univ. Coll.; Merton Coll., Oxford. MA (NZ) 1933; BA Oxon 1st Cl. Eng. Lang. and Lit., 1935; Harmsworth Scholar, Merton Coll., 1935–38; MA, DPhil, 1938, Res. Fellow, The Queen's Coll., Oxford, 1938–47; Head of Research Dept, later Dir, British Information Services, New York, 1940–45; Fellow and Tutor, Magdalen Coll., Oxford, 1947–64; Alexander Lectr, Univ. of Toronto, 1970–71; Vis. Fellow, Australian National Univ., 1976; Corresp. Fellow, Medieval Acad. of America, 1976; Hon. Foreign Mem., American Acad. of Arts and Scis, 1976, Emeritus Leverhulme Fellow, 1978. Gollancz Meml Prize, 1979. Editor of Medium Ævum; Mem. of Council, Early English Text Soc.; Editor, Clarendon Medieval and Tudor Series. *Publications:* The Knight's Tale, 1954; (with H. R. Trevor-Roper) The Poems of Richard Corbett, 1955; Devotional Pieces in Verse and Prose, 1957; The Parlement of Foules, 1957; (ed.) Essays on Malory, 1963; The Humane Medievalist, 1965; (jointly) Early Middle English Verse and Prose, 1966; Chaucer's Book of Fame, 1968; Selections from John Gower, 1968; (ed) Piers Plowman, 1972; Chaucer at Oxford and at Cambridge, 1974; (trans.) Ordo Missæ, 1975; Essays on Gibbon, 1980; The Poetry of the Passion, 1981; articles and reviews in Listener, TLS, Review of English Studies, Landfall (NZ), DNB, Dictionnaire de Spiritualité, etc. *Recreations:* collecting books on Oxford and Cambridge, the study of watermills. *Address:* 10 Adams Road, Cambridge. *T:* Cambridge 355322. *Died 29 Jan. 1981.*

**BENNETT, James;** *b* 18 Dec. 1912; *s* of Samuel and Elizabeth Bennett; *m* 1st, 1936, Dorothy Maclaren (marr. diss. 1980); one *s* one *d*; 2nd, 1980, Lilian Alice Cook. *Educ:* Grove Street Primary and North Kelvinside Secondary Schs., Glasgow. Councillor, Glasgow, 1947–62. Magistrate, 1950–52, Police Judge, 1952–62, JP, 1952–73, Glasgow. MP (Lab) Bridgeton Div. of Glasgow, Nov. 1961–Feb. 1974; PPS to Sec. of State for Scotland, 1964–67. *Recreations:* reading, bowls, gardening. *Address:* 27 Shepley Court, 50 Aldrington Road, SW16 1TT. *Died 17 Sept. 1984.*

**BENNETT, Jill;** actress; Co-founder of Off The Avenue, 1986; *b* Penang, SS, 24 Dec. 1929; *d* of Randle and Nora Bennett; *m* 1st, 1962, Willis Hall (marr. diss., 1965); 2nd, 1968, John Osborne (marr. diss. 1977). *Educ:* Tortington Park; Priors Field. Stratford-upon-Avon, 1949–50. First London appearance in Captain Carvallo, St James's Theatre, 1950; Iras in Anthony and Cleopatra, and Caesar and Cleopatra (Olivier Season), St James's, 1951; Helen Elliot in Night of the Ball, New, 1955; Masha in The Seagull, Saville, 1956; Sarah Stanham in The Touch of Fear, Aldwych, 1956; Isabelle in Dinner with the Family, New, 1957; Penelope in Last Day in Dream Land, Lyric, Hammersmith, 1959; Feemy Evans and Lavinia in Shaw double bill, Mermaid, 1961; Estelle in In Camera, Oxford Playhouse, 1962; Ophelia in Castle in Sweden, Piccadilly, 1962; Hilary and Elizabeth in double bill of Squat Betty and The Sponge Room, Royal Court, 1962; The Countess in A Patriot for Me, Royal Court, 1965; Anna Bowers in A Lily of Little India, St Martin's, 1965; Katrina in The Storm, and Imogen Parrott in Trelawney of the Wells, National, 1966; Pamela in Time Present, Royal Court (and later) Duke of York's, 1968 (won Evening Standard Award and Variety Club's Best Actress Award); Anna in Three Months Gone, Royal Court and Duchess, 1970; West of Suez, Royal Court and Cambridge, 1971; Hedda Gabler, Royal Court, 1972; Leslie in The Letter, Palace, Watford, 1973; Amanda in Private Lives, Globe, 1973; The End of Me Old Cigar, Greenwich, 1975; Loot, Royal Court, 1975; Watch It Come Down, National, 1976; Separate Tables, Apollo, 1977; The Aspern Papers, Chichester, 1978; The Eagle has Two Heads, The Man Who Came to Dinner, Chichester, 1979; Hamlet, Royal Court, 1980; The Little Foxes, Nottingham Playhouse, 1981; Dance of Death, Royal Exchange, Manchester, 1983; Advice (two-man show with Edward Hardwicke), 1985–; Mary Stuart, Edinburgh Festival, 1987; Exceptions, New End, 1988; Poor Nanny, King's Head, 1989; Another Love Story, Leicester Haymarket, 1990. Production for Off The Avenue: Infidelities, Boulevard, 1986. *Films include:* Lust for Life; The Nanny; The Criminal; The Charge of the Light Brigade; Inadmissible Evidence; Julius Caesar (Calpurnia); I Want What I Want; Quilp; Full Circle; For Your Eyes Only; Britannia Hospital; Country; The Old Crowd; The Aerodrome; Lady Jane; Hawks; The Sheltering Sky. TV series: Poor Little Rich Girls, 1984; Paradise Postponed, 1986; numerous TV appearances in classical works, etc. *Publication:* (with Suzanne Goodwin) Godfrey, A Special Time Remembered, 1983. *Recreations:* riding, water ski-ing, ski-ing, looking at paintings. *Address:* Julian House, 4 Windmill Street, W1.                              *Died* 4 *Oct* 1990.

**BENNETT, Joan, MA;** Life Fellow of Girton College, Cambridge; Lecturer in English, Cambridge University, 1936–64; *b* 26 June 1896; *d* of Arthur Frankau and of Julia Frankau (Frank Danby); *m* 1920, Henry Stanley Bennett (*d* 1972), FBA; three *d* (one *s* decd). *Educ:* Wycombe Abbey; Girton Coll., Cambridge. Visiting Lectr in the University of Chicago, 1952, 1955, and 1958. Warton Lecturer (Brit. Acad.), 1958; Rose Mary Crawshay Prize (Brit. Acad.), 1963. Fellow, Folger Library, 1961. *Publications:* Five Metaphysical Poets, 1965 (formerly Four Metaphysical Poets, 1934); Virginia Woolf; Her Art as a Novelist, 1945, 2nd edn enl. 1964; George Eliot: Her Mind and her Art, 1948; Sir Thomas Browne, 1962; The Love Poetry of John Donne (chapter in Seventeenth Century Studies), 1938. *Address:* Church Rate Corner, Cambridge. *T:* Cambridge 353571.                              *Died* 20 *July* 1986.

**BENNETT, Joan Geraldine;** actress (films and plays); *b* 27 Feb. 1910; *d* of Richard Bennett and Adrienne Morrison; *m* 1st, 1926, John Fox (marr. diss., 1928; he *d* 1963); one *d*; 2nd, 1932, Gene Markey (marr. diss., 1936; he *d* 1980); one *d*; 3rd, 1940, Walter Wanger (marr. diss., at Juarez, Mexico, 1965; he *d* 1968); two *d*; *m* 1978, David Wilde. *Educ:* St Margaret's Sch., Waterbury, Conn.; Mlle Lataple's, Versailles, France. *Films include:* (first film) Bulldog Drummond, 1929; Three Live Ghosts; Disraeli; Little Women; Pursuit of Happiness; Private Worlds; The Man in the Iron Mask; Margin for Error; Woman in the Window; Man Hunt; Scarlet Street; Father of the Bride. *Plays include:* (first play) Jarnegan, 1928; Bell, Book and Candle; We're no Angels; Love Me Little; Butterflies are Free; Never too Late, Prince of Wales Theatre, London, 1963. Has appeared on Television: (series) Too Young to go Steady; Dark Shadows. *Publication:* The Bennett Playbill (with Lois Kibbee), 1970. *Recreation:* interior decorating. *Address:* 67 Chase Road North, Scarsdale, NY 10583, USA.
                              *Died* 7 *Dec.* 1990.

**BENNETT, John Sloman,** CMG 1955; *b* 22 Nov. 1914; *y s* of late Ralph Bennett, FRCVS, and Constance Elkington; *m* 1955, Mary, *o c* of Rt Hon. H. A. L. Fisher, OM, and sometime Principal of St Hilda's Coll., Oxford. *Educ:* Royal Liberty Sch., Romford; Magdalene Coll., Cambridge (Schol.). 1st cl. historical tripos, 1935. Entered Colonial Office, 1936; seconded to Office of Minister of State in Middle East, 1941–45; Asst Sec., Colonial Office, 1946; Imperial Defence College, 1953; served Commonwealth Office, subsequently FCO, after merger of Colonial Office in 1966; retired 1976. *Publications:* articles on historical and musical subjects.

*Address:* 25A Alma Place, Oxford OX4 1JW. *Club:* United Oxford & Cambridge University.                  *Died* 22 *July* 1990.

**BENNETT, Sir William Gordon,** Kt 1955; Member of Glasgow Royal Exchange; Member of the Glasgow Trades House. Formerly a Magistrate and Member of Glasgow Corporation. Past President of the Scottish Unionist Association. Contested (C) Shettleston Division of Glasgow, July 1945. MP (C) Woodside Division of Glasgow, 1950–55. Served European War, 1914–18 (wounded); Officer in the Tank Corps. *Address:* 3 Hillside Road, Glasgow G43 1DE.                              *Died* 5 *Oct.* 1982.

**BENNISON, Dr (Robert) John,** FRCGP; medical practitioner; Principal in General Practice, Hatfield Broad Oak, Essex, 1959–88, retired; *b* 4 Feb. 1928; *s* of John Jennings Bennison and Agnes Bennison; *m* 1952, Kathleen Mary Underwood, MB, BChir, MA; two *s* three *d*. *Educ:* Sedbergh Sch.; Corpus Christi Coll., Cambridge (MB, BChir 1951; MA 1953); London Hosp. Med. Coll. DObstRCOG 1957; FRCGP 1972 (MRCGP 1961). Served Med. Br., RAF, 1952–54. General medical practice, 1957–88. Associate Adviser in Gen. Practice, NE Thames Region, 1975–79; Mem., English National Bd for Nursing, Midwifery and Health Visiting, 1983–88. Royal Coll. of General Practitioners: Mem. Council, 1975–84 (Vice-Chm., 1982–83); Chm., Educn Cttee, 1978–81. Med. Editor, Well Being, Channel 4, 1982–85. *Publications:* chapters in med. textbooks; papers and articles in med. jls and lay press, especially on health, and alcohol. *Recreations:* music, drama, wine, France, making things. *Address:* The Old Parsonage, Hampsthwaite, Harrogate, North Yorks.
                              *Died* 24 *March* 1989.

**BENSON, Sir Arthur (Edward Trevor),** GCMG 1959 (KCMG 1954; CMG 1952); *b* 21 Dec. 1907; *s* of late Rev. Arthur H. Trevor Benson, Vicar of Ilam, Staffs, formerly of Castle Connell, Co. Limerick and of St Saviour's, Johannesburg, and Emily Maud Malcolmson, Woodlock, Portlaw, Co. Waterford, late of Hanson Mount, Ashbourne, Derbyshire; *m* 1933, Daphne Mary Joyce, *d* of late E. H. M. Fynn, Serui, near Hartley, S Rhodesia; two *d. Educ:* Wolverhampton Sch.; Exeter Coll., Oxford. Colonial Administrative Service; Cadet, N Rhodesia, 1932; seconded to Colonial Office, 1939; to Prime Minister's Office, 1940–42; to Cabinet Office, 1942–43; to Colonial Office, 1943–44; Northern Rhodesia, 1944–46; Administrative Sec., Uganda, 1946–49; Chief Sec., Central African Council, 1949–51; Chief Sec. to Govt of Nigeria, 1951–54; Governor of Northern Rhodesia, 1954–59. Hon. Fellow, Exeter Coll., Oxford, 1963. JP Devon, 1962–66. KStJ 1954. *Recreation:* fishing. *Address:* Otter Hill, Tipton St John, Sidmouth EX10 0AJ.                              *Died* 15 *Oct.* 1987.

**BENSON, Maj.-Gen. Edward Riou,** CB 1952; CMG 1950; CBE 1945; *b* 4 April 1903; *yr s* of late Brig.-Gen. Riou Philip Benson, CB, CMG, Guildford, Surrey; *m* 1931, Isolda Mary Stuart, *d* of late Gen. Sir John Stuart Mackenzie Shea, GCB, KCMG, DSO; one *s* (one *d* decd). *Educ:* Cheltenham Coll.; RMA Woolwich. 2nd Lieut, Royal Field Artillery, 1923; Lieut, RA, 1925; Capt. 1936; Major 1940; Temp. Lieut-Col 1941; Temp. Brig. 1942; Col 1946; Maj.-Gen. 1951. Served War of 1939–45, North-West Europe, 1944–46. Dep. Dir Mil. Govt (BE), Berlin, 1948–50; Comdr 4 Anti-Aircraft Group, 1951–53; Chief of Staff, GHQ, Middle East Land Forces, 1954–57, retired. Col. Commandant, Royal Artillery, 1960–65. *Address:* Well House, Aldermaston, Berks. *T:* Woolhampton 713347.
                              *Died* 17 *Feb.* 1985.

**BENTON, Gordon William,** CIE 1946; *b* 25 March 1893; *s* of William Benton, Cannock, Staffs; *m* 1st, 1922, Ethel Beatrice (*d* 1971), *d* of George Mark Robinson; no *c*; 2nd, 1973, Vera Alicia, *d* of P. W. J. J. Harman-Harris and widow of H. W. Trussler. *Educ:* Merchant Taylors' Sch. Joined Indian Police, 1912; Indian Army Reserve of Officers, 45th Rattray's Sikhs, Mesopotamia, 1917–19; lent to Govt of HEH the Nizam of Hyderabad for CID, and Dir-Gen., Police and Jails, 1926–33; Deputy Dir, Intelligence Bureau, Home Dept, Govt of India and Mem., two Cttees on aspects of Railway Police admin under the Govt of India Bill then under consideration in parlt, 1935–38; Deputy Inspector-General, Central Provinces and Berar, 1938; retd 1947. Indian Police Medal, 1940; King's Police Medal, 1945. *Address:* 21 Lodge Gardens, Alverstoke, Hants PO12 3PY. *Club:* East India, Devonshire, Sports and Public Schools.
                              *Died* 9 *June* 1983.

**BEOVICH, Most Rev. Matthew,** DD, PhD; Former Archbishop of Adelaide, (RC); *b* 1896; *s* of Matthew and Elizabeth Beovich, Melbourne. *Educ:* Melbourne; Propaganda College, Rome. Ordained Priest, 1922; Asst Priest, N Fitzroy, 1923–24; Inspector, Christian Doctrine, Melbourne Archdiocese Schools, 1924–39; Archbishop of Adelaide, 1940–71. Hon. Sec., Aust. Catholic Truth Soc., 1925–33; Dir, Catholic Education, 1933–39. *Address:* 28 Robe Terrace, Medindie, SA 5081, Australia.     *Died* 24 *Oct.* 1981.

**BERENS, Herbert Cecil Benyon,** MC 1942; Chairman, Evans of Leeds Ltd, since 1972; Director, Allied Irish Investment Bank Ltd, since

1966; *b* 16 Oct. 1908; *s* of Cecil Berens, JP, St Mary Cray, Kent; *m* 1931, Moyra Nancy Mellard; three *s* one *d*. *Educ:* Wellington Coll.; Christ Church, Oxford. Hambro's Bank, 1931–39. Served War of 1939–45; Major, 4th County of London Yeomanry (MC); POW, 1941–43. *Recreations:* racing, shooting. *Address:* Bentworth Hall, Alton, Hants. *T:* Alton 62140. *Clubs:* MCC, I Zingari.

*Died 27 Oct.* 1981.

**BERESFORD, His Honour Eric George Harold;** a Circuit Judge (formerly Judge of County Courts), 1959–76; *b* 19 Nov. 1901; *s* of Henry Beresford, Sutton Coldfield; *m* 1930, Barbara Muriel, *d* of Wallace Edwin Marley, Sutton Coldfield; one *s* one *d*. *Educ:* King Edward's Sch., Birmingham; Emanuel Coll., Cambridge (MA, LLB). Called to Bar, Lincoln's Inn, 1926; practised on Midland Circuit. Chm., Licensed Premises Cttee, New Town of Redditch, 1965. *Recreations:* history and literature. *Address:* Saxbys, Rolvenden, Kent. *T:* Rolvenden 403. *Died 12 April* 1983.

**BERESFORD-STOOKE, Sir George;** *see* Stooke.

**BERGEL, Prof. Franz,** FRS 1959; DPhil. Nat. (Freiburg), PhD (London), DSc (London), CChem, FRSC, FIBiol; Professor Emeritus of Chemistry, University of London; Member, Institute of Cancer Research: Royal Cancer Hospital; *b* Vienna, 13 Feb. 1900; *s* of Moritz Martin Bergel and Barbara Betty Spitz; *m* 1939, Phyllis Thomas. *Educ:* Universities of Vienna and Freiburg im Breisgau. Head of Dept of Medical Chemistry, Inst. Chem., 1927–33, and Privatdoz., Univ. of Freiburg, 1929–33; research worker: Med. Chem. Dept, Univ. of Edinburgh, 1933–36; Lister Inst. of Preventive Med., Dept of Biochemistry, 1936–38; Dir of Research, Roche Products Ltd, Welwyn Garden City, 1938–52; Head, Chemistry Dept, Chester Beatty Res. Inst., 1952–66; Dean, Inst. Cancer Research, 1963–66. Hon. Lectr, Pharmacology Dept, Faculty of Medical Sciences. University Coll., London 1946–73; Consultant: Harvard Med. Sch. and Children's Cancer Research Foundn (now Sidney Farber Cancer Inst.), Boston, Mass, 1959–60, 1967–73; FRSM; FRSA 1957 (Life Mem., 1967–); Member: Soc. Chem. Ind.; Biochem. Soc.; Amer. Assoc. Adv. Sci. (Fellow); Brit. Pharm. Soc. Inst. of Cancer Research, Sutton, named their new library Bergel Library, 1980. *Publications:* Chemistry of Enzymes in Cancer, 1961; All about Drugs, 1970; Today's Carcinochemotherapy, 1970; Alexander Haddow (biographical memoir), 1977; papers and reviews in chemical, biochemical and pharmacological journals. *Recreation:* sketching. *Address:* Magnolia Cottage, Bel Royal, St Lawrence, Jersey, CI. *T:* Jersey 33688.

*Died 1 Jan.* 1987.

**BERGIN, John Alexander,** CB 1980; Deputy Secretary, Lord Chancellor's Department, 1977–80; *b* 25 May 1920; *s* of late B. A. G. and Mrs L. Bergin; *m* 1953, Pierrette Wack, MA. *Educ:* Varndean Sch., Brighton; St Catharine's Coll., Cambridge. BA Hons (Natural Science) 1947. REME, 1940–46 (T/Major, despatches). Asst Principal, Bd of Trade, 1948; HM Customs and Excise, 1954–56; Office of Chancellor, Duchy of Lancaster, 1960; Dept of Economic Affairs, 1964; IDC, 1966; Under-Sec., BoT, 1968–71; Principal Estabt and Finance Officer, Lord Chancellor's Dept, 1971–77. *Recreations:* photography; hybridising *Liliaceae, Amaryllidaceae. Address:* 15 Granard Avenue, SW15 6HH. *Club:* United Oxford & Cambridge University.

*Died 24 May* 1986.

**BERGIN, Kenneth Glenny,** MA, MD Cantab; DPH London; FRAeS; physician; Director, Cavendish Medical Centre, since 1973; President, International Academy of Aviation and Space Medicine, since 1977; *b* 10 June 1911; *er s* of Dr F. Gower Bergin, Clifton, Bristol; *m* 1938, Joan Mary (*d* 1981), *o d* of G. H. Sinnott, Clifton, Bristol and *gd* of Maj.-Gen. N. F. J. Sampson-Way, CB, Henbury, Glos; two *s* one *d*. *Educ:* Clifton Coll.; Queens' Coll., Cambridge; St Bartholomew's Hospital, London. Served with RAF Med. Br., 1939–46 (despatches twice); Flying Trng Bomber (Pathfinder) and Fighter Comds (Wing Comdr, qual. service pilot). BOAC, 1946–64: Dir Personnel and Medical Services, 1959–63; Dir Medical Services, 1963–64. Pres. Airline Med. Directors' Assoc., 1965; Pres., Air League, 1978– (Chm., 1974–77, Vice-Chm., 1960–64); Mem. Council: Brit. Soc. for Internat. Understanding; Aerospace Med. Assoc. (Pres., Internat. Congress, 1978); Member: Airline Personnel Directors' Assoc., 1959–64; Nat. Jt Council for Civil Air Transport, 1959–64; Nat. Jt Adv. Council to Minister of Labour, 1959–64; Bd of Govs, Clifton Coll.; WHO Cttee on Internat. Quarantine; Nat. Aviation Council; Econ. Research Council; Adv. Council, Coll. of Aeronautical and Automobile Engineering; Vice-Chm., Bd of Govs, Coll. of Air Trng, 1962–64; Chm., Air Centre Trust, 1967–70; Master, Guild of Air Pilots and Air Navigators, 1959–61; Custodian, Guild of Air Pilots Benevolent Fund; Freeman and Liveryman, City of London. Hon. Steward, Westminster Abbey. Invitation Lectr., Oxford, Cambridge and Bristol Univs., Brit. Assoc., Royal Soc. of Health, BMA, etc. Dir, Gp Personnel, Cunard Steamship Co. Ltd, 1969–71. FRSocMed; Fellow: Aerospace Medical Assoc.; Internat. Aerospace Med. Assoc. Boothby Award, 1971; Airline

Med. Dirs Award, 1978; Internat. Congress of Aviation and Space Medicine Award, 1979. JP Inner London, 1970–73. OStJ 1959. *Publications:* Aviation Medicine, 1948; numerous others on Aviation Medicine and allied subjects. *Recreations:* fishing, shooting, riding, sailing, flying. *Address:* The Miller's House, Kintbury, Berks RG15 0UR. *T:* Kintbury 292, 99 Harley Street, W1N 1DF. *T:* 01–935 7501. *Clubs:* Athenæum, United Oxford & Cambridge University, Boodle's, Royal Air Force. *Died 26 March* 1981.

**BERGMAN, Ingrid;** actress; *b* 29 Aug. 1915; *d* of Justus and Friedel Bergman; *m* 1937, Petter Lindstrom (marriage dissolved, 1950, Los Angeles; dissolution ruled not valid by a Rome court, 1960); one *d*; *m* 1950 (by proxy, Mexico), Roberto Rossellini (marriage ruled not valid by a Rome court, 1960); one *s* twin *d*; *m* 1958, (in London), Lars Schmidt. *Educ:* Lyceum for Flickor and Sch. of Royal Dramatic Theatre, Stockholm. *Stage:* Liliom, 1940; Anna Christie, 1941; Joan of Lorraine, 1947; Tea and Sympathy (Paris), 1956; Hedda Gabler (Paris), 1962; A Month in the Country, Guildford (Yvonne Arnaud), 1965, and Cambridge Theatre, London; More Stately Mansions, New York, 1967–68; Captain Brassbound's Conversion, Cambridge Theatre, 1971; The Constant Wife, Albery, 1973, and in US, 1974–75; Waters of the Moon, Chichester, 1977, Haymarket, 1978. *Films:* Intermezzo, 1939; Adam Had Four Sons, 1940; Rage in Heaven, 1941; Dr Jekyll and Mr Hyde, 1941; Casablanca, 1942; For Whom the Bell Tolls, 1943; Gaslight, 1944; Saratoga Trunk, 1945; Spellbound, 1945; The Bells of St Mary's, 1946; Notorious, 1946; Arch of Triumph, 1947; Joan of Arc, 1948; Under Capricorn, 1948; Stomboli, 1950; Anastasia, 1957; Elena et les Hommes; The Inn of the Sixth Happiness; Indiscreet, 1958; Goodbye Again, 1961; The Visit, 1963; The Yellow Rolls-Royce, 1964; Cactus Flower, 1970; A Walk in the Spring Rain, 1970; Murder on the Orient Express, 1974; Autumn Sonata, 1978; *television* appearances incl. A Woman Called Golda, 1982 (Emmy awarded posthumously). *Opera:* Joan of Arc at the Stake, 1954. Awarded three Oscars. *Publication:* (with Alan Burgess) My Story, 1980. *Died 29 Aug.* 1982.

**BERGNER, Elisabeth;** actress; *b* Vienna, 22 Aug. 1900; naturalised British subject, 1938; *m* Dr Paul Czinner. Early stage appearances in Austria, Switzerland and Germany included performances with Wedekind in Spring Awakening, Lulu and Schloss Wetterstein; Ophelia in Hamlet, Zürich; Rosalind in As You Like It, Vienna; Katherine in The Taming of the Shrew; Julie in Miss Julie; Viola in Twelfth Night; Juliet in Romeo and Juliet; Joan in Saint Joan; 1924; Mrs Cheyney in The Last of Mrs Cheyney, 1926; Tessa in The Constant Nymph, 1927 (all in Berlin). First London appearance as Gemma Jones in Escape Me Never, Apollo, 1933, NY, 1935; The Boy David, His Majesty's, 1936; The Two Mrs Carrolls, NY, 1943; Duchess of Malfi, NY, 1946; The Gay Invalid, Garrick, 1951; toured Germany and Austria in Long Day's Journey Into Night, 1957; First Love, United States, 1964; The Madwoman of Chaillot, Oxford, 1967. Films include: Der Evangelimann, Ariane, Fräulein Else, Escape Me Never, Dreaming Lips, Catherine the Great, Stolen Life, As You Like It, Pfingstausflug (Berlin Prize, 1979). Schiller Prize, 1963; Goldene Band, International Film Festival, Berlin, 1963 and 1965; Eleonora Duse Prize, Venice, 1983; Ernst Reuter Plakette, Berlin, 1983; Maximilians Orden für Wissenschaft und Kunst, Vienna, 1984; Das Silberne Blatt der Dramatiker Union, Berlin, 1984. Das Grosse Verdienstkreuz mit Stern, Germany; Ehrenmedaille der Bundeshaupstadt Wien, Austria. Daughter of Mark Twain, 1976. *Publication:* Elisabeth Bergner's unordentliche Erinnerungen. *Recreations:* walking, music. *Address:* 42 Eaton Square, SW1. *Died 12 May* 1986.

**BERKELEY, Sir Lennox (Randal Francis),** Kt 1974; CBE 1957; composer; President Emeritus, Cheltenham Festival of Music, since 1984 (President, 1977–83); *b* 12 May 1903; *o s* of Capt. Hastings George Fitzhardinge Berkeley, RN, and Aline Carla (*née* Harris); *m* 1946, Elizabeth Freda Bernstein; three *s*. *Educ:* Gresham's Sch., Holt; Merton Coll., Oxford. BA Oxford, 1926; Hon. DMus Oxford, 1970. Studied music in Paris under Nadia Boulanger, 1927–32. Returned to London, 1935; on staff of BBC Music Dept, 1942–45. Composition Professor, Royal Acad. of Music, 1946–68. Hon. Prof. of Music, Keele Univ., 1976–79. Pres. of Honour, Performing Right Soc., 1975–83; Pres., Composers' Guild of Great Britain, 1975–. Vice-President: Bach Choir, 1978–; Western Orchestral Soc., 1978–; Cttee, Internat. Soc. of Authors and Composers, 1980–82; Pres., Oxford and Cambridge Univ. Musical Club. Hon. Mem., Amer. Acad. and Inst. of Arts and Letters, 1980; Associate, Académie Royale, Belgium, 1983. Hon. Fellow: Merton Coll., Oxford, 1974; Royal Northern Coll. of Music, 1976; Hon. DMus: City, 1983. Awarded Collard Fellowship in Music, 1946; Cobbett Medal 1962; Ordre de Mérite Culturel, Monaco, 1967; KSG 1973. Composer of the Year, Composers' Guild of GB, 1973. *Compositions include: symphony orchestra:* four symphonies; Divertimento; piano concerto; Concerto for Two Pianos; Flute Concerto; Suite: A Winter's Tale; Voices of the Night; orchestration of Poulenc's Flute Sonata; *chamber orchestra:* Violin Concerto; Partita; Windsor Variations; Dialogue for cello and chamber orchestra; Sinfonia Concertante for oboe and orchestra; *string orchestra:* Serenade;

Antiphon; Suite; *vocal/choral music:* Four Poems of St Teresa of Avila for contralto and strings; Stabat Mater for soloists and ensemble; Missa Brevis; Batter My Heart for soprano, choir and chamber orchestra; Four Ronsard Sonnets for tenor and orchestra; Signs in the Dark for choir and strings; Magnificat for choir and orchestra; Three Latin Motets; Hymn for Shakespeare's Birthday; The Hill of the Graces; Judica Me; *chamber music:* many chamber works, including four string quartets; String Trio; Trio for horn, violin and piano; Sextet for clarinet, horn and string quartet; Oboe Quartet; Quintet for wind and piano; various piano works; many songs; carol, I Sing of a Maiden; *opera:* Nelson; A Dinner Engagement; Ruth; Castaway. *Recreations:* reading, walking. *Address:* 8 Warwick Avenue, W2. *Died 26 Dec.* 1989.

**BERLIN, Irving;** author and composer; *b* Russia, 11 May 1888 (as Israel Baline); *s* of Moses Baline and Leah Lipkin; brought to USA, 1893; *m* 1st, 1913, Dorothy Goetz (*d* 1913); 2nd, 1926, Ellin (*d* 1988), *d* of Clarence H. Mackay, NY; three *d*. *Educ:* public schools, NY City, for two years only. First song published, Marie From Sunny Italy, 1907; first complete Broadway score, Watch Your Step, 1914; Music Box Revue, 1921–24; Ziegfeld Follies, 1919, 1920, 1927. Pres. Irving Berlin Music Corp. Served as Sergt Infantry at Camp Upton, LI. Hon. Degrees, Bucknell, Temple, and Fordham Univs; Medal of Merit for This Is The Army; awarded a special Gold Medal by Congress for God Bless America; Legion of Honour, France. Has composed about 800 songs, including: Alexander's Ragtime Band; Oh, How I Hate To Get Up In the Morning; When I Lost You; A Pretty Girl Is Like A Melody; Say It With Music; Always; Remember; Blue Skies; Easter Parade; Heat Wave; Isn't This A Lovely Day; Top Hat, White Tie and Tails; I've Got My Love To Keep Me Warm; White Christmas; This Is The Army, Mr Jones; Anything You Can Do; Doin' What Comes Natur'lly; The Girl That I Marry; There's No Business Like Show Business. Musicals (several of which have been filmed) include: As Thousands Cheer; Face The Music; Louisiana Purchase; Annie Get Your Gun; Miss Liberty; Call Me Madam; Mr President. US Medal of Freedom, 1977. *Address:* Irving Berlin Music Corp., 1290 Avenue of the Americas, New York City, USA. *Clubs:* Lambs, Friars.
*Died 22 Sept.* 1989.

**BERNACCHI, Michael Louis,** CMG 1955; OBE 1952; *b* 5 May 1911; *s* of late Louis Charles Bernacchi, physicist and Antarctic explorer, and late Winifred Edith Harris; *m* 1943, Elaine Chapman; one *s* one *d*. *Educ:* RN Colls Dartmouth and Greenwich; Magdalene Coll., Cambridge. Royal Navy, 1925–34; entered Colonial Service as Cadet, Fiji, 1936; District Commissioner, 1937; acting ADC to Governor of Fiji, 1939; served Royal Navy, 1940–44; Lieut Comdr RN (retd); transferred Malayan Civil Service, 1944; special duty, N Borneo, 1944; Military Administration N Borneo (Col), 1945–46; acting Chief Sec., N Borneo, 1946, Malaya, 1947–52; Class Ic Malayan Civil Service, 1951; (Perak Meritorious Service Medal, 1951); Resident Commissioner, Gilbert and Ellice Islands Colony, 1952–61, retd 1962. *Recreation:* reading. *Address:* 61 Leinster Road, Merivale, Christchurch 1, New Zealand. *Club:* Christchurch (NZ).
*Died 20 Aug.* 1983.

**BERNSTEIN, Cecil (George);** Executive Director, Granada Group Ltd; Chairman: Granada Television International Ltd; Granada Television, 1971–74; *b* 28 July 1904; *s* of Alexander and Jane Bernstein; *m* 1929, Myra Ella, *d* of Rachel and Lesser Lesser; one *s* one *d*. *Educ:* Haberdashers' Aske's. Member, Cinematograph Films Council, 1948–; Pres., Cinema and Television Benevolent Fund. *Address:* 7 Grosvenor Square, W1; Five Trees, Craigweil-on-Sea, Sussex. *Died 18 June* 1981.

**BERNSTEIN, Leonard;** conductor, composer, pianist, lecturer; *b* Lawrence, Mass, 25 Aug. 1918; named Louis Bernstein; *s* of Samuel J. and Jennie (Resnick) Bernstein; *m* 1951, Felicia Montealegre Cohn (*d* 1978); one *s* two *d*. *Educ:* Boston Latin Sch.; Harvard Univ.; Curtis Inst. of Music. Asst to Koussevitzky, Berkshire Music Center, 1942, Head of Conducting Dept, 1951–56; Asst Conductor, NY Philharmonic Orch., 1943–44; Conductor, NYC Symphony, 1945–48; Musical Adviser, Israel Philharmonic Orch., 1948–49; Prof. of Music, Brandeis Univ., 1951–56; Charles Eliot Norton Prof. of Poetry, Harvard Univ., 1973–74; co-conductor (with Dimitri Mitropoulos), NY Philharmonic Orch., 1957–58; Music Dir, NY Philharmonic Orch., 1958–69, then Laureate Conductor; President: English Bach Festival, 1977–; LSO, 1987–. Has conducted all major orchestras of US and Europe in annual tours, 1944–; has toured N and S America, Europe, Near East, USSR and Japan with NY Philharmonic Orch. Festival, Bernstein at 70, produced in his honour by Boston Symphony Orch., Tanglewood, 1988. Tony Award, 1969; Grammy Award for Lifetime Achievement, 1985; Gold Medal, Royal Philharmonic Soc., 1987; Gold Medal for Composition, MacDowell Colony, 1987. Key to Oslo, Norway, 1987; Great Merit Cross of the Order of Merit (FRG), 1987; also holds decorations from: France, Italy, Finland, Chile and Austria. *Works include:* Clarinet Sonata, 1942; Symphony, No 1, Jeremiah, 1942; Song Cycle (I Hate Music), 1943; Seven

Anniversaries for Piano, 1943; Fancy Free, 1944; Hashkivenu, 1945; Facsimile, 1946; Five Pieces for Brass Instruments, 1947; Four Anniversaries for Piano, 1948; Symphony, No 2, The Age of Anxiety, 1949; Song Cycle (La Bonne Cuisine), 1949; songs, Afterthought and Silhouette, 1951; Trouble in Tahiti (one-act opera), 1952; Serenade (after Plato's Symposium) for violin solo, with string orch. and percussion, 1954; Symphony, No 3, Kaddish, 1963; Five Anniversaries for Piano, 1964; Chichester Psalms (a choral work with orchestra), 1965; Mass, a theatre piece for singers, players and dancers, 1971; Score for ballet, Dybbuk, 1974; Suite No 1 from Dybbuk, 1975; Seven Dances from Dybbuk, 1975; Songfest, 1977; A Quiet Place (opera), 1983; Sean Song for voice and strings, 1986; Concerto for orchestra (Jubilee Games), 1986; Trial Song from the Race to Unga, 1987; Missa Brevis for a capella chorus with incidental percussion, 1988; My Twelve Tone Melody, song for voice and piano, 1988; Thirteen Anniversaries for piano, 1988; Arias and Barcarolles for piano four-hands and mixed voices, 1988; Dance Suite for brass quintet, 1990; scores for Broadway musicals including: On the Town, 1944, Wonderful Town, 1953, Candide, 1956, West Side Story, 1957; Score for Film, On the Waterfront, 1954. Has received Hon. Degrees from universities and colleges. *Publications:* The Joy of Music, 1959; Leonard Bernstein's Young People's Concerts for Reading and Listening, 1962; The Infinite Variety of Music, 1966; The Unanswered Question, 1973; Findings, 1982. *Address:* c/o Carson Office, 101 W 55 Street, New York, NY 10019, USA. *Died 14 Oct.* 1990.

**BERRY, Alan Percival,** FBIM; FITD; Barrister-at-Law; Director and Chief Executive, West Midlands Engineering Employers' Association, since 1983; *b* 1 Oct. 1926; *s* of Percy Berry and Winifred Berry; *m* 1952, Audrey Gwendolen, *d* of Douglas E. Spalton, Bramley; one *s* one *d*. *Educ:* Jesus Coll., Oxford (MA). DPA. Called to the Bar, Middle Temple, 1957. HM Factory Inspectorate, 1951–57; Sec., W of England Engrg Employers' Assoc., 1957–63; Dir, Coventry & Dist Engineering Employers' Assoc., 1963–83. Dir, Midland Gp Trng Services Ltd, 1970–; Commissioner, Manpower Services Commn, 1976–79. Member: Coventry Educn Cttee, 1963–; CBI Midlands Council, 1972–; Council, Warwick Univ., 1974–; BBC Midlands Adv. Council, 1977–81 (Chm., 1979–81); BBC Gen. Adv. Council, 1979–81. Governor, Coventry (Lanchester) Polytechnic, 1970– (Chm., 1977–). OStJ 1980. *Publications:* Worker Participation: the European experience, 1974; Labour Relations in Japan, 1979. *Recreation:* sailing. *Address:* 50 Beverley Road, Leamington Spa, Warwicks. *T:* Leamington Spa 23262.
*Died 19 Sept.* 1983.

**BERRY, Hon. Sir Anthony George,** Kt 1983; MP (C) Enfield, Southgate, since 1974 (Southgate, 1964–74); *b* 12 Feb. 1925; *y s* of 1st Viscount Kemsley, GBE; *m* 1st, 1954, Hon. Mary Cynthia Burke Roche (from whom he obtained a divorce, 1966), *er d* of 4th Baron Fermoy; one *s* three *d*; 2nd, 1966, Sarah Anne, *d* of Raymond Clifford-Turner; one *s* one *d*. *Educ:* Eton; Christ Church, Oxford (MA). Served as Lieut, Welsh Guards, 1943–47. Asst Editor, Sunday Times, 1952–54; Editor, Sunday Chronicle, 1954; Dir, Kemsley Newspapers, 1954–59; Managing Dir, Western Mail and Echo Ltd, 1955–59. Dep. Chm., Leopold Joseph & Sons Ltd, 1962–79. PPS to Rt Hon. Peter Walker, Sec. of State, for the Environment, 1970–72, for Trade and Industry, 1972–74; Vice-Chm., Cons. Transport Cttee, 1969–70, 1974–75; Opposition Whip, 1975–79; Vice-Chamberlain of HM Household, 1979–81, Comptroller, 1981–83; Treasurer of HM Household and Govt Dep. Chief Whip, 1983. Pres., Welsh Games Council, 1959–. JP Cardiff, 1961; High Sheriff, Glamorgan, 1962. CstJ. *Publication:* (jt editor) Conservative Oxford, 1949. *Address:* 1 Graham Terrace, SW1. *T:* 01–235 3801; Fox's Walk, Shurlock Row, Twyford, Berkshire. *Clubs:* Portland, White's; Cardiff and County (Cardiff). *Died 12 Oct.* 1984.

**BERRY, Prof. Harry,** BSc London; FPS; CChem, FRSC; Dip. Bact. London; ACT Birmingham; retired; Dean, School of Pharmacy, University of London, 1937–56; Professor of Pharmaceutics, 1944–56; Professor Emeritus, 1956; *b* 6 Oct. 1890; *s* of late William Berry and Lois Robinson Blood; *m* 1918, Agnes May (*d* 1978), *d* of late Robert Boardman; two *s* one *d*. *Educ:* Nantwich and Acton Grammar Sch. Served European War, 1914–19, Royal Fusiliers, RE, RGA (Lieut). Lecturer in Pharmacy, Robert Gordon Colls, Aberdeen, 1919; Head, Dept of Pharmacy, Tech. Coll., Birmingham, 1919–33; Vice-Dean, 1933, Dean, 1937, College of the Pharmaceutical Soc.; Reader in Pharmaceutics, University of London, 1933. Hon. Fellow, School of Pharmacy, Univ. of London, 1956; Mem. Royal Free Hosp. Sch. of Medicine; Hon. Assoc., Coll. of Technology, Birmingham, 1956; Hon. Mem. Guild of Public Pharmacists 1965. Mem. of the British Pharmacopoeia Commission. Examiner for the Universities of London, Glasgow, Manchester, Wales, and the Pharmaceutical Soc.; Member: British Pharmaceutical Codex Revision Cttee; Central Health Services Council Standing Pharmaceutical Advisory Cttee, and Jt Sub-Cttee of Ministry of Health on Definition of Drugs; Cttee of Management of University of London Inst. of Educ.; Chm. Brit. Pharm. Conf., 1951. *Publications:* (jt) Whitla's Pharmacy, Materia Medica and

Therapeutics, 12th edn, 1933; (jt) Penicillin, Fleming, 1st and 2nd edn, 1949; original contributions to Journal of Pharmacy and Pharmacol., Lancet. *Address:* 2 Grange Gardens, Blackwater Road, Eastbourne BN20 7DE. *T:* Eastbourne 640674.

*Died 29 April 1982.*

**BERRY, Col Hon. Julian,** OBE (mil.) 1959; Vice Lord-Lieutenant of Hampshire, since 1983; *b* 24 May 1920; *y* s of 1st Viscount Camrose and Mary Agnes (*née* Corns); *m* 1946, Denise, *d* of Major Leslie Rowan Thompson; one *s* one *d*. *Educ:* Eton. 2nd Lieut, Royal Horse Guards (The Blues), 1939; served War, Middle East and Italy; Captain, 1943; Major, 1945; Lt-Col Commanding Royal Horse Guards, 1958–60; Col Comdg Household Cavalry and Silver Stick in Waiting, 1960–64; retired, 1964. JP 1966, DL 1974, Hants. Bronze Star Medal, USA, 1945. *Recreations:* racing and shooting. *Address:* Old Rectory, Tunworth, Basingstoke, Hants. *T:* Basingstoke 471436. *Clubs:* White's, Jockey (Steward 1970–72); Royal Yacht Squadron. *Died 26 June 1988.*

**BERRY, Michael Francis;** Director of Robert Fleming & Co. Ltd, Merchant Bankers, 1937–77; *b* 17 Oct. 1906; *e* s of C. Seager Berry and Constance, *d* of Rev. D. C. Cochrane; *m* 1939, Prudence, *d* of C. G. Atha, Haverbrack House, Milnthorpe; one *d*. *Educ:* Eton; Hertford Coll., Oxford. Entered City, 1929; served War of 1939–45, Royal Artillery. A Crown Estate Commissioner, 1956–65. High Sheriff Northants 1973. *Publications:* A History of the Puckeridge Hunt, 1950; (with C. M. Floyd) A History of the Eton College Hunt 1857–1968, 1969. *Recreations:* hunting, farming. *Address:* Benefield House, near Peterborough PE8 5AF. *T:* Benefield 219. *Club:* Boodle's. *Died 19 May 1988.*

**BERRYMAN, Lieut-Gen. Sir Frank Horton,** KCVO 1954; CB 1944; CBE 1941; DSO 1919; Company Director since 1961; Director and Chief Executive Officer, Royal Agricultural Society, Sydney, 1954–61; *b* 11 April 1894; *s* of William Berryman; *m* 1925, Muriel Whipp, CBE; one *s* one *d*. *Educ:* Melbourne High Sch.; Sydney Univ.; RMC, Duntroon; Staff Coll., Camberley (psc); Artillery Coll., Woolwich (pac). Served European War, 1915–19 (DSO, despatches twice, wounded); served as regimental officer, battery commander in field artillery, and infantry brigade-major. Army Representative High Commissioner's Office, London, 1931; Brigade-Major 14 Infantry Brigade, Sydney, 1932–34; GSO Operations and Asst Dir Military Operations, Army HQ, Melbourne, 1934–37; GSO1 3 Aust. Div., 1938–39; War of 1939–45; GSO1, 6 Australian Div. at capture of Bardia and Tobruk in 1941 (CBE); CRA 7 Aust. Div. and Comdr Berryforce in Syrian Campaign, 1941 (despatches); Brig. Gen. Staff, 1 Aust. Corps, Aug. 1941, and served in Middle East and Java; Maj.-Gen. General Staff, 1st Australian Army, 1942; Dep. Chief of Gen. Staff, Sept. 1942; DCGS and MCGS on New Guinea Force, Dec. 1942–Oct. 1943; Admin Comd, 2 Aust. Corps, Nov. 1943; Lieut-Gen. GOC 2 Aust. Corps, Finchhaven, Huon Peninsula, New Guinea, Jan. 1944 (CB): GOC 1 Aust. Corps, April 1944; Chief of Staff, Advanced Land Force HQ, South-West Pacific Area, July 1944; served with GHQ SWPA in Hollandia, Leyte, and Manila; present on USS Missouri, Tokyo Bay, at official Japanese surrender ceremony as representative of Australian army, 2 Sept. 1945; Chief of Staff Adv. HQ, AMF, Oct.–Dec. 1945; Chief of Staff HQ Morotai Force, Dec. 1945–March 1946; GOC Eastern Command, Australia, 1946–50, and 1952–53. Awarded Medal of Freedom with Silver Palm by US Govt 1946; Commonwealth Dir Royal Tour (1949), 1948; seconded to Prime Minister's Dept as Dir-Gen. Commonwealth Jubilee Celebrations (1951), and Dir-Gen. Royal Visit (1952), 1951–52; seconded to Prime Minister's Dept as Dir-Gen. Royal Visit (1954), 1953–54; retd list, 1954. Pres., Dr Barnados, Australia, 1966–. Col Comdt, Royal Australian Artillery, 1956–61. *Recreation:* golf. *Address:* 17 Wentworth Street, Point Piper, Sydney, NSW 2027, Australia. *Clubs:* Australian, Royal Sydney Golf (Sydney); Naval and Military (Melbourne). *Died 28 May 1981.*

**BERTHOUD, Sir Eric Alfred,** KCMG 1954 (CMG 1945); DL; MA; retired from HM Foreign Service, 1960; *b* 10 Dec. 1900; 2nd *s* of late Alfred E. Berthoud and Helene Berthoud; *m* 1927, Ruth Tilston (*d* 1988), *d* of Sir Charles Bright, FRSE; two *s* two *d* (and one *s* decd). *Educ:* Gresham's Sch., Holt; Magdalen Coll., Oxford; MA. Demy; Hons in Natural Science; Goldsmith's Exhibnr. Anglo-Austrian Bank Ltd, London, 1922–26; Anglo-Iranian Oil Co. (BP) Ltd, 1926–39; served as board mem. in France, Holland and Germany, war time mandate, 1939–44, denial of oil to Axis. Commercial Sec. to HM Legation, Bucharest, 1939–41; Mem. British military and econ. mission to Soviet Union, 1941–42; Asst Sec., Min. of Fuel and Power (Petroleum Div.), 1942–44; Minister of State's Office, Cairo, 1942–43; Dir Economic Div., Allied Commission for Austria (British Element), 1944–46; Under-Sec., Petroleum Div., Min. of Fuel and Power, 1946–48; Asst Under-Sec., FO, 1948–52; HM Ambassador to Denmark, 1952–56, to Poland, 1956–60. Jt Chairman: International Cttee setting up OEEC in Paris, 1948; Anglo-Polish Round Table Confs, 1963–70. Chm. (part-time) Civil Service Selection Bd, 1963–68. Pres., Colchester

Constituency Liberal Assoc., 1974–76. Member: Council, 1962–73, and Court, Essex Univ.; Council, SSEES, London Univ., 1964–76. Mem. Internat. Council and Governor, Atlantic College, 1962–. Mem., Bd of Visitors, Chelmsford Prison, 1960–75; Pres. (formerly Chm.), Katherine Low Settlement, Battersea; Vice Chm., Sue Ryder Foundn, 1970–72. DL Essex, 1969–. Knight Comdr's Cross with star, Order of Polonia Restituta, 1965; Commander's Order of Merit with Star (Poland), 1985. *Recreation:* international relations. *Address:* Brownings Manor, Blackboys, near Uckfield, Sussex TN22 5HG. *T:* Framfield 259. *Club:* Brooks's.

*Died 29 April 1989.*

**BERTRAM, Prof. Douglas Somerville;** Professor of Medical Entomology and Director of Department of Entomology, London School of Hygiene and Tropical Medicine, 1956–76, later Emeritus; *b* 21 Dec. 1913; *s* of William R. J. Bertram and Katherine Arathoon Macaskill, Glasgow, Scotland; *m* 1st, 1947, Louisa Menzies MacKellar (*d* 1956); two *d*; 2nd, 1973, Muriel Elizabeth (*née* Maas), widow of W. M. Drury. *Educ:* Hillhead High Sch., Glasgow; Univ. of Glasgow. 1st cl. hons BSc (Zoology), 1935, PhD 1940, DSc 1964, Glasgow Univ.; FIBiol; Strang-Steel Scholar, Glasgow Univ., 1935–36. Demonstrator, Dept of Zoology, Glasgow Univ., 1936–38; Lectr, Liverpool Sch. of Tropical Medicine, 1938–40, and 1946–48; Reader in Entomology, London Sch. of Hygiene and Tropical Medicine, 1948–56. Hon. Treas., Royal Society of Tropical Medicine and Hygiene, 1960–73. Overseas work in East and West Africa, India and Ceylon, Central and South America periodically. Served War of 1939–45: Lieut to Major, Royal Army Medical Corps, Middle East, POW Germany, Army Sch. of Health Staff, 1945–46. *Publications:* scientific papers in Annals of Trop. Medicine and Parasitology, Transactions Royal Society Tropical Medicine and Hygiene, Adv. Parasitology, Bulletin WHO, etc. *Recreations:* gardening, painting, travel. *Died 24 Oct 1988.*

**BESSELL, Peter Joseph;** investment consultant and writer; *b* Bath, 24 Aug. 1921; *o* s of Joseph Edgar Bessell and Olive Simons Bessell (*née* Hawkins); *m* 1st, 1942, Joyce Margaret Thomas (*d* 1947), Bath; 2nd, Pauline Colledge (marr. diss. 1978), Saltford, Bristol; one *s* one *d*; 3rd, 1978, Diane, *o* d of Frederick and Doryce Miller, Yardley, Pa, USA. *Educ:* Lynwyd Sch., Bath. Min. of Information Lectr to HM and Allied Forces, 1943–45. Contested (L): Torquay, 1955 and by-election Dec. 1955; Bodmin, 1959; MP (L) Bodmin, 1964–70, retired; Member: Estimates Cttee, 1964–66, 1966–67; Parly Commn to S Vietnam, 1967; Select Cttees on Agriculture, 1967; Vehicle Excise Duty (Allegations), 1969; Procedure, 1964–65. Nat. Pres., Brotherhood Movement, 1967–68. Congregational Lay Preacher, 1939–70. *Publication:* Cover-up (The Jeremy Thorpe Affair), 1981. *Recreations:* music, reading, gardening. *Address:* PO Box 2145, Oceanside, California 92054, USA. *T:* (619) 722–3677.

*Died Nov. 1985.*

**BEST, Rear-Adm. Thomas William,** CB 1966; DL; *b* Hoshangabad, India, 1 Sept. 1915; *s* of late Hon. James William Best, OBE, and Florence Mary Bernarda (*née* Lees); *m* 1942, Brenda Joan, *d* of late F. A. Hellaby, MC, Auckland, New Zealand; two *s* one *d*. *Educ:* Farnborough Sch.; Royal Naval Coll., Dartmouth. Served in NZ Div. of RN (HMS Leander, 1937–41); War of 1939–45 (despatches); Qualified Gunnery Specialist, 1942. Korean War, 1951–52 (despatches); i/c HMS Barrosa, 1952–54; Dep. Dir Naval Ordnance, 1955–58; i/c HMS Ausonia, 1958–60; Capt. Supt, Admiralty Surface Weapons Establishment, 1961–64. ADC to the Queen, 1964; Flag Officer Gibraltar, 1964–66; retd 1967. Governor, Bryanston Sch., 1969–. Chairman: Dorset County Branch NFU, 1976; Dorset Community Council, 1981–84. Member: Royal Bath & West & Southern Counties Soc.; Dorset Naturalists' Trust; Small Industries Cttee for Dorset, CoSIRA, 1973–; West Dorset Beekeepers' Assoc.; Somerset Fruit Growers' Assoc. Dir, Norton Cider Growers' Assoc., 1977–; Governor, Long Ashton Members' Assoc. (formerly Nat. Fruit and Cider Inst.), Long Ashton Res. Station, 1978–. DL Dorset, 1977. *Recreations:* beekeeping, fruit farming. *Address:* Hincknowle, Melplash, Bridport, Dorset. *T:* Netherbury 221. *Club:* Naval and Military. *Died 10 July 1984.*

**BEST-SHAW, Sir John ( James Kenward),** 9th Bt *cr* 1665; Commander (E) RN, retired; *b* 11 June 1895; *s* of Rev. Sir Charles J. M. Shaw, 8th Bt, and Louisa (*d* 1961), *d* of J. W. Bosanquet; *S* father, 1922; assumed the name and arms of Best by Royal Licence, 1956; *m* 1921, Elizabeth Mary Theodora, *e* d of Sir Robert Hughes, 12th Bt; three *s* four *d*. *Educ:* Cheam Sch., Sutton, Surrey; Royal Naval Colls, Osborne and Dartmouth. A lay guardian of the Sanctuary of Our Lady of Walsingham, 1931–78. Served with Royal Navy, Wars of 1914–18 and 1939–45. High Sheriff, Kent, 1961. Pres., Church Union, 1969–71. OStJ. *Heir:* s John Michael Robert Best-Shaw [*b* 28 Sept. 1924; *m* 1960, Jane Gordon, *d* of A. G. Guthrie, Hampton Court House, Farningham, Kent; two *s* one *d* (and *e* s decd)]. *Address:* Boxley Abbey, Sandling, Maidstone, Kent. *T:* Maidstone 52910. *Club:* Naval and Military. *Died 26 Feb. 1984.*

**BESWICK, Baron,** *cr* 1964 (Life Peer); **Frank Beswick,** PC 1968; JP; Chairman, British Aerospace, 1976–80 (Chairman, Organising

Committee, 1975–76); *b* 1912; *m* Dora, *d* of Edward Plumb; one *s* one *d*. Joined RAF, 1940; Transport Command (KCVSA 1944). MP (Lab Co-op.) Uxbridge Div. of Middlesex, 1945–Oct. 1959. PPS to Under-Sec. of State for Air, 1946–49; Parly Sec., Min. of Civil Aviation, 1950–Oct. 1951. UK Govt Observer, Bikini Tests, 1946; Delegate UN General Assembly, 1946. Formerly: Chm., Parly Labour Party Civil Aviation Sub-Cttee; Chm., Co-operative Party Parly Group; a Lord-in-Waiting, 1965; Parly Under-Sec. of State in CO, 1965–67; Captain, Hon. Corps of Gentlemen at Arms, and Govt Chief Whip, House of Lords, 1967–70, Chief Opposition Whip, 1970–74; Minister of State for Industry, and Deputy Leader, House of Lords, 1974–75. Special Adviser to Chm., British Aircraft Corp., 1970–74. Chm. Supervisory Bd, Airbus Industrie, 1978–80. Pres., British Air Line Pilots Assoc., 1978–82 (Vice-Pres., 1965–77). Companion, RAeS, 1978. FRSA 1979. JP Co. of London, 1963. Hon. DSc Cranfield, 1981. *Address:* 27 Margin Drive, SW19.
*Died 17 Aug.* 1987.

**BETHELL, Maj.-Gen. Donald Andrew Douglas Jardine, (Drew);** Warden, Sackville College, since 1981; *b* 6 Feb. 1921; *e s* of D. L. Bethell, Stourbridge, near Birmingham, and L. K. Bethell; *m* 1946, Pamela Mary Woosnam; two *s. Educ:* Sherborne Sch., Dorset. Commnd RA, 1940; Regimental Service, 1940–47; Staff and Regimental appts, 1947–66; CRA, 3rd Div., 1966–68; Dep. Commandant, Staff Coll., 1969–72; Pres., Regular Commissions Bd, 1972–75. Col Comdt, RA, 1978–83. *Recreations:* sailing, fishing, golf, shooting. *Address:* Sackville College, East Grinstead, W Sussex. *T:* East Grinstead 26561; Yacht Acquest. *Club:* Royal Cruising.
*Died 6 Feb.* 1988.

**BETJEMAN, Sir John,** Kt 1969; CBE 1960; CLit 1968; poet and author; Poet Laureate, since 1972; *b* 1906; *s* of late E. E. Betjeman; *m* 1933, Penelope Valentine Hester (author, as Penelope Chetwode, of Two Middle-aged Ladies in Andalusia, 1963, and Kulu, 1972), *d* of Field-Marshal Lord Chetwode, GCB, OM, GCSI; one *s* one *d. Educ:* Marlborough; Oxford. UK Press Attaché, Dublin, 1941–42; Admiralty, 1943. Mem., Royal Commn on Historical Monuments (England), 1970–76. A Governor of Pusey House, Church of England. Hon. Fellow: Keble Coll., Oxford, 1972; Magdalen Coll., Oxford, 1975. Hon. LLD Aberdeen; Hon. DLitt: Oxon, Reading, Birmingham, Exeter, City, Liverpool, Hull, Trinity Coll., Dublin; Hon. ARIBA. *Television:* Time with Betjeman (series), 1983. *Publications: poems:* Mount Zion, 1931; Continual Dew, 1937; Old Lights for New Chancels, 1940; New Bats in Old Belfries, 1945; Selected Poems, 1948 (Heinemann Award); A Few Late Chrysanthemums, 1954 (Foyle Poetry Prize); Poems in the Porch, 1954; Collected Poems, 1958 (Duff Cooper Prize; Foyle Poetry Prize; Queen's Gold Medal for Poetry, 1960); Summoned by Bells (verse autobiography), 1960; Ring of Bells: poems, 1964; High and Low, 1966; A Nip in the Air, 1974; Archie and the Strict Baptists, 1977; Church Poems, 1981; Uncollected Poems, 1982; *non-fiction:* Ghastly Good Taste, 1933, new edn 1971; Shell Guides to Cornwall and Devon; An Oxford University Chest, 1938; Antiquarian Prejudice, 1939; English Cities and Small Towns, 1943; John Piper, 1944; (ed with John Piper): Buckinghamshire Guide, 1948; Berkshire Guide, 1949; Shropshire Guide, 1951; First and Last Loves, 1952; The English Town in the Last 100 Years, 1956; (ed) Guide to English Parish Churches, 1958; (with Basil Clarke) English Churches, 1964; (ed) Pocket Guide to English Parish Churches, 1968; Victorian and Edwardian London, 1969; (with David Vaisey) Victorian and Edwardian Oxford from Old Photographs, 1971; A Pictorial History of English Architecture, 1972; London's Historic Railway Stations, 1972; (contrib.) Westminster Abbey, 1972; (with J. S. Gray) Victorian and Edwardian Brighton from Old Photographs, 1972; West Country Churches, 1973; (with A. L. Rowse) Victorian and Edwardian Cornwall, 1974; Betjeman's Cornwall, 1984; *anthologies:* (ed with late Geoffrey Taylor): An Anthology of Landscape Verse, 1944; English Love Poems, 1957; (ed) Altar and Pew, 1959; A Wealth of Poetry, 1963. *Address:* c/o John Murray Ltd, 50 Albermarle Street, W1X 4BD. *Club:* Beefsteak.
*Died 19 May* 1984.

**BEVAN, Cecil Wilfrid Luscombe, (Bill),** CBE 1965; Principal, University College, Cardiff, 1966–87, retired; Hon. Fellow, since 1982; *b* 2 April 1920; *s* of Benjamin Cecil Bevan and Maud Luscombe; *m* 1st, 1944, Elizabeth Bondfield (*d* 1984), *d* of Henry Dale Bondfield; four *s*; 2nd, 1986, Prof. Beatrice Avalos. *Educ:* University Coll. of Wales, Aberystwyth; University Coll., London. BSc Wales 1940; PhD London 1949; FRSC (FRIC 1957); DSc London 1971. Served Royal Welch Fusiliers and Nigeria Regt, 1940–46 (despatches). Univ. of Exeter, 1949–53; Prof. and Head of Dept of Chemistry, Univ. of Ibadan, 1953–66, Vice Principal and Dep. Vice-Chancellor, 1960–64; Vice-Chancellor, Univ. of Wales, 1973–75 and 1981–83. Member: Tropical Products Inst. Adv. Cttee, 1971–77; Council, University of Cape Coast, Ghana, 1967–74; Welsh Council, 1968–71; Chm., Conciliation Cttee of Wales and SW Race Rel. Bd, 1968–72; Governor Welbeck Coll.; Prof. Associé Univ. de Strasbourg, 1965. Fellow UCL, 1969. Hon. DSc, Univ. of Ibadan, 1973. Officier des Palmes Académiques, France, 1986.

*Publications:* papers, mainly in Jl of Chemical Soc., 1951–. *Recreation:* labouring. *Address:* Flat 7b, The Cathedral Green, Llandaff, Cardiff CF5 2EB; PO Box 241, University of Papua New Guinea, Papua New Guinea. *Clubs:* Royal Commonwealth Society; Cardiff and County (Cardiff); Radyr Golf, Port Moresby Golf.
*Died 19 April* 1989.

**BEVAN, Leonard;** HM Diplomatic Service, retired; *b* 16 Nov. 1926; *s* of Richard (Dick) and Sarah Bevan; *m* 1st, 1953, Muriel Anne Bridger (*d* 1979); 2nd, 1981, Jeanette Elfreda Phillips. *Educ:* Swansea and Gowerton Grammar Schs; UCW, Aberystwyth (BA Hons). RAF, 1948–50. BoT, 1950 (Private Sec. to Parly Sec., 1952–54); UK Trade Comr: Karachi, 1954; Kuala Lumpur, 1957; Principal British Trade Comr and Econ. Adviser to High Comr, Accra, 1959; Nairobi, 1964; Commonwealth Office (later FCO), 1968; Counsellor (Econ. and Commercial), Canberra, 1970; Head, SW Pacific Dept, FCO, 1974; Counsellor (Economic), Brasilia, 1976–79. *Recreations:* bird spotting, clock repairing, flower gardening. *Address:* Tŷ Moryn, Heol Crwys, Trefin, Haverfordwest, Dyfed SA62 5AF. *T:* Croesgoch 490.
*Died 7 Jan.* 1990.

**BEVAN, Percy Archibald Thomas,** CBE 1958; BSc, DEng, FIEE, FIEEE; retired; Director, Engineering, 1954–67, Consultant Engineer, 1967–69, Independent Television Authority (later Independent Broadcasting Authority); *b* 8 Jan. 1909; *s* of late Albert James Bevan, BA, Abertillery, Mon, and Florence Violet Perkins, Worcester; *m* Kathleen Mary, *e d* of late Samuel Hallam and Mary Goodburn. *Educ:* Newport Grammar Sch.; University Coll. and Welsh Coll. of Advanced Technology, Cardiff (now UWIST). Double Diploma Eng. Graduate Apprentice, British Thomson-Houston Company, Rugby, 1930–34; Design Engineer, Studios and Transmitting Stations, BBC, 1934–46; Cambridge Univ., Consultant, Cavendish Laboratory Atomic Energy Cyclotron, 1940–43; involved in RAF airborne radar (night ops), 1941–45; BBC: Senior Television Engineer, Planning and Construction Dept, 1946–50; Chief Planning Engineer, 1950–54. Member: UK Television Adv. Techn. Cttee; Frequency Adv. Cttee, 1955–69; Radio Interference Cttee; UK Rep., Internat. Telecommns Union and Radio Consultative Cttee, 1953–68; Member: UK Space and Radio Research Adv. Cttee, 1960–68; European Broadcasting Union Techn. Cttee; Eurovision and Colour Television Cttees, 1955–68; Mem. of Council IEE and Chm. Electronics Bd, 1967–68; Chm., Prof. Group Sound and Television Broadcasting, 1962–66. Awarded IEE Radio Section Premium, 1947, 1949, Duddell Premium, 1951; Electronics Bd Premium, 1963. Fellow, Royal Television Soc., 1957; Hon. Fellow, British Kinematograph and Television Soc., 1967. *Publications:* many technical and scientific papers in the radio and television broadcasting field. *Recreations:* photography, country life, music, exploring France. *Address:* 8 The Gardens, Fittleworth, Pulborough, West Sussex RH20 1HT. *T:* Fittleworth 380.
*Died 29 Sept.* 1981.

**BEVERLEY, Vice-Adm. Sir (William) York (La Roche),** KBE 1952 (CBE 1947); CB 1949; *b* 14 Dec. 1895; *s* of Major W. H. Beverley; *m* 1931, Maria Teresa Matilde (*d* 1957), *d* of Enrico Palazio, Santa-Margherita-Ligure, Italy; one *s* one *d* (and one *s* decd). *Educ:* Royal Naval Colls, Osborne and Dartmouth. Served throughout European War, 1914–18, and War of 1939–45; ADC to the King, 1947–48; Admiral Supt, Portsmouth, 1949–51; Vice-Adm., 1950; Dir of Dockyards, 1951–54, retired Dec. 1954. *Address:* c/o Grindlays Bank Ltd, 13 St James's Square, SW1Y 4LF.
*Died 19 Nov.* 1982.

**BIBBY, Major Sir (Arthur) Harold,** 1st Bt *cr* 1959; Kt 1956; DSO 1917; DL; LLD (Hon.) Liverpool; President, Bibby Line Ltd; *b* 18 Feb. 1889; *s* of late Arthur Wilson Bibby; *m* 1920, Marjorie (*d* 1985), *d* of late Charles J. Williamson and late The Lady Royden; one *s* three *d* (and one *s* decd). *Educ:* Rugby. Served in RFA (TF), 1908–19; in France and Flanders, 1915–18 (despatches twice, DSO awarded on field of Cambrai). Senior Partner, Bibby Bros & Co., Shipowners and Bankers, 1935–73; Chm., Bibby Line Ltd, 1935–69, Pres., 1969; Director: Sea Insurance Co. Ltd, 1922–68 (Chm., 1930–56); Liverpool & London Steamship Protection & Indemnity Association, 1921–68; LNER, 1924–47; Martins Bank Ltd, 1929–67 (Chm., 1947–62); Suez Canal Co., 1939–57; Member: Mersey Docks & Harbour Board, 1931–65; Governing Body of Rugby Sch., 1932–67; Chairman: Liverpool Steam Ship Owners' Association, 1927 and 1958 (Centenary Year); Employers' Association of Port of Liverpool, 1938–47; Vice-Chm., National Assoc. of Port Employers, 1941–47; Jt Vice-Chm., General Council of British Shipping, 1958–59; President: Training Ship Indefatigable (Chm., 1931–60); Liverpool Sailors' Home (Chm., 1921–51); Liverpool Conservative Assoc., 1959–66; Northwich Conservative Association, 1960–74. DL, Chester, 1937; High Sheriff of Cheshire, 1934–35. Hon. Freeman, City of Liverpool, 1970. *Heir: s* Derek James Bibby, MC. *Address:* Tilstone Lodge, Tarporley, Cheshire CW6 9HT.
*Died 7 March* 1986.

**BIBBY, Dr Cyril;** *b* 1914; *s* of William and Elizabeth Jane Bibby, Liverpool; *m* 1936, Frances (Florence Mabel) Hirst, Mddx; two *s*

two d. Educ: Liverpool Collegiate Sch.; Queens' Coll., Cambridge. Open Major Scholar in natural sciences, 1932; Coll. Prizeman, 1933; Icelandic expedn, 1934; BACantab, 1935. Physics and Chemistry Master, Oulton Sch., Liverpool, 1935–38; Scientific research, Univ. of Liverpool, 1935–40; MACantab, 1939; Sen. Biology Master, Chesterfield Grammar Sch., 1938–40; MSc Liverpool, 1940. Educn Officer to Brit. Social Hygiene Council and then Central Council for Health Educn, 1941–46; Tutor in Biol. (becoming Co-ordinator of Sciences and Sec. to Academic Bd), Coll. of S Mark and S John, London, 1946–59; educational and other research, 1947–59; Principal, Kingston upon Hull Coll. of Educn, 1959–76; Pro-Dir, Hull Coll. of Higher Educn, 1976–78. Visiting Prof., Univ. of Illinois, 1950; PhD London, 1955; Silver Medal of RSA, 1956. Visiting Lecturer at several Univs in USA (also investigatory visits for US Nat. Science Foundn, 1962). Delegate to many internat. congresses, etc., 1947–64. At various periods, Mem. Executive of: Internat. Union of Family Organisations; Fraternité Mondiale; Assoc. of Teachers in Colls and Depts of Educn; Council of Christians and Jews; Eugenics Soc., Nat. Foundn for Educl Research; Soc. for Research into Higher Educn; School Broadcasting Council of UK, etc. Many political activities. FLS, 1942; FRSA, 1954; Hon. Fellow, Hull Coll. of Higher Educn, 1982. *Publications:* Evolution of Man and His Culture, 1938; Heredity, Eugenics and Social Progress, 1939; Experimental Human Biology, 1942; Simple Experiments in Biology, 1943; Sex Education, 1944; How Life is Handed On, 1946; Healthy and Happy, 1948; Story of Birth, 1949; Healthy Day, 1949; Active Human Biology, 1950; Health Education, 1951; Healthy People, 1954; Human Body, 1955; Education in Racial and Intergroup Relations, 1957; T. H. Huxley, 1959; Race, Prejudice and Education, 1959; The First Fifty Years, 1964; Essence of T. H. Huxley, 1968; Biology of Mankind, 1968; T. H. Huxley on Education, 1971; Scientist Extraordinary, 1972; The Art of the Limerick, 1978; Verse Offerings, 1986; papers in various scientific, health, educnl, political, sociological and gen. lit. jls. *Recreations:* reading, writing, walking, sun-bathing, film, theatre, music, travel. *Address:* 11 Beech Grove, Beverley Road, Hull.
*Died 20 June* 1987.

**BIBBY, Major Sir Harold;** *see* Bibby, Major Sir A. H.

**BIBBY, Samuel Leslie,** CBE 1947 (OBE 1945); DL; *b* 19 Jan. 1897; *s* of Samuel Gawith Bibby, Sutton, Surrey; *m* 1923, Eva Margaret Wood, *d* of Dr G. Benington Wood, Sandown, IoW; one *s* one *d* (and one *s* decd). *Educ:* Malvern. Served European War, 1915–19, Capt. RA(TA) (despatches). Mem., London Stock Exchange, 1919–62. Col TA, 1943; Comd 6th (Leatherhead) Bn Surrey Home Guard, 1940–43; Comdt Surrey Army Cadet Force, 1943–49; Chm. Army Cadet Force Sports Council, 1940–49; Military Mem. Surrey T&AFA, 1940–49. DL 1955; High Sheriff of Surrey, 1959. *Address:* Foresters, Deans Lane, Walton-on-the-Hill, Tadworth, Surrey. *T:* Tadworth 2280. *Clubs:* Gresham, MCC. *Died* 2 *May* 1985.

**BIDAULT, Georges;** *b* Moulins, 5 Oct. 1899; *s* of Georges Bidault and Augustine Traverse; *m* 1945, Suzanne Borel. *Educ:* Collège des jésuites de Bollengo; Faculté des Lettres, Paris. Before war of 1939–45 was a professor of history and edited L'Aube, the journal of the Christian Democrats; served in the ranks, was taken prisoner but freed after 12 months; became chm. of the resistance council inside France, 1943; Minister for Foreign Affairs in Provisional Govts of 1944 and 1945; President of Provisional Govt, May 1945; Deputy from the Loire, 1945, re-elected 1946, 1951, 1956, 1958; Premier and Foreign Minister, France, 1946; Minister of Foreign Affairs, 1947–48; Pres. of the Council, 1950 and 1951, Vice-Pres., 1951–52 and 1952; Minister of National Defence, 1951–52; Minister of Foreign Affairs, Jan.–July 1954; Premier, April 1958; Pres., Provisional Bureau of Rassemblement pour L'Algérie française, Oct. 1959; charged with plot against security of the State, July 1962; in Brazil, March 1963–July 1967, Belgium 1967–68; returned to France, June 1968. Delegate to Council of Europe, 1949. Grand' Croix de la Légion d'honneur; Compagnon de la Libération. *Publications:* L'Algérie, l'oiseau aux ailes coupées, 1958; D'une Résistance à l'autre, 1965 (Resistance: the political autobiography of Georges Bidault, 1967); Le Point, 1968. *Address:* 21 rue du Colonel Moll, 75017 Paris, France. *Died 26 Jan.* 1983.

**BIDDULPH, 4th Baron** *cr* 1903; **Robert Michael Christian Biddulph;** *b* 6 Jan. 1931; *s* of 3rd Baron Biddulph and Lady Amy Louise Agar (*d* 1983), *d* of 4th Earl of Normanton; *S* father, 1972; *m* 1958, Lady Mary Maitland, *d* of Viscount Maitland (killed in action, 1943) and *g d* of 15th Earl of Lauderdale; two *s* one *d*. *Educ:* Canford; RMA, Sandhurst. Lt 16/5 The Queen's Royal Lancers, retd. *Recreations:* shooting, fishing. *Heir:* *s* Hon. Anthony Nicholas Colin Maitland Biddulph, *b* 8 April 1959. *Address:* Makerstoun, Kelso, Roxburghshire, Scotland. *Club:* New (Edinburgh).
*Died 3 Nov.* 1988.

**BIDDULPH, Sir Stuart (Royden),** 10th Bt *cr* 1664; retired grazier; *b* 24 June 1908; *s* of Sir Francis Henry Biddulph, 9th Bt, and Janet (*d* 1956), *d* of Walter Bain Hannah, Brisbane; *S* father, 1980; *m* 1939,

Muriel Margaret, 3rd *d* of Angus Harkness, Hamley Bridge, S Australia; one *s* two *d*. *Educ:* Brisbane Grammar School. *Recreation:* gliding. *Heir:* *s* Ian D'Olier Biddulph [*b* 28 Feb. 1940; *m* 1967, Margaret Eleanor, *o d* of late John Gablonski; one *s* two *d*]. *Address:* 119 Watson Street, Charleville, Queensland 4470, Australia.
*Died 8 July* 1986.

**BIERBACH, Martin;** Ambassador of the German Democratic Republic to the Court of St James's, since 1980; *b* 30 Nov. 1926; *m* 1953, Helene Lützel; one *s* one *d*. *Educ:* secondary school; studied foreign politics at university (Diploma in Political Sciences). Entered diplomatic service; leading functions in Min. of Foreign Affairs, German Democratic Republic, 1953–57; Counsellor, GDR Embassy, Peking, People's Republic of China, 1957–59; Consul General, GDR Embassy, Cairo, Arab Republic of Egypt, 1959–62; Head of Near and Middle East Dept, Min. of Foreign Affairs, 1962–66; Ambassador of GDR: Peking, 1966–68; Cairo, 1969–73; Head of South and South East Asia Dept, Min. of Foreign Affairs, 1973–80. Holder of several state awards. *Recreations:* sport, reading. *Address:* Brent Cross House, 124 The Broadway, NW9. *T:* 01–202 3847/9. *Died 9 April* 1984.

**BIERER, Joshua,** MD, DiplIPsychol, DRerPol; FRCPsych; Medical Director, Institute of Social Psychiatry, 1946–82, retired; Consultant Psychiatrist, Runwell Hospital, 1948–67; Founder, 1946, and Medical Director, Marlborough Day-Hospital, 1946–67; Founder, International Association of Social Psychiatry; Co-Founder, International Association of Group Psychotherapy; Editor-in-Chief, International Journal of Social Psychiatry; *b* 1 July 1901; *s* of Dr Josef Bierer, X-Ray specialist; *m* Aliska Frank; *m* 1967, Gilian Moira; one *s* two *d*; *m* Shahin. *Educ:* Vienna Univ. Training in Individual Psychology by Prof. Alfred Adler and Dr A. Neuer (Vienna), 1926–28; Training-Analysis by Dr A. Neuer; private practice as Psychotherapist, 1927–; Lectr, Teaching Inst. of Individual Psychology, Berlin, 1928–29; Research: at Inst. of Physiology, Vienna Univ., 1933; in Psychotherapy and Psychiatry at Mental Hosp., Vienna Univ., 1934–36; at Runwell Hosp., Essex, 1938–40. Psychotherapist, Southend Gen. Hosp. and East Ham Memorial Hosp., 1939–43; Clinical Asst, Guy's Hosp. 1942–43; Visiting Psychotherapist, Runwell Mental Hosp., 1942–43 and 1945–47. Served as Specialist Psychiatrist, Major RAMC, 1944–46. Originated idea of Self-Governed Therapeutic Social Clubs, Day Hosps, Night and Week-end Hosps, Self governed Hostels, Therapeutic Communities, the Total Separation Treatment in Marriage Guidance and a new and revolutionary method in education. Co-Founder, Kibbutz Mishmar Haemek, Israel, 1980–. *Publications:* (jt) Innovation in Social Psychiatry; The Day-Hospital, 1951; (ed) Therapeutic Social Clubs; pioneer research work in problems of social psychiatry, social psychotherapy, group psychotherapy, psychotherapy of psychotics in mental hosps and in out-patient depts in Jl of Mental Science, Lancet, Brit. Med. Jl, Internat. Jl Soc. Psych., etc. *Recreations:* golf, swimming, tennis, table tennis, chess, bridge. *Address:* 140 Harley Street, W1 1AM. *T:* 01–935 1078/2440. *Club:* Garrick. *Died 22 Nov.* 1984.

**BIGG, Wilfred Joseph,** CMG 1948; *b* 20 July 1897; 2nd *s* of late Joseph Henry Bigg; *m* 1925, Ivy Lillian Daniel (*d* 1973); three *d*. *Educ:* Bournemouth Sch. Entered GPO 1912. Served European War, 1914–19. Entered Colonial Office, 1919; Private Sec. to Permanent Under Sec., Dominions Office, 1930–31; returned to Colonial Office, June 1931; Asst Sec., 1943; retired 1957. Member: Commonwealth Shipping Cttee, 1952–57; Bd of Governors, Coll. of Aeronautics, 1955–58; Commonwealth Telecommunications Board, 1955–62. *Recreations:* gardening, motoring. *Address:* Headley, 35 Manwell Road, Swanage, Dorset. *T:* Swanage 2603.
*Died 28 July* 1983.

**BIGGS, Sir Lionel (William),** Kt 1964; *b* 28 May 1906; *s* of William Henry Moore Biggs and Lilian (*née* Bush); *m* 1934, Doris Rose, *d* of late William Davies; one *s*. *Educ:* Manchester Gram. Sch. Served Royal Air Force, 1940–45 (despatches). Lord Mayor of Manchester, 1961–62. JP Manchester 1949. Chm., Aerodrome Owners' Assoc. of GB, 1955. *Recreations:* gardening, swimming. *Address:* Glen Carrig, 151 Richmond Park Road, Bournemouth, Dorset.
*Died 16 Nov.* 1985.

**BIGGS-DAVISON, Sir John (Alec),** Kt 1981; MP (C) Epping Forest, since 1974 (Chigwell, 1955–74 (as Ind C, 1957–58)); *b* 7 June 1918; *s* of late Major John Norman Biggs-Davison, RGA, retd; *m* 1948, Pamela Mary, 2nd *d* of late Ralph Hodder-Williams, MC; two *s* four *d*. *Educ:* Clifton (scholar); Magdalen Coll., Oxford (exhibitioner, MA). Royal Marines, 1939, Lieut 1940; served in RM Brigade and RM Division. Indian Civil Service: Asst Comr, 1942; Forward Liaison Officer, Cox's Bazar, 1943–44; Sub-Divisional Officer, Pindi Gheb, 1946; Political Asst and Comdt, Border Military Police, subsequently Dep. Comr, Dera Ghazi Khan, during and after transfer of Power to Dominion of Pakistan, 1947; retired from Pakistan Administrative Service, 1948. Conservative Research Dept, 1950–55; Sec., Brit. Conservative Delegn to Council of

Europe, 1952, 1953. Contested (C) Coventry South, 1951. Co-founder Pakistan Soc., 1951. Indep. Observer of Malta Referendum, 1956. Mem. Parly Delegations: West Africa, 1956; Guernsey, 1961; Austria, 1964; France, 1965; Canada (Inter-Parly Union Conf.), 1965; Malawi, 1968; Tunisia, Gibraltar, 1969; Portugal, 1973; Cyprus, 1979; Canada, 1984. Vice-Pres., Franco-British Parly Relations Cttee; Chairman: British-Pakistan Parly Gp; Cons. Parly NI Cttee; Vice-Chm., Cons. Parly Foreign and Commonwealth Affairs Cttee. An Opposition Front Bench spokesman on NI, 1976–78. Mem., Parly Assembly, Council of Europe and WEU, 1984–86. Mem. Exec., Cons. and Unionist Members (1922) Cttee. Governor, Clifton Coll., 1972. Hilal-I-Quaid-I-Azam award, Govt of Pakistan, 1988 (posthumous). *Publications:* George Wyndham, 1951; Tory Lives, 1952; The Uncertain Ally, 1957; The Walls of Europe, 1962; Portuguese Guinea: Nailing a Lie, 1970; Africa: Hope Deferred, 1972; The Hand is Red, 1974; Rock Firm for the Union, 1979; The Cross of St Patrick, 1985; contribs to many periodicals. *Recreations:* reading, riding, tennis, walking (Gold Medal London-Brighton Pacesetters' Walk, 1963), took part in parliamentary parachute jump, 1980. *Address:* House of Commons, SW1. *Clubs:* Special Forces, Oxford Union Society.
*Died 17 Sept. 1988.*

**BIGLAND, Ernest Frank,** MBE (mil.) 1945; TD 1946; Chairman, London Trust, 1984; *b* 7 Dec. 1913; *s* of Robert Taylor Bigland and Helen Inglis Scott Bigland (*née* Hannay); *m* 1936, Mary Dalzell; two *s* one *d*. *Educ:* St Edward's Sch., Oxford. FCII. Joined Guardian Assurance Co. Ltd, 1930. Served Royal Artillery, 1939–45 (MBE, despatches); Lt-Col. Guardian Assurance Co. Ltd: Company Sec., 1950; Asst Gen. Manager, 1952; Dep. Gen. Manager, 1957; Gen. Man., 1960; Gp Gen. Man., 1964; Man. Dir, 1966–68; Guardian Royal Exchange Assurance: Man. Dir, 1968–78; Vice-Chm., 1973–78; a Dep. Chm., 1978–83. *Recreations:* shooting, fishing. *Address:* Lucas Green Manor, Lucas Green Road, West End, Woking, Surrey GU24 9LY. *T:* Brookwood 2234. *Clubs:* Brooks's; Leander.
*Died 14 Jan. 1985.*

**BIKANER, Maharaja of; Dr Karni Singhji Bahadur;** *b* 21 April 1924; *e s* of late Lt-Gen. HH Maharaja Sri Sadul Singhji Bahadur of Bikaner, GCSI, GCIE, CVO; *S* father as Maharaja of Bikaner, 1950; *m* 1944, Princess Sushila Kumari, *d* of Maharawal Shri Sir Lakshman Singh Bahadur of Dungapur, *qv*; one *s* two *d*. *Educ:* St Stephen's Coll., Delhi; St Xavier's Coll., Bombay. BA (Hons) (History and Politics); PhD (thesis) Bombay Univ., 1964. Visited Middle East War Front in Nov. 1941 with his grandfather, Maharaja Sri Ganga Singhji Bahadur. Insignia Grand Commander: Order of Vikram Star (Bikaner), Order of Sadul Star (Bikaner), Order of Star of Honour (Bikaner); Africa Star; War Medal; India Service Medal; Arjun Award for Shooting, 1961. Has travelled extensively in Europe, Egypt, USA, Mexico, Honolulu and Far East, etc. Elected to House of People (Parliament of India) as an Independent, 1952; re-elected for 2nd and 3rd terms; elected 4th time, 1967, with largest margin (193,816) in the country; elected 5th time, 1971; left Parliament, 1977; served on various consultative cttees of different ministries. Member: Asiatic Soc. of India; Bombay Natural History Soc. *Publications:* The Relations of the House of Bikaner with the Central Powers 1465–1949, 1974; From Rome to Moscow, 1982 (memoirs). *Recreations:* tennis; shooting (National Champion in clay pigeon traps and skeet for many years; rep. India, clay pigeon shooting, Olympic Games: Rome, 1960, Pre-Olympics, Tokyo, 1963, Tokyo, 1964 (Captain), Mexico, 1968, Munich, 1972, Moscow, 1980; World Shooting Championships: Oslo, 1961; Cairo (Captain), 1962 (2nd in world after tie for 1st place); Wiesbaden, 1966 (Captain); Bologna, 1967; San Sebastian, Spain, 1969; Asian Shooting Championships: Tokyo, 1967; Seoul, 1971 (Captain, Gold Medal); won Clay Pigeon Welsh Grand Prix, 1981, 1984, N Wales Cup, 1981 and NW England Cup, 1981, 1984; Asian Games, Tehran, 1974 (Silver Medal); Kuala Lumpur 1975 (Silver Medal; mem. Indian team which won Team Clay Pigeon Silver Medal, Delhi Asiad, 1982); golf; flying (qualified for private pilot's licence); cricket; mechanics; photography; oil painting. *Address:* Lallgargh Palace, Bikaner 334001, Rajasthan, India. *Clubs:* Clay Pigeon Shooting Assoc., Essex (Hon. Life Vice-Pres.); Willingdon Sports, Cricket Club of India, Bombay Flying, Bombay Presidency Golf, Western India Automobile Association (Bombay); Delhi Golf (Delhi); National Sports Club of India (in all 4 cities).
*Died 4 Sept. 1988.*

**BILAINKIN, George;** diplomatic correspondent; author; lecturer; *b* 12 Feb. 1903; *m* 1940, Dr Lilian Rivlin (marr. diss., 1949); one *d*. *Educ:* Haberdashers' Aske's Sch., NW; Athenée Royal, Belgium. Joint News Ed., Jamaica Daily Gleaner, 1924–25; Special Writer, Leicester Mail, 1925–27; Sub-Ed., Press Association, 1927–29; Ed., Straits Daily Echo, Penang, 1929–30, and Times Correspondent in N Malaya; Asst Literary Ed., Daily Mail, 1934–36; Editorial Staff, News-Chronicle, 1936–38; Diplomatic Correspondent, Allied Newspapers, 1938–40; Special Correspondent, Russia, 1942, for The Star, London, and American newspapers. Special mission to Paris, Berlin, Prague, and Belgrade for Daily Mail, 1945. Delivered 120 lectures in British Univs, clubs, prisons, schools, on Europe, early in 1946. Since then has visited various personalities and countries every year, from Petsamo to Tierra del Fuego. Contributed since 1920 to Encyclopædia Britannica and leading newspapers and reviews. Hon. Mem., Mark Twain Soc. (USA), 1976. *Publications:* Lim Seng Hooi, 1930; Hail Penang, 1932; Within Two Years, 1934; Front Page News-Once, 1937; Changing Opinions, 1938; Poland's Destiny, 1939; Diary of a Diplomatic Correspondent, 1942; Maisky (a biography), 1944; Second Diary of a Diplomatic Correspondent, 1947; Four Weeks in Yugoslavia, 1948; Tito (a biography), 1949; Cairo to Riyadh Diary, 1950; Destination Tokyo, 1965; Four Guilty Britons, 1972; Joseph Kennedy's Fateful Embassy, 1972. *Recreations:* listening; playing with chow-chow and bull-terrier puppies; major diplomatic receptions; reforming the world. Aversions: cats, chain-smokers, solicitors, interrupters, trains. *Club:* Royal Commonwealth Society.
*Died 16 March 1981.*

**BILL, Commander Robert,** DSO 1940; FRICS; FRGS; RN, retired 1955; Consultant, retired 1975; *b* 1 April 1910; *s* of late R. W. Bill, Penn, Staffs; *m* 1st, 1933, Peggy Shaw (marr. diss. 1952), *d* of late Comdr A. R. S. Warden, AM, RN (retd), Paignton, Devon; 2nd, 1952, Wendy Jean (*d* 1962), *d* of late C. P. Booth, Hampstead, NW2; one *s* one *d*; 3rd, 1965, Mrs Nancy Elizabeth Johnson (*d* 1973), *d* of late Major Arthur Edward Phillips, DSO, MFH, Mompesson House, Salisbury; 4th, 1975, Gillian Ruth, 2nd *d* of late Dr Geoffrey Clarke, and *g d* of late Sir William Clarke of Chatteris. *Educ:* RNC, Dartmouth and Greenwich. Specialised in Hydrographic Survey, 1931, and in Electronic Distance Measurement, 1956; Special Director, Vickers Instruments Ltd, 1956–65; Dir and Man. Dir, Tellurometer (UK) Ltd, 1960–66. Lectures and papers on survey by trilateration, UK and Europe. Mem., Chichester DC, 1982–85. Manby Premium, ICE, 1962. *Address:* 2 Bourne Way, Midhurst GU29 9HZ. *T:* Midhurst 4682.
*Died 7 Oct. 1987.*

**BILLAM, John Bertram Hardy,** CB 1979; DFC 1944; Legal Adviser and Deputy Secretary, 1976–82, part-time Assessor, 1982–85, Department of Employment; *b* 20 Oct. 1920; *s* of late John Wilfred Ambrose Billam and Bertha; *m* 1944, Mary (*née* Armitage); one *s* one *d*. *Educ:* Merchant Taylors'; King's Coll., London (LLB 1947). RAF, 1941–46 (Flt-Lt). Called to Bar, Gray's Inn, 1947; Legal Asst, Min. of Labour, 1948; Asst Solicitor, 1967. *Publication:* contrib. Halsbury's Laws of England, 3rd edn (Trade and Labour), 1962. *Club:* Royal Air Force.
*Died 7 July 1986.*

**BILLINGTON, Prof. Ray Allen;** Senior Research Associate, Huntington Library, San Marino, California, since 1963; *b* Bay City, Michigan, USA, 28 Sept. 1903; *s* of Cecil Billington and Nina Allen Billington; *m* 1928, Mabel Ruth Crotty; one *s* one *d*. *Educ:* University of Wisconsin (PhB); University of Michigan (MA); Harvard University (PhD). Instructor and Asst Prof. of History, Clark Univ., Worcester, Mass, 1931–37; Asst Prof., Associate Prof., Prof., Smith Coll., Northampton, Mass, 1937–44; William Smith Mason Prof. of History, Northwestern Univ., 1944–63. Visiting Professor: Western Reserve Univ., 1939; Ohio State Univ., 1942; Harvard Univ., 1948. Dir, Massachusetts Federal Writers' Project, 1936–37; Guggenheim Memorial Fellow, 1943–44; History Editor, The Dryden Press, 1949–56; History Editor, Rinehart & Co., 1956–60; Board of Trustees: The Newberry Library, 1952–63; Occidental Coll., 1971–; Dir., Social Science Research Council, 1952. Harold Vyvyan Harmsworth Prof. of American History, Oxford Univ., 1953–54. Hon. Consultant, Library of Congress, 1974–77. Hon. MA Oxford, 1953; Hon. LittD: Bowling Green Univ., 1958; Redlands Univ., 1965; Adrian Coll., 1979; Hon. LLD: Park Coll., 1961; Occidental Coll., 1969; Univ. of Toledo, 1970; Hon. LHD: Northwestern Univ., 1971; Clark Univ., 1974. *Publications:* The Protestant Crusade, 1938 (reissued 1953); The United States, American Democracy in World Perspective, 1947; Westward Expansion, 1949 (4th edn 1974); The Making of American Democracy, 1950; American History after 1865, 1950; American History before 1877, 1951; The Journal of Charlotte L. Forten, 1953; The Far Western Frontier, 1830–1860, 1956; The Westward Movement in the United States, 1959; Frontier and Section, 1961; The Historian's Contribution to Anglo-American Misunderstanding, 1966; The Frontier Thesis, 1966; America's Frontier Heritage, 1966; America's Frontier Story, 1969; Dear Lady, 1970; Genesis of the Frontier Thesis, 1971; Frederick Jackson Turner, 1973 (Bancroft Prize); People of the Plains and Mountains, 1973; Allan Nevins on History, 1975; America's Frontier Culture, 1977; Westward to the Pacific, 1979; Land of Savagery, Land of Promise, 1980; contribs to historical jls. *Address:* 2375 Lombardy Road, San Marino, Calif, USA. *Clubs:* Wayfarers (Chicago); Westerners, Zamorano (Los Angeles); Athenæum, Valley Hunt (Pasadena).
*Died 7 March 1981.*

**BILNEY, Air Vice-Marshal Christopher Neil Hope,** CB 1949; CBE 1946 (OBE 1940); RAF, retired; *b* 26 Oct. 1898; *s* of late William A. and late Maud H. Bilney, Fir Grange, Weybridge, Surrey; *m* 1926, Nellie G. Perren (*d* 1983); two *d*. *Educ:* Tonbridge Sch. Joined

RNAS, 1917; commissioned 1917; served European War, 1914–18, N Sea and Middle East (despatches); Flt-Lieut RAF, 1926; India, 1925–30 (despatches); Sqdn Leader, 1935, serving at Air Ministry; Wing Comdr, 1939; served War of 1939–45: Boscombe Down, 1939; MAP, 1940–41; Group Capt, 1941; Air Cdre, Vice-Pres. Ordnance Board, 1942; HQ Bomber Comd as Comd Armament Officer, 1944 (despatches); AOC No. 25 Group, 1945 (CBE); Air Ministry, Dir Technical Training, 1947–49 (CB); Air Officer i/c Administration, HQ Maintenance Comd, 1949–51; Dir-Gen. of Technical Services (1), Air Ministry, 1951–52; Pres. Ordnance Board, Ministry of Supply, 1953–54; retd 1954. Took up scouting: District Comr, Andover, 1954; County Comr, Hampshire, 1960–67; awarded Silver Acorn for good service by Chief Scout. *Recreations:* shooting, gardening. *Address:* The Winton Nursing Home, Nether Wallop, near Stockbridge, Hants. *Died 3 July* 1988.

**BILTON, Percy;** Chairman, Percy Bilton Ltd, London, W5, and other companies; *b* 28 Nov. 1896; *s* of Christopher G. Bilton, Ormskirk, Lancs, and Hannah Dunlop, Edinburgh; three *s* two *d*. Founder: Vigzol Oil Co. Ltd, 1919; Percy Bilton Ltd, 1927; and various other property companies. Past Master, Worshipful Co. of Fan Makers, 1959. *Recreations:* yachting, racing, golf, farming (pedigree Jerseys at 5000 acre farm, De Hoek, CP). *Address:* Bilton Towers, W1. *Clubs:* Royal Thames Yacht; Civil Service (Cape Town), etc.
*Died 3 Jan.* 1983.

**BINCHY, Daniel A.;** Senior Professor, Dublin Institute for Advanced Studies, 1950–75; *b* 3 June 1900. *Educ:* Clongowes Wood Coll.; University Coll., Dublin; Munich, Berlin, Paris and The Hague. MA (NUI and Oxford); Dr Phil (Munich). Prof. of Jurisprudence and Legal History, University Coll., Dublin, 1925–45; Senior Research Fellow, Corpus Christi Coll., Oxford, 1945–50, Hon. Fellow, 1971. Envoy Extraordinary and Minister Plenipotentiary for the Irish Free State to Germany, 1929–32. Mem. Council, Royal Irish Academy, 1926, Vice-Pres., 1945. Rhys Lectr, British Academy, 1943; Lowell Lectr, Boston, 1954; Visiting Prof. of Celtic, Harvard Univ., 1962–63; Gregynog Lectr, Univ. of Wales, 1966; O'Donnell Lectr, Oxford, 1967–68. DLitt (*hc*): Dublin, 1956; Wales, 1963; Belfast, 1973; NUI, 1973; DèsL (*hc*) Rennes, 1971. Corresp. Mem., Norwegian Instituttet for Sammenlignende Kulturforsking, 1960; For. Mem., Amer. Acad. of Arts and Sciences, 1962; Corresp. Fellow, British Acad., 1976. *Publications:* Church and State in Fascist Italy, 1941, repr. 1970; Crith gablach, An Early Irish Legal Tract, 1940, repr. 1970; Celtic and Anglo-Saxon Kingship, 1970; Corpus Juris Hibernici, 6 vols., 1979; papers on Old Irish law; various articles in Irish, English, and German reviews. *Address:* Lisnagree, Castleknock, Co. Dublin. *Club:* United Service (Dublin). *Died 4 May* 1989.

**BINGHAM, James;** Chairman, Greater Manchester County Council, 1980–81 (Member, 1974–81); *b* 29 June 1916; *s* of James and Beatrice Bingham; *m* 1940, Jessie Noden. *Educ:* Manchester Central Grammar Sch.; Alsager Teacher Trng Coll.; Manchester Univ. (BSc (Hons) Geology, 1983). Insurance agent, 1938–39. Served War: RA from 1940; commnd 1943; in Eighth Army in N Africa, Italy, Austria; attained rank of Captain. Teacher in local schools, 1946–52; Headmaster: Eccles Parish Sch., 1952–59; St Paul's C of E Sch., Walkden, 1959–78, retired. Worsley UDC: Mem., 1962, 1965–73; last Chm., 1973–74; Chm., Recreation and Arts Cttee, GMC, 1977–80, and mem. other cttees. Member: NW Arts; Royal Exchange Theatre Trust; Hallé Concerts Soc. Cttee; NW Tourist Bd. *Recreations:* geology, keen golfer, cutting and polishing stones, fell walking. *Address:* 30 Ryecroft Lane, Worsley, Manchester M28 4PN. *T:* 061–794 3885.
*Died 15 Oct.* 1990.

**BINGHAM, John;** *see* Clanmorris, 7th Baron.

**BINGHAM, Robert Porter,** CMG 1956; Malayan Civil Service, retired; *b* 3 Jan. 1903; *s* of late Robert William Bingham, Dungannon, Co. Tyrone; *m* 1936, Elizabeth Walker, *d* of late Vincent Andrews Acheson, Castlecaulfield, Co. Tyrone; one *s* one *d*. *Educ:* Royal School, Dungannon; Trinity Coll., Dublin. Entered Malayan Civil Service, 1926; in China, studying Chinese, 1926–28; Protector of Chinese, various parts of Malaya, 1928–41; interned, Singapore, 1942–45; Comr for Labour, Singapore, 1946–50; Sec. for Chinese Affairs, Federation of Malaya, 1950–51; Resident Commissioner, Penang, 1951–57. *Died 29 May* 1982.

**BINNIE, Alfred Maurice,** FRS 1960; FEng 1976; Fellow of Trinity College (1944) and University Reader Emeritus in Engineering, Cambridge; *b* 6 Feb. 1901; *s* of late David Carr Binnie. *Educ:* Weymouth Coll.; Queens' Coll., Cambridge. Jun. Research Engineer, Bridge Stress Cttee, 1923–25; Demonstrator and Lectr, Engrg Lab., Oxford, 1925–44; Rhodes Travelling Fellow, 1932–33; Lectr, Mech. Coll., Oxford, 1933–44; Univ. Lectr, 1944–54, Reader in Engrg, 1954–68, Engrg Lab., Cambridge; Sen. Research Fellow, California Inst. of Technology, 1951–52; Scott Visiting Fellow, Ormond Coll., Univ. of Melbourne, 1966; Vis. Scholar, Univ. of California, Berkeley, 1967–68. FIMechE 1937; FICE 1947.

*Publications:* articles in scientific and engrg jls. *Recreation:* mountaineering. *Address:* Trinity College, Cambridge CB2 1TQ. *T:* 358201. *Club:* Alpine. *Died 31 Dec.* 1986.

**BINNIE, Geoffrey Morse,** FRS 1975; FEng 1976; Consultant to Binnie & Partners, 1973–83; *b* 13 Nov. 1908; *s* of William Eames Binnie and Ethel Morse; *m* 1st, 1932, Yanka Paryczko (*d* 1964); one *s* one *d*; 2nd, 1964, Elspeth Maud Cicely Thompson (*d* 1987). *Educ:* Charterhouse; Trinity Hall, Cambridge (MA); Zurich Univ. FICE, FIWE, FASCE, FGS. Served War of 1939–45, RE (Major). Asst Engr, Gorge Dam, Hong Kong, 1933–37; Chief Asst, Eye Brook Reservoir, Northants, 1937–39; Partner, Binnie & Partners, 1939, resumed practice, 1945; responsible for design and supervision of construction of several water supplies in UK; Sen. Partner 1956–72, resp. for design and supervision of constr. of major projects abroad incl. Dokan dam, Iraq, completed 1960 and Mangla project, W Pakistan, compl. 1970. Chm., Panel advising on design and constr. of 2500 MW Peace River Hydro-electric project, BC, 1962–68. Chief Technical Supervisor, Poechos Dam, Peru, 1972–76; Chm., Advisory Board for Mornos dam, Greece, 1975–76; Chm., Chadwick Trust, 1980–83; Mem., Severn Barrage Cttee, 1978–81; Pres., JInstE, 1955; Vice-Pres., ICE, 1970–72; Fellow Imperial Coll. 1972. Telford Gold Medal, 1968; (1st) Smeaton Gold Medal, 1974. *Publications:* Early Victorian Water Engineers, 1981; Early Dam Builders in Britain, 1987; techn. articles on engrg subjects, papers for World Power Conf., Internat. Commn on Large Dams and ICE. *Recreation:* engineering history. *Address:* St Michael's Lodge, Benenden, Cranbrook, Kent TN17 4EZ. *T:* Cranbrook 240498. *Club:* Athenæum. *Died 5 April* 1989.

**BINNS, Edward Ussher Elliott E.;** *see* Elliott-Binns.

**BINNS, Surgeon Rear-Adm. George Augustus,** CB 1975; ophthalmic medical practitioner; *b* 23 Jan. 1918; *s* of Dr Cuthbert C. H. Binns and Julia Binns (*née* Frommel); *m* 1949, Joan Whitaker; one *s* two *d*. *Educ:* Repton Sch.; St Bartholemew's Hosp. MRCS, LRCP, DO; MCOphth 1988. Casualty House Surgeon, Luton and Dunstable Hosp., 1942. Served War of 1939–45: joined RNVR, Dec. 1942. Served as Specialist in Ophthalmology, 1952, and promoted to Sen. Specialist in Ophthalmology, 1962; subseq. Admiralty Medical Bd, HMS Excellent, and RN Hosp., Gibraltar; MO in Charge, RN Hosp., Plymouth, and Command MO, 1972–75. QHS 1972–75. FRSocMed; Member: BMA, 1942–; Southern Ophthalmological Soc., 1959–; Medical Soc. of London, 1986–; Medical Eye Centre Assoc. Pres., Farnham Br., RN Assoc. Pres., Grayshott Hort. Soc. CStJ 1972. *Recreations:* photography, house and garden maintenance, brewing, wine making, listening to music. *Address:* Netherseal, Hindhead Road, Haslemere, Surrey GU27 3PJ. *T:* Haslemere (0428) 4281. *Clubs:* Naval and Military, Fountain.
*Died 2 April* 1990.

**BINNS, Professor Howard Reed,** CMG 1958; OBE 1948; MA (Cantab), BSc (Edin), MRCVS; *b* 3 Aug. 1909; *s* of Cuthbert Evelyn Binns and Edith Mildred Edwards; *m* 1935, Katharine Vroom Lawson; one *s* one *d*. *Educ:* Bootham Sch., York; St John's Coll., Cambridge; Royal (Dick) Veterinary Coll.; Edinburgh Univ. Veterinary Officer, Nyasaland, 1935–39; Veterinary Research Officer, Palestine, 1940–41; Senior Veterinary Research Officer, Palestine, 1941–47; Dep. Dir of Veterinary Services, Palestine, 1947–48; Director, East African Veterinary Research Organization, 1950–67 (Principal Scientific Officer, EAVRO, 1948–50); Dir, Centre for Internat. Programs, and Prof. of Veterinary Microbiology, Univ. of Guelph, 1969–75; Vis. Prof., Univ. of Guelph, 1975–80; Vis. Lectr on animal diseases exotic to N America, US Dept of Agriculture, 1980, 1983; Vis. Lectr, Animal Path. Divn, Canada Dept of Agric., 1981, 1982; Consultant to Internat. Develt Res. Centre, Ottawa, 1976, 1978; Vis. Prof., Univ. of Saskatchewan, 1980; Vis. Lectr, US Univs, 1980–83. Scientific missions to: USA and Canada, 1939; Syria and the Lebanon, 1945; India, 1946; USA, 1947; South Africa, 1949; Australia, 1960; USA and Germany, 1966; West Indies and S America, 1970; West Africa, 1971; India, 1973; Kenya, 1975, 1976; Carnegie Corp. Grant, 1956; Rockefeller Foundn Grants, 1966, 1970; Commonwealth Foundn Grant, 1971. Consultant to US Nat. Acad. of Sciences, on animal science in tropical Africa, 1959. Mem. Scientific Council for Africa, 1961–65 (Assoc. Mem., 1955–61). Hon. Prof. of Vet. Science in Univ. of East Africa. *Publications:* contribs to scientific jls. *Recreations:* travel, reading, gardening. *Address:* San Diego, Torreguadiaro, Cadiz Province, Spain. *Died 29 April* 1987.

**BINNS, John;** *b* June 1914; *m*; one *s*. *Educ:* Holycroft Sec. Sch., Keighley. Mem., Keighley Borough Council, 1945; Alderman, 1954; Mayor, 1958–59. Joined Labour Party, 1944; MP (Lab) Keighley, 1964–70. Contested (Social Dem.) Keighley, Feb. 1974. Mem. Amalgamated Engineering Union; former Trades Union Officer. *Died 6 Aug.* 1986.

**BINNS, Kenneth Johnstone,** CMG 1960; Under-Treasurer and Commissioner of State Taxes, Government of Tasmania, 1952–76; *b* New South Wales, Australia, 3 June 1912; *s* of late Kenneth Binns,

CBE; *m* 1940, Nancy H. Mackenzie; no *c. Educ:* Melbourne Church of England Grammar Sch.; Queen's Coll., Univ. of Melbourne (MA, BCom); Harvard Univ., USA. First Canberra Scholarship, 1930; Fellow, Commonwealth Fund of NY, 1950. Tasmanian Treasury, 1942–76; Dep. Chm., Tasmanian Govt Insurance Office, 1970–82. Mem., State Library Bd of Tasmania, 1942–80. Fiscal Review Comr to Federal Republic of Nigeria, 1964; with IMF as Adviser to Minister of Finance, Indonesia, 1969. Dir, Comalco Aluminium (Bell Bay) Ltd, 1960–80. Member: State Grants Commn, 1976–80; Retirement Benefits Trust, 1976–82; Launceston Savings Bank Adv. Bd, 1976–83. First Life Mem., Tasmanian Branch, Australian Economic Soc., 1985. *Publications:* Federal-State Financial Relations, Canada and Australia, 1948; Social Credit in Alberta, 1947; various government reports; articles in Economic Record. *Recreations:* fishing, reading. *Address:* 3 Ellington Road, Sandy Bay, Tasmania 7005, Australia. *T:* 25 1863. *Clubs:* Athenæum, Tasmanian, Hobart.        *Died* 1 *Nov.* 1987.

**BIRD, Lt-Gen. Sir Clarence August,** KCIE 1943; CB 1940; DSO 1917; late RE; *b* 5 Feb. 1885; *m* 1919, Dorothea Marian (*d* 1982), MBE 1918, K-i-H 1932, *d* of late Major W. E. Nichols; one *s* (and one *s* died on active service). *Educ:* Cheltenham Coll. Joined Royal Engineers, 1904; served in India, 1907–13, 1917–25, 1930–33, 1939–44; with Indian Expeditionary Force in France, 1914–15; with BEF in France, 1916–17 (Bt Maj.); psc 1921; AHQ India, 1922–25; Army Course, London Sch. of Economics, 1925; Chief Instructor in Fortification, SME, Chatham, 1926–29; Commandant, KGVO Bengal Sappers and Miners, 1930–33; Bt Lieut-Col, 1926; Lieut-Col, 1929; Col, 1933; AQMG Aldershot Command, 1933–35; Chief Engineer, Aldershot Command, 1935–39; Maj.-Gen. 1939; Engineer-in-Chief, Army Headquarters, India, 1939–42; Lieut-Gen. 1941; Master Gen. of Ordnance, India, 1942–44; retd 1944. Col Comdt RE, 1942–52; Col Comdt Indian Electrical and Mechanical Engineers, 1944–48. Dept of Food, Govt of India: Regional Commissioner, NW Region, 1944–45; Special Commissioner, 1945–47; Min. of Food: Divisional Food Officer, North Midland Div., 1947–48; Chm., Rhodesia Railways, 1948–53. FRSA. *Address:* 9 The Drive, Sevenoaks, Kent.        *Died* 30 *July* 1986.

**BIRD, Sir Cyril (Pangbourne),** Kt 1968; Company Director, Perth, Western Australia, retired 1978; *b* 5 April 1906; *s* of late Walter Pangbourne Bird and late Alice Emma Bird; *m* 1st, 1934, Margery Isabel (*d* 1974); two *s* three *d;* 2nd, 1976, Agnes Jarvie. *Educ:* Perth, W Australia. FASA. *Recreations:* fishing, music. *Address:* 4 Riverside Drive, Mosman Park, WA 6012, Australia. *T:* 3846884. *Club:* Royal King's Park Tennis.        *Died* 19 *March* 1984.

**BIRD, Air Vice-Marshal Frank Ronald,** CB 1971; DSO 1945; DFC 1944; AFC 1958; Treasurer, since 1973, Fellow, since 1978, Lady Margaret Hall, Oxford; *b* 18 Nov. 1918; *s* of Frank Bird and Minnie (*née* Robinson); *m* 1943, Joan Dodson, WAAF; two *s. Educ:* Chesterfield Sch., Halton; RAF Coll., Cranwell. Commnd RAF, 1939; Flying Instruction and Experimental Flying, 1940–43; 105 Sqdn Bomber Comd (Pathfinder Force), 1943–45; Empire Test Pilots Sch. and A & AEE, 1945–46; RAF Coll., Cranwell (Cadet Wing), 1946–48; Perm. Commng Bds, Air Min., 1948–50; RAF Staff Coll., Andover, 1950–51; Brit. Jt Services Mission, Washington, USA, 1951–54; A & AEE, Boscombe Down, 1954–57; HQ Bomber Comd (Plans), 1957; CO, RAF Gaydon, 1957–60; Bomber Ops Staff, Air Min., 1960–63; Canadian Nat. Def. Coll., Kingston, Ont., 1963–64; Comdt, A & AEE, Boscombe Down, 1964–68; Director Gen. of Organisation (RAF), 1968–71; Asst Chief of Staff, Automatic Data Processing Division, SHAPE, 1971–73. *Recreations:* fell walking, golf, music, photography. *Address:* 36 North Street, Islip, Oxon. *T:* Kidlington 2808. *Club:* Royal Air Force.        *Died* 20 *Jan.* 1983.

**BIRD, (George William) Terence;** Director: Pilkington Brothers Ltd, 1962–83 (Executive Vice-Chairman, 1971–77); *b* 27 July 1914; *er s* of George Webber Bird and Jane (*née* Hockin); *m* 1942, Hylda Owen Craven; one *d* (one *s* decd). *Educ:* Prescot Grammar Sch.; Imperial Coll. of Science and Technology (BSc, ARCS). FBIM 1972. Pilkington Bros Ltd: Physicist, 1935; Lab. Manager, Triplex Northern Ltd, 1936; Develt Physicist, 1939; Dir, 1962; Chm., Flat Glass Div., 1966. *Publications:* occasional articles in technical jls. *Recreations:* gardening, spectator sports. *Address:* 21 Grange Drive, St Helens, Merseyside WA10 3BG. *Club:* Windermere Motor Boat Racing.        *Died* 15 *July* 1985.

**BIRD, John Louis Warner;** Joint Managing Director, Cable and Wireless plc, since 1982; *b* 18 Jan. 1929; *s* of Sydney Warner Bird and Florence Katherine Byford; *m* 1950, Mary Arnold; one *s* one *d. Educ:* Grammar School. National Cash Register Co. 1950–56; Addressograph-Multigraph Corp., 1956–68; Ultra Electronic Holdings Ltd, 1968–75; Cable & Wireless Ltd, 1975–: Man. Dir, Communications Systems and Services, 1977–81. *Recreations:* golf, caravanning. *Address:* 16 Parkside Drive, Watford, Herts.        *Died* 31 *Oct.*1983.

**BIRD, Terence;** *see* Bird, G. W. T.

**BIRD, Veronica;** Editor, Woman's Realm, 1971–77; *b* 16 Oct. 1932; *o d* of Reginald John Fearn; *m* 1st, 1954, Alec Xavier Snobel (marr. diss. 1974); one *s* one *d;* 2nd, 1974, Michael Bird. *Educ:* Kingsley Sch., Leamington Spa. Editor, Parents magazine, 1963–64; Editor, Mother magazine, 1964–71. *Publications:* Pressing Problems, 1982; Wolf in Sheep's Clothing, 1984. *Recreations:* theatre, cinema. *Address:* 5 Glentham Gardens, SW13 9JN. *T:* 01–748 6344.        *Died* 30 *Aug.* 1986.

**BIRGI, Muharrem Nuri;** Turkish diplomat, retired; *b* Istanbul, 4 Feb. 1908; *o s* of late Ziya Nuri Birgi Pasha, Prof., Faculty of Med., Univ. of Istanbul, later Mem. Grand Nat. Assembly, Turkey, and of Mme Husniye Birgi, *d* of Hassan Rami Pasha, Minister of Marine; *m* (marr. diss.). *Educ:* Lycée Galata Saray, Istanbul; Sch. of Pol. Sciences, Paris (Grad. 1929); Faculty of Law, Geneva (LLB 1931). Entered Turkish For. Min., 1932; 3rd, 2nd and then 1st Sec., Turkish Embassy, Warsaw, 1935–39; Min. for For. Affairs, 1939–41; 1st Sec., Turkish Embassy, Paris-Vichy, 1941; transferred to Madrid, 1942, later promoted Counsellor there. Min. for For. Affairs, Ankara: Co-Dir-Gen. 1st Political Dept, 1944; Dir-General: Dept of Internat. Affairs, 1945; Dept of Co-ordination, 1946; Dept of Consular Affairs, 1946; 2nd Political Dept, 1950; Dep. Sec.-Gen., 1951; Under-Sec. of State, 1952; Sec.-Gen., 1954–57; Turkish Ambassador to Court of St James's, 1957–60. Turkish Permanent Representative to NATO, 1960–72, retired 1972. Hon. Pres., Atlantic Treaty Assoc., 1982– (Pres., 1979–82). *Recreation:* painting. *Address:* Toprakli Sokak 11, Salacak, Üsküdar, Istanbul, Turkey. *T:* Istanbul 3331591.        *Died* 30 *Sept.* 1986.

**BIRKENHEAD, 3rd Earl of,** *cr* 1922; **Frederick William Robin Smith;** Bt 1918; Baron Birkenhead 1919; Viscount Birkenhead 1921; Viscount Furneaux 1922; *b* 17 April 1936; *o s* of 2nd Earl of Birkenhead, TD, and of Hon. Sheila Berry, 2nd *d* of 1st Viscount Camrose; *S* father, 1975. *Educ:* Eton; Christ Church, Oxford. Mem. Council, RSL, 1975–. *Publications:* (as Robin Furneaux): The Amazon, 1969; William Wilberforce, 1974 (Heinemann Award, 1975); *posthumous publication:* (as Earl of Birkenhead) Churchill, 1874–1922, ed Sir John Colville, 1989. *Address:* 48 Arthur Road, Wimbledon, SW19. *T:* 01–947 3983; The Cottage, Charlton, Banbury, Oxon. *T:* Banbury 811224. *Clubs:* Buck's, White's, Portland, All England Lawn Tennis.

       *Died* 16 *Feb.* 1985 (*ext*).

**BIRKETT, George William Alfred,** CBE 1960; CEng, FIEE, FIMechE; Director of Weapons Production, Ministry of Defence (Naval), 1965–70, retired; *b* 16 June 1908; *m* 1939, Doris Lillian Prince; one *s. Educ:* Portsmouth Municipal College. Portsmouth Dockyard, 1929; Techn. Officer, HM Signal Sch., 1938; Prin. Scientific Officer, RNSS, 1946; Sen. Prin. Production Engr, Admty Production Pool, 1953; Supt of Production Pool, Admty, 1956. *Recreation:* sailing. *Address:* 81 Ferndale, Inhurst Wood, Waterlooville, Portsmouth, Hants. *T:* Waterlooville 52695.        *Died* 23 *Jan.* 1988.

**BIRKIN, Sir Charles (Lloyd),** 5th Bt *cr* 1905; *b* 24 Sept. 1907; *s* of late Col Charles Wilfrid Birkin, CMG (4th *s* of 1st Bt); *S* uncle, 1942; *m* 1940, Janet Johnson (*d* 1983); one *s* two *d. Educ:* Eton. Served War of 1939–45, with 112th Regt, 9th Sherwood Foresters. *Publications:* collections of short stories: The Kiss of Death, 1964; The Smell of Evil, 1965; Where Terror Stalks, 1966; My Name is Death, 1966; Dark Menace, 1968; So Cold . . . So Fair, 1970; Spawn of Satan, 1971. *Heir: s* John Christian William Birkin, *b* 2 July 1953. *Address:* West Kella, Sulby, Isle of Man. *T:* Sulby 7544. *Club:* Carlton.        *Died* 8 *Nov.* 1985.

**BIRKIN, Air Commodore James Michael,** CB 1956; DSO 1944; OBE 1951; DFC 1944; AFC 1942; AE 1947; DL; Director, Birkin & Company Limited, New Basford, Nottingham (Lace Manufacturers); *b* 23 April 1912; *s* of late Major H. L. Birkin, Lincoln House, The Park, Nottingham, and late Olive Isobel, *d* of late Rev. H. C. Russell, Wollaton, Notts; *m* 1st, 1956, Antonia Edith (marr. diss. 1977), *d* of late Lt-Col A. F. Stanley Clarke and late Mrs Charles Graves; one *s* one *d;* 2nd, 1980, Susan, *d* of late Edward Mitchell, Ryde, IoW. *Educ:* Harrow; Trinity Coll., Cambridge (MA). London Stock Exchange until 1939; Birkin & Co. Ltd, 1945–. RAFVR, 1938–47; RAuxAF, 1947–63 (Inspector, 1952–62); Hon. Air Commodore, 1956. ADC to the Queen, 1957–63. High Sheriff 1977, DL 1978, Isle of Wight. *Address:* c/o Birkin & Co. Ltd, New Basford, Nottingham. *T:* Nottingham 79351. *Clubs:* Pathfinder, Royal Yacht Squadron, Cowes Corinthian Yacht.

       *Died* 17 *Nov.* 1985.

**BIRKS, Maj.-Gen. (retired) Horace Leslie,** CB 1945; DSO 1941; *b* 7 May 1897; *m* 1920, Gladys Hester (*d* 1957), MBE, *d* of late Lt-Col Hugh Harry Haworth Aspinall, OBE; one *s. Educ:* University College Sch. Enlisted London Rifle Brigade, 1915; 2nd Lieut Machine Gun Corps Heavy Branch, 1917, later Tank Corps; served France, 1915–16 and again 1917 (twice wounded); Instructor RTC

Schools, 1919–24; Staff Coll., Quetta, 1927, 1928; General Staff, Western Command and War Office, 1930–37; Instructor Staff Coll., Quetta, 1937–39; India, 1924–29 and 1937–39; GSO1, 7th Armoured Division, Army of the Nile, 1939–40; 2nd in Command 4th Armoured Bde, 1940–41 (DSO, despatches twice); Commander 11th Armoured Brigade, 1941; Commander 10th Armoured Division, 1942; MG, RAC, CMF, 1944 (CB); retired pay, 1946. Secretary, University College Hospital Medical Sch., 1946–63, retired. *Recreations:* travel, golf. *Address:* c/o Williams and Glyn's Bank, Kirkland House, Whitehall, SW1. *T:* 01–788 7307. *Clubs:* Army and Navy, Roehampton (President).

*Died 25 March 1985.*

**BIRLEY, Sir Robert,** KCMG 1967 (CMG 1950); MA; FSA; Chairman, Central Council of the Selly Oak Colleges, 1969–80; *b* 14 July 1903; *s* of late Leonard Birley, CSI, CIE; *m* 1930, Elinor Margaret, *d* of Eustace Corrie Frere, FRIBA; one *d* (and one *d* decd). *Educ:* Rugby Sch.; Balliol Coll., Oxford (Brackenbury Scholar; Hon. Fellow, 1969). Gladstone Memorial Prize, 1924, 1st Class Hons History. Asst Master, Eton Coll., 1926–35; Headmaster, Charterhouse, 1935–47; Educational Adviser to the Military Governor, CCG, 1947–49; Head Master, Eton Coll., 1949–63; Vis. Prof. of Education, Univ. of the Witwatersrand, 1964–67; Prof. and Head of Dept of Social Science and Humanities, City Univ., London, 1967–71. Mem., Fleming Cttee on Public Schools, 1944; Burge Memorial Lecture, 1948; Reith Lectures, 1949; Clark Lectures, 1961; Chancellor's Lecture, University of Witwatersrand, 1965; Chichele Lectures, All Souls Coll., Oxford, Michaelmas Term, 1967. Gresham Professor in Rhetoric, 1959–. Pres., Bibliographical Soc., 1979–80. Hon. DCL Oxford, 1972; Hon. DSc Aston, 1972; Hon. Doc. Ing, Technical Univ., Berlin, 1949; Hon. LLD: Edinburgh, 1950; Leeds 1950; Liverpool, 1953; Witwatersrand, 1965; City, 1980; Hon. DPhil, Frankfurt Univ., 1959. Grosse Verdienstkreuz (Germany), 1955. *Publications:* The English Jacobins, 1925; Speeches and Documents in American History (selected and edited), 1944; Sunk Without Trace (Clark Lectures), 1962. *Address:* Lomans, West End, Somerton, Somerset. *T:* Somerton 72640. *Club:* Travellers'. *Died 22 July 1982.*

**BIRON, Sir (Moshe Chaim Efraim) Philip,** Kt 1980; Senior Puisne Judge, Tanzania, since 1965; *b* 20 Aug. 1909; *s* of Rabbi Meshillim Zysie Golditch and Sarah Pearl Biron; *m* 1958, Margaret Henderson Colville. *Educ:* Manchester Talmudical Coll., Yeshiva (Rabbi); Manchester Univ. (LLB (Hons)). RAF (volunteered), 1941 (made chairborne because deuteranomalous vision discovered); served as AC2 Gp 4 (misemployed) Technical Branch until 1944 when commnd after being remustered to General Duties Branch; Flt Lt on demobilization, 1946. Called to the Bar, Gray's Inn, 1941; practised at the Bar, N Circuit, until 1949; Resident Magistrate, Colonial Legal Service, Tanganyika, 1949–55; Sen. Resident Magistrate, 1955–56; Actg Judge, 1956–61; Substantive Judge, 1961–. *Recreation:* reading. *Address:* The High Court, PO Box 9004, Dar es Salaam, Tanzania. *Club:* Royal Over-Seas League.

*Died 31 Dec. 1981.*

**BIRSAY, Hon. Lord; Harald Robert Leslie,** KT 1973; CBE 1963 (MBE (mil.) 1945); TD 1944; MA 1927, LLB (Glas.) 1930; QC (Scot.), 1949; DL Orkney, 1965; Hon. LLD: Strathclyde, 1966; Glasgow, 1966; Hon. FEIS 1966; Chairman, Scottish Land Court, 1965–78; *b* 8 May 1905; *s* of Robert Leslie, Master Mariner, Stromness, Orkney, and Margaret Mowat Cochrane, Stromness; *m* 1945, Robina Margaret Marwick, MB, ChB (Edin.), *o d* of ex-Provost J. G. Marwick, FSA (Scot.), Stromness, Orkney; one *s* one *d*. *Educ:* Earlston Public Sch.; Berwickshire High Sch.; Glasgow High Sch.; Glasgow Univ. Served in Glasgow High Sch. (1918–23) and Glasgow Univ. (1923–30) OTCs. Extracted as Solicitor, 1930; called to Scottish Bar, 1937. War of 1939–45 (MBE; despatches); served in the Royal Scots and on HQs 15 (S) Div.; 8 Corps and 21 Army Group; released, 1945, to TARO, as (Hon.) Lieut-Col. Standing Counsel to Dept of Agriculture; Junior Assessor to City of Edinburgh Assessor and Dean of Guild and Burgh Courts, 1949; Senior Assessor, 1960; Advocate-Depute, Scottish Bar, 1947–51; Sheriff of Roxburgh, Berwick and Selkirk, 1956–61; Sheriff of Caithness, Sutherland, Orkney and Zetland, 1961–65. Candidate (Lab) for Orkney and Shetland Constituency, 1950; Chairman: Scottish Advisory Council on the Treatment of Offenders, 1959; Scottish Cttee of British Council, 1963–70; Scottish Joint Council for Teachers' Salaries, 1964; Executive Edinburgh Council of Social Service, 1956–69; Cttee on Gen. Med. Services in the Highlands and Islands, 1964–67; Loaningdale Approved Sch.; Nat. Savings Cttee for Scotland, 1965–72, Pres., 1972–78; Board of Governors, St Hilary's Sch., Edinburgh, 1959–81; Salvation Army Adv. Bd, Edinburgh, 1967–77; Scottish Adv. Cttee on the Travelling People, 1971–77; St Columba's Hospice, Edinburgh, 1971–81, now Vice-Pres.; Hon. President: Glasgow, Orkney and Shetland Association also Edinburgh, Orkney and Zetland Association, 1962; Scottish Council for National Parks until 1965; Hon. Vice-President, Boys' Brigade, 1966– (Hon. Pres., Leith Bn, 1963–); Scottish Council of Boys' Clubs and Youth Clubs, 1962; Shipwrecked Fishermen and

Mariners' Royal Benevolent Society (Scotland), 1966; Orkney Council of Social Service, 1966; Pres., Scottish Nat. Dictionary Assoc., 1968–. Lord High Commissioner to the General Assembly of the Church of Scotland, 1965 and 1966. Hon. Air Cdre, No 2 (City of Edinburgh) Maritime HQ Unit, RAuxAF, 1967–82. *Address:* 27 Queensferry Road, Edinburgh EH4 3HB. *T:* 031–332 3315; Queenafjold, Birsay, Orkney KW17 2 LZ. *T:* (Orkney) Birsay 286. *Clubs:* Royal Scots, Caledonian, Arts (Edinburgh).

*Died 27 Nov. 1982.*

**BISHOP, Maj.-Gen. Sir Alec;** *see* Bishop, Maj.-Gen. Sir W. H. A.

**BISHOP, Ann,** ScD; FRS 1959; *b* 19 Dec. 1899; *o d* of late James Kimberly and Ellen Bishop. *Educ:* Manchester High Sch. for Girls; Manchester Univ.; Cambridge Univ. BSc 1921, DSc 1932, Manchester; PhD 1926, ScD 1941, Cambridge. Hon. Research Fellow, Manchester Univ., 1925–26; Research Asst, Medical Research Council, 1926–29; Beit Memorial Research Fellow, 1929–32; Yarrow Fellow of Girton Coll., Cambridge, 1932–37; Research Fellow of Girton Coll., Cambridge, 1937–66, Life Fellow, 1966; Mem., MRC Staff, 1937–42; Director, MRC Chemotherapy Research Unit at the Molteno Inst., Univ. of Cambridge, 1942–64. *Publications:* articles on the biology of Protozoa, and Chemotherapy, published in Scientific Journals. *Address:* 47 Sherlock Close, Cambridge CB3 0HP. *Died 7 May 1990.*

**BISHOP, Sir Harold,** Kt, *cr* 1955; CBE 1938; FCGI; BSc (Engineering) London; Hon. FIEE, FIMechE; FIEEE; *b* 29 Oct. 1900; 3rd *s* of Henry Thomas Bishop; *m* 1925, Madge Adeline, *d* of Frank Harry Vaus; two *d* (one *s* decd). *Educ:* Alleyn's Sch., Dulwich; City and Guilds Coll. Engineer, HM Office of Works, 1920–22; Engineer, Marconi's Wireless Telegraph Co. Ltd, 1922–23; Senior Supt BBC, 1923–29; Asst Chief Engineer, BBC, 1929–43; Chief Engineer, 1943–52; Dir of Engineering, 1952–63; Consultant, BICC Gp, 1963–68. Hon. FIEE (Pres. 1953–54, Vice-Pres. 1948–53); President: Electrical Industries Benevolent Assoc., 1955–56; Association of Supervising Electrical Engineers, 1956–58; Institution of Electrical and Electronic Techn. Engineers, 1965–69; Royal Television Soc., 1960–62; Fellow, Imperial Coll. of Science and Technology. *Address:* Little Carbis, Harborough Hill, Pulborough, W Sussex. *T:* West Chiltington 3325.

*Died 22 Oct. 1983.*

**BISHOP, Rev. Hugh William Fletcher;** Licensed to officiate, Diocese of London; *b* 17 May 1907; *e s* of John and Mary Bishop, Haughton House, Shifnal, Shropshire. *Educ:* Malvern Coll.; Keble Coll., Oxford (MA). Cuddesdon Coll., Oxford, 1932–33; Deacon, 1933; Priest, 1934. Curate of St Michael's, Workington, 1933–35; Curate of Cuddesdon and Lectr, Cuddesdon, 1935–37. Mem., Community of the Resurrection, Mirfield, (taking name of Hugh), 1940–74; Chaplain to the Forces (EC), 1940–45 (POW, 1942–45); Warden, Hostel of the Resurrection, Leeds, 1946–49; Guardian of Novices, Mirfield, 1949–52; Principal of the College, 1956–65; Father Superior of the Community of the Resurrection, 1965–74, released from the Community of the Resurrection, 1974. *Publications:* The Passion Drama, 1955; The Easter Drama, 1958; Life is for Loving, 1961; (contrib. to) Mirfield Essays in Christian Belief, 1962; The Man for Us, 1968. *Address:* 6 Evelyn Mansions, Carlisle Place, SW1P 1NH. *T:* 01–828 0564. *Died 2 Oct. 1989.*

**BISHOP, Prof. Richard Evelyn Donohue,** CBE 1979; FRS 1980, FEng 1977, FIMechE, FRINA, MRAeS; Vice-Chancellor and Principal, Brunel University, since 1981; Fellow of University College London, since 1964; Director, Bishop, Price & Partners Ltd, since 1975; *b* London, 1 Jan. 1925; *s* of Rev. Dr N. R. Bishop; *m* 1949, Jean Paterson, London; one *s* one *d*. *Educ:* The Roan Sch., Greenwich. RNVR, 1943–46. University Coll., London, 1946–49 (DSc Eng); Commonwealth Fund Fellow in Stanford Univ., California, 1949–51 (MS, PhD). Sen. Scientific Officer, Ministry of Supply, 1951–52; Cambridge Univ.: Demonstrator, 1952; Fellow of Pembroke Coll., 1954; University Lecturer in Engineering, 1955 (MA, ScD); Kennedy Prof. of Mechanical Engrg, Univ. of London, 1957–81. Vis. Prof., Massachusetts Institute of Technology, Summer, 1959; Vis. Lectr, National Science Foundation, USA, Spring, 1961; John Orr Meml Lectr, S Africa, 1971; C. Gelderman Foundn Vis. Prof., Technical Univ., Delft, 1976. Member of Council, Instn of Mechanical Engineers, 1961–64, 1969–70; President, British Acoustical Soc., 1966–68; a Vice Pres., Royal Soc., 1986–88 (Mem. Council, 1986–88); Hon. Member Royal Corps of Naval Constructors, 1968; Originator of Greenwich Forum, 1973. Mem. Senate, London Univ., 1980–81. Liveryman, Shipwrights' Co., 1979–. Hon. Fellow, Portsmouth Polytechnic, 1982. George Stephenson Res. Prize, IMechE, 1959; Thomas Hawksley Gold Medal, IMechE, 1965; Silver Medal of Skoda Works, 1967; Křižík Gold Medal, Acad. Sci. CSSR, 1969; Rayleigh Gold Medal, Brit. Acoustical Soc., 1972; Clayton Prize, IMechE, 1972; RINA Bronze Medals, 1975, 1977; William Froude Gold Medal, RINA, 1988. *Publications:* (with D. C. Johnson) Vibration Analysis Tables, 1956; (with D. C. Johnson) The Mechanics of Vibration, 1960; (with G.

M. L. Gladwell and S. Michaelson) The Matrix Analysis of Vibration, 1965; Vibration, 1965; (with W. G. Price) Probabilistic Theory of Ship Dynamics, 1974; (with W. G. Price) Hydroelasticity of Ships, 1979; (with B. R. Clayton) Mechanics of Marine Vehicles, 1982; many scientific papers. *Recreation:* sailing. *Address:* Brunel University, Uxbridge, Middlesex UB8 3PH. *Club:* Royal Naval and Royal Albert Yacht (Portsmouth) (Chm., 1979–82).
*Died* 12 *Sept.* 1989.

**BISHOP, Ronald Eric,** CBE 1946; FRAeS; Deputy Managing Director, de Havilland Aircraft Co. Ltd, 1958–64; Design Director, de Havilland Aircraft Co. Ltd, Hatfield, 1946–64; *b* 27 Feb. 1903; *m* Nora; two *s.* Joined de Havilland Aircraft Co. Ltd, as an apprentice, 1921; entered Drawing Office, 1923; appointed in charge, 1936. Responsible for following designs: Flamingo, Mosquito, Hornet, Vampire, Dove, Venom, Heron, DH 108, DH 110, Comet Jet Airliner. Gold Medal, RAeS, 1964.
*Died* 11 *June* 1989.

**BISHOP, Rev. William Fletcher;** *see* Bishop, Rev. H.W.F.

**BISHOP, Maj.-Gen. Sir (William Henry) Alexander, (Alec),** KCMG 1964 (CMG 1961); CB 1946; CVO 1961; OBE 1941; psc; psa; *b* 20 June 1897; *s* of Walter Edward and Elizabeth Bishop; *m* 1926, Mary Patricia (*d* 1977), *d* of Henry Corbett, Physician, Plymouth; one *s.* *Educ:* Plymouth Coll.; RMC Sandhurst. Served European War, 1914–19, Mesopotamia and Palestine; with Dorset Regt; Bt Lt-Col 1938; Col 1941; Brig. 1941; Maj.-Gen. 1944. Served in India, 1919–25, War Office, 1933–35 and Colonial Office, 1937–39; served in East Africa, North Africa, and West Africa during War, 1939–44; Director of Quartering, War Office, 1944–45; Chief of Information Services and Public Relations, CCG, 1945–46; Deputy Chief of Staff, CCG, 1946–48; Regional Commissioner, Land North Rhine/Westphalia, 1948–50; Asst Sec., CRO, 1951; Principal Staff Officer to Secretary of State for Commonwealth Relations, 1953–57; British Dep. High Commissioner in Calcutta, 1957–62; Director of Information Services and Cultural Relations, CRO, 1962–64; British High Commissioner, Cyprus, 1964–65, retired. CStJ 1951. Ehren-Nadel, Johanniter Orden, 1951; Comdr, Verdienstkreuz (Germany), 1978. *Recreations:* reading, gardening. *Address:* Combe Lodge, Beckley, Sussex. *T:* Beckley 221. *Died* 15 *May* 1984.

**BISHOP, William Thomas,** CBE 1971; retired; Consultant to Drivers Jonas; *b* 27 March 1901; *s* of Thomas Edward and Hannah B. Bishop; *m* 1st, 1929, Freda Bateman Simes (*d* 1935); one *s* one *d*; 2nd, 1936, Marjorie Bateman Leaver; one *d* (one *s* decd). *Educ:* Andover Grammar Sch.; Aldershot County High Sch. Chartered Surveyor, 1924; FRICS 1931; Mem. Council, RICS, 1960–72 (Hon. Sec. 1963–72). Specialised in Urban Estate Management: 25 yrs with Messrs Clutton, then 26 yrs Drivers Jonas as Partner and Sen. Partner, 1952–71. Appts included Surveyor and Receiver for Crown Estate Comrs (London Estate), Corp. of Trinity House, and Ilchester Estates. Life Vice-Pres., RNLI; Younger Brother of Trinity Hse, 1962. Liveryman, Farmers' Co. *Recreations:* gardening, fishing. *Address:* Bevendean Cottage, Warren Lane, Oxshott, Leatherhead, Surrey. *T:* Oxshott 2007. *Club:* Royal Thames Yacht.
*Died* 16 *Jan.* 1982.

**BISHOPSTON, Baron** *cr* 1981 (Life Peer), of Newark in the County of Nottinghamshire; **Edward Stanley Bishop,** PC 1977; JP; AMRAeS, MIED; Opposition Whip and front-bench spokesman, House of Lords, since 1981; *b* 3 Oct. 1920; *e s* of Frank Stanley Bishop and Constance Camilla Bishop (*née* Dawbney); *m* 1945, Winifred Mary Bryant, JP, *o c* of Frank and Elizabeth Bryant; four *d. Educ:* S Bristol Central Sch.; Merchant Venturers' Technical Coll.; Bristol Univ. Former Aeronautical Design Engineer (British Aircraft Corp.). Member Bristol City Council, 1946–59, 1963–66 (Dep. Leader and Chm. Finance and General Purposes Cttee, 1956–59). JP, City and County of Bristol, 1957–73, Notts 1973–; Visiting Magistrate, HM Bristol Prison, 1959–71. Contested (Lab) Bristol West, 1950; Exeter, 1951; S Gloucester, 1955; MP (Lab) Newark, Notts, 1964–79; Chm., SW Reg. Council, Labour Party, 1953–54; Asst Govt Whip, 1966–67; Opposition Spokesman: on Agric., 1970; on Aviation, Trade and Industry, 1970–74; Parly Sec., MAFF, March–Sept. 1974; Minister of State, MAFF, 1974–79; UK Parly deleg. to N Atlantic Assembly, 1966–74, and Chm., Assembly's Economic Cttee, 1969–72. Promoted Matrimonial Property Bill, 1969–70. Vice-President RDC Assoc., 1965–74; Member: Archbishop of Canterbury's Commn on Organisation of Church by Dioceses in London and SE England, 1965–67; Redundant Churches Fund, 1970–74; Council, Nat. Trust, 1980–. A Church Commissioner, 1968–; Second Church Estates Comr, 1974. FRSA 1982; FAMS. *Recreations:* archæology, genealogy; being with family. *Address:* House of Lords, SW1A 0PW.
*Died* 19 *April* 1984.

**BISS, Godfrey Charles D'Arcy;** retired as Senior Partner, Ashurst Morris Crisp, Solicitors, 1974; *b* 2 Sept. 1909; *s* of Gerald Biss and Sarah Ann Coutts Allan; *m* 1946, Margaret Jean Ellis; two *s. Educ:* St Paul's Sch. (Scholar); Worcester Coll., Oxford (Exhibitioner). 1st Class Jurisprudence, 1932. Solicitor, 1935; Partner in Ashurst, Morris, Crisp, 1947. Royal Artillery, 1940–46; Staff Capt. RA, 23rd Indian Div. Chairman: The Fairey Company Ltd, 1958–70; UKO International (formerly UK Optical & Industrial Holdings Ltd), 1958–78; Director: Siebe Gorman & Co. Ltd, 1963–81; Trafalgar House Ltd, to 1981; International Press Centre Ltd. *Recreations:* gardening, racing. *Address:* c/o Ashurst Morris Crisp, Broadgate House, 7 Eldon Street, EC2M 7HD. *Died* 23 *Jan.* 1989.

**BJÖRNSSON, Henrik Sveinsson,** KBE (Hon.) 1963; Icelandic diplomat, retired; Ambassador to Belgium, Luxembourg and Greece, concurrently accredited to European Economic Community, and Permanent Icelandic Representative to NATO, 1979–84; *b* 2 Sept. 1914; *s* of Sveinn Björnsson (late President of Iceland) and Georgia Hoff-Hansen; *m* 1941, Gróa Torfhildur Jónsdóttir; one *s* two *d. Educ:* Reykjavik Grammar Sch.; Univ. of Iceland. Graduated in Law, 1939. Entered Foreign Service, 1939; served in Copenhagen, Washington, DC, Oslo, Paris and Revkjavik; Secretary to President of Iceland, 1952–56; Secretary-General of Min. of Foreign Affairs, Iceland, 1956–61; Ambassador to: the Court of St James's, 1961–65, also to Royal Netherlands Court, and Minister to Spain and Portugal, 1961–65; Belgium and Permanent Representative to NATO, 1965–67, France, Luxembourg, Yugoslavia, 1965–76, UAR and Ethiopia, 1971–76, and concurrently Permanent Rep. to Council of Europe, 1968–70, and OECD and UNESCO, 1965–76; Permt Under Secretary, Ministry for Foreign Affairs, 1976–79. Kt Comdr of the Order of the Icelandic Falcon, 1963. Holds various foreign decorations. *Address:* Sjafnargata 4, Reykjavik, Iceland. *Died* 21 *Nov.* 1985.

**BLACHE-FRASER, Louis Nathaniel,** HBM 1971; CMG 1959; Chairman, Insurance Brokers West Indies Ltd, 1976; Director: George Wimpey (Caribbean) Ltd; Trinidad Building and Loan Association, 1965; *b* 19 Feb. 1904; *s* of late Winford and Emma Blache-Fraser, Trinidad; *m* 1941, Gwenyth, *d* of George Kent, Grenada; two *s* one *d* (and one *d* decd). *Educ:* Queen's Royal Coll., Trinidad. Joined Trinidad and Tobago Government Service, 1924; Dep. Accountant-General, 1947; Accountant-General, 1948; Dep. Financial Secretary, 1952; Financial Secretary, 1953; Financial Secretary, The West Indies, 1956–60; Chairman, Public Service Commission of The West Indies, 1961–62. Asst Sec., Alstons Ltd, 1962–65, Sec., 1965–70. Past Pres., Trinidad Chamber of Commerce. *Address:* (office) 1–5 Cummins Lane, Port-of-Spain, Trinidad; 14 Coblentz Gardens, St Ann's, Trinidad. *Clubs:* Queen's Park Cricket, Harvard Sports (Trinidad). *Died* 22 *Nov* 1984.

**BLACK, Baron** *cr* 1968 (Life Peer), of Barrow in Furness; **William Rushton Black;** Kt 1958; *b* 12 Jan. 1893; *s* of J. W. and F. M. Black; *m* 1916, Patricia Margaret Dallas (*d* 1976); one *d* (one *s* decd). *Educ:* Barrow Secondary Sch.; Barrow Technical Coll. Apprenticed Vickers Ltd (Engineer), 1908; Works Manager, Vickers Crayford, 1924; General Manager, Weymanns Motor Bodies, 1928; Director and General Manager, Park Royal Vehicles Ltd, 1934, Man. Dir 1939, Chairman 1962–79; Director, Associated Commercial Vehicles Ltd, 1949, Chm. and Managing Dir 1957–78. Chairman: National Research Development Corporation, 1957–69; Leyland Motor Corporation, 1963–67. Pres., SMMT, 1953. *Recreations:* golf, gardening. *Address:* c/o Mr and Mrs John Smyth, Goudie's Farm, Lower Hamswell, Bath, Avon BA1 9DE. *Club:* Royal Automobile.
*Died* 27 *Dec.* 1984.

**BLACK, His Honour George Joseph,** DSO 1944; DFC 1942 and Bar 1944; a Circuit Judge, 1977–84; *b* 24 Jan. 1918; *s* of Tom Walton Black and Nellie Black; *m* 1955; one *s* one *d. Educ:* Queens Coll., Taunton. LLB. Articled Clerk, C. James Hardwick & Co., Solicitors, Cardiff, 1935–39; joined RAF, Sept. 1939; Sgt Pilot 1940; commnd 1942; Sqdn Ldr 1944; fighter bombers, Middle East, Sicily, Italy, 1941–44; Sen. Personnel Staff Officer, 1944–45; released from service, 1946. Admitted Solicitor, 1947; private practice, 1947–49; Legal Dept, New Scotland Yard, 1950–58; Partner, Adams & Black, Cardiff, 1958–77. A Recorder of the Crown Court, 1972–77. *Recreations:* sailing. *Address:* 11 Sealawns, Cold Knap, Barry, S Glamorgan. *Died* 13 *Oct.* 1984.

**BLACK, Prof. Gordon;** Professor of Computation, Faculty of Technology, University of Manchester, 1964–88, later Emeritus; Member, National Electronics Council, 1967–83; *b* 30 July 1923; *s* of Martin Black and Gladys (*née* Lee), Whitehaven, Cumbria; *m* 1953, Brenda Janette, *y d* of H. Josiah Balsom, London; two *s* two *d. Educ:* Workington Grammar Sch.; Hatfield Coll., Durham Univ.; Imperial Coll., London Univ. BSc Durham, 1945; MSc Manchester, 1968; PhD, DIC London, 1954; FInstP 1952; FBCS 1968; CPhys 1984. Physicist, British Scientific Instrument Research Assoc., 1946–56; UKAEA, 1956–66; Principal Sci. Officer, 1956–58; Senior Principal Sci. Officer, 1958–60; Dep. Chief Sci. Officer, 1960–64. Dir, Nat. Computing Centre, 1965–69; Dir, Univ. of Manchester Regional Computing Centre, 1969–83. Dir, Internat. Computers Ltd, 1976–84. Chm., Computer Policy Cttee, Vickers Ltd, 1977–79. Governor, Huddersfield Polytechnic, 1974–80. UN

Computer Consultant, 1983–. *Publications:* scientific papers in learned jls (physics and computers). *Recreations:* piano playing; listening to piano players; old clocks. *Address:* University of Manchester Institute of Science and Technology, Sackville Street, Manchester. *T:* 061–236 3311; Ennerdale, 24 Marlfield Road, Hale Barns, Altrincham, Cheshire WA15 0SQ. *T:* 061–980 4644. *Club:* Athenæum.                                           *Died* 12 *Feb.* 1990.

**BLACK, Sir Harold,** Kt 1970; Deputy Secretary, Northern Ireland Office, Belfast, 1972–74; *b* 9 April 1914; *s* of Alexander and Adelaide Black, Belfast; *m* 1940, Margaret Saxton; one *s* one *d. Educ:* Royal Belfast Academical Institution. Joined Northern Ireland Civil Service, 1934; Asst Sec., NI Cabinet, 1959–63; Dir of Establishments, Min. of Finance, NI, 1963–65; Sec. to the Cabinet and Clerk of the Privy Council, NI, 1965–72. *Recreations:* photography, sailing. *Address:* 19 Rosepark, Belfast BT5 7RG. *T:* Dundonald 2151. *Club:* Strangford Lough Yacht.
*Died* 19 *Jan.* 1981.

**BLACK, Sir Hermann David,** Kt 1974; AC 1986; Chancellor of the University of Sydney, New South Wales, Australia, since 1970; Fellow, University of Sydney, since 1949; Part-time Lecturer in Economics and Education; also a radio commentator on economics and international affairs, in Australia; *b* 1905; *m* Joyce. Former Economic Adviser to the Treasury, NSW; former Pres., Economic Soc. of Australia and NZ; Pres., Australian Instn of Internat. Affairs. Hon. DLitt Univ. of Newcastle, NSW. *Address:* University of Sydney, Sydney, New South Wales 2006, Australia; 99 Roseville Avenue, Roseville, NSW 2069, Australia.            *Died* 1990.

**BLACK, (Ian) Hervey Stuart,** TD 1980; Chairman, General Accident Fire and Life Assurance Corporation Ltd, 1972–79; *b* 8 June 1908; *s* of Archibald Arrol Stuart Black and Edith Mary Macmichael; *m* 1935, Margaret Helen (*d* 1982), *d* of Maj.-Gen. Sir Cecil Pereira and Lady Pereira; two *s* two *d. Educ:* Winchester Coll.; Magdalen Coll., Oxford (3rd Cl. Hons PPE). Commnd Ayrshire Yeomanry, 1930; Captain 1940; served War: WO, 1941–43; Min. of War Transport, N and W Africa, 1943–44, and France, 1944–45. Joined Glasgow Steam Shipping Co. Ltd, 1930, Dir 1933; Dir, Donaldson Line Ltd, and Donaldson Bros & Black Ltd, 1938–68 (Dep. Chm., 1956–68). Gen. Accident Assurance Group: Dir, 1950; Dep. Chm., 1970; chm. or dir, subsid. and assoc. cos, 1950–79. Dir, Scottish United Investors Ltd, 1953–79. Chairman: Scottish Br., Inst. of Dirs, 1976–78; Glasgow Dock Labour Bd, 1946–49; Glasgow & Clyde Shipowners' Assoc., 1952; Glasgow Port Welfare Cttee, 1956–70; Scottish Council, King George's Fund for Sailors, 1950–62 and 1969–73; Glasgow Sea Cadet Corps, 1947–55; Scottish Central Cttee, Royal Life Saving Soc., 1969–72; former Chm., Glasgow Sailors' Home. Dep. Chairman: (former), Clyde Navigation Trust; (former), Clyde Pilotage Authority; Scotland's Garden Scheme, 1947–51. Former Dir, Merchants House, Glasgow. Member: (former), Council, Chamber of Shipping; Scottish Cttee, Council of Indust. Design, 1953–62; Exec. Cttee, Nat. Trust for Scotland, 1979–. Hon. Sec., Lanarkshire and Renfrewshire Foxhounds, 1953–72. OStJ. Medal of Freedom, USA, 1945. *Recreations:* gardening, wine. *Address:* Little Dunbarnie, Bridge of Earn, Perth PH2 9ED. *T:* Bridge of Earn 812205. *Clubs:* White's, Carlton; Western (Glasgow).                             *Died* 14 *Feb.* 1986.

**BLACK, Kenneth Oscar,** MA, MD Cantab, FRCP, BChir, MRCS; Consulting Physician, St Bartholomew's Hospital; *b* 10 Nov. 1910; *s* of late George Barnard Black, Scarborough; *m* 1959, Virginia, *d* of Herbert Lees, Petersham, Surrey; two *d. Educ:* Bootham Sch., York; King's Coll., Cambridge (1st Class Nat. Science Tripos part 1, Senior Exhibitioner); St Bartholomew's Hospital, London. Demonstrator of Physiology and Medical Chief Asst, St Bartholomew's Hospital; Physician, St Bartholomew's Hospital, 1946. MB, BChir 1937; MRCP 1937; MD 1942; FRCP 1946. War service temp. Lt-Col RAMC; served W Africa and India as Medical Specialist and OC Medical Div. Mem., Assoc. of Physicians; Fellow Royal Society Medicine. Examiner in Medicine: University of London, 1953; Soc. of Apothecaries, 1957; for MRCP London, 1967. *Publications:* contributions to journals and textbooks on diabetes and other medical topics. *Recreation:* natural history. *Address:* 28 Palmeira Avenue, Hove, East Sussex BN3 3GB.
*Died* 5 *Aug.* 1987.

**BLACK-HAWKINS, (Clive) David,** MA (Cantab); Head Master, University College School, Hampstead, 1956–75; *b* 2 July 1915; *o c* of late Capt. C. C. R. Black-Hawkins, Hants Regt, and Stella Black-Hawkins (*née* Stein); *m* 1941, Ruth Eleanor (*d* 1977), 3rd *d* of late H. Crichton-Miller, MA, MD, FRCP; one *s* one *d. Educ:* Wellington Coll.; Corpus Christi Coll., Cambridge. Asst Master, University College Sch., 1938; Vice-Master, 1953. Intelligence Corps, Capt., 1940–46; GHQ Middle East, 1942–44. Governor: Westfield Coll., Univ. of London, 1977–; Royal Masonic Instn for Girls, 1975–. *Recreations:* travel, reading memoirs. *Address:* 14A Wedderburn Road, Hampstead, NW3 5QG.            *Died* 17 *April* 1983.

**BLACKALL, Sir Henry (William Butler),** Kt 1945; QC (Cyprus); Hon. LLD (*jd*) (Dublin); Vice-President, Irish Genealogical Research Society; *b* 19 June 1889; *s* of Henry Blackall, Garden Hill, Co. Limerick, and Isabella, *d* of William Butler, JP, High Sheriff Co. Clare 1863, Bunnahow, Co. Clare (descended from Hon. Piers Butler, 2nd *s* of 10th Baron Dunboyne); *m* 1934, Maria, *o d* of D. Severis, MLC, Chairman, Bank of Cyprus. *Educ:* Stonyhurst; Trinity Coll., Dublin. BA (Senior Mod., Gold Medallist); LLB (1st place); 1st of 1st Class Hons Mod. Hist.; 1st Prizeman Roman Law; 1st Prizeman International Law and Jurisprudence (TCD); John Brooke Scholar and Victoria Prizeman (King's Inn); called to Irish Bar, 1912; served in World War I; Crown Counsel, Kenya, 1919; Member Legislative Council, 1920; Sen. Crown Counsel, Nigeria, 1923; Acting Solicitor-General, various periods, 1923–31; Attorney-General, Cyprus, 1932–36; Attorney-General, Gold Coast, 1936–43; MEC, MLC; Governor's Deputy, 1940; Chairman, Cttee of Enquiry into Native Tribunals, 1942; Chief Justice of Trinidad and Tobago, and President of the West Indian Court of Appeal, 1943–46; Chief Justice of Hong Kong, 1946–48; President of the West African Court of Appeal, 1948–51; retired, 1951. *Publications:* The Butlers of Co. Clare; The Galweys of Munster; articles in various historical and genealogical journals. *Recreation:* genealogy. *Address:* PO Box 1139, Nicosia, Cyprus. *T:* Nicosia 76362. *Clubs:* Travellers'; Kildare Street and University (Dublin).            *Died* 1 *Nov.* 1981.

**BLACKBURN, (Evelyn) Barbara;** novelist and playwright; *b* Brampton Brien, Hereford, July 1898; *d* of late E. M. Blackburn, Fairway Cottage, Henley-on-Thames; *m* 1927, Claude Leader; two *s* one *d. Educ:* Eversley, Folkestone. *Publications: novels:* Return to Bondage, 1926; Season Made for Joy, 1927; Sober Feast, 1929; Courage for Martha, 1930; Marriage and Money, 1931; The Club, 1932; The Long Journey, 1933; Lover be Wise, 1934; Good Times, 1935; Abbots Bank, 1948; Georgina Goes Home, 1951; Star Spangled Heavens, 1953; The Briary Bush, 1954; Summer at Sorrelhurst, 1954; The Buds of May, 1955; The Blackbird's Tune, 1957; Spinners Hall (as Barbara Leader), 1957; Green for Lovers, 1958; Story of Alix, 1959; The Little Cousin, 1960; Love Story of Mary Britton, 1961; Doctor and Debutante, 1961; Lovers' Meeting, 1962; Learn Her by Heart, 1962; City of Forever, 1963; Come Back My Love, 1963; (as Frances Castle, with Peggy Mundy Castle) The Sisters' Tale, 1968; as Frances Castle: Tara's Daughter, 1970; The Thread of Gold, 1971; *play:* (with Mundy Whitehouse) Poor Man's Castle; *biography:* Noble Lord, 1949. *Address:* Anchor Cottage, Latchingdon, Chelmsford, Essex. *T:* Maldon 740367.
*Died* 14 *May* 1981.

**BLACKBURN, Fred;** *b* 29 July 1902; *s* of Richley and Mary Blackburn, Mellor; *m* 1930, Marion (decd), *d* of Walter W. and Hannah Fildes, Manchester; two *s. Educ:* Queen Elizabeth's Grammar Sch., Blackburn; St John's Coll., Battersea; Manchester Univ. Teacher. MP (Lab) Stalybridge and Hyde Div. of Cheshire, 1951–70, retired 1970. *Publications:* The Regional Council; Local Government Reform; George Tomlinson. *Address:* 114 Knutsford Road, Wilmslow, Cheshire. *T:* Wilmslow 523142.
*Died* 1 *May* 1990.

**BLACKBURN, Hon. Sir Richard (Arthur),** Kt 1983; OBE (mil.) 1965; Chief Justice, Supreme Court of the Australian Capital Territory, 1977–85; Judge, Federal Court of Australia, 1977–85; *b* 26 July 1918; *s* of late Brig. Arthur Seaforth Blackburn, VC, CMG, CBE, and Rose Ada (*née* Kelly); *m* 1951, Bryony Helen, *d* of H. H. Dutton; one *s* one *d. Educ:* St Peter's Coll., Adelaide; St Mark's Coll., Univ. of Adelaide (BA; Hon. Fellow, 1986); Magdalen Coll., Oxford (BA, BCL; Rhodes Schol. for SA, 1940). Served War, AIF, 1940–45. Called to the Bar, Inner Temple, 1949; Bonython Prof. of Law, Adelaide Univ., 1950–57; in private practice, Adelaide, 1957–66; Judge: NT Supreme Ct, 1966–71; ACT Supreme Ct, 1971–77. Pro-Chancellor, ANU, 1977–84, Chancellor, 1984–. Lt-Col, Adelaide Univ. Regt, 1954–57; Col, 1st Bn Royal SA Regt, 1962–65; Hon. ADC to Governor-Gen. of Australia, 1965–66. Patron, Order of St John, ACT, 1981–; KStJ 1985 (CStJ 1982). *Address:* 29 Custance Street, Farrer, ACT 2607, Australia. *T:* 86–3915.
*Died* 1 *Oct.* 1987.

**BLACKFORD, 4th Baron** *cr* 1935; **William Keith Mason;** Bt 1918; *b* 27 March 1962; *s* of 3rd Baron Blackford, DFC, and of Sarah, *d* of Sir Shirley Worthington-Evans, 2nd Bt; *S* father, 1977. *Educ:* Harrow School. *Address:* 17 The Gateways, Sprimont Place, SW3.
*Died* 15 *May* 1988 (*ext*).

**BLACKIE, John Ernest Haldane,** CB 1959; retired as Chief Inspector of the Department of Education (1951–66); *b* 6 June 1904; *e s* of late Rt Rev. E. M. Blackie, sometime Bishop of Grimsby and Dean of Rochester and late Caroline, *d* of Rev. J. Haldane Stewart of Ardsheal; *m* 1st, 1933, Kathleen Mary (*d* 1941), *d* of F. S. Creswell; no *c*; 2nd, 1942, Pamela Althea Vernon, *d* of A. J. Margetson, HMI; two *s* two *d. Educ:* Bradfield; Magdalene Coll., Cambridge (MA). Asst Master: Lawrenceville Sch., NJ, USA, 1926–27; Bradfield, 1928–33; Asst Director, Public Schools Empire Tour to NZ,

1932–33; HM Inspector of Schools, 1933; District Inspector, Manchester, 1936–47; Divisional Inspector, Eastern Divn, 1947–51; Chief Inspector of: Further Educn, 1951–58; Primary Educn, 1958–66; Secretary of State's Assessor on Central Advisory Council (Plowden), 1963–66. Lectr (part-time), Homerton Coll. of Educn, Cambridge, 1966–70. Mem. Directorate, Anglo-American Primary Project, 1969. Sen. Counsellor, Open Univ., 1970–73. 47th County of Lancaster Home Guard, 1940–44. FRES. *Publications:* Family Holidays Abroad (with Pamela Blackie), 1961; Good Enough for the Children?, 1963; Inside the Primary School, 1967; English Teaching for Non-Specialists, 1969; Inspecting and the Inspectorate, 1970; Changing the Primary School, 1974; Bradfield 1850–1975, 1976; various books and articles on education, travel and entomology. *Recreations:* travel, gardening, natural history. *Address:* The Bell House, Alconbury, Huntingdon, Cambs. *T:* Huntingdon 890270. *Club:* Pitt (Cambridge).                *Died 1 April 1985.*

**BLACKIE, Dr Margery Grace,** CVO 1979; formerly Hon. Consulting Physician to the Royal London Homœopathic Hospital and Dean of the Faculty of Homœopathy; *b* 4 Feb. 1898; *y d* of Robert and Elizabeth Blackie, Trafalgar House, Downham Market, Norfolk. *Educ:* Royal Free Hosp. and Medical School. MB, BS 1926; MD London 1928. Asst Phys., Children's Dept, Royal London Homœopathic Hosp., 1929–36; Asst Phys., Royal London Homœopathic Hosp., 1937–57; Sen. Consultant Phys., 1957–66; Physician to the Queen, 1968–80. Pres., Internat. Homœopathic Congress, 1965. *Publications:* The Place of Homœopathy in Modern Medicine (Presidential address), 1950; The Richards Hughes Memorial Lecture, 1959; The Patient not the Cure, 1975. *Address:* Hedingham Castle, Halstead, Essex. *T:* Hedingham 60435.
                *Died 24 Aug. 1981.*

**BLACKLEY, Travers Robert,** CMG 1952; CBE 1949 (OBE 1946); farmer; *b* 10 March 1899; *o s* of late Travers R. Blackley, Drumbar, Cavan, and of Ethel, *d* of Col E. W. Cuming, Crover, Mount Nugent, Co. Cavan; *m* 1932, Elizabeth, *o d* of late Major A. Deane, Royal Warwickshire Regt, and *g d* of Lt-Col Charles Deane, Gurrane, Fermoy; three *s* two *d* (and one *s* decd). *Educ:* Charterhouse (Scholar); Worcester Coll., Oxford (Senior Exhibitioner). Served European War, 1914–18, in Royal Artillery; joined Sudan Political Service 1922, and served in Blue Nile, Kordofan and Kassala Provinces; seconded for service in Occupied Territory Administrations, 1940. Lt-Col 1940–41; Col 1942; Brig. 1943. Served in Ethiopia and Tripolitania. Chief Administrator, Tripolitania, 1943–51; British Resident in Tripolitania, 1951. Order of the Nile (4th Class), 1936. *Recreations:* farming, shooting, fishing. *Address:* Gurrane, Fermoy, Co. Cork, Eire. *T:* Fermoy 31036. *Club:* Friendly Brothers (Dublin).                *Died 18 Feb. 1982.*

**BLACKLOCK, Captain Ronald William,** CBE 1944; DSC 1917; RN (retired); *b* 21 June 1889; *s* of late J. H. Blacklock, JP, Overthorpe, Banbury; *m* 1920, Aline Frances Anstell (*d* 1975); one *s*. *Educ:* Preparatory Sch.; HMS Britannia. Midshipman, 1906. Specialised in Submarines in 1910. Served European War in Submarines (despatches twice, DSC); Captain 1931; retd owing to ill-health, 1938; War of 1939–45, Director of Welfare Services, Admiralty. *Address:* The Edinburgh Private Clinic, 19 Drumsheugh Gardens, Edinburgh EH3 7RN. *Clubs:* Naval and Military; Royal Yacht Squadron.                *Died 29 Jan. 1987.*

**BLACKMAN, Rear-Adm. Charles Maurice,** DSO 1919; *b* 7 March 1890; 2nd surv. *s* of late Charles W. Blackman; *m* 1917, Brenda Olive (*d* 1969), *y d* of late Lawrence Hargrave; two *d*. *Educ:* Stubbington House, Fareham; HMS Britannia. Lieut, 1910; Lieut-Commander, 1918; Commander, 1924; Captain, 1931; retired list, 1941; promoted to Rear-Adm. for war services, 1946; a Younger Brother of Trinity House; served European War, 1914–18 (DSO); Baltic Operations, 1919–20; lent for service League of Nations, 1925–28; Disarmament Conference, 1932–33; War of 1939–45. *Address:* Ripa, Shore Lane, Bishops Waltham, Hants SO3 1EA. *T:* Bishops Waltham 2329. *Club:* Army and Navy.
                *Died 13 June 1981.*

**BLACKMAN, Prof. Moses,** FRS 1962; Professor of Physics, Imperial College of Science and Technology, London, 1959–76, then Professor Emeritus; Senior Research Fellow, Imperial College, since 1976; *b* 6 Dec. 1908; *e s* of late Rev. Joseph Blackman and Esther Oshry; *m* 1959, Anne Olivia, *d* of late Arthur L. Court, Sydney, Australia. *Educ:* Victoria Boys' High Sch., Grahamstown, SA; Rhodes University Coll., Grahamstown; Universities of Göttingen, London and Cambridge. MSc (SA) 1930; DPhil (Göttingen) 1933; PhD (London) 1936; PhD (Cantab) 1938. Queen Victoria Scholar (University of SA) 1931; Beit Scholar (Imperial Coll.) 1933; DSIR Sen. Res. Scholar, 1935; Member staff Physics Dept, Imperial Coll., 1937–. Mem. British Cttee on Atomic Energy, 1940–41; scientific work for Min. of Home Security, 1942–45. Member Internat. Commn on Electron Diffraction, 1957–66. Member Safety in Mines Research Advisory Board, Min. of Power, 1963–74. *Publications:*

scientific papers on the physics of crystals. *Address:* 48 Garden Royal, Kersfield Road, SW15. *T:* 01-789 1706.
                *Died 3 June 1983.*

**BLACKMAN, Raymond Victor Bernard,** MBE 1970; CEng, FIMarE, FRINA; Editor of Jane's Fighting Ships, 1949–50 to 1972–73 editions; author and journalist; *b* 29 June 1910; *e s* of late Leo Albert Martin Blackman and late Laura Gertrude, *e d* of Albert Thomas; *m* 1935, Alma Theresa Joyce, *y d* of late Francis Richard Hannah; one *s* one *d*. *Educ:* Southern Grammar Sch., Portsmouth. Contrib. to general and technical press, and associated with Jane's Fighting Ships 1930–73; Naval Correspondent, Hampshire Telegraph and Post, 1936–46, Sunday Times, 1946–56. Served Royal Navy, 1926–36 and War of 1939–45, HMS Vernon, Mine Design Dept, Admiralty. Member of The Press Gang. Broadcaster on naval topics. *Publications:* Modern World Book of Ships, 1951; The World's Warships, 1955, 1960, 1963, 1969; Ships of the Royal Navy, 1973; contrib. to The Statesman's Year Book (1949–50 to 1988–89 edns), The Diplomatist, Encyclopædia Britannica Book of the Year, Warships and Navies 1973, The Motor Ship, The Engineer, Navy, Lloyd's List, etc. *Recreations:* seagoing, foreign travel, philately. *Address:* 72 The Brow, Widley, Portsmouth, Hants PO7 5DA. *T:* Cosham 376837. *Clubs:* Anchorites; Press; Seven Seas; Batti-Wallahs; Royal Naval and Royal Albert Yacht (Portsmouth).
                *Died 17 May 1989.*

**BLACKSHAW, James William,** CMG 1951; MBE 1920; Assistant Secretary, Ministry of Supply, 1946–55, retired; *b* 8 June 1895; *s* of Arthur Joseph Blackshaw; *m* 1927, Edith Violet, *d* of George Hansford. *Educ:* Doncaster Grammar Sch. Civil Service from 1911. *Address:* 70 Victoria Avenue, Shanklin, Isle of Wight. *T:* Shanklin 2336.                *Died 19 March 1983.*

**BLACKWELL, Sir Basil Henry,** Kt 1956; JP; President of B. H. Blackwell Ltd (Chairman, 1924–69); Chairman, Basil Blackwell and Mott Ltd, 1922–69, and The Shakespeare Head Press, 1921–69; *b* 29 May 1889; *s* of late Benjamin Henry and late Lydia Blackwell; *m* 1914, Marion Christine (*d* 1977), *d* of late John Soans; one *s* three *d* (and one *s* decd). *Educ:* Magdalen College Sch.; Merton Coll., Oxford. 2nd Class Lit. Hum; studied publishing at the Oxford Press, Amen Corner; joined father in Oxford, 1913; started publishing independently, 1919; formed the Shakespeare Head Press Ltd to carry on and develop the work of the late A. H. Bullen, 1921; formed Basil Blackwell and Mott Ltd (publishers), 1922; succeeded father (the founder of the firm) as Chairman of B. H. Blackwell Ltd (booksellers), 1924; President: International Association of Antiquarian Booksellers, 1925 and 1926; Associated Booksellers of Great Britain and Ireland, 1934 and 1935; The Classical Assoc., 1964–65; William Morris Soc., 1968–79; English Assoc., 1969–70. Hon. Mem., Company of Stationers, 1973. Hon. Freeman of Oxford City. Hon. Fellow, Merton Coll., Oxford; Hon. LLD Manchester Univ., 1965; Hon DCL Oxford, 1979. Officier d'Académie, France. *Recreation:* reading. *Address:* Osse Field, Appleton, Abingdon, Oxon. *T:* Oxford 862436. *Clubs:* Athenæum; Leander.
                *Died 9 April 1984.*

**BLACKWELL, John Kenneth,** CBE 1965; HM Diplomatic Service, retired; *b* 8 May 1914; *s* of late J. W. Blackwell; *m* 1951, Joan Hilary, *d* of late D. W. Field; two *s* one *d*. *Educ:* Roundhay Sch.; Downing Coll., Cambridge (MA). HM Foreign Service, 1938; Vice-consular posts, in China and Mozambique, 1938–45; Second Secretary, British Embassy, Copenhagen, 1946; Consul, Canton, 1947; served in FO, 1950; Consul: Recife, 1952; Basle, 1956; First Secretary and Head of Chancery, British Embassy, Seoul, 1957; served in FO, 1959; First Secretary with UK Delegn to the European Communities in Brussels, 1961; Consul-General: Hanoi, 1962; Lille, 1965; Sen. Trade Comr, Hong Kong, 1969–72; Ambassador to Costa Rica, 1972–74. *Recreations:* linguistics and entomology; walking. *Address:* Oakley Hay, Vincent Road, Selsey, Sussex.
                *Died 14 April 1986.*

**BLACKWELL, Thomas Francis,** MBE (mil.) 1944; DL; Chairman, Turf Newspapers Ltd, since 1955; *b* 31 July 1912; *s* of late Thomas Geoffrey Blackwell and Shirley Maud Lawson-Johnston; *m* 1948, Lisette Douglas Pilkington (marr. diss. 1959); one *s* one *d*. *Educ:* Harrow; Magdalene Coll., Cambridge (MA). Mem. London Stock Exchange, 1935–42. Served War, Coldstream Guards, 1940–45: Bde Major, 5th Gds Armd Bde, 1944–45. Member of Lloyds, 1946. Captain Royal and Ancient Golf Club, 1963; Senior Steward of the Jockey Club, 1965 (Dep. Sen. Steward, 1973–76); Mem., Horserace Betting Levy Board, 1976–78. Chm., St John Council for Suffolk, 1970–82; KStJ 1981. Governor, Harrow School, 1975–82. DL Suffolk, 1974. *Recreations:* racing, shooting, golf. *Address:* Langham Hall, Bury St Edmunds, Suffolk. *T:* Walsham-le-Willows 271. *Clubs:* White's, Pratt's; Jockey (Newmarket).                *Died 18 Dec. 1983.*

**BLACKWOOD, Dame Margaret,** DBE 1981 (MBE 1964); PhD; Senior Associate and Cytogeneticist, University of Melbourne, since 1974; *b* 26 April 1909; *d* of late Robert Leslie Blackwood and Muriel Pearl Henry. *Educ:* Melbourne CofE Girls' Grammar Sch.;

Melbourne Univ. (BSc, MSc 1938); Newnham Coll., Cambridge (PhD 1954). Served War, 1941–46; Wing Officer, WAAAF. University of Melbourne: Lectr, Sen. Lectr, Reader in Botany and Genetics, 1946–74; Dean of Women, Mildura Br., 1946–48; Founder Fellow, First Chm. of Council, Janet Clarke Hall, 1961; Fellow, Trinity Coll., 1980; Mem. Council, 1976–83; Dep. Chancellor, 1980–83. Res. Asst, Univ. of Wisconsin, 1958; Carnegie Travel Fellow, 1958; Hon. Res. Fellow, Birmingham Univ., 1959. Hon. Organising Sec., Melbourne Congress, ANZAAS, 1977; former Sec., Internat. Fedn of Univ. Women (Victoria); Aust.-NZ Chm., Soroptimist Internat., 1957–58; Hon. Mem., SI of SW Pacific. Member: Royal Soc. of Vic; Aust. Genetics Soc.; British Lichen Soc. FANZAAS 1979. Chapman Medal, Inst. of Engrs, 1975. *Publications:* contribs to scientific jls. *Recreations:* music, photography, lichenology. *Address:* 63 Morrah Street, Parkville, Vic 3052, Australia; Botany School, University of Melbourne, Grattan Street, Parkville, Vic 3052. *Club:* Lyceum (Melbourne).
*Died 1 June 1986.*

**BLACKWOOD, Sir Robert (Rutherford),** Kt 1961; Chairman, Dunlop Australia Ltd. 1972–79 (General Manager, 1948–66); *b* Melbourne, 3 June 1906; *s* of Robert Leslie Blackwood and Muriel Pearl (*née* Henry); *m* 1932, Hazel Lavinia McLeod; one *s* one *d*. *Educ:* Melbourne C of E Grammar Sch.; Univ. of Melbourne. BEE 1929, MCE 1932, Melbourne. Senior Demonstrator and Res. Scholar, University of Melbourne, 1928–30; Lecturer in Agric. Engineering, 1931–33; Res. Engineer Dunlop Rubber, Australia Ltd, 1933–35; Tech. Man., 1936–46; Prof. of Mech. Engineering, University of Melbourne, 1947. Chm. Interim Council, Monash Univ., 1958–61; Chancellor, Monash Univ., 1961–68. Member Cttee on Medical Education, Victoria, 1960. Trustee, National Museum of Victoria, 1964–78, Pres. Council, 1971–78; Pres., Royal Soc. of Victoria, 1973–74. FIE Aust, 1948; Hon. LLD Monash, 1971; Hon. DTech Asian Inst. of Technology, Bangkok, 1978. *Publications:* Monash University: the first ten years, 1968; Beautiful Bali, 1970; papers in engrg jls. *Recreation:* painting. *Address:* 8 Huntingfield Road, Melbourne, Victoria 3186, Australia. *T:* 592-5925. *Clubs:* Melbourne, Athenæum (Melbourne). *Died 21 Aug. 1982.*

**BLACKWOOD, Prof. William;** Professor of Neuropathology, University of London, at The Institute of Neurology, The National Hospital, Queen Square, 1958–76, later Professor Emeritus; *b* 13 March 1911; *m* 1940, Cynthia Gledstone; one *s* one *d*. *Educ:* Cheltenham Coll.; Edinburgh Univ. MB, ChB Edinburgh 1934; FRCSEd 1938; FRCPEd 1961; FRCPath (FCPath 1963). Pathologist, Scottish Mental Hospitals Laboratory; Neuropathologist, Edinburgh Royal Infirmary, and Municipal Hospitals, 1939; Senior Lecturer in Neuropathology, University of Edinburgh, 1945; Asst Pathologist, 1947, Pathologist, 1949, The National Hospital, Queen Square, London. *Publications:* Atlas of Neuropathology, 1949; (ed jtly) Greenfield's Neuropathology, 3rd edn, 1976. *Address:* 71 Seal Hollow Road, Sevenoaks, Kent. *T:* Sevenoaks (0732) 454345. *Died 3 Dec. 1990.*

**BLAGDEN, Sir John (Ramsay),** Kt 1970; OBE 1944; TD 1943; Regional Chairman of Industrial Tribunals for East Anglia, 1969–80, retired; *b* Davos, Switzerland, 25 July 1908; *s* of John William Blagden, PhD, MA, and Johanna Alberta (*née* Martin); *m* 1937, Pauline Catherine Robinson; three *d*. *Educ:* Hawtreys; Marlborough; Emmanuel Coll., Cambridge (MA). Joined 7th Bn The Essex Regt TA, 2nd Lieut, 1928; Capt. 1935; Major 1938; called to Bar, Lincoln's Inn, 1934; Practised at Bar, 1934–39; War Service, 1939–45; Lt-Col, CO 64th HAA Regt, RA, 1943; BNAF, 1943; CMF and Land Forces Adriatic, 1944–45; BLA, 1945 (OBE, despatches twice, TD two clasps). Col 1945, Perm. Pres., Mil. Govt Courts, BAOR, Nov. 1945; Judge of Control Commn Courts, Germany, 1947; Sen. Magistrate, Sarawak, 1950; Actg Puisne Judge and Sen. Magistrate, Sarawak, 1951–56; Co-Ed. Sarawak Gazette, 1955; Puisne Judge, Trinidad, 1956–60; Trinidad Ed., West Indian Reports, 1959–60; Puisne Judge, Northern Rhodesia, 1960–64; Justice of Appeal, Northern Rhodesia and Zambia, 1964–65; Chief Justice, Zambia, 1965–69. Grand Cordon of Order of Star of Honour of Ethiopia, 1965. *Recreations:* photography, skiing, riding, walking, tennis, alpinism; watching cricket and motor racing. *Address:* Jackdaws Ford, Chelsworth, Ipswich, Suffolk. *T:* Bildeston 740461. *Club:* Special Forces. *Died 3 June 1985.*

**BLAIR;** *see* Hunter Blair.

**BLAIR, Rev. Andrew Hamish;** Member of the Community of the Resurrection, Mirfield, Yorks, since 1935; *b* 19 June 1901; *s* of Andrew Buchanan Blair, Edinburgh and Banwell, Somerset, and Constance Elizabeth Blair; unmarried. *Educ:* Merchiston Castle; Exeter Coll., Oxford. BA 1923, MA 1926. Deacon, 1924; Priest, 1925; Curate of St Mark, Swindon, 1924; CR Missionary in Borneo, 1936; Subwarden, Hostel of the Resurrection, Leeds Univ., 1937, Warden, 1940; Prior of Mirfield, 1943–49 and 1956–61; Principal, College of the Resurrection, Mirfield, 1949–55; Proctor in Convocation, Wakefield, 1958–61; Prior, St Paul's Priory, Holland

Park, W11, 1963–66. *Publication:* The Why and Wherefore of the Church, 1946. *Recreations:* various. *Address:* House of the Resurrection, Mirfield, West Yorks. *T:* Mirfield 4318.
*Died 25 July 1981.*

**BLAIR, Charles Neil Molesworth,** CMG 1962; OBE (mil.) 1948; Lt-Col; *b* 22 Oct. 1910; *o s* of late Col J. M. Blair, CMG, CBE, DSO, Glenfoot, Tillicoultry, Scotland; *m* 1938, Elizabeth Dorothea, *d* of late Lord Justice Luxmoore, PC; one *d* (one *s* decd). *Educ:* Stowe; RMC Sandhurst. 2nd Lieut The Black Watch, 1930. Served War of 1939–45 in Europe, North Africa and Sicily; Instructor, Army Staff Coll., 1941 and 1944; commanded 1st Black Watch, 1943. Retired from Army on account of war wounds, 1951. Attached FO, 1951–67. *Address:* c/o Lloyds Bank, 6 Pall Mall, SW1Y 5NH. *Club:* Army and Navy. *Died 20 June 1988.*

**BLAIR, David Arthur,** MBE 1943; MC 1944; Director, Distillers Co. Ltd, 1965–79; Chairman, Export Committee (Scotch Whisky), 1965–80, retired; *b* 25 Aug. 1917; *s* of Brig.-Gen. A. Blair, DSO; *m* 1947, Elizabeth Adela Morton; two *s* one *d* (and one *d* decd). *Educ:* Harrow; Sandhurst. Commnd Seaforth Highlanders, 1937; served War of 1939–45, Middle East and Europe; psc, India 1945; resigned commn and entered Distillers Co. Ltd, 1949, as export representative. Chm., United Glass Ltd, 1976–79. *Recreations:* golf, field sports. *Address:* Lilliesleaf House, Lilliesleaf, Roxburghshire. *Clubs:* New (Edinburgh); Royal and Ancient St Andrews (Captain 1978–79). *Died 10 April 1985.*

**BLAIR, Douglas MacColl;** QC 1989; *b* 19 Oct. 1940; *s* of Alexander Edwin Blair and Joan Alexandra Blair (*née* MacColl); *m* 1971, Diana Rosemary Holding-Parsons; one *s* one *d*. *Educ:* Glenalmond Coll., Perthshire, Scotland; Pembroke Coll., Cambridge (BA). Called to the Bar, Inner Temple, 1963; a Recorder, 1986. *Recreation:* golf. *Address:* 88 Camberwell Grove, SE5 8RF.
*Died 16 Feb. 1990.*

**BLAIR, George William S.;** *see* Scott Blair.

**BLAIR, Rev. Canon Harold Arthur,** MA, BD; Canon Residentiary and Chancellor of Truro Cathedral, 1960–75, then Emeritus; *b* 22 Sept. 1902; *s* of Rev. A. A. Blair, SPG Mission, India, some time rector of Saxlingham, Holt, Norfolk; *m* 1933, Honor MacAdam, *d* of Col W. MacAdam, CB, RE; two *s* one *d*. *Educ:* Lancing Coll.; St Edmund Hall, Oxford. BA (2nd cl. Hons Theol.) 1925; MA 1937; BD (Oxon) 1945. Classical Tutor, Dorchester Missionary Coll., 1925–27; Gold Coast Administrative Service, 1927; Asst District Comr, 1928; District Comr, 1935, retd 1939. Ordained Deacon, 1939, Priest, 1940; Asst Curate, Sherborne, 1939–41; Vicar of Horningsham, Wilts, 1941–45; Winterbourne Earls with Winterbourne Dauntsey and Winterbourne Gunner, 1945–54; St James, Southbroom, Devizes, 1954–60. Hon. Canon of Salisbury, 1953 (prebend of Alton Australis); Examining Chaplain: to Bishop of Salisbury, 1952–60; to Bishop of Truro, 1960–81. *Publications:* A Creed before the Creeds, 1954; The Ladder of Temptations, 1960; A Stranger in the House, 1963; essay in Agreed Syllabus of Religious Education (Cornwall), 1964; two essays in Teilhard Re-assessed (symposium), 1970; various articles in Church Quarterly Review. *Recreations:* gardening, cycling, story-telling. *Address:* Beech Cottage, 79 Acreman Street, Sherborne, Dorset DT9 3PH. *T:* Sherborne 812353. *Died 15 Jan. 1985.*

**BLAIR-CUNYNGHAME, Sir James (Ogilvy),** Kt 1976; OBE 1945 (MBE 1943); Chairman, The Royal Bank of Scotland Group plc, 1968–78, Director 1968–82; *b* 28 Feb. 1913; 2nd *s* of late Edwin Blair-Cunynghame and Anne Tod, both of Edinburgh. *Educ:* Sedbergh Sch.; King's Coll., Cambridge (MA). Elected Fellow, St Catharine's Coll., 1939. Served War of 1939–45 (MBE, OBE); RA and Intelligence, Mediterranean and Europe, Lt-Col 1944. FO, 1946–47; Chief Personnel Officer, BOAC, 1947–55; Dir-Gen. of Staff, National Coal Board, 1955–57; Mem. for Staff of Nat. Coal Bd, 1957–59; part-time Mem., Pay Board, 1973–74. Chairman: Royal Bank of Scotland, 1971–76 (Dir, 1960–82); Williams & Glyn's Bank, 1976–78 (Dir, 1969–82); Dep. Chm., Provincial Insurance, 1979–85; Dir, Scottish Mortgage and Trust, 1967–83. Member: Scottish Economic Council, 1965–74; Exec. Cttee Scottish Council Develt and Industry; Council of Industry for Management Educn; Ct of Governors London Sch. of Economics and Political Science; Council Industrial Soc.; Governor, Sedbergh Sch. FBIM; CIPM. Mem., Queen's Body Guard for Scotland. Hon. LLD St Andrews, 1965; Hon. DSc (Soc. Sci.) Edinburgh, 1969. Hon. FRCSEd 1978; FIB 1977. *Publications:* various articles on aspects of personnel management and the economy. *Recreation:* fishing. *Address:* Broomfield, Moniaive, Thornhill, Dumfriesshire. *T:* Moniaive 217. *Clubs:* Savile, Flyfishers'; New, Scottish Arts (Edinburgh).
*Died 4 Jan. 1990.*

**BLAIZE, Rt. Hon. Herbert (Augustus);** PC 1986; Prime Minister of Grenada, since 1984; *b* 26 Feb. 1918. Chief Minister of Grenada, 1960–61, 1962–67; insurance business, 1979–83; Leader, New

National Party, 1984–89. *Address:* Office of the Prime Minister, St George's, Grenada.                              *Died* 19 Dec. 1989.

**BLAKE, Dr Eugene Carson;** retired; General Secretary, World Council of Churches, 1966–72; *b* St Louis, Mo, USA, 7 Nov. 1906; *s* of Orville P. Blake and Lulu (*née* Carson); *m* 1st, 1929, Valina Gillespie; 2nd, 1974, Jean Ware Hoyt. *Educ:* Princeton Univ.; New Coll., Edinburgh; Princeton Theological Seminary. Taught at Forman Christian Coll., Lahore, 1928–29; Asst Pastor, St Nicholas, NYC, 1932–35; Pastor: First Presbyterian Church, Albany, 1935–40; Pasadena Presbyterian Church, 1940–51. Stated Clerk, Gen. Assembly: Presbyterian Church in USA, 1951–58; United Presbyterian Church in USA, 1958–66. National Council of Churches of Christ in USA: Pres., 1954–57; subseq. Mem., Gen. Board; Chm., Commn on Religion and Race. Member: Central Cttee, Exec. Cttee, World Council of Churches, 1954–66. Trustee: Princeton Seminary; Occidental Coll.; San Francisco Theol Seminary. Visiting Lectr, Williams Coll., 1938–40. Has many hon. degrees. *Publications:* He is Lord of All, 1956; The Church in the Next Decade, 1966. *Recreation:* contract bridge. *Address:* 204 Davenport Drive, Stamford, Conn 06902, USA.
                                                                   *Died* 31 *July* 1985.

**BLAKE, Henry E.;** *see* Elliott-Blake.

**BLAKE, John William,** CBE 1972; Professor of History, New University of Ulster, 1972–77, later Emeritus; *b* 7 Dec. 1911; *s* of Robert Gay Blake and Beatrice Mary Blake (*née* Tucket); *m* 1938, Eileen Florence Lord; two *s* one *d. Educ:* Kilburn Grammar Sch.; King's Coll., London (MA). Inglis Student and Derby Scholar, 1933–34; QUB: Asst Lectr, 1934; Lectr, 1944; Sen. Lectr, 1945; served War of 1939–45 in Civil Defence and as Offical War Historian to NI Govt; Prof. of History, Univ. of Keele (until 1962 University Coll. of N Staffs), 1950–64; Acting Principal of University Coll. of N Staffs, 1954–56; Vice-Chancellor, Univ. of Botswana, Lesotho and Swaziland (formerly Basutoland, Bechuanaland Protectorate and Swaziland), 1964–71. Vis. Prof., Univ. of North Carolina at Asheville, 1979. Mem. Staffs Co. Educn Cttee, 1955–61; Mem. Inter-Univ. Council for Higher Educn Overseas, 1955–64; FRHistS. Hon. Fellow, Hist. Soc., Ghana. Hon. DLitt: Keele 1971; Botswana, Lesotho and Swaziland, 1971. *Publications:* European Beginnings in West Africa, 1937; Europeans in West Africa, 2 vols 1942; Official War History of Northern Ireland, 1956; West Africa: Quest for God and Gold, 1977; contribs to historical jls. *Recreations:* gardening, philately. *Address:* Greystones, Northside, Shadforth, Co. Durham.                              *Died* 7 *March* 1987.

**BLAKELY, Colin George Edward;** actor and director since 1957; *b* 23 Sept. 1930; *s* of Victor Charles and Dorothy Margaret Ashmore Blakely; *m* 1961, Margaret Elsa Whiting; three *s. Educ:* Sedbergh School. Manager, Athletic Stores Ltd, Belfast, 1948–57; 1st prof. acting job, Children's Touring Theatre (Gwent), 1957; Group Theatre, Belfast, 1957–59; Cock a Doodle Dandy, Royal Court, 1959; Moon for the Misbegotten, Arts, 1960; The Naming of Murderers Rock, Royal Court, 1960; entered TV and films (Saturday Night and Sunday Morning), 1960–61; Hastings, in Richard III, and Touchstone, in As You Like It, Royal Shakespeare Co., Stratford, 1961; subseq. various films, TV, etc; Nat. Theatre, 1963–68: Pizarro, in Royal Hunt of the Sun; Captain Boyle, in Juno and the Paycock; Proctor, in Crucible; Philoctetes, in Philoctetes; Kite, in Recruiting Officer; Volpone, in Volpone; Hobson, in Hobson's Choice; Captain Shot-over, in Heartbreak House; Astrov, in Uncle Vanya, and Schmidt, in Fire Raisers, Royal Court; Torvald, in A Doll's House, Criterion, 1973; Vukhow, in Judgement, Royal Court, 1976; Dysart, in Equus, Albery, 1976; Dennis, in Just Between Ourselves, Queen's, 1977; Filumena, Lyric, 1977; Enjoy, Vaudeville, 1980; All My Sons, Wyndham's, 1981; Lovers Dancing, Albery, 1983; One for the Road, Duchess, 1985; Daffyd, in Chorus of Disapproval, Nat. Theatre, then Lyric, 1986. *Principal films* include: This Sporting Life; Decline and Fall; Watson, in The Private Life of Sherlock Holmes; The National Health; It Shouldn't Happen to a Vet; The Pink Panther Strikes Again; Equus; Dogs of War; Evil under the Sun; The Little World of Don Camillo; *TV appearances* include: Christ, in Son of Man; Peer Gynt, in Peer Gynt; Antony, in Antony and Cleopatra; Stalin, in The Red Monarch; Landscape, 1983; title rôle in The Father, 1985; The Dumb Waiter, 1985; Operation Julie, 1985; The Birthday Party, 1987. *Recreations:* piano, painting, sketching, golf. *Address:* c/o Leading Artists, 60 St James's Street, SW1. *T:* 01–491 4400.
                                                                   *Died* 7 *May* 1987.

**BLAKEMORE, Alan,** CBE 1976; Member, London Residuary Body, since 1985; Town Clerk and Chief Executive (formerly Town Clerk), Croydon, 1963–82; *b* 17 May 1919; *s* of late John William and Mary Blakemore, Salford; *m* 1956, José Margaret Cavill; two *s. Educ:* North Manchester School. Solicitor, 1943. Articled to Town Clerk, Salford, 1936; RASC (TA), 1939; Army service to 1946; released with hon. rank Lt-Col; Asst Solicitor, Salford, 1946–48; Deputy Town Clerk: Wigan, 1948–52; Bolton, 1952–57; Town

Clerk, Stockport, 1957–63; Officer Adviser: AMC, 1965–74; AMA, 1974–82. Hon. Clerk, General Purposes Cttee, London Boroughs Assoc., 1971–82; Consultant, 1982–. Mem., DHSS Housing Benefits Rev. Cttee, 1984–85. Hon. Freeman, London Bor. of Croydon, 1982. *Address:* Chaseley, 4 Waterfield Drive, Warlingham, Surrey CR3 9HP. *T:* Upper Warlingham 4249. *Club:* Royal Over-Seas League.                              *Died* 28 Oct. 1989.

**BLAKENEY, Frederick Joseph,** CBE 1968; Australian diplomat, retired 1978; *b* Sydney, NSW, 2 July 1913; *s* of Frederick Joseph Blakeney, Sydney; *m* 1943, Marjorie, *d* of John Martin, NSW; one *d. Educ:* Marist Darlinghurst and Mittagong; Univ. of Sydney. AMF, 1940–41; RAAF Flt Lieut (Navigator), 1942–45. Teaching Fellow, Univ. of Sydney, 1946; Dept of External Affairs, Canberra, 1946; 2nd Sec. and 1st Sec., Austr. Embassy, Paris, 1947–49; 1st Sec., then Chargé d'Affaires, Austr. Embassy, Moscow, 1949–51; Dept of Ext. Affairs, Canberra, 1952–53; Counsellor, Austr. Embassy, Washington, 1953–56; Minister to Vietnam and Laos, 1957–59, and to Cambodia, 1957; Asst Sec. (S and SE Asia), Dept of Ext. Affairs, Canberra, 1959–62; Australian Ambassador to Federal Republic of Germany, 1962–68; Australian Ambassador to USSR, 1968–71; First Asst Sec. (Defence), Dept of Foreign Affairs, Canberra, 1972–74; Australian Ambassador to the Netherlands, 1974–77; Australian Ambassador and Perm. Rep. to the UN, Geneva, 1977–78. *Address:* 1 Clissold Street, Mollymook, NSW 2539, Australia.                              *Died* 16 *June* 1990.

**BLAKENHAM,** 1st Viscount *cr* 1963, of Little Blakenham; **John Hugh Hare,** PC 1955; OBE 1945 (MBE 1943); VMH; DL; *b* 22 Jan. 1911; *s* of 4th Earl of Listowel; *m* 1934, Hon. Beryl Nancy Pearson, *d* of 2nd Viscount Cowdray; one *s* two *d. Educ:* Eton Coll. Business, London County Council, Territorial Army, Suffolk Yeomanry, then served during War of 1939–45 in England, North Africa and Italy (despatches, MBE, OBE, Legion of Merit, USA). Alderman LCC, 1937–52; Chm. of London Municipal Soc., 1947–52. MP (C) Woodbridge Div. of Suffolk, 1945–50, Sudbury and Woodbridge Div. of Suffolk, 1950–63. A Vice-Chm. Conservative Party Organisation, (Dec.) 1951–55; Minister of State for Colonial Affairs, Dec. 1955–Oct. 1956; Sec. of State for War, Jan. 1956–Jan. 1958; Minister of Agriculture, Fisheries and Food, Jan. 1958–60; Minister of Labour, 1960–63; Chancellor of the Duchy of Lancaster, also Dep. Leader of the House of Lords, 1963–64; Chairman: Conservative Party Organisation, 1963–65; Council, Toynbee Hall, 1966–; Governing Body, Peabody Trust, 1967–81. Treasurer, Royal Horticultural Soc., 1971–81 (Victoria Medal of Honour, 1974). DL Suffolk, 1968. *Recreations:* golf, gardening. *Heir:* *s* Hon. Michael John Hare. *Address:* 10 Holland Park, W11; Cottage Farm, Little Blakenham, near Ipswich, Suffolk. *T:* Ipswich 830344. *Clubs:* White's, Pratt's.                              *Died* 7 *March* 1982.

**BLAKER, His Honour Nathaniel Robert,** QC 1972; DL; a Circuit Judge, 1976–89, retired; *b* 31 Jan. 1921; *s* of Major Herbert Harry Blaker and Annie Muriel Blaker (*née* Atkinson); *m* 1951, Celia Margaret, *o d* of W. Hedley, DSO, KC, and Mrs Hedley; two *d. Educ:* Winchester; University College, Oxford (MA). Royal Signals, 1940–47. Called to the Bar, Inner Temple, 1948; Bencher, 1971. Dep. Chm., Dorset QS, 1970; a Recorder of the Crown Court, 1972–76. Wine Treasurer, Western Circuit, 1964–76. DL Hants, 1985. *Address:* 2 Culver Road, Winchester, Hants. *T:* Winchester (0962) 69826.                              *Died* 28 *July* 1990.

**BLAKEWAY, John Denys;** HM Diplomatic Service, retired; *b* 27 May 1918; *s* of late Sir Denys Blakeway, CIE; *m* 1946, Jasmine Iremonger; one *s* two *d. Educ:* Rugby (Schol.); Magdalen Coll., Oxford (Schol., MA). British and Indian Army, 1939–46 (wounded). Joined Foreign (subseq. Diplomatic) Service, 1946; served Sofia, Lyons, Athens (twice), Tripoli, FO (twice), Bologna, Rome, Ibadan, The Hague; Consul-Gen., Istanbul, 1975–78. *Recreation:* viticulture. *Address:* Row Farm, Zeals, Warminster, Wilts. *T:* Bourton (Dorset) 840209.                              *Died* 24 *Nov.* 1986.

**BLANCO WHITE, Amber,** OBE; *b* 1 July 1887; *d* of William Pember Reeves and Magdalen Stuart Robison; *m* George Rivers Blanco White; one *s* two *d. Educ:* Kensington High School; Newnham College, Cambridge. Director of Women's Wages, Ministry of Munitions, 1916–19; Member National Whitley Council for Civil Service, 1919–20; University Tutorial Lectr on Moral Science, Morley Coll.; retired 1965. Editor, The Townswoman, 1933; contested Hendon Division, 1931 and 1935. *Publications: as Amber Reeves:* The Reward of Virtue, 1911; A Lady and Her Husband, 1914; Helen in Love, 1916; Give and Take, 1923; *as Amber Blanco White:* The Nationalisation of Banking, 1934; The New Propaganda, 1939; Worry in Women, 1941; Ethics for Unbelievers, 1949; (with H. G. Wells) The Work, Wealth and Happiness of Mankind, 1932; articles on literature and finance. *Address:* 44 Downshire Hill, Hampstead, NW3.                              *Died* 26 *Dec.* 1981.

**BLEASDALE, Raymond John,** CBE 1982; RIBA; Director, Estates and Environment, Scottish Development Agency, since 1976; *b* 3 Sept. 1924; *s* of John William Bleasdale and Rose Bleasdale; *m*

1951, Patricia Feather; two *s* one *d. Educ:* Bradford Grammar Sch.; Leeds Sch. of Architecture. Dipl.Arch 1949; RIBA 1950; FRIAS 1967; AICArb 1967. Served RAF, USA and SE Asia, 1943–47. Development Dept, English Electric Co., 1949–60; Chief Architect, English Electric Gp, 1960–65; Building Dir, Scottish Industrial Estates Corp., 1965–75; joined Scottish Develt Agency, 1975. *Publications:* articles in sundry technical jls. *Recreations:* sailing, walking, painting in oils. *Address:* 9 Kersland Drive, Milngavie, Glasgow G62 8DG. *T:* 041-956 1528. *Club:* Royal Scottish Automobile (Glasgow). *Died* 27 *Nov.* 1982.

**BLELLOCH, Ian William,** CMG 1955; retired; *b* 2 Aug. 1901; *s* of late John Stobie Blelloch and late Christina Macdonald; *m* 1st, 1929, Leila Mary Henderson (*d* 1936); one *s* (and one *s* decd); 2nd, 1946, Margaret Rachel Stevenson. *Educ:* Dunfermline High Sch.; Edinburgh University. MA 1st Class Hons, 1924. Cadet, Federated Malay States, 1926; Class V, 1929; District Officer, Raub, Class IV, 1933; Legal Adviser and Deputy Public Prosecutor, Perak, 1935–37; Sec. to Resident, Negri Sembilan, Class III, 1938; Legal Adviser, Public Prosecutor, Kedah, 1939–41; interned by Japanese, 1942–45; Class II, 1943; Class IB, 1946; Secretary, Resident Commissioner, Perak, 1946–47; Acting British Adviser, Trengganu, 1948–50; British Adviser, Perak, Federation of Malaya, 1951; retired 1957. Perak Meritorious Service Medal, 1953; created Datoh Kurnia Bakti, Perak, 1956; CStJ 1964 (OStJ 1956). *Recreation:* golf. *Address:* The Garth, Blairgowrie, Perthshire. *T:* Blairgowrie 567. *Club:* East India, Devonshire, Sports and Public Schools.
*Died* 25 *March* 1982.

**BLEWETT, Maj.-Gen. Robert Sidney,** OBE 1974; QHP 1987; appointed Director General Army Medical Services, Ministry of Defence, from 1988; *b* 5 Aug. 1931; *s* of late Sidney Blewett and Phylis Augusta Norah (*née* Hamilton); *m* 1958, Elizabeth Maud Lewis; one *s* one *d. Educ:* Truro Sch.; Middlesex Hosp. Med. Sch., Univ. of London. MB BS; MFCM; D(Obst)RCOG; DTM&H. Ho. Surg. and Ho. Phys., W Kent Gen. Hosp., 1955–56. Regtl MO Caribbean Area, 1956–59; Asst Dir of Med. Servs, HQ 53 Welsh Div., 1961–62; Regtl MO 2/2 Gurkha Rifles, 1963–65 (GSMs Brunei, Borneo, Malay Peninsula; mentioned in despatches); D(Obst)RCOG Trainee, BMH Singapore, 1965–66; OC 11 Field Dressing Station, 1966–67; psc 1968; Asst Comdt Royal Army Med. Coll., 1969–71; Commanding Officer: 15 Field Ambulance, 1971–73; BMH Munster, 1973–75; Asst Dir of Med. Servs, HQ 4 Div., 1975–76; Asst Dir Gen. Army Med. Directorate 3/Adjt Gen. 3, 1977–79; CO Cambridge Mil. Hosp., 1979–80; Dep. Comdr Medical, HQ BAOR, 1980–83; Comdr Medical, HQ 1st British Corps, 1983–84; Asst Surg. Gen. (Ops & Plans), MoD (Defence Med. Services Directorate), 1984–85; Comdr Medical, HQ BAOR, 1985–87. OStJ 1984. Chadwick Meml Prize, UCL, 1980. Rhodesia Medal, 1979; Zimbabwe Independence Medal, 1980; Commendation, Comdr Monitoring Force, Rhodesia, 1980. *Recreations:* garden, joinery, tennis. *Address:* c/o Coutts & Co., 23 Hanover Square, W1A 4YE. *Died* 30 *Oct.* 1987.

**BLISS, Kathleen Mary, (Mrs Rupert Bliss),** MA Cantab 1934; Lecturer in Religious Studies, University of Sussex, 1967–72; *b* 5 July 1908; *née* Moore; *m* 1932, Rev. Rupert Bliss; three *d. Educ:* Girton Coll., Cambridge. Educational work in India, 1932–39; Editor, the Christian Newsletter, 1945–49; organized Christian-humanist debate, BBC, 1951–55; Studies of education in industry, 1956–57; General Sec., Church of England Board of Education, 1958–66. Member of Public Schools Commn, 1967–70. Hon. DD (Aberdeen), 1949. Select Preacher before the Univ. of Cambridge, 1967. *Publications:* The Service and Status of Women in the Churches, 1951; We the People, 1963; The Future of Religion, 1969. *Address:* Flat 5, Manormead, Tilford Road, Hindhead, Surrey GU26 6RA. *T:* Hindhead 7274. *Died* 13 *Sept.* 1989.

**BLOCH, Prof. Felix,** PhD; Professor of Physics, Stanford University, USA, 1934–71, Professor Emeritus, since 1971; *b* 23 Oct. 1905; *s* of Gustav Bloch and Agnes Mayer; *m* 1940, Lore Misch; three *s* one *d. Educ:* Zurich, Switzerland. PhD Leipzig, 1928. Asst Zurich, 1928–29; Lorentz Fellow, Holland, 1929–30; Asst Leipzig, 1930–31; Oersted Fellow, Copenhagen, 1931–32; Lecturer, Leipzig, 1932–33; Rockefeller Fellow, Rome, 1933–34; Director-General European Council for Nuclear Research, Geneva, 1954–55. Hon. DSc: Grenoble, 1959; Oxon, 1960; Jerusalem, 1962; Brandeis, 1976; Pavia, 1977; Hon. DPhil Zurich, 1966. Fellow American Phys. Society (Pres., 1965–66); Member: Nat. Academy of Sciences, 1948; Royal Dutch Acad. of Sciences; Hon. Mem., French Physical Soc.; Hon. FRSE; Hon. Fellow, Weizmann Inst., 1958. (Jointly) Nobel Prize for Physics, 1952. Pour le Mérite Order, 1979. *Publications:* about 80 articles on atomic and nuclear physics in various European and American scientific journals. *Recreations:* ski-ing, mountaineering, piano. *Address:* 1551 Emerson Street, Palo Alto, Calif 94301, USA. *T:* 327-8156. *Died* 10 *Sept.* 1983.

**BLOFIELD, Edgar Glanville,** DSO 1940; Lieutenant (E) RN, retired; *b* 1 June 1899; *s* of Shipwright Lieut-Comdr C. Blofield, RN; *m*

1926, Gladys Enid Learmouth; one *d. Educ:* Esplanade House Sch., Portsmouth. Joined Royal Navy, 1915; served in various ships in Home Fleet, Mediterranean and China Stations; was serving in HM Yacht Victoria and Albert on outbreak of war; retired list, 1949; joined Merchant Navy and served in supertankers and cargo liners until 1963. *Recreations:* those connected with country and sea. *Address:* 91 Festing Grove, Southsea, Hants.
*Died* 14 *Feb.* 1981.

**BLOMEFIELD, His Honour Peregrine Maitland;** a Circuit Judge (formerly County Court Judge), 1969–87; *b* 25 Oct. 1917; 2nd *s* of Lt-Col Wilmot Blomefield, OBE; *m* 1941, Angela Catherine, *d* of Major Geoffrey Hugh Shenley Crofton, Heytesbury, Wilts; one *s. Educ:* Repton Sch.; Trinity Coll., Oxford (MA). Royal Signals, 1940–46 (Captain). Called to the Bar, Middle Temple, 1947, Bencher, 1967; Oxford Circuit; Recorder of Burton-on-Trent, 1969; Dep. Chm., Berkshire QS, 1967–71. *Address:* c/o Middle Temple Treasury, Middle Temple Lane, EC4Y 9AT.
*Died* 25 *Feb.* 1988.

**BLOMEFIELD, Sir Thomas Edward Peregrine,** 5th Bt, *cr* 1807; *b* 31 May 1907; *s* of late Commander T. C. A. Blomefield, *e s* of 4th Bt and Margaret, *e d* of E. P. Landon; *S* grandfather, 1928; *m* 1947, Ginette Massart, Paris; one *s. Educ:* Wellington; Trinity Coll., Oxford. Temp. Lieut-Comdt RNVR, 1939–46. *Heir: s* Thomas Charles Peregrine Blomefield [*b* 24 July 1948; *m* 1975, Georgina, *d* of Commander Charles Over; one *s*]. *Address:* 1 Great Lane, Shaftesbury, Dorset. *T:* Shaftesbury 3788.
*Died* 26 *Feb.* 1984.

**BLOOM, Ursula Harvey, (Mrs Gower Robinson);** authoress; *b* Chelmsford, Essex, 11 Dec. 1892; *o d* of late Rev. J. Harvey Bloom, MA; *m* 1st, 1916, Capt. Arthur Brownlow Denham-Cookes, 24th London Regt (Queen's) (*d* 1918); one *s*; 2nd, 1925, Paymaster Comdr Charles Gower Robinson (*d* 1979), RN (retired). *Educ:* privately. First book, Tiger, published privately when seven years old. Writing under the names of Ursula Bloom, Lozania Prole, Sheila Burnes, Mary Essex and Rachel Harvey has published some 500 books. *Publications: include:* The Great Beginning, 1924; Vagabond Harvest, 1925; The Driving of Destiny, 1925; Our Lady of Marble, 1926; The Judge of Jerusalem, 1926; Candleshades, 1927; Spilled Salt, 1927; Base Metal, 1928; An April After, 1928; Tarnish, 1929; To-morrow for Apricots, 1929; The Passionate Heart, 1930; The Secret Lover, 1930; Lamp in the Darkness: a volume of Religious Essays, 1930; Fruit on the Bough, 1931; Packmule, 1931; The Pilgrim Soul, 1932; The Cypresses Grow Dark, 1932; The Log of an NO's Wife, 1932; Wonder Cruise, 1933; Mistress of None, 1933; Rose Sweetman, 1933; Pastoral, 1934; Holiday Mood, 1934; The Questing Trout, 1934; The Gypsy Vans Come Through, 1935; Harvest of a House, 1935; The Laughing Lady, 1936; Laughter on Cheyne Walk, 1936; Three Cedars, 1937; Leaves Before the Storm, 1937; The Golden Venture, 1938; Without Makeup, 1938; The ABC of Authorship, 1938; A Cad's Guide to Cruising, 1938; Lily of the Valley, 1938; Beloved Creditor, 1939; These Roots Go Deep, 1939; The Woman Who Was To-morrow, 1940; Log of No Lady, 1940; The Flying Swans, 1940; Dinah's Husband, 1941; The Virgin Thorn, 1941; Lovely Shadow, 1942; Time, Tide and I, 1942; Age Cannot Wither, 1942; No Lady Buys a Cot, 1943; Robin in a Cage, 1943; The Fourth Cedar, 1943; The Faithless Dove, 1944; No Lady in Bed, 1944; The Painted Lady, 1945; The Changed Village, 1945; Rude Forefathers, 1945; No Lady With a Pen, 1946; Four Sons, 1946; Adam's Daughter, 1947; Three Sisters, 1948; Façade, 1948; No Lady Meets No Gentleman, 1948; Next Tuesday, 1949; Elinor Jowitt, Antiques; No Lady in the Cart; Song of Philomel, 1950; The King's Wife, 1950; Mum's Girl was no Lady, 1950; Pavilion, 1951; Nine Lives, 1951; How Dark, My Lady!, 1951; The Sentimental Family, 1951; As Bends the Bough, 1952; Twilight of a Tudor, 1952; Sea Fret, 1952; The Gracious Lady, 1953; The First Elizabeth, 1953; Hitler's Eva, 1954; Trilogy, 1954; Curtain Call for the Guvnor, 1954; Matthew, Mark, Luke and John, 1954; Daughters of the Rectory, 1955; The Silver Ring, 1955; The Tides of Spring Flow Fast, 1955; Victorian Vinaigrette, 1956; No Lady Has a Dog's Day, 1956; Brief Springtime, 1957; The Elegant Edwardian, 1957; Monkey Tree in a Flower Pot, 1957; He Lit the Lamp, 1958; The Abiding City, 1958; Down to the Sea in Ships, 1958; The Inspired Needle, 1959; Youth at the Gate, 1959; Undarkening Green, 1959; Sixty Years of Home, 1960; The Thieving Magpie, 1960; Prelude to Yesterday, 1961; The Cactus has Courage, 1961; War Isn't Wonderful, 1961; Ship in a Bottle, 1962; Harvest Home Come Sunday, 1962; Parson Extraordinary, 1963; The Gated Road, 1963; Mrs Bunthorpe's Respects, 1963; The House That Died Alone, 1964; The Rose of Norfolk, 1964; The Ring Tree, 1964; The Ugly Head, 1965; The Quiet Village, 1965; Rosemary for Stratford-on-Avon, 1965; Price Above Rubies, 1965; The Dandelion Clock, 1966; The Mightier Sword, 1966; The Old Adam, 1967; A Roof and Four Walls, 1967; Two Pools in a Field, 1967; The Dragon Fly, 1968; Yesterday is To-morrow, 1968; Flight of the Peregrine, 1969; The House of Kent, 1969; The Hunter's Moon, 1970; Rosemary for Frinton, 1970; The

Tune of Time, 1970; The Great Tomorrow, 1971; Perchance to Dream, 1971; Rosemary for Chelsea (autobiog.), 1971; The Caravan of Chance, 1972; The Cheval Glass, 1972; The Duke of Windsor, 1972; The Old Rectory, 1973; Princesses in Love, 1973; Requesting the Pleasure, 1973; The Old Elm Tree, 1974; Miracle on the Horizon, 1974; Royal Baby, 1975; Twisted Road, 1975; Turn of Life's Tide, 1976; Life is no Fairy Tale (autobiog.), 1976; The Great Queen Consort, 1976. *Address:* c/o Newtown House, Walls Drive, Ravenglass, Cumbria. *Died 29 Oct.* 1984.

**BLOOMER, Rt. Rev. Thomas,** DD 1946 (TCD); *b* 14 July 1894; *s* of Thomas and Mary Bloomer; *m* 1935, Marjorie Grace (*d* 1969), *d* of late Rev. David Hutchison; one *s* two *d*; *m* 1973, Marjorie, *widow* of I. M. Orr. *Educ:* Royal Sch., Dungannon, N Ireland; Trinity Coll., Dublin. Ordained to curacy of Carrickfergus, N Ireland, 1918; Curate of: Castleton, Lancs, 1922; Cheltenham, Glos, 1923; Vicar of St Mark's, Bath, 1928; Vicar of Barking, 1935–46; Rural Dean of Barking and Canon of Chelmsford Cathedral, 1943–46; Bishop of Carlisle, 1946–66. Chaplain to: the King, 1944–47; House of Lords, 1953–66. Proctor in Convocation of Canterbury, 1945. Freedom of City of Carlisle, 1966. *Publications:* A Fact and a Faith, 1943; A Fact and an Experience, 1944. *Recreations:* golf, gardening. *Address:* 33 Greengate, Levens, Kendal, Cumbria. *T:* Sedgwick 60771.
*Died 5 Jan.* 1984.

**BLOOMFIELD, Hon. Sir John (Stoughton),** Kt 1967; QC (Victoria) 1965; LLB; Member for Malvern, Legislative Assembly, Victoria, 1953–70, retired; *b* 9 Oct. 1901; *s* of Arthur Stoughton Bloomfield, Chartered Accountant, Melbourne, and Ada Victoria Bloomfield; *m* 1931, Beatrice Madge, *d* of W. H. Taylor, Overnewton, Sydenham, Victoria; one *s* one *d*. *Educ:* Geelong Grammar Sch.; Trinity Coll., Melbourne Univ. Served AIF, 1940–45; Lieut-Col retired. Solicitor, 1927–45; called to Victorian Bar, 1945. Government of Victoria: Minister of Labour and Industry and of Electrical Undertakings, 1955–56; Minister of Education, 1956–67. Mem. Council, University of Melbourne, 1956–70. *Publications:* Company Law Amendments, 1939; Screens and Gowns: Some Aspects of University Education Overseas, 1963; articles in professional journals. *Recreation:* painting. *Address:* 1/22 Mercer Road, Armadale, Victoria 3143, Australia. *T:* 20–2947. *Clubs:* Melbourne, Naval and Military (Melbourne). *Died 30 June* 1989.

**BLOUGH, Roger M(iles);** former Partner, White & Case; former Chairman of the Board of Directors, United States Steel Corporation; *b* 19 Jan. 1904; *s* of Christian E. Blough and Viola (*née* Hoffman); *m* 1928, Helen Martha Decker; twin *d*. *Educ:* Susquehanna Univ. (AB); Yale Law Sch. (LLB). General practice of law with White & Case, New York City, 1931–42; General Solicitor, US Steel Corp. of Delaware, 1942–51; Exec. Vice-President law and Secretary, US Steel Corp., 1951; Vice-Chairman, Director and Member Finance Cttee, US Steel Corp., 1952; General Counsel, 1953–55; Chairman, Chief Exec. Officer and Member Exec. Cttee, 1955–69; Dir and Mem. Finance and Exec. Cttees, 1969–76. Holds numerous hon. degrees. *Publication:* Free Man and the Corporation, 1959. *Address:* (business) 300 Keystone Street, Hawley, Pa 18428, USA; (home) 307 Chestnut Avenue, Hawley, Pennsylvania 18428, USA. *Clubs:* Blooming Grove Hunting and Fishing (Pa); Board Room, Links (NYC); Pine Valley Golf; and numerous others. *Died 8 Oct.* 1985.

**BLUCKE, Air Vice-Marshal Robert Stewart,** CB 1946; CBE 1945; DSO 1943; AFC 1936, Bar 1941; RAF, retired; *b* 22 June 1897; *s* of late Rev. R. S. K. Blucke, Monxton Rectory, Andover, Hants; *m* 1926, Nancy, *d* of late Frank Wilson, Auckland, NZ; one *d* (one *s* decd). *Educ:* Malvern Coll. Dorset Regt and RFC, 1915–18; Mesopotamia, 1916–18; Royal Air Force, 1922; India, 1927–32; Test Pilot Royal Aircraft Establishment, Farnborough, 1933–37; Air Ministry, 1938–42; served in Bomber Comd, 1942–46; AOC No 1 Group RAF, 1945; SASO, AHQ, India, 1947; AOA, Technical Trg Comd, 1947–49; AOA, Far East Air Force, 1949–50; AOC Malaya, 1951; AOC-in-C Transport Comd, 1952; retired 1952. General Manager, National Assoc. for Employment of Regular Sailors, Soldiers and Airmen, 1952–65. *Address:* Harecombe Manor, Southview Road, Crowborough, East Sussex. *T:* Crowborough 661638. *Club:* Royal Air Force. *Died 2 Oct.* 1988.

**BLUETT, Maj.-Gen. Douglas,** CB 1958; OBE 1942; MA, MB; *b* 23 Aug. 1897; *s* of Rev. R. D. Bluett, BD, The Rectory, Delgany, Co. Wicklow, Ireland; *m* 1st, 1940, Johanna Catharine (*d* 1960), *d* of Mr Simpson-Smith, Huddersfield, Yorks; no *c*; 2nd, 1964, Noeline (*d* 1971), *widow* of Col C. Day; 3rd, 1974, Mary (*née* Merrick), *widow* of Francis Power. *Educ:* St Andrews Coll., and Trinity Coll., Dublin. Served European War, 1914–18, in Greek Macedonia, Bulgaria, Serbia, European Turkey and Islands of the Aegean Sea; War of 1939–45, with RAMC, ADMS 10th and 11th Armoured Divs, Western Desert, France and Germany; Lieut-Col, 1943; Col, 1945; Brig., 1953; Maj.-Gen., 1956; QHP 1956–58; retired, 1958. Col Comdt, RAMC, 1958–63. CStJ. Officer, Order of Leopold II avec Palme and Croix de Guerre avec Palme (Belgium), 1945.

*Recreation:* golf. *Address:* c/o Williams & Glyn's Bank Ltd, Kirkland House, Whitehall, SW1; Galtymore, 111 Rochester Road, Aylesford, Kent. *Died 8 Nov.* 1981.

**BLUNDELL, Sir (Edward) Denis,** GCMG 1972; GCVO 1974; KBE 1967 (OBE (mil.) 1944); QSO 1977; Governor-General of New Zealand, 1972–77; *b* 29 May 1907; British; *m* 1945, June Daphne (QSO 1977), *d* of Jack Halligan; one *s* one *d*. *Educ:* Waitaki High Sch. (NZ); Trinity Hall, Cambridge Univ. Called to Bar, Gray's Inn, 1929; admitted as Barrister and Solicitor of the Supreme Court of New Zealand at end of 1929. Served War, 1939–44 with 2nd NZ Div. in Greece, Crete, ME and Italy. Formerly Sen. Partner, Bell, Gully & Co., Barristers and Solicitors, Wellington, NZ. President of the New Zealand Law Society, 1962–68. High Comr for NZ in London, 1968–72. Principal Companion of the Queen's Service Order, 1975–77. Pres., NZ Cricket Council, 1957–60. KStJ 1972. *Recreations:* cricket (cricket Blue Cambridge, 1928, 1929; rep. NZ, 1936–37), golf, swimming, tennis. *Address:* 655 Riddell Road, Glendowie, Auckland, New Zealand. *Clubs:* Wellington; Wellesley, Northern (New Zealand). *Died 24 Sept.* 1984.

**BLUNDEN, Sir William,** 6th Bt, *cr* 1766; RN, retired; *b* 26 April 1919; *s* of 5th Bt and Phyllis, *d* of P. C. Creaghe; *S* father, 1923; *m* 1945, Pamela Mary Purser, 2nd Officer WRNS, *d* of John Purser, Prof. of Civil Engineering, TCD; six *d*. *Educ:* Repton. Lieut-Comdr, RN, 1949; retired 1958. *Heir:* *b* Philip Overington Blunden [*b* 27 Jan. 1922; *m* 1945, Jeanette Francesca (WRNS), *e d* of Captain D. Macdonald, RNR, Portree, Isle of Skye; two *s* one *d*]. *Address:* Castle Blunden, Kilkenny. *T:* Kilkenny 21128.
*Died 28 Oct.* 1985.

**BLUNT, Prof. Anthony (Frederick);** Professor of the History of Art, University of London, and Director of the Courtauld Institute of Art, 1947–Sept. 1974; Surveyor of the Queen's Pictures, 1952–72 (of the Pictures of King George VI, 1945–52); Adviser for the Queen's Pictures and Drawings, 1972–78; *b* 26 Sept. 1907; *y s* of late Rev. A. S. V. Blunt, Vicar of St John's, Paddington. *Educ:* Marlborough Coll.; Trinity Coll., Cambridge. Served War of 1939–45: France, 1939–40; WO, 1940–45. Fellow, Trinity Coll., Cambridge, 1932–36; on staff of Warburg Inst., London, 1937–39; Reader in History of Art, London Univ., and Dep. Dir, Courtauld Inst. of Art, 1939–47. Slade Prof. of Fine Art: Oxford, 1962–63; Cambridge, 1965–66. Hon. Fellow, Trinity Coll., Cambridge, 1967–79. FBA 1950–79; FSA 1960–79; Hon. FRIBA, 1973–79. Hon. DLitt: Bristol, 1961; Durham, 1963; Oxon, 1971; DèsL *hc* Paris, 1966. CVO 1947, KCVO 1956 cancelled and annulled, Oct. 1979, following his exposure as Russian spy during War of 1939–45; Commander: Order of Orange Nassau (Holland), 1948; Legion of Honour (France), 1958. *Publications:* (with Walter Friedlaender), The Drawings of Nicolas Poussin, 1939–75; Artistic Theory in Italy, 1940; François Mansart, 1941; French Drawings at Windsor Castle, 1945; (with Margaret Whinney) The Nation's Pictures, 1951; Rouault's Miserere, 1951; Poussin's Golden Calf, 1951; Art and Architecture in France, 1500–1700, 1953, rev. edn 1981; The Drawings of G. B. Castiglione and Stefano della Bella at Windsor Castle, 1954; Venetian Drawings at Windsor Castle, 1957; Philibert de l'Orme, 1958; The Art of William Blake, 1960; (with H. L. Cooke) The Roman Drawings at Windsor Castle, 1960; (with Phoebe Pool) Picasso: The Formative Years, 1962; Nicolas Poussin: Catalogue raisonné, 1966; Nicolas Poussin (2 vols), 1967; Sicilian Baroque, 1968; Picasso's Guernica, 1969; Supplement to Italian and French Drawings at Windsor, 1971; Neapolitan Baroque and Rococo Architecture, 1975; (with A. Laing *et al*) Baroque and Rococo Architecture and Decoration, 1978; Borromini, 1979; The Drawings of Nicolas Poussin, 1979; articles in Burlington Magazine, Jl of Warburg and Courtauld Insts, Spectator, etc. *Address:* 45 Portsea Hall, Portsea Place, W2.
*Died 26 March* 1983.

**BLUNT, Christopher Evelyn,** OBE 1945; FBA 1965; retired; *b* 16 July 1904; 2nd *s* of Rev. A. S. V. Blunt and Hilda Violet Blunt; *m* 1930, Elisabeth Rachel Bazley (*d* 1980); one *s* two *d*. *Educ:* Marlborough (Foundation Scholar). Entered merchant banking firm of Higginson & Co., 1924; partner, 1947; executive director of successor companies, 1950–64. Served War, 1939–46; 52 AA (TA) Regt; GHQ (Gen. Staff), BEF (despatches), Home Forces, 21 Army Group; SHAEF; retired 1946 (Col). FSA 1936; President: British Numismatic Soc., 1946–50; Royal Numismatic Soc., 1956–61; Wilts Arch. Soc., 1970–74; Soc. of Medieval Archaeol., 1978–80. Medals of Royal, British and Amer. Numismatic Socs. Officer Legion of Merit (USA), 1945. *Publications:* The Coinage of Athelstan, 1974; (with M. M. Archibald) Catalogue of Anglo-Saxon Coins in the British Museum 924–c 973, 1986; contributions to Numismatic Chronicle, British Numismatic Journal, Archæologia, etc. *Recreation:* numismatics. *Address:* Ramsbury Hill, Ramsbury, Marlborough, Wilts. *T:* Marlborough 20358. *Clubs:* Travellers', Pratt's. *Died 20 Nov.* 1987.

**BLUNT, Wilfrid Jasper Walter;** Curator of the Watts Gallery, Compton, 1959–85, then Emeritus; *b* 19 July 1901; *s* of late Rev.

Arthur Stanley Vaughan Blunt and Hilda Violet Master. *Educ:* Marlborough Coll.; Worcester Coll., Oxford; Royal College of Art. Art Master, Haileybury Coll., 1923–38; Drawing Master, Eton Coll., 1938–59. ARCA (London) 1923. Introduced into the Public Schs the craft of pottery (Haileybury, 1927) and Italic handwriting (Eton, 1940). FLS 1969. *Publications:* The Haileybury Buildings, 1936; Desert Hawk, 1947; The Art of Botanical Illustration, 1950; Tulipomania, 1950; Black Sunrise, 1951; Sweet Roman Hand, 1952; Japanese Colour Prints, 1952; Georg Dionysius Ehret, 1953; Pietro's Pilgrimage, 1953; Sebastiano, 1956; Great Flower Books (with Sacheverell Sitwell and Patrick Synge), 1956; A Persian Spring, 1957; Lady Muriel, 1962; Of Flowers and a Village, 1963; Cockerell, 1964; Omar, 1966; Isfahan, 1966; John Christie of Glyndebourne, 1968; The Dream King, 1970; The Compleat Naturalist, 1971; The Golden Road to Samarkand, 1973; On Wings of Song, 1974; 'England's Michelangelo', 1975; The Ark in the Park, 1976; Splendours of Islam, 1976; In for a Penny: a prospect of Kew Gardens, 1978; (with Sandra Raphael) The Illustrated Herbal, 1979; Married to a Single Life: autobiography 1901–1938, 1983; Slow on the Feather: autobiography 1938–1959, 1986. *Recreations:* writing, formerly singing and travel. *Address:* The Curator's House, The Watts Gallery, Compton, near Guildford, Surrey. *T:* Guildford 810437.
*Died 8 Jan.* 1987.

**BLYDE, Sir Henry (Ernest),** KBE 1969 (CBE 1952); former Chairman, Taranaki Harbours Board, for 21 years; Director, Lepperton Dairy Co., for 37 years, and Chairman for 25 years; *b* 25 Oct. 1896; *s* of James Blyde; *m* 1929, Mary, *d* of W. J. McCormick; two *s* two *d*. *Educ:* St Paul's School, St Leonards-on-Sea, Sussex. Formerly Chairman, Taranaki Hospital Bd, for 37 years. JP. *Recreations:* bowling, billiards. *Address:* 233 Carrington Street, New Plymouth, New Zealand. *T:* New Plymouth 88928.
*Died 31 Aug.* 1984.

**BLYTH, Charles Henry,** OBE 1977; Chairman, National Dock Labour Board, 1977–83; *b* 16 Feb. 1916; *s* of Edward Henry Blyth and Emma (*née* Elsey); *m* 1941, Winifred Irene, *d* of Charles and Gertrude Green, Southampton; two *d*. *Educ:* elem. sch., Grimsby, Lincs; Dept of Navigation, University Coll., Southampton. Merchant Navy, 1932–49; Officer, National Union of Seamen, 1949–65. Internat. Transportworkers Federation: Hong Kong Rep., 1965–66; Section Sec., 1966–67; Asst Gen. Sec., 1967–68; elected Gen. Sec. at Wiesbaden Congress, 1968; re-elected at Vienna Congress, 1971, and at Stockholm Congress, 1974; retd, 1977. Pres., Internat. Trade Secretariat's Gen. Conf., 1974–77. Mem., Nat. Ports Council, 1979–81. Mem., Exec. Cttee and Management Cttee, Merchant Seamen's War Meml Soc. *Recreations:* simple cooking, making wooden toys. *Address:* 118 Chiltern Drive, Surbiton, Surrey. *T:* 01–399 7762.
*Died 24 Sept.* 1986.

**BLYTON,** Baron, *cr* 1964 (Life Peer); **William Reid Blyton;** *b* 2 May 1899; *s* of late Charles H. Blyton, retired labourer, and Hannah A. Blyton; *m* 1919, Jane B. Ord; three *d*. *Educ:* Elementary Education Holy Trinity Sch. and Dean Road Sch., South Shields. Served in HM Submarines in European War, 1914–18. Chm., Harton Miners' Lodge, Durham Miners' Assoc., 1928–41, Sec., 1941–45; Mem., Durham Miners' Exec. Cttee, 1930–32, 1942–43. Chm. South Shields Labour Party, 1928–29, 1931–32; Councillor, S Shields Borough Council, 1936–45; Chm. of South Shields Education Cttee, 1943, and of South Shields Electrical Cttee, 1937–40; MP (Lab) Houghton-le-Spring Div. of County Durham, 1945–64; late PPS to Ministry of Civil Aviation; resigned, 1949. Chm. High Sch. Governors and Chm. Secondary and Technical Cttee of South Shields. *Address:* 139 Brockley Avenue, South Shields, Tyne and Wear; Dylan Hotel, 14 Devonshire Terrace, W2.
*Died 25 Oct.* 1987.

**BOAS, Leslie,** OBE 1961; HM Diplomatic Service, retired; *b* Buenos Aires, Argentine, 25 Feb. 1912; *s* of late Gustavus Thomas Boas and late Flora Shield McDonald; *m* 1st, 1944, Margaret Ann Jackson (marr. diss. 1951); one *s*; 2nd, 1951, Patricia Faye Fenning (*d* 1972); 3rd, 1972, Natalie K. Prado (*née* Kitchen). *Educ:* Spain; Gibraltar; Granada University. In business, 1933–39. Joined Coldstream Guards, 1940; commissioned in Royal Ulster Rifles, 1940; invalided out of Army as result of injuries, 1944. Joined Latin American Section of BBC, 1944. Apptd Temp. Press Attaché, Panama, 1946; Temp. First Sec. (Inf.), Bogotá, 1948; Temp. First Sec. (Inf.), Caracas, 1952; estab. as a Permanent First Sec., 1959; Regional Inf. Counsellor, Caracas, 1962–69; Chargé d'Affaires, Panama, April-May 1964; Ambassador to Santo Domingo, 1969–72. Dir, Secretariat of British Bicentennial Liaison Cttee of FCO, 1973–75. *Recreations:* golf, chess, Latin American studies. *Address:* c/o The Royal Bank of Scotland, 97 New Bond Street, W1Y 0EU. *Clubs:* Buck's; Jockey (Bogotá, Colombia).
*Died 16 Aug.* 1988.

**BOASE, Alan Martin,** MA, PhD; Officier de la Légion d'Honneur; *b* 1902; *s* of late W. Norman Boase, CBE, St Andrews; *m* 1931, Elizabeth Grizelle (*d* 1977), *e d* of late Prof. E. S. Forster; four *s*. *Educ:* Eton Coll.; New College, Oxford; Trinity Coll., Cambridge;

Univ. of Paris. Lectr in French, Univ. of Sheffield, 1929–36; Prof. of French, University Coll., Southampton, 1936–37; Marshall Prof. of French, Univ. of Glasgow, 1937–65. Ex-Chm. of Assoc. of Heads of French Depts. Visiting Professor: Univ. of Calif (Berkeley), 1962; Monash Univ., Australia, 1969; Collège de France, 1974. Chm., Consultative Cttee, Inst. Français d'Ecosse. Grand Prix du Rayonnement Français de l'Académie Française, 1979. *Publications:* Montaigne, Selected Essays (with Arthur Tilley), 1934; The Fortunes of Montaigne, 1935, repr. (NY) 1970; Contemporary French Literature (in France: A Companion to French Studies, ed R. L. G. Ritchie), 1937; Les Poèmes de Jean de Sponde, 1950; The Poetry of France, Part III, 1952, Part I, 1964, Part IV, 1969, Part II, 1973; Les Méditations de Jean de Sponde, 1954; La Vie de Jean de Sponde, 1977; Jean de Sponde, œuvres littéraires (ed Corti), 1978; articles and reviews in periodicals. *Recreation:* gardening. *Address:* 39 Inverleith Place, Edinburgh. *T:* 031–552 3005.
*Died 7 Nov.* 1982.

**BOASE, Arthur Joseph,** CMG 1968; OBE 1951; Warden, Ophthalmic Hospital of the Order of St John, Jerusalem, 1956, retired; *b* 23 June 1901; 2nd *s* of William George Boase, medical practitioner; *m* 1929, Alice Mary, *d* of Sir Charles Griffin, QC; four *s* four *d* (and one *s* one *d* decd). *Educ:* Mount St Mary's Coll., Derbyshire; St Thomas' Hosp., London. MRCS, LRCP 1923; DOMS 1933; FRCS 1952. Uganda Med. Service, 1924; Sen. Med. Off., 1937; Specialist (Ophthalmologist), 1945; Sen. Specialist, 1954; retd from Uganda, 1956. Past Pres., E African Assoc. of Surgs. Coronation Medal, 1953. Kt, Order of St Gregory (Papal), 1951; KStJ 1961; Kt, Order of Holy Sepulchre (Greek Orthodox), 1965; Kt, Order of Holy Sepulchre (Armenian), 1969. Istiqlal (Independence) Order, 2nd cl. (Jordan), 1967. *Recreation:* woodworking. *Address:* Linden Cottage, Uckfield, East Sussex TN22 2EH.
*Died 31 Jan.* 1986.

**BODDIE, Donald Raikes;** Consultant in Public Affairs, since 1975; *b* 27 June 1917; *o s* of William Henry and Violet May Boddie; *m* 1941, Barbara Stuart Strong; one *s*. *Educ:* Colston's Sch., Bristol. Joined: London Star, 1942–47; Natal Mercury, Durban, 1947–52; London Evening News, 1953 (held various exec. posts, to Dep. Editor, 1966 and Editor, 1972–74); Dir, Harmsworth Publications Ltd, 1973–74; Vice-Chm., Evening News Ltd, 1974. *Recreations:* travel, theatre, cinematography. *Address:* 87 Regent Street, W1. *T:* 01–439 6992.
*Died 1 Oct.* 1984.

**BODDIE, Prof. George Frederick,** BSc Edinburgh; FRCVS; FRSE; William Dick Chair of Veterinary Medicine, Edinburgh University (in the Royal Dick School of Veterinary Studies), 1953–70; *b* 23 Jan. 1900; *m* 1st, 1926, Daisy (*d* 1968); one *s* two *d*; 2nd, 1971, Margaret. *Educ:* Merchiston Castle Sch.; Edinburgh Univ.; Royal (Dick) Veterinary College, Edinburgh. Clinical Asst Royal (Dick) Veterinary College, 1924; gen. veterinary practice, 1924–30; veterinary inspector local authority; Prof. of Medicine and Pharmacology Royal (Dick) Veterinary College, Edinburgh, 1930. Pres., RCVS, 1964–65, Vice-Pres., 1959–60, 1963–64 and 1965–66. Director: Hill Farm Research Organisation, 1957–66; Scottish Soc. for Prevention of Cruelty to Animals; former Chm. of Cttee, Edinburgh Dog and Cat Home; formerly Hon. Advisory Officer, Highlands and Islands Veterinary Services Scheme. Member: Medicine Commn, 1969–71; Poisons Bd, 1964–76. *Publications:* Diagnostic Methods in Veterinary Medicine, 1944, sixth edn, 1969; An Introduction to Veterinary Therapeutics, 1952; Editor Hoare's Veterinary Materia Medica and Therapeutics (6th edn), 1942 (jointly); many articles in veterinary and scientific jls. *Address:* 8/2 Myreside Court, Edinburgh EH10 5LX.
*Died 19 Aug.* 1985.

**BODLEY SCOTT, Sir Ronald,** GCVO 1973 (KCVO 1964); DM; FRCP; Physician to: the Queen, 1952–73; Florence Nightingale Hospital, since 1958; King Edward VII Hospital for Officers, since 1963; King Edward VII Hospital, Midhurst, since 1965; Principal Medical Officer, Equity and Law Life Assurance Society, since 1952; Senior Medical Adviser, Cavendish Medical Centre, 1975–81; Consulting Physician to: St Bartholomew's Hospital, since 1971 (Physician, 1946; Senior Physician, 1965; Member Board of Governors, 1966–71); Woolwich Memorial Hospital, since 1971 (Physician, 1936–71); British Railways (Eastern Region), since 1957; Royal Navy, since 1963; *b* 10 Sept. 1906; *s* of late Maitland Bodley Scott, OBE, FRCSE, and Alice Hilda Durance George; *m* 1st, 1931, Edith Daphne (*d* 1977), *d* of late Lt-Col E. McCarthy, RMA; two *d*; 2nd, 1980, Mrs Jessie Gaston. *Educ:* Marlborough Coll.; Brasenose Coll., Oxford. BA Oxon, Hons Sch. of Nat. Sci., 1928; MA, BM, BCh, Oxon, 1931; MRCP, 1933; DM Oxon, 1937; FRCP 1943. Chief Asst to Medical Unit, St Bartholomew's Hospital, 1934, Physician 1946–71; Physician, Surbiton Gen. Hosp., 1946–64. Served in Middle East, 1941–45, Lt-Col RAMC; Officer i/c Medical Div. in No 63 and No 43 Gen. Hospitals; Physician to the Household of King George VI, 1949; Hon. Consultant in haematology to the Army at Home, 1957–65, Consulting Physician, 1965–71. Lectures: Langdon Brown, RCP, 1957; Lettsomian, Medical Soc. of London, 1957; Thom Bequest; RCPE, 1965; Croonian, RCP, 1970; Harveian

Orator, RCP, 1976. President: Med. Soc. of London, 1965–66, Trustee, 1972–; British Soc. for Hæmatology, 1966–67 (Hon. Mem. 1977); Chairman: Trustees, Migraine Trust, 1971–73; Medicines Commn, 1973–75; Council, British Heart Foundn, 1975–82; Member: Council, Imperial Cancer Res. Fund, 1968–82; Research Grants Cttee, British Heart Foundn (Chm. 1970–75); Council, RCP, 1963–66 (Censor, 1970–72, Sen. Censor and Sen. Vice-Pres., 1972); Court of Assistants, Soc. of Apothecaries of London, 1964– (Master 1974); Temporary Registration Assessment Bd, GMC, 1973–76; Treasurer, RSoc Med, 1973–76 (Pres., Section of Medicine, 1967–68); Vice-Pres., Coll. of Speech Therapists, 1979; Trustee, Nuffield Medical Benefaction. Formerly Examiner in Medicine, Universities of Oxford, London, Edinburgh, Glasgow, Cairo, Singapore, to the RCP, London and Edinburgh, and to the Conjoint Board. Order of Crown of Brunei, 1970; Order of the Family, Brunei, 1973. Editor: The Medical Annual, 1959–; Price's Textbook of the Practice of Medicine (12th edn, 1978). *Publications:* Cancer: the facts, 1979; various papers in medical jls. *Address:* 79 Dartford Road, Sevenoaks, Kent. *T:* Sevenoaks 452877. *Club:* Boodle's.
*Died 12 May 1982.*

**BOGGON, Roland Hodgson,** MS, MB London; FRCS, LRCP; *b* 11 Aug. 1903; *s* of late Richard Octavius Boggon, OBE, Civil Servant; *m* 1932, Mollie Daphne, *d* of T. H. Newall; one *s* one *d. Educ:* St Paul's Sch. Retired as Consulting Surg. to St Thomas' Hospital, London. Mem. Court of Examiners of the Royal College of Surgeons; Examiner in Surgery, Univ. of London. *Publications:* numerous medical. *Address:* Gittisham Hill House, Honiton, Devon EX14 8TY.
*Died 5 Jan. 1983.*

**BOLAND, Bridget;** author; *b* 13 March 1913; *d* of late John Boland. *Educ:* Sacred Heart Convent, Roehampton; Oxford Univ. (BA 1935). Screenwriter 1937–; numerous films. Served War, 1941–46, in ATS; Senior Comdr. Stage plays: Abca Play Unit productions, 1946; Cockpit, 1948; The Damascus Blade, 1950; Temple Folly, 1952; The Return, 1953; The Prisoner, 1954 (adapted film version, 1955); Gordon, 1961; The Zodiac in the Establishment, 1963; Time out of Mind, 1970. *Publications:* novels: The Wild Geese, 1938; Portrait of a Lady in Love, 1942; Caterina, 1975; *non-fiction:* (with M. Boland) Old Wives' Lore for Gardeners, 1976; Gardener's Magic and Other Old Wives' Lore, 1977; At My Mother's Knee, 1978; The Lisle Letters: an abridgement, 1983 (ed by Muriel St Clare Byrne; selected and arranged by Bridget Boland). *Address:* Bolands, Hewshott Lane, Liphook, Hants.
*Died 19 Jan. 1988.*

**BOLAND, Frederick Henry;** Irish diplomat, retired; Chancellor, Trinity College, Dublin, 1964–82; *b* 1904; 2nd *s* of Henry Patrick Boland and Charlotte (*née* Nolan), Dublin; *m* 1935, Frances Kelly, Drogheda; one *s* four *d. Educ:* Clongowes Wood Coll.; Trinity Coll., Dublin; King's Inns, Dublin. BA; LLB 1925; LLD (jure dignitatis), 1950. University Studentship in Classics, TCD, 1925; Rockefeller Research Fellowship in Social Sciences (Harvard and University of Chicago), 1926–28; 3rd Sec., Dept of External Affairs, 1929; 1st Sec., Paris, 1932; Principal Officer Dept of Industry and Commerce, 1936; Dept of External Affairs: Asst Sec., 1938; Permanent Sec., 1946; Irish rep., Cttee on European Economic Co-operation, Paris, 1947; Irish Ambassador to the Court of St James's, 1950–56; Permanent Representative of Eire at UN, 1956–63 (Pres., 1960); Irish Representative UN Security Council, 1962–63. Dir, Arthur Guinness Son & Co., to 1979. Member: Cttee on Seasonal Migration, 1936; Cttee on Design in Industry, 1938; Royal Irish Acad. Pres., Coll. Historical Soc., TCD. Knight Comdr, Order of St Gregory the Great, 1948; Grand Cross, Order of the North Star of Sweden, 1950. *Recreations:* reading, piano, fishing. *Address:* 60 Ailesbury Road, Dublin, Eire. *T:* Dublin 693599. *Clubs:* Stephens Green; Royal Irish Yacht.
*Died 4 Dec. 1985.*

**BÖLL, Heinrich Theodor;** author; *b* Cologne, 21 Dec. 1917; *s* of Victor Böll and Maria Hermanns; *m* 1942, Annemarie Cech; three *s. Educ:* Gymnasium, Cologne; Univ. of Cologne. Member: German Acad. for Language and Poetry; Bavarian Acad. Fine Arts; Hon. Mem., Union of German Translators. Pres., Internat. PEN, 1971–74; a Founder, World Producers Union, 1970; Mem., Gruppe 47, 1950–. Hon. DSc Aston, 1973; Hon. DTech Brunel, 1973; Hon. LittD TCD, 1973. Winner of numerous prizes and awards, incl. Nobel Prize for Literature, 1972. *Publications:* Auch Kinder sind Zivilisten, 1948 (Children are Civilians Too, 1973); Der Zug war pünktlich, 1949 (The Train was on Time, UK, 1967, 1985); Wanderer, kommst du nach Spa . . ., 1950 (Traveller, if you come to Spa, 1956); Wo warst du, Adam?, 1951 (And Where Were You, Adam?, 1973); Die schwarzen Schafe, 1951; Nicht nur zur Weihnachtszeit, 1952; Und sagte kein einziges Wort, 1953 (Acquainted with the Night, UK, 1954; reprinted as And Never Said a Word, 1978); Haus ohne Hüter, 1954 (The Unguarded House, UK, 1957); Die Waage der Baleks, 1954; Dr Murkes gesammeltes Schweigen und andere Satiren, 1955; Das Brot der frühen Jahre, 1955 (The Bread of those Early Years, 1977); So ward Abend und Morgen, 1955; Unberechenbare Gäste; Erzählungen, 1956; Im Tal der donnernden Hufe, 1957; Irisches Tagebuch, 1957 (Irish Journal); Der Bahnhof

von Zimpren, 1958; Abenteuer eines Brotbeutels, und andere Geschichten, 1958; Brief an einen jungen Katholiken, 1958; Billard um Halbzehn, 1959 (Billiards at Half Past Nine, UK, 1965); Als der Krieg ausbrach, 1961; Als der Krieg zu Ende war, 1962; Anekdote zur Senkung der Arbeitsmoral, 1963; Erzählungen, Hörspiele, Aufsätze, 1961; Ein Schluck Erde (play), 1962; Ansichten eines Clowns, 1963 (The Clown, UK, 1965); Entfernung von der Truppe, 1964 (Absent Without Leave, UK, 1967); Frankfurter Vorlesungen, 1966; Ende einer Dienstfahrt, 1966 (End of a Mission, UK, 1968); Aufsätze, Kritiken, Reden, 1967; Veränderung in Staech, 1969; Hausfriedensbruch, 1970; Aussatz (play), 1970; Gruppenbild mit Dame, 1971 (Group Portrait with a Lady, UK, 1973); Erzählungen 1950–1970, 1972; Gedichte, 1972; Neue politische und literarische Schriften, 1973; Die verlorene Ehre der Katharina Blum, 1974 (The Lost Honour of Katharina Blum, UK, 1975); Berichte zur Gesinnungslage der Nation, 1975; Einmischung erwünscht, 1977; Werke, vols 1–5, 1977, vols 6–10, 1978; Missing Persons and other essays, 1978 (Fürsorgliche Belagerung, 1979 (The Safety Net, 1982); Gesammelte Erzählungen 1947–1980, 1981; Was soll aus dem Jungen bloss werden?, 1981 (What's to Become of the Boy?, UK, 1985); Vermintes Gelände, 1982; Das Vermächtnis, 1982; Die Verwundung, 1983; Mein trauriges Gesicht, 1984; radio plays, translations, etc.; *posthumous publications:* A Sailor's Legacy, 1985; Casualty, 1986; Women in a River Landscape, 1989. *Address:* 5165 Hürtgenwald-Grosshau, an der Nülheck 19, Federal Republic of Germany.
*Died 16 July 1985.*

**BOLS, Hon. Maj.-Gen. Eric Louis,** CB 1945; DSO 1944, and bar 1945; *b* 8 June 1904; *s* of Lt-Gen. Sir Louis Bols, KCB, KCMG, DSO; *m* 1st, 1930, Rosa Vaux (marr. diss., 1947); one *s*; 2nd, 1948, Marion du Plessis (marr. diss., 1965); 3rd, 1967, Barbara Beardshaw (*née* Brown). *Educ:* Wellington Coll.; Royal Military Coll., Sandhurst. 2nd Lieut Devonshire Regt 1924; Capt The King's Regt 1935; Major, 1940; Temp. Lieut-Col 1941; Temp Col 1944; Temp. Brig. 1944; Temp. Maj.-Gen. and War Subs. Col 1945; Comdr 6th Airborne Div., 1945; retd pay, 1948. War Service in Ceylon, UK, and NW Europe. *Address:* Stone Cottage, Peppering Eye, near Battle, East Sussex.
*Died 8 June 1985.*

**BOLSOVER, George Henry,** CBE 1970 (OBE 1947); Director, School of Slavonic and East European Studies, University of London, 1947–76; *b* 18 Nov. 1910; *yr s* of Ernest and Mary Bolsover; *m* 1939, Stephanie Kállai; one *d. Educ:* Leigh Grammar Sch.; Univ. of Liverpool; Univ. of London. BA 1931, MA (Liverpool), 1932, PhD (London), 1933. Univ. of Birmingham, Resident Tutor in Adult Education in Worcs, 1937–38; Asst Lectr in Modern European History, Univ. of Manchester, 1938–43; Attaché and First Sec., HM Embassy, Moscow, 1943–47; Mem. of Editorial Board, Slavonic and East European Review, 1947–63, and Chm., 1958–63; Member: UGC Sub-Cttee on Oriental, African, Slavonic and East European Studies, 1961–71; Treasury Cttee for Studentships in Foreign Languages and Cultures, 1948–58; Inst. of Historical Res. Cttee, 1948–75; Adv. Cttee on Educn of Poles in Gt Britain, 1948–67; Ct of Govs of London Sch. of Economics and Political Science, 1955–77; Council and Exec. Cttee of St Bartholomew's Med. Coll., 1962–76; Council of Royal Dental Hosp. London Sch. of Dental Surgery, 1966–77; Min. of Educn Cttee on Teaching of Russian, 1960–62; Senior Treasurer of University of London Union, 1958–77; Chm., Tutorial Classes Cttee of Council for Extra-Mural Studies of Univ. of London, 1965–76; Chm., Council for Extra-Mural Studies, 1968–76; Mem., 1951–87, Treas., 1966–72, British Nat. Historical Cttee; Mem. Governing Body, GB/East Europe Centre, 1967–78; Governor, Northwood Coll. for Girls, 1963–. *Publications:* essays in: Essays presented to Sir Lewis Namier, 1956, Transactions of Royal Historical Society, 1957; articles in English Historical Review, Journal of Modern History, Slavonic and East European Review, International Affairs, etc. *Recreations:* music, travel. *Address:* 7 Devonshire Road, Hatch End, Mddx HA5 4LY. *T:* 081–428 4282.
*Died 15 April 1990.*

**BOLTE, Dame Edith (Lilian), (Lady Bolte),** DBE 1973 (CBE 1959); *d* of D. F. M. Elder; *m* 1934, Hon. Sir Henry E. Bolte, GCMG. Member State Council: Girl Guide Movement, Victoria; Red Cross, Victoria. *Recreations:* tennis, golf. *Address:* Kialla, Meredith, Vic 3333, Australia. *Clubs:* Alexandra, Liberal Women's, Victoria League.
*Died 14 Aug. 1986.*

**BOLTE, Hon. Sir Henry (Edward),** GCMG 1972 (KCMG 1966); Premier and Treasurer of the State of Victoria, Australia, 1955–72; *b* Skipton, Victoria, 20 May 1908; *s* of J. H. Bolte; *m* 1934, Edith Lilian Elder (Dame Edith Bolte, DBE) (*d* 1986). *Educ:* Skipton State Sch.; Ballarat C of E Grammar Sch. Grazier, with sheep property near Meredith in western district of Victoria. Entered Parliament, 1947; MLA for Hampden, 1947–73; Minister of: Water Supply and Mines, 1948–50; Soil Conservation, 1949–50; Water Supply and Soil Conservation, 1950; Leader of Liberal Party (formerly Liberal and Country Party), 1953–72 (Dep. Leader, Nov. 1950–53). Freedom, City of Melbourne, 1975. Hon. LLD: Melbourne Univ., 1965; Monash Univ., 1967. *Recreations:* golf, shooting, turf.

*Address:* Kialla, Meredith, Victoria 3333, Australia. *Clubs:* Australian, Athenæum (Melbourne); Geelong (Geelong).
*Died 4 Jan.* 1990.

**BOLTON, Col Geoffrey George Hargreaves,** CBE 1960 (MBE 1946); MC 1916; DL; Chairman, North Western Division, National Coal Board, 1951–60 (Marketing Director, 1946–49, Deputy Chairman, 1950–51); *b* 5 Aug. 1894; 4th and *o* surv. *s* of late Henry Hargreaves Bolton, MBE, Newchurch-in-Rossendale, Lancs; *m* 1st, 1919, Ethel (*d* 1942), 2nd *d* of late Rev. James Robinson, Broughton, Preston; one *s* one *d* (and one *s* decd); 2nd, 1943, Margaret, *y d* of late Rev. James Robinson. *Educ:* Clifton Coll., Bristol. Served European War, 1914–18, East Lancs Regt (Gallipoli, Sinai, France); Comd East Lancs Regt TA, 1920–28 (retired 1928). Associated with Coal Industry, 1912–; Dir, Hargreaves Collieries Ltd, 1932–46; Exec. Officer, Lancashire Associated Collieries, 1935–46. DL 1935, JP 1935, Lancaster; High Sheriff, Lancashire, 1962–63. KStJ 1969. *Address:* Fairfield House, Chatburn, Clitheroe, Lancs BB7 4BB. *T:* Clitheroe 41335.
*Died 19 March* 1983.

**BOLTON, Sir George (Lewis French),** KCMG 1950; Hon. Pres., Bank of London and South America since 1970 (Chairman, 1957–70); Chairman: London United Investments Ltd, since 1971; Premier Consolidated Oilfields, 1974–76; Deputy Chairman, Lonrho, since 1973; *b* 16 Oct. 1900; *s* of William and Beatrice Bolton; *m* 1928, May, *er d* of Charles and Amelia Howcroft; one *s* two *d*. Helbert, Wagg & Co. Ltd, 1920; Bank of England to assist in management of Exchange Equalisation Funds, 1933; Tripartite Monetary Agreement, 1936; Adviser to Bank of England, 1941–48; Exec. Director, 1948–57; Director, Bank for Internat. Settlements, 1949–57; UK Alternate Governor of Internat. Monetary Fund, 1952–57 (UK Exec. Director, 1946–52). Director, Bank of England, 1948–68. Director: Canadian Pacific Steamships Ltd; Canadian Pacific Oil & Gas of Canada Ltd. Chm., Commonwealth Development Finance Co., 1968–80. Sheriff of the County of London, 1952 and 1961. Gran Oficial de la Orden de Mayo (Argentina), 1960; Orden del Merito (Chile), 1965. *Publication:* A Banker's World, 1970. *Recreations:* reading, gardening. *Address:* 305 Frobisher House, Dolphin Square, SW1V 3LL.
*Died 2 Sept.* 1982.

**BOLTON, Captain Sir Ian Frederick Cheney,** 2nd Bt *cr* 1927; KBE 1957 (OBE 1946); DL; Captain 3rd Bn Argyll and Sutherland Highlanders; chartered accountant and retired partner, Arthur Young, McClelland, Moores and Co., Glasgow and London; *b* 29 Jan. 1889; *s* of Sir Edwin Bolton, 1st Bart, and Elinor, *d* of Sir John H. N. Graham, 1st Bt; *S* father, 1931. *Educ:* Eton. Served European War, 1914–19 (despatches). Past President Institute of Accountants and Actuaries in Glasgow; Past President Institute of Chartered Accountants of Scotland; Member (part-time) British Transport Commission, 1947–59; Chairman Scottish Area Board, British Transport Commission, 1955–59; President, Scottish Boy Scout Assoc., 1945–58; Lord Dean of Guild, Glasgow, 1957–59. DL Stirling, 1965 (re-appointed, with seniority 1939); HM Lieut of Stirlingshire, 1949–64. Hon. LLD Glasgow Univ., 1955. *Recreation:* Boy Scouts. *Heir:* none. *Address:* West Plean, Stirling FK7 8HA. *TA* and *T:* Bannockburn 812208. *Clubs:* Western (Glasgow); County (Stirling).
*Died 12 Jan.* 1982 (*ext*).

**BOLTON, John,** CB 1985; consulting engineer and arbitrator, since 1986; *b* 30 Dec. 1925; *s* of John and Elizabeth Ann Bolton, Great Harwood, Lancs; *m* 1950, Nell Hartley Mount, *d* of John and Kathleen Mount; three *d*. *Educ:* Blackburn Coll. of Technology and Art. LLB (Hons) London; CEng, FICE, FIMechE, FInstE, FCIArb. Mech. Engrg Apprentice, Bristol Aeroplane Co. Ltd; Civil Engrg Pupil, Courtaulds Ltd; subseq. with English Electric Co. Ltd and NW Gas Board. Entered Health Service as Group Engr, W Manchester HMC, 1954; subseq. Chief Engr to Board of Govs of United Liverpool Hosps, Dep. Regional Engr to Leeds Regional Hosp. Board and Regional Engr to E Anglian Regional Hosp. Board; Chief Engr, 1969–77, Chief Works Officer and Dir Gen. of Works, 1977–86, DHSS. Part-time lectr in building and engrg subjects, 1948–55, Principal, 1955–59, Irlam Evening Inst., Manchester. Liveryman, Co. of Fanmakers. President: CIBSE, 1983–84 (Vice-Pres., 1981–83; Hon. FCIBSE); IHospE, 1985 (Hon. FIHospE); Hon. FIPHE. *Publications:* contribs to: British Hosps Export Council Yearbooks, 1973, 1974, 1975; The Efficient Use of Energy, 1975; papers to internat. confs and to British learned societies; technical articles in various jls. *Recreations:* theatre, music, reading, gardening, swimming. *Address:* Allsprings House, High Street, Little Shelford, Cambs. *T:* Cambridge 842591.
*Died 1 Nov.* 1986.

**BOLTON, Percy,** MA Cantab; *b* 1889; *s* of James Bolton, Blackburn; *m* Florence Madeleine (*d* 1976), 2nd *d* of late Rev. D. L. Scott, MA, LLD Cantab; one *s* one *d*. *Educ:* Blackburn Grammar Sch.; King's Coll., Cambridge (Scholar). Mathematical Tripos, Wrangler, 1911; Natural Science Tripos, Part II, 1912. Asst Master, Cheltenham Coll.; eleven years Head of Physics and Engineering Dept of Oundle

Sch.; Headmaster of Dean Close Sch., Cheltenham, 1924–38; Headmaster of Watford Grammar Sch., 1938–51; retired 1951. *Address:* Brabourne, Kimpton, Hitchin, Hertfordshire. *T:* Kimpton 832362.
*Died 6 Jan.* 1981.

**BOMFORD, Richard Raymond,** CBE 1964; DM Oxon; FRCP; Physician to London Hospital, 1938–70, Consulting Physician since 1970; *b* 15 May 1907; *s* of Raymond Bomford, Evesham, and Evelyn Mary Perkins; unmarried. *Educ:* Bromsgrove Sch.; Wadham Coll., Oxford; London Hospital. Hon. Colonel; late Consultant Physician, 14th Army (despatches); Treasurer, Royal Coll. of Physicians, 1957–70. Mem., Assoc. of Physicians. Hon. FACP. *Publications:* contributions to medical journals and text-books. *Recreation:* gardening. *Address:* 3 Green Lane, Roxwell, Chelmsford CM1 4NA. *T:* Roxwell 321. *Club:* Oriental.
*Died 30 Jan.* 1981.

**BOND, Arthur,** CBE 1972; Chairman, Yorkshire Electricity Board, 1962–71; *b* 19 July 1907; *s* of Rev. A. and Mrs Anne Bond, Darwen, Lancs; *m* 1935, Nora Wadsworth; one *s* one *d*. *Educ:* Darwen Grammar Sch. Solicitor to Cleethorpes Corporation, 1930; Dep. Town Clerk, Luton, 1935; Town Clerk: Macclesfield, 1938; Stockport, 1944; Secretary, Eastern Electricity Board, 1948; Dep. Chairman, Yorkshire Electricity Board, 1952. Solicitor, Legal Member, RTPI; Comp. IEE; CBIM. Hon. Life Mem., Furniture History Soc. *Address:* 5 Linton Road, Wetherby, West Yorks. *T:* Wetherby 62847.
*Died 9 June* 1989.

**BOND, Prof. George,** FRS 1972; Hooker Professor of Botany, University of Glasgow, 1973–76, later Emeritus Professor (Titular Professor, 1965–73); *b* 21 Feb. 1906; *m* 1st, 1931, Gwendolyne Kirkbride (*d* 1960); one *s* one *d* (and one *s* decd); 2nd, 1961, Mary Catherine McCormick (*d* 1986); two *s*. *Educ:* The Brunts Sch., Mansfield; UC Nottingham. BSc, PhD, DSc, FIBiol. Asst Lectr, Dept of Botany, Univ. of Glasgow, 1927; subseq. Lectr, then Reader. Technical Officer, Min. of Food, Dehydration Div., 1942–45. *Publications:* articles in various learned jls on symbiotic fixation of nitrogen. *Recreations:* gardening, church music, draughtsmanship, cricket and tennis. *Address:* 23 Westland Drive, Glasgow G14 9NY. *T:* 041–959 4201.
*Died 5 Jan.* 1988.

**BOND, Maj.-Gen. George Alexander,** CB 1956; CBE 1953 (OBE 1942); late RASC; *b* 31 Dec. 1901; *s* of late Alexander Maxwell Bond, Dover; *m* 1929, Dora Margaret (*d* 1987), *d* of late H. A. Gray; two *s*. *Educ:* Dover Grammar Sch.; RMC. Served War of 1939–45 (despatches, OBE); Brig. 1948; Director of Supplies and Transport, BAOR, 1950–53; DDST, Southern Command, 1953–54; Maj.-Gen. 1955; Inspector RASC, War Office, 1956–57; Dir, Supplies and Transport, 1957, retd. Col Comdt, RASC, 1960–65; Col Comdt, Royal Corps of Transport, 1965–66. *Address:* Coldharbour Hall, Rake, Liss, Hants GU33 7JQ.
*Died 11 Dec.* 1987.

**BOND, Maurice Francis,** CB 1978; MVO 1976; OBE 1955; Clerk of the Records, 1946–81, and Principal Clerk, Information Services, 1974–81, House of Lords; *b* 29 Oct. 1916; *s* of William Francis Bond and Ada Louise Bond (*née* Lightfoot), Windsor; *m* 1954, Shelagh Mary (*d* 1973), *d* of Hulbert Lionel and Katharine Lewis, Northampton. *Educ:* Windsor Boys Sch.; Selwyn Coll., Cambridge (Exhibnr 1933, BA 1936, Cert. of Educn 1937, MA 1941). Head of dept of History and Geography, Beaumont Coll., 1937–46. Clerk, House of Lords, 1946–81. Mem., Royal Commn on Historical MSS, 1981–. Hon. Custodian of the Muniments, St George's Chapel, Windsor Castle, 1947–75; Mem. Council, British Records Assoc., 1948–66 (Chm. Records Preservation section, 1961–66); Mem. Cttee, Windsor and Eton Soc., 1948–63; Hon. Archivist, Borough of Windsor, 1950–80; Mem. Tech. Cttee, Soc. of Archivists, 1956–74; Governor, Windsor Boys' Sch., 1957–; Hon. Gen. Editor: St George's Chapel Monographs, 1960–; Windsor Records Publications, 1966–80; Dir, Simon de Montfort Exhibn, Houses of Parliament, 1965; Mem. Cttee of Management, Inst. of Historical Research, 1968–77; Vice-Pres., Berkshire Archaeological Soc., 1973–; Hon. Consultant, Berks Record Office, 1981–; Dir, Chapel of Kings Exhibn, Windsor Castle, 1975. FSA 1947, FRHistS 1971. Hon. Associate, Royal Holloway Coll., London Univ., 1975–. *Publications:* (ed) The Inventories of St George's Chapel, 1947; The Romance of St George's Chapel, 1947, 13th edn 1983; (ed jtly) The Dictionary of English Church History, 1948; (ed) The Manuscripts of the House of Lords 1710–1714, 2 vols, 1949, 1953, and Addenda, 1514–1714, 1962; (jtly) The Manuscripts of St George's Chapel, 1957; The Seventh Centenary of Simon de Montfort's Parliament, 1965; (with Shelagh Bond) The Chapter Acts of the Dean and Canons of Windsor, 1430, 1523–1672, 1966; Pictorial History of the Houses of Parliament, 1967; Guide to the Records of Parliament, 1971; St George's Chapel, Quincentenary Souvenir Book, 1975; The Diaries and Papers of Sir Edward Dering, 1644–1684, 1976; (with David Beamish) Black Rod, 1976; (with David Beamish) The Lord Chancellor, 1977; (ed) Works of Art in the House of Lords, 1980; contributions to: Eng. Hist. Review; Bulletin of Inst. of Hist. Research; Jl of Eccles. Hist.; The Table; Jl of Soc. of Archivists;

Archives. *Recreations:* travel, music. *Address:* 19 Bolton Crescent, Windsor, Berks. *T:* Windsor 65132. *Club:* National Liberal.
*Died 24 Dec. 1983.*

**BOND, Ralph Norman**, CMG 1953; OBE 1950; *b* 31 Aug. 1900; *s* of Ralph Bond, Morecambe, Lancs; *m* 1929, Dorothy Ward; three *d*. *Educ:* Royal Grammar Sch., Lancaster; St John's Coll., Cambridge. BA Classical Tripos, 1922; MA 1929. Eastern Cadetship in Colonial Service, Dec. 1923; arrived in Ceylon, Jan. 1924; Revenue and judicial posts, 1924–36; Customs (Landing Surveyor and Deputy Collector), 1936–39; Import, Export and Exchange Control, 1939–42; Assistant Chief Secretary, 1942–45; Secretary to C-in-C, Ceylon, 1945–46; Permanent Secretary to Ministry of Posts and Broadcasting, Ceylon, 1947–55; retired, 1955. *Recreations:* formerly Rugby, soccer, hockey, cricket, tennis, swimming and horseriding; then gardening. *Address:* 48 Stuart Avenue, Morecambe, Lancs. *T:* Morecambe 418799. *Died 6 Aug. 1984.*

**BONE, Captain Howard Francis**, CBE 1957; DSO 1940, and Bar 1941; DSC 1940 and Bar, 1942; RN (retired); *b* 20 Oct. 1908; *s* of late Engineer Rear-Adm. H. Bone, CB, and late Mrs A. S. Bone; *m* 1932, Heather Maud Marion Fletcher; one *d*. *Educ:* Felsted; RNC, Dartmouth. Entered RN, 1922; served in submarines, 1930–50. Comdr 1941; Captain, 1947; Dep. Director of Naval Equipment, 1952–54; Captain-in-Charge, Simonstown, and Captain Superintendent, Simonstown Dockyard, 1954–57. ADC to the Queen, Jan. 1956-May 1957. Retired, 1957. *Address:* Inner Meadow, Combe Hay, near Bath, Avon. *T:* Combe Down 833363.
*Died 12 Aug. 1981.*

**BONHAM-CARTER, Sir (Arthur) Desmond**, Kt 1969; TD 1942; Director, Unilever Ltd, 1953–68, retired; *b* 15 Feb. 1908; 2nd *s* of Gen. Sir Charles Bonham-Carter, GCB, CMG, DSO, and Beryl, *née* Codrington; *m* 1st, 1933, Ann Parker Hazelwood (*d* 1972); one *s*; 2nd, 1973, Diane Anastasia, *e d* of Mervyn Madden. *Educ:* Winchester; Magdalene Coll., Cambridge. Served with Royal Tank Regt, 1938–45 (Lt-Col). With Unilever, 1929–68, Dir, 1953–68. Chm., SW Metropolitan RHB, 1968–74; Mem., Camden and Islington AHA, 1974–78. Member: Royal Commission to consider Pay of Doctors and Dentists, 1957–60; Advisory Cttee, Recruitment for the Forces, 1958; Plowden Cttee on Representational Services Overseas, 1962–64; Central Health Services Council, 1965–74. UK Rep., Internat. Hosp. Fedn, 1969–73; Chm., Teaching Hosps Assoc., 1965–72. Trustee, Nightingale Fund, 1961–; Chm., Board of Governors, University College Hospital, 1963–74. *Address:* 15 Ashfield Close, Midhurst, Sussex. *T:* Midhurst 2109.
*Died 18 April 1985.*

**BOOT, Dr Henry Albert Howard;** Senior Principal Scientific Officer, Royal Naval Scientific Service, 1954–77 (Principal Scientific Officer, 1948–54); *b* 29 July 1917; *s* of late Henry James and Ruby May Boot; *m* 1948, Penelope May Herrington; two *s*. *Educ:* King Edward's High Sch., Birmingham (Scholar); Univ. of Birmingham. BSc 1938; PhD 1941. Invention of the cavity magnetron (with Prof. J. T. Randall, FRS), 1939; research on the cavity magnetron at Univ. of Birmingham, 1939–45; Nuffield Research Fellow in Physics at Univ. of Birmingham, 1945–48. Royal Society of Arts Thomas Gray Memorial Prize (with J. T. Randall), 1943; Award by Royal Commission on Awards to Inventors, 1949; John Price Wetherill Medal of the Franklin Institute, 1958; John Scott Award, 1959 (with Prof. J. Randall). *Publications:* various papers on the production of high power ultra high frequency oscillation and controlled thermonuclear fusion, also optical masers. *Recreation:* sailing. *Address:* The Old Mill Cottage, Rushden, near Buntingford, Herts. *T:* Broadfield 231. *Died 8 Feb. 1983.*

**BOOTH, Catherine B.;** *see* Bramwell-Booth.

**BOOTH, Sir Michael Savile G.;** *see* Gore-Booth.

**BOOTHBY, Baron** *cr* 1958, of Buchan and Rattray Head (Life Peer); **Robert John Graham Boothby**, KBE 1953; President, Anglo-Israel Association, 1962–75; *b* 1900; *o s* of late Sir Robert Tuite Boothby, KBE, Beechwood, Edinburgh, and Mabel, *d* of late H. H. Lancaster; *m* 1st, 1935, Diana (marr. diss. 1937), *d* of late Lord Richard Cavendish, PC, CB, CMG; 2nd, 1967, Wanda, *d* of Giuseppe Sanna, Sardinia. *Educ:* Eton; Magdalen Coll., Oxford. BA 1921, MA 1959. Contested Orkney and Shetland, 1923; MP (U) East Aberdeenshire, 1924–58; Parliamentary Private Sec. to the Chancellor of the Exchequer (Rt Hon. Winston S. Churchill, MP), 1926–29; Parliamentary Sec., Ministry of Food, 1940–41; a British delegate to the Consultative Assembly of the Council of Europe, 1949–57; Vice-Chm. Cttee on Economic Affairs, 1952–56; Hon. Pres., Scottish Chamber of Agriculture, 1934. Rector, University of St Andrews, 1958–61; Chm., Royal Philharmonic Orchestra, 1961–63, Hon. Life Mem., 1976; Vice-Pres., Delius Soc. Radner Lectr, Columbia Univ., NY, 1960. Hon. LLD St Andrews, 1959. Hon. Burgess of the Burghs of Peterhead, Fraserburgh, Turriff and Rosehearty. Officer of the Legion of Honour, 1950. *Publications:* The New Economy, 1943; I Fight to Live, 1947; My Yesterday,

Your Tomorrow, 1962; Boothby: recollections of a rebel, 1978. *Address:* 1 Eaton Square, SW1. *Club:* Royal and Ancient (St Andrews). *Died 16 July 1986.*

**BOOTHBY, (Evelyn) Basil**, CMG 1958; HM Diplomatic Service, retired; Tutor, London University Extra-Mural Studies, since 1970; *b* 9 Sept. 1910; *s* of Basil T. B. Boothby and Katherine Knox; *m* 1946, Susan Asquith; two *s* one *d* (and one *s* decd). *Educ:* Winchester; CCC, Cambridge. Student Interpreter, China Consular Service, 1933; appointed a Vice-Consul in China, 1936; served at Shanghai and Hankow (periods Acting Consul); Vice-Consul, Boston, 1940; employed at New York, Dec. 1941–June 1942, when reappointed a Vice-Consul in China and transf. to Chungking; seconded to Govt of India for service in Chinese Relations Office, Calcutta, Oct. 1943–July 1944; Actg Consul Kweilin and Kunming, also Athens, successively, 1944–45; promoted Consul, Sept. 1945; apptd Foreign Service Officer, Grade 7, in Foreign Office, Nov. 1946; promoted Counsellor, Foreign Service Officer, Grade 6, and became Head of UN (Economic and Social) Dept, Sept. 1949; seconded to Commonwealth Relations Office for service in Ontario and attached to Canadian National Defence Coll., Sept. 1950; apptd Counsellor, Rangoon, Nov. 1951 (Chargé d'Affaires, 1952); Counsellor, British Embassy, Brussels, 1954; Head of African Dept, Foreign Office, 1959; British Ambassador to Iceland, 1962–65; Permanent British Rep. to Council of Europe, 1965–69. Lectr, Morley Coll., 1969–70. *Address:* 23 Holland Park Avenue, W11.
*Died 9 Feb. 1990.*

**BOOTHBY, Sir Hugo (Robert Brooke)**, 15th Bt, *cr* 1660; JP; Lieutenant, South Glamorgan, 1974–81 (Vice-Lieutenant of Glamorgan, 1957–74); *b* 10 Aug. 1907; *s* of Sir Seymour William Brooke Boothby, 14th Bt, and Clara Margaret (*d* 1969), *d* of late Robert Valpy; *S* father 1951; *m* 1938, Evelyn Ann, *o d* of H. C. R. Homfray; one *s* two *d*. *Educ:* Lancing; Hertford Coll., Oxford. Served War of 1939–45, Capt. RA 53 (Welsh) Div., 1942–44. Capt. RA (TA). Dir, Wales Tourist Bd, 1965–70; S Wales Regional Dir, Lloyds Bank, 1963–78; Dir, Divisional Bd for Wales, Nationwide Building Soc., 1971–82; Member: Cardiff Rural Dist Council, 1936–58 (Chm. 1948–49 and 1949–50); Representative Body, Church in Wales, 1955–65; National Broadcasting Council for Wales, 1953–56; Glamorgan County Agricultural Executive Cttee, 1953–62; Court and Council, Nat. Museum of Wales, 1955; Civic Trust for Wales, 1973–. Chm., Historic Houses Assoc. in Wales. Fellow, Woodard Corporation, 1961–82. JP 1950, DL 1953, Glamorgan; High Sheriff, Glamorgan, 1953. Hon. Freeman, Borough of Vale of Glamorgan, 1984. *Recreation:* shooting. *Heir: s* Brooke Charles Boothby [*b* 6 April 1949; *m* 1976, Georgiana Alexandra, *d* of Sir John (Wriothesley) Russell, GCVO, CMG; two *d*]. *Address:* Fonmon Castle, Barry, South Glamorgan CF6 9ZN. *T:* Rhoose 710206. *Clubs:* Brooks's; Cardiff and County (Cardiff).
*Died 30 May 1986.*

**BOOTHE, Clare;** *see* Luce, Mrs Henry R.

**BOOTHROYD, Basil;** *see* Boothroyd, J. B.

**BOOTHROYD, (Edith) Hester, (Mrs Francis Boothroyd);** *b* 11 Jan. 1915; *d* of late Stanley John Benham; *m* 1940, Francis Boothroyd; one *d* (and one *d* decd). *Educ:* St Felix Sch., Southwold; Newnham Coll., Cambridge (MA). Min. of Economic Warfare, 1939–44; BoT, 1945–49; Statistician and Prin., Treasury, 1949–64; Asst Sec., DEA, 1965–67, Asst Under-Sec. of State, DEA, 1967–69; Under-Sec., Treasury, 1969–75; Mem., Bd of Crown Agents, 1975–77. Hon. Treasurer, Aldeburgh Festival/Snape Maltings Foundn, 1976–81. Associate Fellow of Newnham Coll., Cambridge, 1981– (Associate, 1975–). *Recreations:* gardening, music, travel. *Address:* Ranworth House, Nayland, near Colchester CO6 4JD. *T:* Nayland 262331.
*Died 7 July 1983.*

**BOOTHROYD, (John) Basil;** writer and broadcaster; *b* 4 March 1910; *m* 1st, 1939, Phyllis Barbara Youngman (*d* 1980); one *s*; 2nd, 1981, June Elizabeth Leonhardt Mortimer. *Educ:* Lincoln Cathedral Choir Sch.; Lincoln Sch. Bank Clerk, 1927. Served with RAF Police, 1941–45; Personal Asst to Provost-Marshal from 1943. Punch contributor continuously from 1938, an Asst Editor, 1952–70, Mem. Punch Table, 1955. Much broadcasting and miscellaneous frivolous journalism; some lecturing and public speaking. Imperial Tobacco Radio Award, best comedy script, 1976. *Television includes:* adaptation of: The Diary of a Nobody, BBC series, 1979; A. J. Wentworth, BA, ITV series, 1982. *Publications:* Home Guard Goings-On, 1941; Adastral Bodies, 1942; Are Sergeants Human? 1945; Are Officers Necessary?, 1946; Lost, A Double-Fronted Shop, 1947; The House About a Man, 1959; Motor If You Must, 1960; To My Embarrassment, 1961; The Whole Thing's Laughable, 1964; You Can't be Serious, 1966; Let's Stay Married, 1967 (and US, 1967); Stay Married Abroad, 1968; Boothroyd at Bay (radio talks), 1970; Philip (an approved biography of HRH the Duke of Edinburgh), 1971 (and US, 1971); Accustomed As I Am, 1975; Let's Move House, 1977; In My State of Health, 1981; (autobiog.) A Shoulder to Laugh On, 1987. *Recreations:* playing the piano,

working. *Address:* Peelers, Church Street, Cuckfield, Sussex. *T:* Haywards Heath 454340/412173. *Club:* Savage.
*Died 27 Feb.* 1988.

**BORDEN, Henry,** OC 1969; CMG 1943; QC 1938; Canadian Lawyer, retired; *b* Halifax, NS, 25 Sept. 1901; *s* of Henry Clifford and Mabel (Ashmere) Barnstead Borden, both of Halifax, NS; *m* 1929, Jean Creelman, *d* of late Dr D. A. MacRae, Toronto, Ont; three *s* two *d. Educ:* King's Coll. Sch., Windsor, NS; McGill Univ.; Dalhousie Law Sch; Exeter Coll., Oxford (Rhodes Schol.). BA Political Science and Economics, McGill, 1921; BA Oxon, 1926. With Royal Bank of Canada, 1921–22. Called to Bar, Lincoln's Inn, 1927; to Bar of Nova Scotia, 1927; to Bar of Ont, 1927. Senior Mem., Borden, Elliot, Kelley, Palmer, 1936–46; Gen. Counsel, Dept of Munitions and Supply, Ottawa, 1939–42; Chairman: Wartime Industries Control Bd, Ottawa, and Co-ordinator of Controls, Dept of Munitions and Supply, Sept. 1942–43; Royal Commission on Energy, 1957–59. Pres., Brazilian Traction Light & Power Co., 1946–63, Chm., 1963–65; Chm. and Pres., Brinco Ltd (formerly British Newfoundland Corporation Ltd), 1965–69; Dir Emeritus, Canadian Imperial Bank of Commerce; Dir, Mem. Exec. Cttee and Past Pres., Royal Agric. Winter Fair. Formerly Lectr, Corp. Law, Osgoode Hall Law Sch; Past President: Canadian Club of Toronto; Lawyers' Club of Toronto. Past Chm., Bd of Governors, Univ. of Toronto. Hon. LLD: St Francis Xavier, 1960; Dalhousie, 1968; Toronto, 1972; Hon. DCL Acadia, 1960. Is an Anglican. Grand Officer, Nat. Order of the Southern Cross (Brazil), 1962; Canada Centennial Medal, 1967. *Publications:* (jtly) Fraser & Borden, Hand Book of Canadian Companies, 1931; ed, Robert Laird Borden: His Memoirs, 1938; ed, Letters to Limbo, by Rt Hon. Sir Robert L. Borden, 1971. *Recreations:* farming, fishing. *Address:* Apt 609, 484 Avenue Road, Toronto M4V 2J4, Canada. *Club:* York (Toronto).
*Died 6 May* 1989.

**BORDER, Hugh William;** *b* 26 Nov. 1890; *s* of William Border and Mary Abbott; *m* 1917, Mabel Evelyn Watts (*d* 1975); one *d. Educ:* Latymer Upper Sch., Hammersmith. Employed in the Ministry of Labour, 1912–14; Consulate-Gen., Rotterdam 1914–20; Probationer Vice-Consul at Colon, July 1920; Acting Consul, 1921 and 1923; Acting Vice-Consul at Constantsa and Braila, 1924; Vice-Consul at Braila, 1924; Acting Consul-Gen., Galatz, 1925 and 1926; Vice-Consul, 1926; Acting Consul-General, Galatz, 1927, 1928 and 1929; Chargé d'Affaires *ai*, Managua, 1930; HM Consul, Managua, July 1930; HM Consul-Gen. (local rank) Havana, 1932; Chargé d'Affaires, Havana, Feb.–June 1933; HM Consul, Havre, 1934–37; HM Consul, Bordeaux, 1937; HM Consul, Nantes, 1939–40; HM Consul-Gen. at Seville, 1945–50; retired, 1950.
*Died 14 Jan.* 1981.

**BORGES, Jorge Luis,** poet; Director, National Library of Argentina, 1955–73; *b* Buenos Aires, 24 Aug. 1899; *s* of late Jorge Borges and of Leonor Acevedo de Borges; *m* 1986, Maria Kodama. *Educ:* Collège de Géneve; Univ. of Cambridge. Prof. of English and N American Literature, Univ. of Buenos Aires, 1955–70. Member: Argentine Nat. Acad., 1955; Uruguayan Acad. of Letters; Goethe Acad. of Sâo Paulo, Brazil; Pres., Argentine Writers' Assoc., 1950–53 (grand prize 1945); Hon. Pres., Argentine branch, Dickens Fellowship of London; Vice-Pres., Amigos de la Literatura Inglesa. Hon. DLitt Oxford 1970; Hon. Dr: Jerusalem 1971; Rome 1984; Hon. LittD Cambridge 1984. Premio de Honor, Prix Formentor (with Samuel Beckett), 1961; Fondo de las Artes, 1963. Hon. KBE; Légion d'Honneur, 1983. *Publications: poems:* Fervor de Buenos Aires, 1923; Luna de Enfrente, 1925; Cuaderno San Martín, 1929; Elogio de la Sombra, 1969 (trans. as In Praise of Darkness, 1975); Selected Poems 1923–1967, 1972; *essays:* Inquisiciones, 1925; El Idioma de los Argentinos, 1928; Evaristo Carriego, 1930; Discusión, 1932; Historia de la Eternidad, 1936; Antología Clásica de la Literatura Argentina, 1942; Nueva Refutación del Tiempo, 1947; Otras Inquisiciones, 1937–52, 1952 (trans. as Other Inquisitions, 1964); *stories:* Historia Universal de la Infamia, 1935; Tlön, Uqbar, Orbis Tertius, 1938; El Jardín de Senderos que se bifurcan, 1941; Ficciones, 1945 (trans. 1962); El Aleph, 1949 (trans. 1973); La Muerte y la Brújula, 1951; (with Adolfo Bioy-Casares) Cronicas de Bustos Domecq, 1967 (trans. as Chronicles of Bustos Domecq, 1982); El Informe de Brodie, 1971 (trans. as Dr Brodie's Report, 1974); El libro de arena, 1975; Obras completas, 1975; (with Adolfo Bioy-Casares) Six Problems for Don Isidro Parodi, 1981; *collections:* El Hacedor, 1960 (trans. as Dreamtigers, 1964); Antología Personal, 1961 (trans. as A Personal Anthology, 1967); Labyrinthe, 1960 (trans. as Labyrinths, 1962); El Libra de los Seres Imaginarios (with Margarita Guerrero), 1967 (trans. as The Book of Imaginary Beings, 1969); Prólogos, 1975; The Book of Sand, 1979; Seven Nights, 1986; *posthumous publication:* (ed jtly) The Book of Fantasy, 1988. *Recreations:* study of Old English and of Old Norse. *Address:* Maipú 994, Buenos Aires, Argentina. *Died 14 June* 1986.

**BORNEMAN, Roy Ernest,** QC 1952; *b* 1904; *s* of Ernest Borneman, London; *m* 1st, 1932, Winifred Dixon, *d* of Dr William Hunter, Aberdeen; two *s*; 2nd, 1973, Sarah Anderson, *d* of Thomas Paterson,

North Berwick. *Educ:* University Coll., Reading; University Coll., London. BA 1924. Called to the Bar, Gray's Inn, 1929; Bencher, 1956; Treasurer, 1972; Vice-Treasurer, 1973. Chm., Board of Referees and Finance Act 1960 Tribunal, 1960–77. Served War of 1939–45, Wing Comdr, Royal Air Force. *Recreations:* golf, music, travel. *Address:* 11 New Square, Lincoln's Inn, WC2; Spindles, Hotley Bottom Lane, Prestwood, Great Missenden, Bucks. *T:* Great Missenden 4858. *Died 1 Nov.* 1983.

**BORRIE, Peter Forbes,** MD, FRCP; retired; Physician in charge of the Skin Department, St Bartholomew's Hospital, 1968–78; Consultant Dermatologist to Moorfields, Westminster and Central Eye Hospitals, 1950–78, and to Barnet General Hospital, 1954–78; *b* 26 March 1918; *s* of late Dr David Forbes Borrie and Martha Ruth Downing; *m* 1942, Helen Patricia, *e d* of Major H. G. Chesney; two *s* two *d. Educ:* Rugby Sch.; Clare Coll., Cambridge; St Bartholomew's Hospital. BA (Nat. Sci. Tripos) 1939; MB, BChir Cantab 1942; MRCP 1948; FRCP 1960; MA Cantab 1950; MD Cantab 1951. House Physician, St Bartholomew's Hospital, 1942; Senior Registrar, Skin Dept, St Mary's Hospital, Paddington, 1948; Chief Asst, Skin Dept, St Bartholomew's Hospital, 1950. Fellow Royal Society of Medicine; Mem. British Association of Dermatology; Lecturer at the Institute of Dermatology. *Publications:* Editor, Roxburgh's Common Skin Diseases, 11th–14th edns, 1959–75; Modern Trends in Dermatology, Series iv, 1971; many articles in medical journals. *Address:* Daymer Dunes, Trebetherick, Wadebridge, Cornwall PL27 6SF. *T:* Trebetherick 2315.
*Died 6 April* 1984.

**BORWICK, Lt-Col Michael George;** JP; farmer; Director, Blair Trust Co.; *b* 27 March 1916; *s* of late Col Malcolm Borwick; *m* 1946, Veronica, *d* of late Lt-Col J. F. Harrison and Hon. Mrs Harrison; two *s* decd. *Educ:* Harrow; in France. Joined Leicestershire Yeomanry, 1935; joined Royal Scots Greys, 1937; joined Middle East Commandos, 1940, fought in Dodecanese Islands and in Crete, 1941 (POW); rejoined Greys, 1945; comd 1954–57. Chm., Royal Scots Greys Assoc., 1963. Joint Master, Eglinton Foxhounds, 1960–63 and 1972–75. Mem., Royal Company of Archers, Queen's Body Guard for Scotland. Mem. Ayrshire CC, 1958–66, resigned; JP Ayrshire, later Strathclyde, 1970; DL Ayrshire, 1960, Vice Lord-Lieut for Ayr and Arran, 1974–83. *Recreations:* hunting, shooting. *Address:* Blair, Dalry, Ayrshire KA24 4ER. *Club:* Cavalry and Guards. *Died 20 April* 1986.

**BORWICK, Lt-Col Sir Thomas Faulkner,** Kt 1946; CIE 1941; DSO 1917; BMechE; FIMechE; late AIF; *b* 1890; *s* of Henry Barton Borwick, Melbourne; *m* 1918, Elsa (*d* 1977), *y d* of Eduardo and Fanny de Ambrosio, Florence; one *s* one *d. Educ:* Scotch Coll. and University, Melbourne. Served European War, 1914–18 (twice wounded, despatches twice, DSO, Croix de Guerre). Worshipful Master, Kitchener Lodge, Simla, 1939. Chm., Indian Advisory Cttee, Institution of Mechanical Engineers, 1950; Dir-Gen. Ordnance Factories, India, 1943–47; Gen. Manager, National Machinery Manufacturers, Ltd, Bombay, 1947–52; joined The Plessey Co., Ilford, 1952; Divisional Manager, 1957; Group Gen. Manager, 1958; Gen. Manager, Swindon Region, 1959–60. Director: The Amar Tool & Gauge Co., 1958–60; Hawley Products Ltd, 1959–60. Chm. of Governors, Farmor's Sch., Fairford, 1967–75. *Address:* Ridgemead House, Englefield Green, Egham, Surrey.
*Died 12 Dec.* 1981.

**BOSANQUET, Charles Ion Carr,** MA; DL; Vice-Chancellor of University of Newcastle upon Tyne, 1963–68 (Rector of King's College, Newcastle upon Tyne, 1952–63); *b* 19 April 1903; *s* of Robert Carr Bosanquet and Ellen S. Bosanquet; *m* 1931, Barbara, *d* of William Jay Schifflein, New York; one *s* three *d. Educ:* Winchester; Trinity Coll., Cambridge (Scholar). Asst Gen. Manager, Friends Provident and Century Life Office, 1933–39; Principal Asst Sec., Ministry of Agriculture and Fisheries, 1941–45; Treasurer of Christ Church, Oxford, 1945–52. Fellow of Winchester Coll., 1951–73; Chm., Reorganisation Commission for Pigs and Bacon, 1955–56; Development Comr, 1956–70; Chm. Min. of Agric. Cttee of Enquiry into Demand for Agricultural Graduates. Hon DCL Durham; Hon LLD Cincinnati; Hon. DLitt Sierra Leone; Hon. DSc City. High Sheriff, 1948–49, DL 1971, Northumberland. Comdr, Order of St Olav. *Address:* White House, Rock Moor, Alnwick, Northumberland. *T:* Charlton Mires 224. *Clubs:* Farmers'; Northern Counties (Newcastle).
*Died 9 April* 1986.

**BOSCH, Baron Jean van den,** Hon. GCVO 1966; Belgian Ambassador to the Court of St James's and Belgian Permanent Representative to the Council of Western European Union, 1966–72; Director, Lloyds Bank International, 1972–78; *b* 27 Jan. 1910; *s* of Baron Firmin van den Bosch and Anne de Volder; *m* 1944, Hélène Cloquet; two *d. Educ:* Ecole Abbatiale, Maredsous; Notre-Dame de la Paix, Namur; Université Catholique de Louvain. Docteur en droit; licencié en sciences historiques; licencié en sciences politiques et diplomatiques. Entered Belgian Diplomatic Service, 1934;

Attaché, London and Paris, 1934; Sec., Pekin, 1937; 1st Sec., Ottawa, 1940; Chargé d'Affaires to Luxembourg Govt in London, 1943; Counsellor, Prince Regent's Household, 1944; Counsellor and Chargé d'Affaires, Cairo, 1948; Counsellor, 1949, Minister, 1953, Paris; Minister, Consul-Gen., Hong Kong, Singapore and Saigon, 1954; Ambassador, Cairo, 1955; accredited Minister, Libya, 1956; Sec.-Gen. of Min. of For. Aff. and For. Trade, 1959–June 1960, and again, Sept. 1960–1965; Ambassador, Congo, July-Aug. 1960. Dir, Lloyds Bank International (Belgium) SA, 1972–78 (Chm., 1973–78). Grand Officier, Ordres Léopold, Couronne, Léopold II. Médaille Civique (1st cl.). Holds foreign decorations. *Address:* 187 Chaussée de Vleurgat, B25, 1050 Brussels, Belgium. *Club:* Anglo-Belgian.
*Died 15 Dec. 1985.*

**BOSE, (L. M.) Vivian;** *b* Ahmedabad, India, 9 June 1891; *s* of late Lalit Mohun Bose and *g s* of late Sir Bipin Krishna Bose; *m* 1930, Irene, *d* of late Dr John R. Mott (winner of Nobel Prize, 1946); one *s* one *d. Educ:* Dulwich Coll.; Pembroke Coll., Cambridge (BA, LLB). Called to Bar, Middle Temple, 1913; practised at the Nagpur Bar; Principal, University Coll. of Law, Nagpur, 1924–30; Govt Advocate and Standing Counsel to the Govt of the Central Provinces and Berar, 1930–36; Additional Judicial Commissioner, Nagpur, for short periods, 1931–34; Puisne Judge, Nagpur High Court, 1936–49; Chief Justice, High Court of Judicature, Nagpur, 1949–51; Puisne Judge, Supreme Court of India, New Delhi, 1951–56, retd; recalled as *ad hoc* Judge, Supreme Court, Sept. 1958–Aug. 1959; Chm., two Government Commissions of Inquiry, 1958–62. Member International Commission of Jurists, 1958–; Pres., 1959–66 (Actg Sec.-Gen. March–Oct. 1963); Hon. Pres. 1966 (toured, on Commission's behalf: Europe, Asia Minor, Australia, Indonesia, Malaya, Burma, East and West Africa, UK, Ireland, Eire, USA, Brazil, 1961 and 1962–63). Hon. Provincial Sec., Boy Scouts Assoc. Central Provinces and Berar, 1921–34; Provincial Commissioner, 1934–37; Chief Commissioner for India, 1948; National Commissioner, 1959–62; Silver Wolf, 1942; Capt. the Nagpur Regt, Indian Auxiliary Force. Volunteer Long Service Medal, 1929; King's Silver Jubilee Medal, 1935; Kaisar-i-Hind Silver Medal, 1936. *Recreations:* photography, wireless, motoring (from and to India, etc), travel; amateur magic, mainly stage illusions. *Address:* Vishranti Farm, Doddakallasandra Post, Bangalore 560 062, India. *T:* 40419. *Died 29 Nov. 1983.*

**BOSTON, Lucy Maria;** writer; *b* 10 Dec. 1892; *d* of James Wood and Mary Garrett; *m;* one *s.* Restored, and lived in, the oldest inhabited Norman house in England, the source of all her books. Carnegie medal, 1960. *Publications: for children* (many translated into seven languages): The Children of Green Knowe, 1954; The Chimneys of Green Knowe, 1958; The River at Green Knowe, 1959; A Stranger at Green Knowe, 1961; An Enemy at Green Knowe, 1964; The Castle of Yew, 1965; The Sea Egg, 1967; Nothing Said, 1971; The Guardians of the House, 1974; The Fossil Snake, 1975; The Stones of Green Knowe, 1976; *novels:* Yew Hall, 1954; Persephone, 1969; *autobiography:* Memory in a House, 1973; Perverse and Foolish, 1979; *poetry:* Time is Undone; *drama:* The Horned Man, 1970. *Address:* The Manor, Hemingford Grey, Huntingdon PE18 9BN.
*Died 25 May 1990.*

**BOSWALL, Sir Thomas H.;** *see* Houstoun-Boswall.

**BOSWORTH, George Simms,** CBE 1968; CEng, FIEE; Director of Newcastle upon Tyne Polytechnic, 1969–77, Hon. Fellow, 1982; *b* 12 Aug. 1916; *s* of George Bosworth and Mabel Anne Simms; *m* 1940, Helen Cowan Rusack; two *s* two *d. Educ:* Herbert Strutt Grammar Sch.; Gonville and Caius Coll., Cambridge. MA (Mechanical Sci. Tripos). Served RAF, Engineer Officer; Sqdn Ldr, 1940–46. English Electric Co., London, 1946–69: Chief of Technical Personnel Administration; Director of Group Personnel Services; Director of Personnel. Hon. DTech Bradford, 1968; Hon. DCL Newcastle upon Tyne, 1978. *Address:* 111 Park Place, Park Parade, Harrogate HG1 5NS. *Club:* Royal Air Force.
*Died 15 May 1986.*

**BOTTRALL, (Francis James) Ronald,** OBE 1949; MA; FRSL; *b* Camborne, Cornwall, 2 Sept. 1906; *o s* of Francis John and Clara Jane Bottrall; *m* 1st, 1934, Margaret Florence (marr. diss., 1954), *o d* of Rev. H. Saumarez Smith; one *s;* 2nd, 1954, Margot Pamela Samuel. *Educ:* Redruth County Sch.; Pembroke Coll., Cambridge. Foundress' Scholar; First Class English Tripos, Parts I and II (with distinction); Charles Oldham Shakespeare Scholarship, 1927. Lector in English, Univ. of Helsingfors, Finland, 1929–31; Commonwealth Fund Fellowship, Princeton Univ., USA, 1931–33; Johore Prof. of English Language and Literature, Raffles Coll., Singapore, 1933–37; Asst Dir, British Inst., Florence, 1937–38; Sec., SOAS, London Univ., 1939–45; Air Ministry: Temp. Admin. Officer, 1940; Priority Officer, 1941; British Council Representative: in Sweden, 1941; in Italy, 1945; in Brazil, 1954; in Greece, 1957; in Japan (and Cultural Counsellor, HM Embassy, Tokyo), 1959; Controller of Educ. 1950–54. Chief, Fellowships and Training Br., Food and Agriculture Org. of UN, 1963–65. Coronation Medal, 1953; Syracuse Internat.

Poetry Prize, 1954. FRSL 1955. KStJ 1972; Kt Comdr, Order of St John of Jerusalem, Malta, 1977. Grande Ufficiale dell'Ordine al Merito della Repubblica Italiana, 1973. *Publications: poetry:* The Loosening and other Poems, 1931; Festivals of Fire, 1934; The Turning Path, 1939; Farewell and Welcome, 1945; Selected Poems, 1946; The Palisades of Fear, 1949; Adam Unparadised, 1954; Collected Poems, 1961; Day and Night, 1974; Poems 1955–73, 1974; Reflections on the Nile, 1980; Against a Setting Sun, 1983; *criticism, anthologies:* (with Gunnar Ekelöf) T.S. Eliot: Dikter i Urval, 1942; (with Margaret Bottrall) The Zephyr Book of English Verse, 1945; (with Margaret Bottrall) Collected English Verse, 1946; Rome (Art Centres of the World), 1968. *Recreations:* music, travel. *Address:* Flat 4, New Cavendish Court, 39 New Cavendish Street, W1M 7RJ. *T:* 01–486 1144. *Died 25 June 1989.*

**BOUGHTON, Michael Linnell Gerald;** Deputy Chairman and Managing Director (Operations), TI Group PLC (formerly Tube Investments), 1984–86 (Chairman, TI Group); Chairman, TI Raleigh Industries Ltd, 1981–85; *b* 14 May 1925; *s* of Edward Morley Westwood Boughton and Iris Dorothy (*née* Linnell); *m* 1954, Barbara Janette, *d* of Sir Ivan Stedeford, GBE; one *s* two *d. Educ:* King Edward's Sch., Birmingham; Rugby Technical Coll. (HNC Product Engrg). Engineering apprentice, B-T-H Co. Ltd, 1942–49; TI Group, 1952–: Man. Dir, Round Oak Steel Works, 1960–61; Jt Man. Dir, Steel Tube Div., 1961–64; Man. Dir, Engrg Div., 1964–74; Man. Dir, Domestic Appliance Div., 1974–83; Director: Condor International, 1969–75; EIS Gp, 1979–84, 1986–. Mem. Bd, PLA, 1986–. *Recreations:* sailing, golf, jobs of construction and destruction. *Address:* Little Heath, Crays Pond, near Pangbourne, Berks RG8 7QG. *T:* Goring-on-Thames (0491) 872622.
*Died 19 May 1990.*

**BOULT, Sir Adrian (Cedric),** CH 1969; Kt 1937; MA; DMus Oxon; Hon. DMus RCM; Vice-President, Council of Royal College of Music, since 1963; *b* Chester, 8 April 1889; *o s* of late Cedric R. Boult, JP, formerly of Liverpool, and Katharine Florence Barman; *m* 1933, Ann, *yr d* of late Capt. F. A. Bowles, RN, JP, Dully, Sittingbourne, Kent. *Educ:* Westminster Sch.; Christ Church, Oxford; Leipzig Conservatorium (now Hochschule). President, Oxford Univ. Musical Club, 1910. Musical Staff, Royal Opera, 1914; Asst Director of Music, 1926. During 1914–18 War, served in War Office and Commission Internationale de Ravitaillement. Teaching staff of Royal College of Music, 1919–30 and 1962–66; Conductor of Patron's Fund, 1919–29; Conductor: Bach Choir, 1928–33; Birmingham Fest. Choral Soc., 1923–30; Musical Director, Birmingham City Orchestra, 1924–30 and 1959–60; Vice-President, City of Birmingham Symphony Orchestra, 1960–; Director of Music, BBC, 1930–42; first Conductor, BBC Symphony Orchestra, 1931–50; assisted Sir Henry Wood and Basil Cameron as conductors of Promenade Concerts in 1942, and took part in nearly every season until 1977; Conductor, London Philharmonic Orchestra, 1950–57, President, 1966–. Since 1922, has conducted in many European countries as well as USA and Canada, introducing British Music wherever possible. Has also directed a number of classes for conductors, especially for BBC and Schools' Music Assoc., and has taken charge of many festivals, notably Petersfield, 1920–39. Assisted at Coronation Services, 1937, 1953, and took part in concerts and services during Westminster Abbey 900th Anniversary Year, 1966. President: Incorp. Society of Musicians, 1928–29; Nat. Youth Orchestra, 1947–57; Schools' Music Assoc., 1947–; Leith Hill Musical Festival, 1955–78; Royal Scottish Academy of Music, 1959–. Hon. Pres., BBC Symphony Club, 1980–. Hon. LLD: Birmingham; Liverpool; Reading; Hon. MusDoc: Edinburgh; Cambridge; Hon. DLitt Oxford, 1979; Hon. RAM; Hon. DMus RCM 1982; Hon. Student, Christ Church, Oxon; FRCM (Vice-Pres.); Hon. Fellow, Manchester Coll., Oxford; Hon. Member Royal Academy of Music, Sweden; Hon. GSM; Hon. TCL (Vice-Pres.); Gold Medal, Royal Philharmonic Soc., 1944; Harvard Medal, with Dr Vaughan Williams, 1956. OStJ. *Publications:* A Handbook on The Technique of Conducting, 1920, rev. edn 1968; (joint) Bach's Matthew Passion, 1949; Thoughts on Conducting, 1963; My Own Trumpet (autobiog.), 1973; (with J. N. Moore) Music and Friends, 1979; contribs on musical subjects to various journals. *Address:* Fox Yard Cottage, West Street, Farnham, Surrey GU9 7EX. *T:* Farnham 715881. *Clubs:* Athenæum (Life Mem.), Royal Commonwealth Society; Leander (Henley).
*Died 22 Feb. 1983.*

**BOULTER, Eric Thomas,** CBE 1978; Director-General, Royal National Institute for the Blind, 1972–80; *b* 7 July 1917; *s* of Albert and Ethel Boulter; *m* 1946, Martha Mary McClure; one *s* one *d. Educ:* St Marylebone Grammar School. World Council for Welfare of Blind: Sec.-General, 1951–59; Vice-Pres., 1959–64; Pres., 1964–69; Hon. Life Mem., 1969. Chm., Council of World Organisations for Handicapped, 1958–61; Mem. Exec., Internat. Council of Educators of Blind Youth, 1962–70; Assoc. Dir, American Foundn for Overseas Blind, 1956–70; Dep. Dir-Gen., RNIB, 1971–72; Sec., British Council for Prevention of Blindness, 1976–. Hon. Life Mem., World Blind Union, 1984. Order of the Andes

(Bolivia), 1960; Silver Medal for service to mankind, City of Paris, 1975; Helen Keller Internat. Award, 1978; Louis Braille Gold Medal, 1978. *Publication:* (with John H. Dobree) Blindness and Visual Handicap—the facts, 1982. *Address:* 40 Snaresbrook Drive, Stanmore, Mddx. *T:* 01–958 8681. *Died 22 Aug.* 1989.

**BOULTING, John Edward;** film producer-director; Joint Managing Director, Charter Film Productions Ltd, since 1937; Director, British Lion Films Ltd, 1958–66; Managing Director, British Lion Films (Holdings) and subsidiaries, 1966–72; *b* 21 Nov. 1913; *s* of Arthur Boulting and Rose Bennett. *Educ:* Reading Sch. Office boy in Wardour Street, 1933. Spent eighteen months selling bad films to reluctant exhibitors; joined independent producer as general factotum on production, 1935; served hard but educative apprenticeship, in small studios. Went to Spain, served in International Brigade, front line ambulance driver, 1937; returned to England. Nov. 1937 formed independent film production company with twin brother Roy. Served War of 1939–45; joined RAF as AC2, 1940; retired Flt-Lieut, 1946. Continued film production; since War has produced Fame is the Spur, The Guinea Pig, Seagulls over Sorrento, Josephine and Men, Brothers in Law; has directed Brighton Rock, Seven Days to Noon, The Magic Box, Lucky Jim (Edinburgh Festival 1957); directed, and co-author of, screen-play Private's Progress, 1955; produced Carlton-Browne of the FO, 1958; directed and co-author screenplay, I'm All Right Jack, 1959; produced The Risk and The French Mistress, 1960; co-author novel and screen-play and director, Heavens Above!, 1962; produced films: The Family Way, 1966; There's a Girl in my Soup, 1970; Soft Beds, Hard Battles, 1974. Former Chm., Local Radio Assoc. *Recreations:* cricket, tennis, reading, film making, horse riding and irritating the conservative minded, particularly those adhering to the extreme political left. *Address:* Warfield Dale House, Warfield Dale, near Bracknell, Berks. *Died 17 June* 1985.

**BOULTON, Edward Henry Brooke,** MC; MA; FIWSc; Timber and Forestry Consultant; Forestry and Timber Counsellor to Marquess of Bath; *b* 1897; *s* of Joseph Henry and Florence Helena Boulton; *m*; one *s*. *Educ:* Portora Royal Inniskillen; St Catherine's Coll., Cambridge. Served with Royal Naval Division, 1915–16, Gallipoli and France; Royal Field Artillery, Capt., 1917–19; School of Forestry, Cambridge, 1920–22; Degree in Forestry and Post-grad. Diploma with Distinction in Timber Technology; University Lecturer in Forestry, 1922–34; Manager Timber Development Assoc. Ltd, 1934; Technical Dir, Timber Development Assoc., Ltd, 1936–48; formed wood preserving company, 1948, and treated many famous buildings incl. Westminster Abbey, Eton Coll., and castles in Scotland; retired 1977 after 22 years as Timber Advr to HMS Victory. Past President and Fellow, Inst. of Wood Science; Past Pres., British Wood Preserving Assoc.; Chm., Bristol Channel and S Wales Timber R&D Assoc. Founder Mem., Internat. Assoc. of Wood Anatomists; Hon. Mem., Timber Res. and Develt Assoc. *Publications:* A Pocket Book of British Trees, 1937, 2nd edn 1941; Timber Houses, 1937; A Dictionary of Wood, 1938; Timber Buildings for the Country, 1938; British Timbers, 1944, 3rd edn 1947; many papers on Forestry and Identification of Timbers. *Recreations:* riding, golf, fishing. *Address:* 78 The Island, Horningsham, Warminster, Wilts. *Died 26 April* 1982.

**BOULTON, Major Sir Edward (John),** 2nd Bt, *cr* 1944; *b* 11 April 1907; *s* of Sir William Whytehead Boulton, 1st Bt and Rosalind Mary (*d* 1969), *d* of Sir John D. Milburn, 1st Bt of Guyzance, Northumberland; *S* father, 1949; unmarried. *Educ:* Eton; Trinity Coll., Cambridge (BA). Joined Staffordshire Yeomanry, 1939. Served War of 1939–45, Middle East, Italy, 1940–44 (despatches); North West Europe (HQ 21 Army Group), 1944–45, Major 1944. Contested Southern Division of Ilford (C), 1945. Retired from membership of London Stock Exchange, 1970. *Heir: b* Sir William Whytehead Boulton, CBE, TD. *Address:* Ouaisné Lodge, Portelet, Jersey, CI. *T:* Jersey 42935. *Died 10 Aug.* 1982.

**BOULTON, Prof. Norman Savage,** DSc, FICE; Emeritus Professor of Civil Engineering, University of Sheffield, since 1964 (Professor, 1955–64); *b* 8 May 1899; *s* of late Professor William Savage Boulton; *m* 1929, Constance (*d* 1968), *d* of late H. Deakin. *Educ:* King Edward's Sch., Birmingham; University of Birmingham. RGA, 1918; BSc (Birmingham), First Class Hons and Bowen Research Schol., 1922; MSc and Dudley Docker Res. Schol., 1923; DSc (Civil Engineering), 1966. Engineering Asst, Public Works Dept, City of Birmingham, 1924–29; University Lecturer in Civil Engineering, King's Coll., Newcastle upon Tyne, 1929–36; Sen. Lecturer in charge of Dept of Civil Engineering, University of Sheffield, 1936–55. Chairman, Yorkshire Assoc. Inst. Civil Engineers, 1947–48 and 1961–62. AMICE, 1927; MICE, 1950. *Publications:* various technical papers in Proc. Instns Civil and Mechanical Engineers, Philosophical Magazine, Jl of Hydrology, Water Resources Research, etc. *Recreations:* music, swimming. *Address:* 68 Endcliffe Vale Road, Sheffield S10 3EW. *T:* Sheffield 661049.

*Died 10 Aug.* 1984.

**BOULTON, Very Rev. Walter,** MA Oxon; *b* 11 July 1901; *s* of Walter and Clara Elizabeth Boulton, Smallthorne, Staffs.; *m* 1932, Kathleen Lorna York Batley; one *s* four *d*. *Educ:* Balliol Coll., Oxford. Exhibitioner of Balliol, 2nd Class Modern History, 1922, BA 1923, MA 1930. Cuddesdon Coll., 1923. Deacon, 1924; Priest, 1925; Curate of St Mark, Woodhouse, Leeds, 1924–27; Asst Chaplain of the Cathedral Church, Calcutta, 1927–34; Chaplain of Lebong, 1934–35. Furlough, 1937. Chaplain, Shillong, 1935–39; St Paul's Cathedral, Calcutta, 1939–45; Canon of Calcutta, 1940–48. Furlough, 1945. Chaplain, Shillong, 1945–47; Vicar of Fleet, Hampshire, 1948–52; Provost of Guildford and Rector of Holy Trinity with St Mary, Guildford, 1952–61; Rector of Market Overton with Thistleton, 1961–72. *Address:* Milton House, Lindfield, Haywards Heath, W Sussex. *Died 27 Nov.* 1984.

**BOURKE, Sir Paget John,** Kt 1957; Judge of the Courts of Appeal, Bahamas and Bermuda, since 1965, British Honduras, since 1968 (President of Courts, 1970–75), Gibraltar, 1970–79; *b* 1906; *s* of H. C. Bourke, Amana, Ballina, Co. Mayo, Ireland; *m* 1936, Susan Dorothy (*née* Killeen); three *s* one *d*. *Educ:* Mount St Mary's Coll., Chesterfield; Trinity Coll., Dublin (Mod. BA, LLB). Barrister-at-law, King's Inn, 1928, Gray's Inn, 1957. Legal Adviser and Crown Prosecutor, Seychelles, 1933; MEC and MLC; Chief Magistrate, Palestine, 1936; Relieving President, District Court, 1941; President, 1945; Judge of Supreme Court of Kenya, 1946; Chief Justice, Sierra Leone, 1955–57; Cyprus, 1957–60. Senior Counsel, Irish Bar, 1961. Acting Chief Justice, Gibraltar, Oct.–Dec., 1965. *Publication:* (ed) Digest of Cases, Seychelles, 1870–1933. *Address:* Box 32, Site 5, Cranbrook Street N, Cranbrook, BC V1C 4H4, Canada. *Club:* Royal St George Yacht (Dun Laoghaire).

*Died 7 Nov.* 1983.

**BOURNE, Baron** *cr* 1964 (Life Peer), of Atherstone; **Geoffrey Kemp Bourne,** GCB 1960 (KCB 1957; CB 1949); KBE 1954 (CBE 1947; OBE 1942); CMG 1952; *b* 5 Oct. 1902; *s* of Col W. K. Bourne, Sway, Hants; *m* 1928, Agnes Evelyn, *d* of late Sir Ernest Thompson, Prestbury, Cheshire; one *s* one *d*. *Educ:* Rugby; RMA Woolwich. Commissioned into RA 1923; served in Hong Kong, 1930–32; Gibraltar, 1933–34; Staff Coll., Camberley, 1935–36; Colchester, 1937; War Office, 1938–41. Served War of 1939–45; Comdr 5th Indian Div., May–Sept. 1946 (Java and India); idc 1947; Head of British Services Mission to Burma, 1948; GOC Berlin (British Sector), 1949–51; GOC 16th Airborne Div. (TA), 1951–52; GOC-in-C, Eastern Command, 1953; GOC Malaya Command and Director of Operations, 1954–56; C-in-C Middle East Land Forces, 1957; Commandant, Imperial Defence Coll., 1958–59; ADC General to the Queen, 1959–60. Col Commandant RA, 1954–67; Hon. Col 10th Bn The Parachute Regt, TA, 1960–65. Retired April 1960. Director-General, Aluminium Federation, 1960–63; Chm., Nat. Building Agency, 1967–73. US Silver Star and Legion of Merit (degree of officer); Duncan Essay Gold Medal, 1935 (RA Institution). *Recreation:* golf. *Address:* Drove House, Cranborne, Wimborne, Dorset. *T:* Cranborne 321. *Club:* Army and Navy.

*Died 26 June* 1982.

**BOURNE, Lt-Col Geoffrey (Howard),** FZS; DPhil, DSc; Vice Chancellor, and Professor of Nutrition, St George's University School of Medicine, Grenada, since 1978; *b* West Perth, Western Australia, 17 Nov. 1909; *s* of Walter Howard Bourne and Mary Ann Mellon; *m* 1935, Gwenllian Myfanwy Jones, BA; two *s*; *m* 1965, Maria Nelly Golarz, PhD. *Educ:* Perth Modern Sch., W Australia; University of Western Australia (BSc 1930, BSc Hons 1931; MSc 1932, DSc 1935); University of Melbourne. DPhil (Oxford), 1943; Hackett Research Student, University of W Australia, 1931–33; Biologist and in charge of Experimental Work, Australian Institute of Anatomy, Canberra, 1933–35; Biochemist Commonwealth of Austr. Advisory Council on Nutrition, 1935–37; Beit Memorial Fellow for Medical Research, Oxford, 1938–41; Mackenzie-Mackinnon Research Fellow of Royal College of Physicians of London and Royal College of Surgeons of England, 1941–44; Demonstrator in Physiology, Oxford, 1941–44, 1946, 1947; in charge of research and development (rations and physiological matters) for Special Forces in South-East Asia, with rank of Major, 1944–45; Nutritional Adviser to British Military Administration, Malaya, with rank of Lt-Col, 1945–46; Reader in Histology, University of London, at the London Hospital Medical Coll., 1947–57; Prof. and Chm. of Anatomy, Emory Univ., Atlanta, Ga, USA, 1957–63; Dir, Yerkes Regional Primate Research Center of Emory Univ., 1962–78. Adjunct Prof. of Health Scis, Georgia State Univ. System, 1986. Member: Soc. Experimental Biology; Nutrition Soc. (foundation Mem.); Anatomical Soc. of GB. and NI, Internat. Soc. for Cell Biology; Aerospace Med. Soc., etc. FRSM. Editor-in-Chief, International Review of Cytology, 1952–; Editor, World Review of Nutrition and Dietetics, 1962–. Sunday May 24th 1981 proclaimed Dr Geoffrey Bourne day by City of Miami Beach. *Publications:* Nutrition and the War, 1940; Wartime Food for Mother and Child, 1942; Cytology and Cell Physiology (ed and part author), 1942, 4th edn 1988; Starvation in Europe, 1943; How Your Body Works, 1949; The Mammalion Adrenal Gland, 1949; Aids to Histology,

1950; (ed) Biochemistry and Physiology of Nutrition, Vols 1, 2; Introduction to Functional Histology; Biochemistry and Physiology of Bone; (ed) The Biology of Ageing; Structure and Function of Muscle; The Division of Labour in Cells; (ed jtly) Muscular Dystrophy in Man and Animals; Atherosclerosis and its origins, 1967; Structure and Function of Nervous Tissue, 1969; The Ape People, 1971; Primate Odyssey, 1974; The Gentle Giants, 1975; (with HSH Prince Rainier III of Monaco) Primate Conservation, 1977; Hearts and Heart-like Organs, 1981; contributor on Famine to Encyclopædia Britannica; contributions to scientific and medical journals. *Recreations:* water ski-ing, tennis, ballet and running (State Mile Championship and Record Holder, Australia). *Address:* St George's University School of Medicine, PO Box 7, St George's, Grenada, West Indies.                      *Died* 19 July 1988.

**BOURNE, Stafford,** MA Cantab; Chairman, 1938–72, President, 1972–79, Bourne & Hollingsworth Ltd (relinquished all connection, on retirement after 57 years service); *b* 20 Feb. 1900; *e s* of late Walter William and Clara Louisa Bourne (*née* Hollingsworth), Garston Manor, Herts; *m* 1940, Magdalene Jane, *d* of Frederick and Anne Leeson; one *s* one *d* (and one *s* decd). *Educ:* Rugby; Corpus Christi, Cambridge; and in France. War of 1939–45, Admiralty Ferry Crews. Co-Founder and First Pres., Oxford Street Assoc., 1958–68. Is actively interested in interchange of young people between UK and W Europe for business and cultural purposes. *Recreations:* yachting, painting, chess. *Address:* Drokes Field Cottage, Beaulieu, Brockenhurst, Hants SO4 7XE. *T:* Bucklers Hard 252. *Clubs:* United Oxford & Cambridge University, Royal Cruising.                                      *Died* 25 Nov. 1986.

**BOUTWOOD, Rear-Adm. Laurence Arthur,** CB 1955; OBE 1940; DL; *b* 7 Sept. 1898; *yr s* of W. A. Boutwood, Luton; *m* 1925, Audrey Winifred, *d* of H. Dale Morris, Polperro; one *s* two *d.* *Educ:* Bedford Sch. BA Open Univ., 1977. Royal Navy, 1916; served European War, 1916–18; Cambridge Univ., 1919–21; HM Ships, in E Indies, Home Fleet, etc., 1921–31; Sec. to Rear-Adm., Aircraft Carriers, 1931–33; Sec. to Third Sea Lord and Controller, 1934–39; HMS Glasgow (despatches), 1939–42; Base Supply Officer, Greenock, 1942–43; Sec. to Fourth Sea Lord, 1943–44; Base Supply Officer, Kilindini, 1944; Fleet Supply Officer, Brit. Pacific Fleet, 1945–46; Asst Dir of Plans, Admty, 1946–48; RN Barracks, Lee-on-Solent, 1948–50; Fleet Supply Officer, Mediterranean Stn, 1950–53; Comd Supply Officer, Portsmouth, 1953–56; retired, 1956. County Comr St John Ambulance Brigade, Cornwall, 1958–71. DL Cornwall, 1965. KStJ 1966. *Address:* Golden Cap, Tideford, Saltash, Cornwall PL12 5HW. *T:* Landrake 237.                          *Died* 29 July 1982.

**BOWATER, Sir Ian (Frank),** GBE 1970; Kt 1967; DSO 1945; TD 1953; one of HM's Lieutenants for the City of London since 1938; *b* 1904; *y s* of late Major Sir Frank Henry Bowater, 1st Bt, TD; *m* 1927, Hon. Ursula Margaret, *d* of late Viscount Dawson of Penn, PC, GCVO, KCB, KCMG, MD; one *s* two *d.* *Educ:* Eton; Magdalen Coll., Oxford. Territorial Commission Berks & Bucks Yeo., 1926–27; rejoined TA, 1938. Served War of 1939–45; Staff Capt. 1st AA Div., London, 1940; E Africa, Madagascar, 1942; CRA Islands area, 1942; CMF Sicily and Italy; Comd 53rd LAA (KOYLI) Regt, 1943–45. Comd 490 (M) HAA Regt (TA), 1947–48; Hon. Col 553 LAA Regt (KOYLI), 1953. Joined family Business, W. V. Bowater & Sons, 1926; later Dir Bowater Sales Co. and subseq. of Bowater Paper Corp. until resignation, 1953; Director, Spicers Ltd, 1953–58; Chairman: Bowater Hotels, 1937–; T. B. Ford Ltd, 1960–68; Carlson/Fords, 1965–68; Dir, GKN Birfield Industries, 1968, retired 1969. Dep. Chm., Country Gentlemen's Assoc., 1957; First Pres., City and Metropolitan Bldg Soc., 1965–72 (Dir 1963–65). Junior Warden, Haberdashers' Company, 1955 and 1961; Master, 1967; Alderman, Coleman Street Ward, 1960–74; Sheriff, City of London, 1965–66; Lord Mayor of London, 1969–70. Chancellor, The City Univ., 1969–70. Hon. DSc The City Univ., 1970. KStJ 1970. *Recreations:* painting, travel, art. *Address:* 38 Burton Court, Franklins Row, SW3 4SZ. *T:* 01-730 2963. *Clubs:* White's, City Livery, Coleman Street Ward, United Wards.
                                                      *Died* 1 Oct. 1982.

**BOWATER, Sir Noël Vansittart,** 2nd Bt, cr 1939; GBE 1954; MC 1917; *b* 25 Dec. 1892; *s* of Sir Frank H. Bowater, 1st Bt and Ethel Anita (*d* 1943), *d* of late Mark Fryar, Burmah; *S* father 1947; *m* 1921, Constance Heiton Bett; one *s* two *d.* *Educ:* Rugby. Commnd Territorial Force RA, 1913; served in France, 1915–19 (MC). Sheriff of City of London, 1948, Lord Mayor, 1953–54; Master, Company of Vintners, 1954–55. KStJ; Kt Comdr Royal Order of the North Star; Kt Comdr Order of Menelik the Second. *Heir: s* Euan David Vansittart Bowater, BA Cantab [*b* 9 Sept. 1935; *m* 1964, Susan Mary Humphrey, *d* of A. R. O. Slater, FCA, and Mrs N. M. Slater; two *s* two *d*]. *Address:* Conifers, St George's Hill, Weybridge, Surrey. *T:* Weybridge 42744; Riscombe, Exford, Somerset. *T:* Exford 280. *Clubs:* City Livery, United Wards, Guildhall.
                                                      *Died* 22 Jan. 1984.

**BOWDELL, Wilfred,** CBE 1973; *b* 28 Nov. 1913; *s* of Harry Bowdell and Sarah Alice Bowdell (*née* Roscoe); *m* 1939, Alice Lord. *Educ:*

Bury High Sch.; Univ. of London (BScEcon); Inst. of Public Finance and Accountancy (Pres., 1972–73). Finance Asst, Bury County Borough Council, 1930–36; Chief Accountancy Asst, Swinton and Pendlebury Borough Council, 1936–39; Chief Accountant, York City Council, 1939–46; Dep. Treas., Enfield Urban District Council, 1946–48; Dep. Treas. 1948–62, Borough Treas. 1962–65, St Marylebone Borough Council; City Treas., Westminster City Council, 1965–74. Member: Public Works Loan Bd, 1975–87 (Dep. Chm., 1980–87); London Housing Staff Commn, 1979–84. *Recreations:* music, photography, gardening. *Address:* 72 Highfield Way, Rickmansworth, Herts. *T:* Rickmansworth 773459.                                      *Died* 17 April 1989.

**BOWDEN, Baron,** *cr* 1963, of Chesterfield (Life Peer); **Bertram Vivian Bowden,** MA, PhD, FIEE, FIEEE, MScTech; Principal, The University of Manchester Institute of Science and Technology (called Manchester College of Science and Technology until May 1966), 1964–76, retired; *b* 18 Jan. 1910; *s* of B. C. Bowden, Chesterfield; *m* 1939, Marjorie Browne (marr. diss., 1954; she *d* 1957); one *s* two *d; m* 1955, Diana Stewart; *m* 1967, Mary Maltby (*d* 1971); *m* 1974, Mrs Phyllis James (marr. diss. 1983; she *m* 1985, R. D. Hetzel). *Educ:* Chesterfield Grammar Sch.; Emmanuel Coll., Cambridge. Worked with late Lord Rutherford, 1931–34; PhD 1934; University of Amsterdam, 1934–35. Physics Master, Liverpool Collegiate Sch., 1935–37; Chief Physics Master, Oundle Sch., 1937–40; Radar Research in England, 1940–43; Radar Research in USA, 1943–46; Sir Robert Watson Watt and Partners, 1947–50; Ferranti Ltd, Manchester (Digital Computers), 1950–53; Dean of the Faculty of Technology, Manchester Univ., 1953–64 and Principal, Manchester Coll. of Science and Technology, 1953–76. Chm. Electronics Research Council of Ministry of Aviation, 1960–64; Minister of State, Dept of Education and Science, 1964–65 (on leave of absence as Principal of Manchester Coll. of Science and Technology). Pres. The Science Masters Assoc., 1962. Pres., Nat. Television Rental Assoc., 1975–82. Hon. FICE 1975; Hon. DS Rennsellaer Polytechnic, USA, 1974; Hon. LLD Manchester, 1976; Hon. DSc Kumasi, Ghana, 1977. Pioneer Award, IEEE Aerospace & Electronic Systems Gp, 1973. *Publications:* Faster Than Thought, 1953; The Development of Manchester College of Science and Technology; numerous papers on education. *Recreations:* listening to music; pottering about. *Address:* Pine Croft, 5 Stanhope Road, Bowdon, Altrincham, Cheshire WA14 3LB. *T:* 061–928 4005. *Club:* Athenæum.                                      *Died* 28 July 1989.

**BOWDEN, Major Aubrey Henry,** DSO 1918; Chairman, Bowden Bros Ltd, 1930–75; *b* 6 June 1895; *e s* of Henry White Bowden, MICE, Great Missenden; *m* 1st, 1918, Helen (*d* 1939), *o d* of late R. G. Modera, Wilbury Lodge, Hove; one *s* one *d*; 2nd, 1941, Andrée Marguerite July; one *s* two *d.* *Educ:* Oundle. Electrical Engineer. Training: Brompton and Kensington Electricity Supply Co.; London Underground Railway; Metropolitan Railway; Oerlikon Co.; from here commissioned: to 11th Service Batt. Royal Warwicks Regt, to Capt. and Brigade Machine Gun Officer, to Machine Gun Corps. *Address:* 28 Berkeley Court, Baker Street, NW1.
                                                      *Died* 30 Dec. 1987.

**BOWDEN, Prof. Kenneth Frank,** DSc, FInstP; Professor of Oceanography in the University of Liverpool, 1954–82, then Emeritus; *b* 23 Dec. 1916; *s* of Frank and Margaret N. Bowden; *m* 1946, Lilias T. M. Nicol; one *d.* *Educ:* Itchen Secondary Sch.; University Coll., Southampton. Scientific Officer, Anti-Submarine Experimental Establishment (Admiralty), 1939–45; Lecturer in Oceanography, University of Liverpool, 1945–52; Principal Scientific Officer, Nat. Inst. of Oceanography, 1952–54; Dean, Faculty of Science, 1959–62, Pro-Vice-Chancellor, 1968–71, Univ. of Liverpool. *Publications:* Physical Oceanography of Coastal Waters, 1983; papers on physical oceanography in various scientific journals. *Address:* Hilbre, 5 Anthony Road, Largs, Ayrshire KA30 8EQ. *T:* Largs 675970.                          *Died* 27 May 1989.

**BOWDEN, Dr Richard Charles,** OBE 1941; PhD, MSc, FRSC, CChem; Consultant, Ministry of Aviation (formerly Ministry of Supply), 1952–60; *b* 31 Aug. 1887; *s* of Richard Charles Bowden, Bristol, and Minnie Clara Thatcher; *m* 1913, Nina Adeline, *er d* of Thomas Fisher, Bristol; no *c.* *Educ:* Merchant Venturers Sch., Bristol; Merchant Venturers Technical Coll., Bristol; Bristol Univ. (Hons, Physical Chemistry). Asst Chemist, Research Dept, Royal Arsenal, Woolwich, 1911; Chemist, Royal Gunpowder Factory, 1912; Chemist 2nd Class, 1915; Chemist in Charge, 1923; Technical Asst (temp.) under Dir of Ordnance Factories, War Office, 1930; Technical Asst, 1932; Chemical Engineer, 1934; Superintendent, Royal Ordnance Factories, 1934–41; Asst Dir of Ordnance Factories (X); Dep Dir of Ordnance Factories (X), 1941; Dir, of Ordnance Factories (X), 1942–52. Patentee or Joint Patentee of various patents relating to chemical processes and chemical plant. Medals: Silver Jubilee, 1935; Coronation, 1937 and 1953. *Publications:* author or joint author of publications in Journal of Chemical Society, 1911, 1912, 1923. *Address:* Villa Maria, 66–68 Croham Road, South Croydon, Surrey CR2 7BB.                          *Died* 5 Sept. 1988.

**BOWDLER-HENRY, Cyril;** *see* Henry.

**BOWEN, Ian;** *see* Bowen, Ivor I.

**BOWEN, Ivor,** CMG 1954; MSc, FRAeS, MIEE; Consultant in Aeronautical Engineering; *b* 21 Feb. 1902; *o s of* James and Barbara Bowen, Oxton, Ches; *m* 1941, Hilda, *o d of* Arthur and Florence Mary Fakes, Cambridge; one *s* one *d. Educ:* Birkenhead Institute; University of Liverpool; Trinity Coll., Cambridge. Oliver Lodge Fellow, University of Liverpool, 1923–24; Research Asst to Sir J. J. Thomson, OM, FRS, 1924–26; Demonstrator in Physics, Cavendish Laboratory, Cambridge, 1925–26; Founder Mem. of Cambridge Univ. Air Squadron, 1925. Lecturer in Air Navigation and Aircraft Instruments, Imperial Coll. of Science, 1938–40; Hon. Sec. Instn of Professional Civil Servants, 1938–40; Dep. Dir of Armament Research, Min. of Aircraft Production, 1940; Dir of Instrument Research and Development, Min. of Supply, 1941–47; Chm. Air Photography Research Cttee, 1945–47; Mem. of Council, British Scientific Instrument Research Assoc., 1945–47; Chief Superintendent, Aeroplane and Armament Experimental Establishment, Boscombe Down, 1947–50; Scientific Adviser to UK High Comr to Australia, and Head of UK Min. of Supply Staff, Australia, 1951–53; Principal Dir of Aircraft Equipment Research and Development, Ministry of Supply, 1953–54; Chm. Air Navigation Cttee of Aeronautical Research Council, 1958–61; Mem. Council, Air League of the British Empire; Mem. Air Traffic Control and Navigation Cttee of Electronics Research Council, 1961–68. Mem., Ct of Common Council, City of London, Ward of Broad Street, 1971–81; Liveryman of Worshipful Company of Carpenters, 1959 (Freeman 1954), and of Worshipful Company of Scientific Instrument Makers. Freeman of City of London, 1955. *Publications:* numerous scientific papers on Physics and Aeronautics. *Recreations:* archæology, arboriculture, shooting. *Address:* Stancote, Kippington Road, Sevenoaks, Kent. *T:* Sevenoaks 52495. *Clubs:* Athenæum, City Livery, Royal Air Force.

*Died 8 Nov. 1984.*

**BOWEN, Prof. (Ivor) Ian,** MA Oxon; *b* Cardiff, 3 Dec. 1908; *s of* Ivor Bowen, KC, later County Court Judge, and Edith May (*née* Dummett); *m* 1st, 1935, Erica Baillie (marr. diss., 1950); one *s* one *d*; 2nd, 1951, Isobel Margaret Lindsay Smith; one *s* one *d. Educ:* Westminster Sch.; Christ Church, Oxford. Fellow, All Souls Coll., 1930–37, and 1968; Lecturer, Brasenose Coll., 1931–40; Chief Statistical Officer, Ministry of Works, 1940–45; Lectr, Hertford Coll., 1946–47; Prof. of Economics and Commerce, Hull Univ., 1947–58; Prof. of Economics, Univ. of WA, 1958–73; Editor, Finance and Development (IMF and World Bank Group), 1974–77. *Publications:* Cobden (Great Lives Series), 1934; Britain's Industrial Survival, 1947; Population (Cambridge Economic Handbooks), 1954; Acceptable Inequalities, 1970; Economics and Demography, 1976. *Recreation:* golf. *Address:* Xalet Verena, La Massana, Andorra. *T:* Andorra 35–2–21. *Club:* Reform.

*Died 20 Nov. 1984.*

**BOWEN, Sir Thomas Frederic Charles,** 4th Bt *cr* 1921; *b* 11 Oct. 1921; *s of* 2nd Bt and May Isobel (*d* 1972), *d of* John Frederick Roberts; *S* brother, 1939; *m* 1947, Jill, *d of* Lloyd Evans, Gold Coast; one *s* two *d. Heir: s* Mark Edward Mortimer Bowen [*b* 17 Oct. 1958; *m* 1983, Kerry Tessa, *d of* Michael Moriarty, Worthing; one *s*]. *Address:* 1 Barford Close, Fleet, Hants GU13 9HJ.

*Died 27 Feb. 1989.*

**BOWER, Sir Frank,** Kt 1960; CBE 1948; *b* 25 Aug. 1894; *s of* Herbert Austin Bower; *m* 1920, Ethel Shaw (*d* 1970); one *s* two *d. Educ:* Lancaster Royal Grammar Sch.; St Catharine's Coll., Cambridge. Served European War of 1914–18; 2/5th King's Own Royal Lancaster Regt, 2/5 Prince Albert Victoria Rajputs, IARO. BA (Classics), 1920; MA 1924. HM Inspector of Taxes, 1920–24; Taxation Officer, Unilever Group, 1924–59. Late Chairman of Tax Cttees of Business Groups; late Director of industrial companies. Past President, Association of British Chambers of Commerce. *Publications:* United Kingdom Volume, World Tax Series, Harvard Law School; contribs to professional journals on tax subjects. *Address:* Flat 3, Highwood, 13 Sunset Avenue, Woodford Green, Essex. *T:* 01-505 7030. *Died 1 Sept. 1982.*

**BOWER, Sir John D.;** *see* Dykes Bower.

**BOWER, Norman;** *b* 18 May 1907. *Educ:* Rugby; Wadham Coll., Oxford. Called to Bar, Inner Temple, 1935; contested West Bermondsey, 1931, North Hammersmith, 1935; MP (C) Harrow West, 1941–51; Member Westminster City Council, 1937–45. *Recreations:* golf, cricket, theatre. *Club:* Carlton.

*Died 7 Dec. 1990.*

**BOWER, Lt.-Gen. Sir Roger (Herbert),** KCB 1959 (CB 1950); KBE 1957 (CBE 1944); *b* 13 Feb. 1903; *s of* Herbert Morris Bower and Eileen Francis Fitzgerald Bower, Ripon; *m* 1939, Hon. Catherine Muriel Hotham, *d of* late Capt. H. E. Hotham, and *y sister of* 7th Baron Hotham, CBE; (one adopted *s*) one *d* (and one *s* decd). *Educ:* Repton; RMC, Sandhurst. Served in India with KOYLI, 1923–30;

Staff Coll., Camberley, 1935–36; Bde Major, Hong Kong, 1937–38. Served War of 1939–45; NW Europe with HQ Airborne Corps, 1944; Comd Air Landing Bdes: 1, Norway, 1945, 6, Palestine, 1945–46 (despatches); Comd Hamburg District, 1948–49, with rank of Maj.-Gen.; Director Land/Air Warfare, War Office, 1950–51; Director of Military Training and Director of Land/Air Warfare, 1951–52; Commander East Anglian District, 1952–55; Chief of Staff, Allied Forces, Northern Europe, 1955–56; GOC and Director of Operations, Malaya, 1956–57; Commander-in-Chief, Middle East Land Forces, 1958–60, retired. Col The KOYLI, 1960–66. Treasurer to HRH Princess Margaret, Nov. 1960–Feb. 1962; Lieut HM Tower of London, 1960–63. Chm., Nat. Fund for Research into Crippling Diseases, 1974–75. US Bronze Star, 1944; King Haakon VII Liberty Cross, 1945. *Address:* Ash House, St Mary Bourne, Andover, Hants. *T:* St Mary Bourne 263. *Clubs:* Army and Navy, Royal Cruising. *Died 9 Jan. 1990.*

**BOWERMAN, Brig. John Francis,** CBE 1946; QPM; Indian Army (retired); *b* 28 Nov. 1893; *s of* John Bowerman, Cullompton, Devon; *m* 1931, Mary Monica Faed Macmillan; one *d. Educ:* Queen Elizabeth's Sch., Crediton. Commissioned West Yorks Regt, 1915; served European War, 1914–18, Mesopotamia, Marri Field Force, 1914–18 (wounded); transferred 129th Duke of Connaught's Own Baluchis, Nov. 1918; active service Afghanistan, 1919, Zhob, 1919–21, Waziristan, 1921–23 and NW Frontier, 1930; Burma Rebellion, 1931–32. Served War of 1939–45, Burma; Chief Liaison Officer, 6th Chinese Army, 1942; Brigadier 1942, as Inspector General Burma Frontier Force; with Chinese-American Forces, Burma, 1943–45; despatches, 1946; retired 1946. King's Police Medal, 1928; American Bronze Star, 1945. *Publications:* Report on exploration, China, Burma, Tibet Border (MacGregor Memorial Medal of United Services Institution, India, 1928); paper on Frontier Areas of Burma (Silver Medal of RSA, 1947). *Recreations:* golf, fishing. *Address:* Tanglewood, Abberton Field, Hassocks Road, Hurstpierpoint, Sussex. *Died 18 Dec. 1983.*

**BOWES, Sir (Harold) Leslie,** KCMG 1968; CBE 1943; Chairman, The Pacific Steam Navigation Company, 1960–65, Managing Director, 1952–65 (Deputy Chairman 1959–60); Chairman, Royal Mail Lines Ltd, 1960–65, Managing Director, 1958–65 (Deputy Chairman 1959–60); *b* 18 Nov. 1893; *m* 1st, 1921; two *s* one *d*; 2nd 1950; one *d*. Served European War, RFC and RAF. The Pacific Steam Navigation Company: Manager for Chile, 1921–48; Director and General Manager, 1949–51. Director: Rea Bros Ltd, 1966–84; Ocean Wilsons (Holdings) Ltd, 1966–84. Member: General Purposes Cttee of Shipping Federation, 1958–61; Central Transport Consultative Cttee, 1959–61; Chairman Liverpool Steam Ship Owners' Assoc., 1954; Chairman General Council of British Shipping, 1954; Chairman Liverpool Port Welfare Cttee, 1955–58; Chairman Liverpool Marine Engineers' and Naval Architects Guild, 1955–56; Chairman Govt Cttee of Inquiry into Canals and Inland Waterways, 1956–58; Member General Cttee of Lloyd's Register of Shipping, 1956–65; Director, "Indefatigable" and Nat. Sea Training Sch. for Boys, 1954–58; Chairman Liverpool Chamber of Commerce, 1957–58; Governor, City of Liverpool College of Commerce, 1958–60; President: Institute of Shipping and Forwarding Agents, 1957–58; Vice-President: British Ship Adoption Society, 1968–75 (Chm. 1958–68); Institute of Transport, 1958–59 (Mem. Council, 1959–; Chairman Shipping Advisory Cttee, 1959–65); Member: Mersey Docks and Harbour Board, 1956–58; Shipping Advisory Council of BTC, 1960–62; Shipping and International Services Cttee of British Railways Board, 1963; Chairman, BNEC Cttee for Exports to Latin America, 1966–67 (Dep. Chm. 1964–66). Member Exec. Cttee: Anglo-Chilean Society, 1960–70 (Vice-Pres., 1970); Anglo-Peruvian Society (Vice-Pres. 1970); Hispanic and Luso-Brazilian Councils, 1960–69 (Vice-Pres. 1969–; Chm. 1963–64 and 1965–66); Anglo-Brazilian Soc.; Member: Cttee of Management, Canning Club; Exec. Cttee, Anglo-Portuguese Society; Vice-Pres., British Mexican Soc., 1974. Liveryman Worshipful Company of Shipwrights (Past Prime Warden). Hon. Citizen of Valparaiso, Chile, 1982. Comdr of Chilean Order of Merit, 1942, Grand Officer, 1952; Comdr, Ecuadorian Order of Merit, 1956; Comdr, Peruvian Order of Merit, 1957, Grand Cross, 1959; Order of Vasco Nuñez de Balboa, 1963; Grand Officer, Orden de Mayo, Argentina, 1964; Grand Cross, Order of San Carlos (Colombia), 1966; Comdr, Cruziero do Sul, Brazil, 1975. *Address:* 7 Chester Row, SW1W 9JF. *T:* 01–730 1523. *Clubs:* Canning, City Livery, Naval and Military.

*Died 29 April 1988.*

**BOWKER, Sir (Reginald) James,** GBE 1961; KCMG 1952 (CMG 1945); *b* 2 July 1901; *yr s of* Lieut-Col F. J. Bowker, Hampshire Regt, and Edith Sophie Mary Elliott; *m* 1947, Elsa, *d of* Michel Gued and Mme Gued Vidal. *Educ:* Charterhouse; Oriel Coll., Oxford. 3rd Secretary, Foreign Office and Diplomatic Service, 1925. Served in Paris, Berlin, Ankara, Oslo and Madrid. British Minister in Cairo, 1945–47; High Commissioner in Burma, 1947–48; Ambassador to Burma, 1948–50; an Asst Under-Secretary of State, FO, 1950–53; Ambassador to Turkey, 1954–58; Ambassador to

Austria, 1958–61; retired from Foreign Service, 1961. *Address:* 3 West Eaton Place, SW1X 8LU. *T:* 01-235 3852. *Clubs:* Brooks's, Buck's.
*Died* 15 *Dec.* 1983.

**BOWLBY, (Edward) John (Mostyn),** CBE 1972; MD; FRCP, FRCPsych, FBPsS; Senior FBA 1989; Hon. Consultant Psychiatrist, Tavistock Clinic, London, since 1972; *b* 26 Feb. 1907; 2nd *s* of late Sir Anthony A. Bowlby, 1st Bt (Pres. Roy. Coll. of Surgeons, 1920–23), and late Maria Bridget, *d* of Rev. Canon Hon. Hugh W. Mostyn; *heir-pres.* to *b* Sir Anthony Hugh Mostyn Bowlby, 2nd Bt; *m* 1938, Ursula, 3rd *d* of late Dr T. G. Longstaff (Pres. Alpine Club, 1947–49) and Mrs D. H. Longstaff, JP; two *s* two *d. Educ:* RNC Dartmouth; Trinity Coll., Cambridge (MA Nat. Scis); UCH (MD). FRCP 1964; FRCPsych (Foundation Fellow) 1971, Hon. Fellow 1980; FBPsS 1945; Mem., Brit. PsychoAnalyt. Soc. Staff Psych., London Child Guidance Clinic, 1937–40; Consultant Psychiatrist: RAMC, 1940–45 (Temp. Lt-Col, 1944–45); Tavistock Clinic, 1946–72 (Chm., Dept for Children and Parents, 1946–68); pt-time Mem., ext. scientific staff, MRC, 1963–72. Consultant: in mental health, WHO, 1950–; Nat. Inst. of Mental Health, Bethesda, Md, 1958–63. Fellow, Center for Advanced Studies in Behavioral Sciences, Stanford, Calif, 1957–58; Vis. Prof. in Psych., Stanford Univ., Calif, 1968; H. B. Williams Trav. Prof., Aust. and NZ Coll. of Psychiatrists, 1973; Freud Meml Vis. Prof., UCL, 1980. Pres., Internat. Assoc. for Child Psych. and Allied Professions, 1962–66; Foreign Hon. Mem., Amer. Acad. of Arts and Sciences, 1981–. Hon. FRSM 1987. Hon. DLitt Leicester, 1971; Hon. ScD Cambridge, 1977; Hon. PhD Regensburg, 1989. Sir James Spence Medal, Brit. Paediatric Assoc., 1974; G. Stanley Hall Medal, 1974, Dist. Scientific Award, 1989, Amer. Psychol Assoc. Distinguished Scientific Contrib. Award, Soc. for Res. in Child Develt. 1981; Salmon Medal, NY Acad. of Medicine, 1984. *Publications:* Personal Aggressiveness and War (with E. F. M. Durbin), 1938; Forty-four Juvenile Thieves, 1946; Maternal Care and Mental Health, 1951 (12 trans); Child Care and the Growth of Love, 1953 (2nd edn 1963); Attachment and Loss (6 trans): Vol. 1, Attachment, 1969, 2nd edn 1982; Vol. 2, Separation: anxiety and anger, 1973; Vol. 3, Loss: sadness and depression, 1980; The Making and Breaking of Affectional Bonds, 1979; A Secure Base, 1988; Charles Darwin: a biography, 1990; papers in Brit. and US jls of psych., psychol. and psychoanalysis. *Recreations:* natural history and outdoor activities. *Address:* Wyldes Close Corner, Hampstead Way, NW11 7JB.
*Died* 2 *Sept.* 1990.

**BOWLBY, Hon. Mrs Geoffrey, (Lettice),** CVO 1937; Extra Woman of the Bedchamber to Queen Elizabeth, the Queen Mother; *b* 24 Sept. 1885; 4th *d* of 11th Viscount Valentia, Bletchington Park, Oxford; *m* 1911, Capt. Geoffrey Vaux Salvin Bowlby, Royal Horse Guards (killed in action, 1915); one *s* one *d.* Commandant of Auxiliary Hospital, 1916–19 (despatches twice); a Lady-in-Waiting to Duchess of York, 1932; Woman of the Bedchamber to the Queen, 1937–45. *Address:* c/o The Countess of Meath, Kilruddery, Bray, Co. Wicklow.
*Died* 13 *Feb.* 1988.

**BOWLBY, John;** *see* Bowlby, E. J. M.

**BOWLBY, Hon. Lettice;** *see* Bowlby, Hon. Mrs Geoffrey.

**BOWLE, John Edward;** historian; *b* 19 Dec. 1905; *o s* of Edward Francis Bowle, Salisbury, and Edith Beatrice, *y d* of late Silas Taunton, Fugglestone, Wilton, Wilts. *Educ:* The Old Malthouse, Langton Matravers; Marlborough Coll. (Council and Keith Rae Exhibitioner); Balliol Coll., Oxford (Brackenbury Scholar, 1924; BA 1927; MA 1932). Senior History Master, Westminster Sch., 1932–40; History Master, Eton, 1940–41. Air Ministry and Foreign Office, 1941–45. Lecturer in Modern History, Wadham Coll., Oxford, 1947–49; Leverhulme Research Fellow, 1949–50; Visiting Prof., Columbia Univ., NY, 1949; Dir, Preparatory Session, College of Europe, Bruges, 1949; Prof. of Political Theory, Bruges, 1950–67. Visiting Professor: Grinnell Coll., Iowa, 1961; Occidental Coll., Los Angeles, 1965; Indiana Univ., 1966; Lecturer, Smith Coll., Northampton, Mass, 1967. Editor, The World To-day, for RIIA, 1949–51. *Publications:* Western Political Thought, 1947 (Arts Council Prize, 1966); The Unity of European History, 1948, rev. edn, 1970; Hobbes and his Critics, 1951; Politics and Opinion in the Nineteenth Century, 1954; Viscount Samuel, a biography, 1957; (ed) The Concise Encyclopædia of World History, 1958, rev. edn 1971; A New Outline of World History, 1963; Henry VIII, a biography, 1964, repr. 1973; England, a portrait, 1966; The English Experience, 1971; The Imperial Achievement, 1974; Napoleon, 1974; Charles I, a biography, 1975; Man Through the Ages, 1977; A History of Europe, 1980; John Evelyn and his World, 1981; (ed) The Diaries of John Evelyn, 1983; contrib. to various periodicals; writes for radio and broadcasts. *Recreations:* travel, painting. *Address:* 24 Woodstock Close, Oxford. *T:* 58379.
*Died* 17 *Sept.* 1985.

**BOWLES, Dame Ann P.;** *see* Parker Bowles.

**BOWLES, Chester;** United States Ambassador to India, 1963–69; *b* Springfield, Mass, 5 April 1901; *s* of Allen Bowles and Nellie Harris; *g s* of Samuel Bowles, Founder of the Springfield Republican; *m* 1934, Dorothy Stebbins Bowles; two *s* three *d. Educ:* Choate Sch., Wallingford, Conn.; Yale Univ., New Haven, Conn. Founded advertising and marketing research agency in NY City with William Benton, 1929; Chm. Board of this agency (Benton & Bowles, Inc.), 1936–41, when sold out interests. Administrator of Office of Price Administration, 1943–46, appointed by President Roosevelt; Mem. of War Production Bd, 1943–46; appointed Dir of Economic Stabilization by President Truman, 1946, and resigned from that post, 1946; Special Asst to UN Sec.-Gen., 1946–48; Governor of Connecticut, 1949–51; American Ambassador to India, and first American Ambassador to Nepal, 1951–53; Mem., 86th Congress, House of Representatives, 1959–60 (2nd Dist. Conn); Under-Sec. of State, USA, Jan.-Nov. 1961; President's Special Representative and Adviser on African, Asian and Latin American Affairs with rank of Ambassador, Nov. 1961–May 1963; Mem. of Congress, US (2nd Dist Conn). Member: Democratic Advisory Council on Foreign Policy; Institute of International Education; American African Soc.; American National Commission for United Nations Economic, Scientific and Cultural Organizations Conference in Paris, 1946; (Internat. Chm.) UN Appeal for Children, 1947; Board of Advisers, Fletcher Sch. of Law and Diplomacy, Medford, Mass; Delivered The Anna Howard Shaw Memorial Lectures at Bryn Mawr Coll., 1953–54; Godkin Lectr, Harvard Univ., 1956; Berkeley Lectr, University of Calif, 1956; Chubb Lectr, Yale Univ., 1957; Rosenfeld Lectr, Grinnell Coll., 1959. Conn Delegate to Democratic Nat. Convention, 1940, 1944, 1948, 1956, 1960; Chm., Platform Cttee, Democratic National Convention, July 1960. Franklin Delano Roosevelt Award for fight against racial discrimination, 1950; Roosevelt Coll. Award for outstanding public service, 1953. Associate Fellow Silliman Coll., Yale Univ.; Hon. DSc The New Sch. for Social Research, New York; Hon. Dr of Laws, Howard Univ., Washington, DC, Hon. Dr of Law: Oberlin Coll., 1957; Bard Coll., 1957; Hon. LLD: American Univ., Washington, DC; Univ. of Rhode Island, 1958; Yale, 1968; Davidson Coll., 1972. *Publications:* Tomorrow Without Fear, 1946; Ambassador's Report, 1954; The New Dimensions of Peace, 1955; American Politics in a Revolutionary World, 1956; Africa's Challenge to America, 1956; Ideas, People and Peace, 1958; The Coming Political Breakthrough, 1959; Conscience of a Liberal, 1962; Makings of a Just Society, 1963; A View from New Delhi, 1969; Promises to Keep: my years in public life, 1941–1969, 1971; and many articles on economic problems and foreign policy. *Recreation:* sailing. *Address:* Hayden's Point, Essex, Conn 06426, USA. *TA:* Essex, Conn. *Clubs:* Essex Yachting (Essex, Conn); Cruising Club of America, Yale (New York).
*Died* 25 *May* 1986.

**BOWMAN, (Thomas) Patrick;** Chairman: PA Management Consultants Ltd, 1966–75; PA International Management Consultants, 1971–75; *b* 25 Sept. 1915; *s* of late Thomas Marshall Bowman and Louisa Hetherington Macfarlane; *m* 1950, Norma Elizabeth Deravin; one *s. Educ:* Oundle Sch.; Hertford Coll., Oxford. Joined Industrial Engineering Div. of Thomas Hedley & Co. (now Proctor & Gamble Ltd), 1937; P A Management Consultants Ltd, 1945 (Dir, 1955; Managing Dir, 1961). Director: London Guardian, 1979–83; Morgan Communications, 1983–85. Member: Monopolies Commn, 1969–72; Council, CBI, 1970–74. Chairman, UK Management Consultants Assoc., 1966, 1974; Founder Member and Fellow of Inst. of Management Consultants; Pres., European Fedn of Management Consultants, 1967–69. Chm., Wimbledon and Putney Conservators Bd, 1976–83. Governor, Sundridge Park Management Centre, 1961–75. FBIM 1959. *Address:* 9 Clement Road, Wimbledon, SW19 7RJ. *T:* 01-946 3828. *Club:* Royal Thames Yacht.
*Died* 6 *Sept.* 1987.

**BOWRING, Edgar Rennie;** *b* 8 Feb. 1899; *yr s* of Henry A. Bowring, St John's, NF, and Liverpool; *m* 1929, Jean Douglas (*d* 1971), *d* of C. A. C. Bruce. *Educ:* Shrewsbury Sch. Formerly Director: C. T. Bowring & Co. Ltd and associated companies; Martins Bank Ltd (a former Dep. Chm. and Chm. of London Bd); Royal Insurance Company Ltd (a former Dep. Chm.); The Liverpool and London and Globe Insurance Co. Ltd; The London and Lancs Insurance Co. Ltd; Cunard Steam-Ship Co. Ltd. Served European War, 1914–18, Lieut RFA. High Sheriff of Cheshire, 1948–49. *Address:* 116 Grosvenor House, Park Lane, W1A 3AA.
*Died* 6 *April* 1982.

**BOX, Sydney;** author and film producer; *b* 29 April 1907; *m* 1st, 1929, Katherine Knight (marr. diss. 1934); 2nd, 1935, Muriel Baker (marr. diss. 1969); one *d*; 3rd, 1969, Sylvia Knowles. In 1939 founded Verity Films Ltd, which produced more than 100 documentary and training films for War Office, Ministry of Information, etc; Producer, Two Cities Films, Denham Studios, 1941–42; Producer, Riverside Studios, 1943–45; Man. Dir and Executive Producer, Gainsborough Pictures, 1946–50. Films include: The Seventh Veil (Academy award for best original screen play, 1946); Quartet; Trio; Holiday Camp; Portrait from Life; The

Years Between; The Man Within; The Passionate Stranger, and The Truth About Women (both with Muriel Box). Author (often in collaboration with Muriel Box) of more than 50 one-act plays, including Not This Man, winner of British Drama League National Festival at Old Vic, 1937. In charge of production London Independent Producers, 1951. Dir, Tyne Tees Television (ITA), 1958–65; Chairman: London Independent Television Producers Ltd, 1963; National Film Corp. Ltd, 1965; Triton Publishing Co. Ltd. Mem., W Australia Arts Council, 1974–77. *Publications:* Diary of a Drop Out, 1969; The Golden Girls, 1971; Alibi in the Rough, 1977; The Lion That Lost Its Way, 1978; Second Only to Murder, 1978. *Address:* 21/71 Mount Street, Perth, WA 6000, Australia.
*Died 25 May 1983.*

**BOXER, (Charles) Mark (Edward), ('Marc');** cartoonist; Editor-in-Chief: Vogue, since 1987; The Tatler, since 1987 (Editor, 1983–87); Editorial Director, Condé Nast Publications, since 1986; *b* 19 May 1931; *s* of Lt-Col Harold Stephen Boxer and Isobel Victoria Hughlings Jackson; *m* 1st, 1956, Lady Arabella Stuart, 3rd *d* of 18th Earl of Moray, MC (marr. diss. 1982); one *s* one *d*; 2nd, 1982, Anna Ford; two *d. Educ:* Berkhamsted Sch.; King's Coll., Cambridge. Editor, Granta, 1952–53; Art Director, Queen, 1957–61; 1st Editor, Sunday Times magazine, 1962–65; Dir, Sunday Times, 1964–66; Editorial Dir, London Life, 1965; Asst Editor, Sunday Times, 1966–79; Dir, Weidenfeld and Nicolson, 1980–83; cartoonist: The Times, 1969–83; Guardian, 1983–86; Daily Telegraph, 1986–; caricaturist: New Statesman, 1970–78; Observer, 1983–; Sunday Telegraph, 1987–. Cartoonist of the Year, 1972. *Publications:* Trendy Ape, 1968; The Times We Live In, 1978; Marc Time, 1984; illus. publications by Clive James: Felicity Fark, 1975, Britannia Bright, 1976, and Charles Charming, 1981. *Recreations:* bridge, chess. *Address:* c/o Vogue, Vogue House, Hanover Square, W1. *Clubs:* Groucho, Portland.
*Died 20 July 1988.*

**BOYCE, Air Vice-Marshal Clayton Descou Clement,** CB 1946; CBE 1944; Assistant Controller of Aircraft, Ministry of Supply, 1957–59, retired; *b* 19 Sept. 1907; *er s* of Col C. J. Boyce, CBE, late IA; *m* 1928, Winifred (*d* 1981), *d* of late J. E. Mead, Castletown, Isle of Man; one *s; m* 1986, Patricia Fielding. *Educ:* Bedford Sch.; Cranwell. Sec.-Gen., Allied Air Forces, Central Europe, 1953; AOC, Cyprus and Levant, 1954–56. *Address:* c/o Lloyds Bank, Cox's and King's Branch, 6 Pall Mall, SW1.
*Died 20 Dec. 1987.*

**BOYCE, Guy Gilbert L.;** *see* Leighton-Boyce.

**BOYD OF MERTON,** 1st Viscount *cr* 1960; **Alan Tindal Lennox-Boyd,** PC 1951; CH 1960; DL; Joint Vice-Chairman of Arthur Guinness, Son & Co. Ltd, 1967–79 (Managing Director, 1960–67); *b* 18 Nov. 1904; 2nd *s* of Alan Walter Lennox-Boyd, and Florence, *d* of James Warburton Begbie; *m* 1938, Lady Patricia Guinness, 2nd *d* of 2nd Earl of Iveagh, KG, CB, CMG, FRS; three *s. Educ:* Sherborne; Christ Church, Oxford (Scholar; MA; Beit Prizeman; Hon. Student, 1968). Pres. of the Oxford Union, 1926. Served with RNVR, 1940–43. Contested Gower Div. of Glamorgan, 1929; MP (C) Mid-Beds, 1931–60; Parliamentary Sec., Ministry of Labour, 1938–39; Parliamentary Sec., Ministry of Home Security, 1939; Parliamentary Sec., Ministry of Food, 1939–40; called to the Bar, Inner Temple, 1941; Parliamentary Sec., Ministry of Aircraft Production, 1943–45; Minister of State for Colonial Affairs, 1951–52; Minister of Transport and Civil Aviation, 1952–54; Sec. of State for the Colonies, 1954–Oct. 1959. Director: Royal Exchange, 1962–70; Tate & Lyle, 1966–74; ICI, 1967–75. President: British Leprosy Relief Assoc., 1960–; Overseas Service Resettlement Bureau, 1962–79; Royal Commonwealth Soc., 1965– (Chm., 1961–64); Overseas Service Pensioners Assoc., 1972–; RNVR Officers' Assoc., 1964–72; Chairman: Voluntary Service Overseas, 1962–64; Brewers Soc., 1965; Maritime Trust, 1976–78; Trustee, BM, 1962–78; Trustee, Natural History Museum, 1963–76; Governor, Sherborne Sch., 1962–, Chm. of Governors, 1968; Mem. Council, Institute of Directors, 1962–. Prime Warden, Goldsmiths' Co., 1964–65. Hon. Fellow, London Sch. of Hygiene and Tropical Medicine, 1977. Hon. LLD Exeter, 1980. Messel Medal, Soc. of Chemical Industry, 1966. DL Beds, 1954–61, Cornwall 1965. DK Brunei, 1971. *Heir: s* Hon. Simon Donald Rupert Neville Lennox-Boyd. *Address:* Ince Castle, Saltash, Cornwall. *T:* Saltash 2274. *Clubs:* Carlton, Pratt's, Buck's, Naval, Royal Automobile, Royal Commonwealth Society; Royal Yacht Squadron, Royal Western Yacht.
*Died 8 March 1983.*

**BOYD, Sir John (McFarlane),** Kt 1979; CBE 1974; General Secretary, Amalgamated Union of Engineering Workers, 1975–82; *b* 8 Oct. 1917; *s* of James and Mary Boyd; *m* 1940, Elizabeth McIntyre; two *d. Educ:* Hamilton St Elem. Sch.; Glencairn Secondary Sch. Engrg apprentice, 1932–37; Engr, 1937–46. AUEW: Asst Div. Organiser, 1946–50; Div. Organiser, 1950–53; Mem. Executive, 1953–75. Pres., Conf. of Shipbuilding and Engineering Unions, 1964; Member: TUC Gen. Council, 1967–75 and 1978–82; Council, ACAS, 1978–82; Director: BSC, 1981–86; UKAEA, 1980–85. Director:

Industrial Trng Services Ltd, 1980–; ICL (UK) Ltd, 1984–88 (then Consultant). A Governor, BBC, 1982–87. Pres., Sorrell Trust for Spastic Children, 1984–. Chm., Labour Party, 1967. Order of the Founder, Salvation Army, 1981. *Recreations:* brass banding, reading. *Address:* 24 Pearl Court, Cornfield Terrace, Eastbourne, Sussex. *Club:* Caledonian.
*Died 30 April 1989.*

**BOYD, Brig. Sir John (Smith Knox),** Kt 1958; OBE 1942; FRS 1951; MD, FRCP, DPH; *b* 18 Sept. 1891; *s* of J. K. Boyd, Largs, Ayrshire; *m* 1st, 1918, Elizabeth Edgar (*d* 1956); 2nd, 1957, Mary Bennett (*d* 1968), *d* of late Denis Harvey Murphy, Northwood. *Educ:* Largs Sch.; Glasgow Univ. (MB, ChB, 1913, Hons, Brunton Meml Prize; MD 1948, Hons, Bellahouston Gold Medal). Entered RAMC 1914; Lieut-Col 1938; Col 1944; Brig. 1945. Served European War, 1914–18; France and Belgium, 1914–15, Salonika, 1916–18. War of 1939–45, Middle East Force, 1940–43, North-West Europe, 1944–45; Dir of Pathology, War Office, 1945–46. KHP 1944–46; retired, 1946. Dir, Wellcome Laboratories of Tropical Medicine, 1946–55. Wellcome Trustee, 1956–66; Scientific Consultant to Wellcome Trust, 1966–68. Mem. of Colonial Medical Research Cttee, 1945–60; Member: Tropical Medicine Research Board, 1961–63; Army Pathology Advisory Cttee, 1946–74. Chairman: Research Defence Soc., 1956–68; Medical Research Council Malaria Cttee and Leprosy Cttee, 1961–63; Royal Society Trop. Diseases Cttee, 1956–64. Hon. Sec., Royal Society of Trop. Medicine and Hygiene, 1946–57, Pres., 1957–59. Hon. FRCPE 1960; Hon. FRCPath, 1968; Hon. LLD Glasgow 1957; Hon. DSc Salford, 1969. Manson Medal, 1968. *Publications:* scientific papers on the pathology of tropical diseases and on bacterial viruses. *Recreation:* golf. *Address:* Mossbank, 6 The Covert, Northwood, Mddx. *T:* Northwood 22437. *Clubs:* Athenæum; Royal and Ancient (St Andrews).
*Died 10 June 1981.*

**BOYD, William,** CC (Canada) 1968; FRSC; *b* 21 June 1885; *s* of Dugald Cameron and Eliza M. Boyd; *m* 1919, Enid G. Christie. *Educ:* Trent Coll., Derbyshire; Edinburgh Univ. MB, ChB 1908; MD Edinburgh (Gold Medal), 1911; Diploma in Psychiatry, Edinburgh, 1912; MRCPE 1912; FRCP 1932; LLD Saskatchewan, 1937; MD Oslo, 1945; DSc Manitoba, 1948; FRCS Canada, 1949; FRCPE 1955; FRCSEd 1966; LLD Queen's 1956. MO, Derby Borough Asylum, Derby, England, 1909–12; Pathologist, Winwick Asylum, Warrington, England, 1912–13; Pathologist, Royal Wolverhampton Hosp., Wolverhampton, 1913–14; Prof. of Pathology, University of Manitoba, Winnipeg, 1915–37; Prof. of Pathology and Bacteriology, University of Toronto, 1937–51, Prof. of Pathology, University of British Columbia, 1951–53. Capt. 3rd Field Ambulance, 46th Div. Imperial Forces, France, 1914–15. *Publications:* With a Field Ambulance at Ypres, 1917; The Physiology and Pathology of the Cerebrospinal Fluid, 1920; Pathology for the Surgeon, 8th edn, 1967; Pathology for the Physician, 7th edn, 1965; Text-Book of Pathology, 8th edn, 1970; Introduction to the Study of Disease, 6th edn, 1971; The Spontaneous Regression of Cancer, 1966. *Recreations:* mountaineering, golf, gardening. *Address:* 40 Arjay Crescent, Toronto, Ont, Canada.
*Died 10 March 1984.*

**BOYD-ROCHFORT, Sir Cecil (Charles),** KCVO 1968 (CVO 1952); Trainer of Racehorses, Newmarket, retired 1968; *b* 16 April 1887; 3rd *s* of late Major R. H. Boyd-Rochfort, 15th Hussars, Middleton Park, Westmeath; *m* 1944, Hon. Mrs Henry Cecil, *d* of Sir James Burnett, of Leys, 13th Bt, CB, CMG, DSO; one *s. Educ:* Eton. Late Capt. Scots Guards (SR); served European War, 1914–18 (wounded, Croix de Guerre). *Relevant publication:* The Captain, by B. Curling, 1970. *Address:* Kilnahard Castle, Ballyheelan, Co. Cavan, Eire. *T:* Ballyheelan 112. *Clubs:* Turf; Kildare Street and University (Dublin).
*Died 18 March 1983.*

**BOYES, Prof. John,** FRCSE, FDS England, FDS Edinburgh; Professor of Dental Surgery, Edinburgh, 1958–77; Hon. Dental Surgeon, Royal Victoria Infirmary, Newcastle; *b* 23 June 1912; *o s* of John and Helen Boyes; *m* 1946, Jean Wood; one *s. Educ:* George Watson's Coll., Edinburgh; Dental Sch. and Sch. of Medicine of the Royal Colleges, Edinburgh. House Surg. and Clinical Asst, Edinburgh Dental Hosp.; House Surg., Middx Hosp.; Res. Surgical Officer and Dental Surg., Plastic and Jaw Unit, Bangour EMS Hosp.; Br. Corresp. of Amer. Dental Assoc.; Mem. of Dental Advisory Cttee of RCSE; Nuffield Prof. of Oral Medicine, University of Durham; Sub-Dean of King's Coll., at Dental Sch.; Dir Newcastle upon Tyne Dental Hospital. *Publications:* Dental Analgesia in A Textbook of Anaesthetics, by Minnitt & Gillies. *Recreations:* book and picture collecting; hill walking. *Address:* 12 Kingsburgh Road, Edinburgh EH12 6DZ. *Clubs:* Oral Surgery; Scottish Arts (Edinburgh); Cairngorm (Aberdeen).
*Died 28 April 1985.*

**BOYLE, Rev. (John) Desmond,** SJ; *b* 29 Aug. 1897; 2nd *s* of late Patrick J. Boyle, Donamon, County Roscommon, Ireland, and Ellen Mary Ryan. *Educ:* Wimbledon Coll.; St Francis Xavier's Coll., Liverpool; Campion Hall, Oxford. Entered the Society of Jesus, 1913;

ordained Priest, 1929; Prefect of Studies, Beaumont Coll., 1931–50; Rector, Beaumont Coll., 1947–50; Rector, Heythrop Coll., 1950–52; Provincial of Eng. Prov. of Soc. of Jesus, 1952–58; Rector of Stonyhurst Coll., 1958–64; Chaplain, Beaumont Coll., 1964–67; Chaplain at St John's, Beaumont, 1967–76. *Address:* St John's, Beaumont, Old Windsor, Berks. *T:* Egham 32428.

*Died 12 Oct. 1982.*

**BOYLE, Sir Lawrence,** Kt 1979; JP; DL; Director: Scottish Mutual Assurance Society, since 1980; Pension Fund Property Unit Trust, since 1980; Partner, Sir Lawrence Boyle Associates, Financial and Management Consultants, Glasgow, since 1980; *b* 31 Jan. 1920; *s* of Hugh Boyle and Kate (*née* Callaghan); *m* 1952, Mary McWilliam; one *s* three *d. Educ:* Holy Cross Acad., Leith, Edinburgh; Edinburgh Univ. BCom, PhD. Depute County Treasurer, Midlothian CC, 1958–62; Depute City Chamberlain, Glasgow, 1962–70; City Chamberlain, Glasgow, 1970–74; Chief Exec., Strathclyde Regional Council, 1974–80. Vis. Prof., Strathclyde Univ. Business Sch., 1979–85. Mem., Public Works Loan Bd, 1972–74. Vice-Pres., Soc. of Local Authority Chief Execs, 1977–78. Member: Cttee of Inquiry into Functions and Powers of Island Councils of Scotland, 1982–84; Cttee of Inquiry into Conduct of Local Government Business, 1985–86. Chm., Scottish Nat. Orch. Soc. Ltd, 1980–83. Member: Council, Scottish Business Sch., 1974–79; Strathclyde Univ. Court, 1980–85; Steering Bd, Strathclyde Univ. Business Sch., 1974–82. IPFA (Mem. Council, and Chm. Scottish Br., 1973–74); CBIM (Mem. Adv. Bd for Scotland, 1973–82). JP Glasgow, 1971; DL Renfrewshire, 1985. *Publications:* Equalisation and the Future of Local Government Finance, 1966; articles and papers in economic jls, etc. *Recreation:* music. *Address:* 24 Broomburn Drive, Newton Mearns, Glasgow. *T:* 041–639 3776.

*Died 27 Dec. 1989.*

**BOYLE, Sir Richard (Gurney),** 4th Bt *cr* 1904; *b* 14 May 1930; *s* of Sir Edward Boyle, 2nd Bt, and Beatrice (*d* 1961), *er d* of Henry Greig, Belvedere House, Kent; *S* to baronetcy of brother, Baron Boyle of Handsworth, 1981; *m* 1961, Elizabeth Anne (marr. diss. 1974), *yr d* of Norman Dennes; three *s. Heir: s* Stephen Gurney Boyle, *b* 15 Jan. 1962. *Address:* Paris Hall Cottage, Hastingwood, Harlow, Essex.

*Died 30 Sept. 1983.*

**BRAADLAND, Erik;** diplomat, retired; *b* 21 Nov. 1910; *m* 1940, Aase Rydtun; one *s* two *d. Educ:* Oslo Univ. (Degree in Economics). Served in Hamburg, Marseille, Stockholm, Berlin; various periods Ministry of Foreign Affairs, Oslo; Acting Head of Military Mission in Berlin, 1949; Chargé d'Affaires at Bonn, 1951; Minister in Belgrade, 1952; Ambassador in Moscow, 1954–58, in London, 1959–61, for Norway; Mem. of Storting, 1961–69. Knight Commander, Order of St Olav; Order of the Yugoslav Flag, 1st Class. *Address:* Ør rute 335, 1750 Halden, Norway. *Clubs:* Norwegian, London; Norske Selskab (Oslo).

*Died 14 July 1988.*

**BRABY, Frederick Cyrus,** CBE 1962; MC 1918; DL; CEng, FIMechE; Hon. Major; retired, from Frederick Braby and Co. Ltd, etc.; *b* 1 May 1897; *e s* of late Cyrus and Mabel Braby (*née* Weddell), of Sutton, Surrey, and High Hurstwood, Sussex; *m* 1931, Margaret Isabel (*d* 1975), *e d* of late F. H. Marshall, Sutton and Hove; no *c. Educ:* Charterhouse; Manchester Univ. (BSc (Eng.)). Served 1915–19 with Lancashire Fusiliers (wounded twice, despatches, MC), and 1921–23 in TA. Apprenticeship with Metropolitan-Vickers Electrical Co. Ltd, Manchester, 1922–24; joined Frederick Braby & Co. Ltd (estab. 1839), 1925, and held various appointments; Director, 1929; Chairman, 1942–65. President: Engineering and Allied Employers' London & District Assoc., 1941–43; Nat. Council, Building Material Producers, 1960–65; Chairman: Industrial Coal Consumers' Council, 1958–65; British Non-Ferrous Metals Res. Assoc., 1958–64. Member of UK Employer/Trade Union Mission to USA, 1941; Vice-President, Engineering and Allied Employers' National Federation, 1952–56; President, 1956–58. County Commissioner (Kent), Boy Scouts Assoc., 1952–67; Member, Sevenoaks RDC, 1963–70; a Governor, Star and Garter Home for Disabled Sailors, Soldiers and Airmen, 1963–73, Vice-Pres., 1974–; Master, Carpenters' Company, 1968–69 (Warden, 1965–68). DL (Kent), 1955. *Recreations:* fishing, photography. *Address:* Three Chimneys, Cooden Beach, East Sussex. *Died 15 July 1983.*

**BRACEWELL-SMITH, Sir Guy,** 3rd Bt *cr* 1947; *b* 12 Dec. 1952; *er s* of Sir George Bracewell Smith, 2nd Bt, MBE, and Helene Marie (*d* 1975), *d* of late John Frederick Hydock, Philadelphia, USA; *S* father, 1976. *Educ:* Harrow. *Heir: b* Charles Bracewell-Smith, *b* 13 Oct. 1955. *Club:* Royal Automobile. *Died 1983.*

**BRADBURY, (Elizabeth) Joyce,** CBE 1970; retired Headmistress; *b* Newcastle upon Tyne, 12 Dec. 1918; *o c* of Thomas Edwin and Anne Bradbury. *Educ:* private sch.; Queen Elizabeth's Grammar Sch., Middleton, near Manchester; Univ. of Leeds. BA (Hons Hist.); Dip. in Educn. Various teaching appts, 1941–57; Dep. Headmistress, Stand Grammar Sch. for Girls, Whitefield, near Manchester, 1957–59; Headmistress: Bede Grammar Sch. for Girls, Sunderland, 1959–67; Pennywell Sch. (co-educnl comprehensive),

1967–72; Thornhill Sch. (co-educnl comprehensive), 1972–78. President, Association of Headmistresses, 1974–76. *Recreations:* travel at home and abroad, walking, pursuing historical interests, music and the theatre, domestic 'arts'. *Address:* 6 Cliffe Court, Roker, Sunderland SR6 9NT. *T:* Sunderland 5487773. *Club:* Soroptimist.

*Died 3 July 1989.*

**BRADDELL, Dorothy Adelaide;** decorative-artist; *b* London, 30 June 1889; *d* of J. L. Bussé; *m* 1914, Darcy Braddell (*d* 1970); one *s* one *d. Educ:* Miss Manville's Sch.; King's Coll., London. Studied art at Regent Street Polytechnic and at Byam Shaw School of Art; won National Gold Medal for decorative design; is chiefly known as a designer of interior decoration and a domestic planner and has been associated largely with all kinds of exhibition work, being responsible for rooms at the Royal Academy Exhibition of Industrial Art, the British Pavilion, Paris Exhibition, 1938, Dorland Hall Exhibitions of British Industrial Art, Ideal Home Exhibitions, the Empire Exhibition, Glasgow, 1938, and Britain Can Make It Exhibition, 1946. *Address:* 8 Lansdowne Road, Holland Park, W11. *T:* 01-727 5487.

*Died 27 April 1981.*

**BRADFORD,** 6th Earl of, *cr* 1815; **Gerald Michael Orlando Bridgeman,** TD; JP; Bt 1600; Baron Bradford, 1794; Viscount Newport, 1815; Captain Shropshire Yeomanry, TARO (retired); Vice-Lieutenant of Shropshire, 1970–74; *b* 29 Sept. 1911; *o s* of 5th Earl of Bradford and Hon. Margaret Cecilia Bruce (*d* 1949), *e d* of 2nd Baron Aberdare; *S* father, 1957; *m* 1946, Mary Willoughby, *er d* of Lt-Col T. H. Montgomery, DSO, Cadogan House, Shrewsbury; two *s* two *d. Educ:* Harrow; Trinity Coll., Cambridge (MA). Served War of 1939–45 (despatches). President, Country Landowners' Assoc., 1955–57; Crown Estate Commissioner, 1956–67. President Timber Growers' Organisation, 1962–64; Chairman: West Midlands Region, Nat. Trust, 1972–80; Forestry Cttee of Great Britain, 1964–66; President, Soil Assoc., 1951–70, Patron, 1970. Chairman of Governors, Harper Adams Agricultural Coll., 1956–73. Freedom of Shrewsbury, 1957. JP 1949, DL 1951, Salop. *Heir: s* Viscount Newport. *Address:* Weston Park, Shifnal, Salop. *T:* Weston-under-Lizard 218; 61d Eaton Square, SW1. *T:* 01-235 4942. *Clubs:* Farmers', MCC.

*Died 30 Aug. 1981.*

**BRADFORD, Ernle;** independent free-lance writer, principally on historical subjects; *b* 11 Jan. 1922; *s* of Jocelyn Ernle Bradford and Ada Louisa (*née* Dusgate); *m* 1957, Marie Blanche Thompson; one *s. Educ:* Uppingham Sch. RNVR, 1940–46 (despatches 1943). Founder Editor, Antique Dealer and Collectors' Guide, 1947. *Publications:* Contemporary Jewellery and Silver Design, 1950; Four Centuries of European Jewellery, 1953 (new edn 1968); The Journeying Moon, 1958; The Mighty 'Hood', 1959 (paperback 1974, new edn 1975); English Victorian Jewellery, 1959 (new edn 1968); The Wind off the Island, 1960; Southward the Caravels: the story of Henry the Navigator, 1961; The Great Siege, 1961 (paperback 1964); The Touchstone, 1962; Antique Collecting, 1963; Companion Guide to the Greek Islands, 1963 (3rd edn 1975); Dictionary of Antiques, 1963; Ulysses Found, 1963, repr. 1985; Three Centuries of Sailing, 1964; The America's Cup, 1964; Drake, 1965; Wall of England, 1966; The Great Betrayal: Constantinople, 1204, 1967 (new edn 1975); The Sultan's Admiral: the life of Barbarossa, 1969; Antique Furniture, 1970; Cleopatra, 1971 (paperback 1974); Gibraltar: the history of a fortress, 1971; Mediterranean: portrait of a sea, 1971; The Shield and the Sword: the Knights of St John, 1973 (paperback 1974); Christopher Columbus, 1973; The Sword and the Scimitar: the saga of the crusades, 1974; Paul the Traveller, 1975; Nelson, 1977; The Year of Thermopylae, 1980; Hannibal, 1982; The Story of the Mary Rose, 1982; Julius Caesar: the pursuit of power, 1984; Siege: Malta 1940–1943, 1985; The Great Ship, 1986. *Recreation:* writing. *Address:* c/o A. M. Heath & Co., 40–42 William IV Street, WC2N 4DD. *Club:* Casino Maltese (Malta).

*Died 8 May 1986.*

**BRADFORD, Rev. Robert John;** MP (OUP) Belfast South since 1974; *b* 1941; *m* 1970, Nora; one *d. Educ:* Queen's Univ., Belfast (BTh). Minister, Suffolk Methodist Church, 1970–74. Worker in Lenadoon area of Belfast, 1970–; contested (Vanguard) Assembly election, Northern Ireland. *Recreation:* formerly Association football (Soccer blue, Queen's Univ.). *Address:* House of Commons, SW1A 0AA; 31 New Forge Lane, Belfast BT9 5NU. *Died 14 Nov. 1981.*

**BRADING, Brig. Norman Baldwin,** CMG 1958; CBE 1945; retired; *b* 25 May 1896; *s* of late Rev. F. C. Brading, Ditton, Kent; *m* Helen Margaret, *d* of G. Gatey, Windermere; one *s* one *d. Educ:* Whitgift; Royal Military College, Sandhurst. 2nd Lieut East Surrey Regt, 1915; served European War, 1914–19 (wounded); War of 1939–45; France, Holland, Germany; despatches, 1945; Lieut-Col 1940, Col 1943, Brig. 1944. Lent to UNO as Dep. Dir for Ops in Brit. Zone of Germany; National Health Services, 1949; lent to Nigerian Govt as House Governor, University Coll. Hospital, Ibadan, Nigeria, 1952. FHA. Knight Comdr Order of Orange Nassau, with swords (Netherlands), 1945. *Recreations:* polo, swimming. *Address:*

Freeland Nursing Home, Freeland, Oxford. *Club:* Royal Over-Seas League.                                                    *Died* 5 June 1990.

**BRADLEY, Harry,** CBE 1951; (First) Director, British Boot, Shoe and Allied Trades Research Association (SATRA), 1922–63, retired; Emeritus President, British Boot and Shoe Institution; *b* 1897; *s* of late George Craven Bradley, Silsden, Yorks; *m* 1921, Bertha Ceridwen, *d* of late Rev. T. Henry Jones, USA and North Wales; one *s* two *d*. *Educ:* Keighley Grammar Sch.; Royal College of Science; Imperial Coll. of Science and Technology. Served European War, 1914–18, RFC and RNVR Anti-submarine Div. On demobilisation completed ARCS (hons), BSc (1st cl. hons); 1 yr research for Admiralty; 1 yr Lectr/Demonstrator, 3rd yr Physics, Royal College of Science. John Arthur Wilson Memorial Lectures, Amer. Leather Chemists' Assoc., 1966. Mem., Royal Institution. *Publications:* many research reports, scientific papers and articles in various jls. *Recreations:* music, gardening, reading; fond of dogs and horses. *Address:* Volta, 38 Piper's Hill Road, Kettering, Northants. *T:* Kettering 513210.                      *Died* 30 Dec. 1982.

**BRADLEY, Air Marshal Sir John Stanley Travers,** KCB 1942; CBE 1941 (OBE 1919); RAF retired; *b* 11 April 1888; *m* (she *d* 1948). Director of Equipment, Air Ministry, 1935–38; Air Commodore, 1935; Air Vice-Marshal, 1938; Air Officer Commanding, Maintenance Command, 1938; Temp. Air Marshal, 1942; Deputy Air Member for Supply and Organisation, Air Ministry, 1942–45; Air Marshal, 1944; retired, 1945. *Address:* Beech Lodge, Rowlands Hill, Wimborne, Dorset. *T:* Wimborne 2709. *Club:* Naval and Military.                                                    *Died* 6 Jan. 1982.

**BRADLEY, General of the Army Omar Nelson,** DDSM (US) 1979; DSM (US) 1943 (with 3 oak leaf clusters); DSM (US Navy); Legion of Merit; Hon. KCB 1944 (Hon. CB 1944); Hon. Chairman, Bulova Watch Company Inc., since 1973 (Chairman, 1958–73); Chairman, Bulova School of Watch Making; *b* 12 Feb. 1893; *s* of John S. and Sarah Elizabeth Hubbard Bradley; *m* 1st, 1916, Mary Quayle (*d* 1965); one *d*; 2nd, 1966, Kitty Buhler. *Educ:* United States Military Academy, West Point. 2nd Lieut US Army, 1915; Lieut-Col, 1936; Brig.-Gen. (temp.), 1941, (perm.) 1943; Maj.-Gen. (temp.), 1942, (perm.) 1944; Lieut-Gen. (temp.), 1943; Gen. (temp.), 1945, (perm.) 1949; General of the Army (perm.), 1950. Commanded II United States Corps in Northern Tunisia and in Sicily, April–Sept. 1943; commanded US troops in invasion of France, June 1944; commanded Twelfth Army Group (American First, Third, Ninth and Fifteenth Armies), 1944; Administrator of Veterans Affairs, 1945–47; Chief of Staff US Army, 1948–49; Chm. of Joint Chiefs of Staff, 1949–53. US rep., standing gp, mil. cttee NATO, 1949–53. Holds hon. doctorates from American and English univs. Freedoms Foundation at Valley Forge George Washington Award, 1971; US Medal of Freedom, 1977; Grand Officer, French Legion of Honour, and many other foreign decorations. *Publication:* A Soldier's Story, 1951; *posthumous publication:* A General's Life: an autobiography (with Clay Blair), 1983. *Recreations:* shooting, golf, fishing. *Address:* PO Box 6670, Fort Bliss, Texas 79906, USA. *Clubs:* Army and Navy, Burning Tree (Washington, DC); El Paso Country; Coronado Country; Wilshire Country; Hillcrest Country; Lakeside Golf (Hollywood); Lotus; AUSA; Hollywood Park Turf; Del Mar Turf; Santa Anita Private Turf.                                *Died* 8 April 1981.

**BRADLEY-WILLIAMS, Col William Picton,** DSO 1919; *b* 9 Oct. 1890; *s* of late Herbert Edward Bradley, The Grange, Bitton, Glos (took name of Williams from late Capt. William Williams, Pontypridd, Glamorgan); *m* 1918, Frances Mary (*d* 1970), *y d* of late John Selwin Calverley of Oulton, near Leeds; two *s* two *d*; *m* 1947, Sylvia Mary Maxwell Jackson, Ferriby, East Yorks (*d* 1969); one *d*. *Educ:* Haileybury. Served European War, 1914–19 (despatches, DSO); Mesopotamia, 1920–21; North West Frontier, India, 1930; Chief Instructor Army Sch. of PT, Aldershot, 1927–30. Commanded 1st Bn The King's Own Yorks Light Infantry, 1936–39; Garrison Comdr, Hull, 1940–41; Commandant Army Physical Training Corps, 1941–44; Comdr No. 1 War Material Reconnaissance Team BAOR, Dec. 1944–June 1945; Army Welfare Officer, HQ Colchester, 1946–54. *Address:* Burstall House, Burstall, near Ipswich, Suffolk IP8 3DP. *T:* Hintlesham 277. *Club:* Naval and Military.                                                *Died* 22 Jan. 1981.

**BRADSHAW, Thornton Frederick;** Chairman, RCA, New York, 1981–86 (Chief Executive Officer, 1981–85); *b* 4 Aug. 1917; *s* of Frederick and Julia Bradshaw; *m* 1st, 1940, Sally Davis (marr. diss. 1974); one *s* two *d*; 2nd, 1974, Patricia Salter West; four step *s*. *Educ:* Phillips Exeter Acad.; Harvard Coll. (BA); Harvard Grad. Sch. of Business (MBA, Dr of Commercial Science). Associate Prof., Sch. of Bus. Admin, Harvard (with time out for Navy service, seven battle stars), 1942–52; Cresap, McCormick & Paget, 1952–56; Atlantic Richfield Co., 1956–81: Vice Pres. and Gen. Man., Finance and Accounting Dept, Jan. 1958; Mem., Bd of Dirs, Feb. 1958; Exec. Vice Pres., 1962; Pres., and Mem. Exec. Cttee of Bd of Dirs, 1964–81; Chm. Exec. Cttee, Jan.–June 1981. Hon. LLD: Pepperdine Univ., 1974; Southampton Coll., 1983; Hon. DSSc: Villanova

Univ., 1975; Claremont Colls, 1981. Many awards, including: Freedom and Justice Award, NAACP, 1976; Amer. Jewish Cttee Human Relations Award, 1976; Business Statesman Award, Harvard Bus. Sch., 1977; Earl Warren Award for 1980, Amer. Soc. for Public Admin, 1981. *Publications:* Corporations and their Critics, 1980; articles and pubns. *Recreations:* boating, tennis, swimming; also a prolific reader, fond of history and biography. *Address:* 435 East 52nd Street, New York, NY 10022, USA; (office) 570 Lexington Avenue, New York, NY 10022. *Clubs:* Mark's; Economic, Harvard, Knickerbocker, River, University (New York); California (LA); Valley Hunt (Pasadena, Calif).
                                                       *Died* 6 Dec. 1988.

**BRADSHAW-ISHERWOOD, Christopher William;** *see* Isherwood, Christopher.

**BRAHMS, Caryl, (Doris Caroline Abrahams);** critic and novelist; journalist specialising in criticism of the theatre arts; ballet critic; writer of film, broadcast and television scripts; *b* Surrey, 8 Dec. 1901. *Educ:* privately and at Royal Academy of Music. Wrote stage versions of: Cindy-Ella, 1962; Sing a Rude Song (stage biography of Marie Lloyd), 1970; Television: The Great Inimitable Mr Dickens, 1970; Ooh! La! La!, adapted series of Feydeau farces, 1973; A Rather Reassuring Programme, 1977; (with Ned Sherrin): Beecham, 1980; The Mitford Girls, 1981. Mem., Nat. Theatre Bd, 1980–. Ivor Novello Award (with Ned Sherrin), 1966. *Publications:* The Moon on my Left, 1930; Footnotes To The Ballet, 1936; Robert Helpmann, Choreographer, 1943; Seat at the Ballet, 1951; Away went Polly, 1952; No Castanets, 1963; The Rest of the Evening's My Own (theatre criticism), 1964; (with S. J. Simon): A Bullet in the Ballet, 1937; Casino for Sale, 1938; The Elephant is White, 1939; Envoy on Excursion, 1940; Don't, Mr Disraeli, 1940 (Evening Standard Book of the Year); No Bed for Bacon, 1941; No Nightingales, 1944 (filmed); Titania Has a Mother, 1944; Six Curtains for Stroganova, 1945; Trottie True, 1946 (filmed); To Hell with Hedda, 1947; You Were There, 1950; (with Ned Sherrin): Cindy-Ella or I gotta Shoe, 1962; Rappel 1910, 1964; Benbow was his Name, 1966; film script: Girl/stroke/Boy, 1971; Paying the Piper (play; adapted from Feydeau), 1972; After You Mr Feydeau, 1975; Gilbert and Sullivan: Lost Chords and Discords, 1975; Nickleby and Me, 1975; Reflections in a Lake, 1976; Enter a Dragon, Stage Centre, 1979. *Recreations:* collecting Edwardian postcards and glass walking-sticks. *Address:* 3 Cambridge Gate, Regent's Park, NW1. *T:* 01-935 6439.          *Died* 5 Dec. 1982.

**BRAILSFORD, Prof. Frederick,** PhD; FIEE; Professor of Electrical Engineering, University College, London, 1951–70, later Emeritus Professor; *b* 22 Sept. 1903; *s* of John James and Frances Ann Brailsford; *m* 1934, Sarah Remington Smyth, Knock, County Down; one *d*. *Educ:* University Coll., Swansea. Whitworth Scholar, 1923; BSc(Eng) London (1st Class Hons), 1927; PhD, London, 1939. Apprentice in HM Dockyard, Pembroke, 1919–23; Electrical Engineer with Metropolitan-Vickers Electrical Co., Manchester, 1926–50. *Publications:* Magnetic Materials, 1960; Physical Principles of Magnetism, 1966; Introduction to the Magnetic Properties of Materials, 1968; various papers to Institution of Electrical Engineers and elsewhere. *Address:* Locks Green, 244 Brooklands Road, Weybridge, Surrey. *T:* Weybridge 47548.
                                                       *Died* 21 Sept. 1985.

**BRAILSFORD, John William;** Keeper, Department of Prehistoric and Romano-British Antiquities, British Museum, 1969–73; *b* 14 July 1918; *o s* of Alfred and Dorothy H. M. Brailsford; *m* 1945, Mary Freeman Boaden; one *s* one *d*. *Educ:* Bedales; Emmanuel College, Cambridge. Sen. Exhibnr and Scholar, BA, MA 1943. Royal Artillery (Survey), 1939–45; Intell. (Air Photo Interpretation), 1945–46. Asst Keeper, Dept of British and Medieval Antiquities, Brit. Mus., 1946; Dep. Keeper, 1963. FMA; FSA 1949; Fellow, German Archaeolog. Inst., 1967. *Publications:* Museum Handbooks to Mildenhall Treasure, 1947; Antiquities of Roman Britain, 1951; Later Prehistoric Antiquities of the British Isles, 1953; Antiquities from Hod Hill in the Durden Collection, 1962; (ed) Hod Hill: Excavations, 1951–58; 1968; Early Celtic Masterpieces from Britain in the British Museum, 1975; papers in learned jls. *Recreations:* various. *Address:* Sunnyside, Brook End, Chadlington, Oxon. *T:* Chadlington 378.                                   *Died* 20 Oct. 1988.

**BRAIN, Ronald,** CB 1967; Chairman, London and Quadrant Housing Trust, 1977–79; *b* 1 March 1914; *s* of T. T. G. Brain, RN, and E. C. Brain (*née* Fruin); *m* 1943, Lilian Rose (*née* Ravenhill); one *s* one *d*. *Educ:* Trowbridge High Sch. Audit Asst, Min. of Health, 1932; Principal, Min. of Health, 1946; Asst Sec., Min. of Housing and Local Govt, 1952; Under-Sec., 1959; Dep. Sec., Dept of Environment (formerly Min. of Housing and Local Govt), 1966–74. *Recreations:* music, chess. *Address:* Flat 4, Badminton, Galsworthy Road, Kingston-upon-Thames, Surrey.          *Died* 27 May 1989.

**BRAINE, John (Gerard);** author; *b* 13 April 1922; *s* of Fred and Katherine Braine; *m* 1955, Helen Patricia Wood; one *s* three *d*.

*Educ:* St Bede's Grammar Sch., Bradford. Furniture-shop asst, bookshop asst, laboratory asst, progress chaser, in rapid succession, 1938–40; Asst, Bingley Public Library, 1940–49; HM Navy, 1942–43; Chief Asst, Bingley Public Library, 1949–51; free-lance writer, London and Yorks, with interval in hospital, 1951–54; Branch Librarian, Northumberland County Library, 1954–56; Branch Librarian, West Riding of Yorks County Library, 1956–57. Writer in Residence, Purdue Univ., 1978. ALA 1950. *Publications:* Room at the Top, 1957 (filmed 1958); The Vodi, 1959; Life at the Top, 1962 (filmed 1965); The Jealous God, 1964; The Crying Game, 1968; Stay with Me till Morning, 1970 (adapted for TV, 1980); The Queen of a Distant Country, 1972 (adapted for TV, 1978); Writing a Novel, 1974; The Pious Agent, 1975; Waiting for Sheila, 1976 (adapted for TV, 1977); Finger of Fire, 1977; J. B. Priestley, 1979; One and Last Love, 1981; The Two of Us, 1984; These Golden Days, 1985. *TV Series:* Man at the Top, 1970, 1972. *Recreations:* walking, talking, Victoriana, and dieting. *Address:* c/o Methuen London Ltd, 11 New Fetter Lane, EC4P 4EE. *Club:* PEN.
*Died 28 Oct. 1986.*

**BRAITHWAITE, Prof. Richard Bevan,** FBA 1957; Emeritus Knightbridge Professor of Moral Philosophy in the University of Cambridge; *b* 15 Jan. 1900; *s* of William Charles Braithwaite, Banbury; *m* 1st, 1925, Dorothea Cotter (*d* 1928), *d* of Sir Theodore Morison; 2nd, 1932, Margaret Mary (*d* 1986), *d* of Rt Hon. C. F. G. Masterman; one *s* one *d. Educ:* Sidcot Sch., Somerset; Bootham Sch., York; King's Coll., Cambridge (Scholar, Prizeman, Research Student). MA Camb. 1926; Fellow of King's Coll., Camb. 1924–; University Lectr in Moral Science, 1928–34; Sidgwick Lectr in Moral Science, 1934–53; Knightbridge Prof. of Moral Philosophy, 1953–67; Tarner Lectr at Trinity Coll., Camb., 1945–46; Pres. Mind Assoc., 1946; Pres. Aristotelian Soc., 1946–47; Annual Philosophical Lectr to British Academy, 1950; Pres. Brit. Soc. for the Philosophy of Science, 1961–63; Deems Lectr, New York Univ., 1962; Forwood Lectr, Liverpool Univ., 1968; Visiting Prof. of Philosophy: Johns Hopkins Univ., 1968; Univ. of Western Ontario, 1969; City Univ. of New York, 1970. Syndic Cambridge Univ. Press, 1943–62; Mem. Gen. Bd of Faculties, 1945–48; Mem. Council Senate, 1959–64. Foreign Hon. Mem., Amer. Acad. of Arts and Scis, 1986. Hon. DLitt Bristol, 1963. *Publications:* Moral Principles and Inductive Policies (British Acad. Lecture, 1950); Scientific Explanation, 1953; Theory of Games as a tool for the Moral Philosopher (Inaugural Lecture), 1955; An Empiricist's view of the nature of Religious Belief (Eddington Lecture), 1955; Introd. to trans. of Gödel, 1962. Articles in Mind, Proc. Aristotelian Soc., etc. *Recreation:* reading novels. *Address:* The Grange, Bottisham, Cambridge. *T:* Cambridge (0223) 811256.
*Died 21 April 1990.*

**BRAMBLE, Courtenay Parker,** CIE 1946; *b* 10 June 1900; *s* of Frank Bramble and Violet, *d* of Col M. G. Totterdell, VD; *m* 1st, 1928, Margaret Louise Lawrence, MBE, 1943, *d* of Sir Henry Lawrence, KCSI; two *s* one *d:* 2nd, 1958, Doreen, *d* of C. E. Cornish, Lytham St Annes, Lancs. *Educ:* St Paul's Cathedral Choir Sch. (Coronation Medal, 1911); Cranleigh Sch.; King's Coll., Cambridge (MA, LLB). Barrister-at-law, Middle Temple; with The Bombay Co. Ltd, India, 1922–33; Senior partner Drennan & Co., Bombay, 1933–52; Silver Jubilee Medal, 1935; Coronation Medal, 1937. Dir, East India Cotton Assoc., Bombay, 1925–33; Mem., Indian Central Cotton Cttee, 1935–50. Mem. of Legislature, Bombay, 1935–50 (Leader, Progress Party); JP and Hon. Magistrate, Bombay; Chm. (appointed by Govt), Children's Aid Soc., Bombay, 1931–39; Pres. Bombay Chamber of Commerce, 1940, 1945–46; Dep. Pres. Associated Chambers of Commerce, India, 1945; Chm. European Assoc., Bombay Branch, 1942–44; Mem., Bombay Presidency War Cttee, 1941–45; Trustee of Port of Bombay, 1949. Music critic, Times of India, 1925–41. Chairman: All India Quadrangular Cricket Cttee, 1935–39; UK Citizens Assoc. (Bombay), 1948–50; National Service Advisory Cttee, 1940–45; Bombay European Hospital Trust, 1943–50; Hon. Lieut, RINVR, 1940–45. Dir (Pres. 1962), Liverpool Cotton Association; Man. Dir, Abercrombie, Bramble & Co. Ltd, 1954–73; Member Council: Cotton Research Corp., 1960–72; Liverpool Sch. of Tropical Medicine, 1974–; a Manager, Royal Liverpool Children's Hospital Sch., 1962–75. *Address:* Cross Trees, Birch Way, Heswall, Merseyside. *T:* 051–342 3873. *Clubs:* United Oxford & Cambridge University; Royal Yacht (Bombay).
*Died 31 Jan. 1987.*

**BRAMWELL-BOOTH, Catherine,** CBE 1971; OF 1983; a Commissioner of the Salvation Army; *b* London, 20 July 1883; *e c* of late General Bramwell Booth. Entered Salvation Army as an Officer, 1903; engaged in training Cadets at International Training Coll., 1907–17; International Sec. for Salvation Army in Europe, 1917; command of Women's Social Work in Great Britain and Ireland, 1926; International Sec. for Europe, 1946–48; retired 1948. Best Speaker award, Guild of Professional Toastmasters, 1978. *Publications:* Messages to the Messengers; A Few Lines; Bramwell Booth, 1933; (compiler) Bramwell Booth Speaks, 1947; Verse, 1947; Catherine Booth, the story of her loves, 1970; Fighting for the King (poems), 1983; (with Ted Harrison) Commissioner Catherine, 1983;

*relevant publication:* Catherine Bramwell-Booth, by Mary Batchelor, 1986.
*Died 4 Oct. 1987.*

**BRANDT, William, (Bill Brandt),** RDI 1978; photographer; *b* 1904; parents of Russian descent; British by birth. *Educ:* studied under Man Ray, Paris, in 1930s. Spent much of early youth in Germany and Switzerland; worked in Paris for many years. At age of 25 became a photo-journalist; settled in London, 1931; towards the end of War of 1939–45 he began to photograph nudes and did portraits and landscapes. Exhibition at Museum of Modern Art, New York, Oct.–Nov. 1969; the Arts Council put on this exhibition at the Hayward Gallery, London, Apr.–May 1970 (Prof. Aaron Scharf wrote introd. to catalogue, Herbert Spencer designed catalogue and poster); subseq. the exhibits were shown at 12 centres outside London and then returned to New York; exhibn of portraits, Nat. Portrait Gall., 1982. Selected The Land exhibition, V and A, 1975–76, Edinburgh, Belfast and Cardiff, 1976. Incl. in TV series on Master Photographers, 1983. Hon. FRPS 1980. Hon. Dr RCA, 1977. Médaille de la Ville de Paris, 1980. *Publications:* The English at Home, 1936; A Night in London, 1938; Camera in London, 1948; Literary Britain, 1951; Perspective of Nudes, 1961; Shadow of Light, 1966, rev. edn 1977; (ed) The Land: twentieth century landscape photographs, 1975; Nudes 1945–1980, 1980; contrib. to magazines in Europe, USA, etc.
*Died 20 Dec. 1983.*

**BRANSON, Col Sir Douglas (Stephenson),** KBE 1954; CB 1950; DSO 1918, and 2 bars; MC 1917; TD; MA; *b* 25 July 1893; *s* of Col George Ernest Branson, JP, Broomgrove, Sheffield; *m* 1st, 1930, Edith Eileen (*d* 1959), *d* of Joseph Bradbury, Sheffield; 2nd, 1961, Ailie (*d* 1981), widow of Brig. John Malcolm Fisher and *d* of late Sir William Bell. *Educ:* Marlborough; New Coll., Oxford. Admitted a Solicitor, 1920 and practised until 1970. Served European War, 1914–18, The Hallamshire Bn York and Lancaster Regt. Col, 1924; Commander 148 Infantry Brigade (TA), 1925–29; Additional ADC to the King, 1927. DL West Riding of Yorks, 1934. High Sheriff of Hallamshire, 1963. *Address:* 6 Paradise Square, Sheffield, S Yorks. *T:* 737346; 385 Fulwood Road, Sheffield S10 3GA. *T:* Sheffield 302149.
*Died 23 Nov. 1981.*

**BRASNETT, Rev. Dr Bertrand Rippington,** DD Oxon, 1935; *b* 22 Jan. 1893; *e s* of Stanley Brasnett, The Manor House, Marham, Norfolk; *g s* of Edward Rowing Brasnett, West Bilney House, Norfolk; unmarried. *Educ:* Oxford High Sch.; private tutor; Keble Coll., Oxford; Cuddesdon Theological Coll. Squire Scholar of the University of Oxford, 1911–15, 2nd class Classical Moderations, 2nd class Literæ Humaniores, BA, MA, Diploma in Theology with Distinction, BD; Deacon, 1916; Priest, 1918; Chaplain and Asst Master, Bradfield Coll., Berks, 1916–18; Priest-in-charge, Coleshill, Bucks, 1918–22; Chaplain and Lecturer, Bishops' Coll., Cheshunt, 1922–25; Vice-Principal, 1925–29, Principal and Pantonian Prof., 1930–42, of the Theological Coll. of the Scottish Episcopal Church, Edinburgh; Hon. Chaplain of St Mary's Cathedral, Edinburgh, 1926–29; Canon, 1930–42, and Chancellor, 1940–42, of St Mary's Cathedral, Edinburgh; Examining Chaplain to the Bishop of Edinburgh, 1930–42; Select Preacher, University of Oxford, 1941–43. *Publications:* The Suffering of the Impassible God, 1928; The Infinity of God, 1933; God the Worshipful, 1935. *Address:* Pleasant View, 15 Jack Straw's Lane, Headington, Oxford OX3 0DL.
*Died 6 Feb. 1988.*

**BRASSEY, Col Sir Hugh (Trefusis),** KCVO 1985; OBE 1959; MC 1944; Lord Lieutenant of Wiltshire, 1981–89; *b* 5 Oct. 1915; *s* of Lieut-Col Edgar Hugh Brassey, MVO, and Margaret Harriet (*née* Trefusis); *m* 1939, Joyce Patricia, *d* of Captain Maurice Kingscote; two *s* two *d* (and one *d* decd). *Educ:* Eton; Sandhurst. Regular Commission, The Royal Scots Greys, 1935–46; served Palestine, Africa, Italy and NW Europe, Lieut-Col Comdg Royal Wilts Yeomanry, 1955–58. ADC (TA) to the Queen, 1964–69; Exon, Queen's Bodyguard, Yeoman of the Guard, 1964–70, Ensign, 1970–79, Lieutenant, 1979–85; Adjutant and Clerk of the Cheque, 1971. Col, The Royal Scots Dragoon Guards, 1973–78. Regional Dir (Salisbury), Lloyds Bank. Chairman, Chippenham Conservative Assoc., 1951–53, 1966–68 (Pres. 1968). Pres., Wilts Assoc. of Boys Clubs, 1968. JP 1951, DL 1955, High Sheriff 1959, Vice Lord-Lieutenant, 1968–81, Wilts. Croix de Guerre (France), 1944. *Recreation:* country. *Address:* Manor Farm, Little Somerford, Chippenham, Wilts SN15 5JW. *T:* Malmesbury 822255. *Club:* Cavalry and Guards.
*Died 10 April 1990.*

**BRATTAIN, Dr Walter H(ouser);** Research Physicist, Bell Telephone Laboratories, Inc., 1929–67; Overseer Emeritus, Whitman College; engaged with others in research investigating the properties of lipid membranes in salt solutions; *b* Amoy, China, 10 Feb. 1902; *s* of Ross R. Brattain and Ottilie Brattain (*née* Houser); *m* 1st, 1935, Keren Gilmore (*d* 1957); one *s*; 2nd, 1958, Emma Jane Miller (*née* Kirsch). *Educ:* Whitman Coll., Walla Walla, Washington; University of Oregon, Eugene, Oregon; University of Minnesota, Minneapolis, Minn. BS 1924, Whitman Coll.; MA 1926, University of Oregon; PhD 1929, University of Minnesota. Asst Physicist,

Bureau of Standards, 1928–29; Technical Staff, Bell Telephone Labs, Inc., 1929–67. Division of War Research, Columbia Univ., 1942–44. Visiting Lecturer, Harvard Univ., 1952–53; Visiting Prof. of Physics (part-time) Whitman Coll., 1963–72. Fellow, Explorers' Club, 1977. Hon. Dr of Science: Portland Univ., 1952; Union Coll., 1955; Whitman Coll., 1955; University of Minnesota, 1957; Gustavus Adolphus Coll., 1963; Hon. LHD Hartwick Coll., 1964. Stuart Ballantine Medal, Franklin Institute, 1952; John Scott Medal, City of Philadelphia, 1955; Nobel Prize for Physics (with J. Bardeen and W. Shockley), 1956. Fellow: American Academy of Arts and Sciences, 1956; National Academy of Sciences, 1959; Hon. MIEEE 1981. *Publications:* many scientific papers on Thermionics and Semiconductors in various physics journals. *Recreation:* golf.

*Died* 13 Oct. 1987.

**BRAUDEL, Prof. Fernand;** Commandeur de la Légion d'Honneur, 1982; Commandeur: Palmes Académiques; l'Ordre National du Mérite; DèsL; Membre de l'Académie Française, 1984; Director of Studies, l'Ecole des Hautes-Etudes en Sciences Sociales, since 1937; Professor, Collège de France, since 1949; Administrator, Fondation de la Maison des Sciences de l'Homme, since 1962; *b* 24 Aug. 1902; *m* 1933, Paule Pradel; two *d. Educ:* Univ. of Paris (LèsL 1921, Agrégé d'histoire 1923). DèsL Univ. of Paris, 1947. Teacher: Lycée d'Alger, 1924–32; Lycées Pasteur, Condorcet and Henri IV, Paris, 1932–35; Professor, Faculty of Letters, São Paulo, Brazil, 1935–37; Pres., Section VI, l'Ecole Pratique des Hautes-Etudes, 1956–72. Corresponding Member: Acad. de la Historia de Buenos Aires, 1947–; British Acad., 1962–; Réal Acad. de la Historia de Madrid, 1963–; Amer. Phil Soc., Heidelberger Akad. des Wissenschaften, and Bäyerische Akad. des Wissenschaften, 1964–; Amer. Acad. of Arts and Sciences, 1970–; Amer. Econ. Soc.; Acad. of Science, Poland; Acad. of Science, Belgrade. Dr *hc* univs of São Paulo, Brussels, Oxford, Madrid, Geneva, Warsaw, Cologne, Chicago, Florence, Padua, Cambridge, Leiden, London, Hull, Edinburgh, E Anglia, St Andrews, Yale and Montreal. Commandeur: Order of Polonia Restituta, 1960; Order of Merit, Italy, 1976. Prix Georges Pompidou, 1980. Mem. Editorial Bd, Annales, Economies, Sociétés, Civilisations, 1947–. *Publications:* La Méditerranée et le monde méditerranéen, 1949, 4th edn 1980 (trans. many langs); (with Ruggiero Romano) Navires et marchandises à l'entrée du port de Livourne, 1547–1611, 1951; (contrib.) La Civilta veneziana del Rinascimento, 1958; (contrib.) Decadenza economica veneziano nel secolo XVII, 1961; Le Monde actuel: les grandes civilisations du monde actuel, 1963; Ecrits sur l'Histoire, 1969; Civilisation matérielle, économie et capitalisme, XVe-XVIIIe siecles, 3 vols, 1980 (trans. many langs); articles in Revue Africaine, Annales ESC, Eventail de l'histoire vivante, and Storia e Economia; *posthumous publication:* The Identity of France, vol. 1, 1988, vol. 2, 1990. *Address:* Fondation de la Maison des Sciences de l'Homme, 54 boulevard Raspail, 75270 Paris, France. *T:* 222–40–24.

*Died* 28 Nov. 1985.

**BRAY, Gen. Sir Robert (Napier Hubert Campbell),** GBE 1966 (CBE 1952); KCB 1962 (CB 1957); DSO 1944, and Bar 1945; retired; late Duke of Wellington's Regiment (Colonel of the Regiment, 1965–75); *b* 1908; *s* of late Brig.-Gen. Robert Napier Bray, CMG, DSO; *m* 1936, Nora, *d* of G. C. G. Gee, Rothley, Leics.; three *s. Educ:* Gresham's Sch., Holt; Royal Military Coll. 2nd Lieut, Duke of Wellington's Regt, 1928. Served War of 1939–45 Norway, Middle East and North Western Europe (despatches, DSO and Bar); Lieut-Col 1941; Brig., 1945; Brig. General Staff British Army of the Rhine, 1950–52; Korea, 1954; Director of Land-Air Warfare, and Director of North Atlantic Treaty Organisation Standardisation, War Office, 1954–57; Maj.-Gen., 1954; General Officer Commanding 56 Infantry Div. (TA), 1957–59; Commander, Land Forces, Arabian Peninsula, 1959; GOC, MELF, 1961; Lieut-Gen. 1961; General Officer Commanding-in-Chief, Southern Command, 1961–63; Commander-in-Chief, Allied Forces, Northern Europe, 1963–67; Dep. Supreme Comdr Allied Powers Europe, 1967–70; General 1965; ADC General to the Queen, 1965–68. *Recreations:* sailing, shooting. *Address:* c/o Lloyds Bank, 6 Pall Mall, SW1Y 5NH. *Clubs:* Army and Navy, Royal Cruising.

*Died* 14 Aug. 1983.

**BRAY, Ronald William Thomas;** mechanical engineer; farmer; Underwriting Member of Lloyd's; *b* 5 Jan. 1922; *s* of William Ernest Bray, mech. engr and co. dir, Earls Court, and Ada Bray, Killington, Westmorland; *m* 1944, Margaret Florence, *d* of James B. Parker, St Margarets-on-Thames; no *c. Educ:* Latymer Upper School. Joined family business, 1938; Man. Dir 1946; pioneered develt of British construction equipment incl. heavy earthmoving equipment, four-wheel-drive tractor shovels; travelled extensively, Europe, N and S Africa, America, Canada, Caribbean and Middle East, developing exports; served on numerous professional and British Standards cttees; resigned 1959. Mem., Woking UDC, 1959–62; Chm./Vice-Chm. of various cttees; Mem., N Yorks CC, 1977–. Contested (C) Stockton-on-Tees, 1964; MP (C) Rossendale, 1970–Sept. 1974; Mem. Parly delegns to India, Malaŵi, Sri Lanka, Sweden. Vice-Chm., Assoc. of Cons. Clubs, 1972–75; Vice-Pres., Lancashire Fedn

of Cons. Clubs. FFB. *Recreations:* swimming, riding, walking. *Address:* Hallbeck, Beckermonds, Buckden, Skipton, N Yorks BD23 5JL. *T:* Kettlewell 832. *Clubs:* Royal Automobile; Royal Automobile Country (Epsom).

*Died* 22 April 1984.

**BRAYBROOKE,** 9th Baron *cr* 1788; **Henry Seymour Neville;** JP; DL; Hon. MA Camb. 1948; Hereditary Visitor of Magdalene College, Cambridge; Patron of two livings; *b* 5 Feb. 1897; *er s* of late Rev. Hon. Grey Neville (2nd *s* of 6th Baron) and late Mary Peele, *e d* of late Canon Francis Slater; *S* cousin, 1943; *m* 1st, 1930, Muriel Evelyn (*d* 1962), *d* of late William C. Manning and widow of E. C. Cartwright; one *s*; 2nd, 1963, Angela Mary (*d* 1985), *d* of late William H. Hollis and widow of John Ree. *Educ:* Shrewsbury Sch. (Scholar); Magdalene Coll., Cambridge. Served European War, 1914–18, in RNA Service and RAF; later held various appointments with Anglo-Iranian and Shell Groups of oil companies. Chm., Diocesan Bd of Finance, Chelmsford, 1950–68. JP Saffron Walden, 1953; DL, 1950–. *Heir:* s Hon. Robin Henry Charles Neville [*b* 29 Jan. 1932; *m* 1st, 1955, Robin Helen (marr. diss. 1974), *d* of late T. A. Brockhoff, Sydney, Australia; four *d* (and one *d* decd); 2nd, 1974, Linda Norman; three *d*]. *Address:* Bruncketts, Wendens Ambo, Saffron Walden, Essex CB11 4JL. *T:* Saffron Walden 40200.

*Died* 12 Feb. 1990.

**BRAYE,** 7th Baron *cr* 1529; **Thomas Adrian Verney-Cave;** JP; DL; Major, late 13/18th Royal Hussars; *b* 26 July 1902; *er s* of 6th Baron Braye and Ethel Mary (*d* 1955), *d* of Capt. Edward Bouverie Pusey, RN; *S* father, 1952; *m* 1934, Dorothea, *yr d* of late Daniel C. Donoghue, Philadelphia; one *d. Educ:* Eton. Major, 13/18th Royal Hussars; formerly Flying Officer, RAF, 1939–46; served on personal staff of The Prince of the Netherlands, 1945–46 (Order of Orange Nassau). Former Dir, George Spencer Ltd. CC Northants, 1952–64. JP Leicestershire, 1953, DL, 1954. *Heir:* d Hon. Penelope Mary [*b* 28 Sept. 1941; *m* 1981, Lt-Col Edward Henry Lancelot Aubrey-Fletcher, Grenadier Guards]. *Address:* Stanford Hall, Lutterworth, Leics LE17 6DH. *T:* Rugby 860250. *Club:* Cavalry and Guards.

*Died* 19 Dec. 1985.

**BRAZENDALE, George William,** CMG 1958; FCA; *b* 1909; *s* of late Percy Ridout Brazendale, and late Edith Mary Brazendale (*née* Maystre); *m* 1938, Madeleine, *o d* of Thomas and Betty Wroe; two *d. Educ:* Arnold Sch., Blackpool, Lancs. Chief Accountant, Colclough China Ltd, Stoke-on-Trent, 1936–41; Asst Area Officer, MAP, 1941–42; Chief Progress Officer, ROF Swynnerton, 1942–43; Secretary, Midland Regional Board, 1943–45; Regional Controller Board of Trade: Northern Region, 1945–46; North-Western Region, 1946–50; Asst Secretary, Board of Trade, 1946; Trade Commissioner for the UK in charge Calcutta, 1950–60. Principal British Trade Commissioner: in the Federation of Rhodesia and Nyasaland, 1961–63; also Economic Adviser to British High Commissioner in Rhodesia, 1964–65; Economic Adviser to Special British Representative in East and Central Africa, 1966–67; retired from HM Diplomatic Service, 1967. ACA 1931. *Recreations:* fishing, gardening. *Address:* 111 Hatherley Court, Hatherley Grove, W2 5RG; 4 Princes Street, Sandy Bay, Hobart, Tas 7005, Australia. *Club:* Oriental.

*Died* 13 April 1990.

**BRAZIER, Rt. Rev. Percy James;** *b* 3 Aug. 1903; *m* 1933, Joan Cooper, MB, BS (*d* 1989); one *s* four *d. Educ:* Weymouth Coll., Dorset; Emmanuel Coll., Cambridge. 2nd class Hist. Trip., Part I, 1924, 2nd class, Part II, and BA, 1925; MA 1939. Ridley Hall, Cambridge, 1925–27, Deacon, 1927; Priest, 1928; Curate of St John the Evangelist, Blackheath, 1927–29; CMS (Ruanda Mission), 1930; Kabale, 1930–34; Kigeme, Diocese of Uganda, 1934–50; Archdeacon of Ruanda-Urundi, 1946–51; Asst Bishop of Uganda for Ruanda-Urundi, 1951–60; Bishop of Rwanda and Burundi, 1960–64 (name of diocese changed when Ruanda-Urundi was granted independence, 1962); retired 1964. Rector of Padworth and Vicar of Mortimer West End, Diocese of Oxford, 1964–70. Chevalier de l'Ordre Royal du Lion (Belgium), 1955. *Recreations:* photography, gardening, ornithology. *Address:* 6 Hillworth House, Hillworth Road, Devizes, Wilts SN10 5EX. *T:* Devizes 71564.

*Died* 30 Nov. 1989.

**BREARLEY, Sir Norman,** Kt 1971; CBE 1965; DSO 1916; MC; AFC; FRAeS; Company Director, Western Australia, retired 1977; *b* Geelong, Vic., 22 Dec. 1890; *s* of late Robert Hillard Brearley, Perth, WA; *m* 1917, Violet, *d* of late Hon. Sydney Stubbs, CMG, MLA, Perth; one *s* one *d. Educ:* state and private schs, Geelong; Technical Coll., Perth, WA. Enlisted, after engineering training. Served War, RFC and RAF, also Major in Liverpool Regt, France and England, 1914–1919 (wounded, despatches, AFC, MC, DSO). War of 1939–45; Gp Capt., RAAF. Founder (1921) of West Australian Airways; was the first airmail contractor to Australian Govt. Pioneer of Australian Air Services. *Publication:* Australian Aviator, 1971. *Recreations:* tennis, golf. *Address:* 6 Esplanade, Peppermint Grove, Cottesloe, WA 6011, Australia. *T:* 312293. *Club:* Weld (Perth, WA).

*Died* 9 June 1989.

**BRECKNOCK, Marjorie Countess of, (Marjorie Minna),** DBE 1967; Superintendent-in-Chief, St John Ambulance Brigade, 1960–70, retired, Chief President, 1972–83; *b* 28 Mar. 1900; *o c* of late Col A. E. Jenkins and of late Mrs Anna Jenkins, Wherwell Priory, Andover, Hants; *m* 1920, Earl of Brecknock (later 5th Marquess Camden; from whom she obtained a divorce, 1941); one *s* (6th Marquess Camden); one *d. Educ:* at home and Heathfield, Ascot. A Lady-in-waiting to Princess Marina, Duchess of Kent, 1937–39. War of 1939–45: Company Asst, ATS, 1940; Junior Commander, 1941; Senior Commander, 1942 (Senior ATS Officer SHAEF, 1944–45); despatches 1945; Bronze Star (USA), 1945. Commanded 310 (Southern Command) Bn WRAC (TA), 1948–54. Joined St John Ambulance Brigade HQ, 1947; appointed Controller Overseas Dept, 1950. GCStJ 1971 (DStJ 1958). Mem. Order of Mercy. *Publication:* Edwina Mountbatten—her life in pictures, 1961. *Recreations:* gardening, shooting, travelling, fishing. *Address:* Wherwell Priory, Andover, Hampshire. *T:* Chilbolton 388.
*Died 24 Aug. 1989.*

**BREDIN, George Richard Frederick,** CBE 1947; MA; Sudan Political Service (retired); Hon. Fellow of Pembroke College, Oxford; *b* 8 June 1899; *s* of late Dr Richard Bredin, Valparaiso, Chile; *m* 1932, Dorothy Wall, *d* of late T. R. Ellison, West Kirby, Cheshire; one *s* one *d. Educ:* Clifton College; Oriel College, Oxford. MA (Oxon) 1925; served European War, Lieut RE (64th Field Company) (despatches), 1917–18. Oriel College, Oxford 1919–21; Hons Degree in Lit. Hum. (Distinction), 1921. Asst District Comr, Sudan Political Service, 1921; District Comr, 1930; Dep. Governor, 1935; Dep. Civil Sec., 1939; Governor Blue Nile Province, Sudan, 1941–48; Mem., Governor-General's Council, 1945–48; Chm., Governing Body of Gordon Meml University Coll., Khartoum, 1945–48; retired, 1948. Asst Registrar, Univ. of Liverpool, 1948–49; Fellow and Bursar, Pembroke Coll., Oxford, 1950–66; a Church Comr, 1951–; Chm., Oxford Diocesan Board of Finance, 1956–58; Chm., Oxford Diocesan Trusts Corp., 1965–70; a Curator of the Oxford Univ. Chest, 1957–69. Chm. of Governors of Abingdon Sch., 1966–72; Vice-Chm., Dorset House Sch. of Occupational Therapy, Oxford; Mem. Exec. Cttee, Gordon Boys School, Woking; Oxford City Councillor, 1965–67. Order of the Nile (3rd Cl.), 1937. *Address:* Rough Lea, Boar's Hill, Oxford. *T:* Oxford 735375.
*Died 30 Sept. 1983.*

**BRENAN, (Edward Fitz-) Gerald,** CBE 1982; MC 1918; author; *b* 7 April 1894; English; *m* 1931, Elisabeth Gamel Woolsey (*d* 1968); one *d. Educ:* self-educated. Served War: Croix de Guerre, 1918. *Publications:* The Spanish Labyrinth, 1943; The Face of Spain, 1950; The Literature of the Spanish People, 1953; South from Granada, 1957; A Holiday by the Sea, 1961; A Life of One's Own (autobiog.), 1962; The Lighthouse Always Says Yes, 1966; St John of the Cross: his life and poetry, 1971; Personal Record (autobiog.), 1974; Thoughts in a Dry Season, 1978. *Recreations:* walking and talking. *Address:* c/o Jonathan Cape, 32 Bedford Square, WC1B 3EL.
*Died 19 Jan. 1987.*

**BRENAN, John Patrick Micklethwait,** MA, BSc Oxon; FLS; FIBiol; Director, Royal Botanic Gardens, Kew, 1976–81; *b* 19 June 1917; *s* of Alexander Richard Micklethwait Brenan, MD, and Jill Fraser Brenan (*née* Parker); *m* 1950, Jean Helen Edwardes; one *s* two *d. Educ:* Tonbridge; Brasenose Coll., Oxford. At Imperial Forestry Inst., Oxford, 1940–48; Mem. Cambridge Botanical Expedn to Nigeria and Cameroons, 1948; apptd Sen. Scientific Officer in the Herbarium, Royal Botanic Gardens, Kew, 1948; Principal Sci. Off., 1954; i/c of Tropical African Section, 1959–65; Keeper of the Herbarium, and Dep. Dir, Royal Botanic Gardens 1965–76. Vis. Prof., Univ. of Reading, 1977. Hon. Botanical Adviser, Commonwealth War Graves Commn, 1978–82; Dir, Internat. Council for Develt of Underutilized Plants, 1981–. Pres., Assoc. for Tropical Biology, 1970–71; Pres., Botanical Soc. of the British Isles, 1981–83 (Vice Pres., 1978–81); Botanical Sec., Linnean Soc. of London, 1965–72; Member: Westonbirt Adv. Cttee, Forestry Commn, 1975– (Chm., 1984); Council, RHS, 1979–; Council, Nat. Trust 1982–. Hon. Mem., Sociedade Broteriana, 1978. FRSA 1978. VMH 1979; Special Medal, South African Assoc. of Botanists, 1982. *Publications:* Check List of the Forest Trees and Shrubs of Tanganyika Territory, 1949 (with Dr P. J. Greenway); contrib. various accounts to Flora of Tropical East Africa, etc.; numerous papers on flowering plants of Europe and Africa in scientific jls. *Recreations:* reading, fishing, natural history, walking. *Address:* 24 Taylor Avenue, Kew Gardens, Richmond, Surrey. *T:* 01–876 6062. *Club:* Athenæum.
*Died 26 Sept. 1985.*

**BRENNAN, Lt-Gen. Michael;** retired as Chief Superintendent of Divisions, Office of Public Works, Dublin; *m* Bridget (decd); one *s* two *d.* Chief of Staff, Irish Army, 1931–40. *Address:* South Hill, Killiney, Co. Dublin.
*Died 24 Oct. 1986.*

**BRENTFORD, 3rd Viscount,** *cr* 1929; Bt, *cr* 1919 and 1956; **Lancelot William Joynson-Hicks;** DL; solicitor; formerly Senior Partner of Joynson-Hicks & Co.; elected Member, Church Assembly, 1934–70; *b* 10 April 1902; 2nd *s* of 1st Viscount Brentford, PC, DL, and Grace Lynn (*d* 1952), *o c* of Richard Hampson Joynson, JP, Bowdon, Cheshire; *S* brother, 1958; *m* 1931, Phyllis (*d* 1979), *o d* of late Major Herbert Allfrey, Newnton House, Tetbury, Gloucestershire; one *s. Educ:* Winchester College; Trinity College, Oxford (MA). Admitted a Solicitor, 1926. Served War of 1939–45 as acting Lt-Comdr, RNVR. MP (C) Chichester Division of West Sussex, 1942–58; Parliamentary Secretary, Ministry of Fuel and Power, Nov. 1951–Dec. 1955. Chairman, Automobile Association, 1956–74. Pres., Southern Regional Assoc. for the Blind, 1972–. DL East Sussex, 1977. *Heir: s* Hon. Crispin William Joynson-Hicks [*b* 7 April 1933; *m* 1964, Gillian Evelyn, *er d* of G. E. Schluter, OBE, Valehyrst, Sevenoaks; one *s* three *d. Educ:* Eton; New College, Oxford]. *Address:* Newick Park, East Sussex.
*Died 25 Feb. 1983.*

**BRETT, George P(latt), jun.;** retired from The Macmillan Company, New York, 1961; *b* Darien, Conn., 9 Dec. 1893; *s* of George Platt and Marie Louise (Tostevan) Brett; *m* 1917, Isabel Yeomans; two *s. Educ:* Collegiate School, New York City; Salisbury School, Salisbury, Conn. Joined staff of The Macmillan Company, Sept. 1913; six months training with competing publishing house, Doubleday, 1915. Served European War, 1914–18, with US Army, private 1916, 2nd Lieut 1917, 1st Lieut Jan. 1918, Capt. July 1918, 16 months service in France, 1918–19; Maj. Reserve Corps until 1940; Lieut-Col, Asst Chief of Staff, NY Guard, 1940–43; Adviser to War Production Board, State Dept, 1943–45. Returned to Macmillan, 1919; Dir and Sales Manager, 1920; Treas., 1920–31; General Manager, 1928–34; Pres., 1931–58; Chairman of the Board, 1959–61. Trustee: Union Square Savings Bank, New York City, 1926–61; Southport (Connecticut) Savings Bank, 1954–58. President: Sasquanaug Assoc. for Southport Improvement, 1954–56; Pequot Library, Southport, Connecticut, 1955–56. *Publications:* occasional contributor to trade journals. *Recreations:* walking, sailing, fishing. *Address:* (home) 240 Main Street, Southport, Connecticut 06490, USA. *Clubs:* Century, Players, Cruising of America (New York); Pequot Yacht (Cdre, 1951–53); Fairfield County Hunt (Conn); Lake Placid (NY); Key Largo Anglers' (Fla).
*Died 11 Feb. 1984.*

**BRETT, Sir Lionel,** Kt 1961; *b* 19 Aug. 1911; 3rd *s* of late Very Rev. H. R. Brett, Dean of Belfast, and Constance Brett (*née* White). *Educ:* Marlborough; Magdalen College, Oxford. BA 1934; MA 1946. Called to Bar, Inner Temple, 1937. War service, 1939–46, released as Major. Joined Colonial Legal Service as Crown Counsel, Nigeria, 1946; Justice, Supreme Court of Nigeria, 1958–68. *Recreations:* reading, walking. *Address:* Lower Ground Floor, 12 Sydney Place, Bath BA2 6NF. *Club:* United Oxford & Cambridge University.
*Died 10 Sept. 1990.*

**BRETT-JAMES, (Eliot) Antony;** author (Military History); Head of War Studies and International Affairs Department, Royal Military Academy Sandhurst, 1970–80 (Deputy Head, 1968–69); *b* 4 April 1920; *er surv. s* of late Norman George Brett-James, MA, BLitt, FSA, Mill Hill, and Gladys Brett-James. *Educ:* Mill Hill Sch.; Paris; Sidney Sussex Coll., Cambridge. 2nd cl. Mod. Langs Tripos, 1947; MA. Served War of 1939–45: Royal Signals, 2nd Lt, 1941; 2nd Air Formation Signals; Lebanon, Syria; 5th Indian Divl Signals, in Alamein Line, 1942; Iraq, India; Capt., 1943; commanded 9th Indian Inf. Bde Signals, Arakan, Imphal, Burma (despatches), 1944; Burma, 1945. Entered publishing: George G. Harrap (mod. langs editor), 1947–52; Chatto & Windus (reader and publicity manager), 1952–58; Cassell, 1958–61 (educl manager, 1960–61). Lectr, then Sen. Lectr, in Mil. Hist., RMA Sandhurst, 1961–67. Helped Field Marshal Montgomery write A History of Warfare, 1964–68; Mil. Advr, BBC TV for Tolstoy's War and Peace, 1971–72. Question setter for Mastermind, BBC TV, 1974–. Mem., RUSI. *Publications:* Report My Signals, 1948; Ball of Fire: the 5th Indian Division in the Second World War, 1951; The Triple Stream, 1953; General Graham, Lord Lynedoch, 1959; Wellington at War, 1794–1815, 1961; (with Lt-Gen. Sir G. Evans) Imphal, 1962; The Hundred Days, 1964; 1812, 1966; The British Soldier 1793–1815, 1970; Europe against Napoleon, 1970; Daily Life in Wellington's Army, 1972; (ed) Escape from the French: Captain Hewson's Narrative, 1981; articles in: Dictionary of National Biography, History Today, Purnell's History of the Second World War; reviews in TLS. *Recreations:* meeting people, watching cricket, restricted gardining from a wheelchair, music. *Address:* Vine Cottage, Steep, Petersfield, Hants. *T:* Petersfield 64927.
*Died 25 March 1984.*

**BREWER, Frank,** CMG 1960; OBE 1953; Foreign and Commonwealth Office (formerly Foreign Office), 1960–76; *b* 1915; *s* of late Lewis Arthur Brewer; *m* 1950, Eileen Marian, *d* of A. J. Shepherd. *Educ:* Swindon Commonweal School; Pembroke College, Oxford (MA). Malayan Civil Service, 1937–59; War Service, 1941–45, Special Forces (POW Sumatra) Chinese Secretariat, Labour Dept; Secretary for Chinese Affairs and Dep. Chief Sec., Fed. of Malaya, 1955–57; Sec. for Defence, 1957–59. *Address:* 18

Forest Way, Tunbridge Wells, Kent. *T:* Tunbridge Wells 24850. *Clubs:* Royal Commonwealth Society, Special Forces.

*Died 21 Dec.* 1987.

**BREWIS, (Henry) John;** Lord-Lieutenant of Wigtown, since 1981; Director, Border Television Ltd, since 1977; Managing Director, Ardwell Estates, Stranraer; farming; *b* 8 April 1920; *s* of Lt-Col F. B. Brewis, Norton Grove, Malton, Yorks; *m* 1949, Faith A. D. MacTaggart Stewart, Ardwell, Wigtownshire; three *s* one *d. Educ:* Eton; New College, Oxford. Served Royal Artillery, 1940–46 (despatches twice); on active service, North Africa and Italy; demobilized with rank of Major. Barrister-at-law, 1946. Wigtownshire County Council, 1955; Convener, Finance Cttee, 1958. MP (C) Galloway, April 1959–Sept. 1974; PPS to The Lord Advocate, 1960–61; Speaker's Panel of Chairmen, 1965; Chm., Select Cttee on Scottish Affairs, 1970; Member British Delegn: to Council of Europe, 1966–69; to European Parlt, Strasbourg, 1973–75; Vice-Chm., Cons. Agric. Cttee, 1971; Chm., Scottish Cons. Gp for Europe, 1973–76. Dist Chm., Queen's Jubilee Appeal, 1976–78. Reg. Chm., Scottish Landowners' Fedn, 1977–80; Chm., Timber Growers Scotland Ltd, 1980–83; Vice-Chm., Forestry Cttee for GB; Mem., Comité Central Propriété Forestière, Brussels, 1979, and other forestry cttees. *Recreations:* golf, tennis, shooting. *Address:* Ardwell House, Stranraer. *T:* Ardwell 227; Norton Grove, Malton, N Yorks. *Clubs:* Caledonian; New (Edinburgh).

*Died 25 May* 1989.

**BREWIS, John Fenwick,** CMG 1962; CVO 1957; HM Diplomatic Service (retired); *b* 26 April 1910; *s* of late Arthur and Mary Brewis; *m* 1948, Rachel Mary, *d* of late Hilary G. Gardner; one *s* one *d. Educ:* Repton; CCC, Camb. Entered China Consular Service in 1933 and served in China till 1944; First Secretary, Baghdad, 1946–49; Consul, Bordeaux, 1950–52; Foreign Office, 1945–46, 1954–55 and 1959–65; Counsellor, Lisbon, 1955–59; Consul-General, Lyons, 1965–67. Tourist and Publicity Officer for Winchester, 1968–75. *Recreations:* gardening, historical reading. *Address:* 49 St Cross Road, Winchester. *T:* Winchester 54187.

*Died 11 Jan.* 1986.

**BREWSTER, Kingman;** Lawyer; Master of University College, Oxford, since 1986; Counsel in London to Winthrop, Stimson, Putnam and Roberts, NYC, since 1981; *b* Longmeadow, Massachusetts, 17 June 1919; *s* of Kingman Brewster and Florence Besse; *m* 1942, Mary Louise Phillips; three *s* two *d. Educ:* Yale University; Harvard University. AB Yale, 1941; LLB Harvard, 1948. Military Service: Lieut (Aviation) USNR, 1942–46. Special Asst Coordinator Inter-American Affairs, 1941; Research Assoc., Dept Economics, Massachusetts Inst. of Technology, 1949–50; Asst. General Counsel, Office US Special Representative in Europe, 1948–49; Cons., Pres. Materials Policy Commn, 1951, Mutual Security Agency, 1952; Asst Prof. of Law, Harvard, 1950–58; Prof. of Law, Harvard, 1953–60; Provost, Yale, 1961–63; Pres., Yale Univ., 1963–77; Ambassador to Court of St James's, 1977–81. Member: President's Commn on Law Enforcement and Administration of Justice, 1965–67; President's Commn on Selective Service, 1966–68; Fulbright Commn, 1986–; Bd of Dirs, Carnegie Endowment Fund for Internat. Peace, 1975–; Internat. Bd, United World Colleges (Chm., 1986–88); American Trust, British Library; Council of Management, Amer. Ditchley Foundn. Trustee, Reuters, 1984–. Member: Council on Foreign Relations; American Philosophical Soc. Lectures: Stevens, Royal Coll. of Med., 1977; St George's House, 1977; Tanner, Clare Hall, 1984; MacDermott, QUB, 1986; Goodman, 1986. Holds many Hon. Degrees; Hon. Fellow, Clare Coll., Cambridge, 1977. Officer, Legion of Honour, 1977. *Publications:* Antitrust and American Business Abroad, 1959, rev. edn (with J. Atwood), 1981; (with M. Katz) Law of International Transactions and Relations, 1960. *Recreation:* sailing. *Address:* Master's Lodgings, University College, Oxford OX1 4BH. *T:* Oxford 276600; (office) Salisbury House, Finsbury Circus, EC2M 5RQ. *Clubs:* Athenæum, Buck's; Metropolitan (Washington); Yale, Century Association (New York); Tavern (Boston, Mass).

*Died 8 Nov.* 1988.

**BREZHNEV, Leonid Ilyich;** Order of Victory; Hero of the Soviet Union (two awards); five Orders of Lenin; two Orders of the Red Banner; Order of Bogdan Khmelnitsky (2nd cl.); Order of the Patriotic War (1st cl.); two Orders of the October Revolution; Order of the Red Star; Hero of Socialist Labour; Chairman of the Presidium, Supreme Soviet of USSR, since 1977 (President, 1960–64); General Secretary (formerly First Secretary) of the Central Committee, CPSU, since 1964; *b* Kamenskoye (now Dnieprodzerzhinsk), Ukraine, 19 Dec. 1906. *Educ:* Institute of Metallurgy, Dnieprodzerzhinsk (graduate). Began career as engineer and was active in social work. Joined Communist Party, 1931; 1st Secretary, Central Cttee, Communist Party of Moldavia, 1950. Elected to Supreme Soviet of USSR, 1950, 1954, 1958, 1962. Central Committee CPSU: Mem., 1952–; Alternate Mem., 1952–57, Mem., 1957–; Presidium; Mem., Party Secretariat, 1952–53, 1956–57, 1963–; Sec., Central Cttee, Communist Party, Kazakhstan, 1954–56.

Maj.-Gen. 1943; Lieut-Gen. 1953. Lenin Peace Prize, 1972; Lenin Prize for Literature, 1979. Karl Marx Gold Medal, USSR Acad. of Scis, 1977. Gold Star, Vietnam, 1980. *Publications:* Little Land, 1978; Rebirth, 1978; Virgin Lands, 1978; Socialism, Democracy and Human Rights, 1981. *Address:* Central Committee, CPSU, Kremlin, Moscow, USSR.

*Died 10 Nov.* 1982.

**BRIANCE, John Albert,** CMG 1960; HM Diplomatic Service, retired; *b* 19 Oct. 1915; *s* of late Albert Perceval and Louise Florence Briance; *m* 1950, Prunella Mary, *d* of Col E. Haldane Chapman; one *s* one *d. Educ:* King Edward VII School. Colonial Police, Palestine, 1936–48; Foreign Office, 1949; British Embassy, Tehran, 1950–52; British Middle East Office, 1953; Foreign Office, 1954–57; Counsellor, British Embassy, Washington, 1958–60; Counsellor, Office of UK Commissioner for SE Asia Singapore, 1961–63; FCO (formerly FO), 1964–70; retired 1970. *Address:* 14 Pitt Street, W8. *Clubs:* Naval and Military, Hurlingham.

*Died 2 Dec.* 1989.

**BRICKER, John William,** LLB; Lawyer, USA; Republican; *b* 6 Sept. 1893; *s* of Lemuel Spencer Bricker and Laura (*née* King); *m* 1920, Harriet Day; one *s. Educ:* State Univ., Ohio. AB 1916; admitted to Bar, Ohio, 1917; LLB 1920. Solicitor, Grandview Heights, 1920–28; Assistant Attorney-General of Ohio, 1923–27; Attorney-General, 1933–37. Governor of Ohio, 1939–41, 1941–43, 1943–45. Candidate (Republican) for US Vice-Presidency, 1944; Senator from Ohio, 1947–58. Member firm of Bricker & Eckler. Member Public Utilities Commission, Ohio, 1929–32. LLD Ohio State University, 1940. Served European War, 1917–18, 1st Lieut. *Address:* 100 East Broad Street, Columbus, Ohio 43215–3670, USA; 2407 Tremont Road, Columbus, Ohio 43221, USA.

*Died 22 March* 1986.

**BRIDGEMAN, 2nd Viscount,** *cr* 1929, of Leigh; **Robert Clive Bridgeman,** KBE 1954; CB 1944; DSO 1940; MC; psc; JP; HM Lieutenant of County of Salop, 1951–Dec. 1969; *b* April 1896; *e s* of 1st Viscount and Caroline Beatrix, DBE (*d* 1961), *er d* of Hon. Cecil Parker; *S* father, 1935; *m* 1930, Mary Kathleen (*d* 1981), 2nd *d* of Baron Bingley, PC; three *d. Educ:* Eton College. 2nd Lieut, The Rifle Bde, 1914; Lieut, 1916; Captain, 1921; Bt Major, 1932; Bt Lieut-Col, 1935, acting Maj.-Gen., 1941; Col and Temp. Maj.-Gen., 1942; served European War (France), 1915–18; Private Secretary to his father when Parliamentary Secretary to Minister of Labour, 1918; Brigade Major, 7th Infantry Brigade, 1932–34; GSO2 War Office, 1935–37; retired pay, 1937; served War of 1939–45 (DSO); Deputy Director, Home Guard, 1941; Director-General, Home Guard and Territorial Army, 1941–44; Deputy Adjt-General, 1944–45. Pres., West Midland TA&VRA, 1968–69. Vice-Chm., Trust Houses Forte Council, 1971–. Alderman, Salop CC, 1951–74. JP Salop, 1951. *Heir: nephew* Robin John Orlando Bridgeman [*b* 5 Dec. 1930; *m* 1966, Harriet Lucy Turton; three *s*]. *Address:* Leigh Manor, Minsterley, Salop SY5 0EX. *T:* Worthen 210. *Club:* Naval and Military.

*Died 17 Nov.* 1982.

**BRIDGES, John Gourlay,** OBE 1954 (MBE 1944); Consultant: Tourism Promotion, Travel and Capital Development; Supervisor, Press, Publicity and Information to Church of Scotland, 1967–72; Director-General, British Travel and Holidays Association, 1945–63, retd; *b* 5 Dec. 1901; *e s* of late David McKay Bridges and late Margaret Gourlay Bridges, Glasgow; *m* 1931, Marion, *d* of late Andrew Bell, MBE, JP, Glasgow; one *s* one *d. Educ:* elementary and secondary schools, Glasgow; Glasgow and West of Scotland Commercial College and School of Accountancy. Secretary, and latterly Director-Secretary, of private Ltd. Co., Glasgow and London, 1922–24; Accountant, Straits Trading Co. Ltd., Singapore and FM States, 1924–30; Sec. at Edinburgh, and later Gen. Sec. for Scotland, of The Overseas League, 1931–35; then Development Sec. of the movement; Development Sec., Overseas League and Gen. Sec., Overseas League in Canada, 1935–38; Gen. Tours Manager, Donaldson Atlantic Line, Great Britain, Canada and USA, 1939. Served in RAF as Embarkation Officer (Personnel) Liverpool, 1940–45; demobilized with rank of Squadron Leader, 1945. Pres. 1960, and Mem., Council of Honour, International Union of Official Travel Organizations (with consultative status UN). Director of Studies and Professor of Tourism, Hawaii Univ., 1964–65. FRGS; Associate Institute of Transport. Member: Association of Scientific Tourism Experts; Exec. Cttee, Scottish Council for Development and Industry; Scottish Tourist Cons. Council. Freeman, City of London, 1962. *Publications:* numerous articles on Travel and allied subjects. *Recreations:* motoring, fishing, gardening. *Address:* 35A Cluny Drive, Edinburgh EH10 6DT. *T:* 031–447 4966. *Club:* Royal Over-Seas League.

*Died 15 Oct.* 1985.

**BRIERLEY, Captain Henry,** CBE 1960 (OBE 1942); MC 1917; House Governor, The London Hospital, 1939–62, retired; *b* 10 Aug. 1897; *s* of James William and Zoe Brierley, Rochdale; *m* 1931, Bettine Ariana (*d* 1969), *d* of Sir William Curtis, 4th Baronet, Caynham, Ludlow, Salop; one *d. Educ:* Shrewsbury. Commissioned Rifle Bde, 1916; served European War, 1914–18, Iraq, 1919–20; Adjt 1st Bn, 1921–24; Adjt London Rifle Brigade, 1925–29; retired 1929. The

London Hospital, 1929; Secretary, 1938. Joint Master Eridge Foxhounds, 1962–68. *Recreation:* foxhunting. *Address:* Stile House, Mark Cross, Crowborough, East Sussex. *T:* Rotherfield 2883.
*Died* 15 *March* 1981.

**BRIGGS, Hon. Sir Francis Arthur,** Kt 1961; a Federal Justice of Supreme Court, Federation of Rhodesia and Nyasaland, 1958–63, retired; *b* 9 July 1902; *yr s* of late William Francis Briggs, Preston, Lancs, and Jane Greig, *yr d* of late Thomas Macmillan, Glasgow; *m* 1953, Edna Dorothy, *d* of late William Thomas Keylock; no *c*. *Educ:* Charterhouse (Schol.); Trinity College, Oxford (Open Classical Schol.). Called to Bar, Inner Temple (Cert. of Honour and Jardine Studentship), 1927. Advocate and Solicitor, FMS, SS and Johore, 1928–40. Served in RAFVR, 1940–46 (despatches), Wing Commander. Colonial Legal Service, 1947; Registrar, Supreme Court, Federation of Malaya, 1948; Puisne Judge, Malaya, 1949; Justice of Appeal, E African Court of Appeal, 1953, Vice-President, 1957. *Address:* Shillingford, La Brecque, Alderney, Channel Islands. *T:* 2019. *Died* 6 *July* 1983.

**BRIGGS, Prof. George Edward,** MA; FRS 1935; Fellow of St John's College, Cambridge (President, 1952–63); Professor Emeritus of Botany, Cambridge University; Professor of Botany, 1948–60, Professor of Plant Physiology, 1946–48, Cambridge University; *b* 25 June 1893; *m* 1920, Nora Burman; one *s* one *d*. *Educ:* Wintringham Grammar School; St John's College, Cambridge. *Publications:* Electrolytes and Plant Cells (with A. B. Hope and R. N. Robertson), 1961; Movement of Water in Plants, 1967. *Address:* 1 Margery Lane, Tewin, Welwyn, Herts AL6 0JP. *T:* Tewin 7419.
*Died* 7 *Feb.* 1985.

**BRIGGS, Maj.-Gen. Raymond,** CB 1943; DSO 1942; psc†; President, Metropolitan Area, Royal British Legion; *b* 19 Jan. 1895; *yr s* of late James Burnett Briggs, Claughton, Cheshire; *m* 1927, Helen Wainwright (*d* 1984), *d* of Charles Edward Kenworthy, Liverpool and New Orleans; one *d*. Served European War, 1914–18, France, Belgium, and Mesopotamia, Liverpool Scottish, King's Own Regt, and MGC, 2nd Lieut, 1915 (wounded twice); Royal Tank Corps, 1920; Bt Major, 1933; Bt Lt-Col, 1938; Colonel, 1941; Acting Brig., 1940; Major-General, 1944. Served War of 1939–45, France and Belgium, 1940 (GSO 1), Middle East and North Africa, 1941–43 (Comd 2 Armd Bde, GOC 1 Armd Division); Director, Royal Armoured Corps, War Office, 1943–47. Member Tank Board, 1943–46 (wounded, despatches twice, DSO, CB, Commander Legion of Merit, USA); retired, 1947. *Address:* 1 Linden Gardens, W2 4HA. *T:* 01–229 3711. *Club:* Army and Navy.
*Died* 4 *April* 1985.

**BRIGHT, Hon. Sir Charles (Hart),** KBE 1980; Chancellor, Flinders University, since 1971; *b* 25 Nov. 1912; *s* of Rev. Charles Bright and Annie Florence Bright; *m* 1940, Elizabeth Holden, *d* of H. B. Flaxman; two *s* one *d*. *Educ:* Scotch Coll.; Univ. of Adelaide (BA, LLB). Called to the Bar of SA, 1934; QC 1960; Judge, Supreme Court of SA, 1963–78, retd. Pres., Law Soc. of SA, 1960–61; Vice-Pres., Law Council of Aust., 1960–61; Chm., SA Health Cttee, 1979–80; Mem., various Royal Commns and Enquiries. Hon. DLitt Flinders, 1983. *Publications:* The Confidential Clerk, 1984; contrib. learned jls. *Recreations:* reading, travelling. *Address:* 1A/97 MacKinnon Parade, North Adelaide, SA 5006, Australia. *T:* 267.3081. *Club:* Adelaide (Adelaide). *Died* 16 *May* 1983.

**BRINCKMAN, Colonel Sir Roderick (Napoleon),** 5th Bt, *cr* 1831; DSO 1940; MC 1941; *b* 27 Dec. 1902; 2nd *s* of Colonel Sir Theodore Brinckman, 3rd Bt, CB; *S* brother 1954; *m* 1st, 1931, Margaret Southam, Ottawa, Canada; two *s*; 2nd, 1942, Rosemary Marguerite Gilbey, *yr d* of late Lt-Col J. C. Hope Vere, Blackwood, Lanarkshire; one *d*. *Educ:* Osborne; Dartmouth. Served in Royal Navy two years (HMS Temeraire, Barham); joined Grenadier Guards in 1922; ADC to Lord Somers (Governor of Victoria), 1926–27; ADC to Lord Willingdon (Governor-General of Canada), 1930–31; served in Egypt, 1931–32, and France, 1940 (DSO, MC, despatches); commanded 2nd (Armoured) Bn Grenadier Guards, 1943; Chief of Staff Military Mission in Moscow, 1944–45; head of British Military Mission to the Netherlands Government in London, 1945–46. *Heir:* *s* Theodore George Roderick Brinckman [*b* 20 March 1932; *m* 1958, Helen Mary Anne, *d* of A. E. Cook, Toronto; two *s* one *d*; *m* 1983, Hon. Mrs Sheira Murray]. *Address:* 7 Mallord Street, Chelsea, SW3 6DT. *T:* 01–352 9935; Cross Keys, Fisher Street, Sandwich, Kent; St Helena, Barbados, BWI. *Club:* White's.
*Died* 16 *April* 1985.

**BRIND, George Walter Richard;** Secretary-General, The Stock Exchange, 1971–75; *b* 13 Oct. 1911; *er s* of late Walter Charles and late Mary Josephine Brind; *m* 1942, Joyce, *er d* of late Matthew and Mary Graham; two *d*. *Educ:* Chiswick. Joined staff of Council of Stock Exchange, London, 1928, and has had no other employment than that with the Exchange. President: English Indoor Bowling Assoc., 1979–80; British Isles Indoor Bowling Assoc., 1983–84. *Recreation:* bowls. *Address:* 7 Amberley Close, Send, Woking, Surrey. *T:* Guildford 223762. *Died* 13 *June* 1988.

**BRINKWORTH, George Harold,** CBE 1960; Legal Adviser and Solicitor to Pay Board, 1973–74; *b* 16 Nov. 1906; *yr s* of George Alban Brinkworth and Hana Mary Brinkworth; *m* 1935, Dorothy Betty Suffield; one *s* one *d*. *Educ:* Wimbledon College; University College, London. LLB (Lond.) 1927. Admitted Solicitor, 1931. Entered Solicitor's Dept, Ministry of Labour, 1935; transf. to Ministry of Nat. Insce, 1945; Asst Solicitor, Min. of Pensions and Nat. Insce, 1948; Principal Asst Sol., DHSS (formerly Min. of Social Security), 1965–71. *Address:* 22 Stevens Parade, Black Rock, Victoria 3193, Australia. *T:* Melbourne 598–6556.
*Died* 11 *Aug.* 1989.

**BRINTON, Denis Hubert,** DM Oxon; FRCP; retired; *b* 9 Dec. 1902; *er s* of Hubert Brinton, Eton College; *m* 1st, 1928, Joan Violet (*d* 1971), *d* of James A. Hood; one *s* (and one *s* decd); 2nd, 1972, Rosemary Cockerill. *Educ:* Eton; New College, Oxford University; St Mary's Hospital, London University. MRCS, LRCP 1927; BM, BCh, 1928; MRCP 1929; DM Oxon 1937; FRCP 1938. Served War of 1939–45 (despatches), Air Commodore, RAF, Consultant in Neuropsychiatry. Member Internat. Neurological Congress, London, 1935; Physician-in-charge, Department of Nervous Diseases, St Mary's Hospital, 1935–63; Dean, St Mary's Hospital Medical School, 1946–51; Physician, National Hospital for Nervous Diseases, 1935–65; Council RCP, 1956–59. Member Assoc. British Neurologists; Member Assoc. Physicians Great Britain; Ed. Quart. Jl Med., 1954–68. *Publications:* Cerebrospinal Fever, 1941; articles in medical jls. *Address:* Bromfields, Burley, near Ringwood, Hants BH24 4HH. *T:* Burley 2319. *Died* 13 *March* 1986.

**BRINTON, Major Sir (Esme) Tatton (Cecil),** Kt 1964; President, Brintons Ltd, Kidderminster, since 1981 (Joint Managing Director, 1952–81, Chairman, 1968–81); *b* 4 Jan. 1916; *o s* of Colonel Cecil Charles Brinton, JP, and Cathleen Cecil Brinton (*née* Maude); *m* 1st, 1938, Mary Elizabeth Fahnestock (*d* 1960); four *s* one *d*; 2nd, 1961, Mrs Irene Sophie Borthwick (*d* 1978); 3rd, 1979, Mrs Mary Ellen Cappel. *Educ:* Eton; Caius College, Cambridge; and in Vienna and Paris. Served with XIIth R. Lancers, France, Desert, Italy, 1939–45. Technical Intelligence, Germany, 1945–46. Contested (C) Dudley, 1945; MP (C) Kidderminster, 1964–Feb. 74; Mayor of Kidderminster, 1953–54; High Sheriff of Worcestershire, 1961–62; President: Kidderminster Conservative Assoc., 1981– (Chm., 1955–56 and 1958–61); W Midlands Cons. Union, 1972–75 (Treasurer, 1958–61; Chm., 1962–64); Jt Treasurer of Conservative Party, 1966–74. Pres., Fedn of British Carpet Manufrs, 1974–76 (Chm., Home Exec. Cttee, 1960–64); Pres., British Carpet Manufrs Assoc., 1976; Chm British Carpets Promotion Council, 1960–66. High Steward of Kidderminster, 1978–. DL Worcs, 1968–81. OStJ 1962. *Address:* 35D Queens Gate, SW7. *Club:* Carlton.
*Died* 26 *Sept.* 1985.

**BRISCOE, Captain Henry Villiers,** CIE 1945; OBE 1943; RN (retd); *b* 9 Nov. 1896; *s* of late Maj. A. V. Briscoe, late RA, and G. M. Briscoe; *m* 1925, Lily Miller, widow (decd); one *s*; *m* 1948, Adaline Mary, *d* of Adam McIntosh, South Bantaskine, Falkirk, Stirling. *Educ:* Yarlet Hall, Staffs; RN Colleges, Osborne and Dartmouth. Royal Navy, 1909–22; Commercial Employment, 1922–31. Colonial Civil Servant, 1931–51; recalled to RN 1941–45; retd from Colonial Service, 1951. *Address:* 1 Thanet House, 4 Vernon Square, Ryde, IoW PO33 2JG. *Died* 22 *Oct.* 1983.

**BRISTOL, 6th Marquess of,** *cr* 1826; **Victor Frederick Cochrane Hervey;** Baron Hervey, 1703; Earl of Bristol, 1714; Earl Jermyn, 1826; *b* 6 Oct. 1915; *s* of 5th Marquess of Bristol; *S* father 1960; *m* 1st, 1949, Pauline Mary (marr. diss. 1959), *d* of late Herbert Coxon Bolton; one *s*; 2nd, 1960, Lady Anne Juliet Wentworth Fitzwilliam (marr. diss. 1972), *o c* of 8th Earl Fitzwilliam, DSC, and of Olive Countess Fitzwilliam, Co. Wicklow; one *s*; 3rd, 1974, Yvonne Marie, *d* of Anthony Sutton; one *s* two *d*. *Educ:* Eton; Royal Military College. The Hereditary High Steward of the Liberty of St Edmund; Grand Master, High Stewards' Assoc.; Hereditary Lord High Interrogator; Patron of 30 Livings; had estates in W, N and E Suffolk, Lincs, Essex, Dominica. Former owner of Ickworth Stud. Founder and first Pres., Nat. Yacht Harbour Assoc.; Vice Pres., Income Tax Payers' Union; Member: West India Cttee; Monday Club; Inst. of Dirs; European Atlantic Group. Mem., Royal Celtic Soc.; Chancellor and Ambassador-at-Large, Monarchist League; Life Governor, Royal Soc. of St George. Director of 30 other companies. Formerly: an expert on Central American Affairs and adviser to Govts; Chm., de Jersey & Co. (Finland) Ltd; Mil. Advr to Finnish Govt (1960). Sen. Mem., Niadh Nask; a Knight of Mark Twain; Kt Grand Cross, Mil. Order of St Lazarus of Jerusalem; Grand Officer, Royal Order of St Alexander (1292 AD) with Cordon. *Recreations:* power yachting, shooting, antiques, beautiful women. *Heir:* *s* Earl Jermyn. *Address:* Le Formentor, Avenue Princesse Grace, Monte Carlo, Monaco; (seat) Ickworth, Bury St Edmunds, Suffolk. *Clubs:* Hurlingham, Eccentric, Marks, House of Lords Motoring; Guards Polo; Royal Worlington Golf; House of Lords Yacht, Royal Thames Yacht (courtesy mem.); Monte Carlo Yacht,

Monte Carlo Country, Monte Carlo Motor (Monaco).
*Died* 10 *March* 1985.

**BRITTEN, Brig. Charles Richard**, OBE 1966; MC 1916; DL, JP; Extra Gentleman Usher to the Queen, since 1955; *b* 25 June 1894; 2nd *s* of late Rear-Admiral R. F. Britten and Hon. Blanche Cecile Colville, *o d* of 11th Baron Colville of Culross; *m* 1st, 1915, Dorothy (*d* 1970), *d* of late Hon. P. Allsopp; one *s*; 2nd, 1971, Pamela, *yr d* of E. G. Attenborough. *Educ:* Eton; RMC Sandhurst. Served European War, 1914–19 (served France, wounded Sept. 1916 and Nov. 1917), and War of 1939–45; Grenadier Guards, 1914; Capt. 1917; Lieut-Col 1935; Bt Col 1937; Col 1938; Brig. 1939; Comdg Grenadier Guards, 1937–39, and 1st (London) Infantry Bde, 1937–41; attached RAF Regiment, 1942; retired, 1946. Pres., Worcs and Hereford Branch, Gren. Guards Assoc. Mem., Worcs CC, 1946–74 (CA 1963); Mem., Martley RDC, 1948–74. DL 1947, JP 1946, High Sheriff 1952, Worcs. *Recreations:* shooting, hunting (former Chm., Wyre Forest Beagles) and fishing. *Address:* Kenswick Manor, Worcester. *T:* Worcester 640210. *Clubs:* Cavalry and Guards; Union and County (Worcester).                          *Died* 17 *Jan.* 1984.

**BRITTON, Prof. Karl William**; Professor of Philosophy, University of Newcastle upon Tyne, 1951–75; *b* Scarborough, Yorks, 12 Oct. 1909; *s* of Rev. J. Nimmo Britton and Elsie Clare Britton (*née* Slater); *m* 1936, Sheila Margaret Christie; one *s* two *d* (and one *s* one *d* decd). *Educ:* Southend High School; Clare College, Cambridge. Pres. Cambridge Union Society, 1931. Choate Fellow at Harvard University, USA, 1932–34; Lecturer in Philosophy: University College of Wales, 1934–37; University College of Swansea, 1937–51. War of 1939–45, Regional Commissioner's Office, Reading, 1941–45. Public Orator, Durham University, 1959–62; Dean of the Faculty of Arts, Newcastle upon Tyne, 1961–63 and 1966–69. Examiner, Moral Sciences Tripos: 1949, 1954, 1955, 1964, 1966. Mill Centenary Lectr, Toronto Univ., 1973. Sec., Mind Assoc., 1948–60, Pres. 1963. Hon. DLitt Durham, 1976. *Publications:* Communication: A Philosophical Study of Language, 1939, repr. 1971; John Stuart Mill, 1953, repr. 1969; Philosophy and the Meaning of Life, 1969; Communication and Understanding, 1978; A Memoir of C. D. Broad, 1978; contrib. to: The Times, Proc. Aristotelian Society, Mind, Philosophy, Analysis, Jl of Philosophy, Cambridge Review, etc. *Address:* Harthope, Millfield Road, Riding Mill, Northumberland. *T:* Riding Mill 354.
*Died* 23 *July* 1983.

**BROADBENT, Sir William Francis**, 3rd Bt, *cr* 1893; *b* 29 Nov. 1904; *s* of Sir John Francis Harpin Broadbent, MD, FRCP, Bt and Margaret Elizabeth Field (*d* 1958); *S* father 1946; *m* 1st, 1935, Veronica Pearl Eustace (*d* 1951); 2nd, 1982, Miranda Hamilton. *Educ:* Winchester College; Trinity College, Oxford (MA). Solicitor, 1933–72, retired. *Heir: cousin* George Walter Broadbent [*b* 23 April 1935; *m* 1962, Valerie Anne, *o d* of C. F. Ward; one *s* one *d*]. *Address:* Flat 43, Ritchie Court, 380 Banbury Road, Oxford. *Club:* United Oxford & Cambridge University.
*Died* 29 *March* 1987.

**BROADLEY, Sir Herbert**, KBE 1947 (CBE 1943); Representative in Britain of United Nations Children's Fund, 1958–68; *b* 23 Nov. 1892; *s* of late Stephenson S. Broadley, Louth, Lincs; *m* 1927, Kathleen May, *d* of late Alfred J. Moore, Camden Square, London; no *c. Educ:* King Edward VI Grammar Sch., Louth; Birkbeck Coll., Univ. of London. Pres. Students' Union; Editor, Coll. Magazine Lodestone, 1922–23. Civil Service, 1912; served in India Office (Military Dept), 1912–1920; served in BoT, 1920–26; Sec., Imperial Customs Conf., 1921, German (Reparations) Act Cttee, 1921, and Imperial Economic Cttee, 1925–26; Asst Sec., Anglo-Soviet Commercial Treaty, 1924; Sec., Anglo-German Commercial Treaty, 1925; Asst Sec., Imperial Econ. Conf., 1932; resigned from Civil Service, 1926, and joined firm of W. S. Crawford Ltd (Advertising Agents), 1927; Dir, W. S. Crawford Ltd and Man. Dir of their Berlin Branch, 1927–32; i/c Distribution and Res. Dept, W. S. Crawford Ltd, London, 1932–39; Fellow and Mem. Council, Inst. of Incorp. Practitioners in Advertising and Chm., Res. Cttee, 1936–39; joined Ministry of Food at outbreak of War, 1939; Asst Sec., Nov. 1939; Principal Asst Sec., 1940; Dep. Sec., 1941; Second Sec., 1945–48; Leader, UK Delegn to Internat. Wheat Confs, 1947 and 1948; UK repr. at UNFAO Confs: Quebec, 1945; Copenhagen, 1946; Dep. Dir-Gen., UNFAO, 1948–58 (Acting Dir-Gen., 1955–56), retd. Trustee, UK Nat. Freedom from Hunger (Mem. Cttee, 1960–). Hon. Freeman of Louth (Lincs) 1961. Hon. Fellow, Birkbeck Coll., Univ. of London, 1963; a Governor, Birkbeck Coll., 1965–. Haldane Meml Lecture on Food and People, Univ. of London, 1964. Commander of the Order of the Crown of Belgium, 1948. *Publication:* The People's Food (with Sir William Crawford), 1938. *Address:* Hollingsworth, Redlands Lane, Ewshot, Farnham, Surrey GU10 5AS. *T:* Aldershot 850437. *Club:* Naval and Military.                                            *Died* 2 *June* 1983.

**BROATCH, James**, CBE 1961; Deputy Chairman of the Cotton Board, 1963; Deputy Chairman, Textile Council, 1967–68; *b* 13

May 1900; *s* of Alfred and Mary Broatch; *m* 1927, Mary Booth (*d* 1984). *Educ:* Manchester Grammar School; University College, Oxford. Editor, Manchester Guardian Commercial, 1930–39; Assistant Secretary, The Cotton Board, 1939–43; Secretary 1943–53; Director-General, 1953–62. *Address:* 5 Lynton Drive, Hillside, Southport, Merseyside. *T:* Southport 67976.
*Died* 30 *June* 1986.

**BROCK, Rear-Admiral Patrick Willet**, CB 1956; DSO 1951; RN retd; Chairman, The Naval Review, 1967–78; *b* 30 Dec. 1902; *e s* of R. W. and M. B. Brock, Kingston, Ontario; *m* 1st, 1931, M. D. Collinson (*d* 1974); 2nd, 1976, Mrs Rosemary Harrison Stanton. *Educ:* Royal Royal Naval College of Canada. Transferred from Royal Canadian Navy to RN, 1921; Commander 1938; Exec. Officer, HMS Mauritius, 1942–44 (despatches); Captain 1944; Senior Naval Officer, Schleswig-Holstein, 1946; commanded HMS Kenya, Far East, 1949–51 (despatches, DSO); Director Operations Div., 1951–53; Rear-Admiral, 1954; Flag Officer, Middle East, 1954–56; Admiralty Material Requirements Committee, 1956–58, retired. Chm., Kipling Soc., 1973–76. Trustee, National Maritime Museum, 1960–74; a Vice-Pres., Soc. for Nautical Research, 1970–. Croix de Guerre (France), 1945; Bronze Star Medal (US), 1951. *Publications:* RUSI Eardley-Wilmot Gold Medal Essay, 1935; (with Basil Greenhill) Steam and Sail in Great Britain and North America, 1973. *Recreations:* gardening, naval history. *Address:* Kiln Cottage, Critchmere, Haslemere, Surrey. *T:* Haslemere 2542.
*Died* 11 *Oct.* 1988.

**BROCKBANK, Prof. (John) Philip**, PhD; Professor of English, since 1979, University of Birmingham; *b* 4 Jan. 1922; *s* of John Brockbank and Sarah Cooper; *m* 1947, Doreen Winterbottom; two *s. Educ:* Oldershaw Grammar Sch., Wallasey; Trinity Coll., Cambridge (MA, PhD). Served RAF, Navigator, 1940–46. Professor of English, Saarbrücken, 1953–54; Asst Lectr, Cambridge, and College Lectr, Jesus Coll., 1954–58; Sen. Lectr, Reading, 1958–62; Prof. of English, York, 1962–79; Dir, Shakespeare Inst., Univ. of Birmingham, 1979–88. General Editor, New Cambridge Shakespeare, 1978–. *Publications:* Marlowe's Dr Faustus, 1961, repr. 1979; ed, Pope, Selected Poems, 1962, repr. 1974; ed, Ben Jonson, Volpone, 1967, repr. 1980; ed, Shakespeare, Coriolanus, 1976; (ed) Players of Shakespeare, 1985; On Shakespeare, 1989; contribs to books on Shakespeare, Milton, Pope, Marvell, and to Shakespeare Survey, TLS, etc. *Recreations:* theatre, water-colours. *Address:* 14 Scholars Lane, Stratford-upon-Avon CV37 6HE. *T:* Stratford-upon-Avon 295058.                                              *Died* 18 *July* 1989.

**BROCKBANK, William**, TD 1946; MA, MD Cambridge; FRCP; Consulting Physician, Royal Infirmary, Manchester, since 1965; Hon. Medical Archivist Manchester University, 1965–75, Hon. Archivist and Keeper, John Rylands University of Manchester Library, since 1975; Hon. Archivist, Manchester Royal Infirmary, 1965–77, Hon. Consultant Archivist, since 1978; *b* Manchester, 28 Jan. 1900; *s* of Edward Mansfield and Mary Ellwood Brockbank; unmarried. *Educ:* Bootham School, York; Caius College, Cambridge; Manchester University. Medical Officer, Manchester Grammar School, 1929–46; Physician, Manchester Royal Infirmary, 1932–65. Lecturer in Medicine, Manchester University, 1933–65; Dean of Clinical Studies, Manchester University, 1939–65. RAMC, Major, 1939–41; Lieut-Colonel, 1941–46. Director, Asthma Clinic, Manchester Royal Infirmary, 1946–65. Fitzpatrick Lecturer, Royal College of Physicians, 1950–51; Chairman Manchester University Medical Library Cttee, 1951–54; Member Council, Royal College of Physicians, 1955–58; President Manchester Medical Society, 1955–56; Vicary Lecturer, Royal College of Surgeons, 1956; Member Hinchliffe Cttee (Cost of Prescribing), 1957–59; Gideon de Laune Lectr, Soc. of Apothecaries, 1963. Dist Comr (now Hon.) Boy Scouts Assoc.; awarded Silver Acorn, 1950. Vice-President, Lancashire CC Club, 1967–. Hon. MSc Manchester, 1972. Special Correspondent for Life for the Manchester Literary and Philosophical Soc., 1981. *Publications:* Portrait of a Hospital, 1952; Ancient Therapeutic Arts, 1954; The Honorary Medical Staff of the Manchester Royal Infirmary 1830–1948, 1965; The Diary of Richard Kay, 1716–51, 1968; The History of Nursing at the Manchester Royal Infirmary, 1752–1929, 1970; numerous papers to the Lancet, mostly on asthma, and to Medical History. *Recreations:* Medical History, archaeology; collecting cricket literature and water colours. *Address:* Elm Grange Hotel, 56 Wilmslow Road, Manchester M20 9GJ. *T:* 061–445 3336. *Club:* National Liberal.
*Died* 12 *March* 1984.

**BROCKLEHURST, Sir John Ogilvy**, 3rd Bt *cr* 1903; *b* 6 April 1926; *s* of Lt-Col Henry Courtney Brocklehurst (2nd *s* of 1st Bt) (killed in action, 1942) and Lady Helen Alice Willington, *d* of 11th Earl of Airlie; *S* uncle, 1975.                                      *Died* 9 *May* 1981 (*ext*).

**BROCKLEHURST, Mrs Mary D.**; *see* Dent-Brocklehurst.

**BROCKWAY, Baron** *cr* 1964 (Life Peer); **(Archibald) Fenner Brockway**; *b* Calcutta, 1 Nov. 1888; *s* of Rev. W. G. Brockway and Frances Elizabeth Abbey; *m* 1914, Lilla (marr. diss. 1945), *d* of Rev.

W. Harvey-Smith; two *d* (and two *d* decd); *m* 1946, Edith Violet, *d* of Archibald Herbert King; one *s*. *Educ:* Sch. for the Sons of Missionaries (now Eltham Coll.). Joined staff Examiner, 1907; sub-editor Christian Commonwealth, 1909; Labour Leader, 1911; editor, 1912–17; secretary No Conscription Fellowship, 1917; sentenced to one month's imprisonment under DORA Aug. 1916, and to three months, six months, and two years hard labour under Military Service Act, Dec. 1916, Feb. 1917, and July 1917; Joint Secretary British Committee of Indian National Congress and editor India, 1919; Joint Secretary Prison System Enquiry Cttee, 1920: Organising Secretary ILP 1922; General Secretary ILP, 1928 and 1933–39; Editor of New Leader, 1926–29, and 1931–46; Labour candidate Lancaster, 1922; Chairman No More War Movement and War Resister's International, 1923–28; Labour candidate Westminster 1924; Exec. Labour and Socialist International, 1926–31; Fraternal Delegate Indian Trade Union Congress and Indian National Congress, 1927; MP (Lab) East Leyton, 1929–31; Chairman ILP, 1931–33; took part in last public Socialist campaign against Hitler in Germany, 1932; Political Secretary ILP, 1939–46; Chairman British Centre for Colonial Freedom, 1942–47; ILP candidate, Upton Division of West Ham, 1934, Norwich, 1935, Lancaster, 1941, and Cardiff East, 1942; ILP Fraternal Delegate Hamburg Trade Union May Day Demonstrations and German Social Democratic Party Conference, Hanover, 1946. Resigned from ILP, 1946, and rejoined Labour Party; MP (Lab) Eton and Slough, 1950–64. Member Internat. Cttee of Socialist Movement for United Europe, 1947–52; first Chairman of Congress of Peoples against Imperialism, 1948–; Fraternal Delegate, Tunisian Trade Union Conf., 1951; Mem. unofficial Fact-finding mission, Kenya, 1952; Chairman: Liberation (formerly Movement for Colonial Freedom), 1954–67 (President, 1967–); British Asian and Overseas Socialist Fellowship, 1959–66; Peace in Nigeria Cttee, 1967–70; Peace Mission to Biafra and Nigeria, 1968; Brit. Council for Peace in Vietnam, 1965–69; Pres., British Campaign for Peace in Vietnam, 1970–; Co-Chm. (with Lord Noel-Baker until 1982), World Disarmament Campaign, 1979–. Hon. LLD Univ. of Lancaster, 1983. *Publications:* Labour and Liberalism, 1913; The Devil's Business, 1915 (proscribed during the war); Socialism and Pacifism, 1917; The Recruit, 1919; Non-Co-operation, 1919; The Government of India, 1920; English Prisons To-day (with Stephen Hobhouse), 1921; A Week in India, 1928; A New Way with Crime, 1928; The Indian Crisis, 1930; Hungry England, 1932; The Bloody Traffic, 1933; Will Roosevelt Succeed?, 1934; Purple Plague (a novel), 1935; Workers' Front, 1938; Inside the Left: a Political Autobiography, 1942; Death pays a Dividend (with Frederic Mullally), 1944; German Diary, 1946; Socialism Over Sixty Years; The Life of Jowett of Bradford, 1946; Bermondsey Story: Life of Alfred Salter, 1949; Why Mau Mau?, 1953; African Journeys, 1955; 1960–Africa's Year of Destiny, 1960; Red Liner (novel in dialogue), 1961; Outside the Right, 1963; African Socialism, 1964; Commonwealth Immigrants: What is the Answer? (with Norman Pannell), 1965; Woman Against the Desert (with Miss Campbell-Purdie) 1967; This Shrinking Explosive World, 1968; The Next Step to Peace, 1970; The Colonial Revolution, 1973; Towards Tomorrow (autobiog.), 1977; Britain's First Socialists, 1980; 98 Not Out (autobiog.), 1986; numerous ILP and Movement for Colonial Freedom pamphlets. *Address:* 31 Ashlyn Close, Bushey, Herts. *T:* Watford 43592.                    *Died 28 April 1988.*

**BRODIE, Peter Ewen,** OBE 1954; QPM 1963; an Assistant Commissioner, Metropolitan Police, 1966–72; *b* 6 May 1914; 2nd *s* of late Captain E. J. Brodie, Lethen, Nairn; *m* 1st, 1940, Betty Eve Middlebrook Horsfall (*d* 1975); one *s*; 2nd, 1976, Millicent Joyce Mellor. *Educ:* Harrow School. Metropolitan Police, 1934–49 (Seconded to Ceylon Police, 1943–47); Chief Constable, Stirling and Clackmannan Police force, 1949–58; Chief Constable, Warwicks Constabulary, 1958–64; HM Inspector of Constabulary for England and Wales, 1964–66. Member: Adv. Cttee on Drug Dependence, 1967–70; Exec. Cttee, Internat. Criminal Police Organisation-Interpol, 1967–70. Chm. Council, Order of St John for Warwicks, 1977–84. CStJ 1978. *Address:* Avonbrook, Sherbourne, Warwick CV35 8AN. *T:* Barford 624348.

*Died 7 Sept. 1989.*

**BRODIE, Very Rev. Peter Philip,** DD; Minister of St Mungo's, Alloa, 1947–87; Minister emeritus since 1987; Moderator of General Assembly of Church of Scotland, May 1978–1979; *b* 22 Oct. 1916; *s* of Robert Brodie and Margaret Jack; *m* 1949, Constance Lindsay Hope; three *s* one *d*. *Educ:* Airdrie Acad.; Glasgow Univ. (MA, BD, LLB, DD); Trinity Coll., Glasgow. Minister, St Mary's, Kirkintilloch, 1942. Church of Scotland: Chm., Gen. Trustees, 1985–; Convener: Gen. Admin Cttee, 1976–80; Judicial Commn of Gen. Assembly, 1982–87. Chm., Whithorn Trust, 1986–. Hon. DD Glasgow, 1975. *Publications:* Four Ways Sunday School Plan, 1964; contrib. jls. *Recreations:* fishing, gardening. *Address:* 13 Victoria Square, Stirling FK8 2RB. *T:* Stirling (0786) 64763. *Clubs:* New, Caledonian (Edinburgh).                    *Died 16 Oct 1990.*

**BROMET, Air Vice-Marshal Sir Geoffrey R(hodes),** KBE 1945 (CBE 1941; OBE 1919); CB 1943; DSO 1917; DL; *b* 28 Aug. 1891; *e s* of

late G. A. Bromet, Tadcaster; *m* 1917, Margaret (*d* 1961), *e d* of late Maj. Ratliffe, Hardingstone, Northampton; (one *d* decd); *m* 1965, Air Comdt Dame Jean Conan Doyle, DBE. *Educ:* Bradfield; Royal Naval Colls, Osborne and Dartmouth. Royal Navy, 1904–14; RNAS, 1914–18; RAF, 1918–38; retired list, 1938; re-employed Sept. 1939; SASO HQ Coastal Command, 1940–41; AOC 19 Group Plymouth, 1941–43; Senior British Officer Azores Force, 1943–45; reverted to retired list, Oct. 1945; Lieutenant-Governor, Isle of Man, 1945–52; a Life Vice-President: Royal Air Force Association; RNLI. DL Kent, 1958. *Address:* Home Green, Littlestone-on-Sea, Kent; 72 Cadogan Square, SW1. *Club:* Royal Air Force.

*Died 16 Nov. 1983.*

**BROMHEAD, Sir Benjamin (Denis Gonville),** 5th Bt, *cr* 1806; OBE 1943; Lieut-Col (Retd) Frontier Force Regt (Indian Army); *b* 7 May 1900; *s* of late Maj. E. G. Bromhead (*er s* of 4th Bt); *S* grandfather, Colonel Sir Benjamin Parnell Bromhead, 4th Bt, CB, 1935; *m* 1938, Nancy Mary, *o d* of late T. S. Lough, Buenos Aires; one *s* two *d*. *Educ:* Wellington College; RMC Sandhurst. Entered Indian Army, 1919; Iraq, 1920 (medal with clasp); Waziristan, 1922–24 (wounded, medal with clasp); NW Frontier of India, 1930 (despatches, medal with clasp); Waziristan, 1937 (despatches); Political Agent, N Waziristan. NW Frontier Province, 1945–47; retd, 1949. *Heir: s* John Desmond Gonville Bromhead [*b* 21 Dec. 1943. *Educ:* Wellington and privately]. *Address:* Thurlby Hall, Aubourn, Lincoln. *Club:* Naval and Military.              *Died 18 March 1981.*

**BROMLEY, Sir Thomas Eardley,** KCMG 1964 (CMG 1955); HM Diplomatic Service, retired; Secretary, Churches Main Committee, Dec. 1970–72; *b* 14 Dec. 1911; *s* of late Thomas Edward Bromley, ICS; *m* 1944, Diana Marion (marr. diss. 1966), *d* of Sir John Pratt, KBE, CMG; (two *s* decd); *m* 1966, Mrs Alison Toulmin. *Educ:* Rugby; Magdalen College, Oxford. Entered Consular Service, 1935; Vice-Consul, Japan, 1938; Asst Private Sec. to the Permanent Under-Secretary of State, 1943, and Private Secretary, 1945; Grade 7, 1945; served in Washington, 1946; Bagdad, 1949; Counsellor, 1953; Head of African Department, Foreign Office, March 1954–Jan. 1956; Imperial Defence College, 1956; Foreign Office Inspectorate, 1957; seconded to Cabinet Office, Oct. 1957; Consul-General at Mogadishu, 1960; Ambassador: to Somali Republic, 1960–61; to Syrian Arab Republic, 1962–64; to Algeria, 1964–65; FO, 1966; Ambassador to Ethiopia, 1966–69. *Address:* 11 Belbroughton Road, Oxford OX2 6UZ.              *Died 18 June 1987.*

**BROMLEY-DAVENPORT, Lt-Col Sir Walter Henry,** Kt 1961; TD; DL; *b* 1903; *s* of late Walter A. Bromley-Davenport, Capesthorne, Macclesfield, Cheshire, and late Lilian Emily Isabel Jane, DBE 1954, JP, *d* of Lt-Col J. H. B. Lane; *m* 1933, Lenette F. (*d* 1989), *d* of Joseph Y. Jeanes, Philadelphia, USA; one *s* one *d*. *Educ:* Malvern. Joined Grenadier Guards, 1922; raised and comd 5 Bn Cheshire Regt, Lt-Col 1939. MP (C) Knutsford Div. 1945–70; Conservative Whip, 1948–51. DL Cheshire, 1949. British Boxing Board of Control, 1953. *Address:* Capesthorne Hall, Macclesfield, Cheshire SK11 9JY. *T:* Chelford 861221; 39 Westminster Gardens, Marsham Street, SW1. *T:* 01–834 2929; Fiva, Aandalsnes, Norway. *Clubs:* White's, Cavalry and Guards, Carlton, Pratt's.

*Died 26 Dec. 1989.*

**BROMMELLE, Norman Spencer;** Secretary-General, International Institute for Conservation of Historic and Artistic Works, 1957–64 and 1966–87, retired; *b* 9 June 1915; *s* of James Valentine Brommelle and Ada Louisa Brommelle (*née* Bastin); *m* 1959, Rosa Joyce Plesters. *Educ:* High Pavement School, Nottingham; University College, Oxford. Scientific research in industry on Metallography and Spectroscopy, 1937–48; Picture Conservation, National Gallery, 1949–60; Keeper, Dept of Conservation, V&A Mus., 1960–77; Dir, Hamilton Kerr Inst., Fitzwilliam Mus., Cambridge, 1978–83 (retd), Technical Adviser (pt-time) 1983–86. Governor, Central Sch. of Art and Design, 1971–77. *Publications:* contributions to: Journal of the Institute of Metals; Studies in Conservation; Museums Journal. *Recreation:* gardening. *Address:* 32 Bogliera, Morra 06010, Città di Castello (PG), Italy. *T:* 75 8574255.

*Died 19 Nov. 1989.*

**BROOK, Caspar;** Director, David Owen Centre for Population Growth Studies, University College Cardiff, since 1974; *b* 24 Aug. 1920; *m* 1948, Dinah Fine; one *s* one *d*. *Educ:* UCW, Cardiff. Royal Tank Regt, Glider Pilot Regt, 1940–46. British Export Trade Research Organisation, 1947; machine tool and electrical engrs, 1947–53; Publications Editor, Economist Intelligence Unit Ltd, 1953–58; Dir, Consumers' Assoc., 1958–64; Man. Dir, Equipment Comparison Ltd, 1964–67; Dir, Industrial Training and Publishing Div., Pergamon Press, 1966–67; Dir, Family Planning Assoc., 1968–74. Mem., Welsh Consumer Council, 1975–79. Social Develt Advr (Sudan), Ministry of Overseas Develt, 1976–; Consultant: UN Fund for Population Activities, 1978–; Internat. Planned Parenthood Fedn, 1981–. *Recreations:* talking, sailing. *Address:* 58 Neville Street, Cardiff CF1 8LS. *T:* Cardiff 44950. *Club:* Reform.

*Died 17 Feb. 1983.*

**BROOK, Prof. George Leslie**, MA, PhD; Professor of English Language 1945–77, and of Medieval English Literature, 1951–77, University of Manchester, later Professor Emeritus; Dean of the Faculty of Arts, 1956–57; Pro-Vice-Chancellor, 1962–65; Presenter of Honorary Graduands, 1964–65; *b* 6 March 1910; 3rd *s* of late Willie Brook, Shepley, Huddersfield; *m* 1949, Stella, *d* of Thomas Maguire, Salford. *Educ:* University of Leeds; Ripon English Literature Prize, 1931. Visiting Professor, University of California, Los Angeles, 1951. *Publications:* An English Phonetic Reader, 1935; English Sound-Changes, 1935; Glossary to the Works of Sir Thomas Malory, 1947; An Introduction to Old English, 1955; A History of the English Language, 1958; English Dialects, 1963; The Modern University, 1965; The Language of Dickens, 1970; Varieties of English, 1973; The Language of Shakespeare, 1976; Books and Book Collecting, 1980; Words in Everyday Life, 1981; edited: The Harley Lyrics, 1948; The Journal of the Lancashire Dialect Society, 1951–54; (with R. F. Leslie) Layamon's Brut, Vol. I, 1963, Vol. II, 1978; (with C. S. Lewis) Selections from Layamon's Brut, 1963. *Address:* 33 Priory Lane, Kents Bank, Grange-Over-Sands, Cumbria LA11 7BH. *T:* Grange-Over-Sands 3732.

*Died 9 July 1987.*

**BROOKE OF CUMNOR**, Baron (Life Peer), *cr* 1966; **Henry Brooke**, PC 1955; CH 1964; *b* 9 April 1903; *y s* of L. Leslie Brooke and Sybil Diana, *d* of Rev. Stopford Brooke; *m* 1933, Barbara (later Baroness Brooke of Ystradfellte), *y d* of Canon A. A. Mathews; two *s* two *d*. *Educ:* Marlborough; Balliol College, Oxford. MP (C) West Lewisham, 1938–45, Hampstead, 1950–66. Deputy Chairman, Southern Railway Company, 1946–48. Member of Central Housing Advisory Committee, 1944–54; Member of London County Council, 1945–55, and of Hampstead Borough Council, 1936–57. Financial Secretary to the Treasury, 1954–57; Minister of Housing and Local Government and Minister for Welsh Affairs, 1957–61; Chief Secretary to the Treasury and Paymaster-General, 1961–62; Home Secretary, 1962–64. Chm., Jt Select Cttee on Delegated Legislation, 1971–73. *Address:* The Glebe House, Mildenhall, Marlborough, Wilts SN8 2LX. *Died 29 March 1984.*

**BROOKE, Vice-Admiral Basil Charles Barrington**, CB 1949; CBE 1947; *b* 6 April 1895; *s* of John C. E. H. Brooke and Hon. Violet M. Barrington; *m* 1925, Nora Evelyn Toppin (*d* 1981); two *s* two *d*. *Educ:* Malvern College. Royal Navy, 1913; Captain, 1938; Rear-Admiral, 1947; retired, 1949. Vice-Admiral (retd), 1950. *Address:* Highfield, Mandeville Road, Saffron Walden, Essex CB11 4 AQ.

*Died 20 Jan. 1983.*

**BROOKE, Maj.-Gen. Frank Hastings**, CB 1958; CBE 1954; DSO 1945; Chief Army Instructor, Imperial Defence College, 1960–62, retd; *b* 1909; *s* of Lt-Col G. F. Brooke, DSO; *m* 1st, 1935, Helen Mary (*d* 1973), *d* of late Major R. Berkeley; two *s*; 2nd, 1974, Mrs S. N. Carson. *Educ:* RMC Sandhurst. 2nd Lieut, The Welch Regt, 1929; Captain 1938. Served NWF, India (Medal and clasp), 1935; staff and regtl appts, 1939–45; Instr Staff College, Camberley, 1945–47; Dep. Comd (Brig.) Burma Mission, 1948–49; WO, 1950–52; Comdr 1st Malay Inf. Bde, 1953–54 (despatches); GOC Federation Army, Malaya, 1956–59. Col, The Welch Regt, 1965–69; Comr, Royal Hosp., Chelsea, 1969–72. Bronze Star Medal, USA, 1945. *Publications:* contrib. on military subjects to Chambers's Encyclopædia. *Recreation:* sailing. *Club:* Army and Navy.

*Died 25 Jan. 1982.*

**BROOKE, Sir George (Cecil Francis)**, 3rd Bt, *cr* 1903; MBE 1949; Major, 17/21 Lancers, retired; *b* 30 March 1916; *s* of Sir Francis Brooke, 2nd Bt, and Mabel (*d* 1982), *d* of Sir John Arnott, 1st Bt; *S* father 1954; *m* 1959, Lady Melissa Wyndham-Quin, *er d* of 6th Earl of Dunraven, CB, CBE, MC; one *s* one *d*. *Educ:* Stowe. Served War of 1939–45 (wounded, despatches twice), in North Africa and Italy. *Heir: s* Francis George Windham Brooke, *b* 15 Oct. 1963. *Address:* Glenbevan, Croom, Co. Limerick. *Clubs:* Calvary and Guards, Pratt's, White's; Kildare Street and University (Dublin).

*Died 27 Dec. 1982.*

**BROOKE, Humphrey;** see Brooke, T. H.

**BROOKE, John;** Chairman, Brooke Bond Liebig Ltd, retired 1971; *b* 7 March 1912; *m* 1936, Bridget (née May); two *s* one *d*. *Educ:* Bedales, Petersfield, Hants. Joined Brooke Bond & Co. Ltd, Oct. 1930, as Trainee Salesman. *Address:* 10 Parsonage Lane, Market Lavington, near Devizes, Wilts. *T:* Lavington 2204.

*Died 12 July 1987.*

**BROOKE, Major Sir John Weston**, 3rd Bt, *cr* 1919; TD; DL; JP; Lovat Scouts; *S* 26 Sept. 1911; *s* of Major Sir Robert Weston Brooke, 2nd Bt, DSO, MC, DL, and Margery Jean, MBE (*d* 1975), *d* of Alex. Geddes of Blairmore, Aberdeenshire; *S* father, 1942; *m* 1st, 1945, Rosemary (marr. diss. 1963; she *d* 1979), *d* of late Percy Nevill, Birling House, West Malling, Kent; two *s*; 2nd, 1966, Lady Macdonald (née Phoebe Napier Harvey) (*d* 1977), MB, FFARCS, DA, *widow* of Sir Peter Macdonald, Newport, IoW. *Educ:* Repton; Trinity College, Cambridge. Apprenticed in engineering trade with

Crompton Parkinsons, Electrical Engineers, Chelmsford; employed previous to hostilities as Constructional Engineer with Associated Portland Cement Manufacturers. DL, Ross and Cromarty, 1964; JP Ross-shire, 1960. *Recreations:* shooting, sailing, ski-ing, farming. *Heir: s* Alistair Weston Brooke, *b* 12 Sept. 1947. *Address:* Midfearn, Ardgay, Ross-shire. *T:* Ardgay 250. *Club:* Royal Ocean Racing.

*Died 19 July 1983.*

**BROOKE, Sir (Norman) Richard (Rowley)**, Kt 1964; CBE 1958; FCA; *b* 23 June 1910; *s* of William Brooke, JP and Eleanor (née Wild), Frodingham, Lincs; *m* 1st, 1948, Julia Dean (marr. diss. 1957); one *s* one *d*; 2nd, 1958, Nina Mari Dolan. *Educ:* Charterhouse School. Joined Guest, Keen & Nettlefolds Ltd, 1935; Commnd TA, 1937; demobilised 1940 on return to GKN; Dir, Guest, Keen & Nettlefolds Ltd, 1961–67; Dir and/or Chm. of several GKN subsidiary cos until retirement in 1967; Director: Eagle Star Insurance Co. (Wales Bd), 1955–80; L. Ryan Hldgs Ltd, 1972–78; a Founder Dir, Develt Corp. for Wales, 1958–67, Hon. Vice-Pres., 1967–83. Founder Mem. and Dep. Chm., British Independent Steel Producers Assoc., 1967. Hon. Life Vice-President, Wales Conservative and Unionist Council, 1966; President, Cardiff Chamber of Commerce, 1960–61; Member Exec. Cttee and Council, British Iron and Steel Federation, to 1967 (Joint Vice-Pres., 1966–67); Vice-Pres., University College, Cardiff, 1965–81, Mem. Council, 1982–86. JP Glamorgan, 1952–64, 1970–74. OStJ 1953. *Recreations:* bridge, music, reading. *Address:* New Sarum, Pwllmelin Lane, Llandaff, Cardiff. *T:* Cardiff 563692. *Club:* Cardiff and County (Cardiff). *Died 21 Sept. 1989.*

**BROOKE Lt-Col Ralph**, OBE 1940; PhD, MS, FRCS, MB, LRCP; late RAMC, TA; Hon. Consulting Orthopædic Surgeon, Royal Sussex County Hospital; formerly: Hon. Surgeon and Hon. Orthopædic Surgeon, Hove Hospital; Hon. Surgeon and Hon. Orthopædic Surgeon, Royal West Sussex Hospital; Hon. Orthopædic Surgeon, Royal Sussex County Hospital; Hon. Surgeon, Worthing Hospital; Consulting Surgeon, Bognor War Memorial Hospital; Consulting Surgeon, Midhurst Hospital; also Barrister-at-law, Inner Temple; *b* Bexhill-on-Sea, 2 April 1900; *s* of Herbert Brooke and E. Bones; *m* Marjorie, *d* of H. W. Lee, Managing Director, Messrs Stones, Ltd, Engineers; one *s* three *d*. *Educ:* Christ's College; Guy's Hospital. Late Demonstrator, Anatomy, Physiology, Operative Surgery, Guy's Hospital; late Medical Officer Hackney Hospital. *Publications:* A Shorter Orthopædics; papers in the professional journals. *Address:* Woodend, Linbrook, Ringwood, Hants.

*Died 16 Aug. 1982.*

**BROOKE, Sir Richard;** see Brooke, Sir N. R. R.

**BROOKE, Sir Richard Christopher**, 9th Bt, *cr* 1662; *b* 8 Aug. 1888; *s* of 8th Bt and Alice, *d* of J. S. Crawley, Stockwood Park, Luton; *S* father, 1920; *m* 1st, 1912, Marian Dorothea (*d* 1965), *o d* of late Arthur Charles Innes, MP, of Dromantine, Co. Down; one *s* one *d*; 2nd, 1967, Kathleen Enda, *d* of Francis Gildea, Dun Laoghaire, Dublin. *Educ:* Eton; Christ Church, Oxford. MA. Late Scots Guards. High Sheriff of Worcestershire, 1931; Worcestershire CC, 1928–46; Vice-Chairman Worcestershire War Emergency Cttee for Civil Defence, 1939; Chairman Bewdley Division, Conservative Association, 1945–46. Late JP and DL Worcestershire. *Recreations:* racing, horse breeding, fishing. *Heir: s* Richard Neville Brooke, late Scots Guards; Chartered Accountant [*b* 1 May 1915; *m* 1st, 1937, Lady Mabel Kathleen Jocelyn (marr. diss., 1959), *yr d* of 8th Earl of Roden; two *s*; 2nd, 1960, Jean Evison, *d* of Lt-Col A. C. Corfe, DSO]. *Address:* Oaklands, St Saviour, Jersey, Channel Islands. *T:* Jersey 62072. *Clubs:* Cavalry and Guards; Kildare Street and University (Dublin); Jockey Club Rooms (Newmarket).

*Died 1 Feb. 1981.*

**BROOKE, (Thomas) Humphrey**, CVO 1969 (MVO 1958); Secretary, Royal Academy of Arts, Piccadilly, W1, 1952–68; *b* 31 Jan. 1914; *y s* of late Major Thomas Brooke, Grimston Manor, York, and late B. Gundreda, *d* of Sir Hildred Carlile, 1st and last Bt; *m* 1946, Countess Nathalie Benckendorff, *o d* of Count Benckendorff, DSO; one *d* (one *s* one *d* decd). *Educ:* Wellington Coll.; Magdalen Coll., Oxford. 1st Cl. Hons Mod. History Oxon, 1935; BLitt 1937. Asst Keeper, Public Record Office, 1937. Served War of 1939–45; commissioned KRRC, 1943. Dir of Archives, Sub-Commn for Monuments, Fine Arts and Archives, Allied Control Commn, Italy, 1944–45; Controller, Monuments and Fine Arts Branch, Allied Commission for Austria, 1946; Dep. Director, Tate Gallery, 1948; Ministry of Town and Country Planning, 1949; Resigned from Civil Service on appointment to Royal Acad., 1951. Founded first rosarium in GB in Suffolk for the preservation and conservation of roses, 1971. Member Order of Santiago (Portugal), 1955; Commander Ordine al Merito della Republica Italiana, 1956; Officier de l'Ordre de l'Etoile Noire (France), 1958. *Recreations:* shooting, fishing, gardening. *Address:* Flat 3, 11 Onslow Square, SW7. *T:* 01–589 5690; Lime Kiln, Claydon, Suffolk. *T:* Ipswich 830334. *Club:* Chelsea Arts.

*Died 24 Dec. 1988.*

**BROOKEBOROUGH**, 2nd Viscount *cr* 1952, of Colebrooke; **John Warden Brooke**, PC (NI) 1971; DL; Bt 1822; Member (UPNI) for

North Down, Northern Ireland Constitutional Convention, 1975–76; *b* 9 Nov. 1922; *s* of 1st Viscount Brookeborough, KG, PC, CBE, MC, and Cynthia Mary, DBE 1959 (*d* 1970), *d* of late Captain Charles Warden Sergison; *S* father, 1973; *m* 1949, Rosemary Hilda Chichester; two *s* three *d*. *Educ*: Eton. Joined Army, 1941; Captain 10th Royal Hussars; wounded, Italy, 1942; subseq. ADC to Field Marshal Alexander in Italy and to Gen. Sir Brian Robertson in Germany; ADC to Viceroy of India, Field Marshal Lord Wavell, 1946; invalided, 1947. Fermanagh County Councillor, 1947–73, Chairman, 1961–73; pioneered streamlining of local govt by voluntary amalgamation of all councils in the county, 1967. MP (U) Lisnaskea Div., Parlt of NI, 1968–73; Mem. (U), N Down, NI Assembly, 1973–75; Parly Sec. to Min. of Commerce with special responsibilities for tourism, Apr. 1969; Parly Sec. to Dept of the Prime Minister (still retaining Commerce office), with responsibility for general oversight of Government's publicity and information services, Jan. 1970; Minister of State, Min. of Finance and Govt Chief Whip, 1971–72. DL Co. Fermanagh, 1967. *Recreations*: shooting, fishing, riding. *Heir*: *s* Hon. Alan Henry Brooke [*b* 30 June 1952; *m* 1980, Janet, *o d* of John Cooke, Doagh, Co. Antrim. Commissioned 17/21 Lancers, 1972; Captain, UDR, 1977]. *Address*: Ashbrooke, Brookeborough, Enniskillen, Co. Fermanagh. *T*: Brookeborough 242.                    *Died* 5 *March* 1987.

**BROOKER, William,** ARA 1980; painter; Principal, Wimbledon School of Art, 1969–81; *b* 26 June 1918; *s* of Charles Frederick Brooker and Winifred Victoria Colverson; *m* 1975, Katina Montesinos Belón; two *d* by a previous marriage. *Educ*: Royal Masonic Sch.; Croydon Sch. of Art; Chelsea Sch. of Art. Served War, 1940–46: Captain, RA and Staff Officer III; served in NW Europe campaign from Normandy until end of war in 86th Anti-Tank Regt, RA (5th Bn Devonshire Regt). Sen. Asst, Bath Acad. of Art, 1949–53; Senior Lecturer in Painting: Willesden and Harrow Schs of Art, 1953–60; Ealing Sch. of Art, 1960–65; Central Sch. of Art and Design, 1965–69. One-man exhibitions: Arthur Tooth & Sons, 1955, 1962, 1964, 1967, 1968, 1971, 1975; Arts Centre, Lusaka, Zambia, 1968; Villiers, NSW, 1971; Thos Agnew & Sons Ltd, 1979; group exhibitions: numerous, incl. London Gp, John Moore's Biennial (Liverpool), Edinburgh Open 100, British Council, Royal Academy, Royal Soc. of British Artists, Leicester Galls and Thos Agnew & Sons Ltd; works in public collections: Tate Gall.; National Gallery of: Canada; NZ; S Australia; Castle Museum, Nottingham; Aberdeen Art Gall.; Manchester City Art Gall.; Glynn Vivian Museum, Swansea; Southampton Art Gall.; contemporary Art Soc.; Museum of Modern Art, Belo Horizonte, Brazil; City Art Gall., Rotherham; Laing Art Gall., Newcastle; Oldham Art Gall.; Arts Centre, Lusaka, Zambia; works in numerous private collections incl. in USA, Far East and Australasia. *Recreations*: listening to music, reading poetry, playing Russian Roulette without a revolver. *Address*: 5 Bankside Close, Carshalton Beeches, Surrey. *T*: 01–669 5168. *Club*: Muriel's.                    *Died* 8 *May* 1983.

**BROOKES, Air Vice-Marshal Hugh Hamilton,** CB 1954; CBE 1951; DFC 1944; RAF retd; *b* 14 Oct. 1904; *s* of late W. H. Brookes and of Evelyn, *d* of J. Forster Hamilton (she married 2nd Sir John Simpson, KBE, CIE); *m* 1932, Elsie Viola Henry; one *d*. *Educ*: Bedford School; Cranwell. Bomber Command, 1924; 84 Sqdn Iraq, 1929; Staff College, 1933; Sqdn Bomber Command, 1937; Iraq, 1938; Western Desert, 1939; Aden, 1941; Station Bomber Command, 1943; Iraq, 1946; Director of Flying Training, 1949; AOC Rhodesia, 1951; AOC Iraq, 1954; AOC No 23 Group, Flying Training Command, 1956–58, retd. *Club*: Royal Air Force.
                    *Died* 16 *March* 1988.

**BROOKS, Oliver;** Deputy Chairman, Electricity Council, since 1982; *b* 22 Jan. 1920; *s* of late Percy Albert Victor Brooks and of Winifred Brooks; *m* 1944, Lillian Reeve; one *d*. *Educ*: St John's Primary Sch., Fulham; Wandsworth Commercial Sch. ACIS. Various appts, 1937–47; Gray Dawes & Co. Ltd, 1947–70; Financial Dir, Inchcape & Co. Ltd, 1970–73; Financial Dir, The Peninsular and Oriental Steam Navigation Co., 1973–79, a Man Dir, 1979–83; Dir, Burmah Oil Co. Ltd, 1975–; Chm., Family Assurance Soc., 1983–. *Recreations*: family life, work. *Address*: The West Penthouse, Cardinal Court, Grand Avenue, Worthing, West Sussex BN11 5NL.                    *Died* 15 *June* 1985.

**BROOKS GRUNDY, Rupert Francis;** *see* Grundy, R. F. B.

**BROOKSBANK, Col Sir (Edward) William,** 2nd Bt, *cr* 1919; TD 1953; DL; Yorkshire Hussars; *b* 15 June 1915; *e s* of late Col Edward York Brooksbank and Hazel, *d* of late H. F. Brockholes Thomas; *S* grandfather, 1943; *m* 1943, Ann, 2nd *d* of Col T. Clitherow; one *s*. *Educ*: Eton. Colonel, Comdg Queen's Own Yorkshire Yeomanry, 1957. Hon. Col, Queen's Own Yorkshire Yeomanry (TA), 1963–69, T&AVR, 1969–71, 1972–75. DL East Riding of Yorks, and City and County of Kingston upon Hull, 1959. *Heir*: *s* Edward Nicholas Brooksbank, late Captain, Blues and Royals [*b* 4 Oct. 1944; *m* 1970,

Emma, *o d* of Baron Holderness, PC, DL; one *s*]. *Address*: Menethorpe Hall, Malton, North Yorks. *Clubs*: Turf; Yorkshire.
                    *Died* 28 *March* 1983.

**BROOKSBANK, Kenneth,** DSC and Bar, 1944; Chief Education Officer, Birmingham, 1968–77; *b* 27 July 1915; *s* of Ambrose and Ethel Brooksbank; *m* 1939, Violet Anne Woodrow; two *d*. *Educ*: High Storrs Gram. Sch., Sheffield; St Edmund Hall, Oxford; Manchester University. Asst Master, Hulme Gram. Sch., Oldham, 1937–41; Royal Navy, 1941–46; Dep. Educn Off., York, 1946–49; Sen. Admin. Asst, Birmingham, 1949–52; Asst Sec. for Educn, NR Yorks CC, 1952–56; Dep. Educn Off., Birmingham, 1956–68. Leader, Unesco Educn Planning Mission to Bechuanaland, Basutoland and Swaziland, 1964. Chairman: Management Cttee, Adult Literacy Unit, Nat. Inst. of Adult Educn, 1978–80, Adult Literacy and Basic Skills Unit, 1980–88; Council for Environmental Educn, 1978–85; Community Educn Centre, 1981–87; Member: Engineering Ind. Trng Bd, 1970–79; Ind. Trng Service Bd, 1974–77. President: Educnl Equipment Assoc., 1970–71; Soc. of Educn Officers, 1971–72. Mem. Council, Aston Univ., 1968–84; Vice-Chm., West Hill Coll., 1983–. Hon. Fellow, Birmingham Univ., 1981; Fellow, Birmingham Polytechnic, 1988. Hon. DSc Aston, 1985. *Publications*: (ed) Educational Administration, 1980; (with J. Revell) School Governors, 1981; (ed jtly) County and Voluntary Schools, 1982. *Address*: 29 Wycome Road, Hall Green, Birmingham B28 9EN. *T*: 021–777 4407.                    *Died* 4 *Feb.* 1990.

**BROOKSBANK, Col Sir William;** *see* Brooksbank, Col. E. W.

**BROTHERSTON, Sir John (Howie Flint),** Kt 1972; Professor of Community Medicine, University of Edinburgh, 1977–80, Emeritus Professor, since 1981; President, Faculty of Community Medicine, 1978–81; Hon. Physician to the Queen, 1965–68; *b* Edinburgh, 9 March 1915; *s* of late William Brotherston, WS, Edinburgh, and Dr Margaret M. Brotherston, MBE, Edinburgh; *m* 1939, Elizabeth Irene Low; two *s* two *d*. *Educ*: George Watson's College, Edinburgh; University of Edinburgh. Graduated: MA 1935, MB, ChB 1940, MD 1950, Edinburgh Univ.; FRCPE 1958; FRCPGlas 1964; FFCM 1973; FRCP 1978; DrPH Johns Hopkins University 1952. DPH London University, 1947. Served War of 1939–45 with RAMC, 1941–46. Rockefeller Fellow in Preventive Medicine, 1946–48; Lecturer in Social and Preventive Medicine at Guy's Hospital Medical School and London School of Hygiene and Tropical Medicine, 1948–51; Senior Lecturer, subsequently Reader, Public Health, London School of Hygiene and Tropical Medicine, 1951–55; Prof. of Public Health and Social Medicine, University of Edinburgh, 1955–64; Dean of the Faculty of Medicine, University of Edinburgh, 1958–63; Chief MO, Scottish Home and Health Dept, 1964–77. Mem. MRC, 1974–77. Hon. FRSH 1967. Hon. LLD Aberdeen, 1971; Hon. MD Bristol, 1981. Bronfman Prize, 1971. *Publications*: Observations on the early Public Health Movement in Scotland, 1952; various contribs to medical and other jls on social medicine and medical education. *Address*: 26 Mortonhall Road, Edinburgh EH9 2HN. *T*: 031–667 2849.

                    *Died* 12 *May* 1985.

**BROUGH, Prof. John,** MA, DLitt; FBA 1961; Professor of Sanskrit, University of Cambridge, since 1967; Fellow of St John's College; *b* 1917; *er s* of Charles and Elizabeth Brough, Maryfield, Dundee; *m* 1939, Marjorie Allan, *d* of Dr W. A. Robertson; one *d*. *Educ*: High School, Dundee; University of Edinburgh; St John's College, Cambridge. First Class Hons in Classics, Edinburgh, 1939; First Class in Classical Tripos, Part II, 1940; First Class in Oriental Langs Tripos, Parts I and II, 1941 and 1942; Fellow St John's College, Cambridge, 1945–48. DLitt Edinburgh, 1945. Worked in agriculture, 1940–43, and as asst in agricultural research, 1943–44. Asst Keeper, Dept of Oriental Printed Books and MSS, British Museum, 1944–46; Lecturer in Sanskrit, SOAS, Univ. of London, 1946–48; Prof. of Sanskrit in the University of London, 1948–67. *Publications*: Selections from Classical Sanskrit Literature, 1951; The Early Brahmanical System of Gotra and Pravara, 1953; The Gāndhārī Dharmapada, 1962; Poems from the Sanskrit, 1968; articles in Chambers's Encyclopædia and Encylopædia Britannica; and in specialist journals. *Recreations*: music, gardening. *Address*: 5 Thorn Grove, Bishop's Stortford, Herts CM23 5LB. *T*: Bishop's Stortford 51407.                    *Died* 9 *Jan.* 1984.

**BROWN;** *see* Clifton-Brown.

**BROWN;** *see* George-Brown.

**BROWN, Baron** *cr* 1964 (Life Peer); **Wilfred Banks Duncan Brown,** PC 1970; MBE 1944; lately Chairman, The Glacier Metal Co. Ltd (1939–65), and Director, Associated Engineering Ltd; *b* 29 Nov. 1908; British; *m* 1939, Marjorie Hershell Skinner; three *s*. *Educ*: Rossall Sch. Joined The Glacier Metal Co. Ltd, 1931; Sales Manager, 1935; Director, 1936; Joint Managing Director, 1937; Managing Director and Chairman, 1939–65. A Minister of State, Board of Trade, 1965–70. Mem., Industrial Develt Adv. Bd, 1975; Chm., Machine Tool Adv. Cttee, 1975. Pro-Chancellor, Brunel

University, 1966–80. Hon. Degrees: DTech Brunel, 1966; Doctor of Laws Illinois, 1967; DSc Cranfield, 1972. *Publications:* (with Mrs W. Raphael) Managers, Men and Morale, 1947; Exploration in Management, 1960; Piecework Abandoned, 1962; (with Elliott Jaques) Product Analysis Pricing, 1964; (with Elliott Jaques) Glacier Project Papers, 1965; Organization, 1971; The Earnings Conflict, 1973; (with Wolfgang Hirsh-Weber) Bismarck to Bullock, 1983. *Recreation:* golf. *Address:* 9 Blenheim Road, NW8 0LU. *T:* 01–624 1446. *Club:* Reform.                       *Died* 17 *March* 1985.

**BROWN, Sir (Charles) James Officer,** Kt 1969; Consultant Thoracic Surgeon: Alfred Hosp.; St Vincent's Hosp.; Queen Victoria Memorial Hosp.; Austin Hosp. (all in Melbourne); *b* 24 Sept. 1897; *s* of David Brown; *m* 1932, Esme Mai Frankenberg; two *d. Educ:* Scotch Coll., Melbourne; Melbourne Univ. MB BS 1920, MD 1922, FRCS 1924, FRACS 1928. Surgeon, Alfred Hosp., 1929–57; Surgeon, Austin Hosp., 1926–67. Mem. Council, Royal Australian Coll. of Surgeons, 1956–68; Pres., National Heart Foundation (Victorian Division), 1966–72. *Publications:* papers in surgical journals. *Recreation:* golf. *Address:* 2/1 Monaro Road, Kooyong, Victoria 3144, Australia. *T:* (03) 2097944. *Clubs:* Melbourne, Royal Melbourne Golf (Melbourne); Victoria Racing.
                                                    *Died* 22 *Aug.* 1984.

**BROWN, Admiral Charles Randall,** Bronze Star 1943; Legion of Merit 1944; Presidential Unit Citation, 1945; DSM 1960; United States Navy, retired, 1962; *b* Tuscaloosa, Alabama, USA, 13 Dec. 1899; *s* of Robison Brown and Stella Seed Brown; *m* 1921, Eleanor Green, Annapolis, Maryland; two *s. Educ:* US Naval Academy; US Air University; US Naval War College. Graduated from US Naval Academy, 1921. During War served on original US Joint Chiefs of Staff and US-British Combined Chiefs of Staff organisations; later, Captain of USS Kalinin Bay and USS Hornet and Chief of Staff of a Fast Carrier Task Force. Commander, US Sixth Fleet, Mediterranean, 1956; C-in-C, Allied Forces Southern Europe, 1959–61. Vice-President for European Affairs, McDonnell Aircraft Corp. of St Louis, Mo, 1962–65. *Recreation:* gardening. *Address:* 4000 Massachusetts Avenue NW, Apartment 1428, Washington, DC 20016, USA. *Clubs:* Army and Navy, Army and Navy Country (Washington, DC); The Brook, New York Yacht (NY).
                                                    *Died* 8 *Dec.* 1983.

**BROWN, Rt. Rev. David Alan;** Bishop of Guildford, since 1973; *b* 11 July 1922; *s* of Russell Alan Brown and Olive Helen Brown (*née* Golding); *m* 1954, Elizabeth Mary Hele, BA, DipEd (London); two *s* one *d. Educ:* Monkton Combe Sch.; London Coll. of Divinity; Sch. of Oriental and African Studies. Univ. of London: BD (1st Cl. Hons) 1946; MTh (Hebrew, Aramaic and Syriac), 1947; BA (1st Cl. Hons Classical Arabic), 1951. ALCD (1st Cl. Hons with distinction), 1948. Jun. Tutor, London Coll. of Divinity, 1947–49; Asst Curate, Immanuel, Streatham Common, 1948–51; Liskeard Lodge, CMS Training Coll., 1951–52; Missionary, CMS, 1952: District Missionary, Yambio, Sudan, 1952–54; Bishop Gwynne Coll., Mundri, Sudan, 1954–61 (Principal 1955); Canon Missioner, Khartoum Cathedral, and Bishop's Commissary (South), 1961–62; research studies at London, Khartoum and Amman Univs, 1962–65; Missionary, Dio. of Jordan, Lebanon and Syria, 1965–66; Asst Curate, St John the Evangelist, Bromley, 1966; Vicar of Christ Church, Herne Bay, 1967–73; Rural Dean of Reculver, 1972–73; Chairman: Canterbury Diocesan Council for Mission and Unity, 1972–73; British Council of Churches Working Party on Islam in Britain, 1974–78, Cttee for Relations with People of Other Faiths, 1978–, C of E Bd for Mission and Unity, 1977–; Chm., Consultative Cttee on Islam in Europe, 1980. Warden, St Augustine's Coll., Canterbury, 1975–79. *Publications:* A Manual of Evangelism, 1958; The Way of the Prophet, 1960; Preaching Patterns, 1961; A Catechism for Enquirers, Catechumens and Confirmation Candidates, 1961; Jesus and God, 1967; The Christian Scriptures, 1968; The Cross of the Messiah, 1969; The Divine Trinity, 1969; Mission is Living, 1972; A Guide to Religions, 1975; A New Threshold, 1976; God's To-morrow, 1977; Meet the Bible, 1978; All Their Splendour, 1982; contribs to Theology, New Fire. *Recreations:* gardening, reading, walking. *Address:* Willow Grange, Woking Road, Guildford GU4 7QS. *T:* Guildford 73922.
                                                    *Died* 13 *July* 1982.

**BROWN, Derek Ernest D.;** *see* Denny-Brown.

**BROWN, Douglas James,** MBE 1959; HM Diplomatic Service, retired; *b* 6 May 1925; *s* of James Stephen Brown and Hilda May (*née* Hinch); unmarried. *Educ:* Edinburgh Univ. (MA). HMOCS, Nigeria, 1951–62 (Private Sec. to Governor-General, 1955–58); joined Diplomatic Service, 1962; Private Sec. to Comr-Gen. for SE Asia, 1962–63; FO, 1963, 1966; Asst to Special Representative in Africa, 1966–67; British High Commn, Nairobi, 1967–68; British Embassy, Djakarta, 1968–71; Inspector, FCO, 1971–73; Counsellor and Consul-Gen., Algiers, 1974–77; Consul-Gen., St Louis, 1977–80. Sec. to Medical Coll., St Bartholomew's Hosp., 1980–88. *Address:* 9

Amherst Avenue, Ealing, W13 8NQ. *T:* 01–997 7125; Via Privata Oliveta 41/18, 16035 Rapallo, Italy.          *Died* 2 *April* 1989.

**BROWN, Edwin Percy,** CBE 1981; Director of Social Services, North Yorkshire County Council, 1973–82; *b* 20 May 1917; *s* of late James Percy Brown and Hetty Brown; *m* 1958, Margaret (*née* Askey); one *s* one *d. Educ:* Mundella Grammar Sch., Nottingham; Nottingham Univ. (Certif. in Social Studies); Teesside Polytechnic (BA Hons 1986). Social worker, Nottinghamshire CC, 1951–54; Sen. social worker, Lancashire CC, 1954–59; Children's Officer: Southampton CC, 1959–65; Wiltshire CC, 1965–71; Dir of Social Services, N Riding CC, 1971–74. Mem., Supplementary Benefits Commn, 1976–80. Adviser to Assoc. of county Councils, 1974–81; President: Assoc. of Directors of Social Services, 1977–78; Nat. Assoc. of Nursery and Family Care, 1984–88. *Recreations:* local history, liberalism, watching cricket, reading. *Address:* Larkfield, 5 Woodland Way, Eastwood, Notts NG16 3BU. *T:* Langley Mill (0773) 714461. *Clubs:* National Liberal; Nottingham and Notts United Services; Nottinghamshire County Cricket.
                                                    *Died* 27 *May* 1990.

**BROWN, Dr Gordon,** OBE 1964; CEng, FIMechE, FInstE; Counsellor, Atomic Energy, Tokyo, 1983–85; *b* 1 Aug. 1921; *s* of Lilian Brown and late John Thomas Brown; *m* 1950, Agnes Dorothy Lloyd; one *s* two *d. Educ:* Wigan Grammar Sch.; Wigan and District Mining and Technical Coll. (Diploma in Engrg, BScEng, London External 1st Cl. Hons); City and Guilds Coll., Imperial Coll. of Science and Technology (DIC, PhD). RAE, 1943–46; Demonstrator, Imperial Coll., 1946–49; Dept of Atomic Energy, Min. of Supply (later UKAEA), 1949; Senior Designer later Asst Chief Engr, Calder Hall Reactor, 1953–56; Chief Engr, Windscale AGR, 1958–62; Dep. Dir, Industrial Power, 1962–63, Reactor Design, 1963–64, Dir, Gas Cooled Reactors, 1964–65. Atomic Power Constructions Ltd: Tech. Dir, 1965; Dep. Man. Dir, 1966; Man. Dir 1967–69; British Nuclear Design and Constructions, 1970–71; Associate Dir, Business Develt, Humphreys and Glasgow, 1971–74; British Nuclear Fuels Ltd: Chief Engr, Fuel Plants, Reprocessing Div., 1974; Chief Engr Enrichment Div. and Dir, Urenco, 1977, Head of Safety, 1979–83; seconded to UKAEA, on loan to FCO, 1983–85. Member: Nuclear Energy Gp Cttee, IMechE, 1975–83; Reprocessing Study Gp, Adv. Cttee on Safety of Nuclear Installations, 1979–83; Council, Inst. of Energy, 1981–83; Bulleid Meml Lectr, Nottingham Univ., 1971; Past Pres., British Nuclear Energy Soc., 1975–77; Chm., Planning Cttee, European Nuclear Soc., 1976–83. Water Arbitration Prize, IMechE, 1966; FInstD; FAm Nuc Soc. *Publications:* papers on nuclear engineering, safety of Calder Hall, pressure vessels, containment buildings, materials, AGR and high temperature reactor inc. process applications, reliability, safety principles. *Recreations:* gardening (roses), swimming, spectator Rugby Union. *Address:* 1 Baycliffe, Lymm, Cheshire WA13 0QF. *Club:* Royal Automobile.
                                                    *Died* 31 *March* 1985.

**BROWN, Gilbert Alexander M.;** *see* Murray-Brown.

**BROWN, Herbert Macauley Sandes;** a Judge of the High Court of Nigeria, 1945–58, retd; *b* Dublin, Feb. 1897; *o s* of late William Herbert Brown, KC, sometime County Court Judge, of Glenfern, Blackrock, Co. Dublin, and Elizabeth Rose (*née* Sandes); *m* 1928, Catherine Mary (*née* Hutchinson) (*d* 1971); one *d. Educ:* The Abbey, Tipperary; Trinity College, Dublin. Served War of 1914–18 in Royal Marines. Called to the Irish Bar, 1921. Entered Administrative Service, Nigeria, 1924; Magistrate, 1934; Assistant Judge, 1943; Puisne Judge, 1945. *Address:* Ashfield, 1 Chamberlain Road, Edinburgh EH10 4DL.                            *Died* 19 *Dec.* 1987.

**BROWN, Prof James Alan Calvert,** MA; Professor of Applied Economics, Oxford University, and Fellow of Merton College, since 1970; *b* Bury, Lancs, 8 July 1922; *s* of Harry and Mary Brown. *Educ:* Bury Grammar Sch.; Emmanuel Coll., Cambridge (BA 1946, MA 1951); MA Oxon 1970. War Service, 1942–46. Min. of Agriculture, Fisheries and Food, 1947–52; Research Officer, Dept of Applied Economics, Cambridge Univ., 1952–65, Fellow of Queen's Coll., 1961–65; Prof. of Econometrics, Bristol Univ., 1965–70. Mem., SW Electricity Bd, 1966–72. *Publications:* monographs: (with J. Aitchison) Lognormal Distribution, 1957; (with R. Stone) Computable Model of Economic Growth, 1962; Exploring, 1970; contribs to econ. and statistical lit. *Recreation:* travel. *Address:* Institute of Economics and Statistics, Manor Road, Oxford OX1 3UL. *T:* Oxford 49631.                    *Died* 21 *Aug.* 1984.

**BROWN, Sir James Officer;** *see* Brown, Sir (Charles) James Officer.

**BROWN, John Cecil,** CBE 1977; Chairman, Yorkshire Water Authority, 1973–78; *b* 21 Jan. 1911; *s* of John Smith Brown and Ady Mary (*née* Little); *m* 1938, Winifred Metcalfe; two *s. Educ:* Univ of Durham, 1931–34 (BSc 1st Cl. Hons). Richardsons Westgarth (Marine Engrs), Hartlepool, 1926–31; Imperial Chemical Industries Ltd, 1934–73: Division Dir of Engrg, 1952, Techn. Man. Dir, 1959; Chm., Mond Div., 1967; Dir, Main Bd, 1970; retd 1973. *Publications:*

various, in techn. and water industry jls. *Recreations:* horticulture, sea cruising. *Address:* Wayside, Firs Lane, Appleton, Warrington WA4 5LD. *T:* Warrington 63275. *Club:* Cruising Association.
*Died 15 May 1983.*

**BROWN, John Francis Seccombe,** AO 1977; MC 1942; Agent-General for Queensland, 1984–88; *b* 2 May 1917; *s* of George Edward Brown and Ruth Seccombe; *m* 1946, Elwyn Phillips; one *s* one *d*. *Educ:* Queensland, Aust. Committee of Direction of Fruit Marketing, 1939–64; Man. Dir and Chief Exec., Golden Circle Cannery, 1964–82; director of six Queensland public companies, 1975–84. Inaugural and Past Pres., Queensland Confedn of Industry; Trustee, Brisbane Grammar Sch., 1974–84. Freedom of City of London, 1985. *Recreations:* social golfer, fishing, boating. *Clubs:* East India, Royal Automobile; Queensland, United Services, Royal Queensland Golf (Qld). *Died 8 Sept. 1989.*

**BROWN, Maj.-Gen. Llewellyn;** see Brown, Maj.-Gen. R. L.

**BROWN, Ormond John;** retired Government Servant; *b* 30 Jan. 1922; *s* of Herbert John Brown and Janie Lee; *m* 1949, Margaret Eileen Beard; two *d*. *Educ:* Gourock High Sch.; Greenock High Sch. Served War, 1941–45: Outer Hebrides, N Africa, Italy, Greece, Austria. Entered Civil Service by Open Competitive Exam., 1938. Sheriff Clerk Service, Scotland, 1939; Trng Organiser, Scottish Ct Service, 1957; Sheriff Clerk of Perthshire, 1970; Principal Clerk of Justiciary, Scotland, 1971; Principal Clerk of Session and Justiciary, Scotland, 1975–82. Hon. Sheriff of Tayside, Central and Fife at Stirling, 1982. *Recreations:* music, golf, gardening. *Address:* Ormar, 29 Atholl Place, Dunblane, Perthshire. *T:* Dunblane 822186. *Club:* Dunblane New Golf (Dunblane). *Died 7 Dec. 1989.*

**BROWN, Rev. Canon Oscar Henry,** CIE 1947; OBE 1938; BA, LLB; Barrister-at-Law; *b* 4 July 1896; *s* of Frank and Winifred Brown; *m* 1918, Daisy Conway (*d* 1967); two *s* three *d*; *m* 1973, Margaret Roggendorf, Dr phil. *Educ:* Cathedral High School, St Xavier's Coll., and Govt Law Coll., Bombay; Gray's Inn, London. Barrister-at-Law, and Advocate of High Court of Bombay; Presidency Magistrate, 1929; Chief Presidency Magistrate, and Revenue Judge, Bombay, 1941–51. Ordained Priest, 1969. Hon. Canon, St Thomas's Cathedral, Bombay, 1970. *Recreations:* yachting, golf, philosophy. *Address:* Arenbergstrasse 13, 5353 Mechernich, West Germany.
*Died 11 March 1982.*

**BROWN, Prof. Reginald Francis,** PhD; (First) Cowdray Professor of Spanish Language and Literature in the University of Leeds, 1953–75, retired; *b* 23 April 1910; *m* 1939, Rica Eleanor Jones; one *s* one *d*. *Educ:* Lancaster Royal Grammar School; Liverpool University. BA First Class Hons. Spanish, 1932; PhD, 1939; University Fellowship, Liverpool, 1934. On Staff of Spanish Departments in Universities of Liverpool, Columbia, and New York, NYC, and Dartmouth College, NH, USA, 1939–43. War of 1939–45: service in RAF Intelligence (FO). Head of Dept of Spanish, University of Leeds, 1945–53. Vis. Prof. of Spanish, Princeton Univ., 1958–59. Pres., Modern Language Assoc., 1970. Leverhulme Emeritus Fellow, 1980–81. Diamond Jubilee Gold Medal, Inst. of Linguists, 1972. Encomienda of Order of Alfonso el Sabio, 1977. *Publications:* Bibliografia de la Novela Española, 1700–1850, (Madrid) 1953; Spanish-English, English-Spanish Pocket Dictionary, (Glasgow) 1954, 2nd edn, 1956; Spain, A Companion to Spanish Studies (ed. E. Allison Peers), 5th edn revised and enlarged, 1956; D. F. Sarmiento, Facundo, ed. Boston, 1960. Articles in Bulletin of Hispanic Studies, Hispania, Hispanic Review, Modern Languages, Year's Work in Modern Language Studies. *Address:* Rivington House, Clarence Road, Horsforth, near Leeds. *T:* Leeds 582443. *Died 25 April 1985.*

**BROWN, Maj.-Gen. (Reginald) Llewellyn,** CB 1950; CBE 1941; MA; FRICS (Council 1950–53); late RE; Hon. Colonel 135 Survey Engineer Regt TA, 1954–60; Consultant Surveyor; *b* 23 July 1895; *m* 1928, Nancy Katharine Coleridge; one *s*. *Educ:* Wellington College; Royal Military Acad. European War, pow, 1914–18. Served in Middle East, North Africa, Italy, 1939–45. Director of Military Survey, War Office, 1946; Director-General, Ordnance Survey, 1949–53. MA Oxon by decree, 1954 (Member of New College). Senior Lecturer in Surveying, 1954–55. FRGS. (Hon. Vice-President, 1969). Consultant to: the Times Atlas, 1955–59; Spartan Air Services of Ottawa, 1956–71. Chm. Meridian Airmaps Ltd. President: Photogrammetric Society, 1957–59; International Society for Photogrammetry, 1956–60 (Vice-President, 1960–64). Founder's Medal, RGS, 1978. Legion of Honour (USA), 1945. FRPSL 1975. *Recreations:* golf, philately. *Address:* Cricket Hill Cottage, Cricket Hill Lane, Yateley, Camberley, Surrey GU17 7BA. *T:* Yateley 872130. *Club:* Naval and Military. *Died 17 July 1983.*

**BROWN, Rt. Rev. Russel Featherstone;** *b* Newcastle upon Tyne, 7 Jan. 1900; *s* of Henry John George Brown and Lucy Jane Ferguson; *m* 1940, Priscilla Marian Oldacres (*d* 1948); three *s*. *Educ:* Bishop's Univ., Lennoxville, PQ, Canada. BA (Theo.) 1933. RAF, 1918–19; business, 1919–29; University, 1929–33; Deacon, 1933; Priest,

1934; Curate, Christ Church Cathedral, Montreal, 1933–36; Priest-in-Charge, Fort St John, BC, 1936–40; Rector of Sherbrooke, PQ, 1940–54; Canon, Holy Trinity Cathedral, Quebec, 1948; Rector, St Matthew's, Quebec, PQ, 1954–60; Archdeacon of Quebec, 1954–60; Bishop of Quebec, 1960–71; subsequently teaching in Papua New Guinea. Assistant Bishop of Montreal, 1976–83. Hon. DCL Bishop's Univ., Lennoxville, 1961; Hon. DD, Montreal Diocesan Theological College, 1968. *Address:* Fyfield Manor, Benson, Oxon OX9 6HA. *T:* 0491–35184. *Died 7 Jan. 1988.*

**BROWN, Prof. Thomas Julian,** MA; FSA; FBA 1982; Professor of Palæography, University of London, since 1961; *b* 24 Feb. 1923; *s* of Tom Brown, land agent, Penrith, Cumberland, and Helen Wright Brown, MBE; *m* 1st, 1959, Alison Macmillan Dyson (marr. diss. 1979); two *d*; 2nd, 1980, Sanchia Mary David (*née* Blair-Leighton). *Educ:* Westminster School (KS); Christ Church, Oxford. 2nd class, Class. Hon. Mods, 1942, and Lit.Hum., 1948. The Border Regt, 1942–45, mostly attached Inf. Heavy Weapons School, Netheravon. Asst Keeper Dept of MSS, British Museum, 1950–60. FSA 1956. Member, Inst. for Advanced Study, Princeton, NJ, 1966–67. Lyell Reader in Bibliography, Univ. of Oxford, 1976–77; Vis. Fellow, All Souls Coll., Oxford, 1976–77. Chm. of Cttee and Trustee, Lambeth Palace Library, 1979–; Pres., Bibliographical Soc., 1986–87. FKC, 1975. *Publications:* (with R. L. S. Bruce-Mitford, A. S. C. Ross, E. G. Stanley and others) Codex Lindisfarnensis, vol. ii, 1960; Latin Palæography since Traube (inaugural lecture), Trans. Camb. Bibliographical Society, 1963; The Stonyhurst Gospel (Roxburghe Club), 1969; The Durham Ritual, 1969; Northumbria and the Book of Kells (Jarrow Lect.), 1972; (with C. D. Verey and E. Coatsworth) The Durham Gospels, 1980. *Address:* King's College, Strand, WC2R 2LS. *T:* 01–836 5454; 1 Edenbridge Road, E9 7DR. *T:* 01–986 0692. *Died 19 Jan. 1987.*

**BROWN, Air Cdre Sir Vernon,** Kt 1952; CB 1944; OBE 1937; MA; CEng; FRAeS; *b* 10 Jan. 1889; *s* of Ernest J. Brown and H. M. Messent, Blackheath; *m* 1st, 1914, Constance Mary (*d* 1967), *d* of late F. E. Duckham (Port of London Authority) and Maud McDougall, Blackheath; one *d*; 2nd, 1971, Sheila Rigby, *d* of late T. M. Rigby and Agnes Carter. *Educ:* Eastbourne College; Jesus College, Cambridge (MA). Gas Engineering prior to 1915, then RFC/RAF (French Croix de Guerre). Served in UK, France, and after war in Iraq and Egypt. Retired 1937 and became Chief Inspector of Accidents, Air Ministry and later Ministry of Civil Aviation; retired as Permanent Civil Servant, 1952. Hon. FSLAET. *Recreation:* music. *Address:* Eastholme, Station Road, Yarmouth, Isle of Wight PO41 0QT. *T:* Yarmouth (IoW) 760189. *Clubs:* Naval and Military; Royal Solent Yacht. *Died 26 Aug. 1986.*

**BROWN, Walter Graham S.;** see Scott-Brown.

**BROWN, Maj.-Gen. William Douglas Elmes,** CB 1967; CBE 1962 (OBE 1945; MBE 1941); DSO 1945; Secretary, The Dulverton Trust, since 1969; *b* 8 Dec. 1913; *s* of late Joseph William Brown, Manor House, Knaresborough, Yorks; *m* 1947, Nancy Ursula (*d* 1980), *d* of Colonel W. F. Basset, Netherton, nr Andover. *Educ:* Sherborne; RMA, Woolwich. 2nd Lieut, RA, 1934. Served War of 1939–45, E Africa, and N Africa (50 (Northumbrian) Div.) (despatches). Seconded to Royal Iraqi Army, 1947–50; Chief of Staff, Northern Ireland, 1961–62; Commandant, School of Artillery, 1962–64; ADC to the Queen, 1963–64; Director of Army Equipment Policy, 1964–66; Dep. Master-Gen. of the Ordnance, 1966–69. Lt-Col 1955; Brigadier, 1961; Major-General, 1964. Col Comdt, RA, 1970–78. *Recreations:* shooting, fishing, golf. *Address:* Gunner's Cottage, Littlewick Green, Maidenhead, Berks. *T:* Littlewick Green 2083. *Clubs:* Army and Navy; Hon. Co. of Edinburgh Golfers. *Died 2 June 1984.*

**BROWNE, Major Alexander Simon Cadogan,** JP; DL; *b* 22 July 1895; *e s* of late Major Alexander Browne of Callaly Castle, Northumberland; *m* 1918, Dorothy Mary (*d* 1979), *d* of late Major F. J. C. Howard, 8th Hussars of Moorefield, Newbridge, Co. Kildare and Baytown, Co. Meath; one *d*. *Educ:* Eton; RMC Sandhurst. Major 12th Royal Lancers; served European War, 1914–18; retired, 1925; re-employed, 1939–45; served HQ 23rd (Northumbrian) Div., BEF, 1940 (despatches) and with BLA 1945. Secretary to the Duke of Beaufort's Fox Hounds, 1928–38; Joint Master, Percy Fox Hounds, 1938–46. Pres., Berwick-upon-Tweed Conservative Assoc., 1970–73. Chairman, Rothbury RDC, 1950–55; CC, 1950–67, CA, 1967–74, Hon. Alderman, 1974, Northumberland; High Sheriff of Northumberland, 1958–59; JP 1946, DL 1961, Northumberland. *Address:* South Wing, Callaly Castle, Alnwick, Northumberland NE664TA. *T:* Whittingham (Northumberland)663. *Clubs:* Cavalry and Guards; Northern Counties (Newcastle upon Tyne).
*Died 26 May 1987.*

**BROWNE, Brig. Dominick Andrew Sidney,** CBE 1945 (OBE 1943); *b* 29 Feb. 1904; *s* of Major Dominick S. Browne, DL, JP, and Naomi, *d* of Hon. R. Dobell, Quebec; *m* 1930, Iris (*d* 1977), *d* of Major G. H. Deane, Littleton House, Winchester; one *s* three *d*. *Educ:* Eton; RMC Sandhurst. 1st Bn Royal Scots Fusiliers, 1924; retired 1929;

Jt Master Co. Galway Hounds, 1933–36. Served War of 1939–45 (CBE). *Recreations:* shooting, fishing. *Address:* Amesbury Abbey, Amesbury, Wilts. *Clubs:* Boodle's; Kildare Street and University (Dublin). *Died 9 Sept. 1982.*

**BROWNE, Sir (Edward) Humphrey,** Kt 1964; CBE 1952; FEng; Chairman, British Transport Docks Board, 1971–82; Deputy Chairman, Haden Carrier Ltd, 1973–84; retired; *b* 7 April 1911; *m* 1934, Barbara Stone (*d* 1970); two *s*. *Educ:* Repton; Magdalene College, Cambridge (BA 1931, MA 1943); Birmingham University (Joint Mining Degree). Manager, Chanters Colliery; Director and Chief Mining Engineer, Manchester Collieries Ltd, 1943–46; Production Director, North-Western Divisional Coal Board, 1947–48; Director-General of Production, National Coal Board, 1947–55; Chm., Midlands Div., NCB, 1955–60; Dep. Chm., NCB, 1960–67; Chairman: John Thompson Group, 1967–70; Woodall Duckham Gp, 1971–73 (Dep. Chm., 1967–71); Bestobell Ltd, 1973–79 (Dir, 1969). Mem., Commonwealth Develt Corp., 1969–72. President: The British Coal Utilisation Research Assoc., 1963–68; Inst. of Freight Forwarders, 1976–77. Director, National Industrial Fuel Efficiency Service, 1960–69; Pres., Institution of Mining Engineers, 1957. Pro-Chancellor, Univ. of Keele, 1971–75. *Address:* Beckbury Hall, near Shifnal, Salop. *T:* Ryton 207. *Club:* Brooks's. *Died 20 Feb. 1987.*

**BROWNE, Hablot Robert Edgar,** CMG 1955; OBE 1942; HM Diplomatic Service, retired; employed in Commonwealth Office (formerly CRO), 1959–67; *b* 11 Aug. 1905; *s* of Dr Hablot J. M. Browne, Hoylake, Cheshire; *m* 1933, Petra Elsie, *d* of Peter Tainsh, OBE; one *d*. *Educ:* St George's, Harpenden; Christ's College, Cambridge. Colonial Administrative Service, Nigeria, 1928; Assistant Colonial Secretary, Barbados, 1939; Asst Secretary, Jamaica, 1943; Deputy Colonial Secretary, Jamaica, 1945; acted as Colonial Secretary on various occasions, 1945–49; Admin. Officer, Class I, Nigeria, 1950; Civil Secretary, Northern Region, Nigeria, 1951–55; Actg Lieut Governor, Northern Region, Nigeria, Sept. 1954; Actg Governor, Northern Region, Nigeria, Oct. 1954; retired from Colonial Administrative Service, 1955. Assistant Adviser to the Government of Qatar, Persian Gulf, 1956–57. *Recreation:* watching cricket. *Address:* 85 Bishop's Mansions, Bishop's Park Road, SW6. *T:* 01–731 3209. *Clubs:* Travellers', MCC. *Died 14 March 1984.*

**BROWNE, Sir Humphrey;** see Browne, Sir E. H.

**BROWNE, Rev. Laurence Edward,** DD (Cantab); MA (Manchester); Emeritus Professor, University of Leeds, since 1952; Vicar of Highbrook, Sussex, 1957–64; *b* 17 April 1887; *s* of late E. Montague Browne, Solicitor, Northampton; *m* 1st, 1920, Gladys May Dearden; one *s* two *d*; 2nd, 1938, Margaret Theresa Wingate Carpenter (*d* 1982); two *d*. *Educ:* Magdalen College School, Brackley; Sidney Sussex College, Cambridge. Lecturer and Fellow of St Augustine's College, Canterbury, 1913–20; Lecturer at Bishops' College, Calcutta, 1921–25; studying Islam in Cairo, Constantinople and Cambridge, 1926–29; Lecturer at the Henry Martyn School of Islamic Studies, Lahore, 1930–34; Rector of Gayton, Northants, 1935–46; Prof. of Comparative Religion at the University of Manchester, 1941–46; Professor of Theology, University of Leeds, 1946–52; Vicar of Shadwell, near Leeds, 1952–57. Examining Chaplain to Bp of Peterborough, 1937–50, to Bp of Ripon, 1946–57. Hulsean Lecturer, Cambridge, 1954; Godfrey Day Lectr, Trin. Coll., Dublin, 1956. *Publications:* Parables of the Gospel, 1913; Early Judaism, 1920 and 1929; Acts, in Indian Church Commentaries, 1925; From Babylon to Bethlehem, 1926, 1936 and 1951 (Telugu translation, 1932, Chinese translation 1935); The Eclipse of Christianity in Asia, 1933, New York, 1967; Christianity and the Malays, 1936; Prospects of Islam, 1944; Where Science and Religion Meet, 1951; The Quickening Word (Hulsean Lectures), 1955; contrib. to New Peake's Commentary, 1962. *Address:* Firgrove Nursing Home, Keymer Road, Burgess Hill, Sussex. *Died 29 May 1986.*

**BROWNE, Stanley George,** CMG 1976; OBE 1965; MD, FRCP, FRCS, DTM, FKC; retired; Director, Leprosy Study Centre, London, 1966–80; Consultant Adviser in Leprosy, Department of Health and Social Security and Hon. Consultant in Leprosy, UCH, 1966–79; Medical Consultant, Leprosy Mission, 1966–78 (Vice-President: England and Wales, since 1982; International, since 1985); Consultant Leprologist to: St Giles' Homes; Order of Charity; Association of European Leprosy Associations; All-Africa Leprosy Training and Rehabilitation Centre, Addis Ababa, 1966–81; President, Baptist Union, 1980–81; *b* 8 Dec. 1907; *s* of Arthur Browne and Edith Lillywhite; *m* 1940, Ethel Marion Williamson, MA (Oxon); three *s*. *Educ:* King's Coll. and KCH, London Univ. (Fellow, KCH Med. Sch., 1977); Inst. de Méd. Tropicale Prince Léopold, Antwerp. MRCS, LRCP, MB, BS (London) (Hons, Dist. in Surg., Forensic Med., Hygiene), AKC, 1933, FKC 1976; MRCP 1934 (Murchison Schol. RCP); FRCS 1935; DTM (Antwerp), 1936; MD (London), 1954; FRCP 1961.

Leverhulme Res. Grant for investigating trng of African med. auxiliaries, 1954; Consultant, WHO Expert Cttee on Trng of Med. Auxiliaries; WHO Travel Grant to visit Leprosy Res. Instns, 1963. Med. Missionary, Baptist Miss. Soc., Yakusu, Belg. Congo, 1936–59 (Hon. Life Mem., 1984); Médecin Directeur, Ecole agréée d'Infirmiers, Yakusu, 1936–59; Léproserie de Yalisombo, 1950–59; Mem. several Govt Commns concerned with health in Belgian Congo; Sen. Specialist Leprologist and Dir of Leprosy Res. Unit, Uzuakoli, E Nigeria, 1959–66; Associate Lectr in Leprosy, Ibadan Univ., 1960–65, 1968–; Vis. Lectr in leprosy in univs and med. schs in many countries. Med. Sec., British Leprosy Relief Assoc., 1968–73; Sec.-Gen., Internat. Leprosy Congress, London, 1968, Bergen, 1973, Mexico City, 1978, New Delhi, 1984. Associate Editor and Dir, Internat. Jl of Leprosy of Internat. Leprosy Assoc., Inc., 1966–84. FRSocMed; Mem. Council, 1967–71, and Fellow, Royal Soc. Trop. Med. Hygiene (Vice-Pres., 1971–73; Pres., 1977–79); Fellow, Hunterian Soc., 1974. President: Christian Med. Fellowship, 1969–71; Ludhiana British Fellowship, 1974–; Internat. Assoc. of Physicians for the Overseas Services, 1978–85; Med. Missionary Assoc., 1982–; Co-founder and first Chm., Christian Med. Fellowship of Nigeria; Chairman: Internat. Congress of Christian Physicians, 1972–75 (Vice-Pres., 1975–82, Pres., 1982–); Editorial Board of Leprosy Review, 1968–73 (Consulting Editor, 1973–); Founder Member: Internat. Filariasis Assoc.; Internat. Soc. of Tropical Dermatology (and Mem., Bd of Dirs, 1976–79, Mem., Advisory Council, 1982–84, Vice-Pres., 1984–). Member: Leprosy Expert Cttee, WHO (Chm., 1976); Assoc. de Léprologues de langue française (Conseiller technique); Section Dermatology, RSM; Medical Policy Cttee, Methodist Missionary Soc.; Medical Adv. Cttee and Gen. Cttee, Baptist Missionary Soc.; British Council, Dr Schweitzer's Hosp. Fund; Comité de Directeurs, Assoc. Internat. du Dr Schweitzer; Medical Commn, European Co-ordinating Cttee of Anti-Leprosy Assocs, 1966– (Chm., 1971–74); Med. Cttee, Hosp. for Tropical Diseases, London, 1966–79; Editorial Bd, Tropical Doctor; Soc. for Health Educn; Acid-Fast Club. Pres., London Baptist Missionary Union, 1983–84; Vice-Pres., LEPRA, 1984–. Hon. Vice-Pres., Internat. Leprosy Assoc.; Mem. (Sec. Treas., 1966–84). Hon. Member: Assoçião Brasileira de Leprologia; Sociedade Argentina de Leprologia; Korean Leprosy Assoc.; Sociedade Mexicana de Dermatologia, 1975; Sociedad Mexicana de Leprologia, 1976; Dermatol. Soc. of S Africa; Hon. Life Mem., Nigeria Soc. of Health; Hon. Foreign Mem., Belgian Royal Acad. of Med., 1980. Lectures: A. B. Mitchell Meml, QUB, 1967; Godfrey Day Meml, Dublin, 1974; Kellersberger Meml, Addis Ababa, 1978; Rendle Short Meml, Christian Medical Fellowship, 1978; Gandhi Meml, New Delhi, 1978; Maxwell Meml, Med. Missionary Soc., 1985. Sir Charlton Briscoe Prize for Research, 1934; Medal, Royal African Soc., 1970 (Life Mem.); Stewart Prize for Epidemiology, BMA, 1975; Ambuj Nath Bose Prize in Tropical Medicine, RCPE, 1977; Damien-Dutton Award, USA, 1979; Special Appreciation prize, Nihon Kensho-kai, 1979; Silver Medal of St Lazarus of Jerusalem, 1981. J. N. Chowdury Gold Medallist and Orator, Calcutta, 1978. Holds foreign orders incl.: Chevalier de l'Ordre Royal du Lion, 1948; Officier de l'Ordre de Léopold II, 1958; Comdr, Order of Malta, 1973; Commandeur, Ordre de Léopold, 1980. KLJ 1984. *Publications:* As the Doctor sees it — in Congo, 1950; Leprosy: new hope and continuing challenge, 1967; numerous articles on trop. diseases, esp. leprosy and onchocerciasis, and on med. educn in learned jls; booklets on med. missionary work, med. ethics, etc. *Relevant publications:* Bonganga: experiences of a missionary doctor, by Sylvia and Peter Duncan, 1958; Mister Leprosy, by Phyllis Thompson, 1980. *Recreations:* photography, reading, writing. *Address:* 16 Bridgefield Road, Sutton, Surrey SM1 2DG. *T:* 01–642 1656. *Died 29 Jan. 1986.*

**BROWNE, Sir Thomas Anthony G.;** see Gore Browne.

**BROWNING, Dame Daphne, (Lady Browning);** see du Maurier, Dame Daphne.

**BROWNING, Colonel George William,** OBE 1946; Welsh Guards, retired; *b* 1 Sept. 1901; *e s* of Rev. B. A Browning; *g s* of Col M. C. Browning, Brantham Court, Suffolk; *m* 1937, Rosemary Sybil, *y d* of Hubert Edgar Hughes, Flempton, Bury St Edmunds, Suffolk, *g d* of Sir Alfred Collingwood Hughes, Bt, East Bergholt, Suffolk; one *s* two *d*. *Educ:* Repton; RMC, Sandhurst. Commissioned Suffolk Regt, 1922; transf. Grenadier Guards, 1924; transf. Welsh Guards, 1939. Served War of 1939–45 (wounded); Comd 3rd Bn Welsh Guards, 1941; psc 1942; Comd 1st Bn Welsh Guards, 1944; AQMG, London District, 1945–48; Comd Welsh Guards 1945–51; retired, 1951. DL Pembrokeshire, 1955. *Address:* Weatherhill Farm, Icklingham, Bury St Edmunds, Suffolk. *T:* Culford 258. *Club:* Army and Navy. *Died 14 March 1981.*

**BRUCE, Alastair Henry,** CBE 1951; DL; Chairman and Managing Director, The Inveresk Paper Company Ltd, 1964–68; Member, Monopolies Commission, 1964–68; Chairman, Paper and Paper Products Industry Training Board, 1968–71; *b* 14 April 1900; *s* of Patrick Chalmers Bruce and Lucy Walmsley Hodgson. *Educ:*

Cargilfield, Midlothian; Uppingham. President British Paper and Board Makers Association, 1938–42 and 1948–51; President British Paper and Board Research Association, 1948–51. DL Midlothian, 1943–.                                    *Died 24 March 1988.*

**BRUCE, Prof. Frederick Fyvie,** MA Aberdeen, Cantab, Manchester, DD Aberdeen; FBA 1973; Rylands Professor of Biblical Criticism and Exegesis, University of Manchester, 1959–78, now Emeritus; *b* 12 Oct. 1910; *e s* of late P. F. Bruce, Elgin, Morayshire; *m* 1936, Betty, *er d* of late A. B. Davidson, Aberdeen; one *s* one *d. Educ:* Elgin Acad.; Univs of Aberdeen, Cambridge, Vienna. Gold Medallist in Greek and Latin; Fullerton Schol. in Classics, 1932; Croom Robertson Fellow, 1933; Aberdeen Univ.; Scholar of Gonville and Caius Coll., Camb., 1932; Sandys Student. Camb., 1934; Ferguson Schol. in Classics, 1933, and Crombie Scholar in Biblical Criticism, 1939, Scottish Univs; Diploma in Hebrew, Leeds Univ., 1943. Asst in Greek, Edinburgh Univ., 1935–38; Lectr in Greek, Leeds Univ., 1938–47; Professor of Biblical History and Literature, University of Sheffield, 1955–59 (Head of Dept, 1947–59); Dean of Faculty of Theology, Univ. of Manchester, 1963–64. Lectures: John A. McElwain, Gordon Divinity School, Beverly Farms, Massachusetts, 1958; Calvin Foundation, Calvin Coll. and Seminary, Grand Rapids, Michigan, 1958; Payton, Fuller Theolog. Seminary, Pasadena, Calif, 1968; Norton, Southern Baptist Theolog. Seminary, Louisville, Kentucky, 1968; Smyth, Columbia Theological Seminary, Decatur, Ga, 1970; Earle, Nazarene Theological Seminary, Kansas City, Mo, 1970; N. W. Lund, N Park Theological Seminary, Chicago, 1970; Thomas F. Staley, Ontario Bible Coll., Toronto, 1973; Moore Coll., Sydney, 1977; Griffith Thomas, Wycliffe Hall, Oxford, 1982; Griffith Thomas, Dallas Theol Seminary, Texas, 1983. Examr in Biblical Studies: Leeds University, 1943–47, 1957–60, 1967–69; Edinburgh University, 1949–52, 1958–60; Bristol University, 1958–60; Aberdeen University, 1959–61; London University, 1959–60; St Andrews University, 1961–64; Cambridge University, 1961–62; University of Wales, 1965–68; Sheffield University, 1968–70; Newcastle University, 1969–71; Keele Univ., 1971–73; Dublin Univ., 1972–75. President: Yorkshire Soc. for Celtic Studies, 1948–50; Sheffield Branch of Classical Association, 1955–58; Victoria Inst., 1958–65; Manchester Egyptian and Oriental Society, 1963–65; Soc. for Old Testament Study, 1965; Soc. for New Testament Studies, 1975. Hon LittD Sheffield, 1988. Burkitt Medal, British Acad., 1979. Editor: Yorkshire Celtic Studies, 1945–57; The Evangelical Quarterly, 1949–80; Palestine Exploration Quarterly, 1957–71. *Publications:* The NT Documents, 1943; The Hittites and the OT, 1948; The Books and the Parchments, 1950; The Acts of the Apostles, Greek Text with Commentary, 1951, rev. edn 1990; The Book of the Acts, Commentary on English Text, 1954, rev. edn 1988; Second Thoughts on the Dead Sea Scrolls, 1956; The Teacher of Righteousness in the Qumran Texts, 1957; Biblical Exegesis in the Qumran Texts, 1959; The Spreading Flame, 1958; The Epistle to the Ephesians, 1961; Paul and his Converts, 1962; The Epistle of Paul to the Romans, 1963, rev. edn 1985; Israel and the Nations, 1963; Commentary on the Epistle to the Hebrews, 1964, rev. edn 1990; Expanded Paraphrase of the Epistles of Paul, 1965; New Testament History, 1969; This is That, 1969; Tradition Old and New, 1970; St Matthew, 1970; The Epistles of John, 1970; First and Second Corinthians (Century Bible), 1971; The Message of the New Testament, 1972; Jesus and Christian Origins outside the New Testament, 1974; Paul and Jesus, 1974; First-Century Faith, 1977; Paul: Apostle of the Free Spirit, 1977; The Time is Fulfilled, 1978; History of the Bible in English, 1979; The Work of Jesus, 1979; Men and Movements in the Primitive Church, 1980; In Retrospect, 1980; The Epistle to the Galatians, 1982; First and Second Thessalonians, 1982; Paternoster Bible History Atlas, 1982; Commentary on Philippians, 1983; The Gospel of John, 1983; The Hard Sayings of Jesus, 1983; Commentary on Colossians, Philemon and Ephesians, 1984; The Pauline Circle, 1985; The Real Jesus, 1985; The Canon of Scripture, 1988; contribs to classical and theological journals. *Recreation:* foreign travel. *Address:* The Crossways, Temple Road, Buxton, Derbyshire SK17 9BA. *T:* Buxton (0298) 23250.                                    *Died 11 Sept. 1990.*

**BRUCE, Hon. Mildred Mary;** *see* Bruce, Hon. Mrs Victor.

**BRUCE of Sumburgh, Robert Hunter Wingate,** CBE 1967; Lord-Lieutenant for Shetland (formerly for the County of Zetland), 1963–82; *b* 11 Oct. 1907; *s* of John Bruce of Sumburgh and Isobel Abel; *m* 1935, Valmai Muriel, *d* of Charles Frederick Chamberlain and Lillian Muriel Smith; no *c. Educ:* Rugby School; Balliol College, Oxford. LMS Railway, 1930–46; on loan to Min. of Economic Warfare, 1941–43; Manager, Northern Counties Rly, Belfast, 1943–46. Retired from LMS to manage Shetland property, 1946. Rep. Rio Tinto Co. in N and S Rhodesia and S Africa, Africa, 1952–57. Member Zetland CC, 1948–52, 1958–61. Member: Advisory Panel on Highlands and Islands, 1948–52, 1957–65; Crofters Commn, 1960–78. Chairman, Highland Transport Board, 1963–66. Medal of Freedom with Silver Palm, USA, 1948. *Recreations:* farming, reading history, golf, convivial argument.

*Address:* Sand Lodge, Sandwick, Shetland ZE2 9HP. *T:* Sandwick 209. *Clubs:* New (Edinburgh); Hon. Co. of Edinburgh Golfers (Gullane).                                    *Died 17 Aug. 1983.*

**BRUCE, Hon. Mrs Victor, (Mildred Mary),** FRGS; *b* 10 Nov. 1895; *d* of Lawrence Joseph Petre, Coptfold Hall, Essex; *m* 1926, Hon. Victor Bruce (marr. diss. 1941), *y s* of 2nd Baron Aberdare. *Educ:* Convent of Sion. Travelled furthest north into Lapland by motor car; held record for Double Channel Crossing, Dover to Calais, by motor boat; 17 World Records, motoring, and of 24–hour record; single-handed drive, covered longest distance for man or woman, 2164 miles, in 24 hours; Coupe des Dames, Monte Carlo Rally, 1927. Flying records: first solo flight from England to Japan, 1930; longest solo flight, 1930; record solo flight, India to French Indo-China, 1930; British Air refuelling endurance flight, 1933. 24 hour record by motor boat, covering 674 nautical miles, single handed, 1929; first crossing of Yellow Sea. Show Jumping, 1st Royal Windsor Horse Show, 1939. Order of the Million Elephants and White Umbrella (French Indo-China). Fellow, Ancient Monuments Society. *Publications:* The Peregrinations of Penelope; 9000 Miles in Eight Weeks; The Woman Owner Driver; The Bluebird's Flight; Nine Lives Plus. *Address:* Croftway House, Croftway, NW3 7AQ. *Clubs:* Royal Motor Yacht, British Racing Drivers (Life Hon. Mem.), Rolls Royce Enthusiasts'.            *Died 21 May 1990.*

**BRUCE-CHWATT, Prof. Leonard Jan,** CMG 1976; OBE 1953; FRCP; FIBiol; Professor of Tropical Hygiene and Director of Ross Institute, London School of Hygiene and Tropical Medicine, University of London, 1969–74, now Emeritus Professor; *b* 9 June 1907; *s* of Dr Michael Chwatt and Anna Marquitant; *m* 1948, Joan Margaret Bruce; two *s. Educ:* Univ. of Warsaw (MD); Paris (Dipl. Méd. Col.); Univ. of London (DTM&H); Harvard (MPH). Wartime service Polish Army Med. Corps and RAMC, 1939–45; Colonial Medical Service (Senior Malariologist, Nigeria), 1946–58; Chief Research and Technical Intelligence, Div. of Malaria Eradication, WHO, Geneva, 1958–68. Mem. Expert Cttee on Malaria, WHO, Geneva, 1956–. Consultant, Wellcome Tropical Inst. (formerly Wellcome Mus. of Med. Science), 1975–. Duncan Medal, 1942; North Persian Forces Memorial Medal, 1952; Darling Medal and Prize, 1971; Macdonald Meml Medal, 1978; Laveran Medal, 1983, 1987; John Hull Grundy Medal, RAMC, 1984; Leuckart Medal, 1987. KStJ 1975. *Publications:* Terminology of Malaria, 1963; chapter on malaria in Cecil and Loeb Textbook of Medicine, 1967 and 1970; Dynamics of Tropical Disease, 1973; The Rise and Fall of Malaria in Europe, 1980; Essential Malariology, 1980, 2nd edn 1985; Chemotherapy of Malaria, 1981, French edn 1984; numerous papers in medical jls. *Recreations:* travel, music, walking. *Address:* 21 Marchmont Road, Richmond, Surrey. *T:* 01–940 5540.
                                    *Died 18 May 1989.*

**BRUCE-GARDYNE, Baron** *cr* 1983 (Life Peer), of Kirkden in the District of Angus; **John, (Jock), Bruce-Gardyne;** *b* 12 April 1930; 2nd *s* of late Capt. E. Bruce-Gardyne, DSO, RN, Middleton, by Arbroath, Angus and Joan (*née* McLaren); *m* 1959, Sarah Louisa Mary, *o d* of Comdr Sir John Maitland and Bridget Denny; two *s* one *d. Educ:* Winchester; Magdalen College, Oxford. HM Foreign Service, 1953–56; served in London and Sofia; Paris correspondent, Financial Times, 1956–60; Foreign Editor, Statist, 1961–64. MP (C): South Angus, 1964–Oct. 1974; Knutsford, March 1979–1983; PPS to Secretary of State for Scotland, 1970–72; Minister of State, HM Treasury, 1981; Economic Sec. to HM Treasury, 1981–83. Vice-Chm., Cons. Parly Finance Cttee, 1972–74, 1979–80. Columnist, Sunday Telegraph, 1979–81, 1984–; editorial writer, Daily Telegraph, 1977–81, 1984–. Consultant, Northern Engineering Industries, 1979–81, 1985–. Director: Central Trustee Savings Bank, 1983–85; Trustee Savings Bank plc, 1985–; TSB England and Wales plc, 1985–; London & Northern Gp plc, 1985–87. *Publications:* Whatever happened to the Quiet Revolution?, 1974; Scotland in 1980, 1975; (with Nigel Lawson) The Power Game, 1976; Mrs Thatcher's First Administration: the prophets confounded, 1984; Ministers and Mandarins: inside the Whitehall village (autobiog.), 1986. *Address:* 13 Kelso Place, W8; The Old Rectory, Aswardby, Spilsby, Lincolnshire.
                                    *Died 15 April 1990.*

**BRUCE LOCKHART, John Macgregor,** CB 1966; CMG 1951; OBE 1944; *b* 9 May 1914; *e s* of late John Harold Bruce Lockhart and Mona Brougham; *m* 1939, Margaret Evelyn, *d* of late Rt Rev. C. R. Hone; two *s* one *d. Educ:* Rugby School (Captain XV); St Andrews University (Harkness Scholar). MA (Hons) French and German, 1937. Asst Master, Rugby School, 1937–39; TA Commission, Seaforth Highlanders, 1938; served War of 1939–45, in UK, Middle East, North Africa, Italy (Lt-Col); Asst Military Attaché, British Embassy, Paris, 1945–47; Control Commission Germany, 1948–51; First Secretary, British Embassy, Washington, 1951–53; served Foreign Office, London, until resignation from the Diplomatic Service, 1965; in charge of planning and development, Univ. of Warwick, 1965–67; Head of Central Staff Dept, Courtaulds Ltd, 1967–71. Visitor, HM Prison Onley, 1972–76. Advisor on Post

Experience Programme, City Univ. Business Sch., 1971–80 (Hon. Fellow, City Univ., 1980); Chm., Business Educn Council, 1974–80; Member: Schools Council, 1975–80; Naval Educn Adv. Cttee, 1973–80. Vis. Scholar, St Andrews Univ., 1981; Vis. Lectr, Rand Afrikaans Univ., 1983. President: Flecknoe Cricket Club, 1966–76; Rugby Football Club, 1972–76. *Publications:* articles and lectures on strategic studies at RCDS, RUSI, Kennedy Inst. of Politics, Harvard and Georgetown Univ., Washington, DC. *Recreations:* music, real tennis, golf, pictures. *Address:* 37 Fair Meadow, Rye, Sussex TN31 7NL. *Clubs:* Reform; Rye Dormy.

*Died* 1 *May* 1990.

**BRUCE LOCKHART, Rab Brougham,** MA Cantab; Headmaster, Loretto School, Musselburgh, Edinburgh, 1960–76, retired; *b* 1 Dec. 1916; *s* of late J. H. Bruce Lockhart; *m* 1941, Helen Priscilla Lawrence Crump; one *s* one *d* (and one *s* decd). *Educ:* Edinburgh Academy; Corpus Christi College, Cambridge. BA (Mod. Lang.) 1939; MA 1946. Assistant Master, Harrow, 1939. Served War of 1939–45: Commissioned RA, 1940; Middle East, 1942–44; Major RA 1944; Intelligence, Italy and Austria, 1945. Assistant Master, Harrow, 1946–50; Housemaster, Appleby College, Oakville, Ont, Canada, 1950–54; Headmaster, Wanganui Collegiate School, Wanganui, New Zealand, 1954–60. *Recreations:* squash, golf and photography; formerly: a Scotland cricket XI, 1935; Scotland XV, 1937, 1939; Rugby "Blue" 1937, 1938. *Address:* Saul Hill, Burneside, near Kendal, Cumbria LA8 9AU. *T:* Selside (053983) 646.

*Died* 1 *May* 1990.

**BRUFORD, Walter Horace,** MA; FBA 1963; *b* Manchester, 1894; *s* of Francis J. and Annie Bruford; *m* 1925, Gerda (*d* 1976), *d* of late Professor James Hendrick; one *s* two *d*. *Educ:* Manchester Grammar School; St John's College, Cambridge; University of Zürich. BA Cambridge, 1915 (1st Class Hons Med. and Mod. Langs). Bendall Sanskrit Exhibitioner; Master Manchester Grammar School; served Intelligence Division, Admiralty, with rank of Lieut RNVR. On demobilisation, research in University of Zürich; Lecturer in German, University of Aberdeen, 1920, Reader, 1923; Professor of German, University of Edinburgh, 1929–51. Seconded to Foreign Office, 1939–43. Schröder Professor of German, University of Cambridge, 1951–61. Corresponding member Deutsche Akademie für Sprache und Dichtung, 1957; Goethe-Medal in Gold, of Goethe-Institut, Munich, 1958; President: Mod. Lang. Assoc., 1959; Mod. Humanities Research Assoc., 1965; English Goethe Soc., 1965–75; Corresponding Member, Sächsische Akademie der Wissenschaften, Leipzig, 1965. Hon. LLD Aberdeen, 1958; Hon. DLitt: Newcastle, 1969; Edinburgh, 1974. *Publications:* Sound and Symbol (with Professor J. J. Findlay); Germany in the eighteenth century; Die gesellschaftlichen Grundlagen der Goethezeit; Chekhov and His Russia; two chapters in Essays on Goethe (ed. by W. Rose); Theatre, Drama and Audience in Goethe's Germany; Literary Interpretation in Germany; Goethe's Faust (introd., revised and annotated, Everyman's Library); Chekhov (Studies in Modern European Literature and Thought); The Organisation and Rise of Prussia and German Constitutional and Social Development, 1795–1830 (in Cambridge Modern History, New Series, Vols VII and IX); Culture and Society in Classical Weimar; Deutsche Kultur der Goethezeit; Annotated edition and interpretation of Goethe's Faust, Part I; The German Tradition of Self-Cultivation: *Bildung* from Humboldt to Thomas Mann; articles and reviews in modern language periodicals. *Address:* The Old Vicarage, East Horrington, Wells, Somerset.

*Died* 28 *June* 1988.

**BRUHN, Erik Belton Evers;** Danish Ballet Dancer; actor; choreographer; teacher; Artistic Director, National Ballet of Canada, since 1983 (Resident Producer, 1973–76); *b* Copenhagen, Denmark, 3 Oct. 1928; *s* of Ernst Emil Bruhn, CE, and Ellen (*née* Evers); unmarried. *Educ:* Royal Danish Theatre, Copenhagen. Started at Royal Danish Ballet School, 1937; dancer with Danish Ballet, 1946–61, Amer. Nat. Ballet Theatre, 1949–58; Dir, Royal Swedish Ballet, 1967–73; guest appearances with many major companies. Principal rôles include those in: Giselle, Swan Lake, Carmen, La Sylphide, Les Sylphides, The Sleeping Beauty, Miss Julie, Night Shadow, Spectre de la Rose, A Folk Tale; also classical pas de deux and various abstract ballets. Character rôles for National Ballet of Canada: Madge in La Sylphide; Dr Coppélius in Coppélia; Peppo in Napoli. Choreographed for National Ballet of Canada: La Sylphide, 1964; Swan Lake, 1967 (also for CBC TV); Les Sylphides, 1973; Coppélia, 1975; Here We Come, 1983. Copenhagen Critic's Theatre Cup, 1962; Nijinsky Prize, 1963; Knight of Dannebrog, 1963; elected to roll of honour of Students' Assoc. of Denmark, 1963; Dancemagazine award, 1968; Diplôme d'honneur (Canada), 1974; Litteris et Artibus medal, 1980. *Publication:* Bournonville and Ballet Tecnic. *Relevant publication:* Erik Bruhn— Danseur Noble, by John Gruen. *Address:* National Ballet of Canada, 157 King Street East, Toronto, Ontario M5C 1G9, Canada.

*Died* 1 *April* 1986.

**BRUNNER, Sir Felix (John Morgan),** 3rd Bt, *cr* 1895; Director of various companies, retired; *b* 13 Oct. 1897; *o s* of Sir John Brunner,

2nd Bt, and Lucy Marianne Vaughan (*d* 1941), *d* of late Octavius Vaughan Morgan, MP; *S* father 1929; *m* 1926, Dorothea Elizabeth, OBE 1965, JP, *d* of late Henry Brodribb Irving and Dorothea Baird; three *s* (and two *s* decd). *Educ:* Cheltenham; Trinity College, Oxford (MA). Served European War, 1916–18, as Lieut RFA; contested (L) Hulme Division Manchester, 1924, Chippenham, Wilts, 1929, and Northwich, Cheshire, 1945. Chairman, Henley Rural District Council, 1954–57. Chairman, Commons, Open Spaces and Footpaths Preservation Society, 1958–70. President, Liberal Party Organisation, 1962–63. *Heir: s* John Henry Kilian Brunner [*b* 1 June 1927; *m* 1955, Jasmine Cecily, *d* of late John Wardrop-Moore; two *s* one *d*]. *Address:* Greys Court, Henley-on-Thames, Oxon. *T:* Rotherfield Greys 296. *Club:* Reform. *Died* 2 *Nov.* 1982.

**BRUNSKILL, Catherine Lavinia Bennett,** CBE 1919; *b* 15 Aug. 1891; *d* of Robert Bennett, Eastbourne; *m* 1918, Brig. George Stephen Brunskill, CBE, MC (from whom she obtained a divorce, 1946); one *d*. Private Secretary to Adjutant-General to the Forces, War Office, 1916–18; and to Commissioner of Metropolitan Police, New Scotland Yard, 1918–19. Defence Medal London Ambulance Service, 1945. *Address:* Flat 3, 65 Cadogan Gardens, SW3.

*Died* 15 *July* 1981.

**BRUNSKILL, Brig. George Stephen,** CBE 1941; MC 1914; *b* 26 Aug. 1891; *s* of late Major Arthur Stephen Brunskill, The King's Own Regt and West India Regt, of Buckland Tout Saints, S Devon, and Annie Louisa Churchward; *m* 1st, 1918, Catherine Lavinia Bennett, CBE (marr. diss. 1946); one *d*; 2nd, 1947, Moira Wallace (*née* Wares); one *s* one *d*. *Educ:* Eastbourne College; Royal Military College, Sandhurst; Staff College, Camberley (psc). Commissioned into Indian Army, 1911, and joined 47th Sikhs; served European War, 1914–18, in France, where twice severely wounded, and Italy as DAAG (MC, Corona d'Italia and Order of St Maurice and Lazarus, Brevet Major); transferred to King's Shropshire Light Infantry, 1918; commanded First Battalion, 1934; Colonel 1937, and served on the staff as Temp. Brigadier in Palestine (CBE), in the Greece and Crete campaigns of 1941 (despatches twice, Greek MC, 1939–43 Star, N African Star, Defence Medal, Czecho Slovak Order of White Lion, 3rd class); and on the Congo-Cairo War Supply Route, 1942–43; retired, 1945. Agent, Slingsby Estate, 1948–66. Councillor, Nidderdale RDC, 1950–66. *Address:* Cob Cottage, Woolstone, Faringdon, Oxon. *T:* Uffington 283.

*Died* 10 *Nov.* 1982.

**BRUNT, Robert Nigel Bright,** CBE 1947; *b* 13 April 1902; *s* of Henry Robert and Mary Madeline Brunt, Leek, Staffs, afterwards of Belle Isle, Co. Fermanagh; *m* 1943, Joan *er d* of Sir Richard Pierce Butler, 11th Bt, Ballin Temple, Co. Carlow; two *s* one *d*. *Educ:* Repton; King's College, Cambridge. Served in India and Pakistan with Burmah-Shell Oil Companies and Associates, 1922–50; a Director in London, 1951–55. Chairman, Punjab Chamber of Commerce, 1940–41; Chairman, National Service Advisory Cttee, Delhi Area, 1939–42; Adviser to Government of India for Petroleum Products, 1941–45; Member, Advisory Cttee for Development of New Delhi, 1940–45; a Trustee of Port of Karachi, 1949–50. A Governor of Queen Charlotte's and Chelsea Hospitals, 1962–65. *Address:* Oak Cottage, Knowle Lane, Cranleigh, Surrey GU6 8JN.

*Died* 1 *Jan.* 1982.

**BRUSH, Lt-Col Edward James Augustus Howard, (Peter),** CB 1966; DSO 1945; OBE 1946; *b* 5 March 1901; *s* of Major George Howard Brush, Drumnabreeze, Co. Down; *m* 1937, Susan Mary, *d* of Major F. H. E. Torbett, Britford, Salisbury; one *d*. *Educ:* Clifton Coll.; RMC. Commnd Rifle Brigade, 1920. Served War of 1939–45 (France; wounded; prisoner of war); retired 1946. Chairman, T&AFA, Co. Down, 1954–65. Mem., NI Convention, 1975–76. JP, DL Co. Down, 1953–74; Vice-Lieutenant, 1957–64; High Sheriff, 1953. Member, Irish Nat. Hunt Steeplechase Cttee. *Publication:* The Hunter Chaser, 1947. *Address:* Drumnabreeze, Magheralin, Craigavon, N Ireland. *T:* Moira 611284.

*Died* 22 *July* 1984.

**BRYAN, Sir Andrew (Meikle),** Kt 1950; DSc; Hon. LLD (Glasgow); FEng, FIMinE, FICE, FRSE; Consulting Mining Engineer; Member of National Coal Board, 1951–57; *b* 1 March 1893; 2nd *s* of John Bryan, Burnbank, Hamilton, Lanarkshire; *m* 1st, 1922, Henrietta Paterson (*d* 1977), *y d* of George S. Begg, Allanshaw, Hamilton; one *s*; 2nd, 1980, Mrs Winifred Henderson Rutledge, widow. *Educ:* Greenfield School; Hamilton Acad.; Glasgow University, graduated 1919 with Special Distinction. Served in University OTC and HM Forces, 1915–18. Obtained practical mining experience in the Lanarkshire Coalfield; HM Junior Inspector of Mines in the Northern Division, 1920; Senior rank, 1926; Dixon Professor of Mining, University of Glasgow, Professor of Mining, Royal College of Science and Technology, Glasgow, 1932–40; Gen. Manager, 1940, Dir, 1942, Managing Director, 1944, Shotts Iron Co. Ltd; also Director Associated Lothian Coal Owners Ltd; Deputy-Director of Mining Supplies, Mines Department, 1939–40; Chief Inspector of Mines, 1947–51. Mem. Council, IMinE

(Hon. Treas.; Hon. Mem., 1957; Pres., 1950 and 1951; Inst. Medal, 1954); Mem., Mining Qualifications Bd, 1947–62, Chm., 1962–72; former Mem. Council, Inst. Mining and Metallurgy, 1951; Hon. Member: Nat. Assoc. of Colliery Managers, 1957 (Futers Gold Medal, 1937; former Mem. Council; Past Pres.); Geol Soc. of Edinburgh; former Mem. Council and Past Pres., Mining Inst. of Scotland; John Buddle Medal, N England Inst. of Mining and Mech. Engrs, 1967. Fellow, Imperial College of Science and Technology. *Publications:* St George's Coalfield, Newfoundland, 1937; The Evolution of Health and Safety in Mines, 1976; contribs to technical journals. *Address:* 3 Hounslow Gardens, Hounslow, Mddx TW3 2DU.                              *Died 27 June* 1988.

**BRYAN, Denzil Arnold**, CMG 1960; OBE 1947; HM Diplomatic Service, retired; *b* 15 Oct. 1909; *s* of James Edward Bryan; *m* 1965, Hope Ross (*née* Meyer) (*d* 1981). *Educ:* in India; Selwyn Coll., Cambridge. Appointed to Indian Civil Service in 1933 and posted to Punjab. Dep. Commissioner, Hissar, 1938; Registrar, Lahore High Court, 1939–41; Dep. Comr, Dera Ghazi Khan, 1941–44; Sec. to Prime Minister, Punjab, 1944–47; and to Governor of Punjab, 1947; retired from ICS, 1947. Appointed to UK Civil Service, Bd of Trade, as Principal, 1947; Asst Sec., 1950; Under Secretary, 1961; served as a Trade Comr in India, 1947–55; UK Senior Trade Comr: in New Zealand, 1955–58; in Pakistan, 1958–61; in South Africa, 1961; Minister (Commercial, later Economic), S Africa, 1962–69. *Address:* 29 Wildcroft Manor, Wildcroft Road, SW15; c/o Lloyds Bank, 6 Pall Mall, SW1.                              *Died 2 Oct.* 1987.

**BRYAN, Willoughby Guy**, TD 1945; Director: Barclays Bank, 1957–81 (Vice-Chairman, 1964–70, Deputy Chairman, 1970–74); Barclays Bank Trust Company Ltd, 1970–81 (Chairman, 1970–74); Barclays Unicorn Group Ltd, 1977–81; *b* 16 Jan. 1911; *e s* of late C. R. W. Bryan; *m* 1936, Esther Victoria Loveday, *d* of late Major T. L. Ingram, DSO, MC; one *d*. *Educ:* Winchester; Hertford College, Oxford. Barclays Bank Ltd, 1932; various appointments including: Local Director, Oxford, 1946; Local Director, Reading, 1947; Local Director, Birmingham, 1955; Chm. Local Bd, Birmingham, 1957–64. Served War of 1939–45, Queen's Own Oxfordshire Hussars. *Recreation:* golf. *Address:* 28 Crooked Billet, Wimbledon Common, SW19 4RQ. *T:* 01–946 5645. *Clubs:* Army and Navy; Rye Golf, Royal Wimbledon Golf.                              *Died* 11 *June* 1987.

**BRYANT, Sir Arthur**, Kt 1954; CH 1967; CBE 1949; Hon. LLD: Edinburgh; St Andrews; New Brunswick; MA (Oxon); FRHistS; FRSL; Council, Society of Authors; Royal Literary Fund; Trustee: Historic Churches Preservation Trust; English Folk Music Fund; Member, Architectural Advisory Panel, Westminster Abbey; President, Friends of the Vale of Aylesbury; *b* 18 Feb. 1899; *e s* of late Sir Francis Bryant, CB, CVO, CBE, ISO, JP, The Pavilion, Hampton Court; *m* 1st, 1924, Sylvia Mary (marr. diss. 1939; she *m* 2nd, F. D. Chew, and *d* 1950), *d* of Sir Walter Shakerley, Bt, Somerford Park, Cheshire; 2nd, 1941, Anne Elaine (marr. diss. 1976), *y d* of Bertram Brooke (HH Tuan Muda of Sarawak). *Educ:* Harrow; BEF France; Queen's Coll., Oxford. Barrister-at-law, Inner Temple. Principal, Cambridge School of Arts, Crafts and Technology, 1923–25; Lectr in History to Oxford Univ. Delegacy for Extra-Mural Studies, 1925–36; Watson Chair in American History, London Univ., 1935; Corres. Member of La Real Academia de la Historia de Madrid; succeeded G. K. Chesterton as writer of Our Note Book, Illustrated London News, 1936–. Chairman: Ashridge Council, 1946–49; Soc. of Authors, 1949–53; St John and Red Cross Library Dept, 1945–74. President: English Association, 1946; Common Market Safeguards Campaign. Chesney Gold Medal, RUSI; Gold Medal, RICS. Hon. Freedom and Livery, Leathersellers' Company; Hon. Member: Southampton Chamber of Commerce; Rifle Brigade Club; Light Infantry Club. KGStJ. *Publications:* King Charles II, 1931; Macaulay, 1932; Samuel Pepys, the Man in the Making, 1933; The National Character, 1934; The England of Charles II, 1934; The Letters and Speeches of Charles II, 1935; Samuel Pepys, the Years of Peril, 1935; George V, 1936; The American Ideal, 1936; Postman's Horn, 1936; Stanley Baldwin, 1937; Humanity in Politics, 1938; Samuel Pepys, the Saviour of the Navy, 1938; Unfinished Victory, 1940; English Saga, 1940; The Years of Endurance, 1942; Dunkirk, 1943; Years of Victory, 1944; Historian's Holiday, 1947; The Age of Elegance, 1950 (Sunday Times Gold Medal and Award for Literature); The Turn of the Tide, 1957; Triumph in the West, 1959; Jimmy, 1960; The Story of England: Makers of the Realm, 1953; The Age of Chivalry, 1963; The Fire and the Rose, 1965; The Medieval Foundation, 1966; Protestant Island, 1967; The Lion and the Unicorn, 1969; Nelson, 1970; The Great Duke, 1971; Jackets of Green, 1973; Thousand Years of British Monarchy, 1975; Pepys and the Revolution, 1979; The Elizabethan Deliverance, 1980; Spirit of England, 1982; Set in a Silver Sea, 1984, vol. 1 of a history of Britain and the British people; prologue and epilogue to David Fraser's Alanbrooke, 1982; *relevant publication:* Arthur Bryant: portrait of a historian, by Pamela Street, 1979; *posthumous publication:* The Search for Justice, 1990. *Address:* Myles Place, The Close, Salisbury, Wilts. *Clubs:*

Athenæum, Beefsteak, Grillion's, Pratt's, Saintsbury, MCC.
                                        *Died* 22 *Jan.* 1985.

**BRYDEN, Sir William (James)**, Kt 1978; CBE 1970; QC (Scot.) 1973; Sheriff Principal of the Lothians and Borders, 1975–78; Sheriff of Chancery in Scotland, 1973–78; *b* 2 Oct. 1909; *y s* of late James George Bryden, JP and late Elizabeth Brown Tyrie; *m* 1937, Christina Mary, *e d* of late Thomas Bannatyne Marshall, CBE, JP; two *s* one *d*. *Educ:* Perth Academy; Brasenose College, Oxford; Edinburgh University. Barrister-at-Law, Inner Temple, 1933; Advocate of the Scottish Bar, 1935; External Examiner in English Law, Edinburgh University, 1937–40; served in RNVR, 1940–45; Hon. Sheriff-Substitute of Dumfries and Galloway, 1946; Sheriff-Substitute of Lanarkshire at Hamilton, 1946–53; Sheriff-Substitute, later Sheriff, of Lanarkshire at Glasgow, 1953–73; Sheriff Principal, Lothians and Peebleshire, 1973–75. Member: Law Reform Cttee for Scotland, 1957–61; Scottish Adv. Council on the Treatment of Offenders, 1959–63; Deptl Cttee on Adoption of Children, 1969–72; Grieve Cttee on Admin of Sheriffdoms, 1981–82; Chm., Working Gp on Identification Procedure under Scottish Criminal Law, 1976–78. *Address:* Craigowan, Ballinluig, Perthshire PH9 0NE. *Club:* New (Edinburgh).                              *Died* 27 *May* 1986.

**BRYHER, (Annie) Winifred;** author; *b* 2 Sept. 1894; *d* of Sir John Reeves Ellerman, 1st Bt, CH, and late Hannah Ellerman (*née* Glover); *m* 1st, 1921, Robert McAlmon (marr. diss., 1926); 2nd, 1927, Kenneth Macpherson (marr. diss., 1947); no *c*. *Educ:* Queenwood, Eastbourne. *Publications:* Development, 1920, etc; The Fourteenth of October, 1952; The Player's Boy, 1953; Roman Wall, 1954; Beowulf, 1956; Gate to the Sea, 1958; Ruan, 1960; The Heart of Artemis, 1963; The Coin of Carthage, 1964; Visa for Avalon, 1965; This January Tale, 1966; The Colors of Vaud, 1970; The Days of Mars, 1972. *Recreations:* travel, the sea, archæology. *Address:* Kenwin, Burier, Vaud, Switzerland.                  *Died* 28 *Jan.* 1983.

**BUCHAN, 16th Earl of,** *cr* 1469; **Donald Cardross Flower Erskine;** Lord Auchterhouse, 1469; Lord Cardross, 1606; Baron Erskine, 1806; *b* 3 June 1899; *s* of 6th Baron Erskine and Florence (*d* 1936), *y d* of Edgar Flower; *S* father, 1957 (as Baron Erskine); and kinsman, 1960 (as Earl of Buchan); *m* 1927, Christina, adopted *d* of Lloyd Baxendale, Greenham Lodge, Newbury; one *s* two *d*. *Educ:* Charterhouse; Royal Military College, Sandhurst. Lieut 9th Lancers, 1918; Captain, 1928; retired, 1930; re-employed, 1939; Lieut-Colonel, 1943. *Heir: s* Lord Cardross. *Address:* Little Orchard, Moreton-in-Marsh, Gloucestershire. *T:* Moreton-in-Marsh 50274.
                                        *Died* 26 *July* 1984.

**BUCHAN, Norman Findlay;** MP (Lab) Paisley South, since 1983 (Renfrewshire West, 1964–83); *b* Helmsdale, Sutherlandshire, 27 Oct. 1922; *s* of John Buchan, Fraserburgh, Aberdeenshire; *m* 1945, Janey Kent, sometime Member of European Parliament; one *s*. *Educ:* Kirkwall Grammar School; Glasgow University. Royal Tank Regt (N Africa, Sicily and Italy, 1942–45). Teacher (English and History). Parly Under-Sec., Scottish Office, 1967–70. Opposition Spokesman on Agriculture, Fisheries and Food, 1970–74; Minister of State, MAFF, March-Oct. 1974 (resigned); Opposition Spokesman on: social security, 1980–81; food, agriculture and fisheries, 1981–83; the arts, 1983–87. Chm. Bd, Tribune, 1985–. Vice-Pres., Poetry Soc., 1981–. *Publications:* (ed) 101 Scottish Songs; The Scottish Folksinger, 1973; The MacDunciad, 1977. *Address:* 72 Peel Street, Glasgow G11 5LR. *T:* 041–339 2583.
                                        *Died* 23 *Oct.* 1990.

**BUCHANAN, Most Rev. Alan Alexander;** Archbishop of Dublin and Primate of Ireland, 1969–77; *b* 23 March 1907; *m* 1935, Audrey Kathryn, *d* of W. A. Crone, Knock, Belfast; two *d*. *Educ:* Trinity College, Dublin. Exhibitioner, Moderator, 1928, TCD Deacon, 1930; Priest, 1931. Assistant Missioner, Church of Ireland Mission, Belfast, 1930–33, Head Missioner, 1933–37; Incumbent of Inver, Larne, 1937–45; Incumbent of St Mary, Belfast, 1945–55; Rural Dean of Mid-Belfast, 1951–55; Rector of Bangor, Co. Down, 1955–58; Canon of St Patrick's Cathedral, Dublin, 1957–58; Bishop of Clogher, 1958–69. Chaplain to the Forces, Emergency Commission, 1942–45. *Address:* Kilbride, Castleknock, Co. Dublin.                              *Died* 4 *Feb.* 1984.

**BUCHANAN, Major Sir Charles James**, 4th Bt, *cr* 1878; HLI; retired; *b* 16 April 1899; *s* of 3rd Bt and Constance (*d* 1914), *d* of late Commander Tennant, RN; *S* father, 1928; *m* 1932, Barbara Helen, *o d* of late Lieut-Colonel Rt Hon. Sir George Stanley, PC, GCSI, GCIE; two *s* two *d*. *Educ:* Harrow; Sandhurst. Served in North Russian Relief Force, 1919; with BEF France, 1939–40 and with AMG in Italy, 1943–44; retired 1945. ADC to Governor of Madras, 1928–32. A member of the Queen's Body Guard for Scotland (Royal Company of Archers); County Commissioner Nottinghamshire, Boy Scouts Association, 1949–62. JP 1952; DL 1954, Notts; High Sheriff of Nottinghamshire, 1962. *Recreations:* fishing and gardening. *Heir: s* Andrew George Buchanan. *Address:* St Anne's Manor, Sutton Bonington, Loughborough. *Club:* Lansdowne.
                                        *Died* 25 *May* 1984.

**BUCHANAN, George (Henry Perrott);** poet; *b* 9 Jan. 1904; 2nd *s* of Rev. C. H. L. Buchanan, Kilwaughter, Co. Antrim, and Florence Moore; *m* 1st, 1938, Winifred Mary Corn (marr. diss. 1945; she *d* 1971); 2nd, 1949, Noel Pulleyne Ritter (*d* 1951); 3rd, 1952, Hon. Janet Hampden Margesson (*d* 1968), *e d* of 1st Viscount Margesson, PC, MC; two *d*; 4th, 1974, Sandra Gail McCloy, Vancouver. *Educ:* Campbell College; Queen's University, Belfast. On editorial staff of The Times, 1930–35; reviewer, TLS, 1928–40; columnist, drama critic, News Chronicle, 1935–38; Operations Officer, RAF Coastal Command, 1940–45; Chm. Town and Country Development Cttee, N Ireland, 1949–53; Member, Exec. Council, European Soc. of Culture, 1954–. *Publications:* Passage through the Present, 1932; A London Story, 1935; Words for To-Night, 1936; Entanglement, 1938; The Soldier and the Girl, 1940; Rose Forbes, 1950; A Place to Live, 1952; Annotations, 1970; Naked Reason, 1971; The Politics of Culture, 1977; *poetry:* Bodily Responses, 1958; Conversation with Strangers, 1961; Minute-book of a City, 1972; Inside Traffic, 1976; Possible Being, 1980; Adjacent Columns, 1982; *plays:* A Trip to the Castle, 1960; Tresper Revolution, 1961; War Song, 1965; *autobiography:* Green Seacoast, 1959; Morning Papers, 1965. *Address:* 18A Courtnell Street, W2 5BX. *T:* 01–229 2927. *Club:* Savile. *Died 28 June 1989.*

**BUCHANAN, Major Sir Reginald Narcissus M.;** *see* Macdonald-Buchanan.

**BUCHANAN-DUNLOP, Captain David Kennedy,** DSC 1945; RN retired; *b* 30 June 1911; *s* of Colonel Archibald Buchanan-Dunlop, OBE and Mary (*née* Kennedy); *m* 1945, Marguerite, *d* of William Macfarlane; no *c. Educ:* Loretto; RNC, Dartmouth. Served as young officer in submarines in Mediterranean and Far East, then Specialist in Fleet Air Arm. Served War of 1939–45 (despatches) in aircraft-carriers world-wide. Asst Naval Attaché, Paris, 1949–52; Dep. Director Nav. Air Org. Naval Staff, 1954–56; Staff of NATO Defence College, Paris, 1957–59; Naval and Military Attaché, Santiago, Lima, Quito, Bogotá and Panama, 1960–62; Captain, Royal Naval College, Greenwich, 1962–64, Commodore President, 1964. *Recreation:* fishing. *Address:* 5 Avenue de la Bourdonnais, 75007 Paris, France. *T:* 551 73 06. *Died 15 Sept. 1985.*

**BUCK, Leslie William;** Director, British Aerospace (plc), 1981–82 (Member, British Aerospace, 1977–80; Member Organising Committee, 1976–77); *b* 30 May 1915; *s* of Walter Buck and Florence Greenland; *m* 1941, Dorothea Jeanne Bieri; two *s. Educ:* Willesden County Grammar Sch. Apprentice panel beater; shop steward; Nat. Union of Sheet Metal Workers and Braziers: District Officer, 1957–60; Dist Sec., 1960–62; Gen. Sec., Nat. Union of Sheet Metal Workers, Coppersmiths, Heating and Domestic Engineers, 1962–77. Member: Confedn of Shipbuilding and Engineering Unions Executive, 1964–77, Pres., 1975–76; Engrg Industry Trng Bd, 1964–79; General Council, TUC, 1971–77. *Recreations:* music, gardening, reading. *Address:* 178 Meadvale Road, Ealing, W5. *T:* 01–998 3943. *Died 23 Dec. 1984.*

**BUCKEE, His Honour Henry Thomas,** DSO 1942; a Circuit Judge (formerly Judge of County Courts), 1961–79; *b* 14 June 1913; *s* of Henry Buckee; *m* 1939, Margaret Frances Chapman; two *d. Educ:* King Edward VI School, Chelmsford. Called to Bar, Middle Temple, 1939. Served RNVR, 1940–46; Lieut-Comdr 1944. *Address:* Rough Hill House, East Hanningfield, Chelmsford, Essex. *T:* Chelmsford 400226. *Died 8 July 1989.*

**BUCKINGHAM, George Somerset;** retired; *b* 11 May 1903; *s* of Horace Clifford Buckingham, Norwich; *m* 1927, Marjorie Lanaway Bateson (*d* 1981); one *s* (one *d* decd). *Educ:* Norwich Sch.; Faraday House Electrical Engrg Coll. (Gold Medallist; Dipl.). BSc (Eng); CEng; FIEE; CBIM. Asst Engr, Yorks Electric Power Co., Leeds, 1924–26; District Engr and Br. Man., Birmingham, for Pirelli-General Cable Works Ltd of Southampton, 1928–48; Midlands Electricity Board: Chief Purchasing Officer, 1948–57; Chief Engr, 1957–62; Dep. Chm., 1962–64; Chm., 1964–69. Member: Electricity Council, 1964–69; Electricity Supply Industry Trng Bd, 1965–69; W Midlands Sports Council, 1966–71; Mem. Council, Univ. of Aston in Birmingham; Mem. Council, Electrical Research Assoc., 1967–72; various sci. and profl Instns and Cttees; Pres. Birmingham Branch, Institute of Marketing, 1967–68. Chairman: South Midland Centre, IEE, 1966–67; Midland Centre, Council of Engineering Instns, 1968–70; Past President, Council of Birmingham Electric Club, 1965; Past President, Faraday House Old Students' Assoc., 1962; Vice-President, Outward Bound Schs Assoc. (Birm. and Dist), 1964–72. *Publications:* papers, articles and reviews in scientific and electrical engrg jls and works of professional engrg bodies. *Recreations:* walking, bridge. *Address:* Alveston Leys Nursing Home, Kissing Tree Lane, Alveston, Stratford-upon-Avon, Warwickshire CV35 7QN. *Died 19 Dec. 1989.*

**BUCKINGHAM, John,** CB 1953; Director of Research Programmes and Planning, Admiralty, 1946–Dec. 1959, retired; *b* 23 Dec. 1894; *e s* of late John Mortimer Buckingham, South Molton, N Devon; unmarried. *Educ:* Berkhamsted Sch.; St John's Coll., Cambridge

(MA). Joined Admiralty scientific staff for anti-submarine duties under Lord Fisher, 1917, and was, until 1959, engaged continuously upon scientific work for the Admiralty; Deputy Director of Scientific Research, 1932; apptd Chief Scientific Officer in RN Scientific Service on its formation in 1946. *Publications:* Matter and Radiation, 1930; various publications in scientific journals. *Address:* 71 Pall Mall, SW1. *T:* 01-930 4152. *Clubs:* Travellers', United Oxford & Cambridge University. *Died 23 Nov. 1982.*

**BUCKINGHAMSHIRE, 9th Earl of,** *cr* 1746; **Vere Frederick Cecil Hobart-Hampden;** Bt 1611; Baron Hobart of Blickling, 1728; *b* 17 May 1901; *s* of Arthur Ernest and Henrietta Louisa Hobart-Hampden; *S* cousin, 1963; *m* 1972, Margot Macrae, *widow* of F. C. Bruce Hittmann, FRACS, Sydney, Australia. *Educ:* St Lawrence College, Ramsgate; Switzerland. Left England for Australia via Canada, 1919; sheep farming and wool business. Served in Royal Australian Air Force, 1942–46; returned to England, 1949. Company Director. *Heir: cousin* (George) Miles Hobart-Hampden [*b* 15 Dec. 1944; *m* 2nd, 1975, Alison Wightman (*née* Forrest); two step *s. Educ:* Univ. of Exeter (BA Hons History); Birkbeck Coll. and Inst. of Commonwealth Studies, Univ. of London (MA Area Studies)]. *Address:* House of Lords, SW1. *Died 19 April 1983.*

**BUCKLEY, Rear-Adm. Peter Noel,** CB 1964; DSO 1945; retd; Head of Naval Historical Branch, Ministry of Defence, 1968–75; *b* 26 Dec. 1909; *s* of late Frank and Constance Buckley, Hooton, Cheshire; *m* 1945, Norah Elizabeth Astley St Clair-Ford, *widow* of Lt-Comdr Drummond St Clair-Ford; one *d* (and two step *s* one step *d*). *Educ:* Holmwood School, Formby, Lancs; RNC, Dartmouth. Midshipman, HMS Tiger, 1927, HMS Cornwall, 1928–30; Lieut: qual. 1931. Submarine Service, 1931–38, in submarines; Lieut-Comdr, CO of HMS Shark, 1938. War of 1939–45 (despatches); POW Germany, 1940–45. Comdr 1945; HMS: Rajah and Formidable, 1946; Siskin, 1947; Glory, 1949; RN Barracks, Portsmouth, 1951; Capt. 1952; Capt. D, Plymouth, 1953; Capt. of Dockyard, Rosyth, 1954; Chief Staff Officer to Flag Officer Comdg Reserve Fleet, 1957; Capt of Fleet, Med. Fleet, 1959; Rear-Adm. 1962; Dir-Gen., Manpower, 1962–64; retd 1965. *Address:* Forest Cottage, Sway, Lymington, Hants. *T:* Lymington 682442. *Died 21 Feb. 1988.*

**BUCKLEY, Hon. Dame Ruth (Burton),** DBE 1959; JP; *b* 12 July 1898; 4th *d* of 1st Baron Wrenbury, PC. *Educ:* Cheltenham Ladies' College. Called to Bar, Lincoln's Inn, 1926. E Sussex County Council: Member of Council, 1936–74; Alderman, 1946–74; Vice-Chm. 1949–52; Chm. 1952–55. Member of South Eastern Metropolitan Regional Hospital Board, 1948–69; Part-time member of Local Govt Boundary Commn for England, 1958–66. JP Sussex, 1935–. Hon. LLD Sussex, 1977. *Address:* Brooklands, Dallington, near Heathfield, E Sussex. *Died 11 July 1986.*

**BUCKLEY, Lt-Col William Howell,** DL; Landed Proprietor; Chairman, Buckleys Brewery Ltd, Llanelly, 1947–72, President, since 1972; *b* 7 Feb. 1896; *s* of William Joseph Buckley and Muriel Howell; *m* 1st, 1920, Karolie Kathleen Kemmis; one *s* one *d*; 2nd, 1952, Helen Josephine Turner; one *d. Educ:* Radley. 2nd Lieut Glamorgan Imperial Yeomanry, 1914; Lieut The Inniskillings (6th Dragoons), 1915; Capt. 5th Inniskilling Dragoon Guards, 1926; Capt. 1930; served War of 1939–45, 6th Cavalry Bde, Palestine, 1939; Deputy Provost Marshal S Area, Palestine, Malta, Western Command. High Sheriff of Carmarthenshire, 1950–51; DL Carmarthen, 1955. Master: Carmarthenshire Fox Hounds, 1931–62; Tivyside Fox Hounds, 1964–66. *Recreation:* hunting. *Address:* Castell Gorfod, St Clears, Dyfed, S Wales. *TA:* St Clears. *T:* St Clears 230210. *Clubs:* Cavalry and Guards, Buck's, Leander. *Died 5 April 1981.*

**BUCKNILL, Peter Thomas,** QC 1961; *b* 4 Nov. 1910; *o s* of late Rt Hon. Sir Alfred Bucknill, PC, OBE; *m* 1935, Elizabeth Mary Stark; three *s* two *d* (and one *d* decd). *Educ:* Gresham's Sch., Holt; Trinity Coll., Oxford (MA). Called to the Bar, Inner Temple, 1935 (Bencher, 1967). Ordinand, Chichester Theol. Coll., 1939; Deacon, 1941; Priest, 1942; received into RC Church, 1943; resumed Bar practice. Appointed Junior Counsel to the Treasury (Admiralty), 1958; resigned on becoming QC. On rota for Lloyd's Salvage Arbitrators, Wreck Commissioner, 1962–78, retired from practice, 1978. *Publications:* contributed to Halsbury's Laws of England, shipping vol., 2nd and 3rd edns. *Recreation:* gardening. *Address:* High Corner, The Warren, Ashtead, Surrey KT21 2SL. *Died 11 Jan. 1987.*

**BUDAY, George,** RE 1953 (ARE 1939); wood engraver; author on graphic arts subjects; *b* Kolozsvar, Transylvania, 7 April 1907; *s* of late Prof. Arpad Buday, Roman archaeologist, and Margaret Buday. *Educ:* Presbyterian Coll., Kolozsvar; Royal Hungarian Francis Joseph Univ., Szeged (Dr). Apptd Lectr in Graphic Arts, Royal Hungarian F. J. Univ., 1935–41; Rome Scholar, 1936–37; won travelling schol. to England (and has stayed permanently) 1937. Broadcaster, BBC European Service, 1940–42; in a Dept of Foreign Office, 1942–45. Dir, Hungarian Cultural Inst., London, 1947–49, resigned. Illustrated numerous folk-tale and folk-ballad collections, vols of classics and modern authors, publ. in many countries. Since 1938 exhib. Royal Acad., Royal Soc. of Painter-Etchers and Engravers, Soc. of Wood Engravers, and in many countries abroad. Works represented in: Depts of Prints and Drawings, Brit. Mus.; Victoria and Albert Mus.; Glasgow Univ.; New York Public Library; Florence Univ.; Museums of Fine Arts, Budapest, Prague, Warsaw; Phillips Memorial Gall., Washington, DC; etc. Grand Prix, Paris World Exhibn, 1937 (for engravings); subsequently other art and bibliophile prizes. Officer's Cross, Order of Merit (Hungary), 1947. *Publications:* Book of Ballads, 1934; The Story of the Christmas Card, 1951; The History of the Christmas Card, 1954 (1964); (wrote and illustr.): The Dances of Hungary, 1950; George Buday's Little Books, I-XII, incl. The Language of Flowers, 1951; The Cries of London, Ancient and Modern, 1954; Proverbial Cats and Kittens, 1956 (1968); The Artist's Recollections, for a volume of his 82 Selected Engravings, 1970; Multiple Portraiture: Illustrating a Poetical Anthology, 1981; contrib. articles to periodicals. *Relevant publication:* George Buday by Curt Visel, in Illustration 63, 1971. *Recreations:* bibliophile hand-printing on his 1857 Albion hand-press and collecting old Christmas cards (probably most representative collection of Victorian cards extant). *Address:* PO Box 150, Coulsdon, Surrey CR3 1YE. *Died 12 June 1990.*

**BUDD, Stanley Alec;** Scottish Representative, Commission of the European Communities, 1975–87; *b* 22 May 1931; *s* of Henry Stanley Budd and Ann Mitchell; *m* 1955, Wilma McQueen Cuthbert (*d* 1985); three *s* one *d. Educ:* George Heriot's Sch., Edinburgh. Newspaper reporter, feature writer and sub-editor, D. C. Thomson & Co, Dundee, 1947–57 (National Service, 1949–51). Research writer, Foreign Office, 1957–60; 2nd Secretary, Beirut, Lebanon, 1960–63; 1st Sec., Kuala Lumpur, Malaysia, 1963–69; FO, 1969–71; Dep. Head of Information, Scottish Office, 1971–72; Press Secretary to Chancellor of Duchy of Lancaster, 1972–74; Chief Information Officer, Cabinet Office, 1974–75. *Publication:* The EEC—A Guide to the Maze, 1986. *Recreations:* music, painting, oriental antiques, bridge. *Address:* 2 Bellevue Crescent, Edinburgh EH3 6ND.
*Died 4 Oct. 1989.*

**BUFFEY, Brig. William,** DSO 1940; TD 1940; DL; *b* 24 Sept. 1899; *s* of late William Buffey, Bromley, Kent; *m* 1926, Dorothy Wensley, *d* of late William Rogers, Nelson, New Zealand; two *d. Educ:* St Dunstan's College, Catford. Served War of 1939–45, Cmd 91st Fd Regt RA, France, Belgium (DSO), India, Persia, 1939–43; CRA 5 Div. Middle East, Italy, BLA, 1943–45 (despatches thrice); Hon. Col 291st Airborne Fd Regt RA (TA), 1946–55. Governor, St Dunstan's College, 1954–79. DL Co. London, subseq. Greater London, 1954–82. *Recreation:* gardening. *Address:* 7 Broad Oak, Groombridge, Tunbridge Wells, Kent. *T:* Groombridge 309.
*Died 24 Jan. 1984.*

**BUHLER, Robert,** RA 1956 (ARA 1947); painter; Hon. Fellow, Royal College of Art; tutor, RCA, 1948–75; *b* London, 23 Nov. 1916; *s* of Robert Buhler, journalist; *m* Evelyn Rowell (marr. diss. 1951); one *s*; *m* 1962, Prudence Brochocka (*née* Beaumont) (marr. diss. 1972); two *s*, and one step *d. Educ:* Switzerland; Bolt Court; St Martin's School of Art; Royal College of Art. Trustee, Royal Academy, 1975–. Exhibited at: Royal Academy, New English Art Club, London Group, London galleries. Work in permanent collections: Chantrey Bequest; Stott Fund; provincial art galleries; galleries in USA, Canada, Australia, NZ, France and Switzerland. *Address:* Flat 5, 38 Onslow Square, SW7 3NS. *T:* 01–589 0797; (studio) 3 Avenue Studios, Sydney Close, SW3. *T:* 01–589 4983.
*Died 20 June 1989.*

**BUIST, Comdr Colin,** CVO 1961 (MVO 1927); RN (Retired); Extra Equerry to the Queen since 1952 (to King George VI, 1937–52); President, Coalite Group Ltd (Chairman, Coalite and Chemical Products Ltd, 1953–70); *b* 10 April 1896; *s* of Col Frederick Braid Buist; *m* 1928, Gladys Mary (*d* 1972), 4th *d* of late Sir William Nelson, Bt. *Educ:* RN Colleges, Osborne and Dartmouth. Served European War, 1914–18; also 1939–44. *Address:* Highmoor Farm, Henley-on-Thames RG9 5DH. *T:* Nettlebed 641275.
*Died 19 May 1981.*

**BÜLBRING, Edith,** MA Oxon; MD Bonn; FRS 1958; Professor of Pharmacology, Oxford University, 1967–71, later Emeritus (University Reader, 1960–67) and Honorary Fellow, Lady Margaret Hall, 1971; *b* 27 Dec. 1903; *d* of Karl Daniel Bülbring, Professor of English, Bonn University, and Hortense Leonore Bülbring (*née* Kann). *Educ:* Bonn, Munich and Freiburg Universities. Postgraduate work in Pharmacology Department of Berlin University, 1929–31; Pediatrics, University of Jena, 1932; Virchow Krankenhaus University of Berlin, 1933; Pharmacological Laboratory of Pharmaceutical Society of Great Britain, University of London, 1933–38; Pharmacology Dept, University of Oxford, 1938–71. Research work on: autonomic transmitters, suprarenals, smooth muscle, peristalsis. Schmiedeberg-Plakette der Deutschen Pharmakologischen Gesellschaft, 1974. Honorary Member:

Pharmaceutical Soc., Torino, Italy, 1957; British Pharmacological Soc., 1975; Deutsche Physiolgische Gesellschaft, 1976; Physiol Soc., 1981. Hon. Dr med: Univ. of Groningen, Netherlands, 1979; Leuven, Belgium, 1981; Homburg (Saar), W Germany, 1988. Wellcome Gold Medal in Pharmacology, 1985. *Publications:* mainly in Jl of Physiology, Brit. Jl of Pharmacology and Proc. Royal Soc. of London, Series B. *Recreation:* music. *Address:* 15 Northmoor Road, Oxford. *T:* Oxford (0865) 57270; Lady Margaret Hall, Oxford. *Died 5 July 1990.*

**BULL, Amy Frances,** CBE 1964; Head Mistress, Wallington County Grammar School for Girls, 1937–64, retired; *b* 27 April 1902; *d* of Herbert Bull, Head Master of Pinewood Preparatory Sch., Farnborough, until 1919, and Ethel Mary Atkinson. *Educ:* Roedean Sch.; Somerville Coll., Oxford. Asst Mistress, Cheltenham Ladies' Coll., 1925–32; Head of History Dept, Portsmouth Northern Secondary Sch., 1932–37; Pres. Head Mistresses' Assoc., 1960–62; Member: Surrey Educn Cttee, 1946–60; National Youth Employment Council, 1959–68; Secondary School Examination Council, 1960–64; Exec. Cttee Central Council for Physical Recreation, 1963–73; Fountain and Carshalton Gp Management Cttee, 1964–74; Sutton Borough Education Cttee, 1966–74; St Helier Hosp. House Cttee; Women's Nat. Commn, 1969–76. Governor: St Michael's Sch., Limpsfield, 1965–81; Queen Mary's and Fountain Hospital Schs, 1972–79; St Ebba's, Brooklands and Ellen Terry Hospital Schs, 1972–82. *Recreations:* gardening, walking in mountains, watching games. *Address:* Firtree Lodge, 16 Broomfield Park, Westcott, Dorking, Surrey. *Clubs:* University Women's, English-Speaking Union. *Died 6 Aug. 1982.*

**BULL, Sir George,** 3rd Bt *cr* 1922, of Hammersmith; Senior Partner of Bull & Bull, Solicitors, 11 Stone Buildings, Lincoln's Inn, and 4 Castle Street, Canterbury; *b* 19 June 1906; 2nd *s* of Rt Hon. Sir William Bull, 1st Bt, and late Lilian, 2nd *d* of G. S. Brandon, Oakbrook, Ravenscourt Park, and Heene, Worthing, Sussex; *S* brother 1942; *m* 1933, Gabrielle, 2nd *d* of late Bramwell Jackson, MC, Bury St Edmunds; one *s* one *d. Educ:* RN Colleges, Osborne and Dartmouth; Paris; Vienna. Admitted Solicitor, 1929. Served War of 1939–45 in RNVR; Comdr, 1942. Chm., London Rent Assessment Cttees, 1966–78. Vice-Chm. Governors, Godolphin and Latymer Sch.; Governor, Latymer Foundation; Trustee Hammersmith United Charities; Member, Hammersmith Borough Council, 1968–71. Chm., Standing Council of the Baronetage, 1977–80. Liveryman Fishmongers' Company; Freeman of City of London; Hon. Solicitor, Royal Society of St George. Pres., London Corinthian Sailing Club. *Recreations:* sailing, travelling. *Heir:* *s* Simeon George Bull [*b* 1 Aug. 1934; *m* 1961, Annick, *y d* of late Louis Bresson and of Mme Bresson, Chandai, France; one *s* two *d*]. *Address:* 3 Hammersmith Terrace, W6. *T:* 01–748 2400; 11 Stone Buildings, Lincoln's Inn. *T:* 01–405 7474. *Clubs:* 1900, MCC, Arts.
*Died 9 Sept. 1986.*

**BULL, Sir Graham (MacGregor),** Kt 1976; retired; *b* 30 Jan. 1918; *s* of Dr A. B. Bull; *m* 1947, Megan Patricia Jones (see M. P. Bull); three *s* one *d. Educ:* Diocesan Coll., Cape Town; Univ. of Cape Town (MD). FRCP. Tutor in Medicine and Asst, Dept of Medicine, Univ. of Cape Town, 1940–46; Lecturer in Medicine, Postgraduate Medical Sch. of London, 1947–52; Professor of Medicine, The Queen's Univ., Belfast, 1952–66; Mem., MRC, 1962–66; Dir, MRC Clinical Research Centre, 1966–78. Research Fellow, SA Council for Scientific and Industrial Research, 1947; Chairman: CIBA Foundn Exec. Cttee, 1977–83; Appropriate Health Resources & Technologies Action Gp Ltd, 1978–80; 2nd Vice-Pres., RCP, 1978–79. *Publications:* contrib. to medical journals. *Address:* 29 Heath Drive, NW3 7SB. *T:* 01–435 1624.
*Died 14 Nov. 1987.*

**BULL, Prof. Hedley Norman,** MA, BPhil (Oxon); BA (Sydney); FBA 1984; Montague Burton Professor of International Relations, University of Oxford, and Fellow of Balliol College, Oxford, since 1977; *b* Sydney, 10 June 1932; *s* of J. N. Bull, Sydney; *m* 1954, Frances Mary, *d* of F. A. E. Lawes; one *s* two *d. Educ:* Fort Street High Sch.; Univ. of Sydney; University Coll., Oxford. Asst Lectr, Internat. Relations, London Sch. of Economics, 1955–57, Lectr 1959; also Rockefeller Fellow, Harvard Univ., 1957–58; Research Associate, Princeton Univ., 1963; Reader in Internat. Relations, London Sch. of Economics, 1963; Dir, Arms Control and Disarmament Research Unit, Foreign Office, London, 1965–67; Prof. of Internat. Relns, Aust. Nat. Univ., 1967–77. Member Council: Inst. for Strategic Studies, London, 1968–77, 1981–; RIIA, 1980–. Res. Dir, Aust. Inst. of Internat. Affairs, 1968–73. Visiting Professor: Polit. Sci., Columbia Univ., 1970–71; Jawaharlal Nehru Univ., New Delhi, 1974–75; Vis. Fellow, All Souls Coll., Oxford, 1975–76. FASSA 1968. *Publications:* The Control of the Arms Race, 1961; The Anarchical Society, 1977; (with Adam Watson) The Expansion of International Society, 1984. *Recreation:* walking. *Address:* Balliol College, Oxford OX1 3BJ. *Club:* Travellers'.
*Died 18 May 1985.*

**BULL, James William Douglas**, CBE 1976; MA, MD, FRCP, FRCS, FRCR; retired; Honorary Consultant Radiologist (diagnostic): National Hospital for Nervous Diseases, Queen Square; Maida Vale Hospital for Nervous Diseases; St Andrew's Hospital, Northampton; St George's Hospital; University Hospital, West Indies; Teacher, Institute of Neurology (University of London); Consultant Adviser in Diagnostic Radiology, Department of Health and Social Security, until 1975; Consultant Neuroradiologist to Royal Navy, until 1975; *b* 23 March 1911; *o s* of late D. W. A. Bull, MD, JP, Stony Stratford, Bucks; *m* 1941, Edith (*d* 1978), *e d* of late Charles Burch, Henley-on-Thames; one *s* one *d*; *m* 1981, Nora Wells. *Educ:* Repton; Gonville and Caius Coll., Cambridge; St George's Hospital. Entrance schol., 1932. Usual house appts; Asst Curator of Museum, Med. registrar, St George's Hospital, Rockefeller Travelling Schol. (Stockholm), 1938–39. Served War, 1940–46, Temp. Major RAMC (POW Singapore). Dean, Inst. of Neurology, Univ. of London, 1962–68. President: 4th Internat. Symposium Neuroradiologicum, London, 1955; British Inst. of Radiology, 1960; Section of Radiology, 1968–69, Section of Neurology, 1974–75, RSM; Pres., Faculty of Radiologists, 1969–72 (Vice-Pres., 1963). Member: Assoc. of British Neurologists; Brit. Soc. of Neuroradiologists; Pres., European Soc. of Neuroradiology, 1972–75. Examiner in Diagnostic Radiology: Conjoint Board, 1957; Univ. of Liverpool, 1959; for Fellowship, Faculty of Radiologists, London, 1965. Watson Smith Lectr, RCP, 1962; Skinner Lectr, Faculty of Radiologists, 1965; Dyke Meml Lectr, Columbia Univ., New York, 1969; Mackenzie Davidson Meml Lectr, Brit. Inst. Radiol., 1972; Langdon Brown Lectr, RCP, 1974. Member: Council, RCP London, 1964–67; Council, RCS, 1968–73. Hon. Fellow: Royal Soc. of Medicine, 1984; American Coll. of Radiologists; Italian Neuroradiological Soc.; Brazilian Radiological Soc.; Royal Australian Coll. of Radiology; Fac. Radiol. RCSI; Radiological Soc. of N America. Hon. Member: Canadian Neurological Soc.; American Neurological Assoc.; French Radiological Soc.; Amer. Soc. of Neuroradiology. *Publications:* Atlas of Positive Contrast Myelography (jointly), 1962. Contrib. to A. Feiling's Modern Trends in Neurology; various papers in medical journals, mostly connected with neuroradiology. *Recreations:* golf, travel. *Address:* 80 King's Road, Henley-on-Thames RG9 2DQ. *T:* Henley-on-Thames 5374. *Club:* United Oxford & Cambridge University.
*Died 5 July 1987.*

**BULLARD, Major-General Colin**, CB 1952; CBE 1943; *b* 23 Feb. 1900; *s* of late Canon J. V. Bullard, MA; *m* 1932, Evelyn May Spencer; one *s. Educ:* Sedbergh; Ellesmere; Richmond, Yorks; Univ. of Liverpool (BEng). Engineer; apprenticeship, Cammell Laird, Birkenhead. RAOC and REME, 1925–53; retired, 1953. Principal, Royal Technical Coll. of East Africa, 1953–57. ADC to the King during 1950; Maj.-Gen., 1950. CEng; FIMechE; FIEE. *Address:* 2 The Orchard, Church Street, Willingdon BN20 9HS. *T:* Eastbourne 51057.
*Died 15 July 1981.*

**BULLEY, Rt. Rev. Sydney Cyril**; *b* 12 June 1907; 2nd *s* of late Jethro Bulley, Newton Abbot, Devon; unmarried. *Educ:* Newton Abbot Grammar Sch.; Univ. of Durham. BA 1932; MA 1936; DipTh 1933; Van Mildert Scholar, Univ. of Durham, 1932; Hon. DD Dunelm 1972. Deacon, 1933; priest, 1934; Curate of Newark Parish Church, 1933–42; Director of Religious Education, Diocese of Southwell, 1936–42; Vicar of St Anne's, Worksop, 1942–46; Chaplain to High Sheriff of Notts, 1943; Hon. Canon of Southwell Minster, 1945; Vicar and Rural Dean of Mansfield, 1946–51; Proctor in Convocation of York, 1945–51; Vicar of Ambleside with Rydal, 1951–59; Archdeacon of Westmorland and Dir Religious Education, Diocese Carlisle, 1951–58; Archdeacon of Westmorland and Furness, 1959–65; Suffragan Bishop of Penrith, 1959–66; Hon. Canon of Carlisle Cathedral, 1951–66; Examining Chaplain to the Bishop of Carlisle, 1952–66; Bishop of Carlisle, 1966–72; Chaplain and Tutor, All Saints' Coll., Bathurst, NSW, 1973–74; Hon. Asst Bishop, Dio. Oxford, 1974. Chaplain to the Queen, 1955–59. Chairman: Southwell Diocese Education Cttee, 1942–51; Worksop Youth Cttee, 1943–45; Mansfield Youth Cttee, 1947–48; Member: Southwell Diocese Board of Finance, 1942–51; Central Council of the Church for Education, 1951–54; Westmorland Education Cttee, 1951–64. Gov. Derby Training Coll., 1938–51, Ripon Training Coll., 1953–58, Lancaster Coll. of Education, 1953–69; Chairman of Governing Body: Casterton Sch., 1962–72; St Chad's Coll., Durham Univ., 1969–83 (Hon. Fellow, 1987); St Mary's Sch., Wantage, 1979–84. *Publications:* The Glass of Time (autobiog.), 1981; Faith, Fire and Fun (verse), 1985; Glimpses of the Divine, 1987. *Address:* 3 Upper Cross Lane, East Hagbourne, Didcot, Oxon. *Died 20 Nov. 1989.*

**BULLOCH, Rev. James Boyd Prentice**; Chaplain to the Queen in Scotland, since 1980; *b* 22 Sept. 1915; *s* of James Prentice Bulloch and Elizabeth MacGregor Boyd; *m* 1953, Louise Ellen Campbell MacLennan. *Educ:* Allan Glen's School; Univ. of Glasgow (MA 1935, BD 1939); Univ. of Edinburgh (PhD 1955). Assistant Minister, Glasgow Cathedral, 1938–42; Minister: Tranent Old Parish Church, 1942–53; Stobo and Drumelzier, 1953–80, with Tweedsmuir,

1960–80, and Broughton and Skirling, 1977–80. FSAScot 1943. Hon. DD Glasgow, 1971. *Publications:* Adam of Dryburgh, 1958; The Kirk in Scotland, 1960; The Scots Confession: a modern rendering, 1960; The Life of the Celtic Church, 1963; The Church of Scotland, 1977; Pilate to Constantine, 1981; (ed) The Third Statistical Account of Scotland: Peebles, 1964; (with late A. L. Drummond): The Scottish Church, 1688–1843: The Age of the Moderates, 1973; The Church in Victorian Scotland, 1843–1874, 1975; The Church in Late Victorian Scotland, 1874–1900, 1978. *Recreation:* the old fashioned roses. *Address:* Upper Loanside, Caledonian Road, Peebles EH45 9DJ. *T:* Peebles 22257.
*Died 13 April 1981.*

**BULLOCK, Prof. Kenneth**, PhD, MSc, CChem, FRSC, MChemA, FPS; Professor of Pharmacy, Manchester University, 1955–70, Emeritus 1970; *b* 27 Dec. 1901; *s* of late James William Bullock, Wigan, Lancashire; *m* 1926, Winifred Mary, *d* of late Rev. F. Ives Cater. *Educ:* Wigan Grammar Sch.; Manchester Univ. Research and Technical Chemist, 1925–32; joined teaching staff of Pharmacy Dept, Manchester Univ., 1932; Lecturer, 1937; Senior Lecturer, 1946; Reader, 1950. Chairman, British Pharmaceutical Conf., 1956. Formerly Examiner for Univs of Dublin, London, Nottingham, and Manchester and for Pharmaceutical Socs of Great Britain and Ireland. *Publications:* original contributions to science, mainly in Journal of Pharmacy and Pharmacology. *Recreations:* gardening and biology. *Address:* 39 Knutsford Road, Wilmslow, Cheshire SK9 6JB. *T:* Wilmslow 522892.
*Died 14 July 1985.*

**BULLOUGH, Geoffrey**, MA; FBA 1966; Emeritus Professor, University of London; *b* 27 Jan. 1901; *s* of James Arthur Bullough and Elizabeth Ford; *m* 1928, Doris Margaret Wall; one *s* one *d. Educ:* Stand Grammar Sch., Whitefield; Manchester Univ. BA 1922, MA 1923 (Vict.), Teachers' Diploma 1923, Gissing Prize 1921, Withers Prize in Education 1923, John Bright Fellowship in English Literature, 1923–24; studied in Italy. Master, Grammar Sch. of Queen Elizabeth in Tamworth, 1924–26; Asst Lecturer in English Literature, Manchester Univ., 1926–29; Lecturer, Edinburgh Univ., 1929–33; Professor of English Literature, Univ. of Sheffield, 1933–46; Professor of English Language and Literature, KCL, 1946–68. Vice-Chm., Sheffield Repertory Co., 1938–46; Governor of Chelsea Coll. of Science and Technology, 1952–68. FKC 1964; Hon. Fellow, Chelsea Coll., 1973. Hon. LittD: Manchester, 1969; Glasgow, 1970; Alfred Univ., NY, 1974; Ghent, 1980. *Publications:* Philosophical Poems of Henry More, 1931; The Oxford Book of Seventeenth-Century Verse (with Sir H. J. C. Grierson), 1934; The Trend of Modern Poetry, 1934, 1949; Poems and Dramas of Fulke Greville, 1939; ed (with C. L. Wrenn) English Studies Today, 1951; ed Essays and Studies, 1953; Narrative and Dramatic Sources of Shakespeare, 1957–75; Milton's Dramatic Poems (with D. M. B.), 1958; Mirror of Minds, 1962; reviews and articles. *Recreations:* music, painting, travel. *Address:* 182 Mayfield Road, Edinburgh EH9 3AX.
*Died 12 Feb. 1982.*

**BULSTRODE, David Wilton;** Chairman, St James Corporate Services Ltd, since 1982; *b* 22 Sept. 1940; *s* of Norman Wilton Bulstrode and Vera Bulstrode; *m* 1965, Maria Sylvia Da Prato; one *s* one *d. Educ:* Haberdashers' Aske's Sch. ACIB. Lloyds Bank, 1957–72; Director: Slater Walker (Jersey), 1972–76; Lazard Brothers & Co. (Jersey), 1976–82; Chairman: Marler Estates, 1978–; Charterhall Properties, 1982–; B.O.M. Holdings, 1986–; Dir, UK Land, 1985–. Mem., Inst. of Directors, 1978–. *Recreations:* football, cricket, Rugby. *Address:* Le Nid Solitaire, Rue des Charrières, St Martin, Jersey, Channel Islands. *T:* Jersey 54626. *Club:* Lord's Taverners'.
*Died 1 Sept. 1988.*

**BUMSTEAD, Kenneth**, CVO 1958; CBE 1952; *b* 28 April 1908; *s* of Ernest and Nellie Bumstead; *m* 1940, Diana, *e d* of Archibald Smollett Campbell; three *s. Educ:* Wallasey Grammar Sch.; Emmanuel Coll., Cambridge. Entered China Consular Service, 1931; served Peking, Tsingtao, Canton, Chungking, Shanghai, 1932–42 (Consul 1939); Madagascar, 1943; London, 1944; Chicago, 1945–48; Shanghai, 1949–52 (Consul-General, 1950); Seattle, 1953–56; Consul-General, Rotterdam, 1957–61; FO Res. Dept, 1963–72, retired. Commander, Order of Oranje Nassau. *Address:* 4 Perry Way, Hilland, Headley, Bordon, Hants GU35 8NE.
*Died 5 Dec. 1987.*

**BUNBURY, Brig. Francis Ramsay St Pierre**, CBE 1958; DSO 1945, Bar 1953; *b* 16 June 1910; *s* of late Lt-Col Gerald Bruce St Pierre Bunbury, Indian Army, and Frances Mary Olivia (*née* Dixon); *m* 1933, Elizabeth Pamela Somers (*née* Liscombe) (*d* 1969); one *s* one *d. Educ:* Rugby and Sandhurst. Commissioned into The Duke of Wellington's Regiment, 1930; Staff Coll., 1941; commanded 1st Bn, The King's Own Royal Regt, Italian Campaign, 1944–45 (despatches, DSO); commanded 1st Bn The Duke of Wellington's Regt, 1951–54, Germany, Korea (Bar to DSO), Gibraltar; AAG, War Office, 1954–56; commanded 50 Independent Infantry Brigade, Cyprus, 1956–59 (despatches, CBE). Dep. Adjt-Gen., Rhine Army, 1959–61; retired 1962.
*Died 28 April 1990.*

**BUNBURY, Sir (John) William Napier**, 12th Bt, *cr* 1681; *b* 3 July 1915; *s* of Sir Charles H. N. Bunbury, 11th Bt, and Katherine (*d* 1965), *d* of H. E. Reid; *S* father, 1963; *m* 1940, Pamela, *er d* of late T. Sutton, Westlecott Manor, Swindon; three *s* (and one *s* decd). *Educ:* Eton; Jesus Coll., Cambridge. 2nd Lieut (TA), 1936. Commissioned, KRRC, 1940; Capt. 1942. High Sheriff of Suffolk 1972. *Recreations:* golf, fishing. *Heir: e* surv. *s* Michael William Bunbury [*b* 29 Dec. 1946; *m* 1976, Caroline, *d* of Col A. D. S. Mangnall; one *s* one *d*]. *Address:* Hollesley House, Hollesley, Woodbridge, Suffolk. *T:* Shottisham 411250. *Club:* Army and Navy. *Died 28 Aug.* 1985.

**BUNN, Dr Charles William**, FRS 1967; Dewar Research Fellow of the Royal Institution of Great Britain, 1963–72; *b* 15 Jan. 1905; *s* of Charles John Bunn and Mary Grace Bunn (*née* Murray); *m* 1931, Elizabeth Mary Mold; one *s* one *d. Educ:* Wilson's Grammar Sch., London, SE; Exeter Coll., Oxford. BA, BSc, (Oxon), 1927; DSc (Oxon), 1953; FInstP, 1944. Mem. Research Staff, Imperial Chemical Industries, Winnington, Northwich, Cheshire (now Mond Div.), 1927–46; transf. to ICI Plastics Div., 1946 (Div. Leader of Molecular Structure Div. of Research Dept, and later of Physics Div.); retd 1963. Chm., X-Ray Analysis Group of The Inst. of Physics and The Physical Soc., 1959–62. Amer. Physical Soc. Award in High Polymer Physics (Ford Prize), 1969. *Publications:* Chemical Crystallography, 1945 (2nd edn 1961); Crystals, Their Role in Nature and in Science, 1964; papers in: Proc. Royal Society; Trans. Faraday Soc.; Acta Crystallographica. *Recreations:* music and horticulture. *Address:* 6 Pentley Park, Welwyn Garden City, Herts. *T:* Welwyn Garden (0707) 323581. *Died 13 April* 1990.

**BUNTING, Basil;** poet; *b* 1 March 1900; *s* of T. L. Bunting, MD, and Annie Bunting (*née* Cheesman); *m* 1st, 1930, Marian Culver; two *d* (one *s* decd); 2nd, 1948, Sima Alladadian; one *s* one *d. Educ:* Ackworth Sch.; Leighton Park Sch.; Wormwood Scrubbs; London Sch. of Economics. Has had a varied undistinguished career. President: The Poetry Soc., 1972–76; Northern Arts, 1973–76. Hon. Life Vis. Prof., Univ. of Newcastle upon Tyne. FRSL. Hon. DLitt Newcastle upon Tyne, 1971. Cholmondeley Award, Soc. of Authors, 1982. *Publications:* Redimiculum Matellarum, 1930; Poems, 1950; The Spoils, 1965; Loquitur, 1965; First Book of Odes, 1965; Briggflatts, 1966; Collected Poems, 1968, 2nd edn 1978; (ed) Joseph Skipsey, Selected Poems, 1976. *Died 17 April* 1985.

**BUÑUEL, Luis;** film director; *b* Calanda, Spain, 22 Feb. 1900; *s* of Leonardo and Maria Buñuel; *m* Jeanne Rucar; two *s. Educ:* Univ. of Madrid; Académie du Cinéma, Paris. Grand Cross, Order of Isabel la Católica (Spain), 1983. *Films include:* Un Chien Andalou, 1929; L'Age d'Or, 1930; Las Hurdes (Land Without Bread), 1936; España, 1936; Gran Casino, 1947; El Gran Calavera, 1949; Los Olivados (The Young and the Damned), 1950 (Best Dir Award, Cannes Film Festival, 1951); Subida al Cielo (Mexican Bus Ride), 1952 (best avant-garde film, Cannes, 1952); El (This Strange Passion), 1952; Abismos de Pasión, 1952; The Adventures of Robinson Crusoe, 1953; Ensayo de un Crimen (The Criminal Life of Archibald de la Cruz), 1955; Cela S'Appelle l'Aurore, 1955; La Mort en ce Jardin, 1956; Nazarin, 1958 (Special Internat. Jury Prize, Cannes, 1959); La Jeune Fille, 1959; La Fièvre Monte à El Pau, 1960; The Young One, 1960; The Republic of Sin, 1960; Viridiana, 1961 (jtly, Golden Palm Award, Cannes, 1961); Island of Shame, 1961; El Angel Exterminador, 1962 (Best film, Cannes, 1962); Le Journal d'une Femme de Chambre, 1964; Simon of the Desert, 1965; Belle de Jour, 1966 (Golden Lion of St Mark Award, Venice Film Festival, 1967); La Voie Lactée, 1969; Tristana, 1970; The Discreet Charm of the Bourgeoisie, 1972; Le Fantôme de la liberté, 1974; Cet Obscur Objet du Désir, 1978. *Posthumous publication:* My Last Breath (autobiog.), 1984. *Address:* c/o Greenwich Film Production, 72 avenue des Champs-Elysées, 75008 Paris, France. *Died 29 July* 1983.

**BURBIDGE, Prof. Percy William**, CBE 1957; MSc NZ; BARes Cambridge; Professor Emeritus of Physics, University of Auckland; *b* 3 Jan. 1891; *s* of R. W. Burbidge and Agnes Mary Edwards; *m* 1923, Kathleen Black, Wellington; one *s* three *d. Educ:* Wellington Boys' Coll.; Victoria Univ. Coll., Wellington; Trinity Coll., Cambridge. Took 1st class honours in Physics (NZ); gained 1851 Exhibition Research Scholarship, 1913; volunteered NZEF, 1917; took BA Research at Cavendish Laboratory, 1920; Carnegie Corporation Travel Grants, 1933, 1951; Mem. NZ Defence Scientific Advisory Cttee, 1940–47. *Publications:* papers on Fluctuations of Gamma Rays, Absorption of X-Rays, Humidity, Frictional Electricity, Photoconduction in Rock Salt; A Lightning Phenomenon (jt paper). *Address:* University, Auckland, NZ. *Died 1 July* 1984.

**BURCH, Cecil Reginald**, CBE 1958; FRS 1944; BA; DSc; Research Associate, 1936–44 and Fellow, since 1944, of H. H. Wills Physics Laboratory, Bristol University; Warren Research Fellow in Physics, 1948–66; *b* 12 May 1901; *s* of late George James Burch, MA, DSc, FRS, and of Constance Emily Jeffries, sometime Principal of

Norham Hall, Oxford; *m* 1937, Enid Grace (*d* 1981), *o d* of Owen Henry Morice, Ipswich; one *d. Educ:* Oxford Preparatory School; Oundle Sch.; Gonville and Caius Coll., Cambridge. Physicist, Research Dept, Metropolitan Vickers Co., Trafford Park, Manchester, 1923–33; Leverhulme Fellow (in Optics), Imperial Coll. of Science and Technology, 1933–35. Rumford Medal, Royal Society, 1954. *Publications:* A Contribution to the Theory of Eddy Current Heating (with N. Ryland Davis); scientific papers on various subjects in physics and technology in Phil. Mag., Proc. Royal Society, etc. *Recreation:* walking. *Address:* 2 Holmes Grove, Henleaze, Clifton, Bristol BS9 4EE. *T:* Bristol 621650. *Died 19 July* 1983.

**BURCH, Maj.-Gen. Geoffrey**, CB 1977; consultant in human resources and in European defence procurement, since 1988; *b* 29 April 1923; *s* of late Henry James Burch, LDS, RCS (Eng); *m* 1948, Jean Lowrie Fyfe; one *s. Educ:* Felsted Sch. Served War: commissioned 2/Lt RA, 1943; served in Italy, 1943–45. India, 1946–47; ptsc 1951; psc 1953; British Defence Liaison Staff, Ottawa, 1962–65; Comd Flintshire and Denbighshire Yeomanry, 1965–66. Programme Director UK/Germany/Italy 155mm project, 1968–71; Dep. Commandant, Royal Military Coll. of Science, 1971–73; Dir-Gen. Weapons (Army), 1973–75; Dep. Master-General of the Ordnance, 1975–77; Mem., ROF Bd, 1975–77. Dir of Management Develt, Courtaulds, 1977–88. Col Comdt, RA, 1978–85. FInstD, FBIM, FIPM. *Recreations:* squash, tennis, bridge. *Clubs:* Royal Automobile, MCC. *Died 13 Oct.* 1990.

**BURDEN, Sqn Ldr Sir Frederick Frank Arthur**, Kt 1980; *b* 27 Dec. 1905; *s* of A. F. Burden, Bracknell, Berks; *m* Marjorie Greenwood; one *d. Educ:* Sloane Sch., Chelsea. Served War of 1939–45, RAF: first with a Polish unit, later with SE Asia Command, and on the staff of Lord Louis Mountbatten. MP (C) Gillingham, Kent, 1950–83. Pres., Textile Distributors Assoc., 1981–. Freeman of Gillingham, 1971. *Recreation:* fishing. *Address:* The Knapp, Portesham, Dorset. *T:* Abbotsbury 366. *Died 6 July* 1987.

**BURDEN, Major Geoffrey Noel**, CMG 1952; MBE 1938; *b* 9 Dec. 1898; *s* of late A. G. Burden, Exmouth, Devon; *m* 1927, Yolande Nancy, *d* of late G. H. B. Shaddick, Kenilworth, Cape Town; one *s* one *d. Educ:* Exeter Sch.; Royal Military College, Sandhurst. Served European War, 1914–18, Devon Regt, 1915–18; Indian Army, 1918–23. Joined Colonial Administrative Service, Nyasaland, 1925; Director of Publicity, 1936; Nyasaland Labour Officer to S Rhodesia, 1937–38; Nyasaland/N Rhodesian Labour Officer in the Union of South Africa, 1939; Chief Recruiting Officer, Nyasaland, 1940. War of 1939–45: military service in Somaliland, Abyssinia, and N Rhodesia, King's African Rifles, 1941–43. Asst Chief Sec., Nyasaland, 1945–46; Commissioner of Labour, Gold Coast, 1946–50; Chief Commissioner, Northern Territories, Gold Coast, 1950–53. Nyasaland Govt Representative in S Rhodesia, 1954–63. Voluntary service under SSAFA (Farnham/Frensham area), 1963–79. *Address:* Flat 17, Merlswood, 33 Meads Road, Eastbourne, Sussex BN20 8ES. *T:* Eastbourne (0323) 33371. *Died 10 May* 1990.

**BURDER, Sir John Henry**, Kt 1944; ED; *b* 30 Nov. 1900; *s* of late H. C. Burder; *m* 1929, Constance Aileen Bailey; two *d. Educ:* Eton College. Joined Jardine Skinner & Co., 1920; Chm., Jardine Henderson Ltd, 1939–47. Chm., Indian Tea Market Expansion Bd, 1939; President: Local Board, Imperial Bank of India, 1943–44; Bengal Chamber of Commerce, 1943–44; Associated Chambers of Commerce of India, 1943–44; Royal Agricultural and Horticultural Soc. of India, 1938–41; Calcutta Soc. for the Prevention of Cruelty to Animals, 1939–41; Lt-Col Commanding Calcutta Light Horse, 1944; Member of Council of State, 1943–44. *Address:* Plovers, Westhall Hill, Fulbrook, Oxon. *T:* Burford 2287. *Club:* Oriental. *Died 19 March* 1988.

**BURGE, James Charles George**, QC 1965; a Recorder, 1972–75; *b* 8 Oct. 1906; *s* of George Burge, Masterton, New Zealand; *m* 1938, Elizabeth, *d* of Comdr Scott Williams, RN, Dorset; two *s* one *d. Educ:* Cheltenham Coll.; Christ's Coll., Cambridge. Barrister, 1932, Master of the Bench, 1949, Inner Temple; Yarborough Anderson Scholar, Profumo Prizeman, Paul Methuen Prizeman. Pilot Officer RAFVR, 1940; Sqdn Ldr; Dep. Judge Advocate, 1941–44. Formerly Prosecuting Counsel, GPO, at CCC; Deputy Chairman, West Sussex Quarter Sessions, 1963–71. *Address:* Monte Puchol 151, Jávea 03730 (Alicante), Spain. *Died 6 Sept.* 1990.

**BURGESS, Sir John (Lawie)**, Kt 1972; OBE 1944; TD 1945; DL; Chairman, Cumbrian Newspapers Group Ltd, since 1945; *b* 17 Nov. 1912; *s* of late R. N. Burgess, Carlisle and Jean Hope Lawie, Carlisle; *m* 1948, Alice Elizabeth, *d* of late F. E. Gillieron, Elgin; two *s* one *d. Educ:* Trinity Coll., Glenalmond. Served War of 1939–45, Border Regt, France, Middle East, Tobruk, Syria, India and Burma; comd 4th Bn, Chindit Campaign, Burma, 1944 (despatches, OBE); Hon. Col 4th Bn The Border Regt, 1955–68. Chm., Reuters Ltd, 1959–68; Dir, Press Assoc. Ltd, 1950–57 (Chm. 1955); Mem. Council, Newspaper Soc., 1947–82; Chm., Border

Television Ltd, 1960–81, Vice-Chm. 1981–82. Mem. Council, Commonwealth Press Union. DL Cumberland, 1955; High Sheriff of Cumberland, 1969; JP City of Carlisle, 1952–82. *Recreations:* dowsing; anything to do with Cumbria. *Address:* The Limes, Cavendish Terrace, Carlisle, Cumbria. *T:* Carlisle 37450. *Clubs:* Garrick, Army and Navy. *Died* 10 *Feb.* 1987.

**BURGHARD, Rear-Adm. Geoffrey Frederic,** CB 1954; DSO 1946; retired; *b* 15 Oct. 1900; *m* 1931, Constance Louise Sheppard (*d* 1981); one *s* one *d. Educ:* RN Colleges, Osborne and Dartmouth. Naval Cadet, 1913; Captain, 1942; Rear-Admiral, 1952; Deputy Controller Electronics, Min. of Supply, 1952–55; retired list, 1955. MIEE 1956–61. *Address:* Edgehill, Pastens Road, Limpsfield, Surrey RH8 0RE. *Died* 7 *May* 1981.

**BURKE, Sir Aubrey (Francis),** Kt 1959; OBE 1941; Vice-Chairman and Deputy Managing Director, The Hawker Siddeley Group Ltd, retired from executive duties, 1969; *b* 21 April 1904; *m* 1936, Rosalind Laura, *d* of Rt Hon. Sir Henry Norman, 1st Bt, PC, OBE, and Hon. Lady Norman, CBE, JP; one *s* three *d* (and one *d* decd). Pres., SBAC, 1958–1959–1960. FCIT; FRSA. High Sheriff of Hertfordshire, 1966–67. *Recreations:* shooting, fishing, sailing. *Address:* Rent Street Barns, Bovingdon, Hertfordshire. *Club:* Royal Automobile. *Died* 8 *March* 1989.

**BURKE, Desmond Peter Meredyth,** MA Oxon; Headmaster, Clayesmore School, 1945–66; *b* 10 May 1912; *s* of late Maj. Arthur Meredyth Burke. *Educ:* Cheltenham Coll.; Queen's Coll., Oxford. Honours, Modern Greats, 1933. Housemaster and Senior Modern Language Master, Clayesmore School, 1936–40; served in Army Intelligence Corps at home, Belgium and Germany, 1940–45. *Recreations:* the theatre, travel, tennis, bridge. *Address:* The Old Lodge, 92 Alumhurst Road, Bournemouth West. *T:* Westbourne 762329. *Died* 9 *Jan.* 1987.

**BURKE, John Barclay;** Deputy Chairman, Royal Bank of Scotland plc, since 1982; Director, Royal Bank of Scotland Group; Chairman, Loganair Ltd; Vice-Chairman, Lloyds and Scottish Ltd; *b* 12 Feb. 1924; *m* 1953, Evelyn Petrie; one *s* one *d. Educ:* Hutchesons' Boys' Grammar Sch., Glasgow. Joined former National Bank of Scotland Ltd, 1941. Served Royal Navy, 1942–46. Gen. Manager, Nat. Commercial & Schroders Limited, 1965–66; General Manager and Director: Nat. Commercial Bank of Scotland Ltd, 1968–69; Royal Bank of Scotland Ltd, 1969–70; Managing Director: Royal Bank of Scotland, 1970–82; Royal Bank of Scotland Gp, 1976–82; Dir, Williams & Glyn's Bank plc. Chm., Cttee of Scottish Clearing Bankers, 1970–73, 1977–79; Pres., The Inst. of Bankers in Scotland, 1973–75. Jt Hon. Treasurer: The Earl Haig Fund (Scotland); Officers' Assoc. (Scottish Branch); Chm. Exec. Cttee, Scottish Council of Social Service. OStJ. FIB(Scot); FBIM. *Recreations:* golf, hill walking, flying. *Address:* 3 Cammo Gardens, Edinburgh EH4 8EJ. *T:* 031-339 2872. *Clubs:* Caledonian; New (Edinburgh); Royal and Ancient (St Andrews). *Died* 12 *Nov.* 1983.

**BURKE, Sir Thomas (Stanley),** 8th Bt, *cr* 1797; *b* 20 July 1916; *s* of Sir Gerald Howe Burke, 7th Bt and Elizabeth Mary (*d* 1918), *d* of late Patrick Mathews, Mount Hanover, Drogheda; *S* father, 1954; *m* 1955, Susanne Margaretha (*d* 1983), *er d* of Otto Salvisberg, Thun, Switzerland; one *s* one *d. Educ:* Harrow; Trinity Coll., Cambridge. *Heir: s* James Stanley Gilbert Burke [*b* 1 July 1956; *m* 1980, Laura, *d* of Domingo Branzuela; one *s* one *d*]. *Address:* 18 Elmcroft Avenue, NW11 0RR. *T:* 01-455 9407. *Died* 2 *April* 1989.

**BURKE-GAFFNEY, Maj.-Gen. (Hon.) Edward Sebastian,** CBE 1944; RA, retired; *b* 17 Aug. 1900; *s* of Francis Sebastian Burke-Gaffney; *m* 1926, Margot Lawrence; one *s* one *d. Educ:* Downside Sch.; RMA, Woolwich. 2nd Lieut RA 1920; Captain, 1933; Major, 1938; Col, 1945; Brig., 1949; Maj.-Gen. 1954; Officer Co. Gentleman Cadets, 1933; Staff Coll., Camberley, 1935–36; AHQ, India, 1937; General Officer Commanding, Aldershot District, 1953–54; retired 1954. *Recreations:* cricket, hockey, golf, shooting. *Address:* 29 Fore Street, Kingsbridge, Devon TQ7 1PG. *Died* 24 *May* 1981.

**BURLEIGH, Very Rev. John H. S.,** DD, BLitt; Professor of Ecclesiastical History, Edinburgh University, 1931–64, Emeritus, since 1964; Dean of the Faculty of Divinity, 1956–64; Moderator of the General Assembly of the Church of Scotland, May 1960–May 1961; *b* Ednam, Kelso, 19 May 1894; *s* of Rev. J. Burleigh; *m* 1926, Mary (*d* 1985), *d* of Rev. C. Giles; one *s* one *d. Educ:* Kelso High Sch., George Watson's Coll. and Univ., Edinburgh; Strasbourg; Oxford. Parish Minister of Fyvie, Aberdeenshire, and St Enoch's, Dundee. Principal, New Coll., Edinburgh, 1956–64. *Publications:* Christianity in the New Testament Epistles; City of God: a Study of St Augustine's Philosophy; St Augustine: Earlier Writings; A Church History of Scotland. *Address:* 21 Kingsmuir Drive, Peebles EH45 9AA. *T:* Peebles 20224. *Died* 22 *March* 1985.

**BURN, Duncan (Lyall);** economist, historian; *b* 10 Aug. 1902; *s* of Archibald William and Margaret Anne Burn; *m* 1930, Mollie White; two *d. Educ:* Holloway County Sch.; Christ's Coll. (Scholar), Cambridge. Hist. Tripos, Pts I and II, Cl. I, Wrenbury Schol. 1924;

Bachelor Research Schol. 1924, Christ's Coll., Cambridge. Lecturer in Economic History: Univ. of Liverpool, 1925; Univ. of Cambridge, 1927. Min. of Supply (Iron and Steel Control), 1939; Member US-UK Metallurgical Mission, New York and Washington, 1943; leader writer and Industrial Correspondent of the Times, 1946–62. Director of the Economic Development Office set up by AEI, English Electric, GEC, and Parsons, 1962–65. Visiting Professor of Economics: Manchester Univ., 1967–69; Bombay Univ., 1971. Member: Advisory Cttee on Census of Production, 1955–65; Exec. Cttee, Nat. Inst. of Econ. and Social Research, 1957–69; Econ. Cttee, DSIR, 1963–65; Specialist Adviser, House of Commons Select Cttee on Energy, 1980–. *Publications:* Economic History of Steelmaking, 1867–1939, 1940; The Steel Industry, 1939–59, 1961; The Political Economy of Nuclear Energy, 1967; Chemicals under Free Trade, 1971, repr. in Realities of Free Trade: Two Industry Studies (with B. Epstein), 1972; Nuclear Power and the Energy Crisis: politics and the atomic industry, 1978; ed and contrib. The Structure of British Industry, 2 vols, 1958; also contrib. to Journals, Bank Reviews, etc. *Recreations:* walking, gardening. *Address:* 5 Hampstead Hill Gardens, NW3 2PH. *T:* 01-435 5344. *Club:* United Oxford & Cambridge University. *Died* 9 *Jan.* 1988.

**BURN, Joshua Harold,** FRS 1942; MA, MD, Cantab; Emeritus Professor of Pharmacology, Oxford University, Emeritus Fellow of Balliol College; *b* 6 March 1892; *s* of J. G. Burn, Barnard Castle; *m* 1st, 1920, Margaret Parkinson (*d* 1927); 2nd, 1928, Katharine F. Pemberton (*d* 1971); two *s* four *d*; 3rd, 1971, Mrs Elizabeth Haslam-Jones. *Educ:* Barnard Castle Sch.; Emmanuel Coll., Cambridge (Scholar); 1st Class Pt 2 Natural Science Tripos; Michael Foster Student and Raymond Horton-Smith Prizeman; temp. Lieut RE, 1914–18; Guy's Hospital, 1918–20; member of staff of Medical Research Council, 1920–25; Director of Pharmacological Laboratories of Pharmaceutical Soc., 1926–37; Dean of Coll. of Pharmaceutical Soc. and Prof. of Pharmacology, Univ. of London, 1933–37; Prof. of Pharmacology, Oxford Univ., 1937–59. Member of 1932 Pharmacopœia Commn; Hon. Fellow, Indian Nat. Science Acad.; Hon. Member Soc. of Pharmacology and Therapeutics of Argentine Medical Assoc. Abraham Flexner Lecturer, Vanderbilt Univ., 1956; Nathanson Memorial Lecturer, Univ. of Southern California, 1956; Dixon Memorial Lecturer, Royal Soc. of Medicine, 1957; Herter Lecturer, Johns Hopkins Univ., 1962; Visiting Prof. to Washington Univ., St Louis, 1959–68. Hon. DSc: Yale, 1957; Bradford, 1971; Hon. MD Johannes Gutenberg Univ., Mainz, 1964; Dr (*hc*), Univ. of Paris, 1965; Hon. Pres., Internat. Union of Pharmacology, 1975; Hon. Member: Deutsche Pharmakologische Gesellschaft (Schmiedeberg Plakette); British Pharmacological Society (first Wellcome Gold Medal in Pharmacology, 1979); Deutsche Akademie der Naturforscher (Leopoldina); Czechoslovak Medical Society J. E. Purkyně. Gairdner Foundation Prize, 1959. *Publications:* Methods of Biological Assay, 1928; Recent Advances in Materia Medica, 1931; Biological Standardization, 1937; Background of Therapeutics, 1948; Lecture Notes on Pharmacology, 1948; Practical Pharmacology, 1952; Functions of Autonomic Transmitters, 1956; The Principles of Therapeutics, 1957; Drugs, Medicines and Man, 1962; The Autonomic Nervous System, 1963; Our most interesting Diseases, 1964; A Defence of John Balliol, 1970. *Address:* 3 Squitchey Lane, Oxford. *T:* Oxford 58209. *Died* 13 *July* 1981.

**BURN, Rodney Joseph,** RA 1962 (ARA 1954); artist; *b* Palmers Green, Middlesex, 11 July 1899; *s* of Sir Joseph Burn, KBE, and Emily Harriet Smith; *m* 1923, Dorothy Margaret, *d* of late Edward Sharwood-Smith; one *s* two *d. Educ:* Harrow Sch. Studied art at Slade Sch.; Asst Teacher at Royal Coll. of Art, South Kensington, 1929–31 and 1946–; Director of School of the Museum of Fine Arts, Boston, Mass, USA, 1931; returned to England, 1934; Asst Master, City & Guilds of London Art Sch.; Tutor, Royal Coll. of Art, 1947–65. Hon. Secretary New English Art Club until 1963; Member Royal West of England Academy, 1963; Hon. Fellow Royal Coll. of Art, 1964; Fellow University Coll. London, 1966; Hon. Mem., Soc. of Marine Artists, 1975. *Address:* 1 The Moorings, Strand on the Green, Chiswick, W4. *T:* 01-994 4190. *Died* 11 *Aug.* 1984.

**BURNET, Sir (Frank) Macfarlane,** OM 1958; AK 1978; KBE 1969; Kt 1951; FRS 1942; MD, ScD (Hon.) Cambridge, 1946; DSc (Hon.) Oxford, 1968; FRCP 1953; Past Director, Walter and Eliza Hall Institute for Medical Research, Melbourne, and Professor of Experimental Medicine, Melbourne University, 1944–1965 (Assistant Director, 1928–31 and 1934–44); Emeritus Professor, Melbourne University, 1965; Chairman, Commonwealth Foundation, 1966–69; *b* 3 Sept. 1899; *s* of Frank Burnet, Traralgon, Victoria; *m* 1st, 1928, Edith Linda (*d* 1973), *d* of F. H. Druce; one *s* two *d*; 2nd, 1976, Hazel Jenkin (*née* Foletta). *Educ:* Geelong Coll., Melbourne Univ. (MD). Resident Pathologist, Melbourne Hosp., 1923–24; Beit Fellow for Medical Research at Lister Institute, London, 1926–27; Visiting worker at National Institute for Medical Research, Hampstead, 1932–33; Dunham Lecturer Harvard Medical Sch., Jan. 1944; Croonian Lecturer, 1950 (Royal Society); Herter Lecturer, 1950 (Johns Hopkins Univ.); Abraham Flexner

Lecturer (Vanderbilt Univ.), 1958. Pres., Australian Acad. of Science, 1965–69. Hon. FRCS 1969. Royal Medal of Royal Society, 1947; Galen Medal in Therapeutics, Society of Apothecaries, 1958; Copley Medal, Royal Society, 1959; Nobel Prize for Medicine, 1960. *Publications:* Biological Aspects of Infectious Disease, 1940 (4th edn (with D. O. White) Natural History of Infectious Disease, 1972); Virus as Organism, 1945; Viruses and Man (Penguin), 1953; Principles of Animal Virology, 1955; Enzyme Antigen and Virus, 1956; Clonal Selection Theory of Acquired Immunity, 1959; Integrity of the Body, 1962; (with I. R. Mackay) Autoimmune Diseases, 1962; Changing Patterns (autobiography), 1968; Cellular Immunology, 1969; Dominant Mammal, 1970; Immunological Surveillance, 1970; Genes, Dreams and Realities, 1971; Walter and Eliza Hall Institute 1915–65, 1971; Auto-immunity and Auto-immune Disease, 1972; Intrinsic Mutagenesis, 1974; Immunology, 1976; Immunity, Aging and Cancer, 1976; Endurance of Life, 1978; Credo and Comment, 1979; technical papers. *Address:* 48 Monomeath Avenue, Canterbury, Victoria 3126, Australia.

*Died 31 Aug.* 1985.

**BURNETT, Lt-Col Maurice John Brownless,** DSO 1944; JP; DL; *b* 24 Sept. 1904; *o s* of late Ernest Joseph Burnett, MBE, JP, The Red House, Saltburn-by-the-Sea, Yorks, and late Emily Maud Margaret, 2nd *d* of John Brownless, Whorlton Grange, Barnard Castle and Dunsa Manor, Dalton; *m* 1930, Crystal, *d* of late Col H. D. Chamier, The Connaught Rangers; one *s. Educ:* Aysgarth Sch.; Rugby Sch.; RMA, Woolwich; Staff Coll., Camberley. 2nd Lieut RA 1924; psc 1937; Lt-Col 1942; served 1939–45; comd 127th (Highland) Field Regt in 51st Highland Division, Normandy to the Rhine; retd 1948. JP, 1957, DL, 1958, N Yorks. Member: N Riding Yorks Education Cttee, 1956–69; NR Yorks Standing Joint Cttee, and York and NE Yorks Police Cttee, 1958–74; Richmond, Yorks, RDC 1958–74 (Chm., 1967–69); N Riding CC, 1962–74 (Chm., Civil Protection Cttee, 1969–74); N Yorks CC, 1974–85 (Vice Chm., 1981–84; Chm., 1984–85; Hon. County Alderman, 1986); Church Assembly, 1955–70, General Synod, 1970–80; Ripon Diocesan Bd of Finance, 1953–85 (Vice-Chm. 1956–79); Exec. Cttee, N Riding Yorks Assoc. of Youth Clubs, 1950–71 (Chm. 1952 and 1965, Pres. 1971–84, Patron 1984–). Governor, Barnard Castle Sch., 1959–63, 1973–85; Chm. of Governors, Richmond Sch., 1970–86; District Comr, Scouts Assoc., (formerly Boy Scouts Assoc.), NR Yorks, 1950, County-Comr, 1961–69. Sec., N Riding Yorks Territorial and Auxiliary Forces Assoc., 1950–68. *Recreations:* country sports and pursuits, interest in local government and youth work. *Address:* Dunsa Manor, Dalton, Richmond, N Yorks DL11 7HE. *T:* Darlington 718251. *Club:* Army and Navy.

*Died 5 Dec.* 1988.

**BURNEY, Sir Anthony (George Bernard),** Kt 1971; OBE 1945; MA, FCA; *b* 3 June 1909; *o s* of Theodore and Gertrude Burney; *m* 1947, Dorothy Mary Vere, *d* of Col Clements Parr; no *c. Educ:* Rugby; Corpus Christi Coll., Cambridge (Hon. Fellow 1975). MA; FCA. Served War of 1939–45, Army: RE and RASC, Europe (Lt-Col). Partner, Binder, Hamlyn & Co., Chartered Accountants, 1938–71. Chm., Debenhams Ltd, 1971–80 (Dir, 1970–80). Dir, Commercial Union, to 1980; Dir of Reorganisation, The Cotton Bd, 1959–60; Mem. Shipbuilding Inquiry Cttee, 1965–66; Chm., Freight Integration Council, 1968–75; Mem. National Ports Council, 1971; Pres., Charities Aid Foundn. Hon. Fellow, LSE, 1987. *Publication:* Illustrations of Management Accounting in Practice, 1959. *Recreations:* gardening, photography. *Address:* 6 Greville Place, NW6. *T:* 01-624 4439. *Clubs:* Buck's, Garrick.

*Died 7 Jan.* 1989.

**BURNHAM, Forbes;** *see* Burnham, L. F. S.

**BURNHAM, James;** Writer; an Editor, National Review, since 1955; *b* 22 Nov. 1905; *s* of Claude George Burnham and Mary May Gillis; *m* 1934, Marcia Lightner; two *s* one *d. Educ:* Princeton Univ.; Balliol Coll., Oxford Univ. Prof. of Philosophy, New York Univ., 1932–54. *Publications:* (jtly) A Critical Introduction to Philosophy, 1932; The Managerial Revolution, 1941, rev. edn 1972; The Machiavellians, 1943; The Struggle for the World, 1947; (jtly) The Case for De Gaulle, 1948; The Coming Defeat of Communism, 1950; Containment or Liberation, 1953; The Web of Subversion, 1954; Congress and the American Tradition, 1959; Suicide of the West, 1964; The War We Are In, 1967. *Address:* Fuller Mountain Road, Kent, Conn 06757, USA. *T:* Kent, Conn, 203–927–3117.

*Died 28 July* 1987.

**BURNHAM, (Linden) Forbes (Sampson),** OE (Guyana) 1973; SC (Guyana); first Executive President of Co-operative Republic of Guyana, since 1980; Leader, People's National Congress, since 1957; *b* 20 Feb. 1923; *s* of J. E. Burnham, Headteacher of Kitty Methodist Sch., and Rachel A. Burnham (*née* Sampson); *m* 1st, 1951, Sheila Bernice Lataste; three *d*; 2nd, 1967, Viola Victorine Harper; two *d. Educ:* Kitty Methodist Sch., Central High Sch., Queen's Coll.; London Univ. British Guiana Scholarship, 1942; BA (London) 1944; Best Speaker's Cup at Univ. of London, 1947; Pres.

W Indian Students Union (Brit.), 1947–48; Delegate, Internat. Union of Students, Paris and Prague, 1947, 1948; LLB (Hons) 1947. Called to the Bar, 1948; QC (British Guiana), 1960, SC 1966. Entered local politics, 1949; Co-founder and Chm., People's Progressive Party, 1949; Minister of Education, 1953; re-elected to Legislature, 1957 and 1961; Founder and Leader, People's Nat. Congress, 1957; Leader of Opposition, 1957–64; Prime Minister of British Guiana, 1964–66, of Guyana, 1966–70, of Co-operative Republic of Guyana, 1970–80. Pres. Kitty Brotherhood, 1947–48, 1949–50; Town Councillor, 1952; Mayor of Georgetown, 1959, 1964; Pres. Bar Association, 1959; Pres. Guyana Labour Union, 1953–56, 1963–65, Pres. General, 1982 (Pres. on leave, 1965–). Patron: Guyana Lawn Tennis Assoc.; Soc. for the Blind; Red Cross Soc. Hon. LLD Dalhousie Univ., Nova Scotia, 1977. Star of Pleninay, Bulgaria, 1984; Order of Red Star, Yugoslavia, 1985. *Publication:* A Destiny to Mould, 1970. *Recreations:* horse-riding, swimming, fishing, hunting, chess (Pres., Guyana Chess Assoc.); special interest, farming. *Address:* Presidential Secretariat, Vlissengen Road, Georgetown, Guyana. *Clubs:* Demerara Cricket, Malteenoes Sports, Guyana Sports, Cosmos Sports, Georgetown Cricket, Non Pareil, Park Tennis, Guyana Motor Racing (Patron) (all in Guyana).

*Died 6 Aug.* 1985.

**BURNS, Arthur F.;** economist; Distinguished Scholar in Residence, American Enterprise Institute, since 1985; *b* Stanislau, Austria, 27 April 1904; *s* of Nathan Burns and Sarah Juran; *m* 1930, Helen Bernstein; two *s. Educ:* Columbia Univ. AB and AM 1925, PhD 1934. Rutgers Univ.: Instructor in Economics, 1927–30; Asst Prof., 1930–33; Associate Prof., 1933–43; Prof., 1943–44; Columbia Univ.: Vis. Prof., 1941–44; Prof., 1944–59; John Bates Clark Prof., 1959–69, now Prof. Emeritus. Nat. Bureau of Econ. Research: Res. Associate, 1930–31; Mem. Res. Staff, 1933; Dir of Res., 1945–53; Pres., 1957–67; Chm. of Bureau, 1967–69; Counsellor to the President of the US, 1969–70; Chm., Bd of Governors of Fed. Reserve System in the US, 1970–78; Alternate Governor, IMF, 1973–78; Distinguished Professorial Lectr, Georgetown Univ., 1978–81; Distinguished Scholar in Residence, Amer. Enterprise Inst., 1978–81; Consultant, Lazard Frères, 1978–81; Mem., Trilateral Commn, 1978–81; Ambassador of USA to FRG, 1981–85. Dir and Trustee of various orgs; Member (or Past Mem. or Consultant) of govt and other advisory bds. Chm., President's Coun. of Economic Advisors, 1953–56; Mem., President's Adv. Cttee on Labor-Management Policy, 1961–66, etc. Fellow: Amer. Statistical Assoc.; Econometric Soc.; Philos. Soc.; Amer. Acad. of Arts and Sciences; Amer. Econ. Assoc. (Pres. 1959); Acad. of Polit. Sci. (Pres., 1962–68); Phi Beta Kappa. Many hon. doctorates, 1952–. Alexander Hamilton Medal, Columbia Univ.; Dist. Public Service Award, Tax Foundn. Mugungwha Decoration, S Korea. Commander, French Legion of Honour; Decoration (1st class), Order of the Rising Sun, Japan; Grand Cross, Order of Merit, FRG. *Publications:* Production Trends in the United States since 1870, 1934; Economic Research and the Keynesian Thinking of our Times, 1946; (jtly) Measuring Business Cycles, 1946; Frontiers of Economic Knowledge, 1954; Prosperity Without Inflation, 1957; The Management of Prosperity, 1966; The Business Cycle in a Changing World, 1969; Reflections on an Economic Policy Maker, 1978; The United States and Germany: a vital partnership, 1986. *Address:* 1150 17th Street NW, Washington, DC 20036, USA. *Clubs:* Century Association (New York); Cosmos, City Tavern (Washington).

*Died 26 June* 1987.

**BURNS, Bryan Hartop;** Hon. Consulting Orthopædic Surgeon: St George's Hospital; St Peter's Hospital, Chertsey; Heatherwood Hospital, Ascot; *b* 14 Dec. 1896; *s* of Hartop Burns, Grendon, Northampton; *m* 1938, Hon. Dorothy Garthwaite, *d* of late Lord Duveen. *Educ:* Wellingborough Sch.; Clare Coll., Cambridge; St George's Hospital Medical Sch. Allingham Scholarship in surgery, St George's Hospital, 1924. 2nd Lieut Northamptonshire Regt, 1915; served France; Captain 1917. Orthopædic Surgeon, Royal Masonic Hospital, 1945–61. Ex-Pres. Orthopædic Section, Royal Society Med.; Mem. of Court of Examiners, Royal College of Surgeons, 1943–46; Emer. Fellow, British Orthopædic Association; Member Société Internationale de Chirurgie Orthopédique. *Publications:* Recent Advances in Orthopædic Surgery, 1937 (jointly); articles on orthopædic subjects. *Address:* 6 Chesterfield Hill, W1. *T:* 01–493 3435. *Clubs:* Boodle's, Brooks's.

*Died 6 Dec.* 1984.

**BURNS, Sir Charles (Ritchie),** KBE 1958 (OBE 1947); MD, FRCP; FRACP; retired; Consulting Physician and Consulting Cardiologist, Wellington Hospital, since 1958; Director, Clinical Services, National Society on Alcoholism (Inc.), NZ, 1970; Consulting Physician, National Society on Alcoholism and Drug Dependence, 1970–81; *b* Blenheim, Marlborough, NZ, 27 May 1898; *s* of Archibald Douglas Burns, Lands and Survey Dept, NZ; *m* 1st, 1935, Margaret Muriel (decd 1949), *d* of John Laffey, Dunedin, NZ; one *s* one *d*; 2nd, 1963, Doris Ogilvy, *d* of Keith Ramsay (sen.), Dunedin, New Zealand. *Educ:* St Mary's Sch., Blenheim, NZ; Marlborough and Nelson Colls, NZ. MB, ChB

(NZ) 1922 (with distinction and Med. Travelling Scholarship; Batchelor Memorial Medal); MRCP 1925; MD (NZ) 1925; Foundation Fellow RACP 1937; FRCP (Lond.) 1943; FMANZ 1979. Med. Registrar Dunedin Hospital, and Medical Tutor Otago Univ., 1925–27; Asst Phys., Dunedin Hospital, 1927–37; Senior Phys. and Cardiologist, Wellington Hospital, NZ, 1940–58; Phys., Home of Compassion, Island Bay, NZ, 1940–68; Mem. Med. Council, NZ, 1943–55; Examr in Medicine, Univ., of NZ, 1947–53, 1959, 1963. Mem. NZ Bd of Censors for RACP, 1954–61; Corresp. Mem. Brit. Cardiac Soc., 1952–71; Life Mem. Cardiac Soc. of Australia and NZ, 1972 (Mem., 1952–72; Mem. Council, 1956–58; Chm. 1964–65); Member: Council and NZ Vice-Pres., RACP, 1956–58; NZ Lepers' Trust Bd, 1958–; Advisory Cttee, The Nat. Soc. on Alcoholism (NZ); Council, Wellington Med. Research Foundn; President: NZ Nutrition Soc., 1967–70; NZ Med. Soc. on Alcohol and Alcoholism, 1978–80; Chm., Industry Cttee, Alcohol Liquor Adv. Council, 1977–80; Patron: NZ Asthma Soc.; NZ Diabetic Soc. (Wellington Br.); Deaf Children's Parents Soc. (Wellington Br.); Soc. for Promotion of Community Standards. Sixth Leonard Ball Oration, Melbourne, 1973. Mem., Guild of Sts Luke Cosmas and Damian, 1954– (Pres., 1966–69). Served War, 1944–47, Military Hospitals, 2nd NZEF, Italy and Japan (OBE). Hon. DSc Otago, 1975. KSG 1977. *Publications:* contrib. medical journals and jls of anciliary medical services. *Recreations:* walking and medical writing. *Address:* 42 Northcote Road, Takapuna, Auckland 9, New Zealand. *T:* Wellington 849–249.

*Died 8 Feb. 1985.*

**BURNS, Lt-Gen. Eedson Louis Millard,** CC (Canada) 1967; DSO 1944; OBE 1935; MC; idc; *b* 17 June 1897; *m* 1927, Eleanor Phelan; one *d. Educ:* Royal Military Coll., Kingston, Canada; Staff Coll., Quetta. Served European War, 1916–18 (France, Belgium) with Royal Canadian Engineers, Signals, Staff; Can. Perm. Force, 1918–39. War of 1939–45; GOC 2nd Can. Div., 1943 (Maj.-Gen.); 5th Can. Div., 1944; 1st Can. Corps, 1944. Dir-Gen. of Rehabilitation, Dept Veteran Affairs, 1945–46, Asst Dep. Minister, 1946–50, Dep. Minister, 1950–54. Chief of Staff, UN Truce Supervision Organisation, Palestine, 1954–56; Comdr UN Emergency Force, 1956–59; Adviser to Govt of Canada on Disarmament, 1960–69, retd; Leader of Canadian Delegation to 18–Nation Disarmament Conference, Geneva, 1962–68. Res. Fellow, Carleton Univ., 1970–71, Prof. of Strategic Studies, 1971–73. Nat. Pres. UNA, Canada, 1952–53 (Altern. Deleg. to UN, 1949). Officier Légion d'Honneur. *Publications:* Manpower in the Canadian Army, 1939–45, 1955; Between Arab and Israeli, 1962; Megamurder, 1966; General Mud, 1970; A Seat at the Table, 1972; Defence in the Nuclear Age, 1976. *Address:* RR 1, Box 132, Manotick, Ont. KOA 2NO, Canada. *Died 13 Sept. 1985.*

**BURNS, Sir Malcolm (McRae),** KBE 1972 (CBE 1959); Principal, Lincoln Agricultural College, New Zealand, 1952–74; *b* 19 March 1910; *s* of J. E. Burns and Emily (*née* Jeffrey); *m* 1936, Ruth, *d* of J. D. Waugh, St Louis, USA; one *s* two *d. Educ:* Rangiora High Sch.; Univs of Canterbury (NZ), Aberdeen and Cornell. Plant Physiologist, DSIR, NZ, 1936; Sen. Lectr, Lincoln Agric. Coll., 1937–48; Dir, NZ Fert. Manuf. Res. Assoc., 1948–52. Chairman: Physical Environment Commn, 1968–70; Fact-finding Gp on Nuclear Power, 1976–77; Member: Nat. Develt Council, 1969–74; Nat. Museum Council, 1974–; Beech Forests Council, 1972–78; Trustee, Norman Kirk Meml, etc. FNZIC; FNZIAS; FRSNZ; FAAAS. Chm., DSIR Research Council, 1959–62. NZ Representative, Harkness Fellowships, 1961–76. Hon. DSc Canterbury, 1974. *Publications:* articles in scientific jls. *Recreations:* bowls, fishing, gardening. *Address:* 7 Royds Street, Christchurch 1, New Zealand. *Died 17 Oct. 1986.*

**BURNS, Sir Wilfred,** Kt 1980; CB 1972; CBE 1967; MEng, PPRTPI, MICE; Deputy Chairman and Member, Local Government Boundary Commission for England, since 1982; *b* 11 April 1923; *m* 1945, Edna Price; one *s* one *d. Educ:* Ulverston Grammar Sch.; Liverpool Univ. Admty, 1944–45; Leeds Corp., 1946–49; Prin. Planning Officer, Coventry Corp., 1949–58; Dep. Planning Officer, Surrey CC, 1958–60; City Planning Officer, Newcastle upon Tyne, 1960–68; Chief Planner, 1968–82, and Dep. Sec., 1971–82, DoE (formerly Min. of Housing and Local Govt). Hon. DSc, Univ. of Newcastle upon Tyne, 1966. *Publications:* British Shopping Centres, 1959; New Towns for Old, 1963; Newcastle upon Tyne: A Study in Planning, 1967. *Address:* 29a Sydenham Hill, SE26. *T:* 01-670 3525. *Died 4 Jan. 1984.*

**BURNTWOOD, Baron** *cr* 1970 (Life Peer), of Burntwood, Staffs; **Julian Ward Snow;** *b* 24 Feb. 1910; *s* of late H. M. Snow, CVO, Mottingham, Kent; *m* 1948, Flavia (*d* 1980), *d* of late Sir Ralph Blois, 9th Bt, and Lady Blois, Cockfield Hall; one *d. Educ:* Haileybury. Royal Artillery, 1939–45. A member of the Union of Shop Distributive and Allied Workers. MP (Lab) Portsmouth Central, 1945–50, Lichfield and Tamworth Div. of Staffs, 1950–70; Vice-Chamberlain to the Household, 1945–46; a Lord Comr of HM Treasury, 1946–50; Parliamentary Secretary: Min. of Aviation,

1966–67; Min. of Health, 1967–68; Parly Under-Sec. of State, Dept of Health and Social Security, 1968–69. *Address:* 37 Chester Way, SE11. *Died 24 Jan. 1982.*

**BURRELL, Vice-Adm. Sir Henry Mackay,** KBE 1960 (CBE 1955); CB 1959; RAN retired; now a retired grazier; *b* 13 Aug. 1904; British (father *b* Dorset; mother *b* Australia, of Scottish parents); *m* 1944, Ada Theresa Weller (*d* 1981); one *s* two *d. Educ:* Royal Australian Naval Coll., Jervis Bay, Australia. Cadet-Midshipman, 1918; specialist in navigation, psc Greenwich, 1938; Commands: HMAS Norman, 1941–42 (despatches); Bataan, 1945; Dep. Chief of Naval Staff, Navy Office, Melbourne, 1947–48; HMAS Australia, 1949; idc 1950; HMAS Vengeance, 1953–54; Second Naval Mem., Australian Commonwealth Naval Board, 1956–57; Flag Officer Commanding HM Australian Fleet, 1955 and 1958; Chief of the Australian Naval Staff, 1959–62. *Publication:* Mermaids Do Exist (autobiog.), 1986. *Address:* 49 National Circuit, Forrest, Canberra, ACT 2603, Australia. *Club:* Commonwealth (Canberra, ACT).

*Died 9 Feb. 1988.*

**BURRELL, John;** *see* Burrell, R. J.

**BURRELL, His Honour John Glyn,** QC 1961; a Circuit Judge (formerly County Court Judge), 1964–80; *b* 10 Oct. 1912; *o s* of Lewis Morgan Burrell and Amy Isabel Burrell; *m* 1941, Dorothy, 2nd *d* of Prof. T. Stanley Roberts, MA Cantab, Aberystwyth; two *d. Educ:* Friars Sch., Bangor; Univ. Coll. of Wales. Called to Bar, Inner Temple, 1936. Practised Northern Circuit (Liverpool); Recorder of Wigan, 1962–64; Chm., Radnorshire QS, 1964–71. Army service, 1940–45. *Address:* The Lodge, Spittal, Haverfordwest, Dyfed. *Died 6 March 1984.*

**BURRELL, Joseph Frederick,** CVO 1976; Partner, Farrer & Co., Lincoln's Inn Fields, 1938–76; Solicitor to the Duchy of Cornwall, 1972–76; *b* 27 July 1909; *s* of Arthur J. T. Burrell and Marie Birt; *m* 1940, Diana Margaret Beachcroft, *d* of Cyril Beachcroft and Vivien Hughes. *Educ:* Eton; Trinity College, Cambridge. Sapper, TA, 1938–40; Gunner, 1940–45. Governor and Mem. Bd of Management, Royal Hosp. and Home for Incurables, 1978–; Mem. Council, DGAA, 1978–; Trustee, Grants Cttee of Florence Nightingale Fund for Aid in Sickness, 1978–. *Address:* 54 Murray Road, Wimbledon, SW19. *Club:* Travellers'.

*Died 20 March 1983.*

**BURRELL, (Robert) John,** QC 1973; *b* London, 28 Nov. 1923; *s* of late Robert Burrell, QC; *m* 1948, Thelma Louise Mawdesley Harris; no *c. Educ:* Rugby; Trinity Hall, Cambridge (MA). Served War, Royal Navy, 1942–46: Fleet Minesweepers and Motor Torpedo Boats, English Channel and Adriatic; participated in D Day landings, 1944; demobilised, 1946, Lieut RNVR. Called to Bar, Inner Temple, 1948; Bencher, Inner Temple, 1980; Member: Senate of Inns of Court and the Bar, 1983–85; Council of Legal Educn, 1984–. Mem., Paddington Borough Council, 1949–56 (Chm. Housing Cttee, 1953–56); Chairman: Plant Varieties and Seeds Tribunal, 1974–; Pres., Ligue Internationale contre la Concurrence Déloyale (Paris), 1980–82 (Vice-Pres., 1978–80); Mem., EEC Working Cttee, EEC Trade Mark Law, 1975–77. *Recreations:* music (piano), mountain walking. *Address:* 1 Essex Court, Temple, EC4Y 9AR. *T:* 01–353 8507. *Died 24 Oct. 1985.*

**BURRELL, Sir Walter (Raymond),** 8th Bt, *cr* 1774; CBE 1956 (MBE 1945); TD; DL; Trustee Royal Agricultural Society of England, since 1948, President 1964, Chairman of Council, 1967–72; *b* 11 Dec. 1903; *er s* of Sir Merrik Burrell, 7th Bt, CBE; *S* father 1957; *m* 1931, Hon. Anne Judith Denman, OBE, *o d* of 3rd Baron Denman, PC, GCMG, KCVO; two *s* two *d. Educ:* Eton. Major 98th Field Regt (Surrey and Sussex Yeo.), Royal Artillery (TA), 1938; Lt-Col (Chief Instructor) 123 OCTU, 1942; Lt-Col BAS (Washington), 1943; Comd 3 Super Heavy Regt, RA 1945 (MBE). Pres. Country Landowners' Assoc., 1952–53; Pres., South of England Agricultural Soc., 1974–. DL Sussex, 1937, West Sussex 1974; County Alderman, 1950; Vice-Chm. West Sussex County Council, 1953. *Heir:* s John Raymond Burrell [*b* 20 Feb. 1934; *m* 1st, 1959, Rowena Pearce (marr. diss. 1971); one *s* one *d*; 2nd, 1971, Margot Lucy, *d* of F. E. Thatcher, Sydney, NSW; one *s* one *d. Educ:* Eton]. *Address:* Knepp Castle, West Grinstead, Horsham, West Sussex. *T:* Coolham 247. *Club:* Boodle's. *Died 4 May 1985.*

**BURROW, Prof. Harold,** MRCVS, DVSM; Professor of Veterinary Medicine, Royal Veterinary College, University of London, 1944–63; Professor Emeritus since 1963; *b* 24 Aug. 1903; *s* of Henry Wilson and Elizabeth Jane Burrow, Hest Bank Lodge, near Lancaster; *m* 1933, Frances Olivia, *d* of Orlando Atkinson Ducksbury, MRCVS, and Mrs Frances Mary Ducksbury, Lancaster; one *d. Educ:* Lancaster Royal Grammar Sch.; Royal (Dick) Veterinary Coll., Edinburgh. Asst Veterinary Officer, City of Birmingham, 1927–30; Chief Veterinary Officer: Birkenhead, 1930–35; Derbyshire CC, 1935–38; Divisional Veterinary Officer, Min. of Agriculture, 1938–42; Private Veterinary Practice, 1942–44. Examiner: to Royal Coll. of Veterinary Surgeons, 1937–44; to

Univs. of Liverpool, London, Reading, Edinburgh, Bristol and Ceylon (various dates). Pres. Old Lancastrian Club, 1953; Member of Council, Royal Society Health, 1950–64 (Chairman, 1956–57, Vice-Pres. 1958–65, Life Vice-Pres., 1965). *Publications:* numerous contributions to veterinary scientific press. *Recreation:* gardening. *Address:* Forge Cottage, Combrook, Warwick. *T:* Kineton 641424.
*Died 31 Oct.* 1987.

**BURROW, Prof. Thomas,** MA, PhD; FBA 1970; Boden Professor of Sanskrit in the University of Oxford, and Fellow of Balliol College, 1944–76; Emeritus Fellow of Balliol, 1976; *b* 29 June 1909; *e s* of Joshua and Frances Eleanor Burrow; *m* 1941, Inez Mary (*d* 1976), *d* of Herbert John Haley. *Educ:* Queen Elizabeth's Sch., Kirkby Lonsdale; Christ's Coll., Cambridge. Research Fellow of Christ's Coll., Cambridge, 1935–37; Asst Keeper in Dept of Oriental Printed Books and Manuscripts, British Museum, 1937–44. Leverhulme Research Fellow, 1957–68. Fellow, Sch. of Oriental and African Studies, 1974. *Publications:* The Language of the Kharoṣṭhī Documents from Chinese Turkestan, 1937; A Translation of the Kharoṣṭhī Documents from Chinese Turkestan, 1940; (with S. Bhattacharya) The Parji Language, 1953; The Sanskrit Language, 1955; (with M. B. Emeneau) A Dravidian Etymological Dictionary, 1961, Supplement, 1968, 2nd rev. edn 1984; (with S. Bhattacharya) The Pengo Language, 1970; The Problem of Shwa in Sanskrit, 1979. *Address:* 1 Woodlands, Kidlington, Oxford OX5 2ER. *T:* Kidlington 5283.
*Died 8 June* 1986.

**BURROWS, Harold Jackson,** CBE 1967; MD; FRCS, FRACS; Civil Consultant to Royal Navy in Orthopaedic Surgery, since 1949 (Honorary since 1977); Hon. Consulting Orthopaedic Surgeon: St Bartholomew's Hospital; Royal National Orthopaedic Hospital; *b* 9 May 1902; *s* of late Harold Burrows, CBE, and Lucy Mary Elizabeth (*née* Wheeler); unmarried. *Educ:* Cheltenham Coll.; King's Coll., Cambridge (MA); St Bartholomew's Hosp. Served War of 1939–45 as Surgeon Comdr RNVR. Beaverbrook Res. Scholar, RCS, 1930–31; Hunterian Prof., RCS, 1932; Asst Orthopaedic Surgeon, 1937, Orthopaedic Surgeon, 1946 and Surgeon i/c Orthopaedic Dept and Clinical Lectr on Orthopaedic Surgery, St Bartholomew's Hosp., 1958–67; Asst Surgeon, 1946, and Orthopaedic Surgeon, Royal Nat. Orthopaedic Hosp., 1948–67; Orthopaedic Surgeon, Nat. Hosp. for Diseases of the Nervous System, 1937–46; Consultant Adviser in Orthopaedics to Min. of Health 1964–71; Orthopaedic Surgeon, The Heritage, Chailey, 1937–70; Dean, Inst. of Orthopaedics, British Postgraduate Med. Fedn, Univ. of London, 1946–64, 1967–70. Nuffield Vis. Fellow to British WI on behalf of CO, 1955; Samuel Higby Camp Vis. Prof., Univ. of Calif., San Francisco, 1963. Chm., British Editorial Bd, Jl of Bone and Joint Surgery, 1961–73 (Asst Ed., 1948–49; Dep. Ed., 1949–60). Fellow: RSM (Hon. Mem. and Past Pres., Orthopaedic Section); Assoc. of Surgeons of Great Britain and Ireland; British Orthopaedic Assoc. (Past Pres.). Member: Council, RCS, 1964–72; Soc. Internat. de Chirurgie Orthopédique et de Traumatologie; Standing Adv. Cttee on Artificial Limbs, 1957–71 (Chm., 1964–71); Corresp. Member: Australian Orthopaedic Assoc.; Amer. Orthopaedic Assoc.; Hon. Member: NZ Orthopaedic Assoc.; Internat. Skeletal Soc. Robert Jones Gold Medal, British Orthopaedic Assoc., 1937. *Publications:* papers on surgical subjects. *Address:* 16 Wood Lane, Highgate, N6. *Died 5 Feb.* 1981.

**BURROWS, Very Rev. Hedley Robert;** Dean Emeritus of Hereford; Dean of Hereford, 1947–61, resigned in Oct. 1961; *b* 15 Oct. 1887; *s* of late Rt Rev. L. H. Burrows; *m* 1921, Joan Lumsden (*d* 1964), *d* of late Rt Rev. E. N. Lovett, CBE; one *s* (*er s* died on active service, 1945) two *d*. *Educ:* Charterhouse; New Coll., Oxford; Wells Theological Coll. Deacon, 1911; Priest, 1912; Curate of Petersfield, Hants, 1911–14; Temp. CF European War, 1914–16, invalided; Hon. CF; Priest in charge St Columba's, Poltalloch, Argyll, 1917–18; Domestic Chaplain to Dr Lang, when Archbishop of York, 1918–19; Curate in charge Dock Street Mission, Southampton, 1919–21; Rector of Stoke Abbott, Dorset, 1921–25; Vicar of St Stephen's, Portsea, 1925–28; Hon. Chaplain to 1st Bishop of Portsmouth, 1927–28. Vicar of Grimsby and Rural Dean of Grimsby and Cleethorpes, 1928–36; Vicar of St Peter's, Bournemouth, 1936–43; Rural Dean of Bournemouth, 1940–43; Prebendary and Canon of Sutton-in-Marisco, Lincoln Cathedral, 1933–43; Archdeacon of Winchester, and Residentiary Canon of the Cathedral, 1943–47. Chm., Midland Region Religious Cttee of the BBC, 1952–57 (ex-officio: Member Midland Council of BBC and Member Headquarters Council of BBC Central Religious Cttee, London). Elected a Church Commissioner for England, and Member Board of Governors, 1952–58. OStJ 1947. *Publication:* Hereford Cathedral, 1958. *Address:* Brendon House, Park Road, Winchester, Hants SO23 7BQ. *Club:* Athenæum. *Died 27 Oct.* 1983.

**BURROWS, Sir (Robert) John (Formby),** Kt 1965; MA, LLB; Solicitor; *b* 29 May 1901; *s* of Rev. Canon Francis Henry and Margaret Nelson Burrows; *m* 1926, Mary Hewlett (*d* 1986), *y d* of Rev. R. C. Salmon; one *s* one *d*. *Educ:* Eton Coll. (Scholar); Trinity Coll., Cambridge (Scholar); Harvard Law Sch. Pres. of The Law

Soc., 1964–65. *Recreation:* small-scale forestry. *Address:* Ridlands Cottage, Limpsfield Chart, Surrey. *T:* Oxted 723288.
*Died 7 Sept.* 1987.

**BURSTALL, Prof. Aubrey Frederic;** Professor of Mechanical Engineering, University of Newcastle upon Tyne (formerly King's College, University of Durham), 1946–67, then Emeritus; Dean of Faculty of Applied Science, 1955–57; *b* 15 Jan. 1902; *s* of Prof. Frederic William Burstall of Univ. of Birmingham and Lilian Maud Burstall (*née* Adley); *m* 1923, Nora Elizabeth (*née* Boycott); two *s* one *d*. *Educ:* King Edward VI Grammar Sch., Birmingham, Univ. of Birmingham; St John's Coll., Cambridge. BScEng Birmingham, 1922, First Class Hons; MScEng Birmingham, 1923; PhD Cantab 1925; DSc Melbourne; Hon. DSc (NUI), 1959. Research student, St John's Coll., Cambridge, 1923–25. Employed on the staff of Synthetic Ammonia and Nitrates Ltd (later merged into ICI Ltd) as research engineer, asst chief engineer and works engineer at Billingham Factory, 1925–34; Aluminium Plant and Vessel Co., London, as Technical Adviser to the Board responsible for design of chemical plant, 1934–37; Prof. of Engineering and Dean of Faculty of Engineering, Univ. of Melbourne, Australia, 1937–45. Developed mechanical respirators for infantile paralysis epidemic, 1937–38; gas producers for motor vehicles, and built new workshops at the Univ.; part-time Comr of State Electricity Commn of Victoria, 1941–43; leave of absence to work for British Min. of Supply in Armaments Design Dept, Fort Halstead, Kent, 1943–44. Member of Nat. Advisory Cttee on Technical Educ., 1948; Chm. North Eastern Branch IMechE, 1956; Member Board of Governors, United Newcastle upon Tyne Hospitals, 1964–67; Member Council of Univ. of Durham, 1964–67; Fellow, NEC Inst. Engineers and Shipbuilders; FIMechE. *Publications:* A History of Mechanical Engineering, 1963; Simple Working Models of Historic Machines, 1968; numerous in engineering journals in Britain and Australia. *Address:* The Firs, Kilmington, Axminster, Devon EX13 7SS. *T:* Axminster 32385. *Died 25 June* 1984.

**BURT, Clive Stuart Saxon,** QC 1954; a Metropolitan Magistrate, 1958–73; *b* 11 June 1900; *m* 1st, 1926, Edith Benning, Montreal; 2nd, 1939, Lilian Bethune, Glasgow; one *s* three *d*. *Educ:* Eton; Oxford Univ. Served War, 1940–45 (despatches). Called to the Bar, Gray's Inn, 1925; Western Circuit. Chairman, The Performing Right Tribunal, 1957–58. Croix de Guerre. *Address:* Townley House, Woodbridge, Suffolk. *Club:* Garrick.
*Died 30 Sept.* 1981.

**BURT, Leonard James,** CVO 1954; CBE 1957; Commander of Special Branch, New Scotland Yard, 1946–58, retired; *b* 20 April 1892; *s* of Charles Richard Burt; *m* 1918, Grace Airey; one *s*. *Educ:* Totton High Sch., Hants. CID, 1919–40; Chief Superintendent, CID, 1940; Intelligence Corps (Lieut-Col) 1940–46. Officer Legion of Honour, 1950; Officer Order of Orange Nassau, 1951; Chevalier Order of Danebrog, 1951. *Publication:* Commander Burt of Scotland Yard, 1959. *Address:* Flat 1, Hedley Court, 67/69 Putney Hill, SW15. *T:* 01-788 4598. *Died 3 Sept.* 1983.

**BURT-ANDREWS, Stanley George,** CMG 1968; MBE 1948; retired; *b* 1 Feb. 1908; *s* of Major Charles and Menie Celina Burt-Andrews; *m* 1937, Vera Boyadjieva; one *d*. *Educ:* Lindisfarne Coll., Westcliff-on-Sea; St Andrew's Coll., Bloemfontein, S Africa. Vice-Consul, 1946–47, Consul, 2nd Secretary, Sofia, 1948; Consul, Barranquilla, 1949–52; Commercial Secretary, British Embassy, Buenos Aires, 1952–53; Consul: Baltimore, 1953–59; Bilbao, 1959–62; Venice, 1962–64; Consul-General, St Louis, Mo., 1965–67. *Recreation:* fishing. *Address:* Villa Verial, 1 Aldwick Place, Fish Lane, Aldwick, Bognor Regis, W Sussex. *Club:* Bognor Regis Golf.
*Died 28 Oct.* 1990.

**BURTON, Neil Edward David;** Secretary, Monopolies and Mergers Commission, 1981–86; retired; *b* 12 May 1930; *s* of late Edward William Burton and Doris Burton; *m* 1954, Jane-Anne Crossley Perry; three *s*. *Educ:* Welwyn Garden City Grammar Sch.; City of London Sch.; Trinity Coll., Oxford (MA). Asst Principal, Min. of Supply; Asst Sec., MAFF, 1966, subseq. CSD and Price Commn; Asst Dir, Office of Fair Trading, 1976; Dir, Restrictive Trade Practices, 1976; Dir of Competition Policy, 1977–81. *Address:* 29 Brittains Lane, Sevenoaks, Kent TN13 2JW. *T:* Sevenoaks (0732) 455608. *Died 6 June* 1990.

**BURTON, Richard,** CBE 1970, stage and film actor; *b* Pontrhydfen, South Wales, 10 Nov. 1925; *m* 1st, Sybil Williams (marr. diss., 1963; she *m* 1965, Jordan Christopher); two *d*; 2nd, 1964, Elizabeth Taylor (marr. diss., 1974, remarried 1975, marr. diss., 1976); 4th, 1976, Susan Hunt (marr. diss. 1982); 5th, 1983, Sally Hay. *Educ:* Port Talbot Secondary Sch.; Exeter Coll., Oxford. Hon. Fellow, St Peter's Coll., Oxford, 1972. First appeared on stage as Glan in Druid's Rest, Royal Court Theatre, Liverpool, 1943; played same rôle, St Martin's, London, 1944. Served with Royal Air Force, 1944–47. Returned to stage in Castle Anna, Lyric, Hammersmith, 1948; subsequent stage appearances include: Richard in the Lady's Not For Burning, Globe, 1949, New York, 1950; Cuthman in The Boy

With a Cart, Lyric, Hammersmith, 1950. Played Hamlet with Old Vic Company, Edinburgh Festival, 1953, and subsequently; has also appeared with Old Vic Company in King John, The Tempest, Twelfth Night, Coriolanus, etc. Old Vic Season, 1955–56; Othello, Iago, Henry V; Time Remembered, New York, 1957–58; Camelot, New York, 1960, throughout US, 1980–81; Hamlet, New York, 1964; Equus, NY, 1976; (with Elizabeth Taylor) Private Lives, NY, 1983. *Films include*: The Last Days of Dolwyn; My Cousin Rachel; The Desert Rats; The Robe; The Prince of Players; Alexander the Great; The Rains of Ranchipur; Sea Wyf and Biscuit; Bitter Victory; Look Back in Anger; Bramblebush; Ice Palace; Cleopatra; The VIP's; Becket; Hamlet (from Broadway prod.); The Night of the Iguana; The Sandpiper; The Spy Who Came in from the Cold; Who's Afraid of Virginia Woolf; The Taming of the Shrew; Dr Faustus; The Comedians; Boom; Where Eagles Dare; Candy; Staircase; Anne of the Thousand Days; Villain; Hammersmith is Out; Raid on Rommel; Under Milk Wood; The Assassination of Trotsky; Bluebeard; The Kinsman; Massacre in Rome; Exorcist II; The Heretic; Equus; The Medusa Touch; The Wild Geese; Wagner; Nineteen Eighty Four. *Relevant publication*: Richard Burton, by J. Cottrell and F. Cashin, 1971. *Address*: c/o Major Donald Neville-Willing, 85 Kinnerton Street, SW1. *T*: 01–235 4640.    *Died 5 Aug. 1984.*

**BURTON-CHADWICK, Sir Robert, (Sir Peter Burton-Chadwick),** 2nd Bt, *cr* 1935; *b* 22 June 1911; *s* of Sir Robert Burton-Chadwick, 1st Bt and Catherine Barbara (*d* 1935), *d* of late Thomas Williams; *S* father 1951; *m* 1st, 1937, Rosalind Mary (marr. diss., 1949), *d* of Harry John Stott; two *d*; 2nd, 1950, Beryl Joan, *d* of Stanley Frederick J. Brailsford; one *s* one *d*. *Educ*: St George's Sch., Harpenden, Herts. Served War of 1939–45, with NZMF, N Africa, Italy, 1942–45. *Heir*: *s* Joshua Kenneth Burton-Chadwick, *b* 1 Feb. 1954. *Address*: 102 Meadowbank Road, Remuera, Auckland 5, New Zealand.    *Died 28 Aug. 1983.*

**BURY, Hon. Leslie Harry Ernest,** CMG 1979; MHR (Lib) for Wentworth, NSW, 1956–74; *b* London, 25 Feb. 1913; *s* of late Rev. E. Bury, Bournemouth, England; *m* 1940, Anne Helen, *d* of late C. E. Weigall; four *s*. *Educ*: Queens' Coll., Cambridge (MA). Bank of NSW, 1935–45. Served War of 1939–45, AIF, 12th Aust. Radar Det. Commonwealth Dept of External Affairs, i/c Economic Relations, 1945–47; Treasury, 1948–51; Alternate Dir, IBRD, IMF, 1951–53, Exec. Dir, 1953–56. Minister: for Air, 1961–62; for Housing, 1963–66; for Labour and Nat. Service, 1966–69; Treasurer, 1969–71; Minister for Foreign Affairs, March-Aug. 1971, resigned. Aust. Rep., Commonwealth Finance Ministers' internat. meetings, etc. *Recreations*: carpentry, gardening, home repairs. *Address*: 85 Vaucluse Road, Vaucluse, NSW 2030, Australia. *Clubs*: Union, Royal Sydney Golf (Sydney).    *Died 7 Sept. 1986.*

**BUSH, Hon. Sir Brian Drex,** Kt 1976; **Hon. Mr Justice Bush;** a Judge of the High Court, Family Division, since 1976; *b* 5 Sept. 1925; *s* of William Harry Bush; *m* 1954, Beatrice Marian Lukeman (*d* 1989); one *s* one *d*. *Educ*: King Edward's Sch., Birmingham; Birmingham Univ. (LLB). Served, RNVR, 1943–46. Called to the Bar, Gray's Inn, 1947, Bencher, 1976. Dep. Chm., Derbyshire Quarter Sessions, 1966–71; a Circuit Judge, 1969–76; Presiding Judge, Midland and Oxford Circuit, 1982–85. Chm., Industrial Tribunal, 1967–69; Member: Parole Bd, 1971–74; W Midlands Probation and After Care Cttee, 1975–77. *Recreations*: sailing, golf. *Address*: Royal Courts of Justice, Strand, WC2. *Clubs*: Flyfishers', Royal Naval Sailing Association, Bar Yacht.    *Died 3 April 1989.*

**BUSH, Douglas;** *see* Bush, J. N. D.

**BUSH, Captain Eric Wheler,** DSO 1940 (and Bars 1942 and 1944); DSC 1915; RN; psc; *b* 12 Aug. 1899; *s* of late Rev. H. W. Bush, Chaplain to the Forces, and Edith Cornelia (*née* Cardew); *m* 1938, Mollie Noël, *d* of Col B. Watts, DSO; two *s*. *Educ*: Stoke House, Stoke Poges; Royal Naval Colleges, Osborne and Dartmouth. Midshipman in HMS Bacchante, 1914; present at Battle of Heligoland Bight, 28 Aug. 1914; took part in defence of Suez Canal Jan.-March 1915; present at original landing at Anzac, Gallipoli, 25 April 1915, and subsequent operations, also original landing at Suvla Bay 1915 (despatches twice, DSC); Midshipman HMS Revenge 1916 and present at Battle of Jutland, 31 May 1916; Sub-Lieut 1917; Lieut 1920; Qualified Interpreter in Hindustani, 1924; Lt-Comdr 1927; Qualified RN Staff Coll., 1931; Commander, 1933; Captain, 1939; Chief of Staff and afterwards Captain Auxiliary Patrol, Dover Command, 1939–40 (DSO); HMS Euryalus in Command, Mediterranean, 1941–43 (Bar to DSO); Senior Officer Assault Group S3, invasion of Normandy, 1944 (2nd Bar to DSO), afterwards in Command of HMS Malaya; Chief of Staff, Naval Force 'W', SEAC, 1945 (despatches twice); in Command HMS Ganges, Boys' Training Establishment, Shotley, Suffolk, 1946–48; Sec. Sea Cadet Council, 1948–59. Gen. Manager, Red Ensign Club, Stepney, 1959–64. School Liaison British-India Steam Navigation Co. Ltd, 1965–71. Retired list, 1948. *Publications*: How to Become a Naval Officer (Special Entry); Bless our Ship; The Flowers of the Sea; How to Become a Naval Officer (Cadet Entry); Salute the Soldier; Gallipoli. *Address*: Flat 2, Bishops Croft, Camden Park, Tunbridge Wells, Kent. *T*: Tunbridge Wells 21768.    *Died 17 June 1985.*

**BUSH, Prof. Ian (Elcock),** MA; PhD; MB, BChir; Research Professor of Psychiatry and Physiology, Dartmouth Medical School, USA, since 1977 (Senior Research Associate, 1974–77); Associate Chief of Staff, Research and Development, Veterans' Administration Hospital, White River Junction, Vermont, since 1977; *b* 25 May 1928; *s* of late Dr Gilbert B. Bush and of Jean Margaret Bush; *m* 1st, 1951, Alison Mary Pickard (marr. diss., 1966); one *s* two *d*; 2nd, 1967, Joan Morthland (marr. diss. 1972); one *s* one *d*; 3rd, 1982, Mary Calder Johnson. *Educ*: Bryanston Sch.; Pembroke Coll., Cambridge BA 1949. Natural Sciences Tripos, 1st class I and II; MA, PhD 1953; MB, BChir. 1957. Medical Research Council Scholar (Physiology Lab. Cambridge; National Institute for Medical Research), 1949–52; Commonwealth Fellow 1952 (University of Utah; Mass. General Hospital); Part-time Research Asst, Med. Unit, St Mary's Hosp. London and med. student, 1953–56; Grad. Asst, Dept Regius Prof. of Med., Oxford, 1956–59; Mem. ext. Scientific Staff, Med. Research Council (Oxford), 1959–61. Hon. Dir Med. Research Council Unit for research in chem. pathology of mental disorders, 1960; Bowman Prof. of Physiology and Dir of Dept of Physiology, Univ. of Birmingham, 1960–64; Senior Scientist, The Worcester Foundation for Experimental Biology, 1964–67; Chm. of Dept and Prof. of Physiology, Medical Coll. of Virginia, 1967–70; Pres. and Dir of Laboratories, Cybertek Inc., New York, 1970–72, and Prof. of Physiology, New York Univ. Med. Sch., 1970–77. Fellow, Amer. Acad. of Arts and Sciences, 1966. *Publications*: Chromatography of Steroids, 1961; The Siberian Reservoir, 1983; contribs to: Jl Physiol.; Biochem. Jl; Jl Endocrinol.; Nature; The Analyst; Jl Biolog. Chem.; Brit. Med. Bulletin; Acta Endocrinologica; Experientia; Biochem. Soc. Symposia, etc. *Recreations*: music, chess, sailing, fishing, philosophy. *Address*: c/o Dartmouth Medical School, Hanover, NH 03755, USA.    *Died 1 Nov. 1986.*

**BUSH, (John Nash) Douglas;** Professor of English, Harvard University, 1936–66, Gurney Professor, 1957–66; *b* Morrisburg, Ontario, Canada, 21 March 1896; *s* of Dexter C. and Mary E. Bush; *m* 1927, Hazel Cleaver; one *s*. *Educ*: Univ. of Toronto, Canada; Harvard Univ., USA. Sheldon Fellow in England, 1923–24; Instructor in English, Harvard, 1924–27; Department of English, Univ. of Minnesota, 1927–36; Guggenheim Fellow, in England, 1934–35; Member American Philosophical Society; Pres. Modern Humanities Research Association, 1955; Corr. Fellow, British Academy, 1960. Hon. LittD: Tufts Coll., 1952; Princeton Univ., 1958; Toronto Univ., 1958; Oberlin Coll., 1959; Harvard Univ., 1959; Swarthmore Coll., 1960; Boston Coll., 1965; Michigan State Univ., 1968; Merrimack Coll., 1969; Hon. LHD: Southern Illinois Univ., 1962; Marlboro Coll., 1966. *Publications*: Mythology and the Renaissance Tradition in English Poetry, 1932 (revised edition, 1963); Mythology and the Romantic Tradition in English Poetry, 1937; The Renaissance and English Humanism, 1939; Paradise Lost in Our Time, 1945; English Literature in the Earlier Seventeenth Century, 1600–1660 (Oxford History of English Literature), 1945 (revised edition 1962); Science and English Poetry, 1950; Classical Influences in Renaissance Literature, 1952; English Poetry: The Main Currents, 1952; John Milton, 1964; Prefaces to Renaissance Literature, 1965; John Keats, 1966; Engaged and Disengaged, 1966; Pagan Myth and Christian Tradition in English Poetry, 1968; Matthew Arnold, 1971; Jane Austen, 1975; Editor: The Portable Milton, 1949; Tennyson: Selected Poetry, 1951; John Keats: Selected Poems and Letters, 1959; (with A. Harbage) Shakespeare's Sonnets, 1961; Complete Poetical Works of John Milton, 1965; Variorum Commentary on Milton, vol. 1, Latin and Greek Poems, 1970, vol. 2 (with A. S. P. Woodhouse and E. Weismiller), Minor English Poems, 1972. *Address*: 3 Clement Circle, Cambridge, Mass 02138, USA.    *Died 2 March 1983.*

**BUSH, Ronald Paul,** CMG 1954; OBE 1946; Colonial Administrative Service, retired; *b* 22 Aug. 1902; *s* of late Admiral Sir Paul Bush; *m* 1938, Anthea Mary Fetherstonhaugh; two *s* one *d*. *Educ*: Marlborough Coll. Appointed to Colonial Administrative Service, 1925; service in Northern Rhodesia: confirmed as District Officer, 1927; promoted Provincial Commissioner, 1947, Sec. for Native Affairs, 1949; retired, 1954; on Commission to enquire into Local Government in Basutoland, 1954. *Recreation*: battling with bindweed and ground elder. *Address*: Ash House, Churt, near Farnham, Surrey. *T*: Headley Down 714493. *Club*: Royal Commonwealth Society.    *Died 18 Aug. 1986.*

**BUSHE-FOX, Patrick Loftus,** CMG 1963; *b* 4 May 1907; *o s* of late Loftus Henry Kendal Bushe-Fox and of Theodora Bushe-Fox (*née* Willoughby). *Educ*: Charterhouse; St John's Coll., Cambridge (MA, LLM). 1st Class Historical Tripos, Pt II, and Whewell Schol. in Internat. Law, 1928. Called to the Bar, Inner Temple, 1932. Ministry of Economic Warfare, 1941–45; HM Embassy, Washington, 1945;

Control Office for Germany and Austria, 1945–47; Foreign Office (German Section), 1947–50; Asst Legal Adviser, Foreign Office, 1950–60; Legal Counsellor, Foreign Office, 1960–67; retired, 1967. *Address:* Flat 3E, Artillery Mansions, 75 Victoria Street, SW1H 0HZ. *T:* 01-222 5002. *Clubs:* Athenæum, United Oxford & Cambridge University. *Died 2 June 1982.*

BUSK, Sir Douglas Laird, KCMG 1959 (CMG 1948); *b* 15 July 1906; *s* of late John Laird Busk, Westerham, Kent, and Eleanor Joy; *m* 1937, Bridget Anne Moyra, *d* of late Brig.-Gen. W. G. Hemsley Thompson, CMG, DSO, Warminster, Wilts; two *d. Educ:* Eton; New Coll., Oxford; Princeton Univ., USA (Davison Scholar). Joined Diplomatic Service, 1929; served in Foreign Office and Tehran, Budapest, Union of S Africa (seconded to United Kingdom High Commission), Tokyo, Ankara, Baghdad; Ambassador to Ethiopia, 1952–56; to Finland, 1958–60; to Venezuela, 1961–64. *Publications:* The Delectable Mountains, 1946; The Fountain of the Sun, 1957; The Curse of Tongues, 1965; The Craft of Diplomacy, 1967; Portrait d'un guide, 1975. *Recreations:* mountaineering and ski-ing. *Address:* Broxton House, Chilbolton, near Stockbridge, Hants. *T:* Chilbolton (026474) 272. *Clubs:* Alpine, Lansdowne.
*Died 11 Dec. 1990.*

BUTEMENT, William Alan Stewart, CBE 1959 (OBE 1945); DSc (Adel.); retired as Chief Scientist, Department of Supply, Australia, 1967; *b* Masterton, NZ, 18 Aug. 1904; *s* of William Butement, Physician and Surgeon, Otago, and Amy Louise Stewart; *m* 1933, Ursula Florence Alberta Parish; two *d. Educ:* Scots Coll., Sydney; University Coll. Sch., Hampstead, London; University Coll., London Univ. (BSc). Scientific Officer at Signals Exptl Estabt, War Office Outstation, Woolwich (now SRDE, Christchurch, Hants), 1928–38; Senior Scientific Officer Bawdsey Research Stn, War Office Outstation; later, under Min. of Supply, Radar Research, 1938–39 (Station moved to Christchurch, Hants, 1939; now RRE, Malvern); Prin. Scientific Officer, Sen. Prin. Scientific Officer, Asst Dir of Scientific Research, Min. of Supply, HQ London, 1940–46; Dep. Chief Scientific Officer of party to Australia under Lt-Gen. Sir John Evetts to set up Rocket Range, 1947; First Chief Supt of Long Range Weapons Estabt (now Weapons Research Establishment), of which Woomera Range is a part, 1947–49; Chief Scientist, Dept of Supply, in exec. charge Australian Defence Scientific R&D, incl. Rocket Range at Woomera, 1949–67. Dir, Plessey Pacific, 1967–81. FIEE, CEng, FInstP, FAIP, FIREE (Aust.), FTS. *Publications:* Precision Radar, Journal IEE, and other papers in scientific journals. *Address:* 5a Barry Street, Kew, Victoria 3101, Australia. *T:* 861 8375. *Died 25 Jan. 1990.*

BUTLAND, Sir Jack (Richard), KBE 1966; Founder and Chairman: J. R. Butland Pty Ltd, 1922; NZ Cheese Ltd, 1926–80; Butland Tobacco Co. Ltd, 1936–82; Butland Industries Ltd, 1949–81; Chairman: Greenacres (Morrinsville) Ltd; Blandford Lodge Ltd; Rothmans (NZ) Ltd, 1956; *e s* of late Henry Butland, Westport, NZ; *m* Gretta May Taylor (*d* 1962); two *s* one *d*; *m* Joan Melville Bull. *Educ:* Hokitika High Sch. Chairman: NZ Honey Control Board, 1933–38; NZ Packing Corp., 1953–60. Pres., Food Bank of NZ, 1970; Dir, Rothmans Industries, 1971. Hon. LLD Auckland, 1967. *Address:* (home) 542 Remuera Road, Remuera, Auckland, NZ; (office) J. R. Butland Pty Ltd, Queen Street, Auckland, NZ. *Club:* Northern (Auckland). *Died 22 Dec. 1982.*

BUTLER OF SAFFRON WALDEN, Baron *cr* 1965 (Life Peer); Richard Austen Butler, KG 1971; CH 1954; PC 1939; MA; Master of Trinity College, Cambridge, 1965–78; *b* Attock Serai, India, 9 Dec. 1902; *e s* of late Sir Montagu S. D. Butler, KCSI; *m* 1st, 1926, Sydney (*d* 1954), *o c* of late Samuel Courtauld; three *s* one *d*; 2nd, 1959, Mollie, *d* of late F. D. Montgomerie and widow of Augustine Courtauld. *Educ:* Marlborough; Pembroke Coll., Cambridge. President, Union Society, 1924; Fellow, Corpus Christi Coll., Cambridge, 1925–29 (Double First Class; Modern Language Tripos French Section, 1924; Historical Tripos Part II, 1925, First Division First Class). Hon. Fellow: Pembroke Coll., Cambridge, 1941; Corpus Christi Coll., Cambridge, 1952; St Anthony's Coll., Oxford, 1957; Hon. LLD: Cambridge, 1952; Nottingham, 1953; Bristol, 1954; Sheffield, 1955; St Andrews, 1956; Glasgow, 1959; Reading, 1959; Hon. DLitt Leeds, 1971; Hon. DCL: Oxon, 1952; Durham, 1968; Calgary, 1968; Liverpool, 1968; Witwatersrand, 1969. MP (C) Saffron Walden, 1929–65; Under-Secretary of State, India Office, 1932–37; Parliamentary Secretary, Ministry of Labour, 1937–38; Under-Secretary of State for Foreign Affairs, 1938–41; Minister of Education, 1941–45; Minister of Labour, June–July 1945; Chancellor of the Exchequer, 1951–55; Lord Privy Seal, 1955–59; Leader of the House of Commons, 1955–61; Home Secretary, 1957–62; First Secretary of State, July 1962–Oct. 1963; Deputy Prime Minister, July 1962–Oct. 1963; Minister in Charge of Central African Office, 1962–Oct. 1963; Secretary of State for Foreign Affairs, 1963–64. Chairman: Conservative Party Organisation, 1959–61; Conservative Research Dept, 1945–64; Conservative Party's Advisory Cttee on Policy, 1950–64. Mem., Indian Franchise Cttee, 1932; Chm., Scientific Advisory Cttee and

Engineering Advisory Cttee, 1942; Chairman of Council of National Union of Conservative Associations, 1945–56, President, 1956–. Chm., Home Office Cttee on Mentally Abnormal Offenders, 1972–75. President: Modern Language Assoc.; National Assoc. of Mental Health, 1946–; Royal Society of Literature, 1951–; Rector of Glasgow Univ., 1956–59; High Steward, Cambridge Univ., 1958–66; High Steward, City of Cambridge, 1963–; Chancellor of Sheffield Univ., 1960–78; Chancellor of Univ. of Essex, 1962–. Azad Memorial Lecture, Delhi, 1970. Freedom of Saffron Walden, 1954. *Publications:* The Art of the Possible, 1971; (ed) The Conservatives: a history from their origins to 1965, 1977; The Art of Memory, 1982. *Recreations:* travel, shooting, agriculture. *Address:* Spencers, Great Yeldham, Halstead, Essex CO9 4JG. *T:* Great Yeldham 237255; Flat 81A, Whitehall Court, SW1. *T:* 01-930 0847 and 01-930 3160. *Clubs:* Carlton, Farmers', Beefsteak, Grillions.
*Died 8 March 1982.*

BUTLER, Rt. Rev. (Basil) Christopher, OSB, MA; Auxiliary Bishop to the Cardinal Archbishop of Westminster since Dec. 1966; President, St Edmund's College, Ware, 1968–85, and Chairman of the Board of Governors, 1969–85; Titular Bishop of Nova Barbara; Hon. Fellow, St John's College, Oxford; *b* 1902; 2nd *s* of late W. E. Butler, Reading. *Educ:* Reading Sch.; St John's Coll., Oxford (White Schol.; Craven Schol.; Gaisford Greek Prose Prize; prox. acc. Hertford Schol.; 1st Class Classical Mods Greats and Theology). Tutor of Keble Coll., Oxford; Classical Master, Brighton Coll., 1927; Downside Sch., 1928; received into Catholic Church, 1928; entered the noviciate at Downside, 1929; Priest, 1933; Headmaster of Downside Sch., 1940–46; Abbot of Downside, 1946–66. Abbot-President of English Benedictine Congregation, 1961–66. Chm., Editorial Bd, Clergy Review, 1966–80; Mem., Editorial Bd, New English Bible, 1972–. Former Chm., English Anglican/Roman Catholic Cttee; Member: Anglican/Roman Catholic Preparatory Commn, 1967–69; Anglican-Roman Catholic Internat. Commn, 1970–81. President, Social Morality Council, 1968–. Consultor, Congregation for Catholic Education, 1968–73; Member, Congregation for the Doctrine of the Faith, 1968–73. Assistant to the Pontifical Throne, 1980–. Hon. LLD: Notre Dame Univ.; Catholic Univ. of America. *Publications:* St Luke's Debt to St Matthew (Harvard Theological Review, 1939); The Originality of St Matthew, 1951; The Church and Infallibility, 1954; Why Christ?, 1960; The Church and the Bible, 1960; Prayer: an adventure in living, 1961; The Idea of the Church, 1962; The Theology of Vatican II, 1967, 2nd enlarged edn, 1981; In the Light of the Council, 1969; A Time to Speak, 1972; Searchings, 1974; The Church and Unity, 1979; An Approach to Christianity, 1981; articles in Dublin Review, Downside Review, Journal of Theological Studies, Clergy Review. *Address:* St Edmund's College, Old Hall Green, Ware, Herts SG11 1DS. *Club:* Athenæum. *Died 20 Sept. 1986.*

BUTLER, Esmond Unwin, OC 1986; CVO 1972; Canadian Public Servant, retired 1988; *b* 13 July 1922; *s* of Rev. T. B. Butler and Alice Lorna Thompson; *m* 1960, Georgiana Mary North; one *s* one *d. Educ:* Weston Collegiate; Univs of Toronto and Geneva; Inst. Internat. Studies, Geneva. BA, Licence ès Sciences politiques. Served RCN, 1942–46. Journalist, United Press, Geneva, 1950–51; Asst Sec.-Gen., Internat. Union of Official Travel Organizations, Geneva, 1951–52; Information Officer, Dept of Trade and Commerce, Dept of Nat. Health and Welfare, 1953–54; Asst Sec. to Governor-Gen., 1955–58; Asst Press Sec. to Queen, London, 1958–59 and Royal Tour of Canada, 1959; Sec. to Governor-Gen., 1959–85; Sec.-Gen., Order of Canada, 1967–85, and Order of Military Merit, 1972–85; Canadian Ambassador to Morocco, 1985–87. CStJ 1967. *Recreations:* fishing, shooting, collecting Canadiana, ski-ing. *Clubs:* Zeta Psi Fraternity (Toronto); White Pine Fishing. *Died 18 Dec. 1989.*

BUTLER, Frank Chatterton, CBE 1961; MA 1934; retd from HM Diplomatic Service, 1967, and re-employed in Foreign Office Library until 1977; *b* 23 June 1907; *s* of late Leonard Butler and late Ada Chatterton Rutter; *m* 1945, Iris, *d* of late Ernest Strater and of Ida Mary Vinall; two *s. Educ:* Central Secondary Sch., Sheffield; Gonville and Caius Coll., Cambridge (Scholar); University of Grenoble. 1st Class Hons, Modern and Medieval Langs Tripos; Exhibitioner of the Worshipful Company of Goldsmiths, 1927, German Prize Essayist, 1928 and 1929. Consular Service, 1930 (head of list); Vice-Consul: Paris, 1931; New York, 1932; Mexico City, 1933–36; Panama, 1936–39; Naples, 1939–40; Barcelona, 1940–43; Consul, Barcelona, 1943–45; First Secretary (Commercial), Bogota, 1945–47; Consul General, Düsseldorf, 1948–52; Consul, Bordeaux, 1952–54; Consul General, Dakar, 1955, and Frankfurt, 1956–60; Counsellor at Shanghai, 1960–62; Consul-General at Cape Town, 1962–67. Fellow, Royal Commonwealth Soc. *Recreations:* golf, riding, motoring. *Address:* Wedgwood, Knowl Hill, Woking, Surrey. *Died 31 July 1984.*

BUTLER, Maj.-Gen. Geoffrey Ernest, CB 1957; CBE 1955; *b* Quetta, 1 Jan. 1905; *s* of Major E. G. Butler, W Yorks Regt; *m* 1934, Marjorie Callender (*née* Laine); one *d. Educ:* Appleby Grammar

Sch.; Leeds Univ. ICI, 1928–30; Lieut, RAOC, 1930; Asst Inspector of Armaments, 1936; Asst Supt of Design, 1937; British Supply Board, N America, 1939–40; British Army Staff, Washington, 1940–43; Asst Chief Supt, Armaments Design, 1943–44; Comdt 3 Base Workshop, REME, 1944–47; Dep. Dir (Production), War Office, 1947–49; Comdt, REME Training Centre, 1949–53; Dir of Mechanical Engineering, Northern Army Group, 1953–56; Inspector, REME, 1956–57; Commandant Base Workshop Group, REME, 1957–60. *Recreations:* golf, gardening. *Address:* Cornerways, 7 Ashley Road, New Milton, Hants BH25 6BA.
*Died 5 Aug. 1981.*

**BUTLER, Lionel Harry,** FRHistS; MA; DPhil; Principal, Royal Holloway College, University of London, since 1973; *b* 17 Dec. 1923; *yr s* of late W. H. and M. G. Butler, Dudley, Worcs; *m* 1949, Gwendoline Williams (author of novels and detective stories), *o d* of A. E. Williams, Blackheath; one *d. Educ:* Dudley Grammar Sch.; Magdalen Coll., Oxford (exhibitioner). Royal Air Force, 1941–43; First Class, Modern History, Oxford, 1945; Sen. Mackinnon Scholar and Junior Lectr, Magdalen Coll., Oxford, 1946; Fellow of All Souls Coll., 1946 (re-elected, 1953); University of St Andrews: Prof. of Mediaeval History, 1955–73; Dean, Fac. of Arts, 1966–71; Mem. General Council, 1956–; Mem., Univ. Ct, 1968–73; Vice-Principal, 1971–73; Hon. Regent, St Salvator's Coll., 1981–. Chatterton Lectr, British Acad., 1955; Leverhulme Lectr, Royal Univ. of Malta, 1961–62; Visiting Prof. of History, Univ. of Pennsylvania, Pa, 1964; Dir, Historical Assoc. Vacation Sch., 1965, 1966 and 1978. Convener, Scottish Univs Council on Entrance, 1968–73. Mem., Scottish Cert. of Educn Exam. Bd, 1969–73; Mem., Cttee of Vice-Chancellors and Principals, 1979–. Member, Management Committee: Inst. of Latin American Studies, Univ. of London, 1974–; Warburg Inst., Univ. of London, 1977–; Member: Extra-Mural Council, Univ. of London, 1976–; Standing Conf. on Univ. Entrance, and SCUE Executive, 1976–; UGC Steering Gp on Library Res., 1977–; Chairman: Centre of Internat. and Area Studies, Univ. of London, 1974–80; Library Resources Co-ordinating Cttee, London Univ., 1975–; Audio-Visual Centre Cttee, London Univ., 1978–; Entrance Requirements Cttee, London Univ., 1979–; Pres., Soc. for Mediterranean Studies, 1979–; Governor, Strode's Coll., Egham, 1973–. Librarian, Order of St John in the British Realm, 1969–; a Trustee, Lambeth Palace Library, 1978–; Historical Dir, 13th Council of Europe Exhibn (on Order of St John in Malta), 1970 (introd. and contribs to Catalogue on Exhibn). FRSA. KStJ 1969. *Publications:* trans. (with R. J. Adam) R. Fawtier, The Capetian Kings of France, 1960; (with C. Given-Wilson) Medieval Monasteries of Great Britain, 1979; The Siege of Rhodes in 1480, 1980; articles in journals and reviews. *Address:* Royal Holloway College, Egham, Surrey. *Club:* Royal and Ancient (St Andrews).
*Died 26 Nov. 1981.*

**BUTLER, Reg, (Reginald Cotterell Butler);** sculptor; *b* Buntingford, Herts, 28 April 1913. ARIBA 1937. Gregory Fellow in Sculpture, Leeds Univ., 1951–53; Associé, Académie Royale des Sciences, des Lettres et des Beaux-Arts de Belgique, 1965. First one-man show, London, 1949. Winner International Competition, The Unknown Political Prisoner, 1953. Retrospective Exhibition: J. B. Speed Art Museum, Louisville, USA, 1963. Pierre Matisse Gallery, New York. *Publication:* Creative Development, 1962. *Address:* Ash, Berkhamsted Place, Berkhamsted, Herts. *T:* Berkhamsted 2933.
*Died 23 Oct. 1981.*

**BUTTIGIEG, Dr Anton;** President of the Republic of Malta, 1976–82; *b* Gozo, 19 Feb. 1912; *s* of Saviour Buttigieg and Concetta (*née* Falzon); *m* 1st, 1944, Carmen Bezzina (decd); two *s* one *d*; 2nd, 1953, Connie Scicluna (decd); 3rd, 1975, Margery Patterson. *Educ:* Royal Univ. of Malta (BA, LLD). Notary Public 1939; Advocate 1941. Police Inspector during Second World War; Law Reporter and Leader Writer, Times of Malta, 1944–48; Actg Magistrate 1955; Editor, The Voice of Malta, 1959–70. MP, 1955–76; Pres., Malta Labour Party, 1959–61, Dep. Leader, 1962–76; Dep. Prime Minister, 1971–76; Minister of Justice and Parly Affairs, 1971–76. Deleg., Malta Constitutional Confs, London, 1958 and 1964; Rep. to Consult. Assembly, Council of Europe, 1966–71, Vice-Pres., 1967–68. Mem., Acad. of Maltese Language. 1st Prize for poetry, Govt of Malta, 1971; Guze Muscat Azzopardi Prize for poetry, 1972; Silver Plaque for poetry, Circolo Culturale Rhegium Julii, Reggio, Calabria, 1975; Internat. Prize for Poetry, Centro di Cultura Mediterranea, Palermo, 1977; First Prize and Special Diploma for Poetry, Centro Culturale Artistico Letterario, Brindisi, 1979; Malta Literary Award (First Prize), 1979; Medal for Poetry, Accad. Pontiana, Naples, 1980. *Publications: lyrical poetry:* Mill-Gallerija ta' Zghoziti (From the balcony of my youth), 1945; Fanali bil-lejl (Lamps in the night), 1969; Qasba mar-Rih (A reed in the wind), 1968; Fl-Arena (In the Arena), 1970; *humorous poetry:* Ejjew Nidhku Ftit (Let us laugh a little), 1963; Ejjew nidhku ftit iehor (Let us laugh a little more), 1966; *Haikus and Tankas:* Il-Muza bil-Kimono (The Muse in Kimono), 1968 (English and Japanese trans); Ballati Maltin (Maltese Ballads), 1973; Il Mare di Malta, 1974, new edn 1980; Il-Ghanja tas-Sittin (The song of the sixty year old), 1975;

The Lamplighter, 1977; Poeziji Migbura-L-Ewwel Volum (Collected Poems, vol. 1), 1978; Qabas el Misbah, 1978; Der Laternenanzünder, 1979; *autobiog.:* Toni, the Seaman's Son, vol. 1, 1978; L-Ghazla tat-Trieq (The Choice of the Way), vol. 2, 1980. *Recreations:* horse racing, gardening. *Address:* The White Lodge, Kappara, Malta.
*Died 5 May 1983.*

**BUTTLE, Prof. Gladwin Albert Hurst,** OBE (mil.) 1942; MA, MB Cantab; FRCP; Wellcome Professor of Pharmacology, School of Pharmacy, London University, 1946–66, and Professor, St Bartholomew's Hospital Medical School, 1948–60, then Emeritus Professor; *b* 11 April 1899; *s* of William and Mary Buttle; *m* 1936, Eva Korella; one *s. Educ:* Whitgift Sch.; St John's Coll., Cambridge; MRCS, LRCP, 1924; MA 1927; BCh 1967; FRCP 1970; MD Louvain, 1945. Qualified University Coll. Hospital, 1924; Pharmacologist, Wellcome Physiological Research Laboratories for 14 years. RMA Woolwich, 1917; Lieut RE, 1918. Served War of 1939–45, British Army (Lt-Col); adviser in Blood Transfusion, MEF and BLA, 1940–45. Expert, FAO, Mexico City, 1967–69; Professor of Pharmacology: Addis Ababa, 1972–74; Riyadh Univ., 1974–78. FRSocMed (PP Section of Therapeutics and Exp. Med.); Past Member: British Pharmacopoeia Codex Action and Uses Cttee; MRC Drug Safety Cttee; Colonial Office Leprosy Cttee; Min. of Agric. Food Additives Cttee; Med. cons to MoD. Co-founder and Dep. Chm., Buttle Trust for Children. *Publications:* contribs on chemotherapy and pharmacology to medical jls. *Recreations:* gardening, tennis. *Address:* 12 Ewhurst, Kersfield Road, SW15. *T:* 01-789 8030; 300 Vauxhall Bridge Road, SW1. *T:* 01-828 7311.
*Died 3 May 1983.*

**BUTTROSE, Murray;** a Deputy Circuit Judge, 1975–77; *b* 31 July 1903; *s* of William Robert and Frances Buttrose, both British; *m* 1935, Jean Marie Bowering; one *s. Educ:* St Peter's Coll. and Adelaide Univ., South Australia. Admitted and enrolled as a barrister and solicitor of the Supreme Court of S Australia, 1927; apptd to HM Colonial Legal Service, 1946; Crown Counsel, Singapore, 1946, Senior Crown Counsel, 1949, and Solicitor-General, Singapore, 1955; Puisne Judge, Singapore, 1956–68, retired. Admitted and enrolled as a solicitor of the Supreme Court of Judicature in England, 1955; a Recorder of the Crown Court, 1972–74. Formerly Temp. Dep. Chm. (part time), London QS. Served with Royal Air Force (RAFVR), 1940–45. *Recreations:* reading, tennis, and golf. *Address:* 64 Palmer Place, North Adelaide, SA 5006, Australia.
*Died 8 Sept. 1987.*

**BUXTON, Major Desmond Gurney,** DL; 60th Rifles, retired; retired as Local Director (Norwich) Barclays Bank, 1958; Member Norfolk County Council, 1958–74; *b* 4 Jan. 1898; *e s* of late Edward G. Buxton, Catton Hall, Norwich, and late Mrs Buxton, The Beeches, Old Catton, Norwich; *m* 1930, Rachel Mary, *yr d* of late Colonel A. F. Morse, Coltishall Mead, Norwich; two *s* three *d* (and one *d* decd). *Educ:* Eton; RMC Sandhurst. 60th Rifles, 1917–39; France and Belgium, 1917–18; NW Europe, 1945. Lieut-Colonel Royal Norfolk Regt (TA), 1939–40; AQ Appointments, 1941–44. Sheriff of Norwich, 1936; High Sheriff, Norfolk, 1960; DL Norfolk, 1961–86. CStJ 1972. *Recreations:* forestry, chess, bridge. *Address:* Hoveton Hall, Wroxham, Norwich NR12 8RJ.
*Died 29 Sept. 1987.*

**BUXTON, Dame Rita (Mary),** DBE 1969 (CBE 1955; OBE 1944); *b* 1900; *d* of Charles James Neunhoffer and Alice Neunhoffer (*née* O'Connor), Melbourne, Australia; *m* 1922, Leonard R. Buxton; three *d. Educ:* Sacré-Coeur Convent. Interested in philanthropic work. Member of the Victoria League. *Recreations:* golf, tennis, bridge. *Address:* 48 Hampden Road, Armadale, Victoria, Australia. *T:* 50-3333; Glynt, Mount Martha, Victoria, Australia. *T:* Mount Martha 741-216. *Clubs:* English-Speaking Union; Alexandra (Melbourne); Metropolitan Golf, Peninsula County Golf, Frankston Golf.
*Died 22 Aug. 1982.*

**BUXTON, St John Dudley,** MB, BS (London), FRCS; Hon Consultant Orthopædic Surgeon to King's College Hospital, and Emeritus Lecturer in Orthopædics to the Medical School; Hon. Consultant Orthopædic Surgeon to the Ministry of Pensions; formerly Consultant Orthopædic Surgeon to the Army, Orthopædic Surgeon to Royal Masonic Hospital, Queen Mary's Hospital, Roehampton and Chairman, Standing Advisory Committee on Artificial Limbs; *b* 26 Dec. 1891; 2nd *s* of late Dudley W. Buxton, MD; *m* Winifred, 2nd *d* of Picton Warlow; one *s* one *d. Educ:* St Peter's Coll., Radley; University Coll. Hospital. Served European War 1914–18 in BEF and Salonika Exp. Force (Croix de Guerre); BEF, 1940 and MEF, 1941–42, Brig. Consultant Orthopædic Surgeon. Regional Adviser to EMS; formerly Lecturer in Orthopædic Surgery and Examiner in Surgery, Univ. of London; Past Pres. Med. Defence Union; Past Pres. Brit. Orthopædic Assoc.; Examiner for Diploma in Phys. Medicine, RCP and RCS; Hunterian Prof. RCS; Past Pres. Section of Orthopædics, Royal Soc. of Medicine; Mem. Soc. International Chirurg. Orth. Traumatol., Hellenic Surg. Soc. and French and Hellenic Soc. Orth. Surg. and Traumatology. Silver Cross of Royal Order of Phœnix (Greece). *Publications:* Arthroplasty; (jointly)

Surgical Pathology; Orthopædics, in Post-Graduate Surgery, ed by R. Maingot; Two Visits to Greece; Amputations, in Butterworth's British Encycl. Med. Practice; Memoirs, in RCS library; articles in Lancet, Proc. Royal Soc. of Med., etc. *Recreations:* writing, gardening. *Address:* Tollgate, 35 Church Road, Shanklin, IoW PO37 6QY. *T:* 2506.                                    *Died 6 Feb.* 1981.

**BUZZARD, John Huxley; His Honour Judge Buzzard;** a Circuit Judge at the Central Criminal Court, since 1974; *b* 12 Aug. 1912; *s* of late Brig.-Gen. Frank Anstie Buzzard, DSO, and Joan, *d* of late Hon. John Collier; *m* 1946, Hilary Ann Courtney Buzzard (*née* Antrobus); two *s* one *d. Educ:* Wellington Coll.; New Coll., Oxford. Open Classical Scholar, New Coll., 1931; commissioned 4th Queen's Own Royal West Kent Regt, TA, 1931; transferred to TA Reserve of Officers, 1935. Called to Bar, 1937 (Master of the Bench, Inner Temple, 1965). Served with RAFVR, in UK, Iceland, and SE Asia, 1940–45 (despatches). Recorder: Great Yarmouth, 1958–68; Dover, 1968–71; Crown Court, 1971–74; Second Sen. Prosecuting Counsel to the Crown, 1964–71, First Sen. Prosecuting Counsel, 1971–74. Consultant Editor, Archbold's Criminal Pleading; Jt Editor, Phipson on Evidence. *Recreations:* mountaineering, ski-ing, sailing. *Address:* Central Criminal Court, Old Bailey, EC4. *Clubs:* Alpine, Lansdowne, Climbers', Cruising Association.
                                    *Died 28 Jan.* 1984.

**BYAM SHAW, Glencairn Alexander,** CBE 1954; a Director, Sadler's Wells, 1966–81; *b* 13 Dec. 1904; *s* of Byam Shaw, artist, and Evelyn Pyke-Nott; *m* 1929, Angela Baddeley, CBE (*d* 1976); one *s* one *d. Educ:* Westminster Sch. First stage appearance, Pavilion Theatre, Torquay, 1923; Mem. J. B. Fagan's Company at Oxford Repertory Theatre; played Trophimof, in The Cherry Orchard, New York; Konstantin Treplev, in The Seagull and Baron Tusenbach, in The Three Sisters, London. Was in Max Reinhardt's production of The Miracle. Went to S Africa with Angela Baddeley in repertory of plays. Played Darnley in Queen of Scots and Laertes in John Gielgud's production of Hamlet; was mem. of company for Gielgud's season at Queen's Theatre. Produced plays in London, New York and Stratford-upon-Avon. A Director of Old Vic Theatre Centre; a Governor, Royal Shakespeare Theatre, 1960–; Mem. Directorate, English Nat. Opera, 1974–81. Co-Dir, with Anthony Quayle, of Shakespeare Memorial Theatre, Stratford-upon-Avon, 1952–56; Director, 1956–59; directed: Ross, Haymarket, 1960; The Lady From the Sea, Queen's, 1961; The Complaisant Lover and Ross, New York, 1961; The Rake's Progress and Idomeneo, Sadler's Wells, 1962; The Tulip Tree, Haymarket, 1962; Cosi fan Tutte, Der Freischütz, Hansel and Gretel, Sadler's Wells, 1963; Where Angels Fear to Tread, St Martin's, 1963; The Right Honourable Gentleman, Her Majesty's, 1964; Faust, Sadler's Wells, 1964; A Masked Ball, Sadler's Wells, 1964; You Never Can Tell, Haymarket, 1966; Die Fledermaus, Sadler's Wells, 1966, Coliseum, 1980; The Rivals, Haymarket, 1966; The Dance of Death, National Theatre, 1967; Orpheus and Eurydice, Sadler's Wells, 1967; The Merchant of Venice, Haymarket, 1967; The Wild Duck, Criterion, 1970; Duke Bluebeard's Castle, 1972; with John Blatchley: The Mastersingers of Nuremberg, 1968; The Valkyrie, 1970; Twilight of the Gods, 1971; The Rhinegold, 1972; Siegfried, 1973; The Ring Cycle, 1973; Tristan und Isolde, 1981. In the Royal Scots during War of 1939–45. Hon. DLitt Birmingham, 1959. *Address:* Barn Acre, Loddon Drive, Wargrave, Berks. *Club:* Reform.                *Died 29 April* 1986.

**BYERS, Baron** *cr* 1964 (Life Peer); **Charles Frank Byers,** PC 1972; OBE 1944; DL; Liberal Leader, House of Lords, since 1967; Chairman of the Liberal Party, 1950–52, 1965–67 (Vice-President, 1954–65); Liberal Chief Whip, 1946–50; MP (L) North Dorset, 1945–50; *b* 24 July 1915; *e s* of late C. C. Byers, Leacing, Sussex; *m* 1939, Joan Elizabeth Oliver; one *s* three *d. Educ:* Westminster; Christ Church, Oxford (MA Hons); Exchange Scholar at Milton Acad., Mass, USA. Blue for Athletics, Oxford, 1937, 220 yds Hurdles; Pres. OU Liberal Club, 1937. Enlisted Sept. 1939, RA; commissioned March 1940; served MEF, CMF, 1940–44; GSO1 Eighth Army, Lt-Col, 1943; served NW Europe, 1944–45, GSO1 HQ, 21 Army Group (despatches thrice); Chevalier Legion of Honour, Croix de Guerre (palmes). Chm., Company Pensions Information Centre, 1973–. FBIM 1965. DL Surrey, 1974. *Address:* Hunters Hill, Blindley Heath, Lingfield, Surrey.
                                    *Died 6 Feb.* 1984.

**BYFORD, Donald,** CBE 1963; Founder D. Byford & Co. Ltd, retired 1971; *b* 11 Jan. 1898; 4th *s* of Charles Watson Byford, JP, Clare, Suffolk; *m* 1922, Marjorie Annie, *d* of Ald. W. K. Billings, JP, Leicester (Lord Mayor, 1933–34); two *s* one *d. Educ:* Bishop's Stortford Coll. 2nd Lieut, Royal Tank Corps, 1917–19. Hosiery Manufacturer, 1919–71. Past President: Leicester Hosiery Manufacturers' Assoc.; Nat. Fedn Hosiery Manufacturers. Past Master: Worshipful Co. Framework Knitters; Worshipful Co. Gardeners. Past Treasurer, Corp. of the Sons of the Clergy.

*Recreations:* shooting, farming. *Address:* Paddock Close, Old Gate Road, Thrussington, Leicester LE7 8TL. *Club:* Farmers'.
                                    *Died 23 Nov.* 1981.

**BYRNE, Muriel St Clare,** OBE 1955; writer and lecturer; Editor of The Lisle Letters (1533–40); *b* 31 May 1895; *o c* of Harry St Clare Byrne, Hoylake, Ches, and Artemisia Desdemona Burtner, Iowa, USA. *Educ:* Belvedere, Liverpool (GPDST); Somerville Coll., Oxford (Hon. Fellow, 1978). English Hons, 1916, BA and MA 1920. Teaching: Liverpool Coll., 1916–17; S. Hampstead High Sch., 1917–18; English Lectr in Rouen, Army Educn (YMCA), 1918–19; Temp. Asst English Tutor, Somerville, 1919, and English coaching for Final Hons at Oxford, 1920–25; Oxford and London Univ. Extension Lectr, 1920–37; Lectr, Royal Academy of Dramatic Art, London, 1923–55; Eng. Lectr, Bedford Coll., 1941–45; Leverhulme Res. Grant, 1945; Bedford Coll. Research Fellowship, 1965; Brit. Acad. Pilgrim Trust Res. Grants, 1958 and 1959; Phoenix Trust Res. Grant, 1970; Twenty Seven Foundn Res. Grant, 1971; British Acad. Research in the Humanities Grant, 1964, 1965, 1966; Leverhulme Research Fellowship, 1968. Examr, London Univ. Dipl. in Dramatic Art, 1951–60. Hon. Sec., Malone Soc., 1926–37; Mem. Council, Bibliographical Soc., 1932–39; Mem. Bd, 1952–, Exec., 1959–, Friends of Girls' Public Day Sch. Trust; Mem., Cttee of Soc. for Theatre Research; History Selection Cttee, Nat. Film Archive, 1968; Mem. Council, RADA, 1973. Governor: Royal Shakespeare Theatre, 1960; Bedford Coll., 1968. Mem., Literary Advisory Panel, Shakespeare Exhibn 1564–1964. FSA 1963. *Publications:* History of Somerville College (with C. H. Godfrey), 1921; Elizabethan Life in Town and Country, 1925 (8th revised edn 1961, American edn 1962, Polish edn 1971): The Elizabethan Home, 1925 (3rd rev. edn 1949); The Elizabethan Zoo, 1926; Letters of King Henry VIII, 1936, 2nd edn 1968, US edn 1968; Common or Garden Child, 1942; (ed) The Lisle Letters 1533–40, 6 vols, 1981; (ed) Selected Lisle Letters, 1982; contributed: Shakespeare's Audience, to Shakespeare in the Theatre, 1927; The Social Background, to A Companion to Shakespeare Studies, 1934; Queen Mary I, to Great Tudors, 1935; History of Stage Lighting and History of Make-Up, to Oxford Companion to the Theatre, 1951; The Foundations of Elizabethan Language, to Shakespeare in his own Age, 1964; Elizabethan Life in the Plays, to The Reader's Encyclopedia of Shakespeare, 1966; Dramatic Intention and Theatrical Realization, to The Triple Bond; essays in honor of Arthur Colby Sprague, 1975; edited: Anthony Munday's John a Kent (Malone Society), 1923; Massinger's New Way to Pay Old Debts, 1949; The French Litleton of Claudius Holyband, 1953; Essays and Studies, Vol. 13 (Eng. Assoc.), 1960; 4-vol. paper-back illustr. edn of Granville Barker's Prefaces to Shakespeare, with Introd. and Notes, 1963; plays produced: England's Elizabeth, 1928 and 1953; "Well, Gentlemen . . ." (with Gwladys Wheeler), 1933; Busman's Honeymoon (with Dorothy L. Sayers), 1936 (American edn, 1981); No Spring Till Now (Bedford Coll. Centenary Play), 1949; Gen. Ed. Pubns for Soc. for Theatre Research, 1949–59; Eng. edit. rep. of and contrib. to Enciclopedia dello Spettacolo, 1955–58; prep. Arts Council's exhibn and Catalogue, A History of Shakespearian Production in England, 1947 (repr. USA 1970); contributor to: The Times, TLS and Times Educ. Suppt; The Library; Review of Eng. Studies; Mod. Lang. Review; Shakespeare Survey; Shakespeare Quarterly; Drama; Theatre Notebook; Sunday Times; Theatre Research; Essays and Studies Vol. 18 (Eng. Assoc.), etc. *Recreations:* play-going and all theatrical activities. *Address:* 28 St John's Wood Terrace, NW8. *T:* 01–722 0967.
                                    *Died 2 Dec.* 1983.

**BYRON,** 11th Baron *cr* 1643; **Rupert Frederick George Byron;** farmer and grazier since 1921; *b* 13 Aug. 1903; *er s* of late Col Wilfrid Byron, Perth, WA, and of Sylvia Mary Byron, 12 College Street, Winchester, England, *o d* of late Rev. C. T. Moore; *S* kinsman, 1949; *m* 1931, Pauline Augusta, *d* of T. J. Cornwall, Wagin, W Australia; one *d. Educ:* Gresham's Sch., Holt. Served War of 1939–45, Lieut RANVR, 1941–46. *Heir: kinsman,* Richard Geoffrey Gordon Byron, DSO [*b* 3 Nov. 1899; *m* 1st, 1926, Margaret Mary Steuart (marr. diss. 1946); 2nd, 1946, Dorigen, *o c* of P. Kennedy Esdaile; two *s. Educ:* Eton]. *Address:* 16 Barnsley Road, Mount Claremont, WA 6010, Australia. *Club:* Naval and Military (Perth, WA).                                    *Died 1 Nov.* 1983.

**BYRON,** 12th Baron *cr* 1643; **Richard Geoffrey Gordon Byron,** DSO 1944; retired; *b* 3 Nov. 1899; *s* of Col Richard Byron, DSO (*d* 1939), and Mabel Mackenzie (*d* 1962), *d* of Charles Albert Winter; *S* kinsman, 1983; *m* 1st, 1926, Margaret Mary Steuart (marr. diss. 1945); 2nd, 1946, Dorigen Margaret (*d* 1985), *o d* of Percival Kennedy Esdaile; one *s* (and one *s* decd). *Educ:* Eton; Sandhurst. Joined 4th Royal Dragoon Guards, 1918; ADC to Governor of Bombay, 1921; Mil. Sec. to Gov.-Gen. of NZ, 1937; comd 4/7th Dragoon Guards, Normandy, 1944; retired, 1948. *Heir: s* Hon. Robert James Byron [*b* 5 April 1950; *m* 1979, Robyn Margaret, *d* of John McLean, Hamilton, NZ; three *d*]. *Address:* 62 Burton Court, SW3. *T:* 01–730 2921.                *Died 15 June* 1989.

# C

**CABLE-ALEXANDER, Sir Desmond William Lionel,** 7th Bt (1809); *b* 4 Oct. 1910; *s* of Sir Lionel Alexander, 6th Bt and Noorouz Weston, *e d* of 1st Baron Cable; assumed addtl name of Cable before that of Alexander, by deed poll, 1931; *S* father, 1956; *m* 1st, 1935, Mary Jane (who obtained a divorce, 1941), *d* of James O'Brien, JP, Enniskillen; one *s*; 2nd, Margaret Wood, *d* of late John Burnett, Dublin; two *d. Educ:* Harrow; Oxford. *Heir: s* Patrick Desmond William Cable-Alexander, Lt-Col Royal Scots Dragoon Guards [*b* 19 April 1936; *m* 1961, Diana Frances Rogers (marr. diss. 1976); two *d*; *m* 1976, Jane Mary, *d* of Dr Anthony Arthur Gough Lewis, MD, FRCP, of York; one *s*]. *Address:* c/o Barclays Bank, 16 Whitehall, SW1.                           *Died* 27 *April* 1988.

**CACCIA,** Baron *cr* 1965 (Life Peer), of Abernant; **Harold Anthony Caccia,** GCMG 1959 (KCMG 1950; CMG 1945); GCVO 1961 (KCVO 1957); *b* 21 Dec. 1905; *s* of late Anthony Caccia, CB, MVO; *m* 1932, Anne Catherine, *d* of late Sir George Barstow, KCB; two *d* (one *s* decd). *Educ:* Eton; Trinity Coll., Oxford (OU RFC XV, 1926). Laming Travelling Fellowship, Queen's Coll., Oxford, 1928, Hon. Fellow, 1974. Entered HM Foreign Service as 3rd Sec., FO, 1929; transferred to HM Legation, Peking, 1932; 2nd Sec., 1934; FO 1935; Asst Private Sec. to Sec. of State, 1936; HM Legation, Athens, 1939; 1st Sec. 1940; FO 1941; seconded for service with Resident Minister, North Africa, 1943, and appointed Vice-Pres., Political Section, Allied Control Commission, Italy; Political Adviser, GOC-in-C Land Forces, Greece, 1944; Minister local rank, HM Embassy, Athens, 1945; Asst Under-Sec. of State, 1946, Dep. Under-Sec. of State, 1949, Foreign Office; British Ambassador in Austria, 1951–54, and also British High Comr in Austria, 1950–54; Dep. Under-Sec. of State, FO, 1954–56; British Ambassador at Washington, 1956–61; Permanent Under-Sec. of State, FO, 1962–65; Head of HM Diplomatic Service, 1964–65, retired. Provost, Eton Coll., 1965–77. Chairman: Standard Telephones & Cables, 1968–79; ITT (UK) Ltd, 1979–81; Director: Orion Bank (Chm., 1973–74); Westminster, later Nat. Westminster Bank, 1965–75; Prudential Assurance Co., 1965–80; F & C Investment Trust, 1965–78; F & C Eurotrust Ltd, 1972–84. Mem. Adv. Council, Foseco Minsep plc, 1972–87. Chm., Gabbitas-Thring Educational Trust, 1967–73. Mem., Advisory Council on Public Records, 1968–73. Pres., MCC, 1973–74. Hon. Fellow, Trinity Coll., Oxford, 1963. Lord Prior of the Order of St John of Jerusalem, 1969–80; GCStJ. *Address:* Abernant, Builth-Wells, Powys LD2 3YR. *T:* Erwood (09823) 233; 9 Pembroke Court, South Edwardes Square, W8 6HN.                        *Died* 31 *Oct.* 1990.

**CADBURY, Jocelyn Benedict Laurence;** MP (C) Birmingham Northfield, since 1979; *b* 3 March 1946; *s* of Laurence Cadbury, OBE and Joyce, *d* of Lewis O. Mathews, Birmingham. *Educ:* Eton; Trinity Coll., Cambridge (BA Econs and Anthropology). Industrial Relations Officer, Joseph Lucas, Birmingham, 1970-74; Prodn Foreman on shift-work at Cadbury Ltd, Somerdale, 1974-76; Prodn Manager at Cadbury's Bournville Factory, 1976-79. Co-opted Mem., Birmingham Educn Cttee, 1976-78. PPS to Min. of State for Industry, 1981–. *Publication:* (with others) British Gas: a prospectus (Bow Group), 1980. *Recreations:* travel, tennis, reading (esp. anything to do with India). *Address:* The Davids, Northfield, Birmingham B31 2AN. *T:* 021-475 1441. *Club:* Leander (Henley-on-Thames).                          *Died* 31 *July* 1982.

**CADBURY, Laurence John,** OBE 1919; *b* 1889; *s* of late George Cadbury; *m* 1925, Joyce, *d* of Lewis O. Mathews, Birmingham; two *s* one *d* (and two *s* one *d* decd). *Educ:* Leighton Park Sch.; Trinity Coll., Cambridge (MA). Economics Tripos. Man. Dir, Cadbury Bros Ltd and associated cos, 1919-59; Chm., Cadbury Bros Ltd, 1944–49 and of J. S. Fry & Sons Ltd, 1952–59; Dir, Bank of England, 1936-61. Director: British Cocoa & Chocolate Co. Ltd, 1920-59; Nation Proprietory Co. Ltd, Tyne Tees Television Ltd, 1958-67; Daily News Ltd; News Chronicle, 1930-60 and Star, 1930-60; Cocoa Investments Ltd, 1937-64; EMB Co. Ltd; Chm., Bournville Village Trust, 1954-78; Treasurer, Population Investigation Cttee, 1936–76. Trustee, Historic Churches Preservation Trust (Exec. Cttee); Head, Economic Section, Mission to Moscow, 1941. High Sheriff of County of London, 1947-48 and 1959-60. Hon. LLD Birmingham, 1970. Mons Medal; 1914 Star; Croix de Guerre. *Publications:* This Question of Population; numerous contribs to the press and periodicals on economics and demographic subjects. *Address:* The Davids, Northfield, Birmingham. *T:* 021-475 1441. *Clubs:* United Oxford & Cambridge University; Leander (Henley); Hawks (Cambridge).                             *Died* 5 *Nov.* 1982.

**CADBURY, Paul Strangman,** CBE 1948; Chairman, Cadbury Bros Ltd, 1959-65; *b* 3 Nov. 1895; *s* of late Barrow Cadbury; *m* 1919, Rachel E. Wilson; two *s* two *d. Educ:* Leighton Park Sch., Reading. Friends' Ambulance Unit, 1915-19; Chm. Friends Ambulance Unit, 1939-48. Hon. DSc Aston, 1971. *Publication:* Birmingham—Fifty Years On, 1952. *Address:* Low Wood, 32 St Mary's Road, Harborne,

Birmingham B17 0HA. *T:* 021-427 1636.
                                        *Died* 24 *Oct.* 1984.

**CADZOW, Sir Norman (James Kerr),** Kt 1959; VRD 1943; *b* 21 Dec. 1912; *s* of late William Cadzow and Jessie, *d* of James Kerr. *Educ:* Sedbergh Sch., Yorkshire. President, Unionist Party in Scotland, 1958; contested (U) Bothwell Div. of Lanarkshire, 1950 and 1951. Rector's Assessor, Glasgow Univ., 1959-63. Joined RNVR 1931, active service, 1939-45 (despatches). *Recreations:* golf and bridge. *Address:* Arden, Bothwell, Glasgow. *T:* Bothwell 853164.
                                        *Died* 21 *June* 1981.

**CAFFYN, Brig. Sir Edward (Roy),** KBE 1963 (CBE 1945; OBE 1942); CB 1955; TD 1950; DL; Chairman, County of Sussex Territorial and Auxiliary Forces Association, 1947–67; Vice-Chairman, Council of Territorial and Auxiliary Forces Associations, 1961–66; *b* 27 May 1904; *s* of Percy Thomas Caffyn, Eastbourne; *m* 1st, 1929, Elsa Muriel, *d* of William Henry Nurse, Eastbourne; two *s*; 2nd, 1946, Delphine Angelique, *d* of Major William Chilton-Riggs. *Educ:* Eastbourne and Loughborough Colleges. Commissioned RE (TA), 1930. Raised and commanded an Army Field Workshop, 1939; served with 51st Highland Division in France, 1940; Brigadier, 1941; a Deputy Director, War Office, on formation of REME, 1942; served on Field Marshal Montgomery's staff as Director of Mechanical Engineering (despatches twice), 1943–45. JP Eastbourne, 1948, transferred East Sussex, 1960; Chairman, Hailsham Bench, 1962–74; DL Sussex, 1956; Chairman, Sussex Agricultural Wages Board, 1951–74. CC for East Sussex, 1958–69, Alderman, 1964, Vice-Chairman 1967; Chm., Sussex Police Authy, 1971–74. *Recreations:* shooting, fishing. *Address:* Norman Norris, Vines Cross, Heathfield, East Sussex. *T:* Horam Road (025672) 2674.                                  *Died* 17 *June* 1990.

**CAGE, Edward Edwin Henry;** General Manager, Craigavon Development Commission, 1966–73; *b* 15 May 1912; *s* of Edward H. Cage and A. M. Windiate; *m* 1938, Hilda W. M. Barber; no *c. Educ:* Cannock House Sch., Eltham; King's Coll., London. Articles, Chartered Accts, 1929–34; Kent CC, 1935–41; Borough Councils: Dagenham, 1941–42; Willesden, 1942–44; Treas., Eton RDC, and Clerk, Jt Hosp Bd, 1944–47; Local Govt BC, 1947–48; Crawley Development Corp.: Chief Finance Officer, 1948–58, Gen. Manager, 1958–61; Chief Finance and Development Officer, Commn for New Towns, 1961–66. *Publications:* contrib. professional, etc., jls and newspapers. *Recreations:* golf, gardening. *Address:* Charters, Pitney Lortie, Langport, Somerset. *Club:* Sherborne Golf.                            *Died* 24 *Dec.* 1984.

**CAHAL, Dr Dennis Abraham;** Senior Principal Medical Officer, Department of Health and Social Security (formerly Ministry of Health), 1963-81; *b* 1 Oct. 1921; *s* of Henry Cahal and Helen Wright; *m* 1948, Joan, *d* of Allan and Laura Grover; one *s. Educ:* Bradford Grammar Sch.; Univ. of Leeds. MB, ChB (Hons) Leeds, 1953; MD (Dist.) Leeds, 1959; MRCP 1968. RA, Indian Artillery and Special Allied Airborne Reconnaissance Force, 1939-46. Hospital appointments and general practice, 1953-55; Lecturer in Pharmacology, Univ. of Leeds, 1955-59; industrial research into drugs, 1959-62. Vis. Prof. of Pharmacology and Therapeutics, St Mary's Hosp. Med. Sch., London, 1967-69. Med. Assessor, Cttee on Safety of Drugs, 1963-70. *Publications:* various articles on drugs in scientific jls. *Recreations:* reading, cricket, rugby football, horses. *Address:* 207 Merryhill Road, Bushey, Herts. *Club:* MCC.
                                        *Died* 25 *Feb.* 1983.

**CAHILL, Patrick Richard,** CBE 1970 (OBE 1944); *b* 21 Feb. 1912; *er s* of late Patrick Francis and Nora Christina Cahill; *m* 1st, 1949, Gladys Lilian May Kemp (*d* 1969); one *s*; 2nd, 1969, Mary Frances Pottinger. *Educ:* Hitchin Grammar Sch. Joined Legal & General Assurance Soc. Ltd, 1929; Pensions Manager, 1948; Agency Manager, 1952; Asst Manager, 1954; Asst General Manager, 1957; Gen. Manager, 1958; Chief Exec., 1969–71; Mem. Board, 1969–77. Served War with RASC, 1940–45 (despatches, OBE); N Africa, Italy, and N Europe, 1st, 7th and 11th Armd Divs; rank of Lt-Col. Managing Dir, Gresham Life Assurance Soc. Ltd and Dir, Gresham Fire and Accident Insurance Soc. Ltd, 1958–72. A Vice-Pres., Chartered Insurance Inst., 1961–63, Pres., 1969; Pres., Insurance Charities, 1965–66; Chm., London Salvage Corps, 1964–65; Chm., British Insurance Assoc., 1967–69. *Address:* Flat G, 47 Beaumont Street, W1. *T:* 01–935 2608; Thorndene, Pluckley, Kent. *T:* Pluckley 306.                                *Died* 20 *March* 1990.

**CAHN, Charles Montague,** CBE 1956; *b* 27 Dec. 1900; *yr s* of Gottfried Cahn and Lilian Juliet Cahn (*née* Montague); *m* 1939, Kathleen Rose (*d* 1981), *d* of Auguste and Kathleen Thoumine; two *d. Educ:* Westminster Sch.; Christ Church, Oxford. BA 1923; MA 1968. Called to the Bar, Inner Temple, 1924. Served War of 1939–45 in Army (France and Middle East). Deputy Judge Advocate, 1945; Asst Judge Advocate-General, 1946; Deputy Judge Advocate-General, BAOR and RAF Germany (2 TAF), 1957–60; Vice Judge Advocate-General, 1963–67, retired 1967. Legal Chairman, Pensions Appeal Tribunals, 1967–77. *Recreation:* walking up and down hills. *Address:* 8 Crundwell Court, East Street, Farnham, Surrey GU9 7TB. *T:* Farnham 724558. *Died* 16 *Aug.* 1985.

**CAIRD, Rev. George Bradford,** MA(Cantab), DPhil, DD(Oxon); FBA 1973; Dean Ireland's Professor of Exegesis of Holy Scripture, Oxford, since 1977; Fellow, Queen's College, Oxford, since 1977; *b* 19 July 1917; *s* of George Caird and Esther Love Caird (*née* Bradford), both of Dundee; *m* 1945, Viola Mary Newport; three *s* one *d. Educ:* King Edward's Sch., Birmingham; Peterhouse, Cambridge; Mansfield Coll., Oxford. Minister of Highgate Congregational Church, London, 1943-46; Prof. of OT Lang. and Lit., St Stephen's Coll., Edmonton, Alberta, 1946-50; Prof. of NT Lang. and Lit., McGill Univ., Montreal, 1950-59; Principal, United Theological Coll., Montreal, 1955-59; Sen. Tutor, 1959-70, Principal, 1970-77, Mansfield Coll., Oxford; Reader in Biblical Studies, Oxford Univ., 1969-77. Grinfield Lecturer on the Septuagint, Oxford Univ., 1961-65. Moderator of General Assembly of URC, 1975-76. Hon. Fellow, Mansfield Coll., 1977. Hon. DD: St Stephen's Coll., Edmonton, 1959; Diocesan Coll., Montreal, 1959; Aberdeen Univ., 1966. Burkitt Medal, British Acad., 1981. *Publications:* The Truth of the Gospel, 1950; The Apostolic Age, 1955; Principalities and Powers, 1956; The Gospel according to St Luke, 1963; The Revelation of St John the Divine, 1966; Our Dialogue with Rome, 1967; Paul's Letters from Prison, 1976; The Language and Imagery of the Bible, 1980 (Collins Bi-Ennial Religious Award, 1982); contribs to: Interpreter's Dictionary of the Bible; Hastings Dictionary of the Bible; Jl of Theological Studies; New Testament Studies; Expository Times. *Recreations:* birdwatching, indoor games, theatre, music. *Address:* The Queen's College, Oxford.
*Died* 21 *April* 1984.

**CAIRNS,** 5th Earl, *cr* 1878; **David Charles Cairns,** GCVO 1972 (KCVO 1969); CB 1960; Rear-Admiral; DL; Baron Cairns, 1867; Viscount Garmoyle, 1878; Her Majesty's Marshal of the Diplomatic Corps, 1962-71; Extra Equerry to the Queen, since 1972; *b* 3 July 1909; *s* of 4th Earl and Olive (*d* 1952), *d* of late J. P. Cobbold, MP; *S* father, 1946; *m* 1936, Barbara Jeanne Harrisson, *y d* of Sydney H. Burgess, Heathfield, Altrincham, Cheshire; two *s* one *d. Educ:* RNC Dartmouth. Served War of 1939–45 (despatches); Dep. Dir, Signal Dept, Admiralty, 1950, comd 7th Frigate Sqdn, 1952; HMS Ganges, 1953–54; Student Imperial Defence Coll., 1955; comd HMS Superb, 1956–57; Baghdad Pact Plans and Training Div., Admiralty, 1958; Pres., RNC Greenwich, 1958–61; retired. Pres., Navy League, 1966–77. Formerly: Dir, Brixton Estate Ltd; Governor, Nuffield Nursing Home Trust. Prime Warden, Fishmongers' Co., 1972. DL Suffolk, 1973. *Heir:* s Viscount Garmoyle. *Address:* The Red House, Clopton, near Woodbridge, Suffolk. *T:* Grundisburgh 262. *Club:* Turf.
*Died* 21 *March* 1989.

**CAIRNS, Rt. Hon. Sir David (Arnold Scott),** PC 1970; Kt 1955; a Lord Justice of Appeal, 1970–77; *b* 5 March 1902; *s* of late David Cairns, JP, Freeman of Sunderland, and late Sarah Scott Cairns; *m* 1932, Irene Cathery Phillips; one *s* two *d. Educ:* Bede Sch., Sunderland; Pembroke Coll., Cambridge (Scholar) (Hon. Fellow, 1973); Senior Optime. MA, LLB (Cantab); BSc (London); Certificate of Honour, Bar Final, 1925. Called to Bar, Middle Temple, 1926; Bencher 1958. KC 1947. Liberal Candidate at By-election, Epsom Div., 1947. Mem. of Leatherhead UDC, 1948–54; Chm., Liberal Party Commn on Trade Unions, 1948–49; Mem. of Liberal Party Cttee, 1951–53; Chm., Monopolies and Restrictive Practices Commn, 1954–56; Recorder of Sunderland, 1957–60; Comr of Assize, 1957 (Midland Circuit), May 1959 (Western Circuit), Nov. 1959 (Wales and Chester Circuit); Judge of the High Court, Probate, Divorce and Admiralty Div., 1960–70. Chairman: Statutory Cttee of Pharmaceutical Soc. of Great Britain, 1952–60; Executive of Justice (British Section of International Commn of Jurists), 1959–60; Minister of Aviation's Cttee on Accident Investigation and Licence Control, 1959–60; Govt Adv. Cttee on Rhodesian Travel Restrictions, 1968–70. *Recreations:* swimming, gardening. *Address:* Applecroft, Ashtead, Surrey. *T:* Ashtead 74132. *Died* 8 *Sept.* 1987.

**CAIRNS, Sir Joseph Foster,** Kt 1972; JP; Lord Mayor of Belfast, 1969-72; *b* 27 June 1920; *s* of Frederick and Janette Cairns; *m* 1944, Helena McCullough; one *s* one *d.* Joined Family Business, 1935; Managing Director, J. Cairns Ltd, 1945–; Chm., Lynley Develt Co. Ltd, 1964-. Member (Unionist), Belfast Corporation, Clifton Ward, 1952–; Dep. Lord Mayor, 1964-65; Member: Senate of Northern Ireland, 1969-72; Senate, QUB, 1969-72. Contested (Unionist): Belfast Central, 1953; Oldpark, 1969. JP Belfast, 1963; High Sheriff of Belfast, 1963. *Recreations:* family life, travel. *Address:* Amaranth, Craigdarragh Road, Helens Bay, Northern Ireland. *T:* Helens Bay 852813. *Died* 2 *May* 1981.

**CAIRNS, Julia, (Mrs Paul Davidson);** writer and lecturer; Vice-President: London and Overseas Flower Arrangement Society; Society of Women Writers and Journalists; *b* 2 Sept. 1893; *o c* of late H. W. Akers, Oxford; *m* 1st, 1915, Frank H. James, The Royal Scots; 2nd, 1925, Capt. Paul Davidson, late 12th Royal Lancers (*d* 1942). *Educ:* Oxford. Entered journalism as a free-lance; Woman Editor of The Ideal Home, 1924; House and Home Director of Woman's Journal, 1927; Editor-in-Chief Weldons Publications, 1929–55; Home Editor, The Queen, 1956–58. President Women's Press Club of London Ltd, 1947 and 1948. *Publications:* Home-Making, 1950; How I Became a Journalist, 1960. *Recreation:* gardening. *Club:* University Women's. *Died* 12 *Dec.* 1985.

**CAKOBAU, Ratu Sir George (Kadavulevu),** GCMG 1973; GCVO 1977; OBE 1953; Royal Victorian Chain, 1982; Governor-General of Fiji, 1973–83; *b* 1911; *s* of Ratu Popi Epeli Seniloli Cakobau; *m* Lealea S. Balekiwai, *d* of Vilikesa Balekiwai. *Educ:* Queen Victoria Sch.; Newington Coll., Australia; Wanganui Technical Coll., NZ. Served War, 1939–45; Captain, Fiji Military Forces. Member: Council of Chiefs, Fiji, 1938–72; Legislative Council, Fiji, 1951–70; Minister for Fijian Affairs and Local Government, 1970–71; Minister without Portfolio, 1971–72. KStJ 1973. *Address:* Bau Island, Tailevu, Fiji. *Died* 25 *Nov.* 1989.

**CALDECOTT, (John) Andrew,** CBE 1990; Chairman, M & G Group PLC, since 1979 (Director, since 1966); Vice Chairman, Kleinwort Benson Ltd, 1974–83; *b* 25 Feb. 1924; *s* of Sir Andrew Caldecott, GCMG, CBE and Lady Caldecott; *m* 1951, Zita Ursula Mary Belloc; three *s* one *d. Educ:* Eton; Trinity Coll., Oxford (2nd Cl. BA Hons Jurisprudence). Qualified Solicitor, 1951. Served War, KRRC, 1942–46. Druces & Attlee, Solicitors, 1951–69 (Partner, 1954–69). Director: Kleinwort Benson Ltd, 1970–83; Kleinwort Benson Gp (formerly Kleinwort, Benson, Lonsdale Ltd), 1974–90; Chloride Group PLC, 1981–89; Whitbread and Company PLC, 1983–; Electronic Rentals Group plc, 1983–88; Blue Circle Industries PLC, 1983–; Blick plc, 1986–. Mem., Bd of Banking Supervision, 1986–. *Recreations:* fishing, music. *Address:* 137B Ashley Gardens, Thirleby Road, SW1P 1HN. *T:* 071–834 0122. *Club:* Boodle's.
*Died* 14 *July* 1990.

**CALDER;** *see* Ritchie-Calder.

**CALDERBANK, Prof. Philip Hugh;** Professor of Chemical Engineering, University of Edinburgh, 1960–80, later Emeritus; *b* 6 March 1919; *s* of Leonard and Rhoda Elizabeth Calderbank; *m* 1941, Kathleen Mary (*née* Taylor); one *s* one *d. Educ:* Palmer's Sch., Gray's, Essex; King's Coll., London Univ. Research and Development Chemist: Ministry of Supply, 1941–44; Bakelite Ltd, 1944–47. Lecturer in Chemical Engineering Dept, University Coll., London University, 1947–53; Professor in Chem. Engineering Dept, University of Toronto, 1953–56; Senior Principal Scientific Officer, Dept of Scientific and Industrial Research, 1956–60. *Publications:* contributor: Chemical Engineering Progress; Transactions Instn of Chemical Engineers; Chemical Engineering Science. *Recreations:* various crafts. *Died* 16 *March* 1988.

**CALDICOTT, Hon. Sir John Moore,** KBE 1955; CMG 1955; *b* 1900; *m* 1945, Evelyn Macarthur; one *s* two step *d. Educ:* Shrewsbury School. Joined RAF 1918. Came to Southern Rhodesia, 1925; farmed in Umvukwes District until 1970. President: Rhodesia Tobacco Assoc., 1943–45; Rhodesia National Farmers' Union, 1946–48. MP for Mazoe, S Rhodesia Parliament, 1948; Minister of Agriculture and Lands, 1951, of Agriculture, Health and Public Service, 1953, of Economic Affairs, 1958–62, of The Common Market, 1962, and of Finance, until 1963, Federation of Rhodesia and Nyasaland. *Address:* 24 Court Road, Greendale, Harare, Zimbabwe. *Club:* Harare (Harare, Zimbabwe).
*Died* 31 *Jan.* 1986.

**CALDWELL, Erskine;** author; Editor of American Folkways, 1940–55; Member: Authors' League; American PEN; (Hon.) American Academy and Institute of Arts and Letters; *b* 17 Dec. 1903; *s* of Ira Sylvester Caldwell and Caroline Preston Bell; *m* 1st, 1925, Helen Lannigan; two *s* one *d*; 2nd, 1939, Margaret Bourke-White; 3rd, 1942, June Johnson; one *s*; 4th, 1957, Virginia Moffett Fletcher. *Educ:* Erskine Coll.; Univ. of Virginia. Newspaper reporter on Atlanta (Ga) Journal; motion picture screen writer in Hollywood; newspaper and radio correspondent in Russia. Order of Cultural Merit (Poland), 1981; Comdr, Order of Arts and Letters (France), 1983. *Publications:* The Bastard, 1929; Poor Food, 1930; American Earth, 1931; Tobacco Road, 1932; God's Little Acre, 1933; We Are the Living, 1933; Journeyman, 1935; Kneel to the Rising Sun, 1935; Some American People, 1935; You Have Seen Their Faces, 1937; Southways, 1938; North of The Danube, 1939; Trouble in July, 1940; Jackpot, 1940; Say! Is This the USA?, 1941; All-Out on the Road to Smolensk, 1942; Moscow Under Fire, 1942; All Night Long, 1942; Georgia Boy, 1943; Tragic Ground, 1944; Stories, 1945; A House in the Uplands, 1946; The Sure Hand of God, 1947; This Very Earth, 1948; Place Called Estherville, 1949; Episode in Palmetto, 1950; Call It Experience, 1951; The Courting of Susie Brown, 1952; A Lamp for Nightfall, 1952; The Complete Stories of Erskine Caldwell, 1953; Love and Money, 1954; Gretta, 1955; Gulf Coast Stories, 1956; Certain Women, 1957; Molly Cottontail, 1958 (juvenile); Claudelle Inglish, 1959; When You

Think of Me, 1959; Jenny By Nature, 1961; Close to Home, 1962; The Last Night of Summer, 1963; Around About America, 1964; In Search of Bisco, 1965; The Deer at Our House (juvenile), 1966; In the Shadow of the Steeple, 1966; Miss Mamma Aimee, 1967; Writing In America, 1967; Deep South, 1968; Summertime Island, 1968; The Weather Shelter, 1969; The Earnshaw Neighborhood, 1971; Annette, 1973; Afternoons in Mid-America, 1976; Stories of Life: North & South, 1983; With All My Might: an autobiography, 1987. *Address:* c/o McIntosh & Otis Inc., 310 Madison Avenue, New York, NY 10017, USA. *T:* New York: MU 9–1050; (home) PO Box 4550, Hopi Station, Scottsdale, Arizona 85258, USA. *Clubs:* Phoenix Press (Phoenix, Arizona); San Francisco Press (San Francisco, Calif). *Died* 11 *April* 1987.

**CALDWELL, Godfrey David;** Under-Secretary, Department of Health and Social Security, 1970–75; *b* 7 Jan. 1920; *er s* of Dr J. R. Caldwell, Milnthorpe, Westmorland; *m* 1959, Helen Elizabeth, *d* of J. A. G. Barnes; one *d*. *Educ:* Heversham Grammar Sch., Westmorland; St Andrews Univ. (MA). Home Office, 1942; transferred to Min. of Nat. Insurance, 1945; Dept of Health and Social Security, 1968–75. *Address:* Low Ludderburn, Cartmel Fell, Windermere, Cumbria. *T:* Crosthwaite 428. *Club:* National Liberal.
*Died* 25 *March* 1985.

**CALDWELL, Janet Miriam Taylor, (Mrs W. R. Prestie);** *see* Caldwell, Taylor.

**CALDWELL, John Foster,** CB 1952; *b* 3 May 1892; *er s* of Charles Sproule Caldwell, Solicitor, Londonderry, and Jeannie Hamilton Foster; *m* 1921, Flora (decd), *yr d* of H. P. Grosse, AMIEE, Belfast and Portrush; one *d*. *Educ:* Foyle Coll., Londonderry; Trinity Coll., Dublin; King's Inns, Dublin. Called to the Bar, 1925; KC (N Ireland) 1946. First Parliamentary Draftsman to the Govt of Northern Ireland, 1945-56; Consolidator of Statute Law, N Ireland, 1956-59; former Member County Court Rules Cttee and Statute Law Cttee, N Ireland; Chief Parliamentary Counsel, Jamaica, 1959-61; Senior Legal Asst, Colonial Office, 1961-62. LLM *hc* Queen's Univ. of Belfast, 1957. *Died* 8 *May* 1981.

**CALDWELL, Taylor, (Janet Miriam Taylor Caldwell; Mrs W. R. Prestie),** FIAL; writer; *b* Prestwich, Manchester, England, 7 Sept. 1900; Scots parentage; citizen of USA; *m* 1st, William Fairfax Combs (marr. diss.; he *d* 1972); one *d*; 2nd, Marcus Reback (*d* 1970); one *d*; 3rd, 1972, William E. Stancell (marr. diss. 1973); 4th, 1978, William Robert Prestie. *Educ:* Univ. of Buffalo, Buffalo, NY. Wrote many years before publication. Formerly Sec. of Board of Special Inquiry, US Dept of Immigration and Naturalization, Buffalo, NY. Dr in lit. hum., St Bonaventure, 1977. Many awards and citations, national and international, including National Award, Nat. League of American Penwomen (gold medal), 1948, Grande Prix, Prix Chatrain, Paris, 1956, Award of Merit, Daughters of the American Revolution, 1956; McElligott Medal, Marquette Univ., Milwaukee. *Publications:* Dynasty of Death, 1938, repr. 1973; The Eagles Gather, 1939; The Earth is the Lord's, 1940; The Strong City, 1941; The Arm and the Darkness, 1942; The Turnbulls, 1943; The Final Hour, 1944; The Wide House, 1945; This Side of Innocence, 1946; There Was a Time, 1947; Melissa, 1948; Let Love Come Last, 1949; The Balance Wheel, 1951; The Devil's Advocate, 1952; Never Victorious, Never Defeated, 1954; Tender Victory, 1956; The Sound of Thunder, 1957; Dear and Glorious Physician, 1959; The Listener, 1960, (Engl. edn) The Man Who Listens, 1961; A Prologue to Love, 1962; To See the Glory, 1963; The Late Clara Beame, 1964; A Pillar of Iron, 1965; Dialogues with the Devil, 1968; Testimony of Two Men, 1968; Great Lion of God, 1970; On Growing up Tough, 1971; Captains and the Kings, 1973; Glory and the Lightning, 1974; Ceremony of the Innocent, 1976; Bright Flows the River, 1978; Answer as a Man, 1981. *Recreations:* just work; occasionally gardening. *Address:* Ivanhoe Lane, Greenwich, Conn 06830, USA. *Clubs:* American Legion, National League of American Penwomen (Buffalo, NY); League of Women Voters (Amherst Township, Erie County, NY); PEN (New York, NY); Women's National Republican (Washington, DC). *Died* 30 *Aug.* 1985.

**CALLAGHAN, Morley (Edward),** CC (Can.) 1983; Canadian novelist; *b* Toronto, 22 Sept. 1903; *s* of Thomas Callaghan and Mary (*née* Dewan); *m* 1929, Lorrete Florence (*d* 1984), *d* of late Joseph Dee; two *s*. *Educ:* St Michael's Coll., Univ. of Toronto (BA); Osgoode Hall Law School. Holds Hon. Doctorates. Canadian Council Prize, 1970; $50,000 Royal Bank of Canada Award, 1970. *Publications:* Strange Fugitive, 1928; Native Argosy, 1929; It's Never Over, 1930; No Man's Meat, 1931; Broken Journey, 1932; Such Is My Beloved, 1934; They Shall Inherit the Earth, 1935; My Joy in Heaven, 1936; Now That April's Here, 1937; Just Ask for George (play), 1940; Jake Baldwin's Vow (for children), 1948; The Varsity Story, 1948; The Loved and the Lost, 1951; The Man with the Coat, 1955 (MacLean's Prize, 1955); A Many Coloured Coat, 1960 (UK 1963); A Passion in Rome, 1961 (UK 1964); That Summer in Paris, 1963; Morley Callaghan, vols 1 and 2, 1964; A Fine and Private Place,

1976; Close to the Sun Again, 1977; No Man's Meat and The Enchanted Pimp, 1978; A Time for Judas, 1983; Our Lady of the Snows, 1985; The Man with the Coat, 1987; The Wild Old Man on the Road, 1988. *Recreation:* sports. *Address:* 20 Dale Avenue, Toronto, Ont M4W 1K4, Canada. *Died* 25 *Aug.* 1990.

**CALLOW, Robert Kenneth,** FRS 1958; MA, DPhil, BSc; Member of Staff, Rothamsted Experimental Station, 1966-72; Member of Scientific Staff, Medical Research Council, 1929-66; *b* 15 Feb. 1901; 2nd *s* of late Cecil Burman Callow and Kate Peverell; *m* 1937, Nancy Helen, *d* of J. E. Newman; one *s* one *d*. *Educ:* City of London Sch.; Christ Church, Oxford. Exhibitioner, 1919, and Research Scholar, 1927, of Christ Church. Served in RAF, 1940-45; relief of Datta Khel, 1941 (despatches). Mem. of Editorial Board, Biochemical Journal, 1946-53 (Dep. Chm., 1951-53); Chm., Biological and Medical Abstracts Ltd, 1955-61; Mem. of Council, Bee Research Association, 1962-74 (Chm., 1963-68; Vice-Pres., 1974-); Visitor, Royal Instn of GB, 1970-73. *Publications:* papers (many jointly) in jls of learned societies. *Recreations:* gardening, stamp-collecting, natural history. *Address:* Marrinagh, Ballajora, Maughold, Isle of Man. *Died* 12 *April* 1983.

**CALTHORPE, Brig. Sir Richard (Hamilton) A. G.;** *see* Anstruther-Gough-Calthorpe.

**CALVINO, Italo;** Italian writer; *b* 15 Oct. 1923; *s* of Mario Calvino and Eva Mameli; *m* 1964, Chichita Singer; one *d*. Hon. Member, American Academy and Institute of Arts and Letters, 1975; Oesterreichisches Staatspreis für Europäische Literatur, 1976; Grande Aigle d'Or du Festival du Livre de Nice, 1982. *Publications:* Il sentiero dei nidi di ragno (The Path of the Spider's Nest), 1947; Ultimo viene il corvo, 1949 (selection pubd as Adam, One Afternoon, 1957, repr. 1983); Il visconte dimezzato (The Cloven Viscount), 1951; Fiabe italiane (Italian Folktales), 1956; Il barone rampante (The Baron on the Trees), 1957; Il cavaliere inesistente (The Nonexistent Knight), 1959; Cosmicomiche (Cosmicomics), 1965; Il castello dei destini incrociati (The Castle of Crossed Destinies), 1969; Le città invisibli (Invisible Cities), 1972; Se una notte d'inverno un viaggiatore (If on a Winter's Night a Traveller), 1979; Palomar, 1983 (Mr Palomar, 1985); Difficult Loves, 1984. *Address:* c/o G. Einaudi Editore SpA, via Gregoriana 38, Rome, Italy.
*Died* 19 *Sept.* 1985.

**CAMBRIDGE,** 2nd Marquess of, *cr* 1917; **George Francis Hugh Cambridge,** GCVO 1933 (KCVO 1927); Earl of Eltham, 1917; Viscount Northallerton, 1917; late Lieut Reserve Regiment 1st Life Guards and Shropshire Yeomanry; Capt. 16th Bn London Regt and RASC, TA; *b* London, 11 Oct. 1895; *er s* of 1st Marquess and Lady Margaret Evelyn Grosvenor (*d* 1929), 3rd *d* of 1st Duke of Westminster; *S* father, 1927; *m* 1923, Dorothy, 2nd *d* of late Hon. Osmond Hastings; one *d*. Royal Trustee, British Museum, 1974-73. *Heir:* none. *Address:* The Old House, Little Abington, Cambs.
*Died* 16 *April* 1981 (*ext*).

**CAMDEN,** 5th Marquess *cr* 1812; **John Charles Henry Pratt;** Baron Camden, 1765; Earl Camden, Viscount Bayham, 1786; Earl of Brecknock, 1812; DL, JP; Major, Reserve of Officers; late Scots Guards; *b* 12 April 1899; *er s* of 4th Marquess Camden, GCVO and Lady Joan Marion Nevill, CBE 1920 (*d* 1952), *d* of 3rd Marquess of Abergavenny; *S* father, 1943; *m* 1st, 1920, Marjorie, DBE 1967 (who obtained a divorce, 1941), *o c* of late Col A. E. Jenkins and Mrs Anna Jenkins, Wherwell Priory, Andover, Hants; one *s* one *d*; 2nd, 1942, Averil (*d* 1977), *er d* of late Col Henry Sidney John Streatfeild, DSO; one *s*; 3rd, 1978, Rosemary, *yr d* of late Brig. Hanbury Pawle, CBE, DL. *Educ:* Ludgrove, New Barnet, Herts; Eton Coll.; RMC Sandhurst. ADC to Gen. Lord Jeffreys, GOC London Dist, 1920-24. Raised and formed 45th Battery 16th Light AA Regt RA, 1938, and commanded during early part of war of 1939-45, then rejoined Scots Guards; late Hon. Col 516th LAA Regt, RA: Gold Staff at Coronation of King George VI and Queen Elizabeth, 1937. DL, JP, Kent. Conservative Peer: Younger Brother of Trinity House. Dir, Darracq Motor Engineering Co., Bayard Cars Ltd and late Dir of many cos; Dir. Nat. Sporting Club, 1937-40; Director: RAC Buildings Co. Ltd; RAC Country Club Ltd; RAC Travel Service Ltd; President: Tonbridge Area League of Mercy; Tunbridge Wells Area of RSPCA; SE Counties Agricultural Soc., 1948 (and Mem. Council); Tunbridge Wells Amateur Dramatic and Operatic Soc.; Royal Agricultural Soc. of England; Joint Pres. Royal Tunbridge Wells Civic Assoc.; Chm. Bd of Trustees, Living of King Charles-the-Martyr, Tunbridge Wells; Pres. St Pancras Almshouse; a Vice-Pres. and Mem. Cttee of Management of Royal Nat. Life-Boat Inst.; Mem. Council of Boy Scouts Assoc. for County of Kent; Hon. Pres., RAC Motor Sport Council. Late President: Women's Lying-in Hosp., Vincent Sq., SW1; Kent and Sussex Hosp., Tunbridge Wells; late Vice-Pres. Royal Northern Hospital, N7; late Trustee Kent Playing Fields Association. FMI. *Recreations:* shooting, boxing, motor-car racing, yachting, motor-boat racing; interests: farming and forestry. *Heir:* *s* Earl of Brecknock. *Address:* Bayham Manor, Lamberhurst, Kent. *T:* Lamberhurst 890 500; 42

Limerston Street, SW10. *T*: 01-352 7838. *Clubs*: Brooks's (Life Mem.), Cavalry and Guards, Pratt's, Turf, Royal Automobile (Senior Vice-Chm., 1952, Vice-Pres., 1978-), British Automobile Racing, MCC; Royal Yacht Squadron (Vice-Cdre 1954-65); House of Lords Yacht (Vice-Cdre); Royal Motor Yacht (Vice-Adm.); Marine Motoring Assoc. (Vice-Pres.); Royal Naval Sailing Assoc. (Hon. Mem.); Yachtsmen's Assoc. of America (Hon. Mem.), etc.
*Died 22 March 1983.*

**CAME, William Gerald,** CIE 1944; BSc (Bristol); retired civil engineer; *b* 8 Dec. 1889; *s* of late John Mathew and Elizabeth Bessie Came, Woodhuish Barton, Brixham, Devon; *m* 1st, 1916, Ada Coombs; one *s* one *d*; 2nd, 1937, Gertrude Marie Farmer; one *s*. Chief Engineer and Sec. to Govt (Roads and Buildings Dept), Bihar, India, 1942–45; retired 1945; re-appointed as Chief Engineer and Secretary of the I and E Depts, 1945–48. Appointed to PWD (B and O) in 1913; previously with T. B. Cooper & Co., Civil Engineers, Bristol. Old Totnesian and an Associate of Univ. Coll., Bristol. *Address*: Somerley View, Ringwood, Hants. *T*: Ringwood 3733.
*Died 17 March 1984.*

**CAMERON OF BALHOUSIE,** Baron *cr* 1983 (Life Peer), of Balhousie in the District of Perth and Kinross; **Marshal of the Royal Air Force Neil Cameron,** KT 1983; GCB 1976 (KCB 1975; CB 1971); CBE 1967; DSO 1945; DFC 1944; AE 1968; Principal of King's College, London, 1980–July 1985, Fellow, since 1980; *b* 8 July 1920; *s* of Neil and Isabella Cameron, Perth, Scotland; *m* 1947, Patricia Louise, *d* of Major Edward Asprey; one *s* one *d*. *Educ*: Perth Academy. Fighter and Fighter Bomber Sqdns, 1940–45; Directing Staff, Sch. of Land/Air Warfare, Old Sarum, 1945–48; Student, RAF Staff Coll., 1949; DS, RAF Staff Coll., 1952–55; CO, Univ. of London Air Sqdn, 1955–56; Personal Staff Officer, Chief of Air Staff, 1956–59; CO, RAF Abingdon, 1959–62; Imperial Defence Coll., 1963; Principal Staff Officer, Dep. Supreme Comdr, SHAPE, Paris, 1964; Asst Comdt, RAF Coll., Cranwell, 1965; Programme Evaluation Gp, MoD, 1965–66; Assistant Chief of Defence Staff (Policy), 1968–70; SASO Air Support Comd, 1970–72; Dep. Comdr, RAF Germany, 1972–73; AOC 46 Gp, RAF, 1974; Air Member for Personnel, MoD, 1974–76; Chief of the Air Staff, 1976–77; Chief of the Defence Staff, 1977–79. Air ADC to the Queen, 1976–77. Chm. Council, Chest, Heart & Stroke Assoc., 1983–. President: Scottish Flying Club; Military Commentators' Circle; Soldiers and Airmens Scripture Readers' Assoc.; Vice-Pres., Officers' Christian Union; Chm. Trustees, Project Trident. Regional Dir, Greater London Regional Bd, Lloyds Bank, 1980–. Hon. Companion, RAeS, 1981. Hon. LLD Dundee, 1981. *Publications*: articles in defence jls; *posthumous autobiography*: In the Midst of Things, 1986. *Recreations*: reading, defence affairs, Rugby football. *Address*: House of Lords, SW1. *Clubs*: Athenæum, Caledonian, Royal Air Force (Pres.).
*Died 29 Jan. 1985.*

**CAMERON, Lt-Gen. Sir Alexander (Maurice),** KBE 1952; CB 1945; MC; retired; *b* 30 May 1898; *s* of late Major Sir Maurice Alexander Cameron, KCMG; *m* 1922, Loveday (*d* 1965), *d* of Col W. D. Thomson, CMG. *Educ*: Wellington Coll. 2nd Lieut Royal Engineers, 1916. Served European War, France and Belgium (wounded, despatches, MC, 2 medals); S Persia (medal and clasp); Iraq and Kurdistan (two clasps); psc 1929. Brevet Lieut-Col, 1939; RAF Staff Coll., 1939; Brig., 1940; Maj.-Gen. 1943; SHAEF, 1944–45; Dep. QMG, 1945–48; Maj.-Gen. i/c Administration, MELF, 1948–51; GOC East African Comd, 1951–53; retired 1954; Director of Civil Defence South-Eastern Region (Tunbridge Wells), 1955–60. *Club*: Army and Navy. *Died 25 Dec. 1986.*

**CAMERON, Prof. Gordon Campbell;** Professor of Land Economy, Cambridge University, since 1980 (Head of Department of Land Economy, 1980–89); Master, Fitzwilliam College, Cambridge, since 1988; *b* 28 Nov. 1937; *s* of Archibald Arthur Cameron and Elizabeth Forsyth; *m* 1962, Brenda; one *s* one *d*. *Educ*: Quarry Bank High Sch., Liverpool; Hatfield Coll., Univ. of Durham (BA Hons). Res. Asst, Univ. of Durham, 1960–62; Univ. of Glasgow: Asst Lectr in Polit. Econ., 1962–63; Lectr in Applied Econs, 1963–68, Sen. Lectr 1968–71, Titular Prof. 1971–74; Prof. of Town and Regional Planning, 1974–79, Dean of Social Sciences, 1979; Fellow, Wolfson Coll., Cambridge, 1980–88, Hon. Fellow, 1988. Res. Fellow, Resources for the Future, Washington, DC, and Vis. Associate Prof., Pittsburgh Univ., 1966–67; Vis. Prof., Univ. of Calif, Berkeley, 1974. Parly Boundary Comr for Scotland, 1976–83. Chm., Inner City Res. Panel, SSRC, 1980–82; Member: Cttee of Enquiry into Local Govt Finance (Layfield Cttee), 1974–76; Bd, Peterborough Develt Corp., 1981–88; Financial Bd, 1987–, Gen. Bd, 1989–, Univ. of Cambridge; Bd, Letchworth Garden City Corp., 1988–; DoE Property Adv. Gp, 1988–. Consultant on Urban Policy, Scottish Develt Dept, 1975–79; Economic Consultant to Sec. of State for Scotland, 1977–80; Consultant on Urban Finance, OECD, 1977–80, on Land Markets, 1986–89. Consultant, Coopers & Lybrand, 1977–88. Governor, Centre for Environmental Studies, London, 1975–82. Editor, Urban Studies Jl, 1968–74. FRSA 1978; Hon. RICS 1982. *Publications*: Regional Economic Development—

the federal role, 1971; (with L. Wingo) Cities, Regions and Public Policy, 1974; (ed) The Future of the British Conurbations, 1980; (ed) A Development Strategy for New Industrial Growth in the Cambridge Sub-Region, 1989. *Recreations*: tennis, all kinds of music, theatre. *Address*: Department of Land Economy, 19 Silver Street, Cambridge CB3 9EP; Fitzwilliam College, Huntingdon Road, Cambridge CB3 0DG. *Club*: United Oxford & Cambridge University.
*Died 14 March 1990.*

**CAMERON, James;** *see* Cameron, M. J. W.

**CAMERON, Brigadier John S.;** *see* Sorel Cameron.

**CAMERON, (Mark) James (Walter),** CBE 1979; journalist and author; *b* 17 June 1911; *s* of William Ernest Cameron, MA, LLB, and Margaret Douglas Robertson; *m* 1st, 1938, Eleanor Mara Murray (decd); one *d*; 2nd, 1944, Elizabeth O'Conor (marr. diss.); one *s* (and one step *s*); 3rd, 1971, Moneesha Sarkar; one step *s* one step *d*. *Educ*: erratically, at variety of small schools, mostly in France. Began journalism, in Dundee, 1928; after leaving Scotland joined many staffs and wrote for many publications, travelling widely as Foreign Correspt in most parts of the world; finally with (late) News Chronicle. Hon. DLitt: Lancaster, 1970; Bradford, 1977; Essex, 1978; Hon. LLD Dundee, 1980. Granada Award, Journalist of the Year, 1965; Granada Foreign Correspt of the Decade, 1966; Hannen Swaffer Award for Journalism, 1966; Gerald Barry Award for distinguished services to journalism, 1980. *Television*: prod. numerous films on contemporary subjects; initiated travel series, Cameron Country, BBC 2, 1967–68, 1984; script for series, The Spanish Civil War, Channel 4, 1983; James Cameron: Once Upon a Lifetime, BBC2, 1984. *Publications*: Touch of the Sun, 1950; Mandarin Red, 1955; "1914", 1959; The African Revolution, 1961; "1916", 1962; Witness in Viet Nam, 1966; Point of Departure, 1967; What a Way to Run a Tribe, 1968; An Indian Summer, 1974; The Best of Cameron, 1982; Cameron in the Guardian 1974–84, 1985; *Play*: The Pump, 1973 (radio, 1973, TV, 1980; Prix Italia 1973). *Recreations*: private life, public houses. *Address*: 3 Eton College Road, NW3. *T*: 01–586 5340. *Club*: Savile.
*Died 26 Jan. 1985.*

**CAMILLERI, His Honour Sir Luigi A.,** Kt 1954; LLD; Chief Justice and President of the Court of Appeal, Malta, 1952–57, retired; *b* 7 Dec. 1892; *s* of late Notary Giuseppe amd Matilde (*née* Bonello); *m* 1914, Erminia, *d* of Professor G. Cali'; five *s* three *d*. *Educ*: Gozo Seminary; Royal Univ. of Malta (LLD). Called to the Bar, 1913. Consular Agent for France in Gozo, Malta, 1919–24; Malta Legislative Assembly, 1921–24; Magistrate, 1924–30; Visitor of Notarial Acts, Chairman Board of Prison Visitors, Chairman Licensing Board, Magistrate in charge of Electoral Register, 1927–30; Judicial Bench, 1930; Royal Univ. of Malta representative on General Council of the Univ., 1933–36; Chairman Emergency Compensation Board, 1940–41; Court of Appeal, 1940–57; President Medical Council, Malta, 1959–68; Member Judicial Service Commission, 1959–62. Examiner in Criminal, Roman and Civil Law, Royal Univ. of Malta, 1931–70. Silver Jubilee Medal, 1935; Coronation Medals, 1937 and 1953. Knight of Sovereign Military Order of Malta, 1952. *Recreation*: walking. *Address*: George Borg Olivier Street, Sliema, Malta. *T*: Sliema 513532. *Club*: Casino Maltese (Malta).

**CAMM, John Sutcliffe;** Chairman and Chief Executive, DRG plc, 1978–85; *b* 18 Jan. 1925; *s* of late Thomas Howard Camm and of Mary Ethel Sutcliffe; *m* 1956, Barbara Kathleen Small; three *s* three *d*. *Educ*: Wycliffe Coll.; Bristol Univ. (BA). RAF pilot, 1943–47. Schoolmaster, Wycliffe Coll., 1950–53. Dir, E. S. & A. Robinson (Holdings), 1963; DRG (formerly Dickinson Robinson Group Ltd): Dir, 1967; Jt Man. Dir, 1972; Man. Dir, 1974; Dep. Chm., 1977. Director: Bristol & West Building Soc., 1982–; Kohler Ltd, South Africa, 1983–. Member Council: CBI, 1981; Bristol Univ.; Chm. of Governors, Wycliffe Coll., 1982. *Recreations*: gardening, cricket, country pursuits. *Address*: Bushy Farm, Breadstone, Glos GL13 9HG. *T*: Dursley 811013. *Clubs*: Naval and Military, MCC.
*Died 18 Sept. 1985.*

**CAMPBELL, Alan Johnston,** CMG 1973; retired grazier, Roma, Qld; President, Australian Country Party, Queensland, 1943-51; Federal and State Trustee, Australian Country Party, 1954-68; *b* Dubbo, NSW, 31 July 1895; *s* of Charles Campbell, Dalrymple, Scotland, and Sarah Ann Eliza (*née* Occleston); *m* 1965, Barbara Jane Dunn, Brisbane. *Educ*: Toowoomba Grammar Sch., Queensland. Served War, 1914-19, in 2nd Australian Light Horse Regt, in Gallipoli and Palestine. Owner of, and controlled, several sheep and cattle stations in Western Queensland from 1920 till retired in 1950, to live in Brisbane. Played active executive parts in various Grazing Industry organisations, 1922-35. Chairman: Charles Campbell & Sons Pty Ltd, of Merino Downs and Cooinda, Roma, Qld, 1918-50; The Countryman Newspaper Pty Ltd, 1947-68. Chm., Gallipoli Fountain of Honour Cttee, Brisbane, 1976–80. Member: Royal Society of Queensland, 1950-; Australian Inst. of Internat. Affairs, 1950-78; directed various campaigns in grazing industry, 1929-36, incl. Roma

Wool Plan, 1930-32; Pres., Aust. Woolgrowers' Assoc., 1932-34; Life Member: United Graziers Assoc. of Qld, 1952 (Mem. Council, 1929-33); Maranoa Graziers Assoc., 1952. Life Fellow: RGS (London), 1972; RGS (Australasia), 1956. *Publications:* The History of the Charles Campbell Clan 1781-1974, 1975; Memoirs of the Country Party 1920-74, 1975. *Recreations:* politics, photography, world travel. *Address:* Queensland Club, GPO Box 4, Brisbane, Queensland 4001, Australia. *T:* Brisbane 221.7072; (residence) 378.1477. *Clubs:* Queensland (Life Mem.), Tattersall's, Queensland Turf (Life Mem.), Royal Automobile (Qld) (all in Brisbane).
*Died 5 March* 1982.

**CAMPBELL, Archibald Hunter,** LLM, BCL, MA, of Lincoln's Inn, Barrister-at-Law; Regius Professor of Public Law, University of Edinburgh, 1945-72, and Dean of the Faculty of Law, 1958-64; *b* Edinburgh, 1902; *o c* of late Donald Campbell, MA. *Educ:* George Watson's Coll., Edinburgh (Dux); Univ. of Edinburgh (MA, Mackenzie Class. Schol., Ferguson Class. Schol.); University Coll., Oxford (Class. Exhibitioner). 1st Class in Hon. Mods, Lit. Hum., Jurisprudence and BCL; Sen. Demy of Magdalen Coll., 1927-28; Sen. Student of Oxford Univ., 1928; Fellow of All Souls, 1928-30 and 1936-; Stowell Civil Law Fellow, University Coll., Oxford, 1930-35; Barber Professor of Jurisprudence, Univ. of Birmingham, 1935-45. Vice-President Society of Public Teachers of Law, 1961-62, President 1962-63. President Classical Assoc. of Scotland, 1963-. Hon. LLD Aberdeen, 1963. *Address:* Portree Nursing Home, 13-15 Blantyre Terrace, Edinburgh. *Club:* New (Edinburgh).
*Died 7 June* 1989.

**CAMPBELL of Achalader, Brig. Archibald Pennant,** DSO 1945; OBE 1939; psc 1930; retired, 1947; Ninth Chief of Baronial House of Campbell of Achalader since 1963; *b* 26 Jan. 1896; *s* of Brig.-Gen. J. C. L. Campbell of Achalader (*d* 1930); *m* 1st, 1926, Phyllis (*d* 1953), *d* of late Sir Henry Bax-Ironside, KCMG; one *d*; 2nd, 1961, Elsie, widow of Dr Howard Clapham, and *d* of late J. Thompson. *Educ:* Malvern; RMA. 2nd Lieut, RFA, 1914. Served European War, 1914-18, with RA 22nd Div. (despatches). Silver Staff Officer at Jubilee of HM King George V, 1935. GSO 2, HQ (British Troops), Egypt, 1937; Bt Lt-Col, 1939; temp. Brig., 1941; Col, 1943. Served War, 1939-45 (Egypt, UK, and NW Europe) as BGS 8 Corps Dist, CRA 47 Div., CCRA 2 Corps Dist and Comdr 8 AGRA. Served in Palestine as Comdr North Palestine Dist, 1945-46; Comdr Suez Canal South, 1946-47. Dist Comr, Boy Scouts Assoc., 1955; British Consular Agent, Moji, Japan, 1957-58. *Recreations:* shooting (big and small game), fishing, hunting. *Address:* 6 Rockley Road, South Yarra, Victoria 3141, Australia. *T:* Melbourne 248300. *Club:* Naval and Military (London).
*Died 3 Oct.* 1983.

**CAMPBELL, Ian George Hallyburton,** TD; QC 1957; Lord Chancellor's Legal Visitor, 1963-79; *b* 19 July 1909; *s* of late Hon. Kenneth Campbell and Mrs K. Campbell; *m* 1949, Betty Yolande, *d* of late Somerset Maclean and widow of Lt-Col Allan Bruno, MBE; one adopted *s* one adopted *d*. *Educ:* Charterhouse, Trinity Coll., Cambridge. Barrister, Inner Temple and Lincoln's Inn, 1932. Served Artists Rifles and Rifle Brigade, 1939-45; Col 1945. Appts include: GSO2, HQ 1st Army; Chief Judicial Officer, Allied Commission, Italy; Chief Legal Officer, Military Govt, Austria (British zone). *Address:* Flat 26, The Abbey, Amesbury, Wilts. *T:* Amesbury 22612.
*Died 16 Oct.* 1986.

**CAMPBELL, Prof. Ian McIntyre,** MA; Professor of Humanity, University of Edinburgh, 1959-82, later Emeritus; *b* 14 Jan. 1915; *s* of late John Campbell and Janet Donaldson; *m* 1945, Julia Margaret Mulgan; two *s* one *d*. *Educ:* Spier's Sch., Beith; Univ. of Glasgow; Balliol Coll., Oxford. First cl. Hons Classics, Glasgow Univ., 1936; First cl., Class. Mods, 1938. Served in Intelligence Corps, Captain, 1939-45; Hon. War Memorial Research Student, Balliol Coll., 1946; Lecturer in Humanity and Comparative Philology, Glasgow Univ., 1947-54; Prof. of Latin, Univ. Coll. of S Wales and Monmouthshire, 1954-59. *Publications:* articles and reviews in learned journals. Jt Editor of Archivum Linguisticum, 1949-. *Recreation:* music. *Address:* 70 Thirlestane Road, Edinburgh EH9 1AR. *T:* 031-447 8994.
*Died 29 Nov.* 1982.

**CAMPBELL, James Grant,** CMG 1970; Consultant to Atlantic Division, Alcan Aluminium Ltd; *b* Springville, NS, Canada, 8 June 1914; *s* of John Kay Campbell and Wilna Archibald Campbell (*née* Grant); *m* 1941, Alice Isobel Dougall; one *d*. *Educ:* Mount Allison Univ., Canada. BSc, 1st cl. hons (Chem.). Chemical Engineer, Aluminium Co. of Canada, Arvida, Que, 1937-41; Demerara Bauxite Co. Ltd, Guyana, Gen. Supt, 1941-50; Aluminium Laboratories Ltd, London, England, 1950 (Headqrs for team investigating hydro power, bauxite and aluminium smelting in Asia, Africa and Europe); on staff of Dir of Operations, Aluminium Ltd, Montreal (concerned with world supply of raw materials for Aluminium Ltd), 1951-55; Managing Dir and Chm., Demerara Bauxite Co., Guyana, 1955-71; Vice-Pres., Alcan Ore Ltd, 1971-77; Overseas Representative, Alcan International Ltd, Montreal, 1977-79. Mem. Bd of Regents, Mount Allison Univ., 1972. Hon.

LLD Mount Allison Univ., 1966. *Recreation:* golf. *Address:* 45 Eaton Square, SW1W 9BD. *Clubs:* Brooks's, Travellers', Oriental; University (New York); University (Montreal).
*Died 21 May* 1989.

**CAMPBELL, Sir (James) Keith,** Kt 1982; CBE 1972; FCA; Chief Executive since 1964, and Chairman since 1974, Hooker Corporation Ltd; Deputy Chairman, Network Finance Ltd, since 1972; *b* 4 March 1928; *s* of late Edward Colin and Amanda Maud Campbell; *m* 1951, Marjorie Elizabeth (*née* Burford); one *s* three *d*. *Educ:* Homebush High Sch.; Australian Accountancy Coll. Chartered Accountant, 1950-62. Chairman, CitiNational Holdings Ltd, 1971-80; Director: Australian Industries Development Corp., 1974-80; IBM (Australia) Ltd, 1969-80; Chm., Australian Financial System Inquiry, 1979-81. Governor, Science Foundn, Sydney Univ., 1971-; Mem. Council: Univ. of NSW, 1981-; Salvation Army, 1981-; Chm., Shepherd Centre (Deaf), 1972-. *Publication:* Final Report of the Committee of Inquiry—Australian Financial System, 1981. *Recreations:* golf, surfing, music. *Address:* 8 Hopetoun Avenue, Mosman, NSW 2088, Australia. *T:* 969.3316. *Clubs:* Union, Elanora Golf (Sydney).
*Died 16 March* 1983.

**CAMPBELL, Prof. James Reid,** PhD, FRCVS; William Dick Professor of Veterinary Surgery, Royal (Dick) School of Veterinary Studies, University of Edinburgh, since 1978; *b* 19 Sept. 1930; *s* of Andrew and Margaret Campbell; *m* 1957, Marette (*née* Martin); two *s* two *d*. *Educ:* Bentinck Primary Sch., Kilmarnock; Kilmarnock Acad.; Glasgow Univ. (BVMS, PhD). FRCVS 1968. House Surg., Univ. of Glasgow Vet. Hosp., 1954-55; Asst in Practice, Fife, 1955-57; Lectr in Vet. Surgery, Univ. of Glasgow Vet. Hosp., 1957-67, Sen. Lectr, 1968-78; seconded to Univ. of Ont, 1958; Sen. Lectr, Faculty of Vet. Science, University Coll., Nairobi, 1964-65. *Publications:* contrib. vet. jls. *Recreations:* golf, music, reading. *Address:* Glamis Cottage, Carberry, Musselburgh EH21 8RZ. *T:* 031-665 2036.
*Died 9 March* 1985.

**CAMPBELL, Sir John Johnston,** Kt 1957; General Manager, Clydesdale Bank Ltd, 1946-58, retired (Director, 1958-75); *b* 11 Dec. 1897; *s* of William Campbell, Stewarton, Ayrshire; *m* 1927, Margaret Fullarton (*d* 1967), *d* of John Brown, Dalry, Ayrshire; one *s* one *d*. *Educ:* Stewarton Secondary Sch. Joined service of The Clydesdale Bank at Stewarton, Ayrshire, 1913. Served with Royal Scots Fusiliers in Palestine, France, and Germany, 1916-19. London Manager, Clydesdale Bank, 1944. Pres., Institute of Bankers in Scotland, 1953-55; Chm.: Development Securities Ltd, 1958-67; Cttee of Scottish Bank Gen. Managers, 1955-57. *Address:* 22 Saffrons Court, Compton Place Road, Eastbourne, E Sussex. *T:* 29271.
*Died 7 Dec.* 1983.

**CAMPBELL, Dame Kate (Isabel),** DBE 1971 (CBE 1954); Medical Practitioner; Specialist Pædiatrician, 1937-76; *b* April 1899; *d* of late Donald Campbell and late Janet Campbell (*née* Mill); unmarried. *Educ:* Hawthorn State Sch.; Methodist Ladies' Coll., Melbourne; Melbourne Univ. MB, BS, 1922; MD 1924; FRCOG 1961; Resident MO: Melbourne Hosp., 1922, Children's Hosp., 1923, Women's Hosp., 1924; Lecturer in Neo-Natal Pædiatrics, Melbourne Univ., 1927-65. Hon. Phys. to Children's Dept, Queen Victoria Hosp., Melbourne, 1926-60; Hon. Pædiatric Consultant in active practice, Queen Victoria Hospital, 1960-66; Hon. Pædiatric Consultant, 1966-; Hon. Neo-Natal Pædiatrician, Women's Hosp., Melbourne, 1945-59; First assistant in Pædiatrics, Professorial Unit, Dept of Obstetrics, Melbourne Univ., 1960-65; Gen. Med. Practice, 1927-37. Consultant to Dept of Infant Welfare, Victoria, 1961-76. Associate, Dept of Paediatrics, Monash Univ., 1971-; Hon. Consultant Paediatrician, Royal Women's Hosp., 1979-. Hon. LLD 1966. Hon. FRACO, 1978. *Publications:* (co-author with late Dr Vera Scantlebury Brown) Guide to the care of the young child, 1947 (last edn 1972); section on The Newborn, in Townsend's Obstetrics for Students, 1964; articles on medical subjects in Medical Journal of Australasia (incl. one on retrolental fibroplasia, 1951) and Lancet. *Recreation:* theatre. *Address:* 1293 Burke Road, Kew, Melbourne, Victoria 3101, Australia. *T:* 80 2536. *Club:* Lyceum (Melbourne).
*Died 12 July* 1986.

**CAMPBELL, Mungo,** CBE 1946; MA; retired shipowner; former director, Barclays Bank Ltd, Newcastle upon Tyne; *b* 5 June 1900; 2nd *s* of late James Campbell, The Manor House, Wormley, Herts; *m* 1st, 1944, Esther McCracken (*d* 1971); one *d* decd; 2nd, 1976, Betty Kirkpatrick. *Educ:* Loretto; Pembroke Coll., Cambridge. Ministry of War Transport, 1939-46 (Dir Ship Repair Div., 1942-46). Hon. DCL Newcastle, 1972. Comdr Order of Orange Nassau (Netherlands), 1947. *Address:* Rothley Lake House, Morpeth, Northumberland NE61 4JY. *Club:* Bath.
*Died 13 April* 1983.

**CAMPBELL, Sir Ralph Abercromby,** Kt 1961; Chief Justice of the Bahamas, 1960-70; *b* 16 March 1906; 2nd *s* of Major W. O. Campbell, MC; *m* 1st, 1936, Joan Childers Blake (marr. diss., 1968); one *s* one *d*; 2nd, 1968, Shelagh Moore. *Educ:* Winchester; University Coll., Oxford. Barrister-at-Law, Lincoln's Inn, 1928;

Western Circuit; Avocat à la Cour, Egypt, 1929; Pres. Civil Courts, Baghdad, Iraq, 1931–44; British Military Administration, Eritrea, Pres. British Military Court and Italian Court of Appeal, 1945; Resident Magistrate, Kenya, 1946; Judge of the Supreme Court, Aden, 1952 (redesignated Chief Justice, 1956)-1960. *Publications:* editor: Law Reports of Kenya and East African Court of Appeal, 1950; Aden Law Reports, 1954–55; Bahamas Law Reports, 1968. *Recreations:* golf, fishing. *Address:* 12 Frere Avenue, Fleet, Hants GU13 8AP. *T:* Fleet 615364. *Died 10 Oct. 1989.*

**CAMPBELL, Robin Francis,** CBE 1978; DSO 1943; Director of Art, Arts Council of Great Britain, 1969–78; *b* 1912; *s* of Rt. Hon. Sir Ronald Hugh Campbell, GCMG and Helen, *d* of Richard Graham; *m* 1st, 1936, Hon. Mary Hermione Ormsby Gore (marr. diss. 1945); two *s*; 2nd, 1945, Lady Mary Sybil St Clair Erskine (marr. diss. 1959); 3rd, 1959, Susan Jennifer Benson; two *s*. *Educ:* Wellington Coll.; New Coll., Oxford. Reuters correspondent, Berlin, Warsaw, 1936–39. Served N Africa, No 8 Commando and GHQ, Cairo, 1940–41; POW, 1941–43. Arts Council of GB, 1960–78. Hon. Dr RCA, 1978. Officier de l'Ordre des Arts et des Lettres, France, 1979. *Address:* 6 Noel Road, N1 8HA. *T:* 01–226 1009. *Died 18 Oct. 1985.*

**CAMPBELL, Rt. Hon. Sir Ronald Ian,** GCMG 1947 (KCMG 1941; CMG 1932); CB 1937; PC 1950; Director of Royal Bank of Scotland, 1950-65 (Extra-ordinary Director, 1965-68); *b* 7 June 1890; *s* of Lieut-Col Sir Guy Campbell, 3rd Bt, and Nina, *d* of late Frederick Lehmann, 15 Berkeley Square, W1. *Educ:* Eton Coll.; Magdalen Coll., Oxford. Entered Diplomatic Service, 1914; Third Sec., Washington, 1915-20; Second and First Sec., Paris, 1920-23; Foreign Office, 1923-27; First Sec., Acting Counsellor and Counsellor, Washington, 1927-31; Counsellor, Cairo, 1931-34; Counsellor in Foreign Office, 1934-38; Minister Plenipotentiary, British Embassy, Paris, 1938-39; Minister at Belgrade, 1939-41; Minister in Washington, 1941-45; an Asst Under-Sec. of State in the Foreign Office, 1945-46; Dep. to Sec. of State for Foreign Affairs on Council of Foreign Ministers, 1945-46; British Ambassador to Egypt, 1946-50; retired, 1950. Grand Officer of Legion of Honour. *Address:* 20 Sidegate, Haddington, East Lothian. *Clubs:* Brooks's, MCC; New (Edinburgh). *Died 22 April 1983.*

**CAMPBELL, Maj.-Gen. Victor David Graham,** CB 1956; DSO 1940; OBE 1946; JP; DL; *b* 9 March 1905; *s* of late Gen. Sir David G. M. Campbell, GCB; *m* 1947, Dulce Beatrix, *d* of late G. B. Goodwin, and *widow* of Lt-Col J. A. Goodwin. *Educ:* Rugby; RMC Sandhurst. 2nd Lieut The Queen's Own Cameron Highlanders, 1924; AQMG and DA&QMG HQ AFNEI, 1945–46; Lt-Col Comdg 1st Bn The Gordon Highlanders, 1949; Brig. Comdg 31 Lorried Infantry Brigade, 1951; Chief of Staff, HQ Scottish Command, 1954–57; psc 1938; idc 1953. DL and JP, 1962, High Sheriff, 1968, County of Devon; Chairman: Totnes RDC, 1971–72; Totnes Petty Sessional Div., 1972–75. *Address:* Beggars Bush, South Brent, South Devon. *Died 4 June 1990.*

**CAMPBELL-PRESTON, Hon. Mrs Angela;** Chairman, 1953–74 (Director, 1945–74) Westminster Press and subsidiary companies; *b* 27 Feb. 1910; 3rd *d* of 2nd Viscount Cowdray; *m* 1st, 1930, George Antony Murray (killed in action, 1945); one *s* (subseq. 10th Duke of Atholl) (and two *s* decd); 2nd, 1950, Robert Campbell-Preston of Ardchattan, OBE, MC; one *d*. *Educ:* home. Chm., S London Hosp. for Women, 1932-48; Chm., Lambeth Gp Hosp. Man. Cttee, 1961-64 (Vice-Chm., 1948-61); Mem., SW London Hosp. Man. Cttee, 1964-70; Sec. of various cttees of King Edward VII Hosp. Fund for London, 1942-50; Past Member: Glasgow Regional Hosp. Bd; Oban Hosps Bd of Management. Dir, Fisher's Hotel Ltd; Chm., Blair Construction Co Ltd. *Recreation:* renovating houses. *Address:* 31 Marlborough Hill, NW8. *T:* 01-586 2291; Ardchattan Priory, Connel, Argyll, Scotland. *T:* Bonawe 274. *Died 11 June 1981.*

**CAMPBELL-PURDIE, Cora Gwendolyn Jean, (Wendy);** founded Tree Crops as demonstration and research project, Greece, 1981; *b* 8 June 1925; *d* of Edmund Hamilton Campbell Purdie and Janie Theodora Williams. *Educ:* Woodford House, New Zealand. Worked with Red Cross Transport Corps in Auckland, 1943–46. English Asst at Lycées in France and Corsica, 1954–56; worked simultaneously and subseq. full-time with British timber firm in Corsica, 1954–58; FAO, Rome, on Mediterranean Reafforestation Project, Aug. 1958. Has been planting trees in N Africa, 1959 onwards; Co-founder with Rev. Austen Williams as Chm., Sahara Re-afforestation Cttee, 1965, registered with Charity Comrs as Bou Saada Trust, 1969 (Dir, 1969–78, when Trust wound up); now expects at least 75 per cent success; planted: 1000 trees (given by Moroccan Min. of Agric.) in Tiznit, 1960 and again in 1961; 10,000 trees (given by Algerian Min. of Agric.) planted by local agricl authorities at Bou Saada, 1964, by 1970 approx. 130,000 trees established on 260 acres; grain, fruit trees and vegetables now also grown, and bees and hens kept. Has planted many more thousands of trees (money given by: Men of the Trees; War on Want; St

Martin-in-the-Fields; the Bishop of Southwark's Diocesan Fund; CORSO (New Zealand), etc). Film made of Bou Saada project, 1970; since then has travelled with film, discussing re-afforestation and forestry techniques, in Commonwealth, USA, Africa, Near and Middle East. Attended: World Food Conf., Rome, 1974; Sahel Drought Conf., Senegal, 1975; began planting Forest of Peace with help of 8th Army veterans, El Alamein, March 1979; work carried on by Commonwealth War Graves Commn after breaking hip in Nov. *Publications:* (in collaboration with Fenner Brockway) Woman against the Desert, 1967; contrib. The Ecologist. *Recreation:* classical music. *Address:* Kardamyli, Messenia, Greece. *Died 20 Jan. 1985.*

**CAMPBELL-SMITH, Walter;** *see* Smith.

**CANDAU, Marcolino Gomes,** MD, DPH; Director-General Emeritus, World Health Organization, Geneva, since 1973; *b* Rio de Janeiro, 30 May 1911; *s* of Julio Candau and Augusta Gomes; *m* 1936, Ena de Carvalho; two *s*; *m* 1973, Sita Reelfs. *Educ:* Univ. of Brazil, Rio de Janeiro; Johns Hopkins Univ., USA. Various posts in Health Services of State of Rio de Janeiro, 1934–43; Asst Superintendent, Servico Especial de Saude Publica, Min. of Education and Health, 1944–47, Superintendent 1947–50; World Health Organization: Dir, Div. of Org. of Public Health Services, Geneva, 1950–51; Asst Dir-General, Dept of Advisory Services, Geneva, 1951–52; Asst Dir, Pan-American Sanitary Bureau, Dep. Reg. Dir for the Americas, Washington, 1952–53; Dir-Gen., Geneva, 1953–73. Hon. Dr of Laws: Univ. of Michigan; Johns Hopkins Univ.; Univ. of Edinburgh; The Queen's Univ. of Belfast; Seoul Univ., Korea; Royal Univ. of Malta; Hon. Dr of Medicine: Univ. of Geneva; Karolinska Inst., Stockholm; Hon. Dr: Univ. of Brazil; Univ. of Sao Paulo, Brazil; Univ. of Bordeaux; Charles Univ., Prague; Inst. of Medicine and Pharmacy, Bucharest; Univ. of Abidjan; Hon. Dr of Science: Bates Coll., Maine, USA; Univ. of Ibadan; Semmelweis Univ. of Medicine, Budapest; Univ. of Cambridge; FRCP, Hon. FRSocMed, and Hon. FRSH (all GB), and various other hon. fellowships in America and Europe; Mem., Royal Soc. of Tropical Medicine and Hygiene, GB; For. Member USSR Acad. of Med. Sciences; Foreign Associated Mem., Nat. Acad. of Medicine, Paris. Mary Kingsley Medal of Liverpool Sch. of Tropical Medicine; Gold Medal of RSH, London, 1966; Harben Gold Medal, RIPH&H, London, 1973; Léon Bernard Medal and Prize, World Health Assembly, 1974; also prizes and medals for services to public health. *Publications:* scientific papers. *Address:* Le Mas, Route du Jura, 1296 Coppet, Vaud, Switzerland. *Died 25 Jan. 1983.*

**CANDY, Air Vice-Marshal Charles Douglas,** CB 1963; CBE 1957; Air Member for Personnel, RAAF, 1966–69, retired; *b* 17 Sept. 1912; *s* of late C. H. and late Mrs Candy; *m* 1938, Eileen Cathryn Mary (*née* Poole-Ricketts); one *d*. Served War of 1939–45; Command and Staff appointments in Australia, the United Kingdom, West Africa and South-West Pacific Area; AOC North-Eastern Area, RAAF, 1946; Joint Services Staff Coll., 1947; Dept of Defence, Commonwealth of Australia, 1948–50; Director of Organisation and Staff Duties, HQ, RAAF, 1950–52; Imperial Defence Coll., 1953; SASO No. 3 Group Bomber Command, RAF, 1954–56; Deputy Chief of the Air Staff, RAAF, 1956–58 (Air Vice-Marshal, 1957); AOC Home Command, RAAF, 1958–59; Sen. Air Staff Officer, Far East Air Force, Royal Air Force, 1959–62; AOC Support Command, RAAF, 1962–66. *Recreation:* golf. *Address:* PO Box 128, Kingston, ACT 2604, Australia. *Clubs:* Commonwealth, Royal Canberra Golf (Canberra); Royal Singapore Golf (Singapore). *Died 4 March 1985.*

**CANFIELD, Cass;** Senior Editor, Harper & Row, Publishers; *b* 26 April 1897; *s* of August Cass and Josephine Houghteling; *m* 1st, 1922, Katharine Emmet; two *s*; 2nd, 1938, Jane White Fuller; 3rd, Joan Hone King. *Educ:* Groton Sch.; Harvard Univ. (AB); Oxford Univ. Harris, Forbes & Co. 1921–22; NY Evening Post, 1922–23; Foreign Affairs (a quarterly magazine), 1923–24; Manager, London (England) office, Harper & Bros, 1924–27; Harper & Bros, NY City, 1927; President, Harper & Bros, 1931–45; Chairman of the Board, 1945–55; Chairman Exec. Cttee, 1955–67. Served European War, 1917–18, commissioned. President National Assoc. of Book Publishers, 1932–34; Trustee, Woodrow Wilson National Fellowship Foundation; Mem. Exec. Cttee, John Fitzgerald Kennedy Library; Chairman, Governing Body, International Planned Parenthood Federation, 1966–69, now Chm. Emeritus. During War of 1939–45 with Board of Economic Warfare, Washington, DC; special advisor to American Ambassador, London, in charge of Economic Warfare Division, 1943; Director, Office of War Information, France, 1945. Albert D. Lasker Award, 1964. Hon. Phi Beta Kappa. *Publications:* The Publishing Experience, 1969; Up and Down and Around, 1972; The Incredible Pierpont Morgan, 1974; Samuel Adams' Revolution, 1976; The Iron Will of Jefferson Davis, 1978; Outrageous Fortunes, 1981; The Six, 1983. *Address:* 10 East 53 Street, New York, NY 10022, USA. *T:* 593–7200. *Clubs:* Century Association (New York); Porcellian (Cambridge, Mass). *Died 27 March 1986.*

CANHAM, Brian John; Metropolitan Stipendiary Magistrate, since 1975; a Recorder, since 1989; b 27 Dec. 1930; s of late Frederick Ernest and of Nora Ruby Canham; m 1955, Rachel, yr d of late Joseph and Martha Woolley, Bank House, Longnor, Staffs; three s one d. Educ: City of Norwich Sch.; Queens' Coll., Cambridge. MA, LLM. Called to Bar, Gray's Inn, 1955. Army Legal Services, BAOR: Staff Captain, 1956, Major, 1958. Private practice as barrister on SE Circuit, 1963–75. Recreations: gardening, sailing, swimming. Address: Thames Magistrates' Court, 58 Bow Road, E3 4DJ.
*Died 10 Sept. 1990.*

CANHAM, Erwin Dain; Editor in Chief, The Christian Science Monitor, 1964–74, then Editor Emeritus; President of The Mother Church, The First Church of Christ, Scientist, in Boston, 1966; b 13 Feb. 1904; s of Vincent Walter Canham and Elizabeth May Gowell; m 1st, 1930, Thelma Whitman Hart; two d; 2nd, 1968, Patience Mary, yr d of Lt-Col Robson Daltry, Bexhill-on-Sea. Educ: Bates Coll.; Oxford Univ. (Rhodes Scholar). Reporter, The Christian Science Monitor, 1925; covered League of Nations Assembly, Geneva, 1926–28; Correspondent at League of Nations, Geneva, 1930–32; Chief of Monitor's Washington Bureau, 1932; General News Editor in Boston, 1939; Managing Editor, 1942–45; Editor, 1945–64; Chm. Board of Directors, Federal Reserve Bank of Boston, 1963, 1964, 1965, 1966, 1967. Presidential Commission: Plebiscite Comr, N Mariana Is, April–June 1975; Resident Comr, N Mariana Is, 1976–78. Awarded numerous hon. degrees by universities and colleges in the USA, from 1946 onwards. Officer, Order of Southern Cross (Brazil), 1951; Commander, Order of Orange-Nassau (Netherlands), 1952; Order of George I (Greece), 1954; Officier, Légion d'Honneur (France), 1958 (Chevalier, 1946); Grand Distinguished Service Cross of Order of Merit (German Federal Republic), 1960; Hon. Comdr, Order of British Empire (CBE), 1964. Publications: Awakening: The World at Mid-Century, 1951; New Frontiers for Freedom, 1954; Commitment to Freedom: The Story of the Christian Science Monitor, 1958; Man's Great Future, 1959. Co-author, The Christian Science Way of Life, 1962. Address: One Norway Street, Boston, Mass 02115, USA. T: 262-2300; (home) Box 229, Capitol Hill, Saipan, North Mariana Islands 96950. Clubs: Gridiron (Washington, DC); Tavern, Harvard, Saturday (Boston).
*Died 3 Jan. 1982.*

CANN, Robert John, MS London, FRCS; Surgeon Emeritus, Ear, Nose and Throat Department, Guy's Hospital (Surgeon, 1938–66); formerly Consulting Ear, Nose and Throat Surgeon, Caterham District Hospital and East Surrey Hospital, Redhill; b Wimbledon, 2 Feb. 1901; e s of Frederick Robert Cann; m 1929, Gwendolen Chambers; one s two d. Educ: Richmond County Sch.; Guy's Hospital Med. Sch.; Bordeaux Univ. MRCS, LRCP 1924; MB, BS 1926; MS (Gold Medal, Lond.) 1930; FRCS 1949. Ear, Nose and Throat Dept, Guy's Hospital: Chief Clinical Asst and Registrar, 1926; Asst Surgeon, 1934; Mem., Medical Staff Cttee, 1934–66 (Chm., 1961–66). Out Patient and Statistical Registrar, Central London ENT Hosp., 1926–34; Otologist to LCC Fever Hospitals, 1934–39; formerly Consulting Surgeon ENT: Evelina Hosp. for Children; Wimbledon Hosp.; Bromley Hosp.; St Helier Hosp.; EMS. Late Examiner, ENT: Univ. of London; RCS; RCP. Member: Bd of Governors, Guy's Hosp., 1960–74; Council of Governors, Guy's Hosp. Med. Sch., 1961–80 (Chm., 1968–74). Mem., Visiting Assoc. of ENT Surgeons of GB, 1947–66 (Pres., 1962). FRSM (Pres. Laryngology Section, 1957). Liveryman, Worshipful Soc. of Apothecaries; Freeman, City of London. Publications: Endoscopic Methods; Heredity of Deafness; Report on Diphtheria Carriers, etc. Recreations: collecting English literature, producing colour in a garden. Address: Cairngorm, North Street, South Petherton, Somerset. T: South Petherton 40881. Club: Athenæum.
*Died 17 Feb. 1983.*

CANNING, Victor; author; b 16 June 1911; m 1934, Phyllis McEwen; two d; m 1976, Mrs Adria Irving Bell. Major, RA, 1940–46. Publications: Mr Finchley Discovers His England, 1934; The Chasm, 1947; Golden Salamander, 1948; Forest of Eyes, 1949; Venetian Bird, 1951; House of the Seven Flies, 1952; Man from the "Turkish Slave", 1953; Castle Minerva, 1954; His Bones are Coral, 1955; The Hidden Face, 1956; Manasco Road, 1957; The Dragon Tree, 1958; Young Man on a Bicycle and other short stories, 1959; The Burning Eye, 1960; A Delivery of Furies, 1961; Black Flamingo, 1962; The Limbo Line, 1963; The Scorpio Letters, 1964; The Whip Hand, 1965; Doubled in Diamonds, 1966; The Python Project, 1967; The Melting Man, 1968; Queen's Pawn, 1969; The Great Affair, 1970; Firecrest, 1971; The Runaways, 1972; The Rainbird Pattern, 1972; Flight of the Grey Goose, 1973; The Finger of Saturn, 1973; The Painted Tent, 1974; The Mask of Memory, 1974; The Kingsford Mark, 1975; The Crimson Chalice, 1976; The Doomsday Carrier, 1976; The Circle of the Gods, 1977; The Immortal Wound, 1978; Birdcage, 1978; The Satan Sampler, 1979; Fall from Grace, 1980; The Boy on Platform One, 1981; Vanishing Point, 1982; Raven's Wind, 1983; Birds of a Feather, 1985. Recreations: fishing, golf. Address: The Thatched Cottage, Ewen, near Cirencester, Glos

GL7 6BU. T: Kemble 350. Club: Flyfishers'.
*Died 21 Feb. 1986.*

CANNON, Air Vice-Marshal Leslie William, CB 1952; CBE 1945; retired; b 9 April 1904; s of late Captain W. E. Cannon, Beds, and Herts Regiment, and of Cathleen Mary (née Jackson), Bedford; m 1930, Beryl (née Heyworth). Educ: Hertford Grammar Sch.; RAF Coll., Cranwell. RAF boy mechanic, 1920–23; Officer Cadet, 1923–25; Pilot Officer, No 2 (AC) Squadron, 1925–27; Flying Officer: No 441 Flight Fleet Air Arm, China Station, 1927; No 2 (AC) Squadron, 1928; Flying Instructor RAF Coll., Cranwell, 1929; F/O and Flight-Lt: Officer Engr. Course, RAF Henlow, 1929–31; Flight-Lt: Engr. Officer RAFMT Depôt, Shrewsbury, 1931–32 and RAF Coll., Cranwell, 1932–33; Engr. SO, Air HQ, India, 1933–35; Flight Comdr No 60 (B) Squdn, Kohat, India, 1935–37 (despatches); Sqdn Ldr: OC No 5 (AC) Sqdn, India, 1937; Personnel SO, HQ Training Command, 1938; Student RAF Staff Coll., Andover, 1939. Served War of 1939–45 (despatches thrice, CBE, American Silver Star): Staff Officer Directorate of Operations, Air Ministry, 1939–40; Wing Comdr: Engr. SO, HQ Bomber Command, 1940; Chief Technical Officer, No. 21 Operational Training Unit, 1941; Group Captain: Directing SO RAF Staff Coll., 1942; OC Bomber Stations in No 2 (B) Group, 1942–43. Part of 2nd TAF (England, France, Belgium, Germany); GC and Air Commodore: AO i/c Admin. HQ No 2 (B) Group, 1943–46; AOC No 85 Group, Hamburg, 1946; idc, 1947; Asst Comdt and Comdt, RAF Staff Coll., Andover, 1948–49; Director of Organisation (Establishments), 1949–51; Commander-in-Chief, Royal Pakistan Air Force, 1951–55; Director-General of Organisation, Dec. 1955–Nov. 1958, retired. At CRO, 1959. Rolls-Royce Senior Representative, India, 1960–65. Recreations: represented RAF at athletics, boxing, pistol shooting. Address: 6 Stockwells, Berry Hill, Taplow, Maidenhead, Berks SL6 0DB. T: Maidenhead 30684. Clubs: Royal Air Force, Victory Services; Phyllis Court (Henley-on-Thames).
*Died 27 Jan. 1986.*

CANT, Rev. Canon Reginald Edward; Canon and Chancellor of York Minster, 1957–81, now Canon Emeritus; b 1 May 1914; 2nd s of late Samuel Reginald Cant; unmarried. Educ: Sir Joseph Williamson's Sch., Rochester; CCC, Cambridge; Cuddesdon Theological Coll. Asst Curate, St Mary's, Portsea, 1938–41; Vice-Principal, Edinburgh Theological Coll., 1941–46; Lecturer, Univ. of Durham, 1946–52 (Vice-Principal, St Chad's Coll. from 1949); Vicar, St Mary's the Less, Cambridge, 1952–57. Publications: Christian Prayer, 1961; part-author, The Churchman's Companion, 1964; (ed jtly) A History of York Minster, 1977. Address: 7 Sykes Close, St Olave's Road, York YO3 6HZ. T: York 23328. Clubs: Royal Commonwealth Society; Yorkshire (York).
*Died 21 May 1987.*

CAPOTE, Truman; author; b New Orleans, USA, 30 Sept. 1924; s of Joseph G. Capote and Nina (née Faulk). Educ: St John's Academy and Greenwich High School (New York). O. Henry Memorial Award for short story, 1946; Creative Writing Award, Nat. Inst. of Arts and Letters, 1959. Publications: Other Voices, Other Rooms (novel), 1948; Tree of Night (short stories), 1949; Observations, 1949; Local Color (travel essays), 1950; The Grass Harp (novel), 1951 (dramatised, 1953); The Muses are Heard (essay), 1956; Breakfast at Tiffany's (short stories), 1958; Selected Writings, 1964; In Cold Blood, 1966; A Christmas Memory, 1966; (with H. Arlen), House of Flowers, 1968; The Thanksgiving Visitor, 1969; The Dogs Bark, 1973; Music for Chameleons, 1981; short stories and articles (both fiction and non-fiction) contributed to numerous magazines. Address: c/o Random House Inc., 201 East 50th Street, New York, NY 10022, USA.
*Died 25 Aug. 1984.*

CARADON, Baron (Life Peer) cr 1964; Hugh Mackintosh Foot, PC 1968; GCMG 1957 (KCMG 1951; CMG 1946); KCVO 1953; OBE 1939; b 8 Oct. 1907; s of late Rt Hon. Isaac Foot, PC; m 1936, Florence Sylvia Tod (d 1985); three s one d. Educ: Leighton Park Sch., Reading; St John's Coll., Cambridge. Pres. Cambridge Union, 1929; Administrative Officer, Palestine Govt, 1929–37; attached to the Colonial Office, 1938–39; Asst British Resident, Trans-Jordan, 1939–42; British Mil. Administration, Cyrenaica, 1943; Colonial Secretary: Cyprus, 1943–45, Jamaica, 1945–47; Chief Sec., Nigeria, 1947–51. Acting Governor: Cyprus, 1944, Jamaica, Aug. 1945–Jan. 1946, Nigeria, 1949 and 1950. Capt.-Gen. and Gov.-in-Chief of Jamaica, 1951–57; Governor and Comdr-in-Chief, Cyprus, Dec. 1957–60; Ambassador and Adviser in the UK Mission to the UN and UK representative on Trusteeship Council, 1961–62, resigned; Minister of State for Foreign and Commonwealth Affairs and Perm. UK Rep. at the UN, 1964–70. Consultant, Special Fund of the United Nations, 1963–64. Mem., UN Expert Group on South Africa, 1964; Consultant to UN Develt Programme, 1971–75. Visiting Fellow: Princeton, Harvard and Georgetown Univs, 1979. KStJ 1952. Hon. Fellow, St John's Coll., Cambridge, 1960. Publication: A Start in Freedom, 1964. Address: House of Lords, SW1; 203 Drake House, Dolphin Square, SW1.
*Died 5 Sept. 1990.*

**CARD, Wilfrid Ingram,** MD, FRCP; Professor Emeritus, University of Glasgow; Diagnostic Methodology Research Unit, Southern General Hospital, Glasgow; *b* 13 April 1908; *e s* of Henry Charles Card; *m* 1934, Hilda Margaret Brigstocke Frere (*d* 1975); one *s* two *d. Educ:* Tonbridge Sch.; St Thomas's Hospital Medical Sch. MB, BS, 1931; MD Lond. 1933; MRCP 1934; FRCP 1944, FRCPE 1953, FRCPGlas 1967. Formerly: Beit Research Fellow; Physician to Out-Patients, St Thomas' Hospital, 1939–48. Physician in Charge, Gastro-intestinal Unit, Western General Hospital, Edinburgh; Reader in Medicine, Edinburgh Univ., 1948–66; Prof. of Medicine in relation to Mathematics and Computing, Univ. of Glasgow, 1966–74; Physician to HM the Queen in Scotland, 1965–75. Member: Association of Physicians of GB; Scottish Soc. of Experimental Medicine. *Publications:* Diseases of the Digestive System; (ed) Modern Trends in Gastro-Enterology, Vols 3 and 4; contrib. to: Principles and Practice of Medicine; articles on gastro-enterological subjects in Gut, Gastro-enterology, and articles relating mathematical methods to medicine in Mathematical Biosciences, Methods of Information in Medicine, etc. *Recreation:* sailing. *Address:* 10 Bowmont Gardens, Glasgow G12 9LW. *Club:* Savile.
*Died 12 Jan.* 1985.

**CARDEW, Michael Ambrose,** CBE 1981 (MBE 1965); potter, since 1923; *b* 26 May 1901; *s* of Arthur Cardew and Alexandra Rhoda (*née* Kitchin); *m* 1933, Mary-Ellen Baron Russell; two *s* (and one *s* decd). *Educ:* King's College Sch., Wimbledon; Exeter Coll., Oxford (BA (Lit. Hum.) 1923). Apprentice at Leach Pottery, St Ives, Cornwall, 1923–26; founded: Winchcombe Pottery, Glos, 1926; Wenford Bridge Pottery, Cornwall, 1939; Ceramist, Achimota Coll., Ghana, W Africa, 1942; founded Volta Pottery, Vume, Ghana, 1945; Pottery Officer, Nigeria, 1950–65; Vis. Lectr, Univ. of New South Wales, 1968; Workshops and Lectures: New Zealand, 1968; USA and Canada, 1967, 1971, 1972, 1976, 1978, 1980, 1981; Lectures, Nigeria and Ghana, 1973; Film (with A. Hallum), 1973. Hon. Dr RCA, 1982. *Publications:* Pioneer Pottery, 1969, (New York 1971); contribs to Pottery Qly, Ceramic Rev., Studio Potter (USA), Ceramics Monthly (USA). *Recreation:* writing. *Address:* Wenford Bridge Pottery, St Breward, Bodmin, Cornwall. *T:* Bodmin 850471.
*Died 11 Feb.* 1983.

**CARDIFF, Brig. Ereld Boteler Wingfield,** CB 1963; CBE 1958 (OBE 1943); *b* 5 March 1909; *m* 1932, Margaret Evelyn, *d* of late Major M. E. W. Pope, Ashwicke Hall, Marshfield; two *d. Educ:* Eton, 2nd Lieut, Scots Guards, 1930. Served War of 1939–45: (despatches thrice); 2nd Bn Scots Guards, 201 Guards Bde; 7th Armoured Div., Western Desert. Served Italy, France, Germany, Far ELF, 1955–58; SHAPE, 1958–63. Brig. 1958; retired, Nov. 1963. Chevalier, Order of Leopold, and Croix de Guerre, 1944. *Recreations:* shooting, fishing. *Address:* Easton Court, Ludlow, Salop. *T:* Tenbury Wells 475. *Clubs:* Cavalry and Guards, White's, Pratt's.
*Died 9 Oct.* 1988.

**CARDINALE, Most Rev. Hyginus Eugene,** DD, JCD; Papal Nuncio to Belgium and Luxembourg, since 1969 and to the European Economic Community, since 1970; Titular Archbishop of Nepte, since 1963; *b* 14 Oct. 1916; *s* of late Gaetano Cardinale and Uliana Cimino Cardinale. *Educ:* St Agnes Academy, Coll. Point, USA; Pontifical Roman Seminary, Rome; St Louis Theological Faculty, Naples; Pontifical Ecclesiastical Academy, Rome. Sec. of Apostolic Delegation in Egypt, Palestine, Transjordan and Cyprus, 1946–49; Auditor of Apostolic Internunciature to Egypt, 1949–52; Counsellor of Nunciature, 1952–61; Chief of Protocol of the Secretariat of State, 1961–63; Apostolic Delegate to Great Britain, Gibraltar, Malta and Bermuda, 1963–69; Special Envoy of the Holy See to the Council of Europe (Strasbourg), 1970–74. Under-Sec. of Techn. Organiz. Commn of Ecumenical Vatican Council II; Ecumenical Council Expert. Doctor of Theology, Canon Law; Diplomatic Sciences; Doctor (*hc*) Belles Lettres and Philosophy. Holds Grand Cross and is Knight Comdr in many orders. *Publications:* Le Saint-Siège et la Diplomatie, 1962; Chiesa e Stato negli Stati Uniti, 1958; La Santa Sede e il Diritto Consolare, 1963; Religious Tolerance, Freedom and Inter-Group Relations, 1966; Signs of the Times and Ecumenical Aspirations, 1967; The Unity of the Church, 1968; The Holy See and the International Order, 1976; Orders of Knighthood, Awards and the Holy See, 1983; contrib. to The Vatican and World Peace, 1969. *Address:* Avenue des Franciscains 9, 1150 Brussels, Belgium. *Died 24 March* 1983.

**CARDWELL, Sir David,** KCB 1981 (CB 1974); Chief of Defence Procurement, Ministry of Defence, since 1980; *b* 27 Nov. 1920; *yr s* of George Cardwell; *m* 1948, Eileen Tonkin, *d* of late Dr F. J. Kitt; one *s* one *d. Educ:* Dulwich Coll.; City and Guilds Coll., London Univ. BSc (Eng.) London. Royal Aircraft Estab., 1942–51; Min. of Supply Headquarters, 1951–56; Military Vehicles and Engrg Estab. (formerly Fighting Vehicles Research and Development Estab.), 1956–76, Dir, 1967–76; Dep. Controller, Estabts and Res. B, and Chief Scientist (Army), and Mem. Army Bd, MoD, 1976–78. Dir, AWRE, MoD, 1978–80. Imperial Defence Coll., 1965. CEng, FCGI, FIMechE, FRAeS; FEng 1978. *Recreation:* gardening.

*Address:* Chief of Defence Procurement, Ministry of Defence, Main Building, Whitehall, SW1. *Club:* Athenæum.
*Died 19 June* 1982.

**CAREW, Major Robert John Henry,** MC; JP, DL; *b* 7 June 1888; *s* of late Col R. T. Carew, DL, of Ballinamona Park, Waterford, and Constance, *d* of Maj.-Gen. William Creagh; *m* 1st, 1915, Leila Vernon (*d* 1934), *d* of late Sir Arthur V. Macan; 2nd, 1936, Dorothea Petrie (*d* 1968), *d* of late Col G. R. Townshend, RA; one *d. Educ:* Marlborough Coll.; RMC Sandhurst. Joined Royal Dublin Fus, 1908; served European War as Staff Captain and DAQMG; retired, 1920. *Recreations:* mechanical work; was Hon. Sec. of the Waterford Hunt, 1926–33. *Address:* Ballinamona Park, Waterford. *T:* Waterford 74429. *Club:* Army and Navy.
*Died 15 Nov.* 1982.

**CAREW, William Desmond;** *b* Sligo, Ireland, 19 Nov. 1899; *s* of Dr W. K. Carew, Colonial Medical Service; unmarried. *Educ:* Clongowes Wood Coll., Ireland; Trinity College, Dublin. 2nd Lieut Duke of Connaught's Own Lancers, Indian Army. Joined Colonial Service, 1921, and served as follows: Fiji, 1921–34; New Hebrides, 1935–40; Malaya, 1941–45 (interned by Japanese at Singapore, 1942–45); Nigeria, 1947; Fiji, 1948. Indian Gen. Service Medal, Bar 1919, Afghanistan Campaign. Puisne Judge, Supreme Court of Fiji, and Chief Justice of Tonga, 1948–55; retired, 1955. Deputy Administrator of Martial Law, Singapore, 1942. Appointed Commissioner to review salaries of Fiji Civil Service and Police Force, 1956; Judge, Court of First Instance, Gibraltar, 1961, retd, 1963. *Recreations:* fishing, golf. *Address:* 7 Donald Lane, Cambridge, New Zealand.
*Died 1 March* 1981.

**CAREW, William James,** CBE 1937; Retired as Clerk of the Executive Council and Deputy Minister of Provincial Affairs, Newfoundland; *b* 28 Dec. 1890; *s* of late James and Johanna Carew; *m* 1920, Mary Florence Channing (decd); one *s* (Titular Archbishop of Telde; Apostolic Pro-Nuncio to Japan) three *d. Educ:* St Patrick's Hall (Christian Brothers), St John's, Newfoundland. Newspaper work, 1908–09; staff of Prime Minister's Office, 1909; Sec., 1914–34; acted as Sec. to Newfoundland Delegate to Peace Conference, 1919; Sec. of Newfoundland Delegation to Imperial Conference, 1923, 1926, 1930; Deputy Min. for External Affairs, 1932; Sec. Newfoundland Delegation to Imperial Economic Conference, Ottawa, 1932; Sec. Cttee for Celebration in Newfoundland of Coronation of King George VI, 1937; Sec. Royal Visit Cttees on occasion of visit of King George VI and Queen Elizabeth to Newfoundland, 1939. Hon LLD Newfoundland, 1985. Commemorative Medals of the Royal Jubilee, 1935, the Coronation, 1937 and the Coronation, 1953. Knight Commander, Order of St Sylvester, 1976. *Address:* Apartment C, 1-A King's Bridge Court, St John's, Newfoundland A1C 2R1, Canada.
*Died 5 April* 1990.

**CAREY, Chapple G.;** *see* Gill-Carey.

**CAREY, Denis;** producer and actor; *b* London, 3 Aug. 1909; *s* of William Denis Carey and May (*née* Wilkinson); *m* Yvonne Coulette. *Educ:* St Paul's Sch.; Trinity Coll., Dublin. First appearance as Micky in The Great Big World, Royal Court, 1921; subseq. appeared in Dublin, 1929–34, London and New York, 1935–39; Pilgrim Players, 1940–43; Glasgow Citizens' Theatre, 1943–45; Arts Council Theatre, Coventry, 1945–46; in Galway Handicap, Men without Shadows, Lyric Hammersmith, 1947. First production, Happy as Larry, Mercury, later Criterion, 1947; Georgia Story, The Playboy of the Western World, London, 1948; Assoc. Producer, Arts Theatre, Salisbury, 1948; Dir, Bristol Old Vic Company, 1949–54; London and other productions include: Two Gentlemen of Verona (from Bristol), An Italian Straw Hat, Old Vic, 1952; Henry V (from Bristol), Old Vic, 1953; The Merchant of Venice, Stratford-on-Avon, 1953; Twelfth Night, The Taming of the Shrew, Old Vic, 1954; Salad Days (from Bristol), Vaudeville, 1954; Twelfth Night, Théatre Nat. de Belgique, Brussels, 1954; A Kind of Folly, Duchess, 1955; Follow That Girl, Vaudeville, 1960; Twelfth Night, Regent's Park, 1962. First Director, American Shakespeare Theatre, Stratford, Conn., 1955; prod Julius Cæsar, The Tempest. Director: Bristol Old Vic tour (British Council), India, Pakistan, Ceylon, 1963; The Golden Rivet, Phœnix Theatre, Dublin, 1964; Armstrong's Last Good-Night, Citizen Theatre, Glasgow, 1964; The Saints Go Cycling, Dublin Festival, 1965; African tour for British Council, 1964–65; Juno and the Paycock, Gaiety Theatre, Dublin, 1966; Hamlet, Dubrovnik Festival, Homecoming, Atelje 212, Belgrade, 1967–69; Hamlet, Kentner Theatre, Istanbul, 1968; Troilus and Cressida, Athens, USA 1969; Androcles and the Lion, Stanford, USA, 1969; Julius Caesar, Kano, Nigeria, 1974–75. Played: Teleyegin in Uncle Vanya, Royal Court, 1970; Egeus and Quince in RSC world tour of A Midsummer Night's Dream, 1972–73; Gunga Din in Chez Nous, Globe, 1974; Da in Da, Liverpool Playhouse, 1975. *Recreations:* walking and gardening. *Address:* c/o Vernon Conway, 19 London Street, Paddington, W2 1HL.
*Died 28 Sept.* 1986.

**CAREY, Lionel Mohun,** TD, MA; JP; Headmaster of Bromsgrove School, 1953–71; *b* 27 Jan. 1911; 4th *s* of late G. M. Carey; *m* 1943, Mary Elizabeth Auld, MBE; two *s. Educ:* Sherborne Sch.; Corpus Christi Coll., Cambridge. Teaching Diploma Institute of Education, London, 1934. Assistant Master, Bolton Sch., Lancs., 1934–37; Christ's Hospital, 1937–53, Housemaster 1940–53. JP Sherborne. *Recreations:* walking, gardening, people, contemplation of eternity. *Address:* Westbury Cottage, Sherborne, Dorset.
*Died 5 June* 1988.

**CAREY, Very Rev. Michael Sausmarez;** Dean of Ely, 1970–82; *b* 7 Dec. 1913; *s* of Rev. Christopher Sausmarez and Jane Robinson Carey; *m* 1945, Muriel Anne Gibbs; one *s* one *d. Educ:* Haileybury Coll.; Keble Coll., Oxford (MA 1941). Ordained, 1939, Curate St John's Waterloo Rd, SE1; Chaplain Cuddesdon Coll., 1941–43; Mission Priest, Gambia, 1943–44; Rector of Hunsdon, Herts, 1945–51; Rector of Botley, Hants, 1951–62; Archdeacon of Ely, 1962–70, and Rector of St Botolph's, Cambridge, 1965–70. Exam. Chap. to Bp of Portsmouth, 1953–59. Hon. Canon, Portsmouth, 1961–62. MA Cantab Incorp. 1967. *Publication:* The Giver of Life, 1979. *Recreations:* music, painting, golf. *Address:* 33 Northwold, Ely, Cambs CB6 1BG. *Died 29 Oct.* 1985.

**CAREY EVANS, Lady Olwen (Elizabeth),** DBE 1969; *b* 3 April 1892; *d* of 1st Earl Lloyd-George of Dwyfor, PC, OM, and Margaret, GBE, *d* of Richard Owen, Mynydd Ednyfed, Criccieth; *m* 1917, Sir Thomas John Carey Evans, MC, FRCS (*d* 1947); two *s* two *d. Publication:* Lloyd George was My Father, 1985. *Address:* Eisteddfa, Criccieth, Gwynedd. *Died 2 March* 1990.

**CARGILL, Sir (Ian) Peter (Macgillivray),** Kt 1981; MBE 1942; Senior Vice President, International Bank for Reconstruction and Development (World Bank), 1978–80; *b* 29 Sept. 1915; *s* of William Macgillivray and Ethel Mary Chestney Cargill; m. 1st, 1939, Margaret Freeling (marr. diss. 1945); one *s*; 2nd, 1951, Inge Haure-Petersen (*d* 1965); 3rd, 1978, Margaret Eileen Gonzalez. *Educ:* Malvern Coll.; Corpus Christi Coll., Oxford. Indian CS, 1938–47; Colonial Office, 1948–50; HM Treasury, 1950–52; IBRD, 1952–80. *Recreation:* golf. *Address:* 2727 31st Street, NW, Washington, DC 20008, USA. *Clubs:* Oriental, Travellers'; F Street (Washington, DC). *Died 10 July* 1981.

**CARLESTON, Hadden Hamilton,** CIE 1947; OBE 1944; *b* Pretoria, SA, 25 July 1904; *m* 1946, Eirene Leslie, *d* of Rev. H. L. Stevens, Torquay, S Devon; two *s* one *d. Educ:* St Olave's Sch., Southwark; Trinity Hall, Cambridge (MA). Indian Civil Service, 1927–47; Dist Magistrate of Civil and Military Station, Bangalore, 1939–43, and of various districts in Madras Presidency, including Vizagapatam, 1944–46, and The Nilgiris, 1947. Civil Liaison Officer with 19th and 25th Indian Inf. Divs, 1944. Sec. of St Cuthbert's Soc., Univ. of Durham, 1948–52; Admin. Sec., Cambridge Univ. Sch. of Veterinary Medicine, 1952–71. *Address:* Selborne, Cae Mair, Beaumaris, Gwynedd. *T:* Beaumaris 810586.
*Died 29 Dec.* 1986.

**CARLISLE, Kenneth Ralph Malcolm,** TD; *b* 28 March 1908; *s* of late Kenneth Methven Carlisle and Minnie Marie Donner; *m* 1938, Hon. Elizabeth Mary McLaren, *d* of 2nd Baron Aberconway; one *s* three *d. Educ:* Harrow; Magdalen Coll., Oxford (BA). Binder, Hamlyn & Co., Chartered Accountants, 1931–32; Liebig's Extract of Meat Co. Ltd, Argentina, Paraguay, Uruguay, 1933–34; Liebig's Companies on Continent of Europe, 1935–37. Major, Rifle Bde, 1939–45. Distinguished Service Medal (Greece); Chevalier de l'Ordre de Leopold (Belgium), 1960. *Recreation:* reading. *Address:* (private) Laurie House, 16 Airlie Gardens, W8 7AW. *T:* 01-229 1714; Wyken Hall, Stanton, Bury St Edmunds, Suffolk IP31 2DW. *Club:* Boodle's. *Died 23 July* 1983.

**CARLYON, Thomas Symington,** CMG 1968; OBE 1940; Managing Director, T. S. Carlyon & Co. Pty Ltd, since 1950; *b* Ballarat, 27 April 1902; *s* of late T. S. Carlyon, Melbourne; *m* 1950, Marie Pichoir, *d* of Edward de Launay; one *s* one *d* (by a previous *m*). *Educ:* Geelong Grammar Sch. Hotel Training, Bellevue Stratford Hotel, USA; General Manager, Hotel Australia, Sydney, 1939–40 and 1946. Member Housing and Catering Cttee, 1956 Olympic Games. Served RAAF, 1940–45 (Sqdn Leader). *Recreations:* golf, racing. *Address:* 82/390 Toorak Road, South Yarra, Vic. 3141, Australia. *Clubs:* Melbourne Cricket, All Racing (Victoria); Metropolitan Golf. *Died 14 March* 1982.

**CARMICHAEL, Dr James Armstrong Gordon,** CB 1978; Chief Medical Adviser (Social Security), Department of Health and Social Security, 1973–78; *b* 28 July 1913; 2nd *s* of Dr Donald Gordon Carmichael and Eileen Mona Carmichael; *m* 1936, Nina Betty Ashton (*née* Heape) (*d* 1981); two *s. Educ:* Epsom Coll.; Guy's Hospital. FRCP, MRCS. Commnd RAMC, 1935; Consultant Physician, MELF, 1953–55; Consultant Physician and Prof. of Tropical Medicine, Royal Army Medical Coll., 1957–58, retd; Hon. Colonel 1958. MO 1958, SMO 1965, Min. of Pensions and Nat. Insce; PMO, Min. of Social Security, 1967; Dep. Chief Medical Advr, DHSS, 1971–73. *Publications:* contrib. to BMJ, Jl of RAMC. *Address:* Rossett Green Nursing Home, Rossett Green Lane, Harrogate, North Yorks HG2 9LL. *T:* Harrogate 873431.
*Died 28 Jan.* 1990.

**CARNARVON, 6th Earl of,** *cr* 1793; **Henry George Alfred Marius Victor Francis Herbert;** Baron Porchester, 1780; Lieut-Colonel 7th Hussars; *b* 7 Nov. 1898; *o s* of 5th Earl and Almina (who *m* 2nd, 1923, Lieut-Colonel I. O. Dennistoun, MVO; she *d* 1969), *d* of late Frederick C. Wombwell; *S* father, 1923; *m* 1st, 1922, Catherine (who obtained a divorce, 1936, and *m* 2nd, 1938, Geoffrey Grenfell (decd), and *m* 3rd, 1950, D. Momand), *d* of late J. Wendell, New York, and Mrs Wendell, Sandridgebury, Sandridge, Herts; one *s* one *d*; 2nd, 1939, Ottilie (marr. diss.), *d* of Eugene Losch, Vienna. *Educ:* Eton. Owns about 4000 acres. *Publications:* No Regrets (memoirs), 1976; Ermine Tales, 1980. *Heir:* s Lord Porchester, KCVO, KBE. *Recreations:* racing and shooting. *Address:* Highclere Castle, near Newbury, Berks. *TA:* Carnarvon Highclere. *T:* Highclere 253204. *Club:* White's. *Died 22 Sept.* 1987.

**CARNE, Colonel James Power,** VC 1953; DSO 1951; DL; *b* 11 April 1906; *s* of late G. N. Carne, Garras, Falmouth; *m* 1946, Mrs Jean Gibson, *widow* of Lt-Col J. T. Gibson, DSO, The Welch Regt; one *step s. Educ:* Imperial Service Coll.; Royal Military Coll., Sandhurst. Commissioned Gloucestershire Regt, 1925; seconded King's African Rifles, 1930–36; Adjutant 1st Bn Gloucestershire Regt, 1937–40. Served War of 1939–45: with KAR and on Staff, Madagascar, 1942, Burma, 1944; CO 6th and 26th Bns KAR, 1943–46. CO 5th Bn (TA) 1947–50, 1st Bn Gloucestershire Regt, 1950–51. Served Korean War of 1950–53 (DSO, VC). Freedom of Gloucester, 1953; Freedom of Falmouth, 1954. DSC (US), 1953. DL County of Gloucester, 1960. *Recreation:* fishing.
*Died 19 April* 1986.

**CARNER, Dr Mosco;** Music Critic of The Times, 1961–69; Member of the BBC Score Reading Panel, 1944–72; *b* 15 Nov. 1904; *m* 1962, Dr Elisabeth Bateman (*d* 1970); *m* 1976, Hazel, *d* of late Mr and Mrs John Sebag-Montefiore. *Educ:* Vienna Univ. and Vienna Music Conservatory. Conductor at Danzig State Theatre, 1929–33. Resident in London since Autumn 1933, where active as conductor, musical author, critic and broadcaster. Music Critic of Time and Tide, 1949–62; Music Critic of The Evening News, 1957–61. Hon. Mem., The Critics' Circle, 1977. Puccini Prize, 1984. Silver Medal of the Italian Government, 1964. *Publications:* A Study of 20th-Century Harmony, 1942; Of Men and Music, 1944; The History of the Waltz, 1948; Puccini, A Critical Biography, 1958, 2nd rev. edn, 1974 (Ital. edn, 1961, Japanese edn 1968, French edn 1984); (ed) The Letters of Giacomo Puccini, 1974; Alban Berg: the man and his work, 1975, rev. and enlarged edn, 1983 (rev. French edn, 1979, Ital. edn, 1985); Madam Butterfly, 1979; Major and Minor, 1980; Hugo Wolf Songs, 1982; Tosca, 1985; *contribs to:* New Oxford History of Music, 1974; 6th edn of Grove's Dictionary of Music and Musicians; *symposia on:* Schubert, 1946; Schumann, 1952; The Concerto, 1952; Chamber Music, 1957; Choral Music, 1963. *Recreations:* reading, motoring and swimming. *Address:* 14 Elsworthy Road, NW3. *T:* 01–586 1553. *Died 3 Aug.* 1985.

**CARNEY, Most Rev. James F.,** DD; Archbishop of Vancouver (RC), since 1969; *b* Vancouver, BC, 28 June 1915. *Educ:* Vancouver College; St Joseph's Seminary, Edmonton, Alta. Ordained, 1942; Vicar-General and Domestic Prelate, 1964; Auxiliary Bishop of Vancouver, 1966. *Address:* 150 Robson Street, Vancouver, BC V6B 2A7, Canada. *T:* 683–0281. *Died 16 Sept.* 1990.

**CARNEY, Admiral Robert Bostwick,** Hon. CBE 1946; DSM (US), 1942 (and Gold Stars, 1944, 1946, 1955); and numerous other American and foreign decorations; United States Navy; retired; *b* Vallejo, California, 26 March 1895; *s* of Robert E. and Bertha Carney; *m* 1918, Grace Stone Craycroft, Maryland; one *s* one *d. Educ:* United States Naval Acad., Annapolis, Md (BS). Served European War, 1914–18; Gunnery and Torpedo Officer aboard USS Fanning in capture of Submarine U-58 off coast of Ireland; War of 1939–45; North Atlantic, 1941–42; Commanding Officer, USS Denver, serving in Pacific, 1942–43; Chief of Staff to Admiral William Halsey (Commander, S Pacific Force), 1943–45, participating in nine battle engagements. Deputy Chief of Naval Operations, 1946–50; President of US Naval Inst., 1950–51, 1954–56; Commander Second Fleet, 1950; Commander-in-Chief, United States Naval Forces, Eastern Atlantic and Mediterranean, 1950–52; Commander-in-Chief, Allied Forces, Southern Europe (North Atlantic Treaty Organisation), 1951–53; Chief of Naval Operations, 1953–55; retired 1955. Chm., Bath Iron Works (Ship Building), 1956–67. Hon. LLD, Loras Coll., 1955. *Publications:* various professional. *Recreations:* field sports, music. *Address:* 2801 New Mexico Avenue (NW), Washington, DC 20007, USA. *Clubs:* Chevy Chase Country, Alibi (Washington, DC); The Brook (NY).
*Died 25 June* 1990.

**CARNOCHAN, John Golder;** Lay Reporter, Town and Country Planning (Scotland) Act 1972, since 1972; *b* Old Kilpatrick, 12 Sept.

1910; *s* of N. and M. G. Carnochan; *m* 1938, Helen Dewar, *y d* of A. A. and A. Ferguson, Doune; one *s*. Chartered Accountant; Entered Ministry of Food, 1942; Dep. Accountant-General, 1948; Asst Secretary, 1949; Under-Secretary, Min. of Agriculture, Fisheries and Food, 1965–70. *Address:* Hillcrest, 14 Venachar Avenue, Callander, Perthshire FK17 8JQ. *Club:* Scottish Liberal (Edinburgh). *Died* 2 *Sept.* 1981.

**CARNOCK,** 3rd Baron, *cr* 1916, of Carnock; **Erskine Arthur Nicolson,** DSO 1919; JP; 13th Bt of Nova Scotia, *cr* 1637; Captain, RN, retired; *b* British Legation, Athens, 26 March 1884; 2nd *s* of 1st Lord Carnock and Mary Catherine (*d* 1951), *d* of Captain Arch. Rowan Hamilton, Killyleagh, Co. Down; *S* brother, 1952; *m* 1919, Katharine (*d* 1968), *e d* of 1st Baron Roborough; one *s* (and one *s* killed in action 1942; one *d* decd). *Educ:* HMS Britannia; RN Staff Coll., 1913. War Staff Officer to the Light Cruiser Forces, 1914–19 (DSO, Légion d'honneur, St Anne with Swords, Crown of Italy); retired list, 1924. *Recreation:* hunting. *Heir: s* Hon. David Henry Arthur Nicolson, *b* 10 July 1920. *Address:* Devonia House, Leg o' Mutton Corner, Yelverton, South Devon PL20 6DJ.
*Died* 2 *Oct.* 1982.

**CARÖE, Sir (Einar) Athelstan (Gordon),** Kt 1972; CBE 1958; President, Trustee Savings Banks, since 1976; Hon. President, EEC Savings Bank Group, since 1979 (Vice-Chairman, 1973–76; President and Chairman, 1976–78); Director, London Board, Norwich Union Group, 1968–78; Grain Merchant and Broker, W. S. Williamson and Co., Liverpool, 1935–73; Consul for Denmark, in Liverpool, 1931–73, also for Iceland, 1947–84; *b* 6 Oct. 1903; *s* of Johan Frederik Caröe and Eleanor Jane Alexandra Caröe (*née* Gordon); *m* 1st, 1934, Frances Mary Lyon (*d* 1947); two *s*; 2nd, 1952, Doreen Evelyn Jane Sandland; one *s* one *d*. *Educ:* Eton Coll. (King's Scholar); Trinity Coll., Cambridge (Scholar, BA). Chairman: Liverpool Savings Bank, 1947–48; Trustee Savings Banks Assoc., 1966–76 (Dep. 1951–66); Vice-Pres., National Savings Cttee, 1971–78. President, Liverpool Consular Corps, 1952; Chairman, Liverpool Chamber of Commerce, 1950–51. Pres., Minton Ltd, Stoke-on-Trent, 1970– (Chm. 1956–70); Chairman: Maritime Insurance Co. Ltd, Liverpool, 1951–68; Liverpool Corn Trade Assoc., 1963–67; Richards-Campbell Tiles Ltd, 1967–68. Pro-Chancellor, Liverpool Univ., 1966–75 (Dep. Treas., 1948–57; Treas., 1957–66; Pres., 1966–72); President, Lancashire County Lawn Tennis Assoc., 1953; Member Lawn Tennis Assoc. Council, 1954–66; President: Nat. Federation of Corn Trade Assocs, 1957–60; Internat. Savings Banks Inst., 1960–69 (Hon. Pres., 1969–). Hon. LLD, Liverpool, 1976. Officer, 1st Class, Order of Dannebrog, 1957 (Officer, 1945); Kt Commander, Order of Icelandic Falcon, 1974 (Officer 1958); Comdr, Order of Crown of Belgium, 1966; Comdr, Order of Leopold (Belgium), 1978. King Christian X Liberty Medal, 1946; Spanish Medal, Al Merito del Ahorro, 1973. *Recreations:* lawn tennis (Lancashire doubles champion, 1933); philately (Fellow RPS(L) 1939; Roll of Distinguished Philatelists, 1972). *Address:* Pedder's Wood, Scorton, near Preston, Lancs PR3 1BE. *T:* Garstang 4698. *Clubs:* British Pottery Manufacturers (Stoke-on-Trent) (Hon. Mem.); Liverpool Racquet Club.
*Died* 19 *April* 1988.

**CAROE, Sir Olaf (Kirkpatrick),** KCSI 1945 (CSI 1941); KCIE 1944 (CIE 1932); FRSL 1959; DLitt Oxon; late ICS and Officer Indian Political Service; Vice-President, Conservative Commonwealth Council, 1969 (Deputy Chairman, 1966–69); *b* 15 Nov. 1892; *e s* of late William Douglas Caroe and of Grace Desborough, *d* of John Rendall; *m* 1920, Frances Marion (Kaisar-i-Hind Gold Medal, 1947) (*d* 1969), *d* of late Rt Rev. A. G. Rawstorne, Bishop of Whalley; two *s*. *Educ:* Winchester; (Demy) Magdalen Coll., Oxford, Captain 4th Bn, The Queen's Regt (TF), 1914–19; entered ICS, 1919; served in Punjab till 1923, when posted to NW Frontier Province as Officer of Political Department; served as Deputy Commissioner, various Frontier Districts, including Peshawar, up to 1932; Chief Secretary to the Govt, of the NWFP, 1933–34; Deputy Secretary, Foreign and Political Dept, Government of India, 1934; officiated as Political Resident in the Persian Gulf, Resident in Waziristan, and as Agent to the Governor-General in Baluchistan, 1937–38 (despatches); Revenue Commissioner in Baluchistan, 1938–39; Secretary, External Affairs Dept, 1939–45; Governor North-West Frontier Province, India, 1947–47; left India Aug, 1947. Vice-Chairman Overseas League, 1951; visited US for British Information Services, 1952; first Pres., Tibet Soc. of the UK, 1959–77; Hon. Vice-Pres., RSAA; Lawrence of Arabia Meml Medal, Royal Soc. for Asian Affairs, 1973. *Publications:* Wells of Power, 1951; Soviet Empire, 1953 (republished 1966); The Pathans, 1958; From Nile to Indus (with Sir Thomas Rapp and Patrick Reid), 1960; Poems of Khushhal (with Sir Evelyn Howell), 1963; introd. new edn of Canbul, by Mountstuart Elphinstone, 1972; articles in The Round Table, Asian Affairs, and other journals. *Address:* Newham House, Steyning, Sussex. *T:* Steyning 812241. *Club:* Lansdowne.
*Died* 23 *Nov.* 1981.

**CARPENTER, John McG. K. K.;** *see* Kendall-Carpenter.

**CARPENTER, Trevor Charles;** Mail Consultant, British Caledonian Airways; *b* 23 March 1917; *s* of late Walter Edward Carpenter and Florence Jane Carpenter, Newport, Mon.; *m* 1940, Margaret Lilian, *d* of late Frederick James and May Ethel Day; one *s* five *d*. *Educ:* Alexandra Road Primary Sch., Newport; Newport High Sch. Exec. Officer, GPO, 1936; Higher Exec. Officer, 1947; Principal, 1951; Private Secretary to PMG, 1962; Dep. Director, Scotland, 1964; Director of Postal Personnel, GPO, 1967–70; Director of Posts, Scotland, 1970–72; Chm., Scottish Postal Bd, 1972–77. *Recreations:* Gaelic singing, watching Rugby football. *Address:* 26 Learmonth Terrace, Edinburgh EH4 1NZ. *T:* 031–332 8000.
*Died* 27 *Feb.* 1986.

**CARR, Sir Bernard;** *see* Carr, Sir F. B.

**CARR, Cyril Eric,** CBE 1980; Senior Partner, Cyril Carr & Carr, Solicitors, Liverpool, since 1970; Lord Mayor of Liverpool, since May 1981; *b* 19 July 1926; *s* of late Henry Carr and of Bertha Carr; *m* 1952, Hilary; one *s* one *d*. *Educ:* Liverpool Coll.; Clifton Coll.; Bishop Ridley Coll., Canada; Liverpool Univ. (LLB Hons 1950). Royal Signals, 1942–44 (Signalman). Qual. solicitor, 1951. Mem. Liverpool City Council (1st Liberal Mem. elected since 1939), 1962; Vice-Chm., Liberal Party Nat. Exec., 1968–72, Chm. of Liberal Party, 1972–73; Chm., Liberal Party Housing Panel, 1978–; Chm., Assoc. Liberal Councillors, 1971–73; contested Wavertree Div., 1964, 1966, 1970, Feb. 1974; Leader, Liberal Gp, Liverpool CC, 1962–75; Mem. Merseyside CC, 1973–77; 1st and only Chm., Liverpool Metrop. DC, 1973–74; Leader, Liverpool MDC, 1973–74, and Liverpool Met. City Council, 1974–75 (resigned leadership for health reasons). Pres., Liverpool Liberal Party; Pres.-elect for 1982–83, Liberal Party; Vice-Pres., Liberal Friends of Israel; Mem. NW Econ. Planning Council, 1973–78. Mem. Liverpool University Court and Council; Pres., Speke Boys' Club. FCIArb 1974. *Publication:* Let Every Englishman's Home be his Castle (with Andrew Ellis), 1978. *Recreations:* politics, Liverpool Football Club, good food and good conversation. *Address:* The Bridge, Ibbotsons Lane, Liverpool L17 1AN. *T:* 051-724 3101. *Clubs:* National Liberal; Racquets (Liverpool). *Died* 1 *Nov.* 1981.

**CARR, Denis Edward Bernard;** UK Permanent Delegate to UNESCO, since 1976, Minister since 1978; *b* 19 June 1920; *s* of Bernard J. Carr, art master and critic, and Violet M. Carr, Sheffield; *m* 1952, Josephine Pruden; two *s* one *d*. *Educ:* Mount St Mary's Coll.; Sheffield Univ.; Jesus Coll., Cambridge. Called to the Bar, Gray's Inn, 1958; called to NSW Bar, 1961. Served War, 1940–46: Captain RA; served UK, E Africa and SE Asia. HM Colonial Service, Uganda, 1946–63: Principal, Nsamizi Trng Centre, Entebbe, 1958–63; Principal, Min. of Overseas Develt, 1963–70; seconded to HM Diplomatic Service as First Sec. (Aid), Nairobi, 1970–75; Head, UN Dept, Min. of Overseas Develt, 1976; Leader, UK Delegn to Industrial Develt Bd, UNIDO, 1976. Languages: French, Swahili. *Recreations:* travel, walking, tennis. *Address:* c/o Lloyds Bank, Cox's & King's Branch, 6 Pall Mall, SW1Y 5NH. *Clubs:* Royal Over-Seas League; Nairobi (Kenya).
*Died* 10 *Jan.* 1981.

**CARR, Edward Hallett,** CBE 1920; FBA 1956; *b* 28 June 1892; *m* 1925, Anne Howe, widow, *d* of T. H. Ward; one *s*. *Educ:* Merchant Taylors' Sch., London; Trinity Coll., Cambridge. Temporary Clerk Foreign Office, 1916; attached to the British Delegation to the Peace Conference, 1919; Temporary Sec. at British Embassy, Paris, for work with the Conference of Ambassadors, 1920–21; 3rd Sec. and transferred to Foreign Office, 1922; 2nd Sec. and transferred to HM Legation at Riga, 1925; transferred to Foreign Office, 1929; Asst Adviser on League of Nations Affairs, 1930–33; First Sec., 1933; resigned, 1936; Wilson Prof. of International Politics, University Coll. of Wales, Aberystwyth, 1936–47. Director of Foreign Publicity, Min. of Information, Oct. 1939–April 1940. Asst Ed. of The Times, 1941–46. Tutor in Politics, Balliol Coll., Oxford, 1953–55; Fellow, Trinity Coll., Cambridge, 1955–; Hon. Fellow, Balliol Coll., Oxford, 1966. Hon. LittD: University of Manchester, 1964; University of Cambridge, 1967; University of Sussex, 1970; Hon. Dr of Law, University of Groningen, 1964. *Publications:* Dostoevsky, 1931; The Romantic Exiles, 1933; Karl Marx: A Study in Fanaticism, 1934; International Relations since the Peace Treaties, 1937; Michael Bakunin, 1937; The Twenty Years' Crisis, 1919–39, 1939; Britain: A Study of Foreign Policy from Versailles to the Outbreak of War, 1939; Conditions of Peace, 1942; Nationalism and After, 1945; The Soviet Impact on the Western World, 1946; Studies in Revolution, 1950; A History of Soviet Russia: The Bolshevik Revolution, 1917–23, Vol. I, 1950, Vol. II, 1952, Vol. III, 1953; The Interregnum, 1923-24, 1954; Socialism in One Country, 1924–26, Vol. I, 1958; Vol. II, 1959, Vol. III (in 2 parts), 1964; Foundation of a Planned Economy, 1926–29, Vol. I (in 2 parts, in collaboration with R. W. Davies), 1969, Vol. II, 1971, Vol. III, parts 1 and 2, 1976, part 3, 1978; German-Soviet Relations Between the Two World Wars, 1919–39, 1951; The New Society, 1951; What is

History?, 1961; 1917: Before and After, 1968; The Russian Revolution: Lenin to Stalin, 1979; From Napoleon to Stalin, and other essays, 1980. *Address:* Trinity College, Cambridge; Dales Barn, Barton, Cambs. *Died 3 Nov.* 1982.

**CARR, Sir (Frederick) Bernard,** Kt 1946; CMG 1944; *b* 5 April 1893; *s* of F. W. Carr; *m* 1933, Doreen Dadds; two *d*. *Educ:* Whitgift. TA Artists' Rifles and Middx Regt, 1911–18; seconded Royal West African Frontier Force, 1917–18; active service, Gibraltar, Egypt, France, East Africa. Colonial Administrative Service, 1919 (Nigeria); Chief Comr, Eastern Provinces, Nigeria, 1943; retired from Colonial Service, 1949. Chief Sec., Eritrea, 1949–50. *Address:* 5 Old Coast Guard Road, Sandbanks, Poole, Dorset BH13 7RL.
*Died 3 May* 1981.

**CARR, Henry Lambton,** CMG 1945; LVO 1957; retired 1961; *b* 28 Nov. 1899; *e s* of Archibald Lambton and Ella Carr, Archangel; *m* 1924, Luba (*d* 1975), *d* of John George Edmund Eveleigh, London; two *s*. *Educ:* Haileybury Coll. Served N Russian Exped. Force (2nd Lieut), 1919. Foreign Office, 1920. HBM Passport Control Officer for Finland, 1927–41; Attaché at British Legation, Stockholm, 1941–45; Foreign Office, 1945; First Sec., HM Embassy, Copenhagen, 1955; Foreign Office, 1958. Chevalier (First Grade) of Order of Dannebrog, Denmark, 1957. *Recreation:* walking. *Address:* Huntington House, Headley Road, Hindhead, Surrey GU26 6BG. *T:* Hindhead 4720; c/o Barclays Bank, East Grinstead, West Sussex. *Club:* Danish. *Died 19 March* 1988.

**CARR, Herbert Reginald Culling,** MA; Headmaster, The Grammar School, Harrogate, Yorks, 1934–60; retired; *b* 16 July 1896; *s* of late Reginald Childers Culling Carr, OBE (ICS), and Enid Agnes Kenney Herbert; *m* 1927, Evelyn Dorothy Ritchie; one *d*. *Educ:* St Paul's Sch.; Pembroke Coll., Oxford (Open Scholar). Hons Modern History (2nd Class); Diplomas in Educn and Econs. Asst Master, Alleyn's Sch., Dulwich, 1927–31; Headmaster, Penrith Grammar Sch., Cumberland, 1931–34. Sub-Lieut RNVR, 1915–19; Flt-Lieut RAFVR, 1940–44 (Africa Star). *Publications:* The Mountains of Snowdonia, 1925; The Irvine Diaries: the enigma of Everest 1924, 1979. *Recreation:* antiques. *Address:* c/o Michael O'Mahony & Partners, Solicitors, 8 Park Street, Cirencester, Glos. *Club:* Alpine.
*Died 23 April* 1986.

**CARR, Sir James (Henry Brownlow),** Kt 1982; Chairman: J. H. B. Carr Pty Ltd, since 1960; Australian Jockey Club, 1974–83 (Vice-Chairman, 1969–74); *b* 17 April 1913; *s* of James Carr and Jessie Amelia Carr; *m* 1943, Audrey Mathews; one *s* three *d*. *Educ:* Beecroft Grammar School, Sydney, Australia. Served War, 1st Armoured Div., AIF, 1941–43. Director, New South Wales Local Board, Colonial Mutual Life Assurance Soc. Ltd, 1972–83. Mem. Cttee, Australian Jockey Club, Sydney, 1955–; Australian Jockey Club Representative on Totalizator Agency Board, NSW, 1974–83. *Recreation:* racing. *Address:* Cherryford, Binda, NSW 2583, Australia. *T:* Binda 9 (048–3551). *Clubs:* Union, Royal Sydney Golf (Sydney). *Died 4 Aug.* 1984.

**CARR, Michael;** MP (Lab) Bootle, since May 1990; *b* 27 May 1947; *s* of Thomas and Sarah Carr; *m* 1970, Lyn Carr; three *s* one *d*. *Educ:* St Mary's Coll., Crosby. Stock controller, Liverpool, 1965–67; travelled abroad, 1967–68; factory worker, Fareham, 1968–71; wharfinger, Liverpool Docks, 1971–84; T&GWU Dist Officer, 1984–90. Mem. Exec., NW Lab. Pty, 1980–90; Secretary: Liverpool Dist Lab. Pty, 1987–89; Walton Constit. Lab. Pty, 1989–. Mem., Skelmersdale DC, 1981–82. *Recreation:* reading science fiction. *Address:* 19 Mercer Drive, Liverpool L4 4QQ. *T:* 051–207 2630. *Club:* Pirie Labour (Liverpool). *Died 20 July* 1990.

**CARR, Brig. William Greenwood,** CVO 1971; DSO 1941 and Bar, 1942; DL, JP; Lieutenant of the Queen's Bodyguard of the Yeomen of the Guard, 1970–71; *b* 10 March 1901; *s* of William Carr, DL, JP, Ditchingham Hall, Norfolk; *m* 1928, Donna Nennella, *d* of Général Count Salazar, via Umbria, Rome; one *d*. *Educ:* Eton; University Coll., Oxford. Commnd in 12th Royal Lancers, 1922; Capt. and Adjt, 1925; comdg: 4th Co. of London Yeomanry, 1939; Comdg 22nd Armoured Bde (8th Army), 1941, 4th Lt Armoured Bde, 1942; Comdg RACOCTU, Sandhurst, 1943; Brig. British Staff, GHQ, SW Pacific, 1944–45; retd 1946. Queen's Bodyguard Yeomen of the Guard: Exon, 1950; Ensign, 1954; Lieut, 1970; retired 1971. Represented England at Olympic Games (riding), 1936. JP Norfolk 1953, DL Norfolk 1961. *Recreations:* hunting, shooting, sailing. *Address:* Ditchingham Hall, Bungay, Suffolk NR35 2JU. *T:* Woodton 226. *Clubs:* Cavalry and Guards; Royal Yacht Squadron. *Died 27 Jan.* 1982.

**CARRERAS, Sir James,** KCVO 1980; Kt 1970; MBE 1944; Chairman, Hammer Film Productions, 1949–80; *b* 30 Jan. 1909; *s* of Henry and Dolores Carreras; *m* 1927, Vera St John (*d* 1986); one *s*. Chief Barker, Variety Club of GB, 1954–55; Pres., Variety Clubs Internat., 1961–63 (Chm. Bd for 11 yrs). Vice-Chm., Royal Naval Film Corp. for 22 yrs; Mem. Bd, Services Kinema Corp. for 12 yrs; Trustee Council, Cinema and Television Benevolent Fund for 4 yrs;

Chairman: Cinema Veterans, 1982–83; Friends of the Duke of Edinburgh Award for 15 yrs; Pres., London Fedn of Boys' Clubs for 5 yrs; Trustee: Police Dependants' Trust for 5 yrs; Bowles Outdoor Pursuits Centre. Grand Order of Civil Merit (Spain), 1974. *Recreation:* cooking. *Address:* Queen Anne Cottage, Friday Street, Henley-on-Thames, Oxon. *Died 9 June* 1990.

**CARRINGTON, Charles Edmund,** MC; writer and lecturer; *b* West Bromwich, 21 April 1897; *s* of late Very Rev. C. W. Carrington; *m* 1st, 1932, Cecil Grace MacGregor (marr. diss., 1954); one *d* decd; 2nd, 1955, Maysie Cuthbert Robertson (*d* 1983). *Educ:* Christ's Coll., New Zealand; Christ Church, Oxford. Enlisted, 1914; first commission, 1915; Capt. 5th Royal Warwickshire Regt, 1917; served in France and Italy (MC); Major TA, 1927. BA Oxford, 1921; MA 1929; MA Cambridge, 1929. Asst Master, Haileybury Coll., 1921–24 and 1926–29; Lectr, Pembroke Coll., Oxford, 1924–25; Educational Sec. to the Cambridge Univ. Press, 1929–54. Military service, 1939, France, 1940; Lt-Col Gen. Staff, 1941–45. Prof. of British Commonwealth Relations at Royal Inst. of Internat. Affairs, 1954–62; organised unofficial Commonwealth conferences, New Zealand, 1959, Nigeria, 1962; Visiting Prof., USA, 1964–65. Has served on: LCC Educn Cttee; Classical Assoc. Council; Publishers Assoc. Educational Group; Royal Commonwealth Soc. Council; Inter-Univ. Council; Overseas Migration Board, Islington Soc., etc; Chm., Shoreditch Housing Assoc., 1961–67. *Publications:* An Exposition of Empire, 1947; The British Overseas, 1950; Godley of Canterbury, 1951; Rudyard Kipling, 1955, rev. edn 1978; The Liquidation of the British Empire, 1961; Soldier from the Wars Returning, 1965, repr. 1984; (ed) The Complete Barrack-Room Ballads of Rudyard Kipling, 1973; Kipling's Horace, 1978; Soldier at Bomber Command, 1987; (with J. Hampden Jackson) A History of England, 1932; (under pen-name of Charles Edmonds) A Subaltern's War, 1929; T. E. Lawrence, 1935; contributor to: Camb. Hist. of the British Empire, 1959; An African Survey, 1957; Surveys of International Affairs, 1957–58 and 1959–60, etc. *Recreations:* historical studies, travel. *Address:* 31 Grange Road, N1 2NP. *T:* 071–354 2832. *Club:* Travellers'. *Died 21 June* 1990.

**CARRITT, (Hugh) David (Graham);** Director, Artemis SA, David Carritt Ltd, and other companies, since 1970; *b* 15 April 1927. *Educ:* Rugby; Christ Church, Oxford. Director, Christie's, 1964–70; with Artemis SA, and its subsidiaries, 1970–. *Publications:* numerous articles in Evening Standard (before 1961); occasional articles in Burlington Magazine. *Recreations:* gardening, pre-Romantic music. *Address:* 120 Mount Street, W1Y 5HB. *T:* 01-493 8529; 111 Manor Road, Deal, Kent. *Club:* Travellers'. *Died 3 Aug.* 1982.

**CARROLL, Madeleine;** screen, stage, and radio actress; *b* 26 Feb. 1906; *d* of John Carroll, Co. Limerick, and Hélène de Rosière Tuaillon, Paris; *m* 1st, 1931, Capt. Philip Astley, MC (from whom she obtd a divorce, 1940); 2nd, 1942, Lieut Sterling Hayden, USMC (from whom she obtd a divorce, 1946); 3rd, 1946, Henri Lavorel (marr. diss.); 4th, 1950, Andrew Heiskell (marr. diss.); one *d* decd. *Educ:* private sch.; Birmingham Univ. (BA Hons French). Started theatrical career in touring company, playing French maid in The Lash; subsequently toured with Seymour Hicks in Mr What's his Name; became leading lady in British films as result of first screen test for The Guns of Loos; subsequently made Young Woodley, The School for Scandal, I was a Spy, and The Thirty Nine Steps; came to America in 1936 and made: The Case against Mrs Ames; The General Died at Dawn; Lloyds of London; On the Avenue; The Prisoner of Zenda; Blockade; Café Society; North-West Mounted Police; Virginia; One Night in Lisbon; Bahama Passage; My Favourite Blonde; White Cradle Inn; An Innocent Affair; The Fan. Radio appearances include the leading parts in: Cavalcade; Beloved Enemy; Romance; There's always Juliet. From 1941 until end of War, engaged exclusively in war activities.
*Died 2 Oct.* 1987.

**CARSE, William Mitchell,** CBE 1953; *b* 23 Aug. 1899; *o s* of Robert Allison Carse, Hawkhead, Renfrewshire; *m* 1928, Helen Knox (*d* 1976), *yr d* of J. B. Beaton, Milliken Park, Renfrewshire; one *s*. *Educ:* Glasgow High Sch.; Glasgow Univ.; Wellington Military Coll., Madras; St John's Coll., Cambridge. Passed Examination for RMC Sandhurst, 1917; proceeded to Wellington Military Coll., Madras, 1918; gazetted to Indian Army, 1918; served in South Persia until 1920; resigned Commission; entered HM Consular Service, 1923; served in USA, Guatemala, Germany, Portuguese East Africa, Portugal and Portuguese West Africa; Consul-Gen., Luanda, Angola, 1937–39; Consul at Teneriffe, 1939; Consul-Gen. at Reykjavik, Iceland, 1943; attached to British Political Mission in Hungary, 1945–46; Consul-Gen. at Tabriz, Persia, 1946–47, and at Ahwaz, Persia, 1948; Deputy High Comr for the UK in Peshawar, Pakistan, 1948–51; Consul-Gen., São Paulo, Brazil, 1951–56, retd. Appointed to Distillers Company Ltd (Industrial Group), London, 1957. *Recreations:* yachting, riding, chess. *Address:* Little Dene, 16 St Alban's Road, Reigate, Surrey RH2 9LN.
*Died 26 March* 1987.

**CARSON, Hon. Edward;** Lieutenant Life Guards; *b* 17 Feb. 1920; *yr s* of Baron Carson, a Lord of Appeal in Ordinary; *m* 1943, Heather, *d* of Lt-Col Frank Sclater, OBE, MC; one *s* one *d. Educ:* Eton; Trinity Hall, Cambridge. MP (C) Isle of Thanet Div. of Kent, 1945–53. *Address:* Crossways, Westfield, near Hastings, Sussex. *T:* Hastings 751976. *Clubs:* Wig and Pen, MCC.
*Died 6 March 1987.*

**CARTER, Sir (Arthur) Desmond B.;** *see* Bonham-Carter.

**CARTER, Barry Robin Octavius; His Honour Judge Carter;** a Circuit Judge, since 1980; *b* 20 Jan. 1928; *s* of late Stanley Noel Carter and late Winifred Margaret Carter; *m* 1959, Hermione (née Brock); one *s* one *d. Educ:* Sherborne; Trinity Coll., Cambridge (BA). Commnd in Royal Engrs, 1947. Called to Bar, Gray's Inn, 1953; Bencher, 1978. Dep. Chm., Hampshire QS, Jan. 1971; Temp. Recorder of Salisbury, Oct. 1971; a Recorder of the Crown Court, 1972–80. Wine Treasurer, Western Circuit, 1976–80. *Recreations:* lawn tennis (Cambridge blue, 1949–51, Captain 1950); golf. *Address:* Mayles, The Drive, Cobham, Surrey. *T:* Cobham 2827; 4 Pump Court, Temple, EC4. *T:* 01-353 2656. *Clubs:* Hawks (Cambridge); Hampshire (Winchester); All England Lawn Tennis and Croquet, International Lawn Tennis of Great Britain, St George's Hill Lawn Tennis.
*Died 6 March 1981.*

**CARTER, Hon. Sir Douglas (Julian),** KCMG 1977; High Commissioner for New Zealand in the United Kingdom, 1976–79; *b* 5 Aug. 1908; *s* of Walter Stephen Carter and Agnes Isobel; *m* Mavis Rose Miles. *Educ:* Palmerston North High Sch.; Waitaki Boys' High Sch. Formerly, Executive Member: Federated Farmers of NZ; Primary Production Council; Pig Production Council. MP (National Party) Raglan, 1957–75; Chm., Govt Transport Cttee, 1960–70; Under Sec., Agriculture, 1966–69; Minister of Agriculture, 1969–72. Chm., Urban Transport Council, NZ, 1980–84. FRSA 1978. *Address:* 6 Edwin Street, St Andrews, Hamilton, New Zealand.
*Died 7 Nov. 1988.*

**CARTER, Edward Julian,** MA; ARIBA; FLA; *b* Grahamstown, South Africa, 10 June 1902; *s* of late Rev. Canon F. E. Carter; *m* 1930, Deborah Benson, *e d* of Bernard Howard, Loughton, Essex; one *s* four *d. Educ:* Lancing Coll.; Magdalene Coll., Cambridge; Architectural Assoc. Sch., London. Librarian-Editor, Royal Institute of British Architects, 1930–46. Head of Libraries Div., UN Educational, Scientific and Cultural Organisation (previously in UNESCO Preparatory Commn), 1946–57. Dir, Architectural Assoc., Bedford Square, 1961–67. Governor, Central Sch. of Art and Design, 1968–. Chairman, Assoc. Special Libraries and Information Bureaux, 1940–45. Vice-Chairman, Soc. for Cultural Relations with USSR, 1943–45. Hon. Fellow, Library Assoc., 1962. *Publications:* The Future of London, 1962. *Address:* 4 Belgrave Place, Clifton, Bristol BS8 3DD. *Club:* Athenæum.
*Died 5 June 1982.*

**CARTER, Edward Robert Erskine;** QC (Can.) 1978; Counsel, Borden and Elliot, Barristers and Solicitors; *b* 20 Feb. 1923; *s* of Arthur Norwood Carter, QC, and Edith Ireland; *m* 1947, Verna Leman Andrews; two *s* two *d. Educ:* Univ. of New Brunswick; (after War) Osgoode Hall, Toronto, Ont; Univ. of New Brunswick; Univ. of New Brunswick Law Sch. (BCL 1947); Rhodes Scholar for New Brunswick, 1947; Oxford Univ. (BCL 1949). Served War with Royal Canadian Artillery, 1942–44; on loan to 7th King's Own Scottish Borderers, First British Airborne Div., 1944; PoW, Sept. 1944–April 1945. Read Law with McMillan, Binch, Wilkinson, Berry & Wright, Toronto, Ont; called to Bar of New Brunswick, 1947; Ontario 1951; associated with A. N. Carter, QC in practise of law, St John, NB, 1949–53; Legal Officer, Abitibi Power & Paper Co. Ltd, Toronto, Ont, 1953–54; joined Fennell, McLean, Seed & Carter, 1954; Partner, 1955–58. President and Chief Executive Officer: Patino Mining Corp., later Patino NV, 1958–72; Hambro Canada Ltd, 1973–75. Chm. and Dir, Advocate Mines Ltd; Director: Bank of Montreal; Westroc Industries Ltd; Sun Alliance Insurance Co.; Global Natural Resources Ltd; Imperial General Properties Ltd; British Canadian Resources Ltd. Member, Law Soc. of Upper Canada. Hon. Consul of Norway, 1977–. *Address:* (office) c/o Borden and Elliot, 250 University Avenue, Toronto, Ontario M5H 3E9, Canada.
*Died 16 April 1982.*

**CARTER, Ernestine Marie, (Mrs John Waynflete Carter),** OBE 1964; Associate Editor, The Sunday Times, 1968–72; *b* 10 Oct. 1906; *m* 1936, John Waynflete Carter, CBE (*d* 1975). *Educ:* Pape Sch., Savannah, Georgia; Wellesley Coll., Wellesley, Mass., USA (BA). Asst Curator of Architecture and Industrial Art, The Museum of Modern Art, New York, 1933–35, Curator, 1936–37; Specialist, Display and Exhibns Div., Min. of Information, 1939–41; US Office of War Information, London, 1941–44, in charge of exhibns and displays; Asst in Fashion Section, Britain Can Make It Exhibn, 1946; Fashion Editor, Harper's Bazaar, 1946–49; Contributor to The Observer, 1952–54; Women's Editor, The Sunday Times, 1955–68. Member: Council, Royal Coll. of Art, 1960–61; Nat. Council for Diploma in Art and Design, 1962–68; Selection Panel,

Duke of Edinburgh's Award for Design, 1965–67; Council, RSA, 1976–78. Hon. Dr RCA, 1976. *Publications:* Grim Glory, 1941; Flash in the Pan, 1953 (re-issued 1963); With Tongue in Chic, 1974; 20th Century Fashion: a scrapbook from 1900 to today, 1975; The Changing World of Fashion, 1977; Magic Names of Fashion, 1980; contributor to: Vogue, Telegraph Magazine, Cosmopolitan, Costume, etc. *Recreation:* sleep. *Address:* 113 Dovehouse Street, Chelsea, SW3. *T:* 01-352 4344.
*Died 1 Aug. 1983.*

**CARTER, Prof. Geoffrey William,** MA; FIEE; FIEEE; Professor of Electrical Engineering, University of Leeds, 1946–74, now Emeritus; *b* 21 May 1909; *s* of late Frederick William Carter, FRS; *m* 1938, Freda Rose Lapwood; one *s* one *d. Educ:* Rugby Sch.; St John's Coll., Cambridge. MA 1937. Student Apprentice, British Thomson-Houston Co. Ltd, Rugby, 1932–35, Research Engineer, 1935–45; University Demonstrator in Engineering Science, Oxford, 1946. *Publications:* The Simple Calculation of Electrical Transients, 1944; The Electromagnetic Field in its Engineering Aspects, 1954 (rev. edn 1967); (with A. Richardson) Techniques of Circuit Analysis, 1972; papers in Proc. IEE and elsewhere. *Recreations:* study of medals, winemaking. *Address:* 26 Park Villa Court, Leeds LS8 1EB. *T:* Leeds 665261.
*Died 18 Feb. 1989.*

**CARTER, Harry Graham,** OBE 1951; Archivist to Oxford University Press, 1954–80, retired; *b* 27 March 1901; *s* of Henry and Sarah Addison Carter; *m* 1934, Ella Mary Garratt (*d* 1977); two *s. Educ:* Bedales Sch.; Queen's Coll., Oxford (MA). Called to the Bar, Lincoln's Inn, 1925. Learner of type-design at Monotype Corporation Works, 1928–29; Asst to Manager, Kynoch Press, 1929–37; Production Manager, Nonesuch Press, 1937–38; Postal Censor, England and Palestine, 1939–45; Head of Design Section, HM Stationery Office, 1946–53. Lyell Lectr, 1968. *Publications:* Fournier on Typefounding, 1930; (with Herbert Davis) Moxon's Mechanick Exercises on Printing, 1962; (with Stanley Morison) John Fell, the University Press, and the 'Fell' Types, 1969; Wolvercote Mill, 1957, 2nd edn 1978; A View of Early Typography, 1969; A History of the Oxford University Press, vol. I, 1975; trans. and ed, C. Enschede, Typefoundries in the Netherlands, 1978; articles and reviews in bibliographical jls. *Address:* The Stone House, Kingston Bagpuize, Abingdon OX13 5AH. *T:* Longworth 820391.
*Died 10 March 1982.*

**CARTER, John Somers;** *b* 26 Feb. 1901; *s* of R. Carter. *Educ:* Edinburgh Academy; Bedford Sch.; Balliol Coll., Oxford, 1st Class Hon. Mods., 3rd Class Lit. Hum. Asst Master, Cheltenham Coll., 1924–32; Headmaster: St John's Sch., Leatherhead, 1933–47; Blundell's Sch., 1948–59. *Address:* Gwarffynnon, Blaencwrt, Llanwnen, Lampeter, Dyfed SA48 7LR. *T:* Cwrtnewydd 352.
*Died 14 June 1989.*

**CARTER, Malcolm Ogilvy,** CIE 1943; MC 1918; Secretary, South-Western Regional Hospital Board, 1947–63, retired; *b* 2 July 1898; *s* of late Reginald Carter, MA, formerly Rector of Edinburgh Academy and Headmaster of Bedford Sch., and Mary Ogilvy Boyd; *m* 1921, Gwyneth Elaine, *d* of R. Platts, Bedford; one *d; m* 1944, Iris Cowgill, *d* of late Rev. T. A. Thomson, Shawell, Leicester. *Educ:* Edinburgh Academy; Bedford Sch.; Balliol Coll., Oxford. RFA 1917; served in France and Belgium, 1917–18 (MC); BA (Oxon), 1920; joined ICS in Bengal, 1921; Secretary to the Board of Revenue, 1934–35; District Magistrate, Midnapore and 24 Parganas, 1935–38; Director of Land Records, Aug.–Nov. 1938; Secretary to Floud Land Revenue Commission, Bengal, 1938–40; Director of Land Records, April–July 1940; Secretary to Governor of Bengal, 1940–42; Civil Representative of the Government of Bengal with Eastern Army, 1942–43; Commissioner Chittagong Division, Bengal and Liaison Officer to XIVth Army and Third Tactical Air Force, 1943–47. FHA. *Address:* The Stile House, Vicarage Lane, Haslemere, Surrey. *Clubs:* Royal Commonwealth Society (Bristol and London); Vincent's (Oxford).
*Died 26 April 1982.*

**CARTER, Air Cdre North,** CB 1948; DFC 1935; RAF retired; *b* 26 Nov. 1902; *s* of Lt-Col G. L. Carter, CIE, Indian Army; *m* 1931, Kathleen Graham Machattie; one *s* one *d. Educ:* Wellington Coll.; RAF Coll., Cranwell. Commissioned from RAF Coll., 1922; No 5 Sqdn, India, 1923–27; RAF Depot, Iraq, 1929–32; No 56 Sqdn, North Weald, 1932–34; No 60 Sqdn, India, 1934 and 1935; RAF Staff Coll., 1936; Sqdn Ldr, 1936; Staff Appointments, 1937–40; Wing Comdr, 1938; commanded RAF Stations Dalcross, South Cerney, Pocklington and Castel Benito, 1941–45; Group Captain, 1946; Air Commodore, 1948; AOC Halton, 1949–50; SASO 205 Group Middle East Air Force 15, 1951–53; Provost Marshal and Chief of Air Force Police, 1953–54, retired 1954; Temp. Administrative Officer, Northern Region, Nigeria, 1955–63. *Address:* Gould's Bay, Hawkesbury River, PMB Brooklyn, NSW 2253, Australia.
*Died 13 Oct. 1984.*

**CARTER, Peter Anthony,** CMG 1970; HM Diplomatic Service, retired; *b* 16 Jan. 1914; *s* of Thomas Birchall Carter; *m* 1946, Mary Hutchison Heard; one *s* one *d. Educ:* Charterhouse; Sidney Sussex

Coll., Cambridge. Metropolitan Police Office, 1936–39; Royal Tank Regt (Major), 1939–44; Colonial Office, 1947–60; Nyasaland, 1951–53; CRO, 1960–61; First Secretary, Dar-es-Salaam, 1961–64; Counsellor, Dublin, 1965–68; Head of British High Commission Residual Staff, Rhodesia, 1968–69; British High Commissioner, Mauritius, 1970–73; Senior Clerk, H of C, 1974–76. *Recreations:* golf, bridge, music. *Address:* Forth House, Beech Drive, Kingswood, Surrey. *Club:* Kingswood Golf. *Died* 21 *Feb.* 1983.

**CARTER, His Honour Sir Walker (Kelly),** Kt 1965; QC 1951; an Official Referee of the Supreme Court of Judicature, 1954–71; Chairman, Criminal Injuries Compensation Board, 1964–75; *b* 7 July 1899; *s* of late Walter Carter, CBE, and Annie Elizabeth Carter; *m* 1925, Phyllis Irene (*d* 1984), *d* of late Edward Ernest Clarke, Bank Bldgs, Simla, India; one *d. Educ:* Repton Sch.; Sidney Sussex Coll., Cambridge. RFA, 1918–19; RA, 1939–43. Called to Bar, Inner Temple, 1924; Bencher, 1965. Chairman, Quarter Sessions for Parts of Lindsey, 1945–67, and for Parts of Kesteven, 1961–67. *Address:* 65 Bedford Gardens, W8. *T:* 01–727 9862. *Club:* Reform. *Died* 29 *March* 1985.

**CARTER, William Stovold,** CMG 1970; CVO 1956; retired; Secretary, Council on Tribunals, 1970–76; *b* 10 Oct. 1915; *s* of late R. S. Carter, Bournemouth, Hants; *m* 1944, Barbara Alice Kathleen Dines; two *s* one *d. Educ:* Bec; Christ's Coll., Cambridge. Entered Colonial Administrative Service (Nigeria), 1939; retd as Administrative Officer, Class I (Resident), 1957. Entered Colonial Office, 1959; Asst Sec., 1965; joined Commonwealth Office, 1966; joined Foreign and Commonwealth Office, 1968; Head of Hong Kong Dept, 1965–70. *Recreation:* golf. *Address:* Broad Oak Farm, Chiddingly, near Lewes, East Sussex. *T:* Chiddingly 872267.

*Died* 13 *Dec.* 1985.

**CASE, Air Vice-Marshal Albert Avion,** CB 1964; CBE 1957 (OBE 1943); General Secretary, Hospital Saving Association, 1969–82; *b* Portsmouth, 5 April 1916; *s* of late Group Captain Albert Edward Case and Florence Stella Hosier Case; *m* 1949, Brenda Margaret, *e d* of late A. G. Andrews, Enfield, Middx; one *s* one *d. Educ:* Imperial Service Coll. Commd RAF, 1934; Sqdn Ldr, 1940; Wing Comdr, Commanding No 202 Squadron, 1942; Group Capt., Maritime Ops HQ, ACSEA, 1945; OC, RAF, Koggala, Ceylon, 1945–46; JSSC, 1950–51; OC, RAF, Chivenor, 1953–55; OC, RAF, Nicosia, 1956–57; IDC, 1959; Air Cdre, 1959; Air Min., Dir, Operational Requirements, 1959–62; Air Vice-Marshal, 1962; AOC No 22 Group RAF, Tech. Trg Comd, 1962–66; SASO HQ Coastal Comd, 1966–68; retd. FBIM. *Recreations:* swimming (RAF blue 1946), sailing. *Address:* High Trees, Dean Lane, Winchester. *Clubs:* Royal Air Force; Royal Air Force Yacht. *Died* 1990.

**CASEY, Terence Anthony,** CBE 1977; KCHS 1976; FCP 1982; retired; General-Secretary, National Association of Schoolmasters/Union of Women Teachers, 1975–83 (National Association of Schoolmasters, 1963–75), then Honorary Life Member; *b* 6 Sept 1920; *s* of Daniel Casey and Ellen McCarthy; *m* 1945, Catherine Wills; two *s* three *d. Educ:* Holy Cross, near Ramsgate; Camden Coll. Teacher's Certificate; Diploma in Mod. Hist. Teaching Service, LCC, 1946–63; Headmaster, St Joseph's Sch., Maida Vale, W9, 1956–63. Pres., Nat. Assoc. of Schoolmasters, 1962–63. Member: Burnham Cttee, 1961–83; Council, Open Univ., 1975–; Catholic Educn Council, 1983–; Vice-Chm., "Catch 'em Young" Project Trust, 1983–; Sec. of State's Voluntary Sector Consultative Council, 1984–; formerly Member: Nat. Advisory Cttee on Supply and Training of Teachers; Teachers' Council Working Party; TUC Local Govt Cttee. Treasurer, European Teachers' Trade Union Cttee, 1978–83; Vice Pres., Internat. Fedn of Free Teachers' Unions, 1978–85. Trustee, Westminster Cathedral, 1983–. *Publications:* The Comprehensive School from Within, 1964; contribs to Times Educnl Supplement. *Recreations:* music, opera, motoring. *Address:* 10 Chelsing Rise, Leverstock Green, Hemel Hempstead, Herts. *Club:* Pathfinders'. *Died* 18 *March* 1987.

**CASHMORE, Rt. Rev. Thomas Herbert;** *b* 27 April 1892; *s* of Thomas James and Julia Cashmore; *m* 1919, Kate Marjorie Hutchinson; two *s* two *d* (and one *s* decd). *Educ:* Codrington Coll., Barbados, BWI (BA, Durham). Ordained, Barbados, for Chota Nagpur, India, 1917; SPG Missionary, Ranchi, Chota Nagpur, 1917–24; Principal St James's Coll., Calcutta, 1924–33; Vicar: St James's Parish, Calcutta, 1924–33; Holmfirth, Yorks, 1933–42; Brighouse, Yorks, 1942–46; Hon. Canon of Wakefield Cathedral, 1942–46; Canon Missioner, Diocese of Wakefield, 1946–54; Suffragan Bishop of Dunwich, 1955–67. Examining Chaplain to Bishop of St Edmundsbury and Ipswich, 1955–67. Awarded Kaisar-i-Hind (2nd Class), 1929; Defence Medal (2nd World War). *Recreation:* motoring. *Address:* Lynton, Graham Avenue, Withdean, Brighton BN1 8HA. *T:* Brighton 553005. *Died* 16 *July* 1984.

**CASSELS, His Honour Francis Henry,** TD 1945; Senior Circuit Judge, Inner London Crown Court, 1972–79 (Chairman, SW London Quarter Sessions, 1965–72); *b* 3 Sept. 1910; 2nd *s* of late Sir James Dale Cassels; *m* 1939, Evelyn Dorothy Richardson (*d* 1979); one *s*

one *d. Educ:* Sedbergh; Corpus Christi Coll., Cambridge (MA). Called to the Bar, Middle Temple, 1932. Served Royal Artillery, 1939–45. Dep. Chm., County of London Sessions, 1954–65. *Address:* 14 Buckingham House, Courtlands, Richmond, Surrey. *T:* 01–940 4180. *Club:* Royal Wimbledon Golf. *Died* 12 *Dec.* 1987.

**CASSIE, Arnold Blatchford David,** CBE 1955; Director of Research, Wool Industries Research Association, 1950–67, retired; *b* 17 May 1905; 3rd *s* of late D. A. Morris Cassie and late Mrs Cassie; *m* 1939, Catherine Dufour, *d* of late Surg. Capt. T. D. Halahan, OBE, RN; one *s* two *d. Educ:* Aberdeen Grammar Sch.; Edinburgh Univ.; Christ's Coll., Cambridge. Vans Dunlop Schol., Edin. Univ., 1926–29; Carnegie Research Schol., 1929–30; Post-grad. Research, University Coll., London, 1928–34; Scientific Officer: ICI Ltd, 1934–36, RAE, 1936–38; Chief Physicist, Wool Industries Research Assoc., 1938–50. Warner Memorial Medal 1949, Mather Lecturer 1962, Textile Institute; George Douglas Lectr, Soc. of Dyers and Colourists, 1961. Vice-Pres., Textile Institute, 1962–65; Governor, Bradford Institute of Technology, 1960–66. Hon. D. Tech. Bradford Univ., 1966. *Publications:* numerous in Proc. Royal Society, Trans. Faraday Soc., Jl of Textile Inst., etc. *Recreations:* gardening, golf, music. *Address:* White Heather, Crescent Walk, Ferndown, Dorset. *T:* Ferndown 873705. *Died* 16 *March* 1982.

**CASSIE, W(illiam) Fisher,** CBE 1966; consulting civil engineer; Partner, Waterhouse & Partners, 1970–74; Professor of Civil Engineering, University of Newcastle upon Tyne (formerly King's College, University of Durham), 1943–70, later Emeritus; *b* 29 June 1905; Scottish; *m* 1st, 1933, Mary Robertson Reid (*d* 1980); 2nd, 1982, Doris Emily Puleston. *Educ:* Grove Academy, Dundee; University of St Andrews. BSc (St Andrews), 1925. Asst Engineer, City Engineer and Harbour Engineer, Dundee; Research at University Coll., Dundee; PhD (St Andrews), 1930; first Senior Sir James Caird Scholarship in Engineering, 1930; Research and Study, University of Illinois (USA), 1930–31; MS (Ill.), 1931. Lectured at: QUB and University Coll., Cardiff, UCL, 1931–40; King's Coll., Durham Univ., later Univ. of Newcastle upon Tyne, 1940–70. Past Chm. Northern Counties Assoc. of Instn of Civil Engineers; Founder Chm. Northern Counties Branch Instn of Structural Engineers; Pres. Inst. Highways Engrs, 1967–68; FRSE; FICE; FIStructE; PPInstHE; Hon. LLD Dundee, 1972; Hon. DTech Asian Inst. of Technology, 1979; Mem. Sigma XI. Bronze Medallist, Instn of Struct. Engrs; Gold badge, English Folk Dance and Song Soc. *Publications:* Structural Analysis, 1947 (with P. L. Capper), Mechanics of Engineering Soils, 1949; (with J. H. Napper) Structure in Building, 1952; (with P. L. Capper and J. D. Geddes) Problems in Engineering Soils, 1966; Fundamental Foundations, 1968; Statics, Structures and Stress, 1973; (with T. Constantine) Student's Guide to Success, 1977; contrib. Jls of ICE, IStructE, and other tech. papers. *Recreations:* photography and traditional cultures of England. *Address:* Benachie, Lochinver, by Lairg, Sutherland. *T:* Lochinver 302. *Died* 20 *April* 1985.

**CASTERET, Norbert;** Commandeur de la Légion d'Honneur, 1975 (Officier 1947); Croix de Guerre, 1917; archæologist, geologist, speleologist; *b* 19 Aug. 1897; *m* 1924, Elisabeth Martin (*d* 1940); one *s* four *d. Educ:* Lycée de Toulouse, Haute-Garonne. Bachelier; lauréat de l'Académie Française, 1934, 1936, 1938; lauréat de l'Académie des Sciences, 1935; mainteneur de l'Académie des Jeux Floraux, 1937; Grande Médaille d'Or de l'Académie des Sports, 1923; Médaille d'Or de l'Education Physique, 1947; Commandeur du Mérite de la Recherche et de l'Invention, 1956; Commandeur du Mérite sportif, 1958; Commandeur des Palmes académiques, 1964; Commandeur du Mérite National; "Oscar" du Courage Français, 1973; Médaille de Sauvetage, 1975; Médaille d'or de la Société d'Encouragement au Bien, 1977; Grande Médaille d'Or de la Société de Géographie de Paris, 1979. *Publications:* 45 works translated into 17 languages: Dix ans sous terre (English edn: Ten Years Under the Earth); Au fond des gouffres; Mes Cavernes (English edn: My Caves); En Rampant; Exploration (English edn: Cave Men New and Old); Darkness Under the Earth; Trente ans sous terre (English edn: The Descent of Pierre Saint-Martin), etc.; contributions to L'Illustration, Illustrated London News, Geographical Magazine, etc. *Recreations:* exploring caves and study on bats. *Address:* Castel Mourlon, 31800 Saint-Gaudens, France. *T:* St Gaudens 61.89.15.13. *Died* 20 *July* 1987.

**CASTLE, Norman Henry;** Chairman: Gee & Watson Ltd, since 1978; Paul Developments Ltd, since 1980; Underwriting Member of Lloyds, since 1976; *b* 1 Sept. 1913; *s* of Hubert William Castle, MBE, and Elizabeth May Castle; *m* 1939, Ivy Olive Watson; one *d* decd. *Educ:* Norfolk House; Ludlow Grammar Sch. Joined Hafnia Konserves, Copenhagen, 1931; London: C. & E. Morton Ltd, 1933; Vacuum Packed Produce Ltd, 1938; Vacuum Foods Ltd, 1939. Served War of 1939–45, RAF. General Manager: A. L. Maizel Ltd, 1945; Times Foods Ltd, 1947; Director, Vacuum Foods Ltd, 1951; Managing Dir, Haigh Castle & Co. Ltd, 1956; Man. Dir, Hafnia Ham Co. Ltd, 1956; Chm. and Man. Dir, S. & W. Berisford Ltd, 1971–78 (Dir, 1967); Chairman: Ashbourne Investments Ltd,

1976–82; Wace Ltd, 1978–85; Director: Incentive Investments Ltd, 1976–82; E. S. Schwab & Co. Ltd, 1976–81; Acatos and Hutcheson Ltd, 1979–. *Recreations:* travel, sailing. *Address:* The Penthouse, 39 Courcels, Black Rock, Brighton, E Sussex. *Clubs:* Lloyd's Yacht, Brighton Marina Yacht (Brighton). *Died 11 July 1988.*

**CASTLE-MILLER, Rudolph Valdemar Thor;** a Recorder of the Crown Court, 1972–75; *b* Britain, 16 March 1905; *s* of late Rudolph Schleusz-Mühlheimer, Randers, Denmark; changed name by deed poll, 1930; *m* 1939, Colleen Ruth, *d* of late Lt-Col N. R. Whitaker; one *s* one *d. Educ:* Harrow; Hertford Coll., Oxford (MA). Called to Bar, Middle Temple, 1929. Mem., Gen. Council of the Bar, 1957–60 and 1964–69. Past Master, Loriners' Company, 1968. Flt Lt, Intell. Br., RAF, 1940–46. *Recreations:* motoring, travel. *Address:* 1 Ellesmere Court, Brackley, Northants NN13 6BT. *T:* Brackley 700230. *Died 15 Sept. 1987.*

**CATHIE, Ian Aysgarth Bewley,** MD, BS, MRCP, FRCPath; DL; *b* London, 3 Jan. 1908; 2nd *s* of George Cathie, Ewell, Surrey, and Lilly Pickford Evans; *m* 1938, Josephine (*d* 1982), *o d* of Joseph Cunning, FRCS, Broome Park, Betchworth, Surrey; one *s* three *d. Educ:* Guy's Hospital; Zürich Univ. Asst path. to Ancoats Hospital, Manchester, 1932; demonstrator in path. in Manchester Univ. and registrar in path. to Manchester Royal Inf., 1934; path. and res. Fellow in path., Christie Hospital and Holt Radium Inst., also path. to Duchess of York Hospital for Babies, Manchester, 1936. Clinical Pathologist to The Hospital for Sick Children, Great Ormond Street, London, 1938–58, retired. Pathologist in EMS, 1939; war service in RAMC, 1940–46; captured in Tobruk, POW 1942–43. Hon. Member, British Pædiatric Association. Hon. Fellow, Inst. of Child Health, 1983. Lord of the Manor of Barton-on-the-Heath, Warwickshire; CC Warwicks, 1965–77 (Vice-Chm., 1973–74, Chm., 1974–76). DL Warwicks, 1974. *Publications:* Chapters in Moncrieff's Nursing and Diseases of Sick Children and (in collaboration) Garrod, Batten and Thursfield's Diseases of Children; also papers on pathology and pædiatrics in medical journals. Editor, Archives of Disease in Childhood, 1951–63. *Recreation:* gardening. *Address:* Barton House, Moreton-in-Marsh, Glos. *T:* Barton-on-the-Heath 303. *Clubs:* Chelsea Arts, Saintsbury. *Died 17 Sept. 1989.*

**CATLEDGE, Turner;** Director, The New York Times, 1968–73; *b* 17 March 1901; *s* of Lee Johnson Catledge and Willie Anna (*née* Turner); *m* 1st; two *d*; 2nd, 1958, Abby Izard. *Educ:* Philadelphia (Miss.) High Sch.; Miss. State College. BSc 1922. Neshoba (Miss.) Democrat, 1921; Resident Editor, Tunica (Miss.) Times, 1922; Man. Editor, Tupelo (Miss.) Journal, 1923; Reporter, Memphis (Tenn.) Commercial Appeal, 1923–27; Baltimore (Md) Sun, 1927–29; New York Times: City Staff, 1929; Correspondent, Washington Bureau, 1930–36; Chief Washington News Correspondent, 1936–41; Chicago Sun: Chief Correspondent, 1941–42; Editor-in-Chief, 1942–43; Nat. Correspondent, New York Times, 1943–44; Managing Editor, 1951–64; Executive Editor, 1964–68; Vice-Pres., 1968–70. Member: Pulitzer Prizes Advisory Cttee, 1955–69; AP Managing Editors Assoc., 1954–64; Advisory Board, American Press Inst.; American Soc. of Newspaper Editors (Dir., Pres. 1961); Sigma Delta Chi. Hon. DLitt Washington and Lee Univ.; Hon. Dr of Humane Letters Southwestern at Memphis; Hon. LLD: Univ. of Kentucky; Tulane Univ. *Publications:* The 168 Days (with Joseph W. Alsop, Jr), 1937; My Life and The Times, 1971. *Address:* (office) 229 West 43rd Street, New York, NY 10036, USA. *T:* 556-1234; (home) 2316 Prytania Street, New Orleans, La 70130, USA. *T:* 522-2429. *Clubs:* National Press, Gridiron (Washington); Century, Silurians (New York); Boston (New Orleans), New Orleans Country. *Died 27 April 1983.*

**CATON-THOMPSON, Gertrude,** FBA 1944; Hon. LittD Cantab 1954; former Fellow of Newnham College, Cambridge, Hon. Fellow 1981; *b* 1 Feb. 1888; *o d* of late William Caton-Thompson and Mrs E. G. Moore. *Educ:* Miss Hawtrey's, Eastbourne; Paris. Employed Ministry of Shipping, 1915–19; Paris Peace Conference, 1919; student British School of Archæology in Egypt, 1921–26; excavated at Abydos and Oxyrhynchos, 1921–22; Malta, 1921 and 1924; Qau and Badari, 1923–25; on behalf of the British School in Egypt inaugurated the first archæological and geological survey of the Northern Fayum, 1924–26; continued work as Field Director for the Royal Anthropological Institute, 1927–28; appointed in 1928 by the British Assoc. to conduct excavations at Zimbabwe and other Rhodesian sites; Excavations in Kharga Oasis, 1930–33; South Arabia, 1937–38; Cuthbert Peek award of the Royal Geographical Society, 1932; Rivers Medallist of the Royal Anthropological Institute, 1934; Huxley medallist, 1946. Burton Medal of Royal Asiatic Society, 1954. Former Governor, Bedford Coll. for Women, and School of Oriental and African Studies, University of London; former Member: Council British Inst. of History and Archæology in East Africa. Fellow, UCL, 1984–. *Publications:* contributions to the Encyclopædia Britannica and various scientific journals; The Badarian Civilisation (part author), 1928; The Zimbabwe Culture, 1931 (repr. 1969); The Desert Fayum, 1935; The Tombs and Moon Temple of Hureidha, Hadramaut, 1944; Kharga Oasis in Prehistory,

1952. *Recreation:* idleness. *Address:* Court Farm, Broadway, Worcs. *Died 18 April 1985.*

**CAUNTER, Brigadier John Alan Lyde,** CBE 1941; MC and Bar; *b* 17 Dec. 1889; *er s* of R. L. Caunter, MD, FRCS, and Mrs R. L. Caunter (*née* W. J. von Taysen); *m* 1920, Helen Margaret Napier (*d* 1942), *er d* of late Sir Walter Napier; one *s* one *d*; *m* 1945, Muriel Lilian Murphy (*née* Hicks). *Educ:* Uppingham Sch.; RMC, Sandhurst. 2nd Lieut Gloucestershire Regt, 1909; served European War, 1914–19 (MC and Bar, despatches, Brevet of Major); taken prisoner, 1914; escaped from Germany, July, 1917; operations France, Flanders, Macedonia, Turkey; Iraq Campaign, 1920–21; psc Camberley, 1923; transferred Royal Tank Corps, 1924; DAAG Rhine Army, 1925 and 1926; GSO2 Northern Command, 1927–28; DAA and QMG, N. Ireland, 1929–33; Bt. Lieut-Colonel, 1933; Lieut-Colonel, 1935; Comd 1st Bn (Light) Royal Tank Corps, 1935–39; Colonel and Temp. Brigadier 1939; Comdr 1st Army Tank Bde July–Oct. 1939; Cmdr Armoured Bde, Egypt, 1939–41; W. Desert Campaign, 1940–41, as Comdr 4th Armoured Bde (CBE, despatches); BGS, GHQ, India, 1941–43; retired 1944. Member Cornwall CC, 1952–67; Member for GB, Internat. Cttee of Internat. Game Fish Association (HQ at Fort Lauderdale, Fla, USA). *Publications:* 13 Days, 1918 (An Escape from a German Prison Camp); Shark Angling in Great Britain, 1961. *Recreations:* fishing, shooting, (present); past: Rugby football, cricket, hockey. *Address:* Penlee House, Shutta Road, East Looe, Cornwall. *Club:* Shark Angling of Great Britain (President and Founder); (HQ at Looe). *Died 21 April 1981.*

**CAUTHERY, Harold William,** CB 1969; *b* 5 May 1914; *s* of Joseph Cauthery, Manchester; *m* 1938, Dorothy Constance, *d* of George E. Sawyer, Sutton Coldfield; one *s* one *d* (and one *d* decd). *Educ:* Bishop Vesey's Grammar Sch., Sutton Coldfield; Christ's College, Cambridge. Asst Inspector of Taxes, Inland Revenue, 1936; Asst Principal, Ministry of Health, 1937; Instructor-Lieut, RN, 1942–45; Principal, Ministry of Health, 1944; Asst Secretary: Ministry of Health, 1950; Ministry of Housing and Local Government, 1951; Under-Sec., Min. of Transport, 1960–66; Dep. Sec., Min. of Land and Natural Resources, 1966; Dir and Sec. and Mem., Land Commn, 1967–71; Dep. Under-Sec. of State (Air), MoD, 1971–72; Sec., Local Govt Staff Commn, 1972–74. *Publication:* Parish Councillor's Guide, 10th Edition, 1958. *Recreations:* music, gardening. *Address:* Eastcote, Petworth Road, Haslemere, Surrey. *T:* Haslemere 51448. *Club:* United Oxford & Cambridge University. *Died 6 July 1987.*

**CAVALCANTI, Alberto de Almeida;** film director and producer; *b* Rio de Janeiro, 6 Feb. 1897. *Educ:* Fine Arts Sch., Geneva (Architecture). Came into Films as an Art Director, then became Director in the French Avant-Garde Group. Came to England in 1934 and worked in the Documentary School. Back to fictional films at Ealing in 1940. Films directed in France, 1924–34: Rien que les heures, En Rade, La P'tite Lilie, Yvette, Le Capitaine Fracasse, etc. Films directed or produced in Great Britain, 1934–46: North Sea, Men of the Lightship, The Foreman Went to France, Went the Day Well, Half-Way House, Champagne Charlie, Dead of Night, The Life and Adventures of Nicholas Nickleby, They Made Me a Fugitive, The First Gentleman, For Them That Trespass. Brazilian productions: Caicara, Painel, Terra é sempre Terra and Volta Redonda; directed: Simão o Caôlho; O Canto do Mar, A Mulher de Verdade. Continental films: Brecht's Herr Puntila und sein Knecht Matti; Windrose (with Joris Ivens); Les Noces Venitiennes. Thus Spake Theodor Herzl (in Israel). Compilation, One Man and the Cinema, Parts I and II. For the Stage: Blood-wedding (in Spain); Fuente Ovejuna (in Israel); La Nuit. French TV, Les Empailles; La Visite de la Vieille-Dame. *Publication:* Filme e realidade. *Address:* 4 Villa Dufresne, 75016 Paris, France. *Club:* Garrick. *Died 23 Aug. 1982.*

**CAVAN, 12th Earl of,** *cr* 1647; **Michael Edward Oliver Lambart,** TD; DL; Baron Cavan, 1618; Baron Lambart, 1618; Viscount Kilcoursie, 1647; Vice Lord-Lieutenant, Salop, 1975–87; *b* 29 Oct. 1911; *o s* of 11th Earl of Cavan and Audrey Kathleen (*d* 1942), *o d* of late A. B. Loder; *S* father, 1950; *m* 1947, Essex Lucy, *o d* of Henry Arthur Cholmondeley, Shotton Hall, Hadnall, Shropshire; one *d* (and two *d* decd). *Educ:* Radley College. Served War of 1939–45, Shropshire Yeomanry (despatches). Lt-Col comdg Shropshire Yeomanry, 1955–58. DL Salop, 1959. *Heir:* kinsman Roger Cavan, *b* 1 Sept. 1944. *Address:* The Glebe House, Stockton, Shifnal, Shropshire TF11 9EF. *T:* Norton 236. *Died 17 Nov. 1988.*

**CAVE, Sir Richard (Guy),** Kt 1976; MC 1944; Chairman, Vickers, since 1984; Director: Tate & Lyle Ltd, since 1976; Equity & Law Life Assurance Society, 1972–79 and since 1983; *b* 16 March 1920; *s* of William Thomas Cave and Gwendoline Mary Nicholls; *m* 1957, Dorothy Gillian Fry; two *s* two *d. Educ:* Tonbridge; Gonville and Caius Coll., Cambridge. Joined Smiths Industries Ltd, 1946; Man. Dir, Motor Accessory Div., 1963; Chief Exec. and Man. Dir, 1968–73; Chm., 1973–76; Chm., Thorn Electrical Industries Ltd,

1976–79; THORN EMI plc, 1979–84. Dep. Chm., BRB, 1983–85; Dir, Thames Television Ltd, 1981–84. Chm., Industrial Soc., 1979–83. *Recreation:* sailing. *Address:* Stanny, Priors Hill Road, Aldeburgh, Suffolk IP15 5EP. *T:* Aldeburgh 2774.

*Died 5 Dec.* 1986.

**CAVE, Sir Richard (Philip)**, KCVO 1977 (MVO 1969); CB 1975; Fourth Clerk at the Table (Judicial), House of Lords, 1965–77 and Principal Clerk, Judicial Department, House of Lords, 1959–77; Taxing Officer of Judicial Costs, House of Lords, 1957–77; Crown Examiner in Peerage Cases 1953–77; Secretary, Association of Lieutenants of Counties and Custodes Rotulorum, 1946–59, and 1964–77; Founder and President, Multiple Sclerosis Society of Great Britain and Northern Ireland (Chairman, 1953–76); a Vice-President, International Federation of Multiple Sclerosis Societies, 1967, Emeritus since 1981; *b* 26 April 1912; 4th *s* of late Charles John Philip Cave and late Wilhelmina Mary Henrietta (*née* Kerr); *m* 1936, Margaret Mary (*d* 1981), *e d* of Francis Westby Perceval; one *s*. *Educ:* Ampleforth Coll.; Trinity Coll., Cambridge (MA); Herts Institute of Agriculture; College of Estate Management. A Gold Staff Officer, Coronation of HM King George VI, 1937. Agent for 6th Earl of Craven's Hamstead Marshall Estate, 1938–39. Royal Wilts Yeomanry (L. Corp.), 1939–40; The Rifle Bde (Captain; Officer i/c Cols Comdt's Office, KRRC and Rifle Bde), 1940–45. Territorial Efficiency Medal, 1946. Vice-Chm., Society for Relief of Distress, 1972–85. A Confrater of Ampleforth Abbey, 1971. DL Greater London, 1973–87. Gold Medal, Royal English Forestry Society, 1939; Silver Medal, RASE, 1939. KSG 1966; KCSG 1972; Kt of Honour and Devotion, SMO Malta, 1972; Kt of Justice, Sacred Military Order of Constantine of St George, 1972. *Publications:* Elementary Map Reading, 1941; articles in Atkin's Encyclopedia of Court Forms in Civil Proceedings, 1968 and 1973; Halsbury's Laws of England, 1974. *Recreations:* photography, collecting map postcards. *Address:* Watergate, 34 Ham Common, Richmond, Surrey TW10 7JG. *T:* 01–940 8014. *Clubs:* Royal Commonwealth Society; University Pitt (Cambridge).

*Died 29 March* 1988.

**CAVERHILL, William Melville;** *see* Melville, Alan.

**CAWSTON, (Edwin) Richard**, CVO 1972; documentary film-maker; film and television consultant; Special Projects Director, Video Arts Ltd; *b* 31 May 1923; *s* of Edwin Cawston and Phyllis, *d* of Henry Charles Hawkins; *m* 1st, 1951, Elisabeth Anne (*d* 1977), *d* of Canon R. L. Rhys; two *s*; 2nd, 1978, Andrea, *e d* of Michael and Dora Phillips, Cyprus. *Educ:* Westminster Sch.; Oriel Coll., Oxford. Served Royal Signals, 1941–46; Captain 1945; Major and SO2 HQ Southern Comd, India, 1946. Joined BBC TV, 1947, as Film Editor, then Producer of original Television Newsreel, 1950–54; producer and director of major documentary films, 1955–79; Head of Documentary Programmes, BBC TV, 1965–79. Chm., British Acad. of Film and TV Arts, 1976–79 (Trustee, 1971–; Mem. Council of Management, 1959–). Awards include: British Film Acad. Award, 1959; Screenwriters Guild Award, 1961; Silver Medal, Royal TV Soc., 1961; Guild of TV Producers and Dirs Award, 1962; Italia Prize, 1962; Desmond Davis Award, 1969; Silver Satellite of AWRT, 1970. *Major documentary films include:* This is the BBC, 1959; The Lawyers, 1960; Television and the World, 1961; The Pilots, 1963; Born Chinese, 1965; Royal Family, 1969; Royal Heritage, 1977; All the World's a Stage, 1984. *Recreation:* making things. *Address:* 26 Lansdowne Crescent, W11.

*Died 7 June* 1986.

**CAYZER, Hon. (Michael) Anthony (Rathbone);** *b* 28 May 1920; 2nd *s* of 1st Baron Rotherwick; *m* 1952, Hon. Patricia Browne (*d* 1981), *er d* of 4th Baron Oranmore and Browne and late Hon. Mrs Hew Dalrymple; three *d*; *m* 1982, Baroness Sybille de Selys Longchamps. *Educ:* Eton; Royal Military Coll., Sandhurst. Commissioned Royal Scots Greys: served 1939–44 (despatches). Dep. Chm., British & Commonwealth Shipping Co. Ltd, 1958–87; Chm., Servisair Ltd, 1954–87; Director: Cayzer, Irvine & Co. Ltd; Caledonia Investments Ltd; Former Dir, Sterling Industries Ltd. President: Inst. of Shipping and Forwarding Agents, 1963–65; Chamber of Shipping of the United Kingdom, 1967; Herts Agric. Soc., 1974; Past Vice-Pres., British Light Aviation Centre. Past Mem. Mersey Docks and Harbour Bd. Chm. Liverpool Steamship Owners Assoc. 1956–57. Trustee: Nat. Maritime Museum, 1968–87 (Chm., 1977–87); Maritime Trust, 1975–87; Dep. Chm., Chatham Historic Dockyard Trust, 1984–89. Vice-Pres., Missions to Seamen, 1984– (Treasurer, 1974–84). *Address:* Great Westwood, Kings Langley, Herts. *Clubs:* Boodle's, Royal Yacht Squadron.

*Died 4 March* 1990.

**CAZALET, Vice-Adm. Sir Peter Grenville Lyon**, KBE 1955; CB 1952; DSO 1945, and Bar 1949; DSC 1940; retired; Chairman, Navy League, 1960–67; Vice-President Association of Royal Navy Officers; *b* 29 July 1899; *e s* of late Grenville William Cazalet and Edith Lyon; *m* 1928, Elise, *d* of late J. P. Winterbotham, Cheltenham, Glos; four *s*. *Educ:* Dulwich. Midshipman in HMS Princess Royal,

1918; Lieut 1921; Comdr 1934; Capt. 1941; Rear-Adm. 1950; Vice-Adm. 1953. Served War of 1939–45 (despatches four times); Commanded: HMS Durban, 1941–42; 23rd Destroyer Flotilla, 1944–45; HMS London, 1949; Commodore Administration, Mediterranean Fleet, 1945–46; Dep. Dir of Plans, Naval Staff, 1946–47; Commodore RN Barracks, Chatham, 1949–50; Chief of Staff to Flag Officer Central Europe, 1950–52; Allied Chief of Staff to C-in-C Mediterranean, 1953–55; Flag Officer Comdg Reserve Fleet, 1955–56; retd 1957. ADC to the King, 1950. King Haakon VII Cross, 1946. *Address:* 16 High Hurst Close, Newick, Lewes, East Sussex BN8 4NJ. *T:* Newick 2396.

*Died 17 Feb.* 1982.

**CAZALET-KEIR, Thelma**, CBE 1952; *b* 28 May 1899; *d* of late W. M. Cazalet; *m* 1939, David (*d* 1969), *s* of Rev. Thomas Keir. Member of London County Council for East Islington, 1925–31; Alderman of County of London, 1931; contested by-election, East Islington, 1931; MP (Nat. C) East Islington, 1931–45; Parliamentary Private Secretary to Parliamentary Secretary to Board of Education, 1937–40; Parliamentary Secretary to Ministry of Education, May 1945. Member of Committee of Enquiry into conditions in Women's Services, 1942; of Committee on Equal Compensation (Civil Injuries), 1943; Chairman London Area Women's Advisory Committee, Conservative and Unionist Associations, 1943–46. Chairman Equal Pay Campaign Committee, 1947; Member Cost of Living Committee; Member Arts Council of Great Britain, 1940–49; Member Executive Committee of Contemporary Art Society; Member Transport Users Consultative Committee for London, 1950–52. A Governor of the BBC, 1956–61. Member Committee Royal UK Beneficent Association, 1962. President Fawcett Society, 1964. *Publications:* From the Wings (autobiog.), 1967; (ed) Homage to P. G. Wodehouse, 1973. *Recreations:* music, lawn tennis. *Address:* Flat J, 90 Eaton Square, SW1. *T:* 01–235 7378.

*Died 13 Jan.* 1989.

**CECIL, Lord (Edward Christian) David (Gascoyne)**; CH 1949; CLit 1972; Goldsmiths' Professor of English Literature, Oxford, 1948–69; Fellow of New College, Oxford, 1939–69, then Honorary Fellow; *b* 9 April 1902; *yr s* of 4th Marquess of Salisbury, KG, GCVO; *m* 1932, Rachel (*d* 1982), *o d* of late Sir Desmond MacCarthy; two *s* one *d*. *Educ:* Eton; Christ Church, Oxford (Hon. Student, 1981). Fellow of Wadham Coll., Oxford, 1924–30. Trustee of National Portrait Gallery, 1937–51. President: The Poetry Soc., 1947–48; Jane Austen Soc., 1966–83. Leslie Stephen Lectr, Cambridge Univ., 1935; Clark Lectr, Cambridge, 1941; Rede Lecturer, Cambridge Univ., 1955. Hon. LittD Leeds, 1950; Hon. DLit London, 1957; Hon. LLD: Liverpool, 1951; St Andrews, 1951; Hon. DLitt Glasgow, 1962. *Publications:* The Stricken Deer, 1929; Sir Walter Scott, 1933; Early Victorian Novelists, 1934; Jane Austen, 1935; The Young Melbourne, 1939; Hardy, the Novelist, 1943; Two Quiet Lives, 1948; Poets and Story-Tellers, 1949; Lord M., 1954; The Fine Art of Reading, 1957; Max, 1964; Visionary and Dreamer: Two Poetic Painters—Samuel Palmer and Edward Burne-Jones, 1969; (ed) The Bodley Head Max Beerbohm, 1970; (ed) A Choice of Tennyson's Verse, 1971; The Cecils of Hatfield House, 1973; Library Looking-glass, 1975; A Portrait of Jane Austen, 1978; A Portrait of Charles Lamb, 1983; Some Dorset Country Houses, 1986. *Address:* Red Lion House, Cranborne, Wimborne, Dorset. *T:* Cranborne 244.

*Died 1 Jan.* 1986.

**CECIL-WRIGHT, Air Commodore John Allan Cecil**, AFC, TD, AE; *b* 1886; *s* of Alfred Cecil Wright, Edgbaston; name changed by Deed Poll from Wright to Cecil-Wright, 1957; *m* 1st, 1910, Irene, *d* of A. C. Auster, Barnt Green, Worcs; one *s*; 2nd, 1920, Lillian Annie May, *d* of Robert Braithwaite Palmer Dolman, London; 3rd, 1946, Ethne Monica, *y d* of late Dr W. E. Falconar; one *s*. *Educ:* Winchester. 1st Vol. Bn Royal Warwicks Regt, 1905; served European War, 1914–19; joined RFC in 1916; Squadron Leader 605 (County of Warwick) Bomber Squadron, 1926–36; Comdt, Midland Command ATC, 1941–45; Hon. Air Cdre 605 (County of Warwick) Sq. Royal Aux. AF, 1946–55; Hon. Area Rep., RAF Benevolent Fund; Vice-Chm. (Air) Warwicks T & AFA, 1945–54. Dir, Warne Wright & Rowland, Ltd (Chm., 1920–63); Dir, The Decca Navigator Co. Ltd; Mem. Birmingham City Council, 1934–39; MP (Nat. U) Erdington div. of Birmingham, 1936–45; Pres., Erdington Conservative and Unionist Assoc., 1945–55; Patron, Sutton Coldfield Cons. and U. Assoc.; Mem., Warwicks CC 1958–61; DL, Warwicks, 1933–67; Mem. Exec. Cttee, Animal Health Trust; President: Cruft's Dog Show, 1962–76; Welsh Kennel Club, 1972–; Kennel Club, 1976– (Chm., 1948–73, Vice-Pres., 1973–76); Scottish Kennel Club, 1981–; Alsatian League and Club of GB; Birmingham Dog Show Soc., 1955–; Vice-Pres., Nat. Canine Defence League. Pres., 605 Squadron Assoc. *Address:* 14 Richmond Court, Park Lane, Milford-on-Sea, Lymington, Hants SO4 0PT. *T:* Milford-on-Sea 2606; 33 Ennismore Gardens, SW7. *T:* 01-584 6197. *Clubs:* Royal Air Force, Kennel; Royal Lymington Yacht.

*Died 14 July* 1982.

**CHADWICK, Sir Albert (Edward)**, Kt 1974; CMG 1967; formerly Chairman, Gas and Fuel Corporation of Victoria; *b* 15 Nov. 1897;

*s* of Andrew and Georgina Chadwick; *m* 1924, Thelma Marea Crawley; one *s* one *d*. *Educ*: Tungamah State Sch., Vic.; University High Sch., Vic. European War, 1914–18; served 1915–19 (MSM; despatches 1918); War of 1939–45: served RAAF, 1940–45 (Group Capt.). Engr, Robt Bryce & Co. Ltd, 1920–25; Lubricant Manager, Shell Co. of Aust. Ltd, 1925–35; Asst Gen. Man., Metropolitan Gas Co. Melbourne, 1935–51; Asst. Gen. Man., subseq. Gen. Man., Gas and Fuel Corp. of Vic., 1951–63. Chm., Overseas Telecommunications Commn (Australia), 1962–68. *Publications*: various technical and economic works. *Recreations*: golf, cricket, football, racing. *Clubs*: Athenæum, Victorian Amateur Turf (Melbourne); Riversdale Golf; (Pres. 1964–79) Melbourne Cricket (Life Mem.). *Died* 27 Oct. 1983.

**CHADWICK, Sir John (Edward)**, KCMG 1967 (CMG 1957); HM Diplomatic Service, retired; *b* 17 Dec. 1911; *e s* of late John Chadwick, Barrister, and Edith (*née* Horrocks); *m* 1945, Audrey Joyce, *d* of late Col L. d'E. Lenfestey, CIE; one *s* two *d*. *Educ*: Rugby; Corpus Christi Coll., Cambridge (MA). Dept of Overseas Trade, 1934; Asst Trade Comr, Calcutta, 1938; Eastern Group Supply Council, Simla, 1941; Commercial Secretary, Washington, 1946–48; First Sec., Tel Aviv, 1950–53; Counsellor (Commercial) Tokyo, 1953–56; Minister (Economic), Buenos Aires, 1960–62, (Commercial), Washington, 1963–67; Ambassador to Romania, 1967–68; UK Representative to OECD, Paris, 1969–71. Consultant, Sterling Industrial Securities, 1973; Special Advr, Asian Develt Bank, 1973–83. *Address*: Larkfields, Woodstock Road, Charlbury, Oxford OX7 3ES. *Club*: Travellers'. *Died* 30 Aug. 1987.

**CHADWICK, Sir Robert, (Sir Peter), B.**; *see* Burton-Chadwick.

**CHADWYCK-HEALEY, Sir Charles Arthur**, 4th Bt *cr* 1919; OBE 1945; TD; *b* 27 May 1910; *s* of Sir Gerald Chadwyck-Healey, 2nd Bt, CBE, and Mary Verena (*d* 1957), *d* of George Arthur Watson; *S* brother, 1979; *m* 1939, Viola, *d* of late Cecil Lubbock; three *s* two *d*. *Educ*: Eton; Trinity College, Oxford. BA 1932, MA 1936. Served War of 1939–45, N Africa, Sicily, Italy (despatches twice, OBE); Lt-Col RA (TA). Fellow, SPCK. *Heir*: *s* Charles Edward Chadwyck-Healey [*b* 13 May 1940; *m* 1967, Angela Mary, *e d* of John Metson, Bassingbourn, Herts; one *s* two *d*]. *Address*: The Red House, Clare, Sudbury, Suffolk. *Died* 14 Aug. 1986.

**CHAGALL, Marc**, Grand Cross Legion of Honour, 1977 (Grand Officer 1971; Commander 1965); artist; *b* Vitebsk, Russia, 7 July 1887; *m* 1915, Bella Rosenfeld (decd); one *s* one *d*; *m* 1952, Valentine Brodsky. *Educ*: Vitebsk, Russia. Left Russia, 1910, for Paris; returned to Russia, 1914; left again for Paris, 1922. Worked with Ambroise Vollard, famous art editor; left France for America, 1941; returned to France, 1948; has settled in the South of France. Has painted mural paintings besides easel pictures, ballet and theatre settings and costumes; at present working on ceramics; has done over 300 engravings. Retrospective exhibitions in the museums of London (Tate Gallery, Royal Academy), Paris, Amsterdam, Chicago, New York, Venice, Jerusalem, and Tel Aviv, 1946–; International Prize for engraving, Biennale Venice, 1948; Erasmus Prize, 1960 (with A. Kokoschka). Salle Chagall founded in Paris Musée d'Art Moderne, 1950. *Publications*: Ma Vie, 1931; Illustrations for: Dead Souls, The Fables of La Fontaine, The Bible, The Arabian Nights, Stories from Boccaccio (verve), Burning Lights and the First Meeting, by Bella Chagall. *Address*: La Colline, Quartier les Gardettes, 06570 Saint-Paul-de-Vence, AM, France. *Died* 28 March 1985.

**CHAGLA, Shri Mohomedali Currim**, BA (Oxon); Indian lawyer and administrator; Barrister-at-law; *b* 30 Sept. 1900; *m* 1931, Meher-un-nissa (*d* 1961), *d* of Dharsi Jivraj; two *s* one *d*. *Educ*: St Xavier's High Sch. and Coll., Bombay; Lincoln Coll., Oxford. Hons. Sch. of Modern History, 1922; President: Oxford Asiatic Society, 1921; Oxford Indian Majlis, 1922; called to Bar, Inner Temple, 1922; practised on Original Side of High Court, Bombay, 1922–41; Professor of Constitutional Law, Government Law Coll., Bombay, 1927–30; Hon. Secretary, Bar Council of High Court of Judicature at Bombay, 1931–41; Puisne Judge, Bombay High Court, 1941–47; Chief Justice, 1947–58. Fellow Bombay Univ.; Hon. Fellow Lincoln Coll., Oxford, 1961. Went to New York as one of India's representatives to UNO Session and fought for Cause of Indians in S Africa, 1946; Vice-Chancellor, Bombay Univ., 1947; President, Asiatic Society of Bombay, 1947–58; Chairman Legal Education Cttee, 1948; Member Law Commission, 1955–58; Shri Krishnarajendra Silver Jubilee Lecturer, 1954. Governor of Bombay, 14 Oct.–10 Dec. 1956. *Ad hoc* Judge International Court of Justice, The Hague, 1957–60; Chairman Life Insurance Corporation Enquiry Commission, 1958; Indian Ambassador to the United States, Mexico and Cuba, 1958–61; Indian High Commissioner in London and Ambassador to Ireland, 1962–63; Leader of Upper House of Parlt, India, 1964–67; Education Minister, 1963–66; Minister for External Affairs, Government of India, Nov. 1966–Sept. 1967. Member, Sikh Grievances Enquiry Commission, Sept. 1961. Leader, Indian Delegation to: Security Council for

Kashmir Debate, 1964 and 1965; Commonwealth Conf., Ottawa, 1964; General Conf., UNESCO, 1964; UN General Assembly, 1967. Hon. LLD: University of Hartford, Hartford; Temple Univ., Philadelphia; Boston Univ., Boston; Dartmouth Coll., Hanover, NH; Leningrad Univ.; Panjab Univ.; Banaras Hindu Univ. Unesco award for dist. service to human rights, 1979. *Publications*: The Indian Constitution, 1929; Law, Liberty and Life, 1950; The Individual and the State, 1958; An Ambassador Speaks, 1962; Education and the Nation, 1966; Unity and Language, 1967; Roses in December (autobiog.), 1974. *Recreation*: bridge. *Address*: Pallonji Mansion, New Cuffe Parade, Bombay 5, India. *Club*: Willingdon (Bombay). *Died* 9 Feb. 1981.

**CHALLANS, Mary;** *see* Renault, M.

**CHALLENGER, Frederick**, BSc (London); PhD (Göttingen); DSc (Birmingham); CChem, FRSC; Professor of Organic Chemistry, the University, Leeds, 1930–53, Emeritus Professor, 1953; *b* Halifax, Yorks, 15 Dec. 1887; *s* of Rev. S. C. Challenger; *m* 1922, Esther Yates, MA (*d* 1969); two *d*. *Educ*: Ashville Coll., Harrogate; Derby Technical Coll.; University College, Nottingham; University of Göttingen. 1851 Exhibition Scholar, 1910–12; Asst Lecturer in Chemistry, University of Birmingham, 1912; Lecturer in Chemistry, 1915; Senior Lecturer in Organic Chemistry, University of Manchester 1920; Vice-President of Royal Institute of Chemistry, 1948–51. Sir Jesse Boot Foundn Lectr (mainly on Prof. F. S. Kipping), Univ. of Nottingham, 1980. Hon. Life Mem., Phytochemical Soc. of Europe, 1981. Hon. Governor, Ashville Coll. *Publications*: Aspects of the Organic Chemistry of Sulphur, 1959; chapter in Organometals and Organometalloids: Occurrence and Fate in the Environment, 1978 (dedicated to him); numerous publications, mostly in the Journal of the Chemical Society, Biochemical Journal and Journal of Institute of Petroleum, dealing with organo-metallic compounds (particularly of bismuth), organic thiocyanates and selenocyanates, aromatic substitution, sulphur compounds of shale oil, and other heterocyclic sulphur compounds, microbiological chemistry; mechanism of biological methylation (especially by moulds) as applied to arsenic, tellurium, selenium and sulphur compounds and checked by use of compounds containing isotopic carbon; sulphonium and other compounds of sulphur in plants and animals and in metabolic disturbances (homocystinuria); reviews on the methionine-cystine relationship in mental retardation and on biosynthesis of organometallic and organometalloidal compounds related to environmental pollution; chemical biography. *Address*: 19 Elm Avenue, Beeston, Nottingham. *T*: Nottingham 257686. *Died* 12 Feb. 1983.

**CHALMERS, George Buchanan**, CMG 1978; HM Diplomatic Service, retired; *b* 14 March 1929; *s* of late George and Anne Buchanan Chalmers; *m* 1954, Jeanette Donald Cant. *Educ*: Hutcheson's Grammar Sch.; Glasgow and Leiden Univs. RAF, 1950–52; FO, 1952–54; 3rd Sec., Bucharest, 1954–57; 2nd Sec., Djakarta, 1957–58; 1st Sec., Bangkok, 1958–61; FO, 1961–64; 1st Sec., Seoul, 1964–66; 1st Sec. and subseq. Commercial Counsellor, Tel Aviv, 1966–70; Dir, California Trade Drive Office, 1971; Head of Oil Dept, FCO, 1971–72; Head of S Asian Dept, FCO, 1973–75; Counsellor, Tehran, 1975–76; Minister, Tehran, 1976–79; Consul-General, Chicago, 1979–82. *Recreations*: ski-ing, bridge. *Address*: East Bank House, Bowden, Melrose, Roxburghshire TD6 0ST.

*Died* 19 July 1989.

**CHALMERS, John**, CBE 1978; retired; General Secretary, Amalgamated Society of Boilermakers, Shipwrights, Blacksmiths and Structural Workers, 1966–80; Member of the General Council of the TUC, 1977–80; *b* 16 May 1915; *s* of John Aitken Chalmers and Alexandrina McLean; two *d* (one *s* decd). *Educ*: Clydebank Sen. Secondary Sch. Apprenticeship, Boilermaker-Plater. Trade Union Official, 1954–; Mem., Nat. Exec. Cttee, Labour Party, 1966–77 (Vice-Chm. 1975–76; Chm. 1976–77). Member: Central Arbitration Cttee, 1976–; Lay Mem., Press Council, 1978–81. *Recreations*: reading, gardening, golf. *Address*: 23 Killingworth Drive, West Moor, Newcastle upon Tyne NE12 0ER. *T*: Newcastle upon Tyne 683246. *Died* 19 Aug. 1983.

**CHALMERS, William John**, CB 1973; CVO 1979; CBE 1954; *b* 20 Oct. 1914; *s* of late William Chalmers and Catherine Florence (*née* Munro), Inverness; *m* 1942, Jessie Alexandra Roy, *y d* of late George Johnston McGregor and Erika Amalie (*née* Jensen), Edinburgh; one *s* one *d*. *Educ*: Inverness Royal Academy; Edinburgh University. BL 1937. Staff Commonwealth War Graves Commission, 1938; served Queen's Own Cameron Highlanders, 1939–45; Bde Major 214th Infantry Bde, 1942–43 and 1944–45 (despatches); Commonwealth War Graves Commission, 1945; Assistant Secretary, 1948–56, Sec. and Dir-Gen., 1956–75. Appeal Secretary, The Queen's Silver Jubilee Appeal, 1975–78; Mem. Admin. Council, The Royal Jubilee Trusts, 1978–80; Chm. Trustees, Hereford Cathedral Appeal Fund, 1985–. Croix de Guerre, France, 1944; Coronation Medal, 1953; Jubilee Medal, 1977. *Address*: Holy Well House, Luston, Leominster, Herefordshire HR6 0DN. *T*: Leominster 5767. *Died* 8 Jan. 1986.

**CHAMBERLAIN, Ronald;** Lecturer and Housing Consultant; *b* 19 April 1901; *m* Joan Smith McNeill (*d* 1950), Edinburgh; one *s* one *d*; *m* 1951, Florence Lilian Illingworth, Cricklewood. *Educ:* Owens Sch., Islington; Gonville and Caius Coll., Cambridge (MA). Formerly Secretary to National Federation of Housing Societies and (later) Chief Exec. Officer to the Miners' Welfare Commission; later engaged on administrative work for the National Service Hostels Corporation. MP (Lab) Norwood Division of Lambeth, 1945–50; Member of Middlesex County Council, 1947–52. Governor, Middlesex Hosp., 1947–74. *Recreation:* tennis. *Address:* 145 Hampstead Way, NW11 7YA. *T:* 01–455 1491.

*Died 12 May* 1987.

**CHAMBERS, Sir (Stanley) Paul,** KBE 1965; CB 1944; CIE 1941; Chairman: Liverpool & London & Globe Insurance Co. Ltd, 1968–74; London & Lancashire Insurance Co. Ltd, 1968–74; Royal Insurance Co. Ltd, 1968–74; *b* 2 April 1904; *s* of late Philip Joseph Chambers; *m* 1st, 1926, Dorothy Alice Marion (marr. diss. 1955), *d* of late T. G. B. Copp; 2nd, 1955, Mrs Edith Pollack, 2nd *d* of late R. P. Lamb, Workington, Cumberland; two *d*. *Educ:* City of London Coll.; LSE (BCom 1928; MSc Econ 1934). Mem., Indian Income Tax Enquiry Cttee, 1935–36; Income Tax Adviser to Govt of India, 1937–40; Sec. and Comr, Bd of Inland Revenue, 1942–47; Chief of Finance Div., Control Commn for Germany, British Element, 1945–47; Dir, ICI Ltd, 1947, Dep. Chm., 1952–60, Chm., 1960–68. Director: National Provincial Bank Ltd, 1951–69; National Westminster Bank Ltd, 1968–74. President: Nat. Inst. of Economic and Social Res., 1955–62; British Shippers' Council, 1963–68; Inst. of Directors, 1964–68; Royal Statistical Soc., 1964–65; Advertising Assoc., 1968–70. Chm., Cttee of Inquiry into London Transport, 1953–55; Member: Cttee apptd to review organisation of Customs and Excise, Oct. 1951–Sept. 1953; Cttee on Departmental Records, June 1952–July 1954; NCB, 1956–60; Cttee of Managers, Royal Institution, 1976–. Prepared Report on Organisation of British Medical Assoc. (March 1972). A Vice-Pres., Liverpool Sch. of Tropical Medicine, 1969–74. Pro-Chancellor, Univ. of Kent, 1972–78; Treasurer, Open University, 1969–75. Lectures: Jephcott, 1966; Messel Medal, 1968; (jtly) Granada Guildhall, 1968; Beveridge Memorial, 1969. Hon. DSc Bristol, 1963; Hon. LLD Liverpool, 1967; Hon. DTech Bradford, 1967; DUniv Open Univ., 1975. *Address:* 1A Frognal Gardens, Hampstead, NW3. *Clubs:* Athenæum, Reform.

*Died 23 Dec.* 1981.

**CHAMBERS, Prof. William Walker,** MBE 1945; William Jacks Professor of German, 1954–79, then Emeritus Professor, University of Glasgow (Vice-Principal, 1972–76); Dean of Faculties, University of Glasgow, since 1984; *b* 7 Dec. 1913; *s* of William and Agnes Chambers; *m* 1947, Mary Margaret Best; one *s* one *d*. *Educ:* Wishaw Public Sch.; Wishaw High Sch.; Universities of Glasgow, Paris and Munich. MA (Glasgow) 1936; L. ès L. (Paris) 1940; PhD (Munich) 1939. Served War of 1939–45 (despatches, MBE); 2nd Lieut, RA, 1941; Intelligence Staff, HQ 8th Army, North Africa, Sicily, Italy and Austria, 1942–46; Asst Lecturer in German, University of Leeds, 1946–47, Lecturer 1947–50; Prof. of Modern Languages, University College, N. Staffs, 1950–54. Chm., Conf. of Univ. Teachers of German in GB and Ireland, 1973–75; Pres., Assoc. of Univ. Teachers, 1962–63. Member: General Teaching Council for Scotland, 1973–77; Commonwealth Scholarship Commn in Britain, 1962–66. Vice-Chm., Governors, Jordanhill Coll. of Educn, 1962–67. FEIS, 1964. Verdienstkreuz Erste Klasse, 1967; Ehrensenator, Univ. of Freiburg, 1976. *Publications:* (ed) Paul Ernst, Selected Short Stories, 1953; (ed) Fouqué, Undine, 1956; (ed) Paul Ernst, Erdachte Gespräche, 1958; (with J. R. Wilkie) A Short History of the German Language, 1970. *Recreations:* gardening, music. *Address:* 26A Monreith Road, Glasgow G43 2NY. *T:* 041–632 1000. *Died 7 Oct.* 1985.

**CHAMPION, Baron,** *cr* 1962, of Pontypridd (Life Peer); **Arthur Joseph Champion,** PC 1967; JP; Deputy Speaker and Deputy Chairman of Committees, House of Lords, 1967–81; *b* 26 July 1897; *s* of William and Clara Champion, Glastonbury, Somerset; *m* 1930, Mary E. Williams, Pontypridd; one *d*. *Educ:* St John's Sch., Glastonbury. Signalman; 1914–18 War, 2nd Lieut, Royal Welch Fusiliers. MP (Lab.) Southern Division of Derbyshire, 1945–50, South-East Derbyshire, 1950–Sept. 1959; Parliamentary Private Secretary to Minister of Food, 1949–50, to Secretary of War, 1950–51; Joint Parliamentary Secretary, Ministry of Agriculture and Fisheries, April–Oct. 1951; Minister without Portfolio and Dep. Leader of the House of Lords, 1964–67. Formerly British Delegate to Consultative Assembly at Strasbourg; Govt appointed Director of the British Sugar Corporation, 1960–64, 1967–68. Hon. ARCVS, 1967; Hon. Mem., BVA, 1976. *Address:* 22 Lanelay Terrace, Pontypridd, Mid Glam. *T:* Pontypridd 402349.

*Died 2 March* 1985.

**CHAMPION, Rev. Sir Reginald Stuart,** KCMG 1946 (CMG 1944); OBE 1934; retired as Vicar of Chilham, Kent (1953–61); *b* 21 March 1895; *s* of late Philip Champion and Florence Mary Hulburd; *m*

1920, Margaret, *d* of late Very Rev. W. M. Macgregor, DD, LLD; two *s* one *d*. *Educ:* Sutton Valence Sch. Enlisted West Kent Yeomanry, 1912; Commissioned 3rd Bn E. Surrey Regt, 1913; European War, 1914–18; Occupied Enemy Territory Administration, Palestine, 1917–20; Colonial Administrative Service, 1920; District Officer, Palestine, 1920–28; Political Secretary, Aden, 1928–34; Secretary to Treaty Mission to the Yemen, 1933–34; Financial Adviser, Trans-Jordan, 1934–39; Dist Commissioner, Galilee, 1939–42; Political Mission to the Yemen, 1940; Chief Secretary, Aden, 1942–44, Gov. and C-in-C, 1944–51; retired from Colonial Service, 1951; ordained Deacon, Jan. 1952; Priest, Dec. 1952; Curate, All Saints', Maidstone, 1952. *Address:* 46 Chancellor House, Mount Ephraim, Tunbridge Wells, TN4 8BT. *T:* Tunbridge Wells 20719. *Died 9 Oct.* 1982.

**CHAMSON, André;** Member of the French Academy; Grand Croix de la Légion d'Honneur; Grand Officier de l'Ordre du Mérite; Curator of the Petit Palais since 1945; Directeur Général des Archives de France, since 1959; International President of the Pen, 1956; *b* 6 June 1900; *s* of Jean Chamson and Madeleine Aldebert; *m* 1924, Lucie Mazauric; one *d*. *Educ:* Ecole des Chartes. Joint Curator, Palais de Versailles, 1933–39. Served War of 1939–45 (Croix de Guerre, Médaille de la Résistance); Captain, Staff of 5th Army, 1939–40; Chef de bataillon, Bde Alsace Lorraine, 1944–45. Près., Collège des Conservateurs du Musée et Domaine de Chantilly. Docteur *hc* Université Laval, Quebec. Grand Officier de l'Ordre de Léopold; Commandeur de la Couronne, Belgium; Officier of Saint Sava, Norway; Officer of Merit, Italy; Grand Officier de l'Ordre du Soleil du Pérou; Grand Officier de l'Etoile Polaire de Suède; Grand Officier de l'Ordre National de la Côte d'Ivoire. *Publications:* Roux le bandit, 1925; Les Hommes de la route, 1927; Le Crime des justes, 1928; Les Quatre Eléments, 1932; La Galère, 1938; Le Puits des miracles, 1945; Le Dernier Village, 1946; La Neige et la fleur, 1950; Le Chiffre de nos jours, 1954; Adeline Vénician, 1956; Nos Ancêtres les Gaulois, 1958; Le Rendez-vous des Espérances, 1961; Comme une Pierre qui Tombe, 1964; La Petite Odyssée, 1965; La Superbe, 1967; La Tour de Constance, 1970; Les Taillons, ou la terreur blanche, 1974; La Reconquête, 1944–45, 1975; Suite guerrière, 1976; Sans peur et les brigands aux visages noirs, 1977; Castanet, le Camisard de l'Aigoual, 1979; Catinat, 1982. *Address:* 35 rue Mirabeau, 75016 Paris, France. *Club:* Pen (Pres.).

*Died 9 Nov.* 1983.

**CHANCE, Major Geoffrey Henry Barrington,** CBE 1962; *b* 16 Dec. 1893; *s* of Ernest Chance, Burghfield, Berks; *m* 1st, 1914, Hazel Mary Louise Cadell (decd); two *d*; 2nd, 1933, Daphne Corona Wallace; one *s* one *d*. *Educ:* Eton. Engineering, 1913–14. Army, 1914–19. Qualified Chartered Accountant, 1928, practised, 1930–40; HM Treasury, 1941–45. Company director. CC, Alderman (Wilts), 1955–67; Chairman Chippenham Conservative Assoc., 1955–62; High Sheriff of Wiltshire, 1965. *Recreations:* fishing, shooting. *Address:* Flat 2, Hatton's Lodge, Braydon, Swindon, Wilts.

*Died 11 July* 1987.

**CHANCE, Ivan Oswald,** CBE 1971; Chairman, Christies International Ltd, 1973–76 (Chairman, Christie, Manson and Woods Ltd, 1958–74); Consultant, 1976–80; *b* 23 June 1910; *s* of Brig.-Gen. O. K. Chance, CMG, DSO, and Fanny Isabel, *d* of Sir George Agnew, 2nd Bt; *m* 1936, Pamela Violet (*d* 1981), *d* of Everard Martin Smith. *Educ:* Eton. Joined Christie's, 1930; became a partner, 1935. Served War of 1939–45: 58 Middx AA Bn (TA), and Coldstream Guards (despatches, 1945). Mem. Council, Nat Trust, 1977–80 (Mem., Exec. Cttee, 1976–80; Chm., Properties Cttee, 1976–80); Chm., 1968–80, Pres. 1980–, Georgian Group. FRSA. *Recreations:* travel, gardening. *Address:* 38 Belgravia Court, Ebury Street, SW1; Colby Lodge, Stepaside, Narberth, Dyfed SA67 8PP. *Clubs:* Beefsteak, Brooks's, White's; Brook (New York). *Died 28 Dec.* 1984.

**CHANCE, Sir Roger (James Ferguson),** 3rd Bt, *cr* 1900; MC; *b* 26 Jan. 1893; *e s* of George Ferguson Chance (2nd *s* of 1st Bt) and Mary Kathleen, *d* of Rev. Henry Stobart; *S* uncle, 1935; *m* 1921, Mary Georgina (*d* 1984), *d* of Col William Rowney, and Kate, *d* of Maj.-Gen. Fendall Currie; one *s* two *d* (and one *s* decd). *Educ:* Eton; Trinity Coll., Cambridge (MA); London University (PhD). Served European War, Aug. 1914–April 1918; Capt. and Adjutant 4th (RI) Dragoon Guards, 1916–17; Capt. 1st Batt. The Rifle Brigade, 1918 (twice wounded, despatches twice, MC); Editor, Review of Reviews, 1932–33; Press Attaché, British Embassy, Berlin, 1938; Sqdn Leader RAFVR, 1940–41. *Publications:* Until Philosophers are Kings (political philosophy), 1928; Conservatism and Wealth (with Oliver Baldwin, politics), 1929; Winged Horses (fiction), 1932; Be Absolute for Death (fiction), 1964; The End of Man (theology), 1973; Apple and Eve (a Cambridge symposium). *Heir:* *s* (George) Jeremy (ffolliott) Chance [*b* 24 Feb. 1926; *m* 1950, Cecilia Mary Elizabeth, *d* of Sir (William) Hugh (Stobart) Chance, CBE; two *s* two *d*]. *Address:* Royal Bank of Scotland, Whitehall, SW1. *Club:* Athenæum. *Died 23 April* 1987.

**CHANCE, Sir (William) Hugh (Stobart),** Kt 1945; CBE 1958; DL; *b* 31 Dec. 1896; 2nd *s* of George Ferguson Chance, Clent Grove, near

Stourbridge, Worcs; *b* of Sir Roger Chance, 3rd Bt, MC; *m* 1st, 1926, Cynthia May (marr. diss.), *er d* of Major A. F. Baker-Cresswell, Cresswell and Harehope, Northumberland; two *s* three *d*; 2nd, 1961, Rachel Carr, *d* of Cyril Cameron, (killed in action, 1915), RHA, and of Mrs Stormonth-Darling. *Educ:* Eton; Trinity Coll., Cambridge (MA). Dir, Chance Brothers Ltd, 1924–64. Served European War, 1914–18, Lieut Worcs Regt and Royal Flying Corps; Smethwick Borough Council, 1940–45; Chm. Smethwick Education Cttee, 1943–45; Worcs County Council, 1946–74, Vice-Chm., 1949–53; Chm. Education Cttee 1958–64; Pres. Assoc. of Technical Institutions, 1948–49; Chm. West Midlands Advisory Council for Further Education, 1949–61; Mem. of "Percy" Cttee on Higher Technological Education; Willis Jackson Cttee on Technical Teachers; Lord Chancellor's Cttee on Intestacy, 1951; Mem. Royal Commn. on Scottish Affairs, 1952; Pres. West Midlands Union of Conservative Associations, 1957–67. High Sheriff of Worcs, 1942; DL Worcs; Alderman Worcs CC 1953; Pres. Worcs Red Cross, 1958–67; Hon. Col (TA) Parsons Memorial Medal, 1946. *Recreation:* archery. *Address:* The Clock House, Birlingham, Pershore, Worcs WR10 3AF. *T:* Evesham 750223. *Club:* Leander.
*Died 17 May 1981.*

**CHANCELLOR, Sir Christopher (John),** Kt 1951; CMG 1948; MA; *b* 29 March 1904; *s* of late Sir John Robert Chancellor, GCMG, GCVO, GBE, DSO; *m* 1926, Sylvia Mary (OBE 1976), *e d* of Sir Richard Paget, 2nd Bt, and Lady Muriel Finch-Hatton, *d* of 12th Earl of Winchilsea and Nottingham; two *s* two *d. Educ:* Eton Coll.; Trinity College., Cambridge (1st class in History). Joined Reuters in 1930; Reuters' Gen. Manager and Chief Corresp in Far East with headquarters in Shanghai, 1931–39; Gen. Manager of Reuters, Ltd, 1944–59, Trustee, 1960–65; Chairman: Daily Herald, 1959–61; Odhams Press Ltd, 1960–61 (Vice-Chm., 1959–60); Chm. and Chief Executive, The Bowater Paper Corporation Ltd and associated cos, 1962–69. Director: Northern and Employers Assurance Co. Ltd, 1946–64; Bristol United Press Ltd, 1958–74; Observer Ltd, 1961–64. Chm., Madame Tussaud's, 1961–72. Mem. Court, London Univ., 1956–62; Chm. Exec. Cttee of The Pilgrims Soc. of Great Britain, 1958–67; Mem. Board of Regents, Memorial Univ. of Newfoundland, 1963–68; Vice-Pres., National Council of Social Service, 1959–71; Dep.-Chm., Council of St Paul's Cathedral Trust, 1954–62; Chm., Appeal and Publicity Cttee, King George VI National Memorial Fund, 1952–54; Dep.-Chm., Exec. Cttee, 1955–56; Chm., Bath Preservation Trust, 1969–76. King Haakon VII Liberty Cross, 1947; Officer Order of Orange Nassau, 1950; Comdr Royal Order of Danebrog, 1951; Officer, Legion of Honour, 1951; Comdr Order of Civil Merit (Spain), 1952; Cross of Comdr Order of Phœnix, 1953; Comdr Order of Vasa, 1953; Comdr Order of Merit (Italy), 1959. *Address:* The Priory, Ditcheat, Shepton Mallet, Somerset. *Club:* Travellers'.                *Died 9 Sept. 1989.*

**CHANDRA, Ram;** *see* Ram Chandra.

**CHANNING WILLIAMS, Maj.-Gen. John William,** CB 1963; DSO 1944; OBE 1951; jssc; psc; *b* 14 Aug. 1908; *s* of late W. A. Williams, Inkpen, Berks; *m* 1936, Margaret Blachford, *d* of late A. J. Wood, Maidenhead, Berks; three *s. Educ:* Trent Coll.; RMC Sandhurst. Commissioned 2nd Lieut, N. Staffs Regt, 1929. Served War of 1939–45 (despatches, DSO): BEF, France, 1939–40; Instructor, Senior Officers' School, 1942–43; GSO1, Staff Coll., Camberley, 1943–44; CO 4th Bn Welch Regt, 1944; served in France, 1944–45, India and Burma, 1945–46. Asst Instructor, Imperial Defence Coll., 1946–48; AA and QMG, 40th Inf. Div., Hong Kong, 1949–50; Colonel General Staff, HQ Land Forces, Hong Kong, 1951–52; Colonel, 1954; BGS (Operations and Plans), GHQ, MELF, 1955–58; Director of Quartering, War Office, 1960–61; Director of Movements, War Office, 1961–63; retired; Brigadier, 1957; Maj.-Gen., 1960. *Recreations:* shooting, fishing. *Address:* Amesbury Abbey, Amesbury, Wiltshire SP4 7EX.          *Died 26 May 1990.*

**CHANTLER, Philip,** CMG 1963; Director of Economic Planning, Cyprus, 1969–70, Swaziland, 1970–71; *b* 16 May 1911; *s* of Tom and Minnie Chantler; *m* 1938, Elizabeth Margaret Pentney; one *d. Educ:* Manchester Central High Sch.; Manchester Univ.; Harvard Univ Commonwealth Fund Fellow, 1934–36; Asst Lectr in Public Admin., Manchester Univ., 1936–38; Tariffs Adviser, UK Gas Corp. Ltd, 1938–40. Served War of 1939–45: RA 1940–41; War Cabinet Secretariat, 1941–45; Economic Adviser, Cabinet Office, 1945–47; Economic Adviser, Ministry of Fuel and Power, 1947–60 (seconded as Economic Adviser, Government of Pakistan Planning Board, 1955–57); Under-Sec., Electricity Div., Min. of Power, 1961–65; Chm., North-West Economic Planning Bd, 1965–69. *Publication:* The British Gas Industry: An Economic Study, 1938. *Recreations:* gardening, cine-photography, Victorian architecture, industrial archæology, domestic odd-jobbing. *Address:* 2 Duchy Road, Harrogate, N Yorks HG1 2EP; 2 The Mill, Rockcliffe, Galloway.                                   *Died 10 Feb. 1988.*

**CHAPLIN, 3rd Viscount,** *cr* 1916, of St Oswalds, Blankney, in the county of Lincoln; **Anthony Freskyn Charles Hamby Chaplin;** Flight Lieutenant RAFVR; *b* 14 Dec. 1906; *er s* of 2nd Viscount and late Hon. Gwladys Alice Gertrude Wilson, 4th *d* of 1st Baron Nunburnholme; *S* father, 1949; *m* 1st, 1933, Alvilde (marr. diss., 1951; she *m* 1951, James Lees Milne), *o d* of late Lieut-Gen. Sir Tom Bridges, KCB, KCMG; one *d*; 2nd, 1951, Rosemary, *d* of 1st Viscount Chandos, KG, PC, DSO, MC; two *d. Educ:* Radley. Occupied with Natural History and Music. Mem. Council, Zoological Soc. of London, 1934–38, 1950–; Sec., 1952–55. Voyage to New Guinea, to collect zoological material, 1935–36. Studied musical composition in Paris with Nadia Boulanger, 1936–39. Served RAF, 1940–46. *Publications:* 3 Preludes for piano; Toccata on a fragment of D. Scarlatti for piano; Cadenza for Mozart's piano concerto in C minor K. 491; various contributions to zoological journals. *Heir:* none. *Address:* Wadstray House, Blackawton, near Totnes, S Devon.                          *Died 18 Dec. 1981 (ext).*

**CHAPLING, Norman Charles,** CBE 1954; Managing Director, Cable and Wireless Ltd, 1951–65, retd; *b* 11 Feb. 1903; *s* of late Charles Chapling; *m* 1933, Lenora, *d* of late Ernest Hedges; one *s*. Past Man. Dir: Cable & Wireless (Mid-East) Ltd; Cable & Wireless (West Indies) Ltd; Direct West India Cable Co. Ltd; Eastern Extension Australasia & China Telegraph Co. Ltd; Eastern Telegraph Co. Ltd; Eastern Telegraph Co. (France) Ltd; Halifax & Bermudas Cable Co. Ltd; Mercury House Ltd; West Coast of America Telegraph Co. Ltd; Western Telegraph Co. Ltd. Past Dir, SA Belge de Câbles Télégraphiques. *Address:* 1 Boscawen, Cliff Road, Falmouth, Cornwall TR11 4AW.
*Died 29 April 1986.*

**CHAPMAN, (Anthony) Colin (Bruce),** CBE 1970; RDI 1979; Chairman, Group Lotus Car Cos Ltd; Designer of sports and racing cars; *b* 19 May 1928; *s* of late S. F. Kennedy Chapman; *m* 1954, Hazel Patricia Williams; one *s* two *d. Educ:* Stationers' Company's Sch., Hornsey; London Univ. (BSc Eng). Served as Pilot, RAF, 1950. Structural Engineer, 1951; Civil Engineer, Development Engineer, British Aluminium Co., 1952. Formed own Company, Lotus Cars, manufacturing motor cars, 1955; Holder of Don Ferodo Trophy in perpetuity after three wins (1956, 1965, 1978); Winner of Formula 1 World Constructors Championship (1963, 1965, 1968, 1970, 1972, 1978). FRSA 1968; Fellow, UCL, 1972; Hon. Dr RCA 1980. *Recreation:* flying. *Address:* Lotus Cars Ltd, Norwich, Norfolk NR14 8EZ. *Clubs:* British Racing Drivers, British Automobile Racing; British Racing and Sports Car.
*Died 16 Dec. 1982.*

**CHAPMAN, Prof. Brian;** Professor of Government, University of Manchester, since 1961, and Dean, Faculty of Economic and Social Studies, 1967–71; *b* 6 April 1923; *s* of B. P. Chapman; *m* 1st, 1949, Jean Margaret Radford (marr. diss.); two *s*; 2nd, 1972, Christina Maria, *d* of Neville and Edna O'Brien, Altrincham; one *s. Educ:* Owen's Sch., London; Magdalen Coll. and Nuffield Coll., Oxford (DPhil, MA). Lieut, RNVR, 1942–45. Dept of Govt, University of Manchester, and Vis. Prof. at several European Univs, 1949–60; Foundn Prof. of Govt and Dir, Public Admin programme, University of W Indies, 1960–61. Member: Council, Manchester Business School; Court, Cranfield Inst. of Technology; Bd of Governors, Police Staff Coll.; Adv. Council on Police Training. Vis. Prof., Queen's Univ., Kingston, Ont, 1972; Vis. Prof., Univ. of Victoria, BC, 1975–76. Gen. Editor, Minerva Series. Knight of Mark Twain, 1979. *Publications:* French Local Government, 1953; The Prefects and Provincial France, 1954; (jtly) The Life and Times of Baron Haussmann, 1956; The Profession of Government, 1959; (jtly) The Fifth Constitution, 1959; British Government Observed, 1963; The Police State, 1970; (jtly) The Resistance in Europe, 1974; (ed jtly) W.J.M.M.: Political Questions, 1974; Introduction to Government, 1977; Canadian Police System, 1977; (contrib.) The Proceedings of the 1978 Cranfield Conference on the Prevention of Crime in Europe, 1979; contributions to internat. learned jls, reviews and newspapers. *Address:* Department of Government, The University, Manchester M13 9PL. *T:* 061-273 7121. *Clubs:* Naval; Manchester Business School (Manchester).
*Died 23 July 1981.*

**CHAPMAN, Very Rev. Clifford Thomas;** Dean Emeritus, Exeter Cathedral, 1980; *b* 28 May 1913; *s* of late Walter and Mabel Mary Chapman; *m* 1939, Nance Kathleen, *d* of late Harold Tattersall; one *s* one *d. Educ:* Sir Walter St John's Sch.; King's College, London University (BA, BD, AKC, MTh, PhD); Ely Theological College. Deacon 1936, Priest 1937; Curate: All Saints, Child's Hill, 1936; Pinner, 1936–38; St Paul's, Winchmore Hill, 1938–39; Pinner, 1939–42; Minister of Church of Ascension Conventional District, Preston Road, Wembley, 1942–45; Vicar of Christ Church, Chelsea, 1945–50; RD of Chelsea, 1946–50; Rector of Abinger, 1950–61; Organizer of Adult Religious Educn, Dio. Guildford, 1952–61; Director of Religious Educn, 1961–63, and of Post-Ordination Training, 1958–68; Examining Chaplain to Bp of Guildford, 1953–73; Canon Residentiary and Sub-Dean of Guildford Cathedral, 1961–73; Dean of Exeter, 1973–80; Proctor in Convocation, 1965–73, Mem. General Synod, 1975–80. FKC 1948.

*Publication:* The Conflict of the Kingdom, 1951. *Recreations:* walking, travel, Greek and Roman antiquities. *Address:* Spring Cottage, Coldharbour, Dorking, Surrey RH5 6HF. *T:* Dorking 6356. *Died 25 May 1982.*

**CHAPMAN, Colin;** *see* Chapman, A. C. B.

**CHAPMAN, Harold Thomas,** CBE 1951; FRAeS; MIMechE; formerly Director, Hawker Siddeley Group, retired 1969; *b* 4 Aug. 1896; 3rd *s* of Henry James and Elizabeth Chapman, Mornington, Wylam-on-Tyne; *m* 1st, 1923, Mabel Annie Graham (*d* 1974); 2nd, 1983, Doris Mary Graham. *Educ:* Rutherford Coll., Newcastle on Tyne. Served European War in RFC and RAF, 1917–19. Joined Armstrong Siddeley Motors Ltd as a Designer, 1926; Works Manager, 1936; Gen. Manager, 1945; Dir, 1946. *Recreations:* fishing, shooting, golfing. *Address:* Ty-Melyn, Rhydspence, Whitney-on-Wye, Hereford. *T:* Clifford 313.

*Died 4 May 1985.*

**CHAPMAN, Kenneth Herbert;** Managing Director, Thomas Tilling Ltd, 1967–73; Director: British Steam Specialities Ltd; Société Générale (France) Bank Ltd; Ready Mixed Concrete Ltd; Goodliffe Garages Ltd; former Director, Royal Worcester Ltd; *b* 9 Sept. 1908; *s* of Herbert Chapman and Anne Bennett Chapman (*née* Poxon); *m* 1937, Jean Martha Mahring; one *s*. *Educ:* St Peter's Sch., York. Articled Clerk, 1926; qual. Solicitor, 1931; private practice, 1931–36; joined professional staff, HM Land Registry, 1936; transf. Min. of Aircraft Prodn, 1940, Private Sec. to Perm. Sec.; transf. Min. of Supply, 1946. Joined Thomas Tilling Ltd, as Group Legal Adviser, 1948; at various times Chm. or Dir of more than 20 companies in Tilling Group. High Sheriff of Greater London, 1974. *Recreations:* Rugby football (Past Pres. and Hon. Treas. of RFU, mem. cttee various clubs), cricket (mem. cttee various clubs), golf. *Address:* 2 Wyndham Lea, Common Hill, West Chiltington, Sussex RH20 2NP. *T:* West Chiltington 3808. *Clubs:* East India, Devonshire, Sports and Public Schools; West Sussex Golf; Harlequin Football. *Died 8 Nov. 1989.*

**CHAPMAN, Sir Robin, (Robert Macgowan),** 2nd Bt *cr* 1958; CBE 1961; TD and Bar, 1947; JP; Partner, Chapman and Partners, Chartered Accountants; Chairman, North Eastern Investment Trust Ltd; *b* Harton, Co. Durham, 12 Feb. 1911; *er s* of 1st Bt and Lady (Hélène Paris) Chapman, JP (*née* Macgowan); *S* father, 1963; *m* 1941, Barbara May, *d* of Hubert Tonks, Ceylon; two *s* one *d*. *Educ:* Marlborough; Corpus Christi Coll., Cambridge (Exhibitioner). 1st Cl. Hons Maths, BA 1933; MA 1937. Chartered Accountant, ACA 1938; FCA 1945. Jt Sec., Shields Commercial Bldg Soc., 1939–83; Partner: Henry Chapman Son and Co., 1939–69; Chapman, Hilton and Dunford, 1969–80; Consultant, Spicer and Pegler, Chartered Accountants, 1980–85. Chairman: Northern Counties Provincial Area Conservative Associations, 1954–57; Jarrow Conservative Association, 1957–60; Pres., Northern Area Conservative Council, 1982–86. Pres., Northern Soc. of Chartered Accountants, 1958–59, Mem. Cttee, 1949–60; Member: Police Authority, Co. Durham, 1955–59, 1961–65; Appeals Cttee, 1955–62; Durham Diocesan Conf., 1953–70; Durham Diocesan Synod, 1971–72; Durham Diocesan Bd of Finance, 1953–71 (Chm. 1966–70); Durham County TA, 1948–68; N England TA, 1968–74; Chm., Durham Co. Scout Council, 1972–82 (Scout Silver Acorn Award, 1973). Governor, United Newcastle Hospitals, 1957–64. TA Army officer, 1933–51; served War of 1939–45: RA Anti-Aircraft Command; GSO 2, 1940; CO 325 LAA regt, RA (TA), 1948–51; Hon. Col 1963; JP 1946, DL, 1952; High Sheriff of County Durham, 1960; Vice Lord-Lieutenant, Tyne and Wear, 1974–84. *Heir: er s* David Robert Macgowan Chapman [*b* 16 Dec. 1941; *m* 1965, Maria Elizabeth de Gosztony-Zsolnay, *o d* of Dr N. de Mattyasovsky-Zsolnay, Montreal, Canada; one *s* one *d*]. *Address:* Pinfold House, 6 West Park Road, Cleadon, Sunderland SR6 7RR. *T:* Wearside 5367451. *Clubs:* Carlton; County (Durham); Hawks (Cambridge).

*Died 2 Aug. 1987.*

**CHAPMAN-MORTIMER, William Charles;** author; *b* 15 May 1907; *s* of William George Chapman-Mortimer and Martha Jane McLelland; *m* 1934, Frances Statler; *m* 1956, Ursula Merits; one *d*. *Educ:* privately. *Publications:* A Stranger on the Stair, 1950; Father Goose, 1951 (awarded James Tait Black Memorial Prize, 1952); Young Men Waiting, 1952; Mediterraneo, 1954; Here in Spain, 1955; Madrigal, 1960; Amparo, 1971. *Address:* Åsenvagen 12, Jönköping 55258, Sweden. *T:* 036–190754.

*Died 13 Dec. 1988.*

**CHAPPLE, Stanley;** Director of Symphony and Opera, University of Washington, now Emeritus; *b* 29 Oct. 1900; *s* of Stanley Clements Chapple and Bessie Norman; *m* 1927, Barbara, *d* of late Edward Hilliard; no *c*. *Educ:* Central Foundation Sch., London. Began his musical education at the London Academy of Music at the age of 8, being successively student, professor, Vice-Principal, Principal until 1936; as a Conductor made début at the Queen's Hall, 1927, and has since conducted Symphony Orchestras in Berlin, Vienna, The

Hague, Warsaw and Boston, St Louis, Washington, DC, and other American and Canadian cities. Assistant to Serge Koussevitzky at Berkshire Music Centre, 1940, 1941, 1942 and 1946; former conductor St Louis Philharmonic Orchestra and Chorus and Grand Opera Association. Hon. MusDoc Colby Coll., 1947. *Address:* 18270 47th Place NE, Seattle, Washington 98155, USA.

*Died 21 June 1987.*

**CHAPUT DE SAINTONGE, Rev. Rolland Alfred Aimé,** CMG 1953; retired; *b* Montreal, Canada, 7 Jan. 1912; *s* of Alfred Edward and Hélène Jeté Chaput de Saintonge; *m* 1940, Barbara Watts; one *s* two *d*. *Educ:* Canada; USA; Syracuse Univ., NY (BA, MA); Geneva Univ. (D ès Sc. Pol.). Extra-Mural Lecturer in International Affairs: University College of the South-West, Exeter, University of Bristol, University College of Southampton, 1935–40; Staff Speaker, Min. of Information, South-West Region, 1940; served Army, 1940–46; Lieut-Col (DCLI); Asst Secretary, Control Office for Germany and Austria, 1946–48; Head of Government Structure Branch, CCG and Liaison Officer to German Parliamentary Council, 1948–49; Head of German Information Dept, FO, 1949–58; UN High Commission for Refugees: Dep. Chief, Information and Public Relations Sect., 1960–64; Rep. in Senegal, 1964–66; Programme Support Officer, 1966–67; Chief, N and W Europe Section, 1967–68; Special Projects Officer, 1968–73. Ordained, Diocese of Quebec, 1975; admitted Community of Most Holy Sacrament, 1976; Bursar, Monastery of Most Holy Sacrament Fathers, Quebec, 1983–87. *Publications:* Disarmament in British Foreign Policy, 1935; British Foreign Policy Since the War, 1936; The Road to War and the Way Out, 1940; Public Administration in Germany, 1961. *Address:* 8 Minley Court, Somers Road, Reigate, Surrey. *Died 20 May 1989.*

**CHARLEMONT,** 13th Viscount *cr* 1665 (Ireland); **Charles Wilberforce Caulfeild;** Baron Caulfeild of Charlemont, 1620 (Ireland); retired Civil Servant, Canada; *b* 10 March 1899; *s* of Charles Hans Caulfeild (*d* 1950) and Ethel Jessie (*d* 1973), *d* of D. G. R. Mann; *S* cousin, 1979; *m* 1930, Dorothy Jessie, *d* of late Albert A. Johnston. *Educ:* Public and High schools, Ottawa, Canada. *Recreations:* formerly curling and lawn bowling. *Heir: nephew* John Day Caulfeild [*b* 19 March 1934; *m* 1st, 1964, Judith Ann (*d* 1971), *d* of James E. Dodd; one *s* one *d*; 2nd, 1972, Janet Evelyn, *d* of Orville R. Nancekivell]. *Address:* 2055 Carling Avenue, Apt 915, Ottawa, Canada K2A 1G6. *Died 14 Sept. 1985.*

**CHARLES, Anthony Harold,** ERD; TD; MA Cantab; MB; FRCS; FRCOG; Consulting Obstetric and Gynæcological Surgeon, St George's Hospital; Consulting Surgeon, Samaritan Hospital for Women (St Mary's); Consulting Gynæcologist, Royal National Orthopædic Hospital; formerly, Hon. Gynæcologist, King Edward VII Hospital for Officers; Consulting Gynæcologist, Caterham and District Hospital; Consulting Surgeon, General Lying-in-Hospital; late Hon. Consultant in Obstetrics and Gynaecology Army; *b* 14 May 1908; 2nd *s* of H. P. Charles; *m* 1962, Rosemary Christine Hubert; three *d*. *Educ:* Dulwich; Gonville and Caius Coll., Cambridge. Examiner in Midwifery and Gynæcology: Univ. of Cambridge; Soc. of Apothecaries; RCOG; Univs of London, Hong Kong and Cairo. Past Mem., Board of Governors, St Mary's Hospital. Past President: Chelsea Clinical Soc.; Sect. of Obstetrics and Gynæcology, RSM. Late Vice-Dean, St George's Hospital Medical Sch.; late Resident Asst Surgeon and Hon. Asst Anæsthetist, St George's Hospital. Colonel AMS; late Hon. Colonel and OC, 308 (Co. of London) General Hospital, T&AVR. Hon. Surgeon to the Queen, 1957–59. Served 1939–45, Aldershot, Malta and Middle-East as Surgical Specialist; Officer-in-Charge, Surgical Division, 15 Scottish General Hospital and Gynæc. Adviser MEF. Past Pres., Alleyn Club. *Publications:* Women in Sport, in Armstrong and Tucker's Injuries in Sport, 1964; contributions since 1940 to Jl Obst. and Gyn., Postgrad. Med. Jl, Proc. Royal Soc. Med., Operative Surgery, BMJ. *Recreations:* golf, boxing (Middle-Weight, Cambridge *v* Oxford, 1930); Past President Rosslyn Park Football Club. *Address:* Consulting Suite, Wellington Hospital, NW8. *T:* 071–586 5959; Gaywood Farm, Gay Street, Pulborough, W Sussex. *T:* West Chiltington (07983) 2223. *Clubs:* Army and Navy, MCC; Hawks (Cambridge). *Died 25 Nov. 1990.*

**CHARLES, Rt. Rev. Harold John;** Bishop of St Asaph, 1971–82; *b* 26 June 1914; *s* of Rev. David Charles and Mary Charles, Carmarthenshire; *m* 1941, Margaret Noeline; one *d*. *Educ:* Welsh Univ. Aberystwyth; Keble Coll., Oxford. BA Wales 1935; BA Oxford 1938, MA 1943. Curate of Abergwili, Carms, 1938–40; Bishop's Messenger, Diocese of Swansea and Brecon, 1940–48; Warden of University Church Hostel, Bangor, and Lecturer at University College, Bangor, 1948–52; Vicar of St James, Bangor, 1952–54; Canon Residentiary of Bangor, 1953–54; Warden of St Michael's Coll., Llandaff, 1954–57; Canon of Llandaff, 1956–57; Dean of St Asaph, 1957–71. ChStJ 1973. *Address:* 53 The Avenue, Woodland Park, Prestatyn, Clwyd. *Died 11 Dec. 1987.*

**CHARLES, Sir John (Pendrill),** KCVO 1975; MC 1945; Partner, Allen & Overy, 1947–78; *b* 3 May 1914; *yr s* of late Dr Clifford

Pendrill Charles and Gertrude Mary (*née* Young); *m* 1st, 1939, Mary Pamela Dudley (marr. diss.); 2nd, 1959, Winifred Marie Heath; two *d*. *Educ:* Tonbridge; Magdalene Coll., Cambridge (MA). Solicitor, 1938. Served War, 1939–45: 11th Regt (HAC) RHA; ME, Sicily and Italy. Steward, British Boxing Bd of Control, 1961–. *Recreations:* travel, fishing, sailing. *Address:* 42 Belgrave Mews South, SW1X 8BT. *T:* 01-235 5792. *Club:* White's.

*Died 9 April 1984.*

**CHARLES, Rev. Canon Sebastian;** Residentiary Canon, Westminster Abbey, since 1978; Steward since 1978, also Treasurer since 1982; Director, Inner City Aid, since 1987; *b* 31 May 1932; *s* of Gnanamuthu Pakianathan Charles and Kamala David; *m* 1967, Frances Rosemary Challen; two *s* two *d*. *Educ:* Madras Univ. (BCom 1953); Serampore Univ. (BD 1965); Lincoln Theological Coll. Curate, St Mary, Portsea, Dio. Portsmouth, 1956–59; Priest-in-charge, St John the Evangelist, Dio. Rangoon, 1959–65; St Augustine's Coll., Canterbury, 1965–66; St Thomas, Heaton Chapel, Dio. Manchester, attached to Industrial Mission Team, 1966–67; Vicar of St Barnabas', Pendleton, 1967–74; Chaplain, Univ. of Salford, 1967–74; Asst Gen. Secretary and Secretary, Div. of Community Affairs, British Council of Churches, 1974–78. Member: Parole Bd, 1980–83; Central Religious Adv. Cttee, BBC/IBA, 1981–86; Charities Aid Adv. Council, 1977–87; Inner City Trust, 1987–; Chm. Internat. Youth Trust (St Pierre Thaon), 1983–. Governor, Westminster Sch., 1984–. Hon. DHL Morningside Coll., Ia, 1988. *Recreations:* reading, tennis. *Address:* 5 Little Cloister, Westminster Abbey, SW1P 3PL. *Died 28 Oct. 1989.*

**CHARLES, William Travers;** Fellow, Faculty of Law, Monash University, 1976–82 (Special Lecturer, 1966–75); Judge of the High Court, Zambia, 1963–66; *b* Victoria, Australia, 10 Dec. 1908; *s* of William James Charles and Elizabeth Esther Charles (*née* Payne); *m* 1940, Helen Gibson Vale; one *s* one *d*. *Educ:* St Thomas Grammar Sch., Essendon, Victoria; University of Melbourne. Admitted to legal practice, Victoria, 1932; practised at bar, 1932–39. Served Australian Army Legal Service including Middle East, 1940–42 (Lieut-Col), seconded AAG (Discipline), AHQ Melbourne, 1942–46. Chief Magistrate and Legal Adviser, British Solomon Islands Protectorate, 1946–51; Judicial Commn, British Solomon Islands, 1951–53; Magistrate, Hong Kong, 1954–56; District Judge, Hong Kong, 1956–58; Judge of the High Court, Western Nigeria, 1958–63. *Recreations:* cricket, football, music, history. *Address:* 2 Burroughs Road, Balwyn, Vic 3103, Australia. *Died 21 Jan. 1990.*

**CHARLES-EDWARDS, Rt. Rev. Lewis Mervyn,** MA, DD; *b* 6 April 1902; *s* of Dr Lewis Charles-Edwards and Lillian Hill; *m* 1933, Florence Edith Louise Barsley; one *s* one *d*. *Educ:* Shrewsbury School; Keble College, Oxford; Lichfield Theological College. Curate: Christ Church, Tunstall, 1925–28; St Paul, Burton on Trent, 1928–31; Pontesbury, 1931–33; Vicar: Marchington, 1933–37; Market Drayton, 1937–44; Newark on Trent, 1944–48; Rural Dean of Hodnet, 1938–44, of Newark, 1945–48; Vicar of St Martin in the Fields, London, WC2, 1948–56; Commissary to Bishop of Honduras, 1945–56; Chaplain to King George VI, 1950–52, to the Queen, 1952–56; Bishop of Worcester, 1956–70. Religious Adviser to Independent Television Authority, 1955–56. Chairman, Midland Region Religious Advisory Committee BBC, 1958–65. Member of Commission on Church and State, 1951. Chaplain and Sub-Prelate Order of St John of Jerusalem, 1965. Select Preacher, University of Cambridge, 1949; Oxford, 1964. *Publication:* Saints Alive!, 1953. *Address:* Brackenwood Cottage, East Tuddenham, Dereham, Norfolk NR20 3NF. *Club:* Athenæum. *Died 20 Oct. 1983.*

**CHARLESON, Ian;** actor; *b* 11 Aug. 1949; *s* of John and Jean Charleson. *Educ:* Parson's Green Primary Sch., Edinburgh; Royal High Sch., Edinburgh; Edinburgh Univ. (MA); LAMDA. *London stage:* 1st professional job, Young Vic Theatre, 1972–74; Hamlet, Cambridge, 1975; Otherwise Engaged, Queen's, 1976; Julius Caesar and Volpone, NT, 1977; The Tempest, Piaf, Taming of the Shrew, Once in a Lifetime, RSC, 1978–80; Guys and Dolls, NT, 1984; Fool for Love, NT, 1985; Cat on a Hot Tin Roof, NT, 1988; *films include:* Jubilee, 1977; Chariots of Fire, 1981; Gandhi, 1982; Car Trouble, 1986; numerous TV appearances. *Address:* c/o Michael Whitehall, 125 Gloucester Road, SW7 4TE. *Died 6 Jan. 1990.*

**CHARLTON, Sir William Arthur,** Kt 1946; DSC; retired as General Marine Superintendent at New York, Furness Withy & Co. SS Lines, 1960; *b* 25 Feb. 1893; *s* of William and Augusta Pauline Charlton; *m* 1919, Eleanor Elcoat (*d* 1978); two *s*. *Educ:* Blyth; Newcastle on Tyne. Master Mariner. DSC for service in N Africa landings, 1943. Younger Brother, Trinity House; Liveryman, Hon. Company of Master Mariners; Fellow, Royal Commonwealth Society. *Address:* Apartment 419, 81 Linden Avenue, Rochester, NY 14610, USA. *Died 29 Oct. 1983.*

**CHARNLEY, Sir John,** Kt 1977; CBE 1970; DSc; FRCS; FACS; FRS 1975; Professor of Orthopædic Surgery, Manchester University, 1972–76, later Emeritus; Consultant Orthopædic Surgeon and Director of Centre for Hip Surgery, Wrightington Hospital, near Wigan, Lancs, 1947–80, retired; *b* 29 Aug. 1911; *m* 1957, Jill Margaret (*née* Heaver); one *s* one *d*. *Educ:* Bury Grammar Sch., Lancs. BSc 1932; MB ChB (Manch.) 1935; FRCS 1936; DSc 1964. Hon. Cons. Orthopædic Surgeon, Manchester Royal Infirmary, 1947. Hon. Lecturer in Clinical Orthopædics, Manchester Univ., 1959; Hon. Lecturer in Mechanical Engineering, 1966, Inst. of Science and Technology, Manchester Univ. Fellow of British Orthopædic Assoc.; Hon. Member: Amer. Acad. of Orthopædic Surgeons; American, French, Belgian, Swiss, Brazilian, and French-Canadian Orthopædic Assocs; S African Medical Assoc. Gold Medal, Soc. of Apothecaries, 1971; Gairdner Foundn Internat. Award, 1973; Olof Af Acrel Medal, Swedish Surgical Soc., 1969; Cameron Prize, Univ. of Edinburgh, 1974; Albert Lasker Medical Research Award, 1974; Lister Medal, RCS, 1975; Albert Medal, RSA, 1978. Hon. MD: Liverpool, 1975; Uppsala, 1977; Hon. DSc: Belfast, 1978; Leeds, 1978. Buccheri-La Ferla Prize, INAIL, Italy, 1977. Freedom of Co. Borough of Bury, 1974. *Publications:* Compression Arthrodesis, 1953; The Closed Treatment of Common Fractures, 1950 (German trans., 1968); Acrylic Cement in Orthopædic Surgery, 1970. *Recreations:* other than surgery, none. *Address:* Birchwood, Moss Lane, Mere, Knutsford, Cheshire. *T:* Knutsford 2267. *Died 5 Aug. 1982.*

**CHASE, Anya Seton;** *see* Seton, A.

**CHASE, Stuart;** author, social scientist; *b* Somersworth, New Hampshire, USA, 8 March 1888; *s* of Harvey Stuart and Aaronette Rowe Chase; *m* 1st, 1914, Margaret Hatfield (divorced, 1929); one *s* one *d*; 2nd, 1930, Marian Tyler. *Educ:* Massachusetts Inst. of Technology; Harvard Univ. SB cum laude, 1910; CPA degree, 1916; four years in Government Service, ending 1921; since 1921 has been chiefly engaged in economic research and writing books and articles; some public lecturing; consulting work for government agencies, business organizations, UNESCO, etc. Member National Inst. of Arts and Letters, Phi Beta Kappa; LittD American Univ., 1949; DHL Emerson Coll., Boston, 1970; DHL New Haven Univ., 1974. *Publications:* The Tragedy of Waste, 1925; Your Money's Worth (with F. J. Schlink), 1927; Men and Machines, 1929; Prosperity: Fact or Myth?, 1929; The Nemesis of American Business, 1931; Mexico, 1931; A New Deal, 1932; The Economy of Abundance, 1934; Government in Business, 1935; Rich Land, Poor Land, 1936; The Tyranny of Words, 1938; The New Western Front, 1939; Idle Money, Idle Men, 1940; A Primer of Economics, 1941; The Road We Are Travelling, 1942; Goals for America, 1942; Where's the Money Coming From?, 1943; Democracy under Pressure, 1945; Men at Work, 1945; Tomorrow's Trade, 1945; For This We Fought, 1946; The Proper Study of Mankind, 1948 (revised, 1956); Roads to Agreement, 1951; Power of Words, 1954; Guides to Straight Thinking, 1956; Some Things Worth Knowing, 1958; Live and Let Live, 1960; American Credos, 1962; Money to Grow On, 1964; The Most Probable World, 1968; Danger—Men Talking, 1969; articles for Harpers, Atlantic, The Saturday Review, etc. *Recreation:* sketching. *Address:* Georgetown, Conn 06829, USA. *Club:* Harvard (New York). *Died 16 Nov. 1985.*

**CHATTERTON, Rev. Sir Percy,** KBE 1981 (OBE 1972); CMG 1977; *b* 8 Oct. 1898; *s* of Henry Herbert Chatterton and Alice Macro; *m* 1924, Christian Ritchie Finlayson (*d* 1975). *Educ:* City of London Sch.; Univ. of London. LCP. Teacher, Friends Sch., Penketh, 1921–23; London Missionary Society, Papua: Teacher, 1924–39; Minister, 1939–64; Member for Moresby, Papua New Guinea House of Assembly, 1964–72; retired. Hon. LLD Papua New Guinea, 1972. *Publication:* Day that I have Loved: Percy Chatterton's Papua, 1972. *Recreations:* hockey, chess. *Address:* PO Box 1808, Port Moresby, Papua New Guinea. *T:* Port Moresby 255945. *Died 26 Nov. 1984.*

**CHATWIN, (Charles) Bruce,** FRSL; writer; *b* 13 May 1940; *s* of Charles Leslie and Margharita Chatwin; *m* 1966, Elizabeth Chanler, NY. *Educ:* Marlborough College. Director, Sotheby & Co., 1965–66; archaeological studies, 1966; journalist, Sunday Times Magazine, 1972–74; full time writer, 1975–. *Publications:* In Patagonia, 1977; The Viceroy of Ouidah, 1980; On the Black Hill, 1982; The Songlines, 1987; Utz, 1988; *posthumous publication:* What Am I Doing Here?, 1989. *Recreations:* walking, wind surfing. *Address:* c/o Aitken and Stone, 29 Fernshaw Road, SW10 0TG. *T:* 01–351 7561. *Died 18 Jan. 1989.*

**CHAU, Hon. Sir Sik-Nin,** Kt 1960; CBE 1950; JP 1940; Hon. Chairman, Hong Kong Chinese Bank Ltd; Chairman or Director of numerous other companies; President, Firecrackers and Fireworks Co. Ltd (Taiwan); State Trading Corporation (Far East) Ltd; *b* 13 April 1903; *s* of late Cheuk-Fan Chau, Hong Kong; *m* 1927, Ida Hing-Kwai, *d* of late Lau Siu-Cheuk; two *s*. *Educ:* St Stephen's Coll., Hong Kong; Hong Kong Univ.; London Univ.; Vienna State Univ. MB, BS, Hong Kong, 1923; DLO, Eng., 1925; DOMS 1926. LLD (Hon.), Hong Kong 1961. Member Medical Board, Hong Kong, 1935–41; Mem. Urban Council, 1936–41; Chm. Po Leung Kuk, 1940–41; MLC, Hong Kong, 1946–59; MEC,

1947-62. Dep. Chm., Subsid. British Commonwealth Parliamentary Assoc., Hong Kong, 1953-59. Chief Delegate of Hong Kong to ECAFE Conference in India, 1948, in Australia, 1949; Chairman ECAFE Conference in Hong Kong, 1955; Leader, Hong Kong Govt Trade Mission to Common Market countries, 1963; Asian Fair, Bangkok, 1967; first Trade Mission to USA, 1970. Fellow, Internat. Academy of Management; Pres. Indo-Pacific Cttee, 1964-67; Chairman: Hong Kong Trade Develt Council, 1966-70; Hong Kong Management Assoc., 1961-69; Fedn of Hong Kong Inds, 1959-66; Cttee for Expo '70, 1969-70; United Coll., Chinese Univ. of Hong Kong, 1959-61; Hong Kong Productivity Council, 1970-73. President, Japan Soc. of Hong Kong; Mem., Textiles Adv. Bd, 1962-74; Foreign Corresp. Nat. Ind. Conf. Bd Inc.; Member: Advisory Board to Lingnan Inst. of Business Administration; British Universities Selection Cttee, 1945-64; Council and Court of University of Hong Kong, 1945-64; Senior Member Board of Education Hong Kong, 1946-60; Chairman Hong Kong Model Housing Society; Vice-President, Hong Kong Anti-Tuberculosis Assoc.; Hon. Steward Hong Kong Jockey Club, 1974 (Steward 1946-74). Hon. President or Vice-President of numerous Assocs; Hon. Adviser of Chinese General Chamber of Commerce; Permanent Dir Tung Wah Hospital Advisory Board. Coronation Medal, 1937; Defence Medal, 1945; Coronation Medal, 1953; Silver Jubilee Medal, 1977; Freedom of New Orleans, 1966; San Francisco Port Authority Maritime Medal, 1968; 3rd Class Order of Sacred Treasure, Japan, 1969; granted permanent title of Honourable by the Queen, 1962. *Address:* c/o Hong Kong Chinese Bank, 61-65 Des Voeux Road, Central District, Hong Kong.

CHAUNCY, Major Frederick Charles Leslie, CBE 1958 (OBE 1953); *b* 22 Dec. 1904; *o s* of late Col C. H. K. Chauncy, CB, CBE, Indian Army; *m* 1932, Barbara Enid Miller, *e d* of late W. H. A. Miller, MA, Imperial Forest Service; one *s. Educ:* Radley; Sandhurst. Commissioned British Army, 1924; transf. IA (45th Rattray's Sikhs), 1928; transf. IPS, 1930; served Persian Gulf, NWF India, Indian States; retired 1947; re-employed under HM's Foreign Office, 1949, as Consul-General at Muscat; retired 1958; appointed by Sultan of Muscat and Oman as his Personal Adviser, 1961-70. *Recreations:* Rugby football (Sandhurst); athletics (Sandhurst, Army, England, also UK in Olympic Games). *Address:* 10 Egmont Drive, Avon Castle, Ringwood, Hants BH24 2BN. *Club:* Naval and Military. *Died 4 June 1986.*

CHAVAN, Yeshwantrao Balvantrao; Chairman, Eighth Finance Commission, India, since 1982; *b* 12 March 1913; *m* 1942, Venubai, *d* of late R. B. More, Phaltan, district Satara. *Educ:* Rajaram Coll., Kolhapur; Law Coll., Poona Univ. (BA, LLB). Took part in 1930, 1932 and 1942 Movements; elected MLA in 1946, 1952, 1957 and 1962; Parly Sec. to Home Minister of Bombay, 1946-52; Minister for Civil Supplies, Community Developments, Forests, Local Self Govt, 1952-Oct. 1956; Chief Minister: Bombay, Nov. 1956-April 1960; Maharashtra, May 1960-Nov. 1962; Defence Minister, Govt of India, 1962-66; Minister of Home Affairs, 1966-70; Minister of Finance, 1970-74; Minister of External Affairs, 1974-77; Leader, Congress Parly Party, 1977-81; Dep. Prime Minister and Home Minister, 1979. Elected Member: Rajya Sabha, 1963; Lok Sabha, 1964, 1967, 1971, 1977, 1980. Mem. Working Cttee of All India Congress Cttee. Pres., Inst. for Defence Studies and Analyses. Hon. Doctorate: Aligarh Univ.; Kanpur Univ., Marathwada Univ., Shivaji Univ. *Publication:* India's Foreign Policy, 1979. *Address:* 1 Racecourse Road, New Delhi 11, India. *T:* 376588.
*Died 25 Nov. 1984.*

CHAVASSE, Michael Louis Maude, MA; QC 1968; His Honour Judge Chavasse; a Circuit Judge, since 1971; *b* 5 Jan. 1923; 2nd *s* of late Bishop C. M. Chavasse, OBE, MC, DD, MA and Beatrice Cropper Chavasse (*née* Willink); *m* 1951, Rose Ethel, 2nd *d* of late Vice-Adm. A. D. Read, CB and late Hon. Rosamond Vere Read; three *d. Educ:* Dragon Sch., Oxford; Shrewsbury Sch.; Trinity Coll., Oxford (Schol). Enlisted in RAC, Oct. 1941; commnd in Buffs, 1942; served in Italy with Royal Norfolk Regt, 1943-45 (Lieut). 2nd cl. hons (Jurisprudence) Oxon, 1946. Called to Bar, Inner Temple, 1949. A Recorder of the Crown Court, 1972-77. *Publications:* (jtly) A Critical Annotation of the RIBA Standard Forms of Building Contract, 1964; (with Bryan Anstey) Rights of Light, 1959. *Recreations:* shooting, photography. *Address:* 2 Paper Buildings, Temple, EC4; Park House, Chevening, Sevenoaks, Kent. *T:* Knockholt 2271. *Died 12 Aug. 1983.*

CHECKLAND, Prof. Sydney George, MA, MCom, PhD; FRSE 1980; FBA 1977; Professor of Economic History, University of Glasgow, 1957-83, later Emeritus; Senior Research Fellow, University of Glasgow, since 1983; *b* 9 Oct. 1916; *s* of Sydney Tom and Fanny Selina Savory Checkland, Ottawa; *m* 1942, Édith Olive, *d* of Robert Fraser and Édith Philipson Anthony; two *s* three *d. Educ:* Lisgar Collegiate Inst., Ottawa; Birmingham Univ. Associate, Canadian Bankers' Assoc., 1937; BCom 1st Cl. 1941, MCom 1946, Birmingham; PhD Liverpool, 1953; MA Cambridge, 1953; Pres. Nat. Union of Students, 1941-42, Internat. Union of Students,

1942-43. Served in British and Canadian Armies; Lieut, Gov.-Gen.'s Foot Guards, Normandy (severely wounded), Parly cand. (Commonwealth Party), Eccleshall, 1945. Asst Lecturer, Lecturer and Senior Lecturer in Economic Science, University of Liverpool, 1946-53; Univ. Lecturer in History, Cambridge, 1953-57; Lector in History, Trinity Coll., 1955-57. A Senate Assessor, and Mem. Finance Cttee, etc, Univ. Court, Glasgow, 1970-73. Vis. Fellow, ANU, 1981; Vis. Prof., Monash Univ., 1981; Vis. Distinguished Prof., Univ. of Alberta, 1984; Vis. Prof., Keio Univ., Tokyo, 1984. Member: Inst. for Advanced Study, Princeton, 1960, 1964; East Kilbride Develt Corp., 1964-68; SSRC, 1979- (Mem. Econ. Hist. Cttee, 1970-72, 1979-82; Chm., Industry and Employment Cttee, 1982-84). Chm., Bd. of Management, Urban Studies, 1970-74; Pres., Scottish Econ. and Social History Soc., 1984-; Vice-Pres., Business Archives Council of Scotland, 1964-67; Member: Scottish Records Adv. Council, 1970-; Nat. Register of Archives (Scotland) (Chm. 1971); Econ. Hist. Soc. Council, 1958- (Pres., 1977-80; Hon. Vice Pres., 1980-). *Publications:* The Rise of Industrial Society in England, 1815-1885, 1964; The Mines of Tharsis, 1967; The Gladstones: a family biography, 1764-1851, 1971 (Scottish Arts Council Book Award); ed (with E. O. A. Checkland) The Poor Law Report of 1834, 1974; Scottish Banking, a history, 1695-1973, 1975 (Saltire Soc. Prize); The Upas Tree: Glasgow, 1875-1975, 1976, enl. edn as 1875-1980, 1982; British Public Policy 1776-1939, 1983; (jtly) Industry and Ethos: Scotland 1832-1914, 1984; contribs to various vols; articles and reviews in economic and historical journals. *Recreations:* painting, gathering driftwood. *Address:* 18 Ferry Path, Cambridge CB4 1HB. *T:* Cambridge 67581.
*Died 22 March 1986.*

CHEESEMAN, Eric Arthur, BSc (Econ), PhD (Med) (London); Professor of Medical Statistics, The Queen's University of Belfast, 1961-77, then Emeritus; *b* 22 Sept. 1912; 1st *s* of late Arthur Cheeseman and Frances Cheeseman, London; *m* 1943, Henriette Edwina Woollaston; one *s. Educ:* William Ellis Sch.; London Univ. Mem. staff of Statistical Cttee of MRC, 1929-39. Served War of 1939-45, RA (TA); GSO3 21 Army Group, 1945. Research Statistician on staff of Statistical Research Unit of MRC and part-time lectr in Med. Statistics, London Sch. of Hygiene and Tropical Medicine, 1946-48; Lectr, later Reader, and Vice-Pres. (Finance), The Queen's Univ. of Belfast, 1948-77; Prof., 1961; Dep. Dean, Faculty of Medicine, 1971-75. Statistical Adviser to Northern Ireland Hospitals Authority, 1948-73; Mem. of Joint Authority for Higher Technological Studies, 1965-70. Consulting Statistician to Northern Ireland Tuberculosis Authority, 1950-59; Mem., Statistical Cttee of Medical Research Council, 1950-61. Fellow Royal Statistical Soc.; Mem., Soc. for Social Medicine (Chm. 1976, Hon. Mem., 1979); Hon. Associate Mem., Ulster Med. Soc. Silver Jubilee Medal, 1977. *Publications:* Epidemics in Schools, 1950; (with G. F. Adams) Old People in Northern Ireland, 1951; various papers dealing with medical statistical subjects in scientific journals. *Recreation:* cricket. *Address:* 43 Beverley Gardens, Bangor, Co. Down, N Ireland. *T:* Bangor 472822. *Died 21 Feb. 1987.*

CHEEVER, John; writer, USA; *b* Quincy, Mass, 27 May 1912; *s* of Frederick Lincoln Cheever and Mary Liley Cheever, *m* 1941, Mary Winternitz; two *s* one *d. Educ:* Thayer Academy. Pulitzer Prize, 1979; Nat. Medal for Literature, 1982. *Publications: novels:* The Wapshot Chronicle, 1957 (Nat. Book Award for fiction); The Wapshot Scandal, 1964 (Howell's Medal for fiction); Bullet Park, 1969; World of Apples, 1973; Falconer, 1977; Oh What a Paradise It Seems, 1982; *short stories:* The Way Some People Live, 1943; The Enormous Radio, 1953, new edn, 1965; The Housebreaker of Shady Hill, 1958; Some People, Places and Things that will not appear in my next novel, 1961; The Brigadier and the Golf Widow, 1964; The Stories of John Cheever, 1979. *Recreations:* practically everything excepting big game. *Address:* Cedar Lane, Ossining, New York, USA. *Club:* Century (New York). *Died 18 June 1982.*

CHEGWIDDEN, Sir Thomas (Sidney), Kt 1955; CB 1943; CVO 1939; MA Oxon; Chevalier Légion d'Honneur, 1956; *b* 7 Feb. 1895; *s* of late Thomas Chegwidden, 8 Wimborne Road, Bournemouth; *m* 1st, 1919, Kathleen Muriel, *d* of A. O. Breeds; 2nd, 1934, Beryl Sinclair (*d* 1980), *d* of A. H. Nicholson; one *d. Educ:* Plymouth Coll.; Maidstone Grammar Sch.; Worcester Coll., Oxford. RMA Woolwich, 1916; Lieut RE, 1917-18. Resigned Commission and entered Upper Div. Civil Service, 1919; Asst Private Sec. to Dr T. J. Macnamara, Sir Montague Barlow, Mr Tom Shaw and Sir Arthur Steel-Maitland; Principal Private Sec. to Mr Oliver Stanley and Mr Ernest Brown; Under-Sec., Min. of Production, 1942-46; Civilian Dir of Studies, Imperial Defence Coll., 1946-47; Chm. of Public Services Bd and of Police Advisory Bd, S Rhodesia, 1947-53; Chm., Interim Federal Public Service Commission, Federation of Rhodesias and Nyasaland, 1953-55; Pres., Assoc. of Rhodesian Industries, 1958-61; Mem. Council, Univ. of Rhodesia, 1970-76; Fellow, Rhodesian Inst. of Management. *Publication:* The Employment Exchange Service of Great Britain (with G. Myrddin-Evans), 1934. *Address:* Huntington House, Hindhead, Surrey. *T:* Hindhead 4600. *Club:* Athenæum. *Died 4 Jan. 1986.*

**CHELWOOD**, Baron cr 1974 (Life Peer), of Lewes; **Tufton Victor Hamilton Beamish**, Kt 1961; MC 1940; DL; b 27 Jan. 1917; o surv. s of late Rear-Admiral T. P. H. Beamish, CB, DL; m 1950, Janet Stevenson (marr. diss. 1973); two d; m 1975, Mrs Pia McHenry (née von Roretz). Educ: Stowe Sch.; RMC, Sandhurst. 2nd Lieut Royal Northumberland Fusiliers, 1937; Active Service, Palestine, 1938–39; War of 1939–45 (wounded twice, despatches, MC); served in France, Belgium, 1940; Malaya, 1942; India and Burma front, 1942–43; North Africa and Italy, 1943–44; Staff Coll., Camberley, 1945. Hon. Col (TA), 1951–57. Mem. Church of England Council on Inter-Church Relations, 1950–60. MP (C) Lewes Div. of E Sussex, 1945–Feb. 1974. Delegate to Council of Europe and Chm. Assembly Cttee, 1951–54; Vice-Chairman: British Group IPU, 1952–54; 1922 Cttee, 1958–74; Chm. Cons. For. Affairs Cttee, 1960–64; an Opposition defence spokesman, 1965–67; Chm., Cons. Gp for Europe, 1970–73; Jt Dep. Leader, British Delegn to European Parlt, 1973–74. Pres., Cons. Middle East Council, 1980–. Pres., Lewes Cons. Assoc., 1977–85; Vice-Pres., ACC, 1986–87. Vice-Pres., Officers Pension Soc., 1980–. Member: Monnet Action Cttee for United States of Europe, 1971–76; Council, RSPB, 1948–61 (Pres., 1967–70; Vice-Pres., 1976–, Gold Medal, 1984); Vice President: Soc. for Promotion of Nature Conservation, 1976–84; Nature Conservancy Council, 1978–84; BVA Animal Welfare Assoc., 1988–. President: Sussex Trust for Nature Conservation, 1968–78; Soc. of Sussex Downsmen, 1975–81; Sussex Ornithol Soc., 1989–. Governor, Stowe Sch., 1966–79; Pres., Old Stoic Soc., 1983. DL East Sussex, 1970–. Hon. Freeman, Lewes, 1970. Golden Cross of Merit, 1944; Polonia Restituta, Poland; Comdr, Order of the Phoenix, Greece, 1949; Order of the Cedar, Lebanon, 1969. Mem. of the Soc. of Authors. Publications: Must Night Fall?, an account of Soviet seizure of power in Eastern Europe, 1950; Battle Royal, a new account for the 700th Anniversary of Simon de Montfort's struggle against Henry III, 1965; Half Marx: a warning that democracy in Britain is threatened by a Marx-influenced Labour Party, 1971; (with Guy Hadley) The Kremlin's Dilemma: the struggle for human rights in Eastern Europe, 1979. Recreations: gardening, bird-watching, music. Address: Plovers' Meadow, Blackboys, Uckfield, Sussex TN22 5NA. Club: Brooks's.
*Died 6 April 1989.*

**CHENEY, Christopher Robert**, CBE 1984; FBA 1951; Professor of Medieval History, University of Cambridge, 1955–72; Fellow, Corpus Christi College, Cambridge, 1955; b 1906; 4th s of George Gardner and Christiana Stapleton Cheney; m 1940, Mary Gwendolen Hall; two s one d. Educ: Banbury County Sch.; Wadham Coll., Oxford (Hon. Fellow, 1968). 1st class Modern History Sch., 1928; Asst Lectr in History, University Coll., London, 1931–33; Bishop Fraser Lectr in Ecclesiastical History, University of Manchester, 1933–37; Fellow of Magdalen Coll., Oxford, 1938–45; Univ. Reader in Diplomatic, 1937–45; Joint Literary Dir of Royal Historical Society, 1938–45; Prof. of Medieval History, Univ. of Manchester, 1945–55. Hon. Fellow, Wadham Coll., Oxford. Corresp. Fellow, Mediaeval Acad. of America; Corresp. Mem., Monumenta Germaniae Historica. Hon. DLitt: Glasgow, 1970; Manchester, 1978. Publications: Episcopal Visitation of Monasteries in the 13th Century, 1931, revd edn 1983; English Synodalia of the 13th Century, 1941; Handbook of Dates, 1945; English Bishops' Chanceries, 1950; (with W. H. Semple) Selected Letters of Pope Innocent III, 1953; From Becket to Langton, 1956; (with F. M. Powicke) Councils and Synods of the English Church, Vol. II, 1964; Hubert Walter, 1967; (with M. G. Cheney) Letters of Pope Innocent III concerning England and Wales, 1967; Notaries Public in England in the XIII and XIV Centuries, 1972; Medieval Texts and Studies, 1973; Pope Innocent III and England, 1976; (with M. G. Cheney) Studies in the Collections of XII Century Decretals, ed from papers of W. Holtzmann, 1979; The Papacy and England, 12th-14th Centuries (Variorum Reprints), 1982; The English Church and its Laws, 12th-14th Centuries (Variorum Reprints), 1982; (with B. E. A. Jones and Eric John) English Episcopal Acta II and III: Canterbury 1162–1205, 2 vols, 1986; articles and reviews in Eng. Hist. Rev., etc. Address: 17 Westberry Court, Grange Road, Cambridge CB3 9BG. T: Cambridge 351892.
*Died 19 June 1987.*

**CHERNIAVSKY, Mischel**; cellist; b Uman, South Russia, 2 Nov. 1893; became British subject, 1922; m 1919, Mary Rogers (d 1980), Vancouver, BC; four s (and one s decd). Educ: privately. Studied violoncello under David Popper and Herbert Walenn. Played before the Czar, Nicholas II, when seven years old; at age of twelve performed Saint-Saëns concerto in presence of composer; toured the world with his brothers, Leo (violinist) and Jan (pianist), who with him formed the Cherniavsky Trio, 1901–23. Since 1925 has appeared in most countries of the world in recital and as soloist with orchestra. Entertained the Forces in Great Britain, 1939–42; organised concerts in Canada in aid of Mrs Churchill's Aid to Russia Fund, 1942–45; toured Union of South Africa, 1953; last public appearance in London, 1958, with Sir Thomas Beecham. Recreations: golf, tennis, antique collecting. Address: Ferme des

Moines, Bourg-Dun, 76740 Fontaine-le-Dun, France. T: (35) 830147. Club: Dieppe Golf.
*Died 21 Feb. 1982.*

**CHESHAM, 5th Baron cr 1858; John Charles Compton Cavendish**, TD; PC 1964; b 18 June 1916; s of 4th Baron and Margot, d of late J. Layton Mills, Tansor Court, Oundle; S father, 1952; m 1937, Mary Edmunds, 4th d of late David G. Marshall, White Hill, Cambridge; two s two d. Educ: Eton; Zuoz Coll., Switzerland; Trinity Coll., Cambridge. Served War of 1939–45, Lieut Royal Bucks Yeomanry, 1939–42; Capt. RA (Air OP), 1942–45. JP Bucks 1946, retd. Delegate, Council of Europe, 1953–56. A Lord-in-Waiting to the Queen, 1955–59; Parly Sec., Min. of Transport, 1959–64. Chancellor, Primrose League, 1957–59. Executive Vice-Chm. Royal Automobile Club, 1966–70; Chairman: British Road Federation, 1966–72 (Vice-Pres., 1972); Internat. Road Fedn, Geneva, 1973–76; Pres., British Parking Assoc., 1972–75; Fellowship of Motor Industry, 1969–71; Hon. Sec., House of Lords Club, 1966–72; Hon. FInstHE, 1970; Hon FIRTE, 1974 (Pres., 1971–73). Heir: s Hon. Nicholas Charles Cavendish [b 7 Nov. 1941; m 1st, 1965, Susan Donne (marr. diss. 1969), e d of Dr Guy Beauchamp; 2nd, 1973, Suzanne, er d of late Alan Gray Byrne, Sydney, Australia; two s]. Address: Manor Farm, Preston Candover, near Basingstoke, Hants. T: Preston Candover 230. Club: Carlton.
*Died 23 Dec. 1989.*

**CHESTER, Sir (Daniel) Norman**, Kt 1974; CBE 1951; MA; Warden of Nuffield College, Oxford, 1954–78; Official Fellow of Nuffield College, 1945–54, Hon. Fellow, 1978; b 27 Oct. 1907; s of Daniel Chester, Chorlton-cum-Hardy, Manchester; m 1936, Eva (d 1980), d of James H. Jeavons. Educ: Manchester Univ. BA Manchester, 1930, MA 1933; MA Oxon, 1946. Rockefeller Fellow, 1935–36, Lecturer in Public Administration, 1936–45, Manchester Univ.; Mem. of Economic Section, War Cabinet Secretariat, 1940–45. Editor of jl of Public Administration, 1943–66. Mem. Oxford City Council, 1952–74. Chairman: Oxford Centre for Management Studies, 1965–75; Police Promotion Examinations Bd, 1969–82; Cttee on Association Football, 1966–68; Football Grounds Improvement Trust, 1975–80; Dep. Chm., Football Trust, 1980–; Vice-Pres. (ex-Chm.), Royal Inst. of Public Administration; Past Pres., Internat. Political Science Assoc. Hon. LittD Manchester, 1968. Corresp. Mem., Acad. des Sciences Morales et Politiques, Institut de France, 1967. Chevalier de la Légion d'Honneur, 1976. Publications: Public Control of Road Passenger Transport, 1936; Central and Local Government: Financial and Administrative Relations, 1951; The Nationalised Industries, 1951; (ed) Lessons of the British War Economy, 1951; (ed) The Organization of British Central Government, 1914–56; (with Nona Bowring) Questions in Parliament, 1962; The Nationalisation of British Industry, 1945–51, 1975; The English Administrative System 1780–1870, 1981; Economics, Politics and Social Studies in Oxford 1900–85, 1986; articles in learned journals. Address: 136 Woodstock Road, Oxford. Club: Reform.
*Died 20 Sept. 1986.*

**CHESTERMAN, Sir Clement (Clapton)**, Kt 1974; OBE 1919; Consulting Physician in Tropical Diseases, retired; b 30 May 1894; 5th s of late W. T. Chesterman, Bath, and Elizabeth Clapton; m 1917, Winifred Lucy (d 1981), d of late Alderman F. W. Spear; three s two d. Educ: Monkton Combe Sch.; Bristol Univ. MD London 1920; DTM and H, Cantab, 1920; FRCP 1952. Served European War, 1914–18 (despatches, OBE): Capt. RAMC (SR), 1917–19, Middle East. Medical Missionary, Belgian Congo, 1920–36; MO and Secretary, Baptist Missionary Soc., 1936–48. Lecturer in Tropical Medicine, Middlesex Hospital Medical Sch., 1944; Lecturer in Tropical Hygiene, University of London Institute of Education, 1956. Member Commn Royale Belge pour la Protection des Indigènes; Mem. Colonial Advisory Medical Cttee; Past Vice-Pres. Royal Society Tropical Medicine and Hygiene; Pres. Hunterian Society, 1967–68; Hon. Mem. Belgian Royal Society of Tropical Medicine. Occasional broadcasts on Medical Missions and Tropical Diseases. Hon. FRAM, 1972. Serbian Red Cross Medal, 1915; Chevalier, Ordre Royal du Lion, 1938. Publications: In the Service of Suffering, 1940; A Tropical Dispensary Handbook (7th edn), 1960; articles in Transactions of Royal Society of Tropical Medicine and Hygiene, British Encyclopædia of Medical Practice, etc. Recreation: golf. Address: Kestrel Grove, Hive Road, Bushey Heath, Herts. T: 01-950 4329. Clubs: Royal Commonwealth Society; Highgate Golf.
*Died 20 July 1983.*

**CHETWYND, Sir George Roland**, Kt 1982; CBE 1968; Board Member, BSC (Industry) Ltd, since 1976; b 14 May 1916; s of George Chetwynd and Anne Albrighton; m 1939, Teresa Reynolds Condon; two d. Educ: Queen Elizabeth Grammar Sch., Atherstone; King's Coll., London University. BA Hons History, 1939; Postgraduate Scholarship; enlisted Royal Artillery, 1940; commissioned Army Educational Corps, 1942. MP (Lab) Stockton-on-Tees, 1945–62; Parliamentary Private Secretary to Minister of Local Government and Planning, 1950–51 (to Chancellor of Duchy of Lancaster, 1948–50); Director: North East Development Council, 1962–67; Northern and Tubes Group, BSC, 1968–70; Board

member, BSC, 1970–76. Delegate to Consultative Assembly, Council of Europe, 1952–54; Member: Nature Conservancy, 1950–62; General Advisory Council, ITA, 1964; North-East Advisory Cttee for Civil Aviation, 1964; Northern Economic Planning Council, 1964–; Board, BOAC, 1966–74; Northern Industrial Develt Bd, 1972–81; Chairman: Northern RHA 1978–82 (Vice-Chm., 1973–76); Cleveland AHA, 1977–78; Dep. Chm., 1967–70, Chm., 1970–71, Land Commn; Chm., Council, BBC Radio Cleveland, 1976–78. Chm. of Governors, Queen Mary's Hosp., Roehampton, 1952. Freedom of Borough of Stockton-on-Tees, 1968. *Recreations:* walking, sea fishing. *Address:* The Briars, Thorpe Larches, Sedgefield, Stockton-on-Tees, Cleveland. *T:* Sedgefield 30336.
*Died 2 Sept. 1982.*

**CHEVRIER, Hon. Lionel,** CC (Canada) 1967; PC (Can.) 1945; QC (Can.); lawyer for Ontario and Quebec, in private practice in Montreal; *b* 2 April 1903; *s* of late Joseph Elphège Chevrier and late Malvina DeRepentigny; *m* 1932, Lucienne, *d* of Thomas J. Brulé, Ottawa; *three s three d. Educ:* Cornwall College Institute; Ottawa Univ.; Osgoode Hall. Called to bar, Ontario, 1928; KC 1938; called to Bar, Quebec, 1957. MP for Stormont, Canada, 1935–54; MP for Montreal-Laurier, 1957–64. Dep. Chief Government Whip, 1940; Chm., Special Parly Sub-Cttee on War Expenditures, 1942; Parliamentary Asst to Minister of Munitions and Supply, 1943; Minister of Transport, 1945–54; Pres., St Lawrence Seaway Authority, 1954–57; Minister of Justice, 1963–64; High Commissioner in London, 1964–67. Delegate, Bretton Woods Conf., 1945; Chm., Canadian Delegn, UN General Assembly, Paris, 1948; Pres., Privy Council, Canada, 1957. Comr-Gen. for State Visits to Canada, 1967; Chairman: Canadian Economic Mission to Francophone Africa, 1968; Mission to study Canadian Consular Posts in USA, 1968; Seminar to study river navigation for Unitar, Buenos Aires, 1970. Hon. degrees: LLD: Ottawa, 1946; Laval, 1952; Queen's, 1956; Concordia, 1984; DCL, Bishops', 1964. *Publication:* The St Lawrence Seaway, 1959. *Recreations:* walking and reading. *Address:* 615 Belmont Street, Lavalin Building, Montreal, Que H3B 2L8, Canada. *Died 8 July 1987.*

**CHIBNALL, Albert Charles,** PhD (London); ScD (Cantab); FRS 1937; Fellow of Clare College, Cambridge; Fellow of the Imperial College of Science and Technology, London; *b* 28 Jan. 1894; *s* of G. W. Chibnall; *m* 1st, 1931 (wife *d* 1936); two *d;* 2nd, 1947, Marjorie McCallum Morgan; one *s* one *d. Educ:* St Paul's Sch.; Clare Coll., Cambridge; Imperial Coll. of Science and Technology; Yale Univ., New Haven, Conn. 2nd Lieut, ASC 1914; Capt., 1915; attached RAF, 1917–19, served Egypt and Salonika. Huxley Medal, 1922; Imperial Coll. Travelling Fellow, 1922–23; Seessel Fellow, Yale Univ., 1923–24; Hon. Asst in Biochemistry, University Coll., London, 1924–30; Asst Prof. 1930–36, Prof. 1936–43, Emeritus Prof. 1943, of Biochemistry, Imperial Coll.; Sir William Dunn Prof. of Biochemistry, Univ. of Cambridge, 1943–49. Silliman Lectr, Yale Univ., 1938; Bakerian Lectr, Royal Society, 1942. Hon. Mem., Biochem. Soc.; Vice-Pres., Bucks Record Soc.; FSA 1977. Hon. DSc St Andrews, 1971. *Publications:* Protein Metabolism in the Plant, 1939; Richard de Badew and the University of Cambridge, 1315–1340, 1963; Sherington, fiefs and fields of a Buckinghamshire village, 1965; Beyond Sherington, 1979; papers in scientific journals on plant biochemistry. *Address:* 6 Millington Road, Cambridge. *T:* Cambridge 353923. *Died 10 Jan. 1988.*

**CHILCOTT, C. M.;** *see* Fordyce, C. M.

**CHILD, Ven. Kenneth;** Archdeacon of Sudbury since 1970; *b* 6 March 1916; *s* of late James Child, Wakefield; *m* 1955, Jane, *d* of late G. H. B. Turner and Mrs Turner, Bolton; one *s* two *d. Educ:* Queen Elizabeth's School, Wakefield; University of Leeds (BA); College of the Resurrection, Mirfield. Deacon 1941, Priest 1942, Manchester; Curate of St Augustine, Tonge Moor, 1941–44; Chaplain to the Forces, 1944–47; Vicar of Tonge Moor, 1947–55; Chaplain of Guy's Hospital, 1955–59; Rector of Newmarket, 1959–69; Rector of Great and Little Thurlow with Little Bradley, 1969–80; Rural Dean of Newmarket, 1963–70. Proctor in Convocation, 1964–; Hon. Canon of St Edmundsbury, 1968–. Hon. CF, 1947. *Publications:* Sick Call, 1965; In His Own Parish, 1970. *Recreation:* travel. *Address:* 6/7 College Street, Bury St Edmunds, Suffolk. *T:* Bury St Edmunds 703035. *Club:* Subscription Rooms (Newmarket).
*Died 25 Oct. 1983.*

**CHILDS, Most Rev. Derrick Greenslade;** *b* 14 Jan. 1918; *er s* of Alfred John and Florence Theodosia Childs; *m* 1951, Elizabeth Cicely Davies; one *s* one *d. Educ:* Whitland Grammar Sch., Carmarthenshire; University Coll., Cardiff (BA Wales, 1st cl. Hons History; Fellow 1981); Sarum Theol College at Wells. Deacon 1941, priest 1942, Diocese of St David's; Asst Curate: Milford Haven, 1941–46; Laugharne with Llansadwrnen, 1946–51; Warden of Llandaff House, Penarth (Hall of Residence for students of University Coll., Cardiff), 1951–61; Gen. Sec., Provincial Council for Education of the Church in Wales, 1955–65; Director of Church in Wales Publications, 1961–65; Chancellor of Llandaff Cathedral,

1964–69; Principal of Trinity Coll. of Education, Carmarthen, 1965–72; Canon of St David's Cathedral, 1969–72; Bishop of Monmouth, 1972–86; Archbishop of Wales, 1983–86. Member: Court University College, Cardiff; Council, St David's Univ. College, Lampeter; Court, Univ. of Wales; Chm., Church in Wales Provincial Council for Educn, 1972–83; Chm. of Council, Historical Soc. of Church in Wales, 1972; Vice-Chm., National Society, 1973; Chm. Bd, Church in Wales Publications, 1974–83. Sub-Prelate, Order of St John of Jerusalem, 1972. *Publications:* Editor: Cymry'r Groes, 1947–49, Province, 1949–68, and regular contributor to those quarterly magazines; contrib.: E. T. Davies, The Story of the Church in Glamorgan, 1962; Religion in Approved Schools, 1967. *Recreations:* music, walking, and watching cricket and Rugby football. *Address:* 30 Birchwood Road, Penylan, Cardiff CF2 5LJ. *T:* Cardiff 483214. *Died 18 March 1987.*

**CHILDS, Hubert,** CMG 1951; OBE 1943; *b* 6 July 1905; 3rd *s* of late Dr W. M. Childs, first Vice-Chancellor of the University of Reading. *Educ:* Oakham Sch.; University College, Oxford. Colonial Administrative Service, Nigeria, 1928–46, Sierra Leone, 1946–58. On Military service, 1941–46. Chief Comr, Protectorate, Sierra Leone, 1950–58. UK Plebiscite Administrator for Southern Cameroons, 1960–61. *Address:* c/o National Westminster Bank, Newbury, Berks. *Died 28 Sept. 1983.*

**CHILDS, Leonard,** CBE 1961 (OBE 1946); DL; JP; Chairman, Great Ouse River Authority, 1949–74; *b* 1 April 1897; *s* of Robert R. Childs, Grove House, Chatteris; *m* 1924, Mary M., *d* of John Esson, MIMinE, Aberdeen; three *s. Educ:* Wellingborough. Served European War, 1914–18, in Royal Flying Corps and Artists' Rifles. County Councillor, Isle of Ely, 1922 (Chairman, 1946–49); Custos Rotulorum, 1952–65; High Sheriff, Cambs and Hunts, 1946; DL Cambs, 1950; JP Isle of Ely, 1932. *Recreation:* shooting. *Address:* South Park Street, Chatteris, Cambridgeshire. *T:* Chatteris 2204.
*Died 31 March 1982.*

**CHILSTON, 3rd Viscount** *cr* 1911, of Boughton Malherbe; **Eric Alexander Akers-Douglas;** Baron Douglas of Baads, 1911; *b* 17 Dec. 1910; *s* of 2nd Viscount and Amy (*d* 1962), *d* of late J. R. Jennings-Bramly, RHA; *S* father, 1947; *m* 1955, Marion (*d* 1970), *d* of late Capt. William Charles Howard, RE. *Educ:* Eton; Trinity Coll., Oxford. Formerly Flight Lieut RAFVR. *Publications:* part author, Survey of International Affairs, 1938, Vol. III, Hitler's Europe, Realignment of Europe (Royal Institute of International Affairs); Chief Whip: The Political Life and Times of A. Akers-Douglas, 1st Viscount Chilston, 1961; W. H. Smith, 1965. *Heir: cousin* Alastair George Akers-Douglas [*b* 6 Sept. 1946; *m* 1971, Juliet Lovett; three *s*]. *Address:* Chilston Park, Maidstone, Kent ME17 2BE. *T:* Lenham 214. *Club:* Brooks's. *Died 10 April 1982.*

**CHILVER, Prof. Guy Edward Farquhar,** MA, DPhil; Professor of Classical Studies, University of Kent at Canterbury, 1964–76, later Emeritus Professor; *b* 11 Feb. 1910; *er s* of late Arthur Farquhar Chilver and late Florence Ranking; *m* 1st, 1945, Sylvia Chloe (marr. diss. 1972), *d* of late D. P. Littell; 2nd, 1973, Marie Elizabeth, *d* of W. J. Powell. *Educ:* Winchester; Trinity Coll., Oxford. Harmsworth Sen. Scholar, Merton Coll., 1932–34. Queen's Coll., Oxford: Fellow and Prælector in Ancient History, 1934–63; Dean, 1935–39; Sen. Tutor, 1948–63; Emeritus Fellow, 1964–; Dep. Vice-Chancellor, Kent Univ., 1966–72; Dean of Humanities, 1964–74. Min. of Food, 1940–45; British Food Mission, Washington, 1943–45. Member Hebdomadal Council, Oxford Univ., 1949–63; Visiting Prof., University of Texas, 1963; Vice-Pres., Society for Promotion of Roman Studies, 1964–. *Publications:* Cisalpine Gaul, 1941; trans. (with S. C. Chilver), and annotated, Unesco History of Mankind, Vol. II, 1965; Historical Commentary on Tacitus' Histories I and II, 1979; articles in learned journals. *Recreation:* bridge. *Address:* Oak Lodge, Boughton, near Faversham, Kent. *T:* Canterbury 51246. *Clubs:* Reform; Kent and Canterbury (Canterbury).
*Died 7 Sept. 1982.*

**CHILVER, Richard Clementson,** CB 1952; *b* 1912; *yr s* of Arthur Farquhar Chilver; *m* 1937, Elizabeth Chilver. *Educ:* Winchester; New Coll., Oxford. Entered HM Civil Service, 1934; Under-Sec., Air Ministry, 1946; Deputy Sec., Cabinet Office, 1955; MoD, 1957; Min. of Transport, 1960; DOE, 1965–72. Administrative Director, Insurance Technical Bureau, 1972–76. *Address:* 108 Clifton Hill, NW8. *T:* 01–624 2702. *Died 20 Oct. 1985.*

**CHISHOLM, Sir Henry,** Kt 1971; CBE 1965; MA, FCA; CBIM; Chairman, Corby Development Corporation (New Town), 1950–76; *b* 17 Oct. 1900; *e s* of late Hugh Chisholm and of Eliza Beatrix Chisholm (*née* Harrison); *m* 1st, 1925, Eve Hyde-Thomson (decd); one *s* (decd); 2nd, 1940, Audrey Viva Hughes (*née* Lamb); two *s;* 3rd, 1956, Margaret Grace Crofton-Atkins (*née* Brantom). *Educ:* Westminster (Schol.); Christ Church, Oxford (Scholar). 2nd Mods, 2nd Lit. Hum., BA 1923, MA 1960. Manager, Paris Office, Barton Mayhew & Co., Chartered Accountants, 1927–32; Partner, Chisholm Hanke & Co., Financial Consultants, 1932–38; Overseas Mills Liaison Officer, Bowater Group, 1938–44; Dir, Bowater-Lloyd

(Newfoundland) Ltd, 1940–44; Mem. and Chm. of Departmental Cttees on Organisation of Naval Supply Services, Admiralty, 1942–45; Dir and Financial Controller, The Metal Box Co. Ltd, 1945–46; Joint Managing Dir, A. C. Cossor Ltd, 1947–60; Chm. Ada (Halifax) Ltd, 1961–74. Mem. Adv. Council, Industrial Estates Ltd (Nova Scotia), 1968–75. Mem., Monopolies Commn, 1966–69. Pres., London Flotilla, RNVSR, 1947–53 (Vice-Pres., 1975–); Chm., Whitley Council for New Towns Staff, 1961–75; a Governor of Westminster Sch., 1954–; Founder Mem. British Institute of Management. *Recreations:* sailing (Captain, Solent Sunbeams, 1964–75, Commodore 1975–), gardening, travel. *Address:* Scott's Grove House, Chobham, Woking, Surrey. *T:* Chobham 8660. *Clubs:* Athenæum, Naval (Hon. Life Mem.), Royal Yacht Squadron, Royal Ocean Racing, Royal London Yacht.

*Died 20 July 1981.*

**CHITTY, Letitia,** MA (Cantab); FRAeS, MICE; *b* 15 July 1897; *d* of Herbert Chitty, FSA and Mabel Agatha Bradby. *Educ:* mostly privately and Newnham Coll., Cambridge. Maths Tripos Part I, 1917; Mech. Science Tripos 1921. Associate of Newnham Coll. 1927–43 and 1958–70. Air Ministry, 1917–19; Airship Stressing Panel, 1922; Bristol Aeroplane Co., 1923–24; Asst to Prof. R. V. Southwell, 1926–32; Airship Analysis, 1933; Asst then Lectr, Civil Engrg, Imperial Coll., 1934–62; work on arch dams for Instn of Civil Engineers and Construction Industry Research and Information Assoc., 1962–69. Telford Gold Medal, ICE, 1969. Fellow, Imp. Coll. of Science and Technology, 1971. FRAeS 1934; AMICE 1947. *Publications:* Abroad: an Alphabet of Flowers, 1948; technical contributions (mostly in collaboration) to Aerto R. and M., Proc. Royal Society, Phil. Mag., RAeS Journal and Journal of ICE. *Address:* Flat 9, Imperial Court, 6 Lexham Gardens, W8. *T:* 01-370 1706.

*Died 29 Sept. 1982.*

**CHLOROS, Prof. Alexander George;** Judge of the Court of Justice of the European Communities, at Luxembourg, since 1981; *b* Athens, 15 Aug. 1926; *yr s* of late George Chloros and of Pipitsa Chloros (*née* Metaxas, now Salti), Athens; *m* 1st, 1951, Helen Comninos, London (*d* 1956); one *d*; 2nd, 1965, Jacqueline Destouche, Marseilles (marr. diss.); one *d*; 3rd, 1979, Katerina Meria, Athens. *Educ:* Varvakeion Model Sch., Athens; University Coll., Oxford. BA Oxon 1951; MA Oxon 1955; LLD London 1972; FKC 1981. Asst Lectr in Law, 1951–54, and Lectr in Law, 1954–59, University Coll. of Wales, Aberystwyth; University of London, King's College: Lectr in Laws, 1959–63; Reader in Comparative Law, 1963–66, Prof., 1966–81; Dir, Centre of European Law, 1974–81; Hon. Vis. Prof., 1981–82. Hayter Scholar, Inst. of Comparative Law, Belgrade, Yugoslavia, 1963–64; Vice-Dean, Internat. Univ. of Comparative Sciences, Luxembourg, 1962–66; Dean of the Faculty of Laws, King's Coll., London, 1971–74; Adviser to Seychelles Government, for: recodification and reform of Code Napoléon, 1973; recodification and reform of Commercial Code, 1975. Visiting Professor: (Professeur associé), Faculty of Law, Univ. of Paris I, 1974–75; Uppsala Univ., 1976; Fribourg, 1977; Athens Univ., 1978–80. Member: Soc. of Public Teachers of Law; UK Cttee on Comparative Law, Inst. Advanced Legal Studies; Brit. Inst. Internat. and Comparative Law; UK deleg. and Vice-Pres., Council of Europe Sub-Cttee on Fundamental Legal Concepts; UK deleg., Conf. of European Law Faculties, Council of Europe, Strasbourg, 1968; Leader of UK delegn to 2nd Conf., 1971, 1st Vice-Pres., 3rd Conf., 1974, Pres., 4th Conf., 1976; exch. Lecturer, Faculty of Law, Univ. of Leuven, Belgium; Director: Brit. Council scheme for foreign lawyers; Student Exchange Scheme with Univ. of Aix-en-Provence; UK deleg. representing Cttee of Vice-Chancellors and Principals at Preparatory Cttee, European Inst. in Florence, and UK Mem., Prov. Academic Cttee. Mem., Central Negotiating Cttee, Entry of Greece in the European Communities. Hon. Bencher, Gray's Inn, 1981; Hon. Vis. Prof., King's Coll., London, 1981–82. Corresp. Member: Acad. of Athens, 1976; Royal Uppsala Acad., 1977. Associate Mem., Internat. Acad. of Comparative Law, 1976. Medal of Univ. of Zagreb, Yugoslavia, 1972. Chevalier 1st cl., Royal Order of Polar Star, Sweden, 1977; Officier, Ordre des palmes académiques, 1979. Gen. Editor, European Studies in Law, 1976–. *Publications:* Editor, Vol. IV (Family Law) and contributor to Internat. Encyc. of Comparative Law, Max Planck Inst. of Internat. and For. Law, Hamburg; Ch. 2 in Graveson, Law and Society, 1967; Yugoslav Civil Law, 1970; ed, A Bibliographical Guide to the Law of the United Kingdom, the Channel Is and Isle of Man, 2nd edn, 1973; ed jtly (with K. H. Neumayer) Liber Amicorum Ernst J. Cohn, CH, 1975; Codification in a Mixed Jurisdiction, 1977; The EEC Treaty (Greek trans.), 1978; (ed) The EEC Treaty and the Act of Accession of Greece (official texts), 1981; contrib. various British and foreign learned periodicals on Comparative Law and legal philosophy. *Recreations:* photography, swimming, travel, European history, coins, icons. *Address:* The Court of Justice of the European Communities, BP 1406, Kirchberg, Luxembourg. *T:* 43031. *Clubs:* Athenæum, Royal Commonwealth Society; Fondation Universitaire (Brussels).

*Died 15 Nov. 1982.*

**CHOLMELEY, Francis William Alfred F.;** *see* Fairfax-Cholmeley.

**CHOLMONDELEY,** 6th Marquess of, *cr* 1815; **George Hugh Cholmondeley,** GCVO 1977; MC 1943; DL; Bt 1611; Viscount Cholmondeley, 1661; Baron Cholmondeley of Namptwich (Eng.), 1689; Earl of Cholmondeley, Viscount Malpas, 1706; Baron Newborough (Ire.), 1715; Baron Newburgh (Gt Brit.), 1716; Earl of Rocksavage, 1815; late Grenadier Guards; Lord Great Chamberlain of England since 1966; *b* 24 April 1919; *e s* of 5th Marquess of Cholmondeley, GCVO, and Sybil (CBE 1946) (*d* 1989), *d* of Sir Edward Albert Sassoon, 2nd Bt; *S* father, 1968; *m* 1947, Lavinia Margaret, *d* of late Colonel John Leslie, DSO, MC; one *s* three *d*. *Educ:* Eton; Cambridge Univ. Served War of 1939–45: 1st Royal Dragoons, in MEF, Italy, France, Germany (MC). Retd hon. rank Major, 1949. DL Chester, 1955. *Heir: s* Earl of Rocksavage, *b* 27 June 1960. *Address:* Cholmondeley Castle, Malpas, Cheshire. *T:* Cholmondeley 202. *Clubs:* Turf, White's.

*Died 13 March 1990.*

**CHOPE, His Honour Robert Charles;** a Circuit Judge (formerly Judge of County Courts), 1965–85; *b* 26 June 1913; *s* of Leonard Augustine and Ida Florence Chope; *m* 1946, Pamela Durell; one *s* two *d*. *Educ:* St Paul's Sch.; University Coll., London (BA Hons 1st Cl.) Called to Bar, Inner Temple, 1938. Served Royal Artillery, 1939–45 (Hon. Captain). Dep. Chm., Cornwall QS, 1966–71. *Address:* Carclew House, Perranarworthal, Truro, Cornwall; 12 King's Bench Walk, Temple, EC4.

*Died 17 Oct. 1988.*

**CHORLEY, (Charles) Harold,** CB 1959; Second Parliamentary Counsel, 1968–69; *b* 10 June 1912; *o s* of late Arthur R. Chorley; *m* 1941, Audrey (*d* 1980), *d* of R. V. C. Ash, MC; two *d*. *Educ:* Radley; Trinity Coll., Oxford. Called to Bar (Inner Temple), 1934. Joined Office of Parliamentary Counsel, 1938; one of the Parliamentary Counsel, 1950–68. *Address:* Paddock Wood, Tisbury, Salisbury, Wilts. *T:* Tisbury (0747) 870325.

*Died 22 Dec. 1990.*

**CHOWDHURY, Abu Sayeed;** President of Bangladesh, 12 Jan. 1972-24 Dec. 1973; unanimously elected President of People's Republic of Bangladesh from April 1973, for five year term, resigned December 1973; Member, United Nations Sub-Commission on Prevention of Discrimination and Protection of Minorities, since 1978, re-elected 1981, 1983 (Chairman, Working Group on Slavery Practices, since 1978); *b* 31 Jan. 1921; *s* of late Abdul Hamid Chowdhury (formerly Speaker, the then East Pakistan Assembly); *m* 1948, Khurshid Chowdhury; two *s* one *d*. *Educ:* Presidency Coll.; Calcutta Univ. (MA, BL). Called to the Bar, Lincoln's Inn, 1947. Gen.-Sec., Presidency Coll. Union, 1941–42; Pres. British Br. of All India Muslim Students' Fedn, 1946. Mem., Pakistan Delegn to Gen. Assembly of the UN, 1959; Advocate-Gen., E Pakistan, 1960; Mem., Constitution Commn, 1960–61; Judge, Dacca High Court, July 1961–72; Chm., Central Bd for Develt of Bengali, 1963–68; Leader, Pakistan Delegn to World Assembly of Judges and 4th World Conf. on World Peace through Law, Sept. 1969; Vice-Chancellor, Dacca Univ., Nov., 1969–72, in addition to duties of Judge of Dacca High Court; Mem., UN Commn on Human Rights, 1971, 1982 and 1986– (Chm., 1985–86); Special Rep. for Govt of Bangladesh, designated by Bangladesh Govt as High Comr for UK and N Ireland, 1971, and Head of the Bangladesh Missions at London and New York, April 1971–11 Jan. 1972; Chancellor, all Bangladesh Univs, 1972–73. Special Rep. of Bangladesh, 1973–75; Leader, Bangladesh Delegns: Conf. on Humanitarian Law, Geneva, 1974, 1975 (Chm., Drafting Cttee); World Health Assemblies, Geneva, 1974, 1975; Internat. Labour Confs, Geneva, 1974, 1975 (Chm., Human Resources Cttee); Confs on Law of the Sea, Caracas, 1974, Geneva, 1975; Gen. Conf. Internat. Atomic Energy Agency, Vienna, 1974; UN Special Session, Sept. 1975, NY; 30th Session of Gen. Assembly, UN, 1975; Conf. of IOC, Jeddah, 1975; led goodwill missions to: Saudi Arabia, Egypt, Syria, Lebanon and Algeria, 1974; Turkey, 1975; Japan, 1983. Vis. Prof., Franklin Pierce Law Center, USA, 1983. Hon. Fellow, Open Univ., 1977. Hon. Deshikottama Viswabharati (Shantiniketan), India, 1972; Hon. LLD Calcutta, 1972. *Recreations:* reading, gardening. *Address:* Rosendale, 103 Mymensingh Road, Dhaka-2, Bangladesh. *T:* 402424. *Clubs:* Athenæum, Royal Over-Seas League, Royal Commonwealth Society; (Hon.) Rotarian, Rotary (Dacca).

*Died 1 Aug. 1987.*

**CHRIMES, Prof. Stanley Bertram,** MA, PhD, LittD; Professor of History and Head of Department of History, University College, Cardiff, 1953–74; later Emeritus; Director, University College, Cardiff, Centenary History Project, 1975–81; Deputy Principal, 1964–66; Dean of Faculty of Arts, 1959–61; *b* 23 Feb. 1907; *yr s* of late Herbert Chrimes and Maude Mary (*née* Rose); *m* 1937, Mabel Clara, *o d* of late L. E. Keyser. *Educ:* Purley County Sch., Surrey; King's Coll. London (Lindley Student, BA, MA); Trinity Coll., Cambridge (Research Studentship, Senior Rouse Ball Student, PhD, LittD). Lectr, 1936, Reader, 1951, in Constitutional History, University of Glasgow. Temp. Principal, Ministry of Labour and National Service, 1940–45. Alexander Medal, Royal Hist. Society,

1934. *Publications*: English Constitutional Ideas in the XVth century, 1936 (American repr. 1965, 1976); (translated) F. Kern's Kingship and Law in the Middle Ages, 1939 (repr. 1948, 1956; paperback edn 1970); (ed and trans.) Sir John Fortescue's De Laudibus Legum Angliæ, 1942 (repr. 1949); English Constitutional History, 1948 (4th rev. edn 1967; edn in Japan, 1963); (ed) The General Election in Glasgow, February 1950, 1950; An Introduction to the Administrative History of Mediæval England, 1952 (3rd rev. edn 1966); Some Reflections on the Study of History, 1954; (ed and cont. 7th edn) Sir W. Holdsworth's History of English Law, Vol. I, 1957; (ed, with A. L. Brown) Select Documents of English Constitutional History, 1307–1485, 1961; Lancastrians, Yorkists, and Henry VII, 1964 (2nd rev. edn 1966); King Edward I's Policy for Wales, 1969; ed (with C. D. Ross and R. A. Griffiths) and contrib., Fifteenth-Century England, studies in politics and society, 1972; Henry VII, 1972, repr. 1977; articles and reviews in Trans Royal Hist. Soc., English Historical Review, Law Quarterly Review, etc. *Address*: 24 Cwrt-y-vil Road, Penarth, South Glamorgan.

*Died 21 July 1984.*

**CHRISTENSEN, Arent Lauri, (A. Lauri Chris);** Norwegian painter and etcher; *b* 30 April 1893; *m* 1933, Hjordis Charlotte Lohren (Lill Chris), painter. *Educ*: The Royal Drawing Sch., Oslo. Began career as etcher and painter in Oslo; later travelled in the South, especially in Provence and Italy, and made a series of decorative landscape-etchings, which were exhibited in several countries; his interest in classic antiquity—especially the Grecian and Egyptian culture—inspired him to make various figure-compositions with incidents from the life in the antiquity and from Homer's Iliad; these compositions have been exhibited throughout Europe and America. Decorated Asker High Sch. with wall-paintings. Invented a new graphic method Chrisgrafia. The following museums have bought his works: British Museum, Victoria and Albert Museum, National Galleriet, Oslo, New York Free Arts Library Museum, Bibliothèque Nationale, Paris, Brooklyn Museum, Brooklyn, etc; Mem. of the Soc. of Graphic Art, London, 1926. *Address*: Villa Chriss, Fjeldstadvn 16, Nesbru, Norway. *Died 3 Feb. 1982.*

**CHRISTENSEN, Christian Neils,** CBE 1970; ERD; *b* 10 Dec. 1901; *m* 1928, Elsie Florence Hodgson; one *s* one *d*. Army service, France, N Africa, Sicily, Italy, 1939–45 (Lt-Col, despatches twice); Officer, Legion of Merit, USA, 1944); Man. Dir, North Western Transport Services Ltd and Dir, Transport Services (BTC) Ltd, 1945–49; Road Haulage Executive: Eastern Divisional Man., 1950–55; Midland Divisional Man., 1955–63; Man. Dir, British Road Services Ltd, and Chm., BRS (Contracts) Ltd, 1963–68; Chm., Road Air Cargo Express (International) Ltd, 1968–71, retired. FCIT. *Recreation*: gardening. *Address*: Ellesmere, 22 Greensleeves Avenue, Broadstone, Dorset, BH18 8BL. *T*: Broadstone 694501.

*Died 28 Dec. 1982.*

**CHRISTIANSEN, Michael Robin;** bookseller; *b* 7 April 1927; *e s* of late Arthur and of Brenda Christiansen; *m* 1st, 1948, Kathleen Lyon (marr. diss.); one *s* one *d*; 2nd, 1961, Christina Robinson; one *s* one *d*. *Educ*: Hill Crest, Frinton; St Luke's, Conn., USA. Reporter, Daily Mail, 1943; Royal Navy, 1945–47; Chief Sub-Editor: Daily Mail, 1950; Daily Mirror, 1956; Dep. Editor, Sunday Pictorial, 1960; Asst Editor, Daily Mirror, 1961–64; Editor, Sunday Mirror, 1964–72; Dep. Editor, Daily Mirror, 1972–74, Editor, 1975. *Recreations*: golf, coarse cricket. *Address*: 2 Armstrong Close, Danbury, Essex. *Died 12 June 1984.*

**CHRISTIE, Ronald Victor,** MD (Edin.); MSc (McGill); DSc (London); FACP; FRCP(C); FRCP; Professor of Medicine and Chairman of the Department, McGill University, 1955–64, then Emeritus Professor; Dean of the Faculty of Medicine, 1964–68; formerly Director Medical Professorial Unit and Physician, St Bartholomew's Hospital; Professor of Medicine, University of London, 1938–55; *b* 1902; *s* of late Dr Dugald Christie, CMG; *m* 1st, 1933, Joyce Mary Ervine (*d* 1967); one *s* one *d*; 2nd, 1976, Manette S. Loomis. *Educ*: in China and later at George Watson's Coll.; Edinburgh Univ. House Physician and House Surg., Royal Infirmary, Edinburgh; Asst in Medicine, Rockefeller Institute for Medical Research, NY; Asst in Dept of Pathology, Freiburg Univ.; Research Associate, McGill Univ. Clinic, Royal Victoria Hosp., Montreal; Asst Dir of the Med. Unit and Asst Physician, London Hosp. Harveian Orator, RCP, 1969. Hon. FRCPEd; Hon. ScD, Dublin, 1962; Hon. DSc: Edinburgh, 1970; McGill, 1978; Hon. LLD Otago, 1975. *Publications*: papers in medical and scientific journals. *Address*: 5775 Toronto Road, Apt 903, Vancouver, BC V6T 1X4, Canada. *Died 27 Sept. 1986.*

**CHRISTIE, Walter Henry John,** CSI 1948; CIE 1946; OBE 1943; *b* 17 Dec. 1905; *s* of late H. G. F. Christie and Mrs L. M. Christie (*née* Humfrey); *m* 1934, Elizabeth Louise, *d* of late H. E. Stapleton; two *s*. two *d*. *Educ*: Eton (KS, Newcastle Medallist); King's Coll., Cambridge (Winchester Reading Prize; MA). Joined Indian Civil Service, 1928 and served in Bengal and New Delhi; Joint Private Sec. to the Viceroy, 1947; Adviser in India to Central Commercial

Cttee, 1947–52; Vice-Chm., British India Corp. Ltd, 1952–58; Commonwealth Develt Finance Co. Ltd, 1959–68; Adviser, E. African Develt Bank, 1969–70. Pres., Upper India Chamber of Commerce, 1955–56; Vice-Pres., Employers' Federation of India, 1956; Pres., UK Citizens Assoc., 1957; Steward, Indian Polo Assoc., 1951. *Publications*: Morning Drum, 1983; contribs to Blackwood's Magazine. *Address*: The Lawn House, Quarry Road, Oxted, Surrey. *T*: Oxted 2447. *Clubs*: East India, Devonshire, Sports and Public Schools; Achilles. *Died 25 Aug. 1983.*

**CHRISTIE, Sir William,** KCIE 1947 (CIE 1941); CSI 1945; MC; retired as Chairman, Bailey Meters & Controls Ltd Croydon and Cornhill Insurance Co. Ltd; former Director, Thomas Tilling Ltd; *b* 29 Feb. 1896; *s* of late Rev. Alexander Mackenzie Christie; *m* Marjorie Haughton, 2nd *d* of late Henry Hall Stobbs; one *s* one *d*. *Educ*: Perth Acad., Perth; Bell Baxter Sch., Cupar, Fife; St Andrews Univ.; Clare Coll., Cambridge. Served Royal Scots, 1914–19 (MC). Joined Indian Civil Service, 1920; Finance Sec., UP, 1938–44; Chief Sec., UP, 1944–45; Chief Comr, Delhi, 1945–47. *Address*: 3 Hartley Court, East Common, Gerrards Cross, Bucks. *T*: Gerrards Cross 882246. *Club*: Caledonian. *Died 15 Oct. 1983.*

**CHRISTY, Ronald Kington,** CB 1965; HM Chief Inspector of Factories, 1963–67; *b* 18 Aug. 1905; *s* of William and Edna Christy; *m* 1931, Ivy, *y d* of W. Hinchcliffe, Whitchurch, Salop; one *s* one *d*. *Educ*: Strand Sch.; King's Coll., Univ. of London. Appointed HM Inspector of Factories, 1930; HM Superintending Inspector of Factories, 1953–59; HM Dep. Chief Inspector of Factories, 1959–63. Mem., Nuclear Safety Advisory Cttee, 1963–67. *Recreations*: gardening, travelling. *Address*: The Garden, Thicket Road, Houghton, Huntingdon, Cambs PE17 2BQ. *T*: St Ives 301384.

*Died 29 Aug. 1987.*

**CHURCHILL, Hon. Gordon,** PC (Canada); DSO 1945; ED; QC; Canadian barrister, retired; *b* Coldwater, Ont, 8 Nov. 1898; *s* of Rev. J. W. and Mary E. Churchill; *m* 1922, Mona Mary, *d* of C. W. McLachlin, Dauphin, Man.; one *d*. *Educ*: Univ. of Manitoba. MA 1931, LLB 1950. Served European War, 1916–18, France; served War of 1939–45 (DSO), commanded First Canadian Armoured Carrier Regt, NW Europe. Principal of a Manitoba High Sch., 1928–38; Mem. Manitoba Legislature, 1946–49; called to Manitoba Bar, 1950; Member Federal Parlt for Winnipeg South Centre, 1951–68, retired; Federal Minister: for Trade and Commerce, 1957–60; of Veterans' Affairs, 1960–63; of National Defence, Feb.–April 1963. Hon. LLD Winnipeg 1976. *Died 3 Aug. 1985.*

**CHURCHILL, Very Rev. John Howard;** Dean of Carlisle, 1973–87; pre-retirement adviser, Diocese of Norwich, since 1988; *b* 9 June 1920; *s* of John Lancelot and Emily Winifred Churchill; *m* 1948, Patricia May, *d* of late John James and Gertrude May Williams; one *s* two *d*. *Educ*: Sutton Valence Sch.; Trinity Coll., Cambridge (Exhibitioner); Lincoln Theological Coll. BA 1942, MA 1946. Deacon, 1943; priest, 1944; Asst curate: St George, Camberwell, 1943–48; All Hallows', Tottenham, 1948–53; Chaplain and Lectr in Theology, King's Coll., London, 1953–60; Vicar of St George, Sheffield, 1960–67; Lectr in Education, Univ. of Sheffield, 1960–67; Canon Residentiary of St Edmundsbury, 1967–73; Director of Ordinands and Clergy Training, Diocese of St Edmundsbury and Ipswich, 1967–73. Lady Margaret Preacher, Univ. of Cambridge, 1969; Proctor in Convocation, 1970–87; Mem., Dioceses Commn, 1978–86. Fellow of King's Coll., London, 1982. *Publications*: Prayer in Progress, 1961; Going Up: a look at University life, 1963; Finding Prayer, 1978; Finding Communion, 1987; Putting Life Together, 1989. *Recreation*: writing. *Address*: 34 Newmarket Road, Norwich NR2 2LA. *T*: Norwich (0603) 633878.

*Died 29 April 1990.*

**CHURCHILL, Maj.-Gen. Thomas Bell Lindsay,** CB 1957; CBE 1949; MC; *b* 1 Nov. 1907; 2nd *s* of late Alec Fleming Churchill, of PWD, Ceylon and Hong Kong, and late Elinor Elizabeth (*née* Bell); *m* 1st, 1934, Gwendolen Janie (*d* 1962), *e d* of late Lewis Williams, MD; one *s* one *d*; 2nd, 1963, Elizabeth Deirdre (marr. diss. 1967), *yr d* of late Bruce R. Campbell, Goorianawa, NSW; 3rd, 1968, Penelope Jane Ormiston (marr. diss. 1974). *Educ*: Dragon Sch., Oxford; Magdalen Coll. Sch., Oxford; RMC Sandhurst. Gained Prize Cadetship to RMC Sandhurst, 1926; Prize for Mil. Hist., 1927. 2nd Lieut, Manchester Regt, 1927; Burma Rebellion, 1930–31 (despatches, MC); Adjt, 1931–34; instructor in interpretation of air photographs, RAF Sch. of Photography, 1934–39; Company Comdr, France, 1939–40; GSO1 Commandos, Sicily and Salerno Landings, 1943; comd 2nd Commando Bde, Italy, 1943; with Marshal Tito and Yugoslav Partisans, 1944 (Partisan Star with Gold Wreath); Albania, 1944; comd 11th and 138th Inf Bdes, Austria, 1945–46; Zone Comdr, Austria, 1947–49; student, Imperial Def. Coll., 1952; Maj.-Gen. i/c Admin., GHQ, Far ELF, 1955–57; Vice-Quartermaster-Gen. to the Forces, 1957–60; Deputy Chief of Staff, Allied Land Forces, Central Europe, 1960–62, retd. Col The Manchester Regt, 1952–58; Col The King's Regt (Manchester and Liverpool), 1958–62. A Vice-President: Commando Assoc., 1950–;

British-Jugoslav Soc., 1975–. *Publications:* Manual of Interpretation of Air Photographs, 1939; The Churchill Chronicles, 1986; Commando Crusade, 1987; articles to Yorks Archæolog. Jl, 1935, to Army Quarterly and to Jl of RUSI. *Recreations:* genealogy, heraldry; fine arts. *Address:* Treedown Farm, Spreyton, Crediton, Devon EX17 5AS. *T:* Bow 671. *Died* 19 *Feb.* 1990.

**CHWATT, Professor Leonard Jan B.;** *see* Bruce-Chwatt.

**CILENTO, Sir Raphael West,** Kt 1935; MD, BS (Adelaide); DTM&H (England); (life) FRSanI (London); FRHistSoc, Queensland; Director-General of Health and Medical Services, Queensland, Australia, 1934–45; Hon. Professor of Tropical and Social Medicine, University of Queensland, 1937–45; Barrister Supreme Court, Queensland, since 1939; *b* 2 Dec. 1893; *s* of Raphael Ambrose Cilento and Frances Ellen Elizabeth West; *m* 1920, Phyllis Dorothy, *d* of late C. T. McGlew; three *s* three *d*. *Educ:* Adelaide High Sch.; Prince Alfred Coll., South Australia; Univ. of Adelaide. Colonial Medical Service (Federated Malay States), 1920–21; Duncan and Lalcaca medals, London Sch. of Tropical Medicine, 1922; Dir, Australian Inst. of Tropical Medicine, Townsville, North Queensland, 1922–28; Dir of Public Health, New Guinea, 1924–28; Rep. (Brit.) League of Nations Mission on Health Conditions in the Pacific with Dr P. Hermant (French rep.), 1928–29; Dir for Tropical Hygiene, Commonwealth of Australia, and Chief Quarantine Officer (General) NE Div., 1928–34, Brisbane, Qld; Pres., Royal Society Qld, 1933–34; Chm., State Nutritional Advisory Board, 1937; Pres., Med. Board of Qld, 1939; Assessor, Med. Assessment Tribunal, 1940; Senior Administrative Officer, Commonwealth Dept of Health, Canberra, ACT; Mem., Army Medical Directorates Consultative Cttee, 1941–45; Chm., National Survey, Health of Coal Miners, Australia, 1945; UNRRA Zone Dir, British occupied area Germany, Maj.-Gen., with assimilated status, BAOR, 1945–46; Dir, Div. of Refugees, 1946, of Div. of Social Activities, 1947–50, UN, NY. Pres., Royal Hist. Soc. of Queensland, 1934–35, 1943–44, 1953–68; Pres., Nat. Trust of Queensland, 1967–71. *Publications:* Malaria, 1924; White Man in the Tropics, 1925; Factors in Depopulation; NW Islands of the Mandated Territory of New Guinea, 1928; Health Problems in the Pacific, 1929; Anne MacKenzie Oration, 1933; Second Sir Herbert Maitland Oration, 1937; Tropical Diseases in Australasia, 1940 (and 1942); Blueprint for the Health of a Nation, 1944; (jtly) Triumph in the Tropics, 1959; Medicine in Queensland, 1961; (contrib.) History of the Australian Army Medical Service, 1930 (ed. A.G. Butler). *Recreations:* international affairs, reading history. *Address:* Altavilla, 56 Glen Road, Toowong, Queensland 4066, Australia. *Clubs:* Johnsonian (Brisbane); Australasian Pioneers (Sydney). *Died* 15 *April* 1985.

**CITRINE, 1st Baron** *cr* 1946, of Wembley; **Walter McLennan Citrine,** GBE 1958 (KBE 1935); PC 1940; Comp. IEE; *b* Liverpool, 22 Aug. 1887; *m* 1913, Doris Slade (*d* 1973); two *s*. Mersey District Sec. of Electrical Trades Union, 1914–20; Pres., Fed. Engineering and Shipbuilding Trades, Mersey District, 1917–18; Sec., 1918–20; Asst Gen. Sec., Electrical Trades Union, 1920–23; Asst Sec., TUC, 1924–25, Gen. Sec., 1926–46; Mem., Nat. Coal Board, 1946–47; Chm., Miners' Welfare Commn, 1946–47. Pres., Internat. Fed. of Trade Unions, 1928–45; Dir. Daily Herald (1929) Ltd, 1929–46; Mem., Nat. Production Advisory Council, 1942–46 and 1949–57; Past Mem., Reconstruction Jt Advisory Council; Treasury Consultative Council; Visiting Fellow, Nuffield Coll., 1939–47; Trustee of Imperial Relations Trust, 1937–49; Nuffield Trust for the Forces, 1939–46; Mem. of Cinematograph Films Council, 1938–48; Exec. Cttee of Red Cross, and St John War Organisation, 1939–46; Chm. of Production Cttee on Regional Boards (Munitions), 1942; Mem., Royal Commission on W Indies, 1938; Pres., British Electrical Development Assoc., 1948–52; Chm. Central Electricity Authority, 1947–57; Pres., Electrical Research Assoc., 1950–52 and 1956–57; Pres. (1955) and Mem. of Directing Cttee, Union Internationale des Producteurs et Distributeurs d'Energie Electrique; Part-time Mem., Electricity Council, 1958–62. Part-time Mem. of UK Atomic Energy Authority, 1958–62. Hon. LLD, Manchester. *Publications:* ABC of Chairmanship; The Trade Union Movement of Great Britain; Labour and the Community; I Search for Truth in Russia, 1936 and 1938; My Finnish Diary; My American Diary, 1941; In Russia Now, 1942; British Trade Unions, 1942; Men and Work, 1964; Two Careers, 1967, etc. *Heir: s* Hon. Norman Arthur Citrine. *Address:* Gorse Cottage, Victoria Road, Brixham, Devon. *Died* 22 *Jan.* 1983.

**CIVIL, Alan,** OBE 1985; Principal Horn, BBC Symphony Orchestra, 1966–88, retired; *b* 13 June 1929; *m* Shirley Jean Hopkins; three *s* three *d*. *Educ:* Northampton, various schools. Principal Horn, Royal Philharmonic Orchestra, 1953–55; Philharmonia Orchestra, 1955–66. Guest Principal, Berlin Philharmonic Orchestra; international horn soloist; Prof. of Horn, Royal Coll. of Music, London; composer; founder of Alan Civil Horn Trio. Member: London Wind Soloists; London Wind Quintet; Music Group of London. Pres., British Horn Soc., 1979–. Internat. Horn Concours

Adjudicator, Munich, Stockholm, Liège, Luxembourg and Oregon. *Recreations:* brewing, swimming, Baroque music. *Address:* The Kings Arms, High Street, Brasted, near Westerham, Kent. *T:* Westerham 62975. *Clubs:* Savage, London Sketch. *Died* 19 *March* 1989.

**CLAGUE, Ven. Arthur Ashford;** Archdeacon of the Isle of Man, 1978–82; Vicar of Lezayre, 1969–82; *b* 12 Jan. 1915; *s* of John James and May Clague; *m* 1940, Kathleen Louise (*née* Delaney); one *d*. *Educ:* King William's Coll., Isle of Man; St John's Coll., Durham Univ. (BA 1938, MA 1941). Deacon 1938, priest 1939, Manchester; Curate, St Mary, Crumpsall, Manchester, 1938–40; Lecturer, Bolton Parish Church, 1940–44; Rector, Christ Church, Harpurhey, Manchester, 1945–49; Rector of Golborne, Dio. Liverpool, 1949–69. Rural Dean of Ramsey, 1972; Diocesan Canon, 1977. *Recreation:* golf. *Address:* The Old Coach House, Northumberland Street, Alnmouth, Alnwick, Northumberland NE66 2RJ. *Clubs:* Royal Commonwealth Society; Raven (I of M). *Died* 13 *Aug.* 1983.

**CLAGUE, Col Sir (John) Douglas,** Kt 1971; CBE (mil.) 1946 (OBE (mil.) 1943); MC 1942; QPM 1968; CPM 1966; TD 1954; JP; *b* 13 June 1917; 2nd *s* of Alfred Ernest and Hannah Clague, Isle of Man; *m* 1947, Margaret Isolin Cowley; one *s* two *d*. *Educ:* King William's College, Isle of Man. Served War, 1939–46, in the Far East: Hong Kong, China, India, Burma, Siam, finishing with rank of Colonel. Since 1947 involved in business and politics, Hong Kong; Chm., Hutchinson International Ltd Group of Cos, 1952–76. Unofficial Mem., Exec. Council of Hong Kong, 1961–74. JP Hong Kong, 1952. Commendatore dell' Ordine al Merito della Republica Italiana, 1969. *Recreations:* golf, swimming, racing. *Address:* Kam Tsin Lodge, Kam Tsin, New Territories, Hong Kong. *T:* Hong Kong 12-900325. *Clubs:* Junior Carlton, The Royal Commonwealth Society; Royal and Ancient (St Andrews); Sunningdale Golf; MCC; Hong Kong, Royal Hong Kong Jockey (Steward) (Hong Kong). *Died* 11 *March* 1981.

**CLAIR, René;** writer and film director; Member of the French Academy, since 1960; Commandeur de la Légion d'Honneur; *b* 11 Nov. 1898; *m* 1928, Bronia Perlmutter; one *s*. Hon. LLD Cambridge, 1956; Hon. Dr RCA, 1967. *Films include:* Paris qui dort, 1923; Entr'acte, 1924; Un chapeau de paille d'Italie, 1927; Sous les Toits de Paris, 1930; Le Million, 1931; A Nous la Liberté, 1932; Quartorze Juillet, 1933; Le Dernier Milliardaire, 1934; The Ghost Goes West, 1935; Flame of New Orleans, 1940; I Married a Witch, 1942; It Happened Tomorrow, 1943; Le Silence est d'Or, 1946; La Beauté du Diable, 1949; Les Belles de Nuit, 1952; Les Grandes Manœvres, 1955; Porte des Lilas, 1956; Tout l'Or du Monde, 1961; Les Fêtes Galantes, 1965. *Publications:* Adams (Star Turn), 1926; La Princesse de Chine, 1951; Réflection faite (Reflection on the Cinema), 1951; Comédies et Commentaires, 1959; Discours de Reception à l'Académie Française, 1962; Cinéma d'hier et d'aujourd'hui (Cinema Yesterday and Today), 1970; L'Etrange Ouvrage des Cieux, 1971; Jeux du hasard (short stories), 1976. *Address:* 11 bis Avenue de Madrid, 92200 Neuilly sur Seine, France.
*Died* 15 *March* 1981.

**CLANMORRIS, 7th Baron** (Ireland), *cr* 1800; **John Michael Ward Bingham;** *b* 3 Nov. 1908; *o s* of 6th Baron Clanmorris; *S* father, 1960; *m* 1934, Madeleine Mary (*d* 1988), *d* of late Clement Ebel, Copyhold Place, Cuckfield, Sussex; one *s* one *d*. *Educ:* Cheltenham Coll.; France and Germany. *Publications:* as John Bingham: My Name is Michael Sibley, 1952; Five Roundabouts to Heaven, 1953; The Third Skin, 1954; The Paton Street Case, 1955; Marion, 1958; Murder Plan Six, 1958; Night's Black Agent, 1960; A Case of Libel, 1963; A Fragment of Fear, 1965; The Double Agent, 1966; I Love, I Kill, 1968; Vulture in the Sun, 1971; The Hunting Down of Peter Manuel, 1974; God's Defector, 1976; The Marriage Bureau Murders, 1977; Brock, 1981; Brock and the Defector, 1982. *Heir: s* Hon. Simon John Ward Bingham [*b* 25 Oct. 1937; *m* 1971, Gizella Maria, *d* of Sandor Zverkó; one *d*]. *Address:* c/o Coutts & Co., 10 Mount Street, W1. *Died* 7 *Aug.* 1988.

**CLANWILLIAM, 6th Earl of,** *cr* 1776; **John Charles Edmund Carson Meade;** Bt 1703; Viscount Clanwilliam, Baron Gilford, 1766; Baron Clanwilliam (UK), 1828; Major Coldstream Guards (retired); HM Lord-Lieutenant for Co. Down, 1975–79 (HM Lieutenant, 1962–75); *b* 6 June 1914; *o s* of 5th Earl of Clanwilliam; *S* father, 1953; *m* 1948, Catherine, *y d* of late A. T. Loyd, Lockinge, Wantage, Berks; six *d*. *Educ:* Eton; RMC Sandhurst. Adjt, 1939–42; Staff Coll., Haifa, 1942; Bde Major, 201 Guards Motor Brigade, 1942–43; Bde Major, 6 Guards Tank Brigade, 1944; Command and Gen. Staff Sch., Fort Leavenworth, USA, 1944; served in Middle East and France (despatches twice); retd, 1948. *Heir: cousin* John Herbert Meade [*b* 27 Sept. 1919; *m* 1956, Maxine, *o d* of late J. A. Hayden-Scott; one *s* two *d*]. *Address:* Rainscombe Park, Oare, Marlborough, Wilts. *T:* Marlborough 63491. *Clubs:* Carlton, Pratt's. *Died* 30 *March* 1989.

**CLAPHAM, Prof. Arthur Roy,** CBE 1969; FRS 1959; MA, PhD (Cantab); FLS; Professor of Botany in Sheffield University, 1944–69, Professor Emeritus 1969; Pro-Vice-Chancellor, 1954–58, Acting Vice-Chancellor, 1965; Member of the Nature Conservancy, 1956–72 (Chairman, Scientific Policy Committee, 1963–70); Chairman, British National Committee for the International Biological Programme, 1964–75; President, Linnean Society, 1967–70; *b* 24 May 1904; *o s* of George Clapham, Norwich; *m* 1933, Brenda North Stoessiger; one *s* two *d* (and one *s* decd). *Educ:* City of Norwich Sch.; Downing Coll., Cambridge (Foundation Scholar). Frank Smart Prize, 1925; Frank Smart Student, 1926–27; Crop Physiologist at Rothamsted Agricultural Experimental Station, 1928–30; Demonstrator in Botany at Oxford Univ., 1930–44. Mem., NERC, 1965–70; Trustee, British Museum (Natural History), 1965–75. Hon. LLD Aberdeen, 1970; Hon. LittD, Sheffield, 1970. Linnean Gold Medal (Botany), 1972. *Publications:* (with W. O. James) The Biology of Flowers, 1935; Flora of the British Isles (with T. G. Tutin and E. F. Warburg, 1952, 1962; with T. G. Tutin and D. M. Moore, 1987); Excursion Flora of the British Isles, 1959, 3rd rev. edn 1981; (with B. E. Nicholson) The Oxford Book of Trees, 1975; various papers in botanical journals. *Address:* Cottage Flat, Holly House, 94 Main Street, Hornby, Lancaster LA2 8JY. *T:* Hornby (05242) 21206. *Died* 18 *Dec.* 1990.

**CLARINGBULL, Sir (Gordon) Frank,** Kt 1975; BSc, PhD; FGS; CPhys, FInstP; FMA; Director, British Museum (Natural History), 1968–76; *b* 21 Aug. 1911; *s* of William Horace Claringbull and Hannah Agnes Cutting; *m* 1st, 1938, Grace Helen Mortimer (*d* 1953); one *s* one *d*; 2nd, 1953, Enid Dorothy Phyllis, *d* of late William Henry Lambert. *Educ:* Finchley Grammar Sch.; Queen Mary Coll., Univ. of London (Fellow 1967). British Museum (Natural Hist.): Asst Keeper, 1935–48; Princ. Scientific Officer, 1948–53; Keeper of Mineralogy, 1953–68. Explosives res., Min. of Supply, 1940–43; special scientific duties, War Office, 1943–45. Mineralogical Soc.: Gen. Sec., 1938–59; Vice-Pres, 1959–63; Pres., 1965–67; For. Sec., 1967–71; Managing Trustee, 1969–77; Gemmological Assoc.: Vice-Pres., 1970–72, Pres., 1972–. Mem., Commn on Museums and Galleries, 1976–83. *Publications:* Crystal Structures of Minerals (with W. L. Bragg); papers in journals of learned societies on mineralogical and related topics. *Recreations:* craftwork, photography. *Address:* Westering, South Esplanade, Burnham-on-Sea, Somerset TA8 1BU. *T:* Burnham-on-Sea (0278) 780096. *Died* 23 *Nov.* 1990.

**CLARK, Baron** *cr* 1969 (Life Peer); **Kenneth Mackenzie Clark,** OM 1976; CH 1959; KCB 1938; CLit 1974; FBA 1949; *b* 13 July 1903; *o s* of late Kenneth McKenzie Clark and Margaret Alice McArthur; *m* 1st, 1927, Elizabeth Martin (*d* 1976); two *s* one *d*; 2nd, 1977, Mme Nolwen de Janzé-Rice. *Educ:* Winchester; Trinity College, Oxford (Hon. Fellow, 1968). Worked for two years with Mr Bernard Berenson, Florence; Keeper of Dept of Fine Art, Ashmolean Museum, Oxford, 1931–33; Director of National Gallery, 1934–45; Surveyor of the King's Pictures, 1934–44; Director of Film Div., later Controller, Home Publicity, Ministry of Information, 1939–41; Slade Professor of Fine Art, Oxford, 1946–50, and October 1961–62; Prof. of the History of Art, Royal Academy, 1977–. Chancellor, Univ. of York, 1969–79. Chairman: Arts Council of Great Britain, 1953–60; ITA, 1954–57. Former Trustee, British Museum. Member: Conseil Artistique des Musées Nationaux; Amer. Academy; Swedish Academy; Spanish Academy; Florentine Acad.; French Acad., 1973; Institut de France. Hon. Mem., American Inst. of Architects. Hon. Degrees from Universities: Oxford, Cambridge, London, Glasgow, Liverpool, Sheffield, York, Warwick, Bath, Columbia (NY), Brown (Rhode Island). Hon. FRIBA; Hon. FRCA. Serena Medal of British Academy (for Italian Studies), 1955; Gold Medal and Citation of Honour New York University; US Nat. Gall. of Arts Medal, 1970; Gold Medal, NY City, 1977; Gold Medal, Academie des Beaux-Arts. HRSA. Comdr, Legion of Honour, France; Comdr, Lion of Finland; Order of Merit, Grand Cross, 2nd Cl., Austria. *Publications:* The Gothic Revival, 1929; Catalogue of Drawings of Leonardo da Vinci in the collection of His Majesty the King at Windsor Castle, 1935; One Hundred Details in the National Gallery, 1938; Leonardo da Vinci, 1939, new edn 1967; Last Lectures by Roger Fry, edited with an introduction, 1939; L. B. Alberti on Painting, 1944; Constable's Hay Wain, 1944; (Introduction to) Praeterita, 1949; Landscape into Art, 1949; Piero della Francesca, 1951; Moments of Vision, 1954; The Nude, 1955; Looking, 1960; Ruskin Today, 1964; Rembrandt and the Italian Renaissance, 1966; A Failure of Nerve, 1967; Civilisation, 1969; Looking at Pictures, 1972; (jtly) Westminster Abbey, 1972; The Artist Grows Old (Rede Lecture), 1972; The Romantic Rebellion, 1973; Another Part of the Wood (autobiog.), 1974; Henry Moore Drawings, 1974; The Drawings by Sandro Botticelli for Dante's Divine Comedy, 1976; The Other Half (autobiog.), 1977; Animals and Men, 1977; An Introduction to Rembrandt, 1978; The Best of Aubrey Beardsley, 1979; Feminine Beauty, 1980. Numerous TV programmes, 1965–68; TV series: Civilisation, 1969; Romantic versus Classic Art, 1973; Moments of Vision (collected works), 1981; The Art of Humanism, 1983. *Address:* The Garden House, Castle Road, Saltwood, Hythe, Kent. *Died* 21 *May* 1983.

**CLARK, (Agnes) Elisabeth, (Mrs Edward Clark);** *see* Lutyens, A. E.

**CLARK of Herriotshall, Arthur Melville,** MA (Hons); DPhil; DLitt; FRSE; FRSA; Reader in English Literature, Edinburgh University, 1946–60; *b* 20 Aug. 1895; 4th *s* of late James Clark and Margaret Moyes McLachlan, Edinburgh. *Educ:* Stewart's Coll., Edinburgh; Edinburgh University (Sibbald Bursar and Vans Dunlop Scholar); Oriel Coll., Oxford (Scholar); MA First Class Hons and twice medallist, DLitt Edinburgh; DPhil Oxford. Lectr in English Language and Literature, Reading, 1920; Tutor to Oxford Home Students, 1921; Sec. of Oxford Union Soc., 1923; Pres. of Speculative Soc., 1926–29; Lectr in English Literature, Edinburgh Univ., 1928–46; Dir of Studies, Edinburgh Univ., 1931–47; Editor of Edinburgh University Calendar, 1933–45; External Examiner in English, St Andrews Univ., 1939–43, and Aberdeen Univ., 1944–46. Pres. of Scottish Arts Club, 1948–50. Pres. of Edinburgh Scott Club, 1957–58. Exhibitor RSA, SSA. Knight's Cross, Order of Polonia Restituta, 1968; GCLJ 1977. *Publications:* The Realistic Revolt in Modern Poetry, 1922; A Bibliography of Thomas Heywood (annotated), 1924; Thomas Heywood, Playwright and Miscellanist, 1931; Autobiography, its Genesis and Phases, 1935; Spoken English, 1946; Studies in Literary Modes, 1946; Two Pageants by Thomas Heywood, 1953; Sonnets from the French, and Other Verses, 1966; Sir Walter Scott: The Formative Years, 1969; Murder under Trust, or The Topical Macbeth, 1982; contribs to Encyc. Brit., Collier's Encyc., Encyc. of Poetry and Poetics, Cambridge Bibl. of Eng. Lit., Library, Mod. Lang. Review, Classical Review, etc. *Recreations:* walking, pastel-sketching. *Address:* 3 Woodburn Terrace, Edinburgh EH10 4SH. *T:* 031-447 1240; Herriotshall, Oxton, Berwickshire. *Clubs:* New, Scottish Arts (Edinburgh); Union Society (Oxford). *Died* 21 *March* 1990.

**CLARK, Col Charles Willoughby,** DSO 1918; OBE 1945; MC 1916; DL; *b* 6 April 1888; *m* 1916, Athie Maria (Dickie) (*d* 1981); (one *s* one *d* decd). *Educ:* Atherstone Grammar Sch. Apprentice, Alfred Herbert Ltd, Coventry, 1904; Dir, 1934 (Chm. 1958–66). Served European War, 1914–18, France, Machine Gun Corps, Royal Tank Corps (MC, DSO, despatches twice). Chm. Coventry Conservative Assoc., 1945–48; Pres. Coventry Chamber of Commerce, 1951–53; Chm. Manufacturers' Section Cttee of Machine Tool Trades Assoc., 1946–55. Mem. Bd of Trade Machine Tool Advisory Council, 1957–66. Freeman of the City of London. Fellow Royal Commonwealth Society; FInstD; Mem. Inst of Export. DL Warwickshire, 1965. *Recreations:* shooting, fishing, travelling. *Address:* Flat 41, Regency House, Newbold Terrace, Leamington Spa, Warwickshire. *T:* Leamington Spa 24004; Brooklands Close, Ablington, near Bibury, Glos. *T:* Bibury 326. *Club:* Royal Automobile. *Died* 1 *March* 1988.

**CLARK, Colin Grant,** MA, DLitt (Oxon); Corresponding Fellow, British Academy; Research Consultant, Queensland University; Director of Institute for Research in Agricultural Economics, Oxford, 1953–69; Fellow of the Econometric Society; *b* 2 Nov. 1905; *s* of James Clark, merchant and manufacturer, Townsville and Plymouth; *m* 1935, Marjorie Tattersall; eight *s* one *d*. *Educ:* Dragon Sch.; Winchester; Brasenose Coll., Oxford; MA 1931, DLitt 1971; MA Cantab 1931; took degree in chemistry; Frances Wood Prizeman of the Royal Statistical Soc., 1928; Asst to late Prof. Allyn Young of Harvard; worked on the New Survey of London Life and Labour, 1928–29, and Social Survey of Merseyside, 1929–30; on Staff of Economic Advisory Council, Cabinet Offices, 1930–31; University Lectr in Statistics, Cambridge, 1931–37. Contested (Lab): North Dorset, 1929; Wavertree (Liverpool), 1931; South Norfolk, 1935. Visiting Lectr at Univs of Melbourne, Sydney, and Western Australia, 1937–38. Under-Sec. of State for Labour and Industry, Dir of Bureau of Industry, and Financial Adviser to the Treasury, Qld, 1938–52. Hon. ScD, Milan; Hon. DEcon: Tilburg; Queensland, 1985; Hon. DEc Monash, 1983. *Publications:* The National Income, 1924–31, 1932; (with Prof. A. C. Pigou) Economic Position of Great Britain, 1936; National Income and Outlay, 1937; (with J. G. Crawford) National Income of Australia, 1938; Critique of Russian Statistics, 1939; The Conditions of Economic Progress, 1940 (revised edns 1951 and 1957); The Economics of 1960, 1942; Welfare and Taxation, 1954; Australian Hopes and Fears, 1958; Growthmanship, 1961; Taxmanship, 1964; (with Miss M. R. Haswell) The Economics of Subsistence Agriculture, 1964; Economics of Irrigation, 1967, 2nd rev. edn (with Dr D. I. Carruthers), 1981; Population Growth and Land Use, 1967; Starvation or Plenty?, 1970; The Value of Agricultural Land, 1973; Regional and Urban Location, 1982; other pamphlets and numerous articles in Economic periodicals. *Recreations:* walking, gardening. *Address:* Department of Economics, University of Queensland, St Lucia, Qld 4067, Australia. *Club:* Johnsonian (Brisbane). *Died* 4 *Sept.* 1989.

**CLARK, David Allen Richard;** *b* 18 July 1905; *s* of David Richard Clark and Sarah Ann Clark (*née* Clark); *m* 1932, Mary Kathleen, *y d* of Samuel Finney and Mary Ellen Finney (*née* Bagnall), Burslem, Stoke-on-Trent; three *s*. *Educ:* West Felton, Oswestry, C of E Sch.; Oswestry Boys' High Sch.; Oswestry Technical Coll.; Faculty of Technology, Manchester Univ. Stoney Prizeman, 1930; BScTech 1931; MScTech 1932. Apprentice fitter and turner, GWR Co., Oswestry Works, 1921–27; Asst. Surveyor's Office, Oswestry RDC, 1929; Draughtsman, Sentinel Steam Wagon Co. Ltd., Shrewsbury, 1930; Part-time Lectr, Manchester Coll. of Technology, 1931–32; Lectr, Heanor Mining and Technical Coll., 1932–36; Senior Lectr, Kingston-upon-Thames Technical Coll., 1936–39; Head of Engineering Dept, Luton Technical Coll., 1939–47; Principal, Constantine Technical Coll., Middlesbrough, 1947–55; Principal, Nottingham Regional Coll. of Technology, 1955–65. CEng, FIMechE. *Publications:* Materials and Structures, 1941; Advanced Strength of Materials, 1951; articles in technical and educational journals. *Recreation:* collection of old English pottery and porcelain, historical documents, autographs, etc. *Address:* 50 Manor Drive, Upton, Wirral, Merseyside.                                    *Died* 15 Feb. 1986.

**CLARK, Elisabeth, (Mrs Edward Clark);** *see* Lutyens, A. E.

**CLARK, Sir Fife;** *see* Clark, Sir T. F.

**CLARK, Sir (Gordon Colvin) Lindesay,** AC 1975; KBE 1968; CMG 1961; MC; BSc; MME; Mining Engineer, Australia; *b* 7 Jan. 1896; *s* of late Lindesay C. Clark, Launceston, Tas.; *m* 1922, Barbara Jane, *d* of A. C. Walch; one *s* two *d*. *Educ:* Church of England Grammar Sch., Launceston, Tasmania; Universities of Tasmania and Melbourne. Deputy-Controller of Mineral Production, Dept of Supply, Australia, 1942–44. Chairman: Western Mining Corp. Ltd, 1952–74 (Dir, 1974–78); Central Norseman Gold Corp. NL, 1952–74; Gold Mines of Kalgoorlie (Aust.) Ltd, 1952–74; BH South Ltd, 1956–74 (Dir, 1974–78); Alcoa of Australia Ltd, 1961–70, Dep. Chm. 1970–72; Director: Broken Hill Associated Smelters Pty Ltd, 1944–67; North Broken Hill Ltd, 1953–71; Beach Petroleum NL, 1964–72. Pres., Australasian Inst. of Mining and Metallurgy, 1959. Life Mem., Nat. Gallery of Victoria. Pres., The Art Foundn of Victoria, 1976–. Hon. DEng, Melbourne Univ., 1961; Hon. LLD, Monash Univ., 1975. Australasian Inst. of Mining and Metallurgy Medal, 1963; Kernot Meml Medal, Melbourne Univ., 1964. *Publication:* Built on Gold: recollections of Western Mining, 1983. *Recreation:* golf. *Address:* 8 Moralla Road, Kooyong, Victoria 3144, Australia. *T:* 20.2675. *Clubs:* Melbourne, Australian (Melbourne); Tasmanian (Hobart); Weld (Perth); Explorers' (New York).                                    *Died* 3 Jan. 1986.

**CLARK, Most Rev. Howard Hewlett,** CC (Canada) 1970; DD; Chancellor, University of Trinity College, Toronto, since 1972; *b* 23 April 1903; *s* of Douglass Clark and Florence Lilian Hewlett; *m* 1935, Anna Evelyn Wilson; one *s* three *d*. *Educ:* University of Toronto; Trinity College, Toronto. BA 1932. Christ Church Cathedral, Ottawa: Curate 1932; Priest-in-Charge, 1938; Rector 1939–54; Canon 1941; Dean of Ottawa, 1945; Bishop of Edmonton, 1954, Archbishop of Edmonton 1959–61; Primate of Anglican Church of Canada, 1959–70; Metropolitan and Archbishop of Rupert's Land, 1961–69; Episcopal Canon of St George's Collegiate Church, Jerusalem, 1964–70. DD (*jure dignitatis*) Trinity College, Toronto, 1945; subsequently awarded numerous honorary doctorates in divinity and in civil law, both in Canada and abroad. *Publication:* The Christian Life According to the Prayer Book, 1957. *Address:* 252 Glenrose Avenue, Toronto, Ont M4T 1K9, Canada.
                                    *Died* 21 Jan. 1983.

**CLARK, John Anthony,** DL, JP; *b* 19 July 1908; *s* of John Bright Clark and Caroline Susan (*née* Pease); *m* 1930, Eileen Mary Cousins; three *s* two *d*. *Educ:* Leighton Park School; New Coll., Oxford. Director, 1931–74, Chairman, 1967–74, C. & J. Clark Ltd and subsidiary companies, retired. Somerset County Council: Councillor, 1952–; Alderman, 1965; Vice-Chm., 1968 (Chm., Agriculture Cttee and Police Authority). Governor, Millfield Sch., 1953 (Chm. of Governors, 1965). JP 1934, DL 1971, High Sheriff 1970, Somerset. Hon. LLD Bath, 1972. *Recreations:* hunting, golf, farming. *Address:* Home Orchard, Street, Somerset BA16 0HX. *T:* Street 42042. *Club:* Somerset County.                                    *Died* 27 Feb. 1985.

**CLARK, Leonard,** OBE 1966; poet and author; retired HM Inspector of Schools; *b* 1 Aug. 1905; *m* Jane, *d* of William Mark Callow, New Cross, and Annie Maria Callow (*née* Graham); one *s* one *d*. *Educ:* Monmouth Sch.; Normal Coll., Bangor. Teacher in Glos and London, 1922–28, 1930–36; Asst Inspector of Schools, Bd of Educn, 1936–45; HM Inspector of Schools, Min. of Educn (later DES), 1945–70; worked in SW, E and W Ridings, and Metropolitan Divisions; visits to Germany, Malta, Mauritius. Home Guard (Devon Regt), 1940–43. Consultant on Poetry for Seafarers' Educn Service, 1940–54; Mem., Literature Panel, Arts Council of GB, 1965–69. Mem., Westminster Diocesan Schools Commn, 1970–76; Adviser for Secondary Schools, Diocese of London, 1970–72. Liveryman of Haberdashers' Co., 1965; Freeman, City of London,

1965. Hon. Life Mem., NUT, 1970. FRSL 1953; Hon. ALAM 1972; Hon. FCP 1981. (Jtly) International Who's Who in Poetry Prize, 1972; Children's Literature Association Award, 1979. Kt, Order of St Sylvester, 1970. *Publications:* Poems, 1925; (ed) The Open Door: anthology of verse for juniors, 1937; Passage to the Pole, 1944; (ed) The Kingdom of the Mind: essays and addresses of Albert Mansbridge, 1945; (ed) Alfred Williams: his life and work, 1945; Rhandanim, 1945; XII Poems, 1948; The Mirror (poems), 1948; English Morning (poems), 1953; Walter de la Mare, a checklist, 1956; Sark Discovered, 1956, rev. edns 1972, 1978; (ed) Andrew Young: prospect of a poet, 1957; (trans. jtly) Edmond de Goncourt, The Zemganno Brothers, 1957; Selected Poems, 1958; (ed) Quiet as Moss, 36 poems by Andrew Young, 1959; Walter de la Mare: a monograph, 1960; (ed) Collected Poems of Andrew Young, with bibliographical notes, 1960; (comp.) Drums and Trumpets: poetry for the youngest, 1962; Green Wood (autobiography), 1962; reissue 1978; Daybreak (poems), 1963; When They Were Children, 1964; (comp.) Common Ground: an anthology for the young, 1964; Who Killed the Bears?, 1964; Andrew Young, 1964; (comp.) All Things New: anthology, 1965; (comp.) The Poetry of Nature, 1965; A Fool in the Forest (autobiography), 1965; Robert Andrew Tells a Story, 1965; Robert Andrew and the Holy Family, 1965; Robert Andrew and Tiffy, 1965; Robert Andrew by the Sea, 1965; Robert Andrew and the Red Indian Chief, 1966; Robert Andrew and Skippy, 1966; Robert Andrew in the Country, 1966; Fields and Territories (poems), 1967; Prospect of Highgate and Hampstead, 1967; Grateful Caliban (autobiography), 1967; Flutes and Cymbals: an anthology for the young, 1968; (ed) Sound of Battle, 1969; (introd) Life in a Railway Factory by Alfred Williams, 1969; Near and Far (poems), 1969; Here and There (poems), 1969; (ed jtly) The Complete Poems of Walter de la Mare, 1970; (ed) Longmans Poetry Library (64 titles), 1970; Walking With Trees (poems), 1970; (comp.) Poems by Children, 1970; All Along Down Along, 1971; Singing in the Streets (poems), 1972; Secret as Toads (poems), 1972; Poems of Ivor Gurney (comp.), 1973; Mr Pettigrew's Harvest Festival, 1974; Great and Familiar (anthology), 1974; Complete Poems of Andrew Young (comp.), 1974; The Hearing Heart (poems), 1974; Tribute to Walter de la Mare (with Edmund Blunden), 1974; Mr Pettigrew's Train, 1975; The Broad Atlantic (poems), 1975; Four Seasons (poems), 1976; Mr Pettigrew and the Bell Ringers, 1976; Collected Poems and Verses for children, 1976; The Inspector Remembers (autobiog.), 1976; Twelve Poems from St Bartholomew's, 1978; Silence of the Morning (poems), 1978; Stranger than Unicorns (poems), 1979; The Tale of Prince Igor (poem), 1980; The Singing Time (poems for the young), 1980; The Way the Wind Blows (anthology of verse for the young), 1980; The Way it Was (poems), 1980; An Infinite Landscape (poems), 1981; Burnt Siena (poems), 1981; contrib. poems and articles to learned jls in GB and USA. *Recreations:* gardening, music, book collecting, writing. *Address:* 50 Cholmeley Crescent, Highgate, N6 5HA. *T:* 01-348 0092. *Clubs:* Highgate Literary, MCC.                                    *Died* 10 Sept. 1981.

**CLARK, Sir Lindesay;** *see* Clark, Sir G. C. L.

**CLARK, Marjorie, (pen-name, Georgia Rivers);** journalist, writer of fiction; *b* Melbourne; *d* of George A. and Gertrude M. Clark. *Educ:* Milverton Girls' Grammar Sch. *Publications:* Jacqueline, 1927; Tantalego, 1928; The Difficult Art, 1929; She Dresses for Dinner, 1933; 12 full-length serials, numerous short stories and articles. *Recreation:* music. *Address:* Flat 2, 374 Auburn Road, Hawthorn, Victoria 3122, Australia. *Club:* PEN (Melbourne Centre).
                                    *Died* 15 Aug. 1989.

**CLARK, Gen. Mark Wayne,** DSC (US); DSM (3 Oak Leaf Clusters) (US Army); DSM (US Navy); US Army, retired; President Emeritus, The Citadel, Military College of South Carolina (President, 1954–65); *b* Madison Barracks, New York, USA, 1 May 1896; *s* of Col Charles Carr and Rebecca Clark; *m* 1st, 1924, Maurine Doran (*d* 1966); 2nd, 1967, Mrs Mary Millard Applegate, Muncie, Ind. *Educ:* United States Mil. Acad. (BS 1917); Infantry Sch. (grad. 1925); Comd and Gen. Staff Sch. (grad. 1935); Army War Coll. (grad. 1937). Served European War, 1917–18 (wounded); Dep. Chief of Staff, Civilian Conservation Corps, 1936–37; Mem. Gen. Staff Corps, March–June 1942; Chief of Staff for Ground Forces, May 1942; C-in-C Ground Forces in Europe, July 1942; led successful secret mission by submarine to get information in N Africa preparatory to Allied invasion, 1942; Comdr Fifth Army in Anglo-American invasion of Italy, 1943, capture of Rome, June 1944; Commanding Gen. 15th Army Group, Dec. 1944; Gen., 1945; US High Commissioner and Comdg Gen. US Forces in Austria, 1945–47; dep. US Sec. of State, 1947; sat in London and Moscow with Council of Foreign Ministers negotiating a treaty for Austria, 1947; Comdg Gen. 6th US Army, HQ San Francisco, 1947–49; Chief, US Army Field Forces, Fort Monroe, Virginia, 1949–52; 1952–53: Comdr-in-Chief, United Nations Command; C-in-C, Far East; Commanding Gen., US Army Forces in the Far East; Governor of the Ryukyu Islands. Thanks of US House of Representatives, 1945. Hon. KCB 1955; Hon. KBE 1944. Hon.

DCL Oxford, 1945; many other awards and honours, both American and foreign. *Publications:* Calculated Risk, 1950; From the Danube to the Yalu, 1954. *Recreations:* fishing, hunting, golfing and hiking. *Address:* 17 Country Club Drive, Charleston, South Carolina 29412, USA. *T:* 795-5333. *Died 17 April 1984.*

**CLARK, Michael Lindsey**, PPRBS; sculptor; *b* 1918; *s* of late Phillip Lindsey Clark, DSO, FRBS, and Truda Mary Calnan; *m* 1942, Catherine Heron (*d* 1987); five *s* three *d. Educ:* Blackfriars Sch.; City of London Art School. ARBS 1949; FRBS 1960; Pres., RBS, 1971–76. Otto Beit Medal for Sculpture, 1960 and 1978, and Silver Medal, 1967, RBS. *Address:* Barford Court Farm, Lampard Lane, Churt, Surrey GU10 2HJ. *Died 24 Jan. 1990.*

**CLARK, Percy**, CBE 1970; Principal, Stainforth-Clark PR; *b* 18 May 1917; *s* of Perceval Harold Clark and Grace Lilian Clark; *m* 1st, 1941, Nan Dalgleish (*d* 1970); two *s* two *d*; 2nd, 1972, Doreen Stainforth. Early career in newspapers: owner South Lancs News Agency, 1936–47. Labour Party: Publications Officer, 1947; Regional Publicity Dir, 1957; Dep. Dir, Information, 1960, Dir, 1964–79. MIPR. *Recreation:* music. *Address:* Barrow Moor, Longnor, Buxton, Derbyshire SK17 0QP. *T:* Buxton 83292. *Club:* MCC. *Died 25 Nov. 1985.*

**CLARK, His Honour Reginald**, QC 1949; Judge of Clerkenwell, Middlesex, County Court Circuit 41, 1955–66, retired; *b* 18 March 1895; *y s* of J. T. Clark, Manchester; *m* 1923, Joan Marguerite, *y d* of R. Herbert Shiers, Bowdon, Ches.; three *d. Educ:* Trinity Hall, Cambridge. Called to Bar, Lincoln's Inn, 1920; Northern Circuit, 1920–23; practised Rangoon Bar, 1924–41; Judge, High Court, Madras, 1944; resigned from Madras High Court, 1948. Chm., N Midland District Valuation Board, Coal Nationalisation Act, 1948–49; Chm., Road and Rail Appeal Tribunal, 1949. Comr of Assize, North-Eastern, Western and South-Eastern Circuits, 1949; a County Court Judge, Circuit 58, Ilford, etc, 1950–55. Served in TF, European War, 1914–18, Gallipoli and France. Served in Army in Burma and India, 1942–44. *Recreations:* fishing and golf. *Address:* 4 Trumpeters House, Old Palace Yard, Richmond, Surrey. *T:* 01-940 2829. *Club:* East India, Devonshire, Sports and Public Schools. *Died 15 Jan. 1981.*

**CLARK, Stuart Ellis**; *b* 6 Feb. 1899; *s* of Robert and Susanah Clark, Dartford, Kent; *m* 1st, 1923, Mabel Olive Winspear (*d* 1932); one *s*; 2nd, 1935, Joan Bulley. *Educ:* Wilson's Sch. Acting Sec., Southern Rly Co., 1944; Asst Docks and Marine Manager, Southern Rly Co., Southampton Docks, 1947; Sec., Docks Executive, 1948; Sec., Docks and Inland Waterways Board of Management, British Transport Commission, 1950–55. *Recreations:* golf, swimming. *Address:* Knapp Cottage, Wambrook, near Chard, Somerset. *T:* Chard 2442.

**CLARK, Sir (Thomas) Fife**, Kt 1965; CBE 1949; retired; formerly Director General, Central Office of Information; *b* Thornaby-on-Tees, 29 May 1907; *m* 1945, Joan (*d* 1977), *d* of late Captain James Mould, DSO, MC; two *s* one *d. Educ:* Middlesbrough High Sch. (North Riding Scholar). Reporter, sub-editor, Parly lobby corresp. and diplomatic correspondent, Westminster Press provincial newspapers, 1924–39; Public Relations and Principal Press Officer, Min. of Health, 1939–49 (resp. for national publicity on diphtheria immunisation scheme and gen. health educn, and the launching of the NHS); Controller, Home Publicity, COI, 1949–52; Adviser on Govt Public Relations and Adviser on Public Relations to Prime Ministers Sir Winston Churchill and Sir Anthony Eden, 1952–55; Advr on Public Relations to Earl Marshal, Coronation, 1953; as Dir Gen, COI, 1954–71, responsible on behalf of FCO for organisation of British Pavilions at World Exhibitions in Brussels, 1958, Montreal, 1967 and Osaka, 1970; acted as Chief Officer, Nov. 1956–March 1957, to first Cabinet Minister, Dr Charles Hill, to co-ordinate Govt inf. services home and overseas. Consultant on External Relations to Crown Agents for Overseas Govts and Administrations, 1971–75, and to Trident Television Gp of Cos, 1976–78. First Pres., 1955–57, Mem. Emeritus, 1978, Internat. Public Relations Assoc. Fellow and Past Pres., Inst. of Public Relations (President's Medal, 1967); Pres., Civil Service Horticultural Fedn, 1959–70. Mem., Coun. of Management, Brighton Arts Festival, 1966–. *Publication:* The Central Office of Information, 1971. *Recreations:* gardening, walking, watching ships and horses. *Address:* Wave Hill, Nevill Road, Rottingdean, Sussex. *T:* Brighton 33020. *Died 28 March 1985.*

**CLARK, William Donaldson**; President, International Institute for Environment and Development, since 1980; *b* 28 July 1916; *y s* of John McClare Clark and Marion Jackson; unmarried. *Educ:* Oundle Sch.; Oriel Coll., Oxford (MA; 1st class Hons Mod. Hist., Gibbs Prize; Hon. Fellow, 1985). Commonwealth Fellow and Lectr in Humanities, Univ. of Chicago, 1938–40; Min. of Information, and Brit. Inf. Services, Chicago, 1941–44; Press Attaché, Washington, 1945–46; London Editor, Encyclopædia Britannica, 1946–49; Diplomatic Corresp., Observer, 1950–55; Public Relations Adviser to Prime Minister, 1955–56; toured Africa and Asia for

BBC and Observer, 1957; Editor of "The Week" in Observer, 1958–60; Dir, Overseas Development Inst., 1960–68; Dir of Information and Public Affairs, IBRD, 1968–73; International Bank for Reconstruction and Development (World Bank): Dir, External Relns, 1973–74; Vice-Pres. for External Relns, 1974–80; an independent Dir, Observer, 1981–. Frequent broadcasts and television appearances, including original Press Conference series (BBC), and Right to Reply (ATV). *Publications:* Less than Kin: a study of Anglo-American relations, 1957; What is the Commonwealth?, 1958; Number 10 (novel and (with Ronald Miller) play), 1966; Special Relationship (novel), 1968; Cataclysm: the North-South conflict of 1987 (novel), 1984. *Recreations:* writing, talking, travel. *Address:* IIED, 10 Percy Street, W1P 0DR; K5, Albany, W1. *T:* 01–734 1182; The Mill, Cuxham, Oxford OX9 5NF. *T:* Watlington 2381; Biniparell, Menorca, Baleares, Spain. *T:* (3471) 367683. *Clubs:* Athenæum, Savile.
*Died 27 June 1985.*

**CLARK-KENNEDY, Archibald Edmund**, MD (Cantab); FRCP; Fellow of Corpus Christi College, Cambridge, since 1919; Physician to the London Hospital, 1928–58; Dean of the London Hospital Medical College, 1937–53; *b* 23 April 1893; *s* of late Rev. A. E. Clark-Kennedy (RN retired), Rector of Ewhurst, Surrey; *m* 1918, Phyllis (*d* 1978), *d* of late Charles Howard Jeffree, Howard Lodge, Clapham Park; one *s* one *d. Educ:* Wellington Coll.; Corpus Christi Coll., Cambridge (exhibitioner; scholar). 1st class hons in Natural Science Tripos. Lieut, Queen's Royal West Surrey Regt (5th Territorial Bn), Aug. 1914; served as a combatant officer in India, then in Mesopotamia with IEF, D; returned to England, 1917; obtained diploma of MRCS and LRCP; commd in RAMC, 1918; served in France as MO to 158th Army RFA Bde. MRCP 1922; FRCP 1930. *Publications:* Stephen Hales, DD, FRS, an Eighteenth Century Biography, 1929; Medicine (two vols): Vol. I, The Patient and his Disease, 1947; Vol. II, Diagnosis, Prognosis and Treatment; Medicine in its Human Setting, 1954; Patients as People, 1957; Human Disease (a Pelican medical book), 1957; How to Learn Medicine, 1959; Clinical Medicine, The Modern Approach, 1960; The London: A Study in the Voluntary Hospital System (two vols): Vol. I, The First Hundred Years, 1740–1840, 1962; Vol. II, The Second Hundred Years, 1840–1948, 1963; Edith Cavell, Pioneer and Patriot, 1965; Man, Medicine and Morality, 1969; Attack the Colour! the Royal Dragoons in the Peninsula and at Waterloo, 1975; A Victorian Soldier, 1980; Cambridge to Botany Bay, 1983; papers in medical and scientific journals. *Recreations:* mountaineering, sailing, hunting. *Address:* 7 Maitland House, Barton Road, Cambridge. *T:* Cambridge 352323. *Died 2 Sept. 1985.*

**CLARKE, Brig. Arthur Christopher Lancelot S.**; *see* Stanley-Clarke.

**CLARKE, Captain Arthur Wellesley**, CBE 1946; DSO 1943; RN; *b* 16 April 1898; *s* of late Captain Sir Arthur W. Clarke, KCVO, KBE, and Lady Clarke; *m* 1926, Kate Cicely Lance; one *s. Educ:* Merton Court Prep. Sch.; RN Colls Osborne and Dartmouth; Emmanuel Coll., Cambridge (6 months 1919). Midshipman, 1914; Lieut 1918; Comdr 1933; Captain 1939; retired list, 1948 and re-employed at Admiralty. Served at sea throughout European War, 1914–18; Dardanelles, 1915 (despatches); Battle of Jutland, 1916; Atlantic and North Sea convoys. Between wars qualified as Navigating and Staff Officer; served at sea including in command at home and abroad; Asst Sec., Cttee of Imperial Defence, 1933–36. War of 1939–45: War Cabinet office, 1940, and later Addtl Naval Attaché, USA; commanded HMS Sheffield, Atlantic, North Russian and Malta convoys, N African landings and Barents Sea battle, 1941–43; Chief of Staff to Governor and C-in-C Malta, and later Naval Liaison Officer to Comdr, 8th Army, 1943; Chief of Staff to Head of Brit. Admty Delegn USA, 1944–46; comd HMS Ocean, 1946–48; Chief of Naval Information, Admty, 1948–57. Vice-President: King George's Fund for Sailors; Younger Brother, Trinity House. Officer, Legion of Merit (USA), 1946. *Recreation:* gardening. *Address:* 16 Yarborough Road, Southsea, Hants. *T:* Portsmouth 24539. *Club:* Naval (Hon. Mem.). *Died 3 Jan. 1985.*

**CLARKE, Charles Edward**, CBE 1960; Directing Actuary, Government Actuary's Department, 1970–74; *b* 8 July 1912; *s* of late Edward James Clarke and late Lucy Ann Clarke (*née* Hunniball); *m* 1941, Ethel Arbon; two *s. Educ:* Thetford Grammar School. FIA 1940. Entered Govt Actuary's Dept, 1929. *Publication:* Social Insurance in Britain, 1950. *Recreations:* walking, travel, photography, do-it-yourself jobs at home. *Address:* 14 Ashmere Avenue, Beckenham, Kent. *T:* 01-658 1360.
*Died 21 March 1981.*

**CLARKE, Denzil Robert Noble;** Chairman, British-American Tobacco Co. Ltd, 1966–70 (Director, 1954–70; Vice-Chairman, 1962); Director, Sun Life Assurance Society, 1966–79; *b* 9 July 1908; *er s* of late R. T. Clarke, ICS, LLD and late Mrs M. M. G. Clarke (*née* Whyte); *m* 1942, Ismay Elizabeth, *e d* of late Lt-Col Hon. R. M. P. Preston, DSO; one *s* two *d. Educ:* Stonyhurst Coll. Articled Clerk, Singleton Fabian & Co., Chartered Accountants, 1926; ACA 1932;

FCA 1960. Joined British-American Tobacco Co. Ltd, 1932. War service, 1941–45; Far East; Lt-Col 1944. *Recreation:* gardening. *Address:* Puffins, South Drive, Wokingham, Berks. *T:* Wokingham 780975. *Clubs:* Special Forces, Army and Navy.
*Died 30 July 1985.*

**CLARKE, Maj.-Gen. Desmond Alexander Bruce,** CB 1965; CBE 1961 (OBE 1944); *b* 15 July 1912; *yr s* of late R. T. Clarke, ICS, LLD, Weybridge and late Mrs R. T. Clarke (*née* Whyte), Loughbrickland, Co. Down; *m* Madeleine, 2nd *d* of Rear-Adm. Walter Glynn Petre, DSO, Weybridge; three *s* two *d*. *Educ:* Stonyhurst Coll.; RMA Woolwich. Commissioned RA, 1932. Served War of 1939–45 (OBE; despatches 4 times); Middle East, India, France, Germany; AA and QMG, 59 (Staffs) Div., 1943; AA and QMG, 43 (Wessex) Div., Dec. 1944. Brig. i/c Administration, Southern Command, 1960–62; Dir of Personal Services, War Office, 1962–64; Dir of Personal Services (Army), Min. of Defence, 1964–66; retd Oct. 1966. Chevalier, Order of the Crown (Belgium), 1945; Croix de Guerre (Belgium), 1945. *Address:* Elm Cottage, Caldbeck, near Wigton, Cumbria. *T:* Caldbeck 433.
*Died 22 Nov. 1986.*

**CLARKE, His Honour Edward;** QC 1960; a Circuit Judge (Judge of the Central Criminal Court), 1964–81; *b* 21 May 1908; *s* of William Francis Clarke; *m* 1948, Dorothy May, *d* of Thomas Leask, Richmond, Surrey; three *s* one *d*. *Educ:* Sherborne Sch.; King's Coll., London. Called to Bar, Lincoln's Inn, 1935. Served War, 1943–46 in France, Belgium, Holland and Germany, Lieut-Col, Judge Advocate-General's Staff. Bencher, 1955, Treasurer, 1973, Lincoln's Inn; Dep. Chm., Herts Quarter Sessions, 1956–63; Dep. Chm., London Quarter Sessions, 1963–64. FKC, 1965. President: King's Coll. London Assoc., 1972–73, 1978–79; Old Shirburnian Soc., 1975–76. *Publications:* (with Derek Walker Smith) The Life of Sir Edward Clarke; Halsbury's Laws of England (Criminal Law). *Recreation:* criminology. *Address:* 19 Old Buildings, Lincoln's Inn, WC2. *T:* 01–405 2980. *Clubs:* Garrick, MCC.
*Died 21 Feb. 1989.*

**CLARKE, Gerald Bryan,** CMG 1964; ISO 1954; Secretary to the Cabinet and Secretary to the Prime Minister, Rhodesia, 1955–70, retired; *b* Gwelo, Rhodesia, 1 Nov. 1909; *s* of Francis Joseph Clarke and Margaret Shiel; *m* 1946, Eleanor, widow of B. C. Catella; one *s* one *d* (and one step *s*). *Educ:* St George's Coll., Bulawayo, Zimbabwe. Joined Southern Rhodesian Civil Service, 1927; Treasury, 1927–40. Served War, 1940–45: S Rhodesia Armoured Car Regt, E Africa and Abyssinia; Pretoria Regt, 6th SA Armoured Div., Italy. Chief Clerk, Treasury, 1945–48; Asst Sec., Public Services Board, 1948; Under-Sec., Cabinet Office, 1950. Attended Constitutional Confs on HMS Tiger, Dec. 1966, and HMS Fearless, 1968, as Mem. of Rhodesian Delegn. Comr of Oaths, Zimbabwe. Coronation Medal, 1952; Independence Decoration, 1970. *Recreation:* rearing trees. *Address:* 7 Grantchester Close, Sandringham Park, Mount Pleasant, Salisbury, Zimbabwe. *T:* Salisbury 304520. *Club:* Umtali (Umtali).
*Died 24 Aug. 1981.*

**CLARKE, Sir Henry O.;** *see* Osmond-Clarke.

**CLARKE, Paul (Henry Francis); His Honour Judge Paul Clarke;** a Circuit Judge since 1974; *b* 14 Oct. 1921; *s* of late Dr Richard Clarke, FRCP, Clifton, Bristol; *m* 1955, Eileen Sheila (*d* 1987), *d* of late Lt-Col J. K. B. Crawford, Clifton Coll.; two *s* one *d*. *Educ:* Clifton Coll.; Exeter Coll., Oxford (MA). Served War, Gloucester Regt and Royal Engineers, 1940–46. Called to Bar, Inner Temple, 1949, practising as Barrister from Guildhall Chambers, Bristol, 1949–74. *Address:* Saffron House, Chudleigh, Devon TQ13 0EE.
*Died 23 Jan. 1989.*

**CLARKE, Reginald Arnold,** CMG 1962; OBE 1960; DFC 1945; Director of Compensation, International Bank for Reconstruction and Development (World Bank), Washington, DC, 1979–87; *b* 6 May 1921; *s* of late John Leonard Clarke; *m* 1st, 1949, Dorithea Nanette Oswald; three *s* one *d*; 2nd, 1979, Serena Kwang Ok Han. *Educ:* Doncaster Grammar Sch. Royal Air Force, 1939–46; Provincial Administration, Nigeria, 1947–52; Financial Secretary's Office, Nigeria, 1952–57; Federal Ministry of Finance, Nigeria, 1957, Permanent Sec., 1958–63, retd. Asst Dir of Administration, IBRD, 1964–70, Dir of Personnel, 1970–79. *Recreations:* travel, tennis, bridge. *Address:* c/o Midland Bank, Gosforth, Cumbria; 2512 NW 202 Street, Seattle, Washington, DC 98117, USA.
*Died 18 Dec. 1989.*

**CLARKE, Roger Simon Woodchurch,** JP; Chairman, The Imperial Tobacco Co. Ltd, 1959–64; *b* 29 June 1903; *s* of late Charles S. Clarke, Tracy Park, Wick, Bristol; *m* 1936, Nancy Lingard (*d* 1980), *d* of late William Martin, formerly of St Petersburg; no *c*. *Educ:* RN Colleges, Osborne and Dartmouth. Joined The Imperial Tobacco Co., 1922; Dir, 1944–68. Pro-Chancellor, Bristol Univ., 1975–83. JP Bristol, 1964. Hon. LLD Bristol, 1975. *Address:* The Little Priory, Bathwick Hill, Bath. *T:* Bath 63103.
*Died 22 Aug. 1988.*

**CLARKE, Thomas Ernest Bennett,** OBE 1952; screenwriter; *b* 7 June 1907; 2nd *s* of late Sir Ernest Michael Clarke; *m* 1932, Joyce Caroline Steele (*d* 1983); one *d* (one *s* decd). *Educ:* Charterhouse; Clare Coll., Cambridge. Staff writer on Answers, 1927–35; editorial staff Daily Sketch, 1936; subsequently free-lance journalist. Wrote screen-plays of films: Johnny Frenchman, Hue and Cry, Against the Wind, Passport to Pimlico, The Blue Lamp, The Magnet, The Lavender Hill Mob (Academy and Venice Awards), The Titfield Thunderbolt, The Rainbow Jacket, Who Done It?, Barnacle Bill, A Tale of Two Cities, Gideon's Day, The Horse Without a Head. Other screen credits include For Those in Peril, Halfway House, Champagne Charlie (lyrics), Dead of Night, Train of Events, Encore, Law and Disorder, Sons and Lovers, A Man Could Get Killed. *Play:* This Undesirable Residence. *Publications:* Go South-Go West, 1932; Jeremy's England, 1934; Cartwright Was a Cad, 1936; Two and Two Make Five, 1938; What's Yours?, 1938; Mr Spirket Reforms, 1939; The World Was Mine, 1964; The Wide Open Door, 1966; The Trail of the Serpent, 1968; The Wrong Turning, 1971; Intimate Relations, 1971; This is Where I Came In (autobiog.), 1974; The Man Who Seduced a Bank, 1977; Murder at Buckingham Palace, 1981; Grim Discovery, 1983. *Recreations:* racing, travel. *Address:* 13 Oakleigh Court, Oxted, Surrey.
*Died 11 Feb. 1989.*

**CLASEN, Andrew Joseph,** Hon. GCVO 1968; Grand Cross, Adolphe Nassau; Commander Order of the Oaken Crown; Grand Cross: Order of Orange Nassau; Iceland Falcon; Luxembourg Ambassador in London, 1955–71 (Minister, 1944–55); *b* 5 Sept. 1906; *yr s* of late Bernard Clasen and Claire Duchscher; *m* 1944, Joan Mary Luke; one *s* one *d*. *Educ:* Beaumont Coll.; Univs of Oxford, London and Aix-la-Chapelle. DrIng, BSc; ARSM; Hon. FIC. Acting Sec.-Gen. Luxembourg Foreign Affairs Ministry, Counsul-Gen., Chargé d'Affaires, 1940–44. Luxembourg Delegate to Red Cross, UNRRA, European Council, UN, NATO and WEU. Grand Officer, Order of Tunisian Republic. *Address:* The Manor House, Rotherfield, Sussex. *Club:* Turf.
*Died 14 May 1984.*

**CLAUDE, Prof. Albert;** creating a Cancer Research Laboratory, L'Université Libre de Bruxelles; Professor, Catholic University of Louvain; *b* Longlier, Belgium, 24 Aug. 1898; an American citizen. *Educ:* Liège Univ. Med. Sch. (Dr in Med. and Surgery, 1928); Inst. für Krebsforschung, Berlin Univ.; Kaiser Wilhelm Inst., Berlin-Dahlem. Rockefeller Inst. for Medical Research (later University): Volunteer, 1929–31; Asst, 1931–38; Associate, 1938–47; Associate Mem., 1947–49, resigned; Adjunct Prof., 1972–76; Emeritus Prof., 1976; Prof., Univ. Libre de Bruxelles, 1948, Emeritus, 1969; Dir, Jules Bordet Inst., later Lab. de Biologie Cellulaire et Cancérologie, Brussels, 1948–71, now Emeritus. Vis. Res. Prof., Johnson Res. Foundn, 1967. Founder of modern cell biol.; first to isolate a cancer virus by chemical analysis and characterize it as a RNA virus. Member: Royal Acad. of Medicine, Belgium; Nat. Acad. of Medicine, France; Internat. Soc. of Cell Biology; Associate Member: Royal Acad. of Scis, Letters and Fine Arts, Belgium; Inst. de France; Hon. Member: Amer. Acad. of Arts and Sciences; Koninklijke Acad. voor Geneeskunde, Belgium; Soc. Française de Microscopie Electronique; Amer. Assoc. for Cancer Res.; French Biol. Soc.; Belgian Soc. of Cell Biol. Hon. doctorates: Modena, 1963; J. Purkinje Univ., Brno, 1971; Rockefeller, 1971; Liège, 1975; Univ. Catholique de Louvain, 1975; Rigksuniv. of Gent, 1975. Prix Baron Holvoet, Fonds Nat. de la Recherche Scientifique, 1965; Medal, Belgian Acad. of Medicine, 1965; Louisa G. Horowitz Prize, Columbia Univ., 1970; Paul Ehrlich and Ludwig Darmstädter Prize, Frankfurt, 1971; (jtly with Prof. Christian de Duve and Prof. George Emil Palade) Nobel Prize for Medicine or Physiology, 1974 (he carried out initial work and they developed his findings). Grand Cordon, Order of Léopold II (Belgium); Comdr, Palmes académiques (France). *Address:* Laboratoire de Biologie Cellulaire, rue des Champs Elysées 62, 1050 Brussels, Belgium; Rockefeller University, 1230 York Avenue, New York, NY 10021, USA.
*Died 22 May 1983.*

**CLAY, Charles John Jervis;** *b* 19 March 1910; *s* of late Arthur J. Clay and Bridget Clay (*née* Parker-Jervis); *m* 1935, Patricia Agnes, *d* of late James and Dorothy Chapman; one *s* two *d*. *Educ:* Eton; New College, Oxford; Pitmans Business College. Served War, 1939–45, Rifle Bde (Officer), and PoW (despatches). Antony Gibbs & Sons Ltd, 1933–70 (Man. Dir, 1952–70); Dir, Internat. Commodities Clearing House Ltd, 1952–84, Man. Dir, 1971–75, Dep. Chm., 1975–77; Dir, R. J. Rouse & Co. Ltd, 1961–74; Dir-Gen., Accepting Houses Cttee, 1971–76. Chairman: Anton Underwriting Agencies Ltd, 1958–76; Wool Testing Services International Ltd, 1961–74; Automated Real-Time Investments Exchange Ltd, 1972–82; London Bd, National Mutual Life Assoc. of Australasia Ltd, 1969–83; Quality Control International Ltd, 1974–84; Mem. London Cttee, Ottoman Bank, 1955–84; Dir, A. P. Bank Ltd, 1977–86. Member: Public Works Loans Bd, 1958–70; ECGD Adv. Council, 1965–70. Mem. Executive Cttee, BBA, 1973–76; Mem. Council, CBI, 1972–76. *Publications:* Modern Merchant Banking, 1976; papers and speeches on Commodity Futures Trading and Clearing.

*Recreations:* sailing, archery, gardening. *Address:* Lamberts, Hascombe, Godalming, Surrey. *T:* Hascombe 240. *Clubs:* Brooks's, MCC. *Died* 1 *June* 1988.

**CLAY, Sir Henry Felix, 6th Bt** *cr* 1841; consultant to McLellan and Partners, Consulting Engineers; *b* 8 Feb. 1909; *s* of Sir Felix Clay, 5th Bt, and late Rachel, *er d* of Rt Hon. Henry Hobhouse; *S* father, 1941; *m* 1933, Phyllis Mary, *yr d* of late R. H. Paramore, MD, FRCS; one *s* two *d*. *Educ:* Gresham's Sch.; Trinity Coll., Cambridge. *Heir: s* Richard Henry Clay [*b* 2 June 1940; *m* 1963, Alison Mary, *o d* of Dr J. Gordon Fife; three *s* two *d*]. *Address:* Wheelwrights, Cocking, Midhurst, Sussex GU29 0HJ. *Died* 8 *June* 1985.

**CLAYDEN, Rt. Hon. Sir (Henry) John,** PC 1963; Kt 1958; *b* 26 April 1904; *s* of Harold William and Florence Hilda Clayden; *m* 1948, Gwendoline Edith Lawrance. *Educ:* Diocesan Coll., Capetown; Charterhouse; Brasenose Coll., Oxford. Called to Bar, Inner Temple, 1926; Advocate, South Africa, 1927; practised Johannesburg. Served War with S African Engineer Corps and SA Staff Corps, 1940–45. Apptd KC 1945; Judge, Supreme Court of South Africa, Transvaal Provincial Div., 1946–55, 1964–65. Judge of Federal Supreme Court, 1955; Chief Justice, Federation of Rhodesia and Nyasaland, Dec. 1960–April 1964. Chm., Industrial Tribunals, 1967–77. Chm. Southern Rhodesia Capital Commission, 1955; Federal Delimitation Commission, 1958; Hammarskjöld Accident Commission, 1962. Acting Gov.-Gen., Federation of Rhodesia and Nyasaland, May-June 1961. Hon. LLD Witwatersrand. *Address:* 8 Walton Street, SW3 1RE. *T:* 01–589 1300. *Clubs:* Athenæum; Rand (Johannesburg); Harare (Zimbabwe). *Died* 11 *July* 1986.

**CLAYSON, Sir Eric (Maurice),** Kt 1964; DL; *b* 17 Feb. 1908; *yr s* of late Harry and Emily Clayson; *m* 1933, Pauline Audrey Wright; two *s*. *Educ:* Woodbridge Sch. Chartered Accountant, 1931; Birmingham Post & Mail Group Ltd: Dir, 1944–74; Man. Dir, 1947; Jt Man. Dir, 1957; Chm., 1957–74; Director: Associated TV Ltd, 1964–75; ATV Network Ltd, 1966–78; Sun Alliance & London Insurance Group, 1965–75 (Chm., Birmingham Area Bd, 1967–80); Birmingham Reg. Bd, Lloyds Bank Ltd, 1966–78. President: Birmingham Publicity Assoc., 1948–49 (Chm., 1947–48); W Midlands Newspaper Soc., 1949–50; The Newspaper Soc., 1951–52 (Hon. Treasurer, 1956–60); Birmingham Branch, Incorporated Sales Managers' Assoc., 1953–54; Birmingham and Midland Inst., 1967–68. Vice-Pres., Fédération Internationale des Editeurs de Journaux et Publications, 1954–67. Chairman: Exec. Cttee, British Industries Fair, 1956–57; Midlands Regular Forces Resettlement Cttee, 1961–70 (Mem., 1958–70). Director: The Press Assoc. Ltd, 1959–66 (Chm., 1963–64); Reuters Ltd, 1961–66. Member: Council, Birmingham Chamber of Industry and Commerce, 1951– (Vice-Pres., 1953–54, Pres., 1955–56); Gen. Council of the Press, 1953–72; BBC Midland Regional Adv. Council, 1954–57; W Midland Regional Economic Planning Council, 1965–68. Governor, The Royal Shakespeare Theatre, Stratford-upon-Avon, 1963–83 (Mem. Exec. Council, 1963–74); Life Governor, Birmingham Univ., 1956–, Mem. Council, 1959–71. President: Radio Industries Club of the Midlands, 1965–69; Midland Counties Golf Assoc., 1960–62; Vice-Pres., Professional Golfers' Assoc., 1959–83. Guardian, Standard of Wrought Plate in Birmingham, 1969–84. DL West Midlands, 1975–84. *Recreation:* reading newspapers. *Address:* Clare Park, near Farnham, Surrey. *Died* 4 *Oct.* 1989.

**CLAYTON, Sir Arthur Harold,** 11th Bt of Marden, *cr* 1732; DSC 1945; Lt-Comdr RNR; *b* 14 Oct. 1903; *s* of Sir Harold Clayton, 10th Bt, and Leila Cecilia (*d* 1976), *d* of Francis Edmund Clayton; *S* father, 1951; *m* 1st, 1927, Muriel Edith (*d* 1929), *d* of late Arthur John Clayton; 2nd, 1931, Alexandra Andreevsky (marr. diss. 1954); one *s* one *d*; 3rd, 1954, Dorothy (Jill) (*d* 1964), *d* of Arthur John Greenhalgh; 4th, 1965, Diana Bircham, *d* of late Charles Alvery Grazebrook. *Educ:* Haileybury Coll. In business in London, 1923–41, 1946–50. Served War of 1939–45, RNVR, 1941–46 (despatches, DSC). *Recreation:* continental driving. *Heir: s* David Robert Clayton [*b* 12 Dec. 1936; *m* 1971, Julia Louise, *d* of late C. H. Redfearn; two *s*]. *Address:* Colonsay, Kingswear, Dartmouth, Devon. *T:* Kingswear 243. *Clubs:* Royal Naval Sailing Association Portsmouth; Royal Yachting Association; Brixham Yacht (Brixham); Royal Dart Yacht (Kingswear); Shore Line (Lifeboat). *Died* 6 *Aug.* 1985.

**CLAYTON, Adm. Sir Richard (Pilkington),** GCB 1980 (KCB 1978); with General Electric Co., since 1981; *b* July 1925; *s* of late Rear-Adm. John Wittewronge Clayton and Florence Caroline Schuster. *Educ:* Horris Hill, Newbury; RNC Dartmouth. Midshipman, HMS Cumberland, 1942–43; various destroyers, 1944; Home Fleet destroyers, 1944–46; HMS Comus, Far East, 1946–49; Trng Sqdn destroyers, 1949–53; HMS Striker, Suez, 1956; psc 1957; comd HMS Puma, 1958–59; Admty, 1959–61; HMS Lion, 1962–64; MoD, 1964–66; Captain of Dockyard, Gibraltar, 1967–68; comd HMS Kent and HMS Hampshire, 1968–69; MoD, 1970–72; Flag Officer Second Flotilla, 1973–74; Sen. Naval Mem., Directing Staff, RCDS, 1975; Controller of the Navy, 1976–79; C-in-C Naval Home

Command, 1979–81; Flag ADC to the Queen, 1979–81. *Recreations:* winter sports, motor cycling. *Address:* c/o Coutts & Co., 1 Cadogan Place, Sloane Street, SW1X 9PX. *Club:* Royal Naval and Royal Albert Yacht (Portsmouth). *Died* 15 *Sept.* 1984.

**CLAYTON, Prof. Sir Stanley (George),** Kt 1974; MD, MS London; FRCP; FRCS; FRCOG; FKC 1976; Professor of Obstetrics and Gynæcology, King's College Hospital Medical School, 1967–76, now Emeritus; Hon. Consulting Surgeon: King's College Hospital; Queen Charlotte's Hospital; Chelsea Hospital for Women; *b* 13 Sept. 1911; *s* of Rev. George and Florence Clayton; *m* 1936, Kathleen Mary Willshire (*d* 1983); one *s* one *d*. *Educ:* Kingswood Sch.; King's Coll. Hosp. Med. Sch. Qualified, 1934; FRCS 1936; Sambrooke Schol., Jelf Medal, Hallett Prize. Surg. EMS; Major RAMC. Obstetric Surg., Queen Charlotte's Hosp., 1946; Surg., Chelsea Hosp. for Women, 1953; Obstetric and Gynæcological Surg., King's Coll. Hosp., 1947–63; Prof. of Obst. and Gyn., Postgrad. Inst. of Univ. of London, 1963–67. Vice-Pres., RCOG, 1971, Pres., 1972–75; Chm., Conf. of Royal Colls, 1975; Mem. Council, RCS, 1975–78; Chm., Adv. Cttee on Distinction Awards, 1976–84. Pres., Nat. Assoc. of Family Planning Doctors, 1974–76; Vice-Pres., FPA, 1976. Mem., Adv. Cttee on Med. Training, EEC, 1976–81. Examiner, Univs of London, Oxford, Cambridge, Birmingham, Dublin, Wales, Hong Kong, Singapore, W Indies and RCOG. Editor, Jl of Obstetrics and Gynaecology, 1963–75. Hon. Fellow, Amer. Assoc. of Obstetricians and Gynecologists, 1975; Hon. FCOG (SA); Hon. Fellow, S Atlantic Assoc. of Obst. and Gyn., 1973; Hon. FRSM 1985; Hon. FRACOG 1985; For. Mem., Belgian Soc. of Obst. and Gyn., 1965; Beecham Lectr, Inst. of Obst. and Gyn., 1973; Joseph Price Orator, Amer. Assoc. Obst. & Gyn., 1974; Simpson Orator, RCOG, 1978. *Publications:* Pocket Gynaecology, 1948, 10th edn 1984; Pocket Obstetrics, 10th edn 1984; jointly: Queen Charlotte's Text-Book, 11th edn 1965; Ten Teachers' Obstetrics, 13th edn 1980, 14th edn 1985; Ten Teachers' Gynaecology, 13th edn 1980, 14th edn 1985; British Obstetric and Gynæcological Practice, 3rd edn 1964; contrib. Encyclopædia Britannica, 1974; articles in med. jls. *Address:* Fir Tree Lodge, Fir Tree Road, Leatherhead, Surrey. *Died* 12 *Sept.* 1986.

**CLEALL, Ven. Aubrey Victor George;** Archdeacon of Colchester, 1959–69, then Archdeacon Emeritus; *b* 9 Dec. 1898; *s* of late George and Cecilia Cleall, Crewkerne, Somerset. *Educ:* Selwyn Coll., Cambridge; Wells Theological Coll. BA 1922, MA 1926, Cambridge. Deacon, 1924; Priest, 1925; Curate of Crewkerne, 1924–28; Vicar of Waltham Abbey, 1929–59. Diocesan Inspector of Schools (Chelmsford Dio.), 1932–46. Saint Antholin's Lecturer (City of London), 1937–57. Officiating CF, 1940–46; Comd 6th Cadet Bn, The Essex Regt (Actg Major TARO), 1942–44. Rural Dean of Chigwell, 1946–59; Hon. Canon of Chelmsford Cathedral, 1949–59; Rector of Wickham St Paul with Twinstead, 1959–63. Member: Convocation of Canterbury and Church Assembly, 1965–69; Essex County Education Cttee, 1951–59 and 1961–67. Governor, Colchester Royal Grammar Sch., 1963–67. *Address:* 189 Seaside, Eastbourne, E Sussex BN22 7NP. *T:* Eastbourne 639816. *Died* 6 *May* 1982.

**CLEARY, Frederick Ernest,** CBE 1979 (MBE 1951); FRICS; Founder, 1943, and President, since 1983, Haslemere Estates Ltd (Chairman, 1943–83); Chairman and Founder, City & Metropolitan Building Society, 1948, President since 1972; *b* 11 April 1905; *s* of Frederick George and Ada Kate Cleary; *m* 1st, 1929, Norah Helena (decd); two *d*; 2nd, 1968, Margaret Haworth (decd). *Educ:* Dame Alice Owen's Sch. FRICS 1929. Common Councilman, Corporation of London (Coleman Street Ward), 1959–; Deputy Mayor, Borough of Hornsey, 1951; Chairman, Metropolitan Public Gardens Assoc., 1954–; Past Master, Worshipful Co. of Gardeners, 1969–70. Hon. Fellow, Magdalene Coll., Cambridge, 1975. President: Dover and Deal Constituency Cons. Assoc.; Council, CPRE (Kent). Officier de la Légion d'Honneur, 1976. *Publications:* Beauty and the Borough, 1949; The Flowering City, 1969, 8th edn 1982; I'll Do It Yesterday (autobiog.), 1979. *Recreations:* lawn tennis, swimming, the environment. *Address:* 33 Grosvenor Square, W1. *T:* 01-499 2717; South Sands House, St Margaret's Bay, near Dover, Kent. *T:* Dover 852106. *Clubs:* MCC, City Livery (Pres., 1956–66). *Died* 17 *June* 1984.

**CLEGG, Sir Alec, (Alexander Bradshaw Clegg),** Kt 1965; Chief Education Officer, West Riding County Council, 1945–74, retired; *b* 13 June 1909; *s* of Samuel and Mary Clegg, Sawley, Derbs; *m* 1940, Jessie Coverdale Phillips, West Hartlepool; three *s*. *Educ:* Long Eaton Gram. Sch.; Bootham Sch., York; Clare Coll., Cambridge (BA); London Day Training Coll.; King's Coll., London (MA), FKC 1972. Asst Master, St Clement Danes Gram. Sch., London, 1932–36; Admin. Asst Birmingham Educn Cttee, 1936–39; Asst Educn Officer, Ches CC, 1939–42; Dep. Educn Officer, Worcs CC, 1942–45; West Riding, Jan.-Sept. 1945. Chm. of Governors, Centre for Information and Advice on Educational Disadvantage, 1976–79. Hon LLD Leeds, 1972; Hon DLitt: Loughborough, 1972; Bradford, 1978. Chevalier de l'ordre de L'Etoile Noire, 1961.

*Publications:* The Excitement of Writing, 1964, USA 1972; (with B. Megson) Children in Distress, 1968; (ed) The Changing Primary School, 1972; About our Schools, 1981. *Address:* Saxton, Tadcaster, N Yorks. *T:* Barkston Ash 288.          *Died 20 Jan.* 1986.

**CLEGG, Sir Cuthbert (Barwick),** Kt 1950; TD; JP; *b* 9 Aug. 1904; *s* of Edmund Barwick Clegg, DL, JP, Shore, Littleborough, Lancs; *m* 1930, Helen Margaret, *y d* of Arthur John Jefferson, MD; one *s*. *Educ:* Charterhouse; Trinity Coll., Oxford (MA). Pres., British Employers Confederation, 1950–52; JP Lancs, 1946, Sheriff, 1955; Sheriff of Westmorland, 1969; Major (retired), Duke of Lancaster's Own Yeomanry. Member: Cotton Industry Working Party, 1946; Cotton Manufacturing Commission, 1947–49; Anglo-American Council on Productivity, 1948–52; Economic Planning Bd, 1949–53; British Productivity Council, 1952–54; Leader, UK Cotton Industry Mission to India, Hong Kong and Pakistan, 1957. Hon. Life Governor, The Cotton, Silk and Man-Made Fibres Research Association (Pres., 1962–67); President: UK Textile Manufacturers' Assoc., 1960–69; Overseas Bankers' Club, 1966–67; Inst. of Bankers, 1968–69. Chm., Martins Bank Ltd, 1964–69; Dir Barclays Bank Ltd, 1968–75; Dep. Chm., Barclays Bank Trust Co. Ltd, 1969–76; Vice-Chm., Halifax Building Soc., 1971–76 (Dir, 1960–76). *Address:* Cottage No 1, Greysfield, Great Barrow, Chester. *T:* Tarvin 40044.          *Died 9 Jan.* 1986.

**CLEGG, Hugh Anthony,** CBE 1966; MA, MB Cantab; Hon. MD (TCD); Hon. DLit QUB; FRCP; retired; *b* 19 June 1900; *s* of Rev. John Clegg and Gertrude, *d* of John Wilson; *m* 1932, Baroness Kyra Engelhardt, *o d* of late Baron Arthur Engelhardt, Smolensk, Russia; one *s* one *d*. *Educ:* Westminster Sch. (King's Schol.); Trinity Coll., Cambridge (Westminster Exhibr, Senior Schol., in Nat. Science); St Bartholomew's Hospital. 1st Class Hons Part 1 Nat. Sci. Tripos; House Physician at St Bartholomew's Hosp.; House Physician at Brompton Hosp. for Diseases of the Chest; Medical Registrar, Charing Cross Hosp.; Sub-editor, British Medical Journal, 1931–34; Deputy Editor, 1934–46; Editor, 1947–65; Dir, Office for Internat. Relations in Med., RSM, 1967–72; Founder and Editor, Tropical Doctor, a jl of med. practice in the Tropics, 1971–72. Hon. Fellow: American Medical Assoc.; Alpha Omega Alpha Honor Med. Soc. Late Chm., UNESCO Cttee on Co-ordination of Abstracting in the Medical and Biological Sciences. Initiator and Sec., First World Conf. on Med. Educn, London, 1953, and Ed. of its Proceedings, 1954; Editor, Medicine a Lifelong Study (Proceedings of the Second World Conf. on Med. Educn, Chicago, 1959). Vice-Pres., L'Union Internationale de la Presse Médicale, and Pres. of its Third Congress, 1957; Member: Med. Panel, British Council to 1965; Council, World Medical Assoc., 1957–61 (Chm., Cttee on Medical Ethics and author of first draft of code of ethics on human experimentation, subsequently modified as Declaration of Helsinki); RCP Cttees on air pollution and health, and smoking tobacco and health, 1969–77. Gold Medal of BMA, 1966. *Publications:* What is Osteopathy? (jointly), 1937; Brush up your Health, 1938; Wartime Health and Democracy, 1941; contributed medical terms Chambers's Technical Dictionary, 1940; How to Keep Well in Wartime (Min. of Information), 1943; Medicine in Britain (British Council), 1944; revised Black's Medical Dictionary, 1940–44; Advisory Editor medical section of Chambers's Encyclopædia. *Recreation:* reading reviews of the books I should like to read but haven't the time to. *Address:* 42 Cloncurry Street, Fulham, SW6 6DU. *T:* 01-736 3445.          *Died 6 July* 1983.

**CLEMENTI, Air Vice-Marshal Creswell Montagu,** CB 1973; CBE 1968 (OBE 1946); Administrator, Sion College, since 1979; *b* 30 Dec. 1918; *s* of late Sir Cecil Clementi, GCMG and Lady Clementi, MBE; *m* 1940, Susan, *d* of late Sir Henry Pelham, KCB and Hon. Lady Pelham; two *s* one *d*. *Educ:* Winchester; Magdalen Coll., Oxford (MA). Commnd in RAFVR, 1938; served War of 1939–45 as pilot in Bomber Comd and Air Armament specialist; CO, No 214 (FMS) Sqdn, 1946–48; RAF Staff Coll., 1949; Air Min. (Bomber Ops Directorate), 1950–52; Wing Comdr i/c Flying, RAF Sylt, Germany, 1953–54; jssc, Latimer, 1955; Directing Staff, 1955–57; attended nuclear weapons trials at Christmas Island, 1958; comd RAF Stn Bassingbourn, 1958–61; Gp Capt. Ops/Plans/Trng, Near East Air Force, Cyprus, 1961–63; idc 1964; Dir of Air Staff Plans, MoD (Air Force Dept), 1965–67; AOC No 19 Gp, RAF Mount Batten, Plymouth, 1968–69; Senior RAF Mem., RCDS (formerly IDC), 1969–71; AOA, Air Support Comd, RAF Upavon, Jan.–Aug. 1972; AOA, Strike Comd. 1972–74; retired 1974. Administrator, The Richmond Fellowship, 1974–76. Gen. Comr for Income Tax, 1977–. A Governor: St Paul's Schs, 1974–; Abingdon Sch., 1979–. Mem., Court of Assistants, Mercers' Co., 1973–, Master, 1977–78. *Recreations:* walking, riding, travel. *Address:* 8 Chiswick Staithe, W4 3TP. *T:* 01-995 9532. *Club:* Royal Air Force.          *Died 26 Aug.* 1981.

**CLEMENTS, Clyde Edwin,** CMG 1962; OBE 1958; Director: C. E. Clements & Co. Pty Ltd, since 1926; C. E. Clements (Holdings) Ltd; President, Clements Peruana SA; *b* 2 Aug. 1897; *e s* of late Edwin Thomas Clements and late Mrs Clements; *m* 1919, Doris

Gertrude Garrett; one *d*. *Educ:* Devonport Grammar Sch., Tasmania; Queen's Coll., Hobart, Tas. Served European War, 1914–18. Vice-Pres. Young Christian Workers, 1943–66; Dir Young Christian Workers Co-operative Soc. Ltd, 1948–62. Pres. Austr. AA, 1956–57; Mem. Bd, Austr. Nat. Travel Assoc., 1956–57; Mem. Bd, Tourist Develt Authority of Victoria, 1958–69; Vice-Pres. (OTA) World Touring Organization, 1958; Chm., British Motoring Conf., 1964–69. Mem. Board of Management, Sir Colin MacKenzie Sanctuary, Healesville, Vic, 1962. Hon. Consul of Peru. Hon. FAIEx. *Recreations:* golf, angling. *Address:* 11 Cosham Street, Brighton, Vic 3186, Australia. *T:* 92.3974. *Clubs:* Royal Automobile of Victoria (Vice-Pres. 1942–44, 1952–53; Pres. 1955–61); RACV Country; Victoria Golf; West Brighton (Vic).          *Died 25 Sept.* 1983.

**CLEMENTS, Sir John (Selby),** Kt 1968; CBE 1956; FRSA; Actor, Manager, Producer; *b* 25 April 1910; *s* of late Herbert William Clements, Barrister-at-Law, and Mary Elizabeth (*née* Stephens); *m* 1st, 1936, Inga Maria Lillemor Ahlgren (marr. diss. 1946); 2nd, 1946, Dorothy Katharine (Kay Hammond) (*d* 1980), *d* of late Sir Guy Standing, KBE, and Dorothy Frances Plaskitt. *Educ:* St Paul's Sch.; St John's Coll., Cambridge. British Actors' Equity: Mem. Council, 1948, 1949; Vice-Pres., 1950–59; Trustee, 1958. Member: Arts Council Drama Panel, 1953–58; Council, RADA, 1957–. First stage appearance, Out of the Blue, Lyric, Hammersmith, 1930; subsequently appeared in: She Stoops to Conquer, Lyric; The Beaux' Stratagem, Royalty, 1930; The Venetian, Little, 1931; Salome, Gate Theatre, 1931; many Shakespearian parts under management of late Sir Philip Ben Greet; founded The Intimate Theatre, Palmers Green, London, 1935, and ran it as weekly repertory theatre until 1940, directing most of and appearing in nearly 200 plays; produced Yes and No, Ambassadors, 1937; appeared in: Skylark, Duchess, 1942; They Came to a City, Globe, 1943; (also produced) Private Lives, Apollo, 1944; (with Old Vic Co.) played Coriolanus, Petruchio and Dunois, New, 1947–48; appeared in Edward My Son, Lyric, 1948–49; as Actor-Manager-Producer, has presented and played in: The Kingmaker; Marriage à la Mode, St James's, 1946; The Beaux' Stratagem, Phoenix and Lyric, 1949–50; Man and Superman, New and Princes, 1951; (also author) The Happy Marriage, Duke of York's, 1952–53; Pygmalion, St James's 1953–54; The Little Glass Clock, Aldwych, 1954–55; personal management of Saville Theatre, 1955–57, where presented and played in: The Shadow of Doubt; The Wild Duck, 1955–56; The Rivals, 1956; The Seagull; The Doctor's Dilemma; The Way of the World, 1956–57; Adviser on Drama to Associated Rediffusion Ltd, 1955–56, where produced films including: A Month in the Country; The Wild Duck; played in: (also co-presented and directed) The Rape of the Belt, Piccadilly, 1957–58; (also presented) Gilt and Gingerbread, Duke of York's, 1959; The Marriage-Go-Round, Piccadilly, 1959–60; produced Will You Walk a Little Faster?, Duke of York's, 1960; played in: J. B., Phœnix, 1961; The Affair, Strand, 1961; The Tulip Tree, Haymarket, 1962; Old Vic American tour, 1962; played in: (also co-presented and directed) The Masters, Savoy, 1963; Robert and Elizabeth, Lyric, 1964; dir and played in, The Case in Question, Haymarket, 1975. Director, Chichester Festival Theatre, 1966–73; 1966 season, presented: The Clandestine Marriage; (also played in) The Fighting Cock (subseq. Duke of York's); The Cherry Orchard; (also played) Macbeth; 1967 season, directed: The Farmer's Wife; (also played Shotover) Heartbreak House (subseq. Lyric); presented: The Beaux' Stratagem; An Italian Straw Hat; 1968 season, presented: The Unknown Soldier and His Wife; The Cocktail Party (subseq. Wyndham's); (played Prospero) The Tempest; The Skin of our Teeth; 1969 season, presented: The Caucasian Chalk Circle; (also directed and played in) The Magistrate (subseq. Cambridge); The Country Wife; (also played Antony) Antony and Cleopatra; 1970 season, presented: Peer Gynt; Vivat! Vivat! Regina!; (also directed) The Proposal; Arms and the Man; The Alchemist; 1971 season presented: (also directed and played in) The Rivals; (also played in) Dear Antoine (subseq. Piccadilly); Caesar and Cleopatra; Reunion in Vienna; 1972 Season, presented: The Beggar's Opera; (also directed and played in) The Doctor's Dilemma; 1973 Season, presented: (also directed and played in) The Director of the Opera; (also directed) Dandy Dick; dir, Waters of the Moon, Chichester, 1977; The Devil's Disciple (General Burgoyne), The Importance of Being Earnest (Canon Chasuble), Chichester, 1979; entered films, 1934; films include: Things to Come; Knight Without Armour; South Riding; Rembrandt; The Four Feathers; Convoy; Ships With Wings; Undercover; They Came to a City; Train of Events; The Silent Enemy; The Mind Benders; Oh What a Lovely War!; Admiral Nelson; Gandhi. *Address:* Rufford Court, 109 Marine Parade, Brighton, E Sussex BN2 1AT. *T:* Brighton 603026. *Club:* Garrick.          *Died 6 April* 1988.

**CLEMITSON, Rear-Adm. Francis Edward,** CB 1952; retired; *b* 9 Nov. 1899; *s* of William David and Helen Louisa Clemitson; *m* 1933, Kathleen Farquhar Shand; two *d*. *Educ:* Christ's Hospital. Entered Royal Navy as Cadet, 1917; Lieut (E), 1921; Commander (E), 1933;

Capt. (E), 1943; Rear-Adm. (E), 1949; Deputy Engineer-in-Chief of the Fleet (Admin.), Admiralty, 1950–53; retired Oct. 1953. *Recreations:* tennis, golf, philately. *Address:* Tanhurst, Bramley, Surrey. *T:* Guildford 893148. *Died 27 Nov.* 1981.

**CLEMO, George Roger,** DSc; FRS 1937; FRSC; Professor of Organic Chemistry, King's College, University of Durham, 1925–54, Professor Emeritus, 1954; Director of Department of Chemistry, 1932–54; *b* 2 Aug. 1889. *Educ:* University Coll., Exeter; Queen's Coll., Oxford. Late asst to Prof. W. H. Perkin at Oxford; was in charge of the Research Department of the British Dyestuffs Corporation, Manchester. *Address:* Cherryburn, Mickley, Stocksfield, Northumberland NE43 7DD.
*Died 2 March* 1983.

**CLEVERDON, (Thomas) Douglas (James);** publisher and former radio producer; *b* 17 January 1903; *er s* of Thomas Silcox Cleverdon, Bristol; *m* 1944, Elinor Nest, *d* of Canon J. A. Lewis, Cardiff; two *s* one *d* (and one *s* decd). *Educ:* Bristol Grammar Sch.; Jesus Coll., Oxford. Bookseller, and publisher of fine printing, Bristol, 1926–39. Free-lance acting and writing for BBC West Region, 1935–39; joined BBC (Children's Hour), 1939; W Regional Features Producer, 1939–43; Features Producer, London, 1943, until retirement in 1969; free-lance producer, 1969–80. Devised and co-produced BBC Brains Trust, 1941. BBC War Corresp. in Burma, 1945; from 1947, mainly concerned with productions for Third Programme including radio works by Max Beerbohm, J. Bronowski, Bill Naughton, George Barker, David Gascoyne, Ted Hughes, David Jones, Stevie Smith, Henry Reed, Dylan Thomas (Under Milk Wood), Peter Racine Fricker, Elizabeth Poston, Humphrey Searle and other poets and composers. Directed first stage prods of Under Milk Wood, in Edinburgh and London, 1955, and in New York, 1957. Directed: Poetry Festivals, Stratford-upon-Avon, 1966–70; Cheltenham Festival of Literature, 1971. Compiled exhibition of paintings, engravings and writings of David Jones, NBL, 1972. Publisher, Clover Hill Edns (illustrated by contemporary engravers), 1964–. Pres., Private Libraries Assoc., 1978–80. *Publications:* Engravings of Eric Gill, 1929; Growth of Milk Wood, 1969; (ed) Sixe Idyllia of Theocritus, 1971; (ed) Under Milk Wood (Folio Soc.), 1972; (ed) Verlaine, Femmes/Hombres, 1972; The Engravings of David Jones: a survey, 1981. *Recreations:* book-collecting; visual arts. *Address:* 27 Barnsbury Square, N1. *T:* 01–607 7392. *Clubs:* Savile, Double Crown. *Died 1 Oct.* 1987.

**CLEWES, Howard Charles Vivian;** novelist; *b* York, 27 Oct. 1912; British parentage; *m* 1946, Renata Faccincani; one *d*. *Educ:* Merchant Taylors' Sch. Various advertising agents, 1931–37. Served War of 1939–45, infantry company Comdr Green Howards, then Major G2; Chief Press and Information Officer, Milan, Italy, 1945–47. Professional novelist, resident Florence, Rome, London, 1948–. *Publications:* (in UK, USA, etc) Dead Ground, 1946; The Unforgiven, 1947; The Mask of Wisdom, 1948; Stendhal, 1949; Green Grow the Rushes, 1950; The Long Memory, 1951; An Epitaph for Love, 1952; The Way the Wind Blows, 1954; Man on a Horse, 1964; I, the King, 1978; *plays:* Quay South, 1947; Image in the Sun, 1955; *films:* The Long Memory, Steel Bayonet, The One that Got Away, The Day They Robbed the Bank of England, Mutiny on the Bounty, The Holiday, Up from the Beach, William the Conqueror, The Novice, The 40 Days of Musa Dagh, etc. *Recreations:* writing, fishing. *Address:* Wildwood, North End, NW3. *T:* 01–455 7110. *Died 29 Jan.* 1988.

**CLIFFORD OF CHUDLEIGH, 13th Baron** *cr* 1672; **(Lewis) Hugh Clifford,** OBE 1962; DL; Count of The Holy Roman Empire; farmer and landowner; President: Devon Branch, Country Landowners Association, 1973–75; Devon Branch, Royal British Legion, 1969–80; *b* 13 April 1916; *s* of 12th Baron and Amy (*d* 1926), *er d* of John A. Webster, MD; *S* father, 1964; *m* 1945, Hon. Katharine Vavasseur Fisher, 2nd *d* of 2nd Baron Fisher; two *s* two *d*. *Educ:* Beaumont Coll.; Hertford Coll., Oxford (BA). 2nd Lieut, Devonshire Regt, 1935. Served War of 1939–45: North Africa; Major, 1941 (prisoner of war, escaped). Retd, 1950. Lieut-Col, 1959; Col, 1961. ADC(TA), 1964–69. Hon. Col, The Royal Devon Yeomanry/1st Rifle Volunteers, RAC, T&AVR (formerly the Devonshire Territorials, RAC), 1968–71; Dep. Hon. Col, The Wessex Yeomanry, 1971–72, Hon. Col D Sqdn, 1972–83. Pres., Devon Co. Agricultural Assoc., 1973–74. DL Devon, 1964–84. *Recreations:* shooting, sailing. *Heir: s* Hon. Thomas Hugh Clifford [*b* 17 March 1948; *m* 1980, Suzanne Austin, *yr d* of Mrs Campbell Austin, Limerick, Eire; one *s* one *d*. Commnd Coldstream Guards, 1967, retired 1977 (Captain)]. *Address:* La Colline, St Jacques, St Peter Port, Guernsey, Channel Islands; Morella, Montrose, Vic 3765, Australia. *Clubs:* Army and Navy; Royal Yacht Squadron.
*Died 17 March* 1988.

**CLIFFORD, Sir (Geoffrey) Miles,** KBE 1949 (OBE 1939); CMG 1944; ED; Médaille de la Résistance Française avec Rosette; *b* 1897; *m* 1st, 1920, Ivy Dorothy ("Peta") (decd), *y d* of Arthur Robert Eland, Thrapston, Northants; no *c*; 2nd, Mary, *e d* of late Thomas

Turner, Shelbyville, Ill., USA. *Educ:* privately. Diploma in Anthropology, UCL; Fellow, UCL. Served European War (France and Flanders), 1914–18; Army of the Rhine, 1919–20. Comd Nigerian European Defence Force, 1938–40 (Special Duty, 1941–42). Entered Colonial Administrative Service (Nigeria), 1921; Acting Resident, Adamawa, 1934–37; Principal Asst Sec., 1938–41; seconded as Colonial Sec., Gibraltar, 1942–44; Senior Resident, Nigeria, 1944; Chm. Salaries Commn, Cyprus, 1945; attached CO, 1946; Governor and C-in-C of Falkland Islands, 1946–54. Chief Warden, Westminster, 1954–57; Mem., LCC, 1955–58; Hon. Organiser, Mental Health Research Fund, 1954–56; Dir, Leverhulme Trust, 1956–65; Cttee of Management, Trans-Antarctic Expedition, 1954; Mem., Antarctic Sub-Cttee, International Geophysical Year; Chm., British National Cttee on Antarctic Research, 1964–78; Cttee of Management, British Trans-Arctic Expedn, 1967; a Vice-Pres., RGS, 1956–62; St Paul's Cathedral Trust Council, 1962–78; a Trustee of Toc H; Vice-Pres., African Medical and Research Foundn; Life Gov., Imperial Cancer Research Fund; Trustee, E Grinstead Res. Trust, 1960–82; Mem., Management Cttee (co-opted), Inst. of Basic Med. Sciences; Hon. Treasurer, Soc. for Health Educn; Mem., Porritt Working Party on Med. Aid to Developing Countries and Chm. Anglo-Amer. Conf. on same theme, Ditchley, 1966; Chm. Planning Cttee, Chelsea Group of Post-graduate Hospitals; Chm. Cttee of Management, Inst. Latin American Studies, London Univ., 1964–78; Mem. Council Voluntary Service Overseas. Chm., Nigerian Electricity Supply Corp., 1957–77. A Governor, Sutton Valence Sch., 1957–77. MInstD; Hon. FRCS; Hon. FDS, RCS; Mem., Ct of Patrons, RCS. *Publications:* A Nigerian Chiefdom; Notes on the Bassa-Komo Tribe; book reviews and occasional contribs to the Press. *Address:* Kingswood Lodge, Trinity Close, Tunbridge Wells, Kent. *Clubs:* Athenæum; Antarctic (Hon. Mem.); Explorers' (New York) (Fellow Emeritus). *Died 21 Feb.* 1986.

**CLIFFORD, Graham Douglas,** CMG 1964; FCIS; Director, The Institution of Electronic and Radio Engineers, 1937–78, Hon. Fellow 1978; *b* 8 Feb. 1913; *s* of John William Clifford and Frances Emily Reece; *m* 1937, Marjory Charlotte Willmot; two *d* (one *s* decd). *Educ:* London schs and by industrial training. Molins Machine Co. Ltd, 1929; Columbia Graphophone Co. Ltd, 1931; American Machinery Co. Ltd, 1934; Dir, Taycliff Investments, 1962–82; formerly dir of other cos. Sec., Radio Trades Exam. Bd, 1942–65 (Hon. Mem. 1965); Jt Founder and Hon. Sec., Nat. Electronics Council, 1961–70 (Hon. Treasurer, 1971–78). For 40 years Editor of The Radio and Electronic Engineer and Electronics Rev. Hon. Mem., Assoc. of Engineers and Architects, Israel, 1966; Hon. Treasurer, UK Cttee for the Gandhi Centenary, 1969–78; Hon. Sec. and Governor, Nehru Meml Trust, 1971–78. Comdr, Order of Merit, Research and Invention, France, 1967. *Publications:* A Twentieth Century Professional Institution, 1960; (ed) Nehru Memorial Lectures, annually 1972–78; contribs to various technical journals. *Recreations:* photography, genealogy, music, but mainly work. *Address:* 45 West Park Lane, West Worthing, W Sussex BN12 4EP. *T:* Worthing 41423. *Died 22 Oct.* 1989.

**CLIFFORD, Sir Miles;** *see* Clifford, Sir G. M.

**CLIFFORD, Sir Roger (Charles Joseph Gerrard),** 6th Bt *cr* 1887; Manager, Rod Weir & Co. Ltd, Waikanae Stock and Station Agents, retired 1979; *b* 28 May 1910; *s* of Charles William Clifford, *d* 1939 (3rd *s* of 1st Bt) and Sicele Agnes (*d* 1948), *d* of Sir Humphrey de Trafford, 2nd Bt; *S* brother, 1970; *m* 1st, 1934, Henrietta Millicent Kiver (*d* 1971); two *s* one *d*; 2nd, 1973, Gretchen Patrice Pollock. *Educ:* Beaumont College, Old Windsor; Harper Adams Agricultural College. *Heir: er s* Roger Joseph Clifford [*b* 5 June 1936; *m* 1968, Joanna Theresa, *d* of C. J. Ward, Christchurch, NZ; one *d*]. *Address:* 8 Kea Street, Waikanae, New Zealand.
*Died 5 July* 1982.

**CLIFTON-BROWN, Anthony George,** TD; late Major RA; formerly Director: Royal Exchange Assurance; Westminster Bank Ltd; Westminster Foreign Bank Ltd; Bank of New South Wales (London Board); one of HM Lieutenants for City of London, 1950–60; *b* 11 Feb. 1903; *y s* of late Edward Clifton-Brown; *m* 1st, 1930, Delia Charlotte (*d* 1947), *y d* of late George Edward Wade; three *d*; 2nd, 1949, Phyllis Adrienne McCulloch, (Bridget) (*d* 1977), *d* of late Francis Harvey, Dublin. *Educ:* Eton; Trinity Coll., Cambridge. Mem. of Court of Assistants, Merchant Taylors' Company (Master, 1945–46; First Upper Warden, 1955–56); Sheriff of the City of London, 1957–58; Alderman of Broad Street Ward, 1950–60. Chm., Management Cttee, Royal London Homœopathic Hosp., 1948–61. Commendatore of Order of Merit of Italian Republic. *Address:* Via del Moro 7, 00153 Rome, Italy. *Died 9 Feb.* 1984.

**CLIFTON-BROWN, Lt-Col Geoffrey Benedict;** *b* 25 July 1899; *m* 1927, Robina Margaret (*d* 1979), *d* of late Rowland Sutton; two *s* (one *d* decd). *Educ:* Eton; RMC Sandhurst. 2nd Lieut 12th Lancers, 1918; Major, 1935; Lt-Col, 1940; served with 12th Lancers in France and Belgium, 1939–40, evacuated Dunkirk (despatches).

MP (C) Bury St Edmunds Div. of West Suffolk, 1945–50. *Address:* Little Bradley House, near Haverhill, Suffolk. *T:* Thurlow 261.
*Died 17 Nov. 1983.*

**CLIFTON-TAYLOR, Alec,** OBE 1982; FSA; architectural historian and critic; *b* 2 Aug. 1907; *o s* of Stanley E. Taylor and E. E. Clifton Hills. *Educ:* Bishop's Stortford Coll.; Queen's Coll., Oxford (MA); Courtauld Inst. of Art, London (BA 1st Cl. Hons History of Art); Sorbonne, Paris (Dip.). FSA 1963; Hon. Brother, Art Workers Guild, 1976; Hon. FRIBA, 1979. Served War, Admiralty, 1940–46: Private Sec. to Parly Sec., 1943–46. Lectr, Univ. of London Inst. of Educn, and RCA, 1934–39; extra-mural lectr, London, 1946–57; Ferens Lectr in Fine Art, Univ. of Hull, 1981; since 1956 has lectured extensively all over Britain and (for univs, museums and art galls, British Council, and E-SU) in every continent, incl. 32 states of USA; occasional talks and television progs for BBC. Pres., Kensington Soc., 1979–; Vice-President: Men of the Stones; Soc. for Italic Handwriting; Patron, Avoncroft Mus. of Buildings; Trustee, Historic Churches Preservation Trust. *Publications:* The Pattern of English Building, 1962 (3rd edn 1972); The Cathedrals of England, 1967; English Parish Churches as Works of Art, 1974 (also transcribed into Braille); (with R. W. Brunskill) English Brickwork, 1977; *based on BBC TV series:* Spirit of the Age (contrib.), 1975; Six English Towns, 1978; Six More English Towns, 1981; Another Six English Towns, 1984; (with A. S. Ireson) English Stone Building, 1983; contribs to over 20 books and to art jls, esp. The Connoisseur. *Recreations:* gazing at mountains, quizzing old churches and houses, painting, gardening, writing limericks, looking up other people in Who's Who. *Address:* 15 Clareville Grove, SW7 5AU. *T:* 01–373 7222. *Club:* Oxford Union (Oxford).
*Died 1 April 1985.*

**CLINTON, (Francis) Gordon,** FRCM; Hon. RAM; FBSM; ARCM; baritone; *b* 19 June 1912; *s* of Rev. F. G. Clinton, Broadway, Worcs; *m* 1939, Phyllis Jarvis, GRSM, ARCM; two *s* one *d*. *Educ:* Evesham Grammar Sch.; Bromley Sch. for Boys. Open Schol. RCM, 1935; Vicar Choral, St Paul's Cathedral, 1937–49; served War of 1939–45 in RAF; demobilised as Flt-Lieut. Appearances at over 2,000 major concerts and festivals (50 in Royal Albert Hall, 30 in Festival Hall, inc. inaugural concerts), 1946–; soloist, Beecham 70th birthday concert, 1949; Mem. staff, RCM, 1949–82 (Mem. Bd of Professors, 1975–82); Principal, Birmingham Sch. of Music, 1960–74; Chorus Master and Co-founder, City of Birmingham Symph. Orch. Chorus, 1974–80. Examr to Associated Board, 1956–83. Tours of America, Canada, Europe, Africa, Australasia, Scandinavia, Far East (singing, adjudicating, lecturing). Hon. Life Mem., Royal Soc. of Musicians. *Recreations:* sport, wild-life. *Address:* 42 Pembroke Croft, Hall Green, Birmingham. *T:* 021–744 3513.
*Died 16 June 1988.*

**CLINTON-THOMAS, Robert Antony,** CBE 1965; HM Diplomatic Service, retired; *b* 5 April 1913; *s* of late Brig. R. H. Thomas, CSI, DSO, and Lady Couchman; *m* 1949, Betty Maria Clocca. *Educ:* Haileybury; Peterhouse, Cambridge (MA). Indian Civil Service, 1937–47; Foreign Office, 1947–49; 1st Sec. and Consul, Manila, 1949–53; Head of Chancery, HM Embassy, Tripoli, 1953–56; FO, 1956–57; Counsellor and Head of Chancery, HM Embassy, Addis Ababa, 1957–59; Counsellor and Head of Chancery, Political Office with the Near East Forces, Cyprus, 1959–61; Political Adviser to the C-in-C Middle East Comd, Aden, 1961–62; Counsellor, HM Embassy, Oslo, 1962–65; FCO (formerly FO), 1965–70; Consul-Gen., Antwerp, 1970–73. *Address:* Flat 21, Bluegates, 4 Belvedere Drive, Wimbledon. *Died 6 Oct. 1981.*

**CLITHEROE, 1st Baron** *cr* (June) 1955, of Downham; Bt *cr* 1945 (succeeded to Btcy Sept. 1955); **Ralph Assheton,** PC 1944; KCVO 1977; KStJ; FSA; JP; DL; Lord-Lieutenant of Lancashire, 1971–76 (Vice-Lieutenant, 1956–71); High Steward of Westminster since 1962; *b* 24 Feb. 1901; *o s* of Sir Ralph Assheton, 1st Bt; *m* 1924, Hon. Sylvia Benita Frances Hotham, FRICS, FLAS, *d* of 6th Baron Hotham; two *s* one *d*. *Educ:* Eton (Oppidan Schol.); Christ Church, Oxford (MA). Called to Bar, Inner Temple, 1925; MP (Nat. U) Rushcliffe Div. of Notts, 1934–45; City of London, 1945–50; Blackburn West, 1950–55. Parly Sec., Min. of Labour and Min. of National Service, 1939–42; Parly Sec., Min. of Supply, 1942–43; Financial Sec. to the Treasury, 1943–44; Chm. Conservative Party Organisation, 1944–46; Chm. Public Accounts Cttee, 1948–50; Chm. Select Cttee on Nationalised Industries, 1951–53; Mem. Royal Commission on West Indies, 1938–39. Chm., Borax (Holdings) Ltd, 1958–69 (Dir, 1947–); Deputy Chairman: (Jt) National Westminster Bank Ltd until 1971 (formerly a Dep. Chm. National Provincial Bank); John Brown & Co. Ltd until 1971; Director: The Mercantile Investment Trust Ltd (Chm. 1958–71); Coutts & Co., 1955–71; formerly Director: Tube Investments Ltd (Dep. Chm.); Rio Tinto Zinc; Tanganyika Concessions Ltd; and other cos. Pres., NW of England and IoM TAVR, 1973–75. DL 1955, JP 1934, Lancashire; Mem. Council, Duchy of Lancaster, 1956–77. *Heir:* s Hon. Ralph John Assheton [*b* 3 Nov. 1929; *m* 1961, Juliet, *d* of Christopher Hanbury; two *s* one *d*. *Educ:* Eton; Christ

Church (Scholar), Oxford (MA)]. *Address:* 17 Chelsea Park Gardens, SW3. *T:* 01-352 4020; Downham Hall, Clitheroe, Lancs. *T:* Chatburn 210. *Clubs:* Carlton, Royal Automobile, MCC.
*Died 18 Sept. 1984.*

**CLITHEROW, Rt. Rev. Richard George,** MA Cantab; *b* 1 Oct, 1909; *s* of H. G. Clitherow, MRCS, and Elizabeth Willis Clitherow; *m* 1941, Diana, *d* of H. St J. Durston; two *s* one *d*. *Educ:* Dulwich College; Corpus Christi College, Cambridge; Wells Theological College. Asst Curate, St Augustine, Bermondsey, 1936–40. Chaplain to the Forces, 1942–46 (despatches). Canon Residentiary, Guildford Cathedral, 1946–58; Bishop Suffragan of Stafford, 1958–74. Proctor in Convocation, Guildford, 1951–58, Lichfield, 1967–72. *Recreations:* fishing and gardening. *Address:* 37 Fairbanks Walk, Swynnerton, Stone, Staffs. *Died 7 Nov. 1984.*

**CLOSE-SMITH, Charles Nugent,** TD 1953; Underwriting Member of Lloyd's (Deputy Chairman, 1970); *b* 7 July 1911; 2nd *s* of Thomas Close Smith, Boycott Manor, Buckingham, and Mary Morgan-Grenville, *d* of 11th Baroness Kinloss; *m* 1946, Elizabeth Vivien, *d* of late Major William Kinsman, DSO, Dublin; three *s*. *Educ:* Eton; Magdalene Coll., Cambridge. Entered Lloyd's, 1932; 2nd Lt, Royal Bucks Yeomanry, 1938. Served War of 1939–45 France and Burma (despatches); retd as Lt-Col, RA. Chairman Lloyd's Non-Marine Underwriters Assoc., 1965; elected to Committee of Lloyd's, 1967–70. *Recreation:* horticulture. *Address:* The Heymersh, Britford, Salisbury, Wilts. *T:* Salisbury 336760. *Clubs:* Boodle's, Gresham.
*Died 22 Sept. 1988.*

**CLOSS, Prof. August,** MA, DPhil; Professor of German and Head of German Department, University of Bristol, 1931–64, later Emeritus; Dean of the Faculty of Arts, 1962 and 1963; *b* 9 Aug. 1898; 4th *s* of late A. Closs; *m* 1931, Hannah Margaret Mary (*d* 1953), novelist and art-critic, *d* of late Robert Priebsch, Prof. and Medievalist at UCL; one *d*. *Educ:* Berlin, Vienna, Graz, London. Lectured at Sheffield Univ., 1929–30; at University Coll., London, 1930–31. Guest-Prof. at univs of Amsterdam, Ghent, Berlin, Heidelberg, Frankfurt A/M, Bern, Vienna, Rome, Florence, etc, and in the USA at Univs of Columbia, Princeton, Yale, California and at Canadian and Indian Univs. Hon. Fellow: Hannover Univ.; Bristol Univ., 1989; Korresp. Mitglied der Deutschen Akademie; Membre Corresp. de l'Institut International des Arts et des Lettres (Zürich); Fellow of PEN. FRSL. Patron, Inst. of Germanic Studies, London Univ., 1986–. Hon. DLitt Bristol, 1987. Hon. Citizen, Hannover, 1987. Comdr, Cross of Order of Merit, West Germany, Austrian Cross of Merit *Litteris et Artibus. Publications:* Medieval Exempla: (Dame World) Weltlohn, 1934; The Genius of the German Lyric, 1938 (enlarged 2nd edn 1962, paperback edn 1965); German Lyrics of the Seventeenth Century, 1940, 1947; Hölderlin, 1942, 1944; Tristan und Isolt, 1944, 1974; Die Freien Rhythmen in der deutschen Dichtung, 1947; Novalis-Hymns to the Night, 1948; Die neuere deutsche Lyrik vom Barock bis zur Gegenwart, 1952, 1957; Deutsche Philologie im Aufriss; Woge im Westen, 1954; Medusa's Mirror; Reality and Symbol, 1957; The Harrap Anthology of German Poetry, 1957, new edn 1969; Reality and Creative Vision in German Lyrical Poetry (Symposium), 1963; (ed) Introductions to German Literature (4 vols), 1967–71, also wrote vol. 4, Twentieth Century German Literature, 1969, 2nd edn 1971; The Sea in the Shell, 1977; (ed) Briefwechsel, 1979; (contrib.) The Love-Potion as a Poetic Symbol in Gottfried's Tristan, in, Tristan Symposium, 1990; contribs to Times Literary and Educ. Supplements, German Life and Letters, Modern Lang. Rev., Euphorion, Reallexikon, Deutsches Literatur-Lexikon, Aryan Path, Germanistik, Universitas, and American journals. *Recreations:* music, collecting first editions. *Address:* 40 Stoke Hill, Stoke Bishop, Bristol BS9 1EX. *Club:* University of Bristol. *Died 21 June 1990.*

**CLOTWORTHY, Stanley Edward,** CBE 1959; Chairman, Alcan Aluminium (UK) Ltd, 1969–74; *b* 21 June 1902; *s* of Joseph and Fanny Kate Clotworthy; *m* 1927, Winifred Edith, *d* of J. Mercer Harris; one *s* one *d*. *Educ:* Peter Symonds Sch., Winchester; University Coll., Southampton. Student apprenticeship with B. T. H. Ltd, Rugby, 1923–26; Macintosh Cable Co., Liverpool, 1926–27; Alcan Industries Ltd (formerly Northern Aluminium Co.), 1927–67. Pro-Chancellor, Southampton Univ., 1972–. Hon. DSc Southampton, 1969. *Recreations:* shooting, gardening. *Address:* Kemano, Warreners Lane, St George's Hill, Weybridge. Surrey. *T:* Weybridge 42904. *Died 6 Dec. 1983.*

**CLOUSTON, Air Cdre (retd) Arthur Edmond,** CB 1957; DSO 1943; DFC 1942; AFC and Bar, 1939; RAF retd; *b* 7 April 1908; *s* of R. E. Clouston, mining engineer, Motueka, Nelson, NZ; *m* 1937, Elsie, *d* of late S. Markham Turner, Farnborough, Hants; two *d. Educ:* Rockville Sch.; Bainham Sch. Joined Royal Air Force, 1930. Record Flight, London–Capetown–London, 1937 (Seagrave Trophy); Record Flight, London–NZ–London, 1938 (Britannia Trophy). Served War of 1939–45 (DFC, DSO), engaged in Research Test Flying, Fighter Comd, Coastal Comd; Comdt, Empire Test-Pilots Sch., Farnborough, 1950–53; AOC, Singapore, 1954–57; Comdt,

Aeroplane and Armament Experimental Establishment, Boscombe Down, Amesbury, 1957–60. Group Capt. 1947; Air Cdre 1954. *Publication:* The Dangerous Skies (autobiography), 1954. *Address:* Wings, Constantine Bay, Padstow, Cornwall.

*Died* 1 *Jan.* 1984.

**CLUTTERBUCK, Maj.-Gen. Walter Edmond,** DSO 1943; MC; *b* 17 Nov. 1894; *s* of E. H. Clutterbuck, JP, Hardenhuish Park, Chippenham, Wilts; *m* 1919, Gwendolin Atterbury (*d* 1975), *o d* of H. G. Younger, JP, Benmore, Argyllshire; one *s* three *d*. *Educ:* Horris Hill; Cheltenham Coll.; RMC Sandhurst. Commissioned Royal Scots Fusiliers, 1913; served European War, 1914–19, France, Gallipoli, Egypt, Palestine, and S Russia (wounded twice, MC and bar, Crown of Italy, 1914 Star and clasp, despatches twice); Bt Lt-Col 1939; War of 1939–45 commanded: 1st Royal Scots Fusiliers, 1939–40; 10th Inf. Bde, 1940–41; 1st Div., 1941–43, N Africa and Pantellaria (DSO, Legion of Honour); an Inf. Div. Home Forces, 1943. Chief of British Military Mission to Egypt, 1945–46; retired pay, 1946. *Recreations:* hunting, fishing, shooting. *Address:* Hornby Castle, Bedale, N Yorks. *T:* Richmond 811579. *Club:* Naval and Military. *Died* 2 *Feb.* 1987.

**CLUVER, Eustace Henry,** ED; MA; DM, ChB Oxon; DPH London; FRSH; Emeritus Professor of Medical Education, University of the Witwatersrand, Johannesburg, SA, since 1963; *b* 28 Aug. 1894; *s* of late Dr F. A. Cluver, Stellenbosch; *m* 1929, Eileen Ledger; three *d*. *Educ:* Victoria Coll., Stellenbosch; Hertford Coll., Oxford (Rhodes scholar). 1st class Final Hon. Sch. of Physiology, 1916. Elected to a Senior Demyship at Magdalen Coll., 1917; King's Coll. (Burney Yeo Scholarship, 1918). Served European War, 1914–18 (Capt. S Af. Med. Corps, BEF, France); War of 1939–45 (Col Dir of Pathology, S Af. Med. Corps). Prof. of Physiology, Univ. of the Witwatersrand, Johannesburg, 1919–26; Sec. for Public Health and Chief Health Officer for the Union of South Africa, 1938–40; Dir of S African Inst. for Med. Research and Prof. of Preventive Medicine, Univ. Witwatersrand, 1940–59. LLD (*hc*) Witwatersrand, 1974. KStJ. *Publications:* Public Health in South Africa, 1934 (Textbook), 6th edn 1959; Social Medicine, 1951; Medical and Health Legislation in the Union of South Africa, 1949, 2nd edn 1960; papers in scientific and medical journals. *Address:* Mornhill Farm, PO Box 226, Walkerville, Transvaal, 1876, South Africa.

*Died* 1 *June* 1982.

**CLWYD, 2nd Baron** *cr* 1919; **John Trevor Roberts;** Bt, 1908; Assistant Secretary of Commissions, Lord Chancellor's Department of House of Lords, 1948–61; *b* 28 Nov. 1900; *s* of 1st Baron and Hannah (*d* 1951), *d* of W. S. Caine, MP; *S* father, 1955; *m* 1932, Joan de Bois (*d* 1985), *d* of late Charles R. Murray, Woodbank, Partickhill, Glasgow; one *s* one *d*. *Educ:* Gresham's Sch.; Trinity Coll., Cambridge. BA 1922. Barrister, Gray's Inn, 1930. JP County of London, 1950. *Recreation:* fishing. *Heir: s* Hon. (John) Anthony Roberts [*b* 2 Jan. 1935; *m* 1969, Geraldine, *yr d* of C. E. Cannons, Sanderstead; three *s*]. *Address:* 15 Aubrey Road, W8. *T:* 01–727 7911; Trimmings, Gracious Street, Selborne, Hants.

*Died* 30 *March* 1987.

**COAKER, Maj.-Gen. Ronald Edward,** CB 1972; CBE 1963; MC 1942; *b* 28 Nov. 1917; *s* of late Lieut-Col Vere Arthur Coaker, DSO, and Cicely Annie Coaker (*née* Egerton), Richard's Hill, Battle, Sussex; *m* 1946, Constance Aimée Johanna, *d* of Francis Newton Curzon, Lockington Hall, Derby; one *s* two *d*. *Educ:* Wellington; RMC, Sandhurst. 2nd Lieut IA (Skinner's Horse), 1937; served War of 1939–45, Middle East, Italy and Burma; transf. 17th/21st Lancers, 1947; Lt-Col 1954; GSO1, 7th Armoured Div., 1954–56; comd 17th/ 21st Lancers, 1956–58; Col GS to Chief of Defence Staff, 1958–60; Brig. 1961; Commandant RAC Centre, 1961–62; Dir of Defence Plans (Army), 1964–66; Assistant Chief of Staff (Intelligence), SHAPE, 1967–70; Dir of Military Operations, MoD, 1970–72. Maj.-Gen. 1966; retired 1972. Col 17th/21st Lancers, 1965–75. DL Rutland, 1973; High Sheriff of Leicestershire, 1980. *Recreations:* agriculture, field sports, bridge. *Address:* Daleacre House, Lockington, Derby DE7 2RH. *T:* Kegworth 3339. *Club:* Cavalry and Guards. *Died* 11 *Oct.* 1983.

**COATE, Maj.-Gen. Sir Raymond Douglas,** KBE 1967; CB 1966; Chairman, Royal Homes for Officers' Widows and Daughters, Queen Alexandra's Court, Wimbledon, since 1969; *b* 8 May 1908; *s* of Frederick James and Elizabeth Anne Coate; *m* 1939, Frances Margaret Varley; two *s*. *Educ:* King Edward's Sch., Bath; RMC Sandhurst. Commissioned into Devonshire Regt, 1928; transferred to Royal Army Pay Corps, 1937; Paymaster-in-Chief, 1963–67; Col Comdt, RAPC, 1970–74. *Address:* 18 Roehampton Close, SW15 5LU. *Died* 8 *March* 1983.

**COATES, Edith,** OBE 1977; Principal Dramatic Mezzo-Soprano, Royal Opera, Covent Garden, 1947; *b* Lincoln, 31 May 1908; *d* of Percy and Eleanor Coates, Leeds; *m* 1933, Harry Powell Lloyd. *Educ:* Trinity Coll. of Music, London. Principal Mezzo, Sadler's Wells, 1935 (Carmen, Delilah, Azucena, Ortrud, Amneris, etc); Principal Mezzo, Covent Garden, 1937 (first appearance there

under Sir Thomas Beecham, and in The Ring under Furtwängler, in Coronation season and 1938, 1939); Sadler's Wells, New Theatre and provinces, singing many roles during War of 1939–45 and in Germany after war. Created role of Auntie in Britten's Peter Grimes, Sadler's Wells, 1945, and afterwards sang it at Paris Opera, Monnaie, Brussels and Covent Garden; has sung over 60 roles in opera; many oratorios, Royal Albert Hall, BBC and Provinces; many concerts and broadcasts; sang title role at Covent Garden in Tchaikowsky's Queen of Spades under Kleiber, 1950–51; sang in first English performances of Berg's Wozzeck, 1952; sang in first performance of Tippett's Midsummer Marriage, Covent Garden, 1955, Janacek's Jenufa, Covent Garden, 1956, and John Gardner's Moon and Sixpence, Sadler's Wells, 1957; played in Candide (Hillman-Bernstein after Voltaire), Saville, 1959; Countess in Queen of Spades, Covent Garden, 1961; sang in first performances of Grace Williams' Opera, The Parlour, Welsh National Opera, Cardiff, 1966; English Opera Group, 1963, 1965, 1967. Hon. FTCL. *Recreations:* reading, walking. *Address:* Montrose, Cross Lane, Findon, Worthing, West Sussex. *T:* Findon 2040. *Club:* Lansdowne. *Died* 7 *Jan.* 1983.

**COATES, Patrick Devereux;** Editor (part-time) of Chinese-language records, for British Academy, at Public Record Office, 1978–87; *b* 30 April 1916; *s* of late H. H. Coates, OBE, and late Mrs F. J. Coates; *m* 1946, Mary Eleanor, *e d* of late Capt. Leveson Campbell, DSO, RN and late Mrs Campbell; one *s* one *d*. *Educ:* Trinity Coll., Cambridge. Entered Consular Service and served at Peking, Canton and Kunming, 1937–41; attached to Chinese 22nd Div. in Burma (despatches) and to Chinese forces in India, 1941–44; Actg Consular Sec. to HM Embassy in China, 1944–46; 1st Sec., Foreign Office, 1946–50; transf. to Min. of Town and Country Planning, 1950; Asst Sec., Min. of Housing and Local Govt, 1955; Asst Under-Sec. of State, Dept of Economic Affairs, 1965–68, Min. of Housing and Local Govt, 1968–70, Dept of the Environment, 1970–72. Hon. Vis. Fellow, SOAS, Univ. of London, 1973–76. *Publication:* The China Consuls, 1988. *Recreations:* reading, writing, pottering. *Address:* Lewesland Cottage, Barcombe, near Lewes, Sussex BN8 5TG. *T:* Barcombe (0273) 400407. *Died* 28 *Oct.* 1990.

**COATES, Sir Robert (Edward James Clive) M.;** *see* Milnes Coates.

**COBBOLD, 1st Baron** *cr* 1960, of Knebworth; **Cameron Fromanteel Cobbold,** KG 1970; PC 1959; GCVO 1963; DL; Lord Chamberlain of HM Household, 1963–71; Chancellor of the Royal Victorian Order, 1963–71; Governor of Bank of England, 1949–61; one of HM Lieutenants for the City of London; *b* 14 Sept. 1904; *s* of late Lt-Col Clement Cobbold; *m* 1930, Lady (Margaret) Hermione (Millicent) Bulwer-Lytton, *er d* of 2nd Earl of Lytton, KG, PC, GCSI, GCIE; two *s* one *d*. *Educ:* Eton; King's Coll., Cambridge. Entered Bank of England as Adviser, 1933; Exec. Dir, 1938; Dep. Governor, 1945. Director: BIS, 1949–61; British Petroleum, 1963–74; Hudson Bay Co., 1964–74; Guardian Royal Exchange, 1963–74. Chairman: Chemical Bank New York Adv. Commn, 1969–74; Italian International Bank, 1971–74. A Permanent Lord in Waiting to the Queen, 1971–. Vice-Pres., British Heart Foundn (Pres. to 1976); Chm., Middlesex Hosp. Board of Governors and Med. Sch. Council, 1963–74. High Sheriff of County of London for 1946–47. Hon. Fellow Inst. of Bankers, 1961; Fellow of Eton, 1951–67; Steward of the Courts, Eton, 1973–. Chm. Malaysia Commission of Enquiry, 1962. Hon. LLD, McGill Univ., 1961. Hon. DSc (Econ.), London Univ., 1963. DL Herts, 1972. *Heir: s* Hon. David Antony Fromanteel Lytton-Cobbold [*b* 14 July 1937; assumed by deed poll, 1960, the additional surname of Lytton; *m* 1961, Christine Elizabeth, 3rd *d* of Major Sir Dennis Frederic Bankes Stucley, 5th Bt; three *s* one *d*]. *Address:* Lake House, Knebworth, Herts. *T:* Stevenage 812310.

*Died* 1 *Nov.* 1987.

**COBHAM, Ven. John Oldcastle,** MA; Archdeacon of Durham and Canon Residentiary of Durham Cathedral, 1953–69, now Archdeacon Emeritus; Licence to Officiate, Diocese of Exeter, since 1982, Diocese of Oxford, since 1986; *b* 11 April 1899; *s* of late Ven. John Lawrence Cobham; *m* 1934, Joan (*d* 1967), *d* of late Rev. George Henry Cobham; no *c*. *Educ:* St Lawrence Coll., Ramsgate; Tonbridge Sch.; Corpus Christi Coll., Cambridge; Univ. of Marburg; Westcott House, Cambridge; Académie Goetz. Served in Royal Field Artillery, 1917–19; Curate at St Thomas', Winchester, 1926–30; Vice-Principal of Westcott House, Cambridge, 1930–34; Principal of The Queen's Coll., Birmingham, 1934–53; Vicar of St Benet's, Cambridge, 1940–45; Recognised Lectr, Dept of Theology, Birmingham Univ., 1946–53; Hon. Canon, Derby Cathedral, 1950–53. Chaplain to the Forces (EC), 1943–45. Select Preacher: Univ. of Cambridge, 1933 and 1940; Univ. of Birmingham, 1938; Univ. of Oxford, 1952–53; Examining Chaplain to the Bishop of Durham, 1953–66, to the Bishop of Wakefield, 1959–68; licensed to officiate dio. St Edmundsbury and Ipswich, 1969–82. Member: Liturgical Commn, 1955–62; Archbishop of Canterbury's Commn on Roman Catholic Relations, 1964–69. George Craig Stewart Memorial Lecturer, Seabury-Western Theological Seminary,

Evanston, Ill., 1963. *Publications:* Concerning Spiritual Gifts, 1933; co-translator of K. Barth in Revelation, a Symposium, 1937; contributor to: The Parish Communion, 1937; No Other Gospel, 1943; The Significance of the Barmen Declaration for the Oecumenical Church, 1943; DNB 1931–40 (E. C. Hoskyns), 1949; Theological Word Book of the Bible, 1950. *Recreation:* sketching. *Address:* The Old Vicarage, Moulsford, near Wallingford, Oxon OX10 9JB.                                        *Died 20 May 1987.*

**COCHRANE OF CULTS,** 3rd Baron *cr* 1919; **Thomas Charles Anthony Cochrane;** *b* 31 Oct. 1922; *s* of 2nd Baron Cochrane of Cults, DSO, and Hon. Elin Douglas-Pennant (*d* 1934), *y d* of 2nd Baron Penrhyn; *S* father, 1968. *Educ:* privately. Founder and Trustee, The Gardeners' Memorial Trust, 1980–. *Heir: b* Hon. (Ralph Henry) Vere Cochrane [*b* 20 Sept. 1926; *m* 1956, Janet Mary Watson, *d* of late Dr W. H. W. Cheyne; two *s*]. *Address:* Crawford Priory Estate, Cupar, Fife, Scotland; (residence) East Craigard, East Church Street, Buckie, Banffshire.                       *Died 15 June 1990.*

**COCHRANE, Dr Robert Greenhill,** CMG 1969; MD, FRCP, DTM&H; Regional Leprosy Officer, Shinyanga Region, Tanzania, 1969–72; Medical Superintendent, Kola Ndoto Leprosarium, Tanzania, 1969–72; retired; *b* 11 Aug. 1899; *s* of Dr Thomas Cochrane and Grace Hamilton Cochrane (*née* Greenhill); *m* 1st, 1927, Ivy Gladys Nunn (*d* 1966); two *s* one *d*; 2nd, 1968, Dr Martha Jeane Shaw. *Educ:* Sch. for Sons of Missionaries, Blackheath (now Eltham Coll.); Univ. of Glasgow; St Bartholomew's Hosp., London; London Sch. of Tropical Medicine. Med. Sec., BELRA (now LEPRA), 1928–33; Med. Supt, Leprosy Hosp., Chingleput, S India, 1933–44 and 1948–51; Dir, Leprosy Campaign and Dir of Leprosy Research, Madras State, India, 1941–51; Dir and Prin. Prof. of Medicine and Dermatology, and Dir, Rural Medicine, Christian Med. Coll., Vellore, S India, 1944–48; Adviser in Leprosy to Min. of Health, London, 1951–65; Vis. Med. Officer, Homes of St Giles, E Hanningfield, Essex, 1951–66; Tech. Med. Adviser, Amer. Leprosy Mission, Inc., 1953–64; Dir, Leprosy Study Centre, London, 1953–65; Med. Supt, Leprosy Hosp., Vadathorasalur, S Arcot, Madras, 1966–68. Pres., Internat. Leprosy Assoc., 1963–68, since when Pres. Emeritus. Kaisar-i-Hind gold medal (India), 1935; Damien-Dutton Award, 1964. *Publications:* A Practical Textbook of Leprosy, 1947; Leprosy in Theory and Practice, 1959, 2nd edn, 1964; Biblical Leprosy, A Suggested Interpretation, 1961; contribs to Internat. Jl of Leprosy, Leprosy Review. *Address:* 606 Swede Street, Norristown, Pa 19401, USA. *Club:* Royal Commonwealth Society.                                        *Died 3 Aug. 1985.*

**COCKAYNE, Dame Elizabeth,** DBE 1955; Chief Nursing Officer, Ministry of Health, 1948–58, retired; *b* 29 Oct. 1894; *d* of William and Alice Cockayne, Burton-on-Trent. *Educ:* Secondary Sch., Burton-on-Trent, and privately. Gen. Hospital Training, Royal Infirmary, Sheffield; Fever Training, Mount Gold Hospital, Plymouth; Midwifery Training, Maternity Hospital, Birmingham. Former experience includes: Supervisor of Training Sch., LCC; Matron of West London Hosp., St Charles' Hosp., Royal Free Hosp. *Recreation:* gardening. *Address:* Rushett Cottage, Little Heath Lane, Cobham, Surrey.                       *Died 4 July 1988.*

**COCKBURN, Claud;** journalist; *b* 12 April 1904; *s* of Henry Cockburn, CB, and Elizabeth Stevenson; *m* 1940, Patricia Arbuthnot; three *s*. *Educ:* Berkhamsted Sch.; Keble Coll., Oxford; Universities of Budapest and Berlin. Travelling Fellow of The Queen's College, Oxford; Correspondent of The Times in New York and Washington, 1929–32; Editor, The Week, 1933–46; Diplomatic and Foreign Correspondent, the Daily Worker, 1935–46; since 1953 has written principally for Punch, New Statesman and Private Eye; Atlantic Monthly, 1968–; weekly columnist, Irish Times. *Publications:* High Low Washington, 1933; Reporter in Spain, 1936; Beat the Devil, 1952; Overdraft on Glory, 1955; (autobiog.) In Time of Trouble, 1956; Nine Bald Men, 1956; Aspects of History, 1957; (autobiog.) Crossing the Line, 1958; (autobiog.) View from the West, 1961; (autobiog.) I, Claud, 1967; Ballantyne's Folly, 1970; Bestseller, 1972; The Devil's Decade, 1973; Jericho Road, 1974; Union Power: the growth and challenge in perspective, 1976; Cockburn Sums Up, 1981. *Recreation:* travel. *Address:* Rock House, Ardmore, Co. Waterford, Ireland. *T:* 024-4196.                 *Died 15 Dec. 1981.*

**COCKER, Prof. Ralph,** CBE 1968; MB, ChB, LDS (Victoria University Manchester); FRCS, FDSRCS; Professor Emeritus of Dental Surgery in the University of London, ex-Director of Dental Studies, and Sub-Dean, King's College Hospital Medical School, University of London, 1947–73, Consultant Dental Surgeon and Director of Dental Department, King's College Hospital, 1947–73, Hon. Consultant Dental Surgeon, since 1973; *b* 18 April 1908; *er s* of Frank Barlow Cocker and Mary Wildman; *m* 1942, Margaret (*née* Jacques); one *s* two *d*. *Educ:* William Hulme's Grammar Sch., Manchester; Manchester Univ. Preston Prize and Medallist, Manchester Univ., 1930. Private Practice, 1930–36; Asst Hon. Dental Surg., Manchester Dent. Hosp., 1933–36; Lectr in Clin. Dental Surg., Manchester Univ., 1936–45; Industrial Health Service

(ICI Ltd), 1940–45; Lctr in Periodontia, Manchester Univ., 1945–47; Actg Cons. Dental Surg., Manchester Royal Infirmary, 1945–47; Past Examr in Dental Sugery, Univs of Manchester, London, Birmingham, Bristol, Sheffield, St Andrews; Chm. Bd of Examrs for Statutory Exam. (GDC), 1964–73; Member: Bd of Faculty, RCS, 1955–71 (Vice-Dean, 1964–65) and Examr to Coll. for Dipl. and Final Fellowship in Dental Surgery; Standing Dental Adv. Cttee of Dept. of Health and Social Security, 1963–74 (Vice-Chm. 1965–74); GDC, 1963–74 (Chm., Educn Cttee, 1970–74, Chm. Central Examining Bd for Dental Hygienists, 1967–74); Sec., Odontolog. Section, RSM, 1961–63 (Vice-Pres. 1970–73); Mem., Dental Educn Adv. Coun. of Gt Brit., 1947–73 (Chm., 1956–57; Treas., 1957–73; Sec., 1967–73); Mem. and Chm., Assoc. of British Dental Hospitals, 1947–73; Mem., Dental Industry Standards Cttee (BSI); Founder Mem., King's Coll. Hosp. Med. Sch. Council and King's Coll. Hosp. Bd of Govs, 1948–73; Mem. Bd of Dental Studies, London Univ., 1948–73 (Chm., 1966–71); Adviser in Dental Surgery to Dept. of Health and Social Security, 1968–74; Temp. Adviser, WHO, 1970–72. FKCHMS 1981; FKC 1985. *Recreations:* mountaineering, ski-ing, photography, ornithology. *Address:* Broad Mead, Westwell Leacon, Charing, Kent TN27 0EN. *T:* Charing 2437. *Club:* Alpine.                       *Died 29 July 1986.*

**COCKER, Sir William Wiggins,** Kt 1955; OBE 1946; JP; MA; LLD; Director of Cocker Chemical Co. Ltd; President, British Tar Products Ltd; a Lloyd's Underwriter; *b* 17 Oct. 1896; *s* of Wiggins Cocker, Accrington; *m* 1922, Mary Emma Bowker, Accrington (*d* 1965); one *s* one *d*; *m* 1970, Mrs Rhoda Slinger, Accrington. Freedom of Borough of Accrington, 1958. *Address:* 384 Clifton Drive North, St Annes-on-Sea, Lancs.               *Died 21 July 1982.*

**COCKERELL, Sydney (Morris),** OBE 1980; FSA; bookbinder; Senior Partner in Cockerell Bindery (formerly D. Cockerell & Son), since 1946; *b* 6 June 1906; *er s* of late Douglas Cockerell and Florence Arundel; *m* 1932, Elizabeth Lucy Cowlishaw; one *s* two *d*. *Educ:* St Christopher Sch., Letchworth. Partnership with Douglas Cockerell, 1924. Vis. Lectr, Sch. of Library, Archive and Information Studies, UCL, 1945–76. Assisted with repair and binding of Codex Sinaiticus Manuscript at British Museum, 1934; has repaired and bound many early and medieval manuscripts including Codex Bezae Book of Cerne, Book of Deer, Thornton Romances, Fitzwilliam Virginal Book, Handel's Conducting Score of Messiah, and repaired and treated, amongst others, papers of Wordsworth, Milton, Tennyson, Isaac Newton, Captain Cook's First Circumnavigation of the Globe; mounted Hereford Mappa Mundi; designed and made numbers of tooled bindings for collectors. Revived and developed craft of marbling paper; designed and made tools and equipment for binding and marbling. Visited Ceylon, Ethiopia, Italy, Canada, Tunisia, Portugal, USA, Greece and Jordan to advise on book conservation. Hon. Member: Soc. of Scribes and Illuminators, 1956; Double Crown Club (Pres., 1976–77); Fellow International Institute for Conservation of Historic and Artistic Works, 1959; Master, Art Workers Guild, 1961. Hon. LittD Cantab, 1982. *Publications:* Marbling Paper, 1934, 4th edn 1985; Appendix to Bookbinding and the Care of Books, 1943, revised and repr. 1973; The Repairing of Books, 1958; contributor to: The Calligrapher's Handbook, 1956, 2nd edn 1985; Encyclopædia Britannica, 1963. *Recreation:* keeping the house up and the weeds down. *Address:* Riversdale, Grantchester, Cambridge. *T:* Cambridge 840124.

                                            *Died 6 Nov. 1987.*

**COCKING, Prof. John Martin,** MA; Leverhulme Emeritus Research Fellow, 1975–77; Fellow, since 1965 and Emeritus Professor, since 1975, King's College, University of London; *b* 9 Nov. 1914; *s* of Matthew Maddern Bottrell Cocking and Annie Cocking; *m* 1941, May Parsons Wallis; one *s*. *Educ:* Penzance County Sch. for Boys; King's Coll., London; Sorbonne; British Institute in Paris. BA (Hons) French, 1935; Teacher's Diploma (London), 1936; Diplôme d'Etudes Universitaires (Sorbonne), 1937; MA (London), 1939. Lecturer in English Literature, British Institute in Paris, 1937–38, Lecturer in English and Asst to the Dir, 1938–39; Asst Lecturer in French, King's Coll., London, 1939–46 (including 5 years' absence on war service in the Army); Lecturer in French, 1946–52, Prof. of French Lang. and Literature, 1952–75, King's Coll., London. Officier de l'ordre national du mérite (France), 1973. *Publications:* Marcel Proust, 1956; Proust: collected essays on the writer and his art, 1982; articles in journals and reviews. *Address:* 8 Marlborough Court, Pinehurst, Grange Road, Cambridge CB3 9BQ. *T:* Cambridge 351740.                       *Died 28 Jan. 1986.*

**COCKRAM, Ben,** CMG 1948; OBE 1944; Jan Smuts Professor of International Relations, University of the Witwatersrand, 1961–70, Emeritus Professor, since 1971; *b* 1903; *s* of B. B. Cockram, St Helier's, Jersey, Channel Islands; *m* 1928, Doris Mary Holdrup; one *d*. *Educ:* Victoria Coll.; Taunton's Sch.; Queen's Coll., Oxford. BA (London); MA (Oxon); PhD (Michigan, USA). Asst Principal, Dominions Office, 1926; Private Sec. to Parly and Permanent Under-Secs of State, 1929–34; Principal, 1934–39; Political Sec. to UK High Comr in Union of S Africa, 1939–44; Counsellor, British

Embassy, Washington, DC, 1944–49; Asst Sec., CRO, 1949–51; Dep. High Comr for the UK in Australia, 1952–54, and Acting High Comr, May–Oct. 1952; Dir of Information, CRO, 1954–57, Dir of Information Services, 1957–62. Adviser to UK delegs to Assembly and Council of League of Nations, 1935, 1936, 1937 and 1938, to Brussels Conference, on Far East, 1936, to San Francisco Conference, 1945, to Councils of UNRRA and FAO, to Peace Conference, Paris, 1946, the Assembly, Security, Economic and Social, and Trusteeship Councils of UN, 1946, 1947 and 1948; to Unesco Conferences, Paris, 1958 and 1960. Mem. of Far Eastern Commission on Japan, 1946–48; Mem. UK Delegation to Commonwealth Educational Conferences: at Oxford, 1959; at Delhi, 1962; Leader, UK Delegations to Unesco Confs on SE Asia, at Bangkok, 1960; on Latin America, at Santiago, Chile, 1961; on Africa, at Paris, 1962. South African Rep. at Nuclear Proliferation Conf., Toronto, 1966. *Publications:* Seen from South Africa, 1963; Problems of Southern Africa, 1964; The Conduct of British Foreign Policy, 1964; Rhodesia and UDI, 1966; The Population Problem and International Relations, 1970. *Recreation:* swimming. *Address:* 198 Main Road, Muizenberg, CP, South Africa.

*Died 9 July 1981.*

**COCKS, Sir (Thomas George) Barnett,** KCB 1963 (CB 1961); OBE 1949; Clerk of the House of Commons, 1962–73, retired; *b* 1907; *m* 1952, Iris Mary Symon (*née* Coltman); one *s* one step *d. Educ:* Blundells Sch.; Worcester Coll., Oxford. Clerk in the House of Commons, from 1931; temporarily attached Min. of Home Security, 1939. Hon. Sec. and later a Trustee of the History of Parliament; Mem., Assoc. of Secretaries-General of Parliaments, 1959–73; Pres., Governing Bd, Internat. Centre of Parliamentary Documentation, Geneva, 1972; Vice-Pres., Westminster Pastoral Foundn, 1984–. Hon. Officer, Saskatchewan Parlt, 1977. *Publications:* The Parliament at Westminster, 1949; (with Strathearn Gordon) A People's Conscience, 1952; The European Parliament, 1973; Mid-Victorian Masterpiece, 1977; Editor: Erskine May's Parliamentary Practice, 15th, 16th, 17th and 18th edns; Council of Europe Manual of Procedure, seven edns. *Address:* 13 Langford Green, SE5 8BX. *T:* 01–274 5448. *Died 6 Feb. 1989.*

**CODRINGTON, Kenneth de Burgh;** Professor Emeritus of Indian Archæology in University of London (Institute of Archæology and School of Oriental and African Studies); *b* 5 June 1899; *o s* of late Col H. de B. Codrington, IA; *m* 1927, Philippa Christine, *y d* of late E. V. Fleming, CB; one *s* one *d. Educ:* Sherborne Sch.; Cadet Coll., Wellington, India; Corpus Christi Coll., Cambridge; Wadham Coll., Oxford. Indian Army, 33rd QVO Light Horse, 1917; invalided, 1921; BA 1921; MA 1926. RAF Educational Staff, Cranwell, 1922; Prof. of Archæology and Fellow of the Graduate Sch., Univ. of Cincinnati, USA, 1925–26; Hon. Lecturer, University Coll., London and School of Oriental and African Studies, 1931; Prof., 1948–66. Mem. Cttee of Management, Inst. of Archæology, 1944–67; Keeper, Indian Section, Victoria and Albert Museum, South Kensington, 1935–48. London Division RNVR, 1924–39; Commander (S) retd, 1946. Joined J. Hackin, Dir of the French Archæological Delegation in Afghanistan, 1940; Dir, Anaradhapura Excavations, Sri Lanka, 1972. Catalogued and hung Burlington Fine Arts Club Exhibn of Indian Art (with Laurence Binyon), 1930; organised Tagore Society's Exhibn of Indian Art, London, 1944; Mem. Selection and Hanging Cttee, Royal Academy Exhibn of Art of India and Pakistan, Burlington House, 1947. Served on Councils of the Royal Asiatic Soc., Royal Anthropological Inst. (Sec., India Res. Cttee, 1927–39), and Museums Assoc.; Hon. Fellow, School of Oriental and African Studies. Chm., Civil Service Retirement Fellowship, SE Kent. Served on County Youth Cttee (Training). Mem., Geographical Club, 1944; Hon. Mem., Mark Twain Soc., 1977. *Publications:* Ancient India, 1926; An Introduction to the Study of Medieval Indian Sculpture, 1929; rev. edns of Vincent Smith's History of Indian Fine Art, 1930, 1961, 1969; An Introduction to the Study of Islamic Art in India (India Soc.), 1934; The Wood of the Image, 1934; Cricket in the Grass, 1959; Birdwood and the Arts of India (Birdwood Lecture, RSA), 1969; papers on art, archæology and anthropology, incl. The Origin of Coinage (Archæological Bull. no 4, 1964), Art for Archaeologists (Bull. of John Rylands Liby vol. 48 no 1, 1965), The Basis of Coinage (Archaeological Bull. no 6, 1967). *Address:* Rose Cottage, Appledore, Kent. *T:* Appledore 388.

*Died 1 Jan. 1986.*

**COE, Peter Leonard;** Artistic Director, Churchill Theatre, Bromley, since 1983; *b* 18 April 1929; *s* of Leonard and Gladys Coe; *m* 1st, 1952, Maria Caday; 2nd, 1958, Tsai Chin; 3rd, 1962, Suzanne Fuller; two *d*; 4th, 1977, Ingeborg; one *s* two *d. Educ:* Latymer Upper Sch., Hammersmith; Coll. of St Mark and St John, Chelsea; LAMDA. Actor, 1952–54; Lectr in Drama, 1954–56; Theatre Dir, 1956–; Artistic Director at: Her Majesty's, Carlisle, 1956; Arts, Ipswich, 1957–58; Queen's, Hornchurch, 1958–59; Mermaid, London, 1959–60; Bubble, London, 1975; Citadel, Canada, 1978–81; Amer. Shakespeare Th., Stratford, Connecticut, 1981–82. Notable musical productions in West End: Oliver; Lock Up Your Daughters; Pickwick; On the Twentieth Century; Barnum; plays

directed in West End: The World of Suzie Wong; The Miracle Worker; Castle in Sweden; Caligula; In White America; The King's Mare; In the Case of J. Robert Oppenheimer; World War 2½; Mister Lincoln; The Sleeping Prince; plays directed at Chichester Festival Theatre: An Italian Straw Hat; The Skin of Our Teeth; The Caucasian Chalk Circle; Peer Gynt; Tonight We Improvise; Feasting with Panthers; Treasure Island; The Sleeping Prince; Jane Eyre; The Prisoner of Zenda; operas directed at English National Opera: Ernani; The Love of Three Oranges; The Angel of Fire. Plays directed in NY: A Life (Tony nomination, Best Dir, 1981); Othello (Tony Award, Best Revival, 1982); Oliver; Pickwick; The Rehearsal; Mister Lincoln; Next Time I'll Sing to You; Six (musical); productions of Shakespeare include: Twelfth Night (India); Julius Caesar (Israel); Macbeth (Stratford, Ontario); Hamlet (London); The Black Macbeth (Roundhouse); Richard III (Denmark); Henry V, Othello, Henry IV, Hamlet (USA). Plays written and performed: Treasure Island, Mermaid, Chichester; Woman of the Dunes, Cleveland, Ohio; Story Theatre, India; Decameron '73, Roundhouse; The Trials of Oscar Wilde, Oxford, Chichester; Cages, The Great Exhibition, The Trial of Marie Stopes, Bubble; Lucy Crown, tour; Great Expectations, Old Vic; Jane Eyre, Chichester. *Recreation:* tennis. *Address:* The Old Barn, East Clandon, Surrey. *Died 25 May 1987.*

**COFFEY, John Nimmo;** Stipendiary Magistrate, Greater Manchester (sitting at Manchester), since 1975; a Recorder of the Crown Court, since 1972; *b* 20 Feb. 1929; *s* of late Samuel Coffey, DSc, FRIC, and of Ruth (*née* Stevenson); *m* 1953, Anne Hesling Bradbury, LLB, JP; three *d. Educ:* Stockport Grammar Sch.; Victoria Univ. of Manchester (LLB). Called to Bar, Gray's Inn, 1951. *Recreations:* sailing, music, gardening. *Address:* 9 Highfield Park, Heaton Mersey, Stockport, Cheshire. *T:* 061-432 4185.

*Died 26 June 1981.*

**COGHILL, John Percival,** CBE 1951; Foreign Service, retired; Minister to Republic of Honduras, 1954–55; *b* 29 Nov. 1902; *s* of Percy de Geiger Coghill and Dr Agnes Irene Sinclair Coghill. *Educ:* Loretto Sch.; Cheltenham Coll.; Emmanuel Coll., Cambridge. Served at various Foreign Service posts in China. *Recreation:* walking. *Club:* Royal Commonwealth Society.

*Died 12 Sept. 1984.*

**COGHILL, Sir Joscelyn (Ambrose Cramer),** 7th Bt *cr* 1778; retired; *b* 30 Sept. 1902; 3rd *s* of Sir Egerton Bushe Coghill, 5th Bt and Elizabeth Hildegarde Augusta (*d* 1954), *d* of Lt-Col Thomas Henry Somerville; *S* brother, 1981; *m* 1st, 1926, Elizabeth Gwendoline Atkins (marr. diss. 1949; she *d* 1980); one *s* one *d*; 2nd, 1949, Louise Berdonneau (marr. diss. 1971; she *d* 1978); three *d*. (one *s* decd). *Educ:* Osborne; RNC Dartmouth; Haileybury; Sandhurst. 1st Lt South Wales Borderers (24th Foot), 1922–25; tea and coffee planting, Kenya, 1926–28; Colonial Service, Kenya, 1929–32; as Lt-Comdr RNVR, served in Aden, Beirut and S France, 1940–46; UNO, London, 1946–47; Allied Control Commission, Germany, 1947–50; also engaged in various businesses and in film acting. *Heir: s* Egerton James Nevill Tobias Coghill [*b* 26 March 1930; *m* 1958, Gabriel Nancy, *d* of Major Dudley Claud Douglas Ryder; one *s* one *d*]. *Address:* Bishopmill House, Elgin, Morayshire.

*Died 6 June 1983.*

**COGHILL, Sir (Marmaduke Nevill) Patrick (Somerville),** 6th Bt *cr* 1778; TD 1947; DL Herts; Lieut-Col RA (TA), retd; *b* 18 March 1896; *s* of 5th Bt and Elizabeth Hildegarde Augusta, *d* of late Col Thomas Henry Somerville, Drishane, Skibbereen; *S* father, 1921. *Educ:* Haileybury. Joined RA 1915; served in France until Armistice and afterwards in Turkey and Iraq; Commanded 86th (Hertfordshire Yeomanry), Fd Regt RA TA, 1939–41, and served in Middle East, 1941–45 (despatches). Col, Arab Legion, Jordan, 1952–56. Order of Istiqlal, 2nd Class, Jordan, 1956. OStJ 1957. *Heir: b* Joscelyn Ambrose Cramer Coghill, *b* 30 Sept. 1902. *Address:* Savran House, Aylburton, Lydney, Glos GL15 6DF. *Died 6 Jan. 1981.*

**COHEN, Sir Jack,** Kt 1965; OBE 1951; JP; Alderman, Borough of Sunderland, 1935–74, and Councillor, 1929; Mayor, 1949–50; *b* 2 Nov. 1896; *s* of Samuel Cohen, Sunderland; *m* 1921, Kitty, *d* of Abraham Sinclair, Glasgow; one *s* one *d*. Served European War, 1914–18. JP Sunderland, 1939. *Address:* 16 Barnes Park Road, Sunderland, Tyne and Wear SR4 7PE. *T:* Sunderland 226593.

*Died 7 Feb. 1982.*

**COHEN, Prof. John,** PhD; Professor of Psychology, University of Manchester, 1952–78, then Emeritus; *b* 20 Jan. 1911; *s* of Joseph and Rebecca Cohen, Tredegar, Mon.; *m* 1st, 1939; one *s* one *d*; 2nd, 1955, Rosemarie Loss; three *s. Educ:* Tredegar Elementary and County Schs.; University Coll., London (MA, PhD). Research at: University Coll., London, 1933–40; Institute of Experimental Psychology, Oxford, 1940. RAC, 1940–41; attached to Offices of War Cabinet and Central Statistical Office, 1941–48; Joint Sec., Expert Cttee on Work of Psychologists and Psychiatrists in the Services, 1942–45; Mem., Working Party on Recruitment and Training of Nurses, 1946–47; Tech. Sec., Internat. Preparatory

Commn for World Congress on Mental Health, 1948; Mem., Inter-professional Advisory Cttee to World Fedn for Mental Health, 1949–52; Consultant to UNESCO, 1948, 1950, 1967; Lectr in Psychology, Univ. of Leeds, 1948–49; Prof. of Psychology, Univ. of Jerusalem, 1949–51; Lectr in Psychology, Birkbeck Coll., Univ. of London, 1951–52. Mem. of Council, Brit. Psychological Soc., 1956–59. Hon. MA (Manchester), FBPsS 1943. Fellow, World Academy of Art and Science; Corr. Mem., Centre de Recherches de Psychologie Comparative. Member: Internat. Editorial Bd of Medikon; Editorial Cttee of IKON Revue Internationale de Filmologie; Adv. Bd, Internat. Soc. for Study of Time. *Publications:* Human Nature, War and Society, 1946; Report on Recruitment and Training of Nurses, 1948; co-editor: Human Affairs, 1937; Educating for Democracy, 1939; co-author: Risk and Gambling, 1956; Humanistic Psychology, 1958; Chance, Skill and Luck, 1960; Readings in Psychology (ed), 1964; Behaviour in Uncertainty, 1964; Human Robots in Myth and Science, 1966; A New Introduction to Psychology, 1966; Psychological Time in Health and Disease, 1967; Psychology: An Outline for the intending Student (ed), 1967; Causes and Prevention of Road Accidents (with B. Preston), 1968; (with I. Christensen) Information and Choice, 1970; Elements of Child Psychology, 1970; Homo Psychologicus, 1971; Psychological Probability, 1972; Everyman's Psychology, 1973; (with J. H. Clark) Medicine, Mind and Man, 1979; The Lineaments of Mind, 1980; numerous papers in psychological, medical, psychiatric and other learned jls. *Recreations:* travel, music. *Address:* 15 Didsbury Park, Didsbury, Manchester M20 0LH. *T:* 061–445 3024.
*Died 19 Dec. 1985.*

**COHEN, John Michael,** FRSL 1957; critic and translator; *b* 5 Feb. 1903; *s* of late Arthur Cohen and Elizabeth (*née* Abrahams); *m* 1928, Audrey Frances Falk; four *s. Educ:* St Paul's Sch.; Queens' Coll., Cambridge. After short spell in publishing, joined family manufacturing business, 1925–40; war-time Schoolmaster, 1940–46; writing and translating from that date. *Publications: translations:* Don Quixote, 1950; Rousseau's Confessions, 1953; Rabelais, 1955; Life of Saint Teresa, 1957; Montaigne's Essays, 1958; Pascal's Pensées, 1961; Bernal Diaz, The Conquest of New Spain, 1963; The Spanish Bawd, 1964; Zarate, The Discovery and Conquest of Peru, 1968; The Four Voyages of Christopher Columbus, 1969, 2nd edn 1988; Sent off the Field, 1974; *criticism and biography:* Robert Browning, 1952; History of Western Literature, 1956; Life of Ludwig Mond, 1956; Poetry of This Age, 1959 (2nd, revised edn, 1966); Robert Graves, 1960; English Translators and Translations, 1962; The Baroque Lyric, 1963; En tiempos difíciles (a study of the new Cuban poetry), 1971; J. L. Borges, 1974; Journeys down the Amazon, 1975; (with J.-F. Phipps) The Common Experience, 1979; *anthologies:* Penguin Book of Comic & Curious Verse, 1952; More Comic & Curious Verse, 1956; Penguin Book of Spanish Verse, 1956, 3rd updated edn, 1988; Yet More Comic & Curious Verse, 1959; Latin American Writing Today, 1967; Writers in the New Cuba, 1967; A Choice of Comic and Curious Verse, 1975; Rider Book of Mystical Verse, 1983; *dictionaries:* (with M. J. Cohen) Penguin Dictionary of Quotations, 1960; (with M. J. Cohen) Penguin Dictionary of Modern Quotations, 1971, rev. edn 1981; other translations. *Recreations:* Buddhism, listening to music; gardening. *Address:* 14 The Moors, Pangbourne, Berks. *T:* Pangbourne 2738.
*Died 19 July 1989.*

**COHEN, Comdr Kenneth H. S.,** CB 1954; CMG 1946; RN; European Adviser to United Steel Companies, 1953–66; Vice-President: European League for Economic Co-operation, since 1972; Franco-British Society, since 1973 (Chairman, 1967–72); *b* 15 March 1900; *s* of late Herman Cohen, Barrister-at-Law, Inner Temple; *m* 1932, Mary Joseph, *d* of late Ernest Joseph, CBE, FRIBA; one *s* one *d. Educ:* Elstree Sch.; Eastbourne Coll. "Special Entry" RN Cadet, 1918, Midshipman, HMS Iron Duke; specialised in Torpedo Duties, 1926; RN Staff Coll., 1932; interpreter in French and Russian; retired (Lt-Comdr), 1935; appointed HMS President, 1939; Comdr 1940. Attached Foreign Office, 1945. Councillor, RIIA, Chatham House, 1963–75. Officier de la Légion d'Honneur; Croix de Guerre avec palmes (France); Legion of Merit, Degree of Officer (USA); Officier de la Couronne (Belgium); Order of the White Lion (Czechoslovakia); Commandeur de l'Etoile Noire (France), 1960. *Publications:* articles in national press on problems of European integration. *Address:* 33 Bloomfield Terrace, SW1. *T:* 01-730 3228. *Club:* Garrick.
*Died 19 Sept. 1984.*

**COHEN, Nat;** Chairman, EMI Films Ltd, 1970–78; *b* 1905; *m* 1932 (wife *d* 1949); one *d* (and one *d* decd). Entered film industry, 1930. Director: EMI Film Productions Ltd, 1970–79; EMI Film & Theatre Corporation Ltd, 1970–79. *Films produced include:* Carry On Sergeant, and 12 other Carry On films; A Kind of Loving; Billy Liar; Darling; Far From the Madding Crowd; Murder on the Orient Express; Death on the Nile; Clockwise. *Address:* 24 St James's Place, SW1A 1NH.
*Died 9 Feb. 1988.*

**COHEN, Percy,** CBE 1936; Joint Director, Conservative Research Department, 1948–59; *b* London, 25 Dec. 1891; *e s* of late M.

Cohen; *m* 1917, Rosa Abrams (*d* 1973); one *s* one *d. Educ:* Central Foundation Sch., London. Entered service of Conservative Central Office, 1911; Head of Library and Information Dept, 1928–48. Served first European War, France. Worked in 12 General Elections; Editor, Constitutional Year Book, 1929–39; Editor, Notes on Current Politics, 1942–59. Sec. to several post-war problems Cttees, 1944–45. *Publications:* British System of Social Insurance, 1932; Unemployment Insurance and Assistance in Britain, 1938; (ed) Conservative Election Handbook, 1945; (ed) Campaign Guide, 1950, 1951, 1955 and 1959. *Recreation:* walking. *Address:* Sunridge Court, 76 The Ridgeway, NW11. *T:* 01–455 5203. *Club:* St Stephen's Constitutional.
*Died 15 Oct. 1987.*

**COHEN, Reuben K.;** *see* Kelf-Cohen.

**COHEN, Sir Rex (Arthur Louis),** KBE 1964 (OBE 1944); *b* 27 Nov. 1906; *s* of Rex David Cohen, Condover Hall, Shrewsbury; *m* 1932, Nina Alice Castello; one *d. Educ:* Rugby Sch.; Trinity Coll., Cambridge (BA). Served KSLI, 1938–45. Past Mem., BoT Cttee for Consumer Protection. Past Chairman: Lewis's Investment Trust Group, 1958–65 (Joint Man. Dir, 1945); NAAFI, 1961–63; Higgs & Hill Ltd, 1966–72; Meat and Livestock Commn, 1967–72. Officer, Order of Orange Nassau (Netherlands), 1944. *Recreations:* racing, horse breeding, shooting. *Address:* Ruckmans Farm, Oakwood Hill, near Dorking, Surrey. *T:* Oakwood Hill 255. *Clubs:* White's; Jockey (Newmarket).
*Died 29 Feb. 1988.*

**COIA, Jack Antonio,** CBE 1967; LLD 1970; BArch; FRIBA 1941; RSA 1962; MRTPI; RGI; architect; Commissioner, Royal Fine Art Commission for Scotland, 1969–78; *b* 17 July 1898; *m* 1939, Eden Bernard; three *d. Educ:* St Aloysius Coll.; Glasgow Sch. of Art; Strathclyde Univ. Works include: immense contribution to RC Church Architecture in Scotland, 1936– (St Anne's Church, Glasgow); Catholic Pavilion, Post Office and Industry North Pavilion for the Empire Exhibition, Glasgow, 1938; Shipbuilding and Railways Section for the Festival of Britain Exhibition, Glasgow, 1951. Senior Partner of Gillespie Kidd and Coia whose works include: Flats at East Kilbride (Saltire Award 1953); and among several awards: from Civic Trust, Bellshill Maternity Hospital, 1962, Old Persons Housing and Home at Dumbarton, 1969; from RIBA: Bronze Medal and Regional Awards for Architecture in Scotland: St Bride's Church, East Kilbride, Church of Our Lady of Good Counsel, Dennistoun, 1966, St Peter's College at Cardross, 1967, Halls of Residence, The Lawns, Cottingham, for Hull University, 1968. Pres., Royal Incorpn of Architects in Scotland, 1967–68. Royal Gold Medal for Architecture, 1969. *Recreation:* golf. *Clubs:* Glasgow Art (Glasgow); Scottish Arts (Edinburgh).
*Died 14 Aug. 1981.*

**COKE, Gerald Edward,** CBE 1967; JP; DL; *b* 25 Oct. 1907; *o s* of late Major the Hon. Sir John Coke, KCVO, and late Hon. Mrs Coke; *m* 1939, Patricia, *e d* of late Rt Hon. Sir Alexander Cadogan, PC, OM, GCMG, KCB; two *s* one *d* (and one *s* decd). *Educ:* Eton; New Coll., Oxford (MA). Served War of 1939–45, Lieut-Col. Treas., Bridewell Royal Hosp. (King Edward's Sch., Witley), 1946–72; Chm., Glyndebourne Arts Trust, 1955–75; Dir, Royal Acad. of Music, 1957–74; Dir, Royal Opera House, Covent Garden, 1958–64; a Governor, BBC, 1961–66. Director: Rio Tinto-Zinc Corp., 1947–75 (Dep. Chm. 1962–66; Chm. Rio Tinto Co., 1956–62); S. G. Warburg & Co., 1945–75; United Kingdom Provident Instn, 1952–74. JP 1952, DL 1974, Hants. Hon. FRAM 1968. *Publication:* In Search of James Giles, 1983. *Recreations:* music, gardening, collecting. *Address:* Jenkyn Place, Bentley, Hants GU10 5LU. *T:* Bentley 23118. *Club:* Brooks's.
*Died 9 Jan. 1990.*

**COKER, Dame Elizabeth,** DBE 1979; DL; Chairman: Mid-Essex District Health Authority (formerly Essex Area Health Authority), since 1973; Basildon Development Corporation, 1981–86 (Member, 1971–86; Deputy Chairman, 1980); *b* 1915; *d* of William Lowe and Ellen Elizabeth (*née* Winnington); *m* 1947, Frank L. Coker, LDS RCS; one *d. Educ:* Grove Park Sch., Wrexham; Queen Mary Coll., Univ. of London (BSc Hons). Member: Essex CC, 1959–81 (Chm., 1971–74); Exec. Cttee, Assoc. of Educn Cttees, 1965–74 (Vice-Pres., 1972–74); County Councils Assoc., 1968–74; Assoc. of County Councils, 1974–81 (Chm., Exec. Council, 1976–79); Council of Local Educn Authorities, 1974–79 (Chm., 1974–75); Eastern Electricity Bd, 1973–77; Chm., Harlow Development Corporation, 1979–80. Mem. Council, Essex Univ., 1965– (Treasurer, 1982–); Governor: Felsted Sch., 1967–; Brentwood Sch., 1968–; Queen Mary Coll., 1977– (Fellow, 1975–); United World Coll. of the Atlantic, St Donats, 1980–. DL Essex, 1974. *Recreation:* travel. *Address:* Winnington House, Danbury, Chelmsford, Essex. *T:* Danbury 2555.
*Died 9 Oct. 1988.*

**COLBURN, Oscar Henry,** CBE 1981; JP; DL; farmer; *b* 14 Jan. 1925; *m* 1950, Helen Joan (*née* Garne); one *s* two *d.* Crown Estates Commissioner, 1976–; Chairman, Grasslands Research Institute, 1976–84; (Hon. Fellow, 1984); Chairman, Consultative Board of Joint Consultative Organization for Research and Development in Agriculture and Food, 1981–84; Former Chm., Regional Panel,

MAFF; former Mem., Northfield Cttee (author, Minority Report); Hon. Fellow 1982, past Mem. Council, RASE. Pioneer breeder of Poll Hereford cattle; during 1960s developed Colbred sheep, first new British breed of sheep for over a century. JP Northleach (Chm., 1976–86); High Sheriff of Glos, 1980–81; DL Glos, 1982. FRAgS 1986. Summers Trophy, NFU Glos Br., 1956; George Hedley Meml Award, for services to Sheep Industry, 1963; Farmers' Club Trophy, 1982; Laurent-Perrier Award for Wild Game Conservation, 1987; instituted Colburn Trophy for annual competition by Gloucestershire Constabulary, 1982. *Publication:* Farmers Ordinary, 1989. *Address:* Crickley Barrow, Northleach, near Cheltenham, Glos GL54 3QA. *Clubs:* MCC, Farmers', Brooks's.

*Died 19 Aug. 1990.*

**COLDSTREAM, Sir William (Menzies),** Kt 1956; CBE 1952; painter; Slade Professor of Fine Art, at University College, University of London, 1949–75; Vice-Chairman, Arts Council of Great Britain, 1962–70 (Member, 1953); Fellow of University College, London; Senior Fellow, Royal College of Art; *b* 28 Feb. 1908; *yr s* of George Probyn Coldstream, MB, CM, and Lilian Mercer Tod; *m* 1st, 1931, Nancy Culliford Sharp (marr. diss. 1942); two *d*; 2nd, 1961, Monica Mary Hoyer, *d* of A. E. Monrad Hoyer; one *s* two *d*. *Educ:* privately; Slade Sch. of Fine Art, University Coll., London. Member: London Artists Assoc:, 1931; London Group, 1933; work represented in exhibitions of: World's Fair, NY, 1938; British Art Since Whistler, Nat. Gallery, 1939; UN Internat. Exhibition, Paris, 1946; Painting and Sculpture of a Decade, Tate Gallery, 1964; retrospective exhibition, South London Gall., 1962; exhibited Anthony d'Offay Gall., 1976; one-man exhibns, Anthony d'Offay Gall., 1978, 1984. Pictures in the collections of: Tate Gallery, National Gallery of Canada, National Museum of Wales, Ashmolean Museum, Imperial War Museum, Arts Council, British Council, Bristol Art Gallery, etc. Works purchased by Contemporary Art Soc. and Chantrey Bequest, 1940. In association with Claude Rogers and Victor Pasmore founded the Sch. of Drawing and Painting, Euston Road, 1937. Served War of 1939–45 with RE; official War Office Artist, Middle East and Italy, 1943–45. Trustee of National Gallery, 1948–55, 1956–63; Trustee of Tate Gallery, 1949–55, 1956–63; a Dir of Royal Opera House, Covent Garden, 1957–62; Chairman: Art Panel of Arts Council, 1953–62; Nat. Adv. Council on Art Education, 1958–71; British Film Institute, 1964–71. Hon. DLitt: Nottingham, 1961; Birmingham, 1962; London, 1984; Hon. DEd CNAA, 1975. *Address:* University College London, Gower Street, WC1. *T:* 01–387 7050. *Clubs:* Athenæum, MCC.

*Died 18 Feb. 1987.*

**COLE, Dr Herbert Aubrey,** CMG 1967; Controller, Fisheries Research and Development, Ministry of Agriculture, Fisheries and Food, 1972–74; *b* 24 Feb. 1911; *s* of Edwin Aubrey Cole, farmer; *m* 1936, Elizabeth Lloyd; two *s* one *d*. *Educ:* Friars Sch., Bangor, N Wales; Univ. Coll. of N Wales. Entire career in Fishery Research, Min. of Agric., Fisheries and Food, Dir of Fishery Research, 1959–72. *Publications:* numerous articles in learned jls. *Recreation:* gardening. *Address:* Forde House, Moor Lane, Hardington Mandeville, Yeovil, Somerset BA22 9NW. *T:* West Coker 2090.

*Died 23 July 1984.*

**COLE, John Sydney Richard,** QC (Somaliland); MA; FIArb; Barrister-at-Law; Senior Lecturer, Law School, University of Dublin, 1966–77; *b* 24 Jan. 1907; *o s* of late Rev. R. Lee Cole, MA, BD, Dublin; *m* 1st, 1931, Doreen Mathews (*d* 1966); one *s* one *d*; 2nd, 1968, Mrs Deirdre Gallet. *Educ:* Methodist Coll., Belfast; Cork Gram. Sch.; Trinity Coll., Dublin (Scholar and Moderator). Master, Royal Coll., Mauritius, 1930–36; Education Officer, Nigeria, 1936–40; Crown Counsel, Nigeria, 1940–46; Attorney-Gen., Bahamas, 1946–51, Somaliland Protectorate, 1951–56; Attorney-Gen. and Minister for Legal Affairs, Tanganyika, 1956–61; retired, 1961. English Legal Draftsman to Government of Republic of Sudan, 1962–65. Reid Prof. of Penal Legislation, Univ. of Dublin, 1965–66. *Publication:* (with W. N. Denison) Tanganyika—the Development of its Laws and Constitution, 1964; Irish Cases on the Law of Evidence, 1972, 2nd edn 1979; Irish Cases on Criminal Law, 1975. *Recreations:* walking, swimming. *Address:* 2 Rus in Urbe, Glenageary, Dublin. *T:* 801993. *Club:* Kildare Street and University (Dublin).

*Died 15 Aug. 1989.*

**COLE, Leslie Barrett,** MA, MD Cantab, FRCP; Hon. Consultant Physician, Addenbrooke's Hospital, Cambridge; Fellow of King's College, Cambridge, 1949–66; Dean of Post Graduate Medical School, University of Cambridge, 1957–65; *b* 23 Feb. 1898; *s* of Samuel Barrett Cole and Annie Gammon; *m* 1927, Mary, *d* of late Surg. Capt. H. W. Finlayson, DSO; three *s*. *Educ:* Leighton Park Sch.; King's Coll., Cambridge (Exhibitioner). Served European War, 1916–18, RFA, India and Mesopotamia; RAMC 1939–41, BEF France. St Thomas's Hosp. (Medical Registrar and Resident Asst Physician; Mead Medal and Toller Prize); formerly Physician: W Suffolk Hosp.; Papworth Hosp. Assessor, MD Cttee, Univ. of Cambridge, 1958–65; Late Examiner: Medicine for MRCP and to Univs of Oxford, Cambridge and Bristol, also Conjoint Board; in Pharmacology, to Univ. of Cambridge; in Pathology to Conjoint Board. Royal College of Physicians: Councillor, 1950; Censor, 1960–62; Sen. Censor and Sen. Vice-Pres., 1964–65. Hon. Lt-Col RAMC. *Publications:* Dietetics in General Practice, 1939; numerous contribs to medical journals on cardiology, diabetes and general medical subjects and on tetanus to Quart. Jl of Medicine, Index of Treatment, British Encyclopædia of Medical Practice and Surgery of Modern Warfare. *Recreations:* riding, sailing. *Address:* 57 De Freville Avenue, Cambridge. *T:* Cambridge 50836. *Club:* Athenæum.

*Died 26 June 1983.*

**COLE, Robin John,** PhD; Head of Life Sciences, Technology, Planning and Research Division, Central Electricity Generating Board, since 1986; *b* 6 Aug. 1935; *s* of John Richard Cole and Amy Cole (*née* Collins); *m* 1956, Jane Legg; three *d*. *Educ:* East Grinstead Grammar School; University College London (BSc); King's College London (PhD). Research at Univ. of Glasgow, 1961–65; Lectr, Sch. of Biological Scis, Univ. of Sussex, 1965, Reader in Developmental Genetics, 1972, Professor, 1976; Dep. Chief Scientist, DHSS, 1982–85. Mem., ESRC, 1984–85. *Publications:* original papers in developmental biology, experimental haematology, genetic toxicology. *Recreations:* fine and decorative arts; contemporary crafts, especially ceramics. *Address:* c/o CERL, Kelvin Avenue, Leatherhead, Surrey KT22 7SE. *T:* Leatherhead 374488.

*Died 29 July 1988.*

**COLEMAN, Laurence Vail;** Director Emeritus, American Association of Museums, since 1958; *b* 19 Sept. 1893; *s* of Thaddeus Vail Coleman and Kate Pratt; *m* 1917, Martine Weeks (decd); three *s*; *m* 1939, Susannah Armstrong. *Educ:* B. S. College of City of New York, 1915; MA Yale Univ., 1919; grad. work, Harvard Univ., 1919. Research Asst, NY State Commn on Ventilation, 1915; Asst in public health, American Museum Natural History, 1916; Asst in Zoology, Peabody Museum Natural History, 1917; US Army, 1918; Chief of Exhibits, American Museum Natural History, 1919–21; Dir, Safety Inst. America, 1921–23; Exec. Sec., American Assoc. of Museums, 1923–26; Dir, 1927–58. Trustee, Edward MacDowell Assoc., 1939–47; Hill-Stead Museum Trust, Connecticut, 1946–49; Mem. Executive Cttee, Internat. Museums Office, Paris, 1930–36; Jt Cttee on Materials for Research of American Council of Learned Societies and Social Science Research Council, 1931–40; Nat Cttee of USA on Intellectual Co-operation of the League of Nations, 1932–46; Cttee on Conservation of Cultural Resources, of National Resources Planning Board, 1941–43; US Nat. Cttee of Internat. Council of Museums, 1948–51. Hon. Fellow, The Museums Assoc. (British); Fellow, Rochester Museum Assoc.; Mid-west Museums Conf., USA; Charter Mem., Nat. Trust for Historical Preservation. Surveys of Museums in: USA, 1924 and 1932–34; Europe, 1927 and 1938; South America, 1928 and 1937; Canada, 1942. Received Alumni Service Medal, 1933, and Townsend Harris Medal, 1944, of College of City of New York; Distinguished Service Award of American Assoc. of Museums, 1940. *Publications:* Manual for Small Museums, 1927; Museums in South America, 1929; Historic House Museums, 1933; The Museum in America (3 vols), 1939, repr. 1970; College and University Museums, 1942; Company Museums, 1942; Museum Buildings (vol. 1), 1950; (with Beardsley Rum) Manual of Corporate Giving, 1952; contribs to educational magazines in US and Europe. *Address:* 1600 S Eads Street, 321-N, Arlington, Va 22202, USA. *Clubs:* Cosmos (Emeritus Mem.) (Washington); Lake Placid (NY State).

*Died 21 July 1982.*

**COLERIDGE, 4th Baron** *cr* 1873, of Ottery St Mary; **Richard Duke Coleridge,** KBE 1971 (CBE 1951; OBE 1944); DL; Captain Royal Navy, retired; *b* 24 Sept. 1905; *e s* of 3rd Baron Coleridge and Jessie Alethea Mackarness (*d* 1957); *S* father, 1955; *m* 1936, Rosamund, *er d* of Admiral Sir W. W. Fisher, GCB, GCVO; two *s*. *Educ:* RNC Osborne and Dartmouth. Entered RN, 1919; RN Staff Course, 1938; invalided off Med. station and retd, 1939; rejoined, 1940, Offices of War Cabinet and of Minister of Defence, with appt to GQG Vincennes, France; War Cabinet Office in London, July 1940–May 1941; Jt Staff Mission, Washington, May 1941; Brit. Jt Staff and Combined Chiefs of Staff, 1942–45, and attended the Confs of Washington, Quebec (1942 and 1943), Cairo, Malta and Yalta; Council of Foreign Ministers, London Conf., Sept. 1945; UN Assembly in London, Jan. 1946; Mil. Staff Cttee of UN, New York, 1946–48; Brit. Jt Services Mission in Washington, 1948, and also Chief Staff Officer to Marshal of the RAF Lord Tedder (Chm. of Brit. Chiefs of Staff Cttee and Brit. Rep. on Standing Gp of NATO, 1950–51); rep. Brit. Chiefs of Staff on Temp. Cttee of Council of NATO, in Paris, 1951; attended Lisbon Conf., 1952; Exec. Sec., NATO, 1952–70. Chairman: Devon and Exeter Savings Bank, 1971–75; SW Trustee Savings Bank, 1975–80 (Pres., 1980–). Chm., Devon Historic Churches Trust, 1972–. DL Devon 1973. US Legion of Merit. *Heir: s* Hon. William Duke Coleridge, Major Coldstream Guards, retired [*b* 18 June 1937; *m* 1962, Everild, (Judy) (marr. diss. 1977), *o d* of Lt-Col and Mrs Beauchamp Hambrough, Wisper's Farm, Nairobi; one *s* two *d*]. *Address:* The Chanter's

House, Ottery St Mary, S Devon. *T:* Ottery St Mary 2417. *Club:* Army and Navy. *Died* 20 *May* 1984.

**COLES, Captain (RNR retired) Arthur Edward,** RD (with clasp); Commodore, Orient Line, retired; *b* 2 July 1902; *s* of late Arthur Coles, FCIS, and Ella May Coles; *m* 1940, Dorothy Blanche (*d* 1981), widow of G. A. Griffin; no *c. Educ:* King Edward's Sch., Bath, Somerset. Cadet in Macandrew's Line, 1918. Joined RNR as probationary Sub-Lieut, 1927; joined Orient Line, 1928. Served Royal Navy, 1938–46; War of 1939–45 (despatches thrice, 1940; Dieppe, 1942; Normandy, 1944): HMS Malaya, 1939; Fleet Minesweepers; 9th Flotilla, 1941–42, 18th Flotilla, 1943–44; HMS Lochinvar (Trg Comdr), 1945–46. In command Orient Line ships, 1951–62, Cdre 1960–62. Younger Brother of Trinity House, 1951–. *Recreations:* motoring, photography. *Address:* Engleberg, 80 Dagger Lane, West Bromwich, West Midlands B71 4BS. *T:* 021-553 0827. *Club:* Birmingham. *Died* 8 *Feb.* 1982.

**COLES, Sir Arthur (William),** Kt 1960; *b* 6 Aug. 1892; *s* of George and Elizabeth Coles; *m* 1919, Lilian Florence Knight; two *s* three *d* (and one *s* decd). *Educ:* State Sch.; Geelong Coll. Served European War, 1914–18: 6th Bn, 1914, Gallipoli and France; commissioned, 1916; wounded thrice. Original partner in retail firm of G. J. Coles & Co., 1919; Dir and Gen. Man. on formation of Company, 1921; Managing Dir, 1931–44. JP 1934; Mem. Melbourne City Council, 1934–44; Lord Mayor of Melbourne, 1938–39–40; MP, Henty, Vic., 1940, resigned, 1946. Mem. Commonwealth War Workers Housing Trust, 1941–45; Chairman: Commonwealth War Damage Commn, 1942–48; Commonwealth Rationing Commn, 1942–50; Austr. Nat. Airlines Commn, 1946–50; British Commonwealth Pacific Airlines, 1946–50; Geelong Coll. Council, 1939–69; Austr. Trustees, Northcote Trust Fund, 1952–75. Vice-Chm., Trusts Corp. of Presbyterian Church of Vic., 1957–77; Mem., Commonwealth Immigration Planning Council, 1948–68; Part-time Mem. of Executive, CSIRO, 1956–65; Mem. Advisory Council, CSIRO, 1965–70; Australian Delegations to Commonwealth Agricultural Bureaux: Quinquennial Conf., London, 1960; Leader Delegn, 1965. *Recreation:* golf. *Address:* 3 Majella Court, Kew, Victoria 3101, Australia. *Clubs:* Athenæum, Peninsula Country Golf (Victoria, Australia). *Died* 24 *June* 1982.

**COLES, Sir Edgar (Barton),** Kt 1959; Director, G. J. Coles & Co. Ltd, Melbourne; *b* St James, Vic, 3 June 1899; *s* of George Coles, Horsham, Vic; *m* 1927, Mabel Irene Johnston (Dame Mabel Coles, DBE); one *s* two *d. Educ:* Scotch Coll., Launceston, Tasmania. Bank of NSW, 1916–19; G. J. Coles & Co.: joined, 1919; Sec., 1921–34; Dir, 1930–; Joint Managing Dir, 1940–44; Sole Managing Dir, 1944–61, Controlling Managing Dir, 1961–67, and Deputy Chm., 1958–61; Vice-Chm., 1961–63; Chm., 1963–68. Pres., Retail Traders Assoc. of Vic, 1946–48 and 1951–54. Pres., Australian Council of Retailers, 1952–54; Councillor of Royal Agricultural Soc., 1957–. *Recreations:* golf, photography. *Address:* Hendra, Mt Eliza, Vic 3930, Australia. *T:* Mt Eliza 71291; 236 Bourke Street, Melbourne, Vic 3000, Australia. *Clubs:* Athenæum (Melbourne); Victoria Racing; Victoria Amateur Turf; Melbourne Cricket; Lawn Tennis Assoc. of Victoria; Peninsula Golf.

*Died* 19 *Feb.* 1981.

**COLES, Sir Kenneth (Frank),** Kt 1957; Chairman, G. J. Coles & Co. Ltd, 1956–63; *b* 19 April 1896; *s* of George and Elizabeth Coles; *m* 1925, Marjorie Evelyn Tolley; one *s* two *d.* Entered G. J. Coles & Co. Ltd, 1921; London Manager, 1927–28; State Manager for NSW, 1933–53; Dir, 1926–76; Dep. Chm., 1945–56; Chm., Aust. Oil and Gas Corp., 1954–67. Pres., Internat. Soc. for Welfare of Cripples, 1957–60. *Recreation:* golf. *Address:* 81A Victoria Road, Bellevue Hill, Sydney, Australia. *T:* 327 4728. *Clubs:* Australian, Elanora Country, Royal Sydney Golf (Sydney). *Died* 2 *April* 1985.

**COLES, Sir Norman (Cameron),** Kt 1977; Chairman, G. J. Coles & Co. Ltd, Melbourne, 1968–79; *b* 10 Sept. 1907; *s* of George Coles and Annie Cameron Coles; *m* 1932, Dorothy Verna Deague; one *s* one *d. Educ:* Launceston C of E Grammar Sch., Tas; Trinity Grammar Sch., Kew, Vic. FASA, FCIS. Joined G. J. Coles & Co. Ltd, Australia, 1924: Company Secretary, 1933; Director, 1949–79; Finance Dir, 1963–67; Man. Dir, 1967–75. Mem., Victorian Plastic Surgery Unit, 1978–. *Recreations:* golf, gardening. *Address:* (office) G. J. Coles & Co. Ltd, 236 Bourke Street, Melbourne, Vic 3000, Australia. *T:* 667–4651; (home) 28 Somers Avenue, Malvern, Vic 3144, Australia. *Clubs:* Athenæum (Melbourne), Probus (Melbourne) (Foundn Pres. 1983–84); Melbourne Cricket, Victoria Racing, Peninsula Golf (all Victoria). *Died* 23 *Nov.* 1989.

**COLEY, (Howard William) Maitland;** Stipendiary Magistrate for Wolverhampton (formerly South Staffordshire), 1961–77; *b* 14 July 1910; *s* of late W. Howard Coley; *m* 1940, Cecile Muriel (from whom he obtained a divorce, 1966), *d* of C. C. H. Moriarty, CBE; one *d*; *m* 1968, Jill Barbour-Simpson; one *s. Educ:* Rugby; Christ's Coll., Cambridge. Called to Bar, Middle Temple, 1934. Served RAF, 1940–45. Recorder of Wenlock, 1946; Recorder of Burton upon Trent, 1956–61; Dep. Chm., Staffordshire QS, 1959–71; Dep.

Circuit Judge, 1972. *Recreations:* golf, sailing. *Address:* New House Farm, Mamble, near Kidderminster, Worcs. *T:* Clows Top 236.

*Died* 10 *April* 1981.

**COLGATE, Dennis Harvey,** MM 1944; Registrar of Family Division of Supreme Court, 1975–84; *b* 9 Oct. 1922; *s* of Charles William and Marjorie Colgate; *m* 1961, Kathleen (*née* Marquis); one *d. Educ:* Varndean Sch., Brighton; Univ. Coll. of South West, Exeter; King's Coll., London (LLB). HM Forces, 1942–47; Principal Probate Registry, 1947–64 (Estabt Officer 1959–64); District Probate Registrar of High Court, Manchester, 1964–75. Consulting Editor, Tristram and Coote's Probate Practice, 1975–84. *Publications:* (ed jtly) Rayden on Divorce, 7th edn 1958 and 8th edn 1960; (ed jtly) Atkin's Court Forms (Probate), 2nd edn 1974, rev. 1985. *Recreations:* walking, do-it-yourself. *Address:* 10 Frogmore Close, Hughenden Valley, High Wycombe, Bucks HP14 4LN. *T:* Naphill (024024) 2659. *Died* 17 *June* 1990.

**COLLAR, Prof. (Arthur) Roderick,** CBE 1964; MA, DSc; FRS 1965; FEng 1976; Sir George White Professor of Aeronautical Engineering, University of Bristol, 1945–73, then Emeritus; Pro-Vice-Chancellor, 1967–70, Vice-Chancellor, 1968–69; *b* 22 Feb. 1908; *s* of late Arthur Collar, JP, and Louie Collar; *m* 1934, Winifred Margaret Moorman; two *s. Educ:* Simon Langton Sch., Canterbury; Emmanuel Coll., Cambridge (Scholar). Aerodynamics Dept, Nat. Physical Laboratory, 1929–41; Structural and Mechanical Engineering Dept, Royal Aircraft Establishment, 1941–45. Pres., Royal Aeronautical Soc., 1963–64; Chairman: Aeronautical Research Council, 1964–68; Chm. Council, Rolls-Royce Technical Coll., 1969–83; Mem. Adv. Council, Royal Military Coll. of Science, Shrivenham, 1964–80, Chm., 1970–78. Member: Clifton Coll. Council, 1969–79; Council, Royal Society, 1971–73; Bd of Governors, United Bristol Hosps, 1968–74; Academic Adv. Council, Cranfield Inst. of Technology, 1970–75; SW Regional Hosp. Bd, 1969–74. Liveryman, Guild of Air Pilots and Air Navigators. Hon. LLD Bristol, 1969; Hon. DSc: Bath, 1971; Cranfield, 1976. R38 Memorial Prize (joint), 1932; George Taylor Gold Medal, 1947; Orville Wright Prize, 1958; J. E. Hodgson Prize, 1960, 1979; Gold Medal, RAeS, 1966; Hon. FRAeS 1973; Hon. FCASI 1980; Hon. FAIAA 1984. *Publications:* Elementary Matrices (joint), 1938; (joint ed.) Hypersonic Flow; (with Prof. A. Simpson) Matrices and Engineering Dynamics, 1986; numerous papers in technical press. *Recreations:* sport (onlooker), poetry, music. *Address:* 14 The Cedars, Woodside, Hazelwood Road, Sneyd Park, Bristol BS9 1QA. *T:* Bristol 681491. *Clubs:* Royal Commonwealth Society; Bristol Savages. *Died* 12 *Feb.* 1986.

**COLLARD, Prof. Patrick John,** JP; MD, FRCP; Professor of Bacteriology and Director of Department of Bacteriology and Virology, University of Manchester, 1962–80, later Professor Emeritus; *b* 22 April 1920; *s* of Rupert John Collard; *m* 1st, 1948, Jessie Robertson (marr. diss. 1955); one *s* one *d*; *m* 2nd, 1956, Kathleen Sarginson; one *s* one *d. Educ:* St Bartholomew's Medical Coll., Univ. of London. Qualified MB, BS, 1942; MD 1951. House Appts, 1942–44. RAMC, 1944–48. Registrar, Westminster Hospital, 1948–50; Lectr, Guy's Hosp. Med. Sch., 1950–54; Prof. of Bacteriology, University Coll., Ibadan, Nigeria, 1954–62; Visiting Professor: London Sch. of Hygiene and Tropical Medicine, 1979; Univ. of Jordan, 1982. FRCP 1972. JP Manchester, 1973. *Publications:* The Development of Microbiology, 1976; papers in: BMJ, Lancet, Jl Soc. Gen. Microbiol., Jl of Hygiene, West African Med. Jl, etc. *Recreations:* talking, reading, playing chess, bookbinding. *Address:* Honor Oak Cottage, Kingham, Oxford. *T:* Kingham 335. *Club:* Athenæum. *Died* 17 *June* 1989.

**COLLENS, John Antony;** an Assistant Auditor General, National Audit Office, since 1984; *b* 19 Nov. 1930; *s* of John Collens and Emily Charlotte Collens (*née* Gomm); *m* 1957, Josephine Stark; three *s. Educ:* Harrogate Grammar Sch. Mem. CIPFA, 1979. National Service, 1950–52. Exchequer and Audit Department: Asst Auditor, 1949; Sen. Auditor, 1962; Dep. Dir of Audit, 1973; Dir of Audit, 1977; Dep. Sec., Exchequer and Audit Dept, 1979–83. *Recreations:* cricket, tennis, walking. *Address:* 141 Park Avenue, Orpington, Kent BR6 9ED. *T:* Orpington 29133.

*Died* 15 *July* 1988.

**COLLETT, Rear-Adm. George Kempthorne,** CB 1957; DSC 1942; *b* 25 Jan. 1907; *s* of William George and Ruth Lilian Collett; *m* 1937, Rongnye, *e d* of Sir Charles A. Bell, KCIE, CMG; one *s* one *d. Educ:* RNC Osborne and Dartmouth. Comdr, 1939; Liaison Officer with Gen. de Gaulle, 1940; Executive Officer, HMS Trinidad, 1941–42; Staff Officer, Home Fleet, 1942–44; Naval Asst to First Sea Lord, 1944–45; CO, HMS Cardigan Bay, 1946–48; Min. of Supply, 1948–50; Joint Services Staff Coll., 1950–52; CO, HMS Bermuda, 1952–54; Vice Naval Deputy, SHAPE, Paris, 1955–57; retd 1958. Legion of Honour (officer), 1945. *Recreation:* gardening. *Address:* Coombe Farm, Churt, Farnham, Surrey. *T:* Headley Down 712533. *Club:* Army and Navy. *Died* 11 *May* 1982.

**COLLETT, Sir (Thomas) Kingsley,** Kt 1968; CBE 1956; formerly Director, Adams Bros & Shardlow Ltd (Creative Printers), London and Leicester, retired 1971; *b* 7 March 1906; 6th *s* of late Sir Charles Collett, 1st Bt, Bromley, Kent (Lord Mayor of London, 1933–34); *m* 1930, Beatrice Olive (*d* 1986), *d* of late Thomas H. Brown, Bickley, Kent. *Educ:* Bishop's Stortford Coll. HM Lieut for City of London, 1958. Freeman, City of London, 1930; Liveryman, Worshipful Co. of Distillers, 1934 (Master, 1960–61); Mem., Ct of Common Coun., City of London (Ward of Bridge), 1945–83; Chairman: City of London Freemen's Sch. Cttee, 1949–52; Port of London Health Authority, 1953; City Lands Cttee and Chief Commoner, 1955; Special Cttee, 1956–66; Policy and Parly Cttee, 1967–70. Corp. of London Rep. on Bd of Port of London Authority, 1959–67; Mem., Pollution Control Cttee, PLA, 1966–73; Chm., Lord Mayor's Appeal Cttee; Kennedy Mem. Fund, 1964; Churchill Fund, 1965; Vice-Chm., Lord Mayor's Appeal Cttee: cleaning St Paul's Cath, 1963–64; Attlee Meml Fund, 1967. Governor, Royal Hospitals; Chm., Governing Council, Bishop's Stortford Coll., 1964–76; Life Mem., Court of The City Univ., 1970–84, Hon. DLitt 1980. Chm., East India and Sports Club, 1959–66; Past Pres., City Pickwick Club. Dep. Governor, Irish Soc., 1975. Chevalier, Mil. Order of Christ (Portugal), 1956. *Recreation:* shooting. *Club:* East India, Devonshire, Sports and Public Schools.          *Died 26 June 1987.*

**COLLEY, Thomas,** MB, ChB (Victoria); MRCS, LRCP, FRCSE; DOMS; Emeritus Cons. Ophthalmologist, Wessex Regional Hospital Board; late Director of Ophthalmology to West Dorset Group of Hospitals; late Hon. Surgeon to Weymouth and Dorset County Royal Eye Infirmary; late Hon. Ophthalmic Surgeon to Dorset County Hospital, Dorchester and Weymouth and District Hospital; Ophthalmic Surgeon to EMS Hospital, Portwey, Weymouth (War Years); late Cons. Oculist to the Dorset CC and Weymouth Education Committee; *b* Dec. 1894; *s* of Thomas and Esther Colley, Preston; *m* Eleanor Mary, *e d* of late Rev. D. J. Thomas, OBE, MA, JP; two *d. Educ:* privately; Manchester Univ. (Dumville Surgical Prize, Medical Clinical Prize); Edinburgh University. House appointments, Royal Infirmary, Manchester, Central Branch Royal Infirmary, Manchester, Hospital for Sick Children, Great Ormond Street, London, Royal London Ophthalmic Hospital (Moorfields). Chm., W Dorset Group Med. Adv. Cttee, 1948–54; Member: Med. Adv. Cttee to SW Metropolitan Regional Hosp. Bd, 1949–51, (Mem., Med. Adv. Cttee of Western Area, 1948–53); W Dorset Group Hospitals Management Cttee, 1948–61. FRSM (Mem. of Council, Section of Ophthalmology, 1938–42); Mem. of Ophthalmological Soc., BMA, etc. *Publications:* papers in medical journals. *Recreation:* philately. *Address:* Anchor House, Eaton Crescent, Clifton, Bristol.          *Died 17 Dec. 1983.*

**COLLICK, Percy Henry;** Assistant General Secretary, Associated Society of Locomotive Engineers, 1940–57 (Organising Secretary, 1934–40); *b* 16 Nov. 1899. Contested (Lab) Reigate Division of Surrey, 1929 and 1931; MP (Lab) West Birkenhead, 1945–50, Birkenhead, 1950–64. General Purposes Cttee, TUC, 1930–34; National Executive, Labour Party, 1944; Joint Parly Sec., Min. of Agriculture, 1945–47. Mem. Council, Royal College of Veterinary Surgeons, 1949–53. Hon. Freeman of Birkenhead, 1965. *Address:* 142 Hendon Way, NW2.          *Died 24 July 1984.*

**COLLIER, Air Vice-Marshal Sir (Alfred) Conrad,** KCB 1947 (CB 1943); CBE 1941; retired as Chief Executive, Guided Weapons Division, English Electric Aviation Ltd, 1960; *b* 16 Nov. 1895; *m* 1st, 1920, G. M. C. Luis (*d* 1961); two *s* one *d*; 2nd, 1963, Kathleen, *d* of late Joseph Donaghy, JP, Londonderry. *Educ:* Sherborne Sch. 2nd Lieut 9th King's Own (RL) Regt, 1914; RFC, 1915 with subsequent continuous service in RFC and RAF; Air Attaché, Moscow, 1934–37; Dep. Dir of Plans, Air Min., 1938; Dir of Allied Air Co-operation, Air Min., 1940; Head of Air Section, British Military Mission to Moscow, 1941; Air Officer i/c Administration, AHQ, India, 1942–43; Deputy AOC-in-C Transport Comd, 1943–45; AOC No. 3 Group, Bomber Comd, 1946; Dir-Gen. of Technical Services, Min. of Civil Aviation, 1946–47; Air Vice-Marshal, 1946; Controller of Technical and Operational Services, Min. of Civil Aviation, 1947, resigned, 1948. A Governor, National Hospitals for Nervous Diseases, 1961–64. DL Kent, 1952–64. FRAeS. Order of White Lion, 2nd Class (Czechoslovakia); Grand Officer, Order of Orange Nassau (Netherlands); Officer, Legion of Honour, and Croix de Guerre (France). *Address:* c/o Lloyds Bank, Walton-on-Thames, Surrey. *Club:* Royal Air Force.
          *Died 16 Sept. 1986.*

**COLLIER, Dr William Adrian Larry;** District Medical Officer for Falmouth, Jamaica, since 1980; *b* 25 Nov. 1913; *s* of Hon. Gerald Collier, 2nd *s* of 2nd Baron Monkswell, and Lily Anderson; *S* uncle as 4th Baron Monkswell, 1964; disclaimed title, 7 April 1964; *m* 1945, Helen (*née* Dunbar, now Mrs Kemp); two *s*; *m* 1951, Nora Selby; one *s* one *d. Educ:* Fellowship Sch.; Odenwald Schule; Summerhill; Univs of Queensland, Edinburgh, London and Cambridge. IB 1937; MB, ChB Edinburgh 1943; DPH London 1947, PHLS (Trainee), 1947–50. Mem., Halstead UDC, 1954–67;

Essex CC, 1958–61. General Practitioner: Halstead, Essex, 1951–69; Hackney, 1970. Member: Amenity Cttee, Nat. Assoc. River Authorities, 1970–72; Council, Forest School Camps; Council, Centreprise 1973. *Publications:* World Index of Imprints used on Tablets and other Solid Dose Forms, 1964, 6th edn (now known as IMPREX), 1976; contribs to Lancet, Pharmaceutical Journal, Drug Intelligence and Clinical Pharmacy (Washington DC). *Recreations:* swimming, camping, kids, local government, Essex River Authority. *Heir (to disclaimed barony):* s Gerard Collier, *b* 28 Jan. 1947. *Address:* 1 Brett Manor, Brett Road, E8. *T:* 01-986 8837; Falmouth Health Centre (Hospital), Trelawny, Jamaica. *T:* 0 954 2346; (home) 0 954 2284.          *Died 27 July 1984.*

**COLLINGS, Maj.-Gen. Wilfred d'Auvergne,** CB 1946; CBE 1941; *b* Guernsey, 8 Aug. 1893; 5th *s* of C. d'Auvergne Collings, MD, and Laura Josephine Williams; *m* 1928, Nancy Draper Bishop (*d* 1983); two *s* one *d. Educ:* Elizabeth Coll., Guernsey; RMC Sandhurst. Commissioned ASC 1914. Served in France, Gallipoli and Mesopotamia, 1914–18 (despatches twice); seconded for service with Egyptian Army, 1923–24 and Sudan Defence Force, 1925–30; on active service in Palestine, 1937–39; Dep. Dir of Supplies and Transport, Western Desert Force, 1940, British Forces in Greece, 1941, Eighth Army, 1941; Dir of Supplies and Transport, Persia and Iraq Force, 1942–43, 21st Army Group, 1944–45, and British Army of the Rhine, 1945–46; retired 1948. Chief of Supply and Transport Div., UN Relief and Works Agency in the Near East, 1949–53. Maj.-Gen. 1944. Commander, Order of Leopold II (Belgium); MC of Greece, Croix de Guerre of France and Belgium. *Address:* La Verdure, Clifton, St Peter Port, Guernsey. *Club:* Army and Navy.          *Died 13 April 1984.*

**COLLINGWOOD, Adrian Redman,** CBE 1975; TD 1953; Chairman of the Eggs Authority, 1971–78; *b* Driffield, Yorks, 26 Feb. 1910; *s* of Bernard Joseph Collingwood and Katherine Mary Collingwood; *m* 1939, Dorothy Strong; two *d. Educ:* Hull Technical College. FIB. Served War of 1939–45, E Yorks Regt (50th Div.) (Major; despatches, 1944); wounded in Western Desert; POW for a year, then escaped by means of tunnel. Midland Bank: Asst Man., Whitefriargate Branch, Hull, 1947–51; Branch Supt, 1951–55; Gen. Manager's Asst, 1955–59; Asst Gen. Manager, 1959–66; Gen. Manager (Agriculture), 1966–71; retd from bank, 1971. *Publications:* lectures. *Recreations:* previously rugger, cricket, tennis; now golf, bridge, fishing. *Address:* Flat 6, Burrells, 25 Court Downs Road, Beckenham, Kent. *T:* 01–650 2265. *Clubs:* Farmers'; (Pres.)Langley Park Golf.          *Died 1 May 1987.*

**COLLINGWOOD, Lt-Gen. Sir George;** *see* Collingwood, Lt-Gen. Sir R. G.

**COLLINGWOOD, Lawrance Arthur,** CBE 1948; *b* 14 March 1887; *s* of J. H. Collingwood; *m* 1914, Anna Koenig, St Petersburg, Russia; two *s* two *d. Educ:* Westminster Abbey Choir Sch.; Exeter Coll., Oxford; St Petersburg Conservatoire. For 50 years associated with work for EMI (HMV); for 25 years associated with work of The Old Vic and Sadler's Wells, first as repetiteur, then conductor; musical dir of Sadler's Wells Opera Co., 1940–47. *Address:* Annalac, Rynachulig, Killin, Perthshire, Scotland.
          *Died 20 Dec. 1982.*

**COLLINGWOOD, Lt-Gen. Sir (Richard) George,** KBE 1959 (CBE 1951); CB 1954; DSO 1944; *b* 7 Oct. 1903; 4th *s* of Col C. G. Collingwood, Lilburn Tower and Glanton Pyke, Northumberland. *Educ:* RN Colls Osborne and Dartmouth; RMC Sandhurst. Entered Cameronians, 1923; Brigadier, 1944; served in Middle East and Burma. GOC 52 Lowland Division and Lowland District, Oct. 1952–55; Maj.-Gen. 1953; GOC, Singapore District, 1957–58; GOC-in-C, Scottish Command, 1958–61; Gov. of Edinburgh Castle, 1958–61; retired, 1961. Col, The Cameronians (Scottish Rifles), 1964–68. A Mem. of the Jockey Club (Steward, 1960). Knight Grand Cross, Order of the Sword (Sweden), 1964. *Recreations:* hunting, shooting, racing. *Address:* Abbey Lands, Alnwick, Northumberland. *T:* Alnwick 602220. *Club:* Boodle's.
          *Died 21 April 1986.*

**COLLINGWOOD, Brig. Sydney,** CMG 1957; CBE 1945; MC 1917; retired; *b* 10 July 1892; *s* of late Sir William Collingwood, KBE, MICE, JP, Dedham Grove, near Colchester, Essex; *m* 1st, 1915, Charlotte Annie (decd), *d* of Colonel James Charles Oughterson, late 18th Royal Irish, Greenock; two *s* one *d*; 2nd, 1940, Eileen Mary (*d* 1977), *widow* of late Major W. D. G. Batten, 3rd Gurkha Rifles, and *d* of A. Willson, Waldegrave Park, Twickenham. *Educ:* Liverpool Coll.; Royal Military Academy. 2nd Lieut, RA, 1912. Served European War, 1914–18. Major, 1930; Bt Lieut-Col 1934; Col, 1938; Brig., 1940; BGS, Southern Command, 1940–42; DDPS, War Office, 1942–46; retd, 1946. Regional Dir, Southern Region, Imperial War Graves Commission (Headquarters, Rome), 1946–57. Croix de Guerre, 1917. *Recreation:* rural preservation. *Address:* Cliffordine House, Rendcomb, Cirencester, Glos.
          *Died 12 Jan. 1986.*

**COLLINS, Bernard John,** CBE 1960; town planner, retired; Controller (formerly Director) of Planning and Transportation, Greater London Council, 1969–74; *b* 3 July 1909; *s* of late John Philip and Amelia Bounevialle Collins; *m* 1937, Grete Elisabeth, *e d* of H. A. Piehler; one *s* three *d*. *Educ:* Ampleforth. Served Royal Artillery, 1939–45, North Africa (despatches) and Italy. Ryde Memorial Prizeman, RICS, 1937. President: Royal Town Planning Inst., 1957–58; International Fedn of Surveyors, 1967–69; Mem. Bureau, Internat. Fedn for Housing and Planning, 1962–66; Vice-Pres., 1968–73, Sen. Vice-Pres., 1973–74, Pres., 1974–75, RICS; Mem. Board of Governors, Coll. of Estate Management, 1959–69; Vice-Chm. of Executive, Town and Country Planning Assoc., 1951–62; Chm., Assoc. of County Planning Officers, 1954–58; County Planning Officer, Middx, 1947–62; Sec. and Chief Exec. Commn for the New Towns, 1962–64; Dir of Planning, GLC, 1964–69; responsible for preparation of Greater London Develt Plan, 1969. Chairman, Technical Panel: Conf. on London and SE Regional Planning, 1964–74; Greater London and SE Regional Sports Council, 1966–74; advised on reorganisation of planning system, City of Jerusalem, 1971. Described by William Hickey of Daily Express as probably the world's top town planner. Pres. Honoraire, Fédération Internationale des Géomètres, 1970–; Hon. Mem., Deutscher Verein für Vermessungswesen (German Soc. of Surveyors), 1965–; Membre d'honneur, Union Belge des Géomètres-experts Immobiliers, 1976–. *Publications:* Development Plans Explained (HMSO), 1951; Middlesex Survey and Development Plan, 1952; numerous addresses, articles and papers on town planning. *Address:* Foxella, Matfield, Kent TN12 7ET. *Club:* Athenæum.

*Died 25 July 1989.*

**COLLINS, Sir Charles Henry,** Kt 1947; CMG 1941; *b* 10 Feb. 1887; *s* of late C. H. Collins, Torquay; *m* 1913, Florence E. Campkin (*d* 1968); one *d* (one *s* and one *d* decd). *Educ:* King's Coll., Univ. of London. BA 1909. Entered Ceylon Civil Service, 1910; Dep. Chief Sec., 1940; Acting Financial Sec. in 1935, 1936, 1937, 1940, and 1943; Acting Chief Sec. in 1944, 1945 and 1947; adviser to govt on changes in administration and procedure in connection with introduction of new constitution, 1946; retired, 1948. *Publications:* Public Administration in Ceylon, 1951; Public Administration in Hong Kong, 1952. *Recreations:* historical and archæological studies. *Address:* Devoncroft, Clandon Road, West Clandon, Guildford, Surrey GU4 7TL. *T:* Guildford 222542. *Club:* Royal Over-Seas League.

*Died 8 March 1983.*

**COLLINS, Sir David (Charles),** Kt 1975; CBE 1969; Immediate Past Chairman, Westland Aircraft PLC; *b* 23 Jan. 1908; *s* of Richard and Margaret Collins; *m* 1936, Dorothy Bootyman. Joined Westland Aircraft Ltd as Works Dir, 1951; Dep. Man. Dir, 1959; Man. Dir, 1965; Chief Exec. and Chm. subsidiary cos, 1968; Chm., 1970–77. FEng, FIMechE, FIProdE, FRAeS. Hon. DSc. *Recreations:* golf, fishing. *Address:* Little Gables, Redwood Road, Sidmouth, Devon EX10 9AB. *T:* Sidmouth 6756. *Club:* Honiton Golf.

*Died 7 June 1983.*

**COLLINS, Sir Geoffrey Abdy,** Kt 1952; *b* 5 June 1888; *y s* of Philip George and Susan Kate Collins; *m* 1936, Joan Mary, 2nd *d* of Albert Edward and Margaret Alice Ratcliffe; one *s* four *d*. *Educ:* Rugby; Christ's Coll., Cambridge (BA, LLB). Admitted solicitor, 1913. Served European War, 1914–18, in The Rifle Brigade (Capt.). Member: Royal UK Beneficent Assoc. Cttee, 1926–54 (Chm., 1950–54); Council of The Law Society, 1931–56, Pres., 1951–52. Past Master, Tylers and Bricklayers Co. *Address:* Mullion, 20 Ballard Estate, Swanage, Dorset. *T:* Swanage 422030.

*Died 2 Nov. 1986.*

**COLLINS, Vice-Adm. Sir John (Augustine),** KBE 1951; CB 1940; RAN retired; *b* Deloraine, Tasmania, 7 Jan. 1899; *s* of Michael John Collins, MD; *m* 1930, Phyllis Laishley, *d* of A. J. McLachlan; one *d*. *Educ:* Royal Australian Naval Coll. Served European War with Grand Fleet and Harwich Force, 1917–18; thereafter in various HM and HMA Ships abroad and in Australian waters; Squadron Gunnery Officer, HMA Squadron; Liaison Officer for visit of Duke and Duchess of York to Australia; in command HMAS Anzac; staff course; Asst Chief of Naval Staff, Australia; Capt. HMAS Sydney (CB), 1939–41; Asst Chief of Staff to C-in-C, China, 1941 (despatches); Cdre comdg China Force, 1942 (Comdr of Order of Orange Nassau); Capt. HMAS Shropshire, 1943–44; Cdre comdg HM Australian Sqdn (wounded), 1944–46; idc 1947; Chief of Naval Staff and First Naval Mem., Australian Commonwealth Naval Bd, Melbourne, 1948–55; Australian High Comr to New Zealand, 1956–62. Officer of Legion of Merit (US); Royal Humane Society's Certificate for Saving Life at Sea. *Publication:* As Luck Would Have It, 1965. *Address:* Unit 31, Trebartha, 69 Roslyn Gardens, Elizabeth Bay, Sydney, NSW 2011, Australia. *Club:* Royal Sydney Golf.

**COLLINS, Gen. (retd) J(oseph) Lawton,** DSM 1942 (Oak Leaf Cluster, 1943, 1944, 1953); Silver Star, 1943 (Army Oak Leaf Cluster, and Navy Gold Star, 1944); Legion of Merit, 1943 (Oak Leaf Cluster, 1945); Bronze Star Medal, 1944; Director, Chas Pfizer & Co. Inc.,

1957–72; Vice-Chairman, Pfizer International Subsidiaries 1957–72; *b* New Orleans, La, 1 May 1896; *s* of Jeremiah Bernard Collins and Catherine Lawton; *m* 1921, Gladys Easterbrook; one *s* two *d*. *Educ:* Louisiana State Univ.; US Military Academy. 2nd Lieut, Infantry, 1917; 22nd Infantry, Fort Hamilton, NY, until Jan. 1918; graduated Inf. Sch. of Arms, Fort Sill, Oklahoma, 1918; went overseas and took command of bn of 18th Inf., Coblenz, 1919; Asst Chief of Staff, Plans and Training Div., American Forces in Germany, until 1921; Instr, US Mil. Acad., 1921–25; graduated: Inf. Sch., Fort Benning, Ga, 1926; Advanced Course, Field Artillery Sch., Fort Sill, Oklahoma, 1927; Instr, Inf. Sch., 1927–31; student, Comd and Gen. Staff Sch., Fort Leavenworth, Kansas, 1931–33; with 23rd Bde (Philippine Scouts), Fort William McKinley, and Asst Chief of Staff, Ops and Mil. Intell., Philippine Div., until 1936; Student: Army Industrial Coll., 1936–37; Army War Coll., 1937–38; Instr there, 1938–40. Served War of 1939–45: Office of Sec., War Dept Gen. Staff, 1940–41; Chief of Staff, VII Army Corps, 1941; Chief of Staff, Hawaiian Dept, 1941; Comdg Gen., 25th Inf. Div. in Guadalcanal ops, New Georgia Campaign, 1942–43; comd VII Army Corps, European Theater, for Invasion of France, 1944; and subseq. campaigns to end of hostilities, 1945; Dep. Comdg Gen. and Chief of Staff, HQ, Army Ground Forces, 1945; Dir of Information, War Dept, 1945; Dep. Chief of Staff, US Army, 1947, and Vice Chief of Staff (upon creation of that post), 1948; Chief of Staff, US Army, 1949–53; US Rep., Standing Group, NATO and US Mem. Mil. Cttee, 1953–56; US Special Rep. in Viet Nam with personal rank Ambassador, Nov. 1954–May 1955. Holds hon. degrees. Army of Occupation Medal, Germany, European War, 1914–18, and War of 1939–45; American Defense Service Medal; Asiatic-Pacific Medal; European-African-Middle Eastern Campaign Ribbon. (In addition to above US decorations) Hon. CB (British) 1945; Order of Suvorov, 2nd Class, twice (Russian); Croix de Guerre with Palm, Legion of Honor, Degree of Grand Officer (French); Order of Leopold II, Grand Officer Croix de Guerre with Palm (Belgian). *Address:* 4000 Massachusetts Avenue, NW, Washington, DC 20016, USA. *T:* 362–0971. *Club:* Chevy Chase (Md).

*Died 12 Sept. 1987.*

**COLLINS, Rear-Adm. Kenneth St Barbe,** CB 1959; OBE 1945; DSC 1942; *b* 9 June 1904; *s* of late Charles Bury Collins, Col RE and late Ethel St Barbe; *m* 1932, Helen Mary Keen; one *s* one *d*. *Educ:* Lydgate House Sch., Hunstanton, Norfolk; RN Colls Osborne and Dartmouth. Midshipman, HMS Warspite, 1922, Vimiera, 1923; Sub-Lt, HMS Fitzroy, 1925; Lt and Lt-Comdr surveying ships, 1927–37; Seaplane Carrier, HMS Albatross, 1939; (as Comdr) Staff of Allied Naval Expeditionary Force, North Africa, 1942; staff of Allied Naval Expeditionary Force, Europe, 1943; surveying, 1947–54; Hydrographer of the Navy, 1955–60; Rear-Adm., 1957; retd 1960. Consultant to the Survey and Mapping Branch of Dept of Mines and Technical Surveys, Ottawa, 1960–63. *Address:* The Old Parsonage, Bentley, near Farnham, Surrey. *T:* Bentley 3227.

*Died 3 Dec. 1982.*

**COLLINS, Rev. Canon Lewis John;** President, International Defence and Aid Fund, since 1964; Canon of St Paul's Cathedral, 1948–81, then Emeritus; *b* 23 March 1905; *s* of Arthur Collins and Hannah Priscilla; *m* 1939, Diana Clavering Elliot; four *s*. *Educ:* Cranbrook Sch.; Sidney Sussex Coll. and Westcott House, Cambridge. Curate of Whitstable, 1928–29; Chaplain, Sidney Sussex Coll., Cambridge, 1929–31; Minor Canon of St Paul's Cathedral, 1931–34; a Dep. Priest-in-Ordinary to HM the King, 1931–34, Priest-in-Ordinary, 1934–35; Vice-Principal, Westcott House, Cambridge, 1934–37; Chaplain RAFVR, 1940–45; Dean of Oriel Coll., Oxford, 1938–48; Fellow Lecturer and Chaplain, 1937–48. St Paul's Cathedral: Chancellor, 1948–53; Precentor, 1953–70; Treasurer, 1970–81. Chairman: Campaign for Nuclear Disarmament, 1958–64; Martin Luther King Foundn, 1969–73; President, Christian Action, 1959– (Chairman, 1946–73). Order of Grand Companion of Freedom, Third Div., Zambia, 1970; Commander, Order of the Northern Star, Sweden, 1976. Gold Medal of UN Special Cttee against Apartheid, for significant contribution to internat. campaign against apartheid, 1978. *Publications:* The New Testament Problem, 1937; A Theology of Christian Action, 1949; Faith Under Fire, 1966; contributor, Three Views of Christianity, 1962. *Address:* Mill House, Chappel Road, Mount Bures, Bures, Suffolk.

*Died 31 Dec. 1982.*

**COLLINS, Norman Richard;** former Director: Associated Communications Corporation (formerly Deputy Chairman, Associated Television Corporation); ATV Network Ltd; Independent Television News Co.; Governor, Sadler's Wells Foundation; Chairman, Loch Ness Investigation Bureau; *b* 3 Oct. 1907; *s* of late Oliver Norman Collins; *m* 1931, Sarah Helen, *d* of Arthur Francis Martin; one *s* two *d*. *Educ:* William Ellis Sch., Hampstead. At Oxford Univ. Press, 1926–29; Asst Literary Editor, News-Chronicle, 1929–33; Dep. Chm., Victor Gollancz Ltd, publishers, 1934–41. Controller Light Programme, BBC, 1946–47; late Gen. Overseas Service Dir, BBC; Controller Television, BBC, 1947–50, resigned. Governor, British Film Inst., 1949–51; Governor,

Atlantic Inst., 1965–69; Member: Council, English Stage Co.; Exec. Cttee, Nat. Book League, 1965–69. General Comr of Taxes, 1967–. President: Appeals Cttee, Nat. Playing Fields Assoc., 1967–69; Adoption Cttee for Aid to Displaced Persons, 1962–70; Radio Industries Club, 1950; Pitman Fellowship, 1957; Regent Advertising Club, 1959–66. Chairman: Age Action Year, 1976; British Foundn for Age Res., 1977; Central Sch. of Speech and Drama, until 1982. *Publications:* The Facts of Fiction, 1932; Penang Appointment, 1934; The Three Friends, 1935; Trinity Town, 1936; Flames Coming Out of the Top, 1937; Love in Our Time, 1938; "I Shall not want", 1940; Anna, 1942; London belongs to Me, 1945 (TV series, 1977); Black Ivory, 1947; Children of the Archbishop, 1951; The Bat That Flits, 1952; The Bond Street Story, 1958; The Governor's Lady, 1968; The Husband's Story, 1978; Little Nelson, 1981; The Captain's Lamp (play), 1938. *Address:* Mulberry House, Church Row, NW3. *Clubs:* Carlton, Turf, Beefsteak, MCC.

*Died 6 Sept.* 1982.

**COLLINSON, Richard Jeffreys Hampton; His Honour Judge Collinson;** a Circuit Judge, since 1975; *b* 7 April 1924; *s* of Kenneth Hampton Collinson and Edna Mary Collinson; *m* 1955, Gwendolen Hester Ward; two *s* two *d*. *Educ:* Heath Grammar Sch., Halifax; Wadham Coll., Oxford (BCL, MA). Sub-Lieut, RNVR, 1944–46. Called to Bar, Middle Temple, 1950; Northern Circuit. Councillor, then Alderman, Wallasey County Borough Council, 1957–74, Leader of Council, 1965–72. *Address:* Merehaven, 2 Mere Lane, Wallasey, Merseyside L45 3HY. *T:* 051-639 5818.          *Died 9 April* 1983.

**COLLIS, John Stewart;** author; *b* 16 Feb. 1900; *s* of W. S. Collis and Edith (*née* Barton), Irish; *m* 1929, Eirene Joy; two *d*; *m* 1974, Lady Beddington-Behrens. *Educ:* Rugby Sch.; Balliol Coll., Oxford (BA). FRSL. *Publications:* include: Shaw, 1925; Forward to Nature, 1927; Farewell to Argument, 1935; The Sounding Cataract, 1936; An Irishman's England, 1937; While Following the Plough, 1946; Down to Earth, 1947 (Heinemann Foundation Award); The Triumph of the Tree, 1950; The Moving Waters, 1955; Paths of Light, 1959; An Artist of Life, 1959; Marriage and Genius, 1963; The Life of Tolstoy, 1969; Bound upon a Course (autobiog.), 1971; The Carlyles, 1972; The Vision of Glory, 1972; The Worm Forgives the Plough, 1973; Christopher Columbus, 1976; Living with a Stranger: a discourse on the human body, 1978; (contrib) Holroyd: The Genius of Bernard Shaw, 1979. *Recreation:* tennis. *Address:* Park House, Abinger Common, Dorking, Surrey. *T:* Dorking 730412.                          *Died 2 March* 1984.

**COLLISON, Lewis Herbert,** TD; MA; Headmaster of Liverpool College, 1952–70; *b* 30 July 1908; *s* of late Mr and Mrs W. H. Collison; *m* 1934, Edna Mollie Ivens; two *d*. *Educ:* Mill Hill Sch.; St John's Coll., Cambridge. Asst Master of Sedbergh Sch., 1931–40; Major in King's Own Royal Regt, 1940–45; Housemaster of Sedbergh Sch., 1946–52. Mem. Council, University of Liverpool, 1963–69. JP Liverpool, 1958–70. *Recreations:* pottery, sailing. *Address:* 22 Riverview, Melton, near Woodbridge, Suffolk IP12 1QU. *Club:* Hawks (Cambridge).          *Died 21 Nov.* 1988.

**COLTART, James Milne; Chairman:** Scottish Television Ltd, 1969–75 (Managing Director, 1957–61, Deputy Chairman, 1961–69); Highland Printers Ltd, since 1959; Deputy Chairman: The Thomson Organisation Ltd, 1964–76 (Managing Director, Thomson Newspapers Ltd, 1959–61); Thomson Television (International) Ltd, since 1962; The Scotsman Publications Ltd, since 1962 (Managing Director, 1955–62); Director, Thomson Printers Ltd and various other newspaper and television companies in Britain and overseas; Chairman of Trustees, The Thomson Foundation, since 1969 (Trustee since 1962); *b* 2 Nov. 1903; *s* of Alexander Coltart and Alice Moffat; *m* 1927, Margaret Shepherd (*d* 1956); one *s*; *m* 1961, Mary Fryer; one *s* one *d*. *Educ:* Hamilton Cres., Glasgow. Accountant: Ioco Rubber Co. Ltd, 1926; Weir Housing Co. Ltd, 1927; Dir and Sec., Marr Downie & Co. Ltd, 1937; Man. Dir, Reid Bros Ltd, 1939; Asst Gen. Manager, Scottish Daily Express, 1950; Gen. Manager, Evening Citizen Ltd, 1955. Hon. LLD Strathclyde Univ., 1967. *Recreations:* golf, fishing. *Address:* (business) Thomson Foundation, Regent's College, Regent's Park; Manor Cottage, Smithwood Common, Cranleigh, Surrey. *T:* Cranleigh 3633.

*Died 6 Sept.* 1986.

**COLTON, Cyril Hadlow,** CBE 1970; *b* 15 March 1902; *yr s* of Albert Edward Colton and Kate Louise; *m* 1932, Doree Beatrice Coles; one *s* two *d*. *Educ:* Reigate Grammar School. Man-made fibres industry from 1921: Fabrique de Soie Artificiel de Tubize, 1921; British Celanese Ltd, 1923: Dir, 1945; Chm., 1964; Pres., 1968; Courtaulds Ltd, 1957: Marketing Dir, 1962–67; Dir, Samuel Courtauld Ltd, 1959–64; Dir, Courtaulds SA, 1962–68; Consultant, Courtaulds Ltd, 1967–78. Chm., Rayon Allocation Cttee, 1940–49; Member: Council, British Rayon Research Assoc., 1946–61; BoT Utility Cloth Cttee, 1950–52; BoT Mission to Middle East, 1954; Pres., Textile Inst., 1954–55. Chairman: British Man-Made Fibres Fedn, 1961–75 (Pres., 1976); British Man-Made Fibres Producers Cttee, 1965–72; Silk and Man-Made Fibres Users Assoc., 1968–70;

BSI Textile Div., 1969–72; Pres., Bureau International pour la Standardisation de la Rayonne et des Fibres Synthetiques, 1969–72; Vice-Pres., Cttee Internat. des Fibres Synthetiques, 1969–72; Pres., British Display Soc., 1966–79; Mem. Council, Cotton, Silk and Man-Made Fibres Research Assoc. (Shirley Inst.), 1969–72; Dep. Chm., Textile Council, 1967–72; Mem., Crowther Cttee on Consumer Credit, 1968–71. CompTI; FRSA; FInstM. Liveryman, Worshipful Co. of Weavers. *Address:* Appin House, Cobham, Surrey. *T:* Cobham 4477.                          *Died 13 Nov.* 1988.

**COLTON, Gladys M.;** Head Mistress, City of London School for Girls, 1949–72; *b* 1909; *er d* of William Henry Colton. *Educ:* Wycombe High Sch.; University Coll., London. BA Hons, History; Postgrad. DipEd, London. Asst Mistress: Slepe Hall, St Ives, 1932–37; Beaminster Grammar Sch., 1937–41; Senior History Mistress, Ealing Girls' Grammar Sch., 1941–49. Mem. Governing Body, City of London Coll., 1957–62. Mem., St Bartholomew's Hosp. Nurse Educn Cttee, 1962–72. FRSA 1953 (Mem. Council, 1969–73). *Recreations:* music, gardening. *Address:* Four Winds, Westleton, Saxmundham, Suffolk. *T:* Westleton 402.

*Died 24 April* 1986.

**COLVILLE, Sir Cecil;** *see* Colville, Sir H. C.

**COLVILLE, Maj.-Gen. Edward Charles,** CB 1955; DSO 1944, Bar, 1945; JP; DL; retired; *b* 1 Sept. 1905; *s* of late Admiral Hon. Sir Stanley Colville, GCB, GCMG, GCVO, and of The Lady Adelaide Colville (*d* 1960), *d* of 4th Earl Clanwilliam, GCB, KCMG, RM; *m* 1934, Barbara Joan Denny; two *d*. *Educ:* Marlborough; Sandhurst. Commnd Gordon Highlanders, 1925, Adjt 1st Bn, 1938, Comdr 2nd Bn, 1943–44; ADC to Governor-Gen., Canada, 1932–34; Brigade Comd, 1944–46 (despatches); Military Adviser to UK High Comr, Canada, 1946–47; Comd Inf. Bde, TA, 1949–52; BGS, HQ Northern Army Group, 1952–54; Chief of Staff, Far East Land Forces, 1954–55; Comdr 51st Highland Div., 1956–59; retired, 1959. JP West Sussex, 1960; DL West Sussex, 1962. *Address:* Old Bartons, Stoughton, near Chichester, West Sussex. *T:* Compton 278. *Club:* Army and Navy.                          *Died 10 Jan.* 1982.

**COLVILLE, Sir (Henry) Cecil,** Kt 1962; MS (Melbourne); FRACS; private surgical practice, Melbourne; *b* 27 Aug. 1891; *s* of John William Colville and Mary Newman; *m* 1916, Harriet Elizabeth Tatchell; two *d*. *Educ:* Melbourne Church of England Grammar Sch. MB, BS (Melbourne) 1914; MS (Melbourne) 1920; FRACS 1931. War service, RAMC and AAMC, 1915–17. Pediatric Surg., Alfred Hospital, Melbourne, 1924–51. Pres., Federal Council of BMA, 1955–62; Pres. AMA, 1962–64. *Address:* 1045 Burke Road, Hawthorn, Vic 3123, Australia. *T:* Melbourne 82-5252. *Club:* Naval and Military.                          *Died 15 April* 1984.

**COLVILLE, Sir John (Rupert),** Kt 1974; CB 1955; CVO 1949; Director: Provident Life Association; London Committee, Ottoman Bank; Eucalyptus Pulp Mills Ltd; *b* 28 Jan. 1915; *s* of late Hon. George Colville and Lady Cynthia Colville; *m* 1948, Lady Margaret Egerton; two *s* one *d*. *Educ:* Harrow; Trinity Coll., Cambridge (1st Class Hons, History Tripos, and Sen. Scholar). Page of Honour to King George V, 1927–31. 3rd Sec., Diplomatic Service, 1937; Asst Private Sec. to Mr Neville Chamberlain, 1939–40; to Mr Winston Churchill, 1940–41 and 1943–45, and to Mr Clement Attlee, 1945. Served War of 1939–45, Pilot, RAFVR, 1941–44. Private Sec. to Princess Elizabeth, 1947–49; 1st Sec., British Embassy, Lisbon, 1949–51; Counsellor, Foreign Service, 1951; Joint Principal Private Sec. to the Prime Minister, 1951–55. Exec. Dir, Hill Samuel Ltd, 1955–80. President: New Victoria Hospital, 1978–85; Prayer Book Soc., 1981–84; Vice-Pres., National Assoc. of Boys' Clubs. Hon. Fellow, Churchill Coll., Cambridge, 1971. Officier, Légion d'Honneur. *Publications:* Fools' Pleasure, 1935; contrib. to Action This Day-Working with Churchill, 1968; Man of Valour, 1972; Footprints in Time, 1976; The New Elizabethans, 1977; The Portrait of a General, 1980; The Churchillians, 1981; Strange Inheritance, 1983; The Fringes of Power, 1985; *posthumous publication:* Those Lambtons!, 1988. *Address:* The Close, Broughton, near Stockbridge, Hampshire SO20 8AA. *T:* Romsey 301331. *Clubs:* White's, Pratt's.                          *Died 19 Nov.* 1987.

**COLVIN, Brigadier Dame Mary Katherine Rosamond,** DBE 1959 (OBE 1947); TD; Extra Lady in Waiting to the Princess Royal, 1964–65 (Lady in Waiting, 1962–64); *b* 25 Oct. 1907; *d* of Lt-Col F. F. Colvin, CBE. Commissioned 1939; Commanded Central Ordnance Depot, ATS Gp, Weedon, Northants, 1943–44; subsequently held staff appointment in Military Government, Germany; Comdt WRAC Sch. of Instruction, 1948–51; Asst Dir, WRAC, HQ. Scottish Comd, 1951–54; Inspector of Recruiting (Women's Services), War Office, 1954–56; Dep. Dir, WRAC, HQ Eastern Command, 1956–57; Dir of the Woman's Royal Army Corps, 1957–61. Hon. ADC to the Queen, 1957–61, retd. *Address:* Pasture House, North Luffenham, Oakham, Rutland LE15 8JU.

*Died 23 Sept.* 1988.

**COMAY, Michael;** Research Fellow, Leonard Davis Institute for International Relations, Jerusalem, since 1976; *b* Cape Town, 17 Oct. 1908; *s* of Alexander and Clara Comay; *m* 1935, Joan Solomon; one *d* (one *s* decd). *Educ:* Univ. of Cape Town (BA, LLB). Barrister, 1931–40. Served with S African Army, Western Desert and UK, 1940–45 (Major). Settled Palestine as representative S African Zionist Fedn, 1945; Adviser, Political Dept Jewish Agency, 1946–48; Dir, British Commonwealth Div., Israel Foreign Min., 1948–51; Asst Dir-Gen., Israel For. Min., 1951–53 and 1957–59; Minister, then Ambassador to Canada, 1953–57; Perm. Rep. and Ambassador of Israel to UN, 1960–67; Political Adviser to For. Minister and Ambassador-at-Large, 1967–70; Ambassador of Israel to the Court of St James's, 1970–73. Associate Gen. Chm., Chaim Weizmann Centenary. *Recreations:* walking, painting. *Address:* 47 Harav Berlin Street, Jerusalem 92505, Israel.
*Died 6 Nov.* 1987.

**COMINO, Demetrius,** OBE 1963; FRSA, FBIM; President, Dexion-Comino International Ltd, 1973 (Chairman, 1947–73); *b* Australia, 4 Sept. 1902; *s* of John and Anna Comino, Greek origin, naturalized British; *m* 1935, Katerina Georgiadis; one *d*. *Educ:* University Coll., London (BSc 1st cl. hons Engrg 1923; Fellow, 1971). Student Apprentice with The British Thompson Houston Co. Ltd, Rugby, until 1926; started own business, Krisson Printing Ltd, 1927; started present company, 1947; set up, with daughter Anna Comino-James, the Comino Foundn, 1971, aims to promote in all stages of educn learning and application of skills in getting results and solving problems, and an understanding of fundamental importance of industry to our society, one of outcomes being initiation by RSA of Industry Year 1986. FRSA 1971. Golden Cross, King George I (Greece), 1967. *Publications:* contribs to official jl of Gk Chamber of Technology and to New Scientist. *Recreation:* thinking. *Address:* Silver Birches, Oxford Road, Gerrards Cross, Bucks. *T:* Gerrards Cross (0753) 883170.
*Died 27 Sept.* 1988.

**COMPSTON, Nigel Dean,** CBE 1981; MA, MD, FRCP; Consulting Physician, retired; Royal Free Hospital, 1954–83; Royal Masonic Hospital, 1960–82; St Mary Abbot's Hospital, 1957–73; King Edward VII Hospital for Officers, 1965–72; *b* 21 April 1918; *s* of George Dean Compston and Elsie Muriel Robinson; *m* 1942, Diana Mary (*née* Standish); two *s* one *d*. *Educ:* Royal Masonic Sch.; Trinity Hall, Cambridge; Middlesex Hospital. BA Cantab 1939; MRCS, LRCP 1942; MB, BCh Cantab 1942; MRCP 1942; MA, MD Cantab 1947; FRCP 1957. RAMC, 1942–47 (Temp. Lt-Col). Research Fellow, Middlesex Hosp. Medical Sch., 1948–51; E. G. Fearnsides Scholar, Cambridge, 1951; Mackenzie Mackinnon Research Fellow, RCP, 1951; Asst Prof. Medicine, Middlesex Hosp., 1952–54; Treasurer, RCP, 1970–85 (formerly Asst Registrar). Examiner: Pharmacology and Therapeutics, Univ. of London, 1958–63, Medicine, 1968; Medicine, RCP, 1965–; Medicine, Univ. of Cambridge, 1971–81. Vice-Dean, Royal Free Hosp. Sch. of Medicine, 1968–70; Mem. Bd of Governors, The Royal Free Hosp., 1963–74. Hon. FFCM 1986. Hon. Editor Proc. RSM, 1966–70. *Publications:* Multiple Sclerosis (jtly), 1955; Recent Advances in Medicine (jtly), 1964, 1968, 1973, 1977, 1981, 1984; contribs to learned jls. *Address:* High Haven, Walton Hill, Littlehaven, near Haverfordwest, Dyfed.
*Died 17 Oct.* 1986.

**COMPTON, Eric Henry,** CVO 1954; Retired Commissioner, New Zealand Police; *b* 14 March 1902; *s* of William Henry Compton and Harriet Compton (*née* Morgon); *m* 1925, Nona Audrey Muriel Cole; five *s* one *d*. *Educ:* Hastings High Sch., NZ. Joined NZ Police Force, 1923; Detective Sergt, 1939, Chief Detective, 1946; Sub-Insp., 1952, Asst Comr, 1952, Comr, 1953; retired on superannuation, 1956. Chm., British Sailors' Soc., Wellington, 1952–; Dep. Chm., NZ British Sailors' Soc., 1952–; Management Cttee, Christian Business Men's Assoc., 1951; Hon. Sec., NZ Fellowship of Peruvian Bible Schs. Lady Godley Medal 1919; Coronation Medal 1953. *Recreation:* bowls (indoor).
*Died 2 April* 1982.

**COMPTON, Robert Herbert K.;** *see* Keppel-Compton.

**COMPTON, Air Vice-Marshal William Vernon C.;** *see* Crawford-Compton.

**CONCANNON, Terence Patrick,** JP; Clerk to the Governors and Foundation Governor, Pope Pius X High School, Wath-upon-Dearne; Director, South Yorkshire Training Trust Ltd, since 1989; *b* 24 Oct. 1932; *s* of late Leo Martin Concannon and Minnie (*née* Foster); *m* 1965, Pauline Marie (*née* Flynn) (*d* 1976); two *s* one *d*. *Educ:* De La Salle College, Sheffield; Sheffield University. DPA. Nat. Service, 1951–53. Local Govt Finance, West Riding CC, 1948–54; Rotherham CBC, 1954–73; Rotherham MBC, 1974–82, retired as Principal Officer; Mem., S Yorks CC, 1973–86 (Chm., 1984–85). Life Mem., NALGO, 1948. Mem., Rotherham Community Health Council, 1978–89; Rotherham Crime Prevention Panel, 1987–. Trustee, S Yorks Racing Apprentice Sch., 1986–. JP Rotherham, 1971. *Recreations:* music, reading, crosswords. *Address:* 195 Hague Avenue, Rawmarsh, Rotherham,

South Yorks S62 7PZ. *T:* Rotherham (0709) 522560. *Clubs:* Labour (Rawmarsh); South Yorkshire County (Barnsley).
*Died 15 Feb.* 1990.

**CONDLIFFE, John Bell,** KCMG (Hon.) 1978; MA, DSc, LLD, LittD; retired; Consultant, Stanford Research Institute, Menlo Park, 1959–74; Professor of Economics, 1940–58, then Emeritus, University of California, Berkeley; *b* Melbourne, Australia, 23 Dec. 1891; *s* of Alfred B. and Margaret Condliffe; *m* 1916, Olive Grace, *d* of Charles Mills; two *s* one *d*. *Educ:* Canterbury Coll., University of NZ; Gonville and Caius Coll., Cambridge (Sir Thomas Gresham Research Student). Prof. of Economics, Canterbury Coll., 1920–26; Research Sec., Institute of Pacific Relations, 1927–31; Visiting Prof. of Economics, Univ. of Mich., 1930–31; Economic Intelligence Service, League of Nations, 1931–36; Univ. Prof. of Commerce, LSE, 1936–39; Associate-Dir, Div. of Economics and History, Carnegie Endowment for International Peace, 1943–48; Research Associate, Institute of International Studies, Yale Univ., 1943–44; Fulbright Research Scholar, Cambridge Univ., 1951; Consultant, Reserve Bank of New Zealand, 1957; Adviser, National Council of Applied Economic Research, New Delhi, 1959–60; Henry E. Howland Memorial Prize, 1939; Wendell L. Willkie Memorial Prize, 1950; Sir James Wattie Prize, 1972. FRSA, 1949; Fellow Amer. Assoc. for the Advancement of Science, 1953. Gold Cross, Royal Order of Phœnix (Greece), 1954. *Publications:* The Life of Society, 1922; A Short History of New Zealand, 1925; Problems of the Pacific, 1928; New Zealand in the Making, 1930 (rev. edn, 1959); Problems of the Pacific, 1929, 1930; China To-day-Economic, 1933; World Economic Survey, 1931–32, 1932–33, 1933–34, 1934–35, 1935–36, 1936–37; The Reconstruction of World Trade, 1940; Agenda for a Post-War World, 1942; The Common Interest in International Economic Organization (with A. Stevenson), 1944; The Commerce of Nations, 1950; Point Four and the World Economy, 1950; The Welfare State in New Zealand, 1958; Foreign Aid Re-examined, 1963; The Development of Australia, 1964; Foresight and Enterprise, 1965; Economic Outlook for New Zealand, 1969; Te Rangi Hiroa: the life of Sir Peter Buck, 1971; Defunct Economists, 1974; articles in journals, etc. *Address:* 1641 Canyonwood Court No 1, Walnut Creek, Calif 94595, USA. *Clubs:* Bohemian (San Francisco); Faculty (Berkeley); Cosmos (Washington).
*Died 23 Dec.* 1981.

**CONEY, Rev. Canon Harold Robert Harvey,** MA Oxon; *b* 28 Oct. 1889; *s* of John Harvey and Hope Josephine Coney; *m* 1925, Edith Mary Carpenter; three *s* one. *d*. *Educ:* Keble Coll., Oxford; Cuddesdon Coll. Formerly an Architect; served in France, 1915–17, Civil Service Rifles (despatches); Meritorious Service Medal, 1916; deacon, 1920; priest, 1921; Curate of Bermondsey, 1920–23; Warden of Caius Coll. Mission, Battersea, 1923–28; Vicar of Felkirk, 1928–37; Canon Missioner of Wakefield Cathedral, 1937–40; Champney Lecturer in Christian Evidence, 1937–40; Campden Lecturer, Wakefield Cathedral, 1937–40; Rector of Thornhill, Dewsbury, 1940–61 and Rural Dean of Dewsbury, 1947–61; Hon. Canon of Wakefield Cathedral, 1937–61, Canon Emeritus, 1961; Curate of Coonamble, NSW, Australia, 1961–63; Permission to officiate, Bath and Wells, 1963–69, Brisbane, 1969–75. *Recreation:* laughing. *Address:* Manormead Nursing Home, Hindhead, Surrey.
*Died 6 Sept.* 1982.

**CONNELL, Sir Charles (Gibson),** Kt 1952; formerly Partner, Connell & Connell, WS, 10 Dublin Street, Edinburgh; *b* 11 March 1899; *s* of late Sir Isaac Connell, SSC, and Mary Jane (*née* Gibson); *m* 1927, Constance Margaret Weir (*d* 1976); one *s* one *d*. *Educ:* Melville Coll., Edinburgh; Edinburgh Univ. Officer Cadet and 2nd Lieut RFA, 1917–19. WS 1923; BL Edinburgh, 1923. JP City of Edinburgh, 1933. Secretary: Royal Scottish Agricultural Benevolent Instn, 1935–66; Scottish Agricultural Arbiters Assoc., 1935–66; Dir, The Edinburgh Building Soc., 1937–79; Life Governor, Melville Coll. Trust. Member: Nature Conservancy, 1961–73 (Chm., Scottish Cttee, 1961–72); Deptl Cttee on Registration of Title to Land in Scotland, 1963; Pres., Scottish Wildlife Trust; Hon. Vice-Pres., Selborne Soc. Pres., Scottish Unionist Assoc., 1944–45 (Joint Hon. Sec., 1938–54); Hon. Pres., Scottish Ornithologists Club. Hon. FRZSScot 1979. Hon. LLD Dundee, 1976. Long Service Award with Merit, National Parks Congress of IUCN, 1982. *Publications:* (ed) 3rd, 4th and 5th Edns (1961) of Connell on the Agricultural Holdings (Scotland) Acts. *Recreations:* wildlife conservation, gardening. *Address:* 12 Abbotsford Park, Edinburgh EH10 5DZ. *T:* 031–447 2026. *Clubs:* New, Caledonian (Edinburgh).
*Died 26 Feb.* 1985.

**CONNER, Cyril,** JP; *b* 26 Feb. 1900; *m* 1st, 1930, Mary Stephanie Douglass; two *d*; 2nd, 1946, Margaret Isobel Hunt (*née* Murison); one *d* (one step *s* adopted). *Educ:* Haileybury; Merton Coll., Oxford. MA Greats and Law. Commn in RGA 1918. Called to Bar, Inner Temple, and practised at Common Law Bar, London, 1924–38; Arbitrator for Milk Marketing Board, 1934–38; BBC Dir for NE England, 1938; Head of BBC's Commonwealth and Foreign Relations, 1941–60, except Jan.–July 1953, when BBC Controller for Northern Ireland. Mem., Administrative Council of European Broadcasting Union, 1951–60. Delegate to Commonwealth Broadcasting Confs, 1946, 1952, 1956, 1960. Chm. of Frances Martin Coll., London, 1950 and 1951. Dep. Chm., West Sussex QS, 1963–71; JP West Sussex, 1963–. Chm., Rent Assessment Cttee for Surrey and Sussex, 1966–73. Company Director, 1973–. *Publications:* contributions to Juridical Review and other legal journals. *Address:* Lovehill House, Trotton, near Rogate, West Sussex. *T:* Midhurst 3665. *Clubs:* Athenæum, Special Forces.

*Died 4 April 1981.*

**CONNOLLY, Sir Willis (Henry),** Kt 1971; CBE 1962; Chairman, State Electricity Commission of Victoria, 1956–71; *b* 25 Nov. 1901; *s* of Joseph John Connolly and Adelaide May Connolly (*née* Little); *m* 1927, Mary Milton Clark; one *s* one *d*. *Educ:* Benalla High Sch. (Matriculation Cert.); Univ. of Melbourne (BEE, BCom). Whole Career spent with SEC of Victoria, 1921–71: Engr and Manager, Electricity Supply, 1937–49; Asst to Gen. Manager, 1949–51; Asst Gen. Manager, 1951–56. Pres. Victoria Inst. of Colleges, 1967–74, 1978–. Chm., Aust. Nat. Cttee, World Energy Conf., 1958–78 (Pres., World Energy Conf., 1962–68); Past Pres., Electricity Supply Assoc. of Australia; former Chm., Electrical Research Bd. Kernot Meml Medal, 1957; "The Australasian Engineer" Award, 1960; Peter Nicol Russell Meml Medal, 1968. Hon. Mem. Australasian Inst. of Mining and Metallurgy, 1970. Hon. DEng Monash, 1967; Hon. DEd, Victoria Inst. of Colleges, 1974. *Recreations:* tennis, photography, music, reading. *Address:* 16 Monkstadt Street, St Kilda, Victoria 3182, Australia. *T:* 91 2670. *Clubs:* Australian, Melbourne (Melbourne). *Died 13 Feb. 1981.*

**CONRAN, (George) Loraine,** FMA; Director, Manchester City Art Galleries, 1962–76; *b* 29 March 1912; *o s* of Col George Hay Montgomery Conran; *m* 1st, 1938, Jacqueline Elspeth Norah Thullier O'Neill Roe (marr. diss. 1970); one *s* one *d* (and one *d* decd); 2nd, 1970, Elizabeth Margaret Johnston; one *d*. *Educ:* RNC Dartmouth. Museum and Art Gallery, Birmingham, 1935; Walker Art Gallery, Liverpool, 1936; Southampton Art Gallery, 1938; Curator, The Iveagh Bequest, Kenwood, 1950. Pres., Museums Assoc. (Hon. Sec., 1959–64); Hon. Sec., Contemporary Art Soc., 1959–65. Chm., Jt Cttee of Museums Assoc. and Carnegie UK Trust; Member: British Nat. Cttee, Internat. Council of Museums, 1959–71; Ct, RCA. Hon. MA Manchester, 1973. Served War of 1939–45 (despatches). *Address:* 31 Thorngate, Barnard Castle, Co. Durham DL12 8QB. *Died 25 Nov. 1986.*

**CONSTANTINE, Prof. Tom,** CEng, FICE, FIMunE; Professor of Civil Engineering since 1967, and Chairman of Civil Engineering Department since 1969, Salford University; *b* 10 Sept. 1926; *s* of Arthur Constantine and Jane Alice Constantine (*née* Fenton); *m* 1949, Mary Moss; one *s* one *d*. *Educ:* Haslingden Grammar Sch.; Burnley Technical Coll.; Manchester Univ. BSc (Eng) London Univ., PhD Manchester. Asst Experimental Officer, Road Research Lab., 1946–48; Engineering Asst, City of Bradford, 1948–50; Asst Engineer, Oldham County Borough, 1950–52; Sen. Asst Engineer, St Helens Co. Borough, 1952–55; Lectr in Civil Engineering: Univ. of Manchester, 1955–61; Univ. of Newcastle upon Tyne, 1961–66; Visiting Prof. and Research Engr, Univ. of California, 1964; Sen. Lectr in Civil Engrg, Univ. of Sheffield, 1966–67; Pro-Vice-Chancellor, Salford Univ., 1975–81, Acting Vice-Chancellor, 1981. IMunE: Bronze Medals, 1956 and 1963; Rees Jeffreys Prizeman, 1961; ICE: Crampton Prizeman, 1963. *Publications:* Passenger Transport Integration, Pilot Study, Sheffield Area, Vols I and 2, 1966; (with W. Fisher Cassie) Student's Guide to Success, 1977; numerous technical papers in Fluid Mechanics and Transport Engrg and Planning. *Recreations:* gardening, music, running. *Address:* 50 Fleetwood Road, Southport, Merseyside PR9 0JZ. *T:* 35321.

*Died 30 Aug. 1981.*

**CONWAY, Hugh Graham,** CBE 1964; FEng; *b* 25 Jan. 1914; *s* of G. R. G. Conway; *m* 1937, Eva Gordon Simpson (*d* 1980); two *s*. *Educ:* Merchiston Castle Sch., Edinburgh; Cambridge Univ. Joined aircraft industry, 1938; Man. Dir, Bristol Engine Division, Rolls Royce Ltd, 1964–70; Dir, Rolls-Royce Ltd, 1966–70, Rolls-Royce (1971) Ltd, 1971; Gp Managing Dir, Gas Turbines, Rolls-Royce Ltd, 1970–71. Member: Decimal Currency Board, 1967–71; Design Council, 1971–76 (Dep. Chm., 1972–76). *Publications:* Engineering Tolerances, 1948; Fluid Pressure Mechanisms, 1949; Landing Gear Design, 1958; Bugatti, 1963; Grand Prix Bugatti, 1968. *Recreation:* vintage motoring. *Address:* 33 Sussex Square, W2.

*Died 27 Nov. 1989.*

**COOK, Alexander Edward,** CMG 1955; *b* 3 April 1906; *s* of Edward Arthur Cook and M. J. Cook (*née* Wreford); *m* 1936, Ethel Catherine Margaret (*née* Mayo); one *s* two *d*. *Educ:* Imperial Service Coll., Windsor; Pembroke Coll., Cambridge. Entered Colonial Service as a Cadet, Nigeria, 1928; Asst District Officer, District Officer, Asst Sec.; Financial Sec., Gibraltar, 1945; Financial Sec., Eastern Region, Nigeria, 1953; Permanent Sec., Ministry of Finance, Eastern Region, Nigeria, 1954; retired 1956; Mem., British

Caribbean Federal Capital Commn, 1956. Attached Fed. Govt of UK of Libya as Economic Adviser, under auspices of UN Tech. Assistance Admin., 1959–60. *Recreations:* fishing and golf. *Address:* The White Cottage, Whitby Road, Milford-on-Sea, near Lymington, Hants. *T:* Milford-on-Sea 3526. *Club:* United Oxford & Cambridge University. *Died 20 July 1984.*

**COOK, Arthur Herbert,** DSc, PhD; FRS 1951; FRSC; Director, Brewing Industry Research Foundation, Nutfield, Surrey, 1958–71 (Assistant Director, 1949–58), retired 1971; *b* London, 10 July 1911; *s* of Arthur Cook, London. *Educ:* Owen's Sch., Islington, London; Universities of London (Imperial Coll. of Science and Technology) and Heidelberg. Joined staff of Imperial Coll., 1937; Asst Prof. and Reader in the University, 1947–49. Hon. DSc Heriot-Watt. *Publications:* (with late Prof. F. Mayer) Chemistry of the Natural Colouring Matters. Numerous articles, mainly in Journal of Chemical Soc. Editor, The Chemistry and Biology of Yeasts, 1958; Barley and Malt: Biology, Biochemistry, Technology, 1962. *Recreations:* gardening, photography. *Address:* Merrylands, Lympstone, Devon. *Club:* Athenæum. *Died 26 July 1988.*

**COOK, Bernard Christopher Allen,** CMG 1958; OBE 1945; *b* 20 July 1906; *s* of late Sir Edward Cook, CSI, CIE; *m* 1933, Margaret Helen Mary, *d* of Rt Rev. C. E. Plumb, DD; two *d* (and one *s* decd). *Educ:* Radley Coll. (Open Scholarship); Brasenose Coll., Oxford (Open Scholarship). ICS 1929; held various posts in UP; Govt of India: Finance and Commerce Cadre, 1938; Custodian of Enemy Property, 1939–41; Actg Joint Sec., Finance Dept, and Mem. Central Legislative Assembly, 1946; Indian Trade Comr, London, 1946–47; Foreign Service, 1947; Control Commn, Germany (currency reform), 1948–49; Political Adviser, Asmara, 1949–51; First Sec. (Commercial), Paris, 1951–53; Counsellor (Commercial), Rangoon, 1953–57; Counsellor (Commercial), HBM Embassy, Mexico City, 1957–59; HM Consul-General, Barcelona, 1959–66; retired, 1966; re-employed, 1967–69; Financial Observer for Central America attached HBM Embassy, San Salvador and temp. Consul, Guatemala, for 2 months; retired permanently, 1969. *Address:* 11 Priory Court, Granville Road, Eastbourne BN20 7ED.

*Died 10 June 1985.*

**COOK, Air Vice-Marshal Eric,** DFC 1945; Fellow, Hughes Hall, Cambridge, since 1975; *b* 30 April 1920; *s* of late Thomas Cook and Sara Elizabeth Cook (*née* Hunnam); *m* 1953, Thelma, *o d* of late Alfred and Isabelle Burns Withnell, Chorley, Lancs; one *s*. *Educ:* Sunderland Technical Coll. MA Cantab. Served War, Bomber Command Sqdns, 1940–45 (despatches twice). Command, MEAF VIP Sqdn, 1951; Staff, HQ Transport Comd, 1953; Sqdn Comdr, Training Comd, 1955–57; Sen. Personnel Staff Officer, MEAF, 1959–60; Chief Instr, Jet Provost Wing, 1961; Sen. Air Staff Officer, Ghana Air Force, 1963; AOA, RAF Germany, 1968–71; Dir of Flying Training, 1971–72; Dir-Gen. RAF Training, 1972–75. *Recreations:* outdoor activities, music. *Address:* Hawkwood, Madeley Court, Hemingford Grey, Cambridgeshire. *T:* St Ives 63647. *Clubs:* Royal Air Force, MCC. *Died 4 March 1985.*

**COOK, Eric William;** HM Diplomatic Service, retired; *b* 24 Feb. 1920; *s* of Ernest Gordon Cook and Jessie (*née* Hardy); *m* 1949, Pauline Elizabeth Lee; one *s*. *Educ:* various private estabts. RAF, 1940–46. GPO, 1947–49; FO (later FCO), 1949–; Consul, Belgrade, 1961–64; Vice-Consul, Leopoldville, 1964–65; Consul, Cleveland, Ohio, 1967–69; also served at Rome, Moscow, Peking and Djakarta; Consul Gen., Adelaide, 1974–76; FCO, 1977–80. *Recreations:* music, writing and photography. *Address:* 11 St Ann's Court, Nizells Avenue, Hove, East Sussex BN3 1PR. *T:* Brighton (0273) 776100.

*Died 5 June 1990.*

**COOK, Vice-Adm. Eric William L.;** *see* Longley-Cook.

**COOK, Sir (Philip) Halford,** Kt 1976; OBE 1965; retired; *b* 10 Oct. 1912; *s* of Rev. R. Osborne Cook and May Cook; *m* 1945, Myra V., *d* of M. A. Dean; one *s* one *d*. *Educ:* Wesley Coll., Melbourne; Queen's Coll., Univ. of Melbourne; University Coll., Univ. of London; Columbia and Kansas Univs, USA. MA Melbourne, 1938; PhD Kansas, 1941. FBPsS 1943; FAPsS 1968, Hon. FAPsS 1972. Lectr, Industrial Relations, Univ. of Melbourne, 1945–46, Lectr, Indust. Admin, 1947–50; Professional Staff, Tavistock Inst. of Human Relations, London, 1950–51; Asst Sec., 1952–63, First Asst Sec., 1963–68, Sec., 1968–72, Aust. Dept of Labour and Nat. Service; Ambassador and Special Labour Advr in Europe, Australian Permanent Mission, Geneva, 1973–77. Chm., Governing Body, ILO, 1975–76. Fellow, Queen's Coll., Univ. of Melbourne, 1972. *Publications:* Theory and Technique of Child Guidance, 1944; Productivity Team Technique, 1951; articles in jls on psychology and on indust. relations. *Recreations:* reading and travel. *Address:* 11 Boisdale Street, Surrey Hills, Victoria 3127, Australia. *T:* Melbourne (03) 898 4793. *Club:* Athenæum (Melbourne).

*Died 4 Jan. 1990.*

**COOK, Sir William (Richard Joseph),** KCB 1970 (CB 1951); Kt 1958; FRS 1962; Director, Buck & Hickman Ltd, 1970–83; *b* 10 April

1905; *s* of John Cook; *m* 1929, Grace (*née* Purnell); one *d*; *m* 1939, Gladys (*née* Allen); one *s* one *d*. *Educ*: Trowbridge High Sch.; Bristol Univ. Entered CS, 1928; various scientific posts in Research Estabs of WO and Min. of Supply, 1928–47; Dir of Physical Research, Admiralty, 1947–50; Chief of Royal Naval Scientific Service, 1950–54; Deputy Dir, Atomic Weapons Research Establishment, Aldermaston, 1954–58; Mem. for Reactors, Atomic Energy Authority, 1961–64 (Mem. for Development and Engineering, 1959–61, for Engineering and Production, 1958–59); Dep. Chief Scientific Adviser, Ministry of Defence, 1964–67; Chief Adviser (Projects and Research) MoD, 1968–70. Director: Rolls-Royce (1971) Ltd, 1971–76; GEC-Marconi Electronics Ltd, 1972–79; Chm., Marconi International Marine Co., 1971–75. FInstP 1967; FINucE 1984. Hon. DSc: Strathclyde, 1967; Bath, 1975. *Address*: Adbury Springs, Newbury, Berks. *T*: Newbury 40409. *Club*: Athenæum. *Died 16 Sept. 1987.*

**COOKE, Dr Arthur Hafford,** MBE 1946; Warden of New College, Oxford, 1976–85, Hon. Fellow, 1985; Pro-Vice-Chancellor, University of Oxford, 1982–85; *b* 13 Dec. 1912; *er s* of late Sydney Herbert Cooke and Edith Frances (*née* Jee); *m* 1939, Ilse (*d* 1973), *d* of late Prof. Hans Sachs; two *s*. *Educ*: Wyggeston Grammar Sch., Leicester; Christ Church, Oxford (MA, DPhil). Research Lectr, Christ Church, 1939. Radar research for Admiralty, 1940–45. Fellow of New Coll., Oxford, 1946–76; University Lectr in Physics, 1944–71; Reader in Physics, 1971–76. Member: Gen. Bd of the Faculties, 1962–72 (Vice-Chm., 1969–71); Hebdomadal Council, 1969–83. Hon. DSc Leicester, 1979. *Publications*: articles in scientific jls on magnetism and low temperature physics. *Address*: 9 Benson Place, Oxford OX2 6QH. *T*: Oxford 52528.

*Died 31 July 1987.*

**COOKE, Rev. Canon Greville (Vaughan Turner),** MA, MusB Cantab; FRAM; FSA; Canon Emeritus, Peterborough Cathedral, since 1956; composer, author, poet, broadcaster; Adjudicator at Musical Festivals; *b* 14 July 1894; *s* of William Turner Cooke, Chief Clerk of Central Office of Royal Courts of Justice, London, and Adeline Hannah, *d* of David Johnson, MD. *Educ*: Hamilton House, Ealing; Royal Academy of Music (Schol., Exhibitioner, Prizewinner); Christ's Coll., Cambridge (Stewart of Rannoch Schol.), 1913, Organ Schol.); Ridley Hall, Cambridge (Theol. Studentship); ARAM 1913; BA 1916; MusBac 1916; MA 1920. Ordained, 1918; Curate, Tavistock, 1918, Ealing, 1920; Dep. Minor Canon of St Paul's Cathedral, 1920–21; Vicar of Cransley, Northants, 1921–56; Rector of Buxted, 1956–71. Canon Non-residentiary of Peterborough Cathedral, 1955. Prof., Royal Academy of Music, 1925–59, FRAM 1927; FSA 1962. Elected FRSA by Council, 1958; Mem., Athenæum, 1931–53. Dir of Music, London Day Training Coll. Examiner for LRAM Diploma, Associated Board Exams, 1927; Lectr for London Univ., Royal Institution of Great Britain, League of Arts, Music Teachers' Association, Sussex Archæological Soc. (Mem. Council), London Appreciation Soc., RSCM, RSA; Lectr in Good English for Shell-Mex and IBM. *Publications*: The Theory of Music, 1928; Art and Reality, 1929; Tonality and Expression, 1929; Poems, 1933; Cransley Broadcast Sermons, 1933; The Light of the World, 1949 (USA 1950, paperback 1965); A Chronicle of Buxted, 1960 (paperback 1965); The Grand Design, 1964; Thus Saith the Lord: a Biblical anthology, 1967; Jenny Pluck Pears, 1972; Night Fancies and other poems, 1976; The Heresies of Orthodoxy, 1980; Who Wrote the Fourth Gospel?, 1981; An Easter Offering, 1982; musical publications include: *orchestral*: Prelude for Strings; *songs*: Three Songs; Day-dreams; The Shepherdess; Bereft; Eileen Aroon; But Yesterday; Your Gentle Care; My Heaven; Weep you no more; The Bells of Heaven; Shepherd Boy's Song; *choral*: Nobody Knows; Deep River; Jillian of Berry; Oh, to be in England; How can I help England; Claribel; Oh, Hush Thee My Baby; Cobwebs; *anthems*: Drop, Slow Tears; Let us with a gladsome mind; This Joyful Eastertide; Bread of the World; Lo! God is Here; *pianoforte*: High Marley Rest; Time Keepers; Meadowsweet; La Petite; Pets' Corner; Up the Ladder; A Day at the Sea; Bargain Basement; Reef's End; Cormorant Crag; Song Prelude; Whispering Willows; Haldon Hills; In the Cathedral; Gothic Prelude; *violin and piano*: High Marley Rest; *'cello and piano*: Sea Croon; *hymns*: Tune Bank No 1, 1987; contributor to Hymns Ancient and Modern, 1950, BBC Hymn Book, Baptist Hymn Book, Methodist Hymn Book, etc. *Address*: Holtwood, Bishops Caundle, Sherborne, Dorset.

*Died 7 Nov. 1989.*

**COOKE, Sir John F.;** *see* Fletcher-Cooke.

**COOKE, Sir Robert (Gordon),** Kt 1979; MA (Oxon); Special Adviser on the Palace of Westminster to the Secretary of State for the Environment, since 1979; *b* 29 May 1930; *er s* of late Robert V. Cooke, FRCS, and Dr Elizabeth Mary Cowie; *m* 1966, Jenifer Patricia Evelyn, *yr d* of Evelyn Mansfield King; one *s* one *d*. *Educ*: Harrow; Christ Church, Oxford. Pres., Oxford Univ. Conservative Assoc., 1952; Editor, Oxford Tory, 1952–53. Councillor, City and Co. of Bristol, 1954–57; contested Bristol SE at Gen. Election, 1955; MP (C) Bristol West, March 1957–1979; Parliamentary Private

Secretary to: Minister of State, Home Office, 1958–59; Minister of Health, 1959–60; Minister of Works, 1960–62; introduced: Fatal Accidents Act, 1959; Historic Buildings Bill, 1963; Motorways Commn Bill, 1968; Owner Occupiers Under-occupied Housing Bill, 1973 and 1974. State Dept Foreign Leader Visitor in USA, 1961. Chairman: Cons. Broadcasting and Communications Cttee, 1962–64, 1973–76; Arts and Heritage Cttee of Cons. Party, 1970–79 (Vice-Chm., 1959–62 and 1964–70); House of Commons Administration Cttee, 1974–79; a Commissioner, 1978; Vice-Chm., Media Cttee, 1976–79; Member: Services Cttee, House of Commons, 1967–79; Select Cttee on Wealth Tax, 1974–75 (Chm. Nat. Heritage Sub-Cttee); Select Cttee, Broadcasting Proceedings of Parlt, 1977–79; Parly delegn to Brazil, 1975; Sudan, 1978; Hungary, 1978; Council of Europe, Athens, 1976; Historic Buildings Council for England, 1970–80; Board, BTA, 1980– (Chm., British Heritage Cttee, 1981–). Pres., Dorset Tourism Assoc., 1983–. Trustee: Nat. Heritage Meml Fund, 1980–; Primrose League; Royal Botanic Gardens, Kew, 1986–. Director, Westward Television, 1970–81. Chm., Parish Meeting of Athelhampton. FRSA. *Publications*: West Country Houses, 1957; Government and the Quality of Life, 1974; *posthumous publication*: Palace of Westminster: Houses of Parliament, 1987. *Recreations*: architecture, building, gardening. *Address*: Athelhampton, Dorchester, Dorset. *T*: Puddletown 363. *Clubs*: Carlton, Pratt's, Farmer's, Garrick, MCC. *Died 6 Jan. 1987.*

**COOKE, Brig. Robert Thomas,** CBE 1943; psc†; *b* 23 Jan. 1897; *o s* of Capt. Robert George Cooke and Sarah Louisa, *d* of Thomas Connolly, Dundalk, Co. Louth; *m* 1922, Löie Howard (*d* 1979), *d* of Frank Shawcross-Smith, Buxton, Derbyshire; two *d*. *Educ*: Warwick Sch.; RMC Sandhurst; Staff Coll., Camberley. 2nd Lieut ASC, 1915; Capt., 1926; Bt Major, 1937; Major, 1938; Lieut-Col, 1940; Col, 1942; Brig., 1943. Served France, Belgium, Egypt and Syria, 1914–19 (severely wounded twice). Staff Coll., 1930–31; Staff Appointments: Aldershot Command, 1932–34; Southern Command, 1934–36; Active Service, Palestine Rebellion, 1937–38; GSO2, War Office, 1938–40. AA&QMG, Narvik, March 1940; AA&QMG 54 Div., July 1940; AQMG (ops) Eastern Command, 1941; DQMG 1st Army, Aug. 1942; DQMG, AFHQ, N Africa, Dec. 1942; DA&QMG 9 Corps BNAF, March 1943; Brig. "Q" 15 Army Group, July 1943; DA&QMG 5 Army, Italy, Sept. 1943; Brig. i/c Administration, HQ L of C 21st Army Group, Nov. 1943–Feb. 1945; Col i/c Admin S Wales District, 1945–46; Brig. "Q" GHQ, Middle East, 1946–47; Brig. i/c Administration, British Troops in Egypt, 1947; invalided out of Army as result of war wounds, 1949. Croix de Guerre, 1944. *Address*: c/o Mrs Thom, Kernick House, 2 Poltair Road, St. Austell PL25 4LR; c/o Lloyds Bank Ltd, Bournemouth, Dorset. *Died 29 Sept. 1984.*

**COOKE, Tom Harry;** Group Editorial Director, St Regis Newspapers Ltd (publishers of the Bolton Evening News, and weekly newspapers in Lancashire, South Yorkshire and north-east England), 1979–81, retired; *b* 26 March 1923; *er s* of Tom Cooke and Dorothy Cooke; *m* 1952, Jean Margaret Taylor; four *d*. *Educ*: Bacup and Rawtenstall Grammar Sch. Served RAF, 1942–47. Journalist on weekly, evening and morning papers in Lancs, 1939–51; Parly and Lobby Corresp. with Kemsley (now Thomson) Newspapers, 1951–59; Asst Editor, Evening Telegraph, Blackburn, 1959–64; Dep. Editor, The Journal, Newcastle upon Tyne, 1964–65; Editor-in-Chief, Bolton Evening News and Lancashire Journal Series, 1965–79. Pres., Guild of Brit. Newspaper Editors, 1975–76; Mem., Press Council, 1976–83. *Recreations*: music, esp. opera; travel, reading. *Address*: MG-CA 268, Carrasquetes, Javea 03737, Alicante, Spain. *T*: (96) 579–39–48. *Club*: Royal Over-Seas League. *Died 5 Oct. 1987.*

**COOPER OF STOCKTON HEATH,** Baron *cr* 1966, of Stockton Heath (Life Peer); **John Cooper,** MA; General Secretary and Treasurer, National Union of General and Municipal Workers, 1962–73; National Water Council, 1973–77; *b* 7 June 1908; *s* of late John Ainsworth Cooper and of Annie Lily Cooper (*née* Dukes); *m* 1934, Nellie Spencer (marr. diss. 1969); three *d*; *m* 1969, Mrs Joan Rogers. *Educ*: Stockton Heath Council Sch.; Lymm Grammar Sch., Cheshire. Employed Crosfields Soap Works, Warrington, 1924–28; NUGMW, 1928–73. District Sec., Southern Dist, 1944–61; Chm., 1952–61. Member: Manchester CC, 1936–42; LCC, 1949; Alderman, 1952–53; London Labour Party Executive; MP (Lab) Deptford, 1950–51; PPS to Sec. of State for Commonwealth Relations, 1950–51. Member: NEC Labour Party, 1953–57; TUC Gen. Council, 1959–73 (Pres., TUC, 1970–71). Chm., British Productivity Council, 1965–66; Mem., Thames Conservancy, 1955–74. Governor various instns, etc. MA Oxon. Prix de la Couronne Française, 1970. *Address*: 23 Kelvin Grove, Chessington, Surrey. *T*: 01-397 3908. *Died 2 Sept. 1988.*

**COOPER, Sqdn Ldr Albert Edward,** MBE 1946; formerly: Managing Director, Dispersions Ltd; Director, Ault & Wiborg International Ltd; *b* 23 Sept. 1910; *s* of Albert Frederick Smith and Edith Alice Cooper, Withernsea, Yorks; *m* 1st, 1933, Emily Muriel (*decd*), *d* of William John Nelder, Launceston; one *d*; 2nd, 1978, Margaret de

Gignac, d of Edward Gerrard Rabette, Portarlington, Queen's Co., Eire. Educ: London Coll. for Choristers; Australia. Entered politics, 1935, when elected to Ilford Borough Council; Chairman: Electricity and Lighting Cttee; Education (Finance) and Legal and Parliamentary Cttees; Alderman, 1947. Served War of 1939–45; enlisted in RAF, 1940, and served as navigator in Coastal Command. Contested (C) Dagenham, Gen. Election, 1945; MP (C)Ilford South, 1950–66, 1970–Feb. 1974; PPS to President of the Board of Trade, 1952–54. Recreations: cricket, swimming, bridge, and motoring. Address: 74 John Aird Court, W2. Died 12 May 1986.

COOPER, (Arthur William) Douglas; art historian and critic; Slade Professor of Fine Art, Oxford University, 1957–58; b London, 20 Feb. 1911. Educ: various European Univs. Dep.-Dir, Monuments and Fine Arts Branch, Control Commn for Germany, 1944–46; Lectr, Courtauld Institute of Art; Flexner Lectr, Bryn Mawr, 1961; Mem. Real Patronato of Prado Mus., Madrid; Fellow (hc), Fogg Mus., Harvard Univ.; Chevalier de la Légion d'Honneur. Publications: Letters of Van Gogh to Emile Bernard, 1937; The Road to Bordeaux, 1940; Paul Klee, 1949; Turner, 1949; Juan Gris, 1949; Leger, 1949; Degas Pastels, 1954; Catalogue of the Courtauld Collection, 1954; Van Gogh Water Colours, 1955; Toulouse-Lautrec, 1956, Graham Sutherland, 1961; De Staël, 1962; Picasso: Les Déjeuners, 1962; Picasso: Theatre, 1968; The Cubist Epoch, 1971; Braque: The Great Years, 1973; Juan Gris: catalogue raisonné, 1977; The Letters of Paul Gauguin to the Brothers Van Gogh, 1983; (with Gary Tinterow) The Essential Cubism, 1983. Address: Monte Carlo Star, Monte Carlo.
Died 1 April 1984.

COOPER, Sir Charles (Eric Daniel), of Woollahra, 5th Bt, cr 1863; b 5 Oct. 1906; s of Sir Daniel Cooper, 4th Bt, and Lettice Margaret, y d of 1st Viscount Long; S father, 1954; m 1st, 1931, Alice Estelle (d 1952), y d of late William Manifold, Victoria, Australia; 2nd, 1953, Mary Elisabeth, e d of Capt. J. Graham Clarke, Frocester Manor, Glos; two s. Educ: Harrow; RMC Sandhurst. Lieut 1st The Royal Dragoons, 1926; Capt., 1935; Major, 1945. Served War of 1939–45. Recreations: hunting and shooting. Heir: s William Daniel Charles Cooper, b 5 March 1955. Address: Cranbourne Grange, Sutton Scotney, Winchester SO21 3NA. Club: Cavalry and Guards.
Died 14 May 1984.

COOPER, Lady Diana, (Diana, Viscountess Norwich); b 29 Aug. 1892; 3rd d of 8th Duke of Rutland, KG (d 1925), and Violet Lindsay (d 1937); m 1919 (as Lady Diana Manners) A. Duff Cooper, 1st Viscount Norwich (cr 1952), PC, GCMG, DSO (d 1954); one s. Nurse at Guy's Hospital during European War, 1914–18. Took leading part in Max Reinhardt's play, The Miracle, that showed, on and off, for 12 years in London and provincial towns, in USA (New York and all the great cities), and on the Continent (Prague, Buda-Pest, Vienna, Dortmund, Salzburg). Pres., Order of Charity. Publications: The Rainbow Comes and Goes, 1958; The Light of Common Day, 1959; Trumpets from the Steep, 1960. Address: 10 Warwick Avenue, W2. Died 16 June 1986.

COOPER, Douglas; see Cooper, A. W. D.

COOPER, Sir Francis Ashmole, (Sir Frank), 4th Bt cr 1905; Chairman, Ashmole Investment Trust Ltd, 1969–74; b 9 Aug. 1905; s of Sir Richard Ashmole Cooper, 2nd Bt. and Alice Elizabeth (d 1963), d of Rev. E. Priestland, Spondon; S brother, 1970; m 1933, Dorothy F. H., d of Emile Deen, Berkhamstead, and Maggie Louise Deen; one s two d (and one d decd). Educ: Lancing Coll.; King's Coll., Cambridge (MA); University Coll., London (PhD). Joined Cooper, McDougall and Robertson Ltd, 1926; on leave to University College, 1931–36; Technical Director, 1940–62; retired, 1962. Recreation: yachting. Heir: s Richard Powell Cooper [b 13 April 1934; m 1957, Angela Marjorie, e d of Eric Wilson, Norton-on-Tees; one s two d]. Address: La Bastide de la Maraouro, 06490 Tourrettes sur Loup, France. Clubs: Carlton, Royal Thames Yacht, Royal Motor Yacht (Sandbanks, Poole). Died 17 June 1987.

COOPER, Sir Gilbert (Alexander), Kt 1972; CBE 1964; ED 1943; MLC, Bermuda, 1968–72, retired; b 31 July 1903; s of Alexander Samuel and Laura Ann Cooper. Educ: Saltus Grammar Sch., Bermuda; McGill Univ., Canada (BCom). Mem., Corp. of Hamilton, Bermuda, 1946–72; Mayor of Hamilton, 1963–72. Mem., House of Assembly, 1948–68 (Chm. House Finance Cttee, 1959–68). Recreations: music, painting, sailing, swimming. Address: Shoreland, Pembroke, Bermuda HMO5. T: 295–4189. Club: Royal Bermuda Yacht. Died 28 May 1989.

COOPER, Sir Henry; see Cooper, Sir W. H.

COOPER, Joshua Edward Synge, CB 1958; CMG 1943; retired from the Foreign Office; b 3 April 1901; e s of late Richard E. Synge Cooper and Mary Eleanor, y d of William Burke; m 1934, Winifred, d of Thos F. Parkinson; two s. Educ: Shrewsbury; Brasenose Coll., Oxford; King's Coll., London. Civil Service, 1925; Trans. Air Min. (attached FO), 1936; returned to FO, 1943; retired, 1961. Publications: Russian Companion, 1967; Four Russian Plays, 1972.

Address: Kingsfield, Cobbler's Hill, Great Missenden, Bucks. T: Great Missenden 2400. Died 14 June 1981.

COOPER, Maj.-Gen. Kenneth Christie, CB 1955; DSO 1945; OBE 1943; psc; idc; retired; b 18 Oct. 1905; 4th s of E. C. Cooper; m 1933, Barbara Harding-Newman; one s one d. Educ: Berkhamsted Sch. 2nd Lieut, Royal Tank Corps, 1927; India, 1930–34; Adjt, 6 RTR, Egypt, 1935–38; Staff Coll., 1939; Bde Major, 23 Armd Bde, 1939–40; CO Fife and Forfar Yeomanry, 1941–42; GSO1, 9 Corps, N Africa, 1942–43; BGS, AFHQ, N Africa-Italy, 1943–44; Comdr, 7 Armoured Bde, 1945–46; Brig., Royal Armoured Corps, N Comd, 1947–48; Chief of Staff, West Africa Comd, 1948–50; idc 1951; Asst Comdt, Staff Coll., 1952–53. GOC 7th Armoured Div., Dec. 1953–March 1956; Chief of Staff to the Comdr-in-Chief Allied Forces, Northern Europe, 1956–59; retired, 1959. Recreations: Rugby, hockey, lawn tennis, shooting. Address: West End House, Donhead St Andrew, Shaftesbury, Dorset. Club: Army and Navy.
Died 4 Sept. 1981.

COOPER, Dr Leslie Hugh Norman, OBE 1973; FRS 1964; CChem, FRSC, FIBiol, FGS; formerly Deputy Director, Marine Biological Laboratory, Plymouth, retired 1972; b 17 June 1905; s of Charles Herbert Cooper and Annie Cooper (née Silk), Prestatyn, Clwyd; m 1935, Gwynedd Daloni Seth Hughes, Bangor, Gwynedd; four s one d. Educ: John Bright Grammar Sch., Llandudno; University Coll. of North Wales, Bangor. PhD 1927, DSc 1938, Univ. of Wales. Chemist, Rubber Research Assoc., 1927–29; Chemist, Imperial Chemical Industries, 1929–30; Chemist at the Marine Biological Laboratory, Plymouth, engaged on the study of the physics and chemistry of the ocean as a biological environment, 1930–72; continuing research at Plymouth on quaternary oceanography and on the application of plate tectonics to biological problems. Hon. DSc Exon, 1974. Publications: numerous papers on oceanography. Address: 2 Queens Gate Villas, Lipson, Plymouth PL4 7PN. T: Plymouth 661174. Died 20 Sept. 1985.

COOPER, Prof. Malcolm McGregor, CBE 1965; Emeritus Professor, University of Newcastle upon Tyne, since 1972; b Havelock North, New Zealand, 17 Aug. 1910; s of Laurence T. Cooper, farmer, and Sarah Ann Cooper; m 1937, Hilary Mathews, Boars Hill, Oxford; three d. Educ: Napier Boys High Sch., NZ; Massey Agricultural Coll., Palmerston North, NZ; University Coll., Oxford. BAgrSc (NZ), 1933; Rhodes Scholarship, 1933; Oxford, 1934–37; Diploma Rural Econ., 1935; BLitt in Agric. Economics, 1937. Returned to NZ 1937. Mem. of Staff, Dept of Scientific and Industrial Research, till 1940, when appointed Lecturer in Dairy Husbandry at Massey Agric. Coll. Served War of 1939–45, with NZ Mil. Forces, 1941–46; in Italy with 2 NZ Div. in an Infantry battalion, 1943–45; rank of Major on demobilisation; returned to Massey as Head of Dept of Dairy Husbandry, 1946; Prof. of Agriculture, Univ. of London, 1947–54; Prof. of Agriculture and Rural Economy, and Dean, Fac. of Agriculture, Univ. of Newcastle upon Tyne, 1954–72; Pro-Vice-Chancellor, Univ. of Newcastle upon Tyne, 1971–72. Nat. Res. Coordinator, Instituto Nacional Investigaciones Agrarias, Spain, 1972–75. President: British Grassland Soc., 1958–59; British Soc. of Animal Production, 1972–73; formerly Member: Nature Conservancy Council; Agricultural Advisory Council; Advisory Board, Pig Industry Development Authority; Agricultural Research and Advisory Cttee for Government of Sudan; Scientific Advisory Panel of the Minister of Agriculture; Agricultural Cttee of UGC; Chm., Beef Recording Assoc. (UK) Ltd. Hon. Life Mem., British Soc. of Animal Production, 1979. FRSE 1956, Hon. FRASE 1969. Hon. Fellow, Wye Coll., London Univ., 1979. Massey Ferguson Award for services to agriculture, 1970. Hon DSc Massey Univ., NZ, 1972. Publications: (in collaboration) Principles of Animal Production (New Zealand), 1945; Beef Production, 1953; Competitive Farming, 1956; Farm Management, 1960; Grass Farming, 1961; Sheep Farming, 1965; (with M. B. Willis) Profitable Beef Production, 1972; technical articles on agricultural topics. Recreations: Rugby football (Rugby Blue, 1934, 1935 and 1936; Capt. OURFC 1936, and Sec. 1935; capped for Scotland, 1936); summer sports, reading, farming. Address: Holme Cottage, Longhoughton, Alnwick, Northumberland. Club: Farmers'.
Died 1 Sept. 1989.

COOPER, Martin Du Pré, CBE 1972; Music Editor of the Daily Telegraph, 1954–76; b 17 Jan. 1910; s of late Cecil Henry Hamilton Cooper, and late Cecil Stephens; m 1940, Mary, d of late Lieut-Col Douglas Stewart, DSO, and late Mabel Elizabeth Ponsonby; one s three d. Educ: Winchester; Oxford (BA). Studied music in Vienna, 1932–34, with Egon Wellesz; Asst Editor, Royal Geographical Soc. Journal, 1935–36; Music Critic: London Mercury, 1934–39; Daily Herald, 1945–50; The Spectator, 1946–54; joined music staff of Daily Telegraph, 1950; Editor of Musical Times, 1953–56. Pres., Critics' Circle, 1959–60. Mem., Editorial Bd of New Oxford History of Music, 1960–. Hon. FTCL; Hon. FRAM 1976. Publications: Gluck, 1935; Bizet, 1938; Opéra Comique, 1949; French Music from the death of Berlioz to the death of Fauré, 1950; Russian Opera, 1951; Les Musiciens anglais d'aujourd'hui, 1952; Ideas and

Music, 1966; Beethoven—the Last Decade, 1970; *translations:* C. M. von Weber: Writings on Music, 1981; Mikhail Drustin: Igor Stravinsky, 1983; Writings of Pierre Boulez, 1986. *Address:* 34 Halford Road, Richmond, Surrey.          *Died* 15 *March* 1986.

**COOPER, Wilfred Edward S.;** *see* Shewell-Cooper.

**COOPER, Sir (William) Henry,** Kt 1985; CBE 1965; ED 1956; Chancellor, University of Auckland, 1968–74, retired; *b* 2 Oct. 1909; *s* of Walter and Ruth Cooper; *m* 1936, Elizabeth McLaren (*d* 1984); one *d* (and one *s* decd). *Educ:* Auckland Grammar Sch.; Univ. of Auckland (MA); Assistant Master: Dilworth Sch., 1933–34; Auckland Grammar Sch., 1935–54; Headmaster, Auckland Grammar Sch., 1954–72; Pro Chancellor, Univ. of Auckland, 1961–67; Mem. Council, Univ. of Auckland, 1955–82. President: Univ. of Auckland Foundn, 1984; Auckland Med. Res. Foundn, 1985. Hon. LLD Auckland, 1974. *Recreations:* golf, music, gardening. *Address:* 22 Ridings Road, Remuera, Auckland 5, New Zealand. *T:* 5200.858. *Club:* Grammar (Auckland).
                                                      *Died* 4 *Sept.* 1990.

**COOPER-KEY, Sir Neill,** Kt 1960; *b* 26 April 1907; *er s* of late Captain E. Cooper-Key, CB, MVO, Royal Navy; *m* 1941, Hon. Lorna Harmsworth, *er d* of 2nd Viscount Rothermere, and of Margaret Hunam (*née* Redhead); one *s* one *d*. *Educ:* RNC, Dartmouth. Served War of 1939–45, Irish Guards. Consultant and Dir of cos, formerly Vice-Chm., Associated Newspapers Group Ltd (Dir, 1944–72). Mem., Cttee of Management, RNLI, 1957–67. MP (C) Hastings, 1945–70. *Clubs:* Carlton, White's.
                                                      *Died* 5 *Jan.* 1981.

**COORAY, His Eminence Thomas Benjamin, Cardinal,** OMI; BA, PhD, DD; Archbishop of Colombo (RC), 1947–76, then Archbishop Emeritus; *b* 28 Dec. 1901. *Educ:* St Joseph's Coll., Colombo; University Coll., Colombo; St Bernard's Seminary, Colombo; The Angelicum, Rome. Prof. of Botany and Latin, St Joseph's Coll., Colombo, 1931; Superior of Oblate Seminary, Colombo, and Prof. of Moral Theology, Pastoral Theology and Canon Law, St Bernard's Seminary, Colombo, 1937; Pres., Sri Lanka Bishops' Conference, 1947–76; created Cardinal, 1965; Member, Pontifical Commn for Revision of Canon Law, 1968–82. Founder Mem., Fedn of Asian Bishops' Confs (FABC), 1970–. *Publications:* booklets on religious matters. *Address:* Cardinal's Residence, Tewatta, Ragama, Sri Lanka. *T:* 538.208.                        *Died* 29 *Oct.* 1988.

**COPE, John Wigley,** MA, MB, BChir Cantab, FRCS; retired; formerly Surgeon in charge Ear, Nose and Throat Department, St Bartholomew's Hospital; *b* 1 Nov. 1907; *o s* of J. J. Cope, Widney Manor, Warwicks; *m* 1937, Muriel Pearce Brown, Reading; two *s* one *d*. *Educ:* King Edward's Sch., Birmingham; Trinity Coll., Cambridge; St Bartholomew's Hosp., London. Demonstrator in Anatomy, St Bartholomew's Med. Coll., 1935. Served with RAFVR (Med. Branch) as Aural Specialist, 1940–45 (Sqdn-Ldr). Aural Surgeon, Royal Waterloo Hosp., 1946; Surgeon, Royal National Throat, Nose and Ear Hosp., 1946. Dean, St Bartholomew's Hosp. Med. Coll., 1962–68. Royal Society of Medicine: Pres., Section of Otology, 1970–71 (formerly Sec.); Hon. Mem., Section of Laryngology, 1983. *Recreations:* shooting, rock-climbing, gardening, golf. *Address:* Owls Hatch Cottage, Seale, near Farnham, Surrey. *T:* Runfold 2456.                           *Died* 15 *June* 1987.

**COPESTAKE, Dr Thomas Barry;** Chief Engineer and Scientist, Department of Economic Development, Northern Ireland, since 1985; *b* 19 Feb. 1930; *s* of Thomas Albert Copestake and Lucy Irene Maddox; *m* 1955, Mavis Adelaide Enser; three *s* one *d*. *Educ:* Longton High Sch., Stoke-on-Trent; Manchester Univ. (BSc, PhD). Research Fellow, National Research Council, Ottawa, 1953; Hirst Research Centre, GEC, Wembley, 1955; Min. of Technology, 1967; Programmes Analysis Unit, Harwell, 1972; Dept of Trade and Industry, 1977. *Publications:* papers on photochemistry and radiation chemistry. *Recreations:* opera, photography, collecting pottery. *Address:* Department of Economic Development, IDB House, Chichester Street, Belfast BT1 4JX. *T:* Belfast 234488.
                                                      *Died* 31 *Jan.* 1989.

**COPLAND, Aaron;** American composer; *b* Brooklyn, NY, 14 Nov. 1900; *s* of Harris M. Copland and Sarah Mittenthal; unmarried. *Educ:* Boys' High Sch., Brooklyn, NY; studied music privately; Fontainebleau Sch. of Music, France; Paris (with Nadia Boulanger). Guggenheim Fellow, 1925, 1926. Lecturer on music, New School for Social Research, NY, 1927–37; organised Copland-Sessions Concerts, which presented American music, 1928–31; tour of Latin-American countries, as pianist, conductor and lecturer in concerts of American music, 1941 and 1947; Charles Eliot Norton Prof. of Poetry, Harvard Univ., 1951–52. *Principal works:* Symphony for Organ and Orchestra, 1924; First Symphony (orch.), 1928; Short Symphony (No. 2), 1933; El Salon Mexico (orch.), 1936; Billy the Kid (ballet), 1938; Piano Sonata, 1941: Lincoln Portrait (speaker and orch.), 1942; Rodeo (ballet), 1942; Sonata for Violin and piano, 1943; Appalachian Spring (ballet, Pulitzer Prize), 1944; Third

Symphony, 1946; Clarinet Concerto, 1948; Piano Quartet, 1950; Twelve Poems of Emily Dickinson, 1950; The Tender Land (Opera), 1954; Symphonic Ode (1929, rev. 1955); Piano Fantasy, 1957; Orchestral Variations, 1958; Nonet, 1960; Connotations for Orchestra, 1962; Dance Panels, 1962; Music for a Great City, 1964; Emblems for Symphonic Band, 1964; Inscape for Orchestra, 1967; Duo for flute and piano, 1971; Three Latin-American Sketches, 1972; various film scores. Pres., American Acad. Arts and Letters, 1971; Member: National Institute of Arts and Letters; American Academy of Arts and Sciences; President of the Edward MacDowell Assoc., 1962; American Soc. of Composers, Authors and Publishers; Hon. Mem., Accademia Santa Cecilia, Rome; Hon. Mem., RAM, 1959; Hon. Dr of Music, Princeton Univ., 1956, Harvard Univ., 1961; Hon. Dr of Humane Letters, Brandeis Univ., 1957. FRSA 1960. Presidential Medal of Freedom, Washington, 1964; Howland Prize, Yale Univ., 1970; Haendel Medallion, NY, 1970; Chancellor's Medal, Syracuse Univ., 1975; Creative Arts Award, Brandeis Univ., 1975; *Publications:* What to listen for in music, 1939 (revised 1957); Our New Music, 1941; Music and Imagination, 1952; Copland on Music, 1960; The New Music 1900–1960, 1968. *Address:* c/o Boosey and Hawkes, 24 West 57 Street, New York, USA. *Clubs:* Harvard, Century Association (New York).                  *Died* 2 *Dec.* 1990.

**CORBET, Air Vice-Marshal Lancelot Miller,** CB 1958; CBE 1944; RAF retired; *b* Brunswick, Vic, Australia, 19 April 1898; *s* of late John Miller and late Ella Beatrice Corbet, Caulfield, Vic, Australia; *m* 1924, Gwenllian Elizabeth, *d* of late Thomas Powell and late May Maria Bennett, Claremont, Western Australia; one *s*. *Educ:* Melbourne High Sch.; Scotch Coll., Melbourne; Melbourne Univ. (MB, BS 1922). RMO, Perth (WA) Hospital, 1922–23, Perth Children's Hospital 1923; Hon. Asst Anæsthetist, Perth Hospital, 1931; Clinical Asst to Out-Patient Surgeon, Perth Hospital, 1931–32. Was Major AAMC; commanded 6th Field Hygiene Sect., 1930–32; entered RAF 1933; served in UK and India, 1933–37; Principal MO, W Africa, 1941–43; Principal MO, Transport Command, RAF, 1943–45; Principal MO, Malaya, 1945–46; Principal MO, British Commonwealth Air Forces, Japan, 1946–48; OC, RAF Hospital, Nocton Hall, 1949–52; Principal MO, HQBF, Aden, 1952–54; Principal MO, 2nd Tactical Air Force, 1954–56; Dep. Dir-Gen. of Medical Services, Air Ministry, 1956–58, retired. Hon. Life Member: BMA; AMA; Aviation Med. Soc. of Aust. and NZ; RAAF Assoc. KStJ. *Recreations:* lacrosse, tennis, squash, golf, etc. *Address:* Unit 201 Ventura House, Air Force Memorial Estate, Bull Creek Drive, Bull Creek, WA 6155, Australia. *T:* Perth 310 1004.
                                                      *Died* 30 *Jan.* 1990.

**CORBETT, Rupert Shelton,** MA, MChir Cantab; FRCS; retired 1961; *b* 11 Feb. 1893; 2nd *s* of late Henry Shelton Corbett. *Educ:* Diocesan Coll., South Africa; Stubbington House, Hampshire; Cambridge Univ.; St Bartholomew's Hosp., London. MRCS, LRCP 1917; FRCS; MA Cantab 1922; BCh 1922; MB 1923; MChir 1927; formerly: Surgeon, St Bartholomew's Hosp.; Surgeon, St Andrew's Hosp., Dollis Hill; Consulting Surgeon, Chalfonts and Gerrards Cross Hosp.; Examiner in Surgery, Universities of Cambridge and London; Mem. of Examining Board, Royal Coll. of Surgeons; Mayo Lectr, Ann Arbor, USA, 1955; First Gordon-Watson Memorial Lectr, 1958; Mem. Council, Assoc. of Surgeons of Great Britain and Ireland, 1957–59; Pres., Chiltern Medical Soc., 1960–61. Chm., Jersey District Nursing Assoc. Central Cttee, 1971–. Pres., Jersey Branch, Royal Commonwealth Soc.; Vice-Pres., St John Ambulance Assoc., Jersey. OStJ 1977 (SBStJ 1971). *Publications:* contributions in British Surgical Practice; various articles in med. jls. *Address:* Katrina, Beaumont Hill, St Peter, Jersey. *T:* Central 20065.
                                                      *Died* 28 *Jan.* 1985.

**CORBETT, Lt-Gen. Thomas William,** CB 1941; MC and Bar; psc; *b* 2 June 1888; *m* 1st, 1915, Flora Margaret Macdonell (*d* 1951); 2nd, 1952, S. N. E., widow of Lt-Col H. H. C. Withers, DSO, RE; one *d*. Served with Hodson's Horse and 2nd Royal Lancers: 2nd Lieut, Indian Army, 1908; Captain, 1915; Bt Major, 1919; Major, 1922; Bt Lt-Col, 1930; Lt-Col, 1933; Col, 1935; Maj.-Gen., 1940; served European War, 1914–19 (MC); a Corps Comdr, Middle East, 1942; CGS, Middle East, 1942; retired, 1943. *Recreation:* painting. *Address:* Panthill, Barcombe, E Sussex. *T:* Barcombe 400305. *Club:* Hurlingham.                              *Died* 28 *Dec.* 1981.

**CORBETT ASHBY, Dame Margery (Irene),** DBE 1967; LLD; Hon. President, International Alliance of Women; Hon. President, British Commonwealth League; *b* 19 April 1882; *d* of C. H. Corbett, sometime MP for E Grinstead, Woodgate, Danehill, Sussex, and Marie, *d* of George Gray, Tunbridge Wells; *m* 1910, Arthur Brian Ashby (*d* 1970), barrister, Inner Temple; one *s*. *Educ:* home; Newnham Coll., Cambridge. Sec. to the National Union of Suffrage Societies on leaving college; lectured on education and land questions from Liberal platforms; Liberal candidate, 1918, 1922, 1923, 1924, 1929 General Elections; 1937 and 1944 by-elections; substitute delegate for UK to Disarmament Conference, 1931–35; travelled and lectured all over Europe, in India, Pakistan, Near East, United States and Canada, speaking in English, French, and German.

Recreations: gardening and travelling. Address: Wickens, Horsted Keynes, West Sussex. T: Chelwood Gate 264. Club: University Women's. Died 15 May 1981.

**CORBETT-WINDER, Col John Lyon,** OBE 1949; MC 1942; JP; Lord-Lieutenant of Powys, 1974–86 (of Montgomeryshire, 1960–74); b 15 July 1911; o s of Major W. J. Corbett-Winder, Vaynor Park, Berriew, Montgomery (Lord Lieutenant of Montgomeryshire, 1944–50); m 1944, Margaret Ailsa, d of Lt-Col J. Ramsay Tainsh, CBE, VD; one s two d. Educ: Eton; RMC Sandhurst. 2nd Lieut, 60th Rifles, 1931; Lt-Col, 1942. Served War of 1939–45, Western Desert and N Africa, 1939–43 (despatches twice); Commanded: 44 Reconnaissance Regt; 1st Bn 60th Rifles; GSO1 Infantry Directorate, WO, 1944–47; commanded 2nd Bn 60th Rifles, Palestine, 1947–48 (despatches); AAG, HQ Southern Command, 1948–51; GSO1, HQ 53 Welsh Inf. Div., 1952–55; Col Gen. Staff, SHAPE Mission to Royal Netherlands Army, 1955–57; Dep. Mil. Sec., HQ, BAOR, 1957–58; retd 1958; RARO, 1958–69. Mem., Parly Boundary Commn for Wales, 1963–79. Pres., TA & VR Assoc. for Wales, 1977–81. Chm., Dyfed-Powys Police Authority, 1978–80 (Vice-Chm., 1976–78). JP Powys (formerly Montgomeryshire), 1959. Commander, Order of Orange Nassau, 1958. KStJ 1970 (CStJ 1966). Recreations: gardening, forestry. Address: Vaynor Park, Berriew, Welshpool, Powys SY21 8QE. T: Berriew (068685) 204.
Died 20 Dec. 1990.

**CORCORAN, Percy John; His Honour Judge Corcoran;** a Circuit Judge (formerly County Court Judge), since 1970; b 26 Nov. 1920; s of Michael Joseph and Sarah Corcoran, Macclesfield, S Australia; m 1949, Jean, JP, MSc, LCST; one s one d. Educ: Christian Brothers' Coll., Adelaide. Royal Australian Air Force, 1941–47. Called to Bar, Gray's Inn, 1948; practised as Barrister, 1948–70; Deputy Judge Advocate, 1953–57; Asst Recorder: Blackpool, 1959–70; Blackburn, 1962–70; Chm., Mental Health Tribunal, NW Area, 1962–70. Pres., Caterham District Scout Council. Recreations: golf, walking, music. Address: 18 Stanstead Road, Caterham, Surrey. T: Caterham 42423. Died 5 Oct. 1984.

**CORDEAUX, Lt-Col John Kyme,** CBE 1946; b 23 July 1902; yr s of late Col E. K. Cordeaux, CBE; m 1928, Norah Cleland (who obtained a divorce, 1953); one s (and one s decd); m 1953, Mildred Jessie Upcher. Educ: Royal Naval Colleges Osborne and Dartmouth. Served Royal Navy 1916–23; transf. Royal Marines (Lieut), 1923; RN Staff Coll., 1937. Served War, 1939–46; Naval Intelligence Div., 1939–42; Major, 1940; Actg Lieut-Col 1941; temp. Col, 1942; seconded to Foreign Office, 1942–46; Lieut-Col 1946. Contested (C), Bolsover Div. of Derbyshire, 1950 and 1951; prospective Conservative Candidate, North Norfolk Div., 1952–53; MP (C), Nottingham Central, 1955–64; promoted, as Private Member's Bill, Landlord and Tenant Act, 1962. Commander, Order of Orange-Nassau (Netherlands), 1944; Commander, Order of Dannebrog (Denmark), 1945; Haakon VII Liberty Cross (Norway), 1946. Publication: Safe Seat (novel), 1967. Recreations: Association football, cricket. Address: 11 Hyde Park Gardens, W2.
Died 4 Jan. 1982.

**CORI, Prof. Carl Ferdinand;** Biochemist, Department of Biochemistry, Harvard Medical School, Boston, Mass, since 1967; Professor of Biochemistry, Washington University School of Medicine, St Louis, Mo, 1931–67; b Prague, Czechoslovakia, 5 Dec. 1896; s of Carl Cori and Maria Lippich; went to US, 1922; naturalised, 1928; m 1920, Gerty T. (d. 1957), d of Otto Radnitz; one s; m 1960, Anne Fitz-Gerald Jones. Educ: Gymnasium, Trieste, Austria; (German) University of Prague (MD). Asst in Pharmacology, University of Graz, Austria, 1920–21; Biochemist State Inst. for Study of Malignant Disease, Buffalo, NY, 1922–31. Mem. Nat. Acad. of Sciences, Royal Society etc. Hon. ScD: Western Reserve, 1946, Yale, 1946, Boston Univ., 1948, Cambridge, 1949; Brandeis, 1965; Gustavus Adolphus Coll., 1965; Washington Univ., 1966; St Louis Univ., 1966; Monash, 1966; Granada, 1967; Univ. of Trieste, 1971. Shared Nobel Prize in Physiology and Medicine, 1947. Mid-West Award, 1946; Squibb Award, 1947; Sugar Research Foundation Award, 1947 and 1950; Willard Gibbs Medal, 1948. Publications: articles in scientific journals. Address: Department of Biochemistry, Harvard Medical School, Boston, Mass 02115, USA; (home) 1010 Memorial Drive, Cambridge, Mass 02138, USA.
Died 19 Oct. 1984.

**CORISH, Brendan;** TD Wexford, 1945–82, retired; Member of Council of State, 1964–77; b 19 Nov. 1918; m 1949; three s. Educ: Christian Brothers' Sch., Wexford. Vice-Chm. of Labour Party, Republic of Ireland, 1946–49; Party Chm., 1949–53; Parly Party Whip, 1947–54; Parly Sec. to Minister for Local Govt and Defence, 1948–51; Minister for Social Welfare, 1954–57; Party Leader, 1960–77; Tanaiste (Deputy Prime Minister) and Minister for Health and Social Welfare, 1973–77. Mem., Wexford CC, 1979–86; Alderman, Wexford Corp., 1979–81. Address: Belvedere Road, Wexford, Ireland. Died 17 Feb. 1990.

**CORMIE, (John) David,** MA, FCA; Chief Executive, building and home improvement product area, Reed International plc, since 1981; b 8 Dec. 1930; s of John George Cormie and Barbara Evelyn Cormie; m 1956, Margaret Killer; two s two d. Educ: City of London Sch.; Cambridge Univ. (MA). FCA 1958. National Service, 2nd Lieut RA. Articled Clerk, J. H. Hugill & Co., 1954–57; Procter & Gamble Ltd, 1957–60; Unilever, 1960–76: Commercial Dir, Lever Brothers Ltd, 1968; Chief Accountant, Unilever, 1970; Chm. and Chief Exec., Batchelors Foods, 1973; Finance Dir, Reed Internat. Ltd, 1976–81. Part-time Mem., British Telecom Bd 1981–. Inst. of Chartered Accountants in England and Wales: Mem. Council, 1971–; Dep. Pres., 1982–83. Governor, Royal Vet. Coll., 1980–. Recreations: theatre, golf, badminton, sailing, gardening, reading. Address: Colneford House, Earls Colne, Colchester CO6 2LG. T: Earls Colne 2026. Died 20 Feb. 1983.

**CORNER, George Washington;** Editor, American Philosophical Society, Philadelphia, Pennsylvania, since 1977; b 12 Dec. 1889; s of George Washington Corner, Jr, and Florence Elmer (née Evans); m 1915, Betsy Lyon Copping (d 1976), d of Rev. Bernard Copping and Cora (née Lyon); one s (one d decd). Educ: Boys' Latin Sch., Baltimore; Johns Hopkins Univ., Baltimore (AB 1909, MD 1913). Asst in Anatomy, Johns Hopkins Univ., 1913–14; Resident House Officer, Johns Hopkins Hosp., 1914–15; Asst Prof. of Anatomy, University of Calif., 1915–19; Associate Prof. of Anatomy, Johns Hopkins, 1919–23; Prof. of Anatomy, Univ. of Rochester, 1923–40; Dir, Dept of Embryology, Carnegie Instn of Washington, Baltimore, 1940–55; Historian, Rockefeller Inst., New York, 1956–60; Exec. Officer, Amer. Philosophical Soc., 1960–77. George Eastman Visiting Prof., Oxford, and Fellow, Balliol Coll., 1952–53; Vicary Lectr, RCS, 1936; Vanuxem Lectr, Princeton, 1942; Terry Lectr, Yale, 1944. Passano Award, 1958. Member: United States National Academy of Sciences (Vice-Pres., 1953–57); American Philosophical Soc. (Vice-Pres. 1953–56). Hon. Fellow Royal Society, Edinburgh; Foreign Mem., Royal Society, London. Dr (hc) Catholic Univ., Chile, 1942; Hon. DSc: Rochester, 1944; Boston, 1948; Oxford, 1950; Chicago, 1958; MA (by decree) Oxford, 1952; Hon. ScD Thomas Jefferson Univ., 1971; Hon. LLD: Tulane 1955; Temple, 1956; Johns Hopkins, 1975; Hon. DMedScience, Woman's Med. Coll., 1958; Hon. LittD Pa, 1965. Publications: Anatomical Texts of Earlier Middle Ages, 1927; Anatomy (a history), 1930; Hormones in Human Reproduction, 1942; Ourselves Unborn, 1944; ed. The Autobiography of Benjamin Rush, 1948; Anatomist at Large, 1958; George Hoyt Whipple and His Friends, 1963; Two Centuries of Medicine, 1965; History of the Rockefeller Institute, 1965; Doctor Kane of the Arctic Seas, 1972; numerous articles on histology, embryology, physiology of reproduction, history of medicine. Recreation: travel. Address: 1302 Deans Drive, Huntsville, Ala 35802, USA. Club: Franklin Inn (Philadelphia).
Died 28 Sept. 1981.

**CORNISH, Rt. Rev. (John) Vernon (Kestell);** Bishop-designate of Tasmania, since 1981; b 13 Oct. 1931; s of Henry Kestell Cornish and Eunice Ellen Harland; m 1960, Dell Judith, d of Samuel John Caswell; three s. Educ: Ipswich Grammar School, Queensland; Univ. of Queensland (BA 1st cl. Philosophy); St Francis' Theol. Coll. (ThL). Journalist on Queensland Times, 1949–54. Deacon 1957, priest 1958; Chaplain, St John's Univ. Coll., 1959; Diocesan Youth Chaplain, 1960–61; Chaplain, Southport School, 1961–66; Rector, St Matthew's, Sherwood, 1966–71; Hon. Canon, St John's Cathedral, Brisbane, 1971–73; Rector, St Luke's, Toowoomba, 1971–76; Archdeacon of the Downs, 1973–76; Dean of Perth, 1976–79; Asst Bishop, dio. Perth, 1979–81. Mem., Anglican Orthodox Jt Doctrinal Commn, 1980–. Publications: The Dean and the Dragons, 1976; A for Anglican, 1977. Recreations: reading, music, bush walking, watching cricket. Address: Bishopscourt, 26 Fitzroy Place, Sandy Bay, Tasmania 7005, Australia. Club: Rotary (Perth, WA). Died 26 Jan. 1982.

**CORNISH, Prof. Ronald James;** b Exeter, Devon, 30 Dec. 1898; s of William Henry Cornish and Eva Maud Eliza (née Horrell); m 1927, Edith Oliver Oliver; twin d. Educ: Hele's Sch., Exeter; Exeter Sch., Exeter; Manchester Univ. RGA, 1917–19; engineer, Messrs Mather & Platt, Ltd, Manchester, 1922–25; Manchester University: Asst Lecturer, 1925–29; Lecturer, 1929–34; Head of Dept of Municipal Engineering, 1934–53; Prof. of Municipal Engineering, 1953–61; Prof. Emeritus, 1966; seconded, Jan.-June 1960, as Prof. of Engineering in University Coll. of Ibadan, Nigeria; Prof. of Civil Engineering, Indian Institute of Technology, Hauz Khas, New Delhi, 1961–66 (Disting. Service Award, 1985); Head of Civil Engrg Dept, Malta Coll. of Arts, Science and Technology, 1966–70. Consultant, Allott and Lomax, 1970–79. FICE (Ex-Mem. Council); FIStructE (Ex-Mem. Council, Hon. Librarian, 1972–74, Lewis E. Kent award, 1974); MIMechE; FIE (Ind.). Hon. FIPHE; FRSH (Ex-Mem. Council). Jubilee Medal, 1977. Publications: papers in Proc. Royal Soc., Philosophical Magazine, Jls of Engineering Instns. Recreations: photography, walking, gardening. Address: 20 Oakdene Road, Marple, Stockport SK6 6PJ. T: 061–427 2768.
Died 8 May 1986.

**CORNISH, Rt. Rev. Vernon;** *see* Cornish, Rt Rev. J. V. K.

**CORNWALL, Gen. Sir J. H. M.;** *see* Marshall-Cornwall.

**CORNWALL, Rt. Rev. Nigel Edmund,** CBE 1955; Assistant Bishop, Diocese of Winchester, and Canon Residentiary of Winchester Cathedral, 1963–73; retired; *b* 13 Aug. 1903; *s* of late Alan Whitmore Cornwall, priest, sometime Archdeacon of Cheltenham; *m* 1959, Mary (*d* 1981), *d* of Rev. C. R. Dalton. *Educ:* Marlborough Coll; Oriel Coll., Oxford. BA, 3rd class History, 1926; MA 1930. Cuddesdon Theological Coll., 1926–27; Deacon, Diocese of Durham, 1927; Curate, St Columba's, Southwick, Sunderland, 1927–30; Priest, Durham, 1928; Chaplain to Bishop of Colombo, 1931–38; Curate, St Wilfred's, Brighton, 1938–39; Missionary Priest of Diocese of Masasi, 1939–49; Headmaster, St Joseph's Coll., Chidya, 1944–49; Bishop of Borneo, 1949–62. Commissary to Bishop of Kuching, in England, 1963–. *Address:* The Hermitage, Cheriton Road, Winchester. *T:* Winchester 55837.
*Died 19 Dec. 1984.*

**CORNWALLIS, 2nd Baron,** *cr* 1927, of Linton, Kent, in County of Kent; **Wykeham Stanley Cornwallis,** KCVO 1968; KBE 1945; MC; DL; Lord Lieutenant of Kent and Custos Rotulorum, 1944–72; HM's Lieutenant for City and County of Canterbury, 1944–72; one of HM's Lieutenants for City of London; President: Whitbread Fremlin's Ltd; Isherwood, Foster & Stacey; former Director: Royal Insurance Co. (Chairman, London Board; Local Director and Chairman, Kent Board); Barclays Bank (Local Director Maidstone and Canterbury Districts); Whitbread Investment Co.; former Chairman, Albert E. Reed & Co.; *b* 14 March 1892; *s* of 1st Baron and Mabel (*d* 1957), *d* of O. P. Leigh, Belmont Hall, Cheshire; *S* father, 1935; *m* 1st, 1917, Cecily Etha Mary (*d* 1943), *d* of Sir James Walker, 3rd Bt of Sand Hutton; one *s* (one *d* decd); 2nd, 1948, Esmé Ethel Alice (*d* 1969), *widow* of Sir Robert Walker, 4th Bt, Sand Hutton. *Educ:* Eton; RMC Sandhurst. Served European War, 1914–18, Royal Scots Greys and General Staff, France and Belgium (wounded, despatches, MC). Hon. Colonel: 5th Bn The Buffs, E Kent Regt, 1956–67; 415 Coast Regt RA (TA), 1935–56; 8th Bn (Territorial), The Queen's Regt, 1967–68. Pro-Chancellor, Univ. of Kent at Canterbury, 1962–72. President: Inst. of Packaging, 1961–64; (former) Kent County Boy Scouts Assoc.; Kent County Playing Fields Assoc.; (former) Kent County Agricultural Soc.; Kent Assoc. of Workmen's Clubs; Kent Squash Raquets Assoc.; Marden and District Commercial Fruit Show; Vice-Pres., Kent Co. Royal British Legion; Patron: Kent Assoc. of Boys' Clubs; Folkestone Race Course; Vice-Patron: Kent County Society; Assoc. of Men of Kent and Kentish Men; Life Vice-Pres. and formerly Trustee of MCC (Pres. 1948); Trustee RASE; Kent County Council: Vice-Chm., 1931–35; Chm., 1935–36, late Alderman; Patron, Kent Mayors' Assoc.; Chm. Kent War Agricultural Executive Cttee, 1939–46; DL, JP Kent; former Vice-Pres., SE District T&AVR. Hon. DCL Univ. of Kent at Canterbury, 1968. Freeman, City of London. Hon. Freeman, Borough of Maidstone. Formerly: Provincial Grand Master, Masonic Province of East Kent; Provincial Grand Master, Kent and West Kent. Grand Master's Order of Service to Masonry. Edward Hardy Gold Medal, for service to County of Kent. KStJ. Knight Comdr, Order of Dannebrog (Denmark); Knight, Order of Mark Twain (USA). *Recreations:* Kent Cricket XI, 1919–26 (Captain, 1924–25–26; PP and Hon. Life Mem., Kent Co. Cricket Club). *Heir:* *s* Hon. Fiennes Neil Wykeham Cornwallis, OBE. *Address:* Ashurst Park, Tunbridge Wells, Kent TN3 0RD. *T:* Fordcombe 212; Dundurn House, St Fillans, Perthshire. *Clubs:* Cavalry and Guards, East India, Devonshire, Sports and Public Schools, MCC (Pres. 1948); (Patron) Kent County (Maidstone), etc.
*Died 4 Jan. 1982.*

**CORRY, Sir James Perowne Ivo Myles,** 3rd Bt, *cr* 1885; a Vice-President of King George's Fund for Sailors, The Royal Alfred Merchant Seamen's Society, and of Royal Merchant Navy School; *b* 10 June 1892; *s* of 2nd Bt and Charlotte, *d* of late J. Collins; *S* father, 1926; *m* 1st, 1921, Molly Irene (marr. diss., 1936), *y d* of late Major O. J. Bell; one *s* two *d*; 2nd, 1946, Cynthia, *widow* of Capt. David Polson, and *o d* of late Capt. F. H. Mahony and Mrs Francis Bliss; one *d*. *Educ:* Eton; Trinity Coll., Cambridge. *Heir:* *s* Lt-Comdr William James Corry, RN retd [*b* 1924; *m* 1945, Diana (*née* Lapsley); four *s* two *d*]. *Address:* Dunraven, Fauvic, Jersey, CI.
*Died 17 Feb. 1987.*

**CORYTON, Air Chief Marshal Sir (William) Alec,** KCB 1950 (CB 1942); KBE 1945; MVO 1919; DFC 1922; RAF retired; *b* 16 Feb. 1895; 3rd *s* of late William Coryton, Pentillie Castle, Cornwall; *m* 1925, Philippa Dorothea, *e d* of late Daniel Hanbury, Castle Malwood, Lyndhurst, *g d* of Sir Thomas Hanbury of La Mortola, Italy; three *d*. *Educ:* Eton; Cambridge. Rifle Brigade; wounded, 1915; RAF 1917; Flying Instructor to the Duke of York, 1919 (MVO); India N-WF 1920 (DFC); Dir of Operations (Overseas), Air Ministry, 1938–41 (CB); AOC Bomber Group, 1942–43; Air Ministry, 1943–44, Asst Chief of the Air Staff (Operations); Air Comdr, Third Tactical Air Force, and Bengal, Burma, SEAC,

1944–45 (KBE); Controller of Supplies (Air) Min. of Supply, 1946–50; Chief Exec. Guided Weapons, Min. of Supply, 1950–51; retired list, 1951. Managing Dir Engine Div., Bristol Aeroplane Co. Ltd 1951; Chm. and Man. Dir Bristol Aero-Engines, Ltd, 1955; Dep. Chm. (Resident in Bristol), Bristol Siddeley Engines Ltd, 1950–64, retired. *Address:* Two Leas, Langton-Matravers, Dorset BH19 3EU.
*Died 20 Oct. 1981.*

**COSBY, Brig. Noel Robert Charles,** CIE 1945; MC; Indian Army, retired; *b* 26 Dec. 1890; *s* of Robert Parkyn Cosby; *m* 1st, 1938, May Margrit Kellersberger (*d* 1942), Berne, Switzerland; no *c*; 2nd, 1960; Margaret Esther Remon Bunting. *Educ:* HMS Worcester, Greenhithe, Kent, for competitive entry to RN. Commissioned Indian Army, Jan. 1915 and posted 5th Royal Gurkas FF in Egypt; served Turkish attack on Suez Canal, 1915; Gallipoli, May–Dec. 1915 (evacuated wounded, despatches twice, MC); Mesopotamia, 1917–19 (despatches); almost continuous service on NW Frontier, India, regimentally and with Frontier Corps, 1921–45; Mohmand Ops, 1935 (despatches); Waziristan Ops, 1939–40 (wounded, despatches); retired 1945 after four years as Inspector-Gen. Frontier Corps with rank of Brig. *Recreation:* gardening. *Address:* Houmet Herbé, Alderney, CI.
*Died 27 Jan. 1981.*

**COSLETT, Air Marshal Sir (Thomas) Norman,** KCB 1963 (CB 1960); OBE 1942; CEng, FIMechE; idc; psc; *b* 8 Nov. 1909; *s* of Evan Coslett; *m* 1938, Audrey Garrett. *Educ:* Barry Grammar Sch.; Halton; Cranwell. Dep. Dir of Engineering Plans, Air Ministry, 1954; Senior Technical Staff Officer, HQ Coastal Command, 1957; Commandant, No 1 School of Technical Training, 1958–61; AOC No 24 Group, 1961–63; AOC-in-C, RAF Maintenance Command, 1963–66. Air Cdre, 1957; Air Vice-Marshal, 1962; Air Marshal, 1963; retired, 1966. *Recreation:* farming. *Address:* c/o Barclays Bank, Sandton City, Sandton, Republic of South Africa.
*Died 9 Nov. 1987.*

**COSSLETT, Dr Vernon Ellis,** FRS 1972; Reader in Electron Physics, University of Cambridge, 1965–75, then Emeritus; Fellow of Corpus Christi College, Cambridge, since 1963; *b* 16 June 1908; *s* of Edgar William Cosslett and Anne Cosslett (*née* Williams); *m* 1st, 1936, Rosemary Wilson (marr. diss. 1940); 2nd, 1940, Anna Joanna Wischin (*d* 1969); one *s* one *d*. *Educ:* Cirencester Grammar Sch.; Bristol Univ. BSc Bristol 1929; PhD Bristol 1932; MSc London 1939; ScD Cambridge 1963. Research at: Bristol Univ., 1929–30; Kaiser-Wilhelm Institut, Berlin, 1930–31; University Coll., London, 1931–32; Research Fellow, Bristol Univ., 1932–35; Lectr in Science, Faraday House, London, 1935–39; Research (part-time), Birkbeck Coll., London, 1936–39; Keddey-Fletcher-Warr Research Fellow of London Univ. (at Oxford), 1939–41; Lectr in Physics, Electrical Laboratory, Oxford Univ., 1941–46; ICI Fellow, Cavendish Laboratory, Cambridge, 1946–49; Lectr in Physics, Univ. of Cambridge, 1949–65. Past Pres., Royal Microscopical Soc.; Past Vice-Pres., Inst. of Physics; Past Pres., Assoc. of Univ. Teachers. Hon. DSc Tübingen, 1963; Hon. MD Gothenburg, 1974. Royal Medal, Royal Soc., 1979; Röntgen Medal (Remscheid), 1984. *Publications:* Introduction to Electron Optics, 1946 (1951); Practical Electron Microscopy, 1951; X-ray Microscopy (with W. C. Nixon), 1960; Modern Microscopy, 1966; many scientific papers. *Recreations:* gardening, mountain walking, listening to music. *Address:* 31 Comberton Road, Barton, Cambridge. *T:* Cambridge (0223) 262428.
*Died 21 Nov. 1990.*

**COSTAIN, Sir Albert (Percy),** Kt 1980; *b* 5 July 1910; *s* of William Percy Costain and Maud May Smith; *m* 1933, Joan Mary, *d* of John William Whiter; one *s* one *d*. *Educ:* King James, Knaresborough; Coll. of Estate Management. Production Dir on formation of Richard Costain Ltd, 1933; Chm., Richard Costain Ltd, 1966–69; Chm., Pre-stressed Concrete Development Group, 1952. MP (C) Folkstone and Hythe, 1959–83; Author of Home Safety Act, 1961; Parliamentary Private Secretary: to Minister of Public Bldg and Works, 1962–64; to Minister of Technology, 1970; to Chancellor of Duchy of Lancaster, 1970–72; to Sec. of State for the Environment, 1972–74. Member: Cttee of Public Accts, 1961–64, 1974–83; Estimates Cttee, 1960–61, 1965–70; Estimates Sub-Cttee on Building and Natural Resources, 1965–83; Chairmen's Panel, House of Commons, 1975–83. Joint Vice-Chm., Conservative Party Transport Cttee, 1964. Jt Sec., Conservative Housing and Local Govt Cttee, 1964–65, Jt Vice-Chm., 1965–66; All Party Tourists and Resorts Cttee: Sec., 1964–66; Vice-Chm., 1966–69; Chm., 1970–71; Vice-Chm., Conservative Party Arts, Public Building and Works Cttee, 1965–70; Chm., Cons. Party Horticulture Cttee, 1976–77. London Treas., Nat. Children's Home, 1950–60. FCIOB. *Recreations:* sailing, golf. *Address:* Inwarren, Kingswood, Surrey. *T:* Mogador 832443; 2 Albion Villas, Folkestone, Kent CT20 1RP. *Clubs:* Carlton; Walton Heath Golf.
*Died 5 March 1987.*

**COTT, Hugh Bamford,** ScD Cantab, DSc Glasgow; FRPS, FZS; Fellow of Selwyn College, Cambridge, since 1945; *b* 6 July 1900; *s* of late Rev. A. M. Cott, Ashby Magna; *m* 1928, Joyce Radford (decd); one *s* one *d*. *Educ:* Rugby Sch.; RMC, Sandhurst; Selwyn

Coll., Cambridge. Joined 1st Bn the Leics Regt; served in Ireland, 1919–21. 2nd class, Nat. Sciences Tripos, Pt I, 1925. Carried out zoological expeditions to SE Brazil, 1923; Lower Amazon, 1925–26; Zoological Society's Expedition to the Zambesi, 1927, Canary Islands, 1931, Uganda, 1952, Zululand, 1956, Central Africa, 1957; Lecturer in Hygiene, Bristol Univ., 1928–32; Asst and Lecturer in Zoology, Glasgow Univ., 1932–38; Strickland Curator and Lectr in the University of Cambridge, 1938–67; Lectr, 1945–67, and Dean, 1966–67, of Selwyn Coll., Cambridge. Founder Member, Soc. Wildlife Artists. War of 1939–45: Mem. Advisory Cttee on Camouflage, 1939–40; Capt. and Major (RE) MEF; served Western Desert, 1941 (despatches); Chief Instructor, Middle East Camouflage Sch., 1941–43; GSO 2 (Cam) Mountain Warfare Trg Centre, 1943–44. *Publications:* Adaptive Coloration in Animals, 1940; Zoological Photography in Practice, 1956; Uganda in Black and White, 1959; Looking at Animals: a zoologist in Africa, 1975; various scientific papers on adaptive coloration, feeding habits of tree frogs, camouflage, edibility of birds, ecology of crocodiles, etc published in Trans and Proc. of Zool Soc. London, Proc. R. Ent. Soc. London, Photographic Jl, Engineers' Jl etc. *Recreations:* travel, pen drawing, photography. *Address:* 10 Stoke Water House, Beaminster, Dorset DT8 3LW. *T:* Beaminster 862798.
*Died 18 April* 1987.

**COTTON, Prof. Harry,** MBE 1918; DSc; *b* 17 June 1889; *s* of John Thomas and Sophia Cotton; *m* 1915, Lilian Hall (decd); one *s*. *Educ:* Manchester Univ., resident at Hulme Hall. Asst Lecturer in Electrical Engineering and in Physics at Technical Coll., Huddersfield; Lecturer in Electrical Engineering at Technical Sch., St Helens; Lecturer at University Coll., Nottingham; Emeritus Prof. of Electrical Engineering at Nottingham Univ.; retired 1954; three years in France with the Meteorological Section RE during the war; practical training in Electrical Engineering at the Hanley Power Station and with the Westinghouse Electrical Co. Ltd. *Publications:* Electricity Applied to Mining; Mining Electrical Engineering; Design of Electrical Machinery; Advanced Electrical Technology; Electrical Transmission and Distribution; Electric Discharge Lamps; Principles of Illumination; Applied Electricity; Vector and Phasor Analysis of Electric Fields and Circuits; Basic Electrotechnology; Memoirs of an Army Meteorologist 1914–18 (in archives of Imperial War Museum and Meteorological Office); contributor to Journal of Institution of Electrical Engineers, World Power, Electrician, Electrical Review and Electrical Times. *Recreations:* music, painting. *Address:* St George's Lodge, Cherry Tree Road, Woodbridge, Suffolk. *T:* 3081.
*Died 27 July* 1985.

**COTTON, Henry;** *see* Cotton, T. H.

**COTTON, Michael James,** CBE 1979; ARIBA, MRTPI; Deputy Chairman, International Military Services Ltd (formerly Millbank Technical Services Ltd), since 1974 (Chief Executive, 1974–80); *b* 22 Dec. 1920; *s* of Clifford Cotton and Mildred L. (*née* Palmer); *m* 1945, Dorsey Jane (*née* Thomas); one *d*. *Educ:* School of Architecture and Dept of Civic Design, Liverpool University. War Service, 1940–46, Royal Marines 42 Commando (Captain). Asst Town Planner, Staffs CC, 1949–50; Architect Planner, Stevenage Development Corp., 1950–52; Asst Town Planner, Fedn of Malaya, 1952–54; Architect and Sen. Architect, Public Works Dept, Singapore, 1954–59; Sen. Architect, Directorate of Works, WO, 1959–64; Chm. Joint Post Office/MPBW R&D Group, 1964–66; Chief Architect, Scottish Office, 1966–67; Asst Dir Overseas Services, MPBW, 1967–69; Dir of Defence Services II, MPBW, later DoE, 1969–72; Dir, Home Estate Management, DoE, 1972–74. *Recreation:* golf. *Address:* Applecroft, Stoatley Rise, Haslemere, Surrey. *T:* Haslemere 51823. *Died 28 March* 1981.

**COTTON, (Thomas) Henry,** MBE 1946; late Flight Lieutenant RAFVR (invalided, 1943); golfer; Professional Golf Correspondent of Golf Monthly; Director and Founder Golf Foundation for development of youthful golfers; Golf Course Architect; *b* Holmes Chapel, Cheshire, 26 Jan. 1907; *m* 1939, Mrs Maria Isabel Estanguet Moss (*d* 1982). *Educ:* Alleyn's Sch. Played in first Boys' Golf Championship, 1921; asst at Fulwell, 1924; Rye, 1925; Cannes, 1926; professional Langley Park, 1927; Waterloo, Brussels, 1933; Ashridge, 1936; won Kent Professional Championship, 1926–27–28–29–30; Belgian Open, 1930, 1934, 1938; Mar del Plata, 1930; Dunlop Tournament, 1931, 1932, 1953, runner-up, 1959; News of the World Tournament, 1932 and 1939; British Open, 1934, 1937 and 1948 (1934 was First British win for 11 years); Italian Open, 1936; German Open, 1937–38–39; Silver King Tournament, 1937; Czechoslovak Open, 1937–38; Harry Vardon Trophy, 1938; Daily Mail £2000 Tournament, 1939; Penfold Tournament, 1939 and 1954; News Chronicle Tournament, 1945; Star Tournament, 1946; Prof. Golfers' Match Play Champion, 1946; French Open Champion, 1946 and 1947; Vichy Open Champion, 1946; represented Great Britain v America, 1929, 1937, 1947, 1953; Ryder Cup Team Capt., 1939, 1947 and 1953; Spalding Tournament, 1947; visited USA in 1929, 1931, 1947, 1948,

1956 and 1957; led US Open Qualifying, 1956; visited Argentine 1929, 1948, 1949 and 1950. Collected over £70,000 for Red Cross and other war charities in 130 matches organised by himself. Golf Consultant: Penina Golf Hotel, Portugal, 1968–75; Penina and Vale do Lobo Golf Clubs, 1978. Architect of golf courses: Abridge, Felixstowe, Canons Brook, Ampfield; Megéve and Deauville (France); Penina, Val de Lobo, Golf de Monte Gorda, and Monte Velho, Algarve (Portugal); Campo de Lagoa (Madeira); Castle Eden Golf Club, Eaglescliffe, Stirling, Gourock, Windmill Hill, Bletchley, Sene Valley, Folkestone, Ely, etc. Hon. Life Mem., Professional Golf Assoc. Vice-President: National Golf Clubs Advisory Bureau; Golf Writers' Assoc. *Publications:* Golf, 1932; This Game of Golf, 1948; My Swing, 1952; (Henry Cotton's) My Golfing Album, 1960; Henry Cotton Says, 1962; Studying the Golf Game, 1964; The Picture World of Golf, 1965; Golf in the British Isles, 1969; A History of Golf, 1973; Thanks for the Game, 1980. *Recreations:* painting, photography.
Knight Bachelor, New Year's Honours List, 1988.
*Died 22 Dec.* 1987.

**COUCHMAN, Dame Elizabeth (May Ramsay),** DBE 1961 (OBE 1941); JP; BA; *b* 19 April 1876; *d* of late Archibald Tannock and Elizabeth Ramsay Tannock; *m* 1917, Claude Ernest Couchman (decd). *Educ:* University of Western Australia (BA). President, Australian Women's National League, 1927–45; Mem., Australian Broadcasting Commission, 1932–42; Senior Vice-Pres., Royal Commonwealth Soc., 1950–61; office-bearer in many educational, patriotic and social-service organisations. Life Member: National Council of Women (Vic); Liberal Party (Vic). *Publications:* articles in the press on Liberal politics and current topics. *Club:* Australian Women's Liberal (Melbourne). *Died 18 Nov.* 1982.

**COUCHMAN, Adm. Sir Walter (Thomas),** KCB 1958 (CB 1954); CVO 1953; OBE 1939; DSO 1942; *b* 1905; *s* of Malcolm Edward Couchman, CSI, and Emily Elizabeth Ranking; *m* 1st, 1937, Phyllida Georgina Connellan (marr. diss. 1965); one *s* two *d*; 2nd, 1965, Mrs Hughe Hunter Blair (*d* 1972), widow of Lieut-Col D. W. Hunter Blair; 3rd, 1972, Mrs Daphne Harvey, widow of Captain E. H. N. Harvey, RN. *Educ:* RN Colleges Osborne and Dartmouth. Specialised in Naval Aviation, 1928; Staff Coll., 1935; Comdr 1938; Captain 1942; qualified Naval Pilot; comd HMS Glory, 1946; Dir of Naval Air Org. and Trg. Admty, 1947; Flag Officer Flying Trg, 1951; Rear-Adm., 1952; Flag Officer, Aircraft Carriers, 1954; Deputy Controller of Supplies (Air), Ministry of Supply, 1955–56; Vice-Adm. 1956; Flag Officer Air (Home), 1957–60; Adm. 1959; Vice-Chief, Naval Staff, Admiralty, 1960. *Address:* The Old Vicarage, Bulmer, Sudbury, Suffolk. *Died 2 May* 1981.

**COUGHTRIE, Thomas,** CBE 1958; Chairman, Bruce Peebles Industries Ltd, and Bruce Peebles Ltd, Edinburgh, 1961–67; *b* 28 Oct. 1895; *m* 1918, Mary Morrison; one *s* two *d*. *Educ:* Royal Coll. of Science, Glasgow. Founded Belmos Co. Ltd, Elect. Engrs, 1919 (merged with Bruce Peebles & Co. Ltd, Edinburgh, 1961); Mem. Royal Fine Art Commn for Scotland, 1962–67; Chm. Valuation Appeals Cttee, Co. Lanark, 1956–71; Director: Ailsa Investment Trust Ltd; Alva Investment Trust Ltd, 1958–63. JP Lanark, 1959. Hon. LLD Glasgow, 1959; Hon. DSc Heriot-Watt, 1968. *Recreations:* golf, gardening, reading. *Address:* Orchard House, Crossford, Carluke, Lanarkshire. *T:* Crossford 203. *Club:* East India, Devonshire, Sports and Public Schools.
*Died 29 Oct.* 1985.

**COULSHAW, Rev. Leonard,** CB 1949; MC 1917; FKC; Chaplain of the Fleet and Archdeacon of the Royal Navy, 1948–52; *b* 24 Feb. 1896; *s* of late Percy Dean Coulshaw and late Alice Maud Hatt; *m* 1932, Yvonne Cecilia Joan, *d* of Rev. C. Hanmer-Strudwick, Rector of Slawston, Leics; no *c*. *Educ:* Southend-on-Sea High Sch. for Boys; King's Coll., London; Ely Theological Coll. Served European War, 1914–18, Essex Regiment, 1914–20 (MC, despatches); left Army with rank of Captain. Ordained, 1923; Curate, St Andrew's, Romford, Essex; commissioned as Chaplain, RN, 1927; served in HMS Cyclops, 1927–29; RN Barracks, Portsmouth, 1929; HMS Iron Duke, 1929–30; HMS Effingham (Flagship East Indies Station), 1930–32; Royal Hospital Sch., Holbrook, 1932–34; Senior Chaplain HMS Ganges, 1934–37; HMS Royal Sovereign, 1937 (present at Coronation Review, Spithead); HMS Revenge, 1937. Chaplain Royal Naval Hospital, Malta, 1937–40; RM Depot, Lympstone, 1940–42; Senior Chaplain, RN Base, Lyness, 1942–44; Chaplain HM Dockyard, Sheerness, 1944–46; RM Barracks, Portsmouth, 1946–47; KHC, 1948–52; QHC, 1952; Vicar of: West End, Southampton, 1952–54; Frensham, 1954–65. *Address:* 4 Ashurst Court, Alverstoke, Gosport, Hants PO12 2TZ. *T:* Gosport 582467.
*Died 22 July* 1988.

**COULSON, Prof. John Metcalfe;** Professor of Chemical Engineering, University of Newcastle upon Tyne (formerly University of Durham), 1954–75 (on leave of absence to Heriot-Watt University, 1968–69), then Emeritus; *b* 13 Dec. 1910; *m* 1943, Clarice Dora Scott (*d* 1961); two *s*; *m* 1965, Christine Gould; one *d*. *Educ:* Clifton

Coll.; Christ's Coll., Cambridge; Imperial Coll. Royal Arsenal, Woolwich, 1935–39; Asst Lectr, Imperial Coll., 1939; Ministry of Supply (Royal Ordnance Factories), 1939–45; Lectr in Chem. Engineering, Imperial Coll., 1945–52; Reader, 1952–54. Hon. DSc Heriot-Watt, 1973. Davis Medal, IChemE, 1973. *Publications:* Chemical Engineering Vol. I and Vol. II (with Prof. J. F. Richardson), 1954 and 1955, 3rd edn 1977; contrib. Instn of Chem. Eng, Chem. Eng Science, etc. *Recreations:* chess, photography. *Address:* Flat 2, Wheatlands Court, 42 Wheatlands Road East, Harrogate, N Yorks.                                    *Died 6 Jan.* 1990.

**COULSON, Prof. Noel James,** MA; Professor of Oriental Laws, since 1967, and Head of Law Department, since 1981, School of Oriental and African Studies, University of London; *b* 18 Aug. 1928; *s* of George Frederick and Marjorie Elizabeth Coulson; *m* 1951, Muriel Ivatts; two *d. Educ:* Wigan Grammar Sch.; Keble Coll., Oxford (MA). Called to the Bar, Gray's Inn, 1961. Lieut, Parachute Regt, 1950–52. Lectr, 1954, and Reader, 1964, in Islamic Law, SOAS; Dean of Faculty of Law, Ahmadu Bello Univ., Nigeria, 1965–66; Visiting Professor of Comparative Law at Law Schools of American Universities: UCLA, 1961 and 1977; Chicago, 1968; Pennsylvania, 1970; Utah, 1977; Harvard, 1979, 1984. Chm., Bd of Studies in Laws, 1980–82, Dean, Faculty of Laws, 1984–86, Univ. of London. *Publications:* A History of Islamic Law, 1964, repr. 1971, 1979; Conflicts and Tensions in Islamic Jurisprudence, 1969; Succession in the Muslim Family, 1971; Commercial Law in the Gulf States, 1984; numerous articles in jls of Law and Islamic Studies. *Recreation:* golf (Captain, Effingham Golf Club, 1976). *Address:* Oak Tree Cottage, Chase Lane, Haslemere, Surrey. *T:* Haslemere 2994.
                                    *Died 30 Aug.* 1986.

**COULSON, Maj.-Gen. Samuel M.;** *see* Moore-Coulson.

**COULTER, Robert,** MC 1945; Controller, BBC Scotland, 1973–75, retired 1976; *b* 15 June 1914; *s* of John and Margaret Coulter, Glasgow; *m* 1940, Flora Macleod Bell; no *c. Educ:* Irvine Royal Academy; Glasgow Univ. MA Hons English Lit. and Lang. 1st Bn Royal Scots Fusiliers, India, UK, Madagascar and Burma, 1939–46 (Major). Principal English Master, Ayr Grammar Sch., 1946–48; Educn Administration, Belfast, 1948–53; BBC Northern Ireland, 1953–67: radio and TV producer; TV organiser; Asst Head of Programmes; Dir of Television, Uganda, 1967–69; Head of Programmes, BBC Scotland, 1969–73. IBA Res. Fellow at QUB, 1978 (Signposts report on youth employment and radio/TV special output, 1980). *Recreation:* recollections in tranquillity. *Address:* 91A Bentinck Drive, Troon, Ayrshire KA10 6HZ. *T:* Troon 315022.
                                    *Died 14 Nov.* 1987.

**COULTHARD, Alan George Weall; His Honour Judge Alan Coulthard;** a Circuit Judge since 1981; *b* Bournemouth, 20 Jan. 1924; *s* of late George Robert Coulthard and Cicely Eva Coulthard (*née* Minns); *m* 1948, Jacqueline Anna, *d* of late Dr T. H. James, Fishguard; two *s* two *d. Educ:* Watford Grammar Sch. Pilot, RAF, 1941–46 (Flt-Lt); 1st Officer, BOAC, 1946–48; Pilot and Staff Officer, RAF, 1948–58. Called to Bar, Inner Temple, 1959; practised at Bar, Swansea, 1959–81; Asst Recorder, 1970; a Recorder of the Crown Court, 1972–81; Hon. Recorder of Borough of Llanelli, 1975–81. Chm., Medical Appeals Tribunal for Wales, 1976–81. Contested (L) Pembrokeshire, 1964. Pres., Swansea Festival Patrons' Assoc., 1974–80. BBC sound and TV broadcasts, 1960–. *Recreations:* music, motor sport, ornithology, country life. *Address:* 9 Burlington Road, N10 1NJ. *T:* 01–883 6200. *Club:* Royal Air Force.
                                    *Died 25 June* 1988.

**COUNSELL, John William,** OBE 1975; Managing Director of the Theatre Royal, Windsor, since 1938; *b* 24 April 1905; *s* of Claude Christopher Counsell and Evelyn Counsell (*née* Fleming); *m* 1939, Mary Antoinette Kerridge; twin *d. Educ:* Sedbergh Sch.; Exeter Coll., Oxford. Mem. of the OUDS, 1923–26; formerly engaged as a tutor. First appearance on professional stage, Playhouse, Oxford, 1928; two tours of Canada with Maurice Colbourne in Shavian Repertory, 1928–29; leading juvenile, Northampton and Folkestone Repertory Cos, 1929–30; Stage Manager for Baliol Holloway's production of Richard III, New, 1930; Stage Dir, Scenic Artist and eventually Producer, Oxford Repertory Company, 1930–33; Producer and Joint Man.-Dir, Windsor Repertory Company, 1933–34; Lover's Leap, Vaudeville, 1934; toured as Tubbs in Sweet Aloes, 1936; toured S Africa in The Frog, 1936–37; refounded Windsor Repertory Co., 1938. Called to the Colours as Territorial reservist, 1940; served in N Africa, France and Germany, 1942–45; Mem. planning staff of SHAEF; demobilised, 1945, rank of Lieut-Col. Resumed direction of Theatre Royal, Windsor. Has, in addition, produced: Birthmark, Playhouse, 1947; Little Holiday, 1948; Captain Brassbound's Conversion, Lyric, Hammersmith, 1948; The Man with the Umbrella, Duchess, 1950; Who Goes There!, Vaudeville, 1951; His House in Order, 1951; Waggon Load of Monkeys, Savoy, 1951; For Better for Worse, Comedy, 1952; Anastasia, St James's, 1953; Grab Me a Gondola, Lyric, 1956; Three Way Switch, Aldwych, 1958; How Say You?, Aldwych, 1959.

*Publications:* Counsell's Opinion (autobiography), 1963; Play Direction: a practical viewpoint, 1973. *Recreations:* gardening, photography. *Address:* 3 Queen's Terrace, Windsor, Berks. *T:* Windsor 65344.                                    *Died 23 Feb.* 1987.

**COURAGE, Edward Raymond,** CBE 1964; *b* 29 Sept. 1906; *er s* of Raymond Courage; *m* 1948, Hermione Mary Elizabeth, *er d* of Lt-Col Sir John Reynolds, 2nd Bt, MBE; one *s. Educ:* Eton; Trinity Coll., Cambridge. High Sheriff of Northants, 1953–54. *Recreations:* racing, shooting, fishing. *Address:* Edgcote, Banbury, Oxfordshire; 31 Abbotsbury House, Abbotsbury Road, W14. *Clubs:* Garrick, Jockey.                                    *Died 3 July* 1982.

**COURATIN, Rev. Canon Arthur Hubert;** Sixth Canon and Chapter Librarian, Durham Cathedral, 1962–74, Canon Emeritus since 1974; *b* 1902; *s* of Arthur Louis and Marian Couratin. *Educ:* Dulwich Coll.; Corpus Christi Coll., Oxford (Scholar); S Stephen's House, Oxford. 1st Cl. Classical Moderations; 2nd Cl. Literae Humaniores; 2nd Cl. Hons Sch. of Theology; BA 1925; MA 1927. Deacon, 1926; priest, 1927; Asst Curate, S Saviour's, Roath, 1926–30 (in charge of S Francis', Roath, 1927–30); Vice-Principal, Queen's Coll., Birmingham, 1930; Asst Curate, S Stephen's, Lewisham (in charge of Church of the Transfiguration, Lewisham), 1930–35; Chaplain, S Stephen's House, Oxford, 1935–36, Vice-Principal, 1936, Principal, 1936–62; Junior Chaplain, Merton Coll., Oxford, 1936–39. Hon. Canon of Christ Church, 1961–62. *Address:* 7 Pimlico, Durham DH1 4QW. *T:* Durham 64767.
                                    *Died 9 July* 1988.

**COURNAND, André Frédéric,** MD; Professor Emeritus of Medicine, Columbia University College of Physicians and Surgeons, New York, since 1964 (Professor of Medicine, 1951–60); *b* Paris, 24 Sept. 1895; *s* of Jules Cournand and Marguérite Weber; *m* 1st, Sibylle Blumer (*d* 1959); three *d* (one *s* killed in action, 1944); 2nd, 1963, Ruth Fabian (*d* 1973); 3rd, 1975, Beatrice Berle. *Educ:* Sorbonne, Paris. BA Faculté des Lettres, 1913; PCB Faculté des Sciences, 1914; MD Faculté de Médecine, 1930. Interne des Hôpitaux de Paris, 1925–30. Came to US in 1930; naturalized American Citizen since 1941. Director, Cardio-Pulmonary Laboratory, Columbia University Division, Bellevue Hospital, 1952; Visiting Physician, Chest Service, Bellevue Hospital, 1952. Member: American Physiological Soc.; Assoc. of Amer. Physicians; National Acad. of Sciences (USA), 1958; Amer. Acad. of Arts and Sciences, 1975; Académie des Sciences et Belles Lettres et Arts, Lyon, 1982. Hon. Member: British Cardiac Soc.; Swedish Soc. Internal Medicine; Swedish Cardiac Soc.; Soc. Médicale des Hôpitaux, Paris; Foreign Mem., Académie Royale de Médecine de Belgique, 1970; Foreign Member: Académie des Sciences, Institut de France, 1957; Académie Nationale de Médecine, Paris, 1958. Laureate: Andreas Retzius Silver Medal of Swedish Soc. Internal Medicine, 1946; Award, US Public Health Assoc., 1949. Croix de Guerre (1914–18) France, three stars; Commandeur de la Légion d'Honneur, 1970 (Officier, 1957). Nobel Prize for Medicine and Physiology (jointly), 1956; Jimenez Diaz Fondacion Prize, 1970; Trudeau Medal, 1971. Doctor (*hc*): University of Strasburg, 1957; University of Lyons, 1958; Université libre de Bruxelles 1959; University of Pisa, 1961; University of Birmingham, 1961; Gustaphus Adolphus, Coll., Minnesota, 1963; University of Brazil, 1965; Columbia Univ., 1965; Univ. of Nancy, 1968. *Publications:* Cardiac Catheterization in Congenital Heart Disease, 1949; L'Insuffisance cardiaque chronique, 1950; Shaping the Future, 1974; From Roots—to Late Budding, (autobiog.), 1986; numerous articles on human physiopathology of lungs and heart and on the relation between science and society. *Recreations:* Groupe de la Haute Montagne du Club Alpin Français, 1929, and American Alpine Club. *Address:* 142 East 19th Street, New York, NY 10003, USA. *T:* 473 3660. *Club:* Century Association (New York).
                                    *Died 19 Feb.* 1988.

**COURTENAY, Hon. Sir (Woldrich) Harrison,** KBE 1973 (OBE 1950); LLD; QC 1974; Speaker, House of Representatives, Belize, (formerly British Honduras), 1963–74 (of Legislative Assembly, 1961–63); Chancellor of Anglican Diocese, since 1956, Registrar since 1946; Barrister-at-Law; *b* Belize City, 15 July 1904; *s* of William and Sarah Courtenay; *m* 1929, Josephine Robinson; four *s* one *d. Educ:* Belize High Sch., British Honduras; Lincoln's Inn, London. Mem. Civil Service, Belize (British Honduras Secretariat), 1920–37; acted on several occasions as Clerk of Legislative and Exec. Councils, and as Head of Educn Dept, 1930; Sec.-Accountant, British Honduras Govt Marketing Agency, 1925–33; also Sec. of Stann Creek Develt Bd. Left for UK, Nov. 1933, to read for the Bar; called to Bar, Lincoln's Inn, 1936; returned to British Honduras and resumed duty, July 1936; resigned, 1937, and entered into private practice; admitted Solicitor of Supreme Court, Belize, 1937; Magistrate, Belize, 1938–41. Has for many years Diocesan Sec. and Mem. Synod, 1926–; Dio. Brit. Honduras; Diocesan Treas.; and Sec.-Treas., Bd of Governors of St Hilda's Coll. (Elected) MLC, 1945–54; MEC, 1947–54; Past Mem., Electricity Bd; also served on several other Bds and Cttees. British Honduras rep. to Conf. on

Closer Assoc. of the BWI, Montego Bay, 1947, also to 2nd and 3rd WI confs; Leader of first delegn from Legislative Council to Colonial Office on Constitutional Reform and Economic Develt, 1947. Member: Standing Closer Assoc. Cttee, which prod. first Federal Constitution, 1948–51; Brit. Section, Caribbean Commn, 1948–52; Alternate Mem., 1952–55; BWI Regional Economic Cttee, 1951–54; Council of University Coll. of the WI; Finance and General Purposes Cttee, Bd of Extra-Mural Studies, and Bd of Inst. of Social and Economic Research, 1948–58; Chm., constitutional Reform Commn, 1949–51; Fiscal Revision Cttee, 1952–53. Representative: at Installation of Princess Alice as Chancellor of University Coll. of WI, 1950; CPA Confs, NZ 1950 and Canada 1952; on visits to Australia, Canada, Jamaica, etc, 1950–52; for visit of the Queen and the Duke of Edinburgh to Jamaica, 1953; to Sugar Conf., Grenada, 1950, and Trade Promotion Conf., Trinidad, 1954; (for BWI) on UK delgn to Conf. of Commonwealth Finance Ministers, Sydney, 1954; Chm., BWI Regional Parly Conf., Jamaica, 1952; Chm. and Constitutional Adviser to United Front Political delgn to London for constitutional talks, 1960; Chm., NEDC, 1962–66; Constitutional Adviser to Political delegn to London for constitutional talks, 1963; Adviser, British Honduras delegn to tripartite confs on Anglo-Guatemalan Dispute, and with Mediator in the dispute, 1962–67. Hon. LLD (Univ. of WI), 1972; Hon. Citizen of San Juan, Puerto Rico, 1948. *Recreations:* travel, reading, music. *Address:* Cloverleaf Park, Northern Highway, (PO Box 636) Belize. *Club:* Royal Commonwealth Society.

*Died 26 June 1982.*

**COURTNEY, Comdr Anthony Tosswill,** OBE 1949; RN; author and lecturer; Managing Director, New English Typewriting School Ltd, since 1969; *b* 16 May 1908; *s* of Basil Tosswill Courtney and Frances Elizabeth Courtney (*née* Rankin); *m* 1st, 1938, Elisabeth Mary Cortlandt Stokes (*d* 1961); no *c*; 2nd, 1962, Lady (Elizabeth) Trefgarne (marr. diss. 1966); 3rd, 1971, Mrs Angela Bradford. *Educ:* Royal Naval Coll., Dartmouth. Midshipman, HMS Ramillies, 1925; world cruise in HMS Renown with the Duke and Duchess of York, 1927; Sub-Lieut HMS Cornwall, 1930; Lieut HMS Malaya, 1931–33; qualified as Interpreter in Russian after language study in Bessarabia, 1934; qualified in Signals and W/T at Signal Sch., Portsmouth, 1935; served at Admiralty and on staff of C-in-C, Plymouth, 1936; Flag Lieut to Rear-Adm. comdg Third Cruiser Sqdn, Mediterranean Fleet, 1937–39; Staff of Adm. comdg 3rd Battle Squadron and N Atlantic Escort Force, 1939–41; Naval Mission in Russia, 1941–42; Flag Lieut and Signals Officer to Adm. comdg Aircraft Carriers, 1943; Staff of Adm. comdg S Atlantic Station, 1944; Staff of Rear-Adm., Gibraltar, 1945; Intelligence Div., Naval Staff, Admiralty, 1946–48; Chief Staff Officer (Intelligence) Germany, 1949–51; qualified as Interpreter in German; Intelligence Div., Naval Staff, Admiralty, 1952–53; retd with rank of Comdr, 1953. Entered business as Export Consultant (ETG Consultancy Services), until 1965. Contested (C) Hayes and Harlington, 1955. MP (C) Harrow East, 1959–66. Vice-Chm. Conservative Navy Cttee, 1964. Chm. Parliamentary Flying Club, 1965; Chm., Wilts Monday Club, 1977. Chm. of Governors, Urchfont Sch., 1982–. *Publication:* Sailor in a Russian Frame, 1968. *Recreations:* shooting, music, fishing. *Address:* Mulberry House, Urchfont, Devizes, Wilts. *T:* Chirton 357. *Club:* White's.

*Died 24 Jan. 1988.*

**COUSIN, Prof. David Ross;** Emeritus Professor of Philosophy, University of Sheffield; *b* 28 Jan. 1904; *s* of John William Cousin and Marion Miller Young; *m* 1930, Beatrice Elizabeth Connell; three *s. Educ:* Merchiston Castle Sch., Edinburgh; The Queen's Coll., Oxford (BA). Class. Mods. 1925; Lit. Hum. 1927; Philosophy, Politics and Economics, 1928. Asst, Dept of Logic, University of Glasgow, 1928; Lecturer, 1930; Senior Lecturer, 1948. Board of Trade (temp. Principal), 1941–45. Prof. of Philosophy, Univ. of Sheffield, 1949–69; Dean of Faculty of Arts, 1958–61. Vis. Prof., Dept of Philosophy, Univ. of Edinburgh, Oct.–Dec., 1974. *Publications:* contributions to learned jls. *Address:* 16 Cobden Crescent, Edinburgh EH9 2BG. *Died 23 March 1984.*

**COUSINS, Rt. Hon. Frank,** PC 1964; Chairman, Community Relations Commission, 1968–70; *b* Bulwell, Notts, 8 Sept. 1904; *m* 1930, Annie Elizabeth Judd; two *s* two *d. Educ:* King Edward Sch., Doncaster. Mem. Institute of Transport; Organiser, Rd Transport Section, TGWU, 1938; Nat. Officer (Rd Tr. Section), 1944; Nat. Sec. (Rd Tr. Section), 1948; Asst Gen. Sec. TGWU, 1955; General Secretary, TGWU, 1956–69 (seconded, as Minister of Technology, Oct. 1964–July 1966). MP (Lab) Nuneaton, Jan. 1965–Dec. 1966. Elected Mem., Gen. Council of TUC, 1956–69. Member: British Transport Jt Consultative Council, 1955; Min. of Labour Nat. Jt Advisory Council, 1956; Exec. Council Internat. Transport Workers Federation, 1956 (Pres., 1958–60, 1962–64); Colonial Labour Advisory Cttee, 1957–62; London Travel Cttee, 1958–60; Political Economy Club, 1957; Council for Scientific and Industrial Research, 1960–64; National Economic Development Council; Central Advisory Council for Science and Technology, 1967–; Nat. Freight Corp., 1968–73; Governor, Nat. Inst. of Economic and

Social Research, 1958; Chm., Central Training Council, 1968–. *Relevant publication:* The Awkward Warrior, by Geoffrey Goodman, 1979. *Recreations:* gardening, reading. *Address:* 5 Frances Drive, Wingerworth, Chesterfield, Derbyshire. *T:* Chesterfield 35653.

*Died 11 June 1986.*

**COUSINS, Norman;** Adjunct Professor, University of California at Los Angeles Medical School, since 1978; *b* 24 June 1915; *s* of Samuel and Sara Cousins; *m* 1939, Ellen Kopf; four *d. Educ:* Teachers Coll., Columbia Univ. Educational Editor, New York Evening Post, 1935–36; Managing Editor, Current History Magazine, 1936–39 (World War II edn, USA); Editor, Saturday Review, 1940–71, 1973–78. Chm., Conn Fact-Finding Commission on Education, 1948–51. Vice-Pres. PEN Club, American Center, 1952–55; National Press and Overseas Press Clubs; co-Chm., National Cttee for a Sane Nuclear Policy, 1957–63. Chm., Nat. Educational Television, 1969–70; US Govt Rep. at dedication Nat. Univ., Addis Ababa, 1962; apptd by Pres. John F. Kennedy to Adv. Cttee on Arts, Nat. Cultural Center, 1962; co-Chm., Citizens' Cttee for a Nuclear Test-Ban Treaty, 1963; Chm., Cttee for Culture and Intellectual Exchange, for International Co-operation Year, 1965; US Presidential Rep. at Inauguration of Pres. of Philippines, 1966; US Govt Rep. at Internat. Writers Conf., Finland, 1966. Chm. Mayor's Task Force on Air Pollution, NYC, 1966–. Holds 53 hon. doctorates of letters, medicine, science and law. Awards include: Benjamin Franklin Award for Public Service in Journalism, 1956; Eleanor Roosevelt Peace Award, 1963; Overseas Press Club Award for best interpretation of foreign affairs in magazine writing, 1965; Family of Man Award, 1968; Carr Van Anda Award for Enduring Contribs to Journalism, Ohio Univ., 1971; Peace Medal of UN, 1971; Nat Arts Club Gold Medal for Literature, 1972; Univ. of Missouri Honor Award for Conspicuous Contribs to Journalism, 1972; Drexel Univ. Distinguished Achievement Award, 1972; Irita Van Doren Book Award, 1972; Magazine Publishers Assoc. Award, 1973; Human Resources Award, Nightingale-Conant Corp., 1973; Delbert Clark Award, West Georgia Coll., 1974; Canadian Govt Environment Award, 1975; Medal of Amer. Coll. of Cardiology, 1978; Author of the Year, Soc. of Authors and Journalists, 1980; Physicians for Social Responsibility, 1980; Niwano Peace Award, 1990; Johns Hopkins Med. Sch. Albert Schweitzer Award, 1990. *Publications:* The Good Inheritance, 1942; The Democratic Chance, 1942; (ed) A Treasury of Democracy, 1942; Modern Man is Obsolete, 1946; (ed jtly) Poetry of Freedom, 1948; Talks with Nehru, 1951; Who Speaks for Man?, 1953; Saturday Review Treasury (ed. sup.), 1957; (ed) In God We Trust, 1958; (ed) Writing for Love or Money, 1958; March's Thesaurus (ed. sup.), 1958; Dr Schweitzer of Lambaréné, 1960; In Place of Folly, 1961; Present Tense, 1967; (ed) Great American Essays, 1967; (ed) Profiles of Gandhi, 1969; The Improbable Triumvirate, 1972; Celebration of Life, 1974; (ed) Memoirs of a Man: Grenville Clark, 1975; Anatomy of an Illness, 1979; Human Options, 1981; (ed) The Physician in Literature, 1982; The Healing Heart, 1983; (ed) The Words of Albert Schweitzer, 1984; Albert Schweitzer's Mission: healing and peace, 1985; The Human Adventure: a camera chronicle, 1986; The Pathology of Power, 1987; (ed) The Republic of Reason, 1988; K. Jason Sitewell's Book of Spoofs, 1989; Head First: the biology of hope, 1989. *Recreations:* music (especially organ), sports, reading, chess. *Address:* (office) Dean's Office, School of Medicine, 12–138 CHS, University of California, Los Angeles, Calif 90024, USA; (home) 2644 Eden Place, Beverly Hills, Calif 90210, USA.

*Died 1 Dec. 1990.*

**COUTTS, Frederick,** CBE 1967; General of The Salvation Army, 1963–69; *b* 21 Sept. 1899; British; *m* 1st, 1925, Bessie Lee (*d* 1967); one *s* three *d*; 2nd, 1969, Olive Gatrall. *Educ:* Leith Academy and Whitehill. RFC, 1917–18. Officer, The Salvation Army, 1920. Literary Sec. to the General, 1952. Training Principal, International Training Coll., 1953–57; Territorial Comdr, Eastern Australia, 1957–63. Hon. DD Aberdeen, 1981. *Publications:* The Timeless Prophets, 1944; He had no Revolver, 1944; The Battle and the Breeze, 1945; Portrait of a Salvationist, 1955; Jesus and Our Need, 1956; The Call to Holiness, 1957; Essentials of Christian Experience, 1969; The Better Fight: the history of the Salvation Army 1914–1946, 1973; No Discharge in This War, 1975; No Continuing City, 1976; Bread for my Neighbour, 1978; In Good Company, 1980; More Than One Homeland, 1982; The Splendour of Holiness, 1983. *Recreations:* reading, music. *Address:* 3 Dubrae Close, St Albans, Herts. *T:* St Albans 59655. *Died 6 Feb. 1986.*

**COUTTS, Sir Walter (Fleming),** GCMG 1962 (KCMG 1961; CMG 1953); Kt 1961; MBE 1949; retired; Director: The Farmington Trust, 1971–78; Inchcape (East Africa) Ltd, 1970–78; Assam Investments, 1964–78; Chairman, Grindlays (Commercial) Holdings, 1974–78; *b* Aberdeen, 30 Nov. 1912; *s* of late Rev. John William Coutts, MA, DD, and Mrs R. Coutts, Crieff; *m* 1942, Janet Elizabeth Jamieson, CStJ, 2nd *d* of late Mr and Mrs A. C. Jamieson; one *s* one *d. Educ:* Glasgow Academy; St Andrews Univ.; St John's Coll., Cambridge. MA St Andrews, 1934. District Officer Kenya, 1936; Secretariat Kenya, 1946; District Commissioner, 1947;

Administrator, St Vincent, 1949; Minister for Education, Labour and Lands, Kenya, 1956–58, Chief Sec., 1958–61; Special Commissioner for African Elections, Feb. 1955; Governor of Uganda, Nov. 1961–Oct. 1962; Governor-Gen. and C-in-C, Uganda, 1962–63. Sec. to Dulverton Trust, 1966–69; Asst Vice-Chancellor (Administration), Univ. of Warwick, 1969–71. Chm., Pergamon Press, 1972–74. *Recreation:* gardening. *Address:* 19 Malindi Street, Willetton, WA 6155, Australia. *T:* Perth 457 2995.
*Died 4 Nov. 1988.*

**COWAN, Maj.-Gen. David Tennant,** CB 1945; CBE 1945; DSO 1942, Bar 1944; MC; Indian Army (retired); late RARO; *b* 8 Oct. 1896; *s* of Charles Thomas and Kate Cowan; *m* 1st, 1920, Anne Elliot Dunlop (*d* 1973); one *d* (one *s* killed in action); 2nd, 1973, Frances Elisabeth Newall, *widow* of Lt-Col F. H. A. Stables. *Educ:* Reading; Glasgow Univ. 2nd Lieut Argyll and Sutherland Highlanders, 1915; Capt. 1920; Maj.-Gen. 1942. Served European War, 1914–18 with 2nd Bn, The Argyll and Sutherland Highlanders (despatches, MC); 3rd Afghan War; Waziristan Ops, 1919–20 (despatches) and 1937 (despatches). 6th Gurkha Rifles, 1917–40; Staff Coll., Quetta, 1927–28; Chief Instructor, Indian Military Academy, 1932–34; Comdt 1/6 Gurkha Rifles, 1939–40; DDMT GHQ, India, 1941; Offg DMT, GHQ, India, 1941–42. War of 1939–45 in Burma (despatches, DSO and bar, CB). GOC 17th Indian Div., 1942–45, and British and Indian Div., British Commonwealth Occupation Force, Japan, 1945–46. Retd 1947, RARO 1948. Commandant, Devon Army Cadet Force, 1948–58. Chm. Approved Sch., Devon, 1951–60; Sec. (part-time) Assoc. of Managers of Approved Schs, 1963–73. DL Devon, 1953–63. Captain and Manager, Indian Army Hockey Team, NZ and Australia Tour, 1926; Hon. Commandant Empire Village, VIth British Empire and Commonwealth Games, Wales, 1958. *Recreations:* games, fishing. *Address:* Ridgecoombe, Penton Grafton, Andover, Hants SP10 0RR. *Club:* Army and Navy. *Died 15 April 1983.*

**COWAN, Prof. Ian Borthwick,** PhD; FRHistS; Professor in Scottish History, University of Glasgow, since 1983; *b* 16 April 1932; *s* of late William McAulay Cowan and Annie Borthwick; *m* 1954, Anna Little Telford; three *d. Educ:* Dumfries Acad.; Univ. of Edinburgh (MA, PhD). FRHistS 1969. Served RAF, Educn Officer, 1954–56. Asst Lectr in Scottish Hist., Univ. of Edinburgh, 1956–59; Lectr in Hist., Newbattle Abbey Coll., 1959–62; Univ. of Glasgow: Lectr in Scottish Hist., 1962–70; Sen. Lectr, 1970–77; Reader, 1977–83. Mem., Royal Commn on Historical MSS, 1990–; Hon. Treasurer, Scottish Hist. Soc., 1965–88; Vice-Pres., Historical Assoc., 1982–. Editor, Scottish Historical Rev., 1983–88. *Publications:* Blast and Counterblast, 1960; Parishes of Medieval Scotland, 1962; (with A.I. Dunlop) Calendar of Scottish Supplications to Rome 1428–32, 1970; The Enigma of Mary Stuart, 1971; (with D.E. Easson) Medieval Religious Houses: Scotland, 1976; The Scottish Covenanters 1660–1688, 1976; Regional Aspects of the Scottish Reformation, 1978; The Scottish Reformation—Church and Society, 1982; (with D. Shaw) Renaissance and Reformation in Scotland, 1983; (with P. H. R. MacKay and A. Macquarrie) The Knights of St John of Jerusalem in Scotland, 1983; Ayrshire Abbeys: Crossraguel and Kilwinning, 1986; Mary Queen of Scots, 1987; articles and papers in learned jls. *Address:* 119 Balshagray Avenue, Glasgow G11 7EG. *T:* 041–954 8494. *Died 22 Dec. 1990.*

**COWANS, Harry Lowes;** MP (Lab) Tyne Bridge, since 1983 (Newcastle Central, Nov. 1976–1983); *b* 1932; *m* Margaret; one *s* three *d.* Was a Technician Officer, Signals and Telecommunications Dept, British Rail. Branch Sec., NUR; Mem. Exec. Cttee, Labour Party Northern Region. Member: Gateshead Metropolitan DC (Chm., Housing Cttee); Tyne and Wear Metropolitan CC (Mem. Management, Finance and Transport (Cttees). Mem., Select Cttee for Transport (Chm., 1984–); Opposition Whip, N Region and transport; Sec., Northern Group Labour MPs. *Address:* House of Commons, SW1A 0AA; 4 Station Cottages, Elysium Lane, Bensham, Gateshead NE8 2XH. *Died 3 Oct. 1985.*

**COWDRY, Rt. Rev. Roy Walter Frederick;** Assistant Bishop of Port Elizabeth, since 1970; Rector of St Cuthbert's, Port Elizabeth, since 1964; *b* 28 April 1915; *s* of Frederick William Thomas Cowdry and Florence Emma (*née* Roberts); *m* 1964, Elizabeth Melene, *d* of Rt Rev. B. W. Peacey; two *s. Educ:* King's Coll., London. Deacon, 1941; Priest, 1942. Asst Curate: St Nicholas, Perivale, 1941–44; Christ Church, Ealing, 1944–50; Domestic Chaplain to Archbishop of Cape Town, 1950–58; Asst Bishop of Cape Town, 1958–61; Bishop Suffragan of Cape Town, 1961–64; Asst Bishop of Grahamstown, 1965–70. Chaplain, Cape Town Gaol, 1951–57. Chaplin, OStJ, 1961. *Address:* St Cuthbert's Rectory, 43 Conyngham Street, Parsons Hill, Port Elizabeth, 6001, S Africa. *T:* 332526. *Club:* Port Elizabeth. *Died 6 Nov. 1984.*

**COWEN, Alan Biddulph,** CMG 1961; OBE 1945; retired as Deputy Chairman of Standards Association of Rhodesia and Nyasaland; *b* 26 Sept. 1896; *m*; two *s. Educ:* St John's Coll., Johannesburg, S Africa; Sch. of Mines and Technology. Formerly Chm., Southern

Rhodesian Electricity Supply Commission; Mem. of Federal Power Board. CEng; FIEE; F(SA)IEE. *Died 12 Sept. 1989.*

**COWEN, John David,** MC 1943; TD 1944; MA; FSA; Director, Barclays Bank Ltd, 1965–74; *b* 16 Nov. 1904; *e s* of John Edward Cowen, Minsteracres, Northumberland; *m* 1944, Rhoda Susan Harris; one *s* two *d. Educ:* Rugby (scholar); Hertford Coll., Oxford (scholar). Final Law Soc. Exams (Hons), 1931. Entered Barclays Bank Ltd, 1931; Gen. Manager (Staff), 1948–49; Gen. Manager, 1950–65. Fellow, Inst. of Bankers (Mem. Council, 1950–59); Chairman: Inter-Bank Cttee on Electronics, 1955–61; Inter-Bank Working Party on Negotiating Machinery in Banking, 1965–67. Joined Northumberland Hussars Yeomanry, 1929; Major, 1942; served in North Africa, Sicily (despatches), France and Germany. Dir, Newcastle upon Tyne and Gateshead Gas Co., 1934–47 (Chm. 1947). Mem., Standing Commn on Museums and Galls, 1966–73; Governor, Museum of London, 1965–67; Vice-Pres., Soc. of Antiquaries of London (Treasurer, 1964–71); Pres., The Prehistoric Soc., 1966–70; Pres. Soc. of Antiquaries of Newcastle upon Tyne, 1966–68 (Hon. Curator, 1933–39, 1947–48); Hon. Mem. German Archaeolog. Inst.; Hon. DCL (Durham), 1961. *Publications:* articles in banking and archaeological jls (Brit. and foreign). *Recreations:* prehistory, travel. *Address:* Over Court, Bisley, near Stroud, Glos GL6 7BE. *T:* Bisley 209. *Died 17 Feb. 1981.*

**COWERN, Raymond Teague,** RA 1968 (ARA 1957); RWS; RE; ARCA; RWA; painter, etcher and draughtsman; *b* 12 July 1913; *s* of George Dent Cowern and Elsie Ellen Teague; *m* Margaret Jean Trotman; one *s* two *d. Educ:* King Edward's Grammar Sch., Aston, Birmingham. Studied Central Sch. of Art, Birmingham, Royal Coll. of Art, London. Worked with Sakkarah Expedition of the Oriental Institute of Chicago; Rome Scholar in Engraving, 1937–39; commissioned by Pilgrim Trust Scheme for Recording Britain. Served in the Army, Infantry, Camouflage and Intelligence Corps, 1940–46. Principal, Brighton Coll. of Art, 1958–70; Associate Dir, and Dean of Faculty of Art and Design, Brighton Polytechnic, 1970–74. Represented by work at British Museum, V&A, Imperial War Mus. and in public collections Glasgow, Liverpool, Manchester, Birmingham, Oxford, Cambridge, Bristol and museums abroad. *Address:* 41 Irish Street, Whitehaven, Cumbria CA28 7BY. *T:* Whitehaven 61734. *Died 8 June 1986.*

**COWLES, Virginia,** OBE 1947; writer; *b* USA, 24 Aug. 1910; *2 d* of Florence Wolcott Jaquith and Edward Spencer Cowles; *m* 1945, Aidan M. Crawley, MBE; two *s* one *d. Educ:* privately. Newspaper correspondent, 1937–41 and 1943–45; Special Asst to the American Ambassador, American Embassy, London, 1942–43. *Publications:* Looking for Trouble, 1941; How America is Governed, 1944; No Cause for Alarm, 1949; Winston Churchill: The Era and the Man, 1953; Edward VII and His Circle, 1956; The Phantom Major, 1958; The Great Swindle, 1960; The Kaiser, 1963; 1913: The Defiant Swan Song, 1967; The Russian Dagger, 1969; The Romanovs, 1971; The Rothschilds, 1973; The Last Tsar and Tsarina, 1977; The Astors, 1979; The Great Marlborough and his Duchess, 1983. *Recreation:* politics. *Address:* 19 Chester Square, SW1. *T:* 01-730 3030. *Died 16 Sept. 1983.*

**COWLES-VOYSEY, Charles,** FRIBA, retired; *b* 24 June 1889; *e s* of Charles Francis Annesley Voysey, FRIBA, architect; *m* 1912, Dorothea Denise Cowles (*d* 1980); no *c. Educ:* private sch.; University Coll., London. Architect for Worthing Civic Centre; White Rock Pavilion, Hastings; the Guildhall, Cambridge; Watford Town Hall; Bromley (Kent), Town Hall Extensions; Bridgeton Halls, Glasgow; Municipal Offices, High Wycombe; Kingsley Hall, Bow; Bognor Regis Municipal Offices; Hampshire County Council Offices, Winchester, and other public buildings and private houses; Consulting Architect to various local authorities. *Recreation:* landscape painting. *Address:* 2 Bunkers Hill, Wildwood Road, NW11 6XA. *T:* 01-455 7274. *Died 10 April 1981.*

**COWLEY, Denis Martin;** AE 1945; QC 1965; a Recorder of the Crown Court, since 1974; *b* 30 Jan. 1919; *s* of late Sir William Percy Cowley, CBE; *m* 1940, Margaret Hazel, *d* of Hugo Teare, Ramsey, Isle of Man; one *s* two *d. Educ:* Radley Coll.; Exeter Coll., Oxford (MA (Hons Jurisprudence)). Served RAFVR, 1939–45. Called to Bar, Inner Temple, 1946; Bencher, 1972. Midland and Oxford Circuit. Dep. Sen. Judge, 1969–82, Sen. Judge, 1982–84, Sovereign Base Areas, Cyprus. Mental Health Appeal Tribunal, 1984. *Recreations:* shooting, sailing. *Address:* Ellan Vannin, The Quay, Castletown, Isle of Man. *T:* Castletown 3532; Francis Taylor Buildings, Temple, EC4. *T:* 01–353 9942. *Club:* United Oxford & Cambridge University. *Died 28 June 1985.*

**COWLING, Richard John,** ARICS; Deputy Chief Valuer, Inland Revenue Valuation Office, 1972–74; *b* 2 Feb. 1911; *s* of Sydney George and Madge Prentice Cowling, late of East Grinstead; *m* 1936, Doris Rosa (decd), *o d* of Albert James Puttock, Guildford; one *s. Educ:* Skinners' Company's Sch. Articles and private practice as a surveyor, 1928–35; War Office Lands Branch, 1936; Inland Revenue Valuation Office, 1937. TA Commission, Green Howards,

1942. *Recreations:* golf, bridge, sailing. *Address:* 18 Gateways, Epsom Road, Guildford, Surrey GU1 2LF. *T:* Guildford 573473.
*Died 30 March* 1987.

**COWLING, Thomas George,** FRS 1947; Professor of Applied Mathematics, Leeds University, 1948–70, later Professor Emeritus; *b* 17 June 1906; *s* of George and Edith Eliza Cowling; *m* 1935, Doris Moffatt; one *s* two *d. Educ:* Sir George Monoux Sch., Walthamstow; Oxford Univ. Teacher of mathematics, Imperial Coll. of Science, University Coll., Swansea, University Coll., Dundee, Manchester Univ., and at University Coll., Bangor (Prof. of Mathematics, 1945–48). Pres., Royal Astronomical Soc., 1965–67. Hon. Fellow, Brasenose Coll., Oxford, 1966. Halley Lectr, Oxford Univ., 1969. Gold Medallist, Royal Astronomical Soc., 1956; Bruce Gold Medallist, Astronomical Soc. of the Pacific, 1985; Hughes Medal, Royal Soc., 1990. *Publications:* (with S. Chapman) The Mathematical Theory of Non-Uniform Gases, 1939, 3rd edn 1970; Molecules in Motion, 1950; Magneto-hydrodynamics, 1957, 2nd edn 1976; also a number of papers, chiefly astronomical and gas-theoretic. *Recreations:* gardening, crosswords. *Address:* 19 Hollin Gardens, Leeds LS16 5NL. *T:* (0532) 785342.
*Died 19 June* 1990.

**COWPER, Brig. Anthony William,** CBE 1964 (OBE 1945); company director; *b* 10 May 1913; *s* of Walter Taylor Cowper, solicitor, Southgate, London, and West Burton, Yorks; *m* 1949, Margaret Mary, *d* of Clarence W. Fry, Upminster, Essex; no *c. Educ:* Merchant Taylors' Sch. Joined Christie's, Fine Art Auctioneers, 1932. Commissioned from TA (HAC) into West Yorks Regt, Nov. 1939; War Service in India, Burma, Ceylon and Singapore, 1940–45 (OBE). Granted regular commn, 1947; served overseas almost continuously (mainly Far East) in Regtl and Staff appts (despatches, Malayan Emergency, 1954); Col 1961; Brig. 1965; Defence Adviser to British High Comr in Malaysia, 1967; retd 1969. Freeman of City of London. *Recreations:* fly fishing, small boat sailing, antiques, Far East affairs. *Address:* 97 Kingsway Gardens, 38 Kings Park Road, Perth, West Australia 6005. *T:* 3213373. *Died 7 May* 1983.

**COWPER, Sir Norman (Lethbridge),** Kt 1967; CBE 1958; *b* 15 Sept. 1896; *yr s* of Cecil Spencer de Grey Cowper; *m* 1925, Dorothea Huntly, *d* of Hugh McCrae; three *d. Educ:* Sydney Grammar Sch.; University of Sydney (BA, LLB). Served War of 1939–45, 2nd AIF, Lt-Col. Solicitor, Supreme Court of NSW, 1923. Partner, Allen, Allen & Hemsley, 1924–70. Dir, Australian Inst. of Polit. Science, 1932–69; Australian Inst. of Internat. Affairs: NSW Br. Pres., 1947–49; Commonwealth Pres., 1949–50; Mem. Council, Australian National Univ., 1955–74; Mem. Board of Trustees, Sydney Grammar Sch., 1935–75 (Chm., 1951–75); Chm., Council on New Guinea Affairs, 1965. *Publications:* occasional articles: Australian Quarterly, Australian Outlook, Australian Dictionary of Biography. *Recreations:* reading, gardening. *Address:* Wivenhoe, Millewa Avenue, Wahroonga, Sydney, Australia. *T:* 48 2336. *Club:* Australian (Sydney) (Pres., 1968–72). *Died 9 Sept.* 1987.

**COX, Sir Christopher (William Machell),** GCMG 1970 (KCMG 1950; CMG 1944); *b* 17 Nov. 1899; *e s* of late A. H. Machell Cox, Chevin Close, St Audries, Somerset. *Educ:* Clifton Coll.; Balliol Coll., Oxford. 2nd Lieut RE (Signals), 1918; 1st class Classical Moderations; 1st class Lit. Hum., 1923; War Memorial Student, Balliol Coll., 1923–24; Craven Fellow, Oxford Univ., and Senior Demy, Magdalen Coll., 1924–26; archæological exploration in Turkey, 1924, 1925, 1926, 1931; Fellow of New Coll., Oxford, 1926–70, Hon. Fellow, 1970. Sub-Warden, 1931; Dean, 1934–36; visited Africa, 1929; Persia, 1936; Dir of Education, Anglo-Egyptian Sudan, and Principal of Gordon Coll., Khartoum, 1937–39; Mem. of Governor-General's Council, 1938–39; Educational Adviser to the Sec. of State for the Colonies, 1940–61; Educational Adviser: Dept of Technical Co-operation, 1961–64; ODM, 1964–70. Pres., Education Sect., British Assoc., 1956. Hon. DLit Belfast, 1961; Hon. LLD: Hong Kong, 1961; Chinese Univ. of Hong Kong, 1969; Hon. LLD Leeds, 1962; Hon. DCL Oxford, 1965. *Publications:* Monumenta Asiae Minoris Antiqua, Vol. V (with A. Cameron), 1937; occasional papers. *Recreations:* travel, formerly skiing, reading. *Address:* New College, Oxford. *Clubs:* Athenæum, MCC. *Died 6 July* 1982.

**COX, Harry Bernard,** CBE 1956; Deputy Chairman, Thos Wyatt Nigeria Ltd, 1967–83; Consultant, Knight, Frank & Rutley, 1967–83; retired; *b* 20 Nov. 1906; *e* surv. *s* of Rev. Charles Henry Cox, BScc; *m* 1955, Joan, *e d* of P. Munn, Brighton; one *s* one *d. Educ:* Upholland Grammar Sch.; Keble Coll., Oxford. Colonial Administrative Service, Nigeria, 1930; Dir of Commerce and Industries, Nigeria, 1949; Acting Development Sec., Nigeria, 1953–54; Acting Commissioner for Nigeria, 1955; Principal Sec. to the Commissioner for Nigeria in the United Kingdom, 1955. John Holt & Co. (Liverpool) Ltd, 1958; Chm., John Holt (Nigeria) Ltd, 1962. Leader, Westminster Chamber of Commerce Mission to Nigeria, 1974. *Address:* 5 Arundel House, 22 The Drive, Hove BN3

3JD. *T:* Brighton 738798. *Clubs:* Oriental; Hove.
*Died 5 Dec.* 1989.

**COX, Ian Herbert,** CBE 1952; MA; FRGS; FZS; *b* 20 Feb. 1910; *e s* of late Herbert Stanley Cox and Elizabeth Dalgarno; *m* 1st, 1932, Katherine Alice Burton (marr. diss. 1938); one *s*; 2nd, 1945, Susan Mary (*d* 1983), *d* of late Lieut Comdr N. G. Fowler Snelling and widow of Flt Lieut D. S. S. Low; one *s* one *d*, and one step *d. Educ:* Oundle; Magdalene Coll., Cambridge (Exhibnr). Geologist, Oxford Univ. Hudson Straits Expedition, 1931; research, Dept of Geology, Cambridge, 1932–36; with BBC 1936–39; served War of 1939–45 (Comdr RNVR); BBC 1946; Science Corresp., London Press Service, 1947–48; Dir of Sci., Festival of Britain Office, 1948–51; Shell Internat. Pet. Co., 1952–70 (Hd Sc. and Develt TR Div., Convener Shell Grants Cttee). Consultant, OECD, 1971–. Mem. Council: RGS, 1953–57, 1959–62; Overseas Develt Inst., 1966–74; BAAS, 1960–70 (Gen. Treasurer, 1965–70); Chelsea Coll., Univ. of London, 1968–74; Mem. Management Cttee, Scott Polar Research Inst., 1955–57; Vice-Pres., Geol. Soc., 1966–68; Mem., Bd of Governors, and Vice-Pres., Exec. Cttee, European Cultural Foundn (Amsterdam), 1972–82. Pres., Arctic Club, 1961. *Publications:* papers on geology and palæontology of the Arctic; (ed) The Queen's Beasts, 1953; The Scallop, 1957; monographs in World Land Use Survey. *Recreations:* working with wood and stone; gardening. *Address:* The Old Post Office, School Hill, Seale, Farnham, Surrey GU10 1HY. *T:* Runfold 2481. *Club:* Athenæum.
*Died 11 Jan.* 1990.

**COX, Sir John (William),** Kt 1951; CBE 1946; Member, 1930–68, and Speaker of the House of Assembly, Bermuda, 1948–68; *b* 29 April 1900; *s* of Henry James and Ellen Augusta Cox; *m* 1st, 1926, Dorothy Carlyle (*d* 1982), *d* of J. D. C. Darrell; three *s*; 2nd, 1984, Joan Maitland Cooper. *Educ:* Saltus Grammar Sch., Bermuda. Merchant; Pres., Pearman, Watlington & Co. Ltd, Hamilton, Bermuda, General and Commission Merchants. Comdr, Royal Netherlands Order of Orange Nassau, 1956. *Address:* The Grove, Devonshire Parish, Bermuda. *T:* 292–0303. *Clubs:* Royal Bermuda Yacht, Royal Hamilton Amateur Dinghy, Mid Ocean (Bermuda).
*Died 11 Dec.* 1990.

**COX, Air Vice-Marshal Joseph,** CB 1957; OBE 1950; DFC 1940; retired; *b* 25 Oct. 1904; *m* 1933, Dorothy Thomas; one *d. Educ:* Peter Symond's Sch., Winchester, Hants. Commissioned, RAF, 1928; various appts at home and abroad, 1929–39. War of 1939–45: Examining Officer (flying), Central Flying Sch., 1939–40; comd No 15 (Bomber) Sqdn, May-Dec. 1940; Chief Instructor No 33 Service Flying Training Sch., Canada, 1941–42; commanded No 31 Bombing and Gunnery Sch., Canada, 1942–43; commanded No 12 Advanced (Pilot) Flying Unit, and Stn Comdr RAF Spitalgate (Grantham), 1943–45. Comd No 8302 Air Disarmament Wing in Germany, 1945–46; comd RAF Fuhlsbuttel (Hamburg), 1946–48; Senior Personnel Staff Officer, HQ Maintenance Comd, 1948–51; Stn Comdr RAF Finningley, 1951–52; AOC, RAF, Ceylon, 1952–55; Senior Air Staff Officer, Flying Training Command, 1955–58; retired, 1958. *Recreations:* (in younger days) tennis, swimming, cricket, soccer, hockey, squash, badminton, water polo, riding. *Address:* 45 Ellesmere Close, Derby Road, Caversham, Reading RG4 0HG. *T:* Reading 472761. *Clubs:* MCC, Victory Services, Royal Air Force; Adastrian Cricket.
*Died 22 April* 1986.

**COX, Sir Robert;** *see* Cox, Sir W. R.

**COX, Thomas Richard Fisher,** CMG 1955; Bursar, St Andrew's College, Dublin, 1962–79; *b* 21 Feb. 1907; *s* of late Rev. James Fisher Cox; *m* 1st, 1933, Doreen Alice Rae; one *s* two *d*; 2nd, 1968, Rowena Mary Figgis; three *s. Educ:* Portora Royal Sch.; TCD; University Coll., Oxford. Provincial Admin., Uganda, 1930; acted as Sec. for African Affairs, 1949–50; Chm. Languages Board, Uganda, 1950–60; Provincial Comr, Uganda, 1950–61. *Publications:* articles in Uganda Jl and Jl of African Admin. *Recreations:* gardening; formerly boxing (boxed for Oxford Univ. *v* Cambridge Univ., 1930). *Address:* 21 Hyde Park, Dalkey, Co. Dublin. *T:* 859551; Ballinahinch, Ashford, Co. Wicklow. *T:* Wicklow 4112.
*Died 12 May* 1986.

**COX, Maj.-Gen. William Reginald,** CB 1956; DSO 1945; Director Territorial Army, Cadets and Home Guard, 1958–60, retired; *b* 13 June 1905; *e s* of late Major W. S. R. Cox; *m* 1947, Dorothy Irene Cox; no *c. Educ:* Wellington Coll. Commissioned KSLI, 1925; Adjutant, 2nd Bn, 1932–35; Staff Coll., Camberley, 1938; served War of 1939–45: Bde Major 114 Inf. Bde, 1940; Instr, Staff Coll., Camberley, 1941; GSO 1 Northern Comd, York, 1942; comd 1 Worcs. Regt, 1942–43; GSO 1, 21 Army Gp, 1943–44; comd 7 Green Howards, 1944; 131 Lorried Inf Bde, 1944; 129, 146 and 31 Inf. Bdes, 1944–45; BGS Western Comd, 1948; idc 1949; DAG, GHQ, MEF, 1950–52; Dep. Dir Infty, War Office, 1952–54; Chief of Staff, Southern Command, 1954–55; GOC 53rd (Welsh) Div., TA, and Mid-West District, 1955–58. Col, KSLI, 1957–63. Order of White Lion of Czechoslovakia (3rd Cl.); Military Cross of

Czechoslovakia, 1945. *Recreation:* golf. *Address:* Amesbury Abbey, Amesbury, Wilts. *T:* Amesbury 24401. *Club:* Naval and Military.
*Died 12 June* 1988.

**COX, Sir (William) Robert,** KCB 1976 (CB 1971); Chief Executive (Second Permanent Secretary), Property Services Agency, Department of the Environment, since 1974; *b* 2 Jan. 1922; *s* of late William Robert and Berthe Marie Cox, Winchester; *m* 1948, Elizabeth Anne Priestley Marten; one *s* one *d. Educ:* Peter Symonds' Sch., Winchester; Christ's Coll., Cambridge. Foreign Office (German Sect.), 1946; Min. of Town and Country Planning, 1950; Min. of Housing and Local Govt, 1952–69 (Under-Sec., 1965); Asst Under-Sec. of State, Office of Sec. of State for Local Govt and Regional Planning, 1969–70; Dep. Under-Sec. of State, Home Office, and Dir-Gen. of Prison Service, 1970–73; Dep. Chief Exec. III, Property Services Agency, DoE, 1974. Member: UN Cttee on Crime Prevention and Control, 1972–74; Bureau of the European Cttee on Crime Problems, 1972–73. *Recreation:* music. *Address:* Church Cottage, Viney Hill, Lydney, Glos GL15 4LZ. *Clubs:* Athenæum, Royal Commonwealth Society.
*Died 28 June* 1981.

**COXWELL-ROGERS, Maj.-Gen. Norman Annesley,** CB 1944; CBE 1943 (OBE 1933); DSO 1940; *b* 29 May 1896; *s* of late Henry Annesley Coxwell-Rogers, Asst Inspector-General Royal Irish Constabulary, Dowdeswell, Glos, and late Mary Georgina, *d* of Edmund Waller, Dundrum and Bray, Co. Dublin; *m* 1928, Diana Coston; one *s* one *d. Educ:* Cheltenham Coll.; Royal Military Academy, Woolwich. 2nd Lieut Royal Engineers, 1915; service at home, Gibraltar and India; served France and Belgium, 1915–18 (wounded, despatches twice); NW Frontier, Mohmand Operations, 1933, served as Field Engineer in charge of construction of Gandab Road (OBE, despatches); Mohmand Operations, 1935, as CRE (Bt Lieut-Col); War of 1939–45, BEF, France, Sept. 1939–June 1940, N Africa, Sicily, and Italy, 1943, Chief Engineer Allied Armies in Italy (despatches twice, DSO, CBE, CB, Legion of Merit (USA)); Colonel, 1941; Maj.-Gen. 1943; retired pay, 1946. Col Comdt RE, 1956–61. *Recreation:* field sports. *Address:* Rossley Manor, near Cheltenham, Glos. *T:* Andoversford 233. *Club:* Naval and Military.
*Died 13 Feb.* 1985.

**CRAIG, Very Rev. Archibald Campbell,** MC 1918; DD (Hon.); *b* 3 Dec. 1888; *yr s* of Rev. Alexander McRae Craig; *m* 1950, Mary Isobel Laidlaw (*d* 1985), *d* of Rev. John Laidlaw; no *c. Educ:* Kelso High Sch.; Edinburgh Univ.; New Coll., Edinburgh. Served European War, 1914–18, 13th Royal Scots and Intelligence Corps, 1914–19. Pastorates in Galston and Glasgow, 1921–30; Chaplain to University of Glasgow, 1930–39; Sec. to the Churches' Commn of Internat. Friendship and Social Responsibility, 1939–42; Gen. Sec., British Council of Churches, 1942–46; Asst Leader, Iona Community, 1946–47; Lecturer in Biblical Studies, Glasgow Univ., 1947–57. Moderator of the Gen. Assembly of the Church of Scotland, May 1961–62. Hon. DD: Edinburgh, 1938; Glasgow, 1961; Dublin, 1961. *Publications:* University Sermons, 1937; Preaching in a Scientific Age (Warrack Lectures), 1954; God Comes Four Times, 1957. *Recreation:* gardening. *Address:* St John's, Doune, Perthshire. *T:* Doune 841386. *Died 26 Aug.* 1985.

**CRAIG, Clifford,** CMG 1951; radiologist; *b* 3 Aug. 1896; *s* of Dr W. J. Craig, Box Hill, Victoria, Australia; *m* 1927, Edith Nance Bulley; two *s* one *d. Educ:* Scotch Coll., Melbourne; University of Melbourne. MB, BS, 1924; MD Melbourne, 1926; MS Melbourne, 1930; FRACS 1930; DDR 1954. Surgeon Superintendent, Launceston General Hospital, 1926–31; Hon. Surgeon, Launceston General Hospital, 1932–41; Surgeon Superintendent, 1941–51. Pres., Tasmanian Branch, BMA, 1941; Mem. Federal Council, BMA, 1941–47. Pres. Rotary International, Launceston, 1950; Pres., Medical Council, Tasmania, 1954–66; Chairman, Tasmanian Cancer Cttee; President: Nat. Trust of Aust. (Tasmania), 1963–72; Aust. Cancer Soc., 1970–73. Gold Medal, Aust. Cancer Soc., 1981. Served European War, 1914–18, 1st AIF (Palestine), 1916–18; War of 1939–45, RAAF, 1940–45. *Publications:* The Engravers of Van Diemen's Land, 1961; History of the Launceston General Hospital, 1963; Old Tasmanian Prints, 1964; (jtly) Early Colonial Furniture in New South Wales and Van Diemen's Land, 1972; A Bibliographical Study of the Van Diemen's Land 'Pickwick Papers', 1973; Mr Punch in Tasmania, 1981; More Old Tasmanian Prints, 1984; articles in medical jls. *Recreations:* Cricket Blue, Melbourne Univ.; tennis, golf. *Address:* 21 High Street, Launceston, Tasmania 7250, Australia. *T:* 319025. *Club:* Launceston (Launceston).
*Died 5 Sept.* 1986.

**CRAIG, Hamish M.;** *see* Millar-Craig.

**CRAMER, Dame Mary (Theresa),** DBE 1971; Past President of the Mater Hospital Auxiliary, Sydney, New South Wales, Australia; *d* of William M. Earls; *m* 1922, Hon. Sir John (Oscar) Cramer; two *s* two *d.* Has been for many years in public life and interested in charitable activities; was closely associated with the Red Cross movement; during War of 1939–45 she was the first area officer of

Women's Aust. Nat. Services on the North Shore. *Address:* Unit 2, 5 Morton Street, Wollstonecraft, NSW 2065, Australia.
*Died 23 Sept.* 1984.

**CRANE, Sir Harry (Walter Victor),** Kt 1966; OBE 1949; JP; Industrial Relations Consultant since 1965; *b* 12 Feb. 1903; *s* of William and Ann Crane; *m*, 1st, 1930, Winefride Mary (*d* 1978), *d* of Thomas and Lucy Wing; one *s; m* 2nd, 1982, Catherine Elizabeth, *d* of Corby Garland Bevan, Haywards Heath. *Educ:* Nottingham. Engineer Fitter. NUGMW: District Officer, 1934; Nat. Officer, 1943; District Sec., 1957; retd from Union service, 1965. Member: Catering Commn, 1950–52; Catering Hygiene Cttee, 1949–52; Food Hygiene Adv. Coun., 1952–78; Workers' Travel Assoc. (now Galleon World Travel Assoc.) Management Cttee, 1960–; (pt-time) E Midlands Electricity Bd, 1965–73; Milk Marketing Bd, 1966–72. Director (part-time), Transport Holding Co., Ministry of Transport, 1966–73. Hon. Pres., Galleon World Travel, 1973–81. Chairman: Labour Party Conference Arrangements Cttee, 1954–65; Industrial Injuries Advisory Council, 1967–73; Sec. or Chm. of Joint Industrial Councils during Trade Union career. FREconS 1944. JP 1961. *Recreations:* swimming, gardening, reading. *Address:* Riverain, 22 Cliff Drive, Radcliffe-on-Trent, Nottingham. *T:* Radcliffe-on-Trent 2683. *Clubs:* Royal Commonwealth Society, Civil Service.
*Died 6 Dec.* 1986.

**CRANE, Morley Benjamin,** FRS 1947; Hon. FLS; VMH; formerly Deputy Director and Head of Pomology Department of the John Innes Horticultural Institution; *b* 17 March 1890. *Publications:* (with Sir Daniel Hall) The Apple, 1933; (with W. J. C. Lawrence) The Genetics of Garden Plants, 4th edn 1952; many research papers on origin, genetics and breeding of cultivated fruits and plants. Hon. Freedom, Fruiterer's Co., 1949; Freedom of City of London, 1949. *Address:* Plovers Dip, 22 Fishponds Way, Haughley, Suffolk.
*Died 22 Sept.* 1983.

**CRANE, Prof. William Alfred James,** MD; FRCP, FRCPGlas, FRCPath; Joseph Hunter Professor of Pathology, University of Sheffield, since 1965; Dean of Sheffield Medical School, 1976–79; Hon. Consultant Pathologist, since 1959; Hon. Director of Cancer Research, since 1968; *b* 27 June 1925; *s* of late William Crane and Margaret McGechie; *m* 1952, Yvonne Elizabeth Dann; one *s* one *d. Educ:* Univ. of Glasgow (MB ChB, MD Hons and Bellahouston Gold Medal). FRCPath 1971 (MRCPath 1963); FRCPGlas 1972 (MRCPGlas 1965); FRCP 1975 (MRCP 1967). RAMC, 1948–50; Hansen Scholar and Lectr, Univ. of Glasgow, 1951–56; Asst Prof., Univ. of Chicago, 1956–57; Lectr in Pathology, Univ. of Glasgow, 1957–59; Sen. Lectr in Pathology, Univ. of Sheffield, 1959–64; Associate Prof., Univ. of Chicago, 1962. Member: MRC Bd, 1970–76; Council, RCPath, 1970–73; Med. Sub-Cttee, UGC, 1979; GMC, 1979–; Sec., Path. Soc. of GB and Ire., 1969–74. Hon. Mem., Dutch Path. Soc., 1976. *Publications:* papers in scientific and med. jls on endocrinology and hypertension. *Recreations:* gardening, music. *Address:* 56 Stumperlowe Crescent Road, Fulwood, Sheffield S10 3PR. *Died 29 Dec.* 1982.

**CRANKSHAW, Edward,** TD; FRSL; writer; Correspondent on Soviet Affairs for The Observer, 1947–68; *b* 3 Jan. 1909; *s* of Arthur and Amy Crankshaw; *m* 1931, Clare, *d* of late E. A. Carr. *Educ:* Bishop's Stortford Coll. Commissioned 4th Bn Queen's Own Royal West Kent Regt (TA), 1936; seconded to Mil. Intell., 1940–45 (GSO1 attached Brit. Mil. Mission, Moscow, 1941–43); Lt-Col, 1942. Ehrenkreuz für Wissenschaft und Kunst, 1st Class (Austria), 1964. *Publications:* Joseph Conrad: Aspects of the Art of the Novel, 1936; Vienna: the Image of a Culture in Decline, 1938; Britain and Russia, 1945; Russia and the Russians, 1947; Russia by Daylight, 1951; Gestapo: Instrument of Tyranny, 1956; Russia without Stalin, 1956; Krushchev's Russia, 1959; The Fall of the House of Habsburg, 1963; The New Cold War: Moscow v. Pekin, 1963; Krushchev: a Biography, 1966; Maria Theresa, 1969; The Habsburgs, 1971; (introd. and commentary) Kruschev Remembers, 1971; Tolstoy: the making of a novelist, 1974; The Shadow of the Winter Palace: the drift to revolution, 1825–1917, 1976 (Yorkshire Post Prize, 1976; Heinemann Award, 1977); Bismarck, 1981 (Whitbread Prize, 1982); Putting up with the Russians, 1984; *novels:* Nina Lessing, 1938; What Glory?, 1939; The Creedy Case, 1954; many translations from German and French, incl. five plays by Ernst Toller; contribs to many periodicals and symposia on Russia, music and painting in UK, USA and worldwide. *Recreations:* fishing, music. *Address:* Church House, Sandhurst, Hawkhurst, Kent. *Club:* Brooks's.
*Died 30 Nov.* 1984.

**CRANSTONE, Bryan Allan Lefevre;** Curator, Pitt Rivers Museum, Oxford, 1976–85; *b* 26 Feb. 1918; *s* of late Edgar Arnold Cranstone and late Clarice Edith Cranstone; *m* 1941, Isabel May, *d* of W. Gough-Thomas; one *s. Educ:* Bootham Sch., York; St Catharine's Coll., Cambridge (MA). Hampshire Regt, 1939–46. Asst Keeper, Dept of Ethnography, BM, 1947–69; field work, New Guinea, 1963–64; Dep. Keeper, Dept of Ethnography, BM (later Museum of Mankind), 1969–76. Vis. Lectr, University Coll., London,

1955–71. Fellow, Linacre Coll., Oxford, 1976. Vice-Pres., RAI, 1980–83. *Publications:* Melanesia: a short ethnography, 1961; The Australian Aborigines, 1973; (with D. C. Starzecka) The Solomon Islanders, 1974; Arte de Nueva Guinea y Papua, 1977; articles in learned jls and encyclopaedias. *Address:* 38 Granville Court, Cheney Lane, Headington, Oxford OX3 OHS. *Died* 4 *Sept.* 1989.

**CRAVEN, 7th Earl of,** *cr* 1801; **Thomas Robert Douglas Craven;** Viscount Uffington, 1801; Baron Craven, 1665; *b* 24 Aug. 1957; *e s* of 6th Earl of Craven and of Elizabeth (*née* Johnstone-Douglas); *S* father, 1965. *Heir: b* Hon. Simon George Craven, *b* 16 Sept. 1961. *Address:* Hamstead House, Hamstead Marshall, Newbury, Berks. *Died* 22 *Oct.* 1983.

**CRAVEN, 8th Earl of,** *cr* 1801; **Simon George Craven;** Baron Craven, 1665; Viscount Uffington, 1801; *b* 16 Sept. 1961; *s* of 6th Earl of Craven and of Elizabeth (*née* Johnstone-Douglas); *S* brother, 1983; *m* 1988, Teresa Maria Bernadette, *d* of George Arthur John Downes; one *s. Educ:* Douai. *Recreation:* sailing. *Heir: s* Viscount Uffington, *b* 13 June 1989. *Address:* Peelings Manor, near Pevensey, Sussex BN24 5AP. *Club:* Royal Ocean Racing.

*Died* 30 *Aug.* 1990.

**CRAVEN, Marjorie Eadon,** RRC 1941 (1st Class); *b* 21 March 1895; *yr d* of late John Alfred Craven and Susannah Eadon Craven, Sheffield, Yorks. *Educ:* Roedean Sch. SRN; SCM; RNT; Diploma in Nursing, Leeds Univ.; Health Visitor. Mem. St John VAD, 1915–17; Leeds Gen. Infirmary, 1917–26; studied nursing administration: Bedford Coll., London, Royal College of Nursing, 1926; Teachers' Coll., Columbia Univ., NY City, 1927–28. Matron, West London Hospital, 1929–38 and 1947–53; Matron and Principal Matron, TANS, 1939–44; Matron-in-Chief, British Red Cross Soc. and Joint Cttee, Order of St John and BRCS, 1953–62, retd. Vice-Pres., W. L. H. Nurses' League; Vice-Pres., National Florence Nightingale Memorial Cttee. Officer (Sister) Order of St John, 1957. Florence Nightingale Medal, 1961. *Recreation:* music. *Address:* Green Finches, 33 North Park, Gerrards Cross, Bucks SL9 8AT. *T:* Gerrards Cross 882349. *Died* 4 *July* 1983.

**CRAWFORD, Sir (Archibald James) Dirom,** Kt 1957; Hon. Treasurer Western Area Conservative and Unionist Association since 1959 (President, 1956–59; Chairman, 1951–56); *b* 1899; *s* of Malcolm M. Crawford and Ethel Elizabeth Crawford, *d* of Andrew Wernicke; unmarried. *Educ:* Winchester; RMC Sandhurst. Served as Subaltern, 6th Inniskilling Dragoons, then RARO; invalided out of Service, 1939. Chairman: Bridgwater Div. Conservative and Unionist Assoc., 1948–51; Somerset County Federation of Conservative and Unionist Assocs, 1950–51. Pres., Somerset County Cttee, British Legion, Dec. 1957– (Hon. Treasurer, 1953–57). *Address:* Park House, Over Stowey, Bridgwater, Somerset. *T:* Nether Stowey 269. *Club:* Cavalry and Guards.

*Died* 10 *Jan.* 1983.

**CRAWFORD, David Gordon,** CMG 1981; HM Diplomatic Service; Ambassador to Bahrain, since 1981; *b* 10 June 1928; *m* 1953, Anne Sturgeon Burns; one *s* three *d. Educ:* Ashford Grammar School, Kent; London School of Economics. Served HM Forces, 1947–55. Joined Diplomatic Service, 1956; FO, 1956; MECAS, 1957–59; Taiz, 1959; Bahrain, 1959–62; FO, 1962–64; First Sec., New York, 1964–67; First Sec. and Head of Chancery, Amman, 1967–69; Consul-Gen., Oman, 1969–71; Head of Accommodation and Services Dept, FCO, 1971–74; Ambassador to Qatar, 1974–78; Consul-General, Atlanta, 1978–81. *Address:* c/o Foreign and Commonwealth Office, SW1. *Died* 6 *Sept.* 1981.

**CRAWFORD, Sir Dirom;** *see* Crawford, Sir A. J. D.

**CRAWFORD, Brig. Sir Douglas Inglis,** Kt 1964; CB 1952; DSO 1945; TD 1942; first Lord-Lieutenant, MetropolitanCounty of Merseyside, 1974–79; Vice-Chairman, United Biscuits, 1962–74; Life President: D. S. Crawford Ltd; William Crawford & Sons Ltd, 1981; *b* 22 March 1904; *e s* of Archibald Inglis and Mary Forsyth Crawford; unmarried. *Educ:* Uppingham; Magdalene Coll., Cambridge. Served War of 1939–45 in Field Artillery; Comd 87 (Field) Army Group RA (TA), 1947–51; Chm., W Lancs T&AFA, 1951–66; Dir, Royal Insurance Co. Ltd, 1951–74. High Sheriff of the County Palatine of Lancaster, 1969–70; DL Lancs, 1951. Hon. LLD Liverpool, 1976. KStJ 1974. *Recreation:* shooting. *Address:* Fernlea, Mossley Hill, Liverpool L18 8BP. *T:* Allerton 2013. *Clubs:* White's, Boodle's; Royal and Ancient, Hon. Company of Edinburgh Golfers. *Died* 13 *Oct.* 1981.

**CRAWFORD, Hugh Adam,** RSA 1958 (ARSA 1938); painter; *b* 28 Oct. 1898; *s* of John Cummings and Agnes Crawford; *m* 1934, Kathleen Mann, ARCA, *d* of late Archibald and Rosamond Mann, Old Coulsdon, Surrey; two *s* (one *d* decd). *Educ:* Garelochhead Public Sch.; Glasgow Sch. of Art. Served in European War, 1915–19. Dipl. Glasgow Sch. of Art, 1923; studied in London, 1923–25. Runner-up, Prix de Rome, 1926. Lectr, 1926, Head of Drawing and Painting Dept, 1936, Glasgow Sch. of Art; Head of Gray's Sch. of Art, Aberdeen, 1948; Princ., Duncan of Jordanstone Coll. of Art,

Dundee, 1953. Commissions include portraits of: Lord Strathclyde; Lord Hughes; Sir Hector Maclennan; Sir Patrick Dolan; Sir Alexander King, etc.; also portraits for War Records. *Publications:* contribs to Scottish Library Review of criticisms of books on art. *Recreation:* study of magnetism. *Address:* Carronmor, Blanefield, Stirlingshire. *T:* Blanefield 512. *Clubs:* Savile, Chelsea; Scottish Arts (Edinburgh); Art (Glasgow). *Died* 2 *March* 1982.

**CRAWFORD, James,** CBE 1956; Full-time Member National Coal Board, 1957–62 (Part-time Member, 1956–57), retired; Member, General Council of Trades Union Congress, 1949–57; Chairman, British Productivity Council, 1955–56; *b* Maybole, 1 Aug. 1896; *s* of late James Crawford; *m* 1st, 1929, Mary McInnes (*d* 1944), *d* of James McGregor; two *s*; 2nd, 1945, Agnes Crossthwaite, *d* of William Sheal; one *s. Educ:* Cairn Sch.; Carrick Academy, Maybole. Served European War, 1914–18, 6th Highland Light Infantry, and 2nd and 10th Cameronians. Mem. of Glasgow City Council, 1930–38; Magistrate, 1935–38. Contested (Lab.) Kilmarnock Div. of Ayr and Bute, 1935; Mem. Advisory Council, Dept of Scientific and Industrial Research, 1950–55; Gen. Pres., National Union of Boot and Shoe Operatives, 1944–57. *Recreation:* bowls. *Address:* 5 Woburn Close, Thorpe Acre, Loughborough, Leics. *T:* Loughborough 68346. *Died* 15 *July* 1982.

**CRAWFORD, Sir John (Grenfell),** AC 1978; Kt 1959; CBE 1954; MEc (Sydney); FAIAS; Chancellor, Australian National University, 1976–84; Director, Australia-Japan Economic Research Project; *b* 4 April 1910; *s* of Henry and Harriet Crawford, Sydney; *m* 1935, Jessie Anderson Morgan; one *d. Educ:* Sydney Univ.; Harvard Univ.; Research Fellow, University of Sydney, 1933–35; Lectr, Agricultural Economics, University of Sydney (Part-time), 1934–41; Commonwealth Fund Fellow, USA, 1938–40; Economic Adviser, Rural Bank of NSW, 1935–43; Director, Commonwealth Bureau of Agricultural Economics, 1945–50; Sec., Dept of Commerce and Agriculture, 1950–56; Sec., Dept of Trade, Commonwealth of Australia, 1956–60; resigned from Civil Service, 1960. Dir and Prof. of Economics, Research Sch. of Pacific Studies, Australian National Univ., 1960–67, and Fiscal Adviser to the Univ.; Vice-Chancellor, ANU, 1968–73; Chancellor, Univ. of Papua and New Guinea, 1972–75. Vice-Chm., Commonwealth Cttee of Economic Enquiry, 1962–64, 1966–67. Mem. World Bank Economic Mission to India, 1964–65; Sen. Agricl Adviser to World Bank, Washington, 1967–81. Chairman: Technical Adv. Cttee to Consultative Gp of Internat. Agricultural Res., 1971–76; Australian Develt Adv. Board, 1975–77; Bd, Internat. Food Policy Res. Inst., 1976–; Mem. Bd, Internat. Fertilizer Develt Center, 1977–. Pres., ANZAAS, 1967–68 (Medallist, 1971). Hon. DSc Newcastle, NSW, 1966; Hon. DEc New England, NSW, 1969; Hon. LLD: Tasmania, 1971; Papua New Guinea, 1975; ANU, 1976; Hon. DSc Econ Sydney, 1972. *Publications:* Australian National Income (with Colin Clark), 1938; Australian Trade Policy 1942–1966, 1968; A Commission to Advise on Assistance to Industries (report to Aust. Govt), 1973; Report on Structural Adjustment in Industry, 1979; Report on Revitalisation of Australian Shipping, 1981; articles in Economic Record, Journal of Public Administration, Australian Outlook; several edited books on Australian Economic Affairs and several published lectures on trade and educn policy. *Recreation:* reading. *Address:* 32 Melbourne Avenue, Deakin, ACT 2600, Australia. *Clubs:* Commonwealth (Canberra); Melbourne (Melbourne). *Died* 28 *Nov.* 1984.

**CRAWFORD, Captain John Stuart,** DSO 1940; OBE 1970; Royal Navy, retired; HM Consul, Tromsö, Norway, 1956–70, retired; *b* 24 March 1900, *s* of late John Crawford, MD, BS, and late Christian Patricia Blackstock; *m* 1927, Katherine Macdonald (*d* 1981); one *d* (and one *s* decd). *Educ:* Dollar Academy; RNC, Osborne and Dartmouth, Midshipman, 1916–18; HMS Valiant; Lieut. 1920; Lieut-Comdr, 1928; Comdr, 1934; Capt., 1940. Naval Attaché Angora, 1946–48; retired list, 1950. County Civil Defence Officer, Northants, 1951; Asst Commissioner of Police (in charge of Marine Police Branch), Malaya, 1951–55, Younger brother of Trinity House, 1961–. *Address:* The Gardens, West Stafford, Dorchester, Dorset. *Club:* Naval and Military. *Died* 9 *Sept.* 1985.

**CRAWFORD-COMPTON, Air Vice-Marshal William Vernon,** CB 1965; CBE 1957; DSO 1943, Bar 1945; DFC 1941, Bar, 1942; RAF retired, 1969; *b* 2 March 1915; *s* of William Gilbert Crawford-Compton; *m* 1st, 1949, Chloe Clifford-Brown (marr. diss. 1978); two *d*; 2nd, 1978, Dolores Perle Goodhew, widow. *Educ:* New Plymouth High Sch., New Zealand. Joined RAF, 1939; served War of 1939–45 (DFC and Bar, DSO and Bar); 11 Group and 2nd TAF Group Capt., 1955; SASO, 11 (Fighter) Group; Student, Imperial Defence Coll., 1961; Air Officer in Charge of Administration, Near East Air Force, 1962–63; SASO 1963–66. Air Vice-Marshal, 1963. Legion of Honour (France); Croix de Guerre (France); Silver Star (USA). *Recreations:* golf, tennis, fishing. *Address:* Mother Friday's House, Newtown, Alderney, CI. *T:* Alderney 2578.

*Died* 2 *Jan.* 1988.

**CRAWSHAW OF AINTREE,** Baron *cr* 1985 (Life Peer), of Salford in the County of Greater Manchester; **Lt-Col Richard Crawshaw,** OBE 1958; TD 1958; MA, LLB; DL; Barrister-at-Law; *b* 25 Sept. 1917; *s* of Percy Eli Lee Crawshaw and Beatrice Lavinia (*née* Barritt); *m* 1960, Audrey Frances Lima; no *c. Educ:* Pendleton Gram. Sch.; Tatterford Sch.; Pembroke Coll., Cambridge (MA); London Univ. (LLB). Clerk, 1929–31; Engineer, 1933–36; Theological Student, 1936–39; Royal Artillery and Parachute Regt, 1939–45; Pembroke Coll., Cambridge, 1945–47; called to Bar, Inner Temple, 1948; Northern Circuit. Liverpool City Council, 1948–65. Commanded 12/13th Bn, The Parachute Regt, TA, 1954–57. MP Toxteth, Liverpool, 1964–83 (Lab, 1964–81, SDP, 1981–83); Mem., Speaker's Panel of Chairmen, 1971–79; Dep. Chm. of Ways and Means and Deputy Speaker, 1979–81. Contested (SDP) Liverpool, Broadgreen, 1983. Estd world non-stop walking record of 255.8 miles, 1972; estd world non-stop walking record (literally non-stop) of 231 miles, 1974. DL Merseyside, 1970. *Recreations:* climbing, walking, free fall parachuting and youth activities. *Address:* The Orchard, Aintree Lane, Liverpool L10 8LE. *T:* 051–526 7886.

*Died 16 July 1986.*

**CRAWSHAW, Philip,** CBE 1959 (MBE 1948); Director-General, Royal Over-Seas League, 1959–79; *b* 25 Nov. 1912; twin *s* of R. Crawshaw; *m* 1947, June Patricia, *d* of E. D. K. Mathews; two *d. Educ:* Repton. Travelling Sec., Over-Seas League, 1936; Asst Sec., 1940; Sec., 1946; Sec.-Gen., 1956. *Address:* 14 Champs Beulai, Longy Road, Alderney, CI. *Clubs:* Royal Over-Seas League; Alderney Golf.

*Died 25 July 1984.*

**CREAGH, Maj.-Gen. Edward Philip Nagle,** CB 1954; retired; *b* 29 Feb. 1896; *s* of late P. W. Creagh, Fermoy, Co. Cork and Mrs S. H. Creagh; *m* 1927, Ethel Frances Montgomery (*d* 1973); one *s* one *d. Educ:* St Augustine's Coll., Ramsgate; University Coll. of Cork, NUI. MB, BCh 1917; MRCP 1931. Commissioned RAMC, 1917; Captain 1918; Major 1929; Lt-Col 1943; Col 1948; Brig., 1951; Maj.-Gen., 1953; QHP 1953. War of 1939–45 (despatches). Retired, Feb. 1956. Col Comdt, RAMC, 1956–63. *Recreations:* amateur rider (up to 1927); trout fishing, golf. *Address:* Old Vicarage, Thriplow, near Royston, Cambs. *T:* Fowlmere 272.

*Died 15 July 1981.*

**CREASEY, Gen. Sir Timothy (May),** KCB 1978 (CB 1975); OBE 1966; Deputy Commander-in-Chief and Chief of Defence Staff, Sultan of Oman's Armed Forces, 1981–85; Personal Military Adviser to HM Sultan of Oman, since 1985; *b* 21 Sept. 1923; *s* of late Lt-Col G. M. Creasey and late Phyllis Creasey, *d* of Vice-Adm. F. C. B. Robinson, RN; *m* 1951, Ruth Annette, *y d* of Major J. I. H. Friend, OBE, MC, DL, JP, Northdown, Kent; one *s* one *d* (and one *s* decd). *Educ:* Clifton Coll. Commissioned Baluch Regt, IA, 1942. Served War: Far East, Italy, Greece, 1942–45. Transf. to Royal Norfolk Regt, 1946; Instructor, Sch. of Infantry, 1951–53; Bde Major, 39th Infantry Bde, Kenya and Ireland, 1955–56; Instr, Army Staff Coll., 1959–61; Instr, RMA, Sandhurst, 1963–64; commanded: 1 Royal Anglian, Aden and BAOR, 1965–67; 11th Armoured Bde, 1969–70; Student, IDC, 1971; Comdr, Sultan's Armed Forces, Oman, 1972–75; Dir of Infantry, 1975–77; GOC Northern Ireland, 1977–79; C-in-C, UKLF, 1980–81. Dep. Col, Royal Anglian Regt, 1976–81, Col, 1982–. Colonel Commandant: The Queen's Div., 1977–81; Small Arms Sch. Corps, 1977–81. Pres., Indian Army Assoc., 1986–. Governor, Clifton Coll., 1979–. Jordanian Order of Independence, 1st class, 1974; Order of Oman, 2nd class, 1975. *Recreations:* shooting, golf, fishing. *Address:* c/o Royal Bank of Scotland, Holt's Branch, Whitehall, SW1. *Clubs:* MCC, Army and Navy.

*Died 5 Oct. 1986.*

**CREASY, Sir Gerald Hallen,** KCMG 1946 (CMG 1943); KCVO 1954; OBE 1937; *b* 1 Nov. 1897; *y s* of Leonard and Ellen Maud Creasy; *m* 1925, Helen Duff, *y d* of Reginald B. Jacomb; one *s* one *d. Educ:* Rugby. On Military Service (RA), 1916–19; entered Colonial Office, 1920; Chief Sec. to the West African Council, 1945–47; Governor and C-in-C, Gold Coast, 1947–49; Governor and C-in-C, Malta, 1949–54, retired 1954. GCStJ 1970 (KStJ 1949). LLD (*hc*) Royal University of Malta, 1954. *Address:* 2 Burlington Court, Eastbourne, East Sussex. *T:* Eastbourne 27147.

*Died 9 June 1983.*

**CREED, Albert Lowry,** MA; *b* 16 July 1909; *s* of Rev. Albert H. Creed; *m* 1943, Joyce Marian (*née* Hunter), Leeds; two *s* one *d. Educ:* Kingswood Sch.; Downing Coll., Cambridge. MA Cantab 1931. Asst Master: Stretford Grammar Sch., 1932–35; Bishop's Stortford Coll., 1935–39; Housemaster, Christ's Hospital, 1939–42; Headmaster: Staveley-Netherthorpe Grammar Sch., 1942–46; Truro Sch., Cornwall, 1946–59; Kingswood Sch., 1959–70; Volunteer with Botswana Min. of Educn, 1973–74. Chm., West Cornwall Hospital Management Cttee, 1957–59; Vice-Pres., Methodist Conf., 1962–63; a Dir, The Methodist Recorder, 1961–86. Pres., Kingswood Old Boys' Assoc., 1975–76. Hon. Sec., UK-Botswana Soc., 1981–83. *Address:* Greggs House, 73 Manchester Road, Chapel-en-le-Frith, near Stockport, Cheshire SK12 6TH. *T:*

Chapel-en-le-Frith 814121. *Club:* Royal Commonwealth Society.

*Died 3 Feb. 1987.*

**CREMIN, Cornelius Christopher;** Chairman, Irish delegation to 3rd UN Conference on the Law of the Sea, 1973–79; *b* 6 Dec. 1908; 2nd *s* of D. J. Cremin and Ann (*née* Singleton), Kenmare, Co. Kerry; *m* 1st, 1935, Patricia Josephine (decd), Killarney; one *s* three *d*; 2nd, 1974, Dr Mary Eta Murphy, Beare Island. *Educ:* National Univ. of Ireland. BComm 1930; MA (Classics) 1931. Travelling studentship (Classics), NUI, 1931–34; Brit. Sch. at Athens and Rome, 1932; Dipl. in Class. Archaeol., Oxford, 1934; 3rd Sec., Dept of External Affairs, 1935; 1st Sec., Irish Legation, Paris, 1937–43; Chargé d'Affaires, Berlin, 1943–45; Chargé d'Affaires, Lisbon, 1945–46; Couns., Dept of External Affairs, Dublin, 1946–48; Asst Sec., 1948–50; Minister to France, March-Sept. 1950; Ambassador to France, 1950–54; Head of Irish Delegn, OEEC, 1950–54, and Vice-Chm. of OEEC Council (official), 1952–54; Ambassador to the Holy See, 1954–56; Sec. of the Dept of External Affairs, Dublin, 1958–62; Irish Ambassador to Britain, 1963–64 (and 1956–58)); Irish Permanent Representative at UN, 1964–74. LLD *hc* National Univ. of Ireland, 1965. Grand Officer of the Legion of Honour, 1954; Knight Grand Cross of the Order of Pius, 1956; Grand Cross of Merit (Fed. Germany), 1960. *Recreations:* golf, boating. *Address:* Tuosist, Killarney, Ireland. *Died 18 April 1987.*

**CRESSWELL, William Foy,** CBE 1956; Senior Official Receiver in Bankruptcy, 1948–56; *b* 2 Nov. 1895; *s* of Edward Cresswell and Annie Maria (*née* Foy); *m* 1922, Olive May Barham; two *d. Educ:* Portsmouth Secondary Sch. Entered Civil Service as Boy Clerk, 1911. Served with Hon. Artillery Company 2nd Inf. Bn in France, Italy and Austria, 1916–19. Appointed to Bankruptcy Department, Board of Trade, 1921; Asst Official Receiver, High Court, 1931; Official Receiver, Swansea and district, 1934; Official Receiver, Bradford, Yorks, 1936; recalled to London to assist with BoT War Damage Insurance Schemes, 1941. Retired, Dec. 1956. *Address:* 27 Sullington Gardens, Worthing, West Sussex. *T:* Findon 2065.

*Died 21 Dec. 1981.*

**CRESWELL, Sir Michael Justin,** KCMG 1960 (CMG 1952); Ambassador to Argentine Republic, 1964–69; retired; *b* 21 Sept. 1909; *s* of late Col Edmund William Creswell, RE; *m* 1st, 1939, Elizabeth Colshorn; one *s*; 2nd, 1950, Baroness C. M. thoe Schwartzenberg; one *s. Educ:* Rugby; New Coll., Oxford. Laming Travelling Fellow, Queen's Coll., Oxford, 1932. Entered Foreign Service, 1933; 3rd Sec., Berlin, 1935–38; 2nd Sec., Madrid, 1939–44, Athens, 1944; Foreign Office, 1944–47; Counsellor, Tehran, 1947–49; Singapore, 1949–51; Minister, British Embassy, Cairo, 1951–54; Ambassador to Finland, 1954–58; Senior Civilian Instructor, Imperial Defence Coll., 1958–60; Ambassador to Yugoslavia, 1960–64. Chm., Surrey Amenity Council, 1974–83; Member: Waverley DC, 1974–85; Waverley BC, 1985–; Surrey CC, 1977–85. *Recreations:* travel, wild life. *Address:* Copse Hill, Ewhurst, near Cranleigh, Surrey. *T:* Cranleigh 277311.

*Died 25 April 1986.*

**CRESWICK, Sir Alexander Reid, (Sir Alec Creswick),** Kt 1974; company director and pastoralist, Australia; Chairman, Victoria Racing Club Committee, 1969–77 (Member, since 1959); *b* 1912; *s* of late H. F. Creswick; *m* 1st, Claudia, *d* of C. B. Palmer; two *s*; 2nd, Dinah Bingham Meeks, *d* of Anthony Hordern; two *d. Educ:* Melbourne Church of England Grammar Sch.; St John's Coll., Oxford. Served War of 1939–45, Australian Army Service Corps. Past Pres.: Victoria Polo Assoc.; Equestrian Fedn of Aust. Formerly: Master of Melbourne Hounds; Manager of Aust. Olympic Equestrian Teams: Rome, Stockholm, Montreal. Life Mem., Council of Royal Agricultural Soc. of Victoria. Director, Carlton and United Breweries Ltd, retd 1979. *Address:* Allanvale, Avenel, Victoria 3664, Australia; c/o 422 Collins Street, Melbourne, Vic. 3000, Australia. *Clubs:* VRC, Melbourne (Melbourne).

*Died 10 June 1983.*

**CRESWICK, Harry Richardson,** MA; Librarian Emeritus of Cambridge University; *b* 1902; *m* Agnes Isabel (*d* 1982), *d* of late J. W. Stubbings. *Educ:* Barnet Grammar Sch.; Trinity Coll., Cambridge. On staff of University Library, Cambridge, 1926–38; Deputy Librarian, Bodleian Library, Oxford, 1939–45; Bodley's Librarian and Student of Christ Church, 1945–47; Librarian of Cambridge Univ. and Professorial Fellow of Jesus Coll., 1949–67, Emeritus Fellow, 1976. Hon. LittD, Trinity Coll., Dublin.

*Died 14 Oct. 1988.*

**CRICHTON, Sir (John) Robertson (Dunn),** Kt 1967; Judge of the High Court of Justice, Queen's Bench Division, 1967–77; *b* 2 Nov. 1912; *s* of Alexander Cansh and Beatrice Crichton, Wallasey, Ches; *m* 1944, Margaret Vanderlip, *d* of Col Livingston Watrous, Washington, DC, and Nantucket, Mass, USA; two *s* one *d. Educ:* Sedbergh Sch.; Balliol Coll., Oxford. Called to the Bar, Middle Temple, 1936; Bencher, 1959. Served War of 1939–45, RA (TA). KC 1951; QC 1952. Recorder of Blackpool, 1952–60; Judge of Appeal of the Isle of Man, 1956–60; Recorder of Manchester and

Judge of Crown Court at Manchester, 1960–67. *Recreations:* gardening, painting. *Address:* Hempfield, Dunham Massey, Altrincham, Cheshire. *T:* 061–928 6101. *Club:* United Oxford & Cambridge University. *Died* 12 *July* 1985.

**CRICHTON, Col Walter Hugh,** CIE 1941; MB, ChB Edinburgh 1919; DPH London 1934; IMS (retired); *b* 24 July 1896; *m* 1920, Dorothy Martindale, Trinity, Edinburgh; one *s* one *d.* Apptd Indian Medical Service, 1920; Foreign Political Dept, 1930; Vice-Consul, Seistan, Persia; Agency Surgeon Kurram Valley, NWFP, 1932; MOH, Simla, 1934; Chief Health Officer, Delhi Prov., 1936; on active service Paiforce, 1941; ADMS, Basra, 1942; Mil. Gov., CMF, 1943; Dir PH Mil. Gov., 21 Army Group, BLA, 1944–45; Dir Public Health, CP and Behar, 1945–47; MOH Kent Co. Dists, 1948–50; Chief WHO Mission, Korea, 1950; PH Administrator WHO East Med. Region, until 1956; ACMO Norfolk; Freeman Naples City, 1944; Cross of Merit (1st Class) Order of Malta, 1944; Kt Comdr Order of Orange-Nassau, 1946. *Address:* Westbury House, West Meon, Petersfield, Hants. *Club:* Naval and Military.
*Died* 16 *Feb.* 1984.

**CRIDLAND, Charles Elliot Tapscott;** Vice-Chairman, The Aero Group, 1969–70; *b* Glos, 21 July 1900; *s* of S. L. Cridland; *m* 1st, 1923, Kathleen (*d* 1957), *d* of Capt. Bell, Cheltenham; two *d*; 2nd, 1948, Louise Simmons (marr. annulled); 3rd, 1968, Joan Gardiner, *d* of late G. A. McLennan and Mrs. E. Coy. *Educ:* Trent Coll., Long Eaton; Faraday House Engineering Coll., London. Chm. and Managing Director: Rye & Co., Lincoln, 1927–30; Eclair Doors Ltd, 1937–47; Aldis Bros Ltd, 1946–57; Automatic Changers Ltd, 1956–57; Chairman: Hawkes & Snow (Curtaincraft) Ltd, 1949–63; Portable Balers Ltd, 1953–61; Aero Heat Treatment Ltd, 1947–69; Hard Coating Ltd, 1951–69; Chisholm, Gray and Co. Ltd, 1956–69; Aerotaps Ltd, 1958–69; Aerocoldform Ltd, 1956–69; Broadstone Ballvalve Co. Ltd, 1959–69; Bendz Ltd, 1962–69; Quality Machined Parts, Ltd, 1964–69; Kinsman Ltd, 1965–69. Vice-Chm., Mercian Builders Merchants Ltd, 1965–67. Dir, A. D Foulkes Ltd, 1958–65. Mem. Org. Cttee, Birmingham Productivity Assoc., 1955–63. Chm. Organisation Cttee, National Farmers' Union, Glos Branch, 1946; Chm., Steel Rolling Shutter Assoc., 1945–46. Scientific Instrument Manufacturers' Assoc. of Gt Brit. Ltd: Mem. Council, 1949–57, Vice-Pres., 1953 and 1957, Pres., 1954–56; Chm., Transport Users' Consultative Cttee, W Midlands Area, 1960–69; Mem., Central Transport Consultative Cttee, 1963–69. Mem. Court of Assistants, The Worshipful Co. of Scientific Instrument Makers, 1955; elected Master, 1956 and 1957; Freeman, City of London, 1955. *Ex-officio* Mem. Bd of Govs, Faraday House Engrg Coll., 1961–63; Vice-Pres. and Hon. Treas. Faraday House Old Students Assoc., 1960, Pres. 1962–63. Served War, RAF, 1918–19. *Recreations:* golf (played for Warwicks and Glos), and farming. *Address:* c/o National Westminster Bank Ltd, Prospect Hill, Douglas, Isle of Man.
*Died* 3 *March* 1983.

**CRISHAM, Air Vice-Marshal William Joseph,** CB 1953; CBE 1944; RAF, retired; *b* 19 Nov. 1906; *m* 1946, Maureen Teresa Bergin, Dublin; three *s* three *d. Educ:* in Ireland. Served War of 1939–45; Nos 13 and 23 Sqdns; Comdt, Central Fighter Establishment, 1950–53; AOC No 12 Group Fighter Command, 1953–56; AOC RAF Levant MEAF, 1956–58; AOC RAF Germany (2nd TAF), 1958–61; retired 1961. *Club:* Royal Air Force.
*Died* 24 *July* 1987.

**CRISP, Prof. Dennis John,** CBE 1978; ScD; FRS 1968; Professor in Department of Marine Biology, University College of North Wales, 1962–83, later Professor Emeritus; Hon. Director, Natural Environment Research Council Unit of Marine Invertebrate Biology, 1965–83; *b* 29 April 1916; *m* 1944, Ella Stewart Allpress; one *s* one *d. Educ:* St Catharine's Coll., Cambridge. Research Asst, Dept of Colloid Science, Univ. of Cambridge, 1943–46; ICI (Paints Div.), i/c of Marine Paints Res. Stn, Brixham, Devon, 1946–51; Dir, Marine Science Laboratories, University Coll. of N Wales, 1951–70. Hon. FNA, 1984. *Publications:* (ed) Grazing in Terrestrial and Marine Environments, 1964; (ed) 4th European Marine Biology Symposium Volume (1969), 1971; papers in Proc. Royal Soc., Jl Marine Biol. Assoc., Jl Experimental Biology, Jl Animal Ecology, etc. *Recreations:* travel, photography. *Address:* Craig y Pin, Llandegfan, Menai Bridge, Gwynedd LL59 5TH. *T:* Menai Bridge 712775. *Died* 18 *Jan.* 1990.

**CRISP, Prof. Leslie Finlay;** Professor of Political Science, Australian National University, 1950–77, then Emeritus Professor; Member since 1974, Chairman, since 1975, Board of Commonwealth Banking Corporation; *b* Melbourne, 19 Jan. 1917; *s* of Leslie Walter and Ruby Elizabeth Crisp; *m* 1940, Helen Craven Wighton; one *s* two *d. Educ:* St Peter's Coll., Adelaide; St Mark's Coll., Univ. of Adelaide (MA); Balliol Coll., Oxford (Rhodes Schol., MA). Australian Public Service, 1940–50: Dir-Gen., Dept of Post-War Reconstruction, 1949–50. Chm., Canberra Hosp. Bd, 1951–55; Mem., Prime Minister's Cttee on Future of Nat. Library and Archives, 1956; Chm., Prime Minister's Cttee on Integration of

Data Bases, 1973–74. *Publications:* Parliamentary Government of the Commonwealth of Australia, 1949; Australian Federal Labour Party, 1955; Ben Chifley, 1961; Australian National Government, 1965; Peter Richard Heydon 1913–1971, 1972, etc. *Address:* 16 Norman Street, Deakin, Canberra, ACT 2600, Australia. *T:* 81 3828. *Club:* Royal Canberra Golf. *Died* 21 *Dec.* 1984.

**CRISP, Hon. Sir (Malcolm) Peter,** Kt 1969; retired; a Justice of the Supreme Court of Tasmania, 1952–71; Senior Puisne Judge, 1968–71; *b* Devonport, Tasmania, 21 March 1912; *s* of late T. M. Crisp, Burnie, (legal practitioner), and Myrtle May (*née* Donnelly); *m* 1935, Edna Eunice (*née* Taylor); two *d. Educ:* St Ignatius Coll., Riverview, Sydney; Univ. of Tasmania (LLB). Admitted legal practitioner, Tas, 1933; Crown Prosecutor, 1940. Served AIF, 1940–46 (in Australia, UK and Borneo, 2/1 Tank Attack Regt and Staff appts; rank of Colonel on discharge). Crown Solicitor, 1947–51; Solicitor-Gen. and KC, 1951. Lecturer in Law of Real Property, Univ. of Tasmania, 1947–52; Mem. Univ. Council, 1948–55; Chairman: State Library Bd, 1956–77; Council, Nat. Library of Aust., 1971 (Mem., 1960–71); Australian Adv. Council on Bibliographical Services, 1973–; Pres., Library Assoc. of Aust., 1963–66; Royal Commissioner, Fluoridation of Public Water Supplies, 1966–68. *Recreations:* cruising, angling. *Address:* 10 Anglesea Street, Hobart, Tasmania. *T:* Hobart 235639. *Clubs:* Tasmanian, Royal Yacht Club of Tasmania (Hobart).
*Died* 13 *Feb.* 1984.

**CROCKER, Antony James Gulliford,** CB 1973; retired as Under-Secretary, Family Support Division, Department of Health and Social Security (1974–78); *b* 28 Oct. 1918; *s* of late Cyril James Crocker and Mabel Kate Crocker; *m* 1st, 1943, E. S. B. Dent; 2nd, 1949, Nancy Wynell, *d* of late Judge Gamon and Eleanor Margaret Gamon; two *s* one *d. Educ:* Sherborne Sch. (Scholar); Trinity Hall, Cambridge (Major Scholar, MA). Served War, 1939–46, Dorsetshire Regt (Major). Asst Princ. 1947, Princ. 1948, Min. of Nat. Insurance. Sec., Nat. Insce Advisory Cttee, 1955–56; Asst Sec., Min. of Pensions and Nat. Insce, 1956; Under-Secretary; War Pensions Dept, 1964 (Min. of Social Security, 1966–68); Supplementary Benefits Commn, 1968; Tax Credits Div., 1972; New Pensions Scheme, 1974. *Recreations:* horticulture, philately. *Address:* The Plot, 35 Guildown Avenue, Guildford, Surrey. *T:* 66555.
*Died* 22 *Feb.* 1988.

**CROFT, Sir Bernard Hugh (Denman),** 13th Bt *cr* 1671; *b* 24 Aug. 1903; *s* of Sir Hugh Matthew Fiennes Croft, 12th Bt and Lucy Isabel, *e d* of Frederick Taylor, Terrible Vale, near Uralla, NSW; *S* father, 1954; *m* 1931, Helen Margaret, *d* of H. Weaver; three *s* two *d. Educ:* Armidale Sch., NSW. Rep. NSW Rugby Union in NZ, 1928. *Recreations:* foothall, tennis, golf. *Heir:* *s* Owen Glendower Croft [*b* 26 April 1932; *m* 1959, Sally, *d* of Dr T. M. Mansfield, Brisbane, Queensland; one *s* two *d*]. *Address:* Salisbury Court, Uralla, NSW 2358, Australia. *T:* Uralla 24. *Died Feb.* 1984.

**CROFT, Major Sir John (Archibald Radcliffe),** 5th Bt *cr* 1818; Army Officer, retired 1956; *b* 27 March 1910; *s* of Tom Radcliffe Croft, OBE (*d* 1964) (6th *s* of 2nd Bt) and Louise (*d* 1964), *d* of Francis Sales; *S* cousin, 1979; *m* 1953, Lucy Elizabeth, *d·* of late Major William Dallas Loney Jupp, OBE; one *s. Educ:* King's School, Canterbury. Commissioned The West Yorkshire Regt (PWO), 1935; served India, Burma, 1936–44; France and Germany, 1945. *Recreations:* shooting, fishing, golf. *Heir:* *s* Thomas Stephen Hutton Croft, *b* 12 June 1959. *Address:* The Barn House, Rayham Farm, South Street, Whitstable, Kent. *Clubs:* Army and Navy; Kent and Canterbury (Canterbury). *Died* 16 *Nov.* 1990.

**CROFT, (John) Michael,** OBE 1971; Founder of National Youth Theatre, 1956; *b* 8 March 1922. *Educ:* Plymouth Grove Elem. Sch. and Burnage Gram. Sch., Manchester; Keble Coll., Oxford (BA Hons). War Service in RAF and RN, 1940–45. After short career as actor, took up teaching, 1949; Asst English Master, Alleyn's Sch., 1950–55 (prod. series of Shakespeare plays with large schoolboy cos); founded Youth Theatre with group from Alleyn's Sch., 1956; this grew rapidly into nat. organisation with provincial branches; rep. Gt Brit. at Paris Festival, 1960 and W Berlin Festival, 1961; appeared at Old Vic, 1965. Also Dir Shakespeare for leading cos in Belgium and Holland, 1960–65; founded Dolphin Theatre Co., Shaw Theatre, 1971; productions include: Devil's Disciple, 1971; Romeo and Juliet, 1972; Antony and Cleopatra, 1977; Richard II, 1980; Nat. Youth Theatre Productions include: Zigger Zagger, Strand, 1968, Berlin Festival, 1968, Holland Festival, 1970, Shaw, 1981; Little Malcolm and his Struggle, Holland Festival, 1968; Fuzz, Berlin Festival, 1970; a series of plays by Peter Terson and Barrie Keeffe, during 1970s; Good Lads at Heart, tour of Canada, 1978; Brooklyn, NY, 1979; The Bread and Butter Trade, Shaw, 1982; Hamlet, 1983. *Publications:* (novel) Spare the Rod, 1954; (travel book) Red Carpet to China, 1958. *Recreations:* sport, travel. *Address:* 74 Bartholomew Road, NW5. *Club:* Savile.
*Died* 15 *Nov.* 1986.

**CROFTON,** 6th Baron *cr* 1797; **Charles Edward Piers Crofton;** Bt 1758; Master Mariner, since 1978; *b* 27 April 1949; *s* of 5th Baron Crofton and of Ann, *e d* of Group Captain Charles Tighe, The Mill House, Kilbride, Co. Wicklow; *S* father, 1974; *m* 1976, Maureen Jacqueline, *d* of S. J. Bray, Taunton, Somerset; one *d*. Ship Master, with Buries Markes (Ship Management) Ltd, 1979–. Mem., Nautical Institute, 1978. *Heir: b* Hon. Guy Patrick Gilbert Crofton [*b* 17 June 1951; *m* 1985, Gillian, *o d* of Harry Godfrey Mitchell Bass, CMG. Commissioned 9/12 Royal Lancers, 1971]. *Address:* Briscoe Cottage, Ford Street, near Wellington, Somerset.
*Died 27 June 1989.*

**CROFTON, Sir Patrick Simon,** 7th Bt *cr* 1801; *b* 2 Dec. 1936; *o s* of Major Morgan G. Crofton (*d* 1947); *S* grandfather, 1958; *m* 1967, Mrs Lene Eddowes, *d* of Kai Augustinus, Copenhagen, and Mrs R. Tonnesen, Port Elizabeth, SA; one *d*. *Educ:* Eton Coll. 2nd Lieut Welsh Guards, 1955–57. Entered Steel Industry, 1957; became Public Relations Consultant, 1961. Joint Managing Dir, Crofton Mohill Holdings Ltd; Dir, Blair Eames Suslak, Sir Patrick Crofton Ltd, Advertising Agents; Managing Dir, Sir Patrick Crofton Developments Ltd. *Recreations:* ski-ing, motoring, music, political argument. *Heir: uncle* Hugh Denis Crofton, *b* 10 April 1937. *Clubs:* Cavalry and Guards, East India, Devonshire, Sports and Public Schools.
*Died 15 May 1987.*

**CROMARTIE,** 4th Earl of, *cr* 1861 (re-creation, revival of peerage forfeited 1745/46); **Roderick Grant Francis Mackenzie,** MC 1945; TD 1964; JP; DL; Major Seaforth Highlanders, retired; Viscount Tarbat of Tarbat, Baron Castlehaven and Baron MacLeod of Leod, *cr* 1861; Chief of the Clan Mackenzie; *b* 24 Oct. 1904; *er* surv. *s* of Lt-Col Edward Walter Blunt-Mackenzie, DL (*d* 1949) and Countess of Cromartie, (3rd in line); *S* mother, 1962, having discontinued use of surname of Blunt, for himself and son, and reverted to Mackenzie; *m* 1st, 1933, Mrs Dorothy Downing Porter (marr. diss. 1945), *d* of Mr Downing, Kentucky, USA; two *d*; 2nd, 1947, Olga (Mendoza) (marr. diss. 1962), *d* of late Stuart Laurance, Paris; one *s*; 3rd, 1962, Lilias Richard, MB, ChB, *d* of Prof. (James) Walter MacLeod, OBE, FRS, FRSE. *Educ:* Charterhouse; RMC Sandhurst. Commissioned to 1st Bn Seaforth Highlanders in Ireland, 1924; transferred to 2nd Bn Seaforth Highlanders, in India, 1925; seconded to Nigeria Regt of RWAFF, 1928–29; rejoined 2nd Seaforth Highlanders, 1930; Operations North-West Frontier, India, 1930–31; in France in 1940 with 4th Seaforth Highlanders (MC). Sec., Scottish Peers Assoc., House of Lords. JP Ross and Cromarty, 1937, DL Ross and Cromarty, 1976; CC Ross and Cromarty, 1963–77 (Vice-Convener, 1970–71, Convener, 1971–75); Hon. Sheriff (formerly Hon. Sheriff Substitute); Convener, Ross and Cromarty District Council, 1975–77. FSAScot. Freeman of Ross and Cromarty, 1977. *Publication:* A Highland History, 1980. *Heir: s* Viscount Tarbat, *b* 12 June 1948. *Address:* Castle Leod, Strathpeffer, Ross and Cromarty, Scotland. *Clubs:* Army and Navy, Pratt's.
*Died 13 Dec. 1989.*

**CROMARTIE, (Ronald) Ian (Talbot),** CMG 1983; HM Diplomatic Service, retired; Ambassador and Leader, UK Delegation to Conference on Disarmament, Geneva, 1982–87; *b* 27 Feb. 1929; *s* of late Ronald Duncan Cromartie and of Mrs Margaret Talbot Cromartie; *m* 1962, Jennifer Frances, *er d* of late Captain Ewen Fairfax-Lucy and Mrs Margaret Fairfax-Lucy; two *s* one *d*. *Educ:* Sherborne; Clare Coll., Cambridge (MA, PhD). Scientific research at Univs of Cambridge and Tübingen, 1950–58; Univ. Demonstrator in Organic Chemistry, Cambridge, 1958–60. Entered Foreign (later Diplomatic) Service, 1961; served in: FO, 1961–62; Saigon, 1962–64; FO, 1964–67; UK Disarmament Delegn, Geneva, 1967–69; FCO, 1969–72; Counsellor, 1972–75, Counsellor (Scientific), 1975–78, Bonn; UK Resident Rep. to IAEA and UN Orgs in Vienna, 1978–82, with personal rank of Ambassador, 1981–82. Chm., *Ad Hoc* Cttee on chemical weapons, Conf. on Disarmament, 1986–87. *Publications:* papers in Jl of Chem. Soc. and other scientific periodicals. *Recreations:* walking, sailing, shooting. *Address:* 61 Ashley Gardens, SW1. *Club:* United Oxford & Cambridge University.
*Died 18 Oct. 1987.*

**CROMPTON-INGLEFIELD, Col Sir John (Frederick),** Kt 1963; TD; DL; *b* 1904; *e s* of Adm. Sir F. S. Inglefield, KCB, DL; *m* 1st, 1926, Rosemary (*d* 1978), *d* of Adm. Sir Percy Scott, 1st Bt, KCB, KCVO, LLD; three *d*; 2nd, 1979, Madeline Rose, *widow* of W. E. Dodds and *d* of Col Conyers Alston, Seven Rivers, Cape Province, South Africa. *Educ:* RN Colls Osborne and Dartmouth. Retired from Royal Navy, 1926. Derbyshire Yeomanry (Armoured Car Co.), Lieut 1936, Major 1939. Served War of 1939–45, with 1st Derbyshire Yeo. and 79th Armoured Div. (despatches) Africa and Europe. Lt-Col Comdg Derbyshire Yeo., 1950–53; Bt Col 1954; Hon. Col, Leics and Derbyshire Yeo., 1962–70. Chm. W Derbyshire Conservative and Unionist Assoc., 1951–66; Vice-Chm., 1957–64, Chm., TA, Derbyshire, 1964–69. CC 1932–55, JP 1933, DL 1953, and High Sheriff, 1938, Derbyshire. OStJ. *Address:* 73 Oakwood Court, Addison Road, W14. *T:* 01–602 1979. *Died 31 Oct. 1988.*

**CROMWELL,** 6th Baron *cr* 1375 (called out of abeyance 1923); **David Godfrey Bewicke-Copley;** Senior Government Broker, since 1981 (Second Government Broker, 1973–81); Mem. London Stock Exchange, since 1956; Partner in Mullens & Co. since 1960; *b* 29 May 1929; *s* of 5th Baron Cromwell, DSO, MC, and Lady Cromwell (*d* 1979), (Freda Constance, *d* of Sir F. W. B. Cripps, DSO); *S* father, 1966; *m* 1954, Vivian Penfold, *y d* of late H. de L. Penfold, Isle of Man; two *s* two *d*. *Educ:* Eton; Magdalene Coll., Cambridge. Called to the Bar, Inner Temple, 1954. *Heir: s* Hon. Godfrey John Bewicke-Copley, *b* 4 March 1960. *Address:* The Manor House, Great Milton, Oxfordshire. *T:* Great Milton 230.
*Died 18 Aug. 1982.*

**CRONIN, Archibald Joseph,** MD (Glasgow), MRCP, DPH London; novelist; *b* 19 July 1896; *s* of Patrick Cronin and Jessie Montgomerie; *m* Agnes Mary Gibson, MB, ChB; three *s*. *Educ:* Glasgow Univ. Served European War, Surgeon Sub-Lieut, RNVR; graduated MB, ChB, with hons, 1919; Physician to Out-Patients Bellahouston War Pensions Hospital; Medical Superintendent Lightburn Hospital, Glasgow; general practice South Wales, 1921–24; Medical Inspector of Mines for Great Britain, 1924; MD (hons) 1925; Report on First-Aid Conditions in British Coal Mines, 1926, published by HM Stationery Dept, also Report on Dust Inhalation in Haematite Mines; practised medicine in London, 1926–30; in 1930 decided to give up medicine, follow natural bent and devote himself to literature; first novel, Hatter's Castle, published in 1931, was instantaneous success; first play, Jupiter Laughs, produced 1940. Hon. DLitt: Bowdoin Univ.; Lafayette Univ. *Publications:* Hatter's Castle, 1931; Three Loves, 1932; Grand Canary, 1933; The Stars Look Down, 1935; The Citadel, 1937; The Keys of the Kingdom, 1942; The Green Years, 1944; Shannon's Way, 1948; The Spanish Gardener, 1950; Adventures in Two Worlds, 1952; Beyond this Place, 1953; Crusader's Tomb, 1956; The Northern Light, 1958; The Judas Tree, 1961; A Song of Sixpence, 1964; A Pocketful of Rye, 1969; The Minstrel Boy, 1975; The Lady with Carnations, 1976; Creator of Dr Finlay's Casebook. *Recreations:* golf, tennis, gardening, fishing. *Address:* Champ-Riond, Baugy sur Clarens, Vaud, Switzerland. *Clubs:* Pilgrims, University, Links (New York).
*Died 6 Jan. 1981.*

**CRONIN, John Desmond,** FRCS; Consultant Surgeon; *b* 1 March 1916; *s* of John Patrick Cronin and Beatrice Cronin (*née* Brooks); *m* 1941, Cora, *d* of Rowland Mumby-Croft; one *s* two *d*. *Educ:* London Univ. MRCS, LRCP 1939; MB, BS (London) 1940; FRCS 1947. House Surgeon, St Bartholomew's Hosp., 1939–40; Surgeon EMS, Royal Free Hosp., 1941–42. Served RAMC, 1942–46, France, Germany and Burma campaigns; Surgical Specialist, Major (Actg Lt-Col 1945). Orthopædic Surgeon, Prince of Wales's Hosp., 1947–51; Orthopædic Surgeon, French Hosp., 1948–. Vice-Chm., North St Pancras Labour Party, 1950. Member LCC, 1952–55. MP (Lab) Loughborough, 1955–79; Opposition Whip, House of Commons, 1959–62; Front Bench Spokesman on aviation, 1961–64. Director: Racal Electronics Ltd, 1965–; Knight Wegenstein Ltd, 1969–70. Officier, Légion d'Honneur, 1967 (Chevalier, 1960). *Publications:* contributions to British Med. Journal and Proceedings Royal Soc. Medicine, and to the national press; Report on the Medical Services of Malta (pub. Central Office of Information, Govt of Malta). *Recreations:* riding, aerobics, walking, cooking. *Address:* 14 Wimpole Street, W1. *T:* 01–580 2460; Ashers Top, Stoney Cross, Lyndhurst, Hants. *Clubs:* Brooks's; Royal Lymington Yacht (Lymington), House of Commons Yacht.
*Died 3 Jan. 1986.*

**CRONIN, John Walton;** Regional Chairman of Industrial Tribunals, 1972–85, part-time, 1985–88; *b* 14 Oct. 1915; *s* of John and Alice Cronin; *m* 1947, Eileen Veronica Bale (*née* Rector); one *d*; one step *s*. *Educ:* Xaverian Coll., Manchester; Manchester Univ. Solicitor. Served War, 1940–46, Major, Indian Army, latterly Staff appt, DAQMG. Private practice, 1946–55; Resident Magistrate, High Court Registrar, Acting Sheriff, Registrar-General Patents, Trade Marks and Designs, Sen. Resident Magistrate, Acting High Court Judge, Adv. Comr to Governor on Detained Persons, N Rhodesia/Zambia, 1955–65; Stipendiary and Circuit Magistrate, Grand Bahama, 1965–71. SBStJ 1969, OStJ 1977. *Address:* 6 Chelsea Court, South Road, Hythe, Kent CT21 6AH. *T:* Hythe (Kent) (0303) 267879. *Club:* Commonwealth Trust.
*Died 11 May 1990.*

**CRONNE, Prof. Henry Alfred;** Professor of Medieval History in the University of Birmingham, 1946–70, then Emeritus Professor; Dean of the Faculty of Arts, 1952–55; *b* 17 Oct. 1904; *o c* of late Rev. James Kennedy Cronne, Portaferry. Co. Down, N Ireland; *m* 1936, Lilian Mey, *er d* of E. F. Seckler, Bishops Tawton, Barnstaple; one *d*. *Educ:* Campbell Coll., Belfast; Queen's Univ. of Belfast; Balliol Coll., Oxford; Inst. of Historical Research, MA Belfast; MA Oxon; MA Birmingham, *jure officii*. Asst Lecturer in History, QUB, 1928–31; Lecturer in Medieval History, King's Coll., London, 1931, and subsequently Lecturer in Palaeography and Reader in Medieval History. War of 1939–45, served in LDV, Home Guard and Somerset

Special Constabulary. *Publications:* Bristol Charters, 1378–1499, 1946; (ed with Charles Johnson) Regesta Regum Anglo-Normannorum, Vol. II, 1100–1135, 1956, (ed with R. H. C. Davis), Vol. III, 1135–1154, 1968, and Vol. IV, Facsimiles and Diplomatic, 1135–54, 1969; The Reign of Stephen, 1970; contribs to historical jls. *Recreations:* writing, drawing. *Address:* Winswood Cottage, Cheldon, Chulmleigh, Devon EX18 7JB. *T:* Chulmleigh (0769) 80567.                                                              *Died 27 Sept* 1990.

**CROOK, 1st Baron** *cr* 1947, of Carshalton, Surrey; **Reginald Douglas Crook;** *b* 2 March 1901; *s* of Percy Edwin Crook; *m* 1922, Ida G. Haddon (*d* 1985); one *s. Educ:* Strand Sch. Local Govt Service; Organising Sec. of Poor Law Officers' Union and Editor, Poor Law Gazette, 1920–24; Gen. Sec., Min. of Labour Staff Assoc., 1925–51, and Editor, Civil Service Argus, 1929–51; Sec., Fedn of Min. of Labour Staff, 1944–51; Mem., National Whitley Council for Civil Service, 1925–51; Mem., Min. of Labour Departmental Whitley Council, 1925–51; Chm., N Islington Lab. Party, 1924–26 (and Chm., N Islington Lab. Party Candidates for 1925 Guardians Election); Hon. Sec., Labour Parliamentary Assoc., 1945–47; a Dep. Chm. of Cttees, House of Lords, 1949–75; Mem., Ecclesiastical Cttee of Parliament, 1949–75; Chm. of Interdeptl Cttee of Enquiry as to Optical Services, appointed by Min. of Health, 1949–52, leading to Opticians Act, 1958; Mem., Parl. Delegn to Denmark, 1949; Deleg. to Finland, 1950; Mem., Police Wages Council, 1951; Chm., National Dock Labour Board, 1951–65, also Chm., National Dock Labour Board (Nominees) Ltd and Chm., National Dock Labour Board Pensions Trustees Ltd; Member: London Electricity Board, 1966–72, General Practice Finance Corp., 1972–76; Chm., London Electricity Consultative Council, 1966–72; Delegate, United Nations General Assembly, 1950; Mem., United Nations Administrative Tribunal, 1951–71, Vice-Pres., 1952–71; Mem., UK Goodwill Mission to 350th Anniversary of Virginia, 1957; President: (also Fellow) Brit. Assoc. of Industrial Editors, 1953–61; Assoc. of Optical Practitioners, 1959–84 (Mem., 1959–); Cystic Fibrosis Research Foundation Trust, 1964; The Pre-Retirement Assoc.; Sutton Talking Newspaper, 1975–; Vice-Pres., Royal Soc. for the Prevention of Accidents; Vice-Pres. and Fellow, Inst. of Municipal Safety Officers. Mem., Inst. of Neurology. Master, Worshipful Co. of Spectacle Makers, 1963–65; an Apothecary, 1951–, and Freeman, 1948–, of City of London. Warden, 1968, Senior Warden, 1971, Master, 1972, Guild of Freemen of City of London. JP Surrey. KStJ 1955. Mem. Chapter-Gen. of St John, 1957–. *Heir: s* Hon. Douglas Edwin Crook [*b* 19 Nov. 1926; *m* 1954, Ellenor Rouse; one *s* one *d*]. *Address:* c/o House of Lords, SW1.          *Died 10 March* 1989.

**CROOKE, Eric Ashley,** FRCS; Consulting Surgeon; *b* 25 April 1894; *s* of Thomas Ashley and Emma Daisy Crook; *m* 1924, Elizabeth Grace Garratt (*d* 1978); one *s* one *d. Educ:* Winchester; New Coll., Oxford (MA, MCh). FRCS 1922. Cons. Surgeon: Charing Cross Hosp., Gordon Hosp., Putney Hosp., Royal Masonic Hosp. Served European War, 1914–18, Surg. Lieut, RN. *Address:* The Old Rectory, Sixpenny Handley, near Salisbury, Wilts.
                                                              *Died 31 March* 1984.

**CROOKS, Very Rev. Samuel Bennett,** OBE 1981; TD 1964; SCF 1963; Dean of Belfast, 1970–85, retired; *b* 20 Jan. 1920; 3rd *s* of Rev. S. B. Crooks, Rector of St Stephen's, Belfast; *m* 1945, Isabel Anne (*née* Kennedy), Belfast; one *s* one *d. Educ:* Down High Sch., Downpatrick, Co. Down; Trinity Coll. Dublin. BA 1943, MA 1947; DLitt Univ. of Ulster, 1986. Dean's Vicar, 1943–47, Vicar Choral, 1947–49, Minor Canon, 1952–61, Belfast Cathedral. Rector of St John's, Orangefield, Belfast, 1949–63; Rural Dean of Hillsborough, 1953–63; Rector of Lurgan, 1963–70; Archdeacon of Dromore, 1964–70. Chaplain to the Houses of Parliament, 1970–74. ChStJ 1976. *Address:* 15 Killard Road, Ballyhornan, Downpatrick, Co. Down. *T:* Strangford 665.                          *Died 21 Aug.* 1986.

**CROOM, Sir John (Halliday),** Kt 1975; TD 1946; FRCP, FRCPE; *b* 2 July 1909; *s* of David Halliday Croom and Eleanor Addey Blair Cunynghame; *m* 1940, Enid Valerie Samuel, actress (known as Valerie Tudor); one *s* one *d. Educ:* Trinity Coll., Glenalmond; Gonville and Caius Coll., Cambridge; Univ. of Edinburgh. BA Cantab, MB, ChB Edin.; FRCPE 1940 (MRCPE 1936), FRCP 1972, FFCM 1972. Served War, RAMC (Lt-Col), France, ME, Malta, Italy, 1939–45 (despatches). Consultant Phys.: Royal Infirmary, Edinburgh, 1946–74; Chalmers Hosp., Edin., 1960–66. Royal Coll. of Phys., Edin.: Sec., Councillor and Vice-Pres., 1950–70; Pres., 1970–73. Principal MO, Standard Life Ass. Co., 1946–78; Med. Adviser: Royal Bank of Scotland, 1965–78; Northern Lighthouse Bd, 1952–78; Hon. Cons. Phys. to Army in Scotland, 1970–75. Chairman: Scottish Cttee of Action on Smoking and Health, 1972–77; Scientific Adv. Gp, 1975–78, and Cancer Programme Planning Gp, 1976–79, of Planning Council, Scotland; Scottish Health Services Scientific Council, 1972–75; Scottish Council for Postgrad. Medical Education, 1974–79; Edinburgh Crematorium Bd, 1972–80. Has served on numerous NHS cttees. Hon. FRACP 1972; Hon. FACP 1973. *Publications:* several articles in sci. jls. *Recreations:* racing, fishing, golf. *Address:* 27 Learmonth

Terrace, Edinburgh EH4 1NZ. *Clubs:* Army and Navy; New (Edinburgh), Hon. Company of Edinburgh Golfers.
                                                              *Died 12 April* 1986.

**CROOT, Sir (Horace) John,** Kt 1965; CBE 1962; Member and Medical Chairman, Pensions Appeal Tribunals, since 1970; *b* 14 Oct. 1907; *s* of Horace Croot, LDS, RCS and Winifred Croot; *m* 1st, 1944, Ruth Martyn; 2nd, 1955, Irene Linda Louvain Burley; no *c. Educ:* Haileybury; Guy's Hosp. Med. Sch. MRCS, LRCP and MB, BS (London), 1930. Resident Posts, Guy's Hospital etc, 1930–32; medical practice, Hong Kong and Canton, 1932–36; Surgeon, Chinese Maritime Customs, 1935–36; post-grad. study, London, FRCS, 1938. Lt-Col RAMC, 1940–46, mainly India and Burma (despatches), 1944. Sen. Lectr in Surgery, Univ. of Bristol, and Hon. Consultant Surgeon, United Bristol Hosps, 1946–50; Prof. of Surgery, Univ. of E Africa, 1951–58; Mem., Legislative Council, Uganda, 1955–61; Minister of Health and Labour, Uganda, 1958–61; Sen. Consultant Surgeon, Mulago Hosp., Kampala, 1961–69. Pres., Assoc. of Surgeons of E Africa, 1956 and 1962. *Address:* 29 Knole Wood, Devenish Road, Sunningdale, Berks. *T:* Ascot 23651.                                   *Died 22 May* 1981.

**CROSBY, John Michael,** CMG 1988; LVO 1976; HM Diplomatic Service; High Commissioner in Belize, 1984–87; *b* 2 Aug. 1940; *s* of Rev. B. Crosby and Norah Crosby (*née* Copeland); *m* 1963, Mary Collinge Smethurst; one *s* one *d. Educ:* Kingswood Sch., Bath; Magdalene Coll., Cambridge (MA). Social work in North Kensington and for SCM in Schools, 1962–65; entered Diplomatic Service, 1965; Third, later Second, Secretary, Addis Ababa, 1966–70; Second, later First, Secretary, FCO, 1970–73; seconded to Cabinet Office, 1973; First Secretary and Head of Chancery: Luxembourg, 1973–76; Mexico City, 1977–79; First Secretary, FCO, 1979–81; Counsellor and Dep. High Comr, Dar es Salaam, 1981–84. *Recreations:* sport, history, travel. *Address:* c/o Foreign and Commonwealth Office, SW1A 2AH. *Club:* United Oxford & Cambridge University.                              *Died 22 Jan.* 1988.

**CROSS OF CHELSEA, Baron** *cr* 1971 (Life Peer), of the Royal Borough of Kensington and Chelsea; **(Arthur) Geoffrey (Neale) Cross,** PC 1969; Kt 1960; a Lord of Appeal in Ordinary, 1971–75; Chairman, Appeals Committee, Takeover Panel, 1976–81; *b* 1 Dec. 1904; *e s* of late Arthur George Cross and Mary Elizabeth Dalton; *m* 1952, Joan, *d* of late Major Theodore Eardley Wilmot, DSO, and widow of Thomas Walton Davies; one *d. Educ:* Westminster; Trinity College, Cambridge. Craven Scholar, 1925. Fellow of Trinity College, 1927–31, Hon. Fellow, 1972; called to the Bar, Middle Temple, 1930, Master of the Bench, 1958, Reader, 1971; QC 1949. Chancellor of the County Palatine of Durham, 1959. A Judge of the High Court of Justice, Chancery Div., 1960–69; a Lord Justice of Appeal, 1969–71. *Publications:* Epirus, 1932; (with G. R. Y. Radcliffe) The English Legal System (6th edn 1977). *Address:* The Bridge House, Leintwardine, Craven Arms, Shropshire. *T:* Leintwardine 205.                                *Died 4 Aug.* 1989.

**CROSS, Sir Cecil Lancelot Stewart, (Sir Lance Cross),** Kt 1984; CBE 1977; *b* 12 Nov. 1912; *s* of Cecil Thomas Cross; *m* 1940, Amy, *d* of Albert Taylor; two *d. Educ:* Timaru Boys' High School; Canterbury University. Fellow, Phys. Ed. Soc., NZ. Served RNZAF, war of 1939–45. Dir, Phys. Educn, YMCA, 1933–39; NZ Supt, Phys. Welfare and Recreation, 1939–52; Head of Sports Broadcasts, 1953–75, of Sporting Services, 1976–77, NZ Broadcasting Council. Chairman: NZ Olympic and Commonwealth Games Assoc., 1967–82 (Pres., 1982–); NZ Sports Council, 1977–84; Mem., IOC, 1969–; Pres., Oceania Assoc. of Nat. Olympic Cttees, 1980–; Vice-Pres., Internat. Basketball Fedn, 1972–. *Address:* 1 Otaki Street, Wellington 3, New Zealand. *Club:* Wellesley (Wellington).
                                                              *Died 13 May* 1989.

**CROSS, Rt. Rev. (David) Stewart;** *b* 4 April 1928; *s* of Charles Stewart and Constance Muriel Cross; *m* 1954, Mary Margaret Workman Colquhoun; one *s* two *d. Educ:* Trinity Coll., Dublin (MA 1956). Deacon 1954, priest 1955; Curate of Hexham, 1954–57; on staff of Cathedral and Abbey Church of St Alban, St Albans, Herts, 1957–63; Precentor, 1960–63; Curate of St Ambrose, Chorlton-on-Medlock and Asst Chaplain to Manchester Univ., 1963–67; BBC Producer in religious broadcasting, 1968–76 (Religious Broadcasting Assistant, BBC North, 1968–71, then Religious Broadcasting Organiser, Manchester Network Production Centre, 1971–76); Bishop Suffragan of Doncaster, 1976–82; Bishop of Blackburn, 1982–88. Chairman: Local Radio Council, BBC Radio Sheffield, 1980–82; Churches Adv. Cttee on Local Broadcasting, 1980–82; British Churches' Cttee for Channel Four, 1981–85; New Media Partnership Trust, 1987–88. Chm., Sandford St Martin Trust, 1986–88. *Recreations:* photography, making music and exchanging puns. *Address:* Honeybee House, Brigsteer, Kendal, Cumbria LA8 8AP.                                          *Died 6 April* 1989.

**CROSS, Sir Eugene,** Kt 1979; MBE 1954; MM 1918; retired steel works manager; *b* 13 Sept. 1896; *s* of Eugene and Hannah Cross; *m* 1923, Ada M. Caswell; one *s. Educ:* local school, Ebbw Vale. Served

War of 1914–18, Fifth Army, 1st Welsh Field Ambulance (Gallipoli, 101st Bridge, France). Iron and Steel Works Manager, 1936, until retirement. (The first Hot Strip and Cold Reduction Mills in the world (outside USA) built at Ebbw Vale commenced rolling Oct. 1939). Elected Mem. Ebbw Vale Hospital Cttee, 1926 (during National Strike); Trustee, Chm. of the Trusteeship, and Chm. Hosp. Bd and Medical Fund, Ebbw Vale, 1934; Mem. Wales Hosp. Bd, 1949, for 19 years (Vice-Chm.). JP Ebbw Vale 1941, served 27 years, Chm. 18 years. *Recreations:* Rugby, cricket, etc. *Address:* Ty Coed, Hospital Drive, Ebbw Vale, Gwent NP3 6PW.
*Died 27 Nov. 1981.*

**CROSS, Frederick Victor,** CMG 1949; Director: Navcot Shipping Holdings; Sitmar Line (London) Ltd; Navigation & Coal Trade Co. Ltd; Alva Shipping (Holdings) Ltd; Alva Star Shipping Co. Ltd; *b* 19 April 1907; *m* 1932, Gwendoline Horton; one *s* one *d*. *Educ:* RNC Greenwich. INA scholarship, 1927. Shipping Attaché, British Embassy, Washington, DC, 1946–49; Asst Sec., MoT, 1949–51. Officer: Order of Orange Nassau, 1947; Order of the Crown of Belgium, 1948. *Address:* 21 Durham Avenue, Bromley, Kent.
*Died 1 June 1981.*

**CROSS, Prof. Kenneth William,** MB, DSc, FRCP; Professor of Physiology, London Hospital Medical College, 1960–81, then Emeritus; Hon. Physiologist to The London Hospital; *b* 26 March 1916; *s* of late George Cross, Ealing; *m* 1942, Joyce M. Wilson (*née* Lack, *d* 1970); one step *d*; *m* 1970, Dr Sheila R. Lewis. *Educ:* St Paul's Sch.; St Mary's Hospital Medical Sch. Qualified, 1940; House appointments in St Mary's Hospital Sector; graded Physician EMS Amersham Emergency Hosp. 1945; Friends' Ambulance Unit, China, 1946–47. Lecturer in Physiology, 1947, Reader, 1952, St Mary's Hosp. *Publications:* contrib. to Journal of Physiology.
*Died 10 Oct. 1990.*

**CROSS, Sir Lance;** *see* Cross, Sir C. L. S.

**CROSS, Brig. Lionel Lesley,** CBE 1950; *b* 7 June 1899; *yr s* of Charles Frederick Cross, FRS, and Edith, *d* of Maj.-Gen. Charles Stainforth, CB; *m* 1940, Rose Blanche Margaret (*d* 1976), *d* of Sir Robert Taylor, Kytes, Herts; no *c. Educ:* Wellington Coll.; RMA Woolwich. Commissioned RFA, 1918; France and Belgium, 1918. Adjutant Bucks and Berks Yeo. Artillery, 1925–29; retd 1929. Rejoined Army, 1939; Staff Capt. RA 1939; France and Belgium, 1940; Major 1941; Lieut-Col 1942; Asst Dir of Public Relations, War Office, 1942–46; Brig. 1946; Dep. Dir of Public Relations, War Office, 1946–50; Chief of Public Information, SHAPE, 1954–58 (Dep., 1951–54); retired, 1958. Sec., Commonwealth Press Union, 1959–70. *Recreations:* racing, bridge. *Address:* 15 Cedar House, Marloes Road, W8. *T:* 01–937 0112. *Club:* Army and Navy.
*Died 6 March 1984.*

**CROSS, Rt. Rev. Stewart;** *see* Cross, Rt. Rev. D. S.

**CROSSLEY, Sir Christopher John,** 3rd Bt *cr* 1909; Lieutenant-Commander Royal Navy, retired; Middle East business consultant; *b* 25 Sept. 1931; *s* of late Lt-Comdr Nigel Crossley, RN (*s* of late Eric Crossley, OBE, 2nd *s* of 1st Bt); *S* great uncle (Sir Kenneth Crossley, 2nd Bt), 1957; *m* 1959, Carolyne Louise (marr. diss. 1969), *d* of late L. Grey Sykes; two *s*; *m* 1977, Lesley, *e d* of late Dr K. A. J. Chamberlain. *Educ:* Canford Sch. Entered Royal Navy, 1950. *Recreations:* royal tennis, squash. *Heir: s* Nicholas John Crossley, *b* 10 Dec. 1962. *Address:* PO Box 100, Heliopolis, Egypt.
*Died 10 July 1989.*

**CROSSLEY, Prof. Eric Lomax;** Professor of Dairying, University of Reading, 1947–68, later Professor Emeritus; *b* 15 Sept. 1903; British; *m* 1933, Janet Hircombe Sutton; one *s. Educ:* Nottingham High Sch.; High Pavement Sch., Nottingham; University Coll., Nottingham. Research work bacteriology and biochemistry at University Coll., Nottingham and Nat. Inst. for Research in Dairying, Shinfield, Reading, 1923–25; Advisory Dairy Bacteriologist, Min. of Agriculture, at Harper Adams Agricultural Coll., Newport, Salop, 1925–29; Chief scientific and technical adviser, dir of laboratories, Aplin & Barrett Ltd, Yeovil, Som and associated Cos, 1929–47. Has been engaged in scientific investigation (particularly bacteriology) of milk processing and manufacture of dairy and other food products. Part-time Consultant, FAO. President: Soc. Dairy Technology, 1953–54; Internat. Commn for Dried and Condensed Milks, 1960–65; Inst. of Food Science and Technology, 1967–69. Technical Mission to Peru, ODM, 1970. Gold Medal, Soc. of Dairy Technol., 1975. *Publications:* The United Kingdom Dairy Industry; original papers in scientific journals. *Recreations:* entomology and music. *Address:* Cliffdene, Shooters Hill, Pangbourne, Berks. *T:* Pangbourne 2967.
*Died 13 June 1982.*

**CROSSLEY, Wing-Comdr Michael Nicholson,** DSO 1940; OBE 1946; DFC; Fighter Command; farming in South Africa since 1955; *b* 29 May 1912; *s* of late Major E. Crossley, OBE; *m* 1957, Sylvia Heyder (*d* 1975); one *s* two *d*; *m* 1977, Moyra Birkbeck, *widow* of Maj.-Gen. T. H. (John) Birkbeck. *Educ:* Eton Coll.; Munich. Commissioned

in RAF, 1935; comd 32 Sqdn during Battle of Britain. *Address:* Loughrigg, White River 1240, E Transvaal, S Africa. *Clubs:* Army and Navy; Rand (Johannesburg).
*Died 7 Dec. 1987.*

**CROSSMAN, Sir (Douglas) Peter,** Kt 1982; TD 1944; DL; *b* 25 Sept. 1908; *s* of late Percy Crossman, Gt Bromley Hall, Colchester; *m* 1st, 1932, Monica, *d* of late C. F. R. Barnett; two *s* one *d*; 2nd, 1939, Jean Margaret, *d* of late Douglas Crossman, Cokenach, Royston. *Educ:* Uppingham; Pembroke Coll., Cambridge. Commission Warwicks Yeomanry, 1934–45. Chairman: Mann Crossman Paulin Ltd, 1961–65; Watney Mann Ltd, 1965–70. President: Licensed Victuallers' Sch., 1958; Shire Horse Soc., 1958; Beer and Wine Trade Benev., 1960; Licensed Victuallers' Nat. Homes, 1963; Hunts Agricultural Soc., 1965; Chairman: Govs, Dame Alice Owen's Sch., 1951–65; Hunts Conservative Assoc., 1954–61; Eastern Area, Nat. Union of Conservative Party, 1965; Nat. Union of Conservative Party, 1969. Master, Brewers' Co., 1950. Chairman, Brewers' Soc., 1968, 1969. DL Huntingdonshire, 1958. Master: Essex and Suffolk Foxhounds, 1938–40; Cambridgeshire Foxhounds, 1947–49. *Recreations:* hunting, shooting, fishing, gardening. *Address:* Tetworth Hall, Sandy, Beds. *T:* Gamlingay 212. *Club:* Cavalry and Guards.
*Died 15 May 1989.*

**CROSTHWAITE, Sir (Ponsonby) Moore,** KCMG 1960 (CMG 1951); *b* 13 Aug. 1907; *o s* of late P. M. Crosthwaite, MICE, and late Agnes Alice, *y d* of J. H. Aitken, Falkirk, Stirlingshire. *Educ:* Rugby; CCC, Oxford. Laming Fellowship, Queen's Coll., 1931. Entered Diplomatic Service, 1932; served in Bagdad, Moscow, Madrid, Athens and Foreign Office; Deputy UK Representative to United Nations, New York, 1952–58; Ambassador to the Lebanon, 1958–63; Ambassador to Sweden, 1963–66. *Recreations:* travel, the arts. *Address:* 17 Crescent Grove, SW4. *Club:* Athenæum.
*Died 27 April 1989.*

**CROUT, Dame Mabel,** DBE 1965; JP; Alderman, London Borough of Greenwich, 1964–71; *b* 6 Jan. 1890. Member of Woolwich Borough Council, 1919–64 (Mayor, 1936–37); Mem. of London Borough of Greenwich, 1964–71. JP, London, 1920–. Mem. of London County Council, 1949–55. Freeman of Woolwich, 1959. *Address:* 17 Beulah Road, Tunbridge Wells, Kent.
*Died 8 Feb. 1984.*

**CROWDER, Michael;** Visiting Professor: Amherst College, USA, since 1986; Institute of Commonwealth Studies, University of London, and General Editor, British Documents on the End of Empire Project, since 1986; Fellow, Woodrow Wilson Center for International Scholars, Washington, DC, since 1988; *b* 9 Jan. 1934; *s* of Henry Cussons Crowder and late Molly Gladys Elizabeth Crowder (*née* Burchell). *Educ:* Mill Hill Sch.; Hertford Coll., Oxford (BA 1st Cl. Hons PPE, MA). 2/Lieut, Middx Regt, seconded to Nigeria Regt, 1953–54. Editor, Nigeria Magazine, Lagos, 1959–62; Secretary, Inst. of African Studies, Univ. of Ibadan, Nigeria, 1962–64; Vis. Lectr in African History, Univ. of Calif, Berkeley, 1964–65; Director, Inst. of African Studies, Fourah Bay Coll., Univ. of Sierra Leone, 1965–67; Research Prof. and Dir, Inst. of African Studies, Univ. of Ife, Nigeria, 1968–71; Prof. of History, Ahmadu Bello Univ., 1971–75 (Head, Dept of History, Kano Campus, 1971–74; Dean, Faculty of Arts and Islamic Studies, 1972–73; Dir, Univ. Centre for Nigerian Cultural Studies, 1972–75); Research Prof. in History, Centre for Cultural Studies, Univ. of Lagos, 1975–78; Editor, 1979–81, Consultant Editor, 1981–, History Today; Prof. of History, Univ. of Botswana, 1982–85. Mem. Exec. Council, 1979–, Jt Hon. Dir, 1981–82, Internat. African Inst.; Jt Editor, Journal of African History, 1985–. Visiting Professor: Columbia Univ., 1964, 1965; Ibadan Univ., 1967, Georgetown Univ., 1970; Amherst Coll., USA, 1987; Vis. Fellow, Centre for Internat. Studies, LSE, 1981–82; Vis. Distinguished Prof., Univ. of Calif, Berkeley, 1985; Sen. Associate Mem., St Antony's Coll., Oxford, 1986. Hon. Exec. Sec., Internat. Congress of Africanists, 1962–68 (jtly with Prof. Lalage Bown, 1965–68); Member Council: African Studies Assoc. of UK, 1979–82; Minority Rights Gp, 1980–86; Mem. Exec. Council, International African Inst., 1979– (Chm., Publication Cttee, 1979–82). General Editor, Hutchinson University Library for Africa, 1976–. Officer, National Order of Senegal, 1964. FRHistS, 1979. *Publications:* The Story of Nigeria, 1962, 4th edn 1977; Senegal: a study in French assimilation policy, 1962, 2nd edn 1967; West Africa under Colonial Rule, 1968; ed jtly, West African Chiefs, 1970; West African Resistance, 1971, 2nd edn 1981; ed jtly, History of West Africa, vol. I 1971, 3rd edn 1986, vol. II 1974, 2nd edn 1987; Revolt in Bussa: a study in British 'Native' Administration in Nigerian Borgu 1902–1936, 1973; Colonial West Africa: collected essays, 1978; Nigeria: an introduction to its history, 1979; West Africa: 1000 AD to the present day, 1980; The Flogging of Phinehas McIntosh: a study in colonial folly and injustice, Bechuanaland 1933, 1988; Jt Gen. Editor: Cambridge Encyclopaedia of Africa, 1981; Historical Atlas of Africa, 1985; (ed) Cambridge History of Africa, vol. VIII, 1984. *Recreations:* music, travelling, gardening. *Address:* 13 Addington Square, SE5 7JZ. *T:* 01–703 8938; Dar

Demdam, rue Merrouche, Casbah, Tangier, Morocco. *Club:* Travellers'. *Died* 14 *Aug.* 1988.

**CROWE, Sir Colin Tradescant**, GCMG 1973 (KCMG 1963; CMG 1956); HM Diplomatic Service, retired; *b* 7 Sept. 1913; *s* of late Sir Edward Crowe, KCMG; *m* 1938, Bettina Lum (*d* 1983). *Educ:* Stowe Sch.; Oriel Coll., Oxford. Served at HM Embassy, Peking, 1936–38 and 1950–53; Shanghai, 1938–40; HM Embassy, Washington, 1940–45; Foreign Office, 1945–48, 1953–56; UK Delegn to OEEC, Paris, 1948–49; HM Legation, Tel Aviv, 1949–50; Imperial Defence Coll., 1957; Head, British Property Commn, Cairo, 1959; British Chargé d'Affaires, Cairo, 1959–61; Deputy UK Representative to the UN, New York, 1961–63; Ambassador to Saudi Arabia, 1963–64; Chief of Administration, HM Diplomatic Service, 1965–68; High Comr in Canada, 1968–70; UK Permanent Rep. to UN, 1970–73. Supernumerary Fellow, St Antony's Coll., Oxford, 1964–65. Dir, Grindlay's Bank Ltd, 1976–84. Chm., Marshall Aid Commemoration Commn, 1973–85. Chm. Council, Cheltenham Ladies Coll., 1974–86. *Address:* Pigeon House, Bibury, Glos. *Club:* Travellers'. *Died* 19 *July* 1989.

**CROWE, Prof. Ralph Vernon**, FRIBA; Professor Emeritus, School of Architecture, Newcastle-upon-Tyne University, since 1981 (Professor of Architecture and Head of Department, 1976–81); subsequently in private practice; *b* 30 Sept. 1915; *s* of Sidney John Crowe and Sarah Emma (*née* Sharp); *m* 1943, Nona Heath Eggington; two *s* one *d*. *Educ:* Westminster City Sch.; Architectural Assoc., London (AA Dipl. Hons); Sch. of Planning and Res. for Reg. Develt. MA Newcastle upon Tyne; ARIBA 1945; MRTPI 1949. War Service, 1941–45: Captain, RE. Govt Architect and Planning Officer, Govt of Barbados, BWI, 1947–50; teaching, Arch. Assoc., 1950–52; Basildon New Town, 1952–53; LCC, 1953–58; County Architect: Shropshire, 1958–66; Essex, 1966–76. *Publications:* contribs to professional and tech. jls. *Recreations:* music (flute), hill walking. *Address:* Holly Hall Barn, Sandhoe, Hexham, Northumberland NE46 4LX. *Died* 20 *Nov.* 1990.

**CROWLEY, Sir Brian Hurtle**, Kt 1969; MM; Chairman, 1962–74 (Member 1944–74), Australian Jockey Club Committee; *b* 18 Feb. 1896; *m* 1922, Dorothy, *d* of L. Sweet; one *s* two *d*. *Educ:* Scots College, Sydney. Served with Aust. Imperial Forces, 1916–19. *Address:* 3 Bedford Crescent, Collaroy, NSW 2097, Australia. *Clubs:* Union, Australian, Elanora Country (all Sydney). *Died* 25 *April* 1982.

**CROWLEY, Thomas Michael**, CMG 1970; Assistant Secretary, Ministry of Defence, 1971–77; *b* 28 June 1917; *s* of late Thomas Michael Crowley; *m* 1965, Eicke Laura, *d* of late Carl Jensen; one *s* two *d*. *Educ:* Forres Acad.; Aberdeen Univ. Entered Civil Service in 1940; Assistant Secretary: Min. of Technology, 1953–70; DTI, 1970; Min. of Aviation Supply, 1970–71. *Address:* 116 Barnett Wood Lane, Ashtead, Surrey. *Died* 19 *April* 1988.

**CROWTHER, Francis Harold**; retired from Diplomatic Service, 1966; *b* Umtali, Southern Rhodesia, 25 May 1914; *s* of A. D. Crowther; *m* 1952, Mary Eleanor, *d* of F. G. Forman; two *d*. *Educ:* Plumtree Sch., Southern Rhodesia; Univ. of Cape Town; Christ Church, Oxford. Entered Consular Service, Japan, 1938; served in Japan, India, Ceylon, Singapore, Indochina, Korea, Foreign Office, Yugoslavia, Morocco, Mozambique and the Netherlands. *Address:* 59 Sloane Gardens, SW1. *Died* 5 *Oct.* 1984.

**CROWTHER, Sir William (Edward Lodewyk Hamilton)**, Kt 1964; CBE 1955; DSO 1919; VRD; FRACP; medical practitioner; President of Medical Council of Tasmania, 1953–54; *b* 9 May 1887; *s* of Edward L. Crowther, MD; *m* 1915, Joyce Nevett Mitchell, Tunallock, NSW; one *s*. *Educ:* Buckland's School; Ormond Coll., University of Melbourne. Late CO 5th Field Ambulance AIF (despatches, wounded, DSO, 1914–15 star, two medals). Pres., Tasmanian Br., BMA, 1934–42. Hon. Consulting Physician, Hobart Gen. Hosp. Halford Oration, 1933; Archibald Watson Memorial Lecture, 1951; Roentgen Oration, 1953. Hon. Adviser, Australian Bibliography Library Bd, State Library of Tasmania, 1965. *Publications:* series on the extinct Tasmanian race and on history of medicine in Tasmania, to scientific journals. *Recreations:* yachting, historical research. *Address:* 190 Macquarie Street, Hobart, Tasmania 7000. *T:* 23.6003. *Clubs:* Tasmanian (Life Mem.), Naval and Military (Hobart). *Died* 30 *May* 1981.

**CROWTHER-HUNT, Baron** *cr* 1973 (Life Peer), of Eccleshill in the West Riding of the County of York; **Norman Crowther Crowther-Hunt**, PhD; Rector, Exeter College, Oxford, since 1982; *b* 13 March 1920; *s* of late Ernest Angus Hunt, and of Florence Hunt, Bradford, Yorks; *m* 1944, Joyce, *d* of late Rev. Joseph Stackhouse, Walsall Wood, Staffs; three *d*. *Educ:* Wellington Road Council Sch.; Belle Vue High Sch., Bradford; Sidney Sussex Coll., Cambridge. Exhibitioner, 1939–40, Open Scholar, 1945–47, Sidney Sussex Coll.; MA 1949, PhD 1951; Hon. Fellow, 1982. Served RA, 1940–45; War Office (GSO3), 1944–45. First Cl. Hist. Tripos, 1946 and 1947; Res. Fellow, Sidney Sussex Coll., 1949–51; Commonwealth Fund Fellow,

Princeton Univ., USA, 1951–52; Fellow and Lectr in Politics, 1952–82, Domestic Bursar, 1954–70, Exeter Coll., Oxford. Deleg., Oxford Univ. Extra-Mural Delegacy, 1956–70; Vis. Prof., Michigan State Univ., 1961. Constitutional Adviser to the Govt, March-Oct. 1974; Minister of State: DES, 1974–76; Privy Council Office, 1976. Member: Cttee on the Civil Service (Fulton Cttee), 1966–68 (Leader of Management Consultancy Group); Commn on the Constitution, 1969–73 (principal author of the Memorandum of Dissent); Civil Service Coll. Adv. Council, 1970–74. Chm., BBC Gen. Adv. Council, 1986–. Mem. Council, Headington Sch., Oxford, 1966–74. Hon. DLitt Bradford, 1974; Hon. LLD Williams Coll., Mass., 1985. *Publications:* Two Early Political Associations, 1961; (ed) Whitehall and Beyond, 1964; (ed with Graham Tayar) Personality and Power 1970; (with Peter Kellner) The Civil Servants, 1980. *Recreations:* playing tennis, squash and the piano; broadcasting. Cambridge Univ. Assoc. Football XI, 1939–40. *Address:* 14 Apsley Road, Oxford. *T:* Oxford 58342; Exeter College, Oxford. *T:* Oxford 244681 and 247422. *Died* 16 *Feb.* 1987.

**CRUICKSHANK, Andrew John Maxton**, MBE 1945; FRSAMD; actor; *b* 25 Dec. 1907; *m* 1939, Curigwen Lewis; one *s* two *d*. *Educ:* Aberdeen Grammar Sch. Hon. DLitt St Andrews, 1977. With Baynton Shakespearean Company, 1929; appeared in Richard of Bordeaux, New York, 1934; Mary Tudor, London Playhouse, 1935; Lysistrata, Gate, 1936; Macbeth, Old Vic, 1937 (Mem. of Old Vic Company, 1937–40). Served Royal Welch Fus., and GS, 1940–45. Spring 1600, Lyric, Hammersmith, 1945–46; The White Devil, Duchess, 1947; The Indifferent Shepherd, Criterion, 1949; Memorial Theatre, Stratford (Parts included Wolsey, Kent and Julius Caesar), 1950; St Joan, Cort Theatre, New York, 1951; Dial M for Murder, Westminster Theatre, 1952; Dead on Nine, Westminster, 1955; The House by the Lake, Duke of York's, 1956; Inherit The Wind, 1960; Look Homeward Angel, 1960; The Lady From the Sea, Queen's, 1961; The Master Builder, Ashcroft Theatre, Croydon, 1963; Alibi for a Judge, Savoy, 1965; Lloyd George Knew my Father, Savoy, 1973; When We Dead Awaken, Haymarket Leicester, 1975; The Thrie Estates, Edinburgh, 1984; Beyond Reasonable Doubt, Queen's, 1987; *National Theatre:* The Woman, 1978; Strife, 1978; The Fruits of Enlightenment, 1979; The Wild Duck, 1980; Sisterly Feelings, 1980. Has appeared in many films, also in radio and on television; TV series, Dr Finlay's Casebook; author of play, Games, 1975. *Publications:* The Infinite Guarantee, 1971; A Scottish Bedside Book, 1977; After the Wager, the Dice and the Games, 1984; *posthumous publication:* An Autobiography, 1988. *Address:* 33 Carlisle Mansions, Carlisle Place, SW1. *Club:* Garrick. *Died* 29 *April* 1988.

**CRUICKSHANK, Charles Greig**, MA, DPhil; FRHistS; author; *b* 10 June 1914; *s* of late George Leslie Cruickshank, Fyvie; *m* 1943, Maire Kissane; three *s*. *Educ:* Aberdeen Grammar Sch.; Aberdeen Univ.; Hertford Coll., Oxford; Edinburgh University. Min. of Supply, 1940–46; BoT, 1946–51; Trade Comr, Ceylon, 1951–55 (economic mission to Maldive Is, 1953); Canada, 1955–58; Sen. Trade Comr, NZ, 1958–63; Exec. Sec., Commonwealth Econ. Cttee, 1964–66; Dir, Commodities Div., Commonwealth Secretariat, 1967–68; BoT (Regional Export Dir, London and SE), 1969–71; Inspector, FCO, 1971–72; CAA, 1972–73; Asst Sec., DTI, 1973. *Publications: non-fiction:* Elizabeth's Army, 1966; Army Royal, 1969; The English Occupation of Tournai, 1971; (jtly) A Guide to the Sources of British Military History, 1971; The German Occupation of the Channel Islands (official history), 1975; Greece 1940–41, 1976; The Fourth Arm: psychological warfare, 1938–45, 1977; Deception in World War II, 1979; SOE in the Far East (official history), 1983; SOE in Scandinavia (official history), 1986; History of the Royal Wimbledon Golf Club, 1986; *fiction: novels:* The V-Mann Papers, 1976; The Tang Murders, 1976; The Ebony Version, 1978; The Deceivers, 1978; Kew for Murder, 1984; Scotch Murder, 1985; contrib. to English Historical Review, Army Quarterly, History Today, Punch, War Monthly, DNB, History of Parliament, etc. *Recreation:* golf. *Address:* 15 McKay Road, Wimbledon Common, SW20 0HT. *T:* 01–947 1074. *Club:* Royal Wimbledon Golf. *Died* 19 *Feb.* 1989.

**CRUICKSHANK, John Merrill**, CMG 1951; OBE 1937; *b* 4 Sept. 1901; *s* of J. P. and J. E. Cruikshank (*née* Crombie); *m* 1930, Elaine Strong; one *s*. *Educ:* McGill Univ. (MD, CM, DPH). Colonial Medical Service; Surgeon, Bahamas, 1928–30; Chief Medical Officer, Bahamas, 1930–40; DMS Bahamas Military Forces, 1939–41; RCAF, 1941–46; Asst Medical Adviser, Colonial Office, 1946–48; Insp.-Gen., S Pacific Health Service, and DMS, Fiji, 1948–56; WHO Area Representative for S Pacific, 1956–59. Dir, Alexander Sanitarium, Belmont, Calif, 1959–64, retd. Certificate Tropical Medicine, London; Fellow: Amer. Coll. Surgeons; Amer. Coll. Physicians; Royal Sanitary Inst. OStJ 1950. *Publications:* articles in medical journals. *Recreation:* electronics. *Address:* 401–33 Avenue SW, Calgary, Alberta T2S 0S8, Canada. *T:* 2436691. *Club:* Corona. *Died* 21 *Dec.* 1984.

**CRUTCHLEY, Adm. Sir Victor Alexander Charles**, VC 1918; KCB 1946 (CB 1945); DSC 1918; RN retired; DL; *b* 2 Nov. 1893; *s* of

late Percy Edward Crutchley and late Hon. Frederica Louisa, 2nd *d* of 3rd Baron Southampton; *m* 1930, Joan Elizabeth Loveday (*d* 1980), *y d* of late William Coryton, Pentillie Castle, Cornwall, and late Mrs William Coryton; one *s* one *d*. *Educ*: Osborne and Dartmouth. Served European War in HMS Centurion, Battle of Jutland; in HMS Brilliant in attempt to block Ostend Harbour, 22–23 April 1918 (DSC); in HMS Vindictive in similar attempt, 9–10 May 1918 (VC, Croix de Guerre); commanded HMS Diomede, New Zealand; Senior Officer, First Minesweeping Flotilla, 1935–36; Capt. Fishery Protection and Minesweeping Flotilla, 1936–37; commanded HMS Warspite, 1937–40; Commodore RN Barracks, Devonport, 1940–42; commanded Australian Naval Squadron, 1942–44; Flag Officer Gibraltar, 1945–47; retired, 1947, as Adm. DL Dorset, 1957. Chief Comdr Legion of Merit (USA), 1944; Polonia Restituta, 1942. *Address*: Mappercombe Manor, Nettlecombe, Bridport, Dorset DT6 3SS.
*Died 24 Jan.* 1986.

**CUBITT, James William Archibald**, MBE 1945; FRIBA; architect, sculptor; Senior Partner of James Cubitt and Partners, London, Nigeria, Malaya, since 1948; *b* 1 May 1914; *s* of James Edward and Isabel Margaret Cubitt; *m* 1st, 1939, Ann Margaret Tooth (marr. diss. 1947); one *s* one *d*; 2nd, 1950, Constance Anne (*née* Sitwell) (marr. diss. 1972; she *d* 1981); one *s*; 3rd, 1973, Eleni Collard (*née* Kiortsis). *Educ*: Harrow; Brasenose Coll., Oxford; Architectural Association Sch. of Architecture. BA Oxon 1935; ARIBA 1940; FRIBA 1955. Army, 1940–45. In private practice as architect from 1948. Main works in England: exhibition and shop design; schools for Herts CC, W Riding CC, LCC, Leeds Corporation. Has also designed many public buildings, schools, offices and private houses in Ghana; now works in Nigeria, Brunei and Libya. Architect for the Universities of Libya and Nigeria; photographs and drawings of Univ. of Garyounis, Benghazi, Libya exhibited at Venice Biennale, 1982 and RIBA Heinz Gall., 1983. Chm., Mortimer and Burghfield Local Labour Party, 1974–. Writes articles and reviews. Council of Architectural Assoc., 1960– (Pres., 1965–66). Sculpture: one-man show, John Whibley Gallery, 1962; Burgos Gallery, NY, 1966; Ellingham Mill Art Soc. exhibn, 1978. *Address*: 25 Gloucester Place, W1. *T*: 01–935 0288.
*Died 16 Dec.* 1983.

**CUDMORE, Derek George**, CBE 1972 (OBE 1969); HM Overseas Civil Service, retired; *b* 9 Nov. 1923; *s* of late Harold Thomas Cudmore and of Winifred Laura Cudmore; *m* 1952, Vera Beatrice (*née* Makin); no *c*. *Educ*: Slough Grammar Sch.; Regent Street Polytechnic. Served War, Royal Navy, 1942–46 (Lt RNVR). Joined Colonial Service as Administrative Officer, 1947; Nigeria and Southern Cameroons, 1947–56; Northern Rhodesia, 1956–57. Consecutively Dist. Comr, Sen. Asst. Sec. and Dep. Financial Sec., British Solomon Islands, 1957–67; Asst Resident Comr, Gilbert and Ellice Islands, 1967–71; Governor, BVI, 1971–74; Development Officer, Kingdom of Tonga, 1975–77. Chief Sec., British Nat. Service, New Hebrides, 1979–80. *Recreations*: golf, travel, sailing. *Address*: Perhams, Honiton, Devon. *T*: Honiton 2310. *Clubs*: Royal Over-Seas League; Honiton Golf.
*Died 20 Dec.* 1981.

**CULLINGFORD, Rev. Cecil Howard Dunstan**, MA; FRSA; *b* 13 Sept. 1904; *s* of Francis James and Lilian Mabel Cullingford; *m* 1st, 1933, Olive Eveline (*d* 1971), *d* of Lt-Col P. H. Collingwood, Clifton, Bristol; one *s* one *d*; 2nd, 1972, Penelope Wood-Hill, *e d* of Dr H. Wood-Hill, Beccles. *Educ*: City of London Sch.; Corpus Christi Coll., Cambridge (Foundation Scholar). 1st Class Hons in Classical Tripos, Parts 1 and 2, and Historical Tripos, Part 2. VIth Form Master, Brighton Coll., 1928–32; Vice-Principal, Clifton Theological Coll., 1932–34; Chaplain of Oundle Sch., 1935–46. Army Chaplain, 1939–45; Guards Armoured Div., 1939–43; Staff Chaplain, 21st Army Group, 1943–44; Senior Chaplain, 79th Armoured Div., 1944–45. Headmaster of Monmouth Sch., 1946–56; Lectr in Naval History at Britannia RNC Dartmouth, 1957–60; Chaplain: St John's Sch., Leatherhead, 1960–64; St Michael's Sch., Limpsfield, 1964–67; Vicar of Stiffkey with Morston, 1967–72; Rural Dean of Beccles, 1973–76. Pres., Silleren Ski Club, 1966; Vice-Pres., Wessex Cave Club; Hon. Member: Cave Res. Group of GB; British Speleological Assoc.; British Cave Res. Assoc. *Publications*: Exploring Caves, 1951; (ed) British Caving: an Introduction to Speleology, 1953 (2nd edn 1961); (ed) A Manual of Caving Techniques, 1969; The Thornhill Guide to Caving, 1976; (ed) The Science of Speleology, 1976. *Recreations*: hockey, pot-holing, music, archæology. *Address*: The Staithe, Beccles, Suffolk NR34 9AV. *T*: Beccles (0502) 712182.
*Died 6 July* 1990.

**CULLWICK, Prof. Ernest Geoffrey**, OBE 1946; Captain (L) RCN(R), retired; MA, DSc, FIEE, FRSE; Watson-Watt Professor of Electrical Engineering in the University of Dundee, 1967–73 (University of St Andrews, Queen's College, Dundee, 1949–67), later Professor Emeritus; Hon. Professor, University of Kent at Canterbury, since 1974; *b* Wolverhampton, 24 May 1903; *s* of late Herbert Ernest Cullwick and Edith Ada Ascough; *m* 1929, Mamie Ruttan, *o d* of G. B. Boucher, Peterborough, Ontario; one *d* (and one *s* decd). *Educ*: Wolverhampton Grammar Sch.; Downing Coll.,

Cambridge (Mathematical Scholar, Foundation Scholar in Engineering). Mathematical and Mechanical Sciences Tripos, Industrial Bursar of the Royal Exhibition of 1851; with British Thomson Houston Co. and Canadian General Electric Co.; Asst Prof. of Electrical Engineering, Univ. of British Columbia, Vancouver, 1928–34; Lectr in Electrical Engineering, Military Coll. of Science, Woolwich, 1934–35; Associate Prof. of Electrical Engineering, Univ. of British Columbia, 1935–37; Prof. and Head of Dept of Electrical Engineering, Univ. of Alberta, Edmonton, 1937–46; Dir of Electrical Engineering, RCN, 1942–47; Dir. Electrical Research Div. Defence Research Board, Ottawa, 1947–49. Dean: Faculty of Applied Science, Univ. of St Andrews, 1955–60, 1965–67; Fac. of Engineering and Applied Science, Univ. of Dundee, 1967–71. Coun., Royal Soc. of Edinburgh, 1958–61; Chm. Scottish Centre IEE, 1961–63. Life Mem., Engineering Inst. of Canada. *Publications*: The Fundamentals of Electromagnetism, 1939; Electromagnetism and Relativity, 1957; technical, scientific and educational papers. *Recreations*: genealogy, bookbinding, painting, philately. *Address*: 20 Riverdale, River, Dover, Kent.
*Died 13 May* 1981.

**CULVER, Roland Joseph**, OBE 1980; actor; *b* 31 Aug. 1900; *s* of Edward Culver and Florence Tullege; *m* 1st, 1934, Daphne Rye (marr. diss.); two *s*; 2nd, 1947, Nan Hopkins. *Educ*: Highgate Coll.; Royal Academy of Dramatic Art. First appearance on stage, Hull Rep. Theatre, as Paul, in Peter and Paul, 1925; first London appearance, Century Theatre, with Greater London Players, 1925; there followed continuous parts in plays in West End theatres. Played Lieut-Comdr Rogers, in French Without Tears, Criterion, Nov. 1936 until 1939; Ford, in Believe It or Not, New, 1940; Viscount Goring, in An Ideal Husband, Westminster, 1943; George Wayne, in Another Love Story, Phoenix, 1944. First English actor to go to Hollywood after end of 1939–45 War; on returning to England appeared as Ronald Knight, MA, in Master of Arts, Strand, 1949; Oscar, in Who is Sylvia?, Criterion, 1950; William Collyer, in The Deep Blue Sea, Duchess, 1952; prod revival of Aren't We All?, Haymarket, 1953. First appearance on New York stage at Coronet, 1953, as Philip, in The Little Hut; Simon Foster in Simon and Laura, Strand, London, 1954; Stanley Harrington in Five Finger Exercise, Comedy Theatre, London, 1958, New York and US tour, 1959–61; Sir Richard Conynham, PC, MP, in Shout for Life, Vaudeville, 1963; Dr Parker in Carving a Statue, Haymarket, 1964; Lebedyev in Ivanov, Phœnix, 1965, New York and United States tour 1966; Getting Married, Strand, 1967; Hay Fever, Duke of York's, 1968; His, Hers and Theirs, Apollo, 1969; My Darling Daisy, Lyric, 1970; Trelawny, Prince of Wales, 1972; The Bedwinner, Royalty, 1974; Polonius, in Hamlet, Nat. Theatre, 1975; Agamemnon in Troilus and Cressida, Nat. Theatre, 1976. Wrote and appeared in his own play, A River Breeze, 1956. Has appeared on BBC TV and ITV; since 1972 various television plays and serials including: Wives and Daughters; Cranford; The Pallisers (as The Duke of Omnium); Way Up to Heaven; The Inquisitor, in Shaw's St Joan. Entered films, 1931, and has appeared in numerous successful pictures. *Films include*: French without Tears, On Approval, The First of the Few, Secret Mission, To Each His Own, Down to Earth, Emperor Waltz, Trio, Quartette, The Greek Tycoon, No Longer Alone. *Publications*: A River Breeze (play), 1957; Not Quite a Gentleman (memoirs), 1979. *Recreations*: painting, golf, hacking and writing. *Address*: 18A Maunsel Street, SW1. *T*: 01–828 1484. *Clubs*: Garrick, Green Room, MCC, Lord's Taverners.
*Died 1 March* 1984.

**CUMBERBATCH, Arthur Noel**, CMG 1953; CBE 1942 (MBE 1933); Minister (Commercial), Cairo, 1948–54, retired from Foreign Service, 1954; *b* 25 Dec. 1895. *Educ*: King's Coll. Sch.; Paris. Served European War, 1914–18 (despatches). Employed in Commercial Secretariat, Athens, 1920; Asst to the Commercial Sec., Athens, 1931; Commercial Secretary, Athens, 1934. Served, later, in Cairo, Tehran and again in Athens. *Address*: 64 Chesterfield House, Chesterfield Gardens, W1. *T*: 01–493 7148.
*Died 22 Dec.* 1982.

**CUMING, Mariannus Adrian**, CMG 1962; retired; Chairman, Cuming Smith & Co. Ltd, Melbourne, 1945–78, and formerly associated fertiliser companies; formerly Director: Broken Hill Pty Co. Ltd and subsidiaries; Imperial Chemical Industries of Australia and New Zealand Ltd; *b* 26 Nov. 1901; *s* of J. Cuming, Melbourne; *m* 1926, Wilma Margaret, *d* of W. C. Guthrie; three *s* one *d*. *Educ*: Melbourne Grammar Sch.; Melbourne Univ. (BSc); Imperial Coll., London (Dip.). FTS. Dir, Alfred Hospital, Melbourne, 1945–76. *Recreations*: golf, fishing. *Address*: 29 Stonnington Place, Toorak, Vic 3142, Australia. *T*: Melbourne 20 5319. *Clubs*: Australian, Melbourne, Royal Melbourne Golf (Melbourne); Weld (Perth).
*Died 26 Feb.* 1988.

**CUMINGS, Sir Charles (Cecil George)**, KBE 1951; *b* 30 March 1904; *s* of late Capt. C. E. G. Cumings and E. M. Cumings, OBE; *m* 1942, Enid Gethen; one *s* one *d*. *Educ*: St Andrew's Coll. and Rhodes University Coll., Grahamstown, S Africa; New Coll., Oxford.

Called to the Bar, Inner Temple, 1927; Sudan Political Service, 1927–30; Legal Dept, Sudan Govt, 1930; Advocate-Gen., 1943; Chief Justice, 1945; Legal Sec., 1947–54. Lectr in Law, Rhodes Univ., 1953–55; Resident Dir in Africa, British South Africa Co., 1958–59; Personal Asst to Principal and Lectr in Law, Univ. of Rhodesia, 1962–77. *Address:* 17 Elkedra Close, Hawker, ACT 2614, Australia. *Died 22 July* 1981.

**CUMMING, Lt-Col Malcolm Edward Durant,** CB 1961; OBE 1945; attached War Office, 1934–65; *b* 27 Sept. 1907; *m* 1972, Mrs Mary Macnutt. *Educ:* Eton; Royal Military Coll., Sandhurst. Served with 60th Rifles, 1927–34. *Recreations:* fishing and rural interests generally. *Address:* c/o Lloyds Bank Ltd, Cox & King's Branch, 6 Pall Mall, SW1. *Club:* Greenjackets. *Died 27 April* 1985.

**CUMMING, Lt-Col Sir Ronald Stuart,** Kt 1965; TD; Chairman, Distillers Company Ltd, 1963–67 (Dir 1946–67); *b* April 1900; *s* of John F. Cumming, OBE, DL, JP, Aberlour, Banffshire; *m* 1925, Mary, OBE 1953, *d* of late Col Wm Hendrie, Hamilton, Canada; two *d. Educ:* Uppingham; Aberdeen Univ. Grenadier Guards, 1918–19; Dir, John Walker & Sons Ltd, 1931–39; Joint Man. Dir, James Buchanan & Co. Ltd, 1939–46; served Seaforth Highlanders (TA), 1939–45; Man. Dir, James Buchanan & Co. Ltd, 1946–51; Chm., Booth's Distilleries Ltd, 1953–63; Chm., John Walker & Sons Ltd, 1957–63; Chm. Council, Scotch Whisky Assoc., 1961–67. Hon. LLD Strathclyde, 1967. *Recreations:* fishing, shooting, golf. *Address:* Sourden, Rothes, Morayshire. *Clubs:* Boodle's; New (Edinburgh). *Died 17 Nov.* 1982.

**CUMMING, Ronald William,** ME; FTS; Director, Caulfield Institute of Technology, 1979–82, retired; *b* 9 April 1920; *s* of John Borland Cumming and Muriel Cumming (*née* Hackford); *m* 1945, Betty Lovell Gent; two *s* two *d. Educ:* Sydney Univ. (BEAero); Univ. of Michigan (AMPsychol); Univ. of Melbourne (ME). Research Scientist, Aeronautical Research Labs, Melbourne, 1941–55; Head, Human Engineering Gp, Aero Res. Labs, 1956–66 (research on human factors in aviation); set up Human Factors Cttee of Aust. Road Research Bd, 1962 (Chm. to 1969); Reader in Mechanical Engrg, Univ. of Melbourne, 1966–71; Prof. of Psychology, Monash Univ., 1971–78. Vis. Prof., Dept of Mech. Engrg, Univ. of Melbourne, 1982–85. Pt-time Comr, Road Safety & Standards Authority, 1975–76; Member, Adv. Council, CSIRO, 1973–78. Pres., Australian Psychological Soc., 1972–73. Hon. DEng Melbourne, 1983. *Publications:* various research papers in jls. *Recreation:* classical music. *Address:* 46 Westbrook Street, East Kew, Victoria 3102, Australia. *Died 31 Dec.* 1986.

**CUMMING, Roualeyn Charles Rossiter,** CIE 1942; KPM 1940; *b* 2 Nov. 1891; *e s* of Roualeyn Charles Cumming, Calne, Wilts; *m* 1st, 1916, Pauline Grace (*d* 1952), *y d* of Edward Hagarty Parry, Stoke Poges; 2nd, 1958, Eileen Mary, *née* Steel (*d* 1975), widow of Comdr E. D. Michell, DSC, RN. *Educ:* St Paul's Sch. Entered Indian Police, 1911; Personal Assist to Chief Comr of Assam, 1914–16; Political Officer, NE Frontier, India, 1926–30: Deputy Inspector-Gen. of Police, Assam, 1935–37; Inspector Gen. of Police and Joint Sec. in Home Dept, Govt of Assam, 1937–46. *Recreation:* golf. *Address:* Post Mead, Bishop's Waltham, Hampshire. *Club:* East India, Devonshire, Sports and Public Schools.
*Died 6 Feb.* 1981.

**CUMMING, William Richard,** CVO 1954; Chairman, Public Lending Right Committee, Department of Home Affairs and Environment, Australia, since 1976; *b* 15 Oct. 1911; *e s* of late George Cumming, Coorparoo, Qld; *m* 1939, Evelyn Joyce, *o d* of late George Paul, Epping, NSW; one *s* one *d. Educ:* Gregory Terr., Brisbane; Univs of Queensland and Sydney. BA Queensland, LLB, DipPubAd Sydney. Admitted to NSW Bar, 1941. Enlisted in AIF and served War of 1939–45 with AAPC, Major. Adviser, Federal Taxation Dept, 1947–51; part-time Lectr, Commercial Law, Political Science, Canberra University Coll., Univ. of Melbourne, 1949–53; Prime Minister's Dept, Australia: Senior Exec. Officer, 1951–55, Asst Secretary, 1955–60, and 1966–70; Official Sec., Australian High Commn, London, 1960–66, 1970–73, and acting Dep. High Comr; (various periods); Cultural Counsellor, Aust. High Commn, London, 1973–74; Chm., Aust. Musical Soc., London, 1973–74; Consultant, Australia Council, 1974–76. Extra Gentleman Usher to the Queen, 1962–66, 1971–74; Dir, Royal Visits, ACT, 1953–54, 1956, 1957–58; Dir-Gen., Australia, Royal Visit, 1959. Secretary: Commonwealth Literary Fund, 1955–60, 1966–70; Commonwealth Historic Memorials Cttee, 1955–60, 1966–70; Commonwealth Art Advisory Bd, 1955–60, 1966–70; Commonwealth Assistance to Australian Composers, 1967–70; Council, Australian Nat. Gallery, 1968–70; Member: Council, Nat. Library of Australia, 1967–70; Council, Australian Inst. of Aboriginal Studies, 1969–70. S. H. Ervin Gall. Cttee, 1978–; Norman Lindsay Gall. Cttee, 1978–. *Recreations:* collecting antiques and Australian art, Australiana, motoring. *Address:* 2 Eric Street, Wahroonga, NSW 2076, Australia. *Club:* Oriental. *Died 17 Aug.* 1984.

**CUNARD, Major Sir Guy (Alick),** 7th Bt *cr* 1859; *b* 2 Sept. 1911; *s* of Captain Alick May Cunard (*d* 1926) (*s* of William Samuel Cunard, *g s* of 1st Bt) and Cecil Muriel (*d* 1964), *d* of late Guy St Maur Palmes, Lingcroft, York; *S* brother, 1973; unmarried. *Educ:* Eton; RMC, Sandhurst. Gazetted 16/5th Lancers, 1931; transferred to 4/7th Royal Dragoon Guards, 1933; Captain, 1939; Major, 1946; active service France and Belgium, 1940, and Western Desert; retired, 1949. *Recreations:* steeplechasing, point-to-pointing, hunting, cricket. *Heir:* none. *Address:* The Garden House, Wintringham, Malton, N Yorks. *T:* Rillington 286.
*Died 17 Jan* 1989 (*ext*).

**CUNDIFF, Major Frederick William;** former Director: Chesters Brewery Co. Ltd (Chairman 1960–61); on merger, Threlfalls Brewery Co. Ltd (Dep. Chm., 1964–67); National Gas and Oil Engine Co.; *b* 1895; *s* of late Sir William Cundiff. *Educ:* Manchester Univ. Commnd RA; seconded to RFC, 1917; also served War, 1939–45. MP (C) Rusholme Div. of Manchester, 1944–45; Withington Div. of Manchester, 1950–51. *Address:* Grenaway, Chelford Road, Prestbury, Macclesfield, Cheshire SK10 4PT.
*Died 7 Aug.* 1982.

**CUNINGHAME, Sir William Alan F.;** *see* Fairlie-Cuninghame.

**CUNLIFFE, Prof. Marcus Falkner;** University Professor, George Washington University, Washington DC, since 1980; *b* 5 July 1922; *s* of Keith Harold and Kathleen Eleanor Cunliffe; *m* 1st, 1949, Mitzi Solomon (marr. diss. 1971); one *s* two *d*; 2nd, 1971, Lesley Hume. *Educ:* Oriel Coll., Oxford. Commonwealth Fund Fellow, Yale Univ., 1947–49; Lectr in American Studies, 1949–56, Sen Lectr, 1956–60, Prof. of Amer. Hist. and Instns, 1960–64, Univ. of Manchester; Prof. of Amer. Studies, Univ. of Sussex, 1965–80. Fellow, Center for Advanced Study in the Behavioral Sciences, Stanford, Calif., 1957–58; Vis. Prof. in American History, Harvard Univ., 1959–60; Vis. Prof., Michigan Univ., 1973; Fellow, Woodrow Wilson Internat. Centre, Washington DC, 1977–78. Member: Massachusetts Historical Soc.; Soc. of American Historians. Hon. Dr Humane Letters: Univ. of Pennsylvania, 1976; New England Coll., 1979. *Publications:* The Literature of the United States, 1954, 4th edn 1986; George Washington: Man and Monument, 1958, rev. edn 1982; The Nation Takes Shape, 1789–1837, 1959; (ed) Weems' Life of Washington, 1962; Soldiers and Civilians: The Martial Spirit in America, 1775–1865, 1968; American Presidents and the Presidency, 1969, rev. edn 1987; (ed with R. Winks) Pastmasters: Some Essays on American Historians, 1969; (ed) Sphere History of Literature: vol. 8, American Literature to 1900, 1974, rev. edn 1986, vol. 9, American Literature from 1900, 1975, rev. edn 1987; The Age of Expansion 1848–1917, 1974; (ed) The Divided Loyalist: Crèvecoeur's America, 1978; Chattel Slavery and Wage Slavery, 1979. *Recreation:* the pursuit of happiness. *Address:* 1823 Lamont Street NW, Washington, DC 20010, USA. *T:* 202–387–4459.
*Died 2 Sept.* 1990.

**CUNLIFFE, Captain Robert Lionel Brooke,** CBE 1944; Royal Navy, retired; *b* 15 March 1895; *s* of Col Foster Cunliffe and Mrs Cunliffe (*née* Lyon); *m* 1st, 1926, Barbara Eleanor Cooper (*d* 1970); three *d*; 2nd, 1971, Christina Cooper (*d* 1989). *Educ:* RN Colls Osborne and Dartmouth. Comdr 1930; Capt. 1936; commanded HMS Milford, 1938–39; RNC Dartmouth, 1939–42; Commodore, Dover, 1942; commanded HMS Illustrious, 1942–44 (despatches); Cdre, RN Barracks, Devonport, 1944–46; Retd, 1946. Naval Asst to UK High Comr, Canada, 1946–48. Grand Officer Order of Leopold II, Belgium, 1948. *Recreations:* cricket, shooting. *Address:* The Garden House, Pakenham, Bury St Edmunds, Suffolk. *T:* Pakenham (0359) 30236. *Died 29 Nov.* 1990.

**CUNLIFFE-OWEN, Sir Dudley (Herbert),** 2nd Bt, *cr* 1920; *b* 27 March 1923; 2nd (but *o* surv.) *s* of Sir Hugo Cunliffe-Owen, 1st Bt and Helen Elizabeth Cunliffe-Owen (*d* 1934), *d* of James Oliver, New York; *S* father, 1947; *m* 1st, 1947, Mary Maud (*d* 1956), *e d* of R. R. Redgrave; 2nd, 1956, Hon. Juliana Nettlefold (*née* Curzon) (marr. diss. 1962), 3rd *d* of 2nd Viscount Scarsdale, TD; one *d*; 3rd, 1964, Jean, *o d* of late Surg. Comdr A. N. Forsyth, RN; one *s* one *d. Educ:* RN Coll., Dartmouth. Served War, 1939–46 (despatches); Lieut Royal Navy; retired 1947. *Recreation:* yachting. *Heir:* *s* Hugo Dudley Cunliffe-Owen, *b* 16 May 1966. *Address:* Eyreton House, Quarterbridge, Douglas, Isle of Man. *T:* Douglas 4545. *Club:* Royal Thames Yacht. *Died 17 July* 1983.

**CUNNINGHAM, Gen. Sir Alan Gordon,** GCMG 1948; KCB 1941 (CB 1941); DSO 1918; MC 1915; LLD; *b* 1 May 1887; *s* of Prof. D. J. Cunningham, FRS, and Elizabeth Cumming Browne; *m* 1951, Margery, *widow* of Sir Harold Edward Snagge, KBE. *Educ:* Cheltenham; Royal Military Academy, Woolwich. First commission, 1906; served European War, France, 1914–18; Brigade Major and Gen. Staff Officer 2nd Grade (despatches 5 times, DSO and MC); Gen. Staff Officer, Straits Settlements, 1919–21; passed Naval Staff Coll., 1925; Brevet Lt-Col 1928; Instructor, Machine Gun Sch., 1928–31; Lt-Col 1935; Imperial Defence Coll., 1937; Comdr Royal Artillery, 1st Div., 1937–38; Maj.-Gen., 1938; Comdr

5th Anti-Aircraft Div. TA, 1938; commanded 66th, 9th and 51st Divs, 1940; GOC East Africa Forces, 1940–41; GOC-in-C 8th Imperial Army in Middle East, 1941; Commandant Staff College, Camberley, 1942; Lt-Gen. 1943; GOC Northern Ireland, 1943–44; GOC-in-C Eastern Command, 1944–45; Gen., 1945; High Commissioner and C-in-C for Palestine, 1945–48; Col Commandant Royal Artillery, 1944–54. Pres., Council of Cheltenham Coll., 1951–63. Comdr American Legion of Merit, 1945; Brilliant Star of Zanzibar (1st class), 1941; Ordre de la Couronne (1st class), Belgium, 1950; Order of Menelik (1st Class), 1954, etc. *Recreations:* gardening, fishing. *Club:* Army and Navy.

*Died 30 Jan. 1983.*

**CUNNINGHAM, Air Cdre Alexander Duncan,** CB 1941; CBE 1919 (OBE 1919); late RAF; *b* 18 July 1888; *m* 1918, Hilda Carter (*d* 1954); *m* 1965, Mrs Gladys Way, September Cottage, Bourne End. Served European War, 1914–19 (despatches, OBE, CBE); Air Commodore, 1933; retired list, 1938. Re-employed, 1939–45 (despatches), Air Vice-Marshal, 1940. *Address:* c/o Ministry of Defence (Air), Whitehall, SW1. *Died 3 Feb. 1981.*

**CUNNINGHAME GRAHAM of Gartmore, Adm. Sir Angus (Edward Malise Bontine),** KBE 1951 (CBE 1944); CB 1947; JP: Lord Lieutenant of Dunbartonshire, 1955–68; Keeper of Dumbarton Castle, since 1955; *b* 1893; *s* of Comdr C. E. F. Cunninghame Graham, MVO, Royal Navy; *m* 1924, Mary Patricia, *d* of late Col Lionel Hanbury, CMG; one *s* one *d*. *Educ:* Osborne and Dartmouth. HM Yacht Victoria and Albert, 1914; served in Grand Fleet, 1914–18; SNO West River, China, 1936–38; Capt. of HM Signal Sch., 1939–41; Capt. of HMS Kent, 1941–43; Commodore Royal Naval Barracks, Chatham, 1943–45; ADC to King George VI; Rear-Adm, 1945; Rear-Adm. Comdg 10th Cruiser Squadron, and 2nd in Comd Home Fleet, 1945–46; Flag Officer, Scotland, 1950–51, and Admiral Superintendent, Rosyth, 1947–51; Vice-Adm. 1948; retd list, 1951; Adm., 1952. A Captain in Royal Company of Archers (Queen's Body Guard for Scotland), 1969–. Hon. Sheriff 1959. Vice-President: RNLI; Earl Haig Fund, Scotland; Trustee for National Library of Scotland; Commissioner of Queen Victoria Sch. A Vice-Pres. National Trust for Scotland. JP Dunbartonshire, 1955. *Address:* Ardoch, Cardross, Dunbartonshire, Scotland. *T:* Dumbarton 62905. *Clubs:* Royal Yacht Squadron (Naval Member); New (Edinburgh). *Died 14 Feb. 1981.*

**CUNYNGHAME, Sir James Ogilvy B.;** *see* Blair-Cunynghame.

**CURLEWIS, His Honour Judge Sir Adrian (Herbert),** Kt 1967; CVO 1974; CBE 1962; retired as Judge of the District Court, New South Wales, Australia, (1948–71); *b* 13 Jan. 1901; *s* of late Judge Herbert R. Curlewis and late Ethel Turner, Authoress; *m* 1928, Beatrice Maude Carr; one *s* one *d*. *Educ:* Sydney Church of England Grammar Sch.; Univ. of Sydney. Called to Bar of NSW, 1927. Served War of 1939–45, Capt. 8 Div. AIF, Malaya. President: Surf Life Saving Assoc. of Australia, 1933–75 (Life Governor, 1975); International Surf Life Saving Council, 1956–71; Patron, World Life Saving, 1971–74; Life Patron, NSW RSL Youth Clubs, 1978; Chairman: Australian Outward Bound Trust (Founder and Past Pres.), 1956–; National Fitness Council, New South Wales, 1948–71; National Co-ordinator, Duke of Edinburgh's Award in Australia, 1958–73; Pres., Royal Humane Soc. (NSW), 1968–. Youth Policy Adv. Cttee to NSW Government, 1961–63. Chm. and Royal Commissioner on various Government Enquiries. *Recreations:* surfing, gardening. *Address:* 5 Hopetoun Avenue, Mosman, NSW 2088, Australia. *T:* 969–8365. *Club:* University (Sydney).

*Died 16 June 1985.*

**CURRAN, Desmond,** CBE 1961; FRCP, FRCPsych; Emeritus Professor of Psychiatry, St George's Hospital Medical School, University of London; Emeritus Civil Consultant in Psychiatry to the Royal Navy; Hon. Consulting Psychiatrist, St George's Hospital, since 1967; Lord Chancellor's Medical Visitor, 1967–75; *b* 14 Feb. 1903; *s* of late J. P. Curran; *m* 1938, Marguerite (*née* Gothard); two *s*. *Educ:* Wellington Coll.; Trinity Coll., Cambridge; St George's Hosp.; Johns Hopkins Hosp., Baltimore. MB, BChir Cambridge, 1928; MRCP 1928, FRCP 1937; MRCS, LRCP 1927; DPM London 1930; House jobs, St George's, 1927–28; HP, Bethlem, 1928–29; RMO and Registrar, Maida Vale Hosp. for Nervous Diseases, 1929–30; Intern, Phipps Clinic, Baltimore, 1930–31; Rockefeller Travelling Fellowship, 1930–31; AMO, Maudsley Hosp., 1931–34 (and later part-time); Gaskell Gold Medal Psychological Medicine, 1933. Consultant Psychiatrist: St George's Hosp., 1934–67; Maida Vale Hosp. for Nervous Diseases, 1934–46. War of 1939–45: Consultant in Psychological Medicine to Royal Navy (Temp. Surg. Capt. RNVR), 1939–46. Mem. SW Metropolitan Hosp. Bd, 1948. Croonian Lecturer, RCP 1948. President: Psychiatric Section, RSM, 1951–52; Royal Med. Psychological Assoc., 1963–64. Member: (Franklin) Deptl Cttee on Punishments, Prisons and Borstals, etc, 1948–51; (Wolfenden) Deptl Cttee on Homosexuality and Prostitution, 1954–57; (Representative RCP), Gen. Med. Council, 1961–67. Examiner in Psychiatry: RCP; Univs of London,

Edinburgh, Newcastle; NUI. Distinguished Fellow, Amer. Psychiatric Assoc., 1966. Hon. FRCPsych, 1972. *Publications:* (jointly) Psychological Medicine, 1943, 9th rev. edn (by P. B. Storey), 1980; articles and papers in medical text books and journals. *Address:* 51 Cottesmore Court, Stanford Road, W8 5QW. *T:* 01–937 4763. *Club:* United Oxford & Cambridge University.

*Died 26 Sept. 1985.*

**CURRAN, Harry Gibson,** CMG 1953; *b* 1901; *s* of late James P. and Jessie M. Curran; *m* 1962, Betty, *d* of Harold Beazley. *Educ:* Royal Naval College, Dartmouth; University College, Oxford (MA). Served War of 1914–18 in Grand Fleet; served War of 1939–45, Middle East (despatches). Treasury Representative, South Asia, India, 1946–53; Canada, 1953–56; Head of Economic Mission, Ecuador, 1956–58; Representative World Bank, India, 1959–61; Dep. Dir, European Office, World Bank, 1961–66. *Address:* Fairmile, St Mark's Avenue, Salisbury, Wilts. *Club:* Travellers'.

*Died 29 Dec. 1986.*

**CURRAN, Rt. Hon. Sir Lancelot (Ernest),** PC (N Ireland) 1957; Kt 1964; BA, LLB (QUB); Lord Justice of Appeal, Supreme Court of Judicature, Northern Ireland, 1956–75; *b* 8 March 1899; 4th *s* of late Miles Curran, Myrtlefield Park, Belfast; *m* 1st, 1924, Doris Lee; two *s* (one *d* decd); 2nd, 1976, Mrs Margaret P. Curran. *Educ:* Royal Belfast Academical Institution. Barrister, King's Inns, 1923; QC (NI) 1943; Bencher, Inn of Court of N Ireland, 1946. MP Carrick Div., Co. Antrim, NI Parlt, April 1945 (re-elected June 1945)–1949; Parly Sec., Min. of Finance and Chief Whip, 1945. Served European War, 1917–18, RFC and RAF; War of 1939–45, Major, Army. Lecturer in Contract and Tort, Queen's Univ., Belfast; Chm. Court of Referees and Dep. Umpire under Unemployment Pensions Acts, 1926–45; Senior Crown Prosecutor for Co. Down; Attorney-Gen., NI, 1947–49; Judge of High Courts of Justice, NI, 1949–56. *Recreation:* golf. *Address:* Rock Cottage, Tullyard, Co. Down. *T:* Drumbo 600. *Club:* Royal Co. Down Golf.

*Died 20 Oct. 1984.*

**CURREY, Ronald Fairbridge,** MC; MA, Hon. LLD; *b* 23 Oct. 1894; *s* of late Hon. H. L. Currey and Ethelreda (*d* 1942), *d* of late C. A. Fairbridge; *m* 1924, Dorothy White (decd); three *s*. *Educ:* Diocesan Coll., Rondebosch; S Andrews Coll., Grahamstown; Rhodes Univ. Coll., Grahamstown; Trinity Coll., Oxford; Rhodes Scholar, 1912. Served 1914–18, Argyll and Sutherland Highlanders (attached Black Watch), France and Belgium (MC and Bar); Asst Master, Rugby Sch., 1920–21; S Andrews Coll., Grahamstown, 1922–26; Joint Headmaster, Ridge Preparatory Sch., Johannesburg, 1927–30; Rector of Michaelhouse, Balgowan, Natal, 1930–38; Headmaster of S Andrews Coll., Grahamstown, S Africa, 1939–55; Headmaster, Ruzawi Sch., Marandellas, S Rhodesia, 1956–61; Lectr in Classics, Rhodes Univ., Grahamstown, until 1965. *Publications:* (with others) Coming of Age-Studies in South African Politics, Economics, and Citizenship, 1930; Some Notes on The Future of the South African Church Schools, 1942; Rhodes: a Biographical Footnote, 1946; (with others) The South African Way of Life, 1953; S Andrews College, 1855–1955, 1955; Rhodes University, 1904–1970, 1970. *Address:* 34 Hill Street, Grahamstown, South Africa.

*Died 13 May 1983.*

**CURRIE, Sir Alick Bradley,** 6th Bt *cr* 1847; retired; *b* 8 June 1904; *s* of George Hugh Currie (*d* 1951) (*g s* of 1st Bt) and Grace, *d* of A. F. Miller, Farmington, New Mexico, USA; *S* kinsman, Sir Walter Mordaunt Cyril Currie, 5th Bt, 1978. Formerly in Radio Communications with US Navy and Federal Aviation, 1923–50; US Representative, ICAO, 1945–50, attending numerous world-wide confs. *Heir:* nephew Donald Scott Currie [*b* 1930; *m* 1st, 1948, Charlotte (marr. diss. 1951), *d* of Charles Johnstone; one *s* two *d*; 2nd, 1952, Barbara Lee, *d* of A. P. Garnier; one *s* two *d*]. *Address:* Tenacre Ranch, 13467 County Road 501, Bayfield, Colorado 81122, USA. *Died 26 Feb. 1987.*

**CURRIE, Sir George (Alexander),** Kt 1960; retired as Vice-Chancellor, University of New Zealand (May 1952–Dec. 1961); *b* Banffshire, Scotland, 13 Aug. 1896; *s* of George Currie, farmer, and Mary Currie; *m* 1923, Margaret, *d* of Alexander Smith; two *s*. *Educ:* University of Aberdeen (BscAg, DSc). War Service, Gordon Highlanders, 1915–18. Manager, Salter Estate Co. Ltd, N Queensland, 1923–26; Scientific Officer, Dept Agric., Queensland, 1926–29; Principal Research Officer, Council for Scientific and Industrial Research, Australia, 1929–39; Prof. of Agriculture, University of Western Australia, 1939–40; Vice Chancellor, Univ. of Western Australia, 1940–52. Chm. Commn on Higher Educn for Papua and New Guinea, 1963–64. Hon. LLD: Aberdeen, 1948; Melbourne, 1954; Dalhousie, Canada, 1958; Papua, New Guinea, 1967. Hon. DLitt, University of Western Australia, 1952. *Publications:* The Origins of CSIRO, 1901–26, 1966; some 20 bulletins, pamphlets and articles on scientific research; articles on univ. educn and admin. *Address:* 20 Chermside Street, Canberra, ACT 2600, Australia. *Died 4 May 1984.*

**CURRIE, Sir James,** KBE 1967 (OBE 1950); CMG 1958; retired from HM Diplomatic Service, 1967; *b* 6 May 1907; *o s* of Charles Howat Currie and Rebecca Ralston, Glasgow; *m* 1945, Daisy Mowat; one *s*. *Educ:* Glasgow Academy; Glasgow Univ.; Balliol Coll., Oxford; London School of Economics. Did not take up appt at UCL, 1931; William Hollins & Co. Ltd, 1931–34; National Milk Publicity Council, 1934–39; taught Working Mens' Coll.; Ministry of Economic Warfare, 1939. Commercial Secretary: Rio de Janeiro, 1941; Ankara, 1944; First Secretary (Commercial), Istanbul, 1945; Santiago, Chile, 1947; British Rep., ECLA, 1948–49; Commercial Counsellor, Washington, 1949; Commercial Counsellor and Consul-General, Copenhagen, 1952; Consul-General: São Paulo, 1956; Johannesburg, 1962. Commonwealth Foundn, 1967–70; Civil Service Commn, 1967–77; London Council of Univ. of Witwatersrand, 1969–78; Community Relations Commn, 1970–73. FRSA 1955. *Publications:* Professional Organisations in the Commonwealth, 1970; reviews for TLS, The Times and other jls. *Recreations:* fishing and golf. *Address:* Juniper House, Tostock, Bury St Edmunds, Suffolk. *Club:* Reform.

*Died 24 Dec. 1983.*

**CURSON, Bernard Robert,** CMG 1967; HM Diplomatic Service, retired; *b* 14 Nov. 1913; *e s* of late Robert and Mabel Curson; *m* 1949, Miriam Olive Johnson (*d* 1986), Lynchburg, Virginia; one *s*. *Educ:* University Coll. Sch. Asst Private Sec. to Sec. of State for India, 1943–44, and 1945–46; Mem., UK Delegn to UN Assembly, 1946, 1947, 1948; Private Sec. to Sec. of State for Commonwealth Relations, 1948–50; Office of High Comr, Ceylon, 1950–52; Mem., UK Delegn to UN Wheat Conf., Geneva, 1956; Mem., UK Delegn to Colombo Plan Consultative Cttee, Wellington, 1956, and Saigon, 1957; British Information Services, Canada, 1958–64; Consul-Gen., Atlanta, USA, 1970–73. *Address:* 3804 Peachtree Road, NE, Atlanta, Ga 30319, USA. *Club:* Travellers'.

*Died 31 Dec. 1988.*

**CURTIN, Rt. Rev. Mgr. Canon Jeremiah John,** DD; Priest-Director and Ecclesiastical Adviser, Universe Enquiry Bureau, since 1953; Canon of Southwark Diocesan Chapter, 1958; Domestic Prelate to HH Pope John XXIII, 1961, Protonotary Apostolic, 1972; Canon Theologian, Metropolitan Chapter, 1981; *b* Sileby, Leics, 19 June 1907; *e s* of late Jeremiah John Curtin and Mary Bridget Curtin (*née* Leahy). *Educ:* Battersea Polytechnic; Wimbledon Coll.; St Joseph's Coll., Mark Cross; St John's Seminary, Wonersh; Gregorian Univ., Rome. BA London 1927; DD Rome 1933 (Gregorian Univ.). Priest, 1931; Prof. of Philosophy and Theology, St John's Seminary, Wonersh, 1933–48; Vice-Rector, 1947–48; Parish Priest, St Paul's, Hayward's Heath, 1948–56; Parish Priest, Our Lady of Ransom, Eastbourne, 1956–61; Rector, Pontificio Collegio Beda, Rome, 1961–72. *Recreations:* archæology, music. *Address:* 48 Castle Street, Farnham, Surrey GU9 7JQ. *T:* Farnham 714659.

*Died 2 Nov. 1988.*

**CURTIS, Brig. Francis Cockburn,** CBE 1945; MA; MIEE; Fellow Emeritus, Trinity Hall, Cambridge, since 1961; *b* 2 May 1899; *s* of late Lieut-Col J. G. C. Curtis, Oxford and Bucks Light Infantry, Walmer, Kent; *m* 1933, Dorothy Joan Grant; two *s* one *d*. *Educ:* Bedales Sch.; RMA, Woolwich; King's Coll., Cambridge (entered 1924; Starred First in Mech. Scis Tripòs, 1926). Commissioned RE 1917; served in Flanders (despatches), Iraq and Palestine; transferred to Royal Signals, 1923; served on General Staff in War Office and Aldershot Command, and in Home Office (ARP Dept), and Office of the Lord Privy Seal; OC 38th (Welsh) Divisional Signals, 1940–41; Army Council Secretariat (Secretary Standing Cttee on Army Administration), 1941; Joint Planning Staff, 1942; Colonel 1943; Dep. Director of Military Operations, 1943–44; Director of Post-Hostilities Plans, War Office, 1944; Brigadier, General Staff (Plans and Ops), GHQ, MELF, 1945–48 (GSM); Director for European Inter-Allied Planning, War Office, 1948–51; retired 1951; Fellow and Bursar, Trinity Hall, Cambridge, 1952–59; Treasurer, 1959–61. Former Mem., Eagle Ski Club. *Recreation:* fishing. *Address:* 16 Marlborough Court, Cambridge CB3 9BQ. *T:* Cambridge 350664.

*Died 24 Sept. 1986.*

**CURTIS, John S.;** *see* Sutton Curtis.

**CURTIS, Percy John,** CB 1960; CBE 1955; Secretary, Exchequer and Audit Department, 1955–63; *b* 3 Oct. 1900; *s* of J. H. Curtis, Trimdon, Co. Durham; *m* 1st, 1924, Dorothy Hilda Ford Hayes (*d* 1954); one *s*; 2nd, 1958, Joyce Irene Potter. *Educ:* Rye Grammar Sch. Entered Exchequer and Audit Dept, 1920. *Address:* 2 Rigault Road, SW6. *T:* 01–736 4072. *Club:* Reform.

*Died 26 March 1985.*

**CURTIS, Richard James Seymour,** OBE 1962; *b* 22 Oct. 1900; *s* of late Sir George Curtis, KCSI, ICS, and of late Lady Curtis, OBE, La Frégate, Dinard, France; *m* 1929, Mary Margaret, *o d* of late Rev. and Mrs H. J. Boyd, St Paul's Vicarage, St Leonards-on-Sea; one *s* one *d*. *Educ:* Haileybury; King's Coll., Cambridge; University of Caen. Hons degree in History, Cambridge, 1922. Appointed Assistant Anglais at Lycée Corneille, Rouen, by Board of Education,

Oct. 1922; Asst Master, Hurst Court, Sept. 1923, Partner, 1926, Headmaster, 1933–61. Incorporated Assoc. of Preparatory Schools (Vice-Chm. IAPS, 1946; Chm. 1957). Asst Sec. and Sec., Common Entrance Examination Board, 1961–67. Mem. Hastings Borough Council, 1952–61; President Soc. of Schoolmasters, 1962. *Publications:* (with A. R. Slater) Latin and French Revision Papers, 1948. Translator of The Revolutionaries, by Louis Madelin; Russia Unveiled, by Panait Istrati; Murder Party, by Henry Bordeaux; The Corsairs of St Malo, by Dupont. *Address:* The Wychert, Haddenham, Bucks. *T:* Haddenham 291136.

*Died 7 Feb. 1985.*

**CURTIS, Wilfred Harry,** CB 1953; CBE 1950; *b* 23 May 1897; retired as Assistant Under-Secretary of State, War Office, 1958. *Educ:* Summerleaze, Harptree, Somerset. JP County of London, 1950–58. *Address:* Rose Cottage, Hindon, Salisbury, Wilts SP3 6DP.

*Died 24 Oct. 1988.*

**CURTIS-RALEIGH, Nigel Hugh; His Honour Judge Curtis-Raleigh;** a Circuit Judge (formerly Judge of County Courts), since 1966; *b* 8 Nov. 1914; *s* of late Capt. H. T. R. Curtis-Raleigh; *m* 1964, Jean Steadman, MB, MRCPsych; five *s*. *Educ:* Wellington; Queen's Coll., Oxford (History Exhibitioner, Kitchener Scholar). Called to the Bar, Middle Temple (Harmsworth Law Scholar), 1939. Served HAC, 1939–40. *Recreations:* music, chess, poker.

*Died 1 Sept. 1986.*

**CURZON, Sir Clifford (Michael),** Kt 1977; CBE 1958; Hon. DMus; FRAM; pianist; *b* 18 May 1907, of British parents; *m* 1931, Lucille Wallace (*d* 1977), American harpsichordist; two adopted *s*. *Educ:* Royal Academy of Music (Thalberg Scholar and Potter Exhibitioner); studied under Prof. Chas Reddie at Royal Academy of Music, Schnabel (Berlin), Katherine Goodson, and Landowska and Boulanger (Paris); concert tours in England, Europe and USA; in 1936 and 1938 toured Europe under the auspices of the British Council; Soloist at the Royal Philharmonic, BBC and Promenade Concerts, etc.; also Colonne and Société Philharmonique Concerts, Paris. 1st performance of Alan Rawsthorne's Piano Concerto No 2, commnd by Arts Council for Festival of Britain, 1951. Formed (with Szigeti, Primrose and Fournier) the Edinburgh Festival Piano Quartet, 1952. American Tours, 1948–70, including solo appearances with New York Philharmonic Orchestra under Bruno Walter, the Philadelphia Orchestra, Pittsburgh and Toronto Orchestras, etc.; Soloist Holland Festival, 1953; Zürich Festival, 1953; tour of Continent as soloist with BBC Symphony Orchestra under Sir Malcolm Sargent, 1954; Soloist Bergen and Munich Festivals, 1954. Soloist Beethoven Festival, Bonn, Salzburg, Edinburgh and Prades Festivals. Hon. Fellow, St Peter's Coll., Oxford, 1981. Hon. DMus Leeds, 1970; Hon. DLitt Sussex, 1973. Royal Philharmonic Soc. Gold Medal, 1980. *Recreations:* gardening and swimming. *Address:* The White House, Millfield Place, Highgate, N6 6JP. *T:* 01–340 5348; The Close, Glenridding, Cumbria.

*Died 1 Sept. 1982.*

**CUTHBERT, Vice-Adm. Sir John (Wilson),** KBE 1957 (CBE 1945); CB 1953; JP; DL; *b* 9 April 1902; *s* of William Cuthbert, Glasgow; *m* 1928, Betty Wake, CBE, *d* of Guy Shorrock; no *c*. *Educ:* Kelvinside Acad.; RN Colleges. Midshipman, 1919; Commander, 1936; Captain, 1941; Rear-Adm., 1951; Vice-Adm., 1954. Commanded: HMS Glasgow, 1942; Ajax, 1944–46; Vengeance, 1949–50; Joint Planning Staff, London, 1942–44; Deputy Controller Admiralty, 1951–53; Flag Officer Flotillas, Home Fleet, 1953–54. Admiral Commanding Reserves, 1955–56; Flag Officer, Scotland, 1956–58. Retired List, 1958. Member Royal Company of Archers (Queen's Body Guard for Scotland); JP Hants 1959; DL Hants 1977. *Address:* Ibthorpe Manor Farm, Hurstbourne Tarrant, near Andover, Hants. *T:* Hurstbourne Tarrant 237.

*Died 7 Dec. 1987.*

**CUTHBERT, William Moncrieff;** DL; Chairman: Clyde Shipping Company, since 1988 (Managing Director, 1971–88); Scottish Amicable Life Assurance Society, since 1985 (Director, since 1976); Chairman of Council and Executive Committee, National Trust for Scotland, since 1984; *b* 22 June 1936; *s* of late Alan Dalrymple Cuthbert and of Elspeth Moncrieff Cuthbert (*née* Mitchell); *m* 1960, Caroline Jean Balfour Mitchell; two *s* one *d*. *Educ:* Shrewsbury School. Dir, the Murray Johnstone managed Investment Trusts, 1982–. Member: Bd, Lloyd's Register of Shipping, 1982–; Council, Royal Glasgow Inst. of Fine Arts, 1981–; Gov., Glasgow School of Art, 1987–. Mem., Royal Co. of Archers (Queen's Body Guard for Scotland, 1968–). FRSA 1987. DL Stirling and Falkirk, 1984. *Address:* 78 Carlton Place, Glasgow G5 9TG. *T:* 041–429 2181.

*Died 15 May 1989.*

**CUTHBERTSON, Sir David (Paton),** Kt 1965; CBE 1957; MD, DSc Glasgow; FRSE, FRCPE; Hon. Senior Research Fellow in Pathological Biochemistry, Glasgow University, and Hon. Consultant in the Biochemical Department of the Royal Infirmary, Glasgow; late Director Rowett Research Institute, 1945–65; *b* 9 May 1900; *s* of John Cuthbertson, MBE, Kilmarnock; *m* 1928, Jean

Prentice (*d* 1987), *d* of late Rev. Alexander P. Telfer, MA, Tarbet, Dunbartonshire; two *s* one *d*. *Educ:* University of Glasgow. BSc 1921; MB, ChB, 1926; DSc, 1931; MD, 1937. Bellahouston Gold Medallist. 2nd Lieut (temp.) Royal Scots Fusiliers, 1919. Lecturer in Pathological Biochemistry and Clinical Biochemist, Royal Infirmary and University of Glasgow, 1926–34; Grieve Lecturer in Physiological Chemistry, University of Glasgow, 1934–45; Arris and Gale Lecturer Royal College of Surgeons, 1942. Lieut-Col and Zone Medical Advisor (No. 1) Glasgow Home Guard, 1941–43; seconded to Administrative Headquarters, Medical Research Council, 1943–45. Consultant Director Commonwealth Bureau of Animal Nutrition, 1945–65; Hon. Consultant in Physiology and Nutrition to the Army, 1946–65. Member: UK Agricultural Mission to Canada, 1950; Tech. Cttee, Scottish Agricultural Improvement Council, 1951–64; Advisory Cttee on Pesticides and other Toxic Chemicals, 1966–71. Chairman: General and Organising Cttees, 9th International Congress of Animal Production, 1966; ARC Tech. Cttee on Nutrient Requirements of Livestock, 1959–65. President: International Union of Nutritional Sciences, 1960–66 (Hon. Pres., 1972–); Sect. I (1953) and Sect. M (1958) of British Assoc.; Nutrition Soc., 1962–65; British Soc. of Animal Production, 1966–67. Scientific Governor, British Nutrition Foundn, 1968–76 (Pres., 1976–79; Hon. Pres., 1979–82). Sir David Cuthbertson Foundn (charitable trust for research), founded by industry, 1985. Baxter Lectr, American Coll. of Surgeons, 1959; 1st W. H. Sebrell Jr Internat. Nutrition Lectr, 1974; Mackdougall-Brisbane Prize Lectr, RSE, 1975; 2nd Jonathan E. Rhoads Lectr, Amer. Soc. Parenteral and Enteral Nutrition, 1979. Hon. Member: European Soc. of Parenteral and Enteral Nutrition, 1981 (Sir David Cuthbertson Lectureship founded 1979); American Institute of Nutrition; Society Biochemistry, Biophysics et Microbiol. Finland; British Soc. of Animal Production; British Nutrition Soc.; Assoc. of Clinical Biochemists. Hon. DSc Rutgers, 1958; Hon. LLD: Glasgow, 1960; Aberdeen, 1972; Dr *hc* Zagreb, 1969. Hon. FRCSE 1967; Hon. FRCPath 1970; Hon. FRCPS Glas; Hon. FIFST 1972. Gold Medal, Czechoslovak Acad. of Agriculture, 1969. *Publications:* Dominions No 4 Report on Nutrition in Newfoundland, with specific recommendations for improvement, 1947; papers on Physiology of Protein Nutrition and Metabolism and on Metabolic Response to Injury (bas-relief in bronze erected to acknowledge researches on this, 1926–34, Glasgow Royal Infirmary, 1987), Ruminant Digestion, etc. *Recreations:* watercolour painting and golf. *Address:* Glenavon, 11 Willockston Road,

Troon, Ayrshire. *T:* Troon 312028. *Club:* Athenæum.
                                                            *Died* 15 *April* 1989.

**CUTHBERTSON, Prof. Joseph William,** DSc, FIM, CEng, FIEE; retired as Cripps Professor of Metallurgy, University of Nottingham (1954–66), later Emeritus Professor; *b* 27 Feb. 1901; *s* of late William Edward Cuthbertson, MRCS, LRCP, and late Kathleen Cuthbertson; *m* 1933, Milly Beatrix Nelson (*d* 1980); no *c*. *Educ:* Manchester Grammar Sch., University of Manchester. Asst, ultimately Senior Lecturer, Dept of Metallurgy, Manchester Univ., 1939–44; seconded to Ministry of Supply, 1942–46; Asst Director of Research, Tin Research Institute, 1944–54. *Publications:* numerous scientific papers, progress reviews, and articles on metallurgy and electro-metallurgy. *Recreations:* motoring, gardening. *Address:* Flat 1, Belvedere, The Esplanade, Grange-over-Sands, Cumbria LA11 7HH. *T:* Grange-over-Sands 3344.                    *Died* 7 *Feb.* 1984.

**CUTNER, Solomon;** *see* Solomon.

**CYRIAX, James Henry,** MD; Visiting Professor in Orthopaedic Medicine, University of Rochester, New York, USA, since 1975; *b* 27 Oct. 1904; *s* of Edgar Ferdinand Cyriax, MD, and Anna Kellgren, LRCP; *m* 1947, Patricia Jane McClintock; three *s* one *d*. *Educ:* University College Sch., London; Gonville and Caius Coll., Cambridge; St Thomas's Hosp., London. LRCP 1929, MD 1938, MRCP 1954. Orthopaedic Physician, St Thomas' Hosp., London, 1947–69. Civil Consultant: Min. of Aviation; BA. First Fellow., British Assoc. of Manipulative Medicine; Patron, Irish Soc. of Orthopaedic Medicine; Président d'Honneur, Societé française de Medicine Orthopédique; Hon. Pres., Cyriax Foundn; Hon. Member: Norwegian Soc. of Manual Medicine; Swedish Soc. of Manual Medicine; North American Acad. of Manipulative Medicine; Purkyne Med. Soc. of Czechoslovakia; Hon. Fellow: NZ Soc. of Physiotherapy; Amer. Physical Medicine Assoc.; CSP; Freeman, City of London; Liveryman, Worshipful Co. of Apothecaries. *Publications:* Textbook of Orthopaedic Medicine (two vols), 1947, vol. I, 8th edn, 1982, vol. II, 10th edn, 1980; Hydrocortisone, 1956; The Shoulder, 1957; Cervical Spondylosis, 1971; The Slipped Disc, 1970, 3rd edn 1980; Manipulation: past and present, 1975; Illustrated Manual of Orthopaedic Medicine, 1983; contrib. BMJ, Lancet, Jl of Bone and Joint Surgery. *Recreation:* sailing. *Address:* Clarence Cottage, Park Village West, NW1. *T:* 01–388 2226. *Club:* Faculty (Rochester, NY, USA).
                                                            *Died* 17 *June* 1985.

# D

**DAENIKER, Dr Armin;** Swiss Ambassador to the Court of St James's, 1957–63, retired; *b* 24 Feb. 1898; *m* 1938; no *c*. *Educ:* Universities of Zürich, Berne, Geneva, London Sch. of Economics (doctor juris utriusque, Zürich). Vice-Consul, Riga, 1927; Shanghai, 1930; Swiss Chargé d'Affaires, Tokio, 1933, Teheran, 1936; Head of Administrative Div., Federal Political Dept, Berne, 1946; Swiss Minister, New Delhi, 1948, and concurrently in Bangkok, 1950; Swiss Minister, Stockholm 1952; Swiss Mem., Neutral Nations Commn for Repatriation of Prisoners of War in Korea, 1953–54; Swiss Minister to the Court of St James's, 1955; Mem. Council, Swiss Winston Churchill Foundation. *Died 14 Jan.* 1983.

**D'AETH, Air Vice-Marshal Narbrough Hughes,** CB 1951; CBE 1943; Licentiate to Officiate, Diocese of Bath and Wells, 1976; *b* 7 Jan. 1901; *s* of late Capt. Reginald Hughes D'Aeth and late Lady Nina Hughes D'Aeth; *m* 1934, Mary Colbeck (*d* 1984), *d* of late E. W. Davis; three *d*. *Educ:* Royal Naval Colls, Osborne and Dartmouth. Served European War, 1914–18, with Grand Fleet, 1917–19; transferred to RAF, 1920; Malta, 1924; China, 1926–28; British Arctic Air Route Expedn in E Greenland, 1930–31; Polar Medal, 1932; Aden, 1934–36; War of 1939–45 in UK and N Africa (despatches thrice, CBE); AOC, RAF, Malta, 1949–52 (CB); AO i/c Administration at HQ, Technical Training Command, 1952–54; SASO, HQ Home Command, 1954–56. Group Capt., 1941; Air Commodore, 1943; Air Vice Marshal, 1950; retired, 1956. Lincoln Theological Coll., 1956–57. Ordained Deacon, Dec. 1957; Curate, St John the Baptist, Crowthorne, Dec. 1957–59; Rector: East Langdon with Guston, Kent, 1959–60; Flinders Islands, 1960–67; Priest-in-Charge, Midland and Swan Parishes, Perth, 1967–71; Licentiate to Officiate: dio. of Perth, 1971–72; dio. of Exeter, 1972–76. American Legion of Merit, 1945; Czechoslovak Medal of Merit, 1945. *Died 21 Jan.* 1986.

**DAHL, Roald;** writer; *b* 13 Sept. 1916; *s* of Harald Dahl and Sofie Magdalene Hesselberg; *m* 1st, 1953, Patricia Neal (marr. diss. 1983); one *s* three *d* (and one *d* decd); 2nd, 1983, Mrs Felicity Ann Crosland (*née* d'Abreu). *Educ:* Repton. Public Schools Exploring Soc. expedn to Newfoundland, 1934; Eastern Staff of Shell Co., 1934–39, served in Dar-es-Salaam; RAF flying trng, Nairobi and Habbanyah, 1939–40; No 80 Fighter Sqdn, Western Desert, 1940 (wounded); Greece, 1941; Syria, 1941; Asst Air Attaché, Washington, 1942–43; Wing Comdr, 1943; British Security Co-ordination, N America, 1943–45. Edgar Allan Poe Award, Mystery Writers of America, 1954 and 1959. *Publications: short stories:* Over to You, 1945; Someone Like You, 1953; Kiss Kiss, 1960; Switch Bitch, 1974; Tales of the Unexpected, 1979; More Tales of the Unexpected, 1980; The Best of Roald Dahl, 1983; Roald Dahl's Book of Ghost Stories, 1983; Two Fables, 1986; *novels:* Sometime Never (A Fable for Supermen), 1948; My Uncle Oswald, 1979; *autobiography:* Boy: Tales of Childhood, 1984; Going Solo, 1986; Ah Sweet Mystery of Life, 1989; *children's books:* (with Walt Disney) The Gremlins, 1943; James and the Giant Peach, 1962; Charlie and the Chocolate Factory, 1964 (staged, Sadler's Wells, 1986); The Magic Finger, 1966; Fantastic Mr Fox, 1970; Charlie and the Great Glass Elevator, 1972; Danny, the Champion of the World, 1975 (filmed 1989); The Wonderful Story of Henry Sugar and Six More, 1977; The Enormous Crocodile, 1978; The Twits, 1980; George's Marvellous Medicine, 1981; Revolting Rhymes, 1982; The BFG, 1982 (filmed 1989); Dirty Beasts, 1983; The Witches, 1983 (Whitbread Award; filmed 1989); The Giraffe and The Pelly and Me, 1985; Matilda, 1988; Rhyme Stew, 1989; Esio Trot, 1990; *play:* The Honeys, 1955; *screenplays:* You Only Live Twice, 1967; Chitty Chitty Bang Bang, 1968; Willy Wonka and the Chocolate Factory, 1971; *television series:* Tales of the Unexpected, 1979; contrib. New Yorker, Harper's Magazine, Atlantic Monthly, Saturday Evening Post, Colliers, etc. *Recreations:* playing Blackjack, picking wild mushrooms. *Address:* Gipsy House, Great Missenden, Bucks HP16 0PB. *Died 23 Nov.* 1990.

**DAHLGAARD, Tyge;** Comdr, Order of the Dannebrog, 1971; Ambassador of Denmark to the Court of St James's, since 1981; *b* 8 April 1921; *s* of Bertel Dahlgaard and Dorthea (*née* Poulsen); *m* 1947, Tove (*née* Jørgensen); two *d*. *Educ:* Copenhagen Univ. (graduated in Econs and Polit. Science, 1947). Joined Min. of Agriculture, 1947 and Min. for Foreign Affairs, 1949; Perm. Deleg., UN, Geneva, 1949–50; Min. for For. Affairs, Copenhagen, 1950–57; Econ. Counsellor, Danish OEEC Mission, Paris, 1957–59, and Danish Embassy, Washington, 1959; Ambassador to EEC, Euratom and ECSC, 1964–Sept. 1966; Minister of Commerce and for Nordic Affairs and Eur. Market Affairs, 1966–67; Ambassador: Belgrade, 1968–Sept. 1972 (also accredited in Tirana, 1970); Tokio and Seoul, 1972–Nov. 1976; The Hague, 1976–Feb. 1981. *Recreations:* music in particular. *Address:* Royal Danish Embassy, 55 Sloane Street, SW1X 9SR. *T:* 01–235 1255. *Died 20 Dec.* 1985.

**DALDRY, Sir Leonard (Charles),** KBE 1963 (CBE 1960); Chairman, St Loye's College for the Disabled, Exeter, 1969–84; *b* 6 Oct. 1908; *s* of Charles Henry Daldry; *m* 1938, Joan Mary (*d* 1976), *d* of John E. Crisp; no *c*; *m* 1976, Monica Mary, *d* of late G. E. Benson and of Helen Benson, Moretonhampstead, Devon; one *s* one *d*. Joined Barclays Bank DCO 1929; Kenya and New York, 1936–52; Local Dir in W Africa at Lagos, 1952–63; Chm., Nigeria Bd, 1961–63. ACIB (Assoc. Inst. of Bankers, 1936); FInstD. Mem. Nigerian Railway Corp., 1955–60; Special Mem., Nigerian House of Reps, 1956–59; Senator, Federal Legislature, Nigeria, 1960–61. *Address:* Prospect House, Budleigh Salterton, Devon EX9 6NZ. *Clubs:* Athenæum, Royal Over-Seas League. *Died 21 Oct.* 1988.

**DALGETTY, James Simpson,** MA, LLB; Solicitor to Secretary of State for Scotland and Solicitor in Scotland to HM Treasury, 1964–71; *b* 13 Aug. 1907; *s* of late Rev. William Dalgetty and Elizabeth Reid Dalgetty (*née* Simpson); *m* 1936, Mary Macdonald; one adopted *d*. *Educ:* George Watson's Coll., Edinburgh; Edinburgh Univ. Legal Asst, Dept of Health for Scotland, 1937; Asst Solicitor, 1944; Asst Solicitor, Office of Solicitor to Sec. of State for Scotland, 1946; Senior Legal Draftsman to Govt of Nyasaland, and acting Solicitor-Gen., 1962–64. *Recreations:* photography, travel, reading. *Address:* 42 Palmerston Place, Edinburgh EH12 5BJ.
*Died 4 Jan.* 1981.

**DALI, Salvador (Felipe Jacinto);** Marqués de Dali y de Pubol, 1982; Spanish painter; stage-designer; book-illustrator; writer; interested in commercial art and films; *b* Figueras, Upper Catalonia, 11 May 1904; *s* of Salvador Dali, notary and Felipa Dome (Doménech); *m* 1935, Gala (*d* 1982) (*née* Elena Diaranoff); she *m* 1st, Paul Eluard. *Educ:* Academy of Fine Arts, Madrid; Paris. First one-man show, Barcelona, 1925; became prominent Catalan painter by 1927; began surrealist painting in Paris, 1928; first one-man show, Paris, Nov. 1929; first one-man show, New York, Nov. 1933; visited United States, 1934, 1939, 1940; lectured in Museum of Modern Art, New York, 1935; later, came to London; first visited Italy, 1937. Designer of scenery and costumes for ballet, etc., also of film scenarios. Has held exhibitions of paintings in many American and European Cities; Exhibition of jewels, London, 1960; major exhibition, Rotterdam, 1970; retrospective, Paris, and Tate Gallery, 1980, Madrid and Barcelona, 1983. *Publications:* Babaouo (ballet and film scenarios), 1932; Secret Life of Salvador Dali, 1942; Hidden Faces (novel), 1944; Fifty Secrets of Magic Craftsmanship, 1948; Diary of a Genius, 1966; The Unspeakable Confessions of Salvador Dali, 1976. *Address:* Hotel St Regis, 5th Avenue, and 55th Street, New York, NY 10022, USA; Port-Lligat, Cadaqués, Spain.
*Died 23 Jan.* 1989.

**DALLARD, Berkeley Lionel Scudamore,** CMG 1948; FCA; JP; *b* Waikari, Christchurch, New Zealand, 27 Aug. 1889; *s* of Geo. Joseph Dallard, Settler, born Tewkesbury, England, and Sarah Maria, born Cheltenham, England; *m* 1915, Agnes Rowan Inglis; three *d*. *Educ:* Waikari Public Sch.; Rangiora High Sch.; Victoria University Coll. Entered Civil Service, NZ, 1907; served in Stamp Office, Audit Office, Board of Trade, Public Service Commissioner's Office (Asst Public Service Commr, 1929), Justice Dept; Controller Gen. of Prisons, and Chief Probation Officer, NZ, 1925–49; Under Sec. for Justice and Registrar Gen., NZ, 1934–49, retd, 1949. Govt Mem. of Govt Service Tribunal, 1949–60, retd. City Councillor, Wellington, 1949–62. Chairman: Wellington Hospital Board, 1962–66; Combined Purchasing Cttee for NZ Hosps, 1963–71. *Publications:* Fettered Freedom, 1980; miscellaneous brochures on Criminology and Law. *Address:* 94 Upland Road, Kelburn, Wellington, NZ. *TA* and *T:* Wellington 759209. *Clubs:* (Past Pres.) Savage, (Past Pres.) Rotary (Wellington, NZ).
*Died 5 Sept.* 1983.

**DALLING, Sir Thomas,** Kt 1951; FRCVS, FRSE; lately Veterinary Consultant with the United Nations Food and Agriculture Organisation; *b* 23 April 1892. *Educ:* George Heriot's Sch., Edinburgh; Royal (Dick) Veterinary College. MRCVS 1914; Fitzwygram and Williams Memorial Prizes. Served with RAVC in France, 1916–18 (despatches), Major. Joined Staff of Glasgow Veterinary Coll., 1919, and later became Chief Investigator of Animal Diseases Research Assoc.; Veterinary Superintendent, Wellcome Physiological Research Laboratories, 1923; Prof. of Animal Pathology, University of Cambridge, 1937 (MA); Dir, Ministry of Agriculture and Fisheries Laboratories, Weybridge, 1942; Chief Veterinary Officer, Ministry of Agriculture and Fisheries, 1948–52; Hon. FRCVS, 1951; Hon. degrees: DSc Belfast, 1951; LLD Glasgow, 1952; DSc Bristol, 1952; LLD Edinburgh, 1959. Dalrymple-Champneys Cup and Medal, 1935; John Henry Steele Memorial Medal in gold, 1950; Thomas Baxter Prize, 1951. Hon. Associate Royal Coll. of Veterinary Surgeons (Mem. Council, 1938–57; Pres., 1949–50, 1950–51; Vice-Pres., 1951–52, 1952–53); late Mem. Agricultural Research Council. *Publications:* many veterinary and scientific articles. *Address:* 77 Howdenhall Road, Edinburgh EH16 6PW. *Died 23 May* 1982.

**DALRYMPLE, Ian Murray,** FRSA; Film Producer, Writer and Director; *b* 26 Aug. 1903; *s* of late Sir William Dalrymple, KBE, LLD; *m* 2nd, Joan Margaret, *d* of late James Douglas Craig, CMG, CBE; one *s* and one *d* of previous marriage and two *s*. *Educ:* Rugby Sch.; Trinity Coll., Cambridge (Editor of The Granta, 1924–25). Executive Producer, Crown Film Unit, Min. of Information, 1940–43; subseq. op. through Wessex Film Productions Ltd and Ian Dalrymple (Advisory) Ltd. Chm. Brit. Film Acad., 1957–58. Film Editor, 1927–35. Screen writer, 1935–39, films including The Citadel, South Riding, Storm in a Teacup, The Lion Has Wings. Produced for Crown Film Unit; Fires Were Started, Western Approaches, Coastal Command, Ferry Pilot, Close Quarters, Wavell's 30,000, Target for To-Night, London Can Take It, etc. Independent productions: The Woman in the Hall, Esther Waters, Once a Jolly Swagman, All Over The Town, Dear Mr Prohack, The Wooden Horse, Family Portrait, The Changing Face of Europe (series), Royal Heritage, Raising a Riot, A Hill in Korea. Commissioned productions include: The Heart of the Matter, The Admirable Crichton, A Cry from the Streets, Bank of England (Educational Films), The Boy and the Pelican. Film Adviser, Decca Ltd, 1967–68. Supervising Film Projects, Argo Record Co. (Div. of Decca Ltd), 1969. Prod Chaucer's Tale, 1970. *Address:* 3 Beaulieu Close, Cambridge Park, Twickenham TW1 2JR.
*Died 28 April 1989.*

**DALRYMPLE-SMITH, Captain Hugh,** RN (retired); *b* 27 Sept. 1901; *s* of late Arthur Alexander Dalrymple-Smith and late Mary Glover; *m* 1939, Eleanor Mary Hoare; two *s* one *d*. *Educ:* Ovingdean; Osborne; Dartmouth. Midshipman, 1917; Ronald Megaw Prize for 1921–22; qualified gunnery 1925, advanced course, 1928. Capt. 1941 (despatches); Admiralty Operations Div., 1942–43; commanding HMS Arethusa, including Normandy landings, 1943–45 (despatches). Naval Attaché, Nanking, 1946–48; commanding HMS King George V, 1948–49. Retired, Dec. 1950, and recalled as Actg Rear-Adm.; Chief of Staff to C-in-C Allied Forces, Northern Europe, 1951–53; retired as Captain. Dir, Television Audience Measurement Ltd, 1958–66. *Recreation:* painting. *Address:* Dale Cottage, Bridge Street, Wickham, Hants PO17 5JE. *T:* Wickham 833103.
*Died 20 Sept. 1987.*

**DALTON, Maj.-Gen. Sir Charles (James George),** Kt 1967; CB 1954; CBE 1949 (OBE 1941); *b* 28 Feb. 1902; *s* of late Maj.-Gen. James Cecil Dalton, Col Comdt, RA, and late Mary Caroline, *d* of late Gen. Sir George Barker, GCB; *m* 1936, Daphne, *d* of Col Llewellyn Evans, and late Mrs F. A. Macartney; one *s* two *d* (and one *s* decd). *Educ:* Aysgarth Sch., Yorks; Cheltenham Coll.; RMA Woolwich. Commissioned, RA, 1921; Staff Coll., Camberley, 1935–36; served in Egypt and India, 1922–39; staff appts in India and Burma, 1939–45 (CRA 26 Ind. Div., BGS 33 Ind. Corps, CRA 14 Ind. Div.); served with CCG, 1946; War Office (Brig. AG Coordination), 1946–49; Comdr 8 AA Bde, 1949–51; Services Relations Adviser to UK High Comr Control Commn for Germany, 1951–54; Dir of Manpower Planning, War Office, 1954–57, retired. Capt. 1934, Major 1939, Lt-Col 1946, Col 1947, Brig. 1951, Maj.-Gen. 1954. Col Comdt RA, 1960–65. Dir-Gen. of Zoological Soc. of London, 1957–67. High Sheriff of Yorks 1972. CStJ. *Recreations:* shooting and fishing. *Address:* The Hutts, Grewelthorpe, Ripon, North Yorks. *T:* Kirkby Malzeard 355.
*Died 6 Jan. 1989.*

**DALTON, Maj.-Gen. John Cecil D'Arcy,** CB 1954; CBE 1948; Vice Lord-Lieutenant North Yorkshire, since 1977; *b* 2 March 1907; *yr s* of late Maj.-Gen. J. C. Dalton, Col Comdt RA, and of late Mrs Dalton; *m* 1942, Pamela Frances, *d* of late Brig.-Gen. W. H. E. Segrave, DSO; two *s*. *Educ:* Cheltenham Coll.; RMA Woolwich, 2nd Lieut RA, 1926; psc 1939; served War of 1939–45; France and Flanders, 1940; N Africa, 1942–43; NW Europe, 1944. COS, British Commonwealth Forces, Korea, 1952–54; Maj.-Gen., 1958; Maj.-Gen. i/c Administration, Gen. HQ, Far East Land Forces, 1957–59; Dir of Quartering War Office, 1959–60; Vice-Quartermaster-Gen., War Office, 1960–62, retired 1962. CC N Riding Yorks, 1964–70, DL North Riding Yorks, 1967, High Sheriff, Yorkshire, 1970–71. *Address:* Hauxwell Hall, Leyburn, North Yorks. *Club:* Army and Navy.
*Died 15 Nov. 1981.*

**DALTON, Philip Neale;** Vice President, Immigration Appeal Tribunal, 1970–82; *b* 30 June 1909; *o s* of late Sir Llewelyn Dalton, MA; *m* 1947, Pearl, *d* of Mark Foster, Kenya; one *s* two *d*. *Educ:* Downside Sch.; Trinity Coll., Cambridge. Barrister-at-law. Inner Temple, 1933; Resident Magistrate, Ghana, 1937; military service, 1939–45; Crown Counsel, Ghana, 1945–51; Solicitor-Gen., Fiji, 1951–53; Attorney-Gen., British Solomon Islands, and Legal Adviser, Western Pacific High Commission, 1953–56; Attorney-Gen., Zanzibar, 1957–63; Puisne Judge, Kenya, 1963–69. Order of the Brilliant Star (second class) Zanzibar, 1963. *Recreations:* cricket, golf. *Address:* Spring Lane, Aston Tirrold, Oxon. *Clubs:* Commonwealth Trust; Nairobi (Nairobi).
*Died 4 Nov. 1989.*

**DALY, Dame Mary Dora,** DBE 1951 (CBE 1949; OBE 1937); Victorian President of Catholic Welfare Organisation since 1941;

Federal President, Australian Association of Ryder-Cheshire Foundations, 1976–78; *b* Cootamundra, NSW; *d* of late T. P. MacMahon, Darling Point, Sydney; *m* 1923, Dr John J. Daly, Melbourne; one *s* one *d*. *Educ:* Loreto Abbey, Ballarat, Vic. War of 1939–45; Mem. of finance and advisory cttees, Australian Comforts Fund; Mem. executive cttees, Lord Mayor of Melbourne's appeals for food for Britain, toys for Britain, Victorian Government fat for Britain drive. Member: National Council, Aust. Red Cross Soc., 1959–76 (Long Service Medal and Bar, 1950; Hon. Life Mem., 1971); Executive, and Council 1936–79, Victorian Div., Red Cross Soc.; Council, Nat. Heart Foundn of Australia (Victorian Div.); Victorian Council, Assoc. of Ryder-Cheshire Foundns; Council and Executive, Ryder-Cheshire Foundn (Victoria); Victorian Council Girl Guides Assoc., 1954; Anti-Cancer Council (Victoria); Lady Mayoress's (Melbourne) Cttee for Metropolitan Hosps and charities; Foundation Mem., Cttee of the Most Excellent Order of the British Empire (Victorian Assoc.); Patron: Nat. Boys Choir; Yooralla Hosp. Sch., for Crippled Children (Pres., DMD Cttee); Wattle Day Child Care Soc.; Austral Salon for advancement of music, literature and fine arts. Pres., Australian Catholic Relief, Archdiocese of Melbourne, 1966–75. Comr for Affidavits, State of Victoria. Cross, Pro Ecclesia et Pontifice, 1952. *Publications:* Marie's Birthday Party, 1934; Cinty, 1961; Timmy's Christmas Surprise, 1967; Holidays at Hillydale, 1974; articles in several magazines. *Recreations:* music, reading, gardening. *Address:* 6 Henry Street, Kew, Vic 3101, Australia; Finavarra, Stevens Street, Queenscliff, Vic 3225, Australia.
*Died 11 June 1983.*

**DANCKWERTS, Prof. Peter Victor,** GC 1940; MBE 1943; FRS 1969; FEng; Shell Professor of Chemical Engineering, Cambridge University, 1959–77, then Emeritus; Fellow of Pembroke College, Cambridge, 1959–77, then Emeritus; *b* 14 Oct. 1916; *s* of late Vice-Adm. V. H. Danckwerts, CMG, and Joyce Danckwerts; *m* 1960, Lavinia, *d* of late Brig.-Gen. D. A. Macfarlane, CB, DSO, KOSB. *Educ:* Winchester Coll.; Balliol Coll., Oxford; Massachusetts Inst. of Technology. BA (chemistry) Oxon, 1938; SM (Chemical Engineering Practice), MIT, 1948; MA Cantab 1948. RNVR, 1940–46. Commonwealth Fund Fellow, MIT, 1946–48; Demonstrator and Lecturer, Dept of Chemical Engineering, Cambridge Univ., 1948–54; Deputy Director of Research and Development, Industrial Group, UK Atomic Energy Authority, 1954–56; Prof. of Chemical Engineering Science, Imperial College of Science and Technology, 1956–59. MIChemE 1955 (President, 1965–66); Hon. FIChemE. Hon. DTech Bradford, 1978; Hon. DSc: Loughborough, 1981; Bath, 1983. For. Hon. Mem., Amer. Acad. of Arts and Scis, 1964; For. Associate, Nat. Acad. of Engineering, USA, 1978. *Address:* The Abbey House, Abbey Road, Cambridge CB5 8HQ. *T:* Cambridge 357275.
*Died 25 Oct. 1984.*

**DANIEL, Adm. Sir Charles (Saumarez),** KCB (CB 1945); CBE 1941; DSO 1939; *b* 23 June 1894; *s* of late Lieut-Colonel C. J. Daniel, CBE, DSO; *m* 1919, Marjory Katharine (*d* 1958), *d* of Arthur C. Wilson, MB, ChB, Formby; one *d*; *m* 1963, Mrs Pares Wilson, The Manor House, Little Shelford, Cambridge. *Educ:* Southcliffe Sch., Filey; RN Colleges, Osborne and Dartmouth. HMS Orion, Home Fleet and Grand Fleet, 1912–18 (despatches, Jutland, 1914–15 Star, 2 medals); specialised in Signals and Wireless, 1918; Commander, 1928; Experimental Commander HM Signal Sch., 1928–30; passed RN and RAF Staff Colleges, 1931–32; Commander HMS Glorious, 1933–34; Captain, 1934; passed Imperial Defence Coll., 1935; Plans Div., Admiralty, for Joint Planning Cttee, 1936–38; Captain D 8th Destroyer Flotilla, 1938–40, European War (DSO); Director of Plans, Naval Staff, Admiralty, 1940–41 (CBE); In Command HMS Renown, 1941–43; Rear-Adm. 1943. Flag Officer, Combined Operations, 1943; Vice-Adm. (Admin.) British Pacific Fleet, Rear-Adm. Commanding 1st Battle Squadron, British Pacific Fleet, 1944–45 (CB); Third Sea Lord and Controller of the Navy, 1945–49 (KCB); Vice-Adm. 1946; Commandant Imperial Defence Coll., 1949–51; Admiral 1950; retired list, 1952. Chairman, Television Advisory Cttee, 1952–62. A Director of Blaw Knox Ltd, 1953–66. *Address:* The Old Manor, Whitehouse Green, Sulhamstead, Reading, Berks RG7 4EA. *T:* Burghfield Common 2423.
*Died 11 Feb. 1981.*

**DANIEL, Prof. Glyn Edmund,** MA, LittD; FBA 1982; Fellow of St John's College, Cambridge, since 1938; Disney Professor of Archæology, University of Cambridge, 1974–81, Emeritus Professor since 1981 (Lecturer, 1948–74); *b* 23 April 1914; *o s* of John Daniel and Mary Jane (*née* Edmunds); *m* 1946, Ruth, *d* of late Rev. R. W. B. Langhorne, Exeter. *Educ:* Barry County Sch.; University College, Cardiff; St John's Coll., Cambridge (Scholar; BA 1st Class Hons with Distinction, Archaeological and Anthropological Tripos); Strathcona Student, 1936; Allen Scholar, 1937; Wallenberg Prizeman, 1937; Research Fellowship, St John's Coll., 1938; PhD 1938; MA 1939; LittD 1962. Intelligence Officer, RAF, 1940–45; in charge Photo Interpretation, India and SE Asia, 1942–45 (despatches); Wing Comdr, 1943. Faculty Asst Lectr in Archaeology, 1945–48; Steward of St John's Coll., 1946–55; Leverhulme Research

Fellow, 1948–50; Leverhulme Emeritus Fellow, 1985–87. Lecturer: Munro, Archaeology, Edinburgh Univ., 1954; Rhŷs, British Acad., 1954; O'Donnell, Edinburgh Univ., 1956; Josiah Mason, Birmingham Univ., 1956; Gregynog University College, Wales, 1968; Ballard-Matthews, University Coll. of North Wales, 1968; George Grant MacCurdy, Harvard, 1971. Visiting Prof., Univ. Aarhus, 1968; Ferrens Prof., Univ. Hull, 1969. Pres., South Eastern Union of Scientific Socs, 1955. President: Bristol and Gloucestershire Archaeological Soc., 1962–63; RAI, 1977–79; Somerset Archaeol and Nat. Hist. Soc., 1984–85. Chm., Duchy of Cornwall Adv. Cttee on Archaeology, 1983–. Fellow: UC Cardiff, 1981; Royal Danish Acad. of Science and Letters, 1984. Hon. Mem. Istituto Italiano di Preistoria e Protostoria; Corresponding Fellow, German Archaeological Institute; Corresponding Mem., Jutland Archaeological Soc.; Foreign Hon. Mem., Archaeol Inst. of Amer. Editor, Ancient Peoples and Places, 1955–, and of Antiquity, 1958–86. Director: Anglia Television, Ltd, 1959–81; Antiquity Publications Ltd; Trustee, Cambridge Arts Theatre. FSA 1942. Knight (First Class) of the Dannebrog, 1961. *Publications:* The Three Ages, 1942; A Hundred Years of Archaeology, 1950; The Prehistoric Chamber Tombs of England and Wales, 1950; A Picture Book of Ancient British Art (with S. Piggott), 1951; Lascaux and Carnac, 1955; ed Myth or Legend, 1955; Barclodiad y Gawres (with T. G. E. Powell), 1956; The Megalith Builders of Western Europe, 1958; The Prehistoric Chamber Tombs of France, 1960; The Idea of Prehistory, 1961, rev. edn (with Colin Renfrew), 1986; The Hungry Archaeologist in France, 1963; New Grange and the Bend of the Boyne (with late S. P. O'Riordain), 1964; (ed with I. Ll. Foster), Prehistoric and Early Wales, 1964; Man Discovers his Past, 1966; The Origins and Growth of Archaeology, 1967; The First Civilisations, 1968; Archaeology and the History of Art, 1970; Megaliths in History, 1973; (ed jtly) France before the Romans, 1974; A Hundred and Fifty Years of Archaeology, 1975; Cambridge and the Back-Looking Curiosity: an inaugural lecture, 1976; A Short History of Archaeology, 1981; (ed) Towards a History of Archaeology, 1981; Some Small Harvest (memoirs), 1986; and articles in archaeological journals; *festschrift:* (ed John D. Evans, Barry Cunliffe and Colin Renfrew) Antiquity and Man, 1981. *Recreations:* travel, walking, food, wine, writing detective stories (The Cambridge Murders, 1945; Welcome Death, 1954). *Address:* The Flying Stag, 70 Bridge Street, Cambridge. *T:* 356082; La Marnière, Zouafques-par-Tournehem, 62890 France. *T:* Calais 35.61.40. *Club:* United Oxford & Cambridge University.

*Died 13 Dec. 1986.*

**DANIELLI, Prof. James Frederic,** FRS 1957; PhD, DSc, MIBiol; Director, Danielli Associates, since 1980; *b* 13 Nov. 1911; *s* of James Frederic Danielli; *m* 1937, Mary Guy; one *s* one *d. Educ:* Wembley County Sch.; London, Princeton and Cambridge Univs. Commonwealth Fund Fellow, 1933–35; Beit Medical Research Fellow, 1938–42; Fellow of St John's Coll., Cambridge, 1942–45; Physiologist to Marine Biological Assoc., 1946; Reader in Cell Physiology, Royal Cancer Hospital, 1946–49; Prof. of Zoology, King's Coll., London, 1949–62; Chm., Dept of Biochemical Pharmacology, Univ. of Buffalo, 1962–65; Provost for Faculty of Natural Sciences and Mathematics, 1967–69; Dir, Center for Theoretical Biol., 1965–74, and Asst to Pres., 1969–72, State Univ. of NY at Buffalo (formerly Univ. of Buffalo, NY); Prof. and Chm., Life Scis Dept, Worcester Polytechnic Inst., Mass, 1974–80. *Publications:* Permeability of Natural Membranes (with H. Davson), 1943; Cell Physiology and Pharmacology, 1950; Cytochemistry: a critical approach, 1953; Editor: Journal of Theoretical Biology; Jl of Social and Biol Structures; Internat. Review of Cytology; Progress in Surface and Membrane Science. *Address:* Danielli Associates Inc., 185 Highland Street, Worcester, Mass 01609, USA; Tangnefedd, Dinas Cross, Dyfed SA42 0SF.

*Died 22 April 1984.*

**DANIELS, David Kingsley,** CBE 1963 (OBE 1945); retired as Secretary-General, Royal Commonwealth Society (1958–67); *b* 17 Feb. 1905; *y s* of late E. Daniels and Anne M. Daniels; unmarried. *Educ:* Kent Coll., Canterbury; St Edmund Hall, Oxford. Colonial Administrative Service, Tanganyika, 1928; King's African Rifles, 1940; Chief Staff Officer, Military Admin., Somalia, 1941 (despatches); Senior Civil Affairs Officer, Reserved Areas, Ethiopia, 1943–45 (OBE); Chief Secretary (Colonel), Military Administration, Malaya, 1945–46; Principal Asst Secretary, Singapore, 1947–49; Under Secretary, Singapore, 1950–52; Dep. Chief Secretary, Federation of Malaya, 1952–55; Dir, Malayan Students Dept in UK, 1956–58. *Address:* Paines Manor, Pentlow, Sudbury, Suffolk CO10 7JT. *Clubs:* Royal Commonwealth Society, MCC.

*Died 27 July 1986.*

**DANIELS, Jeffery;** Director, Geffrye Museum, London, since 1969; *b* 13 July 1932; *s* of John Henry and Edith Mary Daniels. *Educ:* Milford Haven Grammar Sch.; Balliol Coll., Oxford. Read Modern History; MA Oxon. Heal & Son Ltd, 1953–56; Teaching (ILEA), 1956–69. Member: Internat. Consultative Cttee for Mostra di Sebastiano Ricci, Udine, 1976–84; History of Art and

Complementary Studies Bd, CNAA, 1975–80; Hon. Sec., London Fedn of Museums and Art Galls, 1976–85. Member: AICA (Pres., British Section, 1980–83); Assoc. of Art Historians; Cttee, Thirties Soc., 1979–85 (Patron, 1985–). Cavalier, Order of Merit of the Republic, Italy, 1980. *Publications:* Architecture in England, 1968; Biography and catalogue raisonné of Sebastiano Ricci, 1976 (Italian edn, L'Opera Completa di Sebastiano Ricci, 1976); Michelangelo, 1982; contrib. to: The Times, The Connoisseur, Apollo, The Burlington Magazine, The Listener, Collector's Guide, Art News (USA). *Recreations:* opera, ballet, Venice. *Address:* 5 Edith Grove, Chelsea, SW10 0JZ. *T:* 01–352 7692. *Club:* Society of Authors.

*Died 3 Feb. 1986.*

**DANN, Howard Ernest,** CBE 1965; Director, Snowy Mountains Engineering Corporation, 1970–74, and Commissioner, Snowy Mountains Hydro-Electric Authority, 1967–74; *b* 27 April 1914; *m* 1946, Marjorie Bush; two *s. Educ:* Brighton Grammar Sch. (Dux); University of Melbourne (BMechE). AIF, 1940–44; Major RAEME. Supt. Engineer, Electric Authority of NSW, 1946–50; Member Commonwealth and States Snowy River Cttee, 1946–49 (NSW Representative, Techn. Cttee); Chief Engineer Investigations, Snowy Mountains Hydro-Electric Authority, prior to Associate Comr, Snowy Mountains Hydro-Electric Authority, 1959–67. FIEAust, MASCE. *Publications:* papers in journals of Instn of Engrs (Australia) and American Society of Civil Engineers. *Recreation:* golf. *Address:* 18 Rookwood Street, North Balwyn, Vic 3104, Australia. *T:* 859.4428.

*Died 18 April 1986.*

**DANNATT, Sir Cecil,** Kt 1961; OBE 1943; MC 1917; FIEE; MIMechE; Director, Associated Electrical Industries, 1954–63, retired (Vice-Chairman, 1960–62); *b* 21 Sept. 1896; *s* of late Mark and Hannah Dannatt; *m* 1925, Winifred Ethel Flear; two *s. Educ:* Burton-on-Trent Grammar Sch.; Durham Univ. DSc University of Durham, 1936. Research Engineer, 1921–40; Prof. of Electrical Engineering, Birmingham Univ., 1940–44. Managing Director Metropolitan-Vickers Electrical Co., 1954–60. *Publications:* Electrical Transmission and Interconnection, 1926; prize papers, IEE. *Recreation:* golf. *Address:* The Willows, Oxshott, Surrey. *T:* Oxshott 2424. *Club:* Royal Automobile.

*Died 18 Dec. 1981.*

**DANNAY, Frederic;** co-author with Manfred B. Lee, under pseudonym of Ellery Queen; *b* 1905; *m;* two *c.* Visiting Professor at University of Texas, 1958–59. *Publications:* Roman Hat Mystery, 1929; French Powder Mystery, 1930; Dutch Shoe Mystery, 1931; Greek Coffin Mystery, Egyptian Cross Mystery, 1932; American Gun Mystery, Siamese Twin Mystery, 1933; Chinese Orange Mystery, Adventures of Ellery Queen, 1934; Spanish Cape Mystery, 1935; Halfway House, 1936; Door Between, 1937; Devil to Pay, Four of Hearts, Challenge to the Reader, 1938; Dragon's Teeth, 1939; New Adventures of Ellery Queen, 1940; 101 Years' Entertainment, 1941; Calamity Town, The Detective Short Story (a bibliography), Sporting Blood, 1942; There Was an Old Woman, Female of the Species, 1943; Misadventures of Sherlock Holmes, Best Stories from Ellery Queen's Mystery Magazine, 1944; Case Book of Ellery Queen, Murderer Is a Fox, Rogues' Gallery, 1945; The Queen's Awards (1946), To the Queen's Taste, 1946; The Queen's Awards (1947), Murder By Experts, 1947; 20th Century Detective Stories, The Queen's Awards (1948), Ten Days' Wonder, 1948; The Queen's Awards (1949), Cat of Many Tails, 1949; The Queen's Awards (Fifth Series), Literature of Crime, Double, Double, 1950; Origin of Evil, Queen's Quorum, The Queen's Awards (Sixth Series), 1951; Calendar of Crime, King is Dead, The Queen's Awards (Seventh Series), 1952; Scarlet Letters, The Queen's Awards (Eighth Series), 1953; Glass Village, Ellery Queen's Awards (Ninth Series), 1954; QBI: Queen's Bureau of Investigation, Ellery Queen's Awards (Tenth Series), 1955; Inspector Queen's Own Case, Ellery Queen's Awards (Eleventh Series), 1956; In the Queens' Parlor, Ellery Queen's Awards (Twelfth Series), 1957; The Finishing Stroke, Ellery Queen's 13th Annual, 1958; Ellery Queen's 14th Mystery Annual, 1959; Ellery Queen's 15th Mystery Annual, 1960; Ellery Queen's 16th Mystery Annual, 1961; Quintessence of Queen, To Be Read Before Midnight, 1962; Player on the Other Side, Ellery Queen's Mystery Mix, 1963; And On the Eighth Day, Double Dozen, 1964; Queens Full, The Fourth Side of the Triangle, Ellery Queen's 20th Anniversary Annual, 1965; Ellery Queen's Crime Carousel, Study in Terror, 1966; Poetic Justice, Ellery Queen's All-Star Line-up, Face to Face, 1967; Ellery Queen's Mystery Parade, QED: Queen's Experiments in Detection, House of Brass, 1968; Cop Out Minimysteries, Ellery Queen's Murder Menu, 24th Mystery Annual, 1969; The Last Woman in His Life, Ellery Queen's Grand Slam, 1970; A Fine and Private Place, Ellery Queen's Headliners, 26th Mystery Annual, The Golden 13, 1971; Ellery Queen's Mystery Bag, 1972; Ellery Queen's Crookbook, 1974; Ellery Queen's Murdercade, 1975; (ed) Ellery Queen's Christmas Hamper, 1975; Ellery Queen's Crime Wave, 1976; Four Men Called John, Ellery Queen's Searches and Seizures, 1977; Ellery Queen's Masks of Mystery, 1979; co-author with late Manfred B. Lee, *as Barnaby Ross:* Tragedy of X, Tragedy of Y, 1932; Tragedy of Z, Drury Lane's Last Case, 1933 (all four Barnaby Ross publications reissued

as by Ellery Queen, 1940–46); co-author with late Manfred B. Lee, of Ellery Queen, Jr juvenile mysteries and of Radio and Television Programs (Adventures of Ellery Queen); co-editor with late Manfred B. Lee: 21 collections of short stories by Dashiell Hammett, Stuart Palmer, John Dickson Carr, Margery Allingham, Roy Vickers, O. Henry, Erle Stanley Gardner, Lawrence Treat, Edward D. Hoch, Michael Gilbert, Stanley Ellin and Julian Symonds; Ellery Queen's Mystery Magazine (37th year of publication); as *Daniel Nathan:* The Golden Summer, 1953. The following address is for all names Frederic Dannay, Ellery Queen, Barnaby Ross, Daniel Nathan). *Address:* 29 Byron Lane, Larchmont, New York 10538, USA.
*Died 3 Sept.* 1982.

**DARBISHIRE, David Harold,** JP; Chairman, FMC plc, 1975–83; Director, ACC Ltd, since 1972; *b* 23 Oct. 1914; *s* of H. D. Darbishire and Hester E. Bright (*g d* of Rt Hon. John Bright, MP); *m* 1939, Phebe Irene Lankester, *d* of Captain Felix Lankester, MC; three *d. Educ:* Sidcot; Wye Agric. Coll. (Wye DipAgric). Farmer; Vice-Pres., NFU, 1971–74. Mem., Metrication Bd, 1970–77. *Recreations:* hunting, fishing. *Address:* Manor Farm, Wormleighton, Leamington Spa CV33 0XW. *Club:* Farmers'. *Died 6 Aug.* 1986.

**D'ARCY, Surgeon Rear-Adm. Thomas Norman,** CB 1953; CBE 1950; retired; *b* 12 Feb. 1896; *s* of Dr S. A. D'Arcy, Rosslea, County Fermanagh, Ireland; *m* 1922, Eleanor Lennox Broadbent (*d* 1982); two *s* two *d. Educ:* Royal School, Cavan; RCS Dublin. Qualified, 1919; Surgeon Probationer RNVR, 1915–18; Surgeon Lieut RN, 1919; Surgeon Lieut-Comdr 1925; Surgeon Comdr 1930; Surgeon Capt. 1943; Surgeon Rear-Adm., 1951; Medical Officer in Charge, RN Hospital, Plymouth, and Command Medical Officer, 1951–54. KHS 1951; QHS 1952–54. CStJ 1953. Gilbert Blane medal, 1929. *Publications:* surgical articles to Jl of RN Medical Service (Co-Editor, 1946–47). *Recreation:* hockey (old Irish International). *Address:* South Wind, Witley, Surrey GU8 5RB. *T:* Godalming 5751. *Died 17 Jan.* 1987.

**DARESBURY,** 2nd Baron, *cr* 1927, of Walton, Co. Chester; **Edward Greenall,** Bt, *cr* 1876; late Life Guards; *b* 12 Oct. 1902; *o* surv. *s* of 1st Baron Daresbury, CVO, and late Frances Eliza, OBE 1945, *d* of Capt. Wynne-Griffith, 1st Royal Dragoons; *S* father, 1938; *m* 1st 1925, Joan Madeline (*d* 1926), *d* of Capt. Robert Thomas Oliver Sheriffe, of Goadby Hall, Melton Mowbray; 2nd, 1927, Josephine (*d* 1958), *y d* of Brig.-Gen. Sir Joseph Laycock, KCMG, DSO; one *s*; 3rd, 1966, Lady Helena Hilton Green (*née* Wentworth-Fitzwilliam) (*d* 1970), 4th *d* of 7th Earl Fitzwilliam. *Educ:* Wixenford; Eton. *Heir: s* Hon. Edward Gilbert Greenall [*b* 27 Nov. 1928; *m* 1952, Margaret Ada, *y d* of late C. J. Crawford and of Mrs Crawford, Wayside, St Andrews; three *s* one *d*]. *Address:* Altavilla, Askeaton, Co. Limerick, Eire. *T:* Limerick 64281.
*Died 15 Feb.* 1990.

**DARKIN, Maj.-Gen. Roy Bertram,** CBE 1969; Commander Base Organisation RAOC, 1971–73, retired; *b* 3 Sept. 1916; *s* of late Bertram Duncan and of late Isobel Doris Darkin, Aylsham, Norfolk; *m* 1945, Louise Margaret, *d* of late Francis Charles Sydney Green and Lilian Green, Buckden, Hunts, and *widow* of Sqn Ldr J. C. D. Joslin, RAF (killed in action); no *c. Educ:* Felsted School. Commnd Baluch Regt, IA, 1940; war service, NW Frontier, Iraq, Persia (despatches); psc 1943; G2 HQ ALFSEA service, Burma; DAQMG India Office, 1945; transf. RAOC, 1946; Sen. Instructor, RAAOC Sch., Melbourne, 1952–54; DAQMG HQ Aldershot District, 1954–55; jssc 1955; AA&QMG Land Forces, Hong Kong, 1960–62; AAG (Col) MoD, 1962–65; Sen. Provision Officer, COD Bicester, 1965–66; Dir of Ordnance Services, FARELF (Brig.), 1966–69; Dep. Dir Ordnance Services MoD, 1969–71. Hon. Col, RAOC, T&AVR, 1971–73; Col Comdt, RAOC, 1975–79. FBIM. *Recreation:* travel. *Clubs:* MCC; Hankley Common Golf.
*Died 3 April* 1987.

**DARKU, Nana Sir Tsibu;** *see* Tsibu Darku.

**DARLING OF HILLSBOROUGH,** Baron *cr* 1974 (Life Peer), of Crewe; **George Darling,** PC 1966; journalist; *b* 1905; *s* of F. W. Darling, Co-operative shop asst; *m* 1932, Dorothy, *d* of T. W. Hodge, farmer; one *s* one *d. Educ:* Elementary Sch., Crewe; Liverpool and Cambridge Univs. MP (Co-op and Lab), Hillsborough Div. of Sheffield, 1950–Feb. 1974. Minister of State, BoT, 1964–68. Engineer; market research executive; newspaper reporter; BBC Industrial Correspondent, 1945–49; author. Pres., Inst. of Trading Standards Admin. *Recreation:* gardening. *Address:* 17 Amersham Road, Beaconsfield, Bucks. *T:* Beaconsfield 3352.
*Died 18 Oct.* 1985.

**DARLING, Prof. Arthur Ivan,** CBE 1971; Emeritus Professor of Dental Medicine, University of Bristol, 1982; *b* 21 Nov. 1916; *s* of John Straughan Darling and Henrietta Jeffcoat; *m* 1948, Kathleen Brenda Pollard; one *s* three *d. Educ:* Whitley Bay and Monkseaton Grammar Sch.; King's Coll., Univ. of Durham, LDS Dunelm, 1937, BDS Dunelm, 1938; Parker Brewis Research Fellow, 1938–41; MDS Dunelm, 1942; LRCP, MRCS 1947; FDSRCS 1948; DDSc

Dunelm 1957; FFDRCSI 1964; FRCPath 1967. Univ. of Durham: Lectr in Operative Dental Surgery, 1941; Lectr in Oral Anatomy, 1943; Lectr in Dental Materia Medica, 1945; Univ. of Bristol: Prof. of Dental Surgery, 1947–59; Prof. of Dental Medicine, 1959–82; Dir of Dental Studies, 1947–82; Dean of Med. Faculty, 1963–66; Pro-Vice-Chancellor, 1968–72. Mem., Avon AHA (Teaching); Vice-Dean, Bd of Dental Faculty, RCS, 1977–78. Hon. Dir, Dental Unit of MRC, 1961–82. Hon. DSc Wales, 1981; Hon. Dr Univ. of René Déscartes, Paris, 1982. *Publications:* scientific papers on professional subjects in journals. *Recreations:* cabinet making, music. *Address:* 7 Rylestone Grove, Bristol BS9 3UT. *Club:* Athenæum. *Died 22 Dec.* 1987.

**DARLINGTON, Cyril Dean,** DSc; FRS 1941; Sherardian Professor of Botany, University of Oxford, 1953–71, later Emeritus; Keeper, Oxford Botanic Garden, 1953–71; Fellow of Magdalen College, 1953–71; Hon. Fellow, 1971; *b* 19 Dec. 1903; *m* Margaret Upcott; one *s* three *d* (and one *s* decd); 2nd, Gwendolen Harvey (*née* Adshead). *Educ:* St Paul's Sch.; Wye Coll. Rockefeller Fellow in Pasadena, 1932, in Kyoto, 1933. Royal Medal of Royal Society, 1946; Pres. Genetical Soc., 1943–46. Pres. Rationalist Press Assoc., 1948; Dir, John Innes Horticultural Institution, 1939–53; Fellow of Wye Coll. For. Mem. Acc. Lincei and Royal Danish Academy of Sciences. Pres., Internat. Chromosome Conferences, 1964–80. Joint Founder and Editor of Heredity, 1947. *Publications:* Chromosomes and Plant Breeding, 1932; Recent Advances in Cytology, 3rd edn 1965; Evolution of Genetic Systems, 1939, 1958; The Conflict of Science and Society, 1948; The Facts of Life, 1953; Chromosome Botany and the Origins of Cultivated Plants, 1956, 3rd edn 1973; Darwin's Place in History, 1959; Genetics and Man, 1964; The Evolution of Man and Society, 1969; The Little Universe of Man, 1978; (jointly): The Handling of Chromosomes, 1942, 6th edn 1976; Chromosome Atlas of Flowering Plants, 1945, 1956; The Elements of Genetics, 1949; Genes, Plants and People, 1950; edited: Teaching Genetics, 1963; Chromosomes Today, 1966–72. *Recreation:* gardening. *Address:* Botany School, Oxford; Pin Farm Cottage, Barleycott Lane, South Hinksey, Oxon.
*Died 26 March* 1981.

**DART, Raymond Arthur;** United Steelworkers of America Professor of Anthropology, The Institutes for the Achievement of Human Potential, Philadelphia, since 1966; Emeritus Professor since 1959, Professor of Anatomy, 1923–58, and Dean of the Faculty of Medicine, 1925–43, University of the Witwatersrand, Johannesburg; *b* Toowong, Brisbane, Australia, 4 Feb. 1893; *s* of Samuel Dart and Eliza Anne Brimblecombe; *m* 1936, Marjorie Gordon Frew, Boksburg, Transvaal; one *s* one *d. Educ:* Ipswich Grammar Sch., Queensland (Scholarship holder); University of Queensland (Scholarship holder and Foundation scholar); graduated BSc (Hons) 1913; MSc 1915; Sydney Univ., 1914–17; graduated MB, ChM (Hons) 1917; MD 1927; Demonstrator of Anatomy and Acting Principal of St Andrew's Coll., Sydney, 1917; House Surgeon at Royal Prince Alfred Hospital, Sydney, 1917–18; Capt., AAMC, Australia, England, France, 1918–19; Senior Demonstrator of Anatomy, University Coll., London, 1919–20; Fellow of Rockefeller Foundation, 1920–21; Senior Demonstrator of Anatomy and Lecturer in Histology, University Coll., London, 1921–22; Capt., SAMC, 1925; Major, 1928; Lieut-Col Reserve Officers, 1940; Pres. of Anthropological Section SAAAS, 1926 (Gold Medal, 1939); Vice-Pres., SAAAS, 1952; Vice-Pres. of Anthropological Section, BAAS, Johannesburg, 1929; Mem. of International Commission on Fossil Man since 1929; FRSSAF 1930, Hon. FRSSAF 1983 (Mem. of Council, 1938, Vice-Pres. 1938–39, 1939–40, 1950–51); Mem. Board, SA Institute for Medical Research, 1934–48; Mem. SA Med. Council, 1935–48, Executive Cttee, 1940–48; Mem. SA Nursing Council from its inception in 1944 until 1951; Mem. Medical Advisory Cttee, SA Council for Scientific and Industrial Research, 1946–48; Pres. Anthropological Section, First Pan-African Congress of Prehistory, 1947–51; guest-lecturer at The Viking Fund Seminar, New York, and public lecturer of The Lowell Inst., Boston, 1949; Inaugural Lecturer, John Irvine Hunter Memorial, Univ. of Sydney, NSW, 1950; Woodward Lecturer, Yale Univ., USA, 1958; Inaugural Van Riebeeck Lecturer; R. J. Terry Meml Lectr, Washington Univ. Sch. of Medicine, St Louis, 1971. SA Broadcasting Corp., 1959. Pres. SA Archaeological Soc., 1951; Pres. SA Assoc. for Advancement of Science, Bulawayo, S Rhodesia, 1953; Vice-Pres., Fourth Pan-African Congress of Prehistory, 1959–62; Pres. SA Museums Assoc., 1961–62; Vice-Pres., Assoc. Scientific and Technical Socs of S Africa, 1961–62, 1962–63, Pres., 1963–64; Pres. SA Soc. of Physiotherapy, 1961–68, Hon. Life Vice-Pres., 1968–; Mem., Internat. Primatological Cttee, 1963–; Mem., Municipal Library Advisory Cttee, Johannesburg, 1964–. Coronation Medal, 1953; Sen. Capt. Scott Memorial Medal, SA Biological Soc., 1955; Viking Medal and Award for Physical Anthropology, Wenner-Gren Foundation of New York, 1957; Simon Biesheuvel Medal (Behavioural Sciences), 1963; Gold Medal, SA Nursing Assoc., 1970; Silver Medal, SA Medical Assoc., 1972. Hon. DSc: Natal, 1956; Witwatersrand, 1964; La Salle, 1968. Fellow Odontological

Soc. of SA, 1937; Fellow Institute of Biology, 1964; For. Fellow, Linnaean Soc., 1974; Hon. FSA 1986. Raymond Dart Lectureship in Institute for Study of Man in Africa, estab. 1964; Museums of Man and Science, Johannesburg, initiated 1966, Board of Governors, 1968. Life Mem., S African Soc. for Quaternary Res., 1983; Hon. Life Member: Dental Assoc. of South Africa, 1958, Medical Assoc. of South Africa, 1959, Anatomical Society of Great Britain and Ireland, 1961, Anatomical Soc. of Southern Africa, 1970, S African Nursing Assoc., 1970; Archaeological Soc. of SA, 1973; NY Acad. of Scis, 984; Hon. Fellow, Coll. of Medicine of SA, 1985. *Publications:* Racial Origins, chapter in The Bantu-speaking Tribes of South Africa, 1937; chapters on genealogy and physical characters, in Bushmen of the Southern Kalahari, 1937; (ed) Africa's Place in the Human Story, 1954; The Oriental Horizons of Africa, 1955; Adventures with the Missing Link, 1959; Africa's Place in the Emergence of Civilisation, 1960; Beyond Antiquity, 1965; over 250 articles on anthropological, archaeological, neurological and comparative anatomical subjects in scientific and lay periodicals. *Recreations:* swimming, music. *Address:* 20 Eton Park, Eton Road, Sandhurst, Sandton, Transvaal, 2196, South Africa. *Clubs:* Associated Scientific and Technical, Country (Johannesburg); Explorers' (NY) (Hon. Mem.). *Died 22 Nov.* 1988.

**DARVALL, Frank Ongley,** CBE 1954; retired from HM Diplomatic Service, 1970; a Governor: Sulgrave Manor; Haileybury; Imperial Service College; *b* 16 April 1906; 5th *s* of late R. T. Darvall and Annie E. Johnson, Reading; *m* 1931, Dorothy (*d* 1979), *er d* of Harry Edmonds and late Jane Quay, NY City; one *s* decd. *Educ:* Dover Coll.; Reading (BA); London (BA, PhD); Columbia (MA). President Nat. Union of Students, 1927–29; Commonwealth Fund Fellow, 1929–31; Assoc. Sec. for Internat. Studies, Internat. Students Service, 1931–32; Dir, Geneva Students Internat. Union, 1933. Lecturer in Economics and History, Queen's Coll., Harley Street, 1933–36; Director Research and Discussion, English-Speaking Union, 1936–39; Dep. Director American Div., Ministry of Information, 1939–45; British Consul, Denver, 1945–46; 1st Secretary HM Embassy, Washington, 1946–49; Vice-Chairman Kinsman Trust, 1949–56; Editor, The English-Speaking World, 1950–53; Director-General, English-speaking Union of the Commonwealth, 1949–57; Chairman, Congress of European-American Assoc., 1954–57. European Editor, World Review, 1958–59. Hon. Dir, UK Cttee, Atlantic Congress, 1959; Attached British High Commn, Cyprus, 1960–62; Dir, British Information Services, Eastern Caribbean, 1962–66; attached, British Consulate-Gen., Barcelona, 1966; Consul, Boston, 1966–68; FCO (formerly CO), 1968–70. Dean of Academics, Alvescot Coll., 1970–71, Vice-Pres., 1971–72. Contested (L) Ipswich, 1929, King's Lynn, 1935, Hythe bye-election, 1939. Extension Lecturer and Tutorial Classes Tutor, Cambridge and London Universities, 1933–39. *Publications:* Popular Disturbances and Public Order in Regency England, 1934; The Price of European Peace, 1937; The American Political Scene, 1939. *Address:* c/o Lloyds Bank, 1 Butler Place, SW1.
*Died 21 May* 1987.

**DARWEN, 2nd Baron,** *cr* 1946, of Heys-in-Bowland; **Cedric Percival Davies;** Publisher; *b* 18 Feb. 1915; *e s* of 1st Baron and M. Kathleen Brown; *S* father, 1950; *m* 1934, Kathleen Dora, *d* of George Sharples Walker; three *s* one *d*. *Educ:* Sidcot; Manchester Univ. BA Hons English Lit. and Language, Manchester, 1947. Engaged in Cotton Industry, 1932–40. On staff of school for Maladjusted Children, 1942–44. Manchester Univ., 1944–48, Teaching Diploma, 1948. Warden of Letchworth Adult Education Centre, 1948–51; Secretary to Training and Education Dept of National Assoc. for Mental Health, 1951–53; Founded Darwen Finlayson Ltd, Publishers, 1954, Chm., and Man. Dir, 1954–73; Dep. Editor of John O'London's, 1959–62. Chm., Hollybank Engineering Co. Ltd., 1957–70. Is a Quaker. *Publications:* designed and ed, Illustrated County History Series. *Recreations:* sailing, painting, cinéphotography. *Heir:* s Hon. Roger Michael Davies, [*b* 28 June 1938; *m* 1961, Gillian Irene, *d* of Eric G. Hardy, Bristol; two *s* three *d*]. *Died 9 Dec.* 1988.

**DASH, Sir Roydon Englefield Ashford,** Kt 1945; DFC; Hon. LLD London; FRICS; Chairman of the Stevenage Development Corporation, 1953–62; *b* 3 March 1888; *s* of late Roland Ashford Dash, FSI; *m* 1933, Joan Pritchett Harrison. *Educ:* Haileybury Coll., Herts. Chief Valuer, Board of Inland Revenue, retired 1951. *Recreations:* golf and motoring. *Address:* 52 The Shimmings, Boxgrove Road, Guildford, Surrey. *Died 6 April* 1984.

**DAVENPORT, Rear-Adm. Dudley Leslie,** CB 1969; OBE 1954; *b* 17 Aug. 1919; *s* of Vice-Adm. R. C. Davenport, CB, Catherington, Hants; *m* 1950, Joan, *d* of Surg. Comdr H. Burns, OBE; two *s*. *Educ:* RNC, Dartmouth. Served in Destroyers, Mediterranean and Atlantic, 1939–45; commanded HMS Holmes, 1945 and HMS Porlock Bay, 1946; served in HMS Sheffield, 1947–48; at HMS Ganges, 1949–51; Naval Staff Course, 1951; Naval Instructor, Indian Defence Services Staff Coll., 1951–53; comd HMS Virago, 1954–55; NATO Defence Course, 1955–56; Comdr RN Barracks, Chatham, 1956–57; Captain, 1957; Staff of Admiral Comdg

Reserves, 1958–60; Captain Inshore Flotilla Far East, 1960–62; Director Naval Officers Appointments (Seaman Officers), 1962–64; comd HMS Victorious, 1964–66; Rear-Admiral, 1967; Flag Officer, Malta, 1967–69; retd, 1969. *Address:* 2 Anchor Mews, Lymington, Hants SO41 9EY. *T:* Lymington (0590) 678166. *Club:* Army and Navy. *Died 27 Dec.* 1990.

**DAVENPORT, Lt-Col Sir Walter Henry B.;** *see* Bromley-Davenport.

**DAVENTRY, 2nd Viscount,** *cr* 1943; **Robert Oliver Fitz Roy,** Captain RN; retired; *b* 10 Jan. 1893; *er s* of late Captain Rt Hon. Edward Algernon Fitz Roy, MP and of 1st Viscountess Daventry, CBE; *S* mother, 1962; *m* 1916, Grace Zoë (*d* 1978), *d* of late Claude Hume Campbell Guinness; three *d* (and two *d* decd). *Educ:* Royal Naval Colleges, Osborne, Dartmouth. Joined Royal Navy, 1906; Captain, 1936. Served European War, 1914–18; served War of 1939–45: comd HMS Rodney (despatches). High Sheriff, Rutland, 1956–57. *Heir: nephew* Francis Humphrey Maurice FitzRoy Newdegate. *Address:* 82 Swan Court, SW3. *T:* 01–352 7200. *Club:* Carlton. *Died 19 Jan.* 1986.

**DAVID, Brian Gurney,** CBE 1986; Deputy Receiver for the Metropolitan Police District, 1976–86; *b* 25 Jan. 1926; *s* of Constantine and Gladys Emma David; *m* 1950, Jean Valerie (*née* Young). *Educ:* Alleyn's School, Dulwich. Joined Metropolitan Police Office, 1946; Private Secretary to Receiver for the Metropolitan Police District, 1958; Asst Secretary (Director of Finance), 1973. *Recreations:* cats, cooking, crossword puzzles. *Address:* 26 Woodwarde Road, Dulwich, SE22 8UJ.
*Died 27 June* 1990.

**DAVIDSON, Dowager Viscountess; Frances Joan Davidson;** Baroness (Life Peer), *cr* 1963, under title of **Baroness Northchurch;** DBE 1952 (OBE 1920); *b* 29 May 1894; *y d* of 1st Baron Dickinson, PC, KBE; *m* 1919, 1st Viscount Davidson, PC, GCVO, CH, CB (*d* 1970); two *s* two *d*. MP (U) Hemel Hempstead Division of Herts, 1937–Sept. 1959. *Recreations:* gardening, walking. *Address:* 16 Lord North Street, Westminster, SW1. *T:* 01–222 2167.
*Died 25 Nov.* 1985.

**DAVIDSON, Hon. Sir Charles (William),** KBE 1964 (OBE 1945); retired; *b* 14 Sept. 1897; *s* of Alexander Black Davidson and Marion Perry; *m* 1929, Mary Gertrude Godschall Johnson; one *s* two *d*. *Educ:* Townsville Grammar Sch., Townsville. Served European War, 1914–18: 42 Bn AIF, 1916–19; Lieut; France (wounded); served War of 1939–45: 42 Bn AIF, 1939–44; Lt-Col; Hon. Colonel 42 Inf. Bn, 1955. Dairy farmer, 1921–25; sugar farming from 1925. MHR for Capricornia (Queensland), 1946–49, and for Dawson (Queensland), 1949–63, retired; Postmaster-General, 1956–63; Minister for Navy, 1956–58; Dep. Leader, Parliamentary Country Party, 1958–63. *Recreations:* bowls, golf, fishing, gardening. *Address:* 439 Brisbane Corso, Yeronga, Brisbane, Qld 4104, Australia. *T:* Brisbane 48.4264. *Clubs:* United Service, Masonic (Brisbane); Mackay Civic. *Died 29 Nov.* 1985.

**DAVIDSON, Ian Douglas,** CBE 1957; *b* 27 Oct. 1901; *s* of Rev. John Davidson, JP, and Elizabeth Helen (*née* Whyte); *m* 1st, 1936, Claire Louise (*d* 1937), *d* of E. S. Gempp, St Louis, Missouri; one *d*; 2nd, 1938, Eugenia, *d* of late Marques de Mohernando and Lorenza, Marquesa de Mohernando; one *d*. *Educ:* King William's Coll. Royal Dutch Shell Group of Companies, 1921–61; President: Mexican Eagle Oil Co., 1936–47; Cia Shell de Venezuela, 1953–57; Canadian Shell Ltd, 1957–61. Order of St Mark (Lebanon), 1957; Orden del Libertador (Venezuela), 1957. *Address:* One Benvenuto Place, Apt 105, Toronto, Ontario M4V 2L1, Canada. *Clubs:* Caledonian (London); York (Toronto); Links (NY).
*Died 30 July* 1989.

**DAVIDSON, James,** MB, ChB, FRCP Edinburgh; FSAScot.; late Senior Lecturer on Pathology, University of Edinburgh and Consultant Pathologist to the Edinburgh Southern Hospitals and The Royal Victoria and Associated Hospitals; *b* 3 Feb. 1896; *s* of James Davidson and Isabella Slater Shaw; *m* 1927, Constance Ellen Cameron; two *d*. *Educ:* University of Edinburgh. House Physician, Royal Infirmary, Edinburgh; Tutor in Clinical Medicine, University of Edinburgh; Lecturer on Morbid Anatomy and Senior Asst to Prof. of Pathology, University of Edinburgh; Senior Pathologist to Royal Infirmary, Edinburgh; Asst to Prof. of Medical Jurisprudence, University of Edinburgh; Lecturer on Forensic Medicine, London Hospital Medical Coll.; Director of Metropolitan Police Laboratory, Hendon, NW9. *Publications:* various papers on subjects dealing with Pathology and Forensic Science; (joint) text-book, Practical Pathology, 1938. *Recreations:* gardening, golf and fishing. *Address:* Linton Muir, West Linton, Peebles-shire.
*Died 17 May* 1985.

**DAVIDSON, Julia, (Mrs Paul Davidson);** *see* Cairns, J.

**DAVIDSON, Maj.-Gen. Kenneth Chisholm,** CB 1948; MC; psc; late Infantry; *b* 4 July 1897; *m* 1934, Diana Blanche Wilson; one *s* one *d*. *Educ:* Newbury Grammar Sch. 2nd Lieut Gordon Highlanders,

1915; served European War, 1914–19 (wounded twice); War of 1939–45, Persia and Iraq Force (despatches), Sicily (despatches), Italy (despatches). Lieut-Col, 1942; Col, 1942; Brig., 1947; actg Maj.-Gen., 1946; retired pay, 1949 (with hon. rank of Maj.-Gen.). *Address:* Rooklands, Tangley, near Andover, Hants. *T:* Chute Standen 612. *Died 9 April* 1985.

**DAVIDSON, Sir (Leybourne) Stanley (Patrick),** Kt 1955; FRSE; Professor of Medicine, University of Edinburgh, 1938–59, retired; Physician to the Queen in Scotland, 1952–61, an Extra Physician to HM in Scotland, since 1961; *b* 3 March 1894; 2nd *s* of late Sir L. F. W. Davidson; *m* Isabel Margaret (*d* 1979), *e d* of late Hon. Lord Anderson; no *c. Educ:* Cheltenham Coll.; Trinity Coll., Cambridge; Edinburgh Univ.; BA (Cambridge), MB, ChB 1919, Edinburgh Univ., 1st class hons, MD, awarded gold medal for thesis; MD Oslo; FRCP (London), 1940; FRCP (Edinburgh), 1925. Pres., 1953–56; LLD (Edinburgh Univ.) 1962. Regius Prof. of Medicine, University of Aberdeen, 1930–38; Sen. Phys. Royal Infirmary, Aberdeen, 1932–38, etc. Hon. Physician to King George VI in Scotland, 1947–52. Hon. LLD Aberdeen, 1970. *Publications:* Pernicious Anæmia, monograph (with Prof. G. L. Gulland), 1930; A Textbook of Medical Treatment (with D. M. Dunlop and Stanley Alstead), 1963; The Principles and Practice of Medicine (with Staff of Edinburgh Univ. Dept. of Medicine), 1963; Human Nutrition and Dietetics (with R. Passmore), 1963; articles in medical journals. *Recreations:* tennis, golf, fishing, shooting. *Address:* 28 Barnton Gardens, Davidson's Mains, Edinburgh EH4 6AE.
*Died 22 Sept.* 1981.

**DAVIDSON, Roger Alastair McLaren,** CMG 1947; Secretary of the Scottish Universities Entrance Board, 1953–66; *b* 6 Feb. 1900; *s* of late Rev. R. S. Davidson, The Manse, Kinfauns, Perthshire; *m* 1928, Elsie Stuart (*d* 1979), *d* of late J. A. Y. Stronach, Edinburgh; one *s* one *d. Educ:* Fettes Coll., Edinburgh; University of Edinburgh. Served European War, 1914–18, 2nd Lieut Royal Highlanders, 1918–19; entered Colonial Education Service, 1924; Nigeria, 1924–37; Asst Dir of Education, Tanganyika, 1937–40; seconded to Colonial Office, 1941–43; Asst Dir of Education, Southern Provinces, Nigeria, 1943–44; Dir of Education, Nigeria, 1944–51; Inspector-Gen. of Education, Nigeria, 1951–53. *Address:* 6 Hope Street, St Andrews. *T:* St Andrews 72345. *Club:* Royal and Ancient (St Andrews). *Died 9 Aug.* 1983

**DAVIDSON, Sir Stanley;** *see* Davidson, Sir L. S. P.

**DAVIDSON, William Bird;** a Deputy Chairman, National Westminster Bank Ltd, 1973–76 (Director and Chief Executive, 1970–72); Chairman, Lombard North Central, 1973–76; Director, Allied London Properties Ltd, 1976–84; *b* 18 May 1912; 2nd *s* of late J. N. Davidson; *m* 1941, Christina M. Ireton (*d* 1984); two *s. Educ:* Queen Elizabeth Grammar Sch., Penrith. War Service, Royal Artillery, 1939–45. Entered Nat. Provincial Bank, 1929; Jt Gen Manager, 1961; Chief Gen. Manager, 1967–68; Dir, 1968; Dir and Jt Chief Executive, Nat. Westminster Bank, 1968–70. FCIB. *Recreation:* golf. *Address:* 1 Petworth Close, Coulsdon, Surrey CR5 3EW. *T:* Downland (0737) 553687. *Died 11 Sept.* 1990.

**DAVIE, Rev. Sir (Arthur) Patrick;** *see* Ferguson Davie.

**DAVIE, Cedric Thorpe,** OBE 1955; FRSE 1978; FRSAMD 1978; FRAM; Master of Music, 1945–78, and Professor of Music, 1973–78, University of St Andrews, then Emeritus Professor; composer (especially for film, theatre, radio); *b* 30 May 1913; *s* of Thorpe and Gladys Louise Davie; *m* 1937, Margaret Russell Brown (*d* 1974); two *s. Educ:* High Sch. of Glasgow; Royal Scottish Academy of Music; Royal Academy of Music; Royal College of Music. Member: Scottish Arts Council, 1965–74; Arts Council of Great Britain, 1968–74. FRAM, 1949. Hon. Mem., Royal Scottish Acad., 1977. Hon. LLD Dundee, 1969. *Publications:* Musical Structure and Design, 1949; Oxford Scottish Song Book, 1969; Robert Burns: writer of songs, 1975; Scotland's Music, 1980; Catalogue of the Finzi Music Collection in the University Library, St Andrews, 1982; articles and reviews in learned jls. *Recreations:* eating and drinking; travel Northwards in search of sunshine. *Address:* 66 Main Street, Dalry, Castle Douglas DG7 3UW. *T:* Dalry (Kirkcudbrightshire) 293. *Died 18 Jan.* 1983.

**DAVIE, Sir Paul (Christopher),** Kt 1967; *b* 30 Sept. 1901; *s* of Charles Christopher Davie and Beatrice Paulina Mabel (*née* Walrond); *m* 1938, Betty Muriel, *d* of late Captain Ronald Henderson, MP for Henley div. of Oxfordshire, 1924–32, of Studley Priory, Oxon; one *s* one *d. Educ:* Winchester; New Coll., Oxford. Called to Bar, Lincoln's Inn, 1925; 2nd Asst Legal Advisor, Home Office, 1936; Asst Legal Advisor, 1947. Remembrancer, City of London, 1953–67. Chairman: Nat. Deaf Children's Soc., 1970–74; Council and Gen. Develt Services Ltd, 1971–82. *Publications:* Silicosis and Asbestosis Compensation Schemes, 1932; Joint Managing Ed., Encyclopædia of Local Government Law and Administration, 1934. *Recreations:* history, gardening. *Address:* The Old Rectory, Bentley, Farnham,

Surrey GU10 5HU. *T:* Bentley 23128. *Club:* Travellers'.
*Died 25 Jan.* 1990.

**DAVIES;** *see* Llewelyn-Davies.

**DAVIES OF LEEK, Baron** *cr* 1970 (Life Peer), of Leek, Staffordshire; **Harold Davies,** PC 1969; Member, Executive Committee, Inter-Parliamentary Union, since 1975; *b* 31 July 1904; *m* Jessie Elizabeth Bateman, BSc (*d* 1979); one *d. Educ:* Lewis Grammar Sch., Pengam, Glam. Trained for teaching; Schoolmaster and Tutor in Adult Education; several lecture tours in USA and Canada; Lecturer to various organisations and Labour Movement. MP (Lab) Leek Div. of Staffs, 1945–70; formerly Member several Parliamentary Cttees; Joint Parliamentary Secretary, Ministry of Social Security, 1966–67 (Ministry of Pensions and National Insurance, 1965–66). Special Envoy (of Prime Minister) on Peace Mission to Hanoi, 1965. FRGS. Pres., Chatterly Whitfield Mining Museum, 1978–. Has travelled in most countries of Far East, SE Asia, Europe and Africa. *Publications:* various Press articles on Social and Educational Problems, etc.; numerous writings and pamphlets on Far East, SE Asia, etc. *Recreations:* was keen on all sports and played most of them, now interested in foreign affairs (Far East), agriculture, education, economic affairs. *Address:* 81 Trentham Road, Longton, Stoke-on-Trent, Staffs. *T:* Stoke-on-Trent 319976; 13 Shepherds Hill, Highgate, N6 5QJ. *T:* 01–340 5497. *Died 28 Oct.* 1985.

**DAVIES, Air Commodore Adolphus Dan,** CB 1953; CBE 1947; psa; *b* 14 Oct. 1902; *m* 1925, Kathleen Hobbs (*d* 1969); one *d.* Cranwell, 1921–23; Air Ministry, Dep. Directorate War Organisation, 1938; Commanded Scampton, Bomber Command, 1943; Fiskerton, Bomber Command, 1944; Air Ministry, Directorate Gen. of Manning, 1944; Air Officer Commanding Royal Air Force, Hong Kong, 1948; Air Cdre 1949; Air Officer in charge of Administration, Coastal Command, 1951–54; retired Aug. 1954. *Address:* 22 Ravenswood Park, Northwood, Mddx. *T:* Northwood 24290.
*Died 5 Jan.* 1984.

**DAVIES, Alun Bennett O.;** *see* Oldfield-Davies.

**DAVIES, Sir Arthur;** *see* Davies, Sir D. A.

**DAVIES, Carlton Griffith,** CMG 1953; MC 1915; *b* 2 Aug. 1895; *o* surv. *s* of late Walter Davies, MBE, Calcutta and Ealing; *m* 1926, Florence Evelyn (*d* 1981), *y d* of late Robert MacSymon, Greenock and Liverpool; two *s* (and one *s* one *d* decd). *Educ:* Rugby Sch.; Exeter Coll., Oxford. Served European War, 1914–19, London Regt (The Queen's), and Machine-Gun Corps (MC, despatches). Asst District Comr, Sudan Political Service, 1920; Comr, Gezira Area, 1930; Asst Civil Sec., 1935–36; Asst Financial Sec., 1936–40; seconded to Sudan Defence Force, 1940–41 (despatches). Governor, Upper Nile Province, 1941–45; Sudan Agent in London, 1951–55. 4th Class Order of the Nile (Egypt), 1930; Officer of the Order of Leopold (Belgium), 1949. *Recreations:* golf, sailing, gardening. *Address:* Three Lanes End Farm, Wisborough Green, Billingshurst, West Sussex RH14 0EF. *T:* Wisborough Green 375. *Clubs:* Royal Over-Seas League, Royal Commonwealth Society.
*Died 19 Aug.* 1981.

**DAVIES, Sir (David) Arthur,** KBE 1980; Secretary-General Emeritus, World Meteorological Organization, Geneva, Switzerland, since 1980 (Secretary-General, 1955–79); Vice-President, since 1983 and Honorary Consultant, since 1982, Welsh Centre for International Affairs; *b* 11 Nov. 1913; *s* of Garfield Brynmor Davies and Mary Jane (*née* Michael); *m* 1938, Mary Shapland; one *s* two *d. Educ:* University of Wales (MSc) (1st cl. Hons Maths; 1st cl. Hons Physics); Fellow, University Coll., Cardiff, 1985. Technical Officer, Meteorological Office, 1936–39. War Service, RAF, 1939–47 (despatches). Principal Scientific Officer, Met. Office, 1947–49; Dir, E African Met. Dept, Nairobi, 1949–55; Pres. World Meteorological Organization Regional Assoc. for Africa, 1951–55. Vice-Pres., Hon. Soc. of Cymmrodorion, 1986–. Mem., NY Acad. of Scis, 1988–; Hon. Member: Amer. Meteorological Soc., 1970; Hungarian Meteorol Soc., 1975. FInstP, FRMet Soc. Dr *hc* Univ. of Bucharest, 1970; Dr *hc* Univ. of Budapest, 1976; Dr ès Sc *hc* Swiss Fed. Inst. of Technology, 1978; Hon. DSc Wales, 1981. Gold Medal of Merit, Czech. Acad. of Scis, 1978; Silver Medal, Royal Swedish Acad. of Science, 1979; UN Peace Medal, 1979; Cleveland Abbe Award, Amer. Meteorol Soc., 1985; Internat. Meteorological Orgn Prize, WMO, 1985. *Publications:* various meteorological papers and articles. *Recreations:* music, Listener crossword. *Address:* 2 Ashley Close, Patcham, Brighton, East Sussex BN1 8YT. *T:* Brighton (0273) 509437. *Clubs:* Anglo-Belgian, Commonwealth Trust; Explorers' (New York). *Died 13 Nov.* 1990.

**DAVIES, David Lewis,** CBE 1982; DM; Medical Director, The Newington Unit, Ticehurst House, since 1977; *b* 16 April 1911; *s* of late Harry Davies and Anne Davies; *m* 1945, Celia Marjorie Rapport, MB, FFA RCS; three *s. Educ:* Manchester Grammar Sch.; St John's Coll., Oxford (Scholar). BA Oxford (1st Cl. Hons Physiology), 1933; BM, BCh 1936; DPMEng 1943; MA 1944; DM 1948; MRCP 1964; FRCP 1970; FRCPsych 1971. RAMC (Temp.

Major), 1942–46. Physician, Bethlem Royal and Maudsley Hosp., 1948, now Emeritus; Dean, Institute of Psychiatry, University of London, 1950–66. Med. Dir, Alcohol Educn Centre, 1973–80; Mem., Adv. Cttee on Alcoholism to DHSS; Chairman, Attendance Allowance Bd, 1976–82; Pres., Soc. for Study of Addiction. Patron, The Helping Hand Orgn. Hon. Mem., Venezuelan Psychiatric Association, 1964. Hon. FRCPsych 1982. Jellinek Meml Award (jtly), for res. into treatment of alcoholism, 1979. *Publications:* (ed jtly) Psychiatric Education, 1964; (ed jtly) Studies in Psychiatry, 1968; papers on psychiatric subjects in med. jls. Chapters in Louis Wain: the man who drew cats, 1968. Wrote script and commentary for film, Victorian Flower Paintings, 1967. *Recreations:* gardening, travel. *Address:* 152 Harley Street, W1N 1HH. *T:* 01–935 2477; 8 Tollgate Drive, College Road, SE21. *T:* 01–693 9380.
*Died 24 Oct.* 1982.

**DAVIES, Prof. David Richard Seaborne,** MA Cantab; LLB Wales; JP; Dean of the Faculty of Law, University of Liverpool, 1946–71, Professor of the Common Law, 1946–71, then Emeritus, Public Orator, 1950–55, Pro-Vice Chancellor, 1956–60, Warden of Derby Hall, 1947–71; *b* 26 June 1904; *er s* of late David S. and Claudia Davies, Pwllheli. *Educ:* Pwllheli Gram. Sch.; University Coll., Aberystwyth; St John's Coll., Cambridge. (McMahon and Strathcona Studentships). First Class Hons LLB (Wales); Law Tripos, 1927 (Class I, Div. I); Yorke Prize, Cambridge Univ., 1928; Lecturer, and later Reader, in English Law in University of London at London Sch. of Economics, 1929–45; Nationality Div., Home Office, 1941–45; Sec. of the Naturalization (Revocation) Cttee, 1944–48; Member: Oaksey Departmental Cttee on Police Conditions, 1948–49; Standing Cttee on Criminal Law Revision, 1959–72; Chm., Departmental Cttee on Agricultural Diploma Education in Wales, 1956; MP (L) Caernarvon Boroughs, April–July 1945. Pres., Soc. of Public Teachers of Law, 1960–61. Lucien Wolf Memorial Lecturer, 1952. British delegate, SEATO Universities Conference, Pakistan, 1961. Cooley Lecturer, University of Mich., 1962. BBC (Wales) Annual Lecture, 1967. Examiner for many Universities, The Law Society, the Civil Service, etc. Chm., Liverpool Licensing Planning Cttee, 1960–63. Pres., Nat. Eisteddfod of Wales, 1955, 1973, 1975. Pres., Student Council, Univ. of Wales and UCW Aberystwyth; Hon. Life Pres., Liverpool Univ. Legal Soc.; Hon. Life Mem., Univ. Guild of Undergraduates; former Governor: Liverpool College; Rydal School; Life Pres., Liverpool Univ. RFC; Vice-Pres., London Welsh RFC; President: Pwllheli Sports Club, 1972–82; Pwllheli Choral Soc. JP Liverpool, later Caernarvonshire (Gwynedd); High Sheriff of Caernarvonshire, 1967–68. *Publications:* articles in Law Quarterly Review, Modern Law Review, Nineteenth Century, The Annual Survey of English Law, 1930–41. Journal of the Soc. of Public Teachers of Law, etc. *Recreation:* gardening. *Address:* Y Garn, Pwllheli, N Wales. *T:* Pwllheli 2109.
*Died 21 Oct.* 1984.

**DAVIES, Duncan Sheppey,** CB 1982; Consulting Technical Director, Unilever, US National Bureau of Standards, etc; Chairman, BCR Ltd, since 1984; Governor, Technical Change Centre, since 1982; *b* 20 April 1921; *o s* of Duncan S. Davies and Elsie Dora, Liverpool; *m* 1944, Joan Ann Frimston, MA; one *s* three *d*. *Educ:* Liverpool Coll.; Trinity Coll., Oxford (Minor Scholar). MA, BSc, DPhil. CEng, FIChemE, Hon. FIMechE. Joined ICI Dyestuffs Div., 1945; Research Dir, Gen. Chemicals Div., 1961; first Dir, ICI Petrochemical and Polymer Lab., 1962; Dep. Chm., Mond Div., 1967; Gen. Manager, Research, ICI, 1969–77; Chief Engineer and Scientist, DoI, 1977–82; Consulting Technical Dir, BCR Ltd, 1982–84. Member: SERC (formerly SRC), 1969–73, 1977–82; SRC/SSRC, 1973–79 (Chm.); Adv. Bd for Res. Councils, 1977–82; Adv. Council on Applied R&D, NERC, 1977–82; Swann Manpower Working Gp, 1964–66; Council, Liverpool Univ., 1967–69; Council, QEC London, 1975–78; President: R & D Soc., 1983–; SCI, 1986–87. Visiting Professor: Imperial Coll., 1968–70; Univ. of York, 1983–; Vis. Fellow, St Cross Coll., Oxford, 1970; Vis. Prof. Fellow, UC Swansea, 1974–79. DUniv Stirling, 1975; DUniv Surrey, 1980; Hon. DSc Bath, 1981. Castner Medal, SCI, 1967. Foreign Associate, Nat. Acad. of Engineering, USA, 1978. Hon. DSc Technion, Haifa, 1982. *Publications:* (with M. C. McCarthy) Introduction to Technological Economics, 1967; The Humane Technologist, 1976; various papers in engineering and economics, pure and applied chemistry jls. *Recreations:* music, writing. *Address:* 3 Broadlands Close, N6 4AF. *T:* 01–341 2421. *Club:* United Oxford & Cambridge University.
*Died 25 March* 1987.

**DAVIES, Elwyn,** MA; Hon. LLD Wales; MSc, PhD Manchester; President, National Library of Wales, since 1977 (Treasurer, 1959–64; Vice-President, 1970–77); *b* 20 Sept. 1908; *s* of late Rev. Ben Davies, Llandeilo, Dyfed; *m* 1940, Margaret (*d* 1982), *o d* of late Matthew Henry Dunlop, Bury, Lancs; no *c*. *Educ:* Llandysul and Llandeilo Grammar Schs; Universities of Wales (Aberystwyth Coll.) and Manchester. Asst Lectr and Lectr in Geography, University of Manchester, 1934–45, seconded Intelligence Div. Naval Staff, 1941–45; Sec. to the Council, University of Wales, Sec. of the University Press Board and the Board of Celtic Studies,

1945–63; Sec. University Bd for Training Colls, 1945–48, and Univ. Educn Bd, 1948–49; Sec., Univ. Extension Bd, 1945–61; Permanent Sec., Welsh Dept, Min. of Educn, 1963–64; Sec. for Welsh Educn, DES, 1964–69. Chairman: Library Adv. Council (Wales), 1973–79; Wales Regional Library Scheme, 1973–84; Welsh Folk Museum, 1974–. A Governor: National Museum of Wales, 1957– (Mem. Council, 1959–); University College of Wales, Aberystwyth, 1965– (Mem. Council, 1965–); Univ. of Wales, 1966–; Mem. Council, Univ. of Wales Coll. of Medicine (formerly Welsh Nat. Sch. of Medicine), 1978–. Member: Bd of Celtic Studies, Univ. of Wales, 1972–; Local Govt Boundary Commn for Wales, 1974–79 (Dep. Chm., 1978–79); Adv. Council, British Library, 1975–79; Pilkington Cttee on Broadcasting, 1960–62; Standing Commission on Museums and Galleries, 1960–64. *Publications:* Cyfarwyddiadau i Awduron (A Guide for Authors), 1954; (ed) A Gazetteer of Welsh Place-Names, 1957–75; (ed) Celtic Studies in Wales, 1963; (ed with Alwyn D. Rees) Welsh Rural Communities, 1960; papers in anthropological and geographical periodicals. *Address:* 4 Trefor Road, Aberystwyth, Dyfed SY23 2EH.
*Died 18 Sept.* 1986.

**DAVIES, Eryl Oliver,** MA, BLitt (Oxon); HM Chief Inspector of Schools (Wales), since 1972; *b* 5 Dec. 1922; 2nd *s* of late John Edwyn Davies and Elisabeth Oliver Davies, Taimawr, Merthyr Tydfil; *m* 1952, Dr Joyce Crossley, Bradford; one *s* one *d*. *Educ:* Cyfarthfa Castle, Merthyr; Jesus Coll., Oxford. Served War, 1942–46: commissioned South Wales Borderers; served 2nd Bn KSLI, in Normandy (despatches), and War Office, Directorate of Infantry (Major). Asst Master, Bradford Grammar Sch., 1948; HM Inspector, Welsh Dept, Min. of Educn, 1956; Staff Inspector, 1967; Asst Sec., Welsh Office, 1970. Member: Sch. Broadcasting Council of the UK; Schools Council; Open Univ. Adv. Cttee for Wales. *Publications:* articles and poetry in literary jls. *Recreations:* reading, walking. *Address:* 203 Cyncoed Road, Cardiff. *T:* Cardiff 752047. *Club:* National Liberal.
*Died 31 May* 1982.

**DAVIES, Rev. Canon George Colliss Boardman,** DD; retired; Proctor in Convocation, Diocese of Worcester, 1964–75; Canon Residentiary of Worcester, 1963–77, Canon Emeritus, 1977, Vice Dean, 1970–74 and Treasurer, 1970–77; *b* 7 Dec. 1912; *y s* of late Ven. George Middlecott Davies and Berta Mary, *d* of late Admiral F. R. Boardman, CB; *m* 1951, Edith Mavis, *d* of late J. D. Maitland-Kirwan; one *d*. *Educ:* Monkton Combe Sch.; St Catharine's Coll., Cambridge, 2nd cl. Historical Tripos pt 1, 1934; MA 1938; BD 1947; DD 1951; Curate of Woking, 1937–39; permission to officiate Diocese of Ely, 1939–40; Rector of St Clement with St Edmund and St George, Colegate, Norwich, 1940–42; Rector of North Tamerton, 1942–51; Rector of Kingham, 1951–56; Beresford Prof. of Ecclesiastical History, Trinity Coll., Dublin, 1956–63, and Professor of Pastoral Theology, 1960–63; Canon and Treasurer of St Patrick's Cathedral, Dublin, 1962–63. Mem. Gen. Synod of Ch. of Ireland, 1961–63. Commissary to Bp of Kimberley and Kuruman, 1968–76; Dir, Post Ordination Studies and Examining Chaplain to Bp of Worcester, 1971–75. Mem., Exec. Cttee, CMS, 1964–73. Lectr in Church History, Wycliffe Hall, Oxford, 1978–. Governor: Malvern Girls' Coll., 1968–; Dean Close, Cheltenham, 1974–. Trinity Coll., Dublin, MA and DD (*ad eund*), 1959; DD Oxon (by incorp.), 1981. *Publications:* The Early Cornish Evangelicals, 1951; Henry Phillpotts, Bishop of Exeter, 1954; Men for the Ministry: The History of the London College of Divinity, 1963. Contribs to The Church Quarterly Review, The Churchman. *Address:* 53 Blenheim Drive, Oxford OX2 8DL. *T:* Oxford 56297. *Club:* Royal Commonwealth Society.
*Died 21 April* 1982.

**DAVIES, George Peter H.;** *see* Humphreys-Davies.

**DAVIES, Harold Haydn,** CB 1956; MC 1917; Chairman Welsh Board of Health, 1952–57; retired; *b* 27 Dec. 1897; *s* of late John Davies, Ammanford, and London; *m* 1926, Cecilia, *er d* of late Morgan Michael, Pontardulais, Glam.; one *s* one *d*. *Educ:* London; Pembroke Coll., Cambridge. Asst Secretary (Dep. Establishment Officer) Ministry of Housing and Local Govt, 1951; Ministry of Health, 1921–51. Gazetted to Royal Northumberland Fusiliers, 1917; served European War, 1914–18; BEF, France, 1917–18 (MC; prisoner of war, March 1918). Vice Chm., Holloway Sanatorium Hospital Gp, 1958–68; Mem., NW Surrey Hospital Management Cttee, 1968–74. OStJ 1957. *Address:* Woodlands, Coombe Park, Kingston Hill, Surrey. *T:* 01–546 2030.
*Died 13 July* 1982.

**DAVIES, Rev. Canon Hywel Islwyn,** BA; PhD; Rector of Collyweston, 1969–76; Rural Dean of Barnack, 1973–76; *b* 14 Feb. 1909; *s* of Rev. H. J. Davies and Mary Davies, Loughor, Swansea; *m* 1st, 1940, Beti Lewis Beynon (decd); one *d*; 2nd 1956, Glenys Williams. *Educ:* Gowerton Grammar Sch.; University of Wales; Gonville and Caius Coll., Cambridge; St Michael's Coll., Llandaff. BA 1st Class Philosophy, 1932 Pierce Scholar; PhD University of Cambridge; Lord Rhondda Scholar, 1936. Ordained, 1936; Curacy, Methyr Tydfil; Lecturer, 1940, Tutor 1942, St David's Coll., Lampeter; Vicar, Llanstephan, Carms, and Tutor, Trinity Coll., Carmarthen, 1945; Director Adult Education, Diocese of St David's,

1946; Examining Chaplain Bishop of Monmouth; Vicar Llanbadarn Fawr and Lecturer, University College of Wales, Aberystwyth, 1947; Vicar of Llanelly and Canon of St David's Cathedral, 1950; Dean of Bangor, 1957–61; Head of Dept of Religion and Philosophy, Univ. of Ife, 1961–69, Prof. 1966–69, Mem. Univ. Council and Dean of Faculty of Arts, 1963–69. Examining Chaplain to Archbishop of Wales and to Bishop of Bangor, 1957. Public Preacher: Dio. Lagos, Ibadan, and N Nigeria; Examining Chaplain to Bishops of Ibadan and Northern Nigeria; Canon, St James's Cathedral, Ibadan, 1966, Canon Emeritus 1969. Governor, Immanuel Theological Coll., Ibadan. Examiner: Univ. of Ibadan; Univ. of Lagos. Mem. Adv. Panel, W African Sch. Certificate. *Publications:* various, in philosophical, theological, Welsh, English, and African journals. *Recreation:* Celtic Bygones. *Address:* 39 Ambergate Road, Liverpool L19 9AU. *T:* 051–427 4689. *Club:* Royal Commonwealth Society. *Died 19 Feb.* 1981.

**DAVIES, Ifor;** MP (Lab) Gower since Oct. 1959; *b* 9 June 1910; *s* of Jeffrey and Elizabeth Jane Davies; *m* 1950, Doreen Griffiths; one *s* one *d. Educ:* Gowerton; Swansea Technical; Ruskin Coll., Oxford. Oxford Diploma, Economics and Politics. Accountant, 1931–39; Personnel Officer, ICI, 1942–47; Ministry of Labour, Statistics Dept, 1947–48; Personnel Officer, Aluminium Wire and Cable Co. Ltd, 1948–59; Opposition Whip (Welsh), 1961–64; a Lord Commissioner of the Treasury and Govt Whip, 1964–66; Parly Under-Sec. of State, Welsh Office, 1966–69; Sec., Welsh Labour Gp, 1960–66; Chm., Welsh Parly Party, 1970–71. Executive Member South Wales District, WEA, 1950–60; Secretary Gowerton Welsh Congregational Chapel, 1948; Hon. Secretary Gower Constituency Labour Party, 1948–59; Member: Glamorgan County Council, 1958–61; Civic Trust for Wales, 1972–; President: S Wales and Mon Br., Urban District Councils Assoc., 1970–; Gower Soc., 1971–; Chm. Council, University Coll. of Swansea, 1971–; Chairman: Welsh Grand Cttee, 1971–; Welsh Labour Gp MPs, 1973–; Mem., Speaker's Panel of Chairmen. Hon. Mem., Gorsedd of Bards National Eisteddfod, 1970. Hon. LLD Univ. of Wales, 1980. *Recreations:* walking and listening to music. *Address:* Ty Pentwyn, Three Crosses, Swansea, W Glam. *T:* Gowerton 2222.
*Died 6 June* 1982.

**DAVIES, Iforwyn Glyndwr;** Formerly Senior Principal Medical Officer, Ministry of Health; QHP 1957–59; *b* 11 June 1901; *s* of Richard and Margaret Davies, Porth, South Wales; *m* 1930, Lilian May, *d* of Evan James, Cardiff, South Wales; one *s. Educ:* The County Sch., Porth; University College, Cardiff; St Bartholomew's Hospital, London. MRCS, LRCP, 1923; MB, BS London, 1924; MD London, 1944; MRCP, 1926; FRCP, 1954. Formerly: Tuberculosis Physician, City of Nottingham, 1933; Deputy MOH, City and County of Bristol, 1937; Lecturer in Public Health, University of Bristol, 1937; Dep. Director, Preventive Medicine Laboratories; Prof., of Public Health, University of Leeds, 1947, also Medical Officer of Health and School Medical Officer, City of Leeds. *Publications:* Text-Book: Modern Public Health for Medical Students, 1955 (2nd edn, 1963); contrib. to Lancet, Medical Officer, Public Health. *Recreation:* music. *Address:* Amberley, Well Meadows, Shaw, Newbury, Berks. *T:* Newbury 42055.
*Died 12 Jan.* 1984.

**DAVIES, Rev. John Gordon,** MA, DD; Edward Cadbury Professor of Theology and Head of Department of Theology, University of Birmingham, 1960–86, later Emeritus; Director of Institute for Study of Worship and Religious Architecture, University of Birmingham, 1962–86; *b* 20 April 1919; *s* of late Mr and Mrs A. G. Davies, Chester; *m* 1945, Emily Mary Tordoff; one *s* two *d. Educ:* King's Sch., Chester; Christ Church, Oxford; Westcott House, Cambridge. Curate of Rotherhithe, Dec. 1943–Sept. 1948; Univ. of Birmingham: Asst Lecturer in Theology, 1948–50; Lecturer, 1950–57; Senior Lecturer, 1957–59; Reader, 1959–60; Dean of Faculty of Arts, 1967–70. BA Oxon., 1942; MA 1945; BD 1946; DD 1956; MA (Official) Birmingham, 1952; Hon. DD St Andrews, 1968. Hereditary Freeman, City of Chester; Brother of Ancient and Worshipful Company of Skinners and Felt Makers. Bampton Lecturer, 1958. Hon. Canon, Birmingham, 1965–86; Canon Emeritus, Birmingham, 1986. Hon. Mem., Guild for Religious Architecture, USA. Conover Memorial Award, New York, 1967. *Publications:* The Theology of William Blake, 1948 (USA 1966); The Origin and Development of Early Christian Church Architecture, 1952 (USA 1953); Daily Life in the Early Church: Studies in the Church Social History of the First Five Centuries, 1952 (repr. 1955); Daily Life of Early Christians, 1953; Social Life of Early Christians, 1954; The Spirit, the Church, and the Sacraments, 1954; Members One of Another: Aspects of Koinonia, 1958; He Ascended into Heaven: a Study in the History of Doctrine (Bampton Lectures, 1958), 1958 (USA 1958); The Making of the Church, 1960, repr. 1983; Intercommunion, 1961; The Architectural Setting of Baptism, 1962; Holy Week, a Short History, 1963 (USA 1963); The Early Christian Church, 1965 (USA 1965); A Select Liturgical Lexicon, 1965 (USA 1965); Worship and Mission, 1966 (USA 1967; Japan, 1968); Dialogue with the World, 1967; The Secular Use of Church Buildings, 1968 (USA 1968); Every Day God: encountering the Holy in World and Worship, 1973; Christians, Politics and Violent Revolution, 1976 (USA 1976); New Perspectives on Worship Today, 1978; Temples, Churches and Mosques: a guide to the appreciation of religious architecture, 1982 (USA 1982); Liturgical Dance: an historical, theological and practical handbook, 1984; Pilgrimages Yesterday and Today: why? where? how?, 1988 (USA 1988); *translated editions include:* French, German, Italian, Spanish, Finnish, Japanese, Norwegian, Portuguese, Swedish; *co-author:* An Experimental Liturgy, 1958; *translator:* Essays on the Lord's Supper, 1958; The Eucharistic Memorial Vol. I, 1960, Vol. II, 1961; Mission in a Dynamic Society, 1968; *editor:* A Dictionary of Liturgy and Worship, 1972; Worship and Dance, 1975; The Recreational Use of Churches, 1978; A New Dictionary of Liturgy and Worship, 1986; *contributor to:* Becoming a Christian, 1954; The Teachers' Commentary, 1955; The Concise Encyclopædia of Living Faiths, 1959; Making the Building Serve the Liturgy, 1962; The Modern Architectural Setting of the Liturgy, 1964; A Manual for Holy Week, 1967; Preface to Christian Studies, 1971; Journal of Theological Studies; Journal of Hellenic Studies; Vigiliae Christianae; Harvard Theological Review; Encyclopædia Britannica; Theologische Realenzyklopädie, etc. *Recreation:* cooking. *Address:* 28 George Road, Edgbaston, Birmingham B15 1PJ. *T:* 021–454 6254. *Died 13 Dec.* 1990.

**DAVIES, Prof. John Tasman,** PhD, DSc London; MA, ScD Cantab; Professor of Chemical Engineering and Head of Department, University of Birmingham, 1960–83, Research Professor since 1983; *b* 1 May 1924; *m* 1948, Ruth Batt; two *s. Educ:* Boys' High Sch., Christchurch, NZ; Canterbury University Coll.; London Univ. MA Cantab. 1955; PhD London 1949; DSc London 1955; ScD Cantab 1967. Worked with Sir Eric Rideal, FRS, Royal Institution London, 1946–48; Research Associate and Bristol-Myers Fellow, Stanford Univ., Calif. (USA) (worked with late Prof. J. W. McBain, FRS), 1948–49; Beit Mem. Fellow for Medical Research, Royal Instn and KCL, 1949–52; Lectr in: Chemistry, KCL, 1952–55; Chemical Engineering, Cambridge Univ., 1955–60. Overseas guest lecturer at Gordon Conference, USA, 1956, 1980. Visiting Professor: Univ. of Minnesota, 1963; Univ. of Auckland, NZ, 1976, 1980. Member: UN Consultative Commn to Indian Inst. of Petroleum, 1967–71; UNESCO Advisory Group on Petroleum Technology, Arab States, 1967; (part-time) West Midlands Gas Board, 1968–72. Member Sigma-Xi, 1949 (USA), FIChemE. *Publications:* (with Sir Eric Rideal, FRS) Interfacial Phenomena, 1961; The Scientific Approach, 1965, 2nd edn 1973; Turbulence Phenomena, 1972; many on Surface Phenomena and Chemical Engineering. *Address:* Department of Chemical Engineering, The University, Birmingham B15 2TT. *T:* 021–472 1301. *Died 30 Sept.* 1987.

**DAVIES, Kenneth;** see Davies, S. K.

**DAVIES, Michael John,** CMG 1961; OBE 1957; Secretary, Imperial College of Science and Technology, and Clerk to the Governing Body, 1962–79, Fellow, since 1979, on retirement; *b* 7 Oct. 1918; *y s* of late David Alexander Davies; *m* 1949, Elizabeth Eve Burridge; two *s* one *d. Educ:* Diocesan Coll., Cape Town; University of Cape Town; Trinity Coll., Oxford. (MA) as a Rhodes Scholar. Appointed to Colonial Service in Tanganyika, as an Administrative Officer, 1940. Private Secretary to the Governor, 1943–47; seconded to the Colonial Office, 1947–49. Assistant Special Representative for Tanganyika at Trusteeship Council of United Nations, 1958 and 1959; Minister: for Constitutional Affairs in Tanganyika, 1959; for Security and Immigration, 1959–60; for Information Services, 1960–61 (until date of Self Government in Tanganyika, May 1st). Acting Chief Secretary May–Aug., 1960; retired from HM Overseas Civil Service, 1962. Médaille de la Belgique Reconnaissante (for services to Belgian Refugees), 1961. *Recreations:* watching Rugby football (Welsh International, 1938 and 1939); playing golf; gardening. *Address:* Barfield Cottage, Waldron, Heathfield, East Sussex. *T:* Heathfield 3704. *Died 8 July* 1984.

**DAVIES, Oswald Vaughan L.;** see Lloyd-Davies.

**DAVIES, Roy Dicker Salter,** CBE 1967; a Chief Inspector of Schools, Department of Education and Science, 1958–68, retired; *b* 24 March 1906; *yr s* of Ernest Salter Davies, CBE, and Evelyn May Lile. *Educ:* Tonbridge Sch.; Magdalen Coll., Oxford (MA). Served RE, 1939–40, RA, 1940–45. Appointed HM Inspector of Schools, 1934; Staff Inspector, 1951. Mem., Departmental Cttee on Adult Educn, 1969–73. *Recreations:* watching Rugby football; cricket. *Address:* Wick House, Stogumber, Taunton, Somerset. *T:* Stogumber 422.
*Died 6 May* 1984.

**DAVIES, (Stanley) Kenneth,** CBE 1951; Chairman, Wire Ropes Ltd, Wicklow; *b* 25 April 1899; 2nd *s* of late Sir John Davies, CBE, JP; *m* 1938, Stephanie Morton (*d* 1979); one *s* one *d. Educ:* Christ Coll., Brecon; Blundell's; Royal Military Academy, Woolwich. Commnd RA, 1918; served France and Germany, 1918–19. Chairman and Managing Director: George Elliot & Co. Ltd; Bridgwater Wire Ropes Ltd; Somerset Wire Co. Ltd; Terrells Wire Ropes Ltd; Yacht

and Commercial Rigging Co. Ltd; Hartlepool Wire Rope Co.; Excelsior Ropes Ltd (for varying periods between 1929 and 1960, when they were incorp. in British Ropes Ltd, now Bridon Ltd, or in GKN Ltd). Founder Member, Cardiff Aeroplane Club, 1929. Private pilot's licence, 1931–61. Formed Cambrian Air Services Ltd, 1935, Managing Director, 1935–51. Member Cttee Royal Aero Club of United Kingdom, 1935 (Vice-Chm., 1948–51, Chm. 1952–58, Vice-Pres., 1958–); Member Board British European Airways Corporation, 1951–67; Dep. Chairman BEA Helicopters Ltd, 1965–67; Chairman Welsh Advisory Council for Civil Aviation, 1948–60; Chairman Cardiff Airport Consultative Cttee, 1956–63; Member Welsh Cttee of Arts Council of Great Britain, 1954–67; Member Consultative Cttee, Sadler's Wells Trust, 1962–; Chairman of Contemporary Art Society of Wales, 1966–72; Liveryman of the Guild of Air Pilots and Air Navigators; Vice-President, FAI (Fédération Aéronautique Internationale), rep. UK; Member Cttee, Dublin Theatre Festival, 1967; Mem. Ct of Governors, National Theatre of Wales. Life Member: Iron & Steel Institute; S Wales Inst. of Engineers; Royal Agricultural Society; Royal Dublin Society. FRSA; FCIT. Coronation medal, 1953. *Recreations:* aviation and gastronomy (Vice-Pres., Internat. Wine and Food Society). *Address:* Killoughter, Ashford, Co. Wicklow. *T:* Wicklow 4126; Collingdon Road, Cardiff. *T:* 21693. *Clubs:* Athenæum, Brooks's, Naval and Military, Royal Automobile (among remaining 10 longest members); County (Cardiff); Kildare Street and University (Dublin); Bristol Channel Yacht (Swansea).
*Died 24 March* 1987.

**DAVIES, Dr Wyndham Roy;** Consultant to the Pharmaceutical Industry; *b* 3 June 1926; *s* of late George Edward Davies, LLB, Llangadock, Carms, and of Ellen Theresa (*née* Merris), Treaford Hall, Birmingham. *Educ:* King Edward's, Birmingham; Birmingham and London Universities. LRCP 1948; MB, ChB, 1949; DPH 1958; DIH 1959. House Surgeon, General Hospital, Birmingham, 1949; Receiving Room Officer, Children's Hospital, Birmingham, 1949; Resident Medical Officer, Little Bromwich Hospital, Birmingham, 1950. Entered RN, 1950; HMS Surprise, 1950–51; HMS St Angelo, 1951–53; Squadron Medical Officer, 4th Destroyer Sqdn, Home Fleet, 1953–54; Research Assistant, St George's Hospital Medical Sch. (MRC), 1955; Admiralty Medical Board and HMS Dauntless (WRNS), 1956–57; stood by building of HMS Albion, HMS Malcolm, 1957; HMS Glory, 1957; London School of Hygiene and Tropical Medicine, 1958; RN Medical Sch., 1958–59; habitability trials, HMS Centaur and HMS Bulwark, 1959–60; Joint Services Amphib. Warfare Centre, 1960–63; qual. shallow water diver, 1960; Chemical Defence Exper. Establishment, 1963; retired as Surgeon Lieut-Comdr, 1963. Adopted Prospective Parliamentary Candidate for Birmingham Perry Barr Div., 1963; MP (C) Perry Barr Div. of Birmingham, 1964–66; Joint Secretary, Party Educn and Sci. Cttee, 1965–66; Vice-President, Birmingham Cons. and Unionist Assoc., 1965–71. Dir, Medical Economic Res. Inst., 1968; Min. of Overseas Develt, Bahamas, 1969–72; Research on Immunology and Cancer, Rice Univ. and Univ. of Texas, 1976–78. Hon. Medical Adviser, British Sub-Aqua Club, 1959–66; Hon. Medical Adviser, British Safety Council, 1962–64; Governor, Royal Humane Society, 1962–; Chairman Organizing Cttee, World Congress of Underwater Activities, 1962; Cttee, Poole and Dorset Adventure Centre, 1961–64; Island Comdr for Sea Scouts, Malta, 1951–53; ADC, Boy Scouts, City of Westminster, 1957–62; Founder Member Old Edwardians BP Guild, 1948–; Hon. Secretary, Houses of Parliament BP Guild, 1964–66. Medical Officer British Schools Exploring Society Exped. to Labrador, 1958; Medical Commn on Accident Prevention, 1971–70; Founder, Society for Underwater Technology; BMA Rep., 1968–70, 1972–74; Exec. Council, Monday Club, 1965–69; Chairman: Health Cttee, 1965–69; University Liaison Cttee, 1967–68. Mem., Medical Cttee, SW Metropolitan Reg. Hosp. Bd, 1972. Dir, Brit. Cellular Therapy Soc., 1974; Mem., Deutsch Gesellschaft für Zelltherapie, 1972. Editor, Fellowship for Freedom in Medicine Bulletin, 1972–74. *Publications:* Expired Air Resuscitation, 1959; Skin Diving, 1959; Collectivism or Individualism in Medicine, 1965; Reforming the National Health Service, 1967; The Pharmaceutical Industry, A Personal Study, 1967; Health—or Health Service?, 1972; The Present Status of Cell Therapy, 1974; articles in The Practitioner and Physiological Journal. *Recreations:* all sports on, in or under water, travel, exploring, painting. *Died 4 Dec.* 1984.

**d'AVIGDOR-GOLDSMID, Maj.-Gen. Sir James (Arthur),** 3rd Bt *cr* 1934; CB 1975; OBE 1955; MC 1944; *b* 19 Dec. 1912; *yr s* of Sir Osmond d'Avigdor-Goldsmid, 1st Bt, and Alice Lady d'Avigdor-Goldsmid; *S* brother, 1976; unmarried. *Educ:* Harrow; RMC, Sandhurst. 2nd Lieut 4th/7th Royal Dragoon Guards, 1932. Served War of 1939–45, France and Germany (wounded). Commanded: 4th/7th Royal Dragoon Guards, 1950–53; 20th Armoured Brigade Group, 1958–61; Director, Royal Armoured Corps, War Office, subseq. Ministry of Defence, 1962–65; President, Regular Commissions Board, Feb.-Sept. 1965; Director TA and Cadets, 1966–68; Col of 4th/7th Royal Dragoon Guards, 1963–73; Chm.,

SE TA&VRA, 1974–78; Hon. Col The Mercian Yeomanry, T&AVR, 1972–77. MP (C) Lichfield and Tamworth, 1970–Sept. 1974; Mem., Select Cttee on Estimates, 1971–74. Chairman: Racecourse Security Services Ltd, 1976–80; Tattersall's Cttee, 1980–; Exec. of Governors, Corps of Commissionaires, 1980–; Member: Horserace Betting Levy Bd, 1974–77; Council, Winston Churchill Meml Trust. Comr Royal Hosp. Chelsea, 1972–78. *Heir:* none. *Address:* 101 Mount Street, W1. *T:* 01–499 1989. *Clubs:* Cavalry and Guards, Turf, Jockey. *Died 6 Sept.* 1987 (*ext*).

**DAVIN, Daniel Marcus, (Dan Davin),** CBE 1987 (MBE (mil.) 1945); Oxford Academic Publisher, and Deputy Secretary to Delegates of the Oxford University Press, 1974–78, retired; *b* 1 Sept. 1913; *s* of Patrick and Mary Davin; *m* 1939, Winifred Kathleen Gonley; three *d. Educ:* Marist Brothers Sch., Invercargill, NZ; Sacred Heart Coll., Auckland; Otago Univ. (MA); Balliol Coll., Oxford (First in Greats, 1939, MA 1945). Served War: Royal Warwickshire Regt, 1939–40; 2 NZEF, 1940–45; served in Greece and Crete (wounded 1941); Intell. GHQ, ME, 1941–42; NZ Div., N Africa and Italy, 1942–45 (despatches thrice, MBE). With Clarendon Press, 1945–78. Fellow of Balliol Coll., 1965–78, subseq. Emeritus. FRSA. Hon. DLitt Otago Univ., 1984. *Publications: novels:* Cliffs of Fall, 1945; For the Rest of Our Lives, 1947; Roads from Home, 1949; The Sullen Bell, 1956; No Remittance, 1959; Not Here, Not Now, 1970; Brides of Price, 1972; *short stories:* The Gorse Blooms Pale, 1947; Breathing Spaces, 1975; Selected Stories, 1981; *miscellaneous prose:* Introduction to English Literature (with John Mulgan), 1947; Crete (Official History), 1953 (Wellington, War Hist. Br., Dept of Internal Affairs); Writing in New Zealand: The New Zealand Novel (Parts One and Two, with W. K. Davin), 1956; Katherine Mansfield in Her Letters, 1959; Closing Times (Recollections of Julian Maclaren-Ross, W. R. Rodgers, Louis MacNeice, Enid Starkie, Joyce Cary, Dylan Thomas, Itzik Manger), 1975; *editions:* New Zealand Short Stories, 1953; English Short Stories of Today: Second Series, 1958; Katherine Mansfield, Selected Stories, 1963; Short Stories from the Second World War, 1982; (ed jtly) From Oasis to Italy, 1983; The Salamander and the Fire (collected war stories), 1987. *Recreations:* reading, writing, talking. *Address:* 103 Southmoor Road, Oxford OX2 6RE. *T:* Oxford (0865) 57311. *Died 28 Sept.* 1990.

**DAVIS, Bette Ruth Elizabeth;** actress; *b* Lowell, Mass, 5 April 1908. *Educ:* Cushing Academy, Ashburnham, Mass. Stage experience in Wild Duck, Broken Dishes, Solid South; entered films, 1930. Pictures she has appeared in: Of Human Bondage, 1934; Border Town; Dangerous (Academy Award of 1935 won 1936); The Petrified Forest, The Golden Arrow, 1936; Marked Woman, Kid Galahad, It's Love I'm After, That Certain Woman, 1937; Jezebel (Academy Award of 1938 won 1939); The Sisters, 1938; Dark Victory, Juarez, The Old Maid, Private Lives of Elizabeth and Essex, 1939; All This and Heaven Too, 1940; The Letter, The Great Lie, The Bride came COD, The Man who came to Dinner, The Little Foxes, 1941; In This our Life, Watch on the Rhine, Old Acquaintance, 1942; Mr Skeffington, 1944; The Corn is Green, 1945; A Stolen Life, Deception, 1946; Winter Meeting, 1948; June Bride, 1948; The Story of a Divorce; All about Eve, 1950; Payment on Demand, 1951; Phone Call from a Stranger, 1952; Another Man's Poison, 1952; The Star, 1953; The Virgin Queen, 1955; Storm Center, 1956; The Catered Affair, 1956; John Paul Jones, 1956; Wedding Breakfast; The Scapegoat, 1959; Pocketful of Miracles, 1961; Whatever Happened to Baby Jane?, 1962; Dead Ringer, 1964; Painted Canvas, 1963; Where Love Has Gone, 1964; Hush . . . Hush, Sweet Charlotte, 1964; The Nanny, 1965; The Anniversary, 1967; Connecting Rooms, 1969; Bunny O'Hare, 1970; Madam Sin, 1971; The Game, 1972; Burnt Offerings, 1977; Death on the Nile, 1978; Watcher In The Woods, 1980; The Whales of August, 1988. *TV Movies:* Sister Aimee, 1977; The Dark Secret of Harvest Home, 1978; Strangers, The Story of a Mother and Daughter, 1979 (Emmy Award); White Mama, 1980; Skyward, 1980; Family Reunion, 1981; A Piano for Mrs Cimino, 1982; Little Gloria, Happy at Last, 1982; Right of Way, 1983; Hotel, 1983; Murder with Mirrors, 1984; As Summers Die, 1985; *Plays:* The Night of the Iguana, 1961; Miss Moffitt, 1974. Life Achievement Award, Amer. Film Institute, 1977; Rudolph Valentino Life Achievement Award, 1982; Life Achievement Award, Amer. Acad. of Arts, 1983; Dept of Defense Medal for Distinguished Public Service, 1983; Women in Films Crystal Award, 1983; César Award, French Cinema, 1986; Kennedy Center Honors Medallion, 1987. Order of Arts and Letters, France, 1986; Legion of Honour, France, 1987. *Publications:* The Lonely Life, 1963; This 'N' That, 1987. *Relevant Publication:* Mother Goddam by Whitney Stine, 1975 (footnotes by Bette Davis). *Recreations:* swimming and horseback riding. *Address:* c/o Gottlieb Schiff Bomser & Sendroff, PC, 555 Fifth Avenue, New York, NY 10017, USA.
*Died 6 Oct.* 1989.

**DAVIS, Brian;** *see* ffolkes, Michael.

**DAVIS, Brig. Cyril Elliott,** CBE 1941; *b* 15 March 1892; *y s* of late O. J. H. Davis, Ford Park, Plymouth, Devon; *m* 1st, 1918, Fay (*d* 1957), *y d* of Leathes Prior, Eaton, Norwich; two *s*; 2nd, 1958,

Helen, *widow* of Rev. T. V. Garnier, OBE. *Educ:* Alton Sch.; Plymouth Coll. Regular Commission in ASC, 1912, from 3rd DCLI (SR); served European War, 1914–18, France, Belgium, Greek Macedonia, Serbia, Bulgaria, European Turkey, Egypt, Palestine (1914 Star and Clasp, BWM and Victory Medal); Palestine Campaign, 1937 (Palestine Gen. Service Medal); Lieut-Col 1939 and posted to Singapore. Temp. Col 1940; Col 1941; Dep. Dir of Supplies and Transport, Malaya Command (acting Brig.), 1941; transferred to S Western Pacific Command, Java, Jan. 1942; Ceylon, March 1942; retired April 1946. A General Comr of Income Tax, 1958–67. King George V Jubilee Medal, 1935; Comdr Order of Leopold II (Belgium), 1951. *Address:* Stour View Bridge, Sturminster Newton, Dorset. *T:* Sturminster Newton 72832.

*Died 29 June 1986.*

**DAVIS, Harold Sydney,** FRCP; retired; Consultant Physician: Royal Free Hospital, London, 1954–73; King Edward VII Hospital, Windsor, 1945–73; Hampstead General Hospital, 1946–73; formerly Consultant Physician, Florence Nightingale Hospital, London; Hon. Physician to the Queen, T&AVR, 1967–68; *b* 6 Aug. 1908; *s* of Harold Adamson Davis and Edith May Davis, Jamaica, WI; *m* 1940, Molly, *d* of Herbert Percy Stimson, London; one *d*. *Educ:* Jamaica Coll., WI; Dulwich Coll., London; Gonville and Caius Coll., Cambridge; Charing Cross Hosp., London (Exhibr). BA 1930, MB, BChir 1935, MA 1936, Cantab.; LRCP, MRCS 1933; MRCP 1936; FRCP 1954. Held usual resident appts in various London hosps, 1933–39. Commissioned into RAMC, March 1939 (Lieut); seconded as Physician, Ashridge Hosp. (EMS), 1940. OC 308 (Co. London) Gen. Hosp. RAMC/AER, 1964 (Col). Examr in Medicine, London Univ.; Lectr in Medicine, Royal Free Hosp. Sch. of Medicine, London Univ., 1962; Mem. Bd of Govs, Royal Free Hosp., 1963. Pres., Eagle Ski Club, 1960–63. *Publications:* contrib. learned jls. *Recreations:* ski-mountaineering, gardening. *Address:* Fingest Hill Cottage, Skirmett, near Henley-on-Thames, Oxon RG9 6TD. *T:* Turville Heath 275. *Clubs:* Ski Club of Gt Britain (Vice-Pres. 1964; Chm., 1966–68), Kandahar Ski; Leander (Henley-on-Thames). *Died 6 Nov. 1988.*

**DAVIS, Air Chief Marshal Sir John (Gilbert),** GCB 1968 (KCB 1964; CB 1953); OBE 1945; psc 1946; idc 1955; RAF, retired; Lieutenant-Governor and Commander-in-Chief of Jersey, 1969–74; *b* 24 March 1911; *e s* of late John Davis, Whitby, Yorks; *m* 1937, Doreen, *d* of Arthur Heaton, Hinckley, Leics; one *s* one *d*. *Educ:* Whitby Grammar Sch.; Queens' Coll., Cambridge, MA 1937. First Commnd RAF, 1934; served Bomber Sqdns 142 and 57, 1934–36; Instructor No 10 Flying Training Sch., 1936–37; Navigation Staff duties, 1938–39; served war of 1939–45 on anti-submarine duties in Mediterranean, Iceland, Azores, UK (seconded to Turkish Air Force as navigation instructor, 1940–41). Instructor RAF Staff Coll., 1948–50; Gp Captain Plans HQ MEAF, 1951–53; OC RAF Station, Topcliffe, 1953–54; Dir of Plans, Air Ministry, 1955–58; SASO, Bomber Command HQ, 1958–59; Air Officer Commanding No 1 Group, Bomber Command, 1959–61; Air Officer Commanding Malta, and Dep. Comdr-in-Chief (Air), Allied Forces Mediterranean, 1961–63; Air Mem. for Supply and Organisation, MoD, 1963–66; Air Officer Commanding-in-Chief: Flying Trng Comd, 1966–68; Trng Comd, 1968–69. Air ADC to the Queen, 1967–69. KStJ 1969. *Recreations:* ornithology, fishing. *Address:* The Stone House, Ruswarp, near Whitby, North Yorks. *Clubs:* Royal Air Force; Union Society (Cambridge). *Died 3 Feb. 1989.*

**DAVIS, Morris Cael,** CMG 1970; MD, FRACP; Consultant Physician, 110 Collins Street, Melbourne; *b* 7 June 1907; *s* of David and Sarah Davis; *m* 1933, Sophia Ashkenasy (*d* 1966); two *s*. *Educ:* Melbourne High Sch.; Univ. of Melbourne. MB, BS (1st cl. hons) Melbourne, 1930; MD 1932; MRCP 1938; FRACP 1946. Univ. of Melbourne: Prosector in Anatomy, 1927; Beaney Schol. in Pathology, 1932–33; Lectr in Pathology, 1933; Lectr in Medicine, Dental Faculty, 1940–63; Bertram Armytage Prize for Med. Res., 1934 and 1942; Fulbright Smith Mundt Schol., 1953–54. Alfred Hosp., Melbourne: Acting Pathologist, 1933–35; Physican to Out-Patients, 1938–46; Phys. to In-Patients, 1946–67; Cons. Phys., 1967–; Foundn Chm., Cardiovascular Diagnostic Service, 1959–67; Dir and Founder, Dept of Visual Aids, 1954–67 (Producer of a number of bed-side clinical teaching charts, heart models, cinefilms incl. Routine Examination of the Heart, film strips on mitral stenosis, aortic regurgitation, congenital heart disease, also heart contours of fluoroscopy of heart: all these now in the archives of Monash Univ. Sch. of Medicine, Melbourne); Chm. Drug Cttee, 1960–67. Med. Referee, Commonwealth Dept of Health. Travelled Nuffield Sponsorship, 1954; Litchfield Lectr, Oxford Univ., 1954; Hon. Consultant, Dental Hosp., Melbourne, 1946–. Mem., Curricular Planning Cttee, RMIT; Hon. Pres., Medico-Clerical Soc. of Victoria. Pres., Victorian Friends of Hebrew Univ., Jerusalem, 1953–64; Federal Pres., Australian Friends Hebrew Univ., 1964; Alternate Governor, Hebrew Univ., 1961–63, Governor, Bezalel Acad. of Art and Design, Israel. Founder, Australian Medical Assoc. Arts Group (Pres. 1959–82; creator, twelve fused glass windows in E Melbourne Synagogue, 1977); Hon.

Life Pres., Bezalel Fellowship of Arts. Vice-Pres., Aust. Kidney Foundn Appeal, 1971; Mem., Epworth Hosp. Appeal Cttee, 1975–76. *Publications:* History of the East Melbourne Hebrew Congregation 1957–1977, 1977; papers on medicine, medical philosophy and medical educn in Australian Med. Jl, Australian Dental Jl, student jls. *Recreations:* ceramics, painting, music, book collecting, garden. *Address:* 177 Finch Street, Glen Iris, Vic. 3146, Australia. *T:* Melbourne 509.2423. *Died 11 Oct. 1987.*

**DAVIS, Prof. Norman,** MBE 1945; FBA 1969; Merton Professor of English Language and Literature, University of Oxford, 1959–80; Emeritus Fellow, Merton College, Oxford, since 1980; *b* Dunedin, NZ, 16 May 1913; *s* of James John and Jean Davis; *m* 1944, Magdalene Jamieson Bone (*d* 1983); no *c*. *Educ:* Otago Boys' High Sch., Dunedin; Otago Univ.; Merton Coll., Oxford. MA NZ 1934; BA Oxon 1936, MA 1944; NZ Rhodes Scholar, 1934. Lecturer in English, Kaunas, Lithuania, 1937; Sofia, Bulgaria, 1938. Government service mainly abroad, 1939–46. Lecturer in English Language, Queen Mary Coll., University of London, 1946; Oriel and Brasenose Colls., Oxford, 1947; Oxford Univ. Lectr in Medieval English, 1948; Prof. of English Language, University of Glasgow, 1949. Hon. Dir of Early English Text Soc., 1957–83. Jt Editor, Review of English Studies, 1954–63. R. W. Chambers Meml Lecturer, UCL, 1971. Hon. DLitt Otago, 1984. *Publications:* Sweet's Anglo-Saxon Primer, 9th edn 1953; The Language of the Pastons (Sir Israel Gollancz Memorial Lecture, British Academy, 1954), 1955; Paston Letters (a selection), 1958; Beowulf facsimile ed. Zupitza, 2nd edn 1959; English and Medieval Studies (ed with C. L. Wrenn), 1962; The Paston Letters (a selection in modern spelling), 1963, rev. edn 1983; Glossary to Early Middle English Verse and Prose (ed J. A. W. Bennett and G. V. Smithers), 1966; rev. edn, Tolkien-Gordon: Sir Gawain, 1967; Non-Cycle Plays and Fragments (EETS), 1970; Paston Letters and Papers of the Fifteenth Century, Part I, 1971, Part II, 1977; (jtly) A Chaucer Glossary, 1979; Non-Cycle Plays and the Winchester Dialogues (facsimiles), 1979; reviews and articles in jls. *Address:* 191b Woodstock Road, Oxford OX2 7AB. *T:* Oxford 59634. *Died 2 Dec. 1989.*

**DAVIS, Most Rev. William Wallace;** *b* 10 Dec. 1908; *s* of Isaac Davis and Margaret Dixon; *m* 1933, Kathleen Aubrey Acheson (*d* 1966); two *s* two *d*; *m* 1968, Helen Mary Lynton. *Educ:* Bishop's Univ., Lennoxville, PQ. BA 1931, BD 1934; Deacon, 1932; Priest, 1932; Curate, St Matthew's, Ottawa, 1932–36; Rector, Coaticook, PQ, 1936–38; Rector, St Matthew's, Quebec, 1938–52; Archdeacon of Quebec, 1947–52; Dean of Nova Scotia, and Rector of the Cathedral Church of All Saints, Halifax, NS, 1952–58; Bishop Coadjutor of Nova Scotia, 1958–63; Bishop of Nova Scotia, 1963; Archbishop of Nova Scotia and Metropolitan of Ecclesiastical Province of the Atlantic, Canada, 1972–75. DD University of King's Coll., Halifax, 1954; Hon. DCL Bishop's Univ., Lennoxville, PQ, 1960; Hon. LLD St Francis Xavier Univ., Antigonish, Nova Scotia, 1974. *Address:* Apt 712, 1465 Baseline Road, Ottawa, Ont K2C 3L9, Canada. *Died 29 May 1987.*

**DAVIS, Adm. Sir William (Wellclose),** GCB 1959 (KCB 1956; CB 1952); DSO 1944, and Bar, 1944; DL; *b* 11 Oct. 1901; *s* of late W. S. Davis, Indian Political Service; *m* 1934, Lady Gertrude Elizabeth Phipps (*d* 1985), 2nd *d* of 3rd Marquis of Normanby; two *s* two *d*. *Educ:* Summerfields, Oxford; Osborne and Dartmouth Naval Colls. Midshipman, 1917; Lieut, 1921; Comdr, 1935; Capt., 1940; Rear-Adm., 1950; Acting Vice-Adm. and Vice-Adm., 1953; Adm. 1956, Dep. Dir of Plans and Cabinet Offices, 1940–42; commanded HMS Mauritius, 1943–44; Dir of Under Water Weapons, Admiralty, 1945–46; Imperial Defence Coll., 1947; Chief of Staff to C-in-C Home Fleet, 1948–49. The Naval Sec., Admiralty, 1950–52; Flag Officer 2nd in Command Mediterranean, 1952–54; Vice-Chief of the Naval Staff, Admiralty, 1954–57; Comdr-in-Chief, Home Fleet, and NATO Comdr-in-Chief, Eastern Atlantic Area, 1958–60; First and Principal Naval ADC to the Queen, 1959–60, retired. Vice-Pres., King George's Fund for Sailors; Member: Royal Institution of GB (Vice-Pres.); Royal United Service Institution; European-Atlantic Group (Vice-Pres.); British Atlantic Cttee; Gloucestershire Community Council; President: Gloucestershire Outward Bound; Gloucestershire County Scouts; Forest of Dean District Scouts; Treasurer, Friends of Gloucester Cathedral; Mem., St Helena Assoc.; Past Chm., Cheltenham Ladies' College and various educational authorities. DL Glos 1963. *Recreations:* fishing, shooting. *Address:* Coglan House, Longhope, Glos. *T:* Gloucester 830282. *Clubs:* Naval and Military; Ends of the Earth. *Died 29 Oct. 1987.*

**DAVISON, Sir John Alec B.;** *see* Biggs-Davison.

**DAVISON, His Honour William Norris;** a Circuit Judge (formerly a County Court Judge), 1971–86; *b* 20 Aug. 1919; *s* of late Dr W. H. Davison; *m* 1947, Margaret, *d* of late G. H. Bettinson; one *s* two *d*. *Educ:* King Edward's High School, Birmingham; Trinity College, Dublin. RNVR, 1939–43; Royal Indian Naval Volunteer Reserve, 1943–46. Called to the Bar (Middle Temple), 1949; practised

Midland Circuit, 1949–71. *Recreation:* collecting. *Address:* The Homestead, The Green, Hook Norton, Oxon. *T:* Hook Norton 730136.                                            *Died* 16 *Sept.* 1986.

**DAVITT, Cahir;** President of the High Court, Eire, 1951–66, retired (Hon. Mr Justice Davitt); *b* 15 Aug. 1894; *s* of Michael Davitt and Mary Yore; *m* 1925, Sarah Gertrude Lynch; four *s* one *d. Educ:* O'Connell Sch. and University Coll., Dublin, BA, NUI, 1914; LLB, 1916; Barrister, King's Inns, Dublin, 1916, Bencher, 1927. Judge of the Dail Courts, 1920–22; Judge-Advocate Gen., Irish Free State Defence Forces, 1922–26; Temp. Judge, Circuit Court, 1926–27; Circuit Judge, City and County of Dublin, 1927–45; (Puisne) Judge of the High Court, 1945–51. Mem. of Judiciary Cttee, 1923–24, to advise Irish Free State Executive in relation to the establishment of Courts of Justice under the IFS Constitution; Chairman: Civil Service Compensation Board, 1929–66; Commission of Inquiry into Derating, 1930; Med. Bureau of Road Safety, 1969–74. President: Irish Rugby Football Union, 1936–37; Irish Squash Rackets Assoc., 1936. *Address:* Our Lady's Manor, Dalkey, Co. Dublin. *Clubs:* Milltown Golf, Fitzwilliam Lawn Tennis (Dublin).
                                                       *Died* 1 *March* 1986.

**DAVY, Brig. George Mark Oswald,** CB 1945; CBE 1943; DSO 1941; US Legion of Merit; Gold Cross of Merit with Swords, Poland; Sculptor; Painter of horses in oils and of landscapes and seascapes in watercolours; Vice-President, Chelsea Art Society; Associate Member, National Society of Painters, Sculptors and Printmakers; *b* 22 Sept. 1898; *s* of late Capt. G. C. H. Davy; *m* 1932, Isabel Gwendolen (*d* 1970), *d* of late E. Alan Hay, Bengeo House, Hertford; one *s*. European War, 1914–18, France and Belgium: RFA and RHA; transferred to 3rd Hussars, 1931; Staff Coll., Camberley, 1932–33; Bde Major, 150 Inf. Bde, 1935–36; Company Comdr RMC, Sandhurst 1937–38; Naval Staff Coll., Greenwich, 1939; France and Belgium, 1939–40; Western Desert, 1940–41; Greece, April 1941; commanded 3rd and 7th Armoured Bdes in Desert, 1941; Director of Military Operations GHQ, Middle East, 1942–44; Dep. Asst Chief of Staff (Operations), AFHQ Algiers, 1944; commanded Land Forces Adriatic, 1944–45; War Office representative with the Polish Forces, 1945–47; retd 1948; recommissioned for military service, 1956; retd again 1959. *Publication:* The Seventh and Three Enemies, 1953. *Recreation:* fishing. *Address:* Jordanstone House, Alyth, Blairgowrie, Perthshire. *Clubs:* Cavalry and Guards; New (Edinburgh).
                                                       *Died* 16 *June* 1983.

**DAWES, Charles Ambrose William,** MC 1942; Member of Lloyd's since 1950; Fruit Farmer since 1961; Director, East Kent Packers, 1972–81 (Vice Chairman, 1974–80); *b* 30 March 1919; *s* of Edwyn Sandys Dawes and Joan Prideaux (*née* Selby); *m* 1940, Mary Neame Finn; one *s* three *d. Educ:* Stowe. Joined W. A. Browne & Co., Chartered Accountants, 1938. 2nd Lieut (TA), 97th (Kent Yeomanry) Field Regt, RA, 1939; served in France and Middle East, 1939–42; RA Training Regt, Cromer, 1943–46; Captain, 1942. Joined J. B. Westray & Co. Ltd, 1946: Director, 1949; joined New Zealand Shipping Co. Ltd, 1953: Director, 1955; Dep. Chairman, 1961; Chairman, 1966–70. Dir, 1966–72, Dep. Chm., 1971–72, P&OSN Co. Director: Australian and New Zealand Banking Group Ltd, 1971–76; Mercantile & General Reinsurance Co. Ltd, 1963–; Bain Dawes Group Ltd, 1970–72; Shepherd Neame Ltd, Brewers, Faversham, 1974–; Dawes and Henderson (Agencies) Ltd, 1974–. Hon. Treasurer, King George's Fund for Sailors, 1977– (Dep. Chm., 1970–76); Mem. Gen. Council, Barnardo's, 1973–81 (Hon. Treasurer, 1978–81). *Recreations:* shooting, gardening. *Address:* Mount Ephraim, near Faversham, Kent. *T:* Boughton 310. *Clubs:* Farmers', City of London.                       *Died* 12 *Jan.* 1982.

**DAWNAY, Lt-Col Christopher Payan,** CBE 1946 (OBE 1943; MBE 1940); MVO 1944; *b* 1909; *s* of late Maj.-Gen. Guy P. Dawnay, CB, CMG, DSO, MVO, and Mrs Cecil Dawnay; *m* 1939, Patricia, *d* of Sir Hereward Wake, 13th Bt, CB, CMG, DSO; two *s* two *d. Educ:* Winchester; Magdalen Coll., Oxford. With Dawnay Day & Co. Ltd, Merchant Bankers, 1933–39 and 1946–50. War service with Coldstream Guards and in various staff appointments, 1939–45. Partner, Edward de Stein & Co., Merchant Bankers, 1951–60; Director, Lazard Bros & Co. Ltd, 1960–74; Chairman: Guardian Assurance Co., 1967–68; Guardian Royal Exchange Assurance Co., 1970–74. One of HM Lieutenants, City of London. US Legion of Merit. *Recreations:* fishing, shooting. *Address:* Ropers, Longparish, Andover, Hants. *T:* Longparish 204. *Club:* Brooks's.
                                                       *Died* 29 *Jan.* 1989.

**DAWNAY, Hon. George William ffolkes,** MC 1944; DL; Coldstream Guards; Director, Barclays Bank Ltd, 1956–79; Local Advisory Director, Barclays Bank Ltd, Norwich, retired 1979; *b* 20 April 1909; *s* of 9th Viscount Downe, CMG, DSO and Dorothy, *o c* of Sir William ffolkes, 3rd Bt; *m* 1945, Rosemary Helen (*d* 1969), *d* of late Lord Edward Grosvenor and of late Lady Dorothy Charteris; two *s* two *d. Educ:* Eton. DL Norfolk, 1961–84. *Address:* Hillington Hall,

King's Lynn, Norfolk. *T:* Hillington (0485) 600304.
                                                       *Died* 9 *Aug.* 1990.

**DAWNAY, Captain Oliver Payan,** CVO 1953; *b* 4 April 1920; *s* of late Maj.-General Guy Payan Dawnay, CB, CMG, DSO, MVO; *m* 1st, 1944, Lady Margaret Dorothea Boyle (marr. diss. 1962), *y d* of 8th Earl of Glasgow, DSO; two *s* one *d*; 2nd, 1963, Hon. Iris Irene Adele Peake, *e d* of 1st Viscount Ingleby, PC; one *d. Educ:* Eton; Balliol Coll., Oxford. Parliamentary and Press section, Ministry of Economic Warfare, 1939–40. Served War of 1939–45: Coldstream Guards, 1940–46; Adjt 1st Batt., 1943–44 (despatches 1944); seconded to Foreign Office, Conference Dept, 1945–46; demobilised, as Captain, 1946. Messrs Dawnay Day and Co., Merchant Bankers, 1946–50. Private Secretary and Equerry to Queen Elizabeth the Queen Mother, 1951–56; Extra Equerry, 1956–62. Partner, Grieveson, Grant & Co., Stockbrokers, 1961–80. *Address:* Flat 5, 32 Onslow Square, SW7; Wexcombe House, Marlborough, Wilts. *Clubs:* Brooks's, MCC.                     *Died* 18 *March* 1988.

**DAWNAY, Vice-Adm. Sir Peter,** KCVO 1961 (MVO 1939); CB 1958; DSC 1944; DL; Royal Navy, retired; an Extra Equerry to the Queen since 1958; *b* 14 Aug. 1904; *s* of Maj. Hon. Hugh and Lady Susan Dawnay; *m* 1936, Lady Angela Montagu-Douglas-Scott, *d* of 7th Duke of Buccleuch; one *s* one *d. Educ:* Osborne and Dartmouth. Legion of Merit (USA). In command HMS Saintes and 3rd Destroyer Flotilla, 1950–51; in command HMS Mercury (HM Signal Sch.), 1952–53; in command HMS Glasgow, 1954–56. Deputy Controller of the Navy, Admiralty, 1956–58; Flag Officer, Royal Yachts, 1958–62; retired, 1962. Pres., London Assoc. for the Blind, 1968–. High Sheriff, Hants, 1973; DL Hants 1975. *Address:* The Old Post Cottage, Wield, Alresford, Hants SO24 9RS. *T:* Alton 63041.                                         *Died* 1 *July* 1989.

**DAWSON, Christopher William,** CMG 1947; *b* 31 May 1896; *s* of Rev. H. Dawson, MA, and Tertia Dean; *m* 1924, Jill, *d* of Prof. R. G. McKerron, Aberdeen Univ.; no *c. Educ:* Dulwich Coll.; Brasenose Coll., Oxford. Joined East Surrey Regt, 1915; served in India (NW Frontier) and Mesopotamia; demobilised with rank of Captain, 1919. Joined Malayan Civil Service 1920 and served in various parts of Malaya until 1942. Called to Bar, Gray's Inn, 1929. Secretary for Defence Malaya, 1941–42; interned by Japanese in Singapore, 1942–45; Chief Secretary and Officer Administering the Govt, Sarawak, 1946–50; retired, 1950; Deputy Chief Secretary, British Administration, Eritrea, 1951–52. President: British Assoc. of Malaya, 1957–58; Sarawak Assoc., 1962. *Address:* 11 Festival Court, Chichester, W Sussex. *T:* Chichester 780638.
                                                       *Died* 2 *March* 1983.

**DAWSON, Sir (Hugh Halliday) Trevor,** 3rd Bt *cr* 1920; *b* 6 June 1931; *s* of Sir Hugh Trevor Dawson, 2nd Bt, CBE, and Vera Anne Loch (*d* 1982), *d* of late Sir Frederick Loch Halliday, CIE, MVO; *S* father, 1976; *m* 1955, Caroline Jane, *d* of William Antony Acton; two *s. Educ:* Harrow; RMA, Sandhurst. Joined Scots Guards, 1949; Major 1960; retired 1961. Dir, Arbuthnot Latham Holdings, 1969–81; Chairman: Arbuthnot Securities, 1976–81; Arbuthnot Govt Securities Trust, 1979–81. Mem., Exec. Cttee, Unit Trusts' Assoc., 1980. *Recreations:* racing, shooting. *Heir: s* Hugh Michael Trevor Dawson, *b* 28 March 1956. *Address:* 31 Eaton Square, SW1; China House, Pewsey, Wilts. *Clubs:* White's, Pratt's, Cavalry and Guards, Buck's, Turf, City of London, Royal Aero, MCC; Bembridge Sailing (IoW).                                      *Died* 14 *Feb.* 1983.

**DAWSON, James Lawrence,** CEng, FICE; Director of Civil Engineering Services, Property Services Agency, 1979–83; *b* 1 April 1924; *s* of Albert Lawrence Dawson and Margaret (*née* Howell); *m* 1947, Olive Joan (*née* Turner); three *s. Educ:* Sale High Sch.; Royal Naval Engineering Coll.; City Univ. (BSc). Engineer Cadet and RNVR, 1942–45. Engineer and Agent, West's Piling & Construction Co. Ltd, 1945–47; Civil Engineer, Air Ministry Works Directorate and Ministry of Public Building and Works, various positions in Iraq, Libya, Malta and UK, 1948–72; Suptg Engr, Roskill Commission on Third London Airport, 1968–70; Director of Naval Base Develt, Property Services Agency, 1972–79. *Publications:* papers to Instn of Civil Engrs and other professional bodies. *Recreations:* sailing, tennis, bridge, gardening. *Address:* Property Services Agency, Lunar House, 40 Wellesley Road, Croydon CR9 2EL.                                      *Died* 14 *Feb.* 1984.

**DAWSON, John Alexander,** CBE 1942; FICE; *b* 24 March 1886; *s* of Alexander Dawson, Aberdeen; *m* 1910, Margaret (decd), *er d* of late Alexander M. Cruickshank, Bloemfontein, SA; two *s* one *d. Educ:* Robert Gordon's Coll., Aberdeen; Aberdeen and Glasgow Universities, BSc (Engineering) Glasgow. Entered Admiralty as Asst Civil Engineer, 1912; served at Portsmouth, Admiralty, Ostend (1919) and Rosyth; transferred to Air Ministry, 1921; served at Air Ministry, Inland Area, Singapore, Coastal Command; Chief Engineer Air Defence of Great Britain; Chief Engineer Bomber Command; Dep. Director of Works, 1938; Director of Works, Air Ministry, 1940–46, Ministry of Civil Aviation, 1946–48; Chief Resident Engineer, London Airport, 1948–54, retired 1954. *Address:*

Belle Causey, Bishops Tawton Road, Barnstaple, North Devon EX32 9EF. *T:* Barnstaple 71112. *Died* 11 *Feb.* 1985.

**DAWSON, Sir Trevor;** *see* Dawson, Sir H. H. T.

**DAWSON, Wilfred;** retired; Under Secretary, Director, Manpower and Management Services, Departments of the Environment and Transport, 1978–80; *b* 11 Jan. 1923; *s* of Walter and Ivy Dawson; *m* 1944, Emily Louise Mayhew; two *d. Educ:* Riley High Sch., Hull. Civil Service: Air Min., 1939–49; Min. of Town and Country Planning, 1949; Principal, Min. of Housing and Local Govt, 1963; Asst Sec., DoE, 1970; Under-Sec., DoE, 1974–76; Under Sec., Dept of Transport, 1976–78. *Recreations:* walking, woodworking. *Address:* Reydon Grange, Wangford, Beccles, Suffolk.
*Died* 17 *March* 1984.

**DAY, James Wentworth;** FRSA; author, journalist and publicist; Chairman and Managing Director of News Publicity Ltd; *b* Marsh House, Exning, Suffolk, 21 April 1899; *s* of late J. T. Wentworth Day, Lacies Court, Abingdon, Berks, and Martha Ethel Staples of Landwade Hall, Exning and Wicken; *m* 1943, Marion Edith, *d* of late Hamish McLean, Mount Hutt Estates, S Island, NZ, and of Mrs Hamish McLean, Christchurch, NZ; one *d. Educ:* Newton Coll.; Cambridge (extra mural; English under Prof. Sir Arthur Quiller-Couch). Served European War, 1917–18; Daily Express, Publicity Manager and personal assistant to Lord Beaverbrook, 1923; Asst Editor Country Life, 1925; acting Editor of the Field, 1930–31; Dramatic Critic, Sunday Express, 1932, and Editor of English Life; as Personal Representative of Lady Houston, 1933–34, was on exec. of Houston-Mount Everest flight, negotiated purchase of Saturday Review (editor, 1934), conducted High Tory campaign in nine bye-elections. Editor, Illustrated Sporting and Dramatic News, 1935–36–37; Propaganda Adviser to Egyptian Government, 1938–39; Publicity Adviser to Anglo-Turk Relief Cttee, 1940; War Correspondent in France for Daily Mail and BBC, 1940, and with minesweepers; Near East Correspondent to BBC, 1941. Invalided out, 1943; fought press and parly campaign against extravagance and injustices of War Agricl Exec. Cttee system, which led to release of 17,000 acres of govt controlled farms in E Anglia and setting up of Land Appeal Tribunals; drafted Amendment to Pests Act 1954, which made it criminal offence to spread myxomatosis. Dir-Gen., 1100th Anniversary Festival, Bury St Edmunds. Contested (C) Hornchurch Div. of Essex, 1950 and 1951 (reducing Labour maj. from 11,000 to 134 votes). Editor, East Anglia Life, 1962–66; Country Correspondent, Daily Mail. Member Society of Authors; Member Inst. of Journalists; owns a large part of Adventurers' Fen and a few good Old Masters, mainly of the Wentworth family. Founded Essex Wildfowlers' Assoc., 1924; Hon. Life Mem., Wildfowlers' Assoc. of GB and Ireland. *Publications:* The Lure of Speed, 1929; The Life of Sir Henry Segrave, 1930; Speed, the Life of Sir Malcolm Campbell, 1931; My Greatest Adventure (for Sir Malcolm Campbell), 1932; Kaye Don—the Man, 1934; The Modern Fowler, 1934; A Falcon on St Paul's, 1935; King George V as a Sportsman, 1935; Sporting Adventure, 1937; The Dog in Sport, 1938; Sport in Egypt, 1939; Farming Adventure, 1943; Harvest Adventure, 1945; Gamblers' Gallery, 1948; Wild Wings, 1949; Coastal Adventure, 1949; Inns of Sport, 1949; Marshland Adventure, 1950; Broadland Adventure, 1951; The New Yeomen of England, 1952; Rural Revolution, 1952; The Modern Shooter, 1953; Norwich and the Broads, in quest of the Inn, 1953; The Wisest Dogs in the World, 1954; A History of the Fens, 1954; Ghosts and Witches, 1954; They Walk the Wild Places, 1956; Poison on the Land, 1957; The Angler's Pocket Book, 1957; The Dog Lover's Pocket Book, 1957; Lady Houston, DBE—The Woman Who Won the War, 1958; A Ghost Hunter's Game Book, 1958; Newfoundland—The Fortress Isle (for Newfoundland Govt; travelled further north than any British writer), 1959; HRH Princess Marina, Duchess of Kent (The First Authentic Life Story), 1962; The Queen Mother's Family Story, 1967 (republished 1979); Portrait of the Broads, 1967; In Search of Ghosts, 1969; Rum Owd Boys, 1975. Edited Best Sporting Stories (anthology). Contributions to Great Georgians; The English Counties; 50 Great Ghost Stories, 1966; 50 Great Horror Stories, 1969; Treasures of Britain (Readers Digest), 1968; Essex Ghosts, 1974; Norwich Through the Ages, 1976; King's Lynn and Sandringham Through the Ages, 1977; James Wentworth Day Book of Essex, 1980; has broadcast and written many articles on politics, the Near East, field sports, natural history, agriculture, dogs, flying, motoring, racing, shipping, etc, in the leading newspapers and journals. *Recreations:* taking the Left Wing intelligentsia at its own valuation; shooting (especially wildfowling), riding, fishing, sailing, natural history, and old furniture. *Address:* Ingatestone, Essex. *T:* Ingatestone 3055. *Clubs:* United Oxford & Cambridge University, Press, 1900.
*Died* 4 *Jan.* 1983.

**DAYMOND, Douglas Godfrey;** Civil Service Commissioner, 1975–80; *b* 23 Nov. 1917; *s* of Samuel Kevern and Minnie Daymond; *m* 1945, Laura Vivien (*née* Selley); one *s* one *d. Educ:* Saltash Grammar Sch.; London Univ. LLB Hons 1947. Called to Bar, Gray's Inn,

1952. Inland Revenue, 1935; Customs and Excise, 1939; War Service with Royal Engineers in Egypt, Greece and Crete, POW 1941–45; Inland Revenue, 1947; Asst Sec., Royal Commn on Taxation, 1951–55; Sec., Tithe Redemption Commn, 1959–60; Dep. Dir, CS Selection Bd, 1970; Under-Sec., Civil Service Dept, 1973. *Recreations:* gardening, theatre, music. *Address:* 2 Fenten Park, Saltash, Cornwall PL12 6DQ. *T:* Saltash (07555) 5081; Flat 73, Fort Picklecombe, near Millbrook, Cornwall PL12 6DQ. *T:* Plymouth (0752) 845081. *Died* 27 *Oct.* 1990.

**DAYSH, Prof. George Henry John,** CBE 1973; MLitt Oxon; DCL; Deputy Vice-Chancellor of University of Newcastle upon Tyne and Professor of Geography in the University, 1963–66; Emeritus Professor, since Oct. 1966 (Professor of Geography, King's College, University of Durham, Newcastle upon Tyne, 1943–63; Sub Rector, King's College, 1955–63); *b* 21 May 1901; *s* of Alfred John Daysh and Margaret (*née* Campbell); *m* 1927, Sheila Guthrie (*d* 1971), *er d* of Dr A. F. A. Fairweather; one *s* one *d. Educ:* Eggars Grammar Sch.; University College, Reading; Wadham Coll., Oxford. Housemaster, Pocklington Sch., E. Yorks, 1924–27; Lecturer in Geography, Bedford Coll., University of London, 1927–29; Lecturer-in-charge, Dept of Geography, 1930–38, Reader of Geography, 1938–43, King's Coll., Newcastle upon Tyne. Seconded for special duties with Dist Comr for special area of Cumberland, 1938; Major, 4th Northumberland Bn HG, 1940–43; Senior Research Officer, Ministry of Town and Country Planning, 1943–45. Member of Exec. of NE Development Board, 1934–39, Vice-President NE Industrial and Development Assoc.; Chairman Research Cttee of NEIDA; Secretary Commn on Ports of International Geographic Union, 1947–51; Chairman University of Durham Matriculation and Sch. Examination Board, 1953–63. Part-time Member Northern Gas Board, 1956–70. Chairman, Newcastle upon Tyne Hospital Management Cttee, 1968–71. Visiting Prof. Fouad I Univ., 1951. Chairman, Triennial Grants Cttee, University College of Sierra Leone, 1960. Consultant to Cumberland Development Council, 1966–69. Chm., Tyne Tees Television, 1968–71; Dep. Chm., Trident Television Ltd, 1970–72; Dir, Solway Chemicals Ltd. Hon. DCL (Newcastle), 1964. FRSA; FRGS (Victoria Medal 1972). *Publications:* Southampton-Points in its Development, 1928; A Survey of Industrial Facilities of the North-East Coast, 1936 (rev., 1940 and 1949); West Cumberland with Alston-a Survey of Industrial Facilities, 1938 (revised 1951); (ed) Studies in Regional Planning, 1949; (ed) Physical Land Classification of North-East England, 1950; (with J. S Symonds) West Durham, 1953; (ed) A Survey of Whitby, 1958; contribs to Geographical Journal, Geography, Economic Geography, Geographical Review, etc. *Recreations:* gardening, field sports. *Address:* 2 Dunkirk Terrace, Corbridge, Northumberland. *T:* Corbridge-on-Tyne 2154. *Died* 28 *April* 1987.

**DEACON, Lt-Col Edmund Henry;** JP; *b* 1902; *s* of late Col E. Deacon, DL, Sloe House, Halstead; *m* 1927, Betty (*d* 1979), *d* of late Brig.-Gen. J. E. C. Livingstone-Learmonth, CMG, DSO; one *d. Educ:* Wellington; Trinity Coll., Cambridge. Master Newmarket and Thurlow Hounds, 1934–42; Joint Master East Essex Hounds, 1947–50. Commanding 15 Bn Essex Home Guard, 1952; Chairman of Governors of Felsted Sch., 1952–65. DL 1953–78, JP 1954, Essex. *Address:* The Old Rectory, Oxhill, Warwick CV35 0QR. *Club:* Cavalry and Guards. *Died* 20 *Oct.* 1982.

**DEACON, Sir George (Edward Raven),** Kt 1971; CBE 1954; FRS 1944; FRSE 1957; FRAS; FRGS; DSc; Director, National Institute of Oceanography, 1949–71; Foreign Member, Swedish Royal Academy of Sciences, 1958; *b* 21 March 1906; *m* 1940, Margaret Elsa Jeffries (*d* 1966); one *d. Educ:* City Boys' Sch., Leicester; King's Coll., London. FKC. Vis. Prof. of Chemistry of the Environment, KCL, 1974. Served on Scientific Staff of the Discovery Cttee, in England and in the Royal Research Ships William Scoresby and Discovery II, 1927–39. Governor: Bridewell Royal Hosp., 1958–; King Edward's Sch., Witley, 1958–; Charterhouse Sch., 1959–81. Royal Society's National Committees: Oceanic Research, 1959–81 (Chm.); Geodesy and Geophysics, 1949–71 (Chm., 1955–60); Internat. Geophysical Year, 1953–60; Antarctic Research, 1959–81. Pres., Royal Inst. of Navigation, 1961–64; Vice-Pres., RGS, 1965–70. Hon. Member: Royal Soc. of NZ, 1964; Marine Biol Assoc. of UK, 1975; Scottish Marine Biol Assoc., 1977 (Vice-Pres., 1984); RMetS, 1982. Hon. DSc: Liverpool, 1961; Leicester, 1970. Polar Medal, 1942; Alexander Agassiz Medal, US National Academy of Sciences, 1962; Royal Medal, Royal Soc., 1969; Founder's Medal, RGS, 1971; Scottish Geographical Medal, 1972. *Publications:* Oceanographical papers in the Discovery Reports, etc. *Address:* Flitwick House, Milford, Surrey. *T:* Godalming 5929. *Died* 16 *Nov.* 1984.

**DEADMAN, Ronald Thomas A.;** Tutor in Adult Education, Brent and Ealing, since 1985; *b* 28 May 1919; *s* of Thomas Deadman and Margaret Healey; *m* 1952, Joan Evans; no *c. Educ:* Hinguar Street Sch., Shoeburyness; Oakley Coll., Cheltenham. Served RAF, 1937–45. Teaching, 1950–66; Features Editor, The Teacher,

1966–67; Editor: Everyweek, 1967–68; Teachers' World, 1968–76. Leverhulme Res. Fellow, 1975–77. Mem., Press Council, 1969–75. Watchkeeper, M/T Aro, River Blackwater, 1977–78; Fishery Bailiff, Barn Elms Reservoir, 1978–79; Fishery Warden, Kempton Park Reservoir, 1980–84. *Publications:* Enjoying English, Bk 1, 1966; Bk 2, 1968; Bk 3 (Contrasts), 1971; Bk 4 (Perception), 1972; (novels for children): The Happening, 1968; Wanderbodies, 1972; The Pretenders, 1972; (ed, short stories) The Friday Story, 1966; Words in Your Ear, vols 1 and 2, 1972; Going My Way, vols 1, 2 and 3, 1973; (with Arthur Razzell) Ways of Knowing, 1977; Grandma George, 1977; Breadwinners, 1978; Firebirds, 1979; (ed) Round the World Folk Tales, Bks 1–12, 1981; English Language Tests, vols 1–3, 1982; contribs to New Statesman, The Times, British Clinical Jl, Guardian, BBC, Where magazine, Education and Training. *Recreation:* brooding. *Address:* Flat 1, Dawley House, 91 Uxbridge Road, Ealing, W5. *T:* 01–840 3627. *Club:* British Legion.
*Died May* 1988.

**DEAKIN, Rt. Rev. Thomas Carlyle Joseph Robert Hamish;** Bishop Suffragan of Tewkesbury, since 1973; *b* 16 Feb. 1917; *s* of Rev.Thomas Carlyle Deakin (Rector of Uley, Glos, 1943–57), and Harriet Herries Deakin; *m* 1942, Marion, *d* of E. J. and Mrs E. Anson Dyer, Stratford Abbey, Stroud; one *s* (and one *s* decd). *Educ:* Wadham Coll., Oxford (MA); Wells Theological Coll. Deacon 1940, priest 1941, Dio. of Gloucester. Curate of St Lawrence, Stroud, 1940–44; Vicar of Holy Trinity, Forest of Dean, 1944–49; Vicar of Charlton Kings, 1949–73; Rural Dean of Cheltenham, 1963–73; Hon. Canon of Gloucester, 1966–73. *Address:* Green Acre, 166 Hempsted Lane, Gloucester GL2 6LG. *T:* Gloucester 21824.
*Died 3 Aug.* 1985.

**DEAN, Barbara Florence;** Headmistress, Godolphin and Latymer School, Hammersmith, 1974–85; *b* 1 Sept. 1924; *d* of Albert Sidney and Helen Catherine Dean. *Educ:* North London Collegiate Sch.; Girton Coll., Cambridge (MA); London Inst. of Educn (Teachers' Dipl.). Asst History Mistress, Roedean Sch., 1947–49; Godolphin and Latymer School: Asst History Mistress and Head of Dept, 1949–70; Deputy Headmistress, 1970–73. *Address:* 9 Stuart Avenue, Ealing, W5 3QJ. *T:* 01–992 8324.
*Died 22 Sept.* 1989.

**DEAN, Col Donald John,** VC 1918; OBE 1961; TD; DL; JP; *b* 1897; *m* 1923, Marjorie, *d* of late W. R. Wood; one *s* one *d*. Served European War, 1914–18 (despatches, VC); War of 1939–45 (despatches). JP 1951, DL 1957, Kent. Comdr Royal Danish Order of the Dannebrog. *Address:* 1 Park Avenue, Sittingbourne, Kent ME10 1QX.
*Died 9 Dec.* 1985.

**DEAN, Sir John (Norman),** Kt 1957; *b* 13 Dec. 1899; *s* of late George Dean; *m* 1st, 1922, Ivy Dorothy (marr. diss. 1935), *d* of Ernest William Andrews; one *s* decd; 2nd, 1935, Charlotte Helen Audrey (*d* 1973), *d* of Thomas Atkinson Walker; 3rd, 1974, Isabel Bothwell-Thomson. *Educ:* Felsted; King's Coll., London University. BSc London (Hons Chemistry). Flying Officer, RNAS and RAF, 1916–19. Chairman: The Telegraph Construction and Maintenance Co. Ltd, 1954–61; Submarine Cables Ltd, 1960–63; Asst to President, General Cable Corporation of New York, USA, 1964–69, retd. ARIC; FIRI; Comp. IEE. *Publications:* various, to technical and scientific bodies. *Address:* Kiln Ridge, Ide Hill, Sevenoaks, Kent TN14 6JH. *T:* Ide Hill 245.
*Died 5 Jan.* 1988.

**DEAN, Rt. Rev. Ralph Stanley;** Rector, Church of the Redeemer, Greenville, South Carolina, 1979–81, retired; *b* London, 1913; *m* 1939, Irene Florence, *er d* of late Alfred Bezzant Wakefield. *Educ:* Roan Sch., Greenwich; Wembley County Sch.; London Coll. of Divinity, BD London 1938; ALCD 1938; MTh 1944. Deacon 1938; Priest 1939; Curate of St Mary, Islington, 1938–41; Curate-in-charge, St Luke, Watford, 1941–45; Chaplain and Tutor, London Coll. of Divinity, 1945–47, Vice-Principal, 1947–51; Principal, Emmanuel Coll., Saskatoon, Canada, 1951–56; Incumbent of Sutherland and Hon. Canon of Saskatoon, 1955–56; Bishop of Cariboo, 1957; Anglican Executive Officer, 1964–69; Archbishop of Cariboo and Metropolitan of British Columbia, 1971–73; Theological Consultant, Christ Church, Greenville, SC, 1973–79. Episcopal Secretary, Lambeth Conference, 1968. Hon. DD: Wycliffe Coll., Toronto, 1953; Emmanuel Coll., Saskatoon, 1957; Anglican Theolog. Coll., Vancouver, 1965; Huron Coll., Ont, 1965; Hon. STD, Hartford Coll., Conn, 1966. *Publications:* In the Light of the Cross, 1961; article on Anglican Communion, Encyclopædia Britannica. *Address:* South Carolina Episcopal Retirement Cty, Still Hopes, Box 169, West Columbia, South Carolina 29169, USA.
*Died 23 Aug.* 1987.

**DEAN, Dr William John Lyon,** OBE 1959; Chairman, Commission of Enquiry into the Isle of Man Fishing Industry, 1982–84; *b* 4 Nov. 1911; *s* of William Dean, Lossiemouth; *m* 1st, 1938, Ellen Maud Mary (*d* 1977), *d* of Charles Weatherill, CBE; two *s* one *d*; 2nd, 1979, Rachel Marian, *e d* of Humphrey and Rebecca Lloyd, Wotton-under-Edge, Glos. *Educ:* Elgin Academy; Aberdeen Univ. (MB, ChB). Served RAF, 1935–43. Gen. med. practice, 1943–66. Provost of Lossiemouth, 1949–58; Chm., Jt CC of Moray and Nairn,

1964–71; Mem. NE Regional Hosp. Bd, 1947–58. Member: Cttee for Scotland and Northern Ireland White Fish Authority, 1954–81; White Fish Authority, 1963–81; Mem., Herring Industry Bd, 1963, Chm. 1971, until dissolution in 1981. *Publication:* Safety at Sea in Fishing Vessels, 1969 (FAO/ILO/WHO). *Recreation:* fishing (lobster, salmon, trout). *Address:* 6 Ravelston Heights, Edinburgh EH4 3LX. *T:* 031–332 9172.
*Died 8 March* 1990.

**DEARE, Ronald Frank Robert,** CMG 1988; Minister and UK Permanent Representative to UN Food and Agricultural Organisation, Rome, 1985–88, retired; *b* 9 Oct. 1927; *s* of late Albert and Lilian Deare; *m* 1952, Iris Mann; one *s*. *Educ:* Wellington Sch., Somerset. RAF Service, 1945–48. CO 1948; Second Sec., UK Commn, Singapore, 1959; CO, 1962; Dept of Technical Cooperation, 1963; Principal, Min. of Overseas Develt, 1965; Private Sec. to Minister of Overseas Develt, 1971; Asst Sec., 1973; Counsellor (Overseas Develt), Washington, and Alternate Exec. Dir, World Bank, 1976–79; Head of W Indian and Atlantic Dept, FCO, 1980–81; Head of Central and Southern Africa Dept, ODA, FCO, 1981–83; Head of Bilateral Co-ord. and Consultancies Dept, ODA, FCO, 1983–84. *Recreations:* reading, gardening. *Address:* Conifers, Oakhurst, Haywards Heath, West Sussex RH16 1PD. *T:* Haywards Heath 450590.
*Died 19 Aug.* 1989.

**DEARNLEY, Gertrude,** MD, BS London; FRCOG; Gynæcological Surgeon, retired; *b* 17 Aug. 1884; *d* of late Rev. T. W. Dearnley, MA Oxon. *Educ:* Liverpool High Sch.; London (Royal Free Hospital) School of Medicine for Women. *Recreation:* gardening.
*Died 14 March* 1982.

**DEAS, (James) Stewart,** MA, BMus, Hon. FTCL; James Rossiter Hoyle Professor of Music in the University of Sheffield, 1948–68, Emeritus Professor, since 1969; Dean of the Faculty of Arts, University of Sheffield, 1955–58; *b* 19 June 1903; *e s* of John Mackenzie Deas, Asst Keeper HM General Register House, Edinburgh and Elizabeth Bryce Cooper; *m* 1936, Hilda Jamieson; one *s* two *d*. *Educ:* George Watson's Coll.; Edinburgh Univ. MA 1924, BMus 1929, Bucher Scholar, 1926–30, in Berlin with Georg Szell, and Basle. Studied with Sir Donald Tovey and Felix Weingartner. Conductor Edinburgh Opera Co., 1931–33; music critic, Glasgow Evening Times, 1934–35; Director of South African Coll. of Music and Prof. of Music, University of Cape Town, 1935–38; war service Foreign Office and BBC (Caversham); music critic, The Scotsman, London, 1939–44, Edinburgh (Editorial Staff), 1944–48; Conductor Edinburgh Chamber Orchestra, 1946–48; Member BBC Scottish Music Advisory Cttee, 1947–48; Member Council, Programme Cttee, Edinburgh International Festival, 1946–48; has been Guest Conductor of various orchestras including Hallé (series of four concerts for Barbirolli), London Symphony (début, Albert Hall, 1930), Royal Philharmonic, BBC Scottish, Cape Town Municipal and Hovingham Festival. Conductor, Sheffield Chamber Orchestra, 1951–68; Chairman, Sheffield Bach Society, 1959–63. Contributor, weekly music page, Country Life, 1966–73. Hon. Music Adviser, Southern Orchestral Concert Soc., 1979–83 (Vice Pres. 1983). *Publications:* In Defence of Hanslick, 1940, 2nd edn 1973; Or Something, 1941; contrib. symposium, Felix Weingartner, 1976; articles in Music and Letters and other periodicals; occasional contribs to Country Life and Supplement of Oxford English Dictionary. *Address:* 1 The Slade, Froxfield, near Petersfield, Hants. *T:* Hawkley 346. *Club:* Savile.
*Died 18 May* 1985.

**de BEAUVOIR, Simone (L. E. M. B.);** *see* Beauvoir.

**de BEER, Esmond Samuel,** CBE 1969; FBA 1965; FSA, FRSL, FRHistSoc; historical scholar, specialising in seventeenth-century English history; engaged in editing John Locke correspondence; *b* 15 Sept. 1895; *s* of I. S. de Beer and Emily, *d* of Bendix Hallenstein, Dunedin, NZ. *Educ:* Mill Hill Sch.; New Coll., Oxford (MA); University College, London (MA). Studied under late Sir Charles Firth. A Trustee, National Portrait Gallery, 1959–67. Independent Member, Reviewing Cttee on Export of Works of Art, 1965–70. Fellow University College, London, 1967. Hon. Fellow: New Coll., Oxford; Warburg Inst.; Hon. DLitt (Durham, Oxford); Hon. LittD (Otago). Hon. Vice-Pres., the Historical Association; Pres., Hakluyt Society, 1972–78 (Hon. Vice-Pres., 1966); Vice-Pres., Cromwell Assoc., 1980. *Publications:* first complete edition of Diary of John Evelyn, 1955; (ed) The Correspondence of John Locke, vols I-VII, 1976–82; articles and reviews in learned periodicals, etc. *Address:* Stoke House, Stoke Hammond, Milton Keynes MK17 9BN. *Club:* Athenæum.
*Died 3 Oct.* 1990.

**de BROGLIE,** 7th Duc; **Louis Victor de Broglie;** Member of the Institut de France, Académie Française since 1944, Académie des Sciences since 1933; Professor, Faculté des Sciences, Paris, since 1932; Foreign Member Royal Society (London) since 1953; *b* Dieppe, 15 Aug. 1892; *s* of Victor, Duc de Broglie; *S* brother, Maurice, 1960; unmarried. *Educ:* Lycée Janson de Sailly, Paris. Licencié ès Lettres, 1910; Licencié ès Sciences, 1913; served Radio-télégraphie Militaire, 1914–19; Docteur ès Sciences, 1924; Maître de Conférences, Faculté des Sciences, Paris, 1928. Permanent Sec., Académie des Sciences, 1942–75. Prizes include: Nobel Prize for Physics, 1929; Kalinga Prize, 1952. *Publications:* Thèse de doctorat sur la théorie des quanta, 1924; (with Maurice de Broglie) Introduction à l'étude des rayons X et gamma, 1928; La physique nouvelle et les quanta, matiére et lumiére, 1937; Continu et discontinu, 1941; Physique et micro-physique, 1947; Savants et découvertes, 1951; Nouvelles perspectives en microphysique, 1957; Sur les sentiers de la science, 1966; La réinterpretation de la mécanique ondulatoire, 1972; Recherches d'un demi-siècle (souvenirs), 1976; Jalons pour une nouvelle microphysique, 1978. *Address:* 94 Perronet, 92 Neuilly-sur-Seine, France. *T:* Maillot 76.09. *Died 19 March 1987.*

**de BUNSEN, Sir Bernard,** Kt 1962; CMG 1957; MA Oxon; Principal of Chester College, Chester, 1966–71; *b* 24 July 1907; *s* of late L. H. G. de Bunsen, and late Victoria de Bunsen (*née* Buxton); *m* 1975, Joan Allington Harmston, MBE. *Educ:* Leighton Park Sch.; Balliol Coll., Oxford. Schoolmaster, Liverpool Public Elementary Schools, 1930–34; Asst Director of Education, Wiltshire CC, 1934–38; HM Inspector of Schools, Ministry of Education, 1938–46; Director of Education, Palestine, 1946, until withdrawal of British administration, 1948; Professor of Education, Makerere University College, East Africa, 1948, acting Principal, Aug. 1949, Principal, 1950–64, Hon. Fellow, 1968. Vice-Chancellor of University of East Africa, 1963–65; Chairman: Africa Educational Trust, 1967–87; Archbishops' Working Party on Future of Theological Colleges, 1967–68; Africa Bureau, 1971–77; Council for Aid to African Students, 1976–; Vice-President: The Anti-Slavery Soc., 1975–; Royal African Soc., 1977. Hon LLD St Andrews, 1963. *Address:* 3 Prince Arthur Road, NW3. *T:* 071–435 3521. *Died 4 June 1990.*

**de CANDOLE, Eric Armar Vully,** CMG 1952; CBE 1950; MA; Sudan Political Service (retired); *b* 14 Sept. 1901; *e s* of late Rev. Armar Corry Vully de Candole, Rector of Ayot Saint Lawrence, Hertfordshire and late Edith Hodgson; *m* 1932, Marian Elizabeth Pender, *d* of Maj. H. Constable Roberts, DSO, MVO; three *s. Educ:* Colet Court; Aldenham Sch.; Worcester Coll., Oxford (Exhibitioner). Class II Modern History, 1923, BA 1924, MA 1946. Joined Sudan Political Service, 1923; served in Education Dept as Tutor, Gordon Coll., 1923–27; Acting Warden, 1927–28; Berber, Khartoum and Darfur Provinces as Dist Comr and Magistrate, 1928–36; Resident, Dar Masalit, 1936–44; Bimbashi, SADF, 1940–44; Dep.-Governor, Northern Province, 1944–46; seconded to British Military Administration as Chief Secretary, Cyrenaica, 1946–48; Chief Administrator, Somalia, 1948; Chief Administrator, Cyrenaica, 1948–49; HBM's Resident in Cyrenaica, 1949–51. With Kuwait Oil Co. Ltd, 1952–66, BP Co. Ltd, 1966–69. Order of the Nile, Egypt (4th class), 1934; Order of Istiqlal, Libya (1st class), 1954. *Publications:* The Life and Times of King Idris of Libya, 1988; articles on Middle East. *Recreations:* gardening, travel. *Address:* Shootwood, Burley, Hants. *T:* Burley 2330. *Died 7 July 1989.*

**de CLIFFORD,** 26th Baron *cr* 1299; **Edward Southwell Russell,** OBE 1955; TD; psc; Colonel (retired) REME; *b* 30 Jan. 1907; *o s* of 25th Baron and Evelyn Victoria Anne, *d* of Walter Robert Chandler (she *m* 2nd, 1913, Capt. Arthur Roy Stock (*d* 1915); 3rd, George Vernon Tate, MC); *S* father, 1909; *m* 1st, 1926, Dorothy Evelyn Meyrick (marr. diss. 1973); two *s*; 2nd, 1973, Mina Margaret, *o d* of George Edward Sands and Comtesse Sands de Sainte Croix. *Educ:* Eton; Engineering Coll. of London Univ. *Heir:* *s* Hon. John Edward Southwell Russell [*b* 8 June 1928; *m* 1959, Bridget Jennifer, *yr d* of Duncan Robertson, Llangollen, Denbs]. *Address:* The Birches, Silvington, Cleobury Mortimer, Kidderminster, Worcs. *Died 3 Jan. 1982.*

**DE COURCY-IRELAND, Lt-Col Gerald Blakeney,** LVO 1917; MC 1916; The Worcestershire Regt; *b* 1895; *m* 1924, Helen Beresford, *e d* of late John Stapleton-Martin, MA, barrister-at-law, and late Mrs Stapleton-Martin, Wood Hall, Norton, Worcester; one *d. Educ:* Sherborne; Clare Coll., Cambridge. Temp. 2nd Lieut King's Royal Rifle Corps, 1914; temp. Lieut 1915; temp. Captain, 1916; Acting Major, 1917; Adjutant, 9th Service Batt., 1918; relinquished Commission, 1920; Lieut The Worcestershire Regt, 1916; Captain, 1925; Major, 1938; retired pay, 1946, with hon. rank of Lt-Col. *Recreation:* shooting. *Address:* North Lodge, High Street, Newick, East Sussex BN8 4LG. *T:* Newick 3605. *Died 28 March 1986.*

**DEDIJER, Vladimir,** DJur, MA Oxon; Order of Liberation, of Yugoslavia, etc; Yugoslav Author; *b* 4 Feb. 1914; *m* 1st, Olga Popović (*d* 1943); one *d* (one *s* decd); 2nd, 1944, Vera Krizman; one *s* one *d* (and one *s* decd). *Educ:* Belgrade Univ. Served War from 1941, Tito's Army, Lieut-Colonel; Yugoslav Delegate to Peace Conference, Paris, 1946, and to UN General Assemblies, 1945, 1946, 1948, 1949, 1951, 1952. Member Central Cttee, League of Communists of Yugoslavia, 1952–54, when expelled (defended right

of M. Djilas to free speech, 1954; sentenced to 6 months on probation, 1955). Prof. of Modern History, Belgrade Univ., 1954–55. Simon Senior Fellow, Manchester Univ., 1960; Research Fellow, St Antony's Coll., Oxford, 1962–63; Research Associate, Harvard Univ., 1963–64; Visiting Prof.: Cornell Univ., 1964–65; MIT, 1969; Brandeis, 1970; Michigan, 1971, 1973, 1974, 1982–83, 1987. Hon. Fellow, Manchester Univ. President International War Crimes Tribunal, 1966; Hon. Pres., Internat. Tribunal on Afghanistan, 1981. Member, Serbian Acad. of Science. *Publications:* Partisan Diary, 1945; Notes from the United States, 1945; Paris Peace Conference, 1948; Yugoslav-Albanian Relations, 1949; Tito, 1952; Military Conventions, 1960; The Beloved Land, 1960; Road to Sarajevo, 1966; The Battle Stalin Lost, 1969; History of Jugoslavia, 1972; History of Spheres of Influence, 1979; Novi prilozi za biografiju Josipa-Broza Tita, 1982 (New Documents for a Biography of J. B. Tito; banned in Army Libraries in Yugoslavia); Vatican-Jasenovac, 1987; contrib. to Acta Scandinavica. *Address:* Sipar 3, 51475 Savudrija, Istria, Yugoslavia. *T:* 053–59–504. *Died 1 Dec. 1990.*

**DEE, Philip Ivor,** CBE 1946 (OBE 1943); FRS 1941; MA Cantab; Professor of Natural Philosophy at University of Glasgow, 1943–72, later Professor Emeritus; *b* Stroud, Glos, 8 April 1904; *s* of Albert John Dee, Stroud; *m* 1929, Phyllis Elsie Tyte; two *d. Educ:* Marling Sch., Stroud; Sidney Sussex Coll., Cambridge (Scholar). Stokes Student at Pembroke Coll., Cambridge, 1930–33; Lecturer in Physics at Cavendish Laboratory and Fellow of Sidney Sussex Coll., Cambridge, 1934–43; Superintendent, Tele-communications Research Establishment, Ministry of Aircraft Production, 1939–45. Advisory Council DSIR, 1947–52. Hughes Medal of Royal Society, 1952. Hon. DSc Univ. of Strathclyde, 1980. *Publications:* scientific papers in Proceedings of Royal Society, etc. *Address:* Speedwell, Buchanan Castle Estate, Drymen, Stirlingshire. *T:* Drymen 60283. *Died 17 April 1983.*

**DEER, Mrs Olive Gertrude;** Member of Grimsby Borough Council, 1964–67; *b* Grimsby, 31 July 1897; *m* 1916, George Deer, OBE (*d* 1974); one *s* one *d. Educ:* Barcroft Street Sch., Cleethorpes, Lincs. Member: Min. of Labour Exchange Cttees, 1921–45; Bd of Guardians, 1922–25; Bracebridge Mental Hosp. Cttee, 1933–47; Lincoln City Council, 1945–49; Sheffield Regional Hosp. Bd, 1948–50; Bd of Nat. Hosp., Queen Square, 1950; S Eastern Metrop. Regional Hosp. Bd, 1957. Dir, 1940–50, Chm., 1946–48, Lincoln Co-operative Soc. Alderman, LCC, 1952–58; Councillor, LCC (Shoreditch and Finsbury), 1958–64. Chm. LCC Welfare Cttee, 1955–62; Chm. of the London County Council, 1962–63. *Address:* Medina, Carlton Road, Manby, Louth, Lincs. *T:* S Cockerington 386. *Died 20 April 1983.*

**de FERRANTI, Basil Reginald Vincent Ziani;** Member (C) Hampshire Central, European Parliament, since 1984 (Hampshire West, 1979–84) (a Vice-President, 1979–82); Hon. President, Ferranti International Signal plc, since 1988 (Chairman, Ferranti, 1982–87); *b* 2 July 1930; *yr s* of Sir Vincent de Ferranti, MC, FIEE, and of Dorothy H. C. Wilson; *m* 1st, 1956, Susan Sara (from whom he obtained a divorce, 1963; she *m* 1963, Peter Henriques), *d* of late Christopher and Lady Barbara Gore; three *s*; 2nd, 1964, Simone (marr. diss. 1971; she *m* 1971, Sir Frederick Archibald Warner, GCVO, KCMG), *d* of late Col and of Mrs H. J. Nangle; one *d*; 3rd, 1971, Jocelyn Hilary Mary, *d* of late Wing Comdr and Mrs A. T. Laing. *Educ:* Eton; Trinity Coll., Cambridge. Served 4th/7th Royal Dragoon Guards, 1949–50. Man., Domestic Appliance Dept, Ferranti Ltd, 1954–57. Contested Exchange Div. of Manchester, Gen. Election, 1955; MP (C) Morecambe and Lonsdale Div. of Lancaster, Nov. 1958–Sept. 1964. Dir of overseas operations, Ferranti Ltd, 1957–62; Parliamentary Sec., Ministry of Aviation, July-Oct. 1962. Dep. Man. Dir, Internat. Computers and Tabulators, Sept. 1963 until Managing Dir, 1964; Dir, International Computers Ltd until 1972. Mem., Economic and Social Cttee, European Communities, 1973–79 (Chm., 1976–78); Chm., European Movement (British Council), 1980–82. Pres., British Computer Soc., 1968–69; Vice-Pres., Kangaroo Gp, 1982–. Hon. DSc City, 1970. *Publications:* In Europe, 1979; contrib. Brit. Computer Soc. Jl, Proc. IFIP, Proc. Royal Instn of GB. *Recreations:* ski-ing, sailing. *Address:* Ferranti International Signal plc, Millbank Tower, Millbank, SW1. *T:* 01–834 6611; The Old Manor, Church Lane, Ellisfield, Hants RG25 2QR. *Club:* Royal Yacht Squadron. *Died 24 Sept. 1988.*

**DEFFERRE, Gaston;** Officier de la Légion d'honneur; Minister for Planning and Regional Development, France, since 1984; Mayor of Marseilles, 1944–45 and since 1953 (re-elected six times); *b* 14 Sept. 1910; *s* of Paul and Suzanne Defferre; *m* 1st, 1935, Andrée Aboulker; 2nd, 1946, Marie-Antoinette Swaters; 3rd, 1973, Edmonde Charles-Roux, journalist. *Educ:* Lycée de Nîmes; Aix-en-Provence Univ. In practice as lawyer, Marseilles, 1931–51. During War, 1939–45, involved in resistance movement (Croix de guerre, Rosette de la Résistance). Dir, Le Provençal, 1951–. Deputy for Bouches-du-Rhône, 1946–58, 1962–81, re-elected June 1981; Senator, 1959–62;

Sec. of State, Présidence du Conseil, 1946; Under Sec. of State, France Overseas, 1946–47; Minister: Merchant Marine, 1950–51; France Overseas, 1956–57; Leader, Socialist Group, Nat. Assembly, 1967–81; Minister of State, 1981–83; Minister for the Interior and for Decentralisation, 1981–84. *Publications:* Un nouvel horizon, 1977; Si demain la gauche..., 1977. *Address:* Hôtel de Ville, 13002 Marseille, France. *Died 7 May* 1986.

**de FISCHER-REICHENBACH, Henry-Béat,** Dr jur.; Swiss Ambassador to the Court of St James's, 1964–66; *b* 22 July 1901; *s* of Henry B. de Fischer-Reichenbach, architect, bailiff-delegate of the Sov. Order of Malta in Switzerland, and Caroline Falck-Crivelli; *m* 1949, Madeleine de Graffenried, sculptress; three *d. Educ.:* Stella Matutina Jesuit Coll., Feldkirch; Universities of Fribourg, Munich, Paris and Berne (Dr jur. 1926). Entered Federal Political Dept, Berne, 1929; Attaché, Swiss Legation, The Hague, 1931; Second Secretary, Buenos-Aires and Montevideo, 1933; First Secretary: Warsaw, 1939; Bucharest, 1940; Chargé d'affaires successively Riga, Kowno, Reval, Helsinki, 1940; Counsellor: Bucharest, 1941; Cairo and Beirut, 1947; Minister: Cairo, 1949; Ethiopia, 1952; Lisbon, 1954; Ambassador, Vienna, 1959–64. Mem. Board of Patrons, C. G. Jung Inst., Zürich, 1931–71. President: Fondation pour l'histoire des Suisses à l'étranger, 1969–79; Swiss Assoc., Knights of Malta, 1968–79; Comité exécutif international pour l'assistance aux lépreux de l'Order de Malte, 1976–84; European Anti-Leprosy Assoc., 1969–70; Soc. des Amis suisses de Versailles, 1968–69; Head, Delegn of Sovereign Order of Malta to Diplomatic Conference on Humanitarian Law Applicable on Armed Conflicts, Geneva 1974–77; Lecture, The Sovereign Order of Malta, Hague Acad. of Internat. Law, The Hague, 1979. *Publications:* Contributions à la connaissance des relations suisses-égyptiennes, 1956; Dialogue luso-suisse, 1960 (Camões Prize, 1961); 2000 ans de présence suisse en Angleterre, 1980. *Recreations:* history, architecture, psychology. *Address:* Le Pavillon, Thunplatz 52, Berne. *T:* 031 44.15.09; Clos Soleil, Vufflens-le-Château, Vaud, Switzerland. *Clubs:* Travellers'; Grande Société (Berne).
*Died 22 Aug.* 1984.

**de FONBLANQUE, Maj.-Gen. Edward Barrington,** CB 1948; CBE 1945; DSO 1944; *b* 29 May 1895; *s* of Lester Ramsay de Fonblanque and Constance Lucy Kerr; *m* 1934, Elizabeth Sclater; two *s* one *d. Educ.:* Rugby. Joined Royal Artillery 1914; served European War, 1914–18 (despatches); Instructor Equitation Sch., Weedon, 1921–25; Capt., Royal Horse Artillery, 1923–31; Instructor, Staff Coll., Quetta, 1934–38; Commanded B/O Battery RHA, 1938–39; Commanded 2 RHA, 1939–40; GSO 1, 2 Div., 1940; CRA 45 Div., 1940–41; Chief of Staff 10 Corps and 10 Army, 1941–43 (despatches); CCRA 5 Corps, 1944–45; Chief of Staff I Corps, 1946; Chief Administrative Officer, Control Commission Germany, 1947; ADC to the King, 1947; Comdr, Salisbury Plain District, 1948–51; retired, 1951. Asst Comr, Civil Defence, Malaya, 1951; Inspector-Gen., Federal Home Guard, Malaya, 1952–58. Col Comdt, RA 1952; Representative Col Comdt 1959; retd 1960. Comdr, Legion of Merit. *Address:* The Cottage, Bank, near Lyndhurst, Hants. *T:* Lyndhurst 2214; c/o Lloyds Bank, 6 Pall Mall, SW1.
*Died 17 Sept.* 1981.

**de FREITAS, Rt. Hon. Sir Geoffrey (Stanley),** PC 1967; KCMG 1961; Barrister-at-law, Lincoln's Inn (Cholmeley Schol.); President, International Social Service, Geneva, since 1979; Chairman, European Consultants Ltd, since 1979; *b* 7 April 1913; *s* of Sir Anthony Patrick de Freitas, OBE, and Maud, *d* of Augustus Panton Short; *m* 1938, Helen Graham, *d* of Laird Bell, Hon. KBE, Hon. LLD Harvard, of Illinois, USA; three *s* one *d. Educ.:* Haileybury (Governor); Clare Coll., Cambridge (Hon. Fellow); Yale Univ. (Mellon Fellow). Pres. of Cambridge Union, 1934. Shoreditch Borough Council (Lab), 1936–39; Bar Council, 1939. RA 1939, RAF, 1940–45. MP (Lab) Central Nottingham, 1945–50, Lincoln, 1950–61, Kettering, 1964–79; Parliamentary Private Sec. to Prime Minister, 1945–46; Under-Sec. of State for Air, 1946–50; Under-Sec. of State, Home Office, 1950–51; Shadow Minister of Agriculture, 1960–61; Mem. Privileges Cttee, 1964–67; Chm., Select Cttee on Overseas Develt, 1974–79. British High Comr in Ghana, 1961–63; designated (1963) British High Comr in East African Federation when formed; British High Comr in Kenya, 1963–64. Pres., Assembly of Council of Europe, 1966–69; Vice-Pres., European Parlt, 1975–79; Delegate to UN, 1949 and 1964; Pres., N Atlantic Assembly, 1976–78 (founder Mem. 1955). Chairman: Gauche Européenne, 1966–78; Labour Cttee for Europe, 1965–72; Attlee Foundn, 1967–76; Party's Defence Cttee, 1964–71, 1974–76; Soc. of Labour Lawyers, 1955–58; Univ. of East Anglia's Annual Atlantic Community Seminar, 1978– ; Vice-Chairman: Nature Conservancy, 1954–58; British Council, 1964–68; Churches Social Responsibility Cttee, 1956–61; Council: Churchill Trust, 1967–77; Agricultural Cooperative Association, 1964–69. Pres. Inland Waterways Assoc., 1978– . Farmed at Bourn, Cambs, 1953–69. Dir, Laporte Industries, 1968–78. *Recreations:* the countryside; formerly games and athletics (full blue CUAC). *Address:* 34 Tufton Court, Tufton Street, SW1.

*T:* 01-799 3770. *Clubs:* Reform, Garrick, Guild of Air Pilots (Liveryman); Hawks (Cambridge). *Died 10 Aug.* 1982.

**de FREITAS-CRUZ, Joao Carlos Lopes Cardoso;** Grand Cross, Order of Prince Henry the Navigator, 1981; Ambassador of Portugal to Spain, since 1984; *b* 27 March 1925; *s* of Jose A. de Freitas-Cruz and Maria A. L. C. de Freitas-Cruz; *m* 1955, Maria de Lourdes Soares de Albergaria; three *s. Educ.:* Univ. of Lisbon (law degree). Joined Portuguese Foreign Service, 1948; Secretary, Portuguese Embassy, London, 1950–52; Portuguese Delegate to NATO, in Paris, 1952–57; Foreign Office, Lisbon, 1957–59; Sec., Portuguese Embassy, Pretoria, 1959–60; Chargé d'Affaires, Madagascar, 1960–62; Consul-General, New York, 1963–65; Consul-Gen., Salisbury, Rhodesia, 1965–70; Ambassador: to OECD, Paris, 1970–71; in Bonn, 1971–73; Dir-Gen. for Political Affairs, FO, Lisbon, 1973–74; Ambassador, Permanent Representative to NATO, Brussels, 1974–78; Minister for Foreign Affairs, 1978–80; Ambassador to UK, 1980–84. Grand Cross, Order of Merit, Fed. Republic of Germany; Comdr, San Silvester, Holy See; Grand Officer, Légion d'Honneur, France; Grand Cross, Order of Flag, Hungary, and other foreign orders. *Recreations:* golf, hunting, reading. *Address:* Pinar, 1 - Madrid 28006, Spain. *T:* 261–78–00. *Clubs:* Financiero Genova, Real Club Puerta de Hierro.

**de GALE, Sir Leo (Victor),** GCMG 1974; CBE 1969; Governor-General of Grenada, 1974–78; *b* 28 Dec. 1921; 3rd *s* of late George Victor and late Marie Leonie de Gale, Grenada; *m* 1953, Brenda Mary Helen (*née* Scott), Trinidad; five *s* two *d. Educ.:* Grenada Boys' Secondary Sch.; Sir George Williams Univ., Canada. Dip. Accountancy, Dip. Business Admin, Qual. Land Surveyor. Served with 1st Canadian Survey Regt, 1940–45. Co-founder firm de Gale & Rapier, Auditors, 1949. Dir, Brit. Red Cross Br., Grenada, 1960–65; Chm. and Mem., Grenada Breweries Ltd, 1964–74; Dep. Chm., Grenada Banana Soc., 1965–69; Chm. Bd of Governors, Grenada Boys' Secondary Sch., 1960–65; Mem., West Indies Associated States Judicial and Legal Service Commn, 1970–73. *Recreations:* golf, fishing, reading. *Address:* 181 Memorial Road, Hanham, Bristol BS15 3LH. *T:* Bristol 671143. *Clubs:* St George's Men's (Grenada); Grenada Yacht. *Died 22 March* 1986.

**de GEX, Maj.-Gen. George Francis,** CB 1964; OBE 1949; Director, Royal Artillery, 1964–66, retired; *b* 23 April 1911; *s* of late Brig.-Gen. F. J. de Gex, CB, CMG; *m* 1946, Ronda Marianne (*d* 1982), *d* of late C. F. Recaño; one *d. Educ.:* Wellington Coll., Berks; Trinity Hall, Cambridge (MA). 2nd Lieut RA 1931; served War of 1939–45: BEF, 1940 (despatches); NW Europe, 1944. Lt-Col 1953; Col 1954; Brig. 1959; Comd 1 AGRA, 1958–59; DMS(B), War Office, 1959–60. Comd Artillery, Northern Army Group, 1961–64. Col Comdt, RA 1967–76. DSC (USA), 1945. *Recreations:* shooting, sailing. *Address:* Hyde House, Pilton, Shepton Mallet, Somerset. *Club:* Army and Navy. *Died 16 Aug.* 1986.

**de HAVILLAND, Maj.-Gen. Peter Hugh,** CBE 1945; DL; *b* 29 July 1904; *s* of late Hugh de Havilland, JP, CA, The Manor House, Gt Horkesley, Essex; *m* 1st, 1930, Helen Elizabeth Wrey (*d* 1976), *d* of late W. W. Otter-Barry, Horkesley Hall, Essex; two *s*; 2nd, 1981, Mrs Angela Hoare. *Educ.:* Eton; RMA, Woolwich. 2nd Lieut, RA, 1925; Lieut RHA, 1933–36; Adjt 84th (East Anglian) Field Bde, RA (TA), 1936–38; served War of 1939–45 (despatches thrice, CBE); France, Middle East, N Africa, NW Europe; Brig. i/c Administration, 1 Corps, 1945–47; Dep. Regional Comr, Land Schleswig Holstein, 1948; Dep. Head, UK Deleg. Five Power Military Cttee, 1949; UK Mil. Rep., SHAPE, 1951; Chief of Staff, Northern Comd, 1953–55, retd 1955. DL Essex, 1962. Comdr Order of Leopold II, 1945. *Recreations:* shooting, flying (pilot's licence since 1977). *Address:* Horkesley Hall, Colchester. *T:* Colchester 271 259. *Club:* Army and Navy. *Died 15 Dec.* 1989.

**de LACRETELLE, Jacques;** French Writer; Member of Académie Française, since 1936; *b* 14 July 1888; *m* 1933, Yolande de Naurois; three *c*. First book published in 1920; Prix Femina, 1922; Grand Prix du roman de l'Académie Française, 1927. *Publications:* La Vie inquiète de Jean Hermelin, 1920; Silbermann, 1922; La Bonifas, 1925; Histoire de Paola Ferrani, 1929; Amour nuptial, 1929; Le Retour de Silbermann, 1930; Les Hauts Ponts (4 vols), 1932–35; L'Ecrivain public, 1936; Croisières en eaux troubles, 1939; Le Demi-Dieu ou le voyage en Grèce, 1944; Le Pour et le Contre, 1946; Une visite en été (play), 1952; Deux cœurs simples, 1953; Tiroir secret, 1959; Les Maîtres et les Amis, 1959; Grèce que j'aime, 1960; La Galerie des amants, 1963; L'Amour sur la place, 1964; Talleyrand, 1964; Racine, 1970; Portraits d'autrefois, figures d'aujourd'hui 1973; Journal de bord, 1974; Les Vivants et leur ombre, 1977; translation of Precious Bane by Mary Webb and Wuthering Heights by Emily Brontë. *Address:* 49 rue Vineuse, 75016 Paris, France. *T:* 553–79.87; Château d'O, 61570 Mortrée, France. *T:* (33) 35.33.56. *Died 2 Jan.* 1985.

**de la MARE, Prof. Peter Bernard David,** MSc NZ; PhD London; DSc London; FRSNZ; Professor of Chemistry, University of Auckland, New Zealand, 1967–82, then Emeritus (Head of Department,

1967–81); *b* 3 Sept. 1920; *s* of late Frederick Archibald and Sophia Ruth de la Mare, Hamilton, NZ; *m* 1945, Gwynneth Campbell, *yr d* of late Alexander and Daisy Gertrude Jolly, Hastings, NZ; two *d*. *Educ:* Hamilton High Sch., Hamilton, NZ; Victoria University Coll. (University of NZ); University Coll., London. BSc NZ, 1941; MSc NZ, 1942; PhD London, 1948; DSc London, 1955. FRSNZ 1970. Agricultural Chemist, NZ Govt Dept of Agriculture, 1942–45; Shirtcliffe Fellow (University of NZ) at University Coll. London, 1946–48; University Coll. London: Temp. Asst Lecturer, 1948; Lecturer, 1949; Reader, 1956; Prof. of Chemistry, Bedford Coll., University of London, 1960–67. Mem., NZ Universities Entrance Bd, 1972–82. Hon. DSc Victoria Univ. Wellington, 1983. Hector Meml Medal, RSNZ, 1985. *Publications:* (with J. H. Ridd) Aromatic Substitution-Nitration and Halogenation, 1959; (with W. Klyne) Progress in Stereochemistry 2, 1958, 3, 1962; (with R. Bolton) Electrophilic Addition to Unsaturated Systems, 1966, 2nd edn 1982; Electrophilic Halogenation, 1976; scientific papers and reviews. *Recreations:* chess, table tennis, stamp collecting, etc. *Address:* 65 Grant's Road, Opotiki, New Zealand. *Died* 13 Dec. 1989.

**de la MARE, Richard Herbert Ingpen;** President, Faber & Faber (Publishers) Ltd, since 1971 (Chairman, Faber & Faber Ltd, 1960–71); Chairman, Faber Music Ltd, 1966–71; *b* 4 June 1901; *e s* of late Walter John de la Mare, OM, CH, and Constance Elfrida Ingpen; *m* 1930, Amy Catherine (*d* 1968), *er d* of late Rev. S. A. Donaldson, DD, Master of Magdalene College, Cambridge; three *s* one *d*. *Educ:* Whitgift Sch., Croydon; Keble Coll., Oxford. Joined Faber & Gwyer Ltd, 1925, Dir 1928; succeeded by Faber & Faber Ltd, 1929, Dir 1929–45, Vice-Chm. 1945–60. *Publications:* essays and addresses on typography. *Recreations:* reading history and archaeology, listening to music, oriental art, gardening. *Address:* Tithe Barn House, High Street, Cumnor, Oxford OX2 9PE. *T:* Oxford 863916. *Club:* Athenæum. *Died* 22 March 1986.

**de la RUE, Sir Eric (Vincent),** 3rd Bt, *cr* 1898; *b* 5 Aug. 1906; *s* of Sir Evelyn Andros de la Rue, 2nd Bt, and Mary Violet (*d* 1959), *e d* of John Liell Francklin of Gonalston, Notts; *S* father, 1950; *m* 1st, 1945, Cecilia (*d* 1963), *d* of late Lady Clementine Waring; two *s*; 2nd, 1964, Christine Schellin, Greenwich, Conn, USA; one *s*. *Educ:* Oundle. Served War of 1939–45. Capt. Notts Yeomanry, 1942–45. *Heir: s* Andrew George Ilay de la Rue [*b* 3 Feb. 1946; *m* 1984, Tessa D., *er d* of David Dobson]. *Address:* Caldra, Duns, Scotland. *T:* Duns 83294. *Died* 5 Dec. 1989.

**DE LA WARR, 10th Earl** *cr* 1761; **William Herbrand Sackville, DL;** Baron De La Warr, 1299 and 1572; Viscount Cantelupe, 1761; Baron Buckhurst (UK), 1864; *b* 16 Oct. 1921; *e s* of 9th Earl De La Warr, PC, GBE, and Diana (*d* 1966), *d* of late Gerard Leigh; *S* father, 1976; *m* 1946, Anne Rachel, *o d* of Geoffrey Devas, MC, Hunton Court, Maidstone; two *s* one *d*. *Educ:* Eton. Lieut Royal Sussex Regt, 1941–43; Lieut Parachute Regt, 1943; Capt. 1945–46. Contested (C) NE Bethnal Green, 1945; Chm. London Young Conservatives, 1946, Pres. 1947–49. Man. Dir, Rediffusion Ltd, 1974–79 (Dir, 1968–79); Director: British Electric Traction Co. Ltd, 1970–79; Wembley Stadium Ltd, 1972–79; Portals Hldgs Ltd, 1974–; Kent & Sussex Courier, 1982–; Essex Chronicle Series Ltd, 1981–; Chm, Redifon, 1978–79; Dep. Chm., Windsor Television Ltd, 1983–. Pres., Gen. Council and Register of Osteopaths, 1985–. Hon. Col Sussex ACF, 1969–; Vice-Chm., South East TAVR Assoc. (and Chm. Co. of Sussex Cttee), 1968–74 and 1978–83; Chairman: Sussex County Playing Fields Assoc., 1956–71; London and SE Resettlement Cttee for Ex-Regulars, 1969–74. DL East Sussex, 1975. *Heir: s* Lord Buckhurst. *Address:* Buckhurst Park, Withyham, East Sussex. *T:* Hartfield 346, (Estate Office) Hartfield 220; 93 Eaton Place, SW1. *T:* 01–235 7990, (office) 01–235 9227. *Clubs:* White's, Pratt's. *Died* 9 Feb. 1988.

**DELAY, Professeur Jean,** Commandeur de la Légion d'Honneur; Grand Officier de l'Ordre national du Mérite; Member of the Académie de Médecine since 1955; Member of the Académie Française, since 1959; *b* Bayonne, Pyrénées Atlantiques, 14 Nov. 1907; *m* 1933, Marie-Madeleine Carrez; two *d*. *Educ:* Faculté de Médecine and Faculté des Lettres Sorbonne. DèsL Sorbonne. Prof. of Mental Diseases, Faculté de Médecine de Paris, 1946–70; Director, L'Institut de Psychologie, Sorbonne, 1951–70. Pres., First Internat. Congress of Psychiatry, 1950. Mem. French Section Unesco. Hon. Member, Royal Society Med.; Mem., Royal Soc. of Sciences of Uppsala; Distinguished Fellow, APA, 1977. Dr hc Univs of Zürich, Montreal and Barcelona. Médaille d'Or, Congrès Mondial de Psycho-Pharmologie, 1971. *Publications:* scientific: Les Dissolutions de la mémoire, 1942; Les Dérèglements de l'humeur, 1946; Les Maladies de la mémoire, 1947; La Psycho-Physiologie humaine, 1945; Aspects de la psychiatrie moderne, 1956; Etudes de psychologie médicale, 1953; Méthodes biologiques, 1950, psychométriques, 1956, chimiothérapiques, 1961, en psychiatrie; Introduction à la médecine psychosomatique, 1961; Abrégé de psychologie, 1962; Les démences tardives, 1962; L'électroencéphalographie clinique, 1966; Le syndrome de Korsakoff, 1969; literary: La Cité grise, 1946; Hommes sans nom,

1948; Les Reposantes, 1947; La Jeunesse d'André Gide (grand prix de la Critique), Vol. 1, 1956, Vol. 2, 1957; Une Amitié (André Gide et Roger Martin du Gard), 1968; La Correspondance de Jacques Copeau et Roger Martin du Gard, 1972; Avant Mémoire: d'une minute à l'autre, vol. 1, 1979, vol. 2, 1980, La Fauconnier, vol. 3, 1982, D'un siècle à l'autre, vol. 4, 1986. *Address:* 53 avenue Montaigne, 75008 Paris. *T:* 4359 77–07.
*Died* 29 May 1987.

**DELBRÜCK, Prof. Max;** Professor of Biology, California Institute of Technology, 1947–77, then Board of Trustees Emeritus Professor; *b* 4 Sept. 1906; *s* of Hans Delbrück and Lina Thiersch; *m* 1941, Mary Bruce; two *s* two *d*. *Educ:* Univs of Tübingen, Berlin, Bonn and Göttingen. PhD 1930. Visiting Prof., 1956, and Acting Prof., 1961–63, Cologne Univ. Mem., Nat. Acad. of Sciences; Fellow: Leopoldina Acad., Halle; Royal Danish Acad.; Foreign Mem., Royal Soc. Kimber Gold Medal (Genetics), US Nat. Acad. of Sciences; Nobel Prize for Physiology or Medicine (jtly), 1969. Hon. PhD: Copenhagen; Chicago; Harvard; Heidelberg; Univ. of S California. *Address:* 1510 Oakdale Street, Pasadena, California 91106, USA. *Died* 10 March 1981.

**de LOTBINIÈRE, Seymour Joly,** CVO 1956; OBE 1953; *b* 21 Oct. 1905; *s* of late Brig.-Gen. H. G. Joly de Lotbinière, DSO; *m* 1944, Mona Lewis; one *s*. *Educ:* Eton; Trinity Coll., Cambridge. Called to Bar, Lincoln's Inn. On BBC staff, 1932–67. Governor, Bristol Old Vic Trust, 1963–67. CC West Suffolk, 1970–74. *Recreation:* gunflint research. *Address:* Brandon Hall, Brandon, Suffolk. *T:* Thetford 810227. *Died* 6 Nov. 1984.

**de MANIO, Jack,** MC 1940; broadcaster; *b* 26 Jan. 1914; *s* of Jean and Florence de Manio; *m* 1st, 1935, Juliet Gravaeret Kaufmann, New York (marr. diss., 1946); one *s*; 2nd, 1946, Loveday Elizabeth Matthews (*widow, née* Abbott). *Educ:* Aldenham. Served War of 1939–45, Royal Sussex Regt; 7th Bn, BEF, 1939–40; 1st Bn, Middle East Forces, 1940–44; Forces Broadcasting, Middle East, 1944–46. Joined Overseas Service, BBC, 1946; BBC Home Service, 1950; resigned to become freelance, 1964. Presenter BBC programmes: Today, 1958–71; Jack de Manio Precisely, 1971–78; With Great Pleasure, 1971–73; broadcast 1st interview given by HRH The Prince of Wales, 1969; contributor Woman's Hour, 1979–. Assists with fund raising for Assoc. of Friends of Queen Charlotte's and Chelsea Hosp. for Women, 1980–. Radio Personality of Year Award, Variety Club of GB, 1964; Radio Personality Award of Year, British Radio Industries Club, 1971. *Publications:* To Auntie with Love, 1967; Life Begins Too Early, 1970; contribs to Punch and numerous other periodicals. *Recreation:* fishing. *Address:* 105 Cheyne Walk, SW10. *T:* 01–352 0889. *Club:* MCC.
*Died* 28 Oct. 1988.

**DEMANT, Rev. Vigo Auguste,** MA, DLitt Oxford; BSc, Hon. DD Durham; *b* 8 Nov. 1893; *s* of late T. Demant, linguist, of Newcastle on Tyne, and Emily Demant; *m* 1925, Marjorie, *d* of late George Tickner, FZS, Oxford; one *s* two *d*. *Educ:* Newcastle on Tyne; Tournan, France; Armstrong Coll., Durham Univ.; Manchester Coll. and Exeter Coll., Oxford; Ely Theological Coll. Curacies: S Thomas, Oxford, S Nicholas, Plumstead, S Silas, Kentish Town; Dir of Research to Christian Social Council, 1929–33; Vicar of S John-the-Divine, Richmond, Surrey, 1933–42; Canon Residentiary, 1942–49, Treasurer, 1948–49, of St Paul's Cathedral; Canon of Christ Church and Regius Professor of Moral and Pastoral Theology in Oxford University, 1949–71. Ex-Mem. Departmental Cttee on Homosexual Offences and Prostitution. Gifford Lecturer, St Andrews, 1957–58. *Publications:* This Unemployment, 1931; God, Man and Society, 1933; Christian Polity, 1936; The Religious Prospect, 1939; Theology of Society, 1947; Religion and the Decline of Capitalism, 1952; A Two-way Religion, 1957; Christian Sex Ethics, 1963. *Recreation:* carpentry. *Address:* 31 St Andrew's Road, Old Headington, Oxford. *T:* Oxford 64022.
*Died* 3 March 1983.

**de MARGERIE, Roland Jacquin,** CVO 1938; Ambassador of France; Hon. Conseiller d'Etat; *b* 6 May 1899; *s* of late P. de Margerie, KBE, French Ambassador in Berlin, 1922–31, and Jeanne Rostand, sister of the Playwright Edmond Rostand, Mem. of the French Academy; *m* 1921, Jenny, *d* of Edmond Fabre-Luce, Vice-Chm. of the Crédit Lyonnais; two *s* one *d*. *Educ:* Sorbonne; Ecole des Sciences Politiques, Paris. Joined Foreign Office, 1917; Lieut 17th Bn of Chasseurs Alpins, 1918–21; Attaché to French Embassy, Brussels, 1921; Sec., Berlin, 1923; 1st Sec. to the French Embassy, London, 1933–39; mem. of the mission attached to their Majesties during their State visit to France, 1938; Counsellor, 1939; Captain 152nd Regt of the Line, Sept. 1939–Feb. 1940; ADC to Gen. Gamelin, Feb.-March 1940; Private Sec. to the Minister for Foreign Affairs, March 1940; French Consul-Gen., Shanghai, 1940–44; Chargé with the office of the French Embassy in Peking, 1944–46. Asst deleg. negotiations for Brussels Pact, 1948; Minister plenipotentiary, 1949; Director-Gen. of Political Affairs, France, 1955; French Ambassador to the Holy See, 1956–59; to Spain,

1959–62; to the Federal Republic of Germany, 1962–65; Conseiller d'Etat, 1965–70. Comdr Legion of Honour; various foreign orders. *Address:* 14 rue St Guillaume, 75007 Paris, France. *Club:* Jockey (Paris). *Died 13 July* 1990.

**de MOURGUES, Prof. Odette Marie Hélène Louise,** PhD, DLitt; Palmes Académiques 1964; Ordre National du Mérite 1973; Professor Emerita University of Cambridge; Fellow, Girton College, Cambridge, since 1946; *b* 14 May 1914; *d* of Dr Pierre de Mourgues and Hélène Terle; *m* 1934 (marr. diss. 1943); one *s* decd. *Educ:* Lycée du Le Puy; Univs of Grenoble and Aix-en-Provence. Licence en droit, diplôme d'études supérieures de droit, LèsL, agrégation d'anglais; PhD, DLitt Cantab. Teaching posts, Valence, Digne and Marseille, 1942–45; Asst Lectr, Univ. of Aix-en-Provence, 1944–46; Lectr, Girton Coll., 1946, Lectr in French, 1952–68, Reader, 1968–75, Prof. of French, 1975–80, Univ. of Cambridge. *Publications:* Metaphysical, Baroque and Précieux Poetry, 1953; Le Jugement Avant-dernier (fiction), 1954; L'Hortensia Bleu (fiction), 1956; La Fontaine: Fables, 1960; O Muse, fuyante Proie, 1962; An Anthology of French 17C Poetry, 1966; Racine or the Triumph of Relevance, 1967; Autonomie de Racine, 1967; Two French Moralists: La Rochefoucald and La Bruyère, 1978; articles, contribs to Festschriften, published lectures, and revs. *Recreations:* travel, gardening. *Address:* 1 Marion Close, Cambridge. *T:* Cambridge 356865. *Died* 1 *July* 1988.

**DEMPSEY, James;** JP; MP (Lab) Coatbridge and Airdrie since Oct. 1959; *b* 6 Feb. 1917; *s* of late James Dempsey; *m* 1945, Jane, *d* of late John McCann; five *s* one *d*. *Educ:* Holy Family Sch., Mossend; Co-operative Coll., Loughborough; National Council of Labour Colls. Served War of 1939–45; Auxiliary Military Pioneer Corps. Member Hospital Board of Management and Board for Industry and Executive Council, National Health Service, National Assistance Board. JP Lanarkshire, 1954; CC Lanarkshire, 1945–. *Address:* The House of Commons, SW1; 113 Thorndean Avenue, Bellshill, Lanarkshire. *T:* 2712. *Died* 12 *May* 1982.

**DENBY, Sir Richard Kenneth,** Kt 1978; DL; President of the Law Society of England and Wales, 1977 (Vice-President, 1976); Consultant, A. V. Hammond & Co., Bradford, since 1985 (Senior Partner, 1972–85); *b* 20 March 1915; *s* of John Henry and Emily Denby; *m* 1939, Eileen (*d* 1974), *d* of M. H. Pickles, CBE; one *s* two *d*. *Educ:* Ackworth School; Leeds Univ. (LLB). Admitted Solicitor, 1937 (First Cl. Hons and Clifford's Inn Prize). Served War of 1939–45: 2nd Lt, The Green Howards, 1940; AFHQ N Africa, 1942; War Office, DAMS MS1(b), 1944; AMS, Lt-Col Northern Command, 1945 (despatches). Pres., Bradford & Bingley Building Soc., 1982–85; Chairman: Parkland Textile (Holdings) Ltd, 1979–85; Pennine Radio (Bradford Community Radio Ltd), 1975–85. Dir, Opera North Ltd, 1981. Mem., Criminal Injuries Compensation Bd, 1979–. Chm., Mental Health Review Tribunal, NE Region. DL W Yorks, 1982. *Recreations:* fishing, fell-walking. *Address:* 7 Goodwood, Ilkley, W Yorks LS29 0BY. *T:* Ilkley 609076. *Clubs:* Army and Navy, Carlton; Bradford.

*Died* 16 *Dec.* 1986.

**DENHOLM, Sir John (Carmichael),** Kt 1955; CBE 1947; *b* 24 Dec. 1893; *s* of John Denholm and Jane Miller, Greenock, Scotland; *m* 1926, Mary Laura (*d* 1978), *d* of Peter Kerr, Greenock; no *c*. *Educ:* Greenock Acad. Joined family firm, J. & J. Denholm Ltd, 1910; Dir 1922; succeeded father as Chm., 1936–66 (when firm celebrated its centenary with only two Chairmen from inception). RNVR: Midshipman, 1910; Sub-Lieut, 1912; Lieut temp. 1915, perm. list 1917; Lieut-Comdr, 1925; resigned 1926; served European War, 1914–18; RN Div. Antwerp and Gallipoli, 1914–15; RN HMS Ladybird, 1916–19 (despatches); Regional Shipping Rep. for West Coast Scotland, Ministry of Shipping and Min. of War Transport, 1940–45. Council of Chamber of Shipping: Mem. 1936; Vice-Pres, 1953; Pres. 1954–55. Chm., David Macbrayne Ltd, 1963–64. *Recreation:* golf. *Address:* 3 Octavia Terrace, Greenock. *T:* Greenock 20940. *Club:* Royal Scottish Automobile (Glasgow).

*Died* 25 *Oct.* 1981.

**DENHOLM, Col Sir William (Lang),** Kt 1965; TD; DL; Chairman, J. & J. Denholm Ltd, 1966–74; Chairman, Shipping Federation, 1962–65; Joint Chairman, National Maritime Board, 1962–65; President, International Shipping Federation, 1962–67; *b* 23 Feb. 1901; *s* of John Denholm and Jane Miller, Greenock; *m* 1925, Dorothy Jane, *d* of Robert Ferguson, Greenock; two *s* one *d*. *Educ:* Greenock Academy; Greenock Collegiate. Joined family firm J. & J. Denholm Ltd, 1918. 2nd Lieut 77th (H) Field Regt, RA (TA), 1921; in command, 1939–40; Hon. Col 1945–60. Mem. Gen. Cttee, 1935–76 and Scottish Cttee, 1935–77, Lloyd's Register of Shipping. Mem. Council, Shipping Federation, 1936; Vice-Chm., 1950–62. Vice-Chm., Glasgow Royal Infirmary and Assoc. Hospitals, 1949–60; Chm., 1960–64. DL County of Renfrew, 1950. Chevalier of the Order of St Olav (Norway). *Recreation:* golf. *Address:* Glenmill, Kilmacolm, Renfrewshire. *T:* Kilmacolm 2535. *Club:* Royal Scottish Automobile (Glasgow). *Died* 9 *Aug.* 1986.

**DENNELL, Prof. Ralph;** Emeritus Professor of Zoology, University of Manchester, 1975; Beyer Professor of Zoology, 1963–74; *b* 29 Sept. 1907; *m* 1932, Dorothy Ethel Howard; no *c*. *Educ:* Leeds Grammar Sch.; University of Leeds. Demonstrator in Zoology, University of Leeds, 1929; Grisedale Research Student, University of Manchester, 1932; Asst Lecturer in Zoology, University of Manchester, 1935; Asst Lecturer in Zoology, and Lecturer in Zoology, Imperial Coll., 1937–46; Reader in Experimental Zoology, 1946–48, Prof. of Experimental Zoology, 1948–63, University of Manchester. *Publications:* papers on crustacea, insect physiology, and arthropod integuments, in various zoological periodicals.

*Died* 16 *Feb.* 1989.

**DENNING, Lt-Gen. Sir Reginald (Francis Stewart),** KCVO 1975; KBE 1946; CB 1944; Chairman, SSAFA, 1953–74; Vice-President, Liverpool School of Tropical Medicine, 1967–77; *b* 12 June 1894; 2nd *s* of Charles and Clara Denning, Whitchurch, Hants; *m* 1927, Eileen Violet (OBE 1969), *d* of late H. W. Currie, 12 Hyde Park Place, W2; two *s* one *d*. *Educ:* privately. 2nd Lieut Bedfordshire Regt, 1915; European War, 1914–18 (severely wounded, despatches). Adjutant, 1st Bedfs and Herts Regt, 1922–25; Adjutant, 2 Bedfs and Herts Regt, 1926–29; Student Staff Coll., Camberley, 1929–30; Bt Major, 1934; Bt Lt-Col, 1939; Brig., 1941; Subst. Col, 1942; Acting Maj.-Gen., 1943; Maj.-Gen., 1944; Lieut-Gen., 1949; Maj.-Gen. i/c Administration South-Eastern Command, 1943–44; Principal Administrative Officer to the Supreme Allied Commander, South-East Asia, 1944–46; Chief of Staff, Eastern Command, 1947–49; GOC Northern Ireland, 1949–52; retired pay, 1952. Col, Bedfs and Herts Regt, 1948 3rd East Anglian Regt (16th/44th Foot), 1958, Royal Anglian Regt, 1964–66 (formed Regt, 1964). DL, County of Essex, 1959–68. CStJ 1946; Commander Legion of Merit (USA), 1946. *Recreations:* hunting, polo, riding. *Address:* Delmonden Grange, Hawkhurst, Kent TN18 4XJ. *T:* Hawkhurst (05805) 2286. *Clubs:* Army and Navy, MCC.

*Died* 23 *May* 1990.

**DENNIS, Nigel Forbes;** writer; *b* 16 Jan. 1912; *s* of Lieut-Col M. F. B. Dennis, DSO, and Louise (*née* Bosanquet); *m* 1st, Mary-Madeleine Massias; 2nd, 1959, Beatrice Ann Hewart Matthew; two *d*. *Educ:* Plumtree Sch., S Rhodesia; Odenwaldschule, Germany. Secretary, Nat. Bd of Review of Motion Pictures, NY, 1935–36; Asst Editor and Book Reviewer, The New Republic, NY, 1937–38; Staff Book Reviewer, Time, NY, 1940–58; Dramatic Critic, Encounter, 1960–63; Staff Book Reviewer, Sunday Telegraph, 1961–82; Joint Editor, Encounter, 1967–70. FRSL 1966. Swansong for Seven Voices, BBC radio play, 1985. *Publications:* Boys and Girls Come out to Play, 1949; Cards of Identity, 1955; Two Plays and a Preface, 1958; Dramatic Essays, 1962; Jonathan Swift, 1964 (RSL Award, 1966); A House in Order, 1966; Exotics (poems), 1970; An Essay on Malta, 1971. *Plays:* Cards of Identity, Royal Court, 1956; The Making of Moo, Royal Court, 1957; August for the People, Royal Court and Edinburgh Festival, 1962. *Recreation:* gardening. *Address:* c/o A. M. Heath & Co., 40 William IV Street, WC2.

*Died* 19 *July* 1989.

**DENNIS SMITH, Edgar;** *see* Smith.

**DENNY, Sir J(onathan) Lionel P(ercy),** GBE 1966; Kt 1963; MC 1918; Hon. DSc; JP; Lord Mayor of London for 1965–66; *b* 5 Aug. 1897; *s* of J. Percy Denny, Putney; *m* 1920, Doris, *d* of R. George Bare, FSI, Putney; one *s*. *Educ:* St Paul's Sch. Served European War, 1915–19, Lieut E Surrey Regt; active service in France (wounded thrice, MC); Sqdn Leader RAFVR and RAF Regt, 1940–45. Mem. Court of Common Council, for Billingsgate Ward, 1941, Deputy 1951, Chief Commoner 1954, Alderman 1957–70. One of HM Lieuts for the City of London, 1951–70; JP Co. of London, 1951–; JP City of London, 1957–. Livery Companies: Barber-Surgeons (Master, 1938–39); Vintners' (Master, 1960–61); Company of Watermen and Lightermen (Master, 1967). Chm. London Court of Arbitration, 1958–59. Sheriff, City of London, 1961–62. First Chancellor, The City Univ., London, 1966; Hon. DSc. Jt Hon. Col 254 (City of London) Regt RA (TA), 1965–66. KStJ 1966 (OStJ 1961). Vicary Lecturer, RCS, 1972. Chevalier, Légion d'Honneur, 1967 and other orders from Liberia, Ivory Coast, Senegal, Austria and Jordan. *Address:* 901 Grenville House, Dolphin Square, SW1. *T:* 01–834 4048. *Clubs:* City Livery. Press. 1959–60), Eccentric, Royal Thames Yacht. *Died* 5 *Aug.* 1985.

**DENNY-BROWN, Derek Ernest,** OBE 1942; MD NZ; DPhil Oxon; FRCP; J. J. Putnam Professor of Neurology, Emeritus, Harvard University, since 1972; Hon. Col RAMC; *b* 1901; *s* of Charles Denny-Brown; *m* 1937, Sylvia Marie, *d* of late Dr J. O. Summerhayes, DSO; four *s*. *Educ:* New Plymouth High Sch., NZ; Otago Univ., NZ; Magdalen Coll., Oxford (Hon. Fellow, 1976). Beit Memorial Research Fellow, 1925–28; Rockefeller Travelling Fellow, 1936; formerly Neurologist to St Bartholomew's Hosp., London, Asst Physician National Hosp., Queen Square, and sometime Registrar to Dept for Nervous Diseases, Guy's Hosp.; former Dir, Neurol. Unit, Boston City Hosp. Harvard University: Prof. of Neurology,

1941–46, and 1967–72; J. J. Putnam Prof. of Neurology, 1946–67. Fogarty Internat. Scholar, Nat. Insts of Health, Bethesda, Maryland, 1972–73. Hon. Fellow, RSM, 1958. Gran Oficier, Order of Hippolite Unanue (Peru), 1963. Sherrington Medal, Royal Society Mecicine London, 1962; Jacoby Award, Amer. Neurol. Assoc., 1968. Hon. AM Harvard; Hon. LLD Wayne, 1959; Hon. LLD Glasgow, 1971; Dr *hc* Brazil; Hon. DSc Otago, 1969; Hon. DLit Jefferson, 1977. *Publications:* Selected Writings of Sir Charles Sherrington, 1939; Diseases of Muscle (part author), 1953; The Basal Ganglia, 1962; Cerebral Control of Movement, 1966; Centennial Vol., Amer. Neurol. Assoc., 1975; papers on neurological subjects in scientific journals. *Address:* 3 Mercer Circle, Cambridge, Mass 02138, USA.
*Died 20 April* 1981.

**de NORMANN, Sir Eric,** KBE 1946; CB 1941; Chairman, Ancient Monuments Board for England, 1955–64; *b* 26 Dec. 1893; *s* of Albert de Normann and Irene Wood; *m* 1921, Winifred Leigh (*d* 1968); one *s. Educ:* Château du Rosey, Switzerland; University Coll. of South Wales (Fellow, 1981). Served European War, 1915–19 (despatches twice); Office of Works, 1920; Imperial Defence Coll., 1935. Dep. Sec., Ministry of Works, 1943–54. FSA. *Address:* Aylesham, Old Avenue, Weybridge, Surrey. *T:* Weybridge 42682. *Club:* Athenæum. *Died 25 Jan.* 1982.

**DENT, Major Leonard Maurice Edward,** DSO 1914; High Sheriff of Berkshire, 1948–49; *b* 18 June 1888; *s* of Edward and Mabel P. Dent; *m* 1920, Hester Anita (*d* 1976), *d* of Col Gerard Clark; one *s* two *d* (and two *d* decd). *Educ:* Eton; Trinity Coll., Cambridge, BA. Served European War, 1914–18 (wounded, despatches 4 times, DSO, Chevalier Légion d'Honneur, 1919); Major R of O, retd. Chm. and Man. Dir, Abco Products Ltd, 1936–75. Berks CC, 1946–58. Member: Council, Queen's Coll., London, 1935–83 (Chm., 1953–80); Court, Grocers' Co., 1935–82 (Master, 1935–36); Berks Br., CPRE (Chm., 1950–64); Court, Univ. of Reading (Treas., 1959–63); King's Coll. Hosp. Bd of Governors, 1950–63; Chairman: Belgrave Hosp. for Children, 1947–63; Exec. Cttee, City and Guilds of London Inst., 1937–70; City and Guilds of London Art Sch. Cttee, 1958–70. *Recreations:* photography, music, art collecting (especially Rowlandsons). *Address:* Hillfields, Burghfield Common, near Reading RG7 3BH. *T:* Burghfield Common 2495. *Club:* United Oxford & Cambridge University.
*Died 20 July* 1987.

**DENT, Sir Robert (Annesley Wilkinson),** Kt 1960; CB 1951; *b* 27 Jan. 1895; *e s* of late R. W. Dent, JP, Flass, Maulds Meaburn, Penrith, and late Edith Vere, OBE, *d* of Rev. F. H. Annesley Clifford Chambers, Glos; *m* 1927, Elspeth Muriel, *d* of Sir Alfred Tritton, 2nd Bt, Upper Gatton Park, Reigate; one *s* three *d. Educ:* Eton; Trinity Coll., Cambridge. Served European War, 1914–18, with King's Royal Rifle Corps (Lieutenant) in France and Flanders, (wounded, despatches). Rejoined 1940 and served War of 1939–45, with GHQ Home Forces and at the War Office AQMG (Temporary Lieut-Col), 1943–45. Asst Clerk, House of Commons, 1920; Clerk of Public Bills, 1948–59. High Sheriff, Westmorland, 1960. *Recreation:* gardening. *Address:* Lyvennet Bank, Maulds Meaburn, Penrith, Cumbria CA10 3HN. *T:* Ravensworth (Penrith) 225.
*Died 17 Nov.* 1983.

**DENT-BROCKLEHURST, Mrs Mary,** JP; *b* 6 Feb. 1902; *d* of late Major J. A. Morrison, DSO, and late Hon. Mary Hill-Trevor; *m* 1924, Major John Henry Dent-Brocklehurst, OBE (*d* 1949), Sudeley Castle, Glos; three *d* (one *s* decd). *Educ:* at home. JP and CC, 1949, CA 1958, Glos; High Sheriff, County of Gloucester, 1967. *Recreations:* gardening, beekeeping, travelling, archæology. *Address:* Hawling Manor, Andoversford, Cheltenham, Glos GL54 5TA. *T:* Guiting Power 362. *Died 4 March* 1988.

**d'ENTRÈVES, Alexander Passerin;** Professor Emeritus, University of Turin; *b* 26 April 1902; 4th *s* of Count Hector Passerin d'Entrèves et Courmayeur; *m* 1931, Nina Ferrari d'Orsara; one *s* one *d. Educ:* University of Turin, Italy; Balliol Coll., Oxford. Doctor of Law, Turin, 1922; DPhil Oxon, 1932; Lecturer, University of Turin, 1929; Prof. University of Messina, 1934, Pavia, 1935, Turin, 1938; Prefect of Aosta, April-May 1945; Mem. of Council of Val d'Aosta, Dec. 1945. Serena Prof. of Italian Studies, University of Oxford, 1946–57; Fellow Magdalen Coll., Oxford, 1946–57; Prof. of Political Theory, Univ. of Turin, 1958–72. Vis. Prof., Harvard Univ., 1957; Yale Univ., 1960–64. FRHistS; Fellow, Amer. Acad. Arts and Sciences; Member: Société Académique St Anselme, Aosta; Accademia delle Scienze, Turin; Accademia dei Lincei, Rome; Académie de Savoie, Chambéry. Hon. MA Yale, 1961; Dr *hc* Sorbonne, 1978. *Publications:* The Medieval Contribution to Political Thought, 1939; Reflections on the History of Italy, 1947; Aquinas, Selected Political Writings, 1948; Alessandro Manzoni, 1949; Natural Law, An Introduction to Legal Philosophy, 1951; Dante as a Political Thinker, 1952; The Notion of the State, An Introduction to Political Theory, 1967; other publications in Italian and French. *Recreation:* rambling in the Alps. *Address:* Strada ai

Ronchi 48, Cavoretto, Torino 10133, Italy; Castello di Entrèves, Courmayeur, Val d'Aosta, Italy. *Died 15 Dec.* 1985.

**de PASS, Col Guy Eliot,** DSO 1918; OBE 1945; late 4th Dragoon Guards; *b* 30 Oct. 1898; *yr s* of late John de Pass; *m* 1925, Winifred Dorothy, *d* of late Westcot Featherstonehaugh and late Mrs Featherstonehaugh, Durban, Natal; three *d. Educ:* St Andrews, Eastbourne; Eton; Sandhurst. Served European War, 1914–18 (despatches, DSO), 4th Royal Dragoon Guards; Major 4th Batt. Oxford Bucks Light Infantry (TA), 1938; Military Asst to the Quartermaster-Gen. of the Forces, 1940; 2nd in Command 4th Bn Oxford and Bucks Light Infantry, 1939–40; Asst Commandant, Donnington, Salop, 1941; Sub-Area Comdr, Preston, 1943; Dep. Dir Labour 2nd Army (HQ), May 1943–45, NW Europe Campaign (OBE). *Recreation:* shooting. *Address:* Upper House Farm, Harpsden, near Henley-on-Thames, Oxfordshire. *T:* Rotherfield Greys 378. *Club:* Cavalry and Guards. *Died 16 Aug.* 1985.

**de PEYER, Charles Hubert,** CMG 1956; retired Under-Secretary, Ministry of Fuel and Power (served with Foreign Office, with rank of Minister in United Kingdom Delegation to European Coal and Steel Community, 1952–56); *b* 24 Oct. 1905; 2nd *s* of Everard Charles de Peyer and Edith Mabel Starkey; *m* 1st, 1930, Flora Collins, singer, New York; one *s* one *d*; 2nd, 1953, Mary Burgess (*d* 1974); two *s* one *d*; 3rd, 1975, Joan, widow of Wilfred Fienburgh, MP. *Educ:* Cheltenham Coll.; Magdalen Coll., Oxford (Hons PPE). Entered Civil Service, Mines Dept, 1930. *Recreations:* gardening, music. *Address:* 348 Chambersbury Lane, Leverstock Green, Hemel Hempstead, Herts. *Club:* Reform. *Died 29 Nov.* 1983.

**de POLNAY, Peter;** author; *b* 8 March 1906; *m* 1942, Margaret Mitchell-Banks (*d* 1950); one *s*; *m* 1952, Daphne Taylor; *m* 1955, Maria del Carmen Rubio y Caparo. *Educ:* privately in England, Switzerland and Italy. Farmed in Kenya. First began to write in Kenya in 1932; was in Paris when Germans entered, worked with early French Resistance, escaped back to England after imprisonment under Vichy Government. *Publications:* Angry Man's Tale, 1938; Children My Children!, 1939; Boo, 1941; Death and Tomorrow, 1942; Water on the Steps, 1943; Two Mirrors, 1944; The Umbrella Thorn, 1946; A Pin's Fee, 1947; The Moot Point, 1948; Into an Old Room, a Study of Edward Fitzgerald, 1949; Somebody Must, 1949; An Unfinished Journey, 1952; Death of a Legend: The True Story of Bonny Prince Charlie, 1953; Fools of Choice, 1955; Before I Sleep, 1955; The Shorn Shadow, 1956; The Clap of Silent Thunder, 1957; Peninsular Paradox, 1958; The Crack of Dawn, 1960; The Gamesters, 1960; Garibaldi, 1961; No Empty Hands, 1961; The Flames of Art, 1962; A Man of Fortune, 1963; Three Phases of High Summer, 1963; The Plaster Bed, 1965; The World of Maurice Utrillo, 1967; Aspects of Paris, 1968; A Tower of Strength, 1969; The Patriots, 1969; A Tale of Two Husbands, 1970; Napoleon's Police, 1970; The Permanent Farewell, 1970; A T-Shaped World, 1971; A Life of Ease, 1971; The Grey Sheep, 1972; The Loser, 1973; The Price You Pay, 1973; The Crow and the Cat, 1974; Indifference, 1974; A Clump of Trees, 1975; None Shall Know, 1976; The Stuffed Dog, 1976; Driftsand, 1977; The Other Shore of Time, 1978; My Road (autobiog.), 1978; The Autumn Leaves Merchant, 1979; Make-Believe, 1980; The Talking House, 1980; A Minor Giant, 1981; Sea Mist, 1982; Of Venison and Victims, 1983; The Lost Stronghold, 1984; *posthumous publication:* The Guest House, 1985. *Recreation:* French history. *Address:* c/o A. M. Heath & Co. Ltd, 40–42 William IV Street, WC2N 4DD.
*Died 21 Nov.* 1984.

**DERHAM, Prof. Sir David (Plumley),** KBE 1977 (MBE 1945); CMG 1968; BA, LLM Melbourne; Vice-Chancellor of the University of Melbourne, 1968–82; *b* 13 May 1920; *s* of late Dr A. P. Derham, CBE, MC, ED, MD, FRACP; *m* 1944, Rosemary, *d* of late Gen. Sir Brudenell White, KCB, KCMG, KCVO, DSO; one *s* two *d. Educ:* Scotch Coll., Melbourne; Ormond Coll., Melbourne Univ. AIF, 1941–45 (Major). Solicitor, 1948; Barrister, 1948–51; Melbourne University: Tutor in Law, Queen's Coll., and Independent Lectr, Constitutional Law, 1949–51; Prof. of Jurisprudence, 1951–64; Vis. Fellow, Wadham Coll., Oxford, 1953; Carnegie Trav. Fellow, 1953–54; Constitutional Consultant, Indian Law Inst., 1958–59; Sen. Res. Fellow and Vis. Lectr, Chicago Univ. Law Sch., 1961; Vis. Prof. Northwestern Univ. Law Sch., 1961; Dean of Faculty of Law, Monash Univ., 1964–68. Member: Victorian Chief Justice's Law Reform Cttee, 1951–68; Victorian Council of Legal Educn, 1951–68; Bd of Management, Royal Melbourne Hosp., 1958–83; Commonwealth Cttee on Teaching Costs of Medical Hosps, 1961–65; Commonwealth Cttee on Future of Tertiary Educn in Australia, 1962–64; Australian Univs Commn, 1965–68; Bd of Management, Walter & Eliza Hall Inst. of Med. Res., 1968–82. Chairman: Overseas Service Bureau, 1965–81; Melbourne Theatre Co. Bd of Management, 1973–82; Aust. Vice-Chancellors' Cttee, 1975–76. President: Medico-Legal Soc., Vic., 1963–64; Australasian Univs Law Schs Assoc., 1964–65. Fellow, Australian Acad. of Social Scis, 1964. Hon. LLD: Monash, 1968; Melbourne, 1982. *Publications:* (Ch. 1) Legal Personality and

Political Pluralism, 1958; (Ch. 6) Essays on the Australian Constitution, 2nd edn 1961; Paton, Textbook of Jurisprudence (ed) 3rd edn 1964, 4th edn 1972; (with F. K. H. Maher and Prof. P. L. Waller) Cases and Materials on the Legal Process, 1966, 4th edn 1984; (with F. K. H. Maher and Prof. P. L. Waller) An Introduction to Law, 1966, 4th edn 1982; articles in legal and other jls. *Recreations:* golf, tennis, lawn tennis. *Address:* 13 Selborne Road, Toorak, Vic 3142, Australia. *T:* 241–9329. *Clubs:* Naval and Military (Melbourne); Royal Melbourne Golf, Barwon Heads Golf.
*Died 1 Sept. 1985.*

**de ROS,** 27th Baroness (in her own right; Premier Barony of England) *cr* 1264; **Georgiana Angela Maxwell;** *b* 2 May 1933; *er d* of Lieut-Comdr Peter Ross, RN (killed on active service, 1940) and *g d* of 26th Baroness de Ros (*d* 1956); *S* grandmother, 1958 (on termination of abeyance); *m* 1954, Comdr John David Maxwell, RN; one *s* one *d*. *Educ:* Wycombe Abbey Sch., Bucks; Studley Agricultural Coll. Warwicks. NDD 1955. *Heir:* s Hon. Peter Trevor Maxwell, *b* 23 Dec. 1958. *Address:* Old Court, Strangford, N Ireland.
*Died 21 April 1983.*

**DERRY, Warren,** MA; *b* 19 Oct. 1899; *e s* of late Rev. W. T. Derry, Wesleyan minister; *m* 1930, Lorna Adeline (*d* 1985), *yr d* of Reginald H. Ferard; one *s* two *d*. *Educ:* Kingswood Sch., Bath; Magdalen Coll., Oxford (Demy). 2nd Class Hons Classical Moderations, 1920; 1st Class Hons. Final Sch. of English Language and Literature, 1922; Passmore Edwards Scholar, 1922; Asst Master, the Edinburgh Academy, 1922–28; Headmaster Wolverhampton Grammar Sch., 1929–56. *Publications:* Dr Parr, a Portrait of the Whig Dr Johnson, 1966; (ed) Journals and Letters of Fanny Burney, vols IX and X, 1982. *Address:* 11 Abbey Court, Edward Street, Bath.
*Died 9 July 1986.*

**DERWENT,** 4th Baron *cr* 1881; **Patrick Robin Gilbert Vanden-Bempde-Johnstone,** CBE 1974; Bt 1795; *b* 26 Oct. 1901; *y s* of late Hon. Edward Henry Vanden-Bempde-Johnstone, 2nd *s* of 1st Baron and Hon. Evelyn Agar-Ellis (*d* 1952), *d* of 5th Viscount Clifden; *S* brother, 1949; *m* 1929, Marie-Louise (*d* 1985), *d* of late Albert Picard, Paris; one *s*. *Educ:* Charterhouse; RMC, Sandhurst. Commissioned KRRC, 1921; Major, KRRC. Formerly Director: Yorkshire Insurance Co.; National Safe Deposit and Trustee Co. Ltd; past Chm., Reinsurance Corp.; ex-Mem., Horserace Totalisator Bd, Tote Investors Ltd; past Chm., British Road Fedn. Junior Opposition Whip in House of Lords, 1950–51; Minister of State, Bd of Trade, 1962–63; Minister of State, Home Office, 1963–64; Deputy Speaker, House of Lords, 1970–. *Recreations:* shooting and fishing. *Heir:* s Hon. Robin Evelyn Leo Vanden-Bempde-Johnstone, MVO 1957 [*b* 30 Oct. 1930; *m* 1957, Sybille de Simard de Pitray, *d* of Vicomte de Simard de Pitray and Madame Jeannine Hennessy; one *s* three *d*]. *Address:* Hackness Hall, Scarborough, North Yorks; 48 Cadogan Place, SW1. *Club:* Beefsteak.
*Died 2 Jan. 1986.*

**DESHMUKH, Sir Chintaman Dwarkanath,** Kt 1944; CIE 1937; President: India International Centre, New Delhi, since 1959; Council for Social Development, since 1969; *b* Bombay Presidency, 14 Jan. 1896; *s* of D. G. Deshmukh, lawyer; *m* 1st, 1920, Rosina, *d* of Arthur Silcox, London; one *d*; 2nd, 1953, Srimathi Durgabai (*d* 1981). *Educ:* Elphinstone High Sch.; Elphinstone Coll., Bombay; Jesus Coll., Cambridge (Hon. Fellow 1962). National Science Tripos, pt 1, Frank Smart Prize in Botany, BA, 1917; first in Indian Civil Service Examination, London (open competitive), 1918; passed UK Bar Examination in 1919 and was called to Bar, Inner Temple, 1963. Asst Commissioner, 1920–24; Under Sec. to CP Government, 1924–25; Deputy Commissioner and Settlement Officer, 1926–30; Joint Sec. to 2nd Round Table Conference, 1931; Revenue Sec. to CP Govt, 1932–33; Financial Sec. to Govt of CP and Berar, India, 1933–39; Joint Sec. to the Government of India; Dept of Education, Health and Lands; Officer on Special Duty, Finance Dept, Govt of India; Custodian of Enemy Property, 1939; Sec. to Central Board of Reserve Bank of India, Bombay, 1939–41; Deputy-Governor, 1941–43; Governor, 1943–49, retired, 1949. Pres., Indian Statistical Inst., Calcutta, 1945–64. India's delegate to the World Monetary Conference at Bretton Woods, 1944. Governor, World Bank and Fund, for India, Washington, 1946; Financial Rep. in Europe and America of Govt of India, 1949–50; Chm. Joint Board of Governors of World Bank and International Monetary Fund, 1950; Mem. Planning Commn, 1950; Minister of Finance, Govt of India, 1950–56, resigned 1956. Chairman: University Grants Commission, India, 1956–60; Administrative Staff Coll. of India, 1959–73; Indian Institute of Public Administration, 1964; Central Sanskrit Bd, 1967–68; Pres., Institute of Economic Growth, 1962–73; Mem. Bd of Trustees, UN Inst. for Trng and Res., 1965–70. Pres., Population Council of India, 1970–75. Vice-Chancellor, Univ. of Delhi, 1962–67. Holds hon. doctorates from US, UK and Indian Univs. Ramon Magsaysay Award (Philippines), 1959. *Publications:* Economic Developments in India, 1957; In the Portals of Indian Universities, 1959; On the Threshold of India's Citizenhood, 1962; Sanskrit Kāvyā-Mālikā, 1968; Reflections on

Finance, Education and Society, 1972; Aspects of Development, 1972; The Course of My Life, 1973; Bhagavatgita, 1976; Amarakosa, 1981. *Recreation:* gardening. *Address:* India International Centre, 40 Lodi Estate, New Delhi, India; CTI, Hyderabad 500768.
*Died 2 Oct. 1982.*

**de SOLOVEYTCHIK, George Michael;** *see* Soloveytchik.

**de TRAFFORD, Sir Rudolph Edgar Francis,** 5th Bt *cr* 1841; OBE 1919; *b* 31 Aug. 1894; *s* of Sir Humphrey Francis de Trafford, 3rd Bt and Violet Alice Maud (*d* 1925), *d* of James Franklin; *S* brother, 1971; *m* 1st, 1924, June (who obtained a divorce, 1938), *o d* of late Lieut-Col Reginald Chaplin; one *s*; 2nd, 1939, Katherine, *e d* of W. W. Balke, Cincinnati, USA. *Educ:* Downside Sch.; Trinity Coll., Cambridge, BA. Served European War, 1914–18; Intelligence Corps and Gen. Staff GHQ. *Heir:* s Dermot Humphrey de Trafford, VRD. *Address:* 70 Eaton Square, SW1. *T:* 01-235 1823. *Club:* White's.
*Died 16 Aug. 1983.*

**de VESCI,** 6th Viscount, *cr* 1776; **John Eustace Vesey;** *b* 25 Feb. 1919; *s* of Lt-Col Hon. Thomas (Eustace) Vesey (*d* 1946) (*b* of 5th Viscount), and Lady Cecily (Kathleen) Vesey (*d* 1976) (a Lady-in-Waiting to the Duchess of Gloucester, 1947–51, a Woman of the Bedchamber to Queen Mary, 1951–53, and an Extra Lady-in-Waiting to the Duchess of Gloucester from 1953), *d* of 5th Earl of Kenmare; *S* uncle, 1958; *m* 1950, Susan Anne, *d* of late Ronald (Owen Lloyd) Armstrong Jones, MBE, QC, DL, and of Anne (later Countess of Rosse), *o d* of Lt-Col Leonard Messel, OBE; one *s* two *d* (and one *d* decd). *Educ:* Eton; Trinity Coll., Cambridge. Served War of 1939–45 with Irish Guards, Narvik (wounded), North Africa and Italy. Followed career of Land Agent; now managing own property. FLAS(O), FRICS. Kt of Honour and Devotion, Sovereign Mil. Order of Malta. *Heir:* s Hon. Thomas Eustace Vesey, *b* 8 Oct. 1955. *Address:* Abbeyleix, Ireland. *T:* Abbeyleix 31162. *Club:* White's.
*Died 13 Oct. 1983.*

**DEVLIN, William;** Actor; *b* Aberdeen, 5 Dec. 1911; *y s* of William John Devlin, ARIBA, and Frances Evelyn Crombie; *m* 1936, Mary Casson (marr. diss.); one *d*; *m* 1948, Meriel Moore (*d* 1981). *Educ:* Stonyhurst Coll.; Merton Coll., Oxford (BA). Sec. OUDS, 1932–33; studied at Embassy Theatre Sch., 1933–34. New Theatre with John Gielgud, 1934–35 (Hamlet and Noah); Old Vic Company, 1935–36 (Peer Gynt, Cassius, Richard III, Leontes, Lear, etc); except for war period has appeared for Old Vic in every year, 1935–53 (Shylock, Macbeth, Claudius, Brutus, Dogberry, Fluellen, etc.). Parnell in The Lost Leader, Abbey Theatre, Dublin, 1937; Zola, Clemenceau, Gladstone in biogr. plays about them, 1937–38; Ransom in Ascent of F6 and Seth in Mourning becomes Electra, New Theatre, 1938. Joined HM Forces, Sept. 1939, as a Trooper in Horsed Cavalry; commnd in Royal Wilts Yeom. and served with 8th Army in Africa and Italy for 4½ years; released as Major, Nov. 1945. Leading man with Old Vic at Theatre Royal, Bristol, 1945–48. Memorial Theatre, Stratford-on-Avon, seasons 1954 and 1955. First appeared in New York as Bohun, QC in You Never Can Tell, Martin Beck Theatre, 1948; subseq. at Boston as Lear and Macbeth. Played Clemenceau in The Tiger, the first play to be televised in 1936, and has appeared regularly in this medium and also in Sound Broadcasting. Mem., Equity Council, 1957–65. Mem., Monksilver Parish Council, 1967, Chairman 1971, and 1973–74. *Recreations:* golf and fishing. *Address:* Bird's Hill Cottage, Monksilver, Taunton, Som TA4 4JB. *T:* Stogumber 56389.
*Died 25 Jan. 1987.*

**DEVONSHIRE, Dowager Duchess of, (Mary Alice),** GCVO 1955; CBE 1946; Mistress of the Robes to The Queen, 1953–66; Chancellor of the University of Exeter, 1956–70; *b* 29 July 1895; *d* of 4th Marquis of Salisbury, KG, PC, GCVO, and Lady Cicely Alice Gore (*d* 1955), 2nd *d* of 5th Earl of Arran; *m* 1917, as Lady Mary Cecil, 10th Duke of Devonshire, KG; one *s* (see 11th Duke of Devonshire) two *d* (er *s* killed in action, 1944). *Address:* 107 Eaton Square, SW1W 9AA. *T:* 01-235 8798; Moorview, Edensor, Bakewell, Derbyshire. *T:* Baslow 2204.
*Died 24 Dec. 1988.*

**DEWAR, Brig. Michael Preston Douglas,** CB 1958; CBE 1956; retired; *b* 1 Oct. 1906; *s* of late Vice-Admiral R. G. D. Dewar, CBE, and Mrs S. E. Dewar (née Churchill); *m* 1935, Winifred Elizabeth, née Murphy (*d* 1971); one *s* one *d*. *Educ:* Winchester Coll. Commissioned 2nd Lieut, The Buffs, 1926; Captain, 1938; Staff Coll., 1939; Major, 1943; OC Home Counties Bde Trg Centre, 1946–47; GSO 1, 6th Airborne Div., 1947–48; Lt-Col, 1948; Jt Services Staff Coll., 1948–49; Col GS, E Africa, 1949–51; Col, 1951; Col Administrative Plans, GHQ, MELF, 1951–52; Dep. Dir Manpower Planning, War Office, 1952–55; Brig., 1955; UK Nat. Military Rep., SHAPE, 1955–58, retired 1959. *Recreations:* gardening, bridge. *Address:* Great Maytham Hall, Rolvenden, near Cranbrook, Kent. *T:* Cranbrook 241375.
*Died 14 Dec. 1984.*

**DEWES, Sir Herbert (John Salisbury),** Kt 1973; CBE 1954; DL; JP; Chairman, Cheshire County Council, 1968–74; *b* 30 June 1897; *s* of John Hunt Dewes, solicitor, Tamworth, Staffordshire; *m* 1923,

Kathleen (decd), *d* of W. Matthews, Nuneaton; two *s. Educ:* Aldenham. County Alderman for Cheshire, 1950; JP 1951, DL 1966, Cheshire. Presidential Award, RSA, 1973. *Address:* 2 Curzon Park North, Chester CH4 8AR. *T:* Chester 679798.
*Died 17 July 1988.*

**DEWHURST, Keith Ward; His Honour Judge Dewhurst;** a Circuit Judge, since 1972; *b* 11 March 1924; *s* of James Dewhurst, solicitor, and Mildred Catherine Dewhurst; *m* 1952, Norah Mary Hodgson (marr. diss. 1970); two *d. Educ:* Shrewsbury School; Trinity College, Oxford. Called to the Bar, Inner Temple, 1947. Practised on Northern Circuit. *Recreations:* reading, bridge. *Address:* 277 Garstang Road, Fulwood, Preston, Lancs. *T:* Preston 716850.
*Died 4 March 1984.*

**DEWHURST, Comdr Ronald Hugh,** DSO 1940; RN retired; *b* 10 Oct. 1905; *s* of late Robert Paget Dewhurst, ICS, and late Florence Frances Maud Dewhurst; *m* 1928, Torquilla Macleod Lawrence (*d* 1953); one *s* one *d*; *m* 1954, Marion Isabel Dahm; one *d. Educ:* Abberley Hall; Osborne; Dartmouth. Joined Royal Navy, 1919; served in submarines, 1927–53; commanded HM submarines H. 33, Seahorse, and Rorqual (DSO and two Bars); Amphion, Taciturn, and RN Detention Quarters, 1953–55; retired to New Zealand, 1955. *Recreations:* fishing, bridge. *Address:* 2/15 Hodgkins Street, Rotorua, New Zealand. *Died 29 Jan. 1990.*

**DEWING, Maj.-Gen. Richard Henry,** CB 1941; DSO 1917; MC 1915; psc; retired; *b* 15 Jan. 1891; *e* surv. *s* of Rev. R. S. Dewing and Dora, *d* of R. J. Pettiward, of Finborough Hall, Suffolk; *m* 1920, Helen (*d* 1976), *e d* of Lieut-Col A. J. Wogan-Browne, 33rd Cavalry; one *s* (and *e s* killed in action in Libya, 2nd *s* decd, *o d* decd). *Educ:* Haileybury, Commd in RE, 1911; joined 2nd QVO Sappers and Miners, 1914; Capt., 1917; Bt Major, 1919; Major, 1926; Bt Lieut-Col, 1930; Lieut-Col, 1934; Col, 1936; Maj.-Gen., 1939; served in Mesopotamia and Persia, 1915–19 (DSO, MC); Peace Service India, 1913–14, 1920–21; GSO 2 Royal Military Coll., Kingston, Canada, 1927–29; OC 54th Field Co., Bulford; GSO2 Southern Command, 1931–33; Imperial Defence Coll., 1934; Gen. Staff Officer, 1st Grade, War Office, 1936–37; Army Instructor Imperial Defence Coll., 1937–39; Dir of Military Operations, 1939–40; Chief of Staff, Far East, 1940–41; Military Mission, Washington, 1942; Chief of Army-RAF Liaison Staff, Australia, 1943–44; SHAEF Mission to Denmark, 1945. Grand Cross Order of Dannebrog (Denmark); Officer Legion of Merit (USA). *Address:* The Hollies, Kildary, Invergordon, Ross-shire. *Died 21 Sept. 1981.*

**de WOLFF, Brig. Charles Esmond,** CB 1945; CBE 1919 (OBE 1919); LLB; *b* 25 Nov. 1893; *s* of C. L. de Wolff; *m* 1920, Ada Marjorie, *d* of Henry Arnold, Hatch End. Served: European War, 1914–19 (despatches four times, OBE, CBE, Russian Order of Vladimir); Dardanelles and Salonika, South Russia, 1919; 2nd Lieut Royal Sussex Regiment, 1914; transferred RAOC War of 1939–45 (CB); France and Italy; retd pay, 1946. OStJ 1952. *Clubs:* Army and Navy; Union (Malta). *Died 12 Oct. 1986.*

**DEXTER, John;** freelance stage director; Director of Production, 1974–81, Production Adviser, 1981–84, Metropolitan Opera, New York; *b* 2 Aug. 1925. Actor in repertory, television and radio, until 1957; Associate Dir, National Theatre, 1963–66, 1971–75. Best Dir of Drama Award, 1975; Shakespeare Prize, 1978. *Plays directed:* 15 plays, 1957–72, Royal Court, incl. The Old Ones, 1972; Pygmalion, Albery, 1974; Valmouth, Chichester Fest., 1982; *National Theatre:* Saint Joan, 1963; Hobson's Choice, Othello, Royal Hunt of the Sun, 1964; Armstrong's Last Goodnight, Black Comedy, 1965; A Bond Honoured, The Storm, 1966; A Woman Killed With Kindness, Tyger, The Good Natur'd Man, 1971; The Misanthrope, Equus, The Party, 1973; Phaedra Britannica, 1975; As You Like It, 1979; The Life of Galileo, 1980; The Shoemakers' Holiday, 1981; *other London theatres:* The Portage to San Cristobal of A. H., Mermaid, 1982; The Devil and the Good Lord, Lyric, Hammersmith, 1984; Gigi, Lyric, 1985; productions by New Theatre Company (Co-Founder, 1985): The Cocktail Party, Phoenix, 1986; M. Bufferfly, Shaftesbury, 1989; *provinces:* Portraits, Malvern, 1987; season at Haymarket, Leicester, 1988; *New York:* Chips With Everything, 1963; Do I Hear a Waltz?, 1965; Black Comedy and White Lies, The Unknown Soldier and His Wife, 1967; Equus, 1974; The Glass Menagerie, 1983; The Threepenny Opera, 1989; *Los Angeles:* Pygmalian, Ahmanson Th., 1979; *film:* The Virgin Soldiers, 1968; *opera:* Benvenuto Cellini, Covent Garden, 1966; House of the Dead, Boris Godunov, Billy Budd, Ballo in Maschera, I Vespri Siciliani, Hamburg; The Devils of Loudon, Sadler's Wells; La Forza Del Destino, 1975, Paris; L'enfant et les sortilèges, and The Nightingale, Covent Garden, 1983; La Buone Figliola, Buxton Fest., 1985; Nabucco, Zurich, 1986; Madam Butterfly, NY, 1988; *opera for Metropolitan, NY:* I Vespri Siciliani, Aida, 1976; Le Prophète, Dialogues of the Carmelites, Lulu, Rigoletto, 1977; Don Pasquale, Billy Budd, The Bartered Bride, 1978; Don Carlo, Rise and Fall of the City of Mahagonny, Die Entführung aus dem Serail, 1979; Le Rossignol, Le Sacre du Printemps, Oedipus Rex (triple bill), 1981;

Parade, 1981. *Recreations:* work, garden. *Address:* 142A Portland Road, W11. *Died 23 March 1990.*

**DEXTER, Dr Keith,** CB 1978; Second Crown Estate Commissioner, since 1983; *b* 3 April 1928; *yr s* of Arthur William Dexter, farmer, and Phyllis Dexter; *m* 1954, Marjorie Billbrough; no *c. Educ:* Dixie Grammar Sch., Market Bosworth; Univs of Nottingham and Illinois. BSc London 1948; MS Illinois 1951; PhD Nottingham 1954; Nat. Diploma in Agric. 1948. Hon. Associate RICS, 1986; FRAgS 1986. Asst Agric. Economist, Nottingham Univ., 1948–50; Booth Fellow, Illinois Univ., 1950–51; Fulbright Trav. Schol., 1950–51; Res. Schol. and Agric. Economist, Nottingham Univ., 1951–54; Agric. Economist, Min. of Agriculture, 1954–62; Grade I Adviser, Nat. Agric. Adv. Service, 1962–64; Admin. Staff Coll., Henley, 1963; Sen. Principal Agric. Economist, 1964–68; Dep. Dir of Econs and Statistics, 1968–70; Head of Fatstock Div., 1970–71; Under-Sec. (Meat and Fatstock), MAFF, 1971–75; Dep. Sec. (Agricultural Science) and Dir-Gen., ADAS, 1975–83. Mem., ARC, 1975–84. Mem. Court, Cranfield Inst. of Technology, 1980–; Governor, Coll. of Estate Management, Reading, 1984–. Mem. Duke of Edinburgh's 3rd Commonwealth Study Conf., Australia, 1968. *Publications:* (with Derek Barber) Farming for Profits, 1961, 2nd edn 1967; contribs to Jl Agric. Econs. *Recreations:* gardening, fishing. *Address:* Crown Estate Office, 13–15 Carlton House Terrace, SW1Y 5AH. *T:* 01–210 4231. *Club:* Farmers'.
*Died 8 April 1989.*

**d'EYNCOURT;** *see* Tennyson -d'Eyncourt.

**de ZULUETA, Sir Philip Francis;** *see* Zulueta.

**DIAMOND, George Clifford,** OBE 1955; MA; Head Master, Cardiff High School for Boys, retired 1966; *b* 27 Nov. 1902; *s* of George Labbett and Jessie Diamond; *m* 1928, Beryl Jones (decd); two *s. Educ:* Cardiff High Sch.; The Leys Sch., Cambridge; Queens' Coll., Cambridge (Scholar). English Tripos, Class I, History Tripos, Part II, Class II Div. I. Asst Master, Mill Hill Junior Sch., 1926–27; Senior English Master, The Leys Sch., 1927–34. Pres., Welsh Secondary Schools' Assoc., 1957. *Address:* Flat 9A, The Cathedral Green, Llandaff, Glamorgan. *Died 9 Oct. 1985.*

**DIAMOND, Prof. Jack,** CBE 1969; Whitworth Scholar, MSc (Cambridge and Manchester); FCGI; FIMechE; Beyer Professor of Mechanical Engineering, Manchester University, 1953–77, later Emeritus; *b* 22 June 1912; *s* of late Alfred John Diamond and Jessie M. Kitchingham; *m* 1943, Iris Evelyn Purvis; three *d. Educ:* Chatham Technical Sch.; Royal Dockyard School, Chatham; City and Guilds Coll., London; St John's Coll., Cambridge. Engineering apprenticeship, HM Dockyard, Chatham, 1928–32; Whitworth Scholar, 1932; BSc, ACGI, Wh. Sch. (sen.), 1935. Research in Heat Transfer, University Eng. labs and St John's, Cambridge, 1935–37; MSc 1937; Univ. Demonstrator in Engineering, Cambridge, 1937–39. RN (temp. Engr Officer), 1939–44. RN Scientific Service on loan to Ministry of Supply in Canada and at AERE, Harwell, 1944–53. Member: Governing Board of Nat. Inst. for Research in Nuclear Science, 1957–60; UGC, 1965–73; NRDC, 1966–71; Council, IMechE, 1958–70 (Vice-Pres. 1967–70); Pres., Section G, British Assoc., 1970. Pro-Vice-Chancellor, Manchester Univ., 1970–77. FCGI 1968. Hon. DSc Heriot-Watt, 1975. *Publications:* various, in engineering publications. *Address:* 5 Chelford Road, Somerford, Congleton, Cheshire CW12 4QD. *Club:* Athenæum.
*Died 27 June 1990.*

**DIBBS, (Arthur Henry) Alexander,** CBE 1983; Director, National Westminster Bank, 1970–83; Joint Deputy Chairman, British Airways, 1981–85; *b* 9 Dec. 1918; *s* of H. J. Dibbs and P. L. Dibbs (*née* Baker); *m* 1948, Helen Pearl Mathewson; two *d. Educ:* Dover Coll.; Whitgift Middle Sch., Croydon. FIB. AMP, Harvard Univ., 1963. Served with Army, 1939–46. Joined Westminster Bank Ltd, 1935; Manager, Croydon Br., 1960; Asst Gen. Man., 1963; Jt Gen. Man., 1966; National Westminster Bank Ltd: Gen. Man., Domestic Banking Div., 1968; Chief Exec. 1972–77; a Dep. Chm., 1977–82. Mem., NEB, 1979–81. Mem. Bd of Governors, E-SU, 1976–. *Recreations:* golf; watching all sports. *Address:* The Orchard, Deans Lane, Walton on the Hill, Tadworth, Surrey. *Clubs:* Caledonian, MCC (Pres., 1983; Mem. Finance Cttee), Royal Automobile.
*Died 28 Nov. 1985.*

**DICK, Alick Sydney;** industrial consultant; Purchasing Consultant to: Volkswagenwerk AG, Wolfsburg, Germany, since 1968; Audi NSU Auto Union AG, Ingolstadt, Germany, since 1968; *b* 20 June 1916; *s* of Dr W. Dick, Chichester, Sussex; *m* 1940, Betty Melinda Eileen Hill; three *s. Educ:* Chichester High Sch.; Dean Close, Cheltenham. Managing Dir, Standard Triumph International Ltd, Coventry, 1954–61. Pres. of Soc. of Motor Manufacturers and Traders, 1957. Governor: University of Birmingham, 1959–80; Coll. of Aeronautics, Cranfield, 1960–63. Benjamin Franklin Medal (RSA), 1961. Governor, Dean Close Sch., Cheltenham, 1964. *Recreation:* boats. *Address:* The Thatched Cottage, Hill Wootton, Warwick CV35 7PP. *T:* Kenilworth 54416. *Died 8 March 1986.*

**DICK, Clare L.;** *see* Lawson Dick.

**DICK, Commodore John Mathew,** CB 1955; CBE 1945; VRD; RNVR, retired; Solicitor to Secretary of State for Scotland, 1946–64 (and in Scotland to Treasury); *b* 2 Aug. 1899; *s* of late Mathew Dick, Campbeltown, Argyll, and Margaret Barr; *m* 1930, Anne Moir (*d* 1959), *d* of late Ralph Hill Stewart, Edinburgh; one *s. Educ:* Campbeltown Grammar Sch.; Edinburgh Academy. Entered Royal Naval Volunteer Reserve, 1917; served in Mediterranean and Grand Fleet, 1917–19 (despatches, Order of Crown of Roumania); Lieut RNVR 1924; Comdr 1935 (commanded Edinburgh RNVR 1927–39); Capt. 1940 (Coastal Forces and Admiralty); Commodore 1943; RNVR ADC to the King, 1943–45; retired list, 1946. *Address:* 35 Dick Place, Edinburgh. *Club:* New (Edinburgh).
*Died 4 Feb.* 1981.

**DICK-LAUDER, Sir George Andrew;** *see* Lauder.

**DICKENS, Frank,** MA Cambridge, DSc, PhD London; DIC; FRS 1946; FIBiol; *b* 1899; *s* of late John Dickens and Elizabeth Dickens, Northampton; *m* 1925, Molly, *o d* of late Arthur W. and Norah Jelleyman, Northampton; two *d. Educ:* Northampton Grammar Sch.; Magdalene Coll., Cambridge (Scholar). Res. in Organic Chemistry at Imperial Coll. of Science, 1921–23; Lectr in Biochemistry, Middlesex Hospital Medical Sch., whole-time worker for MRC, 1929; Mem. Scientific Staff, MRC, 1931; Research Dir North of England Council of British Empire Cancer Campaign, 1933–46; Philip Hill Professor of Experimental Biochemistry, Middlesex Hosp. Med. Sch., 1946–67, now Emeritus; Dir, Tobacco Research Council Labs, Harrogate, 1967–69. Research for Royal Naval Personnel Cttee of MRC, Nat. Inst. for Medical Research, 1943–44. An Editor of Biochemical Journal, 1937–47; Chm., Biochemical Soc., 1950, Hon. Mem., 1967. Formerly Mem. Scientific Advisory Cttee of the British Empire Cancer Campaign. Chm., British Nat. Cttee for Biochemistry. Hon. Fellow: King's Coll. (University of Newcastle); Leeds Univ. Hon DSc Newcastle upon Tyne, 1972. *Publications:* Chemical and Physiological Properties of the Internal Secretions (with E. C. Dodds); translation of the Metabolism of Tumours (by O. Warburg); ed, Oxygen in the Animal Organism (with E. Neil); Carbohydrate Metabolism and its Disorders (with P. J. Randle and W. J. Whelan); Essays in Biochemistry (with P. N. Campbell); numerous scientific papers mainly in Biochemical Jl. *Recreations:* fishing, photography. *Address:* 15 Thakeham Drive, Goring-by-Sea, Worthing, West Sussex BN12 5AX. *T:* Worthing 43970.
*Died 25 June* 1986.

**DICKENS, Sir Louis (Walter),** Kt 1968; DFC 1940; AFC 1938; DL; *b* 28 Sept. 1903; *s* of C. H. Dickens; *m* 1939, Ena Alice Bastable (*d* 1971); one *s* one *d. Educ:* Clongowes Wood Coll.; Cranwell Cadet Coll. Bomber Sqdn, 1923–27; Flying Trng, 1927; Egypt, 1932; Personnel, Air Min., 1932–35; subseq. Flying Instructor, Cranwell; Bomber Comd, France, 1940; Flying Instructor, Canada, 1941–42; Bomber Comd, 1943–44; SHAEF France, 1944–45; retired, 1947. Member: Berkshire CC, 1952–74 (Chm., 1965–68, Co. Alderman, 1959–73); Wokingham DC, 1974– (Chm., 1974–76). DL Berks, 1966. *Recreation:* golf. *Address:* Copperfield, Beech Lea, Meysey Hampton, near Cirencester, Glos. *Club:* Royal Air Force.
*Died 30 Aug.* 1988.

**DICKINS, Aileen Marian,** MD, FRCOG; Consultant Gynaecological and Obstetric Surgeon, University College Hospital, London, 1967–83, retired; *b* 17 Nov. 1917; *d* of Arthur George Dickins and Marian Helen Dickins. MD; FRCOG 1958. Obstetrician and Gynaecologist: Windsor Gp of Hosps, 1952–64; Ealing Hosp. and Perivale Maternity Hosp., 1951–82. Jun. Vice Pres., RCOG, 1978–80, Sen. Vice-Pres., 1980–81. FRSM; Mem. Women's Visiting Gynaecological Club. *Publications:* contrib. to BMJ and Jl of Obs and Gyn. of Brit. Commonwealth. *Recreations:* skiing, gardening. *Address:* Driscoll's Cottage, Broughton, near Stockbridge, Hants SO20 8BD. *Died 24 July* 1987.

**DICKINSON, Rear-Adm. (retired) Norman Vincent,** CB 1953; DSO 1942, and Bar, 1944; DSC 1920; *b* 29 May 1901; *s* of late Dr Thomas Vincent Dickinson, MD, and Beatrice Frances Evans; *m* 1930, Rosamond Sylvia, *d* of late Vice-Admiral L. W. Braithwaite, CMG; two *s. Educ:* RN Colls, Osborne and Dartmouth. Midshipman, HMS Royal Sovereign, 1917–20; Lieut S Africa Station, 1923–25; specialised in Physical Training, 1926; Training Special Entry Cadets, HMS Erebus, 1927; Term Lieut RNC Dartmouth, 1931; 1st Lieut Boys' Training Establishment, HMS Ganges, 1934; Comdr, 1936; Asst Dir Physical Training Admiralty, 1937; served War of 1939–45 (despatches thrice); Atlantic Convoys, 1940; Capt., 1942; North Africa landing, 1942; Sicily landing, 1943; Salerno landing, 1943; Sen. Officer Inshore Sqdn, Corsica, 1943; Senior Naval Officer, Northern Adriatic, 1944; Senior Officer 18 Minesweeping Flotilla operating from Southern Ireland, 1945; Head of Naval Branch, Berlin, 1947; HMS Victorious (Training Squadron), 1948; Capt. of Royal Naval Coll., Dartmouth, 1949–51; Rear-Adm., 1951; Flag Officer (Flotillas) Indian Fleet, 1951–53;

retired, 1954. Chevalier Légion d'Honneur, 1944; Croix de Guerre with Palm, 1944; Officer, Legion of Merit, 1944. *Recreation:* gardening. *Address:* Dials Close, Lower Wield, near Alresford, Hants. *T:* Preston Candover 269. *Club:* Special Forces.
*Died 13 May* 1981.

**DICKINSON, Reginald Percy,** OBE 1964; retired Under Secretary, Ministry of Defence; *b* 13 Feb. 1914; *s* of Percy and Nellie Dickinson; *m* 1943, Marjorie Ellen Lillistone; two *s. Educ:* Grammar school. BScEng London Univ., 1943; FRAeS, CEng. Air Min., Martlesham Heath, 1936; RAE, 1937; Aircraft and Armament Exper. Estabt, 1942: Supt of Performance, 1953, Supt Weapon Systems, 1962; Dir, Aircraft Develt (B), MoD, Project Dir, Lightning, Hercules, Victor, Buccaneer, Hawk etc, 1965–73; Dir Gen. Mil. Aircraft Projects, 1974–75. Chm., Flight Panel, AGARD, 1963–65; Mem., ARC and RAeS Cttees. Alston Medal for achievements in Flight Testing, 1961. *Recreations:* sailing, golf. *Address:* 1A Lingwood Avenue, Mudeford, Christchurch, Dorset BH23 3JS. *T:* Christchurch 482781. *Clubs:* Highcliffe Sailing; Highcliffe Castle Golf.
*Died 9 Sept.* 1987.

**DICKINSON, Prof. Robert Eric;** Professor of Geography, University of Arizona, 1967–75, retired; formerly Professor of Geography, University of Leeds, 1958, and Research Professor, 1963; *b* 9 Feb. 1905; *m* 1941, Mary Winwood; no *c. Educ:* Upholland Grammar Sch., near Wigan; Leeds University. BA Hons (1st Cl. Geog.), Leeds, 1925; DipEd, Leeds, 1926; MA (Geog.), Leeds, 1928; PhD London, 1932. Asst Lectr in Geography, University Coll., Exeter, 1926–28; University Coll., London: Asst Lectr, 1928–32, Lectr, 1932–41, Reader in Geog., 1941–47; Prof. of Geog., Syracuse Univ., NY, 1947–58. Visiting Prof. at Univs of: California, 1960–61; Washington, 1963; Nebraska, 1963; Kansas State Univ., 1964; Arizona, 1967; Laval, 1968. Rockefeller Fellow, 1931–32 (USA), 1936–37 (Europe); Guggenheim Fellow, 1957–58. *Publications:* Making of Geography, 1932, repr. 1977; The German Lebensraum, 1943; The Regions of Germany, 1944; City, Region and Regionalism, 1945; The West European City, 1951; Germany: A General and Regional Geography, 1952; The Population Problem of Southern Italy, 1955; City and Region, 1964; City and Region in Western Europe, 1967; Makers of Modern Geography, 1969; Regional Ecology, 1970; Regional Concept, 1975; Environments of America, 1975. *Address:* 636 Roller Coaster Road, Tucson, Arizona 85704, USA.
*Died Sept.* 1981.

**DICKINSON, Ronald Arthur,** CMG 1964; Chairman, Exim Credit Management and Consultants, 1971–80; *b* 7 Nov. 1910; *s* of J. H. Dickinson, JP, Cartmel and Oldham, Lancs; *m* 1939, Helen, *d* of Joseph Severs, Oldham, Lancs. *Educ:* schools and univs. Joined ECGD, Under-Sec., 1965–70. Governor, Sports Foundn, 1976–. Order of Merit, Admiral Class, Brazil, 1971. *Recreation:* any sport. *Address:* 86 Regency Lodge, NW3 5EB. *T:* 01–722 2655. *Club:* Overseas Bankers.
*Died 31 July* 1986.

**DICKINSON, Ronald Sigismund Shepherd,** CMG 1967; Secretary, Air Travel Reserve Fund Agency, since 1975; *b* 30 March 1906; *o s* of Walter Sigismund Dickinson and Janet (*née* Shepherd); *m* 1932, Vida Evelyn, 4th *d* of Roger Hall and Maud (*née* Seaton); one *d. Educ:* Dulwich Coll.; London Sch. of Economics. AIB 1936. Min. of Aircraft Production, 1941; Principal, 1943; Civil Aviation Dept, Air Min., 1944; Min. of Civil Aviation, 1946; Asst Sec., 1947; Rees-Jeffreys Post-Graduate Research Student, LSE, 1950–51; Civil Air Attaché, British Embassy, Washington, 1952–54; Civil Aviation Adviser to Fedn of W Indies, Trinidad, 1961–62; UK Representative on Council of ICAO, Montreal, 1962–69. 1st Vice-Pres. of Council of ICAO, 1966–67. *Address:* Flat 1, 3 Sandrock Road, Tunbridge Wells, Kent TN2 3PX.
*Died 28 Dec.* 1984.

**DICKINSON, Prof. Thorold (Barron),** CBE 1973; Professor of Film in the University of London (Slade School of Fine Art), 1967–71, later Emeritus; *b* Bristol, 16 Nov. 1903; *s* of Ven. Charles Henry Dickinson, sometime Archdeacon of Bristol, and Beatrice Vindhya (*née* Thorold); *m* 1929, Irene Joanna Macfadyen, AA Dipl., RIBA (*d* 1979). *Educ:* Clifton Coll.; Keble Coll., Oxford. Entered film industry, 1926; film editor, subseq. film director and script writer. Directed (among others): Gaslight, 1940; The Next of Kin, 1941. Organised Army Kinematograph Service Production Group and produced 17 military training films, 1942–43. Directed Men of Two Worlds, 1944–45; collab. scripts of: Mayor of Casterbridge; Then and Now; directed: The Queen of Spades, 1949; Secret People, 1951; Hill 24 Doesn't Answer, 1953–55. Produced Power Among Men, 1958–59, and many short films for UN. Vice-Pres., Assoc. of Cine-Technicians, 1936–53. Mem. of Cttee, Nat. Film Archive, 1950–56; Chm., Brit. Film Acad., 1952–53; Mem., Cttee administering Brit. Film Inst. Experimental Fund, 1952–56; Chief, Film Services Office of Public Information, UN, NY, 1956–60; Senior Lecturer in Film, Slade School of Fine Art, UCL, 1960–67. Consultant to Amer. Film Inst., 1968; Hon. film consultant, CNAA, 1973–76; Vis. Prof. of Film, Univ. of Surrey, 1975–77. Mem. Board, New York Film Council, 1958–60. Pres., International Federation

of Film Societies, 1958–66 (Hon. Pres., 1966); Hon. Mem., Assoc. of Ciné and TV Technicians, 1977; Hon. Life Member: British Univs Film Council, 1978–; Le Centre Internationale de Liaison des Ecoles de Cinéma et de Télévision (CILECT), 1978–. PhD Fine Arts/Film, University of London, 1971; DUniv Surrey, 1976. *Publications:* (with Catherine de la Roche) Soviet Cinema, 1948; A Discovery of Cinema, 1971; contribs to periodicals: Sight and Sound, Bianco e Nero, Geog. Mag., Soviet Studies, Screen Digest, Times Higher Educn Supplement, Film Comment (NY). *Recreations:* theatre, film, walking, reading. *Address:* Wing Cottage, Sheepdrove, Lambourn, Berks RG16 7UT. *T:* Lambourn 71393.
*Died 14 April 1984.*

**DICKSON, Bertram Thomas,** CMG 1960; BA, PhD; *b* Leicester, 20 May 1886; *s* of J. T. Dickson, Leciester; *m* 1910, Florence (decd), *d* of W. Roberts; one *s* one *d. Educ:* Queen's Univ., Kingston, Ontario (BA); Cornell Univ.; McGill Univ., Montreal (PhD). Served European War, 1914–18: Agricultural Officer, 1st British Army, 1917–18; Commandant, 1st British Army Sch. of Agriculture, 1918–19. Professor of Economic Botany, McGill Univ., 1919–26; Prof. of Plant Pathology, McGill Univ., 1926–27; Chief, Division of Plant Industry, CSIRO, Canberra, 1927–51; Delegate, 2nd Session, FAO Conference, Copenhagen, 1946; Mem., UNESCO Arid Zone Advisory Cttee, 1952–57; UN Adviser, Desert Research Institute of Egypt, 1958–59. Pres., Canberra Repertory Soc., 1932–41; Exec. Mem., Australian National Research Council, 1932–47; Pres., Legacy Club, Canberra, 1933; Pres., Australian Institute of Agricultural Science, 1945–46 (Vice-Pres., 1935–39); Chm., Canberra Univ. Coll., 1954–60. *Address:* c/o Dr F. P. Dickson, 38 Trevellyan Street, Cronulla, NSW 2230, Australia.
*Died 22 July 1982.*

**DICKSON, Dr David,** CB 1969; *b* 1 Nov. 1908; *s* of Robert and Elizabeth Dickson, Crieff, Perthshire; *m* 1935, Isabella Sword Grant, *d* of A. P. Grant, Easterhouse, Lanarkshire; one *s. Educ:* Morrison's Acad., Crieff; University of Edinburgh. Asst Classics Teacher, Royal High Sch., Edinburgh, 1931–38; Principal Classics Teacher, Alloa Acad., 1938–40; HM Inspector of Schools, 1940; HM Chief Inspector of Schools, 1955; HM Senior Chief Inspector of Schools, Scottish Educn Dept, 1966–69. *Recreations:* golf, gardening. *Address:* 7 Albert Place, Stirling. *T:* Stirling 4760.
*Died 4 Feb. 1982.*

**DICKSON, (Horatio Henry) Lovat,** OC 1978; FRSC 1982; writer and publisher; *b* 30 June 1902; *s* of Gordon Fraser Dickson and Josephine Mary Cunningham; *m* 1934, Marguerite Isabella, *d* of A. B. Brodie, Montreal; one *s. Educ:* Berkhamsted Sch.; University of Alberta (MA). Lecturer in English, Univ. of Alberta, 1927–29; Associate Editor, Fortnightly Review, 1929–32; Editor of Review of Reviews, 1930–34; Managing Dir of Lovat Dickson Ltd (Publishers), 1932–38; Director: Macmillan & Co. (publishers), 1941–64; Pan Books Ltd, 1946–64; Reprint Soc., 1939–64. Hon. LLD Alberta, 1968; Hon. DLitt: Western Ontario, 1976; York Univ., Toronto, 1981. *Publications:* The Green Leaf, 1938; Half-Breed, The Story of Grey Owl, 1939; Out of the West Land, 1944; Richard Hillary, 1950; two vols of autobiog.: Vol. I, The Ante-Room, 1959; Vol. II, The House of Words, 1963; H. G. Wells, 1969; Wilderness Man, 1973; Radclyffe Hall at the Well of Loneliness, 1975; The Museum-Makers, 1986. *Address:* Apt 808, 21 Dale Avenue, Toronto, Ont M4W 1K3, Canada. *Club:* Arts and Letters (Toronto).
*Died 2 Jan. 1987.*

**DICKSON, Ian Anderson,** WS; Sheriff of South Strathclyde, Dumfries and Galloway, formerly Lanarkshire, at Hamilton, 1961–77; *b* Edinburgh, 1905; *s* of Robert Anderson Dickson, DDS, and Marie Anne Morris; *m* 1943, Margaret Forbes (*d* 1981), *o d* of James John and Annabella Florence Ross, Glenfuir, Falkirk; four *s. Educ:* Edinburgh Academy; Harrow; Edinburgh Univ. (BL). A practising Solicitor, first in Edinburgh and, 1934–61, in Coatbridge; Mem. Coatbridge Town Council, 1937–44; Burgh Prosecutor, Coatbridge, 1944–60; Hon. Sheriff-Substitute of Lanarkshire at Airdrie, 1955–61. *Recreations:* motoring, bridge, pottering, formerly Scouting (for 50 years) and golf. *Address:* 9 Cleveden Gardens, Glasgow G12 0PU. *T:* 041-339 7731; Rockview, Elie, Fife. *T:* Elie 330234. *Clubs:* Western (Glasgow); Royal Burgess Golfing Society (Edinburgh); Golf House (Elie).
*Died 10 April 1982.*

**DICKSON, Lovat;** *see* Dickson, H. H. L.

**DICKSON, Marshal of the Royal Air Force Sir William (Forster),** GCB 1953 (KCB 1952; CB 1942); KBE 1946 (CBE 1945; OBE 1934); DSO 1918; AFC 1922; idc; psa; *b* 24 Sept. 1898; *s* of late C. C. Forster Dickson, Chancery Registrar's Office, Royal Courts of Justice, and of late Agnes Nelson Dickson, Northwood, Mddx; *m* 1932, Patricia Marguerite, *d* of late Sir Walter Allen, KBE; one *d* (and one *d* decd). *Educ:* Bowden House, Seaford; Haileybury Coll. Royal Naval Air Service, 1916–18 (DSO, despatches thrice); transferred to RAF, 1918; Permanent Commn in RAF, 1919; employed on Naval Flying work, 1919–21; Test Pilot, RAE, 1921–22; Air Ministry, 1923–26; No 56 (Fighter) Sqdn, 1926–27;

RAF Staff Coll., Andover, 1927–28; posted to India, 1929; served on NW Frontier, 1929–30 and at HQ RAF Delhi (despatches); commanded RAF Station, Hawkinge, and No 25 (Fighter) Squadron, 1935–36; Directing Staff, Staff Coll., 1936–38; Imperial Defence Coll., 1939; Dir of Plans, Air Ministry, 1941–42; commanded Nos 9 and 10 Groups in Fighter Comd, 1942–43; commanded No 83 Group in TAF, 1943–44; commanded Desert Air Force, 1944; Asst Chief of Air Staff (Policy), Air Ministry, 1945–46; Vice-Chief of Air Staff, Air Council, Air Ministry, 1946–48; C-in-C, MEAF, 1948–50; Mem. for Supply and Organisation, Air Council, 1950–52; Chief of the Air Staff, 1953–56; Chm. of the Chiefs of Staff Cttee, 1956–59; Chief of Defence Staff, 1958–59. President: Royal Central Asian Soc., 1961–65; Ex-Services Mental Welfare Soc., 1960–76; Haileybury Soc., 1962; Forces Help Society and Lord Roberts Workshops, 1974–81. Master, The Glass Sellers' Co., 1964. Russian Order of Suvarov, 1944; USA Legion of Merit. *Address:* Foxbriar House, Cold Ash, Newbury, Berks. *Club:* Royal Air Force.
*Died 12 Sept. 1987.*

**DIGBY, George F. Wingfield;** retired Keeper Emeritus, Victoria and Albert Museum; *b* 2 March 1911; 2nd *s* of late Col F. J. B. Wingfield Digby, DSO; *m* 1935, Cornelia, *d* of Prof. H. Keitler, University of Vienna; one *s* (decd). *Educ:* Harrow; Trinity Coll., Cambridge; Grenoble Univ.; Sorbonne; Vienna. Asst Keeper, Dept of Textiles, Victoria and Albert Museum, 1934; seconded to Education Office, Jamaica (Jamaica Coll.), 1941–45; Asst Keeper (1st class), Victoria and Albert Museum, 1946; Keeper of Dept of Textiles, 1947–72; retired 1973. *Publications:* The Work of the Modern Potter in England, 1952; Meaning and Symbol in Three Modern Artists, 1955; Symbol and Image in William Blake, 1957; (jtly) History of the West Indian Peoples (4 vols for schools), 1951–59; (part author) The Bayeux Tapestry, 1957; (contributor) Brussels Colloque International: La Tapisserie flamande au XVII-XVIII siècle, 1959; (contributor) Colston Research Soc. Papers: Metaphor and Symbol, 1960; Elizabethan Embroidery, 1963; The Devonshire Hunting Tapestries, 1971; Tapestries, Mediaeval and Renaissance, 1980; (trans. with Cornelia Wingfield Digby) Islamic Carpets and Textiles in the Keir Collection, 1977. *Recreations:* oriental ceramics and contemporary hand-made pottery. *Address:* Raleigh Lodge, Castleton, Sherborne, Dorset DT9 3SA.
*Died 8 Jan. 1989.*

**DIGGINES, Christopher Ewart,** CMG 1974; HM Diplomatic Service, retired; British High Commissioner, Port of Spain, Trinidad and Tobago, 1973–77; British High Commissioner (non-resident), Grenada, 1974–77; *b* 2 July 1920; *s* of late Sir William Diggines; *m* 1946, Mary Walls; one *s* one *d. Educ:* Haileybury Coll.; Trinity Coll., Oxford. Army, 1940–46. Senior History Master, Birkenhead Sch., 1948–49; apptd to CRO, 1949; Office of the UK High Comr in India (Madras), 1952–56; Canadian National Defence Coll., 1958–59; UK Mission to UN (1st Sec.), 1959–62; British Deputy High Commissioner, Kingston, Jamaica, 1962–64; Foreign and Commonwealth Office (formerly Commonwealth Office), 1964–69; Counsellor (Commercial), Lusaka, 1969–73. *Address:* St Clare Lodge, Grams Road, Walmer, Deal, Kent CT14 7NT. *Club:* Commonwealth Trust.
*Died 18 March 1990.*

**DIKE, Prof. Kenneth Onwuka,** CON; MA, PhD; President Anambra State University of Technology, Nigeria, since 1981; *b* 17 Dec. 1917; *s* of late Nzekwe Dike, merchant; *m* 1953, Ona Patricia, *d* of R. R. Olisa, MBE; two *s* three *d* (and one *d* decd). *Educ:* Dennis Memorial Grammar Sch., Onitsha; Achimota Coll., Ghana; Fourah Bay Coll., Sierra Leone; Univ. of Durham (BA); Univ. of Aberdeen (MA); London Univ. (PhD). Appointed Lectr in History, UC, Ibadan, 1950–52; Sen. Res. Fellow, W African Inst. of Social and Economic Res., 1952–54; University Coll., Ibadan: Sen. Lectr, Dept of History, 1954–56; Prof. of History, 1956–60; Vice-Principal, 1958–60; University of Ibadan: Vice-Chancellor, 1960–67; Dir, Inst. of African Studies, 1962–67; Chm., Planning Cttee, Univ. of Port Harcourt, 1967–71; Harvard University: Prof. of History, 1971–73; Andrew W. Mellon Professor of African History, 1973–81. Founder and Dir, Nat. Archives of Nigeria, 1951–64; Chm. Nigerian Antiquities Commn, 1954–67; Pres., Historical Soc. of Nigeria, 1955–67; Chm., Assoc. of Commonwealth Univs, 1965–66. Chm., Commn for Review of Educational System in Eastern Region; Mem., Ashby Commn on Higher Educn in Nigeria; Chm. Organising Cttee, Internat. Congress of Africanists. FKC 1962. FRHistS 1956; Fellow Amer. Acad. of Arts and Scis, 1972. Hon. LLD: Aberdeen, 1961; Northwestern, 1962; Leeds, 1963; London, 1963; Columbia, 1965; Princeton, 1965; Michigan, 1979; Hon. DLitt: Boston, Mass, 1962; Birmingham, 1964; Ahmadu Bello, 1965; Ibadan; Ghana, 1979; Hon. DSc Moscow, 1963. *Publications:* Report on the Preservation and Administration of Historical Records in Nigeria, 1953; Trade and Politics in the Niger Delta 1830–1885, 1956; A Hundred Years of British Rule in Nigeria, 1957; The Origins of the Niger Mission, 1958; also articles in learned journals on Nigerian and West African history. *Address:* Anambra State University of Technology, Private Mail Bag 1660, Enugu, Anambra State of Nigeria, Nigeria. *Clubs:* Royal

Commonwealth Society; Metropolitan (Lagos, Nigeria); Odd Volumes (Boston, Mass). *Died* 26 *Oct.* 1983.

**DILLON,** 21st Viscount *cr* 1622, of Costello Gallen, Co. Mayo, Ireland; **Charles Henry Robert Dillon;** Count in France, 1711; designer; *b* 18 Jan. 1945; *s* of 20th Viscount Dillon and of Irène Marie France, *d* of Renê Merandon du Plessis, Whitehall, Mauritius; *S* father, 1979; *m* 1972, Mary Jane, *d* of late John Young, Castle Hill House, Birtle, Lancs; one *s* one *d*. *Educ:* Downside School; RMA Sandhurst; Royal College of Art. *Heir: s* Hon. Henry Benedict Dillon, *b* 6 Jan. 1973. *Address:* 83 Talfourd Road, SE15. *T:* 01-701 5931. *Died* 15 *Sept.* 1982.

**DILLON, Sir Robert William Charlier,** 8th Bt *cr* 1801; Baron of the Holy Roman Empire, 1782; *b* 17 Jan. 1914; *s* of Robert Arthur Dillon (*d* 1925) and Laura Maud (*d* 1915), widow of J. Lachlin McCliver, New Zealand; *S* kinsman, 1925; *m* 1947, Synolda, *d* of late Cholmondeley Butler Clarke and of Mrs Cholmondeley-Clarke, late of Holy Cross, Co. Tipperary. *Heir:* none. *Address:* Overdene, Wentworth Place, Co. Wicklow, Ireland.

*Died* 25 *Dec.* 1982 (*ext*).

**DINEEN, Ven. Frederick George K.;** *see* Kerr-Dineen.

**DINGWALL, Eric John,** MA, DSc (London), PhD (London, Faculty of Science); anthropologist; Hon. Assistant Keeper, The British Library (Reference Division); Hon. Vice-President, Magic Circle; *b* 1890; *s* of Alexander Harvey Dingwall, Ceylon; *m* 1st, Doris Dunn; 2nd, Dr Margaret Davies (decd). *Educ:* privately; Pembroke Coll., Cambridge. Formerly on staff, Cambridge Univ. Library; Dir, Dept of Physical Phenomena, American Soc. for Psychical Research, New York, 1921; Research Officer, Soc. for Psychical Research, 1922–27, investigating many American and European mediums in New York, Boston, Paris, Copenhagen, Warsaw, Munich, Gratz, etc, publishing results in Proc. and Jl of the SPR; toured Spain, 1935; went to the West Indies, 1936, to study special social and religious conditions in Trinidad and Haiti with reference to abnormal mental phenomena; went to Poland, S America, W Indies, and USA, 1937. Attached to Ministry of Information and to a Dept, Foreign Office, 1941–45. *Publications:* Joint Editor, Revelations of a Spirit Medium, 1922; Studies in the Sexual Life of Ancient and Mediæval Peoples, I, Male Infibulation, 1925; How to Go to a Medium, 1927; Ghosts and Spirits in the Ancient World, 1930; The Girdle of Chastity, 1931; Artificial Cranial Deformation, 1931; How to Use a Large Library, 1933; Editor of English edn of Woman (Ploss-Bartels), 1935; Racial Pride and Prejudice, 1946; Some Human Oddities, 1947; Very Peculiar People, 1950; (with K. M. Goldney and T. H. Hall) The Haunting of Borley Rectory, 1956; (with J. Langdon-Davies) The Unknown—is it nearer?, 1956; The American Woman, 1956; (with T. H. Hall) Four Modern Ghosts, 1958; The Critics' Dilemma, 1966; Editor of and contributor to: Abnormal Hypnotic Phenomena, 1967–68; contributions to English and foreign publications. *Recreation:* studying rare and queer customs. *Address:* 171 Marine Court, St Leonards-on-Sea, East Sussex. *Club:* National Liberal. *Died* 7 *Aug.* 1986.

**DINGWALL, Walter Spender,** MA; Secretary, Chichester Diocesan Fund, 1946–61, retired; *b* 14 Dec. 1900; *s* of late Rev. Walter Molyneux Dingwall and Sophia Spender; *m* 1932, Olive Mary Loasby (*d* 1983); no *c*. *Educ:* Marlborough Coll.; Christ Church, Oxford. Sixth Form Master at St Edward's Sch., Oxford, 1923–37; nine years Bursar of the Sch., ten years Housemaster; Headmaster, Hurstpierpoint Coll., Sussex, 1937–45; Hon. Sec. and Treasurer, Public Schools Bursars' Assoc., 1931–38. Comr of Income Tax, 1962–75. *Address:* 2 Gatehouse Lodge, Terrys Cross, Henfield, BN5 9SX. *T:* Henfield (0273) 493350. *Died* 28 *Aug.* 1990.

**DINKEL, Ernest Michael,** RWS 1957; ARCA 1924; ARWA 1979; FSGE 1981; painter, glass engraver and sculptor; Head of The School of Design, Edinburgh College of Art, 1947–60, retired; *b* 24 Oct. 1894; *s* of Charles and Lucy Dinkel; *m* 1st, 1929, Kathleen Hanks (*d* 1936); 2nd, 1941, Emmy Keet, ARCA, ARWA; two *s* two *d* (and one *s* decd). *Educ:* Huddersfield Sch. of Art. War Service abroad, 1916–19, on the Somme (general and war service medals). Student, Royal Coll. of Art, 1921–25. RIBA Owen Jones Scholarship, 1926. Asst to Prof. Robert Anning Bell and Prof. Tristram, at Royal Coll. of Art, 1925–40; Head of Stourbridge Sch. of Art, 1940–47; Exhibitor: Royal Academy, Royal Scottish Academy, Royal Society of Painters in Water Colours, Royal West Acad. and private exhbns; designer, Royal Hunt Cup and Topham Trophy; work in Tate Gallery, Laing Art Gall., Newcastle upon Tyne, Dudley Art Gall. *Recreations:* pottery; wide interest in art subjects and music. *Address:* The Grange, Bussage, near Stroud, Glos GL6 8AT. *T:* Brimscombe 882368. *Died* 3 *June* 1983.

**DIPLOCK,** Baron (Life Peer) *cr* 1968, of Wansford; **(William John) Kenneth Diplock,** PC 1961; Kt 1956; a Lord of Appeal in Ordinary since 1968; *b* 8 Dec. 1907; *s* of W. J. Hubert Diplock, Croydon; *m* 1938, Margaret Sarah, *d* of George Atcheson, Londonderry. *Educ:* Whitgift; University Coll., Oxford. Barrister, Middle Temple, 1932,

Bencher, 1956, Dep. Treas., 1973, Treas., 1974. Sec. to Master of the Rolls, 1939–48. Served War of 1939–45, RAF, 1941–45. KC 1948; Recorder of Oxford, Dec. 1951–Jan. 1956. Judge of High Court of Justice, Queen's Bench Div., 1956–61; a Lord Justice of Appeal, 1961–68. Judge of Restrictive Practices Court, 1960–61 (Pres., 1961). Mem., Lord Chancellor's Law Reform Cttee, 1952–69. Hon. Fellow of University Coll., Oxford, 1958. Pres., Nat. Assoc. of Parish Councils, 1962–66; Vice-Pres., Brit. Maritime Law Assoc., 1964, Pres., 1975–77; Chm., Inst. of Advanced Legal Studies, 1973–77. Chairman: Permanent Security Commn, 1971–82; Advisory Bd (Comparative Law), Brit. Inst. of Internat. and Comparative Law, 1959–67; Council of Legal Education, 1969–70 (Chm., Bd of Studies, 1963–69); Law Advisory Cttee, Brit. Council, 1966–80; Dep. Chm., Boundary Commn for England, 1958–61. Hon. Pres., Assoc. of Law Teachers, 1971–75; Pres., Inst. of Arbitrators, 1977–80. Hon. Fellow, American Bar Foundation, 1969. Hon. LLD: Alberta, 1972; London, 1979; Hon. DCL Oxon, 1977. *Address:* 1 Crown Office Row, Temple, EC4. *Club:* Athenæum. *Died* 14 *Oct.* 1985.

**DIRAC, Prof. Paul Adrien Maurice,** OM 1973; FRS 1930; BSc Bristol, PhD Cantab; Lucasian Professor of Mathematics, Cambridge, 1932–69, later Professor Emeritus; Fellow of St John's College, Cambridge; Professor of Physics, Florida State University, since 1971; *b* 8 Aug. 1902; *m* 1937, Margit Wigner, Budapest. Mem. Pontifical Academy of Sciences, 1961. Nobel Prize in Physics for 1933; Royal Medal of Royal Society, 1939; Copley Medal of Royal Society, 1952. *Publications:* Principles of Quantum Mechanics, 1930, new edn 1982; Development of Quantum Theory, 1971; General Theory of relativity, 1975; Directions in Physics, 1978; papers on quantum theory. *Address:* Department of Physics, Florida State University, Tallahassee, Florida 32306, USA; St John's College, Cambridge. *Died* 20 *Oct.* 1984.

**DITCHBURN, Robert William,** FRS 1962; Professor of Physics, University of Reading, 1946–68, then Emeritus; *b* 14 Jan. 1903; *e s* of William and Martha Kathleen Ditchburn; *m* 1929, Doreen May, *e d* of Arthur Samuel Barrett; one *s* three *d*. *Educ:* Bootle Secondary Sch.; Liverpool Univ.; Trinity Coll., Cambridge (Entrance and Senior Scholar, Hooper Prizeman, Isaac Newton Student). Fellow of Trinity Coll., Dublin, 1928–46; Prof. of Natural and Experimental Philosophy in Dublin Univ., 1929–46; Temp. Principal Experimental Officer, Admiralty, 1942–45. Mem. of Royal Irish Academy, 1931; Registrar for Social Studies, Trinity Coll., Dublin, 1940–44; Vice-Pres. Physical Soc., 1958; Vice-Pres. Inst. of Physics and Physical Soc., 1960–62. FInstP. Mees Medal, Optical Soc. of America, 1983. *Publications:* Light, 1952; Eye-Movements and Visual Perception, 1973; and scientific papers. *Recreation:* music. *Address:* 21 Park Close, Oxford OX2 8NP.

*Died* 8 *April* 1987.

**DIVINE, Arthur Durham, (David Divine),** CBE 1976 (OBE 1946); DSM 1940; author and journalist; formerly War Correspondent and Defence Correspondent, Sunday Times (until 1975); *b* 27 July 1904; 2nd *s* of Arthur Henry and Mabel Divine, Cape Town; *m* 1931, Elizabeth Ann, 2nd *d* of Sir Ian MacAlister; two *d*. *Educ:* Rondebosch High Sch., Cape Town; Kingswood Coll., Grahamstown, S Africa. Cape Times, 1922–26 and 1931–35, where founded daily column of World Comment; has travelled extensively in Europe, Africa, Asia, N and S America, and the Pacific. *Publications:* Sea Loot, 1930; They Blocked the Suez Canal, 1936; The Pub on the Pool, 1938; Tunnel from Calais, 1943, new edn 1975; many other thrillers; The Merchant Navy Fights, The Wake of the Raiders, Behind the Fleets, 1940, in conjunction with Ministry of Information; Destroyer's War, 1942; Road to Tunis, 1944; Navies in Exile, 1944; Dunkirk, 1945, and many boys' books. Under pseudonym of David Rame: Wine of Good Hope, 1939; The Sun Shall Greet Them, 1941. Under name of David Divine: The King of Fassarai, 1950; Atom at Spithead, 1953; The Golden Fool, 1954; Boy on a Dolphin, 1955; The Nine Days of Dunkirk, 1959, new edn 1976; These Splendid Ships, 1960; The Iron Ladies, 1961; The Daughter of the Pangaran, 1963; The Blunted Sword, 1964; The Broken Wing, 1966; The Stolen Seasons, 1967; The Key of England, 1968; The North-West Frontier of Rome, 1969; The Three Red Flares, 1970; Mutiny at Invergordon, 1970; Certain Islands, 1972; The Opening of the World, 1973; *Films:* Atom at Spithead; Boy on a Dolphin; Dunkirk. *Address:* 24 Keats Grove, Hampstead, NW3 2RS. *T:* 01–435 6928. *Died* 30 *April* 1987.

**DIXEY, Sir Frank,** KCMG 1972 (CMG 1949); OBE 1929; DSc; FRS 1958; FEng; FGS; Geological Adviser and Director of Colonial Geological Surveys, Colonial Office, 1947–59; British Technical Aid Consultant to Water Development Department, Cyprus, 1967–73; Consultant Hydrologist, 1960–74, including service overseas with UN organisations and on geology and hydrogeology of Cyprus; *b* 7 April 1892; *m* 1919, Helen Golding (*d* 1961); one *d* decd; *m* 1962, Cicely Hepworth. *Educ:* Barry Grammar Sch.; University of Wales; Fellow, University Coll., Cardiff, 1981. Served European War, 1914–18, RGA, 1915–18; Govt Geologist, Sierra Leone, 1918–21;

Dir of Geological Survey, Nyasaland, 1921–39; Dir of Water Development, N Rhodesia, 1939–44; Dir of Geological Survey, Nigeria, 1944–47. Geological Soc. Murchison medallist, 1953; Geol. Soc. S Africa Draper medallist, 1945 and Hon. Mem., 1959; Corresponding Mem. Geological Soc., Belgium, 1947, Hon. Mem., 1958. Alexander du Toit Memorial Lecturer, Johannesburg, 1955. Hon. Fellow, Inst. Min. and Met., 1958; Founder Fellow, Fellowship of Engineering, 1976. *Publications:* Practical Handbook of Water Supply, 1931, 2nd edn 1950; official reports and scientific papers on geology, geomorphology, and mineral resources of African States. *Address:* Woodpecker Cottage, Bramber, Steyning, West Sussex BN4 3WE. *T:* Steyning 812313. *Club:* Athenæum.

*Died* 1 *Nov.* 1982.

**DIXON, Bernard;** Chairman, Dixon Group of Malting and Light Industrial Companies, Pampisford, Cambs, since 1960; *b* Redcar, Yorks, 23 Dec. 1906; 3rd *s* of late Capt. Thomas Robert Dixon and Lily Jane (*née* Barry), Thriplow Place, near Royston, Herts; *m* 1930, Olive Marie, *d* of G. H. Watts, Cambridge; four *d*. *Educ:* Campbell Coll., Belmont, Belfast, NI; British Sch. of Malting and Brewing; University of Birmingham. Chm. and Man. Dir, Flowers Breweries Ltd, 1947–58. Sometime examiner, Institute of Brewing, Mem. Publications Cttee, Journal of Inst. of Brewing, Chm. London Section, Inst. of Brewing, 1939–40. Winner numerous awards at home and abroad for brewery products, including championship, London, 1929 and 1930 and Grand Prix, Brussels, Prague, Pilsen. Patentee of inventions used throughout brewing industry. Formerly Hon. Sec. Bedfordshire Brewers' Assoc. and Mem. Brewers' Soc. Cttee on Replanning. Commissioned, Cambs Regt, 1929; Sports Officer, 1930; commissioned, Home Guard, 1940. Breeder of pure-bred Arabian Horses which have been exported to Government studs in all parts of the world; a Governor of the Arab Horse Soc. Past Pres. Old Campbellian Soc. *Publications:* technical papers to various sections of Institute of Brewing and Incorporated Brewers' Guild. *Recreations:* hunting, farming, golf. *Address:* Pampisford Place, Pampisford, Cambs CB2 4EW. *Clubs:* Naval & Military, Royal Automobile; Kildare Street and University (Dublin).

*Died* 30 *March* 1983.

**DIXON, Sir (Francis Wilfred) Peter,** KBE 1959 (CBE 1952); MB, BS; FRCS; Air Vice-Marshal retired; Consultant in Surgery to the RAF, retired 1966; *b* 4 Oct. 1907; *s* of late Frederick Henry Dixon, New Norfolk, Tas.; *m* 1940, Pamela Ruby, *d* of late Brig. Charles C. Russell, MC, RA (Retd), London; two *s* one *d*. *Educ:* Newman Coll.; Melbourne Univ. MB, BS, Melbourne, 1930; FRCS Ed. 1937; FRCS 1949; DO Oxford, 1936. House Surgeon, St Vincent's Hosp., Melbourne. Joined RAF 1930; Wing-Comdr 1943; served War of 1939–45 (despatches); Aden, Normandy, SW Pacific; Air Cdre 1949; Air Vice-Marshal, 1957. Civilian Consultant in Surgery, RAF, 1966–. Hon. Surgeon to King George VI, 1949–52, to Queen Elizabeth II, 1952–66. Lady Cade Medal, RCS, 1963. *Publications:* contribs to medical journals. *Recreation:* sailing. *Address:* Alde Cottage, Park Road, Aldeburgh, Suffolk IP15 5ER. *T:* Aldeburgh 3772.

*Died* 22 *Nov.* 1988.

**DIXON, Sir John George,** 3rd Bt *cr* 1919; *b* 17 Sept. 1911; *s* of Sir John Dixon, 2nd Bt and Gwendolen Anne (*d* 1974), *d* of Sir Joseph Layton Elmes Spearman, 2nd Bt; *S* father, 1976; *m* 1947, Caroline, *d* of late Charles Theodore Hiltermann; one *d*. *Educ:* Cranleigh. *Heir:* nephew Jonathan Mark Dixon [*b* 1 Sept. 1949; *m* 1978, Patricia Margaret, *d* of James Baird Smith; two *s* one *d*]. *Address:* Avenue Ed. Muller 3, 1814 La Tour de Peilz, Vaud, Switzerland.

*Died* 7 *Oct.* 1990.

**DIXON, Prof. Kendal Cartwright,** MA, MD, PhD, FRCPath; Professor of Cellular Pathology, University of Cambridge, 1973–78, then Emeritus; Fellow of King's College, Cambridge, since 1937; *b* 16 Feb. 1911; *s* of late Prof. Henry H. Dixon, ScD, FRS, Dublin Univ., and Dorothea, *d* of late Sir John Franks, CB, Blackrock, Co. Dublin; *m* 1938, Anne, *d* of late F. D. Darley, Stillorgan, Co. Dublin; one *s* one *d*. *Educ:* St Stephen's Green Sch., Dublin; Haileybury; Trinity Coll., Dublin; King's Coll., Cambridge (Scholar); Dun's Hosp., Dublin; St Bartholomew's Hosp., London. 1st cl. Pt 1 1932, 1st cl. Pt 2 (Biochem.) 1933, Nat. Scis Tripos Cantab; MB, BChir Cantab 1939. Asst to Prof. of Physiol., Dublin Univ., 1936; RAMC, 1940–45, Specialist in Pathology; Univ. of Cambridge: Official Fellow of King's Coll., 1945; Univ. Demonstrator in Chem. Path., 1946, Lectr 1949; Tutor for Advanced Students, King's Coll., 1951–59; Dir of Studies in Medicine, King's Coll., 1959–73; Reader in Cytopathology, 1962–73. Vis. Prof. of Pathology, Columbia Univ., NY, 1978. Mem. European Soc. Pathology. *Publications:* Cellular Defects in Disease, 1982; chapters in books and articles in med. jls principally on cellular disorder and death, fatty change, and neuronal metabolism. *Recreation:* the mountains of Kerry. *Address:* King's College, Cambridge.

*Died* 17 *Dec.* 1990.

**DIXON, Leslie Charles G.;** *see* Graham-Dixon.

**DIXON, Malcolm,** FRS 1942; MA, PhD, ScD Cantab; Emeritus Professor of Enzyme Biochemistry, Cambridge University, since 1966; *b* 18 April 1899; *s* of Allick Page Dixon and Caroline Dewe Dixon (*née* Mathews). *Educ:* Emmanuel Coll., Cambridge. BA 1920; began research in biochemistry under Sir F. G. Hopkins, 1921; 1851 Exhibition Senior Student, 1924–27; Senior Demonstrator in Biochemistry, University of Cambridge, 1923–27; University Lecturer in Biochemistry, 1928–44; Reader in Enzyme Biochemistry, Cambridge University, 1945–65; Prof. of Enzyme Biochemistry, 1966; Dir of Sub-Dept of Enzyme Biochemistry, Cambridge Univ., 1945–66; Fellow of King's Coll., Cambridge, 1950–66, Hon. Fellow, 1968–. Pres. of the Commission on Enzymes of the Internat. Union of Biochemistry, 1956–61. *Publications:* Manometric Methods, 1934, 3rd edn 1951; Multi-enzyme Systems, 1949 (also Japanese edn); Enzymes (with Prof. E. C. Webb), 1958, 2nd edn 1964 (also Russian, Japanese and Italian edns), 3rd edn (with Prof. E. C. Webb, Dr C. J. R. Thorne and Prof. K. F. Tipton), 1979; numerous papers dealing with the subject of enzymes, with special reference to biological oxidation processes and cell-respiration. *Recreation:* music. *Address:* Biochemical Laboratory, Cambridge. *T:* Cambridge 51781. *Club:* Athenæum.

*Died* 7 *Dec.* 1985.

**DIXON, Michael George,** OBE 1964; Chief Passport Officer, Foreign and Commonwealth Office, 1967–80, retired; *b* 10 March 1920; *s* of Sidney Wilfrid and Elsie Dixon. *Educ:* Enfield Grammar Sch. Foreign Office, 1937. HM Forces, 1940–46 (POW, Far East). MInstTM. *Recreation:* gardening. *Address:* 9 Ridge Crest, Enfield, Mddx EN2 8JU. *T:* 081–363 3408.

*Died* 23 *April* 1990.

**DIXON, Sir Peter;** *see* Dixon, Sir (F. W.) P.

**DIXON-NUTTALL, Major William Francis,** DSO 1916; TD; late RE (TF); JP; retired as Director United Glass Ltd, 8 Leicester Street, WC2 (1926–54), Dec. 1954; Commissioner for Income Tax; *b* 1885; *e s* of late F. R. Dixon-Nuttall, JP; *m* 1917, Gladys Lena (*d* 1975) *a d* of W. Henry Gregory, Caldecott, Aughton, and Glenorchy Lodge, Dalmally; one *s*. *Educ:* Repton. Joined W Lancs RE (TA), 1904; served War of 1914–18, Major 1915. Former Dir, Cannington, Shaw & Co., and Nuttall & Co. (St Helens). JP Lancs, 1933. *Address:* Esher Place Avenue, Esher, Surrey. *Club:* Carlton.

*Died* 12 *March* 1981.

**DOBBIE, Mitchell Macdonald,** CB 1951; *b* 2 Oct. 1901; *s* of James Dobbie, Ayr, and Jean Macdonald; *m* 1931, Evelyn Willison (*d* 1967), *e d* of R. W. Grieve, Edinburgh. *Educ:* Ayr Academy; University of Edinburgh (MA, LLB). Called to Bar, Gray's Inn, 1927. Entered Inland Revenue Dept, 1925; Ministry of Labour, 1928; Private Sec. to Parl. Sec., 1934; transferred to Dept of Health for Scotland, 1938; Asst Sec., 1939; Principal Asst Sec., 1945; seconded to Ministry of Home Security as Principal Officer, Scotland Civil Defence Region, 1943–45; Under-Sec., Min. of Housing and Local Govt, 1948; Principal Establishment Officer, 1956–63; retd 1963, and re-employed in Scottish Development Dept, 1963–66; Secretary of Commissions for Scotland, 1966–72. JP City of Edinburgh. *Address:* 13 Eton Terrace, Edinburgh EH4 1QD. *T:* 031-332 3150. *Clubs:* New, Scottish Arts (Edinburgh).

*Died* 30 *Oct.* 1982.

**DOBSON, Maj.-Gen. Anthony Henry George,** CB 1968; OBE 1953; MC 1944; BA Cantab; *b* 15 Dec. 1911; *s* of late Col Arthur Curtis Dobson, DSO, Royal Engineers, and late Susanna (*née* Oppenheim); *m* 1945, Nellie Homberger; two *s* two *d*. *Educ:* Cheltenham Coll.; Royal Military Academy, Woolwich; Clare Coll., Cambridge. Commissioned Royal Engineers, 1931; hons degree (mech. science), Cambridge, 1934; service in UK, 1934–37; seconded to RAF for survey duties, Iraq, 1938–39. Served War of 1939–45: Middle East (Egypt, Turkey, Iraq), 1939–42; Prisoner of War, Italy, 1942–43; interned in Switzerland after escape, 1944; North-West Europe (Holland and Germany), 1945. Germany, 1945–50; Manpower planning Dept, War Office, 1950–53; in comd, Engineer Regt, Hong Kong, 1953–56; Engr branch, War Office, 1956–59; Chief Engr, HQ Eastern Comd, UK, 1959–62; DQMG, HQ BAOR, 1962–64; Chief Engr, HQ North AG/BAOR, 1964–67, retd. Lt-Col 1945; Col 1956; Brig. 1959; Maj.-Gen. 1964. Planning Inspectorate, DoE, 1969–78. *Recreations:* travel, gardening. *Address:* Ramillies, Compton Way, Moor Park, Farnham, Surrey. *T:* Runfold 2350. *Clubs:* Army and Navy, Ski Club of Great Britain; Kandahar Ski; International Lions.

*Died* 12 *March* 1987.

**DOBSON, Prof. Eric John,** MA, DPhil Oxon; FBA 1973; Professor of English Language, Oxford University, 1964–80; *b* 16 Aug. 1913; *o s* of John and Lottie Frances Dobson; *m* 1940, Francis Margaret Stinton; two *s* one *d*. *Educ:* North Sydney High Sch.; Wesley Coll., Sydney Univ.; Merton Coll., Oxford. BA (1st cl. Hons English) Sydney, 1934; 1st in Final Hon. Sch. of English 1937, DPhil 1951, Oxford. Tutor in English, Sydney Univ., 1934–35; Wentworth Travelling Fellow of Sydney Univ., 1935–38; Harmsworth Sen. Schol. of Merton Coll., 1938–40; Lecturer in English, University of Reading, 1940–48. Served in Intelligence Div., Naval Staff,

Admiralty, 1943–45. Lecturer in English, Jesus Coll. and St Edmund Hall, Oxford, 1948–54; Reader in English Lang., Oxford Univ., 1954–64 (title of Prof. from 1960); Professorial Fellow of Jesus Coll., Oxford, 1954–80, Emeritus Fellow, 1980–. Hon. Treas., Philological Soc., 1974–80. *Publications:* English Pronunciation 1500–1700, 1957, 2nd edn 1968; The Phonetic Writings of Robert Robinson, 1957; Edition of Hymn to the Virgin in Trans. of Cymmrodorion Soc., 1954; The Affiliations of the MSS of Ancrene Wisse, in English and Medieval Studies, 1962; The Date and Composition of Ancrene Wisse (Gollancz Memorial Lecture, Brit. Acad., 1966); The English Text of the Ancrene Riwle (MS Cleopatra C. vi), 1972; Moralities on the Gospels, 1975; The Origins of Ancrene Wisse, 1976; (with F. Ll. Harrison) Medieval English Songs, 1979; (with S. R. T. O. d'Ardenne) Seinte Katerine, 1981; articles and reviews in journals. *Address:* 50A Davenant Road, Oxford OX2 8BY. *T:* Oxford 56222.
*Died 30 March 1984.*

**DOBSON, Commodore John Petter,** CBE 1961; DSC 1940; RD 1940; RNR (retired); *b* 2 Sept. 1901; *s* of Lieut-Comdr John Dobson, RNR and Alice Martha (*née* Petter); *m* 1942, Edith Agnes Ferguson (*d* 1979); one *d. Educ:* Middlesbrough High Sch.; Liverpool Coll.; HMS Conway. Midshipman, RNR, 1917; Cadet, Canadian Pacific, 1919; Submarines, 1924; Navigator, RMS Empress of Australia; with Royal trip to Canada and US; subsequently called up, 1939. Minesweeping, 1939–42; Cdre of Convoys, 1942–44, including Normandy Landings; Admiralty Berthing Officer, Sydney, NSW, 1944–45. In command CPS, 1946–61; Master, Empress of Canada (Flagship of Canadian Pacific Steamships Ltd), 1961–62; retired, 1962. Mem., Hon. Company of Master Mariners. Freeman and Liveryman of City of London. *Address:* Sea View Cottage, Sandsend, Whitby, North Yorks. *T:* Whitby 83222. *Club:* Whitby Conservative.
*Died 7 Jan. 1985.*

**DODD, Rev. Harold,** MB, ChM (Liverpool), FRCS, LRCP; Hon. Curate, All Soul's Church, W1, 1970–81, retired; Emeritus Surgeon to: St Mary's Hospital Group, Paddington; King George Hospital, Ilford; Royal Hospital, Richmond; Royal London Homoeopathic Hospital; *b* 13 March 1899; *e s* of Alfred Ledward Dodd and Annie Elizabeth Marshall; *m* 1945, Mary, *yr d* of late R. H. Bond; one *s. Educ:* University of Liverpool; Guy's Hosp. RAF (pilot), 1917–19; MB, ChB (Distinction in Surgery) Liverpool, 1922, O. T. Williams Prizeman for 1923; House Surgeon, House Physician, Surgical Tutor and Registrar, Liverpool Royal Infirmary, 1923–26; Asst Medical Superintendent, St Luke's Hosp., Chelsea, 1926 28; Resident Medical Officer, Royal Northern Hosp., N7, 1928–30. Past Pres., Assoc. of Consultants and Specialists of Reg. Bd Hosps. Fellow, Assoc. of Surgeons of Great Britain; FRSM (Ex-Pres. Section of Proctology). *Publications:* (with F. B. Cockett) Pathology and Surgery of the Veins of the Lower Limb, 1956, 2nd edn, 1976; surgical papers in medical journals. *Address:* 8 Park Close, Ilchester Place, W14 8ND. *T:* 01–602 3024.
*Died 28 March 1987.*

**DODD, Prof. James Munro,** DSc, PhD; FRS 1975; FRSE; Professor of Zoology, University College of North Wales, 1968–81, later Emeritus; Leverhulme Emeritus Fellowship, 1982–83; *b* 26 May 1915; *m* 1951, Margaret Helen Ingram Macaulay (*née* Greig), BSc (Aberdeen), PhD (Harvard); three *s. Educ:* The White House Sch., Brampton, Cumberland; Univ. of Liverpool. BSc hons (Cl. 1) 1937; DipEd 1938. PhD St Andrews, 1953; DSc St Andrews, 1968. Biology Master, Cardigan Grammar Sch., 1938–40. Royal Air Force (Navigator and Staff Navigator), 1940–46. Asst in Zoology, Univ. of Aberdeen, 1946–47; Lectr in Zoology, Univ. of St Andrews, in charge of Gatty Marine Laboratory, 1947–57; Reader in Zoology, Univ. of St Andrews, and Dir of Gatty Marine Laboratory, 1957–60; Prof. of Zoology, Leeds Univ., 1960–68. Chm., British Nat. Cttee for Biology, 1976–81 (Chm., Zoology Sub-Cttee, 1972–76). Member Council: Freshwater Biol Assoc.; Scottish Marine Biol Assoc. Assessor, ARC, 1981–82. Trustee, BM (Natural History), 1975–82. Royal Society Representative: Internat. Trust for Zool Nomenclature; Court, Univ. of Wales. Hon. Member: British Soc. for Endocrinology; European Soc. for Comparative Endocrinol. FRSE 1957. Editor in Chief, General and Comparative Endocrinology, 1973–78; Associate Editor: Proceedings of the Royal Soc., series B; Philosophical Trans of the Royal Soc., series B, 1978–83, 1985–. Frink Medal, Zool Soc. of London, 1982. *Publications:* contributor to Marshall's Physiology of Reproduction (3rd and 4th edns), The Thyroid Gland, The Pituitary Gland, The Ovary, and to zoological and endocrinological jls. *Recreations:* fishing, photography, music. *Address:* Weirglodd Wen, Bulkeley Road, Bangor, Gwynedd LL57 2BP.
*Died 15 Dec. 1986.*

**DODD, Rev. William Harold Alfred;** *see* Dodd, Rev. Harold.

**DODDS, Gladys Helen,** MD; FRCS, FRCSE, FRCOG; Hon. Consultant Obstetrician and Gynæcologist, Queen Charlotte's and North East Metropolitan Hospitals, London, retired; *b* Kirkcaldy, Fife, 1898; *d* of James Dodds and Elizabeth Paterson. *Educ:* High Sch., Dunfermline; Univ. of Edinburgh. House Surg., Royal Maternity Hosp. and Royal Hosp. for Sick Children, Edinburgh;

1st Asst, Obstetric Unit, University Coll. Hosp., London. *Publications:* Gynecology for Nurses, 1946; Midwives' Dictionary; contributions to the Encyclopædia of Medical Practice and to medical journals.
*Died 5 Sept. 1982.*

**DODS, Sir Lorimer (Fenton),** Kt 1962; MVO 1947; Emeritus Professor of Child Health, University of Sydney, since 1960; Chairman, Children's Medical Research Foundation, Sydney, since 1966 (Hon. Director, 1960–66); *b* 7 March 1900; British; *m* 1927, Margaret Walsh; one *s* one *d. Educ:* Sydney Church of England Gram. Sch., N Sydney; St Paul's Coll., University of Sydney (1918–23). Served 1st AIF, 1918. Gen. Med. Practice, 1926–37; Pædiatric Practice, 1937–39 and 1945–49 (served 2nd AIF, AAMC, Lt-Col, Middle East and New Guinea, 1939–45). Prof. of Child Health, University of Sydney, and Dir of Commonwealth Inst. of Child Health, 1949–60. *Publications:* various pædiatric contribs. *Address:* 8 Albert Street, Edgecliff, NSW 2027, Australia. *T:* 32 2152. *Club:* Union (Sydney).
*Died 7 March 1981.*

**DOGGART, James Hamilton,** MA, MD, FRCS; Consulting Surgeon, Moorfields, Westminster and Central Eye Hospital and Hospital for Sick Children, Great Ormond Street; Past Chairman, British Orthoptic Board; Livery of the Society of Apothecaries of London; Ophthalmological Society, Société belge d'Ophtalmologie, Société française d'Ophtalmologie; Hon. Member: Australian, NZ and Peruvian Ophthalmological Societies; Oto-Neuro-Ophth. Soc. of the Argentine; Canadian Ophthalmological Society; formerly: Lecturer, Institute of Ophthalmology; Examiner: for British Orthoptic Board; (in Fellowship of Ophthalmology) RCSI; Faculty of Ophth. representative on Council of RCS; Examiner in Ophthalmology, Royal Coll. of Surgeons and Physicians, University of Belfast, and for FRCS, 1954–60; formerly Pres. and Mem. Council, Faculty of Ophthalmologists and Fellow and Councillor, Hunterian Society; Hon. Secretary, Editorial Committee, British Journal Ophthalmology; surgeon-oculist in London, 1929–72; *b* 22 Jan. 1900; *s* of late Arthur Robert Doggart, Bishop Auckland; *m* 1st, 1928, Doris Hilda Mennell; one *d;* 2nd, 1938, Leonora Sharpley Gatti; one *s. Educ:* Bishop's Stortford Coll.; King's Coll., Cambridge (Scholar); St Thomas's Hospital. FRCS; FRSM; FCOphth 1988. Surg. Sub-Lt, RNVR, 1918; Schol., King's Coll., Cambridge, 1919–22; Mem. Anglo-American Physiological Exped. to Andes, 1921; Ophth. Ho. Surg., St Thomas's Hosp., 1923–24; Ho. Surg., Casualty Officer, Royal Northern Hosp., 1925–26; appts at Royal Westminster Ophthalmic Hosp.: Clinical Asst, Refraction Asst, Chief Clin. Asst and Pathologist, 1926–30; appts at Moorfields Eye Hosp.: Clin. Asst, Refraction Asst, Chief Clin. Asst, 1927–34, Asst Med. Officer to Physico-Therapy Dept, 1930–31, Lang Research Schol., 1930–33; Clin. Asst, London Hosp., 1929–34; Ophth. Surg., East Ham Memorial Hosp., 1930–31; appts at St George's Hosp.: Asst Ophth. Surg., 1931–46, Ophth. Surg., 1946–49; Lectr in Ophthalmology, St George's Hosp. Med. Sch., University of London, 1931–49; Ophth. Surg., Lord Mayor Treloar Hosp., 1932–37; Asst Surgeon, Central London Ophthalmic Hosp., 1934–38; Ophth. Surg., Hosp. for Sick Children, Great Ormond Street, 1936–63; Lectr in Ophth., Inst. of Child Health, 1936–63; Hon. Secretary: Section of Ophthalmology, RSM, 1935–37; Ophthalmological Soc., 1939–40, 1946–47. Chm., Cttee of Horatian Soc., 1965–69. Sq/Ldr, W/Cdr, RAF, Med. Br., 1940–45. CStJ 1962. *Publications:* Diseases of Children's Eyes, 1947, 2nd edn, 1950; Children's Eye Nursing, 1948; Ocular Signs in Slit-Lamp Microscopy, 1949; Ophthalmic Medicine, 1949; Chapters in: Moncrieff's Nursing of Sick Children, 1948; Garrod Batten and Thursfield's Diseases of Children, 1949; Stallard's Modern Practice in Ophthalmology, 1949; Berens' Diseases of the Eye, 1949; Parsons and Barling's Diseases of Children, 1954; Treves and Rogers' Surgical Applied Anatomy, 1952; Gaisford and Lightwood's Pædiatrics for the Practitioner, 1955; Thérapeutique Médicale Oculaire; articles in British Encyclopædia of Medical and Surgical Practice; papers in Brit. Jl Ophth., etc. *Recreations:* walking, reading. *Address:* Albury Park, Albury, Guildford, Surrey. *T:* Shere 3289. *Clubs:* English-Speaking Union; Hawks (Cambridge).
*Died 15 Oct. 1989.*

**DOGGETT, Frank John,** CB 1965; retired; Deputy Chairman, UKAEA, 1971–76; Director, National Nuclear Corporation, 1973–76; *b* 7 Jan. 1910; *s* of Frank Hewitt and Charlotte Doggett; *m* 1st, 1940, Clare Judge (*d* 1956); one *d;* 2nd, 1957, Mary Battison. *Educ:* Mathematical Sch., Rochester; University of London (LLB). Inland Revenue, 1929; Air Ministry, 1938; MAP, 1940; MOS, 1946, Under-Sec., 1957–59; Under-Sec., Min. of Aviation, 1959–66, Dep. Sec., 1966–67; Dep. Sec. (A), Min. of Technology, 1967–70; Under-Sec., Dept of Trade and Industry, 1970–71. *Address:* The Jays, Ridgeway Road, Dorking, Surrey. *T:* Dorking 885819.
*Died 4 March 1988.*

**DOIG, Sir James (Nimmo Crawford),** Kt 1970; Director, UEB Industries Ltd; *b* 21 Aug. 1913; *s* of David Dickson Doig; *m* 1943, Rita Elizabeth Lowe; two *s* one *d;* *m* 1976, Irene Evelyn Godden. *Educ:* Alan Glen's School and Royal Technical College, Glasgow. Managing Director, UEB Industries Ltd, 1948–73, Chairman,

1965–79. *Recreations:* yachting, painting. *Address:* c/o UEB Industries, 1–11 Short Street, PO Box 37, Auckland, New Zealand. *Clubs:* Northern, Royal NZ Yacht Squadron (NZ); Royal Sydney Yacht Squadron.                          *Died* 1 *Dec.* 1984.

**DOISY, Prof. Edward A.;** Professor Emeritus of Biochemistry and Director Emeritus of Edward A. Doisy Department of Biochemistry, St Louis University School of Medicine, since 1965; *b* Hume, Ill., 13 Nov. 1893; *s* of Edward Perez and Ada Alley Doisy; *m* 1st, 1918, Alice Ackert (*d* 1964); four *s*; 2nd, 1965, Margaret McCormick. *Educ:* Univ. of Illinois (AB 1914, MS 1916); Harvard (PhD 1920). Hon. ScD: Yale, 1940; Washington, 1940; Chicago, 1941; Central Coll., 1942; Illinois, 1960; Gustavus Adolphus Coll., 1963; Hon. Dr, Paris, 1945; Hon. LLD, St Louis, 1955. Asst in Biochemistry, Harvard Medical Sch., 1915–17; Army Service, 1917–19; Instructor, Associate and Associate Prof. in Biochemistry, Washington Univ. Sch. of Medicine, 1919–23; Prof. of Biochemistry and Chm. of Dept, St Louis Univ. Sch. of Medicine, 1923–65, Distinguished Service Prof., 1951–65. Member: American Soc. of Biological Chemists (Pres. 1943–45); American Chem. Soc.; Endocrine Soc. (Pres. 1949–50); American Assoc. for the Advancement of Science; Soc. for Experimental Biology and Medicine (Pres. 1949–51); National Academy of Sciences; American Philosophical Soc.; Amer. Acad. Arts and Sci.; Pontifical Acad. of Sci.; Foundation or Memorial Lectr at New York, Kansas, Pittsburgh, Chicago, Cleveland, Minnesota, Rochester; several medals and awards; shared the Nobel Prize in Physiology and Medicine for 1943 with Dr Henrik Dam. *Publications:* more than 100 papers in medical and scientific journals. *Recreations:* golf, hunting and fishing. *Address:* Apt 4b, Colonial Village Apartments, Webster Groves, Mo 63119, USA; St Louis University School of Medicine, 1402 South Grand Boulevard, St Louis, Missouri 63104. *T:* 664–9800 ext. 121.
                          *Died* 23 *Oct.* 1986.

**DOLIN, Sir Anton,** Kt 1981; dancer and choreographer; *b* Slinfold, Sussex, 27 July 1904; *s* of H. G. Kay and Helen Maude Kay (*née* Healey); changed name from Patrick Healey-Kay. Joined Diaghilev's Russian Ballet Company in 1923, creating a number of roles; in 1927 danced with Karsavina at the London Coliseum in Le Spectre de la Rose; and later in the year founded the Nemchinova-Dolin Ballet with Nemchinova; rejoined the Diaghilev Company in 1929 (prominently associated with the Camargo Soc.); principal dancer with the Vic-Wells Ballet Company, 1931–35; with Markova-Dolin Ballet Co., 1935–37; organised (with Julien Braunsweg) London's Festival Ballet, 1950; led Festival Ballet in 19-week tour of United States and Canada, 1954–55, and in tour of Europe, 1958; Indiana Univ., 1970–73; has danced principal rôle in all classical and many modern works; has worked also for films, and in revue, etc. His choreographic works for the ballet include: Hymn to the Sun, The Nightingale and the Rose, Rhapsody in Blue, Espagnol, The Pas de Quatre, Variations for Four, Ravel's Bolero, The Swan of Tuonela (Sibelius); choreography (with Lindsay Dolan) The Mitford Girls, Chichester, 1981. Guest Dir of Ballet, Rome Opera. Produced Nutcracker, Giselle, Swan Lake in many countries. The Queen Elizabeth Coronation award, 1954. Awarded The Order of The Sun by the Pres. of Peru, 1959. *Publications:* Divertissement, 1930; Ballet Go Round, 1939; Pas de Deux, 1950; Markova, 1953; Autobiography, 1960; The Sleeping Ballerina, 1966. *Recreation:* travel. *Address:* 3 Orme Court, W2 4RL. *T:* 01-727 1451.
                          *Died* 25 *Nov.* 1983.

**DOLLAR, Jean Marguerite,** FRCS; retired as Surgeon Royal Eye Hospital; Ophthalmic Surgeon: Elizabeth Garrett Anderson Hospital; Royal Free Hospital; St Olave's Hospital, Bermondsey; *b* 23 July 1900. *Educ:* London Sch. of Medicine for Women. MRCS, LRCP 1926; MB, BS 1927; DOMS 1929; MS London 1935; FRCS 1936. Formerly: Surgical Registrar, Royal Eye Hosp.; House Surgeon, Elizabeth Garrett Anderson Hospital, and King Edward VII Hospital, Windsor; Hunterian Professor, Royal College of Surgeons of England. *Publications:* contribs to medical press.
                          *Died* 20 *April* 1982.

**DOLLEY, Michael,** MRIA, FSA, FRHistS; Associate Professor in History, University of New England, Armidale, Australia, 1981, retired (Lecturer, 1978; Senior Lecturer, 1980); *b* 6 July 1925; *s* of late A. H. F. Dolley and Margaret (*née* Horgan); *m* 1950, (Phyllis) Mary Harris; two *s* four *d*. *Educ:* Wimbledon Coll.; King's Coll., Univ. of London (BA). MRIA 1964; FSA 1955; FRHistS 1965. Assistant Keeper: Nat. Maritime Museum, 1948–51; BM, 1951–63; Queen's Univ. of Belfast: Lectr in Med. Hist., 1963–69; Reader, Dept of Mod. Hist., 1969–75; Prof. of Historical Numismatics, 1975–78. Foreign Corresp. Mem., Royal Swedish Acad. of Letters, Hist. and Antiquities, 1970; Foreign Mem., Danish Acad. of Scis and Letters, 1979. *Publications:* Anglo-Saxon Pennies, 1964; Viking Coins of the Danelaw and of Dublin, 1965; The Hiberno-Norse Coins in the British Museum, 1966; The Norman Conquest and the English Coinage, 1966; Anglo-Norman Ireland, 1972; Medieval Anglo-Irish Coins, 1972; vols of jt authorship; approaching 900 papers in jls, mainly numismatic. *Recreations:* conversation and

Irish and Manx history. *Address:* Mavis Bank, 33 Higher Brimley Road, Teignmouth, Devon. *T:* Teignmouth 2994.
                          *Died* 29 *March* 1983.

**DOMVILLE, Sir Gerald Guy,** 7th Bt *cr* 1814; Lieut-Comdr RNVR; *b* 3 March 1896; 3rd *s* of late Rear-Adm. Sir William Cecil Henry Domville, CB, 4th Bt, and Moselle (*d* 1957), *d* of Henry Metcalf Ames, Linden, Northumberland; *S* brother, 1930; *m* 1920, Beatrice Mary (who obtained a divorce, 1930), *o c* of late Brig.-Gen. R. S. Vandeleur, CB, CMG; no *c*. *Educ:* Wellington Coll. Served European War, 1915–19 and War of 1939–45. *Heir:* none. *Address:* 60 Knightsbridge, SW1. *T:* 01-235 2121. *Clubs:* Royal Thames Yacht, Portland, MCC.                *Died* 10 *Oct.* 1981 (*ext*).

**DON, Kaye Ernest;** Chairman and Managing Director, US Concessionaires Ltd, retired 1965; *b* 10 April 1891; *s* of Charles Frederick Don; *m* 1932, Eileen (marr. diss.), *d* of Leonard F. Martin, New York; two *s* one *d*; *m* 1954, Valerie Evelyn, *d* of Ronald Farquar Chapman. *Educ:* Wolverhampton Grammar Sch. Commenced career in the rubber industry, with which was associated until 1915, when joined HM Forces; demobilised, 1919; first served in the Army Service Corps and was discharged on medical grounds; rejoined Royal Flying Corps as pilot in 1916; after serving on the Western Front was posted to British Mission; before the War, raced motor cycles, and took up motor car racing in 1920 and high speed motor boat racing in 1931; British Motor Racing Champion, 1928, 1929; World Water Speed Records: Buenos Aires, 103–104 mph, 1931; Italy, 110 mph, 1931; Loch Lomond, 119 mph, 1932; Internat. Motor Yachting Union Medal, 1931; travelled extensively in America, South America, Australia, South Africa and Europe. *Recreation:* golf. *Address:* Marton, Chobham, Surrey. *T:* Chobham 8256.                          *Died* 29 *Aug.* 1981.

**DON-WAUCHOPE, Sir Patrick (George);** see Wauchope.

**DONALD, David William Alexander,** OBE 1946; TD 1950; General Manager and Actuary, The Standard Life Assurance Company, 1970–79; *b* 3 Feb. 1915; *s* of David Donald and Wilhelmina Ewan. *Educ:* High Sch. of Dundee. FFA 1936. Commnd TA, 1937; served War of 1939–45, Black Watch (RHR), Britain and India; GSO2, Staff Duties, WO, 1943; GSO1, Staff Duties GHQ India, 1944; DAA&QMG 155 (L) Inf. Bde TA, 1949–56. Joined Standard Life Assce Co., 1932: Sen. Asst Actuary, 1946; Jt Actuary, 1949; Actuary, 1962; Dep. Gen. Man., 1969. Dir, Hammerson Property and Develt Corp. plc (formerly Hammerson's Property and Investment Trust Ltd), 1970–85. Pres. Faculty of Actuaries, 1969–71; Chm. Associated Scottish Life Offices, 1974–76; Chm. Bd of Governors, Red House Home, 1966–74; Mem. Council, Edinburgh Festival Soc. Ltd, 1977–81; Dir, Scottish Nat. Orchestra Soc. Ltd, 1977–85. *Publications:* Compound Interest and Annuities-Certain, 1953; contrib. actuarial jls. *Recreations:* music, golf, wine and food. *Address:* 15 Hermitage Drive, Edinburgh EH10 6BX. *T:* 031-447 2562. *Clubs:* New, Hon. Company of Edinburgh Golfers (Edinburgh); Royal and Ancient (St Andrews).
                          *Died* 25 *April* 1986.

**DONALD, Prof. Ian,** CBE 1973 (MBE 1946); MD; FRCSGlas; FRCOG; FCOG(SA); Regius Professor of Midwifery, University of Glasgow, 1954–76, later Emeritus Professor; Hon. Research Consultant, National Maternity Hospital, Dublin, since 1977; *b* 27 Dec. 1910; British; *m* 1937, Alix Mathilde de Chazal Richards; four *d*. *Educ:* Warriston Sch., Moffat; Fettes Coll., Edinburgh; Diocesan Coll., Rondebosch, Cape. BA Cape Town, 1930; MB, BS London, 1937; MD London, 1947; MRCOG 1947; FRCOG 1955; FRCSGlas 1958; FCOG(SA) 1967; Hon. FACOG 1976. Served War of 1939–45 with Royal Air Force (Medical), 1942–46 (despatches). Reader in Obstetrics and Gynæcology, St Thomas's Hosp. Medical Sch., 1951; Reader, University of London, Inst. of Obstetrics and Gynæcology, 1952; Leverhulme Research Scholar, 1953; Blair Bell Memorial Lecturer, RCOG, 1954. Hon. FRCOG 1982; Hon. FRCR 1983; Hon. FRCP Glas 1984. Hon. DSc: London, 1981; Glasgow, 1983. Eardley Holland Gold Medal, 1970; Blair Bell Gold Medal, RSM, 1970; Victor Bonney Prize, RCS, 1970–72; MacKenzie Davidson Medal, BIR, 1975. Order of Fiuh with Gold Star, Yugoslavia, 1982. *Publications:* Practical Obstetric Problems, 1955, 5th edn 1979; articles on respiratory disorders in the newborn, in Lancet and Jl of Obst. and Gynæc. Brit. Empire, and on ultrasonics in diagnosis, in Lancet. *Recreations:* sailing, music, painting. *Address:* Cobblers Row, East End, Paglesham, Essex SS4 2ER. *T:* Canewdon 616.
                          *Died* 19 *June* 1987.

**DONALDSON, Sir Dawson,** KCMG 1967; BSc; CEng, FIEE; Chairman, Commonwealth Telecommunications Board, 1962–69, retired; *b* 29 Dec. 1903; *s* of Dawson Donaldson and Ada M. Gribble; *m* 1928, Nell Penman; two *s* two *d*. *Educ:* Auckland Grammar Sch.; New Zealand Univ. New Zealand Post and Tels Dept, 1922–62; Executive Engineer, 1928–48; Superintending Engineer, 1948–54; Dep. Dir Gen., 1954–60; Dir Gen., 1960–62. *Recreations:* bowls and garden. *Address:* Kirkpatrick House, Duart Road, Havelock North, New Zealand.        *Died* 1990.

**DONCASTER, John Priestman,** CBE 1967; MA; formerly Keeper, Department of Entomology, British Museum (Natural History), 1961–68, retired; *b* 20 Nov. 1907; *s* of Charles Doncaster and Hilda Priestman; *m* 1938, Frances Julia Gaynesford Walter; one *d. Educ:* St Catharine's Coll., Cambridge. Joined British Museum as Asst Keeper in charge of Exhibition Section, 1937; entered Dept of Entomology, 1951. *Address:* 3 Devonshire Road, Harpenden, Herts AL5 4TJ.                                          *Died* 29 *April* 1981.

**DONERAILE,** 9th Viscount, *cr* 1785; **Richard St John St Leger;** Baron Doneraile, 1776; *b* 29 Oct. 1923; *o s* of 8th Viscount and of Sylvia St Leger; *S* father, 1957; *m* 1945, Melva Jean Clifton; three *s* two *d. Educ:* George Washington Sch., USA. In lumber business and real estate. *Heir:* s Hon. Richard Allen St Leger [*b* 17 Aug. 1946; *m* 1970, Kathleen Mary, *e d* of N. Simcox, Co. Cork; one *s* one *d* ].
                                                          *Died* 22 *Oct.* 1983.

**DONNER, Frederic Garrett;** Chairman of the Board of Trustees, Alfred P. Sloan Foundation, 1968–75, retired; Director, General Motors Corporation, 1942–74 (Chairman, 1958–67); *b* 4 Oct. 1902; *s* of Frank Donner and Cornelia (*née* Zimmerman); *m* 1929, Eileen Isaacson; one *d* (and one *s* decd). *Educ:* University of Michigan, Ann Arbor, Michigan, USA. General Motors Corporation, 1926; Dir, Communications Satellite Corporation, 1964–77; Trustee, Sloan-Kettering Inst. for Cancer Research, NY, 1964–75. Holds hon. doctorates and foreign decorations. *Address:* 40 West Elm Street, Apt 5D, Greenwich, Conn 06830, USA. *Clubs:* Links, University (NY City); North Hempstead Country (Long Island, NY).                                             *Died* 28 *Feb.* 1987.

**DONNER, Sir Patrick William,** Kt 1953; MA; DL; *b* 1904; *s* of late Ossian Donner and Violet Marion McHutchen, Edinburgh; *m* 1938, Hon. Angela Chatfield (*d* 1943), *er d* of 1st Baron Chatfield, GCB, OM, KCMG, CVO, Admiral of the Fleet; *m* 1947, Pamela *y d* of Rear Adm. Herbert A. Forster, MVO; one *s* two *d. Educ:* abroad and Exeter Coll., Oxford. Studied Imperial development and administration, 1928–30; MP (C) West Islington, 1931–35; Basingstoke Div. of Hants, 1935–55; Hon. Sec., India Defence League, 1933–35; Parliamentary Private Sec. to Sir Samuel Hoare, Home Sec., 1939; Mem. Advisory Cttee on Education in the Colonies; Parliamentary Private Sec. to Col Oliver Stanley, Sec. of State for the Colonies, 1944; Dir, National Review Ltd, 1933–47; Mem. Executive Council Joint East and Central African Board, 1937–54. Volunteered RAFVR 1939; served at HQ Fighter Command; Acting Sqdn Leader, 1941. Chm. Executive Cttee of the Men of the Trees, 1959–62. Mem., Art Panel of the Arts Council, 1963–66. High Sheriff of Hants, 1967–68; DL Hants 1971. *Publication:* Crusade: a life against the calamitous twentieth century, 1984. *Recreations:* music, travel, landscape gardening. *Address:* Hurstbourne Park, Whitchurch, Hants. *T:* Whitchurch 2230.
                                                          *Died* 19 *Aug.* 1988.

**DONNET OF BALGAY,** Baron *cr* 1978 (Life Peer), of Balgay in the district of the City of Dundee; **Alexander Mitchell Donnet,** CBE 1975; FCIT 1979; JP; Chairman, Scottish Transport Group, 1978–80 (Member, 1969–80); *b* Dundee, 26 June 1916; *m* 1945, Mary, *d* of Gavin Mitchell Black; two *s* one *d. Educ:* Harris Academy, Dundee. Mem., G&MWU, 1935–; Regional Sec., Scottish Region, 1959–78; Nat. Chm., 1970–76; Pres., Scottish TUC, 1970–71; Mem. Gen. Council, TUC, 1972–76. An Asst Comr, Commn on the Constitution, 1969–73. Member: Scottish Economic Council, 1968–81; Forestry Commn, 1973–78; Price Commn, 1977–79; Greater Glasgow Health Bd; Scottish Develt Agency, 1979–82. JP Glasgow, 1961. *Address:* 8 Jordanhill Drive, Glasgow G13 1SA.                                     *Died* 14 *May* 1985.

**DONOUGHMORE,** 7th Earl of (*cr* 1800), **John Michael Henry Hely-Hutchinson;** Baron Donoughmore, 1783; Viscount Suirdale, 1800; Viscount Hutchinson (UK), 1821; *b* 12 Nov. 1902; *er s* of 6th Earl of Donoughmore, KP, PC, and Elena (*d* 1944), *d* of late M. P. Grace, New York; *S* father, 1948; *m* 1925, Dorothy Jean (MBE 1947), *d* of late J. B. Hotham; two *s* one *d. Educ:* Winchester; Magdalen Coll., Oxford. MP (C) Peterborough Div. of Northants, 1943–45. Grand Master, Freemasons' Grand Lodge of Ireland, 1964. *Heir:* s Viscount Suirdale. *Address:* Knocklofty, Clonmel, Ireland. *Club:* Kildare Street and University (Dublin).
                                                          *Died* 12 *Aug.* 1981.

**DONOVAN, Hedley (Williams);** *b* 24 May 1914; *s* of Percy Williams Donovan and Alice Dougan Donovan; *m* 1941, Dorothy Hannon (*d* 1978); two *s* one *d. Educ:* University of Minnesota; Hertford Coll., Oxford (Hon. Fellow, 1977). BA (*magna cum laude*) Minn., 1934; BA Oxon. 1936. US Naval Reserve, active duty, 1942–45 (Lieut-Comdr). Reporter, Washington Post, 1937–42; Writer and Editor, 1945–53, Managing Editor, 1953–59, Fortune; Editorial Dir, Time Inc., 1959–64, Editor in Chief, 1964–79, Consultant, 1979–84. Senior Advisor to the President, 1979–80. Trustee, Nat. Humanities Center. Fellow, Faculty of Govt, Harvard Univ., 1981–87; Vis. Res. Fellow, Nuffield Coll., Oxford, 1986. Fellow, Amer. Acad. of Arts and Sciences. Phi Beta Kappa; Rhodes Scholar. Hon. LittD:

Pomona Coll., 1966; Mount Holyoke, 1967; Boston, 1968; Hon DHL: South-Western at Memphis, 1967; Rochester, 1968; Transylvania, 1979; Hon LLD: Carnegie-Mellon, 1969; Lehigh, 1976; Allegheny Coll., 1979. *Publications:* Roosevelt to Reagan: a reporter's encounters with nine Presidents, 1985; Right Places, Right Times: forty years in journalism, not counting my paper route, 1989. *Address:* Harbor Road, Sands Point, NY 11050, USA. *Clubs:* University, Century (New York); Metropolitan (Washington DC); St Botolph (Boston); Manhasset Bay Yacht (Long Island).
                                                          *Died* 13 *Aug.* 1990.

**DORÁTI, Antal,** Hon. KBE 1983; composer and conductor; Conductor Laureate for life: Royal Philharmonic Orchestra, 1978 (Principal Conductor, 1975–78); Detroit Symphony Orchestra, 1981 (Musical Director, 1977–81); Stockholm Philharmonic, 1981; *b* Budapest, 9 April 1906; *s* of Alexander Doráti and Margit (*née* Kunwald); *m* 1st, 1929, Klara Korody; one *d*; 2nd, 1971, Ilse von Alpenheim. *Educ:* Royal Academy of Music, Budapest; University of Vienna. Conductor: Royal Opera House, Budapest, 1924–28; Münster State Opera, 1929–32; Musical Director: Ballet Russe de Monte Carlo, 1932–40; Ballet Theatre, NY, 1940–42; New Opera Co., NY, 1942–43; Musical Dir and Conductor: Dallas Symph. Orch., 1944–49; Minneapolis Symph. Orch., 1944–60; Chief Conductor: BBC Symphony Orchestra, 1963–66; Stockholm Philharmonic Orch., 1966–74; Musical Dir, Nat. Symphony Orch., Washington, DC, 1970–77. Guest conductor of major orchestras of the world, Salzburg, Holland, Venice, Lucerne, Berlin Festivals, etc; London Symphony, New Philharmonia, London Philharmonic, Royal Philharmonic, Israel Philharmonic orchestras, etc. Holder of 26 recording awards in America and Europe. DrMus: Macalister Coll., St Paul, 1958; George Washington Univ., 1975; Dr (hc) Humanities: Maryland, 1976; Wayne State Univ., Detroit, 1982. Member: Swedish Acad., 1967; Royal Swedish Academy of the Arts; Hon. Prof., Music Acad., Budapest, 1981. Comdr, Order of Vasa; Chevalier of Arts and Letters, France; Order of Letters and Arts, Austria; Order of the Flag, Hungary. Compositions include: The Way (dramatic cantata); Symphony I; Missa Brevis; The two enchantments of Li-Tai-Pe; String Quartet; Cello Concerto; Nocturne and Capriccio for oboe and strings; Magdalena (ballet); Seven Pictures for Orch.; Madrigal Suite; String Octet; Largo Concertato for String Orch.; 'Chamber-Music', Song Cycle for Sopr. and small orch.; Night Music for Flute and small orch.; Variations on a theme of Bartok for piano, Piano Concerto; Threni for String Orch., American Serenades for String Orch.; Ötének; Divertimento for Oboe and Orch.; The Voices (song cycle) for bass voice and Orch.; In the Beginning (five meditations) for baritone, oboe, cello and percussion; Sonata for Assisi for two flutes; String Quartet; Five Pieces for Oboe; Three Studies for Mixed Choir; Of God, Man and Machine for Mixed Choir; Four Choruses for Female Choir; Duo Concertante for Oboe and Piano; The Chosen (opera); Querela Pacis (fantasy for orch.); Triptych for Oboe, Oboe d'amore and English Horn with string orch. *Publication:* Notes of Seven Decades, 1979. *Recreations:* painting sketching, reading, art collecting.
                                                          *Died* 13 *Nov.* 1988.

**DORWARD, Ivor Gardiner Menzies Gordon,** ARSA, FRIBA, FRIAS, RGI; Architect Principal in private practice, since 1960; Member, Royal Fine Art Commission for Scotland, since 1976; *b* 18 Oct. 1927; *s* of William Gordon Dorward and Jean Lawson Dorward (*née* Skinner); *m* 1954, Priscilla Purves Tindal, DA Edin.; two *d. Educ:* Royal High Sch., Edinburgh; Blackpool Grammar Sch.; Edinburgh Coll. of Art. DA 1953; FRIBA 1969. Served RAF, 1945–48. Various travelling scholarships in Europe and Africa, 1951, 1952 and 1953. Architect in private practice, Dorward, Matheson, Gleave & Partners, 1960–. Principal works include university, hospital, and both local and central government buildings. Royal Scottish Acad. Medal for Architecture, 1971. RGI 1978; ARSA 1979. *Recreations:* drawing, sailing, Bull Terriers. *Address:* 50 Sherbrooke Avenue, Glasgow G41 4SB. *T:* 041-427 1771; Kerryfern, Strone, Argyll PA23 8RR. *T:* Dunoon 84416. *Club:* Glasgow Art (Glasgow).
                                                          *Died* 5 *June* 1983.

**DOSSOR, Rear-Adm. Frederick,** CB 1963; CBE 1959; *b* 12 March 1913; *s* of John Malcolm Dossor and Edith Kate Brittain; *m* 1951, Pamela Anne Huxley Newton; two *d. Educ:* Hymers Coll., Hull; Loughborough Coll. BSc(Eng.) London; FIEE. Post Graduate Apprentice and Junior Engineer, Metropolitan Vickers Electrical Co., Manchester, 1935–39; Dept of Dir of Electrical Engineering, Admiralty, 1939–50; Electrical Specialisation, Royal Navy, 1950–65; Chief Staff Officer (Technical), staff of Comdr-in-Chief, Portsmouth, 1961–63; Polaris Project Officer in the Ministry of Technology, 1963–67; Dir of Hovercraft, DTI (formerly Min. of Technology), 1968–71. Retired from Royal Navy, 1965. *Recreation:* gardening. *Address:* 1a Lynch Road, Farnham, Surrey GU9 8BZ. *Club:* Commonwealth Trust.                          *Died* 4 *Oct.* 1990.

**DOUBLEDAY, John Gordon,** OBE 1975; HM Diplomatic Service, retired; HM Ambassador to Liberia, 1978–80; *b* 27 Nov. 1920; *s* of late Douglas Collins Doubleday and Edith Doubleday; *m* 1961,

Ruth Helen (*née* Walls); one *s* two *d. Educ:* Alleyn Court Prep. Sch.; Bedford Sch.; St John's Coll., Cambridge. RAFVR, 1941–46. Colonial Administrative Service, Northern Rhodesia, 1949–65; entered HM Diplomatic Service, 1965; Dep. British High Comr, Bahamas, 1973–76; Dep. British High Comr, Sri Lanka, 1976–78. *Recreations:* most outdoor sports, bridge. *Address:* 1 Nightingale Avenue, Cambridge. *Clubs:* MCC; Gog Magog Golf (Cambridge). *Died* 27 *April* 1982.

**DOUGHTY, Dame Adelaide (Baillieu)**, DBE 1971 (CBE 1964); *b* 2 Dec. 1908; *d* of E. H. Shackell, Melbourne, Australia; *m* 1931, Charles John Addison Doughty, QC (*d* 1973); one *s* one *d. Educ:* St Catherine's Sch., Melbourne; St Hilda's Coll., Oxford (BA). Chm., Nat. Women's Advisory Cttee, Conservative Party, 1963–66; Chm., 1967, Pres., 1978, Nat. Union of Conservative and Unionist Party; Governor, English-Speaking Union, 1958–72 (Dep.-Chm. 1971–72). Mem. Council, Cancer Res. Campaign, 1974. *Address:* Flat 4, 89 Onslow Square, SW7 3LT. *T:* 01–584 5126.

*Died* 12 *Aug.* 1986.

**DOUGLAS, Dr Alexander Edgar**, FRS 1970; FRSC 1954; Principal Research Officer, National Research Council of Canada, since 1973 (Director, Division of Physics, 1969–73); *b* 12 April 1916; *s* of Donald Douglas and Jessie F. Douglas (*née* Carwardine); *m* 1945, Phyllis H. Wright; two *s* one *d. Educ:* Univ. of Saskatchewan; Pennsylvania State University. BA 1939, MA 1940, Saskatchewan; PhD Penn 1948. Nat. Research Council of Canada: Research Scientist, Acoustics Lab., 1942–46; Spectroscopy Lab., 1948; Assoc. Dir., Div. of Pure Physics, 1967. Fellow, American Physical Soc., 1970; Pres., Canadian Assoc. of Physicists, 1975. *Publications:* numerous articles on spectroscopy and molecular structure. *Address:* 150 Blenheim Drive, Rockcliffe Park, Ottawa, Ont K1L 5B5, Canada. *T:* 996.1688. *Died* 26 *July* 1981.

**DOUGLAS, Lord Cecil Charles**; late Lt KOSB and RFC; *b* 27 Dec. 1898; 2nd *s* of 10th Marquess of Queensberry; *m* 1927, Ruby St B. Kirkley, 2nd *d* of De Vere Fenn; one *d. Educ:* Lancing; RMC Sandhurst. Served European War, 1914 (wounded). *Address:* 42 Green Street, W1. *T:* 01–499 3343. *Clubs:* White's, Puffin's (Edinburgh). *Died* 26 *Feb.* 1981.

**DOUGLAS, David Charles**, MA Oxon; Hon. DLitt Wales; Hon. DLitt Exeter; Docteur *hc*, Caen; FBA 1949; Emeritus Professor of History, Bristol University, since 1963; Hon. Fellow, Keble College, Oxford; *b* London, 5 Jan. 1898; *o s* of Dr J. J. Douglas and Margaret E. Peake; *m* 1932, Evelyn Helen, *o d* of Dr B. M. Wilson; one *d. Educ:* Sedbergh; Keble Coll., Oxford (Louisa Wakeman Scholar). 1st Class Hons in Modern History, Oxford, 1921; University Research Scholar in Medieval History and Thought, Oxford, 1922–24; Lecturer in History, Glasgow Univ., 1924–34; Prof. of History, University Coll. of the South West, 1934–39; Prof. of Medieval History, Leeds Univ., 1939–45; Prof. of History, Bristol Univ., 1945–63; Dean of the Faculty of Arts, 1958–60; Trustee of London Museum, 1945–70; David Murray Lectr to University of Glasgow, 1946, Sir Walter Raleigh Lectr to Brit. Acad., 1947; Ford's Lectr in English History, Oxford Univ., 1962–63; Lewis Fry Memorial Lectr, Bristol Univ., 1969. Vice-Pres., Royal Historical Soc., 1953–57; Pres., Bristol and Glos Archæological Soc., 1956. *Publications:* The Norman Conquest, 1926; The Social Structure of Medieval East Anglia, 1927; The Age of the Normans, 1928; Feudal Documents from the Abbey of Bury St Edmunds, 1932; The Development of Medieval Europe, 1935; English Scholars, 1939 (James Tait Black Memorial Prize); Domesday Monachorum, 1944; The Rise of Normandy, 1947; William the Conqueror, 1964; The Norman Achievement 1050–1100, 1969; The Norman Fate 1100–1154, 1976; Time and the Hour, 1977; General Editor, English Historical Documents, 1953, etc.; articles in English Historical Review, Times Lit. Supplt, History, Economic History Review, Revue Historique, French Studies, etc. *Recreation:* book-collecting. *Address:* 4 Henleaze Gardens, Bristol. *Club:* United Oxford & Cambridge University. *Died* 12 *Sept.* 1982.

**DOUGLAS, Donald Wills;** President Douglas Aircraft Co. Inc., 1928–57, Chairman, 1957–67, Hon. Chairman since 1967; *b* 6 April 1892; *s* of William Edward Douglas and Dorothy Locker; *m* 1916, Charlotte Ogg; four *s* one *d*; *m* 1954, Marguerite Tucker. *Educ:* United States Naval Acad.; MIT (BSc 1914). Asst Instructor in aero-dynamics, Mass. Inst. of Tech., 1914–15; Chief Engineer, G. L. Martin Co., Los Angeles, 1915–16; Chief Civilian Aero Engineer, US Signal Corps, 1916; Chief Engineer, G. L. Martin Co., Cleveland, 1916–20; Pres., Douglas Co., 1920–28. President's Certificate of Merit, 1947; Guggenheim Medal, 1939; Collier Trophy, 1940; Comdr, Order of Orange-Nassau, 1950; Chevalier, Legion of Honour, 1950. *Recreations:* yachting, fishing, hunting. *Address:* 377 Camino Sur, Palm Springs, Calif 92262, USA. *Club:* Los Angeles Yacht (Wilmington, Calif). *Died* 1 *Feb.* 1981.

**DOUGLAS, Very Rev. Hugh Osborne**, KCVO 1981; CBE 1961; DD, LLD; Dean of the Chapel Royal in Scotland, 1974–81; Chaplain to The Queen, 1959–81, Extra Chaplain to The Queen, since 1981;

Minister at Dundee Parish Church (St Mary's), 1951–77; Moderator of the General Assembly of the Church of Scotland, 1970–71; *b* Glasgow, 11 Sept. 1911; *s* of Rev. Robert Baillie Douglas, DD, missionary in W India, and Mary Isabella Osborne; *m* 1939, Isabel Crammond, *d* of William Rutherford, Coldstream, Berwicks; one *s* two *d. Educ:* Glasgow Academy; Glasgow Univ.; Trinity Coll., Glasgow. MA 1st Cl. Hons (Classics), 1932. Licensed to preach by Presbytery of Glasgow, 1935; Asst, Govan Old Parish Church, 1935–39; Ordained, Glasgow, 1937; Minister: St John's Leven, 1939; North Leith, Edinburgh, 1942. Member: Legal Aid Central Cttee of Law Soc. of Scotland, 1955–80; Scottish Religious Advisory Cttee of BBC, 1956–58; Gen. Advisory Council of BBC, 1966–69; Convener of Gen. Assembly's Special Cttee on Fourth Centenary of the Reformation, 1955–60; Convener of Gen. Assembly's Special Cttee on Religious Education, 1960–64. Centenary Preacher, St Andrew's Church, Brisbane, 1962, Guest Preacher, 1977. Visiting Lectr, Christian Council of Ghana, 1967. Hon. Governor, Glasgow Acad., 1971. Hon. DD St Andrews, 1958; Hon. LLD Dundee, 1971. *Publications:* Coping with Life, 1964; various pamphlets and articles. *Recreation:* golf. *Address:* Broomlea, 7A Windmill Road, St Andrews. *T:* St Andrews 73232. *Club:* Royal and Ancient Golf (St Andrews). *Died* 4 *Jan.* 1986.

**DOUGLAS, James Albert Sholto**, CMG 1966; Director, IDA/IBRD Education Project Implementation Unit, 1969–79; *b* 23 April 1913; *s* of Dr James Henry Sholto Douglas and Cécile Anne (*née* Brotherson); *m* 1945, Marjorie Lucille (*née* Reynolds); two *s. Educ:* privately in Guyana (Brit. Guiana); Culford Sch., England. Entered Brit. Guyana CS in Commissary's Dept 1932; various posts in Dist Admin, 1933–48; Asst Dist Comr, 1948; Dist Comr, 1953; seconded as a Local Govt Comr, 1957; Dep. Comr of Local Govt, 1960; Permanent Sec., Community Develt and Educn, 1961, Home Affairs 1961–66; Min. of Education, 1966; retired from Guyana Civil Service, 1972. *Recreations:* swimming, riding. *Address:* 93 Duke Street, Georgetown, Guyana. *T:* 61403. *Club:* Royal Commonwealth Society. *Died* 15 *April* 1981.

**DOUGLAS, Sir Sholto (Courtenay Mackenzie)**, 5th Bt, *cr* 1831; MC 1918; *b* 27 June 1890; *s* of Donald Sholto Mackenzie Douglas (*d* 1928), and Edith Elizabeth Anne (*d* 1933), *o d* of George Robinson, Bagatelle, Mauritius; *S* cousin, 1954; *m* 1929, Lorna Tichborne, *d* of Captain Hugh Nangle; two *d*. Served European War, 1914–18 (MC) and War of 1939–45 with Seaforth Highlanders. *Heir:* none. *Address:* 192 Cooden Drive, Cooden, Sussex.

*Died* 9 *June* 1986 (*ext*).

**DOUGLAS-HOME, Charles Cospatrick;** Editor, The Times, since 1982; *b* 1 Sept. 1937; *s* of late Hon. Henry Douglas-Home and of Lady Margaret Spencer; *m* 1966, Jessica Violet Gwynne; two *s. Educ:* Eton (King's Scholar). Commissioned, Royal Scots Greys, 1956–57; ADC to Governor of Kenya, 1958–59; Military Correspondent, Daily Express, 1961–62, Political and Diplomatic Corresp., 1962–64; The Times: Defence Corresp., 1965–70; Features Editor, 1970–73; Home Editor, 1973–78; Foreign Editor, 1978–81; Deputy Editor, 1981–82. Dir, Times Newspapers Ltd, 1982–. Hon. FRCM (Councillor, 1975–). *Publications:* The Arabs and Israel, 1968; Britain's Reserve Forces, 1969; Rommel, 1973; Evelyn Baring: the last Proconsul, 1978. *Recreations:* outdoor sports, music, books. *Address:* 18 Mortimer Crescent, NW6 5NP. *T:* 01–624 6424. *Club:* Caledonian. *Died* 29 *Oct.* 1985.

**DOVE, Maj.-Gen. Arthur Julian Hadfield**, CB 1948; CBE 1946 (MBE 1937); *b* Marton, New Zealand, 25 Aug. 1902; *s* of late Rev. J. Ll. Dove; *m* 1948, Betty Eyre Godson Bartholomew; one *d. Educ:* Haileybury Coll.; RMA, Woolwich. 2nd Lieut RE, 1922; served Palestine, 1936–38 (MBE, despatches, Bt Major). Served War of 1939–45, France, 1940; Dep. Director HQ, 1942; CRE Guards Armoured Div., 1942–43; Chief Engineer, Combined Ops., 1943–44; Dep. Director of Military Ops, 1944–47; WO rep. with Council of Foreign Ministers and at Peace Conference, 1946–47; Dep. Adjutant General, BAOR, 1948–50; Brigadier, General Staff (Staff Duties), GHQ, MELF, 1951–53; Director of Quartering, War Office, 1954–57; Technical Director, FBI, 1957–61; retired 1957. Colonel Comdt RE, 1961–66. *Recreation:* fencing. *Address:* 77 West Street, Reigate, Surrey. *T:* Reigate 45436. *Club:* Royal Commonwealth Society. *Died* 25 *May* 1985.

**DOVE, Sir Clifford (Alfred)**, Kt 1967; CBE 1960 (MBE 1944); ERD 1963; FCIT; Chairman, British Transport Docks Board, 1970–71; Director-General and Member, Mersey Docks and Harbour Board, Liverpool, 1965–69 (General Manager, 1962); Member: National Ports Council, 1967–71; Council Institute of Transport, 1963–66 (Vice-President, 1964–65); Chairman Merseyside and District Section, Institute of Transport, 1964–65; Council, Dock and Harbour Authorities Assoc., 1970–71 (Executive Committee, 1962–69, Chairman, 1965–67, Vice-President, 1971); *b* 1 Dec. 1904; *e s* of Frederick George Dove and Beatrice Dove (*née* Warren); *m* 1936, Helen Taylor, *d* of Captain James Wilson; no *c. Educ:* Russell

Sch.; West Ham Municipal Coll.; London School of Economics. Joined Port of London Authority, 1921; Asst Port Director, Calcutta, 1945–46; Asst to Gen. Manager, Tees Conservancy Comrs, 1947–52; Gen. Manager, Ports, Nigeria and British Cameroons, 1952–54; Chm. and Gen. Manager, Nigeria Ports Authority, 1954–61; Mem. Nigeria Railway Corp., 1955–61; Mem. Nigeria Coal Corp., 1956–61; Comr of St John, Nigeria, 1956–61; Vice-Chm., Nat. Stadium Board of Nigeria, 1959–61; First Chm., Inst. of Transport, Nigeria Sect., 1959–61. Member: NW Economic Planning Council, 1965–69; Economic Develt Cttee for Movement of Exports, 1965–69; Exec. Cttee, Nat. Assoc. of Port Employers, 1968–69. Served War, 1939–46 (despatches, MBE): enlisted RE as 2nd Lieut, 1939; BEF, 1940; Middle East, 1941–44; Military Dock Supt., Alexandria, 1942–44; Dep. Asst Director of Transportation, MEF, 1944; AQMG (Movements) India and Embarkation Comdt, Calcutta, 1946; Demob., as Lt-Col. Joined Suppl. Reserve, 1947; retd, 1956, as Lt-Col. OStJ 1956. FRSA 1967. *Publication:* (with late A. H. J. Bown) Port Operation and Administration, 1950. *Recreation:* golf. *Clubs:* East India, Devonshire, Sports and Public Schools; Royal Lymington Yacht.                *Died 11 March 1988.*

**DOVENER, John Montague,** QC 1972; *b* 7 Dec. 1923; *s* of John Reginald Dovener and Pinky (*née* Wilmott); *m* 1973, Shirley (*née* Donn). *Educ:* Shrewsbury. Pilot, RAF, 1941–47; 5 years Captain RA/TA, 470 Regt RA/TA. Called to Bar, Middle Temple, 1953. Author. *Publications:* (as Montague Jon): The Wallington Case; A Question of Law. *Address:* 2 Pump Court, Temple, EC4Y 7AH.
                                                            *Died 4 Aug. 1981.*

**DOW, James Findlay;** Consulting Physician, St George's Hospital, SW1 (Consultant Physician, 1948–76); Physician to King Edward VII Hospital for Officers, 1960–76; *b* 13 May 1911; *s* of John Archibald Dow and Jetta Findlay; *m* 1952, Dr Jean Millbank; two *s* two *d. Educ:* Strathallan; St John's Coll., Cambridge; Middlesex Hospital. Resident posts at Middlesex and Brompton Hospitals until 1947; Consultant Physician, St George's Hospital, SW1, 1947–76. MB, BChir Cantab., MRCP 1938, FRCP 1948. Major, RAMC, 1947–49. Examiner in Medicine, Cambridge and London Universities, 1950–63. Member: Board of Governors, St George's Hospital, 1962; Assoc. of Physicians; British Society of Gastro-Enterology. *Publications:* papers in medical journals on gastroenterology. *Recreations:* golf, fishing. *Address:* 149 Harley Street, W1. *T:* 01–935 4444. *Clubs:* Caledonian, MCC.
                                                            *Died 24 Sept. 1983.*

**DOW, His Honour R(onald) Graham;** a Circuit Judge (formerly County Court Judge), 1959–80, retired; *b* 7 Dec. 1909; *s* of John Graham Dow and Bessie Graham Dow; *m* 1937, Dorothy May Christie; two *s. Educ:* Kelvinside Academy; Uppingham Sch.; University Coll., Oxford. Called to Bar, 1932. Military Service, 1939–45. *Recreations:* golf and gardening. *Address:* 2 Kirkwick Avenue, Harpenden, Herts. *T:* Harpenden 2006.
                                                            *Died 11 Dec. 1983.*

**DOWD, (Eric) Ronald,** AO 1976; voice consultant; tenor; Artistic Director and Co-Founder (with Maggie Niven), first National Summer School for Singers, Australia, since 1987; *b* Sydney, Australia, 23 Feb. 1914; *s* of Robert Henry Dowd and Henrietta (*née* Jenkins); *m* 1938, Elsie Burnitt Crute (English born) (decd); one *s* (one *d* decd). *Educ:* Sydney. Prior to Army service in Australia, New Guinea and the Celebes, was a bank officer. Upon discharge, adopted full-time singing and performed for various opera organisations and Australian Broadcasting Commission in the Commonwealth. Came to UK for Sadler's Wells, 1956, and returned to Australia by arrangement with Elizabethan Theatre Trust; then rejoined Sadler's Wells, 1959, remaining for a year. Since then has been fully engaged in concerts and opera singing with leading conductors and organisations, including Royal Opera House. Toured NZ and Australia for Australian Broadcasting Commission, 1964; toured Continent with Sadler's Wells, 1963 and 1965; with Aust. Opera Co., 1972–78. Chm., opera panel, Australian Council for the Arts, 1973–; Mem., Sydney Cultural Council, 1982. *Address:* 171 Albion Street, Surry Hills, NSW 2010, Australia. *Club:* Savage (London).                                          *Died March 1990.*

**DOWER, E. L. G.;** *see* Gandar Dower.

**DOWLING, Sir Hallam (Walter),** KBE 1978 (CBE 1968); barrister and solicitor, since 1933; Senior Partner, Dowling, Wacher & Co., Barristers and Solicitors, Napier, NZ; *b* 18 Aug. 1909; *s* of Walter Dowling, Bristol, and Catherine (*née* Shorney), Weston Super Mare; *m* 1936, Dorothea Agnes (*née* Nolan); two *s* two *d. Educ:* Wellington Coll.; Victoria Univ. of Wellington, NZ (LLB). Chairman, Hawke's Bay Hosp. Bd, to 1980 (Mem. Bd, 1944–80); Pres. and Chm., Hawke's Bay Med. Research Foundn Inc.; former Vice-Pres. and Councillor, Hosp. Bds Assoc. of NZ; Member: (representing all NZ hosps) Nursing Council of NZ; NZ Nurses Educn Adv. Cttee; Vice-Chm. and Foundn Trustee, Princess Alexandra Hosp. Trust Bd; Trustee, Hawke's Bay Alcohol and Drug Addiction Trust; Pres. and Chm., AA (Hawke's Bay) Inc., 1954– (Mem. Council, 1944–);

Foundn Pres., NZ AA; Foundn Trustee and past Pres., Eastern and Central Savings Bank; former Councillor: NZ Law Soc.; Hawke's Bay Dist Law Soc. (also past Pres.); past Dep. Mayor and Councillor, Napier City Council; former Exec. Mem., No 5 (Hawke's Bay) Dist Roads Bd; Director: AA Mutual Insce Gp; NZ Motor World. *Recreations:* golf, trout fishing. *Address:* 48 Avondale Road, Taradale, Napier, New Zealand. *T:* (home) Napier 442–040. *Club:* Hawke's Bay (Napier, NZ).                        *Died 5 Feb. 1983.*

**DOWN, Norman Cecil Sommers,** CMG 1955; Senior Principal Inspector of Taxes, Inland Revenue, 1946–56, retired; *b* 9 Sept. 1893; *s* of late James Erskine Down; *m* 1st, 1917, Edith Gertrude (*née* Steddy) (*d* 1961); two *d*; 2nd, 1962, Agnes (*née* Sandham). *Educ:* St Lawrence Coll., Ramsgate. Inland Revenue since 1912; served European War, 1914–19, in 4th Gordon Highlanders, 51st Div. (Captain, despatches, wounded thrice). *Publications:* Temporary Heroes, 1918; Temporary Crusaders, 1919. *Address:* Binnlands, Swan Lane, Edenbridge, Kent TN8 6AJ. *T:* Edenbridge 863129.                                         *Died 14 March 1984.*

**DOWNER, Hon. Sir Alexander (Russell),** KBE 1965; MA; High Commissioner for Australia in the United Kingdom, 1964–72; *b* Adelaide, 7 April 1910; *s* of late Hon. Sir John Downer, KCMG, KC, MP, Adelaide, a founder of the Australian Commonwealth and a former Premier of S Australia; *m* 1947, Mary I., *d* of late Sir James Gosse, Adelaide; one *s* three *d. Educ:* Geelong Grammar Sch.; Brasenose Coll., Oxford (MA, Dip. of Economics and Political Science). Called to Bar, Inner Temple, 1934; admitted South Australian Bar, 1935. Served 8th Div. AIF, 1940–45 (Prisoner-of-War, Changi Camp, Singapore, for 3½ years). Member Board Electricity Trust of South Australia, 1946–49; MP (Liberal) Angas, Australia, 1949–64; Australian Minister for Immigration, 1958–63. Member: Australian Parliamentary Foreign Affairs Cttee, 1952–58; Australian Constitution Review Cttee, 1956–59; Commonwealth Parliamentary Delegation to Coronation, 1953; Board of National Gallery, S Australia, 1946–63; Pres. Royal Over-Seas League, S Australia Branch, 1946–62; a Governor, E-SU, 1973. Freeman, City of London, 1965. FRSA 1968. Hon. LLD Birmingham, 1973. *Recreations:* travelling, collecting antiques, reading. *Address:* Martinsell, Williamstown, South Australia 5351. *Clubs:* Brooks's, (Hon.) Cavalry and Guards; Adelaide (Adelaide); Union (Sydney).
                                                            *Died 30 March 1981.*

**DOWNES, Dr Ronald Geoffrey,** CB 1979; FTS; Scientific Consultant since 1979; Deputy Chancellor, University of Melbourne, since 1984; *b* 3 Jan. 1916; *s* of Albert John Downes and Florence Maude Downes (*née* Davis); *m* Gwenyth Edith Dodds; three *s. Educ:* Univ. of Melbourne (BAgrSc 1937, MAgrSc 1939, DAgrSc 1972). CSIRO, Div. of Soils, 1939–50; Soils Adviser, US Corps of Engineers, New Guinea, 1942–43; Member, Soil Conservation Authority, Victoria, 1950–53, Dep. Chairman, 1953–61, Chm., 1961–73; Dir and Perm. Head, Min. for Conservation, 1973–79. Mem., Admin. Appeals Tribunal, 1981–. Consultant, UN FAO: Israel, 1960, 1965; Iran, 1967; Lebanon, 1967; Algeria, 1972; Rome, 1969, 1974, 1979, 1980; Morocco, 1981; Brazil, 1982. Harkness Fellow in US, 1954–55; Fellow: Aust. Inst. Agric. Sci., 1961; Soil Conservation Soc. America, 1965; Aust. Inst. of Management, 1977; (Foundn Fellow) Aust. Acad. of Technol Scis, 1976. Prescott Medal, Aust. Soc. Soil Sci., 1976; Aust. Medal of Agric., 1978; Hugh Hammond Bennett Award, Soil Conservation Soc. of Amer., 1981. Coronation Medal, 1953; Jubilee Medal, 1977. *Publications:* contribs to scientific jls, also separate publications and chapters in books on soils, land-use, and the ecological basis for conservation of natural resources and resource development. *Recreations:* lawn bowls, orchid and bonsai growing, model ships. *Address:* 3/84 The Righi, Eaglemont, Victoria 3084, Australia. *T:* (03) 458 2683 Melbourne. *Clubs:* Melbourne, Sciences (Melbourne).                        *Died 2 May 1986.*

**DOWNIE, Prof. Allan Watt,** FRCP 1982; FRS 1955; Professor of Bacteriology, Liverpool University, 1943–66, now Emeritus Professor; *b* 5 Sept. 1901; *s* of William Downie, Rosehearty, Aberdeenshire; *m* 1936, Nancy McHardy; one *s* two *d. Educ:* Fraserburgh Academy, Aberdeen Univ. MB, ChB, Aberdeen Univ., 1923; MD, 1929; DSc, 1937. Lecturer Aberdeen Univ., 1924–26, Manchester Univ., 1927–34; Senior Freedom Research Fellow, London Hospital, 1935–39; Member Scientific Staff, Nat. Institute Medical Research, 1939–43. Voluntary Asst, Rockefeller Inst. Med. Research, New York City, USA, 1934–35. Vis. Prof., Medical Sch., Univ. of Colorado, Denver, 1966–69, 1971, 1973. Founder Fellow, RCPath. Hon. LLD Aberdeen Univ., 1956. *Publications:* (Jt) Virus and Rickettsial Diseases of Man, 1950; numerous articles in scientific journals. *Recreations:* golf, fishing, ornithology. *Address:* 10 College Close, Birkdale, Merseyside. *T:* Southport 67269.
                                                            *Died 26 Jan. 1988.*

**DOWNMAN, Prof. Charles Beaumont Benoy,** PhD; Emeritus Professor of Physiology, University of London; Sophia Jex-Blake Professor of Physiology, University of London, at the Royal Free Hospital School of Medicine, 1960–80; *b* 1916; *s* of Rev. Leonard

Charles and Sarah Alice Downman; *m* 1947, Thais Hélène Barakan; one *s* one *d*. *Educ:* City of London Sch.; St Thomas's Hospital Medical Sch. MRCSEng, LRCP, 1941; PhD London, 1953. FRSocMed; Mem., Physiological Society. *Publications:* papers in medical journals. *Address:* 4 Wendover Drive, New Malden, Surrey KT3 6RN. *Died 4 Jan. 1982.*

**DOWNS, Brian Westerdale,** MA Cantab; Fellow (Master, 1950–63) of Christ's College, Cambridge; Professor of Scandinavian Studies, 1950–60; *b* 4 July 1893; *s* of late James Downs, OBE, JP; *m* Evelyn Wrangham (*née* Doubble) (*d* 1977). *Educ:* Abbotsholme Sch.; Christ's Coll., Cambridge (Entrance Scholar). First Class Honours (with distinction), Medieval and Modern Languages Tripos, 1915; Charles Oldham Shakespeare Scholar, 1914, and Allen Scholar, 1918. Lecturer in Modern Languages and English, Christ's Coll., Cambridge, 1918; Fellow, 1919, Tutor, 1928; Member of Council of Senate, Univ. of Cambridge, 1939–44, and 1954–60; Vice-Chancellor of Univ. of Cambridge, 1955–57; Founder Trustee, Churchill Coll., Cambridge. Representative of the British Council in the Netherlands, 1945–46. DLitt (*hc*), Hull. Commander, Royal Swedish Order of the North Star, 1954; Officier de la Légion d'Honneur, 1957; Chevalier, Royal Danish Order of Dannebrog, 1971. *Publications:* Cambridge Past and Present, 1926; Richardson, 1928; Ibsen, the Intellectual Background, 1946; (with Miss B. M. Mortensen) Strindberg, 1949; A Study of Six Plays by Ibsen, 1950; Norwegian Literature, 1860–1920, 1966; translations from the French, Dutch and German; editions of Shamela and Richardson's Familiar Letters. *Recreation:* walking. *Address:* 20 Marlborough Court, Grange Road, Cambridge CB3 9BQ; Christ's College, Cambridge CB2 3BU. *Club:* Athenæum.
*Died 3 March 1984.*

**DOWNSHIRE, 7th Marquess of,** *cr* 1789; **Arthur Wills Percy Wellington Blundell Trumbull Sandys Hill;** Viscount Hillsborough, Baron Hill, 1717; Earl of Hillsborough, Viscount Kilwarlin, 1751; Baron Harwich (Great Britain), 1756; Earl of Hillsborough and Viscount Fairford, 1772; Hereditary Constable of Hillsborough Fort; late Lieut Berks Yeomanry; *b* 7 April 1894; *s* of 6th Marquess and Katherine, 2nd *d* of Hon. Hugh Hare, Forest House, Bracknell, Berks, and *g d* of 2nd Earl of Listowel; *S* father, 1918; *m* 1953, Mrs Noreen Gray-Miller (*d* 1983), *d* of late William Barraclough. *Heir: nephew* (Arthur) Robin Ian Hill [*b* 10 May 1929; *m* 1957, Hon. Juliet Mary Weld-Forester, *d* of 7th Baron Forester, and of Marie Louise Priscilla, CStJ, *d* of Sir Herbert Perrott, 6th Bt, CH, CB; two *s* one *d*]. *Address:* 81 Onslow Square, SW7. *Died 28 March 1989.*

**DOWSE, Maj.-Gen. Sir Maurice Brian,** KCVO 1953; CB 1952; CBE 1947 (OBE 1940); retired; *b* 10 Sept. 1899; *s* of late Bishop Charles Dowse, and of Mrs Charles Dowse; unmarried. *Educ:* Wellington Coll.; RMC, Sandhurst. 2nd Lieut 1918; Lieut 1920; Captain, 1927; Major, 1936; Lt-Col, 1941; Brigadier, 1943; Maj.-Gen. 1951. Served Royal Welch Fusiliers and on Staff at home and overseas, 1918–44; on Staff at home and Far East, 1944–53; retired, 1953. *Address:* 39 Hyde Park Gate, SW7. *Club:* Travellers'.
*Died 24 Sept. 1986.*

**DOWSON, Maj.-Gen. Arthur Henley,** CB 1964; CBE 1961 (OBE 1945); Director-General, Ordnance Survey, 1961–65, retired; *b* 7 Dec. 1908; *s* of late Kenneth Dowson and Beatrice Mary (*née* Davis); *m* 1933, Mary Evelyn, *d* of Col. A. J. Savage, DSO; one *d*. *Educ:* Haileybury; RMA; King's Coll., Cambridge (BA). Commissioned in RE, 1928; War Service in NW Europe, N Africa, Italy. Director of Military Survey, War Office and Air Ministry, 1957. ADC to the Queen, 1958–61; Maj-Gen. 1961. Chm., Norfolk Broads Consortium Cttee, 1966–71. FRICS 1949. Bronze Star (USA) 1945. *Address:* Flat 1, 36A Northgate, Hunstanton, Norfolk PE36 6DR. *Died 15 Dec. 1989.*

**DOYLE, Rear-Adm. Alec Broughton,** CBE 1937; Royal Australian Navy; *b* 5 Oct. 1888; *s* of James H. and Rebekah Doyle, Invermien, Scone, NSW; *m* 1917, Charlotte Madge, *d* of Dr Herbert Lillies, Armadale, Victoria, Australia; two *s*. *Educ:* Scone Grammar Sch., NSW; The King's Sch., Parramatta, NSW; Sydney Univ., NSW. Bachelor of Engineering, 1911; joined Royal Australian Navy, 1912; sea service, 1914–18; Squadron Engineer Officer, 1929–32; Engineer Manager, Royal Australian Naval Dockyard, Garden Island, and General Overseer, Naval Shipbuilding and Repair, Sydney, 1933–42; Engineer Captain, 1934; Director of Engineering (Naval), 1942–43; Engineer Rear-Admiral, 1943; Third Naval Member Australian Commonwealth Naval Board, Navy Office, Melbourne, and Chief of Construction, 1943–48; retired 1948. *Recreation:* reading. *Address:* Malgarai, Boggabilla, NSW 2409, Australia. *Clubs:* Union, University (Sydney).
*Died 30 June 1984.*

**DOYLE, Sir John (Francis Reginald William Hastings),** 5th Bt, *cr* 1828; *b* 3 Jan. 1912; *s* of Col Sir Arthur Havelock James Doyle, 4th Bt, and Joyce Ethelreda (*d* 1961), 2nd *d* of Hon. Greville Howard; *S* father, 1948; *m* 1947, Diana (*d* 1980), *d* of late Col Steel, Indian Army; one *d*. *Educ:* Eton; RMC Sandhurst. Served Palestine, 1938

(medal with clasp); War of 1939–45, in France, Italy, Greece; Major, Cameronians and Royal Irish Fusiliers; retired, 1950. *Address:* Glebe House, Camolin, Co. Wexford.
*Died 10 Feb. 1987 (ext).*

**DOYLE, William Patrick,** QC (NI) 1968; **His Honour Judge Doyle;** a County Court Judge, Northern Ireland, since 1979; *b* 9 April 1927; *s* of John Joseph Doyle and Mary Doyle; *m* 1954, Nora Frances Morley; two *d*. *Educ:* Christian Brothers, Belfast; Coleraine Academical Instn; QUB (LLB 1947). Student, Gray's Inn, 1947–48; Inn of Court of NI, 1944–48; called to Bar of NI 1948. *Recreations:* fishing, golf, bridge. *Address:* 5 Broomhill Park, Belfast BT9 5JB. *T:* (Law Courts) Belfast 35111. *Clubs:* Lansdowne; University Common Room (Belfast). *Died 16 Jan. 1983.*

**D'OYLY, Sir John (Rochfort),** 13th Bt, *cr* 1663; Commander, RN retired; *b* 19 April 1900; *s* of Sir (Hastings) Hadley D'Oyly, 11th Bt, and Beatrice, *d* of late Francis Bingham Clerk, JP; *S* brother, Sir Charles Hastings D'Oyly, 12th Bt, 1962; *m* 1930, Kathleen (marr. diss.; she *d* 1978), *er d* of late Robert Brown Gillespie, Halgolle, Yatiyantota, Ceylon; two *d* (one *s* decd). *Educ:* Hill Brow, Eastbourne; Eastmans Royal Naval Academy, Southsea; HMS Conway. Served European War, 1916–18, with Grand Fleet; Baltic Operations, 1919. Gonville and Caius Coll., Cambridge, 1920–21. Specialised in physical and recreational training, 1921–22; Mediterranean, 1923–25; Term Officer at Royal Naval Coll., Dartmouth, 1925–27; East Indies, 1928–30; HMS St Vincent Boys' Training Establishment, 1930–32; Fleet Physical and Recreational Training Officer, Mediterranean, 1932–35; Asst Superintendent, RN Sch. of Physical and Recreational Training, Portsmouth, 1936–38. Served European War, 1939–45: Comdr of the Coll., RNC, Greenwich; Atlantic; East Indies; Pacific; retd, 1946. *Heir: half-brother,* Nigel Hadley Miller D'Oyly [*b* 6 July 1914; *m* 1940, Dolores (*d* 1971), *d* of R. H. Gregory; one *s* two *d*]. *Address:* c/o Lloyds Bank, 39 Piccadilly, W1. *Club:* Royal Naval and Royal Albert Yacht (Portsmouth). *Died 29 April 1986.*

**D'OYLY CARTE, Dame Bridget,** DBE 1975; Managing Director, Bridget D'Oyly Carte Ltd, since 1961; *b* 25 March 1908; *d* of late Rupert D'Oyly Carte and Lady Dorothy Milner Gathorne-Hardy; *m* 1926, 4th Earl of Cranbrook, CBE (marr. diss. 1931); resumed maiden name by deed poll, 1932. *Educ:* privately in England and abroad, and at Dartington Hall, Totnes (Dance-Drama Group). Savoy Hotel, 1933–39; evacuated nursery schools and child welfare work, 1939–47; Man. Director of D'Oyly Carte Opera Company, Director of Savoy Hotel Ltd and Savoy Theatre Ltd, 1948; Founder and Trustee of D'Oyly Carte Opera Trust Ltd, 1961. *Recreations:* country living and gardening; reading, theatre and music. *Address:* 1 Savoy Hill, WC2R 0BP. *T:* 01–836 4343.
*Died 2 May 1985.*

**DRABBLE, His Honour John Frederick,** QC 1953; retired; a Circuit Judge (formerly County Court Judge), 1965–73; *b* 8 May 1906; *s* of late Joseph and Emily Drabble, Conisbrough, Yorks; *m* 1933, Kathleen Marie Bloor; one *s* three *d*. *Educ:* Mexborough Grammar Sch.; Downing Coll., Cambridge (MA). Called to Bar, 1931. Served War of 1939–45, RAF, 1940–45, finally as Sqdn Leader. Recorder of Huddersfield, 1955–57; of Kingston-upon-Hull, 1957–58. *Publications:* Death's Second Self, 1971; Scawsby, 1977. *Address:* St Mary's, Martlesham, Woodbridge, Suffolk. *T:* Ipswich 622615.
*Died 19 Dec. 1982.*

**DRAKE, Antony Elliot,** CBE 1967 (OBE 1945); *b* 15 June 1907; *s* of Francis Courtney Drake and Mabel Grace (*née* Drake); *m* 1935, Moira Helen Arden Wall; one *s* one *d*. *Educ:* Aldenham Sch.; New Coll., Oxford. Indian Civil Service, 1930; Bihar and Orissa, 1931–37; seconded to Indian Political Service, 1937; served Rajputana, 1937–39; Baluchistan, 1939–43; Mysore (Sec. to Resident), 1943–46; Rajkot (Political Agent, E Kathiawar), 1946–47; appointed to Home Civil Service, HM Treasury, 1947; Asst Sec., 1950; on loan to UK Atomic Energy Authority as Principal Finance Officer, 1957; transferred permanently to UKAEA, 1960; Finance and Programmes Officer, 1964–69; retd, 1969. Member: Hosp. Management Cttee, Royal Western Counties Hosp. Group, 1970–74; Regl Fisheries Adv. Cttee, SW Water Authority, 1975–87. *Recreation:* fishing. *Address:* Badgers, Windmill Lane, West Hill, Ottery St Mary, Devon EX11 1JP. *Club:* Flyfishers'. *Died 16 Oct. 1990.*

**DRAKE, Sir James,** Kt 1973; CBE 1962; Director, Fairclough Construction Group Ltd (formerly Leonard Fairclough Ltd), 1972–77; *b* 27 July 1907; *s* of James Drake and Ellen (*née* Hague); *m* 1937, Kathleen Shaw Crossley; two *d*. *Educ:* Accrington Grammar Sch.; Owens Coll.; Manchester Univ. (BSc). FEng, FICE, PPInstHE. Jun. Engrg Asst, Stockport Co. Borough, 1927–30; Sen. and Chief Engrg Asst, Bootle Co. Borough, 1930–37; Blackpool Co. Borough: Dep. Engr and Surveyor, 1937–38; Borough Engr and Surveyor, 1938–45; County Surveyor and Bridgemaster, Lancs CC, 1945–72 (seconded to Min. of Transport as Dir of NW Road Construction Unit, 1967–68). Hon. Fellow, Manchester Polytechnic,

1972. Hon. DSc Salford, 1973. *Publications:* Road Plan for Lancashire, 1949; Motorways, 1969. *Recreation:* golf. *Address:* 11 Clifton Court, St Annes-on-Sea, Lancs. *T:* St Annes 721635. *Clubs:* Royal Automobile; Royal Lytham and St Annes Golf.

*Died 1 Feb.* 1989.

**DRAKE, James Mackay Henry M.;** *see* Millington-Drake.

**DRAKELEY, Thomas James,** CBE 1952; DSc, PhD; FRIC, FPRI; *b* Barwell, Leicester, 17 Dec. 1890; *o s* of late Thomas Drakeley; *m* 1915, Margaret (*d* 1957), *e d* of late Frank T. Hill. *Educ:* Sir Walter St John's Sch.; University Coll., London. Senior Lecturer in Chemistry, at the Wigan and District Mining and Technical Coll., 1912–19; Head of Dept of Chemistry and Rubber Technology at Northern Polytechnic, 1919–31; Principal, Northern Polytechnic, 1932–55 and 1958–61; Dir, National Coll. of Rubber Technology, Holloway, N7, 1948–55 and 1958–61; Deleg. for UK on International Dairy Federation; Ed. Transactions of Instn of the Rubber Industry, 1925–50; Mem. of Council of Chemical Soc., 1930–33; Mem. of Appeals Tribunal (England and Wales) for further Education and Training Scheme, Ministry of Labour and National Service, 1945–52; Pres. Assoc. of Principals of Technical Institutions, 1946–47; Mem. Regional (London and Home Counties) Advisory Council for Higher Technological Education, 1947–55; Vice-Chm. Regional (London and Home Counties) Academic Board, 1947–52, Chm. 1952–55; Mem. Nat. Advisory Council on Education for Industry and Commerce, Min. of Education, 1948–55; Chm. Northern Group Hosp. Management Cttee, 1956–60. Hancock Medal, Instn of the Rubber Industry, 1952, Life Vice-Pres. 1958–, Chm. of Council, 1962–65, Pres., 1966–68; Vice-Pres., Royal Assoc. of British Dairy Farmers, 1972. *Publications:* research contributions. *Address:* 101 Barrington Court, Pages Hill, N10 1QH. *T:* 01–883 3667.

*Died 16 June* 1981.

**DRAPER, Charles;** *see* Draper, R. C.

**DRAPER, Col Gerald Irving Anthony Dare,** OBE 1965; a Chairman of Industrial Tribunals, 1965–86, retired; Barrister-at-law; *b* 30 May 1914; *o s* of late Harold Irving Draper and Florence Muriel Short; *m* 1951, Julia Jean, *e d* of late Captain G. R. Bald, RN. *Educ:* privately, and by late Hubert Brinton; King's Coll., London Univ. (Law Prizeman, 1933; LLB Hons 1935); LLM London 1938. Admitted Solicitor, 1936; called to the Bar, Inner Temple, 1946. Irish Guards, Ensign and Subaltern, 1941–44; seconded to Judge-Advocate-General's Office, 1945–48; Mil. Prosecutor (War Crimes Trials, Germany), 1945–49; Legal Advr, Directorate of Army Legal Staff, 1950–56; retd as Col, 1956. Lectr in Internat. Law, 1956, Reader, 1964, Univ. of London; Reader, 1967–76, Prof. of Law, 1976–79, Univ. of Sussex; Professor Emeritus, 1979. Vis. Prof., Cairo, 1965; Titular Prof., Internat. Inst. of Humanitarian Law, S Remo, 1976; Lionel Cohen Lectr, Hebrew Univ., Jerusalem, 1972; Vis. Lectr at UK Staff Colls, and Defence Acads, Vienna, Hamburg, Newport RI, and Tokyo. UK Deleg., Internat. Red Cross Confs, 1957–73; Legal Advr to UK Delegn, Diplomatic Conf. on Law of War, 1974–77. Mem., Medico-Juridical Commn, Monaco, 1977. Fellow of NATO, 1958. Hon. Mem., Faculty of US Army Judge-Advocate-General Sch. of Mil. Law. Mem. Editorial Bd, British Year Book of Internat. Law. *Publications:* Red Cross Conventions, 1958; Hague Academy Lectures, 1965, 1979; Civilians and NATO Status of Forces Agreement, 1966; (with HRH Prince Hassan) A Study on Jerusalem, 1979; (with HRH Prince Hassan) Palestinian Self-determination, 1981; articles in learned journals, incl. British Year Book of Internat. Law, Internat. Affairs, Internat., Comp. Law Qly, The Month, Acta Juridica. *Recreations:* Egyptology, history of Penitentials; (for leisure) sitting in the sun. *Address:* 16 Southover High Street, Lewes, Sussex BN7 1HT. *T:* Lewes 472387; 2 Hare Court, Temple, EC4. *Clubs:* Beefsteak; Cercle de la Terrasse (Geneva).

*Died 3 July* 1989.

**DRAPER, (Reginald) Charles,** FIED, MInstPI; a Senior Design Technician for Thames Barrier, since 1968; *b* 25 May 1932; *s* of Cecil Charles and Ada Beatrice Draper; *m* 1954, Diane Valerie (*née* Bunker) (*d* 1982); *m* 1983, Betty Winifred (*née* Harding). *Educ:* Enfield Technical Coll.; Westminster Technical Coll. Trainee draughtsman under agreement with Rendel, Palmer and Tritton, Cons. Engrs, 1949–53. National Service with RM and RE, 1953–55. Re-employed by Rendel, Palmer and Tritton on detailing many major bridges for Burma Railway, 1955–57; upgraded to Designer Draughtsman, developing and designing Radar Aerials, 1957–58; designing portions of large power stations, colliery winder towers and a slipway cradle, 1958–60; *designed:* off-shore oil loading manifold, from which present single buoy mooring manifold was developed, 1961; motorway bridge for BR at Knutsford, 1962; all operating machinery for Bascule Bridge at Kidderpore, Calcutta; invented new constant mesh gear-box and a new tail locking device for bascule bridges, 1963; *designed:* various lock and dock gates and operating machinery for Belfast, Leith, Grangemouth, Haldia, India, 1964–67. Initial member of Thames Barrier design group; inventor of Rising Sector Gate, 1970. Engineer of the Year award

from Engineering News Record in New York, for Thames Barrier Gates, 1978. Freeman of City of London, 1982. *Publications:* two papers in Thames Barrier Design Symposium at Instn of Civil Engrs, 1977; various articles in technical jls. *Recreations:* swimming, walking, pot-holing, tennis, gardening, snooker, reading, painting. *Address:* 20 Brookfield Way, Billingshurst, West Sussex RH14 9AN. *T:* Billingshurst 3706. *Club:* Horsham (W Sussex).

*Died 5 Nov.* 1983.

**DRAYSON, George Burnaby;** *b* 9 March 1913; *s* of late Walter Drayson, Stevenage, Herts; and Dorothy Dyott, *d* of late Captain Hugo Burnaby, RN; *m* 1939, Winifred Heath (marr. diss., 1958); one *d*; *m* 1962, Barbara Radonska-Chrzanowska, Warsaw. *Educ:* Borlasse Sch. Entered City, 1929; Mem. Stock Exchange, 1935–54; Company Director. Commnd Essex Yeomanry, 1931, Captain, 1938; served RA in Western Desert (TD, despatches, prisoner of war, June 1942–Sept. 1943, escaped twice, finally walked 500 miles to freedom). MP (C) Skipton, 1945–79. Member: Inter-Parliamentary Union Delegn to Turkey, 1947; CPA delegns to Caribbean, 1967, Ceylon, 1970, N Zealand, 1974; Leader, gp of parliamentarians to Morocco, 1979. Mem., Expenditure Cttee, 1970–74. Formerly: Chairman: Parly All Party East/West Trade Cttee; British-Polish Parly Gp; Vice-Chairman, British-Argentine, British-Bulgarian, British-Romanian, British-Czechoslovakian, British-Hungarian, British-German Democratic Republic, and British-Venezuelan Parly Gps; Sec., British-Equadorial Gp. *Recreations:* fishing, walking (completed London to Brighton walk, 1939); foreign travel. *Address:* 131A Hamilton Terrace, NW8 9QR. *T:* 01–624 7302; Linton House, Linton-in-Craven, Skipton, N Yorks. *T:* Grassington 752362.

*Died 16 Sept.* 1983.

**DRENNAN, Alexander Murray,** MD Edinburgh 1924; MB, ChB 1906; FRCPE 1914; FRSE 1932; Professor of Pathology, Edinburgh, 1931–54, retired; Professor Emeritus; *b* Jan. 1884; *s* of late Alexr Drennan, Dunalwyn, Helensburgh; *m* 1909; one *s* two *d*. *Educ:* Larchfield, Helensburgh; Kelvinside Academy, Glasgow; Edinburgh Univ. Professor of Pathology, Otago Univ., Dunedin, NZ, 1914–28; Professor of Pathology, Queen's Univ. Belfast, 1928–31; Lieut RAMC 1936; Temporary Acting Lt-Comdr, RNVR (Sp.), 1942–47. *Publications:* (jtly) Atlas of Histopathology of the Skin, 1947; various articles on pathological subjects, etc. *Recreations:* fishing, motoring, sailing. *Address:* Lochard Cottage, Kinlochard, Stirling FK8 3TL. *Club:* Royal Scottish Automobile (Glasgow).

*Died 29 Feb.* 1984.

**DRENNAN, John Cherry,** CBE 1959; JP; Senator, Northern Ireland, 1961–72; HM Lieutenant for Co. Londonderry, 1965–74; *b* 1899; *s* of late John Wallace Drennan, Carse Hall, Limavady, Co. Londonderry; *m* 1926, Margaret (*d* 1979), *d* of late Charles Macfarlane, West Hartlepool; two *d* (one *s* decd). *Educ:* Foyle Coll., Londonderry. JP 1923, High Sheriff, 1955, DL 1955, Co. Londonderry. *Address:* Deerpark, Limavady, Co. Londonderry, N Ireland. *T:* Limavady 2321.

*Died 28 Dec.* 1982.

**DREW, Brig. Cecil Francis,** DSO 1918; *b* 1890; *o s* of late Albert Francis Drew, JP of Foston, Farnham Royal, Bucks; *m* 1915, Elizabeth Seymour Hawker (*d* 1983); one *s* (and one *s* decd). *Educ:* Highgate and Royal Milit. Acad.; Joined The Cameronians, 1910; served European War (despatches twice, DSO); temp. Lt-Col, 1917–19; Brevet Lt-Col, 1932; Lt-Col, 1936; Col, 1938; Brigadier, 1939; GSO 3, War Office, 1919–22; GSO 3, Scottish Command, 1924; DAA and QMG Highland Area, 1925–27; DAQMG South China Command, 1927–28; GSO 51st (Highland) Division, 1929–33; commanded 1st Bn The Cameronians, 1936–38; AAG War Office, 1938–39; Comd East Lancs Area, 1939–40; Comd 183 Inf. Brigade, 1940–42; Brigadier i/c Administration, 1st Corps District, 1942; AAG Southern Command, 1943; Gen. Staff, GHQ Home Forces, 1944–45; retired pay, 1945. JP Bucks, 1949. *Address:* Gatehouse Cottages, Framfield, near Uckfield, East Sussex. *Club:* Army and Navy.

*Died 11 Dec.* 1987.

**DREW, Charles Edwin,** LVO 1952; VRD 1960; FRCS; Hon. Consultant Thoracic Surgeon: St George's Hospital (Surgeon, 1954–79); Westminster Hospital (Surgeon, 1951–82); Hon. Consulting Thoracic Surgeon, King Edward VII Hospital, Midhurst; *b* 1916; *s* of Edwin Frank Drew, Croydon; *m* 1950, Doreen, *d* of Frederick James Pittaway, Stocksfield, Northumberland; one *s* one *d*. *Educ:* Westminster City Sch.; King's Coll., London. MB, BS London 1941; MRCS, LRCP 1941; FRCS 1946. Served War of 1939–45, RNVR (Surgeon-Comdr 1957). Formerly: Chief Asst and Surg. Registrar, Westminster Hosp.; Chief Surgical Asst, Brompton Hosp.; Civilian Consultant in Thoracic Surgery to RN; Hon. Consultant in Thoracic Surgery to Army. Mem. Soc. Thoracic Surgeons; FRSocMed. *Publications:* papers in med. jls. *Address:* The Cottage, 24 Dover Park Drive, Roehampton, SW15 5BG. *T:* 01–788 7030.

*Died 31 May* 1987.

**DREW, Sir Ferdinand (Caire),** Kt 1960; CMG 1951; FASA; Under-Treasurer, South Australia and Chairman State Grants Committee,

1946–60, retired; *b* Adelaide, S Aust., 1 May 1895; *s* of late Charles H. Drew, Adelaide; *m* 1934, Chrissie A., *d* of George M. McGowan; one *s* two *d*. *Educ:* Rose Park Public Sch.; Muirden Coll. Asst Auditor-Gen., 1936–39; Asst Under-Treasurer, 1939–46. Chm. Supply and Tender Board, 1943–49; Mem. Industries Development Cttee, 1942–49; Board Member: State Bank of South Australia, 1948–73 (Dep. Chm. 1963); Adelaide Steamship Co. Ltd, 1962–70; Cellular Aust. Ltd, 1948–59; Director: Unit Trust of SA; United Insurance Co. Ltd; Chrysler Aust. Ltd, 1963–74; Chm., Board of Electricity Trust, South Australia, 1949–70 (Mem., 1949–74). *Address:* 614 Anzac Highway, Glenelg East, SA 5045, Australia.
*Died 23 May 1986.*

**DREW, Harry Edward,** CB 1970; Director, Quality Audit and Advisory Services, since 1973; Chairman, Vision Broadcasting International Ltd, since 1986; *b* 18 Jan. 1909; 2nd *s* of W. H. Drew and F. E. Drew (*née* Brindley), Gillingham, Kent; *m* 1937, Phyllis (*née* Flippance) (decd); one *s*. *Educ:* Wesleyan Sch., Gillingham; RAF Apprentice Sch., Flowerdown, RAF, 1924–37; Air Min. Research Stn, Bawdsey, 1937; Works Man., Radio Prodn Unit, Woolwich, Min. of Supply, 1943; Officer i/c, Research Prototype Unit, W. Howe, Bournemouth, Min. of Aircraft Prodn, 1946; Asst Dir, 1951, Dir, 1959, Electronic Prodn, Min. of Supply, London; Dir of Techn. Costs, Min. of Aviation, London, 1964; Dir-Gen. of Quality Assurance, Min. of Technology, 1966–70; Chief Exec., Defence Quality Assurance Bd, MoD, 1970–72. FIProdE 1951; Hon. FIERE 1985 (Mem. Charter Council; Pres., 1981–83); Hon. FIIM 1981 (Nat. Chm., 1966–68, Vice-Pres., 1969–79, Pres., 1979–81). Hon. CGIA 1974. Past Master, Worshipful Co. of Scientific Instrument Makers, 1980– (Master, 1978–79). *Publications:* papers on training and quality and reliability. *Recreations:* photography, reading, gardening. *Address:* 18 Marten's Close, Shrivenham, Swindon, Wilts SN6 8BA. *Club:* Civil Service.
*Died 9 Dec. 1988.*

**DREW-SMYTHE, Henry James;** *see* Smythe.

**DREWE, Geoffrey Grabham,** CIE 1947; CBE 1958 (OBE 1942); *b* 3 May 1904; 2nd *s* of late Alfred John Drewe, Bournemouth; *m* 1934, Christine Evelyn Isabel Young; two *d*. *Educ:* Cheltenham Coll.; Pembroke Coll., Oxford. Entered ICS, 1928; served in various parts of Sind and Bombay Provinces; Collector and Dist. Magistrate, Ahmedabad, 1938–43; Home Sec. to Government of Bombay, 1944–47; retired from Indian Civil Service, 1947. Asst to Hon. Treasurers of Cons. Party, 1948–70; Manager, Cons. Party Bd of Finance, 1965–70. *Recreation:* gardening. *Address:* Westering, Haven Road, Canford Cliffs, Poole, Dorset. *Club:* East India, Devonshire, Sports and Public Schools.
*Died 28 Jan. 1986.*

**DRING, (Dennis) William,** RA 1955 (ARA 1944); RWS; *b* 26 Jan. 1904; *s* of William Henry Dring; *m* 1931, Grace Elizabeth Rothwell (*d* 1990); one *s* two *d*. *Educ:* Slade Sch. of Fine Art. Portrait and landscape painter; during the war official war artist to Ministry of Information, Admiralty, and Air Ministry. *Address:* Windy Ridge, Compton, Winchester, Hants. *T:* Twyford, Hants (0962) 712181.
*Died 27 Sept. 1990.*

**DRIVER, Sir Arthur (John),** Kt 1962; solicitor; *b* 1900; *s* of Percy John Driver, East Sheen, and Mary Amelie Driver; *m* 1937, Margaret, *d* of Hugh Semple McMeekin, Carnmoney, Northern Ireland; one *s* one *d*. Served in Royal Air Force, 1918. Pres. of Law Soc., 1961–62. Mem. Council, 1965–, and Hon. Dep. Kt Principal, 1986–, Imperial Soc. of Knights Bachelor. Hon. LLD University of Buckingham, 1983. JP Supplementary List. *Address:* Frogmore Cottage, East Clandon, Surrey. *Club:* Reform.
*Died 10 March 1990.*

**DRIVER, His Honour Major Arthur Robert,** AMIEA; *b* Albany, W Australia, 25 Nov. 1909; *s* of late Henry and Mary Driver, Western Australia; *m* 1st, 1936; one *s* one *d*; 2nd, 1949, Marjorie Campbell, *d* of George Leighton, Wodonga, Victoria; one *d*. *Educ:* Hale Sch., Perth, Western Australia; University of Western Australia. Civil Engineer, PWD of WA, 1928–39. War of 1939–45, AMF; Regimental Officer 2/4 Aust. Pioneer Bn, Bde Major, 23rd Aust. Inf. Bde, GSO II (Ops.), Advanced HQ, AMF, 1940–45. Administrator of the Northern Territory and President of Legislative Council of N Territory, Australia, 1946–51; Australian Chief Migration Officer, Rome, 1951–54; Austria and Germany, 1954–56; Chief of Operations, Inter-Governmental Cttee for European Migration, Geneva, 1956–60. Company Dir, 1960–72, retired. *Recreations:* golf, fishing. *Address:* 35 Amaroo Drive, Buderim, Qld 4556, Australia. *Clubs:* Naval and Military, United Services; Headland Golf (Buderim).
*Died 18 May 1981.*

**DRIVER, Thomas;** General Secretary, National Association of Teachers in Further and Higher Education, 1976–77, retired; *b* 9 Sept. 1912; *s* of Joseph and Eliza Driver; *m* 1936, Thora Senior (*d* 1985); one *s* one *d*. *Educ:* Sheffield Univ. (BA, DipEd). FEIS 1977. Barnsley Central Sch., 1937–42; Keighley Jun. Techn. Sch., 1942–45; Barnsley Techn. Sch., 1945–47; Doncaster Coll. of Technology, 1947–68. Gen. Sec., Assoc. of Teachers in Technical Institutions, 1969–76. Hon. Fellow: Polytechnic of City of Sheffield, 1976; NE London Polytechnic, 1978. *Recreations:* listening to music, reading. *Address:* 29 Mercel Avenue, Armthorpe, Doncaster DN3 3HS.
*Died 4 Nov. 1988.*

**DROGHEDA, 11th Earl of,** *cr* 1661 (Ireland); **Charles Garrett Ponsonby Moore,** KG 1972; KBE 1964 (OBE 1946); Baron Moore of Mellifont, 1616; Viscount Moore, 1621; Baron Moore of Cobham (UK), 1954; Chairman of the Financial Times Ltd, 1971–75 (Managing Director, 1945–70); *b* 23 April 1910; *o s* of 10th Earl of Drogheda, PC, KCMG; *S* father, 1957; *m* 1935, Joan (*d* 1989), *o d* of late William Henry Carr; one *s*. *Educ:* Eton; Trinity Coll., Cambridge. 2nd Lieut Royal Artillery (TA), 1939; Captain 1940. On staff of Ministry of Production, 1942–45. Chairman: Newspaper Publishers' Assoc., 1968–70; Royal Opera House, Covent Garden Ltd, 1958–74. Pres., Institute of Directors, 1975–76. Trustee: British Museum, 1974–77; St John's, Smith Square. Chm., London Celebrations Cttee, Queen's Silver Jubilee, 1977. Chm., Royal Ballet Sch. 1978–82. Director: The Economist Newspaper, 1941–; Henry Sotheran, 1977– (Chm., 1977–88); Clifton Nurseries, 1979–86 (Chm.); Times Newspapers Hldgs Ltd, 1981–; Earls Court & Olympia Ltd. Governor, Royal Ballet. Commander: Legion of Honour (France), 1960; Ordine al Merito (Italy), 1968; Grand Officier de l'Ordre de Léopold II (Belgium), 1974. *Publications:* Double Harness (memoirs), 1978; (jtly) Covent Garden Album, 1981. *Heir:* *s* Viscount Moore, *b* 14 Jan. 1937. *Address:* Parkside House, Englefield Green, Surrey. *Clubs:* White's, Army and Navy.
*Died 24 Dec. 1989.*

**DRONFIELD, John,** OBE 1971; MA Cambridge; JP; Headmaster of St Peter's School, York, 1937–67; *b* Heather, Leics, 23 Dec. 1898; *er s* of late Matthew H. Dronfield, Heather, Leics; *m* 1939, Sheila Mary Ross, *e d* of F. W. Williams, Greystones, Co. Wicklow; two *s* two *d*. *Educ:* Ashby-de-la-Zouch; Emmanuel Coll., Cambridge. War Service, 1917–19; 2nd Lieut in 2nd Hampshire Regt 1918; Asst Master and House Tutor at Stanley House Sch., Edgbaston, 1923–26; Asst Master at Worksop Coll., 1926–37; Housemaster of Talbot's House in 1927, and for six years Senior Housemaster and Sixth form Mathematical Master at Worksop; Acting Headmaster of Worksop, Aug.–Dec. 1935. JP City of York, 1942. *Address:* Askham Bryan, York. *T:* York 705757.
*Died 8 March 1983.*

**DROWLEY, Air Vice-Marshal Thomas Edward,** CB 1947; CBE 1943 (OBE 1933); *b* 23 March 1894; *m* Dorothy Mary (*d* 1979); one *d*. Director of Equipment, RAF delegation, Washington, 1941–46; Director-General of Equipment, Air Ministry, 1946–49; retd 1949. Legion of Merit (Commander) USA. *Address:* Cedarwood, Christmas Lane, Farnham Common, Slough, Bucks. *T:* Farnham Common 4151.
*Died 2 March 1985.*

**DRUMALBYN, 1st Baron,** *cr* 1963; **Niall Malcolm Stewart Macpherson,** PC 1962; KBE 1974; *b* 3 Aug. 1908; 3rd *s* of late Sir T. Stewart Macpherson, CIE, LLD, Newtonmore, Inverness-shire and Lady (Helen) Macpherson, K-i-H (*née* Cameron); *m* 1st, 1937, Margaret Phyllis (*d* 1979), *d* of late J. J. Runge and late Norah Cecil Runge, OBE (she *m* 2nd, Dr T. A. Ross); two *d* (and one *d* decd); 2nd, 1985, Mrs Rita Edmiston. *Educ:* Edinburgh Academy; Fettes Coll.; Trinity Coll., Oxford (Scholar). First Class Honour Mods. 1929; First Class Litt Hum. 1931; MA; Rugby Football Blue, 1928. Business training with J. & J. Colman Ltd; Manager Turkish branch, 1933–35; Export branch, London, 1936–39. Commissioned Queen's Own Cameron Highlanders, TA June 1939: Staff Coll., 1942; Temp. Major 1942; MP (Nat L) 1945–50 (Nat L and U), 1950–63, Dumfriesshire. Scottish Whip, 1945–55; Chm., Commonwealth Producers' Organisation, 1952–55, Pres., 1967–70. Dep. Pres., Assoc. of British Chambers of Commerce, 1970. Member BBC General Advisory Council, 1950–55. Joint Under-Sec. of State for Scotland, 1955–60; Parly Sec., Board of Trade, 1960–62; Minister of Pensions and National Insurance, 1962–63; Minister of State, BoT, 1963–64; Minister without Portfolio, 1970–74. Chairman: Advertising Standards Authority, 1965–70, and 1974–77; Assoc. of Conservative Peers, 1975–80. *Heir:* none. *Address:* Claytons, Beeches Hill, Bishop's Waltham, Southampton SO3 1FU. *Club:* Royal Automobile. *Died 11 Oct. 1987 (ext).*

**DRUMMOND, Lieut-Gen. Sir Alexander;** *see* Drummond, Lieut-Gen. Sir W. A. D.

**DRUMMOND, Dame (Edith) Margaret,** DBE 1966 (OBE 1960); MA; Director of the Women's Royal Naval Service, 1964–67; *b* 4 Sept. 1917; *d* of Prof. Robert James Drummond and Marion (*née* Street). *Educ:* Park Sch., Glasgow; Aberdeen Univ. Joined WRNS, April 1941 and progressed through various ranks of the Service. *Recreations:* gardening, reading, concerts and friends. *Address:* Somersham Cottage, Saxlingham, Holt, Norfolk. *Club:* University Women's.
*Died 21 April 1987.*

**DRUMMOND, Lieut.-Gen. (Retd) Sir (William) Alexander (Duncan),** KBE 1957 (CBE 1951; OBE 1945); CB 1954; SPk 1969; Director-General, Army Medical Services, War Office, 1956–61 (Deputy Director-General, 1954–56); late RAMC; *b* 16 Sept. 1901; *m* 1929, Mabel Fullegar. *Educ:* Dundee Univ. MRCS, LRCP 1924; DLO Eng. 1932; FRCS 1947. Joined RAMC, 1925. Formerly: Registrar, Throat, Nose and Ear Hospital, Golden Square; Registrar, Throat, Nose and Ear Dept, Charing Cross Hosp. Served War of 1939–45 (despatches five times, OBE). Col Comdt RAMC, 1961–66. Formerly HM Comr, Royal Hospital, Chelsea. KStJ, 1959. Hon. LLD: Birmingham, 1959; Punjab, 1960. *Publications:* contributions to medical journals. *Address:* c/o Grindlay's Bank, 13 St James's Square, SW1; Chase Lodge, 27 Clapham Common North Side, SW4. *Died 20 Sept. 1988.*

**DRUMMOND-WOLFF, Henry;** *b* 16 July 1899; *s* of late Cecil Drummond-Wolff (*s* of Rt Hon. Sir Henry Drummond-Wolff, PC, GCB, GCMG), and Zaida Drummond-Wolff, Caplanne, Billère, Pau, BP, France; *m* 1933, Margaret, *d* of late Gibson Fahnestock, Newport, Rhode Island, USA; one *d*. *Educ:* Radley (Scholar); RMC Sandhurst (Prize Cadet). Served with Royal Flying Corps, 1917; retired from Royal Air Force, 1919; contested Rotherham Feb. 1933; MP (C) Basingstoke Division of Hants, 1934–35. Life Mem., Commonwealth Parliamentary Assoc. Member of: Grand Council of Primrose League; Migration Council, 1951; Cttee of Empire Economic Union, 1934– (Vice-Chm. 1949; President 1952); Council of Empire Industries Association, 1934–; Council of Empire Industries Association and British Empire League. Has travelled extensively in Europe, USA, and Commonwealth. *Publications:* British Declaration of Independence, 1947; Declaration of Independence and Interdependence, 1948; Commonwealth, 1949; Sovereignty and Fiscal Freedom, 1952; Commonwealth Development and Defence, 1953; Constructive Conservation, 1953; The Rule of Reciprocity, 1954; Europe and the Commonwealth, 1961; The Commonwealth, 1962; Commonwealth, 1966; The Common Market, 1971; The Five Principles, 1980. *Recreation:* travel. *Address:* Beau Rivage, Lausanne, Switzerland; Newport, Rhode Island, USA. *Clubs:* Carlton, Pratt's, Royal Air Force, 1900; Clambake (Newport, USA). *Died 8 Feb. 1982.*

**DRURY, (Alfred) Paul (Dalou),** PPRE; etcher and painter; Principal, Goldsmiths' College School of Art, 1967–69, retired; *b* London, 14 Oct. 1903; *s* of late Alfred Drury, RA; *m* 1937, Enid Marie, painter, *o c* of late Victor Solomon; one *s*. *Educ:* King's Coll. Sch.; Bristol Grammar Sch.; Westminster Sch.; Goldsmiths' Coll. Sch. of Art (British Institution Scholarship in Engraving, 1924). Served War, 1939–45; Plaster (Orthopaedic) Dept, Queen Mary's Hosp., Roehampton. Since 1923 has exhibited etchings, paintings and drawings at the Royal Academy, galleries in England, and prints at representative exhibitions of British Art in Paris, Vienna, Florence, Stockholm, Buenos Aires, Tokyo, etc., and in Canada and the USA; etchings and drawings acquired by the Print Room, British Museum, Ashmolean, Imperial War Museum, Contemporary Art Soc., Boston, USA, and by various museums and galleries in the provinces and abroad. Fellow, Royal Soc. of Painter-Etchers and Engravers, 1926, President, 1970–75. Mem., Faculty of Engraving, British Sch. at Rome, 1948–74. Governor, West Surrey Coll. of Art, 1969–74. *Recreations:* music, writing. *Address:* Rangers Cottage, Nutley, Uckfield, East Sussex TN22 3LL. *T:* Nutley 2857. *Club:* Arts. *Died 19 May 1987.*

**DRYSDALE, Sir (George) Russell,** AC 1980; Kt 1969; Australian artist; Director, Pioneer Sugar Mills Ltd; *b* Bognor Regis, Sussex, 7 Feb. 1912; *s* of late George Russell Drysdale; *m* 1st, 1935, Elizabeth (*d* 1963), *d* of J. Stephen; one *d* (one *s* decd); 2nd, 1965, Maisie Joyce Purves-Smith. *Educ:* Grange Sch., Sussex; Geelong Grammar Sch.; George Bell Art Sch., Melbourne; Grosvenor Sch. of Art, London; La Grande Chaumière, Paris. Mem., Commonwealth Art Adv. Bd, 1962–73. *Exhibitions include:* Leicester Galleries, 1950, 1958, 1965, 1972; NSW Art Gallery, 1960; Queensland Art Gallery, 1961. Represented in permanent collections: Tate Gallery; Metropolitan Museum, NY; National Galleries of Queensland, NSW, W Australia, S Australia, Victoria. *Publication:* (jt author) Journey among Men, 1962. *Recreations:* natural history, pre-history, travelling about the inland of Australia. *Address:* Bouddi Farm, Kilcare Heights, Hardy's Bay, NSW 2256, Australia. *Clubs:* Union, Australasian Pioneers (Sydney). *Died 28 June 1981.*

**DUBUFFET, Jean;** artist (exclusively since 1942); *b* Le Havre, 31 July 1901; *s* of George S. Dubuffet and Jeanne (*née* Paillette); *m* 1st, 1927, Paulette Bret (marr. diss., 1935); one *d*; 2nd, 1937, Emilie (Lili) Carlu. *Educ:* art schs, Paris. Settled at Vence, 1955, after travels. *Exhibitions include:* Galerie René Drouin, Paris, 1944, 1947; Pierre Matisse Gall., NY, 1947–78 and 1981; Cercle Volney and Galerie Rive Gauche, Paris, 1954; ICA, London, 1955, 1966; Tooth, London, 1958, 1960; Daniel Cordier, Paris, 1959, 1960, 1962; Milan, 1960, 1961; Musée des Arts Décoratifs, Paris, 1960–76; Museum of Modern Art, NY, 1962, 1968, 1972; Robert Fraser, London, 1962, 1964, 1966; Venise, 1964; Tate Gall., London, 1966; Guggenheim

Museum, NY, 1966–67, 1973 and 1981; Galerie Jeanne Bucher, Paris, 1964–71 and 1982; Galerie Claude Bernard, Paris, 1964, 1978; Galerie Beyeler, Bâle, 1968, 1975, 1976; Pace Gall., NY, 1968–79 and 1983; Montréal, retrospective, 1969; Galerie Moos, Geneva, 1970; Centre national des arts contemporains, Paris, 1970, 1975; Kunsthalle and Kunstmuseum, Bâle, 1970; Arts Inst., Chicago, 1970; Waddington Gall., London, 1972, 1975, 1980; Grand Palais, Paris, 1973; Kröller-Müller, Holland, 1974; Städtische Kunsthalle, Düsseldorf, 1974; Fundacion Juan March, Madrid, 1976; Musée des Beaux Arts, Le Havre, 1977; Badischer Kunstverein, Karlsruhe, 1977; Galerie Rudolf Zwirner, Cologne, 1977, 1980; FIAT, Turin, 1978; Richard Gray Gall., Chicago, 1979 and 1981; Akad. der Kunste, Berlin, 1980; Mus. moderner Kunst Mus. des XX Jahrhunderts, Vienna, 1980–81; Joseph Haubrich Kunsthalle, Cologne, and Centre Georges Pompidou, Paris, 1981; Seibu Mus. of Art, Tokyo, Nat. Mus. of Art, Osaka, and Studio d'Arte, Milan, 1982; Kunsthalle, Tübingen, Kunstmus., Hanover, Staatl. Graphische Samlung, Munich, Hokin Gall., Palm Beach, and Kunsthaus, Zug, 1983. *Publications:* Prospectus aux amateurs de tout genre, 1946; Prospectus et tous écrits (2 vols), 1967; Asphyxiante culture, 1968; Edifices, 1968; L'homme du commun à l'ouvrage, 1973; La botte à nique, 1973; Catalogue intégral des travaux de Jean Dubuffet, 1982. *Address:* 51 rue de Verneuil, 75007 Paris, France. *Died 12 May 1985.*

**DU CANE, Comdr Peter,** CBE 1964 (OBE 1942); CEng, FIMechE; FRINA; AFRAeS; FRSA; Royal Navy, retired; Consultant, Vosper Ltd, Shipbuilders, Portsmouth, (Managing Director, 1931–63; Deputy Chairman, 1963–73); *b* 18 March 1901; *s* of H. C. Du Cane, DL, Braxted Park, Essex, and Dorothy Blenkinsopp (*née* Coulson), Newbrough Park, Northumberland; *m* 1929, Victoria Geraldine Pole Carew; one *s* two *d*. *Educ:* RNC, Osborne, Dartmouth, Keyham and Greenwich. Served as midshipman afloat, European War, 1917–18; Fleet Air Arm as pilot and technical officer, 1940–41. Specialised design and construction high speed craft including Bluebird II, holder of world's unlimited water speed record at 141.7 mph, for which awarded Segrave Medal for year 1939, also John Cobb's Crusader, first boat to exceed 200 mph, 1952. Designs include many Motor Torpedo Boats used by Royal Navy, Royal Barge, and High Speed Rescue Launches for RAF, also Tramontana, winner of Daily Express Internat. Offshore Power Boat Race, 1962; I and II winners of All British Daily Express Cowes/Torquay, 1964. *Publications:* High Speed Small Craft, 1951, 4th edn, 1974; An Engineer of Sorts, 1972. *Address:* 15 Abbey Mews, Amesbury, Wilts. *Clubs:* White's; Royal Yacht Squadron (Cowes). *Died 31 Oct. 1984.*

**DUCAT, David;** Chairman, The Metal Box Co. Ltd., 1967–70, retired (Managing Director 1949–66; Vice-Chairman 1952–66; Deputy Chairman 1966–67); *b* 1 June 1904; *s* of William John and Amy Ducat; *m* 1933, Hilary Mildred Stokes; three *s* one *d*. *Educ:* Merchant Taylors' Sch.; Gonville and Caius Coll., Cambridge (MA). ACIS 1935. Min. of Production, 1942–45. British Tin Box Manufacturers Fedn: Chm., 1952–61; Vice-Chm., 1961–69. Mem. Court of Assts, Merchant Taylors' Co., 1956– (Master, 1964). Vice-Pres., British Inst. of Management (Council Chm., 1966–68); Mem. Coun., City University, 1966–71. FCIS 1967. *Address:* Morar, 16 Sandy Lodge Road, Moor Park, Rickmansworth, Herts. *T:* Rickmansworth 773562. *Died 13 Feb. 1989.*

**DUCK, Leslie;** Director, Financing of the Budget, Commission of the European Communities, Brussels, 1982–85; *b* 14 Jan. 1935; *s* of John Robert Duck and Elizabeth Duck; *m* 1st, 1961, Maureen Richmond (marr. diss. 1980); one *s* one *d*; 2nd, 1981, Catherina von Tscharner; two step *s*. *Educ:* Acklam Hall Grammar Sch., Middlesbrough; Leeds Univ. National Service, 2nd Lieut Green Howards, 1955–57. Joined Civil Service (HM Customs and Excise), 1958; Principal, 1965; seconded to Secretariat, EFTA, Geneva, 1967–70; HM Treasury, 1970–72; Asst Sec., 1972; HM Customs and Excise, 1972–73; Head of Div., Taxation Directorate, Commn of Eur. Communities, Brussels, 1973–82. *Recreations:* sailing, skiing, music, reading. *Address:* Chemin du Beau-Soleil 8, 1206 Geneva, Switzerland. *T:* 46.66.23. *Died 18 Sept. 1989.*

**DUCKHAM, Prof. Alec Narraway,** CBE 1950 (OBE 1945); Professor of Agriculture, University of Reading, 1955–69, Professor Emeritus, since 1969; *b* 23 Aug. 1903; *e s* of Alexander Duckham, FCS, and Violet Ethel Duckham (*née* Narraway); *m* 1932, Audrey Mary Polgreen (*d* 1969), St Germans, Cornwall; one *s* two *d*. *Educ:* Oundle Sch.; Clare Coll., Cambridge. MA (Hons) Cantab.: Cambridge Dip. Agric. Sci. (dist. in Animal Husbandry), 1926; FIBiol; Silver Research Medallist, Royal Agricultural Society, England, 1926. Research and Advisory work on Animal Husbandry at Cambridge, Aberdeen, Belfast, 1927–39. Chm. Home and Overseas Agric. Supplies Cttees and Dir of Supply Plans Div., Min. of Food, 1941–45. Agric. Attaché, Brit. Embassy, Washington, and Agric. Adviser to UK High Comr, Ottawa, 1945–50. Asst Sec. to Min. of Agriculture and Fisheries, 1950–54. Liaison Officer (SE Region), to the Minister of Agriculture, Fisheries and Food, 1965–70. Vice-

Chm., Alex. Duckham and Co. Ltd, 1945–68. *Publications:* Animal Industry in the British Empire, 1932; American Agriculture, 1952 (HMSO); The Fabric of Farming, 1958; Agricultural Synthesis: The Farming Year, 1963; (with G. B. Masefield) Farming Systems of the World, 1970; (ed with J. G. W. Jones and E. H. Roberts) Food Production and Consumption, 1976. *Recreations:* painting and music. *Address:* Little Park House, Brimpton, Berks. *Club:* Royal Automobile. *Died 22 Sept.* 1988.

**DUCKWORTH, (George) Arthur (Victor),** JP; *b* 3 Jan. 1901; *e s* of Major A. C. Duckworth of Orchardleigh Park, Frome; *m* 1927, Alice, 3rd *d* of John Henry Hammond, New York; three *d*; *m* 1945, Elizabeth, *o d* of Alfred Ehrenfeld, Bridgeham Farm, Forest Green, Surrey; two *d*; *m* 1968, Mary, *y d* of Archdeacon Edmund Hope, and *widow* of Captain K. Buxton. *Educ:* Eton; Trinity Coll., Cambridge (BA). MP (C) Shrewsbury Div. of Salop, 1929–45; Parliamentary Private Sec. to Rt Hon. Sir Geoffrey Shakespeare, 1932–39. Served War of 1939–45, 36th (Middlesex) AA Bn RA, 1939–41. CC Somerset, 1949–64; JP Somerset, 1957. *Address:* Orchardleigh Park, Frome, Somerset BA11 2PH. *T:* Frome 830306. *Clubs:* Travellers', Garrick. *Died 14 Nov.* 1986.

**DUCKWORTH, Captain Ralph Campbell Musbury,** CBE 1946 (OBE 1943); CEng; RN, retired; *b* 11 June 1907; 2nd *s* of Major Arthur Campbell Duckworth, DL, JP, Orchardleigh Park, Frome, Som; *m* 1945, Ruby Cortez, 2nd Officer WRNS (*d* 1979), *o d* of A. W. Ball, Sydenham, London. *Educ:* Royal Naval Colleges, Osborne and Dartmouth. War of 1939–45: served as Lieut-Comdr and Torpedo Officer of HMS Illustrious, 1940–41; Comdr 1941 and staff of C-in-C Mediterranean and C-in-C Levant, 1941–43; OBE for duties in planning and execution of operations for capture of Sicily; Dep. Chief of Staff (acting Capt.) to Vice-Adm. Administration, British Pacific Fleet, 1944–45 (CBE); Captain 1946; Dep. Dir Underwater Weapons Dept, Admiralty, 1946–48; Naval Attaché, British Embassy, Rio de Janeiro, 1949–51; Imperial Defence Coll., 1952; Capt., 1st Destroyer Sqdn, 1953–54; Staff of C-in-C, Mediterranean, 1954–55. Member: Northern Ireland Development Council, 1956–65; Dollar Exports Council, 1956–59; Manager, Industrial Engineering, Morgan Crucible Co. Ltd, 1956–58; Commercial Manager Elliott Bros (London) Ltd, 1959–61; Dir, British Mechanical Engrg Fedn, 1963–68. *Recreations:* gardening and travelling. *Address:* Westbury House, West Meon, near Petersfield, Hampshire. *Died 24 Feb.* 1983.

**DUDDING, Sir John (Scarbrough),** Kt 1964; DL; Her Majesty's Overseas Civil Service, retired; *b* 28 Nov. 1915; *s* of Col Thomas Scarbrough Dudding, OBE, MRCS, LRCP, RAMC, and Maude Campbell Dudding; *m* 1945, Enid Grace Gardner, The Old Hall, Tacolneston, Norwich; one *s* one *d*. *Educ:* Cheltenham Coll.; Jesus Coll., Cambridge (BA Hons). Entered Colonial Service, posted to Nigeria, 1938. War service with Nigeria Regt of Royal West African Frontier Force, in Nigeria, India and Burma, 1940–45. Dep. Comr of the Cameroons and Actg Comr, 1956–58; Permanent Sec., Ministries Federal Nigerian Govt with responsibilities for Works, Surveys, Transport, Aviation, and Communications, 1959–63; retd, 1964. Chairman: Scunthorpe HMC, 1967–74; Humberside AHA, 1974–82; Lincolnshire Cttee VSO, 1966–73; Lincolnshire and Humberside Arts Assoc. (formerly Lincolnshire Regional Arts Assoc.), 1970–73, 1980–82; Pres., Winterton Agricl Soc.; former Pres., S Humberside Br., CPRE. Lindsey CC, 1967–74; DL Lincoln, 1971–, Humberside 1974. FRSA 1971. Hon. LLD Hull, 1981. *Recreations:* gardening, local history and book-collecting. *Address:* Paddock House, Silver Street, Winteringham, Scunthorpe, South Humberside DN15 9ND. *T:* Scunthorpe 732 393. *Club:* Royal Commonwealth Society. *Died 26 June* 1986.

**DUDGEON, Alastair;** *see* Dudgeon, J. A.

**DUDGEON, Henry Alexander,** CMG 1976; HM Diplomatic Service, retired; *b* 12 Aug. 1924; *er s* of late John Brown Dudgeon and late Alison Dudgeon (*née* Winton); *m* 1952, Marjorie Patricia, *d* of Joseph Harvey, MD; no *c*. *Educ:* Knox Academy, Haddington; Magdalene Coll., Cambridge. Served in HM Forces, 1943–47; entered HM Foreign Service, 1949; served at: FO, 1949–52; Sofia, 1952–54; Amman, 1954–58; FO, 1958–61; 1st Sec. and Head of Chancery, Madrid, 1961–66; Counsellor and Head of Chancery, Havana, 1966–69; Civil Service Research Fellow at Glasgow Univ., 1969–70; Head of Marine and Transport Dept, FCO, 1970–74. Dep. Leader, UK Delegn to Third UN Conf. on Law of the Sea, 1974–75; Minister, Canberra, 1976–80. *Address:* 295 Fir Tree Road, Epsom Downs, Surrey. *T:* Burgh Heath 61983. *Died 2 Nov.* 1984.

**DUDGEON, Prof. (John) Alastair,** CBE 1977; MC 1942 and Bar 1943; TD 1947; DL; Consultant Microbiologist, Hospital for Sick Children, Great Ormond Street, 1960–81, Honorary Consulting Microbiologist, 1982; Professor of Microbiology, Institute of Child Health, University of London, 1972–81, Emeritus Professor 1982; *b* 9 Nov. 1916; *yr s* of late Prof. L. S. Dudgeon; *m* 1st, 1945, Patricia Joan Ashton (*d* 1969); two *s*; 2nd, 1974, Joyce Kathleen Tibbetts. *Educ:* Repton Sch.; Trinity Coll., Cambridge; St Thomas's Hosp.,

London. MB, BCh 1944; MA, MD Cantab 1947; FRCPath 1967; MRCP 1970; FRCP 1974. Served in London Rifle Bde and 7th Bn Rifle Bde, 1936–43; transf. to RAMC, 1944; Specialist in Pathology RAMC, 1945; served TA and TAVR, 1947–58; Col RAMC (TA), retd. Asst Pathologist, St Thomas's Hosp., 1947; Asst Pathologist, 1948, Hon. Consultant Virologist, 1953, Hosp. for Sick Children, Gt Ormond St; Sen. Lectr, St George's Hosp. Med. Sch., 1953; Head of Virus Research, Glaxo Labs, 1958. Mem. Cttee of Management, 1966–81, Dean, 1974–81, Inst. of Child Health (Univ. of London); Mem. Bd of Governors, Hosp. for Sick Children, Gt Ormond St, 1962–69 and 1970–81. Hon. Consultant in Pathology to Army, 1977–81. Mem., SE Kent DHA, 1981–. Chm., Res. Funds Cttee, 1981–, Mem. Council, 1982–87, British Heart Foundn. Mem. Court of Assts, 1974, Sen. Warden, 1984–85, Master, 1985–86, Soc. of Apothecaries of London. DL Greater London, 1973. OStJ 1958, FRSA 1986. *Publications:* Modern Trends in Paediatrics (contrib.); Immunization Procedures for Children; Viral Infections of the Fetus and Newborn (co-author). *Recreation:* sailing. *Address:* Cherry Orchard Cottage, Bonnington, Ashford, Kent TN25 7AZ. *T:* Aldington 310. *Clubs:* Army and Navy; Aldeburgh Yacht. *Died 9 Oct.* 1989.

**DUDLEY-WILLIAMS, Sir Rolf (Dudley),** 1st Bt, *cr* 1964; *b* 17 June 1908; *s* of Arthur Williams, Plymouth; assumed and adopted surname of Dudley-Williams, by Deed Poll, 1964; *m* 1940, Margaret Helen, *er d* of F. E. Robinson, OBE, AMIMechE; two *s*. *Educ:* Plymouth Coll.; Royal Air Force Coll., Cranwell. Gazetted, 1928, Flying Officer, 1930; Central Flying Sch., 1933, invalided from service, 1934. Founded Power Jets Ltd, 1936, to develop Whittle system of jet propulsion; Managing Dir, 1941. Mem. Council Soc. of British Aircraft Constructors, 1944; Companion Royal Aeronautical Society, 1944. Contested (C) Brierley Hill, 1950. MP (C) Exeter, 1951–66; PPS to Sec. of State for War, 1958; PPS to Minister of Agriculture, 1960–64. Chm., Western Area of National Union of Conservative Assocs, 1961–64. *Heir: s* Alastair Edgcumbe James Dudley-Williams [*b* 26 Nov. 1943; *m* 1972, Diana Elizabeth Jane, twin *d* of R. H. C. Duncan; three *d*]. *Address:* The Old Manse, South Petherton, Som. *T:* South Petherton 40143. *Club:* Royal Air Force. *Died 8 Oct.* 1987.

**DUDMAN, George Edward,** CB 1973; *b* 2 Dec. 1916; *s* of William James Dudman and Nora Annie (*née* Curtis); *m* 1955, Joan Doris, *d* of late Frederick John Eaton; one *s* one *d*. *Educ:* Merchant Taylors' Sch., London; St John's Coll., Oxford (MA). Churchill Coll., Cambridge, 1982–84. Royal Artillery, 1940–46; Control Commn, Germany, 1946–49. Called to Bar, Middle Temple, 1950. Law Officers' Dept, 1951; Legal Sec., Law Officers' Dept, 1958; Legal Advr, DES, 1965–77; Editor, Statutes in Force, 1977–81. *Recreations:* painting, gardening, cooking, playing chess, studying philosophy. *Address:* 10 Viga Road, Grange Park, N21. *T:* 01–360 5129. *Died 2 July* 1984.

**DUDMAN, Ven. Robert William;** Archdeacon of Lindsey and Fourth Canon Residentiary of Lincoln Cathedral since 1971, Treasurer since 1975; *b* 4 Dec. 1925; *s* of late Robert and Jane Dudman, Basingstoke; *m* 1954, Betty Shannon; one *s* two *d*. *Educ:* King's Coll., Taunton; Lincoln Theol Coll.; Univ. of Hull (BA). Able Seaman, RN, 1944–47. Deacon, 1952; Priest, 1953. Curate: Shiregreen, Sheffield, 1952–53; Wombwell, 1953–55; Frodingham, Scunthorpe, 1955–57; Industrial Chaplain to Bp of Lincoln, 1957–71; Rector of Scotton, 1960–71; Canon and Prebend of Norton Episcopi, Lincoln Cath., 1968. *Address:* The Archdeaconry, Cantilupe Chantry, Lincoln LN2 1PX. *T:* Lincoln 25784. *Died 29 Sept.* 1984.

**DUESBERY, Rev. Canon Julian Percy T.;** *see* Thornton-Duesbery.

**DUFFERIN AND AVA,** 5th Marquess of, *cr* 1888; **Sheridan Frederick Terence Hamilton-Temple-Blackwood;** Baron Dufferin and Clandeboye, Ireland, 1800; Baron Clandeboye, UK, 1850; Earl of Dufferin, Viscount Clandeboye, 1871; Earl of Ava, 1888, and a Bt; *b* 9 July 1938; *o s* of 4th Marquess (killed in action, 1945) and Maureen (she *m* 1948, Major Desmond Buchanan, MC, from whom she obtained a divorce, 1954; *m* 1955, John Cyril Maude, QC), 2nd *d* of late Hon. (Arthur) Ernest Guinness; *S* father, 1945; *m* 1964, Serena Belinda Rosemary, *d* of Group Capt. (Thomas) Loel Evelyn Bulkeley Guinness, OBE. *Educ:* Eton Coll.; Christ Church, Oxford. Trustee: Wallace Collection, 1973–; Nat. Gall., 1981–. Dir, Arthur Guinness PLC, 1979–. *Heir* (to Barony of Dufferin and Clandeboye): Sir Francis Blackwood, 7th Bt. *Address:* 4 Holland Villas Road, W14. *T:* 01–603 8910; Clandeboye, Co. Down, Northern Ireland. *Died 29 May* 1988.

**DUFFUS, Hon. Sir William (Algernon Holwell),** Kt 1971; Justice of the Courts of Appeal for Bahamas, and the Turks and Caicos Islands, since 1975; *b* Jamaica, 13 Aug. 1911; *s* of William Alexander Duffus, JP, and of Emily (*née* Holwell); *m* 1938, Helen Hollinsed; two *s* one *d*. *Educ:* Cornwall Coll. and Titchfield Sch., Jamaica. Solicitor, Supreme Court, Jamaica, 1933. In private practice in Jamaica. Legal Service, Jamaica, 1935; Magistrate, Jamaica, 1943;

Magistrate, Nigeria, 1949, Chief Magistrate, 1953. Called to the Bar, Gray's Inn, 1954; Chief Registrar of the Federal Supreme Court, Nigeria, 1955; Judge of High Ct, W Nigeria, 1957; Justice of Ct of Appeal for E Africa, 1964, Vice-Pres., 1969, Pres., 1970–75. *Address:* Cudworth Cottage, Great Wilbraham, Cambridge CB1 5JD. *T:* Cambridge 880530. *Died 19 Feb. 1981.*

**DUFFY, Hugh Herbert White;** *b* 24 Aug. 1917; *y s* of late Hugh Duffy and Catherine Duffy (*née* White); *m* 1946, Hylda, *y d* of of Stanley Swales, Fleetwood; one *s*. *Educ:* Stonyhurst Coll.; Durham Univ. (LLB). Commnd 9th Bn, Durham LI (TA), 1937; BEF, 1940; wounded France, 1940; discharged owing to wounds, 1942. Admitted solicitor, 1943. Joined Public Trustee Office (Manchester Br.), 1944, transf. London, 1956; Chief Admin. Officer, 1970–73; Asst Public Trustee, 1973–75; Public Trustee, 1975. *Recreations:* reading, motoring, watching sport on TV. *Address:* One Stone, 19 Loughrigg Park, Ambleside, Cumbria. *T:* Ambleside 2478. *Died 6 May 1983.*

**DUFFY, Terence;** President, Amalgamated Union of Engineering Workers, since 1978; *b* 3 May 1922; *s* of John and Anne Duffy; *m* 1957, Joyce Sturgess; one *s* one *d*. *Educ:* St Joseph's RC Sch., Wolverhampton. Served War, Infantry, 1940–46 (1939–45 Star; African, Italian, Victory Decorations). Amalgamated Union of Engineering Workers: Divl Officer (full-time), Birmingham, 1969; Mem., Exec. Council, 1976. Member: TUC General Council, 1978–; NEDC, 1980–; BOTB, 1984–. *Recreations:* gardening, golf. *Address:* 9 Sunningdale Road, Bickley, Kent.
*Died 1 Oct. 1985.*

**DUGMORE, Rev. Prof. Clifford William,** DD; Member, Advisory Editorial Board, The Journal of Ecclesiastical History, since 1979 (Founder, and Editor, 1950–78); British Member of Editorial Board of Novum Testamentum, 1956–76; *b* 9 May 1909; *s* of late Rev. Canon William Ernest Dugmore, MA, RD, and late Frances Ethel Dugmore (*née* Westmore); *m* 1st, 1938, Ruth Mabel Archbould Prangley (*d* 1977); one *d*; 2nd, 1979, Kathleen Mary Whiteley. *Educ:* King Edward VI Sch., Birmingham (foundation scholar); Exeter Coll., Oxford; Queens' Coll., Cambridge. Oxford: BA (Hons Sch. of Oriental Studies), 1932; MA and James Mew Rabbinical Hebrew Scholar, 1935; BD 1940; DD 1957. Cambridge: BA (by incorporation) 1933; MA 1936; Norrisian Prizeman 1940; Select Preacher 1956; Hulsean Lecturer, 1958–60. Deacon 1935, Priest 1936; Asst Curate of Holy Trinity, Formby, 1935–37; Sub-Warden St Deiniol's Library, Hawarden, 1937–38; Rector of Ingestre-with-Tixall, 1938–43; Chaplain of Alleyn's Coll. of God's Gift, Dulwich, 1943–44; Rector of Bredfield and Dir of Religious Education, dio. St Edmundsbury and Ipswich, 1945–47; Sen. Lecturer in Ecclesiast. Hist., University of Manchester, 1946–58; Tutor to Faculty of Theology, 1958; Prof. of Ecclesiastical History, King's Coll., Univ. of London, 1958–76, Emeritus Prof., 1976–. Chm. of British Sous-Commission of Commission Internationale d'Histoire Ecclésiastique, 1952–62; Pres. of the Ecclesiastical History Soc., 1963–64; Mem. of the Senate, 1964–71, Proctor in Convocation, 1970–75, Dean, Univ. Faculty of Theology, 1974–76, University of London. Permission to officiate, Dio. of Guildford, 1966–. FKC 1965; FRHistS 1970. *Publications:* Eucharistic Doctrine in England from Hooker to Waterland, 1942; The Influence of the Synagogue upon the Divine Office, 1944 (2nd edn 1964); (ed) The Interpretation of the Bible 1944 (2nd edn 1946); The Mass and the English Reformers, 1958; Ecclesiastical History No Soft Option, 1959. Contributor to: Chambers's Encyclopædia, 1950 (Advisory Editor, 1960–); Weltkirchenlexikon 1960; Studia Patristica IV, 1961; Neotestamentica et Patristica, 1962; The English Prayer Book, 1963; A Companion to the Bible, 2nd revised edn, 1963; Studies in Church History I, 1964 (also ed); Studies in Church History II, 1965; Eucharistic Theology then and now, 1968; Man and his Gods, 1971; Aspects de l'Anglicanisme, 1974; Thomas More: through many eyes, 1978; Gen. Editor, Leaders of Religion, 1964–76; articles and reviews in Journal of Theological Studies, Journal of Ecclesiastical History, Theology, History, etc. *Recreations:* motoring and philately. *Address:* 77 The Street, Puttenham, Surrey GU3 1AT. *T:* Guildford (0483) 810460. *Died 25 Oct. 1990.*

**du HEAUME, Sir (Francis) Herbert,** Kt 1947; CIE 1943; OBE 1932; KPM 1924; Indian Police Medal; *b* 27 May 1897; *s* of George du Heaume, OBE; *m* 1923, Blanche Helen Learmonth Tainsh (*d* 1981); two *s*. Served European War, 1914–18, Captain, 15th London Regt; joined Indian Police, 1920; Principal, Police Training Sch., Punjab, 1934–42; Deputy Inspector-Gen. of Police, 1942–47. *Address:* c/o Grindlay's Bank, 13 St James's Square, SW1.
*Died 16 March 1988.*

**DUKE, Robin Antony Hare,** CVO 1975; CBE 1970 (OBE 1961); *b* 21 March 1916; *s* of late Reginald Franklyn Hare Duke, CBE, and Diana (*née* Woodforde); *m* 1945, Yvonne (*d* 1984), *d* of late R. W. O. Le Bas, OBE; four *s* one *d*. *Educ:* Lancing Coll.; Brasenose Coll., Oxford (MA). Royal Artillery, 1939–46 (staff, ME, Italy, Greece, 1942–45; Political Adviser's Office, Athens, 1945–46). Joined British

Council, 1947; Budapest, 1948–50; Dir, British Inst., Salonika, 1950–51; Athens, 1951–52; Dep. Dir, Visitors Dept, 1952–55; Representative, Chile, 1955–61; Dep. Controller, Books, Arts and Science Div., 1961–66; Controller, 1966–67; Rep., Japan, 1967–77, retd. Order of Sacred Treasure (Japan), 3rd Cl., 1975. *Publications:* introductions to Pillow Book of Sei Shonagon, 1979; The English Governess at the Court of Siam, 1980. *Recreations:* gardening, travel, theatre. *Address:* The Red House, Cavendish, Sudbury, Suffolk CO10 8BH. *T:* Glemsford 280058. *Club:* Army and Navy.
*Died 27 Nov. 1984.*

**DUKES, Dame Marie;** *see* Rambert, Dame M.

**DULY, Surgeon Rear-Adm. (D) Philip Reginald John,** CB 1982; OBE 1971; Director of Naval Dental Services, 1980–83; *b* 3 April 1925; *s* of Reginald and Minnie Duly; *m* 1948, Mary Walker Smith; two *s* one *d*. *Educ:* The London Hospital. LDSRCS 1947. Joined Royal Navy, Surgeon Lieut(D), 1948; Officer in Charge, Dental Training, 1965–70; Asst to Director of Naval Dental Services, 1970–72; Director of Dental Trng and Research, 1972–76; Comd Dental Surgeon: to Flag Officer Naval Air Comd, 1976–77; to C-in-C Naval Home Comd, 1977–80. Chairman of Examiners, General Dental Council Central Examining Board for Dental Hygienists, 1977–80. QHDS 1978–83. FRSM. *Recreations:* music, esp. church organ playing; DIY repairs on lost causes. *Address:* 13 The Avenue, Alverstoke, Gosport, Hants PO12 2JS. *T:* Gosport 580532. *Club:* Army and Navy. *Died 12 Sept. 1989.*

**du MAURIER, Dame Daphne, (Lady Browning),** DBE 1969; writer; *b* 13 May 1907; 2nd *d* of late Sir Gerald du Maurier; *m* 1932, Lieut-Gen. Sir Frederick A. M. Browning, GCVO, KBE, CB, DSO (*d* 1965); one *s* two *d*. *Educ:* privately; in Paris. Began writing short stories and articles in 1928; first novel appeared 1931. *Publications:* The Loving Spirit, 1931; I'll Never Be Young Again, 1932; The Progress of Julius, 1933; Gerald, a Portrait, 1934; Jamaica Inn, 1936; The du Mauriers, 1937; Rebecca, 1938; Frenchman's Creek, 1941; Hungry Hill, 1943; The King's General, 1946; The Parasites, 1949; My Cousin Rachel, 1951; The Apple Tree, 1952; Mary Anne, 1954; The Scapegoat, 1957; The Breaking Point, 1959; The Infernal World of Branwell Brontë, 1960; Castle Dor (continuation of MS left by late Sir Arthur Quiller-Couch (Q)), 1962; The Glassblowers, 1963; The Flight of the Falcon, 1965; Vanishing Cornwall, 1967; The House on the Strand, 1969; Not After Midnight, 1971; Rule Britannia, 1972; Golden Lads: a study of Anthony Bacon, Francis and their Friends, 1975; The Winding Stair: Francis Bacon, his Rise and Fall, 1976; The Rendezvous and other stories, 1980; The Rebecca Notebook and Other Memories, 1981; *autobiography:* Growing Pains, 1977; *drama:* The Years Between, 1945; September Tide, 1948; *edited:* The Young George du Maurier, 1951. *Recreations:* walking and swimming. *Address:* Kilmarth, Par, Cornwall. *Died 19 April 1989.*

**DUNBAR, Maj.-Gen. Charles Whish,** CBE 1968; *b* 2 June 1919; *s* of late Dr J. Dunbar, FRCS, Auchterarder, Scotland; *m* 1941, Jean Elinor Kerr Morton; two *s* one *d*. *Educ:* Glasgow High Sch.; Glasgow Univ. Commnd 2nd Lieut into Royal Northumberland Fusiliers, 1940; served with Maritime RA, 1940–43; served with Para. Regt 1944–48; transf. to RA 1945; transf. to Highland Light Inf., 1946; Co. Comdr with a Para. Bn and DAA&QMG and Bde Major, Para. Bde Palestine, 1945–48; Staff Coll., 1949; Co. Comdr with HLI, N Africa, Malta and Egypt, 1951–53; Bde Major, Para. Bde, Cyprus; Suez, 1956; 2 i/c Para. Bn, 1957; Jordan, 1958; comd Depot RHF, 1958–59; comd 1 RHF in Aden, Malta and Libya, 1960–62; comd Inf. Bde Gp, Germany, 1962–65; IDC, 1966; Brig. Gen. Staff, HQ, MELF, Aden, 1967; GOC North West District, 1968–70; Director of Infantry, 1970–73, retired 1973; Col, Royal Highland Fusiliers, 1969–78. Vice-Pres., ACF Assoc. (Scotland), 1976–78. Dir, British Red Cross Soc., Perth and Kinross, 1977–. Mem., Royal Company of Archers (Queen's Body Guard for Scotland). *Recreation:* general sport. *Address:* Milton, Auchterarder, Perthshire PH3 1DP. *T:* Auchterarder 2242. *Clubs:* Army and Navy; Royal Golfing Society (Perth). *Died 28 July 1981.*

**DUNCAN, Sir Arthur (Bryce),** Kt 1961; Convener, Dumfriesshire County Council, 1961–68, retired; *b* 27 Aug. 1909; 2nd *s* of J. B. Duncan, Newlands, Dumfries; *m* 1936, Isabel Mary Kennedy-Moffat; four *s* one *d*. *Educ:* Rugby; St John's Coll., Cambridge. Chm., The Nature Conservancy, 1953–61, retd. Chm. of Dirs, Crichton Royal Hospital Bd, 1958–72. DL, Dumfriesshire, 1967–69, Lord Lieutenant 1967–69. *Recreations:* ornithology, entomology and shooting. *Address:* Castlehill, Kirkmahoe, Dumfries DG1 1RD.
*Died 2 Nov. 1984.*

**DUNCAN, James Stuart,** CMG 1946; Hon. Air Commodore; company director; *b* 1893; *m* 1936, Victoria Martinez Alonso, Cordoba, Spain; one *s* two *d*. *Educ:* Coll. Rollin, Paris. Joined Massey-Harris Ltd, Berlin, 1909; went to Canada, 1911. Served with UK Forces in 1914–18 War, rising to be Capt. and Adjutant of 180th Brigade 16th Irish Divisional Artillery. Apptd Gen. Manager Massey-Harris Co., 1936; Pres. 1941; Chm. and Pres. 1949 until his

resignation in 1956. Apptd Actg Dep. Minister of Defence for Air, 1940, when he took over leadership of Brit. Commonwealth Air Trg Plan; declined invitation of Prime Minister, in summer 1940, to join Federal Cabinet as Minister of Air. Chm., Combined Agricl & Food Cttee of UNRRA, 1941–42; Mem. Nat. Res. Council, Ottawa, during War Years. Past Chm.: Toronto Bd of Trade, Toronto Community Chest, Canadian Council of Internat. Chambers of Commerce, Montreal; Hon. Pres., Toronto section, "Free Fighting French"; Chm. Dollar Sterling Trade Council, 1949–61. First Canadian chosen by Nat. Sales Exec. Organization as "Canadian Businessman of the Year," 1956; Chm., Nat. Conf. on Engrg, Sci. and Tech. Manpower, NB, 1956; organizer and Dep. Chm. Canadian Trade Mission to the UK, 1957. On accepting Chairmanship of Hydro-Electric Power Commn of Ont., Nov. 1956, resigned from bd of many Canadian cos incl. Argus Corp. Ltd, Canada Cement, Ltd, Canadian Bank of Commerce, Internat. Nickel of Canada, Ltd, Page-Hersey Tubes; resigned from Chmship Hydro-Electric Power Commn of Ont., 1961. Upon establishing residence in Bermuda, Aug. 1961, resigned from Gov., University Toronto; Chm., Dollar Sterling Trade Coun.; Chm., Australian-Canadian Assoc.; Dir, Industrial Foundn on Educn; Dir, Atomic Energy of Canada, Ltd; Chm., Royal Conservatory of Music Cttee. Hon. LLD, Dartmouth Coll., NH, USA, 1957. Chevalier, French Legion of Honour; Croix de Lorraine; King Haakon VII Cross of Liberation. *Publications:* Russia's Bid for World Supremacy, 1955; The Great Leap Forward, 1959; Russia Revisited, 1960; In The Shadow of the Red Star, 1962; A Businessman Looks At Red China, 1965; Not a One-Way Street (autobiography), 1971. *Address:* Somerset House, Paget, Bermuda. *Club:* Sotogrande (Spain).
*Died 20 Dec. 1986.*

**DUNCAN, Maj.-Gen. Nigel William,** CB 1951; CBE 1945; DSO 1945; DL; *b* 27 Nov. 1899; *s* of George William and Edith Duncan, Earlston, Guildford; *m* 1928, Victoria Letitia Troyte, *d* of late Capt. J. E. Acland, Wollaston House, Dorchester, Dorset; three *d. Educ:* Malvern Coll.; RMC Sandhurst. 2nd Bn The Black Watch, 1919; transf. Royal Tank Corps, 1923; Captain, 1931; Major, 1938; Lieut-Col, 1940; Col, 1943; Brig. 30 Armoured Bde, 1943, 2nd Armoured Bde, 1946; Comdr Royal Armoured Corps Centre, 1947; Maj.-Gen., 1949; Dir Royal Armoured Corps, WO, 1949–52; retired pay, 1952. Col Comdt Royal Tank Regt, 1952–58. Lieut-Governor Royal Hospital, Chelsea, 1953–57. DL Dorset, 1959. *Address:* Marley House, Winfrith Newburgh, Dorchester DT2 8JR. *Club:* Army and Navy.
*Died 24 March 1987.*

**DUNCAN, Ronald Frederick Henry;** *b* 6 Aug. 1914; *s* of Reginald John and Ethel Duncan; *m* 1941, Rose Marie Hansom; one *s* one *d. Educ:* Switzerland; Cambridge Univ. Editor, Townsman, 1938–46; founded Devon Festival of the Arts, 1953. The English Stage Company, 1955. This way to the Tomb, first produced 1945 at Mercury Theatre, London; The Eagle has Two Heads, London, Sept. 1946; The Rape of Lucretia, Glyndebourne, 1946; Stratton, Theatre Royal, Brighton, 1949; Nothing Up My Sleeve, Watergate, 1950; Our Lady's Tumbler, Salisbury Cathedral, 1951; Don Juan, 1953; The Death of Satan, 1954; The Catalyst, 1956; Abelard and Heloïse, 1960 and 1975; Christopher Sly, 1962, Pforzheim Opera House; The Seven Deadly Virtues, 1968; Schubert, London and Nottingham, 1981. *Publications:* The Dull Ass's Hoof, 1941; Postcards to Pulcenella, 1942; Journal of a Husbandman, 1944; This Way to the Tomb, 1946; The Rape of Lucretia, 1946; Home Made Home, 1947; Ben Jonson, 1947; Songs and Satires of the Earl of Rochester, 1948; Stratton, a play, 1948; Jan's Journal, 1948; The Typewriter, a play, 1948; Beauty and the Beast, 1948; Pope's Letters, 1948; The Cardinal, 1949; The Mongrel and other Poems, 1950; Tobacco growing in England, 1950; Our Lady's Tumbler, 1951; Selected Writings of Mahatma Gandhi, 1951; The Blue Fox, 1951; Don Juan, 1952; Jan at the Blue Fox, 1952; Where I Live, 1953; Jan's Journal, 1953; The Death of Satan, 1954; Selected Poems, 1958; Auschwitz, 1958; The Solitudes and other poems, 1960; Judas, 1960; St Spiv, 1960; Abelard and Heloïse, 1961; Anthology of Classical Songs, 1962; All Men Are Islands (Vol i, autobiog.), 1964; The Catalyst, 1965; O-B-A-F-G, 1965; How to Make Enemies (Vol. ii, autobiog.), 1968; The Perfect Mistress and other stories, 1969; Unpopular Poems, 1969; Man, Part I of poem, 1970, Part II, 1972, Part III, 1973, Parts IV and V, 1974; Collected Plays, Vol. 1, 1971; A Kettle of Fish and other stories, 1971; Torquemada, 1971; Dante's *De Vulgari Eloquentia*, 1973; Obsessed (Vol. iii, autobiog.), 1977; Mr and Mrs Mouse, 1977; For the Few, 1977; Encyclopaedia of Ignorance, 1977; The Ward (poems), 1978; Selected Poems, 1978; Auschwitz, 1979; (jt compiler) Lying Truths, 1979; The Uninvited Guest (short stories), 1981; The Tale of Tails (fairy stories), 1981; Collected Poems, 1981; A Memoir of Benjamin Britten, 1981; (ed jtly) Marx Refuted, 1982; Schubert, a play, 1982; Lenin, a play, 1982. *Address:* Welcombe, near Bideford, Devon. *T:* Morwenstow 375. *Club:* Garrick.
*Died 3 June 1982.*

**DUNCAN, Sir William (Barr McKinnon),** Kt 1983; CBE 1973; FEng; FIMechE; FRSE; Chairman 1978; Rolls-Royce Ltd, since 1983 (Director since 1982; Chief Executive, 1983–84); *b* 16 Dec. 1922; *m*

1951, Christina Boyd Worth; one *s* two *d. Educ:* Ardrossan Acad.; Glasgow Univ.; Royal Coll. of Science and Technology (1st Cl. Hons Mech Eng). Joined ICI, 1941; engrg duties, Billingham Div., 1950; Chief Engr and Engrg Dir, Agricl Div., 1961; Gp Gen. Manager, Man Services, 1964; Pres., ICI America, 1966; Dir, Can. Ind. Ltd, 1968; Pres. and Chief Exec., ICI North America Ltd, 1970; Dir, Fib. Ind. Inc., 1970; Dir, ICI Ltd, 1971; Chm., ICI Americas Inc., 1974; Dep. Chm., ICI Ltd, 1977–83; Director: NEB, 1975–78; Legal & General Gp, 1979; Bank of Scotland. Dep. Chm., Horserace Betting Levy Bd, 1983–. Pres., Soc. of Chemical Industry, 1980–81 (Vice-Pres., 1977); Gold Medallist, 1983. Vis. Prof., Strathclyde Univ., 1978–. Mem. Council, Fellowship of Engrg, 1981–84. Hon. LLD Strathclyde, 1978. *Recreations:* golf, horse-racing, music, bridge. *Address:* Rolls-Royce Ltd, 65 Buckingham Gate, SW1E 6AT.
*Died 5 Nov. 1984.*

**DUNCAN-SANDYS, Baron** *cr* 1974 (Life Peer); **Duncan Edwin Duncan-Sandys,** CH 1973; PC 1944; Founder, Civic Trust and President, since 1956; President, Lonrho Ltd, since 1984 (Chairman 1972–84); *b* 24 Jan. 1908; *o s* of Captain George Sandys, formerly MP for Wells, and Mildred, *d* of Duncan Cameron, Ashburton, New Zealand; *m* 1st, 1935, Diana (marr. diss. 1960; she *d* 1963), *d* of late Rt Hon. Sir Winston Churchill; one *s* two *d*; 2nd, 1962, Marie-Claire, *d* of Adrien Schmitt, Paris, and formerly Viscountess Hudson; one *d. Educ:* Eton; Magdalen Coll., Oxford (MA). Entered Diplomatic Service, 1930; served in Foreign Office and British Embassy, Berlin; MP (C) Norwood Div. of Lambeth, 1935–45, Streatham, 1950–Feb. 1974; Political Columnist of Sunday Chronicle, 1937–39; Member Nat. Exec. of Conservative Party, 1938–39; Commissioned in Territorial Army (Royal Artillery), 1937; Co-founder, Air Raid Protection Inst. (later Inst. of Civil Defence), 1938; served in Expeditionary Force in Norway, 1940; Lt-Col 1941; disabled on active service, 1941; Financial Sec. to War Office, 1941–43; Parly Sec., Ministry of Supply, responsible for armament production, 1943–44; Chm., War Cabinet Cttee for defence against German flying bombs and rockets, 1943–45; Minister of Works, 1944–45; Minister of Supply, Oct. 1951–Oct. 1954; Minister of Housing and Local Govt, Oct. 1954–Jan. 1957; Minister of Defence, Jan. 1957–Oct. 1959; Minister of Aviation, Oct. 1959–July 1960; Secretary of State for Commonwealth Relations, July 1960–Oct. 1964, and also Secretary of State for the Colonies, July 1962–Oct. 1964. Founded European Movement, 1947, Chm. International Executive until 1950; Chm., Parly Council of European Movement, 1950–51 (Pres. of Honour, European Movement, 1980–); Mem. Parly Assembly of Council of Europe and of WEU, 1950–51, 1965– (Leader British Delegns, 1970–72); Pres., Europa Nostra, 1969–84 (Hon. Life Pres., 1984); Chm. British Section, Franco British Council, 1972–78; Chm. Internat. Organising Cttee, European Architectural Heritage Year, 1975. Mem., Gen. Adv. Council, BBC, 1947–51. Director, Ashanti Goldfields Corporation, 1947–51 and 1966–72. Vice-Pres., Assoc. of District Councils, 1979–. Hon. Vice-Pres., Nat. Chamber of Trade, 1951–. Hon. MRTPI, 1956; Hon. FRIBA, 1968. Mem. of Magic Circle. Freeman of Bridgetown, Barbados, 1962. Grand Cross, Order of Merit, Italy, 1960; Order of Sultanate of Brunei, 1973; Medal of Honour, City of Paris, 1974; Gold Cup of European Movement, 1975; Goethe Gold Medal, Hamburg Foundn, 1975; Grand Cross of Order of Crown, Belgium, 1975; Commandeur, Légion d'Honneur, France, 1979; Grand Cross, Order of Merit, Fed. Rep. of Germany, 1981. *Publications:* European Movement and the Council of Europe, 1949; The Modern Commonwealth, 1961. *Recreation:* abstract painting. *Address:* Flat T, 12 Warwick Square, SW1. *T:* 01–834 5886. *Club:* Pratt's.
*Died 26 Nov. 1987.*

**DUNDAS, Robert Giffen,** CBE 1961; HM Diplomatic Service, retired 1969; *b* 4 March 1909; *s* of James Dundas and Grace Haxton Giffen; *m* 1938, Pauleen Gosling; three *s* one *d. Educ:* Edinburgh Univ. Entered Levant Consular Service, 1931; Vice-Consul: Beirut, 1931; Cairo, 1932; Third Sec., Alexandria, 1934; Vice-Consul: Casablanca, 1936; Alexandria, 1938; Suez, 1939; Baghdad, 1941; Consul, Tangier, 1944; assigned to Foreign Office, 1947; Consul, Kermanshah, 1949; Consul-General: Tabriz, 1950; Salonika, 1952; New Orleans, 1955; Stuttgart, 1958; Alexandria, 1961; HM Counsellor and Consul-Gen., Benghazi, 1963–66; Consul-Gen., Amsterdam, 1966–69. *Publications:* The House on the Vecht, 1979; contrib. (fiction) to Argosy etc. *Address:* 43 Imber Close, Ember Lane, Esher, Surrey KT10 8ED. *T:* 01–398 7040.
*Died 22 Dec. 1984.*

**DUNDAS, Sir Robert (Whyte-Melville),** 6th Bt, *cr* 1821; JP; *b* 31 Oct. 1881; *o surv. s* of Sir George Whyte Melville Dundas, 5th Bt, and Matilda Louisa Mary (*d* 1945), *d* of Minden J. Wilson; *S* father, 1934; *m* 1926, Dorothea (*d* 1963), *er d* of late A. W. Wiseman, MA, MusBac, Monmouth; no *c. Educ:* Trinity Coll., Glenalmond; Keble Coll., Oxford, MA. Administrative Officer, Nigeria, 1911–30. JP Perthshire, 1940. *Recreation:* cricket. *Address:* Comrie House, Comrie, Perthshire. *T:* Comrie 330. *Club:* New (Edinburgh).
*Died 10 Oct. 1981 (ext).*

**DUNDEE,** 11th Earl of, *cr* 1660 (Scotland); **Henry James Scrymgeour-Wedderburn,** PC; LLD; JP, DL; Viscount Dudhope and Lord Scrymgeour, *cr* 1641 (Scotland); Lord Inverkeithing, *cr* 1660 (Scotland); Lord Glassary, *cr* 1954 (UK); Hereditary Royal Standard-Bearer for Scotland; *b* 3 May 1902; *s* of Col Henry Scrymgeour-Wedderburn, *de jure* 10th Earl and Edith (*d* 1968), *d* of John Moffat, CE, Ardrossan, and Jessie Fulton Arthur; *S* father, 1924 (claim admitted by Cttee for Privileges, House of Lords, as Viscount, 1952, as Earl, 1953); *m* 1946, Patricia Katherine, *widow* of Lt-Col W. D. Faulkner, Irish Guards, and of Lieut-Col (Hon.) David Scrymgeour-Wedderburn, and *d* of late Col Lord Herbert Montagu Douglas Scott; one *s* and two step *d. Educ:* Winchester; Balliol Coll., Oxford. Pres. Oxford Union, Oct. 1924; MP (U) Western Renfrew, 1931–45; Parliamentary Under-Sec. of State for Scotland, 1936–39; served with 7th Black Watch, 1939–41; Additional Parl. Under-Sec. of State, Scottish Office 1941–42. Minister without Portfolio, 1958–61; Minister of State for Foreign Affairs, 1961–64; Asst Dep. Leader, 1960–62, Dep. Leader, 1962–64, House of Lords. Hon. LLD St Andrews, 1954. *Heir: s* Lord Scrymgeour. *Address:* Coultra Farm House, Newport-on-Tay, Fife. *T:* Gauldry 258. *Clubs:* Carlton, Travellers', White's, Pratt's; New (Edinburgh). *Died 29 June 1983.*

**DUNDERDALE, Comdr Wilfred Albert,** CMG 1942; MBE 1920; RNVR, retired; *b* 24 Dec. 1899; *s* of late Richard Albert Dunderdale, Shipowner, and Sophie Dunderdale; *m* 1st, June Morse (marr. diss.); 2nd, 1952, Dorothy Brayshaw Hyde (*d* 1978); 3rd, 1980, Deborah, *d* of Eugene B. Jackson, Boston, Mass and *widow* of Harry McJ. McLeod. Trained as Naval Architect, 1914–17; served with Mediterranean Fleet, 1918–22 (despatches twice); Lieut RNVR, 1920; transferred to British Embassy, Constantinople, 1922–26; Paris, 1926–40; Comdr, 1939. Russian Order of St Anne; Polonia Restituta; French Legion of Honour (Officer); French Croix de Guerre with palm; United States Legion of Merit (Officer). *Clubs:* Boodle's; Knickerbocker (New York); Royal Harwich Yacht (Harwich). *Died 13 Nov. 1990.*

**DUNDONALD,** 14th Earl of, *cr* 1669, **Ian Douglas Leonard Cochrane;** Lord Cochrane of Dundonald, 1647; Lord Cochrane of Paisley and Ochiltree, 1669; Chairman, Duneth Securities Ltd and associated companies; a Representative Peer for Scotland, 1959–63; *b* 6 Dec. 1918; *s* of late Hon. Douglas Robert Hesketh Roger Cochrane (2nd *s* of 12th Earl) and of Hon. Mrs Douglas Cochrane (*d* 1960), Hawkhurst, Kent; *S* uncle, 1958; *m* 1960, Aphra Farquhar (*d* 1972), *d* of late Comdr George Fetherstonhaugh; one *s* one *d*; *m* 1978, Ann Margaret, *d* of late Sir Joseph Harkness, and of Lady Harkness, Tenterden, Kent. *Educ:* Wellington Coll.; RMC, Sandhurst. Joined 1 Battalion The Black Watch, 1938; Adjutant, 16 DLI, 1940–41; Staff Capt. 139 Inf. Bde, 1941–42; Staff Coll., Camberley, 1942 (psc); Asst Mil. Landing Officer, 51 (H) Div., 1943; GSO 3 and GSO 2, HQ Eighth Army, 1943; Company Comdr 6 Bn The Black Watch, 1944–45; Bde Major, 180 Inf. Bde, 1946–47; GSO 2, Army Air Transport Development Centre, 1947–49; Company Comdr 1 Bn The Black Watch, 1949–51; DAQMG, SHAPE, 1951; GSO 2, SD3, War Office and GSO 2, Army Council Secretariat, 1952–53; retired 1953. North American Representative, Atlantic Shipbuilding Co., 1953–54. Mem., UK Delegn to NATO Citizens Convention, Paris, 1962. Chm. Anglo-Chilean Soc., 1958–65. Pres., Ayr and Bute Assoc. of Youth Clubs. Vice-Pres., Royal Caledonian Schs. *Recreations:* shooting, sailing. *Heir: s* Lord Cochrane. *Address:* Beau Coin, La Haule, Jersey, Channel Islands. *Club:* Carlton. *Died 4 Oct. 1986.*

**DUNHAM, Cyril John;** Director, Nationwide (formerly Co-operative Permanent) Building Society, since 1944 (President, 1959–69); *b* 22 April 1908; *m* 1936, Vera Georgia; one *s* two *d. Educ:* Watford Gram. Sch.; Coll. of Estate Management. FRICS 1929. Technical Adviser, War Damage Commn, 1941; Vice-Chm., Peterborough New Town Develt Corp., 1968–73; Vice-President: Building Societies Assoc. (Chm., 1961–63); Internat. Union of Building Socs. (Hon. Life Mem., 1980–). Has also served on: Wembley Borough Council; Nat. House-Builders Registration Council; Town and Country Planning Assoc. FRSA. *Address:* 15 Turner Close, Hampstead, NW11 6TU. *T:* 01–455 8348. *Died 30 Jan. 1986.*

**DUNICAN, Peter Thomas,** CBE 1977; FEng, FICE, FIStructE, FIEI; Consultant, Ove Arup Partnership, since 1984 (Chairman and Director, 1977–84); Chairman: The Arup Partnerships, 1977–85 (Director, 1977–87); Ove Arup & Partners, 1959–77; National Building Agency, 1978–82 (part-time Director, 1964–82); *b* 15 March 1918; *s* of Peter Dunican and Elsie Alice McKenzie; *m* 1942, Irene May Jordan; two *s* one *d* (and one *d* decd). *Educ:* Central Sch., Clapham; Battersea Polytechnic. FICE 1971, FIStructE 1959, FIEI 1970. Asst, S. H. White & Son, Civil Engineers, 1936–43; Structural Engr, Ove Arup & Partners, Consulting Engineers, 1943–49, Sen. Partner 1956–78. Instn of Structural Engineers: Mem. Council, 1964–78; Vice-Pres., 1971–77; Pres., 1977–78. Member: LCC Adv. Cttee on London Bldg Act and Byelaws, 1957; Min. of

Housing Working Party to revise Model Bldg Byelaws, 1960; Bldg Regulations Adv. Cttee, 1962–65; Council, Architect. Assoc., 1968–69; Chm., Ground and Structures Res. Cttee, BRE, 1979–83. Univ. Science and Technol. Bd of Science Research Council: Mem., Aeronaut. and Civil Eng Cttee, 1968–71; Mem., National Jt Consultative Cttee, 1974–77; Chm., Jt Bldg Gp, 1973–76. FEng 1978 (Mem. Council, 1983–86). *Publications:* professional, technical and philosophical papers to jls dealing with construction industry in general and struct. engrg in particular. *Recreations:* working in the garden and going to the opera. *Address:* Charlwood House, Legsheath Lane, East Grinstead, W Sussex RH19 4JW. *T:* Sharpthorne 810088. *Clubs:* Athenæum, Danish. *Died 18 Dec. 1989.*

**DUNK, Sir William (Ernest),** Kt 1957; CBE 1954; retired as Chairman Commonwealth of Australia Public Service Commission (1947–62); formerly Commissioner, British Phosphates Commission and Christmas Island Phosphates Commission; Director, General Television Corporation and other companies; *b* S Australia, 11 Dec. 1897; *s* of Albert L. Dunk; *m* 1922, Elma K. Evans; one *s* one *d. Educ:* Kapunda High Sch., Australia. Australian Public Service from 1914; Auditor-General's Office, 1914–39, Adelaide, New Guinea, London, Sydney; Treasury, 1939–45, as Asst Sec., Special War Services, Dir Reverse Lend Lease, 1943–45; Permanent Sec., Dept of External Affairs, 1945–46. *Address:* 7 Tintern Avenue, Toorak, Victoria 3142, Australia. *Club:* Melbourne (Melbourne). *Died 12 Jan. 1984.*

**DUNKERLEY, Harvey John,** CBE 1953; Controller, Midland Region, BBC, 1948–64, retired; *b* 10 Oct. 1902; *s* of Joseph Braithwaite Dunkerley and Rose Maria (*née* Harvey); *m* 1st, 1928, Kay Hargreaves (*d* 1958); 2nd, 1961, Thelma Couch; one *s* three *d. Educ:* Owen's Sch., London; Magdalen Coll., Oxford (2nd class Hons Mod. Hist.). Announcer, BBC, Savoy Hill, 1924; Asst, BBC Relay Station, Liverpool, 1924; Education Officer, BBC, Manchester, 1928; Programme Dir, BBC Midland Region, 1933; BBC European Service, Sept. 1939, latterly as Dep. to Controller. *Recreation:* country life. *Address:* Gallipot House, Broadway, Worcs. *T:* Evesham 830395. *Died 21 March 1985.*

**DUNKLEY, Philip Parker,** MC and Bar 1944; Executive Chairman, 1978–82, Chairman and Chief Executive, since 1982, Mitchell Cotts plc; *b* 23 March 1922; *s* of late Frederick and Rachel Dunkley; *m* 1948, Barbara Patricia Baxter; one *d. Educ:* King's School, Macclesfield, Cheshire. Served War, 1940–46 (despatches); commnd 10th Gurkha Rifles, 1942; Burma Campaign, 1942–46 (Major). F. Dunkley & Co., 1946–56; Man. Dir, John Shields & Co., 1956–59; joined Mitchell Cotts Group Ltd, 1959; Dir 1963; Man. Dir 1965; Dep. Chm. 1973. Director: Bestobell Ltd, 1971–84 (Dep. Chm., 1976–84); Consolidated Gold Fields Ltd, 1979– (Dep. Chm., 1983–); Samuel Montagu & Co. Ltd, 1980–. *Recreations:* fishing, shooting. *Address:* Hamptons Farm House, Shipbourne, near Tonbridge, Kent. *T:* Plaxtol 547. *Club:* Oriental. *Died 27 Sept. 1985.*

**DUNLOP, Agnes Mary Robertson;** *see* Kyle, Elisabeth.

**DUNLOP, Cdre David Kennedy B.;** *see* Buchanan-Dunlop.

**DUNLOP, Prof. Douglas Morton;** Professor of History, Columbia University, New York, 1963–77, later Emeritus; *b* 25 Feb. 1909; *o s* of Rev. H. Morton Dunlop and Helen Oliver, *e d* of W. D. Dunn; *m* 1948, Margaret Sinclair, *y d* of Major A. R. Munro, TD, Hillend, Edinburgh. *Educ:* Glasgow Academy; Glasgow Univ.; University Coll., Oxford. Scholar, 1928–32; Vans Dunlop Scholar in Medicine, Edinburgh Univ., 1933; Trinity Coll., Glasgow, 1934–37; Brown Downie Fellow, 1937; Maclean Scholar, 1937 and 1938; University of Bonn, 1937–39; BA Oxon 1939, MA 1960. Trinity Hall, Cambridge (MA) 1950; DLitt Glasgow, 1955. Travelled in Turkey and Syria, 1938; Syria (Jabal Ansariyah), 1939; Asst to Prof. of Hebrew, Glasgow Univ., 1939–46. NFS 1942–44. Asst to Prof. of Oriental Langs, 1947–48, Lectr in Semitic Langs, 1948–50, St Andrews Univ.; Mem. CCG, 1948; Lectr in Islamic History, Cambridge Univ., 1950–62. Visiting Prof. of History, Columbia Univ., 1962–63. FRAS; FIAL. *Publications:* The History of the Jewish Khazars, 1954; The Fusul al-Madani (Aphorisms of the Statesman) of al-Farabi, 1961; Arabic Science in the West, 1965; Arab Civilization to AD 1500, 1971; The Muntakhab Siwan al-Hikmah of Abu Sulaiman al-Sijistani, 1979; original papers and reviews in British and foreign Orientalist publications, and articles in encyclopædias. *Recreations:* hill-walking, Scottish history. *Address:* 46 Owlstone Road, Cambridge. *T:* 354147. *Club:* Royal and Ancient (St Andrews). *Died 3 June 1987.*

**DUNLOP, Sir John (Wallace),** KBE 1971; Australian Company Director; Director, Australian Bank Ltd; Senior Adviser on Australian Affairs, Banque Paribas, Paris; *b* 20 May 1910; *s* of late W. P. Dunlop, Sydney; *m* 1st, 1932, Phyllis Haley; one *s* one *d*; 2nd, 1960, Patricia Lloyd Jones. *Educ:* Tudor House; Geelong Grammar Sch.; Univ. of Sydney. *Address:* 17 O'Connell Street, Sydney, NSW

2000, Australia. *T:* 20222. *Clubs:* Australian, Union, Royal Sydney Golf (Sydney).              *Died* 16 *Oct.* 1983.

**DUNLOP, Roy Leslie,** CMG 1965; The Clerk of the Parliament, Queensland, 1954–68; *b* 14 April 1899; *s* of E. J. D. Dunlop; *m* 1925, Olive M. F. Black; one *s. Educ:* Rockhampton. Parliamentary service, 1920–68; 2nd Clerk-Asst, 1920–32; Clerk-Asst and Sergeant-at-Arms, 1933–54. Hon. Sec., Commonwealth Parliamentary Assoc., 1954–68. *Address:* 30 Ralston Street, Wilston, Queensland 4051, Australia. *T:* (07) 356–3914.
             *Died* 7 *Dec.* 1981.

**DUNMORE,** 10th Earl of, *cr* 1686; **Reginald Arthur Murray;** Viscount Fincastle, Lord Murray, 1686; Baron Dunmore (UK), 1831; *b* 17 July 1911; *s* of Arthur Charles Murray (*d* 1964) (*g g s* of 4th Earl), and Susan Maud (*d* 1922), *d* of Edward Richards, Tasmania; *S* kinsman, 1980; *m* 1948, Patricia Mary, *d* of Frank Coles; two *d. Heir: b* Kenneth Randolph Murray [*b* 6 June 1913; *m* 1938, Margaret Joy, *d* of late P. D. Cousins; two *s*]. *Address:* Kooringal, 27 Beach Road, Gravelly Beach, West Tamar, Tasmania 7251, Australia.
             *Died* 14 *June* 1981.

**DUNN, James Anthony;** *b* 30 Jan. 1926; *s* of James Richard Dunn and Margaret (*née* McDermott); *m* 1954, Dorothy (*née* Larkey); two *s* two *d. Educ:* St Teresa's Sch., Liverpool; London Sch. of Economics and Political Science. MP Liverpool, Kirkdale, 1964–83 (Lab, 1964–81; SDP, 1981–83); Opposition Whip, 1971–74; a Lord Comr, HM Treasury, 1974–76; Parly Under-Sec. of State, Northern Ireland Office, 1976–79. Formerly Member: Estimates Cttee; House of Commons Services Cttee; House of Commons Select Cttee on Defence, 1981–83. Sec., Anglo-Manx Commonwealth Parly Gp, 1976–83. Pres., Merseyside Chinese Community Co-ordinating Cttee, 1977–. *Address:* 45 Lisburn Lane, Liverpool L13 9AF. *T:* 051–226 6054.            *Died April* 1985.

**DUNN, Brig. Keith Frederick William,** CBE 1941; DL; retired; *b* 31 July 1891; *s* of Brig.-Gen. R. H. W. Dunn, DL, Althrey, Wrexham, and Constance, *d* of Maj.-Gen. G. E. Erskine; *m* 1st, 1915, Ava (*d* 1938), *d* of Brig.-Gen. H. F. Kays, CB; one *s* one *d* (and one *s* decd); 2nd, 1946, Joan, *d* of Sir Frank Beauchamp, 1st Bt, CBE and widow of Major Claude de Lisle Bush. *Educ:* Wellington Coll.; RMA 2nd Lieut RA 1911. Served European War, 1914–19 (despatches). Equitation Sch., Weedon, 1922–25; Adjt RMA, 1926–29; Lieut-Col 1938; served in North West Europe, 1939; Brig. 1939; CRA, 1st Cavalry Div., 1939–40; comd 5th Cavalry Bde, MEF, 1940–41; retd 1942; re-employed, comd Glos Sub-District, 1942–45. Chief Training Officer, Min. of Agriculture and Fisheries, 1946–47. Mem., Pony Club Orgn Cttee, 1948–66; Chm., Pony Club Trng Cttee, 1954–66. DL Glos, 1960. *Recreations:* hunting, golf. *Address:* Bencombe House, Uley, Dursley, Glos. *T:* Dursley 860255. *Club:* Army and Navy.          *Died* 14 *Feb.* 1985.

**DUNN, Prof. Thomas Alexander;** Professor of Literature and Head of Department of English Studies, University of Stirling, since 1966; *b* 6 March 1923; *s* of James Symington Dunn and Elizabeth Taylor; *m* 1947, Joyce Mary Armstrong; two *s* one *d. Educ:* Dumfries Academy; Edinburgh Univ. (MA, PhD). Served War, Pilot, Fleet Air Arm, Sub-Lt (A) RNVR, 1942–45. Univ. of Ghana, 1953, Prof., 1960; Prof., Univ. of Lagos, 1964–65; Visiting Prof., Univ. of Western Ontario, 1965–66; University of Stirling: Mem., Academic Council, 1966–, Univ. Court, 1968–72; Chm., Board of Studies for Arts, 1975–81; Chm., MacRobert Arts Centre, 1973–82. Member: Inter-Univ. Council for Higher Educn Overseas, 1967–75; Scottish Univs Council on Entrance, 1968–74, 1979–81; Consultative Cttee on the Curriculum, 1968–76. Member: Scottish Arts Council, 1969–76; Arts Council of Gt Britain, 1971–73; Broadcasting Council for Scotland, 1972–76; Films of Scotland, 1972–82; Culture Cttee, UK Nat. Commn for UNESCO, 1983–85; Chairman: Univs Cttee on Scottish Literature, 1970–; Drama Cttee, 1972–76; Grants to Publishers Panel, 1975–78; Pres., Assoc. for Scottish Literary Studies, 1972–76. *Publications:* Philip Massinger: the man and the playwright, 1957; (with D. E. S. Maxwell) Introducing Poetry, 1966; Massinger and Field: The Fatal Dowry, 1969; (ed) Universitas (Ghana), 1955–63; (ed) Fountainwell Drama Texts. *Recreations:* gardening, theatre and arts generally. *Address:* Coney Park, 121 Henderson Street, Bridge of Allan, Stirling FK9 4RQ. *T:* Stirling 833373. *Club:* Stirling and County (Stirling).
            *Died* 31 *March* 1988.

**DUNNE, Irene Marie, (Mrs F. D. Griffin),** Hon. Doctor of Music, Hon. LLD; *b* Louisville, Kentucky, USA, 20 Dec. 1898; *d* of Joseph A. Dunne and Adelaide A. Henry; *m* 1927, Dr Francis D. Griffin (*d* 1965); one adopted *d. Educ:* Loretta Academy, St Louis, Mo., USA; Chicago Musical Coll., Chicago. Acted in the original Show Boat, 1929. Entered motion pictures, 1931; first film Cimarron. Films include: Back Street, Awful Truth, Roberta, Anna and the King of Siam, Life with Father, I Remember Mama, The Mudlark (as Queen Victoria), Never a Dull Moment. Laetare Medal, University of Notre Dame. Mem. Defence Advisory Cttee, US, to advise on welfare matters in the women's services, 1951; Mem. US Delegation

to United Nations 12th Gen. Assembly. *Recreation:* golf. *Address:* 461 North Faring Road, Moment, Los Angeles, Calif 90077, USA.
             *Died* 4 *Sept.* 1990.

**DUNNE, Most Rev. Patrick,** DD; Auxiliary Bishop of Dublin, (RC), 1946; Titular Bishop of Nara; Parish Priest of St Mary's Haddington Road, Dublin; Dean of the Metropolitan Chapter; Vicar-General; *b* Dublin, 3 June 1891. *Educ:* Holy Cross Coll., Clonliffe, Dublin; Irish Coll., Rome. Ordained in Rome, 1913; Sec. to Archbishops of Dublin, 1919–43; Parish Priest, Church of the Holy Family, Aughrim Street, Dublin, 1943–47; Domestic Prelate, 1943. *Address:* St Mary's, Haddington Road, Dublin.
             *Died* 16 *March* 1988.

**DUNNETT, Sir George Sangster,** KBE 1952; CB 1950; *b* 12 May 1907; *e s* of late Sir James Dunnett, KCIE; *m* 1938, Margaret Rosalind (*d* 1977), *er d* of David Davies, MD, Tunbridge Wells; one *s* three *d. Educ:* Edinburgh Academy; Corpus Christi Coll., Oxford. Bd of Educn, 1930; Treasury, 1931; Min. of Civil Aviation, 1946; Dep. Sec., Min. of Agriculture and Fisheries, 1947–56; Chm., Sugar Board, 1956–70. *Recreations:* golf, philosophy. *Address:* Basings Cottage, Cowden, Kent. *T:* Cowden 398. *Club:* Athenæum.
             *Died* 16 *May* 1984.

**DUNPHY, Rev. Thomas Patrick Joseph,** SJ; Assistant Priest, Corpus Christi, Boscombe, since 1987 (Parish Priest, 1980–86); *b* Donnybrook, Dublin, 17 Aug. 1913; *o s* of Thomas Joseph Dunphy and Agnes Mary (*née* Rogers), Dublin. *Educ:* Wimbledon Coll. Joined Soc. of Jesus, 1932; Priest, 1946. Headmaster of St John's (preparatory sch. of Beaumont Coll.), 1949–64; Rector, Beaumont Coll., 1964–67; Socius to the Provincial of the Society of Jesus, 1967–71; Rector, Stonyhurst Coll., 1971–77; Vicar for Religious Sisters in Devon and Dorset, 1977–79; Spiritual Father, St Mary's Hall, Stonyhurst, 1979–80. *Address:* Corpus Christi, 757 Christchurch Road, Boscombe, Bournemouth BH7 6AN. *T:* Bournemouth 425286.            *Died* 23 *July* 1989.

**DUNTZE, Sir George (Edwin Douglas),** 6th Bt, *cr* 1774; CMG 1960; *b* 1 June 1913; *o s* of Sir George Puxley Duntze, 5th Baronet, and Violet May, *d* of late Henry M. Sanderson; *S* father, 1947; *m* 1st, 1941, Joan, *d* of late Major F. E. Bradstock, DSO, MC (marr. diss. 1966); one *d*; 2nd, 1966, Nesta, *e d* of late Thomas R. P. Herbert, Newport, Mon. *Educ:* Shrewsbury Sch.; Trinity Coll., Oxford. (MA). Entered Colonial Administrative Service, 1936. Provincial Comr, Uganda, 1952–61. *Heir: kinsman,* John Alexander Duntze [*b* 13 Nov. 1909; *m* 1935, Emily Ellsworth, *d* of Elmer E. Harlow, USA]. *Address:* 25 Ennismore Gardens, SW7. *Clubs:* Hurlingham; Leander.            *Died* 20 *May* 1985.

**DUNTZE, Sir John Alexander,** 7th Bt *cr* 1774; of Tiverton, Devon; Mechanical Engineer, retired; *b* 13 Nov. 1909; *s* of John Alexander Ralph Duntze (*d* 1950) and Carrie Fairchild Godfrey (*d* 1927); *S* kinsman, Sir George Edwin Douglas Duntze, 6th Bt, CMG, 1985; *m* 1935, Emily Ellsworth, *d* of Elmer E. Harlow, New Bedford, Mass, USA. *Educ:* Pratt Inst., Brooklyn, NY (grad. 1930, Industrial Mech. Engrg). With R. T. Vanderbilt Co., Rubber Lab., E Norwalk, Conn, 1931–40; Mem. NY Rubber Gp of Amer. Chem. Soc.; Federal Tel. & Radio (IT&T), Transformer Div., Belville, NJ, 1941–44; Mem. Amer. Soc. of Mil. Engrs; Dictaphone Corp., Bridgeport, Conn, 1944–59; two patents bearing his name assigned to company on equipment used in sound recording and reproduction (method of rubber sealing for use in tropical humidity and Magnetic Sheet Machine); Perkin-Elmer Corp., Instrument Div., Norwalk, Conn, 1962–69 (a Sen. Manfg Engr); Manager of Engineering, Connecticut Engineering & Instrument Corp., Norwalk, Conn (optical equipment for US govt), 1975–78. Chief Officer, Westport Aux. Police, 1951–60. *Recreations:* German language; old musical shows, scores, recordings and revivals; steam locomotive "buff". *Heir: cousin* Daniel Evans Duntze [*b* 4 April 1926; *m* 1954, Marietta Welsh; one *s* two *d*]. *Address:* St John's Place, Westport, Conn 06880, USA. *T:* 1–203–227–6954.      *Died* 23 *Aug.* 1987.

**DUPONT-SOMMER, André;** Member of the Institut de France (Secrétaire Perpétuel de l'Académie des Inscriptions et Belles-Lettres) since 1961; Hon. Professor: the Collège de France; the Sorbonne; Director of Studies, Ecole des Hautes Etudes, since 1938; *b* 23 Dec. 1900. Gen. Sec., Collège de France, 1934; Pres., Institut d'Etudes Sémitiques, University of Paris, 1952. Member: Accademia dei Lincei, 1972; Österreichische Akademie der Wissenschaften, 1974. Officier de la Légion d'Honneur; Comdr des Palmes académiques. *Publications:* Le Quatrième Livre des Machabées, 1939; La Doctrine gnostique de la lettre "Wâw", 1946; Les Araméens, 1949; Aperçus préliminaires sur les manuscrits de la mer Morte, 1950 (publ. Eng. The Dead Sea Scrolls, a Preliminary Survey, 1952); Nouveaux Aperçus sur les manuscrits de la mer Morte, 1953 (publ. Eng. The Jewish Sect of Qumran and the Essenes, 1954); Le Livre des Hymnes découvert près de la mer Morte, 1957; Les inscriptions araméennes de Sfiré, 1958; Les écrits esséniens découverts près de la mer Morte, 1959 (Eng. trans., The Essene Writings from Qumran); articles in Revue d'Assyriologie,

Revue d'Histoire des Religions, Semitica, Syria, Jl of Semitic Studies, Vetus Testamentum, etc. *Address:* 25 Quai de Conti, 75006 Paris, France. *T:* 329.55.10.                    *Died* 14 *May* 1983.

**du PRÉ, Jacqueline Mary,** OBE 1976; British violoncellist; *b* 1945; *m* 1967, Daniel Barenboim. *Educ:* studied with William Pleeth both privately and at Guildhall Sch. of Music, with Paul Tortelier in Paris, and with Rostropovich in Moscow. Concert début at Wigmore Hall at age of sixteen, followed by appearances on the continent and with principal English orchestras and conductors. Soloist in London and at Bath and Edinburgh Festivals. N American début, 1965. Continued studies in Moscow with Rostropovitch, 1966, returning later to USSR as soloist with BBC Symphony Orchestra. Toured N America, and appeared New York and at World Fair, Montreal; subseq. concerts, major musical centres, 1967. Awarded Suggia Gift at age of ten; Gold medal, Guildhall Sch. of Music, and Queen's Prize, 1960; City of London Midsummer Prize, 1975; Musician of the Year Award, Incorporated Soc. of Musicians, 1980; FGSM, 1975; FRCM, 1977; Hon. FRAM, 1974. Hon. Fellow, St Hilda's Coll., Oxford, 1984. Hon. DMus: London, 1979; Sheffield, 1980; Leeds, 1982; Durham, 1983; Oxford, 1984; Hon. DLit Salford, 1978; DUniv Open, 1979. *Address:* c/o Harold Holt Ltd, 31 Sinclair Road, W14 0NS.                    *Died* 19 *Oct.* 1987.

**DURANT, Rear-Adm. Bryan Cecil,** CB 1963; DSO 1953; DSC 1945; *b* 17 June 1910; *o s* of Francis Durant and Dulce, *d* of Fraser Baddeley; *m* 1st, 1939, Pamela (*d* 1963), *yr d* of Brig.-Gen. William Walter Seymour; three *d* (and one *s* decd); one *d*, 1967, Rachel, *d* of late Col Hon. David Bruce, and Hon. Mrs David Bruce. *Educ:* Radley. Entered Royal Navy, 1929; specialised in navigation, 1935. War of 1939–45; actions in HMS Dorsetshire in Atlantic and Indian Oceans including sinking of Bismarck, 1940–42; sunk by Japanese aircraft, 1942 (despatches); actions in HMS Victorious off North Norway, Sabang, Palembang, Okinawa and Japan, 1942–45; suicide Bomber attacks, 1945 (DSC). Comdr 1945; Capt. 1951; Comd 4th Frigate Sqdn in Korean War, 1952–54 (DSO). Dir, Ops Div., Admlty, 1957; Captain of the Fleet, Home Fleet, 1959; Chief of Staff Far East Station, 1961–63; retired list, 1963. Dir-Gen., Navy League, 1964–75. ADC to the Queen, 1960. Liveryman, Fishmongers Co. DL Greater London, 1970–78. Commendador Henriquina (Portuguese), 1960. *Address:* The Old House, Bighton, near Alresford, Hants. *Club:* Army and Navy.

*Died* 12 *April* 1983.

**DURANT, William James,** BA, MA, PhD; engaged in writing; *b* North Adams, Mass, 5 Nov. 1885; *s* of Joseph Durant and Mary Allors, of French-Canadian stock; *m* 1913, Ida Kaufman (Ariel Durant) (*d* 1981); one *s* one *d*. *Educ:* St Peter's Coll., Jersey City, NJ; Columbia Univ., New York. Prof. of Latin and French, Seton Hall Coll., South Orange NJ, 1907–11; Instructor in Philosophy, Columbia Univ., 1917; Dir of Labour Temple Sch., 1914–27. Presidential Medal of Freedom, 1977. *Publications:* Philosophy and the Social Problem, 1917; The Story of Philosophy, 1926; Transition, 1927; The Mansions of Philosophy, 1929; Adventures in Genius, 1931; The Story of Civilization (11 vols): Our Oriental Heritage, 1935; The Life of Greece, 1939; Cæsar and Christ, 1944; The Age of Faith, 1950; The Renaissance, 1953; The Reformation, 1957; (with Ariel Durant) The Age of Reason Begins, 1961; The Age of Louis XIV, 1963; The Age of Voltaire, 1965; Rousseau and Revolution, 1967 (Pulitzer Prize, 1968); The Age of Napoleon, 1975; A Dual Autobiography, 1977; The Lessons of History, 1968; Interpretations of Life, 1970. *Recreations:* none. *Address:* 5608 Briarcliff Road, Los Angeles, Calif 90068, USA.

*Died* 7 *Nov.* 1981.

**DURLACHER, Sir Esmond (Otho),** Kt 1972; Consultant to Wedd Durlacher Mordaunt & Co. since 1967; *b* 8 Oct. 1901; 2nd *s* of Frederic Henry Keeling Durlacher and Violet Mabel, *d* of Sir Reginald Hanson, 1st Bt, Thorpe Satchville, Leics; *m* 1st, 1930, Lady Sheila Jackson (marr. diss. 1947); two *s* one *d*; 2nd, 1953, Mrs Elizabeth Steele. *Educ:* Repton; Trinity Hall, Cambridge. Member of Stock Exchange, London, 1926–77; Senior Partner, F. & N. Durlacher, Stock-Jobbers, 1936, then Senior Partner, Durlacher Oldham Mordaunt Godson & Co., retd 1966. Mem. Bd of Governors, St George's Hosp., 1944–71; Chm., Bd of Governors, Allhallows Sch., Rousdon, Devon, 1972–77; Chm., Victoria Hosp. for Children, Tite Street, 1957–67. *Address:* Wootton Fitzpaine Manor, Bridport, Dorset. *T:* Charmouth 60455. *Clubs:* Buck's, Portland.

*Died* 28 *May* 1982.

**DURLACHER, Adm. Sir Laurence (George),** KCB 1961 (CB 1957); OBE 1943; DSC 1945; retired; *b* 24 July 1904; *s* of late Frederick Henry Keeling Durlacher and V. M. Durlacher (*née* Hanson); *m* 1934, Rimma, *d* of late R. V. Sass-Tissovsky; one *s* one *d*. *Educ:* RNC Osborne and Dartmouth. Lieut 1927; Comdr 1939; Capt. 1945; Cdre 1st Class, 1952; Rear-Adm. 1955; Vice-Adm. 1958; Adm. 1961. On Staff of Adm. of the Fleet Viscount Cunningham of Hyndhope during N Africa, Sicily and Italian Campaigns (despatches); commanded HMS Volage, 1944–45; Admiralty,

1945–47; commanded 3rd Destroyer Flotilla, Mediterranean, 1949–50; commanded Admiralty Signals and Radar Establishments, 1950–52; Chief of Staff to C-in-C Far East Station, 1952–54; Dep. Chief of Naval Personnel (Personal Services), at Admiralty, 1955–57; Flag Officer Commanding Fifth Cruiser Squadron and Flag Officer Second-in-Command, Far East Station, 1957–58; Dep. Chief of Naval Staff and Fifth Sea Lord, 1959–62; retired, 1962. US Legion of Merit, 1945. *Address:* Mas Tournamy, 06250 Mougins, France.                    *Died* 16 *Jan.* 1986.

**DURNFORD-SLATER, Adm. Sir Robin (Leonard Francis),** KCB 1957 (CB 1955); *b* 9 July 1902; *s* of Captain L. Slater, Royal Sussex Regiment (killed in action, 1914), and Constance Dorothy Durnford-Slater; *m* 1936, Mary Alice Hilleary, *d* of late Col E. H. Gregson, CMG, CIE; one *s* one *d*. *Educ:* Osborne; Dartmouth. Comdr, 1938; Capt., 1944; Rear-Adm., 1953; Vice-Adm., 1956; Adm., 1959. Served War of 1939–45; Executive officer, HMS Hermes, HMS Vernon; Senior Officer, 42nd and subseq. 7th Escort Grp Western Approaches; Trg Capt. Western Approaches; Dir of Underwater Weapons, Admiralty (Bath). Post War: Senior Officer 1st Escort Flotilla, Far East; Commandant Sch. of Amphibious Warfare; Capt. HMS Gambia; Dep. Controller, Admiralty, 1953–56; Flag Officer, 2nd in Command, Mediterranean Fleet, 1956–58; Commander-in-Chief, The Nore, 1958–61; retd. Flag Officer Naval Brigade, Coronation, 1953. Comdr of the Legion of Honour, 1958. *Address:* Four Chiltley Lane, Liphook, Hants.

*Died* 28 *June* 1984.

**DURRANT, Albert Arthur Molteno,** CBE 1945; CEng; FIMechE; FCIT; FRSA; retired from London Transport Board; *b* 11 Sept. 1898; *s* of late Sir Arthur I. Durrant, CBE, MVO; *m* 1922, Kathleen (*d* 1977), *d* of Arthur J. Wright; no *c*. *Educ:* Alleyn's Sch., Dulwich. Joined London Gen. Omnibus Co., 1919; Chief Engineer (Buses and Coaches), London Passenger Transport Bd, 1935–40; Director of Tank Design, Ministry of Supply, 1940–45; Chief Mechanical Engineer (Road Services) London Transport, 1945–65. *Address:* c/o Williams and Glyn's Bank, Holts Branch, 22 Whitehall, SW1.

*Died* 14 *Aug.* 1984.

**DURRANT, Maj.-Gen. James Thom,** CB 1945; DFC 1941; City Councillor, Johannesburg, 1969–77; *b* 1913; *s* of late J. C. Durrant, Hertford and Johannesburg; *m* 1939, Jean Lucy, *d* of G. Harding, Pretoria; two *s*; *m* 1970, Margaret, *d* of late Archie White, Johannesburg. Commanded a group in Air Command, South-East Asia, 1945; Dir-Gen. South African Air Force, 1947–51; retired, 1952. *Address:* 71 First Avenue East, Parktown North, Johannesburg, South Africa.                    *Died* 15 *Oct.* 1990.

**DURRELL, Lawrence George,** FRSL 1954; lately Director of Public Relations, Government of Cyprus; *b* 27 Feb. 1912; *m* 1st, 1935, Nancy Myers (marr. diss. 1947); one *d*; 2nd, 1947, Eve Cohen (marr. diss.); one *d* decd; 3rd, 1961, Claude Forde (*d* 1967); 4th, 1973, Ghislaine de Boysson (marr. diss. 1979). *Educ:* College of St Joseph, Darjeeling, India; St Edmund's Sch., Canterbury. Formerly: Foreign Service Press Officer, Athens and Cairo; Press Attaché, Alexandria; Dir of Public Relations, Dodecanese Islands; Press Attaché, Belgrade, Yugoslavia; Dir of British Council Institutes of Kalamata, Greece, and Cordoba, Argentina. Mellon Lectr in Humanities, Calif. Inst. of Technology, Pasadena, 1975. *Publications:* (novel, under pseudonym Charles Norden) Panic Spring, 1937; The Black Book, 1938 (France and USA), 1973 (England); Private Country (poetry), 1943; Prospero's Cell, 1945; (trans) Four Greek Poets, 1946; Cities, Plains and People, 1946; Cefalu, 1947 (republished as The Dark Labyrinth, 1958); On Seeming to Presume, 1948; (trans) Pope Joan, 1948; Sappho (verse play), 1950; Reflections on a Marine Venus, 1953; The Tree of Idleness, 1955; Selected Poems, 1956; Bitter Lemons, 1957 (Duff Cooper Memorial Prize); White Eagles Over Serbia (juvenile), 1957; The Alexandria Quartet: Justine, 1957, Balthazar, 1958 (Prix du Meilleur Livre Etranger, Paris), Mountolive, 1958, Clea, 1960; Esprit de Corps, 1957; Stiff Upper Lip, 1958; (ed) The Best of Henry Miller, 1960; Collected Poems, 1960, new edn with additions and revisions, 1968; An Irish Faustus (verse play), 1963; The Ikons, 1966; The Revolt of Aphrodite: Tunc, 1968, Nunquam, 1970; Spirit of Place: letters and essays on travel, 1969; The Red Limbo Lingo: a poetry notebook for 1968–70, 1971; Vega and other poems, 1973; The Avignon Quintet: Monsieur, or the Prince of Darkness, 1974 (James Tait Black Memorial Prize), Livia or Buried Alive, 1978, Constance or Solitary Practices, 1982; Sebastian or Ruling Passions, 1983; Quinx or the Ripper's Tale, 1985; The Best of Antrobus, 1975; Selected Poems, 1976; Sicilian Carousel, 1976; The Greek Islands, 1978; Collected Poems, 1980; Smile in the Mind's Eye, 1980; Antrobus Complete, 1985; Caesar's Vast Ghost: aspects of Provence, 1990. *Recreation:* travel. *Address:* c/o Grindlay's Bank, 13 St James's Square, SW1.                    *Died* 7 *Nov.* 1990.

**DÜRRENMATT, Friedrich;** Swiss author and playwright; *b* Konolfingen, Switzerland, 5 Jan. 1921; *s* of Reinhold Dürrenmatt, pastor, and Hulda (*née* Zimmermann); *m* 1946, Lotti Geissler; one s two *d*; *m* 1984, Charlotte Kerr. *Educ:* Gymnasium, Bern; University of Bern; University of Zürich. Prix Italia, 1958; Schillerpreis, 1960; Grillparzer-Preis, Osterreichische Akademie der Wissenschaften, 1968; Grosser Literaturpreis der Stadt Bern, 1969; Osterreichischer Staatspreis für europäische Literatur, 1984; Bayerischer Literaturpreis, 1985; Premio Letterario Internationale Mondello, 1986; Georg-Büchner-Preis, Deutsche Akademie für Sprache und Dichtung, 1986; Ehrenpreis des Schiller-Gedächtnispreises, 1986; Ernst-Rober-Curtius-Preis für Essayistik, 1989. Hon DLitt, Temple Univ. Philadelphia, 1969; Dr (*hc*): Hebrew Univ. of Jerusalem, 1977; Univ. of Nice, 1977; Univ. of Neuchâtel, 1981; Univ. of Zürich, 1983. Buber-Rosenzweig Medaille, Frankfurt, 1977. *Films:* Es geschan am hellichten Tag, 1957; Der Richter und sein Henker, 1957. *Publications: plays:* Es steht geschrieben, 1947 (comedy version, as Die Wiedertäufer, 1967); Der Blinde, 1948; Romulus der Grosse, 1949; Die Ehe des Herrn Mississippi (The Marriage of Mr Mississippi), 1952 (produced New York, Fools Are Passing Through, 1958; filmed, 1961); Nächtliches Gespräch mit einem verachteten Menschen, 1952; Ein Engel kommt nach Babylon (An Angel Comes to Babylon), 1953 (opera version, music by Rudolf Kelterborn, 1977); Der Besuch der alten Dame, 1956 (The Visit, prod New York, 1958, London, 1960; Eng. trans. by Patrick Bowles, 1962; opera version, music by Gottfreid von Einem, 1971, filmed 1980); Frank V—Oper einer Privatbank, 1959 (filmed, 1966); Die Physiker, 1962 (The Physicists, prod Aldwych Theatre, London, 1963); Der Meteor, 1966 (The Meteor, prod Aldwych Theatre, London, 1966); König Johann, nach Shakespeare, 1968; Play Strindberg, 1969; Titus Andronicus, nach Shakespeare, 1970; Urfaust/Woyzeck, zwei Bearbeitungen, 1970–72; Porträt eines Planeten, 1970 (Portrait of a Planet, prod London, 1973); Der Mitmacher, 1973; Die Frist, 1977; Dichterdämmerung, 1980; Achterloo, 1983; (with Charlotte Kerr) Rollenspiele, 1986; Achterloo IV, 1988; *plays for radio:* Aus den Papieren eines Wärters; Der Doppelgänger; Der Prozess um des Esels Schatten; Nächtliches Gespräch mit einem verachteten Menschen; Stranitzky und der Nationalheld; Herkules und der Stall des Augias; Das Unternehmen der Wega; Die Panne (also Die Panne, Komödie, 1979, prod as The Deadly Game, Savoy, London, 1967); Abendstunde im Spätherbst; *essays and criticism:* Theaterprobleme, 1955; Vom Sinn der Dichtung in unserer Zeit, 1956; Friedrich Schiller, 1959; Theatre-Schriften und Reden, 1966; Israels Lebensrecht, 1967; Persönliches über Sprache, 1967; Tschechoslowakei, 1968; Monstervortrag über Gerechtigkeit und Recht, 1968; Sätze aus Amerika, 1970; Dramaturgisches und Kritisches, 1972 (Eng. trans., Writings on Theatre and Drama, 1977); Gespräch mit Heinz Ludwig Arnold, 1976; Zusammenhänge: Essay über Israel, 1976; Der Mitmacher: ein Komplex, 1976; Über Toleranz, 1977; Dürrenmatt-Lesebuch, 1978; Albert Einstein, 1979; Nachgedanken, 1980; Stoffe I–III, 1981; Vorgedanken über die Wechselwirkung, 1982; Versuche, 1988; *novels/prose:* Die Falle/Pilatus, 1947; Der Nihilist, 1950; Der Hund, 1951; Der Tunnel, 1952; Die Stadt, 1952; Der Richter und sein Henker, 1950 (Eng. trans., by Therese Pol, The Judge and his Hangman, 1955; filmed, 1966); Griecke sucht Griechin, 1955 (Eng. trans., Once a Greek, 1966); Die Panne, 1956 (Eng. trans., by Eva H. Morreale, The Quarry, 1962); Mister X macht Ferien, 1957; Der Sturz, 1971; Abu Chanifa und Anan, 1976; Minotaurus, 1985 (trans., Minotaur, 1987); Justiz, 1985 (trans., The Execution of Justice, 1989); Der Auftrag, 1986 (trans., The Assignment, 1988); Durcheinandertal, 1989; *art:* Die Heimat im Plakat, 1963; Bilder und Zeichnungen, 1976; Das zeichnerische Werk/Oeuvres graphiques, 1985. *Recreations:* painting and astronomy. *Address:* Pertuis-du-Sault 34, Neuchâtel, Switzerland. *Died 14 Dec.* 1990.

**DUVAL, Sir Francis (John),** Kt 1977; CBE 1970; Chairman: Arafura Mining Co. Pty Ltd; Duval Pastoral Co. Pty Ltd; Dover Fisheries Pty Ltd; Duval and Co. (Japan); *b* Narrandera, NSW, Australia, 31 Aug. 1909; *s* of late Francis William Duval; *m* 1960, Chieko, *d* of late Isakichi Hanada. *Educ:* Chatswood High, NSW. Served War, 1939–45: Major AIF, ME, Ceylon, New Guinea and Japan. *Recreations:* golf, deep sea game fishing. *Address:* Churinga House, 1 Old Beach Road, Old Beach, Tasmania 7402, Australia. *T:* Hobart 49–1155. *Clubs:* Royal Automobile, Imperial Service, Australian Jockey (Sydney); Commonwealth (Canberra); Tokyo (Tokyo, Japan). *Died 31 May* 1981.

**DWYER, Most Rev. George Patrick,** MA, DD, PhD; former Archbishop of Birmingham; *b* 25 Sept. 1908; *s* of John William and Ima Dwyer. *Educ:* St Bede's Coll., Manchester; Ven. English Coll., Rome; Christ's Coll., Cambridge. PhD 1929, DD 1934, Gregorian Univ., Rome; ordained Priest, 1932; BA Mod. and Med. Lang. Trip. Cambridge (Lady Margaret Scholar, Christ's Coll.). Teaching, St Bede's, Manchester, 1937–47; Catholic Missionary Society, 1947; Editor of Catholic Gazette, 1947–51; Superior, Catholic Missionary Society, 1951–57; Bishop of Leeds, 1957–65; Archbishop of Birmingham, 1965–81; Apostolic Administrator, 1981–82. Pres., RC Bishops' Conference of England and Wales, 1976–79. Hon. Fellow, St Edmund's House, Univ. of Cambridge, 1980. Hon. DLitt:

Keele, 1979; Warwick, 1980. *Publications:* The Catholic Faith, 1954; Mary-Doctrine for Everyman (with Rev. T. Holland, DD), 1956. *Address:* St Paul's Convent, Selly Park, Birmingham B29 7LL. *Died 17 Sept.* 1987.

**DWYER, Air Vice-Marshal Michael Harington,** CB 1961; CBE 1955; retired; *b* 18 Sept. 1912; *s* of late M. H. Dwyer, Royal Garrison Artillery; *m* 1936, Barbara, *d* of late S. B. Freeman, CBE; one *s* one *d*. *Educ:* Oundle Sch. Entered RAF, 1931; served India, 1933–36; UK and NW Europe, 1939–45; Middle East, 1949–51; Air Officer Commanding No 62 Group, 1954–56; SASO No 3 Group, RAF, 1956–57; Student at Imperial Defence Coll., 1958; Air Officer Commanding No 3 Group, 1959–61; AOA, HQ Bomber Command, 1961–65; Regional Dir of Civil Defence, North-West Region, 1966–68. Chm., Harington Carpets, 1973–74. *Address:* Island House, Rambledown Lane, West Chiltington, Sussex. *Died 15 May* 1989.

**DYALL, Valentine;** actor; *b* 7 May 1908; *s* of late Franklin Dyall; *m* 1936, Marjorie Stonor (decd), *d* of Hon. Maurice Stonor; *m* 1940, Babette Holder (decd), adopted *d* of N. F. Holder; two *s*; *m* Kay Woodman; one *d*. *Educ:* Harrow; Christ Church, Oxford. Began acting career at the Old Vic, 1930 and continued regularly on the West End stage until 1938; subsequently mainly in films and broadcasting. First appeared in films, 1941, and has acted in numerous pictures. Took the role of The Man in Black in a radio series. *Publications:* Unsolved Mysteries, 1954; Famous Sea Tragedies, 1955; Flood of Mutiny, 1957. *Recreations:* fishing, golf. *Address:* c/o Essanay Ltd, 75 Hammersmith Road, W14 8UZ. *Died 24 June* 1985.

**DYBALL, Maj.-Gen. (Hon.) Antony John,** CBE 1970 (OBE 1966); MC 1945; TD; Director, Printers' Charitable Corporation, since 1979; *b* 10 July 1919; *s* of John Francis Dyball; *m* 1941, Elizabeth Margaret Siddle; one *d*. *Educ:* Downsend; Epsom College. London Irish Rifles (TA); joined Depot RUR, Armagh, 1939; 1st Bn RUR, part of 6th Airborne Div., NW Europe, 1945 (MC); Trng Major, RUR Depot at Ballymena, 1954–56; comd Queen's Univ. OTC, Belfast, 1956–58; Bde Major, 124 Inf. Bde (TA), 1958–60; CO, London Irish Rifles (TA), 1960–62; AAG, Middle East Comd, 1963–65; Bde Comdr, 107 Independent Inf. Bde (TA), 1965–67; Chief of Staff, HQ Northern Ireland, 1967–69, and Dep. Dir Ops, 1969–70 (acting Maj.-Gen.); Dep. Comdr, Northumberland District, 1970–73, retired; Hon. Maj.-Gen., 1973. *Recreations:* golf, racing. *Address:* 49 Palewell Park, East Sheen, SW14. *T:* 01–878 0394. *Died 12 Feb.* 1985.

**DYKE, Sir Derek William H.;** *see* Hart Dyke.

**DYKES BOWER, Sir John,** Kt 1968; CVO 1953; Hon. DMus Oxon, 1944; MA, MusB Cantab; Hon. RAM; FRCM; Hon. FRCO; Hon. FTCL; FRSCM; Hon. Secretary, Royal College of Organists, 1968–81; Organist of St Paul's Cathedral, 1936–67; *b* 13 Aug. 1905; 3rd *s* of late Ernest Dykes Bower, MD, Glos; unmarried. *Educ:* Cheltenham Coll.; Corpus Christi Coll., Cambridge (Organ Scholar; Hon. Fellow, 1980). John Stewart of Rannoch Scholar in Sacred Music, 1922–28; Organist and Master of the Choir of Truro Cathedral, 1926–29; Succentor, 1929; Organist of New Coll., Oxford, 1929–33; of Durham Cathedral, 1933–36; Conductor of the Oxford Harmonic Soc., 1930–33; Lecturer in Music at University of Durham, 1934; Fellow of Corpus Christi Coll., Cambridge, 1934–37; Associate Dir of Royal Sch. of Church Music, 1945–52; Pres., Incorporated Association of Organists, 1949–50; Pres. of the Royal College of Organists, 1960–62. Master, Worshipful Co. of Musicians, 1967–68. RAFVR 1940–45, with rank of Squadron Leader. *Address:* Ivor Newton House, Edward Road, Bromley, Kent BR1 3NQ. *Club:* Athenæum. *Died 29 May* 1981.

**DYSON, Edith Mary Beatrice,** OBE 1946; RRC 1948, Bar to RRC 1952; *b* 18 June 1900. *Educ:* Greenhead, Huddersfield. Student Nurse, Royal Free Hospital, London, 1919–24; joined Army Nursing Service, 1924, Germany (with the Army of Occupation, 1926), also India, Burma; served War of 1939–45, i/c nursing units Hong Kong; Prisoner of War, 1941–45; War Office, 1946–48; Col, Queen Alexandra's Royal Army Nursing Corps and Deputy Dir Army Nursing Services, 1951–52; retired 1952. *Died 14 Sept.* 1986.

**DYSON, Fred;** General Secretary, National Union of Dyers, Bleachers and Textile Workers, 1973–79; *b* 28 Sept. 1916; *s* of James Dyson and Jane Anne Dyson (née Ashwood); *m* 1946, Beatrice Lilian (née Goepel); one *d*. *Educ:* Nields Council School. MIWP. Served with RAFVR, 1940–46. Woollen Spinner, 1934–39 and 1946–53; National Union of Dyers, Bleachers and Textile Workers: Organiser, 1953; Work Study Officer, 1958; No 4 District Sec., Manchester Area, 1970; Asst Gen. Sec., 1972. Mem. TUC General Council, 1975–79. Member: Garment and Allied Industries Requirements Bd, 1976–79; Industrial Injuries Adv. Council, 1977–81; Central Arbitration Cttee, 1976–79; Industrial Disputes Tribunals, 1974–86; Council, British Textile Confedn, 1973–79; co-opted Mem., Northumberland Co. Highways and Transport Cttee, 1981–; Governor: Tweedmouth First Sch., 1981–; Tweedmouth Middle Sch., 1981–. *Recreations:* landscape painting, swimming. *Address:* 6 Lindisfarne Gardens, Berwick-upon-Tweed, Northumberland TD15 2YA. *T:* Berwick 2176. *Clubs:* Slaithwaite Working Men's (Slaithwaite); Shipley Trades Hall (Shipley); Lidgett Green Working Men's (Bradford).                    *Died* 24 *April* 1987.

**DYSON, Dr James,** FRS 1968; Deputy Chief Scientific Officer, National Physical Laboratory, 1975–76; retired 1976; *b* 10 Dec. 1914; *s* of George Dyson and Mary Grace (*née* Bateson); *m* 1st, Ena Lillian Turner (marr. diss. 1948); one *d*; 2nd, 1948, Marie Florence Chant (*d* 1967); 3rd 1975, Rosamund Pearl Greville Shuter. *Educ:* Queen Elizabeth Sch., Kirkby Lonsdale; Christ's Coll., Cambridge. BA 1936; MA 1960; ScD 1960. Student Apprentice, BT-H Co., Rugby, 1936–39; Research Engr, BT-H Co., Rugby, 1939–46; Consultant (Optics), AEI Research Lab., Aldermaston, 1946–63; Supt, Div. of Mech. and Optical Metrology, NPL, 1963–74. FInstP 1960; Hon. Fellow Royal Microscopical Soc., 1969. *Publications:* Interferometry, 1969; papers on applied optics in learned jls. *Recreations:* astronomy, mechanical occupations, music, people, deploring the motor-car and Women's Lib. *Address:* 6 Rectory Close, Tadley, Basingstoke, Hants RG26 6PH.

*Died* 22 *Jan.* 1990.

**DYSON, Richard George;** Director, Commonwealth Development Finance Co. Ltd, 1968–81; *b* 17 July 1909; 2nd *s* of late Charles Dyson and late Ellen Gwendoline Dyson (*née* Barrington-Ward), Huddersfield, Yorks; *m* 1940, Lorna Marion, *d* of late H. H. Elkin, Alexandria, Egypt, and Port Lincoln, Australia; four *s* (two *d* decd). *Educ:* Charterhouse (Sen. Schol.); Christ Church, Oxford (Open Classical Exhibn). MA 1st cl. Hons in Hon. Mods and Greats. Joined Barclays Bank Ltd, 1933; transf. to Barclays Bank DCO, 1936; served overseas in Egypt, Sudan and E Africa until 1945; apptd an Asst Gen. Manager, 1951, a Gen. Manager, 1959, a Vice-Chm., 1967, and the Dep. Chm., 1968–76 (Bank renamed Barclays Bank International Ltd, 1971); Dir, Barclays Bank Ltd, 1972–80; Dep. Chm., Antony Gibbs Holdings Ltd, 1976–80; Chm., Lombard Assoc., 1962–63. Vice-Pres. Council, Inst. of Bankers, 1974– (Mem. 1963–74, Dep. Chm. 1970, Pres. 1972–74); Governor: Sutton's Hosp. in Charterhouse, 1968–84; Charterhouse Sch., Godalming, 1968–84. FCIB(FIB 1960). *Recreations:* cricket, gardening. *Address:* Brickfields, Chobham, Surrey. *T:* Chobham 8150. *Clubs:* MCC; Free Foresters.                    *Died* 23 *Aug.* 1987.

# E

**EAGLESHAM, Eric John Ross,** MA, BEd, LLB; Professor of Education, Durham University, 1947–66, retired; Professor Emeritus, 1966; *b* 29 Oct. 1905; 3rd *s* of late Reverend David Eaglesham, Chapelknowe, Canonbie, Dumfriesshire; *m* 1957, Nancy, *yr d* of late J. F. Rintoul; three *s* one *d. Educ:* Dumfries Acad.; Edinburgh Univ., 1923–27, 1930–31. Asst Teacher, Gretna Sch., 1927–30; Asst Teacher, Lockerbie Academy, 1931–35; Lecturer, Education Dept, Manchester Univ., 1936–38; Master of Method, Jordanhill Training Centre, Glasgow, 1938–40; RAF, rank Flight Lieut, on planning staff of Air Ministry dealing with questions of International Law, 1941–42; Principal Master of Method, Jordanhill Training Centre, Glasgow, 1942–43; Depute Dir of Studies, Jordanhill Training Centre, 1944–46. *Publications:* From School Board to Local Authority, 1956; Morant on the March (Yearbook of Education), 1957; The Foundations of Twentieth Century Education in England, 1967; articles in various learned journals. *Address:* Westfield, Gelt Road, Brampton, Cumbria CA8 1QH.                                                             *Died* 22 *Sept.* 1988.

**EAGLETON, Guy Tryon;** *b* 1 July 1894; *s* of late John Eagleton and of Violet Marion Eagleton; *m* 1947, Amy Rubina Gothard (*d* 1987); no *c. Educ:* Aldenham Sch. Solicitor, 1919; Asst Clerk Haberdashers' Company, 1925; Clerk of the Haberdashers' Company, 1931–50, retired. *Address:* 10 Bradbourne Park Road, Sevenoaks, Kent TN13 2DD. *T:* Sevenoaks 454781. *Club:* Royal Blackheath Golf (Captain General, Sen. Past Captain).                                     *Died* 26 *Aug.* 1988.

**EAKER, Gen. Ira Clarence,** Hon. KCB 1945; Hon. KBE 1943; DSM, US Army (2 Oak Leaf Clusters), US Navy; DFC (Oak Leaf Cluster); Silver Star; Legion of Merit; Wright Brothers Trophy, 1977; Special Congressional Gold Medal, 1979; *b* Field Creek, Texas, 13 April 1896; *s* of Y. Y. Eaker and Dona Lee; *m* Ruth Huff Apperson; no *c. Educ:* South Eastern State Teachers' Coll., Durant, Okla; University of Southern California; Columbia Univ., 2nd Lieut of Infantry, Regular Army, 1917; Capt. 1920; Major, 1935; Lieut-Col (temp.) 1937; Lieut-Col 1940; Col (temp.), 1941; Brig.-Gen. (temp.) Jan. 1942; Maj.-Gen. (temp.) Sept. 1942; Lieut-Gen. (temp.) 1943; permanent Brig.-Gen. RA 1944; Gen. 1985. Served in Philippines, 1919–22; pilot of one of planes of Pan-American Flight round South America, 1926–27 (DFC); chief pilot of Airplane Question Mark on refuelling endurance flight, 1929, establishing a new world flight endurance record (Oak Leaf Cluster for DFC). In command of VIII Bomber Command in European Theatre of Operations, 1942; commanded Eighth Air Force, 1942–44 and also US Army Air Forces in UK, 1943–44; comd. Mediterranean Allied Air Forces in Italy, 1944; Dep. Comdg Gen. Army Air Forces and Chief of Air Staff, US, 1945–47; retired 1947. Vice-President: Hughes Tool Co., 1947–57; Douglas Aircraft, 1957–61. Founding Pres., US Strategic Inst., 1972 (Vice-Chm., 1974). Author, syndicated weekly column on subjects in nat. security area, 1962–. DSM 1981, awarded by USAF for exceptionally meritorious service, 1957–81. French Legion of Honour (Grand Officer) and many other foreign decorations. *Publications:* (with Gen. Arnold): Army Flyer, This Flying Game, Winged Warfare. *Address:* 2202 Decatur Place NW, Washington, DC 20008, USA.                                 *Died* 6 *Aug.* 1987.

**EARLE, Air Chief Marshal Sir Alfred,** GBE 1966 (KBE 1961; CBE 1946); CB 1956; *b* 1907; *s* of late Henry Henwood Earle, and Mary Winifred Earle, Beaworthy, Devon; *m* 1st, 1934, Phyllis Beatrice (*d* 1960), *o d* of W. J. Rice, Watford; one *s* one *d*; 2nd, 1961, Rosemary (*d* 1978), widow of Air Vice-Marshal F. J. St G. Braithwaite, and *d* of late G. Grinling Harris, Clifford's Inn; 3rd, 1979, Mrs Clare Newell, widow of Rev. Gp Captain Ivor Newell and *d* of Dr Thomas Yates, DD. *Educ:* Shebbear Coll., Beaworthy, Devon. Graduated from Royal Air Force Coll., Cranwell, 1929. Served in Bomber Squadrons in United Kingdom and Iraq and as instructor at RAF Sch. of Photography, 1930–38; psa 1939; Training Command, 1940; Air Ministry, in Directorate of Plans, 1941–42; Comd No 428 RCAF Sqdn and stations in Bomber Comd, 1942–43; Offices of War Cabinet and Minister of Defence (attended Cairo and Yalta Confs), 1943–45; AOC No 300 Transport Grp (Austr.) and No 232 Transport Grp (Far East), 1945–46; Directing Staff, RAF Staff Coll., 1946–49; idc 1950; Comd RAAF Staff Coll., 1951–53; Air Ministry, Dir of Policy (Air Staff), 1954; Asst Chief of Air Staff (Policy), 1955–57; AOC No 13 Group, 1957–59; Deputy Chief of Defence Staff, 1960–62; AOC-in-C, Technical Training Command, 1962–64; Vice-Chief of Defence Staff, 1964–66; retd 1966; Dir Gen. of Intelligence, Min. of Defence, 1966–68. Chm., Waveney DC, 1974–76. *Recreation:* gardening. *Address:* 3 Buttermere Gardens, Alresford, Hants. *Club:* Royal Air Force.

*Died* 27 *March* 1990.

**EARLE, Lt-Col Charles,** DSO 1945; OBE 1943; jssc; psc; *b* 23 Nov. 1913; *s* of late Col Maxwell Earle, CB, CMG, DSO; *m* 1st, 1939, Marguerite (marr. diss., 1956), 2nd *d* of Herbert Carver; one *s* two *d*; 2nd, 1957, Fenella, *o d* of late H. C. Whitehouse. *Educ:*

---

Wellington; RMC. Grenadier Guards, 1933; Lt-Col 1953, Retired 1958. Sec.-Gen., Internat. Cargo Handling Assoc., 1961–72. Served War of 1939–45 in NW Europe, Africa and Italy. Adjt RMA Sandhurst, 1948. Croix de Guerre with palm, France, 1943. *Address:* Elliscombe House Nursing Home, Holton, near Wincanton, Somerset BA9 8EA.                                     *Died* 22 *March* 1989.

**EASSON, Rt. Rev. Edward Frederick;** *b* 29 July 1905; *s* of Edward Easson and Ada Jessie Easson (*née* Betsworth); *m* 1937, Mary Forbes Macdonald; two *s. Educ:* Morgan Academy, Dundee; St Andrews Univ.; Edinburgh Theological College. Maths and Science Master at Lasswade Secondary School, 1929–31; Assistant Curate of St Peter's, Lutton Place, 1933–36, with charge of St Aidan's, Craigmillar, 1936–39; Rector of St Peter's, Peterhead, and Chaplain to HM Prison, 1940–48; Diocesan Inspector of Schools, 1945–55; Canon of St Andrew's Cathedral, Aberdeen, 1946; Rector of St Devenick's, Bieldside, 1948–56; Dean of Aberdeen and Orkney, 1953–56; Bishop of Aberdeen and Orkney, 1956–72. Hon. DD St Andrews, 1962. *Address:* 25 Corbiehill Avenue, Davidsons Mains, Edinburgh EH4 5DX.                                    *Died* 11 *Feb.* 1988.

**EASSON, Prof. Eric Craig,** CBE 1978; FRCPGlas, FRCR; Hon. FFRRCSI; Director of Radiotherapy, Christie Hospital and Holt Radium Institute, Manchester, 1962–79; Professor of Radiation Therapeutics, University of Manchester, 1973–79, later Emeritus Professor; Consultant Adviser in Radiotherapy to Department of Health, 1974–79; *b* 28 Jan. 1915; *s* of William Easson and Helen (*née* Whitton); *m* 1938, Moira McKechnie Greig; two *s* one *d. Educ:* Glasgow Univ. (MB ChB 1938; MD 1958); MSc Manchester 1977. Served War, RAF, UK and SE Asia, 1939–45. Christie Hospital, 1946–79; Regional Advsr in Radiotherapy, NW RHA, 1962–79; Chm., Regional Adv. Cttee on Oncological Services, 1973–79. Past Mem. Council and Radiobiol. Sub-cttee, British Inst. of Radiology; Vice-Pres., Hon. Treas., Examiner and Mem. Council, Faculty of Radiologists, 1957–70; Knox Lectr, 1967; Pres., RCR, 1975–77; Mem., MRC Leukaemia Working Party, 1960–70; Mem./Chm. various WHO Expert Cttees on Cancer, 1962–74; Mem. Council and Exec. Cttee, Internat. Union Against Cancer and Chm., Cancer Control Commn, 1966–74; Mem. Council, Nat. Soc. for Cancer Relief; Hon. FFRRCSI 1976; Fellow: RSM; Manchester Med. Soc.; Hon. Fellow, Manchester Polytechnic, 1979. *Publications:* co-author, The Curability of Cancer in Various Sites, 1968; ed and co-author, Cancer of the Uterine Cervix, 1973; many papers, leading articles and chapters in learned jls and books in UK and abroad, all on various aspects of cancer. *Recreations:* bee-keeping, fly fishing, current affairs. *Address:* Sheriffmuir, 105 Buxton Old Road, Disley, via Stockport, Cheshire SK12 2BN. *T:* Disley 2541.

*Died* 18 *Oct.* 1983.

**EASTAUGH, Rt. Rev. Cyril;** *see* Easthaugh.

**EASTAUGH, Rt. Rev. John (Richard Gordon);** Bishop of Hereford, since 1973; *b* 11 March 1920; *s* of Gordon and Jessie Eastaugh; *m* 1963, Bridget Nicola, *y d* of Sir Hugh Chance, CBE; two *s* one *d. Educ:* Leeds Univ.; Mirfield. Curate of All Saints, Poplar, 1944; Rector: of W. Hackney, 1951; of Poplar, 1956; Commissary of Bp of Polynesia, 1962; Vicar of Heston, 1963; Archdeacon of Middlesex, 1966–73; Vicar of St Peter, Eaton Square, 1967–74. Sub Prelate, Order of St John, 1978–. *Recreations:* theatre, music. *Address:* Bishop's House, The Palace, Hereford HR4 9BN.

*Died* 16 *Feb.* 1990.

**EASTERBROOK, Prof. William Thomas James,** FRSC 1957; Professor of Economics, University of Toronto, Canada, 1956–77, then Professor Emeritus; Chairman, Department of Political Economy, University of Toronto, 1961–70; *b* 4 Dec. 1907; *s* of W. J. Easterbrook and Emily McKerr; *m* 1937, Dorothy Mary Walker; two *s* one *d. Educ:* Universities of Manitoba, Toronto, and Harvard. BA (Hon.) Manitoba, 1933; University of Toronto Sch. of Grad. Studies, 1933–36; MA 1935; Harvard Univ., 1936–37; PhD, University of Toronto, 1937. Dept Economics, Univ. of Manitoba, 1938–40 and 1942–47; Guggenheim Fellow, 1940–41; Research Associate, Research Center in Entrepreneurial History, Harvard Univ., 1949 (leave of absence from Toronto). Vice-Pres. Economic History Assoc. (US), 1959–61; Trustee, Business History Inc., 1959–; Mem. Research Cttee on Culture and Communications (Ford Foundation), 1953–55. Pitt Prof. of American History and Institutions, Cambridge Univ., 1955–56; Marshall Lecturer, University of Cambridge, 1956; Professorial Fellow of Jesus Coll. Cambridge, 1955–56; MA Cantab. 1956. Economic Adviser, Ministry of Economic Affairs and Develt Planning, Tanzania, 1966–67. LLD Manitoba, 1963. *Publications:* Agricultural Credit in Canada, 1937; Canadian Economic History (with H. Aitken), 1955; Approaches to Canadian Economic History (with M. H. Watkins), 1968; articles contrib. to Canadian Jl of Economics and Political Science, Jl of Economic History, American Economic Review, etc.; also to Canada (ed George Brown) UN Series, and The Progress of Underdeveloped Countries (ed B. Hoselitz). *Address:* 50 Prince

Arthur Avenue, Apt 1901, Toronto 5, Canada. *Club:* University Faculty (Toronto).                                     *Died* 27 *March* 1985.

**EASTHAUGH, Rt. Rev. Cyril,** MC 1917; MA (Oxon); *b* 22 Dec. 1897; *y s* of late Robert Wilgress Eastaugh; adopted spelling of Easthaugh, 1983; *m* 1948, Lady Laura Mary Palmer, *d* of 3rd Earl of Selborne, PC, CH; one *s* two *d*. *Educ:* Christ Church, Oxford; Cuddesdon College. Served European War, 1914–18, S Staffs Regt. Chaplain, Cuddesdon Coll., 1930–34; Vice-Principal, 1934–35; Vicar of St John the Divine, Kennington, 1935–49; Suffragan Bishop of Kensington, 1949–61; Bishop of Peterborough, 1961–72. Hon. Canon of Southwark, 1945; Proctor in Convocation, 1943. Chaplain and Sub-Prelate of the Order of St John of Jerusalem, 1961–. *Address:* Blackmoor House, Liss, Hants. *T:* Bordon 3777.
*Died* 16 *Dec.* 1988.

**EASTICK, Brig. Sir Thomas (Charles),** Kt 1970; CMG 1953; DSO 1942; ED 1939; CSS 1946; KCSA 1975; Chairman, Standing Committee, "Call to the People of Australia", 1951–54; President, El Alamein Group (SA), 1946–60; Chairman of Trustees, Poppy Day Fund (Inc.), 1950–77; President of Australia Day Council, S Australian Branch (Federal), 1962–65 and 1976–78; Chairman of Trustees, Services Cemeteries Trust; Deputy Chairman, World War II Fund; *b* 3 May 1900; *s* of Charles William Lone and Agnes Ann Eastick; *m* 1925, Ruby Sybil Bruce; five *s*. *Educ:* Goodwood Sch., Australia. Senior Cadets, 1914–18; Citizen Forces, 1918 (Artillery); Lieut 1922, Capt. 1926, Major 1930, Lieut-Col 1939. Served War of 1939–45 (despatches, ED, DSO); raised and commanded 2/7 Aust. Fd Regt 1940–43; Middle East, Alamein; Brig., CRA 7 Aust. Div., 1943; CRA 9 Aust. Div., 1944; Comdr Kuching Force, 1945; took Japanese surrender and relieved Kuching Prisoner Compound; administered comd 9 Aust. Div., Dec. 1945–Feb. 1946, when Div. disbanded. Hon. ADC to Governor-Gen. of Australia, 1950–53; Mem., Betting Control Board, 1954–65; State Pres. Returned Sailors, Soldiers and Airmen's Imperial League of Australia, S Australia, 1950–54–61–72; Comdr HQ Group Central Command, 1950–54. Pres., SA Womens Meml Playing Fields, 1954–80. Col Comdt, Royal Australian Artillery, 1955–60. Pres. Engine Reconditioners Assoc. of Austr., 1958–61. FAIM. Rotary Club of Adelaide Service Award, 1969–70. *Recreation:* photography. *Address:* c/o Dr B. C. Eastick, PO Box 163, Gawler, SA 5118, Australia.                                     *Died* 16 *Dec.* 1988.

**EASTON, Admiral Sir Ian,** KCB 1975; DSC 1946; Commandant, Royal College of Defence Studies, 1976–77; retired 1978; *b* 27 Nov. 1917; *s* of Walter Easton and Janet Elizabeth Rickard; *m* 1st, 1943, Shirley Townend White (marr. diss.); one *s* one *d*; 2nd, 1962, Margharetta Elizabeth Martinette Van Duyn de Sparwoude (marr. diss.); one *d*; 3rd, Irene Victoria Christensen; one *s* one *d*. *Educ:* The Grange, Crowborough; RNC, Dartmouth. Entered Royal Navy, 1931, and, as an actg Sub-Lt, qualified as a pilot, 1939. During War of 1939–45 served as pilot in HM Ships Glorious, Ark Royal and Formidable and as Direction Officer HMS Indefatigable; Comdr, 1952; Naval Staff Coll., 1953; on staff of BJSM, Washington, 1955–57; Staff Direction Officer, on Staff of Flag Officer Aircraft Carriers, 1957–59; JSSC, 1959; Captain, 1960; Asst Dir of Tactical and Weapons Policy Div., 1960–62; two years exchange service with RAN, in command of HMAS Watson, 1962–64; Naval Asst to Naval Member of Templer Cttee, 1965; Dir of Naval Tactical and Weapons Policy Div., 1966–68; Comdg Officer of HMS Triumph, Far East, 1968–69; Asst Chief of the Naval Staff (Policy), 1969–71; Flag Officer, Admiralty Interview Bd, 1971–73; Head of British Defence Staff and Defence Attaché, Washington, 1973–75. Dir, British Americas Cup Challenges, PLC, 1986–. *Recreations:* boats, books, gardening. *Address:* c/o Lloyds Bank, Freshwater, Isle of Wight. *Clubs:* Royal Thames Yacht; Royal Solent Yacht (Yarmouth, IoW).                                 *Died* 14 *June* 1989.

**EASTON, Air Cdre Sir James (Alfred),** KCMG 1956; CB 1952; CBE 1945; RAF retired; *b* 11 Feb. 1908; *s* of late W. C. Easton, Winchester; *m* 1st, 1939, Anna Mary (*d* 1977), *d* of Lieut-Col J. A. McKenna, Ottawa; one *s* one *d*; 2nd, 1980, Jane Walker, *d* of late Dr J. S. Leszynski and *widow* of Mr William M. Walker Jr, both of Detroit. *Educ:* Peter Symonds' Sch., Winchester; RAF Coll., Cranwell. Joined RAF 1928; served NWF India, 1929–32, Egypt, 1935–36, and Canada, 1937–39, as Air Armament Adviser to Dept of National Defence; despatches, 1940; Group Capt., 1941; Air Cdre, 1943; Dir in Air Staff Branch, Air Ministry, 1943–45, and then in RAF Delegation, Washington; retired, 1949; attached Foreign Office, 1954–58; HM Consul-Gen., Detroit, 1958–68. Res. Consultant on Trade Develt of Great Lakes Area, USA, 1968–71; Dep. Chm., Host Cttee for 1974 World Energy Conf., 1972–75; Associate Mem., Overseas Advisory Associates Inc., Detroit, 1975–82. Officer, Legion of Merit (US). *Publication:* The Transportation of Freight in the Year 2000, 1970. *Recreations:* travel and travel literature, gardening, golf. *Address:* 390 Chalfonte Avenue, Grosse Pointe Farms, Mich 48236, USA. *Clubs:* Royal Air Force; Country, Detroit; Grosse Pointe (Detroit).
*Died* 19 *Oct.* 1990.

**EASTWOOD, Christopher Gilbert,** CMG 1947; Assistant Under-Secretary of State, Colonial Office, 1947–52, and 1954–66; *b* 21 April 1905; *s* of late W. Seymour Eastwood, West Stoke House, Chichester, and Cecil Emma Eastwood; *m* 1934, Catherine Emma, *d* of late John Douglas Peel, Stonesfield Manor, near Oxford; one *s* three *d*. *Educ:* Eton (Schol.); Trinity Coll., Oxford. Entered Home Civil Service, 1927; appointed to Colonial Office; Private Sec. to High Commissioner for Palestine, 1932–34; Sec. of International Rubber Regulation Cttee, 1934; Private Sec. to Lord Lloyd and Lord Moyne when Secs of State for Colonies, 1940–41. Prin. Asst Sec. Cabinet Office, 1945–47; Commissioner of Crown Lands, 1952–54. *Address:* Stonesfield Manor, Oxford OX7 2PT. *T:* Stonesfield 222.
*Died* 14 *Oct.* 1983.

**EASTWOOD, Sir Eric,** Kt 1973; CBE 1962; FRS 1968; Consultant, GEC-Hirst Research Centre, from 1974; *b* 12 March 1910; *s* of George Eastwood and Eda (*née* Brooks); *m* 1937, Edith (*née* Butterworth); two *s*. *Educ:* Oldham High Sch.; Manchester Univ.; Christ's Coll., Cambridge, PhD 1935; MSc 1932; FIEE 1951 (Pres., IEE, 1972–73); FInstP 1968. Academic work, 1936–41. Sqdn Ldr, RAF, 1941–46 (despatches). Head of Radiation Laboratory, NelsonResearch Lab., English Electric Co., 1946–48; Dep. Dir of Research, Marconi Wireless Telegraph Co., 1948–54; Dir, 1954–62. Dir of Research, English Electric, 1962–68; Dir of Research, General Electric-English Electric Companies, 1968–74. Consultant, GEC-Marconi Electronics Ltd, 1974–81. Mem., SRC, 1968–74. Hon. DSc: Exeter, 1969; Cranfield, 1971; Aston, 1975; City, 1976; Heriot-Watt, 1977; Hon. DTech Loughborough, 1970; Hon. FUMIST, 1971; Hon. FIEE, 1979. Wakefield Medal, RAeS, 1961; Glazebrook Medal, Inst. of Physics and Physical Soc., 1970; Sir James Alfred Ewing Medal, ICE, 1976. *Publications:* Radar Ornithology, 1967; various papers on spectroscopy, radar techniques, radar meteorology, radar ornithology in Proc. Physical Soc., Proc. Royal Society, Nature, etc. *Recreation:* music ('cello). *Address:* 5 The Ryefield, Little Baddow, Danbury, Essex. *T:* Danbury 3240.                                     *Died* 6 *Oct.* 1981.

**EASTWOOD, Major Sir Geoffrey (Hugh),** KCVO 1965 (CVO 1956); CBE 1945; *b* 17 May 1895; *s* of late John Edmund Eastwood. Served 1914–19, 3rd King's Own Hussars. Hon. Attaché, Brit. Emb., Paris, 1919–21; Clerk and Prin. Clerk, House of Lords, 1924–58. Comptroller to Gov.-Gen. of Canada, 1941–46; Comptroller to the Princess Royal, 1959–65; Extra Equerry to the Queen, 1965; Chief Steward, Hampton Court Palace, 1970–75. *Address:* Wilderness House, Hampton Court Palace, Surrey. *T:* 01-977 5550. *Clubs:* Brooks's, MCC.                                     *Died* 1 *Aug.* 1983.

**EATON, Vice-Adm. Sir John (Willson Musgrave),** KBE 1956; CB 1953; DSO 1941; DSC 1941; RN retired; *b* Nov. 1902; 2nd *s* of Dr Walter Musgrave Eaton and Margaret Emily (*née* Ibbetson); *m* 1945, Cynthia Mary Hurlstone, *widow* of Major Gerald Tatchell, The Royal Lincolnshire Regiment; (two *step-d*). *Educ:* Temple Grove, Eastbourne; RNC Osborne and RNC Dartmouth. HMS Barham, Midshipman, 1919–21; HM Destroyers, 1922–25; HM Submarines, 1925–28; HMS Malaya, 1928–30; HM Destroyers, 1930–38; Student RN Staff Coll., 1939; HM Destroyers, 1939–43; HMS Sheffield, 1945; HMS St Vincent, 1946–48; idc, 1948–49; Dir of RN Staff Coll., Greenwich, 1949–51; Flag Officer Commanding HM Australian Fleet, Oct. 1951–53; Flag Officer Commanding Reserve Fleet, 1954–55; C-in-C America and West Indies Station, 1955–56; Dep. Supreme Allied Comdr Atlantic, Oct. 1955–Dec. 1957. *Recreations:* golf, shooting. *Address:* Dolphins, Church Street, Kelvedon, Essex CO5 9AH. *T:* Kelvedon 283.
*Died* 21 *July* 1981.

**EBOO PIRBHAI, Diwan Sir,** Kt 1952; OBE 1946; Director of Companies; *b* 25 July 1905; *m* 1925, Kulsambai; two *s* three *d* (and one *s* decd). *Educ:* Duke of Gloucester Sch., Nairobi. Representative of HH The Aga Khan. Member, Nairobi City Council, 1938–43. MLC Kenya, 1952–60; Member of various other official bodies; Past President Central Muslim Association; Chm., HH Prince Aga Khan Shia Imami Ismaili Leader's Internat. Council, 1987–. Given title of Count, 1954 and title of Diwan, 1983, both created by HH The Aga Khan. Brilliant Star of Zanzibar, 1956; Order of Crescent Cross of the Comores, 1966. *Address:* PO Box 40898, Nairobi, Kenya. *T:* (home) 767133; (office) 338177. *Clubs:* Reform, Lansdowne, Commonwealth Trust; Nairobi, Muthaiga (Kenya).
*Died* 4 *Jan.* 1990.

**ECCLESHARE, Colin Forster;** publisher; formerly London Manager, Cambridge University Press; Founder Member, PuMA (Publishers Management Advisers), since 1984; *b* 2 May 1916; *yr s* of Albert and Mary Alice Eccleshare, Derby; *m* 1942, Elizabeth, *e d* of late H. S. Bennett, FBA, and Joan Bennett; one *s* two *d* (and one *d* decd). *Educ:* Bemrose Sch., Derby; St Catharine's Coll., Cambridge (MA). Joined Cambridge Univ. Press, 1939. War Service, 1940–46; commissioned RE; Captain Survey Directorate, War Office, 1944; Major, HQ, ALFSEA, 1945. Rejoined Cambridge Univ. Press, 1946; Asst London Manager, 1948; London Manager, 1963–72; Dir

Group Projects, 1972–77. Publishing Consultant, British Library, 1977. Acting Sec., Athlone Press, Univ. of London, 1978–79. Director: Educational Associates Ltd (Hong Kong); John Wiley & Sons Ltd, 1979–85. Mem. Council, Publishers Assoc., 1965–71; Treasurer, 1971–73; Pres., 1973–75; Vice Pres., 1975–77. Member: Publishers' Advisory Cttee, British Council, 1964–85; Bd, Book Development Council, 1968–70 and 1975–79 (Chm., 1975–77); Exec. and Internat. Cttees, Internat. Publishers' Assoc., 1975–77; Groupe des Editeurs du Livre de la CEE, 1973–75; Adv. Cttee, British Library Bibliographical Services Div., 1975–78; British Nat. Bibliography Res. Fund Cttee, 1978–85; UK Nat. Commn UNESCO, 1978–85; Chairman: Other-Media Cttee, Internat. Scientific, Technical and Medical Publishers, Soc. of Bookmen, 1977–80. Missions (for Publishers Assoc., BDC, Brit. Council) to: Hungary, USSR, 1964; Philippines, Japan, 1968; Pakistan, 1971; USSR, Australia, 1974; Saudi Arabia, 1976; Israel, 1977. *Publications:* The Society of Bookmen: an informal history, 1984; regular contributor to The Bookseller, 1950–62. *Address:* 4 Branch Hill, NW3. *T:* 01–794 3496; Tyddyn Pandy, Barmouth. *T:* Barmouth 280315. *Club:* Garrick. *Died* 11 *Dec.* 1989.

**EDDEN, Vice-Adm. Sir (William) Kaye,** KBE 1960 (OBE 1944); CB 1956; DL; *b* 27 Feb. 1905; *s* of late Major H. W. Edden, The Cameronians, and late Mrs H. W. Edden (*née* Neilson); *m* 1936, Isobel Sybil Pitman (*d* 1970), Bath, *g d* of Sir Isaac Pitman; one *s*. *Educ:* Royal Naval Colls, Osborne and Dartmouth. Comdr, 1938; Admiralty, 1938–40; served War of 1939–45: HMS London, 1941–42; Staff C-in-C, Eastern Fleet, 1942–44 (OBE); Capt. 1944, Admty, 1944–47; RNAS Yeovilton, 1947–49; Capt. (D) 6th Destroyer Sqdn, and HMS Battleaxe, 1949–51; Admiralty, 1951–53; Rear-Adm. 1954; Commandant, Jt-Services Staff Coll., Latimer, 1953–56; Flag Officer Commanding Fifth Cruiser Sqdn and Flag Officer Second-in-Command, Far East Station, 1956–57; Vice-Adm. 1957; Admiral Commanding Reserves, 1958–60, retd 1960. DL West Sussex, 1977. *Address:* Littlecroft, Old Bosham, West Sussex PO18 8LR. *T:* Bosham (0243) 573119. *Club:* Army and Navy. *Died* 14 *Sept.* 1990.

**EDDIE, Sir George (Brand),** Kt 1966; OBE 1948; JP; retired; *b* 14 Nov. 1893; *s* of William and Jessie Eddie, Banchory, Kincardineshire; *m* 1926, Mary, *d* of George Ferguson, Glasgow; one *s* two *d*. *Educ:* Banchory. Secretary/Agent, Blackburn Trades Council and Labour Party, 1920–60; Vice-Chm. and Chm., NW Regional Council of Labour Party, 1940–; Mem., Blackburn Town Council, 1927– (Leader, 1945–68). Freeman, Blackburn Co. Borough, 1960. JP Blackburn, 1946. DL Lancs, 1968–76. *Recreations:* golf, bowls, motoring. *Address:* 7A Billinge View, Tower Road, Blackburn, Lancs. *Died* 16 *Oct.* 1981.

**EDDISON, Rear-Adm. Talbot Leadam,** CB 1961; DSC 1945; *b* 10 June 1908; *e s* (*yr twin*) of late Edwin and Mrs Eddison (*née* Leadam); *m* 1932, Doris (*née* Mavrogordato); one *s* one *d*. *Educ:* Royal Naval Coll., Dartmouth. Entered Dartmouth 1922. Commodore, Royal Naval Barracks, Devonport, 1958–59; Rear-Adm. 1959; served as Vice-Naval Dep. to Supreme Allied Comdr Europe, 1959–62; retired, 1962. *Address:* 4 Halton Close, Bransgore, Christchurch, Dorset BH23 8HZ. *T:* Bransgore 72593. *Club:* Royal Commonwealth Society. *Died* 11 *April* 1983.

**EDEN, Edward Norman,** CB 1980; Consultant; Under Secretary, Metrology, Quality Assurance, Safety and Standards Division, Department of Trade, retired 1982; *b* 5 Nov. 1921; *o s* of late Edward Eden and late Eva Eunice Eden; *m* 1st, 1967, Madge Nina Savory (*d* 1969); 2nd, 1974, Norma Veronica Berringer. *Educ:* Bancroft's Sch.; University Coll. London (BSc(Eng), PhD). Served RN, 1941–46. Senior Scientific Officer, Min. of Fuel and Power, 1953, Senior Principal Scientific Officer 1965, DCSO 1967–71; Head, Fuel Policy Planning Unit, Min. of Technology, later DTI, 1969–71; Under Sec., Metrology, Quality Assurance, Safety and Standards Div., DTI, later Dept of Prices and Consumer Protection, later Dept of Trade, 1971–81. Chairman: Working Party on Metrological Control Systems, 1976–77; Cttee on Metrological Control of Equipment for Use for Trade, 1984–85; Adv. Council, BASEEFA, 1987–90. *Publications:* Report, Metrological Control Systems, 1977; Report, Metrological Control of Equipment for Use for Trade, 1985; articles in learned jls. *Recreations:* walking, bird watching, odd-jobbing. *Address:* 13 Allison Grove, Dulwich, SE21 7ER. *T:* 01–693 7267. *Died* 6 *April* 1990.

**EDGE, Sir Knowles,** 2nd Bt *cr* 1937; JP; *b* 31 Dec. 1905; *s* of Capt. Sir William Edge, 1st Bt, and Ada (*d* 1973), *d* of I. Ickringill, Keighley; *S* father, 1948; *m* 1932, Dorothea Eunice (*d* 1976) *y d* of Robert Walker, Newhaven, Conn, USA; one *s* (and one *s* decd). *Educ:* Bolton Sch.; Trinity Hall, Cambridge. Formerly Chm. and Man. Dir William Edge & Sons Ltd and assoc. cos. Contested Hillsborough Div. of Sheffield, 1950. Mem. of Bolton Town Council, 1931–58. Chm., British Federation of Music Festivals, 1951–76. Mem. Cttee of Management, Royal National Lifeboat Institution. JP Lancs 1955. *Recreation:* yacht cruising. *Heir:* s William Edge [*b* 5 Oct.

1936; *m* 1959, Avril Elizabeth Denson; two *s* two *d*]. *Address:* Fair Lawn, Fair Lawn Road, Lytham, Lancs. *Club:* Athenæum. *Died* 19 *March* 1984.

**EDGEWORTH-JOHNSTONE, Maj.-Gen. Ralph,** CBE 1947; *b* 23 Nov. 1893; *s* of Ralph William Johnstone; *m* 1933, Cecily Margaret Thorp. *Educ:* France and Germany. Enlisted Fort Garry Horse, 1914; served European War, 1914–18 (wounded twice); commissioned Royal North'd Fusiliers, 1915. Retired, 1938, to join Public Relations Directorate War Office; Asst Dir, Lieut-Col, 1940; Dep. Dir, Brig., 1944; Dir, Maj.-Gen., 1946–52. *Address:* c/o Lloyds Bank, 6 Pall Mall, SW1. *Died* 19 *June* 1990.

**EDMUNDS, Christopher Montague,** MusD; *b* 26 Nov. 1899; 2nd *s* of Charles Edmunds; *m* 1923, Kathleen, *d* of Arthur Vaughan-Jones; one *s* one *d*. *Educ:* King Edward VI Sch., Camp Hill, Birmingham; Birmingham Univ.; Manchester Univ.; Birmingham Sch. of Music. 1st Cl. Hons BMus Birmingham, 1922; MusD, Manchester, 1936. Theory Teacher and Dir of opera class, Birmingham Sch. of Music, 1928–45; Principal, Birmingham Sch. of Music, 1945–56; Fellow Birmingham Sch. of Music; Fellow Trinity Coll. of Music (Mem. Corp. and Examiner, 1940–78). *Publications:* compositions include: The Blue Harlequin (opera); chamber and orchestral music; vocal and instrumental music; Romance, 1946 (pianoforte and orchestral work, commissioned by BBC). *Recreation:* gardening. *Address:* Tanyard Cottage, Stonegate, Whixley, N Yorks YO5 8AS. *T:* Borough Bridge 330766. *Died* 2 *Jan.* 1990.

**EDWARDES JONES, Air Marshal (Retd) Sir (John) Humphrey,** KCB 1957 (CB 1954); CBE 1943; DFC 1940; AFC 1941; retired 1961; *b* 15 Aug. 1905; *s* of late G. M. Edwardes Jones, KC and G. R. Johnston; *m* 1935, Margaret Rose Graham; one *s* one *d*. *Educ:* Brighton Coll.; Pembroke Coll., Cambridge. Entered RAF, Sept. 1926; served in Egypt, 4 Flying Training Sch. and 208 Sqdn, 1930–35; Commanded: No 213 Fighter Sqdn, 1937–40; No 56 Op. Trg Unit, 1940; No 56 and 58 OTU's, 1941; Exeter Fighter Sector, 1942; No 323 Fighter Wing, Algiers, Nov. 1942; AOC, No 210 Group, Algiers, 1943; idc 1950; Dir of Plans, Air Ministry, 1951. Commandant, Sch. of Land/Air Warfare, RAF, Old Sarum, Wilts, 1955–57; Comdr-in-Chief, 2nd Tactical Air Force, and Comdr, 2nd Allied Tactical Air Force, 1957–61. Legion of Honour (French), 1946. *Recreation:* golf. *Address:* Old Marks, Holtye, Sussex TN8 7ED. *T:* Cowden 317. *Club:* Royal Air Force.
*Died* 19 *Jan.* 1987.

**EDWARDS, Brig. Arthur Bertie Duncan,** CBE 1943; MC; *b* 29 April 1898; *s* of Joseph Arthur Edwards, Portsmouth, and Rosa May Duncan, Isle of Wight; *m* 1925, Clara Elizabeth (*d* 1989), 3rd *c* of late Edmund Barkworth, JP, Seaton, Devon; three *s*. *Educ:* RMA Woolwich. 2nd Lieut RE 1916; Capt. 1926; Major 1935; Lt-Col 1942; Temp. Col 1943, Temp. Brig. 1943; Col 1945; Brig. 1949. Served France, 1917–18 (BWM and VM); India, 1918–19; Iraq, 1919–20 (MC, BGS with Iraq clasp); India, 1920–22; England, 1922–35; Malta, 1935–39; England, 1939–40; France, 1940 (despatches); Greece, 1940–41; Libya, 1941; CRE Eighth Army Troops Engineers, Libya and Egypt, 1941–42 (despatches twice, OBE, North African Star); Dep. Chief Engineer, N Delta Defences, Egypt, 1942; Chief Engineer, Malta, 1942–43 (CBE); Chief Engineer, British Troops in Egypt, 1943; No 13 CE Works (Construction), Middle East, 1943–44; Engineer Adviser, AA Command, England, 1944; Dep. Dir Works 21 Army Group BLA and BAOR, 1944–48 (despatches); Kt Comdr of Orange-Nassau with swords); Chief Engineer, Eastern Command, United Kingdom, 1948–51; retired, 1951. *Address:* c/o Lloyds Bank, 6 Pall Mall, SW1. *Died* 3 *Aug.* 1990.

**EDWARDS, Carl Johannes;** stained glass artist; *b* 15 Feb. 1914; *m* 1941, Kathleen Margaret Selina Morgan; two *d*. *Educ:* studied Art under James Hogan, RDI, and at various London Art Schs. Chief Designer Whitefriars Glass Works, 1948; resigned 1952. Governor Harrow Sch. of Art, 1949; Liveryman, Worshipful Company of Glaziers, 1949. Chief works in: Cairo Cathedral; Liverpool Cathedral; House of Lords; Lambeth Palace Chapel; Temple Church; Royal Air Force Church, St Clement Dane's; Portsmouth Cathedral; St David's Cathedral, Wales; Auckland Cathedral, NZ; Westminster Sch., and several works in concrete and glass for England and abroad. *Recreations:* golf and music. *Address:* The Glasshouse, 11 Lettice Street, Fulham, SW6 4EH. *T:* 01–736 3113; 36 Denman Drive South, NW11. *Clubs:* Challoner; Highgate Golf.
*Died* 17 *Jan.* 1985.

**EDWARDS, Geoffrey,** CEng, FICE, FRICS, MConsE, FASCE; Chairman, GEP International Ltd (formerly GEP Consulting Group), since 1966; Westfield Trust Ltd, since 1966; Principal, Edwards Newstead, since 1967; *b* 28 April 1917; *s* of Frank Edwards, boot and shoe manufr, and Gladys Evelyn, *d* of Joseph Downes, mining engr; *m* 1st, 1943, Barbara Henrietta Edwards (*d* 1959); no *c*; 2nd, 1960, Pauline Nancy (marr. diss. 1982; she *d* 1984), *d* of Walter James Edwards, boot and shoe manufr, and Anne Evelyn Gully; two *d*; 3rd, 1984, Joan Hibberd, PhD (marr. diss.

1986). *Educ:* private prep. sch.; St Brendan's Coll., Clifton, Bristol; Merchant Venturers/Bristol Univ. FRICS 1951; CEng, FICE 1956. Defence works, 1939–43; Civil Engr, BOAC, W Africa, 1943–45; various appts, BOAC, 1945–66, incl. Gen. Man. Properties and Services, and Mem. of Exec. Management. Dir and Dep. Chm., N Surrey Water Co., 1962–78; Dir and Dep. Chm., Sutton Dist Water Co., 1970–73; Chm., Thames Water Authority, 1978–83; Founder Chm., Surveyors Holdings Ltd, 1980–82; Mem., National Water Council, 1978–83. Chm., Westminster Chamber of Commerce, 1982–84; formerly Member: Council, RICS; Airport Engrg Bd, ICE; Council, Nat. Fedn of Housing Assocs. Freeman and Liveryman, City of London; Liveryman: Worshipful Co. of Plumbers; Worshipful Co. of Engineers. Founder Chm., World Airports Confs; broadcaster on airport subjects; Founder Chm., World Water Congresses. Underwriting name, Lloyd's of London. Former Steward, Henley Royal Regatta. *Publications:* papers, and contribs to technical jls on airport and water matters. *Recreations:* swimming, shooting, farming. *Address:* 402 Drake House, Dolphin Square, SW1V 3NN. *T:* 071–834 9929; Westbarn, Upton Cheyney Road, Wick, near Bristol BS15 5RJ. *T:* Abson (027582) 2212. *Clubs:* City Livery, Farmers'.                                      *Died* 13 *Aug.* 1990.

**EDWARDS, George,** FFARCS; Consulting Anæsthetist: St George's, General Lying-in (St Thomas'), Samaritan (St Mary's) and Queen Charlotte's Hospitals; *b* 14 Jan. 1901; *m* 1934, Jean Lilian Smith, MD; one *s*. *Educ:* Royal Grammar Sch., Worcester; St George's Hospital (Johnson Anatomy Prize). MRCS, LRCP 1926; DA, RCP and S 1936; FFARCS 1948. Sen. Anaesthetist, 1931, later Hd, Dept of Anaesthetics, St George's Hosp.; retired 1972. RAMC, 1941–44; Lt-Col. Adviser in Anæsthetics, BNAF and CMF. Hon. Mem. (Pres. 1945–46), Sect. Anæsthetics, RSocMed. Mem. of Bd of Faculty of Anæsthetists, RCS, 1948–54; first Hewitt Lectr, RCS, 1950; first Snow Memorial Lectr, Assoc. of Anæsthetists, 1958. *Publications:* articles in medical journals. *Address:* Davenham, Graham Road, Malvern, Worcester WR14 2HY. *T:* Malvern 564338.                                              *Died* 8 *June* 1989.

**EDWARDS, Harold Clifford,** CBE 1945; MS, FRCS, FRCOG, FACS (Hon.); Honorary Colonel RAMC; Consulting Surgeon to King's College Hospital; Emeritus Lecturer, and Director, Department of Surgery, King's College Hospital Medical School, 1956–70, Fellow 1983; Surgeon to Royal Masonic Hospital, 1956–70; Consulting Surgeon to King Edward VII Hospital for Officers, 1956–70; St Saviour's Hospital; Consultant Adviser in Surgery to the Minister of Health, 1956–70; Surgeon Emeritus to the Evelina Hospital for Children; *b* 15 Aug. 1899; *s* of William Evans Edwards and Mary Selina Jones; *m* 1926, Ida Margaret Atkinson Phillips (*d* 1981); two *s*. *Educ:* University Coll., Cardiff; King's College Hospital, London. Served in Royal Engineers, 1917–19; entered University Coll., Cardiff, 1919; MRCS, LRCP, MB, BS 1923; FRCS 1926; MS London Univ., 1928; Hon. Surgeon to King's Coll. Hosp., 1928, and to Evelina Hosp. for Children, 1931; Robert Jones Gold Medal for an Essay upon Injuries to Muscles and Tendons, 1930, and Jacksonian Prize of RCS for a Dissertation on Diverticula of the Intestine, 1932; Hunterian Prof., RCS, 1934; Consulting Surg. Southern Comd, England, 1942–44; Consulting Surg., Central Mediterranean Forces, 1944–46; late Dean of King's College Hosp. Medical Sch. Past Master, Worshipful Soc. of Apothecaries. Mem. Court of Examiners, 1931–60, and Mem. Council, 1955–71, RCS (past Vice-Pres.). Examiner in Surgery, Univs of London, Cambridge, Wales, Birmingham, Dublin and Bristol. Chm., Armed Forces Adv. Cttee on Postgraduate Med. and Dental Officers, 1971–75; President: British Soc. of Gastroenterology, 1961; Assoc. of Surgeons of Gt Brit. and Ireland, 1962; FRCOG 1971; Hon. Fellow: American Surgical Assoc.; Assoc. of Surgeons of W Africa; Assoc. of Surgeons of West Indies; Mem. Académie de Chirurgie. Former Editor of GUT the British Jl of Gastro-enterology. Hon. Gold Medal, RCS, 1972; Eric Farquharson Award, RCSE, 1978. *Publications:* Surgical Emergencies in Children, 1935; Diverticula and Diverticulitis of the Intestine, 1939; Recent Advances in Surgery, 1954; papers in BMJ, Lancet, etc. *Recreation:* tapestry work. *Address:* 17 Grange Court, Pinehurst, Grange Road, Cambridge CB3 9BD. *T:* Cambridge 69512. *Club:* Athenæum.
                                                      *Died* 2 *Aug.* 1989.

**EDWARDS, Air Cdre Sir Hughie (Idwal),** VC 1941; KCMG 1974; CB 1959; DSO 1942; OBE 1947; DFC 1941; Governor of Western Australia, 1974–75; *b* W Australia, 1 Aug. 1914; *s* of late Hugh Edwards; *m* 1942, Cherry Kyrle (*d* 1966), widow of Flight Lieut H. R. A. Beresford; one *s* one *d*; *m* 1972, Mrs Dorothy Carew Berrick. *Educ:* Fremantle, W Australia. Joined Regular Australian Army, 1934; transferred to RAAF, 1935, to RAF, 1936. Served War of 1939–45, in European, Middle and Far East theatres (despatches, DFC, VC, DSO). Commandant, Central Fighter Establishment, 1958–60; ADC to the Queen, 1960–63; idc 1961; Dir of Estabts, Air Ministry, 1962–63, retd. Australian Representative, Selection Trust, 1964–74. KStJ 1974. *Recreations:* squash, cricket. *Address:* 21B Ranelagh, 3 Darling Point Road, Darling Point, NSW 2027,

Australia. *Clubs:* White's, MCC; Union, Imperial Service, Australian Jockey (Sydney).                          *Died* 5 *Aug.* 1982.

**EDWARDS, James Keith O'Neill, (Jimmy Edwards),** DFC 1945; MA (Cantab); MFH; *b* 23 March 1920; *s* of late Prof. R. W. K. Edwards and late Mrs P. K. Edwards; *m* 1958, Valerie Seymour (marr. diss. 1969). *Educ:* St Paul's Cathedral Choir Sch.; King's Coll. Sch., Wimbledon; St John's Coll., Cambridge. Served War of 1939–45, in RAF, 1940–46. Windmill Theatre, London, 1946; Adelphi Theatre, 1950–51, 1952–54, 1954–55 and 1960–61; *Radio and Television:* Take It From Here, BBC, 1948–59; Does The Team Think?, BBC, 1957–77; Whack-O!, BBC Television, 1957–61 and 1971–72; Seven Faces of Jim, 1961–62; Six More Faces of Jim, 1962–63; Bold as Brass, 1964; John Jorrocks, Esq., BBC-2, 1966; Fosset Saga, ATV, 1969; The Glums, LWT, 1979. *Films:* Three Men in a Boat, 1957; Bottoms Up, 1960; Nearly a Nasty Accident, 1961; The Plank, 1979; Rhubarb, 1980; It's Your Move, 1982. *Stage:* Big Bad Mouse, Shaftesbury, 1966–68, Prince of Wales, 1971; Halfway up the Tree, Queen's, 1968; Maid of the Mountains, Palace, 1972; Hulla Baloo, Criterion, 1972; Doctor in the House, 1978; Oh Sir James, 1979; Oliver!, Toronto, 1983. Lord Rector of Aberdeen Univ., 1951–54. *Publications:* Take It From Me, 1952; Oh Sir James (play), 1979; Six of the Best (Memoirs), 1984. *Recreations:* foxhunting, polo, flying, squash, brass bands. *Address:* Riven Oak, Mill Lane, Fletching, Uckfield, East Sussex TN22 3SR. *Club:* Savile.                                            *Died* 7 *July* 1988.

**EDWARDS, John;** Editor, Yorkshire Post, since 1969; *b* 2 Jan. 1932; *s* of late Arthur Leonard Edwards; *m* 1st, 1954, Nancy Woodcock (*d* 1978); one *s* one *d*; 2nd, 1979, Brenda Rankin; one *d*. *Educ:* Wolverhampton Municipal Grammar School. Entered journalism, Wolverhampton Chronicle; subseq. worked on newspapers and magazines in Fleet Street and provinces; from 1961, Yorkshire Post: Dep. Night Editor, Business Editor, Asst Editor and Dep. Editor. Dir, Yorkshire Post Newspapers Ltd. *Address:* 1 Edgerton Road, West Park, Leeds LS16 5JD.           *Died* 20 *March* 1989.

**EDWARDS, Sir John (Arthur),** Kt 1970; CBE 1953; President, London Rent Assessment Panel, 1968–73 (Vice-President, 1965–68); *b* 1 June 1901; *s* of late John Edwards, JP, and Mary Elizabeth Cromar, Rossett; *m* 1932, Dorothy Margaret, *y d* of late Sir Richard Williams, OBE, DL, JP, Bangor, North Wales; two *s*. *Educ:* Grove Park Sch., Wrexham. FRICS. Chartered Surveyor. Articles and various appointments as a Chartered Surveyor and Land Agent, 1919–28; joined Valuation Office, 1929; Dep. Chief Valuer, Valuation Office, Bd of Inland Revenue, 1950–65. *Recreation:* fishing. *Address:* 29 High Firs, Gills Hill, Radlett, Herts. *T:* 6550.
                                                      *Died* 25 *Aug.* 1983.

**EDWARDS, John Braham Scott,** MA (Oxon); **His Honour Judge John Edwards;** a Circuit Judge, since 1977; *b* Bristol, 29 March 1928; *s* of late Lewis Edwards and late Hilda Edwards (*née* Scott); *m* 1963, Veronica Mary, *d* of late Lt-Col Howard Dunbar (killed in action, 1942), and of Mrs Brodie Good; one *s* two *d*. *Educ:* Royal Masonic Schools, Bushey; Merton Coll., Oxford. National service, Army, 1946–48. Teaching Fellow, Univ. of Chicago Law Sch., 1952–53. Called to the Bar, Middle Temple, 1954; Bencher 1973; practised as barrister, London and Western Circuit, 1954–77; a Recorder of the Crown Court, 1972–77. Hon. Secretary-Gen. of Internat. Law Assoc., 1960–85. Churchwarden, St Anne's, Kew, 1973–83. *Recreations:* history, golf, gardening. *Address:* c/o Treasury, Middle Temple, EC4Y 9AT. *T:* (home) 01–940 8734. *Club:* Roehampton.
                                                      *Died* 9 *July* 1987.

**EDWARDS, Prof. Kenneth Charles,** CBE 1970; Professor of Geography in the University of Nottingham (first holder of the Chair), 1948–70, later Emeritus Professor; *b* 2 March 1904; *s* of C. W. Edwards, Southampton; *m* 1937, Barbara Joyce West, Southsea; no *c*. *Educ:* Itchen Grammar Sch.; University Coll., Southampton. Asst Lectr in Geography and Demonstrator in Geology, University Coll., Nottingham, 1927; Indep. Lecturer in Geography and Head of Dept of Geography, University Coll., Nottingham, 1934; Reader in Geography, 1939; seconded to Ministry of Town and Country Planning, as Regional Research Officer for East Midlands, 1944–46; Temp. appt as Acting-Head of Dept of Geography, University Coll., Auckland, NZ, 1951; Dean of Faculty of Law and Social Sciences, Univ. of Nottingham, 1958–61. Founder, and Chm., Editorial Cttee of the East Midland Geographer, 1954. President: Geographical Field Gp, 1946; Section E British Assoc. for the Advancement of Science, 1959; Inst. of British Geographers, 1960; Geographical Assoc., 1963. Visiting Prof., Makerere Univ. Coll., Uganda, 1963; Murchison Grant, RGS, 1964. Mem., East Midlands Economic Planning Council, Dept of Economic Affairs, 1966–72. Founder Mem. and Cttee, Univ. of Nottingham Club, 1952–80. Hon. Mem., Polish Geog. Soc., 1980. Order of the Crown of Oak, and Order of Merit, Grand Duchy of Luxembourg; Cross of the Order of the Restitution of Poland. *Publications:* Sweden; Dalarna Studies, 1940; The Land of Britain; Nottinghamshire, 1944; Luxembourg (NID), 1944; Studies in Regional Planning (ed. G. H.

J. Daysh); The East Midlands, 1949; (with F. A. Wells) A Survey of the Chesterfield Region, 1950; (with H. H. Swinnerton and R. H. Hall) The Peak District, 1962; Nottingham and its Region (ed), 1966; (co-organiser) Atlas du Luxembourg, 1971, rev. edn, 1980; various contribs and research papers to geog. periodicals; Editor, British Landscape Through Maps (Geog. Assoc.), 1960–79. *Recreations:* walking, including field excursions at home and abroad; music. *Address:* 24 Bramcote Drive, Beeston, Notts. *T:* 257309.

*Died 7 May 1982.*

**EDWARDS, Rt Rev. Lewis Mervyn C.;** *see* Charles-Edwards.

**EDWARDS, Sir Martin Llewellyn,** Kt 1974; DL; Solicitor; Consultant with Edwards, Geldard & Shepherd, Cardiff; *b* 21 May 1909; *s* of Charles Ernest Edwards, Solicitor, and Annie Matilda Edwards (*née* Llewellyn); *m* 1936, Dorothy Ward Harrap; one *s* two *d* (and one *d* decd). *Educ:* Marlborough Coll.; Lincoln Coll., Oxford (MA). Admitted Solicitor, 1934. Commnd in RAuxAF, 1937; served 614 (Glamorgan Sqdn RAuxAF, UK), 1937–41; 241 Sqdn, 1941–42; RAF Staff Coll., 1942; Wing Comdr Desert Air Force, HQ Iraq, Persia, and Air Defences Eastern Med., 1942–43; Mem. Directing Staff, ME Jt Staff Coll., Haifa, 1944; Station Comdr, RAF Amman, 1944–45. Mem. Council and Gen. Purposes and Finance Cttees, Glamorgan T&AFA, 1946–68 (Vice-Chm., Air, 1961–68). Mem. Council, Law Society, 1957 (Vice-Pres. 1972–73, Pres., 1973–74; Chm., Educn and Trng Cttee, 1966–69). Pres., Associated Law Socs of Wales, 1960–62; Pres., Incorporated Law Soc. for Cardiff and District, 1969–70. Member: Lord Chancellor's Cttee on Legal Educn, 1967–71. Council, UWIST, 1969–79; Drinking and Driving Cttee, DoE, 1974–76; part-time Chm., Industrial Tribunals, 1975–78. Governor, Coll. of Law, 1967–80 (Chm. of Governors, 1969–72). DL Glamorgan, 1961. *Recreations:* walking, gardening, photography. *Address:* Pentwyn Farm, Graig Llwyn Road, Lisvane, Cardiff CF4 5RP. *T:* Cardiff 751813. *Club:* Army and Navy.

*Died 20 June 1987.*

**EDWARDS, Richard Lionel,** QC 1952; *b* 1 Aug. 1907; *s* of late Lionel T. Edwards, BA, JP, Weston Underwood, Olney, Bucks; *m* 1944, Eleanor Middleton, *d* of late Sir Henry Japp, KBE; no *c*. *Educ:* Rugby Sch.; Oriel Coll., Oxford. Called to English Bar, 1930; Bencher of Lincoln's Inn, 1957. *Recreations:* gardening, Italian painting and fishing. *Address:* Weston Underwood, Olney, Bucks. *T:* Bedford 711312.

*Died 31 May 1984.*

**EDWARDS, Robert;** National Officer of Transport and General Workers' Union, 1971–76; *b* 16 Jan. 1905; *m* 1933, Edith May Sandham (*d* 1970); one *s*. *Educ:* Council Schs and Technical Coll. Served with Republicans in Spain during Spanish civil war. Chm. delegns to Russia, 1926 and 1934. Mem. Liverpool City Council, 1929–32; Nat. Chm., ILP, 1943–48; Founder Pres., Socialist Movement for United States of Europe. Gen. Sec., Chemical Workers' Union, 1947–71; Chm., Chem. Section, ICF, 1971–76; Vice-President: British Section European League for Economic Co-operation; Economic Research Council. Contested (ILP) Chorley 1935, Stretford 1939 and Newport 1945. MP (Lab and Co-op): Bilston, 1955–74; Wolverhampton SE, 1974–87. Vice-Pres., Council of Europe, 1969–70; Dep. Leader, British Delgn to Council of Europe, and Chm., Defence Cttee, WEU Assembly, 1968–72; Leader, British Delegn, N Atlantic Assembly, 1968–69. Pres., Industrial Common Ownership Movement, 1970–87; Chm., Parly Gp for Industrial Common Ownership, 1976–87; Mem., European Parlt, 1977–79; Life Hon. Associate, Parly Assembly of Council of Europe, 1989. Editor, The Chemical Worker. Trustee, Scott Bader Commonwealth, 1969–79. Hon. Fellow, Wolverhampton Polytechnic, 1986. *Publications:* Chemicals—Servant or Master, 1947; Study of a Master Spy, 1962; Multinationals and the Trade Unions, 1978; One Year in the European Parliament, 1979. *Address:* 2 Sheerwater Road, Woking, Surrey GU21 5TT.

*Died 4 June 1990.*

**EDWARDS-MOSS, Sir John (Herbert Theodore),** 4th Bt *cr* 1868; *b* 24 June 1913; *s* of late Major John Edwards-Moss and Dorothy Kate Gwyllyam, *e d* of late Ven. Henry William Watkins, DD; *S* uncle, Sir Thomas Edwards-Moss, 3rd Bt, 1960; *m* 1951, Jane Rebie, *d* of Carteret John Kempson; five *s* one *d*. *Educ:* Downhouse, Rottingdean. *Heir:* *s* David John Edwards-Moss, *b* 2 Feb. 1955. *Address:* Ruffold Farm, Cranleigh, Surrey.

*Died 28 Dec. 1988.*

**EGAN, Dr Harold;** Government Chemist, 1970–81; *b* 23 Dec. 1922; *o s* of late Silas Henry Egan and Jenny Egan (*née* Vanner); *m* 1948, Daphne Marian Downing Cleeland; one *s*. *Educ:* Chiswick County Sch.; Acton Technical Coll.; Imperial Coll. London. BSc, PhD, DIC. St George's Hosp., London (Biochemical Dept), 1940–43; Dept (later Laboratory) of the Government Chemist, 1943–. Visiting Professor: Food Science, Queen Elizabeth Coll., Univ. of London, 1973–77; Chem. Scis, UEA, 1980–; Chem. of the Environment, KCL, 1980–. Member: British Hallmarking Council; ICSU Scientific Cttee on Problems of the Envt, 1979–82; Sec., CHEMRAWN (chemical research applied to world needs) Cttee,

Internat. Union of Pure and Applied Chemistry, 1979–; Pres., Internat. Acad. of Environmental Safety, 1980–81. FRSC, FRSH, FIFST, FRNS. *Publications:* various papers on trace analysis, particularly pesticide residues and other environmental contaminants. *Recreations:* maps, books on London, Home Counties. *Address:* 5 Highland Road, Amersham, Bucks HP7 9AP. *T:* Amersham 28629. *Died 29 June 1984.*

**EISENHOWER, Milton Stover;** President, The Johns Hopkins University, 1956–67, 1971–72, now President Emeritus; *b* 15 Sept. 1899; *s* of David Jacob and Ida Stover Eisenhower; *m* 1927, Helen Elsie Eakin (decd); one *s* one *d*. *Educ:* Kansas State Univ. (BS); Univ. of Edinburgh. City Ed., Abilene (Kan.) Daily Reflector, 1918 and 1920–21; Asst Prof. Journalism, Kansas State Univ., 1924; Amer. Vice-Consul, Edinburgh, 1924–26; Asst to Sec. of Agric., 1926–28; Dir Inf., US Dept of Agric., 1928–41, Land Use Co-ordinator, 1937–42; Dir, War Relocation Authority, 1942; Assoc. Dir, Office of War Inf., 1942–43; Pres., Kansas State Univ., 1943–50; Pres., Pennsylvania State Univ., 1950–56. Mem. Fact-finding Board in Gen. Motors labor-management dispute, 1945; Famine Emergency Relief Ctee, 1946; Exec. Bd Unesco, 1946; President's Cttee on Government Organisation, 1953–60; Nat. Advisory Cttee on Inter-American Affairs, 1960; Special Ambassador and Personal Rep. of US Pres., on Latin Amer. Affairs, 1953, 1957, 1958, 1959, 1960; Chm., US Nat. Commn for Unesco, 1946–48; Deleg., Unesco Confs, 1946–47–48–49. Mem., President's Commn on Higher Educn, 1946; Problems and Policies Cttee, Amer. Council on Educn, 1950–53; Exec. Cttee, Assoc. Land-Grant Colls and Univs, 1944–47, 1950–53, Chm., 1946–47, 1952–53; Pres. Assoc., 1951–52. Chm. Nat. Cttee for The People Act, 1951–53; Director: Fund for Adult Educn, 1953–61; Freedoms Foundn Inc., 1951–; The Geisinger Memorial Hosp., 1952–; Mem., Atlantic-Pacific Interoceanic Canal Study Commn, 1965–70; Chairman, President's Commn on: Causes and Prevention of Violence, 1968–69; Internat. Radio Broadcasting, 1972–73. Also trusteeships, etc both past and present. Holds numerous hon. degrees (including LLD Johns Hopkins), foreign orders, etc. *Publications:* The Wine is Bitter, 1963; The President is Calling, 1974; ed many publications for US Dept of Agric.; articles for Scholar, Sat. Evening Post, Colliers, Country Gentlemen, etc. *Address:* Evergreen House, 4545 North Charles Street, Baltimore, Md 21210, USA. *T:* 338–7670. *Clubs:* Johns Hopkins, Elkridge (Baltimore).

*Died 2 May 1985.*

**EKIN, Maj.-Gen. Roger Gillies,** CIE 1946; IA, retired; *b* 18 Nov. 1895; *yr s* of T. C. Ekin, MInstCE; *m* 1st, 1923, Phyllis Marian (*d* 1967), *er d* of Maj.-Gen. Sir Henry Croker, KCB, CMG; one *s* two *d*; 2nd, 1972, Mona de Hamel (*d* 1979), *widow* of Etienne Bruno de Hamel. *Educ:* Westminster; RMC Sandhurst. First Commissioned, 1914; Palestine campaign, 1916–19; on Operations in Waziristan, 1920–21; Operations NWFP, 1930; Brevet Lt-Col 1936; Comdt 5th Bn FF Rifles, 1937–40; Comd Kohat Bde Ahmedzal Ops, 1940; Col 1939; Comdt Tactical Sch., India, 1940–41; Comd 46 Inf. Bde, Burma campaign, 1941–42; Nowshera Bde, 1942–45; Kohat (Independent) Bde, 1945–46. Despatches five times. GOC Bihar and Orissa Area, India, 1946–47; retired, 1947; Sec., Hereford Diocesan Board of Finance, 1947–61. *Address:* c/o Lloyds Bank, 6 Pall Mall, SW1Y 5NH. *Died 6 March 1990.*

**ELATH, Eliahu,** PhD; President Emeritus, Hebrew University, Jerusalem; Israeli diplomatist; Chairman, Board of Governors, Israel Afro-Asian Institute; *b* 30 July 1903; *s* of Menachem and Rivka Epstein (Elath); *m* 1931, Zehava Zalel. *Educ:* Hebrew Univ., Jerusalem; American Univ., Beirut, Lebanon. Reuter's Corresp. in Syria and Lebanon, 1931–34. Mem. Political Dept of Jewish Agency for Palestine in Jerusalem, 1934–45; Dir Political Office of Jewish Agency for Palestine in Washington, 1945–48; Special Representative of Provisional Govt of Israel in USA, 1948; Ambassador of Israel to USA, 1948–50; Minister of Israel, 1950–52, Ambassador, 1952–59, to the Court of St James's. Pres., Israel Oriental Soc. Vice-Pres., Jewish Colonization Assoc. (ICA). Hon. PhD: Brandeis; Wayn; Hebrew Union Coll.; Dropsie Coll., USA. *Publications:* The Bedouin, Their Customs and Manners, 1933; Trans-Jordan, 1934; Israel and her Neighbours, 1960; The Political Struggle for Inclusion of Elath in the Jewish State, 1967; San Francisco Diary, 1971; British Routes to India, 1971; Zionism and the Arabs, 1974; Zionism and the UN, 1977; The Struggle for Statehood, 1982; contribs to Quarterly of Palestine Exploration Fund, Jl of Royal Central Asian Society, Encyclopædia Britannica. *Address:* 17 Bialik Street, Beth Hakerem, Jerusalem, Israel. *T:* 524615. *Died 24 June 1990.*

**ELBORNE, Sydney Lipscomb,** MBE 1918; Chairman of Hunts Quarter Sessions, 1947–63; *b* 6 July 1890; *e s* of late William Elborne, MA, Wootton House, Peterborough; *m* 1925, Cavil Grace Mary (*d* 1984), *d* of late George E. Monckton, Fineshade Abbey, Northants; one *s* one *d*. *Educ:* King's Sch., Peterborough; Trinity Coll. Cambridge (MA). Asst Inspector of High Explosives (Technical), The Royal Arsenal, Woolwich, 1914–18; called to Bar, Inner

Temple, 1919; Mem. Midland Circuit; Mem. Gen. Council of the Bar, 1940–47; Asst Recorder of Birmingham, 1953. Mem. Hunts CC, 1930–45; JP Hunts, 1932. Pres. Soc. of Chairmen and Dep. Chm. of Quarter Sessions, 1955. Mem. Mr Justice Austen Jones's Cttee on County Court procedure, 1947; formerly Trustee and Mem. Council, Northants Record Soc.; formerly Trustee of Peterborough Museum Soc. and Maxwell Art Gallery; Mem. Area Cttee (No 11) Legal Aid, 1950–69. Contested (C) Leicester (Bosworth Div.), 1929 and Manchester (Ardwick), by-election, 1931. Formerly FGS, ARIC. *Address:* Water Newton, Peterborough. *T:* Peterborough 233223. *Club:* Carlton.                    *Died* 29 *Dec.* 1986.

**ELDER, Hugh**, MA; *b* 1905; *s* of late Rev. Hugh Elder, MA, Edinburgh; *m* 1939, Winifred Mary, *o d* of late Col M. Stagg, OBE, RE; one *s* (and one *s* decd). *Educ:* Edinburgh Academy; Edinburgh Univ. (Scholar); Corpus Christi Coll., Oxford. MA Hons Classics, Edinburgh, 1927; BA, Lit. Hum. 1929, MA 1934, Oxford. Asst Master at Sherborne Sch., 1929–35; Asst Master at Fettes Coll., 1935–38; Headmaster of Dean Close Sch., Cheltenham, 1938–46; Headmaster of Merchant Taylors' Sch., 1946–65. *Recreations:* music, golf. *Address:* Millbrook, Huish Episcopi, Langport, Somerset.                                       *Died* 7 *Feb.* 1986.

**ELDER-JONES, His Honour Thomas;** retired Circuit Judge (formerly Judge of County Courts), 1953–76; *b* 4 Oct. 1904; *o s* of late David Jones, JP, Foxcote Grange, Andoversford, shipowner, and late Anne Amelia (Roberts); *m* 1948, Hon. Diana Katherine Taylor (*née* Russell) (*d* 1978), *o d* of 25th Baron de Clifford; one adopted *d* one step *s*. *Educ:* Shrewsbury; Trinity Coll., Oxford (MA). Barrister-at-law, Inner Temple, 1927. Served 1939–43, 2nd Royal Gloucestershire Hussars, retired, rank of Hon. Major. Sec. National Reference Tribunal for Coal Mining Industry, 1943–53; Judge of County Courts Circuit 34 (Brentford and Uxbridge), 1953–57, Circuit 52 (Bath-Swindon), 1957–76. At Bar practised in Common Law and Coal Mining matters. *Recreation:* fox-hunting. *Address:* The Dower House, Somerford Keynes, Cirencester, Glos. *T:* Cirencester 861296.                                        *Died* 10 *Dec.* 1988.

**ELDIN-TAYLOR, Kenneth Roy,** CVO 1955; *b* 27 Sept. 1902; *s* of late Thomas Taylor, Welbourn, Lincoln; *m* 1st, 1926, Katharine Mary (*d* 1984), *er d* of late Frederick Ernest Taylor, FRCS, LRCP, Brancaster, Norfolk; three *s*; 2nd, 1985, Mrs Nellie Gladys Midgley (decd). *Educ:* Lincoln School; Selwyn College, Cambridge (MA, LLM, Exhibitioner and Univ. Squire Law Schol.). Called to the Bar, Lincoln's Inn, 1970. Solicitor for Affairs of HM Duchy of Lancaster, 1942–67; Chm., Industrial Appeals Tribunals, 1967–74; Sec., Diocesan Conf., 1966–68; former Member of Council, British Records Association; Chairman: Portsmouth Diocesan Parsonages Bd; Clergy Sustentation Fund. *Recreations:* literature, rowing, racing. *Address:* 5 Yardley Court, Milton Road, Harpenden, Herts. *T:* Harpenden (05827) 60164. *Clubs:* Leander; Royal Naval and Royal Albert Yacht (Portsmouth).          *Died* 28 *Sept.* 1990.

**ELDRIDGE, Lt-Gen. Sir John;** *see* Eldridge, Lt-Gen. Sir W. J.

**ELDRIDGE, Lt-Col William James,** OBE (mil.) 1944; DL; Vice Lord-Lieutenant, Isle of Wight, since 1986; *b* 14 Feb. 1917; *s* of R. J. Eldridge; *m* 1941, Joan Cecily, *d* of late F. W. Fidgeon and of D. M. Fidgeon; one *s* three *d*. *Educ:* Sherborne School. Served War, 2nd Lieut, Royal Hampshire Regt, 1940–41; various Staff appts until GSO1 (Ops): 10 Corps, 1944; AFHQ Greece, 1945–46. Solicitor (Partner), James Eldridge & Sons, IoW, 1947–83. *Recreation:* gardening. *Address:* Cypress Cottage, St John's Road, Newport, Isle of Wight. *T:* Newport 522722.

                                                *Died* 7 *April* 1987.

**ELDRIDGE, Lt-Gen. Sir (William) John,** KBE 1954 (CBE 1941); CB 1944; DSO 1919; MC; Chairman, Kearney and Trecker, CVA Ltd, 1957–68; *b* 2 March 1898; *s* of late William Henry Eldridge; *m* 1954, Violet Elizabeth (*d* 1956), *e d* of John Cane, Wrexham. 2nd Lieut RA 1915; served European War, France and Belgium, 1916–18 (wounded, despatches twice, DSO, MC); Iraq Operations, 1919–20; War of 1939–45 (despatches, CBE, Bar to DSO). Dir-Gen. of Artillery, Ministry of Supply, 1945–48; Comdt Mil. Coll. of Science, 1948–51; GOC Aldershot District, 1951–53; Controller of Munitions, Min. of Supply, 1953–57, retired. Col Comdt: RA, 1951–61; Glider Pilot Regt, Glider Pilot and Parachute Corps, 1951–57. *Address:* Mais House, 18 Hastings Road, Bexhill-on-Sea, Sussex. *Club:* Royal Air Force.              *Died* 3 *Nov.* 1985.

**ELEY, Sir Geoffrey (Cecil Ryves),** Kt 1964; CBE 1947; *b* 18 July 1904; *s* of late Charles Cuthbert Eley, JP, VMH, East Bergholt Place, Suffolk, and of Ethel Maxwell Eley (*née* Ryves); *m* 1937, Penelope Hughes, *d* of late Adm. Sir Frederick Wake-Walker, KCB, CBE; two *s* two *d*. *Educ:* Eton; Trinity Coll., Cambridge (BA 1925; MA 1933); Harvard Univ. (Davison Scholar), 1925–26. On Editorial Staff of Financial News, 1926–28; banking, finance and brokerage in England, France, Switzerland and the USA, 1928–32; London Manager of Post and Flagg, members of New York Stock Exchange, 1932–39; Naval Intelligence Div., Admiralty, 1939–40; Capital

Issues Cttee, 1940–41; Min. of Supply as Dir of Contracts in charge of Capital Assistance to Industry, 1941–46; Min. of Supply as Dir of Overseas Disposals, 1946–47. Mem., London Electricity Bd, 1949–59. Chairman: British Drug Houses Ltd, 1948–65; Richard Crittall Holdings Ltd, 1948–68; Dep. Chm. and Chm., Brush Group, 1953–58; Chairman: Richard Thomas & Baldwin's Ltd, 1959–64; Thomas Tilling Ltd, 1965–76 (Dir, 1950–76); Heinemann Group of Publishers Ltd, 1965–76; Dep. Chm., British Bank of the Middle East, 1952–77 (Dir, 1950–77); Vice-Chm., BOC International Ltd, 1964–76 (Dir, 1959–76); Director: Bank of England, 1949–66; Equity & Law Life Assurance Soc., 1948–80. Leader, UK Trade Mission to Egypt, Sudan and Ethiopia, 1955. Vice-Pres., Middle East Assoc., 1962–85. Member: Cttee, Royal UK Benevolent Assoc., 1957–85; Council, Friends of Tate Gall., 1977–85; Court, Univ. of Essex, 1967–85. High Sheriff, Co. of London, 1954–55; High Sheriff of Greater London, 1966. *Recreations:* gardening, the arts, foreign travel. *Address:* The Change House, Great Yeldham, Essex CO9 4PT. *T:* Great Yeldham (0787) 237260.

                                                *Died* 17 *May* 1990.

**ELGOOD, Captain Leonard Alsager,** OBE 1919; MC 1915; DL; JP; FRSE; Director, The Distillers Co. Ltd, 1943–60; Chairman, United Glass Ltd, 1951–61; Director, Royal Bank of Scotland, 1946–66, Extraordinary Director, 1966–68; Chairman of Committee on Natural Resources of Scotland (Scottish Council for Development and Industry), 1958–62; *b* 13 Dec. 1892; *s* of late William Alsager Elgood, Dundee, and late Mrs Elgood; *m* 1917, Jenny Coventry Wood (*d* 1984), *d* of late R. A. Harper Wood and late Mrs Wood, Perth; two *s*. *Educ:* Dundee High Sch. Served with the Black Watch (Capt.), 1914–19 (despatches thrice); retd, 1919. Chartered Accountant, 1919; Sec., John Dewar & Sons Ltd, Perth, 1936; Sec., The Distillers Co. Ltd, 1939. DL 1948, JP 1943, County of the City of Edinburgh. *Address:* 16 Cumlodden Avenue, Edinburgh EH12 6DR. *T:* 031–337 6919.                     *Died* 31 *Jan.* 1987.

**ELIOTT OF STOBS, Sir Arthur Francis Augustus Boswell,** 11th Bt *cr* 1666; Chief of the Clan Elliot; *b* 2 Jan. 1915; *s* of Sir Gilbert Alexander Boswell Eliott, 10th Bt, and Dora Flournoy Adams Hopkins (*d* 1978), Atlanta, Georgia, USA; *S* father, 1958; *m* 1947, Frances Aileen, *e d* of late Sir Francis McClean, AFC; one *d*. *Educ:* Harrow; King's Coll., Cambridge. BA 1936, MA 1949. 2nd Lieut, King's Own Scottish Borderers (TA), 1939, Major, 1944. Served in East Africa and Burma with King's African Rifles, 1941–45. Member of Queen's Body Guard for Scotland, Royal Company of Archers. FSAScot 1986. *Publication:* The Elliots, the story of a Border Clan, 1974. *Heir:* cousin Charles Joseph Alexander Eliott [*b* 9 Jan. 1937; *m* 1959, Wendy Judith, *d* of Henry John Bailey; one *s* four *d* (and one *s* decd)]. *Address:* Redheugh, Newcastleton, Roxburghshire. *T:* Liddesdale 213. *Clubs:* New (Edinburgh); Leander.                                      *Died* 6 *April* 1989.

**ELKINS, Vice-Adm. Sir Robert (Francis),** KCB 1958 (CB 1954); CVO 1952; OBE 1942; *b* 12 Jan. 1903; *er s* of Dr F. A. Elkins, Leavesden, Kings Langley; *m* 1940, Gwendolen Hurst Flint. *Educ:* RNC, Osborne and Dartmouth. Qualified as Interpreter (German), 1928; specialised in Gunnery, 1929; Commander, 1937; in comd HMS Bideford, 1939–40 (despatches, 1940); Prisoner of War, 1940; Comdr, HMS Renown, 1940; Capt. Dec. 1942; in comd HMS Dido, 1944–45; idc 1949; in comd HMS Ocean, 1949–50; in comd HMS Excellent, 1950–52; ADC to King George VI, 1952; ADC to the Queen until July 1952; Rear-Adm. 1952; Vice-Adm. 1955; Flag Officer, 2nd in Comd, Far East Station, 1955–56; Admiral, British Joint Staff Mission, Washington, 1956–58, retired 1959. *Recreations:* all outdoor sports. *Address:* Branlea, Foreland Road, Bembridge, IoW. *T:* Bembridge 82522.                    *Died* 27 *April* 1985.

**ELLES, Robin Jamieson,** CBE 1974 (OBE 1945; MBE 1942); JP; County Director, Dunbartonshire British Red Cross Society, 1968–80; *b* 4 Jan. 1907; *er s* of late Bertram Walter Elles, Malayan Civil Service, and late Jean Challoner Elles; *m* 1932, Eva Lyon Scott Elliot (*d* 1984), *d* of Lt-Col William Scott Elliot; one *s*. *Educ:* Marlborough Coll.; Trinity Hall, Cambridge. BA 1928, MA 1950. Sudan Political Service, 1929–34; J. & P. Coats Ltd, India and China, 1935–40; Army, 1940–45: OETA Abyssinia, 1941; Sudan Defence Force, 1942–45, Libya and Tripolitania, Temp. Lt-Col Comdg 10 SDF Inf. Bn, 1944–45; J. & P. Coats Ltd, Personnel, 1946–66, retd 1966. Chm. of Governors, Paisley Coll. of Technology, 1966–76 (Governor, 1950–76); Chairman: Scottish Adv. Cttee, Nat. Youth Employment Council, 1962–71; Nat. Youth Employment Council, 1971–74. JP Dunbartonshire, 1952. *Publications:* various papers. *Recreations:* fishing, rowing (Cambridge Blue, 1927 and 1929; rowed for Leander, 1929). *Address:* Rogart, Garelochhead, Dunbartonshire. *T:* Garelochhead 810304. *Club:* Leander (Henley-on-Thames).                                     *Died* 18 *June* 1987.

**ELLIOT, Sir John,** Kt 1954; High Sheriff of Greater London, 1970–71; *b* London, 6 May 1898; 2nd *s* of R. D. Blumenfeld; assumed Christian name as surname by Deed Poll, 1922; *m* 1924, Elizabeth, *e d* of late Dr A. S. Cobbledick; one *s* one *d*. *Educ:* Marlborough;

Sandhurst. European War in 3rd Hussars; after four years in journalism joined former Southern Rly, 1925, in charge public relations (first in UK). Visited USA, Canada, frequently; Deputy General Manager, Southern Rly, 1937, Gen. Manager, 1947; Chief Regional Officer: Southern Region, British Railways, 1948–49; London Midland Region, Euston, 1950–51; Chairman: Railway Exec., 1951–53; London Transport, 1953–59; Pullman Car Co., 1959–63; Thos. Cook & Son Ltd, 1959–67; Willing & Co. Ltd, 1959–70; London and Provincial Poster Group Ltd, 1965–71. Director: Commonwealth Development Corp., 1959–66; Railway Air Services, Channel Islands Airways, 1933–48; Thomas Tilling Ltd, 1959–70; British Airports Authority, 1965–69; Cie Internationale des Wagons-Lits, 1960–71. Vice-Pres., Internat. Union of Railways (UIC), 1947 and 1951–53. Formerly Col. (Comdg) Engineer and Railway Staff Corps, Royal Engineers, 1956–63. Visited Australia, 1949 (at invitation of Govt of Victoria, to report on rail and road transport), 1966, 1970, and E Africa, 1969 (on transport study (World Bank)). FInstT (Pres., 1953–54). Mem. Société de l'histoire de Paris, 1958–74. Officier, Légion d'Honneur; American Medal of Freedom. *Publications:* The Way of the Tumbrils (Paris during the Revolution), 1958; Where our Fathers Died (Western Front 50 years after), 1964; On and Off the Rails, 1982; regular newspaper feature, Speaking of That . . . ; book reviews in Daily Telegraph and Sunday Times; many papers on transport. *Recreations:* military history, gardening, cricket (Vice-Pres. Essex CCC). *Address:* 3 Duchess of Bedford House, Duchess of Bedford Walk, W8 7QL. *Clubs:* Cavalry and Guards, MCC.
　　　　　　　　　　　　　　　　　　　　　*Died* 18 *Sept.* 1988.

**ELLIOT, Captain Walter,** DSC 1944; RN Retd; *b* 17 Feb. 1910; *s* of John White Elliot and Frances Hampson; *m* 1936, Thelma Pirie Thomson (*d* 1988); four *d*. *Educ:* HMS Conway; Royal Naval Coll. Joined RN, 1929; specialised in Naval Aviation. Served War of 1939–45 (DSC, despatches); retired, 1958. Took Economics Degree, London Univ., 1958 (BSc Econ). In business, 1958–60. MP (C) Carshalton and Banstead, 1960–Feb. 1974. *Recreations:* fencing, fishing, tennis. 　　　　　　　　　　　　*Died* 8 *Sept* 1988.

**ELLIOTT, Sir Hugh (Francis Ivo),** 3rd Bt *cr* 1917; OBE 1953; Editor, Technical Publications, and Research Consultant, International Union for Conservation of Nature, 1970–80, retired; *b* 10 March 1913; *er s* of Sir Ivo Elliott, 2nd Bt; *S* father, 1961; *m* 1939, Elizabeth Margaret, *er d* of A. G. Phillipson; one *s* two *d*. *Educ:* Dragon Sch.; Eastbourne Coll.; University Coll., Oxford. Tanganyika Administration, 1937; Administrator, Tristan da Cunha, 1950–52; Permanent Sec., Min. of Natural Resources, Tanganyika, 1958; retired, 1961. Commonwealth Liaison Officer for International Union for Conservation of Nature, 1961–66; acting Sec.-Gen., 1962–64, Sec.-Gen., 1964–66, Sec. Ecology Commn, 1966–70. Trustee, British Museum (Natural History), 1971–81; Hon. Sec., British Ornithologists' Union, 1962–66, Vice-Pres. 1970–73, Pres., 1975–79; Chm., British Nat. Sect., Internat. Council for Bird Preservation, 1980–81. Comdr, Order of Golden Ark (Netherlands), 1980. *Publications:* (ed) Proc. 2nd World Conf. on Nat. Parks, Yellowstone, 1972; (jtly) Herons of the World, 1978; contributor to Ibis and various ornithological and conservation jls. *Recreations:* ornithology, travel. *Heir:* s Clive Christopher Hugh Elliott, PhD [*b* 12 Aug. 1945; *m* 1975, Marie-Thérèse, *d* of H. Ruttimann; two *s*]. *Address:* 173 Woodstock Road, Oxford OX2 7NB. *T:* Oxford 515469. 　　　　　　　　　　　　　*Died* 21 *Dec.* 1989.

**ELLIOTT, Maj.-Gen. James Gordon,** CIE 1947; retd; *b* 6 April 1898; *s* of late Dr William Elliott, Welshpool, Montgomeryshire; *m* 1931, Barbara Eleanor (*d* 1979), *y d* of William Douglas, Malvern; one *s* one *d*. *Educ:* Blundell's Sch. Commissioned, Indian Army, 1916; 1st Punjab Regt, 1922; GSO2 Staff Coll., Quetta, 1935–37; Dir Military Training, India, 1942–43; Bde Comdr, 1943–44; Dep. Welfare Gen., India, 1945–46; Dep. Sec. (Mil.), Defence Cttee, India, 1947–48; retired 1948. *Publications:* Administrative Aspect of Tactics and Training, 1938; The Story of the Indian Army, 1939–45, 1965; The Frontier 1839–1947, 1968; Field Sports in India 1800–1947, 1973; India, 1976. *Recreation:* gardening. *Address:* c/o National Westminster Bank, 11 Rolle Street, Exmouth, Devon. *Club:* Naval and Military. 　　　　　　　　*Died* 27 *June* 1990.

**ELLIOTT, Michael Paul,** OBE 1980; Resident Artistic Director, Royal Exchange Theatre Company, Manchester, since 1973; *b* 26 June 1931; *s* of Canon W. H. Elliott and Edith Elliott; *m* 1959, Rosalind Marie Knight; two *d*. *Educ:* Radley Coll.; Keble Coll., Oxford (BA Hons). Staff producer, BBC TV Drama (over 50 TV plays), 1956–60; freelance, theatre, TV and films, 1960; Associate Dir, RSC, As You Like It, with Vanessa Redgrave, Stratford and London, 1961; John Mortimer's Two Stars for Comfort, with Trevor Howard, Garrick, 1962; last Dir, Old Vic Th., Peer Gynt, with Leo McKern, 1962–63; freelance, 1963–68; Miss Julie, with Albert Finney and Maggie Smith, National Th., 1965; formed 69 Theatre Co., Manchester Univ. Th., 1968; productions incl.: When We Dead Awaken, 1968, with Wendy Hiller (also Edin. Fest. and BBC TV); Daniel Deronda, 1969, with Vanessa Redgrave; Peer Gynt,

1970, with Tom Courtenay; co-producer: She Stoops to Conquer, Garrick, 1969; Catch My Soul, Princes, 1971; became first Resid. Artistic Dir of 69 Theatre Co. (subseq. called Royal Exchange Th. Co.), 1973; opened new Royal Exch. Th., 1976; productions include: Uncle Vanya, 1977, with Albert Finney and Leo McKern; The Ordeal of Gilbert Pinfold, 1977, with Michael Hordern; Twelfth Night, 1978, Crime and Punishment, 1978, with Tom Courtenay; Family Reunion, 1979, with Edward Fox; Lady From the Sea, 1978, with Vanessa Redgrave; Dir, 3 plays in Roundhouse season, 1979, The Family Reunion, transf. to Vaudeville, London; The Dresser, Queen's, 1980, NY, 1981; Philoctetes, 1982; After the Lions, 1982; Moby Dick, 1983. Member: Arts Council, 1972–75 (Mem. Panels, and Chm., 1963–70); NT, Bldg Cttee, 1963–66; BBC Adv. Council, 1963–66. Interviewer and broadcaster on BBC Sound and TV; TV Producer for British and Norwegian TV; CBS Special Prodn for coast-to-coast Amer. TV, 1964. Hon. Fellow, Manchester Polytechnic, 1977; Hon. MA Manchester, 1980. *Recreations:* photography, painting. *Club:* Savile. 　　　*Died* 30 *May* 1984.

**ELLIOTT, Ralph Edward;** *b* 7 May 1908; *y s* of late Frederick Worsley Elliott, Ruckinge, Kent; *m* 1934, Phyllis, 2nd *d* of late William Douglas Craig, Kingsnorth, Kent; two *s* one *d*. *Educ:* Ashford Gram. Sch. Entered Westminster Bank Ltd, later National Westminster Bank Ltd, Rochester, 1926; Chief Gen. Man., 1966–68; Jt Chief Exec., 1968–70; Dir, 1969–76; Dep. Chm., 1970–73. Trustee, Leonard Cheshire Foundn, 1972–. FIB. *Address:* Little Hendra, Shire Lane, Chorleywood, Herts. *T:* Chorleywood 2223.
　　　　　　　　　　　　　　　　　　　　　*Died* 23 *Dec.* 1981.

**ELLIOTT, Sydney Robert;** Editor of the Daily Herald, 1953–57; *b* 31 Aug. 1902; *o surv. s* of Robert Scott Elliott and Helen Golden; *m* 1927, Janet Robb Johnston; two *s* one *d* (one *s* decd). *Educ:* Govan High Sch., Glasgow. Managing Editor, Reynolds News, 1929; Editor, Evening Standard, 1943; Political Adviser, Daily Mirror, 1945; Managing Dir, The Argus and Australian Post, Melbourne, 1949; Gen. Manager, Daily Herald, 1952. Collaborated with author of George Wigg by Lord Wigg, 1972. *Publications:* Life of Sir William Maxwell, 1922; Co-operative Storekeeping; Eighty Years of Constructive Revolution, 1925; England, Cradle of Co-operation, 1937. *Address:* 5 Frognal Close, Hampstead, NW3. *T:* 01–435 4149. 　　　　　　　　　　　　　　　　*Died* 9 *Oct.* 1987.

**ELLIOTT-BINNS, Edward Ussher Elliott,** CB 1977; Under-Secretary, Scottish Home and Health Department, 1966–78; *b* 24 Aug. 1918; *e s* of Leonard and Anna Elliott-Binns; *m* 1942, Katharine Mary McLeod, *d* of late Dr J. M. Caie; one *d*. *Educ:* Harrow; King's Coll., Cambridge. Served with Army, 1939–46; Leics Regt and Special Forces (Major). Asst Principal, Scottish Home Dept, 1946; Principal, 1948; Asst Sec., Royal Commn on Capital Punishment, 1949–53; Private Sec. to Minister of State, Scottish Office, 1956–57; Asst Sec., 1957. *Address:* 22 Wilton Road, Edinburgh EH16 5NX. *T:* 031–667 2464. *Club:* Special Forces. 　　　*Died* 14 *Feb.* 1990.

**ELLIOTT-BLAKE, Henry,** TD 1955, and Bar; MA; FRCS, FRCSE; Hon. Plastic Surgeon, St George's Hospital; Emeritus Consultant Plastic Surgeon, St Helier Hospital, Carshalton; *b* 25 Dec. 1902; *s* of Henry Thomas Blake, MIWE, CC, JP, of Herefordshire, and Maud Blake; *m* 1945, Mary, Baroness Swaythling, *d* of Hon. Mrs Ionides. *Educ:* Dean Close, Cheltenham; Queens' Coll., Cambridge (hockey Blue 1931); St Thomas's Hospital, London. MRCS; LRCP 1929; MA, MB, BChir (Cambridge) 1931; FRCS 1941; FRCSE 1941; late Major (surg. specialist), RAMC (TA); served France (Dunkirk) and India; invalided. Founder Mem. British Assoc. Plastic Surgeons; FRSocMed (late Pres., Section of Plastic Surgery). Sometime Consultant Plastic Surgeon: Victoria Hosp. for Children, Tite Street; Royal Alexandra Hosp. for Sick Children, Brighton, Royal Sussex County Hosp., Brighton, Westminster Hosp. Gp (Queen Mary's Hosp., Roehampton, and Carshalton), and Senior Surgeon to the Ministry of Pensions (Roehampton and Stoke Mandeville). Founder Mem. Medical Art Soc. Exhibited: Royal Soc. of Portrait Painters; Royal Academy of Arts; ROI; Armed Forces Art Soc. Founder Mem., Cambridge Senior Soc. *Publications:* four chapters in: Operative Surgery (ed Prof. Charles Rob and Rodney Smith); Butterworths Operative Surgery-Service Vol. 3(b), The Reconstruction of the Penile Urethra in Hypospadias; articles in medical journals. *Recreation:* golf. *Address:* 17 Cadogan Square, SW1X 0HT. *Clubs:* Boodle's; Hawks (Cambridge); Dunkirk Veterans' Assoc.; Royal St George's Golf (Sandwich); Royal Ashdown Forest Golf (Life Mem.); Berks Golf (Ascot); Senior Golfing Society. 　　　　　　　　　　　　　　*Died* 7 *Oct.* 1983.

**ELLIS, Amabel W.;** *see* Williams-Ellis.

**ELLIS, Harold Owen,** CMG 1958; OBE 1952; CEng; FIEE; *b* 11 April 1906; *s* of Owen Percy Ellis, accountant, and Kate Beatrice Ellis, Plymouth; *m* 1932, Phyllis Margaret Stevenson (decd); *m* 1954, Ella Stewart Mathieson. *Educ:* Sutton Secondary Sch., Plymouth. Apprentice, Devonport Dockyard. Engineering Inspector, Post Office, 1926; Executive Engineer, 1940. Served Army, 1944–47, Col. Asst Controller-Gen., Posts and Telegraphs,

Control Commn, Germany, 1947; Postmaster-Gen., Nyasaland, 1949; Dir of Posts and Telegraphs, Federation of Nigeria, 1954; Postmaster-Gen., E Africa, 1958; retd Colonial Service, 1962; Administrative Consultant, 1962–66. Has attended many internat. conferences on telecommunications, sometimes representing Britain. *Publications:* technical articles and papers. *Recreations:* sailing, swimming, photography. *Address:* Turbruad, Banchory, Kincardineshire AB3 4AE.　　　　　　　　　*Died* 1 *March* 1981.

**ELLIS, Dr Mary Jenny Lake,** FRCPsych; DPM; Senior Medical Officer, HM Borstal Institution, Feltham, since 1965; *b* 1 Jan. 1921; *d* of John Reginald Taylor and Beatrice Violet Lake Taylor; *m* 1947, Norman William Warr Ellis; two *s* one *d*. *Educ:* The Hall Sch. (later at Bratton Seymour); London Sch. of Medicine for Women, Royal Free Hosp. MB BS 1946; MRCS LRCP 1944: FRCPsych 1977 (MRCPsych 1972); DPM 1964. Neurosurgical and gen. surgical, Ho. Surgs, Enfield and Royal Free Hosp., 1944–45; Res. Surgical Officer, EMS Neurosurgery Unit of SW, 1945–48; Family Planning Clinics, Southend and Basildon New Town, 1951–61; Divl Surg., SJAB, Droitwich, 1961–63; Jun. Dr, then Registrar, Powick Hosp., Worcs, 1961–64; Locum Registrar, Horton Hosp., 1964; Locum Consultant, Runwell Hosp., Wickford, 1965; SMO, HM Borstal, Feltham, 1965– (seniority merit award, 1973); Consultant to Windsor Probation Hostel, 1975–82; Cropwood Fellow, Inst. of Criminology, Cambridge, 1974. Editor, Prison Med. Jl, 1970–76, 1978–82. Mem. Exec., Assoc. of Psychiatric Study of Adolescents, 1973–, Chm., 1978–81; Organiser, APSA Conf., Adolescent and the Law, 1977; Mem., NACRO working party, Children in Prison, 1976–77. *Publications:* articles in New Society, New Behaviour, Prison Med. Jl. *Recreations:* propagating plants and ideas, working with problems of triangular relationships, them, us and those, the management of crisis, watching birds when there is time from watching human behaviour. *Address:* HM Borstal, Bedfont Road, Feltham, Mddx TW13 4ND. *T:* 01-890 0061.
　　　　　　　　　　　　　　　　　　　*Died* 19 *April* 1983.

**ELLIS, Sir Thomas Hobart,** Kt 1953; *b* 11 Oct. 1894; *s* of late Rev. Herbert Ellis. *Educ:* Manchester Grammar Sch.; Queen's Coll., Oxford. Entered Indian Civil Service, 1919; Additional Judge of High Court, Calcutta, 1944–47; Judge of High Court of East Bengal, 1947–53; Chief Justice, 1953–54. Acting Governor of East Bengal, Sept.–Dec. 1954. Officer on Special Duty, Government of Pakistan, 1955–57. *Recreations:* photography, trekking. *Address:* c/o Grindlays Bank, 13 St James's Square, SW1.
　　　　　　　　　　　　　　　　　　　*Died* 12 *Dec.* 1981.

**ELLIS, Wilfred Desmond,** OBE 1952; TD; Manager: Conversion Executive, Gas Council, 1965–68; Customer Service and Conversion, British Gas Corporation, 1968–73, retired; Lay Member, Press Council, 1969–76; *b* 7 Nov. 1914; 2nd *s* of late Bertram V. C. W. Ellis and late Winifred Dora Ellis; *m* 1947, Effie Douglas, JP, *d* of late Dr A. Barr, Canonbie, Scotland; one *s* two *d*. *Educ:* Temple Grove; Canford. Commissioned as 2nd Lt, Middlesex Regt, 1937. Served War of 1939–45 at home and NW Europe with Middlesex Regt (despatches, 1944). Rejoined TA, 1947, retiring as Dep. Comdt 47 (L) Inf. Bde, 1962; County Comdt, Mddx Army Cadet Force, 1958–62; ADC to the Queen, 1966–69. Joined Gas Industry, 1932; Uxbridge, Maidenhead, Wycombe & Dist. Gas Co. until War of 1939–45; returned to Company until nationalisation; served with North Thames Gas Bd in various appts until joining Gas Council Research Station, Watson House, 1963, as Asst, and then Dep. Dir; transf. to Gas Council, 1966, as Manager, Conversion Executive. Freeman, City of London, 1936; Liveryman, Merchant Taylors' Co., 1936–. DL (Greater London), 1964–79. Vice-Chm., Greater London TAVR, 1965–67. Fellow, Inst. of Marketing. *Recreations:* shooting, local affairs. *Address:* Lea Barn, Winter Hill, Cookham Dean, Berkshire SL6 9TW. *T:* Maidenhead (0628) 4230. *Club:* Naval and Military.　　　　　　　　*Died* 30 *Dec.* 1990.

**ELLISON, Randall Erskine,** CMG 1960; ED 1946; *b* 6 March 1904; 2nd *s* of late Rev. Preb. J. H. J. Ellison, CVO, Rector of St Michael's, Cornhill, EC, and Mrs Ellison; unmarried. *Educ:* Repton Sch.; New Coll., Oxford (MA). Superintendent of Education, Northern Provinces, Nigeria, 1928; seconded to British Somaliland as Dir of Education, 1938–43; Military Service with British Somaliland and Nigerian Forces, 1940–43; Asst Dir of Education, Tanganyika, 1945; Deputy Dir, 1946; Deputy Dir of Education, Northern Region, Nigeria, 1955; Dir of Education, 1956; Adviser on Education, 1957. Chm., Public Service Commission, Northern Region, Nigeria, 1958, retired 1961. Asst Sec., Church Assembly, Dean's Yard, SW1, 1962–63. Chm., Africa Cttee of CMS, 1969–73; Mem. Council, Westfield Coll., London Univ., 1964–78 (Chm., 1967–68; Hon. Treasurer, 1969–76; Hon. Fellow, 1978). Hon. Steward, Westminster Abbey, 1964. *Publication:* An English-Kanuri Sentence Book, 1937. *Recreations:* choral singing, chamber music. *Address:* 32 Oppidans Road, Hampstead, NW3 3AG. *Clubs:* United Oxford & Cambridge University, Royal Commonwealth Society.
　　　　　　　　　　　　　　　　　　　*Died* 23 *April* 1984.

**ELLMANN, Richard,** MA Oxon; PhD Yale; FBA 1979; Woodruff Professor, Emory University, since 1982; Extraordinary Fellow, Wolfson College, Oxford, since 1984; *b* Highland Park, Michigan, 15 March 1918; *s* of James Isaac Ellmann and Jeanette (*née* Barsook); *m* 1949, Mary Donahue; one *s* two *d*. *Educ:* Highland Park High Sch.; Yale Univ. (MA, PhD); Trinity Coll., Dublin (LittB). Served War of 1939–45, Office of Strategic Services, USNR, 1943–46. Instructor at Harvard, 1942–43, 1947–48; Briggs-Copeland Asst Prof. of Eng. Composition, Harvard, 1948–51; Prof. of English, Northwestern Univ., 1951, Franklin Bliss Snyder Prof., 1963–68; Prof. of English, Yale, 1968–70; Goldsmiths' Prof. of English Lit. and Fellow, New Coll., Oxford Univ., 1970–84, Hon. Fellow, New Coll., 1987. Rockefeller Fellow, 1946–47; Guggenheim Fellow, 1950, 1957, 1970; Kenyon Review Fellow Criticism, 1955–56; Fellow, Sch. of Letters, Indiana Univ., 1956, 1960; Senior Fellow, 1966–72; Frederick Ives Carpenter Vis. Prof., Univ. of Chicago, 1959, 1968, 1975, 1976, 1977; Grantee, Nat. Endowment for the Humanities, 1977–78. Mem., US-UK Educnl Commn, 1970–. Mem. Editorial Committee: Publications of the Modern Language Assoc., 1968–73; American Scholar, 1968–74. FRSL; Fellow, Amer. Acad. and Inst.; National Book Award, 1960. Hon. DLitt: NUI, 1976; Boston Coll., 1979; Emory Univ., 1979; Northwestern, 1980; McGill, 1986; Hon. PhD Gothenburg, 1978; Hon. DHL Rochester, 1981. Wilbur Cross Medal, Yale Univ., 1987. *Publications:* Yeats: The Man and the Masks, 1948; The Identity of Yeats, 1954; James Joyce: a biography, 1959 (Nat. Book Award for non-fiction, 1960), revd edn 1982 (Duff Cooper Meml Prize, James Tait Black Prize, 1983); Eminent Domain, 1967; Ulysses on the Liffey, 1972; Golden Codgers, 1973; The Consciousness of Joyce, 1977; James Joyce's Hundredth Birthday, 1982; Oscar Wilde at Oxford, 1984; W. B. Yeats's Second Puberty, 1985; Samuel Beckett: Nayman of Noland, 1986; Four Dubliners: Wilde, Yeats, Joyce and Beckett, 1987; Oscar Wilde, 1987 (Pulitzer Prize); *edited:* Selected Writings of Henri Michaux (trans.), 1951; My Brother's Keeper, by Stanislaus Joyce, 1958; (with others) Masters of British Literature, 1958; Arthur Symons: The Symbolist Movement in Literature, 1958; (with Ellsworth Mason) The Critical Writings of James Joyce, 1959; Edwardians and late Victorians, 1959; (with Charles Feidelson, Jr) The Modern Tradition, 1965; Letters of James Joyce (Vols II and III), 1966; James Joyce: Giacomo Joyce, 1968; The Artist as Critic: Oscar Wilde, 1970; Oscar Wilde: twentieth century views, 1970; (with Robert O'Clair) Norton Anthology of Modern Poetry, 1973; Selected Letters of James Joyce, 1975; New Oxford Book of American Verse, 1976; (with Robert O'Clair) Modern Poems, 1976; Oscar Wilde, The Picture of Dorian Gray and Other Writings, 1982; *posthumous publication:* A Long the Riverrun: selected essays, 1988. *Address:* 39 St Giles', Oxford OX1 3LW. *Clubs:* Athenæum; Signet (Harvard); Elizabethan (Yale).　　　　*Died* 13 *May* 1987.

**ELLWOOD, Captain Michael Oliver Dundas,** DSO 1940; *b* 13 July 1894; *s* of late Rev. C. E. Ellwood, Cottesmore, Rutland. *Educ:* Cheam Sch., Surrey; RN Colls, Osborne and Dartmouth. Entered Royal Navy, 1907; retired as Comdr, 1934; rejoined as Capt. on retired list, 1939; reverted to retired list, Sept. 1946. *Club:* Army and Navy.　　　　　　　　　　　　　　　*Died* 21 *Nov.* 1984.

**ELMHIRST, Air Marshal Sir Thomas (Walker),** KBE 1946 (CBE 1943); CB 1945; AFC 1918; RAF retired; Lieutenant-Governor and Commander-in-Chief of Guernsey, 1953–Oct. 1958; *b* 15 Dec. 1895; 4th *s* of late Rev. W. H. Elmhirst, Elmhirst, near Barnsley, Yorks; *m* 1st, 1930, Katharine Gordon (*d* 1965), 4th *d* of William Black, Chapel, Fife; one *s* one *d*; 2nd, 1968, Marian Louisa, *widow* of Col Andrew Ferguson and *d* of late Lt-Col Lord Herbert Montagu-Douglas-Scott. *Educ:* RN Colls, Osborne and Dartmouth. RN, 1908–15, Dardanelles and Dogger Bank in HMS Indomitable; RN Air Service, 1915–18; RAF as Major, Comdg Naval Airship Patrol Station, Anglesey, 1918 (AFC); RAF Staff Coll., 1925; commanded No. 15 Bomber Squadron and Abingdon Wing, 1935–37; 1st British Air Attaché to HM Embassy, Ankara, 1937–39; Dep. Dir Intelligence Air Ministry and Air Cdre HQ Fighter Comd, 1940 (Battle of Britain); RAF mem. of British Mission for Staff conversations with Turkish Gen. Staff, Ankara, 1941; AOC RAF Egypt, 1941 (despatches twice); 2nd in Comd Desert Air Force (Alamein campaigns), 1942 (CBE); Air Officer i/c Administration NW Africa, TAF, 1943 (despatches, CB, Tunis and Sicily campaigns); 2nd in Comd British Air Forces in NW Europe, Normandy-Germany campaign (KBE, despatches), 1944–45; Asst Chief of Air Staff (Intelligence), 1945–47; Chief of Inter-Service Administration in India, 1947; first C-in-C Indian Air Force, 1947–50; retd, 1950. Hon. Air Marshal in the Indian Air Force, 1950. Fife County Councillor, 1950; Civil Defence Controller Eastern Zone, Scotland, 1952–53. DL, County of Fife, 1960–70. Comdr, US Legion of Merit; Grand Officer, Crown of Belgium and Croix de Guerre; Comdr, Legion of Honour and French Croix de Guerre. KStJ 1954. *Recreations:* grandchildren and fishing. *Address:* The Cottage, Dummer, Basingstoke, Hants. *Club:* Royal Air Force.　　　　　　　　　　　　　　　*Died* 6 *Nov.* 1982.

**EL-SADAT, Mohamed Anwar;** President of the Arab Republic of Egypt, since 1970; *b* 25 Dec. 1918; *s* of Mohamed El-Sadat; *m* 1949,

Jehan El-Sadat; one *s* three *d. Educ:* Military Coll., Cairo (graduated 1938). Signal Officer, 1938; excommunicated from Army for underground work against British Occupation, 1942; efforts to liberate Egypt led him to prison many times; Mem., Free Officers Underground Orgn, 1951; Editor-in-Chief, Al-Gomhouria newspaper, 1953; Sec., Islamic Conf. and National Union, 1957; Head of Parliament, 1960; Head of Afro-Asian Solidarity Council, 1961; Vice-Pres. of Egypt, 1969. Nobel Peace Prize (jtly, with Menachem Begin), 1978. US Medal of Freedom (posthumous), 1984. Decorations from: Yugoslavia, 1956; Greece, 1958; German Democratic Republic, 1965; Bulgaria, 1965; Rumania, 1966; Finland, 1967; Iran, 1971; Saudi Arabia, 1974. *Publications:* Unknown Pages, 1955; The Secrets of the Egyptian Revolution, 1957; The Story of Arab Unity, 1957; My Son, This is your Uncle Gamal, 1958; The Complete Story of the Revolution, 1961; For a New Resurrection, 1963; In Search of Identity, 1978. *Recreations:* reading literary works and watching films. *Address:* The Presidential Palace at Abdeen, Cairo, Arab Republic of Egypt.
*Died 6 Oct.* 1981.

**ELSMORE, Geoffrey William;** Chief Inspector, HM Inspectorate of Schools, since 1981; *b* 29 Oct. 1925; *s* of George Frederick Elsmore and Edith Elsmore; *m* 1953, Diana Gwynneth Allen; three *s* three *d. Educ:* City of Worcester Coll. of Educn (qualified teacher). Served RAF, 1943–47. Schoolmaster, Kidlington Jun. Sch., 1950–56; Headmaster, West Kidlington Primary Sch., 1956–63 (also occasional Tutor and Lectr, Oxford Univ. Dept and Inst. of Educn); HM Inspector of Schs, NW Div., 1963–73; HM Staff Inspector, Primary Educn, 1973–81. *Recreations:* sailing, painting, music. *Address:* Department of Education and Science, Elizabeth House, York Road, SE1 7PH. *T:* 01–928 9222. *Died 12 April* 1985.

**ELSTUB, Sir St John (de Holt),** Kt 1970; CBE 1954; BSc, FEng, FIMechE, FInstP; Chairman, IMI plc, 1972–74 (Managing Director, 1962–74); *b* 16 June 1915; *s* of Ernest Elstub and Mary Gertrude (*née* Whitaker); *m* 1939, Patricia Arnold; two *d. Educ:* Rugby Sch.; Manchester Univ. Joined ICI, Billingham, 1936. Served War of 1939–45 as RAF Bomber Pilot; Supt, Rocket Propulsion Dept, Ministry of Supply, 1945. Joined ICI Metals Div., 1947, Prod. Dir, 1950, Man. Dir, 1957, Chm., 1961; Director: Royal Insurance Co., 1970–76; The London & Lancashire Insurance Co., 1970–76; The Liverpool, London & Globe Insurance Co., 1970–76; British Engine Insurance Ltd, 1970–84; Rolls Royce Ltd, 1971–85; Averys Ltd, 1974–79; Hill Samuel Group Ltd, 1974–82; Regional Dir, W Midlands and Wales, Nat. Westminster Bank Ltd, 1974–79; Dir, TI Gp PLC, 1974–85, Dep. Chm., 1979–85. Past Pres., British Non-Ferrous Metals Federation. Chm., Jt Government/Industry Cttee on Aircraft Industry, 1967–69; Member: Plowden Cttee on Aircraft Industry, 1964–65; Engrg Industry Trng Bd, 1964–72; Midlands Electricity Bd, 1966–75; Review Bd for Govt contracts, 1969–75; Pres., IMechE, 1974–75. A Guardian, Birmingham Assay Office; Governor, Administrative Staff Coll., Henley, 1962–74; Mem. Council, Univ. of Aston in Birmingham, 1966–72 (Vice-Chm. 1968–72); Life Governor, Univ. of Birmingham. Hon. DSc Univ. of Aston in Birmingham, 1971. Verulam Medal, Metals Soc., 1975. *Recreations:* landscape gardening, travel, DIY, old motor cars. *Address:* Haynes Green Farm, Broadwas-on-Teme, Worcester WR6 5NX. *T:* Knightwick 21116. *Club:* Army and Navy.
*Died 24 Jan.* 1989.

**ELTON, John Bullen;** Senior Master of the Supreme Court, Queen's Bench Division, and Queen's Remembrancer, since 1982 (Master since 1966); *b* 18 Jan. 1916; *s* of Percy Maden Elton, company director; *m* 1939, Sonia (*née* Mandelkorn); three *d. Educ:* Bishop's Stortford Coll.; Brasenose Coll., Oxford. Called to the Bar, Inner Temple, 1938, Bencher, 1982. RNVR, 1943–46. *Recreation:* sailing. *Address:* 3 Ailsa Road, St Margaret's, Twickenham, Middx. *Club:* Royal Victoria Yacht. *Died 9 Oct.* 1983.

**ELWORTHY-JARMAN, Air Cdre Lance Michael,** DFC 1940; RAF (retired); Director, Engineering Industries Association, 1958–73, retired; *b* 17 Aug. 1907; *s* of Hedley Elworthy and Mary Elizabeth Jarman (*née* Chatterway-Clarke); *m* 1940, Elizabeth Evelyn Litton-Puttock (*d* 1978); one *s* one *d. Educ:* Christchurch High Sch., NZ; Canterbury Coll., Univ. of NZ. Commissioned, RAF, 1929; No 12 Bomber Sqdn, Andover, 1930; No 14 Bomber Sqdn, Amman, 1931; Officers' Engineering Course, Henlow, 1932–35; RAF, Abukir, Atbara, Sudan, Cairo, 1935–38; Maintenance Command, 1938. Served War of 1939–45: Nos 214 and 9 Bomber Sqdns, 1939; Chief Flying Instructor, Nos 11–20 and 23 Operational Training Units, 1940; CO, No 27 OTU, Lichfield, 1941; SASO, No 93 Bomber Gp, 1942; CO, RAF Stations, Kidlington and Wyton, 1943; SASO, No 205 Gp, Italy, 1945, qualified as Pathfinder; OC RAF Stations, Oakington and Abingdon, 1947; Senior Officer Administration, RAF, No 42 Gp, 1949; OC, RAF Jet Training Stations, Full Sutton and Merryfield, 1951; Chief of Staff, Royal Pakistan Air Force, 1952; attached Nellis Air Force Base to test T33 and F86E, 1953; official observer, atomic explosions at Yucca Flat and Nevada, 1955; AO Defence Research Policy Staff, Cabinet Office, 1955–56;

RAF Rep., Commonwealth Conf. on Defence Sci., Canada; AOA, NATO, Channel and Atlantic Commands, 1957; retired from RAF, 1958. CEng, MIMechE, AFRAeS, MBIM, MAIE. *Publications:* Editor, Engineering Industries Jl. *Recreation:* sailing; lectr, offshore and ocean navigation; examr, RYA/DTI yachtmaster certificate. *Address:* Merryfield, 9 Newenham Road, Lymington, Hants. *T:* Lymington 74577. *Clubs:* Royal Air Force, Royal Ocean Racing; RAF Yacht (Hamble); Royal New Zealand Yacht Squadron.
*Died 30 Oct.* 1986.

**ELWYN-JONES,** Baron *cr* 1974 (Life Peer), of Llanelli and Newham; **Frederick Elwyn-Jones,** PC 1964; CH 1976; Kt 1964; Lord High Chancellor of Great Britain, 1974–79; a Lord of Appeal, since 1979; *b* 24 Oct. 1909; *s* of Frederick and Elizabeth Jones, Llanelli, Carmarthenshire; *m* 1937, Pearl Binder; one *s* two *d. Educ:* Llanelli Grammar Sch.; University of Wales, Aberystwyth; Gonville and Caius Coll., Cambridge (Scholar, MA, Pres. Cambridge Union); Hon. Fellow, 1976. Called to Bar, Gray's Inn, 1935, Bencher, 1960, Treasurer, 1980; QC 1953; QC (N Ireland) 1958; Hon. Bencher, Inn of Court of N Ireland, 1981. Major RA (TA); Dep. Judge Advocate, 1943–45. MP (Lab) Plaistow Div. of West Ham, 1945–50, West Ham South, 1950–74, Newham South 1974, 1974; PPS to Attorney-Gen., 1946–51; Attorney General, 1964–70. Recorder: of Merthyr Tydfil, 1949–53; of Swansea, 1953–60; of Cardiff, 1960–64; of Kingston-upon-Thames, 1968–74. Member of British War Crimes Executive, Nuremberg, 1945. UK Observer, Malta Referendum, 1964. Mem., Inter-Departmental Cttee on the Court of Criminal Appeal, 1964. Mem. of Bar Council, 1956–59. President: University Coll., Cardiff, 1971–88; Mental Health Foundn, 1980–89. FKC, 1970. Hon. LLD: University of Wales, 1968; Ottawa Univ., 1975; Columbia Univ., NY, 1976; Warsaw, 1977; Univ. of Philippines, 1979; Law Soc. of Upper Canada, 1982. Hon. Freeman: Llanelli; London. *Publications:* Hitler's Drive to the East, 1937; The Battle for Peace, 1938; The Attack from Within, 1939; In My Time (autobiog.), 1983. *Recreation:* travelling. *Address:* House of Lords, SW1. *Died 4 Dec.* 1989.

**EMELEUS, Prof. Karl George,** CBE 1965; MA, PhD; FInstP; MRIA; Professor of Physics, Queen's University, Belfast, 1933–66; *b* 4 Aug. 1901; *s* of Karl Henry Emeleus and Ellen Biggs; *m* 1928, Florence Mary Chambers; three *s* one *d. Educ:* Hastings Grammar Sch.; St John's Coll., Cambridge. Fellow, Amer. Physical Soc. Hon. ScD Dublin; Hon. DSc: NUI; Queen's Univ., Belfast, 1983; Ulster, 1986. *Address:* c/o Queen's University of Belfast, Belfast BT7 1NN. *Died 18 June* 1989.

**EMERY, Rt. Rev. Anthony Joseph;** Bishop of Portsmouth (RC), since 1976; *b* Burton-on-Trent, 17 May 1918. Ordained 1953. Auxiliary Bishop of Birmingham (Titular Bishop of Tamallula), 1968–76. Chm., Catholic Educn Council, 1968–84. *Address:* Bishop's House, Edinburgh Road, Portsmouth PO1 3HG.
*Died 5 April* 1988.

**EMERY, Sir (James) Frederick,** Kt 1957; JP; Company Director; *b* 17 Dec. 1886; *s* of William Joseph and Ruth Emery; *m* 1912, Florence Beatrice Gradwell; one *d. Educ:* Manchester Univ. MP (U) West Salford, 1935–45; Member of Salford City Council, 1921–35 (Councillor 1921–33, Alderman, 1933–35); Pres. North Fylde Conservative Association; Mayor of Salford, 1932–33. JP Salford 1927. *Address:* Rathmines, 189 Victoria Road West, Cleveleys, near Blackpool, Lancs. *T:* Cleveleys 3090.
*Died 30 Oct.* 1983.

**EMETT, (Frederick) Rowland,** OBE 1978; FCSD; artist and inventor; *b* 22 Oct. 1906; *m* 1941, Mary; one *d.* Contributor to Punch for many years. In 1951 The Far Twittering to Oyster Creek Railway forsook the pages of Punch and appeared full-blown and passenger-carrying at The Festival Gardens, for The Festival of Britain. The impact of this led to a succession of large three-dimensional, Gothick-Kinetic, fully-working inventions of ever-increasing complexity, which have been exhibited all over the world. Constructed the Edwardian inventions for the film Chitty Chitty Bang Bang, 1968. Built his first permanent construction The Rhythmical Time Fountain, for the City of Nottingham Victoria Centre, 1974. The fully-working three-dimensional inventions include: the Exploratory Moon-probe Lunacycle "Maud"; the Borg Warner Vintage Car of the Future, permanently in the Museum of Science and Industry, Chicago; SS Pussiewillow II, personal air-and-space vehicle, commnd by and housed in Nat. Mus. of Air and Space, Smithsonian Instn, Washington DC. The Featherstone Kite Openwork Basket-weave Gentleman's Flying Machine, together with seven other inventions, have been acquired by Ontario Science Centre, Toronto. Pussiewillow III, a celestial cats'-cradle, commnd by Basildon New Town. Dawn Flight: mist clearing, mallard rising, and the early Up Slow Surprised, acquired by Tate Gallery for permanent collection, 1985. *Publications:* (with Mary Emett) Anthony and Antimacassar, 1943; collections from Punch incl. Engines, Aunties and Others, 1943, Sidings and Suchlike, 1946, Home Rails Preferred, 1947,

Saturday Slow, 1948 and Far Twittering, 1949; The Early Morning Milk Train, 1978; Alarms and Excursions, 1978; two signed limited-edn prints, 1978. *Address:* Wild Goose Cottage, 113 East End Lane, Ditchling, Hassocks, West Sussex BN6 8UR. *T:* Hassocks (0273) 2459; 137 Nell Gwynn House, Sloane Avenue, SW3 3AX.
*Died 13 Nov. 1990.*

**EMMERSON, Sir Harold Corti**, GCB 1956 (KCB 1947; CB 1942); KCVO 1953; *b* 1896; *m* 1931, Lucy Kathleen Humphreys; two *s* three *d. Educ:* Warrington Secondary Sch. Served War of 1914–18 in Royal Marine Artillery. Ministry of Labour, 1920; Secretary Government Mission on Industrial Conditions in Canada and United States, 1926–27; Secretary Royal Commn on Unemployment Insurance, 1930–32; Principal Private Secretary to Ministers of Labour, 1933–35; Secretary Department of Commissioner for Special Areas, 1938–39; Principal Officer, Civil Defence, Northern Region, 1939–40; Under-Secretary Ministry of Home Security, 1940–42; Chief Industrial Commissioner, Ministry of Labour, 1942–44; Deputy-Secretary and Director General of Man Power, 1944–46; Permanent Secretary: Ministry of Works, 1946–56; Ministry of Labour, 1956–59. Member: Security Inquiry Cttee, 1961; Council on Prices, Productivity and Incomes, 1960–62; War Works Commission, 1960–64; Council on Tribunals, 1961–64. Chairman, London Government Staff Commn, 1963–65. Hon. MA Liverpool. *Publication:* The Ministry of Works, 1956. *Address:* 26 Millfield, Berkhamsted, Herts. *Club:* Arts.
*Died 2 Aug. 1984.*

**EMMERSON, Dr Thomas**, MInstP; *b* 28 Aug. 1909; *s* of James Emmerson and Agnes McCartney; *m* 1938, Dorothy (*d* 1979), *d* of C. J. R. Tipper; two *s. Educ:* Leeds Grammar Sch.; Leeds Univ. (Schol.), BSc, PhD (Physics). Radio Valve Industry, 1933–36; Adm. Scientific Service, 1936–45; GKN Group, 1945–78: Dir of Research, 1949–68; Corporate Staff Dir of Research and Products, 1968–70; Consultant, 1971–78. Mem., Industrial Grants Cttee, DSIR, 1953–63; Mem. Council: Brit. Welding Res. Assoc., 1963–68; Welding Inst., 1968–74. British Association for the Advancement of Science: Chm., W Midlands Br., 1964–74; Mem. Council, 1962–78; Gen. Sec., 1974–78. Member: Appts Bd, Univ. of Leeds, 1966–71; Glazebrook Cttee, 1966–68; Bessborough Cttee of Enquiry on Res. Assocs, 1972–73; Mem., latterly Chm., Adv. Council on R & D for Steel Ind. (ACORD), 1968–75. *Recreations:* lawn tennis, music, landscape gardening. *Address:* Highfield, Trysull, near Wolverhampton WV5 7JB. *T:* Wombourne 893387.
*Died 13 March 1981.*

**EMMINGER, Otmar**, Dr oec. publ.; Chairman, Deutsche Pfandbriefanstalt, since 1980; director of companies and member of international advisory boards; Governor, Deutsche Bundesbank (Federal Bank), 1977–79; *b* Augsburg, 2 March 1911; *s* of Erich Emminger, Senatspräsident (Reichsminister der Justiz, 1923–24) and Maria Scharff; *m* 1966, Dr *rer. pol.* Gisela Boden; two *s. Educ:* in Law and Economics, at Univs of Berlin, Munich, Edinburgh, and London Sch. of Economics. Mem. and Div. Chief, Inst. for Business Research (Institut für Konjunkturforschung), Berlin, 1935–39. Served War of 1939–45. Div. Chief, Bavarian Min. of Economics, 1947–49; Mem. German Delegn to OEEC, Paris, 1949–50; Dir, Research and Statistics Dept, Bank deutscher Länder, 1951–53; Mem. Bd of Governors, Deutsche Bundesbank (Federal Bank), 1953–69, Dep. Governor, 1970–77; Exec. Dir, IMF, Washington, 1953–59, a Governor, 1977–80. Dep. Chm., Monetary Cttee, EEC, 1958–77; Chm., Monetary Cttee of OECD, 1969–77; Chm., Deputies of Group of Ten, 1964–67; Mem., Group of Thirty, 1978–. *Publications:* Die englischen Währungsexperimente der Nachkriegszeit, 1934; Deutschlands Stellung in der Weltwirtschaft, 1953; Währungspolitik im Wandel der Zeit, 1966; Zwanzig Jahre deutsche Geldpolitik, 1968; Verteidigung der D Mark, 1980. *Recreations:* ski-ing, hiking. *Address:* Hasselhorstweg 36, D6000 Frankfurt am Main, West Germany. *T:* 684354.
*Died 2 Aug. 1986.*

**EMMS, John Frederick George**, FIA; a Deputy Chairman, Commercial Union Assurance Company Ltd, 1983–88 (Vice-Chairman, 1979–83); *b* 2 Sept. 1920; *s* of late John Stanley Emms and Alice Maud Emms (*née* Davies); *m* 1942, Margaret Alison Hay; one *s* one *d* (and one *s* decd). *Educ:* Harrow County Sch.; Latymer Upper Sch. FIA. Served War RA/RCS, 1939–46. Joined Commercial Union Assurance Co. Ltd, 1938; Investment Manager, 1968–70; Chief Investment Manager, 1970–72; Dir, 1972; Exec. Dir, 1974; Chief General Manager, 1977–82. Director: Barclays Bank UK, 1981–86; British Technol. Gp., 1979–85. Mem., NEB, 1979–85. Mem., British Red Cross Finance Cttee, 1973–86. Mem. Adv. Panel, British Coal (formerly NCB) Superannuation and Pension Schemes, 1973–; Chm. Trustees, PO Staff Superannuation Scheme, 1983–86. Chm. of Govs, Latymer Upper Sch., 1987–. *Recreations:* sport, reading. *Address:* Oakhurst, Silverwood Copse, West Chiltington, Pulborough, W Sussex RH20 2NQ. *T:* West Chiltington (07983) 2838.
*Died 9 Oct 1990.*

**EMPSON, Sir Charles**, KCMG 1956 (CMG 1943); Foreign Service, retired; *b* 24 April 1898; *s* of late Arthur Reginald Empson, Yokefleet, East Yorks; *m* 1931, Monica, *d* of late Canon J. W. S. Tomlin; one *s* one *d. Educ:* Harrow; Magdalene Coll., Cambridge. War Service, 1917–19 (Mesopotamia); joined staff of Civil Commissioner, Bagdad, 1920, and remained on staff of High Commissioner, Bagdad, until 1934 (Consul, 1924–32, Commercial Secretary, 1932–34); Commercial Agent for Palestine, 1934–38; Commercial Secretary HM Embassy, Rome, 1938–39; Commercial Counsellor, HM Embassy, Cairo, 1939–46; Minister (Economic), Special Commission in SE Asia, 1946–47; Minister (Commercial) HM Embassy, Rome, 1947–50; Minister (Commercial) HM Embassy, Washington, 1950–55; Ambassador to Chile, 1955–58. Rural District Councillor, Bridge-Blean, 1960–74. *Address:* Seatonden, Ickham, Canterbury, Kent. *Club:* English-Speaking Union.
*Died 17 Aug. 1983.*

**EMPSON, Sir William**, Kt 1979; FBA 1976; Professor of English Literature, Sheffield University, 1953–71, then Emeritus; *b* 27 Sept. 1906; *s* of late A. R. Empson, Yokefleet Hall, Howden, Yorks, and Laura (*née* Micklethwait); *m* 1941, Hester Henrietta Crouse; two *s. Educ:* Winchester; Magdalene Coll., Cambridge. Chair of English Literature, Bunrika Daigaku, Tokyo, 1931–34; Professorship in English Literature, Peking National University, then part of the South-Western Combined Universities, in Hunan and Yunnan, 1937–39; BBC Chinese Editor, 1941–46, after a year in BBC Monitoring Dept; returned to Peking National Univ., 1947, Prof., Western Languages Department. Hon. LittD East Anglia, 1968; Hon. DLitt Bristol, 1971; Hon. LittD: Sheffield, 1974; Cambridge, 1977. *Publications:* Seven Types of Ambiguity, 1930; Poems, 1935; Some Versions of Pastoral, 1935; The Gathering Storm (verse), 1940; The Structure of Complex Words, 1951; Collected Poems, 1955; Milton's God, 1961; (ed with D. Pirie) Selected Poems of Coleridge, 1972; *posthumous publications:* Using Biography, 1984; Collected Poems, 1985. *Address:* Studio House, 1 Hampstead Hill Gardens, NW3.
*Died 15 April 1984.*

**ENDERL, Dr Kurt H.;** Ambassador of Austria to the Court of St James's, 1975–78, retired 1979; *b* 12 April 1913; *s* of Hugo Enderl and Karoline Enderl; *m* 1967, Adele Leigh. *Educ:* Vienna Univ. (Dr of Law). 3rd Sec., Austrian Legation, London, 1946–47; Chargé d'Affaires, Aust. Legation, New Delhi, 1950–53; Austrian Minister in Israel, 1955–58; Head of Multilateral Economic Dept, Min. of Foreign Affairs, Vienna, 1958–61; Austrian Ambassador: in Poland, 1962–67; in Hungary, 1967–72; Chief of Protocol, Vienna, 1972–74. *Recreations:* tennis, ski-ing. *Address:* Linke Wienzeile 12, 1060 Vienna, Austria.
*Died 25 March 1985.*

**ENDERS, Dr John Franklin;** Chief, Virus Unit, Division of Infectious Diseases, Children's Medical Center, Boston, Mass, since 1972 (Chief of Research Division, 1947–72); University Professor Emeritus, Harvard University, since 1967; *b* 10 Feb. 1897; *s* of John Ostrom Enders and Harriet Goulden Whitmore; *m* 1927, Sarah Frances Bennett (*d* 1943); one *s* one *d*; 1951, Carolyn Bernice Keane; one step *s. Educ:* St Paul's Sch., Concord, NH; Yale Univ. (BA 1919); Harvard Univ. (MA 1922, PhD 1930). USNR Flying Corps, 1917–20. Teaching and research in field of infectious diseases of man, 1927–. Member Faculty Harvard Medical Sch., 1929–67; Civ. Cons. to Secretary of War on Epidemic Diseases in Army, 1942–46; Member Commn on Virus Dis, US Army, 1949–68; Member WHO Expert Advisory Panel on Virus Diseases, 1958. Passano Award, 1953; Lasker Award, 1954; Nobel Laureate, 1954, in Physiology or Medicine; Cameron Prize, 1960; Ricketts Award, 1962; Robert Koch Medal, 1963; Galen Award, Soc. of Apothecaries, 1981. US Presidential Medal of Freedom, 1963; Commander of the Republic of Upper Volta, 1965. Member: National Academy of Sciences (US); American Philosophical Society; Academie Nat. de Med. (France); Deut. Akad. d. Naturforsch. (Leopoldina); Hon. Member: RSM (England); Acad. Roy. de Med. (Belgium); Foreign Mem., Royal Soc. (England); Associé honoraire étranger, Académie des Sciences, Inscriptions et Belles-Lettres de Toulouse; Associé étranger, Académie des Sciences de l'Institut de France. Fellow American Academy of Arts and Sciences. Hon. FACS. Holds several honorary degrees. *Publications:* (joint) Immunity: Principles and Application in Medicine and Public Health, 1939; papers in scientific journals. *Recreations:* fishing, sailing. *Address:* 64 Colbourne Crescent, Brookline, Mass 02147, USA. *T:* Longwood 6–3539. *Clubs:* Country (Brookline); Harvard, Saturday (Boston, Mass).
*Died 8 Sept. 1985.*

**ENERGLYN, Baron** *cr* 1968 (Life Peer), of Caerphilly; **William David Evans**, MSc, DSc, PhD; DL; Professor of Geology, University of Nottingham, 1949–78; formerly Dean of the Faculty of Pure Science; *b* 25 Dec. 1912; *s* of Councillor D. G. Evans; *m* 1941, Jean Thompson Miller; no *c. Educ:* Caerphilly Grammar Sch.; University Coll., Cardiff. Geologist to HM Geological Survey of Great Britain, 1939; Member of Regional Survey Board of Ministry of Fuel and Power for South Wales Coalfield, 1945; Senior Lecturer in Geology, University College of South Wales and Monmouthshire, 1947.

Discoverer of vitricin, the antibiotic in coal; initiator of pyrochromotography, photogrammetry and membrane colorimetry. FGS 1939; FRGS 1944; FLS 1945; MIME 1952; MIMM 1949. MSc Wales, 1938; PhD London, 1940. DL Notts, 1974. Hon. Fellow, Mark Twain Soc. of America, 1976. *Publications:* Through the Crust of the Earth, 1974; research papers in Trans and Proc. of Geol Society of London, Royal Geog. Society, Institute of Mining and Metallurgy, etc, on geology of older rocks of Wales, and Cornwall, and cause of dust diseases among coalminers and metalliferous miners. *Address:* 7 The Dentons, Denton Road, Eastbourne, E Sussex BN20 7SW. *Club:* Royal Automobile.
*Died 27 June 1985.*

**ENGELS, Johan Peter;** Chairman, Philips Electronic and Associated Industries Ltd, 1964–73; *b* Rotterdam, Holland, 6 March 1908; *m* 1935, Christina Pieternella van Hoeflaken (*d* 1980); three *s* one *d*. *Educ:* Holland. Joined Philips, in Holland, 1928. Moved to England and appointed Managing Director of Philips Electrical Ltd, 1961; appointed Director of Philips Electronic & Associated Industries Ltd, 1962, and Chairman, 1964. Officer, Order of Orange Nassau (Holland), 1968. *Recreations:* golf, swimming, reading, gardening. *Address:* c/o Philips Electronic and Associated Industries Ltd, Arundel Great Court, 8 Arundel Street, WC2R 3DT.
*Died 15 Feb. 1981.*

**ENGHOLM, Sir Basil Charles,** KCB 1968 (CB 1964); Director: Sadler's Wells Theatre Trust, since 1975; New Sadler's Wells Opera, 1987–89; *b* 2 Aug. 1912; *o s* of late C. F. G. Engholm; *m* 1936, Nancy, *er d* of Lifford Hewitt, St Anthony, Rye; one *d*. *Educ:* Tonbridge Sch.; Sorbonne, Paris; Sidney Sussex Coll., Cambridge (Law Tripos, MA). Member of Gray's Inn; Metal business, New York, 1933–34; entered Ministry of Agriculture and Fisheries, 1935; War of 1939–45: part-time NFS; Principal Private Secretary to Minister of Agriculture and Fisheries, 1943–45; Asst Secretary, 1945; Under-Secretary, 1954; Fisheries Secretary, 1960–62; Dep. Secretary, 1964–67; Permanent Sec., MAFF, 1968–72. Dir, Comfin Ltd, 1973–85 (Consultant, 1985–86). Chm., BFI, 1978–81; Trustee, Theatre Trust, 1977–84. *Recreations:* reading, painting, opera, ballet, films, looking at pictures. *Address:* Hunters, Langton Road, Langton Green, Tunbridge Wells TN3 0BA. *T:* Tunbridge Wells (0892) 27480. *Club:* United Oxford & Cambridge University.
*Died 12 June 1990.*

**ENGLEDOW, Sir Frank Leonard,** Kt 1944; CMG 1935; FRS 1946; MA, BSc; Fellow of St John's College, Cambridge; Drapers' Professor of Agriculture, Cambridge University, 1930–57; *b* 1890; *m* Mildred (*d* 1956); four *d*. *Educ:* St John's Coll., Cambridge. The Queen's Own (Royal West Kent Regt), 1914–18; Adjutant, 5th Batt. Mesopotamian Expeditionary Force; retiring rank Lt-Col; asst Director of Agriculture, Mesopotamia, 1918–19. *Publication:* (ed) Britain's Future in Farming. *Address:* The Hope Nursing Home, Brooklands Avenue, Cambridge CB2 2BQ. *T:* Cambridge 59087.
*Died 3 July 1985.*

**ENNALS, John Arthur Ford;** Chairman, British Yugoslav Society, since 1982; Director, United Kingdom Immigrants Advisory Service, 1970–83; *b* Walsall, 21 July 1918; *e s* of Arthur Ford Ennals, MC, and Jessie Edith Ennals (*née* Taylor); one *s* one *d*. *Educ:* Queen Mary's Grammar Sch., Walsall; St John's Coll., Cambridge. MA (History and Psychology). Rotary Travelling Schol. to USA, 1935. Pres., British Univs League of Nations Soc., and Cttee, Cambridge Union, 1938–39. Lectr for British Council, Roumania and Yugoslavia, 1939–40; War Corresp., Greece, Yugoslavia, Albania, 1941; on staff of British Embassy, Madrid, 1941–42, and Foreign Office, 1942–43. Served War: Egypt, Italy and Yugoslavia, 1943–45. Mem., S Bucks DC, 1983–87. Contested (Lab): Walsall South, 1955, 1959; Thames Valley, European Parly elecns, 1979. Secretary-Gen., World Fedn of UN Assocs, 1946–56; Gen.-Sec. and Tutor in Internat. Relations, Ruskin Coll., Oxford, 1956–66; Dir-Gen., UN Assoc., 1966–70 (Vice-Pres., 1978–); Hon. Pres., World Fedn of UN Assocs, 1977–; Member: OXFAM Exec., 1965–75; Exec. Council, Assoc. of Supervisory Staffs, Executives and Technicians, 1960–69. Trustee, Assoc. of Scientific Technical and Managerial Staffs, 1969–; Chm., Anti-Apartheid Movement, 1968–76; Member: Community and Race Relations Unit, British Council of Churches, 1971–79; Exec. Cttee, British Refugee Council, 1981–83; CPRE, 1974–. Parish Councillor: Kidlington, 1961–67; Hedgerley, 1976–. Yugoslav Star with Golden Wreath, 1984; Peace Medal (India), 1986. *Recreations:* travelling in Europe, Asia and Africa; walking in Wales; cricket. *Address:* 3 Village Lane, Hedgerley, Bucks SL2 3UY. *T:* (home) Farnham Common 4302. *Club:* India.
*Died 14 Sept. 1988.*

**ENNISKILLEN, 6th Earl of,** *cr* 1789; **David Lowry Cole,** MBE 1955; Baron Mountflorence, 1760; Viscount Enniskillen, 1776; Baron Grinstead (UK), 1815; farmer, Kenya and N Ireland; *b* 10 Sept. 1918; *er s* of Hon. Galbraith Lowry Egerton Cole (*d* 1929) (3rd *s* of 4th Earl of Enniskillen) and Lady Eleanor Cole (*d* 1979), *d* of 2nd Earl of Balfour; *S* uncle, 1963; *m* 1st, 1940, Sonia Mary Syers (from

whom he obtained a divorce, 1955; she *d* 1982); one *s* one *d*; 2nd, 1955, Nancy Henderson MacLennan, former American Vice Consul. *Educ:* Eton; Trinity Coll., Cambridge. BA Agric. 1940. Served War of 1939–45, Captain Irish Guards: Kenya Emergency, 1953–55, Provincial Comdt, Kenya Police Reserve (MBE). MLC for North Kenya, 1961–63. Formerly: Member Kenya Meat Commn; Member Exec., Kenya National Farmers Union; Vice-Chairman Kenya Stockowners Council; Member Exec., Kenya Board of Agriculture; Member Board: Land and Agric. Bank of Kenya; East African Diatomite Syndicate Ltd. Captain, Ulster Defence Regt, 1971–73. Mem., Fermanagh CC, 1963–69; DL 1963–78, JP 1972–78, Co. Fermanagh. *Recreations:* shooting, golf, fishing. *Heir: s* Viscount Cole. *Address:* Kinloch House, Amulree, Dunkeld, Perthshire PH8 0EB; PO Box 30100, Nairobi, Kenya. *Clubs:* Carlton, Turf, Cavalry and Guards; New (Edinburgh); Muthaiga Country (Nairobi).
*Died 30 May 1989.*

**ENSOR, Alick Charles Davidson, (David);** solicitor, journalist and author; *b* 27 Nov. 1906; *s* of Charles William Ensor, MRCS, LRCP, and Helen Margaret Creighton Ensor; *m* 1st, 1932, Norah Russell (marr. diss.); one *s* two *d*; 2nd, 1944, Frances Vivienne Mason. *Educ:* Westminster Sch. Solicitor, 1928; Prosecuting Solicitor, Newcastle upon Tyne, 1932; Prosecuting Solicitor, Metropolitan Police, 1935; Law Lecturer, Police Coll., Hendon, 1935; Deputy Clerk of Peace, Middlesex, 1937; Clerk of Peace, London, 1938. War service with Army in France, Africa, Far East, 1939–44. Practised as Solicitor in Brussels, 1945–47. Retired from Law and farmed in Dorset, 1948. MP (Lab) Bury and Radcliffe, 1964–70; PPS to Ministers of Agriculture. Mem., Select Cttee on Estimates, 1964–69; Chairman: Private Bill Cttee, 1967–70; House of Commons Catering Cttee, 1969–70; Anglo-Soviet Parly Cttee and other Gps; Leader of many delegations all round the world including Mauritius, Pakistan, Spain and GDR. Has broadcast regularly for radio and television since 1957. Films include: The Trials of Oscar Wilde; The Pot Carriers; Death and the Sky Above. TV Series, The Verdict is Yours. Vice-Pres., Mark Twain Soc. of America, 1977–. Has travelled extensively in Eastern Europe, Middle and Far East. *Publications:* Thirty Acres and a Cow, 1955; I was a Public Prosecutor, 1958; Verdict Afterwards, 1960; With Lord Roberts through the Khyber Pass, 1963; contributions to Local Government Law in England and Wales, Journal of Criminal Law. *Recreation:* studying French history. *Address:* L'Etoile d'Or, 66701 Argelès-sur-Mer, France.
*Died 5 Feb. 1987.*

**ENTERS, Angna;** mime; dancer; painter; sculptor; author; dramatist; composer; choreographer; scene and costume designer for the theatre; *b* NYC, US, 28 April 1907; *o c* of Edward Enters and Henriette Gasseur-Styleau; *m* Louis Kalonyme. *Educ:* privately and self-educated in US; Europe; Egypt; Greece. Theatre début New York, 1924, presenting in solo performance a new theatre form in which she combined for the first time the arts of mime, dance, music, costume, scenic design; originated phrase dance-mime now in Amer. dictionaries; first performer to be presented in a theatrical performance, 1943, by Metropolitan Museum of Art, NYC; presented for her 25th Broadway (NY) season, 1959; a nationwide television broadcast, in US, presented a composite portrait of her work in theatre, painting, writing, 1959. London début, St Martin's Theatre, 1928; many subseq. British seasons including television. Paris début, 1929; Am. Rep. in Internat. Theatre season presented by C. B. Cochran, Queen's Theatre, 1931. Rep. Am. Nat. Theatre and Acad., at Internat. Arts Festival, Berlin, and tour of W Germany. Guggenheim Foundation Fellowships, 1934 and 1935 (research in Greece, Egypt, Near East). Début exhibn of painting, NY, 1933, many subseq. Début exhibn of paintings in London, Eng., 1934 and subseq. Début exhibn of sculpture, New York, 1945; subseq. one-woman shows of painting and sculpture in US and Canada. Works are in Metropolitan Museum of Art, New York, etc. Painted mural, modern Penthouse Theatre of University of Washington, Seattle, 1950. Rep. in Exhibns, NY Museum of Modern Art, 1953. First work in Ceramics exhibited in New York and Los Angeles, 1953. Lecture tours US, 1954–. Prof. of Acting, Baylor Univ., Waco, Texas, and Director of plays, Dallas Theatre Center, Dallas, Texas, 1961–62. Fellow: Center for Advanced Studies, Wesleyan Univ., Middletown, Conn, 1962–; Pennsylvania State Univ., 1970. Films based on her original stories: Lost Angel, Tenth Avenue Angel, Silly Girl, 1944–47; You Belong to Me, 1950. Created and staged Commedia dell' Arte (play within play seq.) in film Scaramouche, 1951; Dir, also designer of stage settings and costumes, for play, Yerma, by G. Lorca (Broadway, NY, etc.), 1958. Plays produced: Love Possessed Juana, 1946; The Unknown Lover-A Modern Psyche, 1947. *Publications:* First Person Plural (self-illustr.), 1937, new edn 1978; Love Possessed Juana (self-scored and illustr. play), 1939; Silly Girl (self-illustr. autobiog.), 1944; Among the Daughters (novel), 1955 (publ. London, 1956, as A Thing of Beauty); Artist's Life (self-illustrated), 1957; Artist's Life (publ. London, 1959); (trans. with L. Kalonyme) Chantecler, by E. Rostand, 1960; Angna Enters on Mime, 1965; also illustrated Best American Short Stories of 1945; article on Pantomime, Encyclopædia Britannica.
*Died 28 Feb. 1989.*

**ENTHOVEN, Roderick Eustace,** FRIBA; FSA; architect in private practice; Consultant, Enthoven Architects (formerly Enthoven & Mock), since 1978; *b* 30 May 1900; *o* surv. *s* of late Ernest James Enthoven, Great Ote Hall, Wivelsfield, Sussex, and Rosaline Mary Eustace Smith; *m* 1933, Cecilia Mary Le Mesurier; three *s*. *Educ:* Clifton College. Received architectural education at Architectural Association Sch., 1919–24, qualifying with SADG Medal, Architectural Association Diploma. Partner in Enthoven & Mock; Partner in Pakington & Enthoven until war of 1939–45. Civil Camouflage Officer to Air Ministry, 1940–44; served in Italy as Captain, Monuments, Fine Arts and Archives Officer, 1944–45. Pres. Architectural Association, 1948–49; Vice-Pres. RIBA, 1951–53. Master of the Art Workers' Guild, 1976; Liveryman, Goldsmiths' Co. Commissions include: Khartoum Univ.; Goldsmiths' Coll.; City of London Polytechnic; Royal Foundn of St Katharine; Queen Elizabeth House, Oxford. *Publications:* contributor to various architectural journals. *Recreations:* theatre, foreign travel. *Address:* 3 Berkeley Gardens, Kensington Church Street, W8 4AP. *T:* 01–229 1482; 113 Old Street, EC1V 9JR. *T:* 01-253 1540. *Club:* Athenæum.      *Died 24 Nov.* 1985.

**ERSKINE, Sir (Robert) George,** Kt 1948; CBE 1945; Adviser to and former Director of Morgan Grenfell & Co. Limited; former Director, London & Provincial Trust Ltd (Chairman 1954–71); Member of London Advisory Committee, Scottish Council (Development and Industry); Former Member Council, RAF Benevolent Fund; *b* 5 Nov. 1896; *s* of late John Erskine, Kirkcudbright; unmarried. *Educ:* Kirkcudbright Academy; Edinburgh Univ. (BL). On staff of National Bank of Scotland, 1913–29, when joined Morgan Grenfell; Director, 1945–67; former Director: GKN Ltd; British-Commonwealth Shipping Co. Ltd, etc. Served European War, 1914–18. Dep. Chm. NAAFI, 1941–52; Vice-Pres. Institute of Bankers (Pres., 1954–56); Master of Glaziers' Company, 1960–61; Mem. Jenkins Cttee on Company Law, 1959–62. High Sheriff of Surrey, 1963–64. Mem., Law Soc. of Scotland. Fellow, Inst. of Directors; FRGS. Freeman, City of London; Past Grand Senior Deacon, United Grand Lodge of England. *Address:* Busbridge Wood, Godalming, Surrey. *T:* Hascombe 378.      *Died 10 May* 1984.

**ERSKINE-HILL, Sir Robert,** 2nd Bt, *cr* 1945; Member of the Royal Company of Archers, Queen's Body Guard for Scotland; Chartered Accountant; Director, Life Association of Scotland, 1951–87 (Chairman, 1960–86); *b* 6 Feb. 1917; *er s* of Sir Alexander Galloway Erskine-Hill, 1st Bt, KC, DL, and Christian Hendrie, MBE (*d* 1947), *o d* of John Colville, MP, Cleland, Lanarkshire; *S* father, 1947; *m* 1942, Christine Alison, *o d* of late Capt. (A) Henry James Johnstone of Alva, RN; two *s* two *d*. *Educ:* Eton; Trinity Coll., Cambridge (BA). Served War of 1939–45, in RNVR. Partner, Chiene & Tait, CA, Edinburgh, 1946–80. *Heir: s* Alexander Roger Erskine-Hill [*b* 15 Aug. 1949; *m* 1984, Sarah Anne Sydenham Clarke, *er d* of late Dr R. J. Sydenham Clarke and of Mrs Charles Clarke; one *s* one *d*]. *Address:* Quothquhan Lodge, Biggar, Lanarkshire. *T:* Tinto 332.      *Died 10 July* 1989.

**ERSKINE-LINDOP, Audrey Beatrice Noël;** novelist; *b* London, 26 Dec. 1920; *d* of late Lt-Col A. H. Erskine-Lindop, MC, and Ivy Monck-Mason; *m* 1945, Dudley Gordon Leslie, scriptwriter and playwright. *Educ:* Convent of Our Lady of Lourdes, Hatch End, Middx; Blackdown Sch., Wellington, Somerset. Started career in Worthing Repertory Company; became scriptwriter (England and Hollywood). Books have been published in numerous countries. Freeman of City of London, 1954. *Plays:* Beware of Angels (in collaboration with Dudley Leslie), prod Westminster Theatre, 1959; Let's Talk Turkey, prod 1955. *Publications:* In Me My Enemy, 1948; Soldiers' Daughters Never Cry, 1949; The Tall Headlines, 1950; Out of the Whirlwind, 1951; The Singer Not the Song, 1953 (Book Society choice; filmed, 1961); Details of Jeremy Stretton, 1955; The Judas Figures, 1956; I Thank a Fool, 1958; The Way to the Lantern, 1961; Nicola, 1966; I Start Counting, 1966 (Prix Roman Policier, France, 1968); Sight Unseen, 1969; Journey into Stone, 1973; The Self-Appointed Saint, 1975. *Recreations:* history (particularly collecting relics of favourite historical characters); anything to do with birds and cats; very fond of the wilder type of countryside. *Address:* Southcliffe Cottage, Sandrock Road, Niton Undercliff, IoW PO38 2NQ. *T:* Niton 730291.      *Died 7 Nov.* 1986.

**ERTZ, Susan, (Mrs J. R. McCrindle),** FRSL; writer; *b* 13 Feb. 1887; *d* of Charles Edward Ertz and Mary Gertrude Le Viness of New York; *m* 1932, Major J. Ronald McCrindle, CMG, OBE, MC (*d* 1977). *Publications:* Novels: Madam Claire; Nina; Afternoon; Now East, Now West; The Galaxy; Julian Probert, Face to Face (short stories); The Proselyte, 1933; Now We Set Out, 1934; Woman Alive, 1935; No Hearts to Break, 1937; Big Frogs and Little Frogs (short stories), 1938; Black, White, and Caroline (for children), 1938; One Fight More, 1940; Anger in the Sky, 1943; Two Names upon the Shore, 1947; The Prodigal Heart, 1950; The Undefended Gate, 1953; Charmed Circle, 1956; In the Cool of the Day, 1961; Devices and Desires, 1972; The Philosopher's Daughter, 1976;

contributions to various periodicals. *Recreations:* painting, gardening, travel. *Address:* Fir Tree Cottage, Newenden, Hawkhurst, Kent. *T:* Northiam 2196.      *Died 11 April* 1985.

**ESCRITT, (Charles) Ewart,** OBE 1970; MA; Secretary, Oxford University Appointments Committee, 1947–70; Fellow, Keble College, Oxford, 1965–70; *b* 26 Aug. 1905; *s* of late Rev. Charles Escritt; *m* 1939, Ruth Mary, *d* of late T. C. Metcalf; two *s* one *d*. *Educ:* Christ's Hospital; Keble Coll., Oxford. Asst Master, Bromsgrove Sch., 1928; Staff of Tootal Broadhurst Lee Co. Ltd, 1933–46. Served War of 1939–45: 42 Div. RASC (TA), 1939; 18 Div. RASC, Capt. 1940; POW, Singapore and Thailand, 1942–45. *Recreation:* Japanese studies. *Address:* 32 Portland Road, Oxford. *T:* Oxford (0865) 57072.      *Died 31 Oct.* 1990.

**ESDAILE, Philippa Chichele,** DSc, FLS; Reader in Biology, University of London, and Head of Biology Department, King's College of Household and Social Science, 1921–51; *b* 1888; *y d* of late George Esdaile, Manchester and late Georgina, *d* of George Doswell, Somerset. *Educ:* Manchester High Sch. for Girls. Graduated Univ. of Manchester, 1910; Research Fellow of University of Manchester and University Coll., Reading; Acting Head of Zoology Dept, Bedford Coll., University of London, 1915–20; Senior Lecturer in Zoology, Birkbeck Coll., University of London, 1920–21; Vice-Pres. of Linnean Soc. of London, 1932–33; Member: Makerere-Khartoum Education Commission, 1937; Advisory Committee on Education, Colonial Office, 1933–38; Committee on Nutrition in the Colonial Empire, Econ. Adv. Coun., 1933; Federation of Univ. Women; Crosby Hall. Formerly Member: Coun. of Girls' Public Day Sch. Trust, Ltd; Governing Body of Hatfield Sch., Herts. *Publications:* Economic Biology for Students of Social Science, Parts 1 and 2; various scientific papers. *Address:* St Audrey's, Church Street, Old Hatfield, Herts. *T:* Hatfield 61990.
     *Died 17 Dec.* 1989.

**ESHELBY, Prof. John Douglas,** FRS 1974; Professor of the Theory of Materials, University of Sheffield, since 1971; *b* 21 Dec. 1916; *s* of Alan Douglas and Doris Mason Eshelby; unmarried. *Educ:* privately; Univ. of Bristol. BSc, MA, PhD. Temp. Exper. Officer, HMS Vernon, 1939–40; RAF, 1940–46; res. worker, Univ. of Bristol, 1946–52; Res. Assoc., Univ. of Illinois, 1952–54; Lectr, Univ. of Birmingham, 1954–64; res. worker, Cavendish Lab., Univ. of Cambridge, 1964–66; Fellow of Churchill Coll., 1965–66; Reader, Univ. of Sheffield, 1966–71. Vis. Prof., Technische Hochschule, Stuttgart, 1963. *Publications:* articles on lattice defects and continuum mechanics in various learned jls. *Address:* 9 Beech Court, Beech Hill Road, Sheffield S10 2SA. *T:* Sheffield 681723.
     *Died 10 Dec.* 1981.

**ESMONDE, Sir Anthony Charles,** 15th Bt, *cr* 1629; *b* 18 Jan. 1899; 3rd *s* of Dr John Esmonde, MP; *S* brother (Capt. Sir John Lymbrick Esmonde, Bt), 1958; *m* 1927, Eithne Moira Grattan, *y d* of Sir Thomas Grattan Esmonde, 11th Bt; three *s* three *d*. *Educ:* Clongowes Wood Coll.; Germany. Surgeon Lieut, RN, 1921–25; LRCS & P Ireland, 1921. TD Wexford, 1951–73; Consultative Assembly, Council of Europe, 1954 (Cttees of Agriculture and Non-represented nations); Mem. Irish National Health Council, 1956. Mem. Catholic Truth Soc. of Ireland, 1936. Mem. Royal Dublin Soc., 1938. Knight of Honour and Devotion, Order of Malta, 1957. *Recreations:* agriculturist; fishing, shooting, etc. *Heir: e s* John Henry Grattan Esmonde, SC (His Honour Judge Esmonde) [*b* 27 June 1928; *m* 1957, Pamela Mary, *d* of late Francis Stephen Bourke, FRCPI; three *s* two *d*. SC 1971; TD (Fine Gael) Wexford, 1973–77; a Circuit Court Judge, 1977–]. *Address:* Ballynastragh, Gorey, Co. Wexford, Eire. *T:* Arklow 7182.      *Died 17 March* 1981.

**ESMONDE, Sir John Henry Grattan,** 16th Bt *cr* 1629; SC; **His Honour Judge Esmonde;** Circuit Court Judge, Western Circuit, since 1977; *b* 27 June 1928; *s* of Sir Anthony Charles Esmonde, 15th Bt, and of Eithne Moira Grattan, *y d* of Sir Thomas Grattan Esmonde, 11th Bt; *S* father, 1981; *m* 1957, Pamela Mary, *d* of late Francis Stephen Bourke, FRCPI; three *s* two *d*. *Educ:* Blackrock College, Dublin; University Coll., Dublin; King's Inns, Dublin. BComm, NUI. Member of the Irish Bar, 1949; Senior Counsel, 1971. TD (Fine Gael) Wexford, 1973–77. *Heir: s* Thomas Francis Grattan Esmonde, *b* 14 Oct. 1960. *Address:* 6 Nutley Avenue, Dublin 4. *T:* Dublin 693040. *Club:* Galway County.      *Died 16 May* 1987.

**ESPLEN, Sir William Graham,** 2nd Bt, *cr* 1921; former Shipowner; *b* 29 Dec. 1899; *s* of 1st Bt and Laura Louise (*d* 1936), *d* of late John Dickinson, Sunderland; *S* father, 1930; *m* 1928, Aline Octavia (marr. diss. 1951), *y d* of late A. Octavius Hedley; one *s*. *Educ:* Harrow; Cambridge. Joined Royal Naval College, Keyham, 1918; retired, 1922. *Recreation:* fishing. *Heir: s* John Graham Esplen [*b* 4 Aug. 1932; *m* 1956, Valerie Joan, *yr d* of Maj.-Gen. A. P. Lambooy, CB, OBE, and late Doris Lambooy; one *s* three *d*]. *Address:* c/o Alldens Cottage, Thorncombe Street, Bramley, Surrey GU5 0NA.
     *Died 29 April* 1989.

**ESSEX, 9th Earl of,** *cr* 1661; **Reginald George de Vere Capell,** TD; Baron Capel, 1641; Viscount Malden, 1661; *b* 9 Oct. 1906; *o s* of 8th

Earl of Essex and Mary Eveline (*d* 1955), *d* of late W. R. Stewart Freeman; *S* father, 1966; *m* 1st, 1937, Mrs Mary Reeve Strutt (marr. diss. 1957), *d* of Gibson Ward, Bermuda; 2nd, 1957, Nona Isobel (*née* Miller), Christchurch, NZ (*widow* of Frank Smythe). *Educ:* Eton; Cambridge. Lt-Col, 1947; Commanded 16th Airborne Div., Signals Regt (TA), 1948. Hon. Col 47 Signals Regt, Mddx Yeo., 1957. *Heir: kinsman* Robert Edward de Vere Capell [*b* 13 Jan. 1920; *m* 1942, Doris Margaret, *d* of G. F. Tomlinson; one *s*]. *Address:* Floyds Farm, Wingrave, Aylesbury, Bucks. *T:* Aston Abbotts 220. *Clubs:* Bath, MCC.                                *Died 18 May 1981.*

**ESSEX, Rosamund Sibyl**, MA; free-lance journalist, since 1979; *b* 26 July 1900; *d* of late Rev. Herbert J. Essex and late Rachel Watson; unmarried; one adopted *s*. *Educ:* Bournemouth High Sch. for Girls; St Hilda's Coll., Oxford. Editorial staff of the Church Times, 1929–47; Asst Ed., 1947–50; Editor, 1950–60; Member of Staff, Christian Aid, British Council of Churches, 1960–78. Chm. Religious Press Group, 1952–53 and 1957–58. Commissioned and licensed a Reader in the Church of England, dio. St Albans, 12 July 1969. *Publications:* (with Sidney Dark) The War Against God, 1937; Into the Forest, 1963; Woman in a Man's World (autobiog.), 1977. *Recreation:* photography. *Address:* 32 Holywell Hill, St Albans, Herts AL1 1BZ. *T:* St Albans 53424. *Club:* Royal Commonwealth Society.                                *Died 11 April 1985.*

**ESSLEMONT, Mary**, CBE 1955; MA, BSc, MB, ChB, DPH, LLD, JP; *b* 1891; *d* of late George Birnie Esslemont, MP for South Aberdeen. *Educ:* Aberdeen High Sch. for Girls; Aberdeen Univ. Asst, Botany Dept, University of Aberdeen, 1915–17; Science Lecturer, Stockwell Training Coll., London, 1917–19; Asst MOH, Keighley, Yorks, 1924–29; Gen. Practitioner, Aberdeen, 1929, until retirement. Fellow: BMA, 1959; RCGP, 1969. Mem., Aberdeen Univ. Court, 1947–74. Hon. LLD, University of Aberdeen, 1954. JP for District Council of Aberdeen. Freedom, City of Aberdeen, 1981. *Recreation:* travel. *Address:* Mile End House, 30 Beechgrove Terrace, Aberdeen AB2 4ED. *T:* 633601. *Club:* Soroptimist Headquarters.                                *Died 25 Aug. 1984.*

**ESTCOURT, Maj.-Gen. Edward Noel Keith**, DSO 1944; OBE 1945; psc; *b* 17 Dec. 1905; *s* of E. A. Estcourt, Gloucester and B. M. Carr-Calthorp, Norfolk; *m* 1938, Pamela Wellesley; two *s* one *d*. *Educ:* Cheltenham Coll.; RMA Woolwich. Commissioned RA, 1925. Served War of 1939–45: N Africa, Italy and Greece. Staff Coll., Camberley, 1940; GSO1 1st Inf. Div., 1944–45; GSO1 4th Inf. Div., 1945–46. Dep. Dir Mil. Ops, War Office, 1951–55; Dep. Comdt, NATO Defence Coll., 1955–57; Commandant, NATO Defence Coll., Paris, 1958. Principal, Ashridge Coll., 1958–62. Bronze Star, USA, 1945. *Recreations:* shooting, fishing, golf. *Address:* Trip The Daisy, Idstone, Swindon, Wilts SN6 8LL.
                                *Died 26 May 1982.*

**ESTES, Elliott M(arantette)**; President and Chief Operating Officer, General Motors Corporation, Detroit, USA, 1974–81; *b* Mendon, Mich, 7 Jan. 1916. Joined Gen. Motors Corp., 1956; Exec. Vice-Pres., Ops and Staff Dir, 1972–74. Director: Kellogg Co. Inc.; Owens-Illinois Inc.; Communications Satellite Corp. *Address:* c/o General Motors Corporation, 3044 West Grand Boulevard, Detroit, Mich 48202, USA.                        *Died 25 March 1988.*

**ETHERTON, Ralph (Humphrey)**, MA; Barrister-at-Law; *b* 11 Feb. 1904; *o s* of late Louis Etherton and Bertha Bagge; *m* 1944, Johanne Patricia, *y d* of late Gerald Cloherty, Galway, Ireland; one *s* one *d*. *Educ:* Charterhouse; Trinity Hall, Cambridge. Called to Bar, Inner Temple, 1926, and joined Northern Circuit, practised at Common Law Bar until 1939; Municipal Reform Candidate LCC election, N Camberwell 1931, and W. Fulham 1937; served in RAFVR (Special Duties), Flt Lt, 1940–42; MP (Nat. C) for Stretford div. of Lancs, 1939–45; contested (Nat. C) Liverpool (Everton div.), 1935, Stretford div. of Lancs, 1945; engaged in commerce and farming, since 1945. Chm. of Coningsby Club, 1933–34; Mem. of Parliamentary Delegation to Australia and New Zealand, 1944. *Recreations:* travel, riding. *Address:* Greentree Hall, Balcombe Forest, W Sussex RH17 6JZ. *T:* Balcombe 811319. *Clubs:* Carlton, Pratt's.
                                *Died 10 Dec. 1987.*

**ETON, Robert;** *see* Meynell, L. W.

**ETTLINGER, Prof. Leopold David;** Professor of History of Art, University of California, Berkeley, 1970–80; *b* 20 April 1913; *s* of Dr Emil Ettlinger, University Librarian, and Dora (*née* Beer); *m* 1st, 1939, Amrei (*née* Jacoby) (*d* 1955); 2nd, 1959, Madeline (*née* Noirot); 3rd, 1973, Helen (*née* Shahrokh). *Educ* Stadtgymnasium Halle; Universities of Halle and Marburg. Social Worker for Refugee Children from Germany, 1938–41; Asst Master, King Edward VI Grammar Sch., Five Ways, Birmingham, 1941–48; Asst Curator, Photographic Collection, Warburg Institute, University of London, 1948–51; Curator of Photographic Collection, 1951–56; Lectr, Warburg Inst., 1956–59; Durning Lawrence Prof. of History of Art, Univ. of London, 1959–70. Fellowship, Inst. for Advanced Study, Princeton, 1956; Vis. Professor: Yale Univ., 1963–64; Univ. of Calif, Berkeley, 1969; Univ. of Bonn, 1975–76, 1981–82, 1984–85; Univ. of Victoria, BC, 1980; Stanford Univ., 1983–85; Univ. of Melbourne, 1983; Kress Prof., Nat. Gall. of Art, Washington DC, 1980–81; Johnson Prof., Middlebury Coll., 1982; Scholar-in-Residence, Univ. of Puget Sound, Tacoma, Washington, 1986. FSA 1962–. British Academy award, 1963. *Publications:* (with R. G. Holloway) Compliments of the Season, 1947; The Art of the Renaissance in Northern Europe, in New Cambridge Modern History, Vol. I, 1957; Kandinsky's "At Rest", 1961; Art History Today, 1961; The Sistine Chapel before Michelangelo: Religious Imagery and Papal Politics, 1965; (with Helen S. Ettlinger) Botticelli, 1976; Antonio and Piero Pollaiuolo, 1978; (with Helen S. Ettlinger) Raphael, 1987; contribs to Journal of Warburg and Courtauld Insts, Burlington Magazine, Architectural Review, Connoisseur, Italian Studies and other jls.                        *Died 4 July 1989.*

**ETZDORF, Hasso von;** *b* 2 March 1900; *s* of Rüdiger von Etzdorf-Neumark and Agnes Maria Lorentz; *m* Katharina Otto-Margonin. *Educ:* Universities of Berlin, Göttingen, Halle (LLD). German Foreign Office, 1928; served in Berlin, Tokyo, Rome, Genoa (Consul-Gen.); Dep. Head, German Office for Peace Questions, Stuttgart, 1947–50; FO, Bonn, 1950–53; Head of German Delegn at Interim Cttee for Eur. Def. Community in Paris, rank of Minister, 1953; Dep. Sec.-Gen., WEU, London, 1955; Ambassador of German Federal Republic to Canada, 1956–58; Dep. Under-Sec. and Head of Western Dept, FO, Bonn, 1958–61; Ambassador of German Fed. Rep. to Court of St James's, 1961–65. GCVO (Hon.) 1964; Order of Merit with Star, Federal Republic of Germany, 1957. *Address:* Eichtling, D-8018 Grafing bei München, Germany. *T:* Glonn (08093) 1402. *Clubs:* Travellers'; Anglo-Belgian.
                                *Died 7 July 1989.*

**EUGSTER, General Sir Basil (Oscar Paul)**, KCB 1970 (CB 1966); KCVO 1968; CBE 1962; DSO 1945; MC 1938, and Bar, 1940; DL; *b* 15 Aug. 1914; *er s* of late Oscar Louis Eugster, DSO, Kempston Hoo, near Bedford; *m* 1939, Marcia Elaine, *er d* of late Air Commodore Sir Percy Smyth-Osbourne, CMG, CBE; two *s*. *Educ:* Beaumont; Christ Church, Oxford (MA). 2nd Lieut Irish Guards, 1935. Served War of 1939–45 in Narvik, Italy and NW Europe; Bde Maj., HQ 140 Inf. Bde, 1943–44; GSO 2 (Ops); HQ 5 Corps CMF, Oct.–Nov., 1944; OC 3rd Bn IG, Jan.–Feb., 1945; GSO 1, Guards Div., Dec. 1945–Jan. 1947; OC 2nd Bn, Irish Guards, 1947; JSSC, 1950; OC 1st Bn, Irish Guards, 1951–54; AAG War Office, 1954–56; Comdt, Eaton Hall Officer Cadet Sch., 1956–58; Comdt Mons Officer Cadet Sch., 1958; IDC 1959; Comd, 3rd Inf. Bde Gp, and Dhekelia Area, Cyprus, 1959–62; Comdt Sch. of Infantry, Warminster, 1962–63; GOC 4 Div., BAOR, 1963–65; GOC London Dist, and Maj.-Gen. Comdg Houshold Bde, 1965–68; Commander, British Forces, Hong Kong, 1968–70; GOC-in-C, Southern Comd, 1971–72; C-in-C, UKLF, 1972–74. ADC (Gen.), 1973–74; retired 1974; Col, Irish Guards, 1969, Hon. Col 1974–80, London Irish Co., N Irish Mil. (V). DL Devon, 1977. *Address:* Holmedown, Exbourne, N Devon. *T:* Exbourne 241. *Clubs:* White's, Buck's.
                                *Died 5 April 1984.*

**EUWE, Dr Machgielis;** Commandeur, Order of Oranje Nassau, 1979 (Officer 1936); Ridder van de Nederlandse Leeuw, 1971; President, International Chess Federation, 1970–78; *b* 20 May 1901; *m* 1926, Carolina Elizabeth Bergman; three *d*. *Educ:* Amsterdam Univ. Mathematical: University, 1918; Final proof, 1923; Dissertation (doctor-degree), 1926; Chess: Champion of Holland, 1921, Amateur Champion of the World, 1928, World Champion (Universal) being still amateur, by winning a match against Alekhine (15½–14½), 1935, lost the title in the return match against Alekhine (9½–15½), 1937; several wins in tournaments, especially in British tournaments. Chm. Cttee installed by Euratom which studied process of human thinking with particular relation to chess, 1961–63. Dir Netherlands Automatic Information Processing Research Centre, 1959–64; Prof., Univ. of Tilburg, 1964–71 (Extraordinary Prof. in Automation at Univ. Rotterdam, 1964–71). Commandeur, Order of Orange Nassau (Netherlands), 1979. *Publications:* Dutch: Practische Schaaklessen, 1927; Schaakopeningen, 1937; Eindspelen, 1940; Positiespel en Combinatiespel, 1949; Middenspelen, 1951; English: Strategy and Tactics, 1936; From my Games, 1938; Judgment and Planning, 1953; The Logical Approach to Chess (with U. Blaine and J. F. S. Rumble), 1958; A Guide to Chess Endings (with David Hooper), 1959; Master against Amateur (with Prof. W. Meiden), 1963; Road to Mastery (with Prof. W. Meiden), 1963; The Development of Chess Style, 1966; Master against Master (with Prof. W. Meiden), 1977; Fischer and his Predecessors, 1977; Bedrijfsvoering met de Computer, 1969; several other publications on automatic data processing. *Address:* Mensinge 40, 1083 HC Amsterdam, Netherlands. *T:* 020–441340.
                                *Died 26 Nov. 1981.*

**EVANG, Karl**, MD; Norwegian physician; Director-General, Norwegian Health Services, 1939–72; *b* 19 Oct. 1902; *s* of Jens Ingolf Evang and Beate (*née* Wexelsen); *m* 1929, Gerda Sophie

Landmark Moe; one s three d. Educ: Oslo Univ. (MD). On Staff, Oslo Municipal Hosp., 1932–34; MO, State Factor, Inspection Office, 1937–38; represented Norway at UNRRA, FAO, and WHO, 1943–. Pres., 2nd World Health Assembly, 1949; Chm., WHO Exec. Bd, 1966; Member: WHO Panel on Public Health Administration; Norwegian Soc. of Hygiene. Vis. Prof. of Social Medicine, Univ. of Tromsø, 1973. Hon. FRSM. Hon. Fellow, Amer. Public Health Assoc. (Bronfman Prize, 1970). Léon Bernard Medal and Prize, WHO, 1966. *Publications:* Birth Control, 1930; Norwegian Medical Dictionary, 1933; Race Policy and Reaction, 1934; Education to Peace, 1947; The Rehabilitation of Public Health in Norway, 1947; The Public Health Services, 1948; Sexual Education, 1951; Health Service, Society and Medicine, 1958; Health Services in Norway, 1960, 4th edn 1976; Use and Abuse of Drugs, 1966; Current Narcotic Problems, 1967; Health and Society, 1974. *Address:* Måltrostveien 11B, Oslo 13, Norway. *Died 3 Jan. 1981.*

**EVANS OF HUNGERSHALL,** Baron *cr* 1967 (Life Peer), of Borough of Royal Tunbridge Wells; **Benjamin Ifor Evans,** Kt 1955; MA, DLit London; FRSL; *b* London, 19 Aug. 1899; *y s* of Benjamin Evans; *m* 1923, Marjorie Ruth, *d* of late John Measures, Ifield; one *d. Educ:* Stationers' Company's Sch.; University Coll., London. Prof. of English at Southampton, Sheffield and London; Principal, Queen Mary Coll. (University of London), 1944–51; Provost, University Coll., London, 1951–66. Educational Dir of the British Council, 1940–44; Vice-Chm. of Arts Council, 1946–51; Chairman: Educational Advisory Council, Thames Television; Linguaphone Institute. Vice-Pres., RSL, 1974, Chm. 1975–77. Fellow: UCL; Queen Mary Coll. Hon. Dr of Letters, University of Paris; Hon. LLD, University of Manchester. Officer of the Legion of Honour; Chevalier, Order of the Crown of Belgium; Comdr, Order of Orange Nassau; Comdr, Order of Dannebrog. *Publications:* Encounters, 1926; English Poetry in the Later Nineteenth Century, 1933; The Limits of Literary Criticism, 1933; Keats, 1934; edns, with W. W. Greg, of The Commody of Susanna, and Jack Juggler, 1937; Tradition and Romanticism, 1940; A Short History of English Literature, 1940; English Literature (for British Council), 1944; In Search of Stephen Vane, 1946; The Shop on the King's Road, 1947; Literature Between the Wars, 1948; A Short History of English Drama, 1948; The Church in the Markets, 1948; (with Mary Glasgow) The Arts in England, 1948; The Use of English, 1949; (with Marjorie R. Evans) A Victorian Anthology, 1949; The Language of Shakespeare's Plays, 1951; Science and Literature, 1954; English Literature: Values and Traditions, 1962; Portrait of English Literature, 1979. *Address:* House of Lords, SW1. *Club:* Athenæum. *Died 28 Aug. 1982.*

**EVANS, Albert;** *b* 10 June 1903; *s* of Moses Richard Evans; *m* 1929, Beatrice Joan, *d* of F. W. Galton. *Educ:* LCC Sch.; WEA. MP (Lab) West Islington, Sept. 1947–Feb. 1950, South-West Islington, 1950–70; retired; Member: Islington Borough Council, 1937–47; LCC, 1946–49. *Address:* Abbey Lodge, 3 Hooks Hill Road, Sheringham, Norfolk. *Died 4 Dec. 1988.*

**EVANS, Alfred Thomas, (Fred Evans);** BA; *b* 24 Feb. 1914; *s* of Alfred Evans, Miner, and Sarah Jane Evans; *m* 1939, Mary (*née* O'Marah); one *s* two *d. Educ:* Primary and Grammar Schs; University of Wales. Head of Dept, Grammar Sch., Bargoed, Glam, 1937–49; Headmaster, Bedlinog Secondary Sch., Glam, 1949–66; Headmaster, Lewis Boys Grammar Sch., Pengam, Mon, 1966–68. Contested (Lab) Leominster, 1955, Stroud, 1959; MP (Lab) Caerphilly, July 1968–1979. Organising Agent, Caerphilly Constituency Labour Party, 1962–66. Chm., Welsh Parly Lab. Party, 1977; a Chm., Private Bills Cttee, 1975. *Address:* 8 Dilwyn Avenue, Hengoed, Mid Glam CF8 7AG. *T:* Hengoed 812069. *Clubs:* Aneurin Labour (Caerphilly); Labour (Bargoed). *Died 13 April 1987.*

**EVANS, Sir Arthur Trevor,** Kt 1954; Controller of Death Duties, 1951–57; *b* 7 Nov. 1895; *er s* of Benjamin Evans; *m* 1925, Mary Dagmar (*d* 1977), *d* of J. H. Powell, JP, Aberdare, Glam; one *s* one *d. Educ:* Stationers' Company's Sch.; King's Coll., London. LLB. Asst Controller of Death Duties, 1944. Dep. Controller, 1947. *Address:* Flat 1, Cliff Court, Rottingdean, Brighton BN2 7JD. *Died 1 Jan. 1983.*

**EVANS, Sir Athol (Donald),** KBE 1963 (CBE 1954; MBE 1939); retired as Secretary for Home Affairs, Government of the Federation of Rhodesia and Nyasaland (Sept. 1953–Dec. 1963); *b* 16 Dec. 1904; *s* of Henry Evans; *m* 1931, Catherine Millar Greig; one *s* two *d. Educ:* Graeme Coll. and Rhodes Univ., Grahamstown, S Africa (BA, LLB). Joined S Rhodesia Public Service, 1928: consecutively Law Officer, Legal Adviser, Mem. of Public Services Board, and Sec. for Internal Affairs. Chairman of: Board of Trustees, National Gallery of Zimbabwe; Zimbabwe National Trust; Nat. Council for Care of Aged. Past District Governor, Rotary International. Gold Cross of St Mark (Greece), 1962. *Recreations:* tennis, shooting. *Address:* 8 Harvey Brown Avenue, Harare, Zimbabwe. *T:* 725164. *Died 9 June 1988.*

**EVANS, Sir Bernard,** Kt 1962; DSO 1941; ED 1944; FRAIA; architect; Consultant, Bernard Evans & Partners Pty Ltd, since 1972 (Governing Director, 1946–72, retired); Director, Sun Alliance & London Insurance Group, Victoria; Managing Director, Withalit Pty Ltd; *b* 13 May 1905; *s* of Isaac Evans and Lucy (*née* Tunnicliffe); *m* 1929, Dorothy May Evans (*née* Ellis), *d* of William and Mary Ellis; one *s* two *d. Educ:* private sch.; Melbourne Technical Coll. Raised 2/23rd Bn, AIF, War of 1939–45; 24th Bde 9th Div.; served Tobruk, El Alamein (Brig.), Lae and Finschhaven (despatches thrice, DSO, ED). Architect; notable buildings: London Ct, Perth, WA; CRA and Legal & General Assurance Society Pty Ltd, Melbourne, Vic. Lord Mayor of Melbourne, 1959–61 (Councillor, Gipps Ward, 1949–75). Comr Melb. and Metropolitan Bd of Works; Pres. Royal Melbourne Institute of Technology, 1958–60; Pres. Princes Hill Village, 1958–75; Pres. Royal Commonwealth Society, Victorian Br., 1960–77; Past Nat. Pres. Royal Commonwealth Society. Mem. Inst. of Dirs, London. Cavaliere dell' Ordine della Stella della Solidarieta Italiana, 1971. *Recreation:* artist in oils. *Address:* Warrawee, 735 Orrong Road, Toorak, Victoria 3142, Australia. *T:* 24–5591. *Clubs:* Athenæum, Naval and Military (Melbourne); VRC, VATC, RACV, Kelvin, West Brighton (all Melbourne, Australia). *Died 19 Feb. 1981.*

**EVANS, Charles;** *see* Evans, W. C.

**EVANS, Vice-Adm. Sir Charles (Leo Glandore),** KCB 1962 (CB 1958); CBE 1953; DSO 1941; DSC 1940; *b* 2 Aug. 1908; *o s* of Major S. G. Evans, MC; *g s* of Gen. Leopold Evans and Col John Crosbie; *m* 1942, Kyriakoula, 3rd *d* of Gen. Doulcaris, Athens, Greece. Entered Royal Naval Coll., 1922; specialised as a pilot, 1930; served as fighter pilot in Aircraft Carriers in Norwegian, Dunkirk, Mediterranean and Middle East campaigns and in North Sea, Mediterranean and Pacific theatres in War of 1939–45 (despatches thrice, DSC, DSO); Naval Air Attaché in USA, 1946 and 1947; Dir of Air Warfare Division, Naval Staff, The Admiralty, 1950–51; Commanding HMS Ocean (CBE) in Mediterranean and Korea, 1951 and 1952; student Imperial Defence Coll., 1953; Commodore, RN Barracks, Portsmouth, 1954 and 1955; Flag Officer, Flying Training, 1956–57; Deputy Chief of Naval Personnel and Head of Directorate of Officer Appointments, 1957–59; Flag Officer, Aircraft Carriers, 1959–60; NATO Deputy Supreme Allied Commander, Atlantic, 1960–62, retired. Pres., Fleet Air Arm Officers Assoc. 1963. Dir-Gen., British Film Producers' Assoc., 1964–67; Vice-Pres., Film Production Assoc. of GB, 1967–68; Chm., Central Casting Ltd, 1967–68; former Chm. of various British and foreign cos. *Club:* Army and Navy. *Died 27 Dec. 1981.*

**EVANS, Collis William,** CB 1958; CBE 1949; Under Secretary, Ministry of Civil Aviation, 1948–59; *b* 27 May 1895; *s* of late W. J. Evans, Folkestone; *m* 1st, 1938, Annie Urquhart (*d* 1957); 2nd, 1970, Hilda Stewart. Served European War, 1914–18, Yeomanry and RFA, Middle East, Macedonia and France. Exchequer and Audit Dept, 1914; Principal, Air Ministry, 1938; Financial Adviser to HQ RAF, Middle East and North Africa, 1938–43; Adviser on Administration and Finance, Transport Command, 1943; Asst Sec., Dept. of Civil Aviation, 1944. *Address:* Ringle Crouch, Nash, near Bletchley, Bucks MK17 0EP. *T:* Milton Keynes 501785. *Died 16 Oct. 1984.*

**EVANS, His Honour David Carey Rees Jones,** MA, BCL Oxon; Judge of County Courts, 1946–71; Deputy Chairman, Quarter Sessions, Norfolk, retired; *b* 3 March 1899; *s* of late Sir David W. Evans; *m* 1937, Margaret Willoughby Gale; one *d. Educ:* Sherborne Preparatory Sch.; Sherborne Sch.; Jesus Coll., Oxford (Scholar); Gray's Inn (Holt Scholar). Called to Bar, 1923; S Wales and Chester Circuit, practising at Cardiff; formerly part-time Lecturer in Law at University Coll. of S Wales and Mon, Cardiff. Chm. of Ministry of Labour Tribunals for Breconshire and Merthyr, 1937–46; Recorder of Merthyr Tydfil, 1945–46. 2nd Lieut RGA 1918–19. *Address:* 16 Cross Street, Hoxne, Diss, Norfolk. *Died 8 Dec. 1982.*

**EVANS, His Honour David Eifion Puleston,** QC 1954; Member Foreign Compensation Commission, 1963–75; *b* 8 Dec. 1902; *s* of late John Owain Evans, CBE and Margaret Anne Evans; *m* 1933, Roberta (*d* 1966), *y d* of Sir Robert McAlpine, 1st Bt. *Educ:* Towyn Sch.; University Coll. of Wales, Aberystwyth; Downing Coll., Cambridge (Foundation Schol., MA, LLB). Barrister, Gray's Inn, 1926, practised London, Wales and Chester Circuit; commissioned RASC 1940; Office of Judge Advocate Gen., 1941–45, Major; resumed practice, 1945; Mem. General Council of the Bar, 1955–56; Chm., Radnorshire Quarter Sessions, 1959–62; Deputy Chm., Brecknock Quarter Sessions, 1960–62; County Court Judge, Circuit No 28 (Mid-Wales and Shropshire), 1956–62. *Address:* 104 Westhill, Putney, SW15 2UQ. *Club:* Reform. *Died 22 April 1984.*

**EVANS, Prof. Sir David (Gwynne),** Kt 1977; CBE 1969; FRS 1960; Demonstrator, Sir William Dunn School of Pathology, University of Oxford, 1976–79, retired; *b* 6 Sept. 1909; *s* of Frederick George Evans, Atherton, Manchester; *m* 1937, Mary (*née* Darby); one *s* one *d. Educ:* Leigh Grammar Sch.; University of Manchester. BSc,

1933; MSc, 1934; PhD, 1938; DSc, 1948. Demonstrator and Asst Lecturer in Chemistry, Dept of Bacteriology, University of Manchester, 1934; Mem. of Scientific Staff, Dept of Biological Standards, Nat. Inst. for Medical Research, London, 1940; Reader in Chemical Bacteriology, Dept of Bacteriology, University of Manchester, 1947; Head of Biological Standards Control Laboratory, Nat. Inst. for Medical Research, London, 1955–58; Dir, Dept of Biological Standards, 1958–61; Prof. of Bacteriology and Immunology, 1961–71, now Emeritus, London Sch. of Hygiene and Tropical Medicine; Dir, Lister Inst. of Preventive Medicine, 1971–72; Dir, Nat. Inst. for Biological Standards and Control, 1972–76. Member: WHO Expert Panel on Biological Standardization, 1956–77; Governing Body, Animal Virus Res. Inst., Pirbright, 1964–75; MRC, 1965–69; Northumberland Cttee on Foot-and-Mouth Disease, 1968–69; Cttee on Safety of Medicines, 1973–77; British Pharmacopœia Commn, 1973–77; Investigation into the Birmingham Smallpox Occurrence, 1978–79. Chm., Veterinary Adv. Cttee, Horserace Betting Levy Bd, 1973–79. Pres., Soc. for General Microbiology, 1972–75. FRCPath, 1965. BMA Stewart Prize Award, 1968; Buchanan Medal, Royal Soc., 1977. DUniv Surrey, 1982. *Publications:* numerous scientific papers, mainly on bacteriology and immunology. *Recreations:* gardening, music, travel. *Address:* 4 Craig Wen, Rhos-on-Sea, Colwyn Bay, Clwyd LL28 4TS. *T:* Colwyn Bay 46662. *Club:* Athenæum.
*Died 13 June 1984.*

**EVANS, Sir David (Lewis),** Kt 1958; OBE 1947; BA, BLitt, Hon. DLitt Wales; Keeper of Public Records, Jan. 1959–Oct. 1960, retired (Deputy Keeper of the Records, 1954–58); Commissioner, Historical MSS Commission, 1954–80; *b* 14 Aug. 1893; *s* of Rev. David Evans and Margaret Lewis; *m* 1923, Marie Christine (*d* 1966), *d* of Edwin Austin, JP; two *d. Educ:* Bridgend County Sch.; University Coll. of Wales, Aberystwyth; Jesus Coll., Oxford. Lieut, Duke of Wellington's Regt, 1915–19, France and Belgium (despatches). Entered Public Record Office, 1921; Principal Asst Keeper, 1947. Lectr, Administrative History and Archive Administration, Sch. of Librarianship and Archives, University Coll. London, 1947–54. FRHistS (Vice-Pres. 1956–60); Council, Hon. Soc. of Cymmrodorion; Member: Advisory Council on Public Records, 1959–65; History and Law Cttee, Bd of Celtic Studies; Exec Committee: Internat. Council on Archives, 1953–68 (Vice-Pres. 1956–60); Pres. 4th Internat. Congress of Archivists, Stockholm, 1960; Governor: British Film Institute, 1961–64; Nat. Library of Wales, 1961– (Council, 1962–80); Nat. Museum of Wales, 1965–. *Publications:* Flintshire Ministers' Accounts, 1328–1352, 1929; History of Carmarthenshire: Chapter on Later Middle Ages, 1935; (part author) Notebook of John Smibert, Painter, Mass Hist. Soc., 1969; articles, reviews, in Cymmrodorion Transactions, Eng. Hist. Review, Nat. Lib. of Wales Jl, Virginia Hist. Soc. Trans, etc. *Address:* Whitegates, Stratton-on-the-Fosse, Somerset. *Club:* National Liberal. *Died 23 April 1987.*

**EVANS, David M.;** *see* Moule-Evans.

**EVANS, His Honour (David) Meurig;** a Circuit Judge (formerly County Court Judge), 1957–79, retired; *b* 9 Sept. 1906; *s* of H. T. Evans, Aberayron, Cards; *m* 1933, Joyce Diedericke Sander (decd), St Albans; two *s* two *d; m* 1969, Mrs Anne Balsham. *Educ:* Cardiff High Sch.; Aberayron County Sch.; Cardiff Technical Coll. Journalist on staff of Western Mail and The Economist, 1925–31. Called to Bar, Gray's Inn, 1931; practised on Wales and Chester Circuit, 1932–57; Chairman, Cardigan QS, Denbigh QS, Dep. Chm., Anglesey and Caenarvon QS, 1958–71. Served 1940–45, Lieut-Comdr RNVR. Chm., Medical Appeal Tribunal for Wales, 1952–57; Jt Pres., Council of HM Circuit Judges, 1974–75. *Recreations:* golf and yachting. *Address:* Rivendell, Menai Bridge, Gwynedd. *T:* Menai Bridge 712253. *Clubs:* Royal Welsh, Royal Anglesey, etc. *Died 7 March 1983.*

**EVANS, Prof. Dennis Frederick,** FRS 1981; Professor in Inorganic Chemistry, Imperial College, London, since 1981; *b* 27 March 1928; *s* of George Frederick Evans and Gladys Martha Taylor; one *d. Educ:* Nottingham High Sch.; Lincoln Coll., Oxford (open scholar); Gibbs Univ. Scholar, 1949; MA, DPhil. ICI Res. Fellow, Oxford, 1952–53 and 1954–56; Res. Associate, Univ. of Chicago, 1953–54; Lectr in Inorganic Chemistry, Imperial Coll., London, 1956–63; Sen. Lectr, 1963–64, Reader, 1964–81. *Publications:* articles in various scientific jls. *Recreations:* wine, travel. *Address:* 64A Cathcart Road, SW10 9JQ. *T:* 071–352 6540.
*Died 6 Nov. 1990.*

**EVANS, Edward Walter,** CMG 1931; *b* 1890; 2nd *s* of late Arthur Evans; *m* 1923, Margaret, *d* of late J. K. Young, Barrister-at-Law; two *s* one *d. Educ:* Marlborough Coll.; Corpus Christi Coll., Oxford (Classical Scholar). 1st Class Classical Mods, 1st Class Lit. Hum.; appointed to Colonial service, 1914; served in various dependencies in East Africa and Caribbean area before retiring from post of Colonial Sec., Mauritius, in 1939, after administering the Government of Mauritius on various occasions; during 1939–45

War served in Gibraltar and on Overseas Services of BBC; served on Control Commission for Germany, 1945–46; employed in History Dept Bristol Univ., 1946–55. *Publications:* contrib. Mind, vol LXXX. *Address:* Medway Farm, Askerswell, Dorchester, Dorset.
*Died 25 Feb. 1985.*

**EVANS, Prof. (Emyr) Estyn,** CBE 1970; Emeritus Professor of Geography, and Hon. Fellow, Institute of Irish Studies, Queen's University of Belfast; Leverhulme Emeritus Fellow, 1970–72; *b* 29 May 1905; 4th *s* of Rev. G. O. and Elizabeth Evans, Shrewsbury; *m* 1931, Gwyneth Lyon, *e d* of Prof. Abel Jones, Aberystwyth; four *s. Educ:* Welshpool County Sch.; University Coll. of Wales, Aberystwyth. BA Geography and Anthropology, 1925, MA 1931, DSc 1939. Independent Lecturer in Geography, QUB, 1928–44; Reader, 1944–45; Prof., 1945–68; Dir, Inst. of Irish Studies, 1965–70; Dean of the Faculty of Arts, 1951–54; Mem. of Senate. Tallman Visiting Professor: Bowdoin Coll., Maine, 1948–49; Visiting Professor: Indiana Univ., 1964; Louisiana State Univ., 1969. Mem., Historic Monuments Council (NI) (former Chm.); former Mem. Adv. Council, Republic of Ireland; first President: Ulster Folk Life Soc.; Ulster Archæological Soc.; Ulster Architectural Heritage Soc.; former Chm. of Trustees, Ulster Folk and Transport Museum and Trustee, Ulster Museum; Hon. Mem. and former Vice-Pres., Prehistoric Soc. Former Member: Executive Cttee, NI Council of Social Service; NI Tourist Bd; Pres. Sect. E 1958 and Sect. H 1960, Brit. Assoc. for the Advancement of Science (first Chm. NI Area Cttee); Sir James Frazer Memorial Lectr, 1961; Sir Everard im Thurn Memorial Lectr, 1966; Wiles Lectr, 1971. Chm., Northern Ireland Government Cttee on Itinerants; Vice-Chm., Cttee on Nature Conservation. FSA; MRIA; Hon. MRTPI; Hon. Life Mem., Royal Dublin Soc., 1981. Hon. ScD Bowdoin, 1949; Hon. LittD Dublin, 1970; Hon. LLD QUB, 1973; Hon. DLitt: NUI, 1975; Wales, 1977; Hon. DSc NUU 1980. Victoria Medal, RGS, 1973. Hons Award, Assoc. of Amer. Geographers, Pa, 1979. *Publications:* France, A Geographical Introduction, 1937; (joint) Preliminary Survey of the Ancient Monuments of Northern Ireland, 1940; Irish Heritage, 1942; A Portrait of Northern Ireland (Festival of Britain) 1951; Mourne Country, 1951, rev. edn 1967; Lyles Hill: A Late Neolithic Site in County Antrim, 1953; Irish Folk Ways, 1957; Prehistoric and Early Christian Ireland, 1966; (ed) Facts from Gweedore, 1971; The Personality of Ireland (Wiles Lectures), 1973, revd edn 1981; The Personality of Wales (BBC Wales Annual Lecture), 1973; (ed) Harvest Home: the last sheaf, 1975; (ed) Ireland's Eye, the photographs of R. J. Welch, 1977; The Irishness of the Irish (essays), 1986; papers in scientific journals. *Address:* 98A Malone Road, Belfast. *T:* 668510. *Club:* Ulster Arts (Hon. Member) (Belfast). *Died 12 Aug. 1989.*

**EVANS, Evan Stanley,** CBE 1951; FRCS; Medical Superintendent, Lord Mayor Treloar Hospital, Alton, 1946–69, retired; President, Queen Elizabeth's Foundation for the Disabled, Leatherhead, since 1982 (Chairman, 1942–81); former Chairman, Treloar Trust; *b* 2 July 1904; *e s* of David Evans; *m* 1934, Muriel Gordon, *y d* of Peter Henderson; five *s. Educ:* St Bartholomew's Hospital. MRCS, LRCP, 1927; FRCS 1931; MB, BS London 1932; House Surg. and House Surg. (orthop.), St Bartholomew's Hosp., 1928; Medical Supt, Heatherwood Hosp., Ascot, 1932; Medical Supt, Queen Mary's Hosp., Carshalton, 1942. Hon. Cons. Orthop. Surgeon: Treloar Orthop. Hosp.; Lord Mayor Treloar Trust; Queen Elizabeth's Foundn for Disabled; Farnham Hosp. Fellow Brit. Orthop. Assoc.; Founder Mem. Exec. Cttee of British Council of Rehabilitation; formerly Chm. Exec. Cttee, Central Council for the Disabled; Vice-Pres., Jt Examination Board for orthopædic nursing. *Publications:* articles on non-pulmonary tuberculosis and cerebral palsy, in medical journals and books. *Address:* Highfield, Derby Road, Haslemere, Surrey GU27 1BP. *T:* Haslemere 51934.
*Died 27 Aug. 1982.*

**EVANS, Sir Francis (Edward),** GBE 1957; KCMG 1946 (CMG 1944); DL; Agent for the Government of N Ireland in Great Britain, 1962–66; *b* 4 April 1897; *s* of late Thomas Edward Evans, Belfast; *m* 1920, Mary (*d* 1976), *d* of late Rev. Prof. James Dick, MA, DD, Belfast; no *c. Educ:* Royal Academy, Belfast; London Sch. of Economics. Served European War, Lieut Royal Irish Rifles, 1915–19; Consular Service, 1920; Vice-Consul in New York, 1920–26, Boston, 1926–29, Colon, Panama, 1929–32, and Boston, 1932–34; Consul at Los Angeles, 1934–39; in Foreign Office, 1939–43; Consul at New York, 1943; Consul-Gen., 1944–50; Asst Under-Sec. of State, FO, 1951; British Ambassador to Israel, 1952–54 (Minister, 1951–52); British Ambassador to the Argentine, 1954–57. Dep. Chm. Northern Ireland Development Coun., 1957–65. Pres., Central Council, Ulster 71 Festival. Hon. Col, 6th (T) Bn Royal Ulster Rifles, 1961–67, (T&AVR), 1967–71. Hon. LLD Queen's Univ., Belfast; Hon. DCL Ripon Coll., Wisconsin; Hon. DLitt New University of Ulster. DL Belfast, 1959. KStJ. *Clubs:* Travellers'; Ulster (Belfast). *Died 21 Aug. 1983.*

**EVANS, Fred;** *see* Evans, Alfred T.

**EVANS, Lt.-Gen. Sir Geoffrey (Charles),** KBE 1954 (CBE 1945); CB 1946; DSO 1941 (bars 1942, 1944); retired, 1957; *b* 13 March 1901; *s* of late Col C. R. Evans, DSO; *m* 1928, Ida Louise, *d* of late H. R. Sidney; no *c. Educ:* Aldenham Sch.; Royal Military Coll., Sandhurst. 2nd Lieut The Royal Warwickshire Regt, 1920; Adjutant: 1st Bn, 1926–29; 7th Bn (TA), 1934–35; Staff Coll., 1936–37. Served War of 1939–45 (despatches five times): Bde Major, N Africa and Eritrea, 1940–41; OC 1st Bn Royal Sussex Regt, N Africa, 1941–42; Comdt Staff Coll., Quetta, 1942; Brig. Comdt, India, 1943; Brig., Gen. Staff 4 Corps, Burma, 1943–44; Bde Commander, Burma, 1944; GOC 5 and 7 Indian Divs, Burma, 1944–45; GOC Allied Land Forces, Siam, 1945–46; GOC 42 (Lancs) Div. and North-West District, 1947–48; Dir of Military Training War Office, 1948–49; GOC 40 Div., Hong Kong, 1949–51; Temp. Comd. (Lt-Gen.), British Forces, Hong Kong, 1951–52; Asst Chief of Staff (Org. and Trng), Supreme HQ, Allied Powers, Europe, 1952–53; GOC-in-C, Northern Command, 1953–57; retired. Hon. Col 7th Bn The Royal Warwickshire Regt, 1959–64. A Vice-Pres., Nat. Playing Fields Assoc.; Chairman: London and Middlesex Playing Fields Association, 1959–70; Anglo-Thai Soc., 1967–71. Comr, Royal Hosp., Chelsea, 1968–76. DL Greater London, 1970–76. *Publications:* The Desert and the Jungle, 1959; (with A. Brett-James) Imphal, 1962; The Johnnies, 1964; Slim as Military Commander, 1969; Tannenberg 1410:1914, 1971; Kensington, 1975; contrib. chapters: The Decisive Battles of the 20th Century, 1975; War Lords, 1976; articles for Purnell's History of the Second World War, History Today, The Field, The Antique Collector, reviews. *Address:* 11 Wellington Square, SW3.
*Died 27 Jan.* 1987.

**EVANS, George Ewart;** author, lecturer, and broadcaster, since 1948; *b* 1 April 1909; *s* of William and Janet Evans, Abercynon, Glamorgan; *m* 1938, Florence Ellen Knappett; one *s* three *d. Educ:* Abertaf Sch.; Mountain Ash Grammar Sch.; UC Cardiff. BA Hons Classics Wales, 1930; DipEd 1931. Writer of short stories, verse, radio and film scripts; specialized in history and folk life of the village. Univ. of Essex: Major Burrows Lectr, 1972; Vis. Fellow, 1973–78; Hon. DU 1982; Hon. DLitt Keele, 1983. Pres., Section H (Anthropology), British Assoc. for Advancement of Science, Swansea, 1971. *Publications:* The Voices of the Children, 1947; Ask the Fellows who Cut the Hay, 1956; (ed) Welsh Short Stories, 1959; The Horse in the Furrow, 1960; The Pattern Under the Plough, 1966; The Farm and the Village, 1969; Where Beards Wag All, 1970; (with David Thomson) The Leaping Hare, 1972; Acky, 1973; The Days That We Have Seen, 1975; Let Dogs Delight, 1975; From Mouths of Men, 1976; Horse Power and Magic, 1979; The Strength of the Hills (autobiography), 1983; Spoken History, 1987. *Recreations:* walking, gardening, watching Rugby football. *Address:* 19 The Street, Brooke, Norwich NR15 1JW. *T:* Brooke 50518.
*Died 11 Jan.* 1988.

**EVANS, Sir Harold,** 1st Bt, *cr* 1963; CMG 1957; OBE 1945; *b* 29 April 1911; *s* of Sidney Evans and Gladys Mary Lythgoe; *m* 1945, Elizabeth Jaffray; one *d* (one *s* decd). *Educ:* King Edward's Sch., Stourbridge. Editorial staff of newspapers in Worcs and Sheffield, 1930–39; Freelance Journalism, 1939–40; British Volunteers in Finland, 1940; Staff of British Legation, Helsinki, 1940–42; Min. of Information Rep. in W Africa (Staff of Resident Minister), 1942–45; Dep. Public Relations Officer, Colonial Office, 1945–53; Chief Information Officer, Colonial Office, 1953–57; Public Relations Adviser to the Prime Minister, 1957–64; Head of Information and Research, Independent Television Authority, 1964–66; Adviser on Public Relations to Bd, Vickers Ltd, 1966–76; Chm., Health Educn Council, 1973–76. *Publications:* Men in the Tropics, Anthology, 1949; Vickers: against the odds 1956–77, 1978; Downing Street Diary, 1981; various contributions. *Address:* 3 Challoners Close, Rottingdean, East Sussex. *T:* Brighton 33397.
*Died 21 April* 1983 (*ext*).

**EVANS, (Harry) Lindley,** CMG 1963; Pianist; Composer; retired as Professor of Pianoforte, NSW State Conservatorium of Music, Sydney, Australia, 1928–66, a Governor, 1966–73; *b* 18 Nov. 1895; British; *m* 1926, Marie Florence Stewart. *Educ:* St George's Grammar Sch., Capetown, South Africa. Pianist with Dame Nellie Melba, 1922–31. Celebrated a 40-year partnership in giving two-piano recitals, 1964. Melody Man in Children's Hour (ABC) since its inception, 1940. Pres., Musical Assoc. of NSW (life Mem.); Past Pres., Fellowship of Australian Composers (Life Mem.). *Publications:* many musical compositions. *Recreations:* bowls, yachting. *Address:* 47/84 St George's Crescent, Drummoyne, NSW, Australia. *T:* 81–3896. *Club:* Savage (Sydney) (Life Mem.; Pres. 13 yrs).
*Died 2 Dec.* 1982.

**EVANS, Maj.-Gen. Henry Holland,** CB 1972; *b* Harrogate, 18 Nov. 1914; *o s* of Major H. Evans; *m* 1939, Norah Mary, *d* of F. R. Lawson, Wolstanton, Staffs; one *s* one *d. Educ:* King James Grammar Sch., Almondbury, near Huddersfield; Manchester Univ. Commissioned Duke of Wellington's Regt (TA), 1936; Regular Army Commission in AEC, 1939; Officer Instructor, Duke of York's

Royal Mil. Sch., 1939–41; Staff Officer: 43 (Wessex) Div., 1942–45; War Office, 1945–48; Chief Educn Officer, Malta and Libya, 1948–51; various RAEC appts, incl. Headmaster DYRMS and Chief Inspector of Army children's schools, to 1963; CEO, Northern Comd, 1963–65; CEO, BAOR, 1965–68; Dir of Army Educn, 1969–72. Sec., Council for Accreditation of Corresp. Colls, 1973–75. Mem., Sevenoaks Town Council, 1973–77. *Address:* c/o Royal Bank of Scotland, Whitehall, SW1.
*Died 2 Jan.* 1987.

**EVANS, Hubert John Filmer,** CMG 1958; LLD; HM Diplomatic Service, retired; Central Asian Research Centre, 1965–70; *b* 21 Nov. 1904; *y s* of late Harry Evans and Edith Gwendoline Rees; *m* 1948, Marjory Maureen Filmer (*née* Carrick), widow of Col R. A. M. Tweedy. *Educ:* City of London Sch.; Jesus Coll., Oxford (Classical Scholar); Montpellier. Studied oriental languages with Ross, Minorsky, and in the East. Entered Indian Civil Service, 1928; served as Magistrate in various districts of United Provinces, 1929–37; Deputy Commissioner of Delhi, and Pres., Delhi Municipal Council, 1938–42; Sec. Delhi Administration, 1942–45; Collector of Agra, 1945–47; appointed to Foreign Service, 1947; at the Foreign Office, 1948–50; Financial Adviser to Persian Gulf Residency, 1950–51; Consul-Gen. at Meshed, 1951; Ambassador to Nicaragua, 1952–54; Consul-Gen., Rotterdam, 1955–56; HM Ambassador to Korea, 1957–61. Hon. Sec., Royal Central Asian Soc. and Chm. Ed. Board 1965–70. Hon. MRAS; Hon. LLD Korea, 1960; Freedom of Seoul, 1960. *Publications:* Islam in Iran (trans. from Russian), 1985; Looking Back on India, 1987; contribs to encyclopaedias and various articles in oriental jls. *Recreations:* the Persian Poets, and travel. *Address:* Manoir d'Arlette, Fatouville, 27210 Beuzeville, France; Le Vert Feuillage, Honfleur, France. *Club:* Athenæum.
*Died 28 June* 1989.

**EVANS, Sir Hywel (Wynn),** KCB 1976 (CB 1972); Deputy Chairman, Prince of Wales Committee, since 1986 (Member, since 1981); Vice President, University College of Swansea, since 1986; Permanent Secretary, Welsh Office, 1971–80; *b* 30 May 1920; *s* of late Dr T. Hopkin Evans, MusDoc and Adelina Evans; *m* 1949, Jessie Margaret Templeton; one *d. Educ:* Liverpool Collegiate Sch.; Liverpool Univ. RA and Intell. Corps, 1940–46 (despatches). Joined Min. of Labour, as Asst Principal, 1947; seconded to FO, 1952–54; Commonwealth Fellow, 1957–58; Private Sec. to Ministers of Labour, 1959–60; Sec., NEDC, 1964–68; Asst Under-Sec. of State, Welsh Office, 1968–71. Chm., Welsh Arts Council, 1981–86; Mem., Arts Council of GB, 1981–86. Member: Court of Govs: Nat. Mus. of Wales, 1981–; Court, Univ. of Wales, 1985–; Council, WNO, 1986–; Gorsedd of Bards of Wales. US Bronze Star, 1945. *Publication:* Governmental Regulation of Industrial Relations, 1960 (USA). *Recreations:* opera, watching rugby. *Address:* Coed-yr-Iarll, St Fagans, Cardiff, S Wales CF5 6DU. *T:* Cardiff 565214.
*Died 2 June* 1988.

**EVANS, Sir Ian William G.;** *see* Gwynne-Evans.

**EVANS, Ioan (Lyonel);** JP; MP (Lab and Co-op) Cynon Valley, since 1983 (Aberdare, Feb. 1974–1983); *b* 1927; *m* 1949, Maria Evans, JP (*née* Griffiths); one *s* one *d. Educ:* Llanelli Grammar Sch.; University Coll., Swansea. Has held various Co-op (incl. Sec. Birm. and Dist Co-op Party) and Labour Party offices. MP (Lab and Co-op) Birmingham Yardley, 1964–70; PPS to Postmaster-Gen., 1965–66; Asst Govt Whip, 1966–68; Comptroller of HM Household, 1968–70. Formerly Vice-Chm. West Midlands Parly Labour Group of MP's; Chm., PLP For. Affairs Gp, 1981–; Vice-Chairman: PLP Disabled Gp, 1974–; PLP Prices and Consumer Protection Gp, 1974–; PLP Trade Group, 1974–; Co-op Parly Gp, 1974–; Hon. Secretary: Welsh Lab. MPs Gp; Welsh Parly Party; Mem., Welsh Select Cttee, 1980–82; Front Bench Spokesman on Europe and EEC, 1982–83, on Wales, 1983–. Formerly Vice-Chm., UK Parly delegn to Consultative Assembly of Council of Europe; formerly Mem., UK Delegn to Assembly of WEU; Vice-Chairman: Parly Assoc. for World Govt, 1980–; Parliamentarians for World Order, 1980–; Mem. Exec. Cttee, British Branch, IPU. Co-opted Mem., W Bromwich Educn Cttee; Governor, W Bromwich Grammar Sch.; Lectr for WEA and NCLC; Dir, Internat. Defence and Aid Fund, 1970–74; Member: Exec. Cttee, Wales Council of Labour; Exec. Cttee, Christian Action Council. Chm., Justice for Rhodesia, 1973–. JP: Birmingham, 1960–70; Middlesex, 1970–. *Address:* 169 Eastcote Road, Ruislip, Middx. *T:* Ruislip 75251.
*Died 10 Feb.* 1984.

**EVANS, Lindley;** *see* Evans, H. L.

**EVANS, Dr Luther Harris;** retired librarian and government official; *b* near Sayersville, Bastrop County, Texas, USA, 13 Oct. 1902; *s* of George Washington and Lillie Johnson Evans; *m* 1925, Helen Murphy; one *s. Educ:* University of Texas; Leland Stanford Univ., USA. AB 1923, MA 1924 Texas; PhD Stanford, 1927; Doctor of Humane Letters, Yale, 1946; LLD Pa Mil. Coll., 1948, British Columbia Univ., 1948; DL Loyola Coll., 1950; Denison Univ., 1961; DLitt Brown Univ., 1953; LLD Columbia, 1953; LLD Dartmouth Coll., 1956; Doctor of the Humanities Washington

Univ., 1959; Marietta Coll. 1962; Dr of Literature Adelphi Coll., 1960. Instructor in freshman orientation course in problems of citizenship, Stanford Univ., 1924–27; Instructor in Government, New York Univ., 1927–28; Instructor in Political Science, Dartmouth Coll., 1928–30; Asst Prof. of Politics, Princeton Univ., 1930–35; Dir, Historical Records Survey of Work Projects Administration, 1935–39; Dir of Legislative Reference Service, Library of Congress, 1939–40; Chief Asst Librarian, on occasion Acting Librarian of Congress, 1940–45; Librarian of Congress, 1945–53. Member: UNESCO Executive Board, 1949–53; US Nat. Commission for UNESCO, 1946–52 (Chm. 1952); (adviser, London Conference on an international educational and cultural organisation, 1945; deleg. or adviser, General Conf., UNESCO, 1947–53); Dir-Gen. United Nations Educational, Scientific and Cultural Organisation, 1953–58; Mem. US National Commission for UNESCO, 1959–63; Senior Staff Mem. Brookings Instn, Washington, DC, 1959–61; Dir Nat. Educn Assoc. Project on Educational Implications of Automation, Washington, DC, 1961–62; Dir, Internat. Collections, Columbia Univ., New York, 1962–71. Vis. Prof. in Library Studies, Univ. of Puerto Rico, 1972. Chm., Washington Area Cttee on Refugees, 1960–62; Chm., US Cttee for Refugees, 1962–71; Member Nat. Board: UNA of USA, 1964–69; Amer. Civil Liberties Union, 1964–69; Hon. Vice-Chm., Commn to Study Organisation of Peace; Pres., World Federalists, USA, 1971–76. Hon. Vice-Pres. Library Association (Eng.); Hon. Mem., Association of Special Libraries and Information Bureaux (Eng.); Member: American Library Assoc. (life-mem.); Nat. Education Assoc. (life mem.); Soc. for Internat. Development. Decorations awarded by: Brazil, France, Japan, Lebanon and Peru. *Publications:* The Virgin Islands, from naval base to new deal, 1945; (with others) Survey of Federal (US) Departmental Libraries, 1961; The Decade of Development: problems and issues (with others), 1966; The United States and UNESCO, 1971; articles and book reviews in professional journals. *Address:* 8702 Village Drive 1304, San Antonio, Texas 78217, USA.                     *Died 23 Dec.* 1981.

EVANS, **Maurice Hubert;** Legion of Merit (US) 1945; Actor-manager; *b* Dorchester, Dorset, 3 June 1901; *s* of Alfred Herbert Evans, JP (Dorset). *Educ:* Grocers' Company Sch. Commenced theatrical career at Festival Theatre, Cambridge; later in a series of plays at Wyndham's, London; made his first successes in John van Druten's Diversion and R. C. Sherriff's Journey's End; following several years of appearances in West End became leading man at the Old Vic, where he was seen as Hamlet, Richard II, Petruchio, Benedick, etc.; went to America, 1936, to play Romeo to Katharine Cornell's Juliet; also appeared as the Dauphin in St Joan, Napoleon in St Helena. Produced and played title role Richard II, New York City, 1937; uncut Hamlet, 1938–39; produced and played Falstaff in Henry IV (Part 1), 1939; appeared as Malvolio in Twelth Night with Helen Hayes, 1940–41; produced and played title role in Macbeth, New York City, 1941–42; in each play toured provinces extensively. Went on a lecture tour in aid of British War Relief, 1941. US Citizen, 1941; Captain US Army, 1942; disch. with rank of Major, 1945. Played Hamlet in own GI version, 1945–46, New York; 1946–47, in provinces (acting version published Doubleday & Co., 1947). Produced and starred in Man and Superman, New York, 1947–48, establishing record New York run for play of Bernard Shaw; toured provinces, 1948–49; produced, and co-starred with Edna Best in Terence Rattigan's Browning Version, 1949; starred in Shaw's The Devil's Disciple, New York, and toured provinces, 1950; revived Richard II at NY City Center, 1951; starred in Dial 'M' for Murder, New York, 1952–54, and toured provinces, 1954; starred in Shaw's The Apple Cart, New York and provinces, 1956–57; produced and starred in Shaw's Heartbreak House, New York, 1959–60; starred in Tenderloin (musical), New York, 1960–61; The Aspern Papers, New York, 1961–62; with Helen Hayes in Shakespeare Revisited, A Program For Two Players, at Stratford (USA) and on tour, 1962–63; Holiday, Los Angeles, 1980; On Golden Pond, Florida, 1981; produced The Teahouse of the August Moon (Pulitzer-Critics' prize), 1953; No Time for Sergeants, 1955; Artistic Supervisor, New York City Center Theatre Company, 1949–51. Made first American picture 1950, co-starring with Ethel Barrymore in Kind Lady; also made Androcles and the Lion, Warlord, Jack of Diamonds, Planet of the Apes, Rosemary's Baby, Thin Air, Planet of the Apes Revisited, and, in England, Gilbert and Sullivan, 1952 and Macbeth, 1960. Became United States citizen, 1941. Hon. doctorates: Univ. of Hawaii; Lafayette Coll., Penn.; Brandeis Univ. *Clubs:* Oriental; Players (New York).
                                                        *Died 12 March* 1989.

EVANS, **His Honour Meurig;** *see* Evans, His Honour D. M.

EVANS, **Lady Olwen (Elizabeth) C.;** *see* Carey-Evans.

EVANS, **Dr Philip Rainsford,** CBE 1968; Physician-Paediatrician to the Queen, 1972–76; Physician, The Hospital for Sick Children, Great Ormond Street, 1946–75; *b* 14 April 1910; 2nd *s* of Charles Irwin Evans, headmaster of Leighton Park Sch., and Katharine Evans; *m* 1935, Dr Barbara Dorothy Fordyce Hay-Cooper; three *s*

one *d. Educ:* Sidcot Sch., Winscombe, Som; Leighton Park Sch., Reading; Manchester University. BSc 1930, MSc 1941, MB, ChB 1933, MD 1941, Manchester; MRCP 1935, FRCP 1945, London. Rockefeller Travelling Research Fellow, 1937–38; Asst Pædiatrician, Johns Hopkins Hosp., Baltimore, 1938–39; Asst Physician to Children's Dept, King's Coll. Hosp., London, 1939–46; Dir, Dept of Paediatrics, Guy's Hosp., 1946–71; Dir, British Tay-Sachs Foundn, 1971–74. Served War of 1939–45, RAMC, N Africa and Italy, 1942–46 (despatches); Hon. Col AMS. Editor, Archives of Disease in Childhood, 1947–54. Hon. Mem., British, French and American Pædiatric Socs. Member, Cttee on Milk Composition, 1957–59, Ministry of Agriculture, Fisheries and Food. FRSM (Pres., Section of Pædiatrics, 1968–69, Section of Comparative Medicine, 1982–83); Hon. Sec. British Pædiatric Assoc., 1954–59; Hon. Consultant to the Army in Pædiatrics, 1962–66; formerly Visiting Prof., Makerere, Saigon, Sheffield, Beirut; late Examr Universities of Bristol, Leeds, Birmingham, Cambridge, Jordan, and RCP; Mem. Council, RCP, 1962–65; Censor, RCP, 1972–74. (Jointly) Dawson Williams Prize, BMA, 1969; Moxon Medal, RCP, 1987. *Publications:* (joint) Infant Feeding and Feeding Difficulties, 1954; Jt Editor, Garrod, Batten and Thursfield's Diseases of Children, 1953; original papers in med. journals. *Address:* 24 Abbey Road, NW8 9AX. *T:* 071–624 1668.                     *Died 5 July* 1990.

EVANS, **Phyllis Mary Carlyon,** MA; Headmistress, St Swithun's School, Winchester, 1952–73; *b* 17 April 1913; *d* of L. L. C. Evans, late Headmaster of Swanbourne House Sch., Bletchley, Bucks, and of Mrs M. Evans (*née* Gore-Browne). *Educ:* Wycombe Abbey Sch., Bucks; St Hugh's Coll., Oxford. Lit Hum, 1935. Classics mistress, St Mary's, Calne, 1935–39; Yates Theology Scholar St Hugh's Coll., Oxford, 1939–40; Degree in Theology, 1940; MA 1940. Senior Classics mistress, The Alice Ottley Sch., Worcester, 1940–45; Head Mistress, Wellington Diocesan Sch. for Girls, Marton, New Zealand, 1946–51. Representative of Winchester Diocese in Church Assembly, 1957–70; Lay Reader. *Address:* April Cottage, 13 St Swithun's Street, Winchester.                     *Died 27 Oct.* 1990.

EVANS, **Very Rev. Raymond Ellis;** Dean of Monmouth and Vicar of St Woolos, Newport, Gwent, 1953–75; *b* 10 Aug. 1908; *m* 1944, Alice Craigie, *d* of John and Alice Logan, Stirling, Scotland; two *c*. *Educ:* St David's Coll., Lampeter; St John's Coll., Oxford (MA). Deacon, 1934; Priest, 1935; Curate of Penmaen, 1934–36, of St John the Evangelist, Newport, 1936–44; Vicar of St Andrew's, Newport, 1944–47; Examining Chaplain to Bishop of Monmouth, 1946; Vicar of Blackwood, 1947–52; Sec. Monmouth Diocesan Conf., 1951; Vicar of St Mark, Newport, 1952–53. *Address:* 23 Stelvio Park Drive, Newport, Gwent NPT 3EL.
                                                        *Died 30 Dec.* 1983.

EVANS, **Very Rev. Seiriol John Arthur,** CBE 1969; Dean of Gloucester, 1953–72; *b* 22 Nov. 1894; *er s* of Rev. John Arthur Evans, DD, Sible Hedingham, Essex, and Amelia Annie Price; *m* 1928, Selina Georgiana (*d* 1983), *d* of Rev. Charles Francis Townley, CBE, Fulbourn Manor, Cambridge; no *c. Educ:* King's Sch., Worcester; King's Coll., Cambridge; Salisbury Theological Coll. Asst Master at Felsted Sch., 1917–19; Deacon, 1920; Priest, 1921; Curate of St Mary and All Saints, Kidderminster, 1920–22; Minor Canon and Sacrist of Gloucester Cathedral and Assistant Master at King's Sch., Gloucester, 1922–23; Precentor of Ely Cathedral and Headmaster of the Choir Sch., 1923–29; Rector of Upwell-Christchurch 1929–47; Chaplain RNVR, 1940–45; Proctor in Convocation for Diocese of Ely, 1940–47; Archdeacon of Wisbech, 1945–53; Rector of Upwell-St Peter, 1947–53. Chairman: Council for the Care of Churches, 1954–71; Bishop's Adv. Cttee for Care of Churches, 1974–84. Mem. of the Royal Commission on Historical Manuscripts, 1957; Church Commissioner, 1958–68; Mem., Cttee of Inquiry into Sale of Works of Art, 1963–65; Trustee, National Portrait Gallery, 1963–70. FSA 1935; FRHistS 1940; Fellow, St Michael's Coll., Tenbury, 1958. *Publications:* A Short History of Ely Cathedral, 1925; The Mortification of the Manor of Nepal (EHR vol. 51 no 201), 1936; Ely Chapter Ordinances (Camden Misc.: Vol. XVII), 1940; The Medieval Estate of Ely Cathedral Priory: a preliminary survey, 1973. *Address:* The Old Manor, Fulbourn, near Cambridge. *Club:* Athenæum.
                                                        *Died 29 June* 1984.

EVANS, **Sir (Sidney) Harold;** *see* Evans, Sir Harold.

EVANS, **Very Rev. Sydney Hall,** CBE 1976; Dean of Salisbury, 1977–86; *b* 23 July 1915; *s* of William and Winifred Evans; *m* 1941, Eileen Mary (*née* Evans); two *s* one *d. Educ:* Bristol Grammar Sch.; St Chad's Coll., Durham. MA 1940, BD 1945, Durham. Deacon 1939, priest 1940; Curate of Bishop Auckland, Co. Durham, 1939–41; Curate of Ferryhill, Co. Durham, 1941–43. Chaplain RAFVR, 1943–45. Chaplain and Lecturer, King's Coll., London, 1945–48; Warden of King's Coll. post-graduate coll. at Warminster, 1948–56; Dean of King's Coll., London, 1956–77; Hon. Canon of Southwark, 1959–77; Preacher of Gray's Inn, 1960–77; formerly Exam. Chaplain to Bishops of Southwark, Chelmsford, Truro, Durham, London. Public Orator, Univ. of London, 1972–74. FKC

1955; FSA 1986. Hon. Bencher, Gray's Inn, 1977. Hon. DD: Lambeth, 1978; London, 1978. *Recreations:* walking and bird-watching. *Address:* 18 Cripstead Lane, St Cross, Winchester.
*Died 6 Jan.* 1988.

**EVANS, Sir Trevor (Maldwyn),** Kt 1967; CBE 1963; Director, Beaverbrook Newspapers Ltd, 1954–69; Industrial Consultant, Beaverbrook Group, since 1967; *b* 21 Feb. 1902; *s* of late Samuel Evans and late Margaret Evans, Abertridwr, Glam; *m* 1930, Margaret, *d* of late J. B. Gribbin and late S. J. Gribbin, Heaton Moor, Ches; one *s* one *d. Educ:* Pontypridd Gram. Sch. Journalist, Glamorgan Free Press, Pontypridd, 1922–24; South Wales News, 1924–26; Daily Dispatch, 1926–28; Daily Mail, 1928–30; Daily Express, 1930–70 (Industrial Correspondent, 1930–67). Dir, Internat. Press Centre. Mem. Press Council, 1964–75. *Publications:* Strange Fighters, We British, 1943; Ernest Bevin, biography, 1946; The Great Bohunkus, biography of Ian Mackay, 1953. *Recreations:* watching Rugby and cricket; listening to discussion groups. *Address:* 17 Wolsey Close, Kingston Hill, Surrey. *T:* 01-942 6016. *Clubs:* Reform, Press. *Died 10 June* 1981.

**EVANS, William,** MD, DSc, FRCP; Consulting Physician: to Cardiac Department, London Hospital; to National Heart Hospital; and to Institute of Cardiology; Consulting Cardiologist to Royal Navy, 1946–67; Hon. Cardiologist to Royal Society of Musicians; *b* 24 Nov. 1895; *s* of late Eben Evans, Tregaron, Cardiganshire; *m* 1936, Christina (*d* 1964), *d* of late John Lessels Downie, Kirkcaldy. *Educ:* University Coll. of Wales, Aberystwyth; London Hospital; London Univ., MB, BS (London) 1925, hons in Surgery; MD (London) 1927; FRCP 1937; DSc (London) 1944; K. E. D. Payne Prize in Pathology, 1927; Hutchinson Triennial Prize in Clinical Surgery, 1929; Liddle Triennial Prize in Pathology, 1931; Sydney Body Gold Medal, 1954; Strickland Goodall Lect., 1942; Finlayson Lect., 1947; St Cyres Lect., 1952; Gerrish Milliken Lect., University of Philadelphia, 1954; First Rufus Stolp Memorial Lect., University of Evanston, Ill., 1954; Carbutt Memorial Lect., 1957; Schorstein Lect., 1961; Wiltshire Lect., 1961. First Leonard Abrahamson Memorial Lecture, Royal College of Surgeons in Ireland, Dublin, 1963; Sir Thomas and Lady Dixon Lecture, Belfast, 1965. Formerly Asst Dir to Medical Unit, Paterson Medical Officer and Chief Asst to Cardiac Dept, London Hosp. Served European War, 1914–18, Combatant Officer, Lancs Fusiliers, and Battalion Education Officer. Hon. DSc (Wales), 1961. Mem. American Heart Assoc.; Hon. Mem. British Cardiac Soc.; Hon. Mem. Soc. of Phys. in Wales; Hon. FRSM, 1976. Guest Lecturer at Centenary Meetings of Royal Melbourne Hospital, 1948. High Sheriff of Cardiganshire, 1959. Hon. Mem. Order of Druids, 1960. *Publications:* Student's Handbook of Electrocardiography, 1934; Cardiography (2nd edn, 1954); Cardiology (2nd edn, 1956); Cardioscopy, 1952; Diseases of the Heart and Arteries, 1964; Journey to Harley Street, 1969; Diary of a Welsh Swagman, 1975; various papers on medical and cardiological subjects in Quarterly Jl of Med., Lancet, BMJ and Brit. Heart Jl. *Recreations:* fishing, gardening, farming. *Address:* Bryndomen, Tregaron, Dyfed, West Wales. *T:* Tregaron 404.
*Died 20 Sept.* 1988.

**EVANS, William Campbell,** OBE 1976; General Manager, Redditch Development Corporation, 1976–79; *b* 13 Jan. 1916; *s* of Frank Randolph Evans and Elizabeth Evans; *m* 1939, Sarah A. Duckworth; one *s* one *d. Educ:* Calday Grange Grammar Sch., West Kirby, Cheshire; Bury High Sch., Bury, Lancs. IPFA; FCA. Served RASC and RE, 1939–42. Local Govt Finance: Bury, 1932–38; Newton-le-Willows, Lancs, 1938–39 and 1942–44; Wolverhampton, 1944–53; Dep. Borough Treas., Northampton, 1953–58; Borough Treas., West Bromwich, 1958–64; Chief Finance Officer, Redditch Develt Corp., 1965–76. Mem. Council, IMTA/CIPFA, 1969–79, Vice-Pres., 1976–77, Pres., 1977–78. *Recreations:* gardening, music, watching sport.
*Died 9 Jan.* 1990.

**EVANS, Prof. (William) Charles,** PhD; FRS 1979; FRSC, FIBiol; Professor and Head, Department of Biochemistry and Soil Science, University College of North Wales, Bangor, 1951–79, later Emeritus; *b* 1 Oct. 1911; *s* of Robert and Elizabeth Evans; *m* 1942, Dr Irene Antice Woods; three *s* one *d. Educ:* Caernarfon Higher Grade and County Schs; University Coll. of N Wales, Bangor (John Hughes Entrance Scholar; 1st Cl. Hons Chemistry, 1932; MSc Org. Chem., 1934); Med. Sch., Univ. of Manchester (Platt Physiol Scholar; PhD Physiol., 1936). FRIC 1948; FIBiol 1955. Demonstr in Biochem., Sch. of Medicine, Univ. of Leeds, 1937, Dir of Blood Transfusion Labs, 1940; res. staff, Inoculation Dept (Wright-Fleming Inst.), St Mary's Hosp. Med. Sch., London, 1944; Special Lectr in Biochem. and Animal Health, University Coll., Aberystwyth, 1946. *Publications:* contrib. to Jl Chem. Soc., Biochem. Jl, Nature, MRC Reports, Brit. Jl Exp. Path., Brit. Vet. Jl, and Bot. Jl Linnean Soc. *Recreations:* cross country and middle distance running (when younger), farming and out-of-door pursuits, Rugby football. *Address:* Cae Ocyn, Llangaffo, Ynys Mon, Gwynedd LL60 6LY; Department of Biochemistry and Soil Science, University

College of North Wales, Deiniol Road, Bangor. *T:* Bangor 351151, ext. 411. *Died 24 July* 1988.

**EVANS, William Edis Webster;** *b* London, 26 Aug. 1908; *yr s* of late Rev. William Evans, Rector of Brondesbury; *m* 1956, Jean Hilda, *widow* of Andrew Allan and *d* of late Robert Smith Marshall, Forfar, Angus. *Educ:* Merchant Taylors' Sch., London. Editorial staff, John o' London's Weekly, 1928–39; Dep. Editor, 1951; Editor, 1953–54. Asst Editor, PTO, 1939; Gen. Editor, Country Life Books, 1954–67. Served RAF, 1940–47; Middle East, Italy, Germany; Wing Comdr (despatches). *Publications:* Editor (with Tom Scott) of In Praise of Golf, 1949; The Golfers' Year, 1950 and 1951; Rubs of the Green, 1969; The Encyclopaedia of Golf, 1971, 3rd edn 1980. *Recreations:* golf, reading. *Address:* 16 Chatterton Court, Kew Road, Richmond, Surrey TW9 2AR. *T:* 01-940 7789. *Club:* Royal Mid-Surrey Golf.
*Died 5 March* 1982.

**EVANS, William Ewart;** Judge of the High Court of Lesotho, 1967–73 (Acting Chief Justice, 1968); Judge of High Court of Northern Rhodesia and of the Rhodesia and Nyasaland Court of Appeal, 1953–62; *b* 24 May 1899; *s* of late John William Evans and Catherine Evans, Swansea, S Wales; *m* 1919, Agnes May Wilson (*d* 1981); one *s* four *d. Educ:* Swansea Grammar Sch. Served European War, 1917–19, in King's Royal Rifle Corps and Royal Army Service Corps. Called to Bar, 1934; practised on South Wales Circuit; Colonial Legal Service, 1938; acted in various judicial capacities; Resident Magistrate, Lusaka, Livingstone, N'Dola, Broken Hill, and Luanshya, 1940. *Recreation:* gardening. *Address:* 1 Van Riebeeck Street, Bedford, Cape Province, South Africa.
*Died 6 Jan.* 1990.

**EVANS, William John;** retired as General Secretary of Associated Society of Locomotive Engineers and Firemen (Oct. 1960–July 1963); Civil Representative, National Association for Employment of Regular Sailors, Soldiers and Airmen, 1963–69; *b* 4 Oct. 1899; *m* 1919, Ellen Tonks (*d* 1980); one *s. Educ:* Bucknell Sch. Joined LNW Railway, 1916. Royal Navy Service, 1916–21. Great War and Victory Medals; Mine Clearance Service Medal. Served as Executive Cttee Mem. of Trade Union, 1934–39; Pres. of Executive Cttee, 1937–38–39; Organising Sec., 1939–56; Asst Gen. Sec., 1956–60. Mem., Eastern Region Railways Board, 1963–66. Mem., Eccles Town Council, 1932–34. *Recreations:* boxing, bowling, and Association football. *Address:* 29 Gorsefield Road, Shard End, Birmingham, West Midlands B34 7AN.
*Died 23 Aug.* 1983.

**EVELING, Walter Raphael Taylor,** CBE 1960; Chartered Surveyor, retired, 1968; Deputy Chief Valuer, Inland Revenue, 1965–68 (Assistant Chief Valuer, 1951); *b* 8 March 1908; *s* of late Raphael Eveling, Hampstead Garden Suburb; *m* 1935, Annie Ferguson Newman, Belfast; one *s. Educ:* Paradise House Sch., Stoke Newington. Joined the Valuation Office, Inland Revenue, 1935. FRICS. *Address:* 12 Cooil Ny Marrey, Waterloo Road, Ramsey, Isle of Man. *Died 15 Nov.* 1987.

**EVERALL, John (Harold);** Hon. Fellow, Royal Agricultural Society of the Commonwealth (Hon. Treasurer, 1966–75); *b* 12 Oct. 1908; *s* of late William and Anne Heynes Everall, Shrawardine Castle, Shrewsbury; *m* 1935, Breda, *d* of late Gerald J. Sherlock, Ballsbridge, Dublin; one *s* one *d. Educ:* Malvern Coll. FRICS; Chartered Surveyor (Agriculture) and Pedigree Cattle Breeder (retired). War of 1939–45, Intelligence Officer (Captain), 4 Salop Bn, HG. Past President: Hereford Herd Book Soc.; Nat. Cattle Breeders' Assoc.; Shropshire and Montgomeryshire Agric. Valuers' Assoc.; Shropshire Chamber of Agric.; Vice-Pres., Shropshire and W Midland Agric. Soc., 1964–. Vice-Chairman: Hants and Winchester Br. E-SU, 1974–76; Shrewsbury Div. Conservative Assoc., 1946–50; Livestock Cttee of Brit. Agric. Export Council, 1967–70; (rep. BAEC at Santarem, Portugal, Fairs, 1967 and 1969). Former Mem. Exec. Cttee: Farmers' Club; Royal Smithfield Club; former Hon. Sec., Shropshire, Herefordshire and Mid-Wales branch, RICS. Mem. Council, Royal Agric. Soc. of Eng., 1949–70 (resigned). Rep. UK: World Confs of Pedigree Hereford Cattle Breeders, Hereford 1951, Kansas City, USA, 1960 and Dublin 1964; Royal Agric. Soc. of the Commonwealth Confs (as one of three delegs) at Sydney 1963, Toronto 1967, Nairobi 1969, Christchurch (NZ), 1973. Mem., Stapledon Trust Memorial Cttee, 1969–83. Internat. Judge of Pedigree Hereford Cattle and owner of Shrine herd (dispersed 1968). Judged: Palermo, Argentina, 1944 and 1963; Sydney, 1963; Nairobi (Borans), 1969; also at Royal of England, Royal Highland, Royal Welsh and Royal Dublin Shows. Director, QMP Ltd, 1958–65. Freeman of Kansas City, USA, and City of London (Liveryman). *Recreations:* fishing, beagling (Chm., Meon Valley Beagles Hunt Cttee, 1972–79); formerly fox-hunting (Mem. S Shropshire Hunt Cttee, 1953–68); shooting. *Address:* Shrine Lodge, Church Stretton, Shropshire SY6 7AS. *T:* Church Stretton 722979. *Club:* Travellers'. *Died 17 May* 1984.

**EVERARD, Lt-Col Sir Nugent Henry,** 3rd Bt, *cr* 1911; late The Duke of Wellington's Regiment (W Riding); *b* 28 Feb. 1905; *er s* of 2nd

Bt and Louisa Cole, *d* of R. H. Metge, MP, Athlumney, Navan; *S* father, 1929; *m* 1933, Frances Audrey (*d* 1975), *y d* of J. C. Jesson; one *s* one *d*. Retired with the hon. rank of Lt-Col, 1958. *Heir: s* Robin Charles Everard [*b* 5 Oct. 1939; *m* 1963, Ariel Ingrid, *e d* of late Col Peter Cleasby-Thompson, MBE, MC; one *s* two *d*].
*Died* 15 *Dec.* 1984.

**EVEREST, Arthur Ernest**, DSc, PhD, FRSC; Fellow of the Society of Dyers and Colourists; retired; *b* 1888; *m* 1914, Annie Kathleen Broome (*d* 1982); two *d*. *Educ:* Wrekin Coll.; University of Birmingham and on the Continent. Formerly Managing Director John W. Leitch & Co. Ltd and associated companies; Vice-Pres. of Royal Institute of Chemistry, 1936–39. Mem. of Council, 1933–36 and 1945–48; Mem. of Council of Assoc. of Brit. Chemical Manufacturers, 1934–54; Mem. of Governing Council Wrekin Coll., 1934–74. *Publications:* two books and various memoirs on chemical and allied subjects. *Address:* 18 Stanton Road, Ludlow, Shropshire SY8 2LR. *Died* 24 *Feb.* 1983.

**EVERETT, Rear-Adm. Douglas Henry**, CB 1950; CBE 1946 (MBE 1919); DSO 1940; *b* 16 June 1900; *s* of Douglas and Blanche Everett, Park House, Broadlands, Romsey; *m* 1932, Margery Annette Yeldham (*d* 1982); three *s* one *d*. *Educ:* Oakham Sch.; Cadet HMS Conway, 1913; RN Coll., Dartmouth. Served European War, 1916–18; War of 1939–45 (despatches twice); Flag Officer, Ground Training, 1949–51; Pres. Admiralty Interview Board, 1951–52; retired list, 1952. Chilean Order of Merit, 1939. *Address:* Gillinghams, Milford-on-Sea, Lymington, Hants. *T:* Lymington 2368. *Died* 26 *Aug.* 1986.

**EVERINGTON, Geoffrey Devas**, QC 1968; Barrister-at-Law; *b* 4 May 1915; *s* of late Herbert Devas Everington, MB and Muriel Frances Everington, Sanderstead; *m* 1951, Laila Nissen Hovind; four *s* three *d*. *Educ:* Westminster. Called to Bar, Gray's Inn, 1939, Bencher 1976; commenced practice at Bar, 1945. *Recreations:* music, tennis. *Address:* South Gable, Granville Road, Limpsfield, Oxted, Surrey. *T:* Oxted 4000. *Died* 23 *Feb.* 1982.

**EVERS, Claude Ronald**; MA; Headmaster of Sutton Valence School, 1953–67; *b* 17 Jan. 1908; *s* of late C. P. Evers (formerly housemaster at Rugby Sch.); *m* 1935, Marjorie Janet Ironside Bruce; four *s*. *Educ:* Rugby; Trinity Coll., Oxford. Asst Master, Wellington Coll., 1931–35; Asst Master, Rugby Sch., 1936–40; Headmaster of Berkhamsted Sch., 1946–53. Warden of Pendley Residential Centre of Adult Education, 1967–73. War service (Royal Warwicks Regt), 1940–45. Old Stager. *Publication:* Rugby (Blackie's Public School Series), 1939. *Address:* 20 Richmond Court, Osmond Road, Hove BN3 1TD. *T:* Brighton 723721. *Died* 26 *Nov.* 1988.

**EVERY, Sir John (Simon)**, 12th Bt, *cr* 1641; *b* 24 April 1914; *er s* of Sir Edward Oswald Every, 11th Bt and Lady (Ivy Linton) Every (*d* 1976); *S* father, 1959; *m* 1st, 1938, Annette Constance (marr. diss., 1942), *o c* of late Major F. W. M. Drew, Drewscourt, Co. Cork; 2nd, 1943, Janet Marion, *d* of John Page, Blakeney, Norfolk; one *s* two *d*. *Educ:* Harrow. Served War of 1939–45. Capt., Sherwood Foresters. Business Co. Dir, 1954–60, Dir of private companies. *Recreations:* cricket, tennis, shooting. *Heir: s* Henry John Michael Every [*b* 6 April 1947; *m* 1974, Susan Mary, *er d* of Kenneth Beaton, Hartford, Hunts; three *s*]. *Address:* Egginton, near Derby. *T:* Etwall 2245. *Club:* MCC. *Died* 3 *Nov.* 1988.

**EVETTS, Lt-Gen. Sir John (Fullerton)**, Kt 1951; CB 1939; CBE 1937; MC; *b* 30 June 1891; *s* of late Lieut-Col J. M. Evetts, Tackley Park, Oxon; *m* 1916, Helen Phyllis (*d* 1980), *d* of late Captain C. A. G. Becher, Burghfields, Bourton on the Water, Glos; one *s*. *Educ:* Temple Grove; Lancing; Royal Military Coll., Sandhurst; Staff Coll., Camberley. Entered Army, 1911; joined The Cameronians (Scottish Rifles); served European War, 1914–18 (MC, despatches); Lieut 1913; Captain 1915; temp. Major Machine Gun Corps, 1916; Bt-Major 1929; Substantive, 1929; Bt Lt-Col 1931; Substantive Lt-Col Royal Ulster Rifles, 1934; Col 1935; Maj.-Gen. 1941; employed with Iraq Army, 1925–28; DAAG War Office, 1932; Commander British Troops in Palestine, 1935; GSO1 Palestine, 1936; Brig. Comd. 16th Inf. Bde, Palestine and Trans-Jordan, 1936–39 (despatches); BGS, HQ, Northern Command, India, 1939–40; Comdr Western (Indept) Dist, India, 1940–41; Divl Comdr, 1941 (despatches); Asst CIGS, 1942; Senior Military Adviser to Minister of Supply, 1944–46; retired pay, 1946; Head of British Ministry of Supply Staff in Australia, 1946–51, and Chief Executive Officer Joint UK-Australian Long Range Weapons, Board of Administration, 1946–49. Managing Dir, 1951–58, Chm., 1958–60, Rotol Ltd and Brit. Messier. OStJ. Legion of Honour (US), 1943. *Address:* Pepper Cottage, Kemerton, near Tewkesbury, Glos. *Club:* Army and Navy. *Died* 21 *Dec.* 1988.

**EWALD, Paul P.**, DrPhil; FRS 1958; Professor Emeritus of Physics, Polytechnic Institute of Brooklyn, since 1959; Professor of Physics, 1949–59, and Head of Department, 1949–57, Polytechnic Institute of Brooklyn; *b* Berlin, Germany, 23 Jan. 1888; *s* of Paul Ewald, Historian (Univ. Berlin), and Clara Ewald, Portrait-Painter; *m*

1913, Ella (Elise Berta) (*née* Philippson); two *s* two *d*. *Educ:* Victoria Gymnasium, Potsdam; Univs of Cambridge, Göttingen and Munich (DrPhil 1912). Asst to D. Hilbert (Mathematics, Göttingen), 1912–13; Asst to A. Sommerfeld (Theor. Physics, Munich), 1913–21; X-ray mechanic, German army, 1915–18; Lecturer in Theoretical Physics, Univ. of Munich, 1918; Prof. of Theoretical Physics, TH Stuttgart, 1921–37; Res. Fellow., Cambridge Univ., 1937–39; Lecturer, later Prof. of Mathematical Physics, The Queen's Univ., Belfast, 1939–49. Corresp. Mem. Acad. Göttingen, 1937; Fellow Amer. Acad. Arts and Sci., US, 1954; Membre d'honneur Société Française de Minéralogie et de Cristallographie, 1955; Ehrenmitglied, Deutsche Mineralog. Ges., 1958. Mem. Exec. Cttee. Internat. Union of Crystallography, 1948–66, Pres., 1960–1963. Corresp. Mem. Bavarian Acad. Sci., 1962; Fellow, Deut. Akad. d. Naturforscher (Leopoldina), 1966. Hon. Mem., Cambridge Philosophical Soc., 1968. Dr *hc*; TH Stuttgart, 1954; Univ. de Paris, 1958; Adelphi Univ., 1966; Univ. Munich, 1968; Polytechnic Inst., Brooklyn, 1972. Max Planck Medal, Deutsche Physikal Gesellschaft, 1978; Gregory Aminoff Medal, Swedish Acad., 1979. *Publications:* Kristalle und Röntgenstrahlen, 1923 (Germany); Handbuch der Physik, 1923 (Berlin); 50 Years of X-ray Diffraction, 1962 (Oosthoek, Holland). Contrib. Thermodynamics and Physics of Matter, 1955 (USA), etc. Editor: Zeitschrift für Kristallographie, 1923–37; Acta Crystallographica, 1948–59. *Address:* 108 Sheldon Road, Ithaca, NY 14850, USA. *Died* 22 *Aug.* 1985.

**EWART EVANS, George;** *see* Evans, G. E.

**EWART JAMES, His Honour William Henry;** a Circuit Judge, 1974–83; *b* 15 Dec. 1910; *e s* of Rev. David Ewart James; *m* 1941, Esmé Vivienne, *y d* of Edward Lloyd, Liverpool and Gresford; two *s* one *d*. *Educ:* Bishop's Stortford Coll.; Worcester Coll., Oxford. MA (Mod. Hist.). Private Sec. to J. H. Morgan, KC, Counsel to the Indian Princes, 1936; Asst. Sec. European Gp, Bengal Legislature, 1937–38; travelled Far East and America, 1936–39. Served War: in Grenadier Guards, Royal Welch Fusiliers and 1st Airborne Div., Sept. 1939–Dec. 1945. Called to the Bar, 1948; Counsel to the Post Office, Western Circuit, 1957–70; Dep. Chm., Devon QS, 1968–71; a Recorder of the Crown Court, 1972–74. Mem., Hants CC, 1952–74; Alderman, 1965; Chm., Local Govt Cttee, 1963–74. *Recreations:* travel, butterflies. *Address:* Springfield, Greywell, Basingstoke, Hants. *T:* Odiham 2644.
*Died* 17 *March* 1988.

**EWBANK, Maj.-Gen. Sir Robert Withers**, KBE 1964 (CBE 1954); CB 1957; DSO 1945; MA; late Royal Engineers; retired; President Emeritus, Association of Military Christian Fellowships; *b* 20 July 1907; *s* of late Brig.-Gen. W. Ewbank, CB, CIE, RE and Mrs Ewbank, *d* of late Col Barrow, IMS; *m* 1932, Isobel Joyce Forster; one *s* two *d*. *Educ:* Weymouth Coll.; Royal Military Academy, Woolwich (King's and Pollock Medals, Armstrong Memorial Prize for Science); Christ's Coll., Cambridge (Scholar; MA 1st Class Hons Mech. Sciences Tripos). Garrison Engineer, Trincomalee, Ceylon, 1934–36; Adjt, Kent Fortress RE TA, 1936–39; GSO2 War Office, 1939–41; Instructor Staff Coll., Camberley, 1941–42; GSO1 War Office, 1942–44; Comdr, Royal Engineers, 50 Northumbrian Division, BLA, 1944–46; Col Q (Movements) War Office, 1946–49; Student Imperial Defence Coll., 1950; Sec. Chiefs of Staff Cttee, Ministry of Defence, 1951–53; Chief of Staff, British Army Staff, Washington, USA, 1954–56; Dir of Movements, War Office, 1956–58; Chief of Staff, HQ Northern Army Group, 1958–60; Commandant, Royal Military Coll. of Science, 1961–64; retd 1964. Pres., Officers' Christian Union of GB, 1965–76. *Recreations:* photography, climbing, travel. *Address:* 5 Petworth Court, Overstrand, Rustington, West Sussex BN16 2LF. *T:* Rustington 6345. *Died* 28 *April* 1981.

**EWING, Air Vice-Marshal Vyvyan Stewart**, CB 1954; CBE 1951; RAF Medical Branch, retired; Principal Medical Officer, Home Command, 1953–55; *b* 4 Oct. 1898; *m* Ethel Nancy (*d* 1975). MB, ChB (St Andrews); Diploma in Public Health. Air Vice-Marshal, 1951; retired, 1955. CStJ. *Address:* 19 Lauder Close, Southbourne, Emsworth, W Sussex. *T:* Emsworth 4002.
*Died* 8 *April* 1981.

**EXETER, 6th Marquess of**, *cr* 1801, **David George Brownlow Cecil,** KCMG 1943; Baron Burghley, 1571; Earl of Exeter, 1605; DL; Hereditary Grand Almoner; Lord Paramount of the Soke of Peterborough; *b* 9 Feb. 1905; *e s* of 5th Marquess of Exeter, KG, CMG; *S* father, 1956; *m* 1st, 1929, Lady Mary Theresa Montagu-Douglas-Scott (marr. diss. 1946), 4th *d* of 7th Duke of Buccleuch; three *d*; 2nd, 1946, Diana Mary Forbes, *widow* of Col David Forbes and *er d* of late Hon. Arnold Henderson; one *d*. *Educ:* Eton; Le Rosey; Magdalene Coll., Cambridge, MA. Lieut Grenadier Guards, retired 1929, re-employed 1939; served War of 1939–45: Staff Captain, 1940; Major, Dep. Asst Dir, 1941, Lt-Col, Asst Dir, Tank Supply, 1942; Controller of Aircraft Repairs and Overseas Supplies, Min. of Aircraft Production, 1942–43; Hon. Colonel: 5th Bn Northants Regt, 1939–48; Bermuda Militia, 1945–46. MP (U)

Peterborough Div., Northants, 1931–43; Parly Private Secretary to: late Lord Hailsham for World Economic Conf.; Parly Sec. at Min. of Supply, 1939–41; Chm. Economy Cttee, Raw Materials, 1939–43; Governor and C-in-C of Bermuda, 1943–45. Leader, UK Industrial Mission to Pakistan, 1950, and to Burma, 1954. Rector of St Andrews Univ., 1949–52. Mayor of Stamford, 1961. President: Amateur Athletic Assoc., 1936–76; Internat. Amateur Athletic Fedn, 1946–76; British Olympic Assoc., 1966–77 (Chm., 1936–66); Mem., Internat. Olympic Cttee, 1933–, Vice-Pres., 1952–66, now Doyen. Chairman: Propaganda Cttee, Nat. Fitness Council, 1938; Organising and Exec. Cttee for 1948 Olympic Games in London; Fedn of Chambers of Commerce of British Commonwealth, 1952–54; President: Young Britons Assoc., 1933–37; Junior Imperial League, 1939 (Chm., 1933–37); Council, Radio Industry, 1952; English Tourist Bd, 1966; BTA, 1966–69. Director: National Westminster Bank Ltd; Lands Improvement Co., 1938–75; Firestone Tyre & Rubber Co. Ltd; L&NER, 1930–46; BOAC, 1946–56; Chairman: A. C. Cossors, 1946–53; Birmid Qualcast, 1946–76; Trustee, Trust Houses Forte. Mem. Exec. Cttee, King George VI Nat. Memorial Fund. Pres., CUAC, 1926–27; Winner of: Oxford v Cambridge 120 yards hurdles and 220 yards hurdles, 1925, 1926, 1927; eight British Championships, 1928; Olympic 400 metres hurdles, 1928; 5th, 110 metre hurdles, 4th, 400 metre hurdles, and 2nd, 4 × 400 metres, Olympic Games, 1932; 1st three times, Empire Games, 1930; many other races at home and abroad. Hunted own private pack of foxhounds, 1935–39; Joint-Master: E Sussex, 1939–53; Old Berkshire Hunt, 1953–57; Burghley Hunt, 1957–67; Pres., BHS, 1963. Pres., Junior Carlton Club, 1956–77. DL Northants, 1937–46, Huntingdon and Peterborough, 1965–. Hon. FRCS. Hon. LLD St Andrews, 1942. KStJ. *Recreations:* hunting, shooting, fishing, athletics. *Heir: b* Lord (William) Martin Alleyne Cecil. *Address:* Burghley House, Stamford, Lincs. *Clubs:* Pratt's, Carlton. *Died* 21 *Oct.* 1981.

**EXETER,** 7th Marquess of, *cr* 1801; **William Martin Alleyne Cecil;** Baron Burghley, 1571; Earl of Exeter, 1605; *b* 27 April 1909; 2nd *s* of 5th Marquess of Exeter, KG, CMG and Hon. Myra Rowena Sibell Orde-Powlett, *d* of 4th Baron Bolton; *S* brother, 1981; *m* 1st, 1934, Edith Lilian Csanady de Telegd (*d* 1954); one *s*; 2nd, 1954, Lillian Jane Johnson; one *d* (and one *d* decd). *Educ:* Royal Naval Coll., Dartmouth. *Publications:* Being Where You Are, 1977; On Eagles' Wings, 1977; Beyond Belief, 1986. *Heir: s* Lord Burghley. *Address:* PO Box 8, 100 Mile House, British Columbia V0K 2E0, Canada. *T:* 604–395–2323. *Died* 12 *Jan.* 1988.

**EXHAM, Maj.-Gen. Robert Kenah,** CB 1952; CBE 1949 (OBE 1946); MC 1940; Director Land/Air Warfare, War Office, 1957–60, retired;

*b* 25 Jan. 1907; *s* of late Col Frank Simeon Exham, DSO; *m* 1940, Avril Mary, *d* of late Major F. Langley Price; two *s. Educ:* Radley Coll. Served North-West Frontier of India, 1935 (despatches twice, medal with clasp); War of 1939–45 (despatches, MC). Maj.-Gen. late Duke of Wellington's Regt (West Riding). *Address:* Tall Trees, Beech Hill, Mayford, Woking, Surrey GU22 0SB. *T:* Woking 62783. *Died* 31 *Jan.* 1985.

**EXTON-SMITH, Prof. Arthur Norman,** CBE 1981; MD; FRCP; Director, Geriatric Neurophysiology Unit, Whittington Hospital, London, since 1985; Professor of Geriatric Medicine, University College Hospital Medical School, London, 1973–84; *b* 7 Jan. 1920; *s* of Arthur and Ethel Exton-Smith; *m* 1951, Jean Barbara Belcher; one *s* one *d. Educ:* Nottingham High Sch.; Pembroke Coll., Cambridge (MA, MD). FRCP 1964. Consultant Physician: Whittington Hosp., London 1951–65; UCH, 1965–73. Hon. DM Nottingham, 1984. Lord Cohen of Birkenhead Medal, British Soc. for Res. in Ageing, 1984; Moxon Medal, RCP, 1984; Dhole-Eddlestone Meml Prize, British Geriatrics Soc., 1986; Sandoz Prize for Gerontological Res., Internat. Assoc. of Gerontology, 1987. *Publications:* Medical Problems of Old Age, 1955; Geriatrics (with P. W. Overstall), 1979; (ed with M. Weksler) Practical Geriatric Medicine, 1986; contrib. Lancet, BMJ. *Address:* 6 North Grove, Highgate, N6 4SL. *T:* 01–341 4433. *Died* 29 *March* 1990.

**EYTON, Lt-Col Robert Charles Gilfrid M.;** *see* Morris-Eyton.

**EYTON, Mrs Selena Frances W.;** *see* Wynne-Eyton.

**EZARD, Clarence Norbury,** CBE 1954 (OBE 1942); Retired as Ambassador to Costa Rica; *b* 6 Oct. 1896; *m* 1936, Olive Lillian Vaneus. *Educ:* Carlisle Grammar Sch.; Emmanuel Coll., Cambridge. Probationer Vice-Consul in General Consular Service, 1924; Acting Vice-Consul, Havana, 1926; Chargé d'Affaires, May-Oct. 1928; Sec. to Special Mission at Inauguration of Pres. of Republic of Cuba, with Temp. rank of 3rd Sec. in Diplomatic Service, 1929; Subst. rank of Vice-Consul, 1929; Vice-Consul at Bogotá, 1930; local rank of 2nd Sec. in Dipl. Service, 1930; in charge of Consulate at Havana, March-June 1931, of Legation April-June 1931. Transferred to New York, 1932, to Piræus, 1934. Acting Consul at Athens, 1935 and 1936; Consul at Beira, 1938; Montevideo, 1945, with rank of Consul and 1st Sec.; Consul-Gen., Gdansk, 1946; Consul-Gen., Haifa, 1949; Minister to Costa Rica, 1953; Ambassador to Costa Rica, 1956; retired, 1957. *Address:* Three Fields, Mayfield, East Sussex. *Club:* Carlton.
*Died* 8 *Nov.* 1986.

# F

**FAGG, Bernard Evelyn Buller,** MBE 1962; MA; FSA; FMA; Curator, Pitt Rivers Museum, Oxford, 1963–75; b 8 Dec. 1915; s of late W. P. Fagg and Mrs L. Fagg; m 1942, Mary Catherine, d of G. W. Davidson; one s two d (and two s decd). Educ: Dulwich Coll.; Downing Coll., Cambridge. Nigerian Admin. Service, 1939–47. War service with West African Engineers, East African Campaign, 1939–43. Dept of Antiquities, Republic of Nigeria, 1947–63 (Dir, 1957–63); Lincoln Coll., Oxford, 1964; Fellow of Linacre Coll., 1965–75, Emeritus Fellow, 1976. Publications: Nok terracottas, 1977; contribs to learned jls. Address: 45 Woodstock Road, Oxford. T: 54875. Club: Leander.                      Died 14 Aug. 1987.

**FAIRBAIRN, Douglas Chisholm,** CIE 1945; CBE 1956; MA; retired; formerly Director, Thomas Hamling & Co. Ltd, St Andrew's Dock, Hull; b 1904; s of late Rev. R. T. and Mrs Fairbairn; m 1938, Agnes, d of late Rev. William amd Mrs Arnott; two s. Educ: George Heriot's, Edinburgh; Edinburgh Univ. (MA). Formerly: Secretary Bengal Chamber of Commerce and Industry, Calcutta, 1938–56, also in that capacity Sec. Associated Chambers of Commerce of India; Chm., Hull Fishing Vessel Owners and Hull Fishing Industry Associations, 1957–62. JP, City and County of Kingston-upon-Hull, 1966–71. Recreation: gardening. Address: Vikings, 29 Hampden Hill, Beaconsfield, Bucks HP9 1BP. T: Beaconsfield 4670.

Died 5 Feb. 1987.

**FAIRBAIRN, Sir Robert (Duncan),** Kt 1975; JP; Chairman, Clydesdale Bank plc, 1975–85 (Director, 1967–85; General Manager, 1958–71; Vice-Chairman, 1971–75); b 25 Sept. 1910; s of late Robert Fairbairn and Christina Fairbairn; m 1939, Sylvia Lucinda, d of late Rev. Henry Coulter; two s one d. Educ: Perth Academy. Joined service of The Clydesdale Bank at Perth, 1927; Beckett & Whitehead Prizeman, Inst. of Bankers, 1934; Midland Bank, 1934. Lt-Comdr (S) RNVR, 1939–46. Asst Gen. Manager, Clydesdale & North of Scotland Bank, 1951. Chm., Clydesdale Bank Industrial Finance Ltd, 1981–85; Director: Commercial Union Assurance Group (Local Board), 1958–85; Midland Bank Finance Corp. Ltd, 1967–74; Clydesdale Bank Finance Corp. Ltd, 1967–85; Clydesdale Bank Insurance Services Ltd, 1970–85; Newarthill Ltd, 1972–; Midland Bank Ltd, 1975–85; Chairman: Scottish Computer Services Ltd, 1971–85; Scottish Amicable Life Assce Soc., 1976–78 (Dir to 1981); A Dir, British Nat. Oil Corp., 1976–79. Glasgow Chamber of Commerce (Vice-Pres., 1970–76). Pres., Inst. of Bankers in Scotland, 1961–63; Vice-Pres., Scottish Economic Soc. (Pres. 1966–69); Chairman: Scottish Industrial Develt Advisory Bd, 1972–81; Cttee of Scottish Bank General Managers, 1963–66; Vice-Chm., Inst. of Fiscal Studies (Scotland), 1976–85; Vice-Pres., British Bankers Assoc., 1966–68; Member: Scottish Council (Develt and Industry), Vice-Pres., 1967–68; Scottish Council of CBI. Chm., Cystic Fibrosis Research Investment Trust plc, 1981–85. FCIB, FIB (Scot); FRSA; CBIM; Hon. FSIAD. JP Glasgow, 1962. Recreations: golf, fishing. Address: The Grange, Hazelwood Road, Bridge of Weir, Renfrewshire. T: Bridge of Weir 2102. Clubs: Caledonian, MCC; Western (Glasgow); Corinthian Casuals; Royal and Ancient (St Andrews).

Died 26 March 1988.

**FAIRBANK, Alfred John,** CBE 1951; FRSA; calligrapher; b 12 July 1895; er s of Alfred John and Emma Fairbank; m 1919, Elsie Kneeshaw; one s (one d decd). Entered Civil Service, 1911; Senior Executive Officer, Admiralty, 1949–55; retired from Civil Service, 1955. Pres. Soc. of Scribes and Illuminators, 1951–63; Vice-Pres. of Soc. for Italic Handwriting; Member: Soc. of Designer Craftsmen; Art Workers Guild; The Double Crown Club. Leverhulme Research Awards, 1956 and 1957. Designer and responsible for production of The Books of Remembrance of the Royal Air Force, Church of St Clement Danes. Publications: A Handwriting Manual, 1932, 9th edn 1975; A Book of Scripts, 1949, 3rd edn 1977; Editor and calligrapher of Beacon Writing Books I–VI, 1958; (with Berthold Wolpe) Renaissance Handwriting, 1960; (with Dr. R. W. Hunt) Humanistic Script of the Fifteenth and Sixteenth Centuries, 1960; A Roman Script for Schools, 1961; (with Prof. Bruce Dickins) The Italic Hand in Tudor Cambridge, 1962; The Story of Handwriting, 1970; Augustino da Siena, 1975. Relevant publication: Calligraphy and Palæography: Essays presented to Alfred Fairbank on his seventieth birthday, 1965. Address: 27 Granville Road, Hove, East Sussex BN3 1TG. T: Brighton 733431.

Died 14 March 1982.

**FAIRBANKS, Maj-Gen. Cecil Benfield,** CB 1950; CBE 1946 (MBE 1940); retired 1958; Administrative Secretary, National Council of Social Service, 1958–65; b 12 June 1903; s of F. C. Fairbanks, Montreal, Canada; m 1936, Rosamonde Beryl Fisher; one s one d. Educ: Marlborough Coll.; Keble Coll., Oxford. Commissioned with The Sherwood Foresters, Jan. 1924; Adjutant 1st Foresters, 1935–38; Adjutant 5th Foresters TA, 1938–40. Served UK, 1924–35; West Indies, 1935–38; War of 1939–45, France, 1939–40; Middle East,

1941–45 (Irak, 1943, Italy, 1945); France and Germany, 1945–46. OC 14th Foresters, 1943; Comd Inf. Bde, 1944–46; BGS 1947; idc 1948; Dir of Inf., 1948–49; GOC Nigeria Dist, 1949–52; Chief Army Instructor, Imperial Defence Coll., 1953–54; GOC Rhine District, British Army of the Rhine, 1955–58, retd. Col The Sherwood Foresters, 1958–65. Address: Candy Lane House, Fen Street, Nayland, Colchester, Essex.                      Died 5 March 1982.

**FAIRFAX, Sir Warwick (Oswald),** Kt 1967; MA; Director: John Fairfax & Sons Ltd (The Sydney Morning Herald, The Sun Herald, The Sun, The Australian Financial Review, The National Times, and other publications); Vice President, Australian Elizabethan Theatre Trust; owns Harrington Park; b 1901; o s of Sir James Oswald Fairfax, a Proprietor and Dir of John Fairfax and Sons, Ltd, and Mabel, d of Capt. Francis Hixson, RN; m 1928, Marcie Elizabeth, o d of David Wilson, Barrister of Sydney; one s one d; m 1948, Hanné Anderson, 2nd d of Emil Bendixsen, Copenhagen; one d; m 1959, Mary, o d of Kevin Wein; one s. Educ: Geelong Grammar Sch., St Paul's Coll., Sydney Univ.; Balliol Coll., Oxford. 2nd Class Hons in Sch. of Philosophy, Politics and Economics; joined staff of John Fairfax and Sons, Ltd, 1925; Dir, 1927; Managing Dir 1930; Cttee of One with admin. and management powers, 1970–76; Chairman of Dirs, 1956–76. Plays: A Victorian Marriage, Vintage for Heroes, The Bishop's Wife, performed Sydney 1951, 1952, 1956. Publications: Men, Parties, and Policies, 1943; The Triple Abyss: towards a modern synthesis, 1965; ed, A Century of Journalism (The Sydney Morning Herald), 1931. Recreations: the arts, philosophy, motoring and vintage cars. Address: John Fairfax & Sons Ltd, Box 506, GPO Sydney, Australia; Fairwater, 560 New South Head Road, Double Bay, Sydney, NSW 2028, Australia; Harrington Park, Narellan, NSW 2567. Clubs: Carlton, Oriental, Australian, Union, Pioneers, Royal Sydney Yacht Squadron (Sydney).                      Died 14 Jan. 1987.

**FAIRFAX-CHOLMELEY, Francis William Alfred,** CBE 1960; Director: Barclays Bank Ltd, 1957–73; Barclays Bank SA, France, 1968–75 (Chairman, 1968–70); b 20 Sept. 1904; e s of Hugh Charles Fairfax-Cholmeley, JP of Brandsby, York, and of Alice Jane (née Moverley); m 1940, Janet Meta, e d of Sir John Ogilvy-Wedderburn, 11th and 5th Bt; two d (one s decd). Educ: Eton; Magdalene Coll., Cambridge (MA). Joined Barclays Bank Ltd, 1926; Local Dir, 54 Lombard Street, 1939–48; Resident Dir in Paris, Barclays Bank (France) Ltd, 1948–64, Chm., 1964–68; Local Dir, Foreign Branches, 1964–66, and Pall Mall East, 1966–68; Hon. Dir, Banque de Bruxelles SA. Served RA, 1939–45 (Major). Address: Struie, Forfar Road, Kirriemuir, Angus.                      Died 7 April 1983.

**FAIRHURST, William Albert,** CBE 1961; Chairman, Bridge Design Consultants Pty Ltd, Sydney; Consultant to W. A. Fairhurst & Partners, Glasgow (formerly F. A. Macdonald & Partners), Consulting Civil Engineers, since 1971 (Senior Partner, 1940–71); b 21 Aug. 1903; s of John Robert Fairhurst and Elizabeth Ann Massey, Alderley Edge, Cheshire; m 1937, Elizabeth Robertson Jardine; one s one d. Educ: Cavendish Road Sch., W. Didsbury; Manchester Coll. of Technology. FICE; FIStructE; FNZIE; FInstHE; Mem. Soc. Civil Engrs, France. Designer of many bridges, including Queen's Bridge, Perth, Howford Bridge, Ayrshire, Kingston Bridge, Glasgow, and new Tay Road Bridge. Mem. of Royal Fine Art Commission for Scotland, 1963–72. Pres. of Scottish Chess Assoc., 1957–69; British Chess Champion, 1937; eleven times Scottish Chess Champion and seventeen times West of Scotland Chess Champion; awarded title of International Chess Master by Internat. Federation of Chess, 1951. Chess Correspondent, Glasgow Herald, 1959–69. FRSA. Hon. LLD St Andrews, 1968. Publications: Arch Design Simplified; (jointly) Design and Construction of Reinforced Concrete Bridges; numerous papers on bridges and structural engineering to engineering institutions. Recreations: bridge, art, chess. Address: 1 Lynedoch Terrace, Glasgow G3 7XQ. T: 041-332 8754; 4 Four Trees, Howick, Auckland, New Zealand. Clubs: Royal Automobile; Glasgow Art.

Died 13 March 1982.

**FAIRLEY, Alan Brand;** Deputy Chairman of Grand Metropolitan Hotels Ltd, 1970–73; First President of Mecca Ltd since 1972; b Edinburgh, s of James Fairley and Jane Alexander; m 1942, Roma Josephine Haddow; one d. Educ: George Watson's Coll., Edinburgh. Joined family catering business (Fairleys of Edinburgh) from college, 1919; opened Dunedin dance hall where broadcast bands and cabaret artists, 1923; opened Piccadilly Club (first night club in Glasgow), internat. stars and bands, 1926; formed a number of Scottish cos to run dance halls, 1934–37; partnership with Carl Heimann to run dance halls all over UK, 1936 (until his death, 1968). Served War of 1939–45, Army Catering Corps, 1940–45, Major. Acquired lease of Café de Paris, London, 1943, and re-opened it, 1948, presenting Noel Coward, Marlene Dietrich, Maurice Chevalier and many others. Created Mecca Ltd, now notable for its promotion of Miss World, TV Come Dancing and Carl-Alan award for outstanding contributions to ballroom dancing, after the Christian names of its founders; Jt Chm. with Carl

Heimann, Mecca Ltd, 1952, Chm. Mecca Ltd 1968; Mecca Ltd merged with Grand Metropolitan Hotels Ltd, 1970. Member: Variety Club of Great Britain and Réunion des Gastronômes (both in London). *Recreations:* swimming, golf. *Address:* 5 Mount Rule House, Braddan, Isle of Man. *T:* Marown 852702. *Club:* Saints and Sinners.
*Died 19 July* 1987.

**FAIRLEY, Prof. Barker,** OC 1979; MA Leeds, PhD Jena; Hon. LittD: Leeds; Waterloo (Canada); Toronto; Carleton; York (Canada); Western; Hon. LLD Alberta; RCA 1980; FRSC; Emeritus Professor of German in University College, University of Toronto; *b* Barnsley, Yorks, 21 May 1887; *s* of Barker and Charlotte Fairley; *m* 1914, Margaret Adele Keeling (*d* 1968), Bradford, Yorks; one *d*. *Educ:* Universities of Leeds and Jena. Lektor in English at University of Jena, 1907–10; Lecturer in German at University of Alberta, 1910; Henry Simon Prof. of German Language and Literature, Manchester Univ., 1932–36. Corresp. Fellow, British Acad., 1971. *Publications:* Charles M. Doughty, 1927; Goethe as revealed in his Poetry, 1932; A Study of Goethe, 1947; Goethe's Faust, 1953; Heinrich Heine, An Interpretation, 1954; Wilhelm Raabe, an Introduction to his Novels, 1961; (trans.) Goethe, Faust, 1970; Poems of 1922, 1972. *Address:* 90 Willcocks Street, Toronto, Canada. *Club:* Arts and Letters (Toronto).
*Died 11 Oct.* 1986.

**FAIRLIE-CUNINGHAME, Sir William Alan,** 15th Bt *cr* 1630; MC; BE (Sydney); retired as Research Officer, National Standards Laboratory, Sydney; *b* 31 Jan. 1893; *s* of 13th Bt and Georgiana Maud, *d* of late Edward Hardman Macartney; *S* brother, 1939; *m* 1929, Irene Alice (*d* 1970), *d* of late Henry Margrave Terry; one *s*. *Educ:* Sydney Univ. Served European War, 1915–19 (MC). Res. Officer, Metrology Div., Commonwealth Scientific and Industrial Res. Orgn, 1943–58. *Heir:* *s* William Henry Fairlie-Cuninghame [*b* 1 Oct. 1930; *m* 1972, Janet Menzies, *d* of late Roy Menzies Saddington; one *s*]. *Address:* 62 Farrer Brown Court, Nuffield Village, Castle Hill, NSW 2154, Australia.
*Died 15 Dec.* 1981.

**FAIRMAN, Prof. Herbert Walter;** Emeritus Professor of Egyptology, University of Liverpool (Brunner Professor of Egyptology, 1948–74); Special Lecturer in Egyptology, University of Manchester, 1948–69; *b* 9 March, 1907; *s* of Rev. W. T. Fairman, DD; *m* 1937, Olive Winnifred Nicholls; one *s* one *d*. *Educ:* Goudhurst Sch. for Boys, Goudhurst, Kent; University of Liverpool. Excavations of the Egypt Exploration Soc. at Armant and Tell el Amarna (Egypt), 1929–36, and Sesebi and Amarah West (Sudan), 1936–48. Field Dir, Egypt Exploration Society's Nubian Expedition, 1937–48. *Publications:* The Triumph of Horus, 1974; chapters on the inscriptions in: Mond and Myers, The Bucheum, 1934; Frankfort and Pendlebury, The City of Akhenaten II, 1933; (also editor) Pendlebury, The City of Akhenaten III, 1950; articles in Journal of Egyptian Archæology, Annales du Service des Antiquités de l'Egypte and Bulletin de l'Institut français d'archéologie orientale. *Recreations:* swimming, walking. *Address:* 6 Garth Drive, Mossley Hill, Liverpool L18 6HW. *T:* 051-724 2875.
*Died 16 Nov.* 1982.

**FAIRN, (Richard) Duncan;** Assistant Under-Secretary of State, Home Office, 1964–67; *b* 1 June 1906; *s* of Percy Frederick and Mary Fairn; *m* 1930, Marion Cristina (*d* 1985), *d* of James M. Sturrock; one *s* decd. *Educ:* Elementary Sch.; Battersea County (now Henry Thornton) Sch.; failed Bank of England entrance; London Sch. of Economics, BSc (Econ). Voluntary prison teacher and visitor, 1926–30. Education Officer, Pettit Farm Settlement, Dagenham, 1929–30; Joint Warden, The Settlement, York, 1930–38; Dep. Governor, Manchester Prison, 1938–39; Dep. Governor, Wakefield Prison, 1939–42; Governor, Rochester Borstal, 1942–45; First Principal, Prison Service Staff Coll., Wakefield, 1945–48; Asst Comr of Prisons, 1948–55; a Comr of Prisons, 1955–63, when Prison Commn was dissolved; Dir of Prison Administration, 1952–60; Chief Dir, Prison Dept, Home Office, 1960–64; Training Officer, Lord Chancellor's Office, 1967–72. Visited various parts of the world to advise on prison administration, 1955–69; Chm. Cttee on Detention Camps in Kenya, 1959. Swarthmore Lectr, Society of Friends, 1951; Vis. Lectr, UN Inst. at Fuchū, Tokyo, 1967; visited Nigeria to advise on prison admin, 1973. Pres., Pinner Branch of UNA, 1970–; Vice-Pres., Nat. Assoc. of Prison Visitors, 1970–; Member: Council of National Book League, 1951–77; European Cttee on Crime Problems (Strasbourg), 1964–67; Internat. Penal and Penitentiary Foundn, 1965–67; UK delegn to UN Social Develt Commn, 1967–71; Parole Bd, 1967–71; UN Adv. Cttee of Experts on Prevention of Crime and Treatment of Offenders, 1970–72; Peter Bedford Project, 1974–76. Governor, Leighton Park Sch., 1961–76. Chairman: Management Cttee, E London Family Service Unit, 1958–78; Bd of Governors, Bedales Sch., 1963–65; John Bellers Ltd, 1974–82; Peter Bedford Trust, 1977–83; Civil Service Selection Bds, 1972–76. Associate Mem., BFI. *Publications:* Quakerism, a faith for ordinary men, 1951; The Disinherited Prisoner (Eleanor Rathbone Memorial Lecture), 1962; contrib.: Changing Concepts of Crime

and its Treatment, 1966; various criminological jls; DNB Supplement, 1961–70. *Recreations:* reading, walking, log-splitting, music and people. *Address:* Lavender Cottage, 82 Paines Lane, Pinner, Mddx HA5 3BL. *T:* 01–866 9650. *Club:* Authors'.
*Died 12 April* 1986.

**FALCONER, Prof. Alexander Frederick,** VRD; BLitt, MA; FRSL; Professor of English in the University of St Andrews, 1955–78; *s* of Alexander W. Falconer and Emily Henrietta Carlow Falconer. *Educ:* Universities of Glasgow, St Andrews and Oxford (Magdalen Coll.). Lecturer, St Salvator's Coll., St Andrews, 1935–39. Served in Home and Eastern Fleets, rank of Lieut, and Lt-Comdr RNVR, 1940–45. Senior Lecturer in Univ. of St Andrews, 1946. Mem. of group of editors for Boswell's correspondence at Yale, 1952–. Folger Fellow, 1958. Jt Gen. Editor, Percy Letters Series, 1964. Naval Officer i/c, St Andrews Univ. Unit, RNR. Trustee, Nat. Library of Scotland, 1956–. Mem., Royal Inst. of Navigation. *Publications:* A. Spir, Right and Wrong (trans.), 1954; The Percy Letters, Vol. IV, 1954, Vol. VI, 1960; Shakespeare and the Sea, 1964; A Glossary of Shakespeare's Sea and Naval Terms, 1965; articles and reviews. *Address:* 6 Alexandra Place, St Andrews. *T:* St Andrews 73457. *Clubs:* Naval, Mayfair.
*Died 3 May* 1987.

**FALCONER, Lieut-Col Sir George Arthur,** KBE 1947; CIE 1942; DL; *b* 3 June 1894; *s* of late E. J. Falconer; *m* 1925, Esther, K-i-H, *d* of late Major M. Boyd-Bredon; (one *s* decd). Served in Great War, 1914–17, with 4th Hussars; 2nd Lieut 1916; Indian Army, Cavalry, 1917; Capt. 1921; Major, 1935; Lt-Col 1943; Asst Consul-Gen. Meshed, 1919–21; Indian Political Service, 1923; Under Sec. Persian Gulf Residency, 1924–26; Asst Resident, Aden, 1927–29, Kashmir, 1929–31; Sec. to Resident, Kolhapur, 1932–33, Baroda, 1933–36; HM Consul, Kerman (Persia), 1937–42; Pol. Agent, Bhopal, 1942–44; HM Minister in Nepal, 1944–47; United Kingdom Ambassador to Nepal, 1947–51; retired 1951. CC, W Suffolk, 1955–74 (Vice-Chm., 1965–70; CA, 1966); DL, High Sheriff, Suffolk, 1964. Mem. Church Assembly, 1955–70. OStJ. *Address:* Orchard House, Monks Eleigh, near Ipswich, Suffolk IP7 7AU. *T:* Bildeston 740296. *Club:* Army and Navy.
*Died 18 Sept.* 1981.

**FALCONER, Sir James Fyfe,** Kt 1973; MBE 1944; JP; Town Clerk of Glasgow, 1965–75; *b* 18 Nov. 1911; *m* 1938, Jessie Elizabeth Paterson; two *s* two *d*. *Educ:* Queen's Park Secondary Sch.; Glasgow University. Law Apprentice, 1926–32; Solicitor, 1932–48; Town Clerk Depute, 1948–59; Senior Town Clerk Depute, 1959–65. JP Glasgow, 1962. *Recreations:* gardening, golf, bowling. *Address:* 101 St Andrew's Drive, Glasgow G41 4RA. *T:* 041–423 0681.
*Died 30 Dec.* 1983.

**FALKINER, Lt-Col Sir Terence (Edmond Patrick),** 8th Bt of Annmount, Cork, *cr* 1778; DL; late Coldstream Guards; retired 1956; *b* 17 March 1903; *s* of 7th Bt and Kathleen (*d* 1948), *e d* of Hon. Henry Robert Orde-Powlett, 2nd *s* of 3rd Baron Bolton; *S* father, 1917; *m* 1925, Mildred, *y d* of Sir John Cotterell, 4th Bt; two *s* three *d*. *Educ:* St Anthony's, Eastbourne; The Oratory Sch., Edgbaston. DL, Herefordshire, 1965. KStJ. *Heir:* *s* Edmond Charles Falkiner [*b* 24 June 1938; *m* 1960, Janet Iris, *d* of Arthur E. B. Darby, Bromyard, Herefordshire; two *s*]. *Address:* c/o Edmond Falkiner, 111 Wood Street, Barnet, Herts EN5 4BX. *T:* 01–440 2426.
*Died 19 Feb* 1987.

**FALKLAND,** 14th Viscount *cr* 1620; **Lucius Henry Charles Plantagenet Cary;** Lord Cary, 1620; *b* 25 Jan. 1905; *e s* of 13th Viscount Falkland and Ella Louise (*d* 1954), *e d* of E. W. Catford; *S* father, 1961; *m* 1st, 1926, Joan Sylvia (who obtained a divorce, 1933), *d* of Capt. Charles Bonham Southey, of Frinton-on-Sea; two *d*; 2nd, 1933, Constance Mary, *d* of late Capt. Edward Berry; one *s*; 3rd, 1958, Charlotte Anne (marr. diss. 1974), *e d* of late Bevil Granville, Chadley, Wellesbourne, Warwick. *Educ:* Eton. Flying Officer RAFVR, 1941–45 (invalided). *Heir:* *s* Master of Falkland. *Address:* 18 Tower Park, Fowey, Cornwall. *T:* Fowey 3211. *Clubs:* Carlton, Royal Commonwealth Society.
*Died 16 March* 1984.

**FALSHAW, Sir Donald (James),** Kt 1967; retired; *b* 22 Jan. 1905; *s* of James and Martha Falshaw; *m* 1937, Jessie Louise Taylor; no *c*. *Educ:* Lancaster Royal Gram. Sch.; Sidney Sussex Coll., Cambridge. Indian Civil Service (Punjab), 1928–66: District and Sessions Judge, 1932–46; Judge, Lahore High Court, 1946–47; Judge, Punjab High Court, India, after partition, 1947–66, Chief Justice, Dec. 1961–May 1966. *Recreations:* cricket, racing. *Address:* 125 Kenilworth Court, Lower Richmond Road, Putney, SW15. *T:* 01–788 8058. *Club:* East India, Devonshire, Sports and Public Schools.
*Died* 1984.

**FALVEY, Sir John (Neil),** KBE 1976; QC 1970; barrister, Fiji; *b* 16 Jan. 1918; *s* of John Falvey and Adela Falvey; *m* 1943, Margaret Katherine, *d* of Stanley Weatherby; three *s* two *d* (and one *d* decd). *Educ:* Eltham and New Plymouth Convent Schs; Whangarei High Sch.; Otago Univ. (BA); Auckland Univ. (LLB). Colonial Admin. Service (incl. mil. service, Fiji and Gilbert and Ellice Is), 1940–48; private legal practice, 1949–70. Mem., Legislative Council, 1953–72;

Attorney-General, 1970–77; Senator and Leader of Govt Business, 1972–79. Hon. Danish Consul, 1950–70. Chevalier (First Cl.), Royal Order of Dannebrog, 1968. *Recreation:* golf. *Address:* PO Box 1056, Suva, Fiji. *T:* 301–817. *Clubs:* Fiji, Defence, Fiji Golf.
*Died* 1990.

**FAREED, Sir Razik,** Kt 1951; OBE 1948; Sri Lanka Moor by race and Muslim by religion; Member of Ceylonese Parliament, from 1952; *b* 1895; Member of Senate, Ceylon, 1947–52; Member, State Council of Ceylon until Ceylon Independence Act, 1947; Member, Colombo Municipal Council, 1930–; Founder, only Muslim Ladies' College in Ceylon; Founder and President, Moors' Islamic Cultural Home (Inc.); Life Pres., All Ceylon Moors Assoc. Patron: Sri Lanka Moor Youth League; Orchid Circle of Sri Lanka; President: Islamia Home for Needy and Orphan Children; Sri Lanka Sufi Study Circle; Sri Lanka Kennel Club. *Address:* Hajara Villa, 27/1 Fareed Place, Colombo 4, Sri Lanka. *T:* 88357 and 28928. *Clubs:* Ceylon Turf (Vice-Pres.), Ceylon Poultry. *Died* 23 *Aug.* 1984.

**FARIDKOT, Col HH Farzand-i-Saadat Nishan Hazrrat-i-Kaisar-i-Hind, Raja Sir Har Indar Singh Brar Bans Bahadur, Ruler of,** KCSI 1941; *b* 29 Jan. 1915; *S* father as Raja, 1919; *m* 1933. *Educ:* Aitchison Chiefs Coll., Lahore. Full Ruling Powers, 1934; is one of Ruling Princes of India; Hon. Col Sikh LI; Hon. Col Bengal Engineer Group; MLA Pepsu LA. Salute, 11 guns. Formerly Mem. National Defence Council of India and of Standing Cttee of Chamber of Princes. Past Grand Master (Hon.), 1974, OSM 1971, Grand Lodge of India; Dist. Grand Master for N India, 1977, United Grand Lodge of England. *Address:* Faridkot, Punjab, India. *Died* 16 *Oct.* 1989.

**FARMAR, Hugh William,** MVO 1973; Clerk to the Drapers' Company, 1952–73; Member of the Court of the Company since 1974; Governor, Queen Mary College, University of London, 1952–83 (Treasurer 1952–73), Hon. Fellow, 1967; *b* 6 June 1908; *o s* of late Col H. M. Farmar, CMG, DSO, and Violet, *y d* of late Sir William Dalby and Hyacinthe Wellesley; *m* 1944, Constantia, *o d* of late Rt Hon. Sir Horace Rumbold, 9th Bt, GCB, and late Etheldred, Lady Rumbold, CBE; two *s. Educ:* Eton; Balliol Coll., Oxford. 2nd class clerk, Charity Commn, 1937; RAFVR, 1939–46 (on staff, Resident Minister, Accra, 1942–43; Asst Private Sec. to Sec. of State for Air 1945–46). Principal clerk, Charity Commn, 1946. Hon. LLD William and Mary Coll., Virginia, 1968. *Publications:* The Cottage in the Forest, 1949; A Regency Elopement, 1969; articles and broadcasts on travel and country subjects. *Recreations:* country pursuits. *Address:* Wasing Old Rectory, Aldermaston, Reading, Berks. *T:* Tadley 4873. *Clubs:* Brooks's, Pratt's.
*Died* 6 *July* 1987.

**FARMER, Rev. Herbert Henry,** MA Cantab, Hon. DD Glasgow; Emeritus Professor of Systematic Theology 1935–60, in Westminster College, Cambridge; *b* 27 Nov. 1892; *s* of William Charles Farmer and Mary Ann Buck; *m* 1923, Gladys Sylvie Offord; one *s* two *d. Educ:* Owen's Sch., Islington; Peterhouse, Cambridge (1st cl. Moral Sciences Tripos; Burney Studentship in the Philosophy of Religion, University of Cambridge); Westminster Coll., Cambridge. Minister of Presbyterian Church, Stafford, 1919–22; Minister of St Augustine's Presbyterian Church, New Barnet, 1922–31; Carew Lecturer, Hartford Seminary Foundation, USA, 1930; Riley Prof. of Christian Doctrine, Hartford Seminary Foundation, USA, 1931–35; Barbour Prof. of Systematic Theology, Westminster Coll. (Presbyterian), Cambridge, 1935–60; Norris-Hulse Prof. of Divinity, Cambridge University, 1949–60; Fellow of Peterhouse, Cambridge, 1950–60. Stanton Lecturer in the Philosophy of Religion, University of Cambridge, 1937–40; Warrack Lecturer, 1940; Lyman Beecher Lecturer, Yale Univ., 1946; Gifford Lecturer, Glasgow Univ., 1950–51. *Publications:* Things Not Seen, 1927; Experience of God, 1929; The World and God, 1935; The Healing Cross, 1938; The Servant of the Word, 1941; Towards Belief in God, 1942; God and Men, 1948; Revelation and Religion, 1954; The Word of Reconciliation, 1967. *Address:* 78 Braemore Road, Hove, Sussex BN3 4HB. *Died* 13 *Jan.* 1981.

**FARNHILL, Rear-Adm. Kenneth Haydn,** CB 1968; OBE 1945; Secretary, Defence, Press and Broadcasting Committee, 1973–80; *b* 13 April 1913; *s* of late H. Haydn Farnhill, Bedford; *m* 1938, Helen May, *d* of late W. Houghton, Southsea; one *s* one *d. Educ:* Bedford. Joined RN, 1930. Served 1939–45: Home Fleet, Admty, Eastern Fleet. Sec. to Controller of Navy, 1953–56; Captain, RN Supply Sch., 1958–59; IDC 1960; Dir of Management and Support of Intelligence, MoD, 1966–69. Comdr 1948; Captain 1957; Rear-Adm. 1966; retd 1969. *Address:* 1 Christchurch Gardens, Widley, Portsmouth, Hants. *T:* Cosham 377187. *Died* 6 *Dec.* 1983.

**FARNSWORTH, John Windsor;** Chairman, East Midlands Economic Planning Board, 1965–72; *b* 5 May 1912; *yr s* of late Arthur Claude and Annie Farnsworth, Derby; *m* 1938, Betty Mary Bristow; two *s. Educ:* Hanley High Sch.; Balliol Coll., Oxford; Univ. of Birmingham. Asst Comr, Nat. Savings Cttee, 1935; transf. to Min. of Nat. Insurance, 1948; Regional Controller, N Midland Region,

Min. of Pensions and Nat. Insurance, 1961; transf. to Dept of Economic Affairs, 1965; Min. of Housing and Local Govt, later Dept of the Environment, 1969. Pres., Nottingham and E Mids Group, Royal Inst. of Public Administration, 1966–68. *Recreations:* painting, foreign travel. *Address:* 143 Melton Road, West Bridgford, Nottingham. *T:* Nottingham 231937. *Died* 6 *July* 1987.

**FARQUHAR, Lt-Col Sir Peter (Walter),** 6th Bt, *cr* 1796; DSO 1943 (and Bar 1944); OBE 1982; JP; 16th/5th Lancers; RAC Reserve of Officers, retired; *b* 8 Oct. 1904; *s* of 5th Bt and Violet (*d* 1959), *d* of Col Charles Seymour Corkran, late Grenadier Guards; *S* father, 1918; *m* 1937, Elizabeth Evelyn, (*d* of late Francis Cecil Albert Hurt; three *s. Educ:* Eton; RMC, Sandhurst. Served War of 1939–45, France, Middle East and Italy (wounded twice, DSO and Bar). Past Pres., Swindon Council of Boys' Clubs; Vice-Pres., Nat. Assoc. of Boys' Clubs, 1970–. Joint-Master of Portman Hounds, 1947–59. JP Dorset, 1955. *Heir:* s Michael Fitzroy Henry Farquhar [*b* 29 June 1938; *m* 1963, Veronica Geraldine, *e d* of Patrick Hornidge, Newton Ferrers, and of Mrs M. F. L. Beebee, Walton, Radnorshire; two *s*]. *Address:* West Kington House, Chippenham, Wiltshire SN14 7JE. *T:* Castle Combe 782331.
*Died* 2 *June* 1986.

**FARQUHARSON-LANG, William Marshall,** CBE 1970; Member, National Health Service (Scotland) Staff Commission, 1972–77; *b* 2 July 1908; *s* of late Very Rev. Marshall B. Lang, DD, sometime Moderator, Gen. Assembly of Church of Scotland, and Mary Eleanor Farquharson Lang; *m* 1937, Sheila Clive Parker; one *d. Educ:* Edinburgh Acad.; Edinburgh Univ. (MA); London Univ. Sudan Political Service (Educn), 1931–55; Dep. Dir of Educn (Sudan Govt), 1950–55. Mem., 1959, Chm., 1965–72, NE Regional Hosp. Board; Vice-Chm., Scottish Health Services Council, 1964–66; Chm., Cttee on Admin. Practice of Hosp. Bds in Scotland, 1966; Rector's Assessor and Mem., Aberdeen Univ. Court, 1965–76. Mem., Kincardine CC, 1956–59. Laird of Finzean, Aberdeenshire, 1938–61. Hon. LLD Aberdeen, 1972. Coronation Medal, 1953. Sudan Republic Medal, 1977. *Publication:* The Manse and the Mansion, 1987. *Recreations:* fishing, country activities. *Address:* Balnahard House, Finzean, Aberdeenshire. *T:* Feughside 270. *Club:* New (Edinburgh). *Died* 20 *Feb.* 1988.

**FARRANT, Maj.-Gen. Ralph Henry,** CB 1964; retd; Chairman, Royal National Lifeboat Institution, 1975–79; *b* 2 Feb. 1909; *s* of late Henry Farrant, MICE, Rye, Sussex; *m* 1932, Laura Bonella (*d* 1984), *d* of late Lieut-Col G. Clifford M. Hall, CMG, DSO; two *d. Educ:* Rugby; RMA, Woolwich. 2nd Lieut, RA 1929; Field and Mountain Artillery till 1938. War of 1939–45: Tech. Appts in Min. of Defence (1) and HQ, MEF, 3rd British Inf. Div., 1944. Lieut-Col 1950, Min. of Supply; Col 1954; Brig. 1957; Dir of Munitions, Brit. Jt Services Mission, Washington, 1955–58; Sen. Mil. Officer, Armament R&D Estabt, 1958–61; Maj.-Gen. 1961; Vice-Pres., Ordnance Board, 1961–63; Pres. of Ordnance Bd, War Office, 1963–64. Yachtsman's Award, RYA, 1973. *Recreation:* sailing. *Address:* 3 Meadow View Close, Wareham, Dorset. *Clubs:* Army and Navy, Royal Yacht Squadron, Royal Motor Yacht, Royal Ocean Racing, Royal Artillery Yacht. *Died* 15 *Feb.* 1988.

**FARRELL, Arthur Acheson,** CB 1962; *b* Portadown, 29 July 1898; *s* of late Arthur T. Farrell, Portadown, solicitor, and of Ellen Moorcroft, *d* of late Hugh Anderson, Belfast; *m* 1st, 1925, Margaret Kerr (*d* 1945), *d* of Archibald Irwin, JP, Belfast; three *s*; 2nd, 1954, Wilhelmina (*d* 1973) (*sister* of 1st wife). *Educ:* Campbell Coll., Belfast; Trinity Coll., Dublin. Royal Artillery, 1917–19. Chartered Accountant, 1922; Registrar of Claims Tribunal, 1923; Civil Service, Northern Ireland: Ministry of: Finance, Asst Principal, 1924; Home Affairs, Dep. Principal, 1928, Principal, 1935, Asst Sec., 1939; Public Security, 1940; Commerce, 1945–58. Comptroller and Auditor-Gen. for Northern Ireland, 1959–63, retired. *Recreations:* photography, bowls, carpentry.
*Died* 27 *Aug.* 1983.

**FARRELL, Arthur Denis,** CMG 1970; *b* 27 Jan. 1906; *s* of Joseph Jessop Farrell, CBE; *m* 1953, Margaret Madeline (*née* Cox); one *s. Educ:* St Paul's Sch.; Balliol Coll., Oxford. Sixth Form (Classical) Master, Sedbergh Sch., 1929–30, Bradford Grammar Sch., 1930–36; called to the Bar, Middle Temple, 1937; Sixth Form (Classical) Master, Bedford Sch., 1939–41; served RAF, 1941–46. Squadron-Leader; Crown Counsel, Singapore, 1947–51: Legal Draftsman, Fedn of Malaya, 1951–56; Solicitor-Gen., Fedn of Malaya, 1956–58; QC 1957; Puisne Judge, Kenya, 1958–69 (Acting Chief Justice, 1968). Chm., Med. Appeal Tribunals, 1974–78. Coronation Medal, 1953. *Recreations:* golf, photography, music. *Address:* 64 East Avenue, Bournemouth, Dorset. *T:* Bournemouth (0202) 761878.
*Died* 18 *Dec.* 1990.

**FARRER, Sir (Walter) Leslie,** KCVO 1948; solicitor (retired); *b* 30 Jan. 1900; 2nd *s* of late Bryan Farrer, Binnegar Hall, Wareham, Dorset; *m* 1926, Hon. Marjorie Laura Pollock (*d* 1981), *d* of 1st Viscount Hanworth; one *s* one *d. Educ:* Rugby; Balliol. Admitted a Solicitor, 1926; Partner Messrs Farrer & Co., 1927–64; Mem.

Council of Law Soc., 1945–52; Mem. Disciplinary Cttee under Solicitors Acts, 1953–63. Private Solicitor to King George VI and to the Queen, 1937–64. Director, London Life Assoc. Ltd, 1942–80 (Pres., 1966–73). Pres. Selden Soc., 1955. Prime Warden, Fishmongers' Co., 1968–69. *Recreations:* reading and sight-seeing. *Address:* Charlwood Place Farm, Charlwood, Surrey. *T:* Norwood Hill 862413.                                    *Died 6 March 1984.*

**FARRIS, Hon. John Lauchlan;** Chief Justice of British Columbia and Administrator of Province of British Columbia, 1973–79; *b* 5 Sept. 1911; *s* of late Senator John Wallace de Beque Farris, QC and late Dr Evlyn Fenwick Farris; *m* 1933, Dorothy Colledge; one *s* two *d*. *Educ:* Univ. of British Columbia (BA); Harvard Law Sch. (LLB). Lectured on commercial law, Univ. of British Columbia, 1945–55. KC (Canada) 1950. Past Pres., Vancouver Bar Assoc.; Past Chm. of Bd of Governors, Crofton House Sch.; Past Pres., Harvard Club of Vancouver; Pres., Canadian Bar Assoc., 1971–72 (Past Vice-Pres. for BC); Fellow, Amer. Coll. of Trial Lawyers. Hon. Member: Amer. Bar Assoc.; Manitoba Bar Assoc.; Law Soc. of Saskatchewan. Senior Partner, Farris Farris Vaughan Wills & Murphy, until 1973. *Recreations:* boating, woodworking. *Address:* 1403 Angus Drive, Vancouver, BC V6H 1V2, Canada. *T:* (604) 738–1264. *Clubs:* Vancouver (Vancouver); Union (Victoria); Royal Vancouver Yacht, West Vancouver Yacht.                      *Died 15 Oct. 1986.*

**FARWELL, Rt. Rev. Gerard Victor;** Abbot of Worth, 1965–88; Abbot President of English Benedictine Congregation, 1967–85; *b* 15 Oct. 1913; 3rd *s* of late Frederick Arthur Farwell and Monica Mary Quin. *Educ:* St Benedict's, Ealing. Entered Downside Abbey, 1932; Housemaster at Downside Sch., 1946–48; Bursar at Worth, 1950–57; Prior of Worth, 1957–65. *Address:* Worth Abbey, Crawley, West Sussex RH10 4SB.                     *Died 23 May 1988.*

**FASSBINDER, Rainer Werner;** film and theatre director, writer, actor; *b* Bad Wörishofen, Bavaria, 31 May 1946. Studied acting, Fridl-Leonhard Studio, Munich. Actor, Munich Action Theatre, 1967; director, writer, actor, Antitheater, Munich, 1967–70; director, Theater am Turm, Frankfurt, 1974–75. Prods for Antitheater include: Katzelmacher, 1968; Pre Paradise sorry now, 1969; Anarchie in Bayern, 1969; Werwolf, 1969; Blut am Hals der Katze, 1971; prods for Theater am Turm include: Uncle Vanya; Miss Julie. Films include: Liebe ist Kälter als der Tod, 1969; Katzelmacher, 1969 (West German Critics Prize, Federal Film Prize, 1969); Götter der Pest, 1969; Warum läuft Herr R. Amok, 1970 (Federal Film Prize, 1970); Rio das Mortes, 1970; Die Niklashauser Fahrt, 1970; Der Amerikanische Soldat, 1970; Whity, 1970; Warnung vor einer heiligen Nutte, 1970; Pioniere in Ingolstadt, 1970; Händler der vier Jahreszeiten, 1971 (TV 1971); Die bitteren Tränen der Petra von Kant, 1972; Die Zärtlichkeit der Wölfe (actor and producer), 1973; Faustrecht der Freiheit, 1974; Effi Briest, 1974; Angst essen seele auf, 1974 (Critics Award, Cannes, 1974); Mutter Küsters' Fahrt zum Himmel, 1975; Angst vor der Angst, 1975; Satansbraten, 1976; Wildwechsel, 1976 (TV 1972); Schatten der Engel (actor and scriptwriter), 1976; The Marriage of Maria Braun, 1979; In A Year with 13 Moons, 1979; The Third Generation, 1979; Berlin Alexanderplatz, 1980; Lili Marleen, 1981; Die Sehnsucht der Veronika Voss, 1982; Lola, 1982; Querelle, 1982; Kamikaze 1989 (actor), 1982. *Address:* c/o New Yorker Films, 43 West 61st Street, New York, NY 10023, USA.
                                        *Died 10 June 1982.*

**FAULKNER, Hon. Arthur James;** MP (Labour) for Roskill, NZ, since 1957; President, New Zealand Labour Party, since 1976; *b* Auckland, NZ, 1921; *m* 1945, May Cox; two *s* three *d*. *Educ:* Otahuhu District High Sch., NZ. Served War of 1939–45 with RAF as Spitfire pilot in UK, N Africa and Europe. Formerly a credit manager. Labour Party organiser for North Island, 1952–57. Contested (Lab) Franklin, 1951; North Shore, 1954. Parliamentary experience on Select Cttees on Defence, Foreign Affairs, Statutes Revision, Local Govt Convener of Labour Caucus Cttees on Defence and Foreign Affairs. Fact-finding missions to South-East Asia, 1963 and 1967; travelled to Europe and UK to discuss EEC matters, 1969. Minister of Defence, Minister i/c War Pensions and Rehabilitation, 1972–74; Minister of Labour and State Services, 1974–75. *Recreations:* fishing, boating, aviation. *Address:* 1 Inverness Avenue, Mt Roskill, Auckland, New Zealand.
                                        *Died 15 May 1985.*

**FAULKNER, Captain George Haines,** CB 1947; DSC 1916; Royal Navy; *b* 27 April 1893; *s* of Rev. Thomas George Faulkner and Kate Nicholls; *m* 1st, 1924, Kathleen (*d* 1947), *d* of Dr Henry Wilson, Cheadle, Cheshire; no *c*; 2nd, 1959, Marjorie Lucy Rowland (*d* 1974), Lustleigh, Devon; 3rd, 1977, Marjorie Charteris Lewin. *Educ:* Lickey Hills Sch., Worcs; RN Colleges, Osborne and Dartmouth. Osborne, 1906; Midshipman, 1910. Served European War, 1914–18, in destroyers (despatches) Battle of Heligoland Bight, special promotion to Lieut; commanded HMS Mystic, Thruster and Patriot, 1918–19; psc 1922–23; served in HMS Hood on Special Service Squadron World Cruise, 1923–24; commanded HMS

Voyager, 1926–28; Comdr 1928; Capt. 1935; commanded HMS Bideford, 1937–38; Chief of Staff and Capt. on Staff of C-in-C the Nore, 1939–41; in command of HMS Berwick, 1941–43; Chief of Staff to C-in-C South Atlantic, with rank of Commodore 2nd class and stationed at Capetown, 1943–45; retired list, 1945; re-appointed. First Naval Mem. of New Zealand Naval Board and Chief of Naval Staff, NZ, with rank of Commodore 2nd Class, 1945–47; reverted to retired list, 1947. *Address:* Grove Cottage, Lustleigh, Devon. *T:* 232.                                  *Died 22 Aug. 1983.*

**FAULKNER, Sir Percy,** KBE 1964; CB 1950; Controller of HM Stationery Office and Queen's Printer of Acts of Parliament, 1961–67; *b* 11 May 1907; *s* of Thomas Faulkner and Margaret A. Faulkner (*née* Hood); *m* 1933, Joyce Rosemary Lois MacDonogh (*d* 1988); one *s* one *d*. *Educ:* Royal Belfast Academical Institution; Trinity Coll., Dublin. Entered Ministry of Transport, 1930; Dep. Sec. (Inland Transport), 1957; Dep. Sec. (Shipping), 1958–61; Chm. British Cttee on Prevention of Pollution of the Sea by Oil, 1953–57; rep. UK at various international conferences on shipping matters, 1947–60. *Address:* Highfield, 11 Green Lane, Aspley Guise, Beds MK17 8EN. *Club:* Athenæum.                    *Died 22 Sept. 1990.*

**FAULKS, Hon. Sir Neville (Major Ginner),** Kt 1963; MBE 1944; TD 1946; Judge of the High Court of Justice, Family Division (formerly Probate, Divorce and Admiralty Division), 1963–77; *b* 27 Jan. 1908; *s* of M. J. Faulks, MA and Ada Mabel Faulks; *m* 1st, 1940, Bridget Marigold Bodley (*d* 1963); two *s* one *d*; 2nd, 1967, Elizabeth (*d* 1982), widow of Rt Rev. A. G. Parham, MC; one step *s* four step *d*. *Educ:* Uppingham Sch. (scholar); Sidney Sussex Coll., Cambridge (Exhibitioner). Called to the Bar, LLB, 1930; QC 1959; Bencher, Inner Temple, 1963. Joined TA; served War of 1939–45 (despatches twice), Alamein. Prosecuting Counsel to Bd of Trade and other ministries at Central Criminal Court, etc., 1946–59. Recorder of Deal, 1957–59; Recorder of Norwich, 1959–63. Chm., Cttee to review Defamation Act, 1952, 1971–74. *Publications:* Fraser on Libel (ed, with late Mr Justice Slade); Investigation into the Affairs of H. Jasper and Company Limited, 1961; No Mitigating Circumstances (autobiog.), 1977; A Law Unto Myself (autobiog.), 1978. *Recreation:* The Times crossword puzzle. *Address:* Wallis's Cottage, Bowden, Dartmouth, South Devon. *T:* Stoke Fleming 770597.                                   *Died 13 Oct. 1985.*

**FAURE, Edgar (Jean);** de l'Académie Française; President, National Assembly, France, 1973–78; Member, European Parliament, since 1979; *b* Béziers, 18 Aug. 1908; *s* of Jean-Baptiste Faure and Claire Faure (*née* Lavit); *m* 1931, Lucie Meyer (*d* 1977); two *d*; *m* 1980, Marie-Jeanne Vuez. *Educ:* Ecole de Langues Orientales, Paris. Advocate, Paris Court of Appeal, 1929; Dir of Legislative Services to the Presidency, Council of French Cttee of Nat. Liberation, 1943–44; Asst Deleg. to War Crimes Trials, Nuremberg, 1945; Deputy for the Jura (Radical-Socialist), 1946–58; Mayor of Port-Lesney (Jura), 1947–70; Pres., General Council of the Jura, 1949–67; Secretary of Finance, 1949–50; Minister of Budget, 1950–51; Minister of Justice, 1951–52; Prime Minister, Jan.-Feb. 1952; Pres, Commn of Foreign Affairs of Nat. Assembly, 1952–53; Minister of Finance and Economic Affairs, 1953–54; Minister of Foreign Affairs, Jan.-Feb. 1955; Prime Minister, Feb. 1955–Jan. 1956; Minister of Finance, May-June 1958; Senator for the Jura, 1959–66; Deputy for Doubs, 1966–72, 1973–; Prof. of Law, Univ. of Dijon, 1962–66; Minister of Agriculture, 1966–68; Minister of Education, 1968–69; Dir of Research, Faculty of Law, Besançon, 1970–72; Pres., Internat. Commn of Develt of Educn, 1971–72; Mayor of Pontarlier, 1971; Minister of State for Social Affairs, 1972–73; Pres., Regional Council, Franche-Comté, 1974–; Senator from Doubs, 1980. *Publications:* La politique française du pétrole, 1939; M Langois n'est pas toujours égal à lui-meme (novel), 1950; Le serpent et la tortue (study of China), 1957; La disgrace du Turgot, 1961; Etude sur la capitation de Dioclétian d'après le panégyrique VIII, Prévoir le present, 1966; Philosophie d'une réforme, 1969; L'âme du combat (essay), 1970; Ce que je crois, 1971; Apprendre à être (Rapport de la Commission internationale sur le développement de l'éducation, Unesco), 1972; Pour un nouveau contrat social, 1973; La Banqueroute de Law, 1978; (memoirs) Avoir toujours raison . . . c'est un grand tort, vol. 1, 1982 (Prix Cazes, 1983). *Address:* 134 rue de Grenelle, 75007 Paris, France; Ermitage de Beaulieu, 77350 France.                                    *Died 30 March 1988.*

**FEARNLEY, John Thorn;** HM Diplomatic Service, retired; *b* 9 Feb. 1921; *o* *s* of Tom Fearnley and Grace Gertrude (*née* Thorn); *m* 1st, 1947, Margaret Ann Davies (marr. diss. 1944), *er* *d* of John Hunter Davies, IPS (*d* 1930 when HM Consul, Kerman, Iran); three *d* two *s*; 2nd, 1974, Wendy R. Grande; two step *s*. *Educ:* Manchester Gram. Sch.; Caius Coll., Cambridge (Scholar). Farm labouring (Norfolk, Kincardineshire, Cheshire) 1940–42. Served with RN, 1942–46 (Submarine Branch). Joined Foreign Service, 1947; FO, 1947–48; New York (UN), 1948–50; Tehran, 1950–52; FO, Civil Service Selection Bd, 1953; Tehran, 1953–56; Berlin, 1956–58; FO, 1958–60; Lagos, 1960–62; Paris, 1962–65. Head of Oil Dept, FO, 1965–69; Senior Officers' War Course, RN Coll., Greenwich, 1969;

Consul-Gen., Frankfurt, 1969–75; Consul-Gen., Sydney, 1975–76. Founder Mem., Foreign (now Diplomatic) Service Assoc. *Recreation:* Monmouth. *Address:* 4 Saint James Street, Monmouth, Gwent NP5 3DL. *T:* Monmouth 3493. *Died 22 May* 1986.

**FEARNLEY SCARR, J. G.;** *see* Scarr.

**FEATHERSTONE, Col (William) Patrick Davies,** MC 1944; TD 1960; Vice Lord-Lieutenant of Staffordshire, since 1976; farmer; *b* 17 Sept. 1919; *s* of late Henry Walter Featherstone, OBE, MD, Hon. LLD, JP, and of Margery Eveline (*née* Harston); *m* Joan Llewellyn, *d* of Lt-Col R. H. Waddy, DSO; two *s* one *d*. *Educ:* Rugby Sch.; Trinity Coll., Cambridge (BA). Served War, 1939–46: RA, France, Belgium, Holland and Germany. Staffs Yeomanry, 1948–62; Lt-Col Comdg, 1959–62; Hon. Col 1972. Member: W Midlands TAVR Assoc.; Lichfield Diocesan Synod and Bd of Finance, 1976–. DL 1963, JP 1967, Staffs; High Sheriff of Staffs, 1969. *Recreations:* shooting, nature conservation. *Address:* Yoxall Lodge, Newchurch, near Burton-on-Trent, Staffs. *T:* Hoar Cross 237.
*Died* 1 *Dec.* 1983.

**FEHILY, Rt. Rev. Mgr Canon Thomas Francis;** Principal RC Chaplain (Army), 1973–77; *b* 16 Nov. 1917; *s* of late Patrick and Mary Fehily, Ballineen, Co. Cork. *Educ:* Capuchin Franciscan Coll., Rochestown, Co. Cork; St Kieran's Coll., Kilkenny. Ordained, 1942; Motherwell Dio., 1943–53. Commissioned Army Chaplain, 1953; served: Germany, 1953–56; Malaya, 1956–59; Germany and Berlin, 1959–63; RMA, Sandhurst, 1963–66. Senior Chaplain: NI, 1966–67; Singapore, 1967–69; HQ 1 Br. Corps, 1969–71; Western Command, 1971; Northern Command, 1972–73. Canon of Motherwell Cathedral Chapter, 1984. *Recreations:* fishing, golf. *Address:* St John's, Blackwood, Kirkmuirhill, Lanarkshire ML11 9RZ. *Died* 16 *Sept.* 1987.

**FEILDEN, Maj.-Gen. Sir Randle Guy,** KCVO 1953; CB 1946; CBE 1944 (OBE 1943); DL; *b* 14 June 1904; *e s* of Major P. H. G. Feilden; *m* 1929, Mary Joyce, *d* of Sir John Ramsden, 6th Bt; two *s* (and one *s* decd). *Educ:* Eton; Magdalene Coll., Cambridge. Coldstream Guards, 1925; ADC GOC London Dist, 1933–36; Regimental Adjutant, 1936–39; Staff Capt. 7 Gds Bde 1939–40; DAQMG 3 Div. April–Sept. 1940; AQMG 5 Corps, 1940–41; AA and QMG Guards Armoured Division, 1941–42; DQMG: Home Forces, Feb.–Aug. 1943; 21 Army Group, Aug. 1943–45; Rhine Army, Aug. 1945–March 1946; VQMG, War Office, 1947–49; retired pay, 1949. Oxfordshire: High Sheriff 1971, DL 1975. A Steward of the Jockey Club, 1952, senior Steward, 1954, 1961, 1965–73; Chm., Turf Board, 1965–. *Recreations:* cricket, shooting, racing. *Address:* Old Manor House, Minster Lovell, Oxford. *T:* Asthall Leigh 228; 3 Kingston House South, SW7. *T:* 01-589 7135. *Clubs:* Pratt's, White's. *Died 27 Oct.* 1981.

**FELL, Charles Percival,** LLD; Hon. Director, Royal Trustco Ltd; Hon. Governor, McMaster University (Chancellor, 1960–65); *b* Toronto, 1894; *s* of I. C. Fell and Sarah (Branton) Fell, both of Toronto, Ont.; *m* 1st, 1925, Grace E. Matthews; three *s*; 2nd, 1976, Marjorie Jane Montgomery. *Educ:* University of Toronto Schs; McMaster Univ. Associated with Dillon, Read & Co., NY, 1921–24; Dominion Securities Corp., Toronto, 1925–29; Chm. Canadian group, Investment Bankers Assoc. of America, 1928. Pres., Empire Life Assurance Co., 1934–68. Mem. Bd of Referees (Excess Profits Tax Act, Canada), Ottawa, 1940–45. Pres., Art Gall. of Toronto, 1950–53; Chm., Bd of Trustees, Nat. Gall. of Canada, Ottawa, 1953–59. Coronation Medal, Canada, 1953. Hon. LLD McMaster Univ., 1957. *Clubs:* York, Toronto, Granite (Toronto).
*Died* 2 *Feb.* 1988.

**FELL, Dame Honor Bridget,** DBE 1963; FRS 1952; medical research worker, Strangeways Research Laboratory, Cambridge, since 1979 (Director, 1929–70); Foulerton Research Fellow, Royal Society, 1941–67; Fellow of Girton College, Cambridge, 1955; *b* 22 May 1900; *d* of Col William Edwin Fell and Alice Fell (*née* Pickersgill-Cunliffe). *Educ:* Wychwood Sch., Oxford; Madras Coll., St Andrews; Edinburgh Univ. BSc (Edinburgh) 1922; PhD (Edinburgh) 1924; DSc (Edinburgh) 1930; MA (Cantab) 1955. Research Student, DSIR, 1922; Research Asst, MRC, 1924; Junior Beit Fellow, 1924; 4th Year Beit Fellow, 1927; Senior Beit Fellow, 1928; Messel Research Fellow, Royal Society, 1931; Royal Society Research Professor, 1963–67; med. res. worker, Dept of Immunology, Univ. of Cambridge, 1970–79. Hon. LLD: Edinburgh, 1959; Glasgow, 1970; Hon. DSc: Oxon, 1964; London, 1967; Hon. ScD: Smith Coll., USA, 1962; Harvard, 1964; Cambridge, 1969; Hon. MD Leiden 1976; Foreign Member: Royal Netherlands Academy, 1964; Serbian Acad. Sci. and Arts, 1975; Hon. Fellow, Somerville Coll., Oxford, 1964; Fellow, King's Coll., London, 1967. Prix Charles-Leopold Mayer, French Academy of Science, 1965. *Publications:* various communications to biological and medical journals. *Recreation:* travel. *Address:* 42b Queen Edith's Way, Cambridge. *T:* Cambridge 247022. *Died 22 April* 1986.

**FELL, Captain William Richmond,** CMG 1957; CBE 1947; DSC 1941; RN retd; Admiralty Marine Salvage Officer, Grade I, 1948–60; *b* 31 Jan. 1897; *s* of Walter Fell, MD Oxon, and Margaret Richmond; *m* 1921, Phyllis (*née* Munday); two *s*. *Educ:* Wellington Coll., New Zealand. Joined RN 1915; Midshipman HMS Warspite, 1916–17 (Jutland); Dover Patrol, 1917–18. Served in submarines, 1918–39; first comd, 1925. War of 1939–45 (despatches, DSC): "Q" boat ops, 1940; Norway, 1941; Combined ops, 1941–42; rejoined submarines, 1942; Comd Human Torpedo ops, 1942–43. Training officer, midget submarines, 1943; Comd of HMS Bonaventure, in rank of Capt. (midget submarines), 1943–47, home and Pacific waters. Boom Defence and Salvage Officer, 1948 (Malta and Med.); retired with rank of Capt., 1948, and joined Admty Salvage; Ship Target Trials home and abroad, 1949–50; Salvage ops at home, 1951–56; Suez, as Principal Salvage Officer, 1956–57. Legion of Merit, Officers' Class, 1947 (US). *Publications:* short stories contributed to Blackwood's, 1945–49; The Sea Surrenders, 1960; The Sea our Shield, 1966. *Recreations:* yachting, fishing. *Address:* Mahina Bay, Eastbourne, Wellington, NZ. *Died 28 Nov.* 1981.

**FELLOWES, Maj.-Gen. Halford David,** CB 1957; DSO 1945; *b* 2 Aug. 1906; *er s* of late Major Halford Le M. Fellowes, 47th Sikhs (retd), Tenterden; *m* 1st, 1932, Angela Mary (marr. diss. 1941), *d* of P. E. Cammiade, ICS (retd); one *d*; 2nd, 1942, Rosemary, *er d* of late Brig.-Gen. Sir Terence Keyes, KCIE, CSI, CMG. *Educ:* St Paul's Sch., London. Royal Marines: 2nd Lieut 1924; Lieut 1927; Capt. 1936; A/Maj. 1940; A/Lt-Col 1940; Bt Major 1941; A/Col 1945; T/Brig. 1945; Major 1946; A/Lieut-Col 1947; Lieut-Col 1948; A/Col 1952; Col 1952; Maj.-Gen. 1954. Served HM Ships Berwick, Resolution, Sheffield, Base Defences Mediterranean, 1935–36; RM Siege Regt, 1940–42; GSO1, Special Service Group, 1943–44; 42 Commando RM (SE Asia), 1944–45 (wounded in Arakan, 1945); HQ 3 Commando Bde, 1945–46; GSO1 (Trg), RM office, 1947–49; Commando Sch., RM, 1949–52; Depot, RM Deal, 1952–54; psc 1943; jssc 1947. Commander Plymouth Group, Royal Marines, 1954–57, retired. *Address:* Cedar Cottage, Brede, Rye, East Sussex TN31 6EH. *T:* Brede 882743. *Club:* Rye Golf.
*Died* 2 *March* 1985.

**FELLOWES, Brig. Reginald William Lyon,** CBE 1943; *b* 6 Aug. 1895; *s* of late Frederick William Fellowes and Mrs Fellowes, The Grange, Hitchin; *m* 1921, Dulcie M. B. H. Peel (marr. diss. 1946); two *s*; *m* 1947, M. G. Joan Beard. *Educ:* Wellington Coll.; RMA Woolwich. 2nd Lieut RFA Aug. 1914; served in France, Belgium, and Italy, 1914–19 (MC and Bar, despatches); psc; retired with rank of Major, 1938; mobilised Sept. 1939, France, Iraq and Persia, Sicily and Italy (CBE, despatches, Legion of Honour); released Aug. 1945, hon. rank Brig. *Address:* Cladich, Dalmally, Argyll. *T:* Dalmally 246. *Club:* New (Edinburgh). *Died* 17 *July* 1982.

**FELLOWES, Sir William (Albemarle),** KCVO 1964 (CVO 1952); Agent to the Queen, Sandringham Estate, 1936–64, retired; Member of firm, Savills (formerly Alfred Savill, Curtis & Henson, before that Alfred Savill & Sons) (Land Agents and Valuers), 1964–77; *b* 10 Sept. 1899; 2nd *surv. s* of Charles Arthur Fellowes and Mary Fellowes; *m* 1924, Jane Charlotte (*d* 1986), *d* of Brig.-Gen. A. F. H. Ferguson; two *s* two *d*. *Educ:* Winchester Coll.; Oriel Coll., Oxford. Agent to: Major W. S. Gosling, Hassobury Estate, Essex, 1925–30; Old Warden Estates, Beds, 1930–36. Became Agent to King George VI, 1936. Served with Scots Guards, 1940–45. DL Norfolk, 1965–81. FLAS 1927; Associate of the Chartered Surveyors, 1923. FRICS 1964. *Recreations:* shooting and fishing. *Address:* Flitcham House, Flitcham, King's Lynn, Norfolk. *T:* Hillington 600346.
*Died* 6 *April* 1986.

**FENDER, Percy George Herbert;** Chairman and Managing Director, London Wine Exchange, since 1968; *b* Balham, 22 Aug. 1892; *e s* of Percy Robert Fender and Lily Herbert; *m* 1st, 1924, Ruth Marian Clapham (*d* 1937); one *s* one *d*; 2nd, 1962, Susan Victoria Gordon (*née* Kyffin) (*d* 1968). *Educ:* St George's Coll., Weybridge; St Paul's Sch. Cricket for Sussex, 1910–13, for Surrey, 1914–35 (Captain, 1921–32); toured Australia for MCC, 1920–21; also South Africa, 1922–23; toured Australia for London Star as First Special Cricket Correspondent for any newspaper, 1928–29. Fastest hundred ever made in first class cricket (35 mins) for Surrey v Northants (world record, 1920); fastest five wickets in first class cricket (in seven consecutive deliveries) for Surrey v Middlesex at Lords (world record, 1927); first cricketer to achieve cricketer's treble: 1,000 runs, 100 wickets and 50 catches in one season (world record, 1921). Contributor to Field, Sporting and Dramatic, Telegraph, etc. Football for Casuals, Corinthians and Fulham. Training in Vale Paper Mills, Lancs, then Papeterie Belge Droogenbosch, Belgium and Bureau Concours Hippique Brussels; joined Crescens Robinson Co. Ltd, 1912, Dir, 1922, Chm., 1943–68, resigned 1973; created Herbert Fender & Co., 1922, retired as Chm. and Man. Dir, 1977. Served War: England, India and Burma, Royal Fusiliers, 1914–15, Royal Flying Corps, 1915 and Royal Air Force, 1915–18; Special Constable, 1926–40; rejoined RAF as Pilot Officer, 1940–46; Sen. Movement Officer, 2nd TAF, Invasion of Europe (despatches), S

Africa, New Zealand, Australia, Phillipines, New Guinea, retired as Wing Comdr, 1945. Mem. LCC for Norwood Div. of Lambeth, 1952–55 and 1955–58. DL County of London, 1958; Greater London, 1965–75. Grant of Arms, 1966. Freeman, City of London, 1960. *Publications:* Defending the Ashes, 1921; Turn of the Wheel, 1929; The Tests of 1930, 1930; Kissing the Rod, 1934; Lonsdale Library on Cricket; ABC of Cricket, 1937, BBC and Television Cricket, etc. *Recreations:* bridge, golf, billiards, snooker, real tennis. *Address:* (home) 6 Cotswold Court, Burford Road, Horsham, Sussex RH13 5SS; (office) West Street, Horsham, Sussex. *Clubs:* Royal Air Force, MCC (Life Mem. 1981); Horsham (Horsham); Surrey County Cricket (Life Mem.; Vice-Pres., 1979).

*Died 15 June 1985.*

**FENNING, Frederick William;** Deputy Director, Atomic Energy Research Establishment, 1979–84, retired; *b* 14 Dec. 1919; *s* of Thomas and Lilian Fenning; *m* 1949, Eileen Mary Lyttle; one *s* two *d. Educ:* Clacton; Cambridge Univ. BA (Hons). Min. of Aircraft Production, 1940; Min. of Supply, Tube Alloys Project, Cambridge, 1942; Montreal, 1943; Chalk River, Ontario, 1945; AERE, Harwell, 1946–58; Chief Physicist, Risley, 1958; Dir, Reactor Technology, Risley, 1960–66; Dep. Dir, Harwell, 1966–77; Dir of Atomic Energy Technical Unit, UKAEA, 1977–79. *Recreations:* gardening, general DIY. *Address:* 21 St Peter's Hill, Caversham, Reading, Berks RG4 7AX. *T:* Reading 472302. *Died 5 April 1988.*

**FENTON, Wilfrid David Drysdale,** CBE 1963; FRSE; BSc, FIEE; Director, Project Development Group (Europe), since 1978; *b* 27 March 1908; *s* of late David Fenton, Edinburgh; *m* 1st, 1955, Isobel Stewart (marr. diss. 1974); no *c*; 2nd, 1974, Elaine Herman, *d* of late Louis Surut, New York; two step *c. Educ:* George Watson's Coll., Edinburgh; Edinburgh Univ. Called to Bar, Middle Temple, 1937. Kennedy and Donkin, Cons. Engrs, London, 1931–33; Central Electricity Bd, London, 1933–38; Personal Asst to Gen. Manager, Midland Counties Electric Supply Co., 1938–44; Commercial Engr, 1944–48, Sec. and Commercial Engr, 1948–55, N of Scotland Hydro-Electric Bd; Chm., 1955–62, Uganda Electricity Bd; Chm., S Wales Electricity Bd, 1962–68; Chm., London Electricity Bd, 1968–72, Dep. Chm., CEGB, 1972–75; Man. Dir, Overseas Consultancy Services, Electricity Council 1975–76 (Dir, 1970–75); Man. Dir, British Electricity International, 1976–77; Consultant, Nat. Utility Services, 1979–81. Director: Uganda Development Corp., 1955–57; Inter G Ltd, 1978–83; Hon. Treas., 1956–57, Vice-Chm., 1957–62, Makerere Univ. Coll.; Chm Mulago Hosp. (Kampala) Autonomy Cttee, 1961. Freeman, City of London, 1970. *Recreation:* golf. *Address:* 31 Cadogan Lane, SW1X 9DR. *Clubs:* Caledonian, Royal Commonwealth Society; Royal Wimbledon Golf.

*Died 4 May 1985.*

**FENWICK, Robert George,** CBE 1975; QPM 1969; HM Inspector of Constabulary, 1967–77; *b* 1913; *s* of late George R. F. Fenwick, Horton Grange, Northumberland; *m* 1943, Eileen Winifreda, *d* of late James Carstairs Dodds, Buenos Aires. *Educ:* Dame Allan's Sch. Barrister-at-Law, Gray's Inn, 1951. Metropolitan Police, 1934–59; seconded to Foreign Office for duties in São Paulo, Brazil, 1957–58; Directing Staff, Police Coll., 1959–60; Asst Chief Constable, Glos, 1960–62; Chief Constable, Shropshire, 1962–67. Adviser to Qatar State Police, 1972–77. *Address:* Ebor House, Kingsland, Shrewsbury, Shropshire. *T:* Shrewsbury 4158.

*Died 16 Jan. 1987.*

**FERGUS, Most Rev. James,** DD; *b* Louisburgh, Co. Mayo, 23 Dec. 1895. *Educ:* St Jarlath's College, Tuam; and at Maynooth. Ordained priest, 1920; studied Dunboyne; Curate, Glenamaddy, 1921, Tuam, 1924; Archbishop's secretary, 1926; Administrator, Westport, 1943; Parish Priest, Ballinrobe, 1944; Bishop of Achonry, 1947–76, retired 1977. *Address:* Ballaghaderreen, Co. Roscommon, Eire.

*Died 24 March 1989.*

**FERGUSON, John,** FIAL; FRSA; President, The Selly Oak Colleges, Birmingham, 1979–86 (Hon. Fellow, 1989); *b* 2 March 1921; *s* of Prof. Allan and Dr Nesta Ferguson; *m* 1950, Elnora Dixon; no *c. Educ:* Bishop's Stortford Coll.; St John's Coll., Cambridge. BD 1st cl. hons London, 1944; BA 1st cl. hons with double distinction Class. Tripos Cantab, 1947; Henry Carrington and Bentham Dumont Koe Studentship, 1947; Denny Studentship, 1947; Kaye Prize, 1951 (for essay in early Church History). Civil Defence, 1941–45; Master at Bishop's Stortford Coll., 1945–46; Lectr in Classics, King's Coll., Newcastle upon Tyne, 1948–53; Sen. Lectr in Classics, Queen Mary Coll., London, 1953–56; Prof. of Classics, Univ. of Ibadan, 1956–66 (Dean, Faculty of Arts, 1958–59, 1960–61); Dean and Dir of Studies in Arts, Open Univ., 1969–79 (Dep. Chm. of Senate, 1969–74). Hill Vis. Prof. 1966–68, Prof. 1968–69, and Hill Vis. Prof. in Classics, 1988, Univ. of Minnesota; Old Dominion Vis. Prof. Humanities, Hampton Inst., Va, 1968–69; Visiting Professor: Univ. of Florida, 1977; Ohio Wesleyan Univ., 1978; Vis. Chair in Contemporary Theology, Lafayette-Orinda Presbyterian Church, 1987; Vis. Theologian-in-Residence Coll. of Wooster, Ohio, 1989; Lectures: Emily Hobhouse Meml, Cape Town, 1961; Alex

Wood Meml, Cambridge, 1971; Kinchin Smith Meml, London, 1972; Herbert Collins Meml, Southampton, 1976; Lady Ardilaun, Dublin, 1976; Rodes-Helm, Bowling Green, Ky, 1977; Montgomery, UK, 1977–79; Carpenter, Delaware, Ohio, 1978; Apothecaries, London, 1983; Dacorum, Hemel Hempstead, 1983; Noel-Baker Meml, London, 1983; Chavasse, Oxford, 1985; Doris Hansen, Cardiff, 1985; Tantur, Jerusalem, 1986; Louis Caplan, Liverpool, 1988. Chm. 1953–56, Vice-Chm. 1978–79, Fellowship of Reconciliation; Trustee, UNA, 1984–(Vice-Chm., 1978–80; Chm., 1980–84); British Council of Churches: Chm., Educn Dept, 1971–74; Community Affairs Div., 1974–78; Chairman: British and Foreign Schools Soc., 1975–86; Birmingham Jt Cttee for Adult Educn Inf. and Advice Services, 1979–86; Mem. Council, Prospect Hall, 1978–86; Governor, Queen's Coll., Birmingham; Vice-Chm., Christian Social and Economic Res. Foundn; President: Friends' Guild of Teachers, 1978–79; London Soc. for Study of Religion, 1978–80; Vice-President: Orbilian Soc., 1973– (Pres., 1972); Nat. Peace Council; Hon. Life Vice-Pres., Assoc. for Reform of Latin Teaching. Chm., Weoley Hill Cricket Club. Hon. Mem., Mark Twain Soc., and Kt of Mark Twain. DUniv Open, 1988; Hon. DLitt New England Coll., NH, 1989. *Publications:* The Enthronement of Love, 1950; (ed) Studies in Christian Social Commitment, 1954; Pelagius, 1956; (jtly) Letters on Pacifism, 1956; Christian Faith for Today, 1956; The UN and the World's Needs, 1957; (ed) Plato Republic X, 1957; Moral Values in the Ancient World, 1958; (jtly) The Emergent University, 1960; (ed) Studies in Cicero, 1962; Foundations of the Modern World, 1963; (jtly) The Enduring Past, 1965; (jtly) Nigeria under the Cross, 1965; Ibadan Verses, 1966; (ed) Ibadan Versions, 1967; The Wit of the Greeks and Romans, 1968; Christian Byways, 1968; (jtly) Africa in Classical Antiquity, 1969; Socrates: A Source-Book, 1970; Religions of the Roman Empire, 1970; American Verses, 1971; Some Nigerian Church Founders, 1971; Sermons of a Layman, 1972; The Place of Suffering, 1972; A Companion to Greek Tragedy, 1972; Aristotle, 1972; The Heritage of Hellenism, 1973; The Politics of Love, 1973; (ed) War and the Creative Arts, 1973; (rapporteur) Non-violent Action: a Christian appraisal, 1973; Clement of Alexandria, 1974; Utopias of the Classical World, 1975; The Open University from Within, 1975; Danilo Dolci, 1975; An Illustrated Encyclopaedia of Mysticism and the Mystery Religions, 1976; O My People, 1977; War and Peace in the World's Religions, 1977; Religions of the World, 1978; (jtly) Political and Social Life in the Great Age of Athens, 1978; (ed) Juvenal The Satires, 1979; Greek and Roman Religion: a source book, 1980; Jesus in the Tide of Time, 1980; The Arts in Britain in World War I, 1980; Callimachus, 1980; (ed) Christianity, Society and Education, 1981; Gods Many and Lords Many, 1981; (jtly) Rome: the Augustan Age, 1981; Disarmament: The Unanswerable Case, 1982; Hymns of a Layman, 1982; (ed) Euripides, Hippolytus, 1984; Catullus, 1985; A Prosopography to the Poems of Juvenal, 1987; Euripides: Medea and Electra, 1987; Catullus, 1988; Give Peace a Chance, 1988; Not Them But Us, 1988; some 25 course-unit books for the Open Univ.; *plays:* The Camp, 1956; The Trial, 1957; The Road to Heaven, 1958; Job, 1961; Editor, Nigeria and the Classics, Vols I-IX; Jt Editor, Reconciliation Quarterly; Sen. Editor, Selly Oak Jl, 1984–86; numerous articles on classical subjects, theology, internat. affairs and literature; also some hymns; *posthumous publications:* Among the Gods, 1989; Morals and Values in Ancient Greece, 1989. *Recreations:* cricket, book-hunting, church architecture, drama, opera, conducting madrigals, travelling in the Graeco-Roman world. *Address:* 102 Oakfield Road, Selly Park, Birmingham B29 7ED. *T:* 021–472 1922. *Clubs:* Penn; MCC; Union (Cambridge).

*Died 22 May 1989.*

**FERGUSON DAVIE, Rev. Sir (Arthur) Patrick,** 5th Bt *cr* 1641 and *re-created* 1847 for General Henry Ferguson, husband of Juliana, *d* of Sir John Davie, 8th Bt of Creedy; TD 1954; Liturgical Adviser to the Anglican Province of Jerusalem and the Middle East, 1976–84; *b* 17 March 1909; *s* of late Lt-Col Arthur Francis Ferguson Davie, CIE, DSO (3rd *s* of 3rd Bt), and late Eleanor Blanche Daphne, *d* of late C. T. Naylor (she *m* 1918, Major J. H. W. Knight-Bruce, who *d* 1951; she *d* 1964); *S* uncle, 1947; *m* 1949, Iris Dawn Cable-Buller, *o d* of Capt. and Hon. Mrs Buller, Downes, Crediton; one *s. Educ:* Wellington Coll.; Lincoln Coll., Oxford (MA). Ely Theological Coll., 1932–34; Deacon, 1934, Priest, 1935. Asst Curate, Littleham-cum-Exmouth, 1934–37; St Augustine's, Kilburn, NW6, 1938–39; CF (TA), 1937–45; Hon. CF 1945; served with 4th Bn Devonshire Regt in UK and Gibraltar, 1939–43; CMF, N Africa and Italy, 1943–45; Vicar of St John's Torquay, 1945–48; Rural Dean of Cadbury, 1966–68; Hon. Chaplain to Bishop of Exeter, 1949–73. *Publication:* The Bishop in Church, 1961. *Heir:* s Antony Francis Ferguson Davie, *b* 23 March 1952. *Address:* Skalatos House, PO Box 129, Girne, Mersin 10, Turkey. *Club:* United Oxford & Cambridge University.

*Died 23 Jan. 1988.*

**FERGUSSON, Ian Victor Lyon;** *b* 22 Jan. 1901; *y s* of late Rev. Dr John Moore Fergusson; *m* 1927, Hannah Grace (*née* Gourlay) (*d* 1978); three *s* one *d. Educ:* Berkhamsted Sch. Joined Evans Medical Ltd. (then Evans Sons Lescher & Webb Ltd), 1919; Dir, 1927; Man.

Dir, 1941; Chm. and Man. Dir, Evans Medical Ltd, 1943–62; Dir, Glaxo Group Ltd, 1961–62; Dir, Carless Capel & Leonard Ltd, 1964–72. Pres., Chemists Federation, 1940–41; Chm., Assoc. British Pharmaceutical Industry, 1946–47. Mem., Liverpool Regional Hospital Board, 1958–61. *Recreations:* fishing, gardening. *Address:* 3 Sycamore Close, Sibford Gower, near Banbury, Oxon OX15 5SB.
*Died 7 Jan 1990.*

**FERGUSSON HANNAY, Lady;** *see* Leslie, Doris.

**FERMOY,** 5th Baron *cr* 1856; **Edmund James Burke Roche;** Chairman, Eddington Bindery Ltd; *b* 20 March 1939; *s* of 4th Baron Fermoy and Ruth Sylvia (Dowager Lady Fermoy); *S* father, 1955; *m* 1964, Lavinia Frances Elizabeth, *o d* of late Capt. John Pitman and of Mrs Pitman, Foxley House, Malmesbury, Wilts; two *s* one *d* (and twin *d* decd). *Educ:* Eton; Sandhurst; RAC, Cirencester. Capt., Royal Horse Guards (The Blues), retd 1967. Trustee, Pheasant Trust. District Councillor (Hungerford), Newbury DC, 1976–79; Mayor of Hungerford, 1983. *Recreation:* steeplechasing. *Heir: s* Hon. Patrick Maurice Burke Roche, *b* 11 Oct. 1967. *Address:* Eddington House, Hungerford, Berks. *T:* Hungerford 82540. *Clubs:* White's, Turf, 1,001. *Died 19 Aug. 1984.*

**FERNALD, John Bailey;** *b* 21 Nov. 1905; *s* of C. B. Fernald and Josephine Harker; *m* 1942, Jenny Laird; one *d. Educ:* Marlborough Coll.; Trinity Coll., Oxford. Pres., OUDS, 1927; Dramatic Editor, The Pall Mall Magazine, 1929; first professional production, Arts Theatre, 1929; subsequently produced plays continuously in London till 1936, when became Associate Producer for Associated British Pictures Corporation; returned to theatre, 1938; on teaching staff of Royal Academy of Dramatic Art, 1934–40. Joined RNVR, 1940 and served almost continuously at sea until 1945; left service with rank of Lieut-Comdr. Dir of Productions, Reunion Theatre, 1946; Dir of the Liverpool Playhouse, 1946–49; subsequently produced: The Love of Four Colonels, Wyndham's; The White Sheep of the Family, Piccadilly; The First Born, Winter Garden; Nightmare Abbey and Dial M for Murder, Westminster; Escapade, Strand; The Devil's General, Savoy; Crime and Punishment (Television); Saint Joan, St Martin's; The Remarkable Mr Pennypacker, New; The House by the Lake, Duke of York's; Jubilee Production of Peter Pan; Tea and Sympathy, Comedy; Hedda Gabler, Nye Teater, Oslo; The Love of Four Colonels, Kansanteatteri, Helsinki; Ghosts, Old Vic; The Tchekov Centenary Production of The Seagull, Edinburgh Festival and Old Vic; The Affair, Henry Miller Theatre, New York; The Schoolmistress, Savoy; The Enchanted, Arts Theatre; Ivanov, Uncle Vanya, The Seagull, and various plays at Arts Theatre and elsewhere; 1st production in England of Bertolt Brecht's The Caucasian Chalk Circle, Vanbrugh Theatre, RADA, Anton Tchekov's The Cherry Orchard at the National Theatre, Pretoria and Johannesburg; Private Lives, Bristol Old Vic.; directed 31st year production of Agatha Christie's The Mousetrap, St Martin's Theatre, 1982. Shute Lectr on the Art of the Theatre, Liverpool Univ., 1948. Principal, Royal Academy of Dramatic Art, 1955–65; Dir, John Fernald Co., Meadowbrook Theatre, Rochester, Mich, and Prof. of Dramatic Art, Oakland Univ., Rochester, Mich, 1966–70; Prof., Dept of Theatre, NY State Univ., 1970–71; returned from USA, 1972, now largely concerned with teaching of acting at drama schs and directing classical revivals at repertory theatres. Mem., Nat. Council for Drama Trng (Vice-Chm., Accreditation Cttee). Awarded Silver Medal of Royal Soc. of Arts, 1966. *Publications:* The Play Produced: a Manual of Stage Production, 1933; Destroyer from America, 1942; Sense of Direction, 1968; contrib. to Encyclopaedia Britannica, 1972. *Recreations:* music, travelling, looking at cats, and producing the plays of Anton Tchekov. *Address:* 2 Daleham Mews, NW3. *T:* 01–435 2992.
*Died 2 April 1985.*

**FERNYHOUGH, Brig. Hugh Edward,** CBE 1956; DSO 1945; retired; *b* 15 April 1904; *s* of late Col Hugh Clifford Fernyhough and Mrs Beatrice Fernyhough; *m* 1943, Mary, *d* of late T. D. and Mrs Moore, Mill Down, Clyst St Mary, Exeter; one *s. Educ:* Wellington Coll., Berks; RMA Woolwich. 2nd Lieut. 1924; Lieut 1927; Capt. 1937; grad. Staff. Coll., Camberley, 1939; GSO2, 12 Corps, 1940; GSO2, Instr, Staff Coll., Camberley, 1941; Comdt (Col) NZ Staff Coll., 1942–43; OC 53 (London) Medium Regt, 1944–45; Comdt (Col) RA, OCTU, 1945–46; CRA (Col) HQ, E Africa, 1947–48; Col i/c Admin, E Africa, 1948–49; AAG, RA, WO, 1949–52; CRA 40 Inf. Div. (Hong Kong), 1952–53; Dep. Dir, RA, 1954–56; retd 1956. Col Comdt, Royal Artillery. *Address:* Mill Down, Clyst St Mary, Exeter. *T:* Topsham 4568. *Club:* Army and Navy.
*Died 10 Jan. 1982.*

**FERRAR, William Leonard;** Principal, Hertford College, Oxford, 1959–64; *b* 21 Oct. 1893; *s* of George William Parsons and Maria Susannah Ferrar; *m* 1923, Edna O'Hara (*d* 1986); one *s. Educ:* Queen Elizabeth's Hospital, Bristol; Bristol Grammar Sch.; Queen's Coll., Oxford. Open Mathematical Schol., Queen's, 1912; Univ. Junior Math. Schol., 1914; Sen. Schol., 1922; MA Oxon 1920; DSc Oxon 1947. Served European War, 1914–18, in ranks, Artillery and

Intelligence, 1914–19. Lecturer, University Coll. of N Wales, Bangor, 1920–24; Sen. Lecturer, Edinburgh, 1924–25; Fellow, Hertford Coll., Oxford, 1925–59, Bursar, 1937–59. Formerly mem. Hebdomadal Council, Gen. Board and the Chest, Oxford Univ.; Sec., London Math. Soc., 1933–38. *Publications:* Convergence, 1938; Algebra, 1941; Higher Algebra for Schools, 1945, Part II, 1948; Finite Matrices, 1951; Differential Calculus, 1956; Integral Calculus, 1958; Mathematics for Science, 1965; Calculus for Beginners, 1967; Advanced Mathematics for Science, 1969; various research papers, 1924–37. *Address:* 21 Sunderland Avenue, Oxford OX2 8DT.
*Died 22 Jan. 1990.*

**FERRARI, Enzo;** President and Managing Director of Ferrari Automobili SpA Sefac, 1940–77; *b* Modena, 20 Feb. 1898; *s* of Alfredo Ferrari and Adalgisa Bisbini; *m* 1923, Laura Garello (*d* 1978); one *s* decd. *Educ:* State sch.; Professional Institute of Technology. Started as tester, Turin, 1918; later with CMN, Milan; tester, driver, sales executive, Alfa Romeo, 1920–39; subsequently Dir, Alfa Corse; Pres. and Managing Dir of Scuderia Ferrari, later of Auto Avio Construzione Ferrari, 1940–60. Builder of racing, sports and gran turismo cars in factory built at Maranello in 1943 and reconstructed in 1946. Commendatore, 1928; Cavaliere del Lavoro, 1952. Hon. doctorate in engineering, Bologna, 1960. *Publication:* Le mie gioie terribili (autobiog.). *Address:* viale Trento Trieste 31, Modena, Italy. *T:* 24081–24082; (office) Maranello, Modena, Italy. *T:* 91161–91162. *Died 14 Aug. 1988.*

**FEYNMAN, Prof. Richard (Phillips);** Professor of Physics, California Institute of Technology, Pasadena, Calif, since 1951; *b* 11 May 1918; *s* of Melville Feynman and Lucille (*née* Phillips); *m* 1960, Gweneth Howarth, Rippenden, Yorks; one *s* one *d. Educ:* MIT; Princeton Univ. Los Alamos, N Mex. Atomic Bomb Project, 1943–46; Cornell Univ., 1946–51. Mem. Brazilian Acad. of Sciences; Fellow (Foreign), Royal Soc., London, 1965. Einstein Award, 1954; Nobel Prize for Physics (jointly), 1965; Oersted Medal, 1972; Niels Bohr Internat. Gold Medal, 1973. *Publications:* The Feynman Lectures in Physics, 1963; The Character of Physical Law, 1965; Statistical Mechanics, 1972; Photon-Hadron Interactions, 1972; Surely You're Joking, Mr Feynman, 1985; QED: the strange theory of flight and matter, 1985; papers in scientific journals on quantum electro-dynamics, liquid helium, theory of beta-decay, quantum chromodynamics. *Recreations:* Mayan Hieroglyphics, opening safes, playing bongo drums, drawing, biology experiments, computer science (none done well). *Address:* 2475 Boulder Road, Altadena, Calif 91001, USA. *T:* 213–797–1262. *Died 15 Feb. 1988.*

**FFOLKES (ffolkes), Michael, (Brian Davis),** FCSD (FSIAD 1966); freelance artist; *b* 6 June 1925; *s* of late Walter Lawrence Davis, MSIAD, and of Elaine Rachel Bostock; *m* 1st, 1952, Miriam Boxer (marr. diss. 1971); two *s*; 2nd, 1972, Irene Ogilvy Kemp (marr. diss. 1978); one *d. Educ:* Leigh Hall Coll., Essex; St Martin's School of Art, 1941–43; Chelsea School of Art, 1946–49 (ND Painting 1948). Served Royal Navy, 1943–46. First drawing in Punch, 1943, and regular contributor, 1946–; Illustrator: Daily Telegraph's Way of the World, 1955–; Punch film column, 1961–72, 1978–; Member, Punch Table, 1978–. Drawings appear in The New Yorker, Playboy, Private Eye, Reader's Digest; exhibitor: Royal Academy, Leicester Galls, Arthur Jeffress Gall., The Workshop; drawings in V&A and BM; has illustrated over fifty books. *Publications:* ffanfare, 1953; How to Draw Cartoons, 1963; Mini Art, 1968; Private Eye Cartoon Library, 1976; ffolkes' ffauna, 1977; ffolkes' Companion to Mythology, 1978; ffundamental ffolkes, 1985. *Recreations:* walking, talking, cinema, music, collecting illustrated books. *Address:* 186 Shaftesbury Avenue, WC2H 8BA. *T:* 01–240 1841. *Clubs:* Savage, Toby, Omar Khayyam. *Died 18 Oct. 1988.*

**FFORDE, Sir Arthur (Frederic Brownlow),** GBE 1964; Kt 1946; MA Oxon; *b* 23 Aug. 1900; *s* of late Arthur Brownlow fforde, Indian Civil Service, and Mary Alice Storer Branson; *m* 1926, Mary Alison, *yr d* of late James MacLehose, printer to University of Glasgow; two *s* one *d. Educ:* Rugby Sch.; Trinity Coll., Oxford. Admitted Solicitor, 1925; Partner in firm of Linklaters & Paines, London, 1928–48; Mem. of Council of Law Soc., London, 1937–48; Deputy Dir-Gen., Ministry of Supply, (Finance) 1940, (Contracts) 1941; Under-Sec., Contracts Finance, Ministry of Supply, 1943; Under-Sec., HM Treasury, 1944–45; Head Master of Rugby Sch., 1948–57; Chm., the British Broadcasting Corporation, 1957–64; Mem., Central Board of Finance of Church of England, 1957–70 (Vice-Chm., 1957–60, Chm., 1960–65); Director, 1957–70: Equity & Law Life Assurance Society Ltd; National Westminster Bank Ltd, and other cos. Hon. LLD University of Wales. *Address:* Apple Tree Corner, The Close, Wonersh, near Guildford, Surrey.
*Died 26 June 1985.*

**FFRENCH, 7th Baron, *cr* 1798; Peter Martin Joseph Charles John Mary ffrench;** Bt 1779; *b* 2 May 1926; *s* of Capt. Hon. John Martin Valentine ffrench (*d* 1946), *s* of 5th Baron, and of Sophia, *d* of late Signor Giovanni Brambilla, Villa Sucota, Como, Italy; *S* uncle, 1955; *m* 1954, Sonia Katherine, *d* of Major Digby Cayley; one *s* two *d. Heir: s* Hon. Robuck John Peter Charles Mario ffrench, *b* 14 March 1956. *Address:* Castle ffrench, Ballinasloe, Co. Galway, Ireland. *Died 30 Jan. 1986.*

**FIDGE, Sir (Harold) Roy,** Kt 1967; JP; Commissioner, 1956–77, Chairman, 1963–77, Geelong Harbor Trust; *b* Warracknabeal, Vic., 24 Dec. 1904; *s* of Edward Fidge, Beulah, Vic.; *m* 1st, 1934, Mavis Melba Jane (*d* 1948), *d* of James Robert Burke, Warracknabeal; one *s* one *d*; 2nd, 1949, Nance (*d* 1979), *d* of George Davidson, Sydney, NSW. *Educ:* Geelong High Sch.; Geelong Coll.; Ormond Coll., University of Melbourne (LLB). Admitted Barrister and Solicitor, Supreme Court of Victoria, 1929. Royal Australian Navy, 1940–45; Lt-Comdr RANR. Councillor, City of Geelong, 1939–40, and 1946–; Mayor of City of Geelong, 1954–56 and 1964–68; Mem., Geelong High Adv. Council, 1940–59, Pres., 1956–59. Hon. Nat. Sec.-Treas., Assoc. of Apex Clubs, 1934–40, 1946–47, Life Governor, 1940; President: East Geelong Br., Aust. Red Cross Soc., 1961–67; Geelong E Techn. Sch. Council, 1960–65; Geelong Law Assoc., 1959–60 (Hon. Sec.-Treas., 1934–40, 1945–54); Member: Exec. Cttee of Municipal Assoc. of Victoria, 1964–; Council, Assoc. of Port and Marine Authorities of Aust., 1968–77. Co-founder with late Captain S. A. Pidgeon, Geelong Navy League Sea Cadets (now TS Barwon), 1931. Victorian Employers' Fedn Community Service Award, 1967. *Recreations:* gardening, woodwork. *Address:* 23 Meakin Street, Geelong, Victoria 3219, Australia. *T:* Geelong 95304. *Clubs:* Geelong, RSL, Ex-Navalmen's Assoc., Legacy, Victoria League, Geelong Rotary (Hon.) (all Australia).
*Died 13 Jan. 1981.*

**FIDLER, Alwyn Gwilym S.;** *see* Sheppard Fidler.

**FIDLER, Michael M.,** JP; President, General Zionist Organisation of Great Britain, since 1973; Founder and National Director, Conservative Friends of Israel, since 1974; Founder and International Director, All Party Friendship with Israel Group, European Parliament, since 1979; Chairman, International Organisation Commission, World Jewish Congress, since 1975; business consultant; Managing Director, Wibye Ltd, since 1968; *b* 10 Feb. 1916; *s* of Louis Fidler and Golda Fidler (*née* Sherr); *m* 1939, Maidie (*née* Davis); one *s* one *d*. *Educ:* Salford Grammar Sch.; Salford Royal Tech Coll. Cllr, Borough of Prestwich, 1951–63; Mayor, 1957–58; Alderman, 1963–74. Pres., Middleton, Prestwich and Whitfield Div. Cons. Assoc., 1965–69; Chm., Divl Educn Exec. (Prestwich, Whitfield and Radcliffe), Lancs CC, 1967–69. MP (C) Bury and Radcliffe, June 1970–Oct. 1974; Sec., Canadian Gp of Cons. Commonwealth Overseas Cttee, 1970–71; Treasurer, Parly Migraine Gp, 1970–74. Lectr, Extra Mural Dept, Manchester Univ., 1966–. Man. Director: H. & L. Fidler Ltd, 1941–70; Michael Lewis Ltd, 1942–70. Member: Grand Council, CBI, 1965–67; Nat. Exec., Nat. Assoc. of British Manufacturers, 1953–65. President: Fedn of Jewish Youth Socs of Gt Britain and Ireland, 1951–; Manchester Union of Jewish Socs, 1964–; Council of Manchester and Salford Jews, 1966–68 (Hon. Sec., 1950–53; Hon. Treasurer, 1953–55; Vice-Pres., 1954–60); Holy Law Congregation, Manchester, 1967–70 (Life Vice-Pres., 1977–84, Life Pres., 1984–); Bd of Deputies of British Jews, 1967–73; Cons. Friends of Israel, Redbridge Area Council, 1982–85; Vice-President: Children and Youth Aliyah Cttee for Gt Britain, 1968–81; Mizrachi, Hapoel-Hamizrachi Fedn of Gt Britain and Ireland, 1968–78; Hillel Foundn of Gt Britain, 1968–; Life Vice-President: Manchester Jewish Bd of Guardians, 1967–; Manchester Jewish Social Services, 1967–; Vice-Chairman: World Conf. on Jewish Educn, 1968–75; World Conf. of Jewish Organisations, 1967–73; Member Exec. Cttee: Council of Christians and Jews, Manchester Branch, 1966–; World Meml Foundn for Jewish Culture, 1968–80; World Conf. on Jewish Material Claims against Germany, 1968–80. Patron, All Party Parly Cttee for release of Soviet Jewry, 1971–74. Governor: Stand Grammar Schools, 1955–74; Inst. of Contemporary Jewry, Hebrew Univ. of Jerusalem, 1967–73; St Peter's RC Grammar Sch., 1968–80; Bury Grammar Schools, 1970–74. President: British Parks Lawn Tennis Assoc., 1952–59; SE Lancs Amateur Football League, 1966–67; Prestwich Heys Amateur Football Club, 1965–; Member: House of Commons Motor Club, 1970–74; Parly Flying Club, 1971–74. JP Co. Lancs, 1958. FRGS, FRAS, FREconS, FIAI. *Publications:* One Hundred Years of the Holy Law Congregation, 1964; articles. *Recreations:* politics, travel, reading, filming, foreign affairs, education. *Address:* 51 Tavistock Court, Tavistock Square, WC1H 9HG. *T:* 01–387 4925; 1 Woodcliffe Lodge, Sedgley Park Road, Prestwich, Manchester M25 8JX. *T:* 061–773 1471; Lower Ground Floor, 45 Westbourne Terrace, W2 3UR. *T:* 01–262 2493. *Clubs:* Embassy; Milverton Lodge (Manchester).
*Died 5 Sept. 1989.*

**FIELD, Sir John (Osbaldiston),** KBE 1967; Kt 1962; CMG 1959; first Governor, Gilbert and Ellice Islands Colony, 1972–73 (Resident Commissioner, 1970–71); *b* 30 Oct. 1913; *s* of late Frank Osbaldiston Field; *m* 1951, Irene Margaret, 2nd *d* of late Harold Godfrey Judd, CBE. *Educ:* Stellenbosch Boys' High Sch. S Africa; Magdalene Coll., Cambridge (MA). Colonial Administrative Service, Nigeria,

1936; Senior District Officer, 1951; Resident, 1954; Commissioner of the Cameroons, 1956; UK Special Representative for British Cameroons at UN Trusteeship Council, 1956–61; Commissioner of Southern Cameroons, 1960–61; Governor and C-in-C of St Helena, 1962–68; Staff Liaison Officer, HM Overseas Civil Service, 1968–69; acting Administrator, Montserrat, 1969. *Recreation:* fishing. *Address:* Little Park, PO Box 35, Himeville 4585, Natal, South Africa. *Clubs:* United Oxford & Cambridge University; Victoria (Pietermaritzburg). *Died 22 Feb. 1985.*

**FIELD, John William,** CMG 1951; JMN 1964; MD; DSc; Colonial Medical Service, retired; *b* 5 Aug. 1899; *s* of late Walter Field, Birmingham, England; *m* 1921, Elsie Mary, *d* of late William Dodd, Cardiff; one *s* three *d*. *Educ:* Oldbury Secondary Sch.; Birmingham Univ. Served European War, 1917–19. MB, ChB (Birmingham), 1924; Medical Officer, Malayan Medical Service, 1925; MD (Birmingham, Hons), 1929; Malaria Research Officer, Inst. for Med. Research, Federation of Malaya, 1931. Chalmers Medal, Royal Society of Tropical Medicine, 1941. Interned by Japanese in Singapore, 1942–45. Dir, Institute for Medical Research, Federation of Malaya, 1949–56. Mem., Expert Adv. Panel on Malaria, WHO, 1956–76. Hon. DSc (Malaya), 1959. *Publications:* various papers on tropical medicine. *Address:* The Knoll, Whitchurch, Ross-on-Wye, Herefordshire. *Died 15 April 1981.*

**FIELD, Stanley Alfred,** CBE 1982; JP; President, William Baird PLC, since 1981 (Chairman, 1961–81); Director: Winterbottom Energy Trust PLC, since 1959 (Chairman, 1962–83); Merchants Trust PLC, since 1964; *b* 1913; *m* 1950, Doreen Plunkett; one *s* two *d*. Senior Partner, W. N. Middleton & Co., 1946–53; Man. Dir, Prestige Group Ltd, 1953–58; Dir, Venesta Ltd, 1956–64 (Chm., 1958–64); Dir, 1966–84, Chm., 1977–83, Expamet Internat. (formerly Expanded Metal Co.). Mem. Cttee, AA, 1965–83. Governor: Christ's Hospital, 1970–; King Edward's Sch., Witley, 1970–. Liveryman, Glass Sellers Company. JP City of London, 1951. *Address:* (office) 79 Mount Street, W1Y 5HJ; (home) Sayer's Cottage, Hoyle Heyshott, Midhurst, West Sussex. *Clubs:* Carlton, City Livery. *Died 7 Jan. 1986.*

**FIELDGATE, Alan Frederic Edmond,** CMG 1945; *b* 20 Nov. 1889; *m* 1915, Dorothy Alice Thomas. *Educ:* Worcester Coll., Oxford (BA). Asst District Commissioner, Gold Coast Colony, 1915; District Commissioner, 1922; Provincial Commissioner, 1934–46. *Address:* Olde Court, Higher Lincombe Road, Torquay, Devon.

**FIELDHOUSE, Arnold;** *see* Fieldhouse, R. A.

**FIELDHOUSE, Bill;** *see* Fieldhouse, W.

**FIELDHOUSE, (Richard) Arnold;** building contractor; *b* 1 Aug. 1916; *m* 1952; one *s*. *Educ:* elem. sch. Elected to Manchester City Council for Levenshulme Ward, 1946: served as Leader of City Council, Chm. Policy Cttee, and Chm. Finance Cttee. Elected to Greater Manchester County Council for Levenshulme Elect. Div., 1973: Leader of Conservative Opposition, 1973–77; Mem., Policy Cttee; Leader of Council, 1977–81. *Recreations:* gardening, sailing. *Address:* Tudor Cottage, Macclesfield Road, Prestbury, Cheshire SK10 4BH. *T:* Prestbury (0625) 828272.
*Died 28 Sept. 1990.*

**FIELDHOUSE, William, (Bill Fieldhouse),** CBE 1978; Director, Fort Howard International, since 1984; *b* 1 Jan. 1932; *o c* of Joseph Fieldhouse and Elsie Broadbent; *m* 1st, 1953, Joan Lomax; one *s* one *d*; 2nd, 1978, Torunn Hassel; one *s* one *d* (and one *d* decd). *Educ:* Wallsend Grammar Sch.; Rutherford Coll., Newcastle upon Tyne. CEng; MIMechE 1967. Parsons Marine, 1949–53; Cunard, 1953–56; Allis-Chalmers, 1956–65; Tarmac, 1965–67; Peter Dixon, 1967–69; Letraset, 1969–81 (Chm., 1973–81); Director: UBM, 1978–80; Carrington Viyella, 1979–83 (Chm., 1980–83); Dalgety, 1980–83; Consoltex Inc., 1981–83 (Chm., 1982–83); Vantona Viyella, 1983 (Dep. Chm., 1983); Aquanautics, 1984. FRSA 1975. *Recreations:* hunting, skiing, tennis. *Address:* Fort Howard International, Chesterfield House, 385 Euston Road, NW1 3AU. *Club:* Royal Automobile. *Died 16 Jan. 1988.*

**FIELDING, Frank Stanley,** OBE 1966; HM Diplomatic Service, retired; Deputy Consul-General, Toronto, 1975–78; *b* 21 Dec. 1918; *s* of John Edgar Fielding and Anne; *m* 1944, Lela Coombs; one *s*. *Educ:* St Albans Sch.; UCL; King's Coll., London. Diploma in Journalism. HM Forces, 1940–46. Control Commn for Germany, 1946–48; Third Sec., Brit. Embassy, Vienna, 1948–50; Second Sec., Brit. Embassy, Beirut, 1950–55; Vice Consul, Cleveland, 1955–56; First Secretary: Brit. Embassy, Djakarta, 1956–60; FO, 1960–62; Consul (Commercial), Cape Town, 1962–65; First Sec., Brit. Embassy, Pretoria, 1965–68; Consul, NY, 1968–69; Dep. High Comr, Brisbane, 1969–72; Counsellor (Commercial), Singapore, 1972–75. *Recreations:* golf, fishing. *Address:* 28 Berkeley Square, Havant, Hants PO9 2RT. *T:* Havant (0705) 482540.
*Died 29 Oct. 1990.*

**FIELDING, Gabriel, (Alan Gabriel Barnsley);** Professor of English, Washington State University, 1967–81, later Professor Emeritus; *b* 25 March 1916; *s* of late George Barnsley, Clerk in Holy Orders, and Katherine Mary (*née* Fielding-Smith), a descendant of Henry Fielding, the novelist; *m* 1943, Edwina Eleanora Cook, Storrington, Sussex; three *s* two *d*. *Educ:* St Edward's Sch., Oxford; Trinity Coll., Dublin; St George's Hospital, London. BA, TCD, 1939. MRCS (Eng.), LRCP (London) 1942. Served with RAMC, 1943–46 (Capt.). Dep. Medical Officer, HM Training Establishment, Maidstone, Kent, 1954–64. Appointed Author in Residence (Prof. of English) to Washington State Univ., USA, 1966–67. Hon. DLitt Gonzaga Univ., Spokane, Washington, 1967. *Publications: poetry:* The Frog Prince and Other Poems, 1952; Twenty-Eight Poems, 1955; Songs without Music, 1979; *novels:* Brotherly Love, 1954; In the Time of Greenbloom, 1956, repr. 1984; Eight Days, 1958; Through Streets Broad and Narrow, 1960, repr. 1986; The Birthday King (W. H. Smith Prize for Literature, 1964; St Thomas More Gold Medal, USA, 1964), 1963, repr. 1985; Gentlemen in Their Season, 1966; Pretty Doll-Houses, 1979; The Women of Guinea Lane, 1986 (USA 1986); *short stories:* New Queens for Old (a novella and nine stories), 1972 (Governor's Literary Award, Washington State, 1972). *Recreations:* my home, painting, cold river swimming, my daily journal, walking. *Address:* 945 Monroe Street, Pullman, Washington 99163, USA. *Died 27 Nov. 1986.*

**FIELDING, Ven. Harold Ormandy;** Archdeacon of Rochdale, 1972–82; Archdeacon Emeritus since 1982; Vicar of St Peter, Bolton, 1965–83; *b* 13 Nov. 1912; *s* of Harold Wolstencroft and Florence Ann Fielding; *m* 1939, Elsie Whillance; three *s* one *d*. *Educ:* Farnworth Grammar Sch.; Magdalene Coll., Cambridge (MA); Ripon Hall, Oxford. Curate: St Mary, Leigh, 1936–40; St Paul, Walkden, 1940–44; Vicar of St James, New Bury, 1944–65; Hon. Canon of Manchester, 1965–72; Rural Dean of Bolton, 1965–72. *Address:* 6 High Meadows, Bromley Cross, Bolton BL7 9AR. *T:* Bolton 594650. *Died 30 Aug. 1987.*

**FIENNES, Gerard Francis Gisborne T. W.;** *see* Twisleton-Wykeham-Fiennes.

**FIFE, Charles Morrison,** CB 1950; MA; *b* 17 Aug. 1903; *s* of Alexander John Fife and Margaret Anne Morrison; *m* 1940, Evelyn Mary Thicthener (*d* 1970); no *c*. *Educ:* King Edward's High Sch., Birmingham; Christ's Coll., Cambridge. Senior Scholar, Christ's Coll., 1922; John Stewart of Rannoch (Univ.) Scholar, 1923; 1st Cl. Classical Trip. Pt I, 1924; Browne (Univ.) Scholar, 1925; 1st Cl. Div. I Classical Trip. Pt II, 1925; 2nd Cl. Hons Economics Trip. Pt II, 1926. Entered Civil Service, War Office, 1926; Private Sec. to Sir Reginald Paterson (Dep. Under Sec. of State), 1934–35; Asst Under-Sec. of State, WO, 1948–64, Ministry of Defence, 1964, retired. Conservator of Wimbledon Common, 1961–68. JP County of London, 1960–65. *Recreation:* Stefano Colonna's. *Address:* 4 Cokers Lane, Croxted Road, SE21 8NF. *Club:* United Oxford & Cambridge University. *Died 14 March 1982.*

**FIFE, His Honour Ian Braham,** MC 1945; TD (2 bars) 1946; a Circuit Judge (formerly County Court Judge), 1965–82 (Judge of Bromley County Court, 1969–82); *b* 10 July 1911; *o s* of late Donald Fulford Fife and Muriel Alice Fife (*née* Pitt); *m* 1947, Pauline, *e d* of T. R. Parsons and Mrs Winifred Parsons, CBE, Cambridge; two *s* two *d*. *Educ:* Monkton Combe Sch. Served, Royal Fusiliers, 1939–47. Called to Bar, Inner Temple, 1948; Mem. Bar Council, 1960–64; Deptl Cttee on Mechanical Recording of Court Proceedings, 1964–70. A Conservator of Wimbledon and Putney Commons, 1982–90. *Publications:* The Offices, Shops and Railway Premises Act, 1963; Agriculture (Safety, Health and Welfare); Redgrave's Factories Acts (edns 20–22); Redgrave's Offices and Shops (edns 1–2); (with E. A. Machin) Health and Safety at Work, 1980, rev. edn 1990; (with E. A. Machin) Redgrave's Health and Safety in Factories (edns 1–2), 1982, rev. edn 1988; (with E. A. Machin) Redgrave's Health and Safety, 1990; contrib. Halsbury's Laws of England, 3rd and 4th edns; Atkin's Court Forms. *Address:* 2 Castello Avenue, Putney, SW15. *T:* 081–788 6475.
*Died 2 June 1990.*

**FIGGURES, Sir Frank (Edward),** KCB 1970 (CB 1966); CMG 1959; *b* 5 March 1910; *s* of Frank and Alice Figgures; *m* 1st, 1941, Aline (*d* 1975), *d* of Prof. Hugo Frey; one *s* one *d*; 2nd, 1975, Ismea, *d* of George Napier Magill and *widow* of Jack Barker. *Educ:* Rutlish Sch.; New Coll., Oxford. Harmsworth Senior Scholar, Merton Coll., Oxford, 1931; Henry Fellow, Yale Law Sch., 1933; Called to Bar, Lincoln's Inn, 1936; Military Service (RA), 1940–46; Joined HM Treasury, 1946; Dir of Trade and Finance, OEEC, 1948–51; Under-Sec., HM Treasury, 1955–60; Sec.-Gen. to EFTA, 1960–65; Third Secretary, Treasury, 1965–68; Second Permanent Secretary, 1968–71; Dir-Gen., NEDO, 1971–73; Chm., Pay Bd, 1973–74. Dir, Julius Baer Bank Internat. Ltd, 1975–81; Mem. Adv. Bd, London Br., Julius Baer, Zurich, 1982–84. Chairman: Central Wagon Co. Ltd, 1976; BBC Gen. Adv. Council, 1978–82. Hon. DSc Aston 1975. *Address:* 7A Spring Lane, Glaston, Uppingham, Rutland

LE15 9BX. *T:* Uppingham (0572) 822777. *Club:* Reform.
*Died 27 Nov. 1990.*

**FILER, Albert Jack,** CB 1954; Past President, Brick Development Association Ltd; *b* 14 Aug. 1898; 2nd *s* of Albert James Shephard Filer and Jessie (*née* Marrison); *m* 1923, Violet D., *o d* of late Edward T. Booth, Bexhill, Sussex; one *d*. *Educ:* County Secondary Sch., Holloway, N. Entered Civil Service, 1914, Office of Works. Served European War of 1914–18 in Civil Service Rifles. Principal, 1940, Min. of Works, Asst Sec., 1943, Under Sec., 1948; Gen. Manager, Directorate Gen. of Works, 1958–60, retired from Civil Service, 1960. *Address:* 1 Heatherwood, Midhurst, West Sussex. *T:* Midhurst 2816. *Died 27 July 1989.*

**FILSON, Alexander Warnock;** consultant in film industry; *b* 23 Aug. 1913; *s* of late J. T. W. Filson, Indian Police; *m* 1941, Judith Henrietta, *d* of late Major R. H. Greig, DSO, and late Mrs Rokeling; one *s* two *d*. *Educ:* Clifton Coll., (Schol.); The Queen's Coll., Oxford (Schol.) (MA). Army, 1939–45 (ex-TA). Asst Sec., Parliamentary Labour Party, 1945–47; Sec. Fabian Soc., 1947–49; Mem. of Kensington Borough Council, 1937–49. Contested (Lab) Brentford and Chiswick, 1955. Director: Fedn of British Film Makers, 1957–66; Film Production Assoc. of GB, 1967–70; Israel Film Industry, London Office, 1971–76. *Publications:* (asst to Prof. G. D. H. Cole) British Trade Unionism Today, 1939; ed (with Prof. G. D. H. Cole) British Working Class Movements, 1789–1875: Select Documents, 1951; Distribution of Films produced in the Countries of the Community (for EEC Commn), 1980; Production and Distribution of Short Films in the Countries of the Community (for EEC Commn), 1981; The Exhibition of Film outside the Mainstream Cinema in the Countries of the Community, 1984 (for EEC Commn). *Recreations:* reading and sightseeing. *Address:* 6 Grosvenor Road, Richmond, Surrey. *T:* 01–940 2072.
*Died 29 March 1986.*

**FINCH, Ven. Geoffrey Grenville;** Vicar of Romsey and Archdeacon Emeritus, since 1982; Archdeacon of Basingstoke, 1971–82; *b* 7 Oct. 1923; *yr s* of late R. A. and E. M. Finch; *m* 1951, Margaret Ann Denniston; one *s* three *d*. *Educ:* Quarry Bank High Sch., Liverpool; St Peter's Hall, Oxford; Wycliffe Hall; Wells Theological Coll. Hon. Sch. of Nat. Sci. and Theology (2nd cl), Oxford, 1942–43; MA 1947. Foreign Office and Allied Commission for Austria, 1944–46; Oxford and Wells, 1947–50; ordained, 1950; Curate, Wigan Parish Church, 1950–54; Vicar, S Peter's, Westleigh, Lancs, 1954–59; Rector, Milton Parish Church, Hants, 1960–71; Vicar of Preston Candover and Bradley, Hants, 1971–76. Proctor in Convocation, 1965–70; Rural Dean of Christchurch, Hants, 1966–71. Member: Gen. Synod, 1973–80; Central Bd of Finance, CofE, 1975–80. *Recreations:* sailing, photography, painting, natural history, pottering. *Address:* The Vicarage, Romsey, Hants SO5 8EP. *T:* Romsey 513125.
*Died 31 March 1984.*

**FINCH, Col John Charles W.;** *see* Wynne-Finch.

**FINCH, Maj.-Gen. Lionel Hugh Knightley,** CB 1941; DSO 1916, Bar 1917; OBE; FLS; *b* 18 July 1888; *o s* of late Capt. E. H. Franklyn Finch, 30th Regt; *m* 1919, Hildegard, *d* of late Dr Gustav Schild, Herford, Germany and late Mrs J. C. A. Sepp-Clésius, Nijmegen, Holland; one *d*. *Educ:* Cheltenham Coll.; Birmingham Univ.; London Univ. Served European War, 1914–18 (DSO and bar, OBE, despatches, Bt Major); Staff Coll., Camberley, 1924–25; GSO3 at HQ, Northern Command, 1926–27; DAA and QMG at HQ Northumbrian Area, 1928–29; Bt Lt-Col, 1929; commanded Depot, Cheshire Regt, 1930–33; Comdr, Landi Kotal Bde, 1934; DAQMG at Army HQ India, 1934; comd 1st Bn Lancs Fusiliers, 1934–36; Asst Adjutant-Gen., War Office, 1936–39; Dep. Dir of Recruiting and Organisation, War Office, 1939; Dir of Recruiting and Organisation, War Office, 1939–40; Dep. Adjutant-Gen., War Office, 1940; Divisional Comdr, 1940; Chm., War Office Committees, 1940–41; District Comdr, Home Forces, 1941–42; retired, 1943; late The Lancs Fusiliers, The Cheshire Regt, and The Royal Sussex Regt. *Address:* National Westminster Bank, Petworth, West Sussex. *Died 23 Oct. 1982.*

**FINDLATER, Richard, (Kenneth Bruce Findlater Bain);** Associate Editor, The Observer, since 1982; Editor, The Author, since 1961; *b* 23 Dec. 1921; *s* of Thomas Bain and Elizabeth Bruce; *m* 1st, 1948, Romany Evens (marr. diss. 1961); three *s* one *d*; 2nd, 1979, Angela Colbert. *Educ:* Archbishop Tenison's Grammar School. Theatre Critic, Tribune, 1948–57; Literary Editor, Tribune, 1950–57; Editor, Books and Art, 1957–58; Literary Editor and Theatre Critic, Sunday Dispatch, 1958–59; Theatre Critic, Time and Tide, 1960–62; Editor, Twentieth Century, 1961–65; Asst Editor, The Observer, 1963–82. Member: BBC Critics, 1953–69; Arts Council Drama Panel, 1953–62 and 1970–74; Housing the Arts Cttee of Inquiry, 1956–61; Theatre Inquiry, 1967–70; Council, English Stage Co., 1978–81; Soc. of Authors, 1978–. *Publications:* The Unholy Trade, 1952; Grimaldi, 1955; Michael Redgrave: Actor, 1956; Emlyn Williams, 1957; Six Great Actors, 1957; Banned, 1967; (ed) Memoirs of Grimaldi, 1968; (ed) Comic Cuts, 1970; The Player Kings, 1971;

(ed) Public Lending Right, 1971; Lilian Baylis, 1975; The Player Queens, 1976; Joe Grimaldi: his life and theatre, 1978; (with Mary Relph Powell) Little Tich, 1979; (ed) At the Royal Court, 1981; These Our Actors, 1983; (ed) Author! Author!, 1984; *pamphlets:* The Future of the Theatre, 1959; What are Writers Worth?, 1963; The Book Writers: Who are They?, 1966. *Address:* Foxholes, Kingham, Oxon. *Club:* Garrick. *Died* 5 *Jan.* 1985.

**FINDLAY, Alexander,** MBE 1983; Member, Mental Welfare Commission for Scotland, since 1986; *b* 9 May 1926; *s* of Alexander and Margaret Findlay; *m* 1951, Margaret Webster Aitken Milne; two *s*. *Educ:* Harris Academy, Dundee. Telecoms engineer, 1942–57; Telecoms executive, 1957–84. Chm., Lothian Health Bd, 1983–86; Member: Children's Panel for Scotland, 1974–79; Penicuik Town Council, 1970–74. Chief Scout's Award for services to Scouting, 1978. *Recreations:* golf, travel. *Address:* 54 Rullion Road, Penicuik, Midlothian. *T:* Penicuik (0968) 73443. *Club:* Royal Over-Seas League. *Died* 25 *July* 1990.

**FINDLAY, Comdr James Buchanan,** CBE 1957; RN (Retd); Director, Bank of Scotland, 1933–71; *b* 7 Jan. 1895; *m* 1923, Mary Sancroft Findlay-Hamilton; three *s* one *d*. *Educ:* Royal Naval Colls, Osborne and Dartmouth. Retired from RN after European War of 1914–18; served in War of 1939–45. *Recreations:* shooting, golf, gardening. *Address:* The Garden House, Carnell, Kilmarnock, Ayrshire. *Club:* Lansdowne. *Died* 26 *Dec.* 1983.

**FINDLAY, Prof. John Niemeyer,** FBA 1956; Borden Parker Bowne Professor of Philosophy, Boston University, since 1978 (University Professor of Philosophy, since 1972); *b* 25 Nov. 1903; 2nd *s* of J. H. L. Findlay, Pretoria, South Africa; *m* 1941, Aileen May, *d* of G. S. Davidson, Wellington, NZ; one *s* one *d* (and one *d* decd). *Educ:* Boys' High Sch., Pretoria; Transvaal Univ. Coll.; Balliol Coll., Oxford (Rhodes Scholar, 1st Lit. hum.); University of Graz. Lecturer in Philosophy, Transvaal University Coll., 1927–33; Prof. of Philosophy, University of Otago, NZ, 1934–44; Prof. of Philosophy, Rhodes University Coll., Grahamstown, S Africa, 1945; Prof. of Philosophy, Natal University Coll., 1946–48; Prof. of Philosophy, King's Coll., Newcastle upon Tyne, Univ. of Durham, 1948–51; University Prof. of Philosophy, King's Coll., Univ. of London, 1951–66. Gifford Lecturer, Univ. of St Andrews, 1964–66. Prof. of Philosophy, Univ. of Texas, 1966–67; Clark Prof. of Moral Philosophy and Metaphysics, Yale Univ., 1967–72. Fellow, Amer. Acad. of Arts and Scis, 1978. FKC 1970. *Publications:* Meinong's Theory of Objects and Values, 1933, new edn, 1963; Hegel: A Re-Examination, 1958; Values and Intentions, 1961; Language, Mind and Value, 1963; The Discipline of the Cave, 1965; The Transcendence of The Cave, 1967; trans. Husserl, Logische Untersuchungen, 1969; Axiological Ethics, 1970; Ascent to the Absolute: metaphysical papers and lectures, 1970; Plato's Written and Unwritten Doctrines, 1974; Plato and Platonism, 1978; Kant and the Transcendental Object, 1981; Wittgenstein: a critique, 1984; Studies in the Philosophy of J. N. Findlay, ed Cohen, Martin and Westphal, replies and autobiog. by J. N. Findlay, 1985; articles in Mind, Philosophy, Philosophy and Phenomenological Research, Proc. of the Aristotelian Soc., etc. *Address:* 14 Lambolle Road, NW3; 96 Bay State Road, Boston, Mass 02215, USA. *Club:* Royal Commonwealth Society. *Died* 27 *Sept.* 1987.

**FINGALL,** 12th Earl of *cr* 1628; **Oliver James Horace Plunkett,** MC; Baron Killeen, 1436; Baron Fingall (UK) 1831; Major, late 17th/21st Lancers; *b* 17 June 1896; *er s* of 11th Earl and Elizabeth Mary Margaret (*d* 1944), *e d* of George Burke, JP, Danesfield, Co. Galway; *S* father, 1929; *m* 1926, Jessica (*d* 1965), *yr d* of late Allan Hughes, Lynch, Allerford, Somerset; *m* 1966, Mrs Clair Richardson, *widow* of Frank Richardson, Geelong, Vic., Aust. *Educ:* Downside. Served European War (MC); retired pay, 1931; in army again, 1939–45. Roman Catholic. *Recreations:* racing and travelling. *Heir:* none. *Address:* The Commons, Dunsany, Co. Meath, Ireland. *TA:* Fingall, Dunsany. *T:* Navan 25193. *Clubs:* Cavalry and Guards; Kildare Street and University (Dublin). *Died* 5 *March* 1984 (*ext*).

**FINLAISON, Brig. (retd) Alexander Montagu,** CBE 1957; DSO 1944; *b* 14 March 1904; *s* of Maj.-Gen. J. B. Finlaison, CMG, late Royal Marines, Dedham, Essex; *m* 1935, Monica Mary Louisa, *d* of T. W. Donald, Grendon, Stirling; one *d* (and one *d* decd). *Educ:* RN Colls Osborne and Dartmouth; RMC Sandhurst. Commissioned Cameronians (Scottish Rifles), 1924; seconded Sudan Defence Force, 1932–38; served War of 1939–45: Greece, Crete, Sicily, Italy; commanded 2nd Wiltshires, 2nd Cameronians, 17 Infantry Brigade, Italy, 1943–44; BGS, HQ Scottish Command, 1954–57; ADC to the Queen, 1955–57; retired, 1957; Commandant, Queen Victoria Sch., Dunblane, 1957–64. *Address:* Gledenholm, Ae, Dumfries DG1 1RF. *T:* Parkgate 242. *Club:* Naval and Military.
*Died* 6 *June* 1989.

**FINLAY, Sir Graeme Bell,** 1st Bt, *cr* 1964; ERD; Barrister-at-Law; Sous Juge d'Instruction and Assistant Judge of Petty Debts Court for Jersey, 1972–77; *b* 29 Oct. 1917; *yr s* of late James Bell Pettigrew Finlay and late Margaret Helena, *d* of John Euston Davies, JP,

Portskewett House, nr Chepstow, Mon.; *m* 1953, June Evangeline, *y d* of Col Francis Collingwood Drake, OBE, MC, DL, late 10th Royal Hussars, Harlow, Essex; one *s* two *d*. *Educ:* Marlborough; University College, London. Served War of 1939–45, 2nd Lieut S Wales Borderers (suppl. res.), 1939; 7th (Croix de Guerre) Bn, 24th Regt (Beach Divs), 1940–41; seconded to 5th Royal Gurkha Rifles (Frontier Force), 1942–45; Martial Law Officer, Upper Sind Force (Hur Rebellion), 1943; Acting Major and DAAG, HQ, NW Army, 1945. Hon. Captain, The Royal Regt of Wales. Called to Bar, Gray's Inn, 1946 (Lord Justice Holker Sen. Exhibr); pupil of Lord Hailsham of St Marylebone; President of Hardwicke Society, 1950–51. Presided over first televised joint debate between Oxford and Cambridge Union Societies, 1950. Contested (C) Ebbw Vale, General Election, 1950; MP (C) Epping Division of Essex, 1951–64; Parliamentary Private Secretary to Rt Hon. Iain Macleod, Minister of Health, 1952–55; Asst Whip (unpaid), 1957–59; Lord Commissioner of the Treasury, 1959–60; Vice-Chamberlain of the Household, 1960–64; Mem., Parly Delegn to Russia, 1960; a Deputy Judge of County Courts, later Circuit Judge, 1967–72; a Dep. Chm., Agricultural Land Tribunal (SE Region), 1971–72. *Publications:* (jt author) Proposals for an Administrative Court, 1970; frequent contributor to Justice of the Peace and Local Government Review. *Recreations:* reading history and painting. *Heir:* *s* David Ronald James Bell Finlay, *b* 16 Nov. 1963. *Address:* La Campagne, Rozel, Jersey, CI. *T:* Jersey 51194; 4 Paper Buildings, Temple, EC4. *T:* 01–353 3366. *Died* 21 *Jan.* 1987.

**FINLAY, Jane Little, (Sheena),** CBE 1985; JP; Deputy Chairman, Equal Opportunities Commission, since 1980; *b* 29 Sept. 1917; *e d* of James Whyte Hepburn and Jean Brown, Langside, Glasgow; *m* 1941, John A. R. Finlay, QC; one *s* two *d* (and one *d* decd). *Educ:* Spier's Sch., Beith; Hutcheson's Girls' Grammar Sch., Glasgow; Glasgow Univ. (MA Hons English and Philosophy, 1940); Jordanhill Coll., Glasgow (Teacher's Trng Cert., 1941). Asst Principal, Bd of Inland Revenue, 1941–45 (Private Office, 1943–45). Teaching: Mayfield County Sch., Putney, 1946; Cooper's Sch., Chislehurst (part-time), 1962–73. Part-time Mem. Value Added Tax Tribunals, 1973–; Mem (Vice-Chm.), Bromley Community Health Council, 1974–76, Chm., 1976–78; Co-Chm., Women's Nat. Commn, 1975–77; Vice-Pres., 1971–74, Pres., 1975–78, British Fedn of University Women; Mem., 1982–, Vice-Pres., 1985–, EEC Adv. Cttee on Equality. UK Deleg., Unesco Conf., Bonn, 1975; Mem., UK delegn to UN European Regional Seminar, Groningen, 1977; EEC Deleg., UN Decade of Women Conf., Nairobi, 1985. JP Bromley, 1966 (Mem. 1967, Chm. 1980–81, Juvenile Panel). *Recreations:* cooking, reading, gardening, sailing. *Address:* Thornhill, Golf Road, Bickley, Bromley, Kent BR1 2JA. *T:* 01–467 3637. *Died* 28 *Nov.* 1985.

**FINLAY, John Alexander Robertson,** QC 1973; **His Honour Judge Finlay;** a Circuit Judge, since 1976; *b* 9 Nov. 1917; *o s* of late Rev. John Adamson Finlay, MA and Mary Hain Findlay; *m* 1941, Jane Little Hepburn, (Sheena), CBE (*d* 1985); one *s* two *d* (and one *d* decd). *Educ:* High Sch. of Glasgow; Glasgow Univ. (Foulis School, John Clerk Schol.); Queen's Coll., Oxford (Schol.). Caird Medal, Melville Medal, MA 1st cl. Philosophy Glasgow, 1939; BA 2nd cl. Jurisprudence 1946, MA 1959, Oxon. Served in RN, 1940–46: Seaman 1940; commnd 1941; Lieut RNVR 1942. Called to Bar, Middle Temple, 1946 (Harmsworth Schol.); Bencher, 1971. Recorder of the Crown Court, 1975–76; Acting Deemster, IoM Court of Appeal, 1975; periodically Judge of High Ct, Chancery Div., 1976–; Judge, Bromley County Ct, 1982–. Member: Bar Council, 1970–74; Senate of Inns of Ct and the Bar, 1984–86; Vice-Pres., Council of HM Circuit Judges, 1988 (Hon. Sec., 1986–). Chm., Crosby Hall, 1975–76. Member: Law Guardian Editorial Adv. Cttee, 1971–72; Renton Cttee on Preparation of Legislation, 1973–75. *Recreations:* music, sailing, garden labour, thinking. *Address:* Thornhill, 10 Golf Road, Bickley, Bromley, Kent. *T:* 01–467 3637; 16 Old Buildings, Lincoln's Inn, WC2. *Club:* Athenæum. *Died* 6 *Jan.* 1989.

**FINLAY, John Euston Bell,** CB 1959; OBE 1946; TD 1947; consultant on indirect taxation, since 1968; *b* 11 Sept. 1908; *e s* of late James Bell Pettigrew Finlay and late Margaret Helena Finlay, Douro Court, Cheltenham; *m* 1942, Zoë Josephine, *d* of late Brigadier Edward Lees, DSO, Whyte Cottage, Selsey, Sussex; one *s* one *d*. *Educ:* Marlborough; Geneva Univ. Junior Legal Asst, Board of Customs, 1933; Senior Legal Asst, 1945. Principal, 1948, Asst Secretary, 1949; Under-Sec., 1954–68; Commissioner and Director of Estab. and Org., 1954–65; Comr i/c Internat. and Tariff Divs, Bd of Customs and Excise, 1965–68; retired, 1968. Chairman, Finance Cttee, Customs Co-operation Council, Brussels, 1967–68. Governor St Dunstan's Educational Foundation, 1964–73. Member Management Cttee, CS Benevolent Fund, 1958–68; Trustee, CS Retirement Fellowship, 1968–. Mem., Chichester DC, 1976–79. Commnd from Trooper Inns of Court Regt to 1st (Rifle) Bn The Mon. Regt TA, 1934. Served, 1939–42, with 38 Div., 53 Div. and at Western Command (ADC to GOC-in-C and GSO2) (ops); psc Staff Coll., Camberley, 1942; seconded 1943–45, AIF; served New

Guinea, Moluccas, Philippines and Borneo as GSO2 and GSO1, Anglo-Australian Special Airborne Forces (OBE). Hon. Lieut-Colonel. FRGS. *Recreations:* gardening, racing. *Address:* Bernards Gate House, 22 Lavant Road, Chichester, Sussex. *T:* Chichester 527369; 38 Sloane Court West, SW3. *T:* 01–730 5955. *Clubs:* Travellers', Special Forces. *Died 6 Nov. 1982.*

**FINLAY, Sheena;** *see* Finlay, J. L.

**FINLAYSON, Maj.-Gen. Forbes;** *see* Finlayson, Maj.-Gen. W. F.

**FINLAYSON, Air-Vice Marshal James Richmond G.;** *see* Gordon-Finlayson.

**FINLAYSON, Maj.-Gen. (William) Forbes,** OBE 1955; Director, Army Dental Service, 1966–70; *b* 12 Oct. 1911; *s* of late Lieut-Colonel W. T. Finlayson, OBE, Army Dental Corps, Edinburgh; *m* Anne McEwen, *d* of Walter Stables Smith, Peebles; one *s* one *d*. *Educ:* George Heriot's Sch., Edinburgh; Royal College of Surgeons, Edinburgh; FDSRCSE 1970. LDS 1933. Lieut, Army Dental Corps, 1935; Captain 1936; Major 1945; Lieut-Colonel 1952; Colonel 1959; Maj.-General 1966. Served in: UK, 1935–39, 1945–50, 1955–59, 1963–70; Far East, 1939–45 (POW); BAOR, 1950–52, 1959–63; MELF, 1952–55. QHDS, 1966–70. CStJ 1970. *Recreations:* Rugby football, golf, tennis, walking. *Address:* 2 Great Sanders House, Hurst Lane, Sedlescombe, E Sussex TN33 0PE.

*Died 23 Dec. 1989.*

**FINLEY, Sir Moses,** Kt 1979; FBA 1971; Master of Darwin College, Cambridge, 1976–82, Hon. Fellow, since 1982; *b* 20 May 1912; became British subject, 1962; *m* 1932, Mary F. Thiers; no *c*. *Educ:* Syracuse Univ., USA; Columbia Univ., USA. BA Syracuse 1927 (*magna cum laude*) (Phi Beta Kappa); MA Columbia, 1929 and PhD 1950. Held various teaching, research, editorial and consulting posts with: Encyclopaedia of the Social Sciences, 1930–33; Inst. of Social Research (then affiliated with Columbia Univ.), 1937–39; City Coll. of New York, 1934–42; Columbia Univ., 1933–34, 1948–54; exec. posts with war relief agencies, 1942–47. Fellow in History, Columbia Univ., 1934–35; Fellow, Amer. Council of Learned Socs, 1948; Lectr, then Asst Prof. of History, Newark Colls of Rutgers Univ., 1948–52; Faculty Fellow, Fund for the Advancement of Educn, 1951–52. Lectr in Classics, Cambridge Univ., 1955–64; Fellow, Jesus Coll., 1957–76, Hon. Fellow, 1977; Reader in Ancient Social and Economic History, Cambridge Univ., 1964–70, Prof. of Ancient History, Cambridge Univ., 1970–79; Librarian, Jesus Coll., 1960–64; Chm., Faculty Bd of Classics, Cambridge Univ. 1967–69; Chm., Social and Political Sciences Cttee, Cambridge Univ., 1973–74. Sather Prof. of Classical Literature, Univ. of California, Berkeley, 1972; Lectures: First Mason Welch Gross, Rutgers Univ., 1972; Jane Harrison Meml, Newnham Coll., Cambridge, 1972; Mortimer Wheeler Archaeol, British Acad., 1974; Collège de France, 1978; British Museum Soc., 1979 (at Nat. Theatre); Wiles, QUB, 1980; J. C. Jacobsen Meml, Danish Acad., 1981; Distinguished Guest, RCPsych, 1986. Sec., Cambridge Philological Soc., 1959–65, Pres., 1974–76; Convener of Ancient Hist. section, Internat. Economic Hist. Conf., Aix-en-Provence, 1962, Munich, 1965; Edinburgh, 1978; Pres., Jt Assoc. of Classical Teachers, 1981–83 (Chm., sub-cttee on Ancient Hist., 1964–71); Pres., Classical Assoc., 1973–74. A Trustee, British Museum, 1977–84. Editor: Views and Controversies in Classical Antiquity, 1960–73; Ancient Culture and Society, 1969–. FRHistS, 1970. For. Member: Royal Danish Acad. of Scis and Letters, 1975; Accademia Nazionale dei Lincei, 1982; Hon. For. Mem., Amer. Acad. of Arts and Sciences, 1979. Hon. DLitt: Leicester, 1972; Saskatchewan, 1979; Sheffield, 1979; Hon. DHumLitt City Coll. of NY, 1982. Wolfson Literary Award in History, 1972. *Publications:* Studies in Land and Credit in Ancient Athens, 1952; The World of Odysseus, 1954, 2nd edn 1977; (ed) The Greek Historians, 1958; (ed) Slavery in Classical Antiquity, 1960; The Ancient Greeks, 1963; (ed) Josephus, 1965; Aspects of Antiquity, 1968; Ancient Sicily, 1968, 2nd edn, 1979; Early Greece: the Bronze and Archaic Ages, 1970, 2nd edn, 1981; The Ancestral Constitution (inaugural lecture), 1971; (ed) Thucydides, 1972; Knowledge for what? (Encyclopaedia Britannica Lecture), 1973; Democracy Ancient and Modern, 1973, 2nd edn 1985; (ed) Problèmes de la terre en Grèce ancienne, 1973; The Ancient Economy, 1973, 2nd edn 1985; (ed) Studies in Ancient Society, 1974; The Use and Abuse of History, 1975, 2nd edn, 1986; (with H. W. Pleket) The Olympic Games: the first thousand years, 1976; (ed) Studies in Roman Property, 1976; (ed) Atlas of Classical Archaeology, 1977; The Idea of a Theatre: the Greek experience, 1980; Ancient Slavery and Modern Ideology, 1980; (ed) The Legacy of Greece: a new appraisal, 1981; Economy and Society in Ancient Greece, 1981; Politics in the Ancient World, 1983; Ancient History: evidence and models, 1985; articles and reviews in classical, historical and legal jls, and in literary weeklies and monthlies in Britain and the US; *posthumous publication:* (ed) Classical Slavery, 1987. *Recreations:* conversation, listening to music, travel. *Address:* 12 Adams Road, Cambridge CB3 9AD. *T:* Cambridge 357784.

*Died 23 June 1986.*

**FINN, Donovan Bartley,** CMG 1946; FRSC, FCIC; Director of Fisheries, Food and Agriculture Organization of the United Nations, 1946–64, retired; *b* Hendon, 1 March 1900; *s* of Edwin Bartley Finn and Eleanor Penton; *m* 1946, Florence Stewart Daly. *Educ:* University of Manitoba (BSc, MSc); Cambridge Univ. (PhD). Director Fisheries Expt. Station, Prince Rupert, BC, of the Fisheries Research Board of Canada, 1925; Director Fisheries Expt. Station, Halifax, NS, of Fisheries Research Board of Canada, 1934; Chairman Salt Fish Board of Canada, 1939; Deputy Minister of Fisheries, Dominion of Canada, 1940–46; Member Economic Advisory Cttee, Dominion of Canada, 1941; Chairman Food Requirements Cttee, 1943–46. Represented Canada as delegate and adviser at various international bodies and conferences during war with respect to fisheries and food matters. *Publications:* scientific journals, on physics and chemistry of food proteins. *Recreations:* mountaineering, music. *Address:* Castello di Sterpeto, Sterpeto d'Assisi, Perugia, Italy. *Clubs:* Rideau, University (Ottawa).

*Died 1 Nov. 1982.*

**FIRBANK, Maj.-Gen. Cecil Llewellyn,** CB 1953; CBE 1951; DSO 1944 and Bar 1945; DL; *b* 18 March 1903; *m* 1st, 1934, Audrey Hobhouse (marr. diss. 1952); one *s*; 2nd, 1952, Marye Brenda Fleetwood-Wilson. *Educ:* Cheltenham Coll.; RMC Sandhurst. Gazetted to 1st Somerset LI, 1924; served Egypt, 1926–29; seconded to Royal West African Frontier Force, 1929–34; served with Somerset LI, 1934–42; on active service, North West Europe, 1944–45, Comd 2nd Lincolns; Comd 71 Infantry Bde, 1945–46; Staff Coll., 1947–48; Commandant School of Infantry, Warminster, 1948–51; GOC SW District and 43rd Wessex Division (TA), 1951–54; Director of Infantry, War Office, 1955–58; retired pay, 1959. Colonel Commandant, Aden Protectorate Levies, 1958–62; Colonel, Somerset and Cornwall Light Infantry, 1963–68; Dep. Colonel, The Light Infantry (Somerset and Cornwall), 1968–70. Hon. Colonel: 4/5th Somerset LI (TA), 1955–60; North Somerset Yeomanry (44th Royal Tank Regt), 1959–64. Dir, Civil Defence for Wales, 1960–65. DL Somerset, 1959. *Recreations:* cricket, field sports. *Address:* The Owls, Charlton Horethorne, near Sherborne, Dorset. *T:* Corton Denham 279. *Club:* Army and Navy.

*Died 19 Aug. 1985.*

**FIRTH, Arthur Percival;** Sports Editor, Daily Mail, since 1986; *b* 13 Aug. 1928; *s* of Arthur and Florence Firth; *m* 1957, Joyce Mary (*née* Fairclough); two *d*. *Educ:* Arnold Sch., Blackpool. Reporter, Lancashire Evening Post, 1950–58; Daily Express: Sub-Editor, 1960; Night Editor, 1969–72; Northern Editor, 1972–78; Dep. Editor, 1978–80; Editor, 1980–81; Asst Editor, Daily Mail, 1982–86. *Recreations:* golf, fishing, cricket. *Address:* Daily Mail, Tudor Street, EC4. *T:* 01–353 6000. *Died 12 Dec. 1987.*

**FISHER, Alan Wainwright;** General Secretary, National Union of Public Employees, 1968–82; *b* 20 June 1922; *s* of Thomas Wainwright Fisher and Ethel Agnes Fisher; *m* 1958, Joyce Tinniswood (marr. diss. 1976); two *s* one *d*; *m* 1978, Ruth Woollerton. *Educ:* Primary and Secondary Schools in Birmingham. National Union of Public Employees: Junior Clerk, 1939; Midlands Divisional Officer, 1953; Asst General Secretary, 1962. Mem., TUC Gen. Council, 1968–82; Chm., TUC, 1980–81. Member: Nat. Jt Council for Local Authorities, Services, 1956– (Chm., 1971–72); Ancillary Staffs Council (Sec. 1965–79) and Gen. Council (Chm. 1966–69) of Whitley Councils for Health Services; Potato Marketing Bd, 1969–70; Bd, Centre for Educnl Develt Overseas (Governor 1970–); Nat. Radiological Protection Bd, 1971; Med. Adv. Cttee, Health and Safety Commn, 1977–; Bd, BOAC, 1970–72; BAB, 1972–82; London Electricity Bd, 1970–80; Dir, Harland and Wolff, Shipbuilders, Belfast, 1975–83. Governor, Henley Administrative Staff Coll., 1977–83. *Recreation:* seismography. *Address:* Plas Farchynys, Bontddu, Gwynedd. *T:* Bontddu 643.

*Died 20 March 1988.*

**FISHER, Prof. Charles Alfred,** MA Cantab; Professor of Geography, School of Oriental and African Studies, University of London, 1964–81; *b* 23 April 1916; *er s* of Rev. Charles and Bertha Fisher (*née* Anderson); *m* 1945, Irene Mary Clarke (*d* 1972), ARCM, GRSM; one *s* one *d*. *Educ:* Strand Sch., London; St Catharine's Coll., Cambridge (Exhibr 1935, Scholar 1938, Junior Librarian 1938–40). Geog. Tripos, Parts I and II (First Class Hons), 1937, 1938; University Bartle Frere Exhibr, 1938, 1939; MA 1942; DLitt Komazawa, Tokyo, 1976. Served War of 1939–45 with RE Malaya Comd HQ. Asst Lecturer in Geography, University College of Leicester, 1946; Lecturer in Geography, University College of Wales, Aberystwyth, 1946–49; Senior Research Officer, Institute of Colonial Studies, Oxford, 1950–51; Lecturer in Geography, University (Coll.) of Leicester, 1951–58, Reader, 1958–59; Professor and Head of the Department of Geography, 1959–64, and Director of Centre of Japanese Studies, 1962–64, University of Sheffield. RGS Travelling Fellowship, 1947; Visiting Lecturer in Geography and Visiting Fellow of Trumbull Coll., Yale Univ., 1953–54. Chairman Assoc. of British Orientalists, 1962–63. Editor, Modern Asian Studies, 1967–70. Victoria Medal, RGS, 1974. *Publications:*

Geographical Essays on British Tropical Lands, 1956 (Joint Editor); South-east Asia: a Social Economic and Political Geography, 1964; Essays in Political Geography, 1968 (Editor); articles, mostly on political geography of Asia, in Geog. Journal, Econ. Geog., International Affairs, Politique Etrangère, etc. *Recreations:* music and foreign travel. *Address:* c/o School of Oriental and African Studies, University of London, Malet Street, WC1E 7HP. *Club:* Geographical. *Died* 7 *Jan.* 1982.

**FISHER, Major (Hon.) Charles Howard Kerridge,** MC 1918; JP; Director of property companies, since 1960; *b* 21 Dec. 1895; *s* of late Charles Henry Fisher, Westbury, Wilts; *m* 1923, Ethel Mary (*d* 1958), *d* of Sidney Redcliffe Chope, JP, Bideford, Devon; one *s* one *d*; *m* 1967, Gertrude Elizabeth, JP, *widow* of William Walter Symper, Harrow. *Educ:* Trowbridge High Sch., Wiltshire. Served European War, 1914–18 (MC); with Hon. Artillery Company and RA in Belgium and France; War of 1939–45: Home Guard and Army Welfare Officer; Hon. Major 1958. Manufacturer ladies' clothing, 1923–59, when retired (Company Dir). Member Acton Borough Council, 1940–45 (Educn Cttee, 1945–65). JP 1947, DL 1961–79, Middlesex (now London). First High Sheriff of Greater London, 1965. Lord Lieutenant's Representative for Acton, 1958–70 (now London Borough of Ealing, 1965–71); Dep. Chairman, Willesden Petty Sessional Division, 1962–69. General Comr of Income Tax, 1965–69. Freeman, City of London, 1947; Liveryman, Haberdashers' Company, 1948; Patron, Local Cadets; Pres., Boy Scouts Assoc.; Vice-President: Acton Branch, British Legion; NW County Met. Area British Legion. Member, War Pension Cttee, Ealing, 1940 (Vice-Chairman 1960). Past Asst Grand Dir of Ceremony, Lodge 766. Silver Jubilee Medal, 1977. *Recreations:* local social activities. *Address:* Arunshead Farm, Green Lane, Shamley Green, Guildford GU5 0RD. *Club:* City Livery.
*Died* 10 *Jan.* 1987.

**FISHER, Hon. Francis Forman,** CBE 1980; MC 1944; Principal, Wolsey Hall, Oxford, since 1980; Master of Wellington College, 1966–80; *b* 25 Sept. 1919; 2nd *s* of late Most Rev. and Rt Hon. Lord Fisher of Lambeth, GCVO; unmarried. *Educ:* Repton; Clare Coll., Cambridge (MA). Commissioned, The Sherwood Foresters, 1940; served War of 1939–45, Middle East, and Western Desert (POW Tobruk, 1942); escaped from Italy and returned to England, 1943; demobilised, rank of Capt., 1946 (MC); returned to Cambridge, 1946; Asst Master, Repton Sch., 1947–54; Housemaster, 1948–54; Warden of St Edward's Sch., Oxford, 1954–66. Incorporated MA Oxford Univ. through Christ Church, 1955. Chm., Headmaster's Conf., 1973. Governor: Repton Sch.; Oundle Sch.; St Catherine's Sch.; Dragon Sch.; Caldicott and Horris Hill Prep. Schs; Chairman of Governors: Mount House Sch.; Greycotes Sch. Dir, Ecclesiastical Insurance Office Ltd, 1981–; Chm., GAP Activities Ltd, 1982–. *Recreations:* cricket, hockey (rep. CUHC *v* Oxford, 1947), and other games. *Address:* New Barn, Cassington Road, Yarnton, Oxford. *T:* Kidlington 6717. *Clubs:* East India, Devonshire, Sports and Public Schools; Hawks (Cambridge). *Died* 27 *Nov.* 1986.

**FISHER, Prof. Frederick Jack,** MA; Professor of Economic History, London School of Economics, University of London, 1954–75; *b* 22 July 1908; *s* of A. H. Fisher, Southend-on-Sea; *m* 1943, Barbara Vivienne, *d* of J. E. Whisstock, Southend-on-Sea; one *s* one *d*. *Educ:* Southend High Sch.; London Sch. of Economics. MA. Served RAF, 1941–46. Asst Lecturer and Lecturer in Economic History, London Sch. of Economics, 1935–47; Reader in Economic History, 1947–54. FRHistS. Wiles' Lectr, QUB, 1973. Hon. DLitt Exeter, 1983. *Publications:* (ed) Essays in the Economic and Social History of Tudor and Stuart England, 1961; (ed) Calendar of Manuscripts of Lord Sackville of Knole, vol II, 1966; contrib. Economica, Economic History Review. *Address:* 22 Lyndale Avenue, NW2.
*Died* 7 *Jan.* 1988.

**FISHER, Sir John,** Kt 1942; Shipowner; *b* 1892; *s* of James Fisher, Barrow-in-Furness; *m* 1947, Maria, *d* of Richard Elsner, Vienna, Austria. *Educ:* Sedbergh; Malvern. President, James Fisher and Sons Limited (Chairman, 1915–76); Chm., Barrow Housing Company Ltd. Mem. Council, Chamber of Shipping of UK, 1935–74; Chm., Coasting & Home Trade Tramp Section, Chamber of Shipping of UK, 1935–39; Mem., Transport Adv. Council, 1934–39; Chm., Coastal Shipping Adv. Cttee, 1957–62; Dir Coasting and Short Sea Shipping, Min. of War Transport, 1939–46; Chm. United Maritime Authority, European Area, 1945–46; Pres. Baltic and International Maritime Conf., 1951–53. FICS. Freeman: Shipwrights' Co.; Borough of Barrow-in-Furness. Served European War, 1914–18, with King's Own Royal Lancaster Regt (Staff Capt. 154 Inf. Brigade, 51st Div., 1915–16). Comdr, Order of Orange Nassau (Netherlands); Officer, Order of Merite Maritime (France); Kt Comdr, Order of Isabel la Católica (Spain); Comdr, Order of Infante Dom Henrique (Portugal). *Address:* Blakeholme Wray, Newby Bridge, Cumbria. *T:* 345. *Club:* Windermere Royal Yacht (Windermere). *Died* 7 *Nov.* 1983.

**FISHER, Ven. Leslie Gravatt;** Archdeacon of Chester and Canon Residentiary of Chester Cathedral, 1965–75; Vice-Dean, 1973–75;

Archdeacon Emeritus since 1975; *b* 18 Aug. 1906; *m* 1935, Dorothy Minnie (*née* Nash); two *d*. *Educ:* Hertford Grammar Sch.; London Coll. of Divinity. ALCD 1933. Deacon, 1933; Priest 1934. Curate of Emmanuel, Northwood, 1933–36; Vicar of St Michael and All Angels, Blackheath Park, 1936–39; Rector of Bermondsey, 1939–47; Curate-in-charge, Christ Church, Bermondsey, 1942–47; Chap., Bermondsey Med. Mission Hosp., 1946–47; Home Sec., CMS, and Licensed Preacher, Diocese of Southwark, 1947–65; Licence to Officiate, Bromley, Dio. of Rochester, 1948–. Chm., Church Information Cttee, 1966–75. *Recreations:* music and photography. *Address:* 14 Lamb Park, Chagford, Newton Abbot, Devon. *T:* Chagford 3308. *Died* 16 *June* 1988.

**FISHER, Rear-Adm. Ralph Lindsay,** CB 1957; DSO 1940; OBE 1941; DSC 1943; *b* 18 June 1903; *s* of F. Lindsay Fisher, CBE, one-time Pres. Inst. of Chartered Accountants, and Ethel Owen Pugh, Caernarvon; *m* 1934, Ursula Carver, Torquay; five *d*. *Educ:* Osborne and Dartmouth. First went to sea, 1920; Commanded: HMS Wakeful, 1940 (Dunkirk, DSO); Musketeer, 1943–45 (sinking of Scharnhorst, DSC); Solebay, 1947–48; Indefatigable, 1952–54. Naval Staff Course, 1934; Jt Services Staff Coll., 1949; Flag Officer Ground Trng (Home Air Comd), 1954–57. Retd, 1957. *Recreation:* sailing. *Address:* Scotnish Cottage, by Lochgilphead, Argyll. *T:* Tayvallich 646. *Clubs:* Naval and Military, Royal Cruising.
*Died* 19 *April* 1988.

**FISHER, Prof. Reginald Brettauer,** CBE 1966; Professor of Biochemistry, University of Edinburgh, 1959–76, Dean of Faculty of Medicine, 1972–75; engaged in research, Medical Research Council, 1976–79, and postgraduate teaching, since 1976; *b* 13 Feb. 1907; *s* of late Joseph Sudbury and Louie Fisher; *m* 1929, Mary, *d* of late C. W. Saleeby; three *d* (one *s* decd). Educ: King Edward VII Sch., Sheffield; St John's Coll., Oxford. MA, DPhil (Oxon), 1933. University Demonstrator in Biochemistry, Oxford, 1933–59; Rockefeller Travelling Fellow, 1939; Research Officer (on secondment), Min. of Home Security, 1942; Air Ministry, 1943–45; Consultant, US War Dept, 1945. Member: Physiological Soc.; Royal Society of Medicine. *Publications:* Protein Metabolism, 1954; contributions to: Biochem. Jl; Jl Physiol.; Jl Biol. Chem.; Am. Jl Physiol., etc. *Address:* University Laboratory of Physiology, Parks Road, Oxford. *Died* 11 *Nov.* 1986.

**FISHER, Prof. William Bayne,** DUP; Professor of Geography, University of Durham, 1956–81, then Emeritus; first Principal of the Graduate Society, Durham University, 1965–81; *b* 24 Sept. 1916; unmarried. *Educ:* Darwen Gram. Sch.; Universities of Manchester, Louvain, Paris. Research Scholar, Univ. of Manchester, 1937; RAF 1940; Liaison Officer to French in Syria and Lebanon, 1944; Asst Lectr, Univ. of Manchester, 1946; Lectr, Univ. of Aberdeen, 1947; Carnegie Fellow, 1951; Reader, Univ. of Durham, 1954; Dir, Centre of Middle Eastern and Islamic Studies, Durham Univ., 1962–65; Vis. Prof., Leuven Univ., 1978–79. Chm. of Governors, Durham High Sch. for Girls, 1981–. Murchison Award, RGS, 1973. *Publications:* Les Mouvements de population en Normandie, 1940; The Middle East, a Physical Social and Regional Geography, 1951; (with H. Bowen-Jones) Spain, a geographical background; (with H. Bowen-Jones and J. C. Dewdney) Malta, 1961; (Ed) The Cambridge History of Iran, Vol I (The Land of Iran), 1968; (with J. I. Clarke) Populations of the Middle East and North Africa, 1972; (with P. W. Kent) Resources, Environment and the Future, 1982; various articles in periodicals and works of reference. *Recreations:* music, travel, geographical gastronomy. *Address:* Abbey View, 42 South Street, Durham. *T:* Durham 64291. *Club:* Royal Commonwealth Society.
*Died* 29 *June* 1984.

**FISK, James B(rown);** Retired; President, Bell Telephone Laboratories, Inc., NJ, USA, 1973–74; *b* 30 Aug. 1910; *s* of Henry James and Bertha Brown Fisk; *m* 1938, Cynthia Hoar; three *s*. *Educ:* Mass. Inst Technology (BS, PhD); Trinity Coll., Cambridge (Proctor Travelling Fellow). Soc. of Fellows, Harvard Univ., 1936–38; Associate Prof. of Physics, University of North Carolina, 1938–39; Gordon McKay Prof. and Senior Fellow, Harvard Univ., 1948–49; Dir of Research, US Atomic Energy Commn, 1947–48; Bell Telephone Laboratories: 1939–47 and 1949–; Vice-Pres. Research, 1954–55; Executive Vice-Pres., 1955–59; Pres., 1959–73. President's Science Advisory Cttee, 1952–60; Consultant, 1960–73; Gen. Advisory Cttee, Atomic Energy Commission, 1952–58; Chm. Geneva Technical Discussions on Nuclear Tests, 1958. Presidental Certificate of Merit, 1946. Industrial Research Inst. Medal, 1963; Fellow: Amer. Acad. of Arts and Sciences; Amer. Phys. Soc.; IEEE; Member: Nat. Acad. of Sciences; Amer. Philosoph. Soc.; Nat. Acad. of Engrg. Washington Award, Western Soc. of Engineers, 1968; Midwest Res. Inst. Citation, 1968; Founder's Medal, Nat. Acad. of Engrg, 1975; Herbert Hoover Medal, 1976. Holds several Hon. Degrees. *Publications:* various scientific and technical articles in: Proceedings Royal Society, Bell System Technical Journal, Physical Review. *Recreations:* gardening, mountain climbing, golf. *Address:* Bell Telephone Laboratories,

Murray Hill, New Jersey 07974, USA. *T:* 201–582–4471 (Murray Hill, NJ). *Clubs:* Harvard (NY City); Ausable (NY); Somerset Hills (NJ). *Died 10 Aug. 1981.*

**FISON, Sir (Frank Guy) Clavering,** Kt 1957; JP; DL; Chairman, Fisons Ltd, 1929–62; *b* 1892; *er surv. s* of late J. O. Fison, of Stutton Hall, Ipswich; *m* 1922, Evelyn Alice (OBE 1964), *er d* of late F. L. Bland Rookwood, Copdock, Ipswich; two *d. Educ:* Charterhouse; Christ Church, Oxford. Served War: Lieut 4 Bn (T), Suffolk Regt, 1914–20 (despatches 1916); Major (Temp.) RAF, 1918; Captain 6 Bn Suffolk Regt, 1939–40. Joined Fisons, 1919; retired 1962. MP (U) Woodbridge Div. of Suffolk, 1929–31. Hon. Life Pres., Fisons Ltd. JP East Suffolk, 1942; High Sheriff 1942, DL 1958, Suffolk. *Address:* Crepping Hall, Stutton, Ipswich, Suffolk IP9 2SZ. *Died 13 April 1985.*

**FITCH, (Ernest) Alan,** JP; DL; *b* 10 March 1915; *e s* of late Rev. and of Mrs E. W. Fitch; *m* 1950, Nancy Maude, *y d* of late R. Kennard Davis; one *s* one *d. Educ:* Kingswood Sch., Bath. Was formerly Mineworker. MP (Lab) Wigan, June 1958–1983; Asst Whip (paid), 1964–66; a Lord Comr of the Treasury, 1966–69; Vice-Chamberlain, HM Household, Oct. 1969–June 1970; Opposition Whip, 1970–71. Mem., Chairmen's Panel, 1971–78; Mem., European Parlt, 1978–79. Chm., North West Regional Council of the Labour Party. Chm., Wigan Groundwork Trust, 1983–. JP Lancs, 1958; DL Greater Manchester, 1985. Hon. Freeman, Co. Borough of Wigan, 1974. *Recreations:* reading, walking. *Address:* 117 The Avenue, Leigh, Lancs WN7 1HR. *T:* Leigh 673992. *Died 7 Aug. 1985.*

**FITTON, James,** RA 1954 (ARA 1944); FSIA; painter; *b* Oldham, Lancs, 1899; *s* of James Fitton and Janet Chadwick; *m* 1928, Margaret Cook; one *s* one *d.* First one man show, Arthur Tooth, New Bond Street, 1933. Member, London Group, 1932–52. Works represented in exhibns: British Art since Whistler, 1939; London Group Jubilee Exhibn, Tate Gallery, 1964. Works in collections of: Contemporary Art Soc.; Chantry Bequest (Tate Gall.); V&A; British Museum; Imperial War Museum; National Gallery of Wales; Manchester, Nottingham, Aberdeen and numerous public and private collections. Chief Assessor to Min. of Educn Nat. Diploma of Design (Pictorial, Painting and Industrial Design), 1940–65. Served on: Arts Council (Art Panel); Colstream Cttee; Summerson Cttee; RCA Council; Chelsea Coll. of Art; Central Coll. of Art and Design; Camberwell Sch. of Art. Mem., latterly Chm., Stamp Adv. Cttee, from 1945 until completion of Definitive Stamp. Drawings and Posters for Min. of Food, 1939–45; London Transport (Underground Posters); Murals for Festival of Britain (Seaside Section). Illustrations for a variety of magazines. Trustee: British Museum, 1968–75; Royal Academy of Arts; Hon. Surveyor, Dulwich Picture Gall.; Governor: Dulwich Coll.; Dulwich Coll. Prep. Sch. Trust. *Publication:* The First Six Months Are the Worst, 1939. *Address:* 10 Pond Cottages, College Road, Dulwich Village, SE21 7LE. *T:* 01–693 1158. *Died 2 May 1982.*

**FITTS, Sir Clive (Hamilton),** Kt 1963; MD Melbourne, FRCP, FRACP, DTM Sydney; retired 1978; formerly Consulting Physician to: Royal Melbourne Hospital; Royal Women's Hospital; Austin Hospital for Chronic Diseases; Victorian Tuberculosis Service; *b* 14 July 1900; *s* of Hamilton Fitts and Katherine Fitts (*née* Pardey); *m* 1939, Yrsa E., *d* of Prof. W. A. Osborne; two *s* three *d. Educ:* Scotch Coll. and Melbourne Church of England Gram. Sch., Melbourne; Trinity Coll., University of Melbourne. Post-Graduate: England, Switzerland, USA; Carnegie Scholarship, 1948. Tudor Edwards Meml Lecture, RCP, 1967. Member: Brit. Cardiac Soc.; Brit. Thoracic Soc.; Med. Soc., London; Pres. Cardiac Soc. of Aust. and NZ, 1960; Vice-Pres. RACP, 1958; Hon. Life Mem., Nat. Heart Foundn of Australia, 1980 (Vice-Pres. and Mem. Exec. Cttee, 1960–65); formerly Mem. Council: University of Melbourne; Melbourne C of E Gram. Sch.; Chm. Felton Bequest Cttee; First Pres., Nat. Gall. Soc.; Hon. Life Mem., Friends of the Baillieu Library, Univ. of Melbourne, 1979; Fellow, Trinity Coll., Univ. of Melbourne, 1980. Formerly Mem. Commonwealth Drug Evaluation Cttee. Major AAMC Reserve. *Publications:* various papers on diseases of heart and lungs in medical journals. *Recreations:* mountaineering, tennis (represented University of Melbourne, and Victoria), fly fishing. *Address:* Tucks Road, Main Ridge, Victoria 3928, Australia. *T:* (059) 89.6003. *Clubs:* Beefsteak; Melbourne, Beefsteak (Melbourne). *Died 7 Feb. 1984.*

**FITZGERALD, Brian Percy Seymour V.;** *see* Vesey-Fitzgerald.

**FITZGERALD, Rev. (Sir) Edward Thomas,** 3rd Bt *cr* 1903; a Roman Catholic priest; *b* 7 March 1912; *S* father, Sir John Joseph Fitzgerald, 2nd Bt, 1957, but does not use title. *Heir: b* Rev. Daniel Patrick Fitzgerald, *b* 28 June 1916. *Died 13 Aug. 1988.*

**FITZGERALD, Terence;** Chief Charity Commissioner, 1975–82; *b* 20 March 1919. *Educ:* Allhallows Sch.; Exeter Coll., Oxford; Middle Temple. Royal Artillery, 1940–46; attached Royal Indian Artillery, 1941–45. Home Office, 1948; Imperial Defence Coll., 1962; HM Treasury, 1963–64; Asst Under-Sec. of State, Home Office, 1964–75.

*Address:* 95 Peaslands Road, Sidmouth, Devon.
*Died 4 July 1985.*

**FitzGERALD, Sir William James,** Kt 1944; MC; QC (N Rhodesia) 1936; *b* Cappawhite, Co. Tipperary, May 1894; *s* of late Joseph FitzGerald, MB, Cappawhite; *m* 1st, 1933, Erica (marr. diss. 1946), *d* of F. J. Clarke, Chikupi Ranch, Northern Rhodesia; one *s*; 2nd, Cynthia Mary Mangnall, *d* of late W. Foster, OBE, Jerusalem; one step *s. Educ:* Blackrock Coll.; Trinity Coll., Dublin (Hon. LLD 1960). Served European War, Durham Light Infantry and XV Corps Mounted Troops (MC and Croix de Guerre); BA 1919; Barrister-at-Law, King's Inns, Dublin, 1922, and Middle Temple; Nigerian Administrative Service, 1920; Police Magistrate, Lagos, 1921; Crown Counsel, Nigeria, 1924; Solicitor-Gen., N Rhodesia, 1932; Attorney-Gen., N Rhodesia, 1933; Palestine, 1937–43; Chief Justice of Palestine, 1944–48. Pres. Lands Tribunal, 1950–65. *Address:* 51 Vicarage Court, Vicarage Gate, W8 4HE. *Club:* Athenæum. *Died 4 July 1989.*

**FitzGIBBON, (Robert Louis) Constantine (Lee-Dillon);** writer; *b* 8 June 1919; *s* of Comdr Francis Lee-Dillon FitzGibbon, RN, and Georgette Folsom, Lenox, Mass, USA; *m* 1967, Marjorie (*née* Steele); one *d*; (by a previous marr. to Marion (*née* Gutmann) one *s*, *b* 1961). *Educ:* Wellington Coll.; Munich Univ.; Sorbonne; Exeter Coll., Oxford. Served War of 1939–45, British Army (Oxford and Bucks Light Infantry), 1939–42; US Army, 1942–46. Schoolmaster, Saltus Gram. Sch., Bermuda, 1946–47; then independent writer. Mem. Irish Acad. of Letters. FRSL; Fellow, Guggenheim Memorial Foundn, 1966. *Publications:* The Arabian Bird, 1949; The Iron Hoop, 1950; Dear Emily, 1952; Miss Finnigan's Fault, Norman Douglas, The Holiday, 1953; The Little Tour, 1954; The Shirt of Nessus, 1955; In Love and War, 1956; The Blitz, 1957; Paradise Lost and More, 1959; When the Kissing had to Stop, 1960, new edn (posthumous), 1989; Going to the River, 1963; Random Thoughts of a Fascist Hyena, 1963; The Life of Dylan Thomas, 1965; (ed) Selected Letters of Dylan Thomas, 1966; Through the Minefield, 1967; Denazification, 1969; High Heroic, 1969; Out of the Lion's Paw, 1969; Red Hand: The Ulster Colony, 1971; The Devil at Work (play), 1971; A Concise History of Germany, 1972; In the Bunker, 1973; The Life and Times of Eamon de Valera, 1973; The Golden Age, 1976; Secret Intelligence, 1976; Man in Aspic, 1977; Teddy in the Tree, 1977; Drink, 1979; The Rat Report, 1980; The Irish in Ireland, 1982; and trans from French, German and Italian. Contributor to Encyc. Brit., newspapers and periodicals in Britain, America and elsewhere. *Address:* Newbridge Mews, Sandymount, Dublin 4, Ireland. *Club:* Beefsteak. *Died 23 March 1983.*

**FITZHERBERT, Cuthbert;** *b* 24 May 1899; British; 4th *s* of William Joseph Fitzherbert-Brockholes, CBE, and Blanche Winifred Mary, 2nd *d* of late Maj.-Gen. Hon. Sir Henry Hugh Clifford, VC, KCMG, CB; *m* 1930, Barbara (*d* 1975), *e d* of Henry Scrope, Danby; three *s* three *d* (and one *s* decd). *Educ:* Oratory Sch.; New Coll., Oxford (BA). Commissioned Coldstream Guards, 1917; served 1917–18 in European War of 1914–18, in 1st Bn Coldstream Guards (wounded). Joined Barclays Bank Ltd, 1922; Union Bank of Manchester, 1923–26; Local Dir, Barclays Bank Ltd, Darlington, 1926; Local Dir, Barclays Bank Ltd, Birmingham, 1939. Served War of 1939–45, with Coldstream Guards, 1940–44. Returned as Gen. Man. (Staff), Barclays Bank Ltd, 1944; a Director: Barclays Bank Ltd (Vice-Chm., 1948–64), 1948–72; Barclays Bank DCO, retd 1971; formerly Dir, London Montrose Investment Trust, retd 1972. *Publications:* Henry Clifford VC, his letters and sketches from the Crimea (ed), 1953; The Prince and the Pedlar (stalking memories), 1977. *Recreations:* shooting, stalking. *Address:* St Wilfrid's, 29 Tite Street, Chelsea, SW3 4JX. *T:* 01–352 3011. *Club:* Cavalry and Guards. *Died 23 July 1986.*

**FitzHERBERT, Sir John (Richard Frederick),** 8th Bt, *cr* 1784; TD; *b* 15 Sept. 1913; *s* of Ven. Henry E. FitzHerbert, sometime Archdeacon of Derby, and Hon. Margaret Elinor (*d* 1957), *d* of 3rd Baron Heytesbury; *S* uncle, Sir William FitzHerbert, 7th Bt, 1963; *m* 1957, Kathleen Anna Rees; no *c. Educ:* Charterhouse; Royal Agricultural Coll., Cirencester. Served War of 1939–45, Sherwood Foresters (TA). FLAS 1950; FRICS 1970. *Heir: nephew* Richard Ranulph FitzHerbert, *b* 2 Nov. 1963. *Address:* Tissington Hall, Ashbourne, Derbyshire. *T:* Parwich 246. *Club:* Derby County (Derby). *Died 21 March 1989.*

**FitzHUGH, His Honour James,** QC 1973; a Circuit Judge, 1976–88; *b* 2 April 1917; *s* of T. J. FitzHugh and S. FitzHugh (formerly Jocelyn); *m* 1955, Shelagh (*née* Bury), *d* of R. W. and B. Bury, Lytham St Annes. *Educ:* St Bede's Coll., Manchester; Manchester Univ. (BA (Admin)); London Univ. (LLB). Commissioned in Supplementary Reserve of Officers, RA, 1938; War of 1939–45: Captain, GSO. Called to Bar, Gray's Inn; Mem., Northern Circuit, 1948–88. *Recreations:* travel, golf. *Address:* 186 St Leonard's Road East, St Annes on the Sea, Lytham St Annes, Lancs. *T:* St Annes 723068. *Club:* Royal Lytham and St Annes Golf.
*Died 27 Feb. 1989.*

**FITZMAURICE, Sir Gerald (Gray),** GCMG 1960 (KCMG 1954; CMG 1946); QC 1957; International Law Consultant; *b* 24 Oct. 1901; *s* of late Vice-Admiral Sir Maurice Fitzmaurice, KCVO, CB, CMG, and Mabel Gertrude, *y d* of late S. W. Gray; *m* 1933, Alice Evelina Alexandra Sandberg; one *s* (and one *s* decd). *Educ:* Malvern; Gonville and Caius Coll., Cambridge (BA, LLB 1924). Called to Bar, Gray's Inn, 1925; Bencher, 1961; practised, 1925–29; 3rd Legal Adviser to Foreign Office, 1929; seconded as Legal Adviser to Ministry of Economic Warfare, 1939–43; 2nd Legal Adviser, FO, 1945–53; Legal Adviser, FO, 1953–60; Judge of Internat. Court of Justice, 1960–73; Judge of European Court of Human Rights, 1974–80. Legal Adviser to UK Delegations, San Francisco UN Charter Conference, 1945; Paris Peace Conference, 1946. UN Assembly, 1946, 1948–59, Japanese Peace Conference, San Francisco, 1951, and Berlin and Manila Confs, 1954; Counsel for HM Govt in several cases before the International Court of Justice at The Hague; Member: Permanent Court of Arbitration, 1954–80; UN Internat. Law Commission, 1955–60 (Pres. 1959); Mem. Inst. International Law (Pres., 1967–69); Pres. Grotius Soc., 1956–60. Hon. Fellow, Gonville and Caius Coll., Cambridge, 1961. Hon. LLD: Edinburgh, 1970; Cantab, 1972; Hon. DJur Utrecht, 1976. *Publications:* articles in British Year Book of International Law, 1931–58, Hague Recueil, 1948 and 1957 and in other legal journals. *Address:* (home) 3 Gray's Inn Square, WC1R 5AH; (professional) 2 Hare Court, Temple, EC4. *Clubs:* Athenæum, United Oxford & Cambridge University.

*Died 7 Sept. 1982.*

**FitzROY, Charles;** late 2nd Lieutenant Royal Horse Guards and Pioneer Corps; *b* 3 Jan. 1904; *o s* of 4th Baron Southampton, OBE, and late Lady Hilda Mary Dundas, *d* of 1st Marquess of Zetland; *S* father, 1958, as 5th Baron Southampton, but disclaimed his title for life, 16 March 1964; *m* 1st, 1927, Margaret (*d* 1931), *d* of Prebendary H. Mackworth Drake, Vicar of Paignton; one *s*; 2nd, 1940, Mrs Joan Leslie (marr. diss., 1944); 3rd, 1951, Rachel Christine, *d* of Charles Zaman, Lille, France. *Educ:* Harrow. Served Royal Horse Guards, 1923–25; re-employed, 1940, with RA, Pioneer Corps, 1941. Joint-master, Grove Fox-hounds, 1930–32. *Heir:* (to disclaimed barony): *s* Hon. Charles James FitzRoy [*b* 12 Aug. 1928; *m* 1951, Pamela Anne, *d* of E. Henniker, Maidenhead, Berks; one *s* one *d* (and one *s* decd)]. *Address:* Preluna Hotel, Sliema, Malta.

*Died 1989.*

**FLAHIFF, His Eminence Cardinal George Bernard,** CC (Canada) 1974; CSB, DD; Former Archbishop of Winnipeg; *b* Paris, Ontario, 26 Oct. 1905; *s* of John James Flahiff and Eleanor (*née* Fleming). *Educ:* St Michael's Coll. (BA); St Basil's Seminary; University of Strasbourg; Ecole des Chartes and Ecole des Hautes Etudes, Paris, 1931–35; Professor of Mediæval History, University of Toronto Graduate School and Pontifical Institute of Mediæval Studies, 1935–54; Superior General, Basilian Fathers, 1954–61; Archbishop of Winnipeg, 1961–82. Cardinal, 1969. Member: Société de l'Ecole des Chartes (Paris); American Catholic Historical Society; Mediæval Academy of America. Hon. LLD: St John Fisher Coll., Rochester, NY, 1964; Seattle, 1965; Notre Dame, 1969; Manitoba, 1969; Windsor, 1970; Toronto, 1972; Hon. DD: Winnipeg, 1972; St Francis Xavier, 1973; Laval, 1974; Univ. of St Thomas, Houston, 1977. *Address:* 81 St Mary Street, Toronto, Ontario M5S 1J4, Canada.

*Died 22 Aug. 1989.*

**FLEETWOOD-HESKETH, Charles Peter F.;** *see* Hesketh.

**FLEMING, Amy Margaret,** MD, DSc, FRCOG; Hon. Consulting Obstetrician and Gynæcologist: St Mary's Hospital, Harrow Road; St Mary Abbot's Hospital, Kensington; Teacher in Queen Charlotte's Hospital, and Institute of Obstetrics and Gynæcology, University of London; *d* of Charles Friskin Fleming and Margaret Burns Elphinstone Waddell. *Educ:* Universities of Glasgow, Vienna, Tübingen. Formerly Prof. of Obstetrics and Gynæcology, University of London; Senior Asst Surgeon Royal Samaritan Hospital for Women, Glasgow, and Royal Maternity and Women's Hospital, Glasgow. *Publications:* papers in Transactions of the Royal Society of Edinburgh, and other medical monographs. *Recreation:* gardening. *Address:* Glentress, Innerleithen Road, Peebles, Scotland EH45 8BE. *T:* Peebles 20518.

*Died 7 Jan. 1981.*

**FLEMING, Dame Celia;** *see* Johnson, Dame C.

**FLEMING, Sir Charles (Alexander),** KBE 1977 (OBE 1964); FRS 1967; Honorary Fellow, Research School of Earth Sciences, Victoria University of Wellington, since 1986; Research Associate, National Museum of New Zealand, since 1983, and New Zealand Geological Survey, since 1986; *b* 9 Sept. 1916; *s* of Geo. H. Fleming, Auckland, NZ; *m* 1941, Margaret Alison, *d* of S. G. Chambers, Auckland; three *d*. *Educ:* King's Coll., Auckland; University of Auckland. Boyhood interest in birds and shell-collecting led to participation in Auckland Mus. expedns, 1933–35; student fieldwork on birds of NZ and Chatham Is (basis of papers publ. 1939); Asst Geologist, NZ Geol Survey, 1940; subseq. Palæontologist, Sen. Palæontologist, and Chief Palæontologist, DSIR, 1953–77. Overseas service as

coastwatcher, Auckland Is, 1942–43. Hon. Lectr in Geology, Victoria Univ. of Wellington, 1974–86. Pres., Ornithol. Soc. NZ, 1948–49; NZ Delegate: Internat. Geol Congresses, 1948, 1960; British Commonwealth Conf. on Geology and Mineral Resources, 1948; Mem. Bd of Trustees: Nat. Art Gall. and National (formerly Dominion) Mus., 1954–76 (Chm., Mus. Council, 1972–75); Nat. Library, 1971–72; NZ Fauna Protection Adv. Council; NZ Nat. Commn for Unesco, 1966–70; Nat. Parks Authority, 1970–81; Environmental Council, 1970–73. President: Internat. Paleont. Union (Oceania Filial), 1964–68; Aust. and NZ Assoc. for Advancement of Science, 1968–70. FRSNZ 1952 (Pres. 1962–66); Fellow, Art Galls and Museums Assoc. of NZ, 1956; Corresp. Fellow, American Ornithologists' Union, 1962; Hon. FGS 1967; For. Mem., Amer. Philosophical Soc., 1973; Hon. FZS 1979; Sen. ANZAC Fellow, 1979. Several scientific prizes and awards. *Publications:* (ed) Checklist of New Zealand Birds, 1953; trans. Hochstetter's Geology of New Zealand, 1959; Marwick's Illustrations of New Zealand Shells, 1966; The Geological History of New Zealand and its Life, 1979; George Edward Lodge: Unpublished Bird Paintings, 1982; geol and palæontol bulletins; about 300 research papers on mollusca, cicadas, birds, geology, palæontology, biogeography. *Recreations:* recorded music, natural history. *Address:* Balivean, 42 Wadestown Road, Wellington, NZ. *T:* Wellington 737–288.

*Died 11 Sept. 1987.*

**FLEMING, Prof. Charles Mann,** CBE 1964; Emeritus Professor of Administrative Medicine, since 1971 (Professor 1960–71), Dean of the Faculty of Medicine, 1959–70, and Dean of Postgraduate Medicine, 1970–72, in University of Glasgow; *b* 1 March 1904; *y s* of John Somerville Fleming and Christina Taylor Gerard, Glasgow; *m* 1930, Margaret Hamilton Barrie, *er d* of George Simpson, Newfoundland; one *d*. *Educ:* Hillhead High Sch; Glasgow Univ. MA 1924, MB, ChB 1929, MD 1933 (Glasgow); MRCPEd 1945, FRCPEd 1952, FRFPS (G.) 1959, FRCP (Glasgow) 1962. Hon. FRCGP 1964. Regional MO, 1937–39, Hospital Officer (Eastern Dist, Scotland), 1939–46, Principal MO, 1946–59, Dept of Health for Scotland. Convener Post-Grad. Med. Board, University of Glasgow, 1959–72; Chm., Western Regional Cttee for Postgrad. Medical Educn, 1967–72; Member: General Medical Council, 1961–73; WHO Expert Advisory Panel on Organisation of Medical Care, 1959–76; Royal Commission on Med. Educn, 1966–68; Central Cttee on Postgraduate Med. Educn (GB), 1967–71; Scottish Council for Postgraduate Med. Educn, 1970–72. Addtl Mem. Gen. Dental Council, 1965–73. *Publications:* contributions to medical journals. *Recreation:* golf. *Address:* 8 Thorn Road, Bearsden, Glasgow. *T:* Bearsden 2810.

*Died 15 March 1985.*

**FLEMING, Hon. Donald Methuen,** PC (Canada) 1957; QC (Ontario) 1944; *b* Exeter, Ont., 23 May 1905; *s* of Louis Charles and Maud Margaret Wright Fleming; *m* 1933, Alice Mildred Watson, Toronto; two *s* one *d*. *Educ:* public schools and Collegiate Inst., Galt; Univ. of Toronto (BA, LLB); Osgoode Hall Law Sch. Called to Bar, Ontario, 1928; subsequently practised in Toronto, 1928–57; Counsel to Blake, Cassels and Graydon, Barristers and Solicitors, Toronto, 1963–67. MP for Toronto-Eglinton, 1945–63; Minister of Finance and Receiver-General, 1957–62; Minister of Justice and Attorney-General of Canada, 1962–63. A Governor, Internat. Bank and IMF, 1957–63; Chairman: Commonwealth Finance Ministers' Conf., Mont Tremblant, Province of Quebec, 1957; Commonwealth Trade and Economic Conf., Montreal, 1958; OECD, 1961, 1962; Leader: delegn of Canadian Ministers to meetings of US-Canada Jt Trade and Economic Cttee, Washington, 1957, 1960, 1961 (Chm. Ottawa meeting, 1959, 1962), and meeting of Canada-Japan Jt Cttee of Ministers, Tokyo, 1963; Canadian delegn to OEEC Confs, Paris, 1960; Canadian delegate: NATO Conf. of Heads of Govt, Paris, 1957; NATO Ministerial Confs, 1958, 1959, 1961; Commonwealth Parly Confs, London, 1948, Ottawa, 1952, Nairobi, 1954. Has taken part in numerous parly, political, municipal and civic welfare activities and in church affairs. Man. Dir, Bank of Nova Scotia Trust Cos; General Counsel to Bank of Nova Scotia in Bahamas, 1968–80; Chm., M&G (Cayman) Ltd. Mem. Senate, 1944–48, Bd of Governors, 1964–68, Univ. of Toronto. Past Pres., Toronto YMCA. Hon. Mem., Canadian Legion; Hon. Life Mem., Canadian Bar Assoc. DCL hc Bishop's Univ., 1960; LLD hc Waterloo Lutheran Univ., 1967. *Publications:* So Very Near (political memoirs), 2 vols, 1985; numerous works and articles on legal subjects; contribs to legal periodicals including Canadian Encyclopedic Digest, Canadian Bar Review, Canadian Abridgement, etc. *Recreations:* all branches of sport. *Address:* 21 Country Lane, Willowdale, Toronto, Ont M2L 1E1, Canada. *Clubs:* Canadian (Pres., 1964), Empire, Granite, National, Queen's, Rosedale Golf, Toronto Cricket (Toronto).

*Died 31 Dec. 1986.*

**FLEMING, Rt. Rev. Launcelot;** *see* Fleming, Rt Rev. W. L. S.

**FLEMING, Prof. Marston Greig,** BSc; PhD; FEng; FIMM; Senior Research Fellow, Imperial College of Science and Technology; Professor of Mineral Technology in the University of London

(Imperial College), 1961–80, Emeritus 1980; Consultant; *b* 10 Jan. 1913; *s* of late Alexander Greig Fleming, Montreal; *m* 1951, E. Box, painter; two *s* one *d* (by a previous marriage). *Educ:* Westmount High Sch.; Queen's Univ., Canada. Metallurgist with Canadian goldmining companies, 1936–41. RCAF navigator, 1941–46; Flight Lieut, 1943; Imperial Coll., Royal Sch. of Mines: Lecturer, 1946–51, Senior Lecturer, 1951–58, Reader, 1958–61; Head of Dept of Mining and Mineral Technology, 1967–74; Dean, 1968–71. Pro-Rector, Imperial Coll., 1974–79; Head of Dept of Mineral Resources Engrg, 1979–80. Mineral processing consultant to governments, mining companies and to HM Govt, at various times, 1946–. Chm., Mineral Processing Cttee, DSIR and Min. of Technology, 1959–66; Member: Cttee on Overseas Geology and Mining, DTC, 1962–63; Steering Cttee, Warren Spring Lab., 1966–68. Chm. Advisory Panel, BCURA, 1961–66; IMM Council, 1962–83, Vice-Pres., 1968–71, Pres., 1971–72; Member: Cttee on Mineral Planning Control, DoE, 1972–75; Chemicals and Minerals Requirements Bd, Dept of Industry, 1972–75. British rep., Scientific Cttee, Internat. Mineral Processing Congress, France, 1963, USA, 1964, USSR, 1968, Czechoslovakia, 1970, London 1973 (Chm., 1973–75), Italy 1975, Poland 1979; Canada 1982; Council of Mining and Metall. Instns, 1969– (Vice-Chm., 1971–76; Chm., 1976–). Dir, UNESCO Regional Course, Benares, 1964; Chm., Brighton Conf. on the Technologist in the Mineral Ind. of the Future, 1969. Member: Governing Body, Imperial Coll., 1968–80 (Fellow, 1982); Ct of Governors, Camborne Sch. of Mines, 1971–82. Hon. ARSM, 1966. 10th Julius Werner Lectr, 1973. IMM Gold Medal, 1981. *Publications:* Identification of Mineral Grains (with M. P. Jones), 1965; papers in a number of scientific and technical journals, etc. *Address:* Zoffany House, 65 Strand-on-the-Green, W4. *Club:* Garrick.

*Died 6 Dec. 1982.*

**FLEMING, Patrick Lyons;** retired Director of Companies; *b* Aberdeen, 3 April 1905; *er s* of late Col Frank Fleming, DSO; *m* 1929, Eleanor (*d* 1970), *d* of late H. G. Tapper; two *d. Educ:* Shrewsbury; Lincoln Coll., Oxford (Schol., MA). Dir of numerous companies, mainly connected with what became the Drayton Gp, 1934–78; Council Member: Inst. of Directors, 1948–75 (Treasurer 1974–75); Aims of Industry, 1952–75; Chm. of Epsom Division Conservative Assoc., 1949–50. *Publications:* sundry contribs to financial jls. *Recreations:* reading, formerly rowing and field sports. *Address:* Lurley Manor, Tiverton, Devon.

*Died 17 Feb. 1985.*

**FLEMING, Rt. Rev. (William) Launcelot (Scott),** KCVO 1976; DD (Lambeth); MA (Cambridge), MS (Yale); FRSE; *b* 7 Aug. 1906; *y s* of late Robert Alexander Fleming, MD, LLD; *m* 1965, Jane, *widow* of Anthony Agutter. *Educ:* Rugby Sch.; Trinity Hall and Westcott House, Cambridge; Yale Univ. (Commonwealth Fund Fellow, 1929–31). Deacon, 1933; Priest, 1934; Expeditions to Iceland and Spitzbergen, 1932 and 1933; Chaplain and Geologist, British Graham Land Expedition to the Antarctic, 1934–37; Polar Medal, 1935–37; Examining Chaplain to Bishop of Southwark, 1937–49, to Bishop of St Albans, 1940–43, to Bishop of Hereford, 1942–49; Fellow and Chaplain, Trinity Hall, Cambridge, 1933–49, Dean, 1937–49; Director of Scott Polar Research Institute, Cambridge, 1947–49; Bishop of Portsmouth, 1949–59; Bishop of Norwich, 1959–71; Dean of Windsor, 1971–76; Register, Order of the Garter, 1971–76; Domestic Chaplain to the Queen, 1971–76. Chaplain RNVR, HMS King Alfred, 1940; HMS Queen Elizabeth, 1940–43; HMS Ganges, 1943–44; Director of Service Ordination Candidates, 1944–46. Chairman: Church of England Youth Council, 1950–61; Archbishops' Advisers for Needs and Resources, 1963–73. Parly Gp for World Govt: Vice-Chm., 1969–71; Chm., Associate Members, 1971–76. Member: Council, Univ. of E Anglia, 1964–71; Royal Commn on Environmental Pollution, 1970–73; Chairman of Governors, Portsmouth Grammar Sch., 1950–59; Canford Sch., 1954–60; Mem., Governing Body, United World Coll. of the Atlantic; Visitor, Bryanston Sch., 1984– (Governor, 1946–83); Pres., Young Explorers Trust, 1976–79; Trustee: Trident Trust, 1972–86; Prince's Trust, 1976–87. Hon. Chaplain, RNR (RNVR 1950). Hon. Fellow, Trinity Hall, Cambridge, 1956; Hon. Vice-President, Royal Geographical Society, 1961. Hon. DCL Univ. of East Anglia, 1976. *Address:* Tithe Barn, Poyntington, near Sherborne, Dorset DT9 4LF. *T:* Corton Denham (096322) 479. *Died 30 July 1990.*

**FLEMMING, Cecil Wood,** CBE 1964 (OBE 1944); FRCS, MCh; Consultant Orthopædic Surgeon, University College Hospital, London, 1933–65; retired; *b* 20 Aug. 1902; *s* of Percy and Elizabeth Flemming; *m* 1931, Elizabeth, *d* of W. Nelson Haden, JP; two *s* one *d. Educ:* Rugby; Trinity Coll., Oxford. FRCS, 1928; MCh Oxford, 1929. Served War of 1939–45, in RAF (Volunteer Reserve), Air Commodore (OBE). *Publications:* contrib. to learned journals on surgical subjects. *Address:* 34 Hanover Gate Mansions, Park Road, NW1 4SL. *T:* 01-724 1694. *Died 18 Sept. 1981.*

**FLEMMING, Sir Gilbert Nicolson,** KCB 1953 (CB 1948); *b* 13 Oct. 1897; *s* of Percy Flemming, FRCS, and E. E. Flemming, MD; *m* 1935, Virginia Coit; two *s* two *d. Educ:* Rugby; Trinity Coll.,

Oxford. Ministry of Education (Board of Education), 1921–59; Permanent Sec. to the Ministry of Education, 1952–59. Mem., Restrictive Practices Court, 1960–64. *Address:* G3 Burton Lodge, Portinscale Road, SW15. *Died 24 Oct. 1981.*

**FLETCHER,** Baron *cr* 1970 (Life Peer), of Islington; **Eric George Molyneux Fletcher,** PC 1967; Kt 1964; LLD London; Solicitor, Consultant to Denton, Hall, Burgin & Warrens; *b* 26 March 1903; *s* of late Clarence George Eugene Fletcher, Town Clerk of Islington; *m* 1929, Bessie Winifred, *d* of late James Butt, Enfield; two *s* one *d. Educ:* Radley; University of London, LLB London, 1923; Admitted Solicitor, 1924; BA London, 1926; LLD London, 1932; FSA 1954; FRHistS. MP (Lab) East Islington, 1945–70; Minister without Portfolio, 1964–66; Chairman of Ways and Means and Deputy Speaker, House of Commons, 1966–68. Mem. LCC for South Islington, 1934–49 (Chm. Finance Cttee); formerly Mem. Exec. Cttee Fabian Soc.; Dep. Chm., Associated British Picture Corp., 1946–64; Commissioner for Public Works Loans, 1946–55; Senator of London Univ., 1946–50 and 1956–74; Mem. Exec. Cttee, Grotius Soc.; Pres. of Selden Soc., 1967–70; Chm., Management Cttee, Inst. of Archaeology, 1968–73; Governor: Birkbeck Coll., 1934–62 (Hon. Fellow, 1983); London Sch. of Economics; Member: Evershed Cttee on Practice and Procedure of Supreme Court; Church Assembly, 1962; Commission on Church and State, 1951; Advisory Council on Public Records, 1959–64; Royal Commission on Historical Manuscripts, 1966–; Statute Law Cttee, 1951–76. A Trustee of the British Museum, 1968–77. Chm., Advisory Bd for Redundant Churches, 1969–74. Pres. British Archæological Assoc., 1960–63. *Publications:* The Students' Conflict of Laws, 1928 (with late E. Leslie Burgin); The Carrier's Liability, 1932; Benedict Biscop (Jarrow Lecture), 1981; Random Reminiscences, 1986; miscellaneous articles on legal historical, and archæological subjects. *Recreations:* golf, swimming. *Address:* 5 Chancery Lane, Clifford's Inn, EC4A 1BU. *T:* 071–242 1212; 51 Charlbury Road, North Oxford OX2 6UX. *T:* Oxford (0865) 52292. *Club:* Athenæum.

*Died 9 June 1990.*

**FLETCHER, Sir Alexander MacPherson, (Sir Alex Fletcher),** Kt 1987; financial adviser and company director; Chairman, Fletcher Scott Ltd; *b* 26 Aug. 1929; *s* of Alexander Fletcher and Margaret Muirhead; *m* 1950, Christine Ann Buchanan; two *s* one *d. Educ:* Greenock High School. Chartered Accountant, 1956. Marketing Exec., internat. co., 1956–64; Man. Dir, 1964–71; private practice as Chartered Accountant, 1971–. Mem. East Kilbride Develt Corp., 1971–73. Contested (C): W Renfrewshire, 1970; Edinburgh Central, 1987. MP (C): Edinburgh N, Nov. 1973–1983; Edinburgh Central, 1983–87. Opposition front bench spokesman on Scottish Affairs, 1977–79; Parly Under Sec. of State, Scottish Office, 1979–83; Minister for Corporate and Consumer Affairs, DTI, 1983–85. Mem., European Parlt, 1976–77. Mem., Scottish Develt Agency, 1988–. *Recreations:* golf, music. *Address:* 8a Symons Street, Sloane Square, SW3 2TJ. *Clubs:* Royal Automobile; New (Edinburgh).

*Died 18 Sept. 1989.*

**FLETCHER, Prof. Basil Alais,** MA, BSc; Emeritus Professor, University of Leeds; Research Fellow, Bristol University, 1971; *b* 10 April 1900; *s* of Walter Henry and Julia Fletcher; *m* 1928, Gerrardine Mary, *d* of William Daly; one *s* one *d. Educ:* Ilford Sch., Essex; University Coll., London. Physics Master, Gresham's Sch., Holt, Norfolk, 1922–26; Fellow Commoner, Sidney Sussex Coll., Cambridge, 1926–27; Senior Science Master, Gresham's Sch., Holt, 1927–30; Albert Kahn Fellow for Great Britain, 1930–31; Headmaster, Chippenham Sch., Wilts, 1932–35; Prof. of Education, Dalhousie Univ., Halifax, Canada, 1935–39; Prof. of Education, University Coll., Southampton, 1939–41; Prof. of Education, Bristol Univ., 1941–55; Vice-Principal of the University Coll. of Rhodesia and Nyasaland, Salisbury, 1956–60. *Publications:* Laboratory Physics (with H. W. Heckstall-Smith), 1926; Youth Looks at the World, 1932; Education and Colonial Policy, 1936; Child Psychology for Parents, 1938; The Next Step in Canadian Education, 1939; Education and Crisis, 1946; A Philosophy for the Teacher, 1961; Universities in the Modern World, 1968; The Challenge of Outward Bound, 1971. *Address:* 4 Belmont, Lansdown, Bath BA1 5DZ. *Died 19 Feb. 1983.*

**FLETCHER, Edward Joseph;** MP (Lab) Darlington since 1964; *b* 25 Feb. 1911; *m* Constance Murial, *d* of George Lee, Whickham, Hants; two *d. Educ:* St Mary's Sch., Handsworth; Fircroft Coll., Bourneville, Birmingham. Joined Labour Party, 1926; has held many offices; Chm., Tribune Group, 1977–78. Member: AEU, 1932 (Mem. Birmingham Dist Cttee); Clerical and Admin. Workers' Union, 1950 (Northern Area Sec., 1949–64); Newcastle City Council, 1952–64 (Chm. Finance Cttee, Dep. Ldr Labour Gp). Chm. N Eastern Assoc. for the Arts, 1961–65. *Address:* House of Commons, SW1. *Died 13 Feb. 1983.*

**FLETCHER, James Thomas,** CBE 1967; (first) Chairman, North Yorkshire County Council, 1973–77 (formerly North Riding of Yorkshire County Council, 1957–73); *b* 3 Dec. 1898; *s* of Thomas

Fletcher; *m* 1933, A. Walburn; two *s* one *d*. *Educ:* St John's Sch., Whitby. Mayor of Borough of Redcar, 1944; Chm., S Tees-side Hosp. Man. Cttee, 1958–74; Mem., N Riding Yorks CC, 1934. *Address:* Glenora, 8 Upgang Lane, Whitby, N Yorks YO21 3EA.
*Died 23 Feb.* 1990.

**FLETCHER, Sir Norman Seymour**, Kt 1977; agriculturalist and pastoralist, Western Australia; *b* Sydney, 20 Sept. 1905; *s* of Thomas Fletcher, Nottingham and Ivy Jeffrey, Goulburn, NSW. Established the Dirk Brook Stud at Keysbrook in 1948 and pioneered the introduction to WA of the Hereford cattle breed. AASA. Past Pres., Western Australia Royal Agricultural Soc.; has given outstanding service to the agricultural and pastoral industries in WA for 30 years; worked hard for advancement and development of cattle and meat industry, both in the southern areas of WA and in the Kimberleys. *Address:* Unit 1, Haddon Place, 39 The Esplanade, South Perth, WA 6151, Australia. *Clubs:* Weld, Western Australian (Perth).
*Died 18 Aug.* 1986.

**FLETCHER, Hon. Sir Patrick Bisset**, KBE 1958; CMG 1953; sometime MP for Matopo (SR); *b* 1901; 3rd *s* of late Hon. R. A. Fletcher, CBE, JP, Bulawayo, S Rhodesia; *m* 1929, Dorothy Maud, *d* of late Col W. Napier, CMG, Bulawayo, S Rhodesia; one *s* two *d*. *Educ:* Rondebosch Boys' High Sch.; Rhodes Univ., Grahamstown. Civil Service, 1923–30; Gold Mine Owner and Farmer; elected to S African Parliament, 1936; Mem., War Supplies and Price Advisory Bds, 1940–44. Minister of Agriculture and Lands, 1945–51 (Southern Rhodesia); Minister of Native Affairs, 1951–58; Minister of Lands, 1956–58; Minister of Irrigation and Surveys, 1957–58. Represented S Rhodesia, Coronation, 1953. President: Rhodesia Assoc. for prevention of Tuberculosis; Central African Trade Fair, 1959–. *Recreation:* golf. *Address:* Fletcher Estates, PO Box 37, Sinoia, Zimbabwe. *Club:* Bulawayo (Zimbabwe).
*Died 31 Aug.* 1981.

**FLETCHER, Richard Cawthorne**, OBE 1981; MA; JP; Headmaster, Worcester College for the Blind, 1959–80; *b* 30 Aug. 1916; *s* of late Philip C. Fletcher, MC, and of Edith Maud (*née* Okell); *m* 1946, Joan Fairlie Woodcock; one *s* one *d*. *Educ:* Marlborough; University Coll., Oxford. Served Army (Emergency Commn), 1939–46. Asst Master, Charterhouse, 1946–Aug. 1959. *Publications:* The Teaching of Science and Mathematics to the Blind (ed), 1973; The College on the Ridge, 1984. *Recreation:* music. *Address:* Yew Tree Cottage, Wick, near Pershore, Worcestershire.
*Died 18 July* 1986.

**FLETCHER-COOKE, Sir John**, Kt 1962; CMG 1952; MA Oxon; *b* 8 Aug. 1911; *er s* of late Charles Arthur and Gwendolen May Fletcher-Cooke; *m* 1st, 1936, Louise Brander (marr. diss. 1948); one *s*; 2nd, 1949, Alice Egner (marr. diss. 1971), Washington, DC; one *s* one *d*; 3rd, 1977, Marie-Louise, *widow* of Louis Vicomte Fournier de la Barre. *Educ:* Malvern Coll. (Barham Schol.); University of Paris (Diplômé, degré supérieur); Oxford Univ. (Kitchener Scholar, Senior Exhibitioner, St Edmund Hall). First Cl. Hons Politics, Philosophy and Economics; economic research, Oxford Univ., 1933; Asst Principal, Colonial Office, 1934; Private Sec. to successive Permanent Under-Secs of State for the Colonies, 1937; Officer Malayan CS, 1937; Asst Sec., FMS, 1938; special duty, FMS, 1939; Magistrate, Singapore, 1939; Sec., Foreign Exchange Control, Malaya, 1939; Dist Officer, FMS, 1940. Served with RAF as intelligence officer, FO, 1942–46; Prisoner of War in Japan, 1942–45. Attached to Colonial Office for special duty and accompanied Constitutional Comr to Malta, 1946; Under-Sec. to Govt of Palestine, 1946–48; Mem. Exec. Council, Palestine, 1947; Special Rep. for Palestine at UN discussions on Palestine, 1948; UK rep. on Special Cttee and later on Trusteeship Council UN, Geneva and Lake Success, 1948–50; Counsellor (Colonial Affairs), Perm. UK Deleg. to UN, New York, 1949–51; Colonial Adviser to UK Deleg. to UN Gen. Assembly, 1948–50 and alternate UK deleg. to UN Gen. Assembly 1949; Colonial Sec., Cyprus, 1951–55. Acted as Governor of Cyprus for various periods, 1951–55. Attached Colonial Office for Special Duty (temp.), 1956; Minister for Constitutional Affairs, Tanganyika, 1956–59; Chief Sec. to the Govt of Tanganyika, 1959–60. Special Rep. of Tanganyika at Ghana Independence Celebrations, 1957, at Economic Commission for Africa, Addis Ababa, 1959, and at Trusteeship Council, UN, New York, 1957, 1958, 1959, 1960 and 1961. Acted as Governor of Tanganyika for various periods, 1959–61; Dep. Governor, Tanganyika, 1960–61. Visiting Prof. (African Affairs) University of Colorado, Boulder, USA, 1961–62, 1966, and 1973–74; Fellow, African Studies Assoc., NY, 1961–. Mem. Constituencies Delimitation Commn for Kenya, 1962; Mem. Exec. Cttee, Overseas Employers' Federation, 1963–67. Contested (C) Luton, Nov. 1963. MP (C) Test Div. of Southampton, 1964–66. Mem. Councils of Royal Commonwealth Society and of United Society for Propagation of the Gospel, 1964–67. Vice-Chm., Internat. Team to review structure and organisation of FAO, Rome, 1967. Dir, Programmes in Diplomacy, Carnegie Endowment for International Peace, New York, 1967–69. Mission for British Govt to Anglo-French Condominium of New Hebrides, 1969. Chm., various Civil Service

Commn Selection Boards, 1971–. *Publications:* The Emperor's Guest, 1942–45, 1971, 3rd edn 1982 (also issued as Talking Book for the Blind, 1982; original diaries donated to Imperial War Museum, 1982); (contrib.) Parliament as an Export, 1966; short stories and contribs to many periodicals. *Recreation:* building dry Cotswold stone walls. *Address:* c/o Lloyds Bank, Stock Exchange Branch, 111 Old Broad Street, EC2N 1AU. *Clubs:* Travellers', Royal Commonwealth Society.
*Died 19 May* 1989.

**FLETT, Sir Martin (Teall)**, KCB 1965 (CB 1953); Director, Siebe Gorman Holdings Ltd, since 1972; *b* 30 July 1911; *s* of late Sir John Smith Flett, KBE, FRS, and of Lady (Mary Jane) Flett (*née* Meason); *m* 1936, Mary, *er d* of Sir Alec Martin; two *s* one *d*. *Educ:* George Watson's Coll.; St Paul's Sch.; St John's Coll., Oxford. 1st Class Modern History, 1933; Home Civil Service, Dominions Office, 1933; HM Treasury, 1934; War Cabinet Office, Ministry of Reconstruction and Lord President's Office, 1944–46; Under-Sec., HM Treasury, 1949–56; Alternate UK Dir, International Bank and Financial Counsellor, British Embassy, Washington, 1953–56; Dep. Sec., Ministry of Power, 1956–61; Dep. Under-Sec. of State, Air Ministry, 1961–63; Permanent Under-Sec. of State: Air Min., 1963–64; (RAF), 1964–68, (Equipment), 1968–71, MoD. Dir, Decca Ltd, 1972–80. Pres., Old Pauline Club, 1976–79. *Address:* 45 Campden Hill Road, W8. *T:* 01-937 9498. *Clubs:* Athenæum, Royal Air Force; Royal Wimbledon Golf.
*Died 25 Feb.* 1982.

**FLINT, Percy Sydney George, (Pip)**; Member, Monopolies and Mergers Commission, since 1986; *b* 23 May 1921; *s* of Percy Benjamin Flint and Nellie Kate Flint; *m* 1946, Joyce Marjorie Peggy Papworth; two *d*. *Educ:* Sir George Monoux Grammar School; Emmanuel College, Cambridge. Called to the Bar, Inner Temple, 1955. Royal Signals (Major), 1941–47; Colonial Administrative Service and HMOCS, Nigeria, 1948–61; Imperial Chemical Industries, 1961–85 (Secretary, 1981–85). *Address:* Courtlands, Kippington Road, Sevenoaks, Kent TN13 2LH. *T:* Sevenoaks (0732) 455638. *Club:* Athenæum.
*Died 19 Sept.* 1990.

**FLORENCE, Philip Sargant**, Hon. CBE 1952; MA (Cantab), PhD (Columbia); Hon. LittD (Hum) (Columbia); Hon. DSocSc (Birmingham); Professor of Commerce, 1929–55, Dean of the Faculty of Commerce and Social Science, 1947–50, University of Birmingham; *b* 25 June 1890; *s* of late Henry Smythe Florence and late Mary Sargant-Florence; *m* 1917, Lella Faye Secor (*d* 1966); two *s*. *Educ:* Rugby Sch.; Caius Coll., Cambridge (History Scholar); 1st Class Economics, 1914, Columbia Univ., New York (Garth Fellow). Organising Sec., British Assoc. Cttee on Fatigue from the Economic Standpoint, 1913–15; Investigator to the Health of Munition Workers' Cttee, 1915–16; Investigator (Associate Sanitarian), US Public Health Service, 1917–21; Lecturer, Bureau of Industrial Research and Bureau of Personnel Administration, New York, 1919–21; University Lecturer in Economics, Cambridge Univ., 1921–29; Staff Lecturer in Economics, Magdalene Coll., Cambridge, 1924–29; Chm., Social Study Cttee, Birmingham Univ., 1930–46; Mem. Council, Royal Economic Society, 1930–61, Vice-Pres., 1972–; Pres. Section F (Economics) British Assoc. for the Advancement of Science, 1937; Visiting Prof. University of Cairo, 1940; Consultant US National Resources Planning Board, 1940–41; Retail Trade Cttee, Board of Trade, 1941; Chm., Greater Birmingham Employment Cttee, 1957–63. Visiting Prof., Johns Hopkins Univ., 1959; Consultant, Jordan Development Bd, 1960–61; Leverhulme Lecturer, University of Malta, 1962; Visiting Prof., University of Rhode Island, 1967, 1968. *Publications:* Use of Factory Statistics in the Investigation of Industrial Fatigue, 1918; US Public Health Bulletin No 106, Comparison of an Eight-Hour Plant and a Ten-Hour Plant (in collaboration), 1920; Economics of Fatigue and Unrest, 1924; Over-Population, Theory and Statistics, 1926; Economics and Human Behaviour, 1927; The Statistical Method in Economics and Political Science, 1929; Uplift in Economics, 1930; The Logic of Industrial Organisation, 1933; (joint) Consumers Co-operation in Great Britain, 1938; (joint) County Town, 1946; Investment Location and Size of Plant, 1947; Labour, 1948; The Logic of British and American Industry, 1953, rev. edn 1971; Industry and the State, 1957; Ownership, Control and Success of Large Companies, 1961; Post-War Investment, Location and Size of Plant, 1962; Economics and Sociology of Industry, 1964, rev. edn 1969; Atlas of Economic Structure and Policies, 1970; (jtly) The Roots of Inflation, 1975; (ed jtly) C. K. Ogden: a collective memoir, 1977; articles, etc, in Economic, Sociological, Statistical and Psychological Journals. *Address:* Highfield, 128 Selly Park Road, Birmingham B29 7LH. *T:* 021–472 0498.
*Died 29 Jan.* 1982.

**FLORY, Prof. Paul John**; J. G. Jackson—C. J. Wood Professor in Chemistry, Stanford University, 1965–75, then Emeritus; *b* 19 June 1910; *s* of Ezra Flory and Martha Brumbaugh Flory; *m* 1936, Emily Catherine Tabor; one *s* two *d*. *Educ:* Manchester Coll., Ind; Ohio State Univ. BSc Manchester Coll. 1931; PhD (Phys Chem.) Ohio 1934. Research Chemist, E. I. DuPont de Nemours & Co., 1934–38;

Res. Associate, Cincinnati Univ., 1938–40; Res. Chemist, Esso Lab., Standard Oil Co., 1940–43; Section Head, Res. Lab., Goodyear Tire & Rubber Co., 1943–48; Prof., Cornell Univ., 1948–56; Exec. Dir of Res., Mellon Inst., 1956–61; Prof., Stanford Univ., 1961–; Chm., Dept of Chem., Stanford Univ., 1969–71. FAAAS; Fellow, Amer. Phys. Soc.; Member: Amer. Chem. Soc.; Amer. Acad. Arts and Scis; Nat. Acad. Scis; Amer. Philos. Soc.; Nat. Res. Council: Chm., Cttee on Macromolecular Chemistry, 1955–59; Chm., Div. of Chem. and Chem. Technology, 1966–68. Holds numerous medals and awards, including: Priestley Medal (Amer. Chem. Soc.) 1974; Nobel Prize for Chemistry, 1974; US Nat. Medal of Science, 1974; Perkin Medal, Soc. of Chem. Industry, 1977; Carl-Dietrich-Harries Medal, German Rubber Soc., 1977; Eringen Medal, Soc. of Engineering Sci., 1978. Hon. ScD: Manchester Coll., 1950; Ohio State, 1970; Hon. DSc Manchester, 1969; Hon. PhD: Weizmann Inst. of Sci., Israel, 1976; Clarkson Coll., 1978. *Publications:* Principles of Polymer Chemistry, 1953 (trans. Japanese, 1955); Statistical Mechanics of Chain Molecules, 1969 (trans. Japanese, 1971, Russian, 1971); numerous papers on phys. chem. of polymers and macromolecules. *Recreations:* swimming, cycling, hiking. *Address:* Department of Chemistry, Stanford University, Stanford, Calif 94305, USA. *T:* 415–497–4574. *Died* 9 *Sept.* 1985.

**FLOWER, Group Capt. Arthur Hyde**, CBE 1939; *b* Bemboka, NSW, 13 Dec. 1892; *s* of late Thomas Flower; *m* 1924, Nina Joan Castleden Whitby (*d* 1976); no *c*; *m* 1977, Margaret June, *d* of late Cecil Vernon Wickens, Adelaide, SA. *Educ:* Tilba, NSW. Served with AIF, Egypt and France, 1915–16; transferred to Royal Flying Corps, 1917; served in No. 42 Squadron, France and Italy, 1917–1918 (French Croix de Guerre with palm); Egypt and Turkey, 1920–23; Egypt, 1926–31 and 1934–36; Palestine, 1937–38 (CBE, despatches); France, Sept. 1939–May 1940; England, 1940–42; SWP Area, Aug. 1942–Nov. 1944; retired May 1945; returned to Australia, 1948. Comdr Order of Leopold (Belgium). *Recreations:* shooting, golf. *Address:* Garden Cottage, 188 Longwood Road, Heathfield, SA 5153, Australia. *Died* 3 *Dec.* 1987.

**FODEN, Air Vice-Marshal Arthur**, CB 1964; CBE 1960; BSc; CEng; FIEE; Consultant, Electronic Systems, since 1985; *b* 19 April 1914; *s* of Henry Foden, Macclesfield, Cheshire; *m* 1938, Constance Muriel Foden (*née* Corkill); one *s* one *d*. *Educ:* Manchester Univ. Electronic Engineer, 1935–37; Education Officer, Royal Air Force, 1937–39; Signals Officer, Royal Air Force, 1939; Dep. Dir, Signals Staff, Min. of Def., 1964–67; Asst Chief of Defence Staff (Signals), 1967–69, retired; Director: (C), Govt Communications HQ, 1969–75; Racal Comsec, 1975–85. *Recreations:* gardening, music. *Address:* Ravenglass, Wargrave, Berks. *T:* Wargrave (073522) 2589. *Died* 23 *Nov.* 1990.

**FODEN, William Bertram**, CB 1945; formerly Assistant Under-Secretary of State, Air Ministry; retired; *b* 19 Sept. 1892; *s* of late W. G. Foden, Newcastle, Staffs; *m* 1920, Zélie, *d* of late G. K. Lemmy, Lewisham; one *s* one *d*. *Educ:* High Sch., Newcastle, Staffs; St John's Coll., Cambridge (scholar). BA 1914; RGA and RE, 1916–18; Research Dept, Woolwich Arsenal, 1918; Air Ministry, 1919–53. *Address:* 2 Westwood Close, Threshers, Crediton, Devon EX17 3NJ. *T:* Crediton 2709.

*Died* 6 *Sept.* 1981.

**FOGARTY, Susan Winthrop**, CB 1983; Under-Secretary, Highways, Department of Transport, since 1978; *b* 16 April 1930; *d* of late Philip Christopher Fogarty and Hilda Spenser Fogarty. *Educ:* Badminton Sch., Bristol; King's Coll., Newcastle. BA Dunelm. Joined Min. of Defence, 1951; joined Scottish Educn Dept, 1955; Private Sec. to Jt Parly Under-Sec. for Scotland, 1957–59; Principal, Scottish Educn Dept, 1959; Min. of Transport, 1960; Asst Sec. 1966; Cabinet Office, 1968; Dept of Environment, 1971; Under Sec., DoE, 1973 (Regional Dir, W Midlands, 1975–78). *Recreations:* reading history and thrillers, swimming, walking. *Address:* 401 Howard House, Dolphin Square, SW1V 3PF. *T:* 01-821 0666. *Club:* Royal Commonwealth Society. *Died* 1 *Dec.* 1983.

**FOGG, Albert**, CBE 1972; DSc; *b* 25 Feb. 1909; *o* *s* of late James Fogg, Bolton; *m* 1937, Barbara Thelma Winifred Davies (marr. diss.); one *s* one *d*. *Educ:* Manchester University. Scientific staff, National Physical Laboratory, 1930–46; first Dir, Motor Industry Research Assoc., 1946–64; Director: Leyland Motor Corporation, 1964–68; British Leyland Motor Corporation Ltd, 1968–74; ENASA (Spain), 1965–74; retired. Hon. DSc Southampton, 1979. Inst. of Mechanical Engineers: T. Bernard Hall Prize, 1945 and 1955; Starley Premium, 1956; James Clayton Prize, 1962; Viva Shield and Gold Medal, Worshipful Company of Carmen, 1962. *Publications:* numerous papers in jls of scientific socs and professional instns. *Address:* 4 Brownsea View Close, Lilliput, Poole, Dorset. *T:* Poole 708788. *Died* 12 *June* 1989.

**FOGGIN, (Wilhelm) Myers**, CBE 1974; Principal, Trinity College of Music, London, 1965–79; *b* 23 Dec. 1908; *m* 1952, Lotte Breitmeyer; one *s* one *d*. *Educ:* Dr Erlich's Sch., Newcastle upon Tyne; Royal Academy of Music. Concert Pianist; Prof. of Piano, RAM, 1936;

Conductor, People's Palace Choral and Orchestral Soc., 1936–49. Intelligence Officer, RAF, 1940–45. Guest Conductor, Carl Rosa Opera, Sadler's Wells Opera and BBC; Dir of Opera, RAM, 1948–65; Conductor, Croydon Philharmonic Soc., 1957–73; Warden, RAM, 1949–65. Dir of Music, Queenswood Sch., 1966–82; Pres., Nat. Fedn of Music Socs, 1967–72; Chm., Royal Philharmonic Soc., 1968–81. Hon. FTCL, FRAM, FRCM, Hon. GSM, FRNCM. *Address:* Medmery, Lock Lane, Birdham, Chichester, W Sussex PO20 7BA. *Club:* Athenæum. *Died* 17 *July* 1986.

**FOLLETT, Sir David (Henry)**, Kt 1967; MA Oxon, PhD London; FInstP; FMA; Director, Science Museum, 1960–73; *b* 5 Sept. 1907; *er* *s* of Septimus and Rose Annie Follett; *m* 1932, Helen Alison Wilson; three *s* decd. *Educ:* Rutlish Sch.; Brasenose Coll. (Hulme Exhibitioner); Birkbeck Coll. (post-graduate). Joined Adam Hilger Ltd, optical instrument manufacturers, 1929. Asst Keeper, Dept of Physics, Science Museum, 1937. Meteorological Branch, RAFVR, 1939. Returned to Science Museum, 1945; Deputy Keeper, Dept of Physics, 1949; Keeper of Dept of Electrical Engineering and Communications, 1957–60. Governor Imperial Coll. of Science and Technology, 1960–73; Trustee Imperial War Museum, 1960–73; Vice-Pres., Institute of Physics and Physical Soc., 1965–69; Mem., Ancient Monuments Board for England, 1966–77. *Publications:* The Rise of the Science Museum under Henry Lyons, 1978; papers in scientific jls. *Recreations:* gardening, sailing. *Address:* 3 Elm Bank Gardens, Barnes, SW13. *T:* 01-876 8302. *Club:* Athenæum.

*Died* 11 *May* 1982.

**FOLLETT, Samuel Frank**, CMG 1959; BSc, CEng, FIEE, FRAeS; *b* 21 March 1904; *o* *s* of Samuel Charles Follett and Kate Bell; *m* 1932, Kathleen Matilda Tupper. *Educ:* Farnham Gram. Sch.; Univ. of London. Electrical Research Assoc., 1924–27; Electrical Engineering Dept, RAE Farnborough, 1927–45; Asst Dir of Instrument R&D (Electrics), Min. of Supply, 1946–50; Dir of Instrument R&D, 1950–54; Dep. Dir-Gen. Aircraft, Equipment, R&D, 1954–56; Dir.-Gen., Min. of Supply Staff, Brit. It Services Mission, Washington, DC, 1956–59; Dep. Dir, RAE Farnborough, 1959–63; Dep. Controller of Guided Weapons, Min. of Aviation, 1963–66; Scientific Adviser to BoT, 1966–69. *Address:* Darby Cottage, St Johns Road, Farnham, Surrey. *T:* Farnham 716610.

*Died* 26 *Aug.* 1988.

**FOLLOWS, Sir (Charles) Geoffry (Shield)**, Kt 1951; CMG 1945; Northern Rhodesia representative on Federal Interim Public Service Commission, 1953–59; *b* 4 July 1896; *m* 1922, Claire Camille, *d* of late Julien Lemarchand. *Educ:* Wellington Sch., Som. 2nd Lieut The King's (Liverpool) Regt 1914; served in France, 1915–18, and in various Staff appts until 1920; Colonial Service, Seychelles, 1920–24; attached Colonial Office, 1925; Gibraltar, 1925–36; N Rhodesia, 1936–45; Chief Financial Adviser to Mil. Admin, Hong Kong, 1945–46; Fin. Sec., Hong Kong, 1946–52; Chm. N Rhodesia Salaries Commn, 1952; Mem. Preparatory Commn on Federation of Rhodesias and Nyasaland, 1952. Mem., Order of the Legion of Merit (Rhodesia), 1979. *Address:* 12 Lanark Road, Harare, Zimbabwe. *Died* 7 *Aug.* 1983.

**FOLLOWS, Sir Denis**, Kt 1978; CBE 1967 (MBE 1950); Chairman, British Olympic Association, since 1977; *b* 13 April 1908; *s* of Amos Follows; *m* 1938, Mary Elizabeth Milner; two *d*. *Educ:* City Sch., Lincoln; Nottingham Univ. (BA). Pres., National Union of Students, 1930–32; Pres., Internat. Confedn of Students, 1932–34; Vice-Pres., 1933, Chm., 1948, Pres., 1972–, Universities Athletic Union. Asst Master, Chiswick Grammar Sch. for Boys, 1932–40. Royal Air Force, Flight Lieut, 1940–46. Sec., British Airline Pilots Assoc., 1946–62. Chm., Nat. Jt Council for Civil Air Transport, 1951–52; Secretary of the FA, 1962–73. Hon. Treasurer, CCPR, 1977–; Chairman: Major Spectator Sports Div. CCPR, 1973–; Sports Adv. Cttee, Nat. Assoc. of Youth Clubs, 1975–; Member: Council, Assoc. of Nat. Olympic Cttees, 1979–; Exec. Cttee, Assoc. of European Nat. Olympic Cttees, 1980–. Silver Medal of the Olympic Order, 1980; Manning Award for non-competitive Sportsman of the Year, Sports Writers' Assoc., 1980. *Recreation:* gardening. *Address:* 70 Barrowgate Road, Chiswick, W4. *T:* 01-994 5782. *Died* 17 *Sept.* 1983.

**FOLLOWS, Sir Geoffry;** *see* Follows, Sir C. G. S.

**FONDA, Henry;** actor, USA; *b* Grand Island, Nebraska, USA, 16 May 1905; *s* of William Brace Fonda and Herberta Jaynes; *m* 1965, Shirlee Adams; one *s* two *d* of previous *m*. *Educ:* University of Minnesota, Minneapolis, Minn. Began acting at Omaha Community Playhouse, Nebraska; subseq. played many parts with touring companies. Made first appearance on New York stage, Guild Theatre, 1929; *stage appearances include:* The Farmer Takes a Wife, 46th Street, 1934; Mister Roberts, Alvin, 1948; Point of No Return, Alvin, 1951; Caine Mutiny Court Martial, Plymouth, 1954; Two for the Seesaw, 1958; Critics' Choice; Silent Night, Lonely Night; A Gift of Time, 1962; Generation, 1965; Our Town; The Time of Your Life; Clarence Darrow (USA and London, 1975); First Monday in October, 1978; The Oldest Living Graduate, 1980;

Showdown at the Adobe Motel, 1981. Entered films, 1935; *films include*: Jesse James, Grapes of Wrath, Mister Roberts, The Wrong Man, 12 Angry Men (also produced), Warlock, The Best Man, A Big Hand for the Little Lady, Trail of the Lonesome Pine, You Only Live Once, Young Mr Lincoln, The Lady Eve, The Ox Bow Incident, The Male Animal, My Darling Clementine, The Rounders, Madigan, Yours, Mine and Ours, The Boston Strangler, Once upon a Time. . . in the West, Too Late the Hero, There Was a Crooked Man, The Cheyenne Social Club, Sometimes a Great Notion, The Serpent, The Red Pony, Ash Wednesday, My Name is Nobody, Mussolini—The Last Days, Midway, Rollercoaster, Last of the Cowboys, Fedora, Home to Stay, The Swarm, Meteor, Roots: the next generation, City on Fire, On Golden Pond (Oscar 1982). Served USN, 1942–45. Hon. DHL, Ursinus Coll., 1966; Hon. Dr Nebraska Univ., 1972. Life Achievement Award, American Film Inst., 1978; Hon. Oscar, 1981. *Publication*: Fonda, My Life (as told to H. Teichmann), 1982. *Address*: c/o John Springer, 667 Madison Avenue, NYC, USA.                           *Died 12 Aug. 1982.*

**FONTANNE, Lynn;** actress; *b* Woodford, Essex, 6 Dec. 1887; *m* 1922, Alfred Lunt (*d* 1977), actor. Began as child in pantomime in Drury Lane; walked on in various London companies with Lewis Waller, Beerbohm Tree, Lena Ashwell; played in touring company with Weedon Grossmith for few seasons, playing name part in Young Lady of 17 and other small parts in various curtain raisers; on tour in Milestones, then revival in London; small parts in My Lady's Dress; then America; many plays with Laurette Taylor; name part in Dulcy, followed by many leads including Goat Song, Strange Interlude, Second Man, Caprice, At Mrs Beams, Pygmalion, The Guardsman, Meteor, Design for Living, Point Valaine, Taming of the Shrew, Idiot's Delight; Amphytrion 38 (NY and London), 1938; There Shall Be No Night (NY and London), 1943; Love in Idleness (O Mistress Mine, in New York); Quadrille (London), 1952; The Great Sebastians (NY), 1956; The Visit (London), 1960; The Sea Gull. Presidential Medal of Freedom, 1964; Antoinette Perry Award; Emmy Award. Holds hon. degrees from 12 universities and colleges.                                           *Died 30 July 1983.*

**FOOTE, Rev. John Weir,** VC 1942; DD, LLD University of Western Ontario, 1947; Minister of Reform Institutions, Government of Ontario, 1950–57; *b* 5 May 1904; *s* of Gordon Foote, Madoc, Ontario; *m* 1929. *Educ*: University of Western Ontario, London, Ont; Presbyterian Coll. (McGill). Served War of 1939–45; Regimental Chaplain with Royal Hamilton Light Infantry (VC). Minister St Paul's Presbyterian Church, Port Hope, Ont. Canadian Army from 1939, Asst Principal Chaplain (P). *Recreations*: golf, fishing. *Address*: Front Road East, Coburg, Ontario, Canada.
                                                  *Died 2 May 1988.*

**FOOTMAN, David John,** CMG 1950; MC 1916; MA 1953; *b* 17 Sept. 1895; *s* of Rev. John Footman and Ella Mary (*née* Kennard); *m* 1927, Joan Isabel (marr. diss. 1936); she *d* 1960), *d* of Edmund Footman; no *c*. *Educ*: Marlborough; New Coll., Oxford. European War, 1914–19, Royal Berks Regt. Levant Consular Service, 1919–29; Foreign Office, 1935–53; Fellow of St Antony's Coll., Oxford, 1953–63, Emeritus Fellow, 1963–. *Publications*: Half-way East, 1935; Pig and Pepper, 1936; Pemberton, 1943; Red Prelude, 1944; The Primrose Path, 1946; Civil War in Russia, 1961; The Russian Revolutions, 1962; Dead Yesterday, 1974. *Address*: 11a Collingham Gardens, SW5. *Club*: Naval and Military.
                                                  *Died 8 Oct. 1983.*

**FORBES, Sir Archibald (Finlayson),** GBE 1957; Kt 1943; Chartered Accountant; President, Midland Bank Ltd, 1975–83 (Director, 1959; Deputy Chairman, 1962–64; Chairman, 1964–75); *b* 6 March 1903; *s* of late Charles Forbes, Johnstone, Renfrewshire; *m* 1943, Angela Gertrude (*d* 1969), *o d* of late Horace Ely, Arlington House, SW1; one *s* two *d*. *Educ*: Paisley; Glasgow Univ. Formerly Mem. of firm of Thomson McLintock & Co., Chartered Accountants. Joined Spillers Ltd as Executive Dir, 1935: Dep. Chm., 1960; Chm., 1965–68; Pres., 1969–80. Mem. of various Reorganisation Commns and Cttees appointed by Minister of Agriculture, 1932–39; Chm., Nat. Mark Trade Cttees for Eggs and Poultry, 1936–39; Dir of Capital Finance, Air Min., 1940; Deputy Sec., Min. of Aircraft Production, 1940–43; Controller of Repair, Equipment and Overseas Supplies, 1943–45 (incl. Operational Control, nos 41 and 43 Gps, RAF and Dir, Gen. Repair and Maintenance, RAF); Mem. of Aircraft Supply Council, 1942–45; Chairman: First Iron and Steel Board from its formation, 1946, to dissolution 1949; Iron and Steel Board from its inception under the Iron and Steel Act, 1953, until 1959; British Millers' Mutual Pool Ltd, 1952–62 (Dep. Chm. 1940–52); Central Mining and Investment Corp., 1959–64; Debenture Corp. Ltd, 1949–79; Midland and International Banks Ltd, 1964–76; Director: Shell Transport & Trading Co. Ltd, 1954–73; English Electric Co. Ltd, 1958–76; Dunlop Holdings Ltd, 1958–76; Rand Mines Ltd, S Africa, 1959–64; Bank of Bermuda Ltd, 1966–75. Pres., FBI, 1951–53; Chm., Cttee of London Clearing Bankers, 1970–72 (Dep. Chm., 1968–70); Pres., British Bankers' Assoc., 1970–71, 1971–72 (Vice-Pres. 1969–70); Dir, 1950–53, Dep.

Chm., 1961–64, Finance Corp. for Industry. Member: Cttee to enquire into Financial Structure of Colonial Develt Corp., 1959; Review Body on Doctors' and Dentists' Remuneration, 1962–65; Governing Body, Imp. Coll. of Science and Technology, 1959–75. Councillor for life, The Conference Board Inc., NY, 1983. Chm., Arthritis and Rheumatism Council, 1983–. Pres., Epsom Coll., 1964–. Hon. JDipMA. *Recreations*: golf and fishing. *Address*: 40 Orchard Court, Portman Square, W1. *T*: 01–935 9304. *Clubs*: Brooks's, Pratt's, Beefsteak.                        *Died 2 June 1989.*

**FORBES of Pitsligo, Sir Charles Edward Stuart-,** 12th Bt *cr* 1626; Building contractor, retired; *b* 6 Aug. 1903; *s* of Sir Charles Hay Hepburn Stuart-Forbes, 10th Bt, and Ellen, *d* of Capt. Huntley; *S* brother, 1937; *m* 1966, Ijah Leah MacCabe (*d* 1974), Wellington, NZ. *Educ*: Ocean Bay Coll. *Recreations*: motoring, football, cricket, hockey, swimming, deep sea fishing, hunting, rowing, launching, tennis. *Heir*: *n* William Daniel Stuart-Forbes [*b* 21 Aug. 1935; *m* 1956, Jannette MacDonald; three *s* two *d*].
                                                  *Died 28 March 1985.*

**FORBES, Charles Harington Gordon,** CBE 1965 (OBE 1941); Registrar, Principal Probate Registry, Somerset House, 1946–64; *b* 20 Feb. 1896; *s* of Harington G. Forbes, OBE; *m* 1927, Jean J. Beith; one *d*. *Educ*: Malvern Coll. Entered service of Principal Probate Registry, 1914. Served European War, 1914–18, with The Honourable Artillery Company. *Address*: Chetwynd, Watermill Lane, Bexhill-on-Sea, East Sussex.                *Died 8 Nov. 1982.*

**FORBES, Dr Gilbert;** Regius Professor of Forensic Medicine, University of Glasgow, 1964–74, later Emeritus; *b* 5 Aug. 1908; *s* of late George and late Jane Gilbert Forbes; *m* 1938, Marian Margaret Macrae Guthrie, Springfield, Fife; one *d*. *Educ*: Hillhead High Sch., Glasgow; Glasgow Univ. (BSc). MB, ChB Glasgow, 1933; Brunton Memorial Prize, 1933; FRFPSG 1935; FRCSE 1935; MD 1945; FRCPath 1966. House posts at Western Infirmary, Glasgow, 1933–34; Demonstrator in Anatomy, University of Glasgow, 1934–36; Lecturer in Anatomy, University of Aberdeen, 1936–37; Police Surgeon to City of Sheffield and Lecturer in Forensic Medicine, University of Sheffield, 1937–48; Senior Lectr in Forensic Medicine, Univ. of Sheffield, 1948–56; Reader in Forensic Medicine, Univ. of Sheffield, 1956–64. Asst Deputy Coroner to City of Sheffield, 1945–59. At various times external examiner in forensic medicine in Univs of Manchester, Birmingham, Leeds, Glasgow, Aberdeen and Edinburgh. *Publications*: original papers on medico-legal subjects in medical and scientific journals. *Recreation*: motoring. *Address*: 18 The Glen, Endcliffe Vale Road, Sheffield S10 3FN.                                              *Died 30 Aug. 1986.*

**FORBES, Hon. Sir Hugh (Harry Valentine),** Kt 1970; Hon. Mr Justice Forbes; a Judge of the High Court, Queen's Bench Division, since 1970; *b* 14 Feb. 1917; *e s* of late Rev. H. N. Forbes, sometime Rector of Castle Bromwich; *m* 1st, 1940, Julia Margaret (marr. diss. 1970), *yr d* of Frank Gilbert Weller; one *s* two *d*; 2nd, 1970, Janet Moir, *o d* of Campbell Andrews, MD, Harrow. *Educ*: Rossall; Trinity Hall, Cambridge (1st cl. Law). Served War of 1939–45: Major, Gordon Highlanders; GSO2 War Office and GHQ India. Called to Bar, Middle Temple, 1946; QC 1966; Bencher, 1970. Chm., Lincs (Kesteven) QS, 1967–71 (Dep. Chm., 1961–67); Dep. Chm., Hunts and Peterborough QS, 1965–70; Additional Judge, Employment Appeal Tribunal, 1976–82. Mem., Parole Bd, 1977–79 (Vice-Chm., 1978–79). Chancellor: Dio. of Ely, 1965–69; Dio. of Chelmsford, 1969–; Pres., Court of Ecclesiastical Causes Reserved, 1985–. Chm. Council, Royal Yachting Assoc., 1971–76. *Publication*: Real Property Law, 1950. *Recreations*: sailing, listening to music. *Address*: Royal Courts of Justice, WC2. *Clubs*: Royal Cruising; Royal Yacht Squadron (Cowes).                                  *Died 13 Dec. 1985.*

**FORBES, Ian Alexander,** PhD; *b* 27 Oct. 1915; *s* of Robert Douglas Forbes and Amy Forbes; *m* 1945, Rosemary Blair, DA; one *s* one *d*. *Educ*: Alloa Acad.; Edinburgh Univ. (BSc 1937, PhD 1939). ICI (Explosives) Ltd, 1939–48 (also seconded to M.A.P. Explosives); Distillers Co. Ltd, 1948–80: Man. Dir, Scottish Grain Distillers Ltd, 1972–80; Man Dir, D.C. (Malt Products) Ltd, 1966–80; Chm., John Watney & Co. Ltd, 1952–80; Dir, Thos Borthwick (Glasgow) Ltd, 1953–80; retd 1980. *Recreation*: golf. *Address*: Blackness, King's Road, Longniddry, East Lothian EH32 0NN. *T*: Longniddry 53136. *Clubs*: Muirfield Golf, Longniddry Golf.
                                                  *Died 19 Nov. 1986.*

**FORBES, Col Sir John Stewart,** 6th Bt of Newe *cr* 1823; DSO; JP; Vice-Lieutenant of Aberdeenshire, 1973–84; *b* 8 Jan. 1901; *o surv. s* of 5th Bt and late Emma Theodora, *d* of Robert Maxwell; *S* father, 1927; *m* 1933, Agnes Jessie, *er d* of late Lt-Col D. L. Wilson-Farquharson, DSO; five *d*. *Educ*: Wellington Coll.; RMA, Woolwich. 2nd Lieut RE, 1920; Temp. Brig. 1948; Col 1949; served Norway Campaign, 1940 (DSO, despatches); Burma, 1944–45 (despatches); Comdt, Indian Coll. of Military Engrg, 1947–48; retired 1953. Hon. Col 51st (H) Div. Engineers, TA, 1960–67. DL 1953, JP 1955, Aberdeenshire. *Heir*: *cousin* Major Hamish Stewart Forbes, MBE, MC [*b* 15 Feb. 1916; *m* 1945, Jacynthe Elizabeth

Mary, o d of late Eric Gordon Underwood; one s three d]. *Address:* Allargue, Corgarff, Aberdeenshire AB3 8YP.
*Died 23 July 1984.*

**FORBES, Robert Brown;** Director of Education, Edinburgh, 1972–75; b 14 Oct. 1912; s of Robert James Forbes and Elizabeth Jane Brown; m 1939, Nellie Shepley; one s one d. *Educ:* Edinburgh Univ. (MA, MEd). Asst Dir of Educn, Edinburgh, 1946, Depute Dir, 1952. Chm., Scottish Council for Research in Educn, 1972. *Address:* 7 Wilton Road, Edinburgh EH16 5NX. *T:* 031–667 1323.
*Died 31 May 1989.*

**FORBES, William Alfred Beaumont,** QC 1972; a Recorder of the Crown Court, since 1974; a Law Commissioner, since 1977; b 29 June 1927; er s of William Forbes, MA, FEIS, Aberdeen; m 1952, Helen Elizabeth (marr. diss. 1979), er d of R. A. Harting, FCA, Hillingdon; one s two d. *Educ:* Aberdeen Grammar Sch.; Galashiels Acad.; George Watson's Boys' Coll., Edinburgh; Univ. of St Andrews (MA, 1st cl. Hons Mod. Hist./Economics); Magdalen Coll., Oxford (BA, 1st cl. Hons Jurisprudence). Jun. Lectr in Law, Magdalen Coll., Oxford, 1953–54, Brasenose Coll., 1954–58. Called to Bar, Gray's Inn, 1953. Junior Prosecuting Counsel, Bot, 1968–72. Mem., Royal Commn on Criminal Procedure, 1978–80. *Recreation:* golf. *Address:* Law Commission, Conquest House, 37/38 John Street, Theobalds Road, WC1N 2BQ. *T:* 01-242 0861. *Clubs:* Caledonian; Denham Golf.
*Died 4 May 1981.*

**FORD, Edmund Brisco,** FRS 1946; MA, DSc Oxon, Hon. DSc Liverpool; Senior Dean, and Fellow, 1958–71, Fellow Emeritus, 1976–77, and Distinguished Fellow and Senior Dean, since 1977, All Souls College, Oxford; Professor of Ecological Genetics, 1963–69, and Director of Genetics Laboratory, Zoology Department, 1952–69, Oxford; Emeritus Professor, since 1969; b 23 April 1901; s of Harold Dodsworth Ford and Gertrude Emma Bennett; unmarried. *Educ:* Wadham Coll., Oxford (Hon. Fellow, 1974). Research worker, Univ. Lectr and Demonstrator in Zoology and Comparative Anatomy, Univ. Reader in Genetics, Oxford; Pres., Genetical Soc. of Great Britain, 1946–49; Mem. of Nature Conservancy, 1949–59; Mem. various scientific (chiefly zoological) societies. Wild Life Conservation Cttee of Ministry of Town and Country Planning, 1945–47 (Cmd Rept 7122). Formerly represented British Empire on Permanent Internat. Cttee of Genetics. Has travelled in USA, NZ, Australia, Near and Far East. Initiated Science of Ecological Genetics. Darwin Medallist, Royal Society, 1954. Delivered Galton Lecture of London Univ., 1939; Woodhall Lectr of the Royal Institution, 1957; Woodward Lectr, Yale Univ., 1959 and 1973. Hon. FRCP 1974; Hon. FRES. Weldon Memorial Prize, Oxford Univ., 1959. Medallist of Helsinki Univ., 1967. Foreign Mem., Finnish Acad. Pres. Somerset Archæological Soc., 1960–61. *Publications:* Mendelism and Evolution, 1931, 8th edn 1965; (with G. D. Hale Carpenter) Mimicry, 1933; The Study of Heredity (Home University Library), 1938, 2nd edn 1950; Genetics for Medical Students, 1942, 7th edn 1973; Butterflies (Vol. I of New Naturalist Series), 1945, 2nd repr. of 4th edn, 1972, pbk 1975, rev. edn 1977; British Butterflies (King Penguin Series), 1951; Moths (New Naturalist Series), 1955, 4th edn 1976; Ecological Genetics, 1964, 4th edn 1975 (trans: Polish 1967, French 1972, Italian 1978); Genetic Polymorphism (All Souls Monographs), 1965; Evolution Studied by Observation and Experiment, 1973; Genetics and Adaptation, 1976; Understanding Genetics, 1979; Taking Genetics into the Countryside, 1981; (with J. S. Haywood) Church Treasures in the Oxford District, 1984; numerous contribs to scientific jls, on genetical and zoological subjects. Festschrift: Ecological Genetics and Evolution, ed E. R. Creed, 1971. *Recreations:* archæology, literature, travel. *Address:* 5 Apsley Road, Oxford; All Souls College, Oxford. *TA:* and *T:* Oxford 279312; Zoology Department, South Parks Road, Oxford. *Club:* Travellers'.
*Died 21 Jan. 1988.*

**FORD, Sir Edward,** Kt 1960; OBE 1945; Professor of Preventive Medicine and Director of the School of Public Health and Tropical Medicine, University of Sydney, 1947–68, then Emeritus; b 15 April 1902; s of Edward John and Mary Ford, South Yarra, Victoria. *Educ:* Univ. of Melbourne, Sydney and London. RMO, Melbourne Hosp., 1930; Lectr in Anatomy, Melbourne Univ., 1933; Sen. Lectr in Anatomy and Histology, Melbourne Univ., 1934–36; Lectr, Sch. of Public Health and Tropical Medicine, Sydney, 1937–39. Served War of 1939–45: in Australian Army Middle East, New Guinea, Burma; Senior Malariologist, AIF, and late Dir of Hygiene and Pathology, Aust. Army; Col AAMC, 1940–45. Rockefeller Fellow, 1946; Dean of Faculty of Medicine and Fellow of Senate, Sydney Univ., 1953–57. Vice-Pres., RACP, 1970–73. *Publication:* Bibliography of Australian Medicine 1790–1900, 1976. *Address:* Cahors, 117 Macleay Street, Potts Point, NSW 2011, Australia. *Club:* Australian (Sydney).
*Died 27 Aug. 1986.*

**FORD, Henry, II;** Member of the Board and Chairman, Finance Committee, Ford Motor Company, Dearborn, Michigan; b Detroit, 4 Sept. 1917; s of Edsel B. and Eleanor (Clay) Ford; m 1st, 1940, Anne McDonnell (marr. diss.); one s two d; 2nd, 1965, Maria

Cristina Vettore Austin (marr. diss. 1980); 3rd, 1980, Kathleen DuRoss. *Educ:* Hotchkiss Sch., Lakeville, Conn; Yale Univ. Dir, Ford Motor Co., 1938–; became employee, 1940; Vice-Pres., 1943; Executive Vice-Pres., 1944; Pres., 1945; Chief Executive Officer, 1945–79, and Chm., 1960–80; retd as officer and employee, 1982. Director: Sotheby's Holdings, Inc., 1983– (Vice-Chm., 1983–86); Manufacturers Trust Co. of Florida, NA, 1983–85. Graduate Mem., Business Council (Mem. 1947–). Trustee, The Ford Foundn, 1943–76; Chm. Trustees, Henry Ford Health Care Corp., 1982–; Mem., St Mary's Hosp. Adv. Bd of Trustees, 1984–. *Address:* (home) Palm Beach, Fla, USA; (office) Dearborn, Michigan, USA.
*Died 29 Sept. 1987.*

**FORD, Sir Henry Russell,** 2nd Bt cr 1929; TD; JP; b 30 April 1911; s of Sir Patrick Ford, 1st Bt, and Jessie Hamilton (d 1962), d of Henry Field, WS, Moreland, Kinross-shire, and Middlebluf, Manitoba; S father, 1945; m 1936, Mary Elizabeth, y d of late Godfrey F. Wright, Whiddon, Bovey Tracy; one s three d. *Educ:* Winchester; New Coll., Oxford. War of 1939–45 served in UK, North Africa and Italy (despatches). Chm., Berwick and E Lothian Unionist Assoc., 1948–50, 1958–60. JP 1951. TD 1960. *Recreations:* golf, gardening. *Heir:* s Andrew Russell Ford [b 29 June 1943; m 1968, Penelope Anne, d of Harry Relph; two s one d]. *Address:* 1 Broadgait Green, Gullane, East Lothian. *T:* Gullane 842214. *Club:* Hon. Company of Edinburgh Golfers (Muirfield).
*Died 22 Dec. 1989.*

**FORD, Air Vice-Marshal Howard,** CB 1959; CBE 1954; AFC 1944; RAF (retd); b 18 Dec. 1905; s of Lewis Ford and Beatrice Ford; m 1936, Marie (d 1974), d of Daniel O'Reilly, Cork, and Agnes Mayne, New York. *Educ:* Blundell's Sch.; Pembroke Coll., Cambridge (BA). Represented Cambridge at ski-ing and athletics, also England and Great Britain at athletics; British Olympic Athletic Team, 1928. Joined Royal Air Force, 1930; served War of 1939–45 (AFC). Transferred to Technical Branch, 1951; Dir, Air Armament R&D, Min. of Supply, 1952–55; Senior Technical Staff Officer, Flying Training Command, 1956–59; Vice-Pres. Ordnance Board, 1960–61, Pres., 1963; retired from RAF, 1963. Group Capt., 1947; Air Cdre, 1953; Air Vice-Marshal, 1960. *Address:* 11 Dalmeny Court, 8 Duke Street, St James's, SW1. *Clubs:* Royal Air Force, Royal Automobile.
*Died 28 March 1986.*

**FORD, Sir Leslie (Ewart),** Kt 1956; OBE 1945; FCIT; General Manager, Port of London Authority, 1948–64; b 27 July 1897; e s of late Elias Ford, OBE; m 1925, Mary Mabel, e d of late Walter Powles, Acocks Green, Warwicks; one d. *Educ:* Cardiff High Sch. Joined GW Railway Co., 1912. Served European War, 1914–18, with Welch Regt and 2nd Bn Monmouthshire Regt. Brunel Medallist, LSE, 1924. Stationed various South Wales Ports, 1923–39; Chief Docks Manager, 1944. Major, Home Guard, 1941–45. Col Engineer and Railway Staff Corps RE (TA), 1957. Freeman: City of London, 1963; Waterman and Lighterman's Co. of River Thames, 1963. CStJ. Commander: Royal Order of North Star (Sweden); Military Order of Christ (Portugal); Order of Dannebrog (Denmark). *Recreation:* golf. *Address:* 26 Bedford Gardens, Campden Hill, W8 7EH. *T:* 01-727 5595.
*Died 22 March 1981.*

**FORD, Percy;** Professor Emeritus, The University of Southampton; b 19 Feb. 1894; 4th s of George Horace Ford, Brighton; m 1921, Grace Lister (d 1981), Long Eaton; one s one d. *Educ:* Varndean Sch.; London Sch. of Economics, University of London (Gerstenberg Scholar). Resident Lecturer, Ruskin Coll.; Lecturer, Amherst Coll., Mass, USA; Lecturer in Dept of Economics, and Sec. of University Extension Board and Tutorial Classes Joint Cttee, King's Coll., Univ. of Durham, 1923–26; Head of Dept and Prof. of Economics, University of Southampton, 1926–59; Sen. Research Fellow, 1959–61. National Service, Ministry of Supply, 1939–46. Hon. LLD Southampton, 1974 (Hon. degrees of LLD conferred on Prof. P. and Mrs G. Ford at the same time). *Publications:* Economics and Modern Industry, 1930; Work and Wealth in a Modern Port, 1934; Incomes, Means Tests and Personal Responsibility, 1939; Economics of Collective Bargaining, 1958; Social Theory and Social Practice, 1969; Parliamentary Papers Series, 1951–62 (with G. Ford): Breviate of Parliamentary Papers, Vol. I, 1900–16; Vol. II, 1917–39, Vol. III, 1940–54; Select List of British Parliamentary Papers, 1833–1899; Hansard's and Catalogue and Breviate of Parliamentary Papers, 1696–1834; editorial work connected with, and selection of, nineteenth century British Parliamentary Papers for 1,000 vol. reprint (complete set presented to Parliament); Select List of Reports of Irish Dail and Senate, 1922–72; Select List of Reports and Other Papers in House of Commons's Journals, 1688–1800; Guide to Parliamentary Papers; Luke Graves Hansard's Diary, 1814–41; (with J. Bound) Coastwise Shipping and the Small Ports, 1951; (with G. Ford and D. Marshallsay) Select List of Parliamentary Papers 1955–64, 1970; (with C. J. Thomas) Industrial Prospects of Southampton, 1951, Shops and Planning, 1953, Housing, 1953, Problem Families, 1955; Ed., Southampton Civic Survey, 1931; Contributor, Britain in Depression, 1935; articles in journals of economics. *Address:* Lane End, Sandgate Lane,

Storrington, Pulborough, West Sussex RH20 3HJ; Little Haven, Debden Purlieu, Hants. *Died* 19 *Sept.* 1983.

**FORD, Maj.-Gen. Sir Peter St C.;** *see* St Clair-Ford.

**FORD, Sir Sidney (William George),** Kt 1967; MBE 1944; President, National Union of Mineworkers, 1960–71; *b* 29 Aug. 1909; *s* of George and Harriet Ford; *m* 1st, 1936, Ivy Elizabeth Lewis (*d* 1964); one *s* two *d*; 2nd, 1965, Sheila Simon. *Educ:* Silver Street Elementary Sch. Joined Staff of Miners' Federation of Great Britain (later NUM), 1925. Mem., Central Transport Consultative Cttee for GB, 1970–71. *Address:* 18 Woodland Way, Winchmore Hill, N21. *T:* 01-886 8837. *Died* 13 *Aug.* 1983.

**FORDE, Rt. Hon. Francis Michael,** PC 1944; Australian High Commissioner in Canada, 1946–53; Dean of the Diplomatic Corps, Ottawa, Canada, 1952–53; *b* 18 July 1890; *m* 1925, Veronica Catherine O'Reilly; three *d* (one *s* decd). *Educ:* Christian Brothers Coll., Toowoomba, Qld, Aust. School teacher; electrical engineer; Mem. of Qld State Parliament, 1917–22; elected to House of Representatives for Capricornia, Qld Gen. Elections, 1922, 1925, 1928, 1929, 1931, 1934, 1937, 1940, 1943; Mem. Jt Select Cttee on Motion Picture Industry in Australia, 1927, and of Royal Commission on same, 1927–28; Mem. of Joint Cttee on Public Accounts, 1929; Acting Minister for Trade and Customs, Australia, 1929–30; Acting Minister for Markets and Transport, 1930–31; Minister for Trade and Customs, 1930–31, 1932; Dep. Leader Federal Parliamentary Labour Party, 1932–46, and Dep. Leader of the Opposition, 1932–41; Dep. Prime Minister, Minister for Army, Mem. and Vice-Chm. of War Cabinet, Australia, 1941–46; Minister for Defence, 1946; Acting Prime Minister, April–July 1944 and Oct. 1944–Jan. 1945; Prime Minister for short period, 1945; Actg Prime Minister (about two months), 1946. Leader of Australian Delegn to UN Conf., San Francisco, April 25 1945. Mem. for Flinders, Qld Parliament, By-Election, March 1955; re-elected, Gen. Election, May 1956. Represented Australia at Gen. Douglas MacArthur's funeral in USA, 1964. LLD (Hon.): Ottawa Univ., 1950; Montreal Univ., 1952; Laval Univ., 1952; Univ. of Qld, Brisbane, 1972. *Recreations:* tennis, golf, bowls. *Address:* 44 Highland Terrace, St Lucia, Brisbane, Queensland 4067, Australia. *T:* Brisbane 370 9447. *Died* 28 *Jan.* 1983.

**FORDER, Prof. Henry George;** Professor of Mathematics, Auckland University, 1934–55; Professor Emeritus since 1955; *b* 27 Sept. 1889; *s* of Henry Forder, Worstead, Norwich; *m* 1921, Dorothy (*d* 1970), *d* of William Whincup, Bingham, Notts; no *c. Educ:* Paston Grammar Sch., N Walsham; Sidney Sussex Coll., Cambridge. Wrangler, 1910. Mathematical Master at Hulme Grammar Sch., Oldham; High Sch., Cardiff; St Olave's Sch.; Hymers Coll. Hector Medal, Royal Society NZ, 1946. Hon. DSc 1959. *Publications:* Foundations of Euclidean Geometry, 1927 (Dover Reprint, 1958, Rumanian trans., 1970); School Geometry, 1930; Higher Course Geometry, 1931; The Calculus of Extension, 1941 (Chelsea Reprint, 1960); Geometry (Hutchinson's University Library), 1950, Turkish translation, 1965; various articles. *Recreations:* walking and talking. *Address:* Lichfield, Selwyn Village, Port Chevalier, Auckland, New Zealand. *Died* 21 *Sept.* 1981.

**FORDHAM, Sir (Alfred) Stanley,** KBE 1964; CMG 1951; JP; *b* 2 Sept. 1907; *e s* of late Alfred Russell Fordham, JP, Melbourn Bury, Cambs, and Caroline Augusta Stanley; *m* 1934, Isabel, *y d* of Juan Ward, Lima, Peru; one *s* one *d. Educ:* Eton; Trinity Coll., Cambridge. Vice-Consul, San Francisco, 1930–33; Lima, 1933–36; Guatemala, 1936–43; Los Angeles, 1943–44; Consul and Chargé d'Affaires, San Salvador, 1944–45; Consul, St Louis, 1945–48; transferred to Foreign Office, 1948, and promoted Counsellor (Head of American Dept), 1949; Warsaw, 1951–52; Stockholm, 1952–54; Minister, HM Embassy, Buenos Aires, 1954–56; HM Ambassador to Cuba, 1956–60; HM Ambassador to Colombia, 1960–64; Mem., UK Delegn to UN General Assembly, 1961. Retired from Foreign Service, 1964. JP 1966, High Sheriff 1973–74, Cambs and Isle of Ely; HM Lieutenant for Cambridgeshire, 1975–77. Grand Cross of San Carlos (Colombia). *Recreations:* gardening, shooting. *Address:* Melbourn Bury, Royston, Herts. *T:* Royston 60206. *Clubs:* MCC; Cambridge County. *Died* 6 *April* 1981.

**FORDHAM, Wilfrid Gurney;** QC 1967; *b* 9 Dec. 1902; *s* of Edward Wilfrid Fordham and Sybil Harriet (*née* Langdon-Davies); *m* 1930, Peta Marshall Freeman; one *s. Educ:* St George's, Harpenden; Magdalene Coll., Cambridge. Called to Bar, Inner Temple, 1929 (Bencher 1981); retired from practice, 1986. Dep. Circuit Judge, 1972–74; a Recorder of the Crown Court, 1974–76. Contested: (L) Bromley, Kent, 1929, 1930; (Lab) Wycombe, Bucks, 1959. *Publications:* various legal books. *Recreation:* travel. *Address:* 4 Paper Buildings, Temple, EC4. *T:* 01-353 2739.

*Died* 1 *Oct.* 1988.

**FORDYCE, Catherine Mary,** MA (London and Oxford); *b* Wareham, Dorset, 18 Dec. 1898; *d* of Ernest Chilcott, MA, Vicar of Elberton, Glos; *m* 1929, Prof. Christian James Fordyce (*d* 1974). *Educ:* St

Mary's Hall, Brighton; Bedford Coll. for Women. London BA Classical Hons Cl. I, 1920; Gilchrist Studentship, 1921; MA (with distinction), 1922; Fellow and Classical Tutor of Lady Margaret Hall, Oxford, 1922–29. *Publications:* articles in Classical Quarterly, 1923; Essay, Myth and Reality, in Adventure, 1927. *Address:* Baxter House, Lowther Terrace, Kirklee, Glasgow G12 0RN.

*Died* 27 *Feb.* 1983.

**FORECAST, Kenneth George,** CB 1985; Under Secretary, Central Statistical Office, Cabinet Office, 1979–85; *b* 21 Aug. 1925; *s* of late George Albert Forecast and Alice Matilda Forecast (*née* Davies); unmarried. *Educ:* William Morris Sch., Walthamstow; SW Essex Techn. Coll. BSc (Econ) London. Statistical Officer, MAP, 1945–48; Economist/Statistician with de Zoete & Gorton, Stock Exchange, London, 1948–51; Statistician: Central Statistics Office, Dublin, 1951–58; BoT, London, 1958–66; Chief Statistician, MoT, 1966–70; Dir of Statistics, DES, 1970–79. Mem. Council, Huguenot Soc. of GB and Ireland. *Publications:* contribs to Review of Internat. Statistical Inst. and to Jl of Statistical and Social Inquiry Soc. of Ireland. *Address:* 9 Mathart Court, The Avenue, Highams Park, E4 9QQ. *T:* 01–527 3023. *Club:* Civil Service.

*Died* 15 *March* 1988.

**FOREMAN, Carl,** CBE (Hon.) 1970; FRSA; screen writer, producer, director; Executive Producer, High Noon Productions, since 1975; *b* Chicago, USA, 23 July 1914. *Educ:* Crane Coll.; Univ. of Illinois; Northwestern Univ., USA. Formerly Man. Dir and Exec. Producer, Open Road Films Ltd. *Film scripts:* So This is New York; Champion (Academy Award nomination); Home of the Brave; The Men (Academy Award nomination); Cyrano de Bergerac; (writer-prod.) High Noon (Academy Award nomination); The Bridge on the River Kwai; (writer-prod.) The Key; (writer-prod.) The Guns of Navarone (Academy Award nomination); (writer-prod.-dir) The Victors; (writer-prod.) Mackenna's Gold; (writer-prod.) Young Winston (Variety Club of GB Show-business Writer Award, 1972; Best Screenplay Award, Writers' Guild of GB, 1972; Academy Award nomination); Executive Producer, films: The Mouse that Roared; Born Free; Otley; The Virgin Soldiers; Living Free. Mem. Bd of Governors: British Film Inst., 1966–71; National Film Sch., 1971–75; Mem. Exec. Council, Film Production Assoc., 1967–75; Pres., Writers' Guild of GB, 1968–75 (Dist. Service Award, 1968); Writers' Guild of Amer. Laurel Award, 1969; Valentine Davies Award, 1977. Comdr, Order of the Phoenix (Greece), 1962. *Publications:* A Cast of Lions, 1966; Young Winston, 1972. *Address:* 1370 Avenue of the Americas, New York, NY 10019, USA. *Clubs:* Savile, Garrick. *Died* 26 *June* 1984.

**FORESTIER-WALKER, Sir Clive Radzivill;** *see* Walker.

**FORMAN, Louis,** MD London; FRCP; Consultant Dermatologist Emeritus, Guy's Hospital and St John's Hospital for Diseases of the Skin; *b* 1901; unmarried. *Educ:* Guy's Hosp., Univ. of London. MRCS, LRCP 1923; MB, BS 1924; MRCP 1925; FRCP 1939. Formerly Dermatologist SE Group, London CC; Medical Registrar, Guy's Hosp. Past President: British Assoc. Dermatology; Section of Dermatology, RSM. Hon. FRSM 1985. *Publications:* various articles in med. jls. *Address:* 22 Harley House, Regent's Park, NW1 5HE. *T:* 01–487 3834. *Died* 13 *Nov.* 1988.

**FORMAN HARDY, Col Thomas Eben,** CBE 1966; MC 1943; TD 1945; Chairman, Forman Hardy Holdings Ltd (including T. Bailey Forman Ltd (newspaper proprietors) and subsidiary cos), since 1939; *b* 30 Aug. 1919; *s* of late William Eben Hardy and Dorothea Kate (*née* Forman); *m* 1946, Marjorie Senior (*née* Edgar); one *s* one *d* (and one *s* decd). *Educ:* Harrow; Trinity Coll., Cambridge. S Notts Hussars Yeo., 1939; served War of 1939–45 with 456 Indep. Light Battery, RA, in N Africa; also served in Sicily, Italy, and was an original mem. of mule-pack 7th Mountain regt, RA; promoted Major and commanded a battery; wounded in action, Italy; commanded S Notts Hussars Yeo., 1958–62; Dep. Bde Comdr, 148 (E Midlands) Inf. Bde, TA 1962–66; Hon. Col, S Notts Hussars Yeo., 1963. ADC (TA) to the Queen, 1966–71. Chm., TAVRA (E Midlands), 1980–85; Former Pres., S Notts Hussars Old Comrades Assoc.; Vice President: Notts Royal British Legion; Nottingham Br., BLESMA. Pres., Newark & Notts Agricl Show, 1965, 1976 and 1988. Jt Master, S Notts Hunt, 1957–65. High Sheriff, 1960, DL 1963, Notts. *Recreations:* shooting, golf. *Address:* Car Colston Hall, Bingham, Notts NG13 8JE. *T:* East Bridgford 20254. *Club:* Cavalry and Guards. *Died* 14 *Sept.* 1989.

**FORRESTER, Rev. William Roxburgh,** MC; Professor of Practical Theology and Christian Ethics, St Mary's College, St Andrews University, 1934–58; Emeritus Professor; *b* 19 Feb. 1892; *s* of Rev. David Marshall Forrester, DD, and Annie Roxburgh; *m* 1922, Isobel Margaret Stewart McColl (*d* 1976); three *s* two *d. Educ:* Glasgow Acad.; Glasgow and Edinburgh Univs. MA (Hons) Edinburgh, 1914; European War: France, Mesopotamia, Persia and India in RFA, 1914–19 (MC 1917); studies at New Coll., Edinburgh; France and Germany, 1919–22; BD, 1924; Minister at Roslin, 1922–28; Minister at Cairns Memorial Church, Edinburgh,

1928–34; Interim Gen. Sec. Scottish National YMCA, 1940–44; DD (Edinburgh) 1939. Cunningham Lecturer, New Coll., Edinburgh, 1947–48–49; LLD St Andrews, 1959. Associate Minister, St Andrew's Presbyterian Church, Nairobi, Nov. 1961–Nov. 1962. *Publications:* Christian Vocation, Studies in Faith and its Relation to Work, 1951; Conversion, 1937, Concern, 1963; The Pen and the Panga, two Addresses on Education and Religion (East Africa), 1965; Your Life and Mine, 1967. *Recreations:* fishing, gardening. *Address:* Roxstone House, 24 Murrayfield Avenue, Edinburgh. *T:* 031–337 2522. *Died 15 Aug. 1984.*

**FORSTER, Walter Leslie,** CBE 1942; Legion of Merit (USA), 1944; BSc; FInstPet; Director, various cos; *b* 30 June 1903; *s* of John Mark Forster, Leeds; *m* 1936, Lorna, *d* of T. L. Bonstow, Coulsdon, Surrey; one *s. Educ:* Leeds Univ. *Address:* 61 Summit Crescent, Westmount, Montreal, Canada. *Clubs:* St James's, Mount Royal (Montreal). *Died 13 Feb. 1985.*

**FORSYTH-THOMPSON, Aubrey Denzil,** CMG 1944; CVO 1947; CBE 1941; *b* 3 Oct. 1897; *s* of Ernest Alfred Thompson; *m* 1924, Kathleen Esther Murray; one *s* one *d. Educ:* Weenen County College, Natal; New College, Oxford. Served European War, France, RFA, Lieut 1917–19; Oxford, 1919–20 (BA); Administrative Officer, Uganda, 1921–37; Asst Resident Commissioner and Govt Secretary, Bechuanaland Protectorate, 1937–42; Resident Commissioner, 1942–46; Resident Commissioner, Basutoland, 1946–51; retired, 1951. *Recreation:* gardening. *Address:* 269 West Street, Pietermaritzburg, Natal, S Africa. *Died 13 June 1982.*

**FORTER, Alexis Kougoulsky,** CMG 1982; OBE 1963; HM Diplomatic Service, retired; Counsellor, Paris, 1977–82; *b* 6 Sept. 1925; *s* of Sqdn Ldr Michael Forter and Suzanne Forter; *m* 1971, Barbara Wood. *Educ:* St Paul's Sch.; Magdalen Coll., Oxford (First Cl. Hons Oriental Studies). Commissioned RAF, 1944; served Middle East, 1945–47. Joined Foreign (later Diplomatic) Service, 1950; 3rd Sec., Tehran, 1951; Vice-Consul, Basra, 1952; Port Said, 1954; FO, 1955; 1st Sec., Baghdad, 1957; FO, 1958; Tehran, 1959; FO, 1964; Saigon, 1966; FCO, 1969; Nairobi, 1971; FCO, 1973. *Recreations:* beagling, music, shooting. *Address:* 146B Ashley Gardens, SW1P 1HG. *Clubs:* Travellers', Beefsteak. *Died 12 July 1983.*

**FORTES, Prof. Meyer,** MA, PhD; FBA 1967; William Wyse Professor of Social Anthropology, University of Cambridge, 1950–73; Fellow of King's College, Cambridge, 1950–78, Honorary Fellow, since 1980; *b* Britstown, Cape, 25 April 1906; *e s* of late Nathan and late Mrs Bertha Fortes, Cape Town, S Africa; *m* 1928, Sonia (*d* 1956), *d* of late N. Donen, Worcester, Cape, SA; one *d*; *m* 1960, Doris Y. Mayer, MD, *d* of late D. S. Yankauer, NY. *Educ:* South African Coll. High Sch., Cape Town; University of Cape Town; University of London. Univ. of Cape Town: Roderick Noble Schol., 1926, Willem Hiddingh Schol., 1927–30; London Sch. of Economics: Ratan Tata Student, 1930–31, Rockefeller Fellow, 1933–34; Fellow, International African Institute, 1934–38; Lectr, LSE, 1938–39; Research Lectr, University of Oxford, 1939–41; National Service, West Africa, 1942–44; Head of Sociological Dept, West African Institute, Accra, Gold Coast, 1944–46; Reader in Social Anthropology, Oxford, 1946–50. President: Section H, Brit. Assoc. for the Advancement of Science, 1953; Section 25, ANZAAS, 1975. Lectures: Josiah Mason, Univ. of Birmingham, 1949; Frazer, Glasgow, 1956; Henry Myers, Royal Anthrop. Inst., 1960; Lewis Henry Morgan, Univ. of Rochester, USA, 1963; Munro, Univ. of Edinburgh, 1964, 1973; Emanuel Miller Meml, Assoc. Child Psychol. and Psychiatry, 1972; Ernest Jones Meml, Brit. Psychoanalytical Soc., 1973; Marett, Oxford, 1974; Huxley Meml, Royal Anthrop. Inst., 1977. Chm., Assoc. Social Anthropologists, 1970–73. For. Mem., American Philosophical Soc., 1972; Foreign Hon. Mem. Amer. Acad. of Arts and Sciences, 1964. Field Research: Northern Territories, Gold Coast, 1934–37; Nigeria, 1941–42; Ashanti Gold Coast, 1945–46; Bechuanaland, 1948. Pres., Royal Anthropological Institute; Hon. Editor, Jl Royal Anthropological Inst., 1947–53; Mem. Exec. Council, International African Institute; Mem. Exec. Cttee, British Sociological Assoc., 1952–55. Visiting Professor: Chicago Univ., 1954, 1973; Univ. of Ghana, 1971 (Leverhulme); Australian Nat. Univ., 1975; Univ. of California, Santa Cruz, 1977; Northwestern Univ., 1978 (M. J. Herskovits); Univ. of Manchester, 1980. Fellow: Center for Advanced Study in Behavioral Science, Stanford, 1958–59, and 1967–68; University Coll., London, 1975. Hon. Fellow, LSE, 1979. Rivers Medal, Royal Anthropological Inst., 1946. Hon. DHL Chicago, 1973; Hon. DLitt Belfast, 1975. *Publications:* The Dynamics of Clanship among the Tallensi, 1945; The Web of Kinship among the Tallensi, 1949; Social Anthropology at Cambridge since 1900, 1953; Oedipus and Job in West African Religion, 1959; Kinship and the Social Order, 1969; Time and Social Structure, 1970; (ed) Marriage in Tribal Societies, 1972; (ed with S. Patterson) Studies in African Social Anthropology, 1975; (ed with M. Bourdillon) Sacrifice, 1980; various papers in psychological and anthropological journals. *Address:* 113 Grantchester Meadows, Cambridge CB3 9JN. *Died 27 Jan. 1983.*

**FORTY, Francis John,** OBE 1952; BSc, FICE, FSA, FRSH, FIMunE; City Engineer, Corporation of London, 1938–64; *b* Hull, Yorks, 11 Feb. 1900; *s* of J. E. Forty, MA Oxon, headmaster, Hull Grammar Sch., and Maud C. Forty; *m* 1st, 1926, Doris Marcon Francis (*d* 1958), *d* of Dr A. G. Francis, BA Cantab, FRCS; one *s* two *d*; 2nd, 1965, Elizabeth Joyce Tofield. *Educ:* Hymers Coll., Hull; Glasgow Univ. (BSc 1923). RNAS, RAF, 1918–19 (Commnd Pilot). Engineering Asst, Hull; Engineering Asst, York; Chief Engineering Asst, Willesden. Deputy Borough Surveyor, Ealing; Borough Engineer and Surveyor, Ealing, 1934–38. War duties, 1939–45, included i/c City of London Heavy Rescue Service (Civil Defence Long Service Medal). Works include: (with Sir Albert Richardson) St Paul's Garden, 1951; (in consultation with Prof. W. F. Grimes) exposure and preservation of section of Town Wall of London, 1951–53; London Wall new route between Moorgate and Aldersgate Street, with car park underneath, 1959; Blackfriars Bridgehead Improvement with underpass, 1962–; multi-storey car park, Upper Thames Street, 1962; Walbrook Wharf Public Cleansing Depot and Wharf (consultant architect, Sir Hugh Casson), 1963. Formerly Member: London Regional Bldg Cttee; Nat. Soc. for Clean Air; Roman and Mediaeval London Excavation Council; Festival of Britain Council for Architecture, Town Planning and Bldg Research; Minister of Transport's Parking Survey Cttee for Inner London; Minister of Housing and Local Govt's Thames Flooding Technical Panel; Sussex Archaeological Trust. Liveryman of the Worshipful Company of Painter-Stainers, of the City of London. *Publications:* Bituminous Emulsions for Use in Road Works (with F. Wilkinson), 1932; Swimming Bath Water Purification from a Public Health Point of View (with F. W. Wilkinson), various contribs technical and other jls; notably contrib. on exposure and preservation of Roman and Mediæval work in the Town Wall of London. *Address:* Flat 8, Emanuel House, 18 Rochester Row, SW1P 1BS. *T:* 071–834 4376. *Clubs:* Athenæum, Royal Air Force. *Died 22 Nov. 1990.*

**FOSTER, Sir Idris (Llewelyn),** Kt 1977; MA Wales and Oxon; FSA; Jesus Professor of Celtic in the University of Oxford, 1947–78, then Emeritus; Fellow of Jesus College, 1947–78, Honorary Fellow, 1978; Hon. RCamA; Member: Royal Commission on Ancient Monuments in Wales and Monmouthshire; Museums and Galleries Commission (formerly Standing Commission on Museums and Galleries), 1964–82; Governing Body, Church in Wales; Vice-President, National Library of Wales; *b* 23 July 1911; *e s* of late Harold L. Foster and Ann J. (Roberts), Carneddi, Bethesda, Bangor, Caerns; unmarried. *Educ:* County Sch., Bethesda; University Coll. of North Wales, Bangor (Hon. Professorial Fellow, 1978); National Univ. of Ireland, Dublin. BA (Wales) with First Class Hons, 1932; University Research Student, 1933–35; MA (Wales) with distinction, 1935; Fellow of University of Wales, 1935; Head of Dept of Celtic, University of Liverpool, 1936–47; Warden of Derby Hall, University of Liverpool, 1946–47; served in Intelligence Div., Naval Staff, Admiralty, 1942–45; Sir John Rhys Memorial Lectr, Br. Acad., 1950; O'Donnell Lectr, Univ. of Edinburgh, 1960, Univ. of Wales, 1971–72; G. J. Williams Lectr., University Coll., Cardiff, 1973; University of Oxford: Select Preacher, 1973–74; James Ford Special Lectr, 1979; President: Soc. for Study of Mediæval Languages and Literature, 1953–58; Cambrian Archaeological Assoc., 1968–69; Court of Nat. Eisteddfod of Wales, 1973–77 (Chm. Council, 1970–73); Irish Texts Soc., 1973–83; Chm., Gwynedd Archaeol Trust, 1974–79, 1983–; formerly Chm., Modern Langs Bd, and Anthropol. and Geography Bd, Oxford; Mem., Council for Welsh Language, 1973–78; Chm., Ancient Monuments Bd for Wales, 1979–83; Hon. Editor, Trans. and publications, Cymmrodorion Soc., 1953–78. *Publications:* (ed with L. Alcock) Culture and Environment, 1963; (ed with Glyn Daniel) Prehistoric and Early Wales, 1965; papers and reviews. *Recreation:* music. *Address:* Cae'ronnen, Carneddi, Bangor, Gwynedd. *Club:* Athenæum. *Died 18 June 1984.*

**FOSTER, Sir John (Galway),** KBE 1964; QC 1950; Barrister-at-Law; *b* 4 Nov. 1904; *s* of late General Hubert John Foster. *Educ:* Eton; New Coll., Oxford. Fellow of All Souls, 1924; Lectr in Private International Law, Oxford, 1934–39; First Sec., British Embassy, Washington, 1939; Brigadier, General Service, 1944. Recorder of Dudley, 1936–38; Recorder of Oxford, 1938–51 and 1956–64. MP (C) Northwich, Cheshire, 1945–Feb. 1974; Parly Under-Sec. of State, CRO, 1951–Oct. 1954. Mem. Council, Aims of Industry, 1974–; Chm., Facts about Business. Hon. Fellow, Wolfson Coll., Oxford, 1981. Legion of Honour; American Legion of Merit; Croix de Guerre (with palms). *Publications:* lectures and articles on constitutional and private international law. *Address:* 2 Hare Court, EC4Y 7BH. *T:* 01-353 2233. *Died 1 Feb. 1982.*

**FOSTER, Sir Peter Harry Batson Woodroffe,** Kt 1969; MBE 1943; TD 1946; a Judge of the Chancery Division of the High Court of Justice, 1969–83; *b* 5 Dec. 1912; *s* of late Frank Foster; *m* 1937, Jane

Hillcoat Easdale, *d* of late James Easdale; one *s* three *d*. *Educ:* Rugby Sch.; Corpus Christi Coll., Cambridge (BA, LLB). Called to the Bar, Inner Temple, 1936; Bencher, Lincoln's Inn, 1963. Fife and Forfar Yeomanry, 1939; War of 1939–45: Dunkirk, 8th Armd Div., Alamein, 18 Army Gp, Tripoli, Col, 21 Army Group, North Western Europe (despatches thrice, MBE). Resumed practice, 1945; QC 1957. Mem., Gen. Council of the Bar, 1956–60; Mem., Senate, 1966–69, 1976–79. Chm., Chancery Bar Assoc., 1963–68; formerly Member Council: Officers' Assoc.; Royal Albert Hall; Steward British Boxing Board of Control. Church Commissioner for England, 1965–69. Reserve Chm., Conscientious Objectors Tribunal, 1965–69; Chm., Performing Right Tribunal, 1969. *Recreations:* golf, travelling. *Address:* 7 Cadogan House, 93 Sloane Street, SW1. *T:* 01–730 1984. *Clubs:* White's; Royal and Ancient Golf (St Andrews); Hawks (Cambridge). *Died 10 May 1985.*

**FOSTER, Robert,** CBE 1963 (OBE 1955; MBE 1949); FCIS; FIB; President, Savings Banks Institute, 1970–75; *b* 4 March 1898; *s* of Robert Foster; *m* 1927, Edith Kathleen (*née* Blackburn); two *d*. *Educ:* Rutherford Coll., Newcastle upon Tyne. RNVR, 1915–19. London Trustee Savings Banks, 1924–63 (Gen. Manager, 1943–63), retired. Mem. Nat. Savings Cttee, 1957–62. Mem. Court, Worshipful Company of Plumbers, 1959– (Master, 1965). *Recreations:* golf, gardening. *Club:* City Livery. *Died 21 Dec. 1989.*

**FOTHERGILL, (Arthur) Brian,** FSA; FRSL; historian and biographer; *b* 3 April 1921; *s* of late John Smirthwaite Fothergill, of Newlands, near Kendal, and late Kathleen Entwisle (she *m* 2nd, 1941, J. M. Somervell, Kendal). *Educ:* Wycliffe; King's College, London (AKC 1942). Army service (Intelligence Corps), 1944–47. Schoolmaster, 1947–57; freelance writer, 1958–. Royal Society of Literature: Fellow, 1970; Mem. Council, 1977–89; Vice-Pres., 1986–; Chm. Council, 1986–89. *Publications:* The Cardinal King, 1958; Nicholas Wiseman, 1963; Mrs Jordan: portrait of an actress, 1965; Sir William Hamilton: envoy extraordinary, 1969 (Heinemann Award 1969, Silver Pen Prize, 1970, trans. German, 1970); The Mitred Earl, 1974; Beckford of Fonthill, 1979 (Heinemann Award, 1980); (ed) Essays by Divers Hands, vol. XLI, 1980; The Strawberry Hill Set, 1983; (contrib.) Vathek and The Escape from Time, 1989; contribs to Encyclopaedia Britannica, TLS. *Recreations:* reading, listening to opera. *Address:* 7 Union Square, N1 7DH. *Clubs:* Royal Over-Seas League, PEN (English Centre).

*Died 6 Aug. 1990.*

**FOULKES, Maj.-Gen. Thomas Herbert Fischer,** CB 1962; OBE 1945; *b* 29 May 1908; *e s* of late Maj.-Gen. C. H. Foulkes, CB, CMG, DSO; *m* 1947, Delphine Elizabeth Smith; two *s*. *Educ:* Clifton Coll., Bristol (Pres., Old Cliftonian Soc., 1963–65); RMA Woolwich; St Catharine's Coll., Cambridge. BA 1930, MA Cantab 1954. Commissioned into RE, 1928; served in India and Burma, 1931–46 (CRE 39 Indian Div., also CRE 17 Indian Div. during Burma campaign); Comdr Corps RE (Brig.) 1 Br. Corps in BAOR, 1956–57; Chief Engr (Brig.) Middle East, 1957–58; Chief Engr (Brig.) Southern Command, UK, 1958–60; Engineer-in-Chief (Maj.-Gen.), War Office, 1960–63. Col Comdt, Royal Engineers, 1963–73. Hon. Col, RE Resources Units, AER, 1964–67; Hon. Col, RE Volunteers (Sponsored Units), T&AVR, 1967–72. President: Instn of Royal Engrs, 1965–70; Royal Bombay Sappers and Miners Officers Assoc., 1982–. Governor: Clifton Coll., 1964; Handcross Park Sch., 1968–. Pres., Aldershot and N Hants Cons. Assoc., 1978–83. Liveryman, Worshipful Co. of Plumbers of City of London, 1960, Master, 1973. CEng, FICE. *Recreations:* travel, fishing, photography. *Address:* Caton, 32 Fitzroy Road, Fleet, Aldershot, Hants GU13 8JW. *T:* Fleet 616650. *Club:* Army and Navy. *Died 29 Dec. 1986.*

**FOURNIER, Pierre;** 'cellist; Officier, Légion d'Honneur; *b* 24 June 1906; *m* 1936, Lydia Antik (*d* 1978); one *s*; *m* 1980, Junko Taguchi. *Educ:* University and Conservatoire, Paris. Formerly teacher at the National Conservatoire, Paris. Concert soloist every season in the European Capitals as well as in USA, South America and Far East; also soloist playing with chief orchestras. Commander, Ordre national du Mérite (France); Commander, Ordre Léopold II (Belgium); Officer, Arts and Letters (Paris); Chevalier with Crown (Luxembourg). *Address:* 14 Château Banquet, 1202 Geneva, Switzerland. *Died 8 Jan. 1986.*

**FOWKE, Sir Frederick (Woollaston Rawdon),** 4th Bt *cr* 1814; *b* 14 Dec. 1910; *e s* of Sir Frederick Ferrers Conant Fowke, 3rd Bt, and Edith Frances Daubeney (*d* 1958), *d* of late Canon J. H. Rawdon; *S* father, 1948; *m* 1948, Barbara (*d* 1982), *d* of late E. Townsend; two *d*. *Educ:* Uppingham. Served War of 1939–45, in Derbs Yeomanry, 1939–43 (wounded). *Recreation:* shooting. *Heir:* *n* David Frederick Gustavus Fowke, *b* 28 Aug. 1950. *Address:* Lower Woolstone Farm, Bishops Tawton, Barnstaple, N Devon. *Died 9 Dec. 1987.*

**FOWLER, Frank James,** CBE 1974 (OBE 1945); TD; *b* 1 Oct. 1911; *s* of James Edward Fowler and Sarah Anne Fowler; *m* 1949, Josephine Kennedy; two *s* one *d*. *Educ:* King Edward's Sch., Birmingham; Univ. of Birmingham. MB, ChB; FRCP, FFCM. Univ. of Birmingham: Union Sec., 1931–32; Sec., Guild of Undergrads,

1933–34; Mem. Ct of Governors, 1934–36. House appts: Gen. Hosp., Birmingham, 1936; Hallam Hosp., W Bromwich, 1937 and 1946–48; Asst MO, City Hosp., Derby, 1938; commnd RAMC (TA), 1938; Unit MO, UK and France, 1939–41; DADMS 9 Corps, UK and N Africa, 1941–43; ADMS 2 Dist Italy, 1943–44; ADMS Ops Allied Forces HQ, 1944–45; ADMS (Adm.) CMF, 1945. Asst Sen. MO, Oxford RHB, 1948–51; Dep. SAMO, NE Met. RHB, 1951–58; SAMO NW Met. RHB, 1958–73; Reg. MO, Yorks RHA, 1973–76; Senior MO, DHSS, 1977–80. Mem. Bd and Treas., Faculty of Community Medicine, 1972–77. *Recreations:* pianoforte and organ playing; gardening, walking. *Address:* 7 Franklin Place, Chichester PO19 1BL. *T:* Chichester 788566.

*Died 2 April 1981.*

**FOWLER, Sir Robert (William Doughty),** KCMG 1966 (CMG 1962); HM Diplomatic Service, retired; *b* 6 March 1914; *s* of William and Martha Louise Fowler; *m* Margaret MacFarquhar (*née* MacLeod); one *s* one *d* (twins). *Educ:* Queen Elizabeth's Grammar Sch., Mansfield; Emmanuel Coll., Cambridge. Burma CS, 1937–48; Burma Army (Military Administration), 1944–46; Additional Sec. to Governor of Burma, 1947; Commonwealth Relations Office from 1948; seconded to Foreign Service for UK Delegn to UN, 1950–53; Fedn of Rhodesia and Nyasaland and High Commn Territories Dept, CRO, 1954–56; Brit. Dep. High Comr: Pakistan, 1956–58; Canada, 1960–62; Nigeria, 1963–64. Attended IDC, 1959. British High Comr to Tanzania, Aug. 1964, until diplomatic relations broken off in Dec. 1965; Ambassador to Sudan from 1966 until break in relations in 1967; reappointed Ambassador, 1968–70 (during the break, Administrator of Gibraltar Referendum and Under-Sec. of State, Commonwealth Office). *Recreations:* gardening, painting, photography. *Address:* 7 Leicester Close, Henley-on-Thames, Oxon. *T:* Henley 2404. *Clubs:* Royal Commonwealth Society; Phyllis Court (Henley).

*Died 29 May 1985.*

**FOX;** *see* Lane-Fox and Lane Fox.

**FOX, Patrick Loftus B.;** *see* Bushe-Fox.

**FOX, Sir (Robert) David (John) S.;** *see* Scott Fox.

**FOX, Sir Theodore (Fortescue),** Kt 1962; MA, MD Cambridge, LLD Glasgow, DLitt Birmingham; FRCP; *b* 26 Nov. 1899; 3rd *s* of late R. Fortescue Fox; *m* 1930, Margaret (*d* 1970), *e d* of late W. S. McDougall, Wallington, Surrey; four *s*. *Educ:* Leighton Park Sch.; Pembroke Coll., Cambridge (scholar); London Hosp. (house physician). Mem. of Friends' Ambulance Unit, BEF, 1918; Ship Surg., 1925; joined staff of The Lancet, 1925; served in RAMC, 1939–42 (late temp. Major); Ed., The Lancet, 1944–64. Dir, Family Planning Assoc., 1965–67. Croonian Lectr, RCP, 1951; Heath Clark Lectr, Univ. of London, 1963; Harveian Orator, RCP, 1965; Maurice Bloch Lectr, Univ. of Glasgow, 1966. Hon. Fellow: Royal Australian Coll. of Gen. Practitioners, 1962; NY Acad. of Medicine, 1984. *Publication:* Crisis in Communication, 1965. *Address:* Green House, Rotherfield, East Sussex. *T:* Rotherfield 2870. *Club:* Athenaeum. *Died 19 June 1989.*

**FOX-PITT, Maj.-Gen. William Augustus Fitzgerald Lane,** CVO 1966 (MVO 1936); DSO 1940; MC 1916; retired; DL; Member of HM Bodyguard of Hon. Corps of Gentlemen-at-Arms, 1947–66; Lieutenant, 1963–66; (Standard Bearer, 1961–63); *b* 28 Jan. 1896; *s* of late Lieut-Col W. A. Fox-Pitt, Presaddfed, Anglesey; *m* 1931, Mary Stewart, *d* of A. H. H. Sinclair, MD, FRCSE; two *s* one *d*. *Educ:* Charterhouse. ADC to the King, 1945–47; joined Cheshire Regt 1914; served with Welsh Gds, 1915–39; Comd, 1st Bn, 1934–37; OC Welsh Guards Regt, 1937–40; Comd Gds Bde BEF, 1940, Armd Bde, 1941–43; Comdr, East Kent Dist as Maj.-Gen., 1943; retired with hon. rank of Maj.-Gen. 1947. Mem. Dorset CC 1952; DL Dorset, 1957. *Recreations:* shooting, golf. *Address:* Marsh Court, Sherborne, Dorset. *T:* Bishops Caundle 230. *Clubs:* Pratt's, Cavalry and Guards. *Died 26 April 1988.*

**FOXELL, Rev. Maurice Frederic,** KCVO 1965 (CVO 1953; MVO 1942); MA; Extra Chaplain to the Queen since 1965; Honorary Minor Canon St Paul's Cathedral; *b* 15 Aug. 1888; 4th *s* of late Rev. W. J. Foxell, PhD, and Annie Harte; *m* 1914, Mariana (*d* 1975), 2nd *d* of late John Morton Fountain, Hillingdon, Middx; two *s* two *d*. *Educ:* Christ's Hospital; Queen's Coll., Oxford. Asst Curate St Paul's, Hammersmith, 1911–15; Friern Barnet, 1915–17; Minor Canon St George's Chapel, Windsor Castle, 1917–21; Minor Canon and Succentor, St Paul's Cathedral, 1921–39; Rector of St James's, Garlickhythe, EC4, 1939–64. Sub-Dean of HM Chapels Royal, Sub-Almoner, Deputy Clerk of the Closet, and Domestic Chaplain to the Queen, 1952–65 (to King George VI, 1948–52). *Publication:* Wren's Craftsmen at St Paul's, 1934. *Recreations:* water-colour, wood-engraving, piano. *Address:* The College of St Barnabas, Lingfield, Surrey. *T:* Dormans Park 508. *Died 7 May 1981.*

**FOXON, Prof. George Eric Howard,** MA, MSc; Professor of Biology, University of London, 1955–72, later Emeritus Professor; Head of

Biology Department, Guy's Hospital Medical School, 1948–72; *b* 1908; *s* of George Thomas Foxon, OBE, and Edith Maud (*née* Lewis); *m* 1932, Joan Burlinson; one *s* one *d* (and one *s* decd). *Educ:* King's Coll. Sch., Wimbledon; Queens' Coll., Cambridge. BA 1930, 1st Cl. Hons Nat. Sci. Tripos Pt II, 1931; MA 1934; MSc (Wales) 1943. Asst in Zoology, University of Glasgow, 1932–37; Asst Lectr and Lectr in Zoology, University Coll., Cardiff, 1937–48; Reader in Biology, University of London, 1948–55. Chm. of the British Univs Film Council, 1959–63, 1967–69. Fellow Cambridge Philosophical Soc., FLS; FIBiol; FZS. *Publications:* various scientific papers, mainly dealing with the comparative study of the heart and blood system of vertebrate animals. *Address:* Thorpe Cloud, Woodfield Lane, Ashtead, Surrey KT21 2BE. *T:* Ashtead 72306.
*Died 16 Nov.* 1982.

**FRAENKEL, Heinrich;** freelance author; *b* 28 Sept. 1897; *s* of Benno Fraenkel and Alwina (*née* Taendler); *m* 1936, Gretel Levy-Ries; two *s. Educ:* German schools and universities. Began career in film trade journalism, Berlin; as screen-writer, went to Hollywood for two years but returned to Germany; continued to write screen plays but increasingly interested in politics; emigrated to avoid arrest in night of Reichstag fire, 1933; went to Paris, then London; still made living writing screen-plays but wrote political books, lectured on German history, the roots of Nazism, etc. At war's end, determined to return to Germany; disillusioned by many long trips made for the New Statesman; sought British nationality, 1949. Has written chess column in New Statesman (as Assiac), 1949–76. Order of Merit (1st class) of Fed. Rep. of Germany, 1967. *Publications:* The German People Versus Hitler, 1940; Help Us Germans to Beat the Nazis, 1941; The Winning of the Peace, 1942; The Other Germany, 1943; A Nation Divided, 1949; The Boy Between, 1956; Farewell to Germany, 1958; with Roger Manvell: Dr Goebbels, 1959; Hermann Goering, 1962; The July Plot, 1964; Heinrich Himmler, 1965; The Incomparable Crime, 1967; The Canaris Conspiracy, 1969; History of the German Cinema, 1971; Rudolf Hess, 1971; Inside Hitler, 1973; Seizure of Power, 1974; Adolf Hitler: the man and the myth, 1977, English enlgd edn, repr. 1982; *as Assiac:* Adventure in Chess, 1950; Delights of Chess, 1960, US, French, Dutch, Spanish and German edns substantially enlgd and revised; (with Kevin O'Connell) Prepared Variations, 1981; (with Kevin O'Connell) Opening Preparation, 1982; More Delights of Chess, 1982, enlarged edn, 1983; More Delights in Chess, 1986; That's Funny, 1986. *Address:* 19 Mayo Court, Northcroft Road, Ealing, W13. *T:* 01–840 5350. *Club:* Authors'. *Died 25 May* 1986.

**FRAMPTON, Meredith,** RA 1942 (ARA 1934); Honorary Retired Academician; *b* 1894; *s* of Sir George Frampton, RA; *m* 1951, Hilda Norman, *d* of late James B. Dunn, RSA, FRIBA, and of Mrs Dunn, Edinburgh. *Educ:* Westminster. Retrospective exhibition, Tate Gall., 1982. *Address:* Hill Barn, Monkton Deverill, Warminster, Wilts. *Club:* Athenæum. *Died 16 Sept.* 1984.

**FRAMPTON, Walter Bennett,** OBE 1945; Metropolitan Magistrate, Marylebone Magistrates' Court, 1952–67, retired; *b* 1 Oct. 1903; *er s* of late Walter Frampton, Recorder of Chichester, and Catherine Bennett; *m* 1928, Gwyneth Davies; one *s* one *d. Educ:* Westminster Sch.; London Univ. Called to Bar, Middle Temple, 1925; joined ROC 1939; RAFVR, 1940–45; Wing-Commander, 1941; Senior Administrative Officer, Nos 16 and 19 Groups, RAF (despatches, OBE). Metropolitan Magistrate, 1947. *Recreation:* cricket. *Address:* Egg Hall Cottage, Birch Street, Nayland, Suffolk CO6 4JA. *T:* Nayland 263116. *Died 29 April* 1981.

**FRANCIS, (Alan) David,** CBE 1959; LVO 1957; *b* 2 Dec. 1900; *m* 1932, Norah Turpin; two *s. Educ:* Winchester; Magdalen Coll., Oxford (MA); Corpus Christi Coll., Cambridge (BA). Passed into General Consular Service, 1923; after course in Economics at Cambridge, appointed Vice-Consul, Antwerp, 1925; served as Vice-Consul at Rotterdam, Panama, Bogota and Prague; was also Lloyds Agent at Prague; served in FO, 1936, appointed Vice-Consul, Brussels, and Consul there, 1937. Attached to Costarican Delegation to Coronation of King George VI. Seconded as Principal in Aliens Dept, Home Office, 1940; Consul at Lisbon, 1941; Barcelona, 1942; First Sec. and Consul, Caracas, 1944; Chargé d'Affaires there, 1946; served in FO, 1947; Consul-Gen. at Danzig, 1949, New Orleans, 1951; Consul-Gen., Oporto, 1955–58; retired, 1958. Mem., Lord Chancellor's Advisory Council on Public Records, 1962–67. FRHistS. *Publications:* The Methuens and Portugal, 1966; The Wine Trade, 1972; The First Peninsular War, 1975; Portugal 1715–1808, 1985; articles in learned periodicals. *Recreation:* walking. *Address:* 21 Cadogan Street, SW3 2PP. *Club:* Travellers'.
*Died 22 June* 1987.

**FRANCIS, Alfred Edwin,** OBE 1952; Consultant to major theatre companies in London, Cardiff and Bristol; *b* 27 March 1909; *er s* of Reginald Thomas Francis and Ellen Sophia Francis, Liverpool; *m* 1941, Joan Quayle Stocker (*d* 1979), Cheshire; one *s. Educ:* Liverpool Coll.; Liverpool Sch. of Architecture. Song writer and stage designer, 1932–39; Hon. Organising Secretary: Liverpool Ballet

Club; ENSA, W Command, 1941–45. Overture commnd by Liverpool Philharmonic Soc., 1943. Dir of Liverpool 1951 Festival, 1950; Admin. Dir (later Chm.), London Old Vic, 1952; Man. Dir (later Vice-Chm.), Television Wales and West, 1959; Exec. Chm. Welsh National Opera (and later Drama) Co., 1968–75. Board Member: London Festival Ballet; D'Oyly Carte Trust; London Old Vic Trust; Cardiff New Theatre Trust; former member: Nat. Theatre Bd; Bristol Old Vic Trust; various Arts Council and Welsh Arts Council cttees; Member: British Council Adv. Panel for Drama (former Chm.); Grand Council, Royal Acad. of Dancing. Pres., Vic-Wells Assoc.; Hon. Vice-Pres., UK Cttee for UNICEF (former Chm.). Whitbread Anglo-American Theatre Award, 1966. *Recreation:* making a fourth at bridge. *Address:* 20 Selwyn Court, Church Road, Richmond, Surrey TW10 6LR. *T:* 01–940 6612. *Clubs:* Garrick (Hon. Life Mem.), Saints and Sinners, Green Room, Arts Theatre; Artists (Liverpool) (Hon. Member and former Pres.).
*Died 19 June* 1985.

**FRANCIS, David;** *see* Francis, A. D.

**FRANCIS, Sir Frank (Chalton),** KCB 1960 (CB 1958); FSA; FMA; Director and Principal Librarian, British Museum, 1959–68; *b* Liverpool, 5 Oct. 1901; *o s* of late F. W. Francis and Elizabeth Chalton; *m* 1927, Katrina McClennon, Liverpool; two *s* one *d. Educ:* Liverpool Inst.; Liverpool Univ.; Emmanuel Coll., Cambridge. Asst Master, Holyhead Co. Sch., 1925–26; British Museum: entered Library, 1926; Sec., 1946–47; Keeper, Dept of Printed Books, 1948–59. Lectr in Bibliography, Sch. of Librarianship and Archives, University Coll., London, 1945–59. David Murray Lectr, Univ. of Glasgow, 1957. Editor, The Library, 1936–53; Jt Editor, Jl of Documentation, 1947–68. Museums Association: Mem. Council, 1960–; Vice-Pres., 1964–65; Pres., 1965–66. Bibliographical Society: Jt Hon. Sec. (with late R. B. McKerrow), 1938–40; Hon. Sec. 1940–64; Pres., 1964–66. Library Association: Council, 1948–59; Chm. Exec. Cttee, 1954–57; Pres., 1965. President: ASLIB, 1957–58; Internat. Fedn of Library Assocs, 1963–69; Chm. Trustees, Nat. Central Library. Vice-Pres., Unesco Internat. Adv. Cttee on Bibliography, 1954–60. Chairman: Circle of State Librarians, 1947–50; Internat. Cttee of Library Experts, UN, 1948; Council, British Nat. Bibliography, 1949–59; Unesco Provisional Internat. Cttee on Bibliography, 1952; Academic Libraries Section, Internat. Fedn of Library Assocs; Anglo-Swedish Soc., 1964–68. Consultant, Council on Library Resources, Washington, DC, 1959–. Trustee, Imp. War Museum; Governor, Birkbeck Coll. Correspondant, Institut de France; Mem., Bibliographical Soc. of America, and other bibliographical socs; Corresp. Mem., Massachusetts Historical Soc.; Hon. Mem., Kungl. Gustav Adolfs Akademien; Foreign Hon. Mem., Amer. Acad. of Arts and Sciences. Master, Clockmakers' Co., 1974. Hon. Fellow: Emmanuel Coll., Cambridge; Pierpont Morgan Library, NY; Hon. FLA. Hon. LittD: Liverpool; TCD; Cambridge; Hon. DLitt: British Columbia; Exeter; Leeds; Oxford; New Brunswick; Wales. *Publications:* Historical Bibliography in Year's Work in Librarianship, 1929–38; (ed) The Bibliographical Society, 1892–1942: Studies in Retrospect, 1945; (ed) Facsimile of The Compleat Catalogue 1680, 1956; Robert Copland: Sixteenth Century Printer and Translator, 1961; (ed) Treasures of the British Museum, 1971; translations from German, including W. Cohn, Chinese Art, 1930; articles and reviews in The Library, TLS, etc. *Recreations:* golf, walking, bibliography. *Address:* The Vine, Nether Winchendon, Aylesbury, Bucks. *Clubs:* Athenæum, Royal Commonwealth Society; Grolier (New York).
*Died 15 Sept.* 1988.

**FRANCIS, Hugh Elvet,** QC 1960; practising at Chancery Bar, 1932–39, and 1945–79; *b* 28 March 1907; *s* of Maurice Evan Francis, JP, Cemmes, Montgomeryshire and Ellen Frances (*née* Jones); *m* 1932, Emma Frances Wienholt, *d* of J. G. W. Bowen, Tyddyn, Llanidloes; three *s* one *d* (and one *s* decd). *Educ:* Machynlleth County Sch.; UCW Aberystwyth; St John's Coll., Cambridge. LLB Wales 1st Cl. Hons, 1929; Schol. St John's Coll., Cambridge, 1930; LLB Cantab 1st Cl. Hons, Macmahon Law studentship, 1931; Arden Schol. and Lord Justice Holker Sen. Schol., Gray's Inn, Certificate of Honour, Bar Final Exams, 1931; Barrister, Gray's Inn, 1932, Bencher, 1956, Treas., 1974; Chancellor of the County Palatine of Durham, 1969–71. Served War of 1939–45 in RA and JAG Dept (despatches). Pres., Iron and Steel Arbitration Tribunal, 1967–74; Chairman: Performing Right Tribunal, 1969–80; Cttee on Rent Acts, 1969–71; Chancery Bar Assoc., 1972–77. Hon. Treas., Bar Council, 1961–64. *Publication:* Jt Ed. Lindley on Partnership, 1950. *Recreations:* fishing, gardening and country pursuits. *Address:* 2 Gray's Inn Square, Gray's Inn, WC1R 5AA. *T:* 01–242 4181; Tyddyn, Llandinam, Powys. *T:* Llanidloes 2448.
*Died 7 June* 1986.

**FRANK, Ilya Mikhailovich;** Professor, Moscow University, since 1940; Director, Laboratory of Neutron Physics, Joint Institute for Nuclear Research, Dubna, since 1957; *b* Leningrad, 23 Oct. 1908; *yr s* of Mikhail Lyudvigovich Frank, Prof. of Mathematics, and Dr

Yelizaveta Mikhailovna Gratsianova; *m* 1937, Ella Abramovna Beilikhis, historian; one *s. Educ:* Moscow University (under S. I. Vavilov's guidance). Engaged by State Optical Inst. in Leningrad after graduation, 1931–34 (DSc 1935), and by P. N. Lebedev Physical Inst., USSR Acad. of Scis, Moscow, 1934, Head of Laboratory of Atomic Nucleus (from 1971 part of Inst. for Nuclear Res.), 1947–. Elected Corr. Mem. USSR Acad. of Sciences, 1946, Mem., 1968. Main works in field of optics and nuclear physics. Has participated from beginning in investigations dealing with Vavilov-Cerenkov radiation; carried out many theoretical investigations into Vavilov-Cerenkov effects and in related problems (The Doppler effect in a refractive medium, transition, radiation, etc.) and continues this research. Under his leadership research pulsed reactors of IBR type, IBR-30 with injector and IBR-2 are being developed as well as res. programmes for these pulsed neutron sources, 1957–. Awarded Nobel Prize for Physics (jointly with P. A. Cerenkov and I. E. Tamm) for discovery and interpretation of Cerenkov effect, 1958. USSR State Prize, 1946, 1954, 1971. Decorated with 3 orders of Lenin and 3 other orders. *Address:* Joint Institute for Nuclear Research, Dubna, near Moscow, USSR.

*Died 22 June* 1990.

**FRANK, Phyllis Margaret Duncan, (Mrs Alan Frank);** *see* Tate, P. M. D.

**FRANK, Sir Robert John,** 3rd Bt, *cr* 1920; FRICS; late Flying Officer, RAFVR; Director, Ashdale Land and Property Co. Ltd, since 1963; *b* 16 March 1925; *s* of Sir Howard Frank, 1st Bt, GBE, KCB, and Nancy Muriel (she *m* 2nd, 1932, Air-Marshal Sir Arthur Coningham, KCB, KBE, DSO), *e d* of John Brooks; *S* brother, killed in action, 1944; *m* 1st, 1950, Angela Elizabeth (marr. diss. 1959), *e d* of Sir Kenelm Cayley, 10th Bt; two *d*; 2nd, 1960, Margaret Joyce Truesdale; one *s. Educ:* Shawnigan Lake, Vancouver Island; Harrow. FRICS 1951. *Heir: s* Robert Andrew Frank, *b* 16 May 1964. *Address:* Ruscombe End, Waltham St Lawrence, near Reading, Berks.                          *Died 22 Feb.* 1987.

**FRANKEL, Dan;** *b* 18 Aug. 1900; *s* of Harris Frankel, Mile End; *m* 1921, Lily, *d* of Joseph Marks, Stepney; one *s.* Mem. LCC for Mile End Division of Stepney, 1931–46; Mayor of Stepney, 1928–29; MP (Lab) Mile End Division of Stepney, 1935–45.

*Died 16 May* 1988.

**FRANKEL, Prof. Joseph;** Professor of Politics, University of Southampton, 1963–78, later Emeritus; *b* 30 May 1913; *s* of Dr I. and Mrs R. Frankel; *m* 1944, Elizabeth A. Kyle (*d* 1985); one *d. Educ:* Univ. of Lwow, Poland (Master of Laws, 1935); Univ. of Western Australia (LLM 1948); Univ. of London (PhD Econ (Internat. Rel.) 1950). Legal Practice, Solicitor, in Poland, 1935–38. Farming in Western Australia, 1938–47; Temp. Asst Lectr, University Coll. London, 1950–51; Lectr and Sen. Lectr, Univ. of Aberdeen, 1951–62. Head of Dept of Politics, 1963–73, Dean, Faculty of Social Sciences, 1964–67, Univ. of Southampton. Res. Associate, RIAA, 1972–73. Vis. Prof., International Christian Univ., Tokyo, 1977; Hon. Fellow, Centre for Internat. Studies, Southampton, 1985–; Sen. Associate Mem., St Antony's Coll., Oxford, 1985–. Hon. Professorial Fellow, Univ. of Wales, 1980–85. Hon. Pres., British Internat. Studies Assoc., 1973–. *Publications:* The Making of Foreign Policy, 1962, 2nd edn 1967; International Relations, 1963, 4th edn (as International Relations in a Changing World) 1988; International Politics: conflict and harmony, 1969; National Interest, 1970; Contemporary International Theory and the Behaviour of States, 1973; British Foreign Policy 1945–1973, 1975; contribs to International Affairs, Brit. Jl Internat. Studies, etc. *Recreations:* gardening, literature, art and music. *Address:* Well Cottage, Lockinge, Wantage, Oxon OX12 8QD. *T:* Abingdon 833114. *Club:* Athenæum.                *Died 13 Jan.* 1989.

**FRANKEN, Rose (Dorothy);** Novelist; Playwright; *b* Texas, 28 Dec. 1895; *d* of Michael Lewin and Hannah (*née* Younker); *m* 1st, 1914, Dr S. W. A. Franken (*d* 1932); three *s*; 2nd, 1937, William Brown Melony (*d* 1970). *Educ:* Ethical Culture Sch., NYC. *Publications: novels:* Pattern, 1925; Twice Born, 1935, new edn 1970; Call Back Love, 1937; Of Great Riches, 1937 (as Gold Pennies, UK, 1938); Strange Victory, 1939; Claudia: the story of a marriage, 1939; Claudia and David, 1940; American Bred, 1941; Another Claudia, 1943; Women in White, 1945; Young Claudia, 1946; The Marriage of Claudia, 1948; From Claudia to David, 1949; The Fragile Years, The Antic Years (as The Return of Claudia, UK), 1952; Rendezvous (as The Quiet Heart, UK), 1954; (autobiography) When All is Said and Done, 1963; You're Well Out of Hospital, 1966; Swan Song, 1976; *plays:* Another Language, 1932; Mr Dooley, Jr: a comedy for children, 1932; Claudia, 1941; Outrageous Fortune, 1944; When Doctors Disagree, 1944; Soldier's Wife, 1945; Hallams, 1948; The Wing, 1971; also short stories in Colliers, Liberty, Cosmopolitan, Harper's Bazaar and anthologies.                *Died 22 June* 1988.

**FRANKENBURG, John Beeching;** Legal Adviser, British Council, since 1964; *b* 19 April 1921; *s* of late Sidney Frankenburg, JP, and of Charis Frankenburg, MA Oxon, SCM, JP; *m* 1952, Pamela

Holmes; two *s. Educ:* Stowe; Balliol Coll., Oxford (MA Hons Jurisp.). Called to the Bar, Inner Temple, 1947. Army, 1940; commnd 1941; POW N Africa, 1942; invalided out, 1945. Treas., World Assembly of Youth, 1949–52; Asst Legal Adviser: Dir of Public Prosecutions, 1958–60; British Council, 1960–63. Member Liberal Party: Council, 1947–55; Nat. Exec., 1947–54; Liberal Party Candidate: S Kensington, 1950; Berwick-on-Tweed, 1951; Nuneaton, 1955. Governor, St Andrews Sch., Pangbourne, 1971–. *Publication:* The Young Lawyer (with J. L. Clay and J. A. Baker), 1955. *Recreations:* watching and playing games, reading. mental autolycism. *Address:* Beechings, Pangbourne, Berks. *T:* Pangbourne 3248. *Club:* Englefield Social (Englefield, Berks).

*Died 11 July* 1981.

**FRANKLIN, Alfred White,** FRCP; Hon. Consulting Physician, Department of Child Health, Saint Bartholomew's Hospital; Hon. Consulting Pædiatrician, Queen Charlotte's Maternity Hospital; *b* 1905; *yr s* of Philip Franklin, FRCS; *m* 1943, Ann Grizel, *er d* of late Rev. Francis Dent Vaisey; two *s* two *d. Educ:* Epsom Coll.; Clare Coll., Cambridge (scholar); St Bartholomew's Hospital. MB, BCh, 1933; FRCP, 1942. Lawrence Scholarship and Gold Medal, 1933 and 1934, St Bartholomew's Hosp.; Temple Cross Research Fellow, Johns Hopkins Hosp., 1934–35. Pædiatrician to Sector III, EMS. Dep. Chm., Attendance Allowance Bd, DHSS, 1970–78; Formerly Chm., Invalid Children's Aid Assoc.; Co-founder, The Osler Club, London. Past Pres., British Pædiatric Assoc.; President: British Soc. for Medical History, 1974–76; Internat. Soc. for Prevention of Child Abuse and Neglect, 1981–82. *Publications:* (ed) Selected Writings of Sir D'Arcy Power, 1931, and of Sir William Osler, 1951; The Care of Invalid and Crippled Children, 1960; Concerning Child Abuse, 1975; Pastoral Paediatrics, 1976; Widening Horizons of Child Health, 1976; (ed) The Challenge of Child Abuse, 1977; (ed) Child Abuse: Prediction, Prevention and Follow-Up, 1977; (ed) Family Matters, 1983; contrib. to books and jls on medical, historical and bibliographical subjects. *Address:* 149 Harley Street, W1N 2DE. *T:* 01-935 4444; The Cottage, Northaw, Herts. *T:* Potters Bar 52184. *Club:* Athenæum.

*Died 20 Sept.* 1984.

**FRANKLIN, George Frederic;** formerly Headmaster, Lincoln School, retired Dec. 1957; *b* Greenwich, 28 Dec. 1897; *s* of John and Alice Franklin; *m* 1926, Edith Kate Young (*d* 1986); one *s* one *d. Educ:* Roan Sch.; King's Coll., Cambridge. Asst Master, Merchant Taylors' Sch., Crosby; Senior Mod. Langs Master, Christ's Hosp. *Publications:* French and German school texts. *Address:* Swan Hill House, Shrewsbury, Salop SY1 1NQ.       *Died 13 April* 1987.

**FRANKLIN, Henry William Fernehough;** Headmaster, Epsom College, 1940–62; *b* 30 June 1901; *s* of Henry Franklin, Schoolmaster; *m* 1931, Phyllis Denham; one *d. Educ:* Christ's Hosp.; Christ Church, Oxford. Asst Master, Radley Coll., 1924–27; Asst Master, Rugby Sch., 1927–39. Chm. of Home Office Departmental Cttee on Punishments in Prisons, Borstals, etc., 1948. Mem., Advertising Standards Authority, 1962–67. *Publications:* Fifty Latin Lyrics, 1955; (with J. A. G. Bruce) Latin Prose Composition, 1937; Latin Reader, 1939. *Recreations:* formerly various games: cricket (OU XI 1924; Essex County XI); Rugby football (OU XV 1923; Barbarian FC), hockey, fives, etc.; also music and change-ringing. *Address:* The Cottage, Westward Lane, West Chiltington, Pulborough, West Sussex. *T:* W Chiltington 2282.                                        *Died 25 May* 1985.

**FRANKLIN, Prof. Norman Laurence,** CBE 1975 (OBE 1963); MSc, PhD; FRS 1981; FEng; Professor of Nuclear Engineering, Department of Chemical Engineering, Imperial College of Science and Technology, University of London, since 1984; part-time Member, UKAEA, since 1971; Director, AMEC plc, since 1985 (Chairman, AMEC Projects and Worley-Santa Fe); *b* 1 Sept. 1924; *s* of William Alexander and Beatrice Franklin; *m* 1949, Bessie Coupland; one *s* one *d. Educ:* Batley Grammar School; University of Leeds. British Coke Res. Assoc., 1945–48; Lecturer in Chemical Engineering, Univ. of Leeds, 1948–55; joined UKAEA, 1955; Mem. for Production, 1969–71. Man. Dir, Chief Executive and Dir, 1971–75, part-time Dir, 1975–85, British Nuclear Fuels Ltd; Chm. and Man. Dir, Nuclear Power Co. Ltd, 1975–80; Man. Dir, National Nuclear Corporation, 1980–84 (Dir, 1974–84). FEng, FIChemE (Pres. 1979). Hon. DSc Leeds, 1976. Chevalier de la Légion d'Honneur, 1984. *Publications:* Statistical Analysis in Chemistry and the Chemical Industry, 1954; The Transport Properties of Fluids, Vol. 4, Chemical Engineering Practice, 1957; Heat Transfer by Conduction, Vol. 7, Chemical Engineering Practice, 1963; papers in Trans Instn of Chemical Engineers, 1953–66. *Recreation:* walking. *Address:* Imperial College of Science and Technology, Exhibition Road, SW7; The Evergreens, Greenacre Close, Knutsford, Cheshire WA16 8NL. *T:* Knutsford 3045. *Club:* East India, Devonshire, Sports and Public Schools.                *Died 7 Nov.* 1986.

**FRANKLIN, Olga Heather,** CBE 1950 (MBE 1919); RRC 1946 (ARRC 1942); *b* 20 Sept. 1895; *e c* of late Robert Francis Franklin,

OBE. *Educ:* St Michael's Lodge, Stoke, Devonport, VAD, 1915–17; WRNS, 1917–19; King's Coll. Hosp., 1923; Queen Alexandra's Royal Naval Nursing Service, 1927–50; Matron-in-Chief, 1947–50; King's Hon. Nursing Sister (the first appointed), 1947–50; retired, 1950. Prisoner of war, Hongkong, 1941–45. *Address:* 57 Dean Court Road, Rottingdean, Brighton BN2 7DL. *T:* Brighton 32202.
*Died 20 April 1987.*

**FRANKLYN, Charles Aubrey Hamilton,** MD Lausanne, MB, BS London, MA *hc* Malaya 1951; MRCS, LRCP 1923; FLS; FSA(Scot); Physician and Genealogical-historian; *b* Brentwood, Co. Essex, 25 Aug. 1896; *er s* of late Major Aubrey Hamilton Franklyn and Ethel Mary, *d* of late Walter Gray. *Educ:* Tonbridge Sch.; St Thomas's Hosp.; Universities of London, Lausanne, Oxford (Exeter Coll.), France, 1916–19. Lieut RA (SR), 1915–20; in practice as physician from 1925; temp. MO, P & O Line, 1933; MO (part-time) HM Prison, Lincoln, 1934–37; in EMS (Grade III) from 1939. Mem. of Standing Cttee, University of London, 1927–61 (Senior mem., 1954–61); Bedell of Convocation, University of London, from 1932; a Provincial Supervisor in Charge of Final Degree Examns (June) 1941–56. Mem. BMA, 1923–48; Life Mem. Oxford Soc. Fellow Philosophical Soc. of England; Mem. Amer. Institute for Philosophical Studies. Hon. Asst to Editor Burke's Landed Gentry, Centenary (15th) edn, 1937, and to Editor Armorial Families, 7th edn, 1929–30 (2 vols). Authority on Academical Dress, University Degrees and Ceremonies, Modern Heraldry and Genealogy, etc. Designer of Official Robes and Academical Dress for Universities: Malaya, Australian National, Southampton, Hull, and New Univ. of Ulster, Coleraine, Co. Londonderry; designed: armorial ensigns and 3 badges, British Transport Commn, 1956; Arms of Borough of Bridgnorth, 1959; Arms of St Peter's Hall (now College), Oxford. MA Malaya 1951, by diploma, *hc*, in absentia; Hon. DLitt: Geneva Theolog. Coll, Vincennes, Ind, 1972; Central Sch. of Religion, Ind. and Redhill, Surrey, 1972. *Publications:* The Bearing of Coat-Armour by Ladies, 1923, repr. with supp. 1973; English and Scottish Heraldry compared and contrasted (Scots. Mag. Jan. 1925); University Hoods and Robes (25 cards), 1926; The Genealogy of the Chavasse Family, 1929; A Genealogical History of The Family of Tiarks of Foxbury, 1929, 2nd edition, rev. and enlarged 1969 (priv. printed); A Genealogical and Heraldic History of Four Families (privately printed), 1932; A Genealogical History of the families of Paulet (or Pawlett), Berewe (or Barrow), Lawrence, and Parker (privately printed), 1964, Supplement, incl. Morgan of Llanfabon, Turner of Oldland in Keymer, Vavasour of Hazlewood, Walwyn of Longford, etc, 1969; A Genealogical History of the Families of Montgomerie of Garboldisham, Hunter of Knap, and Montgomerie of Fittleworth (privately printed), 1967; Academical Dress from the Middle Ages to the Present Day, including Lambeth Degrees (privately printed), 1970; (ed jtly) Haycraft's Degrees and Hoods of the World's Universities and Colleges, 5th edn, 1972; The Genealogy of Anne the Quene (Anne Bullen) and other English Families, 1977; Cuckfield Rural Dist, Official Local Guide (new edn), 1947; A Dedication Service for the Parish Church of St John the Baptist, Mexborough, 1967; contribs to: Enc. Brit.; 5th edn of Grove's Dic. of Music and Musicians; Pears Cyclopædia; Chambers's Enc.; Internat. Enc. of Higher Educn, etc. *Recreations:* music, cats, motoring, travelling, lecturing, and writing, etc. *Address:* 44 Sackville Gardens, New Church Road, Hove, Sussex BN3 4GH. *T:* Brighton 733071; c/o National Westminster Bank Ltd, 1 Lee Road, Blackheath, SE3 9RH; Exeter College, Oxford.
*Died 26 Nov. 1982.*

**FRASER OF ALLANDER;** Barony of (*cr* 1964) title disclaimed by 2nd Baron; *see under* Fraser, Sir Hugh, 2nd Bt.

**FRASER OF NORTH CAPE, 1st Baron,** *cr* 1946, of Molesey; **Admiral of the Fleet Bruce Austin Fraser,** GCB (KCB 1943; CB 1939); KBE 1941 (OBE 1919); Hon. DCL Oxon 1947; Hon. LLD Edinburgh 1953; Hon. LLD Wales; *b* 5 Feb. 1888; *s* of Gen. Alexander Fraser, CB, late RE. *Educ:* Bradfield College. Entered RN 1902; served 1914–18 War, HMS Minerva (Dardanelles and E Indies) and HMS Resolution; Flag Captain; commanded HMS Glorious; Chief of Staff, Mediterranean Fleet, 1938–39; Third Sea Lord and Controller, 1939–42; 2nd-in-Command, Home Fleet, 1942; C-in-C Home Fleet, 1943–44 (in charge of Russian convoys and sinking of the Scharnhorst); Adm. 1944; C-in-C Eastern Fleet, 1944; C-in-C British Pacific Fleet, 1945–46 (British signatory to Japanese surrender); C-in-C Portsmouth, 1947–48; Adm. of the Fleet, 1948; First Sea Lord and Chief of Naval Staff, 1948–51. First and Principal Naval ADC to the King, 1946–48. Hon. Freeman, Shipwrights' Co. Order of Suvarov (Russia), 1944; DSM (USA); Grand Order of Orange Nassau (Netherlands); Chevalier of Legion of Honour and Croix de Guerre with palm (France); Grand Cross, Order of St Olav (Norway). *Heir:* none. *Address:* 18 Wolsey Road, East Molesey, Surrey KT8 9EL. *T:* 01-979 1136.
*Died 12 Feb. 1981 (ext).*

**FRASER OF TULLYBELTON,** Baron *cr* 1974 (Life Peer), of Bankfoot; **Walter Ian Reid Fraser,** PC 1974; a Lord of Appeal in Ordinary, 1975–85; Member of the Queen's Body Guard for Scotland (Royal Company of Archers); *b* 3 Feb. 1911; *o s* of late Alexander Reid Fraser, stockbroker, Glasgow; *m* 1943, (Mary Ursula) Cynthia (Gwendolen), *o d* of Col I. H. Macdonell, DSO (late HLI); one *s. Educ:* Repton; Balliol Coll., Oxford (scholar; Hon. Fellow, 1981). BA Oxon 1932; LLB Glasgow 1935; Advocate, 1936; QC Scotland 1953. Lecturer in Constitutional Law, Glasgow Univ., 1936; and at Edinburgh Univ., 1948. Served Army (RA and staff), 1939–45; UK; Burma. Contested (U) East Edinburgh constituency, Gen. Election, 1955. Chm., University Comrs, 1988–. Mem. Royal Commission on Police, 1960. Dean of the Faculty of Advocates, 1959–64; a Senator of HM Coll. of Justice in Scotland, 1964–74. Hon. LLD: Glasgow, 1970; Edinburgh, 1978. Hon. Master of the Bench, Gray's Inn, 1975. *Publication:* Outline of Constitutional Law, 1938 (2nd edn, 1948). *Recreations:* shooting, walking. *Address:* Tullybelton House, Bankfoot, Perthshire. *T:* Bankfoot 312. *Club:* New (Edinburgh).
*Died 17 Feb. 1989.*

**FRASER, Sir Hugh,** 2nd Bt *cr* 1961, of Dineiddwg; Chairman, since 1982, and Managing Director, since 1985, Sir Hugh & Sir Group; *b* 18 Dec. 1936; *s* of 1st Baron Fraser of Allander, DL, LLD, JP (Bt 1961) and of Kate Hutcheon, *d* of late Sir Andrew Lewis, LLD, JP; *S* to father's Btcy, and disclaimed Barony, 1966; *m* 1st, 1962, Patricia Mary (marr. diss. 1971), *e d* of John Bowie; three *d*; 2nd, 1973, Aileen Ross (marr. diss. 1982; she *d* 1984). *Educ:* St Mary's, Melrose; Kelvinside Academy. Director: Allander Hldgs Ltd; Ettinger Brothers (Tailoring) Ltd; Clan Fraser Knitwear Ltd; Dumbarton Football Club Ltd; Internat. Caledonian Assets Ltd; D & S Shirts Ltd; Black Bear Ltd; Twentieth Century Fashions Ltd; Zucker Textiles Ltd; Air Charter Scotland Ltd; Hebridean Herbals Ltd. Hon. Dr Stirling, 1985. *Recreations:* farming, football. *Address:* Middleton of Mugdock, near Milngavie, Dunbartonshire.
*Died 5 May 1987 (ext).*

**FRASER, Rt. Hon. Sir Hugh (Charles Patrick Joseph),** Kt 1980; MBE; PC 1962; MP (C) Stafford, since 1983 (Stone Division of Staffordshire, 1945–50, Stafford and Stone Division of Staffordshire, 1950–83); *b* 23 Jan. 1918; *s* of 16th Baron Lovat; *m* 1956, Lady Antonia Pakenham (marr. diss. 1977; she *m* 2nd, 1980, Harold Pinter); three *s* three *d. Educ:* Ampleforth Coll.; Balliol Coll., Oxford; The Sorbonne, Paris. Roman Catholic. Ex-Pres. Oxford Union; war service with Lovat Scouts, Phantom and Special Air Service. PPS to Sec. of State for the Colonies, 1951–54; Parly Under-Sec. of State and Financial Sec., War Office 1958–60; Parly Under-Sec. of State for the Colonies, 1960–62; Sec. of State for Air, 1962–64. Pres., West Midlands Conservative and Unionist Assoc., 1967. Director: Sun Alliance; industrial cos. Order of Orange Nassau, Order of Leopold with palm, Belgian Croix de guerre. *Address:* Eilean Aigas, Beauly, Inverness, Scotland; House of Commons, SW1. *Clubs:* Beefsteak, White's.
*Died 6 March 1984.*

**FRASER, Ian Montagu,** MC 1945; Secretary, The Buttle Trust, 1978–86 (Deputy Secretary, 1971–78); *b* 14 Oct. 1916; *s* of Col Herbert Cecil Fraser, DSO, OBE, TD, and Sybil Mary Statter; *m* 1st, 1945, Mary Stanley (*d* 1964); one *s* one *d*; 2nd, 1967, Angela Meston; two *s. Educ:* Shrewsbury Sch.; Christ Church, Oxford. 1st Cl. Class. Hon. Mods, 1937; 1st Cl. Lit Hum 1939. Regular Commn in Frontier Force Rifles, IA, 1939, and served War of 1939–45, NW Frontier, Iraq, Syria and Western Desert (MC, despatches twice, POW); retired 1948. Executive, Guthrie and Co. Ltd, 1948; Gen. Sec., The John Lewis Partnership, 1956–59, Consultant, 1959–64. RARO, Rifle Bde, 1948–. MP (C) Sutton Div. of Plymouth, 1959–66; PPS to Sec. of State for the Colonies, 1962; Asst Govt Whip, 1962–64; Opposition Whip, 1964–66; Conservative Research Dept, 1966–67. Exec. Dir, GUS Export Corp., 1967–70. *Recreations:* flyfishing, sailing. *Address:* How Hatch, Chipstead, Surrey CR3 3LN. *T:* Downland 51944. *Clubs:* Carlton; Royal Western Yacht (Plymouth).
*Died 8 Nov. 1987.*

**FRASER, Col James Douglas,** CBE 1976; TD 1950 (1st clasp 1951, 2nd clasp 1958); DL; retired Insurance Broker and Consultant; Chairman, Strathclyde Valuation Appeal Panel, since 1975; *b* 12 July 1914; *s* of John Fraser and Jessie Victoria McCallum or Fraser; *m* 1st, 1944, Esme Latta (*d* 1964); one *s* one *d*; 2nd, 1966, Nancy McGregor or Stewart; one step *d. Educ:* Glasgow Acad. ACII 1933. Insurance Broker with Stenhouse Holdings Ltd, 1947–69 (Dir, 1954–69); Insurance Consultant, 1969–74. Commnd TA, 1938; War Service, Highland Light Infantry, 1939–46; Comd 5/6th Bn HLI, 1953–56; Dep. Comdr (Colonel), 154 (Highland) Bde, 1956–58; Chm., Lowland TAVRA, 1973–76. DL Dunbartonshire, 1975. OStJ 1980. *Recreations:* golf, reading, music. *Address:* 6B Lennox Court, 22 Stockiemuir Avenue, Bearsden, Glasgow G61 3JN. *T:* 041-942 3020. *Clubs:* Caledonian; Western, Buchanan Castle Golf (Glasgow).
*Died 4 May 1981.*

**FRASER, Very Rev. John Annand,** MBE 1940; TD 1945; DD; Moderator of the General Assembly of the Church of Scotland, May 1958–May 1959; Extra Chaplain to The Queen, in Scotland, since

1964 (Chaplain, 1952–64); *b* 21 June 1894; *er s* of Rev. Charles Fraser, BD, Minister of Croy, Inverness-shire, and Elizabeth Annand; *m* 1925, Leila, *d* of Col Ewen Campbell; one *s* one *d*. *Educ:* Robert Gordon's Coll., Aberdeen; Inverness Royal Academy; Universities of Aberdeen and Edinburgh. MA Aberdeen 1919. Served European War, 1914–18: in ranks 4th Bn Gordon Highlanders, 1915, Commd 7th Bn 1917. CF (TA) 1935; SCF, 52nd (Lowland) Div., 1940; Dep. Asst Chaplain Gen., West Scotland Dist, 1942. Asst Minister, St Matthew's, Edinburgh, 1921; Minister of Humbie, East Lothian, 1923; Minister of Hamilton, Second Charge, 1931, First Charge, 1949; Minister, Aberdalgie and Dupplin, Perth, 1960–70. Convener of Maintenance of Ministry Cttee of Church of Scotland, 1950–54; Convener of Business Cttee, 1962–67; Convener of Gen. Administration Cttee, 1962–66; Chm. of Judicial Commn, 1962–66; Chm. of Church of Scotland Trust, 1962–66; Mem. Broadcasting Council for Scotland, 1963–67. Hon. DD Aberdeen, 1951. *Recreations:* fishing, gardening. *Address:* Flat 3, 4 Gillsland Road, Edinburgh. *Club:* Caledonian (Edinburgh).
*Died 3 Oct. 1985.*

**FRASER, Kenneth Wharton,** CMG 1962; OBE 1945; Advertising and Public Relations executive (retired); formerly Dominion President, New Zealand Returned Services' Association; *b* 1 Nov. 1905; *s* of late William Fraser, Edinburgh, Scotland; *m* 1926, Ione May (*d* 1975), *d* of late William James Moor, Auckland, NZ; two *s* three *d*. *Educ:* Auckland, NZ. War service: 1940–45, 2nd NZEF, Lt-Col; Cmdg Officer, 5 Field Regt, NZ Artillery, 1940–41 (then POW to 1945). Dominion Executive, New Zealand Returned Services' Assoc., 1946–48; Dominion Vice-Pres. (NZRSA), 1949–54; Dominion Pres., 1955–62, retired. *Address:* 11 Karu Crescent, Waikanae, New Zealand. *T:* 5784. *Club:* United Services Officers' (Wellington).
*Died 7 March 1981.*

**FRASER, Louis Nathaniel B.;** *see* Blache-Fraser.

**FRASER, Sir Robert;** *see* Fraser, Sir W. R.

**FRASER, Sir Robert Brown,** Kt 1949; OBE 1944; Chairman, Independent Television News, 1971–74; *b* 26 Sept. 1904; *s* of Reginald and Thusnelda Fraser, Adelaide, South Australia; *m* 1931, Betty Harris; one *d*. *Educ:* St Peter's Sch., Adelaide; Trinity Coll., Univ. of Melbourne (BA); Univ. of London (BSc Econ.). Leader Writer Daily Herald, 1930–39; Empire Div., Ministry of Information, 1939–41; Dir, Publications Div., Ministry of Information, 1941–45; Controller of Production, Ministry of Information, 1945–46; Dir-Gen., Central Office of Information, 1946–54; Dir-General, ITA, 1954–70. Hon. Fellow, LSE, 1965. Hon. Life Mem., Royal Inst. of Public Administration, 1975; Editor, New Whitehall Series, for Royal Inst. of Public Administration, 1951–70. Gold Medal, Royal Television Soc., 1970. *Address:* Flat 5M, Portman Mansions, Chiltern Street, W1. *Club:* Athenæum.
*Died 20 Jan. 1985.*

**FRASER, Rt. Hon. Thomas,** PC 1964; retired; *b* 18 Feb. 1911; *s* of Thomas and Mary Fraser, Kirkmuirhill, Lanarks; *m* 1935, Janet M. Scanlon (*d* 1987), Lesmahagow, Lanarks; one *s* one *d*. *Educ:* Lesmahagow Higher Grade Sch. Left school 1925 and started work in a coal-mine (underground); worked underground, 1925–43; Miners' Union Branch Official, 1938–43; Sec., Lanark Constituency Labour Party, 1939–43; MP (Lab) Hamilton Div. of Lanarks, 1943–67; Joint Parliamentary Under-Sec. of State, Scottish Office, 1945–51; Minister of Transport, 1964–65. Member: Royal Commn on Local Govt in Scotland, 1966–69; Highlands and Islands Develt Bd, 1967–70; Chm., N of Scotland Hydro-Electric Bd, 1967–73; Mem., S of Scotland Electricity Bd, 1967–73; Chairman: Scottish Local Govt Staff Commn, 1973–77; Scottish Local Govt Property Commn, 1976–77; Commn for Local Authority Accounts in Scotland, 1974–79. Freeman of Hamilton, 1964. *Address:* 15 Broompark Drive, Lesmahagow, Lanarks.
*Died 21 Nov. 1988.*

**FRASER, Thomas Cameron,** CB 1966; MBE 1945; TD 1951; Secretary, Engineering Industries Council, since 1976; *b* 21 Jan. 1909; *er s* of late Dr Thomas Fraser, CBE, DSO, TD, DL, LLD, Aberdeen; *m* 1934, Dorothy Graham (*d* 1966), *y d* of late Graham Partridge, East Grinstead; two *s* two *d*. *Educ:* Fettes; University Coll., Oxford. Lloyds Bank Ltd, 1931–39. Served RA (TA), 1939–45; Major (GSO2) War Office, 1942; Lt–Col (GSO1) HQ, AA Command, 1943–45. Temp. Principal, Central Price Regulation Cttee, 1946; Sec. and Dir, Wool Textile Delegation, and Wool (and Allied) Textile Employers' Council, Bradford, 1947–62; Industrial Dir, NEDC, 1962–70; Chm., EDC for Wool Textile Industry, 1970–77; Dir, Commn of Inquiry into Industrial and Commercial Representation, 1970–72; Dir-Gen. (temp.), NEDC, 1973; Principal, Advice Centre on the Organisation of Indust. and Commercial Representation, 1974–81. Mem. British Delegation to International Labour Conferences, Geneva, 1953, 1954, 1956, 1957, 1959, and European Regional Conf., ILO, 1955. Mem., BBC North Regional Advisory Council, 1960–62. *Publications:* articles; Economic Development Committees—A New Dimension in

Government-Industry Relations (Jl of Management Studies), 1967; Chambers of Commerce and Trade Associations (Jl of RSA), 1973. *Recreations:* golf, walking. *Address:* 25 Bedford Gardens, W8. *T:* 01-727 0674. *Clubs:* United Oxford & Cambridge University, Royal Automobile.
*Died 6 Oct. 1982.*

**FRASER, William,** CBE 1969; CEng, FIEE; Chairman, BICC Ltd, 1973–76; *b* 15 July 1911; *e s* of late Alexander Fraser and Elizabeth Williamson Fraser; *m* 1938, Kathleen Mary Moore (*d* 1971), 3rd *d* of late Alderman and Mrs J. W. Moore; two *s* two *d*. *Educ:* Glasgow High Sch.; University Coll. London (BSc Hons). Production Engr, Joseph Lucas Ltd, 1935–37; joined Scottish Cables Ltd, 1937; Dir, 1938; Managing Dir, 1948–62; Chm., 1958–76; Chm., Scottish Cables (S Africa) Ltd, 1950–76; Dir, British Insulated Callender's Cables Ltd, 1959, on entry of Scottish Cables into BICC Group; Exec. Dir (Overseas Cos), 1962–64; Managing Dir (Overseas), 1964–68; Managing Dir (Overseas & Construction Gp), 1968–70; Dep. Chm. and Chief Exec., 1971–73. Vice-Chm., Phillips Cables Ltd (of Canada), 1961–70; Dir and Dep. Chm., Metal Manufactures Ltd (of Australia) and Subsidiaries, 1962–70; Chm., Balfour, Beatty & Co. Ltd, 1969–70; Director: Anglesey Aluminium Ltd, 1971–75; Clydesdale Bank Ltd, 1974–84. Chm., Scottish Council of FBI, 1959–61. Pres., Electrical and Electronics Industries Benevolent Assoc., 1974–75. *Recreations:* fishing, shooting, golf. *Address:* Fenwick Lodge, Ewenfield Road, Ayr. *T:* Ayr 265547.
*Died 28 March 1990.*

**FRASER, Sir (William) Robert,** KCB 1952 (CB 1939); KBE 1944; MA; *b* Hemingford Abbots, St Ives, Hunts, 9 Oct. 1891; *e s* of Garden William Fraser (W. F. Garden) and Ethel Mary Syson; *g g s* of Francis Fraser, Findrack, Aberdeenshire; *m* 1915, Phyllis (*d* 1970), *d* of William Smith, London; three *s* one *d*. *Educ:* Christ's Hosp.; University Coll., Oxford (MA). First Mods 1912; First Lit. Hum. 1914; entered Treasury, 1914; Principal, 1919; Asst Sec., 1932; Princ. Asst Sec., 1934–39; Sec., Dept of Health for Scotland, 1939–43; Sec. War Damage Commn, 1943, and Central Land Bd, 1947; Dep. Chm. and Permanent Sec., 1949–59; Chm. (part-time), 1959–62. Vice-Pres., Lawn Tennis Assoc. (Chm., 1958, Hon. Treasurer, 1962–70); Vice-Pres. Civil Service Sports Council; Pres., Civil Service Lawn Tennis Assoc. *Recreations:* gardening, crosswords, radio, chess, large print books. *Address:* 33 Hollycroft Avenue, NW3. *T:* 01–435 3566. *Clubs:* United Oxford & Cambridge University, All-England Lawn Tennis.
*Died 10 July 1985.*

**FRASER ROBERTS, John Alexander;** *see* Roberts.

**FREARS, John Newton,** CBE 1955; MA; JP; Pro-Chancellor, Leicester University, since 1962; *b* 29 June 1906; *s* of John Russell Frears and Minnie Keighley Frears (*née* Cape); *m* 1st, 1931, Elaine Pochin (*d* 1974); one *s* one *d*; 2nd, 1976, Jennifer Anne Steel. *Educ:* Gresham's Sch., Holt; Trinity Coll., Cambridge. Frears & Blacks Ltd, 1928–70 (Chm., 1937–70); Dir, Nabisco-Frears Biscuits Ltd, 1964–71. Dir of Bakeries for UK, Min. of Food, 1941–45. Hon. LLD Leicester, 1967. *Address:* The Gatehouse, Causeway Lane, Cropston, Leics. *T:* Anstey 2581.
*Died 23 June 1981.*

**FREEMAN, Sir Bernard;** *see* Freeman, Sir N. B.

**FREEMAN, Ifan Charles Harold,** CMG 1964; TD 1961; Registrar, University of Malawi, 1965–72, retired; *b* 11 Sept. 1910; *s* of late C. E. D. W. Freeman; *m* 1937, Enid, *d* of late Edward Hallum; two *d*. *Educ:* Friars Sch., Bangor; Univ. of Wales (MA). Served with Royal Artillery, 1939–46 (Major; despatches). Colonial Service: Kenya, 1946–58; Nyasaland, 1958–65. *Recreation:* gardening. *Address:* Swn y Wylan, Marianglas, Gwynedd. *Club:* Mombasa (Kenya).
*Died 2 Dec. 1990.*

**FREEMAN, Sir (John) Keith (Noel),** 2nd Bt *cr* 1945; Chairman and Managing Director, Garmantex Ltd; Director, Clothworkers' Foundation; *b* 28 July 1923; *o s* of Air Chief Marshal Sir Wilfrid Rhodes Freeman, 1st Bt, GCB, DSO, MC, and Gladys, *d* of J. Mews; *S* father 1953; *m* 1946, Patricia Denison, *yr d* of late C. W. Thomas, Sandown, IoW; one *s* one *d*. *Educ:* Rugby; Christ Church, Oxford. Served War of 1939–45: Flight-Lieut RAF, Europe and Middle East. Joined Courtaulds Ltd, 1946; work study engr, then Asst Manager, Weaving Mill, 1946–53; Glanzstoff-Courtaulds GmbH, Cologne, Germany, 1953–57; Commercial Dir, Courtelle Div., 1957–62; Dir, Viyella International Ltd, 1962; Commercial Dir, then Man. Dir, Monsanto Textiles SA, 1963–67; Regional Dir, International Wool Secretariat, 1967; Dir, LRC International Ltd, 1968–69; Man. Dir, LR Industries Ltd, 1968–69; Chm., Aristoc Ltd, 1971–73; Dir, Associated Leisure Ltd, 1973–75. *Heir:* *s* James Robin Freeman, *b* 21 July 1955. *Address:* c/o Midland Bank Ltd, 151 Hoe Street, Walthamstow, E17.
*Died 5 June 1981.*

**FREEMAN, Sir (Nathaniel) Bernard,** Kt 1967; CBE 1956; Chairman, Metro-Goldwyn-Mayer Pty Ltd, 1967, retired; *b* 1 Sept. 1896; *s* of Adolph and Malvina Freeman; *m* 1926, Marjorie Arabel (*née* Bloom); one *s* one *d*. *Educ:* Public Sch. and Xavier Coll., Melbourne. Served European War, 1914–18: 38th Bn, 3rd Div., First AIF, and Austr. Flying Corps; inaugurated free films to Austr. Troops,

1939–45. Founded Metro-Goldwyn-Mayer Austr., NZ and S Pacific, 1925; Man. Dir, Metro-Goldwyn-Mayer, 1925–66. First Mem. Chm., Motion Picture Distributors' Assoc. of Austr., 1939–41, also 1963. Chm. various cttees, appeals and trusts, 1945–; National Chm., UNICEF, 1952; Chm., World Refugee Year, NSW, 1960; Chm. of Trustees and Internat. Houses Appeal, Univs of Sydney and NSW; Chm., NSW and Canberra, ANZAC Memorial and Forest in Israel; Mem. Exec., Sydney Opera House Trust, 1962–69; mem. of many other cttees; Life Mem., RSL State Br., 1945–; Life Governor: Royal NSW Instn for Deaf and Blind Children; Vic. Ear and Eye Hosp.; Vic. Sch. for Deaf Children. Fellow, Sydney University Internat. House. Library of Univ. of NSW now named Sir Bernard Freeman Library. Paul Harris Award, Sydney Rotary Club, 1981. *Recreations:* swimming, bowls. *Address:* 2/c Hopewood Gardens, 13 Thornton Street, Darling Point, NSW 2027, Australia. *Clubs:* American National (Sydney), City Bowling (Sydney).
*Died 25 Nov. 1982.*

**FREEMAN, Nicholas Hall,** OBE 1985; DL; barrister; a Recorder, since 1985; *b* 25 July 1939; *s* of William Freeman and late Grace Freeman, Leicester. *Educ:* Stoneygate Sch., Leicester; King's Sch., Canterbury. Admitted Solicitor, 1962; called to the Bar, Middle Temple, 1968. Chancellor, Diocese of Leicester, 1979–. Kensington and Chelsea Borough Council: Member, 1968–; Vice-Chm., Town Planning Cttee, 1973, Chm., 1975; Leader, 1977–89; Mayor, 1989–. Vice-Chm., General Purposes Cttee, London Boroughs Assoc., 1978–. Mem., Conservative Central Office Policy Gp for London, 1981–. Contested (C) Hartlepool, Feb. and Oct. 1974. Governor, Emmanuel Sch., Clapham, 1974–78. Freeman, City of London, 1981. DL Gtr London, 1989. *Recreations:* reading, particularly biography, holidays in France, theatre. *Address:* 51 Harrington Gardens, SW7 4JU. *T:* 01–370 3197. *Clubs:* Carlton; Leicestershire (Leicester)
*Died 11 Nov. 1989.*

**FREEMAN, Captain Spencer,** CBE 1942; Co-Founder and Director, Hospitals Trust (1940) Ltd, Dublin; *b* Swansea, S Wales, 10 Dec. 1892; *s* of late A. Freeman; *m* 1924, Hilda Kathleen (*d* 1978), *d* of Charles Simpkin Toler; one *s. Educ:* Johannesburg Coll., S. Africa (scholarship winner); Technical Institute, York, Pa, USA. Up to 1914, Automotive Industry USA; organised entire Mechanical Transport Salvage in France, War of 1914–18; subsequently Consulting Business Engineer; Emergency Services Organisation War of 1939–45, for restoration of production in all munitions factories, Min. of Aircraft Production, Min. of Supply and Admiralty; Min. of Aircraft Production: Dir, 1940–41; Prin. Dir of Regional and Emergency Services Organisation, 1941–44; seconded to Board of Trade on special assignment for restoration of industry to civilian production; Business Mem. Industrial and Export Council, Board of Trade, 1944–45. Member: Radio Board (a Cttee of British War Cabinet); Radio Planning and Production Cttee; Radio Production Executive, 1944–45. Served European War, 1914–19, non-commissioned ranks to Capt. (despatches, Mons Medal). MSAE. Sportsman of the Year, Irish Sports Writers, 1973. *Publications:* Production under Fire, 1967; You Can Get to the Top, 1972; Take your Measure, 1972. *Recreations:* all sports. *Address:* Knocklyon House, Templeogue, Dublin 14, Eire. *T:* Dublin 900234. *Clubs:* Naval and Military; Kildare Street and University (Dublin).
*Died 27 May 1982.*

**FREETH, H. Andrew,** RA 1965 (ARA 1955); RE 1946; PPRWS (RWS 1955); RBA 1949; RP 1966; Portrait Painter and Etcher; on staff of Sir John Cass College, Whitechapel; *b* Birmingham, 29 Dec. 1912; *s* of John Stewart Freeth and Charlotte Eleanor Stace, Hastings; *m* 1940, Roseen Marguerite Preston; three *s* one *d. Educ:* College of Art, Birmingham; British School at Rome, 1936–39 (Rome Scholarship in Engraving). ARE 1938. Served in Intelligence Corps (Major), 1940–46, in Mediterranean theatre; loaned to RAF Middle East as Official War Artist, 1943. Drawings and etchings have been purchased by Contemporary Art Society for British Museum, by Fitzwilliam Museum, by British Council, Bristol, Birmingham and Sunderland Art Galleries, by numerous Oxford and Cambridge Colls, etc; by Nat. Portrait Gall., Ashmolean Museum, Imperial War Museum, and Victoria and Albert Museum; reproduced in various publications. Best known works: (Portraits): Sir Alec Douglas-Home, J. Enoch Powell, W. Somerset Maugham, G. E. Moore, Walter de la Mare, Lord Avon, Sir Bernard Lovell, Lord MacDermott, Lord Chief Justice of N Ireland, Bishops of Dover, London, Peterborough, Derby, Gloucester, St Albans, Lord Edmund-Davies, Sir Anthony Wagner. Pres., RWS, 1974–76. Freeman and Liveryman, Painter-Stainers Co., 1977. *Address:* 13 Burnaby Gardens, Grove Park, Chiswick, W4 3DS.
*Died 26 March 1986.*

**FRERE, Alexander Stewart,** CBE 1946; MA Cantab; *b* 23 Nov. 1892; *m* 1933, Patricia Marion Caldecott, *d* of late Edgar Wallace; two *s* one *d. Educ:* Christ's Coll., Cambridge. Served Royal East Kent Yeomanry, seconded Royal Flying Corps. European War, 1914–18; edited the Granta, Cambridge, 1920–21; on staff of London Evening News, 1922–23; joined William Heinemann Ltd, Publishers, 1923;

Dir, 1926; Man. Dir, 1932–40; Chm., 1945–61; Pres., 1961–62; Mem. of council Publishers Assoc., 1938–39. Assisted organise National Service Campaign, Ministry of Labour and National Service, Jan.–June 1939; Dir of Public Relations, Min. of Labour and National Service, 1940–44. Adviser to HM Govt Delegn to ILO Conf., Columbia Univ., New York, 1941. Chevalier de la Légion d'Honneur, 1953. *Address:* Knoll Hill House, Aldington, Kent. *Clubs:* White's, Garrick, Royal Thames Yacht; Century (NY); Travellers' (Paris).
*Died 3 Oct. 1984.*

**FREUD, Anna,** CBE 1967; Psycho-Analyst; Director of Hampstead Child Therapy Course and Clinic, since 1952; *b* 3 Dec. 1895; *d* of Professor Sigmund Freud and Martha Freud (*née* Bernays). *Educ:* Cottage Lyceum, Vienna. Chm., Vienna Inst. of Psycho-Analysis until 1938; Mem., London Inst. of Psycho-Analysis since then. Hon. degrees: LLD: Clark Univ., USA, 1950; Univ. of Sheffield, 1966; ScD: Jefferson Med. Coll., USA 1964; Univ. of Chicago, 1966; Yale, 1968; Columbia, 1978; Harvard, 1980; MD Univ. of Vienna; DPhil J. W. Goethe Univ., Frankfurt, 1981. *Publications:* Introduction to the Technique of Child Analysis, trans. L. P. Clark (USA), 1928; Psychoanalysis for Parents and Teachers, trans. Barbara Low, 1931; The Ego and Mechanisms of Defence, trans. Cecil Baines, 1937, 3rd edn 1969; (with D. T. Burlingham) Young Children in Wartime, 1942; (with D. T. Burlingham) War and Children, 1944; (with D. T. Burlingham) Infants without Families, 1944; Psychoanalytical Treatment of Children, trans. Nancy Proctor-Gregg, 1946, 2nd edn 1951; (ed jtly) Psychoanalytic Study of the Child, 30 vols, 1945–; (ed with J. Strachey and others) The Standard Edition of the Complete Psychological Works of Sigmund Freud, 24 vols, 1953–56; (with W. D. Wall) The Enrichment of Childhood, 1962; (with T. Bergmann) Children in Hospital (USA), 1966; Normality and Pathology in Childhood, 1966; Indications of Child Analysis, and other papers, 1969; Difficulties in the Path of Psychoanalysis (USA), 1969; Research at the Hampstead Child Therapy Clinic, and other papers 1956–65, 1970; Problems of Psychoanalytic Technique and Therapy, 1973; (with Albert J. Solnit and J. Goldstein): Beyond the Best Interests of the Child, 1973; Before the Best Interests of the Child, 1979; (collected edn) The Writings of Anna Freud , Vols I–VIII, 1975–80; contribs to Internat. Jl of Psycho-Analysis. *Address:* 20 Maresfield Gardens, NW3. *T:* 01-435 2002.
*Died 9 Oct. 1982.*

**FREUDENBERG, Hubertus Friedrich, Prince of L. W.;** *see* Loewenstein-Wertheim-Freudenberg.

**FREW, Sir John Lewtas,** Kt 1981; OBE 1976; MD; FRCP, FRACP; Hon. Consulting Physician, Royal Melbourne Hospital; *b* 10 Sept. 1912; *s* of Captain J. D. Frew; *m* 1940, Joyce M. E., *d* of A. F. Bell; one *s. Educ:* Camberwell Grammar Sch.; Scotch Coll., Melbourne; Ormond Coll., Melbourne Univ. Served War, 1941–45: Captain 13 AGH (POW). Royal Melbourne Hospital: Med. Supt, 1938–41; Sub-Dean, 1947–54; Pres., Cttee of Management, 1973–79 (Vice-Pres., 1968–73). Vis. Specialist, Heidelberg Repatriation Hosp., 1948–79; Comr, Commonwealth Serum Labs, 1967–70. Royal Australasian College of Physicians: Censor-in-Chief, 1966–70; Vice-Pres., 1970–72; Pres., 1972–74. Hon. FACP. *Address:* 34 Queen's Road, Melbourne, Vic 3004, Australia. *Club:* Melbourne (Melbourne).
*Died 8 May 1985.*

**FRICKER, Prof. Peter Racine,** FRCO, ARCM; Corwin Professor of Music, Music Department, University of California, Santa Barbara, since 1986 (Professor of Music, since 1964); Director of Music, Morley College, 1952–64; *b* 5 Sept. 1920; *s* of late Edward Racine Fricker; *m* 1943, Audrey Helen Clench. *Educ:* St Paul's Sch. Royal College of Music, 1937–40. Served War, 1940–46, in Royal Air Force, working in Signals and Intelligence. Has worked as Composer, Conductor, and Music Administrator since 1946. Hon. Professorial Fellow, Univ. of Wales, Cardiff, 1971. Pres. Emeritus, Cheltenham Festival, 1987 (Pres., 1984–86). Hon. RAM, 1966. Hon. DMus (Leeds), 1958. Order of Merit, West Germany, 1965. *Publications:* Four Fughettas for Two Pianos, 1946; Wind Quintet, 1947; Three Sonnets of Cecco Angiolieri da Siena, for Tenor and Seven Instruments, 1947; String Quartet in One Movement, 1948; Symphony No 1, 1948–49; Prelude, Elegy and Finale for String Orchestra, 1949; Concerto for Violin and Orchestra, 1949–50; Sonata for Violin and Piano, 1950; Concertante for Cor Anglais and String Orchestra, 1950; Symphony No 2, 1950; Concertante for Three Pianos, Strings and Timpani, 1951; Four Impromptus for Piano; Concerto for Viola and Orchestra, 1951–53; Concerto for Piano and Orchestra, 1952–54; String Quartet No 2, 1952–53; Rapsodia Concertante for Violin and Orchestra, 1953–54; Dance Scene for Orchestra, 1954; Musick's Empire for Chorus and Small Orchestra, 1955; Litany for Double String Orchestra, 1955; 'Cello Sonata, 1956; Oratorio, The Vision of Judgement, 1956–58; Octet, 1958; Toccata for Piano and Orchestra, 1958–59; Serenade No 1, 1959; Serenade No 2, 1959; Symphony No 3, 1960; Studies for Piano, 1961; Cantata for Tenor and Chamber Ensemble, 1962; O Longs Désirs: Song-cycle for Soprano and Orchestra, 1963; Ricercare for Organ, 1965; Four Dialogues for Oboe and Piano,

1965; Four Songs for High Voice and Orchestra, 1965; Fourth Symphony, 1966; Fantasy for Viola and Piano, 1966; Three Scenes for Orchestra, 1966; The Day and the Spirits for Soprano and Harp, 1967; Seven Counterpoints for Orchestra, 1967; Magnificat, 1968; Episodes for Piano, 1968; Concertante No 4, 1968; Toccata for Organ, 1968; Saxophone Quartet, 1969; Praeludium for Organ, 1969; Paseo for Guitar, 1970; The Roofs for coloratura soprano and percussion, 1970; Sarabande In Memoriam Igor Stravinsky, 1971; Nocturne for chamber orchestra, 1971; Intrada for organ, 1971; A Bourrée for Sir Arthur Bliss for cello, 1971; Concertante no 5 for piano and string quartet, 1971; Introitus for orchestra, 1972; Come Sleep for contralto, alto flute and bass clarinet, 1972; Fanfare for Europe for trumpet, 1972; Ballade for flute and piano, 1972; Seven Little Songs for chorus, 1972; Gigue for cello, 1973; The Groves of Dodona for six flutes, 1973; Spirit Puck, for clarinet and percussion, 1974; Two Petrarch Madrigals, 1974; Trio-Sonata for Organ, 1974; Third String Quartet, 1975; Fifth Symphony, 1975; Seachant for flute and double bass, 1976; Sinfonia for 17 wind instruments, 1976; Anniversary for piano, 1977; Sonata for two pianos, 1977; Serenade for four clarinets, 1977; Laudi Concertati for organ and orchestra, 1979; Serenade No 5, 1979; In Commendation of Music, 1980; Five Short Pieces for organ, 1980; Six Mélodies de Francis Jammes for tenor, violin, cello and piano, 1980; Spells for solo flute, 1980; Bagatelles for clarinet and piano, 1981; For Three, for oboes, 1981; Two Expressions for Piano, 1981; Rondeaux for horn and orchestra, 1982; Whispers at these Curtains (oratorio), 1984; Madrigals for Brass Quintet, 1984; Aspects of Evening for cello and piano, 1985; Concertino for St Paul's (orch.), 1985; Recitative, Impromptu, and Procession for organ, 1985; Concerto for orch., 1986; Second Sonata for Violin and Piano, 1987; Six Diversions for Piano, 1987; Walk by Quiet Waters, for orch., 1988; 2nd Piano Concerto, 1989; A Dream of Winter, cantata for baritone and piano, 1989; also music for film, stage and radio. *Recreation:* travel. *Address:* (home) 5423 Throne Court, Santa Barbara, Calif 93111, USA. *T:* (805) 964-3737; Department of Music, University of California, Santa Barbara, Calif 93106, USA. *Club:* East India, Devonshire, Sports and Public Schools. *Died* 1 Feb. 1990.

**FRISBY, Maj.-Gen. Richard George Fellowes,** CB 1963; CBE 1958; DSO 1944; MC 1939; KL; *b* 17 Dec. 1911; *er s* of late Col H. G. F. Frisby, Royal Hants Regt, and late Mrs R. M. Frisby, Bacton Grange, Herefordshire; *m* 1938, Elizabeth Mary, 2nd *d* of late Col W. G. Murray, 3rd King's Own Hussars, Twyford House, Winchester, and late Mrs M. Murray, Pretoria, South Africa; two *s.* *Educ:* Haileybury Coll.; Royal Military College, Sandhurst. Commissioned Hants Regt, 1931; Mohmand Campaign, 1935; British Army Staff, Washington, 1941–42. Commanded: 4 Bn Welch Regt, 1944–45; 1 Bn Hants Regt, 1945–46; 14 Bn Parachute Regt, 1949–51; 1 Bn R Hants Regt, 1951–53; Tactical Wing Sch. of Infantry, 1953–54; 1 Commonwealth Div., Korea, 1955–56; 24 Independent Brigade, 1957–58; Gen. Staff, HQ Eastern Command, 1959–60; GOC 53 Infantry Div. (TA), 1961–63; Maj.-Gen., 1961; Chief of Staff to the C-in-C, Allied Forces, Northern Europe, Dec. 1963–65; retd. DL Hants, 1981. *Address:* Hampton Hill Cottage, Swanmore, Hants SO3 2QN. *T:* Bishops Waltham 2673. *Club:* Army and Navy. *Died* 7 Feb. 1982.

**FRITH, Brig. Sir Eric (Herbert Cokayne),** Kt 1973; CBE 1945 (MBE 1926); DL; JP; Chairman, Official Side, Police Council for UK, 1966–74; *b* 10 Sept. 1897; *s* of late Brig.-Gen. Herbert Cokayne Frith, CB, Taunton; *m* 1925, Joan Margaret, *yr d* of late Major R. B. Graves-Knyfton; one *s.* *Educ:* Marlborough Coll.; RMC Sandhurst. 2nd Lieut Somerset LI, 1915; served European War, 1914–18 (wounded); psc; served War of 1939–45; retd Dec. 1948. Somerset County Council: Mem. 1949 (Chm. 1959–64, Vice-Chm. 1956–59); Alderman 1957. DL 1953, JP 1953, Somerset. Order of Polonia Restituta (Poland), 1945; Medal of Freedom with Silver Palm (US), 1945. *Recreations:* cricket, Rugby football, hunting, shooting, hockey (in the past). *Address:* The Cottage, Mount Street, Taunton TA1 3QE. *T:* Taunton 84180. *Clubs:* Naval and Military; Somerset Stragglers Cricket. *Died* 30 June 1984.

**FRIZZELL, Edward,** CBE 1981; QPM 1978; HM Chief Inspector of Constabulary for Scotland, 1979–83; *b* 6 Dec. 1918; *s* of late Edward Frizzell and Mary (*née* Cox); *m* 1945, May Russell; one *s* one *d.* *Educ:* Greenhill Primary Sch.; Coatbridge High Sch. Served War, RAF, 1943–45 (Flying Officer). Det. Sgt, 1953, Det. Chief Inspector, 1961, Paisley Burgh Police; Det. Chief Supt, 1968, Asst Chief Constable, 1968, Renfrew and Bute Constab.; Chief Constable: Stirling and Clackmannan Police, 1970; Central Scotland Police, 1975. OStJ 1971. *Recreations:* shooting, golf. *Address:* 24 Alexander Drive, Bridge of Allan, Stirling FK9 4QB. *T:* Bridge of Allan 3846. *Club:* Stirling and County (Stirling). *Died* 25 May 1987.

**FROME, Sir Norman (Frederick),** Kt 1947; CIE 1945; DFC 1918; MSc, FIEE; late Consultant, Messrs Preece, Cardew & Rider, Consulting Engineers; formerly Indian Posts and Telegraphs Department; *b* 23 Sept. 1899; *s* of late John Frome, Bristol; *m* 1928, Edith S. Guyan (*d* 1981). *Educ:* Fairfield Grammar Sch.; University

of Bristol. Served European War, 1914–18, in RFC and RAF, 1917–18. Joined Indian Posts and Telegraphs Dept, 1923; Dir of Telegraphs, 1937; Postmaster-Gen., 1941; Chief Engineer, 1946. *Publications:* articles on telecommunications, 1928–60. *Recreations:* astronomy, ornithology. *Address:* Elmwood, Gussage All Saints, near Wimborne, Dorset BH21 5ET. *Club:* Royal Commonwealth Society. *Died* 29 Oct. 1982.

**FROST, Norman,** CBE 1959; KPM 1950; *b* 18 March 1899; *s* of William Frost and Maud Frost (*née* Strickland); *m* 1927, Ivy Edna (*née* Bush); two *s.* *Educ:* March, Cambs. Royal Engineers (Signals), 1917–20. Peterborough Police, 1926–44; Boston Police, 1944–47; seconded Home Office; Commandant Police Training Sch., 1945–47; Eastbourne Police, 1947–54; Chief Constable of Bristol, 1954–64. OStJ. *Address:* Westovers, Wedmore, Somerset. *T:* Wedmore 712568. *Club:* St John House. *Died* 24 Nov. 1985.

**FRY, Prof. Dennis Butler;** Emeritus Professor of Experimental Phonetics, University College, London, Professor 1958–75; Hon. Research Fellow, University College London; *b* 3 Nov. 1907; *s* of late F. C. B. Fry and Jane Ann (*née* Butler), Stockbridge, Hants; *m* 1937, Chrystabel, *er d* of late Charles Smith, JP, Brighton; one *s* two *d.* *Educ:* Gosport Grammar Sch.; University of London. Asst Master, Tewkesbury Grammar Sch., 1929–31; Asst Master, Kilburn Grammar Sch., 1931–34; Asst Lecturer in Phonetics, University Coll., London, 1934–37; Lecturer and Superintendent of Phonetics Laboratory, 1937–49. Served as Squadron Leader, RAFVR, 1940–45; in charge of Acoustics Laboratory, Central Medical Establishment, RAF, 1941–45. Reader in Experimental Phonetics, University of London, 1948; Head of Dept of Phonetics, UCL, 1949–71. Editor of Language and Speech, 1958–78. Pres., Permanent Internat. Council for Phonetic Sciences, 1961; Hon. Fellow, College of Speech Therapists, 1964; Fellow, Acoustical Soc. of America, 1966; Governor: Sadler's Wells Foundation, 1966. Trustee, Inst. for Cultural Research. FRSA 1970. *Publications:* The Deaf Child (with E. M. Whetnall), 1963; Learning to Hear (with E. M. Whetnall), 1970; Homo Loquens, 1977; The Physics of Speech, 1979; papers on speech and hearing in scientific and linguistic journals. *Recreation:* music, especially singing. *Address:* 18 Lauriston Road, SW19. *T:* 01-946 3046. *Died* 21 March 1983.

**FRY, E(dwin) Maxwell,** CBE 1953; RA 1972 (ARA 1966); BArch; FRIBA, FRTPI; Dist Town Planning; consultant architect and town planner in retirement; active painter; *b* 2 Aug. 1899; *s* of Ambrose Fry and Lydia Thompson; *m* 1927, Ethel Speakman (marr. diss.); one *d*; *m* 1942, Jane B. Drew, FRIBA. *Educ:* Liverpool Inst.; Liverpool Univ. Sch. of Architecture. Practised with Walter Gropius as Gropius and Fry, 1934–36; as Maxwell Fry and Jane Drew, 1945–50, as Fry, Drew, Drake, & Lasdun, 1951–58; now as Fry, Drew, Knight & Creamer. Work includes schools, hospitals, working-class and other flats, houses in England and educational buildings in Ghana and Nigeria. Served with Royal Engineers, 1939–44. Town Planning Adviser to Resident Minister for West Africa, 1943–45; Senior Architect to New Capital Chandigarh, Punjab, 1951–54. One-man show, Drian Gall., 1974. Ex-Mem. Royal Fine Art Commission; Corr. Mem. Académie Flamande, 1956; Hon. FAIA 1963; Council Mem. RIBA (Vice-Pres. 1961–62) and RSA; Royal Gold Medal for Architecture, 1964. Hon. LLD Ibadan Univ., 1966. *Publications:* Fine Building, 1944; (jointly with Jane B. Drew) Architecture for Children, 1944; Tropical Architecture, 1964; Art in a Machine Age, 1969; Maxwell Fry: autobiographical sketches, 1975; contribs to architectural and other papers. *Address:* West Lodge, Cotherstone, Barnard Castle, Co. Durham DL12 9PF. *T:* Teesdale 50217. *Died* 3 Sept. 1987.

**FRY, Sir (Francis) Wilfrid,** 5th Bt *cr* 1894; OBE 1967; CEng; MIME; Mining Engineer, retired; *b* 2 May 1904; *s* of Sir John Pease Fry, 2nd Bt and Margaret Theodora (*d* 1941), *d* of Francis Edward Fox; *S* brother, 1985; *m* 1943, Anne Pease, JP, *e d* of Kenneth Henry Wilson, OBE, JP. *Educ:* Clifton; Trinity Coll., Cambridge (BA). Served 1940–42 as Lieut RE, bomb disposal. Area General Manager for NCB, 1947–67; formerly Mining Agent and director of two companies. JP Co. Durham, 1949–67, N Yorks, 1968–74 (Chm. of Bench, 1971–74). *Recreations:* formerly hunting, fishing, bee-keeping; now light gardening. *Heir:* none. *Address:* Cleveland Lodge, Great Ayton, Middlesbrough, Cleveland TS9 6BT. *T:* Great Ayton 722215. *Died* 26 July 1987 (*ext*).

**FRY, Sir John (Nicholas Pease),** 4th Bt *cr* 1894; *b* 23 Oct. 1897; *s* of Sir John Pease Fry, 2nd Bt and Margaret Theodora (*d* 1941), *d* of Francis Edward Fox, JP; *S* brother, 1971; *m* 1927, Helen Murray (*d* 1981), *d* of late William Gibson Bott, MRCS, JP; one *d* (and one *d* decd). *Educ:* Clifton; Trinity College, Cambridge (BA). Served European War, 1914–18 with Friends Ambulance Unit; War of 1939–45, with Special Constabulary. *Heir:* *b* Francis Wilfrid Fry, OBE [*b* 2 May 1904; *m* 1943, Anne Pease, *e d* of late Kenneth Henry Wilson, OBE, JP]. *Address:* c/o Mrs M. J. Redway, 6 Turners Wood

Drive, Chalfont St Giles, Bucks HP8 4NE.
*Died* 14 *Jan.* 1985.

**FRY, Maxwell;** *see* Fry, E. M.

**FRY, Sir Wilfrid;** *see* Fry, Sir F. W.

**FRYER, James,** QPM 1979; FBIM; Chief Constable of Derbyshire, since 1979; *b* 19 Dec. 1930; *s* of Ronald John Fryer and Winifred Fryer; *m* 1952, Felicia Wyatt; one *s* two *d*. *Educ:* Yorkshire schools. Extension Certificate in Criminology, Univ. of Leeds, 1968. Served Royal Engineers, 1949–51. Police Constable, West Riding Constabulary, 1954; transf. Leeds City Police; PC 1956; Inspector, 1963; Sub-Divisional Command, 1965; Detective Supt, 1968; transf. Derby County and Borough Constabulary; Detective Chief Supt, 1972; transf. West Mercia Constabulary; Asst Chief Constable, 1975; transf. Derbyshire Constabulary; Dep. Chief Constable, 1976. Intermediate Command Course, 1969, Sen. Command Course, 1972, Police Staff College. *Publication:* ed jtly, Moriarty's Police Law, 24th edn, 1980. *Recreations:* walking, reading, shooting, gardening. *Address:* Butterley Hall, Ripley, Derby DE5 3RS. *T:* Ripley 43551. *Club:* Special Forces. *Died* 10 *March* 1981.

**FULFORD, Sir Roger (Thomas Baldwin),** Kt 1980; CVO 1970; *b* 24 Nov. 1902; *o* surv. *s* of late Canon Fulford; *m* 1937, Sibell (*d* 1980), widow of late Rev. Hon. C. F. Lyttelton and *d* of late Charles Adeane, CB. *Educ:* St Ronans; Lancing; Worcester Coll., Oxford. Pres. of Union, 1927; called to Bar, 1931; Liberal Candidate for Woodbridge Div. of Suffolk, 1929; for Holderness Div. of Yorks, 1945; for Rochdale, 1950; joined editorial staff of The Times, 1933; Part-time Lecturer in English, King's Coll., London, 1937–48; Asst. Censor, 1939–40; Civil Asst War Office, 1940–42; Asst Private Sec. to Sec. of State for Air, 1942–45. Pres., Liberal Party, 1964–65. *Publications:* Royal Dukes, 1933; George IV, 1935; The Right Honourable Gentleman, 1945; The Prince Consort, 1949; Queen Victoria, 1951; History of Glyn's, 1953; Votes for Women, 1957; The Liberal Case, 1959; Hanover to Windsor, 1960; C. H. Wilkinson, 1965; Samuel Whitbread, 1967; The Trial of Queen Caroline, 1967; ed (with late Lytton Strachey) The Greville Memoirs, 1937; (ed) The Autobiography of Miss Knight, 1960; (ed) Letters Between Queen Victoria and the Princess Royal: Dearest Child, 1964; Dearest Mama, 1968; Your Dear Letter, 1971; Darling Child, 1976; Beloved Mama, 1981. *Address:* Barbon Manor, Carnforth, Lancs. *Club:* Boodle's. *Died* 18 *May* 1983.

**FULLER, Buckminster;** *see* Fuller, R. B.

**FULLER, Major Sir (John) Gerard (Henry Fleetwood),** 2nd Bt, *cr* 1910; late Life Guards; *b* 8 July 1906; *s* of 1st Bt and Norah Jacintha (who married secondly Col R. Forestier Walker, DSO, and died 1935), *d* of late C. Nicholas Paul Phipps of Charlcot, Westbury, Wilts; *S* father, 1915; *m* 1st, 1931, Lady Fiona Pratt (marr. diss. 1944), *yr d* of 4th Marquess Camden, GCVO; two *s*; 2nd, 1945, Kathleen Elizabeth, MBE, DStJ (*d* 1964), 5th *d* of late Sir George Farrar, Bt, Chichely Hall, Newport Pagnell, Bucks; 3rd, 1966, Mrs Mary Leventon. *Educ:* Uppingham. 2nd Lieut Life Guards, 1927; Captain 1938; Major, 1941; retired, 1946; served War of 1939–45 (despatches). JP Wilts, 1946; Mem. Wilts CC 1947–71; County Alderman, 1961; Joint Master Avon Vale Fox Hounds, 1947–61, and 1962–64. *Heir: s* John William Fleetwood Fuller [*b* 18 Dec. 1936; *m* 1968, Lorna Marian, *o d* of F. R. Kemp-Potter, Findon, Sussex; three *s*. Major, The Life Guards, 1968]. *Address:* Neston Park, Corsham, Wilts. *T:* Hawthorn 810211; Balmore, Cannich, Inverness-shire. *T:* Cannich 262. *Died* 16 *Oct.* 1981.

**FULLER, Richard Buckminster;** American geometer, educator and architect-designer; University Professor Emeritus, Southern Illinois University and University of Pennsylvania; *b* Milton, Mass, 12 July 1895; *s* of Richard Buckminster Fuller and Caroline Wolcott Fuller (*née* Andrews); *m* 1917, Anne Hewlett; one *d* (and one *d* decd). *Educ:* Milton Acad.; Harvard Univ., US Naval Acad. Apprentice machine fitter, Richards, Atkinson & Haserick, 1914; Ensign to Lieut, US Navy, 1917–19; Asst Export Man., Armour & Co., 1919–21; Nat. Accounts Sales Man., Kelly-Springfield Truck Co., 1922; Pres., Stockade Building System, 1922–27; Founder, Pres., 4-D Co., Chicago, 1927–28; Editor and Publisher, Shelter Magazine, Philadelphia, 1930–32; Asst to Dir of Housing Res., Pierce Foundn, NY, and American Radiator & Standard Sanitary Manftg Co., Buffalo, 1930–31; Founder, Dir and Chief Engr, Dymaxion Corp., Bridgeport, 1932–36; Asst to Dir, Res. and Develt, Phelps Dodge Corp., 1936–38; Tech. Consultant, Fortune Mag., 1938–40; Vice-Pres. and Chief Engr, Dymaxion Co. Inc., Delaware, 1940–50; Chief Mech. Engr, US Bd of Econ. Warfare, 1942–44; Special Asst to Dep. Dir, US Foreign Econ. Administration, 1944; Chm. Bd and Chief Engr, Dymaxion Dwelling Machines, 1944–46; Chm. Bd of Trustees, Fuller Research Foundn, Wichita, Kansas, 1946–54; Pres. Geodesics Inc., Forest Hills, 1949–; Pres., Synergetics Inc., Raleigh, NC, 1954–59; Pres. Plydomes Inc., Des Moines, 1957–; Chm. Bd, Tetrahelix Corp., Hamilton, 1959–; Pres., Triton Foundn, Cambridge, Mass, 1967–; Editor-at-large, World Magazine, NY,

1972–75; Internat. Pres., MENSA, Paris, 1975–; Internat. Pres., World Soc. for Ekistics, Athens, 1975–; contrib. Editor, Saturday Review, 1976–; Consultant, Design Science Inst., Philadelphia, 1972–. Charles Eliot Norton Prof. of Poetry, Harvard Univ., 1961–62; Harvey Cushing Orator, Amer. Assoc. of Neuro-Surgeons, 1967; Jahawarlal Nehru Lectr, New Delhi, 1969; Hoyt Fellow, Yale Univ., 1969; World Fellow in Residence, Consortium of Univ. of Pennsylvania, Haverford Coll., Swarthmore Coll., Bryn Mawr Coll., and Univ. City Science Center, 1972–. Holds 25 patents in architecture, transport, cartography (first and only cartography patent awarded in USA) and other fields; *inventions include:* the World Game, Dymaxion house, car, bathroom, map; discovered energetic/synergetic geometry, 1917; geodesic structures, 1947 (over 200,000 geodesic domes erected in 100 countries). *Architect of:* US pavilion for Montreal World Fair, 1967; Samuel Beckett Theatre, St Peter's Coll., Oxford, 1969–; geodesic auditorium, Kfar Menachem Kibutzin, Israel, 1969–; Tri-centennial Pavilion of S Carolina, Greenfield, 1970; Religious Center, Southern Illinois Univ., 1971; Chief Architect, internat. airports at New Delhi, Bombay and Madras, 1973; consultant to Architects Team 3, Penang Urban Center, 1974–. Mem. many professional instns; Hon. Fellow, St Peter's Coll., Oxford, 1970; Hon. FRIBA 1968; FAIA 1975; holds hon. degrees from 43 univs/colleges; awards include Industrial Designers Soc. of Amer. (first) Award of Excellence, 1966; Gold Medal, Architecture, Nat. Inst. of Arts and Letters, 1968; Royal Gold Medal for Architecture, RIBA, 1968; Humanist of the Year Award, Amer. Assoc. of Humanists, 1969; Master Designer Award, McGraw Hill, 1969; Gold Medal, Amer. Inst. Architects, 1970. *Publications:* 4D Timelock, 1927; Nine Chains to the Moon, 1938 (UK 1973); The Dymaxion World of Buckminster Fuller (with Robert Marks), 1960 (rev. edn 1973); No More Second Hand God, 1962; Education Automation, 1963 (UK 1973); Ideas and Integrities (ed Robert Marks), 1963; untitled epic poem on history of industrialization, 1963; World Resources Inventory (6 documents) (with John McHale), 1963–67; Operating Manual for Spaceship Earth, 1969; Utopia or Oblivion, 1969; The Buckminster Fuller Reader (ed James Meller), 1970; I Seem to be a Verb (with Jerome Agel and Quentin Fiore), 1970; Intuition, 1972; Earth Inc., 1973; Synergetics: Explorations in the Geometry of Thinking (with E. J. Applewhite), 1975, Vol. 2, 1979; And It Came to Pass, Not to Stay, 1977; Critical Path, 1981; Tetrascroll, 1982; Grunch of Giants, 1983; (with Anwar Dil) Humans in Universe, 1983; many contribs to jls etc. *Address:* 3501 Market Street, Philadelphia, Pa 19104, USA. *T:* (215) 387-5400. *Died* 1 *July* 1983.

**FULLER-GOOD, Air Vice-Marshal James Laurence Fuller,** CB 1957; CVO 1953; CBE 1951; RAF retired; *b* 20 Sept. 1903; *m* Joan; one *s*. Air Officer Commanding, Air Headquarters, Malaya, 1951–52 (CBE); Director of Personal Services (Air), Air Ministry, 1952–53; Air Officer Commanding No 22 Group, Technical Training Command, 1953–57; Commandant-Gen. of the Royal Air Force Regt and Inspector of Ground Combat Trng, 1957–59, retd. Air Vice-Marshal, 1954. *Club:* Royal Air Force.

*Died* 11 *May* 1983.

**FULTON, Baron,** *cr* 1966, of Falmer (Life Peer); **John Scott Fulton,** Kt 1964; Hon. Fellow, Balliol College, Oxford; *b* 27 May 1902; *y s* of the late Principal A. R. Fulton, Dundee; *m* 1939, Jacqueline, *d* of K. E. T. Wilkinson, York; three *s* one *d*. *Educ:* Dundee High Sch.; St Andrews Univ.; Balliol Coll., Oxford (Exhibitioner). Asst in Logic and Scientific Method, London Sch. of Economics, 1926–28; Fellow, 1928–47, Balliol Coll. Oxford; Tutor in Philosophy, 1928–35; Tutor in Politics, 1935–47; Jowett Lecturer, 1935–38; Jowett Fellow, 1945–47; Rockefeller Fellow, 1936–37; Faculty Fellow, Nuffield Coll., 1939–47; Principal, University Coll. of Swansea, 1947–59 (Hon. Fellow, 1985); Vice-Chancellor: University of Wales, 1952–54 and 1958–59; University of Sussex, 1959–67. Chairman: Inter Univ. Council for Higher Educn Overseas, 1964–68; British Council, 1968–71; Cttee on the Civil Service, 1966–68; a Governor of the BBC, 1965–70 (Vice Chm., 1965–67 and 1968–70). Principal and Asst Sec., Mines Dept, 1940–42; Principal Asst Sec. Min. of Fuel and Power, 1942–44. Dir Wales and Mon Industrial Estates Ltd, 1948–54. Chairman: Board for Mining Qualifications, 1950–62; Universities Council for Adult Educ., 1952–55; Council of Nat. Inst. of Adult Educ., 1952–55; Commn on educational requirements of Sierra Leone, 1954; Selection Cttee for Miners' Welfare Nat. Scholarships, 1949–59; Nat. Adv. Coun. on the Training and Supply of Teachers, 1959–63; Univs Central Coun. on Admissions, 1961–64; Commn on Royal Univ. of Malta, 1962–72; Commn on establishment of a second University in Hong Kong, 1962; BBC Liaison Advisory Cttee on Adult Education Programmes, 1962–65; BBC Further Education Adv. Coun. for the UK, 1965; Institute of Development Studies, 1966–67; ITA Adult Educn Adv. Cttee, 1962–65; Coun. of Inst. of Educn, University of London, 1967–71; Coun. of Tavistock Inst. of Human Relations, 1968–78; Manpower Soc., 1973–76. Member: National Reference Tribunal for Coal Industry of Great Britain, 1957–65; Cttee on University Teaching Methods, 1961–64. Pres., Soc. for Research into Higher Education,

1964–67; Pres., Morley College, 1969–. Hon. LLD: Chinese Univ. of Hong Kong, 1964; California, 1966; Yale, 1967; Sussex, 1967; Wales, 1968; Dundee, 1968; Hon. DLitt: Ife, 1967; Royal Univ. of Malta, 1967; Carleton, 1970; DUniv Keele, 1971. *Publications:* (with C. R. Morris) In Defence of Democracy, 1935; various articles and named lectures. *Recreation:* golf. *Address:* Brook House, Thornton Dale, Pickering, N Yorks. *T:* Pickering 74221. *Club:* Athenæum. *Died* 14 *March* 1986.

**FURLONGE, Sir Geoffrey (Warren)**, KBE 1960 (OBE 1942); CMG 1951; *b* 16 Oct. 1903; *s* of Robert Shekleton Furlonge and Agnes Mary (*née* Hatch); *m* 1952, Anne (*d* 1975), *d* of late E. A. Goldsack; *m* 1975, Vera Kathleen, *widow* of late Major Guy Farquhar. *Educ:* St Paul's Sch.; Emmanuel Coll., Cambridge. Entered Levant Consular Service, 1926; served at Casablanca, 1928–31; Jedda, 1931–34; Beirut, 1934–46; Political Officer with HM Forces in the Levant States, 1941–46. At Imperial Defence Coll., 1947; served in FO, 1948 (Head of Commonwealth Liaison Dept, 1948–50, Head of Eastern Dept, 1950–51); Minister (later Ambassador) to Jordan, 1952–54; Minister to Bulgaria, 1954–56; Ambassador to Ethiopia, 1956–59. *Publications:* The Lands of Barbary, 1966; Palestine is my Country, 1969. *Address:* 7 Heathfield Close, Midhurst, West Sussex GU29 9PS. *Died* 15 *Aug.* 1984.

**FURNEAUX, Robin;** *see* Birkenhead, 3rd Earl of.

**FURNIVALL, Maj.-Gen. Lewis Trevor,** CB 1964; DSO 1943; Director of Medical Services, Far East Land Forces, 1965–66; retired 1967; *b* 6 Sept. 1907; *er s* of late Lt-Col C. H. Furnivall, CMG, and late Mrs D. Furnivall (*née* Macbean); *m* 1941, Audrey Elizabeth Furnivall (*née* Gibbins); three *s* one *d. Educ:* Blundell's Sch.; St Mary's Hosp., London. MRCS, LRCP 1931; House Surg., Worcester Gen. Infirmary, 1931; Lieut, RAMC 1931; NW Frontier of India (Mohmand), 1933 (medal and clasp); Capt. 1934; Major 1941; Lieut-Col 1947; Col 1953; Brig. 1960; Maj.-Gen. 1961. Service in India, 1932–38; DADMS, 1939–. War Service, 1939–45 (UK, MELF, Italy, France, Germany); ADMS, 1944–48 (despatches, 1946); DDMS, HQ, BAOR, 1949–52; ADMS, HQ, Land Forces, Hong Kong, 1953–54; ADMS, HQ, Northumbrian Dist, 1955–57; Dep. Chief Med. Officer, SHAPE, 1957–60; Inspector of Training, Army Med. Services, 1960; Deputy Dir Medical Services, Eastern Command, 1961–65. QHS 1961–67. La Médaille d'Honneur du Service de Santé, 1960. *Address:* Woodside, 80 Lynch Road, Farnham, Surrey. *T:* Farnham 715771. *Died* 12 *July* 1986.

**FYERS, FitzRoy Hubert;** *b* 13 March 1899; *s* of late Major Hubert Alcock Nepean Fyers, MVO, and Evangeline Blanche, *e d* of late Captain Hon. Francis A. J. Chichester and Lady Emily Chichester; *m* 1949, Bryda Hope Collison (*d* 1976), *d* of late Octavius Weir. *Educ:* Eton; RMC, Sandhurst. Entered Rifle Brigade, 1917; served in European War, France, 1918; seconded to Machine Gun Corps, 1920; ADC to Gen. Sir Alex. Godley, British Army of the Rhine, 1922–24, and to Gen. Sir John Du Cane, 1924–25; retired from Army, 1926; Sec. to Sir H. Hesketh Bell, on special mission to Yugoslavia, 1929; Extra-Equerry to the Duke of Connaught, 1929–30; Equerry to The Duke of Connaught, 1930–39, and Comptroller, 1938–41 (MVO 1935, CVO 1939, later rescinded). Rejoined Rifle Brigade on outbreak of War, Sept. 1939; transferred to King's Own Scottish Borderers, Nov. 1939; on Staff of Lt-Gen. Sir Wm Dobbie, Malta, as Military Asst, 1940 (despatches); Major, 1940; Military Liaison Officer to Rear-Adm., Alexandria, 1942–43; Asst Sergeant-at-Arms, House of Commons, 1945–48. OStJ. *Address:* Cromartie House, Strathpeffer, Ross-shire. *T:* Strathpeffer 468. *Clubs:* Travellers'; New (Edinburgh); Royal Scottish Automobile (Glasgow). *Died* 22 *April* 1981.

**FYNN, Sir Basil Mortimer L.;** *see* Lindsay-Fynn.

# G

**GADD, Maj.-Gen. Alfred Lockwood, (David),** CBE 1962 (OBE 1955); *b* 10 July 1912; *s* of late Charles A. Gadd; *m* 1st, 1936, Gwenrudd Eluned (*d* 1965), *d* of late Morgan Edwards; one *s* one *d*; 2nd, 1965, Anna Louisa Margaret (*d* 1977), *d* of late Carl-August Koehler; 3rd, 1980, Agnes Muriel, *widow* of William E. McKenzie-Hill. *Educ:* Harvey Grammar Sch., Folkestone; Peterhouse, Cambridge (Open Scholar, MA). Asst Master: Bedford Sch., 1934–35; King's Sch., Rochester, 1935–39; Marlborough Coll., 1939–40. Commissioned Intelligence Corps, 1941; GSO3 War Office, 1942; Major, 1942; Lt-Col 1944; Chief Instructor 5 Formation Coll., 1945; Comdt No 1 Army Coll., 1946; Chief Education Officer, Far ELF, 1947; various Education Staff appts, 1950–62; Dir of Army Education, WO, 1962–65. *Publications:* (as David Gadd): Georgian Summer: the story of 18th century Bath, 1971; The Loving Friends: a portrait of Bloomsbury, 1974. *Recreations:* reading and writing. *Address:* Flete, Ermington, Ivybridge, Devon PL21 9NZ. *T:* Holbeton 425 and 416. *Died* 15 March 1986.

**GAEKWAD, Lt-Col Dr Fatesinghrao P.;** *b* 2 April 1930; *s* of HH Sir Pratapsingh Gaekwar, GCIE, Maharaja of Baroda; *S* father, 1951; title abolished, 1971; *m* 1950, Padmarati Devi, Princess of Jodhpur (*d* 1984). *Educ:* privately, under English tutor; passed Senior Cambridge Examination, 1947. Entered politics, 1956; elected to Lok Sabha 1957, 1962, 1971, 1977; Parly Sec. to Defence Minister, 1957–62, Mem. Public Accounts Cttee, 1963–64. MP (Congress), Gujarat, 1967–71; Minister for Health, Gujarat Govt, 1967–71. Chancellor, Maharaja Sayajirao Univ., Baroda, 1951–. Chairman: Baroda Rayon Corp. Chm., Bd of Governors, Nat. Inst. of Sports, Patiala, 1962–63; well-known cricketer and sportsman; Manager, Indian Cricket Team to England, 1959 and to Pakistan, 1978, 1982–83; Pres., Bd of Control for Cricket in India, 1963–66; expert commentator for cricket matches both in India and UK, summarises for BBC. Member: CCI, Bombay; MCC, London. FZS London. Internat. Trustee, World Wildlife Fund, for 6 years (Founder Pres., Indian Nat. Appeal); Pres., Indian Soc. of Naturalists; Member: IUCN; Fauna Preservation Soc.; RSPB; Indian Bd for Wildlife; World Poultry Science Assoc. Cultural Dr, World Univ. of USA, 1983; Hon. DHum World Acad. of Arts and Culture of Taipeh, Taiwan Rep. of China, 1984; Baden-Powell World Fellow, 1982. Travelled with four friends by car, India to Europe through Middle East, 1955; also two months safari in Belgian Congo and E Africa, 1955; visited most countries around Globe. *Publications:* Palaces of India, 1980; (contrib.) Quick Singles, ed C. Martin-Jenkins and M. Seabrook, 1986. *Recreations:* photography, cooking, reading, poetry. *Address:* Laxmi Vilas Palace, Baroda 390 001, (Gujarat), India. *Died* 1 Sept. 1988.

**GAFFNEY, Maj.-Gen. (Hon.) Edward Sebastian B.;** *see* Burke-Gaffney.

**GAGE, 6th Viscount,** *cr* 1720; **Henry Rainald Gage,** KCVO 1939; Bt 1622; Baron Gage (Ireland), 1720; Baron Gage (Great Britain), 1790; DL; *b* 30 Dec. 1895; *o s* of 5th Viscount and Leila (*d* 1916), 2nd *d* of Rev. Frederick Peel, MA, and Hon. Adelaide, *d* of 3rd Baron Sudeley; *S* father, 1912; *m* 1st, 1931, Hon. Alexandra Imogen Clare Grenfell (*d* 1969), *yr d* of 1st Baron Desborough, KG, GCVO; two *s* one *d*; 2nd, 1971, Hon. Mrs Campbell-Gray. *Educ:* Eton; Christchurch, Oxford. Served European War, 1914–18 (wounded); War of 1939–45, Coldstream Guards and Staff; Lord-in-Waiting, 1925–29 and 1931–39; PPS to Sec. of State for India, 1925–29. Vice-Pres., National Federation of Housing Societies and various Sussex County Organisations. DL 1927, Vice Lieutenant, 1957–70, Sussex. *Heir:* *s* Hon. George John St Clere Gage [*b* 8 July 1932; *m* 1971, Valerie Ann (marr. diss. 1975), *yr d* of J. E. Dutch, Horam, Sussex]. *Address:* Firle, Lewes, Sussex. *T:* Glynde 256. *Clubs:* Brooks's, White's. *Died* 27 Feb. 1982.

**GAGE, His Honour Conolly Hugh;** a Circuit Judge (formerly Judge of County Courts), 1958–78; Barrister-at-Law; Fellow Commoner, Sidney Sussex College, Cambridge, 1962; *b* 10 Nov. 1905; *s* of William Charles Gage and May Guerney Holmes, *d* of Rt Hon. Lord Justice Holmes; *m* 1932, Elinor Nancy Martyn; one *s* one *d*. *Educ:* Repton; Sidney Sussex Coll., Cambridge. Called to Bar, Inner Temple, 1930; enlisted as Gunner in RA, TA, April 1939; served with First Canadian Army as ADJAG (Br.) (despatches). MP (UU) S Belfast, 1945–52; Recorder of Maldon and Saffron Walden, 1950–52; Chm., Huntingdonshire and Peterborough QS, 1963–71; Dep. Chm., Essex QS, 1955–71. Chm., County Court Rules Cttee, 1974–78. Chancellor, dio. of Coventry, 1948–76, of Lichfield, 1954–76. Member, British Delegns to: Commonwealth Relations Conf., Canada, 1949; Consultative Assembly, Council of Europe, 1949–52. *Recreations:* fishing, shooting, gardening. *Address:* Manor Lodge, Brill, Bucks. *T:* Brill 238213. *Clubs:* Carlton, Ulster (Belfast). *Died* 3 Oct. 1984.

**GAILEY, Thomas William Hamilton,** CBE 1968; Member, Economic and Social Committee, EEC, 1973–78; *b* 7 Oct. 1906; *s* of late

Thomas Andrew Gailey, ISO, and late Mabel Gailey; *m* 1st, 1937, Beryl (*d* 1972), *er d* of late Harold Kirkconnel; one *d*; 2nd, 1973, Mary Diana (*d* 1981), *y d* of late Frederick Priddle. *Educ:* King's Sch., Rochester; University Coll., Oxford (MA). Served with companies in Tilling Bus Group, 1932–59. Served War of 1939–45, with RAF: Wing Comdr, RAF Transp. Comd and psa, 1943. Vice-Chm., Bristol Wing, Air Trng Corps, 1945–56. Mem., Tilling Gp Management Bd, 1960–64; Chm., Tilling Bus Gp, 1965–68; Dir, Passenger Planning, Transp. Holding Co., 1967–68; Mem., Nat. Bus Company, 1968–74, Chief Executive, 1968–71; Mem., Nat. Council for Omnibus Industry, 1960–69; Dir, Bristol Commercial Vehicles and Eastern Coach Works, 1962–71; Director: Leyland National Co. Ltd; Park Royal Vehicles Ltd, 1969–71. Mem., Scottish Transport Gp, 1968–71. Chm., Public Transp. Assoc., 1967–69. Vice-Chm., Road Operators' Safety Council, 1964–68. Transport Advr, English Tourist Bd, 1972–74. FCIT (Vice-Pres., 1966–68); FRSA. Freeman of City of London; Liveryman, Worshipful Co. of Carmen; Governor, British Transp. Staff Coll., 1969–75. *Publications:* various papers for professional institutes and societies. *Address:* Wheatsheaf Pond Cottage, Liphook, Hants. *T:* Liphook 723467. *Clubs:* Travellers'; Bristol Savages (Bristol). *Died* 18 Sept. 1986.

**GAIRDNER, Gen. Sir Charles Henry,** GBE 1969 (KBE 1960; CBE 1941); KCMG 1948; KCVO 1954; CB 1946; Governor of Tasmania, 1963–68; *b* 20 March 1898; *e surv s* of late C. A. Gairdner, Lisbeg House, County Galway; *m* 1925, Hon. Evelyn Constance Handcock, CStJ, *o d* of 5th Baron Castlemaine, Moydrum Castle, Co. Westmeath; no *c*. *Educ:* Repton; RMA, Woolwich. Entered Army in 1916, served in France and Flanders (wounded); Staff Coll., Camberley, 1933–35; commanded 10th Royal Hussars, 1937–40; GSO 1st grade 7 Armoured Division, 1940–41; Deputy Dir of Plans, Middle East, 1941; GOC 6th Armoured Division, 1942; Commandant, Higher Commanders Sch., 1943. GOC 8th Armoured Division, 1943; CGS North Africa, 1943; Maj.-Gen. Armoured Fighting Vehicles, India, 1944; Maj.-Gen., 1941; Lt-Gen., 1944; Head, UK Liaison Mission, Japan, 1945–46. Prime Minister's Special Representative in Far East, 1945–48. Gov., State of W Australia, 1951–63. Col 10th Royal Hussars 1949–52; Hon. Col 10th Light Horse, 1952–68; Hon. Col Royal Tasmanian Regt, 1964–68. Hon. Air Commodore, RAAF. KStJ 1951; Hon. DLitt W Australia, 1956; Hon. LLD, University of Tasmania, 1967. American Medal of Freedom with Silver Palm, 1948. *Recreations:* hunting, polo, golf, yachting. *Address:* 24 The Esplanade, Peppermint Grove, W Australia. *Clubs:* Cavalry and Guards; Weld, West Australian (Perth), Royal Perth Yacht, Royal Freshwater Bay Yacht. *Died* 22 Feb. 1983.

**GAISFORD, Prof. Wilfrid Fletcher,** MD London, MSc Manchester, FRCP; Czechoslovak Military Medal of Merit, 1st class, 1945; First Professor of Child Health and Paediatrics and Director of the Department of Child Health, University of Manchester, 1947–67, later Emeritus; *b* 6 April 1902; *s* of Captain Harold Gaisford, RN, and Annie, *d* of Captain Wm Fletcher, RIN; *m* 1933, Mary, *d* of Captain Wm Guppy; one *s* three *d* (and one *d* decd). *Educ:* Bristol Grammar Sch.; St Bartholomew's Hosp., London, MB London, 1925; MD London, 1928; Post-graduate study in St Louis Children's Hosp., University of Washington, USA, 1928–29; FRCP, 1940; MSc Manchester, 1951. Hon. Asst Physician, East London Children's Hosp., 1932; Mem., British Paediatric Assoc., 1933. Physn, Dudley Road Hosp., Birmingham, 1935–42; Cons. Paediatrician, Warwicks CC, 1942–47; Leonard Parsons Memorial Lecturer, University of Birmingham, 1954–55; Catherine Chisholm Memorial Lecturer, 1965. Hon. Physician, Royal Manchester Children's Hosp. and St Mary's Hosp., Manchester; Hon. Cons. Paediatrician, United Manchester Hosp., 1967. Regional Adviser in Child Health, 1948. Hon. Member: Canadian Paediatric Association, 1949; Swedish Paediatric Association, 1960; Finnish Paediatric Association, 1965; Hon. Fellow, American Acad. of Pediatrics, 1962; Pres., British Paediatric Assoc., 1964–65. Extraord. Mem., Swiss Paediatric Soc., 1965; Pres., Paediatric Section, Manchester Med. Soc., 1966–67. *Publications:* contrib. to the Encyclopædia of British Medical Practice, Lancet, BMJ, Practitioner, Archives of Disease in Childhood, Jl Pediatrics, etc. Joint Editor, Pædiatrics for the Practitioner (Gaisford and Lightwood). *Recreation:* gardening. *Address:* Treloyhan, Church Road, Perran-ar-Worthal, Truro TR3 7QE. *T:* Truro 864664. *Died* 24 March 1988.

**GAITSKELL, Baroness,** *cr* 1963, of Egremont (Life Peer); **Anna Dora Gaitskell;** *b* Russia, 25 April 1901; *d* of Leon Creditor; *m* 1937, Rt Hon. Hugh Todd Naylor Gaitskell, PC, CBE, MP (*d* 1963), *s* of late Arthur Gaitskell, Indian Civil Service; two *d* (and one *s* by a former marriage). Trustee, Anglo-German Foundn, 1974–83. Mem., House of Lords All Party Cttee on Bill of Human Rights, 1977–. *Address:* 18 Frognal Gardens, NW3. *Died* 1 July 1989.

**GAITSKELL, Sir Arthur,** Kt 1970; CMG 1949; Member, Commonwealth (formerly Colonial) Development Corporation,

1954–73, retired; *b* Oct. 1900; *s* of late Arthur Gaitskell, ICS; *m* 1939, Jeanne Stephanie, *d* of Col E. C. Townsend, ICS; one *s* two *d*. *Educ*: Winchester Coll.; New Coll., Oxford. Manager, Sudan Plantations Syndicate, 1945–50; Chm. and Managing Dir, Sudan Gezira Board, 1950–52. Consultant, 1952–53; Member: Royal Commission on East Africa, 1953–54; Tanganyika Agricultural Corp., 1955. Research Fellow, Nuffield Coll., Oxford, 1955–58; Nominee of International Bank on Food and Agriculture Commn, Pakistan, 1959–60; Consultant: to Mitchell Cotts, Ethiopia, to Kenya African National Union, Kenya, and to Ford Foundation, Nigeria, 1961–62. Lecturer at Economic Development Institute, International Bank, Washington, 1963. Consultant to: Euphrates Project Authority, 1965; Sir Alex Gibb and Partners on Indus Basin Survey, 1965–66; World Food Program, Mexico, 1966; FAO for Philippines, 1967, for Thailand, 1968. Member: Coun., Overseas Develt Inst., 1965; Adv. Bd, Mekong River, 1968; ILO Mission to Colombia, 1970; Mission to Jamaica for Agric. Sector, Jamaican Govt, 1973. *Publication*: Gezira, 1959. *Address*: Bicknoller, Taunton, Somerset.                                    *Died* 8 *Nov*. 1985.

**GALBRAITH, Hon. Sir Thomas Galloway Dunlop**, KBE 1982; MP (U) for Hillhead Division of Glasgow since 1948; Member of Queen's Body Guard for Scotland (Royal Company of Archers); a Governor of Wellington College; *b* 10 March 1917; *e s* and *heir* of 1st Baron Strathclyde, PC; *m* 1956, Simone (marr. diss. 1974), *e d* of late Jean du Roy de Blicquy, Bois d'Hautmont, Brabant; two *s* one *d*. *Educ*: Aytoun House, Glasgow; Wellington Coll.; Christ Church, Oxford (MA); Glasgow Univ. (LLB). Served War of 1939–45, in RNVR (Lieut), 1939–46. Contested (U) Paisley, July 1945; East Edinburgh, Oct. 1945; Asst Conservative Whip, 1950; Scottish Unionist Whip, 1950–57; a Lord Commissioner of the Treasury, 1951–54; Comptroller of HM Household, 1954–55; Treasurer of HM Household, 1955–57; Civil Lord of the Admiralty, 1957–59; Joint Parliamentary Under-Sec. of State, Scottish Office, 1959–62; Joint Parliamentary Sec., Ministry of Transport, 1963–64. Chm., Cttee on Nuclear propulsion for Merchant Ships, 1957–59. Pres. Scottish Georgian Soc., 1970–80. *Address*: Barskimming, Mauchline, Ayrshire. *T*: Mauchline 50334; 2 Cowley Street, SW1. *Clubs*: Carlton; Conservative (Glasgow); New (Edinburgh).
*Died* 2 *Jan*. 1982.

**GALE, George Stafford**; journalist, author, broadcaster; *b* 22 Oct. 1927; *e s* of George Pyatt Gale and Anne Watson Gale (*née* Wood); *m* 1st, 1951, Patricia Marina Holley (marr. diss. 1983); four *s*; 2nd, 1983, Mary Kiernan Malone, *o d* of late Dr Louis Dillon Malone and late Dr Eileen Malone, Cannock, Staffs, and Dublin. *Educ*: Royal Grammar Sch., Newcastle upon Tyne; Peterhouse, Cambridge; Göttingen University. 1st cl. hons Historical Tripos, Cantab, 1948 and 1949. Leader writer, reporter, Labour Corresp., Manchester Guardian, 1951–55; Special and Foreign Corresp., Daily Express, 1955–67; Columnist, Daily Mirror, 1967–69; freelance journalist, 1969–70; Editor, The Spectator, 1970–73; columnist, Daily Express, 1976–86, Associate Editor, 1981–86, chief leader writer, 1981–82; freelance, 1986–; columnist: Daily Mirror and Sunday Mirror, 1986–87; Daily Mail, 1987–. Presenter, phone-in programmes, London Broadcasting, 1973–80, 1984–85; commentator, Thames Television, 1977–79; panellist, What's My Line, 1984–87. *Publications*: No Flies in China, 1955; (with P. Johnson) The Highland Jaunt, 1973; (contrib.) Conservative Essays, 1979; countless articles. *Recreations*: looking, brooding, disputing. *Address*: Titlington Hall, Alnwick, Northumberland NE66 2EB. *T*: Powburn (066578) 435. *Club*: Garrick.                        *Died* 3 *Nov*. 1990.

**GALE, Malcolm Ruthven**, CBE 1964 (MBE 1948); HM Diplomatic Service, retired; financial, portfolio and export consultant, since 1970; *b* 31 Aug. 1909; *s* of late George Alfred Gale and late Agnes Logan Gale (*née* Ruthven); *m* 1st, 1932, Doris Frances Wells; 2nd, 1936, Ilse Strauss; one *s* one *d*. *Educ*: Sedbergh; Madrid Univ. Market Officer, Santiago, 1945; Third Sec., Dec. 1947; Second Sec. (Commercial), Caracas, 1948; First Sec. (Commercial), 1952 (negotiated armament contracts with Venezuelan Govt); First Sec. (Commercial), Ankara, 1953; Actg Counsellor (Commercial), 1954; First Sec. (Commercial), Bahrein, 1955; Consul (Commercial), Milan, 1958; Acting Consul-Gen., Milan, 1958 and 1959; Counsellor, 1959; Counsellor (Commercial): Washington, 1960–64 (in charge of British export promotion, British store promotions and "British Weeks" in entire US market); Lisbon, 1964–67; Minister (Commercial) Buenos Aires, 1967–69. *Recreations*: cars, photography. *Address*: Apartado 32, Colares, 2710 Sintra, Portugal. *T*: Lisbon 929.0575.                                  *Died* 23 *Sept*. 1990.

**GALE, General Sir Richard Nelson**, GCB 1954 (KCB 1953; CB 1945); KBE 1950 (OBE 1940); DSO 1944; MC 1918; *b* 25 July 1896; *s* of late Wilfred Gale and Helen Webber Ann, *d* of Joseph Nelson, Townsville, Qld, Australia; *m* 1st, 1924, Ethel Maude Larnack (*d* 1952), *d* of Mrs Jessie Keene, Hove; no *c*; 2nd, 1953, Daphne Mabelle Eveline, *d* of late Francis Blick, Stroud, Glos. *Educ*: Merchant Taylors' Sch.; Aldenham; RMC, Sandhurst. 2nd Lieut Worcestershire Regt, 1915; Captain DCLI 1930; Major, Royal

Inniskilling Fusiliers, 1938; Lt-Col Sept. 1939; Brig. 1941; Maj.-Gen. 1946; act. Lt-Gen. 1945; Lt-Gen. 1947; Gen. 1952; raised and commanded the 1st Parachute Brigade; commanded 6th British Airborne Div.; Deputy Commander 1st Allied Airborne Army, 1945; Commander 1st British Airborne Corps, 1945; 1st Inf. Div. 1946–47; GOC British Troops, Egypt and Mediterranean Command, 1948–49; Dir-Gen. of Military Training, War Office, 1949–52; Commander-in-Chief, Northern Army Group, Allied Land Forces Europe and British Army of the Rhine, 1952–57; retired 1957; re-employed NATO 1958; Dep. Supreme Allied Comdr, Europe, 1958–60. ADC (General) to the Queen, 1954–57; Col, The Worcestershire Regt, 1950–61; Col Comdt, The Parachute Regt, 1956–61. Comdr Legion of Merit (US); Comdr Legion of Honour, Croix de Guerre with palm (France); Grand Officier de La Couronne (Belgium). *Publications*: With the 6th Airborne Division in Normandy, 1948; Call to Arms, 1968; Great Battles of Biblical History, 1969; The Worcestershire Regiment, 1970; Kings at Arms, 1971. *Recreation*: principal interest Eastern and Central Asian affairs. *Address*: Hampton Court Palace, East Molesey, Surrey. *Club*: Army and Navy.                                *Died* 29 *July* 1982.

**GALLAHER, Patrick Edmund**, CBE 1975; Chairman, North West Gas, 1974–82; Part-time Member, British Gas Corporation, 1973–81; *b* 17 June 1917; *s* of late Cormac and Agnes Gallaher; *m* 1947, Louise Hatfield (*d* 1965); one *s* two *d*. *Educ*: St Philip's Grammar School and College of Technology, Birmingham. Chemist and Engineer, City of Birmingham Gas Dept, 1934–46; Asst Engineer, Redditch Gas Co., 1946–49. With West Midlands Gas Board: Engineer and Manager, Redditch, 1949–53; Divisional Engineer, 1953–62; Regional Distribution Engineer, 1962–64; Distribution Controller, 1964–66; Area Construction Engineer, 1966–67; Area Distribution Engineer, 1967–68. Wales Gas Board (later Wales Gas Region): Dep Chm., 1968–70; Chm., 1970–74. Pres., IGasE, 1977–78. *Recreations*: sailing, gardening, travel. *Address*: March, Warrington Road, Mere, Knutsford, Cheshire.
*Died* 25 *Sept*. 1988.

**GALLOWAY, Lt-Col Arnold Crawshaw**, CIE 1946; OBE 1941; *b* 1901; *o s* of late Percy Christopher Galloway; *m* 1946, Mary, *d* of Arthur William Odgers, Oxford; three *s*. *Educ*: Sevenoaks Sch.; City of London Sch.; RMC. 2/10 Gurkha Rifles, 1921–28. Member, Middle Temple. 1st class Interpreter, Persian and Arabic. Entered Indian Political Service, 1928; Under-Sec. Rajputana, 1929–30; Vice-Consul, Ahwaz, Persia, 1930–31; Vice-Consul, Zahidan, Persia, 1932–33; Under-Sec. to Resident, Persian Gulf, 1934; Sec., British Legation, Kabul, Afghanistan, 1935–36; Sec. to Polit. Resident, Persian Gulf, 1937–38; Polit. Agent, Kuwait, Persian Gulf, 1939–41; Polit. Advr to British Forces in Iraq and Persia, 1941–43 (despatches); Consul-Gen., Ahwaz, 1943–44; Polit. Agent, Muscat, 1944–45; Polit. Resident, Persian Gulf, 1945; Polit. Agent, Bahrein, 1945–47; Consul-Gen., Bushire, 1947; Polit. Agent, Kuwait, 1948–49; UK Repres. of Bahrain Petroleum Company Ltd, 1950–68; Chm., Middle East Navigation Aids Service, 1958–68. *Address*: Flat 5, Coker House, East Coker, near Yeovil, Somerset BA22 9HS. *Club*: Flyfishers'.                            *Died* 1 *Aug*. 1988.

**GALPIN, Sir Albert James**, KCVO 1968 (MVO, 4th class 1958; 5th class 1945); CBE 1963 (OBE 1953); Secretary, Lord Chamberlain's Office, 1955–68; Serjeant-at-Arms to the Queen, 1955–68; *b* 1903; *s* of C. A. Galpin; *m* 1930, Vera (*d* 1980); one *s* one *d*. Entered Lord Chamberlain's Office, 1936; Asst Sec., 1941. *Recreation*: scouting. *Address*: Alderman's Cottage, Knowl Hill, Reading, Berks. *T*: Littlewick Green 2637.                                 *Died* 8 *July* 1984.

**GALSWORTHY, Sir Arthur (Norman)**, KCMG 1967 (CMG 1953); HM Diplomatic Service; retired; *b* 1 July 1916; *s* of late Captain Arthur Galsworthy and late Violet Gertrude Harrison; *m* 1st, 1940, Margaret Agnes Hiscocks (*d* 1973); two *s*; 2nd, 1976, Aylmer Jean Martin. *Educ*: Emanuel Sch.; Corpus Christi Coll., Cambridge. Entered Colonial Office as Asst Principal, Administrative Grade, Oct. 1938. On active service, Dec. 1939–Dec. 1945: enlisted Royal Fusiliers, Sept. 1939; commnd in DCLI, 1940; attached Intelligence Corps, 1941; N Africa (First Army), 1942–43; Captain 1942; Sicily and Italy (Eighth Army), 1943–44; Major 1943; GSO1 with HQ, 21 Army Gp, 1944–45. Returned to Colonial Office, Dec. 1945; Asst Sec. in charge of International Relations Dept of Colonial Office, 1947–51; Chief Sec., West African Inter-Territorial Secretariat, Accra, 1951–54; in charge of Colonial Office Finance Dept, 1954–56; Asst Under-Sec. of State, 1956–65; Dep. Under-Sec. of State, Colonial Office, 1965–66, Commonwealth Office, 1966–68, FCO, 1968–69; British High Comr in NZ, 1969–72, in Tonga and W Samoa (non-resident), 1970–73; Governor of Pitcairn, 1970–73; Ambassador to Republic of Ireland, 1973–76. *Recreations*: fishing, bird-watching. *Address*: Bluecoat Farm, Lympsham, near Weston-super-Mare, Somerset. *Club*: United Oxford & Cambridge University.                                        *Died* 7 *Oct*. 1986.

**GAMBLE, Sir David**, 5th Bt *cr* 1897; *b* 5 June 1933; *s* of Sir David Arthur Josias Gamble, 4th Bt and Elinor Mary (*d* 1961), *d* of Henry

E. Cole; *S* father, 1982; *m* 1956, Dawn Adrienne, *d* of late David Hugh Gittins; one *s* two *d*. *Educ:* Shrewsbury. *Heir:* s David Hugh Norman Gamble, *b* 1 July 1966. *Address:* Keinton House, Keinton Mandeville, Somerton, Somerset.                    *Died* 27 *Dec.* 1984.

**GAMBLE, Sir David Arthur Josias,** 4th Bt *cr* 1897; *b* 9 Dec. 1907; *e s* of Sir David Gamble, 3rd Bt and Eveline Frances Josephine (*d* 1952), 2nd *d* of late Rev. Arthur R. Cole; *S* father, 1943; *m* 1st, 1932, Elinor Mary (Molly) (*d* 1961), *o d* of Henry E. Cole, Summers, Long Sutton, Hants; one *s*; 2nd, 1965, Evelyn Gamble. *Educ:* Shrewsbury; Wadham Coll., Oxford. BA 1930, MA 1945. Colonial Service, 1930–32; Farmer, 1932–49. Chm. Cirencester RDC, 1958–59. *Heir:* s David Gamble [*b* 5 June 1933; *m* 1956, Dawn Adrienne Stuart; one *s* two *d*]. *Address:* Wood End, Tregony, near Truro, Cornwall.                    *Died* 9 *Jan.* 1982.

**GAMBLE, Sir (Frederick) Herbert,** KBE 1964; CMG 1955; HM Diplomatic Service, retired; *b* 21 May 1907; *s* of Frederick West Gamble and Edith (*née* Moore); *m* 1942, Janine Corbisier de Cobreville; two *d*. *Educ:* Portora Royal School, Enniskillen; Trinity Coll., Dublin. Entered Levant Consular Service, Nov. 1930; HM Consul, Suez, 1945–46; Commercial Counsellor, Bagdad, 1948–52; Commercial Counsellor, Athens, 1952–55; Ambassador to Ecuador, 1955–59; HM Consul-Gen., Los Angeles, 1959–64; HM Ambassador to Bolivia, 1964–67. *Recreation:* golf. *Address:* Santana, Delgany, Co. Wicklow, Ireland.                    *Died* 21 *June* 1983.

**GAMMANS, Lady, (Ann Muriel);** FRSA; *b* 6 March 1898; *d* of late Frank Paul, Warblington, Hants; *m* 1917, David Gammans, 1st and last Bt, *cr* 1955, MP (*d* 1957). *Educ:* Portsmouth High Sch. Travelled widely in the Far East, Europe and North America. Spent many years of her married life in Malaya and Japan. MP (C) Hornsey, 1957–66. Retired March 1966. Order of the Sacred Treasure, 2nd class (Japan), 1971. *Recreation:* travel. *Club:* (Assoc. Lady Member) Naval and Military.                    *Died* 28 *Dec.* 1989.

**GANDAR DOWER, Eric Leslie,** MA (Law); founder of Aberdeen Airport, Allied Airways (Gandar Dower) Ltd, Aberdeen Flying School Ltd, Aberdeen Flying Club Ltd, and Aberdeen Aerodrome Fuel Supplies Ltd; *b* 1894; 3rd *s* of late Joseph Wilson Gandar-Dower and late Amelia Frances Germaine. *Educ:* Brighton Coll.; Jesus Coll., Cambridge. Trained for stage at RADA. Toured with Alan Stevenson, Cecil Barth and Harold V. Neilson's Companies in Kick In, Betty at Bay, The Witness for the Defence, and The Marriage of Kitty. Played wide range of parts on tour with Sir Philip Ben Greet's Shakespeare Company, including Horatio in Hamlet, Antonio in Merchant of Venice, Sicinius Velutus in Coriolanus, Don Pedro in Much Ado About Nothing and Oliver in As You Like It, also in London Shakespeare for Schools LCC Educational Scheme. Wrote and produced The Silent Husband. Toured under own management as Lord Stevenage in Young Person in Pink. Competed King's Cup Air Race 5 years. Holder of FAI Aviators Certificate. Built Dyce (Aberdeen) Airport. Founded Allied Airways (Gandar Dower) Ltd, 1934; Mem. Exec. Council Aerodrome Owners Assoc., 1934–45; Founder Mem. Air Registration Bd; Pioneered Scottish Air Lines Aberdeen/Edinburgh, Aberdeen/ Glasgow, Aberdeen/Wick/Thurso/Kirkwall/Stromness and Shetland, which operated throughout 1939–45 War. Pioneered first British/Norwegian Air Line, 1937, Newcastle to Stavanger. Founded, May 1939, 102nd Aberdeen Airport Air Training Corps. Served as Flight Lieut RAFVR, 1940–43. First Chm. and Founder, Assoc. of Brit. Aircraft Operators, 1944. MP (C) Caithness and Sutherland, 1945–50. Attached Mau Mau Campaign, Kenya, 1952–53. *Recreations:* ski-ing, squash, tennis, lawn tennis, swimming, poetry, flying, motoring. *Address:* Westerings, Clos des Fosses, St Martin, Guernsey, Channel Islands. *T:* Guernsey 38637. *Clubs:* Royal Automobile; Hawks, Amateur Dramatic, Footlights (Cambridge); Automobile de France (Paris).

                    *Died* 4 *Oct.* 1987.

**GANDELL, Sir Alan (Thomas),** Kt 1978; CBE 1959; FCIT; FIPENZ; Member, National Ports Authority, New Zealand, 1969–81; Chancellor, Order of St John, New Zealand, 1972–81; *b* 8 Oct. 1904; *s* of William Gandell and Emma Gandell; *m* 1933, Edna Marion (*née* Wallis); one *s*. *Educ:* Greymouth Dist High Sch. Mem., Inst. of Engineers, NZ, 1940, now FIPENZ (1982); FCIT 1959. NZ Govt Railways: civil engrg appts, 1920–52; Mem., Bd of Management, 1953–57; Gen. Man., 1955–66, retd. GCStJ 1983 (KStJ 1971). *Recreations:* bowling, gardening. *Address:* Strand Home, Wesleyhaven, Rata Street, Naenae, New Zealand.

                    *Died* 10 *July* 1988.

**GANDELL, Captain Wilfrid Pearse,** CBE 1940; Royal Navy; *b* 1 Nov. 1886; *s* of late T. Pearse Gandell, 16 Earl's Court Square, SW5, Chm. Oxford and Cambridge Club; *m* 1923, Lilian Amabel Marian (*d* 1982) (BEM 1970; Diocesan Pres., Mothers' Union, dio. Chichester, 1943–52; WVS-WRVS Centre Organiser, Horsham Urban and Rural Dists, 1946–74; Long Service Medal and bar 1970), *d* of Maj.-Gen. Maxwell Campbell, RE; one *d* (one *s* decd). *Educ:* Stoke House; HMS Britannia. Went to sea as Midshipman

in 1902; specialised in torpedo; present at battle of Jutland in HMS St Vincent; ns 1922; retired in 1929; recalled Sept. 1939; served as Principal Sea Transport Officer, French Ports, from declaration of war till fall of France (despatches, CBE), then as PSTO Clyde till 1941, both with rank of Commodore; Chief Staff Officer, Plymouth, 1941–44 (US Legion of Merit); Senior Officer Reserve Fleet, Forth Area, 1944–46; reverted to retired list, April 1946. Member: West Sussex CC, 1958–64; Horsham RDC, 1952–64; Asst Chief Warden CD, Horsham Area, 1952–65. RHS medal, 1918. *Address:* Hayes Warren, Slinfold, Horsham, West Sussex RH13 7RF. *T:* Slinfold 790246. *Clubs:* Royal Navy, MCC.                    *Died* 9 *June* 1986.

**GANDER, L(eonard) Marsland;** journalist, war correspondent, author; Television and Radio Correspondent and Critic of The Daily Telegraph 1946–70; *b* London, 27 June 1902; *s* of James Gander and Ellen Marsland; *m* 1931, Hilda Mabel Ellen Rowley (*d* 1980); two *s*. *Educ:* Higher Elementary Sch., Stratford; City of London Coll. Reporter, Stratford Express, West Ham, 1919–24; Chief Reporter, Times of India, Bombay, 1924–26; Acting Editor, Illustrated Weekly of India, 1925; Radio Correspondent of the Daily Telegraph, 1926, Television Critic and Correspondent, 1935; War Correspondent of The Daily Telegraph, 1941–45; covered campaigns in Burma, Dodecanese, Italy, Southern France, Greece, 1943–44; with 6th Airborne Div. and 1st Canadian Army, Europe, 1945. Chm., Press Club, 1959; Fellow of the Royal Television Soc., 1961 (Mem. Council, 1965). Toured United States for Ford Fund for Advancement of Education, 1963. Special Governor, Crossways Trust Old People's Homes, 1972–75. Collaborated with Asa Briggs on Sound and Vision, final vol. of History of Broadcasting in UK, 1979. *Publications:* Atlantic Battle, 1941; Long Road to Leros, 1945; After These Many Quests, autobiography, 1950; Television for All, 1950. *Recreations:* desultory chess, swimming, gardening, washing-up. *Address:* 8 Paddock Green, Rustington, Sussex BN16 3AU. *T:* Rustington 782966. *Clubs:* Press, Savage, Lord's Taverners'.

                    *Died* 6 *March* 1986.

**GANDHI, Mrs Indira (Nehru);** Prime Minister of India, 1966–77 and since 1980; President of the Indian National Congress, since 1978; *b* 19 Nov. 1917; *d* of late Pandit Jawaharlal Nehru and Kamala Kaul; *m* 1942, Feroze Gandhi (*d* 1960); one *s* (and one *s* decd). *Educ:* Visva-Bharati. Founded Vanar Sena (Congress children's organisation), 1929; joined Indian National Congress, 1938; Mem., Working Cttee, 1955; Pres., Congress Party, 1959–60; Chm., Citizens' Central Council, 1962; Mem., Lok Sabha, 1964–77, 1978, 1980–; Minister of Information and Broadcasting, 1964–66; Minister: for Home Affairs, 1970–73; for Atomic Energy, 1967–77, 1980–; for Defence, 1980–82. Dep. Chm., Internat. Union of Child Welfare; Vice-Pres., Indian Coun. of Child Welfare. Chancellor, Visva Bharati Univ., 1966–77, 1982–. Most admired person in world, Gallup Poll, USA, 1971. Hon. DCL Oxon, 1971. *Publications:* The Years of Challenge 1966–69, 1975; The Years of Endeavor 1969–72, 1975; Inde, 1978; India and Bangladesh: selected speeches and statements, 1971, 1979; (with Jean-Louis Nou) India: speeches and reminiscences, 1975; Eternal India, 1980; My Truth, 1981; Peoples and Problems, 1982. *Address:* 1 Safdarjang Road, New Delhi 110 011, India.                    *Died* 31 *Oct.* 1984.

**GANE, Richard Howard;** Chairman of the Board of Directors, George Wimpey & Co. Ltd, 1973–76; *b* 5 Nov. 1912; *s* of Richard Howard Gane and Ada (*née* Alford); *m* 1st, 1939, Betty Rosemary Franklin (*d* 1976); one *s* one *d* (and one *s* decd); 2nd, 1977, Elizabeth Gaymer. *Educ:* Kingston Grammar School. Joined George Wimpey & Co. Ltd, 1934; also Chm. of George Wimpey Canada Ltd, and Dir, Markborough Properties Ltd, Toronto, 1965–73. *Recreations:* golf, shooting. *Address:* Woodlands, Cranley Road, Burwood Park, Walton-on-Thames, Surrey.                    *Died* 18 *May* 1988.

**GARBO, Greta, (Greta Lovisa Gustafsson);** film actress; *b* Stockholm, 18 Sept. 1905; *d* of Sven and Louvisa Gustafsson. *Educ:* Dramatic Sch. attached to Royal Theatre, Stockholm. Began stage career as dancer in Sweden. First film appearance in The Atonement of Gosta Berling, 1924; went to US, 1925; became an American Citizen, 1951. Films include: The Torrent, 1926; The Temptress, 1926; Flesh and the Devil, 1927; Love, 1927; The Divine Woman, 1928; The Mysterious Lady, 1928; A Woman of Affairs, 1929; Wild Orchids, 1929; The Single Standard, 1929; The Kiss, 1929; Anna Christie, 1930 (first talking rôle); Susan Lenox, Her Fall and Rise, 1931; Mata Hari, 1931; Grand Hotel, 1932; As You Desire Me, 1932; Queen Christina, 1933; Anna Karenina, 1935; Camille, 1936; Conquest, 1937; Ninotchka, 1939; Two-Faced Woman, 1941.

                    *Died* 15 *April* 1990.

**GARDENER, Sir (Alfred) John,** KCMG 1954 (CMG 1949); CBE 1944; JP; *b* 6 Feb. 1897; *s* of late G. Northcote Gardener, Exeter; *m* 1st, 1929, Dorothy Caroline (*d* 1967), *d* of late Emile Purgold, Liverpool; no *c*; 2nd, 1968, Marion May (*d* 1977), *d* of Linden E. W. Huish, Exeter; no *c*. *Educ:* Heles Sch., Exeter; Trinity Hall, Cambridge. Served in Army in France and Belgium, 1916–18. Joined Consular Service, 1920, and served in various posts in S

Persia, Morocco, Syria and USA. In June 1941 served as Political Officer during Syrian Campaign with rank of Lieut-Col (subsequently Col). Served in Foreign Office, 1946–49; British Ambassador to Afghanistan, 1949–51, and to Syria, 1953–56; retired, 1957. JP Devon, 1959. *Address:* c/o Barclay's Bank, Exeter, Devon. *Died 16 March* 1985.

**GARDHAM, Arthur John,** MS, FRCS; formerly Senior Surgeon to University College Hospital and Examiner in Surgery to University of London; *b* Leytonstone, Essex, Nov. 1899; 2nd *s* of Arthur and Elizabeth Gardham; *m* 1936, Audrey Glenton, 3rd *d* of late Francis Carr, CBE; one *s* two *d*. *Educ:* Bancroft's Sch.; University College and University College Hospital, London. MRCS, LRCP 1921; MB, BS (London), 1923; FRCS 1924; MS (London), 1926. Served RNVR, 1917–18. Qualified 1921; House appts at UCH; Pearce Gould Scholar, 1925; Asst to Prof. Clairmont at Kantonsspital, Zürich, 1925; Surgical Registrar and later Asst Dir of Surgical Unit, UCH. Surgeon to Hampstead Gen. Hosp. (Royal Free Hosp. Group). Served RAMC, 1940–45; Consulting Surgeon to 14th Army and Eastern Comd, India (despatches). Mem. Court of Examiners of RCS, 1945–51; Examiner in Surgery: to Univ. of Cambridge, 1951–57; to Univ. of Edinburgh, 1957–60; to Univ. of London, 1958–62; associated with Emergency Bed Service of King Edward's Hosp. Fund for London from its foundation in 1938; Hunterian Prof., RCS; Fellow: Royal Society of Medicine (Pres. of Surgical Sect., 1963–64); University Coll., London; Assoc. of Surgeons (late Mem. Council). Late Hon. Sec., Devon and Somerset Stag-hounds. *Publications:* (with Davies) The Operations of Surgery, 1963, Vol. 2, 1969; Sections of Grey Turner's Modern Operative Surgery; various papers on surgical subjects. *Recreations:* field sports. *Address:* Castle Green, Oare, Brendon, near Lynton, Devon. *T:* Brendon 205.
*Died 11 March* 1983.

**GARDINER, Baron** *cr* 1963, of Kittisford (Life Peer); **Gerald Austin Gardiner,** PC 1964; CH 1975; Chancellor, The Open University, 1973–78; *b* 30 May 1900; *s* of late Sir Robert Gardiner; *m* 1st, 1925, Lesly (*d* 1966), *o d* of Edwin Trounson, JP; one *d*; 2nd, 1970, Mrs Muriel Box. *Educ:* Harrow Sch.; Magdalen Coll., Oxford (MA; Hon. Fellow, 1983). 2nd Lieut Coldstream Guards, 1918; Pres. Oxford Union and OUDS, 1924; called to the Bar, 1925; KC 1948. Friends Ambulance Unit, 1943–45. Mem. Cttee on Supreme Court Practice and Procedure, 1947–53; Mem. of Lord Chancellor's Law Reform Cttee, 1952–63. A Master of the Bench of the Inner Temple, 1955; Chm. Gen. Council of the Bar, 1958 and 1959; former Chm., Council of Justice; Mem., Internat. Cttee of Jurists, 1971–. Chm (Jt), National Campaign for Abolition of Capital Punishment. Alderman, London County Council, 1961–63. Lord High Chancellor of Great Britain, 1964–70. BA Open Univ., 1977. Hon. LLD: Southampton, 1965; London, 1969; Manitoba, 1969; Law Soc. of Upper Canada, 1969; Birmingham, 1971; Melbourne, 1973; DUniv York, 1966. *Publications:* Capital Punishment as a Deterrent, 1956; (ed jtly) Law Reform Now, 1963. *Recreations:* law reform and the theatre. *Address:* Mote End, Nan Clark's Lane, Mill Hill, NW7 4HH. *Club:* Garrick. *Died 7 Jan.* 1990.

**GARDINER, Lt-Col Christopher John,** DSO 1940; OBE 1945; TD 1942; DL; RE; late Chairman of Gardiner, Sons and Co. Ltd, Bristol, merchants; *b* 2 June 1907; *s* of Edward John Lucas Gardiner, Clifton, Bristol; *m* 1938, Bridget Mary Taplin; three *s* one *d*. *Educ:* Clifton Coll., Bristol. Commissioned in South Midland RE, TA, in 1926; CRE 48 Div., 59 Div., and 12 Corps Tps RE (despatches thrice). Past Pres., Soc. of Builders Merchants. Governor, Clifton Coll. DL Glos 1953; DL Avon 1974. *Recreations:* Rugby (played for Clifton Coll), fishing. *Address:* 3 Norland Road, Clifton, Bristol BS8 3LP. *T:* 735187. *Died 19 May* 1986.

**GARDINER, Ernest David,** CMG 1968; CBE 1967; Head of Science Department, Melbourne Grammar School, 1948–74; Chairman, Commonwealth Government's Advisory Committee on Standards for Science Facilities in Independent Secondary Schools, 1964–76; *b* 14 July 1909; 2nd *s* of Ernest Edward Gardiner and Isabella Gardiner (*née* Notman), Gisborne, Vic.; *m* 1940, Minnie Amanda Neill (*d* 1983); one *s* one *d*. *Educ:* Kyneton High Sch.; Melbourne Univ. BSc 1931, BEd 1936, Melbourne; FACE 1968. Secondary Teacher with Educn Dept of Vic., 1932–45; Melbourne Grammar Sch., 1946–74. *Publications:* Practical Physics (2 vols), 1948; Practical Problems in Physics, 1959; Problems in Physics, 1969, rev. and enl. edn (with B. L. McKittrick), 1985; Practical Physics, 1972. *Recreations:* music, theatre, swimming, Scottish country dancing. *Address:* c/o Alton Court, 2 McIntyre Drive, Altona, Vic 3018, Australia. *Died 14 Jan.* 1988.

**GARDINER, (Frederick) Keith,** JP; Past President, Neepsend Steel and Tool Corporation, Ltd; *b* Plumstead, Kent, 9 Jan. 1904; *s* of Frederick Gardiner and Edith Mann; *m* 1929, Ruth Dixon (*d* 1985); one *s* (and one *s* decd). Various editorial positions with newspaper companies in the South of England and at Darlington, York, Oxford and Sheffield; Editor, The Sheffield Telegraph, 1937–55. President: Inst. of Journalists, 1950; Hallam Cons. Assoc. Former Vice-Chm.,

Sheffield Wednesday FC. FJI. JP Sheffield; Chm., Magistrates' Courts Cttee; former Vice-Chm., Sheffield Bench. *Recreation:* golf. *Address:* 145 Pencisely Road, Llandaff, Cardiff CF5 1DN. *Club:* Hallamshire Golf (Past Pres.) (Sheffield).
*Died 14 March* 1989.

**GARDINER, Brig. Richard,** CB 1954; CBE 1946 (OBE 1944); *b* 28 Oct. 1900; *s* of Major Alec Gardiner, RE; *m* 1st, 1924, Catherine Dod (*née* Oliver); two *s;* 2nd, 1982, Barbara Mary (*née* Borrow). *Educ:* Uppingham Sch.; Royal Military Academy. Commissioned into RFA, 1920; transferred to RE, 1924; Asst Executive Engineer, E Indian Rly, 1927; Sec. to Agent, E Indian Rly, 1930; Exec. Engineer, 1934; Govt Inspector of Rlys, Burma, 1938; reverted to military duty, 1940; Dir of Transportation, India, 1942; reverted to Home Establishment, 1945; Dir of Transportation, War Office, 1948; Dir of Engineer Stores, War Office, 1950; retired Dec. 1953; Man. Dir, Peruvian Corp., Lima, 1954–63. Surrey CC, 1970–77. ADC to King George VI, 1951–52, to the Queen, 1952–53. FCIT. *Recreations:* music, gardening. *Address:* Botolph House, Botesdale, Diss, Norfolk IP22 1BX. *T:* Diss 898413.
*Died 3 Aug.* 1989.

**GARDINER-HILL, Harold,** MBE, MA, MD (Cantab), FRCP; former Consultant Physician, St Thomas' Hospital; Fellow Royal Society of Medicine; President Section of Endocrinology, 1949–50; Member Association of Physicians, Great Britain; *b* London, 14 Feb. 1891; *e s* of late Hugh Gardiner-Hill, MD; *m* Margaret Helen, *e d* of Sir E. Farquhar Buzzard, 1st Bt, KCVO; three *s*. *Educ:* Westminster Sch.; Pembroke Coll., Cambridge; St Thomas's Hosp. Mem. Cambridge Univ. Golf Team, 1911–12; Medical Registrar, St Thomas' Hospital, 1920; Royal Army Medical Corps, 1915–18; Royal Air Force Medical Service, 1918–19 (despatches); CO RAF Central Hosp., Finchley, 1919; Asst Medical Unit, St Thomas' Hosp., 1925–28; Asst Physician, Royal Free Hosp., 1928–30; Oliver Sharpe Lectr RCP, 1937. *Publications:* Modern Trends in Endocrinology, 1957; Clinical Involvements, 1958; articles in the Quarterly Jl of Medicine, British Jl of Obstetrics and Gynaecology, Lancet, BMJ, Proc. Royal Soc. Medicine, Practitioner and Jl of Mental Science chiefly on endocrine diseases. *Recreations:* golf (Chm. of Rules of Golf Cttee, Royal and Ancient, 1949–52; Captain, Royal and Ancient, 1956), and other games. *Address:* Flat 2, 9 Mount Sion, Tunbridge Wells, Kent. *T:* Tunbridge Wells 42323. *Club:* Royal and Ancient (St Andrews).
*Died 25 March* 1982.

**GARDNER, Dame Frances (Violet),** DBE 1975; FRCP; FRCS; Consulting Physician, Royal Free Hospital, London, since 1978; *b* 28 Feb. 1913; *d* of late Sir Ernest and Lady Gardner; *m* 1958, George Qvist, FRCS (*d* 1981). *Educ:* Headington Sch., Oxford; Westfield Coll., Univ. of London; Royal Free Hospital School of Medicine. BSc London, 1935; MB, BS London, 1940; MD London, 1943; MRCP 1943, FRCP 1952; FRCS 1983. Medical Registrar, Royal Free Hosp., 1943; Clinical Asst, Nuffield Dept of Medicine, Oxford, 1945; Fellow in Medicine, Harvard Univ., USA, 1946; Consultant Physician, Royal Free Hosp., 1946–78; Chief Asst, National Hosp. for Diseases of the Heart, 1947; late Physician: Royal National Throat, Nose and Ear Hosp., London; Hosp. for Women, Soho Sq., London; The Mothers' Hosp., London; former Dean, Royal Free Hosp. Sch. of Medicine; Visitor, Med. Faculty, Khartoum, 1981. Commonwealth Travelling Fellow, 1962; late Examnr, MB, BS, Univ. of London; Rep. Gen. Med. Schools on Senate of Univ. of London, 1967; Mem., Gen. Med. Council, 1971; Pres., Royal Free Hosp. Sch. of Medicine, 1979. Formerly Chm., London/Riyadh Univs Med. Faculty Cttee. *Publications:* papers on cardiovascular and other medical subjects in BMJ, Lancet, and British Heart Jl. *Address:* Fitzroy Lodge, Fitzroy Park, Highgate N6 6JA. *T:* 01–340 5873; Consulting Suite, Wellington Hospital, NW8 9LE. *T:* 01–586 3213. *Died 10 July* 1989.

**GARDNER, Dame Helen (Louise),** DBE 1967 (CBE 1962); FBA 1958; FRSL 1962; DLitt; Emeritus Professor of English Literature, University of Oxford and Hon. Fellow, Lady Margaret Hall and St Hilda's College; *b* 13 Feb. 1908; *d* of late C. H. Gardner and Helen M. R. Gardner. *Educ:* North London Collegiate Sch.; St Hilda's Coll., Oxford. BA Oxford (1st class Hons Sch. of English Lang. and Lit.), 1929; MA 1935; DLitt 1963. Asst Lectr, Royal Holloway Coll., Univ. of London, 1931–34; Lectr, Univ. of Birmingham, 1934–41; Tutor in English Literature, St Hilda's Coll., 1941–54, and Fellow, 1942–66; Reader in Renaissance English Literature, Univ. of Oxford, 1954–66; Merton Prof. of English Literature, Univ. of Oxford and Fellow of Lady Margaret Hall, 1966–75; Vis. Prof., Univ. of California, Los Angeles, 1954; Lectures: Riddell Meml, Univ. of Durham, 1956; Alexander, Univ. of Toronto, 1962; Messenger, Cornell Univ., 1967; T. S. Eliot Meml, Univ. of Kent, 1968; Charles Eliot Norton, Harvard, 1979–80. Delegate, Oxford University Press, 1959–75. Mem., Robbins Cttee on Higher Education, 1961–63; Mem., Council for National Academic Awards, 1964–67; Trustee, National Portrait Gallery, 1967–78. Foreign Hon. Member: Amer. Acad. of Arts and Scis; Amer.

Philosophical Soc.; Bavarian Acad. Hon. DLitt: Durham, 1960; East Anglia, 1967; London, 1969; Birmingham, 1970; Harvard, 1971; Yale, 1973; Warwick, 1976; Hon. LittD Cambridge, 1981; Hon. LLD Aberdeen, 1967. R. M. Crawshay Prize, British Acad., 1952, 1980. *Publications:* The Art of T. S. Eliot, 1949; The Divine Poems of John Donne, 1952, 2nd edn 1978; The Metaphysical Poets (Penguin), 1957; (ed with G. M. Story) The Sonnets of William Alabaster, 1960; The Business of Criticism, 1960; The Elegies and Songs and Sonnets of John Donne, 1965; A Reading of Paradise Lost, 1965; John Donne: Selected Prose (co-ed with T. Healey), 1967; (ed) Shakespearian and Other Studies by F. P. Wilson, 1969; Religion and Literature, 1971; (rev. and ed) F. P. Wilson, Shakespeare and the New Bibliography, 1971; (ed) The Faber Book of Religious Verse, 1972; (ed) The New Oxford Book of English Verse 1250–1950, 1972; The Composition of Four Quartets, 1978; In Defence of the Imagination, 1982. *Recreations:* gardening, foreign travel.                                        *Died 4 June 1986.*

**GARDNER, Hugh,** CB 1966; CBE 1953; *b* 28 March 1910; *yr s* of C. H. Gardner; *m* 1934, Margaret Evelyn Carvalho; one *s* two *d. Educ:* University College Sch.; Merton Coll., Oxford (MA). Served Min. of Agriculture, Fisheries and Food (formerly Min. of Agriculture and Fisheries), 1933–70; Under-Sec., 1953–70, retired; Mem., Sec. of State for the Environment's Panel of Independent Inspectors, 1970–80. Chm., Assoc. of First Div. Civil Servants, 1945–48. *Publication:* Tales from the Marble Mountain, 1967. *Recreations:* golf, gardening, writing, going abroad. *Address:* The Cobb, North Road, Berkhamsted, Herts. *T:* Berkhamsted 5677. *Club:* United Oxford & Cambridge University.                        *Died 5 Aug. 1986.*

**GARDNER, W(alter) Frank,** CBE 1953; Director, The Prudential Assurance Co. Ltd, 1961–71 (Deputy Chairman, 1965–69); *b* 6 Nov. 1900; *s* of late Walter Gardner and Emma Mabel Gardner, Streatham Hill, SW2; *m* 1st, 1925, Constance Gladys (*d* 1945), *d* of late Frederick William and Ellen Haydon, Norwich; one *d*; 2nd, 1949, Kathleen Lilian, *y d* of late George William and Florence Charlotte Smith, Hampton Hill, and *widow* of Dr Frederick Lishman, Bexhill. *Educ:* Dulwich College; Institute of Actuaries. Chief Actuary, Prudential Assurance Co. Ltd, 1945–50; Chief General Manager, 1950–60. Fellow (FIA), 1924; President, 1952–54. FSS 1952. *Publications:* contributions to Journal of Institute of Actuaries. *Recreations:* bowls, cine-photography. *Address:* 8c South Cliff Tower, Eastbourne, East Sussex BN20 7JN. *Clubs:* Carlton; Devonshire (Eastbourne); Eastbourne Bowling.

*Died 16 July 1983.*

**GARDNER, Air Commodore William Steven,** CB 1958; OBE 1945; DFC 1940 and bar 1941; AFC 1943; *b* 16 Dec. 1909; *s* of late Campbell Gardner, JP, Groomsport, Co. Down, Northern Ireland; *m* 1937, Theodora, *d* of W. G. Bradley, Castlerock, Co. Derry; one *s* one *d* (and one *d* decd). *Educ:* Campbell Coll., Belfast. Joined RAF 1935; served in 106, 44 and 144 Squadrons, Bomber Command, 1939–45. Group Capt. 1951; Air Commodore, 1956; Head of Plans and Operations, CENTO, 1957–59; Acting Air Vice-Marshal, 1963; Provost Marshal, 1960–63; Director-General of Personal Services, 1963. *Recreation:* sailing. *Address:* Corner Cottage, Shipton Green, Itchenor, Sussex. *Club:* Royal Ulster Yacht.

*Died 7 Sept. 1983.*

**GARDYNE;** *see* Bruce-Gardyne.

**GARLAKE, Maj.-Gen. Storr,** CBE 1949; *b* 11 April 1904; *yr s* of John Storr Inglesby and Dorothy Eleanor Garlake, Cradock, CP; *m* 1932, Catherine Ellen, *er d* of James Wightman, Cape Town; one *s* one *d. Educ:* St Andrew's Prep. Sch., Grahamstown; RN Colleges, Osborne and Dartmouth. Joined BSAP, 1925; commissioned 1929; transferred to S Rhodesia Staff Corps, 1933; Maj.-Gen. 1953. Served War of 1939–45, ME and India, 1942–45; Commander Military Forces, S Rhodesia, 1947–53; Imp. Defence Coll., 1949; Chief of General Staff, Federation of Rhodesia and Nyasaland, 1953–59. Additional ADC to the Queen, 1952–54; retired 1959. *Address:* Flat 208, Warick House, Montague Avenue, Harare, Zimbabwe. *Club:* Salisbury (Harare, Zimbabwe).                        *Died 4 Feb. 1983.*

**GARLAND, Ailsa Mary, (Mrs John Rollit Mason);** broadcaster on TV and radio; *d* of James Francis Garland and Elsie Elizabeth Langley; *m* 1948, John Rollit Mason; one *s. Educ:* La Retraite, Clapham Park; St Mary's, Woodford Green, Essex. Fashion Editor, Vogue Export Book, 1947–50; Editor, Shopping Magazine, 1952–53; Woman's Editor, Daily Mirror, 1953–59, Assistant Editor, 1959–60; Editor of Vogue, 1960–63; Director, Condé Nast Publications Ltd, 1961–63; Editor in Chief, Woman's Jl, 1963–68; Editor of Fashion, 1963–68; Dir, Fleetway Publications Ltd, 1963–68; Fashion Coordinator, IPC Magazines Ltd, 1970–72. Governor, London College of Fashion, 1961–68. Mem. Consultative Cttee, Coll. of Fashion and Clothing Technology. Vice-Chm., Suffolk Heritage Trust, 1979; Trustee, Suffolk Historic Churches Trust, 1979. *Publication:* Lion's Share (autobiog.), 1970. *Recreations:* gardening, reading, theatre. *Address:* The Little House, Lady Street, Lavenham, Suffolk.                                        *Died 5 Nov. 1982.*

**GARLAND, Prof. Henry Burnard,** JP; MA, PhD, LittD; Professor of German in the University of Exeter, 1948–72, later Emeritus Professor; *b* 30 Aug. 1907; *s* of late William Garland, Dover, and Alice Mary (*née* Jarry); *m* 1949, Hertha Marie Louise (*née* Wiesener); two *d. Educ:* Dover County Sch.; Emmanuel Coll., Cambridge. BA, Mod. & Med. Langs. Tripos, 1st Class with Distinction, 1930; Patterson Prizeman, 1930; Tiarks German Scholar, 1931; Faculty Assistant Lecturer, Cambridge, 1934; MA 1934, PhD 1935, LittD 1970, Cambridge; University Lecturer, Cambridge, 1937. Served War of 1939–45; Cambridge STC, 1940–43; RA, 1943–46, UK, Belgium, Germany (Colonel); Instructor in Gunnery, Sch. of Artillery, 1944. Controller and Chief Editor, Die Welt, Hamburg, 1946; Head German Department, University College, Exeter, 1947; Chairman Arts Faculty, 1947–53; Vice-Principal, 1953–55; Acting Principal, 1953–54; Elector, Schröder Chair of German, Cambridge Univ., 1954–74; Deputy Vice-Chancellor, Exeter Univ., 1955–57; Public Orator, 1956–65. JP Exeter, 1961; Member, State Studentship Selection Cttee, Department of Education and Science, 1965–68, Panel Chairman, 1966–68. Governor, Blundell's Sch., 1969–75. Hon. DLitt Exeter, 1977. Bronze Medal, Univ. of Rennes, 1970; Goethe-Medaille, Goethe-Institut, 1975; (with Mary Garland) J. G. Robertson German Prize, London Univ., 1979. *Publications:* Lessing: The Founder of Modern German Literature, 1937, revd edn 1962; Schiller, 1949, new edn 1978; Storm and Stress, 1952; Schiller Revisited, 1959; Schiller the Dramatic Writer, 1969; A Concise Survey of German Literature, 1970, expanded edn, 1976; (with Mary Garland) The Oxford Companion to German Literature, 1976; German section of The Age of Enlightenment, 1979; The Berlin Novels of Theodor Fontane, 1980; Editions of works by Schiller (3), Lessing, Fontane and H. v. Kleist; Essays on Schiller, Fontane, Schnitzler and the Prussian Army; contributions to Cassell's Encyclopædia of Literature, Collier's Encyclopædia. *Recreations:* music, architectural photography, bird-watching. *Address:* 5 Rosebarn Avenue, Exeter EX4 6DY. *T:* Exeter 55009.

*Died 4 May 1981.*

**GARLICK, Rev. Canon Wilfrid;** *b* 12 Oct. 1910; *s* of late Arthur and Clemence Garlick; *m* 1936, Edith, *d* of late H. Goddard; one *s. Educ:* Oldham Hulme Grammar Sch.; Manchester Univ. (MA *hc* 1968); Egerton Hall Theological Coll. BSc 1931, Manchester. Curate St Andrew, Ancoats, Manchester, 1933–35; Curate St Clement, Chorlton-cum-Hardy, 1935–38; Rector St Nicholas, Burnage, Manchester, 1938–44; Officiating Chaplain to Forces, 1938–44; Vicar of St George, Sheffield, 1944–48; Vicar of St George, Stockport, 1948–75; Rector of Alderley, 1975–82; Hon. Canon of Chester, 1958–82. Hon. Chaplain to the Queen, 1964–80. *Recreations:* golf, travel. *Address:* 10 Glasfryn Avenue, Meliden, Prestatyn, N Wales.                        *Died 29 Oct. 1982.*

**GARNER, Baron** *cr* 1969 (Life Peer), of Chiddingly; **(Joseph John)** Saville Garner, GCMG 1965 (KCMG 1954; CMG 1948); Chairman, Joint Commonwealth Societies Council, since 1981; *b* 14 Feb. 1908; *s* of Joseph and Helena Maria Garner, Highgate, N; *m* 1938, Margaret Beckman, Cedar Lake, Ind, USA; two *s* one *d. Educ:* Highgate Sch.; Jesus Coll., Cambridge. Appointed Dominions Office, 1930; Private Sec. to successive Secretaries of State, 1940–43; Senior Sec., office of UK High Comr Ottawa, 1943–46; Dep. High Comr for the UK, Ottawa, Canada, 1946–48; Asst Under-Sec., Commonwealth Relations Office, 1948–51; Deputy High Commissioner for the UK in India, 1951–53; Deputy Under-Secretary, Commonwealth Relations Office, 1952–56; British High Commissioner in Canada, 1956–61; Permanent Under-Secretary of State, Commonwealth Relations Office, 1962–65, Commonwealth Office, 1965–68; Head of HM Diplomatic Service, 1965–68. Secretary, Order of St Michael and St George, 1966–68 (Registrar, 1962–66). Chairman: Bd of Governors, Commonwealth Inst., 1968–74; Commonwealth Scholarship Commn in the UK, 1968–77; Cttee of Management, Inst. of Commonwealth Studies, 1971–79; Bd of Management, RPMS, 1971–80; London Bd, Bank of Adelaide, 1971–80 (Dir, 1969–80); Treasurer and Chm., Board of Governors, Highgate Sch., 1976–83 (Governor 1962). Member: Council, Voluntary Service Overseas, 1969–74; Security Commission, 1968–73. Bd of Governors, SOAS, Univ. of London, 1968–73. Hon. LLD: Univ. of Brit. Columbia, 1958; Univ. of Toronto, 1959; Hon. Fellow, Jesus College, Cambridge, 1967. President, Old Cholmeleian Society, 1964. *Publications:* The Books of the Emperor Wu Ti (transl. from German), 1930; The Commonwealth Office 1925–68, 1978. *Recreations:* gardening, travel. *Address:* Highdown Farmhouse, Horam, Heathfield, E Sussex TN21 0JR. *T:* Chiddingly 432. *Club:* Royal Automobile.                        *Died 10 Dec. 1983.*

**GARNER, Frank Harold;** farmer since 1971; *b* 4 Dec. 1904; *m* 1929, Hilda May Sheppard; one *d. Educ:* Swindon Technical Sch.; Universities of Cambridge, Oxford, Reading and Minnesota, USA. MA (Cantab), MA (Oxon), MSc (Minnesota, USA); FRAgSs. Assistant to Director of Cambridge University Farm, 1924; University Demonstrator in Agriculture at Cambridge, 1927; University Lecturer (Animal Husbandry) at Cambridge, 1929; Assistant to Executive Officer, Cambridgeshire War Agriculture

Executive Cttee, 1939; County Agricultural Organiser, East Suffolk, 1940; General Manager of Frederick Hiam Ltd, 1944–58; Principal, RAC, Cirencester, Glos, 1958–71. Chairman: Cambridgeshire NFU, 1956–57; Bucks NFU, 1978. Liveryman, Farmers' Livery Co., Master, 1971–72. *Publications:* Cattle of Britain, 1943; The Farmers Animals, 1943; British Dairy Farming, 1946; (with E. T. Halnan and A. Eden) Principles and Practice of Feeding Farm Animals, 1940, 5th edn 1966; (ed) Modern British Farming Systems, 1975; (ed) Farming in Our Lifetime, 1989. *Recreation:* swimming. *Address:* Brooklyn, Park Street, Princes Risborough, Bucks HP17 9AH. *Club:* Farmers'.                            *Died 23 Feb.* 1990.

**GARNETT, David,** CBE 1952; CLit 1977; FRSL; author; *b* 1892; *s* of late Edward and Constance Garnett; *m* 1st, Rachel Alice (*d* 1940), *d* of W. C. Marshall, architect; two *s*; 2nd, 1942, Angelica Vanessa, *o d* of late Clive Bell; four *d*. *Educ:* Royal College of Science, South Kensington. Fellow, Imperial College of Science and Technology, 1956; Hon. DLitt Birmingham, 1977. *Publications:* The Kitchen Garden and its Management; Lady into Fox (Hawthornden and Tait-Black Prizes for 1923); A Man in the Zoo; The Sailor's Return; Go She Must!; The Old Dovecote, 1928; No Love, 1929; The Grasshoppers Come, 1931; A Rabbit in the Air, 1932; Pocahontas, 1933, repr. 1972; Beany-Eye, 1935; War in the Air, 1941; The Golden Echo, 1953; Flowers of the Forest, 1955; Aspects of Love, 1955; A Shot in the Dark, 1958; A Net for Venus, 1959; The Familiar Faces, 1962; Two by Two, 1963; Ulterior Motives, 1966; A Clean Slate, 1971; The Sons of the Falcon, 1972; Purl and Plain, 1973; Plough Over the Bones, 1973; The Master Cat, 1974; Up She Rises, 1977; Great Friends, 1979; edited: The Letters of T. E. Lawrence, 1938; The Novels of Thomas Love Peacock, 1948; The Essential T. E. Lawrence, 1951; The White-Garnett Letters, 1968; Carrington: Letters and extracts from her diaries, 1970. *Recreation:* travel. *Address:* Le Verger de Charry, 46 Montcuq, France. *T:* (65) 31.85.35.                                      *Died 17 Feb.* 1981.

**GARNONS WILLIAMS, Captain Nevill Glennie,** MBE 1919; Royal Navy (Retired); *b* 1899; *s* of late Rev. Arthur Garnons Williams, Abercamlais, Brecon; *m* 1928, Violet (*d* 1979), *d* of late B. G. Tours, CMG; one *d*. *Educ:* RN Colls, Osborne and Dartmouth; Caius Coll., Cambridge. Joined Royal Navy, 1912; served European War, 1914–18, Jutland (despatches); and War of 1939–45; retired as Captain, 1946. DL 1948, JP 1956, Brecknockshire; Vice-Lieutenant, 1959–64, Lord Lieutenant, 1964–74, Brecknockshire. Croix de Guerre (avec Palmes), 1916. KStJ 1973. *Recreations:* forestry, fishing, cricket, scouting. *Address:* Abercamlais, Brecon, Powys. *T:* Sennybridge 206. *Clubs:* Army and Navy, MCC.
                                                 *Died 27 Feb.* 1983.

**GARNSWORTHY, Most Rev. Lewis Samuel,** DD; *b* 18 July 1922; *m* 1954, Jean Valance Allen; one *s* one *d*. *Educ:* Univ. of Alberta (BA); Wycliffe Coll., Toronto (LTh). Asst Curate: St Paul's, Halifax, 1945; St John, Norway Toronto, 1945–48; Rector: St Nicholas, Birchcliff, Toronto, 1948–56; Transfiguration, Toronto, 1956–59; St John's Church, York Mills, Toronto, 1960–68; Suffragan Bishop, Diocese of Toronto, 1968–72; Bishop of Toronto, 1972–79; Archbishop of Toronto, 1979–88; Metropolitan of Ontario, 1979–85. Fellow, Coll. of Preachers, Washington, DC. DD *hc:* Wycliffe Coll., Toronto, 1969; Trinity Coll., Toronto, 1973; Huron Coll., 1976. *Address:* Suite 201, 1210 Don Mills Road, Don Mills, Ontario M3B 2N9, Canada. *Clubs:* Albany, York (Toronto).
                                                 *Died 26 Jan.* 1990.

**GARRARD, His Honour Henry John;** a Circuit Judge (formerly a County Court Judge), 1965–84; *b* 15 Jan. 1912; *s* of late C. G. Garrard; *m* 1945, Muriel, *d* of late A. H. S. Draycott, Stratford-on-Avon; one *s* one *d*. *Educ:* Framlingham Coll., Suffolk. Called to the Bar, Middle Temple, Nov. 1937; Mem. of Oxford Circuit. Served 1939–45, Staffs Yeomanry (QORR) and Worcestershire Regt, East and North Africa, rank of Lieut; prisoner-of-war, 1942–45. Mem. of Mental Health Review Tribunal for Birmingham Area, 1963–65; Recorder of Burton-on-Trent, 1964–65. *Recreations:* family, dogs, country life. *Address:* Birtsmorton, Stowe Lane, Stowe-by-Chartley, Stafford ST18 0NA. *T:* Weston (0889) 270674.
                                                 *Died 18 July* 1990.

**GARRATT, Gerald Reginald Mansel,** MA, CEng, FIEE; FRAeS; retired; Keeper, Department of Aeronautics and Marine Transport, Science Museum, South Kensington, 1966–71; *b* 10 Dec. 1906; *s* of Reginald R. and Florence Garratt; *m* 1931, Ellen Georgina Brooks, Antwerp, Belgium; two *d*. *Educ:* Marlborough Coll.; Caius Coll., Cambridge. International Telephone & Telegraph Laboratories, 1929–30; RAE, Farnborough, 1930–34; Asst Keeper: Dept of Textiles and Printing, Science Museum, 1934; Dept of Telecommunications, 1936; Dep. Keeper 1949. Served RAF 1939–46 (Wing Comdr). Founder Mem., Cambridge Univ. Air Squadron, 1926. Commissioned RAF Reserve of Officers, 1928; retired 1966 (Wing Comdr). *Publications:* One Hundred Years of Submarine Cables, 1950; The Origins of Maritime Radio, 1972; numerous articles on history of telecommunications. *Recreation:*

amateur radio. *Address:* Littlefield, 28 Parkwood Avenue, Esher, Surrey KT10 8DG. *T:* 01–398 1582.           *Died 14 April* 1989.

**GARRETT, Alexander Adnett,** MBE 1934; *b* London, 15 July 1886; *e s* of late Adnett William Garrett and Marion Walker Bruce; *m* 1928, Mildred (*d* 1975), *g d* of L. S. Starrett, Athol, Mass. *Educ:* Owen's Sch., London; London Sch. of Economics (BSc); King's Coll., London (Gilbart Prizeman); Christ's Coll., Cambridge (Economics Tripos). FCIS; attended the 20th Convention of the American Institute of Accountants, St Louis, USA, 1924; Internat. Congresses on Accounting, Amsterdam, 1926, New York, 1929, and Berlin, 1938; Asst Sec., 4th Internat. Congress on Accounting, London, 1933; sometime Hon. Mem., former Soc. of Incorporated Accountants (Sec. 1919–49, retired 1949; Asst Sec., 1913); visited Accountancy Bodies in Canada, USA, Australia, New Zealand, South Africa, 1947–50. Dept of Applied Economics, Cambridge, 1950–59. Hon. Mem., Australian Soc. of Accountants, 1956. Served Royal Naval Reserve, 1915–31; Comdr (S), RNR (retired). *Publication:* History of the Society of Incorporated Accountants, 1885–1957, 1961. *Address:* 7 King's Bench Walk, Temple, EC4. *T:* 01–353 7880. *Clubs:* Athenæum, Reform.

                                                  *Died 5 June* 1986.

**GARRETT, Prof. Stephen Denis,** FRS 1967; Professor of Mycology, 1971–73, later Professor Emeritus (Reader 1961–71), and Director of Sub-department of Mycology, 1952–73, University of Cambridge; Fellow of Magdalene College, Cambridge, since 1963; *b* 1 Nov. 1906; *s* of Stephen and Mary Garrett, Leiston, Suffolk; *m* 1934, Ruth Jane Perkins; three *d*. *Educ:* Eastbourne Coll.; Cambridge Univ.; Imperial Coll., London. Asst Plant Pathologist, Waite Agric. Res. Inst., Univ. of Adelaide, 1929–33; Research Student, Imperial Coll., 1934–35; Mycologist, Rothamsted Experimental Stn, 1936–48; Lectr, later Reader, Botany Sch., University of Cambridge, 1949–71. Hon. Member: British Mycological Soc., 1975; British Soc. for Plant Pathology, 1984. Hon. Fellow, Indian Acad. of Sciences, 1973. *Publications:* Root Disease Fungi, 1944; Biology of Root-infecting Fungi, 1956; Soil Fungi and Soil Fertility, 1963, 2nd edn 1981; Pathogenic Root-infecting Fungi, 1970. *Address:* 315 Lichfield Road, Cambridge CB1 3SH. *T:* Cambridge 247865.
                                                 *Died 26 Dec.* 1989.

**GARROW, Sir Nicholas,** Kt 1965; OBE 1956; JP; retired, 1960; Chairman, Northumbria Tourist Board, since 1974; *b* 21 May 1895; *m* 1919; two *s* one *d*. Chm., Northumberland CC, 1952–67 (CC 1925; CA 1937); JP Northumberland, 1936–; Vice-Pres., Royal National Institute for Blind, 1974– (Mem., 1936–); Foundation and Life Mem., Royal Commonwealth Society for the Blind, 1974; Vice-President: North Regional Assoc. for the Deaf, 1975–; Northumberland Playing Fields Assoc., 1975–; Mem., Church of Christ, 1917–, Senior Elder, 1950–. Hon. Alderman, Northumberland CC, 1974. *Address:* Essendene, Kenilworth Road, Ashington, Northumberland.                        *Died 23 Dec.* 1982.

**GARSIDE, Kenneth;** Director of Central Library Services and Goldsmiths' Librarian, University of London, 1974–78; *b* 30 March 1913; *s* of Arthur Garside and Ada (*née* Speight); *m* 1951, Anne Sheila Chapman; one *s*. *Educ:* Bradford Grammar Sch.; Univ. of Leeds. BA Mod. Langs 1935, DipEd 1936, MA Spanish 1937. War Service, 1941–46: commnd into Intell. Corps; campaign in NW Europe, 1944–45; GSO2 (Intell.) BAOR, 1946. CO, Univ. of London OTC, 1958–63. Asst Librarian, Univ. of Leeds, 1937–45; Dep. Librarian, UCL, 1945–58; Librarian, King's Coll., London, 1958–74 (FKC 1981). Mem., Enemy Wartime Publications (Requirements) Cttee, 1946–48; Jt Hon. Sec., Univ. and Res. Section of Library Assoc., 1948–51; Chm., Assoc. of British Theol and Philos. Libraries, 1961–66; Trustee, Liddell Hart Centre for Military Archives, King's Coll., London, 1963–; Hon. Sec., Council of Mil. Educn Cttees of Univs of UK, 1966–78; Sec, Nat. and Univ. Libraries Sect., Internat. Fedn of Library Assocs, 1967–68, Univ. Libraries Sub-Sect., 1967–73; Mem., Univ. of London Cttee on Library Resources, 1968–71; Mem., CNAA Librarianship Bd, 1971–81; Mem., British Library Adv. Cttee for Reference Division (Bloomsbury), 1975–78; Hon. Keeper, Military Archives, King's Coll., London, 1979–. Vice-Chm., British Theatre Museum Assoc., 1971–77. Editor, LIBER Bull., 1980–. *Publications:* Guide to the Library Resources of the University of London, 1983; contrib. to literature of librarianship. *Recreations:* travel, wine and food, bird watching. *Address:* Pavilion Cottage, 36 New Road, Esher, Surrey KT10 9NU. *T:* Esher 65157. *Clubs:* Arts, Authors' (Chm. 1969–72).            *Died 1 Dec.* 1983.

**GARSIDE, Air Vice-Marshal Kenneth Vernon,** CB 1962; DFC 1942; RAF, retired; *b* 13 Aug. 1913; *s* of late Dyson Garside, Maidenhead, Berks; *m* 1940, Margery June, *d* of late William Henry Miller, Tanworth-in-Arden; one *s* one *d*. *Educ:* Bradfield Coll.; St John's Coll., Oxford (MA). First commissioned RAF, 1937. Served War of 1939–45 (despatches twice, DFC); Sqdn and War Service in Far East, Mediterranean and Indian Ocean theatres, 1938–44; European theatre, 1944–45. Command and staff appts in UK and USA, 1945–57; Air Cdre 1957; AOC No 16 Group, 1957; Dep. COS,

Logistics and Admin., Allied Forces Central Europe, 1958; Dir of Quartering, Air Min., 1959; Air Vice-Marshal 1960; Senior Air Staff Officer, HQ Coastal Command, RAF, 1961–63; AOC No 18 Group, Coastal Command, and Air Officer, Scotland and Northern Ireland, 1963–65. Managing Dir, petro-chemical companies, 1966–69. Liveryman, Worshipful Co. of Horners; Freeman of City of London. *Recreations:* rowing (Blue 1936), swimming (Blue 1935). *Address:* The Garden House, 15 High Street, Thame, Oxon. *Clubs:* Royal Air Force; Vincent's (Oxford); Leander (Henley).

*Died 2 Aug. 1986.*

**GARTRELL, Rt. Rev. Frederick Roy;** *b* 27 March 1914; *s* of William Frederick Gartrell and Lily Martha Keeble; *m* 1940, Grace Elizabeth Wood; three *s* one *d*. *Educ:* McMaster Univ. (BA); Wycliffe Coll. (LTh, BD). Deacon, 1938; Priest, 1939. Curate, St James the Apostle, Montreal, 1938; Rector, All Saints', Noranda, PQ, 1940; Senior Asst, St Paul's, Bloor Street, Toronto, 1944; Rector, St George's, Winnipeg, Manitoba, 1945; Archdeacon of Winnipeg, 1957; Rector, Christ Church Cathedral, Ottawa, and Dean of Ottawa, 1962–70; Bishop of British Columbia, 1970–80. DD (*hc*): Wycliffe Coll., Toronto, 1962; St John's Coll., Winnipeg, 1965. *Recreation:* golf. *Address:* 1794 Barrie, Victoria, BC V8N 2W7, Canada.

*Died 18 May 1987.*

**GARVEY, Sir Terence Willcocks,** KCMG 1969 (CMG 1955); HM Diplomatic Service, retired; *b* Dublin, 7 Dec. 1915; *s* of Francis Willcocks Garvey and Ethel Margaret Ray; *m* 1st, 1941, Barbara Hales Tomlinson (marr. diss.); two *s* one *d*; 2nd, 1957, Rosemary, *d* of late Dr Harold Pritchard. *Educ:* Felsted; University Coll., Oxford (Scholar). BA Oxon (1st Class Philosophy, Politics and Economics), 1938; Laming Fellow of The Queen's Coll., Oxford, 1938. Entered Foreign (subsequently Diplomatic) Service, 1938; has served in USA, Chile, Germany, Egypt and at Foreign Office; Counsellor, HM Embassy, Belgrade, 1958–62; HM Chargé d'Affaires, Peking, 1962–65 and Ambassador to Mongolia, 1963–65; Asst Under-Sec. of State, Foreign Office, 1965–68; Ambassador to Yugoslavia, 1968–71; High Comr in India, 1971–73; Ambassador to the USSR, 1973–75. Senior Associate Mem., St Antony's Coll., Oxford, 1976–. *Publication:* Bones of Contention, 1978. *Recreation:* fishing. *Address:* 11A Stonefield Street, N1 0HW. *Club:* Travellers'.

*Died 7 Dec. 1986.*

**GASCOIGNE, Maj.-Gen. Sir Julian (Alvery),** KCMG 1962; KCVO 1953; CB 1949; DSO 1943; DL; *b* 25 Oct. 1903; *e s* of late Brig.-Gen. Sir Frederick Gascoigne, KCVO, CMG, DSO, and Lady Gascoigne, Ashtead Lodge, Ashtead, Surrey; *m* 1928, Joyce Alfreda (*d* 1981), *d* of late Robert Lydston Newman and Mrs Newman; one *s* one *d*. *Educ:* Eton; Sandhurst. 2nd Lieut Grenadier Guards, 1923; Staff Coll., Camberley, 1938–39; served War of 1939–45, commanding 1st Bn Grenadier Guards, 1941–42; commanding 201 Guards Brigade, 1942–43; North Africa and Italy, 1943 (wounded). Imperial Defence Coll., 1946; Dep. Comdr British Jt Services Mission (Army Staff), Washington, 1947–49. GOC London District and Maj.-Gen. commanding Household Brigade, 1950–53; retired pay, 1953; Mem. of Stock Exchange and Partner in Grieveson Grant & Co., 1955–59; Governor and C-in-C Bermuda, 1959–64; Col Commandant, Hon. Artillery Co., 1954–59. Patron, Union Jack Services Clubs, 1977 (Vice-Pres., 1955–64; Pres., 1964–76); a Comr of the Royal Hospital, Chelsea, 1958–59; Chm. Devon and Cornwall Cttee, The National Trust, 1965–73. JP 1966, DL Devon, 1966. KStJ, 1959. *Address:* Sanders, Stoke Fleming, S Devon. *Club:* Royal Bermuda Yacht.

*Died 26 Feb. 1990.*

**GASH, Robert Walker;** Chief Executive, since 1973, and Clerk to the Lieutenancy, since 1972, Royal County of Berkshire; Clerk, Thames Valley Police Authority, since 1974; *b* 8 Jan. 1926; *s* of William Edward Gash and Elsie Hutton (*née* Armstrong); *m* 1951, Rosamond Elizabeth Brown; two *s*. *Educ:* Carlisle Grammar Sch.; Christ Church, Oxford (MA). Solicitor. Asst Solicitor, Cumberland CC, 1955–58; Asst Clerk of Council, Dep. Clerk of Peace, E Suffolk, 1958–68; Dep. Clerk of Council, Dep. Clerk of Peace, Northamptonshire, 1968–72; Clerk of Council, Royal Co. of Berkshire, 1972–74. Pres., Berks, Bucks and Oxon Incorp. Law Soc., 1984–85. Freeman, City of London, 1984. *Recreations:* Gilbert and Sullivan, crosswords. *Address:* 9 Brocks Way, Shiplake, Henley-on-Thames, Oxon. *T:* Wargrave 3746. *Club:* Leander.

*Died 19 April 1986.*

**GASS, Sir Michael David Irving,** KCMG 1969 (CMG 1960); HM Overseas Civil Service, retired; *b* 24 April 1916; *e s* of late George Irving Gass and Norah Elizabeth Mustard; *m* 1975, Elizabeth Periam, *e d* of late Hon. John Acland-Hood, Wootton House, near Glastonbury. *Educ:* King's Sch., Bruton; Christ Church, Oxford (MA); Queens' Coll., Cambridge (BA). Appointed Colonial Administrative Service, Gold Coast, 1939. Served War of 1939–45 (despatches twice) with The Gold Coast Regt, RWAFF; East Africa, Burma; Major. District Commissioner, Gold Coast, 1945; Asst Regional Officer, Ashanti, 1953–56; Permanent Sec., Ministry of the Interior, Ghana, 1956–58; Chief Sec. to the Western Pacific

High Commission, 1958–65; Acting High Commissioner for the Western Pacific for periods in 1959, 1961, 1963 and 1964; Colonial Secretary, Hong Kong, 1965–69. Actg Governor, Hong Kong, for periods in 1966, 1967, and 1968; High Comr for W Pacific and British High Comr for New Hebrides, 1969–73. Mem., Somerset CC, 1977–81. *Recreation:* ornithology. *Address:* Fairfield, Stogursey, Bridgwater, Som. *T:* Nether Stowey 732251. *Clubs:* East India, Devonshire, Sports and Public Schools; Hong Kong (Hong Kong).

*Died 27 Feb. 1983.*

**GASTAMBIDE, Philippe,** FCIArb; QC 1979; avocat honoraire à la Cour de Paris, 1979; *b* 30 Sept. 1905; *s* of Maurice Gastambide and Marthe (*née* Kullmann); *m* 1st, 1931, Pascale Miraband (decd); one *s* two *d*; 2nd, 1970, Nicole Vingtain. *Educ:* Sorbonne, Paris (Faculty of Law); Christ Church, Oxford. Lic. ès lettres et en droit; MA (Oxon). Avocat à la Cour de Paris, 1933–78, Avocat honoraire 1979; called to the Bar, Lincoln's Inn, 1934. FCIArb 1978. *Recreations:* tennis, bridge, music. *Address:* 4 King's Bench Walk, Temple, EC4Y 7DL. *T:* 01-353 3581; 9 rue d'Anjou, 75008 Paris. *T:* Paris 266 13–44. *Clubs:* United Oxford & Cambridge University; Cercle du Bois de Boulogne (Paris).

*Died 27 May 1984.*

**GASYONGA II, Sir Charles Godfrey,** Kt 1962; Omugabe (Hereditary Ruler) of Ankole, Uganda, since 1944; *b* 1910. Ankole is a Federal State in Uganda and its government has separate legislative powers since the Independence of Uganda on 9th Oct. 1962. *Address:* PO Box 102, Mbarara, Ankole, Uganda.

*Died 1982.*

**GATACRE, Rear-Adm. Galfry George Ormond,** CBE 1960; DSO 1952; DSC 1941 (and Bar 1942); Company Director; *b* Wooroolin, Australia, 11 June 1907; *s* of R. H. W. Gatacre, Bath, Somerset, and Wooroolin, and of C. E. Gordon, Banchory, Scotland; *m* 1933, Wendy May, *d* of E. A. Palmer, Sydney, Australia; one *s* one *d*. *Educ:* Brisbane Boys' Coll.; Royal Australian Naval Coll. Service at sea has been in HM and HMA ships around the world. Lieut 1930; Lieut-Comdr 1938; Comdr 1942; Capt. 1948; Rear-Adm. 1958. Australian Naval Attaché in USA, 1953–55; Command of HMAS Melbourne, 1955–56; Dep. Chief of Naval Staff, 1957–58; Flag Officer Comdg HM Australian Fleet, 1959; Head, Australian Joint Services Staff in USA, 1960–61; Flag Officer East Australian Area, 1962–64. Australasian Representative, Marconi Space & Defence Systems, 1968–. *Publication:* Reports of Proceedings: a naval career 1921–1964, 1982. *Recreations:* golf, tennis. *Address:* 78 Glenhurst Gardens, 11 Yarranabbe Road, Darling Point, Sydney, NSW 2027, Australia. *Club:* Royal Sydney Golf.

*Died 12 Aug. 1983.*

**GATES, Ernest Everard,** MA; retired Company Director; *b* 29 May 1903; *o c* of Ernest Henry Gates, Old Buckenham Hall, Norfolk, and Eva, *y d* of George Siggs, JP, Streatham; *m* 1931, Stella (*d* 1981), *y d* of Henry Knox Simms. *Educ:* Repton; Corpus Christi Coll., Cambridge. Formerly a director, Manchester Chamber of Commerce (1945–51), and various companies. Gazetted Lieut RA Sept. 1939; Major, 1941. MP (C) Middleton and Prestwich Div. of Lancs, May 1940–Oct. 1951. PPS to Rt Hon. W. S. Morrison, Min. of Town and Country Planning, 1943–45. *Recreations:* shooting, fishing, golf, travel. *Address:* Pride's Crossing, Ascot, Berks. *T:* Ascot 22330. *Club:* Portland.

*Died 12 Oct. 1984.*

**GATES, Chm. Thomas S(overeign), Jr;** *b* Philadelphia, 10 April 1906; *s* of Thomas Sovereign Gates and Marie (*née* Rogers); *m* 1928, Millicent Anne Brengle; three *d* (one *s* decd). *Educ:* Chestnut Hill Acad.; University of Pennsylvania (AB). Joined Drexel & Co., Philadelphia, 1928; Partner, 1940–. War Service, 1942–45 (Bronze Star, Gold Star): US Naval Reserve (Capt.). Under-Sec. of Navy, 1953–57; Sec. of the Navy, 1957–59; Dep. Sec. of Defense, 1959; Sec. of Defense, USA, Dec. 1959–Jan. 1961. Director: Morgan Guaranty Trust Co., 1971– (Chm., Exec. Cttee, 1961–62, 1965–68, 1969–71; Pres., 1962–65); Bethlehem Steel Corp.; General Electric Co.; Campbell Soup Co.; Insurance Co. of N America; Philadelphia Contributionship for Insce of Houses from Loss by Fire; Scott Paper Co. Chief of US Liaison Office, Peking, 1976–77. Life Trustee, University of Pennsylvania. Hon. LLD: University of Pa, 1956; Yale Univ. 1961; Columbia Univ. 1961. *Address:* Mill Race Farm, Devon, Pennsylvania, USA. *Clubs:* Philadelphia, Racquet (Philadelphia); The Links (NYC); Metropolitan (Washington, DC); Gulph Mills Golf.

*Died 25 March 1983.*

**GATES, William Thomas George,** CBE 1967; Chairman, West Africa Committee, London, 1961–76; *b* 21 Jan. 1908; *s* of Thomas George and Katherine Gates; *m* 1938, Rhoda (*née* Sellars), *d* of Mrs W. E. Loveless; two *s*. *Educ:* Ilford County High Sch., London Univ. National Bank of New Zealand, London, 1925–30; John Holt & Co. (Liverpool) Ltd, resident Nigeria, 1930–46; Gen. Manager: Nigeria, 1940; Gold Coast, 1947; Liverpool, 1947; Man. Dir, 1956; Dep. Chm., 1964, retired, 1967. MLC, Nigeria, 1940–46; Director: W African Airways Corp, 1941–46; Campbell Co., Louisville, Ky, 1954–67; Edward Bates & Sons (Holdings) Ltd, 1964–70; Edinburgh & Overseas Investment Trust Ltd, Edinburgh, 1964–71. Dist Scout Comr, Northern Nigeria 1940–42; Mem. Liverpool Dist Cttee,

Royal National Life-Boat Instn, 1956–73; Mem. Bd of Govs, United Liverpool Hosps, 1958–70; Gen. Comr of Income Tax, 1967–73; Chm., Liverpool Porterage Rates Panel, 1969–74. Chm., Royal African Soc., 1975–77, Vice-Pres., 1978–87. *Recreations:* golf, fishing, cricket, gardening. *Address:* Masongill, Long Street, Sherborne, Dorset DT9 3DT. *T:* Sherborne (0935) 814214. *Clubs:* MCC; Royal Liverpool Golf (Hoylake).

*Died 23 Nov. 1990.*

**GATTIE, Maj.-Gen. Kenneth Francis Drake,** DSO 1917; MC; DL; *b* 22 April 1890; *s* of late Walter Montagu Gattie and Catherine Anne, *d* of late Rev. T. R. Drake. *Educ:* Tonbridge Sch. Commissioned 3rd Monmouthshire Regt, 1910; served on Western front, 1915-Armistice; Adjutant, 3rd Monmouthshire Regt, 1915; Brigade Major, 75th Infantry Brigade, 1916; Capt. South Wales Borderers, 1917; Gen. Staff, GHQ, 1918 (MC, DSO, despatches five times); Brigade Major, Rhine Army, 1919; served in India, 1919–22 and in 1924; psc, Camberley, 1923; Gen. Staff Officer, War Office, 1924; Brevet Major, 1926; Brigade Major, Rhine Army, 1927; Instructor in Tactics, Sch. of Artillery, 1929; DAA and QMG, Highland Area, 1931; Brevet Lieut-Col, 1931; Major, 1934; GSOII, 43rd (Wessex) Division, 1935–37; Lieut-Col 1937; Commanded 1st Bn Queen's Royal Regt (West Surrey) 1937–38; Col, 1938; Commander 2nd (Rawalpindi) Infantry Brigade, India, 1938 (despatches); acting Maj.-Gen., 1941; temp. Maj.-Gen.; District Commander, India, 1941; retired pay, 1945. DL Brecknock, 1954. Indian NWF Medal 1937–39. *Address:* Tymar, Llyswen, Brecon, Powys. *T:* Llyswen 208. *Died 24 Aug. 1982.*

**GAUNT, Rev. Canon Howard Charles Adie, (Tom Gaunt);** Precentor, Winchester Cathedral, 1967–73; Sacrist, 1963 and Hon. Canon, 1966, Canon Emeritus, since 1974; *b* 13 Nov. 1902; *s* of C. F. Gaunt, Edgbaston; *m* 1st, 1927, Mabel Valery (*d* 1978), *d* of A. E. Bond, Wannerton, near Kidderminster; two *s*; 2nd, 1979, Mary de Lande Long. *Educ:* Tonbridge Sch.; King's Coll., Cambridge. Asst Master: King Edward's Sch., Birmingham, 1928–29; Rugby Sch., 1929–37; Headmaster, Malvern Coll., 1937–53; Chaplain, Winchester Coll., 1953–63. Select Preacher, Universities of Oxford and Cambridge. Hymnwriter. *Publications:* Two Exiles: A School in Wartime, 1946; School: A Book for Parents, 1950; contribs to 100 Hymns for Today and More Hymns for Today, also to numerous hymnbooks in USA, Canada and UK. *Address:* 57 Canon Street, Winchester.

*Died 1 Feb. 1983.*

**GAVEY, Clarence John,** MD, FRCP; Consulting Physician (Cardiologist) to Westminster Hospital, London, Moorfields Eye Hospital and Edenbridge and District War Memorial Hospital; *b* 20 June 1911; 2nd *s* of late Walter John Gavey, Jurat of Royal Court, Guernsey; *m* 1937, Marjorie, *d* of late John Guille, Guernsey; three *d*. *Educ:* Elizabeth College, Guernsey; London Hospital Medical Sch., Buxton Prize in Anat. and Phys.; MRCS LRCP 1934; MB, BS, London 1934. Formerly Emergency Officer, Ho. Phys., Ho. Phys. to Cardiac Dept, Paterson Schol. and Chief Asst, Cardiac Dept, London Hosp.; Chief Med. Asst, Westminster Hosp. MD London 1936, MRCP 1936, FRCP 1948. Past Examnr in Medicine for London Univ., RCP, University Coll. of West Indies. Goulstonian Lecturer, Royal College of Physicians London, 1949; Buckston Brown Medal, Harveian Soc. London 1950; FRSM (Past Mem. Council and Vice-Pres., Section of Medicine); Mem. Assoc. of Physicians of Gt Britain and Ireland; Mem. Internat. Soc. of Internal Medicine; Mem. British Cardiac. Soc.; Mem. London Cardiological Club; Mem. Harveian Soc. of London; Mem. Ophthalmic Soc. of UK. Hon. Lieut-Col RAMC; served MEF, 1942–46. *Publications:* The Management of the "Hopeless" Case, 1952; cardiac articles in French's Differential Diagnosis of Main Symptoms, 1967; various papers in Lancet, Brit. Med. Jl, Brit. Heart Jl, etc. *Address:* Le Carrefour, Les Prevosts Road, St Saviours, Guernsey, Channel Isles. *T:* Guernsey 64942.

*Died 7 Sept. 1982.*

**GAVIN, Malcolm Ross,** CBE 1966 (MBE 1945); MA, DSc, CEng, FIEE, FInstP; Chairman of Council, Royal Dental Hospital School of Dental Surgery, University of London, 1974–81; *b* 27 April 1908; 3rd *s* of James Gavin; *m* 1935, Jessie Isobel Hutchinson; one *s* one *d*. *Educ:* Hamilton Acad.; Glasgow Univ. Mathematics Teacher, Dalziel High Sch., Motherwell, 1931–36; Physicist, GEC Res. Labs, Wembley, 1936–47; HMI, Scottish Education Dept, 1947–50; Head of Dept of Physics and Mathematics and Vice-Principal, College of Technology, Birmingham, 1950–55; Prof. of Electronic Engrg and Head of Sch. of Engrg Sci, University Coll. of N Wales, 1955–65; Principal, Chelsea Coll., Univ. of London, 1966–73; Dir, Fulmer Res. Inst., 1968–73. Member: Electronics Res. Coun., Min. of Aviation, 1960–64; Res. Grants Cttee of DSIR (Chm., Electrical and Systems Sub-Cttee, 1964–65); SRC (Mem. Univ. Sci. and Tech. Bd and Chm. Electrical Sub-Cttee, 1965–69, Chm. Control Engineering Cttee, 1969–73; Mem. Engineering Bd, 1969–73); Inter-Univ. Council for Higher Education Overseas, 1967–74; UGC, Hong Kong, 1966–76; Council, European Physical Soc., 1968–70; Murray Cttee, Univ. of London, 1970–72; Council, N

Wales Naturalist Trust, 1973–77; Council, University Coll. of North Wales, 1974–77; Visitor, Nat. Inst. Industrial Psychology, 1970–74; Pres. Inst. of Physics and Physical Soc., 1968–70 (Vice-Pres., 1964–67). Hon. ACT, Birmingham, 1956; Hon. DSc (Ife), 1970. Hon. Fellow, Chelsea Coll. *Publications:* Principles of Electronics (with Dr J. E. Houldin), 1959. Numerous in Jl of IEE, Brit. Jl of Applied Physics, Wireless Engineer, Jl of Electronics, etc. *Recreations:* gardening, grandchildren. *Address:* Mill Cottage, Pluscarden, Elgin, Morayshire IV30 3TZ. *T:* Dallas 281.

*Died 4 Feb. 1989.*

**GEAKE, Maj.-Gen. Clifford Henry,** CB 1945; CBE 1944; Hon. Maj.-Gen. (retired) RAOC; *b* 3 June 1894; *s* of Thomas Henry Geake; *m* 1915, Brenda Mary, *d* of Dr A. W. F. Sayres; two *s*. Served European War, 1914–18, France and Belgium (wounded, despatches); War of 1939–45, Middle East and Italy (despatches, CBE, CB); retired pay, 1946. Officer, Legion of Merit, USA. *Address:* c/o Barclays Bank Ltd, Friary Branch, Guildford, Surrey. *Died 30 July 1982.*

**GEDDES OF EPSOM,** Baron *cr* 1958, of Epsom (Life Peer); **Charles John Geddes,** Kt 1957; CBE 1950; Chairman, Polyglass Ltd and associated Companies; *b* 1 March 1897; *s* of Thomas Varney Geddes and Florence Louisa Mills; *m* 1920, Julia Burke; one *d*. *Educ:* Blackheath Central Sch. Post Office: boy messenger, telegraph learner, telegraphist. Served European War, 1914–18; RFC; Lieut, 1916–19, Pilot, 1918–19. General Sec. of the Union of Post Office Workers, 1944–57; Member of the General Council of the Trades Union Congress, 1946–57 (Pres. of the TUC, 1954–55); retired, 1957. *Recreations:* television, reading, gardening. *Address:* 5 Cleeve Close, Framfield, Sussex TN22 5PQ. *T:* Framfield 562.

*Died 2 May 1983.*

**GEDDES, Air Cdre Andrew James Wray,** CBE 1946 (OBE 1941); DSO 1943; *b* 31 July 1906; *s* of late Major Malcolm Henry Burdett Geddes, Indian Army, and late Mrs Geddes, Seaford, Sussex; *m* 1929, Anstice Wynter, *d* of late Rev. A. W. Leach, Rector of Leasingham, Lincs; one *s* one *d*. *Educ:* Oakley Hall, Cirencester, Glos; Wellington Coll., Berks; Royal Military Academy Woolwich. 2nd Lt Royal Artillery, 1926; seconded Flying Officer RAF 1928–32; Lieut RA 1929; seconded Flight Lieut RAF 1935–38; Capt. RA 1939; served War of 1939–45 (despatches twice, OBE, DSO, CBE, Commander Legion of Merit, USA); seconded Squadron Leader RAF 1939; Acting Wing Commander RAF 1940; Acting Group Capt., 1942; Acting Air Commodore, 1943; War Subst. Group Capt., 1943; Major RA 1943; Air Commodore Operations and Plans, HQ 2nd TAF for the Invasion. Prepared and signed Treaty for Operation Manna/Chowhound (dropping of food to 3,500,000 Dutch people and allied PoWs), 1945 (nicknamed Man Van Manna and presented with Dutch Erasmus Medal, 1985). Transferred from RA to RAF, 1945; Air Cdre Dir of Organisation (Establishments), Air Ministry, 1945–47 (the 'Geddes Axe'); Group Capt. (subst.), 1947; graduated Imperial Defence Coll., London, 1948; Commanding No. 4 Flying Training Sch. and RAF Station, Heany, S Rhodesia, 1949–51; Dep. Dir of Organisation, Plans, Air Ministry, 1951–54, retd with rank of Air Cdre, 1954; Asst County Civil Defence Officer (Plans), East Sussex County Council, 1957–65; Deputy Civil Defence Officer, Brighton County Borough, 1965–66. Mem., British Hang-gliding Assoc., 1975 (believed to be oldest living person who has flown a hang-glider; first solo when aged 68 years 9 months); qualified instructor/examiner, Nat. Cycling Proficiency Scheme, RoSPA, 1977; Founder Mem., Cuckmere Valley Canoeing Club. Life Pres., Manna Assoc., 1986.

*Died 15 Dec. 1988.*

**GEMMELL, Prof. Alan Robertson,** OBE 1981; Professor of Biology, University of Keele, 1950–77, later Emeritus; *b* 10 May 1913; *s* of Alexander Nicol Gemmell and Mary Robertson; *m* 1942, Janet Ada Boyd Duncanson; two *s*. *Educ:* Ayr Academy; University of Glasgow. BSc (Hons) Glasgow. Commonwealth Fund Fellow, University of Minnesota, 1935–37 (MS); Agricultural Research at West of Scotland Agricultural Coll., 1937–41; PhD Glasgow, 1939; DSc Keele 1986. Lecturer in Botany, Glasgow Univ., 1942–44; Biologist at West Midland Forensic Science Laboratory, 1944–45; Lecturer in Botany, Manchester Univ., 1945–50. Regular broadcaster since 1950. Mem., Adv. Council for Horticultural Therapy, 1981–. Pres., British Agricl and Horticultural Plastics Assoc. *Publications:* Science in the Garden, 1963; Gardeners Question Time Books, 1965, 1967; Developmental Plant Anatomy, 1969; The Sunday Gardener, 1974; The Penguin Book of Basic Gardening, 1975; The Practical Gardener's Encyclopedia, 1977; Basics of Gardening, 1978; (Associate Editor) Chronica Botanica, Vol. I, 1935; many contributions to scientific journals. *Recreations:* golf, gardening, popular science, reading. *Address:* Ornalinn, Knowe Road, Brodick, Isle of Arran KA27 8BY. *T:* Brodick 2248. *Club:* Farmers'.

*Died 5 July 1986.*

**GEOFFREY-LLOYD,** Baron *cr* 1974 (Life Peer), of Broomfield, Kent; **Geoffrey William Geoffrey-Lloyd,** PC 1943; *b* 17 Jan. 1902; *e s* of late G. W. A. Lloyd, Andover House, Newbury. *Educ:* Harrow

Sch.; Trinity Coll., Cambridge (MA); Pres. of the Cambridge Union, 1924. Contested (C) SE Southwark, 1924, Ladywood, 1929; Private Sec. to Rt Hon. Sir Samuel Hoare (Sec. of State for Air), 1926–29; Private Sec. to Rt Hon. Stanley Baldwin (Prime Minister, 1929, subseq. Leader of Opposition), 1929–31; MP (U) Ladywood Div. of Birmingham, 1931–45; PPS to Rt Hon. Stanley Baldwin (Lord Pres. of the Council), 1931–35, (Prime Minister), 1935; Parly Under-Sec., Home Office, 1935–39; Sec. for Mines, 1939–40; Sec. for Petroleum, 1940–42; Chm. Oil Control Board, 1939–45; Minister in charge of Petroleum Warfare Dept 1940–45, and Parly Sec. (Petroleum), Min. of Fuel and Power, 1942–45; Minister of Information, 1945; a Governor of BBC, 1946–49; MP (C) King's Norton, Birmingham, 1950–55; Minister of Fuel and Power, 1951–55; MP (C) Sutton Coldfield, 1955–Feb. 1974; Minister of Education, 1957–Oct. 1959; President Birmingham Conservative and Unionist Assoc., 1946–76. Chm., Leeds Castle Foundn, 1974–. *Address:* 77 Chester Square, SW1W 9DY. *T:* 01-730 0014. *Clubs:* Carlton, Pratt's, Royal Yacht Squadron.

*Died 12 Sept. 1984.*

**GEORGE, Herbert Horace,** CB 1944; MC; *b* 1890; *s* of John George, Clapham; *m* 1913, Emily Rose (*d* 1952), *d* of Thomas Eaton, Clapham; no *c. Educ:* Westminster City Sch.; Trinity Coll., Cambridge. Entered Civil Service, 1913. Served in RA in European War, 1914–19. Under-Sec. for Finance and Accountant-Gen., Ministry of Health, 1946–50; retired, 1950. *Address:* Fouryews, Telham, Battle, East Sussex. *T:* Battle 2927.

*Died 25 Oct. 1982.*

**GEORGE-BROWN, Baron** *cr* 1970 (Life Peer), of Jevington, Sussex; **George Alfred George-Brown,** PC 1951; Director: Commercial Credit (Holdings) Ltd, since 1974; Commercial Credit Services (Holdings), since 1980; *b* 2 Sept. 1914; *s* of George Brown; name changed to George-Brown by deed poll, 1970; *m* 1937, Sophie Levene; two *d.* MP (Lab) Belper Div. of Derbyshire, 1945–70; Parliamentary Private Secretary to Minister of Labour and National Service, 1945–47, to Chancellor of the Exchequer, 1947; Joint Parliamentary Secretary, Ministry of Agriculture and Fisheries, 1947–51; Min. of Works, April-Oct. 1951; First Secretary of State and Secretary of State for Economic Affairs, Oct. 1964–Aug. 1966; Secretary of State for Foreign Affairs, 1966–68. Dep. Leader, Labour Party, 1960–70. Pres., Social Democratic Alliance, 1981–. Productivity Counsellor, Courtaulds Ltd, 1968–73; Chm., Compton Webb Group Marketing Ltd; Dep. Chm., J. Compton, Sons & Webb (Holdings) Ltd, 1980–; Director: British Northrop Ltd, 1978; GT Japan Investment Trust Ltd, 1980–. Order of Cedar of Lebanon, 1971. Biancamano Prize (Italy), 1972. *Publications:* In My Way (memoirs), 1970; The Voice of History, 1979. *Address:* c/o House of Lords, SW1. *Died 2 June 1985.*

**GEORGES-PICOT, Jacques Marie Charles,** KBE (Hon.) 1963; Commandeur, Légion d'Honneur; Hon. Chairman of the Board, Suez Finance Company (Chairman, 1957–70); *b* 16 Dec. 1900; *s* of Charles Georges-Picot and Marthe Fouquet; *m* 1925, Angéline Pelle; five *s. Educ:* Lycée Janson de Sailly, Paris. Inspector of Finance, 1925; Chef de Cabinet, Minister of Budget, 1931; Dir Min. of Finance, 1934; Agent Supérieur in Egypt, of Suez Canal Co., 1937; Asst Dir-Gen. of Suez Canal Co., 1946; Dir-Gen., 1953; Pres., 1957. Dir, Fondation des Sciences Politiques, Paris. *Publication:* La véritable crise de Suez, 1975. *Recreation:* tennis. *Address:* 2 Square Mignot, 75016 Paris, France. *T:* 727–7968. *Club:* Circle Interallié (Paris). *Died 6 Feb. 1987.*

**GERARD, Rt. Rev. George Vincent,** CBE 1944; Assistant Bishop of Sheffield, 1947–71; Residentiary Canon of Sheffield Cathedral, 1960–69; Chairman, House of Clergy, Church Assembly, 1965–70; *b* 24 Nov. 1898; *e s* of late George and late Frederikke Marie Gerard, Snowdon, Canterbury, New Zealand; *m* 1920, Elizabeth Mary Buckley; one *s* one *d. Educ:* Waihi Sch., Winchester, NZ; Christ's Coll., Christchurch, NZ; Brasenose Coll., Oxford. Inns of Court, OTC 1917; 2nd Lieut The Buffs, 1918, Lieut 1918 (MC); demobilised, 1919; BA (Oxon), 1921; MA 1925; deacon, 1922; priest, 1923; Vicar of Pahiatu, 1929–32; Petone, 1932–36; St Matthew, Auckland, 1936–38; Bishop of Waiapu, 1938–44; served as Senior Chaplain to the NZ Forces, 1940–41 (prisoner, but repatriated to England, 1943). Senior NZ Chaplain South Pacific, 1944; Hospital Ship, 1945. Vicar and Rural Dean of Rotherham, 1945–60; Hon. Canon of Sheffield, 1947–60. Proctor in Convocation of York, 1950 and 1952–70. *Address:* 18 Barton Court Avenue, New Milton, Hants BH25 7HD. *Died 14 Jan. 1984.*

**GÉRIN, Winifred Eveleen, (Mrs John Lock),** OBE 1975; MA Cantab; FRSL; author; *b* 7 Oct. 1901; 2nd *d* of F. C. Bourne and Katharine (*née* Hill); *m* 1st, Eugene Gérin (*d* 1945), of Brussels; 2nd, 1954, John Lock; no *c. Educ:* Sydenham High Sch. for Girls; Newnham Coll., Cambridge. War of 1939–45 in Political Intelligence Dept of Foreign Office. James Tait Black Mem. Prize, 1968; RSL Heinemann Prize, 1968; Rose Mary Crawshay Prize, 1968. FRSL 1968; Mem. Council, RSL. *Plays:* My Dear Master, Arts Theatre,

Leeds, 1955; Juniper Hall, BBC TV, 1956. *Publications:* Anne Brontë, 1959; Branwell Brontë, 1961; The Young Fanny Burney, 1961; Charlotte Brontë, 1967; Horatia Nelson, 1970; (ed) Charlotte Brontë, Five Novelettes (from MSS), 1971; Emily Brontë, 1971; Writers and their Work: the Brontës (2 vols), British Council, 1973; Elizabeth Gaskell: a biography, 1976 (Whitbread award); Anne Thackeray Ritchie: a biography, 1981; editorial work. *Recreations:* music, country life, travelling. *Address:* 2 Marlborough Court, Pembroke Road, W8; 3 The Green, Stanford-in-the-Vale, Oxon.

*Died 28 June 1981.*

**GERMAN, Sir Ronald (Ernest),** KCB 1965; Kt 1959; CMG 1953; Director: Securicor Ltd, 1966–80; National Counties Building Society, 1966–80; *b* 19 Oct. 1905; *m* 1931, Dorothy Sparks; no *c. Educ:* HM Dockyard Sch., Devonport. Entered GPO 1925; Asst Dir Posts & Telegraphs Dept, Sudan, 1942; British Post Office, 1945; Postmaster-Gen., East Africa, 1950–58; Dep. Dir Gen. of the Post Office, UK, 1959–60, Dir Gen., 1960–66. Chm. Makerere Coll. Council, 1957–58 (Vice-Chm. 1954). CStJ, 1963. *Address:* Flat 1, 8A Grassington Road, Eastbourne, East Sussex.

*Died 11 May 1983.*

**GERVIS-MEYRICK, Sir George David Eliott Tapps-;** *see* Meyrick.

**GETHIN, Lt-Col (Retd) Sir Richard Patrick St Lawrence,** 9th Bt, *cr* 1665; late REME; *b* 15 May 1911; *s* of Col Sir Richard Walter St Lawrence Gethin, 8th Bt, and Helen (*d* 1957), *d* of W. B. Thornhill; *S* father 1946; *m* 1946, Fara, *y d* of late J. H. Bartlett; one *s* four *d. Educ:* Oundle Sch. Lieut RAOC, 1935; Lieut-Col REME, 1943; Officer Commanding No 11 Vehicle Depot Workshops, until 1957, retired. Restorer of antique furniture. Hon. Research Fellow (Physics), Aston Univ., Birmingham, 1977–81. *Publication:* Restoring Antique Furniture, 1974. *Heir:* *s* Richard Joseph St Lawrence Gethin [*b* 29 Sept. 1949; *m* 1974, Jacqueline, *d* of Comdr David Cox; three *d*]. *Address:* 28 The Maltings, Tewkesbury, Glos GL20 5NN. *T:* Tewkesbury 298180. *Died 26 Dec. 1988.*

**GIAMATTI, (Angelo) Bartlett,** PhD; President, National League of Professional Baseball Clubs, USA, 1986–89; *b* Boston, Mass, 4 April 1938; *s* of Prof. Emeritus Valentine Giamatti and Mary Walton; *m* 1960, Toni Smith; two *s* one *d. Educ:* South Hadley High Sch.; Internat. Sch. of Rome; Phillips Acad., Andover Mass; Yale Univ. (BA *magna cum laude*); Yale Grad. Sch. (PhD). Instructor in Italian and Comparative Literature, Princeton Univ., 1964; Asst Prof., 1965; Asst Prof. of English, Yale Univ., 1966; Associate Professor of: English, 1968, English and Comparative Literature, 1969; Prof. of English and Comparative Literature, Yale Univ., 1971 (Ford chair, 1976–77, but he relinquished to assume newly founded chair); John Hay Whitney Prof. of English and Comparative Lit., Yale Univ., 1977, also (Spring, 1977) Dir of Div. of Humanities, Faculty of Arts and Scis. Master of Ezra Stiles Coll. (a residential coll. of Yale), 1970–72; Dir of Visiting Faculty Program of Yale, 1974–76; Associate Dir of Nat. Humanities Inst., Yale, 1977; Pres., Yale Univ., 1978–86. Guggenheim Fellow, 1969–70. Mem., Council on For. Relations, 1978–. Member: Mediaeval Acad. of America, 1963–; MLA, 1964–; Council for Financial Aid to Educn, 1980–; Amer. Philosophical Soc., 1982–; Bd of Trustees, Ford Foundation, 1983–; Trustee, Mount Holyoke Coll., 1983–; Fellow: Amer. Acad. of Arts and Scis; AAAS, 1980. Hon. LLD: Princeton, 1978; Harvard, 1978; Notre Dame, 1982; Coll. of New Rochelle, 1982; Dartmouth Coll., 1982; Hon. LittD: Amer. Internat. Coll., 1979; Jewish Theol Seminary of Amer., 1980; Atlanta Univ., 1981. Career Achievement Award in Educn, Nat. Italian American Foundn, 1982; Award for outstanding contribution to Higher Educn, Brown Univ. 1985; Comdr, l'Ordre National des Arts et des Lettres, France, 1985; Comdr, Order of Merit (Italy), 1979; Comdr's Cross of Fed. Order of Merit, Germany, 1985. *Publications:* (ed jtly) The Songs of Bernart de Ventadorn, 1962; The Earthly Paradise and the Renaissance Epic, 1966; (ed jtly) Ludovico Ariosto's Orlando Furioso, 1968; (ed jtly) A Variorum Commentary on the Poems of John Milton, vol. 1, 1970; Play of Double Senses: Spenser's Faerie Queene, 1975; The University and the Public Interest, 1981; Exile and Change in Renaissance Literature, 1984; gen. editor, 3 vol. anthology Western Literature, 1971. *Recreations:* interested in sport and ballet. *Died 1 Sept. 1989.*

**GIAUQUE, William (Francis);** Professor of Chemistry, University of California, Berkeley, 1934–62, Emeritus 1962; recalled to active service, 1964–77; continuing research, since 1977; *b* (as US citizen) Niagara Falls, Ont., Canada, 12 May 1895; *s* of William T. S. Giauque and Isabella Jane (*née* Duncan); *m* 1932, Muriel Frances Ashley, BS (Chem.), PhD (Physics); two *s. Educ:* High Sch., Niagara Falls; University of Calif. BS 1920, PhD (Chem., minor Physics) 1922. Faculty of Chemistry, University of Calif.: Instructor, 1922–27; Asst Prof., 1927–30; Assoc. Prof., 1930–34. Government work during War of 1939–45. Member: National Academy of Sciences; Amer. Philosophical Soc.; Amer. Acad. of Arts and Sciences. Hon. DSc Columbia; Hon. LLD Univ. Calif. Nobel prize for Chemistry, 1949; and other awards. *Publications:* about 200 papers in scientific journals. *Address:* 2643 Benvenue Avenue, Berkeley, Calif 94704, USA; University of California, Berkeley, Calif, USA. *Died 29 March* 1982.

**GIBB, Bill;** *see* Gibb, W. E.

**GIBB, George Dutton,** CB 1979; Chief Dental Officer, Department of Health and Social Security and Department of Education and Science, 1971–83; *b* 9 March 1920; *s* of late Dr William Forsyth Gibb and Margaret Jane Gibb (*née* Dutton); *m* 1948, Mary Dupree; two *d. Educ:* St Helen's Coll., Southsea; University Tutorial Coll., London; Guy's Hospital. LDS RCS 1950, FDS RCS 1979. Enlisted RNVR, 1940; commnd (Exec. Br.) 1941. Gen. Dental Practitioner, High Wycombe, 1950–71. Mem., Bucks Exec. Council, 1957–65; Hon. Sec., Bucks Local Dental Cttee, 1957–65; Mem., Standing Dental Adv. Cttee, 1964–71; Mem., Central Health Services Council, 1967–71; Chm. of Council, British Dental Assoc., 1967–71; Mem., GDC (Crown nominee), 1972–83. *Address:* Yenda, 10 Haw Lane, Bledlow Ridge, near High Wycombe, Bucks HP14 4AH. *Died 25 Feb.* 1986.

**GIBB, William Elphinstone, (Bill Gibb);** Company Director, Bill Gibb Ltd, since 1972; Chairman, Bill Gibb Fashion Group Ltd, since 1982; *b* 23 Jan. 1943; *s* of George and Jessie Gibb. *Educ:* Fraserburgh Acad.; St Martin's Sch. of Art (DipAD); Royal Coll. of Art (DesRCA). Fellow, Indust. Arts Soc., 1976. First shop, Alice Paul, 1967; Designer at Baccarat, 1967–79; founded Bill Gibb Ltd, 1972. Created first ballet costumes for Remy Charlip's Mad River, 1972; designed costume for Lynn Seymour as Salomé, 1981. Dress in Cecil Beaton Exhibn, V&A, 1971; 10 yrs Retrospective Fashion show for 7,000 people, Royal Albert Hall, 1977. Nominated for Yardley Award, New York, 1967; Vogue Designer of the Year, 1970 (outfit now in Bath Museum); Silver Heart, Variety Club of GB (for fashion spectacular at London Convention), 1975; award from Today programme (ITV) for best fashion show of 1979. *Recreations:* historical reading, travelling to regenerate inspiration. *Address:* 38 Drayton Court, Drayton Gardens, SW10. *Clubs:* Embassy, Legends, The Gardens, Ritz Casino, Chelsea Arts, Hippodrome. *Died 3 Jan.* 1988.

**GIBBENS, His Honour (Edward) Brian,** MA Oxon; QC 1962; a Circuit Judge, 1973–85; *b* 26 Sept. 1912; *s* of Rev. George Percy Gibbens and Dr Fanny Gibbens; *m* 1939, Kathleen Joan Rosier; two *s* one *d. Educ:* Newcastle-under-Lyme High Sch.; St Catherine's Society, Oxford. Called to the Bar, Gray's Inn, 1934 (Bencher, 1967; Treasurer, 1984); practised on Oxford Circuit from 1934. Served in RA and as staff officer, Nov. 1939–45. Major in Army Officers Emergency Reserve, 1946–. Mem. Gen. Council of the Bar, 1947–52, 1964–68, 1969–73; a Recorder of Crown Courts, 1972–73 (Recorder of West Bromwich, 1959–65, of Oxford, 1965–71); Hon. Recorder, City of Oxford, 1972–85. Dep. Chm. QS, Oxon., 1964–71; Comr of Assize, Bristol, 1970, Oxford, 1971, Birmingham, 1971; Leader of the Oxford Circuit, 1966–71; Jt Leader, Midland and Oxford Circuit, 1972. Conducted Home Office inquiry into corporal punishments at Court Lees approved sch., 1967; conducted public inquiry into automatic level crossings after railway accident at Hixon, Staffs, 1968; leading counsel for the Army in Widgery Tribunal of Inquiry into shooting of civilians in Londonderry, 1972. Hon. Mem., Midland Inst. of Forensic Medicine. Freeman, City of London, 1983. *Recreation:* gardening. *Died 6 Nov.* 1985.

**GIBBENS, Frank Edward Hilary George; His Honour Judge Frank Gibbens;** a Circuit Judge, since 1973; *b* 23 April 1913; *s* of Frank Edward George and Geraldine Edel Gibbens; *m* 1940, Margaret Gertrude Wren; three *d. Educ:* Malvern; Peterhouse, Cambridge (BA). Called to Bar, Inner Temple, 1938. Served War, commission in RAF, 1940–46. Sqdn Leader, rank on demobilisation. On appt as Judge, retired from Bar, 1973. *Recreation:* golf. *Address:* Warren Close, Coombe Hill Road, Kingston-upon-Thames. *Died 7 Feb.* 1987.

**GIBBENS, Prof. Trevor Charles Noel,** CBE 1977 (MBE 1945); MA, MD; FRCP, FRCPsych; Professor of Forensic Psychiatry, Institute of Psychiatry, London University, 1967–78, later Emeritus Professor; Hon. Consultant, Bethlem Royal and Maudsley Hospitals, since 1951; Consultant to London Remand Home for Girls, since 1951; *b* 28 Dec. 1912; *s* of George Gibbens and Sarah Jane Hartley; *m* 1950, Patricia Margaret, *d* of A. E. and E. Mullis; two *s* one *d. Educ:* Westminster Sch.; Emmanuel Coll., Cambridge; St Thomas's Hosp., London. RAMC, 1939; POW, 1940–45. Sen. Lectr, Forensic Psychiatry, 1950–67. Member: Cttee on Business of the Criminal Courts (Streatfield Cttee), 1958; Royal Commn on Penal Reform, 1964–66. President: British Acad. of Forensic Sciences, 1967–68; Internat. Soc. of Criminology, 1967–74. Chm., Inst. for Study and Treatment of Delinquency, 1974–81; Vice-Chm., Howard League, 1975–; Mem., Parole Board, 1972–75. Member: Adv. Gp on Law of Rape (Heilbron Cttee), 1975; Policy Adv. Cttee to Criminal Law Revision Cttee, 1976–79. *Publications:* Shoplifting, 1962; Psychiatric Studies of Borstal Lads, 1963; Cultural Factors in Delinquency, 1966; Medical Remands in Criminal Courts, 1977;

articles in scientific jls. *Address:* c/o Institute of Psychiatry, de Crespigny Park, SE5 8AF. *T:* 01–703 5411.
*Died 27 Oct.* 1983.

**GIBBERD, Sir Frederick,** Kt 1967; CBE 1954; RA 1969 (ARA 1961); FRIBA, FRTPI, FILA; FSIA; practising as an Architect, Town Planning Consultant and Landscape Architect; *b* 7 Jan. 1908; *e s* of late Frederick Gibberd, Kenilworth, Warwicks; *m* 1st, 1938, Dorothy (*d* 1970), *d* of late J. H. Phillips, Hampstead; one *s* two *d*; 2nd, 1972, Patricia Fox Edwards. *Educ:* King Henry VIII Sch., Coventry. Private practice in London since 1930. Principal buildings include: Pullman Court, Streatham; London Airport, Terminal Buildings and Chapel; Bath Technical College; St Neots Bridge; Hinkley Point and Didcot Power Stations; Metropolitan Cathedral, Liverpool (won in open competition); New Monastery, Douai Abbey; Longmans Green Offices, Harlow; Doncaster Law Courts (with L. J. Tucker); Designs for: London Mosque (won in open competition); Arundel Great Court; Coutts Bank, Strand; Inter-Continental Hotel, Hyde Park Corner. Principal town designs, Harlow New Town (Architect-Planner, 1947–80); master plan, Memorial Univ., Newfoundland. Civic Centres for: Doncaster; Harlow; Leamington Spa; Nuneaton and St Albans. Shopping Centres: Lansbury Market; Redcar; Harvey Centre, Harlow; Stratford-upon-Avon. Principal Landscape and Garden Designs: Harlow, overall landscape design and Water Gardens; Queen's Gardens, Hull; Llyn Celyn, Derwent and Kielder Reservoirs; Potash Mine at Boultby; Dinorwic Pump Storage Scheme. Member: Royal Fine Art Commission, 1950–70; Council RIBA, 1959–76; Past President, Building Centre; Past Principal, Architectural Association School of Architecture. Hon. LLD, Liverpool, 1969. RIBA Bronze Medal; Gold Medal, RTPI, 1978; two Festival of Britain Awards; four Housing Medals; five Civic Trust Awards; two European Architectural Heritage Year awards. *Publications:* The Architecture of England, 1938; Town Design, 1953; Metropolitan Cathedral of Christ the King, Liverpool, 1968; The Design of Harlow, 1980; (jtly) Harlow: the story of a new town, 1980. *Recreation:* gardening. *Address:* Marsh Lane, Harlow, Essex CM17 0NA. *Died 9 Jan.* 1984.

**GIBBON, Monk;** *see* Gibbon, W. M.

**GIBBON, (William) Monk,** PhD (Dublin); FRSL; poet and writer; *b* Dublin, 15 Dec. 1896; *o s* of late Rev. Canon William Monk Gibbon, MA, Rural Dean, Taney, Dundrum, Co. Dublin, and Isabel Agnes Pollock (*née* Meredith); *m* 1928, Mabel Winifred, *d* of Rev. Walter Molyneux Dingwall, MA, and Mabel Sophia Spender; two *s* four *d. Educ:* St Columba's Coll., Rathfarnham; Keble Coll., Oxford (Open History Exhibn). Served European War, 1914–18, as Officer, RASC; France, 1916–17; Invalided out, 1918. Taught in Switzerland; master at Oldfeld Sch., Swanage (12 yrs). Silver Medal for Poetry, Tailteann Games, 1928. Tredegar Memorial Lecture, Royal Society of Literature, 1952; Tagore Centenary Lecture, Abbey Theatre, Dublin, 1961. Mem. Irish Acad. of Letters, 1960 (Vice-Pres., 1967). *Publications: poetry:* The Tremulous String, 1926; The Branch of Hawthorn Tree, 1927; For Daws to Peck At, 1929; Seventeen Sonnets, 1932; This Insubstantial Pageant (collected poems), 1951; The Velvet Bow and other poems, 1972; *autobiography:* The Seals, 1935; Mount Ida, 1948; Inglorious Soldier, 1968; The Brahms Waltz, 1970; The Pupil, 1981; *biography:* Netta (Hon. Mrs Franklin), 1960; *novel:* The Climate of Love, 1961; *ballet and film criticism:* The Red Shoes Ballet, 1948; The Tales of Hoffmann, 1951; An Intruder at The Ballet, 1952; *travel:* Swiss Enchantment, 1950; Austria, 1953; In Search of Winter Sport, 1953; Western Germany, 1955; The Rhine and its Castles, 1957; Great Houses of Europe, 1962; Great Palaces of Europe, 1964; *literary criticism:* The Masterpiece and the Man, 1959. The Living Torch (an Æ anthology), 1937. *Recreations:* watching ballet and good films. *Address:* 67 Springhill Park, Killiney, Co. Dublin, Eire. *T:* Dublin 853362. *Died 29 Oct.* 1987.

**GIBBONS, Brig. Edward John,** CMG 1956; CBE 1947 (MBE 1939); *b* 30 Aug. 1906; *s* of Edward Gibbons, Coventry; *m* 1946, Gabrielle Maria (*d* 1982), widow of Capt. P. A. Strakosh; one step *d. Educ:* King Henry VIII Sch., Coventry; Gonville and Caius Coll., Cambridge. Nigerian Administrative Service, 1929. Army Service, 1941–46: Dir of Civil Affairs, South East Asia Command; Brig. Sec. Eastern Provinces, Nigeria, 1948; Commissioner of the Cameroons (under UK Trusteeship), 1949–56; Dept of Technical Cooperation, 1962–64; Min. of Overseas Develt, 1964–68. *Recreation:* wood engraving. *Address:* 6 Grove House, The Grove, Epsom, Surrey. *T:* Epsom (03727) 26657. *Club:* Royal Automobile.
*Died 8 Nov.* 1990.

**GIBBONS, Sir John Edward,** 8th Bt *cr* 1752; Captain (Dorset Regiment); independent; *b* 14 Nov. 1914; *s* of Sir Alexander Doran Gibbons, 7th Bt and Gladys Constance (*d* 1945), *d* of late Rev. Charles Watkins; *S* father 1956; *m* 1937, Mersa Wentworth Foster (marr. diss. 1951), Warmwell House, near Dorchester; one *s* two *d. Educ:* Charterhouse. Asst Regional Dir (Nottingham) of Arts

Council of Great Britain, 1946–50. Dorset Regt, 1939–45; Staff Officer, 1942–43, Iran and Syria. *Heir: s* William Edward Doran Gibbons [*b* 13 Jan. 1948; *m* 1972, Patricia Geraldine Archer, *d* of Roland Archer Howse; one *d*]. *Address:* 2 Malt Cottages, Preston, Weymouth, Dorset. *Club:* MCC. *Died 20 Sept.* 1982.

**GIBBONS, Stella Dorothea, (Mrs A. B. Webb),** FRSL; poet and novelist; *b* London, 5 Jan. 1902; *d* of C. J. P. T. Gibbons, MD; *m* 1933, Allan Bourne Webb (*d* 1959), actor and singer; one *d*. *Educ:* N London Collegiate Sch.; University Coll., London. Journalist, 1923–33; BUP, Evening Standard, The Lady. *Publications:* The Mountain Beast (Poems), 1930; Cold Comfort Farm, 1932 (Femina Vie Heureuse Prize, 1933); Bassett, 1934; The Priestess (Poems), 1934; Enbury Heath, 1935; The Untidy Gnome, 1935; Miss Linsey and Pa, 1936; Roaring Tower (Short Stories), 1937; Nightingale Wood, 1938; The Lowland Venus (Poems), 1938; My American, 1939; Christmas at Cold Comfort Farm (Short Stories), 1940; The Rich House, 1941; Ticky, 1943; The Bachelor, 1944; Westwood, 1946; The Matchmaker, 1949; Conference at Cold Comfort Farm, 1949; Collected Poems, 1950; The Swiss Summer, 1951; Fort of the Bear, 1953; Beside the Pearly Water (short stories), 1954; The Shadow of a Sorcerer, 1955; Here Be Dragons, 1956; White Sand and Grey Sand, 1958; A Pink Front Door, 1959; The Weather at Tregulla, 1962; The Wolves were in the Sledge, 1964; The Charmers, 1965; Starlight, 1967; The Snow Woman, 1969; The Woods in Winter, 1970; *unpublished works:* Verses for Friends; The Yellow Houses; An Alpha. *Recreations:* reading, listening to music.
*Died 19 Dec.* 1989.

**GIBBS, Dennis Raleigh,** CMG 1962; CVO 1966; DSO 1944; CON (Hon.) 1964; Managing Director, Hewanorra Enterprises Ltd, Vieux Fort, St Lucia, 1980–82, retired; *b* 3 March 1922; *e s* of late Gerard Yardley Gibbs, Epping, and Carol Gibbs (*née* Francis); *m* 1952, Barbara Erica Batty, MB, ChB; two *s* one *d*. *Educ:* Bradfield Coll. RAF, 1940–46; CO 82 Sqdn, 1942–44; Wing Comdr Air Staff, Air HQ, Burma, 1945. Seconded FO, 1946; Colonial Admin. Service, 1946–56, then E Nigerian Public Service, 1956–64 (Perm. Sec., Min. of Works, 1958, Adv. to Min. of Economic Planning, 1962–64); Administrator of Montserrat, WI, 1964–71; real estate develt, St Lucia, 1972–77; Man. Dir, Mustique Co., St Vincent, 1977–79. President: Montserrat Nat. Trust, 1983–; Montserrat Legion, 1982–. *Recreations:* outdoor activities. *Address:* Box 479, Plymouth, Montserrat, WI. *Died 19 Sept.* 1985.

**GIBBS, Sir Frank Stannard,** KBE 1954 (OBE 1939); CMG 1949; *b* 3 July 1895; *m* 1944, Sylvia Madeleine Knight; one *s* one *d*. Probationer Vice-Consul, Genoa, 1920; served Madrid, Rio de Janeiro, Paris, Marseilles, Beira, Milan; Vice-Consul, 1923; transferred to China Consular Service with Consular rank, 1935; Actg Consul-Gen., Canton, 1937, Addis Ababa, 1939; served Rosario and Tunis: Consul-Gen., 1946; Foreign Service Officer, Grade 5, 1947; Consul-Gen., Saigon, 1947–51, with personal rank of Minister, 1950–51; Ambassador to the Republic of the Philippines, 1954–55 (Minister, 1951–54), retired 1955. *Address:* El Rincón, High Street, Old Woking, Surrey. *T:* Woking 70147. *Died 22 Oct.* 1983.

**GIBBS, Rt. Hon. Sir Humphrey Vicary,** PC 1969; GCVO 1969 (KCVO 1965); KCMG 1960; OBE 1959; Governor of Rhodesia (formerly S Rhodesia), 1959–69; *b* 22 Nov. 1902; 3rd *s* of 1st Baron Hunsdon; *m* 1934, Molly Peel Nelson (later Dame Molly Gibbs, DBE); five *s*. *Educ:* Eton; Trinity Coll., Cambridge. Started farming near Bulawayo, 1928; ceased farming operations, 1983. Hon. LLD Birmingham, 1969. Hon. DCL East Anglia, 1969. KStJ 1959. *Address:* 22 Dornie Road, Pomona, PO Borrowdale, Harare, Zimbabwe. *T:* Harare 883281. *Clubs:* Bulawayo (Bulawayo, Zimbabwe); Harare (Harare, Zimbabwe).
*Died 5 Nov.* 1990.

**GIBBS, Prof. Norman Henry,** MA, DPhil; Emeritus Fellow, All Souls College, Oxford, since 1977; Chichele Professor of the History of War in the University of Oxford, 1953–77; *b* 17 April 1910; *m* 1941, Joan Frances Leslie-Melville; two *d*; *m* 1955, Kathleen Phebe Emmett (*d* 1989). Open Exhibitioner, Magdalen Coll., Oxford, 1928; Senior Demy, 1931; Asst Lecturer, University Coll., London, 1934–36; Fellow and Tutor in Modern History, Merton Coll., Oxford, 1936. 1st King's Dragoon Guards, 1939; Historical Section, War Cabinet Office, 1943. Former Chm., Naval Education Advisory Cttee; former Member: Internat. Council of Institute for Strategic Studies; Council, Royal United Service Institution; Research Associate, Center for Internat. Studies, Princeton, 1965–66. Visiting Professor: Univ. of New Brunswick, 1975–76; US Military Academy, West Point, 1978–79; Nat. Univ. of Singapore, 1982–84. US Outstanding Civilian Service Medal, 1979. *Publications:* 2nd edition, Keith, British Cabinet System, 1952; The Origins of the Committee of Imperial Defence, 1955; contribs to: Cambridge Modern History (new edn); L'Europe du XIXme et du XXme siècles, (Milan) 1966; (ed) The Soviet System and Democratic Society, 1967; History of the Second World War, Grand Strategy,

Vol. 1, 1976. *Address:* c/o Newland House, 50 Oxford Road, Witney, Oxon. *Died 20 April* 1990.

**GIBBS-SMITH, Charles Harvard;** Keeper Emeritus, Victoria and Albert Museum, since 1971; Research Fellow, Science Museum, since 1976; first Lindbergh Professor of Aerospace History, National Air and Space Museum, Smithsonian Institution, USA, 1978; Adjunct Fellow, Wilson Centre, 1978; aeronautical historian; *b* 22 March 1909; *y s* of late Dr E. G. Gibbs-Smith; *m* 1975, Lavinia Snelling. *Educ:* Westminster; Harvard Univ., USA (Research Fellow and MA). Asst-Keeper, Victoria and Albert Museum, 1932–39, Keeper of Public Relations and Educn Dept, 1947–71; loaned to Ministry of Information, 1939 (Asst-Dir of Photograph Div., 1943, Dir, 1945). Organised photograph libraries of Ministry of Information; Press Censorship; Admiralty Press Div.; USA Office of War Information, London; Radio Times-Hulton Picture Library. Served in ROC 1941–44 (Hon. Mem., 1945). Hon. Companion, and Cttee Mem. History Group, Royal Aeronautical Society; Fellow, Coll. of Psychic Studies; Mem. Soc. for Psychical Res.; Hon. Mem., RPS, 1973. FRSA 1948; FMA 1952. First Chm., Costume Soc., 1965. Mem. Bd of Governors, ESU 1956–59. Mem. Bd of Electors, Internat. Aerospace Hall of Fame, 1975. Hon. Fellow, RCA, 1969. Chevalier, Danish Order of the Dannebrog. *Publications:* V & A Museum Costume Bibliography, 1936; Basic Aircraft Recognition, 1942; German Aircraft, 1943; Aircraft Recognition Manual, 1944 (new edn 1945); Ballooning, 1948; The Great Exhibition of 1851, 1950; Air League Recognition Manual, 1952; A History of Flying, 1953; Balloons, 1956; The Fashionable Lady in the 19th Century, 1960; The Invention of the Aeroplane, 1966; The Bayeux Tapestry, 1973; The Art of Observation, 1973; Pioneers of the Aeroplane, 1975; Early Flying Machines, 1975; Science Museum *monographs:* The Aeroplane: an historical Survey, 1960 (2nd edn as Aviation, etc 1970); Sir George Cayley's Aeronautics, 1962; The Wright Brothers, 1963; The World's First Flights, 1965; A Directory and Nomenclature of the First Aeroplanes, 1966; Leonardo da Vinci's Aeronautics, 1967; Clément Ader, his Flight Claims, 1967; A Brief History of Flying, 1968; The Rebirth of European Aviation, 1974. *Novels:* Operation Caroline, 1953; Yankee Poodle, 1955; Escape and be Secret, 1957; articles and broadcasts on art, crime, aeronautical history, etc. *Recreations:* fencing, classification, travel, parapsychology. *Address:* c/o Science Museum, South Kensington, SW7. *Clubs:* Naval and Military, Royal Aero; Harvard (USA). *Died 3 Dec.* 1981.

**GIBSON, Dr Alan Frank,** FRS 1978; FInstP; Head of Laser Division, Rutherford and Appleton Laboratories, 1977–83; Hon. Research Fellow, Clarendon Laboratory, Oxford; Visiting Professor, University of Essex; *b* 30 May 1923; *s* of Hezeltine Gibson and Margaret Wilson; *m* 1945, Judith Cresswell; one *s* two *d*. *Educ:* Rydal Sch., Colwyn Bay; Birmingham Univ. (BSc, PhD). FInstP 1965. Joined TRE, Malvern, 1944; conducted research and later lead res. groups on aspects of solid state physics and devices, notably semiconductor devices; Dep. Chief Scientific Officer (by individual merit), 1961; Univ. of Essex: first Prof. of Physics, 1963; res. on optical properties of semiconductors using lasers; Chm. of Physics Dept, 1963–69 and 1971–76; Dean of Phys. Sciences, 1964–68; Pro-Vice-Chancellor, 1968–69 and 1974–75. Glazebrook Medal and Prize, Inst. of Physics, 1983. *Publications:* (General Editor) Progress in Semiconductors: Vol. 1, 1956 to Vol. 9, 1965; An Introduction to Solid State Physics and its Applications, 1974 (repr. with corrections 1976); over 70 res. pubns in learned jls. *Address:* Dunstan Lodge, Letcombe Regis, Wantage, Oxon OX12 9JY. *T:* Wantage 66531.
*Died 27 March* 1988.

**GIBSON, Sir John (Hinshelwood),** Kt 1969; CB 1962; TD 1944; QC (Scotland) 1961; *b* 20 May 1907; *y s* of late William John Gibson, Solicitor, Falkirk; *m* 1948, Jane, *o d* of late Captain James Watt; one *s* one *d*. *Educ:* Fettes Coll. (Scholar); University of Edinburgh. MA 1928; LLB 1931. Admitted to Faculty of Advocates, and called to Bar (Scot.), 1932. Entered Lord Advocate's Dept, 1945; Legal Sec. and First Parly Draftsman for Scotland, 1961–69; Counsel to Scottish Law Commn, 1969–77. Member: Editorial Bd, Statutes in Force, 1968–77; Cttee on Preparation of Legislation, 1973–75. TA (Royal Artillery), 1931–45 (War service, 1939–45); hon. Major. *Address:* 3 Tipperlinn Road, Edinburgh EH10 5ET. *T:* 031–447 2792. *Club:* New (Edinburgh). *Died 9 July* 1985.

**GIBSON, Hon. Sir Marcus (George),** Kt 1970; *b* 11 Jan. 1898; *e s* of late Clyde Gibson, Oatlands, Tasmania, and Lucy Isabel (*née* Stanfield); *m* 1929, Iris Lavinia, *d* of A. E. Shone, East Risdon, Tas; one *s* one *d*. *Educ:* Leslie House Sch., Hobart; Univ. of Tasmania. LLB (Tas) 1921; LLM (Tas) 1924. Served European War: Gunner, AIF, 1917–19. Admitted to bar of Supreme Court, Tasmania, 1921; private practice, 1921–29; Solicitor to the Public Trust Office, 1929–38; Police Magistrate, 1939–42; Asst Solicitor-General, 1942–46; KC 1946; Solicitor-General, 1946–51; Puisne Judge, Supreme Court of Tasmania, 1951–68; on several occasions Actg Chief Justice and Administrator, Govt of Tasmania. President: Tasmanian Council on the Ageing, 1964–76; E-SU (Tasmanian

Br.). *Recreations:* theatre, gardening. *Address:* 296 Sandy Bay Road, Hobart, Tas. 7005, Australia. *T:* Hobart 235624. *Club:* Tasmanian (Hobart).                                    *Died* 11 *Sept.* 1987.

**GIBSON, Rt. Hon. Sir Maurice White,** PC 1975; Kt 1975; **Rt. Hon. Lord Justice Gibson;** Lord Justice of Appeal, Supreme Court of Judicature, Northern Ireland, since 1975; Member, Restrictive Practices Court, since 1971; *b* 1 May 1913; 2nd *s* of late William James Gibson, Montpelier House, Belfast, and of Edith Mary Gibson; *m* 1945, Cecily Winifred, *e d* of late Mr and Mrs Dudley Roy Johnson, Cordova, Bexhill-on-Sea, Sussex; one *s* one *d. Educ:* Royal Belfast Academical Institution; Queen's Univ., Belfast (LLB, BA). English Bar Final Exam. First Cl. and Certif. of Honour, 1937; Called to Bar of NI with Special Prize awarded by Inn of Court of NI, 1938; called to Inner Bar, NI, 1956. Puisne Judge, NI High Court of Justice, 1968–75. Apptd Mem. several Govt Cttees on Law Reform in NI; Dep. Chm., Boundary Commn for NI, 1971–75; Chm., SLS Legal Publications (NI). Chm., NI Scout Council. *Address:* 29a Purdysburn Hill, Belfast BT8 8JY. *T:* Drumbo 762. *Club:* Royal Belfast Golf.               *Died* 25 *April* 1987.

**GIBSON, Sir Ronald (George),** Kt 1975; CBE 1970 (OBE 1961); DL; MA Cantab; FRCS, FRCGP; Chairman of Council, British Medical Association, 1966–71; *b* 28 Nov. 1909; *s* of George Edward Gibson and Gladys Muriel, *d* of William George Prince, JP, CC, Romsey, Hants; *m* 1934, Dorothy Elisabeth Alberta, *d* of Thomas Alfred Rainey, Southampton; two *d. Educ:* Mill Hill Sch., St John's Coll., Cambridge; St Bartholomew's Hosp., London. Gen. Practitioner, retired 1977. MO, Winchester Coll. and St Swithun's Sch., Winchester, 1950–77. Lieut-Col RAMC (Emergency Reserve), PMO Italian Somaliland, 1944–45. Mem. Council: BMA, 1950–72 (Chm., Representative Body, 1963–66; Chm. Council, 1966–71); RCS, 1962–67 (FRCS 1968); Mem., GMC, 1974–79. First Provost, SE Eng. Faculty, Royal College of General Practitioners, 1954 (James Mackenzie Lectr, 1967; FRCGP 1967). Member: Central Health Services Council, 1966–76 (Vice-Chm., 1972–76); Personal Social Services Council, DHSS, 1973–76; Standing Med. Adv. Cttee, 1966–76 (Chm., 1972–76); Adv. Council on Misuse of Drugs; Steering Cttee on Barbiturates (Chm.); Adv. Cttee, Drug Surveillance Res. Unit, Southampton Univ. (Chm.); Council, Med. Insurance Agency (Chm. 1977–82); Medical Information Rev. Panel, British Library, 1978–82 (Chm., 1978–82); Tribunal on Alleged Atrocities, NI, 1971. Pres., Brendoncare Foundn. FRSA 1983. Governor, Eastleigh Coll. of Further Educn, 1977–85. Mem. Ct, Univ. of Southampton, 1979–86. High Steward, Winchester Cathedral, 1985–. Mem., Ct of Assts, Worshipful Soc. of Apothecaries of London, 1971 (Liveryman, 1964; Master, 1980). Gold Medallist, BMA, 1970; BMA Winchester Address, 1979 (And Is There Honey Still For Tea). DL Hants 1983. Hon. LLD Wales, 1965; Hon. DM Southampton, 1980. *Publications:* Care of the Elderly in General Practice (Butterworth Gold Medal), 1956; The Satchel and the Shining Morning Face, 1971; The One with the Elephant, 1976; Adolescence, 1978; The Family Doctor, His Life and History, 1981; contrib. Lancet, BMJ, etc. *Recreations:* medicine, music, cricket, gardening. *Address:* 21 St Thomas' Street, Winchester, Hants SO23 9HJ. *T:* Winchester 54582. *Clubs:* Athenæum, MCC.                             *Died* 27 *May* 1989.

**GIBSON, Air Vice-Marshal William Norman,** CBE 1956; DFC; Royal Australian Air Force, retired; Senior Air Staff Officer, Operational Comd, RAAF, 1963–64 and 1966; *b* 28 April 1915; *s* of late Hamilton Ross Gibson; *m* 1938, Grace Doreen, *d* of John Walter Downton, Sydney; one *d. Educ:* NZ; Parramatta High Sch.; Point Cook. RAN, 1936–39; RAAF: CO, Port Moresby, 1942; SASO, RAAF Command, 1943–44; SASO, 1st Tactical Air Force, 1947–48; CO, RAAF East Sale, 1953–54; Dir of Training, 1955–56; Air Cdre, Plans, 1957; CO, RAAF Amberley, 1959–62; SASO, HQ Far East Air Force, 1964–66. ADC to HM the Queen, 1955–58. Legion of Merit (USA). *Address:* 26 Hillcrest Avenue, Mona Vale, NSW 2103, Australia. *Club:* Imperial Service (Sydney).

*Died* 31 *July* 1982.

**GIELGUD, Val Henry,** CBE 1958 (OBE 1942); retired as Head of Sound Drama, BBC, after 35 years; *b* 28 April 1900; *s* of late Frank and Kate Terry Gielgud; *m* 1921, Natalie Mamontoff (marr. diss., 1925); *m* 1928, Barbara Druce (marr. diss.); one *s; m* 1946, Rita Vale (marr. diss.); *m* 1955, Monica Grey (marr. diss.); *m* 1960, Vivienne June Bailey. *Educ:* Rugby Sch.; Trinity Coll., Oxford. Had a somewhat variegated early career, including some time as sec. to an MP, as sub-editor of a comic paper, and as an actor; joined the Radio Times, 1928, and was appointed BBC Dramatic Dir, 1929; since then has written novels, stage plays, broadcast plays, and collaborated in several film scenarios, Death at Broadcasting House, Royal Cavalcade, Café Colette, Talleyrand, and Marlborough. *Publications:* Black Gallantry, 1928; Gathering of Eagles, 1929; Imperial Treasure, 1930; The Broken Men, 1931; Gravelhanger, 1932; Outrage in Manchukuo, 1937; The Red Account, 1939; Beyond Dover, 1940; Confident Morning, 1943; Years of the Locust, autobiog., 1946; How to Write Broadcast Plays;

Radio Theatre 1946; Fall of a Sparrow, 1948; Special Delivery, 1949; One Year of Grace, 1950; The High Jump, 1953; Cat, 1956; British Radio Drama, 1922–1956, A Survey, 1957; Gallows' Foot, 1958; To Bed at Noon, 1960; And Died So?, 1961; The Goggle-Box Affair, 1963; Years in a Mirror, 1965; Cats: a personal Anthology, 1966; Conduct of a Member, 1967; A Necessary End, 1969; The Candle-Holders, 1970; The Black Sambo Affair, 1972; My Cats and Myself, 1972; In Such a Night, 1974; A Fearful Thing, 1975; *plays:* Away from it All; Chinese White; Party Manners; Iron Curtain; The Bombshell; Mediterranean Blue; Not Enough Tragedy; Gorgeous George; (with Holt Marvell) Under London; Death at Broadcasting House; Death as an Extra; Death in Budapest; The Television Murder (with Eric Maschwitz). *Recreations:* reading, especially Milit. History, enjoying the society of Siamese cats, talking and travel. *Address:* Wychwood, Barcombe, near Lewes, East Sussex. *Club:* Savile.               *Died* 30 *Nov.* 1981.

**GIFFORD, J(ames) Morris,** CBE 1973; FCIT; Director-General, National Ports Council, 1963–78 (Member of Council, 1964–78); *b* 25 March 1922; *y s* of Frederick W. Gifford, Dunfermline; *m* 1943, Margaret Lowe Shaw, MA (Hons), Dunfermline; two *s* one *d. Educ:* Dunfermline High Sch. (Dux 1939); Edinburgh Univ. (First Bursar). MA Hons Classics, 1946. Lieut RA, 1942–45. Called to Bar, Middle Temple, 1951. Shipping Fedn, 1946–55: Asst Sec., Mersey, 1948–50 and Thames, 1950–53; Sec., Clyde, 1954–55; Gen. Man., Nat. Assoc. of Port Employers, and Mem. Nat. Dock Labour Bd, 1955–63. Vice-Pres., CIT, 1975, Pres., 1976. *Recreations:* crosswords, reading, gardening. *Address:* 15 Bourne Avenue, Southgate, N14 6PB. *T:* 01–886 1757. *Club:* Oriental (Chm., 1978–79).                             *Died* 27 *Aug.* 1987.

**GILBERT, Carl Joyce;** President, Association of Independent Colleges and Universities in Massachusetts, since 1972; *b* 3 April 1906; *s* of Seymour Parker Gilbert and Carrie Jennings Gilbert (*née* Cooper); *m* 1936, Helen Amory Homans; one *s. Educ:* University of Virginia; Harvard. AB University of Virginia, 1928; LLB Harvard, 1931. Admitted to Mass bar, 1931; Associate Ropes, Gray, Boyden & Perkins, 1931–38; member firm (name changed to Ropes, Gray, Best, Coolidge & Rugg), 1938–49; Treasurer-Vice-Pres., The Gillette Company (formerly Gillette Safety Razor Company), Boston, 1949–56; Pres., 1956–57; Chm. of Board and Chief Exec. Officer, 1957–66; Chm. Exec. Cttee, 1966–68. Special Representative for Trade Negotiations, Washington, DC, in Exec. Office of President, with rank of Ambassador, 1969–71. Hon. LLD Boston Coll., Mass, 1958; Hon. DSc Worcester Polytechnic Inst., 1976; Hon. LHD: Northeastern Univ., 1977; Tufts Univ., 1980. *Address:* Strawberry Hill Street, Dover, Mass 02030, USA. *T:* 785 0311. *Clubs:* Somerset, Dedham Country and Polo (Boston).           *Died* 13 *Nov.* 1983.

**GILBERT, Frederick;** retired as Special Commissioner of Income Tax; *b* North Cornwall, 15 Nov. 1899; *s* of William Gilbert, farmer, and Jessie Cleave; *m* 1st, Ethel (decd), *d* of William Baily, Launceston; three *d;* 2nd, Blanche, *d* of William Banyard, Cambridge. *Recreations:* bowls, painting. *Address:* 2 Grinley Court, Cranfield Road, Bexhill-on-Sea, East Sussex TN40 1QD. *T:* Bexhill 211793.                                    *Died* 9 *Feb.* 1989.

**GILBERT, Brig. Sir William (Herbert Ellery),** KBE 1976 (OBE 1945); DSO 1944; Director, New Zealand Security Intelligence Service, 1956–76, retired; *b* 20 July 1916; *s* of Ellery George Gilbert and Nellie (*née* Hall); *m* 1944, Patricia Caroline Anson Farrer; two *s* one *d. Educ:* Wanganui Collegiate Sch., NZ; RMC, Duntroon, Australia. NZ Regular Army, 1937–56; War Service with 2NZEF, ME and Italy, 1940–45; retd, Brig. Pres., NZ World Wildlife Fund. Bronze Star, USA, 1945. *Recreations:* golf, fishing, gardening. *Address:* 38 Chatsworth Road, Silverstream, New Zealand. *T:* Wellington 286570. *Clubs:* Wellington, Wellington Golf (NZ).

*Died* 25 *Sept.* 1987.

**GILCHRIST, Sir (James) Finlay (Elder),** Kt 1978; OBE 1946; Life President and Director, Harrisons & Crosfield PLC (Chairman, 1962–77); *b* 13 Aug. 1903; *s* of late Thomas Dunlop Gilchrist and Agnes Crawford Elder; *m* 1933, Dorothy Joan Narizzano (*d* 1986); two *s* one *d. Educ:* Glasgow Academy. *Address:* South Cottage, Hapstead Farm, Ardingly, Sussex. *T:* Ardingly 892368. *Club:* East India.                                    *Died* 13 *March* 1987.

**GILCHRIST, John;** a Recorder of the Crown Court, since 1980; *b* 28 Nov. 1929; *s* of late John T. Gilchrist and of Dorothy Gilchrist; *m* Margaret Mercedes Summers, MD, FRCPath; one *s.* Schoolmaster, 1958–64. Called to the Bar, Gray's Inn, 1967. *Recreation:* sailing. *Address:* 10 Ridgeway Avenue, Marford, Clwyd. *Clubs:* Cruising Association; Athenæum (Liverpool); Bar Yacht, Royal Anglesey Yacht.                                  *Died* 12 *June* 1982.

**GILES, Sir Alexander (Falconer),** KBE 1965 (MBE 1946); CMG 1960; HM Colonial Service retired; *b* 1915; *o s* of late A. F. Giles, MA, LLD; *m* 1953, Mrs M. E. Watson, *d* of late Lieut-Col R. F. D. Burnett, MC, and *widow* of Lieut-Col J. L. Watson; two step *s* one step *d. Educ:* The Edinburgh Academy; Edinburgh Univ.; Balliol

Coll., Oxford (BA). Pres. Oxford Union Soc., 1939. 2nd Lieut the Royal Scots, 1940; attached RWAFF, 1941; 81 (WA) Div., 1943; Lieut-Col comdg 5 GCR, 1945 (MBE, despatches). Cadet Colonial Service, Tanganyika, 1947; Administrator, St Vincent, 1955–62; Resident Commissioner, Basutoland, 1962–65; British Govt Representative, Basutoland, 1965–66. Chairman: Victoria League in Scotland, 1968–70; Scottish Council, Royal Over-Seas League, 1969–70, Central Council, 1972–75. Dir, Toc H, 1968–74. Gen. Sec., Scotland, Royal Over-Seas League, 1976–78. *Publications:* articles in service jls. *Recreation:* the printed word. *Address:* 4 Royal Crescent, Edinburgh EH3 6PZ.     *Died 11 April 1989.*

**GILES, Sir (Henry) Norman,** Kt 1969; OBE 1966; *b* Northam, WA, 3 May 1905; *s* of late J. O. Giles, Claremont, WA; *m* 1929, Eleanor, *d* of late S. J. Barker; one *s* one *d*. *Educ:* Christ Church Grammar Sch., WA. Served War of 1939–45: RAAF, 1941–44; Flt-Lt (Aust. and New Guinea). Joined Elder Smith & Co. Ltd, 1922; Asst Manager for WA, 1944–47; Manager for WA, 1947–48; Asst Gen. Manager, Aust., 1948–52; Gen. Manager, Aust., 1952–55; Man. Dir, 1955–62; name changed, on amalgamation, to Elder, Smith, Goldsbrough Mort Ltd; Gen. Manager, 1962–67, Chm., 1967–76. Chm., Commonwealth Develt Bank Exec. Cttee, 1959–77; Director: Commonwealth Banking Corp., 1959–77 (Dep. Chm. 1959–62, 1967–75); Babcock Australian Hldgs Ltd, 1959–76; P&O Australia Ltd, 1959–75 (Chm. 1969–75); Elder Smith Goldsbrough Mort Gp Cos, 1962–76; Gove Alumina Ltd, 1969–72; Reyrolle Parsons of Australia Ltd (Gp), 1971–76; Reyrolle Pty Ltd Gp, 1973–76; Chm., Farming Management Services Ltd (WA), 1977–. Member: Commonwealth Export Develt Council, 1965–70 (Mem. Exec. and Dep. Chm., 1966–70); SA Industrial Adv. Council, 1967–70; Australian Wool Industry Adv. Cttee, 1970–71. Member: SA State Cttee, CSIRO, 1962–71; Australia-Japan Business Co-operation Cttee, 1966–75; Council, Duke of Edinburgh's 3rd Commonwealth Study Conf., 1966; Acad. of Science Industry Forum, 1967–72; Pacific Basin Econ. Council, 1968–75. Vice-Pres. and Mem. Exec. Cttee, WA Chamber of Commerce, 1947–50; Mem. Exec., Nat. Council of Wool Selling Brokers of Australia, WA, 1947–53, SA, 1953–62. Mem. Council, Aust. Admin. Staff Coll., 1950–75; Fellow: Council for C of E Schools, WA, 1933–53; Australia Inst., Rotterdam, 1965–76. *Address:* 31 Strathearn, 16 King's Park Avenue, Crawley, WA 6009, Australia.     *Died 26 May 1983.*

**GILHAM, Harold Sidney,** CB 1956; Asst Comptroller of the Patent Office, Board of Trade, 1955–59, retired; *b* 7 Aug. 1897. Formerly a Superintending Examiner at the Patent Office.
    *Died 28 Nov. 1982.*

**GILL, Austin,** CBE 1955; MA, Licencié-ès-lettres; Marshall Professor of French, University of Glasgow, 1966–71, retired; *b* 3 Sept. 1906; *m* 1939, Madeleine Monier. *Educ:* Bury Municipal Secondary Sch.; Universities of Manchester, Grenoble, Paris. Research Fellow, 1929–30, Faulkner Fellow, 1930–31, and Langton Fellow, 1931–33, Manchester Univ. Asst Lecturer in French, Edinburgh Univ., 1933–34; Lecturer in French, Edinburgh Univ., 1934–43; British Council Representative in French North Africa, 1943–44; British Council Actg Rep. in France, 1944–45; Official Fellow, Tutor in Modern Langs, Magdalen Coll., Oxford, 1945–50 and 1954–66, Emeritus Fellow, 1989; Dir of Brit. Inst. in Paris, 1950–54. *Publications:* (ed) Les Ramonneurs, 1957; (ed) Life and Letters in France, 1970; The Early Mallarmé, vol. I, 1980, vol. II, 1986; articles and reviews in literary and philological journals. *Address:* 15 Beaumont Gate, Glasgow G12 9ED.
    *Died 20 March 1990.*

**GILL, Cecil Gervase H.;** *see* Hope Gill.

**GILL, Cyril James;** Telecommunications Management Consultant, 1972–77; *b* 24 Dec. 1907; *s* of William and Alice Gill; *m* 1931, Dae M. (*née* Bingley); one *s* one *d*. *Educ:* Mundella Gram. Sch., Nottingham. Served Army, Royal Signals, 1942–46, to Col GHQI. Engrg Dept, GPO, 1929–48; Telephone Man., Sheffield, 1949; Princ., Post Office HQ, 1950; Princ. Private Sec. to PMG, 1957; Dep. Dir, External Telecommunications Exec., 1958; Controller of Supplies, 1959; Vice-Dir, ETE, 1964; Dir, External Telecomm. Exec., GPO, 1967–69; Dir, Cable and Wireless Ltd, 1967–69; Chm. Commonwealth Telecomm. Council, 1968–69; Chm. Grading Commn, Nigerian Min. of Communications, 1970–71. *Recreations:* gardening, golf, travel. *Address:* 65 Longton Avenue, Upper Sydenham, SE26 6RF. *T:* 01–699 2745.     *Died 5 April 1990.*

**GILL, Evan William Thistle;** Canadian Ambassador to Ireland, 1965–68; retired; *b* 2 Nov. 1902; *s* of Robert Gill; *m* 1930, Dorothy Laurie; two *s* one *d*. *Educ:* RMC, Kingston, Ont.; McGill Univ., Montreal, PQ. Began career with industrial and commercial organs; served Canadian Army, 1940–46; Cabinet Secretariat, 1946–50; External Affairs, 1950; Canada House, 1950–51; High Comr for Canada to Union of S Africa, 1954–57; High Comr for Canada to Ghana, 1957–59; Asst Under-Sec. of State for External Affairs, 1959–62; High Commissioner for Canada in Australia, 1962–64.

*Address:* St Andrews, New Brunswick E0G 2X0, Canada. *Clubs:* Rideau (Ottawa); University (Toronto).     *Died 5 Feb. 1990.*

**GILL, Frank Maxey;** Director, Gill & Duffus Group Ltd, 1957–80; *b* 25 Sept. 1919; fifth *s* of Frederick Gordon Gill, DSO, and Mary Gill; *m* 1st, 1942, Sheila Rosemary Gordon (decd); three *d*; 2nd, 1952, Erica Margaret Fulcher; one *s*. *Educ:* Kingsmead Prep. Sch., Seaford; Marlborough Coll.; De Havilland Aeronautical Technical Sch. Joined Gill & Duffus Ltd, 1940; served RAF (Flt/Lt), 1940–46; rejoined Gill & Duffus Ltd, 1946; Joint Managing Director, 1959; Chm., 1976–79. Hon. Trustee, Confectioners' Benevolent Fund, 1981– (Pres., 1970). Mem., Surrey Soc. of Model Engineers. *Recreation:* model engineering. *Address:* 6 The Pavilion, Wraymill Park, Batts Hill, Reigate, Surrey RH2 0LQ.
    *Died 30 March 1990.*

**GILL, Maj.-Gen. John Galbraith,** CBE 1943 (OBE 1919); DSO 1918; MC; late RAMC (retired); *b* 6 April 1889; *s* of late R. P. Gill, of Guntur, India; *m* 1915, Madge, *d* of late Rev. George Davidson, BSc, of Edinburgh; no *c*. *Educ:* Brentwood School, Essex; Edinburgh University. MB, ChB, 1912; DPH (Scot. Conjoint), 1923; DTM&H (Cantab), 1924. Retired pay, 1946. *Address:* Forest Oaks, The Rise, Brockenhurst, Hants SO4 7SJ.     *Died 23 Jan. 1981.*

**GILL, Air Cdre Hon. Thomas Francis, (Frank),** CBE 1961; DSO 1941; New Zealand Ambassador to the United States of America and Mexico, since 1980; *b* Wellington, 1917; *s* of T. P. Gill; *m* 1942, Barbara, *d* of I. W. Benson, Mddx; three *d*. *Educ:* St Patrick's Coll., Wellington. psa, jssc, idc. Joined RNZAF, 1937; served War, RAF, 1939–45: France; Battle of Britain; Comdr, NZ Flying Boat Sqdn No 490; 1945–69: served RAF, Singapore; Head, NZ Mil. Mission, Washington; served on NZ Air Bd as DCAS, subseq. as Air Mem. for Personnel, and Air Mem. for Supply; AOC Ops Gp. MP (Nat.) E Coast Bays, NZ, 1969–80; formerly: Chm., Public Expenditure Cttee; Nat. Party Spokesman on Health and Social Welfare; Mem., Nat. Party Policy Cttee; Minister: of Health, and of Immigration, 1975–78; of Defence, of Police, i/c of War Pensions, and i/c of Rehabilitation, 1978–80. *Address:* New Zealand Embassy, 37 Observatory Circle NW, Washington, DC 20008, USA.
    *Died 1 March 1982.*

**GILL-CAREY, Chapple,** FRCS; former Consulting Surgeon, Royal National Throat, Nose and Ear Hospital; former Consulting Ear, Nose and Throat Surgeon: Hospital of St John and St Elizabeth; Surbiton Hospital; Former Member, Council, Royal College of Surgeons; *b* 12 May 1897. MRCS Eng, LRCP London 1918; FRCS Ed. 1923; FRCS Eng 1948. Formerly: Surgeon, Ear, Nose and Throat Department, Hospital of St John and St Elizabeth; Chief Clinical Assistant, Ear, Nose and Throat Department, Guy's Hospital; Assistant Surgeon, Central London Throat, Nose and Ear Hospital; Dean of the Institute of Laryngology and Otology. Fellow Royal Society of Medicine. Ex-President British Association of Otolaryngologists. *Publications:* contributions to medical journals, etc. *Address:* 5 Holly Lodge Gardens, N6 6AA.
    *Died 21 Dec. 1981.*

**GILLAN, Sir (James) Angus,** KBE 1939; CMG 1935; *b* 11 Oct. 1885; *s* of late Rev. James Gillan, DD, and Margaret, *d* of John Wilson; *m* 1917, Margaret Douglas (*d* 1973), *d* of late M. A. Ord-Mackenzie; one *s*. *Educ:* Edinburgh Acad.; Magdalen Coll., Oxford. Rowed for Oxford 19707, 1909; won Stewards and Olympic IVs (Magdalen) 1908; Grand (Magdalen) 1911; Olympic VIIIs (Leander) 1912; Entered Sudan Political Service, 1909; Asst Political and Intelligence Officer, Sudan Western Frontier Force, 1916 (despatches twice, Order of Nile, 4th Class); Governor Kordofan Province, 1928; Asst Civil Sec., 1932; Civil Sec., 1934, retired 1939; Principal Officer, North Midland Civil Defence Region, Nottingham, 1940–41; Controller, Commonwealth and Empire Div., British Council, 1941–49; British Council Representative in Australia, 1949–51. Fellow, King's Coll., University of London (Treasurer, 1955–70). Pres., Royal Over-Seas League; Past Chairman: Conservative Commonwealth Council; Royal Over-Seas League; Sudan Govt British Pensioners' Assoc.; Anglo-Sudanese Assoc., etc. Order of Nile, 2nd Class, 1935. *Publications:* articles in various journals on the Sudan, Commonwealth affairs and cultural relations. *Recreations:* shooting, unskilled gardening and carpentering. *Address:* Sheep Cote Cottage, Leigh, Surrey. *T:* Norwood Hill 862432. *Clubs:* Athenæum, Leander, Royal Over-Seas League.
    *Died 23 April 1981.*

**GILLARD, Hon. Sir Oliver James,** Kt 1975; Judge of the Supreme Court of Victoria, 1962–78; *b* 2 June 1906; *s* of late E. T. V. Gillard, Stawell, Victoria; *m* 1934, Jean Gillon; three *s*. *Educ:* Stawell High; Melbourne Univ. BA, LLB. 2nd AIF, 1941–43, Captain. Teacher, Essendon High, 1923–26; Managing Clerk with Vincent Nolan, Solicitor, 1926–31; Barrister, 1930; Legal Office, Commonwealth Dept of Transport, 1943–44; QC 1950; Mem., Victoria Bar Council, 1957–62 (Chm., 1958–61). Chm., Chief Justice's Law Reform Cttee, 1973–78. Director: Murray Valley Coaches Ltd, 1947–50; Barristers' Chambers Ltd, 1959–62; Vary Bros Pty Ltd, 1954–62. Chancellor, Melbourne Univ., 1978–80. Chairman: Churchill Trust (Victoria), 1966–78; Youth Adv. Council, 1967–72; State Youth Council,

1973–78. Pres., Bayside Area Victoria Boy Scouts Assoc., 1963–71. *Recreations:* reading, golf. *Address:* 18 Asling Street, Brighton, Victoria 3186, Australia. *Died* 7 *Sept.* 1984.

**GILLESPIE, Robert,** CBE 1951; *b* 24 Nov. 1897; *s* of late James Gillespie and Ann Wilson Gillespie; *m* 1928, Isabella Brown (*d* 1980), *d* of late Dr Donald Murray, MP; one *s* one *d. Educ:* Queen's Park Sch., Glasgow. Joined Brit. Tanker Co. Ltd, 1922; Asst Manager, 1936; Gen. Manager, 1944; Dir and Gen. Manager, 1946; Managing Dir, 1950–56; a Dir, 1956–67; a Managing Dir of The British Petroleum Co. Ltd, 1956–58, retired; Mem., Council, Chamber of Shipping of UK, 1943–70. Served European War in Army, 1914–19; in ranks with Cameronians (Scottish Rifles) TF in UK; commnd KOSB, served UK, Palestine and France. War of 1939–45, served as Asst Dir, Tanker Div. of Ministry of War Transport, 1942–43. *Recreation:* contract bridge. *Address:* Craigrathan, Kippford, Dalbeattie, Kirkcudbrightshire. *T:* Kippford 653. *Died* 18 *Nov.* 1986.

**GILLETT, Eric;** Vice-Chairman, Scottish Wildlife Trust, 1982–86; *b* 22 July 1920; *m* 1945, Dorothy; one *s. Educ:* public primary and secondary schs; Downing Coll., Cambridge. Royal Artillery, 1942; Dept of Health for Scotland, 1946; Under-Sec., Scottish Home and Health Dept, 1969–71; Fisheries Sec., Dept of Agric. and Fisheries for Scotland, 1971–76; Sec., Scottish Develt Dept, 1976–80. Comr (Ombudsman) for Local Authority Services in Scotland, 1982–86. Chm., Scottish Assoc. of CAB, 1982–86. *Publication:* Investment in the Environment: a study of environmental policies in Scotland, 1983. *Recreations:* amateur chamber and orchestral music, hill walking, ancient buildings and the modern environment, Citizens' Advice Bureaux. *Address:* 66 Caiystane Terrace, Edinburgh EH10 6SW. *T:* 031-445 1184. *Died* 24 *April* 1987.

**GILLETT, Maj.-Gen. Sir Peter (Bernard),** KCVO 1979 (CVO 1973); CB 1966; OBE 1955; Governor, Military Knights of Windsor, 1980–89; *b* 8 Dec. 1913; *s* of Bernard George Gillett, OBE, Milford on Sea, Hants; *m* 1952, Pamela Graham, *widow* of Col R. J. Lloyd Price and *d* of Col Spencer Graham Walker, Winsley, Wilts. *Educ:* Marlborough Coll.; RMA, Woolwich. Commissioned RA, 1934; apptd to RHA, 1945; service in UK and India to 1944; War Office, 1944; BAOR, 1944–45; Instructor, Staff Coll., 1947–49; staff appts in UK and E Africa to 1955; Comd 5 RHA, 1955; SHAPE, 1958; CRA 3 Inf. Div., 1959; IDC, 1962; Chief of Staff, HQ Eastern Comd, 1962–65; GOC, 48th Div. TA, W Midland District, 1965–68. Sec., Central Chancery of the Orders of Knighthood, 1968–79. Col Comdt, Royal Regt of Artillery, 1968–78. *Recreations:* sailing, shooting and travel. *Address:* 4 Cumberland Lodge Mews, Windsor Great Park, Windsor SL4 2JD. *T:* Egham 72952. *Clubs:* Army and Navy, MCC, Royal Ocean Racing. *Died* 4 *July* 1989.

**GILLIE, Dame Annis Calder, (Dame Annis Smith),** DBE 1968 (OBE 1961); MB, BS London, FRCP; FRCGP; formerly in general medical practice (1925–63); *b* 3 Aug. 1900; *d* of late Rev. Dr Robert Calder Gillie and Emily Japp; *m* 1930, Peter Chandler Smith, MA, FRIBA (*d* 1983); one *s* one *d. Educ:* Wycombe Abbey Sch.; University Coll. and University Coll. Hosp., London. MRCP 1927. Member: BMA Council, 1950–64; Council of Medical Protection Soc., 1946–; Medical Practices Cttee, 1948–60; Med. Women's Federation (Pres. London Assoc., 1942–45, Pres. 1954); Foundn Mem., Royal College of General Practitioners (Chm., 1959–62, Pres., 1964–67); Mem., Central Health Services Advisory Council, 1956–70; North West Regional Hosp. Bd, 1958–63; Mem., Oxford Regional Hosp. Bd, 1964–74. Fellow, UCL, 1969. Hon. MD Edinburgh. *Publications:* contributions to medical jls. *Recreations:* reading, listening. *Address:* Bledington, Kingham, Oxford. *T:* Kingham 360. *Died* 10 *April* 1985.

**GILLIE, (Francis) Blaise,** CB 1958; Consultant in Town and Regional Planning; *b* 29 Feb. 1908; *s* of Rev. R. C. Gillie, Presbyterian Minister, and Emily Japp; *m* 1939, Mary Besly; three *s* one *d. Educ:* Gresham's Sch., Holt; Trinity Hall, Cambridge. Entered Ministry of Health, 1930. Asst Gen. Inspector, 1936, Principal, 1937; transf. to Min. of Works and Planning, 1942; Asst Sec., 1943; transf. to Min. of Town and Country Planning, 1943; Imperial Defence Coll., 1948; transf. to Min of Local Govt and Planning, 1951 (subseq. Dept of Environment); Under-Sec., 1954; Welsh Sec., 1957–63. OECD Consultant on Regional Planning, Turkish Govt, 1963–65; UN appointment, Afghanistan, 1965–67; UN Adviser to Nat. Inst. for Physical Planning and Construction Research, Ireland (An Foras Forbartha), 1967–70; Consultant to Irish Ind. Develt Authy, 1970; Research Associate, Inst. of Social Studies, The Hague, 1971; Sen. Lectr in Town and Regional Planning, American Univ. of Beirut, Lebanon, 1972–76. *Publications:* (pt-author with P. L. Hughes) Some Principles of Land Planning, 1950; Basic Thinking in Regional Planning, 1967; An Approach to Town Planning, 1971. *Recreations:* history, landscape. *Address:* Kennet House, Ramsbury, Wilts. *Died* 25 *May* 1981.

**GILLIES, Sir Alexander,** Kt 1959; FRCSEd, FRACS; MChOrth; Consulting Orthopædic Surgeon, Wellington, Nelson and Dannevirke Hospitals, New Zealand; *b* 1891; *s* of Gilbert Gillies; *m* 1920, Effie Lovica, *d* of James Pearson Shaw, Kamloops, BC; two *d* decd; *m* 1978, Joan Mary, *d* of Francis Joseph Kennedy, Wellington, NZ. *Educ:* Otago Boys' High Sch.; Edinburgh Univ. MB, ChB Ed 1923; DMRE Liverpool 1925; FRCSEd 1926; FRACS 1931; MChOrth Liverpool 1936. Asst Orthopædic Surgeon Robert Jones & Agnes Hunt Hosp., Oswestry, Salop, 1924; Fellow, Mayo Clinic, Rochester, Minnesota, 1928. Sen. Orthop. Surg., Wellington Hosp., NZ, 1929–50. President: NZ Red Cross Soc., 1953–61, later Pres. Emeritus (Counsellor of Honour, 1961); NZ Crippled Children Soc., 1968. Emeritus Fellow, Brit. Orthopædic Assoc., 1966. *Publications:* contrib. med. jls. *Recreation:* golf. *Address:* 10C Herbert Gardens, 186 The Terrace, Wellington C1, New Zealand. *T:* Wellington 729–444. *Died* 19 *Feb.* 1982.

**GILLSON, Thomas Huntington,** OBE 1973; HM Diplomatic Service, retired; *b* 2 July 1917; *s* of Robert and Ellen Gillson; *m* 1st, Margaret Dorothy Mumford (marr. diss.); two *d*; 2nd, 1969, Elizabeth Anne Fothergill (marr. diss.). *Educ:* Emanuel Sch., London. Bd of Educn, 1935; FO, 1937; served with Royal Corps of Signals, 1940–46; Budapest, 1946; FO, 1947; Milan, 1948; Buenos Aires, 1949; Warsaw, 1952; Vice-Consul, Kirkuk, 1953; FO, 1957; 1st Sec., The Hague, 1959; Pretoria, 1962; FO, 1966; Kabul, 1970; Counsellor, Ankara (Cento), 1973. *Recreation:* painting in watercolours (exhibitor RI, RWA, etc). *Address:* 7 Long Copse Court, Long Copse Lane, Emsworth, Hants PO10 7UW. *T:* Emsworth 6260. *Club:* Royal Commonwealth Society. *Died* 14 *Jan.* 1984.

**GILMOUR, Andrew,** CMG 1949; Malayan Civil Service, retired; *b* 18 July 1898; *s* of late James Parlane Gilmour, Solicitor, Burntisland, and late Mima Simpson; *m* Nelle Twigg (*d* 1983); two *s* three *d* (and one *s* killed in action). *Educ:* Royal High Sch., Edinburgh; Edinburgh Univ. (MA Hons Classics, 1920). Served European War, Argyll and Sutherland Highlanders, 1915–17. Appointed to Malayan Civil Service, 1921; Asst Controller of Labour, 1923–26; Head of Preventive Service, Singapore, 1927; Resident, Labuan, 1928–29; District Officer, Jasin, 1929–30, Ulu Kelantan, 1930–36; Asst Colonial Sec., SS, 1936–38; Registrar-Gen. of Statistics, SS and FMS, 1938–39; Shipping Controller, Singapore, 1939–41; Defence Intelligence Officer, Hong Kong, Dec. 1941; interned Hong Kong 1942–45; Sec. for Economic Affairs, Singapore, 1946–52; Staff Grade, MCS, 1947; Chm. N Borneo Rubber Commn, 1949; MEC and MLC Singapore (nominated official); acted as Colonial Sec., Singapore, June-Aug. 1948 and March-April 1952; ret. from Colonial Service, 1953; Planning Economist, UN Technical Assistance Mission, Cambodia, 1953–55; Economic Survey Commissioner, British Honduras, 1956. Secretary: British European Assoc., Singapore, 1956–75; Tanglin Trust Ltd, 1961–75; Raeburn Park School Ltd, 1961–75; Editor, BEAM, 1959–75. *Publications:* My Role in the Rehabilitation of Singapore 1946–53, 1973; An Eastern Cadet's Anecdotage, 1974. *Recreations:* cricket (Hon. Life Pres., Singapore Cricket Club); philately (Patron, Singapore Stamp Club). *Address:* Lorimer House, 491 Lanark Road, Juniper Green, Edinburgh EH14 5DQ. *T:* 031–442 2735. *Clubs:* Royal Over-Seas League; Singapore Cricket (Hon. Life Pres.).

*Died* 11 *July* 1988.

**GILMOUR, John Scott Lennox,** MA, FLS; Director, University Botanic Garden, Cambridge, 1951–73, retired; Fellow of Clare College, Cambridge, since 1951; *b* London, 28 Sept. 1906; *s* of late T. L. Gilmour, CBE, and Elizabeth, *o d* of late Sir John S. Keltie; *m* 1935, Molly, *y d* of late Rev. M. Berkley; three *d. Educ:* Uppingham Sch.; Clare Coll., Cambridge. Curator of the Herbarium and Botanical Museum, Cambridge, 1930–31; Asst Dir of Royal Botanic Gardens, Kew, 1931–46; seconded to Petroleum Div., Min. of Fuel and Power, as Principal Officer, 1940–45. Dir, Royal Horticultural Society's Garden, Wisley, Surrey, 1946–51. Sec., Systematics Assoc., 1937–46, Chm., 1952–55; Pres., Botanical Soc. of the British Isles, 1947–51; Chm. Internat. Commn on Horticultural Nomenclature, 1952–66, and International Cttee on Nomenclatural Stabilization, 1954; Rapporteur, Internat. Commission on the Nomenclature of Cultivated Plants, 1956–65, Chm., 1965–74; Brit. Rep., Council of Internat. Soc. Hort. Sci., 1960–73. Royal Horticultural Society: Victoria Medal of Honour in Horticulture, 1957; Mem. Council, 1957–61, 1962–66, 1968–73; Chm., Orchid Cttee, 1964–73; Veitch Gold Medal, 1966. Cons., new Botanic Garden at Ramat Hanadiv, Israel, 1964–68; Sec.-Treas. the Classification Society, 1964–68, Vice-Pres., 1968–78; Mem. Adv. Cttee Hunt Bot. Library, Pittsburgh, 1961–; Mem. Council, Bibliogr. Soc., 1963–68. Sandars Reader, Cambridge, 1971. First Chm., Cambridge Humanists, 1955–57, Pres., 1974–; Dir, Rationalist Press Assoc., 1961–74, Hon. Associate, 1976. *Publications:* British Botanists, 1944; Wild Flowers of the Chalk, 1947; Wild Flowers (in New Naturalist Series with S. M. Walters), 1954, pbk edn 1972; (ed) Thomas Johnson: Botanical Journeys in Kent and Hampstead, 1972; Some Verses, 1977; contributions to botanical, bibliographical, and rationalist jls, Jt Editor the New Naturalist, since 1943. *Recreations:* music, book-collecting. *Address:* 25 Fitzwilliam Road, Cambridge. *T:* Cambridge 355776. *Died* 3 *June* 1986.

**GILMOUR, Michael Hugh Barrie**; solicitor, retired; Chief Legal Adviser and Solicitor to British Railway Board, 1963–Jan. 1970 (Secretary to Board, Oct. 1965–Jan. 1968); *b* 1 Dec. 1904; *e* surv. *s* of late Thomas Lennox Gilmour, CBE, Barrister, and Elizabeth Hervey, *o c* of late Sir John Scott Keltie, LLD; *m* 1937, Elisabeth, *o d* of late Francis Edward Cuming; one *d*. *Educ:* Leighton Park; abroad. Solicitors Office, Great Western Railway Company, 1929; Solicitor to Company, 1945–47; Solicitor to Railway Executive in Western Region, 1948–49; Chief Solicitor (1949) and Chief Legal Adviser (1951), British Transport Commission, until 1962. Served War of 1939–45, RAFVR, July 1940–Sept. 1941 (Squadron Leader). *Recreations:* walking, reading. *Address:* 55 Strand-on-the-Green, Chiswick, W4 3PD. *Club:* Garrick.                    *Died* 3 *Dec.* 1982.

**GILPIN, John**; dancer; teaching, coaching and mounting ballet productions; *b* 10 Feb. 1930; twin *s* of W. J. and L. M. Gilpin; *m* 1st, 1960, Sally Judd; one *d*; 2nd, 1983, Princess Antoinette of Monaco. *Educ:* Cone-Ripman Sch. (Schol.). Michael, in Peter Pan, 1942, 1943; and other rôles (stage, films and broadcasting) until 1945, when he decided to devote himself exclusively to dancing. Awarded Adeline Genée Gold Medal, 1943. With Ballet Rambert, 1945–48; Roland Petit's Ballets de Paris, 1948–49; Grand Ballet du Marquis de Cuevas, 1950; Leading Dancer, Festival Ballet, 1950–72; guest dancer, Royal Ballet, 1961–62, and with Amer. Ballet Theatre, La Scala, Milan, Chicago Ballet, etc. Created many important rôles incl. Witch Boy; danced all leading classical rôles, incl. Swan Lake, Sleeping Beauty, Nutcracker, Giselle, also Spectre de la Rose, Etudes and special prodns of Carmina Burana, Madrid, 1979; Noël Coward's only ballet, London Morning, was written for him. Artistic Director: Fest. Ballet, 1965–67; Pittsburg Ballet, 1977. Produced: Firebird, Tokyo, 1971; Giselle, Dublin, Invitation to the Dance (première), Canada, 1980; Giselle, Iceland, Nutcracker, Gothenburg and Scottish Ballet's revival of Le Spectre de la Rose, 1982. Prix Vaslav Nijinsky, French Academy of Music and Dance, 1958; Queen Elizabeth II Coronation Award, 1953; Etoile d'Or, Paris, 1964. *Publication:* Dancing with Life (autobiog.), 1982; *relevant publication:* John Gilpin by Cyril Swinson. *Recreation:* music. *Address:* 3 Orme Court, W2.                    *Died* 5 *Sept.* 1983.

**GILPIN, Rt. Rev. William Percy**; *b* 26 July 1902; *e s* of late Percy William and Ethel Annie Gilpin. *Educ:* King Edward's, Birmingham; Keble Coll., Oxford. BA 1st class, Theology, 1925; MA 1928. Curate of Solihull, Warwicks, 1925–28; Vice-Principal of St Paul's Coll., Burgh, 1928–30; Chaplain of Chichester Theological Coll., 1930–33; Vicar of Manaccan with St Anthony, 1933–36; Vicar of St Mary, Penzance, 1936–44; Dir of Religious Education, Gloucester, 1944–51; Canon Missioner of Gloucester, 1946–52; Archdeacon of Southwark, 1952–55; Bishop Suffragan of Kingston-upon-Thames, 1952–70. Examining Chaplain to: Bishop of Truro, 1934–44, Bishop of Gloucester, 1945–52. *Recreation:* general railway matters. *Address:* 50 Lower Broad Street, Ludlow, Shropshire SY8 1PH. *T:* Ludlow 3376.                    *Died* 4 *Jan.* 1988.

**GILROY, John T. Y.**, ARCA, FRSA; artist; portrait and landscape painter; *b* 30 May 1898; *s* of John William Gilroy, artist; *m* 1924, Gwendoline Peri-Short; one *s*; *m* 1950, Elizabeth Outram Thwaite. *Educ:* King's Coll., Newcastle on Tyne; Hon. MA Univ. of Newcastle upon Tyne, 1975; Royal College of Art, London. Served European War, 1916–18, RFA. British Institute Scholar, 1921; RCA Travelling Scholar, 1922. Exhibition, Upper Grosvenor Galls, 1970. Creator of Guinness posters, 1925–60, also of Royle's publications of humour. Painted many famous portraits throughout Canada and America; also portraits of the Duke of Windsor when King Edward VIII; Queen Elizabeth the Queen Mother; Queen Elizabeth II, The Duke of Edinburgh (for RNEC); Princess Margaret; Prince Charles; Princess Anne; Field Marshal Earl Alexander of Tunis (Nat. Portrait Gall.); Earl Mountbatten of Burma; Rt Hon. Edward Heath; Lord Hailsham of Saint Marylebone; Sir Winston Churchill, 1942; Pope John; Sir Aubrey Smith; Sir John Clements; Sir John Gielgud; Sir Malcolm Sargent. Hon. MA Newcastle upon Tyne, 1976. *Publications:* (illustrated) McGill, The Story of a University, 1960; Rough Island Story (News Reel of Depression), 1931–35. *Recreations:* travelling, conversation. *Address:* 6 Ryecroft Street, Fulham, SW6. *T:* 01–736 9916. *Clubs:* Garrick (Life Mem.; Chm., Works of Art Cttee), Green Room.                    *Died* 11 *April* 1985.

**GILSON, John Cary**, CBE 1967 (OBE 1945); Director, Medical Research Council's Pneumoconiosis Research Unit, 1952–76; *b* 9 Aug. 1912; 2nd *s* of late Robert Cary Gilson, MA and late Marianne C. Gilson, MA (*née* Dunstall); *m* 1945, Margaret Evelyn Worthington, MA, *d* of late Robert A. Worthington, OBE, FRCS; two *s* one *d*. *Educ:* Haileybury Sch.; Gonville and Caius Coll., Cambridge. MB, BChir Cantab 1937; MRCP 1940; FRCP 1956; FFOM 1979. 1st Asst, London Hosp.; Staff of RAF Inst. of Aviation Medicine, 1940–46; Mem. Scientific Staff of MRC, 1946–76, at Pneumoconiosis Research Unit, Asst Ed., Brit. Jl Industr. Med., 1955–64, and on Ed. Bd of various other jls; Mem., Govt and internat. cttees on Pneumoconiosis and health hazards of asbestos;

Pres., British Occupational Hygiene Soc., 1960–61; Pres., Occupational Medicine Section, RSM, 1968–69; Hon. Life Mem., NY Acad. of Sciences, 1966. Hon. Fellow, Inst. of Occupational Hygienists, 1988. *Publications:* papers on pulmonary physiology and industrial medicine in scientific jls. *Recreations:* domestic engineering; clouds. *Address:* Hembury Hill Farm, Honiton, Devon EX14 0LA. *T:* Broadhembury 203.                    *Died* 1 *Dec.* 1989.

**GIMSON, (Arthur) Clive (Stanford)**, MBE 1944; MC 1945; Head Master, Blundell's School, 1971–80; *b* 28 June 1919; *s* of Harold Gimson, Leicester and Janet Marjorie Stanford, Aldringham, Suffolk; *m* 1957, Fiona Margaret Walton; three *s*. *Educ:* Uppingham Sch.; Clare Coll., Cambridge (Exhibr, MA). Royal Artillery, 1939–46; Sub-Warden, Mary Ward Settlement, 1947–48; Asst Master: Bradfield Coll., 1948–55; Melbourne Grammar Sch., 1956; Housemaster, Bradfield Coll., 1957–63; Head Master, Sebright Sch., 1963–70. *Recreations:* mountains and monasteries. *Address:* Mansard Cottage, Aldringham, Leiston, Suffolk.
                    *Died* 14 *Dec.* 1982.

**GINGOLD, Hermione Ferdinanda**; actress; *b* 9 Dec. 1897; *d* of James and Kate Gingold; *m* 1st, Michael Joseph (marr. diss.); one *s* (and one *s* decd); 2nd, Eric Maschwitz (marr. diss.). *Educ:* privately. Started as child actress at His Majesty's Theatre with Sir Herbert Tree in Pinkie and the Fairies. Played in Shakespeare at Old Vic and Stratford on Avon. Five years in intimate revue. O Dad, Poor Dad, Piccadilly, 1965; Highly Confidential, Cambridge, 1965; A Little Night Music, Majestic, New York, 1973, Adelphi, London, 1975; Side by Side by Sondheim, 1977–78. *Films:* Bell, Book and Candle, 1958; Gigi, 1959; Jules Verne's Rocket to the Moon, 1967; A Little Night Music. Many US television appearances. Has recorded Façade and Lysistrata. *Publications:* The World is Square: my own unaided work, 1945; Sirens should be Seen and Not Heard, 1963; articles and short stories. *Address:* 405 East 54th Street, New York, NY 10022, USA.                    *Died* 24 *May* 1987.

**GIRDWOOD, John Graham**, CBE 1946; CA; *b* 1890; 2nd *s* of late David Girdwood, Glasgow; *m* 1924, Janet Ellis Kerr (*d* 1976), *d* of late John Hood, Port Glasgow; no *c*. Controller of Canteens, Ministry of Supply, 1941–46; Controller of Admiralty Canteens, 1943–46; Chm. Min. of Health House Building Costs Cttee for England and Wales, 1947–53; Chm. of Aerated Bread Co. Ltd, 1948–58; Chm. of Wm Beardmore & Co. Ltd, 1954–57. Mem. of Council of Inst. of Chartered Accountants of Scotland, 1952–55. *Recreation:* golf. *Address:* 30 Hepburn Gardens, St Andrews, Fife KY16 9DF. *Clubs:* Carlton; Royal and Ancient (St Andrews).
                    *Died* 13 *March* 1981.

**GIVEN, Rear-Adm. John Garnett Cranston**, CB 1955; CBE 1945 (OBE 1943); MIMechE, MIMarE; retired from Royal Navy, June 1955; *b* 21 Sept. 1902; *s* of late J. C. M. Given, MD, FRCP, and Mrs May Given, Liverpool; *m* 1931, Elizabeth Joyce (*née* Payne) (*d* 1985), Brenchley, Kent, and Durban, Natal; one *s* two *d*. *Educ:* King William's Coll., IOM; Charterhouse, Godalming. RNEC Keyham, 1922–25; HMS Hood, 1926; RNC Greenwich, 1928; Admiralty, 1930; HMS Berwick, China Station, 1933; HMS Neptune, 1940; Admiralty, 1942; HMS Howe, East Indies, 1944; Fleet Train, British Pacific Fleet, 1945; Asst Engineer-in-Chief, Admiralty, 1947; Commanding Officer Royal Naval Engineering Coll., Plymouth, 1948–51; idc 1952; Staff of Comdr-in-Chief, The Nore, 1953–55; Managing Dir, Parsons Marine Turbine Co., Wallsend, 1955–62. *Recreations:* fishing and walking. *Address:* c/o National Westminster Bank, 26 The Haymarket, SW1.
                    *Died* 11 *July* 1988.

**GLASGOW, 9th Earl of**, *cr* 1703; **David William Maurice Boyle, CB** 1963; DSC 1941; Baron Boyle, 1699; Viscount of Kelburn, 1703; Baron Fairlie (UK), 1897; Rear-Admiral, retired; *b* 24 July 1910; *e s* of 8th Earl of Glasgow, DSO; *S* father, 1963; *m* 1st, 1937, Dorothea (marriage dissolved, 1962), *o d* of Sir Archibald Lyle, 2nd Bart; one *s* two *d*; 2nd, 1962, Vanda, the Hon. Lady Wrixon-Becher (*d* 1984), 2nd *d* of 4th Baron Vivian. *Educ:* Eton. Served War of 1939–45 in Atlantic, Channel, Arctic and Far East (despatches, DSC). Comdr, 1945; Capt., 1952; Capt. of the Fleet, Home Fleet, 1957–59; Commodore, RN Barracks, Portsmouth, 1959–61; Rear-Adm., 1961; Flag Officer, Malta, 1961–63; retd Sept. 1963. Mem. of the Royal Co. of Archers (Queen's Body Guard for Scotland). *Recreations:* shooting, golf, travel. *Heir:* *s* Viscount of Kelburn. *Address:* Kelburn Castle, Fairlie, Ayrshire. *T:* Fairlie 204. *Club:* New (Edinburgh).                    *Died* 8 *June* 1984.

**GLASGOW, Mary Cecilia**, CBE 1949 (MBE 1942); BA; Director (formerly Chairman), Mary Glasgow Holdings Ltd, Educational Publishers (firm founded 1957); *b* 24 May 1905; *d* of late Edwin Glasgow. *Educ:* Lady Margaret Hall, Oxford (Hons Sch. of French Language and Literature). Inspector of Schs, Bd of Education, 1933–39; Sec.-Gen., The Arts Council of Great Britain (formerly CEMA), 1939–51. Pres., The Opera Players. Fellow, Institute of Linguists, 1978– (Chm., 1975–78; Pres., 1978–81; Diamond Jubilee Medal, 1971); Trustee, Inst. of Linguists Educnl Trust Ltd (Chm.,

1976–82); Chm., Mary Glasgow Language Trust Ltd. Officer, L'Ordre National du Mérite, 1977 (Chevalier, 1968). FRSA 1983. *Address:* 5 Justice Walk, Chelsea, SW3 5DE. *T:* 01-352 7457; Entrechaux, 84340 Malaucène, France. *T:* Entrechaux (90) 36 07 48. *Died 31 Oct.* 1983.

**GLASS, Sir Leslie (Charles),** KCMG 1967 (CMG 1958); HM Diplomatic Service, retired; Chairman, Anglo-Romanian Bank, 1973–81; *b* 28 May 1911; *s* of Ernest Leslie and Kate Glass; *m* 1st, 1942, Pamela Mary Gage; two *s* (one *d* decd); 2nd, 1957, Betty Lindsay Hoyer-Millar (*née* Macpherson); two step *d. Educ:* Bradfield Coll.; Trinity Coll., Oxford (Hon. Fellow, 1982); Sch. of Oriental Studies, London Univ. Indian Civil Service, 1934; Asst Warden, Burma Oilfields, 1937; Settlement Officer, Mandalay, 1939; Far Eastern Bureau Min. of Inf., 1942; Lt-Col Head of Burma Section, Psychological Warfare Div., SEAC; Head of Information Div., Burma Mil. Admin, 1943; Sec. Information Dept, Govt of Burma, 1945; Comr of Settlements and Land Records, Govt of Burma, 1946; joined Foreign Office as 1st Sec. (Oriental Sec.), HM Embassy, Rangoon, 1947; Foreign Office, 1949–50; Head of Chancery, HM Legation Budapest (Chargé d'Affaires, 1951–52), 1950–53; Head of Information Div., British Middle East Office, 1953; seconded to Staff of Governor of Cyprus, 1955–56; Counsellor and Consul-Gen., British Embassy, Washington, 1957–58; Dir-Gen. of British Information Services in the US and Information Minister, British Embassy, Washington 1959–61; Minister employed in the Foreign Office, 1961; Asst Under-Sec. of State, Foreign Office, 1962–65; Ambassador to Romania, 1965–67; Ambassador and Dep. Permanent UK Representative to UN, 1967–69; High Comr in Nigeria, 1969–71, retired; re-employed FCO, 1971–72; Mem., Panel of Chairmen, CSSB, 1973–81. Governing Council, Bradfield Coll., 1973–81. Trustee, Thomson Foundn, 1974–86; Dir, Irvin Great Britain, 1981–. *Publication:* The Changing of Kings: memories of Burma 1934–1949, 1985. *Recreation:* fishing. *Address:* Stone House, Ivington, Leominster, Herefordshire. *T:* Ivington 204. *Club:* East India, Devonshire, Sports and Public Schools.

*Died 17 Dec.* 1988.

**GLASS, Ruth,** MA; Director, Centre for Urban Studies, University College London, since 1958; *b* 30 June 1912; *d* of Eli and Lilly Lazarus; *m* 1st, 1935, Henry Durant (marr. diss. 1941); 2nd, 1942, David V. Glass, FRS, FBA (*d* 1978); one *s* one *d. Educ:* Geneva and Berlin Univs; London Sch. of Economics; Columbia Univ., NY. Sen. Research Officer, Bureau of Applied Social Research, Columbia Univ., 1940–42; Res. Off., Min. of Town and Country Planning, 1948–50; University College London: Dir, Soc. Res. Unit, Dept of Town Planning, 1951–58; Hon. Res. Associate, 1951–71; Vis. Prof., 1972–85; Hon. Res. Fellow, 1986–. Visiting Professor: Essex Univ., 1980–86; London Univ. Inst. of Educn, 1984–87. Chm., Urban Sociol. Res. Cttee, Internat. Sociol Assoc., 1958–75. Editorial Adviser: London Jl; Internat. Jl of Urban and Regional Res.; Sage Urban Studies Abstracts. Hon. FRIBA, 1972. Hon. LittD Sheffield, 1982. *Publications:* Watling, A Social Survey, 1939; (ed) The Social Background of a Plan, 1948; Urban Sociology in Great Britain, 1955; Newcomers, The West Indians in London, 1960; London's Housing Needs, 1965; Housing in Camden, 1969; contributor to: Town Planning Review; Architectural Review; Population Studies; Internat. Social Science Jl; Monthly Review; Trans. World Congresses of Sociology, New Society, etc. *Address:* 10 Palace Gardens Terrace, W8; Eastway Cottage, Walberswick, Suffolk. *Died 7 March* 1990.

**GLAZEBROOK, His Honour Francis Kirkland;** a Circuit Judge (formerly a Judge of County Courts), 1950–72; *b* 18 Feb. 1903; 3rd *s* of late William Rimington Glazebrook; *m* 1930, Winifred Mary Elizabeth Davison (*d* 1984); one *s* two *d. Educ:* Marlborough Coll.; Trinity Coll., Cambridge; Harvard Univ., USA. Called to the Bar, Inner Temple, 1928; Practised in the Common Law. Served War in Army, 1939–45. Croix de Guerre (France); Bronze Star (USA). *Recreations:* fishing, gardening, golf. *Address:* Rectory Park, Horsmonden, Kent. *Died 7 March* 1988.

**GLAZEBROOK, Reginald Field;** formerly Director: Liverpool & London & Globe Insurance Co. Ltd; Liverpool Warehousing Co. Ltd; Liverpool Grain Storage & Transit Co. Ltd; Gandy Belt Ltd; *b* 23 April 1899; *s* of late William Rimington Glazebrook; *m* 1928, Daisy Isabel Broad; four *s. Educ:* Marlborough. Served European War, Lieut RFC, 1916–18. Cotton Merchant; Past Pres. Liverpool Cotton Assoc. *Recreations:* fishing, shooting, gardening. *Address:* Brynbella, Tremeirchion, St Asaph, Clwyd LL17 0UE. *Died 2 March* 1986.

**GLEADELL, Maj.-Gen. Paul,** CB 1959; CBE 1951; DSO 1945; *b* 23 Feb. 1910; *s* of late Captain William Henry and Katherine Gleadell; *m* 1937, Mary Montgomerie Lind, *d* of late Col Alexander Gordon Lind, DSO, and Mrs Lind; two *s* two *d. Educ:* Downside Sch.; Sandhurst. Commissioned in The Devonshire Regt, 1930 (Adjutant 1936–39); DAAG, Rawalpindi Dist, 1940; Staff Coll. (Quetta), 1941; Brigade Major 80th Indian Bde, 1942; Commanded 12th Bn

The Devonshire Regt (6th Airborne Div.), 1944–45; Secretariat, Offices of the Cabinet and Ministry of Defence, 1945–48; Joint Services Staff Coll., 1948; Col (G S Intelligence), GHQ Far East Land Forces, 1949–51; comd 1st Bn The Devonshire Regt (3rd Inf. Div.), 1951–53; Senior Army Instructor, Joint Services Staff Coll., 1953–55; Brigade Comdr, 24th Independent Infantry Brigade, 1955–56; Imperial Defence Coll., 1957; Chief of Staff to Dir of Operations, Cyprus, 1958–59; in command 44th Div. (TA) and Home Counties District, and Dep. Constable of Dover Castle, 1959–62; Dir of Infantry, 1962–65. Clerk to Governors, Rookesbury Park School, 1966–72, Governor, 1973–80. French Croix de Guerre with Palm, 1944. *Address:* Down Wood Lodge, Came, Dorchester, Dorset DT2 8NR. *Clubs:* Naval and Military, Challoner.

*Died 3 Aug.* 1988.

**GLEAVE, Ruth Marjory;** Headmistress, Bradford Girls' Grammar School, since 1976; *b* 29 May 1926; *d* of Harold Gleave and Alice Lillian Dean. *Educ:* Birkenhead High Sch., GPDST; Univ. of Liverpool (BA Hons Geography, DipEd). Head of Geography Dept, Wade Deacon Girls' Grammar Sch., Widnes, 1947–54; Head of Geography Dept and Deputy Head, Withington Girls' Sch., Manchester, 1954–60; Head, Fairfield High Sch., Droylsden, Manchester, 1960–75. *Recreations:* travel, natural history, outdoor activities, the arts—literature and art. *Address:* Bradford Girls' Grammar School, Squire Lane, Bradford BD9 6RB.

*Died 24 Dec.* 1986.

**GLEDHILL, Alan,** MA Cantab, LLD London; Professor Emeritus of Oriental Laws, University of London; Hon. Fellow, School of Oriental and African Studies; *b* 26 Oct. 1895; *s* of late O. Gledhill, Redroofs, Wells Road, Wolverhampton; *m* 1st, 1922, Mercy (*d* 1963), *d* of Victor Harvey, Calcutta; two *s* one *d*; 2nd, 1967, Marion Glover, *d* of late C. W. Watson, Santa Cruz, Argentine. *Educ:* Rugby; Corpus Christi Coll., Cambridge; Gray's Inn. Served European War, 1914–18, Lieut Monmouthshire Regt 1915–16; joined ICS 1920; District and Sessions Judge, 1927; Special Judge, Tharrawaddy, 1930–33; War of 1939–45; Dep. Comr, Cachar, Assam, 1942–43; Dep. Chief Judicial Officer, British Military Administration, Burma, 1944–45 (despatches); Actg Judge High Court Rangoon, Oct. 1945; Puisne Judge, 1946–48; Lecturer in Indian and Burmese Law, Sch. of Oriental and African Studies, 1948–54; Reader in Oriental Laws, 1954–55; Prof. of Oriental Laws, University of London, 1955–63; Lectr in Hindu Law, Inns of Court Sch. of Law, 1955–67. *Publications:* The British Commonwealth: The Development of its Laws and Constitutions, Vol 6, The Republic of India, 1951 (2nd edn, 1964). Vol. 8, The Islamic Republic of Pakistan, 1957 (2nd edn, 1967); Fundamental Rights in India, 1955; The Penal Codes of Northern Nigeria and the Sudan, 1963. *Recreations:* swimming, walking. *Address:* Springwood Residential Home, Duffield, Derby. *Club:* Royal Commonwealth Society. *Died 16 July* 1983.

**GLEDSTANES, Elsie,** RBA 1929 (ARBA 1923); portrait, figure and landscape painter; *b* 21 Jan. 1891; *d* of late Francis Garner Gledstanes, late mem. Stock Exchange Cttee. *Educ:* Eastbourne; Paris. Studied art at Paris, Slade Sch. and Byam Shaw, and Vicat Cole Sch. of Art; served in WRNS, 1917–18; London Auxiliary Ambulance Driver, 1939–45; WVS Transport, 1941–42; Driver Women's Legion, 1942–45; exhibited works in RA, RBA, RPS, NPS, International Soc. and in the Provinces; works in Imperial War Museum, etc. Mem. of Pastel Soc. FRSA. *Address:* 61 Campden Street, W8 7EL. *T:* 01-727 8663; Glan-y-Gors, Prenteg, Portmadoc. *T:* Portmadoc 2510. *Died 23 Nov.* 1982.

**GLENAVY, 4th Baron** *cr* 1921; **Michael Mussen Campbell;** Bt 1916; *b* 25 Oct. 1924; *s* of 2nd Baron Glenavy and Beatrice Moss (*d* 1970), *d* of William Elvery, Rothbury, Foxrock, Co. Dublin; *S* brother, 1980. *Educ:* St Columba's College, Rathfarnham; Trinity Coll., Dublin. Called to the Bar, King's Inns, Dublin, 1947. *Publications:* Peter Perry, 1956; Oh Mary This London, 1959; Across the Water, 1961; The Princess in England, 1964; Lord Dismiss Us, 1967; Nothing Doing, 1970. *Heir:* none. *Address:* 39 Kendal Street, W2.

*Died June* 1984 (*ext*).

**GLENCONNER, 2nd Baron,** *cr* 1911; **Christopher Grey Tennant;** Bt *cr* 1885; *b* 14 June 1899; *s* of 1st Baron and Pamela (*d* 1928), *d* of late Hon. Percy Scawen Wyndham (she *m* 2nd, 1922, 1st Viscount Grey); *S* father, 1920; *m* 1st, 1925, Pamela (who obtained a divorce, 1935), 2nd *d* of Sir Richard Paget, 2nd Bt; two *s*; 2nd, 1935, Elizabeth Mary, *er d* of late Lieut-Col E. G. H. Powell; one *s* two *d. Heir:* *s* Hon. Colin Christopher Paget Tennant. *Address:* Rovinia, Liapades, Corfu, Greece. *Club:* White's. *Died 4 Oct.* 1983.

**GLENDAY, Dorothea Nonita;** MA Oxon; Headmistress, Clifton High School for Girls, 1933–62; President, Association of Headmistresses, 1958–60; *b* 10 May 1899. *Educ:* Girls' Grammar Sch., Bury, Lancs; St Hugh's Coll., Oxford. Hons Degree in English Language and Literature. Senior English Mistress at Francis Holland Church of England Sch., Graham Street, London, 1921–26. International hockey player. Headmistress of Rugby High Sch., 1926–33. Pres.

West of England Branch of Assoc. of Headmistresses, 1946–48; Chm. of Assoc. of Independent and Direct-Grant Schs, 1949–51. *Publication:* Reluctant Revolutionaries, 1974. *Address:* 1 Hayward Road, Oxford. *Club:* University Women's.
*Died 18 May 1982.*

**GLENDINNING, Edward Green;** Chief Executive, City of Edinburgh District Council, 1975–80; *b* 3 Dec. 1922; *yr s* of late George M. Glendinning and Isabella Green; *m* 1944, Jane Rollo Dodds Greig; one *s* one *d. Educ:* Boroughmuir Sch., Edinburgh; Edinburgh Univ. (BL). Lieut RNVR (Air Br., Pilot), 1941–46; Edinburgh Univ., 1940–41 and 1946–48; admitted Solicitor, 1948; Edinburgh Corporation, 1949; Depute Town Clerk, 1959; Town Clerk, City and Royal Burgh of Edinburgh, 1972–75. Comdr, Order of Pole Star (Sweden), 1976. *Recreations:* friends, talking, listening to music, walking (but not too far). *Died 7 July 1984.*

**GLENKINGLAS, Baron** *cr* 1974 (Life Peer), of Cairndow, Argyll; **Michael Antony Cristobal Noble,** PC 1962; *b* 19 March 1913; 3rd *s* of Sir John Henry Brunel Noble, 1st Bt, of Ardkinglas; *m* 1940, Anne, *d* of Sir Neville Pearson, 2nd Bt; four *d. Educ:* Eton Coll.; Magdalen Coll., Oxford. Served RAFVR, 1941–45. Argyll County Council, 1949–51. MP (C) Argyllshire, June 1958–Feb. 1974; PPS to Sec. of State for Scotland, 1959; Asst Govt Whip (unpaid), 1960 (Scottish Whip, Nov. 1960); a Lord Comr of the Treasury, 1961–62; Sec. of State for Scotland, 1962–64; President of the Board of Trade, June–Oct. 1970; Minister for Trade, DTI, Oct. 1970–Nov. 1972. Chm., Unionist Party in Scotland, 1962–63. Chairman: Associated Fisheries, 1966–70; Glendevon Farms (Winchburgh), 1969–70; British Agricultural Export Council, 1973–77; Hanover Housing (Scotland) Assoc., 1978–80; Director: John Brown Engineering Ltd, 1973–77; Monteith Holdings Ltd, 1974–. *Recreations:* gardening, fishing, shooting. *Address:* Strone, Cairndow, Argyll. *T:* Cairndow 284. *Club:* Boodle's. *Died 15 May 1984.*

**GLENN, William James,** CB 1968; BA, BAI, FICE; Director-General, Water Engineering, Department of the Environment, 1971–72, retired; *b* 26 June 1911; *s* of late John Glenn, Londonderry; *m* 1937, Wilhelmina Jane Gibson, MA, *d* of late John Gibson, Dublin; two *s. Educ:* Trinity Coll., Dublin Univ. Entered Air Min. as Asst Civil Engr, Directorate Gen. of Works, 1937; Sen. Civil Engr, Air HQ, W Africa, 1944–45; service in Airfield Construction Br, RAF, BAFO Germany, 1948–50; Chief Engr Flying Trng Comd, RAF, 1952–54; Dep. Dir of Works, 1956–57; Chief Engr, Far East Air Force, 1957–59; Dir of Works, 1962–65; Chief Civil Engr, MPBW, 1965–68; Chief Engineer, Min. of Housing and Local Govt, 1968–71. Mem. Bd, Maplin Develt Authy, 1973–74. Hon. FIPHE. *Recreation:* golf. *Address:* Bucklers, Hungerford Lane, Shurlock Row, near Reading RG10 0NY. *T:* Twyford 343445. *Clubs:* Royal Air Force; East Berkshire Golf.
*Died 31 Jan. 1984.*

**GLENNIE, Alan Forbes Bourne,** CMG 1956; *b* 11 April 1903; *s* of late Vice-Adm. R. W. Glennie, CMG; *m* 1931, Dorothy Sybil, *d* of late J. A. H. Johnston, DSc; one *s* one *d. Educ:* RN Colls Osborne and Dartmouth; Trinity Coll., Cambridge (MA). Joined Provincial Administration, N Rhodesia, 1924; Provincial Commissioner, 1945; Resident Commissioner, Barotseland Protectorate, Northern Rhodesia, 1953–57, retired; Government Sec., St Helena, 1963–65, retired. *Address:* 85 Gibson Road, Kenilworth, 7700, Cape Province, Republic of South Africa. *Club:* Royal Over-Seas League.
*Died 12 Sept. 1984.*

**GLOAG, John (Edwards);** author; *b* 10 Aug. 1896; *s* of Robert McCowan Gloag and Lillian Morgan; *m* 1922, Gertrude Mary (*d* 1981), *d* of late Ven. G. H. Ward; one *s* one *d. Educ:* Battersea Grammar Sch.; largely self-educated. Studied architecture at Regent Street Polytechnic, 1911–13; with studio Thornton-Smith Ltd, 1913–16; served in Essex Regt, 1916; Household Brigade Cadet Battalion, 1917; 2nd Lieut Welsh Guards, 1918; served with 1st Bn BEF, May–Aug. 1918, and invalided home; Technical and Art Ed. of the Cabinet Maker, 1922; Ed., 1927; Dir, Pritchard, Wood & Partners Ltd, 1928–61; Public Rel. Dir, Timber Development Assoc., 1936–38. FSA; Hon. FRIBA; Hon. FSIA; RSA Silver Medal, 1943, Bicentenary Gold Medal, 1958. Member: Utility Furniture Advisory Cttee (Board of Trade), 1943–47; Council of Industrial Design, 1949–55; Council of Royal Society of Arts, 1948–56, 1958–63 (Vice-Pres., 1952–54); Bd of Trustees, Sir John Soane's Mus., 1960–70; Chairman: Internat. Conf. on Industrial Design, 1951; Council of Building Centre, 1950–64; Pres. of the Soc. of Architectural Historians of Great Britain, 1960–64. Broadcast talks and short stories, 1933 onwards; Mem. team in: Men Talking; Design in Modern Life; Brains Trust (occasionally Question Master); a few appearances on TV, before and after 1939–45 war. *Publications: fiction:* To-Morrow's Yesterday, 1932; The New Pleasure, 1933; Winter's Youth, 1934; Sweet Racket, 1936; Ripe for Development, 1936; Sacred Edifice, 1937 (new edn, with foreword by Sir Basil Spence, 1954); It Makes a Nice Change, 1938; Documents Marked Secret, 1938; Manna, 1940; Unwilling Adventurer, 1940; I Want an Audience, 1941; Mr Buckby is Not at Home, 1942; Ninety-nine per cent, 1944; In Camera, 1945; First One and Twenty (omnibus), 1946; Kind Uncle Buckby, 1947; All England at Home, 1949; Take One a Week, 1950; Not in the Newspapers, 1953; Slow, 1954; Unlawful Justice, 1962; Rising Suns, 1964; Ceasar of the Narrow Seas, 1969; The Eagles Depart, 1973; Artorius Rex, 1977; *verse:* Board Room Ballads, 1933; *architecture and design:* Colour and Comfort, 1924; Men and Buildings, 1931 (illustr. edn, 1950); Artifex or the Future of Craftsmanship, 1926; English Furniture (Library of English Art), 1934 (6th edn, 1973); Design in Modern Life (ed.), 1934; Industrial Art Explained, 1934; The Place of Glass in Building (ed), 1942; The Missing Technician in Industrial Production, 1944; The Englishman's Castle, 1944; Plastics and Industrial Design, 1945; House out of Factory (with Grey Wornum, FRIBA), 1945; British Furniture Makers, 1945; Self-training for Industrial Designers, 1947; The English Tradition in Design, 1947 (revised and enlarged edn, 1959); A History of Cast Iron in Architecture (with D. L. Bridgewater, FRIBA), 1948; How to write Technical Books, 1951; A Short Dictionary of Furniture, 1952 (rev. edn, 1965, abridged edn, 1966, enl. rev. edn, 1969); Georgian Grace, 1956, rev. edn, 1967; Guide to Western Architecture, 1958, rev. edn 1969; Introduction to Catalogue of Irwin Untermyer Coll. of Eng. Furniture for Metropolitan Museum of Art, NY, 1958; Victorian Comfort, 1961, rev. edn, 1973; Victorian Taste, 1962, rev. edn, 1972; The English Tradition in Architecture, 1963; Architecture (Arts of Man), 1963; The Englishman's Chair, 1964; Enjoying Architecture, 1965; Introduction to Early English Decorative Detail, 1965; (with Maureen Stafford) Guide to Furniture Styles, English and French, 1972; The Architectural Interpretation of History, 1975; *social history:* Home Life in History, 1927, with C. Thompson Walker; Time, Taste and Furniture, 1925; Word Warfare, 1939; The American Nation, 1942 (revised, enlarged edn, with Julian Gloag, 1954); What About Business?, 1943 (enlarged edn entitled What About Enterprise?, 1948); 2000 Years of England, 1952; Advertising in Modern Life, 1959; A Social History of Furniture Design, 1966; *biography:* Mr Loudon's England, 1970. *Recreation:* reading. *Address:* 3 The Mall, East Sheen, SW14 7EN. *T:* 01-876 4530. *Clubs:* Arts, Garrick. *Died 17 July 1981.*

**GLOVER, Derek Harding,** CBE 1967; Special Duties Director, British Airways Board, 1975–76 retired (Member and Group Financial Director, 1971–74); *b* 17 April 1916; *s* of Harold Harding Glover and Dora McRae; *m* 1947, Joan Marjorie Piper; two *s. Educ:* Hillcrest Prep. Sch., Frinton-on-Sea; Leys Sch., Cambridge. ACA 1937. Services, 1939–46; BOAC, 1946–71. Chm., International Aeradio Ltd, 1971–76 (Dir, 1963–76); Chm., Airways Pension Scheme, 1971–78. *Recreations:* golf, gardening, good food. *Address:* Cockers, Burwash, Etchingham, Sussex. *T:* Burwash 882536.
*Died 2 Nov. 1981.*

**GLOVER, Sir Douglas,** Kt 1960; TD 1945; *b* 13 Feb. 1908; *s* of S. Barnish Glover, Rochdale; *m* 1st, 1934, Agnes May (*d* 1976), *d* of William Brown, JP, Netherlaw, Kirkcudbright, and Longfield, Heaton Mersey; no *c*; 2nd, 1976, Margaret Eleanor Hurlimann, *widow* of Erwin Hurlimann, Schloss Freudenberg, Rotkreuz, Kanton Zug, Switzerland. *Educ:* Giggleswick. TA 1939; 7th Manchester Rgt, 52 Div., NW Europe; Lieut-Col comdg Princess Louise Kensington Regt, 49 Div., 1945; despatches, 1946; comdg 9th Manchester Regt TA 1947–50; Bt-Col 1950; TARO 1950. Contested (C) Blackburn, 1945, Stalybridge and Hyde, 1950 and 1951; MP (C) Ormskirk, 1953–70; Mem. Public Accounts Cttee, 1965–70. Chairman Young Conservatives, North-West Area, 1946; Treasurer, North-West, 1951–54; Mem., Nat. Exec. of Conservative Party, 1951–69; Chm. N Western Area, 1956–60; Chm., Nat. Union of Conservative Assocs, 1961–62. Pres., Cheadle Cons. Assoc., 1974–77. Delegate 10th Commonwealth Parl. Conf., Canberra, 1959. Mem. Mr Speaker's Panel of Chm., 1961; Chm. United and Cecil Club, 1962–65; Deleg. 17th Gen. Assembly of the UN, New York, 1962; Vice-Chm., Lancs and Ches Mems Cttee, 1966; Pres., Lancastrian Assoc., 1966; Chm., Anti-Slavery Soc., 1965–73; Mem. Coun., Nat. Fedn of Housing Assocs, 1966–72; Chm. Pierhead Housing Soc., 1965–76. Governor, Giggleswick School, 1970 (Chm., 1975–77). Knight Officer, Order of Orange Nassau, 1946. *Address:* Schloss Freudenberg, 6343 Rotkreuz, Kanton Zug, Switzerland. *T:* Rotkreuz (042) 641126; 94 Avenue d'Iena, 75116 Paris, France. *T:* 720 0481. *Clubs:* Carlton, Turf. *Died 15 Jan. 1982.*

**GLOVER, Sir Gerald (Alfred),** Kt 1971; Consultant, Glover & Co.; President, Edger Investments Ltd, since 1980; *b* 5 June 1908; *m* 1933, Susan Drage (OBE 1982; Chm., Nat. Adoption Soc. for England); two *d. Educ:* City of London School. Solicitor, 1932. King's Messenger, 1938–40; served War of 1939–45, Mil. Intell., at home and abroad; Major. Conservative Party: Mem. 1935–; Chm. 1963–71, Vice-Pres. 1972–74, Patron 1978–, E Midland Area Exec.; Treas. Kettering Div., 1953–67; President: Kettering Cons. Club, 1970–; Kettering Cons. Assoc., 1971–. Patron, London Branch, Red Cross; Trustee: National Adoption Soc. for England; Bankside Arts Centre; Founder: South Bank Arts Centre and Gallery, Southwark; East Kent Arts Centre and Gallery, Folkestone; Pres., Kettering and District Scouts; Past Pres., Northants Agricultural Soc. (Pres., 1970). CC Northants (Vice-Chm., 1972–74; Chm., Police Authority, 1978–81). Liveryman, Basketmakers' Co. Freeman, City of London. *Recreations:* bloodstock breeding and racing (bred, raced and owns Privy Councillor, winner of 2000 Guineas, 1962), landscape gardening, visual art. *Address:* Pytchley House, Northants. *T:* Kettering 790258. *Clubs:* White's, Boodle's.

*Died 12 Dec. 1986.*

**GLOVER, Harold,** CB 1977; coinage consultant; *b* 29 Jan. 1917; 4th *s* of late George Glover, Wallasey, Ches; *m* 1949, Olive, *d* of late E. B. Robotham, Sawbridgeworth, Herts; two *s. Educ:* Wallasey Gram. Sch. Joined Customs and Excise, 1933; joined Min. of Works, 1949 (now DoE); Controller of Supplies, 1957; Under-Secretary, 1967–70; Dep. Master, Royal Mint, 1970–74; Controller, HMSO, 1974–77. Served RAF, 1940–46 (Flt Lieut Signals). FRSA 1963 (Mem Council, 1974–79; Bicentenary Medal, 1967); Hon. FCSD (Hon. FSIAD 1975). *Recreation:* music. *Address:* 23 Walnut Tree Crescent, Sawbridgeworth, Herts. *T:* Bishops Stortford 723256. *Clubs:* Reform, Royal Air Force. *Died 30 April 1988.*

**GLUBB, Lt-Gen. Sir John Bagot,** KCB 1956; CMG 1946; DSO 1941; OBE 1925; MC; Chief of General Staff, the Arab Legion, Amman, Jordan, 1939–56; *b* 16 April 1897; *s* of late Maj.-Gen. Sir F. M. Glubb, KCMG, CB, DSO; *m* 1938, Muriel Rosemary, *d* of Dr J. G. Forbes; one *s* and one *s* two *d* adopted. *Educ:* Cheltenham; Royal Military Academy, Woolwich, Aug. 1914; 2nd Lieut RE, 1915; served in France (wounded thrice, MC); to Iraq as Lieut RE, 1920; resigned commission, 1926, and became Administrative Inspector, Iraq Govt; transferred Transjordan, 1930; Officer Commanding Desert Area, 1932; Officer Commanding Arab Legion, Transjordan, 1939–56. *Publications:* Story of the Arab Legion, 1948; A Soldier with the Arabs, 1957; Britain and the Arabs, 1959; War in the Desert, 1960; The Great Arab Conquests, 1963; The Empire of the Arabs, 1963; The Course of Empire, 1965; The Lost Centuries, 1967; The Middle East Crisis–A Personal Interpretation, 1967; Syria, Lebanon, Jordan, 1967; A Short History of The Arab Peoples, 1969; The Life and Times of Muhammad, 1970; Peace in the Holy Land, 1971; Soldiers of Fortune, 1973; The Way of Love, 1974; Haroon al Rasheed, 1976; Into Battle: a soldier's diary of the Great War, 1977; Arabian Adventures, 1978; A Purpose for Living, 1979; The Changing Scenes of Life (autobiog.), 1983. *Address:* West Wood, Mayfield, Sussex. *Died 17 March 1986.*

**GLUECKAUF, Eugen,** DrIng, DSc, FRS 1969; Consultant, Atomic Energy Research Establishment, since 1971; *b* 9 April 1906; *m* 1934, Irma E. A. Glueckauf (*née* Tepper); one *d. Educ:* Technische Hochschule, Berlin. Research Asst to Prof. F. A. Paneth, Imperial Coll., London, 1934–39; Res. Associate, Durham Colls, 1939–47; Mackinnon Res. Student of Royal Society, 1942–44. Group-leader and later Branch-head in Chem. Div., AERE, Harwell, 1947–71. *Publications:* Atomic Energy Waste, 1961; contribs in fields of: microgasanalysis of atmospheric gases, theory of ion exchange and chromatography, radio chemistry, electrolyte solution chemistry. *Recreations:* gardening, music. *Address:* Bankside, Chilton, Oxon OX11 0RZ. *T:* Abingdon 834296. *Died 11 Sept. 1981.*

**GLYNN, Prudence Loveday, (The Lady Windlesham);** journalist; editorial staff of The Times, 1966–81 (Fashion Editor, 1966–80); *b* 22 Jan. 1935; *d* of late Lt-Col R. T. W. Glynn, MC, and Evelyn Margaret Vernet Glynn; *m* 1965, 3rd Baron Windlesham; one *s* one *d.* Member: Design Council, 1973–79; selection panel, Duke of Edinburgh's Design prize, 1971–73; CNAA, 1977–; CNAA Cttee for Art and Design, 1972–; Crafts Council, 1977–80; Mem. Council, Royal College of Art, 1969–77. Governor, English-Speaking Union, 1972–78; Trustee, Museum of London, 1981–. FRSA 1974. Cavaliere al merito della Repubblica Italiana, 1975. *Publications:* In Fashion, 1978; Skin to Skin, 1982; Harpers and Queen Faces and Fashion— The Last Sixty Years, 1984; contribs to numerous jls, television etc. *Address:* 26 Powis Terrace, W11 1JH. *T:* 01–229 2975.

*Died 24 Sept. 1986.*

**GLYNN GRYLLS, Rosalie;** *see* Mander, Lady (Rosalie).

**GOADBY, Hector Kenneth,** FRCP; retired; Hon. Consulting Physician, St Thomas' Hospital, London; *b* 16 May 1902; *s* of late Sir Kenneth Goadby, KBE; *m* 1937, Margaret Evelyn (*née* Boggon); one *s* two *d. Educ:* Winchester; Trinity Coll., Cambridge (MA, MD). MRCS, LRCP 1926; FRCP 1936. Physician, St Thomas's Hosp., 1934–67; Cons. Physician, Southern Army and Eastern Comd, India, 1945; Physician, St Peter's Hosp., Chertsey, 1948. *Publications:* contribs to Jl of Physiology, Lancet, Acta Medica Scandinavica. *Recreations:* sailing, golf. *Address:* High House Farm, 54 High House Drive, Rednal, Birmingham B45 8ET. *T:* 021–445 5169. *Club:* Rye Golf. *Died 25 Sept. 1990.*

**GOBBI, Tito;** opera singer, baritone; *b* 24 Oct. 1915; *s* of Giovanni and Enrica Weiss; *m* 1937, Tilde de Rensis; one *d. Educ:* Padua Univ. Scholarship, Scala Opera House, 1936–37. Appeared Rome Opera House, 1939. Repertoire of 100 operas. Has sung in all the major opera houses and concert halls throughout the world. Notably Salzburg Festival: Don Giovanni (under Fürtwangler), 1950; Falstaff (under von Karajan), 1957. Has recorded 30 Complete Operas and made numerous other records; has made many films and appeared on television all over the world. Started as Stage Director, Lyric Opera of Chicago, Oct. 1965; then Royal Opera House, Covent Garden; Master classes in Italy, USA and UK; Director: Opera Workshop, Florence, 1971–81; Studio dell'Opera Italiana, Asolo, 1981–. Mem., The Friends of Covent Garden; Hon. Mem., Univ. of Chicago; Hon. RAM. Dr *hc* Rosary Coll., River Forest, Ill, USA, 1980. Disco d'Oro (Golden Record), 1959; Leopardo d'Oro, 1962. Hon. Officer, NY Police, 1969. Commendatore al Merito della Repubblica Italiana, 1958; Officer of San Jago, Portugal, 1970; Grand Officer, Order of Merit, Italy, 1976. *Publication:* My Life, 1979. *Recreations:* painting, driving, shooting, moulding. *Address:* via Valle della Muletta 47, 00123 La Storta, Rome, Italy. *T:* 3790996. *Clubs:* Arts (London) (Hon. Mem.); Societa Dante Alighieri; (Patron) Verdi Soc. (Liverpool); Roma Libera (Rome); Lyons (Hon. Mem.). *Died 5 March 1984.*

**GODDARD, Maj.-Gen. John Desmond,** MC 1944; *b* 13 Jan. 1919; *s* of late Major J. Goddard, HAC, Bombay and Gerrards Cross, Bucks; *m* 1948, Sheila Noel Vera, *d* of late C. W. H. P. Waud, Bombay and St John, Jersey; three *s* one *d. Educ:* Sherborne; RMA Woolwich. 2 Lieut, RA, 1939. Served War of 1939–45: France, 1939–40; N Africa, 1943; Italy, 1943–45. Brevet Lt-Col 1957; JSSC 1957; CO, 2 Fd Regt, RA, 1960–62; IDC 1964; CRA, 3 Div., 1965–66; BGS, Directorate Mil. Ops, MoD, 1966–69; Dir, Mil. Assistance Office, MoD, 1969–72, retired. Staff Dir, British Leyland Internat., 1972–78. *Recreations:* yachting, riding, shooting, golf, carpentry, gardening. *Address:* Cranford, Pinewood Hill, Fleet, Hants GU13 9AW. *T:* Fleet (0252) 614825. *Clubs:* Army and Navy; Royal Lymington Yacht. *Died 14 Sept. 1990.*

**GODDARD, Air Marshal (retired) Sir (Robert) Victor,** KCB 1947 (CB 1943); CBE 1940; MA Cantab; *b* 6 Feb. 1897; *s* of late Charles Ernest Goddard, OBE, TD, MD; *m* 1924, Mildred Catherine Jane (*d* 1979), *d* of Alfred Markham Inglis; two *s* one *d. Educ:* RN Colls Osborne and Dartmouth; Jesus Coll., Cambridge; Imperial Coll. of Science, London. Served European War, 1914–19, with RN, RNAS, RFC and RAF; War of 1939–45 (despatches, American DSM); Dep. Dir of Intelligence, Air Min., 1938–39; AOA, GHQ, BEF, France, 1939, SASO 1940; Dir of Military Co-operation, Air Ministy, 1940–41; Chief of the Air Staff, New Zealand, and Commander Royal NZ Air Forces, South Pacific, 1941–43; AOA, Air Command, South-East Asia, 1943–46; RAF Representative at Washington, USA, 1946–48; Mem. of Air Council for Technical Services, 1948–51; retd 1951. Principal of the Coll. of Aeronautics, 1951–54. Vice-Pres., Airship Assoc., 1984– (Pres., 1975–84). Governor (Chm. 1948–57), St George's Sch., Harpenden, 1948–64; Governor, Bryanston Sch., 1957–78. Occasional broadcaster, 1934–. *Publications:* The Enigma of Menace, 1959; Flight towards Reality, 1975; Skies to Dunkirk, 1982. *Address:* Meadowgate Lodge, Brasted, Westerham, Kent TN16 1LN. *Died 21 Jan. 1987.*

**GODFREY, Derrick Edward Reid,** MSc, PhD; Director, Thames Polytechnic, 1970–78; *b* 3 May 1918; *s* of Edward Godfrey; *m* 1944, Jessie Mary Richards; three *s* one *d. Educ:* Shooters Hill Grammar Sch.; King's Coll., London. Design and development of aero-engines, with D. Napier & Sons, 1940–45; Lectr and Reader in Applied Mathematics, Battersea Polytechnic, 1945–58; Head of Dept of Mathematics and later Principal, Woolwich Polytechnic, 1958–70. Mem. Council for Nat. Academic Awards, 1964–67. *Publications:* Elasticity and Plasticity for Engineers, 1959; contribs to learned jls, etc, on mathematics and on educational matters. *Recreations:* music, gardening. *Address:* The Oaks, Beech Park, West Hill, Ottery St Mary, Devon EX11 1UG. *T:* Ottery St Mary 2551. *Died 17 Dec. 1989.*

**GODWIN, Prof. Sir Harry,** Kt 1970; FRS 1945; FLS; MA, ScD; Professor of Botany, University of Cambridge, 1960–68, Emeritus 1968; Fellow of Clare College, Cambridge, since 1925; *b* 9 May 1901; *m* 1927, Margaret Elizabeth Daniels; one *s* decd. University Reader in Quaternary Research, Cambridge, Oct. 1948–60. Croonian Lectr, Royal Soc., London, 1960. Pres., Xth International Botanical Congress, 1964. Foreign Member: Royal Danish Acad. of Science and Letters; Royal Scientific Soc. of Uppsala; German Acad. of Science Leopoldina; Amer. Acad. Arts and Scis; Life Mem., Quaternary Research Assoc., 1981; Hon. Mem., Royal Soc. of New Zealand; MRIA. Hon. ScD, Trinity Coll., Dublin, 1960. Hon. DSc: Lancaster, 1968; Durham, 1974. Prestwick Medal, Geol. Soc., London, 1951; Gold Medal, Linnean Soc., London, 1966; Gunnar Erdtman Medal for Palynology, 1980; Albrecht Penck Medal, Deutsche Quartärvereinigung, 1982. *Publications:* Plant Biology, 1930; History of the British Flora, 1956, new edn, 1975; Fenland: its ancient past and uncertain future, 1978; The Archives of the Peat Bogs, 1981; Cambridge and Clare, 1985. *Address:* 30 Barton Road, Cambridge CB3 9LF; Clare College, Cambridge. *T:* Cambridge 350883. *Died 12 Aug. 1985.*

**GOFF, E(ric) N(oel) Porter;** *b* 24 Dec. 1902; *s* of John Richards Goff, Canon of Kildare and Rector of Portarlington, Ireland, and Alice Weir; *m* 1926, Barbara Denman Hodgson (*d* 1975); two *s. Educ:* Trinity Coll., Dublin (Scholar). BA (Senior Moderatorship and Gold Medal), 1924; MA 1929; Deacon 1926; Priest 1927; Curate of Immanuel, Streatham, 1926–29; Christ Church, Westminster, 1929–31; St Michael's, Chester Square, 1931–33; Vicar of Immanuel, Streatham, 1933–39; Provost of Portsmouth, 1939–72. Proctor in Convocation, 1939–72; Church Comr, 1948–72. Select Preacher: Univ. of Oxford, 1952–54; Dublin, 1956, 1959. *Address:* c/o Williams & Glyn's Bank Ltd, Holt's Branch, Kirkland House, Whitehall, SW1A 2DL. *Club:* National Liberal.
　　　　　　　　　　　　　　　　　　　　　　　*Died* 4 *April* 1981.

**GOFFIN, Comr Sir (John) Dean,** Kt 1983; Salvation Army Officer, retired; *b* 9 July 1916; *s* of Henry Charles Goffin and Catherine McLean Goffin; *m* 1939, Marjorie Bertha Barney; three *d* (one *s* decd). *Educ:* Napier Boys' High Sch.; Otago Univ. (MusB). Served War, 2nd NZEF, 1939–45: ME, Crete and Italy (Captain). Salvation Army Officer, NZ, 1952–56 and 1966–83 (GB, 1956–66); Territorial Comdr, 1980–83 (Comr). *Publications:* eighty original choral and brass band compositions, 1939–. *Recreations:* classical music, gardening, fishing. *Address:* 1 Bayview Road, Browns Bay, Auckland 10, New Zealand. *Died* 23 *Jan.* 1984.

**GOLD, Prof. Victor,** FRS 1972; Professor of Chemistry, since 1964, Head of Department of Chemistry since 1971, and Dean of Faculty of Natural Science, 1978–80, King's College, University of London; *b* 29 June 1922; *yr s* of late Dr Oscar and Mrs Emmy Gold; *m* 1954, Jean (*née* Sandiford); one *s* one *d. Educ:* King's Coll. and University Coll., London, Fellow UCL, 1973, FKC, 1975. BSc 1942, PhD 1945, DSc 1958; FRSC. Tuffnell Scholar 1942–44, Ramsay Meml Medal 1944, UCL; King's Coll., London: Demonstrator, 1944–46; Asst Lectr, 1946–47; Lectr in Chemistry, 1947–56; Reader in Physical Organic Chemistry, 1956–64. Res. Fellow and Resident Dr, Cornell Univ., 1951–52; Vis. Professor: Cornell Univ., 1962, 1963, 1965; Univ. of California, Irvine, 1970; Case Western Reserve Univ., 1975; Vis. Sen. Scientist, Brookhaven Nat. Lab., NY, 1962, 1966. Chairman: British Cttee on Chemical Educn, 1977–78; British Nat. Cttee for Chemistry, 1978–84. Mem. Council: Faraday Soc., 1963–66; Chem. Soc., 1971–74; Vice-Pres., Perkin Division, 1983–85. Royal Institution: Manager, 1983–84; Mem. Council and Vice-Pres., 1984–; Chm., Davy-Faraday Lab. Cttee, 1984–. Ingold Medal and Lectureship, RSC, 1984–85. Editor, Advances in Physical Organic Chemistry, 1963–. *Publications:* pH Measurements: their theory and practice, 1956; (with D. Bethell) Carbonium Ions: an introduction, 1967; (ed, with E. F. Caldin) Proton-Transfer Reactions, 1975; scientific papers, chiefly in Jl Chem. Soc. *Recreation:* music. *Address:* Department of Chemistry, King's College London, Strand, WC2R 2LS. *T:* 01–836 5454. *Club:* Athenæum. *Died* 29 *Sept.* 1985.

**GOLDBERG, Arthur J(oseph),** DJur; lawyer, USA; Permanent Representative of US to UN, 1965–68; Ambassador-at-Large, and Chairman of US Delegation, Conference on Security and Co-operation in Europe, 1977–78; lecturer, writer, and visiting professor at various universities; *b* Chicago, Ill, 8 Aug. 1908; *s* of Joseph Goldberg and Rebecca (*née* Perlstein); *m* 1931, Dorothy Kurgans; one *s* one *d. Educ:* City Coll., Chicago; North-western Univ. (JD). Admitted to Bar of Ill., 1929, US Supreme Ct Bar, 1937. Private practice, 1929–48. Gen. Counsel: Congress of Industrial Workers, 1948–55; United Steel workers, 1948–61; Industrial Union Dept, AFL-CIO, 1955–61; Special Counsel, AFL-CIO, 1955–61. Member firm: Goldberg, Devoe, Shadur & Mikva, Chicago, 1945–61; Goldberg, Feller & Bredhoff, Washington, 1952–61; Paul, Weiss, Goldberg, Rifkind, Wharton & Garrison, NY, 1968–71. Sec. of Labor, 1961–62. Associate Judge, US Supreme Court, Washington, 1962–65. Chm., UNA of USA, 1968–70, Hon. Chm., 1970–. Is a Democrat. Charles Evans Hughes Prof., Woodrow Wilson Sch. of Diplomacy, Princeton Univ., 1968–69; Distinguished Prof., Sch. of Internat. Relations, Columbia Univ., 1969–70; Univ. Prof. of Law and Diplomacy, Amer. Univ., 1971–73; Distinguished Prof., Univ. of Calif, SF, 1974–; Distinguished Vis. Prof., Univs of Calif, Alabama, N Dakota, Akron, Boston, Radford, and New Mexico; Judge in Residence, Univs of Colorado and Oklahoma, and Nova Univ. Assoc. Fellow, Morse Coll., Yale Univ., Illinois Univ. Member: Chicago Bar Assoc.; Ill. Bar Assoc.; Amer. Bar Assoc.; DC Bar Assoc.; Assoc. Bar City of NY; Amer. Acad. Arts and Scis. Holds numerous awards and hon. degrees. Presidential Medal of Freedom (US), 1978. *Publications:* Civil Rights in Labor-Management Relations: a Labor Viewpoint, 1951; AFL-CIO-Labor United, 1956; Unions and the Anti-Trust Laws, 1956; Management's Reserved Rights, 1956; Ethical Practices, 1958; A Trade Union Point of View, 1959; Suggestions for a New Labor Policy, 1960; The Role of the Labor Union in an Age of Bigness, 1960; The Defenses of Freedom: The Public Papers of Arthur J. Goldberg, 1966; Equal Justice: the Warren era of the Supreme Court, 1972; contribs to jls and newspapers. *Address:* 2801 New Mexico Avenue NW, Washington, DC 20007, USA.
　　　　　　　　　　　　　　　　　　　　　　　*Died* 19 *Jan.* 1990.

**GOLDFINGER, Ernő,** RA 1975; FRIBA 1963; private architect; *b* Budapest, 11 Sept. 1902; *s* of late Dr Oscar Goldfinger and Regine (*née* Haiman); *m* 1931, Ursula Ruth Blackwell; two *s* one *d. Educ:* Gymnasium Budapest; Le Rosay Rolle, Gstad, Switzerland; Ecole des Beaux Arts, Paris; Inst. d'Urbanisme, Sorbonne, 1927–28. DPLG 1932; RIBA 1946. Main Buildings: Shop, Helena Rubinstein, London, 1926; Monument, Algiers, 1928; House, Broxted, Essex, 1935; Terraced Houses, Willow Road, Hampstead, 1937 (scheduled as bldg of Architect. Interest, 1974); Houses, Bruxelles, 1951; (competition winner) Alex. Fleming House, Min. of Health, 1960 (Civic Trust Award, 1964); French govt's Tourist Offices, London and Paris; houses, flats, schs, neighbourhood units, newspaper bldg offices, warehouse, factories, farm, shops, old people's home, cinema; also Sunlight Studies, 1931 (designed Heliometer Machine). Exhibitions: Sect. of British Pavilion, Internat. Exhibn, Paris, 1937; ICI, Olympia BIF, 1938; MARS Gp, 1938; Grille CIAM, Aix en Provence, 1955; This is Tomorrow, London, 1956; Architectural Assoc., and Royal Acad. of Arts, 1983; Les Premiers Elévès d'Auguste Perret, Institut Français d'Architecture, Paris, 1985. Drawing and models at RIBA Heinz Gall. collection and RA. Lecture tours: English and Amer. univs; France, Spain, Hungary. Hon. Sec., Brit. Sect., Internat. Reunion of Architects, parent body of Internat. Union of Archs (UIA), 1936; 1st Org. Sec., UIA, 1946 (drafted Statutes); RIBA Deleg., UIA Council, Cuba and Mexico, 1963; Deleg., UIA Sports Bldgs Commission: Oslo, 1964; Krakow, 1967; Mexico City, 1968; Moscow, 1970. Member: French Sect., CIAM, 1928 (deleg. Congress, Athens, 1933); MARS Gp, 1934; Architect. Assoc., 1935 (Mem. Council, 1960–63, 1965–68); For. Relns Cttee, RIBA, 1937–45; Council, ARCUK, 1941–49; Bldg Req. Sub-cttee, Sci. Adv. Cttee to MPBW, 1943–45; Council of Industrial Design, 1961–65; Cercle d'Etudes Architecturals, Paris, 1975. Hon. Member: AASTA (now ABT), 1937; Assoc. of Hungarian Architects, 1963. FRSA. British Corresp., Architecture d'Aujourd'hui, 1934–74. *Publications:* County of London Plan Explained (jtly), 1945; British Furniture Today, 1951; contrib. Arch. Rev., RIBA Jl, Jl Inst. Amer. Architects, Architect. Year Book; *relevant publications:* Goldfinger Ernő, by Prof. M. Major, 1973 (Bupapest); Catalogue, 1920–1983, by James Dunnett and Gavin Stamp (Architectural Assoc. exhibn catalogue), 1983; special number Architect. Design (Jan. 1963); articles in Architect. Rev., Archs Jl, Architecture d'Aujourd'hui, Arch. & Urbanism, Tokyo, New Yorker 1957, Contemporary Architects, 1980. *Recreations:* travel, architecture. *Address:* 2 Willow Road, Hampstead, NW3 1TH. *T:* 01–435 6166. *Died* 15 *Nov.* 1987.

**GOLDING, F(rederick) Campbell,** MB, ChM, FRCP, DMRE, FFR; retired; Director, X-Ray Diagnostic Department, Middlesex Hospital, 1956–67; Lecturer in Radiology, Middlesex Hospital Medical School; Hon. Consultant Radiologist, Royal National Orthopædic Hospital; Civilian Consultant in Radiology, RN and RAF; Consultant Radiologist, Arthur Stanley Institute for Rheumatic Diseases; Consultant Radiologist, Chelsea Hospital for Women; *b* 4 June 1901; *o s* of late Frederick Golding, Sydney, Australia, and Nell Campbell, Castlemaine, Victoria; *m* 1942, Barbara Hubbard, *d* of late Charles Hubbard, Nassau and of Mrs Hubbard, 15 Grosvenor Square, W1; two *s. Educ:* Scots Coll., Melbourne; St Andrews Coll., University of Sydney. Late Dir, X-Ray Diagnostic Dept, Royal Marsden Hosp.; Examiner in Radiology, Royal College of Physicians, 1954–57. Watson-Jones Lecturer, Royal College of Surgeons, 1964; Mackenzie Davidson Lecturer, British Institute of Radiology, 1961. *Publications:* (contrib.) Textbook of X-Ray Diagnosis by British Authors; (contrib.) Textbook of Rheumatic Diseases; (Jt) Survey of Radiology of the Chest, British Encyclopædia of Medical Practice, 1956; various other medical publications.*Recreation:* fishing in north of Scotland. *Address:* The Barn, Hursley, Winchester, Hants.
　　　　　　　　　　　　　　　　　　　　　　　*Died* 17 *July* 1984.

**GOLDMAN, Peter,** CBE 1959; Director-General, International Organisation of Consumers Unions, since 1987 (President, 1970–75); *b* 4 Jan. 1925; *o s* of late Captain Samuel Goldman and late Jessie Goldman (*née* Englander); *m* 1st, 1961, Cicely Ann Magnay (marr. diss. 1969; she *d* 1985); 2nd, 1970, Stella Maris Joyce. *Educ:* Pembroke Coll., Cambridge; London Univ. BA 1st cl. hons History 1946, MA 1950, Cantab; Pres., Cambridge Union; Hadley Prize, Pembroke Coll., 1946; BA 1st cl. hons History, London, 1948. Smith-Mundt Fellowship, USA, 1955–56. Joined Conservative Research Dept, 1946; Head of Home Affairs Section, 1951–55; Dir of Conservative Political Centre, 1955–64; Dir, Consumers' Assoc., 1964–87. Mem., LCC Educn Cttee, 1958–59; contested (C) West Ham South, 1959, Orpington, 1962; Chm., Coningsby Club, 1958–59, Treas., 1953–58, 1963–83, Pres., 1983–. A Vice-Pres., Assoc. for Consumer Res., 1987– (Dir, 1964–87); Member: Post Office Users' Nat. Council, 1970–72; Community Relations Commn, 1973–75; Wine Standards Bd, 1973–81; Cttee of Inquiry into the Future of Broadcasting, 1974–77; Royal Commn on Legal Services,

1976–79; Council on Internat. Develt, 1977–79; Council, Bureau Européen des Unions de Consommateurs, 1979–87 (Pres., 1983–87); Consumer Consultative Cttee, EEC, 1979–80; Monopolies and Mergers Commn, 1980–83. FRSA 1970 (Silver Medal, 1969). *Publications:* County and Borough, 1952; Some Principles of Conservatism, 1956; The Welfare State, 1964; Consumerism: art or science?, 1969; Multinationals and the Consumer Interest, 1974. *Address:* 34 Campbell Court, Queen's Gate Gardens, SW7. *T:* 01–589 9464. *Club:* Carlton.                    *Died* 29 Sept. 1987.

**GOLDMANN, Dr Nahum;** President of the World Jewish Congress, 1951–77; *b* 10 July 1895; *s* of Soloman and Rebecca Goldmann; *m* 1934, Alice (*née* Gottschalk); two *s*. *Educ:* Berlin, Marburg, Heidelberg, Germany. Editor of Encyclopædia Judaica in Berlin, 1922–34; Rep. of Jewish Agency for Palestine with League of Nations, Geneva, 1934–40; Pres., Cttee of Jewish Delegations, 1936–; Mem. Exec. Cttee, Jewish Agency for Palestine, 1934–; Chm. Exec. Cttee, World Jewish Congress, 1936–; Rep., Jewish Agency in USA, 1940–; Chm. Admin. Cttee, World Jewish Congress, 1945–51; Chm., Jewish Agency, 1951 (Pres., 1956–68); Pres., Conf. on Jewish Material Claims against Germany, 1950–; Pres., Memorial Foundation for Jewish Culture, 1965–. *Publications:* Memories, 1970; Où va Israel?, 1975; Le Paradoxe Juif, 1977. *Address:* 12 Avenue Montaigne, Paris, France. *T:* 720.23.85; 9 Rehov Rashba, Jerusalem. *T:* 661116.          *Died* 29 Aug. 1982.

**GOLDSMID, Sir James Arthur d'A.;** *see* d'Avigdor-Goldsmid.

**GOLDSMITH, John Herman Thorburn,** CBE 1959; a Manager of the Royal Institution, 1964–67 and 1968–71, Vice President 1969; Part-time Member, NW Area Gas Board, 1955–64; *b* 30 May 1903; *m* 1932, Monica, *d* of late Capt. Harry Simon; one *d*. *Educ:* Marlborough; Magdalen Coll., Oxford. War of 1939–45, Fire Staff Officer, Grade I, National Fire Service. Dep. Chm., Civil Service Selection Bd, 1945; Chm., Civil Service Selection Board, and a Civil Service Commissioner, 1951–63. Haakon Cross, Norway, 1945; Order of Orange Nassau, Netherlands, 1945. *Publications:* Hildebrand (Children's Stories), 1931, 1949; Three's Company, 1932. *Recreation:* fly-fishing. *Address:* 46 Regency House, Newbold Terrace, Leamington Spa, Warwickshire CV32 4HD. *T:* Leamington Spa 39246.                    *Died* 31 *May* 1987.

**GOLDSMITH, Mac;** retired; *b* 3 July 1902; *s* of David and Klara Goldschmidt; *m* 1936, Ruth (*née* Baum); one *s* one *d*. *Educ:* Oberealschule, Marburg; Technical Coll., Mannheim. Founded Mecano GmbH Frankfurt/M, 1925; Metallgummi GmbH Frankfurt/M, 1933; Metalastik Ltd, Leicester, 1937; British Bundy Tubing Co., Welwyn Garden City, 1937; acquired Precision Rubbers Ltd for Metalastik Ltd, 1955, and merged Metalastik Ltd with John Bull Gp of Cos (Dep. Chm. and Man. Dir); merged with Dunlop Ltd, 1958; retd from Dunlop Gp, 1970. Farmer, Normanton House and Manor Farms, Thurlaston, Leics. Trustee: Leicester Theatre Trust; Leics Med. Res. Foundn; Life Mem., Ct and Mem., Council, Leicester Univ.; Member: Leicester and District Disablement Adv. Cttee of Dept of Employment; Leicester Museums, Libraries and Publicity Cttee; Royal cttees, Royal Leicester, Rutland and Wycliffe Soc. for the Blind; Bd of Governors, Jerusalem Coll. of Technology Sch. of Applied Sciences; Life Governor, Hillel House, London; Trustee, Leicester Hebrew Congregation; President: Leicester Maccabi Assoc.; Leicester Symphony Orchestra; Leicester Gramophone Soc.; Vice-Pres., City of Leicester Competitive Festival of Music; Patron, Leics Org. for Relief of Suffering. Hon. LLD Leicester, 1971. Freeman, City of Leicester, 1971. *Recreations:* formerly golf, riding, ski-ing. *Address:* 3 Birkdale Avenue, Knighton Road, Leicester LE2 3HA. *T:* Leicester 708127.                    *Died* 15 *May* 1983.

**GOLDSTEIN, Sydney,** FRS 1937; MA; PhD; Gordon McKay Professor of Applied Mathematics, Harvard University, Emeritus; *b* 3 Dec. 1903; *o s* of Joseph and Hilda Goldstein, Hull; *m* 1926, Rosa R. Sass, Johannesburg; one *s* one *d*. *Educ:* Bede Collegiate Sch., Sunderland; University of Leeds; St John's Coll., Cambridge. Mathematical Tripos, 1925; Smith's Prize, 1927; PhD, 1928; Rockefeller Research Fellow, University of Göttingen, 1928–29; Lectr in Mathematics, Manchester Univ., 1929–31; Lectr in Mathematics in the Univ. of Cambridge, 1931–45; Fellow of St John's Coll., Cambridge, 1929–32, 1933–45; Leverhulme Research Fellow, Calif. Inst. of Technology, 1938–39; Beyer Prof. of Applied Mathematics, Manchester Univ., 1945–50; Prof. of Applied Mathematics, 1950–55; and Chm. Aeronautical Engineering Dept, 1950–54, Technion Institute of Technology, Haifa, Israel, and Vice-Pres. of the Institute, 1951–54. Worked at Aerodynamics Div., National Physical Laboratory, 1939–45; Adams Prize, 1935. Chm., Aeronautical Research Council, 1946–49. Foreign Member: Royal Netherlands Acad. of Sciences and Letters (Section for Sciences), 1950; Finnish Scientific Soc. (Section for maths and phys), 1975. Hon. Fellow: St John's Coll., Cambridge, 1965; Weizmann Inst. of Science, 1971; Hon. FRAeS, 1971; Hon. FIMA, 1972. Hon. DEng Purdue Univ., 1967; Hon. DSc: Case Inst. of Technology, 1967;

The Technion, Israel Inst. of Technology, Haifa, Israel, 1969; Leeds Univ., 1973. Timoshenko Medal of Amer. Soc. of Mech. Engrs (for distinguished contribs to Applied Mechanics), 1965; Hon. Mem., ASME, 1981. *Publications:* (ed) Modern Developments in Fluid Dynamics, 1938; Lectures on Fluid Mechanics, 1960; papers on mathematics and mathematical physics, especially hydrodynamics and aerodynamics. *Address:* 28 Elizabeth Road, Belmont, Mass 02178, USA.                    *Died* 22 *Jan.* 1989.

**GOMES, Sir Stanley Eugene,** Kt 1959; Retired Chief Justice, West Indies Federation; *b* Georgetown, British Guiana, 24 March 1901; *s* of late Mr and Mrs M. Gomes; *m* 1936, Elaine Vera (*née* Wight). *Educ:* St Joseph's Coll., Dumfries, Scotland; Jesus Coll., Cambridge. BA Cantab, 1923; called to Bar, Gray's Inn, 1924. British Guiana: Magistrate, 1929; Asst Attorney-Gen., 1933; Attorney-Gen., Leeward Islands, 1944; QC 1946; Puisne Judge, Trinidad, 1948. Chief Justice: Barbados, 1957–58; Trinidad, 1958; WI Fedn, 1961. Pres., Brit. Caribbean Court of Appeal, 1962. Retd Dec. 1962. *Recreations:* fishing, golf. *Address:* 1 Dalney Lodge, 4th Avenue, Rockley New Road, Christchurch, Barbados, West Indies.
                    *Died* 24 *Sept.* 1985.

**GONZI, Most Rev. Michael,** KBE 1946; DD, ICD, BLit; Archbishop Emeritus of Malta; *b* Vittoriosa, Malta, 13 May 1885; *s* of Joseph Gonzi and Margaret Tonna. *Educ:* Malta Seminary; Malta Univ.; Beda Coll., Rome. Priest, 1908; Prof. of Holy Scripture and Hebrew at the Malta Univ., 1915; Sec. to the Archbishop of Malta, 1921; Mem. of the Senate of the Maltese Parliament, 1921; Canon Theologian of the Malta Cathedral, 1923; Bishop of Gozo, 1924; Coadjutor to Bishop of Malta, 1943; Archbishop of Malta, 1943–76; Assistant at the Pontifical Throne, 1949. Bailiff Grand Cross of the Order of Malta, St John of Jerusalem, 1949. *Address:* Archbishop's Palace, Valletta, Malta GC.                    *Died* 22 *Jan.* 1984.

**GOOCH, Sir Robert Douglas,** 4th Bt *cr* 1866; *b* 19 Sept. 1905; *s* of Sir Daniel Fulthorpe Gooch, 3rd Bt and Mary Winifrid (*d* 1921), *d* of late Edward William Monro; *S* father, 1926; *m* 1st, 1928, Moyra Katharine (marr. diss. 1930), *d* of Charles Howard Saunders, MB; 2nd, 1930, Mary Eileen (*d* 1979), *d* of Colin George Barrett and *widow* of Major H. L. Gifford; one *d*. Heir: *kinsman* Trevor Sherlock Gooch, VRD [*b* 15 June 1915; *m* 1st, Denys Anne (*d* 1976), *d* of Harold Victor Venables; one *s* four *d*; 2nd, 1978, Jean, *d* of late Joseph Wright].                    *Died* 6 *May* 1989.

**GOOD, Air Vice-Marshal James Laurence Fuller F.;** *see* Fuller-Good.

**GOODALE, Sir Ernest (William),** Kt 1952; CBE 1946; MC 1917; Director, 1928, Managing Director, 1930–61, Chairman, 1949–71, and Chairman Emeritus since 1971, Warner & Sons Ltd, textile manufacturers; *b* 6 Dec. 1896; *s* of Wm Thos Goodale, Charter Town Clerk of Barnes, Surrey, and Frances Mary Wheatley; *m* 1st, 1924, Gwendolen Branscombe (*d* 1972), *yr d* of late Sir Frank Warner, KBE; one *s* one *d*; 2nd, 1973, Pamela June, *d* of Stanley A. Bone, Betchworth, Surrey. *Educ:* St Catherine's Coll., Richmond, Surrey; Surrey County Sch., Richmond; King's Coll., London Univ. London Univ. OTC, 1914–15; served European War, 2nd Lieut and Lieut Royal Warwicks Regt, 1916–19, Mesopotamia, Persia, Caucasus, etc. Admitted Solicitor, 1920; Partner, Minet, Pering, Smith & Co., London, retired 1928. Member of: Council for Art and Industry, 1934–39; Council of Industrial Design, 1945–49; Ramsden Cttee on Exhibitions and Fairs, 1945; Bd of Trade Advisory Cttees on Exhibitions and Fairs, 1948–65; Chm. Sub-Cttee on BIF ("Goodale Report"), 1953; Chm. BIF Ltd, 1954–56; Inst. of Export (Vice-Pres., 1956–66); Douglas Cttee on Purchase Tax, 1951; Council, Royal College of Art, 1950–53; Hon. Fellow, Society of Industrial Artists and Designers, 1960; Textile Inst., 1937– (Pres. 1939–40 and 1957–59); Silk and Rayon Controller (Min. of Supply), 1939; Pres., Silk and Man-Made Fibres (formerly Rayon) Users' Assoc. (Inc.), 1945–70; Vice-President: International Silk Assoc., 1949–68; British Man-Made (formerly Rayon and Synthetic) Fibres Federation, 1943–74; Chairman: Furnishing Fabric Fedn, 1945–68; Furnishing Fabrics Export Group, 1940–68; Hon. Pres., Furnishing Fabric Manufacturers' Assoc.; a Vice-Pres. and Mem. Grand Council and Cttees, FBI (Chm. Industrial Art Cttee, 1949–62); Mem. Council, CBI, 1965–74; Mem. Council Royal Society Arts, 1935–83 (Chm., 1949–52, subseq. Hon. Vice-Pres.); Pres. British Colour Council, 1953–70; Mem. Bd of National Film Finance Corp., 1957–69; Mem. Min. of Educn Adv. Council on Art Educn, 1959–66; Mem. for Dorking (North), Surrey CC, 1961–70, Alderman, 1970–74. Liveryman, Worshipful Co. of Weavers, 1929– (Court of Assistants, 1946–. Renter Bailiff, 1956–57, Upper Bailiff, 1957–58); Mem. of Law Soc. *Publications:* Weaving and the Warners, 1971; contributions to trade literature. *Address:* Branscombe, Nutcombe Lane, Dorking, Surrey.
                    *Died* 16 *Nov.* 1984.

**GOODALL, Rev. Dr Norman;** Minister of United Reformed Church, retired; *b* 30 Aug. 1896; *s* of Thomas and Amelia Goodall; *m* 1920, Dr Doris Elsie Florence (*née* Stanton) (*d* 1984); two *s* one *d*. *Educ:* Council sch., Birmingham; Mansfield Coll., Oxford (MA, DPhil,

Hon. Life Fellow 1980). Minister: Trinity Congregational Church, Walthamstow, 1922–28; New Barnet Congregatnl Ch., 1928–36; Foreign Sec., London Missionary Soc., 1936–44; Sec., Internat. Missionary Council, 1944–61; Asst Gen. Sec., World Council of Churches, 1961–63. Chm., Congregatnl Union of England and Wales, 1954–55; Moderator: Internat. Congregatnl Council, 1962–66; Free Ch. Federal Council, 1966–67. Dale Lectr, Mansfield Coll., Oxford, 1965–66; Associate Lectr, Heythrop Coll., 1970–71; Vis. Lecturer: Selly Oak Colls, 1963–66 (Hon. Fellow, 1981); Irish Sch. of Ecumenics, Dublin, 1971–73; Vis. Prof., Pontifical Gregorian Univ., Rome, 1975. *Publications:* With All Thy Mind, 1933; Pacific Pilgrimage, 1941; One Man's Testimony, 1949; History of the London Missionary Society 1895–1945, 1954; The Ecumenical Movement, 1961 (2nd edn 1964); Christian Missions and Social Ferment, 1964; Ecumenical Progress, 1972; Second Fiddle: recollections and reflections, 1979. *Recreations:* friends, music, books. *Address:* 241 Woodstock Road, Oxford OX2 7AD. *T:* Oxford 55099.                                                                    *Died 1 Jan.* 1985.

**GOODALL, Sir Reginald,** Kt 1985; CBE 1975; Conductor, Royal Opera House, since 1947; *b* 13 July 1901; *m* 1932, Eleanor Gipps. RCM, RAM; Hon. DMus: Leeds Univ; Oxford, 1986; Hon. MusD Newcastle Univ. Hon. Freeman, Musicians' Co., 1986. *Address:* Barham Court, Barham, Canterbury, Kent.

*Died 5 May* 1990.

**GOODBODY, Gen. Sir Richard (Wakefield),** GCB 1963 (CB 1953); KBE 1958; DSO 1943; Bath King at Arms, 1965–76; *b* 12 April 1903; *s* of Gerald E. Goodbody, Woodsdown, Co. Limerick; *m* 1929, Mary Eveline Talbot, Provost's House, Edgmond, Newport, Salop; three *s* one *d. Educ:* Rugby; RMA Woolwich. Commissioned RA, 1923; apptd to RHA, 1927; Adjt, HAC, 1936; Bde Major 1st Support Group, 1940; CO 11 RHA, 1942; Comdr 2 Armd Bde, 1943; CRA 7th Armd Div., 1946; Comd 15 Inf. Bde, 1947; Dep. DMT War Office, 1948; Comdt Sch. of Artillery, 1949; GOC 56 (London) Armoured Div., TA, 1951; Dir of Royal Artillery, War Office, 1954; GOC-in-C Northern Comd, 1957–60; Adjt-Gen. to the Forces, 1960–63. Col Commandant: Royal Artillery, 1957–68; Hon. Artillery Co., 1959–66; Royal Horse Artillery, 1960–68; ADC Gen. to the Queen, 1961–63. Retd from the Army, 1963. Mem., Council of St Dunstan's. *Recreations:* shooting, fishing, gardening. *Address:* Broadlea Farm, Sutton Waldron, Blandford, Dorset. *Club:* Naval and Military.                                        *Died 29 April* 1981.

**GOODE, Sir William (Allmond Codrington),** GCMG 1963 (KCMG 1957; CMG 1952); DL; *b* 8 June 1907; *e s* of late Sir Richard Goode, CMG, CBE; *m* 1st, 1938, Mary Armstrong Harding (*d* 1947); 2nd, 1950, Ena Mary McLaren; one *d. Educ:* Oakham Sch.; Worcester Coll., Oxford (Classical exhibitioner). Barrister-at-Law, Gray's Inn, 1936. Joined Malayan Civil Service, 1931; District Officer, Raub, 1936–39; Asst Commissioner for Civil Defence, Singapore, 1940. Mobilised in 1st Bn Singapore Volunteer Corps as Lance-Corporal, 1941 (prisoner of war, Singapore, 1942; moved to Thailand for work on the Burma Railway; released 1945). Dep. Economic Sec., Federation of Malaya, 1948; Chief Sec., Aden, 1949–53; Acting Governor, Aden, 1950–51; Chief Sec., Singapore, 1953–57; Governor of Singapore, Dec. 1957–2nd June 1959; Yang di-Pertuan Negara of the State of Singapore and UK Commissioner, Singapore, 1959; Governor and C-in-C, North Borneo, 1960–63 (Chm., Water Resources Bd, 1964–74. DL Berks 1975. KStJ 1958. *Address:* East Streatley House, Streatley-on-Thames, Berks RG8 9HY. *Club:* East India.                                                          *Died 15 Sept.* 1986.

**GOODENOUGH, Kenneth Mackenzie,** CMG 1949; MC 1918; *b* Bristol, 30 Oct. 1891; 3rd *s* of late W. T. Goodenough, Bristol; *m* 1916, Florence Alda Bolwell (*d* 1971); two *s. Educ:* Fairfield Sch., Bristol. Entered surveying profession and qualified as a Professional Associate of the Surveyors' Institution. Served European War, 1914–18 in Royal Artillery, commissioned 1917 (MC). Took up business appointment in S Rhodesia, 1928. Pres. Bulawayo Chamber of Commerce, 1942 and 1943; Dep. Mayor of Bulawayo, 1944. High Comr for S Rhodesia, 1946–Jan. 1953. Freeman of City of London; Liveryman of Worshipful Co. of Needlemakers. *Address:* 30 North Shore Road, Hayling Island, Hants. *Club:* Bulawayo (Bulawayo).

*Died 12 Feb.* 1985.

**GOODENOUGH, Samuel Kenneth Henry;** Senior Partner: Knight Frank & Rutley, since 1978; KFLH Zimbabwe, since 1980; Chairman, Knight Frank & Rutley (Nigeria) Agricultural Services Ltd, since 1981; *b* 3 April 1930; 3rd surv. *s* of Sir William Goodenough, 1st Bt, and of Dorothea Lady Goodenough, *d* of late Hon. Kenneth Gibbs, one time Archdeacon of St Albans; *m* 1979, Patricia (marr. diss. 1982), *er d* of P. C. Barnett, Prae Wood, St Albans; one step *s* one step *d. Educ:* Eton Coll. (Oppidan Schol.); Christ Church, Oxford. MA Oxon. FRICS. Knight, Frank & Rutley: articled, 1952; Partner, 1961. Partner in family farming enterprise, 1965–. Pres., Agricl Section, Internat. Real Estate Fedn, 1975–78. Governor, London House for Overseas Graduates, 1961– (Vice-Chm., 1980–); Chm., Homœopathic Medical Trust, 1970–.

Mem. Ct of Assts, Goldsmiths' Co., 1981–. FRSA 1980. *Recreations:* shooting, painting, organ playing, gardening. *Address:* Flat 50 Belgravia Court, Ebury Street, SW1. *T:* 01-730 1030; Filkins Hall, Filkins, Lechlade, Glos. *T:* Filkins 413. *Clubs:* Brooks's, Pratt's; New (Edinburgh).                                            *Died 13 July* 1983.

**GOODERSON, Richard Norman;** a Recorder of the Crown Court, since 1972; Reader in English Law, University of Cambridge, since 1967; Fellow, St Catharine's College, Cambridge, since 1948; *b* 3 March 1915; *o s* of late George Gooderson and Clarice Gooderson (*née* Judge); *m* 1939, Marjorie, *yr d* of William Nash; two *s* one *d. Educ:* Northampton Grammar Sch.; St John's Coll., Cambridge (Scholar). BA 1st cl. with distinction Pts I and II Law Tripos; George Long Prizes for Roman Law and for Jurisprudence, Bhaonagar Medal; MA 1948. Called to Bar, Inner Temple, 1946 (certif. of honour). Indian Civil Service, 1938–46; Cambridge Univ.: Lectr, 1949–67; Chm. Faculty of Law, 1970–73; St Catharine's College: Tutor, 1951–65; Senior Tutor, 1965–67; President, 1962–65, 1972–75. Chm., Luton Rent Tribunal, 1960–72; Dep. Chm., Hunts and Peterborough QS, 1970–71. *Publications:* Alibi, 1977; articles in legal jls. *Address:* 1 Newnham Terrace, Cambridge. *T:* Cambridge 58523.                                                     *Died 25 March* 1981.

**GOODFELLOW, Maj.-Gen. Howard Courtney,** CB 1952; CBE 1946 (OBE 1943); retired 1954; *b* 28 July 1898; *yr s* of late Thomas Goodfellow, Plymouth; *m* 1928, Vera St John, *yr d* of late H. St J. Hewitt, Salisbury. *Educ:* Plymouth Coll.; RMC Sandhurst. Commissioned into ASC, 1916; served European War, 1914–18, in France and Italy; seconded to Iraq Army, 1928–32; War of 1939–45, served in Italy and NW Europe, rank of Brig. Order of Rafidain, Class IV (Iraq), 1931. *Address:* Chapel Lodge, Greywell, Hants. *T:* Odiham 2076.                                                      *Died 10 Jan.* 1983.

**GOODSELL, Sir John William,** Kt 1968; CMG 1954; FASA; Company Director, since 1971; Member: State Cancer Council, 1962–78; Council, University of New South Wales, since 1948; Convocation, Macquarie University, since 1965; Chairman: Unisearch Ltd; Winston Churchill Fellowship Trust; *b* 6 July 1906; *s* of late Major S. P. Goodsell, VD, Croix de Guerre (avec Palme), and of late Mrs L. A. Goodsell; *m* 1932, Myrtle Thelma, *d* of late R. H. Austin; three *d. Educ:* Canterbury High Sch., NSW. Member: Public Library Bd, 1948–55; Public Accountants Registration Bd, 1948–55; Under-Sec. and Comptroller of Accounts, New South Wales Treasury, 1948–55; Pres. Metropolitan Water Sewerage and Drainage Board, Sydney, April 1955–Sept. 1960; Chm., NSW Public Service Bd, 1960–71; Member: Council, Australian Soc. of Accountants, 1959–61; Sydney Harbour Transport Board, 1951–55; Appointments Bd, Univ. of Sydney, 1963–71; Prince Henry Hospital Bd, 1960–76 (Chm., 1960–61); Prince of Wales Hospital Bd, 1961–76; Eastern Suburbs Hospital Bd, 1968–76; Chm., Tax Agents Board, 1948–55; Custodian Trustee, Legislative Assembly Members Superannuation Fund, 1948–55; Trustee, Kuring-gai Chase Trust, 1962–64. Hon. DSc Univ. of NSW, 1976. Coronation Medal, 1953. *Recreations:* tennis and fishing. *Address:* 22 King Street, Ashbury, NSW 2193, Australia. *T:* 798 4826.                    *Died 3 July* 1981.

**GOODSON, Alan,** OBE 1978; QPM 1972; Chief Constable of Leicestershire (sometime Leicester and Rutland), 1972–86; Chairman, Post Office Users' Council for Wales, and Member, Post Office Users' National Council, since 1988; *b* 2 June 1927; *m* 1954, Mary Anne Reilly; one *s* two *d. Educ:* Hitchin Grammar Sch.; King's Coll., London (LLB). Royal Navy, 1945–48. Metropolitan Police, 1951–65; Chief Constable of Pembrokeshire, 1965–68; Asst Chief Constable, Dyfed-Powys, 1968; Asst Chief Constable, then Dep. Chief Constable, Essex, 1968–72; idc 1970. Member: Home Secretary's Adv. Council on Penal System, 1975–78; Lord Chancellor's Adv. Cttee on Legal Aid, 1988–; Dyfed Valuation and Community Charge Tribunal, 1989–. UK Rep., Interpol, 1980–82. Assessor, Hon. Mr Justice Popplewell's Inquiry into Crowd Safety and Control at Sports Grounds, 1985. President: Assoc. of Chief Police Officers, 1979–80; Chief Constables Club, 1981–82; Vice-Pres., European Police Sports Union, 1982–86; Chm., Police Athletic Assoc., 1984–86 (Hon. Sec., 1975–84).

*Died 16 May* 1990.

**GOODSON, Lt-Col Sir Alfred Lassam,** 2nd Bt *cr* 1922; *b* 26 Aug. 1893; *er s* of 1st Bt; *S* father, 1940; *m* 1920, Joan (*d* 1939), *d* of C. J. Leyland, Haggerston Castle, Beal, Northumberland; *m* 1941, Enid Clayton Leyland, *d* of late Robert Clayton Swan, Barrowby Grange, Grantham. *Educ:* Radley. Served European War, 1914–19, Captain City of London Yeomanry, TF, 1916; commanded No 1 Bn Northumberland Home Guard, 1940–45. Master, College Valley Foxhounds, 1924–81. *Heir: n* Mark Weston Lassam Goodson [*b* 12 Dec. 1925; *m* 1949, Barbara Mary Constantine, *d* of Surg.-Capt. R. J. McAuliffe Andrews, RN; one *s* three *d*]. *Address:* Corbet Tower, Kelso, Roxburghshire. *T:* Morebattle 203.

*Died 17 Feb.* 1986.

**GOODSTEIN, Prof. Reuben Louis,** PhD, DLit (London); ScD (Cantab); Professor of Mathematics, University of Leicester,

1948–77, then Emeritus; *b* 15 Dec. 1912; 2nd *s* of late Alexander and Sophia Goodstein; *m* 1938, Louba, *d* of late Samuel Atkin; one *s* one *d*. *Educ*: St Paul's Sch. (scholar and sen. scholar); Magdalene Coll., Cambridge (BA, MSc). Scholar and Research Scholar, Magdalene Coll., 1931–35; Lectr in Mathematics, Univ. of Reading, 1935–47; Dean of the Faculty of Science, 1954–57; Pro-Vice-Chancellor, 1966–69, Univ. of Leicester. Hon. Librarian, Mathematical Assoc., 1955–77, Pres., 1975–76; Editor, Mathematical Gazette, 1956–62. Mem. Council, Assoc. for Symbolic Logic, 1965–69. *Publications*: Mathematical Analysis, 1948; Constructive Formalism, 1951, 2nd edn, 1965; The Foundations of Mathematics, 1952; Axiomatic Projective Geometry, 1953, 2nd edn 1962; Mathematical Logic, 1957, 2nd edn 1962 (Russian trans. 1961); Recursive Number Theory, 1957 (Russian trans. 1970); Recursive Analysis, 1961 (Russian trans. 1970); Fundamental Concepts of Mathematics, 1962, 2nd edn 1979; Boolean Algebra, 1963 (Dutch trans. 1965, Japanese trans. 1969); Essays in the Philosophy of Mathematics, 1965; Complex Functions, 1965 (Spanish trans. 1975); Development of Mathematical Logic, 1971 (Japanese trans. 1978); articles in British, continental and American jls. *Address*: Hadfield, Manor Road, Leicester.

*Died 28 March 1985.*

**GOODWIN, Michael Felix James;** Director, Institute for the Study of Conflict, since 1979 (Administrative Director, 1971–79); *b* 31 Jan. 1916; *e s* of late F. W. Goodwin; *m* 1944, Alison, *y d* of Capt. Lionel Trower and Ethel Matheson of Achany; one *s* one *d*. *Educ*: privately. North Reg. Drama Dir, BBC,1938, West Reg. Drama Dir, 1939. Served War of 1939–45, in Royal Artillery, 1939–43. Returned to BBC in Features Dept and Overseas News Service, 1943–47. Dramatic critic, The Weekly Review, 1945–46; succeeded Helen Waddell as Asst Editor, The Nineteenth Century and After, 1945–47; Editor, The Twentieth Century (formerly The Nineteenth Century and After), 1947–52; Editor, Bellman Books, 1952–55; Dir, Contact Publications, 1955–60; Dir, Newman Neame Ltd, 1960–65. Financial Advr, Internat. Assoc. for Cultural Freedom, Paris, 1967–73. *Publications*: Nineteenth Century Opinion, 1949 (Penguin); Artist and Colourman, 1966; Concise Dictionary of Antique Terms, 1967. *Address*: 16 Cope Place, W8. *T*: 01-937 3802. *Club*: Travellers'. *Died 7 Sept. 1988.*

**GOODWIN, Sir Reginald (Eustace),** Kt 1968; CBE 1960; Leader of the Labour Party, Greater London Council, 1967–80, Leader of the Council, 1973–77, Leader of the Opposition, 1967–73 and 1977–80; *b* 3 July 1908; *s* of late Thomas William Goodwin, Streatham, London; *m* 1943, Penelope Mary, *d* of late Capt. R. T. Thornton, MBE, MC, Chepstow, Mon; two *s* one *d*. *Educ*: Strand Sch., London. Tea Buyer in City of London, 1928–34; Asst Gen. Sec., Nat. Assoc. of Boys' Clubs, 1934–45. Served War of 1939–45. Mem., Bermondsey Borough Council, 1937–65 (Leader of Council, 1947–65); Hon. Freeman of the Borough, 1963; Mem. LCC, 1946–65; Alderman, 1961 (Chm. Gen. Purposes Cttee, 1954–58; Establishment Cttee, 1958–60; Housing Cttee, 1960–61; Finance Cttee, 1961–65); Mem., GLC, 1964–81 (Chm. Finance Cttee, 1964–67; Chm. ILEA Finance Sub-Cttee, 1964–67, 1970–73). Dep. Chm., Basildon Develt Corp., 1970–78, Chm. 1979–80. Gen. Sec., Nat. Assoc. of Boys' Clubs, 1945–73. Mem. Ct, Univ. of London, 1968–84. DL County of London, 1958–82. *Recreations*: local government; gardening. *Address*: Twitten Cottage, Marehill, Pulborough, West Sussex. *T*: Pulborough 2202.

*Died 29 Sept. 1986.*

**GOODWIN, Lt-Gen. Sir Richard (Elton),** KCB 1963 (CB 1959); CBE 1954; DSO 1944; DL; Vice Lord-Lieutenant, Suffolk, 1978–83; *b* 17 Aug. 1908; *s* of late Col W. R. P. Goodwin, DSO, and Mrs Goodwin; *m* 1940, Anthea Mary Sampson; three *s*. *Educ*: Cheltenham Coll.; Royal Military Coll., Sandhurst. Commissioned into Suffolk Regt, 1928; served in India, 1930–38; ADC to Governor of Madras, 1935; Adjutant 2nd Suffolk, 1935–38; 2nd i/c 9th Royal Warwickshire, 1941–42; CO 1st Suffolk, 1943–45; College Comdr, RMA Sandhurst, 1947–49; Comdt, Sch. of Infantry, 1951–54; Comdr, 6th Infty Bde, 1954–57; GOC 49th Infty Div. (TA) and N Midland Dist, 1957–60; GOC, E Africa Comd, 1960–63; Comdr 1st (British) Corps, 1963–66; Military Secretary, MoD (Army), 1966–69. Lieutenant, HM Tower of London, 1969–72. Col 1st E Anglian Regt (Royal Norfolk and Suffolk), 1962–64; Dep. Col The Royal Anglian Regt, 1964–66, Col, 1966–71. DL Suffolk 1973. *Recreations*: hunting and other field sports. *Address*: The Old Plough, Denham, Bury St Edmunds, Suffolk IP29 5EW. *Club*: Army and Navy.

*Died 28 Oct. 1986.*

**GOODWIN HUDSON, Rt. Rev. Arthur William;** *see* Hudson.

**GOODYEAR, Prof. Francis Richard David,** FBA 1984; Visiting Professor and Chairman of Governing Committee, Department of Classics, University of the Witwatersrand, since 1984; *b* 2 Feb. 1936; *s* of Francis Goodyear and Gladys Ivy Goodman; *m* 1967, Cynthia Rosalie Attwood; one *s*. *Educ*: Luton Grammar Sch.; St John's Coll., Cambridge. MA, PhD (Cantab). Open schol., St John's

Coll., Cambridge, 1953; Craven schol., Hallam Prize, 1956; Classical Tripos, Pts 1 and 2, cl. 1, 1956–57; Chancellor's Medal, H. A. Thomas Studentship, 1957. Cambridge University: Research Fellow, St John's Coll., 1959–60; Official Fellow, 1960–66, Librarian, 1960–64, Queens' Coll.; London University: Hildred Carlile Prof. of Latin, 1966–83; Hd of Dept of Latin, 1966–83, Dean of Faculty of Arts, 1971–73, Bedford Coll.; Chm., Bd of Studies in Classics, 1977–78. Mem., Accademia Nazionale Virgilian, 1975. Mem., Adv. Editorial Bd, Cambridge Classical Texts and Commentaries, 1974–. *Publications*: Incerti auctoris Aetna, 1965; Appendix Vergiliana (jt editor), 1966; Corippi Iohannidos libri viii (jt editor), 1970; Tacitus, a survey, 1970; The Annals of Tacitus, vol. i, 1972, vol. ii, 1981; papers and reviews in learned jls, contribs to works of reference. *Recreations*: light reading, travel. *Address*: 78 George V Avenue, Pinner, Mddx HA5 5SW; Department of Classics, University of the Witwatersrand, 1 Jan Smuts Avenue, Johannesburg, 2001, South Africa. *Died 24 July 1987.*

**GOOLDEN, Barbara;** novelist; *b* 5 June 1900; *d* of Charles and Isabel Goolden (*née* Armit); one adopted *s* decd. *Educ*: Community of the Holy Family; two private schools. Appeared on TV and spoke on radio. *Publications*: The Knot of Reluctance, 1926; The Sleeping Sword, 1928; Children of Peace, 1928; The Conquering Star, 1929; The Waking Bird, 1929; The Ancient Wheel, 1930; Toils of Law, 1931; Thin Ice, 1931; Sugared Grief, 1932; Eros, 1933; Separate Paths, 1933; Slings and Arrows, 1934; Victory to the Vanquished, 1935; Wise Generations, 1936; The Primrose Path, 1936; Morning Tells the Day, 1937; The Wind My Posthorse, 1937; Within a Dream, 1938; Young Ambition, 1938; Call the Tune, 1939; The Asses Bridge, 1940; The Best Laid Schemes, 1941; Crown of Life, 1941; Men as Trees, 1942; Swings and Roundabouts, 1943; Community Singing, 1944; Ichabod, 1945; Daughters of Earth, 1947; Jig Saw, 1948; From the Sublime to the Ridiculous, 1949; Strange Strife, 1952; Venetia, 1952; The China Pig, 1953; Truth is Fallen in the Street, 1953; Return Journey, 1954; Who is my Neighbour?, 1954; Bread to the Wise, 1955; The World His Oyster, 1955; At the Foot of the Hills, 1956; To Have and to Hold, 1956; The Singing and the Gold, 1956; The Nettle and the Flower, 1957; Through the Sword Gates, 1957; The Linnet in the Cage, 1958; The Ships of Youth, 1958; Sweet Fields, 1958; A Pilgrim and his Pack, 1959; For Richer, For Poorer, 1959; Falling in Love, 1960; New Wine, 1960; Where Love is, 1960; To Love and to Cherish, 1961; One Autumn Face, 1961; Against the Grain, 1961; The Little City, 1962; The Pebble in the Pond, 1962; Marriages are Made in Heaven, 1963; Love-in-a-Mist, 1963; Battledore and Shuttlecock, 1963; Fools' Paradise, 1964; The Gentle Heart, 1964; The Gift, 1964; Blight on the Blossom, 1965; A Finger in the Pie, 1965; The Lesser Love, 1965; Anvil of Youth, 1966; Nobody's Business, 1966; A Time to Love, 1966; Second Fiddle, 1967; A Time to Build, 1967; All to Love, 1968; The Eleventh Hour, 1968; The Reluctant Wife, 1968; A Marriage of Convenience, 1969; Today Belongs to Us, 1969; The Snare, 1970; A Question of Conscience, 1970; Fortune's Favourite, 1971; No Meeting Place, 1971; Before the Flame is Lit, 1971; A Leap in the Dark, 1972; A Law for Lovers, 1973; Time to Turn Back, 1973; The Broken Arc, 1974; Mirage, 1974; The Crystal and the Dew, 1975; Silver Fountains, 1975; Goodbye to Yesterday, 1976; In the Melting Pot, 1976; Unborn Tomorrow, 1977; The Rags of Time, 1978; *for children*: Minty, 1959; Five Pairs of Hands, 1961; Minty and the Missing Picture, 1963; Minty and the Secret Room, 1964; Trouble for the Tabors, 1966; Top Secret, 1969. *Recreation*: reading. *Address*: Stildon, London Road, East Grinstead, West Sussex RH19 1PZ. *Died 29 April 1990.*

**GOOLDEN, Richard Percy Herbert,** OBE 1978; Actor and Broadcaster since 1923; *b* 23 Feb. 1895; *s* of Percy Pugh Goolden Goolden, MA, Barrister-at-Law, and Margarida da Costa Ricci. *Educ*: Charterhouse; New Coll., Oxford. BA 1923, Honour Sch. of Modern Languages (French). Secretary, 1923, OUDS with whom he visited Scandinavia in Loyalties and Mr Pim Passes By, also appeared as Dolon in Doctor Cyril Bailey's production (in Greek) of The Rhesus of Euripides. First professional appearance in 1923 with late J. B. Fagan's newly formed Repertory Company at The (old) Oxford Playhouse, as Mazzini Dunn in Heartbreak House; Shakespearean Season at The (old) Memorial Theatre, Stratford-on-Avon, 1925; from 1926 worked for some time at The Lyric, Hammersmith, under late Sir Nigel Playfair. Varied career in London and Provinces (also Malta and Canada), in diversity of parts ranging from traditional classical repertoire to Farce, Opera Bouffe, Revue, Single Act Variety and Seaside Piers; among several hundred parts played Mole in Toad of Toad Hall (annually for five years 1930–34, Lyric, Savoy, and Royalty Theatres); Prince Paul in Offenbach's The Grand Duchess, Daly's, 1937; Lord Fancourt Babberley in Charley's Aunt, Haymarket, 1938; Professor Cunningham in Grouse in June, Criterion, 1939; The Fool in King Lear (with Donald Wolfit), St James's, 1943; in Captain Carvallo, St James's, 1950; in Sir Laurence Olivier's Festival Productions of Caesar and Cleopatra, and Antony and Cleopatra, St James's, 1951; Lord Hector in Anouilh's Leocadia (Time Remembered), Lyric

Hammersmith and New, 1954–55; Platina in Montherlant's Malatesta, Lyric, Hammersmith, 1957; Nagg in End Game, Royal Court, 1958; The Mayor in Look After Lulu, Royal Court and New, 1959; The White Rabbit in Alice in Wonderland, Winter Garden, 1959–60; Mr Jones in The Cupboard, Arts Theatre Club, 1961; Politic in Lock Up Your Daughters, Mermaid, 1962 and Her Majesty's, 1962–63; has played Mole in Toad of Toad Hall: Westminster, 1960–61; Saville, 1961–62; Comedy (also directed), 1963–64; Queen's, 1964–65; Comedy, 1965–66, 1966–67; Fortune, 1967–68; Duke of York's, 1968–69, 1970–71 and 1971–72; Strand, 1969–70; Jeanetta Cochrane, 1972–73, 1973–74; Haymarket, 1974–75; Duke of York's, 1975–76; Her Majesty's, 1976–77; Cambridge, 1977–78; Piccadilly, 1978–79; Old Vic, 1979–80; in Regent's Park Open Air Theatre: Shallow in Merry Wives of Windsor, 1968; Old Gobbo in Merchant of Venice, 1969; Verges in Much Ado About Nothing, 1970; The Pedant in Taming of the Shrew, 1975; Sir Nathaniel in Love's Labour's Lost, 1976, 1977; King of France in Henry V, 1977; Oxford Playhouse: Old Gobbo in Merchant of Venice, Lob in Dear Brutus, 1973; Bernard in Dirty Linen, Arts Theatre Club, 1976; Broomy in A Conception of Love, Oxford Drama Fest., 1978. Created popular Radio Characters, Mr Chips (the first presentation of this famous character in any medium), Mr Pim, Mr Penny, Old Ebenezer, and The Little Man in Dr L. du Garde Peach's Children's Hour Historical Playlets; has also appeared in films and television plays. Served European War, 1914–18, in France as a private in RAMC; performed continuously throughout War of 1939–45 at Troop Concerts and in shelters and refugee centres (in French), etc. Favourite parts: Mr Pim, Mole, and The Fool in King Lear. Special Variety Club Award, 1976; Variety Club Award, 1977. *Recreations:* household repairs and decoration; arguing; and singing Edwardian music-hall songs. *Address:* 15 Oakley Street, SW3 5NT. *T:* 01–352 7123. *Club:* United Oxford & Cambridge University.      *Died 18 June* 1981.

**GOOSSENS, Léon Jean,** CBE 1950; FRCM; Hon. RAM; Solo Oboist; *b* Liverpool, 12 June 1897; *s* of late Eugène Goossens, musician and conductor; *m* 1st, 1926; one *d*; 2nd, 1933, Leslie (*d* 1985), *d* of Brig. A. Burrowes; two *d*. *Educ:* Christian Brothers Catholic Institute, Liverpool; Liverpool Coll. of Music. Started oboe studies at 10 yrs of age with Charles Reynolds; at 14 studied at RCM, London, and at 16 joined London Symphony Orchestra on tour with Nikisch; same year toured Wales with Sir Henry Wood and Queen's Hall Orchestra as principal oboist, the following year accepting post as permanency. Served in European War, 1915–18 (wounded). Principal oboe, London Philharmonic Orchestra, also at Covent Garden Opera House with Sir Thomas Beecham; Prof. at RCM and RAM; after recitals in London and other English cities, toured USA, 1927 and 1928; Rep. British Music in most European capitals, at NY World Fair, with Sir Adrian Boult; also in Washington with Dr Clarence Raybould; recitals for BBC and lectures in schools, music clubs, univs and on TV. Has produced in England a new school of oboe-playing and promoted the oboe to the ranks of other solo instruments, for which leading composers of the day have written and, in many cases, dedicated their works to this artist; *works include:* concerti by Malcolm Arnold, Arnold Cooke, Dr Vaughan Williams, Rutland Boughton, Cyril Scott, Gordon Jacob, Francesco Ticciati, Ralph Nicholson, Sir Eugène Goossens; solo or chamber works by Dr Walter Stanton, Gustav Holst, Sir Edward Elgar, Sir George Henschel, John Addison, Dame Ethel Smyth, Franz Reizenstein, Thomas Pitfield, Somers Cocks, Gerald Finzi, Sir Arthur Bliss, Sir Arnold Bax, William Wordsworth, Lord Britten, Sigtenhurst Meyer, Alec Templeton, Alec Rowley, Alan Richardson, Francis Poulenc, Morgan Nicholas, Thomas Dunhill and Edwin Roxburgh. Toured Australia and New Zealand, also played in Singapore, 1954; visited Persia and Turkey, also Austria, 1955; toured Jugoslavia, 1954; toured USSR with Music Delegation headed by Master of The Queen's Musick, 1956; Coast to Coast Tour Canada, 1957; toured Scandinavia and Portugal, 1959, USA 1965, Munich 1972, St Moritz and Aberdeen (with Internat. Youth Orch.), 1971–73. Recitals in Malta, 1962–77. Pres., Art Soc., Gordonstoun Schs., 1980–. Belgrade Jurist, Internat. Wind Competition, 1981. Cobbett Medal for services to Chamber Music, 1954. *Publication:* (jtly with Edwin Roxburgh) The Oboe, 1977. *Relevant publication:* Music in the Wind, by Barry Wynne, 1967. *Recreation:* sailing. *Address:* Dulas Court, Dulas, Hereford HR2 0HL. *T:* Golden Valley 240214. *Clubs:* Chelsea Arts, London Corinthian Sailing; Malta Union.      *Died 13 Feb.* 1988.

**GOPALLAWA, William,** MBE 1953; President of Sri Lanka, 1972–77; Chancellor: University of Sri Lanka, Peradeniya; Vidyodaya University of Sri Lanka, Nugegoda; Vidyalankara University of Sri Lanka, Kelaniya; *b* Dullewe, Matale, 17 Sept. 1897; *s* of Tikiri Banda Gopallawa, and Dullewa Gopallawa Tikiri Kumarihamy; *m* 1928, Seila Rambukwella (*d* 1977); two *s* two *d*. *Educ:* Dharmaraja Coll. and St Anthony's Coll., Kandy, Ceylon; Law Coll., Colombo. Teacher, 1918–20; enrolled as Proctor of Supreme Court of Ceylon, 1924; practised in Matale, 1924–39; Mem., Urban Council, Matale, 1927–39 (Chm., 1928–34); Municipal Comr, Kandy, 1939;

Municipal Comr, Colombo, 1952; retired, 1957. Ambassador for Ceylon: in China, 1958; in USA, 1961 (concurrently Ambassador to Cuba and Mexico with residence in Washington); Governor-General of Ceylon, 1962–72. Chm., Arts Council's Panel for folk-songs and folk-dancing, 1954–56; A Founder, Dodandeniya Buddhist Schs, Matale; Founder Member: Vidyartha Coll., Kandy; Social Service League, Matale; Chief Scout for Sri Lanka. Past Pres., Kandy Rotary Club; Hon. Mem., Rotary Club of Colombo. Hon. LLD: University of Ceylon (Peradeniya), 1962; Vidyalankara University, 1962; Hon. DLitt, Vidyodaya Univ., 1962. Religion: Buddhist. *Recreations:* cricket, tennis, golf. *Address:* 128 Dharmapala Mawatha, Matale, Sri Lanka.
     *Died 30 Jan.* 1981.

**GORDON, Lord Adam (Granville),** KCVO 1970 (CVO 1961); MBE 1945; Comptroller to Queen Elizabeth the Queen Mother, 1953–73; Extra Equerry to Queen Elizabeth the Queen Mother, since 1974; *b* 1 March 1909; *s* of late Lt-Col Douglas Gordon, CVO, DSO, and *brother* of 12th Marquess of Huntley; *m* 1947, Pamela, *d* of Col A. H. Bowhill, CBE; two *s*. *Educ:* Eton. Asst Sec., Hurlingham Club, 1936–39. Served War of 1939–45 (despatches, MBE); Hants Yeomanry in GB, N Africa and Italy; retired 1945, with rank of Major. Sec., Brooks's Club, 1945–53. Mem. Queen's Body Guard for Scotland (Royal Co. of Archers). *Address:* Hethersett, Little-worth Cross, Seale, Surrey. *Clubs:* Brooks's, Pratt's, MCC.
     *Died 5 July* 1984.

**GORDON, Donald McDonald,** CMG 1970; HM Diplomatic Service, retired; *b* 14 Aug. 1921; *s* of late Donald McDonald Gordon and late Anabella Gordon (*née* Wesley); *m* 1948, Molly Denise, *o d* of Maurice Norman, Paris; three *s*. *Educ:* Robert Gordon's Coll., Aberdeen; Aberdeen Univ. Served in RA, 1941–47 (despatches). Entered Foreign (later Diplomatic) Service, 1947; FO, 1947; 2nd Sec. (Commercial), Lima, 1950; 2nd, later 1st Sec. (Commercial), Vienna, 1952; FO, 1956; 1st Sec. and Head of Chancery, Rangoon, 1960; 1st Sec., later Counsellor and Head of Chancery, Pretoria/Cape Town, 1962; Imp. Def. Coll., 1966; Counsellor and Consul-Gen., Saigon, 1967–69; Head of SE Asia Dept, FCO, 1969–72; Dep. High Comr, Kuala Lumpur, 1972–75; High Comr, Nicosia, 1975–79; Ambassador to Austria, 1979–81. Hon. LLD Aberdeen, 1982. *Publication:* The Gangrel Fiddler and Other Poems, 1984. *Address:* 23 Kew Green, Richmond, Surrey.      *Died 13 April* 1985.

**GORDON, Dr Hugh Walker,** MC 1917; MA; MB; FRCP; Consulting Physician to Department of Skin Diseases, St George's Hospital; Consulting Dermatologist to Royal Marsden Hospital and West London Hospital; Fellow Royal Society Medicine (Past President of Section of Dermatology); Hon. Member (Past President) British Association of Dermatology; Member of St John's Dermatological Society; *b* Maxwellton, Kircudbrightshire, 5 Aug. 1897; *er s* of late H. Sharpe Gordon, OBE, JP, Dumfries, Scotland and of late John Ann, *d* of Hugh Gilmour, London; *m* 1929, Jean Helen, *d* of late H. W. Robertson, Butterfield and Swire, London; one *s* one *d*. *Educ:* Marlborough Coll.; Pembroke Coll., Cambridge (History Exhibitioner); St George's Hospital (entrance scholar); Paris; Vienna, MB, BCh Cambridge, 1926; MRCS 1925; FRCP 1940. Late Vice-Dean, St George's Hosp. Med. Sch., 1946–51, Actg Dean, 1944–46; Dermatologist EMS Sector VII, 1939–46; Med. Officer i/c St George's Hosp., EMS, 1939–45; late Dermatologist to St John's Hosp., Lewisham, Shadwell Children's Hosp. and East Ham Memorial Hosp. Late Resident Med. Officer, St George's Hosp., and House Surg. and House Physician. Served European War, 1914–18, RFA, 1916–18, invalided out of Army with rank of Capt. *Publications:* chapters in Modern Practice of Dermatology, 1950; articles on dermatology in med. journals. *Recreations:* country pursuits. *Address:* 3 High Street, Kirkcudbright, SW Scotland. *T:* Kirkcudbright 30740. *Club:* Oriental.      *Died 9 Dec.* 1987.

**GORDON, Maj.-Gen. James Leslie,** OBE 1944; Deputy Medical Officer of Health, City of Canterbury, 1965–74, retired; *b* 10 Sept. 1909; *s* of Dr James Leslie Gordon and Annie Laycock; *m* 1939, Dorothy Roberson. *Educ:* Epsom Coll.; Middlesex Hosp. MRCS LRCP 1935, DPH London 1948. Commandant, Army Sch. of Health, 1956. Prof. of Army Health, Royal Army Medical Coll., 1958; Dir of Army Health, War Office, 1962–64 (Ministry of Defence, April-May 1964). Mem., Faculty of Community Medicine, RCP, 1972. *Address:* 28 St Stephen's Hill, Canterbury, Kent. *Club:* Naval and Military.      *Died 6 Nov.* 1985.

**GORDON, Sir John Charles,** 9th Bt, *cr* 1706; *b* 4 Jan. 1901; *s* of 8th Bt and Elizabeth, *d* of Rev. John Maitland Ware; *S* father, 1939; *m* 1928, Marion, 3rd *d* of James Wright, Springfield, Sydney; one *s* one *d*. *Heir: s* Robert James Gordon [*b* 17 Aug. 1932; *m* 1976, Helen, *d* of Margery Perry, Cammeray, Sydney]. *Address:* 61 Farrer-Brown Court, Nuffield Village, Castle Hill, NSW 2154, Australia.
     *Died 1982.*

**GORDON, Kathleen Olivia,** CBE 1966; Director, The Royal Academy of Dancing, 1948–68, Hon. Fellow, 1976; *b* 15 Jan. 1898; *d* of George R. Gordon, OBE, MD and Alice Maude Gordon. *Educ:*

Manchester High Sch. for Girls; King's Coll., London Univ. With Royal Academy of Dancing, 1924–68; Coronation Award, 1964. *Recreations:* reading, theatre, and ballet. *Address:* 23 Addisland Court, W14. *T:* 01–602 0430. *Died 5 July 1985.*

**GORDON, Strathearn,** CBE 1967 (OBE 1953); Librarian of the House of Commons, 1950–67; *b* 3 Sept. 1902; 2nd *s* of Hon. Huntly D. Gordon, Sheriff-Substitute of Ross and Cromarty, and Violet, *d* of John Gaspard Fanshawe, Parsloes; *m* 1934, Elizabeth, *d* of Lovelace Serjeantson; two *s* one *d*. *Educ:* Edinburgh Academy; RMC Sandhurst. Joined 2nd Bn Highland Light Infantry, 1923; invalided 1927. Clerk in the House of Commons, 1930. *Publications:* Our Parliament, 1945; (with T. G. B. Cocks) A People's Conscience, 1952. *Address:* Avoch House, Avoch, Ross-shire IV9 8RF. *T:* Fortrose 20432. *Club:* Army and Navy. *Died 2 April 1983.*

**GORDON-FINLAYSON, Air Vice-Marshal James Richmond,** DSO 1941; DFC 1940; *b* 19 Aug. 1914; *s* of late Gen. Sir Robert Gordon-Finlayson, KCB, CMG, DSO, and late Lady (Mary) Gordon-Finlayson, OBE; *m* 1953, Margaret Ann (*d* 1965), *d* of Col G. C. Richardson, DSO, MC; one *s* one *d* by a former marriage. *Educ:* Winchester; Pembroke Coll., Cambridge (MA). Mem. Inner Temple, 1935; joined RAF, 1936; ADC to Gov. of Kenya, 1938–39; served in Libya, 1940 and 1941–42, Greece, 1940–41 (despatches), Syria, 1941; Sqdn Ldr 1940; OC 211 Sqdn, 1940–41; RAF Staff Coll., 1942; Air Staff, Air Min., 1942–45; RAF Liaison Offr to HQ, US Army Strategic Air Force, Guam, 1945; Air Staff, Air Comd, SEA, 1945–46; SASO, AHQ, Burma, 1946; OC 48 Sqdn, 1946–47; on directing staff, JSSC, Group Captain 1951; Air Staff, Air Min., 1951–54, OC, RAF Deversoir, 1954; OC, RAF Khormaksar, 1954–56; on staff of HQ Bomber Command, 1956, Asst Comdt, RAF Staff Coll., Bracknell; Air Cdre, 1958; Air Vice-Marshal, 1961; Dir-Gen. of Personal Services, Air Ministry, 1960–63; retired, June 1963. Greek DFC, 1941; Sheikh el Bilharith. *Publications:* Epitaph for a Squadron, 1965; Their Finest Hour, 1976; articles on strategic and air and military affairs in various jls; verse. *Recreations:* fishing, sailing, travel and literary interests. *Address:* Avenida del Cobre 9–11, Apartado 187, Algeciras (Prov. de Cadiz), Spain. *Clubs:* Naval and Military, MCC; RAF Yacht. *Died 3 March 1990.*

**GORDON-HALL, Maj.-Gen. Frederick William,** CB 1958; CBE 1945; *b* 28 Dec. 1902; *s* of Col Frederick William George Gordon-Hall and Clare Frances (*née* Taylor); *m* 1930, Phyllis Dorothy Miller (*d* 1985); one *s* one *d*. *Educ:* Winchester Coll.; RMC Sandhurst. Gazetted Royal Tank Corps, 1923; Staff Capt., War Office, 1935–39; Ministry of Supply, 1939–43; HQ Allied Armies in Italy, 1943–45; Military Dir of Studies, Mil. Coll. of Science, 1946–49; Dir of Technical Services (Land), British Joint Staff Mission, Washington, 1950–52; Dir of Inspection of Fighting Vehicles, Ministry of Supply, Dec. 1952–June 1955. Dir-Gen. of Fighting Vehicles, Min. of Supply, 1955–58, retd. *Recreations:* domestic engineering, cabinet making. *Address:* Whitegates, Salisbury Road, Horsham, West Sussex. *T:* Horsham 3304. *Died 23 Feb. 1990.*

**GORDON LENNOX, Rear-Adm. Sir Alexander (Henry Charles),** KCVO 1972; CB 1962; DSO 1942; Serjeant at Arms, House of Commons, 1962–76; *b* 9 April 1911; *s* of Lord Bernard Charles Gordon Lennox and Evelyn (*née* Loch); *m* 1936, Barbara, *d* of Maj.-Gen. Julian Steele; two *s*. *Educ:* Hetherdown, Ascot; RNC Dartmouth. Served as young officer in small ships in Far East and Home Fleet; communication specialist. Served War of 1939–45 (despatches 1943); in ME, East Coast Convoys, Russian Convoys; subsequently commanded HMS Surprise, HMS Mermaid and 2nd Frigate Sqdn, HMS Mercury and HMS Newcastle. Dep. Chief of Supplies and Transport, 1959–62; President, RNC Greenwich, 1961–62. Haakon VII Freedom Medal (Norway), 1946. *Recreations:* shooting, fishing and gardening. *Address:* Quags Corner, Minstead, Midhurst, West Sussex. *T:* Midhurst 3623. *Club:* Naval (Portsmouth). *Died 4 July 1987.*

**GORDON LENNOX, Lieut-Gen. Sir George (Charles),** KBE 1964; CB 1959; CVO 1952; DSO 1943; King of Arms, Order of British Empire, 1968–83; *b* 29 May 1908; *s* of late Lord Bernard Charles Gordon Lennox, 3rd *s* of 7th Duke of Richmond and Gordon and late Evelyn Loch, *d* of 1st Baron Loch; *m* 1931, Nancy Brenda Darell; two *s*. *Educ:* Eton; Sandhurst. Served Grenadier Guards, 1928–52; served with Regt and on Staff, war of 1939–45, in Europe, Africa and Far East; Lieut-Col Commanding Grenadier Guards, Jan. 1951–July 1952; Comdr 1st Guards Brigade, 1952–54; IDC, 1955; BGS (SD and Trg) HQ, BAOR, 1956–57; GOC 3rd Div., 1957–59; Comdt, RMA Sandhurst, 1960–63; Dir-Gen. of Military Training, 1963–64; GOC-in-C Scottish Comd and Governor of Edinburgh Castle, 1964–66. Col, Gordon Highlanders, 1965–78. *Recreations:* field sports. *Address:* Gordon Castle, Fochabers, Morayshire. *T:* Fochabers 820275. *Club:* Cavalry and Guards. *Died 11 May 1988.*

**GORDON WATSON, Hugh;** *see* Watson.

**GORE, John Francis,** CVO 1941; TD; journalist and author; *b* 15 May 1885; *y s* of late Sir Francis Gore, KCB; *m* 1926, Lady Janet Helena Campbell (*d* 1982), *er d* of 4th Earl Cawdor; one *s* two *d*. *Educ:* Radley Coll.; Trinity Coll., Oxford (MA). Barrister-at-Law, Inner Temple, 1909; served European War, 1914–19 (despatches); Captain Bedfordshire Yeomanry; Sec. Training Grants Cttee, Ministry of Labour, 1920; took up journalism, 1923; pen-name The Old Stager, of the Sphere's Newsletter, 1928–64. JP Sussex, 1932–59, Chm. Midhurst Bench, 1944–58. *Publications:* The Trial Stone, 1919; A Londoner's Calendar, 1925; The Way In, 1927; The Ghosts of Fleet Street, 1929; Charles Gore, father and son, 1932; Creevey's life and times, 1934; Nelson's Hardy and his wife, 1935; Sydney Holland, Lord Knutsford, 1936; Geoffrey Colman; Mary, Duchess of Bedford (privately printed), 1938; King George V, 1941 (awarded J. T. Black Memorial Prize, 1941); Creevey, 1948; Edwardian Scrapbook, 1951; Three Howard Sisters (with another), 1955. *Address:* Littlehay, Burley, Ringwood, Hants. *T:* Burley 3306. *Club:* I Zingari. *Died 24 July 1983.*

**GORE-BOOTH,** Baron *cr* 1969 (Life Peer), of Maltby; **Paul Henry Gore-Booth,** GCMG 1965 (KCMG 1957; CMG 1949); KCVO 1961; HM Diplomatic Service, retired; Director: Grindlays Bank, 1969–79; United Kingdom Provident Institution, 1969–79; Registrar, Order of St Michael and St George, 1966–79; *b* 3 Feb. 1909; *m* 1940, Patricia Mary Ellerton; twin *s* two *d*. *Educ:* Eton; Balliol Coll., Oxford. Joined Foreign Service, 1933; FO 1933–36; Vienna, 1936–37; Tokyo, 1938–42; Washington, 1942–45; FO, 1945–49; Head of UN (Economic and Social) and Refugees Depts, 1947–48; Head of European Recovery Dept, Foreign Office, 1948–49; Dir British Information Services in United States, 1949–53; Ambassador to Burma, 1953–56; Dep. Under-Sec. (Economic Affairs), Foreign Office, 1956–60; British High Commissioner in India, 1960–65; Permanent Under-Sec. of State, FO, 1965–69; Head of HM Diplomatic Service, 1968–69. Hot Springs Food Conference, 1943; UNRRA Conference, 1943; Chicago Civil Aviation Conference, 1944; San Francisco Conf., 1945; UN Assembly, 1946 (Sec. of UK Deleg.) Jan. and Oct. and 1947; British Rep., Gp of Four drafting Convention setting up OECD. Chairman: Save the Children Fund, 1970–76; Disasters Emergency Cttee, 1974–77. Chm. Bd of Governors, Sch. of Oriental and African Studies, Univ. of London, 1975–80. Pres., Sherlock Holmes Soc. of London, 1967–79; Chm., Windsor Music Festival, 1971–73. *Publications:* With Great Truth and Respect (autobiog.), 1974; (ed) Satow's Guide to Diplomatic Practice, 5th edn, 1978. *Address:* 70 Ashley Gardens, SW1P 1QG. *Clubs:* Athenæum, Baker Street Irregulars. *Died 29 June 1984.*

**GORE-BOOTH, Sir Michael Savile,** 7th Bt, *cr* 1760; *b* 24 July 1908; *s* of 6th Bt and Mary (*d* 1968), *d* of Rev. S. L'Estrange-Malone; *S* father, 1944. *Educ:* Rugby; Trinity Coll., Cambridge. *Heir: b* Angus Josslyn Gore-Booth [*b* 25 June 1920; *m* 1948, Hon. Rosemary Vane (marr. diss., 1954), *o d* of 10th Baron Barnard; one *s* one *d*]. *Address:* Lissadell, Sligo. *Died 16 March 1987.*

**GORE BROWNE, Sir Thomas (Anthony),** Kt 1981; Senior Government Broker, 1973–81; Treasurer, Imperial Cancer Research Fund, 1980–88; *b* 20 June 1918; 2nd *s* of Sir Eric Gore Browne, DSO; *m* 1946, Lavinia, *d* of Sir (Henry) Charles Loyd, GCVO, KCB, DSO, MC; three *s* one *d*. *Educ:* Eton Coll.; Trinity Coll., Cambridge. Served Grenadier Guards, 1938–48, France, N Africa, Italy. Joined Mullens & Co., 1948, Partner 1949–81. Dir, SW Regional Bd, Nat. Westminster Bank, 1981–84. *Address:* Flat 62, Melton Court, SW7 3JH. *T:* 01–589 0530. *Clubs:* Brooks's, White's, Pratt's. *Died 7 Sept. 1988.*

**GORELL BARNES, Sir William (Lethbridge),** KCMG 1961 (CMG 1949); CB 1956; Deputy Under-Secretary of State, Colonial Office, 1959–63; Deputy Chairman, Royal Group of Insurance Companies, 1972–80 (Director, 1963–80); *b* 23 Aug. 1909; *y s* of late Sir Frederic Gorell Barnes and Caroline Anne Roper Lethbridge; *m* 1935, Barbara Mary Louise, *e d* of late Brig. A. F. B. Cottrell, DSO, OBE; three *d* (one *s* decd). *Educ:* Marlborough Coll.; Pembroke Coll., Cambridge, 1st Cl. Classical Tripos Pt 1, 1st Cl. Mod. Langs Tripos Pt 2. Served in HM Diplomatic Service (Foreign Office, Baghdad and Lisbon), 1932–39; Offices of War Cabinet, 1939–45; Personal Asst to Lord Pres. of the Council, 1942–45; Asst Sec., HM Treasury, 1945–46; Personal Asst to Prime Minister, Oct. 1946–Feb. 1948; Seconded to Colonial Office, 1948; Asst Under-Sec. of State, 1948–59. Mem. UK delegn for negotiations with European Economic Community, 1962. Director: Doulton & Co., 1966–80 (Dep. Chm., 1969–80); Limmer Holdings Ltd, 1966–71 (Chm., 1971); Tarmac PLC, 1971–83; Tarmac Roadstone Hldgs Ltd, 1983–84; Donald Macpherson Gp, 1972–84; Vice-Chm. and Financial Dir, Harvey's of Bristol, 1963–66; Chm., James Templeton & Co., 1967–69. Chm., Cons. Commonwealth and Overseas Council, 1974–75. Mem. Council, Westfield Coll., London Univ., 1970–77 (Hon. Fellow, 1978). *Publication:* Europe and the Developing World, 1967. *Recreations:* gardening, walking, reading. *Address:* Mattishall

Hall, Dereham, Norfolk. *T:* Dereham 858181. *Clubs:* Reform; Norfolk (Norwich). *Died 25 March 1987.*

**GORING-MORRIS, Rex,** OBE 1975; HM Diplomatic Service, retired; *b* 17 Oct. 1926; *s* of late Cecil Goring Morris and Doris Flora Edna (*née* Howell); *m* 1st, 1950, Constance Eularia Heather (*d* 1979), *d* of late Mr and Mrs Cecil Bartram, Oxford; two *s* three *d*; 2nd, 1979, Mrs Mary Poole (*née* King), Aldenham, Herts; one step *s* one step *d*. *Educ:* Chichester High Sch.; New Coll., Oxford; RAF Coll., Cranwell, 1945–46. No 66 (F) Sqdn, 1947–50; Central Flying Sch., 1950; No 6 FTS, 1950–51; French Air Force, Marrakech and Rabat, 1951–53; RAF Odiham, 1954–56; Flt Cdr No 66 (F) Sqdn, 1956–57; HQ Fighter Comd, 1957; HQ RAF Germany, 1957–59; RAF Staff Coll., 1959; Sqdn Cdr, Central Fighter Estabt, 1959–61; Military Agency for Standardisation, NATO, London, 1962–63; Wing Comdr 1963; Air Attaché, Tel Aviv, 1964–67; jssc 1968; Jt Warfare Estabt, 1969; retired from RAF and joined HM Diplomatic Service, 1969; 1st Sec., FCO, 1969–71; 1st Secretary and Head of Chancery: Tunis, 1971–75; Bangkok, 1975–77; Counsellor, Consul-Gen. and Hd of Chancery, Bangkok, 1978–79; Stockholm, 1979–82. *Recreations:* travel, photography; Oxford blue for Association Football, 1944–45. *Address:* Woodlands, High Coppice, Amersham, Bucks HP7 0AW. *T:* Amersham 726528. *Club:* Royal Air Force. *Died 14 May 1988.*

**GORONWY-ROBERTS, Baron** *cr* 1974 (Life Peer), of Caernarvon and of Ogwen in the county of Caernarvon; **Goronwy Owen Goronwy-Roberts,** PC 1968; MA; Fellow, University of Wales, since 1938; *b* 20 Sept. 1913; *yr s* of E. E. and Amelia Roberts, Bethesda, Caernarvonshire; *m* 1942, Marian Ann, *yr d* of David and Elizabeth Evans, Tresalem, Aberdare; one *s* one *d*. *Educ:* Universities of Wales and London; on Continent. Exhibitioner, BA; MA; Univ. of Wales; Research at King's College, London, and on the Continent, 1937–39. Served in Infantry, 1941; Army Reserve, 1941–. Youth Education Officer to Caernarvonshire Education Authority, 1941–44. MP (Lab) Caernarvonshire, 1945–50, Caernarvon, 1950–Feb. 1974; Mem., House of Commons Panel of Chairmen, 1963–64; Minister of State, Welsh Office, 1964–66; Dept of Education and Science, 1966–67; Minister of State, FCO, 1967–69, Bd of Trade, 1969–70; Parly Under-Sec. of State, FCO, 1974–75; Minister of State, FCO, and Dep. Leader, House of Lords, 1975–79. Writes and broadcasts on literary and political matters. Member: Court of Governors of University Coll. of Wales and National Museum of Wales; Fabian Society; Trustee, Oppenheimer Trust for Ex-Servicemen. Chm., Regional Economic Council for Wales, 1965–. Formerly: Chm. Hughes and Son Ltd, Publishers, Wrexham; Lectr in Educn, Univ. Coll., Swansea. FRSA 1968. Hon. Freeman, Royal Borough of Caernarvon, 1972. *Recreations:* walking, music, collecting Year Books. *Address:* House of Lords, SW1. *Died 23 July 1981.*

**GOSLING, Sir Arthur Hulin,** KBE 1955; CB 1950; BSc; FRSE; FRICS; Director-General, Forestry Commission, 1948–62, retired; *b* 26 July 1901; 5th *s* of late C. F. Gosling; *m* 1931, Jane Alexander (*d* 1969), *o d* of late Dr M. Bryson. *Educ:* Bell's Gram. Sch., Coleford, Glos; Edinburgh Univ. District Officer, Forestry Commission, 1928; Divisional Officer, Glasgow, 1938; Asst Comr, Scotland, 1940; Dep. Dir Gen., 1947. Chm. Commonwealth Forestry Assoc., 1963–72. *Address:* The Old Manse, Cerne Abbas, Dorset. *Club:* Athenæum. *Died 8 Aug. 1982.*

**GOSNAY, Maxwell; His Honour Judge Gosnay;** a Circuit Judge, since 1973; *b* 31 July 1923; *o s* of William and Milly Gertrude Gosnay; *m* 1959, Constance Ann, *d* of Ben and Constance Mary Hardy; one *s* one *d*. *Educ:* Leeds Grammar Sch.; Christ Church, Oxford (MA). Called to Bar, Inner Temple, 1945. Asst Recorder, Leeds, 1965–71; Deputy Licensing Authority, Yorks Traffic Comrs, 1965–72; Dep. Chm., WR Yorks QS, 1967–71; a Recorder, 1972–73. *Recreations:* golf, reading. *Address:* 25 Park Lane, Leeds LS8 2EX. *T:* Leeds 663066. *Died 17 May 1986.*

**GOSS, Leonard (Cecil);** Administrative Director, Council of Christians and Jews, since 1984; *b* London, 19 May 1925; *s* of Jack and Sophie Goss; *m* 1978, Mildred, *d* of Hyman and Rebecca Gershon. *Educ:* Raine's Foundn Sch., Stepney, London. Journalist, latterly News Editor, S Wales Evening Post, Swansea, 1944–70; Inf. Officer, University Coll. of Swansea, 1970–75. Jt Chief Exec., 1975–81, Gen. Sec., 1981–84, CCJ. British Jun. Chamber of Commerce: Vice-Pres., 1954–57; National Hon. PRO, 1952–54 and 1957–62; Senator, Jun. Chamber Internat., 1963–; Vice-Chm., IFL, 1969–74, Vice-Pres. Brit. Section, 1975–, Hon. Dir, Internat. Assembly, 1981 (Jubilee Year). Member: Exec. Cttee, Jewish Scout Adv. Council, 1975–84; Bd of Deputies of British Jews, 1976– (Mem. Central Jewish Lecture and Information Cttee, 1979–, Vice-Chm., 1982–); Exec. Cttee, All-Party and Inter-Faith Cttee for Racial Justice, 1977– (founder mem.); Exec. Cttee, Religious Zionist Movement, 1978– (Jt Hon. Sec., 1982–); Gp Relations Cttee, AJEX, 1976–. Hon. Secretary: Golders Green AJEX, 1978–; Religious Weekly Press Gp, 1975–; British Israel Numismatic Soc., 1983–; Jt Hon.

Sec., Guild of Jewish Journalists, 1983–; Mem., Jewish Book Council, 1984–. Hon. Treasurer, Internat. CCJ, 1980–82, Exec. Cttee, 1982–84. Leader, Brit. contingent to World Conf. of Jewish Journalists, Jerusalem, 1977. Formerly: Vice-Chm., Swansea Citizens' Advice Bureau; Chm., Swansea Br., Save the Children Fund and Chm., all-Wales SCF Conf.; Mem. Wales Cttee, Internat. Refugee Year, and Freedom from Hunger Campaign; W Glam County Scout Officer. Scout Movement's Thanks Badge, 1943, and Medal of Merit, 1970; IFL Internat. Badge of Honour, 1974. Editor, Common Ground (CCJ qly), 1975–81. *Publications:* contrib. to Jewish Chronicle, Catholic Herald, and Baptist Times. *Recreations:* theatre, reading. *Address:* Council of Christians and Jews, 1 Dennington Park Road, NW6; 42 Golders Gardens, NW11 9BU. *T:* 01–455 5599. *Died 26 Dec. 1984.*

**GOSS, Brig. Leonard George,** CB 1946; *b* 30 May 1895; *s* of Alfred Herbert Goss, Wellington, NZ; *m* 1920, Ella May, *d* of John Airth Mace, New Plymouth, NZ; one *d*; *m* 1950, Rhoda, *d* of Thomas Lowis, Wellington, NZ. *Educ:* New Plymouth Boys' High Sch. (NZ); RMC of Australia. Commissioned in NZ Staff Corps, Lieut 1916; Captain 1919; Major, 1935; Lt-Col 1939; Temp. Brig. 1942; retired 1948. Legion of Merit (USA), 1944. *Recreations:* Rugby, cricket, swimming, boxing. *Address:* 17 Waitui Crescent, Lower Hutt, NZ. *Club:* United Service (Wellington, NZ). *Died 5 June 1988.*

**GOSTLING, Maj.-Gen. Philip le Marchant Stonhouse S.;** *see* Stonhouse-Gostling.

**GOTLEY, Roger Alwyn H.;** *see* Henniker-Gotley.

**GOUDGE, Elizabeth (de Beauchamp;** FRSL 1945; *b* 24 April 1900; *d* of late Henry Leighton Goudge, Regius Professor of Divinity in the University of Oxford, and late Ida de Beauchamp Collenette; unmarried. *Educ:* Grassendale, Southbourne; Reading Univ. Writer of novels, children's books, short stories and plays. *Publications: novels:* Island Magic, 1932; The Middle Window, 1933; A City of Bells, 1934; Towers in the Mist, 1936; The Bird in the Tree, 1939; The Castle on the Hill, 1942; Green Dolphin Country, 1944; The Herb of Grace, 1948; Gentian Hill, 1950; The Heart of the Family, 1953; The Rosemary Tree, 1956; The White Witch, 1958; The Dean's Watch, 1960; The Scent of Water, 1963; The Child from the Sea, 1970; *collections of short stories:* Make-Believe, 1949; The Reward of Faith, 1950; White Wings, 1952; The Lost Angel, 1971; *plays:* Three Plays, 1937; *children's books:* Smokey House, 1938; Sister of the Angels, 1939; Henrietta's House (in America: The Blue Hills), 1942; The Little White Horse, 1946 (awarded Carnegie Medal for 1947); The Valley of Song, 1951; Linnets and Valerians, 1964; I Saw Three Ships, 1969; *biography:* God so Loved the World (Life of Christ), 1951; St Francis of Assisi, 1959; *autobiography:* The Joy of the Snow, 1974; Anthology of Verse and Prose: A Book of Comfort, 1964; A Diary of Prayer, 1966; 2nd Anthology of Verse and Prose: A Book of Peace, 1967; 3rd Anthology of Verse and Prose: A Book of Faith, 1976. *Recreations:* reading and gardening. *Address:* Rose Cottage, Peppard Common, Henley-on-Thames, Oxon. *Died 1 April 1984.*

**GOUGH, Brig. Guy Francis,** DSO; MC; late Royal Irish Fusiliers; *b* 9 Aug. 1893; *e s* of late Hugh George Gough, Hyderabad, Deccan; *m* 1st, 1914, Dorothy (*d* 1953), *d* of late Edwin Paget Palmer, Patcham House, Sussex; one *s* one *d*; *m* 2nd, 1954, Elizabeth Treharn, *d* of Lewis David Thomas, Newton, near Porthcawl. *Educ:* The Oratory Sch.; RMC Sandhurst. 2nd Lieut, Royal Irish Fusiliers, Aug. 1914; European War, 1914–18. France and Belgium with 1st Royal Irish Fusiliers, and on the Staff (wounded, despatches, MC, 1915 Star); Staff Course, 1916. Commanded 1st Bn Nigeria Regt, 1936–37; War of 1939–45: Commanded ITC Royal Irish Fusiliers, 1st Battalion Royal Irish Fusiliers (in France and Belgium, May 1940), 202nd and 11th Infantry Brigades, Advanced Base I Army (N Africa), North Aldershot Sub-District. DSO, 1939–45 Star, Africa Star (with 1st Army clasp); retd pay, 1946. Control Commission, Germany as a Senior Control Officer, 1947–48. Coronation Medal, 1937. *Address:* Glyn Deri, Talybont-on-Usk, near Brecon, Powys LD3 7YP. *Died 19 Oct. 1988.*

**GOULD, R(alph) Blair,** MB, ChB Sheffield; DA (England); FFARCS; physician, anæsthetist; Fellow Royal Society of Medicine (Member Section of Anæsthetists); Fellow, Internat. College of Anæsthestists, USA; Fellow, Association of Anæsthetists of Great Britain; Hon. Consultant Anæsthetist: St George's Hospital; Royal Throat Nose and Ear Hospital; *b* Edinburgh, 15 May 1904; *o s* of late Maurice Gould, Bournemouth; *m* 1937, Lydia, *e d* of late Robert Geneen, 89 Park Lane, W1; two *s*. *Educ:* King Edward VII Sch., Sheffield; Sheffield Univ. Held Senior Resident appointments at Jessop Hospital for Women, Sheffield; Sheffield Royal Hosp., and West London Hosp., Hammersmith; Surg., Canadian Pacific Steamship Co.; lately: Hon. Asst in the Out-patient Dept, Central London Throat, Nose and Ear Hosp.; Clinical Asst, Central London Ophthalmic Hosp.; Clinical Asst, Aural and Children's Depts, West London Hosp.; Specialist in Anæsthetics: Metropolitan Reg. Hosp.

Bds, etc; EMS for London; Senior Consultant Anæsthetist: German Hosp.; Brentwood Dist Hosp.; Royal Nat. Throat Hosp.; Sch. of Dental Surgery, Royal Dental Hosp. (also Lectr); Anæsthetist to LCC and Royal Eye Hosp.; Hon. Anæsthetist: St John's Hosp., Lewisham; Romford Victoria Hosp.; Queen Mary's Hosp., Sidcup; Editor, Anæsthesia. *Publications:* various communications to the medical journals. *Recreations:* music, photography. *Address:* 25 Briardale Gardens, NW3. *T:* 01–435 2646.

*Died 1 July 1984.*

**GOULD, Sir Ronald,** Kt 1955; General Secretary, National Union of Teachers, 1947–70; (First) President of World Confederation of Organizations of the Teaching Profession, 1952–70; Member, Community Relations Commission, 1968–73; *b* 9 Oct. 1904; *s* of late Fred Gould, OBE; *m* 1st, 1928, Nellie Denning Fish (*d* 1979); two *s*; 2nd, 1985, Evelyn Little. *Educ:* Shepton Mallet Grammar Sch.; Westminster Training Coll. Asst Master Radstock Council Sch., 1924–41; Headmaster Welton County Sch., 1941–46. Dep. Chm., ITA, 1967–72. Chm. Norton Radstock UDC, 1936–46; Pres. NUT, 1943–44; Hon. Fellow; Educational Inst. of Scotland; College of Preceptors, 1965. Hon. MA Bristol, 1943; Hon. LLD: British Columbia, 1963; McGill, 1964; St Francis Xavier, NS, 1969; Leeds 1971; DUniv. York 1972. Officier, Ordre des Palmes Académiques, France, 1969; Das Verdienstkreuz (1st Cl.), Germany, 1979. *Publications:* The Changing Pattern of Education, 1965; Chalk Up the Memory (autobiog.), 1976. *Address:* 12 St John's Avenue, Goring by Sea, Worthing, Sussex BN12 4HU.

*Died 11 April 1986.*

**GOULD, Sir Trevor (Jack),** Kt 1961; Justice of Appeal, Fiji Court of Appeal, since 1965; *b* 24 June 1906; *s* of Percy Clendon and Elizabeth Margaret Gould; *m* 1934, May Milne; one *s* two *d*. *Educ:* Auckland Gram. Sch.; Auckland Univ. Coll., NZ. Barrister and Solicitor, Supreme Court of New Zealand, 1928; Supreme Court of Fiji, 1934; Crown Counsel, Hong Kong, 1938; served War, 1941–45 (prisoner of war). Actg Puisne Judge, Hong Kong, 1946, Puisne Judge, 1948; Acting Chief Justice, Hong Kong, 1953–55; Senior Puisne Judge, Hong Kong, 1953–58; Justice of Appeal, Court of Appeal for Eastern Africa, 1958–63; Vice-Pres. Court of Appeal for Eastern Africa, 1963–65. *Recreation:* sports. *Address:* 21 Mount St John Avenue, Auckland 3, New Zealand. *Club:* The Northern (Auckland). *Died 2 May 1984.*

**GOULDEN, Gontran Iceton,** OBE 1963; TD 1946 (and 3 Clasps); FRIBA; *b* 5 April 1912; *s* of late H. G. R. Goulden, Canterbury, and Alice Mildred Iceton; *m* 1937, Phyllis Nancye, *d* of J. W. F. Crawford, Dublin; two *s* one *d*. *Educ:* St Edmund's Sch., Canterbury; Paris; London Univ. (Dipl.). Commissioned RA (TA) 1931, Capt. 1936, Major 1939; served UK, Ceylon (GSO2 to C-in-C), India and SEAC (CO 6 Indian HAA Regt I Artillery; Comd 13 AA Bde), 1939–45; T/Lieut-Col 1943; A/Brig. 1945 (despatches twice); Lieut-Col 1947, Bt Col 1953. Col 1954; Deputy Commander, 33 AA Brigade, 1954–58; TARO 1960; Hon. Col 452 HAA Rgt RA (TA), 1960–61; Hon. Col 254 Fd Regt RA (TA) 1964–65; Mem. Mddx TA&AFA, 1947–53. Surveyor to Wellcome Archæol. Exped. to Near East, 1934–35; Asst to Graham Dawbarn, 1935–39. Teaching staff of Architectural Association Sch. of Architecture, 1945–46. Chief Tech. Officer and Dep. Dir, the Building Centre, 1947–61, Dir, 1962–68, Dir-Gen., 1968–74; Dep. Chm., Building Centre Gp, 1974–77; Governor, Building Centre Trust, 1974–. Mem. of Council AA, 1949–58 (Pres., 1956–57). Hon. Sec. Modern Architectural Research (MARS) group, 1950–53. Member: Architects Registration Council of the UK, 1954–56, 1963–64, 1971–72; RIBA Council, 1956–57, 1962–65; ARCUK/RIBA Observer Liaison Cttee of Architects of the Common Market, 1963–72; Dir, VIth Congress Intern Union of Architects, 1961; Chm. UIA and Foreign Relations Cttee, RIBA, 1962–65. Treasurer UIA, 1965–75; Mem., Franco-British Union of Architects; Honorary Corresponding Mem. Danish Architectural Assoc., 1965; Pres. International Union of Building Centres, 1962–63, Sec.-Gen. 1969–77; Mem. Council, Modular Soc., 1955–59. Sec., The Architecture Club, 1958–64; Member: Min. of Transport Advisory Cttee on landscaping of trunk roads, 1963–64; Ministry of Public Building and Works Cttee on the Agrément System, 1964–65; General Council of BSI, 1964–67. Governor: St Edmund's Sch., Canterbury; St Margaret's Sch., Bushey, 1949–59. Occasional guest lectr to Serenissima Travel, 1978–82; lectr and broadcaster on architectural subjects. Hereditary Freeman of City of Canterbury. *Publications:* Bathrooms, 1966; regular contrib. to The Times book and travel pages, and to architectural papers. *Recreations:* travel, sailing. *Address:* 28 St Peter's Square, Hammersmith, W6 9NW. *T:* 01–748 6621.

*Died 19 April 1986.*

**GOULDING, Sir Basil;** see Goulding, Sir W. B.

**GOULDING, Lt-Col Terence Leslie Crawford P.;** see Pierce-Goulding.

**GOULDING, Sir (William) Basil,** 3rd Bt *cr* 1904; Director: Fitzwilton Ltd; *b* 4 Nov. 1909; *s* of Sir Lingard Goulding, 2nd Bt, and Nesta

Violet (*d* 1968) (she *m* 2nd, 1938, Stanley Adams, who *d* 1965), *d* of late Hon. Mr Justice Wright, and *g d* of Sir Croker Barrington, 4th Bt; *S* father, 1935; *m* 1939, Valerie Hamilton (Chairman and Managing Director, Central Remedial Clinic, Dublin; Senator, Seanad Eireann; Hon. LLD NUI), *o d* of 1st Viscount Monckton of Brenchley, PC, GCVO, KCMG, MC, QC, and *g d* of Sir Thomas Colyer-Fergusson, 3rd Bt; three *s*. *Educ:* Winchester Coll.; Christ Church, Oxford. War of 1939–45, Wing Comdr RAFVR. Former Dir, Rio-Tinto Zinc Corp. Ltd, 1936–81. *Heir: s* William Lingard Walter Goulding [*b* 11 July 1940. *Educ:* Winchester Coll.; Trinity Coll., Dublin. Headmaster of Headfort School, Kells]. *Address:* Dargle Cottage, Enniskerry, Co. Wicklow, Eire.

*Died 16 Jan. 1982.*

**GOURLAY, Harry Philp Heggie,** JP; DL; MP (Lab) Kirkcaldy, since Feb. 1974 (Kirkcaldy Burghs, 1959–74); *b* 10 July 1916; *s* of William Gourlay; *m* 1942, Margaret McFarlane Ingram; no *c*. *Educ:* Kirkcaldy High Sch. Coachbuilder, 1932; Vehicle Examiner, 1947. Mem. Kirkcaldy Town Council, 1946, Hon. Treasurer, 1953–57; Magistrate, 1957–59; Vice-Chm. Fife Education Cttee, 1958; Mem. Hospital Management Cttee; Sec. Kirkcaldy Burghs Constituency Labour Party, 1945–59; Mem. Estimates Cttee, 1959–64; Chm. Scottish Parly Labour Group, 1963–64 and 1976–77; Government Whip, 1964–66; a Lord Comr of the Treasury, 1966–68; Dep. Speaker and Dep. Chm. of Ways and Means, 1968–70; Mem., Select Cttee on Procedure, 1974–79; Chm., Scottish Grand Cttee, 1979–. DL Fife, 1978. *Recreations:* chess, golf. *Address:* 34 Rosemount Avenue, Kirkcaldy, Fife. *T:* Kirkcaldy 261919.

*Died 20 April 1987.*

**GOW, Ian (Reginald Edward),** TD 1970; MP (C) Eastbourne since Feb. 1974; *b* 11 Feb. 1937; *yr s* of late Dr and Mrs A. E. Gow; *m* 1966, Jane Elizabeth Packe; two *s*. *Educ:* Winchester. Commnd 15th/19th Hussars, 1956. Solicitor 1962. Contested (C): Coventry East, 1964; Clapham, 1966. PPS to the Prime Minister, 1979–83; Minister for Housing and Construction, 1983–85; Minister of State, HM Treasury, 1985. *Recreations:* tennis, cricket, gardening. *Address:* The Dog House, Hankham, Pevensey, East Sussex. *T:* Eastbourne (0323) 763316; 25 Chester Way, Kennington, SE11. *T:* 071–582 6626. *Clubs:* Carlton, Pratt's, Beefsteak, Cavalry and Guards, MCC. *Died 30 July 1990.*

**GOW, Brig. John Wesley Harper,** CBE 1958 (OBE 1945); DL; JP; retired Shipowner; *b* 8 April 1898; *s* of late Leonard Gow, DL, LLD, Glasgow, and Mabel A. Harper, *d* of John W. Harper, publisher, Cedar Knoll, Long Island, NY; *m* 1925, Frances Jean, JP (*d* 1975), *d* of James Begg, Westlands, Paisley; three *s*. *Educ:* Cargilfield; Sedbergh; RMC Sandhurst; Trinity Coll., Oxford. Entered Scots Guards, 1917; severely wounded, France. Late partner, Gow Harrison & Co. Mem. Queen's Body Guard for Scotland (Royal Company of Archers), 1941. MFH, Lanarkshire and Renfrewshire, 1949–54; Pres. Royal Caledonian Curling Club, 1958–60; Chm. West Renfrewshire Unionist Assoc., 1947–60, Pres. 1960–68; Life Vice-Pres., RNLI, 1978 (Chm. Glasgow Branch, 1937–73); Mem. Council, SS&AFA, 1961–73, Hon. Life Mem. 1983 (Pres., West of Scotland Br., 1969–85; Pres., Glasgow Branch, 1955–73); Member Council: Erskine Hosp., 1946–78 (Hon. Pres., 1978); Earl Haig Fund Officers Assoc. (Scotland), 1946–75; Mem. Glasgow TA & AFA, 1947–56. Served War of 1939–45: Scots Guards, RARO; Lt-Col attached RA (LAA), NW Europe; commanded 77 AA Bde, RA (TA), 1947–48; Brig. 1948. Hon. Col 483 HAA (Blythswood) Regt RA, TA, 1951–56; Hon. Col 445 LAA Regt RA (Cameronians) TA, 1959–67, later 445 (Lowland) Regt RA (TA). DL Renfrewshire (formerly City of Glasgow), 1948; JP Renfrewshire, 1952. Lord Dean of Guild, Glasgow, 1965–67. OStJ 1969. Chevalier Order of Crown of Belgium and Croix de Guerre (Belgian), 1945. *Recreations:* curling, hunting, shooting. *Address:* The Old School House, Beith Road, Howwood, Renfrewshire PA9 1AW. *T:* Kilbarchan 2503. *Clubs:* Army and Navy; Western (Glasgow); Prestwick Golf. *Died 27 Dec. 1986.*

**GOWER, Sir (Herbert) Raymond,** Kt 1974; MP (C) Vale of Glamorgan, since 1983 (Barry Division of Glamorganshire, 1951–83); journalist and broadcaster; *b* 15 Aug. 1916; *s* of late Lawford R. Gower, FRIBA, County Architect for Glamorgan, and Mrs Gower; *m* 1973, Cynthia, *d* of Mr and Mrs James Hobbs. *Educ:* Cardiff High Sch.; Univ. of Wales; Cardiff Sch. of Law. Solicitor, admitted 1944; practised Cardiff, 1948–63; Partner, S. R. Freed & Co., Harewood Place, W1, 1964–. Contested (C) Ogmore Division of Glamorgan, general election, 1950. Political Columnist for Western Mail for Cardiff, 1951–64. Parliamentary Private Secretary: to Mr Gurney Braithwaite, 1951–54, to Mr R. Maudling, 1951–52, to Mr J. Profumo, 1952–57, to Mr Hugh Molson, 1954–57, Min. of Transport and Civil Aviation, and to Minister of Works, 1957–60. Member: Speaker's Conf. on Electoral Law, 1967–69, 1971–74; Select Cttee on Expenditure, 1970–73; Select Cttee on Welsh Affairs, 1979–83; Treasurer, Welsh Parly Party, 1966–; Chm., Welsh Cons. Members, 1970–74, 1979–. Jt Founder and Dir, first Welsh Unit Trust. Governor, University Coll., Cardiff, 1951–; Member Court of Governors: National Museum of Wales, 1952–; National Library of Wales, 1951–; University Coll., Aberystwyth, 1953–; Vice-President: National Chamber of Trade, 1956–; Cardiff Business Club, 1952; South Wales Ramblers, 1958–; Sec., Friends of Wales Soc. (Cultural); Mem., Welsh Advisory Council for Civil Aviation, 1959–62; President: Wales Area Conservative Teachers' Assoc., 1962–; Glamorgan (London) Soc., 1967–69. FInstD 1958. *Recreations:* tennis, squash rackets, and travelling in Italy. *Address:* House of Commons, SW1; 45 Winsford Road, Sully, South Glam. *Clubs:* Carlton, Royal Over-Seas League.

*Died 22 Feb. 1989.*

**GOWER-JONES, Ven. Geoffrey;** Archdeacon of Lancaster, 1966–80, Archdeacon Emeritus, since 1981; Vicar of St Stephen-on-the-Cliffs, Blackpool, 1950–80; *b* 30 April 1910; *s* of late Rev. William Gower-Jones; *m* 1938, Margaret, *d* of late John Alexander; one *s* one *d*. *Educ:* Brasenose Coll., Oxford; Wells Theological Coll. Ordained 1934; Curate: St Paul, Royton, 1934–39; Prestwich, 1939–43; Vicar, Belfield, 1943–50. Canon of Blackburn, 1962–66; Rural Dean of Fylde, 1962; Rural Dean of Blackpool, 1963–66. *Address:* 7 Egerton Drive, Hale, Cheshire. *T:* 061–980 3886.

*Died 5 Nov. 1982.*

**GOWING, Rt. Rev. Eric Austin;** *b* 11 March 1913; *s* of late Frederic Lanchester and Beryl Moselle Gowing; *m* 1940, Muriel, *d* of late Rt Rev. Thomas Sherwood Jones, DD; two *s*. *Educ:* North Sydney High Sch.; Sydney Univ.; Oxford Univ. BA Sydney, 1934; BA Oxon, 1938; MA Oxon, 1943; Curate: St Mary, Deane, 1938–42; St Andrew, Plymouth, 1942–45; Vicar of St Peter, Norbiton, 1945–50; Dean of Nelson, NZ, 1950–56; Archdeacon of Christchurch and Vicar of St Mary's, Merivale, NZ, 1956–60; Bishop of Auckland, 1960–78. *Address:* 33 Pohutukawa Road, Beachlands, Auckland, NZ. *T:* Auckland 5366218.

*Died 3 June 1981.*

**GRACE, David Mabe;** QC 1985; *b* 23 May 1945; *s* of Edwin and Evelyn Grace; *m* 1975, Eileen Marian, 5th *d* of Patrick and Joanna Duffy; one *s* two *d*. *Educ:* Birkenhead Sch.; Exeter Coll., Univ. of Oxford (BA). Called to the Bar, Gray's Inn, 1967. *Address:* 3 Essex Court, Temple, EC4Y 9AL. *T:* 01–583 9294.

*Died 9 June 1988.*

**GRACE, Sir John (Te Herekiekie),** KBE 1968; MVO 1953; AE (RNZAF) 1950; New Zealand High Commissioner in Fiji, 1970–73; sheep and cattle station owner since 1958; *b* 28 July 1905; *s* of John Edward Grace, JP and Rangiamohia Herekiekie; *m* 1st, 1940, Marion Linton McGregor (*d* 1962); no *c*; 2nd, 1968, Dorothy Kirkcaldie. *Educ:* Wanganui Boys' Coll.; Te Aute Coll., Hawkes Bay. Served War of 1939–45, Royal NZ Air Force (Sqdn-Ldr). NZ Public Service, 1926–58: Private Sec. to Ministers of the Crown incl. three Prime Ministers, 1947–58; Member: NZ Historic Places Trust, 1952–68; NZ Geographic Bd, 1952–68; Maori Purposes Fund Bd, 1961–68; Maori Educn Foundn, 1962–68; Nature Conservation Coun., 1963–68; Nat. Coun. of Adult Educn, 1964–68; Lake Taupo Forest Trust, 1968–; Fiji Leper Trust Bd, 1972; Rotoaira Forest Trust, 1974–; Tuwharetoa Trust Bd, 1974–; Lake Taupo Reserves Bd, 1975–; Vice-Pres. and Dominion Councillor, NZ Nat. Party, 1959–67. JP 1947. *Publication:* Tuwharetoa, a History of the Maori People of the Taupo District, NZ. *Recreations:* golf, trout fishing, gardening. *Address:* 84 Parkes Avenue, St Johns Hill, Wanganui, New Zealand. *T:* Wanganui 55.323. *Clubs:* Wellesley (Wellington); Wanganui (Wanganui).

*Died 11 Aug. 1985.*

**GRACE, Dr Michael Anthony,** FRS 1967; Reader in Nuclear Physics, Oxford University, 1972–87, now Emeritus Reader; Student and Tutor in Physics, Christ Church, 1959–87, now Emeritus Student; *b* 13 May 1920; *er s* of late Claude Saville Grace, Haslemere, Surrey, and Evelyn Doris (*née* Adams); *m* 1948, Philippa Agnes Lois, *o d* of Sir (Vincent) Zachary Cope, MD, MS, FRCS; one *s* three *d*. *Educ:* St Paul's; Christ Church, Oxford. MA 1948; DPhil 1950. Mine Design Dept, HMS Vernon, 1940–45. ICI Research Fellowship, Clarendon Laboratory, Oxford, 1951; University Sen. Res. Officer, Dept of Nuclear Physics, 1955–72; Lectr in Physics, Christ Church, 1958, Censor, 1964–69; Dr Lee's Reader in Physics, 1972. Governor: St Paul's Schools, 1959; Harrow School, 1969. *Publications:* papers in various jls including Phil. Mag., Proc. Royal Soc., Proc. Phys. Soc., Nuclear Physics. *Recreations:* lawn tennis, swimming. *Address:* 13 Blandford Avenue, Oxford, *T:* Oxford 58464. *Club:* Athenæum.

*Died 17 May 1988.*

**GRACIE, George Handel H.;** *see* Heath-Gracie.

**GRADY, John William,** MA Cantab; Director, Zacharama Ltd, since 1978; *b* London, 6 April 1915; *s* of late John William Grady and Teresa (*née* Moore); *m* 1939, Edith Mary Green; one *s* one *d*. *Educ:* St Olave's Sch. Entered Post Office as Exec. Off., 1935; Higher Exec. Off., 1946; Sen. Exec. Off. in Organisation and Methods Br., 1950; Asst Accountant Gen., 1955; Financial Adviser, External Telecommunications, 1962; Dep. Dir of Finance, 1964; Dir of Giro and Remittance Services, PO, 1965–69. Exec. Dir, Samuel Montagu & Co. Ltd, 1969–75. Mem., Newlon Housing Trust, 1975–.

*Recreations:* music, walking. *Address:* 17 Millers Road, Toft, Cambridge CB3 7RX. *T:* Comberton 3107.

*Died 8 April 1982.*

**GRAEME, Bruce, (pseudonym of Graham Montague Jeffries);** Novelist; *b* 23 May 1900; *s* of late William Henry Jeffries; *m* 1925, Lorna Hélène, *d* of Capt. Hay T. Louch; one *s* one *d*. *Educ:* Privately. Finish of education interrupted by Great War; volunteered for Queen's Westminster Rifles; after demobilization became free-lance journalist; travelled several times to USA and France on various commissions, published short stories, 1921–25; interested in film work; financed, produced and sold one reel comedy, 1919–20; resumed this lifelong interest in films as script writer, and producer, 1942; entered Gray's Inn, 1930. *Publications:* The Story of Buckingham Palace, 1928; The Story of St James's Palace, 1929; A Century of Buckingham Palace, 1937; The Story of Windsor Castle, 1937; Blackshirt, 1925; The Trail of the White Knight, 1926; The Return of Blackshirt, 1927; Hate Ship, 1928; Trouble, 1929; Blackshirt Again, 1929; Through the Eyes of the Judge, 1930; The Penance of Brother Alaric, 1930; A Murder of Some Importance, 1931; Unsolved, 1931; Gigins Court, 1932; Alias Blackshirt, 1932; The Imperfect Crime, 1932; Impeached, 1933; Epilogue, 1933; An International Affair, 1934; Public Enemy No 1, 1934; Satan's Mistress, 1935; Blackshirt the Audacious, 1936; Not Proven, 1935; Cardyce for the Defence, 1936; Blackshirt the Adventurer, 1936; Mystery on the Queen Mary, 1937; Blackshirt takes a Hand, 1937; Disappearance of Roger Tremayne, 1937; Racing Yacht Mystery, 1938; Blackshirt: Counter-Spy, 1938; The Man from Michigan, 1938; Body Unknown, 1939; Blackshirt Interferes, 1939; Poisoned Sleep, 1939; 13 in a Fog, 1940; Blackshirt Strikes Back, 1940; The Corporal Died in Bed, 1940; Seven Clues in Search of a Crime, 1941; Son of Blackshirt, 1941; Encore Allain, 1941; House with Crooked Walls, 1942; Lord Blackshirt, 1942; News Travels by Night, 1943; A Case for Solomon, 1943; Calling Lord Blackshirt, 1944; Work for the Hangman, 1944; Ten Trails to Tyburn, 1944; The Coming of Carew, 1945; A Case of Books, 1946; Without Malice, 1946; A Brief for O'Leary, 1947; No Clues for Dexter, 1948; And a Bottle of Rum, 1948; Tigers Have Claws, 1949; Cherchez la Femme; Dead Pigs at Hungry Farm, 1951; Lady in Black, 1952; Mr Whimset Buys a Gun, 1953; Suspense, 1953; The Way Out, 1954; So Sharp the Razor, 1955; Just an Ordinary Case, 1956; The Accidental Clue, 1957; The Long Night, 1958; Boomerang, 1959; Fog for a Killer, 1960; The Undetective, 1962; Almost Without Murder, 1963; Holiday for a Spy, 1964; Always Expect the Unexpected, 1965; The Devil was a Woman, 1966; Much Ado About Something, 1967; Never Mix Business With Pleasure, 1968; Some Geese Lay Golden Eggs, 1968; Blind Date for a Private Eye, 1969; The Quiet Ones, 1970; The Lady doth Protest, 1971; Yesterday's Tomorrow, 1972; Two and Two Make Five, 1973; Danger in the Channel, 1973; The D Notice, 1974; The Snatch, 1976; Two-Faced, 1977; Double Trouble, 1978; Mather Again, 1979; Invitation to Mather, 1979; Mather Investigates, 1981. *Address:* Gorse Field Cottage, Aldington Frith, near Ashford, Kent. *T:* Aldington 383. *Club:* Paternosters.

*Died 14 May 1982.*

**GRAFFTEY-SMITH, Sir Laurence Barton,** KCMG 1951 (CMG 1944); KBE 1947 (OBE 1932); *b* 16 April 1892; *s* of late Rev. Arthur Grafftey-Smith and late Mabel, *d* of Rev. Charles Barton, Cheselbourne, Dorset; *m* 1930, Vivien (marr. diss., 1937), *d* of G. Alexander Alderson; two *s*; *m* 1946, Evgenia Owen, *d* of late P. H. Coolidge, Berkeley, Calif. *Educ:* Repton; Pembroke Coll., Cambridge. Student Interpreter, Levant Consular Service, 1914. HM Vice Consul, 1920; served at Alexandria, Cairo (Residency), Jeddah, Constantinople; Asst Oriental Sec. at the Residency, Cairo, 1925–35; HM Consul, Mosul, 1935–37; Baghdad, 1937–39; HM Consul-Gen. in Albania, 1939–40; attached British Embassy, Cairo, 1940; Chief Political Adviser, Diego Suarez, May 1942; Chief Political Officer, Madagascar, July 1942; Consul-Gen., Antananarivo, 1943; Minister to Saudi Arabia, 1945–47; High Comr for UK in Pakistan, 1947–51; retired from Govt service on 31 Dec. 1951; UK Rep. on Gov.-Gen.'s Commn, Khartoum, 1953–56. *Publications:* (with Godfrey Haggard) Visa Verses, 1915 (privately printed); Bright Levant, 1970; Hands to Play, 1975. *Address:* Broom Hill House, Coddenham, Suffolk.

*Died 3 Jan. 1989.*

**GRAHAM, Andrew Guillemard;** author and journalist; *b* 1 Feb. 1913; *s* of John Parkhurst Graham and Norah Madeleine (*née* Neal); unmarried. *Educ:* Uppingham Sch. (Rutland Schol.); New Coll., Oxford (BA). Served War with Welsh Guards, 1939–46; NW Europe campaign with 1st Bn, 1944–45; HQ, Guards Div., 1945–46. Sec., Conservative Club, St James's St., 1947–49; rejoined Welsh Guards, 1952; Asst Mil. Attaché, Brit. Legation, Saigon, 1952–54; Mil. Attaché (GSO1) Brit. Embassy, Beirut, 1955–57; Comptroller, Brit. Embassy, Paris, 1959–61. The Times wine correspondent, 1962–71. *Publications:* Interval in Indo-China, 1956; The Club, 1957; A Foreign Affair, 1958; Love for a King, 1959; Mostly Nasty, 1961; Sharpshooters at War, 1964; The Regiment, 1966; The Queen's Malabars, 1970. Regular Correspondent, The Times,

1962–71. *Recreation:* gardening. *Address:* c/o Coutts & Co., 440 Strand, WC2R 0QS. *Club:* Beefsteak.                    *Died* 30 *April* 1981.

**GRAHAM of Gartmore, Adm. Sir Angus (Edward Malise Bontine) C.;** *see* Cunninghame Graham.

**GRAHAM, Maj.-Gen. Frederick Clarence Campbell,** CB 1960; DSO 1945; Lord-Lieutenant of Stirling and Falkirk (Central Region), 1979–83; *b* Ardencaple Castle, Helensburgh, Scotland, 14 Dec. 1908; *s* of Sir Frederick Graham, 2nd Bt, and Lady Irene Graham (*née* Campbell); *m* 1936, Phyllis Mary, *d* of late Maj.-Gen. H. F. E. MacMahon, CB, CSI, CBE, MC; three *s. Educ.:* Eton Coll.; RMC Sandhurst. Commissioned Argyll and Sutherland Highlanders, 1929; served 1st and 2nd Bn Argyll and Sutherland Highlanders in China, India, UK and Palestine, 1929–39; Adjutant 1st Bn, 1937; War of 1939–45, served Palestine, N Africa, Crete, Syria, India, Italy; commanded 1st Bn Argyll and Sutherland Highlanders, 1944–end of war in Europe. Since 1945: GSO1, Home Counties District and Home Counties Div.; Joint Services Staff Coll.; Staff Coll., Camberley (Col); Comdr 61 Lorried Infantry Brigade (Brig.); Asst Commandant, RMA Sandhurst; Dep. Comdr, Land Forces, Hong Kong and Comd (Brig.) 40 Inf. Div.; Adviser in recruiting, MoD; Comdr Highland District and 51st (Highland) Div., TA, 1959–62; retd from HM Forces, 1962. Col, The Argyll and Sutherland Highlanders, 1958–72. Col Comdt, The Scottish Div., 1968–69; Hon. Col, Argyll and Sutherland Highlanders of Canada, 1972–77. Mem. of Royal Company of Archers, The Queen's Body Guard for Scotland, 1958–. Member: Perth CC, 1973–75; Stirling DC, 1976–80 (Vice-Chm., 1977–80). DL Perthshire, 1966. *Address:* Mackeanston House, Doune, Perthshire.                    *Died* 9 *May* 1988.

**GRAHAM, Gerald Sandford,** MA, PhD, FRHistS; Rhodes Professor of Imperial History, London University, 1949–70, later Emeritus; *b* Sudbury, Ontario, 27 April 1903; *s* of Rev. H. S. Graham and Florence Marian Chambers; *m* 1929, Winifred Emily Ware (marr. diss. 1950); one *s*; *m* 1950, Constance Mary Grey, Toronto; one *s* two *d. Educ.:* Queen's Univ., Canada; Harvard, 1926–27; Cambridge, 1927–29; Berlin and Freiburg-im-Breisgau, 1929–30; Instructor in History, and Tutor, Harvard Univ., 1930–36; successively Asst, Associate, and Prof. of History, Queen's Univ., 1936–46; Guggenheim Fellowship to US, 1941; RCNVR, 1942–45; Reader in History, Birkbeck Coll., Univ. of London, 1946–48. Mem., Inst. for Advanced Study, Princeton, 1952. Kemper Knapp Vis. Prof., Univ. of Wisconsin, 1961, Univ. of Hong Kong, 1966; Vis. Prof. of Strategic Studies, Univ. of Western Ontario, 1970–72; Vis. Montague Burton Prof. of Internat. Relations, Univ. of Edinburgh, 1974. FKC 1981. Hon. DLitt Univ. of Waterloo, Ont, 1973; Hon. LLD Queen's Univ., Ont, 1976; Hon. LitD Western Ontario, 1986. Editor: Imperial Studies series, Royal Commonwealth Soc., 1952–70; West Africa History series, 1956–70. *Publications:* British Policy and Canada, 1774–1791, 1930; Sea Power and British North America, 1783–1820, 1941; Empire of the North Atlantic, 1950 (2nd edn 1958); Canada, A Short History, 1950; The Walker Expedition to Quebec, 1711 (Navy Records Soc., and Champlain Soc.), 1953; The Politics of Naval Supremacy, 1965; (with R. A. Humphreys) The Navy and South America, 1807–1823 (Navy Records Soc.), 1962; Britain in the Indian Ocean, 1810–1850, 1967; A Concise History of Canada, 1968; A Concise History of the British Empire, 1970; Tides of Empire, 1972; The Royal Navy in the American War of Independence, 1976; The China Station: War and Diplomacy 1830–60, 1978; contributor to: Newfoundland, Economic, Diplomatic and Strategic Studies, 1946; Cambridge History of the British Empire, vol. III, 1959; Regionalism in the Canadian Community 1867–1967, ed Mason Wade, 1969. *Recreation:* sawing wood. *Address:* Hobbs Cottage, Beckley, Rye, Sussex. *T:* Beckley 308. *Club:* Royal Commonwealth Society.
                    *Died* 5 *July* 1988.

**GRAHAM, Air Vice-Marshal Henry Rudolph,** CB 1958; CBE 1955; DSO 1941; DFC 1942; *b* 28 March 1910; *s* of Major Campbell Frederick Graham, late Cape Mounted Rifles and South African Mounted Rifles, and Frances Elizabeth Cheeseman; *m* 1949, Maisie Frances Butler; two *s*; three *d* by a former marriage. *Educ.:* Rondebosch; SA Trng Ship General Botha, S Africa. Union Castle Line, 1926–31; RAF, 1931–62. National Trust, 1966–69. Military Cross (Czechoslovakia), 1940. *Recreation:* farming. *Address:* Majoro, PO Box 189, Magaliesburg, 2805, South Africa. *Clubs:* Wanderers', RAF Officers' (Johannesburg).
                    *Died* 14 *Feb.* 1987.

**GRAHAM, Lt-Gen. Howard Douglas,** OC 1967; CVO 1973; CBE 1946; DSO 1943 and Bar 1944; ED; CD; QC (Canada); retired as Lieutenant-General Canadian Army; *b* 1898. Served War of 1914–18: Canadian Infantry in France, Germany and Belgium; served War of 1939–45 (DSO and Bar, CBE, UK, France, 1940, Sicily and Italy; Senior Canadian Army Liaison Officer, London, and Army Adviser to the Canadian High Commissioner in London, 1946–48; Vice-Chief of Canadian General Staff, 1948–50; Gen. Officer Commanding Central Command, Canada, 1951–55; Chief

of Canadian Gen. Staff, 1955–58; undertook, on behalf of Canadian Govt, during 1958, a comprehensive survey of all aspects of Canada's civil def. policy and programme. Acted as Canadian Sec. to the Queen, 1959 and 1967. Pres. (retd), Toronto Stock Exchange. Officer, US Legion of Merit; Chevalier Legion of Honour (France); Croix de Guerre with palm (France). *Address:* 33 Colonial Crescent, Oakville, Ont. L6J 4K8, Canada.                    *Died* 28 *Sept.* 1986.

**GRAHAM, Prof. John Macdonald,** CBE 1955; Professor of Systematic Theology, University of Aberdeen, 1937–71, retired; *b* 17 March 1908; *s* of Thomas Graham and Elizabeth Macdonald; *m* 1933, Jessie Huntley Carmichael; two *s* twin *d. Educ.:* Allan Glen's Sch., Glasgow; University of Glasgow. MA. First Cl. Hons. in Mental Philosophy, 1930; Ferguson Scholar in Philosophy, 1931. Minister of Radnor Park, Clydebank, 1933–37. Mem. of Aberdeen Town Council, 1947–64; Lord Provost of the City of Aberdeen, 1952–55 and 1961–64; DL 1956; Hon. DD Glasgow, 1959; Hon. LLD Aberdeen, 1964. FEIS 1964. *Publication:* Christianity, Democracy and Communism, 1958. *Address:* Ruchil House, Comrie, Perthshire. *T:* Comrie 307.                    *Died* 7 *April* 1982.

**GRAHAM, Sir Ralph Wolfe,** 13th Bt *cr* 1629; *b* 14 July 1908; *s* of Percival Harris Graham (2nd *s* of 10th Bt) (*d* 1954) and Louise (*d* 1934), *d* of John Wolfe, Brooklyn, USA; *S* cousin, 1975; *m* 1st, 1939, Gertrude (marr. diss. 1949), *d* of Charles Kaminski; 2nd, 1949, Geraldine, *d* of Austin Velour; two *s. Heir: s* Ralph Stuart Graham [*b* 5 Nov. 1950; *m* 1st, 1972, Roxanne (*d* 1978), *d* of Mrs Lovette Gurzan; 2nd, 1979, Deena Vandergrift]. *Address:* 134 Leisureville Boulevard, Boynton Beach, Fla 33435, USA.                    *Died* 1988.

**GRAHAM, Sir Richard Bellingham,** 10th Bt of Norton Conyers, *cr* 1662; OBE 1946; DL; Wing Commander, RAFVR; Chairman, Yorkshire Television, 1968–81; *b* 17 May 1912; *e s* of Sir Guy Graham, 9th Bt, and Katharine Noel (*d* 1966), *d* of Frank Stobart, Selaby, Darlington; *S* father, 1940; *m* 1939, Beatrice Mary, *o d* of late Michael Seymour Spencer-Smith, DSO; three *s. Educ.:* Eton Coll.; Magdalene Coll., Cambridge. DL N Yorks (formerly NR Yorks), 1961; High Sheriff of Yorkshire, 1961. *Heir: s* James Bellingham Graham, *b* 8 Oct. 1940. *Address:* Norton Conyers, Melmerby, Ripon, North Yorks.                    *Died* 29 *Jan.* 1982.

**GRAHAM, William,** CB 1950; MBE 1920; Acting Secretary-General of the Intergovernmental Maritime Consultative Organisation (IMCO), 1961–63, Deputy Secretary-General, 1959–61; *b* 14 Dec. 1894; *s* of late A. Graham, Bradford, Yorks; *m* 1917, Elizabeth Young Warnock (*d* 1977); one *s* one *d. Educ.:* Bradford. Entered CS, 1911; served in Board of Trade until formation of Ministry of Shipping, 1939; Asst Secretary, Commercial Services Division, Ministry of Transport, 1940–46; Head of British Merchant Shipping Mission in Washington, DC, 1946; Under-Secretary, Ministry of Transport, 1946–59; Vice-Chairman, Maritime Transport Cttee, OEEC, 1948–59. *Address:* 115 Downs Court Road, Purley, Surrey. *T:* 01-660 1263.                    *Died* 1 *July* 1981.

**GRAHAM-DIXON, Leslie Charles,** QC 1950; retired 1956; *b* 17 June 1901; *m* 1926, Dorothy Rivett; two *s. Educ.:* Merchant Taylors' Sch.; St John's Coll., Oxford. Called to the Bar, 1925, Inner Temple. Western Circuit. Vice-Pres., Council, Royal Albert Hall, 1965–. Chm. Council, Charing Cross Hosp. Med. Sch., 1973–81, Pres., 1981–84. *Address:* The Clock Tower, Nutley, E Sussex. *T:* Nutley 2275.                    *Died* 15 *Feb.* 1986.

**GRAHAM DOW, Ronald;** *see* Dow.

**GRAHAM-GREEN, Major Graham John,** CB 1978; TD 1945; FCIArb; Chief Taxing Master of the Supreme Court, 1972–79 (Master, 1953–72); *b* 16 Dec. 1906; *m* 1933, Eirene Mary Baston; one *d. Educ.:* Dulwich. Admitted solicitor, 1929; Partner Kingsford, Dorman & Co., 1935–52; and Director of Companies. Served HAC, 1924–33; RA (TA), 1935–45. Freeman of City of London, 1945; Member: Law Soc., 1929 (Hon. Mem., City of Westminster and Eastbourne Law Socs, 1979); City of London Solicitors Company, 1945; London Maritime Arbitrators' Assoc., 1977. Co-Founder of Catholic Marriage Advisory Council, 1946; Founder Chm., Bd of Trustees, Friends of Osborne House Convalescent Home for Officers, 1979. FCIArb 1984. *Publications:* Cordery's Law Relating to Solicitors, 5th edn, 1961, Supplements 1962, 1963, 1965 and 1966, 6th edn 1968, Supplements 1970, 1974, 7th edn, 1981, Supplement 1984; Criminal Costs and Legal Aid, 1965, 2nd edn 1969, 3rd edn 1973, Supplement 1978, etc. *Recreations:* riding, travelling. *Address:* 7 Osborne House, Courtlands, Richmond, Surrey TW10 5BE. *Club:* Army and Navy.                    *Died* 22 *Aug.* 1985.

**GRAHAM SMITH, Stanley,** CBE 1949; *b* 18 Jan. 1896; *s* of late George and Minnie Elizabeth Graham Smith; *m* 1929, Mrs Blanche Violet Horne (*d* 1974), *widow* (*née* Venning); one *s. Educ.:* Strand Sch., King's Coll., London. Entered Civil Service, 1914 (Admiralty). Served European War as pilot in Royal Naval Air Service, Dec. 1916–Jan. 1919. Rejoined Admiralty, 1919. Private Secretary to Accountant-General of the Navy, 1922–32; Private Secretary to Civil Lord of Admiralty, 1932–35; Head of Air Branch, Admiralty,

1941–49; Under Secretary (Naval Staff), Admiralty, 1950–56; retired from Civil Service, 1956. *Died* 11 *Oct.* 1989.

**GRAINER, Ron;** composer for stage and screen; *b* Atherton, Australia, 11 Aug. 1932; *s* of Ronald Albert and Margaret Grainer; *m* 1966, Jennifer Marilyn Dodd; one *s*. *Educ:* St Joseph's Coll., Nudgee, Brisbane; Sydney Conservatorium. *Compositions include: musicals:* Robert and Elizabeth, 1964; On the Level, 1966; Sing a Rude Song, 1970; *incidental music for stage:* Andorra, Nat. Theatre, 1964; Come As You Are, 1970; *film scores:* Some People; Live Now, Pay Later; Dock Brief; Terminus; The Caretaker; Night Must Fall; A Kind of Loving; The Moonspinners; The Finest Hours; To Sir with Love; Lock up your Daughters; Before Winter Comes; The Omega Man; Cat and Mouse; Second on the Right; *TV themes and incidental music:* Steptoe and Son; Maigret; Comedy Playhouse; Dr Who; Panorama; That Was The Week That Was; Boy Meets Girl; Man in a Suitcase; Thief; Paul Temple; For the Love of Ada; The Train Now Standing; South Riding; Malice Aforethought; Edward and Mrs Simpson; Rebecca; Tales of the Unexpected; Shelley; Born and Bred. *Recreations:* theatre, travel. *Address:* c/o R. K. Records, 34 Windmill Street, W1. *Died* 22 *Feb.* 1981.

**GRAND, Keith Walter Chamberlain;** FCIT; Chairman, Railway Benevolent Institute; *b* 3 July 1900; *m* 1st, 1925, Alice M. (*d* 1969), *d* of late Henry Gates, Brockville, Ont., Canada; one *d* (one *s* decd); 2nd, 1971, Enid M. Wheatley. *Educ:* Rugby. Joined GWR 1919; USA 1926–29; General Manager, British Railways, Western Region, 1948–59. Member (full-time) British Transport Commn, 1959–62; Member Coastal Shipping Advisory Cttee, 1959–62; Chm., Coast Lines, 1968–71. *Recreation:* golf. *Address:* Queen Anne Flat, Little Sodbury Manor, Chipping Sodbury, near Bristol. *Clubs:* Carlton, MCC; Royal Mid-Surrey Golf (Richmond). *Died* 17 *Sept.* 1983.

**GRANDI, Count** (di Mordano) *cr* 1937, **Dino;** retired; President Chamber of Fasci and Corporazioni, Italy, 1939–43; late Member of the Chamber of Deputies and of the Fascist Grand Council; *b* Mordano (Bologna), 4 June 1895; *m* 1924, Antonietta Brizzi; one *s* one *d*. Graduated in Law at the University of Bologna, 1919; volunteered for the war and was promoted to Captain for merit and decorated with silver medal, bronze medal, and three military crosses for valour; journalist and political organiser, after the war led the Fascist movement in the North of Italy and took part in the March on Rome as Chief of the General Staff of the Quadrunvirato; elected member of the Chamber of Deputies, 1921, 1924, 1929, 1934, and 1939; member of the General Direction of the Fascist Party Organisation, 1921–23–24; Deputy President of the Chamber of Deputies, 1924; Italian Delegate to the IV, V, International Labour Conference, 1922, 1923; Under-Secretary of State for the Interior, 1924; Under Secretary of State for Foreign Affairs, 1925–29; Italian Delegate, Locarno Conference, 1925; to Conferences for Settlement of War Debt, Washington, 1925 and London, 1926; and Hague Conference on War Debts, 1929; Head of Italian Delegation, London Naval Conference, 1930; Italian Delegate, Danubian Conference, London, 1932; Head of Italian Delegation, Geneva Disarmament Conference, 1932; Minister of Foreign Affairs, 1929–32; Permanent Italian Delegate to the Council of the League of Nations, 1925–32; Italian Ambassador in London, 1932–39; Keeper of the Seal and Minister of Justice, Italy, 1939–43; Head of Italian Delegation to London Naval Conference, 1936; Italian Representative to London Session of Council of League of Nations, 1936; at London Meeting of Locarno Powers, 1936; and on the London International Cttee for Non-Intervention in Spain, 1936, 1937, 1938, 1939. *Publications:* Origins of Fascism, 1929; Italian Foreign Policy, 1931; The Spanish War in the London Committee, 1939; The Frontiers of the Law, 1941, etc; (autobiog.) Il mio paese: ricordi autobiografici, 1986. *Recreations:* book collecting, riding, gardening, mountaineering. *Address:* I-41030 Albareto Di Modena, Italy. *Died* 21 *May* 1988.

**GRANER, Most Rev. Lawrence L.,** CSC, DD, BA; *b* Franklin, Pa, USA, 3 April 1901; *s* of W. D. Graner. *Educ:* Holy Cross Seminary, Notre Dame, Indiana, USA; Notre Dame Univ.; Holy Cross Coll., Washington, DC, USA. BA (Notre Dame), 1924; member of congregation of Holy Cross, 1921; priest, 1928; missionary, diocese of Dacca, 1928–45; delegate to Gen.-Chapter of the Congregation of Holy Cross, 1945; Vicar-General of Dacca, 1937–45; member of Provincial Council of Congregation of Holy Cross; War of 1939–45, Chaplain to US Air Forces; Bishop of Dacca, 1947–50; Archbishop of Dacca, 1950–67. *Address:* Corby Hall, Notre Dame, Indiana 46556, USA. *Died* 21 *April* 1982.

**GRANT, Alexander Ludovic,** TD 1940; DL; JP; Director, Barclays Bank Ltd, 1945–73 (Chairman, Manchester and Liverpool Local Boards, 1945–73; Local Director, Liverpool, 1930, Manchester, 1940); Director, Barclays Bank (DCO), 1948–72; *b* 26 March 1901; *s* of late John Peter Grant of Rothiemurchus, Aviemore, Inverness-shire, and late Lady Mary Grant, *d* of 3rd Earl Manvers; *m* 1946, Elizabeth Langley, *widow* of Capt. J. G. F. Buxton, Grenadier

Guards, and *d* of late Major Robert Barbour, Bolesworth Castle, Tattenhall, Cheshire; two *d*. *Educ:* Winchester; New Coll., Oxford (MA). Entered Barclays Bank Ltd, 1925; General Manager, Union Bank of Manchester, 1938–39 (Union Bank of Manchester was absorbed by Barclays Bank, 1940). Served Lovat Scouts, 1920–40 (Major 1935), and with Cheshire Home Guard, 1940–45. Cheshire Hunt: Sec., 1940–49; Chm., Cttee, 1949–54. High Sheriff of Cheshire, 1956; DL Cheshire, 1963. *Recreations:* shooting, fishing, gardening. *Address:* Springhill, Marbury, Whitchurch, Salop. *T:* Whitchurch 3710. *Clubs:* Pratt's, MCC. *Died* 6 *March* 1986.

**GRANT, Alexander Thomas Kingdom,** CB 1965; CMG 1949; MA; Fellow of Pembroke College, Cambridge, 1966–73, then Fellow Emeritus; *b* 29 March 1906; *s* of late Harold Allan Grant and Marie F. C. Grant; *m* 1930, Helen Frances, *d* of late Dr and Mrs H. Newsome, Clifton, Bristol. *Educ:* St Olave's Sch.; University Coll., Oxford (Scholar in Modern History). Research on international financial problems at RIIA, 1932–35. Leverhulme Research Fellow, 1935–37. Lectr in Dept of Polit. Econ., UCL, 1938–39. Joined HM Treasury, 1939; Under-Sec., 1956; Under Sec., ECGD, 1958–66. UK member on Managing Board of European Payments Union, 1952–53; Secretary of Faculty of Economics, Cambridge, 1966–71; Senior Research Officer, Dept of Applied Economics, 1971–73. *Publications:* Society and Enterprise, 1934; A Study of the Capital Market in Post-War Britain, 1937; The Machinery of Finance and the Management of Sterling, 1967; The Strategy of Financial Pressure, 1972; Economic Uncertainty and Financial Structure, 1977; miscellaneous articles. *Address:* 11 Marlowe Road, Newnham, Cambridge CB3 9JW. *T:* Cambridge 63119. *Died* 8 *Aug.* 1988.

**GRANT, Cary;** actor; Director: Fabergé Inc.; Metro Goldwyn Mayer Inc.; *b* Bristol, 18 Jan. 1904; *s* of Elias Leach and Elsie Kingdom; became US citizen, 1942; *m* 1st 1934, Virginia Cherill (marr. diss., 1934); 2nd, 1942, Barbara Hutton (marr. diss., 1945); 3rd, 1949, Betsy Drake; 4th, 1965, Dyan Cannon (marr. diss., 1968); one *d*; 5th, 1981, Barbara Harris. *Educ:* Fairfield Academy, Somerset. Dir Emeritus, Western Airlines. Mem., Board of Governors, United Services Orgn, 1976–. Started acting, New York, 1921; appeared in: Golden Dawn; Polly; Boom Boom; Wonderful Night; Street Singer; Nikki. *Films include:* Arsenic and Old Lace; None but the Lonely Heart; The Bishop's Wife; The Bachelor and the Bobby Soxer; Mr Blandings Builds His Dream House; To Catch a Thief; The Pride and the Passion; An Affair to Remember; Indiscreet; North by North-West; Operation Petticoat; A Touch of Mink; Charade; Father Goose; Walk, Don't Run. Special Academy Award for contributions to motion picture industry, 1969. *Recreation:* riding. *Died* 29 *Nov.* 1986.

**GRANT, Rt. Rev. Charles Alexander,** MA; LCL; Bishop of Northampton, (RC), 1967–82, Apostolic Administrator 1982; *b* 25 Oct. 1906; *s* of Frank and Sibylla Christina Grant. *Educ:* Perse Sch., Cambridge; St Edmund's, Ware; Christ's Coll., Cambridge; Oscott Coll., Birmingham; Gregorian Univ., Rome. Curate, Cambridge, 1938; Parish Priest: Ely, 1943; Kettering, 1945. Bishop-Auxiliary of Northampton, 1961–67. *Address:* St John's Convent, Kiln Green, near Reading RG10 9XP. *Died* 24 *April* 1989.

**GRANT, Prof. Colin King,** MA, DPhil; Professor of Philosophy in the University of Durham, since 1959; *b* 22 March 1924; *s* of Edward Harold Stewart Grant and Leila Ellen Grant (*née* King); *m* Alison Stoddart Wallace, MB, MRCS, DMRT, DCH; two *s*. *Educ:* Clayesmore Sch.; Wadham Coll., Oxford. First Class Philosophy, Politics and Economics, 1944; Pollard Student of Wadham Coll., 1944–46; DPhil 1950. Assistant in Moral Philosophy Dept, Univ. of Glasgow, 1946–49; Lecturer in Philosophy, Univ. of Nottingham, 1949–59. Vis. Lectr, Univ. of Chicago, 1950–51; Visiting Professor: Univ. of Maryland, 1964; Univ. of Bergen, 1967. *Publications:* articles in Mind, Philosophy, Proc. of Aristotelian Society, etc. *Recreations:* travel, reading. *Address:* 202 Gilesgate, Durham. *Died* 26 *Feb.* 1981.

**GRANT, Sir Ewan (George) M.;** *see* Macpherson-Grant.

**GRANT, Frank,** CB 1953; OBE 1939; former Under-Secretary, Ministry of Agriculture and Fisheries; *b* 1890; *s* of late J. F. Grant, Evesham; *m* 1926, Eileen, *d* of late T. H. Carey; one *d* (one *s* decd). *Address:* 9 Harefield Gardens, Middleton-on-Sea, Bognor Regis, West Sussex. *T:* Middleton-on-Sea 3511. *Died* 2 *Jan.* 1986.

**GRANT, Isabel Frances,** MBE 1959; LLD (Edinburgh); *b* 21 July 1887; *d* of late Colonel H. G. Grant, CB, late the Seaforth Highlanders; *g d* of late Field Marshal Sir Patrick Grant, KCB, GCMG; unmarried. *Educ:* privately. Founder of the Highland Folk Museum at Kingussie. *Publications:* Everyday Life on an Old Highland Farm, 1922, reprinted 1981; Social and Economic Development of Scotland before 1603, 1929; In the Tracks of Montrose, 1931; Everyday Life in Old Scotland, 1933; Social and Economic History of Scotland, 1934; Lordship of the Isles, 1935;

Highland Folk Ways, 1961; Angus Og of the Isles, 1969; Along a Highland Road, 1980. *Recreation:* reading. *Address:* 22 Lennox Row, Edinburgh EH5 3JW. *Died 19 Sept. 1983.*

**GRANT, James Currie,** CBE 1975; Editor, The Press and Journal, Aberdeen, 1960–75, Associate Editor, 1975–76, retired; *b* 5 May 1914; *s* of Alexander Grant, Elgin; *m* 1940, Lillias Isabella Gordon; one *d. Educ:* Elgin Academy. With the Northern Scot, Elgin, 1930–36; joined The Press and Journal, as reporter, 1936; served with Royal Artillery, 1940–46; Sub-editor, The Press and Journal, 1946, Dep. Chief Sub-Editor, 1947–53, Asst Editor, 1953–56, Dep. Editor, 1956–60. Chm., Editorial Cttee, Scottish Daily Newspaper Soc., 1972–75. *Recreations:* voluntary social work, gardening, swimming. *Address:* 42 Fonthill Road, Aberdeen AB1 2UJ. *T:* 582090. *Died 5 Sept. 1988.*

**GRANT, Sir James Monteith,** KCVO 1969; Marchmont Herald, 1957–69 and since 1981; Lord Lyon King of Arms, 1969–81; Writer to the Signet; *b* 19 Oct. 1903; *m* 1st, 1935, Agnes Winifried Comrie Lorimer (*d* 1955); 2nd, 1958, Yvonne Margaret Wilkinson; one *d. Educ:* The Edinburgh Academy; Univ. of Edinburgh. MA, LLB Edinburgh; WS 1927. Carrick Pursuivant, 1946. Secretary to the Order of the Thistle, 1971–81. FSA (Scot). KStJ 1970 (OStJ 1967). Grand Officer (Class II), Order of the Polar Star, Sweden, 1975. *Address:* 40 Corstorphine Road, Edinburgh EH12 6HS. *T:* 031-337 1209. *Clubs:* New, Scottish Arts (Edinburgh). *Died 1 Dec. 1981.*

**GRANT, Joan, (Mrs Denys Kelsey);** *b* 12 April 1907; *d* of John Frederick Marshall, CBE; *m* 1st, 1927, Arthur Leslie Grant; one *d;* 2nd, 1940, Charles Robert Longfield Beatty; 3rd, 1960, Denys Edward Reginald Kelsey, MB, MRCP. *Publications:* Winged Pharaoh, 1937; Life as Carola, 1939; Eyes of Horus, 1942; The Scarlet Fish and other Stories, 1942; Lord of the Horizon, 1943; Redskin Morning, 1944; Scarlet Feather, 1945; Vague Vacation, 1947; Return to Elysium, 1947; The Laird and the Lady, 1949 (US edn, Castle Cloud); So Moses Was Born, 1952; Time out of Mind (autobiography), 1956 (US edn, Far Memory); A Lot to Remember, 1962; (with Denys Kelsey) Many Lifetimes, 1969; The Collected Works of Joan Grant, 1979; The Blue Faience Hippopotamus, 1984; The Monster Who Grew Small, 1987; translations in Icelandic, Swedish, Finnish, Danish, Dutch, Polish, Hungarian, French, German, Italian, Portuguese. *Address:* c/o A. P. Watt Ltd, 20 John Street, WC1N 2DR. *Died 3 Feb. 1989.*

**GRANT, Captain John Moreau,** CBE 1944; Royal Canadian Navy, retired; *b* 22 July 1895; *s* of late Hon. MacCallum Grant and Laura MacNeil Parker; *m* 1923, Jocelyn Clare Weaver-Bridgman; one *d. Educ:* Heidelberg Coll., Germany; RCN Coll., Halifax, NS. *Address:* 601 Transit Road, Victoria, British Columbia, Canada. *T:* 598–2138. *Died 2 Feb. 1986.*

**GRANT, Sir (Kenneth) Lindsay,** CMT 1969; Kt 1963; OBE 1956; ED 1944; Director, T. Geddes Grant Ltd (Chairman, 1946–64); Chairman, Vice-Chairman, and Director of numerous other companies; *b* Trinidad, 10 Feb. 1899; *s* of T. Geddes Grant (Canadian); *m* 1923, (Edith) Grace Norman; no *c. Educ:* Queen's Royal College, Trinidad; Maritime Business Coll., Halifax, NS. Served European War: (3rd Trinidad Contingent, 1916–17, 5th BWI Regt, 1917, RFC, 1917) 2nd Lieut; (RAF 1917–19) Flying Officer; War of 1939–45: (Trinidad Volunteers) Major, 2nd in Comd, 1944–45. Joined T. Geddes Grant Ltd, 1919; Manager, Office Appliances Dept, 1921; Director, 1927; Chm. and Man. Dir. 1946 (retd as Man. Dir, Sept. 1962; Chm. until 1964; Pres., 1964–68 and 1979–). Pres., 1957–75, Hon. Life Pres., 1975–, Trinidad and Tobago Leprosy Relief Assoc. Past and present activities: Church (Elder, Greyfriars); Boy Scouts; Cadets; Social Service. Chaconia Gold Medal, 1969. *Recreations:* none now; played cricket, Association football, tennis, golf. *Address:* (office) T. Geddes Grant Ltd, Box 171, Port of Spain, Trinidad. *T:* 625 4805; (home) 50 Ellerslie Park, Maraval, Trinidad. *T:* 622 5202, Port of Spain. *Clubs:* Royal Commonwealth Society, Royal Over-Seas League, (Hon. Life) MCC (all London); Union, Country, Queen's Park Cricket, etc (Trinidad). *Died 24 Jan. 1989.*

**GRANT, Ronald Thomson,** OBE; FRS 1934; MD, FRCP, DPH; formerly physician on staff of Medical Research Council; Consultant Physician Emeritus, Guy's Hospital; *b* 5 Nov. 1892; *m;* one *d. Educ:* Glasgow Univ. *Publications:* articles in scientific journals. *Address:* Farley Green Cottage, Shophouse Lane, Albury, Guildford, Surrey GU5 9EQ. *T:* Shere 2164. *Died 7 Nov. 1989.*

**GRANT, Air Vice-Marshal Stanley Bernard,** CB 1969; DFC 1942; bar to DFC 1943; RAF; *b* 31 May 1919; *s* of late Harry Alexander Gwatkin Grant and Marjorie Gladys Hoyle; *m* 1948, Barbara Jean Watts (*d* 1963); one *s* one *d; m* 1965, Christiane Marie Py (*née* Bech); one step *s* two step *d. Educ:* Charterhouse; RAF Coll., Cranwell. Joined RAF, 1937; War of 1939–45; service in UK, Malta, Egypt and Italy. Air Ministry, 1946–47; Flying Training Command, 1948–56; Fighter Command, 1955–56; SEATO,

Bangkok, 1957–59; Fighter Command, 1960–61; idc course, 1962; NATO, Fontainebleau, 1963–64; Directing Staff, IDC, 1965–68; Comdr, British Forces, Gulf, 1968–69; retired 1970. *Address:* 14 rue des Cordeliers, 83170 Brignoles, France. *Club:* Royal Air Force. *Died 4 July 1987.*

**GRANT, Prof. Willis,** DMus, Hon. RAM, FRCO, ARCM; Stanley Hugh Badock Professor of Music, 1958–72, and Dean of Faculty of Arts, 1968–70, Bristol University; later Emeritus Professor; *b* Bolton, 1 May 1907; *o s* of Herbert Grant; *m* Grace Winifred, *d* of C. A. Baker, Moseley, Birmingham. *Educ:* Astley Bridge Sch.; privately. Studied music with several teachers including Sir Edward C. Bairstow, York Minster; Organist and Choirmaster, All Souls' Parish Church, Bolton, 1929–31; Asst Organist, Lincoln Minster, 1931–36; Music Master, South Park High Sch., 1931–36; conducted Gate Burton Choral Soc., 1932–35; Extra-mural lectr for the University of Nottingham, 1936–37; Organist and Master of the Choristers, Birmingham Cathedral, 1936–58; Tutor in Special Music Course for Teachers at Sheffield City Training Coll., 1938–39; Conductor, Birmingham Bach Soc., 1938–58 (subseq. Hon. Life Mem.); Lecturer in Music, Sheffield Univ., 1934–47; Extra-mural lecturer for WEA and Sheffield Univ., 1938–47; Dir of Music, King Edward's Sch., Birmingham, 1948–58; Extra-mural lectr for Birmingham Univ., 1956–58. Rep. of RSCM for Birmingham Dio., 1936–58. Pres. Birmingham Organists' Assoc., 1950–55 (Hon. Life Mem.); Mem., Management and Music Advisory Cttees of City of Birmingham Symphony Orchestra, 1950–58; Special Comr, RSCM, 1953–; Mem. Musical Adv. Board, 1952–55; Mem. Council: RCO; Incorporated Soc. of Musicians, 1956–59, 1960– (Mem. Exec. Cttee, 1958–; Pres., 1974–75); President: Music Masters' Assoc., 1958; Incorporated Assoc. of Organists, 1964–66; Bristol Bach Choir; Incorporated Soc. of Musicians, 1974–75; Chairman: Bristol Opera Co. Mem. Management Cttee, Western Orchestral Soc.; Music Panel, SW Arts Assoc.; Governor: Newton Park Coll., Bath; Birmingham Univ., 1973–. Served with HM Forces, RASC, 1941–42; AEC Major, lecturing on music in India Comd, 1942–46. *Publications:* An Album of Songs; Music in Education. *Recreations:* photography, gardening. *Address:* The Old Rectory, Compton Martin, Somerset BS18 6JP. *T:* West Harptree 350. *Died 9 Nov. 1981.*

**GRANTHAM, Mrs Violet Hardisty;** Member of Newcastle upon Tyne City Council, 1937–74; Alderman of City, 1951–58; *b* 15 Feb. 1893; *o d* of Thomas Taylor, BSc, and Sarah Taylor; *m* John Grantham (*d* 1945) (formerly Sheriff of Newcastle upon Tyne, and Lord Mayor, 1936–37). *Educ:* privately. Dir of Private Companies. Lady Mayoress of Newcastle upon Tyne, 1936–37 and 1949–50; Sheriff of Newcastle upon Tyne, 1950–51 (first woman to hold this office); Lord Mayor, 1952–53 and 1957 (first woman to hold this office); Mem. Newcastle upon Tyne HMC, 1948–72; Founder Mem., and Mem. of Cttee, Percy Hedley Home for Spastic Children. Trustee: St Mary the Virgin Hosp. Trust (Chm.); Mary Magdalene and Holy Jesus Hosp. Trust (Vice-Chm.). Formerly Northern Area Chm. of Women's Junior Air Corps; formerly Pres. Newcastle upon Tyne Branch of Royal College of Nursing; active in Townswomen's Guilds and other women's organisations. Freeman, City and Co. of Newcastle upon Tyne, 1968. *Address:* 74 Mary Magdalene Bungalows, Newcastle upon Tyne 2. *Died 20 May 1983.*

**GRANVILLE, Sir Keith,** Kt 1973; CBE 1958; FCIT; Hon. FRAeS; *b* 1 Nov. 1910; *m* 1st, 1933, Patricia Capstick; one *s* one *d;* 2nd, 1946, Truda Belliss; one *s* four *d. Educ:* Tonbridge Sch. Joined Imperial Airways as Trainee, 1929 and served Italy, Tanganyika, Southern and Northern Rhodesia, Egypt, India. BOAC: Manager African and Middle East Div., 1947; Commercial Dir, 1954; Dep. Managing Dir, 1958–60; Mem. Bd, 1959–72; Dep. Chm., 1964–70; Man. Dir, 1969–70; Chm. and Chief Exec., 1971–72; Mem. Bd, BEA, 1971–72; British Airways Board: Mem., 1971–74; Dep. Chm., 1972–74; Chairman: BOAC Associated Companies Ltd, 1960–64; BOAC Engine Overhaul Ltd, 1971–72; International Aeradio Ltd, 1965–71 (Dep.-Chm., 1962–65). Mem. Bd, Maplin Development Authority, 1973–74. President: Inst. of Transport, 1963–64; IATA, 1972–73. Chm., British Residents' Assoc. of Switzerland, 1979–81. Hon. FRAeS, 1977. *Address:* Speedbird, 1837 Château d'Oex, Switzerland. *T:* (029) 4 76 03. *Died 7 April 1990.*

**GRANVILLE-WEST, Baron,** *cr* 1958 (Life Peer), of Pontypool, in the County of Monmouthshire; **Daniel Granville West;** formerly Senior Partner in the firm of D. Granville West, Chivers & Morgan, Newbridge and Pontypool; *b* 17 March 1904; *s* of John West, Newbridge, Monmouthshire, and Elizabeth West (*née* Bridges); *m* 1937, Vera (JP Monmouthshire, 1956), *d* of J. Hopkins, Pontypool; one *s* one *d.* Admitted a Solicitor, 1929. Served War of 1939–45: Royal Air Force Volunteer Reserve, Flight Lt. MP (Lab) Pontypool Div. of Monmouthshire, July 1946–58. PPS to Home Sec., 1950–51. Mem. of Abercarn Urban District Council, 1934–38 and of Monmouthshire County Council, 1938–47. *Address:* Brynderwen, Abersychan, Pontypool, Gwent. *T:* Talywain 236. *Died 23 Sept. 1984.*

**GRASAR, Rt. Rev. William Eric,** DCL, STL; *b* 18 May 1913. *Educ:* Brigg Grammar School; Panton; English College, Rome. Priest 1937; Vice-Rector, English College, Rome, 1942–46; Chancellor, Nottingham Diocese, 1948–52; Rector of St Hugh's College, Tollerton, 1952–56; Vicar-General, Nottingham Diocese, 1956–62; Bishop of Shrewsbury, 1962–80. *Address:* St Vincent's, Bentinck Road, Altrincham, Cheshire WA14 2BP. *T:* 061-928 1689.
*Died 28 Dec. 1982.*

**GRATTAN-BELLEW, Sir Arthur (John),** Kt 1959; CMG 1956; QC (Tanganyika), 1952; *b* 23 May 1903; *s* of Sir Henry (Christopher) Grattan-Bellew, 3rd Bt, and Lady Sophia Forbes, *d* of 7th Earl of Granard, KP; *m* 1931, Freda Mary Mahony (*d* 1979); one *s* one *d*. *Educ:* Downside Sch.; Christ's Coll., Cambridge (BA). Called to Bar, Lincoln's Inn, 1925; practised in London until 1935, Legal Service, Egyptian Govt, 1936–38; Colonial Legal Service, Malaya, 1938–41. Military Service, 1941–45 (POW 1942–45). Colonial Legal Service; Malaya, 1946–48; Attorney-General: Sarawak, 1948–52; Tanganyika, 1952–56; Chief Sec., Tanganyika, 1956–59; Legal Adviser's Dept, Foreign and Commonwealth Office, retired. Chm., Bellew, Parry and Raven Gp of companies. *Address:* Pledgdon Green, Henham, near Bishop's Stortford, Herts.
*Died 5 Jan. 1985.*

**GRAVES, Robert Ranke;** writer; Hon. Fellow, St John's College, Oxford; *b* London, 1895; *s* of late Alfred Perceval and Amy Graves; *m* 1st, Nancy, *d* of late Sir Wm Nicholson; one *s* two *d* (and one *s* killed in Burma); 2nd, Beryl, *d* of late Sir Harry Pritchard; three *s* one *d*. *Educ:* Charterhouse; St John's Coll., Oxford (Hon. Fellow, 1971). Served in France with Royal Welch Fusiliers; Prof. of English Literature, Egyptian Univ., 1926. Clarke Lecturer at Trinity Coll., Cambridge, 1954. Arthur Dehon Little Memorial Lecturer, Massachusetts Institute of Technology, 1963. Professor of Poetry, Univ. of Oxford, 1961–66. Books (over 137) and manuscripts, on permanent exhibition, at Lockwood Memorial Library, Buffalo, NY. Bronze Medal for Poetry, Olympic Games, Paris, 1924; Gold Medal for Poetry, Cultural Olympics, Mexico, 1968; Gold Medal of Nat. Poetry Soc. of America, 1960; Queen's Gold Medal for Poetry, 1968. Adoptive son of Deyá village, Mallorca, 1968, where resident since 1929. *Publications:* Goodbye to All That, An Autobiography, 1929 (revised 1957); But it Still Goes on, 1930; The Real David Copperfield, 1933; I, Claudius, 1934 (awarded Hawthornden and James Tait Black Memorial Prizes for 1934); Claudius the God, 1934; Antigua Penny Puce, 1936; T. E. Lawrence to his Biographer, 1938; Count Belisarius, 1938 (awarded Stock Prize, 1939); Sergeant Lamb of the Ninth, 1940; The Long Week End: A Social History (with Alan Hodge), 1940; Proceed, Sergeant Lamb, 1941; Wife to Mr Milton, 1943; The Reader Over Your Shoulder (with Alan Hodge), 1943; The Golden Fleece, 1944; King Jesus, 1946; The White Goddess, 1947; Collected Poems, 1948; Seven Days in New Crete, 1949; The Common Asphodel (Collected Essays on Poetry), 1949; The Isles of Unwisdom, 1949; Occupation: Writer, 1950; Poems and Satires, 1951; The Nazarene Gospel Restored (with Joshua Podro), 1953; The Greek Myths, 1955 (new edn, Greek Myths and Legends, 1968, illustrated edn, 1982); Homer's Daughter, 1955; The Crowning Privilege, 1955; Adam's Rib, 1955; Catacrok (stories), 1956; Jesus in Rome (with Joshua Podro), 1957; They hanged my saintly Billy, 1957; (ed) English and Scottish Ballads, 1957; Steps, 1958; Collected Poems, 1959; The Penny Fiddle, 1960; More Poems, 1961; Oxford Addresses, 1962; New Poems, 1962; (with Raphael Patai) Hebrew Myths; Genesis, 1964; Collected Short Stories, 1964; Man Does, Woman Is (poems), 1964; Mammon and the Black Goddess, 1964; Hebrew Myths: Genesis (with Rafael Patai), 1965; Ann at High Wood Hall, 1965; Collected Short Stories, 1965; Love Respelt, 1965; Majorca Observed, 1965; Collected Poems, 1965; Seventeen Poems Missing from Love Respelt, 1966; Two Wise Children, 1966; Colophon, 1967; Poetic Craft and Principle, 1967; The Poor Boy who followed his Star, 1968; Poems 1965–68, 1968; The Crane Bag and other disputed subjects, 1968; Beyond Giving, 1969; Poems 1968–1970, 1970; The Song of Songs (with lithographs by Hans Erni), 1971; The Green-Sailed Vessel, 1971; All Things to all Men (play), 1971; Poems: abridged for dolls and princes, 1971; Poems 1970–72, 1972; Difficult Questions: Easy Answers, 1973; Timeless Meeting, 1973; At the Gate, 1974; Collected Poems 1975, 1975; An Ancient Castle (for children), 1980; *translations:* The Golden Ass, 1949; Alarcón's Infant with the Globe, 1956; Galvan's The Cross and the Sword, 1956; George Sand's Winter in Majorca, 1957; Suetonius's Twelve Cæsars; Lucan's Pharsalia; Homer's Anger of Achilles, 1959; Terence's Comedies, 1962; Rubaiyyat of Omar Khayaam (with Omar Ali-Shah), 1967. *Address:* c/o A. P. Watt Ltd, 26/28 Bedford Row, WC1. *Died 7 Dec. 1985.*

**GRAY, Basil,** CB 1969; CBE 1957; MA; FBA 1966; Keeper of Oriental Antiquities, British Museum, 1946–69, Acting Director and Principal Librarian, 1968; *b* 21 July 1904; *s* of late Surgeon-Major Charles Gray and Florence Elworthy, *d* of Rev. H. v. H. Cowell; *m* 1933, Nicolete, *d* of late Laurence Binyon, CH; two *s* two *d* (and one *d* decd). *Educ:* Bradfield; New Coll., Oxford. British

Academy excavations in Constantinople, 1928; entered British Museum (Printed Books), 1928; transferred to sub-Dept of Oriental Prints and Drawings, 1930; in charge of Oriental Antiquities (including Oriental Prints and Drawings) from 1938; Dep. Keeper, 1940. Mem. of Art Panel of the Arts Council, 1952–57, and 1959–68; President: Oriental Ceramic Soc., 1962–65, 1971–74, 1977–78; 6th Internat. Congress of Iranian Art and Archaeology, Oxford, 1972. Mem., Reviewing Cttee on Export of Works of Art, 1971–79; Chm., Exhibn cttee, The Arts of Islam, Hayward Gallery, 1976. President: Soc. for S Asian Studies (formerly Soc. for Afghan Studies), 1979–; British Inst. of Persian Studies, 1987–; Chm., Societas Iranologica Europaea, 1983–87. A Visitor of Ashmolean Museum, Oxford, 1969–79. Sir Percy Sykes Meml Medal, 1978. *Publications:* Persian Painting, 1930; Persian Miniature Painting (part author), 1933; Chinese Art (with Leigh Ashton), 1935; The English Print, 1937; Persian Painting, New York, 1940; Rajput Painting, 1948; (joint) Commemorative Catalogue of the Exhibition of the Art of India and Pakistan, 1947–48, 1950; Treasures of Indian Miniatures in the Bikanir Palace Collection, 1951; Early Chinese Pottery and Porcelain, 1953; Japanese Screen-paintings, 1955; Buddhist Cave paintings at Tun-huang, 1959; Treasures of Asia; Persian Painting, 1961; (with D. E. Barrett) Painting of India, 1963; An Album of Miniatures and Illuminations from the Bâysongnhori Manuscript of the Shāhnāmeh of Ferdowsi, 1971; The World History of Rashid al-Din, a study of the RAS manuscript, 1979; (ed, and jt author) The Arts of the Book in Central Asia 1370–1506, 1979; (ed, and jt author) The Arts of India, 1981; Sung Porcelain and Stoneware, 1984; Studies in Chinese and Islamic Art, vol. 1, 1985, vol. 2, 1988; (ed) Faber Gallery of Oriental Art and Arts of the East Series. *Address:* Dawber's House, Long Wittenham, Oxon OX14 4QQ. *Club:* Savile. *Died 10 June 1989.*

**GRAY, Charles Herbert,** FRCS; Hon. Consultant Orthopædic Surgeon, Royal Free Hospital; formerly Consulting Orthopædic Surgeon, British Postgraduate Medical School, Hammersmith Hospital, and Connaught Hospital, Walthamstow. *Educ:* Victoria University, Manchester. BSc; MB, ChB (hons) 1932; MRCS, LRCP, 1932; FRCS, 1935. Temp. Lt-Col, Royal Army Medical Corps, Hunterian Prof., Royal College of Surgeons, 1946, 1949. Formerly, Fracture and Orthopædic Registrar, Middlesex Hosp.; Surg. Registrar, Royal Nat. Orthopædic Hospital. Fellow: British Orthopaedic Assoc.; Hunterian Soc.; Membre Société Internationale de Chirurgie, Orthopédie et Traumatologie. *Publications:* various articles in medical jls. *Address:* 8 Upper Wimpole Street, W1. *T:* 01-580 5307; 16 Hamilton Close, NW8.
*Died 1982.*

**GRAY, David;** Secretary-General, International Tennis Federation, since Aug. 1976; *b* 31 Dec. 1927; *s* of David Reginald Gray and Beatrice Gladys (*née* Goodyear); *m* 1962, Margaret Clare Emerson; three *s* one *d*. *Educ:* King Edward VI Grammar Sch., Stourbridge; Birmingham Univ. (BA Hons English). Journalist: Evening Telegraph, Blackburn, 1951–53; News Chronicle, 1953–54. Guardian: Manchester Guardian/Guardian, 1954–76; Midlands Correspondent, 1955–56; Lawn Tennis Correspondent, 1956–76; Sports Editor, 1961–68. Sports Writer of the Year Award, 1975. *Publications:* contrib. to Oxford Companion to Sport and other sports ref. books; *posthumous publication:* Shades of Gray (anthol.), 1988. *Recreations:* theatre, hill climbing. *Address:* 50 Luttrell Avenue, SW15 6PF. *T:* 01-788 4809. *Clubs:* Queen's, International Lawn Tennis (GB, France, Italy, Sweden and USA), Players' Theatre. *Died 6 Sept. 1983.*

**GRAY, George Charles,** DMus (Cantuar) 1968; FRCO 1920; FRSCM 1967; Organist and Master of the Music, Leicester Cathedral, 1931–69; Conductor of Leicester Bach Choir, 1931–69; Senior Lecturer in Music, Leicester College of Education, 1946–76; Lay Canon of Leicester Cathedral, 1942; Examiner, Trinity College of Music, 1958; *b* 1897; *s* of late Charles Wilson Gray and Alice Gray; *m* 1925, Gladys Gofton (*d* 1972), York; two *s* one *d* (and one *d* decd). *Educ:* Rotherham Grammar Sch. MusB (Dunelm) 1927. Articled pupil of late Sir Edward Bairstow at York Minster, 1919–22; Lafontaine Prize winner, Royal Coll. of Organists, 1920, also winner, Worshipful Company of Musicians Silver Medal, 1922; Organist and Choirmaster successively of St Michael-le-Belfry, York, St Martin's, Leeds, and Alnwick Parish Church; Conductor of Alnwick Choral Union, and Wooler Choral Union; Organist and Choirmaster, St Mary le Tower, Ipswich, 1926; Founder and Conductor of Ipswich Bach Choir, 1929–30; Conductor of Ipswich Choral Society, 1928–30; Extra-mural Lecturer in Musical Appreciation at Vaughan Coll., Leicester, 1931–51; Lecturer in Singing, University Coll., 1931–58. Pres. Cathedral Organists' Assoc., 1968–70. Hon. MusM Leicester, 1965. *Recreation:* cricket. *Address:* 8 Knighton Court, Knighton Park Road, Leicester LE2 1ZB. *T:* 705167. *Club:* Rotary. *Died 24 March 1981.*

**GRAY, Gordon;** Chairman Emeritus, National Trust for Historic Preservation; *b* 30 May 1909; *s* of Bowman and Nathalie Lyons Gray; *m* 1938, Jane Boyden Craige (*d* 1953); four *s*; *m* 1956, Nancy

Maguire Beebe; three step *d. Educ:* Woodberry Forest Sch., Woodberry Forest, Va; University of N Carolina, Chapel Hill, NC; Yale Law Sch., New Haven, Conn. Admitted to NY Bar, 1934, and associated with Carter, Ledyard & Milburn, 1933–35; with Manly, Hendren & Womble, Winston-Salem, NC, 1935–37; admitted to North Carolina Bar, 1936; Pres., Piedmont Publishing Company, 1937–47. N Carolina Senate, 1939, 1941, 1945. Enlisted in US Army as private, 1942; Capt., 1945. Asst Sec. of Army, 1947; Under-Sec. of Army, 1949; Sec. of Army, 1949; Special Asst to the President, USA, April–Nov. 1950; Dir, Psychological Strategy Board, July–Dec. 1951. Pres. of Univ. of N Carolina, Feb. 1950–Nov. 1955; Assist Sec. of Defense, International Sec. Affairs, US, 1955–57; Dir, Office of Defense Mobilization, 1957–58; Special Asst to President, USA, for National Security Affairs, 1958–61; Mem., President's Foreign Intelligence Adv. Bd, 1961–77. Chm., Summit Communications, Inc.; Director Emeritus: American Security Bank; Media General, Inc.; Trustee: Brookings Instn, 1961–75; Federal City Council. Pres., Kensington Orchids Inc. Holds several hon. degrees. *Address:* 1224 30th Street NW, Washington, DC 20007, USA; (Office) 1616 H Street NW, Washington, DC 20006, USA. *Clubs:* Alibi, Burning Tree, Metropolitan (all Washington); The Brook (New York).
*Died 26 Nov. 1982.*

**GRAY, Ian;** MA; Managing Director and Chief Executive, Welsh Development Agency, since 1976; Member: Development Corporation for Wales, since 1976; Design Council Wales Advisory Committee, since 1977; *b* 29 Aug. 1926; *er s* of late Henry Gray and Elizabeth Cowan Gray; *m* 1954, Vaudine Angela Harrison-Ainsworth; one *s* one *d. Educ:* Royal High Sch., Edinburgh; Univ. of Edinburgh (MA Econ.). War Service with Royal Scots and Indian Army, 1944–45 (2nd Lieut). Joined BoT, 1948; Private Sec. to successive Parly Secs, 1951–52 and to Pres., 1952–54; British Trade Comr, Wellington, 1954–56; Principal British Trade Comr, Cape Town, 1957–60; BoT, London, 1961–67; BoT Controller for Wales, Cardiff, 1967–69; Dir, Min. of Technology Office for Wales, 1970; Dir for Wales, DTI, 1971; Skelmersdale Develt Corporation: Gen. Manager, 1972–73; Man. Dir, 1973–76. Mem. Bd of Management, Corlan Housing Assoc., 1979–82. Member: Ormskirk District HMC, 1972–74; Lancs AHA, 1973–76. *Recreations:* photography, carpentry, making and drinking wine. *Address:* Welsh Development Agency, Treforest Industrial Estate, Treforest, Mid Glamorgan. *T:* Treforest 2666. *Club:* Cardiff and County.
*Died 11 March 1983.*

**GRAY, Air Vice-Marshal John Astley,** CB 1945; CBE 1943; DFC; GM; retired; *b* 1899. *Educ:* Framlingham Coll. Served European War, 1917–19; War of 1939–45. Air Vice-Marshal 1944; AOC 91 (B) Gp, 1944–46; AOC RAF Mission to Greece, 1947–48; SASO, HQ Transport Comd, 1949–51; AOA, HQ ME Air Force, 1951–54; retired, 1954. *Address:* Bittern, Thorpeness, Suffolk. *Club:* Royal Air Force.
*Died 6 June 1987.*

**GRAY, Very Rev. John Rodger,** VRD 1956; Minister at Dunblane Cathedral, 1966–84, then Minister Emeritus; Moderator of the General Assembly of the Church of Scotland, 1977–78; *b* 9 Jan. 1913; *s* of John Charles Gray, Hartlea, Coatbridge, and Jeannie Gilmour Rodger; *m* 1952, Dr Sheila Mary Whiteside; three *s. Educ:* High Sch. of Glasgow; Glasgow Univ. (MA 1934); Yale Univ. (BD 1938); Princeton Univ. and Seminary (ThM 1939). Pres., Glasgow Univ. Union, 1934–35. Commonwealth Fund Fellow, Yale, 1937–39; Asst Minister, Barony of Glasgow, 1939–41; Chaplain: RN, 1941–46; RNVR, 1946–63; Minister, St Stephen's, Glasgow, 1946–66. Hastie Lectr in Theol., Glasgow Univ., 1947–50; Lectr in Theol., Glasgow Sch. of Study and Trng, 1948; Lectr, Princeton Inst. of Theol., 1949 and 1968. Convener, Church and Nation Cttee, Gen. Assembly of Church of Scotland; Mem., Religious Adv. Cttees, BBC, IBA, and STV. Select Preacher, Univ. of Oxford, 1977. Hon. DD Tulsa, 1979; Hon. LHD Presb. Coll., S Carolina, 1980. *Publications:* The Political Theory of John Knox, 1939; Splintering the Gates of Hell (monograph), 1977; (ed. and contrib.) The Pulpit Digest, 1979–81; chapter in Ministers for the 1980s, 1979; chapter in Grow or Die, 1981; articles, sermons, and book revs in Expository Times, Gen. Practitioner, and Princeton Sem. Jl. *Address:* 7 Glen Court, Dunblane, Perthshire FK15 0DY. *T:* Dunblane 823927. *Club:* New (Edinburgh).
*Died 9 Aug. 1984.*

**GRAY, Mary Elizabeth,** CBE 1946 (OBE 1942); WRVS Administrator, Midland Region, 1949–71; resigned as County Commissioner, Gloucestershire Girl Guides (1949–61); *b* 19 May 1903; *d* of late Edward Wilmot Butler and Ethel Margaret Gray. *Educ:* Lanherne House, Dawlish; Switzerland. Joined WVS 1938; WVS Administrator, Eastern Counties Region 4, 1938–44; Deputy Vice-Chm., WVS , 1944; WVS Administrator SEAC and FE, 1944–48. *Address:* Clanmere Nursing Home, Great Malvern, Worcs.
*Died 18 Aug. 1983.*

**GRAY, Nicol;** *see* Gray, W. N.

**GRAY, Stephen Alexander Reith;** Chairman, Welsh Development Agency, since 1980; *b* 18 June 1926; *er s* of late Alexander Reith Gray and Catherine Mary Thompson. *Educ:* Winchester Coll.; Trinity Coll., Cambridge. Stewarts & Lloyds Ltd, 1950–53; John Summers & Sons Ltd, 1953–68; BSC: Member for Engineering, 1968–70; Man. Dir, Strip Mills Div., 1970–72. Director: Lamberton & Co. Ltd, 1973–; Bertrams Ltd, 1975–; GSK Steel Developments Ltd, 1975–; The Colville Estate Ltd, 1978–; Cursitor Property Co. Ltd, 1978–; UK Provident Instn, 1973–; Salisbury Indep. Hosp. & Med. Services Ltd, 1980–. Member: Clwyd AHA, 1973–79; Wales Health Tech. Services Organisation, 1973–77. High Sheriff of Flints, 1972. *Address:* Lower Soughton, Northop, Mold, Clwyd. *T:* Northop 203. *Club:* Leander.
*Died 12 May 1982.*

**GRAY, Trevor Robert,** MBE 1973; JP; Company Secretary, Gwent Hospitals Contributory Fund, 1948–84; *b* 27 March 1919; *s* of Walter Augustus Gray and Lilian May Gray; *m* 1941, Tessie Patricia Thomas; two *s. Educ:* Alexandra Road Sch.; Belle Vue Central Sch.; Newport Technical Coll. Chm., Wales Leagues of Friends, 1970–84; Vice-Chairman: British Hosps Contrib. Schemes Assoc., 1976 (Mem. Exec. Cttee, 1961–81; Vice-Pres., 1981); Nat. Assoc. of Leagues of Hosp. Friends, 1968 (Mem. Council, 1955–84); Member: Welsh Hosp. Bd, 1968–74; Central Health Services Council, 1976–79; South Gwent Community Health Council, 1974–82 (Chm., 1975–78); Welsh Assoc. of Community Health Councils, 1974–82 (Chm., 1978–80); GMC, 1979–. JP Newport, 1968. *Recreations:* reading, walking. *Address:* The Heights, Forge Lane, Bassaleg, Gwent NP1 9NG. *T:* Rhiwderin 3513.
*Died 10 Aug. 1985.*

**GRAY, William John,** CB 1976; FRCPsych; Member of the Parole Board, Home Office, London, 1976–77, retired; *b* 9 Jan. 1911; *m* 1942, Norma Margaret Morrison; two *d. Educ:* Wishaw High Sch.; Glasgow Univ. (MB, ChB). Dep. Medical Supt, Glengall Hosp., Ayr, 1939–42. Served War: Major, RAMC (Specialist Psychiatrist), 1942–47; Corps Psychiatrist and Staff Officer, Italy, 1943–45. SMO, Wakefield, Maidstone and Liverpool Prisons, 1947–62; First Medical Supt and Governor, HM Prison, Grendon, 1962–75; Sen. PMO and Asst Under-Sec. of State, Home Office, 1971–75. Nuffield Travelling Fellowship, in six European countries, 1957; Lectr in Forensic Psychiatry, Liverpool Univ., 1960–62. *Publications:* several articles on med. and psychiatric treatment and med. care and protection of prisoners. *Recreations:* angling, bridge, gardening. *Address:* 88 Crosshill Terrace, Wormit, Newport on Tay, Fife DD6 8PS. *T:* Newport on Tay 541355. *Club:* Civil Service.
*Died 25 Oct. 1985.*

**GRAY, William Macfarlane,** OBE 1961; JP; FCCA; FCIS; FSAScot; Senior Partner Macfarlane Gray & Co., Stirling, 1934–71, Consultant, 1971–75; Hon. Sheriff for Stirling and Clackmannan since 1964; *b* 28 March 1910; *s* of Peter M. Gray and Isabella Bain Macfarlane; *m* 1938, Muriel Agnes Elizabeth Lindsay, *d* of James R. Lindsay, Glasgow; two *d. Educ:* The High Sch. of Stirling. Provost of Royal Burgh of Stirling, 1958–64; Nat. Pres., Assoc. of Certified and Corporate Accountants, 1954–56; Chm. Stirling Festival of the Arts Cttee, 1958–67; Chm. Stirlingshire Savings Cttee, 1959–76; Member: Court, Univ. of Stirling, 1968–72; Executive Cttee, Scottish Council (Development and Industry), 1961–75; Scottish Tourist Board, 1963–64; Council, National Trust for Scotland, 1962–74; Chairman: PO Advisory Cttee for Stirlingshire and Clackmannan; of Trustees, Smith Art Gallery and Museum, Stirling, 1958–64; Sponsoring Cttee for University of Stirling, 1963–65. Member: South of Scotland Electricity Board, 1961–66; Independent Television Authority (Chm. Scottish Adv. Cttee), 1964–70; Nat. Savings Cttee for Scotland, 1969–78; Exec. Cttee, British Council (Chm. Scottish Adv. Cttee), 1970–76. Hon. Freeman: Royal Burgh of Stirling, 1964; Ville de Saint Valéry-en-Caux, 1960. Hon. DUniv. Stirling, 1968. KStJ; Receiver Gen., Priory of Scotland, Order of St John of Jerusalem, 1978–84; Preceptor of Torphichen, 1984–. *Recreations:* golf, bowling. *Address:* 12 Park Avenue, Stirling FK8 2QR. *T:* Stirling 4776. *Club:* Stirling and County.
*Died 11 July 1984.*

**GRAY, (William) Nicol,** CMG 1948; DSO 1944, Bar, 1945; KPM 1951; FRICS; *b* 1 May 1908; *e s* of late Dr W. Gray, Westfield, West Hartlepool; *m* 1st, 1953, Jean Marie Frances Backhouse (marr. diss. 1966), *o c* of Lieut-Col G. R. V. Hume-Gore, MC and Mrs W. Lyne-Stephens, and widow of Major Sir John Backhouse, Bt, MC; two *d;* 2nd, 1967, Margaret Clare Galpin, widow of Commander Walter Galpin, RN. *Educ:* Trinity Coll., Glenalmond. Royal Marines, 1939–46; GSO II RM Div., no I (Experimental) WOSB; Mil. Instructor, HMS Dorlin; CO 45 RM Commando; Comdt, RM Octu; Inspector-Gen.; Palestine Police, 1946–48; Commissioner of Police, Federation of Malaya, 1948–52. Agent to the Jockey Club, Newmarket, 1953–64. Administrator, MacRobert Trusts, 1970–74. Trustee, Duke of Edinburgh's Award Scheme, 1973–78; Hon. Trustee, 1979–83. *Address:* The Bacchus House, Elsdon, Northumberland. *T:* Otterburn 20665.
*Died 14 Jan. 1988.*

**GRAYSON, Sir Ronald Henry Rudyard,** 3rd Bt of Ravens Point, *cr* 1922; *b* 15 Nov. 1916; *s* of Sir Denys Henry Harrington Grayson, 2nd Bt, and Elsie May (*d* 1973), *d* of Richard Davies Jones; *S* father, 1955; *m* 1st, 1936, Babette Vivienne (marr. diss. 1944), *d* of Count Vivien Hollender; 2nd, 1946, Vicki Serell. *Educ:* Harrow Sch. Engineering apprenticeship Grayson, Rollo & Clover Docks Ltd, 1934. Dir, 1940–49; Emigrated to Australia, 1953. Served War of 1939–45, RAF. *Heir: uncle* Rupert Stanley Harrington Grayson, writer [*b* 22 July 1897; *m* 1st, 1919, Ruby Victoria Banks; 2nd, 1950, Vari Colette O'Shea]. *Recreation:* books. *Address:* 5 Cheero Point Road, Cheero Point, NSW 2254, Australia.
*Died 25 April 1987.*

**GREATBATCH, Sir Bruce,** KCVO 1972 (CVO 1956); Kt 1969; CMG 1961; MBE 1954; *b* 10 June 1917; *s* of W. T. Greatbatch; unmarried. *Educ:* Malvern Coll.; Brasenose Coll., Oxford. Appointed Colonial Service, 1940, Northern Nigeria. War Service with Royal W African Frontier Force, 1940–45, rank of Major, Burma Campaign (despatches). Resumed Colonial Service, Northern Nigeria, 1945; Resident, 1956; Sec. to Governor and Executive Council, 1957; Senior Resident, Kano, 1958; Sec. to the Premier of Northern Nigeria and Head of Regional Civil Service, 1959; Dep. High Comr, Nairobi, Kenya, 1963; Governor and C-in-C, Seychelles, and Comr for British Indian Ocean Territory, 1969–73; Head of British Development Div., Caribbean, 1974–78; freelance consultant, 1978–. KStJ 1969. *Recreations:* shooting, gardening. *Address:* Greenleaves, Painswick, near Stroud, Glos GL6 6TX. *T:* Painswick 813517. *Club:* East India, Devonshire, Sports and Public Schools. *Died 20 July 1989.*

**GREAVES, Maj.-Gen. Charles Granville Barry,** CB 1947; CBE 1945 (OBE 1941); late Royal Engineers; *b* 1900; *s* of late Charles Gregory Heritage Greaves, Inverness; *m* 1926, Maud Frances Mary (*d* 1982), *d* of late Frank Euting, Durban, S Africa; two *s* (and one *s* decd). *Educ:* Inverness Royal Academy; RMA Woolwich. Commissioned RE 1920. Dir of Movements, War Office, 1949–53; retired 1953; American Bronze Star, 1945. *Address:* Devon Lodge, 15 Kimbolton Avenue, Bedford. *T:* 53368. *Died 4 June 1982.*

**GREAVES, Prof. Harold Richard Goring;** Professor of Political Science in the University of London 1960–75, then Emeritus; *b* 17 Nov. 1907; *s* of Harold Frederick Greaves, Derbyshire, and Beatrice Violet (*née* Heather); unmarried. *Educ:* London Sch. of Economics, University of London; Graduate Institute, Geneva. Taught at the London Sch. of Economics and Political Science from 1930; previously worked in business, a bank, and free lance journalism. Visiting Professor, Columbia Univ., New York, 1959–60; Literary Editor, Political Quarterly. Contested (Lab) Camborne, Cornwall, 1935. War-time service BBC and RIIA. *Publications:* The League Committees and World Order, 1931; The Spanish Constitution, 1933; Reactionary England, 1936; Raw Materials and International Control, 1936; The British Constitution, 1938; Federal Union, 1940; The Civil Service and the Changing State, 1947; The Foundations of Political Theory, 1958; Democratic Participation and Public Enterprise (Hobhouse Memorial Lecture), 1964; contrib. to Political Quarterly, Political Science Quarterly, Modern Law Review, The Civil Service in Britain and France, etc. *Address:* The Forge, Stoke by Clare, Suffolk. *Club:* Reform.
*Died 26 Feb. 1981.*

**GREAVES, Prof. Ronald Ivan Norreys,** MD, FRCP; Professor of Pathology, University of Cambridge, 1963–75, later Emeritus Professor; Fellow of Gonville and Caius College, since 1935; *b* 15 July 1908; *s* of late Rt Rev. Arthur I. Greaves, Bishop of Grimsby and Blanche, *d* of late Joseph Meadows; *m* 1936, Anne, *d* of late Philip Bedingfeld; one *d*. *Educ:* Uppingham Sch.; Clare Coll.; Cambridge (Nat. Scis Tripos, 1st Cl. Part I, 1930, 1st Cl Part II (Pathology), 1931, BA 1930, MA, MB, BCh 1935, MD 1946]; Harmsworth Scholar, 1931, St Mary's Hosp., Paddington. Demonstrator in Pathology, Cambridge Univ., 1935; seconded to Med. Research Council, 1939–45 for res. and production of freeze-dried blood plasma for transfusion; Reader in Bacteriology, Cambridge, 1946; Head of Department of Pathology, 1963–75. Past Pres., Soc. for Cryobiology. *Publications:* chapters in books and articles in med. jls, principally on freeze-drying of blood plasma and its transfusion, and on preservation of micro-organisms by freeze-drying. *Recreations:* electronics and gardening. *Address:* 59 Barrow Road, Cambridge CB2 2AR. *T:* Cambridge (0223) 353548.
*Died 29 Aug. 1990.*

**GREAVES, Sir (William) Western,** KBE 1974 (CBE 1960); *b* 29 Dec. 1905; *s* of late John Greaves, solicitor and late Mary Beatrice Aked, Bingley; *m* 1933, Marjorie Nahir Wright, *d* of late Leslie Wright, Alticry, Scotland; one *s* three *d*. *Educ:* Worcester Cathedral Choir Sch.; Ripon Sch. Hon. Pres. of Bd of Governors, Northlands Asociación Civil de Beneficencia (girls' sch.); Pres., La Rueda Finance Co. Chm., British Community Council, 1958–60 and 1971–73, Argentina. Associate, British Hosp. and British and American Benevolent Soc., British Soc. Trust (all Buenos Aires).

*Recreations:* golf, riding (jumping). *Address:* La Rueda, c/o Tortugas Country Club, 1667 Tortuguitas, FCGB, Province of Buenos Aires, Argentina. *T:* Tortuguitas 0320-91214. *Clubs:* Canning, Royal Over-Seas League; English (Buenos Aires); Tortugas Country.
*Died 8 July 1982.*

**GRECH, Herbert Felix,** CVO 1954; *b* 18 May 1899; *m* 1923, Alice Machell (*d* 1969); two *d* (one *s* decd). *Educ:* St Aloysius' Coll., Malta. Served in Army, 1917–20, Lieut King's Own Malta Regt of Militia. Malta Police Force, 1920–54; Commissioner of Police, Malta, 1951–54; retired 1954. *Address:* Flat 1, 27 Creche Street, Sliema, Malta. *T:* Sliema 30086. *Club:* Union (Malta).
*Died 21 Dec. 1982.*

**GREEN, Arthur Eatough,** CIE 1946; OBE 1937; MC 1917; MSc (Leeds); FICE; JP; Chief Engineer, Public Works Department, Bihar, India, retired; *b* 16 Dec. 1892; *s* of late William Green; *m* 1929, Frances Margaret (*d* 1983), *d* of late Col William Henry Savage, CMG; two *s* one *d*. *Educ:* King's Sch., Pontefract; Leeds Univ. Served European War, 1914–18, in 5th Bn West Yorks Regt and RE. Appointed to PWD, India, 1919; served province of Bihar and Orissa, 1919–47; Chief Engineer and Sec. to Govt of Orissa, in PWD, 1942–44, to Govt of Bihar, 1944–47. JP Co. Antrim, 1964. *Recreation:* fishing. *Address:* Drumawillin House, Ballycastle, Co. Antrim, N Ireland. *T:* Ballycastle 62349.
*Died 14 Dec. 1984.*

**GREEN, Sir George (Ernest),** Kt 1963; Past Chairman of Eagers Holdings Ltd; *b* 1892; *s* of Jabez Green, Brisbane, and Catherine Genevieve, *d* of T. Cronin; *m* Ailsa Beatrice, *d* of Charles George Rools Crane. *Educ:* Maryborough Grammar Sch. Pres., Royal National Agricultural and Industrial Assoc. of Qld, 1955–61. *Address:* 35 Markwell Street, Hamilton, Brisbane, Qld 4007, Australia. *Died Oct. 1982.*

**GREEN, Graham John G.;** *see* Graham-Green.

**GREEN, Henry Rupert,** CBE 1960; MA; Legal Senior Commissioner of Board of Control, 1953–60, later Ministry of Health; retired 1977; *b* 29 Dec. 1900; *o s* of late Henry Green, JP, solicitor, and Margaret Helen Green, Stockport, Cheshire; *m* 1937, Marie Elizabeth Patricia Bailey; three *s* one *d*. *Educ:* Charterhouse; Hertford Coll., Oxford (Exhibitioner). Barrister, Lincoln's Inn, 1926; practised on Northern Circuit, 1926–36; Commissioner of Board of Control, 1936. War of 1939–45: commissioned RAF, 1940; served as Operations Staff Officer, Malta, 1941–43; released, 1944. Pres. Governors, St Mary's Sch. for Girls, Gerrards Cross. *Publications:* title: Persons Mentally Disordered (Pts 2 and 3), Halsbury's Laws of England, 3rd Edn, 1960; title: Persons of Unsound Mind, Halsbury's Statutes (Burrows Edn), 1950 and similar title: Encyclopædia of Court Forms, 1949. *Recreation:* carpentry. *Address:* The Square House, Latchmoor Grove, Gerrards Cross, Bucks SL9 8LN. *T:* Gerrards Cross 882316. *Died 28 Dec. 1988.*

**GREEN, Hon. Howard Charles,** PC (Canada); QC (BC); LLD (University of British Columbia); *b* Kaslo, BC, 5 Nov. 1895; *s* of Samuel Howard and Flora Isabel Green; *m* 1st, 1923, Marion Jean (decd), *d* of Lewis Mounce, Vancouver; two *s*; 2nd, 1956, Donna Enid (decd), *d* of Dr D. E. Kerr, Duncan, BC. *Educ:* High Sch., Kaslo; University of Toronto (BA); Osgoode Hall Law Sch. Served European War, 1915–19. Called to Bar of British Columbia, 1922; elected to Federal Parliament, 1935; Minister of Public Works and Govt House Leader, 1957–59; Acting Minister of Defence Production, 1957–58; Dep. Prime Minister, 1957–63; Canadian Sec. of State for External Affairs, 1959–63. Is a Progressive Conservative. *Address:* 4160 W 8th Avenue, Vancouver, British Columbia V6R 1Z6, Canada. *Club:* Terminal City (Vancouver, BC). *Died 26 June 1989.*

**GREEN, (James) Maurice (Spurgeon),** MBE, TD, MA; Editor, The Daily Telegraph, 1964–74 (Deputy Editor, 1961–64); *b* 8 Dec. 1906; *s* of Lieut-Col James Edward Green, DSO; *m* 1st 1929, Pearl (*d* 1934), *d* of A. S. Oko, Cincinnati, USA; 2nd, 1936, Janet Grace, *d* of Maj.-Gen. C. E. M. Norie, CB, CMG, DSO; two *s*. *Educ:* Rugby Sch. (scholar); University Coll., Oxford (scholar, 1st Class, Honour Mods and Lit. Hum.). Editor of The Financial News, 1934–38; Financial and Industrial Editor of The Times, 1938–39 and 1944–53 (served in Royal Artillery, 1939–44); Asst Editor, 1953–61. Pres., Inst. of Journalists, 1976–77. *Recreations:* books, music, fishing. *Address:* The Hermitage, Twyford, near Winchester, Hants. *T:* Twyford 713980. *Club:* Reform. *Died 19 July 1987.*

**GREEN, Maj.-Gen. Kenneth David,** CB 1982; OBE; ED; FICE; Secretary, Premier's Department, Government of Victoria, 1972–82; *b* 20 Nov. 1917; *s* of D. W. Green; *m* 1945, Phyl, *d* of J. Roohan; one *s*. *Educ:* Williamstown High Sch.; Melbourne High Sch.; Melbourne Univ. (BCE). Served 2nd AIF. Joined State Rivers and Water Supply Commn, Vic, 1939; design and exec. engrg appts, 1958–65; Commissioner: State Rivers and Water Supply Commn, Vic, 1965–72; Australian Cities Commn, 1972–75. Fourth Task Force, CMF, 1966–69; Southern Comd Trng Gp, 1969–70; Comdr

3rd Div., CMF, 1970–73; Col Comdt, RAE, Vic, 1976–82. Chairman: State Recreation Council (formerly Nat. Fitness Council), Vic; Duke of Edinburgh's Award Scheme Cttee, Vic, 1971–81; Nat. Water Research Council, 1982–83; Member: Council, Order of Australia, 1974–82; Australia Day Cttee (Vic), 1982–; Film Victoria Bd, 1982. Pres. Council, Chisholm Inst. of Technology, 1982–85; Vice-Pres., Victoria Br., Scout Assoc. of Aust., 1982–. FTS; FASCE; Hon. FIE (Aust). *Publications*: technical papers. *Recreations*: golf, swimming, listening to classical music. *Clubs*: Melbourne, Athenæum, Naval and Military (Melbourne); Melbourne Cricket, Huntingdale Golf, Frankston Golf.

                                                            *Died* 2 *Oct.* 1987.

**GREEN, Leslie William,** CVO 1974; MBE 1953; *b* 1 July 1912; *y s of* late George Green and of Jane E. Green; *m* 1938, Alice Robertshaw; one *s* one *d*. *Educ*: Moseley Grammar Sch., Birmingham; City of Birmingham Commercial Coll. Cert AIB; FCIT. Accountant Officer, RAF, 1940–46 (Flt-Lt); Asst Aiport Man., Heathrow, 1946–47; Airport Man., Croydon, 1947–50; Dep. Airport Man., Heathrow, 1950–55; Airport Man., Heathrow, 1955–62; Admin. Dir, London Airports, 1962–65; Gen. Man., Gatwick, 1965–71; Gen. Man., Heathrow, 1971–73; Special Projects Dir, British Airports Authority, 1973–75. *Recreations*: golf, gardening, watching cricket. *Clubs*: MCC; (Pres.) Chipstead and Coulsdon Cricket; Chipstead Golf.                                          *Died* 21 *July* 1983.

**GREEN, Maurice;** *see* Green, J. M. S.

**GREEN, Paul Eliot,** LittD; writer; *b* 17 March 1894; *s of* William Archibald Green and Betty Lorine Byrd; *m* 1922, Elizabeth Atkinson Lay; one *s* three *d*. *Educ*: Buie's Creek Academy; University of North Carolina; Cornell Univ. Editor of The Reviewer, a literary quarterly, 1925; winner of Pulitzer Prize for best American Play, 1927, In Abraham's Bosom; Guggenheim Fellow for study abroad, 1928–30; Member, National Institute of Arts and Letters; Founder, Inst. of Outdoor Drama. Hon. Degrees from various univs. N Carolina Dramatist Laureate, 1979. *Publications*: *plays*: The Lord's Will and other Plays, 1925; Lonesome Road (one-act plays), 1926; The Field God and In Abraham's Bosom, 1927; In the Valley and Other Plays, 1928; The House of Connelly and Other Plays, 1931; Roll Sweet Chariot, 1935; Shroud my Body Down, 1935; Hymn to the Rising Sun, 1936; Johnny Johnson, 1937; The Lost Colony (symphonic drama), 1937; Out of the South (The Life of a People in Dramatic Form), 1939; The Enchanted Maze, 1939; Native Son (co-author), 1941; The Highland Call (with music), 1941; The Common Glory (symphonic drama), 1948; Peer Gynt (modern adaptation of Ibsen's play), 1951; Wilderness Road (symphonic drama), 1956; The Founders (symphonic drama), 1957; Wings for to Fly (three Negro plays), 1959; The Confederacy (symphonic drama), 1959; The Stephen Foster Story (symphonic drama), 1960; Five Plays of the South, 1963; The Sheltering Plaid, 1965; Cross and Sword (symphonic drama), 1966; Texas (symphonic drama), 1967; Sing All a Green Willow (play with music), 1969; Trumpet in the Land (symphonic drama), 1972; The Honeycomb (folk drama), 1972; Drumbeats in Georgia, 1973, Louisiana Cavalier, 1976, We the People, 1976, The Lone Star, 1977 (symphonic dramas); Palo Duro (sound and light drama), 1978; numerous screen plays; *novels*: The Laughing Pioneer, 1932; This Body the Earth, 1935; *miscellaneous*: Wide Fields (short stories), 1928; The Lost Colony Songbook, 1938; Salvation on a String (stories), 1946; Dog on the Sun (stories), 1949; The Hawthorn Tree (essays), 1943; Forever Growing (essay), 1945; The Common Glory Songbook, 1951; Dramatic Heritage (essays), 1953; Drama and the Weather (essays), 1958; Plough and Furrow (essays), 1963; Texas Songbook, 1967; Words and Ways (stories), 1968; Home to My Valley (stories), 1970; Land of Nod and other Stories (stories), 1976. *Recreations*: music and farming. *Address*: Old Lystra Road, Chapel Hill, North Carolina 27514, USA. *T*: 919-933-8581.

                                                            *Died* 4 *May* 1981.

**GREEN, Roger (Gilbert) Lancelyn;** author; *b* 2 Nov. 1918; *s of* Major G. A. L. Green, MC, RFA, and H. M. P. Sealy; *m* 1948, June, *d of* S. H. Burdett, Northampton; two *s* one *d*. *Educ*: Dane Court Sch., Surrey; Liverpool Coll.; privately; Merton Coll., Oxford (MA, BLitt). Part-time professional actor, 1942–45; Dep. Librarian, Merton Coll., Oxford, 1945–50; William Nobel Research Fellow in Eng. Lit., Liverpool Univ., 1950–52; Mem. Council, Univ. of Liverpool, 1964–70; Andrew Lang Lectr, Univ. of St Andrews, 1968. Editor, Kipling Journal, 1957–79. Mythopoeic Schol. Award (USA), 1975. Hon. DLitt Liverpool, 1981. *Publications*: The Lost July, and other poems, 1945; Tellers of Tales, 1946, rev. edn 1965; The Searching Satyrs, 1946; Andrew Lang: a critical biography, 1946; The Sleeping Beauty, and other tales, 1947; The Singing Rose, and other poems, 1947; From the World's End: a fantasy, 1948, repr. USA 1971; Beauty and the Beast, and other tales, 1948; Poulton-Lancelyn: the story of an ancestral home, 1948; The Story of Lewis Carroll, 1949; The Wonderful Stranger, 1950; The Luck of the Lynns, 1952; A. E. W. Mason: a biography, 1952; The Secret of Rusticoker, 1953; King Arthur and his Knights of the Round Table,

1953, 8th edn 1967; The Diaries of Lewis Carroll, 1953; Fifty Years of Peter Pan, 1954; The Theft of the Golden Cat, 1955; The Adventures of Robin Hood, 1956, 6th edn 1966; Mystery at Mycenae, 1957; Two Satyr Plays (Penguin Classics), 1957; Into Other Worlds: space flight in fiction from Lucian to Lewis, 1957; Old Greek Fairy Tales, 1958; The Land Beyond the North, 1958; The Land of the Lord High Tiger, 1958; Tales of the Greek Heroes, 1958, 8th edn 1973; The Tale of Troy, 1958, 10th edn 1973; Lewis Carroll, 1960; The Saga of Asgard, 1960, 3rd edn as Myths of the Norsemen, 1970; J. M. Barrie, 1960; The True Book About Ancient Greece, 1960; The Luck of Troy, 1961, 4th edn 1973; Mrs Molesworth, 1961; Ancient Greece, 1962; Andrew Lang, 1962; The Lewis Carroll Handbook, 1962; Once, Long Ago, 1962; C. S. Lewis, 1963; Authors and Places, 1963; Ancient Egypt, 1963; Tales of the Greeks and Trojans, 1964; Tales from Shakespeare, 2 vols, 1964–65; A Book of Myths, 1965; Tales the Muses Told, 1965; Myths from Many Lands, 1965; Kipling and the Children, 1965; Andrew Lang: the greatest bookman of his age (Indiana Bookman), 1965; Folk Tales of the World, 1966; Sir Lancelot of the Lake, 1966; Tales of Ancient Egypt, 1967; Stories of Ancient Greece, 1968; Jason and the Golden Fleece, 1968; The Tale of Ancient Israel, 1969; St Andrew's Church, Bebington: a short history, 1969; The Book of Dragons, 1970; Kipling: the critical heritage, 1971; The Book of Magicians, 1973; (with Walter Hooper) C. S. Lewis: a biography, 1974; Holmes, this is Amazing: essays in unorthodox research, 1975; The Book of Other Worlds, 1976; The Tale of Thebes, 1977; (with M. N. Cohen) The Letters of Lewis Carroll, 2 vols, 1979. *Recreations*: book collecting, Greece Ancient and Modern, Greek and Roman theatre. *Address*: Poulton Hall, Poulton-Lancelyn, Bebington, Wirral, Merseyside L63 9LN. *T*: 051–334 2057. *Clubs*: Arts, National Book League.                              *Died* 8 *Oct.* 1987.

**GREEN, Roger James N.;** *see* Northcote-Green.

**GREENE, (Charles) Raymond;** Chevalier of the Legion of Honour; Hon. Consultant Physician, Royal Northern Hospital, Royal Free Hospital and St Luke's Hospital for Clergy; *b* 17 April 1901; *s of* late Charles Henry Greene, MA, FRHistSoc; *m* 1934, Eleanor Craven, *d of* late Hamilton Gamble, St Louis, USA; one *s* one *d*. *Educ*: Berkhamsted; Pembroke Coll., Oxford (Theodore Williams Scholar in Medicine and Senior Open Scholar); Westminster Hospital (Scholar in Anatomy and Physiology), BA (Hons) Oxon, 1924, MA 1927, DM 1935; MRCP, 1943; FRCP 1954; held various appointments at Westminster Hospital, Queen Charlotte's Hospital, and Radcliffe Infirmary, Oxford. Mem. Kamet Expedition, 1931; Mem. Everest Expedition, 1933. Schorstein Research Fellow in Medical Science, University of Oxford, 1932–34; Senior Clinical Asst in charge of the Endocrine Clinic, Westminster Hosp., 1938–45; Physician: Metropolitan Hosp., 1945–54; Whittington Hosp., 1948–66. Dir, Heinemann Medical Books, 1960–80, Chm., 1970–80. Formerly Chm., Nuffield Inst. of Comparative Medicine. Hunterian Professor, RCS of England, 1943 and 1956; Sandoz Lectr, Inst. of Neurology, 1972. Mem. British Pharmacopœia Commission, 1948–53; Vice-Pres., Royal Society of Medicine and Pres. Section of Endocrinology, 1953, Hon. Mem. 1973; Chm. Fourth Internat. Goitre Conf., 1960; Vice-Pres., Fifth Internat. Thyroid Conf., 1965; Vice-Pres., European Thyroid Assoc., 1966; Corresp. Mem., Amer. Thyroid Assoc.; Ex-Pres., Thyroid Club; Vice-Pres., Alpine Club, 1948–49; Hon. Mem., Oxford Univ. Exploration Club and Oxford Univ. Mountaineering Club. FZS (formerly Vice-Pres.). *Publications*: The Practice of Endocrinology, 1948; Myasthenia Gravis, 1969; Human Hormones, 1970; Sick Doctors, 1971; (jtly) Begin Enlargement of the Prostate, 1973; Moments of Being, 1974; (jtly) Colour Atlas of Endocrinology, 1979; many scientific and medical papers on the effects of great altitude and exposure to cold, and on endocrinology. *Recreations*: formerly mountain climbing and travel. *Address*: 10 Cheltenham Terrace, Chelsea, SW3 4RD. *T*: 01-730 1434. *Clubs*: Athenæum, Alpine.

                                                            *Died* 6 *Dec.* 1982.

**GREENE, Edward Reginald,** CMG 1953; FRSA; *b* Santos, Brazil, 26 Nov. 1904; *s of* late Edward Greene and Eva Greene; *m* 1945, Olwen Armstrong Maddocks (marr. diss. 1964); *m* Irmingard Fischges. *Educ*: Bedales Sch.; St John's Coll., Cambridge (BA 1926). After Continental banking experience joined coffee merchant firm E. Johnston & Co. Ltd, 1927; has since travelled and traded in coffee, Brazil, USA, East Africa, Continent; Dir of Coffee, Ministry of Food, 1943, subsequently Dir of Raw Cocoa; resigned 1952; resp. for establishment of London Robusta Coffee Exchange, 1953. Chm., Coffee Fedn, 1952–53; Mem., Commn of Inquiry into Coffee Industry, Uganda Protectorate, 1957. Hon. Vice-Pres., Brazilian Chamber of Commerce, 1968–. Mem., The Cambridge Soc. FRSA 1971. *Recreations*: chess, above all keeping well. *Address*: Orbell House, Castle Hedingham, Essex CO9 3EJ. *T*: Hedingham (0787) 60298. *Clubs*: City of London (Hon. Mem.), Garrick.

                                                            *Died* 13 *Nov.* 1990.

**GREENE, Felix;** freelance writer, broadcaster and film-maker; *b* 21 May 1909; *s of* Edward and Eva Greene; *m* 1945, Elena Lindeman;

one *d*. *Educ:* Sidcot Sch.: Clare Coll., Cambridge. Parliamentary candidate (Nat. Lab), 1931; Talks Dept, BBC, 1933; first BBC foreign rep., N America, 1936; seconded to FO to visit all capitals in S America and prepare report for Cabinet on German and Italian propaganda, 1938; at request of Canadian Govt travelled to all radio stations in Canada and wrote basic draft of constitution of CBC, 1938–39; resigned from BBC, 1940; Amer. Friends Service Cttee (Quaker), 1941; with Aldous Huxley, Gerald Heard and Christopher Isherwood, founded Trabuco Coll., Calif, 1943. Active in US movement against the war in Vietnam and continued non-recognition of People's Republic of China; first visit to China, 1957, frequent visits since; returned to reside UK, 1968. Chm., Soc. for Anglo-Chinese Understanding, 1974, Vice-Pres. 1977–. Produced and directed films (most of which widely shown in western countries, some receiving internat. awards): China!, 1963; The Peking Symphony Orchestra, 1963; Inside North Vietnam, 1967; Cuba Va!, 1968; series of 8 films under gen. title One Man's China, 1972; Freedom Railway (The Tanzam Railway), 1974; Tibet, 1977. Filmed interviews with: Premier Chou En-lai, 1960, 1963, 1972; President Ho Chi Minh, 1965; Chairman Hua Guofeng, 1979; Vice-Premier Deng Xiaoping, 1979; unofficial discussions with, *inter alios*, the Dalai Lama, Robert McNamara, U Thant, Nehru, Pres. Roosevelt, Pres. Truman. Has lectured at all senior univs in US. Member: RIIA; PEN. Hon. LitD, Monmouth Coll., Illinois, 1963. *Publications:* (most of which trans. into other languages): ed, Time to Spare, 1935; What's Really Happening in China?, 1959; The Wall has Two Sides, 1961; Let There be a World, 1963, rev. edn 1982; A Curtain of Ignorance, 1964; Vietnam! Vietnam!, 1966; The Enemy: notes on Imperialism and Revolutionism, 1970; Peking, 1978; articles in Sunday Times, Observer, Life, Paris Match, etc. *Address:* 8 York House, Upper Montagu Street, W1. *T:* 01–262 5905; PO Box 272, San Miguel de Allende Gto, Mexico.
*Died 15 June 1985.*

**GREENE, Sir Hugh (Carleton),** KCMG 1964; OBE 1950; Hon. President, The Bodley Head, since 1981 (Chairman, 1969–81); Chairman, Greene, King & Sons Ltd, Westgate Brewery, Bury St Edmunds, 1971–78; Member, Observer Editorial Trust, 1969–76; *b* Nov. 1910; *s* of late Charles Henry Greene; *m* 1934, Helga Guinness (marr. diss.); two *s*; *m* 1951, Elaine Shaplen (marr. diss.); two *s*; *m* 1970, Tatjana Sais (*d* 1981); *m* 1984, Sarah Grahame. *Educ:* Berkhamsted; Merton Coll., Oxford (MA). Daily Telegraph Berlin staff, 1934; Chief Correspondent, 1938; expelled from Germany as reprisal, May 1939; Warsaw correspondent, 1939; after the outbreak of war reported events in Poland, Rumania, Bulgaria, Turkey, Holland, Belgium, and France. Joined BBC as head of German Service, 1940, after service in RAF; Controller of Broadcasting in British Zone of Germany, 1946–48; BBC East European Service, 1949–50; Head of Emergency Information Services, Federation of Malaya, 1950–51; Asst Controller, BBC Overseas Services, 1952–55; Controller, Overseas Services, 1955–56; Chm. Federal Commn of Inquiry into Organisation of Broadcasting in Fed. of Rhodesia and Nyasaland, 1955; Dir of Administration, BBC, 1956–58; Dir, News and Current Affairs, BBC, 1958–59; Director-General, 1960–69; a Governor, BBC, 1969–71. Vice Pres., European Broadcasting Union, 1963–69; Chm., European-Atlantic Action Cttee on Greece, 1971–74. Reported for Govt of Israel on Israel Broadcasting Authority, 1973; reported for Greek Govt on constitution of Greek broadcasting, 1975. CBIM, 1966. Fellow, BAFTA, 1984. Hon. DCL E Anglia, 1969; DUniv Open Univ., 1973; DUniv York, 1973. Grand Cross, Order of Merit (Germany), 1977. *Publications:* The Spy's Bedside Book (with Graham Greene), 1957; The Third Floor Front, 1969; (ed) The Rivals of Sherlock Holmes, 1970; (ed) More Rivals of Sherlock Holmes: cosmopolitan crimes, 1971; The Future of Broadcasting in Britain, 1972; (ed) The Crooked Counties, 1973; (ed) The American Rivals of Sherlock Holmes, 1976; (ed) The Pirate of the Round Pond and Other Strange Adventure Stories, 1977; (ed) The Complete Rivals of Sherlock Holmes, 1983; (with Graham Greene) Victorian Villainies, 1984. *Address:* Earl's Hall, Cockfield, near Bury St Edmunds, Suffolk.
*Died 19 Feb. 1987.*

**GREENE, Raymond;** *see* Greene, C. R.

**GREENFIELD, Sir Harry,** KBE 1974; Kt 1948; CSI 1946; CIE 1938; *b* 2 Oct. 1898; *m* 1st, 1931, Hilda Adeline Wilkinson (*d* 1977); one *s*; 2nd, 1978, Dorothy Myra Parkes (*née* Spencer). Served European War, Berks Yeomanry and Tank Corps in UK, France and Germany, 1916–19. In Civil Service in India, 1919–47, retiring as Chairman Central Board of Revenue, Govt of India. Delegate of India to Narcotics Commn of UN, 1946; Vice-Pres., 1948–52, Pres., 1953–68, Permanent Central Narcotics Bd (elected to UN under Internat. Convention, 1925, on Dangerous Drugs); Pres., Internat. Narcotics Control Bd, 1968–75; Chm., Inst. for the Study of Drug Dependence, 1968–75. Dir, The Chartered Bank, 1953–73 and of various companies. Until 1974 associated with Internat. Chamber of Commerce for 20 years in furtherance of internat. trade. Governer, Polytechnic of Central London, 1970–80 (Regent Street Polytechnic, 1956–70); Chm. Council, The Leprosy Mission,

1962–74; Chm., Royal Society for India, Pakistan and Ceylon, 1963–75; Vice-Chm., Westminster Chamber of Commerce, 1963–65 and of Commns on Formalities in Internat. Trade, Internat. Chamber of Commerce, 1962–74. Mem. Cttee to review Customs and Excise Organisation, 1951–53. Mem. Advisory Cttee Chelsea Sch. of Art, 1958–64. *Recreations:* gardening and fly-fishing. *Address:* Ruthven, Holmewood Ridge, Langton Green, Kent TN3 0BN. *Club:* Oriental.
*Died 23 April 1981.*

**GREENHILL,** 2nd Baron, *cr* 1950, of Townhead; **Stanley E. Greenhill,** MD, DPH; FRCP(C), FACP, FFCM; Professor Emeritus, Department of Medicine and Community Medicine, University of Alberta, Edmonton, Alberta, 1982; *b* 17 July 1917; *s* of 1st Baron Greenhill and Ida Goodman; *S* father, 1967; *m* 1946, Margaret Jean, *d* of Thomas Newlands Hamilton, Ontario, Canada; two *d*. *Educ:* Kelvinside Academy, Glasgow; California and Toronto Univs. MD Toronto, DPH Toronto; British Informa.ion Services, 1941; RAF, 1944. Prof., Dept of Medicine, University of Alberta, 1952–82. WHO Consultant, 1973–74. *Publications:* contrib. medical journals. *Recreations:* photography, travel. *Heir: b* Hon. Malcolm Greenhill, *b* 5 May 1924. *Address:* 10223, 137th Street, Edmonton, Alta T5N 2G8, Canada. *T:* 403–452–4650; c/o 28 Gorselands, Newbury, Berks. *Club:* Faculty (Edmonton, Alta).
*Died 28 Sept. 1989.*

**GREENLEES, Ian Gordon,** OBE 1963; MA; *b* 10 July 1913; *s* of Samuel Greenlees and Rosalie Stewart. *Educ:* Ampleforth Coll.; Magdalen Coll., Oxford. Reader in English Literature at University of Rome, 1934–36; supervisor of cultural centres of English for the British Council and Acting British Council Representative in Italy, 1939–40; Dir, British Institute, Rome, 1940; commissioned in Army, 1940; served in North African and Italian Campaigns, 1942–45, with rank of Major (despatches). Second Sec. (Asst Press Attaché) at British Embassy, Rome, Jan.-Dec. 1946; Asst British Council Representative, Italy, May 1947–Sept. 1948; Deputy British Council Representative, Italy, 1948–54; Dir, British Inst. of Florence, 1958–81. Medaglia d'Argento ai Benemeriti della Cultura (Italy), 1959; Cavaliere Ufficiale, 1963; Hon. Citizen, Bagni di Lucca, 1972; Commendatore dell' Ordine del Merito della Repubblica Italiana, 1975. *Publication:* Norman Douglas, 1957. *Recreations:* swimming, walking, and talking. *Address:* Casa Mansi, Via del Bagno 20, Bagni di Lucca, Prov. di Lucca, Italy. *T:* 0583 87522. *Club:* Athenæum.
*Died 22 July 1988.*

**GREENSLADE, Brigadier Cyrus,** CBE 1940; psc; *b* 13 May 1892; *s* of late William Francis Greenslade and R. B. Greenslade, St Mary Church, Torquay; *m* 1917, Edith Margaret Johnson (*d* 1975); one *d*. *Educ:* Blundell's Sch., Tiverton. 2nd Lieut Devonshire Regt 1914; Capt. South Staffordshire Regt; Major York and Lancaster Regt; Lieut-Col North Staffordshire Regt; Brevets of Major and Lieut-Col; Instructor at Staff Coll., Camberley, 1932–35; GSO2 Army HQ, India, 1936–37; Col. 1936; Brigadier 1940; served European War, 1914–18, France, Salonica; 1919, The Baltic States (despatches, OBE); War of 1939–45, War Office as AQMG and Dir of Quartering, France, as Dep. QMG (CBE); 2 Corps HQ as DA&QMG. Combined Ops Training Centre as 2nd i/c to Vice-Adm. and Chief Instructor; Middle East, Comdr Eritrea Area and Comdr 2nd Bde Sudan Defence Force, 1942–44 (despatches); Palestine, as Comdr Southern Palestine Area, 1944–46; retd pay, 1946. Dep. Chief, Displaced Persons Operation, UNRRA, Germany and Paris, 1946–47; International Refugee Organisation, Geneva HQ, 1947–48; Chief UK Officer, IRO, 1948–51. Exec. Officer, Royal Commonwealth Society for the Blind, 1953–59. Legion of Merit, USA (Commander). *Address:* Manor Farm House, West Chinnock, near Crewkerne, Somerset. *T:* Chiselborough 395. *Club:* Athenæum.
*Died 30 Oct. 1985.*

**GREENWOOD OF ROSSENDALE,** Baron *cr* 1970 (Life Peer), of East Mersea, Essex; **Arthur William James Greenwood, (Anthony Greenwood),** PC 1964; DL; Director, Britannia Building Society, since 1972 (formerly Leek, Westbourne and Eastern Counties Building Society) (Chairman, 1974–76); company director and consultant; *b* Leeds, 14 Sept. 1911; *s* of late Rt Hon. Arthur Greenwood, CH, MP; *m* 1940, Gillian Crawshay Williams; two *d*. *Educ:* Merchant Taylors' Sch.; Balliol Coll., Oxford (MA). President Oxford Union, 1933. National Fitness Council, 1938–39; Ministry of Information in UK, Russia and Middle East, 1939–42; Intelligence Officer in RAF (Flight Lieut), 1942–46; Allied Reparation Commission, Moscow, Potsdam Conference, Allied Reparation Conference, Paris, 1945; Organising Cttee, Inter-Allied Reparation Agency, 1945–46. Mem. Hampstead Borough Council, 1945–49. MP (Lab), Heywood and Radcliffe, 1946–50, Rossendale, 1950–70. Vice-Chairman Parly Labour Party, 1950, 1951; Parly Cttee of Labour Party, 1951–52 and 1955–60; Vice-Chm., Nat. Exec. Cttee of Labour Party, 1962–63, Chm., 1963–64 (Mem., 1954–70); Sec. of State for Colonial Affairs, Oct. 1964–Dec. 1965; Minister of Overseas Development, Dec. 1965–Aug. 1966; Minister of Housing and Local Government, 1966–70; Chm., House of Lords Select Cttee on Europe, 1977–79. Chm., Labour Parly Assoc.,

1960–71; Member: Commonwealth Develt Corp., 1970–78; Central Lancashire New Town Develt Corp., 1971–76; Chm., UK Housing Assoc., 1972–80, Pres. 1980–; Dep. Chm., Housing Corp., 1974–77; Pres., Housing Centre, 1975–; Chairman: Local Govt Trng Bd, 1975–; Local Govt Staff Commn, 1972–76; Vice-Pres., Assoc. of District Councils, 1974–; President: Urban Dist Councils' Assoc., 1971–72; Essex Assoc. of Local Councils, 1977–; British Trust for Conservation Volunteers, 1974–79; Socialist Educational Assoc., 1963–72; Cremation Soc., 1970–; River Thames Soc., 1971–78; Pure Rivers Soc., 1971–76; River Stour Trust, 1977–; London Soc., 1971–76 and 1979–; Josephine Butler Soc., 1971–76; Assoc. of Metropolitan Authorities, 1974–; Vice-President: Commonwealth Parly Assoc.; Building Societies Assoc., 1971–; RSPCA; Adv. Bd on Redundant Churches, 1975–; British Rheumatic Assoc.; Central Council for Rehabilitation; British Council for Rehabilitation; Mem., Cttee of Inquiry on Rehabilitation of Disabled Persons, 1953; Chm., British Council for Rehabilitation of Disabled, 1975–77. Pro-Chancellor, Univ. of Lancaster, 1972–78. Hon. LLD Lancaster, 1979. JP London, 1950; DL Essex 1974. *Address:* 38 Downshire Hill, Hampstead, NW3; The Old Ship Cottage, East Mersea, Essex. *Clubs:* Savile, Royal Automobile.

*Died 12 April 1982.*

**GREENWOOD, Jack Neville;** General Manager, Stevenage Development Corporation, 1976–80, retired; *b* 17 March 1922; *s* of Daniel Greenwood and Elvina Stanworth; *m* 1947, Margaret Jane Fincher; two *s* two *d. Educ:* Harrow County Sch. Mem., Chartered Inst. of Public Finance and Accountancy. RAF, 1941–46. Ruislip Northwood UDC, 1938–49; Southall Borough Council, 1949–50; Stevenage Develt Corp., 1950–80, Chief Executive Officer, 1967–76. *Recreation:* trying to write short stories, novels, plays. *Address:* 70 Churchill Road, Chipping Norton, Oxon OX7 5HP. *T:* Chipping Norton 3157. *Died 4 June 1989.*

**GREENWOOD, Joan;** Actress; Theatre, Films, Radio, Television; *b* 4 March 1921; *d* of late Earnshaw Greenwood, Artist; *m* 1960, André Morell (*d* 1978); one *s. Educ:* St Catherine's Sch., Bramley, Surrey. First professional stage appearance in Le Malade Imaginaire, 1938; since then has appeared in: Little Ladyship; The Women; Striplings; Damaged Goods; Heartbreak House; Hamlet; Volpone; A Doll's House; Frenzy; Young Wives' Tale; The Confidential Clerk (New York); Peter Pan 1951; The Moon and the Chimney, 1955; Bell, Book and Candle, 1955; Cards of Identity, 1956; Lysistrata, 1957–58; The Grass is Greener, 1959; Hedda Gabler, 1960, 1964; The Irregular Verb to Love, 1961; Oblomov (later Son of Oblomov), 1964; Fallen Angels, 1967; The Au Pair Man, 1969; The Chalk Garden, 1971; Eden End, 1972; In Praise of Love, 1973; The Understanding, 1982. Acted at Chichester Festival, 1962. *Television includes:* Country, 1981; Ellis Island, USA, 1984; Caring, 1985. *Films include:* They Knew Mr Knight, Latin Quarter, Girl in a Million, Bad Sister, The October Man, Tight Little Island, Bad Lord Byron, Train of Events, Flesh and Blood, Kind Hearts and Coronets, The Man in the White Suit, Young Wives Tale, Mr Peek-a-Boo, The Importance of Being Earnest, Monsieur Ripois, Father Brown, Moonfleet, Stage Struck, Tom Jones, The Moonspinners, The Water Babies, Hound of the Baskervilles, Wagner, Little Dorrit, Caring. *Recreations:* reading, ballet, music, painting. *Address:* c/o National Westminster Bank, 352A King's Road, SW3. *Died 27 Feb. 1987.*

**GREENWOOD, Prof. John Neill,** DSc, MMetE; Emeritus Professor, University of Melbourne, since 1965; *b* St Helens, 12 Dec. 1894; *s* of late Ellen and Walter Greenwood; *m* Gladys (marr. diss. 1933), *d* of late Moritz and Bertha Uhland; two *s* one *d*; *m* 1934, Winifred A, *d* of late James and Katherine Borrie; two adopted *d. Educ:* St Helen's Technical Sch. Victoria University, Manchester, 1st class hons metallurgy, 1913–16; Chief Research Asst, Sir W. G. Armstrong Whitworth & Co. (Openshaw), 1916–19; MSc, by thesis, 1917; Chief of Research Dept, Sam. Fox & Co., Ltd, 1919–24; Prof. of Metallurgy, Melbourne Univ., 1924–46. DSc 1922; MMetE (Melbourne), 1931; designing pilot plant for wrought tungsten for Australian Ministry of Munitions, 1942–44; Research Prof. of Metallurgy, 1946–59 (Sen. Prof. of Univ. from 1956), retd; Prof. (personal chair) and Dean of Faculty of Applied Sciences, 1960–64, retd. Past-Pres. and Mem. of Council, 1933–44, Australian Inst. Mining and Metallurgy. Royal Commissioner, King's Bridge Failure, 1962–63. Hon. Life Mem. Victorian Coll. of Optometry, 1964. Hon. FIM, 1979. Hon. DApSc Melbourne, 1968; Hon. DEng Monash, 1974. Silver Medal, Aust. Inst. Metals, 1958; Bronze Medal, Aust. Inst. Mining and Metallurgy, 1961. *Publications:* Glossary of metallographic terms; various original researches in metallurgy and pyrometry, in Journal Iron and Steel Inst., and Journal Institute of Metals, Faraday Soc., Birmingham Met. Soc., Staffs Iron and Steel Institute, Australasian Institute of Mining and Metallurgy. *Address:* 2 Moona Avenue, Mornington, Victoria 3931, Australia. *Died 30 Aug. 1981.*

**GREENWOOD, Robert;** novelist and short-story writer; *b* Crosshills, Yorks, 8 March 1897; *m* 1932, Alice Ross; no c.; *m* 1971, Dorothy

Pantung, SRN. *Publications:* novels: Mr Bunting, 1940; Mr Bunting at War, 1941; The Squad Goes Out, 1943; Wagstaff's England, 1947; Mr Bunting in the Promised Land, 1949; Good Angel Slept, 1953; O Mistress Mine, 1955; A Breeze in Dinglesea, 1957; A Stone from the Brook, 1960; Spring at the Limes, 1963; Summer in Bishop Street, 1965. Books published in England and/or USA and translated into Swedish, Spanish, German, French, Hebrew and Russian; short stories published in England and USA; adapted Bunting novels for the British film, Salute John Citizen. *Address:* Flat 1, 15 Bath Road, Felixstowe, Suffolk. *Died 5 April 1981.*

**GREENWOOD WILSON, J.;** *see* Wilson, John G.

**GREEVES, Rev. Frederic,** MA; LLD; Principal, 1949–67, and Randles Chair of Systematic Theology and Philosophy of Religion, 1946–67, Didsbury College, Bristol, retired 1967; President, Methodist Conference, 1963–64; *b* 1 June 1903; *s* of Rev. Edward Greeves and Mabel Barnsley Greeves; *m* 1929, Frances Marion Barratt; one *s* one *d. Educ:* Merchant Taylors' Sch., Crosby; Manchester Univ. (BA); Didsbury Coll., Manchester; Cambridge Univ. Asst Tutor, Didsbury Coll., Manchester, 1924–28; Methodist Minister, Cheltenham, 1928–30; BA Cambridge, 1932 (MA 1936); Burney Prize, 1933; Minister, Cambridge, 1930–33; Epsom, 1933–39; Oxford, Chaplain to Methodists in Univ., 1939–46. Chm. West Regional Religious Adv. Council, BBC, 1952–57; Fernley-Hartley Lecture, 1956; Cato Lectr, 1960. Hon. LLD (Bristol), 1963. *Publications:* Jesus the Son of God, 1939; Talking about God, 1949; The Meaning of Sin, 1956; Theology and the Cure of Souls, 1960; The Christian Way, 1963. *Address:* 1 Westmorland House, Durdham Park, Bristol BS6 6XH. *T:* Bristol 741594.

*Died 23 Feb. 1985.*

**GREEVES, John Ernest,** CB 1966; Permanent Secretary, Ministry of Home Affairs for Northern Ireland, 1964–70, retired; *b* 9 Oct. 1910; *s* of late R. D. Greeves, Grange, Dungannon, Co. Tyrone; *m* 1942, Hilde Alexandra, *d* of E. Hülbig, Coburg, Bavaria; one *s* one *d. Educ:* Royal School, Dungannon. Entered Min. of Labour, NI, 1928; Asst Sec., 1956–62; Permanent Sec., 1962–64; subseq. Min. of Home Affairs. *Address:* 22 Downshire Road, Belfast BT6 9JL. *T:* 648380. *Died 6 Jan. 1987.*

**GREEVES, Maj.-Gen. Sir Stuart,** KBE 1955 (CBE 1945; OBE 1940); CB 1948; DSO 1944; MC 1917; (ex-Indian Army) Deputy Adjutant General, India, until 1957, retired; *b* 2 April 1897; *s* of late J. S. Greeves; unmarried. *Educ:* Northampton Sch. Served European War, 1914–18 (MC and Bar); War of 1939–45 (DSO and Bar, CBE). *Address:* c/o Lloyds Bank, 6 Pall Mall, SW1; Flat 601, Grosvenor Square, College Road, Rondebosch, Cape Town, S Africa. *Club:* Naval and Military. *Died 11 Oct. 1989.*

**GREG, Barbara,** RE; artist and wood engraver; *b* 30 April 1900; *d* of H. P. and J. E. Greg; *m* 1925, Norman Janes, RWS, RE, RSMA (*d* 1980); one *s* two *d. Educ:* Bedales. Studied at Slade Sch. of Fine Art. Exhibited wood engravings in London, provincial and foreign exhibitions from 1926. ARE 1940; RE 1946. Books illustrated include A Fisherman's Log by Major Ashley Dodd, Enigmas of Natural History and More Enigmas of Natural History by E. L. Grant Watson, The Poacher's Handbook, Fresh Woods, Pastures New, by Ian Niall. *Address:* c/o 15 Crescent Road, N8.

*Died 22 Sept. 1983.*

**GREGORY, Philip Herries,** PhD, DSc London, DIC; FRS 1962; Head of Plant Pathology Department, Rothamsted Experimental Station, Harpenden, Hertfordshire, 1958–67; *b* Exmouth, Devon, 24 July 1907; *s* of late Rev. Herries Smith Gregory, MA and late Muriel Edith Gregory (*née* Eldridge), Hove, Sussex; *m* 1932, Margaret Fearn Culverhouse; one *s* one *d. Educ:* Brighton Technical Coll.; Imperial Coll. of Science and Technology, London. Research in medical mycology, Manitoba Med. Coll., 1931–34; Research plant pathologist, Seale-Hayne Agric. Coll., Newton Abbot, Devon, 1935–40; Rothamsted Experimental Station, Harpenden; Agric. Research Council Research Officer, 1940–47 (seconded for penicillin research to ICI, Manchester, 1945–46); Mycologist, Rothamsted Experimental Station, 1948–54; Prof. of Botany, University of London, Imperial Coll. of Science and Technology, 1954–58. Pres. British Mycological Soc., 1951. *Publications:* The Microbiology of the Atmosphere, 1961, 2nd edn, 1973; papers on mycology, plant pathology, and virology. *Address:* 11 Topstreet Way, Harpenden, Herts AL5 5TU. *Died 9 Feb. 1986.*

**GREGORY, Roderic Alfred,** CBE 1971; FRS 1965; George Holt Professor of Physiology, University of Liverpool, 1948–81, later Emeritus Professor; *b* 29 Dec. 1913; *o c* of Alfred and Alice Gregory, West Ham, London; *m* 1939, Alice, *o c* of J. D. Watts, London; one *d. Educ:* George Green's Sch., London; University Coll. and Hospital, London. BSc Hons Physiology, 1934; MSc Biochemistry, 1938; MRCS, LRCP, 1939, FRCP 1977; PhD Physiology, 1942; DSc Physiology, 1949; Paul Philip Reitlinger Prize, 1938; Schafer Prize, 1939; Bayliss-Starling Scholar, 1935; Sharpey Scholar, 1936–39 and 1941–42; Rockefeller Fellow, 1939–41; Lecturer in

Physiology, University Coll., London (Leatherhead), 1942–45; Senior Lecturer in Experimental Physiology, University of Liverpool, 1945–48; Mem. Biolog. Res. Bd, MRC, 1965–71, Chm. 1969; Mem., MRC, 1967–71; a Vice-Pres., Royal Soc., 1971–73. Hon. Member: Amer. Gastroenterological Assoc., 1967; British Soc. of Gastroenterology, 1974; Physiol. Soc., 1982; Amer. Physiol. Soc., 1982; For. Mem., Amer. Acad. of Arts and Sciences, 1980. Inaugural Bengt Ihre Lecture and Anniversary Medal, Swedish Med. Soc., 1963; Lectures: Purser, TCD, 1964; Waller, Univ. of London, 1966; Meml Lecture, Amer. Gastroenterolog. Assoc., 1966; Ravdin, Amer. Coll. of Surgeons, 1967; Harvey, 1968; William Mitchell Banks, Liverpool Univ., 1970; Finlayson, RCPGlas, 1970; Bayliss-Starling, Physiological Soc. of GB, 1973. Baly Medal, RCP, 1965; John Hunter Medal, RCS, 1969; Beaumont Triennial Prize, Amer. Gastroenterological Assoc., 1976; Royal Medal, Royal Soc., 1978. Fellow, University Coll., London, 1965; Feldberg Foundn Prize, 1966; Feltrinelli Internat. Prize for Medicine, Accademia Nazionale dei Lincei, Rome, 1979. Hon. DSc, Univ. of Chicago, 1966. *Publications:* Secretory Mechanisms of the Gastro-intestinal Tract, 1962; various papers in Jl Physiol., Qly Jl exp. Physiol. and elsewhere since 1935. *Recreation:* music. *Address:* Department of Physiology, University of Liverpool, PO Box 147, Liverpool L69 3BX. *T:* 051–794 5331. *Died 5 Sept. 1990.*

**GREGSON, Maj.-Gen. Guy Patrick,** CB 1958; CBE 1953; DSO 1943 and Bar 1944; MC 1942; retired as General Officer Commanding 1st Division, Salisbury Plain District (1956–59); *b* 8 April 1906; *m* 1st, Oriel Lucas Scudamore; one *s*; 2nd, Iris Crookenden; one *d*. *Educ:* Gresham's Sch., Holt; RMA. 2nd Lieut RA, 1925. Served War of 1939–45 (despatches twice, MC, DSO and Bar, Croix de Guerre); Lt-Col 1942; Brig. 1950. Korea, 1953 (CBE). Regional Dir of Civil Defence, Eastern Region, 1960–68. *Address:* Bear's Farm, Hundon, Sudbury, Suffolk. *T:* Hundon 205.
*Died 10 Dec. 1988.*

**GRESFORD JONES, Rt. Rev. Edward Michael,** KCVO 1968; DD (Lambeth), 1950; *b* 21 Oct. 1901; *s* of Rt Rev. Herbert Gresford Jones; *m* 1933, Lucy, *d* of R. Carr Bosanquet, Rock, Northumberland; three *d*. *Educ:* Rugby; Trinity Coll., Camb. Curate of St Chrysostom's, Victoria Park, Manchester, 1926–28; Chaplain of Trinity College, Cambridge, 1928–33; Vicar of Holy Trinity, South Shore, Blackpool, 1933–39; Rural Dean of the Fylde, 1938–39; Vicar of Hunslet, Leeds, 1939–42; Rector of St Botolph-without-Bishopsgate, 1942–50; Bishop Suffragan of Willesden, 1942–50; Bishop of St Albans, 1950–69; Lord High Almoner, 1953–70; Hon. Asst Bishop of Monmouth, 1970–78. Chairman of C of E Youth Council, 1942–50; Chm. of C of E Moral Welfare Council, 1951–61; Member of Council of Scouts' Assoc., 1955–76. Hon. Freedom of City of St Albans, 1969. *Recreations:* painting, bird watching and fishing. *Address:* Cottage 34, Headbourne Worthy House, Winchester, Hants SO23 7JG. *T:* Winchester 883017. *Died 7 March 1982.*

**GRETTON, 2nd Baron,** *cr* 1944, of Stapleford; **John Frederic Gretton,** OBE 1950; *b* 15 Aug. 1902; *o s* of 1st Baron Gretton, PC, CBE, and Hon. Maud Helen de Moleyns, *y d* of 4th Baron Ventry; *S* father, 1947; *m* 1930, Margaret, *e d* of Capt. H. Loeffler; two *s* two *d*. *Educ:* Eton. MP (C) Burton Div. of Staffs, 1943–45. *Recreations:* yachting, shooting, travelling. *Heir:* *s* Hon. John Henrik Gretton [*b* 9 Feb. 1941; *m* 1970, Jennifer, *o d* of Edmund Moore, York; one *s* one *d*]. *Address:* Stapleford Park, Melton Mowbray. *T:* Wymondham (Leicestershire) 229; 77 Sussex Square, W2. *Club:* Carlton.
*Died 26 March 1982.*

**GRETTON, 3rd Baron** *cr* 1944, of Stapleford; **John Henrik Gretton,** DL; farmer; *b* 9 Feb. 1941; *s* of 2nd Baron Gretton and Margaret, *e d* of Captain Henrik Loeffler; *S* father, 1982; *m* 1970, Jennifer Ann, *o d* of Edmund Moore, York; one *s* one *d*. *Educ:* Shrewsbury. Career in malting and brewing, 1961–74. DL Leicestershire, 1986. *Recreations:* travel, miniature railways, reading, music. *Heir:* *s* Hon. John Lysander Gretton, *b* 17 April 1975. *Address:* Holygate Farm, Stapleford, Melton Mowbray, Leics. *T:* Wymondham 540.
*Died 4 April 1989.*

**GREVILLE, 4th Baron,** *cr* 1869; **Ronald Charles Fulke Greville;** *b* 11 April 1912; *s* of 3rd Baron and Olive Grace (*d* 1959), *d* of J. W. Grace, Leybourne Grange, Kent, and *widow* of Henry Kerr; *S* father, 1952. *Educ:* Eton; Magdalen Coll., Oxford Univ. *Recreations:* music, travel, tennis, gardening, swimming. *Heir:* none. *Address:* 75 Swan Court, Chelsea Manor Street, SW3. *T:* 01–352 3444; Lionsmead House, Shalbourne, near Marlborough, Wilts. *T:* Marlborough 870440. *Club:* Hurlingham.
*Died 9 Dec. 1987 (ext).*

**GREY, Charles Frederick,** CBE 1966; miner; Independent Methodist Minister; *b* 25 March 1903; *m* 1925, Margaret, *d* of James Aspey. Mem. of Divisional Labour Exec. MP (Lab) Durham, 1945–70; Opposition Whip (Northern), 1962–64; Comptroller of HM Household, 1964–66, Treasurer, 1966–69. President: Independent Methodist Connexion, 1971; Sunderland and District Free Church

Council; Mem., Univ. of Durham Council. Freeman of Durham City, 1971. Hon. DCL Durham, 1976. *Address:* 38 Gelt Crescent, Lyons Avenue, Hetton-le-Hole, Tyne and Wear DH5 0HX. *T:* Hetton-le-Hole 2292. *Died 7 Sept. 1984.*

**GREY, Col Geoffrey Bridgman,** CB 1977; CBE 1960; TD 1954; DL, JP; Partner, Messrs Dawkins & Grey, Solicitors, Birmingham, since 1946; *b* 19 Oct. 1911; *s* of Alderman Samuel John Grey (formerly Lord Mayor of Birmingham) and Mrs Jessie Grey; *m* 1939, Betty Francis Mary (*née* Trimingham); two *d*. *Educ:* Mill Hill Sch., London; Brasenose Coll., Oxford Univ. (MA, BCL). Admitted solicitor, 1937. Commnd TA, S Staffs Regt, 1938; served War, 1939–45: European campaign with S Staffs, and York and Lancaster Regts; mentioned in despatches; Major 1943; TA, 1945–: Lt-Col 1950, Col 1954; comd 5th Bn S Staffs Regt, 1950–53; Hon. Colonel: 5th Bn S Staffs Regt, 1957–67; 5/6 (Territorial) Bn Staffs Regt (Prince of Wales), 1967–69; 5th Staffs Cadet Regt, 1963–; ADC, 1963–66; Chm., W Midland TA&VRA, 1970–77. Hon. Legal Adviser, W Midlands Baptist (Trust) Assoc. Pres., Birmingham Consular Assoc., 1965–67 (Vice-Pres., 1963–65); Hon. Consul for the Netherlands, 1959–81; Vice-Consul for Belgium, 1965–. DL Staffs, 1954; JP City of Birmingham, 1966. Officer, Order of Orange Nassau, 1975. *Recreation:* photography. *Address:* 215 Bristol Road, Edgbaston, Birmingham B5 7UB. *T:* 021-440 3080. *Clubs:* Naval and Military; Edgbaston Priory (Birmingham).
*Died 26 March 1983.*

**GREY, (Patrick) Ronald,** QC 1980; a Recorder of the Crown Court, since 1981; *b* 17 March 1927; *s* of Eric Grey and Anna Marie Grey (*née* Baggioli); *m* 1st, 1955, Elisabeth Marguerite Southey (marr. diss. 1971); one *d*; 2nd, 1974, Annabel Hope, 2nd *d* of late Col Max Freeman, OBE, and of Eileen Freeman; one *s*. *Educ:* Abingdon Sch.; private tutors. Commissioned in 5th Royal Gurkha Rifles (FF), 1945; served as Lieut, 3rd Bn, Java and Malaya, until 1947. Called to the Bar, Middle Temple, 1950; Crown Prosecuting Counsel, Cyprus, 1955–57; Sen. Crown Prosecuting Counsel, Cyprus, 1957–59; Sen. Magistrate, Bermuda, 1959–62; Deputy Circuit Judge, 1976–81. *Recreations:* listening to music, photography, gardening. *Address:* 1 Middle Temple Lane, Temple, EC4. *T:* 01–583 0659; 214 Cranmer Court, Sloane Avenue, SW3. *Club:* Hurlingham. *Died 26 Sept. 1985.*

**GREY, Sir Paul (Francis),** KCMG 1963 (CMG 1951); *b* 2 Dec. 1908; *s* of Lt-Col Arthur Grey, CIE, and Teresa (*née* Alleyne); *m* 1936, Agnes Mary, *d* of late Richard Weld-Blundell, Ince-Blundell Hall, Lancs; three *s*. *Educ:* Charterhouse; Christ Church, Oxford. Entered Diplomatic Service, 1933; served in Rome, 1935; Foreign Office, 1939; Rio de Janeiro, 1944; The Hague, 1945; Counsellor, Lisbon, 1949; Minister, British Embassy, Moscow, 1951–54; Assistant Under Sec., Foreign Office, Sept. 1954–57; HM Ambassador to Czechoslovakia, 1957–60; HM Ambassador to Switzerland, 1960–64. *Address:* Holm Wood, Elstead, Godalming, Surrey GU8 6DB. *Died 15 Dec. 1990.*

**GREY, Ronald;** *see* Grey, P. R.

**GREY-TURNER, Dr Elston,** CBE 1980; MC 1944; TD 1955; Vice-President, British Medical Association, since 1982 (Secretary, 1976–79); *b* 16 Aug. 1916; *s* of late Prof. George Grey Turner, LLD, DCh, MS, FRCS, FRCSEd, FRACS, and late Alice Grey Schofield, BSc; *m* 1952, Lilias, *d* of late Col Sterling Charles Tomlinson, Hereford; two *s* one *d*. *Educ:* Winchester Coll.; Trinity Coll., Cambridge; St Bartholomew's Hosp. BA 1938, MA 1942, Cantab; MRCS, LRCP 1942. Ho. Surg., St Bart's Hosp., 1942. Served War in RAMC (N Af., Italy, Germany), 1942–46. Ho. Phys., Addenbrooke's Hosp., 1946; Asst Principal, Min. of Health, 1947–48; Jt Sec., Interdeptl Cttee on Rating of Site Values (Simes Cttee), 1948; Asst Sec., BMA, 1948, Under-Sec. 1960, Dep. Sec. 1964. Sec., Jt Emergency Cttee of the Professions, 1952; Local Sec., Gen. Assembly of World Med. Assoc., 1949; first World Conf. on Med. Educn, 1953; 19th World Med. Assembly, 1965; Sec.-Gen., Standing Cttee of Doctors of the EEC, 1976. Freeman, City of London, 1946; Lt-Col RAMC (TA), 1956; Col RAMC (TA), 1958; QHP, 1960–62; Carmichael Lectr, Royal Coll. of Surgeons in Ireland, 1971; Crookshank Lectr, Faculty of Radiologists, 1973. Grey Turner Lectr, Internat. Soc. of Surgery, 1979. Mem., Court of Assistants, Soc. of Apothecaries of London, 1965– (Master, 1975–76); Hon. Col, 257 (Southern) Gen. Hosp., RAMC(V), 1973–78; Trustee RAMC Historical Museum, 1978–. Dir, Private Patients Plan Ltd (formerly Provident Assoc. for Medical Care Ltd), 1976–; Mem. Council, Medical Insurance Agency Ltd, 1977–; Chm. Med. Bd, St John Ambulance, 1982–. Silver Jubilee Medal, 1977. CStJ 1984. Hon. MD Newcastle, 1980. *Publications:* (with F. M. Sutherland) History of the British Medical Association, vol. II, 1932–1981, 1982; articles in British and foreign med. jls. *Recreation:* gardener-handyman. *Address:* The Manor House, Petersham, Surrey TW10 7AG. *Club:* Carlton. *Died 20 Jan. 1984.*

**GRIBBLE, Leonard Reginald;** Author; *b* 1 Feb. 1908; *s* of late Wilfred Browning Gribble and late Ada Mary Sterry; *m* 1932, Nancy

Mason; one *d*. In 1928 wrote first detective story; literary adviser various London publishers: inaugurated The Empire Bookshelf series for the BBC; judge in two international novel competitions; has devised and written commercial radio programmes and commercial films; founder mem. Paternosters Club; in Press and Censorship Div. of Ministry of Information, 1940–45; co-founder Crime Writers Assoc., 1953. *Publications:* The Gillespie Suicide Mystery, A Christmas Treasury, 1929; The Jesus of the Poets, The Grand Modena Murder, 1930; Is This Revenge?, 1931; The Stolen Home Secretary, 1932; Famous Feats of Detection and Deduction, The Secret of Tangles, 1933; The Riddle of the Ravens, 1934; All The Year Round Stories (with Nancy Gribble), 1935; Riley of the Special Branch; The Case of the Malverne Diamonds, 1936; The Case-book of Anthony Slade, 1937; Tragedy in E flat, 1938; The Arsenal Stadium Mystery (filmed), 1939 and 1950; Heroes of the Fighting RAF, 1941; Death by Design (a film), 1942; Epics of the Fighting RAF, 1943; Heroes of the Merchant Navy, 1944; Toy Folk and Nursery People (verse), 1945; Best Children's Stories of the Year (editor), 1946–50; Profiles from notable Modern Biographies (editor); Atomic Murder, 1947; Hangman's Moon, 1949; They Kidnapped Stanley Matthews, 1950; The Frightened Chameleon, 1951; Murder Out of Season, 1952; Famous Manhunts, 1953; Adventures in Murder, 1954; Triumphs of Scotland Yard, 1955; Death Pays the Piper, 1956; Famous Judges and their Trials, 1957; Great Detective Exploits, 1958; Don't Argue with Death, 1959; Hands of Terror, 1960; Clues that Spelled Guilty, 1961; When Killers Err, 1962; They Challenged the Yard, 1963; Heads You Die, 1964; Such Women are Deadly, 1965; Great Manhunters of the Yard, 1966; Strip Tease Macabre, 1967; Stories of Famous Conspirators, 1968; Famous Stories of Scientific Detection, 1969; Strange Crimes of Passion, 1970; They Got Away with Murder, 1971; Sisters of Cain, 1972; Programmed for Death, 1973; Such was Their Guilt, 1974; They Conspired to Kill, 1975; You Can't Die Tomorrow, 1976; Compelled to Kill, 1977; They Came to Kill, 1979; Crime Stranger than Fiction, 1981; Dead End in Mayfair, 1981; Notorious Killers in the Night, 1983; The Dead Don't Scream, 1983; Notorious Crimes, 1984; Such Lethal Ladies, 1985; also writes fiction (some filmed) under several pseudonyms; translations in fourteen languages; contribs to Chambers's Encyclopædia, Encyclopaedia Americana, DNB; book-reviews, feature articles, short stories and serials to various publications; *posthumous Publication:* They Shot to Slay, 1986. *Recreations:* motoring abroad, watching things grow. *Address:* Chandons, Firsdown Close, High Salvington, Worthing, West Sussex. *T:* Worthing 61976.

*Died 27 Sept. 1985.*

**GRIER, Anthony MacGregor**, CMG 1963; General Manager, Redditch Development Corporation, 1964–76; Member (C), Hereford and Worcester County Council, 1977–85; *b* 12 April 1911; *e s* of late Very Rev. R. M. Grier, St Ninian's House, Perth, Scotland, and late Mrs E. M. Grier; *m* 1946, Hon. Patricia Mary Spens, *er d* of 1st Baron Spens, PC, KBE, QC; two *s* one *d*. *Educ:* St Edward's Sch.; Exeter Coll., Oxford. Colonial Administrative Service, Sierra Leone, 1935; attached to Colonial Office in London and Delhi, 1943–47; North Borneo, now Sabah, Malaysia, 1947–64; Chm., Sabah Electricity Board, 1956–64. Chm. of Governors, King's School, Worcester, 1976–86. *Recreations:* golf, shooting. *Address:* Mulberry House, Abbots Morton, Worcester WR7 4NA. *T:* Inkberrow 792422. *Club:* East India.

*Died 22 Dec. 1989.*

**GRIERSON, Sir Richard Douglas**, 11th Bt *cr* 1685; *b* 25 June 1912; *o s* of Sir Robert Gilbert White Grierson, 10th Bt, and Hilda (*d* 1962), *d* of James Stewart, Surbiton, Surrey; *S* father, 1957. *Educ:* Imperial Service Coll., Windsor. Journalist. *Heir: cousin* Michael John Bewes Grierson [*b* 24 July 1921; *m* 1971, Valerie Anne, *d* of Russell Wright]. *T:* Brighton 736355. *Died 5 May* 1987.

**GRIEVE, Sir (Herbert) Ronald (Robinson)**, Kt 1958; FAMA 1968; Medical Practitioner; *b* 6 June 1896; 2nd *s* of Lieut Gideon James Grieve (killed in action, 1900) and Julia Australia Grieve (*née* Robinson), Sydney, Australia; *m* 1945, Florence Ross Timpson (*d* 1969), formerly of Cheadle Heath, Cheshire; one *s* two *d*; *m* 1972, Margaret Du Vé. *Educ:* Sydney Gram. Sch.; University of Sydney. Grad. in Medicine and Surgery. Resident Medical Officer, Newcastle Gen. Hosp., NSW, 1920–21; House Physician, Manchester Royal Infirmary, 1922–23; Hon. Clinical Asst in Medicine, Royal Prince Alfred Hospital, Sydney, 1941–47. Pres. BMA (NSW Branch), 1947; Mem. NSW Medical Board, 1938–63; Chm. Medical Benefits Fund of Australia, from inception, 1947–75; Pres. Internat. Fedn of Voluntary Health Service Funds, 1968; Mem. Commonwealth of Australia Advisory Cttee on National Health Act, 1953–. MLC, NSW, 1933–34. *Recreations:* angling, the turf; formerly rowing and cricket (rep. Sydney Univ.). *Address:* 113 Homer Street, Earlwood, Sydney, NSW 2206, Australia. *T:* 55–1514. *Clubs:* University, Old Sydneians, Australian Jockey (Sydney).

*Died 1 July 1982.*

**GRIEVE, Thomas Robert**, CBE 1968; MC 1944; Deputy Chairman, Hunterston Development Company Ltd, since 1973; *b* 11 Sept.

1909; *s* of Robert Grieve and Annie Craig (*née* Stark); *m* 1st, 1946, Doreen Bramley Whitehead; two *d*; 2nd, 1978, Mrs R. K. Dimoline (*d* 1985); 3rd, 1986, Mrs M. A. McNeil. *Educ:* Cargilfield and Fettes Coll., Edinburgh. Joined Anglo-Saxon Petroleum Co. Ltd, 1930; served in London, 1930–40. Commissioned 9th Highland Lt Inf. (TA), 1928, seconded Movement Control, Royal Engineers, 1943–45; served NW Europe, rank of Major. Vice-Pres. in charge of Operations, Shell Oil Co. of Canada, 1945; Exec. Asst to Regional Vice-Pres. of Shell Oil Co., Houston, Texas, 1949; Manager of Distribution and Supply Dept, Shell Petroleum Co. Ltd, London, 1951; Director: Shell-Mex and BP Ltd, Shell Refining Co. Ltd, Shell Co. UK Ltd, 1959–65; Shell International Petroleum Co. Ltd, 1963–65; Vice-Chm. and Man. Dir, Shell-Mex and BP Ltd, 1965–71; Chm., United Kingdom Oil Pipelines Ltd, 1965–71; Director: London and Provincial Trust Ltd, 1970–80; Oil and Associated Investment Trust, 1971–84; Viking Resources Trust, 1972–85; Chairman: Hogg Robinson (Scotland) Ltd, 1975–78; Newarthill Ltd, 1977–80. Chm., London Exec. Cttee, Scottish Council, 1971–77. Mem., Management Cttee, AA, 1971–80. Governor, Shiplake Coll., Henley-on-Thames, 1980–. *Recreations:* bridge, travel. *Address:* Gearholm, 84 Bell Street, Henley, Oxon RG9 2BD. *T:* Henley 577901. *Clubs:* Caledonian, MCC. *Died 18 Dec. 1987.*

**GRIFFIN, Sir Francis (Frederick)**, Kt 1971; retired; Director, Ryland Vehicle Group Ltd, 1941–78; *b* 3 June 1904; *s* of James Cecil and Lucy Griffin; *m* 1936, Kathleen Mary Fitzgerald; one *d* (twin *d* and one adopted *s* decd). *Educ:* St Philip's Grammar Sch., Edgbaston. Nat. Deleg., W Midland Div., Motor Agents' Assoc., 1948–54; Mem., Inst. of Motor Industry. Elected to Birmingham City Council, 1949 (Leader of Council, 1964–72). Chm., W Midland Planning Authority Conf., 1966–69; First Chm., W Midland Passenger Transp. Authority, 1969–72; Dir, Nat. Exhibn Centre, 1970–74, 1976–80. Mem., Cons. Gp Metropolitan CC, 1973–(Chm., 1973–75). Freeman, City of Birmingham, 1970. *Publications:* Selling Municipal Houses, 1967; Selling More Council Houses, 1970. *Recreation:* politics. *Address:* 101 Metchley Lane, Harborne, Birmingham B17 0JH. *T:* 021-427 4554. *Club:* Conservative (Birmingham).

*Died 22 July 1982.*

**GRIFFIN, Irene Marie (Mrs Francis D. Griffin)**; *see* Dunne, I. M.

**GRIFFITH, Hon. Sir Arthur Frederick**, Kt 1977; MLC; President, Legislative Council, Western Australia, since 1974; *b* Geraldton, 22 April 1913; *m*; one *c*. *Educ:* public schs in Australia. Served War of 1939–45, RAAF (commnd from ranks). MLA for Canning, WA, 1950–53; MLC (Lib): Suburban, 1953–65; North Metropolitan, 1965–; Minister: for Mines, Housing and Justice, 1959–65; for Mines and Justice, 1965–71, Legislature of Western Australia; Leader of the Opposition, Legislative Council, 1958–59, 1971–74. *Address:* Office of the President, Legislative Council, Perth, Western Australia; 40 Tilton Terrace, City Beach, WA 6015, Australia.

*Died 17 Nov. 1982.*

**GRIFFITH, Grosvenor Talbot**; retired; Warden of Missenden Abbey, 1958–66; *b* 27 Jan. 1899; *s* of late Thomas Wardrop Griffith, CMG, and Louisa, *d* of late Grosvenor Talbot, JP, Leeds; *m* 1934, Hilda Mary (*d* 1980), *d* of late Eric Nisbet, JP Ryton-on-Tyne; one *s* one *d*. *Educ:* Charterhouse; Trinity Coll., Cambridge. 1st Class Historical Tripos Pt 1 1921, 2nd Class Pt 2, 1922. RFA 1917–19; BEF France, 1918 (wounded Nov. 1918); Trinity Coll., Cambridge, 1919–23; Asst Master and Tutor Wellington Coll., 1923–34; called to Bar, Inner Temple, 1934; Headmaster, Oakham Sch., Rutland, 1935–57. Dep. Chm., Rutland Quarter Sessions, 1946–57; Chm. Rutland Magistrates, 1954–57. Mem. Governing Body English-Speaking Union, 1962–73; Governor, Dean Close Sch., 1966–. JP Bucks, 1962–66. *Publication:* Population Problems of Age of Malthus, 1926 (repr. 1967). *Recreation:* painting. *Address:* Old Swindon House, Swindon Village, Cheltenham. *T:* Cheltenham 25565. *Club:* English-Speaking Union. *Died 9 July 1981.*

**GRIFFITH, Guy Thompson**, MA; FBA 1952; Laurence Reader in Classics, Cambridge University, 1951–75; Fellow of Gonville and Caius College, since 1931; Lecturer in Classics, 1937–75; *b* 7 Jan. 1908; *m* 1940, Josephine Marjorie Rainey; three *s* one *d*. *Educ:* The Leys Sch., and Gonville and Caius Coll., Cambridge. Served in RAFVR, 1941–45. Joint Editor Classical Quarterly, 1947–51. *Publications:* The Mercenaries of the Hellenistic World, 1935; (with Michael Oakeshott) A Guide to the Classics, 1936; The Greek Historians, in Fifty Years of Classical Studies (ed M. Platnauer), 1954; (with N. G. L. Hammond) A History of Macedonia, vol. ii, 1979; articles mostly on Greek History in periodicals.

*Died 11 Sept. 1985.*

**GRIFFITH, John Eaton**, CMG 1949; OBE 1941; *b* 1894; *s* of L. J. Griffith, Brondesbury; *m* 1921, Violet Godson (*d* 1958); two *d*. *Educ:* University Coll. RA., 1914–19, Egypt and France; retd disabled, 1919. 1920–50, UK Civil Service; Air Ministry; Ministry of Aircraft Production; Ministry of Production and Ministry of Fuel and Power; Principal Private Sec. to successive Ministers of Aircraft Production, Lord Beaverbrook and Lord Brabazon; Under-Sec.,

Ministry of Supply, 1949–50; retired, 1950. Chm. European Coal Organisation, 1946–47. Organising Cttee XIV Olympiad, 1948; Pres. International Lawn Tennis Federation, 1945, 1953–54 and 1963–64; Life Vice Pres. The Lawn Tennis Assoc., 1969; Life Pres. Bucks Lawn Tennis Assoc. *Address:* St Martins, Grimm's Hill, Great Missenden, Bucks. *T:* Great Missenden 2244. *Club:* All England (Wimbledon). *Died 12 March 1985.*

**GRIFFITH-WILLIAMS, Brig. Eric Llewellyn Griffith,** CBE 1945; DSO 1918; MC and Bar; DL; psc; late RA; 5th *s* of late A. L. G. Griffith-Williams, Highfields, Marlow, Bucks; *b* 2 May 1894; *m* 1938, Delia (*d* 1964), *o c* of late Lt-Col H. S. Follett, CBE, Rockbeare Manor, Devon; one *d. Educ:* Tonbridge Sch.; RMA, Woolwich. Served European War, 1914–19; Bt. Lt-Col, 1937; War of 1939–45; Col 1940; Brig. 1940; retired pay, 1946. High Sheriff of Devonshire, 1966; DL Devon 1966. *Address:* Westcott House, Rockbeare, near Exeter, Devon EX5 2LU. *Club:* Army and Navy.
*Died 5 March 1987.*

**GRIFFITHS, Captain Hubert Penry,** OBE 1953; Assistant Commissioner, City of London Police, 1940–60; *b* 24 April 1894; *yr s* of late Henry Griffiths; *m* 1926, Beryl Rees, *o c* of late I. Newton Rees; one *s* (and one *s* one *d* decd). *Educ:* St Paul's Sch. Gazetted to 5th Special Res. Bn, Middlesex Regt, Oct. 1914; seconded to Nigeria Regt, Royal W African Frontier Force, 1915–20; served German W and E African Campaigns, 1915–18; Second in Command, 2nd Bn, 1918; served Egba Rising, 1918; Asst Comr, Nigeria Police, 1920, Commissioner, 1927; Actg Asst Inspector Gen., Northern Provinces, 1935–36; Police Div., Home Office, 1937; Actg Comr, City of London Police, 1952–53 and again for one year in 1954. Liveryman of Gold and Silver Wyre Drawers Company. OStJ 1952. Commander, Order of North Star (Sweden); Commander Star of Ethiopia. *Address:* 33 Seacliffe Avenue, Takapuna, Auckland 9, NZ. *Club:* City Livery. *Died 8 April 1983.*

**GRIFFITHS, Dr James Howard Eagle,** OBE 1946; President, Magdalen College, Oxford, 1968–79; *b* 6 Dec. 1908; *s* of Rev. James David Griffiths and Olive Arnold (*née* Chataway). *Educ:* Denstone Coll.; Magdalen Coll., Oxford (Demy). 1st cl. Natural Science (Physics), 1930; DPhil 1933; MA 1934. Sec., CVD (Admty), 1943–45. Magdalen Coll., Oxford: Fellow, 1934–68; Sen. Dean of Arts, 1947–50, 1956–60, 1965–66; Vice-Pres., 1951–52; University Demonstrator and Lectr in Physics, 1945–66; Reader in Physics, 1966–68; Vice-Chancellor, University of Malaya, Kuala Lumpur, 1967–68. C. V. Boys Prize, Physical Soc., London, 1951. Mem., Hebdomadal Council, Oxford, 1951–63, 1968–73; Mem., Hale Cttee on Univ. Teaching Methods. Hon. DEd, Univ. of Mindanao, Philippines, 1968. *Publications:* papers in Proc. Royal Soc., Proc. Phys. Soc. London and other physics jls. *Recreations:* music, wine. *Address:* Magdalen College, Oxford. *T:* Oxford 726250. *Club:* Leander (Henley-on-Thames). *Died 28 Aug. 1981.*

**GRIFFITHS, Sir Peter N.;** *see* Norton-Griffiths.

**GRIFFITHS, Richard Cerdin,** CMG 1978; Director, Inter-University Council for Higher Education Overseas, 1970–80; *b* 21 Oct. 1915; *s* of James Griffiths, MBE, and Gwendolen Griffiths, Swansea; *m* 1944, Pamela de Grave Hetherington; three *s* one *d. Educ:* Swansea Grammar Sch.; Jesus Coll., Oxford (Exhibnr, Hon. Schol.). MA. Entered Admiralty as Asst Principal, 1939; Royal Navy (Ord. Seaman), 1940–41; British Admiralty Delegn, Washington, DC, 1941–43. Transf. to HM Treasury, 1946; Private Sec. to Sec. of Treasury (Sir Edward Bridges), 1948–49; Asst Sec., 1949; Treasury Representative in Australia and New Zealand, 1952–53; Imperial Defence Coll., 1957; Head of Arts and Science Div., 1958–63; Under-Sec., Treasury, 1963; Dep. Sec., UGC, 1963–70. Mem., UPGC, Hong Kong, 1967–80; Mem. Council: S Pacific Univ., 1971–73; Queen Elizabeth Coll., Univ. of London; Univ. of East Asia, Macau; Mem., Bd of Governors, Royal Marsden Hosp., 1982–84; Hon. Treasurer: Inst. of Cancer Res., Univ. of London; Ex-Service Fellowship Centres; Vice Chm., Hill Homes, 1971–81; Trustee and Vice-Pres., Highgate Literary and Scientific Instn; Chm., Robert Whipple Trust. Mem. Council, Hon. Soc. of Cymmrodorion. Symonds Award, Assoc. of Commonwealth Univs, 1979. Hon. LLD: Malaya, 1980; Hong Kong, 1981; Hon. DSc Ulster, 1980. *Recreations:* cricket, walking. *Address:* 2 St Albans Villas, NW5 1QU. *T:* 01–485 1862. *Clubs:* Athenæum; MCC.
*Died 2 June 1985.*

**GRIFFITHS, Ward David;** Part-time Member Board, British Steel Corporation, 1970–79; *b* 9 Oct. 1915; *s* of David and Maud Griffiths; *m* 1940, Maisie Edith Williams; three *s* two *d. Educ:* elementary and technical schools. Steelworker, 1936–70. Br. Sec. and subseq. Exec. Mem., Iron and Steel Trades Assoc., 1960–68. Deleg., Tinplate Jt Industrial Council, 1965–68; Employee Dir, S Wales Gp and subseq. Strip Mills Div., British Steel Corp., 1968–70; Director: Grundy Auto Products Ltd, 1975–79; Ruthner Continuous Crop Systems Ltd, 1976–78. *Recreations:* motoring, Rugby football. *Address:* 18 Cambridge Gardens, Ebbw Vale, Gwent NP3 5HG.

*T:* Ebbw Vale 303716. *Club:* Ernest Lever Works (Ebbw Vale).
*Died 1 March 1988.*

**GRIGOROV, Mitko;** Hero of Socialist Labour, 1980; Order of Georgi Dimitrov, 1959, 1970, 1980; Member since 1971, Vice-President, since 1974, State Council of People's Republic of Bulgaria; *b* 9 Sept. 1920; *m* 1956, Stanka Stanoeva; one *d. Educ:* Sofia University. Mem. of Parliament from 1953, Minister without Portfolio, 1962–66; Sec., Central Cttee, Bulgarian Communist Party, 1958–66 (Mem., Politbureau, Central Cttee, 1961–66). Bulgarian Ambassador to the Court of St James's, 1969–71. Mem., Editorial Board of magazine Problems of Peace and Socialism, 1966–69. *Recreation:* mountaineering. *Address:* c/o Durzhaven Suvet (State Council of Bulgaria), Dondoukov 2, Sofia, Bulgaria.
*Died 6 Sept. 1987.*

**GRIGSON, Geoffrey (Edward Harvey),** poet; *b* 2 March 1905; 7th *s* of late Canon W. S. Grigson, Pelynt, Cornwall and of Mary Beatrice Boldero; *m* 1st, Frances Galt (*d* 1937), St Louis, Missouri; one *d*; 2nd, Berta Kunert (marr. diss.); one *s* one *d*; 3rd, Jane Grigson, *d* of G. S. McIntire, CBE; one *d.* Editor of New Verse, 1933–39; formerly on staff of Yorkshire Post, Morning Post (Literary Editor) and BBC. *Publications:* Several Observations, 1939; Under the Cliff and other poems, 1943; Henry Moore, 1943; The Isles of Scilly and other poems, 1946; Samuel Palmer, 1947; The Harp of Aeolus, 1947; Places of the Mind, 1949; The Crest on the Silver, 1950; William Barnes (Muses Library), 1950; John Clare (Muses Library), 1950; Essays from the Air, 1951; A Master of Our Time (Wyndham Lewis), 1951; Gardenage, 1952; Legenda Suecana (poems), 1953; Freedom of the Parish, 1954; The Englishman's Flora, 1955; Gerard Manley Hopkins, 1955; English Drawings, 1955; The Painted Caves, 1957; Art Treasures of the British Museum, 1958; The Three Kings, 1958; A Herbal of All Sorts, 1959; The Cherry Tree, 1959; English Excursions, 1960; Christopher Smart, 1961; The Shell Country Book, 1962; Collected Poems, 1963; Poems of Walter Savage Landor, 1964; (with Jane Grigson) Shapes and Stories, 1964; The Shell Country Alphabet, 1966; A Skull in Salop and Other Poems, 1967; Shapes and Adventures, 1967; Poems and Poets, 1968; A Choice of William Morris's Verse, 1968; Ingestion of Ice-Cream and Other Poems, 1969; Shapes and People, 1969; Notes from an Odd Country, 1970; (ed) Faber Book of Popular Verse, 1971; (ed) A Choice of Southey's Verse, 1971; Discoveries of Bones and Stones and Other Poems, 1971 (Duff Cooper Meml Prize 1972); (ed) Unrespectable Verse, 1971; Rainbows, Fleas and Flowers, 1971; Shapes and Creatures, 1972; Sad Grave of an Imperial Mongoose and Other Poems, 1973; (ed) Faber Book of Love Poems, 1973; (ed) Dictionary of English Plant Names, 1974; Angles and Circles and other Poems, 1974; The Contrary View, 1974; Britain Observed, 1975; (ed) Poet to Poet: Charles Cotton, 1975; (ed) Penguin Book of Ballads, 1975; The Goddess of Love, 1976; Faber Book of Epigrams and Epitaphs, 1977; (ed) Faber Book of Nonsense Verse, 1978; The Fiesta and Other Poems, 1978; (ed) Oxford Book of Satirical Verse, 1980; History of Him and other Poems, 1980; (ed) Faber Book of Poems and Places, 1980; Twists of the Way (poems), 1980; The Cornish Dancer (poems), 1982; The Private Art, 1982; Blessings, Kicks and Curses, 1982; Collected Poems 1963–1980, 1984; Recollections: mainly of writers and artists, 1984; (ed) The Faber Book of Reflective Verse, 1984; Montaigne's Tower and other poems, 1985; *posthumous publication:* Persephone's Flowers, 1986. *Address:* Broad Town Farmhouse, Broad Town, Swindon, Wilts. *T:* Broad Hinton 259. *Died 25 Nov. 1985.*

**GRIGSON, (Heather Mabel) Jane;** Cookery Correspondent, Observer Colour Magazine, since 1968; *b* 13 March 1928; *d* of George Shipley McIntire, CBE, and Doris Berkley; *m* Geoffrey Grigson (*d* 1985); one *d. Educ:* Casterton Sch., Westmorland; Newnham Coll., Cambridge. Editorial Assistant, Rainbird McLean Ltd, and Thames and Hudson Ltd, 1953–55; translator from Italian, 1956–67; cookery writer, 1967–. *Publications:* Charcuterie and French Pork Cookery, 1967; Good Things, 1971; Fish Cookery, 1973; English Food, 1974 (rev. edn 1979); The Mushroom Feast, 1975; Jane Grigson's Vegetable Book, 1978 (Glenfiddich Writer of the Year; André Simon Meml Prize); Food with the Famous, 1979; Jane Grigson's Fruit Book, 1982 (Glenfiddich Writer of the Year; André Simon Meml Prize); The Observer Guide to European Cookery, 1983; The Observer Guide to British Cookery, 1984; Exotic Fruit and Vegetables (with paintings by Charlotte Knox), 1986; *translation:* Of Crimes and Punishments, by Cesare Beccaria, 1964 (John Florio prize). *Address:* Broad Town Farmhouse, Broad Town, Swindon, Wiltshire. *T:* Swindon 731259. *Died 12 March 1990.*

**GRIME, Sir Harold (Riley),** Kt 1959; DL; JP; Chairman and Editor-in-Chief of the West Lancashire Evening Gazette and associated newspapers; Editor of the Blackpool Gazette, 1926–62; *b* 12 May 1896; *s* of late Frederick Alexander Grime, JP, and late Fannie Grime (*née* Riley); *m* 1925, Mary (Mollie) Bowman (*d* 1970), *d* of late W. Powell Bowman, Leeds; two *d. Educ:* Arnold Sch., Blackpool; Bonn, Germany. East Lancs Regt, 1915–17; Indian Army, 1917–20. Yorkshire Evening Post and London Evening

News, 1920–23. Dir, Press Association, 1942–51 (Chm. 1946–47); Dir, Reuters, 1945–47; Founder Mem., British Cttee, Internat. Press Inst., 1951; Chm., Guild of Editors (NW Region), 1957–58; Mem., Gen. Adv. Council, BBC, 1960–64. Hon. Sec., Blackpool Victoria Hosp., 1938–48; Hon. Treas., Blackpool Conservative and Unionist Assoc., 1938–45; Dir, Blackpool Tower and Winter Gardens Cos., 1944–68 (Vice-Chm. 1953–68); President: Preston and District Chamber of Commerce, 1962–67; Blackpool Civic Trust, 1975–; Hon. Life Pres., Blackpool Council for Voluntary Service; Hon. Life Patron, Blackpool Catering Coll. Hon. Freeman of Blackpool, 1950. DL Lancs, 1968. JP for Blackpool, 1943–. *Publications:* The Silver Trumpet, 1942; Sand in My Shoes, 1950. *Address:* 24 Lowcross Road, Poulton-le-Fylde, Lancs.

*Died 31 Aug. 1984.*

**GRIMES, Prof. William Francis,** CBE 1955; DLitt, FSA; FMA; Director of the Institute of Archæology, and Professor of Archæology, University of London, 1956–73; *b* 31 Oct. 1905; *e s of* Thomas George Grimes, Pembroke; *m* 1st, 1928, Barbara Lilian Morgan (marr. diss. 1959); one *s* one *d*; 2nd, 1959, Audrey Williams (*née* Davies) (*d* 1978); 3rd, 1980, Molly Waverley Sholto Douglas (*née* Penn). *Educ:* University of Wales (MA); DLitt Wales, 1961. Asst Keeper of Archæology, National Museum of Wales, Cardiff, 1926–38; Asst Archæology Officer, Ordnance Survey, 1938–45; seconded to Min. of Works to record historic monuments on defence sites, 1939–45; Dir London Museum, 1945–56. Mem. Royal Commn on Ancient Monuments in Wales, 1948–78 (Chm., 1967–78), and of Ancient Monuments Boards, England, 1954–77, Wales, 1959–78; Mem. Royal Commn on Historical Monuments (England), 1964–78. Sec. to Coun. for British Archæology, 1949–54, Pres. 1954–59, Vice-Pres., 1961–65, Treas., 1964–74; Pres. London and Middlesex Archæological Soc., 1950–59, Hon. Vice-Pres., 1976–; Pres. Royal Archæological Institute, 1957–60 (Vice-Pres. 1951–57); Vice-President: Soc. of Antiquaries, 1953–57; Soc. for Medieval Archæology; Prehistoric Soc., 1958–61; Soc. for Roman Studies, 1973–; Hon. Dir of Excavations for the Roman and Mediæval London Excavation Council, 1946–; Chm., London Topographical Soc., 1961–73. Pres., Cambrian Archæological Assoc., 1963–64 (G. T. Clark Prize, 1946); Chm., Faculty of Archæology, History and Letters, British Sch. at Rome, 1963–66; President: Stanmore Archæological Soc., 1962–; Tenby Museum, 1969–; Field Studies Council, 1975– (Chm., 1966–75). Hon. Professorial Fellow, Univ. of Wales, 1961 (University Coll. Swansea); Fellow, University Coll. Cardiff, 1974. *Publications:* Holt, Denbighshire, Legionary Works Depôt (Y Cymmrodor), 1930; Pre-history of Wales, 1951; (ed) Aspects of Archæology in Britain and Beyond, 1951; (with M. D. Knowles) Charterhouse, 1954; (with others) Brooke House, Hackney (London Survey, Vol. XXVIII), 1960; Excavations in Defence Sites, 1939–1945, I, 1960; The Excavation of Roman and Mediæval London, 1968; many papers in learned jls. *Address:* 29 Bryn Road, Swansea, West Glamorgan SA2 0AP. *Died 25 Dec. 1988.*

**GRIMWOOD, Frank Southgate,** BA; DPhil; ABPsS; *b* 14 July 1904; *s* of late Frank Grimwood, Ipswich and Newbury, and Rose Grimwood (*née* Lake), Bucklebury, Berks; *m* 1935, Mary Habberley Price, MA Oxon; one *s* one *d*. *Educ:* Isleworth County High Sch.; Reading Univ. (Wantage Hall); The Queen's Coll., Oxford. DPhil Oxon; BA Hons University of Reading. Sub-Warden and Foreign Student Sec., SCM, 1929–30; Lecturer in Philosophy and Psychology, City Literary Institute, 1930–40; training in Deep Analysis under Drs J. A. Hadfield and R. G. Hargreaves of Tavistock Clinic, London; Welfare Officer (Oxon, Bucks, and Berks), Min. of Labour and Nat. Service, 1940–48. Advanced Student, The Queen's Coll., Oxford, 1948–56, including one year (1951) at Cuddesdon Theological Coll. (thesis on psychotherapy and religion). Lecturer and Tutor, Oxford Univ. Extra-Mural Delegacy, 1956–61; Warden and Director of Studies, Moor Park College, 1961–72; lecturing and tutoring groups for Nat. Marriage Guidance Council, 1965–70; Exec. Sec., Keble Coll., Oxford, Centenary Appeal, 1972–74. Private Consulting Psychotherapist. *Publication:* Journey towards Belief in God, 1986. *Recreations:* painting, walking, biography. *Address:* 69A Jack Straw's Lane, Oxford OX3 0DW. *T:* Oxford 68535. *Died 6 April 1990.*

**GRINKE, Frederick (Otto),** CBE 1979; FRAM; Solo Violinist; Professor of Violin, Royal Academy of Music, London, retired; *b* Winnipeg, Canada, 8 Aug. 1911; *s of* Arthur Grinke, Winnipeg; *m* 1942, Dorothy Ethel Sirr Sheldon; one *s*. *Educ:* Winnipeg; Royal Academy of Music, London (all prizes for solo and chamber music playing). Studied with Adolf Busch in Switzerland, with Carl Flesch in London and Belgium. Was leader and soloist with the Boyd Neel Orchestra for 10 years. Appeared regularly as Soloist with leading orchestras; has played in many countries in Europe also in America, Australia and New Zealand. Has appeared at Festivals: Edinburgh, Bath, Cheltenham, Three Choirs, Salzburg. Has taken part in many Promenade Concerts. A sonata was dedicated to him by Vaughan Williams; has made numerous recordings, including many works with the composers as pianists (such as Rubbra, Ireland, Berkeley, Benjamin). Has acted as mem. of the Jury for several international

violin competitions. FRSA 1979. *Recreations:* music, cooking, wine, reading, the theatre. *Address:* Albion House, 14 Lambeth Street, Eye, Suffolk IP23 7AG. *T:* Eye 870483.

*Died 16 March 1987.*

**GROBECKER, Ven. Geoffrey Frank,** MBE 1959; Archdeacon of Lynn, 1980–87, Archdeacon Emeritus since 1987; *b* 1922; *s of* Archibald Douglas and Ethel May Grobecker; *m* 1949, Audrey Kathleen Bessell; two *d*. *Educ:* St Paul's School; Queens' Coll., Cambridge (BA 1949, MA 1953); Ridley Hall, Cambridge. Deacon 1950, priest 1951, dio. Southwark; Curate of Morden, 1950–52; CF, 1952; Senior Chaplain, RMA, Sandhurst, 1966–69; DACG, 1969–72; ACG, 1972–77; Hon. Chaplain to the Queen, 1973–77; Vicar of Swaffham, 1977–80. *Recreations:* family, walking, gardening, bird-watching. *Address:* 15 Moberly Road, Salisbury, Wilts SP1 3BZ. *Died 27 Feb. 1989.*

**GROMYKO, Andrei Andreevich,** Order of Lenin (four awards); President of the Presidium, Supreme Soviet of the USSR, 1985–88; Member, Politburo, 1973–88; Member, Central Committee, Communist Party of the Soviet Union, 1956–89; *b* 18 July 1909; *m* Lydia D. Grinevich; one *s* one *d*. *Educ:* Agricultural Institute and Institute of Economics, Moscow. Scientific worker (senior), Acad. of Sciences USSR, 1936–39, also lecturing in Moscow Universities. Chief of American Division National Council of Foreign Affairs, 1939; Counsellor, USSR Washington Embassy, 1939–43; Ambassador to USA and Minister to Cuba, 1943–46; Soviet Representative on UN Security Council, 1946–48; Deputy Foreign Minister, 1946–49, 1953–54; 1st Deputy Minister of Foreign Affairs, 1949–52; Soviet Ambassador in London, 1952–53; First Deputy Foreign Minister in Moscow, 1954–57; Minister of Foreign Affairs, USSR, 1957–85; First Dep. Prime Minister, 1983–85. Chm. of Delegates, Conference on Post-War Security, Dumbarton Oaks, USA, 1944. Holds many orders and awards of USSR and other countries. *Publications:* Only for Peace, 1979; Memories (autobiog.), 1989. *Address:* Central Committee, CPSU, Kremlin, Moscow, USSR. *Died 2 July 1989.*

**GRONOW, Alun Gwilym;** Secretary, Association of Metropolitan Authorities, since 1985; *b* 22 Oct. 1931; *s* of Ivor Austin Gronow and Kate Evelyn Gronow; *m* 1977, Kathleen Margaret Hodge; two *s* one *d*. *Educ:* Dorking Grammar School; King's College London (BA Hons). Teacher, 1955–67; Education Administration, 1967–77; Asst Sec., Local Authorities' Conditions of Service Adv. Bd, 1978–81; Under Sec., 1981–83, Dep. Sec., 1983–85, AMA. *Recreations:* theatre, travel, bridge. *Address:* 7 Helford Walk, Woking, Surrey GU21 3PL. *T:* Woking 20953. *Club:* Reform.

*Died 14 Oct. 1989.*

**GROOM, Sir (Thomas) Reginald,** Kt 1961; Chartered Accountant; Partner, Peat, Marwick, Mitchell & Co, Brisbane, Qld, 1932–77; Commissioner, Australian National Airlines Commission, 1961–75; Director: Woodland Ltd (Chairman), 1969–80; Consolidated Rutile Ltd, 1964–78; Mount Isa Mines Holdings Ltd, 1962–77; P & O Australia Ltd, 1958–78; Elder Smith Goldsbrough Mort Ltd, 1966–78; Member of Commonwealth Banking Corporation Board, 1964–74, and of several private companies; *b* 30 Dec. 1906; *s* of Roy Graeme Groom and May Augusta Groom; *m* 1932, Jessie Mary Grace Butcher; two *s* one *d*. *Educ:* Brisbane Grammar Sch.; University of Qld (BA, BCom). Admitted to Institute of Chartered Accountants in Australia, 1932; in public practice, 1932–77. Alderman, Brisbane City Council, 1943–; Lord Mayor of Brisbane, 1955–61. Commissioner, Qld Local Govt Grants Commn, 1977–79. Dir, Australian Elizabethan Theatre Trust. *Recreations:* farming, fishing, golf. *Address:* 39 Ferguson Avenue, Buderim, Qld 4556, Australia. *T:* (office) 221–9411. *Clubs:* Queensland, Johnsonian (Brisbane). *Died 28 June 1987.*

**GROOM, Air Marshal Sir Victor Emmanuel,** KCVO 1953; KBE 1952 (CBE 1945; OBE 1940); CB 1944; DFC 1918, and Bar, 1921; RAF retired; *b* 4 Aug. 1898; *e s of* late William E. Groom; *m* 1st, 1924, Maisie Monica Maule (*d* 1961); one *s* (and one *s* decd); 2nd, 1969, Mrs Muriel Constance Brown (*d* 1990), *widow* of Captain G. S. Brown. *Educ:* Alleyns, Dulwich. Served European War, 1916–18, Artists Rifles, 14 Foot W Yorks Regt; RFC 1917, RAF 1918 (DFC); Egypt, Turkey, Iraq, 1919–22 (bar to DFC); RAF Staff Coll. (psc 1928); India, 1929–34; Bomber Command, 1936–41 (OBE); Directorate of Plans, Air Min., 1941–42; Head of RAF Staff planning the invasion under Chief of Staff to the Supreme Allied Commander, 1942–43; SASO 2nd Tactical Air Force, 1943–45; AOA Flying Trg Command, 1945–46; Dir-Gen. of Manning, Air Ministry, 1947–49; AOC 205 Group RAF, MEAF, 1949–51; C-in-C, MEAF, 1952; AOC-in-C, Technical Training Command, 1952–55, retired 1955. Officer Legion of Honour (France). *Address:* 8 Somerville House, Manor Fields, SW15 3LX. *T:* 081–788 1290. *Club:* Royal Air Force. *Died 6 Dec. 1990.*

**GROSS, Anthony Imre Alexander,** CBE 1982; RA 1980 (ARA 1979); Hon. RE 1979; painter, etcher; *b* 19 March 1905; *s* of Alexander Gross and Isabelle Crowley; *m* 1930, Marcelle Florenty; one *s* one

*d. Educ:* Repton; Slade; Paris; Madrid. Exhibits London, Paris, New York, etc. Has also made films and illustrated books. Lives several months each year in France. *Recreation:* restoring an ancient house. *Address:* 115 King George Street, Greenwich, SE10 8PX.
*Died 8 Sept.* 1984.

**GROSVENOR, Mrs Beatrice Elizabeth Katherine**, CBE 1952; United Kingdom Representative on the Executive Committee of the Programme of the United Nations High Commissioner for Refugees, 1959–60; *b* 6 Nov. 1915; *d* of late Lord Edward Grosvenor and late Lady Dorothy Charteris; *m* 1944 (marr. annulled, 1945), Major Richard Girouard. *Educ:* Holy Child Convent, Cavendish Square, W1. Served War of 1939–45 (despatches), with St John Ambulance Brigade; Asst Superintendent-in-Chief SJAB, 1946–52; Deputy Superintendent-in-Chief, 1952–59; County Pres. for Co. Cork, Eire, SJAB, 1960. DStJ 1958. *Address:* Kenmare House, Killarney, Co. Kerry. *T:* Killarney 41.                                    *Died 15 June* 1985.

**GROTRIAN, Sir John (Appelbe Brent)**, 2nd Bt, *cr* 1934; *b* 16 Feb. 1904; 2nd and *o* surv. *s* of Sir Herbert Brent Grotrian, 1st Bt, KC, JP, and Mary Lilian (*d* 1971), *d* of late Robert Adams, Barrister-at-law of Hamilton, Ont., Canada; *S* father, 1951. *Educ:* Eton Coll.; Trinity Coll., Oxford. Served in War of 1939–45 (despatches). *Heir:* nephew Philip Christian Brent Grotrian [*b* 26 March 1935; *s* of Robert Philip Brent Grotrian (*d* on active service, 1945; *y s* of 1st Bt) and Elizabeth Mary Hardy-Wrigley; *m* 1960, Anne Isabel, *d* of Robert Sieger Whyte, Toronto, Canada; one *s*]. *Address:* Raughmere House, Lavant, Chichester, West Sussex. *T:* Chichester 527120.
*Died 6 Feb.* 1984.

**GROUNDS, George Ambrose**, CBE 1958; DSO 1918 (Bar 1918); TD 1933; DL; retired; *b* 19 Nov. 1886; *s* of Frederick and Elizabeth Grounds; *m* 1950, Kathleen Burton Sale (*d* 1968). *Educ:* St Ives (Hunts) Gram. Sch.; Lowestoft Coll. Banking, 1903–45. Served European War, 1914–18, Royal Tank Corps, France (wounded); served War of 1939–45, RA; Lt-Col 1936. DL Lincs, 1951; Chm. Holland (Lincs) CC, 1963–67; Alderman HCC, 1961–74. *Address:* The Elms, 53 Sleaford Road, Boston, Lincs. *T:* Boston 62772.
*Died 9 Sept.* 1983.

**GROUNDS, Sir Roy (Burman)**, Kt 1969; LFRAIA; Hon. Fellow, AIA; Governing Director, Roy Grounds & Co. Pty Ltd, Architects, since 1963; *b* Melbourne, 18 Dec. 1905; *s* of Herbert Algernon Haslett and Maude Hawksworth (*née* Hughes); *m* 1940, Alice Bettine James; one *s* one *d* (and one *d* decd). *Educ:* Melbourne Grammar Sch.; Univ. of Melbourne. BArch Melbourne, 1947. Partner, Mewton & Grounds, 1932–38; Two Centenary Gold Medal awards for completed bldgs, 1935; practice in Europe and Melbourne, 1938–41. Commissioned RAAF, SW Pacific, 1941–45; Sen. Lectr in Architecture, Univ. of Melbourne, 1945–52; Sen. partner, Grounds, Romberg & Boyd, Architects, Melbourne, 1953–62. RVIA Arch. Award, 1954; RAIA Arch. Award (for Aust. Acad. of Science Bldg, Canberra), 1957; Pan-Pacific Architectural Citation of AIA, 1960; Sulman Award for Arch., 1961; RAIA Gold Medal, 1968; Hon. Life FAIA, 1972. *Address:* 24 Hill Street, Toorak, Victoria 3142, Australia. *T:* 24-3110. *Club:* Commonwealth (Canberra).                                    *Died 2 March* 1981.

**GROVER, Sir Anthony (Charles)**, Kt 1973; Chairman: Lloyd's Register of Shipping, 1963–June 1973; Lifeguard Assurance Ltd, 1964–76; *b* 13 Oct. 1907; *s* of F. J. Grover, Harrow, Middx; *m* 1st, 1931, Marguerite Beatrice Davies; one *s* one *d*; 2nd, 1979, Clarisse, Mrs Grantley Loxton-Peacock. *Educ:* Westminster Sch. War of 1939–45 (despatches): joined Coldstream Guards, 1940; served in Italy, 1942–44; rose to rank of Major. Underwriting Mem. of Lloyd's, 1936– (Dep. Chm., 1958; Chm., 1959–60). Dep. Chm. and Treasurer, Lloyd's Register of Shipping, 1956–58, 1961–63. Comdr, Order of Leopold II, 1967; Comdr, Order of Oranje Nassau, 1968; Comdr, Order of Dannebrog, 1972. *Recreation:* golf. *Address:* 85 Bedford Gardens, Kensington, W8. *T:* 01-727 5286. *Clubs:* White's; Woking Golf; Royal St George's Golf (Sandwich); Honourable Company of Edinburgh Golfers; Swinley Forest Golf.
*Died 3 Sept.* 1981.

**GRUBB, Violet Margaret**, DSc London; retired; *b* Oxton, Notts, 1898; *o d* of Rev. H. Percy Grubb and M. A. Crichton-Stuart. *Educ:* Bournemouth High Sch.; Westfield Coll., University of London. BSc Hons London, 1920; DSc London, 1925; Asst Lecturer in Botany, Westfield Coll., 1923–25; Science teacher in I Fang Sch., Changsha, Central China and Lecturer in Hunan Provincial Univ., 1925–30; Lecturer in Dept of Botany, Westfield Coll., University of London, 1931–37; Headmistress, Westonbirt Sch., Tetbury, Glos, 1937–55; Principal, The Training Coll., Salisbury, 1955–62. Pres., Assoc. Head Mistresses of Boarding Schs, 1943–45. Chm., Assoc. of Independent and Direct Grant Schs, 1950–53; Member: Central Advisory Council for Education (England), 1956–59; Science Museum Advisory Council, 1957–64. *Publications:* Articles on Ecology and Reproduction of Marine Algæ and on distribution of Far Eastern Algæ, in scientific journals in England and abroad.

*Address:* 10 Manor Road, Salisbury SP1 1JS. *T:* Salisbury 28814. *Club:* Royal Over-Seas League.                                    *Died 24 Jan.* 1985.

**GRUENTHER, Gen. Alfred M(aximilian)**; (Hon.) CB (UK) 1943; DSM (US) (with 2 Oak Leaf Clusters) 1943, 1945, 1956; US Army, retired; Member: The Business Council; President's Commission on an All-Volunteer Armed Force, since 1969; Editorial Board, Foreign Affairs Magazine, since 1959; *b* Nebraska, 3 March 1899; *s* of Christian M. Gruenther and Mary Shea; *m* 1922, Grace Elizabeth Crum (*d* 1979); two *s*. *Educ:* Military Academy, West Point (BS). Commissioned, Field Artillery, 1918; routine peacetime assignments, including 8 years as instructor and asst professor chemistry and electricity at West Point; Deputy Chief of Staff, Allied Force Headquarters (London, North African Campaign, Algiers), 1942–43; Chief of Staff, Fifth Army (Italy), 1943–44; Chief of Staff, 15th Army Group (Italian Campaign), 1944–45; Dep. Comdr, US Forces in Austria, 1945; Dep. Comdt, Nat. War Coll. Washington, 1945–47; Dir Jt Staff, Jt Chiefs of Staff, 1947–49; Dep. Chief of Staff for Plans and Operations, Army Gen. Staff, 1949–51; Gen., US Army, 1951; Chief of Staff, SHAPE, 1951–53; Supreme Allied Commander, Europe, 1953–56; retd 1956. Director: Pan American World Airways, 1960–72; New York Life Insurance Co., 1960–73; Dart Industries, 1964–80; Federated Department Stores, 1964–76; Mem., Bd of Trustees, Inst. for Defence Analyses, 1964–78. Member: Presidential Arms Control Gen. Adv. Cttee, 1966–69; Presidential Adv. Cttee on Foreign Assistance, 1965–69. Pres., American Red Cross, 1957–64. Chm., English-Speaking Union of US, 1966–68. Hon. Pres., World Bridge Federation. Several decorations, including Grand Cross of Légion d'Honneur, 1954, and Médaille Militaire, 1956. Hon. degrees from 38 universities including Harvard, Yale, Columbia, Dartmouth and Holy Cross. *Publications:* Famous Hands of the Culbertson-Lenz Match, 1932; Duplicate Contract Complete, 1933. *Address:* Cathedral Apartments, 4101 Cathedral Avenue, NW, Washington, DC 20016, USA.                                    *Died 30 May* 1983.

**GRUNDY, Air Marshal Sir Edouard (Michael FitzFrederick)**, KBE 1963 (OBE 1942); CB 1960; Chairman, Short Brothers and Harland, 1968–76; *b* 29 Sept. 1908; *s* of late Frederick Grundy and Osca Marah Ewart; *m* 1st, 1945, Lucia le Sueur (*née* Corder) (*d* 1973); three *s* (and one *d* decd); 2nd, 1975, Mrs Marie Louise Holder. *Educ:* St Paul's Sch.; RAF Coll., Cranwell. 56 (F) Sqdn 1928; 403 Flight FAA, 1929–31; Signals Specialist Course, 1932; RAF North Weald, 1933 36; RNZAF HQ, 1937–40; OC No 80 (S) Wing, 1941–42; CSO, NW African AF, 1942–43; CSO Mediterranean Allied Tactical Air Forces, 1943–44; CSO, RAF, Middle East, 1944–45; Commandant, Empire Radio Sch., 1945–46; Dep. Dir Air Staff Policy, Air Ministry, 1947–49; Air Adviser, Royal Norwegian AF, 1949–51; Dep. CSO, Supreme HQ Allied Powers Europe, 1951–52; idc 1953; Senior Air Staff Officer, Brit. Jt Services Mission in USA, 1954–55; Chm. NATO Military Agency for Standardisation, 1955–58: Air Officer i/c Administration, FEAF, 1958–61; Commandant-Gen. RAF Regt, 1961–62; Controller, Guided Weapons and Electronics, Ministry of Aviation, 1962–66; retired, 1966. Mem., Engineering Industries Council, 1975–. Pres., SBAC, 1975–76. FRAeS. Chevalier, Royal Norwegian Order of St Olaf, 1953. *Recreations:* usual. *Address:* c/o Lloyds Bank, 6 Pall Mall, SW1. *Club:* Royal Air Force.                                    *Died 15 June* 1987.

**GRUNDY, Fred**, MD; MRCP; DPH; Barrister-at-law; Assistant Director-General, World Health Organization, Geneva, 1961–66; retired; *b* 15 May 1905; *s* of Thomas Grundy, Manchester; *m* 1932, Ada Furnell Leppington, Hessle, Yorks; one *s* one *d*. *Educ:* Leeds and London Univs. MB, ChB (Hons), Leeds; MRCS, LRCP, 1927; DPH, RCPS, 1931; MD Leeds, 1933; MRCP, 1951. Called to the Bar, Inner Temple, 1934. Resident hospital appts and gen. practice, 1927–31; Asst County Medical Officer, E Suffolk, 1931–34; Asst MOH to Borough of Willesden, 1934–35; Deputy MOH to Borough of Luton, 1935–37; MOH to Borough of Luton, 1937–49; Mansel Talbot Prof. of Preventive Medicine, Welsh Nat. Sch. of Medicine, 1949–61. *Publications:* A Note on the Vital Statistics of Luton, 1944; (with R. M. Titmuss) Report on Luton, 1945; Handbook of Social Medicine, 1945; The New Public Health, 1949; Preventive Medicine and Public Health: An Introduction for Students and Practitioners, 1951; papers on public health and scientific subjects. *Recreations:* mountaineering, yachting, golf, etc. *Address:* Weir House, Radyr, near Cardiff.                                    *Died 16 Oct.* 1989.

**GRUNDY, John Brownsdon Clowes**, TD 1951; Officier d'Académie, 1937; MA, PhD, DLit; *b* 21 April 1902; *m* 1939, (Carol) Dorothea, *d* of Enid Pennington; two *s* three *d*. *Educ:* Emanuel Sch.; Fitzwilliam Hall, Cambridge (Exhibitioner); University Coll., London (research). Asst Master, St Paul's Sch., 1923–27; English Lektor, University of Göttingen, 1928; "The Connoisseur", 1928–29; Sen. Mod. Langs Master, Shrewsbury Sch., 1929–39. Served War of 1939–45, The Rangers (KRRC); principally in Gen. Staff (Intell.); Normandy-Germany, 1944; rank at release, temp. Col. First Rep. of Brit. Council in Finland, 1945–49; Dir, Brit. Institute, Cairo, 1949–50; head of mod. langs, Harrow Sch.,

1950–53; Headmaster of Emanuel Sch., 1953–63; Head of Dept of Modern Languages, University Coll. of Sierra Leone, 1964–66. *Publications:* Tieck and Runge, 1929; Brush Up Your German, series, 1931–61; French Style, 1937; Life's Five Windows, 1968; various edns and translations of foreign texts. *Recreations:* antiquities, hills, foreign parts. *Address:* Llyn Du, Llansantffraid, Powys.                                                *Died* 17 *July* 1987.

**GRUNDY, R(upert) F(rancis) Brooks;** consultant engineer; General Manager, Corby Development Corporation, 1950–68, and Industrial Projects Consultant to the Corporation, 1968–70; *b* 6 Sept. 1903; *s* of J. F. E. Grundy, fine art publisher, London and Emily Grundy (*née* Brownsdon); *m* 1938, Heather Mary, *d* of William and Mabel Thomas, Swansea; one *s* one *d*. *Educ:* Emanuel Sch., London; University Coll., London (BSc (Eng.)); Open Univ. (BA 1975). FICE, FIMunE. Municipal Engrg, 1922–44, at Croydon, Bournemouth, Swansea, Carlisle and Harrow; Borough Engr and Surveyor: Mansfield, 1944–45; Wallasey, 1945–49; Wandsworth, 1949–50. Mem., BBC Midlands Region Adv. Coun., 1966–68. *Publications:* Builders' Materials, 1930; Essentials of Reinforced Concrete, 1939, 1948; papers presented to ICE and IMunE. *Recreations:* golf, walking, reading. *Address:* The Mill House, Brigstock, Kettering, Northants. *T:* Brigstock 218.
                                                        *Died* 13 *Jan.* 1988.

**GRÜNEBERG, Prof. Hans,** FRS 1956; PhD Berlin, MD Bonn, DSc London; Professor of Genetics, University College, London, 1956–74, later Emeritus; *b* 26 May 1907; *o s* of late De Levi Gruneberg and Mrs Else Grüneberg (*née* Steinberg), Wuppertal-Elberfeld, Germany; *m* 1st, 1933, Elsbeth (*d* 1944), *d* of late Hugo Capell; two *s*; 2nd, 1946, Hannah (*d* 1962), *d* of late Albrecht Blumenfeld. *Educ:* Städt. Gymnasium, Wuppertal-Elberfeld, Germany. Hon. Research Asst, University Coll., London, 1933–38; Moseley Research Student of Royal Society, 1938–42. Captain, RAMC, 1942–46. Reader in Genetics, University Coll., London, 1946–55. Hon. Dir, MRC Expmtl Genetics Res. Unit, 1955–72. *Publications:* The Genetics of the Mouse, 1943, 1952; Animal Genetics and Medicine, 1947; The Pathology of Development, 1963. Numerous papers in scientific jls. *Recreation:* foreign travel. *Address:* University College, Wolfson House, 4 Stephenson Way, NW1. *T:* 01-387 7050.                           *Died* 23 *Oct.* 1982.

**GRYLLS, Rosalie G.;** *see* Mander, Lady (Rosalie).

**GUDENIAN, Haig,** OBE 1980; Consultant, Stonehart Publications Ltd; *b* 16 April 1918; *s* of Miran and Nevric Gudenian; *m* 1949, Lilian Doreen Leavett. *Educ:* University College Sch., London. Trained as journalist, 1934–40. War service in Army, 1940–46: Middle East, N Africa, Italy, Germany (despatches twice). Chief Sub-Editor and Asst Editor, John Bull Magazine, 1946–52; Asst Editor and Associate Editor, Illustrated, 1952–55; Editor, Ideal Home, 1957–64; Founder-Director, GRM Ltd, Publishing Contractors and Consultants, 1966; joined Stonehart Publications, 1974; Dir, Stonehart & Chantry Ltd, 1978–81; Founder-Editor, Tax & Insurance Letter, 1975–. Vice-Chairman, Muscular Dystrophy Group of Great Britain, 1970– (Chm. Management Cttee, 1961–). *Address:* Westwood, Dunsfold, near Godalming, Surrey. *T:* Dunsfold 252.                                        *Died* 5 *Feb.* 1985.

**GUERISSE, Count Albert Marie Edmond,** GC 1946; Hon. KBE 1979; DSO 1942 (under name of Patrick Albert O'Leary); medical officer; Major-General in the Belgian Army; Director-General, Medical Service, Belgian Forces; retired 1970; *b* Brussels, 5 April 1911; *m* 1947, Sylvia Cooper Smith (*d* 1985); one *s*. *Educ:* in Belgium; Louvain; Brussels University. Medical Officer, Lieut, 1940; after Belgian capitulation embarked at Dunkirk and became, in Sept. 1940, Lieut-Comdr, RN; first officer of "Q" ship, HMS Fidelity (under name of P. A. O'Leary). Engaged on secret work in France from April 1941 until arrest by Gestapo in March 1943 (chief of an escape organisation). After 2 years in Concentration Camps returned to England. After demobilisation from RN rejoined Belgian Army (1st Lancers); joined Belgian Volunteer Bn, 1951, as Chief of Medical Service in Korea. Officier Légion d'Honneur, 1947; Medal of Freedom with golden palm, 1947; Officier Ordre Léopold, 1946, Grand Officier, 1970; French Croix de Guerre, 1945; Polish Croix de Guerre, 1944. Hereditary Nobility with personal title of Count granted by King of the Belgians, 1986. *Address:* Avenue du Roi Soleil 32, 1410 Waterloo, Belgium.          *Died* 26 *March* 1989.

**GUEST, Baron** (Life Peer), *cr* 1961; **Christopher William Graham Guest,** PC 1961; a Lord of Appeal in Ordinary, 1961–71; *b* 7 Nov. 1901; *s* of Edward Graham and Mary Catherine Guest; *m* 1941, Catharine Geraldine Hotham; four *s* one *d*. *Educ:* Merchiston Castle; Cambridge (MA, LLB); Edinburgh (LLB). Called to Scots Bar, 1925, Inner Temple, 1929; Bencher, Inner Temple, 1961. 2nd Lieut Royal Artillery, TA, 1939; Major, Judge Advocate General's Branch, War Office, 1942. QC, Scots Bar, 1945. Contested (U) Kirkcaldy Burghs, 1945; Advocate Depute, 1945; Pres. Transport Arbitration Tribunal, Scotland, 1947–55; Sheriff of Ayr and Bute, 1952–54; Trustee National Library of Scotland, 1952–57; Sheriff of

Perth and Angus, 1954–55; Chm. Building Legislation Cttee, 1954–57; Chm. Scottish Agricultural Wages Board, 1955–61; Chm. Scottish Licensing Law Cttee, 1959–63. Dean of the Faculty of Advocates, 1955–57; a Senator of the College of Justice in Scotland, 1957–61. Hon. Fellow, Clare Coll., Cambridge, 1971. Hon. LLD Dundee, 1973. *Publication:* Law of Valuation in Scotland, 1930. *Address:* 22 Lennox Street, Edinburgh EH4 1QA. *T:* 031-332 4833. *Club:* Buck's.                                       *Died* 25 *Sept.* 1984.

**GUIDOTTI, Gastone,** FRSA; Counsellor of State, Rome, 1968; *b* 29 Sept. 1901; *m* 1931, Raffaellina Betocchi; one *d*. *Educ:* St Carlo's Coll., Modena and University of Siena, Italy. Head of Dept at Ministry of Foreign Affairs, Rome, 1935; First Sec., Belgrade; First Sec., Stockholm; Italian Rep. to Allied Govts, London, 1945; in charge of Italian Legation, Prague, 1945, Athens, 1946; Head of Liaison Office of Min. of Foreign Affairs with Allied Govt, Trieste, 1947; Gen. Dir of Polit. Affs, Italian Min. for For. Affs, Rome, and Mem. various Italian Delegns to Nato Confs, Coun. of Europe Meetings, etc, 1948; Head of Italian Representation to UNO, 1951; Italian Ambassador: Belgrade, 1955; Vienna, 1958; Bonn, 1961; UK, 1964–68. Holds foreign decorations including 4 grand crosses. *Recreations:* shooting, art collecting. *Address:* Via Ettore Petrolini 36, Rome, Italy. *Clubs:* Unione (Florence), Circolo della Caccia (Rome).                                         *Died* 28 *March* 1982.

**GUILD, Surgeon Captain William John Forbes;** CBE 1952; FRCS, MD; RN retd; House Governor, King Edward VII Convalescent Home for Officers, Osborne House, IoW, 1965–71; *b* 30 Aug. 1908; *s* of late William Guild and Jessie Guild, Dundee; *m* 1st, 1942, Joan (*d* 1957), *d* of Charles Innes, Hornsey; one *s* one *d*; 2nd, 1958, Jessie, *d* of John MacLennan, Mallaig. *Educ:* Harris Academy, Dundee; St Andrews Univ. MB, ChB 1930; MD (StA) 1936, FRCSE 1941. Post-grad. House appts, Royal Infirmary, Dundee. Served RN Med. Service, 1933–65: Ophthalmic Specialist and Surgical Specialist; final appt as Med. Officer i/c RN Hosp., Gibraltar; ret. with rank of Surgeon Captain. Sen. Fellow, Assoc. of Surgeons; Mem., Faculty of Ophthalmologists. *Publications:* various papers on naval medical matters. *Recreations:* tennis, gardening, hill-walking. *Address:* The Manse, The Mall, Brading, Isle of Wight. *T:* Brading 316. *Club:* Royal Over-Seas League.                           *Died* 23 *June* 1982.

**GUILLUM SCOTT, Sir John (Arthur),** Kt 1964; TD 1945; *b* 27 Oct. 1910; *e s* of late Guy H. Guillum Scott; *m* 1939, Muriel Elizabeth, *d* of late James Ross; one *d*. *Educ:* King's Sch., Canterbury. Queen Anne's Bounty, 1929–46; Asst Sec., Church Assembly, 1946–48, Sec., 1948–70; Sec.-Gen., General Synod of C of E, 1970–72; Communar of Chichester Cathedral, 1973–79. Inns of Court Regt TA, 1929–53; war service, 1939–45 (despatches); Lieut-Col commanding Inns of Court Regt, 1950–53; Bt Col, 1953. DCL (Lambeth) 1961. *Recreations:* gardening, field sports. *Address:* 5 North Close, St Martins Square, Chichester, West Sussex.
                                                        *Died* 6 *May* 1983.

**GUINNESS, Thomas Loel Evelyn Bulkeley,** OBE 1942; late Irish Guards; *b* 9 June 1906; *s* of late Benjamin S. Guinness; *m* 1st, 1927, Hon. Joan Yarde-Buller (from whom he obtained a divorce, 1936); one *s* decd; 2nd, 1936, Lady Isabel Manners (marr. diss., 1951), *yr d* of 9th Duke of Rutland; one *s* one *d*; 3rd, 1951, Gloria (*d* 1980), *d* of Raphael Rubio, Mexico. *Educ:* Sandhurst. MP (U) City of Bath, 1931–45; Contested Whitechapel, 1929, and By-election, 1930; Group Captain Auxiliary Air Force Reserve. Served War of 1939–45: RAF (despatches five times). Comdr Order of Orange Nassau; Officer Legion of Honour, France; Croix de Guerre. *Address:* Villa Zanroc, Epalinges 1066, Vaud, Switzerland. *Clubs:* White's, Buck's, Turf, Beefsteak; Royal Yacht Squadron (Cowes).
                                                        *Died* 31 *Dec.* 1988.

**GUIRINGAUD, Louis de;** Grand Officier de la Légion d'Honneur, 1976; Minister for Foreign Affairs, France, 1976–78; *b* 12 Oct. 1911; *s* of Pierre de Guiringaud and Madeleine de Catheu; *m* 1955, Claude Mony; one *s*. *Educ:* Lycée Buffon; Lycée Saint Louis; Université de Paris, Sorbonne; Ecole des Sciences politiques, Paris. Degrees in letters, law and political sciences. Joined Staff of Minister for Foreign Affairs, 1936; Diplomatic Service, 1938–78; Attaché, Ankara, 1938–39. Served War of 1939–45: with French forces, 1939–40; assigned to French High Commn, Beirut, 1940–41; with Resistance in France, 1942; Special Asst to French Comr for Foreign Affairs, de Gaulle's Provisional Govt, Algiers, 1943–44; with French forces, Italy and France, 1944–45. First Sec., London, 1946–49; Political Dir, French High Commn in Germany, 1949–52; Consul-Gen., San Francisco, 1952–55; Dep. Rep. to UN Security Council, 1955–57; Amb. to Ghana, 1957; Dir, Dept of Moroccan and Tunisian Affairs, Min. for Foreign Affairs, 1960; Dep. High Comr in Algeria, 1962; Gen.-Inspector, Diplomatic Posts, 1963–66; Amb. to Japan, 1966–72; Permanent Rep. to UN, 1972–76. Holds several other French and foreign decorations, incl. Grand Cross of Rising Sun. *Address:* 2 rue Cognacq-Jay, 75007 Paris, France. *Clubs:* Jockey, Morfontaine, Union Interalliée (Paris).
                                                        *Died* 15 *April* 1982.

**GULL, Sir Michael Swinnerton Cameron,** 4th Bt, *cr* 1872; *b* 24 Jan. 1919; *o s* of 3rd Bt and Dona Eva Swinnerton (*d* 1973), *e d* of late Sir Thomas Swinnerton Dyer, 11th Bt; *S* father, 1960; *m* 1st, 1950, Mrs Yvonne Bawtree (decd), *o d* of Dr Albert Oliver Macarius Heslop, Cape Town; one *s* one *d*; *m* 2nd. *Educ:* Eton. Late 2nd Lieut, Scots Guards (SRO). *Heir: s* Rupert William Cameron Gull [*b* 14 July 1954; *m* 1980, Gillian Lee, *d* of Robert MacFarlaine]. *Address:* Wedgeport, Bertha Avenue, Newlands, Cape Town, S Africa.
*Died 12 April* 1989.

**GULLAND, John Alan,** PhD; FRS 1984; Senior Research Fellow, Centre for Environmental Technology, Imperial College, London, since 1984; *b* 16 Sept. 1926; *s* of late Alan Gulland; *m* 1951, Frances Audrey James; two *s* one *d*. *Educ:* Marlborough Coll.; Jesus Coll., Cambridge (BA 1950, PhD 1971). Scientist at Fisheries Laboratory, Lowestoft, Suffolk, 1951–66; Staff member, Fisheries Dept, FAO, Rome, 1966–84. Adviser to Internat. Whaling Commn, 1964–76, Internat. Commn for Northwest Atlantic Fisheries, 1960–67, and other bodies. Hon. DSc: Rhode Island, 1979; Helsinki, 1984. *Publications:* The Fish Resources of the Ocean, 1972; The Management of Marine Fisheries, 1974; (ed) Fish Population Dynamics, 1977, 2nd edn 1988; Fish Stock Assessment, 1983; papers in scientific jls. *Recreations:* golf, gardening. *Address:* 41 Eden Street, Cambridge CB1 1EL. *T:* Cambridge (0223) 322035.
*Died 24 June* 1990.

**GUNDELACH, Finn Olav;** a Vice-President, Commission of the European Communities, since 1977 (Member, since 1973); *b* Vejle, Denmark, 23 April 1925; *s* of Albert Gundelach and Jenny Hobolt; *m* 1953, Vibeke Rosenvinge; two *s*. *Educ:* Aarhus Univ. Sec., Danish Min. of For. Affairs, 1953–55; Permanent Rep. to UN, Geneva, 1955–59; Dir, Dept of Commercial Policy, GATT, 1959; Asst Gen. Sec., GATT, 1959, Asst Gen. Dir, 1965; Ambassador to EEC, 1967–72. Commander, Order of Dannebrog; Grand Cross (Brazil). *Publications:* articles in foreign trade jls. *Address:* Commission of the European Communities, Rue de la Loi 200, 1040 Brussels, Belgium. *Died 13 Jan.* 1981.

**GUNDRY, Rev. Canon Dudley William,** MTh; Canon of Leicester Cathedral, since 1963, Emeritus since 1987; *b* 4 June 1916; *e s* of late Cecil Wood Gundry and Lucy Gundry; unmarried. *Educ:* Sir Walter St John's Sch.; King's Coll., London. BD (1st cl. Hons) 1939, AKC (1st cl. Hons Theology) 1939, MTh 1941. Deacon, 1939; Priest 1940. Curate of St Matthew, Surbiton, 1939–44; Lectr in History of Religions, University Coll. of North Wales, Bangor, 1944–60; Mem. Senate and Warden of Neuadd Reichel, 1947–60; Dean of Faculty of Theology, 1956–60; Hon. Sec., British Section, Internat. Assoc. for History of Religions, 1954–60; Select Preacher, Trinity Coll., Dublin, 1957; Prof. and Head of Dept of Religious Studies, and Mem. of Senate, University Coll., Ibadan, 1960–63; Canon Residentiary and Chancellor of Leicester Cathedral, 1963–87; Commissary to Bishop of Northern Nigeria, 1963–69; Rural Dean of Christianity, Leicester, 1966–74; Proctor in Convocation, 1970–80. Church Affairs Consultant and Correspondent to Daily Telegraph, 1978–86. Sometime Examining Chaplain to Bishops of Bangor, St Davids and Leicester; Examiner to Universities of Leeds, London, Keele, St David's Coll., Lampeter, Gen. Ordination Examination. Chm. of Governors, Newton's Educnl Foundn, 1977–. *Publications:* Religions: An Historical and Theological Study, 1958; Israel's Neighbours (in Neil's Bible Companion), 1959; The Teacher and the World Religions, 1968; contrib. to: Collins Dictionary of the English Language, 1979; The Synod of Westminster, 1986; many articles and signed reviews in theological and kindred journals; Editor, Leicester Cathedral Qly, 1963–79. *Recreation:* wandering about England and Wales. *Address:* 28 Stoneygate Court, London Road, Leicester LE2 2AH. *T:* Leicester 704133. *Clubs:* Athenæum; Leicestershire (Leicester).
*Died 24 March* 1990.

**GUNLAKE, John Henry,** CBE 1947; FIA; FSS; FIS; consulting actuary, retired; *b* 23 May 1905; *s* of late John Gunlake, MRCS, LRCP, and late Alice Emma Gunlake; unmarried. *Educ:* Epsom Coll. Institute of Actuaries: Fellow, 1933; Hon. Sec., 1952–54; Vice-Pres., 1956–59; Pres., 1960–62. A Statistical Adviser, Min. of Shipping, 1940–47. Member: Cttee on Econ. and Financial Problems of Provision for Old Age, 1953–54; Royal Commn on Doctors' and Dentists' Remuneration, 1957–60; Permanent Advisory Cttee on Doctors' and Dentists' Remuneration, 1962–70. *Publications:* Premiums for Life Assurances and Annuities, 1939. Contrib. to Jl of Inst. of Actuaries. *Recreations:* reading, music, working. *Address:* 120 Clapham Common North Side, SW4 9SP. *T:* 071–228 3008. *Club:* Reform. *Died 11 Sept.* 1990.

**GUNNING, Sir Robert Charles,** 8th Bt, *cr* 1778; gold-mine owner and farmer; *b* 2 Dec. 1901; *o s* of late Charles Archibald John Gunning and Beatrice Constance Purvis; *S* cousin, 1950; *m* 1934, Helen Nancy, *d* of late Vice-Adm. Sir T. J. Hallet, KBE, CB; eight *s* two *d*. *Educ:* St Paul's Sch.; Leeds Univ. Business in the Sudan and Nigeria, 1924–33; prospecting and gold-mining in Nigeria, 1933–38;

pegged first Nigerian lode gold-mine of the least importance, this in 1935 at Bin Yauri; served AA Command, 1939–46, temp. Capt. Emigrated to Alberta, 1948. Chairman: Peace River Hosp. Bd; Peace Region Mental Health Council. *Recreations:* gardening, cricket, and almost any ball game. *Heir: s* Lt-Comdr Charles Theodore Gunning, CD; RCN retd; PEng [*b* 19 June 1935; *m* 1969, Sarah (marr. diss. 1982), *d* of Col Patrick Arthur Easton; one *d*]. *Address:* c/o Postmaster, Peace River, Alberta, Canada.
*Died 7 Dec.* 1989.

**GUNSTON, Major Sir Derrick Wellesley,** 1st Bt, *cr* 1938; MC; *b* 26 Feb. 1891; *s* of late Major Bernard Hamilton Gunston, late 5th Dragoon Guards; *m* 1917, Evelyn (Gardenia), OBE 1944, *d* of Howard St George, Cam House, Campden Hill, W8; one *s* (and *er s* killed in action 1944). *Educ:* Harrow; Trinity Coll., Cambridge. Pres. of the New Carlton Club at Cambridge; joined Irish Guards, Aug. 1914; second in command 1st Battalion Irish Guards at Armistice; War of 1939–45, Major 7th Bn Glos Regt; MP (C) Thornbury Division Glos, 1924–45; Parliamentary Private Sec. to Rt Hon. Sir Kingsley Wood, Parliamentary Sec. to the Ministry of Health in Conservative Government, 1926–29; Parliamentary Private Sec. to Rt Hon. Neville Chamberlain, Chancellor of the Exchequer, 1931–36, to Sir Edward Grigg, Joint Under-Sec. for War 1940–42. *Heir: s* Richard Wellesley Gunston [*b* 15 March 1924; *m* 1st, 1947, Elizabeth Mary (from whom he obtained a divorce, 1956), *e d* of Arthur Colegate, Hillgrove, Bembridge, IoW; one *d*; 2nd, 1959, Mrs Joan Elizabeth Marie Coldicott (marr. diss.), *o d* of Reginald Forde, Johannesburg; one *s*; 3rd, 1976, Veronica Elizabeth (*née* Haines), *widow* of Captain V. G. Loyd]. *Address:* 55 Onslow Square, SW7 3LR. *Clubs:* Carlton; MCC; Royal Yacht Squadron (Cowes); Bembridge Sailing (Bembridge, IoW).
*Died 13 July* 1985.

**GUNTHER, Sir John Thomson,** Kt 1975; CMG 1965; OBE 1954; MB, DTM&H Sydney; Vice-Chancellor, University of Papua and New Guinea, 1966–72; Assistant Administrator, Papua and New Guinea, 1957–66; formerly MEC and MLC, Papua and New Guinea; *b* 2 Oct. 1910; *s* of C. M. Gunther; *m* 1938; one *s* three *d*. *Educ:* King's Sch.; Sydney Univ. Dir of Public Health, Papua and New Guinea, 1949–56; Levers Pacific Plantations Pty Ltd, Brit. Solomon Is, 1935–37; Chm., Med. Bd (Mt Isa, Qld), investigating Plumbism, 1938–41; MO, RAAF, 1941–46; Malariologist, RAAF, 1943; CO 1 Trop. Research Fld Unit, 1944–45; Mem. S Pacific Commn Research Coun. (Chm. 1st meeting); Chm. Select Cttee on Polit. Develt for Papua and NG; Mem. Commn on Higher Educn, Papua and NG. *Publications:* reports to govt of Qld on Plumbism, 1939–40; reports to RAAF on Malaria and Scrub Typhus. *Recreation:* gardening. *Club:* University (Sydney).
*Died 27 April* 1984.

**GURD, Surg. Rear-Adm. Dudley Plunket,** CB 1968; Medical Officer-in-Charge, Royal Naval Hospital, Malta, 1966–69; in private practice, 1969–86; *b* 18 June 1910; *s* of Frederick Plunket Gurd and Annie Jane Glenn; *m* 1939, Thérèse Marie, *d* of John and Frances Delenda, Salonika, Greece; one *s* one *d*. *Educ:* Belfast Royal Academy; Queen's Univ., Belfast, MB, BCh, BAO (Hons) 1932; MD (High Commend) 1942; FRACS 1945; MCh 1959; FRCS (Eng.) 1964. Gilbert Blane Medal, 1943. Sen. Consultant and Adviser in Ophthalmology to the Navy, 1952–66; Hon. Lectr and Examiner in Ophthalmology, Univ. of Hong Kong, 1945–48; Warden, Ophthalmic Hosp. of St John, Jerusalem, Jordan, 1952–55. Joined RN as Surg. Lieut, 1934; Lieut-Comdr 1939; Comdr 1945; Capt. 1958; Rear-Adm. 1966; retired 1969; Served in Royal Naval Hosps at Malta, Barrow Gurney, Hong Kong, Plymouth and Haslar. QHS 1964. KStJ 1967 (CStJ 1954). Hon. DSc QUB, 1969. Chevalier de l'Ordre Nationale du Viet-Nam, 1949; Gold Cross, Order of Holy Sepulchre, 1955. *Publications:* various contribs to ophthalmic literature. *Recreations:* interested in all kinds of sport and athletics, also in languages, religion and medical education. *Address:* Shanklin Lodge, Eastern Villas Road, Southsea, Hants PO4 0SU. *T:* Portsmouth 731496. *Clubs:* Athenæum; Royal Naval and Royal Albert Yacht; Union (Malta). *Died 9 Aug.* 1987.

**GURDEN, Sir Harold Edward,** Kt 1983; *b* 28 June 1903; *s* of late Arthur William and late Ada Gurden; *m* 1st, 1929, Lucy Isabella Izon (*d* 1976); three *d*; 2nd, Elizabeth Joan, *widow* of Arthur Taylor. *Educ:* Lyttelton Sch.; Birmingham Univ. Birmingham City Council, Selly Oak Ward, 1946–56; Pres. Birmingham and Dist Dairyman's Assoc., 1947–50; Chm. Soc. of Dairy Technology, Midland Div.; Pres.-Elect, Nat. Dairyman's Assoc., 1951; Chm., Northfield Div. Conservative Assoc., 1950–52. MP (C) Selly Oak Div. of Birmingham, 1955–Oct. 1974; Mem. of Speaker's Panel, House of Commons, 1966; Chm., Selection Cttee, House of Commons, 1970. Chm., Park Farm Preserves Ltd, 1954–84. Rector's Warden, St Margaret's Westminster, 1973–75, Dep. Rector's Warden, 1975–83, Rector's Warden Emeritus, 1983. Pres., Birmingham Branch RSPCA, 1966–79. *Recreations:* bridge, golf, numismatics. *Address:* 20 Portland Road, Oxford OX2 7EY. *Died 27 April* 1989.

**GUSTAFSSON, Greta Lovisa;** see Garbo, G.

**GUTCH, Sir John,** KCMG 1957 (CMG 1952); OBE 1947; b 12 July 1905; s of late Clement Gutch, MA, King's Coll., Cambridge, and late Isabella Margaret Newton; m 1938, Diana Mary Worsley; three s. Educ: Aldenham Sch.; Gonville and Caius Coll., Cambridge. Classical scholar, 1924; 1st class Classical Tripos, Part I, 1926; 2nd class Classical Tripos, Part II, 1927; BA 1927; MA 1931. Cadet, Colonial Administrative Service, 1928; Asst District Commissioner, Gold Coast, 1928; Asst Colonial Secretary, Gold Coast, 1935; Asst Secretary, Palestine, 1936, Principal Asst Secretary, 1944, Under Sec., 1945; Asst Sec., Middle East Department, Colonial Office, 1947; Chief Secretary, British Administration, Cyrenaica, 1948; Adviser to the Prime Minister, Government of Cyrenaica, 1949; Chief Secretary, British Guiana, 1950–54; High Commissioner for Western Pacific, 1955–60. British Electric Traction Co. Ltd, 1961–69. Governor, Aldenham School, 1964–81; Mem., Cttee of Management, Institute of Opthalmology, 1965–80 (Fellow, 1968). Publications: Martyr of the Islands: the life and death of John Coleridge Patteson, 1971; Beyond the Reefs: the life of John Williams, missionary, 1974. Address: Meadow House, 45 Larkhill Road, Crondall Lane, Farnham, Surrey GU9 7DB. T: Farnham 721456. *Died 11 Feb. 1988.*

**GUTHRIE, Hon. Sir Rutherford (Campbell),** Kt 1968; CMG 1960; b 28 Nov. 1899; s of late Thomas O. Guthrie, Rich Avon, Donald; m 1927, Rhona Mary McKellar, d of late T. McKellar; one s (and one s decd). Educ: Melbourne Church of England Grammar Sch.; Jesus Coll., Cambridge (BA 1921). Farmer and grazier, Skipton, Victoria. Served European War of 1914–18 and War of 1939–45 (wounded, despatches): 9 Australian Div., El Alamein. MP Ripon, Victoria, 1947–50; Minister for Lands and for Soldier Settlement, 1948–50. Recreations: fishing and golf. Address: Jedburgh Cottage, Howey Street, Gisborne, Vic. 3437, Australia. Clubs: Melbourne, Naval and Military; Hawks, Pitt (Cambridge); Leander (Henley on Thames). *Died 20 Feb. 1990.*

**GUTHRIE, William Keith Chambers,** LittD; FBA 1952; Master of Downing College, Cambridge, 1957–72, Hon. Fellow 1972; Laurence Professor of Ancient Philosophy, 1952–73; b 1 Aug. 1906; s of Charles Jameson Guthrie; m 1933, Adele Marion Ogilvy, MA; one s one d. Educ: Dulwich Coll.; Trinity Coll., Cambridge. Browne Scholar, 1927, Craven Student, 1928, Chancellor's Classical Medallist, 1929; Member of expeditions of American Society for Archaeological Research in Asia Minor, 1929, 1930 and 1932; Bye-Fellow of Peterhouse, 1930, Fellow, 1932–57, Hon. Fellow, 1957; University Proctor, 1936–37; Public Orator of the University, 1939–57; P. M. Laurence Reader in Classics, 1947–52; Intelligence Corps, 1941–45 (temp. Major 1945); Messenger Lecturer, Cornell Univ., 1957; James B. Duke Visiting Professor of Philosophy, Duke Univ., 1966; Raymond Prof. of Classics, State Univ. of New York at Buffalo, 1974. President, Classical Assoc., 1967–68. LittD Cambridge, 1959; Hon. DLitt: Melbourne, 1957; Sheffield, 1967. Publications: Monumenta Asiae Minoris Antiqua, IV (with W. M. Calder and W. H. Buckler), 1933; Orpheus and Greek Religion, 1935; Aristotle De Caelo, text, trans., introduction and notes (Loeb Classical Library), 1939; The Greek Philosophers, 1950; The Greeks and their Gods, 1950; F. M. Cornford, The Unwritten Philosophy (edited with a memoir by W. K. C. G.), 1950; Greek Philosophy: The Hub and the Spokes (Inaugural Lecture), 1953; In the Beginning: some Greek views of the origins of life and the early state of man, 1957; A History of Greek Philosophy, Vols 1–5, 1962–78; contributions to various classical journals. Address: 3 Roman Hill, Barton, Cambridge CB3 7AX. T: Comberton 2658. *Died 17 May 1981.*

**GUTHRIE-JAMES, David,** MBE 1944; DSC 1944; author; b 25 Dec. 1919; s of Sir Archibald James, KBE, MC; m 1950, Hon. Jaquetta Digby, y d of 11th Baron Digby, KG, DSO, MC, TD; four s two d. Educ: Eton; Balliol. Served before the mast, Finnish 4-m. barque Viking, 1937–38; Balliol Coll., Oxford, 1938–39. Served War of 1939–45, RNVR, 1939–46; PoW 1943; escaped from Germany to Sweden, 1944. Mem. Antarctic Exped., 1945–46; Polar Adviser, Film Scott of the Antarctic, 1946–48. Joined Burns & Oates Ltd, Publishers, 1951. MP (C) Kemp Town Division of Brighton, 1959–64; MP (C) Dorset North, 1970–79. Council Mem., Outward Bound Trust, 1948–72; Trustee, National Maritime Museum, 1953–65. Knight of Malta, 1962. Publications: A Prisoner's Progress,

1946; Scott of the Antarctic: The Film, 1950; That Frozen Land, 1952; The Life of Lord Roberts, 1954; (ed) Wavy Navy, 1948; (ed) Outward Bound, 1957; (ed) In Praise of Hunting, 1960. Recreations: country pursuits. Address: Torosay Castle, Craignure, Isle of Mull, Scotland. T: Craignure 421. *Died 15 Dec. 1986.*

**GUYMER, Maurice Juniper,** OBE 1982; DL; JP; Metropolitan Stipendiary Magistrate, since 1967; b 29 Aug. 1914; s of Frank and Florence Mary Guymer. Educ: Northcliffe House, Bognor Regis; Westminster School. Admitted Solicitor, 1936. Served with RAF, 1940–45. Chm., Inner London Juvenile Courts, 1967–76. Royal Borough of Kingston upon Thames: Council, 1953; Mayor, 1959–60 and 1960–61; Alderman, 1960–65; JP 1956. DL, Co. Surrey, 1960. Mem., Bd of Visitors, Latchmere House Remand Centre, 1958– (Chm., 1969–82). Chm., Kingston and Malden District Scout Council, 1962–76, Pres., 1976–. Address: Desborough Cottage, 132 Lower Ham Road, Kingston upon Thames, Surrey. T: 01–546 5529. *Died 26 Jan. 1985.*

**GUYMER, Robert,** CBE 1981; FCA; Member (C), Surrey County Council, 1967–81, Leader of the Council, 1977–81; b 30 Nov. 1908; s of William and Harriet Guymer; m 1933, Elizabeth (née Mason); one d (one s decd). Educ: Lancaster Royal Grammar Sch. Qualified as Accountant, 1935; Partner, Parker Edwards & Co., Chartered Accountants, 1938–59; Sales Administrator, United Glass Ltd, 1960–68; Director: Bee Brothers Ltd, 1944–59; Dilworth & Carr Ltd, 1946–60; Ingram Textiles Ltd, 1938–60. Member, Lancashire CC, 1946–60 (Alderman, 1955–60); Chm., Finance Cttee, 1955–58). Chm., Highways and Transport Cttee, Surrey CC, 1973–81. JP Leyland Hundred, Lancs, 1953–60. Recreation: golf (Captain: Preston Golf Club, 1954, Burhill Golf Club, 1968). Address: 11 Chaseley Court, Oatlands Drive, Weybridge, Surrey KT13 9JH. T: Walton on Thames 25192. Club: Burhill Golf (Walton on Thames). *Died 10 July 1981.*

**GWYNNE-EVANS, Sir Ian William,** 3rd Bt, cr 1913; Deputy Chairman, Real Estate Corporation of South Africa Ltd, 1973–79 (Managing Director and Chairman, 1950–73); Director, Grootvlei (Proprietary) Mines Ltd, retired 1982; b 21 Feb. 1909; er s of Sir Evan Gwynne-Evans, 2nd Bt; S father, 1959; m 1st, 1935, Elspeth Collins (marr. diss.); two d; 2nd, 1946, Monica Dalrymple. Educ: Royal Naval College, Dartmouth. Entered Royal Navy as Cadet, 1922; retired as Lieut, 1934. Served War, 1940–45, Lieut, Royal Navy. Recreation: bowls. Heir: b Francis Loring Gwynne-Evans [b 22 Feb. 1914; m 1st, 1937, Elisabeth Fforde (marr. diss., 1958), d of J. Fforde Tipping; two s one d; 2nd, 1958, Gloria Marie Reynolds; one s three d and one adopted s]. Address: Ivy Farm, St John, Jersey, CI. Clubs: Garrick; Victoria (Jersey); Rand, Inanda (Johannesburg). *Died 27 Dec. 1985.*

**GWYNNE-JONES, Allan,** CBE 1980; DSO 1916; RA 1965 (ARA 1955); painter, etcher; b 27 March 1892; s of Ll. Gwynne-Jones; m 1937, Rosemary Elizabeth, d of H. P. Allan; one d. Educ: Bedales Sch. Abandoned study of law for painting; was a student at Slade School for a short time before the first European War, returned as student after war, 1919–23. Served European War, 1914–18: enlisted Army 1914, Public Schools Bn, commissioned 3rd East Surrey Regt (Reserve Bn) France, 1916; posted as 2nd Lt to 1st Cheshire Regt, and with whom awarded DSO, Somme, 1916; transferred to HM Welsh Guards, 1917 (wounded twice, despatches twice). Professor of Painting, Royal College of Art till 1930 when appointed Staff, Slade School, retired from Slade, 1959. Trustee of Tate Gallery, 1939–46. Represented by pictures in the collections of HM The Queen and HM The Queen Mother, and in the Tate Gallery and the public galleries of Birmingham, Newcastle, Leeds, Oldham, Carlisle, Manchester, Sheffield, and Merthyr Tydfil, and the National Galleries of Wales, South Africa and Australia, and in the collections of the Arts Council and Contemporary Art Society; and by drawings, etchings and engravings in the British Museum, Victoria and Albert Museum, and National Museum of Wales; retrospective exhibn, Thomas Agnew, London, 1972. Publications: A Way of Looking at Pictures; Portrait Painters; Notes for art students; Introduction to Still-Life. Address: Eastleach Turville, near Cirencester, Glos. T: Southrop 214. Club: Athenæum. *Died 5 Aug. 1982.*

**GYDE, Sophie Adele;** see Wyss, S.

**GYÖRGYI, Albert S.;** see Szent-Györgyi.

# H

**HACKER, Prof. Louis Morton,** MA (Columbia); Emeritus Professor of Economics, Columbia University, USA, 1967 (Economics Department, 1935; Dean of School of General Studies, 1952–58, Director, 1949–52; Professor of Economics, 1948–67); *b* 17 March 1899; *s* of Morris Hacker; *m* 1st, 1921, Lillian Lewis (*d* 1952); one *s* one *d*.; 2nd, 1953, Beatrice Larson Brennan (*d* 1977). *Educ:* Columbia Coll.; Columbia University. Assistant and contributing Editor of New International Encyclopædia, Social Science Encyclopædia, Columbia Encyclopædia; taught economics and history at University of Wisconsin, Ohio State University, Utah State Agricultural College, University of Hawaii, Yeshiva University, Penn State University, Univ. of Puget Sound, Army War College, National War College. Executive sec. American Academic Freedom Study; Editor, American Century Series; Chairman, Academic Freedom Cttee, American Civil Liberties Union, resigned 1968; Guggenheim Fellow, 1948, 1959; Relm Foundation Fellow, 1967. Harmsworth Professor of American History, Oxford Univ., 1948–49; Lecturer, Fulbright Conference on American Studies, Cambridge, 1952. Visiting Distinguished Professor of Economics, Fairleigh Dickinson, 1967–68. Fellow, Queen's Coll., Oxford, and MA (Oxon); Benjamin Franklin Fellow of RSA; Hon. LLD Hawaii; Hon. LHD Columbia. Students Army Training Corps, 1918. *Publications:* (with B. B. Kendrick) United States since 1865, 1932, 4th edn 1949; The Farmer is Doomed, 1933; Short History of the New Deal, 1934; The US: a Graphic History, 1937; American Problems of Today, 1939; Triumph of American Capitalism, 1940; (with Allan Nevins) The US and Its Place in World Affairs, 1943; The Shaping of the American Tradition, 1947; New Industrial Relations (jointly), 1948; Government Assistance and the British Universities (jointly), 1952; (with H. S. Zahler) The United States in the 20th Century, 1952; Capitalism and the Historians (jointly), 1954; Alexander Hamilton in the American Tradition, 1957; American Capitalism, 1957; Larger View of the University, 1961; Major Documents in American Economic History, 2 vols, 1961; The World of Andrew Carnegie, Part 1, 1861–1901, 1968; The Course of American Economic Growth and Development, 1970; (with M. D. Hirsch) Proskauer: his life and times, 1978; contributions to learned journals and reviews. *Recreations:* walking, bridge, travel. *Address:* 430 W 116th Street, New York, NY 10027, USA. *Clubs:* Athenæum (London); Faculty, Columbia University (New York); Pilgrims (USA).                  *Died 22 March 1987.*

**HADDINGTON, 12th Earl of,** *cr* 1619; **George Baillie-Hamilton,** KT 1951; MC; TD; FRSE; FSAScot; LLD (Glasgow); Baron Binning, 1613; Scottish Representative Peer, 1922–63; HM Lieutenant County of Berwick, 1952–69; *b* 18 Sept. 1894; *s* of Lord Binning (*d* 1917; *e s* of 11th Earl) and Katharine Augusta Millicent (*d* 1952), *o c* of W. Severin Salting; *S* grandfather, 1917; *m* 1923, Sarah, *y d* of G. W. Cook, of Montreal; one *s* one *d*. *Educ:* Eton; Sandhurst. Served European War (Royal Scots Greys), 1915–18 (MC, wounded); late Major 19th (L and BH) Armoured Car Coy. Served European War of 1939–45; Wing Comdr RAFVR, 1941–45; Capt. Queen's Body Guard for Scotland, Royal Company of Archers, 1953–74. Pres. Soc. of Antiquaries of Scotland; Pres. Scottish Georgian Soc.; Chm. of Trustees, National Museum of Antiquities, Scotland; Trustee, National Library of Scotland. *Publications:* verse: The Gathering of the Clans, 1968; I Love Mountains, 1970. *Heir: s* Lord Binning. *Address:* Tyninghame, Dunbar, East Lothian.
                                                            *Died 17 April 1986.*

**HADDON, Eric Edwin,** CB 1965; CChem, FRSC; retired; Director, Chemical Defence Establishment, Ministry of Defence, 1961–68; *b* 16 March 1908; *s* of late William Edwin Haddon, York; *m* 1934, Barbara Fabian, York; no *c*. *Educ:* Archbishop Holgate's Grammar Sch., York; Queen Mary Coll., London Univ. BSc (Special) Chemistry, ARIC 1929; FRIC 1943. Joined Scientific Staff of Admiralty, 1929; Scientific Staff of War Dept, 1929; Sec., Scientific Advisory Council, Min. of Supply, 1945–52; Dir, Chemical Defence Research and Development, Min. of Supply, 1957–61. *Recreations:* electronics, gardening, bridge. *Address:* Knavesmire, St Leonards Road, Thames Ditton, Surrey KT7 0RX. *T:* 01–398 5944.
                                                            *Died 16 March 1984.*

**HADDOW, Sir (Thomas) Douglas,** KCB 1966 (CB 1955); FRSE; Permanent Under-Secretary of State, Scottish Office, 1965–73; *b* 9 Feb. 1913; *s* of George Haddow, Crawford, Lanarkshire; *m* 1942, Margaret R. S. Rowat (*d* 1969); two *s*. *Educ:* George Watson's Coll., Edinburgh; Edinburgh Univ.; Trinity Coll., Cambridge. MA (Edinburgh) 1932; BA (Cambridge) 1934. Department of Health for Scotland, 1935; Private Sec. to Sec. of State for Scotland, 1941–44. Commonwealth Fund Fellow, 1948. Secretary: Dept of Health for Scot., 1959–62; Scottish Develt Dept, 1962–64; Chm., N of Scotland Hydro-Electric Bd, 1973–78; Mem. (pt-time), S of Scotland Electricity Bd, 1973–78; Dir, British Investment Trust, 1978–83. Chm. Court, Heriot-Watt Univ., 1978–84. Hon. LLD Strathclyde Univ., 1967; Hon. DLitt Heriot-Watt Univ., 1971.

*Recreation:* golf. *Address:* The Coach House, Northumberland Street Lane SW, Edinburgh EH3 6JD. *T:* 031–556 3650; Castle View, Dirleton, East Lothian EH39 5EH. *T:* Dirleton 266. *Club:* Royal Commonwealth Society.                       *Died 26 Dec. 1986.*

**HADDRILL, Harry Victor;** County Councillor, West Yorkshire County Council; *b* 15 Nov. 1914; *s* of Harry Charles Haddrill and Sophie Nancy (*née* Davis); *m* 1937, Kathleen Hilda Miller; three *s*. *Educ:* Ninfield; Bexhill. Served War: Royal Sussex Regt, 1939–43; Royal Hampshire Regt, 1943–45; France, N Africa, Italy, Egypt. Elected: W Riding CC, 1956 (West Riding CA, 1968–74); W Yorks Metropolitan CC, 1973; first Conservative Chm., 1977–78; Chairman: Law and Parly Cttee, 1967–71; Fire Service Cttee, 1971–74; Planning Cttee, 1979–81; Jt Dep. Leader of the Opposition, W Yorks CC, 1981–. Pres., Ilkley Cons. Assoc., 1981–. *Recreations:* playing tennis, watching cricket, reading, listening to music, play-going. *Address:* 41 Grange Estate, Ilkley, W Yorks. *T:* Ilkley 608620. *Clubs:* Constitutional; British Legion (Ilkley).
                                                            *Died 11 Sept. 1983.*

**HADEN-GUEST, 3rd Baron** *cr* 1950, of Saling, Essex; **Richard Haden Haden-Guest;** *b* 20 July 1904; *s* of 1st Baron Haden-Guest, MC, and Edith (*d* 1944), *d* of Max Low; *S* brother, 1974; *m* 1st, 1926, Hilda (marr. diss. 1934), *d* of late Thomas Russell-Cruise; one *d*; 2nd, 1934, Olive Maria, *d* of late Anders Gotfrid Nilsson; one *s* decd; 3rd, 1949, Marjorie, *d* of late Dr Douglas F. Kennard. *Educ:* Bembridge. *Heir: half-b* Hon. Peter Haden Haden-Guest [*b* 1913; *m* 1945, Jean, *d* of late Dr Albert George Hindes; two *s* one *d*]. *Address:* 3 Chemin des Cret de Champel, 1206 Geneva, Switzerland. *T:* Geneva 476940.                                     *Died 26 May 1987.*

**HADLEY, Dr George Dickinson;** Emeritus Physician, Middlesex Hospital; *b* 30 June 1908; *s* of Laurence Percival Hadley and Norah Katherine Hadley (*née* Alabaster); *m* 1947, Jean Elinor Stewart; three *d*. *Educ:* King Edward VI Sch., Birmingham; Clare Coll., Cambridge. 1st Class Natural Sciences Tripos, Part II 1930, Part II 1931, Cambridge; MB, ChB Cantab 1934; MRCP 1937; MD Cantab 1939; Elmore Clinical Research Student, University of Cambridge, 1936–38; FRCP 1947. Major RAMC and Medical Specialist, 1939–45 (POW, Germany, 1940–45). Physician, Middlesex Hospital, 1946. Examiner in Medicine: Cambridge Univ., 1955–57; University of London, 1956–60; RCP, 1965–70. *Publications:* articles in various medical journals. *Recreations:* angling, 'cello playing, book-binding. *Address:* 59 Gloucester Crescent, NW1 7EG.                           *Died 14 Aug. 1984.*

**HADRILL, John Michael W.;** *see* Wallace-Hadrill.

**HAFFENDEN, Maj.-Gen. Donald James W.;** *see* Wilson-Haffenden.

**HAGEN, Dr John P(eter),** Presidential Certificate of Merit (US), 1947; DSM (US), 1959; Professor of Astronomy and Head of Department of Astronomy, Pennsylvania State University, 1967–75, later Emeritus; Director, Office of United Nations Conference, National Aeronautics and Space Administration, 1960–62 (Director, Vanguard Division, 1958–60); *b* 31 July 1908; *s* of John T. and Ella Bertha Hagen (*née* Fisher); *m* 1935, Edith W. Soderling; two *s*. *Educ:* Boston, Wesleyan, Yale and Georgetown Univs. Res. Associate, Wesleyan Univ., 1931–35; Supt Atmosphere and Astrophysics Div., US Naval Res. Lab., 1935–58; Dir, Project Vanguard, 1955–58. Lecturer, Georgetown Univ., 1949–52. FRAS 1969; FIEEE; Fellow: Amer. Acad. of Arts and Sciences; Amer. Assoc. for Advancement of Science; Amer. Astronomical Soc. Chairman: Study Gp 2 (Radioastronomy and Space Res.), Comité Consultative Internat. Radio; IUCAF Cttee of ISCU. Hon. ScD: Boston, 1958; Adelphi, Loyola, Fairfield, 1959; Mt Allison, 1960. Phi Beta Kappa. *Publications:* contrib. to Astrophysical Journal and to Proc. Inst. Radio Engrg; contributor to Encyclopædia Britannica. *Address:* 613 W Park Avenue, State College, Pa 16803, USA. *T:* 237–3031. *Club:* Cosmos (Washington, DC).
                                                            *Died 26 Aug. 1990.*

**HAGERTY, James Campbell, (Jim Hagerty);** *b* Plattsburg, 9 May 1909; *s* of James A. Hagerty; *m* 1937, Marjorie Lucas; two *s*. *Educ:* Blair Acad.; Columbia Univ. Joined staff of New York Times, 1934; Legislative Correspondent, 1938–42; Press Sec. to Governor Dewey, 1943–50; Sec. to Governor, 1950–52; Press Sec. to President Dwight D. Eisenhower, 1953–61; Vice-Pres., Corporate Relations, Amer. Broadcasting Cos Inc., 1961–74, retired 1974. *Address:* (home) 7 Rittenhouse Road, Bronxville, NY 10708, USA.
                                                            *Died 11 April 1981.*

**HAGUE, Harry;** a Recorder of the Crown Court, 1972–79; *b* 9 April 1922; *o c* of Harry Hague and Lilian (*née* Hindle), Stalybridge and Blackpool; *m* 1967, Vera, *d* of Arthur Frederick and Sarah Ann Smith, Manchester; two step *d*. *Educ:* Arnold Sch., Blackpool; Manchester and London Univs. LLB London. Army, 1941–44. Called to Bar, Middle Temple, 1946; Northern Circuit. Asst Recorder, Burnley, 1969–71. Contested (L): Blackburn East, 1950; Blackpool North, 1959, 1962 (bye-election) and 1964; Mem. Nat.

Exec., Liberal Party, 1956–59 and 1962–64. *Recreations:* activities concerning animals, motoring, historical buildings.

**HAIDER, Michael Lawrence;** Chairman of the Board, Chief Executive Officer, and Chairman of Executive Committee, Standard Oil Co. (NJ), 1965–69, retired; *b* 1 Oct. 1904; *s* of Michael Haider and Elizabeth (*née* Milner). *Educ:* Stanford Univ. BS 1927. Chemical Engineer, Richfield Oil Co., 1927–29; Carter Oil Co., Tulsa, Okla., 1929–38 (Chief Engineer, 1935–38); Manager, Research and Engineering Dept, Standard Oil Development Co., 1938–45; Standard Oil Co. (NJ): Executive, Producing Dept, 1945–46; Deputy Co-ordinator of Producing Activities, 1952–54; Vice-President, 1960–61; Executive Vice-President, 1961–63; President and Vice-Chairman, Executive Cttee, 1963–65. Was with: Imperial Oil Ltd, Toronto, 1946–52 (Vice-President and Director, 1948–52); International Petroleum Co. Ltd (President and Director), 1954–59. President, American Institute of Mining and Metallurgical Engineers, 1952. *Publications:* (ed) Petroleum Reservoir Efficiency and Well Spacing, 1943; articles in technical journals. *Address:* (office) Room 1250, 1 Rockefeller Plaza, New York, NY 10020, USA; (home) 35 Adam Way, Atherton, Calif 94025, USA.
*Died Aug.* 1986.

**HAIGH, (Austin) Anthony (Francis),** CMG 1954; retired as Director of Education and of Cultural and Scientific Affairs, Council of Europe, 1962–68; *b* 29 Aug. 1907; *s* of late P. B. Haigh, ICS, and Eliza (*d* 1963), *d* of George Moxon; *m* 1st, 1935, Gertrude (marr. diss. 1971), 2nd *d* of late Frank Dodd; two *s* two *d*; 2nd, 1971, Eleanore Margaret, *d* of late T. H. Bullimore and widow of J. S. Herbert. *Educ:* Eton; King's Coll., Cambridge. Entered Diplomatic Service, 1932; served in Foreign Office and at HM Embassies at Rio de Janeiro, Tokyo, Lisbon, Ankara, Cairo and Brussels; Head of Cultural Relations Department, Foreign Office, 1952–62. Chairman Cttee of Cultural Experts, Council of Europe, 1960–61; Chairman, Admin. Board, Cultural Fund of Council of Europe, 1961–62. *Publications:* A Ministry of Education for Europe, 1970; Congress of Vienna to Common Market, 1973; Cultural Diplomacy in Europe, 1974. *Address:* The Furnace, Crowhurst, near Battle, East Sussex. *Club:* Leander.
*Died* 11 *June* 1989.

**HAIGHT, Gordon Sherman,** PhD; Professor of English, Yale University, 1950, Emily Sanford Professor, 1966, Emeritus 1969; General Editor, Clarendon George Eliot, since 1975; *b* 6 Feb. 1901; *s* of Louis Pease Haight and Grace Carpenter; *m* 1937, Mary Treat Nettleton. *Educ:* Yale Univ. BA 1923, PhD 1933. Master in English: Kent Sch., 1924–25; Hotchkiss Sch., 1925–30; taught English at Yale, 1931–69; Master of Pierson Coll., Yale Univ., 1949–53. Visiting Prof. of English: Columbia Univ., 1946–47; Univ. of Oregon, 1949. Guggenheim Fellow, 1946, 1953, 1960. Fellow Royal Society of Literature, Corres. Fellow British Academy. Member: Berzelius; Zeta Psi. Wilbur Cross Medal, Yale, 1977. *Publications:* Mrs Sigourney, 1930; George Eliot and John Chapman, 1940, 1969; George Eliot, A Biography, 1968 (James Tait Black Award, Heinemann Award of Royal Society of Literature, Van Wyck Brooks Award, 1969; Amer. Acad. of Arts and Letters Award, 1970), 3rd rev. edn, 1985; Editor: Miss Ravenel's Conversion (J. W. De Forest), 1939, 1955; Adam Bede, 1948; The George Eliot Letters, 9 vols, 1954–78, one vol. edn 1985; Middlemarch, 1955; The Mill on the Floss, 1961, Clarendon edn, 1980; A Century of George Eliot Criticism, 1965; Portable Victorian Reader, 1971; contribs to various literary jls. *Recreations:* garden, water colours. *Address:* 145 Peck Hill Road, Woodbridge, Conn 06525, USA. *T:* 203–393–0689. *Clubs:* Yale, Century (New York); Elizabethan (New Haven).
*Died* 28 *Dec.* 1985.

**HAILSTONE, Bernard,** RP; painter; *b* 6 Oct. 1910; *s* of William Edward Hailstone; *m* 1934, Joan Mercia Kenet Hastings (*d* 1987); one *s. Educ:* Sir Andrew Judd's Sch., Tonbridge. Trained at Goldsmiths' Coll. and Royal Academy Schs; Practising Artist, 1934–39; NFS, London (Fireman Artist), 1939–42; Official War Artist to Ministry of Transport, 1942–44; Official War Artist to SEAC, 1944–45. Recent portraits include: HM Queen; Prince Charles and Princess Anne; Mrs Anne Armstrong, US Ambassador to UK; Pres. of USA, Jimmy Carter, 1977; HM Queen Elizabeth The Queen Mother, 1980; Prince Andrew, 1981. *Recreation:* tennis. *Address:* 43a Glebe Place, Chelsea, SW3. *T:* 01–352 1309; 49 Roland Gardens, SW7. *T:* 01–373 2970. *Club:* Chelsea Arts.
*Died* 27 *Dec.* 1987.

**HAINE, Reginald Leonard,** VC 1917; MC 1919; Captain HAC; *s* of late H. J. Haine, Clipsham, Ringley Avenue, Horley; *b* 10 July 1896; *m* 1923, Dora Beatrice, *er d* of late E. Holder, Monticello, South Border, Purley; one *d.* Lieut-Col Home Guard. *Address:* Dawslea Cottage, Hollist Lane, Midhurst, West Sussex.
*Died* 12 *June* 1982.

**HAINES, Sir Cyril (Henry),** KBE 1962 (CBE 1953; MBE 1930); Chairman, South West London Rent Tribunal, 1962–66; *b* 2 March 1895; *s* of late Walter John Haines, OBE, formerly Deputy Chief Inspector of Customs and Excise; *m* 1934, Mary Theodora, *d* of late

Rev. J. W. P. Silvester, BD, Hon. CF, Vicar of Wembley; two *d. Educ:* Hele's Sch., Exeter. Apptd to Scottish Education Dept, 1914. On active service with Army, 1915–19. Appt to Foreign Office, Dec. 1919. Called to Bar, Middle Temple, 1926. Asst Brit. Agent to Anglo-Mexican Revolutionary Claims Commn, 1928; Registrar, HM Supreme Court, for China, 1930 (acted as Asst Judge during absences from China of one of Judges); Asst Judge, HM Consular Court in Egypt, and, for Naval Courts, HM Consul at Alexandria, Egypt, 1943; Judge of HM Consular Court in Egypt, 1946. Indep. Referee for War Pension Appeals in Egypt, 1946; Asst Judge of HM Chief Court for the Persian Gulf, 1949–59, and Head of Claims Dept, Foreign Office, 1949–54; Judge of HM Chief Court for the Persian Gulf, 1959–61. Vice Pres., Abbeyfield Orpington Soc., 1985– (Chm., 1962–75; Pres., 1975–85). *Address:* Wood Lea, 6 The Glen, Farnborough Park, Orpington, Kent. *T:* Farnborough, Kent, 54507.
*Died* 22 *Feb.* 1988.

**HAINES, Geoffrey Colton,** OBE 1965; FCA, FSA; Fellow, The Royal Numismatic Society, (Hon. Treasurer), 1930–61); *b* Barrow-in-Furness, 18 Sept. 1899; *e surv. s* of late Harry Colton Haines, FCA, and Margaret Elizabeth Haines (*née* Barnes); *m* Olive (JP, Mayor of Wandsworth, 1956–57, Hon. Freeman 1969), *e surv. d* of late Philip Scott Minor, Solicitor, Manchester; one *d. Educ:* St Paul's Sch. Private and Officer Cadet, Inns of Court, OTC, 1917–18, 2nd Lieut The East Surrey Regt, 1919; Dep. Dist Warden, Putney, 1939–45; Bomb Reconnaissance Officer, Civil Defence, 1943–45; Asst Chief Warden, Civil Defence Corps, Wandsworth, 1954–55. Chief Executive Officer, London Association for the Blind, 1932–64, Vice-Pres., 1965; former Mem. of Executive Cttee of Royal National Institute for the Blind and other Charities for Blind Welfare; Mem. Royal Masonic Benevolent Instn, 1954–78 (Dep. Chm., 1958–76); Mem., Bd of Management, Royal Masonic Hosp., 1962–78. Hon. Mem., Nat. Assoc. of Industries for the Blind & Disabled Inc. (Chm. 1952–53). Hon. Mem., Cambridge Numismatic Soc. *Publications:* revised, The Roman Republican Coinage (by late Rev. E. A. Sydenham), 1952; various papers to Numismatic Chronicle, etc. *Recreations:* archæology, Roman and Byzantine history and numismatics, travel, motoring, walking. *Address:* 31 Larpent Avenue, Putney, SW15 6UU. *T:* 01–788 0132.
*Died* 14 *Sept.* 1981.

**HAKEWILL SMITH, Maj.-Gen. Sir Edmund,** KCVO 1967; CB 1945; CBE 1944; MC; psc; JP; Governor, Military Knights of Windsor, 1951–78; Deputy Constable and Lieutenant-Governor of Windsor Castle, 1964–72; *b* Kimberley, S Africa, 17 March 1896; *s* of George Cecil Smith and Mildred, 2nd *d* of J. B. Currey; *m* 1928, Edith Constance, *e d* of Brigadier-Gen. H. Nelson, DSO, Shovel, Somerset; one *d. Educ:* Diocesan Coll., South Africa; RMC Sandhurst. Commissioned into Royal Scots Fusiliers as 2nd Lieut, 1915; ADC to Governor of Bengal, 1921–22; Adjutant, 2nd RSF, 1927–30; Staff Coll., Quetta, 1930–32; Staff Capt., War Office, 1934–36. Employed Air Staff Duties, RAF, 1936–37; DAAG War Office, 1938–40. Comdr 5 Devons, March–June 1940; Comdr 4/5 RSF, 1940–41; Comd 157 Inf. Bde, 1941–42; Dir of Organisation, War Office (Maj.-Gen.), 1942–43; Comdr 155 Inf. Bde (Brig.), Feb.–Nov. 1943; Comdr 52nd Lowland Div. (Maj.-Gen.), 1943 till disbandment, 1946; Commander, Lowland District, 1946; retired pay, 1949. Served European War, 1915–18 (wounded twice, MC); War of 1939–45 (despatches, CBE, CB. Order of St Olaf, Order of Orange-Nassau). Col, The Royal Scots Fusiliers, 1946–57; Berks County Commandant, Army Cadet Force, 1952–57. Grand Officer of Order of Orange Nassau, 1947; Order of St Olaf, Second Class, 1947. *Address:* Apt 28, Tennis Court Lane, Hampton Court Palace, East Molesey, Surrey.
*Died* 15 *April* 1986.

**HALDANE, Archibald Richard Burdon,** CBE 1968; *b* 18 Nov. 1900; *s* of late Sir Richard Haldane; *m* 1941, Janet Macrae Simpson-Smith; one *s* one *d. Educ:* Edinburgh Academy; Winchester Coll.; Balliol Coll., Oxford; Edinburgh University. LLB Edinburgh, 1926; WS 1926; DLitt Edinburgh, 1950. Dep. Chm., Trustee Savings Banks Assoc., 1959–61; Chm., Trustee Savings Banks Inspection Cttee, 1960–67; Vice-Pres., Trustee Savings Bank Assoc., 1971. *Publications:* By Many Waters, 1940; The Path by the Water, 1944; The Drove Roads of Scotland, 1950, repr. 1973; New Ways through the Glens, 1962, repr. 1973; Three Centuries of Scottish Posts, 1971; By River, Stream and Loch, 1973. *Recreations:* fishing, walking. *Address:* Foswell, Auchterarder, Perthshire. *T:* Auchterarder 2610; 4 North Charlotte Street, Edinburgh. *T:* 031–225 4181. *Club:* New (Edinburgh).
*Died* 18 *Oct.* 1982.

**HALE, Baron** *cr* 1972 (Life Peer), of Oldham; **(Charles) Leslie Hale;** *b* 13 July 1902; *s* of Benjamin George Hale, Managing Director of Stableford & Co. Ltd, Coalville, Leics; *m* 1926, Dorothy Ann Latham (*d* 1971); one *s* one *d. Educ:* Ashby-de-la-Zouch Boys' Grammar Sch. Articled to Evan Barlow, Solicitor, Leicester; practised in Coalville, Nuneaton and London. Mem. Leics County Council, 1925–50. Contested (L) S Nottingham, 1929. MP (Lab) for Oldham, Lancs. 1945–50, West Division of Oldham, 1950–Jan. 1968, resigned. Freedom of Oldham, 1969. *Publications:* Thirty Who

Were Tried, 1955; John Philpot Curran, 1958; Blood on the Scales, 1960; Hanged in Error, 1961; Hanging in the Balance, 1962; None So Blind, 1963. *Recreation:* house painting. *Address:* 92 College Road, SE21.
*Died 9 May 1985.*

**HALE, Comdr John William,** DSO 1940; RN retired; *b* 30 March 1907; 4th *s* of late Warren Stormes Hale and late Cora Hale; *m* 1938, Ada Elizabeth Bowden; one *s* two *d*. *Educ:* Highgate Sch.; RN Coll., Dartmouth. Went to sea as midshipman in HMS Resolution, 1924; Lieut and joined Fleet Air Arm, 1929; Lieut Cdr 1937; at beginning of war of 1939–45, served in HMS Glorious and then HMS Illustrious; took part in attack on Italian Fleet, Taranto, 11 Nov. 1940 (DSO); Commander, 1940; retired, 1957; Freeman of City of London; Past Master of Tallow Chandlers Company. Mem., Historic Houses Assoc. (opens Letheringham Water Mill and Gardens to public during the summer). *Recreation:* gardening. *Address:* Letheringham Mill, Woodbridge, Suffolk.
*Died 12 Nov. 1985.*

**HALE, Joseph;** engineer; formerly Merchant Navy; *b* 28 Oct. 1913; *s* of J. Gordon Tyson Hale and M. Hale (*née* Johnston); *m* 1939, Annie Irene Clowes; one *s* one *d*. *Educ:* elementary and secondary technical schs. Mem. Bolton Town Council until 1950; Junior Whip to Labour Group; Chm. Bolton West Divisional Party, 1949; Mem. Amalgamated Engineering Union District Cttee, 1943–50. MP (Lab) Rochdale, 1950–51. *Recreations:* literature, music. *Address:* 30 Thorpe Street, Bolton, Lancs.
*Died 7 Feb. 1985.*

**HALEY, Philip William Raymond Chatterton,** MBE 1956; HM Diplomatic Service, retired 1976; *b* 18 June 1917; 2nd *s* of late Joseph Bertram Haley and late Lilian Anne Chatterton Haley; *m* 1941, Catherine Skene Stewart, LRAM, LRCM; two *d*. *Educ:* Perse Sch.; London University. HM Services, 1940–47 in KOSB and on Gen. Staff; 2nd Lieut 1941, Lieut 1942, Captain 1943, Major 1945, Lt-Col 1946; Control Commn for Germany, 1947–56, serving also with Internat. Commn for the Saar. HM Diplomatic Service, 1956; Consul, Düsseldorf; Hamburg, 1959; 1st Sec. and Embassy spokesman, Bonn, 1960; Dep. Consul-General, Chicago, 1964; Johannesburg, 1968; Consul-Gen., Hanover, 1973. Hon. PhD Chicago, 1967. Croix de la Libération, 1946. *Recreations:* gardening, painting, senile delinquency (*eg* bird watching), collecting gasteropod molluscs. *Address:* Casa Iris, 6 Calle el Tulipan, San Patricio, Santa Ursula, Tenerife, Canary Isles. *T:* 300814.
*Died 15 March 1987.*

**HALEY, Sir William (John),** KCMG, 1946; Hon. LLD Cambridge 1951, Dartmouth, New Hampshire, 1957, London, 1963, St Andrews, 1965; Hon. Fellow Jesus College, Cambridge 1956; FRSL; Commissioner of Appeal for Income Tax, Jersey, 1971–83; *b* Jersey, CI, 24 May 1901; *s* of Frank Haley, Bramley, Leeds, and Marie Sangan; *m* 1921, Edith Susie Gibbons; two *s* two *d*. *Educ:* Victoria Coll., Jersey. Joined Manchester Evening News, 1922; Chief Sub-Editor, 1925; Managing Editor, 1930; Dir Manchester Guardian and Evening News, Ltd, 1930; Jt Managing Dir, 1939–43; Dir Press Association, 1939–43; Dir Reuters, 1939–43; Editor-in-Chief, BBC, 1943–44; Dir-Gen., BBC, 1944–52; Editor of the Times, 1952–66; Dir and Chief Executive, The Times Publishing Co. Ltd, 1965–66; Chm., Times Newspapers Ltd, 1967; Editor-in-Chief, Encylopædia Britannica, 1968–69. Pres., Nat. Book League, 1955–62; Chm., Jersey Arts Council, 1976–77. Chevalier Legion of Honour, 1948; Grand Officer, Order of Orange Nassau, 1950. *Address:* Beau Site, Gorey, Jersey, Channel Islands. *T:* Jersey 51068.
*Died 6 Sept. 1987.*

**HALL, 2nd Viscount,** *cr* 1946, of Cynon Valley; **(William George) Leonard Hall;** *b* 9 March 1913; *s* of 1st Viscount Hall, PC, and Margaret, *d* of William Jones, Ynysybwl; *S* father, 1965; *m* 1st, 1935, Joan Margaret (*d* 1962), *d* of William Griffiths, Glamorganshire; two *d*; 2nd, 1963, Constance Ann Gathorne (*d* 1972), *d* of Rupert Gathorne Hardy, London; 3rd, 1975, Marie-Colette Bach, St Viatre. *Educ:* Christ Coll., Brecon; University Coll. Hospital. MRCS; LRCP. Asst MOH, Merthyr Tydfil, 1938–40. Surgeon Lt-Comdr, RNVR, 1940–46. Powell Duffryn Group, 1946–60; Dir of Investments, Africa, Asia and ME, Internat. Finance Corp. (affiliate of IBRD), 1962–64; Advisor for Special Projects, Internat. Finance Corp., 1963–64; Chm., Post Office, 1969–70. *Recreations:* country activities. *Address:* Solvain, 41210 St Viatre, Loir et Cher, France. *T:* (54) 83 63 67.
*Died 24 July 1985 (ext).*

**HALL, Arthur Henderson,** RWS 1970; RE 1961; MSIA; ARCA; painter, etcher, freelance illustrator; Head of School of Graphic Design, Kingston Polytechnic, 1965–71 (Senior Lecturer in charge, 1952–65); *b* 25 June 1906; *s* of Charles and Mary Hall; *m* 1942, Frances Bruce (*decd*); one *s* one *d*. *Educ:* Sedgefield; Royal College of Art; British Sch., Rome. Prix de Rome, Engraving, 1931; Glass Designer for Webb & Corbett, 1933–36; Part-time Teacher, Kingston Sch. of Art, 1933–41; Part-time Teacher, London Central Sch. of Art, 1936–39. RAF, 1942–46. Teacher, London Central Sch. of Art, 1946–52; exhibits paintings and etchings at: RA, RWS, RE.

*Publications:* numerous illustrations for children's books and books on gardening. *Recreations:* gardening, travel. *Address:* 15 Church Road, East Molesey, Surrey. *T:* 01–979 5681. *Club:* Nash House.
*Died 7 Jan. 1983.*

**HALL, Dr Cecil Charles,** CB 1968; retired; Director, Warren Spring Laboratory, Ministry of Technology, 1964–68; *b* 10 May 1907; *s* of Frederick Harrington and Alice Hall; *m* 1950, Margaret Rose Nicoll; no *c*. *Educ:* Beckenham Gram. Sch.; London Univ. Jun. Chemist, S Metropolitan Gas Co., 1925–30; BSc 1st Hons Chem. (London), 1929; MSc (London), 1931. Jun. Asst, Fuel Research Stn, DSIR, 1930; PhD (London), 1934. Research in high pressure hydrogenation of coal tar and synthesis of oils and chemicals from coal by catalytic processes. Special Merit Promotion to Sen. Princ. Scientific Off., 1952; Dep. Chief Chemist, Fuel Res. Stn, DSIR, 1953; Dep. Dir, Warren Spring Lab., 1959. Chm. Governors, N Herts Coll., 1978–83. FRSC (FRIC 1944); FInstE (FInstF 1954). *Publications:* (with T. P. Hilditch) Catalytic Processes in Industrial Chemistry, 1937; numerous research and review papers in scientific and techn. jls dealing with chemistry of high pressure hydrogenation processes and with Fischer Tropsch synthesis. *Recreation:* gardening, specialising in iris growing and hybridising (Pres., British Iris Soc., 1967–70). *Address:* 1 The Close, Rectory Lane, Stevenage, Herts SG1 4BU. *T:* Stevenage 353417. *Clubs:* Civil Service; Rotary (Stevenage).
*Died 3 Nov. 1987.*

**HALL, Rt. Rev. Denis Bartlett;** *b* 9 April 1899; *s* of Frank Marshall Hall and Caroline Beatrice Hall (*née* Bartlett), both of Bristol. *Educ:* Tudor House Sch., Henleaze, Bristol; Bristol Grammar Sch.; Bristol Univ. (BA). RNVR, 1917–19. University of Bristol, 1919–23; Ridley Hall, Cambridge, 1923–24. Curate, St Gabriel's Sunderland, 1924–28; Chaplain, HMS Conway Sch. Ship, 1928–30; Vicar of Bishopston, Bristol, 1930–47; Asst Bishop on The Niger, 1947–57; Vicar of St Paul's, Thornton Heath, Surrey, 1957–61; Asst Bishop of Canterbury, 1960–61; Rector of Tormarton with W Littleton, Glos, 1961–66. *Address:* Cowlin House, 26 Pembroke Road, Clifton, Bristol BS8 3BB.
*Died 5 April 1983.*

**HALL, Ven. Edgar Francis,** MA; Archdeacon of Totnes, 1948–62, Archdeacon Emeritus, 1962; Canon Residentiary of Exeter, 1934–62; Treasurer, Exeter Cathedral, 1951–62; *b* 14 Aug. 1888; *s* of Francis R. Hall, Oxford; *m* 1915, Anstice (*d* 1982) *d* of Dr Louis Tosswill, Exeter; three *d*. *Educ:* Oxford High Sch.; Jesus Coll., Oxford (Scholar). Asst Master, Exeter Sch., 1911; Deacon 1914; Priest 1915; Curate of St James', Exeter, 1914; Chaplain of Exeter Sch., 1917; Vicar of Leusden, Devon, 1921; Diocesan Dir of Relig. Education, Exeter, 1934; Proctor in Convocation, 1944; Gen. Sec. Nat. Soc., 1943–47; Chm. Church of England Council for Education, 1949–58 (Sec. 1948–49). Retired, 1962. *Address:* The Old Parsonage, Leusden, Poundsgate, Newton Abbot, Devon. *T:* Poundsgate 329.
*Died 9 Feb. 1987.*

**HALL, Frederick Thomas Duncan;** Chairman, West Midlands County Council, 1977–78 (Member, 1974–82); Lord Mayor of Birmingham, May 1972–May 1973; *b* 12 Jan. 1902; *s* of Frederick James and Catherine Harriett Hall; *m* 1925, Irene Margaret Lawley; one *s*. *Educ:* Bourne Coll., Quinton, Birmingham. Chairman, Hall & Rice Ltd and associated cos. Member: West Bromwich Educn Cttee, 1933–46 (co-opted); Birmingham City Council, 1949–73 (Alderman, 1961); served Cttees: Educn, 1949–73 (Chm., 1966–69); Finance, 1966–73; Gen. Purposes, 1956–74; Jt Consultative, 1969–72 (Chm.); Allotments, 1949–66. Governor: Birmingham Univ., 1967–73; Aston Univ., 1957–80; Handsworth Grammar Sch., 1960–. Member: AMC (Educn) Cttee, 1967–72 (Vice-Chm., 1971–72); Assoc. of Educn Cttees Exec., 1968–72; Chm., Sandwell Ward Conservative Assoc., 1947–65; Pres., Handsworth Div. Conservative Assoc., 1973; Dir, Birmingham Repertory Theatre, 1970–73; formed Handsworth Historical Soc., 1951 (Chm., 1951–65). Vice-Pres., West Bromwich Albion FC, 1979–. *Recreations:* hockey, golf, historical research. *Address:* 32 Englestede Close, Birmingham B20 1BJ. *T:* 021–554 6060. *Clubs:* Aberdovey Golf (Pres., 1967–79); Sandwell Park Golf (Captain, 1948–49).
*Died 10 March 1988.*

**HALL, Maj.-Gen. Frederick William G.;** *see* Gordon-Hall.

**HALL, (Harold) Peter;** Legal Adviser and Solicitor, Crown Estate Commissioners, 1976–80; Solicitor of Supreme Court; *b* 10 Dec. 1916; *s* of Arthur William Henry and Ethel Amelia Hall; *m* 1946, Tessibel Mary Mitchell (*née* Phillips); one *s* one *d*. *Educ:* Bristol Grammar Sch.; Bristol Univ. (LLB Hons). Articled to, and Asst Solicitor with, Burges Salmon & Co., Solicitors, Bristol, 1934–39. Served War of 1939–45: enlisted Somerset Light Inf., Dec. 1939; commnd in E Yorkshire Regt, 1940; service Home and Far East, 1940–45. Asst Provost Marshal (Major), Southern Army, India Command, 1945. Legal Branch, Min. of Agric., Fisheries and Food, 1946–66; Asst Legal Adviser, Land Commn, 1967–71; Asst Solicitor, Dept of the Environment, 1971–76. *Recreations:* reading, photography, walking. *Address:* The Ridings, 9 Steep Hill Court

Road, Ventnor, Isle of Wight PO38 1UH. *Club:* Royal Solent Yacht (Yarmouth, IoW).                                    *Died* 12 *Feb.* 1986.

**HALL, John Edward Beauchamp,** CMG 1959; *b* 9 Dec. 1905; *s* of Henry William Hall, MA, and Emily (*née* Odam); *m* 1936, Jane Gordon (*née* Forbes); two *d. Educ:* Bradfield Coll., Berks; Worcester Coll., Oxford. Foundation Scholar, Bradfield Coll., 1919–24; Exhibitioner, Worcester Coll., Oxford, 1924–28. Appointed to Colonial Administrative Service, Nigeria, 1930; Permanent Sec., Federal Government of Nigeria, 1958–60; retired, 1961. *Recreation:* gardening. *Address:* The Croft, Church Road, Sandhurst, Hawkhurst, Kent TN18 5NS. *T:* Sandhurst 302.

*Died* 17 *Jan.* 1989.

**HALL, Maj.-Gen. Kenneth,** CB 1976; OBE 1962 (MBE 1958); Director of Army Education, 1972–76; *b* 29 July 1916; *s* of Frank Hall and Hannah Hall (*née* Clayton); *m* 1945, Celia Adelaide Elizabeth Francis; two *s. Educ:* Worksop Coll.; St John's Coll., Cambridge (MA). Served War of 1939–45: commissioned in Royal Tank Regt, 1940–49; transf. to Royal Army Educational Corps, 1949; War Office, 1945–52; HQ Malta Garrison, 1953–57; War Office, 1958–62; HQ Aldershot District, 1962–64; Chief Educn Officer, GHQ, MELF, 1965; Comdt Army Sch. of Educn, 1965–66; MoD, 1966–69; Chief Educn Officer, HQ Southern Comd, 1969–71; Comdt RAEC Centre, 1971–72. Col Comdt, RAEC, 1978–82. *Recreations:* boxing (Cambridge Univ. Blue, 1937–38–39), reading, golf. *Address:* 42 Exeter House, Putney Heath, SW15. *T:* 01–788 4794. *Clubs:* Roehampton; Hawks (Cambridge).                     *Died* 12 *Dec.* 1987.

**HALL, Sir Noel (Frederick),** Kt 1957; Principal, Brasenose College, Oxford, 1960–73, Hon. Fellow 1973; *b* 23 Dec. 1902; *s* of late Cecil Gallopine Hall and late Constance Gertrude Upcher; *m* 1st, 1927, Edith Evelyn Pearl Haward (marr. diss. 1944); no *c*; 2nd, 1946, Elinor Hirschhorn Marks; one *s* one *d. Educ:* Royal Grammar Sch., Newcastle on Tyne; Bromsgrove Sch.; Brasenose Coll., Oxford. 1st Class hons Modern History, 1924; Senior Hulme Scholar, 1924–25; Certificate Social Anthropology, 1925; BA 1924; MA 1933. Commonwealth Fund Fellow in Economics, Princeton Univ., 1925–27, AM (Economics) Princeton, 1926; Lecturer in Political Economy, head of Dept of Political Economy, and Civil Service Tutor, University of London, University Coll., 1927–29; Senior Lecturer, 1929–35; Prof. of Political Economy in the University of London (University Coll.) 1935–38; Sec. of Fellowship Advisory Cttee of Rockefeller Foundation for Social Sciences in Great Britain and Ireland, 1930–36; Dir, National Institute for Economic and Social Research, 1938–43; Mem. of International Commission for Relief of Child Refugees in Spain, 1939; Joint Dir, Ministry of Economic Warfare, 1940; Minister in charge of War Trade Department, British Embassy, Washington, 1941–43; Development Adviser West Africa, 1943–45; Principal of the Administrative Staff Coll., Greenlands, Henley-on-Thames, 1946–61. Ford Foundation Distinguished Visiting Prof., New York Univ., 1958 (University Medal, 1958). Hon. Associate, College of Advanced Technology, Birmingham, 1963. Hon. LLD Univ. of Lancaster, 1964. *Publications:* Measures of a National and International character for Raising Standards of Living (Report to Economic Committee of League of Nations, 1938); The Exchange Equalisation Account, 1935; Report on Grading Structure of Administrative and Clerical Staff in the Hospital Service, 1957; The Making of Higher Executives, 1958. *Recreations:* golf, bridge. *Address:* 1 Northfield End, Henley-on-Thames, Oxon. *T:* Henley-on-Thames 3265. *Club:* English-Speaking Union.                              *Died* 29 *March* 1983.

**HALL, Peter;** *see* Hall, H. P.

**HALL, Prof. Philip,** FRS 1942; MA; Sadleirian Professor of Pure Mathematics, Cambridge University, 1953–67, then Emeritus (University Lecturer in Mathematics, 1933–51; Reader in Algebra, 1951–53); Fellow of King's College, Cambridge, 1927; *b* 11 April 1904. *Educ:* Christ's Hosp. Hon. Sec. London Mathematical Soc., 1938–41, 1945–48, Pres., 1955–57. Sylvester Medal, Royal Society, 1961; de Morgan Medal and Larmor Prize of the London Mathematical Soc., 1965. Hon. DSc: Tübingen, 1963; Warwick, 1977. Hon. Fellow, Jesus Coll. Cambridge, 1976. *Address:* 50 Impington Lane, Histon, Cambs.            *Died* 30 *Dec.* 1982.

**HALL, William Telford,** CSI 1947; CIE 1942; *b* 4 June 1895; *s* of John Hall, Edinburgh; *m* 1922, E. Winifred, *d* of late Col Sir George McCrae, DSO, DL; two *s* one *d. Educ:* George Heriot's Sch. Served European War, 1914–18, Capt. Royal Irish Fusiliers and Machine Gun Corps, Salonica and France. Joined Indian Forest Service, 1921; Chief Conservator of Forests, United Provinces, India. *Address:* Ashley Park Retirement Home, Ashley Park, West Clandon, near Guildford, Surrey.            *Died* 26 *Jan.* 1985.

**HALLAND, Col Gordon Herbert Ramsay,** CIE 1931; OBE 1918; HM Inspector of Constabulary for England and Wales, 1938; retired, 1953; *b* 1888; *e s* of late Rev. J. T. Halland, MA, Rector of Blyburgh, Kirton-in-Lindsey, Lincs; *m* 1st, 1916, Helen Claudine Blanche (*d* 1946), *o d* of late Maj.-Gen. J. M. Walter, CB, CSI, DSO; two *d*;

2nd, 1947, Baroness Sigrid von der Recke (*née* von Lutzau), Windau, Latvia. *Educ:* private; Royal Latin Sch., Buckingham. Science Master at Kirton Grammar Sch., Lincs, 1906–08; Entered Indian Police, 1908 and posted to Punjab; served Ambala, Lahore, Rohtak, Hoshiarpur, Rawalpindi, Lyallpur, and Amritsar Districts; on police duty with the King at Delhi Durbar, 1911; Served European War, 1914–18 in Army in India Reserve of Officers (Major and Gen. Staff Officer, 2nd Grade, Army Headquarters, India) (despatches, OBE); Principal, Punjab Police Training Sch., Phillaur, 1921–26; on police duty with Duke of Connaught at Delhi, 1921; on police duty with Prince of Wales at Delhi, 1922; Lt-Col, Army in India Reserve of Officers, 1927; attached Gen. Staff, Headquarters of Shanghai Defence Force and subsequently North China Command, 1927–30; Senior Superintendent of Police, Delhi, 1930–31; Hon. ADC to the Viceroy, 1930, with hon. rank of Col; Chief Constable of Lincs, 1931–34; Dep. Asst Commissioner in charge of the Metropolitan Police Coll., 1934–38; Inspector-Gen. of Police, Ceylon, 1942–44; services lent to Foreign Office, Aug. 1944–Oct. 1947, as Inspector Gen. of Public Safety, CCG (British Element). Mem. County Council for Parts of Lindsey, Nov. 1953–March 1957. DL County of Lincoln, 1954–57. *Publication:* A Clarion Call (poems), 1978. *Recreations:* gardening; (past) shooting, riding, polo, cricket, tennis. *Address:* Broadlands, The Park, Cirencester Road, Minchinhampton, Stroud, Glos GL6 9EQ. *T:* Brimscombe 3969. *Club:* Lincolnshire County.                     *Died* 28 *March* 1981.

**HALLETT, Vice-Adm. Sir Cecil Charles;** *see* Hughes Hallett.

**HALLIDAY, Edward Irvine,** CBE 1973; RP 1952; RBA 1942; ARCA (London) 1925; Immediate Past-President, Royal Society of Portrait Painters; Past-President, Royal Society of British Artists; Vice-President and Chairman, Artists General Benevolent Institution, since 1965; President, Artists League of Great Britain, since 1975; *b* 7 Oct. 1902; *s* of James Halliday and Violet Irvine; *m* 1928, Dorothy Lucy Hatswell; one *s* one *d. Educ:* Liverpool; Paris; Royal College of Art, London; British Sch. at Rome (Rome Scholar 1925). War of 1939–45: service with RAF Bomber Command until seconded for special duties with Foreign Office. Mural paintings in London and Liverpool. Posters of Western Highlands for British Railways. Principal Portraits include: The Queen, for various cities, regiments, etc.; The Queen and The Duke of Edinburgh, for SS Caronia; The Duke of Edinburgh, for Gordonstoun Sch., Baltic Exchange, the Press Club, and Nat. Defence Coll.; The Prince of Wales, for Air Support Comd, RAF, and Naval Club; Queen Elizabeth the Queen Mother; HRH Princess Alice, Countess of Athlone; Admiral of the Fleet the Earl Mountbatten of Burma; Countess Mountbatten of Burma; Pandit Nehru (painted in New Delhi); Sir Edmund Hillary; President Azikiwe (painted in Nigeria); Dr Kaunda (painted in Zambia); King Olaf of Norway; Lord Hunt of Fawley and other doctors. Conversation Pieces include: The Royal Family; The 5th Marquess of Salisbury with his brother and sisters; Undergraduates at Worcester Coll., Oxford, 1937 and 1952. Broadcasts on many subjects. Governor, Fedn of British Artists, 1970–. Gold Medal, Paris Salon, 1953, 1965. FRSA 1970. *Address:* 62 Hamilton Terrace, NW8. *T:* 01–286 7030. *Clubs:* Athenæum, Arts, Chelsea Arts.                         *Died* 2 *Feb.* 1984.

**HALLIDAY, Frank Ernest;** author; *b* 10 Feb. 1903; *s* of James Herbert Halliday, Bradford, and Annie Louisa Anderson, Scarborough; *m* 1927, Nancibel Beth Gaunt, *d* of C. F. Gaunt; one *s. Educ:* Giggleswick Sch.; King's Coll., Cambridge. Asst Master, Cheltenham Coll., 1929–48. Resident in St Ives as a writer, 1948–. Shakespeare Lectr, Stratford, Ont., 1964, and for British Coun. in Portugal and Spain, 1965. *Publications:* Five Arts, 1946; Shakespeare and his Critics, 1949 (rev. edn 1958); A Shakespeare Companion, 1952 (rev. edn 1964); Richard Carew of Antony, 1953; The Poetry of Shakespeare's Plays, 1954; The Legend of the Rood, 1955; Shakespeare in his Age, 1956; Shakespeare, A Pictorial Biography, 1956; The Cult of Shakespeare, 1957; A History of Cornwall, 1959; Indifferent Honest, 1960; The Life of Shakespeare, 1961; Unfamiliar Shakespeare, 1962; Meditation at Bolerium (Poems), 1963; A Concise History of England, 1964; A Cultural History of England, 1967, 1981; A Cornish Chronicle, 1967; Dr Johnson and his World, 1968; Chaucer and his World, 1968; Wordsworth and his World, 1969; Thomas Hardy: his life and work, 1972; The Excellency of the English Tongue, 1975; Robert Browning, 1976. *Address:* 12 Barnaloft, St Ives, Cornwall. *T:* Penzance 766650.

*Died* 26 *March* 1982.

**HALLIDAY, Sir George Clifton,** Kt 1967; Consultant Otolaryngologist, Royal Prince Alfred Hospital and Prince Henry Hospital (Consultant Surgeon, since 1960); *b* 22 April 1901; *s* of late Edward James Halliday, NSW; *m* 1927, Hester Judith Macansh; two *s* one *d. Educ:* The King's Sch., Parramatta; St Paul's Coll., Univ. of Sydney. MB, ChM Sydney Univ., 1925; FRCSE 1934; FRACS 1954. Surg., St George Hosp., 1935; Surg., Royal Prince Alfred Hosp., 1936; Lectr in Otolaryngology, Sydney Univ., 1948–61. Served in AAMC, Middle East, 1940–43 (Lt-Col). Patron, Australian Assoc. for Better Hearing. Hon. Mem., RSM, 1970;

Corresp. Fellow, Amer. Laryngological Assoc., 1970; Hon. Fellow, Aust. Med. Assoc., 1971. Hon. Fellow, Sydney Univ., 1985. *Recreations:* tennis, cricket, golf. *Address:* 67 Cranbrook Road, Rose Bay, NSW 2029, Australia. *T:* 327.2280. *Clubs:* Union, Royal Sydney Golf (Sydney). *Died 25 July 1987.*

**HALLIDAY, James;** *see* Symington, David.

**HALLINAN, Sir Charles (Stuart),** Kt 1962; CBE 1954; solicitor; *b* 24 Nov. 1895; *o s* of John Hallinan and Jane Hallinan (*née* Rees); *m* 1921, Theresa Doris Hallinan, JP (*née* Holman) (decd); three *s* one *d*; *m* 1966, Mme Paule Reboul, *er d* of Count Nicholas Debane, and widow of M. Gabriel Reboul. *Educ:* Monkton House Sch., Cardiff; Ratcliffe Coll., near Leicester; also privately. Solicitor, admitted 1919. Served European War, 1914–18, with Inns of Court OTC (Cav.) RFA and RFC; War of 1939–45: comd 21st Bn (Glam.) Home Guard, Lt-Col. Deputy Lord Mayor of Cardiff, 1945–46, 1960–61, 1969–70, 1971–72, Lord Mayor, 1975–76; Past Chm., Cardiff Transport Cttee. Past Chm. and Life Vice-Pres., Wales Conservative Area Council; Patron, Wales Conservative Club Council; Life Vice-Pres. Assoc. of Cons. Clubs, England and Wales (Badge of Honour); Former Mem. Executive Cttee, Nat. Union of Conservative and Unionist Associations, and Mem. various local Cons. organisations; Pres., Cardiff W Young Conservatives; formerly Mem., Cardiff City Council and Alderman; Mem. Grand Council, Primrose League; Ruling Councillor, Ninian Stuart Habitation Primrose League; Pres., Cardiff West Conservative and Unionist Association; Contested (C) Central Div. Cardiff July 1945 and Cardiff W Div. Feb. 1950. Former Nat. Vice-Pres. Royal British Legion; now Patron, Wales. Past Pres., Cardiff and District Law Society; Vice-Pres., Cardiff Law Students Soc.; Hon. Vice-Pres., University Coll., Cardiff Law Soc. Vice-President: Cardiff Business Club; BLESMA; Cardiff Central (OCA) Rifle Club; Past Captain, Cardiff Municipal Golfing Soc. Hon. Mem., Cardiff 2000; Hon. Rotarian, Cardiff. Past Member Court of Governors: Nat. Museum of Wales; Univ. of Wales; Ex-officio Mem., Court. UWIST; Governor, St Illtyd's Coll., Cardiff; Representative Governor for Cardiff and District Law Soc., Univ. of Wales; Chm. of Governors, Monkton House Cardiff Educn Trust Ltd. President: Old Monktonians Cardiff Assoc.; Salisbury Constitutional Club, Newport; Past Pres., S. Wales Kennel Assoc. Patron, S. Wales Br., Soc. for Protection of Unborn Children. KCSG. OStJ. Hon. Citizen, Minneapolis City, Minn. *Address:* Twin Gables, 9 Cefn Coed Road, Cardiff. *T:* Cardiff 751252. *Club:* County (Cardiff).
*Died 24 Feb. 1981.*

**HALLINAN, Sir Eric,** Kt 1955; *b* 27 Oct. 1900; *s* of Edward Hallinan, Midleton, Co. Cork, and Elizabeth, *d* of Maj.-Gen. Sir Thomas Dennehy; *m* 1936, Monica, *d* of George Waters, Midleton, Co. Cork; one *s* one *d*. *Educ:* Downside; Trinity Coll., Dublin. BA, LLB Dublin, 1924; Barrister-at-Law (King's Inns, 1923; Gray's Inn, 1927). Practised at Irish Bar, 1924–29. Colonial Administrative Service, Nigeria, 1930–36; Colonial Legal Service, Nigeria, 1936–40; Attorney-Gen., Bahamas, 1940–44; Puisne Judge: Trinidad, 1944–48; Nigeria, 1948–52; Chief Justice, Cyprus, 1952–57; Chief Justice of The West Indies, 1958–61; Justice of Appeal, Bahamas and Bermuda, 1966–68. LLD (*jure dig.*) Dublin, 1958. *Club:* Royal Commonwealth Society.
*Died 13 April 1985.*

**HALLIWELL, Leslie;** Film Consultant to ITV and Channel Four, since 1987; *b* 23 Feb. 1929; *s* of James and Lily Halliwell; *m* 1958, Ruth (*née* Turner); one *s* (and one step *s* one step *d*). *Educ:* Bolton Sch.; St Catharine's Coll., Cambridge (MA). Journalist, Picturegoer, 1952; Prog. Manager, specialised cinemas in Cambridge, 1953–55; Exec. Trainee, 1956, Administrator of Publicity Div., 1957, Rank Org.; Film Researcher, Granada Television, 1959; Programme Buyer: Southern Television, 1958; ITV, 1968–87; Granada TV, 1960–87; Channel Four, 1981–87. Daily Mail TV columnist, 1987. TV: devised and presented: Home Front, (series), 1982; What the Censor Saw, 1983; Looks Familiar, 1984; The British at War (series), 1984; Americans at War, 1985; Yesterday's Britain, 1985. Author of plays professionally performed (Harrogate, Bristol, Blackpool, Bolton, Hastings, Leeds etc): Make your own Bed, 1957; A Night on the Island, 1960. *Publications:* The Filmgoer's Companion, 1965, 9th edn 1988; The Filmgoer's Book of Quotes, 1973, 2nd edn 1978; (with Graham Murray) The Clapperboard Book of the Cinema, 1975; Halliwell's Movie Quiz, 1977; Halliwell's Film Guide, 1977, 6th edn 1987; Mountain of Dreams, 1977; Halliwell's Teleguide, 1979, revd edn (with Philip Purser) as Halliwell's Television Companion, 1982, revd edn 1986; Halliwell's Hundred, 1982; The Ghost of Sherlock Holmes (short stories), 1983; Seats in All Parts (autobiog.), 1985; Halliwell's Harvest, 1986; The Dead that Walk, 1986; Return to Shangri-La (novel), 1987; A Demon Close Behind (short stories), 1987; Double Take and Fade Away, 1987; A Demon on the Stair (short stories), 1988; contrib. Spectator, New Statesman, TLS, Sight and Sound, Photoplay, Variety, Television Radio Age, Television Today. *Recreations:*

country driving, travel, collecting, walking. *Address:* Clovelly, 26 Atwood Avenue, Richmond, Surrey. *Died 21 Jan. 1989.*

**HALLOWS, Ralph Ingham,** CMG 1973; MBE 1947; retired from Bank of England, 1973; *b* 4 May 1913; *s* of Ralph Watson Hallows, MA Cantab, TD, and Muriel Milnes-Smith; *m* 1939, Anne Lorna Bond (*d* 1989); one *s* one *d*. *Educ:* Berkhamsted Sch. Indian Police Service, 1932; Indian Political Service, 1937; India Office/Commonwealth Relations Office, 1947; Kuwait Oil Co., 1948; Bank of England, 1954. Specialist Advr to Select Cttee on Overseas Develt, 1974. *Recreations:* golf, fishing, sailing. *Address:* Apple Tree Cottage, Thursley Road, Elstead, Surrey GU8 6DG. *T:* Elstead 702284. *Died 27 March 1990.*

**HALLSTEIN, Walter;** (Professor and Doctor); Grand Cross of Merit, Federal Republic of Germany; President, Commission of the European Economic Community, 1958–67; President, European Movement (international), 1968–74; *b* Mainz, Germany, 17 Nov. 1901; *s* of Jakob Hallstein and Anna Hallstein (*née* Geibel); unmarried. *Educ:* Humanistisches Gymnasium, Darmstadt and Mainz; Bonn, Munich and Berlin Univs. Doctorate of Law, University of Berlin. Prof., Rostock Univ., 1930–41; Prof., 1941–, Dir, 1941–44, Inst. for Comparative Law, Frankfort; Rector, Frankfort Univ., 1946–48; Visiting Prof., Georgetown Univ., Washington, DC, USA; Pres., German Unesco activities, 1949–50; Head, German Schumanplan delegn, Paris, 1950; Staatssekretär: Federal Chancellery, 1950; German Foreign Office, 1951–58. Mem., Bundestag, 1969–72. Adviser, Action Cttee for the United States of Europe, 1969–. Holds eighteen hon. doctorates. Grand Cross of 26 foreign orders, etc.; International Charlemagne Prize of City of Aix-la-Chapelle, 1961; Robert Schuman Prize, 1969. *Publications:* Die Aktienrechte der Gegenwart, 1931; Die Berichtigung des Gesellschaftskapitals, 1942; Wiederherstellung des Privatrechts, 1946; Wissenschaft und Politik, 1949; United Europe—Challenge and Opportunity, 1962; Der unvollendete Bundesstaat, 1969; Europe in the Making, 1972; Die Europäische Gemeinschaft, 1973. *Recreation:* travelling. *Address:* 5439 Rennerod/ Oberwesterwaldkreis, Germany; (office) D7 Stuttgart 1, Klopstockstrasse 29, Germany. *Died 29 March 1982.*

**HALSEY, Reginald John,** CMG 1957; BScEng; FCGI; DIC; CEng; FIEE; *b* 16 Dec. 1902; *s* of Edwin J. Halsey, Portsmouth; *m* 1930, Edna May Tonkin; one *d*. *Educ:* Secondary Sch. and HM Dockyard Sch., Portsmouth; Imperial Coll. of Science and Technology. Entered Post Office, 1927, and engaged on research in telecommunications; Asst Engineer-in-Chief, 1953 58; Dir of Research, 1958–64. Dir, Cable and Wireless Ltd, 1959–73. Chm., Adv. Cttee on Telecommunications, CGLI, 1957–. Hon. Mem., CGLI, 1972. Fellow of Imperial Coll., 1965. *Publications:* many scientific and engineering. *Address:* 11 High Meads, Wheat-hampstead, Herts AL4 SAE. *Died 13 Jan. 1982.*

**HAMER, John,** MBE 1944; VMH 1975; Secretary, Royal Horticultural Society, 1962–75; *b* 14 June 1910; 2nd *s* of late John and Katherine Hamer; *m* 1st, 1940, Marjorie Agnes (*d* 1970), *e d* of late Major A. H. Martin, RE and E. Martin; one *s* one *d*; 2nd, 1980, Joan Edith MacKinlay (*née* Prior) (*d* 1988). *Educ:* University of Leeds (BA, DipEd). Commnd, The Loyal Regt, 1930. Educn Service, 1933–38. Attached S Lancs Regt, 1938–39; War Service, 1939–46 (despatches, MBE): The Loyal Regt, Hertfordshire Regt, Royal Tank Regt; SO2, 20 British Mil. Mission (Free French), DAQMG 36 Brick (18 DLI) Combined Ops, ME, Italy, NW Europe, 1943–45; Lieut-Col, Comd 36 Brick (18 DLI), AAQMG Lille Area, 1945; Food Controller, Price Controller, Controller of Supplies, Singapore, 1945. Joined Malayan Civil Service, 1946: District Officer, Jasin, Malacca, 1948, Klang, Selangor, 1952; British Adviser, Perlis, 1955; Deputy Chm., Rural Industrial Development Authority, Federation of Malaya, 1957; Ministry of Agriculture, 1958; State Sec., Penang, 1958–61. Joined Royal Horticultural Soc., 1961. *Recreation:* gardening. *Address:* Wildacres, Bashurst Copse, Itchingfield, West Sussex RH13 7NZ. *T:* Slinfold 790467.
*Died 28 Feb. 1990.*

**HAMES, Jack Hamawi,** QC 1972; a Recorder of the Crown Court, since 1977; *b* 15 June 1920; *s* of Elie and Edmee Hamawi; *m* 1949, Beryl Julia Cooper; two *s*. *Educ:* English School, Cairo; Queens' Coll., Cambridge (MA, LLM). Called to Bar, Inner Temple, 1948, Bencher, 1979, Master of the Archives, 1986. Vice-Chm. of Governors, John Ruskin Sch., Croydon. *Publication:* contrib. to Solicitors' Jl. *Recreations:* squash, tennis, gardening, painting, music, poetry, history, literature. *Address:* 18 Castlemaine Avenue, South Croydon CR2 7HQ. *T:* 01–688 6326; 10 Old Square, Lincoln's Inn, WC2A 3SO. *T:* 01–405 0758. *Clubs:* Warlingham Sports (former Chm.), Warlingham Squash (former Chm.).
*Died 14 Sept. 1988.*

**HAMILTON OF DALZELL,** 3rd Baron, *cr* 1886; **John d'Henin Hamilton,** GCVO 1987 (KCVO 1981); MC 1945; JP; Lord Lieutenant of Surrey, 1973–86 (Vice-Lieutenant, 1957–73); President, National Association of Probation Officers, 1964–74; a Lord-in-Waiting to the Queen, 1968–81; *b* 1 May 1911; *s* of late Major Hon. Leslie d'Henin Hamilton, MVO, and Amy Cecile, *e d* of late Col Horace Ricardo, CVO; S uncle, 1952; m 1935, Rosemary Olive, d of late Major Hon. Sir John Coke, KCVO; two s one d. Educ: Eton; RMC, Sandhurst. Coldstream Guards, 1931–37 and 1939–45 (Major). Min. of Agriculture's Liaison Officer in South-East, 1960–64. Mem., Council on Tribunals, 1964–72; Chm., Lord Chancellor's Adv. Cttee on Legal Aid, 1972–79. Chairman: Surrey Agricultural Exec. Cttee, 1958–68; Surrey Council of Social Service, 1960–73; Guildford Bench, 1968–78; Guildford Cathedral Council, 1958–69. DL Surrey, 1957; JP Guildford, 1957. KStJ 1973. Heir: s Hon. James Leslie Hamilton [b 11 Feb. 1938; m 1967, Corinna, yr d of late Sir Pierson Dixon, GCMG, CB and Lady Dixon; four s]. Address: Garden Cottage, Snowdenham House, Bramley, Guildford, Surrey GU5 0DB. T: Guildford 892002.

*Died 31 Jan. 1990.*

**HAMILTON, Sir Bruce S.;** see Stirling-Hamilton.

**HAMILTON, Sir (Charles) Denis,** Kt 1976; DSO 1944; TD 1975; Editor-in-Chief, Times Newspapers Ltd, 1967–81 (Chief Executive, 1967–70, Chairman, 1971–80); Chairman, Reuters Ltd, 1979–85; Director, Standard Chartered Bank, 1982–87; b 6 Dec. 1918; er s of Charles and Helena Hamilton; m 1939, Olive, author, yr d of Thomas Hedley Wanless and Mary Anne Wanless; four s. Educ: Middlesbrough High Sch. Editorial Staff: Evening Gazette, Middlesbrough, 1937–38; Evening Chronicle, Newcastle, 1938–39; Editorial Asst to Viscount Kemsley, 1946–50; Editorial Dir, Kemsley (now Thomson) Newspapers, 1950–67; Editor of the Sunday Times, 1961–67; Chm., Times Newspapers Hldgs, 1980–81. Director: Evening Gazette Ltd, 1960–82; Newcastle Chronicle and Journal Ltd, 1960–82; Internat. Thomson Orgn Plc (formerly Kemsley Newspapers, Thomson Newspapers, Thomson British Holdings), 1950–83. Chm., British Cttee, 1972–78, first Pres., 1978–83, Internat. Press Inst.; Pres., Commonwealth Press Union, 1981–83. Member: Council, Newspaper Publishers' Association, 1950–80; Press Council, 1959–81; National Council for the Training of Journalists (Chm., 1957); BOTB, 1976–79; British Library Bd, 1975–87; IBA, 1981–84; Chm., British Museum Publications Ltd; Trustee: British Museum, 1969–; Henry Moore Foundn, 1980–; Visnews, 1981–85; Vice-Pres., Exec. Cttee, GB-China Centre, 1986– (Vice Chm., 1981–84; Chm., 1984–86); Governor, British Inst. Florence, 1974–. Joint Sponsor of exhibitions: Tutankhamun, BM, 1972; China, RA, 1973; 1776–US Bicentennial, Nat. Maritime Mus., 1976; Gold of Eldorado, RA, 1978; Vikings, BM, 1980. Served War of 1939–45, TA, Durham Light Infantry; Lt-Col comdg 11th Bn Durham LI and 7th Bn Duke of Wellington's Regt. Hon. DLitt: Southampton, 1975; City, 1977; Hon. DCL Newcastle upon Tyne 1979. Grande Officiale, Order of Merit (Italy), 1976. Publications: Jt Editor, Kemsley Manual of Journalism, 1952; Who is to own the British Press (Haldane Meml Lecture), 1976; posthumous publication: Editor-in-Chief (autobiog.), 1989. Recreation: military history. Address: 78A Ashley Gardens, Thirleby Road, SW1P 1HG. T: 01–828 0410. Clubs: Garrick, Royal Automobile, Grillions. *Died 7 April 1988.*

**HAMILTON, Cyril Robert Parke,** CMG 1972; Director: Rank Organisation and subsidiary companies, 1963–77; A. Kershaw & Sons Ltd, 1966–77; Rank Xerox Ltd, 1967–77; b 4 Aug. 1903; s of Alfred Parke and Annie Hamilton; m 1st, 1929, Cecily May Stearn (d 1966); one s one d; 2nd, 1971, Betty Emily Brand. Educ: High Sch., Ilford; King's Coll., London Univ. Entered Bank of England, 1923, and retired as Deputy Chief Cashier, 1963, after career mainly concerned with internat. financial negotiations and Exchange Control. Vice-Chm., Standard and Chartered Banking Gp Ltd, 1969–74; Dep. Chm., Standard Bank, 1963–74; Director: Standard Bank of SA, 1963–74; Midland and International Banks, 1964–74; Banque Belge d'Afrique, 1969–74; Chairman: Malta International Banking Corp, 1969–74; Tozer Standard and Chartered Ltd, 1973–74. Recreations: golf, gardening. Address: Peat Moor, Harborough Hill, Pulborough, West Sussex RH20 2PR. T: West Chiltington (07983) 2171. Clubs: Brooks's, MCC.

*Died 6 Sept. 1990.*

**HAMILTON, Sir Denis;** see Hamilton, Sir C. D.

**HAMILTON, Maj.-Gen. Godfrey John,** CB 1966; CBE 1959 (OBE 1956); DSO 1935; b 31 March 1912; s of late Lieut-Col F. A. Hamilton, OBE, DL, JP, and of Mrs Hamilton, Osbaston, Monmouth; m 1st, 1937, Mary Penelope Colthurst; one d; 2nd, 1942, Mary Margaret Kaye, FRSL; two d. Educ: Radley Coll.; RMC, Sandhurst. Commnd, 1932; served in Guides Infantry, IA, 1932–48 (despatches): India, Burma and Malaya; Royal Irish Fusiliers (despatches twice): Palestine, Egypt, Germany, Korea, Kenya, N Ireland, Berlin. Chief, Joint Services Liaison Organization, BAOR, 1963–66. Retired, 1967. Recreations: fishing, painting, gardening. Address: The Old House, Boreham Street, near Hailsham, East Sussex. Club: Army and Navy.

*Died 21 Dec. 1985.*

**HAMILTON, Hamish;** Founder and President, Hamish Hamilton Ltd, Publishers (Chairman, 1931–81, and Managing Director,

1931–72); b Indianapolis, 15 Nov. 1900; o s of James Neilson Hamilton, and Alice van Valkenburg; m 1st, 1929, Jean Forbes-Robertson (marr. diss. 1933), d of Sir Johnston and Lady Forbes-Robertson; 2nd, 1940, Countess Yvonne Pallavicino, of Rome; one s. Educ: Rugby; Caius Coll., Cambridge (Medical Student, 1919). MA (Hons Mod. Langs), LLB. Travelled in USA, 1922–23; called to Bar (Inner Temple), 1925; London Manager Harper and Brothers, Publishers, 1926; founded Hamish Hamilton Ltd, 1931; served in Army, 1939–41 (Holland and France, 1940); seconded to American Division, Ministry of Information, 1941–45; Hon. Sec. Kinsmen Trust, 1942–56; founded Kathleen Ferrier Meml Scholarships, 1954; a Governor, the Old Vic, 1945–75; Member Council, English-Speaking Union; a Governor, British Institute, Florence. Chevalier de la Légion d'Honneur, 1953; Grande Ufficiale, Order of Merit (Italy), 1976. Publications: articles on publishing, Anglo-American relations and sport. Commemorative Anthologies: Decade, 1941, Majority, 1952. Recreations: music, the theatre, travel; formerly rowing (spare stroke Cambridge Eight, 1921; stroked Winning Crews Grand Challenge Cup, Henley, 1927 and 1928, and Olympic Eight, Amsterdam, 1928 (silver medal)), ski-ing, flying, squash. Clubs: Garrick; Leander. *Died 24 May 1988.*

**HAMILTON, Iain (Bertram);** author and journalist; b 3 Feb. 1920; s of John Hamilton and Margaret Laird MacEachran; m 1944, Jean Campbell Fisher; one s one d. Educ: Paisley Grammar Sch. Editorial staff: Daily Record, 1944–45; The Guardian, 1945–52; The Spectator, 1952; Asst Editor, 1953, Associate Editor, 1954–56, The Spectator; Editor-in-Chief, 1957, Editorial Director, The Hutchinson group of publishing cos, 1958–62; Editor of The Spectator, 1962–63. Man. Dir, Kern House Enterprises Ltd, 1970–75; Dir of Studies, Inst. for Study of Conflict, 1975–77; Founder Mem., British Irish Assoc. Has contrib. prose and verse to Radio, Daily Telegraph, Encounter, Illustrated London News, Interplay, Country Life, The Times Educational and Literary Supplements, Spectator, World Review, Twentieth Century, Scots Review and other periodicals. Publications: Scotland the Brave, 1957; The Foster Gang (with H. J. May), 1966; Embarkation for Cythera, 1974; The Kerry Kyle, 1980; Koestler: a Biography, 1982; play: The Snarling Beggar, 1951. Address: 105 Salisbury Road, Leigh-on-Sea, Essex SS9 2JN. T: Southend-on-Sea 77634.

*Died 15 July 1986.*

**HAMILTON, Maj.-Gen. John Robert Crosse,** CB 1957; CBE 1950; DSO 1944; late RE; Fellow, Churchill College, Cambridge (Bursar, 1959–72); b 1 April 1906; s of late Major J. A. C. Hamilton, Fyne Court, Bridgwater, Somerset; m 1938, Rosamond Budd, d of late Richard Hancock, Hong Kong; one s one d. Educ: Radley; Royal Military Academy; Caius Coll., Cambridge. idc 1950. 2nd Lieut RE, 1925. Served War of 1939–45 (DSO), France, Belgium, Germany; acting Brig., 1947; Lt-Col 1948; Col, 1950; Maj.-Gen., 1956. idc 1950. Chief of Staff, HQ Malaya Command, 1955–56; Dir of Military Operations, War Office, 1956–59; retired, 1959. Col Comdt, RE, 1962–71. Address: Peas Hill End, Shipton Gorge, Bridport, Dorset DT6 4LT. Club: Naval and Military.

*Died 8 July 1985.*

**HAMILTON, Prof. Patrick John Sinclair;** Professor of Community Health, University of London, since 1982; b 28 July 1934; s of Rev. John Edmund Hamilton, MC, BA, and Hon. Lilias Hamilton (née Maclay); m 1972, Fiona Elizabeth Hunter; one s one d. Educ: Winchester Coll.; Christ's Coll., Cambridge; Edinburgh Univ.; London Univ. BA Cantab; MB, ChB Edinburgh; DPH, DTM&H London. FFCM; FRCP 1986. National Service, RAMC Bde of Gurkhas, 1960–62. Lecturer, Makerere University Coll. Med. Sch., Uganda, 1963–65; Lectr/Sen. Lectr, Dept of Medical Statistics and Epidemiology, London School of Hygiene and Tropical Medicine, 1967–74; Dir, Pan American Health Organization/WHO Caribbean Epidemiology Centre, Port of Spain, Trinidad, 1975–82. Member, Director General WHO Independent Commn on Onchocerciasis Control Programme, 1979–81. Publications: on epidemiology and control of infectious and non-infectious disease and tropical medicine. Recreations: riding, walking, collecting medical history. Address: 6 Redburn Street, SW3. T: 01–351 3988.

*Died 12 June 1988.*

**HAMILTON, Captain Sir Robert William Stirling-,** 12th Bt, cr 1673; JP, DL; RN, retired; b 5 April 1903; s of Sir William Stirling-Hamilton, 11th Bt, and late Mabel Mary, d of Maj.-Gen. Tyndall; S father 1946; m 1930, Eileen, d of late Rt Rev. H. K. Southwell, CMG; one s two d. Educ: RNC, Dartmouth. Commodore, RN Barracks, Portsmouth, 1952–54, retired 1954. DL, Sussex, 1970–. Heir: s Bruce Stirling-Hamilton [b 5 Aug. 1940; m 1968, Stephanie, e d of Dr William Campbell; one s one d]. Address: Puriton Lodge, Hambrook, Chichester, West Sussex. T: West Ashling 363.

*Died 14 Feb. 1982.*

**HAMILTON, Walter,** MA; Hon. DLitt Durham; FRSL; Master of Magdalene College, Cambridge, 1967–78, Hon. Fellow, since 1978; b 10 Feb. 1908; s of late Walter George Hamilton and Caroline

Mary Stiff; *m* 1951, Jane Elizabeth, *o d* of Sir John Burrows; three *s* one *d*. *Educ:* St Dunstan's Coll.; Trinity Coll., Cambridge (Scholar). 1st Class Classical Tripos, Part I, 1927; Part II, 1929; Craven Scholar, 1927; Chancellor's Classical Medallist, 1928; Porson Prizeman and Craven Student, 1929. Fellow of Trinity Coll., 1931–35; Asst Lecturer, University of Manchester, 1931–32; Asst Master, Eton Coll., 1933–46, Master in Coll., 1937–46, Fellow, 1972–81, Steward of the Courts, 1987–; Fellow and Classical Lecturer, Trinity Coll., 1946–50; Tutor, 1947–50; University Lectr in Classics, 1947–50; Head Master: of Westminster Sch., 1950–57; of Rugby Sch., 1957–66. Editor, Classical Quarterly, 1946–47. Chairman: Scholarship Cttee, Lord Kitchener Nat. Meml Fund, 1953–59, Exec. Cttee, 1967–77; Headmasters' Conference, 1955, 1956, 1965, 1966; Governing Body, Shrewsbury Sch., 1968–81; Governing Bodies Assoc., 1969–74. Member: Exec. Cttee, British Council, 1958–70; Council of Senate of Cambridge Univ., 1969–74. *Publications:* A new translation of Plato's Symposium, 1951; Plato's Gorgias, 1960; Plato's Phaedrus and Letters VII and VIII, 1973; (with A. F. Wallace-Hadrill) Ammianus Marcellinus, the later Roman Empire, 1986; contributions to Classical Quarterly, Classical Review, etc. *Address:* 6 Hedgerley Close, Cambridge. *T:* Cambridge 63202. *Died 8 Feb. 1988.*

**HAMILTON, William Aitken Brown,** CMG 1950; *b* 3 June 1909; *e s* of Brown Hamilton, Milltimber, Aberdeenshire; *m* 1936, Barbara, *e d* of S. T. Gano, Belmont, Massachusetts, USA; one *s* (and one *s* decd). *Educ:* Aberdeen Grammar Sch.; Aberdeen Univ. 1st Class Hons Classics. Administrative Civil Service, Board of Education, 1931; Principal, 1936; Joint Sec., Athlone Cttee on Nursing Services, 1937–39; Ministry of Food, 1939–44; Asst Sec., 1943; Ministry of Education, 1944–49; Dir of Establishments and Under-Sec., 1946; Dir of Establishments and Asst Under-Sec. of State, CRO, 1949; Dir of Personnel, UN, 1959–62; Asst Under-Sec. of State, Commonwealth Office, 1962–67, retired. *Address:* Bonds, Bullingstone Lane, Speldhurst, Kent TN3 0JY. *T:* Langton 3164. *Died 14 May 1982.*

**HAMILTON STUBBER, Lt-Col John Henry;** Lord Lieutenant of Co. Tyrone, since 1979; *b* 1921; *o s* of late Major Robert Hamilton Stubber, DSO, and Lady Mabel Hamilton Stubber, MBE, *d* of 4th Earl of Erne and *widow* of Captain Lord Hugh William Grosvenor; *m* 1953, Fiona Patricia, *d* of late Captain G. W. Breitmeyer, Didmarton, Glos; four *s*. *Educ:* Eton; Trinity Coll., Cambridge. Joined Coldstream Guards, 1941; served France and Germany, 1941–45 (despatches 1945); Captain 1944, retired 1948; Major, Ulster Defence Regt, 1970, retired 1978 with rank of Hon. Brevet Lt-Col. Chairman, Dungannon DC, 1973–79. Formerly JP Gloucestershire. DL 1971, High Sheriff 1972, Co. Tyrone. CStJ 1981. *Address:* Aughentaine, Fivemiletown, Co. Tyrone BT75 0LH, Northern Ireland. *T:* Fivemiletown 271. *Clubs:* Turf, MCC; Ulster (Belfast); Kildare Street and University (Dublin). *Died 3 Oct. 1986.*

**HAMMER, Armand,** MD; Chairman of Board and Chief Executive Officer, Occidental Petroleum Corp., Los Angeles, since 1957; *b* 21 May 1898; *s* of Dr Julius Hammer and Rose Robinson; *m* 1st, 1927, Olga von Root (marr. diss.); one *s*; 2nd, 1943, Angela Zevely (marr. diss.); 3rd, 1956, Frances Barrett (*d* 1989); one *s*. *Educ:* Columbia University (BS 1919; MD 1921, Coll. of Physicians and Surgeons). President: Allied Amer. Corp., 1923–25; A. Hammer Pencil Co., 1925–30; Hammer Galleries Inc., 1930–; J. W. Dant Distilling Co., 1943–54; Pres. and Chm. Board, Mutual Broadcasting System, NY, 1957–58; Chm., M. Knoedler & Co. Inc., 1972–; Mem., Nat. Petroleum Council, 1968–; Member, Board of Directors: Canadian Occidental Petroleum Ltd, 1964–; Cities Service Co., 1982–; Southland Corp., 1983–; Amer. Petroleum Inst., 1975; Founder and Hon. Chm., Armand Hammer Coll. of American West, New Mexico, 1981–; Mem. Court, Mary Rose Trust, 1981–; Chm., Internat. Council, Shakespeare Globe Centre (and Chm., N Amer. Div.), 1982–. Hon. Corresp. Mem., RA, 1975–; Hon. Mem., Royal Scottish Acad. Hon LLD: Pepperdine, 1978; Southeastern, 1978; Columbia, 1978; Aix-en-Provence, 1981; Hon. LHD Colorado, 1979; Hon. DPS Salem, 1979; Hon. DSc S Carolina, 1983. Comdr, Order of Crown, Belgium, 1969; Comdr, Order of Andres Bellos, Venezuela, 1975; Order of Aztec Eagle, Mexico, 1977; Royal Order of Polar Star, Sweden, 1979; Grand Officer, Order of Merit, Italy, 1981; Kt Comdr's Cross, Austria, 1982; Comdr, French Legion of Honour, 1983 (Officer, 1978); numerous awards and distinctions from USA bodies. *Publications:* Quest of the Romanoff Treasure, 1932; (with N. Lyndon) Hammer: witness to history (autobiog.), 1987; *relevant publications:* The Remarkable Life of Dr Armand Hammer, by Robert Considine, 1975, UK edn, Larger than Life, 1976, numerous foreign edns; The World of Armand Hammer, by John Bryson, 1985. *Address:* Occidental Petroleum Corporation, 10889 Wilshire Boulevard, Los Angeles, Calif 90024, USA. *T:* (office) (213) 879 1700. *Clubs:* Los Angeles Petroleum; Jockey (New York). *Died 10 Dec. 1990.*

**HAMMOND, Maj.-Gen. Arthur Verney,** CB 1944; DSO 1943; Indian Army, retired; *b* 16 Oct. 1892; *s* of late Col. Sir Arthur G. Hammond,

VC, KCB, DSO; *m* 1919, Mary Ellen Eaton (marr. diss. 1946); two *d*; *m* 1947, E. Boyes Cooper. *Educ:* Streete Court; Wellington Coll.; Royal Military College, Sandhurst. 2nd Lieut 1911, attached R West Kent Regt; Joined QVO Corps of Guides (Cavalry), 1912; European War, 1914–18 (despatches); NW Persia, 1920–21; Staff Coll., Quetta, 1925–26; Brigade Major, 1928–32; commanded The Guides Cavalry, 1937–39; War Office, London, 1939–40 (Col on the Staff); Brigade Comd 1941–43; served in Burma, 1942–43 (DSO); Maj.-Gen. 1942; ADC to the King, 1942–43; Comdg Lucknow District, 1944–45; retired, 1947. *Died 15 Jan. 1982.*

**HAMMOND, Stanley Alfred Andrew,** CMG 1943; Adviser on Establishment, Organization and Training, Barbados, 1959–64, retired; *b* 24 Oct. 1898; *s* of Alfred Gauntlett Hammond; *m* 1946, Adèle Alice Viola, *d* of William Wallace Cathcart Dunlop. *Educ:* Bancrofts Sch.; Trinity Coll. Oxford. 2nd Lieut RE 1917; Superintendent of Education, Nigeria, 1922; Dir of Education, Jamaica, 1928; Senior Education Commissioner, West Indies, 1936; Educn Adviser to Comptroller for Development and Welfare, West Indies, 1940; Chief Adviser Development and Welfare Organization, West Indies, 1948. Commissioner, Enquiry into Organization of the Civil Service, Leeward Islands, 1951. Adviser with special Duties, Development and Welfare Organisation, West Indies, 1950–53; retired, 1953. Dir of Training, Barbados, 1956. *Address:* c/o Midland Bank Ltd, 52 Oxford Street, W1A 1EG; Little Edgehill, St Thomas, Barbados, West Indies.
*Died 10 Sept. 1981.*

**HAMPER, Rev. Richard John,** JP; General Secretary, Free Church Federal Council, since 1979; *b* 18 Nov. 1928; *s* of Albert Thomas Hamper and Margaret Catherine Hamper; *m* 1954, Madeline Lewis; two *s* two *d*. *Educ:* Price's Sch., Fareham, Hants; Oxford Univ. (MA). Baptist Minister: Botley and Eynsham, Oxon, 1952–56; Bilborough, Nottingham, 1956–61; Queen's Road, Coventry, 1961–79. Free Church Adviser, Central Indep. Television (formerly ATV), 1970–. JP Inner London Juvenile Bench, 1969–. *Recreations:* fell walking, gardening. *Address:* Free Church Federal Council, 27 Tavistock Square, WC1H 9HH. *T:* 01-387 8413.
*Died 25 Feb. 1986.*

**HAMPSHIRE, Sir (George) Peter,** KCMG 1967 (CMG 1963); HM Diplomatic Service, retired; *b* 1 Dec. 1912; *s* of late G. N. Hampshire and Marie Hampshire (*née* West); *m* 1956, Eve Buhler (*née* Rowell); no *c*. *Educ:* Repton; Oriel Coll., Oxford. Apptd to War Office, 1935; Control Office for Germany and Austria and Foreign Office (German Section), 1946–48; Office of UK High Commission, Ottawa, 1948–51; UK Dep. High Comr, Dacca, 1953–55; IDC, 1956; Counsellor, British Embassy, Buenos Aires, 1957–60; Asst Under-Sec. of State, CRO, 1961–64, DSAO, 1965–66; High Comr, Trinidad and Tobago, 1966–70. Mem., Chairmen's Panel, Civil Service Selection Bd, 1970–77. *Address:* Old School House, Risby, Bury St Edmunds, Suffolk. *T:* Bury St Edmunds 810245. *Club:* Travellers'.
*Died 4 July 1981.*

**HAMSON, Prof. Charles John,** QC 1975; Professor of Comparative Law, University of Cambridge, 1953–73; Fellow of Trinity College, since 1934; Barrister-at-Law, Gray's Inn, Bencher, 1956, Treasurer, 1975; Correspondent, Institut de France (Acad. Sci. Mor. et Pol.), since 1961; Doctor *hc* Universities of Grenoble, Nancy, Poitiers, Bordeaux, Brussels, Montpellier, Strasbourg; Hon. Fellow, St Edmund's House, Cambridge, 1976; Chevalier de la Légion d'Honneur; *b* 23 Nov. 1905; *er s* of Charles Edward Hamson (formerly of Constantinople), and of Thérèse Boudon; *m* 1933, Isabella (*d* 1978), *y d* of Duncan Drummond and Grace Gardiner of Auchterarder; one *d*. *Educ:* Downside; Trinity Coll., Cambridge. Entrance and Sen. Scholar in Classics; Classical Tripos Part I 1925, Part II 1927 (distinction); Capt. CU Epée Team, 1928; Davison Scholar, Harvard Law Sch., 1928–29; Linthicum Foundation Prize (North-western Univ.) 1929; Yorke Prize, 1932; LLB 1934; LLM 1935. Asst Lecturer, 1932, Lecturer, 1934, Reader in Comparative Law, 1949; Chm. Faculty Board of Law, 1954–57. Editor, Cambridge Law Jl, 1955–74; Univ. Press Syndic, 1955–69; Library Syndic, 1966–73; Gen. Bd, 1966–69. President: Internat. Acad. of Comparative Law, 1966–79; CU Catholic Assoc., 1964–76; St Edmund's Assoc., 1977–81. Served War of 1939–45; commissioned in Army, 1940; detached for service with SOE; Battle of Crete, 1941; POW Germany, 1941–45. Hamlyn Lectures on Conseil d'Etat, 1954; Visiting Professor: University of Michigan Law Sch. (Ann Arbor), 1957; Paris Faculty of Law, 1959; Univ. of Pennsylvania, 1964; Auckland Univ., 1967; professeur associé, Paris II, 1973–74; Sherill Lectr, Yale Law Sch., 1960; Wiener-Anspach Inaugural Lectr, Univ. of Brussels, 1978. *Address:* Trinity College, Cambridge. *T:* Cambridge 338525. *Died 14 Nov. 1987.*

**HANBURY TENISON, Marika;** Cookery Editor, Sunday Telegraph, since 1967; Deputy Chairman, Sea Fish Industry Authority, since 1981; *b* 9 Sept. 1938; *d* of Lt-Col John Montgomerie Hopkinson and Alexandra Martha Ingeborg Pauline Stiernstedt; *m* 1959, Airling Robin Hanbury-Tenison, OBE, FLS, FRGS; one *s* one *d*. *Educ:*

Francis Holland Sch. for Girls. Freelance journalist, 1966–; Cookery Editor: The Cornish Guardian, 1966–67; Nova, 1967–68; The Spectator, 1977–79. Cornish Food Writer of the Year, 1981. *Publications:* Soups and Hors d'Oeuvres, 1969; Deep Freeze Cookery, 1970; Left Over for Tomorrow, 1971; Marika Hanbury Tenison's Menus for Each Month of the Year, 1972; For Better, For Worse, 1972; Eat Well and Be Slim, 1974; A Slice of Spice, 1974; Best of British Cooking, 1977; Recipes from a Country Kitchen, 1978; The Magimix and Food Processor Cookery Book, 1978; New Fish Cookery, 1979; Teach Yourself Deep Freezing, 1979; Cooking with Vegetables, 1980 (André Simon Meml Fund Book Award); The Cook's Handbook, 1980; Book of Afternoon Tea, 1980; Sunday Telegraph Cook Book, 1980; The Princess and the Unicorn, 1981; Magimix Cookery, 1982; contribs to nat. newspapers, many journals and magazines. *Recreations:* gardening, cooking, travelling, the pursuit of unicorns. *Address:* Maidenwell, Cardinham, near Bodmin, Cornwall PL30 4DW. *T:* Cardinham 224. *Clubs:* Annabel's, Harry's Bar. *Died 24 Oct.* 1982.

**HANCOCK, Lt-Col Sir Cyril (Percy),** KCIE 1946 (CIE 1941); OBE 1930; MC; *b* 18 Sept. 1896; *m* Joyce (*d* 1982), *d* of F. R. Hemingway, ICS; two *s* one *d* (and one *s* decd). *Educ:* Wellington Coll.; RMC, Sandhurst. Commd Indian Army, 114th Mahrattas, 1914; ADC to GOC 1st Corps MEF (Gen. Sir Alexander Cobbe, VC), 1918; GSO 3 at GHQ Baghdad, 1919; transf. to Bombay Political Dept, 1920; Asst Pvte Sec. to Governor of Bombay (Lord Lloyd), 1921; Asst Pvte Sec. to Viceroy (Lord Reading), 1923; Sec., Rajkot Pol. Agency, 1925; Sec. to Resident for Rajputana, 1929; Prime Minister, Bharatpur State, Rajputana, 1932; Dep. Sec., Govt of India (Pol. Dept, i/c War Br.), 1939; Resident: Eastern States, Calcutta, 1941; Western India States and Baroda Rajkot, 1943. *Address:* Woodhayes, Firgrove Road, Yateley, Hants GU17 7NH. *T:* Yateley (0252) 873240. *Club:* Indian Cricket. *Died 6 Nov.* 1990.

**HANCOCK, Prof. Sir (William) Keith,** KBE 1965; Kt 1953; MA; FBA 1950; Emeritus Professor and Hon. Fellow; Professor of History, Australian National University, Canberra, 1957–65; *b* Melbourne, 26 June 1898; *s* of Archdeacon William Hancock, MA; *m* 1st, 1925, Theaden Brocklebank (*d* 1960); 2nd, 1961, Marjorie Eyre. Fellow of All Souls Coll., Oxford, 1924–30; Prof. of Modern History in the University of Adelaide, 1924–33; Prof. of History, Birmingham Univ., 1934–44; Chichele Prof. of Economic History, University of Oxford 1944–49; Dir, Institute of Commonwealth Studies, and Prof. of British Commonwealth Affairs in the University of London, 1949–56; Dir of the Research Sch. of Social Sciences, Australian National Univ., 1957–61; appointed to War Cabinet Offices as Supervisor of Civil Histories, 1941, thereafter editor of series. Fellow: Churchill Coll., Cambridge, 1964; St John's Coll., Cambridge, 1971–72. Hon. Fellow, Balliol Coll., Oxford; Corresp. Mem., Sch. of Oriental and African Studies. FAHA (1st Pres.) 1969. Hon. DLitt (Rhodes, Cambridge, Birmingham, Oxford, Cape Town, Melbourne, ANU, Adelaide, WA). Foreign Hon. Member: American Historical Association; American Academy of Arts and Sciences. Order of Merit of Republic of Italy. *Publications:* Ricasoli, 1926; Australia, 1930; Survey of British Commonwealth Affairs, 1937, 1940, and 1942; Politics in Pitcairn, 1947; (with M. M. Gowing) British War Economy, 1949; Country and Calling, 1954; War and Peace in this Century, 1961; Smuts: The Sanguine Years, 1870–1919, Vol. I, 1962; The Fields of Force, 1919–1950, Vol. II, 1968; Discovering Monaro, 1972; Professing History, 1976; Perspective in History, 1982; Testimony, 1985. *Address:* 49 Gellibrand Street, Campbell, Canberra, ACT 2601, Australia. *Club:* Athenæum. *Died 13 Aug.* 1988.

**HANDLEY, Richard Sampson,** OBE 1946; Surgeon, The Middlesex Hospital, W1, 1946, Surgeon Emeritus, 1974, retired; *b* 2 May 1909; *e s* of late W. Sampson Handley; *m* 1st, 1942, Joan (*d* 1975), *d* of Dr Cyril Gray, Newcastle upon Tyne; one *s* one *d*; 2nd, 1976, Rosemary, *d* of Captain E. Dickinson, Reigate. *Educ:* Uppingham Sch.; Gonville and Caius Coll., Cambridge; The Middlesex Hospital. Entrance Schol., Middx Hosp., 1930; BA Cantab 1930 (Pts 1 and 2, Nat. Sci. Tripos); MRCS, FRCP and MA, MB, BCh Cantab, 1933; University Demonstrator of Anatomy, Cambridge, 1936; Asst Pathologist, 1937, and Surgical Registrar, 1939, Middx Hosp. FRCS 1938; Mem. Council, 1966, Vice-Pres., 1974, RCS; Hon. Sec. RSM, 1967–73, Pres., Surgery Section, 1971; Pres., Assoc. of Surgeons of GB and Ireland, 1973–74. Served, 1939–46 (despatches, OBE); Temp. Major RAMC and Surgical Specialist, serving with BEF, 1939, and MEF, 1940; Temp. Lieut-Col, RAMC, 1944, serving BLA. Late Examiner in Surgery, Cambridge Univ.; late Mem. Court of Examiners, RCS; late Hon. Sec., Assoc. of Surgeons of GB and Ireland. Hon. Member: Hellenic Surgical Soc.; Salonika Med. Soc. Hon. MD Salonika, 1976. *Publications:* papers and lectures on surgical subjects, especially with reference to malignant disease. *Recreations:* sailing, model-making. *Address:* Elmdon Cottage, Chalkpit Lane, Marlow, Bucks SL7 2JE. *T:* Marlow 6155. *Died 16 June* 1984.

**HANDY, Gen. Thomas Troy,** Hon. KBE 1945; DSC (US) 1918; DSM (US) 1945 (Oak Leaf Clusters, 1947 and 1954); Legion of Merit, 1945; formerly Deputy to General Ridgway (Supreme Allied Commander in Europe and Commander-in-Chief US European Command, 1952–53); *b* Tennessee, 11 March 1892; *s* of Rev. T. R. Handy and Caroline (*née* Hall); *m* 1920, Alma Hudson, Va; one *d*. *Educ:* Va Mil. Inst. (BS). Served European War, 1917–18 (DSC, French Croix de Guerre); War of 1939–45; when US a belligerent, 1942, became Asst Chief of Staff, Ops Div.; Dep. Chief of Staff, US Army, 1944; Gen. 1945. Comdg-Gen. 4th Army, Texas, 1947; C-in-C all Amer. Troops in Europe (except in Austria and Trieste), 1949–52; retired 1954. Grand Officer, Legion of Honour, 1951. *Died 14 April* 1982.

**HANES, Prof. Charles Samuel,** FRS 1942; FRSC 1956; Professor of Biochemistry, University of Toronto, 1951–68, then Emeritus; Hon. Fellow of Downing College, Cambridge; *b* 21 May 1903; *m* 1931, Theodora Burleigh Auret, Johannesburg; one *d*. *Educ:* University of Toronto (BA 1925); University of Cambridge, PhD Cantab 1929; ScD Cantab 1952. Lately Reader in Plant Biochemistry, University of Cambridge, and Director, Agricultural Research Council Unit of Plant Biochemistry; previously Dir of Food Investigation, Dept of Scientific and Industrial Research. Flavelle Medal, Royal Society of Canada, 1958. *Address:* 9 Crescent Place, Apt 2414, Toronto, Ontario M4C 5L8, Canada. *T:* 416–699 0900. *Died 6 July* 1990.

**HANKEY, Col George Trevor,** OBE 1945; TD; late RAMC (TA); Consulting Oral Surgeon; *b* London, 15 March 1900; *er s* of J. Trevor Hankey, Lingfield, Surrey; *m* 1933, Norah (*d* 1939), *y d* of late R. H. G. Coulson, Tynemouth; (one *s* decd); *m* 1945, Mary Isobel, *d* of late R. H. G. Coulson, Tynemouth. *Educ:* Oakham Sch; Guy's Hosp. LDSEng, 1922; LRCP, MRCS 1925; elected FDS, RCS, 1948, FRCS 1977; Consultant Dental Surgeon, St Bartholomew's Hospital, 1928–65, retd; Consultant, The London Hosp. Dental Sch., 1928–66; Lectr in Oral Surg., University of London. Fellow, Royal Society of Medicine; Examr in Dental Surgery, RCS England, 1948–54; Examiner in Dental and Oral Surgery, University of London, 1948–56; Pres. Odontological Section, RSM 1957–58 (now Hon. Mem.); Charles Tomes Lecturer, RCS, 1953; Mem. Bd Dent. Faculty RCS, 1958–73; Vice-Dean, 1966–67. John Tomes Prize, RCS, 1960, Mem. Bd Govs, London Hosp., 1954–63, and NE Metrop. Reg. Hosp. Bd, 1959–62; Founder Fellow, Brit. Assoc. Oral Surgeons, Pres., 1963–64; Sprawson Lectr, 1967. Served War, 1917–19; 2nd Lt, RHA; Commissioned RAMC(TA), 1927; OC 141 Field Ambulance, 1939; OC 12 Gen. Hosp., 1952; Hon. Col 1957–62. Served War of 1939–45 (despatches, prisoner, OBE). Officer, Legion of Merit, USA, 1951. *Publications:* chapter on Mandibular Joint Disorders, in Surgical Progress, 1960; contrib. Brit. Dental Jl and British Jl of Oral Surgery; various communications on Oral Surgery and Pathology to Proc. Royal Society of Medicine. *Recreations:* golf, fishing. *Address:* 22 East Hill Road, Oxted, Surrey RH8 9HZ. *T:* Oxted 3553. *Died 4 Jan.* 1987.

**HANKINSON, Cyril Francis James,** Editor of Debrett's Peerage, 1935–62; *b* 4 Nov. 1895; *e s* of late Charles James Hankinson, MBE, JP (pseudonym Clive Holland), of Ealing, W5, and formerly of Bournemouth, and late Violet, *d* of William Downs, CE; *m* 1942, Lillian Louise (*d* 1976), *d* of late Walter Herbert Read, FSI, 29 Castlebar Road, Ealing, W5; one *s*. *Educ:* Queen Elizabeth's Grammar Sch., Wimborne, Dorset. European War, 1915–19 with Kite Balloon Section RFC, France, Belgium and subsequently at Air Ministry; Asst Editor of National Roll of the Great War, 1919–21; Asst Editor of Debrett, 1921–35. *Publications:* My Forty Years with Debrett, 1963; A Political History of Ealing, 1972. Contributor to London, Commonwealth, and American Press, and to Encyclopaedia Britannica and Chambers's Encyclopaedia, of articles regarding Royal Family, Peerage, Heraldry, etc; also lectured and broadcast on these subjects. *Recreations:* reading biographies, watching cricket. *Address:* 13 Welsby Court, Eaton Rise, Ealing, W5. *T:* 01-997 5018. *Club:* MCC. *Died 3 Oct.* 1984.

**HANKINSON, Sir Walter Crossfield,** KCMG 1948 (CMG 1941); OBE 1936; MC; *b* 1894; *y s* of late A. W. Hankinson; *m* 1936, Sheila (*d* 1981), *d* of Dr Frederick Watson, Sydney. *Educ:* Manchester Grammar Sch.; Jesus Coll., Oxford. MA. Served European War, 1914–18 (MC); Colonial Office, 1920; transferred to Dominions Office, 1925; Acting Representative in Australia of HM Govt in the United Kingdom, 1931–32 and 1935–36; Principal Private Sec. to successive Secretaries of State for Dominion Affairs, 1937–39; Principal Sec., Office of High Commissioner for the United Kingdom in Canada, 1939–41; Principal Sec. to United Kingdom Representative to Eire, 1942–43; Dep. High Comr in Australia, 1943–47; Acting High Comr June 1945–June 1946; UK High Commissioner in Ceylon, 1948–51; British Ambassador to Republic of Ireland, 1951–55, retired. *Recreation:* reading. *Address:* 25 Beauchamp Street, Deakin, Canberra, ACT 2600, Australia. *Club:* United Oxford & Cambridge University. *Died 21 Jan.* 1984.

**HANLEY, James;** novelist, short story writer and playwright; *b* 1901. *Publications: novels:* Drift, 1930; Boy, 1931; Ebb and Flood, 1932; Captain Bottell, 1933; Resurrexit Dominus, 1934; The Furys, 1935; Stoker Bush, 1935; The Secret Journey, 1936; Hollow Sea, 1938; Our Time is Gone, 1940; The Ocean, 1941; No Directions, 1943; Sailor's Song, 1943; What Farrar Saw, 1946; Emily, 1948; Winter Song, 1950; House in the Valley (as Patric Shone), 1951, reissued as Against the Stream, 1982; The Closed Harbour, 1952; The Welsh Sonata, 1954; Levine, 1956; An End and a Beginning, 1958; Another World, 1972; A Woman in the Sky, 1973; A Dream Journey, 1976; A Kingdom, 1978; *short stories:* German Prisoner, 1930; A Passion Before Death, 1930; The Last Voyage, 1931; Men in Darkness, 1931, NY 1932; Stoker Haslett, 1932; Aria & Finale, 1932; Quartermaster Clausen, 1934; At Bay, 1935; Half-an-Eye, 1937; People Are Curious, 1938; At Bay and other stories, 1944; Crilley and other stories, 1945; Selected Stories, 1947; A Walk in the Wilderness, 1950; Collected Stories, 1953; The Darkness, 1973; Lost, 1979; *essays:* Grey Children (a sociological study), 1937; Between the Tides, 1939; Don Quixote Drowned, 1953; The Face of Winter, 1969; John Cowper Powys: A Man in the Corner, 1969; Herman Melville: A Man in the Customs House, 1971; *plays:* Say Nothing, 1962; The Inner Journey, 1965; Plays One, 1968; *Recreations:* fishing, music. *Address:* c/o David Higham Associates, 5/8 Lower John Street, Golden Square, W1R 4HA.
*Died 11 Nov.* 1985.

**HANLON, John Austin Thomas,** JP; a Recorder of the Crown Court, 1972–77; *b* 18 Dec. 1905; *s* of late Thomas Peter Hanlon; *m* 1933, Marjorie Edith (Nesta), *d* of late John W. Waltham Taylor, Portsmouth. *Educ:* Portsmouth Grammar Sch. Joined Portsmouth Police, 1924; served through ranks CID, Det. Sgt, Det. Inspector; Dep. Chief Constable, Scarborough, 1934; Chief Constable, Leamington, 1938; Home Office Regional Comr's Staff, 1940; admitted student Gray's Inn, 1934; called to the Bar, 1944; practised NE Circuit. Deputy Chm. of Quarter Sessions: Co. Northumberland, 1955–65; Co. Durham, 1958–65; Chm., Co. Northumberland QS, 1965–71. Chm. of Traffic Comrs, Northern Traffic Area, 1953–75. JP Northumberland, 1954–. *Recreations:* athletics (British Team, Olympic Games, 1928; AAA 220 yds and 440 yds Champion, 1929; many internat. teams and events); fishing, shooting, motoring, music. *Address:* Hartburn, Morpeth, Northumberland NE61 4JB. *T:* Hartburn 269. *Club:* Northern Counties (Newcastle upon Tyne). *Died 17 Oct.* 1983.

**HANNAN, William;** insurance agent; *b* 30 Aug. 1906; *m*; one *d. Educ:* North Kelvinside Secondary Sch. MP (Lab) Maryhill, Glasgow, 1945–Feb. 1974; Lord Commissioner of HM Treasury, 1946–51; an Opposition Whip, Nov. 1951–53; PPS to Rt Hon. George Brown as First Sec. and Sec. of State for Economic Affairs, 1964–66, as Sec. of State for Foreign Affairs, 1966–68; retired from Parliament, General Election, Feb. 1974. Mem., British Delegation to Council of Europe. Town Councillor, Glasgow, 1941–45. Joined SDP, 1981. *Recreation:* music. *Died 6 March* 1987.

**HANNAY, Lady Fergusson;** *see* Leslie, Doris.

**HANNEN, Athene, (Mrs Nicholas Hannen);** *see* Seyler, A.

**HANSON, Rt. Rev. Richard Patrick Crosland,** MA, DD; FBA 1988; MRIA; Professor of Historical and Contemporary Theology, University of Manchester, 1973–82, then Emeritus; Assistant Bishop: Diocese of Manchester, 1973–83; Diocese of Chester, since 1983; *b* 24 Nov. 1916; *s* of late Sir Philip Hanson, CB, and late Lady Hanson; *m* 1950, Mary Dorothy, *d* of late Canon John Powell; two *s* two *d. Educ:* Cheltenham Coll.; Trinity Coll., Dublin. 1st Hons BA in Classics also in Ancient Hist., 1938; BD with Theol. Exhibn, 1941; DD 1950; MA 1961. Asst Curate, St Mary's, Donnybrook, Dublin, and later in Banbridge, Co. Down, 1941–45; Vice-Principal, Queen's Coll., Birmingham, 1946–50; Vicar of St John's, Shuttleworth, dio. Manchester, 1950–52; Dept of Theol., Univ. of Nottingham, Lectr, Sen. Lectr and Reader, 1952–62; Lightfoot Prof. of Divinity, Univ. of Durham, and Canon of Durham, 1962–64; Prof. of Christian Theology, Univ. of Nottingham, 1964–70; Hon. Canon of Southwell, 1964–70; Canon Theologian of Coventry Cathedral, 1967–70; Examining Chaplain to the Bishop of Southwell, 1968; Bishop of Clogher, 1970–73. MRIA 1972. *Publications:* Origen's Doctrine of Tradition, 1954; II Corinthians (commentary, Torch series), 1954; Allegory and Event, 1959; God: Creator, Saviour, Spirit, 1960; Tradition in the Early Church, 1962; New Clarendon Commentary on Acts, 1967; Saint Patrick: his origins and career, 1968; Groundwork for Unity, 1971; The Attractiveness of God, 1973; Mystery and Imagination: reflections upon Christianity, 1976; (ed, abridged and trans.), Justin Martyr's Dialogue with Trypho, 1963; Saint Patrick, Confession et Lettre à Coroticus, avec la collaboration de Cécile Blanc, 1978; Christian Priesthood Examined, 1979; Eucharistic Offering in the Early Church, 1979; (with A. T. Hanson) Reasonable Belief: a Survey of the Christian Faith, 1980; The Continuity of Christian Doctrine, 1981; The Life and Writings of the Historical St Patrick, 1982;

Studies in Christian Antiquity, 1986; (with A. T. Hanson) The Identity of the Church, 1987; The Search for the Christian Doctrine of God: the Arian controversy 318–381, 1988; contribs to: Institutionalism and Church Unity, 1963; The Anglican Synthesis, 1964; Vindications, 1966; (ed) Difficulties for Christian Belief, 1966; (co-ed) Christianity in Britain 300–700, 1968; (ed) Pelican Guide to Modern Theology, 1969–70; contribs to: A Dictionary of Christian Theology, 1969; Lambeth Essays on Ministry, 1969; Le Traité sur le Saint-Esprit de Saint Basile, 1969; Cambridge History of The Bible, vol. 1, 1970; Dogma and Formula in the Fathers (Studia Patristica XIII 2 etc, 1975); The Christian Attitude to Pagan Religions (Aufstieg und Niedergang der römischen Welt II.23.2, 1980); articles in: Jl of Theol Studies, Vigiliae Christianae, Expository Times, Theology, Modern Churchman, The Times; *posthumous publication:* (with A. T. Hanson) The Bible Without Illusions, 1989. *Recreation:* drama. *Address:* 24 Styal Road, Wilmslow, Cheshire SK9 4AG. *Died 23 Dec.* 1988.

**HARBORD, Rev. and Hon. (Charles) Derek (Gardner);** a Judge of the High Court of Tanganyika, and Member, Court of Appeal for East Africa, 1953–59, retired; Earl Marshal's warrant for grant of arms, 1966; *b* 25 July 1902; *yr s* of F. W. Harbord, Birkenhead, and Isabella (*née* Gardner), Sale; *m* Grace Rosalind (*d* 1969), *o d* of A. S. Fowles, Birmingham; two *s* one *d. Educ:* Mount Radford Sch., Exeter; Gray's Inn; St Michael's Theol Coll., Llandaff. Barrister-at-Law, 1925; Deacon, 1925; Priest, 1926; Curate, W Norwood, 1925–27; Streatham, 1927–29; Vicar, Stoke Lyne, 1929; Royal Army Chaplains Dept, 1929; Chaplain i/c Depot RAMC, Crookham, and V Lt Bde RA, Ewshott, 1929–30; Vicar, Hindolveston (where he built a new parish church, the ancient one having collapsed 40 years earlier), 1930–33; Vicar, Good Shepherd, W Bromwich, 1933–35; resigned to become a Roman Catholic, 1935. Practised at English Bar, 1935–40: Central Criminal Court, SE Circuit, Mddx and N London Sess; Sec., Bentham Cttee for Poor Litigants, 1937–40; Army Officers Emergency Reserve, 1938; HM Colonial Legal Service, 1940; Dist Magistrate and Coroner, Gold Coast, 1940–44; Registrar of High Court of N Rhodesia and High Sheriff of the Territory, 1944–46; Resident Magistrate and Coroner, N Rhodesia, 1946–53; Chm., Reinstatement in Civil Employment (Mining Industry) Cttee; Chm., Liquor Licensing Appeal Tribunal for N Rhodesia; admitted to Ghana Bar, 1959; Senior Lecturer, Ghana Sch. of Law, and Editor of Ghana Law Reports, 1959–61. Reconciled with Anglican Communion and licensed to offic. Accra dio., 1959–61; Rector of St Botolph-without-Aldgate (which, with its ancient peal of bells, he restored after extensive damage by fire) with Holy Trinity, Minories, 1962–74; Fellow of Sion College, 1962–74; permission to officiate, dio. Rochester, 1974–. *Publications:* Manual for Magistrates (N Rhodesia), 1951; Law Reports (N Rhodesia), 1952; Law Reports (Ghana), 1960. *Recreations:* keeping track of 29 grand and great grandchildren, reading modern theology and other whodunnits, pottering about. *Address:* College of St Barnabas, Lingfield, Surrey RH7 6NJ. *T:* Dormans Park 706. *Club:* Athenæum. *Died 26 Sept.* 1987.

**HARDIE, John William Somerville,** MA Cantab; Hon. DLitt; Principal, Loughborough College of Education, 1963–73; *b* 21 Aug. 1912; 2nd *s* of late Most Rev. W. G. Hardie, CBE, DD; *m* 1938, Evelyn Chrystal, 5th *d* of J. C. Adkins, Uppingham, Rutland; one *s* two *d. Educ:* St Lawrence Coll., Ramsgate; Trinity Coll., Cambridge. Second Cl. Hon. (Div. I) Modern and Medieval Lang. Tripos. Asst Master St Lawrence Coll., 1933–35; Asst Master Uppingham Sch., 1935–40; Headmaster Cornwall Coll., Montego Bay, Jamaica 1940–42; Headmaster Jamaica Coll., Kingston, Jamaica, 1943–46; Asst Master Blundell's Sch., 1946–47; Headmaster, Canford Sch., 1947–60; Headmaster-Elect, Hesarack Sch., Iran, 1960–61; consultant Voluntary Service Overseas, 1961; Managing Dir, The Broadcasting Company of Northern Nigeria Ltd (seconded by Granada TV Ltd), 1961–62; Head of Information and Research, The Centre for Educational Television Overseas, Nuffield Lodge, 1962–63. Chm., HMC Overseas Cttee, 1958–60. Mem. Council Loughborough Univ. of Technology, 1968–76; a Governor, St Luke's Coll., Exeter, 1974–78. Hon. DLitt Loughborough, 1973. *Recreations:* hockey (Cambridge Univ. Hockey XI, 1931, 1932, Captain 1933; Welsh Hockey XI, 1931, 1932, Captain 1933–39), music, painting. *Address:* 15 Parc-an-Dillon, Portscatho, Truro, Cornwall TR2 5DU.
*Died 9 March* 1987.

**HARDIE, William Francis Ross;** President, Corpus Christi College, Oxford, 1950–69; Hon. Fellow, 1969; *b* 25 April 1902; *s* of late W. R. Hardie, Professor of Humanity, University of Edinburgh; *m* 1938, Isobel St Maur Macaulay; one *s* (and one *s* decd). *Educ:* Edinburgh Academy; Balliol Coll., Oxford. Fellow by Examination, Magdalen Coll., 1925; Fellow and Tutor in Philosophy, Corpus Christi Coll., Oxford, 1926–50. *Publications:* A Study in Plato, 1936; Aristotle's Ethical Theory, 1968, 2nd edn 1980; articles in philosophical journals. *Address:* 28 Turnpike Road, Cumnor Hill,

Oxford OX2 9JQ. *T:* Oxford (0865) 862880.
*Died 30 Sept.* 1990.

**HARDING OF PETHERTON,** 1st Baron *cr* 1958, of Nether Compton; **Field-Marshal Allan Francis, (John), Harding,** GCB 1951 (KCB 1944); CBE 1940; DSO 1941; MC; *b* 10 Feb. 1896; *s* of late Francis E. Harding, Compton Way, S Petherton, Somerset; *m* 1927, Mary G. M. (*d* 1983), *d* of late Wilson Rooke, JP, Knutsford, Cheshire; one *s. Educ:* Ilminster Grammar Sch. Served European War, 1914–19, with TA and Machine Gun Corps (MC); Lieut Somerset Light Infantry 1920; Capt. 1923; psc 1928; Brigade Major British Force, Saar Plebiscite; Bt Major, 1935; Bt Lieut-Col 1938; Lieut-Col 1939; Brig. 1942; Maj.-Gen. 1942; Lieut-Gen. 1943; General, 1949; Field-Marshal, 1953. Served War of 1939–45 (despatches, CBE, DSO and two Bars, KCB). GOC CMF, 1946–47; GOC-in-C Southern Command, 1947–49; C-in-C, Far East Land Forces, 1949–51; Comdr-in-Chief, British Army of the Rhine, 1951–52; Chief of the Imperial Gen. Staff, 1952–55. Governor and Comdr-in-Chief, Cyprus, 1955–Nov. 1957. Director: Nat. Provincial Bank, 1957–69; Standard Bank, 1965–71; Williams (Hounslow) Ltd, 1962–74 (Chm. 1962–71); Plessey Co. Ltd, 1967–70 (Dir, 1962–75; Dep. Chm., 1964–67; Chm., 1967–70). ADC Gen. to King George VI, 1950–52, to the Queen, 1952–53. Col 6th Gurkha Rifles, 1951–61; Col Somerset and Cornwall LI (Somerset LI, 1953–60); Col, The Life Guards, and Gold Stick to the Queen, 1957–64. KStJ. Hon. DCL (Durham). *Recreation:* gardening. *Heir: s* Major Hon. John Charles Harding [*b* 12 Feb. 1928; *m* 1966, Harriet, *yr d* of late Maj.-Gen. J. F. Hare and Mrs D. E. Hare; two *s* one *d*]. *Address:* The Barton, Nether Compton, Sherborne, Dorset. *Clubs:* Army and Navy, Cavalry and Guards, Naval and Military.
*Died 20 Jan.* 1989.

**HARDING, Ann;** retired actress; *b* Fort Sam Houston, San Antonio, Texas, USA, 7 Aug. 1902; *d* of General George Grant Gatley; *m* 1937, Werner Janssen, Symphony Conductor (marr. diss. 1963; Court restored Ann Harding as her legal name); one *d* from a former marriage. *Educ:* American public schs; Baldwin Sch., Bryn Mawr, Penna. First appearance as Madeline in Inheritors, with The Provincetown Players, New York; Tarnish, Trial of Mary Dugan, New York; Candida, London, 1937; Glass Menagerie, California, 1948; Garden District, New York, 1958. *Films include:* Holiday, East Lynne, Life of Vergie Winters, When Ladies Meet, The Fountain, Peter Ibbetson, Gallant Lady, Love From A Stranger (British picture), Mission to Moscow, Janie (Warners), Christmas Eve, It Happened on Fifth Avenue, The Man in the Grey Flannel Suit. *Recreations:* tennis, motoring, knitting, reading.
*Died 1 Sept.* 1981.

**HARDING, Sir Harold (John Boyer),** Kt 1968; FEng, FCGI, FICE; Consulting Civil Engineer; individual practice since 1956; *b* 6 Jan. 1900; *s* of late Arthur Boyer Harding, Elvetham, Hants, and Helen Clinton (*née* Lowe); *m* 1927, Sophie Helen Blair, *d* of E. Blair Leighton, RI; two *s* one *d. Educ:* Christ's Hosp.; City and Guilds (Engrg) Coll.; Imperial Coll. of Science and Technology; BSc, DIC. Joined John Mowlem & Co. Ltd, Civil Engrg Contractors, 1922; Dir, John Mowlem & Co., 1950–56; Dir, Soil Mechanics Ltd 1949–56; Consultant to Channel Tunnel Study Group, 1958–70. Governor: Westminster Techn Coll., 1948–53; Northampton Engrg Coll., 1950–53; Imperial Coll., 1955–75. Mem., Building Res. Bd, 1952–55; Pres., ICE, 1963–64; Mem., Aberfan Disaster Tribunal, 1966–67; Vice-Pres., Parly and Scientific Cttee, 1968–72. James Forrest Lectr, ICE, 1952. Chm., British Tunnelling Soc., 1971–73. Col, Engr & Railway Staff Corps. (RE TA), 1956–65. AMICE 1927; MICE 1939; FCGI 1952; FEng 1976; Fellow, Imperial Coll. of Science and Technology, 1968. Hon. DSc City Univ., 1970. Prix Coiseau, Soc. des Ingénieurs Civils de France, 1964. *Publications:* Tunnelling History and My Own Involvement, 1981; numerous papers to ICE. *Recreations:* varied. *Address:* 37 Monmouth Street, Topsham, Exeter, Devon. *T:* Topsham 3281.
*Died 27 March* 1986.

**HARDING, Maj.-Gen. Reginald Peregrine,** CB 1953; DSO 1940; late 5th Royal Inniskilling Dragoon Guards; *b* 3 July 1905; *s* of late John Reginald Harding, JP, and Elizabeth Margaret Harding; *m* 1941, Elizabeth Mary Baker (marr. diss. 1970); one *s* one *d. Educ:* Wellington Coll. Joined 5th Royal Inniskilling Dragoon Guards, 1925; served Palestine, 1938–39 (despatches); France and Flanders, 1940 (DSO); NW Europe, 1944 (Bar to DSO); Comdr N Midland District and 49 Armoured Div., Dec. 1951–55; Comdr, East Anglian District, 1955–58; retired, 1958. DL Essex, 1958–79. *Recreations:* steeplechasing, hunting, polo, fishing, shooting, raquets. *Address:* Abbots Croft, Chappel, Essex. *T:* Colchester 240232.
*Died 27 Dec.* 1981.

**HARDING, Rosamond Evelyn Mary,** PhD, LittD; *b* 6 April 1898; *d* of late W. A. Harding and Ethel Adela Harding, Madingley Hall, Cambs. *Educ:* Newnham Coll., Cambridge. PhD (Cambridge), 1931. LittD, 1941 (for research on subjects connected with music). Held Airplane Pilot's "A" Licence, 1936–39. *Publications:* A History

of the Piano-Forte, 1933, 2nd edn 1978; edition of the Twelve Piano-Forte Sonatas of L. Guistini di Pistoia, 1732, 1933; Towards a Law of Creative Thought, 1936; Origins of Musical Time and Expression, 1938; An Anatomy of Inspiration, 3rd edn 1948 (corrected repr. of 2nd edn with new preface, 1967); edn of Il Primo Libro d'Intavolaura di Balli d'Arpicordo di Gio, Maria Radino, 1592, 1961; Matthew Locke: thematic catalogue, with calendar of the main events of his life, 1971; The Metronome and its Precursors, 1979; various articles in 4th and 5th edns, Grove's Dictionary of Music. *Address:* Jersey Lodge, 1 Lorne Road, Southwold, Suffolk. *T:* Southwold 722049.
*Died 6 May* 1982.

**HARDINGE,** 5th Viscount *cr* 1846, of Lahore and of King's Newton, Derbyshire; **Henry Nicholas Paul Hardinge;** Senior Vice President, Royal Bank of Canada, since 1983; *b* 15 Aug. 1929; *s* of 4th Viscount Hardinge, MBE, and of Margaret Elizabeth Arnott, *d* of Hugh Fleming, Ottawa; *S* father, 1979; *m* 1st, 1955, Zoë Anne (marr. diss. 1982), *d* of the Hon. H. de M. Molson, OBE, Montreal; three *s*; 2nd, 1982, Baroness Florence von Oppenheim; one *d. Educ:* Harrow School. Commissioned into 7th Queen's Own Hussars, 1949–54. Joined The Royal Bank of Canada, 1954; Chief Exec., 1981–82, Dep. Chm., 1982–83, Orion Royal Bank Ltd. *Recreations:* hunting, shooting, fishing. *Heir: s* Hon. Charles Henry Nicholas Hardinge, *b* 25 Aug. 1956. *Address:* 5 Somerset Square, W14 8EE. *T:* 01–602 5169. *Clubs:* Cavalry and Guards; Mount Royal (Montreal).
*Died 16 July* 1984.

**HARDMAN, Amy Elizabeth;** Matron, The Royal Free Hospital, London, 1953–70; *b* 23 Dec. 1909; *d* of late Charlton James Hardman and Elizabeth Clark. *Educ:* Godolphin and Latymer Sch., Hammersmith; Rosebery Sch. for Girls, Epsom. General Training, St Bartholomew's Hosp., London, 1930–34 (SRN); Midwifery Training, Kingston County Hosp., 1937 (SCM); Asst Matron, Sister Tutor, Metropolitan Hosp., E8, 1937–42; Matron, The Guest Hospital, Dudley, Worcs, 1942–49; Matron, St Margaret's Hospital, Epping, 1949–53. *Publication:* An Introduction to Ward Management, 1970. *Address:* Apple Tree Cottage, Main Street, Northiam, Rye, East Sussex TN31 6LE. *T:* Northiam (07974) 2319.
*Died 2 Nov.* 1990.

**HARDMAN, David Rennie,** MA, LLB; JP; Secretary, Sir Ernest Cassel Educational Trust, 1935–84; Secretary, Stafford Cripps Memorial Appeal and Trustees; *b* 1901; *s* of David Hardman, MSc, and Isobel Rennie, Mansfield House University Settlement; *m* 1928, Freda Mary Riley; one *d*; *m* 1946, Barbara, *er d* of late Herbert Lambert, Bath; one *s* one *d. Educ:* Coleraine Academical Instn; Christ's Coll., Cambridge. Mem. Railway Clerks' Assoc., 1919–21; Pres. Cambridge Union Soc., 1925; Contested (Lab) Cambridge Borough, 1929. Cambridge Borough Councillor and Cambridge County Councillor, 1937–46; late Chm. Cambs Education Cttee; JP Cambridge, 1941–47; MP (Lab) Darlington, 1945–51; Parl. Sec., Min. of Education, 1945–51; contested (Lab) Rushcliffe Div. of Notts, 1955; leader UK delegns UNESCO, Paris 1946, Mexico 1947, Beirut 1948, Paris 1949, Florence 1950, Paris 1951; Vice-Pres. Shaw Soc.; Pres., Holiday Fellowship, 1962–69. Visiting Prof. of English Literature, Elmira, New York, 1964–66. Barclay Acheson Prof. Internat. Studies, Macalester Coll., Minn, 1967. *Publications:* What about Shakespeare?, 1939; Poems of Love and Affairs, 1949; Telscombe: A Sussex Village, 1964; History of Holiday Fellowship 1913–1940, 1981; History of Sir E. Cassel Educational Trust 1919–1982, 1982. *Recreation:* gardening. *Address:* 21 Hassocks Road, Hurstpierpoint, West Sussex BN6 9QH. *T:* Brighton 833194. *Club:* Savile.
*Died 6 Dec.* 1989.

**HARDMAN, Air Chief Marshal Sir (James) Donald Innes,** GBE 1958 (OBE 1940); KCB 1952 (CB 1945); DFC; Royal Air Force retired; *b* 21 Feb. 1899; *s* of James Hardman, MA, Delph, Yorks; *m* 1930, Dorothy, *d* of William Ashcroft Thompson, JP, Larkenshaw, Chobham; two *s* one *d. Educ:* Malvern; Hertford Coll., Oxford. Served European War, 1916–19; joined RAF 1918; Wing Comdr, 1939; Air Commodore, 1941; Air Vice-Marshal, 1945; Air Officer i/c Administration, Air Comd, SE Asia, 1946–47; Asst Chief of Air Staff (Ops), 1947–49; Comdt RAF Air Staff Coll., 1949–51; AOC-in-C, Home Comd, 1951–52; Air Marshal, 1952; Chief of Air Staff, RAAF, 1952–54; Air Chief Marshal, 1955; Air Mem. Supply and Organisation, 1954–57; retired, 1958. *Address:* Dolphin Cottage, St Cross Hill, Winchester, Hants. *Club:* Royal Air Force.
*Died 2 March* 1982.

**HARDWICK, Charles Aubrey,** CMG 1971; QC (Australia); Vice-Patron, Benevolent Society of New South Wales, since 1973 (Director, 1947–73; Vice-President, 1958–61; President, 1961–73); *b* 29 July 1885; 2nd *s* of G. W. Hardwick, Rylstone, NSW; *m* 1922, Maisie Jean (*d* 1971), *er d* of David Fell, MLA, Sydney and Rout's Green, Bledlow Ridge, Bucks; two *s* (and one *s* decd). *Educ:* Rylstone Public Sch.; Univ. of Sydney (evening student). BA 1913, LLB 1915. NSW Dept of Attorney-General and of Justice, 1902–14; called to NSW Bar, 1915, in practice, 1915–76; KC 1934; Actg Judge, Supreme Court of NSW, 1939. Foundn Mem., NSW Inst. of

Hospital Almoners, Treas. 1937–63; Dir, Prince Henry's Hosp., 1936–44; Vice-Chm., Metropolitan Hosps Contribution Fund, 1938–44. Mem., Sydney Cricket Ground, 1909–. *Recreations:* reading, formerly billiards, bowls, lawn tennis, golf, cricket, bridge. *Address:* Wentworth Chambers, 180 Phillip Street, Sydney, NSW 2000, Australia; James Milson Retirement Village, 65 High Street, North Sydney, NSW 2060, Australia. *T:* Sydney 929 2579. *Clubs:* Australian, Australian Jockey (Life Mem.), Sydney Cricket Ground (Hon. Mem.) (Sydney). *Died* 6 March 1984.

**HARDY, Sir Alister (Clavering),** Kt 1957; FRS 1940; MA, DSc Oxon; FLS, FZS; Hon. Fellow of Exeter College, Oxford; Hon. Fellow of Merton College, Oxford (Fellow, 1946–63); Professor Emeritus, University of Oxford; *b* Nottingham, 10 Feb. 1896; *y s* of late Richard Hardy; *m* 1927, Sylvia Lucy, 2nd *d* of late Prof. Walter Garstang; one *s* one *d. Educ:* Oundle Sch.; Exeter Coll., Oxford. Lieut and Capt. 2/1 Northern Cyclist Bn, 1915–19; attached RE, Asst Camouflage Officer, Staff of XIII Army Corps, 1918; Christopher Welch Biological Research Scholar, 1920; Oxford Biological Scholar at the Stazione Zoologica, Naples, 1920; Asst Naturalist in Fisheries Dept, Min. of Agriculture and Fisheries, 1921–24; Chief Zoologist to the Discovery Expedition, 1924–28; Prof. of Zoology and Oceanography, University Coll., Hull, 1928–42; Regius Prof. of Natural History, University of Aberdeen, 1942–45; Linacre Prof. of Zoology, University of Oxford, 1946–61; Prof. of Zoological Field Studies, Oxford, 1961–63; Gifford Lectr, Univ. of Aberdeen, for 1963–65. Founder, and Dir 1969–76, Religious Experience Res. Unit, Manchester Coll., Oxford. Scientific Medal of Zoological Soc., 1939. Hon. LLD Aberdeen; Hon. DSc: Southampton; Hull. Pierre Lecomte du Noüy Prize, 1968. Templeton Prize for Progress in Religion, 1985. *Publications:* The Open Sea, Part I, The World of Plankton, 1956; The Open Sea, Part II, Fish and Fisheries, 1958; The Living Stream, 1965; The Divine Flame, 1966; Great Waters, 1967; (with R. Harvie and A. Koestler) The Challenge of Chance, 1973; The Biology of God, 1975; The Spiritual Nature of Man, 1979; Darwin and the Spirit of Man, 1983; A Cotswold Sketchbook, 1984. *Recreation:* water-colour sketching. *Address:* 7 Emden House, Barton Lane, Old Headington, Oxford OX3 9JU. *T:* Oxford 62775. *Died* 24 May 1985.

**HARDY, Gen. Sir Campbell Richard,** KCB 1957 (CB 1954); CBE 1951; DSO 1944 (and 2 Bars); RM retired; Director of the Coal Utilisation Council, 1960–70; *b* 24 May 1906; *s* of Major Frank Buckland Hardy, OBE; *m* 1931, Phyllis Cole Sutton; one *s* one *d. Educ:* Felsted Sch. 2nd Lieut RM, 1924; HMS Renown, 1927–29; courses, 1929–30; HMS Rodney, 1930–31; Physical Training Officer, Portsmouth Div., RM, 1932–37; RNC Dartmouth, 1937–38; HMS Vindictive, 1938–39; served War of 1939–45; Adjt Ports Div., RM, 1939–40; RM Div., 1940–43; 46 Commando, RM, 1943–44; Comd 3 Commando Bde, 1944–45; Staff, RM Office, 1946–47; Chief Instructor, Sch. of Combined Ops, 1947–48; Comd 3 Commando Bde, 1948–51; CO Depot, RM, Deal, 1951; Chief of Staff Royal Marines, 1952–55; Commandant General of the Royal Marines, 1955–59; retired, 1959; Col Comdt, Royal Marines, 1961–66. *Address:* Bunch Lane Lodge, Haslemere, Surrey. *T:* Haslemere 3177. *Club:* Army and Navy. *Died* 29 July 1984.

**HARDY, Brig. George Alfred,** FRGS; FRICS; Deputy Director and Keeper of the Maproom, Royal Geographical Society, 1977–84; *b* 5 June 1923; *s* of Charles A. Hardy and Caroline A. Hodges; *m* 1946, Olive (*née* Tennant); one *d. Educ:* Duke of York's Royal Military School. 2nd Lieut, RE, 1944; served W African Frontier Force, 1945–46; Survey of India, 1946–47; Sch. of Military Engineering and Sch. of Military Survey, 1948–50; British Schools' Exploring Soc., Norway, 1949; Air Survey Officer, Ordnance Survey, 1953–56; Sen. Instr., Sch. of Mil. Survey, 1956–59; OC 19 Topog. Survey Sqdn, S Arabia, 1959–61; OC 13 Field Survey Sqdn, BAOR, 1961–63; Chief Geographic Officer, Allied Forces N Europe, Oslo, 1964–66; Staff Officer, MoD, 1966–68; Geographic Adviser to Supreme Allied Command, NATO, 1968–70; Dep. Dir, Cartography and Map Production, 1970–73, Dir, Field Survey, 1973–77, Ordnance Survey; ADC to the Queen, 1976–77. *Publications:* contribs to Geographical Jl, RGS. *Address:* c/o Lloyds Bank, Cox's & King's Branch, 6 Pall Mall, SW1. *Died* 18 Feb. 1990.

**HARDY, Sir Harry,** Kt 1956; JP; ATI; chartered textile technologist; *b* 10 Sept. 1896; *e s* of Friend and Elizabeth Ann Hardy, Rods Mills, Morley; *m* 1922, Remie (*d* 1955), *d* of Benjamin Siddle, Morley; *m* 1957, Mollie, *d* of Henry Dixon, Morley. *Educ:* Univ. of Leeds. Retired as chemical and fibre manufacturer. Lectr in Textiles, Dewsbury Technical Coll., 1920–35, Head of Textile Industries Dept, 1925–35; Lecturer in Textiles, Huddersfield Technical Coll., 1922–25; Examiner to City and Guilds of London Institute, 1941–44. Pres. Morley and District Textile Soc., 1936–; Founder Pres. Morley Musical Soc., 1943–58; Chm. Youth Employment Cttee, 1943–70; Chm. Local Employment Cttee, 1950–68; Founder Pres., Rotary Club of Morley, 1949–; Vice-Pres. Textile Inst., 1956–59; Liveryman, Cordwainers' Co., 1946–. Hon. Life Pres., Batley and

Morley Conservative Assoc. (65 years active service). County Councillor, West Riding of Yorks, 1945–49, County Alderman, 1949–70; JP Borough of Morley, 1948–. Hon. Freeman, Borough of Morley, 1972. *Recreations:* education for textiles, science and technology of textiles; youth employment, music and the arts. *Address:* 45 The Roundway, Dartmouth Park, Morley, near Leeds. *T:* Morley 535150. *Died* 5 Jan. 1984.

**HARDY, Sir James (Douglas),** Kt 1962; CBE 1955 (OBE 1953); *b* 8 June 1915; *s* of James Percy Hardy; *m* 1937, Robina, *d* of Robert Bookless; two *s. Educ:* Gonville and Caius Coll., Cambridge. ICS, 1937–47; Pakistan Civil Service, 1947–61. Dist and Sessions Judge and Dep. Comr, Punjab, up to 1952; Jt Sec. to Govt of Pakistan, 1953; served in: Min. of Communications, as Jt Sec. in charge, 1953–56; Cabinet Secretariat; Min. of Law. Apptd Jt Sec. in charge Estabt Div., President's Secretariat, 1959; promoted Sec., Govt of Pakistan President's Secretariat, 1960; retired, 1961. Ford Foundation representative, in N Africa, 1961–67; Project Manager and Chief UN Adviser, UN Special Fund Public Service Reform and Trng Project, Tehran, 1968–75; Chief Project Manager and UN Adviser, Admin. Reform, Govt of Morocco, Rabat, 1975–76. Star of Pakistan (SPk), 1961; Comdr Order of Tunisia, 1967. *Recreations:* riding, golf, motoring. *Address:* c/o Midland Bank, Poultry and Princes Street, EC2. *Died* 28 Feb. 1986.

**HARDY, Col Thomas Eben F.;** *see* Forman Hardy.

**HARE, Geoffrey;** marketing/management consultant; Chief Executive, Scottish Tourist Board, 1986–87; *b* 28 Dec. 1940; *s* of Leslie and Greta Hare; *m* 1971, Joy Margaret Beckley; one *d. Educ:* José Pedro Varela School, Montevideo, Uruguay; Lawrence Sheriff Grammar School, Rugby. Management Trainee, Savoy Hotel, London, Spain, Canary Isles, 1957–59; Hotel Management Trainee, Paris, Jersey, UK, 1960–63; Agricultural/Hotel studies, Israel, 1964–65; Universal Sky Tours, Majorca, 1965–66; Area Manager, Wallace Arnold Tours, Portugal, 1966–67; Trust House Forte Hotels, 1967–77; Dir of Tourism, NW Tourist Bd, 1977–86. *Recreations:* philately, driving, walking, sketching. *Address:* 10/4 Damside, Dean Village, Edinburgh EH4 3BB. *Died* 22 Oct. 1988.

**HARE, Prof. Patrick James;** Grant Professor of Dermatology, University of Edinburgh, 1968–80, then Emeritus Professor; *b* 18 Jan. 1920; *yr s* of John Henry Hare and Isabella McIntyre; *m* 1945, Mary, *yr d* of late Col A. H. Bridges, CB, CIE, DSO, and Dorothea Seth-Smith; two *s. Educ:* Westminster City Sch.; University Coll., London (Andrews Scholar); University Coll. Hosp. Med. Sch.; Johns Hopkins Univ. (Rockefeller Student). MB, BS, 1944; MD Johns Hopkins, 1944; RAMC 1945–48 (Burma, Singapore); Registrar, Dept of Dermatology, 1948; MRCP 1949; FRCP 1964; MRCPE 1968, FRCPE 1971. Travelling Fellow, Univ. of London, 1951 (Paris, Zürich); Consultant Dermatologist, UCH, 1951–68; Research worker and Senior Lecturer in Dermatology, UCH Med. Sch., 1952–59; MD London 1954; Cons. Dermatologist, Whittington Hosp., London, 1959–68. Mem., Jt Cttee for Higher Med. Trng, 1973–78 (Chm., Specialist Adv. Cttee (Dermatology), 1973–78). Editor, British Journal of Dermatology, 1959–67. Sec. Sect. of Dermatology, Royal Society of Medicine, 1961–62 (Pres., 1978–79). *Publications:* The Skin, 1966; Basic Dermatology, 1966; scientific and med. articles in various jls. *Recreations:* gardening, music. *Address:* 81 Cedric Road, Bath BA1 3PE. *T:* Bath 26467. *Died* 5 April 1982.

**HARE, Ronald,** MD (London); Emeritus Professor of Bacteriology in University of London since 1964 and Hon. Consulting Bacteriologist to St Thomas' Hospital since 1951; *b* 30 Aug. 1899; *s* of late Frederick Hare, MD, and Elizabeth Roxby Hare, Esh Winning, Co. Durham; *m* 1932, Barbara Thurgarland Wintle (*d* 1966); one *s. Educ:* Royal Masonic Sch.; Birkbeck Coll.; St Mary's Hosp., London. Scholar, Institute of Pathology and Research, 1925, and asst in Inoculation Dept, St Mary's Hospital, London, 1926–30; first asst in Research Laboratories, Queen Charlotte's Hospital, London, 1931–36; Research Associate in Connaught Laboratories, Univ. of Toronto, and Lectr in Dept of Hygiene and Preventive Medicine, 1936; has carried out extensive researches on the streptococci (Catherine Bishop Harman Prize of BMA and Nicholls Prize of Royal Society of Medicine); largely responsible for the planning and building of the penicillin plant set up in the University of Toronto by the Govt of Canada. Professor of Bacteriology, University of London, 1946–64. Mem. Council: Wright-Fleming Inst., 1952–60; Nuffield Inst. of Comparative Med., 1960–68; Fountains and Carshalton Gp Hospital Management Cttee, 1966–71. Pres., Pathology Sect., 1963–64, and Mem. Council, Royal Society of Medicine, 1965–68; Examr in Universities of: London, Malaya, Birmingham, West Indies, East Africa, Ibadan. *Publications:* Pomp and Pestilence, 1954; An Outline of Bacteriology and Immunity, 1956; Bacteriology and Immunity for Nurses, 1961; The Birth of Penicillin, 1970; many papers in scientific and medical jls. *Recreations:* water-colour painting, the history of pestilence.

*Address:* The Manor, Sibbertoft, near Market Harborough, Leics.
*Died* 13 *March* 1986.

**HARGRAVE, John Gordon,** FRSA; artist and writer; *b* 1894; *s* of
Gordon Hargrave, landscape painter; *m* 1919, Ruth Clark (marr.
diss. 1952); one *s*; *m* 1968, Gwendolyn Gray. *Educ:* Wordsworth's
Sch., Hawkshead. Illustrated Gulliver's Travels, and the Rose and
the Ring at the age of fifteen; chief cartoonist, London Evening
Times, at the age of seventeen; joined the staff of C. Arthur Pearson
Ltd, 1914; enlisted in RAMC, and served with 11th (Irish) Division
in Gallipoli campaign (Suvla Bay Landing), and later in Salonika;
invalided out, end of 1916; Art Manager, C. Arthur Pearson Ltd,
1917–20; founded the Kibbo Kift, 1920 (later Social Credit Party,
The Green Shirts); Hon. Adviser to the Alberta Govt Planning
Cttee, 1936–37; issued the Alberta Report, July 1937; invented the
Hargrave Automatic Navigator for Aircraft, 1937; created animal
character, "Bushy", for The Sketch, 1952. *Publications:* Lonecraft,
1913, and five other handbooks on camping and the outdoor life; At
Suvla Bay, 1916; Harbottle, 1924; Young Winkle, 1925; And Then
Came Spring, 1926; The Pfenniger Failing, 1927; The Confession
of the Kibbo Kift, 1927; The Imitation Man, 1931; Summer Time
Ends, 1935; Professor Skinner alias Montagu Norman, 1939; Words
Win Wars, 1940; Social Credit Clearly Explained, 1945; The Life
and Soul of Paracelsus, 1951; The Paragon Dictionary, 1953; The
Suvla Bay Landing, 1964; The Facts of the Case concerning the
Hargrave Automatic Navigator for Aircraft (privately pr.), 1969;
special articles on Paracelsus, 1971, and L. Hargrave, inventor of
the box-kite, in Encyclopaedia Britannica, 1974; The Confession of
the Kibbo Kift (special request edn), 1979. *Recreation:* work.
*Address:* 3 Rosemary Court, Fortune Green Road, Hampstead,
NW6. *Died* 21 *Nov.* 1982.

**HARGREAVES, Eric Lyde;** Emeritus Fellow since 1963 (Fellow,
1925, Tutor, 1930, Senior Tutor, 1937–56), Oriel College, Oxford; *b*
13 Oct. 1898; *s* of George Harrison and Emily Frances Hargreaves.
*Educ:* St Paul's Sch.; Corpus Christi Coll., Oxford (Scholar).
Wounded and taken prisoner, April 1918; 1st Class Lit. Hum.,
1921; PhD London, 1924; University Lecturer in Economics,
1929–35, and 1954–59; Historian, Official History of Second World
War (Civil Series), 1942–52; Fellow of Royal Economic and Royal
Statistical Societies. *Publications:* Restoring Currency Standards,
1926; National Debt, 1930; (with M. M. Gowing) Civil Industry
and Trade, 1952; essays and articles on economic subjects.
*Recreation:* walking. *Address:* Oriel College, Oxford.
*Died* 20 *Feb.* 1984.

**HARGREAVES, Brig. Kenneth,** CBE 1956 (MBE (mil.) 1939); TD
1942; DL; Lord-Lieutenant, West Yorkshire, 1974–78 (West Riding
of Yorkshire and City of York, 1970–74); *b* 23 Feb. 1903; *s* of late
Henry Hargreaves, Leeds, and late Hope Hargreaves; *m* 1st, 1958,
Else Margareta Allen (*d* 1968); one step *s* one step *d* (both adopted);
2nd, 1969, Hon. Mrs Margaret Packe (*d* 1986); two step *d*. *Educ:*
Haileybury Coll. Lieut-Col comdg 96th HAA Regt RA, 1939–41;
Brig. comdg 3rd Ind. AA Bde, 1942–45; Hon. Col, several TA
regiments, 1947–66; Vice-Pres., Yorks TAVR, 1970–78. Man. Dir,
1938–64, Chm., 1964–74, Hon. Pres., 1974–87, Hargreaves Gp Ltd;
Director: Lloyds Bank Ltd, 1965–73 (Chm., Yorkshire Regional
Bd, 1967–73); Yorkshire Bank, 1969–79; Sadler's Wells Trust Ltd,
1969–75; ENO, 1975–80; Opera North, 1981–84; Pres., Friends of
Opera North, 1978–88, Patron, 1988–. Mem., Royal Commn on
Historical Monuments, 1971–74. Pres., Queen's Silver Jubilee
Appeal, W Yorks, 1977–78. Chairman: Coal Industry Soc., 1933–34,
Pres. 1973–75; Coal Trade Benevolent Assoc., 1958; British
Railways (Eastern) Bd, 1970–73 (Dir, 1964–73). President:
Chartered Inst. of Secretaries, 1956 (FCIS 1930); W Yorks Branch,
BRCS, 1965–74, now Patron; St John Council (W Yorks), 1970–74,
W and S Yorks, 1974–78; Yorks Agricultural Soc., 1972–73;
Haileybury Soc., 1974–75; Vice-Pres., Leeds Chamber of
Commerce, 1946–47; Dep. Chm., Leeds Musical Festival, 1961–70;
Mem. Court, University of Leeds, 1950– (Hon. LLD 1970); Trustee,
York Minster, 1970–; High Steward, Selby Abbey, 1974–; Patron,
Central Yorkshire Scouts, 1978 (former Chm. and Pres.). Contested:
Pontefract, 1945; Keighley, 1950 and 1951; Hon. Treasurer, Yorks
Provincial Area Conservative and Unionist Assoc., 1946–54;
Governor, Swinton Conservative Coll., 1952–70; Lay Reader,
Ripon Diocese, 1954–. Liveryman, Clothworkers' Co., 1938, Master,
1969–70. High Sheriff of Yorks, 1962–63; DL WR Yorks 1956–70,
West Yorks, 1978–. KStJ 1970. *Recreations:* gardening, music.
*Address:* Easby House, Great Ouseburn, York YO5 9RQ. *T:*
Boroughbridge (04233) 30548. *Clubs:* Army and Navy, Carlton.
*Died* 27 *March* 1990.

**HARINGTON, Maj.-Gen. John,** CB 1967; OBE 1958; *b* 7 Nov. 1912;
*s* of late Col Henry Harington, Kelston, Folkestone, Kent; *m* 1943,
Nancy, *d* of late Stanley Allen, Denne Hill, Canterbury; one *s*.
*Educ:* Lambrook, Bracknell; Aldenham Sch.; RMA Woolwich.
Commnd RA, 1933. Served War of 1939–45: BEF, 1939–40; Capt.,
RHA, France and Germany; Major 1943; 1st Airborne Corps; Lt-
Col 1945. GSO1, British and Indian Div., Japan, 1946–47; CO 18th

Regt RA, 1954–55; College Comdr, RMA, Sandhurst, 1956–57;
Head of Defence Secretariat, Middle East, 1958–59; commanded
1st Artillery Brigade, 1960–61; BRA, Far East Land Forces, 1962;
DMS (2), War Office, 1962–64 (Min. of Defence, 1964); Chief of
Staff to C-in-C, Far East Comd, 1964–67, retired. *Recreations:* ski-
ing, shooting, golf, tennis. *Address:* Harkaway, Goodworth Clatford,
Andover, Hants SP11 7RE. *Clubs:* Army and Navy, Ski Club of
Great Britain. *Died* 28 *March* 1989.

**HARINGTON, Sir Richard Dundas,** 13th Bt *cr* 1611; *b* 16 Oct. 1900; *s*
of 12th Bt and Selina Louisa Grace (*d* 1945), *d* of 6th Viscount
Melville; *S* father, 1931. *Educ:* Eton. *Heir: nephew* Nicholas John
Harington, *b* 14 May 1942. *Address:* c/o Coutts & Co., Bankers, 440
Strand, WC2. *Died* 17 *Nov.* 1981.

**HARINGTON HAWES, Derrick Gordon;** *b* 22 May 1907; *s* of late
Col Charles Howard Hawes, DSO, MVO, Indian Army; *m* 1932,
Drusilla Way; one *s* two *d*. *Educ:* Wellington Coll.; RMC Sandhurst.
14th Punjab Regt, IA, 1927–34; Indian Political Service, 1934–47;
King Edward's Hospital Fund for London, 1949–62; Dir Gen.,
Internat. Hospital Fedn, 1962–75. *Address:* 8 Northbrook Road,
Aldershot, Hants GU11 3HE. *Club:* Oriental.
*Died* 7 *Nov.* 1986.

**HARKNESS, Captain Kenneth Lanyon,** CBE 1963; DSC 1940; Royal
Navy; *b* 24 Aug. 1900; *s* of late Major T. R. Harkness, RA, and late
Mrs G. A. de Burgh; *m* 1st, 1932, Joan Phyllis Lovell (*d* 1979); one
*d*; 2nd, 1979, Mary Isabel Powell (*née* Stroud), Brettenham, Suffolk.
*Educ:* RN Colls, Osborne and Dartmouth; Cambridge Univ.
Midshipman, HMS Bellerophon, 1917; Cambridge Univ., 1922;
Qual. Gunnery, 1926; Comdr Admty, 1935; Sqdn Gunnery Off.,
2nd Battle Sqdn, 1937; Comd HMS Winchelsea, 1938; Comd HMS
Fearless, 1939–40; Capt. 1940; Chief of Intell. Service, Far East,
1940–42; Dep. Dir of Naval Ordnance, Admty, 1943–44; Comd
HMS Ceylon, 1945; Comd HMS Sheffield, 1946; Chief of Staff to
C-in-C Portsmouth, 1947; retired from RN, 1949. Civil Defence
Officer, Portsmouth, 1949; Home Office, Asst Chief Trg Off. (CD),
1952; Prin. Off., later Reg. Dir of CD, London Reg., 1954; Temp.
seconded as CD Adviser, Cyprus, 1956; later Regional Dir of Civil
Defence, London Region, 1954–65. *Recreation:* gardening. *Address:*
Far Rockaway, Durford Wood, Petersfield, Hants GU31 5AW. *T:*
Liss 893173. *Died* 12 *Jan.* 1990.

**HARLAND, Rt. Rev. Maurice Henry,** MA, DD; *b* 17 April 1896; *s* of
late Rev. William George Harland and late Clara Elizabeth
Harland; *m* 1923, Agnes Hildyard Winckley, MBE 1967; two *d*.
*Educ:* St Peter's Sch., York; Exeter Coll., Oxford (MA); Leeds
Clergy Sch. DD (Lambeth) 1948. 2nd Lieut West Yorks Regt,
1914–15; 2nd Lieut R Field Artillery, 1915–16; Lieut Royal Flying
Corps and afterwards RAF, 1916–19; Curate St Peter's, Leicester,
1922–27; Priest in Charge St Anne's Conventional District, 1927–33;
Perpetual Curate of St Matthew's Holbeck, Leeds, 1933–38; Vicar
of St Mary's, Windermere, 1938–42; Rural Dean of Ambleside;
Vicar of Croydon, 1942–47; Archdeacon of Croydon, 1946–47;
Hon. Canon of Canterbury, 1942–47; Bishop Suffragan of Croydon,
1942–47; Bishop of Lincoln, 1947–56; Bishop of Durham, 1956–66,
retired. Select Preacher, Oxford Univ., 1949–50. Pres., Edinburgh
Sir Walter Scott Soc., 1940–50; Hon. Fellow, Exeter Coll., Oxford,
1950; Hon. DD Durham Univ., 1956. Introduced to House of Lords,
1954 and again in 1956 on becoming Bishop of Durham. *Recreations:*
fishing, riding. *Address:* Heathfield, West Wittering, Chichester,
West Sussex PO20 8OA. *T:* Birdham 511040.
*Died* 29 *Sept.* 1986.

**HARLAND, Sydney Cross,** DSc (London); FRS 1943; FRSE 1951;
FTI (Hon.) 1954; George Harrison Professor of Botany, Manchester
University, 1950–58, retired, Emeritus Professor, 1958; Member,
Agricultural Research Council, 1950–55; *b* 19 June 1891; *s* of
Erasmus and Eliza Harland, Cliff Grange, Snainton, Yorks; *m* 1st,
1915, Emily Wilson Cameron; two *d*; 2nd, 1934, Olive Sylvia
Atteck; one *s*. *Educ:* Municipal Secondary School, Scarborough;
King's Coll., London. Asst Supt Agric., St Vincent, BWI, 1915;
Asst for Cotton Research, Imp. Dept Agric. for West Indies, 1918;
Head Botanical Dept, British Cotton Industry Res. Assoc.,
Manchester, 1920; Prof. Botany and Genetics, Imperial Coll. Trop.
Agric., Trinidad, 1923; Chief Geneticist, Empire Cotton Growing
Corp., Cotton Research Station, Trinidad, and Cotton Adviser to
Comr of Agric., 1926; Gen. Adviser to State Cotton Industry of Sao
Paulo, Brazil, 1935; Dir, Institute of Cotton Genetics, National
Agricultural Soc., Peru, 1939–50. Mem., UNESCO Mission to
Ecuador, 1962. President: Genetical Soc. of GB, 1953–56; Indian
Cotton Congress, 1956; Fellow: Botanical Soc., Edinburgh, 1953;
New England Inst. of Medical Res., 1963. Hon. Mem., Internat.
Union for R&D, 1964. Hon. MSc Manchester, 1958; Hon. DSc
West Indies, 1973. *Publications:* The Genetics of Cotton, 1939; also
papers on cotton, cocoa, other tropical crops, and applied genetics.
*Recreations:* travel, gardening, human genetics. *Address:* Cliff
Grange, Snainton, Scarborough, Yorks. *T:* Snainton 549. *Club:*
Athenæum. *Died* 8 *Nov.* 1982.

**HARLAND, Prof. William Arthur;** Regius Professor of Forensic Medicine, University of Glasgow, since 1974; *b* 7 March 1926; *s* of Robert Wallace Harland and Elizabeth Montgomery Robb; *m* 1953, Brenda Foxcroft; three *s* one *d*. *Educ:* Methodist Coll., Belfast; Queen's Univ., Belfast. MB, BCh Belfast 1948, MD Belfast 1974; FRCP(C) 1959, PhD London 1964, FRCPath 1967, MRCPGlas 1971, FRCPGlas 1974, FRSE 1980. Demonstrator in Pathology, Emory Univ., 1951–53; Resident Pathologist, Presbyterian Hosp., NY, 1954; Dir of Labs, St Joseph's Hosp., Chatham, Ont, 1955–58; Assoc. Path., Jewish Gen. Hosp., Montreal, 1958–60; Sen. Lectr in Pathology, Univ. of West Indies, 1960–64; Path., MRC Atheroma Res. Unit, Western Infirmary, Glasgow, 1964–66; Sen. Lectr in Pathology, Univ. of Glasgow, 1966–74. *Publications:* various articles in sci. jls on thyroid diseases and on atherosclerosis. *Recreation:* sheep farming. *Address:* Department of Forensic Medicine, University of Glasgow, Glasgow G12 8QQ. *T:* 041–339 8855.
*Died 9 Jan.* 1985.

**HARLECH, 5th Baron** *cr* 1876; **William David Ormsby Gore,** PC 1957; KCMG 1961; *b* 20 May 1918; *e* surv. *s* of 4th Baron Harlech, KG, PC, GCMG, and Lady Beatrice Cecil (Dowager Lady Harlech, DCVO) (*d* 1980); *S* father, 1964; *m* 1st, 1940, Sylvia (*d* 1967), 2nd *d* of late Hugh Lloyd Thomas, CMG, CVO; one *s* three *d* (and one *s* decd); 2nd, 1969, Pamela, *o d* of Ralph F. Colin, New York; one *d*. *Educ:* Eton; New Coll., Oxford. Joined Berks Yeomanry, 1939, Adjutant, 1942; Major (GS), 1945. MP (C) Oswestry Div. of Salop, 1950–61; Parliamentary Private Sec. to Minister of State for Foreign Affairs, 1951; Parliamentary Under-Sec. of State for Foreign Affairs, Nov. 1956–Jan. 1957; Minister of State for Foreign Affairs, 1957–61; British Ambassador in Washington, 1961–65. Dep.-Leader of the Opposition, House of Lords, 1966–67. Dep. Chm., Commn on Rhodesian Opinion, 1972. President: British Bd of Film Censors, 1965–; The Pilgrims (Soc. of UK, 1965–77); Trustee, The Pilgrim Trust, 1965– (Chm., 1974–79); Chairman: Harlech Television; Falcon Resources; Albion Film Investments NV, 1984–; Kennedy Meml Trust; Papworth and Enham Village Settlements; European Movement, 1969–75; RIIA, 1978–84. Director: Morgan Crucible, 1965–; Commercial Bank of Wales, 1972–. Chm., Adv. Cttee, Kennedy Inst., Harvard; Mem., Adv. Cttee, V&A Mus., 1979–83; Trustee, Tate Gallery, 1971–78; Governor, Yehudi Menuhin Sch. Hon. Chm., Shelter, 1969–73, Pres. 1973–78; Chm., Nat. Cttee for Electoral Reform, 1976–84. Hon. Fellow, New Coll., Oxford, 1964. Hon. DCL, Univ. of Pittsburgh, 1962; Hon. LLD: Brown Univ., 1963; New York Univ., 1964; William and Mary Coll., 1965; Manchester, 1966. DL Salop, 1961. KStJ. *Publications:* Must the West Decline?, 1966; (jtly) Europe: the case for going in, 1971. *Heir:* *s* Hon. Francis David Ormsby Gore, *b* 13 March 1954. *Address:* 14 Ladbroke Road, W11. *T:* 01–229 6701; House of Lords, Westminster, SW1; Glyn, Talsarnau, Gwynedd. *T:* Harlech 780338. *Club:* Pratt's. *Died 26 Jan.* 1985.

**HARLEY, Prof. John Laker,** CBE 1979; FRS 1964; FLS; FIBiol; MA, DPhil Oxon; Professor of Forest Science, Oxford University, 1969–79, then Emeritus Professor; Fellow of St John's College, Oxford, 1969–79, then Emeritus Fellow; *b* 17 Nov. 1911; *s* of late Charles Laker Harley and Edith Sarah (*née* Smith); *m* 1938, Elizabeth Lindsay Fitt; one *s* one *d*. *Educ:* Leeds Grammar Sch.; Wadham Coll., Oxford. Open Exhibition, Wadham Coll., 1930, Hon. Scholar 1933, Hon. Fellow, 1972; Christopher Welch Scholar, Oxford, 1933–37; Senior Student 1851 Exhibition, 1937–38. Departmental Demonstrator, Oxford, 1938–44. Served in Royal Signals, 1940–45: attached Operation Research Group No. 1, India, Lieut-Col GSO1. University Demonstrator, Oxford, 1945–62; Browne Research Fellow, Queen's Coll., Oxford, 1946–52; Official Fellow, Queen's Coll., Oxford, 1952–65; Reader in Plant Nutrition, Oxford Univ., 1962–65; Prof. of Botany, Sheffield Univ., 1965–69. Mem., ARC, 1970–80. President: British Mycological Soc., 1967 (Hon. Mem. 1980); British Ecological Soc., 1970–72 (Hon. Mem. 1983); Inst. of Biology, 1984–86. Hon. Fellow: Nat. Acad. of Scis, India, 1981; Wye Coll., 1983. Hon. MA and FilDr Uppsala, 1981; Hon. DSc Sheffield, 1989. Editor, New Phytologist, 1961–83. Linnean Medal for Botany, 1989. *Publications:* Biology of Mycorrhiza, 1969; (with S. E. Smith) Mycorrhizal Symbiosis, 1983; (with E. L. Harley) Check-list of Mycorrhiza in the British Flora, 1987; scientific papers in New Phytologist, Annals of Applied Mycology, Annals of Botany, Biochemical Jl, Plant Physiology, Proc. Royal Soc., Jl of Ecology. *Recreation:* gardening. *Address:* The Orchard, Old Marston, Oxford OX3 0PQ.
*Died 13 Dec.* 1990.

**HARLOCK, Maj.-Gen. Hugh George Frederick,** CBE 1953; *b* 20 Aug. 1900; *s* of James Harlock, Camperdown, Victoria; *m* 1935, Florence Madge, *d* of W. C. Ewing, Sydney, NSW; one *s* one *d*. *Educ:* Wesley Coll., Melbourne; RMC Duntroon. Commnd Aust. Staff Corps, 1921; Regimental and Staff appts in Royal Australian Artillery, 1922–39; Aust. Imperial Force, 1940–47; Staff appts, AHQ, 1947–49; Aust. Army Rep., UK, 1950–52; Brig. i/c Admin, E. Comd, 1953; Maj.-Gen. 1954; Gen. Officer Commanding, Northern Command, Australian Military Forces, 1954–57. *Address:* 2 Holmes

Street, Toowong, Queensland 4066, Australia. *Club:* United Service (Brisbane). *Died 30 July* 1981.

**HARMAN, Sir Cecil W. F. S. K.;** *see* Stafford-King-Harman.

**HARMAN, Ernest Henry,** CBE 1973 (OBE 1961); Chairman, South Western Gas Region (formerly South Western Gas Board), 1964–73; *b* 1908; *m* 2nd, 1958, Dorothy Anne Parsons; (two *d* by 1st *m*). *Educ:* London Univ. BSc (Hons). Sec., 1936, Gen. Manager, 1944, Commercial Gas Co.; Gen. Manager, Sheffield and Rotherham Div., East Midlands Gas Board, 1949; Dep. Chm., East Midlands Gas Board, 1952. *Recreations:* tennis, motoring, music. *Address:* Tall Trees, Court Hill, Church Lench, Evesham, Worcs WR11 4UH. *Died 22 Aug.* 1989.

**HARMER, Cyril Henry Carrington;** *b* 17 Aug. 1903; *s* of Henry Revell Harmer and Edith Annie Harmer; *m* 1935, Elizabeth Boyd Baird; two *d*. *Educ:* Brighton Grammar Sch. Joined H. R. Harmer, 1921; Partner, 1927; Dir, 1946; Chm. and Man. Dir, 1967–76; Pres., 1976–79. Lieut RA, 1939–45; POW, 1941–45. Roll of Distinguished Philatelists, 1969. *Publications:* (with R. E. R. Dalwick) Newfoundland Air Mails, 1953, rev. edn 1984; contribs to philatelic jls. *Recreation:* bowls. *Address:* 20 Wildcroft Manor, SW15 3TS. *T:* 01–788 0710. *Clubs:* Hurlingham; Collectors (New York).
*Died 17 Sept.* 1986.

**HARMOOD-BANNER, Sir George Knowles,** 3rd Bt, *cr* 1924; *b* 9 Nov. 1918; *s* of Sir Harmood Harmood-Banner, 2nd Bt, and Frances Cordelia (*d* 1975), *d* of late George Duberly, JP, Plansworth, Co. Durham; *S* father, 1950; *m* 1947, Rosemary Jane, *d* of Col M. L. Treston, CBE, FRCS, FRCOG, late IMS, and late Mrs Sheila Treston; two *d*. *Educ:* Eton; University of Cambridge. Served War of 1939–45; Lieut Royal Welch Fusiliers, 1942, attached to East African Engineers (SEAC); transferred RASC, 1945. *Recreations:* tennis, ski-ing and swimming. *Heir:* none. *Address:* c/o National Westminster Bank plc, 14 Sloane Square, SW1W 8EQ.
*Died 23 Oct.* 1990 (*ext*).

**HARMSWORTH, 2nd Baron,** *cr* 1939, of Egham; **Cecil Desmond Bernard Harmsworth;** painter; *b* 1903; *e s* of 1st Baron Harmsworth and Emilie Alberta (*d* 1942), *d* of William Hamilton Maffett, Finglas, Co. Dublin; *S* father, 1948; *m* 1926, Dorothy Alexander, *d* of late Hon. J. C. Heinlein, Bridgeport, Ohio, USA; one *d*. *Educ:* Eton Coll.; Christ Church, Oxford (MA); (in drawing) Académie Julian, Paris; (in painting) public galleries. Was successively newspaperman and book publisher before becoming a painter. Exhibitions: Galerie des Quatre-Chemins, Paris, 1933; Wildenstein Gall., London, 1938; Bonestell Gall., New York, 1944; Swedish Modern, Dallas, Texas, 1950; Messrs Roland, Browse & Delbanco, London, 1954; Berkeley Square Gall., London, 1988. Has been regular contributor to Salon d'Automne and group exhibitions in Paris; has exhibited in many London and New York galleries, and at the Phillips Memorial Gallery, Washington, DC. Portraits of Norman Douglas, Havelock Ellis, Lord Inverchapel, James Joyce, Consuelo de Saint-Exupéry, Sir Osbert Sitwell, Swami Nikhilananda, etc. Chairman, Dr Johnson's House Trust. Served in British Information Services, New York, 1940–46. *Publications:* occasional prose and verse contributions to English, Irish, and US periodicals, inc. verse translation of Paul Valéry, Le Cimetière Marin (Adam Internat. Review nos 334–336, 1969); drawings and paintings reproduced in US magazines. *Heir:* *nephew* Thomas Harold Raymond Harmsworth [*b* 20 July 1939; *m* 1971, Patricia Palmer, *d* of late M. P. Horsley; two *s* three *d*]. *Address:* Lime Lodge, Egham, Surrey. *T:* Egham (0784) 32379.
*Died 2 June* 1990.

**HARPER, Sir Arthur (Grant),** KCVO 1959 (CVO 1954); CBE 1954; JP; retired; Chairman: Wareham Associates Ltd; Woolshed Restaurant Ltd; Deputy Chairman, Williams Development Holdings Ltd; *b* 16 July 1898; *s* of William John and Robina Harper; *m* 1925, Hilda Mary Evans (decd); two *s* one *d*. *Educ:* Hastings High Sch. Entered NZ Civil Service, 1914; held various positions; Sec. for Internal Affairs, also Clerk of the Writs, NZ, 1948–58. Chief Electoral Officer, 1945–50; Dir of Royal Tours of NZ, 1953–54, 1956, 1958. Patron, Vice-Pres., Trustee or Mem. of several national and local voluntary organizations. JP 1949. *Recreations:* cricket and hockey, bowls (past); interested in most sports. *Address:* Flat 1, 50 Devonshire Road, Miramar, Wellington, NZ. *T:* 886–425. *Club:* United Services Officers' (Wellington).
*Died 17 May* 1982.

**HARPER, Frank Appleby, (Bill),** CB 1979; MBE 1954; Director of Establishments and Organisation, Department of Education and Science, 1974–80; *b* 11 April 1920; *s* of F. S. and M. E. B. Harper; *m* 1st, 1943, Daphne Margaret (*née* Short) (*d* 1965); one *d*; 2nd, 1968, Mrs Jillian Kate Langstaff (*née* Brooks). *Educ:* Grammar Sch., Birmingham. Regular Army (Royal Engrs) until joined Home Civil Service as Direct Entry Principal, 1964; Under-Sec. 1974.

*Recreation:* home workshop. *Address:* Lochnell, Searle Road, Farnham, Surrey. *T:* Farnham (Surrey) 714127.

*Died* 12 *Oct.* 1983.

**HARPER, George Clifford;** *b* 8 Aug. 1900; *s* of Charles George and Emily Harper, Newcastle upon Tyne; *m* 1st, 1925, Georgette Marie Aimée Guéry (*d* 1977); two *d* (and one *s* decd); 2nd, 1980, Margaret Rose Miriam Benezra. *Educ:* Shrewsbury Sch.; Christ Church, Oxford. Traffic Apprentice LNER; Asst Master at Stowe and Bedford; Headmaster of King Edward VI Sch., Southampton, until 1946; HM Inspector of Schools, 1947–60 (Metropolitan Divisional Inspector, 1952–60); Mem., Anglo-French Mixed Cultural Commn, 1954–60; Chm. and Dir, British Cttee for Interchange of Teachers with USA, 1960–65. Officier d'Académie. *Address:* 4 Trym Bank, Grove Road, Bristol BS9 2RQ. *T:* Bristol 685243.

*Died* 3 *Aug.* 1986.

**HARPER, Norman Adamson;** Vice President, Gemmological Association of Great Britain, since 1978 (Chairman, 1965–78); Founder-Director, Perry Greaves Ltd, 1964; Director: W. A. Perry & Co. Ltd, since 1953; Gemmological Instruments Ltd, since 1965; Managing Director, H. H. Bray Ltd, since 1977; *b* 15 Oct. 1913; *s* of Andrew Adamson Harper, Newcastle-upon-Tyne; *m* 1st, 1935, Priscilla (*d* 1956), *d* of William George Hoverd; three *s* one *d*; 2nd, 1957, Brenda, *d* of Robert Watts; one *s*. *Educ:* Rutherford Coll.; Durham Univ. Dip. Nat. Assoc. Goldsmiths, 1946. FGA 1934; FRGS 1946; FInstD 1953; FBIM 1978. Chm., Nat. Assoc. of Goldsmiths, 1961–63; Guardian of Standard of Wrought Plate in Birmingham, 1963–; Sen. Lectr on Gemstones and Jewellery, City of Birmingham Sch. of Jewellery and Silversmithing, 1946–66; Founder, Course on Gem Diamonds for Jewellers, 1962. Freedom of Goldsmiths' Co. (Special Award), 1947; Freedom of City of London, 1947. Winner of Greenough Trophy, 1946. *Publications:* Introduction to Gemstones, 1955; Handbook on Gem Diamonds, 1965; articles in Jl of Gemmology, British Jeweller, Watchmaker and Jeweller, etc. *Recreations:* keyboard music, historical studies. *Address:* 9 Jury Street, Warwick CV34 4EH. *T:* Warwick 42791. *Clubs:* Athenæum, Naval and Military, Number Ten; Portcullis (Warwick). *Died* 8 *July* 1982.

**HARRAP, (George) Paull (Munro),** CBE 1974; Chairman, Harrap General Books, since 1981; *b* 10 June 1917; *s* of George Steward and Kathleen Mary Harrap; *m* 1959, Alice Foyle. *Educ:* privately. Entered family firm, 1936; Chm., George G. Harrap & Co. Ltd, 1971–81. *Address:* Tile House, Stebbing Green, Essex. *T:* Stebbing 261; 60 Darwin Court, Gloucester Avenue, NW1 7BQ. *T:* 01–267 8571. *Died* 26 *Feb.* 1985.

**HARRIMAN, (William) Averell;** US Ambassador-at-Large, 1965–69; *b* 15 Nov. 1891; *s* of late Edward Henry Harriman and Mary Williamson Averell; *m* 1st, 1915, Kitty Lanier Lawrence (decd); two *d*; 2nd, 1930, Mrs Marie Norton Whitney; 3rd, 1971, Hon. Mrs Leland Hayward, *e d* of 11th Baron Digby, KG, DSO, MC, TD. *Educ:* Groton Sch., Yale Univ., BA 1913. Partner Brown Brothers Harriman & Co. since 1931, Limited partner since 1946; Chairman of the Board, Union Pacific Railroad Co. 1932–46; Mem. Business Advisory Council for the Dept of Commerce since 1933 (Chm., 1937–40). Vice-Pres. in Charge of Purchases and Supplies of Union Pacific Railroad Co., 1914–18; Chm. Board of Merchant Shipbuilding Corp., 1917–25; Chm. Board of W. A. Harriman & Co., Inc. (merged with Brown Brothers, 1931), 1920–30; Chm. Exec. Cttee Ill. Central Railroad Co., 1931–42; National Recovery Administration: Division Administrator of Div. II, Jan.-March 1934, Special Asst Administrator, March-May, 1934, Administrative Officer, Nov. 1934–June 1935; Associated with Industrial Materials Div., National Defense Advisory Commission, 1940; Chief, Materials Branch, Production Div., Office of Production Management, Jan.-March 1941; Pres. Roosevelt's Special Representative in Great Britain with rank of Minister, March 1941; Special Rep. of the Pres. and Chm. of the President's Special Mission to USSR with rank of Ambassador, 1941; US Representative in London of Combined Shipping Adjustment Board, 1942; Mem. London Combined Production and Resources Board, 1942; US Ambassador to USSR, 1943–46; to Britain, 1946; US Sec. of Commerce, 1946–48; US Special Representative in Europe under Economic Co-operation Act of 1948 (with rank of Ambassador) until 1950; US Rep. on N Atlantic Defence, Financial and Economic Cttee, 1949; Special Asst to Pres. Truman, 1950–51; Chm. NATO Commission on Defense Plans, 1951; Dir of Foreign Aid under Mutual Security Act, 1951–53; Governor, State of New York, Jan. 1955-Dec. 1958; US Ambassador-at-Large, Feb.-Dec. 1961 and 1965–69; Asst Sec. of State for Far Eastern Affairs, 1961–63; Under-Sec. for Political Affairs, 1963–65. Negotiated Limited Test Ban Treaty, 1963; US Representative, Vietnam Peace Talks, Paris, 1968–69. Medal for Merit, presented by President Harry S. Truman; Presidential Medal of Freedom, with distinction, presented by President Lyndon B. Johnson, 1969; Foreign Service Cup, American Foreign Service, 1980; Winston Churchill Award, Winston Churchill Foundn, 1981; Four Freedoms Award, 1983.

Hon. LLD: New York, 1947; Columbia, 1954; Yale, 1964; Harvard, 1966; Georgetown, 1970; Yeshiva, 1972; and many other hon. degrees. Democrat. *Publications:* Peace with Russia?, 1960; America and Russia in a Changing World, 1971; (with E. Abel) Special Envoy to Churchill and Stalin 1941–1946, 1975. *Address:* (residence) Willow Oaks, Middleburg, Va 22117, USA.

*Died* 26 *July* 1986.

**HARRIS,** 5th Baron *cr* 1815, of Seringapatam and Mysore, and of Belmont, Kent; **George St Vincent Harris,** CBE 1972; MC; JP; DL; Vice-Lieutenant of Kent, 1948–72; *b* 3 Sept. 1889; *e s* of 4th Baron and Hon. Lucy Ada Jervis, CI (*d* 1930), *d* of 3rd Viscount St Vincent; *S* father, 1932; *m* 1918, Dorothy Mary (*d* 1981) (Order of League of Mercy), *d* of Rev. W. J. Crookes, late Vicar of Borden; one *s*. *Educ:* Eton, Christ Church, Oxford (MA). Capt. late Royal East Kent Imperial Yeomanry; served European War, 1914–18 (MC, wounded, despatches). Grand Master, Mark Master Masons of England, 1954–73; Grand Master, Masonic Knights Templar of England, 1947–73. Commissioner St John Amb. Brigade for Kent, 1940–45; Chm. Kent Police Authority, 1945–64; KStJ 1949. JP 1919, DL 1936, Kent. *Heir: s* Hon. George Robert John Harris, *b* 17 April 1920. *Address:* Belmont Park, Faversham, Kent. *Clubs:* MCC, Carlton, Beefsteak. *Died* 16 *Oct.* 1984.

**HARRIS, Marshal of the Royal Air Force Sir Arthur Travers,** 1st Bt, *cr* 1953; GCB 1945 (KCB 1942; CB 1940); OBE 1927; AFC 1918; *b* 13 April 1892; *m* 1st, 1916; one *s* two *d*; 2nd, 1938, Thérèse Hearne; one *d*. Served European War, 1914–19, 1st Rhodesian Regt, RFC, and RAF; India, 1921–22; Iraq, 1922–24; Egypt, 1930–32; Group Capt. 1933; Air Ministry, Dep. Dir of Plans, 1934–37; Air Commodore, 1937; AOC 4 Bomber Gp, 1937; Head of RAF Mission, USA and Canada, 1938; Air Vice-Marshal, 1939; Air Marshal, 1941; Air Chief Marshal, 1943; AOC, RAF Palestine and Transjordan, 1938–39; AOC, 5 Bomber Group, 1939–40; Deputy Chief of Air Staff, 1940–41; Head of Royal Air Force Delegation to USA, 1941; Commander-in-Chief Bomber Command 1942–45. Marshal of the RAF 1945. Managing Director South African Marine Corporation, 1946–53. Order of Suvorov (1st class) (Russia), 1944, Grand Cross Polonia Restituta (Poland), 1945, Chief Commander Legion of Merit (US), 1944; Grand Cross Order of the Southern Cross (Brazil), 1945; Grand Officier Légion d'Honneur, Croix de guerre avec palme (France), 1945; DSM (US), 1945. Freeman of Honiton and of Chepping Wycombe; Freeman, City of London and Liveryman, Guild of Air Pilots and Air Navigators, 1978. Hon. LLD Liverpool, 1946. *Heir: s* Anthony Kyrle Travers Harris, *b* 18 March 1918. *Address:* The Ferry House, Goring-on-Thames, Oxfordshire RG8 9DX. *Clubs:* Royal Air Force, Army and Navy; Pathfinders; Royal and Ancient (St Andrews).

*Died* 5 *April* 1984.

**HARRIS, Sir Charles Joseph William,** KBE 1961 (CBE 1927); Kt 1952; Private Secretary to successive Parliamentary Secretaries to Treasury, 1919–24, 1924–29 and 1931–61; retired as Assistant Secretary, HM Treasury, 1961; *b* 1901; *m* 1924, Emily Kyle Thompson; one *s* two *d*. *Educ:* Christ Church Sch., Ramsgate; privately. Private Sec. to Conservative Chief Whip, 1924 and 1929–31. Freeman, City of London; Mem., Court of Assistants, Guild of Freemen of City of London; Liveryman, Scriveners' Company. *Address:* 7 Fir Tree Court, Allum Lane, Elstree, Herts WD6 3NF. *T:* 01–953 6618. *Club:* City Livery.

*Died* 14 *Jan.* 1986.

**HARRIS, Euan Cadogan;** Deputy Legal Adviser, Ministry of Agriculture, Fisheries and Food, 1964–71; *b* 6 June 1906; *s* of late Charles Poulett Harris, MD and Violet Harris; *m* 1931, Brenda (*d* 1986), *er d* of late William Turnbull Bowman, OBE and Jessie Bowman; two *d*. *Educ:* Epsom Coll.; Clare Coll., Cambridge. BA 1927; LLM 1928. Admitted Solicitor (Edmund Thomas Child Prize), 1930. Entered Legal Dept of Min. of Agric. and Fisheries, 1935; Asst Solicitor, 1949–64. *Recreations:* walking, swimming, gardening; reading, especially history and psychical research. *Address:* Great Maytham Hall, Rolvenden, Kent TN17 4NE. *T:* Cranbrook 241284. *Died* 4 *May* 1988.

**HARRIS, Sir Jack Alexander S.;** *see* Sutherland-Harris.

**HARRIS, Kenneth Edwin,** MA, MD Cantab; FRCP; Senior Physician and Cardiologist, University College Hospital; Consulting Physician to the Republic of the Sudan in London; Consulting Physician Royal Chest Hospital; Senior Censor, Royal College of Physicians; Examiner in Medicine Universities of Cambridge, London and Bristol, and Conjoint Examining Board of England; *b* 13 May 1900; *s* of late Dr Thomas Harris, MD, FRCP, Physician, Manchester Royal Infirmary, and late I. M. Harris (*née* Brockbank); *m* 1932, Edith I. L. Abbott (*d* 1981), MB, BS (London), DPH (Eng.); no *c*. *Educ:* Shrewsbury Sch.; Gonville and Caius Coll., Cambridge; University Coll. Hospital. BA (Hons); Fellowes Silver Medal for Clinical Medicine; Liston Gold Medal for Surgery; Erichsen Prize for Practical Surgery. Liveryman, Apothecaries Soc.; Vice-Pres. of Cambridge Graduates Medical Club. Freeman of City of London.

Mem., English-Speaking Union. *Publications:* Minor Medical operations (with E. I. L. Harris), 1938; contributions to: Heart, Lancet, BMJ, 1929–. *Recreations:* philately, gardening, colour photography, foreign travel and architecture. *Address:* The White House, 4 Grand Avenue, Worthing, West Sussex BN11 5AN. *T:* Worthing 48056. *Died* 23 *Oct.* 1981.

**HARRIS, Sir Lewis Edward,** Kt 1979; OBE 1960; *b* 25 March 1900; *s* of Joseph Henry Harris and Mable Harris, New Zealand; *m* Myra Nicholson Anderson, *d* of Christopher Nicholson; two *s* one *d*. *Educ:* Hastings School, New Zealand. Knighthood conferred for services to the handicapped in New Zealand. *Address:* Brooklands, Puketapu, Hawkes Bay, RD2, Napier, New Zealand.
*Died* 3 *March* 1983.

**HARRIS, Thomas Maxwell,** FRS 1948; Professor of Botany, University of Reading, 1935–68, Professor Emeritus, 1968; *b* 8 Jan. 1903; *s* of Alexander Charles Harris and Lucy Frances Evans; *m* 1928, Katharine Massey; one *s* three *d*. *Educ:* Bootham, York; Wyggeston Sch., Leicester; University Coll., Nottingham; Christ's Coll., Cambridge (scholar). Natural Science Tripos, Parts I and II, 1st Class Hons; London BSc, 1st Class Hons; ScD Cambridge; Mem. of Danish Expedition to E Greenland, 1926–27; Demonstrator in Botany, 1928; Fellow of Christ's Coll., 1928. Vice-Pres., Royal Society, 1960–61; President, Linnæan Soc., 1961–64; Vice-Pres., 1964. Trustee, Natural History Museum, 1963–73. *Publications:* communications to scientific journals on Palæobotany. *Recreation:* gardening. *Address:* 74 Birdhill Avenue, Reading RG2 7JU. *T:* Reading 84930; Department of Geology, The University, Reading, Berks. *Died* 1 *May* 1983.

**HARRIS, Sir William (Woolf),** Kt 1974; OBE 1961; JP; surveyor and public companies director; *b* London, 19 Aug. 1910; *e s* of Simon Harris and Fanny Harris, London; *m* 1952, Beverly Joyce, *y d* of Howard Bowden, Minneapolis, USA; one *s* two *d*. *Educ:* King's Coll.; Princeton Univ. Chm. of number of companies concerned with residential and industrial building construction. Chm., Bow Street Magistrates Court, 1955–80; Chm., Inner London Juvenile Courts, 1955–75; Member: Inner London Sessions Appeals Court; London Probation Cttee and Home Office Juvenile Courts Consultative Cttee, 1955–72; a General Commissioner of Taxes; Vice-Pres. (former Chm.), Royal Soc. of St George (City of London); former jt Nat. Treas., Trades Adv. Council; Founder 1951, and Chm. until 1963, Addison Boys Club, Hammersmith; Conservative Party: Chairman: Nat. Union of Conservative Assocs, 1971–73; Party Conf., 1972; Standing Adv. Cttee on Candidates, 1971–73; Greater London Area, 1966–69; former London Area, 1963; Mem., Adv. Cttee on Policy, 1965–75 and of other nat. adv. cttees; Mem., Nat. Exec. Cttee and Gen. Purpose Cttee, 1963–75; Chm., S Battersea Conservative Assoc., 1956–63; former Pres. and Chm., Battersea Chamber of Commerce; Branch Chm., NSPCC, 1956–65; Founder and Nat. Chm., Leasehold Reform Assoc., 1956–67. Mem. Council and Ct, City Univ., 1979–. Mem. Council, Imperial Soc. of Knights Bachelor, 1978–. Prime Warden, Worshipful Co. of Basketmakers, 1984–85. Freeman, City of London; High Sheriff of Greater London, 1971–72; JP Bow Street, 1952. *Publications:* papers on problems of juvenile delinquency, child welfare, mental health and penal reform in various jls. *Recreations:* reading history, theatre, travel. *Address:* 6 London House, Avenue Road, NW8 7PX. *T:* 01–586 0707. *Clubs:* Carlton, St Stephen's Constitutional, City Livery. *Died* 23 *Sept.* 1988.

**HARRISON, Alexander,** CBE 1955; CA; *b* 26 Feb. 1890; *s* of John Harrison, CBE, LLD, FRSE, DL, and Helen Georgina Roberts; *m* 1931, Jean Muriel Small; one *s* three *d*. *Educ:* Merchiston Castle Sch. Chartered Accountant, 1914 (Distinction). Chairman: Edinburgh Savings Bank, 1945–54; Edinburgh Investment Trust, 1945–60; Standard Life Assurance Co., 1955–57; Dir, British Linen Bank, 1945–68; Alex Cowan & Sons. Former Vice-Pres., Trustee Savings Bank Assoc. (Dep. Chm., 1947–59). Mem. Edinburgh Town Council, 1946–48. Served European War, 1914–18; temp. Major, Royal Scots, attached Machine Gun Corps in France and Italy, FRSGS. Hon. Pres., Scottish Mountaineering Club. *Address:* 3a Tipperlinn Road, Edinburgh EH10 5ET. *T:* 031–447 7434. *Clubs:* Alpine; New (Edinburgh). *Died* 1 *Dec.* 1988.

**HARRISON, Rev. Cecil Marriott;** Vicar of Aislaby, Diocese of York, 1969–79, retired; *b* 16 March 1911; *s* of late Tom Marriott Harrison, Davidson's Mains, Midlothian; *m* 1944, Phyllis Edith McKenzie. *Educ:* Westminster Sch.; Trinity Coll., Cambridge. 1st Class Classical Tripos Pt I, 1930; Pt II, 1932; BA 1932, MA 1936; Classical Sixth Form Master, Nottingham High Sch., 1932; Dulwich Coll., 1934; Charterhouse, 1936–47. Served War of 1939–45; Royal Signals, 1940–46; Headmaster of Felsted Sch., 1947–51; Headmaster, King's School, Peterborough, 1951–69. Deacon, 1966, Priest, 1967. *Address:* 4 Rosedale Abbey, Pickering, N Yorks YO18 8RA. *T:* Lastingham 569. *Died* 15 *Aug.* 1986.

**HARRISON, Maj.-Gen. Desmond,** CB 1946; DSO 1940; FICE; Civil Engineer; *b* 11 Nov. 1896; *s* of R. J. Harrison, JP; *m* 1920, Kathleen

Harrison (*née* Hazley); one *s* two *d* (*er s* killed 1945 serving in NW Europe). *Educ:* Kilkenny Coll.; Mountjoy Sch., Dublin; RMA, Woolwich; Cambridge Univ. Temp. Maj.-Gen. 1944; Maj.-Gen. 1947; Comdt SME 1942; Engineer-in-Chief, SEAC, 1943; Director of Fortifications and Works, War Office, 1946; retired 1947. Mem. Overseas Food Corp., 1947; resigned 1949. Comdr Legion of Merit, USA. *Recreations:* golf, shooting, fishing. *Address:* 55 Hans Road, SW3. *T:* 01–584 4867. *Club:* Army and Navy.
*Died* 23 *June* 1984.

**HARRISON, Maj.-Gen. Eric George William Warde,** CB 1945; CBE 1943; MC 1915; MA (hon.) Oxford; *b* 23 March 1893; *s* of Major W. C. Warde Harrison, Indian Army; *m* 1961, Mrs Roza M. Stevenson (*d* 1967), widow of J. B. Stevenson. *Educ:* Royal Military Academy, Woolwich. Commissioned Royal Artillery, 1913; European War, France and Belgium, 1914–19, GSOII 58 Div. and III Corps (despatches four times, MC, Crown of Italy, Bt Major); Staff Coll. Camberley, 1925–26; GSOII Lahore District, India, 1928–32; shot in Tanganika, 1930; in Baltistan, British Lahaul, Chamba in Himalayas, and in forests of United and Central Provinces in India; Major, 1932; Bt Lieut-Col 1931; Commanding Oxford Univ. OTC 1934–38; Lieut-Col 1939; Col 1939. War of 1939–45, CRA 12 Div., BRA Northern Ireland, CCRA 9 Corps, MGRA AFHQ, Comdr Surrey and Sussex District. War Service North Africa and Italy, 1943–45 (despatches, CBE, CB); Temp. Maj.-Gen. 1944; ADC to the King, 1945–46; retired pay, 1946. JP 1951, DL 1955, High Sheriff 1958, Cornwall. Chm. St Lawrence's Hospital Management Cttee, 1952–66. *Publications:* Riding, 1949; To Own a Dog, 1951; Gunners, Game and Gardens, 1979. *Recreations:* gardening, painting; Rugby football Mother Country XV 1919, Army 1920; Athletics, represented England in 120 yds Hurdles, 1914 and 1920, Olympic Games, 1924; Master RA Harriers, 1920–24, Staff Coll. Drag 1925–26, Lahore Hounds 1928–31, South Oxon Foxhounds, 1935–38, North Cornwall Foxhounds, 1940–48. *Address:* Swallowfield Park, near Reading, Berks. *Club:* Army and Navy. *Died* 20 *Dec.* 1987.

**HARRISON, Ernest,** CMG 1935; BSc; *b* 30 July 1886; *s* of Thomas Harrison and Louise Goodwin; *m* 1st, 1911, Annie Gladys Anyan (*d* 1920); 2nd, 1925, Josephine ffolliott Highett (*d* 1957); two *s* (and two *s* killed on active service); 3rd, Helen Day Price. *Educ:* Holmes Chapel; Edinburgh Univ.; Ames, Iowa, USA. Lectr, Grootfontein Sch. of Agriculture, Cape Colony, 1910–12; Principal, Sch. of Agriculture, Cedara, Natal, 1913–17; Land Manager, S African Townships, Mining and Finance Corp., 1918–20; Dep. Dir of Agriculture, Kenya Colony, 1921–30; Dir of Agriculture, Tanganyika, 1930–37; Prof. of Agriculture, Imperial Coll. of Tropical Agriculture, Trinidad, BWI, 1938–43, 1943–47. Agricultural Consultant, Lima, Peru. *Address:* 876 Somenos Street, Victoria, BC V8S 4A6, Canada. *Died* 7 *March* 1981.

**HARRISON, Prof. Francis Llewelyn,** FBA 1965; Professor of Ethnomusicology, University of Amsterdam, 1970–76, later Emeritus; *b* Dublin, 29 Sept. 1905; *s* of Alfred Francis and Florence May Harrison; *m* 1966, Joan Rimmer; (two *d* of a former marriage). *Educ:* St Patrick's Cathedral Gram. Sch., Dublin; Mountjoy Sch., Dublin; Trinity Coll., Dublin; Oxford Univ. MusB Dublin, 1926; MusD Dublin, 1929; MA, DMus Oxon, 1952; Hon. LLD Queen's (Canada), 1974. Organist, St Canice's Cath., Kilkenny, 1927; Prof. of Music: Queen's Univ., Kingston, Ontario, 1935; Colgate Univ., 1946; Washington Univ., St Louis, 1947; Lectr in Music, 1952, Sen. Lectr, 1956, Reader in History of Music, 1962–70, University of Oxford; Senior Research Fellow, Jesus Coll., 1965–70. Visiting Professor of Musicology: Yale Univ., 1958–59; Utrecht Univ., 1976–79; Mellon, Univ. of Pittsburg, 1981; Vis. Prof. of Music, Princeton Univ., 1961, 1968–69; Vis. Mem., Inst. for Advanced Study, Princeton, 1957; Vis. Scholar, Queen's Univ, Kingston, 1980; Fellow of Center for Advanced Study in the Behavioral Sciences, Stanford, Calif, 1965–66. General Editor: Early English Church Music, 1961–73; Polyphonic Music of the Fourteenth Century, 1963–73. *Publications:* The Eton Choirbook (3 vols), 1956–61; Music in Medieval Britain, 1958; Collins Music Encyclopaedia (with J. A. Westrup), 1956; Musicology (with M. Hood and C. V. Palisca), 1963; European Musical Instruments (with J. Rimmer), 1964; Polyphonic Music of the Fourteenth Century, vol. V (Motets of French Provenance), 1969, vol. XV (Motets of English Provenance), 1980, (with E. Sanders and P. J. Lefferts) vol. XVI (English Music for Mass and Office), 1983, vol. XVII (Votive Sequences etc.), 1986; Time, Place and Music, 1974; (with E. J. Dobson) Medieval English Songs, 1979; edns of music by William Mundy, John Sheppard and others; contribs to New Oxford History of Music, and to musical jls, etc. *Recreation:* travel. *Address:* 3 Gore Mews, Canterbury, Kent CT1 1JB. *T:* Canterbury 59752. *Died* 29 *Dec.* 1987.

**HARRISON, Sir Geoffrey (Wedgwood),** GCMG 1968 (KCMG 1955; CMG 1949); KCVO 1961; HM Diplomatic Service, retired; *b* Southsea, 18 July 1908; *s* of late Lieut-Comdr Thomas Edmund Harrison, Royal Navy, and Maud, *d* of Percy Godman; *m* 1936,

Amy Katharine, *d* of late Rt Hon. Sir R. H. Clive, PC, GCMG; three *s* one *d. Educ:* Winchester; King's Coll., Cambridge. Entered FO, 1932; served HM Embassy, Tokyo, 1935–37; HM Embassy, Berlin, 1937–39; Private Sec. to Parly Under-Sec., FO, 1939–41; First Sec., FO, 1941–45; Counsellor, HM Embassy, Brussels, 1945–47; Brit. Minister in Moscow, 1947–49; Head of Northern Dept, FO, 1949–51; Asst Under-Sec., FO, 1951–56; Ambassador: to Brazil, 1956–58; to Persia, 1958–63; Dep. Under-Sec. of State, FO, 1963–65; Ambassador to the USSR, 1965–68. Mem., West Sussex CC, 1970–77. Order of Homayoun (1st Class), 1959. *Recreations:* music, gardening. *Address:* West Wood, Mannings Heath, near Horsham, Sussex. *T:* Horsham 40409.

*Died 12 April 1990.*

**HARRISON, Rear-Adm. Hubert Southwood,** CBE 1951; DSC 1941; *b* Glasgow, 7 Aug. 1898; *s* of T. S. Harrison; *m* 1935, Beth Rowson Saynor (*d* 1962). *Educ:* Trinity Coll., Glenalmond. Cadet, RN, 1916; Midshipman, 1917; Sub-Lieut, 1918; Lieut (E), 1920; Lieut-Comdr (E), 1927; Comdr (E), 1930; Capt. (E), 1941; Rear-Adm. (E), 1948; Asst Dir of Dockyards, Admiralty, 1946–52; retired, 1952. *Recreations:* golf, sailing, fishing. *Address:* House in the Wood, Budock Vean, Falmouth. *T:* Mawnan Smith 250337.

*Died 26 June 1985.*

**HARRISON, Maj.-Gen. John Martin Donald W.;** *see* Ward-Harrison.

**HARRISON, Laurence,** CMG 1952, retired; *b* 3 Oct. 1897; *s* of late George Henry Harrison; *m* 1st, 1923, Nellie Florence (Serving Sister of Order of St John; *d* 1963); one *d*; 2nd, 1969, Jenny Margaret Wallace Pritchard (*née* Duncan), Sandown, Johannesburg. *Educ:* St Dunstan's Coll.; Strand Sch. Served BEF France (RE), 1916–19. Entered Min. of Pensions, 1919; transf. to Dept of Overseas Trade, 1930; Asst Trade Commissioner, Johannesburg, 1937, Trade Commissioner (Grade II), 1945, Trade Commissioner (Grade I), New Delhi, 1947, Johannesburg, 1953–57. *Recreation:* field natural history. *Address:* 3 Victoria Court, Barberton, 1300 East Transvaal, South Africa. *Died 5 Oct. 1982.*

**HARRISON, Lloyd Adnitt,** CBE 1977; Chief Executive Officer, Greater Nottingham Co-operative Society Ltd, 1969–77; *b* 15 March 1911; *s* of late Joseph Adnitt Harrison and Frances Louisa Harrison; *m* 1954, Mabel Pauline Hooley. *Educ:* Beeston Higher Sch., Notts; Co-operative Coll. Nottingham Co-op. Soc. Ltd: Admin. Officer, 1956–65; Managing Sec., 1965–69. Director: Co-operative Insurance Soc. Ltd, 1973–75; Co-operative Bank, 1974–75; Co-operative Wholesale Soc. Ltd, 1968–76 (Chm., CWS, 1973–76). Chm., Building and Social Housing Foundn. Vice-Pres., Nottingham Univ. Council. CBIM. Hon. LLD Nottingham, 1983. *Recreations:* music, reading, walking, gardening, local radio (formerly Chm. Local Radio Council, Nottingham). *Address:* 63 Parkside, Wollaton, Nottingham NG8 2NQ. *T:* Nottingham 256452. *Died 23 Aug. 1985.*

**HARRISON, Sir Reginald Carey, (Sir Rex Harrison),** Kt 1989; Commendatore, Order of Merit of the Republic of Italy, 1967; actor; *b* 5 March 1908; *s* of William Reginald and Edith Carey Harrison; *m* 1st, 1934, Marjorie Noel Collette Thomas; one *s*; 2nd, 1943, Lilli Palmer (marr. diss. 1957; she *d* 1986); one *s*; 3rd, 1957, Kay Kendall (*d* 1959); 4th, 1962, Rachel Roberts (marr. diss. 1971); 5th, Hon. Elizabeth Rees Harris (marr. diss. 1976), *d* of 1st Baron Ogmore, PC, TD; 6th, 1978, Mercia Tinker. *Educ:* Birkdale Preparatory Sch.; Liverpool Coll. Made first appearance on the stage at Liverpool Repertory Theatre, 1924; remained until 1927. Toured with Charley's Aunt playing Jack, 1927; also toured at intervals during subsequent years until 1935, and appeared with Cardiff Repertory, and in the West End. First appearance on London stage as Rankin in The Ninth Man, Prince of Wales Theatre, 1931; First appearance on New York stage at Booth Theatre, 1936, as Tubbs Barrow in Sweet Aloes. Played in French Without Tears at Criterion, 1936–37–38, and at Haymarket Theatre, 1939–41, in Design for Living (Leo) and No Time for Comedy (Gaylord Esterbrook). Volunteered RAFVR, 1941, and served till 1944. Released from Forces to make Blithe Spirit (film), and, 1945, Rake's Progress (film). Filmed in Hollywood, 1945–46–47. (Maxwell Anderson's) Anne of the Thousand Days, Schubert Theatre, NY, 1948–49 (Antoinette Perry Award, best actor); in The Cocktail Party, New Theatre, London, 1950; acted in and produced Bell, Book and Candle, Ethel Barrymore Theatre, NY, 1951, and Phœnix Theatre, London, 1954; in Venus Observed, Century Theatre, NY, 1952; directed and played in Love of Four Colonels, Schubert Theatre, NY, 1953; produced Nina, Haymarket Theatre, London, 1955; acted in: My Fair Lady (Henry Higgins), Mark Hellinger Theatre, NY, 1956–57 (Antoinette Perry Award, best actor), and Drury Lane, London, 1958–59; The Fighting Cock, Anta Theatre, NY, 1959; Platonov, Royal Court, 1960 (Evening Standard Award, best actor); August for the People, Edinburgh Festival, 1961, and Royal Court Theatre; The Lionel Touch, Lyric, 1969; Henry IV, Her Majesty's, 1974; Perrichon's Travels, Chichester, 1976; Caesar

and Cleopatra, NY, 1977; The Kingfisher, NY, 1978–79; Heartbreak House, Haymarket, 1983, NY, 1983; Aren't We All?, Haymarket, 1984–85, NY and US tour, 1986; Australian tour, 1986–87; The Admirable Crichton, Haymarket, 1988; The Circle, NY, 1989. Began acting in films in 1929. Best known films: Storm in a Teacup, 1936; St Martin's Lane, 1937; Over the Moon, 1938; Night Train to Munich, Major Barbara, 1940–41; Blithe Spirit, 1944; I Live in Grosvenor Square, 1944; The Rake's Progress, 1945; (Hollywood, 1945) Anna and the King of Siam, 1946; The Ghost and Mrs Muir, 1947; The Foxes of Harrow, 1947; (Galsworthy's) Escape (in England), 1948; Unfaithfully Yours (in America), 1948; The Long Dark Hall, 1951; King Richard and the Crusaders, 1954; The Constant Husband, 1955; The Reluctant Debutante, 1958; Midnight Lace, 1960; The Happy Thieves, 1961; Cleopatra (Julius Caesar), 1962; My Fair Lady, 1964 (Academy Award, best actor); The Yellow Rolls Royce, 1965; The Agony and the Ecstacy, 1965; The Honey Pot, 1967; Doctor Dolittle, 1967; A Flea in her Ear, 1967; Staircase, 1968; The Prince and the Pauper, 1976; Man in the Iron Mask, 1977; Ashanti, 1979; television work includes: Anastasia, 1986. *Publication:* Rex (autobiog.), 1974. *Recreations:* golf, painting. *Address:* 5 Impasse de la Fontaine, Monte Carlo, Monaco 98000. *Clubs:* Beefsteak, Green Room, Garrick; Players' (New York); Travellers' (Paris). *Died 2 June 1990.*

**HARRISON, Prof. Ronald George;** Derby Professor of Anatomy, University of Liverpool, since 1950; *b* 5 April 1921; *s* of James Harrison and Alice Hannah Harrison (*née* Edmondson); *m* 1945, Marjorie Gooding (marr. diss. 1965), Fairfield, St Philip, Barbados; two *s* one *d*; *m* 1966, Dr M. J. Hoey, Southport, Lancs; one *d. Educ:* Ulverston Grammar Sch.; Oxford Univ. BA Oxon, 1942; BM, BCh, Oxon 1944; MA Oxon, 1946; DM Oxon, 1949. Demy, Magdalen Coll., Oxford, 1939–42; Pres., OU Scientific Club, 1942. Junior Gynæcological House Surg., Nuffield Dept of Obstetrics and Gynæcology, Oxford, 1943; Gynæc. and Obst. House Surgeonships, Radcliffe Infirmary, Oxford, 1944–45; Demonstrator and Lecturer, Dept of Human Anatomy, Univ. of Oxford, 1945–49. Lectr in Anatomy, Ruskin Sch. of Drawing and Fine Art, 1946–50; Univ. Demonstrator, Dept of Human Anatomy, Univ. of Oxford, 1949–50; Lectr in Anatomy, Pembroke Coll., Oxford, 1950; Vis. Prof. of Egyptology, Univ. of Cairo, 1972. Sometime External Examr: RCS; RCSI; Univs of: Belfast, Birmingham, Glasgow, Leeds, London, Manchester, Oxford, TCD, Khartoum, Haile Sellassie I, Addis Ababa. Lectures: First Celebrity, British Acad. Forensic Scis, 1970; Sir John Struthers Meml, 1979. BBC TV film, Tutankhamen Postmortem, 1969; ITV film, Tutankhamen Kinship, 1973. Fellow: Eugenics Soc.; Zoological Soc. of London. Chm., Bd of Governors, Liverpool Coll. of Occupational Therapy, 1968; President: Inst. of Science Technology, 1972–76; Liverpool Univ. Med. Sciences Club, 1954–55; Wallasey Med. Soc., 1981–82. For. Corr. Mem., Royal Belgian Soc. of Obstetrics and Gynæcology, 1964–68. Pres., Rotary Club of Liverpool, 1971 (Vice-Pres., 1970). Kt of the Dannebrog (Denmark), 1977. *Publications:* A Textbook of Human Embryology, 1959, 1963; The Adrenal Circulation, 1960; Sex and Infertility, 1977; Clinical Embryology, 1978; Chapters in Cunningham's Textbook of Anatomy, 1964, 1972, 1981; Orthopaedics and Traumatology, 1980; contrib. to various medical and scientific journals. Editor, Studies on Fertility, 1954–58. *Recreations:* riding, egyptology. *Address:* The Stables, Fernhill, Upper Brighton, Wallasey, Merseyside. *T:* 051-639 6327.

*Died 31 Dec. 1982.*

**HARROWBY, 6th Earl of,** *cr* 1809; **Dudley Ryder;** Baron Harrowby, 1776; Viscount Sandon, 1809; Major, late RFA (TAR); *b* 11 Oct. 1892; *e s* of 5th Earl of Harrowby and Hon. Mabel Danvers Smith, DBE (*d* 1956), *y d* of late Rt Hon. W. H. Smith, MP, and 1st Viscountess Hambleden; *S* father 1956; *m* 1922, Lady Helena Blanche Coventry (*d* 1974), *e d* of late Viscount Deerhurst; two *s* one *d. Educ:* Eton; Christ Church, Oxford (BA). Asst Private Sec. to Viscount Milner, Sec. of State for the Colonies, Jan. 1919–Aug. 1920; MP (U) Shrewsbury Division of Salop, Nov. 1922–Nov. 1923, and Oct. 1924–May 1929; Parliamentary Private Sec. to Sir S. Hoare, Sec. of State for Air, Dec. 1922–Nov. 1923; Alderman LCC, 1932–37, Mem. for Dulwich, 1937–40; served European War, Major RA, 1914–19 (wounded); served War of 1939–45. Col Commandant Staffs Army Cadet Force, 1946–50. DL Staffs, 1925; JP Staffs, 1929; Mem. of Royal Commission on Historical Manuscripts, 1935–66. Hon. DLitt Oxon, 1964. *Publications:* England at Worship; (joint) Geography of Everyday Things. *Heir:* *s* Viscount Sandon. *Address:* Sandon Hall, Stafford; Burnt Norton, Chipping Campden, Gloucestershire. *Club:* Travellers'. *Died 7 May 1987.*

**HARRY, Ralph Gordon,** MChemA, CChem, FRSC; *b* 25 June 1908; *s* of Jenkin Campbell Harry and Sarah Harrison; *m* 1938, Dorothy Mary Crafter; two *d. Educ:* Monkton House Sch., Cardiff; University Coll. of S Wales and Monmouthshire. Asst to Public Analyst, Cardiff (Inst. of Prev. Med.), 1934–37; Chief Chemist, J. Campbell Harry & Co., 1937–41; Manager, Toilet Research Dept, Unilever Ltd, 1941–47; Head, Cosmetic and Toilet Preparations Research Dept, Beecham Research, 1947–49; Chief Experimental

Chemist, Maclean Gp of Companies, 1949–53; Chief Research and Develt Chemist and Dep. Chief Chemist (Pharmaceuticals and Cosmetics), Internat. Chemical Co. Ltd (American Home Products Corp.), 1954–73. Devised and published ultra-violet, infra-red, chemical and staining techniques to determine skin penetration; internationally recognised as pioneering recognition of cosmetics by medical profession and govt authorities thoughout world by his publications on post-mortem and living skin and acclaimed by leading dermatologists and cancer specialists. Rep., Gt Britain, Cttee of Honour, 2nd Symposium Internat. des Parfums, Synthetiques et Natural, et de Cosmetologie, Versailles, 1956. Premio Internazionale di Estetica e Cosmetologia 'Guiliana Brambilla', for outstanding contribs to the art and science of cosmetics, 1967. Fellow, RSocMed. Founder Vice-Chm., 1948–50, Hon. Mem., 1973, Soc. of Cosmetic Scientists (formerly Soc. of Cosmetic Chemists of GB). Co-patentee, several British, German, Greek, S American and Swiss patents. *Publications:* The Principles and Practice of Modern Cosmetics: Vol. 1, Modern Cosmeticology, NY 1940, Spanish edns 1954, 7th edn London 1982 (reprinted under title Harry's Cosmeticology); Vol. 2, Cosmetic Materials, their origin, uses and dermatological action, 1948, 2nd edn 1963; contrib. Chambers's Encycl., Br. Jl of Dermatology and Syphilis, The Analyst, Chem. & Ind., Paint Manufacture, Mnfg Chemist, Pharm. Jl, Jl of State Medicine (USA). *Recreations:* cine sound films (Double Star awards 16mm); 35mm technical photography (ARPS 1941); Hi-Fi sound. *Address:* 61 Kimberley Road, Penylan, Cardiff CF2 5DL. *T:* Cardiff 495075. *Club:* Royal Society of Medicine.
*Died 18 Sept. 1984.*

**HART, Sir Byrne,** Kt 1974; CBE 1968; MC; chartered accountant; *b* Brisbane, 6 Oct. 1895; *s* of F. McD. Hart; *m* 1922, Margaret H., *d* of D. Cramond; two *s* (and one *s* decd). *Educ:* Southport Sch.; Brisbane Grammar Sch. FCA. Served Wars of 1914–18 and 1939–45. *Address:* 14 Gerald Street, Ascot, Brisbane, Queensland 4007. *Clubs:* Queensland, Queensland Turf (Brisbane); Union (Sydney).
*Died 19 March 1989.*

**HART, Sir George (Charles),** KBE 1973; BEM 1971; JP 1967; company director, Auckland, New Zealand; Chairman, British Hearing Aids (77) Ltd, Manufacturers of Universal Hearing Aids (chiefly electronic equipment); *b* 1901; *m* Betty (*née* Thomas), Wales. Pioneered manufacture of hearing aids in New Zealand; researched from 1930, into hearing defects; made what is believed to be the world's first electronic hearing aid; his firm exports to many countries. *Address:* British Hearing Aids (77) Ltd, Registered Office and Consulting Rooms, 22 Hobson Street, Auckland, New Zealand; 355 Richardson Road, Mount Roskill, Auckland 4, NZ. *T:* 677418.
*Died 3 Oct. 1981.*

**HART DYKE, Sir Derek William,** 9th Bt *cr* 1677; *b* 4 Dec. 1924; *s* of Sir Oliver Hamilton Augustus Hart Dyke, 8th Bt, and Millicent Zoë (*d* 1975), *d* of Dr Mayston Bond; *S* father, 1969; *m* 1st, 1953, Dorothy Moses, Hamilton, Ont (marr. diss. 1963); one *s* one *d*; 2nd, 1964, Margaret Dickson Elder, Ottawa (marr. diss. 1972). Mem., Royal Canadian Military Inst. *Educ:* Harrow; Millfield. *Heir: s* David William Hart Dyke, *b* 5 Jan. 1955. *Address:* 30 West Avenue North, Apt 611, Hamilton, Ontario L8L 5B8, Canada. *Club:* Hamilton Press.
*Died 14 Sept. 1987.*

**HARTFALL, Prof. Stanley Jack,** TD 1942; BSc, MD; FRCP; Professor of Clinical Medicine, University of Leeds, 1948–64, then Emeritus; *b* 27 Feb. 1899; *m* 1931, Muriel Ann Hunter; two *s* (one *d* decd). *Educ:* University of Leeds; Guy's Hosp. House Surg. and House Physician. Resident Medical Officer, Leeds Gen. Infirmary, 1926–30; Medical Asst to Sir A. Hurst, Guy's Hosp., 1930–32; Leverhulme Research Scholar, Royal College of Physicians, London, 1932–33; Hon. Physician and Consulting Physician, Leeds Gen. Infirmary and Leeds Regional Hosp. Board, Harrogate Royal Bath Hosp., Dewsbury and District Gen. Hosp., Prof. of Therapeutics, University of Leeds, 1937. Lieut-Col RAMC (TA). *Publications:* numerous papers on pathological and clinical subjects, gastro-intestinal diseases, anaemias and blood diseases, arthritis and rheumatism. *Recreations:* cricket and tennis. *Address:* White Gables, Hill Farm Road, Playford, near Ipswich, Suffolk. *T:* Ipswich 623784.
*Died 31 Dec. 1982.*

**HARTLINE, Prof. Haldan Keffer;** Professor of Biophysics, Rockefeller University, New York, 1953–74, then Emeritus; *b* Bloomsburg, Pa, 22 Dec. 1903; *s* of Daniel S. Hartline and Harriet F. Keffer; *m* 1936, Elizabeth Kraus; three *s. Educ:* Lafayette Coll. (BS); Johns Hopkins Univ. (MD), Nat. Res. Fellow, Medicine, Johns Hopkins Univ., 1927–29; Reeves Johnson Trav. Res. Schol., Universities of Leipzig and Munich, 1929–31; University of Pa; Fellow, Med. Physics, 1931–36; Asst Prof. Biophysics, Eldridge Reeves Johnson Foundn for Med. Physics, 1936–40; Assoc. Prof. Physiology, Cornell Univ. Med. Coll., NY, 1940–41; Asst Prof. Biophysics, Johnson Foundn, Univ. of Pennsylvania, 1941–42, Assoc. Prof. Biophysics, 1943–48, Prof. of Biophysics, 1948–49; Prof. Biophysics and Chm. of Dept, Johns Hopkins Univ., 1949–53. Mem., Nat. Acad. of Sciences; For.

Mem., Royal Soc. (London); Hon. Member: Optical Soc., Amer., 1980; Physiol. Soc., 1980. Hon. ScD: Lafayette Coll., 1959; Pennsylvania, 1971; Rockefeller, 1976; Maryland, Baltimore County, 1978; Syracuse, 1979; Hon. Dr of Laws, Johns Hopkins Univ., 1969; Hon. Dr med. Freiburg, 1971. William H. Howell Award (Physiol.), 1927; Howard Crosby Warren Medal, 1948; A. A. Michelson Award, 1964; Nobel Prize in Physiology or Medicine (jointly), 1967; Lighthouse Award, NY Assoc. for the Blind, 1969. *Publications:* contrib. Ratliff: Studies on Excitation and Inhibition in the Retina, 1974; articles in: Amer. Jl Physiol; Jl Gen. Physiol.; Jl Cell. Comp. Physiol.; Cold Spring Harbor Symposia on Quant. Biol.; Jl Opt. Soc. Amer.; Harvey Lectures; Science; Rev. Mod. Physics, etc. *Recreation:* mountain hiking. *Address:* Patterson Road, Hydes, Maryland 21082, USA. *T:* 301 592 8162.
*Died 18 March 1983.*

**HARTNELL, Air Vice-Marshal Geoffrey Clark,** CBE 1955; RAAF, retired; *b* Melbourne, 15 April 1916; *s* of late F. B. Hartnell, Melbourne; *m* 1941, Joyce M., *d* of late J. T. Webster; two *s* one *d. Educ:* Wesley Coll. Cadet RAAF Pt Cook, 1936; service Aust., SW Pacific, UK, 1939–45; Air Staff RAAF HQ, 1946–50; CO RAAF Amberley, Qld, 1951–53; Dir of Air Staff Plans and Policy, RAAF HQ Melbourne, 1953–56; Senior Air Staff Officer, HQ Home Command, 1956–58; idc 1959; Officer Commanding RAAF Butterworth, 1960–62; Dir Gen. of Plans and Policy, Dept of Air, Canberra, 1960–63; Head, Australian Joint Services Staff and RAAF Representative, London, 1964–66; Extra Gentleman Usher to the Royal Household, 1964–66; Dir, Joint Service Plans, Dept of Defence, Canberra, 1966–68. *Recreation:* woodwork. *Address:* 48 Endeavour Street, Red Hill, ACT 2603, Australia.
*Died 16 May 1981.*

**HARTNETT, Sir Laurence (John),** Kt 1967; CBE 1945; BBM (Singapore) 1974; FRSA; MIE (Australia); Industrial Adviser to Singapore Government; industrial consultant, chairman and director of a number of companies; *b* Woking, Surrey, 26 May 1898; *s* of John Joseph Hartnett, MD and Katherine Jane Hartnett; *m* 1925, Gladys Winifred, *d* of Charles Walter Tyler, Bexleyheath, Kent; three *d. Educ:* Kingston Grammar Sch.; Epsom Coll., England. Cadet, Vickers Ltd, England. Served European War, 1914–18, as Flt Sub-Lieut, RNAS and Pilot, RAF; War of 1939–45: Dir of Ordnance Production, Min. of Munitions, and Chm. Army Inventions Bd, Australia. Started own engrg and motor business; Man. Motor Dept, Guthrie & Co. Ltd, Singapore; Zone Man., General Motors, USA; Vice-Pres., General Motors Export Co., NY; Sales Man., General Motors, Nordeska, Sweden; Dir, Vauxhall Motors Ltd, England; Man. Dir, General Motors Holdens, Australia, 1934–46; Regional Dir of the overseas operations; Chm., Ambulance Design Cttee, 1967. Mem. Exec. and Past Pres., Aust. Industries Develt Assoc.; Trustee, Inst. of Applied Sciences, Vic.; Mem. Govt Bd, Corps of Commissionaires. Hon. FAIM. Hon. LLD Melbourne, 1983. *Publication:* Big Wheels and Little Wheels, 1964. *Recreations:* yachting, tennis. *Address:* Rubra, Mt Eliza, Vic. 3930, Australia. *T:* Melbourne 78–71271; Flat 4, 24 Hill Street, Toorak, Vic. 3142, Australia. *T:* Melbourne 245381. *Club:* Canadian Bay (Mt Eliza).
*Died 4 April 1986.*

**HARTWELL, Lady; Pamela Margaret Elizabeth Berry;** *b* 16 May 1914; 2nd *d* of 1st Earl of Birkenhead, PC, GCSI, KC, and of Margaret, Countess of Birkenhead; *m* 1936, Hon. (William) Michael Berry (later Baron Hartwell, MBE, TD); two *s* two *d.* Member: Adv. Council, V&A Museum, 1973–; British Section, Franco-British Council, 1977–; Chm., British Museum Soc., 1977–. Mem., E-SU Selection Bd US Debators, 1973–; Trustee, British Museum, 1979–. *Address:* Oving House, Aylesbury, Bucks; 18 Cowley Street, Westminster, SW1.
*Died 7 Jan. 1982.*

**HARTWELL, Sir Charles (Herbert),** Kt 1960; CMG 1954; *b* 1904; *m* 1st, 1931, Margaret Sheely (*d* 1942); 2nd, 1948, Mary Josephine Keane; one *s* decd. *Educ:* St John's Coll., Cambridge. Ceylon CS, 1927; Administrative Sec., Palestine, 1940; reverted to Ceylon Civil Service, 1942, and became Sec. to the Governor of Ceylon. Dir of Establishments, Kenya, 1947; Deputy Chief Sec. and Mem. for Education and Labour of Legislative Council of Kenya, 1952; Minister for Education, Labour and Lands, Kenya, 1955; Chief Sec., Uganda, 1955–60; retired from Colonial Service, July 1960; assumed duties as Chm. of Public Service Commission and Police Service Commission in Northern Rhodesia, Oct. 1960; retired, 1963; Ministry of Overseas Development, 1963–66; Adviser to the Government of Mauritius, 1966–67; Chm., Public Services Commn, Hong Kong, 1967–71; retired 1972. *Address:* 16 Clifton Place, Brighton, East Sussex. *Club:* East India, Devonshire, Sports and Public Schools.
*Died 31 Aug. 1982.*

**HARTY, (Fredric) Russell;** television and radio broadcaster; journalist; *b* 5 Sept. 1934; *s* of Fred and Myrtle Harty. *Educ:* Queen Elizabeth's Grammar School, Blackburn; Exeter College, Oxford (BA Hons 1957; MA 1961). Taught at Giggleswick School, Settle,

1958–64; Lectr in English Literature, City College, City Univ. of NY, 1964–66; producer: radio programmes, 1967–69; Aquarius, London Weekend TV, 1969–71; presenter: TV programmes, LWT, 1972–80; BBC TV, 1980–; BBC Radio, 1987–. *Publication:* Mr Harty's Grand Tour, 1988. *Recreations:* travel, looking at gardens, thinking about living in Italy, snoozing. *Address:* c/o Armitage, 24 Denmark Street, WC2H 8NJ. *T:* 01–836 3941. *Club:* Garrick.
*Died 8 June* 1988.

**HARVATT, Thomas,** CMG 1960; Secretary and Deputy Director, Council of Legal Education, 1934–68; *b* 5 Nov. 1901; *s* of Thomas Joseph Harvatt, Sheffield; *m* 1931, Nellie Adelaide, *d* of James Stephen Blythe, Sydenham; two *d. Educ:* King Edward VII Sch., Sheffield; University Coll., London; Inner Temple. Personal Asst to Dir of Educn, Sheffield, 1923–27; first Sec. for Educn, NALGO, 1927–34; Sec. to Council of Legal Education, 1934–68, and Dep. Dir of Inns of Court Sch. of Law, 1958–68; Mem. Cttee on Legal Education for Students from Africa, 1960. *Address:* 72 Old Lodge Lane, Purley, Surrey. *Died 17 Jan.* 1984.

**HARVEY, Alexander,** PhD, BSc; CPhys, FInstP; Principal, University of Wales Institute of Science and Technology, 1946–68 (formerly Cardiff Technical College, later Welsh College of Advanced Technology); Pro-Vice-Chancellor, University of Wales, 1967–68; *b* 21 Sept. 1904; *s* of Andrew Harvey, Bangor, Co. Down; *m* 1933, Mona Anderson, Newcastle upon Tyne; one *s* two *d. Educ:* Gateshead Grammar Sch.; Armstrong (King's) Coll., Univ. of Durham. Commonwealth Fund Fellowship, Univ. of California, 1929–31; Scientific Asst, Adam Hilger Ltd, London, 1931–33; Asst Lecturer, Physics Dept, University of Manchester, 1933–34; Head of Physics Dept, Wigan and District Mining and Tech. Coll., 1934–42; Principal, Scunthorpe Tech. Sch., 1942–46. President: Assoc. of Principals of Technical Instns, 1957–58; South Wales Instn of Engineers, 1970–71; Chm. Council of Assoc. of Technical Instns, 1961–62. Hon. LLD Wales, 1970. *Publications:* Science for Miners, 1938; One Hundred Years of Technical Education, 1966; various papers on optical, spectroscopic and educational subjects. *Address:* 110 Pencisely Road, Llandaff, Cardiff. *T:* Cardiff 563795.
*Died 16 Oct.* 1987.

**HARVEY, Ven. Francis William;** Archdeacon of London and Canon Residentiary of St Paul's Cathedral, since 1978; *b* 28 Sept. 1930; *s* of Frank and Clara Harvey; *m* 1955, Mavis Wheeler; one *s* three *d. Educ:* Chester College; Lichfield Theological Coll. Mil. service, RAOC, 1948–50. Teaching service, 1952–60; Curate, St Ann, Rainhill, Liverpool, 1962–65; Vicar, St Mark, Edge Lane, Liverpool, 1965–68; Liverpool Diocesan Planning Adviser, 1967–71; Area Sec., London Diocesan Fund, 1971–75; Pastoral Sec., Diocese of London, 1975–78; Prebendary of St Paul's Cathedral, 1975–78. Examining Chaplain to Bishop of London, 1981–. Member: Gen. Synod Commn on Faculty Jurisdiction, 1980; Gen. Synod, 1984–. Trustee, City Parochial Foundn, 1979–. Freeman, City of London, 1979; Hon. Liveryman, Masons' Co., 1984. MA Lambeth, 1982. *Recreations:* music, reading, photography. *Address:* 2 Amen Court, EC4M 7BU. *T:* 01–248 3312. *Died 10 Nov.* 1986.

**HARVEY, Ian Douglas,** TD 1950; psc 1944; author; public relations consultant; free-lance journalist; Associate, Douglas Stephens Associates Ltd, Management Consultants, 1970–80; *b* 25 Jan. 1914; *s* of late Major Douglas Harvey, DSO, and of late Mrs Bertram Bisgood (*née* Dorothy Cundall); *m* 1949, Clare (legally separated), *y d* of late Sir Basil E. Mayhew, KBE; two *d. Educ:* Fettes Coll.; Christ Church, Oxford. BA, 1937; MA, 1941. President: Oxford Univ. Cons. Assoc., 1935; Oxford Carlton Club, 1936; Oxford Union Soc., 1936. Served War of 1939–45, Adjutant, 123 LAA Regt, RA, 1940; Bde Major, 38 AA Bde, RA, 1943; GSO2 (ops), HQ AA command, 1944; Staff Coll. Camberley, 1944; Bde Major 100 AA Bde, NW Europe, 1945; Lieut-Col Comdg 566 LAA Regt, RA (City of London Rifles) TA, 1947–50. Contested Spelthorne Div. of Mddx, 1945; MP (C) Harrow East, 1950–58; Mem., Parly Select Cttee for reform of Army and Air Force Acts, 1952–54; Sec., 1922 Cttee, 1955–57; Parly Sec., Min. of Supply, 1956–57; Jt Parly Under-Sec. of State, FO, 1957–58. Mem. of Council, Royal Borough of Kensington, 1947–52; Mem. of LCC for S Kensington, 1949–52; Rep. of LCC on County of London TA Assoc. 1949–52; Chairman: Paddington Cons. Assoc., 1980–83; Westminster N Cons. Assoc., 1983; ILEA Tertiary Educn Bd, Div. 1, 1985–; contested (C) Westminster N, ILEA, 1986. Deleg. Advertising Assoc. to Advertising Fedn of America Convention (Detroit), 1950; Chm. Press Relations Cttee of Internat. Advertising Conference (Great Britain), 1951; Member: Advertising Assoc.; Inst. of Public Relations; Adv. Cttee on Publicity and Recruitment for Civil Defence, 1952–56; London Soc. of Rugby Union Football Referees; Rep. of Church Assembly on Standing Cttee of Nat. Soc., 1951–55; Vice-Pres., Campaign for Homosexual Equality, 1972–; Pres., Cons. Gp for Homosexual Equality, 1980–. Director: W. S. Crawford Ltd, 1949–56; Colman, Prentis and Varley Ltd, 1962–63; Advertising Controller, Yardley of London Ltd, 1963–64 (Advertising Dir, 1964–66). Chairman: Coningsby Club, 1946–47; London Old

Fettesian Assoc., 1953–54 (Vice-Pres., 1981–); Dep. Chm., Westminster Play Assoc., 1980–; Secretary: Iain Macleod Meml Trust, 1974–; Selwyn-Lloyd Meml Library Appeal, 1980–81; Subscriptions Manager, Middle East International, 1978–80. Governor: Birkbeck Coll., 1949–52; St George's Sch. (RC), Maida Vale, 1977– (Chm., 1983); Paddington Coll., 1979–; St Mary of the Angels (RC) Sch., 1983–; St Augustine's Sch., Kilburn, 1984–; Quintin Kynaston Sch., St John's Wood, 1985–. Editor, Westminster North Gazette, 1984–. *Publications:* Talk of Propaganda, 1947; The Technique of Persuasion, 1951; Arms and To-morrow, 1954; To Fall Like Lucifer, 1971. *Recreations:* squash, cycling, swimming, tennis. *Address:* 62D St Michael's Street, W2 1QR.
*Died 10 Jan.* 1987.

**HARVEY, Prof. Leslie Arthur;** Professor, 1946–69, and Head of Department of Zoology, 1930–69, University of Exeter; *b* 23 Dec. 1903; *s* of Arthur Harvey; *m* 1925, Christina Clare Brockway; one *s* one *d. Educ:* Bancroft's Sch.; Imperial Coll., London. ARCS 1923; BSc 1923; Beit Mem. Research Student, Imperial Coll., 1923–25; MSc 1925. Asst Lecturer, subsequently Lecturer in Zoology, University of Edinburgh, 1925–30. *Publications:* (with D. St Leger Gordon) Dartmoor, 1952; contributions to various learned journals, 1925–. *Recreations:* gardening, bridge. *Address:* Benhams, The Garrison, St Mary's, Isles of Scilly. *T:* Scillonia 22686.
*Died 19 March* 1986.

**HARVEY, Richard Jon Stanley,** QC 1970; a Recorder of the Crown Court, since 1972; *b* 30 Aug. 1917; *s* of Nehemiah Stanley Harvey, Home Civil Servant, and Alicia Margaret Harvey; *m* 1942, Yvonne Esther, *e d* of A. J. d'Abreu, FRCS, Waterford, Eire; no *c. Educ:* Newtown Sch., Waterford; Mountjoy Sch., Dublin; Trinity Coll., Dublin. 1st cl. sizarship in Irish, 1936; First Scholar of the House, History and Political Science, 1938; 1st cl. Moderatorship History and Political Science, 1940; Pres., Univ. Philosophical Soc., 1940–41; Founder Mem., Students Representative Council, 1941; LLB 1941. Royal Artillery, 1942–45; SUO Tonfanau RA OCTU, 1943; 2nd Lieut RA 1943, subseq. W/Subst. Lieut. Called to the Bar, Gray's Inn, 1947, Holker Scholar, 1947–48, Master of the Bench, 1980. Contested (C): Woolwich East, 1951 and 1952; Romford, 1955 and 1959. Gresham Prof. of Law, 1961–64. Received into Catholic Church, 1952. *Publications:* Harvey on Industrial Relations, 1971; contribs to learned jls; novels and other works written pseudonymously. *Recreations:* music, reading, gardening, swimming, walking, writing novels pseudonymously; formerly cricket and athletics (occasional mem. TCD 1st Cricket XI and Athletics 1st team, 1936–39). *Address:* 3 Raymond Buildings, Gray's Inn, WC1. *T:* 01–405 9420; Francis Taylor Building, Temple, EC4. *T:* 01–353 2182; The Barge, Great Walsingham, Norfolk. *T:* Walsingham 330. *Clubs:* Carlton, Sportsman, Les Ambassadeurs, Newman Association, Catenian Association, Royal Automobile; Royal West Norfolk Golf. *Died 21 Feb.* 1986.

**HARVIE-WATT, Sir George Steven,** 1st Bt, *cr* 1945, of Bathgate; QC 1945; TD 1942 (with three Bars); *b* 23 Aug. 1903; *s* of late James McDougal Watt of Armadale; *m* 1932, Bettie, *o d* of late Paymaster-Capt. Archibald Taylor, OBE, RN; two *s* one *d. Educ:* George Watson's Coll., Edinburgh; Glasgow Univ.; Edinburgh Univ. Called to Bar, Inner Temple, 1930; practised in London and on North Eastern Circuit. Commissioned RE TA 1924, 52nd (Lowland) Scottish Div., 1924–29; 56th (1st London) Div., 1929–38; Bt Major, 1935; Lt-Col Commanding 31st Bn RE TA, 1938–41; promoted Brig. to command 6th AA Bde, 1941; Brig. Commanding 63rd AA Bde TA, 1948–50; Hon. Col 566 LAA Regt, 1949–62. ADC to King George VI, 1948–52; ADC to the Queen, 1952–58; MP (U) Keighley Div. of Yorks, 1931–35; (U) Richmond, Surrey, Feb. 1937–Sept. 1959; PPS to late Rt Hon. Euan Wallace when Parly Sec. to Board of Trade, 1937–38; Asst Government Whip, 1938–40; PPS to Rt Hon. Winston S. Churchill when Prime Minister, July 1941–July 1945; Hon. Treas. UK Branch of Commonwealth Parly Assoc., 1945–51; Mem. UK Deleg. to CPA Confs, Ottawa and Washington, 1949, Australia and New Zealand, 1950; Mem. of Borough Council, Royal Borough of Kensington, 1934–45. Formerly Mem. of City of London TA Association; TA Rep. Council of RUSI, 1948–57; DL: Surrey, 1942; Greater London, 1966–78; JP County of London, 1944–56. President: Consolidated Gold Fields Ltd, 1973–81 (Chief Executive, 1954–69, Dep. Chm., 1954–60, Chm., 1960–69); Printers' Pension Corp., 1956–57; formerly: Chm., Monotype Corp. Ltd; Director: Eagle Star Insce Co.; Standard Bank Ltd; Midland Bank Ltd; Clydesdale Bank Ltd; Great Western Rly Co.; North British Steel Gp. Member of Queen's Body Guard for Scotland, Royal Company of Archers; Hon. Freeman, City of London, 1976. FRSA 1973. Gold Medal, Inst. Mining and Metallurgy (for distinguished service to world-wide mining), 1969. *Publication:* Most of My Life, 1980. *Heir: s* James Harvie-Watt, *b* 25 Aug. 1940. *Recreation:* Territorial Army. *Address:* Sea Tangle, Earlsferry, Leven, Fife KY9 1AD. *T:* Elie 330506. *Club:* Caledonian (Chm. 1953–61, Vice-Pres. 1961–85). *Died 18 Dec.* 1989.

**HARWOOD, (Basil) Antony,** MA; QC 1971; Barrister; a Master of the Supreme Court (Queen's Bench Division), 1950–70; Senior

Master and Queen's Remembrancer, 1966–70; *b* 25 June 1903; 2nd *s* of late Basil Harwood, DMus, Woodhouse, Olveston, Glos; *m* 1929, Enid Arundel (*d* 1990), *d* of late Philip Grove, Quorn House, Leamington; two *s*. *Educ:* Charterhouse; Christ Church, Oxford (MA). Called to the Bar, Inner Temple, 1927. Served War of 1939–45 in Italy. Prosecuting Counsel to Post Office, Western Circuit, 1948–50. Pres. Medico-Legal Soc., 1967–69. Liveryman, Loriners' Co., 1963–. Hon. Mem., Epée Club, 1970 (Mem., 1928–70). *Publication:* Circuit Ghosts, 1980. *Address:* Fernhill House, Almondsbury, Bristol BS12 4LX. *Club:* Royal Automobile.
*Died 30 June 1990.*

**HARWOOD, Elizabeth Jean, (Mrs J. A. C. Royle);** international opera singer; *b* 27 May 1938; *d* of Sydney and Constance Harwood; *m* 1966, Julian Adam Christopher Royle; one *s*. *Educ:* Skipton Girls' High Sch.; Royal Manchester Coll. of Music. FRMCM, GRSM, LRAM. Kathleen Ferrier Memorial Schol., 1960; jt winner, Verdi Competition (Busetto), 1965. Principal operatic roles at Glyndebourne, Sadler's Wells, Covent Garden, Scottish Opera, principal opera houses in Europe incl. Salzburg, Paris and La Scala; toured Australia, 1965, with Sutherland-Williamson Internat. Opera Co. singing principal roles in Lucia de Lammermoor, La Sonnambula and L'Elisir d'Amore; Così Fan Tutte, NY Met. Opera, 1975 (début); 1982; Don Giovanni, 1978; Rosenkavalier, Glyndebourne, 1980; took part in exchange visit to La Scala with Covent Garden Opera, 1976; ABC recital and concert tour, 1986. Has made numerous recordings of oratorio, opera and English songs. *Recreations:* swimming, horse riding. *Address:* c/o Royle House, Wenlock Road, N1 7ST. *T:* 071–253 7654. *Club:* Oriental.
*Died 22 June 1990.*

**HASELDEN, Edward Christopher,** CMG 1952; *b* 14 Aug. 1903; *s* of E. N. Haselden, Minieh, Upper Egypt; *m* 1929, Lily Jewett Foote; two *d*. *Educ:* Cheltenham Coll.; Pembroke Coll., Cambridge. Joined Sudan Political Service, 1925; Sudan Agent in Cairo, 1945–53; retired, 1953. Chm. of Anglo-Egyptian Aid Soc. Cttee, 1960. Order of the Nile (4th Class), 1936. *Address:* 14 Gilston Road, SW10. *Club:* Athenæum.
*Died 18 March 1988.*

**HASSALL, Joan,** OBE 1987; RE 1948; FSIAD 1958; painter and wood engraver; *b* 3 March 1906; *d* of late John Hassall, RI, RWA, and late Constance Brooke-Webb. *Educ:* Parsons Mead, Ashtead; Froebel Educational Institute, Roehampton. Sec. to London Sch. of Art, 1925–27; studied Royal Academy Schs, 1928–33; studied Wood Engraving, LCC Sch. of Photo-engraving and Lithography. Teacher of Book Production (deputy), Edinburgh Coll. of Art, 1940; resumed her own work in London, chiefly wood engraving, 1945. Work represented in: British Museum, Victoria and Albert Museum and collections abroad. Designed the Queen's Invitation Card to her guests for Coronation, 1953. Master, Art Workers Guild, 1972 (Mem., 1964–); Bronze Medal, Paris Salon, 1973. *Publications:* first published engraving in Devil's Dyke, by Christopher Hassall, 1935; The Wood Engravings of Joan Hassall, 1960; Joan Hassall: Engravings and Drawings, 1985. Her engraved and drawn work appears in many classic and contemporary books of prose and poetry, and in advertising. *Recreations:* music, literature and printing. *Address:* Priory Cottage, Malham, Skipton, N Yorks BD23 4DD. *T:* Airton 356.
*Died 6 March 1988.*

**HASSEL, Prof. Odd;** Knight of the Order of St Olav; Guldberg-Waage and Gunnerus Medals; Emeritus Professor of the University, Oslo; *b* 17 May 1897; *s* of Ernst August Hassel and Mathilde Klaveness. *Educ:* Oslo, Munich and Berlin Universities. Lectr, Oslo Univ., 1925, docent 1926, full Professor, 1934; Director, Department of Physical Chemistry of Univ. of Oslo, 1934–64. Hon. Fellow: Chemical Soc., London; Amer. Chem. Soc.; Norwegian Chemical Soc., Oslo; Fellow of Academies in Oslo, Trondheim, Stockholm, Copenhagen, etc. Nobel Prize for Chemistry, 1969. Hon. Dr Phil, Univ. of Copenhagen, 1950; Hon. FilDr, Univ. of Stockholm, 1960. *Publications:* Kristallchemie, 1934, trans. English and Russian; about 250 scientific papers, chiefly on molecular structure problems. *Address:* Chemistry Department, University of Oslo, Blindern, Oslo 3, Norway; (home) Holsteinveien 10, Oslo 8. *T:* 232062.
*Died 11 May 1981.*

**HASTINGS, Hon. Anthea, (Esther), (Hon. Mrs Hastings);** professionally known as Hon. Mrs Michael Joseph; Chairman, Michael Joseph Ltd, since 1978; *b* 6 March 1924; *d* of Rt Hon. Lord Hodson, PC, MC; *m* 1st, 1950, Michael Joseph (*d* 1958); one *s* one *d*; 2nd, 1963, D. E. Macdonald Hastings; one *d*. *Educ:* Queen's Gate School, London. Director, Michael Joseph Ltd, 1950, Dep. Chm., 1962. *Recreations:* cooking, gardening, travel, horseracing. *Address:* Brown's Farm, Old Basing, Hampshire RG24 0DE. *T:* Basingstoke 21057.
*Died 23 Jan. 1981.*

**HASTINGS, Bernard Ratcliffe;** Chairman, North Western Electricity Board, since 1985; *b* 16 March 1930; *s* of Robert Patrick and Mary Frances Hastings; *m* 1956, Mary Roddick Murdoch, BA; one *s* one *d*. *Educ:* Glasgow Univ. BSc Hons. Various posts, latterly Head of Industrial Engrg Dept, Mullard Radio Valve Co., 1955–67;

Management Services Controller, South of Scotland Electricity Bd, 1967–74; Dep. Chm., 1974–77, Chm., 1978–85, Merseyside and N Wales Electricity Bd. *Recreations:* golf, piano, gardening.
*Died 20 June 1989.*

**HASTINGS, Hubert De Cronin;** Chairman, Architectural Press, 1927–74; Editor, Architectural Review, 1927–73; Editor, Architects' Journal, 1932–73; *b* 18 July 1902; *s* of Percy Hastings and Lilian Bass; *m* 1927, Hazel Rickman Garrard; one *s* one *d*. Royal Gold Medal for Architecture, 1971. *Publications:* The Italian Townscape, 1963; Civilia—The End of Sub-Urban Man, 1971; The Alternative Society, 1980. *Address:* 9/13 Queen Anne's Gate, Westminster, SW1. *Clubs:* Arts, National, ICA.
*Died 3 Dec. 1986.*

**HASTINGS, Lt-Col Robin Hood William Stewart,** DSO 1944 (and Bar 1945); OBE (mil.) 1946; MC 1943; despatches twice; Chairman, British Bloodstock Agency Ltd, 1968–86, President, since 1986; *b* 16 Jan. 1917; *s* of Hon. Osmond Hastings and Mary Caroline Campbell Hastings; *c* and *heir-pres.* to 15th Earl of Huntingdon; *m* 1950, Jean Suzanne Palethorpe; one *d*. *Educ:* Stowe Sch.; Christ Church Oxford (Hons History, MA). Commissioned Rifle Brigade, 1939; Commanded: 6th Bn The Green Howards, 1943–44; 2nd Bn KRRC, 1944; GSOI 11th Armoured Div., 1945; commanded 1 Rifle Bde, 1945–46. Employed by BBA Ltd, 1952–; Director, 1954. Rode steeplechasing, 1945–52. *Publications:* The Rifle Brigade 1939–45, 1950; (jtly) The London Rifle Brigade 1919–50, 1952; Without Reserve (autobiog.), 1987. *Recreations:* hunting, shooting. *Address:* The Malt House, Bramdean, Alresford, Hampshire SO24 0LN. *T:* Bramdean 243. *Club:* White's.
*Died 28 March 1990.*

**HATHERTON, 7th Baron** *cr* 1835; **Thomas Charles Tasman Littleton,** TD 1955; *b* 6 Oct. 1907; *s* of 4th Baron Hatherton and Hester Edithe (*d* 1947), *d* of Thomas Tarrant Hoskins, MD, Tasmania; *S* brother, 1973; *m* 1933, Ann Scott, *o d* of late Lt-Comdr Thomas McLeod, RN; one *d*. *Educ:* St Edward's School. Commnd TA, 1934; served War of 1939–45; Captain TARO 1945, retd 1956. *Heir: cousin* Edward Charles Littleton [*b* 1950; *m* 1974, Hilda Maria Robert; one *s* one *d*]. *Address:* Walhouse, Hutton Henry, Castle Eden, Co. Durham. *Club:* Naval and Military.
*Died 28 Sept. 1985.*

**HATTON, Thomas Fielding; His Honour Judge Hatton;** a Circuit Judge, since 1984; *b* 13 Jan. 1931; *s* of late Dr John Hatton, MD, DPH, and Margaret Louise Hatton, RRC (*née* Dixon); *m* 1959, Elizabeth Mary, *d* of late William Edwin Metcalfe and Kathleen Elizabeth Mary Metcalfe, Clifton, York; one *s* three *d*. *Educ:* Epsom College; Worcester College, Oxford (MA). Nat. Service, RA; commissioned 1950, served RA TA (Captain). Called to the Bar, Middle Temple, 1956 (Garraway Rice Prize; Harmsworth Scholar); in practice, Northern Circuit, 1956–84. Mem., County Court Rules Cttee, 1978–82. *Recreations:* reading, walking. *Address:* Warren Cottage, Stanley Road, Hoylake, Wirral. *T:* 051–632 4048; Hilltop, High Road, Chigwell, Essex. *Club:* Royal Liverpool Golf.
*Died 25 June 1989.*

**HAUGHTON, Daniel Jeremiah;** *b* Dora, Walker County, Ala, 7 Sept. 1911; *s* of Gayle Haughton and Mattie Haughton (*née* Davis); *m* 1935, Martha Jean, *d* of Henry Oliver, Kewanee, Ill, a farmer; no *c*. *Educ:* Univ. of Alabama. BS degree in commerce and business administration, 1933. Lockheed Aircraft Corp., 1939–76: first as systems analyst; Works Manager, Vega Aircraft Corp. (a subsidiary), 1943; General Manager, Lockheed-Georgia Co. (a div.), 1952–56; elected: a Lockheed Vice-Pres., 1952, Exec. Vice-Pres., 1956; a Dir, 1958; Pres. of Corp., 1961; Chm. of Bd, 1967–76. Member of many professional societies; active in community and national affairs, including, 1967, Chm. of US Treasury Dept's industrial payroll savings bonds campaign. Chm., Nat. Multiple Sclerosis Soc.; Bd of Trustees, Nat. Security Industrial Assoc. Employer of the Year, Nat. Ind. Recreation Assoc., 1973; Management Man of the Year, Nat. Managing Assoc., 1966; Award of Achievement, Nat. Aviation Club, 1969; 16th Annual Nat. Transportation Award, Nat. Defense Transportation Assoc.; Tony Jannus Award, 1970; Salesman of the Year, Sales and Marketing Assoc., Los Angeles, 1970. Hon. LLD: Univ. of Alabama, 1962; George Washington Univ., 1965; Hon. DSc (Business Admin) Clarkson Coll. of Tech., 1973; Hon. LLD Pepperdine Univ., 1975. *Recreation:* fishing. *Address:* 1890 Battlefield Road SW, Marietta, Ga 30064, USA. *T:* (404) 422 9957. *Club:* Capital City (Atlanta).
*Died 5 July 1987.*

**HAUGHTON, Dr Sidney Henry,** DSc; FRS 1961; FGS 1914; *b* 7 May 1888; *s* of Henry Charles Haughton and Alice Haughton (*née* Aves), London; *m* 1914, Edith Hoal, Cape Town; one *s* one *d*. *Educ:* Walthamstow Technical Institute; Trinity Hall, Cambridge. BA Cantab 1909; DSc Cape Town, 1921. Palæontologist, S African Museum, Cape Town, 1911, Asst Dir, 1914; Sen. Geologist, S African Geological Survey, 1920, Dir, 1934; Chief Geologist, S African Atomic Energy Board, 1948–54. Mem., at various times of Governmental Bds and Commns on Industrial Requirements, Fuel Research, Scientific and Industrial Research, Museums, University

Finances. Hon. LLD Cape Town, 1948; Hon. DSc: Witwatersrand, 1964; Natal, 1967; Corresponding Mem., Geological Soc. Amer., 1948, etc. *Publications:* Stratigraphical Geology of Africa South of the Sahara, 1962; Geological History of Southern Africa, 1969; numerous, on geol., palæontolog. and geograph. subjects, in learned jls; rev. and ed Geology of South Africa, by A. L. Du Toit (3rd edn), 1954. *Recreations:* music, reading, walking; formerly: cricket, hockey, tennis. *Address:* Bernard Price Institute for Palaeontological Research, University of the Witwatersrand, 1 Jan Smuts Avenue, Braamfontein, Johannesburg, 2001, South Africa. *Club:* Country (Pretoria). *Died 24 May 1982.*

**HAVERGAL, Henry MacLeod,** OBE 1965; MA Oxon, BMus Edinburgh; FRCM; FRSAMD; Hon. RAM; *b* 21 Feb. 1902; *er s* of Rev. Ernest Havergal; *m* 1st, 1926, Hyacinth (*d* 1962), *er d* of Arthur Chitty; two *s*; 2nd, 1964, Nina Davidson, Aberdeen. *Educ:* Choristers Sch., Salisbury; St Edward's Sch., Oxford; St John's Coll., Oxford (history exhibnr, also organ exhibnr). Dir of Music, Fettes Coll., Edinburgh, 1924–33; Haileybury Coll., 1934–36; Harrow Sch., 1937–45; Master of Music, Winchester Coll., 1946–53; Principal, Royal Scottish Academy of Music (later Royal Scottish Academy of Music and Drama), 1953–69; Dir, Jamaica Sch. of Music, 1973–75. Pres., ISM, 1949. Hon. DMus Edinburgh, 1958; Hon. LLD Glasgow, 1969. *Recreation:* fishing. *Address:* 3 East Claremont Street, Edinburgh EH7 4HT. *T:* 031–556 6525. *Club:* New (Edinburgh). *Died 13 June 1989.*

**HAWES, Derrick Gordon H.;** *see* Harington Hawes.

**HAWES, Maj.-Gen. Leonard Arthur,** CBE 1940; DSO 1918; MC; MA (Hon.) Oxon; DL; Royal Artillery; *b* Throcking, Herts, 22 July 1892; *s* of C. A. Hawes, Uckfield, Sussex; *m* 1st, 1919, Gwendolen Mary (*d* 1970), *d* of D. H. Grimsdale, JP, Uxbridge, Middlesex; one *d* (one *s* decd); 2nd, 1972, Yolande (*d* 1984), widow of Wyndham Robinson. *Educ:* Bedford; RM Academy, Woolwich. Lieut Royal Garrison Artillery, 1911; Capt., 1916; Temp. Major, 1917; Major, 1929; Bt Lieut-Col 1932; Lieut-Col and Col 1938; served European War, 1914–18 (wounded, CBE, DSO, MC, despatches, Order of Crown of Italy); served War of 1939–45; retired pay, 1945. DL West Sussex, 1977. *Address:* Old Manor House, West Harting, Petersfield, Hants. *Club:* Army and Navy. *Died 7 Aug. 1986.*

**HAWKE, 9th Baron,** *cr* 1776, of Towton; **Bladen Wilmer Hawke;** *b* 31 Dec. 1901; *s* of 8th Baron and late Frances Alice, *d* of Col J. R. Wilmer, Survey of India; *S* father, 1939; *m* 1934, Ina Mary, *e d* of late Henry Faure Walker, Highley Manor, Balcombe, Sussex; seven *d*. *Educ:* Winchester; King's Coll., Cambridge (MA). Bombay Company, India, 1923–38; Temp. Civil Servant, Ministry of Economic Warfare, 1940–43, War Office, 1943–45. Lord-in-Waiting to the Queen and Government Whip, House of Lords, 1953–57. Chm. Conservative Back Bench Peers Assoc., 1949–53; Executive Cttee, National Union Conservatives, 1950–53; Mem., House of Laity, Church Assembly, later Gen. Synod of C of E, 1955–75; Church Commissioner, 1958–73; Chm., Chichester Diocesan Board of Finance, 1962–72. Director: Initial Services Ltd, 1960–78; Ecclesiastical Insurance Office, Ltd, 1961–77. *Recreations:* golf, gardening. *Heir:* *b* Squadron Leader Hon. (Julian Stanhope) Theodore Hawke, Auxiliary Air Force [*b* 19 Oct. 1904; *m* 1st, 1933, Angela Margaret Griselda (marr. diss., 1946), *d* of late Capt. Edmund W. Bury; two *d*; 2nd, 1947, Georgette Margaret, *d* of George S. Davidson; one *s* three *d*]. *Address:* Faygate Place, Faygate, Sussex. *T:* Faygate 252. *Club:* Carlton.
*Died 5 July 1985.*

**HAWKER, Sir Richard (George),** Kt 1965; MA Cantab; *b* 11 April 1907; *s* of late R. M. Hawker; *m* 1940, Frances C., *d* of late S. Rymill; two *s* two *d* (and one *s* decd). *Educ:* Geelong Grammar Sch.; Trinity Hall, Cambridge. Returned SA, 1929; took over management Bungaree Merino Stud, 1932. Mem. Blyth Dist Coun., 1936–42, 1946–70. War service: 9/23 Light Horse Regt, 1939–41; 1st Armoured Div., AIF, 1941–44. Member: Cttee SA Stud Merino Breeders Assoc., 1939–40, 1959– (Pres. 1962–63, 1963–64); Council, Aust. Assoc. of Stud Merino Breeders, 1962–71 (Pres., 1968–71); Australian Wool Industry Conf., 1963–65 (as nominee of Federal Graziers' Council). Chm., Roseworthy Agricultural Coll. Council, 1964–73. Director: Adelaide Steamship Co. Ltd, 1949–79 (Chm. 1952–73); Coal & Allied Industries, NSW, 1961–78; (local bd in SA) Queensland Insurance Co. Ltd, 1955–74; Amalgamated Wireless (Australasia) Ltd, 1971–78. *Recreations:* shooting, fishing. *Address:* Bungaree, Clare, SA 5453, Australia. *T:* Clare (088) 422676. *Clubs:* Oriental; Australian (Sydney); Adelaide (SA).
*Died 12 Nov. 1982.*

**HAWKES, Prof. Leonard,** FRS 1952; Head of Department of Geology, Bedford College, 1921–56; Professor Emeritus since 1956; Fellow of Bedford College, 1971; *b* 6 Aug. 1891; *s* of Rev. Philip Hawkes; *m* 1926, Hilda Kathleen, *d* of late L. V. Cargill; one *s*. *Educ:* Armstrong Coll.; Kristiania Univ. 1851 Exhibitioner, 1914. Served European War, 1914–18, Capt. RAMC, 1917–19 (despatches). Lecturer in Geology, Armstrong Coll., 1919–21. Sec., Geological

Soc. of London, 1934–42 (Pres., 1956–58); Pres. Mineralogical Soc., 1954–57. Murchison Medallist, 1946. Wollaston Medallist, 1962. Geol. Soc. of London. *Publications:* papers dealing with geology of Iceland. *Address:* 26 Moor Lane, Rickmansworth, Herts. *T:* Rickmansworth 72955. *Died 29 Oct. 1981.*

**HAWKINGS, Sir (Francis) Geoffrey,** Kt 1978; Chairman: Stone-Platt Industries Ltd, 1974–80 (Director, 1962; Managing Director, 1967); Chloride Group Ltd, 1977–79 (Director, 1975; Deputy Chairman, 1976); Director, Alliance Investment Co., 1976–81; *b* 13 Aug. 1913; *s* of Harry Wilfred Hawkings and Louise Hawkings, Lymington, Hants; *m* 1940, Margaret Mary, *d* of Alexander Wilson, OBE, MD, DL; one *s* one *d*. *Educ:* Wellington; New Coll., Oxford (MA). Commissioned into Lancashire Fusiliers (TA), 1939; Camberley sc, 1943; Bde Major, Inf. and Air-borne Bdes. Administrative appt, Stewarts & Lloyds Ltd, 1946–49; joined Textile Machinery Makers Ltd, 1950, Dir, 1959, Man. Dir, 1961. Mem., Court of Governors, Manchester Univ., 1964–79; Pres., Engrg Employers' Fedn, 1978–80. *Recreations:* fishing, racing. *Died 31 Oct. 1990.*

**HAWKINS, (Clive) David B.;** *see* Black-Hawkins.

**HAWKINS, Rt. Rev. Ralph Gordon,** CMG 1977; ThD; *b* St John's, Newfoundland, 1911; *s* of late Samuel J. and Alfreda Hawkins; *m* 1938, Mary Edna, *d* of late William James and Grace Leslie, Newport, Mon.; one *s* one *d*. *Educ:* Univ. Memorial Coll., St John's; St Boniface Coll., Warminster; Durham Univ. (Hatfield Coll.). BA, LTh 1934; deacon, 1935, priest, 1936, Bristol. Curate of St Anne's, Brislington, 1935–38; Rector of Morawa, 1938–43; Rector of Wembley-Floreat Park, 1943–49; Chaplain, RAAF, 1943–45; Rector of St Hilda's, N Perth, 1949–56; Canon of Perth, 1954; Archdeacon of Perth, 1957; Bishop of Bunbury, 1957–77. *Address:* 9 Cross Street, Bunbury, WA 6230, Australia.
*Died July 1987.*

**HAWKINS, Vice-Adm. Sir Raymond (Shayle),** KCB 1965 (CB 1963); *b* 21 Dec. 1909; *s* of late Thomas Hawkins and Dorothy Hawkins, Bedford; *m* 1936, Rosalind (marr. diss. 1980), *d* of late Roger and Ada Ingpen; three *s* one *d*. *Educ:* Bedford Sch. Entered Royal Navy, 1927; HMS Iron Duke 1932; HMS Resolution, 1933; served with Submarines, 1935–43; HMS Orion, 1943. Asst Naval Attaché, Paris, 1954; Commanding Officer, HMS St Vincent, 1957; Rear-Adm., Nuclear Propulsion, 1959; Dir of Marine Engineering, 1961–63; Chief Naval Engineering Officer, 1962–63; Vice-Adm., 1964; a Lord Comr of the Admiralty, Fourth Sea Lord and Vice-Controller, 1963–64; Chief of Naval Supplies and Transport and Vice-Controller of the Navy, MoD, 1964–67; retd, 1967. *Address:* The Old Garden, All Saints Road, Lansdown, Bath, Avon.
*Died 18 Oct. 1987.*

**HAWKINS, Rev. Robert Henry;** *b* 3 March 1892; *s* of Rev. Francis Henry Albert Hawkins and Mary Anna Ridley Hawkins (*née* Morris); *m* 1917, Margaret (*d* 1977), *e d* of Rev. T. A. Lacey, DD, Canon of Worcester; two *s* three *d*. *Educ:* Forest Sch., Essex; St Edmund Hall, Oxford. BA 1913, MA 1919. Served European War: commissioned 3rd S Staffs Regt, 1914; France and Salonika, 1915–17; RFC (Flight Comdr), 1917–19. Ordained Deacon, 1919, Priest, 1920; Vicar of: Maryport, Dio. Carlisle, 1923–27; St George, Barrow in Furness, 1927–34; Dalston, 1934–43; Vicar of St Mary, Nottingham, Rural Dean of Nottingham and Hon. Canon of Southwell, 1943–58; Canon of St George's, Windsor, 1958–70. *Address:* Manormead, Tilford Road, Hindhead, Surrey GU26 6RA. *T:* Hindhead 4044. *Died 19 Sept. 1989.*

**HAWLEY, Major Sir David Henry,** 7th Bt, *cr* 1795; MA; FRICS; DL; late KRRC; formerly with firm of Jas Martin & Co., Chartered Surveyors, Land Agents and Valuers, 8 Bank Street, Lincoln; *b* 13 May 1913; *e s* of Capt. Cyril Francis Hawley and Ursula Mary, *d* of late Col L. Gregson; one *s* two *d*. *Educ:* Eton; Magdalene Coll., Cambridge. Served Palestine, 1936–39 (medal and clasp), War of 1939–45 (prisoner, 1939–45 Star, despatches). Hon. Life Mem., Nat. Trust. Chm., Lincoln Dio. Adv. Cttee, 1978–81. Vice-Pres., Lincs Branch, CLA. DL 1952, High Sheriff, 1962–63, Lincs. *Recreations:* shooting, letter writing. *Heir:* *s* Henry Nicholas Hawley, *b* 26 Nov. 1939. *Address:* Tumby Lawn, Boston, Lincs PE22 7TA. *T:* Coningsby 42337. *Died 19 March 1988.*

**HAWORTH, Sir (Arthur) Geoffrey,** 2nd Bt, *cr* 1911; MA; farmer; *b* 5 April 1896; *s* of Sir Arthur Haworth, 1st Bt, and Lily (*d* 1952), *y d* of late John Rigby, Altrincham; *S* father, 1944; *m* 1926, Emily Dorothea (*d* 1980), *er d* of H. E. Gaddum, The Priory, Bowdon; two *s* two *d*. *Educ:* Rugby Sch.; New Coll., Oxford. Served European War, 1914–19, Lieut Queen's Own Royal West Kent Regiment and Machine Gun Corps (despatches). Chm., Hallé Concert Soc., 1965–77; Pres., Manchester Palace Theatre Trust Ltd, 1980– (Chm., 1978–80). FRSA 1969. JP Chester, 1937–70. Hon. MA Manchester, 1972. *Recreation:* music. *Heir:* *s* Philip Haworth [*b* 17 Jan. 1927; *m* 1951, Joan Helen, *d* of late S. P. Clark, Ipswich; four *s* one *d*].

*Address:* The Red Brook, Lower Peover, Cheshire. *Club:* Farmers'. *Died* 7 *April* 1987.

**HAWORTH, Very Rev. Kenneth William;** Dean of Salisbury, 1960–71, Dean Emeritus, since 1971; *b* 21 Jan. 1903; *s* of William Bell and Helen Haworth; *m* 1937, Sybil Mavrojani (*d* 1982); two *s* two *d*. *Educ:* Cheltenham Coll.; Clare Coll., Cambridge; Wells Theological Coll. Curate of St Giles, Willenhall, 1926; Domestic Chaplain 1931, Examining Chaplain, 1937, to Bp of Lichfield; Chaplain of Wells Theological Coll., 1938; CF (4th cl.), 1939; Rector of Stratton w. Baunton, Dio., Gloucester, 1943; Vice-Principal of Wells Theol. Coll., 1946, Principal, 1947–60; Prebendary of Combe II in Wells Cathedral, 1947–60; Exam. Chap. to Bishop of Bath and Wells, 1947; Proctor in Convocation, 1956–59; Exam. Chap. to Bishop of Salisbury, 1962. *Address:* The Common, Woodgreen, Fordingbridge, Hants. *T:* Downton 22239.
*Died* 22 *April* 1988.

**HAWORTH, Robert Downs,** DSc, PhD Victoria, BSc Oxon; FRS 1944; FRSC; Firth Professor of Chemistry, University of Sheffield, 1939–63, then Emeritus; *b* 15 March 1898; *s* of J. T. and Emily Haworth, Cheadle, Cheshire; *m* 1930, Dorothy, *d* of A. L. Stocks, Manchester; one *d*. *Educ:* Secondary Sch., Stockport; University of Manchester, Mercer Scholar, 1919; Beyer Fellow, 1920; 1851 Exhibition Scholar, 1921–23; 1851 Exhibition Sen. Student, 1923–25; Demonstrator in Organic Chemistry, Oxford, 1925–26; Lecturer in Chemistry, King's Coll., Newcastle upon Tyne, 1927–39. Visiting Prof. of Organic Chemistry, University of Madras, 1963–64. Davy Medal, Royal Society, 1956. Hon. DSc Sheffield, 1974. *Publications:* papers on organic chemistry in Journal of Chemical Society. *Address:* 11 Cedar Grove, Bexley, Kent DA5 3DB. *T:* 081–303 9829. *Died* 19 *May* 1990.

**HAWORTH, Hon. Sir William (Crawford),** Kt 1969; Director of companies; *b* 15 April 1905; *s* of Edward Haworth; *m* 1927, Winifred Senior. *Educ:* Essendon; Melbourne Univ.; Victorian Pharmacy Coll. PhC 1925; MPSA. War of 1939–45: Captain, 2nd AIF, 9th Div.; served in Egypt, Tobruk, Palestine and Syria; R of O 1944. Municipal Councillor, S Melbourne, 1923–38; Mem. Bd of Management, Victoria Infectious Diseases Hosp., 1936–38; Mem. Council, S Melbourne Technical Sch., 1939–62 (Pres., 1947–48) MLA for Albert Park, Vic Parliament, 1937–45; Minister for Health and Housing, Vic Govt, Oct.-Nov. 1945. MHR for Isaacs, Aust. Commonwealth Parliament, 1949–69. Mem., Jt Parly Cttee for Foreign Affairs, 1959–66; Leader of Aust. Delegn to Inter-Parly Union Conf., Warsaw, 1959 (Mem. IPU Council, 1959–60); Dep. Chm. of Cttees, 1960–69. *Recreation:* golf. *Address:* 25 Grange Road, Toorak, Vic 3142, Australia. *T:* 241–7055. *Clubs:* Australian (Melbourne); Naval and Military, West Brighton, Victoria Racing, Royal Automobile Club of Victoria, Kingston Heath Golf (Vic).
*Died* 1 *Dec.* 1984.

**HAWSER, His Honour (Cyril) Lewis,** QC 1959; a Circuit Judge, 1978–90; Senior Official Referee, 1985–90; *b* 5 Oct. 1916; *s* of Abraham and Sarah Hawser; *m* 1940, Phyllis Greatrex; one *s* one *d*. *Educ:* Cardiff High Sch.; Balliol Coll., Oxford (Williams Law Scholar; MA). Called to the Bar, 1938, Bencher, 1966, Treasurer, 1987, Inner Temple. Recorder of Salisbury, 1967–69; Recorder of Portsmouth, 1969–71; a Recorder of the Crown Court, 1972–78; Official Referee, 1978. Mem. Council and Vice-Chm. of Exec. Cttee of Justice. *Publication:* (report) Case of James Hanratty, 1975. *Recreations:* tennis, chess, conversation. *Address:* 1 Harcourt Buildings, Middle Temple Lane, EC4. *T:* 071–353 8131.
*Died* 25 *July* 1990.

**HAWTON, Sir John (Malcolm Kenneth),** KCB 1952 (CB 1947); *b* 18 Sept. 1904; *s* of John Francis Hawton; *m* 1935, Hilda Cawley; one *d*. *Educ:* Emanuel Sch.; St John's Coll., Cambridge (1st Class Classical Tripos, Foundation Scholar, Graves Prizeman). Barrister (Middle Temple); entered Ministry of Health, 1927; various duties in that Ministry, concerning local government, housing, water supply, private bill legislation, public health, wartime emergency services, also inception and running of National Health Service; Permanent Sec., Ministry of Health, 1951–60. Chm., British Waterways Board, 1963–68, Vice-Chm., 1968–74. Mem., Advertising Standards Authority, 1962–73. *Recreations:* erstwhile.
*Died* 7 *Jan.* 1982.

**HAWTREY, Stephen Charles,** CB 1966; Clerk of the Journals, House of Commons, 1958–72; *b* 8 July 1907; *s* of Edmond C. Hawtrey; *m* 1934, Leila Winifred (*d* 1982), *e d* of late Lieut-Col Wilmot Blomefield, OBE; two *s* one *d*. *Educ:* Eton; Trinity Coll., Cambridge (MA). Asst Clerk, House of Commons, 1930; Senior Clerk, 1944. Temporarily attached to Min. of Home Security, 1939; to Secretariat of Council of Europe, Strasbourg, France, at various sessions between 1950 and 1964. *Publication:* (With L. A. Abraham) A Parliamentary Dictionary, 1956 and 1964; 3rd edn (with H. M. Barclay), 1970. *Died* 9 *Oct.* 1990.

**HAY, Sir (Alan) Philip,** KCVO 1961 (CVO 1953); TD; Treasurer to the Duke and Duchess of Kent, since 1962; *b* 27 Feb. 1918; *y s* of late E. Alan Hay; *m* 1948, Lady Margaret Katharine Seymour, DCVO (*d* 1975); three *s*. *Educ:* Harrow; Trinity Coll., Cambridge (BA). Herts Yeomanry, TA (135 Field Regt RA), 1939; prisoner, Singapore, 1942–45. Private Sec. to Princess Marina, Duchess of Kent, 1948–68. Director: National Mutual Life Assoc. of Australasia, 1967; Sotheby & Co., 1969. *Address:* Nottingham Cottage, Kensington Palace, W8. *T:* 01–937 5514. *Clubs:* Boodle's, Buck's. *Died* 7 *April* 1986.

**HAY, Sir Frederick Baden-Powell,** 10th Bt of Alderston, *cr* 1703; *b* 24 June 1900; *s* of late Frederick Howard Hay; *S* uncle, 1936; *m* 1935, Henrietta Margaret, *d* of Herbert William Reid; no *c*. *Recreations:* golf, turf, motoring. *Heir:* *b* Ronald Nelson Hay [*b* 9 July 1910; *m* 1940, Rita, *d* of John Munyard; one *s* one *d*]. *Address:* Haddington, 14/32 Mentone Parade, Mentone, Vic 3194, Australia. *T:* 550 3726. *Club:* Royal Caledonian (Melbourne). *Died* 20 *June* 1985.

**HAY, Sir Philip;** *see* Hay, Sir A. P.

**HAY, Robert Edwin, (Roy Hay),** MBE 1970; VMH 1971; formerly Editor, Gardeners' Chronicle (1954–64); *b* 20 Aug. 1910; *o s* of late Thomas Hay, CVO, sometime Superintendent Central Royal Parks; *m* 1st, 1946, Elizabeth Jessie (*d* 1976), *d* of late Rev. H. C. Charter; two *d*; 2nd, 1977, Mrs Frances Perry, MBE, VMH. *Educ:* Marylebone Grammar Sch. Horticultural seed trade, 1928; Asst Editor, Gardeners' Chronicle, 1936; Editor, Royal Horticultural Soc.'s publications, 1939; Min. of Agriculture, 1940; Horticultural Officer, Malta, 1942; Controller of Horticulture and Seed Divs, British zone of Germany, 1945. Officier du Mérite Agricole: Belgium, 1956; France, 1959. *Publications:* Annuals, 1937; In My Garden, 1955; Gardening the Modern Way, 1962; (with P. M. Synge) The Dictionary of Garden Plants, 1969; (jtly) The Dictionary of Indoor Plants in Colour, 1975; (ed) The Complete Guide to Fruit and Vegetable Growing, 1978; (with Frances Perry) Tropical and Subtropical Plants, 1982; Gardener's Calendar, 1983. *Recreations:* reading, crossword puzzles. *Died* 21 *Oct.* 1989.

**HAY, Sir Ronald Nelson,** 11th Bt *cr* 1703, of Alderston; *b* 9 July 1910; *s* of Frederick Howard Hay (*d* 1934) (*g s* of 6th Bt); *S* brother, 1985; *m* 1940, Rita, *d* of John Munyard; one *s* one *d*. *Heir:* *s* Ronald Frederick Hamilton Hay, *b* 1941. *Died* 6 *April* 1988.

**HAY, Roy;** *see* Hay, Robert E.

**HAYCOCKS, Prof. Norman,** CBE 1969; Professor of Education, University of Nottingham, 1946–73; Deputy Vice-Chancellor, University of Nottingham, 1962–66, Pro-Vice-Chancellor, 1969–73; *b* 17 Nov. 1907; *s* of late Aaron and Jessie Haycocks, Salop and Manchester; unmarried. *Educ:* Salford Grammar Sch.; Univs of Manchester (open Schol.), Paris and Grenoble. BA First Cl. Hons in French, Manchester, 1928 (Research Schol.), MA 1929 (by research, Mediaeval French). Lecturer Univ. of Grenoble, 1928–29; Asst Master, North Manchester Sch. (branch of Manchester Gram. Sch.), 1929–33; Lecturer in Education, University of Manchester, 1933–46. Chairman, Standing Conference of National Voluntary Youth Organisations, 1952–70; Mem. Schools Broadcasting Council, 1958–68, and Chm., Secondary I Programme Cttee, 1958–64; Governor, National Coll. for Training of Youth Leaders, 1960–70; Member: Youth Service Development Council, 1963–71; Television Research Cttee, 1963–; Adv. Cttee for Supply and Trng of Teachers, 1973–78. Vice-Chm., Universities' Council for the Education of Teachers, 1967–69, Chm., 1969–73; Acad. Sec., 1973–78. Vis. Prof. of Education, Univ. of East Anglia, 1976–81. Hon. FCP, 1972. Hon. LLD Nottingham, 1974; Hon. DEd CNAA, 1978. Squadron Leader in Intelligence Branch of Royal Air Force, 1941–45 (despatches). *Publications:* articles and papers in educational journals. *Recreations:* theatre and gardening. *Address:* 109 Derby Road, Bramcote, Nottingham NG9 3GZ. *T:* Nottingham 255024. *Club:* National Liberal. *Died* 30 *March* 1982.

**HAYDAY, Sir Frederick,** Kt 1969; CBE 1963; National Industrial Officer, National Union of General and Municipal Workers, 1946–71; Chairman, International Committee, Trades Union Congress; *b* 26 June 1912; *s* of late Arthur Hayday, MP for W Notts; *m*. Member: General Council of the Trades Union Congress, 1950–72 (Chairman, 1962–63, Vice-Chairman, 1964–69); IBA (formerly ITA), 1969–73; British Railways Board, 1962–76. Mem., Police Complaints Bd, 1977–83. *Address:* 42 West Drive, Cheam, Surrey. *T:* 081–642 8928. *Died* 26 *Feb.* 1990.

**HAYDON, Prof. Denis Arthur,** FRS 1975; Professor of Membrane Biophysics, University of Cambridge, since 1980; Fellow, since 1965, Vice-Master, 1978–82, Trinity Hall, Cambridge; *b* 21 Feb. 1930; *s* of late Ernest George Haydon and Grace Violet (*née* Wildman); *m* 1st, 1958, Ann Primrose Wayman (marr. diss. 1986); two *s* one *d*; 2nd, 1987, Ann Juliet Bateman Simon. *Educ:* Dartford Grammar Sch.; King's Coll., Univ. of London (BSc, PhD). MA, ScD Cantab. ICI Res. Fellow, Imperial Coll., London, 1956–58; Asst Dir of Res., Univ. of Cambridge, Dept of Colloid Science,

1959–70, and Dept of Physiology, 1970–74; Dir of Studies in Natural Scis, Trinity Hall, 1965–78; Asst Tutor, Trinity Hall, 1968–73; Tutor for Natural Scientists, Trinity Hall, 1973–74; Reader in Surface and Membrane Biophysics, Univ. of Cambridge, 1974–80. Chem. Soc. Medal for Surface and Colloid Chem., 1976. *Publications:* (with R. Aveyard) An Introduction to the Principles of Surface Chemistry, 1973; papers on surface chemistry and membrane biophysics in Proc. Royal Soc., Trans Faraday Soc., Jl Chem. Soc. and other sci. jls. *Recreations:* climbing, sailing, music. *Address:* Lower Farm, Wicken Bonhunt, Saffron Walden, Essex CB11 3UG. *T:* Saffron Walden 40989. *Died 29 Nov.* 1988.

**HAYES, Thomas William Henry;** *b* 1 Aug. 1912; *s* of Henry Daniel and Joanna Hayes; *m* 1933, Alice Frances; one *s*. *Educ:* Central Foundation Sch., London; London Univ. After 3 years in teaching and 2 in industry joined Prison Service, 1937, as Borstal Housemaster. Served in RA, 1940–45. Dep. Gov. Rochester Borstal, 1945–48; Staff Officer, with British Police and Prisons Mission to Greece, 1948–51; Governor, subseq. of Lewes Prison, Hatfield and Lowdham Grange Borstals, Ashford Remand Centre and Wormwood Scrubs Prison; Asst Dir of Borstals, Home Office, 1964–69; Regional Dir of Prisons, SW Region, 1969–72; Advr to Dir of Prisons, Botswana, 1975–77; Regional Prisons Adviser, British Develt Div., Caribbean, 1978–79, retired. *Recreations:* gardening, contract bridge. *Address:* 58 Harvest Court, Jersey Farm, St Albans, Herts AL4 9QY. *Died 15 Nov.* 1989.

**HAYNES, Sir George (Ernest),** Kt 1962; CBE 1945; *b* 24 Jan. 1902; *e s* of Albert Ernest and Sarah Anne Haynes, Middlewich, Cheshire; *m* 1930, Kathleen Norris Greenhaigh; two *d*. *Educ:* Sandbach Sch.; Liverpool Univ. BSc 1922; school master and educational and social research, 1923–28; Warden of University Settlement, Liverpool, 1928–33; Dir, Nat. Council of Social Service, 1940–67; Mem., Lord Chancellor's Cttee: on Procedure of County Courts, 1948; on Legal Aid, 1944–45 (and Mem., Adv. Cttee, 1950–75); Chm., Standing Conf. on Legal Aid, 1973–75. Chm., Temp. Internat. Council for Educational Reconstruction of UNESCO, 1947–48; Mem. Colonial Office Advisory Cttee, on Social Development, 1947–63. President: Internat. Conf. of Social Work, 1948–56; Standing Conf. for the Advancement of Counselling; Chairman: Preparatory Cttee, World Assembly of Youth, 1947–48; Internat. Congresses at Paris, 1950, Madras, 1952, Toronto, 1954, Munich, 1956; Nat. Children's Bureau, 1963–68; Invalid Children's Aid Association, 1964–69; Rural Industries Loan Fund Ltd, 1949–68; Social Services Cttee, National Association for Mental Health, 1955–58; Standing Conference of British Organisations for Aid to Refugees, 1953–60; Council of British Assoc. of Residential Settlements, 1963–68; Adv. Council, Rural Industries Bureau, 1962–68; Exec. Cttee, British National Conference on Social Welfare, 1950–67; Social Science Cttee, Nat. Fund for Research into Crippling Diseases, 1968–72. Vice-Chm., Family Welfare Assoc., 1961–66. Mem. Council of Brit. Red Cross Soc., 1960–76; Vice-President: Holiday Fellowship; British Assoc. for Disability and Rehabilitation; Assoc. for Spina Bifida; TOC H; Crown Trustee, City Parochial Foundation, 1965–75; Pres., Nat. Assoc. of Citizens Advice Bureaux, 1978–81; Trustee, National Birthday Trust, 1981–82 (Pres., 1966–81). UK Delegate to UN Social Commission, 1962–66, and to UN Commn for Social Develt 1967. René Sand Memorial Award, 1958. *Address:* 103 Richmond Hill Court, Richmond, Surrey. *T:* 01-940 6304. *Died 5 March* 1983.

**HAYNES, Rear-Adm. William Allen,** CB 1968; OBE 1941; retired 1970; *b* 29 Sept. 1913; *s* of late Paymaster Capt. W. F. Haynes, Royal Navy and late Mrs M. W. Haynes (*née* Wilkinson); *m* 1964, Mary Theodosia Peploe; two *d*. *Educ:* Royal Naval Colleges, Dartmouth, Keyham and Greenwich. HMS Leander, 1935–36; HMS Glasgow, 1938–41; HM Dockyard, Chatham, 1941–44; HMS Gabbard, 1944–47; Admty i/c development of steam catapult, 1947–51; HMS Ceylon (Korean War), 1951–53; Apprentice Trng in HMS Fisgard, 1953–55; HM Dockyard, Chatham, 1955–60; Imp. Def. Coll., 1961; Dir of Naval Ship Production, 1962–67; Dir-Gen., Dockyards and Maintenance, 1967–69. Comdr 1947; Capt. 1958; Rear-Adm. 1966. CStJ 1985. *Recreations:* sailing, gardening. *Address:* Bowden House, Dartmouth, Devon. *T:* Stoke Fleming 770234. *Died 30 June* 1985.

**HAYTER, Stanley William,** CBE 1967 (OBE 1959); Hon. RA 1982; artist; *b* 27 Dec. 1901; *s* of William Harry Hayter and Ellen Mercy Palmer; *m* 1st, 1926, Edith Fletcher (marriage dissolved at Reno, Nevada, 1929); one *s* decd; 2nd, 1940, Helen Phillips (marr. diss., Paris, 1971); two *s*. 3rd, Désirée Moorehead. *Educ:* Whitgift Middle Sch.; King's Coll., London. Chemist, Anglo-Iranian Oil Co., Abadan, Iran, 1922–25. Founded Atelier 17, Paris, 1927. Has exhibited since 1927 in various cities of Europe, America and Japan (incl. London: 1928, 1938, 1957, 1962, 1967). Paintings and prints in principal museums in Gt Britain, France, Belgium, Switzerland, Sweden, Italy, Canada, USA, Japan. Foreign Mem., Amer. Acad. of Arts and Scis, 1978. Hon. Dr: Hamline Univ., Minn.; New Sch. for Social Research, NY, 1983. Legion of Honour, 1951;

Commandeur des Arts et Lettres, 1986 (Chevalier, 1967). *Publications:* New Ways of Gravure, 1949 (New York also) (revised edn 1983); Nature and Art of Motion, New York, 1964; About Prints, 1962. *Address:* 12 rue Cassini, 75014 Paris, France. *T:* 43 26 26 60. *Died 4 May* 1988.

**HAYWARD, Sir Alfred,** KBE 1961 (CBE 1960); retired; *b* England, 14 Jan. 1896; *s* of Thomas and Minnie Hayward, Sudbourne, Suffolk; *m* 1st, 1923, Margaret Fromm (*d* 1971); one *s* two *d*. 2nd, 1971, Priscilla Catherine Sansom. Came to New Zealand, 1911. Served European War, 1914–18, in France, 1916–18. Took up farming in Waikato district. Dir, NZ Co-op. Dairy Co., 1933–61. Chm., 1947–61; Deputy Chm., NZ Dairy Board, 1958. JP 1957. *Address:* 34 Melrose House, 159 Waiki Road, Tauranga, New Zealand. *Died 30 Jan.* 1988.

**HAYWARD, Sir Charles (William),** Kt 1974; CBE 1970; Founder and Trustee, Hayward Foundation and Charles Hayward Trust; *b* 3 Sept. 1892; *s* of John and Mary Hayward, Wolverhampton; *m* 1st, 1915, Hilda (*d* 1971), *d* of late John and Alexandra Arnold; one *s*; 2nd, 1972, Elsie Darnell, *d* of late Charles and Kate George. *Educ:* St John's School, Wolverhampton. Mem. of Post Office Advisory Council, 1952. Held Directorships, 1920–, in various companies, public and private, including engineering, farming and horticulture. Vice-Pres., Wildfowl Trust. Pres., Royal Wolverhampton Sch. Liveryman of Barbers' Company; Freeman of the City of London, 1938; Worshipful Company of Masons. Hon. Fellow, Keble Coll., Oxford, 1973, Oriel Coll., Oxford, 1980. Hon. FRCS, 1970; Hon. Fellow, Inst. of Ophthalmology, 1967; Hon. LLD Birmingham, 1975. KStJ 1973. *Address:* Isle of Jethou, PO Box 5, Guernsey, CI. *T:* Guernsey 23844. *Died 3 Feb.* 1983.

**HAYWARD, Sir Edward (Waterfield),** Kt 1961; grazier and company director, Australia; Chairman, Coca Cola Bottlers Ltd, since 1948; Director, Bennett & Fisher Ltd, since 1960; *b* 10 Nov. 1903; *s* of Arthur Dudley Hayward and Mary Anne Hayward; *m* 1935, Ursula (*d* 1970), *y d* of late T. E. Barr Smith; *m* 1972, Jean Katherine Bridges, *widow* of Ernest Bushby Bridges. *Educ:* St Peter's Coll., Adelaide, S Australia. Lt-Col, 2nd AIF, Middle East, New Guinea and Borneo (despatches: 1944 in New Guinea, 1945 in Borneo). Pres., Council of St John in South Australia, 1976– (Chm. 1946–76). Purchased Silverton Park, Delamere, SA 1942, and established Border Leicester Stud and later Hereford Stud. KStJ 1960; Bronze Star Medal, USA, 1945. *Recreations:* polo (represented S Australia, Interstate, 1936–57); golf, swimming. *Address:* 175 North Terrace, Adelaide, SA 5000, Australia. *T:* 212-7560; Carrick Hill, Springfield, SA 5062, Australia. *T:* 79-3886. *Clubs:* Adelaide, Naval, Military & Air Force, Royal Adelaide Golf, Adelaide Polo (Adelaide SA); Melbourne (Melbourne); Australian, Royal Sydney Golf (Sydney, NSW). *Died Aug.* 1983.

**HAZAN, Hon. Sir John (Boris Roderick),** Kt 1988; **Hon. Mr Justice Hazan;** a Judge of the High Court of Justice, Queen's Bench Division, since 1988; *b* 3 Oct. 1926; *s* of Selik and Eugenie Hazan. *Educ:* King's Coll., Taunton; King's Coll., Univ. of London (LLB 1946). Called to Bar, Lincoln's Inn, 1948, Bencher 1977. Prosecuting Counsel to Inland Revenue, South Eastern Circuit, 1967–69; QC 1969; Dep. Chm., Surrey QS, 1969–71; a Recorder of the Crown Court, 1972–82; a Circuit Judge, Central Criminal Ct, 1982–88. Member: Criminal Law Revision Cttee, 1971–; Home Secretary's Policy Adv. Cttee on Sexual Offences, 1976–84; Lord Chancellor's and Home Secretary's Cttee on Fraud Trials, 1984–86; Dept of Trade Inspector, Hartley Baird Ltd, 1973–76. JP Surrey, 1969. Freeman, City of London; Liveryman, Musicians' Co. *Recreations:* music, opera, walking. *Address:* Royal Courts of Justice, Strand, WC2. *Club:* Savile. *Died 19 Aug.* 1988.

**HEAD, 1st Viscount** *cr* 1960, of Throope; **Antony Henry Head;** PC 1951; GCMG 1963 (KCMG 1961); CBE 1946; MC 1940; *b* 19 Dec. 1906; *s* of late Geoffrey Head; *m* 1935, Lady Dorothea Ashley-Cooper, *d* of 9th Earl of Shaftesbury, KP, PC, GCVO, CBE; two *s* one *d* (and one *d* decd). *Educ:* Eton; Royal Military Coll., Sandhurst, Adjt Life Guards, 1934–37; Staff Coll., 1939; Brigade Major 20th Gds Bde, 1940; Asst Sec. Cttee Imperial Defence, 1940–41; Guards Armd Div., 1941–42 (GSO2); representative with Directors of Plans for Amphibious Operations (Brigadier), 1943–45. MP (C) Carshalton Division of Surrey, 1945–60; Sec. of State for War, 1951–56; Minister of Defence, Oct. 1956–Jan. 1957. High Commissioner (first) of the United Kingdom in the Federation of Nigeria, 1960–63; High Commissioner to the new Federation of Malaysia, 1963–66. Trustee of the Thomson Foundation, 1967–75. Pres., RNIB, 1975– (Chm., 1968–75). Col Comdt, SAS Regt, 1968–76. Chm., Wessex Region, National Trust, 1970–76. *Recreations:* sailing, shooting. *Heir: s* Hon. Richard Antony Head [*b* 27 Feb. 1937; *m* 1974, Alicia, *er d* of Julian Salmond, Malmesbury; two *s*. *Educ:* Eton; Royal Military Coll., Sandhurst]. *Address:* Throope Manor, Bishopstone, near Salisbury, Wilts. *Died 29 March* 1983.

**HEAD, Alice Maud;** *b* London, 3 May 1886; *y d* of F. D. Head. *Educ:* privately; North London Collegiate Sch. for Girls. Editor of Woman at Home, 1909–17; Managing Director of the National Magazine Company, Ltd, and editor of Good Housekeeping, 1924–39; rejoined the firm of George Newnes Ltd, 1941–49; Director, Country Life Ltd, 1942–49. *Publications:* It Could Never Have Happened, 1939; contributions to various daily and weekly publications. *Recreations:* travelling, reading, theatre-going. *Address:* 22 Whitelands House, Chelsea, SW3. *T:* 01-730 1967. *Club:* PEN.
*Died 25 July 1981.*

**HEADLAM-MORLEY, Prof. Agnes,** MA, BLit; Montague Burton Professor of International Relations, Oxford University, 1948–71; *b* 10 Dec. 1902; *o d* of late Sir James Wycliffe Headlam-Morley, CBE, Historical Adviser to the Foreign Office. *Educ:* Wimbledon High Sch., GPDST; Somerville Coll., Oxford. Fellow and Tutor, St Hugh's Coll., Oxford, 1932. Adopted Prospective Conservative Candidate, Barnard Castle Div. of Durham, 1936. Hon. Fellow: Somerville Coll., Oxford, 1948; St Hugh's Coll., Oxford, 1970; Mem., St Antony's Coll. Received into the Roman Catholic Church, 1948. Mem., Academic Council, Wilton Park. Founder Mem., Anglo-German Assoc. *Publications:* The New Democratic Constitutions of Europe, 1929; Editor (with K. Headlam-Morley) of Studies in Diplomatic History by J. W. Headlam-Morley, 1930; Arthur Cayley Headlam (a memoir published in The Fourth Gospel as History by A. C. Headlam, 1948); Last Days, 1960; (ed) A Memoir of the Peace Conference of Paris 1919 by J. W. Headlam-Morley, 1972; essay on Gustav Stresemann in The History Makers, ed Sir John Wheeler-Bennett and Lord Longford, 1973; contrib. Longford Report on Pornography, 1976; articles and reviews in Trivium and History Today. *Address:* 29 St Mary's Road, Wimbledon, SW19; St Hugh's College, Oxford. *T:* 01–946 6134.
*Died 21 Feb. 1986.*

**HEADLAM-MORLEY, Kenneth Arthur Sonntag,** OBE 1962; Secretary, The Iron and Steel Institute, 1933–67; *b* 24 June 1901; *o s* of late Sir James Headlam-Morley, CBE (who assumed additional surname of Morley by Royal Licence, 1917), Historical Adviser to the Foreign Office, and Else, *y d* of late Dr August Sonntag, Lüneburg; *m* 1951, Lorna Dione, *d* of late Francis Kinchin Smith; three *s* two *d*. *Educ:* Eton; New Coll., Oxford (Schol.). Staff of Dorman, Long & Co. Ltd, 1924; Secretary: Inst. of Metals, 1944–47; Instn of Metallurgists, 1945–48; Dep. Controller Chrome Ore, Magnesite and Wolfram Control, Foundry Bonding Materials Control and assoc. Controls of Min. of Supply, 1940–43. Hon. Life Member: Amer. Inst. of Mining and Metallurgical Engrs, 1955; Amer. Soc. for Metals, 1955. Hon. Member: l'Assoc. des Ingénieurs sortis de l'Ecole de Liège, 1955; Verein deutscher Eisenhüttenleute, 1955; Soc. Française de Métallurgie, 1956; The Indian Institute of Metals, 1963. Chevalier Order of Vasa (Sweden), 1954; Chevalier Order of the Crown (Belgium), 1955. *Recreation:* gardening. *Address:* Field House, Whorlton, Barnard Castle, Co. Durham DL12 8XA. *T:* Teesdale 27354.
*Died 28 Oct. 1982.*

**HEAKES, Air Vice-Marshal Francis Vernon,** CB 1944; Commander, Legion of Merit (US); RCAF retired; *b* 27 Jan. 1894; *s* of Frank R. Heakes, Architect, and Susie Pemberton Heakes; *m* 1920, Edna Eulalie Watson, BA (*d* 1986); one *s* three *d*. *Educ:* University of Toronto. Canadian Expeditionary Force, Lieut 1916–17; RFC (seconded), 1917–18; RAF 1918–19; CAF 1919; CAF and RCAF since 1923; Air Mem. Permanent Joint Board, Canada and US; Dir Air Personnel, RCAF; Dir Plans & Operations; AOC, RCAF, Newfoundland; AOC Western Air Command, Canada. *Recreations:* sports, all kinds, writing prose and verse, oil painting, musical composition. *Address:* 1449 West 40 Avenue, Vancouver, BC V6M 1V5, Canada.
*Died 13 May 1989.*

**HEALD, Rt. Hon. Sir Lionel Frederick,** PC 1954; Kt 1951; QC 1937; JP; Air Commodore RAF (VR); *b* 7 Aug. 1897; *yr s* of late James Heald, Parrs Wood, Lancs; *m* 1st, 1923, Flavia, *d* of Lieut-Col J. S. Forbes; one *s* one *d*; 2nd, 1929, Daphne Constance, CBE 1976, *d* of late Montague Price; two *s* one *d*. *Educ:* Charterhouse; Christ Church, Oxford (Holford Exhibitioner). BALitt Hum 1920. Served RE (SR) 1916–19 (Italian Bronze Medal); RAF (VR), 1939–45. Borough Councillor (MR), St Pancras, 1934–37. Called to Bar, Middle Temple, 1923, Bencher, 1946; Junior Counsel to Board of Trade in technical matters, 1931–37; additional mem. of Bar Council, 1947. Contested (Nat C) SW St Pancras Div., 1945; MP (C) Chertsey, 1950–70. Governor, Middlesex Hospital, 1946–1953. JP Surrey, 1946. Attorney-Gen., 1951–54. *Address:* Chilworth Manor, Guildford, Surrey. *Club:* Garrick.
*Died 7 Nov. 1981.*

**HEALEY, Sir Charles Arthur C.;** *see* Chadwyck-Healey.

**HEALEY, Donald Mitchell,** CBE 1973; Director, Healey Automobile Consultants Ltd, since 1955; *b* 3 July 1898; *s* of John Frederick and Emmie Mitchell Healey; *m* 1921, Ivy Maud James; three *s*. *Educ:* Newquay Coll. Pupil, Sopwith Aviation Co., 1914; RFC and RAF, 1915–18; Aeronautical Inspection Dept, Air Ministry, 1918–20;

self-employed automobile engr and competitions driver, 1920; Experimental Manager and Technical Dir, Triumph Motor Co. Ltd, 1933–39; Gen. Man., Air Min. Carburettor Co., Humber Co., and RAF, 1939–45; formed Donald Healey Motor Co. Ltd, Manufacturers, Healey, Nash Healey and Austin Healey cars, 1945–73; Chm., Jensen Motors Ltd, 1973. Médaille de l'Education Physique et Sports (ler Cl.), Monaco, 1962. *Recreations:* swimming, motor sport. *Address:* Bridge House, Perranporth, Cornwall TR6 0ES. *T:* Truro 573521. *Club:* Royal Air Force.
*Died 13 Jan. 1988.*

**HEALEY, Rt. Rev. Kenneth;** an Assistant Bishop, Diocese of Lincoln since 1966; *b* 7 Aug. 1899; *s* of late Harry Healey; *m* 1925, Marjorie, *d* of late Harry Wright Palmer, Friday Bridge, Cambs; two *d*. *Educ:* Moulton Grammar Sch. Deacon, 1931; Priest, 1932; Asst Curate, Grantham, 1931; Rector of Bloxholm with Digby, 1935; and Vicar of Ashby de la Launde (in plurality), 1939: Rural Dean of Lafford North, 1938; Vicar of Nocton, 1943; Rector of Algarkirk, 1950–58; Archdeacon of Lincoln, 1951–58; Bishop Suffragan of Grimsby, 1958–65. Proctor in Convocation, 1945–70; Church Commissioner, 1952–72. Chm. (formerly Vice-Chm.) Lindsey and Kesteven Agricultural Wages Cttee, 1945–69. MA Lambeth, 1958. *Address:* Gedney Dyke, Spalding, Lincs. *T:* Holbeach 362030.
*Died 12 Feb. 1985.*

**HEANEY, Brig. George Frederick,** CBE 1943; late Royal Engineers (retd); *b* 1 June 1897; 2nd *s* of late George Robert Heaney, Dublin; *m* 1929, Doreen Marguerite, *e d* of late Lieut-Col R. H. Hammersley-Smith, CBE; one *s* two *d* (and one *s* decd). *Educ:* St Lawrence; RMA Woolwich; Christ's Coll., Cambridge. 2nd Lieut RE 1916; European War in France, 1917–18 (wounded, despatches twice); apptd to Survey of India, 1921; in India and Burma, 1920–41; served in Persia-Iraq Forces, 1941–43 (CBE); D Survey, Allied Land Forces, SEAC, 1944–45; retired from Army, 1948; Surveyor-Gen. of India, 1946–51; Pres. Inst. of Surveyors (India), 1950–51; Managing Dir, North Essex Growers Ltd, 1963–64. *Address:* 16 Park Road, Lymington, Hants SO4 9GN.
*Died 26 Feb. 1983.*

**HEATH, Sir Barrie,** Kt 1978; DFC 1941; Director, RTZ Cement Ltd, since 1980; *b* 11 Sept. 1916; *s* of George Heath and Florence Amina Heath (*née* Jones); *m* 1st, 1939, Joy Anderson (*d* 1980); two *s*; 2nd, 1981, Joan Elizabeth McKee. *Educ:* Wrekin; Pembroke Coll., Cambridge. Trained with Rootes Securities Ltd, 1938–39; fighter pilot, RAF, 1939–45 (Wing Comdr, despatches); Dir, Hobourn Aero Components, Rochester, 1946–50; Man. Dir, Powell Duffryn Carbon Products Ltd, 1950–60; Man. Dir, Triplex Safety Glass Co. Ltd, 1960–68, Chm., 1965–74; non-exec. Dir, GKN Ltd, 1972–74; Group Chm., GKN Ltd, 1975–79; Chm., Hesketh Motorcycles, 1980–82; Director: Pilkington Brothers Ltd, 1967–84; Barclays Bank UK Ltd, 1975–84; Barclays Bank Ltd, 1976–84; Smiths Industries plc, 1970–86. Pres., Soc. of Motor Manufacturers and Traders, 1978–80 (Vice-Pres., 1973–78, Dep. Pres., 1980–81); Vice-President: Engineering Employers' Fedn, 1975–80; Inst. of Motor Industry, 1975–; Pres., German Chamber of Industry and Commerce in UK, 1977–80; Founder Mem., Engineering Industries Council, 1975–80; Chm., Commonwealth Games UK Jt Appeal Cttee, 1977–78; Member: Industrial Democracy Cttee, 1975–77; British Overseas Trade Adv. Council, 1977–80; BOTB, 1977–80; Tenneco European Adv. Council, 1980–84. Governor, and Chm. Vehicle Cttee, Motability, 1977–85. Trustee: Nat. Motor Mus., 1975–; RAF Mus., 1976–; Beaverbrook Foundn, 1984–. Freeman of City of London; Liveryman, Coachmaker and Coach Harness Makers' Co. *Recreations:* yachting, shooting. *Address:* Watercroft, Penn, Bucks HP10 8NX. *Clubs:* Royal Air Force, Royal Ocean Racing, Royal Thames Yacht; Royal Yacht Squadron, Royal London Yacht.
*Died 22 Feb. 1988.*

**HEATH-GRACIE, George Handel,** BMus (Dunelm), 1932; FRCO 1915; Organist and Master of the Choristers, Derby Cathedral, 1933–57; Diocesan Choirmaster, 1936–57; Founder and Conductor, Derby Bach Choir, 1935; Special Commissioner, Royal School of Church Music, 1951–66; *b* 4 June 1892; *m* 1922, Marjory Josephine Knight (*d* 1986). *Educ:* Bristol Grammar Sch.; Bristol Cathedral. Organist of various Bristol Churches, 1909–14; of St John's, Frome, 1914–15; Service with HM forces, 1915–19; Organist of St Peter, Brockley, SE, 1918–33; Cor Juctor South London Philharmonic Soc., 1919–21; Broadcast Cnurch Music Series, 1936–38; Music Dir, Derby Sch., 1938–44; Mem. panel of examnrs, Associated Bd of Royal Schs of Music, 1946–82; Sch. Music Adviser, Derbyshire Educn Cttee, 1944–57; Mem. Council, Incorporated Soc. of Musicians for SW England, 1964–67; Mem. Diocesan Adv. Cttee, to 1957; Mem., Artist selection panel, BBC, 1946–74. Extra-mural Lectr, University Coll., Nottingham; Festival Adjudicator and Lectr. Toured Canada and USA as adjudicator, lecturer and performer, 1949, return visit, 1953; travelled in Asia, and African Tour, 1959; Eastern Tour, Ceylon, Singapore, Malaya, 1960; Tour of W Indies, N and S America and New Zealand, 1966, and New Zealand, 1968. *Publications:* various Church Music and press articles. *Recreations:* gossip, brewing. *Address:* Woodhouse, Uplyme, Lyme Regis, Dorset. *Clubs:* Savage; Exeter and County; (Hon.) Kiwanis (Peterborough, Ont). *Died 20 April* 1987.

**HEATHCOAT AMORY, Sir William,** 5th Bt *cr* 1874; DSO 1942; *b* 19 Aug. 1901; *s* of Sir Ian Murray Heathcoat Amory, 2nd Bt, CBE, and Alexandra Georgina (*d* 1942), *d* of Vice-Adm. Henry George Seymour, CB; *S* to baronetcy of brother, 1st Viscount Amory, 1981; *m* 1933, Margaret Isabel Dorothy Evelyn, *yr d* of Sir Arthur Havelock James Doyle, 4th Bt; two *s* two *d*. *Educ:* Eton; RMC Sandhurst. 2nd Lt KRRC, 1921; served War of 1939–45, Western Desert, Italy and Normandy; Lt-Col 1942; retired, 1948. A Member of HM Body Guard, Honourable Corps of Gentlemen-at-Arms, 1952–66. *Recreations:* hunting, shooting, fishing, ornithology, carving. *Heir: s* Ian Heathcoat Amory [*b* 3 Feb. 1942; *m* 1972, Frances Louise, *d* of J. F. B. Pomeroy; three *s*]. *Address:* Calverleigh Court, Tiverton, Devon. *T:* Tiverton 254033.

*Died 27 Aug.* 1982.

**HEAUME, Sir (Francis) Herbert du;** *see* du Heaume.

**HEAWOOD, Geoffrey Leonard;** *b* 5 Jan. 1893; *s* of late Professor P. J. Heawood, OBE, DCL; *m* 1926, Norah Buchanan (*d* 1975), 2nd *d* of late Rt Rev. J. T. Inskip, DD; one *s* one *d*. *Educ:* Blundell's; Wadham Coll., Oxford (Math. Mods and Lit. Hum.). Capt. 4th Bn Wilts Regt; attached 1st Oxford and Bucks LI; Major, Home Guard. Tutor Knutsford Test Sch., 1919–22; London Sec. Student Christian Movement, 1922–24; Resident Tutor, King's Coll. Hostel, London, 1924–26; Asst Master Alleyns Sch., 1925–29; Headmaster County Sch. for Boys, Bromley, 1929–37; Headmaster Cheltenham Grammar Sch., 1937–53; Sec. of the Central Advisory Council for the Ministry (CACTM), 1953–60, General Sec., 1960–62; retired, 1962. *Publications:* Religion in School; Vacant Possession; Westminster Abbey Trinity Lectures, 1961; The Humanist-Christian Frontier. *Address:* Pendean, West Lavington, Midhurst, West Sussex. *T:* Midhurst 4375. *Died 9 April* 1982.

**HEBB, Prof. Donald Olding,** FRSC 1959; FRS 1966; Professor of Psychology, 1947–72 (part-time appointment, 1972–74), and Chancellor, 1970–74, Professor Emeritus, 1975, McGill University (Chairman of Department, 1948–58; Vice-Dean of Biological Sciences, 1964–66); *b* 22 July 1904; *s* of Arthur Morrison Hebb and Mary Clara Olding; *m* 1st, 1931, Marion Isobel Clark (*d* 1933); 2nd, 1937, Elizabeth Nichols Donovan (*d* 1962); two *d*; 3rd, 1966, Margaret Doreen Wright (*née* Williamson) (*d* 1983). *Educ:* Dalhousie Univ.; McGill Univ.; University of Chicago; Harvard Univ. PhD (Harvard), 1936. Taught in schools, Nova Scotia and Quebec, 1925–34; Instructor, Harvard Univ., 1936–37; Research Fellow, Montreal Neurological Inst., 1937–39; Lectr, Queen's Univ., 1939–42; Research Associate, Yerkes Labs of Primate Biology, 1942–47. Royal Soc. Vis. Prof., UCL, 1974. Hon. Prof., Dalhousie Univ., 1978–. Pres., Canadian Psychol Assoc., 1952; Pres., American Psychol. Assoc., 1960. Hon. DSc: Chicago, 1961; Waterloo, 1963; York, 1966; McMaster, 1967; St Lawrence, 1972; McGill, 1975; Memorial, 1977; Hon. DHL, Northeastern, 1963; Hon. LLD: Dalhousie, 1965; Queen's, 1967; Western Ontario, 1968; Concordia, 1975; Trent, 1976; Victoria, BC, 1976; Hon. DCL Bishop's, 1977. *Publications:* Organization of Behaviour, 1949; Textbook of Psychology, 1958, 3rd edn 1972; Essay on Mind, 1980; papers in technical psychological jls. *Address:* RR1, Chester Basin, Nova Scotia B0J 1K0, Canada. *T:* (902) 275–4367.

*Died 20 Aug.* 1985.

**HEBBLETHWAITE, Sidney Horace,** CMG 1964; HM Diplomatic Service, retired; Hon. Vice-Consul at Florence, since 1978; *b* 15 Nov. 1914; *s* of Sidney Horace Hebblethwaite and Margaret Bowler Cooke; *m* 1942, May Gladys Cook; two *d*. *Educ:* Reale Ginnasio-Liceo, Francesco Petrarca, Trieste, Italy; Pembroke Coll., Cambridge. Third Sec., FO, 1939; transferred to: Rome, 1939; FO, 1940; Lisbon, 1942; Second Sec. 1944; transferred to FO, 1945; Foreign Service Officer, 1948; 1st Sec. (Information), Athens, 1949; transferred to: Rome, 1951; FO, 1955; seconded to Treasury, 1957; transferred to Brussels, 1958; Counsellor: HM Embassy, Stockholm, 1958–62, Rangoon, 1962–65; Counsellor (Information), Washington, 1965–68; retired, in order to take up appt as HM Consul, Florence, 1970–74. *Recreations:* music, reading. *Address:* 10 Via San Egidio, Florence, Italy. *Died 16 Dec.* 1987.

**HECKER, William Rundle,** CBE 1963; MA, BSc, FKC; Headmaster of St Dunstan's College, Catford, 1938–67; *b* 1899; *s* of late W. J. Hecker, Margate, and Elizabeth, *d* of Richard Rundle, Hazelbeech, Northants; *m* 1925, Ione Murray, *d* of late J. P. Topping, MD; one *s*. *Educ:* Chatham House, Ramsgate; King's Coll., London. Served European War, 1914–18, in France; London Regt, 1917–19; Senior Science Master, Boston Gram. Sch., 1924–25; Asst Master, Epsom Coll., 1925–28; Headmaster of Tavistock Gram. Sch., 1928–31, Wilson's Gram. Sch., Camberwell, 1931–38. Pres. Incorporated Assoc. of Headmasters, 1951. Chm. Jt Cttee of the Four Secondary Assoc., 1958–59. *Recreations:* walking, gardening, travel. *Address:*

5 Meadowcourt Road, Oadby, Leicester.

*Died 3 Nov.* 1983.

**HECKLE, Arnold,** CMG 1964; Chairman and President, Rubery Owen Canada Ltd; North American Director, The Rubery Owen Group of Companies; Director: Johnston Equipment Co. Ltd; Delta Benco Cascade Ltd; *b* 4 Dec. 1906; *s* of late James Allison Heckle; *m* 1954, Monique, *d* of late Alfred Choinière, Montreal. *Educ:* Padgate Sch., Lancs; Warrington Technical Coll. Entered Local Govt; subseq. Bd of Trade: Regional Controller, Midlands, 1941; Asst Sec., Bd of Trade; British Trade Comr, Johannesburg, 1957–60; Principal British Trade Comr, PQ, 1960–68. *Recreations:* fly-fishing, golf. *Address:* PO Box 1002, St Sauver-des-Monts, Quebec, Canada. *Clubs:* St James's, Montreal (Montreal).

*Died 18 Jan.* 1982.

**HEDDLE, (Bentley) John;** MP (C) Mid Staffordshire, since 1983 (Lichfield and Tamworth, 1979–83); Consultant Surveyor (partner Elliott Son and Boyton, Chartered Surveyors, since 1980); Underwriting Member of Lloyd's, and director of public and private companies; *b* 15 Sept. 1941; *s* of Oliver Heddle and late Lilian Heddle; *m* 1st, 1964, Judith (marr. diss. 1985; she *d* 1988), *d* of Dr R. H. M. Robinson, Hyde Hall, Rettendon, Essex, and Joy Robinson, Hothfield, Kent; two *s* two *d*; 2nd, 1986, Janet (*née* Stokes), of Hythe, Kent, and Chalvington, Sussex. *Educ:* Bishop's Stortford Coll.; College of Estate Management, London Univ., 1962–64. FCIArb; FInstD, FRSA, and other professional instns. Partner, Heddle Butler & Co., Cons. Surveyors, 1966–70; John Heddle & Co., 1970–80. Member: Internat. Real Estate Fedn, 1972–; Bd of Management, UK Housing Assoc., 1980–. Vice-Pres., Building Socs Assoc. Councillor, Kent CC, 1973–80. Contested (C): Gateshead West, Feb. 1974; Bolton East, Oct. 1974; adopted as parly cand., Lichfield and Tamworth, Nov. 1975. Mem., H of C Select Cttee on the Environment, 1982; Chm., Cons. Parly Environment Cttee, 1983– (Jt Sec., 1979–83). Chairman: Bow Gp Environment Cttee, 1980–82; Cons. Nat. Local Govt Adv. Cttee, 1984–89; Mem., Cons. Party Nat. Union Exec, 1984–89. Industry and Parlt Trust Fellowship, 1979. Deleg. to CPA Conf., Gibraltar, 1981. Freeman, City of London, 1979. Hon. FIAA&S 1987. *Publications:* the Way Through the Woods, 1973; St Cuthbert's Village—an urban disaster, 1976; A New Lease of Life—a solution to Rent Control (CPC), 1975; The Great Rate Debate (CPC), 1980; No Waiting?—a solution to the hospital waiting list problem (CPC), 1982; various contribs on housing, rating, planning and environmental subjects to nat. and profess. press and political jls. *Recreation:* relaxing with family. *Address:* House of Commons, SW1A 0AA. *T:* 01–219 5074; The Old College House, Lichfield, Staffs. *Club:* Carlton. *Died 19 Dec.* 1989.

**HEDGES, Sir John (Francis),** Kt 1962; CBE 1958; retired solicitor in private practice; *b* 1917; *o s* of late Francis Reade Hedges and Nesta Violet (*née* Cavell); *m* 1957, Barbara Mary (*née* Ward), widow of Comdr Richard Scobell Palairet, RN; no *c*. *Educ:* St Andrew's, Eastbourne; Harrow. Commissioned Royal Signals, 1940; served India and SE Asia, TARO, 1950. Chm. Abingdon Conservative Assoc., 1948–60; Chm. Wessex Area, 1954–57 (Hon. Treas. 1960–67); Pres. Berks, Bucks and Oxon Justices' Clerks' Soc., 1955; Pres. Berks, Bucks and Oxon Inc. Law Soc., 1963; Chm. Turner's Court Sch. for Boys, 1955–75; Pres. League of Friends, Wallingford Hosps, 1953–73; Mem. Berks Exec. Council, NHS, 1960–74 (Chm., 1971–74); Chm., Berkshire AHA, 1973–79; Chm., Oxon Diocese Redundant Churches Uses Cttee, 1974–. Hon. Freeman, Borough of Wallingford, 1971. *Recreations:* gardening, music. *Address:* The Coach House, Castle Street, Wallingford, Oxon OX10 8DL. *T:* Wallingford 36217. *Died 14 Dec.* 1983.

**HEDLEY, Hilda Mabel,** CB 1975; Under-Secretary, Department of Health and Social Security (formerly Ministry of Health), 1967–75; *b* 4 May 1918; *d* of late George Ward Hedley, Cheltenham, and late Winifred Mary Hedley (*née* Cockshott). *Educ:* Cheltenham Ladies' Coll.; Newnham Coll., Cambridge. Uncommon Languages Dept., Postal Censorship, 1940–42; Foreign Office, 1942–46; Min. of Health, later DHSS, 1946–75. Sec. to Royal Commn on Mental Health, 1954–57. Nuffield Foundation Travelling Fellowship, 1960–61. Gen. Sec., Cheltenham Ladies' Coll. Guild, 1976–82. *Recreations:* gardening, bird-watching, cooking. *Address:* The Anchorage, Castle Street, Winchcombe, Cheltenham GL54 5JA. *T:* Cheltenham 602314. *Died 29 Jan.* 1988.

**HEDSTROM, Sir (John) Maynard,** KBE 1980; retired; company director; *b* 16 May 1908; *s* of Sir John Maynard Hedstrom and Grace Lambert Hedstrom (*née* Eastgate); *m* 1940, Moira Harwood (*née* Dietrich); two *s*. *Educ:* Geelong Grammar School; Melbourne University. LLB. Joined Morris Hedstrom Ltd, Suva, Fiji, as junior clerk, 1934; retired as General Manager, 1958. Dir, W. R. Carpenter Holdings Ltd; Chm., W. R. Carpenter (South Pacific) Ltd. Knight First Class, Order of Vasa, Sweden, 1964. *Recreation:* learning to grow old. *Address:* 37 Prince's Road, Tamavua, Suva, Fiji. *T:* Suva

381416. *Clubs:* Australian (Sydney); Fiji, Defence, Union (Suva); Royal Suva Yacht. *Died* 15 *Nov.* 1983.

**HEIFETZ, Jascha;** Commander, Legion of Honour, 1957; violinist, soloist; 1st Vice-President of American Guild of Musical Artists, Inc., New York City; Hon. Member: Society of Concerts of Paris Conservatoire; Association des Anciens Elèves du Conservatoire; Cercle International de la Jeunesse Artistique; Hon. Vice-President of Mark Twain Society, USA; Hon. President, Musicians' Fund of America; on music department staff, University of Southern California, Los Angeles; *b* Vilna, Russia, 2 Feb. 1901; father professional violinist and music teacher; *m* 1928, Florence Vidor; one *s* one *d*; *m* 1947, Mrs Frances Spiegelberg; one *s. Recreations:* sailing, ping-pong (table tennis), motoring, reading and dancing. *Address:* Beverly Hills, Calif, USA. *Clubs:* Royal Automobile, Savage; Bohemian (New York); Beaux Arts, Inter-Allied (Paris).
*Died* 10 *Dec.* 1987.

**HEIN, Sir (Charles Henri) Raymond,** Kt 1977; Chevalier de la Légion d'Honneur, 1950; QC 1956; Barrister-at-Law, in practice since 1925; Director of Companies; *b* 26 Sept. 1901; *s* of Jules Hein and Clémence de Charmoy; *m* 1928, Marcelle Piat; four *s* four *d. Educ:* Royal Coll., Mauritius (Scholar, 1920); Wadham Coll., Oxford. MA Oxon. Mem., Council of Govt, 1936-48; Mayor of Port Louis, 1948. Dir, 1937-76, Pres., 1965-76, Mauritius Commercial Bank; Chairman: Swan Insurance Ltd, 1967-; Mauritius Life Assurance, 1972-; Anglo-Mauritius Assce Soc. Ltd, 1973-; New Mauritius Dock Co. Ltd, 1960-70 (Dir, 1937-70); Dir, Reinsurance Co. of Mauritius. Former President: Mauritius Chamber of Agric.; Mauritius Sugar Industry Res. Inst.; Mauritius Turf Club. Pres., Alliance Française, 1948-54. Former Pres., Bar Council. *Publications:* trans. Bernardin de St Pierre's Paul et Virginie, 1977; Le Naufrage du Saint Géran (Légende de Paul et Virginie), 1981. *Recreations:* music, gardening, ancient Greek literature. *Address:* Route de Saint Jean, Quatre Bornes, Mauritius; (chambers) Cathedral Square, Port Louis. *T:* 2-0327. *Club:* Mauritius Turf (Port Louis). *Died* 6 *Jan.* 1983.

**HEINZ, Henry John, II,** Hon. KBE 1977; Chairman, H. J. Heinz Company, since 1959 (President, 1941-59); *b* Sewickley, Pa, USA, 10 July 1908; *s* of Howard and Elizabeth Rust Heinz; *m* 1st, 1935, Joan Diehl (marr. diss. 1942); one *s; m* 1953, Drue English Maher. *Educ:* Yale (BA 1931); Trinity Coll., Cambridge. Salesman, H. J. Heinz Co., Ltd, London, 1932; with H. J. Heinz Co., Pittsburgh, Pa, Pres., 1941-59; Chm., 1959-. Chm., Governing Bd, Yale Univ. Art Gallery; Member: Adv. Cttee, Yale Univ. Economic Growth Centre; Council of Management, British-Ditchley Foundn; Business Cttee for the Arts; Nat. Council (US), WWF; Director: Pittsburgh Symphony Soc.; World Affairs Council, Pittsburgh; Trustee: Carnegie Inst.; Carnegie-Mellon Univ.; Internat. Life Science Inst.; Nutrition Foundn; Cttee for Econ. Develt; US Council, ICC. Commander, Royal Order of the Phœnix, Greece, 1950; Chevalier de la Légion d'Honneur, France, 1950; Comdr of Order of Merit, Italian Republic. OStJ. *Recreation:* ski-ing. *Address:* (residence) Goodwood, Sewickley, Pa 15143, USA. *Clubs:* Buck's, White's; The Brook, River (New York); Duquesne, Rolling Rock, Allegheny Country (Pittsburgh). *Died* 23 *Feb.* 1987.

**HEINZE, Prof. Sir Bernard (Thomas),** AC 1976; Kt 1949; MA, LLD, MusDoc, FRCM; Degré Supérieur Schola Cantorum, Paris; Ormond Professor of Music, University of Melbourne, 1925-57; Director, State Conservatorium, NSW, 1957-66; Conductor Melbourne Philharmonic Society since 1928; Conductor under contract to ABC since 1947; *b* Shepparton, Vic, 1 July 1894; *m* 1932, Valerie Antonia, *d* of late Sir David Valentine Hennessy, of Melbourne; three *s. Educ:* St Patrick's Coll., Ballarat; Melbourne Univ. MA (Melbourne); LLD (Hon.) (Brit. Columbia); FRCM 1931. Won the Clarke Scholarship in 1912 and was sent to England to study at the Royal College of Music; studies interrupted by five years' service as an officer in the Royal Artillery; won the Gowland Harrison Scholarship, 1920; studied at the Schola Cantorum, Paris, under Vincent d'Indy and Nestor Lejeune; studied in Berlin under Willy Hess; returned to Australia, 1923; founded Melbourne String Quartette; Conductor: University Symphony Orchestra, 1924-32; Melbourne Symphony Orchestra, 1933-46. Mem., ABC Music Adv. Cttee; Chairman: Commonwealth Assistance to Australian Composers, 1967-; Music Adv. Cttee, Australian Council for the Arts, 1969-. Dir General for Music, Australian Broadcasting Co. 1929-32. Officier de la Couronne, Belgium, 1938; Polonia Restituta, 1973. *Recreations:* golf and philately. *Address:* 101 Victoria Road, Bellevue Hill, Sydney, NSW 2023, Australia. *Clubs:* Canada (Melbourne); Royal Sydney Golf, American (Sydney).
*Died* 10 *June* 1982.

**HEITLER, Prof. Walter Heinrich,** PhD; FRS 1948; Professor of Theoretical Physics, University of Zürich, 1949-74; *b* 2 Jan. 1904; *m* 1942, Kathleen Winifred; one *s. Educ:* Universities of Berlin and Munich. Doctor's Degree, Munich, 1926; Privatdocent for Theoretical Physics, University of Göttingen, 1929-33; Research

Fellow, University of Bristol, 1933-41; Professor of Theoretical Physics, 1941-49; Dir, School of Theoretical Physics, Dublin Institute for Advanced Studies, 1945-49. Hon. DSc Dublin, 1954; Dr rer nat *hc* Göttingen, 1969; Hon. DPhil Uppsala, 1973. Max Planck Medal, 1968; Marcel Benoist Prize, 1969; Gold Medal, Humboldt Gesellschaft, 1979. *Publications:* (with F. London) Theory of Chemical Bond, 1927; Quantum Theory of Radiation, 1936 (3rd edn 1954); Elementary Wave Mechanics, 1945 (2nd edn 1956); papers on Cosmic Rays, Meson theory, Quantum-electrodynamics; Der Mensch und die Naturwissenschaftliche Erkenntnis, 1961, 4th edn, 1966 (Eng. Trans. Man and Science, 1963); Naturphilosophische Streifzüge, 1970; Naturwissenschaft ist Geisteswissenschaft, 1972; Die Natur und das Göttliche, 1974, 4th edn 1977 (Foundn for Western Thinking Lit. prize); Gottesbeweise?, 1977. *Address:* The University, Zürich, Switzerland; (home) Am Guggenberg 5, Zürich. *Died* 15 *Nov.* 1981.

**HELLINGS, Gen. Sir Peter (William Cradock),** KCB 1970 (CB 1966); DSC 1940; MC 1943; DL; *b* 6 Sept. 1916; *s* of Stanley and Norah Hellings; *m* 1941, Zoya, *d* of Col Bassett; one *d* (one *s* decd). *Educ:* Naut. Coll., Pangbourne. Joined Royal Marines, 1935; Company Cmdr, 40 Commando, 1942; GSO 2, Commando Group, 1944; Comdr 41 and 42 Commandos, 1945-46; Brigade Major, 3 Commando Bde in Malaya, 1949-51; joined Directing Staff of Marine Corps Schs, Quantico, USA, 1954; Comdr 40 Commando, 1958; Brigade Comdr, 3 Commando Bde, 1959; Comdr Infantry Training Centre, Royal Marines, 1960; idc 1962; Dep. Dir, Joint Warfare Staff, 1963; Maj.-Gen., 1964; Chief of Staff to Commandant-Gen., RM, 1964; Group Comdr, HQ Portsmouth Group RM, 1967-68; Lt-Gen., 1968; Comdt-Gen., RM, 1968-71; General, 1970. Col Comdt, Royal Marines, 1977-79, Representative Col Comdt, 1979-80. DL Devon 1973. *Recreations:* shooting, fishing. *Address:* The Leys, Milton Combe, Devon PL20 6HW. *T:* Yelverton (0822) 3355. *Died* 2 *Nov.* 1990.

**HELLMAN, Lillian;** playwright; *b* New Orleans, Louisiana, USA, 20 June 1907; *d* of Max Bernard Hellman and Julia Newhouse; *m* 1925, Arthur Kober (divorced). *Educ:* New York Univ.; Columbia Univ. Worked for Horace Liveright, Publishers, 1925-26. Hon. LLD Wheaton Coll., MA Tufts Univ.; Hon. LLD: Rutgers Univ., 1963, Brandeis Univ., 1965; Yale, 1974; Smith Coll., 1974; New York Univ., 1974; Franklin and Marshall Coll., 1975; Columbia Univ., 1976; Creative Arts Award, Brandeis Univ.; Mem., National Inst. of Arts and Letters (Gold Medal for Drama, 1964); Mem., American Academy of Arts and Sciences. Book reviews, Herald Tribune, wrote short stories. First produced play The Children's Hour, 1934. Wrote movie scenarios The Dark Angel, These Three (screen version of The Children's Hour), Dead End, The Little Foxes, North Star. *Publications:* plays produced: The Children's Hour, 1934; Days to Come, 1936; The Little Foxes, 1939; Watch on the Rhine, 1941; The Searching Wind, 1944; Another Part of the Forest, 1946; adapted from the French, Roblés' play, Montserrat, 1949; The Autumn Garden, 1951; adapted Anouilh's The Lark, 1955; adapted Voltaire's Candide as comic operetta, 1956; Toys in the Attic, 1960; adapted Blechman's novel How Much as play, My Mother, My Father and Me, 1963; edited: The Selected Letters of Anton Chekhov, 1955; (with introduction) Dashiell Hammett, The Big Knockover, 1966; (memoir) An Unfinished Woman, 1969 (National Book Award 1970); Pentimento, 1974; Scoundrel Time, 1976; Maybe, 1980. *Address:* 630 Park Avenue, New York, NY 10021, USA. *Died* 30 *June* 1984.

**HELPMANN, Sir Robert Murray,** Kt 1968; CBE 1964; dancer, actor (stage and films); choreographer; producer; director; *b* 9 April 1909; *s* of James Murray Helpman, Mount Gambia, South Australia, and Mary Gardiner, Mount Shank, SA. *Educ:* Prince Alfred's Coll., Adelaide. First appeared under J. C. Williamson's Management, Australia, 1926-30; Premier Danseur, Sadler's Wells Ballet, 1933-50; Director, Australian Ballet, 1965-76; Artistic Dir, Adelaide Festival, 1970-. Guest dancer, Royal Opera House, 1958; guest artist, Sadler's Wells Royal Ballet, 1977. *Theatre:* Stop Press, Adelphi, 1936; Oberon, A Midsummer Night's Dream, Old Vic, 1937-38; Gremio, The Taming of the Shrew, 1939; title role, Old Vic prodn, Hamlet, New, 1944; Flamineo, The White Devil, 1947; Prince, He Who Gets Slapped, Duchess, 1947; Stratford-on-Avon, 1948 season: Shylock, King John and Hamlet; Sir Laurence Olivier's Shaw-Shakespeare Festival Season, 1951: Apollodorus, Caesar and Cleopatra; Octavius Caesar, Antony and Cleopatra; The Millionairess, New, 1952; Oberon, A Midsummer Night's Dream, Edinburgh Festival, UK and Canada, 1954; Old Vic Australian Tour, 1955: Petruchio, Taming of the Shrew; Shylock, Merchant of Venice; Angelo, Measure for Measure; Old Vic: Shylock, Merchant of Venice, 1956; Launce, The Two Gentlemen of Verona, 1957; Emperor, Titus Andronicus, 1957; Pinch, Comedy of Errors, 1957; King Richard, Richard III, 1957; Georges de Valera, Nekrassov, Edinburgh Festival and Royal Court, 1957; Sebastian, Nude with Violin, London and Australian Tour, 1958; Sarah in America, USA, 1980; Colette, USA, 1982; Valmouth, Chichester, 1982; The Cobra, Australia, 1983; The Merry Widow, Australia, 1985; Il Puritani,

Australia, 1985; *produced:* Madame Butterfly, Royal Opera Hse, Covent Gdn, 1950; Murder in the Cathedral, Old Vic, 1953; Coq d'Or, Royal Opera Hse, 1954, 1956, 1962; After the Ball, Globe, 1954; Antony and Cleopatra, Old Vic, 1957; The Marriage-Go-Round, Piccadilly, 1959; Duel of Angels: New York, 1960; Melbourne, 1961; Old Vic S American Tour, 1962; Peter Pan, Coliseum, 1972, 1973, 1974, Palladium, 1975; *choreographer:* Red Shoes (and Premier Danseur), 1948; Australia, 1964: Comus; Hamlet; The Birds; Miracle in the Gorbals; Adam Zero; The Soldier's Tale; Elektra; The Display; Yugen; Cinderella, Covent Gdn, 1965; Elektra, Australia, 1966; Sun Music, Australia; dir, Camelot, Drury Lane, 1964; *films include:* One of our Aircraft is Missing, Wyecroft in Caravan, Henry V (Bishop of Ely), Tales of Hoffmann, The Iron Petticoat, Big Money, Red Shoes, 55 Days in Pekin, The Soldier's Tale, The Quiller Memorandum, Chitty Chitty Bang Bang, Alice in Wonderland (Mad Hatter), Don Quixote, The Mango Tree, Patrick. Has appeared on TV. Knight of the Northern Star (Sweden); Knight of the Cedar (Lebanon). *Address:* c/o Midland Bank, 16 King Street, WC2; 7 Bayview Avenue, Balmoral, NSW 2088, Australia.                               *Died* 28 *Sept.* 1986.

**HELY, Brig. Alfred Francis,** CB 1951; CBE 1945; DSO 1943; TD 1944; DL; Chief Dental Officer, Cheshire County Council, 1957–68; *b* 3 Aug. 1902; *s* of Alfred Francis Hely; unmarried. *Educ:* St Edward's Coll., Liverpool; Liverpool Univ. Qualified as a Dental Surg., 1923; in private practice, 1923–26. Liverpool Univ. OTC, 1921–25; Cadet Corporal, Duke of Lancaster's Own Imperial Yeomanry, 1925–26; 106 (Lancs Hussars), RHA, 1926–41 (comd, 1937–41); served War of 1939–45 (despatches twice); 60th Field Regt, RA, 1941–42; CRA 7 Ind. Div., 1942–45; Comd 7 Ind. Div. 1945 until end of hostilities in Burma (3 months); war service in Palestine, Western Desert, Greece, Crete, Syria, 1940–42, North-West Frontier, India, 1942, Burma, 1943–45. CRA 42 (Lancs) Inf. Div. (TA), 1947–50. DL Merseyside (formerly County Palatine of Lancaster), 1951. *Recreations:* outdoor country pursuits. *Address:* 27 Bidston Court, Upton Road, Oxton, Birkenhead, Merseyside L43 7PA.                                         *Died* 24 *June* 1990.

**HEMINGFORD, 2nd Baron,** *cr* 1943, of Watford; **Dennis George Ruddock Herbert,** MA; JP; Lieutenant of Cambridgeshire, 1974–75 (Lord Lieutenant of Huntingdon and Peterborough, 1968–74); Vice-President, Africa Bureau (Chairman, 1952–63); *b* 25 March 1904; *s* of 1st Baron Hemingford, PC, KBE; *S* father, 1947; *m* 1932, Elizabeth McClare (*d* 1979), *d* of late Col J. M. Clark, Haltwhistle, Northumberland; one *s* two *d. Educ:* Oundle; Brasenose Coll., Oxford. Master, Achimota Coll., Gold Coast, 1926–39; Headmaster, King's Coll., Budo, Uganda (CMS), 1939–47; Rector Achimota Training Coll., Gold Coast, 1948–51. Mem., London Government Staff Commission, 1963–65. JP Hunts, 1960–65, Huntingdon and Peterborough, 1965–74, Cambs, 1974. Chairman: Hunts CC, 1961–65; Huntingdon and Peterborough CC, 1967–71. *Heir: s* Hon. (Dennis) Nicholas Herbert [*b* 25 July 1934; *m* 1958, Jennifer Mary Toresen Bailey; one *s* three *d*]. *Address:* The Coach House, Hemingford Abbots, Huntingdon. *T:* St Ives, Cambs, 62375. *Clubs:* Royal Commonwealth Society, National.

*Died* 19 *June* 1982.

**HENARE, Sir James Clendon Tau,** KBE 1978 (CBE 1966); DSO 1945; retired farmer, New Zealand; *b* Motatau, NZ, 18 Nov. 1911; *s* of Tau Henare, MP; *m* 1933, Rosie, *d* of Johnson Cherrington; three *s* three *d. Educ:* Motatau Sch., Awanui, Takapuna; Thorndon Normal Sch.; Sacred Heart Coll., Auckland; Massey Coll. (later Univ.). Served War, 2nd NZEF; Private, 1939; commissioned, 1940; finally CO (Lt-Col) Maori Bn (despatches). Member: Waitangi Nat. Trust Bd; Bay of Islands CC; Bay of Islands Maritime and Historic Park Bd; Chm., Taitokerau Trust Bd. Former Member: Rehabilitation Bd; Geographic Bd; Bd of Maori Affairs; Auckland Diocese Synod; Maori Language Runanga, and many other organisations. Awarded KBE for service to the community, especially Maori affairs, New Zealand. *Address:* Moerewa Road 3, Bay of Islands, New Zealand.                                           *Died* 2 *April* 1989.

**HENDEL, Prof. Charles William;** Professor Emeritus of Moral Philosophy and Metaphysics, Yale University; *b* 16 Dec. 1890; *s* of Charles William Hendel and Emma Stolz, American; *m* 1916, Elizabeth Phoebe Jones (*d* 1977); two *s. Educ:* Princeton Univ. LittB 1913; PhD 1917. United States Army, 1917–18, 2nd Lieut Infantry. Instructor, Williams Coll., 1919–20; Asst and Associate Prof., Princeton Univ., 1920–29; MacDonald Prof. of Moral Philosophy, McGill Univ., 1929–40; Chm. of Philosophy, 1929–40; Dean of Faculty of Arts and Science, 1937–40; Clarke Prof. of Moral Philosophy and Metaphysics, Yale Univ., 1940–59; Chm. of Dept, 1940–45 and 1950–59; Prof. Emeritus, 1959–. Gifford Lecturer, University of Glasgow, 1962–63. Hon. MA Yale, 1940. President: American Philosophical Assoc. (Eastern Div.), 1940; American Soc. for Political and Legal Philosophy, 1959–61. *Publications:* Studies in the Philosophy of David Hume, 1925 (2nd edn enlarged with Supplement, 1963); (jointly) Contemporary Idealism in America, 1932; Jean Jacques Rousseau, Moralist, 2 vols

1934 (2nd edn with Preface, 1963); Citizen of Geneva, 1937; Civilization and Religion, 1948; The Philosophy of Kant and our Modern World; John Dewey: Philosophy and the Experimental Spirit, 1959; many translations, joint authorships, and edns of philosophical works. *Recreations:* music, out-of-doors, in woods, fields and mountains.                                     *Died* 12 *Nov.* 1982.

**HENDERSON, 1st Baron,** *cr* 1945, of Westgate in the City and County of Newcastle upon Tyne; **William Watson Henderson,** PC 1950; Director, Alliance Building Society, 1955–75 (Chairman, 1966–72); journalist and political writer; *b* Newcastle upon Tyne, 8 Aug. 1891; *s* of late Rt Hon. Arthur Henderson, MP. *Educ:* Queen Elizabeth Grammar Sch., Darlington. Editorial Sec., Daily Citizen, 1912–14; Parliamentary Correspondent, Labour Press Dept, 1919–21; Lobby Correspondent, Daily Herald, 1919–21; Sec., Press and Publicity Dept, Labour Party, 1921–45; Private Sec. to Rt Hon. John Hodge, MP, Minister of Labour, 1917; Prospective Labour Candidate, Bridgwater Div. of Somerset, 1919–21; MP (Lab) Enfield, 1923–24 and 1929–31; Parliamentary Private Sec. to the Sec. of State for India, 1929–31; Personal Asst to Rt Hon. Arthur Greenwood, MP (Minister without Portfolio and Mem. of the War Cabinet), 1940–42; an additional mem. of the Air Council, 1945–47; a Lord in Waiting to the King, 1945–48; a Parly Under-Sec. of State, FO, 1948–51. A British Representative at Assembly of Council of Europe, 1954 and 1955; Labour Peers representative on Parliamentary Cttee of Parliamentary Labour Party, 1952–55.

*Died* 4 *April* 1984 (*ext*).

**HENDERSON, Rt. Rev. Edward Barry,** DSC 1944; DD (Lambeth) 1960; *b* 22 March 1910; 2nd *s* of late Dean of Salisbury, the Very Rev. E. L. Henderson; *m* 1935, Hester Borradaile Taylor (*d* 1985); one *s* two *d. Educ:* Radley; Trinity Coll., Cambridge. Curate of St Gabriel's, Pimlico, 1934–36; Priest-in-charge, All Saints, Pimlico, 1936–39; Rector of Holy Trinity, Ayr, 1939–47; Chaplain, RNVR, 1943–44; Vicar of St Paul's, Knightsbridge, 1947–55; Rural Dean of Westminster, 1952–55; Bishop Suffragan of Tewkesbury, 1955–60; Bishop of Bath and Wells, 1960–75. Chm., Church of England Youth Council, 1961–69. Chaplain and Sub-Prelate, Order of St John of Jerusalem, 1961. Hon. Freeman, City of Wells, 1974. Hon. DLitt Bath, 1975. *Recreations:* fishing, golf, and sailing. *Address:* Coker House, East Coker, Yeovil, Somerset. *T:* Yeovil 863741.                                       *Died* 13 *June* 1986.

**HENDERSON, Prof. Eugénie Jane Andrina,** FBA 1986; Emeritus Professor of Phonetics in the University of London, since 1982; *b* 2 Oct. 1914; *d* of William Alexander Cruickshank Henderson and Pansy Viola (*née* Schürer); *m* 1941, George Meier; four *s* (one *d* decd). *Educ:* schools in England and Paris; University Coll., London (BA English Hons; Fellow, 1981). Part-time Asst, Adv. Cttee on Spoken English, BBC, 1935–38; Lectr, Dept of Phonetics, UCL, 1937–39; Temp. Asst Principal, Min. of Economic Warfare, 1939–41; School of Oriental and African Studies: Lectr in Phonetics 1942–46; Sen. Lectr in Phonetics 1946–53; Reader in Phonetics 1953–63; Prof. of Phonetics in the Univ. of London, 1964–82 (established Chair from 1966). Vis. Prof., Rangoon, 1954; fieldwork in Burma, 1954; Visiting Lectureships: Univ. of Hawaii, 1970; S Illinois, 1971; Cornell, 1971; Seoul, 1971; Sorbonne (Paris III), 1972; Bangkok (Mahidol Univ.), 1975; Salzburg, 1979; Hong Kong, 1983; Univ. of W Indies, 1984. Chm., Linguistics Assoc. of GB, 1977–80; Pres., Philological Soc., 1984–88. Hon. Fellow, SOAS, 1985. *Publications:* Tiddim Chin: a descriptive analysis of two texts, 1965; The Domain of Phonetics, 1965; The Indispensable Foundation: a selection from the writings of Henry Sweet, 1971; articles in Trans Phil. Soc., Bull. of SOAS, Linguistics of Tibeto-Burman Area, Lingua, SE Asian Ling. Studies, etc. *Address:* 9 Briardale Gardens, Hampstead, NW3 7PN. *T:* 01–794 8862.

*Died* 27 *July* 1989.

**HENDERSON, Rear-Adm. Geoffrey Archer,** CB 1969; retired; *b* 14 Aug. 1913; *s* of late Sir Charles James Henderson, KBE; *m* 1959 Pamela (Rachel), *d* of late Sir Philip Petrides; one *s* one *d. Educ:* Christ's Hosp. Entered RN, 1931. Served War of 1939–45; HMS Onslow, 1941–42 (despatches); Sec. to Asst Chief of Naval Staff (F), 1943–44. HMS Newfoundland, 1952–55; HMS Victorious, 1957–58; Cabinet Office, 1959–61; idc 1962; Director of Naval Officer Appointments (S), 1963–65; Commodore, RN Barracks, Portsmouth, 1965–66; ADC 1966; Naval Mem. of Senior Directing Staff, Imperial Defence Coll., 1966–68; Chief Naval Supply and Secretariat Officer, 1968–70, and Dir, Management and Support Intelligence, MoD, 1969–70. Admin Manager, National Mutual Life Assce Soc., 1970–78. *Address:* Pigeon's Green, St Mary's Platt, Sevenoaks, Kent TN15 8NL. *T:* Borough Green 882462.

*Died* 17 *Nov.* 1985.

**HENDERSON, Sir Guy (Wilmot McLintock),** Kt 1956; BA, LLM Cantab; QC (Uganda) 1949; Chief Justice of the Bahamas, 1951–60, retired; *b* 13 July 1897; *e s* of late Arthur James and Charlotte West Henderson; *m* 1930, Ann (*d* 1980), *d* of late George and Elizabeth Dring-Campion; two *s* one *d. Educ:* Blundell's, Tiverton; Collegiate

Sch., Wanganui, NZ; Trinity Coll., Cambridge. Served European War, 1914–18, Lieut RFA (SR). Barrister-at-Law, Inner Temple, 1923; private practice, Rangoon, Burma, 1924–29; professional clerk, prosecuting staff GPO, London, 1930–32; stipendiary and circuit magistrate, Bahamas, 1932–37; Crown Counsel, Tanganyika Territory, 1937–40; legal draftsman, Nigeria, 1940–45; dep. Chief Legal Adviser, British Military Administration, Malaya, 1945–46; Solicitor-Gen., Colony of Singapore, 1946–48; Attorney-Gen., Uganda Protectorate, 1948–51. *Address:* PO Box N 7776, Lyford Cay, Nassau, Bahamas.                                    *Died* 21 *May* 1987.

**HENDERSON, Prof. John Louis,** MD, FRCPE; Professor of Child Health, University of Dundee, 1967–72, then Emeritus; *b* 25 March 1907; British; *m* 1st, 1938, Agnes Deneson McHarg, MB, ChB (*d* 1963); one *s* three *d*; 2nd, 1964, Helen Nea Carlisle Richards (*née* Attenborough). *Educ:* Leighton Park Sch., Reading; University of Edinburgh. Sen. Pres., Royal Medical Society, Edinburgh 1934–35; Lecturer, Dept of Child Health, University of Edinburgh, 1939–45; Rockefeller Travelling Fellow at Yale and Harvard, USA, 1946; Senior Lecturer, Dept of Child Health, University of Edinburgh, 1947–51; Physician, Royal Edinburgh Hosp. for Sick Children, 1948–51; Prof. of Child Health, University of St Andrews, 1951–67. Member: Scottish Health Services Council, 1953–62; GMC, 1968–; Chm. Standing Med. Adv. Cttee, Dept of Health for Scotland, 1956–62. *Publications:* Cerebral Palsy in Childhood and Adolescence, 1961; articles in medical journals. *Recreations:* golf, ornithology. *Address:* Oranmore, East End, Chirnside, Duns, Berwickshire.                                    *Died* 14 *Feb.* 1985.

**HENDERSON, Keith,** OBE; RWS; RSW; ROI; PS; SWIA; *b* 17 April 1883; *er s* of George MacDonald Henderson and Constance Helen, *d* of James Keith; *m* Helen (*d* 1972), *d* of Charles Knox-Shaw. *Educ:* Marlborough; Paris. Served Aug. 1914 to end of war (despatches twice). Pictures in Public Galleries, Manchester, Preston, Birmingham, Worthing, Newport, Leamington, Dublin, Glasgow, Aberdeen, Lancaster, Carlisle, Dundee, Swansea, Perth, Kirkaldy; many pictures and drawings in American and Canadian collections. War Artist to the Air Force, 1940. Each winter from 1971, off to the Equator to make studies of world's ever diminishing wild life. *Publications:* (also illustrator of) Letters to Helen; Palm-groves and Hummingbirds; Prehistoric Man; Burns by himself; Till 21 (autobiog.); The Labyrinth; The Romaunt of the Rose; The Conquest of Mexico; Green Mansions; No Second Spring; Buckaroo; Christina Strang; Highland Pack; Scotland before History, etc; poems; *plays:* What Gabriel Did; Mélusine; Did Honorius Kill Stilicho?; Gabrina Barizhni, etc. *Address:* Fresh Woods, Elgin, Cape, South Africa.                                    *Died* 24 *Feb.* 1982.

**HENDERSON, Kenneth David Druitt,** CMG 1951; Vice-President, World Congress of Faiths, since 1966; *b* 4 Sept. 1903; *s* of late George Gilfillan Henderson, MA, MB, CM (Edinburgh); *m* 1935, Margery Grant, *d* of John Atkinson, Sydney, NSW; one *s* two *d*. *Educ:* Glenalmond; University Coll., Oxford. Entered Sudan Political Service, 1926; Dept Asst Civil Sec., 1938–44; Sec. to Governor-General's Council, 1939–44, to N Sudan Advisory Council, 1944; Principal Sch. of Administration and Police, Omdurman, 1944; Deputy-Governor, Kassala Province, Sudan, 1945; Asst Civil Sec., 1946–49; Governor, Darfur Province, Sudan, 1949–53. Sec., Spalding Educnl Trust, 1953–86. Officer, Order of the Nile, 1937. *Publications:* History of the Hamar Tribe, 1935; Survey of the Anglo-Egyptian Sudan, 1898–1944, 1945; The Making of The Modern Sudan, 1952; Sudan Republic, 1965; Account of the Parish of Langford, 1973; Younghusband Memorial Lecture (inaugural), 1976; Is Religion Necessary? (Farmington Paper), 1977; Set Under Authority, 1987; contribs to Chambers's Encyclopædia, Encyclopædia Britannica, and Encyclopædia Americana. *Address:* Orchard House, Steeple Langford, Salisbury, Wilts SP3 4NQ. *T:* Salisbury 790388.

                                    *Died* 23 *March* 1988.

**HENDERSON, Sir Malcolm (Siborne),** KCMG 1961 (CMG 1952); HM Diplomatic Service, retired; *b* 21 April 1905; *s* of late Lt-Col Kenneth Henderson; *m* 1933, Paula Elizabeth Wilms; two *d*. *Educ:* Winchester and privately. MA Edinburgh. Vice-Consul, Antwerp, 1927–30, Chicago, 1930–35, New York, 1935–42; Consul, Atlanta, 1942–44; Foreign Office, 1944–47; Counsellor (Commercial) and Consul-Gen., Lisbon, 1947–52; Land Commissioner, Hanover, 1952–55, and Consul-Gen., 1954–55; Ambassador: to Grand Duchy of Luxembourg, 1955–57; to Republic of Uruguay, 1957–61; to Austria, 1961–65. *Address:* 32 Cadogan Place, SW1X 9RX. *Club:* Travellers'.                                    *Died* 11 *May* 1981.

**HENDERSON, Sir Neville (Vicars),** Kt 1975; CBE 1967; Founder of firm of Henderson & Lahey, Solicitors, Brisbane, 1924; retired to become consultant, 1971; grazier and company director, Australia; *b* 21 March 1899; *s* of John Cunningham Henderson, grazier, late of Brougham, Toowong, Brisbane, formerly of Goulburn, NSW, etc, and Ann Janet Henderson, *d* of Capt. Lachlan Macalister, 48th Regt; *m* 1934, Jean Hamilton Brownhill, *d* of David James Brownhill, Sydney, NSW; one *s* two *d*. *Educ:* Southport Sch., Southport, Qld (Pres., Old Southportians Assoc., 1926); Univ. of Qld, Brisbane; Trinity Coll., Univ. of Melbourne, Vic. Final Hons Schol. in Law and Supreme Ct Prizeman (Melb.) 1922; BA, LLM (Melb.) 1922. Barrister and solicitor of Supreme Ct of Vic., 1923, and of High Ct of Aust., 1923; Solicitor of Supreme Ct of Qld, 1923; Notary Public, 1945. Mem. Council, Qld Law Assoc., 1926–27, Sec., 1926–28; collaborated in drafting the first Conveyancing Scale for use in Qld, 1925–26; assisted in drafting Act, 1927, and has taken part in Law Reform since that time; also Sec. Qld Law Soc. Incorp., 1928–54, and Clerk to Statutory Cttee of the Soc., 1928–31, also its delegate at Aust. Law Conf., Sydney (at which Law Council of Aust. was formed), 1932; Council, St John's Coll., Univ. of Qld, 1932–38; Sec., Law Council of Aust., 1939–40. Captain, AMF, 1932. Served War, 1940–44: Judge Advocate on various Courts Martial, 1940–43; Major, 1942, and apptd Dep. Asst Adj.-Gen., Northern Comd; assisted in organising course for rehabilitation of legal ex-Servicemen, and Hon. Lectr in Law of Life Ins., 1945. Sen. Partner, Henderson & Sons, Graziers, Mahrigong Station, Winton, Qld, 1950–79; Pres., Soc. of Notaries of Queensland, 1954–56; Founder and Governor, Henderson Foundn (educnl and charitable instn), 1957. Man. Editor for Annotated Reprint of Qld Statutes (20 vols), 1962; Crises and Change, 1986. Hon. Consul for Austria, Qld, 1957; Dean of Consular Corps of Queensland, 1977. Dist. Service Order in gold of Republic of Austria, Kt Cross First Cl., 1964; Grand Decoration of Honour for services to the Republic of Austria, 1982. *Publications:* Estate Planning (Proc. of Second Commonwealth and Empire Law Conf., Ottawa, 1960), etc. *Address:* Glencraig, 63 Eldernell Avenue, Hamilton, Brisbane, Qld 4007, Australia. *T:* 268–3953. *Clubs:* Queensland, United Service, Journalists', Queensland Turf, Tattersalls (all in Brisbane); Australasian Pioneers' (Sydney).                                    *Died* 15 *Aug.* 1986.

**HENDERSON, Peter,** CB 1965; MD; Senior Principal Medical Officer, Ministry of Education, 1964–69; *b* 16 March 1904; *e s* of Peter and Margaret Henderson, Inverness; *m* 1933, Beatrice Chrissie Pashley, Bridlington, Yorks; no *c*. *Educ:* High Sch. and Royal Academy, Inverness; Aberdeen Univ. MB 1929; MD 1931; DPH London, 1932. Resident MO, Bradford City Sanatorium, 1929–30; House Physician, St Luke's Hospital, Bradford, 1930–31; Resident MO, Inst. of Ray Therapy, London, 1931–32; Asst MO, Somerset CC, 1933–35; Asst MO, St Helens, 1935–36; Dep. MOH, Leyton, 1936–39; MOH, Todmorden, 1939–40; MO, Min. of Educn., 1940–51, PMO, 1951–64. Consultant, WHO. Milroy Lectr, 1968. QHP 1962. *Publications:* various papers on the health and disabilities of children in BMJ, Lancet and Practitioner; contribs to The Theory and Practice of Public Health (ed. W. Hobson), 1961, 5th edn 1979; chapter in The Humanist Outlook (ed A. J. Ayer), 1968; Disability in Childhood and Youth, 1974. *Recreation;* gardening. *Address:* Lythe Ghyll, Merrowcroft, Guildford, Surrey. *T:* Guildford 575353.                                    *Died* 13 *Nov.* 1983.

**HENDERSON, Rupert Albert Geary;** Chairman: Australian Newsprint Mills Ltd, 1960–78; Trustees of Reuters Ltd, 1961–78 (Trustee, 1952–78, Director, 1946–51); Amalgamated Television Services Pty Ltd, 1958–74; *b* 26 Feb. 1896; *s* of late Robert Geary Henderson and Isabel Henderson; *m* 1st, 1914, Helene, *d* of Thomas Mason; one *s*; 2nd, 1939, Hazel, *d* of Herbert Harris; one *d*. *Educ:* Glebe Public Sch., Sydney. Literary staff, The Sydney Morning Herald, 1915; London rep., 1923–26; Advertising Manager, Sydney Mail, 1927; Circulation Manager, Sydney Morning Herald, 1928; Sec. to Gen. Manager, 1934; Gen. Manager, 1938; Chm., Australian Associated Press Pty Ltd, 1940–49; Managing Director: John Fairfax & Sons Pty Ltd, 1949–56; John Fairfax Ltd, 1956–64 (Dir 1964–78); Associated Newspapers Ltd, 1954–64; Pres. Australian Newspaper Proprietors' Association, 1942–47 and 1951–58; Director, Australian Assoc. Press Pty Ltd. *Recreation:* grazier. *Address:* John Fairfax Ltd, 23 Hamilton Street, Sydney, NSW 2000, Australia. *TA:* Herald, Sydney. *T:* 20944. *Clubs:* Union, Royal Prince Alfred Yacht (Sydney).                                    *Died* 9 *Sept.* 1986.

**HENMAN, Philip Sydney,** DL; Founder of Transport Development Group Ltd; FCIT. DUniv Surrey, 1974. Farmer. High Sheriff, Surrey, 1971–72; DL Surrey, 1979. *Address:* 25 Elm Place, Rustington, W Sussex.                                    *Died* 8 *Nov.* 1986.

**HENNESSEY, Robert Samuel Fleming,** CMG 1954; Assistant Research Director, Wellcome Foundation, 1967–70, retired; *b* 8 May 1905; *s* of late W. R. H. Hennessey and late Elizabeth Fleming; *m* 1930, Grace Alberta Coote (*d* 1980); one *s* one *d*. *Educ:* St Andrew's Coll., Dublin; Dublin and London Universities. MD, FRCPI, DipBact, DTM&H. Pathologist, Uganda, 1929; Dep. Director (Laboratories), Palestine, 1944; Dep. Director, Medical Services, Palestine, 1946; Asst Medical Adviser, Colonial Office, 1947; Director of Medical Services, Uganda, 1949–55; Head of the Wellcome Laboratories of Tropical Medicine, London, 1956–58; Head of Therapeutic Research Division, Wellcome Foundation, 1958–66. *Publications:* papers on pathology in scientific jls.

*Recreations:* music, literature. *Address:* 51 Stone Park Avenue, Beckenham, Kent. *T:* 01–650 5336.                              *Died* 31 *May* 1989.

**HENNESSY, Denis William,** OBE 1967; HM Diplomatic Service, retired; *b* 5 Dec. 1912; *s* of Daniel Hennessy and Rosina Gertrude Hennessy (*née* Griffiths); *m* 1937, Lorna McDonald Lappin; three *s* one *d*. *Educ:* private sch. Joined Foreign Office, 1930; served in the Foreign Office and in Prague, Washington, New York, Zürich, Bremen, Miami, Düsseldorf, Accra, and as Consul-Gen., Hanover; Counsellor, Bonn, 1969–72. *Address:* 37 Dean Road, Bateman, WA 6153, Australia. *Club:* Travellers'.                      *Died* 15 *Sept.* 1990.

**HENNESSY, Sir Patrick,** Kt 1941; Chairman: Ford Motor Co. Ltd, 1956–68; Henry Ford & Son Ltd, Cork, Eire, 1955–77; *b* 18 April 1898; *s* of Patrick Hennessy, Ballyvodak House, Midleton, Co. Cork; *m* 1923, Dorothy Margaret (*d* 1949), *d* of Robert Davis, JP, Killaney Lodge, Boardmills, N Ireland; two *s* one *d*. Served European War, 1914–18, Royal Inniskilling Fus. Pres., Soc. of Motor Manufacturers & Traders, 1965 and 1966, Dep. Pres., 1967 and 1968. Formerly Mem. Adv. Council, Min. of Aircraft Production. *Address:* 4 Grafton Street, W1X 4RD; Larkmead, Theydon Bois, Essex. *T:* Theydon Bois 2139. *Club:* Royal Automobile.                                            *Died* 13 *March* 1981.

**HENNIKER-GOTLEY, Roger Alwyn,** MA Oxon; Headmaster of Sebright School, 1938–63, retired; *b* 8 Feb. 1898; 3rd *s* of late Rev. George Henniker-Gotley and late Louisa Sarah Lefroy; *m* 1931, Helen Hope Campbell, *d* of late Rev. Gerald Campbell Dicker; two *s. Educ:* Cheltenham Coll.; Brasenose Coll., Oxford. Served European War, 1914–18, Lancashire Fusiliers. Asst Master and Housemaster, Stamford School, 1924–25; Asst Master and Housemaster, Worksop Coll., 1925–27; Asst Master and Senior English Master, Cranleigh Sch., 1927–38. *Recreations:* cricket, ornithology, gardening. *Address:* Little Orchard, Codford St Mary, Warminster, Wiltshire. *T:* Warminster 50239.

*Died* 28 *Aug.* 1985.

**HENNING, Prof. Basil Duke,** PhD; *b* 16 April 1910; *s* of late Samuel C. Henning and Julia, *d* of Gen. Basil Duke, CSA; *m* 1939, Alison Peake; two *s* one *d. Educ:* Yale Univ. (BA 1932, PhD 1937). Served War: Pacific War, 1943–45; Lieut (JG) USNR, 1942–44; Lieut, 1944–47; Lt-Comdr, 1947–55. Commendation Medal, USA, 1944 and 1945. Yale University: Instr, 1935–39; Sterling Fellow, 1939–40; Instr, 1940–42; Asst Prof., 1945–46; Associate Prof., 1946–70; Master, Saybrook Coll., 1946–75; Colgate Prof. of History, 1970–78. FRHistS 1963. Yale Medal, 1979; William C. DeVane Medal, Phi Beta Kappa Soc. (Yale chapter), 1981. *Publications:* (ed) The Parliamentary Diary of Sir Edward Dering, 1670–1673, 1940; (jtly) Ideas and Institutions in European History, 800–1715, 1948; The Quest for a Principle of Authority, 1715 to Present, 1948; Crises in English History, 1066–1945: select problems in historical interpretation, 1952; The Dynamic Force of Liberty in Modern Europe, 1952; Foundations of the Modern State, 1952; Select Problems in Western Civilization, 1956; (ed) Conflict in Stuart England: essays in honour of Wallace Notestein, 1960; (ed) History of Parliament 1660–1690, 1983. *Recreations:* reading, music. *Address:* 223 Bradley Street, New Haven, Conn 06511, USA. *T:* 203–777–0123; 34 Tavistock Square, WC1H 9EZ. *T:* 01–636 0272. *Clubs:* Garrick; Yale (NY); Lawn (New Haven, Conn).

*Died* 15 *Jan.* 1990.

**HENNINGS, John Dunn,** CMG 1968; HM Diplomatic Service, retired; High Commissioner in Singapore, 1978–82; *b* 9 June 1922; *o c* of Stanley John and Grace Beatrice Hennings, Ipswich, Suffolk; *m* 1953, Joanna Anita, *er d* of J. Thompson Reed, Northampton; two *s. Educ:* Ipswich Sch.; University College, Oxford. Foreign Office and Berlin, 1947–49; Colonial Office, 1949–53 (Sec., British Guiana Constitutional Commn, 1951); W African Inter-Territorial Secretariat, Accra, 1953–55; Colonial Office, 1955–60; Attaché for Colonial Affairs, British Embassy, Washington, DC, 1960–63; Commonwealth Relations Office, 1963; Counsellor, HM Diplomatic Service, 1965; Head, British High Commission, Residual Staff, Salisbury, Rhodesia, 1966–68; Counsellor and Head of Chancery, High Commn, Delhi, 1968–72; Actg High Commissioner, Uganda, 1972; High Comr, Jamaica, and Ambassador (non-resident) to Haiti, 1973–76; Asst Under Sec. of State, FCO, 1976–78. *Recreations:* reading, photography. *Address:* Rest-Harrow, 3 Heathfield, Chislehurst, Kent. *Club:* Travellers'.

*Died* 7 *Oct.* 1985.

**HENRION, Frederic Henri Kay,** OBE 1985 (MBE 1951); RDI; PPSIAD; general consulting designer and lecturer; Founder of Henrion, Ludlow and Schmidt, 1982; *b* 18 April 1914; *m* 1947, Daphne Hardy, sculptress; two *s* one *d*. Textile design in Paris, 1932–33; worked in Paris and London, 1936–39; designed Smoke Abatement Exhibition, Charing Cross Station, and worked on Glasgow Empire Exhibition, 1939, and New York World Fair, 1940–45. Design of all exhibitions for Ministry of Agriculture through Ministry of Information and exhibitions for Army Bureau of Current Affairs (WO), etc., 1943–45. Consultant Designer to US

Embassy and US Office of War Information, 1945; Chief Cons. Designer to Sir William Crawford and Partners, 1946–47; Art Editor of Contact Publication, 1947–48; Art Director BOAC Publications, 1949–51, and of Future Magazine, 1951; Designer, Festival of Britain pavilions (Agriculture and Natural History), 1950–51–54; Art Editor and Designer of the Bowater Papers, 1951–53; subseq. Cons. Designer for many firms. Posters for: GPO; BOAC; LPTB; Council of Industrial Design; exhibitions and permanent collections in Europe, USA and S America. One-man show, Designing Things and Symbols, at Institute of Contemporary Arts, 1960. Vis. Lectr, RCA, 1950–60; Member Council and Vice-President, SIAD (President, 1961–63); Member: Council of Industrial Design, 1963–66; Advisory Council to Governors of London School of Printing; Council, CNAA (Chm. Bd of Graphic Design; Mem. Cttee of Art and Design, 1973–78); Court, RCA, 1975–; President: Alliance Graphique Internationale, 1962–67; ICOGRADA, 1968–70; Past Governor, Central School of Art; Outside Assessor, Scottish Schools of Art; Consultant Designer to: BTC; KLM Royal Dutch Airlines; British Olivetti Ltd; Tate & Lyle Ltd; The Postmaster General; BEA; Blue Circle Group; Courage, Barclay & Simonds Ltd; Financial Times; Volkswagen, Audi, NSU, Porsche, LEB, Penta Hotels, Braun AG. Co-ordinating graphics designer for British Pavilion, Expo 67. Master of Faculty, RDI, 1971–73; Head of Faculty of Visual Communication, London Coll. of Printing, 1976–79. Visiting Professor: Cooper Union, NY, 1984–; Univ. of Essen, 1984–85; lectured in the UK, USA, USSR, Canada, Mexico, Israel, Germany, and Italy, 1982–85 and 1988–89. Sen. Fellow, RCA, 1988. Hon. Dip. Manchester, 1962. SIAD Design Medal, 1976; Icograda Design excellence award, 1989. *Publications:* Design Co-ordination and Corporate Image, 1967 (also USA); Top Graphic Design, 1983; (ed and designed) AGI Annals, 1989; contributor to: Graphis, Gebrauchgraphik, Design Magazine, Architectural Review, Art and Industry, Penrose Annual, Format, Novum Gebrauchsgraphik, The Designer, Print Magazine (USA), Graphic Design, Idea (Tokyo). *Address:* 35 Pond Street, NW3 2PN. *T:* 071–435 7402.                                      *Died* 5 *July* 1990.

**HENRIQUES, Sir Cyril George Xavier,** Kt 1963; QC (Jamaica); LLB; President, Court of Appeal, Jamaica, 1968–74; *b* Kingston, Jamaica, 5 July 1908; *s* of Cyril Charles Henriques and of Mrs Edith Emily Henriques; *m* Marjory Brunhilda (*née* Burrows); two *d. Educ:* St George's Coll., Jamaica; St Francis Xavier's Coll.; University College, London. Called to Bar, Inner Temple, 1936; Crown Counsel, Jamaica, 1939; Resident Magistrate, 1944; Attorney General, British Honduras, 1950; Puisne-Judge, Jamaica, 1955; appointment in British Honduras, 1956; Chief Justice of Supreme Court of Windward Islands and Leeward Islands, 1958; Judge of Appeal, Appeal Court of Jamaica, 1963–68. *Address:* 11 Jacks Hill Road, Kingston 6, Jamaica.                              *Died* 18 *June* 1982.

**HENRY, Hon. Albert (Royle);** First Premier of the Cook Islands, 1965–78 (re-elected 1968, 1972, 1974); *b* 11 June 1907; *s* of Geoffrey Henry and Metua Grace; *m* Elizabeth, 2nd *d* of late Hugh McCrone Connal, Edinburgh; two *s* two *d. Educ:* St Stephen's Coll., Auckland, NZ. Land owner and plantation owner; school teacher, Cook Islands, 1924–36; Chief Clerk, Trading Co., 1937–42; joined Defence Force, 1940–43, no overseas service; Cook Islands Representative, Rugby, cricket and tennis, 1921–40; Official Sec., Cook Islands Progressive Assoc., 1947–64; Official Sec., Cook Islands Co-op. Soc., 1947–50. Hon. Dr of Laws, Univ. of Guam, 1968; Hon. Life Mem., Brazilian Cultural and Literary Union of Writers. KBE 1974, rescinded 1980. *Recreation:* when not sleeping, is working. *Address:* Avarua, Rarotonga, Cook Islands.

*Died* 2 *Jan.* 1981.

**HENRY, Cyril Bowdler, (C. Bowdler-Henry);** Knight (First Class) Royal Norwegian Order of St Olav; Chevalier de la Légion d'Honneur; Officer of Order of Orange Nassau; Czechoslovak Military Medal of Merit (First Class); LRCP, MRCS, FDSRCS (Eng.); Vice-President Royal Society Medicine (President Sect. Odontology, 1954–55, Hon. Member, 1964); Life Governor, Emeritus Hon. Consulting Surgeon, late Senior Surgeon and Lecturer in Oral Surgery, Royal Dental Hospital of London and Chairman of Governing Body of The London School of Dental Surgery (University of London), in Centenary Year of School's foundation; Member Board of Studies in Dentistry, and Examiner in Oral Surgery for Mastership in Dental Surgery, University of London; Life Governor Westminster Hospital; *b* Leire, Leics, 10 Oct. 1893; *s* of late Thomas Henry, Moorgate Park, Retford, and Rose Emily Bowdler, Shrewsbury; *m* 1st, 1920, Dorothy Mildred (*d* 1978), 2nd *d* of late William Henry Bradley, Solicitor; 2nd, 1981, Audrey Mabel, *d* of late Ernest G. Coles, Taunton, Somerset. *Educ:* King Edward VI's Grammar Sch., Retford; Sheffield Univ.; Royal Dental and Westminster Hospitals, and King's Coll., University of London. Lieut RAMC attached 22 CCS, BEF, 1915–16; House Physician, House Surgeon, Resident Obstetric Assistant, Westminster Hospital, 1917–20; in this post conducted deliveries for first ever teaching ciné film on two cases of parturition (normal and breech presentation) (extracts in G. Drummond Robinson's Atlas of Normal Labour, 1921); Assistant Dental Surgeon, Metropolitan

Hospital, 1919–22; Dental Surgeon, Westminster Hospital, 1922–29, Royal Dental Hospital, 1925–59. Oral Surgeon, EMS, Sept. 1939; gave services during Second World War as Hon. Oral Surgeon and Consulting Stomatolgist to: Royal Norwegian Armed Forces in UK; Royal Norwegian Min. of Social Welfare; Polish Min. of Labour and Social Welfare; Netherlands Army; Czechoslovak Armed Forces; Fighting French Forces; Armed Forces of Yugoslavia; Czechoslovak and Polish Red Cross Socs. Introduced into UK, 1945, operation devised by Prof. F. Kostecka of Prague for correction of mandibular prognathism (Hapsburg jaw). Appointed to represent the Royal College of Surgeons at the IInd International Stomatological Congress (Bologna), 1935, and at the IXth International Dental Congress, Vienna, 1936. Arris and Gale Lectr, RCS, 1933–34; Hunterian Prof., RCS, 1935–36; Menzies Campbell Lectr (on dental history), RCS, 1962. A Governor, St George's Hosp., 1954–60. Hon. Fellow, British Assoc. of Oral Surgeons; Fellow, Harveian Soc. of London; Member: BMA; British Dental Assoc.; Hon. Mem., American Dental Soc. of London (President, 1960–61), etc. *Publications:* (with A. W. Marrett-Tims) Tomes' Dental Aanatomy, 8th Edn; A Study of the Mandibular third molar tooth (with G. M. Morant), Biometrika, vol. 28, 1936; Chapters in a System of Dental Surgery by Sir Norman G. Bennett and in Post Graduate Surgery by Rodney Maingot; papers, lectures and reviews upon scientific subjects related to dental medicine, oral surgery, stomatology and dental history. *Address:* 62 Harley Street, W1. *T:* 01-580 1612. *Died 12 Jan. 1981.*

**HENRY, (Ernest James) Gordon,** FCIB; Chairman: Adam & Company PLC, Edinburgh, since 1983; New Scotland Insurance Group, since 1986; Independent Insurance Company, since 1986; *b* 16 June 1919; *s* of Ernest Elston Henry and Dolina Campbell (*née* Smith); *m* 1950, Marion Frew Allan; three *d*. *Educ:* Bellahouston Acad., Glasgow. FCIB 1957. Served War, Army (No 5 Commando), 1939–46. Began career in insurance broking, Glasgow, 1937; founded Gordon Henry & Co., Insurance Brokers, 1952; merged with Matthews Wrightson, 1957; Dep. Chm., Matthews Wrightson Hldgs, 1974; Chm., Stewart Wrightson Holdings Ltd (formerly Matthews Wrightson Holdings Ltd), 1978–81, retd. Dir, Royal Caledonian Schs, Herts. Member: Worshipful Co. of Insurers; Incorporation of Bakers, Glasgow; Merchants House, Glasgow. *Recreations:* golf, fishing, writing. *Address:* Rannoch, Gryffe Road, Kilmacolm, Renfrewshire. *T:* Kilmacolm 3382; 4 Johnstone Court, North Street, St Andrews. *T:* St Andrews 77164. *Clubs:* The Western (Glasgow); Royal & Ancient Golf (St Andrews, Fife); Western Gailes Golf (Ayrshire); Kilmacolm Golf (Renfrewshire). *Died 31 Oct. 1989.*

**HENSBY, Frederick Charles,** OBE 1973; HM Diplomatic Service, retired; *b* 7 Nov. 1919; *s* of late Charles Henry Hensby and Ivy Helen (*née* Lake); *m* 1946, Maud Joyce (*née* Stace). *Educ:* Hendon County Grammar Sch. Joined Foreign Office, 1937. Served War: Devonshire Regt, 1940–42; Intelligence Corps, 1942–46. Returned to FO, 1946; HM Embassy: Rio de Janeiro, 1947–50; Paris, 1950–52; FO, 1952–56; HM Vice Consul, Muscat, 1956–58; Sec. to Allied Kommandantura, Berlin, 1958–59; FO, 1960–62; First Sec. and Consul: Monrovia, 1962–64; Paris, 1965–66; Asst Head of Protocol Dept, FCO, 1967–69; First Sec., British High Commn, New Delhi, 1970–72; Asst Head, Migration and Visa Dept, FCO, 1973–75; Counsellor and Head of Consular Dept, FCO, 1976–77. *Recreations:* gardening, bird-watching, golf. *Address:* Giles Coppice, Woodsdale, Battle, Sussex TN33 0LS. *T:* Battle 2746. *Club:* Royal Commonwealth Society. *Died 6 April 1982.*

**HENTSCHEL, Christopher Carl,** MSc; FLS, FZS, FIBiol; Principal, Chelsea College of Science and Technology, 1962–65, retired; *b* 4 July 1899; *s* of Carl and Bertha Hentschel; unmarried. *Educ:* St Paul's Sch. (Classical Scholar); King's Coll., London. Demonstrator, in Biology, St Bartholomew's Med. Coll., 1923–31; Chelsea Polytechnic, later Chelsea Coll. of Science and Technology: Lectr in Zoology, 1931–53; Head, Dept of Botany and Zoology, 1953–61; Vice-Principal, 1961–62. Mem. of Senate, University of London, 1956–64, 1966–70. Vice-Pres., Linnean Soc. of London, 1943–44, 1950–51, 1952–53; Formerly Governor: Sloane & Rutherford Schs, London; Paddington Technical Coll.; Pent Valley Sch., Folkestone. Hon. FChS. *Publications:* (with W. R. Ivimey Cook) Biology for Medical Students, 1932; papers on parasitic Protozoa. *Recreations:* motoring; continental travel. *Address:* 6 Winchester Drive, Dere Park, Brandon, Durham DH7 8UG. *Died 21 July 1986.*

**HEPPEL, Richard Purdon,** CMG 1959; HM Diplomatic Service, retired; *b* 27 Oct. 1913; 2nd *s* of late Engineer Rear-Admiral Walter George Heppel and Margaret, *d* of late Robert Stevens Fraser; *m* 1949, Ruth Theodora, *d* of late Horatio Matthews, MD; two *s* one *d*. *Educ:* Rugby Sch.; Balliol Coll., Oxford. Laming Travelling Fellow, Queen's Coll., 1935. Entered Diplomatic Service, 1936; Third Sec., Rome, 1939; Second Sec., Tehran, 1942; First Sec., Athens, 1944; Private Sec. to Min. of State, 1946; First Sec., Karachi, 1948, Madrid, 1951; Counsellor, HM Legation, Saigon, 1953–54; Ambassador to Cambodia, 1954–56; Minister at Vienna,

1956–59; Head of South East Asia Dept, Foreign Office, 1959; Head of Consular Dept, Foreign Office, 1961–63; Imperial Defence Coll., 1960; Consul-Gen. at Stuttgart, 1963–69. Administrative Officer, The City Univ. Grad. Business Centre, 1969–70; Appeals Sec. for Beds, Bucks and Herts, Cancer Res. Campaign, 1970–79. MIL 1985. Freeman, Skinners' Company, 1961, Liveryman 1969. *Address:* Barns Piece, Nether Winchendon, Aylesbury, Bucks. *Club:* Travellers'. *Died 17 Nov. 1986.*

**HEPPENSTALL, (John) Rayner;** novelist, critic and criminal historian; *b* 27 July 1911; *s* of Edgar and Lizzie Heppenstall, Huddersfield, Yorks; *m* 1937, Margaret Harwood Edwards, Newport, Mon; one *s* one *d*. *Educ:* in Yorks (variously); Calais; University of Leeds; University of Strasbourg. Graduated (Modern Languages), 1933; schoolmaster, 1934; freelance author, 1935–39. Served War of 1939–45 Army (RA, Field, RAPC), 1940–45. Feature-writer and producer, BBC, 1945–65, Drama producer, 1965–67. *Publications:* First Poems, 1935; Apology for Dancing, 1936; Sebastian, 1937; The Blaze of Noon, 1939, new edn, 1980 (Arts Council Prize, 1966); Blind Men's Flowers are Green, 1940; Saturnine, 1943 (revised as The Greater Infortune, 1960); The Double Image, 1946; Poems, 1933–1945, 1946; The Lesser Infortune, 1953; Léon Bloy, 1954; Four Absentees, 1960; The Fourfold Tradition, 1961; The Connecting Door, 1962; The Woodshed, 1962; The Intellectual Part, 1963; Raymond Roussel: a critical guide, 1966; Portrait of the Artist as a Professional Man, 1969; The Shearers, 1969; A Little Pattern of French Crime, 1969; French Crime in the Romantic Age, 1970; Bluebeard and After, 1972; The Sex War and Others, 1973; Reflections on The Newgate Calendar, 1975; Two Moons, 1977; Tales from the Newgate Calendar, 1981; edited: Existentialism (G. de Ruggiero), 1946; Imaginary Conversations, 1948; Architecture of Truth, 1957; (with Michael Innes) Three Tales of Hamlet, 1950; translated: Atala and René (Chateaubriand), 1963; Impressions of Africa (Roussel) (with Lindy Foord), 1966; A Harlot High and Low (Balzac), 1970; When Justice Falters (Floriot), 1972. *Recreations:* variable. *Address:* Coach Cottage, 2 Gilford Road, Deal, Kent. *T:* Deal 63493. *Died 23 May 1981.*

**HERBERT, Christopher Alfred,** CB 1973; retired; *b* 15 June 1913; *s* of Alfred Abbot Herbert and Maria Hamilton (*née* Fetherston); *m* 1941, Evelyn Benson Scott (*née* Ross) (*d* 1972); one *s* one *d*. *Educ:* Mountjoy Sch., Dublin; Trinity Coll., Dublin (BA (Hons)). Indian Civil Service, 1937–47; Eastern Manager, May & Baker (India) Ltd, 1947–50. MoD, 1950–77, Under Sec., 1971–77. *Recreations:* walking, gardening, reading. *Address:* 41 Woodcote Avenue, Wallington, Surrey. *T:* 01–647 5223. *Club:* East India, Devonshire, Sports and Public Schools. *Died 22 Nov. 1988.*

**HERBERT, Lieut-Gen. Sir (Edwin) Otway,** KBE 1955 (CBE 1944); CB 1942; DSO 1940; retired as General Officer Commanding-in-Chief, Western Command (1957–60); Colonel Commandant, Royal Artillery 1956–66; *b* 18 Nov. 1901; *s* of late Gustavus Otway Herbert; *m* 1925, Muriel Irlam Barlow; one *d*. *Educ:* Felsted Sch.; Royal Military Academy, Woolwich. Commissioned Royal Artillery, 1921: served war of 1939–45; BEF France and Belgium, 1939–40 (despatches, DSO); 1st Army, 78 Div., North Africa, 1942–43 (bar to DSO); 21 Army Group, 1943–45 (despatches, CBE, CB); GOC British Troops, Berlin, and British Commandant, Berlin, 1947–49; Dir Territorial Army and Cadets, War Office, 1949–52; GOC 44 (Home Counties) Div. and District, 1952–53; GOC-in-C, West Africa Command, 1953–56. High Sheriff of Anglesey, 1964–65. Officer of Legion of Merit (USA); Knight Commander Orange Nassau (Netherlands); Commander of Leopold II (Belgium). *Recreations:* most outdoor sports available. *Address:* Llanidan House, Brynsiencyn, Anglesey. *T:* Brynsiencyn 393. *Club:* Army and Navy. *Died 4 April 1984.*

**HERBERT, Major George,** MBE; *b* 1892; *s* of William Herbert, York; *m* 1916, Elsie (*d* 1952), *d* of late G. E. Barton, York; one *s*. Served European War, France, 1914–19 (despatches, MBE) Major; Active Service, 1939–44 (despatches), Food Controller Gibraltar. MP (C) Rotherham, 1931–33; dir of companies. *Publications:* Trade Abroad, 1924; British Empire Ltd, 1926; The Call of Empire, 1927; Can Land Settlement Solve Unemployment?, 1934. *Recreations:* golf, fishing, cricket. *Address:* Hampden House, Duchy Road, Harrogate, North Yorks. *Died 16 June 1982.*

**HERBERT, Lt-Gen. Sir Otway;** *see* Herbert, Lt-Gen. Sir E. O.

**HERCHENRODER, Sir (Marie Joseph Barnabe) Francis,** Kt 1953; QC; Assistant Legal Adviser. Commonwealth Office, retired, 1968; *b* 13 Feb. 1896; 3rd *s* of late Sir Alfred Herchenroder, KC and Lady Herchenroder (*née* Vinton); *m* 1923, Marie Charlotte Paule Geneve; two *d*. *Educ:* Royal College, Mauritius; Middle Temple, London. Called to the Bar, 1919; District Magistrate, Mauritius, 1923; Additional Substitute Procureur and Advocate General, Mauritius, 1934; Substitute Procureur and Advocate General, Mauritius, 1938; KC 1943; Puisne Judge, Supreme Court, Mauritius, 1944; Procureur and Advocate General, Mauritius, 1945; Chief Justice, Mauritius,

1949–60. Coronation Medals, 1937, 1953. *Address:* 11 Pelham Court, Chelsea, SW3. *T:* 01–584 3937.      *Died 9 April* 1982.

**HERKLOTS, Geoffrey Alton Craig,** CBE 1961; MSc, PhD; FLS; FIBiol; VMH; *b* Naini Tal, India, 10 Aug. 1902; *er s* of late Rev. Bernard Herklots, MA; *m* 1932, Iris, *yr d* of late Capt. Philip Walter, RN; two *s* one *d. Educ:* Trent Coll., Derbyshire; University of Leeds; Trinity Hall, Cambridge. Reader in Biology, University of Hong Kong, 1928–45; interned at Stanley Camp, Hong Kong, Jan. 1942–Aug. 1945; Secretary for Development, Hong Kong, 1946–48; Secretary for Colonial Agricultural Research, Colonial Office, London, 1948–53. Principal and Director of Research, Imperial College of Tropical Agriculture, Trinidad, 1953–60, retired 1961. Colombo Plan Botanical Adviser to HM Government of Nepal, 1961–63. Corresp. Member Zoological Society. *Publications:* Common Marine Food Fishes of Hong Kong, 1936, 3rd edn 1961; The Birds of Hong Kong, Field Identification and Field Note Book, 1946; Vegetable Cultivation in Hong Kong, 1941; The Hong Kong Countryside, 1951; Hong Kong Birds, 1953, 2nd edn 1967; Birds of Trinidad and Tobago, 1961; Vegetable Cultivation in South-East Asia, 1973; Flowering Tropical Climbers, 1976. Editor: Hong Kong Naturalist, 1930–41; Journal of Hong Kong Fisheries Research Station, 1940. *Recreations:* drawing, gardening, walking. *Address:* Church View, Somerby, Melton Mowbray, Leicestershire LE14 2PZ. *T:* Somerby 389.      *Died 14 Jan.* 1986.

**HERMES, Gertrude Anna Bertha,** OBE 1982; RA 1971 (ARA 1963); RE; sculptor; wood engraver; Teacher of wood engraving, Royal Academy Schools, W1, until 1976; *b* Bickley, Kent, 18 Aug. 1901; *m* 1926, Blair Hughes-Stanton (marr. diss. 1932); one *s* one *d. Educ:* Belmont, Bickley, Kent; Leon Underwood's Sch., London. Portrait Sculpture and decorative carving for buildings; wood engraving decorations for books; fountain and door furniture, Shakespeare Memorial Theatre, Stratford-on-Avon; Britannia Window, British Pavilion, Paris, 1937; 3 glass panels, British Pavilion, World's Fair, NY, 1939; Engravings for books, for: Cressett Press, Swan Press, Golden Cockerel Press, Penguin Books Ltd, etc.; member of: London Group; Society of Wood-engravers. *Recreations:* swimming and fishing. *Address:* 31 Danvers Street, Chelsea, SW3. *T:* 01–352 4006.      *Died 9 May* 1983.

**HERON-MAXWELL, Sir Patrick Ivor,** 9th Bt of Springkell, *cr* 1683; *b* 26 July 1916; *o s* of 8th Bt and Norah (*d* 1971), *d* of late Hon. Francis Parker; *S* father, 1928; *m* 1942, D. Geraldine E., *y d* of late C. Paget Mellor, Letchworth, Herts, and Victoria, BC; three *s. Educ:* Stowe. *Heir:* s Nigel Mellor Heron-Maxwell [*b* 30 Jan. 1944; *m* 1972, May Elizabeth Angela, *o d* of W. Ewing, Co. Donegal; one *s* one *d*]. *Address:* 9 Cowslip Hill, Letchworth, Herts.      *Died 18 Aug.* 1982.

**HERRICK, Very Rev. Richard William;** Provost of Chelmsford Cathedral, since 1978 (Vice-Provost, 1962–77); Director of Chelmsford Cathedral Centre for Research and Training, since 1973; *b* 3 Dec. 1913; *s* of W. Herrick, Retford, Notts; *m* 1943, Ann L. Sparshott; two *s* one *d. Educ:* King Edward VI Sch., Retford; Leeds University; College of the Resurrection, Mirfield. Civil Servant, 1930–34. BA Leeds, 1937; Deacon, 1939; Priest, 1940; Curate of Duston, 1939–41; Curate of St Mark's, Portsea, 1941–47; Vicar of St Michael's, Northampton, 1947–57; Canon Residentiary of Chelmsford Cathedral, 1957–77; Director of Religious Education for the Diocese of Chelmsford, 1957–67; Chm. of House of Clergy and Vice-Pres., Chelmsford Diocesan Synod, 1970; Dir of Laity Training, 1967–73; Proctor in Convocation and Mem. Gen. Synod, 1970–. *Address:* 208 New London Road, Chelmsford, Essex. *T:* Chelmsford 354318.      *Died 5 May* 1981.

**HERRING, Lt-Gen. Hon. Sir Edmund Francis,** KCMG 1949; KBE 1943 (CBE 1941); DSO 1919; MC; ED; QC; Lieutenant-Governor of Victoria, 1945–72; Chief Justice of Supreme Court of Victoria, 1944–64; Chancellor of Archdiocese of Melbourne, since 1941; *b* Maryborough, Victoria, 2 Sept. 1892; *s* of Edmund Selwyn Herring and Grandfather Stella Fetherstonhaugh; *m* 1922, Dr Mary Ranken Lyle (*see* Dame Mary Ranken Herring); three *d. Educ:* Melbourne Church of England Grammar Sch.; Trinity Coll., Melbourne Univ. (Rhodes Schol., Victoria, 1912); New Coll., Oxford (MA, BCL 1920). Hon. Fellow, 1949; Barrister, Inner Temple, 1920, Hon. Bencher 1963; called to Bar, Melbourne, 1921; KC 1936. King Edward's Horse, July–Dec. 1914; commissioned RFA, Dec. 1914; BEF France and Macedonia, 1915–1919 (DSO, MC, despatches); Australian Citizen Forces, 1923–39; war of 1939–45 (CBE, KBE): AIF, 1939–44 (CRA 6th Div., 1939–41; commanded 6th Div., 1941–42; General Officer Commanding: Northern Territory Force, 1942; 2 Australian Corps, 1942; New Guinea Force, 1942–43; 1 Australian Corps, 1942–44; GMC 1 (Greece) 1941); DSC (USA) 1943. Dir Gen., Recruiting, Australia, 1950–51. Hon. Col. Melbourne Univ. Regt, 1950–. Chm. of Trustees, Shrine of Remembrance, Melbourne, 1945–79; Mem. Bd, Australian War Memorial, Canberra, 1945–74, Chm., 1959–74; President: Toc H, Australia, 1947–; Boy Scouts Assoc. of Victoria, 1945–68; Australian

Boy Scouts Assoc., 1959–77. Vice-Pres., British and Foreign Bible Soc. London. Leader, Australian Coronation Contingent, 1953. Hon. DCL Oxford 1953; Hon. LLD Monash, 1973. KStJ 1953. *Relevant Publication:* Ned Herring: a biography of Lt-Gen. the Hon. Sir Edmund Herring, by Stuart Sayers, 1980. *Recreation:* golf. *Address:* 226 Walsh Street, South Yarra, Vic. 3141, Australia. *T:* 261000. *Clubs:* Melbourne, Naval and Military, Australian (Hon. Mem.), Royal Melbourne Golf (Melbourne); Barwon Heads Golf.      *Died 5 Jan.* 1982.

**HERRING, Dame Mary Ranken,** DBE 1960; *b* 31 March 1895; *d* of late Sir Thomas Lyle, DSc, FRS and Lady Lyle, CBE; *m* 1922, Edmund Francis Herring (*see* Liuet-General Hon. Sir Edmund Francis Herring); three *d. Educ:* Toorak College and Melbourne University. MB, BS Hons, Melbourne, 1921. Medical Officer, Ante-Natal Clinics, Prahran and South Melbourne, 1926–45; Mem. and Vice-Pres., Melbourne District Nursing Soc., 1931–57; Vice-President and President, AIF Women's Association, 1939–47; President, Council of Toorak Coll., 1948–71; Vice-Chairman, British Commonwealth Youth Sunday, 1947–59; Member and Patron: Children's Welfare Assoc. of Victoria; Spastic Children's Soc. of Victoria; Save the Children Fund; Victoria Family Council; Victorian Women's Amateur Sports Council and Hockey Assoc.; Life Member: Victorian Bush Nursing Assoc.; Victoria Council of Social Service; Chairman of Trustees, V. S. Brown Memorial Trust; Dep. President, Victoria League in Victoria, 1945–74; Dep. President, Red Cross in Victoria, 1945–74; Member Advisory Council on Child Welfare, 1956–61. CStJ 1953. *Recreations:* gardening, golf. *Address:* 226 Walsh Street, South Yarra, Victoria 3141, Australia. *T:* 261000. *Clubs:* Lyceum, (Melbourne); Royal Melbourne Golf; Barwon Heads Golf.      *Died 26 Oct.* 1981.

**HERRON, Shaun;** novelist; *b* 23 Nov. 1912; *s* of late Thomas and Mary Herron, Carrickfergus, Co. Antrim; *m*; two *s* two *d.* Northern Irish. Ordained to Ministry of Scottish Congregational Churches, 1940; Minister, United Church of Canada, 1958. Editor, British Weekly, 1950–58; Correspondent in USA, 1960–64, Sen. Leader Writer, 1964–76, Winnipeg Free Press. Has held various lectureships in US and Canada. Finds entries in reference books too dreary to read. *Publications: novels:* Miro, 1968; The Hound and The Fox and The Harper, 1970; Through the Dark and Hairy Wood, 1972; The Whore-Mother, 1973; The Bird in Last Year's Nest, 1974; The Mac Donnell, 1976; Aladale, 1978; The Search for Arthur Barber, 1981; The Blacksmith's Daughter, 1987; At the House on Pine Street, 1987; The Pink Peacock and the Kingdom, 1988. *Recreations:* none. *Address:* Colbert Agency Curtis Brown, 303 Davenport Road, Toronto, Ont M5R 1K5, Canada.      *Died* 1989.

**HERZFELD, Gertrude Marianne Amalia,** MB, ChB, FRCSE; retired; Vice-President: Scottish Society of Women Artists, since 1954; Edinburgh Cripple Aid Society, since 1956; Trefoil School for Physically Handicapped Children, since 1964; *b* 1890; *d* of late Michael Herzfeld. *Educ:* Private School; Edinburgh Univ. MB, ChB, Edinburgh, 1914; Dorothy Gilfillan Prize, 1914; FRCSE, 1920; Wm Gibson Scholarship, 1920–22; formerly House Surgeon, Royal Hospital for Sick Children and Chalmers Hospital, Edinburgh, 1914–17; Surgeon, attached RAMC Cambridge Hospital, Aldershot, 1917; senior House Surgeon, Bolton Infirmary, 1917–19; Consultant Surgeon: Bruntsfield Hospital for Women and Children, 1920–55; Royal Edinburgh Hospital for Sick Children, 1920–45; Surgeon, Edinburgh Orthopaedic Clinic, 1925–55; Univ. Lectr on Surgery of Childhood, 1920–45; Lectr, Edinburgh Sch. of Chiropody, 1924–28. Chairman, City of Edinburgh Div., BMA, 1960–62. Past Pres., Med. Women's Fedn. Pres., Soroptimist Club of Edinburgh, 1929, Hon. Mem., 1955; Hon. Mem., Fedn of University Women, Edinburgh Assoc. *Publications:* various articles on Surgical Conditions of Childhood in the British Medical Jl, Lancet, American Jl of Surgery, etc. *Address:* Ashfield, 1 Chamberlain Road, Edinburgh EH10 4DL. *T:* 031–229 8849.      *Died 12 May* 1981.

**HERZOG, Frederick Joseph,** MC; farmer, retired; *b* 8 Dec. 1890; *s* of late F. C. Herzog, formerly of Mossley Hill, Liverpool; *m* 1918, Constance Cicely Broad (*d* 1983); two *s* one *d. Educ:* Charterhouse; Trinity Coll., Cambridge. BA, Economics tripos, 1911. Served European War in Royal Artillery, 1914–19 (MC); retired with rank of Major. High Sheriff of Denbighshire, 1942; JP Denbighshire since 1946. *Recreations:* sketching, gardening. *Address:* The Grange, Ruthin, North Wales. *T:* Ruthin 2124.      *Died 30 Dec.* 1987.

**HESKETH, (Charles) Peter (Fleetwood) Fleetwood-,** TD 1943, and two Bars; DL; *b* 5 Feb. 1905; 2nd *s* of late Charles Hesketh Fleetwood-Hesketh, and late Anne Dorothea, *e d* of Sir Thomas Brocklebank, 2nd Bt; *m* 1940, (Mary) Monica (*d* 1982), JP Lancs, 2nd *d* of Sir Ralph Cockayne Assheton, 1st Bt; one *d. Educ:* Eton. Studied architecture at London Univ. under Sir Albert Richardson, and at Architectural Association; Student RIBA and Registered Architect. Worked in office of late H. S. Goodhart-Rendel and later with Seely & Paget and other architects. Member of Lloyd's until

1975. Hon. district rep., for National Trust, 1947–68 (Mem., W Midlands Regional Cttee, 1972–81); Member: Covent Gdn Conservation Area Adv. Cttee, 1972–; Archbp's Adv. Bd on Redundant Churches, 1973–78; Cttee, Westminster Soc.; Gen. Synod of Church of England, 1975–80; Prayer Book Soc. (Founder Mem. and Trustee); Cttee of Incorporated Church Building Soc.; Council, Anglo-Rhodesian Soc., 1965–80 (Chm. Lancs and Cheshire Br., 1969–80); Salisbury Gp, 1978–. Hon. Dist Rep., Georgian Group and other societies; Founder Mem., Victorian Society (Secretary, 1961–63, Hon. Architectural Adviser 1963–, Chm., Liverpool Gp, 1968–); Patron, Thirties Soc., 1980–; Mem., Dilettanti Soc., 1983–. Architectural Correspt, Daily Telegraph, 1964–67. President: Widnes, Cheshire, Div., Conservative Assoc., 1971–83; Halton Constituency Cons. Assoc., 1983–. Special Constable in London during Gen. Strike, 1926. 2nd Lieut DLO Yeomanry (Cavalry) 1926, Captain 1938. Served, 1939–45, with DLO Yeomanry; WO, MI (Liaison); in occupied France with 2nd SAS and Maquis; Monuments, Fine Arts and Archives (Austria). High Sheriff, Lancs., 1960–61; DL Lancs, 1961–74, Cheshire, 1974–. A Burgess of Preston; Freeman of Hale. Assisted with The Master Builder magazine in early 1930's. *Publications:* Guide to the Palace of Schönbrunn, 1945; Murray's Lancashire Architectural Guide, 1955; Lancs section of Collins's Guide to English Parish Churches, 1958 (ed. John Betjeman); Life of Sir Charles Barry, in Peter Ferriday's Victorian Architecture, 1963; 1790–1840 section of Ian Grant's Great Interiors, 1967; chapters in: Shell Guide to England (ed John Hadfield), 1970, rev. edn 1981; The Country Seat (ed Howard Colvin and John Harris), 1970; contrib. Good Churches Guide, 1982. Illustrated John Betjeman's Ghastly Good Taste, 1933, extended 1970. Contrib. articles and drawings to Country Life, etc. *Address:* The Manor House, Hale, near Liverpool. *T:* 051–425 3116; 57 Great Ormond Street, WC1. *T:* 01–242 3672. *Clubs:* Travellers', MCC, Royal Automobile (Life Mem.).                    *Died 10 Feb. 1985.*

**HESKETH, Roger Fleetwood,** OBE 1970; TD 1942; *b* 28 July 1902; *e s* of Charles Hesketh Fleetwood-Hesketh, DL; *m* 1952, Lady Mary Lumley, OBE, DStJ, *e d* of 11th Earl of Scarbrough, KG, PC, GCSI, GCIE, GCVO; one *s* one *d* (and one *d* decd). *Educ:* Eton; Christ Church, Oxford (MA). Joined Duke of Lancaster's Own Yeomanry, 1922. Called to the Bar, Inner Temple, 1928. MP (C) for Southport, 1952–59. High Sheriff, Lancs, 1947; DL 1950, Vice-Lieutenant, 1972–77; JP 1950, Lancs; Mayor of Southport, 1950; Freeman of the Borough, 1966. Chairman, Lancashire Agricultural Executive Cttee, 1965–72. Trustee, Historic Churches Preservation Trust. Served War of 1939–45 (despatches, Bronze Star Medal, USA). Hon. Colonel, Duke of Lancaster's Own Yeomanry, 1956–67. *Address:* Meols Hall, Southport, Merseyside. *T:* Southport 28171; H4 Albany, Piccadilly, W1. *T:* 01–734 5320. *Club:* Travellers'.
                                                        *Died 14 Nov. 1987.*

**HETHERINGTON, Roger le Geyt,** CBE 1974 (OBE 1945); retired; *b* 20 Dec. 1908; *s* of late Sir Roger and Lady Hetherington; *m* 1945, Katharine Elise Dawson; one *d*. *Educ:* Highgate Sch.; Trinity Coll., Cambridge (MA). FEng, FICE, FIWEM. Joined Binnie Deacon & Gourley (later Binnie & Partners), as pupil, 1930. Served War, RE, 1940–45. Taken into partnership, Binnie & Partners, 1947, Sen. Partner, 1973. President: Institution of Civil Engineers, 1972–73; Pipeline Industries Guild, 1975–77. *Address:* 38 North Road, Highgate N6 4AX. *T:* 081–340 4203. *Club:* United Oxford & Cambridge University.                                    *Died 1 Aug. 1990.*

**HEWAN, Gethyn Elliot;** Secretary, Surrey Golf Union, since 1977; *b* 23 Dec. 1916; *s* of late E. D. Hewan and Mrs L. Hewan; *m* 1943, Peggy (*née* Allen); one *s* two *d*. *Educ:* Marlborough Coll., Wilts; Clare Coll., Cambridge (Exhibitioner); Yale Univ., USA (Mellon Schol). BA Hons 1938; MA 1943, Cambridge. Served War of 1939–45 (despatches): Middle East; Capt. 3rd Regt RHA 1943; Staff Coll., Camberley, psc 1944; BMRA 51st Highland Div., 1944–45. Asst Master, Wellington Coll., 1946–50; Headmaster, Cranbrook Sch., Bellevue Hill, NSW, 1951–63; Acting Bursar, Marlborough Coll., Wilts, 1963; Asst Master, Winchester Coll., 1963–64, Charterhouse Sch., 1964–65; Headmaster, Allhallows Sch., Rousdon, 1965–74. Sec., NSW branch of HMC of Aust., 1956–63; Standing Cttee of HMC of Aust., 1958–63; Foundation Member, Aust. Coll. of Education, 1958; Exec. Cttee, Australian Outward Bound Foundation, 1958–63. *Recreations:* cricket (Cambridge blue, 1938), golf, fishing; formerly hockey (blue, 1936–37–38, Captain) and billiards (½-blue, 1938). *Address:* Newquay, Nursery Close, Horsell, Woking, Surrey. *T:* Woking 62597. *Clubs:* I Zingari; Free Foresters; Oxford and Cambridge Golfing Society; Worplesdon Golf; Senior Golfers'.
                                                        *Died 1 July 1988.*

**HEWER, Christopher Langton,** MB, BS (London); MRCP; Hon. FFARCS; Consulting Anæsthetist to St Bartholomew's Hospital and to Hospital for Tropical Diseases, London; late Senior Anæsthetist, The Queen's Hospital for Children, Hackney Road; Seamen's Hospital, Royal Albert Dock; St Andrew's Hospital, Dollis Hill; late Anæsthetist to Queen Mary's Hospital,

Roehampton, Ministry of Pensions, Brompton Chest Hospital and Anæsthetic Specialist RAMC; Examiner in Anæsthesia to Royal College of Surgeons of England and Royal College of Physicians; late Consultant Anæsthetist to West Herts Hospital, Hemel Hempstead, to Luton and Dunstable Hospital, and to Harpenden Hospital; *s* of Joseph Langton Hewer, MD, FRCS; *m* 1925, Doris Phœbe, *d* of H. D'Arcy Champney, MA, Bristol; two *s* one *d*. *Educ:* University Coll. Sch; St Bartholomew's Hospital. Junior Scholarship in Anatomy and Physiology in St Bartholomew's Hospital Medical Coll.; MB, BS London degree (distinction in Physiology), 1920; served as House Surgeon and Resident Anæsthetist at St Bartholomew's Hospital; FRSM; Sec. of the Anæsthetic Section of same, 1930 and 1931, Pres., 1936–37; late Vice-Pres. Assoc. of Anæsthetists of Great Britain and Ireland, and Editor Emeritus of the Association's Journal, Anæsthesia; Member Anæsthetics Cttee of MRC and RSM; Pres., Section of Anæsthetics, BMA, 1953; Hon. Member: Liverpool Soc. of Anæsthetists; Canadian Soc. of Anæsthetists; late Member Board of Faculty of Anæsthetists, RCS. Frederic Hewitt Lecturer, 1959. Henry Hill Hickman Medallist, 1966, John Snow Medallist, 1966. *Publications:* Anæsthesia in Children, 1922; (with H. E. G. Boyle) Practical Anæsthetics, 1923; (ed) 1st-13th edns, Recent Advances in Anæsthesia and Analgesia, 1st edn 1932, (ed with R. S. Atkinson) 14th edn 1982; Thoughts on Modern Anæsthesia, 1970; articles in medical journals and reports; Section on Anæsthesia in Post Graduate Surgery, edited by R. Maingot; formerly editor Section on Anæsthesia in Medical Annual. *Address:* 19 Ludlow Way, Hampstead Garden Suburb, N2 0JZ.
                                                        *Died 28 Jan. 1986.*

**HEWETT, Sir John George,** 5th Bt, *cr* 1813; MC 1919; Captain KAR; *b* 23 Oct. 1895; *e* surv. *s* of Sir Harold George Hewett, 4th Bt, and Eleanor (*d* 1946), *d* of Capt. Studdy, RN, and Mrs W. T. Summers; *S* father, 1949; *m* 1926, Yuilleen Maude (*d* 1980), *o c* of Samuel F. Smithson, Lauriston, Camberley; two *s*. *Educ:* Cheltenham. Served European War, 1914–18, British East Africa, 1914–19. *Heir: e s* Peter John Smithson Hewett, MM [*b* 27 June 1931; *m* 1958, Jennifer Ann Cooper, *o c* of Emrys Thomas Jones, Bexhill-on-Sea; two *s* one *d*. *Educ:* Bradfield Coll.; Jesus Coll., Cambridge. Called to the Bar, Gray's Inn, 1954; Advocate in Kenya. Kenya Regt attached Special Branch, Kenya Police, 1957]. *Address:* Lamwia Road, Langata, PO Box 40763, Nairobi, Kenya.                    *Died 17 Oct. 1990.*

**HEWITT, Air Vice-Marshal Joseph Eric,** CBE 1951 (OBE 1940); psa 1934; Royal Australian Air Force (retired); Member Panel of Military Experts, United Nations, since 1952; Chairman and Managing Director, Langate Publishing, since 1980; *b* 13 April 1901; *s* of late Rev. J. H. Hewitt, MA, BD and late Rose Alice Hewitt (*née* Harkness), Melbourne, Vic; *m* 1925, Lorna Pretoria (*d* 1976), *d* of late Alfred Eugene Bishop and late Joanne Bishop (*née* Prismall), Melbourne, Vic; three *d*. *Educ:* Scotch Coll., Melbourne; Royal Australian Naval Coll., Jervis Bay, NSW. Served in RAN, RN, RAAF and RAF, 1915–28; Cadet Midshipman, 1915; Midshipman, 1918; Sub-Lieut 1921; Lieut, 1922. Transferred to RAAF, 1928; Comdg Officer RAAF, HMAS Albatross, 1929–32; RAF Staff Coll., Andover, 1934; Asst Liaison Officer, Australia House, London, 1935; Comdg Officer, No 104 Sqdn, RAF, 1936–38; SASO, RAAF, Richmond, NSW, 1938–39; Sen. Admin. Staff Officer, Southern Area, HQ, 1939–40; DPS, HQ, RAAF, 1940–41; DCAS, RAAF, 1941; Director of Air Operations, Staff of C-in-C. Allied Command, NEI, Java, 1942; ACAS, 1942; Director of Allied Air Intelligence, SW Pacific Area, 1942 and 1944; AOC No 9 Op. Group, 1943 (Battle of Bismarck Sea, 1943); Air member for Personnel, RAAF, HQrs, 1945–48; Australian Defence Representative, London, 1949–51; Air Member for Supply and Equipment, Dept of Air, Melbourne, 1951–56, retired April 1956. Member, Council for Adult Education of Victoria, 1956–66. Manager, Education and Training, Internat. Harvester Co. (Aust.) Pty Ltd, 1956–66; Trustee, Services Canteens Trust Fund, 1957–77. Associate, Aust. Soc. of Authors, 1982; FAIM 1956. *Publications:* Adversity in Success, 1980; The Black One, 1984. *Recreations:* swimming, gardening, reading. *Address:* Unit 1, 24 Oxford Street, South Yarra, Vic 3141, Australia. *Club:* Naval and Military (Melbourne).                                    *Died 1 Nov. 1985.*

**HEWS, (Gordon) Rodney (Donald),** MC 1945; TD 1950; DL; Chairman, Kent Messenger Ltd, 1982–86 (Deputy Chairman, 1980–82); *b* 10 May 1917; *yr s* of late G. R. Hews and Alderman Mrs Evelyn Hews, CBE; *m* 1944, Maureen Sydney Smith, *d* of late Air Cdre Sydney Smith, OBE, DL; two *s* one *d*. *Educ:* Kent Coll., Canterbury. Joined family newspaper, Kentish Gazette, 1935; Editor, 1950–63; Man. Dir, T. F. Pain & Sons Ltd (publishers of East Kent Mercury, Deal), 1953–80; Chm. and Man. Dir, Kent County Newspapers Ltd, 1960–80. Gazetted 2nd Lieut 4th Bn The Buffs, TA, 1936; served War, 1939–45, on Staff and with 2nd Bn The Buffs: France, 1940; ME, Persia/Iraq, 1941–43 (ME Staff Coll., 1942); Burma, 1944–45 (MC); commanded 4th Bn The Buffs, 1953–55, 5th Bn The Buffs, 1955–57; Col 133 Infantry Bde, 1957–66. Gen. Tax Comr, Canterbury Div., 1961– (Chm., 1967–). Mem., Immigration Appeals Tribunal, 1963–65. JP Canterbury, 1955–85

(Chm., 1972–81); Vice Chm., Kent Magistrates' Courts Cttee, 1980–83; DL Kent, 1980. Comdr, Order of the Dannebrog, Denmark, 1955. *Address:* 4 Derringstone Street, Barham, near Canterbury, Kent CT4 6QB. *T:* Canterbury 831238.

*Died 7 March* 1988.

**HEXT, Maj.-Gen. Frederick Maurice,** CB 1954; OBE 1945; CEng; FIMechE; FIEE; *b* 5 May 1901; *s* of Frederick Robert Hext; *m* 1924, Kathleen Goulden; one *s*. *Educ:* Portsmouth Gram. Sch.; RMA, Woolwich. Commissioned RE 1921; served in India, 1925–28, and 1931–34; Instructor, Sch. of Military Engineering, 1939–42; served NW Europe Campaign (despatches) Comdr, REME, 53rd (Welsh) Div., and Dep. Dir of Mechanical Engineering, 12 Corps; DDME, 1 Corps, 1945–46; DDME, Burma Command, 1946–48; AAG, AG 21, War Office, 1949–51; DME, BAOR, 1951–53; Inspector of REME, 1953–56, retired 1956. Hon. Col 53 (Welsh) Inf. Div. REME, 1956–61. Maj.-Gen., 1953. Formerly Member Wessex RHB; Chm. Isle of Wight Group Hospital Management Cttee, 1961–72. FRSA. *Address:* 17 Brettingham Court, Hinton St George, Crewkerne, Somerset. *T:* Crewkerne 73059. *Died 1 May* 1987.

**HEY, Donald Holroyde,** DSc, PhD; FRS 1955; FRSC; Daniell Professor of Chemistry, University of London, 1950–71, now Emeritus Professor; President, Section B, British Association for the Advancement of Science, 1965; *b* Swansea, 1904; 2nd *s* of Arthur Hey, MusB, FRCO, LRAM, and Frances Jane Hey; *m* 1931, Jessie (*d* 1982), MSc (Wales), *d* of Thomas and Katharine Jones; one *s* one *d*. *Educ:* Magdalen Coll. Sch., Oxford; University Coll., Swansea, BSc, MSc Wales; PhD London; DSc Manchester. Asst Lecturer in Chemistry, University of Manchester, 1928–30; Lecturer in Chemistry, University of Manchester, 1930–38; Lecturer in Chemistry, Imperial Coll. of Science and Technology, London, 1939–41; Dir of British Schering Research Institute, 1941–45; University Prof. of Chemistry at King's Coll., London, 1945–50; Asst Principal, King's Coll., 1962–68. Scientific Advr for Civil Defence, SE Region, 1952–58. Vice-Pres. of Chemical Soc. 1951–54 (Tilden Lectr, 1951, Pedler Lectr, 1970, Hon. Secretary, 1946–51, Vice-Pres., Perkin Div., 1971). Reilly Lectr, University of Notre Dame, Indiana, 1952; Visiting Prof. University of Florida, 1967. FKC; Fellow Imp. Coll. of Science and Technology, 1968; Hon. Fellow: Chelsea Coll., 1973; Univ. Coll. Swansea, 1986. Member: Council, KCL, 1955–78; Adv. Council RMCS, 1961–73. Hon. DSc Wales, 1970. Defence Medal 1945. Intra-Science Res. Conf. Award and Medal, Santa Monica, Calif., 1968; Hon. Fellow, Intra-Science Res. Foundn, 1971. *Publications:* articles in scientific journals, mainly in Jl of Chem. Soc. *Recreations:* music, gardening. *Address:* 78 Doods Road, Reigate, Surrey. *Died 21 Jan.* 1987.

**HEYCOCK, Baron** *cr* 1967 (Life Peer), of Taibach; **Llewellyn Heycock,** CBE 1959; DL, JP; *b* 12 Aug. 1905; *s* of late William Heycock and Mary Heycock; *m* 1930, Olive Elizabeth (*née* Rees); one *s* (and one *s* decd). *Educ:* Eastern Sch., Port Talbot. Engine Driver, Dyffryn Yard Loco Sheds, Port Talbot. Glam County Council: Mem., 1937–74; Chm. 1962–63; Chm., Educn Cttee, 1944–74; Chm., West Glamorgan CC, 1973–75. Pres., UWIST, 1968–75; Mem., Council and Court, University of Wales. Formerly: Mem., Council and Court, University Coll. of S Wales and Mon.; Chairman: Schools Museum Service for Wales; Celtic Sea Adv. Cttee; Exec. Cttee, Royal National Eisteddfod of Wales, Port Talbot (1966); Welsh Jt Educn Cttee; President: Coleg Harlech; Assoc. of Educn Cttees (1964–65); Nat. Assoc. of Div. Execs for England and Wales (1954–55, 1965–66); Exec. Mem., County Councils Assoc.; Mem., Adv. Cttee for Educn in Wales under 1944 Butler Act. Hon. Druid, Nat. Eisteddfod of Wales, 1963; Vice-Pres., Nat. Theatre Co. for Wales. Hon. LLD, University of Wales, 1963. Hon. Freedom of Port Talbot, 1961. CStJ. JP Glam; JP Port Talbot; DL Glam 1963. *Recreation:* Rugby football. *Address:* 1 Llewellyn Close, Taibach, Port Talbot, West Glam. *T:* Port Talbot 882565.

*Died 14 March* 1990.

**HEYCOCK, Air Cdre George Francis Wheaton,** CB 1963; DFC 1941; JP; *b* 17 Sept. 1909; *s* of Rev. F. W. Heycock, MA, and Edith Rowlandson; *m* 1938, Betty Boyd; one *s*. *Educ:* Haileybury and Imperial Service Coll.; Cranwell Cadet Coll. Commnd in RAF, 1929; Flying Instructor at RAF Coll., Cranwell and Central Flying Sch., 111 Sqdn, Fleet Air Arm, 1935–37. Test Pilot, Farnborough, 1937–39. Command of 23 and 141 Sqdns, 1940–42. Dir of Ops, Indian Air Force, 1949; Command of RAF Syerston, 1950–52; Air Ministry, 1952–55; Chief of Staff, British Joint Services Mission (RAF Staff), Washington, and Air Attaché, Washington, 1955; Air Attaché, Paris, 1959–64. JP Northants, 1965. Comdr Légion d'Honneur. *Recreation:* golf. *Address:* The Manor House, Pytchley, Northants. *T:* Kettering 790269. *Club:* Royal Air Force.

*Died 27 June* 1983.

**HEYMANSON, Sir (Sydney Henry) Randal,** Kt 1972; CBE 1965 (OBE 1955); Chairman of the Board, American Australian Association, since 1967; *b* 18 April 1903; *s* of Frederick Heymanson

and Elizabeth (*née* McDonnell). *Educ:* Melbourne C of E Grammar Sch.; Melbourne Univ. (MA Hons); London Univ. Australian Newspapers Service: European Corresp., 1928–40; Editor, NY, 1940–69; War Corresp., ETO; Editor and Publisher, Vital News, 1939–42; N American Rep., West Australian Newspapers, 1969–. Pres., Foreign Press Assoc., NY, 1942–43; Pres., Australian Soc. of NY, 1945–46. Exec. Vice-Pres. 1950–65, Pres. 1965–66, American Australian Assoc. *Recreations:* bibliomania, art collecting, travel. *Address:* 7 Mitchell Place, New York, NY 10017, USA. *Clubs:* Overseas Press, Dutch Treat, Ends of the Earth (New York); National Press (Washington). *Died 27 Aug.* 1984.

**HEYS, Derek Isaac,** CBE 1971; TD 1945; Senior Partner in Heys, Wall & Co., Freight Forwarders, 1949–73; Executive with Wingate & Johnston Ltd, Liverpool, 1973–79; *b* 6 Aug. 1911; twin *s* of Isaac and Laura Heys; *m* 1936, Margaret Helena Ashcroft; one *s* one *d* (and one *s* decd). *Educ:* Birkenhead Sch. Late Lt-Col RA (TA). Pres., Internat. Fedn of Forwarding Agents' Assocs (FIATA), 1967–71; Nat. Chm., Inst. of Shipping and Forwarding Agents, 1962–63; Chm., Merseyside Chamber of Commerce and Industry, 1970–71; Chm., first Adv. Cttee of three, apptd by Dirs of Mersey Docks & Harbour Co. to represent interest of holders of Co.'s redeemable subordinated unsecured Loan Stock, 1974; Vice-President: Inst. of Freight Forwarders, 1965–; Assoc. of British Chambers of Commerce, 1975. Consul for Belgium in Liverpool, 1966–77. Chm. of Governors, Birkenhead Sch., 1977–. High Sheriff, Merseyside, 1982. Order of the Crown (Belgium), 1977. *Recreation:* golf. *Address:* Fairway Cottage, Pinfold Lane, West Kirby, Wirral, Merseyside. *T:* 051–632 4242. *Clubs:* Athenæum (Liverpool); Royal Liverpool Golf (Hoylake). *Died 9 May* 1984.

**HEYWOOD, Geoffrey Henry,** CBE 1972; Consultant, Dunlop Heywood & Co., Chartered Surveyors, Manchester, since 1969 (Partner, 1930–69); Chairman, Skelmersdale Development Corporation, 1969–75; President, Manchester Rent Assessment Panel, 1965–74; *b* 22 Aug. 1903; *s* of late Henry Arthur Heywood, Christleton Lodge, Chester; *m* 1931, Magdeleine Jeanne Georgette Marie, *d* of late J. H. Herpin, Paris; one *s* one *d*. *Educ:* Repton School. FRICS. Mem. Council, RICS, 1950–70 (Pres. 1962–63). Mem., Skelmersdale Develt Corp., 1962–75 (Dep. Chm. 1962–69). *Address:* 1 Derrydown, Hook Heath Road, Woking, Surrey GU22 0LD. *T:* Woking 23251. *Died 20 June* 1986.

**HEYWOOD, Very Rev. Hugh Christopher Lempriere,** MA; Provost Emeritus of Southwell; *b* 5 Nov. 1896; *s* of late Charles Christopher Heywood; *m* 1920, Margaret Marion (*d* 1982), *d* of Herbert Vizard; one *s* one *d*. *Educ:* Haileybury; Trinity Coll., Cambridge (Scholar and Stanton Student). Manchester Regt 1914–17 (wounded, despatches); 74th Punjabis IA 1917–23 (Staff Capt., 1919–22); Ordained, 1926; Curate of St Andrew's the Great, Cambridge, 1926–27; of Holy Cross, Greenford, 1927–28; Fellow and Dean, Gonville and Caius Coll., Cambridge, 1928–45; University Lecturer in Divinity, Cambridge, 1937–45; Provost of Southwell and Rector of S Mary, Southwell, 1945–69; Priest-in-charge of Upton, Diocese of Southwell, 1969–76. Examining Chaplain to Bishop of Southwark, 1932–41, and to Bishop of Southwell, 1941–69. Junior Proctor, Cambridge, 1934–35 and 1942–43. *Publications:* The Worshipping Community, 1938; On a Golden Thread, 1960; Finding Happiness in Remembering, 1978; Still on a Golden Thread, 1980; And Still on that Thread, 1982. *Address:* 26 Lyndewode Road, Cambridge.

*Died 8 May* 1987.

**HIBBARD, Prof. Howard,** PhD; Professor of Art History, since 1966, Chairman, Department of Art History and Archaeology, 1978–81, Columbia University; *b* 23 May 1928; *s* of Benjamin Horace Hibbard and Margaret Baker Hibbard; *m* 1951, Shirley Irene Griffith; three *d*. *Educ:* Univ. of Wisconsin (BA 1949, MA 1952); Columbia Univ.; Harvard Univ. (PhD 1958). Fulbright Fellow, Paris, 1949–50; Univ. Fellow, Columbia Univ., 1952–53; Harvard Prize Fellow, 1953–54; Fellow, Amer. Acad. in Rome, 1956–58; Vis. Instr, Univ. of Calif, 1958–59; Asst Prof., 1959–62, Associate Prof., 1962–66, Columbia Univ. Amer. Council of Learned Socs Fellow, Rome, 1962–63; Guggenheim Fellow, Rome, 1965–66 and 1972–73; Sen. Fellow, Nat. Endowment for Humanities, Rome, 1967, 1979–80; Vis. Dist. Scholar, City Coll., City Univ. of NY, 1973–74; Vis. Prof., Yale Univ., 1976; Slade Prof. of Fine Art, Oxford Univ., 1976–77. Phi Betta Kappa Vis. Scholar, 1980–81. Fellow, Amer. Acad. of Arts and Sciences, 1969. Hon. MA Oxon 1977. Editor-in-Chief, Art Bulletin, 1974–78. *Publications:* The Architecture of the Palazzo Borghese, 1962; Bernini, 1965; Bernini e il barocco, 1968; (with J. Nissman) Florentine Baroque Art from American Collections, 1969; Carlo Maderno and Roman Architecture 1580–1630, 1972; Poussin: The Holy Family on the Steps, 1974; Michelangelo, 1975, 2nd edn 1984; Masterpieces of European Sculpture, 1977; The Metropolitan Museum of Art, 1980; Caravaggio, 1983; contrib. Art Bull., Burlington Mag., Jl Soc. Architect. Historians. *Recreations:* gardening, cooking. *Address:* 176 Brewster Road, Scarsdale, NY 10583, USA. *T:* 914–725–3743.

*Died 29 Oct.* 1984.

**HIBBERD, (Andrew) Stuart**, MBE; *b* 5 Sept. 1893; *y s* of late W. H. Hibberd, Canford Magna, Dorset; *m* 1923, Alice Mary, *e d* of late Lieut-Col Gerard Chichester, North Staffs Regt; no *c. Educ:* Weymouth Coll.; St John's Coll., Cambridge (MA). Served European War in 7th and 5th Batt. Dorset Regt; and 46th Punjabis IA; later 2/25th Punjabis IA; served in Gallipoli, Mesopotamia and Waziristan. Joined BBC, at Savoy Hill, 1924; on Headquarter Staff until retirement, 1951; for some years Chief Announcer. Fellow: Royal Society of Arts; Royal Society of St George. *Publication:* This—is London, 1951. *Recreations:* gardening, music. *Address:* 2 West Field, Budleigh Salterton, Devon. *Died* 1 Nov. 1983.

**HIBBERD, Sir Donald (James)**, Kt 1977; OBE 1956; Chairman, Comalco Ltd, 1969–80 (Chief Executive, 1969–78); *b* 26 June 1916; *s* of William James Hibberd and Laura Isabel Hibberd; *m* 1942, Florence Alice Macandie; one *s* one *d. Educ:* Sydney Univ. (BEc). Commonwealth Dept of Trade and Customs, 1939–46; Exec. Asst, Commonwealth Treasury, 1946–53; Mem., Aust. Aluminium Production Commn, 1953–57; First Asst Sec., Banking Trade and Industry Br., Commonwealth Treasury, 1953–57; Exec. Dir, Commonwealth Aluminium Corp., 1957–61; Man. Dir, Comalco Industries Pty Ltd, 1961–69. Director: COR Ltd, 1949–51; G. E. Crane Hldgs Ltd, 1961–78; Conzinc Rio Tinto of Aust. Ltd, 1962–71; Mem., Reserve Bank Bd, 1966–81; Vice Chm., Queensland Alumina Ltd, 1964–80; Chm., Munich Reinsurance Co. of Aust. Ltd, 1970–; Chm., NZ Aluminium Smelters Ltd, 1969–80. Pres., Aust. Mining Industry Council, 1972–73. Mem., Melbourne Univ. Council, 1967–. *Recreations:* golf, reading. *Address:* 193 Domain Road, South Yarra, Vic 3141, Australia. *T:* 264037. *Clubs:* Athenæum (Melbourne); Commonwealth (Canberra); Royal Melbourne Golf, Frankston Golf. *Died* 31 Dec. 1982.

**HIBBERD, Prof. George**, PhD; ARTC, CEng, Hon. FIMinE; FRSE; Dixon Professor of Mining, University of Glasgow, and Professor of Mining, University of Strathclyde, Glasgow, 1947–67, later Emeritus; *b* Muirkirk, NB, 17 May 1901; *e s* of Charles Hibberd and Helen Brown; *m* 1931, Marion Dalziel Robb Adamson (*d* 1989); two *s* two *d. Educ:* Muirkirk Public Sch.; Royal Tech. Coll., Glasgow. Walter Duncan Res. Scholar. Mining official, 1926–28; Coll. Lectr, 1928–46. Past Pres. Mining Inst. of Scotland. Mem. Council, Inst. Mining Engineers. *Publications:* A Survey of the Welsh Slate Industry; A Survey of The Caithness Flagstone Industry; numerous papers on mining and scientific subjects in technical press. (Jointly) A Survey of the Scottish Slate Industry and A Survey of the Scottish Free-Stone Quarrying Industry. *Recreations:* golf, gardening. *Address:* 120 Kings Park Avenue, Glasgow G44 4HS. *T:* 041–632 4608. *Died* 8 Nov. 1989.

**HIBBERD, Stuart;** *see* Hibberd, A. S.

**HIBBERT, Maj.-Gen. Hugh Brownlow**, DSO 1940; *b* 10 Dec. 1893; *s* of late Adm. H. T. Hibbert, CBE, DSO; *m* 1926, Susan Louisa Mary Feilding (*d* 1975); one *s* one *d. Educ:* Uppingham; RMC, Sandhurst. Retired pay, 1946. *Address:* Kilsall Hall, Shifnal, Salop. *Died* 22 June 1988.

**HICHENS, Mrs Mary Hermione**, CBE 1950; ARRC; JP; County Councillor, Oxon, 1937–51, Chairman of Education Committee, 1946–57, Alderman, 1951–74; *b* 15 Oct. 1894; 3rd *d* of Gen. Rt Hon. Sir N. G. Lyttelton, GCB, GCVO; *m* 1919, William Lionel Hichens (Chm. of Cammell Laird; killed by enemy action, 1940); two *s* three *d* (and one *s* killed in action). *Educ:* Alexander Coll., Dublin. Served as Military Probationer QAIMNS in England, 1915; in France, 1916–19 (despatches, ARRC); Mem. of Royal Commission on the Geographical Distribution of the Industrial Population, 1937–39, signed Minority Report; Mem. of Consultative Panel on Post-War Reconstruction to Minister of Works and Buildings; Mem. of Departmental Cttee on Land Utilisation, 1941; Mem. of Departmental Cttee on Training of Teachers, 1942; Commissioner under the Catering Act, 1943–58. Member: County Councils Assoc., 1946–66; Oxon Agric. Exec. Cttee, 1956–61. JP Oxon 1934. *Address:* North Aston Hall, Oxford OX5 4JA. *T:* Steeple Aston 40200. *Died* 27 March 1985.

**HICKEY, Nancy Maureen**, OBE 1979; SRN, SCM, MTD, DN; Chairman, Central Midwives Board for England and Wales, 1979–83, retired; *b* 31 Aug. 1924; *d* of late Timothy Hickey and Elsie Winifred Hickey. *Educ:* Woking Secondary School for Girls. SRN Guy's Hospital, 1948; SCM Sussex Maternity Hosp., 1949; Sister, Guy's Hosp., 1953–55; MTD Royal College of Midwives, 1954; Midwifery Teacher, Guy's Hosp., 1955–57; Midwifery Supt, Pembury Hosp., 1957–65; Diploma in Nursing, London (Obst.), 1957; Matron, Coventry Maternity Hosp., 1965–70; Chief Nursing Officer, Coventry, 1970–74; Area Nursing Officer, Coventry, 1974–79. *Recreations:* light music, walking. *Club:* Coventry Soroptimist (Coventry). *Died* 22 Sept. 1986.

**HICKINBOTHAM, Rev. James Peter**, DD Lambeth, 1979; *b* 16 May 1914; *s* of late F. J. L. Hickinbotham, JP and late Mrs Hickinbotham; *m* 1948, Ingeborg Alice Lydia Manger; two *s* one *d. Educ:* Rugby

Sch.; Magdalen Coll., Oxford; Wycliffe Hall, Oxford. Deacon, 1937; priest, 1938; curate: St John, Knighton, Leicester, 1937–39; St Paul, S Harrow, 1940–42; Chaplain, Wycliffe Hall, Oxford, 1942–45; Vice-Principal, 1945–50. Prof. of Theology, University Coll. of the Gold Coast, 1950–54. Principal, St John's Coll. and Cranmer Hall, Durham, 1954–70; Principal of Wycliffe Hall, Oxford, 1970–79. Examining Chaplain: to Bishop of Manchester, 1947–50; to Bishop of Leicester, 1948–53; to Bishop of Durham, 1955–70. Proctor in Convocation, 1957–70. Hon. Canon, Durham Cathedral, 1959–70. Hon. Curate, Christ Church, Dowend, 1979–84. *Address:* 23 St George's View, Cullompton, Devon EX15 1BA. *T:* Cullompton 33326. *Died* 26 April 1990.

**HICKINBOTHAM, Sir Tom**, KCMG 1953 (CMG 1951); KCVO 1954; CIE 1944; OBE 1939; *b* 27 April 1903; 2nd *s* of James Ryland Hickinbotham, MB, and Beatrice Elliot, *d* of Rev. Theophilus Sharp, MA. *Educ:* Royal Military Coll., Sandhurst. Entered Indian Army, 1923; served North West Frontier, 1924 (medal); posted to 5th Battalion Baluch Regiment, 1924; transferred to Indian Political Service, 1930; served in various appointments in Aden, 1931–32, 1933–35, and 1938–39; Political Agent, Bahrain, 1937, Muscat, 1939–41, Kuwait, 1941–43, Bahrain, 1943–45; Kalat, 1945–47; Chm. of the Aden Port Trust, 1948–51; Governor and Comdr-in-Chief of Colony and Protectorate of Aden, 1951–56, retired from Government Service. Director of various companies, 1956–73. *Publication:* Aden, 1958. *Recreation:* fishing. *Address:* Newburgh, Ettrick, Selkirk TD7 5HS. *Died* 14 Oct. 1983.

**HICKS, Col Sir Denys (Theodore)**, Kt 1961; OBE 1950; TD 1943; DL; Member Council of The Law Society, 1948–69; *b* 2 May 1908; *s* of late Cuthbert Hicks, Bristol; *m* 1941, Irene Elizabeth Mansell Leach; four *d. Educ:* Clifton. Admitted a Solicitor of Supreme Court of Judicature, 1931. Served War of 1939–45; with RA in UK and on staff; Col 1953; Hon. Col, 266 (Gloucester Vol. Artillery) Bty RA (Vols), 1972–75. Vice-President of The Law Society, 1959, Pres., 1960; Chm., Internat. Bar Assoc., 1966–70, Pres., 1970–74, Hon. Life Pres., 1974. Dep. Chm., Horserace Betting Levy Board, 1961–76; Mem., Royal Commission on Assizes and QS, 1967. Hon. Member: Amer. Bar Assoc., 1960; Il Ilustre y Nacional Collegio de Abagados de Mexico, 1964; Virginia State Bar Assoc., 1966. DL Avon (formerly Glos), 1957. *Address:* Damson Cottage, Hunstrete, Pensford, Bristol BS18 4NY. *T:* Compton Dando 464. *Died* 9 Jan. 1987.

**HICKS, Donald**, OBE 1968; MSc (London), FIChemE, FRSC; Director-General, British Coal Utilisation Research Association, 1962–67; *b* 26 June 1902; *e s* of late Benjamin and Matilda Hicks; *m* May, *y d* of late William and Margaret Sainsbury, Shirenewton, Chepstow; no *c. Educ:* Pontypridd Grammar Sch.; Glamorgan Coll. of Technology. Chief Coal Survey Officer, DSIR, S Wales, 1930–45; Supt of Coal Survey Organisation, DSIR, 1946; Dir of Scientific Control, Nat. Coal Bd, 1947–58; Carbonisation and Scientific Dir and Mem. East Midland Divisional Bd of NCB, 1959–62; Dir of Operational Research and Dir of Pneumoconiosis Field Research, Nat. Coal Bd, 1949–62. *Publications:* Primary Health Care: a review, 1976; papers in various scientific and technical jls. *Recreations:* walking and reading. *Address:* 26 St Kingsmark Avenue, Chepstow, Gwent NP6 5LY. *T:* Chepstow 3147. *Died* 30 Jan. 1986.

**HICKS, Sir Edwin (William)**, Kt 1965; CBE 1956; Company Director and consultant; *b* 9 June 1910; *s* of late William Banks Hicks, Melbourne, Victoria; *m* 1st, 1937, Jean (*d* 1959), *yr d* of late Thomas MacPherson, Brighton, Victoria; four *s* one *d*; 2nd, 1961, Lois, *o d* of Norman S. Swindon, Canberra; one *s* one *d. Educ:* Haileybury; Melbourne Grammar Sch.; Canberra Univ. Coll. (BCom 1947). Commonwealth Public Service Bd, 1929–31; Commonwealth Statistican's Branch, 1931–38; Trade and Customs Dept, 1938–48; Senior Inspector, then Actg Asst Comr Commonwealth Public Service Bd, investigating organisation and methods of Commonwealth Govt Depts, 1948–51; Secretary: Dept of Air, Commonwealth of Australia, 1951–56; Dept of Defence, 1956–68; Australia High Comr in NZ, 1968–71, retired from Public Service, 1971. Served 1942–45 with Royal Australian Air Force in South West Pacific Area. *Recreations:* formerly: cricket, football, tennis; latterly golf. *Address:* 73 Endeavour Street, Red Hill, ACT 2603, Australia. *Died* 14 May 1984.

**HICKS, Howard Arthur**, CBE 1981; Founder, 1957, Chairman, 1957–86, Life President, since 1986, IDC Group plc; *b* 3 May 1914; *s* of Ivor Lewis Hicks and Gertrude Freda (*née* Shaw); *m* 1940, Anne Maureen (*née* Lang); one *s* one *d. Educ:* Pontypridd; Polytechnic of Wales (Fellow 1984). DSc Aston in Birmingham, 1976. CEng, FICE, FIProdE, FCIOB, FAmSCE, MSocIS, FIMM, FRSA, CBIM. Civil Engineer, Bridge Dept, Glamorgan CC, 1934–39; served War, Royal Engineers, 1939–46 (Major); Man. Dir, Beecham Reinforced Concrete Engineers, 1947–56; Director: Candover Investments plc, 1980–; Royalty Theatre plc, 1987–. Chm., Aston Technical Management & Planning Services (Aston Univ.) Ltd,

1970–82; President: Inst. of Materials Management, 1977–80; Instn of Production Engrs, 1980–81. Internat. Engrg Achievements Award, Inst. for the Advancement of Engrg, 1981; Distinguished Internat. Archimedes Engrg Achievements Award, Nat. Soc. of Professional Engrs of America, 1980; SME Engrg Citation, Soc. of Manufacturing Engrs of United States, 1982; Internat. Engr of the Year, Inst. for the Advancement of Engrg, LA, Calif, 1983; Space Shuttle Technol. Award, NASA, 1984; Hon. CGIA. *Recreation:* theatre. *Address:* Avonfield, Stratford upon Avon, Warwickshire CV37 6BJ. *T:* Stratford upon Avon 293594. *Clubs:* Athenæum; Cardiff and County; Phoenix (Lima, Peru).

*Died 4 Jan. 1989.*

**HICKS, Lt-Col James Hamilton,** OBE 1966; TD 1945; *b* 21 April 1909; *yr s* of late Major George Hicks, MC, TD, JP, and Elizabeth Young; *m* 1938, Roberta Kirk (*d* 1971), *y d* of late Thomas Boag, Greenock; no *c*. *Educ:* Pannal Ash Coll., Harrogate. 2nd Lieut RA, Territorial Army, 1929; Capt., 1934; Major, 1939; served in War of 1939–45, OC Bute Battery RA; POW (Germany), 1940–45; despatches, 1945; Lieut-Col, 1950. Chm. Buteshire T&AFA, 1950–62; County Cadet Commandant, Bute, 1950–53; DL, JP, Bute, 1949, Vice-Lieut, 1957–75. *Address:* 39 Crichton Road, Rothesay PA20 9JT. *T:* Rothesay 2612. *Died 9 June 1985.*

**HICKS, Ursula Kathleen, (Lady Hicks);** University Lecturer in Public Finance, Oxford, 1947–65; Fellow of Linacre College, since 1965; *b* 17 Feb. 1896; *d* of W. F. and I. M. Webb, Dublin; *m* 1935 Sir John Hicks, FBA. *Educ:* Roedean; Somerville College, Oxford; London Sch. of Economics (Hon. Fellow, 1980). Asst Lecturer, London Sch. of Economics, Oct. 1935 (resigned on marriage); Lecturer in charge of Dept of Economics, Liverpool University, 1941–46; Fiscal Comr, Uganda, 1962, Eastern Caribbean, 1962–63. Hon. Fellow, Inst. of Social Studies, The Hague, 1967; Hon. DSc (Econ.), Belfast, 1966. *Publications:* Finance of British Government, 1920–36, 1938; Taxation of War Wealth, 1941, Standards of Local Expenditure, 1943, The Problem of Valuation for Rating, 1944, and The Incidence of Local Rates, 1945 (with J. R. Hicks); Indian Public Finance, 1952 (UN); Finance and Taxation in Jamaica (with J. R. Hicks), 1955; Public Finance, 1955; British Public Finances, their Structure and Development, 1880–1952, 1954; Development from Below (Local Government and Finance in Developing Countries of the Commonwealth), 1961; Federalism and Economic Growth (with others), 1961; Report of Fiscal Commission Eastern Caribbean (Command Paper No 1991), 1963; Development Finance: Planning and Control, 1965; The Large City: A World Problem, 1974; Federalism, Failure and Success: a comparative study, 1978; Handbuch der Finanz-wissenschaft, 1982; articles in Economic Journal, Economica, Public Administration, etc. *Recreations:* painting, gardening. *Address:* Porch House, Blockley, Glos GL56 9BW. *T:* Blockley 700210. *Died 16 July 1985.*

**HIEGER, Izrael,** DSc (London); Biochemist, Royal Marsden Hospital, 1924–66; *b* Siedletz, Russian-Poland, June 1901; *s* of F. E. Hieger; *m* 1943, Lois Hieger; one *d*. *Educ:* Birkbeck Coll. and University Coll., London. With colleagues, Anna Fuller Memorial Prize for Cancer Research, 1939. *Publications:* One in Six: An Outline of the Cancer Problem, 1955; Carcinogenesis, 1961; papers on the discovery of cancer producing chemical compounds. *Address:* Chester Beatty Research Institute, Royal Marsden Hospital, Fulham Road, SW3. *Died 14 Oct. 1986.*

**HIGGINS, Rev. Canon John Denis P.;** *see* Pearce-Higgins.

**HIGGON, Col Laurence Hugh,** CBE 1958; MC 1916 and Bar 1917; *b* 3 Sept. 1884; 4th (and *o* surv.) *s* of late Capt. J. D. G. Higgon, RA, DL, JP, Scolton, Pembrokeshire; *m* 1922, Neda Kathleen C. (*d* 1987), *er d* of Lieut-Col F. Rennick (killed 1915); two *d*. *Educ:* Cheltenham; RMA, Woolwich. Entered RA 1903; retired, 1927; comd 102nd (Pembroke Yeo.) Bde RA, 1930–35 (Bt Col); Hon. Col 1948; Hon. Comr Toc H in Wales, 1931. Rejoined RA (Lieut-Col), 1939. Home Guard, Pembs (Lieut-Col), 1942–45. DL, JP, Pembrokeshire; JP Haverfordwest. Served European War, 1914–19, France and Flanders (despatches twice, MC and Bar). Chm. Pembroke County War Memorial Hospital 1934–53; Mem. West Wales Hosps Management Cttee, 1948–53; Chm. Standing Joint Cttee, 1949–54; Chm., Pembroke TA Assoc., 1944–47; Lord Lieutenant, Pembrokeshire, 1944–54. OStJ. *Address:* c/o Brig. D. W. H. Birch, CBE, Five Elms Cottage, Woodcutts, Salisbury, Wilts. *Club:* Army and Navy. *Died 5 April 1987.*

**HIGGS, Godfrey Walter,** CBE 1960; Vice-President, Bahamas Senate, 1964–68; *b* 28 Sept. 1907; *yr s* of late Charles Roger Higgs; *m* 1937, Marion Suzanne (marr. diss.), *y d* of Roscoe Hagen, Rochester, NY; three *s*; *m* Eleanor Claire, *y d* of Charles Frederick Beckmann, New York City, USA. *Educ:* Queen's Coll., Taunton. Called to Bahamas Bar, 1929; English Bar, Inner Temple, 1933 (Profumo Prize); Deputy Speaker, House of Assembly, Bahamas, 1937–42; Mem. Executive Council and Leader for the Govt, Bahamas House of Assembly, 1942–45 and 1946–49; Member: Legislative Council, Bahamas, 1950–64; Senate, 1964–68. *Recreations:* yachting,

swimming, golf, shooting, fishing, etc. *Address:* Stanley, PO Box N3247, East Bay Street, Nassau, Bahamas. *Clubs:* Royal Nassau Sailing, Nassau Lawn Tennis. *Died 4 May 1986.*

**HIGGS, Sir John (Walter Yeoman),** KCVO 1986; FSA; Secretary and Keeper of the Records, Duchy of Cornwall, since 1981; *b* 1 Sept. 1923; *s* of Walter Frank Higgs and Cecilia Elizabeth (*née* Yeoman); *m* 1948, Elizabeth Patricia, *d* of Lt-Col H. B. Norcott, Rifle Bde; two *d*. *Educ:* Oundle Sch.; Emmanuel Coll., Cambridge (MA). National Inst. of Agricl Engrg, 1944–46; Agricultural Economics Inst., Univ. of Oxford, 1946–48; Lectr, Faculty of Agric., Univ. of Reading, 1948–57; Keeper, Museum of English Rural Life, 1951–57; Lectr in Agricl Development, Univ. of Oxford, 1957–66; Fellow of Exeter Coll., 1963–73; Finance and Estates Bursar, 1963–68; Sen. Research Fellow, 1969–73; Curator: University Chest, 1963–70; University Theatre, 1963–70. Consultant to UN and FAO and other UN Agencies on rural develt in several countries, 1964–80; Secretary: UN/FAO/ILO World Conf. on Agrarian Reform, 1966; FAO/Unesco/ILO World Conf. on Agricl Educn and Trng, 1970; Chief, Educn and Extension Service, FAO, Rome, 1971–74; Member: Adv. Cttee, Agrarian History of England & Wales, 1956–; Prince of Wales' Council, 1979–; President: British Agricl History Soc., 1974–76; Internat. Assoc. of Agricl Museums, 1974–76; Trustee, Ernest Cook Trust, 1977–. Partner in family farms in Dumfriesshire and Oxfordshire. *Publications:* The Land: a visual history of modern Britain, 1964; ed, People in the Countryside, 1964; ed, Education for Rural Families in Developing Countries, 1977; numerous papers on agricl and rural development in nat. and internat. jls. *Recreations:* fishing, shooting. *Address:* Arkleton, Langholm, Dumfriesshire DG13 0HL. *T:* Ewes 247; 10 Buckingham Gate, SW1. *T:* 01–828 3550. *Clubs:* Brooks's, Farmers'; Leander. *Died 6 June 1986.*

**HIGHTON, Rear-Adm. Jack Kenneth,** CB 1959; CBE 1952; *b* 2 Sept. 1904; *s* of John Henry Highton and Kate (*née* Powers); *m* 1933, Eileen Metcalfe Flack; one *s* two *d*. *Educ:* Bedford Modern Sch. Joined Royal Navy, 1922; Captain 1951; Dir of Welfare and Service Conditions, 1955–57; Rear-Adm. 1957; Chief Staff Officer (Administration) to Commander-in-Chief, Plymouth, 1957–60; retired, 1960. *Recreations:* walking, sailing, gardening. *Address:* c/o National Westminster Bank, Woodbridge, Suffolk.

*Died 17 Feb. 1988.*

**HILDER, Rev. Geoffrey Frank;** Archdeacon of Taunton, 1951–71; Prebendary of Wells Cathedral, 1951–73; Provost of Western Division of Woodard Corporation, 1960–70; *b* 17 July 1906; *s* of Albert Thomas and Lilian Ethel Hilder; *m* 1939, Enid (*d* 1985), *d* of Rev. F. E. Coggin. *Educ:* Uppingham Sch.; Lincoln Coll., Oxford; Inner Temple; Ely Theological Coll. Called to the Bar, 1930. Deacon, 1931; Priest, 1932; Rector of Ruardean, Glos., 1937–41; Vicar of St Stephen's, Cheltenham, 1941–48; Vicar of Hambridge, 1948–59. Prolocutor of Lower House of Convocation of Canterbury, 1955–70; Dir of Ecclesiastical Insurance Office Ltd, 1957–61. *Recreations:* music, gardening. *Address:* 4 Falcon Terrace, Bude, Cornwall EX23 8LJ. *T:* Bude 4532. *Died 6 Feb. 1988.*

**HILDRED, Sir William (Percival),** Kt 1945; CB 1942; OBE 1936; Grand Officer, Order of Orange-Nassau, 1946; Commander Order of Crown of Belgium; MA; Director-General Emeritus International Air Transport Association (Director-General, 1946–66); *b* 13 July 1893; *s* of late William Kirk Hildred; *m* 1920, Constance Mary Chappell, MB, ChB (*d* 1985); two *s* one *d*. *Educ:* Boulevard Sch., Hull; University of Sheffield. Served European War, 1st York and Lancaster Regt, 1914–17; entered Treasury, 1919; Finance Officer, Empire Marketing Board, 1926–34; Head of Special Measures Branch, Ministry of Agriculture and Fisheries, 1934–35; Deputy General Manager, Export Credits Guarantee Dept, 1935–38; Deputy Dir-Gen. of Civil Aviation, Air Ministry, 1938; Principal Asst Sec., Ministry of Aircraft Production, 1940; assisted in formation of RAF Ferry Command, Montreal, 1941; Director-Gen. of Civil Aviation, Ministry of Civil Aviation, 1941–46. Edward Warner Award of ICAO, 1965. Hon. LLD: Sheffield; McGill Univ.; FRSA. Hon. FRAeS. *Recreations:* cycling, music, carpentry. *Address:* Spreakley House, Frensham, Surrey.

*Died 21 Nov. 1986.*

**HILDYARD, Rev. Christopher,** LVO 1966; MA; *b* 28 April 1901; *s* of Lyonel D'Arcy and Dora Hildyard. *Educ:* St George's, Windsor Castle; Repton; Magdalene Coll., Cambridge; Cuddesdon Theological Coll. Curate at Glass Houghton, West Yorks, 1925–27; Curate at Gisborough, North Yorks, 1927–28; Asst Minor Canon, Westminster Abbey, 1928–32; Minor Canon, Westminster Abbey, 1932–73; Chaplain of Westminster Hospital, 1937–58; Custodian, Westminster Abbey, 1945–55; Sacrist, Westminster Abbey, 1958–73, Sacrist Emeritus, 1977. Chairman, Royal Asylum of St Ann's Soc., 1952–76. *Recreation:* painting. *Address:* 2 The Cloisters, Westminster, SW1P 3PA. *T:* 01–222 4982.

*Died 17 May 1987.*

**HILEY, Joseph;** DL; *b* 18 Aug. 1902; *s* of Frank Hiley of Leeds; *m* 1932, Mary Morrison, *d* of Dr William Boyd; three *d. Educ:* West Leeds High Sch.; Leeds Univ., 1920–23. Formerly family business, Hiley Brothers, took over firm of J. B. Battye & Co. Ltd, 1924, Managing Dir 1927–59; Dir, Irish Spinners Ltd, 1952–74. Mem. of Lloyd's, 1966–. MP (C) Pudsey, Oct. 1959–Feb. 1974. Leeds City Councillor, 1930, Alderman, 1949, resigned, 1960; Lord Mayor of Leeds, 1957–58. Past President: Hand-Knitting Assoc.; Leeds Chamber of Commerce; Northorpe Hall Trust. DL West Yorks, 1971. *Recreations:* cricket, theatre. *Address:* Elmaran, Layton Road, Horsforth, Leeds. *T:* Horsforth 584787. *Clubs:* Leeds (Leeds); Pudsey Conservative (Pudsey).                              *Died* 17 *Nov.* 1989.

**HILGENDORF, Sir Charles,** Kt 1981; CMG 1971; JP; farmer; *b* 1908; *s* of Prof. Frederick William Hilgendorf and Frances Elizabeth (*née* Murray); *m* 1936, Rosemary Helen Mackenzie; one *s* one *d. Educ:* Christ's College, Christchurch; Univ. of Canterbury, NZ (MA; Hon. LLD 1978). Held various positions in Federated Farmers of NZ, 1946–61. Member: NZ Meat Producers Board, 1961–80 (Chm., 1972–80); University Grants Cttee (of NZ), 1961–74. *Address:* Sherwood, Ashburton, NZ. *T:* Winchmore 643. *Clubs:* Farmers'; Christchurch, Wellington (both in New Zealand).
                                                               *Died* 17 *Jan.* 1990.

**HILL OF LUTON,** Baron, *cr* 1963 (Life Peer); **Charles Hill,** PC 1955; MA, MD, DPH, LLD; *b* 15 Jan. 1904; *s* of late Charles Hill and Florence M. Cook; *m* 1931, Marion Spencer Wallace; two *s* three *d. Educ:* St Olave's Sch.; Trinity Coll., Cambridge; London Hosp. Formerly: House Physician and Receiving Room Officer, London Hospital; London University Extension Lecturer in Biology; Deputy Medical Supt, Coppice Mental Hospital, Nottingham; Deputy MOH, City of Oxford; Sec., BMA, 1944–50: Pres., World Medical Assoc.; Chm., Central Council for Health Educn; Hon. Sec., Commonwealth Medical Conf. Chm., Chest, Heart and Stroke Assoc., 1974–83 (Vice-Pres., 1983–). MP (L and C) Luton, 1950–63; Parly Sec., Min. of Food, 1951–April 1955; Postmaster-Gen., April 1955–Jan. 1957; Chancellor of the Duchy of Lancaster Jan. 1957–Oct. 1961; Minister of Housing and Local Government and Minister for Welsh Affairs, Oct. 1961–July 1962. Chm., Nat. Jt Council for Local Authorities' Administrative, Professional, Technical and Clerical Services, 1963–78. Chm., Independent Television Authority, 1963–67; Chm. of Governors of the BBC, 1967–72. Chairman: Laporte Industries Ltd, 1965–70; Abbey National Building Soc., 1976–78 (Dir, 1964–78). Hon. Fellow Amer. Medical Assoc. *Publications:* What is Osteopathy? (jointly), 1937; Re-printed Broadcasts, 1941–50; Both Sides of the Hill, 1964; Behind the Screen, 1974. *Recreations:* fishing, walking. *Address:* 9 Borodale, Kirkwick Avenue, Harpenden, Herts AL5 2QW. *T:* Harpenden 64288.                                           *Died* 22 *Aug.* 1989.

**HILL, Rev. Alexander Currie,** CB 1957; Minister Emeritus of Portknockie, Banffshire; Principal Finance Officer, Board of Trade, 1958–64; *b* 23 Jan. 1906; *o s* of late Alexander Hill and Jeanie Currie; unmarried. *Educ:* George Heriot's Sch., Edinburgh; Univ. of Edinburgh; Univ. of Aberdeen (Faculty of Divinity); Christ's Coll., Aberdeen. Entered Administrative Class, Home Civil Service, 1928. Under-Sec., Board of Trade, 1950–58. *Address:* 62a Rubislaw Den North, Aberdeen AB2 4AN. *Club:* Royal Northern (Aberdeen).                                          *Died* 16 *March* 1983.

**HILL, Christopher Pascoe,** CB 1964; CBE 1956; Charity consultant; *b* 6 July 1903; *s* of late Charles Pascoe Grenfell Hill; *m* 1st, 1926, Elizabeth Ridding Oldfield (*d* 1931), *d* of late Lieut-Col H. Oldfield, RMA; one *d*; 2nd, 1934, Joan Elizabeth Smith, *d* of late R. W. Smith; two *s* one *d. Educ:* Merchant Taylors'; St John's Coll., Oxford, Gaisford Prizeman, 1925. Entered Home Office, Asst Principal, 1925; Asst Sec., Ministry of Home Security, 1942; Home Office: Aliens Dept, 1943–47; Children's Dept, 1947–56; Asst Under-Sec. of State, 1957. Attached to Charity Commission, 1956, to prepare Charities Act, 1960; Chief Charity Commissioner, 1960–65; Sec. to Archbishop's Commission on Church and State, 1966–70. Vice Pres., Herts Council of Voluntary Service; Member: Exec. Cttee, Hertfordshire Soc., 1966–79; Standing Conf. on Herts Countryside (Chm., 1967–76); Gen. Adv. Council of BBC; BBC and IBA Central Appeals Adv. Cttees (Chm.), 1969–74; Council, National Trust, 1969–73; Family Welfare Assoc. Inf. Cttee, 1968–78; Legal Bd, Church Assembly, 1966–70; Adv. Council, Christian Orgns Res. and Adv. Trust. Director: WRVS Trustees Ltd, 1966–79; Internat. Standing Conf. on Philanthropy, Geneva. UK correspondent, Foundation News, 1975–. King Haakon VII Liberty Cross, Norway. *Publications:* A Guide for Charity Trustees, 1966, rev. edn 1974; UK section, Trusts and Foundations in Europe, 1972; UK section, Philanthropy in the Seventies, 1973; papers on delinquency and charity subjects in periodicals. *Recreations:* garden, painting, archæology, preserving Herts countryside. *Address:* The Grange, Therfield, Royston, Herts. *T:* Kelshall 358. *Club:* Athenæum.                                          *Died* 22 *April* 1983.

**HILL, Colin de Neufville,** CMG 1961; OBE 1959; Business Manager, University of Sussex, 1964–82; *b* 12 Jan. 1917; *s* of Philip Rowland and Alice May Hill; *m* 1950, Mary Patricia Carson Wilson; two *s. Educ:* Cheltenham Coll.; St Edmund Hall, Oxford. BA. hons in Mod. Langs, Oxford, 1938. Selected for appt to Colonial Service, 1938; Administrative Officer, Colonial Admin. Service, Eastern Nigeria, 1939; served with Provincial and Regional Administration, Eastern Nigeria, 1939–53; transferred to Tanganyika and apptd Sec. for Finance, 1954; Permanent Sec. to the Treasury, Tanganyika Government, 1959–64. *Recreations:* photography, gardening, music. *Address:* Mount Pleasant Farm, Barcombe, near Lewes, East Sussex.                                          *Died* 21 *Jan.* 1989.

**HILL, Sir Denis;** *see* Hill, Sir J. D. N.

**HILL, Douglas William,** CBE 1965; DSc; *b* 3 March 1904; *o s* of Henry and Florence Mary Hill; *m* 1st, 1936, Margaret Eluned (*d* 1956), *y d* of Rev. O. M. Owen; one *s*; 2nd, 1958, Mabel Constance Prothero (*d* 1975), *er d* of James Belford. *Educ:* St George's Sch., Bristol; Univs of Bristol, Liverpool and Illinois, PhD Liverpool, 1926; DSc Bristol, 1936. Research Chemist, Boots Pure Drug Co. Ltd, 1927–30; Commonwealth Fund Fellow, Univ. of Illinois and Rockefeller Inst. for Med. Research, New York, 1930–33; Lectr in Organic Chemistry, UC Exeter and Special Lectr in Biochemistry, Bristol Univ., 1933–37; Asst to Dir, Shirley Inst., 1937–40; Min. of Supply, 1940–43; Combined Production and Resources Board, Washington DC, 1943–44; Dep. Dir, Shirley Inst., 1944–56; Director, 1956–69. Mem. Council RIC, 1948–60 (Chm., Manchester and Dist Sect., 1953–54); Mem. Council, Chemical Soc., 1947–50; Vice-Pres., Parly and Sci. Cttee, 1962–65; Chairman: Cttee of Dirs of Research Assocs, 1960–63; Cttee of Dirs of Textile Research, Assocs, 1964–66; Cttee on Mule Spinners' Cancer; Chm. of Governors, Royal Coll. of Advanced Technology, Salford, 1962–67; Chm. of Council and Pro-Chancellor, Univ. of Salford, 1967–75, Sen. Pro-Chancellor, 1976–82; Member: UGC Cttee on Libraries, 1962–68, Cttee of Management, Science Policy Foundn; Chm., Perkin Centenary Trust; Dir, Shirley Developments Ltd, 1953–74. Chm., Macclesfield Div. Liberal Assoc., 1948–56. Bernard Dyer Memorial Medallist and Lectr, 1962; Mather Lectr, 1970. Hon. DSc Salford, 1969. *Publications:* Insulin: Its Production, Purification and Properties, 1936; Impact and Value of Science, 1944, 2nd edn, 1946; Co-operative Research for Industry, 1946; papers and articles in scientific jls, press and reviews. *Recreations:* sketching, travel, writing and lecturing. *Address:* River Cottage, Cage Lane, Smarden, near Ashford, Kent. *T:* Smarden 588. *Club:* Athenæum.
                                                               *Died* 16 *May* 1985.

**HILL, (Francis) John,** CBE 1976; Hon. DCL UEA, 1982; Hon. FCP 1980; FRSA; County Education Officer for Suffolk, 1973–79 (CEO West Suffolk, 1961–73); Member, Suffolk Area Health Authority, 1979–82; *b* 8 July 1915; *m* Roma Lunn, Stourbridge; one *s. Educ:* King Edward VI Sch., Stourbridge; Univ. of Birmingham (English and Educn); Univ. of Poitiers. Royal Signals, 1940–46, Major (despatches). In Educn Depts of, successively, Wiltshire, Hertfordshire and Cornwall (Deputy Education Officer), prior to appt to West Suffolk. Chairman: Council for Educnl Technology (UK) from inception, 1973–80; Eastern Regional Council for Special Educn, 1976–82; Mem., 1961–, Hon. Member 1980–, Council, Univ. of E Anglia (Chm. Jt Cttee for Academic Staff); Vice-Chm. Governors, Cambridge Inst. of Educn, 1974–80; Trustee, Homerton Coll., Cambridge, 1969– (Vice-Chm., 1980–); Mem. Council and Chm. Educn Cttee, RNIB, 1966–; UK deleg. to World Conf. on Educn of Blind Youth, Boston, USA, 1967; Vice-Chm. Trustees, Central Bureau for Educnl Visits and Exchanges, 1965–77; (first) Chm., UK/USA Schs Exchange Scheme; Member, E-SU Schols Cttee; UK Rep., Commonwealth Educn Conf., Wellington, NZ, 1977; Member Govt Cttees on: Sch. Transport, Educnl Technology, Speech Therapy Sces in Medicine and Educn, Recreation Management Trng; adv. visits to USA (3), Dublin, Gibraltar, France, Austria, Scandinavia. Member: Sports Council for UK, 1975–82 (Chm. Nat. Centres Cttee, Vice-Chm. Finance Cttee); Chairman: Eastern Council for Sport and Recreation, 1965– (Chm., Finance and Grants Cttee, 1976–79; Chm., 1979–82); Governor, Sports Aid Foundn (UK), 1981–; (first) Chm., Sports Aid Foundn (East), 1980–. Hon. Mem., CCPR. Cert. Exceptional Sce to Anglo-Amer. relations, 1975. *Recreations:* most sports, gardening, countryside, imposing democratic solutions. *Address:* Willowfield, Old Newton, Stowmarket, Suffolk. *T:* Stowmarket 673525.                                          *Died* 21 *Oct.* 1984.

**HILL, Sir George (Alfred) Rowley,** 9th Bt *cr* 1779; retired; *b* 11 Oct. 1899; *s* of Alfred Rowley Hill (*d* 1946) (brother of 7th Bt) and Jean (*d* 1943), *d* of J. Cunninghame; *S* cousin, 1980; *m* 1st, 1924, Rose Ethel Kathleen Spratt, MBE (marr. diss. 1938); one *s*; 2nd, 1938; one *s* one *d. Educ:* Melville Coll., Edinburgh. Indian Railways, 1919–37; retired, ill health. Served RNVR, 1915–Jan. 1919, and 1940–45. War Ribbons, 1914–18 and 1939–45, inc. Atlantic Star. *Recreations:* Rugby, golf, shooting, tennis. *Heir:* *s* Richard George Rowley Hill, MBE, Major KOSB, retired [*b* 18 Dec. 1925; *m* 1st, 1954, Angela Mary (*d* 1974), *o d* of Lt-Col Stanley Herbert Gallon, TD; 2nd, 1975, Zoreen Joy, *o d* of late N. Warburton Tippett and

*widow* of Lieut Andrew Marshall, KOSB; two *d*]. *Address:* c/o Barclays Bank, Berwick-upon-Tweed TD15 1AF.
*Died 29 Nov. 1985.*

**HILL, Harold G.;** *see* Gardiner-Hill.

**HILL, Sir Ian (George Wilson),** Kt 1966; CBE 1945; TD; LLD; FRSE; MB; FRCPE; FRCP; Hon. Physician to HM The Queen in Scotland, 1956–70; Professor of Medicine, University of Dundee (formerly University of St Andrews), 1950–69, later Professor Emeritus; *b* 7 Sept. 1904; *s* of late A. W. Hill, JP, and of Mrs J. M. Hill, Edinburgh; *m* 1st, 1933, Audrey (*d* 1966), 2nd *d* of late G. W. Lavender, Stoke-on-Trent; one *s* one *d*; 2nd, 1968, Anna, *o d* of late M. W. Hill. *Educ.:* George Watson's Coll., Edinburgh; Universities of Edinburgh, Michigan and Vienna. MB, ChB (Hons), Edinburgh, 1928; FRCPE 1933; FRCP 1956; Ettles Scholar, Allan Fellow, Shaw-Macfie-Lang Fellow, etc, Univ. of Edinburgh; Rockefeller Travelling Fellow, 1932–33; Lecturer in Medicine, University of Aberdeen, 1933–37; Lectr in Therapeutics, University of Edinburgh, 1937–49; Asst Physician, Edinburgh Royal Infirmary, 1938–50; Physician, Deaconess Hosp., Edinburgh, 1946–50. Served War of 1939–45, Officer i/c Med. Div., Mil. Hosps in UK, MEF and India, 1939–44; Consulting Physician (Brig.), XIVth Army, Burma and ALFSEA, 1944–45; Col, RAMC (TARO) retd; Hon. Col 2nd Scottish Gen. Hosp., 1947–58; Examr in Med., Univs Edinburgh, Glasgow, Birmingham, E Africa, Leeds, Singapore, Hong Kong; Vis. Prof. of Medicine: McGill Univ., 1967; Univ. of Teheran, 1970–71; Vis. Consultant in Medicine, Hong Kong, Malaya, Borneo, etc, 1956 and 1961; Hon. Consulting Physician, Scottish Comd (Army), 1965–70. Dean, Med. Faculty, Haile Selassie I Univ., Ethiopia, 1971–73. Lectures: Gibson RCPE, 1949; Patel, Bombay, 1961; Walker, RCP and S Glasgow, 1962; Centennial, Univ. of Illinois, 1967; Carey Coombs, Univ. of Bristol, 1968; Wilson Meml, Univ. of Michigan, 1968. Former Senior Pres. Royal Medical Soc., Edinburgh; Pres., RCPE, 1963–66; Hon. Member: British Cardiac Soc. (Chm. 1962); Assoc. of Physicians of Great Britain and Ireland (Pres. 1962); Scottish Soc. of Physicians (Pres., 1967). Hon. Member: Cardiac and Endocrinological Socs of India; Cardiac Soc. of Hong Kong; Acad. Med., Singapore, 1966; Cardiological Soc., Columbia, 1968. Hon. FRACP 1966; Hon. FACP 1967. Hon. LLD Dundee, 1970. *Publications:* various contribs to scientific and medical books and journals, principally on cardiology. *Address:* Prior's Croft, 14 Nethergate, Crail KY10 3TY. *Club:* Crail Golfing Society.
*Died 5 May 1982.*

**HILL, John;** *see* Hill, F. J.

**HILL, Sir (John) Denis (Nelson),** Kt 1966; MB, BS; FRCP; FRCPsych; DPM; Professor of Psychiatry, University of London at the Institute of Psychiatry, 1966–79, later Emeritus; *b* 5 Oct. 1913; *s* of late Lieut-Col John Arthur Hill, Orleton Manor, near Ludlow; *m* 1st, 1938, Phoebe Elizabeth Herschel, *o d* of Lieut-Col H. H. Wade; one *s* one *d*; 2nd, 1962, Lorna, *d* of J. F. Wheelan; one *s* one *d*. *Educ.:* Shrewsbury Sch.; St Thomas' Hosp., London. Chief Asst, Dept Psychol Medicine, St Thomas' Hosp., 1938–44; Psychiatric Specialist, Emergency Medical Service, 1939–46; Physician and Lecturer in Psychological Medicine, King's Coll. Hosp., London, 1947–60; Senior Lecturer, Institute of Psychiatry, Maudsley Hosp., London, 1948–60; Hon. Physician, Maudsley Hosp., 1948–60; Prof. of Psychiatry, Middlesex Hosp. Medical Sch., London, 1961–66. Member: MRC, 1956–60; GMC, 1961– (Crown Representative, 1961–79); Mem., Central Health Service Council, 1961–67; Pres. Psychiatry Sect., RSM, 1964–65. Chm., Medical Sickness and Life Assurance Soc., 1981–. Lectures: Adolf Meyer, APA, 1968; Herman Goldman, NY Med. Coll., 1968; Vickers, MHRF, 1972; Maudsley, RCPsych, 1972. Rock Carling Fellow, 1969. *Publications:* Editor: Electro-encephalography: a symposium, 1950; contrib to textbooks on medical subjects and to scientific journals. *Address:* 71 Cottenham Park Road, Wimbledon, SW20; Orleton Manor, near Ludlow, Salop. *Club:* Athenæum.
*Died 5 May 1982.*

**HILL, Norman Hammond,** MD (London), MRCP; Consulting Physician: Belgrave Hospital for Children; Metropolitan and Wembley Hospitals; *b* 10 March 1893; *s* of Lewis Gordon Hill and Amy Caroline Hammond; *m* 1938, Suzanne Mary, *y d* of Rev. H. S. Rees, Christchurch, Mon. *Educ.:* Bradford Grammar Sch.; St Bartholomew's Hosp. MRCS, LRCP 1915. Served in Army, 1915–19, Capt. RAMC (TF); held appointment of House Surgeon, Chief Asst to a Medical Unit, and Casualty Physician St Bartholomew's Hosp. and House Physician and Senior Resident Medical Officer Metropolitan Hosp. *Publications:* articles on medical subjects to Lancet, British Medical Journal, Clinical Journal, and Medical Press and Circular. *Recreations:* golf, photography. *Address:* 22 Acacia Road, NW8. *T:* 01–722 7466.
*Died 6 Jan. 1984.*

**HILL, Sir Robert E.;** *see* Erskine-Hill.

**HILL, Victor Archibald Lord,** MA; *b* 3 July 1905; *o s* of W. E. Hill; *m* 1938, Jean Melicent, *e d* of Dr D. N. Seth-Smith, Bournemouth; two *s*. *Educ.:* Chigwell Sch.; Queen Mary Coll., London (Open Exhibr; University Schol. in Classics; 1st cl. Hons BA); Hertford Coll., Oxford (Open Schol., 1st Cl. Hon. Mods, 3rd Cl. Lit. Hum.). MA (Oxon) 1934. Asst Master, Shrewsbury Sch., 1930–40, 1946–48; Headmaster, Allhallows Sch., 1948–65; Asst Master: Blundell's, 1965–66; Uppingham, 1966–67, 1968–69; Chigwell, 1969–70; Lectr in Classics, Exeter Univ., 1967–68. Served 1940–45, with KSLI and RA (Major). *Recreation:* music. *Address:* Beggars' Roost, Morchard Bishop, near Crediton, Devon. *T:* Morchard Bishop 315.
*Died 12 Feb. 1988.*

**HILLIARD, Christopher Richard; His Honour Judge Hilliard;** a Circuit Judge, since 1980; *b* 12 June 1930; *s* of late Dr Francis Maybury Hilliard and Mrs Gwen Hilliard; *m* 1955, Anne Margaret, *o d* of late Mr and Mrs Mark Maber; one *s* one *d*. *Educ.:* RN Colls, Dartmouth and Greenwich. Served RN, 1947–61: Lieut 1952, Lt-Comdr 1960; retd 1961. Called to the Bar, Middle Temple, 1959; admitted to Cyprus Bar, 1960; practised at the Bar, South Eastern Circuit, 1962–80. A Regular Judge, Central Criminal Court, 1984–. Freeman, Worshipful Co. of Wax Chandlers, 1984. *Recreations:* reading, heraldry, keeping Jacob's sheep. *Address:* Central Criminal Court, Old Bailey, EC4M 7EH. *T:* 01–583 0410. *Clubs:* National, Naval and Military.
*Died 4 Dec. 1985.*

**HILLIER, Arthur,** OBE 1947; retired as Chairman and Managing Director, Sperry Gyroscope Co. Ltd (1938–59); Chairman: Industrial Products (Speco) Ltd, 1949–59; New Holland Machine Co. Ltd, 1954–59; *b* 2 Dec. 1895; *s* of Thomas Hillier and Ann Hillier (*née* Holland); *m* 1st, 1919, Rita Mary (*d* 1955), *d* of John Wakeley; two *d*; 2nd, 1956, Margaret Howard. *Educ.:* Judd Sch., Tonbridge, Kent. Joined Sperry Gyroscope Co. Ltd as Asst Sec., 1916; Sec., 1920; Dir, 1922; Dir and Gen. Manager, 1933; Man. Dir, 1934. Freeman of City of London, 1930; Freeman and Liveryman of: Needlemakers' Company, 1930; Shipwrights' Company, 1951. FCIS 1937; FIN 1953 (was Founder Mem.); JP Middlesex, 1951; High Sheriff County of Middlesex, 1956–57. Comdr, Order of Orange Nassau (Netherlands), 1950; Officer, Legion of Honour (France), 1952; Commendatore, Order of Merit (Italy), 1955. *Recreation:* ancient history. *Address:* Cranmore, Little Forest Road, Bournemouth, Dorset. *T:* Bournemouth 765532. *Clubs:* Royal Automobile, City Livery.
*Died 7 June 1986.*

**HILLIER, Sir Harold (George),** Kt 1983; CBE 1971; President, Hillier Nurseries (Winchester) Ltd, Nurserymen and Seedsmen to the Queen and to the Queen Mother; horticulturalist; *b* 2 Jan. 1905; *s* of Edwin Lawrence and Ethel Marian Hillier; *m* 1934, Barbara Mary Trant; two *s* two *d*. *Educ.:* Peter Symonds Sch., Winchester; King Edward's Grammar Sch., Southampton. Joined Hillier Nurseries, 1922. Gave own arboretum, regarded as one of most complete collections of woody plants hardy in temperate regions, to Hampshire CC; has given plants to leading hardy plant collections in UK, incl. Ventnor Botanic Garden, IoW. FLS; Hon. FRHS 1972 (Mem. Council, 1953–74; a Vice-Pres., 1974–); Hon. Fellow, Japanese Horticultural Soc., 1976. VMH 1957; Veitch Memorial Medal in Gold, 1962; Massachusetts Horticultural Society's Thomas Roland Medal, 1965. *Recreation:* making an arboretum. *Address:* Jermyns House, Ampfield, Romsey, Hants SO5 0QA. *T:* Braishfield 68212.
*Died 8 Jan. 1985.*

**HILLIER, Tristram Paul,** RA 1967 (ARA 1957); painter and writer; *b* 11 April 1905; *s* of Edward Guy Hillier, CMG, and Ada Everett; *m* 1st, 1931, Irene Rose Hodgkins (marr. diss. 1935); two *s*; 2nd, 1937, Leda Millicent Hardcastle; two *d*. *Educ.:* Downside; Christ's Coll., Cambridge. Studied at Slade Sch. and under André Lhôte, Paris. Has held nine one-man exhibitions in London at Lefevre Gall. (3) and Tooth's Gall. (7); other exhibitions: retrospective, Worthing Art Gall., 1960; Galerie Barreiro, Paris; Langton Gall., London, 1974; Pieter Wenning Gall., Johannesburg, 1975; Rep. by official purchases of pictures in following public collections: Tate Gall.; National Galleries of Canada, NSW, and Victoria; Ferens Art Gall., Hull; Contemporary Art Soc.; City Art Galleries: Manchester, Aberdeen, Leeds, Southampton, Nottingham, Belfast, Exeter; Art Galleries of Toronto, Brisbane, Rochdale, Oldham, Kettering; Min. of Works (for Brit. Embassies Fund); Harris Musuem, Preston; Chantrey Bequest; Norton Simon Museum, USA. Served as Lieut RNVR, 1940–45. *Publication:* Leda and the Goose (autobiography), 1954. *Recreations:* riding, walking, swimming. *Address:* c/o Alex Reid & Lefevre, Lefevre Gallery, 30 Bruton Street, W1X 8JD. *T:* 01–629 2250; Yew Tree Cottage, East Pennard, Shepton Mallet, Somerset. *T:* Ditcheat 284.
*Died 18 Jan. 1983.*

**HILLINGDON, 5th Baron** *cr* 1886; **Patrick Charles Mills;** Bt 1868; MC 1945; TD; retired; *b* 4 Nov. 1906; *s* of Comdr the Hon. Geoffrey Mills, RNVR (*d* 1917) (6th *s* of 1st Baron) and Grace Victoria (*née* Boddam) (*d* 1951); *S* cousin, 1978; *m* 1st, 1931, Nancy Elizabeth Nixon (marr. diss. 1939); two *d*; 2nd, 1945, Mary Miriam (*d* 1976), *d* of W. Hoare-Ward. *Educ:* Lancing; St Catharine's Coll., Cambridge. Member, London Stock Exchange, 1934–76; Partner: Marks Bulteel Mills & Co., 1937–63; Greener Dreyfus & Co., 1963–68; Cohen De Smitt Greener Dreyfus, 1968–76. Served Kent Yeomanry, 1936–58; War of 1939–45 with BEF in France, 1939–40; Middle East, 1941–43; Italy, 1944–45; Lt-Col i/c, 1955–58; Bt Col, 1958. *Recreation:* golf. *Heir:* none. *Address:* The Tod House, Seal, Kent. *T:* Sevenoaks 61819. *Clubs:* Knole Park Golf, Rye Golf, Woking Golf, Royal N Devon Golf.

*Died 1 Sept. 1982 (ext).*

**HILLS, Edwin Sherbon,** CBE 1971; FRS 1954; FAA; Professor of Geology, 1944–64, Research Professor, 1964–71, subseq. Hon. Professor and Professor Emeritus, University of Melbourne; *b* Melbourne, 31 Aug. 1906; *s* of Edwin S. Hills, Melbourne; *m* 1932, Claire D. Fox; two *s* one *d*. *Educ:* Univs of Melbourne and London. DSc Melbourne; PhD London; FIC; DSc (Hon.) Dunelm; Hon. FGS (Bigsby Medallist, 1951); David Syme Prize for Scientific Research (Melbourne), 1939. Dep. Vice-Chancellor, Univ. of Melbourne, 1962–71. Fellow, Imperial Coll. of Science and Technology, London, 1967; Hon. Fellow Aust. Inst. of Geographers. Inaugural W. R. Browne Medal, Geol. Soc. Australia, 1979. *Publications:* Outlines of Structural Geology, 1940, new edn 1953; Physiography of Victoria, 1941, new edn 1975; Elements of Structural Geology, 1963, new edn 1971; (ed) Arid Lands: a Geographical Appraisal, 1966. *Address:* 25 Barry Street, Kew, Victoria 3101, Australia. *T:* 862.2079. *Died 1 May 1986.*

**HILLS, Lawrence Donegan;** President, Henry Doubleday Research Association, since 1986; *b* 2 July 1911; *s* of William Donegan and Mabel Annie Hills; *m* 1964, Mrs Hilda Cherry Brooke (*née* Fea) (*d* 1989). *Educ:* at home, owing to ill health. Took up horticulture on medical advice in 1927 and worked for many leading nurseries until 1940. Served War of 1939–45, RAF. Wrote first book, Miniature Alpine Gardening, in hospitals before invalided out on D-Day. Founded Henry Doubleday Research Assoc., 1954, and Pres. of this leading internat. body of gardeners and farmers without chemicals, 1954–86. Gardening Correspondent: Observer, 1958–66; Punch, 1966–70; Countryman, 1970; Garden News, 1981–90; Associate Editor, Ecologist, 1973; Contributing Editor, Organic Gardening, 1988–. Hon. DSc Coventry Poly., 1990. *Publications:* Miniature Alpine Gardening, 1944; Rapid Tomato Ripening, 1946; Propagation of Alpines, 1950; Alpines Without A Garden, 1953; Russian Comfrey, 1953; Alpine Gardening, 1955; Down To Earth Fruit and Vegetable Growing, 1960; Down to Earth Gardening, 1967; Lands of the Morning (Archaeology), 1970; Grow Your Own Fruit and Vegetables, 1971; Comfrey—Its Past, Present and Future, 1976; Organic Gardening, 1977; Fertility Gardening, 1981; Month by Month Organic Gardening, 1983; Fighting Like the Flowers (autobiog.), 1989; The Good Potato Guide, 1990. *Recreations:* reading, thinking, non-gardening writing, classical music. *Address:* Henry Doubleday Research Association, Ryton-on-Dunsmore, Coventry, Warwicks CV8 3ES. *Died 20 Sept. 1990.*

**HILTON, Sir Derek (Percy),** Kt 1966; MBE 1945; *b* 11 April 1908; *o c* of Percy Hilton and Mary Beatrice Hilton (*née* Stott); *m* 1945, Joanna Stott, *er d* of late Sir Arnold Stott, KBE; three *d*. *Educ:* Rugby Sch.; Trinity Hall, Cambridge. Solicitor, 1932; subsequently private practice in Manchester. War of 1939–45, Manchester Regt; seconded to special operations executive, 1941. Mem. Council, Law Soc., 1951; Hon. Sec., Manchester Law Soc., 1950–59; Pres., Manchester Law Soc., 1957; Pres. of the Law Soc., 1965–66. Dir, Abbey National Building Soc., 1966–81; Chm., Lancashire & Yorkshire Revisionary Interest Co. Ltd, 1956–77; Pres., Immigration Appeal Tribunal, 1970–78. Norwegian Liberty Cross, 1945. *Recreations:* gardening, walking, fishing. *Address:* Eaves, Chapel-en-le-Frith, Stockport, Cheshire SK12 6UA. *T:* Chapel-en-le-Frith 812241. *Club:* Special Forces. *Died 10 April 1986.*

**HIM, George,** PhD (Bonn); RDI; FSTD; AGI; designer (freelance) and design consultant; Design Consultant to El Al Israel Airlines, 1952–78; Senior Lecturer, Leicester Polytechnic, 1976–78; *b* 4 Aug. 1900; *m* Shirley Elizabeth (*née* Rhodes). *Educ:* Warsaw, Moscow, Bonn, Leipzig. In practice, first in Germany, then in Poland, from 1928; in London, since 1937. Field of work: book illustration, TV graphics, toys, publicity design; designed Festival Clock in Battersea Park, 1951; *exhibitions:* The Observer Masada Exhibition, 1966; Masada Exhibition, New York, Chicago, Washington, etc, 1967–69, other European cities, 1970–72; retrospective, London Coll. of Printing, 1976; Ben Uri Gall., 1978; Ben Uri Gall. (Him Ancient and Modern), 1981. Chief Designer of Israel Pavilion, Expo 67, Montreal; designed covers for The New Middle East (monthly). Discoverer of the "County of Schweppshire" (with Stephen Potter) 1951–64. Work for TV. *Publications:* Israel, the Story of a Nation, 1957; illustrations to Zuleika Dobson, 1960; Plays for Puritans, 1966; Don Quixote, 1980; For Jerusalem and All Her People, 1981; *children's books:* Locomotive, 1937, The Little Red Engine, 1942 (with J. Le Witt); Squawky (with S. Potter), 1964; Folk Tales (with Leila Berg), 1966; Giant Alexander books (with F. Herrmann),

1964, 1966, 1971, 1972, 1975; Little Nippers (ed by Leila Berg), 1973, 1974; The Day with the Duke (with Ann Thwaite), 1969; Ann and Ben, 1974; The Adventures of King Midas (with Lynn Reid-Banks), 1976; King Wilbur books (with Jim Rogerson), 1976. *Recreation:* work. *Address:* 37B Greville Road, NW6 5JB. *T:* 01–624 6663. *Died 4 April 1982.*

**HIMMELWEIT, Prof. Hildegard Therese, (Hilde);** Professor of Social Psychology, London School of Economics, University of London, 1964–83, Emeritus Professor 1983; *b* Berlin, 20 Feb. 1918; *d* of S. Litthauer and Feodore Litthauer (*née* Remak); *m* 1940, Prof. F. Himmelweit (*d* 1977), MD, FRCPEd; one *d*. *Educ:* Berlin; Hayes Court, Kent; Newnham Coll., Cambridge. Degrees in Mod. Langs and Psych.; qual. Educational and Clinical Psychologist, 1943; PhD London 1945; Clin. Psychologist, Maudsley Hosp., 1945–48; joined LSE, 1949; Reader in Social Psychology, 1954. Dir Nuffield Television Enquiry, 1954–58; Visiting Professor: Univ. of Calif, Berkeley, 1959; Hebrew Univ., Jerusalem, 1974; Stanford Univ., Calif, 1975; Fellowship to Centre for Advanced Study of Behavioral Sciences, Stanford, Calif, 1967 and 1983; Fellow, Van Leer Foundn, Jerusalem, 1978–79; Chm., Academic Adv. Cttee of Open Univ., 1969–74; FBPsS 1952; Member: Council, Brit. Psycholog. Soc., 1961–64; Editorial Bds, Brit. Jl of Soc. and Clin. Psychology, 1962–86, Jl Communications Research, 1972–86. Interdisciplinary Science Reviews, 1976–, Jl of Communication, 1978–, Applied Social Psychology Annual, 1982–, Media, Culture and Society, 1983–; Research Bd, Inst. of Jewish Affairs, 1970–; US SSRC Cttee on TV and Social Behaviour, 1973–79; Annan Cttee on Future of Broadcasting, 1974–77; Adviser, House of Commons Select Cttee on ITA, 1972; Trustee: Internat. Broadcasting Inst., 1974–79; Centre for Contemporary Studies, 1980–; Vice-Pres., Internat. Soc. of Political Psychology, 1978–81 (Nevitt Sanford Award, 1981). Hon. Dr Open Univ., 1976. *Publications:* Television and the Child, 1958; How Voters Decide, 1981, rev. edn 1985; articles and chapters on: rôle, structure and effects of broadcasting; attitude development and change; socialization, rôle of school and other instns; societal influences on outlook and behaviour; political attitudes and their change; voting behaviour. *Address:* London School of Economics, Houghton Street, WC2. *T:* 01–405 7686.

*Died 15 March 1989.*

**HINCHEY, Herbert John,** CMG 1966; CBE 1955; Financial Adviser to Prime Minister of Mauritius, 1967–72; *b* 13 Feb. 1908; *s* of late Edward and late Mary A. Hinchey, Sydney, NSW; *m* 1944, Amy E., *d* of late William and late Caroline Beddows, Vuni Vasa Estate, Taveuni, Fiji; no *c*. *Educ:* Sydney Grammar Sch.; University of Sydney; London Sch. of Economics. Bank of New South Wales, Sydney and Brisbane, 1932–40; Colonial Administrative Service, later HMOCS, 1940–65; Financial Secretary: Western Pacific High Commn, 1948–52; Govt of Mauritius, 1952–57; E Africa High Commn/Common Services Organization, 1957–65. Sometime Member: Mauritius Legislative Coun.; E African Central Legislative Assembly; Chairman: E African Industrial Coun.; E African Industrial Research Bd; E African Currency Bd, E African Airways Bd, etc. *Recreations:* reading, writing, walking. *Address:* 59 Stradbroke Court, 98 Bayview Street, Runaway Bay, Qld 4216, Australia. *Club:* Corona. *Died 4 Aug. 1988.*

**HINDE, Maj.-Gen. (Hon.) Sir (William) Robert (Norris),** KBE 1956 (CBE 1948); CB 1955; DSO 1940 (and 2 Bars); *b* 25 June 1900; *s* of late Major H. Hinde, Fordlands, Northam, N Devon; *m* 1926, Evelyn Muriel Wright (*d* 1980), *d* of late Capt. H. FitzHerbert Wright, Yeldersley Hall, Derby; one *s* three *d*. *Educ:* Wellington Coll.; RMC Sandhurst. 2nd Lieut 15th Hussars, 1919; served War of 1939–45: France, Belgium, 1939–40; Lt-Col 1940; Col 1944; comd 15/19th Hussars, 1940–42; comd 22nd Armd Bde, Libya, Italy, Normandy, 1943–44; Dep. Mil. Governor, Brit. Sector, Berlin, 1945–48; Dep. Comr, Land Niedersachsen, Hanover, 1949–51; Dist Comd, Cyrenaica, 1952–53; Maj.-Gen. 1957; Dir of Operations, Kenya, 1953–56; retd 1957. ADC 1950–56. Col 15th/19th Hussars, 1957–64. *Address:* Shrewton House, Shrewton, Salisbury, Wilts. *T:* Shrewton 233. *Died 13 July 1981.*

**HINDERKS, Prof. Hermann Ernst,** MA, DrPhil; Professor of German in the Queen's University, Belfast, 1954–70; *b* 19 Dec. 1907; *s* of Elrikus Hinderks and Alma Charlotte Jane (*née* Hildebrand); *m* 1935, Ingeborg (*née* Victor); three *d*. *Educ:* Lichtwark Schule, Hamburg; Univs of Hamburg, Freiburg i.Br and Basle (MA, DrPhil 1938). Teacher St George's Cathedral Grammar Sch., Capetown, 1935–37; Head of German Dept, Rhodes University Coll., Grahamstown, S Africa, 1938–39; Lecturer in German, University of Cape Town, 1939–53. *Publications:* Friedrich Nietzsche, ein Menschenleben und seine Philosophie (with H. A. Reyburn and J. G. Taylor), 1st edn 1946, 2nd edn 1947 (Eng. version, Nietzsche, The Story of a Human Philosopher, 1948). Uber die Gegenstandsbegriffe in der Kritik der reinen Vernunft, 1948. *Recreations:* music and walking. *Address:* 8821 Gnotzheim, Spielberg 28, Mittelfranken, W Germany.

**HINDLEY, Henry Oliver Rait;** b 19 June 1906; 3rd s of late Sir Clement Hindley; unmarried. *Educ:* Oundle; Trinity Coll., Cambridge; Dundee School of Economics. Industrial Consultant, 1936–40; Treasury, 1940; Air Min., 1940–45; Dir-Gen., Brit. Air Commission, later British Supply Office, USA, 1945–46; Chairman: Northern Divisional Board of National Coal Board, Sept. 1946–47; Raw Cotton Commission, 1947–51. Canadian Civil Servant, 1961; Sec., Adv. Cttee on Broadcasting, 1965; Asst Under-Sec. of State, 1965–69; Dept of Communications, 1969–75. Sec., Cttee on Telecommunications and Canadian Sovereignty, 1979. *Address:* 200 Rideau Terrace 1114, Ottawa, Ontario, K1M 0Z3, Canada.
*Died 30 Aug.* 1988.

**HINES, Gerald;** *see* Hines, V. G.

**HINES, Robert Henry;** Metropolitan Stipendiary Magistrate, since 1976; b 14 Feb. 1931; s of late Harry Hines and Josephine Hines; m 1957, Shelagh Mary, d of Mathew McKernan; four s. *Educ:* St Edmund's Coll., Ware, Herts. Commnd Army, National Service, 1949–51. Called to the Bar, Lincoln's Inn, 1954; practised at Bar; joined Magistrates' Court's Service, Inner London, 1958; Chief Clerk, Bow Street Magistrates' Court, 1964–76. *Recreation:* music. *Address:* 39 Mount Park Crescent, W5 2RR. *T:* 01–997 2911.
*Died 26 March* 1982.

**HINES, His Honour (Vivian) Gerald,** QC 1964; a Circuit Judge, 1972–79, retired (Chairman, North East London Quarter Sessions, 1965–68, Greater London Quarter Sessions (Middlesex Area), 1969, Greater London Quarter Sessions (Inner London), 1969–71); b 24 Dec. 1912; 2nd s of late John Hines and Lizzie Emily (née Daniells), Essex; m 1st, 1950, Janet Graham, MA (d 1957), e d of late John Graham, Wigtownshire; 2nd, 1960, Barbara, y d of late Herbert Gunton, Colchester. *Educ:* Earls Colne Grammar Sch. Admitted Solicitor, 1935; private practice, 1935–42; Clerk to Colchester Borough Justices, 1942; called to Bar, Inner Temple, 1943; South-Eastern Circuit. Dep. Chairman: Essex QS, 1955–67; County of London QS, 1965; Judge of the Central Criminal Court, 1968–69. Mem., Home Office Adv. Council on the Penal System, 1970–. Member: Council, Magistrates' Assoc., 1967–70; Standing Joint Cttee, Essex, 1962–65. Governor, New Coll., London, 1963–65; Member: Court of Essex Univ., 1966–; Council of Boy Scouts' Assoc., 1961–66; Essex CC, 1946–49. JP Essex, 1955, Greater London, 1965–79. Freeman, City of London, 1975. Liveryman, Fan Makers' Co., 1976. *Publications:* Judicial Discretion in Sentencing, 1982; contrib. to Halsbury's Laws of England, 4th edn (Criminal Law Vol.); articles in British Jl of Criminology, The Magistrate, Reform and other jls. *Address:* 19 Cambridge Road, Colchester, Essex CO3 3NS. *T:* Colchester 576773.     *Died 5 April* 1987.

**HINGLEY, Anthony Capper Moore,** CVO 1954; b 28 Nov. 1908; e s of late Lieut-Col S. H. Hingley and Dorothy, d of Thomas Capper; m 1947, Ruth, d of late C. P. Andrews; two s one d. *Educ:* Rugby Sch.; Trinity Coll., Oxford (MA). Ceylon Civil Service, 1931–47; Asst Establishment Officer, Kenya, 1947–49; Chief Establishment Officer, Nyasaland, 1949–50; Sec. to Governor-Gen., Ceylon, 1950–54; Chief Establishment Officer, Nyasaland, 1954–60; seconded as Mem., Interim Federal Public Service Commn, Fedn of Rhodesia and Nyasaland, 1955–59; Establishments Adviser, Seychelles, 1965. *Recreations:* golf, bridge. *Address:* Jesters', Queen Square, North Curry, Taunton, Som. *Clubs:* East India, Devonshire, Sports and Public Schools; Somerset County.
*Died 22 July* 1983.

**HINKSON, Pamela;** novelist, journalist, writer of travel books and children's books; o d of late H. A. Hinkson, author, Resident Magistrate, Ireland, and late Katharine Tynan Hinkson, poet and prose writer. *Educ:* privately, and by living in France and Germany. During War, 1939–45: worked for Ministry of Information; mem. of Cttee of Shamrock (Irish Service) Club in London; lectured in USA for British Information Service, on India, 1944. Lecture Tours to HM Forces overseas, 1946 and 1947. Lecture Tour to German audiences, Germany, 1947. *Publications:* include: Wind from the West, 1930; The Ladies' Road, 1932; The Deeply Rooted, 1935; Seventy Years Young (collaboration with Elizabeth, Countess of Fingall), 1937; Irish Gold, 1940; Indian Harvest, 1941; Golden Rose, 1944; The Lonely Bride, 1951; contributor to The Fortnightly, Cornhill, Spectator, New Statesman, Time and Tide, Observer, Sunday Times, Guardian, Country Life, etc. *Recreations:* friendship (with adults and children), country life, animals. *Address:* c/o Lloyds Bank, 112 Kensington High Street, W8.
*Died 26 May* 1982.

**HINSLEY, Prof. Frederick Baden,** DSc; FEng; Professor of Mining and Head of Department of Mining Engineering, University of Nottingham, 1947–67, later Emeritus; b 20 May 1900; m 1932, Doris Lucy Spencer; three s two d. *Educ:* Coalville Technical Coll.; University of Birmingham. Lecturer and Vice-Principal, County Technical Coll., Worksop, 1932–39; Lecturer in Dept of Mining, University Coll., Cardiff, 1939–47. Pres. IMinE, 1968. Silver medal, Warwicks and S Staffs Inst. of Mining Engineers, 1940; Gold medal,

South Wales Inst. of Engineers, 1946; Silver medal, Midland Counties Instn of Engineers, 1951; Douglas Hay medal, 1955, Institution Medal, 1971, Instn of Mining Engineers; Van Waterschoot Van der Gracht medal, Royal Geol. and Mining Soc. of the Netherlands, 1962. *Publications:* contribs to: Proc. S Wales Inst. of Engineers; Proc. Nat. Assoc. of Colliery Managers; Trans Instn of Mining Engineers. *Recreations:* writing history of mining, gardening, reading. *Address:* 7 Puller Road, Boxmoor, Hemel Hempstead, Herts HP1 1QL. *T:* Hemel Hempstead 62011.
*Died 7 Feb.* 1988.

**HINTON OF BANKSIDE,** Baron cr 1965 (Life Peer); **Christopher Hinton,** OM 1976; KBE 1957; Kt 1951; FRS 1954; MA; FEng; Hon. FICE; Hon. FIMechE; Hon. FIEE; FIChemE; FRSA; b 12 May 1901; s of late Frederick Henry Hinton, Lacock, Wilts; m 1931, Lillian (d 1973), d of late Thomas Boyer; one d. *Educ:* Chippenham Grammar Sch.; Trinity Coll., Cambridge. Engineering apprenticeship, GWR Co., Swindon, 1917–23; Trinity Coll., Cambridge, 1923–26 (senior scholarship, 1st Class Hons Mech. Sciences Tripos, John Wimbolt Prize, Second Yeats Prize). ICI (Alkali), Northwich, 1926–40 (Chief Engineer, 1931–40); on loan from ICI to Ministry of Supply, 1940–46 (Dep. Dir-Gen. of Filling Factories, 1942–46); Dep. Controller Atomic Energy (Production), Min. of Supply, 1946–54; Mem. of Board for Engineering and Production, and Man. Dir (Industrial Gp), UKAEA, 1954–57; Chairman: Central Electricity Generating Board, 1957–64; Internat. Exec. Cttee of World Energy Conf., 1962–68; Dep. Chm., Electricity Supply Research Coun., 1965–; Special Adviser to the Internat. Bank for Reconstruction and Develt, 1965–70; Chancellor of Bath Univ., 1966–80. President: CEI, 1976–; Fellowship of Engineering, 1976–81. Hon. Fellow of Trinity Coll., Cambridge, 1957; Hon. Associate, Manchester Coll. of Science and Technology. Hon. DEng, Liverpool, 1955; Hon. DSc (Eng), London, 1956; Hon. ScD, Cambridge, 1960; Hon. LLD, Edinburgh, 1958; Hon. DSc: Oxford, 1957; Southampton, 1962; Durham, 1966; Bath, 1966. Albert Medal (RSA), 1957; Melchett Medal, Inst. of Fuel, 1957; Glazebrook Medal and Prize, 1966; Rumford Medal (Royal Soc.); Axel Johnson Prize, Roy. Swedish Acad. of Engrg; Wilhelm-Exner Medal, Österreichischer Gewerbeverein; Castner Medal, Soc. of Chem. Industries; James Watt Internat. Medal, IMechE. Pres., IMechE, 1966–67. Hon. Fellow: Metals Soc.; Instn of Gas Engineers; Inst. of Welding; Welding Soc.; IMunE; Hon. MASME. For. Associate, Amer. Acad. of Engineering; Corresp. Mem., Mexican Acad. of Engineering; Mem., Eur. Acad. of Arts, Sciences and Humanities; Hon. Mem., Eur. Nuclear Soc. Imperial Order of The Rising Sun (Japan), 1966. *Publications:* Engineers and Engineering, 1970; Heavy Current Electricity in the United Kingdom: history and development, 1979. *Address:* Tiverton Lodge, Dulwich Common, SE21 7EW. *T:* 01–693 6447.
*Died 22 June* 1983.

**HINTZ, Orton Sutherland,** CMG 1968; former Editor, The New Zealand Herald, Auckland, New Zealand, 1958–70; Trustee, Woolf Fisher Trust (educational); Patron, Central North Island Wildlife Conservancy Council; b 15 Nov. 1907; s of late Alfred and late Cora Hintz; m 1st, 1931, Flora Margaret McIver (d 1943); 2nd, 1965, Caroline Jean Crawford (née Hutchinson). *Educ:* Mt Albert Grammar Sch., Auckland; Auckland Univ. Joined NZ Herald Staff, 1925; Parly Corresp., 1935–38; War service, Naval Intelligence, 1941–46; Night Ed., NZ Herald, 1946; Assoc. Ed., NZ Herald, 1952; Dir, Wilson & Horton Ltd, 1961; Dir, NZ Press Assoc., 1962 (Chm. 1965–66); Reuters Trustee, 1964–68. Mem. Coun., Outward Bound Trust of NZ, 1961; Delegate, Commonwealth Press Conf., India and Pakistan, 1961. *Publications:* The New Zealanders in England, 1931; HMNZS Philomel, 1944; Trout at Taupo, 1955; (ed) Lord Cobham's Speeches, 1962; Fisherman's Paradise, 1975. *Recreations:* trout fishing (Patron, Lake Taupo Angling Fedn, 1970–81), cricket, Rugby football. *Address:* 36 Oregon Drive, Rainbow Point, Taupo, NZ. *T:* 85–568. *Clubs:* Anglers' (New York); Fly Fishers (Taupo).
*Died 18 Nov.* 1985.

**HIROHITO, Emperor of Japan, (Emperor Showa),** KG 1971; FRS 1971; b Tokyo, 29 April 1901; s of Emperor Yoshihito and Empress Sadako; m 1924, Princess Nagako, d of Prince Kuniyoshi Kuni; two s three d (and two d decd). *Educ:* special tutors; The Peers' School. Became regent because of father's illness, 1921; became emperor, 1926; formally enthroned, 1928. *Publications:* 7 books on marine biology. *Heir:* HIH Crown Prince Akihito [b 23 Dec. 1933; m 1959, Michiko Shoda; two s one d]. *Address:* Imperial Palace, Tokyo, Japan.     *Died 7 Jan.* 1989.

**HIRSCH, Prof. Kurt August;** Emeritus Professor of Pure Mathematics, University of London, Queen Mary College; b Berlin, 12 Jan. 1906; s of Dr Robert Hirsch and Anna (née Lehmann); m 1928, Elsa Brühl; one s two d. *Educ:* University of Berlin; University of Cambridge. Dr phil (Berlin), 1930; PhD (Cambridge), 1937. Asst Lecturer, later Lecturer, University Coll., Leicester, 1938–47; Lecturer, later Sen. Lecturer, King's Coll., Newcastle upon Tyne,

1948–51; Reader, University of London, Queen Mary Coll., 1951–57, Prof., 1957–73. Editor, Russian Mathematical Surveys. *Publications:* (with A. G. Kurosh) Theory of Groups, 2 vols, 2nd English edn 1954; (with F. R. Gantmacher) Theory of Matrices, 2 vols, English edn 1960; (with A. G. Kurosh) Lectures on General Algebra, English edn 1964; (with I. R. Shafarevich) Basic Algebraic Geometry, 1974; contribs to learned jls. *Recreations:* chess, gardening. *Address:* 101 Shirehall Park, NW4 2QU. *T:* 01–202 7902. *Died 4 Nov.* 1986.

**HIRST, Geoffrey Audus Nicholson,** TD 1945; *b* 14 Dec. 1904; *s* of late Col E. A. Hirst, CMG, TD, Ingmanthorpe Hall, Wetherby, Yorks. *Educ:* Charterhouse; St John's Coll., Cambridge. Former Director: Samuel Webster & Sons Ltd; J. Hey & Co. Ltd; Hey & Humphries Ltd; Spinks (Caterers) Ltd; FBI: Mem. Grand Council and Executive Cttee, 1932–40, 1958–65; Mem. Economic Policy Cttee; Mem. Leeds Exec., 1930–46; East and West Riding Council and Exec., 1946–65, Vice-Chm., 1956, Chm., 1958–60. Mem. of Council, CBI: Mem., Economic Cttee, East and West Ridings and Humberside (Yorks) Regional Council, 1965–69. Leeds Chamber of Commerce: Mem. Council, 1932–; Junior Vice-Pres., 1948–49; Senior Vice-Pres., 1949–51; Pres., 1952–54; Mem. Council, Bradford Chamber of Commerce, 1950–70; Vice-Pres., Urban Dist Councils' Assoc., 1951–70; Mem., Nat. Advisory Council for Educn in Industry and Commerce, 1948–51; Chm., Yorks Regional Academic Bd, 1947–49; Mem., Leeds and Hull Academic Board, 1947–53 (Chm., 1949–50); Mem., Yorks Council for Further Educn, 1934–40 and 1949–51; Leeds Coll. of Technology: Mem. Bd of Governors, 1932–40; Vice-Chm., 1932–36 and 1938–40. Member: Leeds Nat. Service Cttee, 1938–40; UK Council of European Movement; Economic League, Central Council, 1934–67. Chm., W Yorks Regional Council and Exec., 1945–50; Mem., Nat. Council, Inst. of Marketing and Sales Management, 1932–35, 1960–62; Leeds Executive: Mem., 1930–; Chm., 1932–33; Pres., 1949–50; Vice-Pres. W Yorks Branch, English-Speaking Union. MP (C) Shipley Div., WR Yorks, 1950–70; Hon. Sec., Conservative Party's Parliamentary Trade and Industry Cttee, 1959–61, Vice-Chm., 1962, Chm., 1963–64. Leader, Assoc. of British Chambers of Commerce Delegn to Holland, 1953; Mem., Parly Delegns to Malta, 1965, Holland, 1966. Member: Leeds Musical Festival Exec., 1934–54; Leeds Philharmonic Soc. Exec., 1930–39. FCS, FSS, FREconS, FInstMSM. TA, 1924–32, rejoined, 1939; served War of 1939–45; Battery Comdr, second in Comd 69th Fd Regt, RA, 1939–44; attached to Staff, 21 Army Gp, 1945. *Publications:* various contribs to the Press. *Recreations:* travel, music, bridge. *Address:* 3 King Gardens, Hove BN3 2PE. *T:* Brighton 727978.
*Died 18 June* 1984.

**HITCHCOCK, Geoffrey Lionel Henry,** CBE 1975 (OBE 1957); External Relations Consultant, Bell Educational Trust, Cambridge, 1977–81; *b* 10 Sept. 1915; *s* of late Major Frank B. Hitchcock, MC, and Mrs Mildred Hitchcock (*née* Sloane Stanley), Danbury, Essex; *m* 1950, Rosemary, *d* of Albert de Las Casas, Tiverton; two *s* one *d*. *Educ:* Oratory Sch., Caversham; Hertford Coll., Oxford (Exhibr, MA). British Council, April-Sept. 1939. Commnd London Rifle Bde, 1939; served with KAR in E Africa and SE Asia; Major 1943. Returned to British Council, 1946; served in London; Germany, 1950–54; Representative in Austria, 1954–59; Representative in Yugoslavia, 1962–67; Controller Home Div., British Council, 1970–73; Rep. of British Council in France and Cultural Counsellor, British Embassy, Paris, 1973–76. *Recreations:* race-going, gardening. *Address:* The Old Post, Shipton-under-Wychwood, Oxfordshire OX7 6BP. *T:* Shipton-under-Wychwood 831474. *Club:* Travellers'. *Died 25 Nov.* 1987.

**HITCHCOCK, Prof. Henry-Russell;** Adjunct Professor, Institute of Fine Arts, University of New York, since 1969; *b* 3 June 1903; *s* of Henry R. Hitchcock and Alice Whitworth Davis. *Educ:* Middlesex Sch., Concord, Mass, USA; Harvard Univ. MA 1927. Asst Prof. of Art, Vassar Coll., 1927–28; Asst, Assoc., Prof., Wesleyan Univ., 1929–48; Lectr in Architecture, Massachusetts Institute of Technology, 1946–48; Prof. of Art, Smith Coll., Mass, 1948–68; Prof. of Art, Univ. of Massachusetts, 1968. Dir, Smith Coll. Museum of Art, 1949–55; Lectr, Inst. of Fine Arts, New York Univ., 1951–57; Lectr in Architecture, Yale Univ., 1951–52, 1959–60, 1970, Cambridge Univ., 1962, 1964. Fellow Amer. Acad. of Arts and Sciences. Hon. Corr. Mem. RIBA; Franklin Fellow, RSA; Pres., Soc. of Architectural Historians, 1952–54; Fellow, Pilgrim Soc.; Founder-Mem., Victorian Soc.; Pres., Victorian Soc. in America, 1969–74. Hon. FRIBA 1986. Hon. DFA New York Univ., 1969; Hon. DLitt Glasgow, 1973; Hon. DHL: Pennsylvania, 1976; Wesleyan, 1979. Award of Merit, AIA, 1978; Benjamin Franklin Award, RSA, 1979. *Publications:* Modern Architecture, 1929, 2nd edn, 1970; J. J. P. Oud, 1931; The International Style (with Philip Johnson), 1932 (2nd edn 1966); The Architecture of H. H. Richardson, 1936 (3rd edn 1966); Modern Architecture in England (with others), 1937; Rhode Island Architecture, 1939 (2nd edn 1968); In the Nature of Materials, the Buildings of Frank Lloyd Wright, 1942 (2nd edn 1973); American Architectural Books, 1946;

Painting towards Architecture, 1948; Early Victorian Architecture in Britain, 1954, 2nd edn 1972; Latin American Architecture since 1945, 1955; Architecture: Nineteenth and Twentieth Centuries, 1958 (4th edn 1977); German Rococo: The Brothers Zimmermann, 1968; Rococo Architecture in Southern Germany, 1968; (with William Seale) Temples of Democracy, 1977; Netherlandish Scrolled Gables of the 16th and early 17th Centuries, 1978; German Renaissance Architecture, 1981; *relevant publication:* In Search of Modern Architecture: a tribute to Henry-Russell Hitchcock (ed Helen Searing), 1982. *Address:* 152 E 62nd Street, New York, NY 10021, USA. *T:* 758–6554. *Died 19 Feb.* 1987.

**HITCHEN, Rt. Rev. Anthony;** Titular Bishop of Othona and an Auxiliary Bishop of Liverpool, (RC), since 1979; *b* 23 May 1930. *Educ:* St Cuthbert's College, Ushaw. Priest, 1955; Administrator of St Mary's, Liverpool, 1969. *Address:* 55 Victoria Road, Freshfield, Liverpool L37 1LN. *Died 10 April* 1988.

**HITCHINS, Francis Eric,** CBE 1954; Member, Australian Wool Realization Commission, 1945–57; President Emeritus, Australian Wool and Meat Producers' Federation; sheep farming, Cranbrook, W Australia; *b* 15 Oct. 1891; *m* 1921, Bessie R. Paltridge; two *s* one *d*. Served European War, 1914–18, AIF, France. Inspector, Agric. Bank of W Australia, 1918–23; Land Valuer, Federal Taxation Dept, 1923–32; resumed sheep farming. Pres., Wool Sect., Primary Producers' Assoc. of WA; Pres., Australian Wool and Meat Producers' Fedn, 1941–52; Wool Grower Rep., Central Wool Cttee, War of 1939–45. Grower Rep., London Wool Confs, 1945 and 1950. *Publications:* Tangled Skeins: A Historic Survey of Australian Wool Marketing, 1956; Skeins Still Tangled: wool events 1952–72, 1972. *Address:* RSL War Veterans Home, Alexander Drive, Mount Lawley, WA, Australia. *Died 8 Dec.* 1983.

**HOARE, Cecil Arthur,** DSc; FRS 1950; FIBiol; *b* 6 March 1892; *m* Marie Leserson. *Educ:* XII St Petersburg Gymnasium; University of Petrograd (BSc 1917); University of London (DSc 1927). Fellow of Petrograd Univ., 1917–20; Lectr at Military Medical Academy, Petrograd, 1918–20; Researcher to Medical Research Council, 1920–23; Head of Protozoological Dept, Wellcome Laboratories of Tropical Medicine, London, 1923–57; Wellcome Research Fellow, 1957–70; Trypanosomiasis Research Institute, Uganda Medical Service, 1927–29; Acting Prof. of Medical Protozoology at London Sch. of Hygiene and Tropical Medicine, 1941–45; Recorder of "Protozoa" in Zoological Record, 1926–57; Mem., Expert Panel, WHO, 1957–73. Hon. Member: Soc. Protozool., USA; Amer. Soc. Parasitol.; Brit. Soc. Parasitol.; Royal Soc. Trop. Med. and Hygiene; Société de Pathologie Exotique, Paris; For. Member: Société Belge de Médecine Tropicale; Soc. Protistol. Franç. G. Vianna Medal, Brazil. Acad. Sci., 1962; Patrick Manson Prize, 1963, Manson Medal, Royal Soc. Trop. Med., 1974. *Publications:* Handbook of Medical Protozoology, 1949; The Trypanosomes of Mammals, 1972; numerous papers dealing with the Protozoa. *Address:* 25 Park Street, Charlton, Malmesbury, Wilts SN16 9DF.
*Died 23 Aug.* 1984.

**HOARE, Rear-Adm. Desmond John,** CB 1962; Vice President, United World Colleges, since 1969; *b* 25 June 1910; *s* of Capt. R. R. Hoare, OBE, Royal Navy; *m* 1941, Naomi Mary Gilbert Scott; one *s* two *d*. *Educ:* Wimbledon Coll.; King's Sch., Rochester. Joined RN, 1929; Engineering training, RNEC Keyham, 1930–33; Advanced engineering course, RNC Greenwich, 1934–36; HMS Exeter, 1936–39; Admiralty, 1939–41; HMS King George V, 1942–44; Admiralty, 1945–48; HMS Vanguard, 1949–51; HMS Condor (apprentice training), 1951–53; idc, 1955; Admiralty, 1956–59; Chief Staff Officer Technical to C-in-C Plymouth, 1960–62; retired, 1962. Headmaster, Atlantic Coll., 1962–69. *Recreations:* sailing, power boats. *Address:* Bally Island House, Skibbereen, Cork, Ireland. *Died 26 April* 1988.

**HOARE, Sir Frederick (Alfred),** 1st Bt, *cr* 1962; Kt 1958; Managing Partner of C. Hoare & Co., Bankers, of 37 Fleet Street, since 1947; Director: Messrs Hoare Trustees, since 1947; Mitre Court Securities Ltd, since 1963; Mitre Court Property Holding Co., since 1980; Grimersta Estate Ltd, since 1969; Tuscan Development Co., since 1972; Hoare's Bank Nominees Ltd, since 1936; *b* 11 Feb. 1913; *s* of late Frederick Henry Hoare, 37 Fleet Street, EC4; *m* 1st, 1939, Norah Mary, OBE (*d* 1973), *d* of A. J. Wheeler; two *d*; 2nd, 1974, Oonah Alice Dew (*d* 1980), *d* of late Brig.-Gen. David Ramsay Sladen, CMG, DSO, and Isabel Sladen (*née* Blakiston-Houston); 3rd, 1984, Sarah Lindsay Bamber (marr. diss. 1986), *widow* of James Henry Bamber and *d* of late Robert Irwin Herald, Glengyle, Belfast. *Educ:* Wellington Coll. Clerk to C. Hoare & Co., 1931; Bankers' Agent, 1936, Managing Partner 1947. Chm., General Practice Finance Corp., 1966–73; Deputy Chairman: Nat. Mutual Life Assurance Soc., 1969–72; St George Assurance Co. Ltd, 1969–73; Dir, TR Property Investment Trust plc, 1972–83. Common Councilman City of London, 1948; Alderman for Ward of Farringdon Without, 1950–71; Sheriff, City of London, 1956; Lord Mayor of London, 1961–62. Formerly one of HM Lieutenants for

City of London; former Governor: Christ's Hosp.; Royal Bridewell Hosp.; Past Chm., St Bride's Institute; Mem., Court of Assistants and Prime Warden of Goldsmiths' Company, 1966–67; Liveryman, Spectacle Makers' Company, 1948–; Mem. Court, City Univ., 1974–. Pres., British Chess Federation, 1964–67; Past President: London Primary Schs Chess Assoc.; Cosmopolitan Banks Chess Assoc.; Upward Bound Young People's Gliding and Adventure Trust; Vice-Pres., Toc H. Trustee: Lady Hoare Thalidomide Appeal; Historic Churches Preservation Trust; Vice-Pres., Anglers' Co-operative Assoc. (Chm., 1977–82); Chm., John Eastwood Water Protection Trust Ltd, 1977–82; Member: Nat. Coun. for Voluntary Organisations; Nat. Council, Noise Abatement Soc.; Chm., Family Welfare Assoc., 1961–68; Vice-Pres., British Rheumatism and Arthritis Assoc., 1979–. Past Grand Deacon, United Grand Lodge of England. KStJ. Knight of Liberian Humane Order of African Redemption, 1962; Grand Officier de L'Ordre National de la République de Côte d'Ivoire, 1962. *Recreations:* chess, fishing, ornithology, photography, philately. *Heir:* none. *Address:* 34 Cadogan Square, SW1X 0JL. *Clubs:* Garrick, City Livery, Flyfishers', Pepys.                                    *Died 24 Nov.* 1986 (*ext*).

**HOBART, Maj.-Gen. Patrick Robert Chamier,** CB 1970; DSO 1945; OBE 1944; MC 1943; *b* 14 Nov. 1917; *s* of Robert Charles Arthur Stanley Hobart and Elsie Hinds. *Educ:* Charterhouse; Royal Military Academy Woolwich; 2nd Lieut, Royal Tank Corps, 1937; served in war of 1939–45 (despatches 4 times); France, Western Desert, Tunisia, Italy, with 2nd Royal Tank Regt, BM 9th Armd Bde, GSO2 30 Corps, GSO1 7th Armd Div; NW Europe, GSO1 Guards Armd Div. and CO 1st RTR; CO 2nd RTR, BAOR and N Africa, 1958–60; Comdr, 20th Armoured Brigade, BAOR, 1961–63; Chief of Staff, 1 (British) Corps, BAOR, 1964–66; Dir Military Operations, MoD, 1966–68; Chief of Staff Army Strategic Command, 1968–70; Dir, RAC, 1970–72; retired; Lieut-Governor, Royal Hosp., Chelsea, 1973–78. Col Comdt, Royal Tank Regt, 1968–78, Representative Col Comdt, 1971–74. ADC to the Queen, 1961–66. *Address:* c/o Royal Bank of Scotland, Kirkland House, Whitehall, SW1.                                   *Died 22 Nov.* 1986.

**HOBART, Lt-Comdr Sir Robert (Hampden),** 3rd Bt *cr* 1914; RN; *b* 7 May 1915; *o s* of Sir (Claud) Vere Cavendish Hobart, 2nd Bt, DSO, OBE and Violet Verve, MBE (*d* 1935), 2nd *d* of late John Wylie; *heir-pres.* to 10th Earl of Buckinghamshire; *S* father, 1949; *m* 1st, 1942, Sylvia (*d* 1965), *d* of H. Argo, Durban, Natal; three *s* one *d*; 2nd, 1975, Caroline Fleur, *d* of Colonel H. M. Vatcher, MC, and widow of 11th Duke of Leeds. *Educ:* Wixenford; RN Coll., Dartmouth. Sub-Lieut, RN, 1935; Lieut-Comdr, 1945; served War of 1939–45 (wounded, two medals, four stars); retired, 1950. Contested (Nat Lib) Hillsborough Div. of Sheffield, 1945, (C and L) Itchen Div. of Southampton, 1950. *Heir: s* John Vere Hobart [*b* 9 April 1945; *m* 1982, Kate Iddles; two *s*]. *Address:* 42 Egerton Gardens, SW3 2BZ. *Clubs:* Travellers', Royal London Yacht; Royal Yacht Squadron; Royal Southern Yacht, Bembridge Sailing.
                                                *Died 14 Nov.* 1988.

**HOBBS, William Alfred,** CB 1973; CBE 1965; Chief Valuer, Board of Inland Revenue, 1972–74; *b* 3 March 1912; *s* of A. V. Getland Hobbs; *m* 1937, Rose Winslade; one *s* one *d*. *Educ:* Brighton, Hove and Sussex Grammar Sch. Chartered Surveyor (FRICS). Private practice, 1928–38; joined Valuation Office, 1938; Dist Valuer (Maidstone), 1945; Superintending Valuer, 1950 (London, Manchester and Birmingham); Asst Chief Valuer, 1958; Dep. Chief Valuer, 1966–71. *Recreations:* fly-fishing, golf. *Address:* 216 Cooden Sea Road, Bexhill-on-Sea, E Sussex. *T:* Cooden 3995.
                                              *Died 16 March* 1984.

**HOBKIRK, Col Elspeth Isabel Weatherley,** CBE 1951; TD 1952; WRAC (retired); Governor of HM Prison and of HM Borstal for Girls, and of HM Young Offenders Institute, Greenock, 1955–69; also appointed Woman Adviser to Scottish Home and Health Department on conditions of detention of Women and Girls in Scotland, 1956, retired from Scottish Prison Service, Aug. 1969; *b* 17 May 1903; *d* of late Brig.-Gen. C. J. Hobkirk, CMG, DSO, Cleddon Hall, Trellech, Mon., and Nora Louisa Hobkirk (*née* Bosanquet). *Educ:* Sandecotes, Dorset; London Sch. of Art. JP Monmouthshire, 1938–49. Joined FANY, 1938; enrolled ATS, 1939; served War of 1939–45, Sen. Comdr, 1942; Chief Comdr, 1945; Controller and Dep. Dir ATS, HQ London District, 1946; Dep. Dir ATS, War Office, 1947–49; commissioned into Women's Royal Army Corps, 1949; Dep. Dir WRAC, War Office, 1949; Dep. Dir WRAC, HQ Eastern Command, 1950–52; Vice-Pres. Regular Commissions Bd, 1950–52; retired, 1952. Head Warden, Bristol Royal Hospital, 1952–54; Governor, HM Prison, Duke Street, Glasgow, 1954–55 (prison moved to Greenock, 1955). Member: Govt Adv. Cttee on Drug Dependence, 1967–70; Parole Board for Scotland, 1970–73; (Chm.) Civil Service Commn Panel of Interviewers, 1969–73; Adv. Council on Social Work (Scotland), 1970–72; Emslie Cttee on Penalties for Homicide, 1970–72; Edinburgh Appeals Cttee, Campaign for Cancer Research, 1970–73; Bd of Governors and Exec. Cttee, St Columba's Hospice, 1976–80;

an Hon. Sec., RUKBA, Edinburgh, 1974–75; Abbeyfield Edinburgh Exec. Cttee, 1975–76 (Chm. Extra Care House); Catholic Social Work Centre Exec. Cttee, 1974–77; Council, Scottish Soldiers', Sailors' and Airmen's Housing Assoc. and Mem., House Cttee, 1979–84. Hon. LLD Glasgow, 1976. *Recreations:* travel, painting, music, gardening; country pursuits generally. *Address:* 8 Moray Place, Edinburgh EH3 6DS.                        *Died 21 Aug.* 1990.

**HOBSON, Alec,** CBE 1962 (OBE 1946); MVO 1955; *b* 29 Oct. 1899; *s* of Frederick Hobson, Esher, Surrey; *m* 1924, Elizabeth Josephine (*d* 1986), *d* of Arthur Newman, Sudbury, Suffolk; one *s* (one *d* decd). Served Inns of Court and Royal West Surrey Regiments, 1918–19. Engaged in pedigree livestock improvement work, 1920–39; joint founder-partner Harry Hobson & Co. (pedigree livestock auctioneers), 1928. Domestic food production work for Min. of Agriculture, 1939–45. Sec., Royal Agricultural Soc. of England and of Nat. Agricultural Examinations Bds, 1946–61; Hon. Sec., Royal Agricultural Society of The Commonwealth, 1957–67, Hon. Fellow, 1977. Founder Mem., Guild of Agricultural Journalists; Founder Pres., Nat. Soc. of Master Thatchers; Liveryman, Past Master, and Court of Assts, Worshipful Co. of Farriers; Freeman, Worshipful Co. of Farmers. *Recreations:* golf, gardening. *Address:* 12 St Michael's Close, Aylsham, Norfolk NR11 6HA. *T:* Aylsham 734274. *Club:* Farmers'.                            *Died 11 Sept.* 1986.

**HOBSON, His Honour (John) Basil,** QC (Kenya, 1950; Nyasaland, 1953); a Circuit Judge (formerly Deputy Chairman, NE London Quarter Sessions), 1968–78; *b* 1905; *s* of late J. D. Hobson, QC, Trinidad, British West Indies, and late Cecilia (*née* Johnstone); *m* 1932, Ursula, *y d* of late William Collie, Trinidad; no *c*. *Educ:* Sherborne. Solicitor, 1929; Dep. Registrar, Supreme Court, Trinidad, 1936; admitted Middle Temple and called to Bar, 1938; Crown Counsel, Uganda, 1939. Served War of 1939–45, King's African Rifles, 1939–41; Dep. Judge-Advocate, East Africa Command, 1941–44; Solicitor-Gen., Kenya, 1947; MLC, Kenya, 1947–51; Chm., Labour Advisory Board, Kenya, 1948–49; Attorney-Gen., MEC and MLC, Nyasaland, 1951–57; acted Chief Justice, April–Nov. 1954; Dep. Chm., Essex QS, 1964–68. Chm. Commn on African Fishing Industry, 1956; Chm. Select Cttee on Non-African Agriculture, 1957. *Recreation:* watching cricket. *Address:* The Chantry, Marston Road, Sherborne, Dorset DT9 4BL. *T:* Sherborne 2582. *Club:* MCC.                                *Died 13 Oct.* 1985.

**HOBSON, Prof. William,** BSc (1st Cl. Hons), MD (Dist.), DPH (Dist.), Leeds; MRCS; LRCP; Consultant in medical education, World Health Organisation, since 1971; *b* 5 Sept. 1911; *s* of William Hobson, The Langdales, Park Lane, Leeds; *m* 1937, Lucy Muriel Wilson; one *s* one *d*; *m* 1953, Heather McMahon Greer; one *d*. *Educ:* Fulneck; Bradford Grammar Sch.; Leeds Univ. Lecturer in Physiology and Hygiene, University of Leeds, 1936–38; Asst Sch. Medical Officer, Leeds, 1938–39; Asst County MO, Hants CC, 1939–40; Medical Officer of Health Borough of Lymington, Hants, 1940–42. Major, RAMC, 1942–46 (despatches). Senior Lecturer in Preventive Medicine, University of Bristol, 1946–48; Prof. of Social and Industrial Medicine, University of Sheffield, 1949–58; Chief, Educn and Training, WHO European Office, 1958–68; Chief of Staff Training, WHO HQ Geneva, 1968–71; Consultant, WHO Regional Office for E Mediterranean, Alexandria, 1971–72. WHO Visiting Prof. to India, 1957–58. Hon. Patron, Western Foundn of Vertebrate Zoology, Los Angeles, 1968. Commandeur de la Confrérie des Chevaliers de Tastevin de Bourgogne, 1963. *Publications:* The Health of the Elderly at Home (with J. Pemberton), 1955 (Ciba Foundn Prize, 1956); (ed) Modern Trends in Geriatrics, 1956; (ed) Theory and Practice of Public Health, 1961, 5th edn 1979 (trans. into Greek, Turkish and Italian), 1974; World Health and History, 1963; contribs to Jl of Hygiene, BMJ, Jl of Phys. Med., Jl of Social Med., Bristol Med. Chir. Jl, Jl Med. Chir. Soc., The Naturalist, etc. *Recreation:* ornithology. *Address:* Strand Cottage, Myrtleville, Co. Cork, Ireland.                          *Died 29 Nov.* 1982.

**HOCHOY, Sir Solomon,** TC 1969; GCMG 1962 (KCMG 1959; CMG 1957); GCVO 1966; OBE 1952; Governor-General and C-in-C of Trinidad and Tobago, 1962–72 (Governor, 1960–62); *b* Jamaica, 20 April 1905; *m* 1935, Thelma Edna Huggins; one adopted *d*. *Educ:* St Mary's Coll., Port-of-Spain, Trinidad. Trinidad Government: Clerk, 1928–44; Labour Officer, 1944–46; Deputy Industrial Adviser, 1946–49; Commissioner of Labour, 1949–55; Deputy Colonial Sec., 1955–56; Chief Sec., Trinidad and Tobago, 1956–60. KStJ 1961. *Recreation:* fishing. *Address:* Blanchisseuse, Trinidad. *Clubs:* Royal Commonwealth Society, Corona; Clipper (International).                                        *Died 14 Nov.* 1983.

**HODGE, John Ernest,** CMG 1962; CVO 1956; QPM 1955; Inspector-General of Police, Republic of Nigeria, 1962–64; *b* 3 Nov. 1911; *s* of late Rev. J. Z. Hodge, DD; *m* 1950, Margaret Henrietta, *d* of late Rev. Hugh Brady Brew, Wicklow; one *s* one *d*. *Educ:* Taunton Sch., Taunton, Som. Jamaica Constabulary, 1931–35; The Nigeria Police, 1935–64. Mem. East Lothian CC, 1972–75. OStJ 1961. CPM 1953. *Recreation:* golf. *Address:* Netherlea, Dirleton, East Lothian,

Scotland. *T:* Dirleton 272. *Club:* North Berwick.
*Died 18 Oct.* 1989.

**HODGKIN, (Curwen) Eliot;** artist and writer; *b* 19 June 1905; *o s* of Charles Ernest Hodgkin and Alice Jane Brooke; *m* 1940, Maria Clara (Mimi) Henderson (*née* Franceschi); one *s. Educ:* Harrow; Royal Academy Schs. Exhibited at Royal Academy and bought under Chantrey Bequest, for Tate Gallery: October, 1936; Undergrowth, 1943; Pink and White Turnips, 1972; One Man Shows: London Leicester Galleries, 1956; New York, Durlacher, 1958; London, Arthur Jeffress Gallery, 1959; New York, Durlacher, 1962; London, Reid Gallery, 1963; Agnew's, 1966. *Publications:* She Closed the Door, 1931; Fashion Drawing, 1932; 55 London Views, 1948; A Pictorial Gospel, 1949. *Address:* 23 Hillcrest, 51–57 Ladbroke Grove, W11 3AX. *Died 30 May* 1987.

**HODGKIN, Thomas Lionel;** lecturer and writer; Emeritus Fellow, Balliol College, Oxford; *b* 3 April 1910; *s* of late R. H. Hodgkin, Provost of Queen's Coll., Oxford, and D. F. Hodgkin, *d* of late A. L. Smith, Master of Balliol; *m* 1937, Dorothy Mary Crowfoot, OM, FRS; two *s* one *d. Educ:* Winchester Coll. (Exhibitioner); Balliol Coll. (Schol). Sen. Demy, Magdalen Coll., 1932–33; Asst Secretary, Palestine Civil Service, 1934–36; Education Officer, Cumberland Friends' Unemployment Cttee, 1937–39; Staff Tutor in North Staffs, Oxford University Tutorial Classes Cttee, 1939–45; Sec. to the Oxford University Delegacy for Extra-Mural Studies, and Fellow of Balliol, 1945–52; Visiting Lecturer: Northwestern Univ., Illinois, 1957; University Coll. of Ghana, 1958; Research Associate, Institute of Islamic Studies, McGill Univ., Montreal, 1958–61; Dir, Institute of African Studies, University of Ghana, 1962–65; Lecturer in Govt of New States, Univ. of Oxford, and Fellow of Balliol, 1965–70. MA Oxon. *Publications:* Nationalism in Colonial Africa, 1956; Nigerian Perspectives, 1960, 2nd edn 1975; African Political Parties, 1961; articles on African affairs. *Recreations:* birdwatching, conversation. *Address:* Crab Mill, Ilmington, Shipston-on-Stour, Warwicks. *T:* Ilmington 233. *Died 25 March* 1982.

**HODGKINSON, Commander Guy Beauchamp,** DSO 1940; RN retired; *b* 11 Jan. 1903; *s* of Commander George Hodgkinson, RN retired, and Helen Blanche Raggett; *m* 1930, Beryl Margaret, *d* of Harry Langley; two *d. Educ:* St Hugh's Sch., Chislehurst; RN Colleges Osborne and Dartmouth. War of 1939–45 (despatches twice, DSO). *Died 23 Aug.* 1981.

**HODGSON, Thomas Charles Birkett,** CVO 1970; OBE 1966; QPM 1969; Chief Constable, Thames Valley Constabulary, 1968–70; *b* 8 Dec. 1907; *s* of late Thomas Edward Birkett Hodgson, Preston, Lancs; *m* 1936, Gwyneth Cosslett Bowles, *d* of Ivor Willans Bowles, Llandaff, Cardiff; one *s* one *d. Educ:* St Peter's, York. Served with Lancashire Constabulary, 1927–55; Asst Chief Constable, Birmingham, 1955–59; Chief Constable, Berkshire, 1959–68. *Address:* Little Newnham, Sutton Veny, near Warminster, Wilts. *T:* Sutton Veny 254. *Died 21 Nov.* 1986.

**HODGSON, Thomas Edward Highton,** CB 1958; *b* 22 Aug. 1907; *e s* of late Sir Edward Hodgson, KBE, CB; *m* 1935, E. Catherine, *d* of T. Robin Hodgson; four *s. Educ:* Felsted Sch.; St John's Coll., Oxford. Asst Master, Felsted Sch., 1931; Board of Trade: Principal, 1941; Asst Sec., 1945; Asst Sec., Ministry of Materials, 1951; Under Secretary: Ministry of Supply, 1954; Ministry of Aviation, 1959; Ministry of Health, 1960–68; Asst Sec., Gen. Register Office, later OPCS, 1968–72. *Address:* 15 Church Street, Sudbury, Suffolk.
*Died 7 Nov.* 1985.

**HODSON, Baron** (Life Peer), *cr* 1960, of Rotherfield Greys; **Francis Lord Charlton Hodson,** PC 1951; Kt 1937; MC; a Lord of Appeal in Ordinary, 1960–71; Member of Permanent Court of Arbitration at The Hague, 1949–73; *b* 17 Sept. 1895; *s* of Rev. Thomas Hodson, MA, late Rector of Oddington, Glos, and Catherine Anne Maskew; *m* 1918, Susan Mary (*d* 1965), *d* of late Major W. G. Blake, DL; one *s* (and *er s* killed in Libya 23 Jan. 1942; one *d* decd). *Educ:* Cheltenham Coll.; Wadham Coll., Oxford (Hon. Fellow). 2nd Lieut 7th Bn Glos Regt, Sept. 1914; served in Gallipoli and Mesopotamia, 1915–17 (MC, Cavaliere of the Order of the Crown of Italy); retired as Captain, 1919; called to Bar, Inner Temple, 1921; Junior Counsel to Treasury (Probate), 1935; KC 1937; Judge of High Court of Justice (Probate Divorce and Admiralty Division), 1937–51; Bencher, Inner Temple, 1938; a Lord Justice of Appeal, 1951–60. Past Pres., Internat. Law Assoc., British Branch. *Address:* Rotherfield Greys, Oxon. *T:* Rotherfield Greys 303. *Club:* Huntercombe Golf (Henley-on-Thames).
*Died 11 March* 1984.

**HODSON, Prof. Cecil John,** MB, BS London; FRCP; FRCR; DMRE; Professor of Uroradiology, School of Medicine, Yale University, 1975–85; *b* 20 Dec. 1915; *s* of Dr J. E. Hodson and Kate Bassnett; *m* (marr. diss.); one *s. Educ:* Eastbourne Coll.; St Mary's Hosp., Paddington. Junior medical posts: St Mary's Hosp. and St Giles Hosp., Camberwell; Brompton Hosp.; Harefield Emergency Hosp. RAMC, 1942–46 (despatches); served in N Africa, Sicily, Italy and Greece; Major, Specialist in Radiology. Dep. Dir, X-Ray Dept, University Coll. Hosp., 1949; Dir, X-Ray Diagnostic Dept, UCH, 1960–70; Radiologist, Queen Elizabeth Hosp. for Children, 1948–70; Hon. Cons. Radiologist, Queen Alexandra Mil. Hosp., Millbank, 1963–70; Prof. of Radiology, Memorial Univ. of Newfoundland, 1970–75. Sec., Faculty of Radiologists, 1959–64, Vice-Pres., 1964–65. Baker Travelling Prof. of Royal Australasian College of Radiology, 1962. William Julius Mickle Fellow, University of London, 1966; FRSM. Member: The Renal Assoc.; Thoracic Soc.; British Paediatric Assoc.; Harveian Soc.; Medical Soc. of London. Hon. FACR 1981. *Publications:* chapters in radiological textbooks; numerous contributions to medical journals. *Recreations:* mountains, sailing, gardening. *Address:* School of Medicine, Yale University, New Haven, Conn 06518, USA; 720 Mt Carmel Avenue, Hamden, Conn 06510, USA. *Clubs:* Alpine Ski; United Hospitals Sailing; Royal Sussex Yacht.
*Died 1 Dec.* 1985.

**HODSON, Donald Manly;** *b* 10 Sept. 1913; 2nd *s* of late Prof. T. C. Hodson; *m* 1940, Margaret Beatson Bell, *er d* of late Sir Nicholas Beatson Bell, KCSI, KCIE; three *s* one *d. Educ:* Gresham's Sch.; Balliol Coll., Oxford. Editorial staff, the Economist, 1935; Leader writer, Financial Times, 1936; Asst Leader Page Editor, News Chronicle, 1937–38; Leader Page Editor, News Chronicle, 1939. BBC European Services: Sub-Editor, 1940; Chief Sub-Editor, 1942; Duty Editor, 1943; European Talks Editor, 1945; Asst Head of European News Dept, 1946; Head of European Talks and English Dept, 1948–51; Asst Controller, European Services, 1951–58; Controller, Overseas Services, 1958–68; Controller of Programmes, External Broadcasting, 1968–70; Dir of Programmes, External Broadcasting, 1971–73, retired. *Address:* Scotland House, Scotland Street, Stoke by Nayland, Suffolk. *T:* Nayland 262102.
*Died 27 March* 1988.

**HODSON, Joseph John,** BDS; PhD; FRCPath; FDSRCS; Professor Emeritus, 1972; Professor of Oral Pathology, University of Sheffield, 1960–72; formerly Hon. Consultant in Oral Pathology to the United Sheffield Hospitals, and to Sheffield Regional Hospital Board; *b* 7 March 1912; *e s* of late Rev. J. J. Hodson, MA, and late Mrs A. Hodson, Birmingham; *m* 1937, Mary Alice, *d* of late John and Florence Whitman, Hull; one *s* one *d. Educ:* Birmingham Univ.; Royal College of Surgeons, Edinburgh. Dental Surgeon to Warwicks CC, 1938–41. War Service, Capt., Royal Army Dental Corps, 1941–45. University of Sheffield: Research Asst, 1947–49, Lectr, 1949–53, Sen. Lectr, 1953–60, in Oral Pathology. Howard Mummery Research Prize, BDA, 1952–57. *Publications:* various papers in Medical and Dental Jls covering research in oral tumours, dental and other diseases of the mouth. *Recreations:* music, gardening. *Address:* 34 Glamis Avenue, Melton Park, Gosforth, Newcastle upon Tyne NE3 5SX. *Died 10 Dec.* 1983.

**HODSON, Leslie Manfred Noel,** CMG 1958; OBE 1953; QC 1943; retired as Advocate of the High Court of Southern Rhodesia (1929–63); *b* 2 Dec. 1902; *s* of late A. Hodson, JP, and Mrs Hodson; *m* 1927, Iona May Mackenzie (*d* 1972); two *s* one *d. Educ:* Boys' High Sch., Salisbury, Rhodesia; University of the Witwatersrand. City Councillor, Salisbury, Rhodesia, 1932–36; contested by-election, Hartley, 1937; MP for Salisbury Central, 1946 and 1948. First Chm. Rhodesia Univ. Assoc., 1945–53, of Inaugural Board, 1953, and of 1st Council, 1954–58, University Coll. of Rhodesia and Nyasaland, 1953–62. MP Federal Assembly of Rhodesia and Nyasaland, 1953–62. Dep. Speaker Legislative Assembly, 1951, 1953. Hon. LLD Rhodesia, 1975. *Recreation:* journalism. *Address:* Ellerton Farm, Harare South, PO Box 3261, Harare, Zimbabwe. *T:* Harare 8943610. *Club:* Harare (Harare). *Died 9 Jan.* 1985.

**HODSON, Rt. Rev. Mark Allin;** an Assistant Bishop of London, since 1974; *b* 1907; *s* of Albert Edgar Hodson, Solicitor; *m* 1959, Susanna Grace, *e d* of late Arthur Hugh Lister, CMG. *Educ:* Enfield Grammar Sch.; University Coll., London (BA), Fellow, 1974; Wells Theological Coll. Ordained 1931; Asst Curate, St Dunstan, Stepney, 1931–35; Missioner St Nicholas, Perivale, 1935–40; Rector of Poplar, 1940–55. Officiating Curate-in-charge of All Hallows, E India Docks, 1942–52; St Stephen, Poplar, 1943–52; St Frideswide, Poplar, 1947–52; Prebendary of Newington in St Paul's Cathedral, London, 1951–55; Suffragan Bishop of Taunton, 1955–61, also Prebendary and Rector of St Michael and All Angels, Dinder, diocese of Bath and Wells, 1956–61; Bishop of Hereford, 1961–73. Chairman: Steering Cttee, SPG, 1950–53; C of E Cttee for Social Work, 1961–67. Exam. Chaplain to Bp of London, 1974–81. Chaplain General, Guild of St Barnabas for Nurses, 1974–76; Pres., Retd Clergy Assoc., 1974–76. Foundn Governor, Enfield Grammar Sch, 1973–81. *Recreation:* travel. *Address:* 150 Marsham Court, Marsham Street, SW1P 4LB. *T:* 01–828 8378. *Club:* Athenæum.
*Died 23 Jan.* 1985.

**HOFFMAN, Anna Rosenberg;** Senior Partner, Anna M. Rosenberg Associates, public and industrial relations consultants, New York; *b* Budapest, Hungary, 19 July 1902; *d* of Albert Lederer and

Charlotte Bacskal; *m* 1919, Julius Rosenberg; one *s*; *m* 1962, Paul Gray Hoffman (*d* 1974). Member: President's Commn on Income Maintenance Programs, 1968–; States Urban Action Center, 1967–; NY Urban Coalition, Inc. of Nat. Urban Coalition, 1967–; Mayor Lindsay's Cttee on Rent Control, 1967–; National Citizens' Commn for Internat. Cooperation; Bd of Directors, United Nations Assoc. of the United States of America, Inc.; Population Crisis Cttee; Franklin Delano Roosevelt Memorial Commission; Board of Trustees, Eleanor Roosevelt Memorial Foundation; Board of Directors of World Rehabilitation Fund, Inc.; also Mem. of other Boards and Cttees, etc., in the United States. Formerly: Asst Sec. of Defense, USA, 1950–53; Regional Director of: War Manpower Commn, 1942–45; Social Security Admin., 1936–42; Office of Defense, Health and Welfare Services, 1941–42; Nat. Recovery Admin., 1934–35, Personal Representative of President Roosevelt, 1944, and of President Truman, 1945, to European Theatre of War; Sec. to President Roosevelt's Labor Victory Board, 1942–45; Member: US Nat. Commn for Unesco, 1946–50; Advisory Commn of the President on Universal Mil. Training, 1946–47; President Roosevelt's Industrial Relations Commn to Great Britain and Sweden etc.; Bd of Education, City of NY, 1961–63; Nat. Adv. Commn on Selective Service, 1966–67. Medal of Freedom, 1945 (first award by Gen. Eisenhower to a civilian); Medal for Merit, 1947; Dept of Defense exceptional Civilian Service Award, 1953; Medallion of City of NY (for work on beautification of City), 1966. Holds Hon. Degrees in USA. *Publications:* chapter, Social Security and the National Purpose, in The Family in a World at War, 1942; article on history and status of American woman in business world, in The Great Ideas Today, 1966. *Recreations:* chiefly indoor gardening; collection of modern French art; antique china. *Address:* (office) 444 Madison Avenue, New York, NY 10022, USA; (home) 2 East 88 Street, New York, NY 10028, USA.

*Died 9 May 1983.*

**HOFSTADTER, Prof. Robert;** Max H. Stein Professor of Physics, Stanford University, 1971–85, later Emeritus; Director, High Energy Physics Laboratory, Stanford University, 1967–74; *b* Manhattan, New York, NY, 5 Feb. 1915; *s* of Louis and Henrietta Hofstadter; *m* 1942, Nancy Givan, Baltimore, Md; one *s* two *d*. *Educ:* City Coll. of New York (BS *magna cum laude*); Princeton Univ. (MA, PhD). Instructor in Physics: University of Pennsylvania, 1940–41; City Coll., New York, 1941–42; Associate Physicist and Physicist, Nat. Bureau of Standards, Washington DC, 1942–43; Asst Chief Physicist, Norden Laboratories Corp., New York, 1943–46; Asst Prof., physics, Princeton Univ., 1946–50; Associate Prof., physics, Stanford Univ., 1950–54; Prof., physics, 1954–. Member, Board of Governors: Weizmann Institute of Science, Rehovoth, Israel, 1967–; Technion, Haifa, Israel, 1977–85. Mem., Bd of Directors, John Fluke Manufacturing Co., Washington, 1979–. Associate Editor: Physical Review, 1951–53; Investigations in Physics, 1958–65; Review of Scientific Instruments, 1954–56; Reviews of Modern Physics, 1958–61. Has held various fellowships; Fellow American Physical Soc.; FPS (London); MNAS; Member: Amer. Acad. of Arts and Sciences; Inst. of Medicine; Amer. Phil Soc.; Amer. Acad. of Achievement. Sigma Xi; Phi Beta Kappa. Hon. LLD, City Univ. of NY, 1962; Hon. DSc: Gustavus Adolphus Coll., Minn, 1963; Carleton Univ., Ottawa, 1967; Seoul Nat. Univ., 1967; Technion, Haifa, Israel, 1985; *Laurea* (hc), Padua, 1965; Dr Univ. (*hc*), Univ. of Clermont, 1967; Dr rer. nat. (*hc*) Julius-Maximilians Univ. of Würzburg, 1982; Dr rer. nat. (*hc*) Johannes Gutenberg Univ. of Mainz, 1982. (Jtly) Nobel Prize in Physics, 1961. *Publications:* (with Robert Herman) High Energy Electron Scattering Tables, 1960 (US); (ed) Nuclear and Nucleon Structure, 1963 (US); (co-ed with L. I. Schiff) Nucleon Structure (Proc. Internat. Conf. at Stanford Univ., 1963), 1964; numerous scientific papers on various aspects of molecular structure, solid state physics, nuclear physics, elementary particles, quantum electrodynamics, laser fusion and review articles on crystal counters, electron scattering, nuclear and nucleon structure and coronary angiography. *Recreations:* ranching, photography. *Address:* Department of Physics, Stanford University, Stanford, Calif 94305–2184, USA.

*Died 1990.*

**HOGAN, Hon. Sir Michael (Joseph Patrick),** Kt 1958; CMG 1953; DSNB 1970; *b* 15 March 1908; *m* 1946, Patricia, *d* of late Thomas Galliford; no *c*. *Educ:* Belvedere Coll., Dublin; Stonyhurst Coll., Lancs; Trinity Coll., Dublin Univ. (BA, Gold Medal, 1st cl. hons; LLB). Admitted Solicitor, Ireland, 1930; admitted to Kenya Bar, 1931; called to Irish Bar (Kings Inns), 1936; Chief Magistrate, Palestine, 1936; Crown Counsel, 1937; Attorney-Gen., Aden, 1945; called to English Bar (Inner Temple), 1946; KC (Aden) 1946; Solicitor-Gen., Palestine, 1947; attached Foreign Office, 1949; Malaya: Solicitor-Gen., 1950, QC (Malaya) 1952; Attorney-Gen., Federation of Malaya, 1950–55; Chief Justice of Hong Kong, 1955–70, and of Brunei, 1964–70; Member, Courts of Appeal: the Bahamas, Bermuda and Belize, 1970–75; Gibraltar, 1970–84; President, Courts of Appeal: Brunei, 1970–73; the Bahamas, 1975–78; Bermuda and Belize, 1975–79; Seychelles, 1977–84. British

Mem., Anglo-Japanese Property Commission (apptd under Peace Treaty), 1960. Hon. LLD Dublin Univ., 1962. KSG 1970. *Publications:* revised edition of the Laws of Aden, 1948. *Recreations:* golf, bridge. *Address:* 2 Carlyle Mansions, Cheyne Walk, SW3. *Clubs:* Athenæum; Kildare Street and University (Dublin); Royal Irish Yacht; Hong Kong and Hong Kong Country.

*Died 27 Sept. 1986.*

**HOGBEN, Herbert Edward;** retired; *b* 21 Dec. 1905; *s* of Herbert Edward Hogben; *m* 1929, Dorothy, *d* of Samuel Eastoe Pearson; three *d*. *Educ:* Borden Gram. Sch., Sittingbourne; King's Coll., London (BSc). Scientific Officer, Admiralty, 1927–; Princ. Scientific Officer, 1943; Sen. Princ. Sci. Off., 1952; Dep. Chief Sci. Off., 1961; Chief Sci. Off., Min. of Def. (Navy), 1965; Dep. Chief Scientist, Admiralty Surface Weapons Establishment, 1965–68; Scientific Adviser to Comdr, British Navy Staff, Washington, 1968–70. *Publications:* ASE monographs and technical notes, articles for Jl Inst. of Navigation. *Recreations:* gardening, travel. *Address:* 12 Portsdown Hill Road, Bedhampton, Havant PO9 3JX.

*Died 10 Nov. 1984.*

**HOGG, Alexander Hubert Arthur,** CBE 1973; Secretary, Royal Commission on Ancient Monuments in Wales and Monmouthshire, 1949–73; *b* 2 May 1908; *s* of A. F. Hogg; *m* 1943, Nellie, *d* of G. P. Henderson, MD; one *s* one *d*. *Educ:* Highgate Sch.; Sidney Sussex Coll., Cambridge (MA). Asst Engineer, Sir R. McAlpine & Sons, 1930–34; Junior Scientific Officer, Roads Research Laboratory, 1934–36; Lecturer, Engineering Dept, King's Coll., Newcastle upon Tyne, 1936–42; Temp. Experimental Officer, Admiralty Undex Works, Rosyth, 1942–45; ICI Fellowship, 1945–47; Lecturer Engineering Laboratory, University of Cambridge, 1947–49. FSA; FSAScot. Hon. DLitt Wales, 1974. *Publications:* Hill-Forts of Britain, 1975; British Hill-forts, an Index, 1979; Surveying for Field Archaeologists, 1980; papers in Philosophical Magazine and in Archæological periodicals. *Address:* Brynfield, Bryn Hendre, Waun Fawr, Aberystwyth SY23 3PP. *T:* Aberystwyth 623479.

*Died 11 Sept. 1989.*

**HOGG, Sir Kenneth Weir,** 6th Bt, *cr* 1846; OBE 1946; Lieutenant-Colonel (retired); *b* 13 Sept. 1894; *s* of Guy Weir Hogg (*d* 1943); *S* to baronetcy of cousin, 4th Baron Magheramorne, 1957; *m* 1936, Hon. Aline Emily Partington, *o d* of 2nd Baron Doverdale. *Educ:* Haileybury; Christ Church, Oxford. Served in European War, 1914–18 and War of 1939–45; Irish Guards, 1915–33. *Recreations:* fishing, ski-ing. *Heir: cousin* Major Arthur Ramsay Hogg, MBE 1945 [*b* 24 Oct. 1896; *m* 1924, Mary Aileen Hester Lee (*d* 1980), *d* of late P. H. Lee Evans; three *s* one *d*]. *Address:* 2 Curzon Place, Park Lane, W1. *Clubs:* White's, Portland.

*Died 25 Jan. 1985.*

**HOGG, Sir William Lindsay L.;** *see* Lindsay-Hogg.

**HOGGER, Rear-Adm. Henry Charles,** CB 1961; DSC 1942; *b* 27 June 1907; *s* of Henry George and Maria Jane Hogger; *m* 1935, Ethel Mary Kreiner (*d* 1973); two *s* one *d*. *Educ:* Portsmouth Grammar Sch. Entered Navy, Special Entry Cadet, 1925; specialised in Engineering at RNE Coll., Keyham and RN Coll., Greenwich. During War of 1939–45, served in HMS Kipling and Jervis, 1941–43. Chief Engineer, Hong Kong Dockyard, 1951–54; Asst Engineer-in-Chief, 1955–57; Manager, Engineering Dept, Portsmouth Dockyard, 1957; retired, 1961. Admiralty Regional Officer, Midlands, 1962; Dep. Head, Royal Naval Engineering Service, 1963–71; Dir, Production and Support Dockyards, 1970–72. *Recreation:* golf. *Address:* 12 Lansdown Crescent, Bath, Avon. *T:* Bath 310108. *Club:* Army and Navy.

*Died 22 July 1982.*

**HOGUE, Oliver Alfred John,** CVO 1954; literary staff, Mirror Newspapers, Sydney, 1962–75 and 1976; Associate News Editor, Daily Mirror, 1968–75; *b* 16 Sept. 1910; *s* of Frank Arthur Hogue and Vida C. Hogue (*née* Robinson), Sydney; *m* 1st, 1936, Mary Barbour May (marr. diss., 1966); four *s*; 2nd, 1966, Mary Elizabeth Mofflin (*d* 1976), *d* of Solomon Merkel, Lithuania. *Educ:* Newcastle (NSW) High Sch. Literary staff, Newcastle Herald, 1930; War Correspondent in Australia, 1940–43; Press Sec. to Hon. J. A. Beasley, Australian Minister for Supply, 1943–45; Political Corresp. for Sydney Sunday Sun, Canberra, 1945–53; literary staff, Sydney Sun, 1954–62. Pres., C'wealth Parly Press Gall., 1947–49. Aust. Govt PRO for Australian visit of the Queen and Prince Philip, 1954. *Address:* 7/34 Archer Street, Chatswood, NSW 2067, Australia. *T:* 4196614. *Club:* Journalists' (Sydney).

*Died 8 June 1987.*

**HOHLER, Thomas Sidney A.;** *see* Astell Hohler.

**HOLBECHE, Brian Harry,** CBE 1972; MA Cantab; Headmaster, King Edward's School, Bath, since 1962; *b* 1920; *s* of Ronald Harry Holbeche, Hillybroom, Essex; *m* 1945, Philippa, *d* of Rev. Canon Robert Hunter Jack; one *s* one *d*. *Educ:* Wyggeston Sch., Leicester; St Catharine's Coll., Cambridge (Scholar). Served War of 1939–45: Sub-Lt RNVR, Submarine Service, Middle East. Sen. English Master and Housemaster, St Peter's Sch., York, 1954–61. Pres., Headmasters' Assoc., 1970; Chairman: Direct Grant Cttee of Headmasters' Conf., 1972–73; Joint Four Secondary Schools'

Assoc., 1974 (Vice-Chm., 1972–73); Jt Council of Heads, 1976. *Address:* Nelson House, Beechen Cliff, Bath, Avon. *Club:* East India, Sports and Public Schools. *Died* 17 *Feb.* 1982.

HOLBURN, James; *b* 1 Dec. 1900; *s* of late Rev. James Holburn, Alyth, Perthshire; *m* 1931, Elizabeth Margaret (*d* 1972), *d* of late Rev. John McConnachie, DD, Dundee; three *s*. *Educ:* Harris Academy, Dundee; University of Glasgow (MA Hons). Editorial staff, the Glasgow Herald, 1921–34; joined The Times, 1934: asst correspondent and actg corresp. Berlin, 1935–39; correspondent Moscow, 1939–40; Ankara, 1940–41; War Correspondent, Middle East, 1941–42; Correspondent New Delhi, 1942–46; United Nations Headquarters, 1946–48; Diplomatic Corresp., 1948–51; Chief Corresp. Middle East, 1952–55; Editor, The Glasgow Herald, 1955–65. *Publications:* contributions to various periodicals. *Recreations:* golf, angling. *Address:* Pitnacree, Johnshill Road, Alyth, Perthshire PH11 8DX. *T:* Alyth 2476. *Club:* Western (Glasgow). *Died* 26 *Feb.* 1988.

HOLDEN, Kenneth Graham; retired; *b* 6 May 1910; *e s* of Norman Neill Holden; *m* 1937, Winifred Frances, *d* of Lt-Col T. F. S. Burridge; two *d*. *Educ:* Wellington Coll.; Pembroke Coll., Cambridge. Admitted Solicitor, 1935. Director: (and sometime Chm.) Hardman & Holden Ltd, Manchester, 1936–64; Williams & Glyn's Bank Ltd (formerly as Williams Deacon's Bank Ltd), 1949–78 (Chm., 1964–72); Royal Bank of Scotland Ltd, 1950–69; Geigy (Holdings) Ltd (later CIBA-Geigy (UK) Ltd), 1955–75; Borax Consolidated Ltd, 1961–64; Haden-Carrier Ltd, 1967–75; The Trustee's Corp. Ltd, 1967–80; Manchester Ship Canal Co., 1968–74; National Commercial Banking Group Ltd, 1969–76; Yorkshire Bank Ltd, 1970–78; The Industrial and General Trust Ltd, 1971–80. Part-time Mem., NW Gas Bd, 1965–72. Formerly Mem. Bd of Management (and sometime Jt Hon. Treasurer), Manchester Royal Infirmary. Governor, Manchester Grammar School. *Address:* 40 Lee Road, Aldeburgh, Suffolk. *T:* Aldeburgh (072885) 3159. *Club:* All England Lawn Tennis. *Died* 5 *Oct.* 1990.

HOLDEN, Sir Michael (Herbert Frank), Kt 1973; CBE 1968; ED 1949; Chief Justice, Rivers State, Nigeria, 1970–76; *b* 19 May 1913; *s* of Herbert Charles Holden, solicitor, Bolton, Lancs, and Mary Clare Holden (*née* Timaeus); *m* 1941, Mabel, *d* of Harry Morgan, Cwt Blethyn, Usk, Monmouthshire, and Ethel Morgan (*née* Jones), Betllan Deg, near Usk; two *s* one *d*. *Educ:* Aldenham Sch., Elstree, Herts. Admitted solicitor, 1937; employed in Lagos, Nigeria, as Asst Solicitor to J. C. Ticehurst, Sept. 1937 to July 1940, when embodied in Nigeria Regt. Served War of 1939–45; demob. rank Captain, 1945. Private practice as solicitor in Jos, Northern Nigeria; apptd Magistrate, Sept. 1955; Chief Magistrate, 1960; Judge, 1961; Sen. Puisne Judge, Kano State, 1970. *Recreations:* photography, electronics, fishing. *Address:* 3 Rushton Road, Wilbarston, Kettering, Northants. *T:* Kettering 761100. *Died* 11 *March* 1982.

HOLDEN, Philip Edward; an Underwriting Member of Lloyd's since 1954; *b* 20 June 1905. *Educ:* King Edward VI Schs, Birmingham. Qualified, CA, 1929; Managing Dir Amalgamated Anthracite Collieries, from 1940. Past Chm., Amalgamated Anthracite Holdings Group of Cos. Has served on Exec. of Monmouthshire and S Wales Coal Owners Assoc., and as Chm. of its Commercial Cttee; also served on Exec. Bd of S Wales Coal Mines Scheme. Pres. Swansea Chamber of Commerce, 1952–53; Vice-Chm. Chamber of Coal Traders, 1953–65; Vice-Chm. Nat. Council of Coal Traders (Chm. 1953–65); Pres. Brit. Coal Exporters' Assoc., 1958–63; Mem. Industrial Coal Consumers' Council, 1958. A Dir of public and private cos (coal, shipping, manufactures, electronics, electro-chemical and general engineering, etc). *Recreations:* Pres. Swansea City AFC Ltd; Vice-Pres. Clyne Golf Club, Ltd. *Address:* La Maison Blanche, Jerbourg Road, St Martin, Guernsey, CI. *T:* Guernsey 37985. *Club:* Royal Automobile. *Died* 15 *Jan.* 1987.

HOLDER, Sir John (Eric Duncan), 3rd Bt, *cr* 1898; late Flight Lieutenant RAFVR; *b* 2 Aug. 1899; *s* of Sir Henry Holder, 2nd Bt, and Evelyn (*d* 1946), *d* of Sir Robert Ropner, 1st Bt; *S* father, 1945; *m* 1st, 1927, Evelyn Josephine (marr. diss.), *er d* of late William Blain; one *s* two *d*; 2nd, Marjorie Emily, *d* of late F. R. Markham. *Educ:* Uppingham; Brasenose Coll., Oxford (MA). *Heir:* *s* John Henry Holder, Royal Armoured Corps [*b* 12 March 1928; *m* 1960, Catharine Harrison, *yr d* of late Leonard Baker; twin *s* one *d*]. *Address:* Mulberry House, 17 Johnsons Drive, Hampton, Middx TW12 2EQ. *Died* 10 *May* 1986.

HOLDERNESS, Rt. Rev. George Edward, ERD (with 2 clasps) 1955; Dean Emeritus of Lichfield; an Assistant Bishop, Diocese of York, since 1980; *b* 5 March 1913; 2nd *s* of A. W. Holderness, Roundhay, Leeds; *m* 1940, Irene Mary, *er d* of H. G. Hird, Bedale, Yorkshire; one *s* two *d*. *Educ:* Leeds Grammar Sch.: Keble Coll., Oxford (MA); Westcott House, Cambridge. Assistant Curate of Bedale, 1936–39; Chaplain and Asst Master, Aysgarth School, Bedale, 1939–47. CF (RARO), 1940; SCF, 81st W African Div., 1943; DACG, India

Command, 1945. Vicar of Darlington, 1947–55; Hon. Canon of Durham Cathedral, 1954; Suffragan Bishop of Burnley, 1955–70; Rector of Burnley, 1955–70; Canon of Blackburn Cathedral, 1955–70; Dean of Lichfield, 1970–79. DACG, TA, Northern Command, 1951–55. *Recreations:* shooting, fishing. *Address:* Riseborough Cottages, Marton, Sinnington, York YO6 6RD. *Clubs:* MCC, Forty, Lord's Taverners', I Zingari.
*Died* 21 *Oct.* 1987.

HOLDSWORTH, Max Ernest, OBE 1944; TD; DL; MA; LLB; Barrister-at-Law; Deputy-Chairman, Court of Quarter Sessions, Gloucestershire, 1954–68; Recorder of Lichfield, 1939–68; Colonel (TA); *b* 6 Nov. 1895; *o s* of late M. F. Holdsworth; *m* 1929, Frances Jessie Corn; one *s* one *d*. *Educ:* King Edward's Sch., Birmingham; Christ's Coll., Cambridge. Served European War, 1915–19; also in War of 1939–45; called to the Bar, Gray's Inn, 1922. DL Warwicks, 1945, Hereford and Worcester, 1974. *Publications:* Law of Transport, 1932. *Address:* 44 Britannia Square, Worcester. *T:* Worcester 23133. *Club:* Union and County (Worcester). *Died* 22 *July* 1982.

HOLE, George Vincer, CBE 1969; ICAO Consultant on Airport Affairs, since 1975; Chief Executive, British Airports Authority, 1965–72; *b* 26 Jan. 1910; *s* of George William Hole and Louisa Hole (*née* Vincer); *m* 1938, Gertraud Johanna Anna Koppe (Baroness von Broesigke); two *s*. *Educ:* Wilson's Grammar Sch., London; London Sch. of Economics. BSc (Econ.) 1933. Asst Auditor, Exchequer and Audit Dept, 1929; passed First Div. Exam., 1935; Under-Sec., 1958; Min. of Aviation, 1959–65; student Imperial Defence Coll., 1948; Chm. First Div. Assoc., 1949–50; Chm. OEEC Productivity Group, on Traffic Engineering and Control, in the United States, 1954; Chm. W European Airports Assoc., 1970; Member: Council, Internat. Bd of Airport Operators, 1970; Bd, Internat. Civil Airports Assoc. (Chm.); Bd, Airport Assocs Co-ordinating Council (first Chm.). FCIT. Hon. Treas., Caravan Club, 1960–66. Dir, J. E. Greiner Co. Ltd, Consulting Engineers, Edinburgh, 1972–75. ICAO Lectr on Airport Affairs, Beirut, 1972–75. Chm. Bd of Governors, Christ's Coll., Blackheath, 1962–83. Officer, Order of Orange Nassau, Netherlands, 1946; Officer, Order of the Crown, Belgium, 1946. *Recreation:* pottering. *Address:* 2 Macartney House, Chesterfield Walk, Greenwich, SE10 8HJ. *T:* 01–858 3917. *Died* 7 *March* 1988.

HOLE, Tahu Ronald Charles Pearce, CBE 1956; Director of Administration and Member, Board of Management, BBC, 1958–60, retired; *b* Christchurch, NZ, 29 March 1908; *s* of Charles Hole and Susan Eliza Hole; *m* Joyce Margaret Wingate. *Educ:* Sydenham School, Christchurch; Canterbury University Coll. (journalism), NZ. Reporter on New Zealand and Australian newspapers, 1926–35; first news editor, Sydney Morning Herald, 1935–37; London corresp. and war corresp., Sydney Morning Herald, 1937–40; special corresp., The Herald, Melbourne, 1940–41; BBC: commentator, 1940–41; joined Overseas Service, 1941; Empire Services, 1942; producer of War Review, 1942–43; Overseas Talks Manager, 1944; Asst Editor, News Div. and Mem., Edtl Bd, 1946; Editor-Controller, News Div. (Home, Overseas and TV news), 1948–58. Member: Adv. Council, Empire Press Union, 1937–41; Edtl Bd, RIIA, 1949–54; Press, Broadcasting and Armed Services (Defence Notice) Cttee, 1945–58; BBC adviser to UK Govt's delegation to UN Information Conf., Paris, 1953; BBC rep. at Internat. Convention of Radio and TV News Directors, Washington, 1954, Miami, 1957; Mem., BBC delegation to Commonwealth Broadcasting Conf., London, 1947, Sydney, 1956; organised with Rank Orgn and Reuter for establishment of British Commonwealth International Newsfilm Agency Ltd (Visnews), 1956, Dep. Chm., 1957, Chm., 1958. First journalist to fly to news assignment in NZ; NZ Journalists' Assoc. Award for best journalism, 1929. Frequently attacked by Nazi propaganda dept for war-time broadcasts, card referring to his activities found in Gestapo HQ files after fall of Berlin. Life Mem., Royal Soc. of St George. *Publications:* Anzacs into Battle, 1941; Experiment in Freedom, 1944; The Responsibilities of Editing News and Current Affairs in Radio and Television, 1957; contribs to The Times, Daily Telegraph, Time and Tide, National Review. *Recreations:* travel, music, reading. *Address:* Iwerne Minster, Blandford Forum, Dorset. *Club:* Carlton. *Died* 22 *Nov.* 1985.

HOLLAND, Sir Jim Sothern, 2nd Bt, *cr* 1917; TD 1950; *b* 31 March 1911; *er s* of Sir R. Sothern Holland, 1st Bt, and Stretta Aimée Holland (*née* Price) (*d* 1949); *S* father, 1948; *m* 1937, Elisabeth Hilda Margaret, *o d* of Thomas Francis Vaughan Prickard, CVO; two *d*. *Educ:* Durnford; Marlborough; Trinity Coll., Oxon (MA). Central Mining and Investment, 1932–64; Dir, Price & Pierce Ltd, 1959–66; a Manager and Alternate Dir, Charter Consolidated Ltd, 1964–69. Joined TA 1939. City of London Yeomanry. Served War of 1939–45; 1942–44, ADC to Field-Marshal Viscount Gort, when Governor of Malta; Major RA, TA, 1946–48. *Recreations:* botany, stalking. *Heir:* *b* Guy Hope Holland, late Royal Scots Greys [*b* 19 July 1918; *m* 1945, Joan Marian, *o d* of late Capt. H. E. Street, 20th

Hussars; two *d. Educ:* Christ Church, Oxford]. *Address:* Dderw, Rhayader, Powys. *T:* Rhayader 810226. *Club:* Bath.

*Died 25 Dec.* 1981.

**HOLLAND, Rt. Rev. John Tristram,** CBE 1975; *b* 31 Jan. 1912; *s of* Rt Rev. H. St B. Holland; *m* 1937, Joan Theodora Arundell, *d of Dr* R. Leslie Ridge, Carlton House, Enfield, Mddx; three *d. Educ:* Durham School; University College, Oxford; Westcott House, Cambridge. BA 1933, MA 1937, Oxford. Deacon, 1935; Priest, 1936; Curate of St Peter's, Huddersfield, 1935–37; Commissary to Bishop of Wellington, 1936–37; Vicar of Featherston, 1938–41; CF (2 NZEF), 1941–45; Vicar of: St Peter's, Upper Riccarton, 1945–49; St Mary's, New Plymouth, 1949–51; Bishop of Waikato, 1951–69; Bishop in Polynesia, 1969–75; Officiating Minister: Diocese of Canterbury, 1975–76; Diocese of Waiapu, 1976–87; Dio. of Waikato, 1987. *Address:* Kerridge House, Selwyn Village, Auckland 2, New Zealand. *Died 9 Oct.* 1990.

**HOLLAND-MARTIN, Edward;** *b* 8 March 1900; *s* of late R. M. Holland-Martin, CB; *m* 1955, Dagny Mary MacLean, *yr d* of late Major J. M. Grant and late Mrs Horace Webber; one *d. Educ:* Eton; Christ Church, Oxford (MA). Director: Bank of England, 1933–48; Bank of London and S America, 1948–70; Dep. Chm., BOLSA, 1951–70. CPRE: Hon. Treasurer, 1928–71, Vice-Pres., 1971–; Hon. Treasurer, Nat. Trust, 1948–68; BHS: Mem. Council, 1948–, Hon. Treasurer, 1956–66, Pres., 1978–80. Prime Warden, Fishmonger's Company, 1959. Sheriff of County of London, 1941; one of HM Lieutenants, City of London, 1933–. Mem. Jockey Club. *Address:* Overbury Court, near Tewkesbury, Glos GL20 7NP. *T:* Overbury 202; St James's Place, SW1. *T:* 01-493 0937. *Club:* White's. *Died 10 March* 1981.

**HOLLIS, Rt. Rev. (Arthur) Michael;** *b* 23 June 1899; *s* of late Rt Rev. George Arthur Hollis, Bishop of Taunton; *m* 1935, Mary Cordelia (*d* 1984), *d* of late Very Rev. Andrew Ewbank Burn, Dean of Salisbury. *Educ:* Leeds Grammar Sch.; Trinity Coll., Oxford (Scholar). Army, 1918–19; BA (2nd class Classical Hon. Mods) 1920; 1st class Lit. Hum., 1922; MA, 1924; BD, 1931; Leeds Clergy Sch., 1922; ordained deacon, 1923; priest, 1924; Curate S Andrew's, Huddersfield, 1923–24; Chaplain and Lecturer in Theology, Hertford Coll., Oxford, Fellow, 1926–31; Lecturer St Peter's Leeds, 1931; SPG Missionary, Bishop's Theological Seminary, Nazareth, diocese of Tinnevelly, India, 1931–37; Perpetual Curate of S Mary's Charlton Kings, diocese of Gloucester, 1937–42; CF 4th class (RARO), 1939–42; Bishop of Madras, 1942–47; Bishop in Madras, 1947–54; Moderator, Church of South India, 1948–54; Professor of Church History, United Theological Coll., Bangalore, 1955–60; Rector of Todwick, 1961–64; Second Assistant Bishop to the Bishop of Sheffield, 1963–66; Asst Bishop, Dio. of St Edmundsbury and Ipswich, 1966–75. Teaching, USA, 1960–61. *Publications:* Paternalism and the Church; The Significance of South India; Mission, Unity and Truth. *Address:* Flat 2, Manormead, Tilford Road, Hindhead, Surrey GU26 6RA. *T:* Hindhead 6951.

*Died 11 Feb.* 1986.

**HOLLIS, Hugh;** part-time Chairman for Civil Service Commission Appointments Board, 1972–77; *b* 25 July 1910; *s* of Ash and Emily Geraldine Hollis; *m* 1939, Muriel Bewick Hollis (*née* Nattrass); two *s. Educ:* Stockton Sec. Sch.; Constantine Techn. College. BSc Hons London; CChem; FRIC. Imperial Chemical Industries, 1928–36; Chemist, War Office, 1936–40; Principal Scientific Officer, Min. of Supply, 1940–56; Army Dept, MoD, 1956–71: Asst Dir Chemical Inspectorate; Dir 1963, title changed to Dir of Quality Assce (Materials), MoD, 1969–71 (CSO 1970), retired 1971. *Publications:* articles in Jl of Oil and Colour Chemists Assoc. and Inst. of Petroleum. *Recreations:* gardening, trout and salmon fishing. *Address:* Green Point, Fossebridge, Cheltenham, Glos. *T:* Fossebridge 463. *Died 6 Oct.* 1986.

**HOLLIS, Rt. Rev. Michael;** *see* Hollis, Rt Rev. A. M.

**HOLLOWAY, Gwendoline Elizabeth,** BA Hons; *b* 9 April 1893. *Educ:* University of Bristol (Hall of Residence, Clifton Hill House). Asst Mistress at Harrogate College for Girls, 1917–26; Vice-Principal, Queen's Coll., 1926–31; Acting Principal, 1931–32; Principal, 1932–40; First woman to be appointed Principal of Queen's Coll.; Lady Principal of Alexandra Coll., Dublin, 1940–61; Headmistress, Lowther Coll., North Wales, 1961–63. President, Federation of Soroptimist Clubs of Great Britain and Ireland, 1948–49; Life Mem., Alumni Assoc., Univ. of Bristol (Pres. 1968–69). *Recreation:* walking. *Died 12 Jan.* 1981.

**HOLLOWAY, Stanley,** OBE 1960; actor, vocalist and monologuist; *b* London, 1 Oct. 1890; *m* 1st, 1913; one *s* three *d*; 2nd, 1939, Violet Marion Lane; one *s*. Formerly seaside concert artist; first West End appearance as Capt. Wentworth in Kissing Time, Winter Garden, 1919; René in A Night Out, Winter Garden, 1920; original member of the Co-Optimists, and remained as one until disbandment, 1927; Bill Smith in Hit the Deck, London Hippodrome, 1927; Lieut Richard Manners in Song of the Sea, His Majesty's, 1928; Cooee,

Vaudeville, 1929; appeared with the revived Co-Optimists, 1929, The Co-Optimists of 1930, London Hippodrome; Savoy Follies, Savoy, 1932; Here We Are Again, Lyceum, 1932; Eustace Titherley in Three Sisters, 1934; first appearance in pantomime, Prince of Wales's, Birmingham, 1934, as Abanazar in Aladdin, and has played same part each succeeding Christmas at Leeds, Golders Green, Edinburgh and Manchester; All Wave, Duke of York's, 1936; London Rhapsody, London Palladium, 1938; All The Best, season at Blackpool, 1938; Saville: in Up and Doing, 1940 and 1941 in Fine and Dandy, 1942; Played First Gravedigger in Festival Production of Hamlet, New Theatre, 1951; Midsummer Night's Dream (with Old Vic at Edinburgh Festival, and subsequently Metropolitan Opera House, New York, followed by tour of USA and Canada); played Alfred Doolittle in New York production of My Fair Lady (musical version of Pygmalion), 1956–58 and in London production, Drury Lane, 1958–59; Burgess in Candida, Shaw Festival, Canada, 1970; Siege, Cambridge Theatre, 1972; William in You Never Can Tell, Shaw Festival, Canada, 1973; The Pleasure of His Company, tour of Australia and Hong Kong with Douglas Fairbanks Jnr, 1977. *Films:* Hamlet (Gravedigger), This Happy Breed, The Way Ahead, The Way to the Stars, Cæsar and Cleopatra, Champagne Charlie, The Perfect Woman, Midnight Episode, One Wild Oat, The Lavender Hill Mob, The Magic Box (Festival Film), Lady Godiva Rides Again, Meet Me To-night, The Titfield Thunderbolt, The Beggar's Opera, Meet Mr Lucifer, A Day to Remember, Fast and Loose, An Alligator Named Daisy, Jumping for Joy, No Trees in the Street, Alive and Kicking, No Love for Johnnie, On The Fiddle, My Fair Lady (Alfred Doolittle), Ten Little Indians, Mrs Brown You Have A Lovely Daughter, Run a Crooked Mile, Private Life of Sherlock Holmes, What's in it for Harry, The Flight of the Doves, Up the Front, Desperate Journey. TV series: Our Man Higgins, Hollywood, 1962–63; Thingamybob, London, 1968; TV film, Dr Jekyll and Mr Hyde, 1973. Variety Club of GB Special Award, 1978. *Publications:* Wiv a Little Bit o' Luck (authobiography), 1967; Monologues, 1979; The Stanley Holloway Monologues, 1980; More Monologues, 1981. *Address:* Pyefleet, Tamarisk Way, East Preston, Sussex. *Died 30 Jan.* 1982.

**HOLLOWOOD, A(lbert) Bernard,** MSc(Econ); FRSA; Editor of Punch, 1957–68; author, economist and cartoonist; contributor of articles and drawings to Punch since 1942; Member of Punch Table since 1945; *b* 3 June 1910; 2nd *s* of Albert and Sarah Elizabeth Hollowood, Burslem, Staffordshire; *m* 1938, Marjorie Duncan, *d* of Dr W. D. Lawrie, Hartshill, Stoke-on-Trent; one *s* two *d. Educ:* Hanley High School; St Paul's Coll., Cheltenham; London University. Lecturer in Economics, School of Commerce, Stoke-on-Trent, and Loughborough Coll., 1932–43; lecturer to HM Forces; on staff of The Economist, 1944–45; Research Officer, Council of Industrial Design, 1946–47; Editor of Pottery and Glass, 1944–50; Pocket cartoonist of Sunday Times, 1957–60, The Times, Sunday Telegraph, etc. Broadcaster from 1939. Visiting Prof. at American Univs. Member, Court of Governors, London School of Economics. Hon. MA Keele, 1968. *Publications:* Direct Economics, 1943; Money is No Expense, 1946; An Innocent at Large, 1947; Britain Inside-Out, 1948; Scowle and Other Papers, 1948; Pottery and Glass, 1949; Poor Little Rich World, 1948; The Hawksmoor Scandals, 1949; Cornish Engineers, 1951; The Story of Morro Velho, 1954; Tory Story, 1964; Pont, The Story of Graham Laidler, 1969; Cricket on the Brain, 1970; Tales of Tommy Barr, 1970; Funny Money, 1975; Pamphlets and Papers on Economics. *Recreations:* chess, village cricket (formerly county cricket: Staffordshire 1930–46). *Address:* Blackmoor Paddock, Haldish Lane, Shamley Green, Surrey. *T:* Bramley 2118.

*Died 28 March* 1981.

**HOLMAN, Dr Portia Grenfell;** Senior Physician in Psychological Medicine, Elizabeth Garrett Anderson Hospital, 1954–69, retired; *b* 20 Nov. 1903; *d* of Hon. William Arthur Holman, KC, Premier of New South Wales, 1914–18, and Ada Augusta Kidgell. *Educ:* The Women's Coll., Sydney, NSW; Newnham Coll., Cambridge. Economics Tripos, 1923–26, BA Cantab, 1926. Research and lecturing at St Andrews Univ., 1927–33; MA Cantab 1923. Medical student, Cambridge and Royal Free Hospital, 1934–39. Consultant Psychiatrist to Twickenham Child Guidance Clinic, 1944, West Middlesex Hospital, 1945, Elizabeth Garrett Anderson Hospital, 1946. MD 1950; Burlingame Prize, 1952; FRCP 1961; FRCPsych 1971. Founder and first Chairman Association of Workers for Maladjusted Children, 1951. *Publications:* Bedwetting, 1954; Psychology and Psychological Medicine for Nurses, 1957; (with Amy Sycamore) Sebastians: hospital school experiment in therapeutic education, 1971; contributions to Journal of Mental Science. *Recreations:* mountain climbing, swimming. *Address:* 2 Prince Albert Road, NW1. *Club:* Royal Society of Medicine.

*Died 16 May* 1983.

**HOLMES, Sir (David) Ronald,** Kt 1973; CMG 1969; CBE 1962 (MBE 1943); MC 1943; ED 1956; Chairman, Public Services Commission, Hong Kong, 1971–77; *b* 26 Dec. 1913; *s* of late Louis James Holmes and late Emily Sutcliffe, Brighouse, W Yorks; *m* 1945, Marjorie

Partner, Lawrence, Gardner & Co., Chartered Accountants, Bristol, 1931–57. 2nd Lieut RE (TA), 1923; CRE 61 Div., 1939–42; DCE Scottish Command, 1942–44; DCE Second Army, 1944–45; Col 1945. Chm., Commn of Enquiry into Port of Aden, 1963. Governor of Clifton Coll., 1954–; Mem. of Court of Univ. of Bristol, 1956–. DL Co. Gloucester, 1950–. *Recreation:* reading. *Address:* Penthouse C, Marklands, Julian Road, Sneyd Park, Bristol BS9 1NP. *T:* Bristol 682615. *Clubs:* Army and Navy; Bath and County (Bath).
*Died 14 Dec. 1986.*

**HOOD PHILLIPS, Owen;** *see* Phillips.

**HOOFT, Willem Adolf Visser 't;** *see* Visser 't Hooft.

**HOOK, Prof. Sidney;** Professor, Department of Philosophy, Graduate School of Arts and Science, New York University, 1939–72, now Emeritus Professor; Senior Research Fellow on War, Revolution and Peace, at Hoover Institution, Stanford University, since 1973; Founder of The New York University Institute of Philosophy; *b* 20 Dec. 1902; *s* of Isaac Hook and Jennie Halpern; *m* 1924; one *s*; *m* 1935, Ann Zinken; one *s* one *d*. *Educ:* College of the City of New York; BS 1923; Columbia Univ. (MA 1926, PhD 1927); Columbia Univ. Fellowship in Philosophy, 1926–27; Guggenheim Research Fellowship in Philosophy for Study Abroad, 1928–29, 1953–; Ford Fellowship for the Study of Asian philosophy and culture, 1958. Teacher, New York City Public Schs, 1923–27; Instr in Philosophy, Washington Square Coll., New York Univ., 1927–32; Asst Prof., 1932–34; Assoc. Prof. and Chm. of Dept of Philosophy, 1933–39; Lectr, New Sch. for Social Research, NYC, 1931–. Vis. Prof., Univ. of California, 1950, Harvard Univ., 1961; Thomas Jefferson Memorial Lectr, Univ. of California at Berkeley, 1961; Regents Prof., Univ. of California at Santa Barbara, 1966; Vis. Prof., Univ. of California at San Diego, 1975. Fellow at Center for Advanced Study in the Behavioral Sciences, Stanford Univ., 1961–62. Butler Silver Medal for distinction in Philosophy, Columbia Univ., 1945. Organiser: conf. on Methods in Philosophy and Sci., conf. on Sci. Spirit and Dem. Faith, and Cttee for Cultural Freedom; Organiser and Co-Chm., Americans for Intellectual Freedom; President: Univ. Centers for Rational Alternatives; John Dewey Foundn (and Treasurer); Mem., American Philosophical Assoc. Vice-Pres., Eastern Div., 1958, Pres., 1959–60, Am. Assoc. Univ. Profs (past Council Mem.); Vice-President: Internat. Cttees for Academic Freedom; Council, Nat. Endowment for the Humanities, 1973–79 (Jefferson Lectr, 1984). Hon. DHL: Univ. of Maine, 1960; Univ. of Utah, 1970; Univ. of Vermont, 1979; Hon LLD: Univ. of California, 1966; Rockford Coll., 1970; Univ. of Florida, 1971. Fellow: American Academy of Arts and Sciences, 1965; Nat. Acad. of Educn, 1968. Presidential Medal of Freedom, 1985. *Publications:* The Metaphysics of Pragmatism, 1927; Towards the Understanding of Karl Marx, 1933; American Philosophy—To-day and To-morrow, 1935; From Hegel to Marx, 1936; Planned Society—Yesterday, To-day, To-morrow, 1937; John Dewey: An Intellectual Portrait, 1939; Reason, Social Myths and Democracy, 1940; The Hero in History, 1943; Education for Modern Man, 1946; Heresy, Yes—Conspiracy No, 1953; The Ambiguous Legacy; Marx and the Marxists, 1955; Common Sense and the Fifth Amendment, 1957; Political Power and Personal Freedom, 1959; The Quest for Being, 1961; The Paradoxes of Freedom, 1962; The Fail-Safe Fallacy, 1963; Religion in a Free Society, 1967; Academic Freedom and Academic Anarchy, 1970; Education and the Taming of Power, 1973; Pragmatism and the Tragic Sense of Life, 1975; Revolution, Reform and Social Justice, 1976; Philosophy and Public Philosophy, 1980; Marxism and Beyond, 1983; Out of Step: an unquiet life in the XXth Century (autobiog.), 1987; Editor of various works; contrib. numerous articles to philosophical journals. *Recreation:* gardening. *Address:* New York University, New York, NY 10003, USA. *T:* 212–598–3262; Hoover Institution, Stanford, Calif 94305, USA. *T:* 415–497–1501.
*Died 12 July 1989.*

**HOOKER, Sir Stanley (George),** Kt 1974; CBE 1964 (OBE 1946); FRS 1962; DSc; DPhil; Technical Adviser to the Chairman, 1977–81, Consultant, since 1981, Rolls-Royce Ltd; *b* 30 Sept. 1907; 5th *s* of William Harry and Ellen Mary Hooker; *m* 1st, 1936, Hon. Margaret Bradbury; one *d*; 2nd, 1950, Kate Maria Garth; one *d*. *Educ:* Borden Grammar Sch.; Imperial Coll., London; Brasenose Coll., Oxford (Hon. Fellow 1980). Scientific and Research Dept, Admiralty, 1935–38; Rolls Royce Ltd, 1938–48; Bristol Aero Engines, 1948–59. Apptd Chief Engr, Engine Div., Bristol Aeroplane Co. Ltd, 1951 and a Dir, 1952; Technical Dir (Aero), Bristol Siddeley Engines Ltd, 1959; Technical Dir, Bristol Engine Div. of Rolls-Royce Ltd, 1966–71; Gp Technical Dir, Rolls-Royce Ltd, 1971–77. FIMechE (Mem. Council, 1958–); FRAeS; Fellow, Imperial Coll.; Hon. Mem. ASME, 1980; Fellow, Amer. Acad of Engineering, 1981; Hon. Prof., Peking Inst. of Aeronautical Scis, 1973. Hon. ScD Cambridge, 1982. British Silver Medal for Aeronautics, awarded by RAeS, 1955; Diplôme Paul Tissandier, by Féd. Aero Internationale, 1955; Thulin Bronze Medal by Swedish Aero. Soc., 1960; Brit. Gold Medal for Aeronautics, by RAeS, 1961; James Clayton Prize (jointly), 1966; Gold Medal, RAeS, 1967;

Churchill Gold Medal, Soc. of Engineers, 1968; Goddard Medal, Amer. Inst. of Aeronautics and Astronautics, 1969; Leverhulme Medal, Royal Soc., 1981; Wilhelm-Exner-Medaille, Österreichen Gewerbeverein, 1982. *Publication:* Not Much of an Engineer (autobiog.), 1984. *Address:* Rolls-Royce Ltd, PO Box 3, Filton, Bristol; Orchard Hill, Milbury Heath, Wotton-under-Edge, Glos. *Clubs:* Athenæum; Wings (NY).
*Died 24 May 1984.*

**HOOKWAY, Reginald John Samuel,** FRTPI; consultant planner; Director of the Countryside Commission, 1971–81; *b* 7 June 1920; *er s* of Charles and Florence Hookway, Bideford, Devon; *m* 1942, Ethel Lylie Ashford; one *s* two *d*. *Educ:* Bideford Grammar Sch.; University Coll. of the South West, Exeter (BSc). Served War, 1940–46 (despatches; commnd RE; served in N Africa, Italy, Jugoslavia, Greece. Devon County Council: Research Officer, 1948–55; Asst County Planning Officer, 1955–58; Dep. County Planning Officer, Norfolk CC, 1958–64; Principal Planning Officer, Countryside Commn, 1965–69; Dep. Chief Planning Officer, Min. of Housing and Local Govt, 1969–71. Mem., Nat. Parks Policies Review Cttee, 1972–74, and many other govt cttees. British Travel Authority: Chm., Caravan and Camping Sub Cttee, 1981–; Mem., Marketing Cttee, 1981–; Adviser to Council for Environmental Consultation, 1982–. Hon. LLD Exeter, 1981. *Publications:* a number of papers on rural and recreational planning, incl. many for Countryside Commn. *Recreations:* walking, swimming. *Address:* 1 Albert Court, Albert Road, Cheltenham, Glos GL52 2TN. *T:* Cheltenham 519483. *Club:* Reform.
*Died 5 Dec. 1982.*

**HOOLEY, Maj.-Gen. St John Cutler,** CB 1958; CBE 1954; *b* 30 Sept. 1902; *s* of late S. P. Hooley, Tharston, Norfolk; *m* 1931, Molly Isobel, *d* of late Dr A. Scott-Turner, MRCS, LRCP, JP, London; one *d*. *Educ:* RMA, Woolwich. Royal Artillery, 2nd Lieut 1923; Captain RAOC, 1934; Dep. Dir Ordnance Services: AA Comd, 1945–46; British Mil. Mission, Greece, 1947–50; HQ Eastern Comd, 1950–52; Dir, Ordnance Services, HQ BAOR and Northern Army Gp, 1952–57; Brig. 1954, Maj.-Gen. 1957; Inspector RAOC, 1957–58; Comdt, Mechanical Transport Organisation, Chilwell, 1958–60, retired. Served War of 1939–45 in Norway, Middle East and India (despatches). *Recreations:* golf, travel, photography. *Address:* Storrington Cottage, Sea Avenue, Rustington, Sussex.
*Died 13 Feb. 1985.*

**HOOPER, Sir Anthony (Robin Maurice),** 2nd Bt *cr* 1962; *b* 26 Oct. 1918; *o s* of Sir Frederic Collins Hooper, 1st Bt, and Eglantine Irene (Bland); *S* father, 1963; *m* 1970, Cynthia (marr. diss. 1973), *yr d* of Col W. J. H. Howard, DSO. *Educ:* Radley; New Coll., Oxford. Royal Artillery, 1939–41; Asst to Hubert Philips, News Chronicle, 1941–42; Political Research Centre, 1942–44; Actor (Liverpool, Windsor, Birmingham, Oxford, London, BBC), 1944–50; temp. Civil Servant, Cabinet Office, 1950–52. Asst Design Manager, Schweppes Ltd, 1952–64; Director, Couper Gallery, 1964–68. *Recreations:* music, conversation and people. *Club:* Savile.
*Died 25 May 1987 (ext).*

**HOOPER, Sir Robin (William John),** KCMG 1968 (CMG 1954); DSO 1943; DFC 1943; HM Diplomatic Service, retired; *b* 26 July 1914; *s* of late Col John Charles Hooper, DSO, and late Irene Annie Palmer Hooper (*née* Anderson), Harewell, Faversham, Kent; *m* 1941, Constance Mildred Ayshford (*d* 1986), *d* of late Lieut-Col Gilbert Ayshford Sanford, DSO, DL, Triley Court, Abergavenny, Mon; three *s*. *Educ:* Charterhouse; The Queen's Coll., Oxford. 3rd Sec., Foreign Office, 1938–40. Served War of 1939–45; on active service with RAF, 1940–44 (Wing-Comdr). Second Sec., HM Embassy, Paris, 1944–47; First Sec., HM Embassy, Lisbon, 1947–49; transferred to FO, 1949; Counsellor, 1950; Head of Personnel Dept, 1950–53; Counsellor, HM Embassy, Bagdad, 1953–56; Head of Perm. Under-Sec.'s Dept, FO, 1956–60; Asst Sec.-Gen. (Political), NATO, 1960–66; Ambassador to Tunisia, 1966–67; Ambassador to Southern Yemen, 1967–68; Dep. Sec., Cabinet Office, 1968–71; Ambassador to Greece, 1971–74. Chm., Anglo-Hellenic League, 1975–78. Dir, Benguela Railway Co., 1976–84. Mem., NATO Appeals Bd, 1977–85. Chevalier, Legion of Honour, 1945. Croix de Guerre, 1939–45 (2 Palms), 1945. *Address:* Brook House, Egerton, near Ashford, Kent TN27 9AP. *Club:* Travellers'.
*Died 14 June 1989.*

**HOOSON, Tom (Ellis);** MP (C) Brecon and Radnor, since 1979; *b* 16 March 1933; *s* of late David Maelor Hooson and Ursula Ellis Hooson. *Educ:* Rhyl Grammar School; University College, Oxford (MA); Gray's Inn. Career in publishing, advertising and marketing in Britain, USA and France. With Benton & Bowles Inc., 1961–76 (Senior Vice-Pres., Dir of European Operations, 1971–76); Dir of Communications, Cons. Party, 1976–78; Dir-Gen., Periodical Publishers Assoc., 1978–. Contested (C) Caernarvon, 1959. Chm., Bow Group and Bow Publications, 1960–62; founded Welsh Farm News, 1957. *Publications:* (jtly) Work for Wales, 1959; (contrib.) Lessons from America, 1973. *Recreations:* walking, sailing, tennis, reading. *Address:* House of Commons, SW1. *Club:* Carlton.
*Died 8 May 1985.*

HOPE, Sir Archibald (Philip), 17th Bt of Craighall, *cr* 1628; OBE 1945; DFC 1940; AE 1943; retired 1977; *b* 27 March 1912; *s* of 16th Bt and Hon. Mary Bruce, OBE, JP Midlothian, *e d* of 10th Lord Balfour of Burleigh; *S* father, 1924; *m* 1938, Ruth (*d* 1986), *y d* of Carl Davis, Fryern, Storrington, Sussex; two *s. Educ:* Eton; Balliol Coll., Oxford. BA 1934; ACA 1939; FCA 1960; Mem. of Queen's Body Guard for Scotland (Royal Company of Archers). Served, RAFO, 1931–35; 601 (County of London) Sqdn AAF, 1935–40 (comdg during Battle of Britain); served War of 1939–45 (despatches twice, DFC, OBE). Wing Comdr (acting Group Capt.), AAF. Joined Airwork, 1945; Dir, 1951; resigned, June 1956; Dir, D. Napier & Son Ltd, 1956–61; Dir, Napier Aero Engines Ltd, 1961–68; Chief Exec., Napier Aero Engines Ltd, 1962–68; English Electric Co., 1968–70; Gp Treasurer, GEC Ltd, 1970–77. Mem., Air Transport Users Cttee, CAA, 1973–79, Dep. Chm. 1974–77, Chm. 1977–79. Chm., The Air League, 1965–68. FRAeS 1968. *Heir:* *s* John Carl Alexander Hope [*b* 10 June 1939; *m* 1968, Merle Pringle, *d* of Robert Douglas, Southside, Holbrook, Ipswich; one *s* one *d*]. *Address:* The Manor House, Somerford Keynes, near Cirencester, Glos GL7 6DL. *T:* Cirencester 861250. *Clubs:* Royal Air Force; New (Edinburgh); Nairobi (Nairobi).                    *Died 27 July 1987.*

HOPE, James Kenneth, CBE 1946; DL; MA (Hon.); Recorder of City of Durham, 1942–74; Clerk of the Peace of County of Durham, Clerk of Durham County Council, and County Registration Officer, 1937–61; County Controller of Civil Defence, 1942–61; Clerk of Durham County Magistrates' Courts Cttee, 1952–61; *b* 12 July 1896; *s* of late J. Basil Hope, OBE, JP, and of Amy L. Hope, Bedford; *m* 1928, Mary Joyce, *yr d* of late Lieut-Col Rouse Orlebar, JP, DL, Hinwick, Beds; three *d. Educ:* Bedford Sch. Served European War, 1915–19: Commissioned Officer, 1st Bn Bedfordshire Regt. Solicitor, 1922; Asst Solicitor, Beds County Council, 1922–27; Dep. Clerk of the Peace and of County Council, Durham, 1927–37; T&AFA, County of Durham, 1937–61. Pres., Durham County Assoc. of Parish Councils, 1963–69. DL, Co. Durham, 1944; High Sheriff of Durham, 1966. *Address:* West Park, Lanchester, Co. Durham. *T:* Lanchester 520339. *Club:* Durham County (Durham).

*Died 1 Feb. 1983.*

HOPE GILL, Cecil Gervase, MA; *b* 14 Dec. 1894; *s* of late Rt Rev. Charles Hope Gill and late Mary Hope Gill (*née* Thorp); *m* 1931, Kiti Colin, *e d* of Dr Alexander Campbell-Smith, Nelson, NZ. *Educ:* Windlesham House, Brighton; King William's Coll., IoM; Brighton Coll.; St John's Coll., Cambridge. Served in Royal Monmouthshire RE (Special Reserve), 1914–19 (wounded, despatches); Major 1919 (CRE Tournai); entered Levant Consular Service, 1920; served at Tangier (Vice-Consul), 1921; Casablanca, 1922; Saffi, 1923; Tetuan, 1923–25; Tangier (Asst Oriental Sec.), 1925–30; Jedda (Head of Chancery and Chargé d'Affaires), 1930–33; Alexandria (Consul), 1933–36; Addis Ababa, 1936–; Imperial Defence Coll., 1937; Seattle, 1938–40; Baghdad (Asst Oriental Sec.), 1941; Léopoldville (Actg Consul-Gen.), 1941–47; Addis Ababa (First Sec.), 1942–44; Foreign Office, 1944–45; Tetuan (Consul-Gen.), 1945–52; retired from HM Foreign Service with rank of Consul-Gen., 1952. *Recreations:* travel, fruit growing, wine making, bee keeping, cinematography. *Address:* Interpares 51, Cerrado de Calderón, Málaga, Spain. *T:* 34 52 298 457. *Club:* Royal Automobile.                                *Died 20 Jan. 1984.*

HOPE-JONES, Sir Arthur, KBE 1964; CMG 1956; Chairman, London Sumatra Plantations plc, since 1978; Director and/or Adviser to companies in UK and abroad, since 1960; *b* 26 May 1911; *s* of William and Dinah Elizabeth Hope-Jones; *m* 1938, Lucile Owen, New York; one *s* one *d. Educ:* Kirkby Lonsdale; Christ's Coll., Cambridge (1st cl. hons Hist. Tripos); Columbia Univ., New York (Commonwealth Fund Fellow); Brookings Inst., Washington, DC. Fellow of Christ's Coll., Cambridge, 1937–46. Served War, 1939–45 (TA Gen. List); seconded for duties at home and abroad; Economic Adviser in Persia to Anglo-Iranian Oil Co. Ltd (later BP), 1944–46; Economic Adviser Govt of Kenya, 1946–48; Mem., later Minister, for Commerce and Industry, Govt of Kenya, 1948–60; Member: Kenya Legislature, 1947–60; East African Legislative Assembly, 1955–60. Pres., Mesopotamia and Paiforce Officers Dinner Club. *Publications:* Income Tax in the Napoleonic Wars, 1939; contribs to learned society and financial periodicals. *Recreations:* walking, fishing, reading. *Address:* 1 Buckland Court, Buckland, Betchworth, Surrey. *T:* Betchworth 2179; PO Box 43561, Nairobi, Kenya, East Africa. *Clubs:* East India; Muthaiga Country, Nairobi (Nairobi).                            *Died 24 Jan. 1984.*

HOPKINS, Admiral Sir Frank (Henry Edward), KCB 1964 (CB 1961); DSO 1942; DSC 1941; DL; Commander-in-Chief, Portsmouth, 1966–67; retired, 1967; *b* 23 June 1910; *s* of late E. F. L. Hopkins and Sybil Mary Walrond; *m* 1st, 1939, Lois Barbara (*d* 1986), *d* of J. R. Cook, Cheam, Surrey; 2nd, 1987, Mrs Georgianna Priest. *Educ:* Stubbington House, Nautical Coll., Pangbourne. Joined Navy as Cadet, 1927; served in HM Ships: London, Tiger, Whitehall, Vortigern, Winchester, Courageous, Furious, 1928–38; War of 1939–45 (despatches, 1941), in No 826 Fleet Air Arm Squadron

(Formidable), 1940–41, and comd No 830 Sqdn, 1941–42, based on Malta; USS Hancock and USS Intrepid, American Pacific Fleet, 1944–45; took part in following operations: Dunkirk, air operations over Europe, Battle of Matapan, evacuation of Crete, bombardment of Tripoli, Malta, Battle of Leyte Gulf; Korean War, Theseus, 1950 (despatches); Capt., 1950; Dir of Air Warfare, Admiralty, comd Myngs, Tyrian, Grenville, and Ark Royal, 1954–58; comd RNC Dartmouth, 1958–60; Rear-Adm. 1960; Flag Officer: Flying Training, 1960–62; Aircraft Carriers, 1962–63; Vice-Adm. 1962; a Lord Comr of the Admiralty, Deputy Chief of Naval Staff and Fifth Sea Lord, 1963–64; Dep. Chief of Naval Staff, MoD, 1964–66; Adm. 1966. DL Devon, 1982. American Legion of Merit, 1948; Comdr, Order of Sword, Sweden, 1954. *Recreations:* sailing, golf. *Address:* Kingswear Court Lodge, Kingswear, S Devon. *Clubs:* Naval and Military, Royal Yacht Squadron; Royal Naval Sailing Assoc.; Britannia Yacht.                        *Died 14 April 1990.*

HOPKINS, Col Harold Leslie, CIE 1946; OBE 1942; *b* 1897; *s* of Walter Hopkins, York; *m* 1927, Louise; one *s. Educ:* York. Served European War, 1914–18; War of 1939–45, in Europe, Middle East and India; Colonel, 1943. General Manager, Bombay Port Trust, 1944–45. Chief Docks Manager, Hull, 1956–59, retd. *Address:* 3 Westbourne Grove, Scarborough, North Yorks. *T:* Scarborough 72993.                                        *Died 2 Jan. 1981.*

HOPKINS, Prof. Harry Geoffrey, MSc, DSc London; MSc Manchester; Professor of Mathematics, University of Manchester Institute of Science and Technology, since 1966; *b* 14 April 1918; *s* of late Charles Thomas and late Violet Florence (*née* Johnson) Hopkins. *Educ:* Enfield Grammar Sch.; Harrow County Sch.; University Coll., London (Fellow, 1977). Scientific Officer, Structural and Mechanical Engrg Dept, RAE, Farnborough, 1940–45; Asst in Mathematics, Queen's Univ., Belfast, 1946; Lectr in Mathematics, Manchester Univ., 1946–52; Fulbright Scholar, 1951, and Vis. Prof. of Applied Mathematics, Brown Univ., Providence, RI, 1951 and 1952–54; Senior Principal Scientific Officer, Basic Research Div., Royal Armament R&D Estabt, Fort Halstead, 1954–59; Dep. Chief Scientific Officer (Appleton, Individual Merit Award), 1959–66; Senior Foreign Scientist Fellow (Nat. Science Foundn), Dept of Physics, Washington State Univ., 1965–66. Editor, Jl of Mechanics and Physics of Solids, 1969–. UMIST: Mem. Ct, 1969–71; Mem. Council, 1974–76; Vice-Principal for Finance, 1974–77; Dep. Principal, 1976; Mem. Ct, Manchester Univ., 1979–81. Chm., Structure Sub-Cttee, 1976–77, Mem., Airframe Materials and Structures Cttee, 1977–80, ARC. FIMA 1964; FRAS 1964; Mem. Acoustical Soc. of America, 1967; Fellow, ASME 1979. *Publications:* theoretical research on the mechanics and physics of solids; contributed to: Progress in Solid Mechanics, 1960; Applied Mechanics Surveys, 1966; Engineering Plasticity, 1968; Trends in Solid Mechanics, 1979; Mechanics of Solids, 1981; papers in Proc. and Phil. Trans Royal Soc., Jl Mech. and Phys. Solids, Rep. and Memo. Aero. Res. Council, and other math. and sci. jls. *Recreations:* music, alpine walking and photography, American history. *Address:* Department of Mathematics, University of Manchester Institute of Science and Technology, PO Box No 88, Sackville Street, Manchester M60 1QD. *T:* 061-236 3311; The Mount, Brookfield Crescent, Goostrey, Crewe, Cheshire CW4 8PQ. *T:* Holmes Chapel 34557.                                        *Died 4 Jan. 1982.*

HOPKINS, John Collier Frederick, CMG 1962; DSc; AICTA; FIBiol; Director and Editor, Commonwealth Mycological Institute, 1956–64 (Assistant Editor, 1954); *b* 12 May 1898; *s* of late William and Edith Hopkins; *m* 1945, Elizabeth Callister, *d* of George and Helen Rothnie, Salisbury, Rhodesia; two *d. Educ:* Emanuel Sch.; King's Coll. and Imperial Coll., London (Vice-Pres., Univ. of London Boat Club, 1922); Imperial Coll. Trop. Agric., Trinidad. DSc (London) 1933; AICTA 1926. Hon. Artillery Co., 1916; RFC, 1916–18; RAF, 1918–19; Royal Rhodesia Regt, 1940–45. Agricultural Officer, Uganda, 1924. Mycologist, 1926, Senior Plant Pathologist, 1933, Chief Botanist and Plant Pathologist, 1946, S Rhodesia. Member: Agric. Res. Council, ODM (formerly Agric. Res. Cttee, Colonial Office), 1956–64; Mycology Cttee MRC, 1956–64. Pres., Rhodesia Scientific Assoc., 1930, 1940–42; Pres., Section C, S African Assoc. for the Advancement of Science, 1940; Chm., London Branch, Inst. Biology, 1961–64. *Publications:* Diseases of Tobacco in Southern Rhodesia, 1931; Common Veld Flowers, 1940; Tobacco Diseases, 1956; numerous papers in scientific journals. *Address:* Riverside, Glen Mona, Maughold, Isle of Man. *T:* Laxey 677.

*Died 1 Oct. 1981.*

HOPKINS, Rev. Canon Leslie Freeman; Canon Residentiary and Treasurer, Liverpool Cathedral, 1964–79; later Canon Emeritus; *b* 1914; *o s* of Joseph Freeman and Mabel Hopkins, London; *m* 1940, Violet, *d* of Edgar Crick, Crayford; three *s* one *d. Educ:* City of London Sch. (Abbott Schol.); Exeter Coll., Oxford (Squire Schol. and Exhib.); Wells Theological Coll. BA 1937, 2nd Cl. Hon. Mods, 2nd Cl. Hons Theology; MA 1940; BD Oxon 1953. Deacon 1938, priest 1939; Curate of Crayford 1938, Nympsfield 1942; Priest-in-Charge, Holy Trinity, Charlton, 1942–45; Vicar of St Chrysostom's,

Peckham, 1945–56; Surrogate, 1946–62; Vicar of All Saints, Battersea Park, 1956–62; Chief Inspector of Schools, Dio. of Southwark, 1954–62; Dir of Religious Education, Dio. of Liverpool, 1962–72; Chaplain of Josephine Butler Coll., 1962–72; Governor of Chester Coll., St Elphin's, Darley Dale and of Grammar Schs; Visiting Lectr in Religious Education; Mem. of Council: Guild of St Raphael, 1944– ; USPG. Liveryman, Glass Sellers Co.; Freeman, City of London. FRSA 1982. *Publications:* contribs to press and Syllabuses of Religious Education. *Recreations:* architecture and music. *Address:* Laurel Cottage, Peasmarsh, Rye, Sussex. *T:* Peasmarsh 559. *Died 20 Feb.* 1987.

**HOPKINS, Maj.-Gen. Ronald Nicholas Lamond,** CBE 1943; Legion of Merit (US) 1944; psc; Australian Regular Army, retired; *b* 24 May 1897; *s* of Dr Wm F. Hopkins and Rosa M. B. Lamond; *m* 1926, Nora Frances Riceman; one *s*. *Educ:* Melbourne Grammar Sch.; RMC, Duntroon. Lieut Aust. Permt Forces, 1 Jan. 1918 and seconded 1st AIF; served with 6th Australian Light Horse Regt, Palestine, 1918; Staff Capt. 3rd Australian Light Horse Bde, 1919; Staff Coll., Quetta, 1927–28; attached Royal Tank Corps, England, 1937–38; 2nd AIF 1940; service in Middle East and New Guinea; Hon. ADC to Governor-Gen., 1943–45; late Dep. Chief of Gen. Staff (Australia). Chief Exec. Officer, Adelaide Festival of Arts, 1959–60. Hon. Fellow, St Mark's Coll., Univ. of Adelaide, 1977. *Publication:* Australian Armour, 1978. *Address:* 24 Wilsden Street, Walkerville, SA 5081, Australia. *Club:* Adelaide (Adelaide). *Died 26 Nov.* 1990.

**HOPKINSON, Maj.-Gen. Gerald Charles,** CB 1960; DSO 1945; OBE 1953; MC 1938; retired; *b* Wellington, Som, 27 May 1910; *s* of Capt. Charles Reginald Hopkinson (killed in action, 1914); *m* 1938, Rhona Marion (*d* 1979), *d* of Henry Turner, Farnham, Surrey; one *d*. *Educ:* Imperial Service Coll.; RMC Sandhurst. Second Lieut, Royal Tank Corps, 1930; served in operations, NW Frontier, India, 1935 and 1937–38; served War of 1939–45 (India, Middle East, Italy and Europe); comd 1st RTR, Korea, 1952–53; 33rd Armoured Bde, BAOR, 1953–57; GOC 4th Div., BAOR, 1958–59; Dir, RAC, War Office, Oct. 1959–62. Lieut-Col 1952; Col 1953; Maj.-Gen. 1958. Order of the Crown and Croix de Guerre (Belgium). *Died 2 June* 1989.

**HOPKINSON, Col (Henry) Somerset (Parnell),** OBE 1944; DL; *b* 16 Oct. 1899; *s* of Col H. C. B. Hopkinson, CMG, CBE, and Hon. M. F. L. Parnell, *d* of 3rd Baron Congleton; *m* 1928, Marie Josephine de Gilibert Addison, *d* of Lieut-Col A. J. B. Addison, Royal Irish Rifles; one *d* (and one *d* decd). *Educ:* Winchester and RMC. 2nd Lt Rifle Brigade, 1919; Major, 1938; Staff Coll., 1933–34; Brig. 1945; served War of 1939–45, Palestine, Burma, India; retd 1948. County Councillor Monmouthshire, 1958–64; JP 1950, DL 1951, High Sheriff 1964, Gwent, formerly Monmouthshire. FSA, FSG. *Recreations:* shooting, foreign travel. *Address:* Llanfihangel Court, Abergavenny, Gwent. *T:* Crucorney 217. *Club:* Army and Navy. *Died 6 Nov.* 1988.

**HOPKINSON, Sir (Henry) Thomas,** Kt 1978; CBE 1967; author, journalist; *b* 19 April 1905; 2nd *s* of late Archdeacon J. H. Hopkinson; *m* 1st, Antonia White; one *d* (and one step *d*); 2nd, Gerti Deutsch; two *d*; 3rd, 1953, Dorothy, *widow* of Hugh Kingsmill. *Educ:* St Edward's Sch., Oxford; Pembroke Coll., Oxford (Scholar). BA, 1927; MA, 1932; Hon. Fellow, 1978. After working as a freelance journalist and in advertising and publicity, was appointed Asst Editor of the Clarion, 1934; Asst Editor, Weekly Illustrated, 1934–38; helped in preparation and launching of Picture Post; Editor, 1940–50; also edited Lilliput, 1941–46; Features Editor, News Chronicle, 1954–56; Editor, Drum Magazine, 1958–61. Dir for Africa of Internat. Press Inst., 1963–66. Senior Fellow in Press Studies, Univ. of Sussex, 1967–69; Vis. Prof. of Journalism, University of Minnesota, 1968–69; Dir, Course in Journalism Studies, UC Cardiff, 1971–75, Hon. Professorial Fellow, 1978. Hon. DLitt Wales, 1990. Hon. FRPS 1976; Silver Progress Medal, RPS, 1984. *Publications:* A Wise Man Foolish, 1930; A Strong Hand at the Helm, 1933; The Man Below, 1939; Mist in the Tagus, 1946; The Transitory Venus (short stories), 1948; Down the Long Slide, 1949; Love's Apprentice, 1953; short life of George Orwell, 1953, in British Council series Writers and Their Work; The Lady and the Cut-Throat (short stories), 1958; In the Fiery Continent, 1962; South Africa, 1964 (New York); (ed) Picture Post, 1938–1950, 1970; (with D. Hopkinson) Much Silence: the life and work of Meher Baba, 1974; Treasures of the Royal Photographic Society, 1980; Of This Our Time (autobiog.), 1982; Under the Tropic (autobiog.), 1984; Shady City (novel), 1987; stories in English and American magazines, and for radio. *Address:* 26 Boulter Street, St Clement's, Oxford OX4 1AX. *T:* Oxford (0865) 240466. *Died 20 June* 1990.

**HOPKINSON, Col Somerset;** *see* Hopkinson, Col H. S. P.

**HOPKINSON, Sir Thomas;** *see* Hopkinson, Sir H. T.

**HOPLEY, Ven. Arthur;** Archdeacon Emeritus of the Diocese of Bath and Wells, since 1977; *b* 17 Oct. 1906; *o s* of Ernest Charles Hopley; *m* 1934, Marjorie Carswell Niven, *d* of John Niven; two *a*. *Educ:* Sir George Monoux Sch.; Wells Theological Coll. Asst Curate, St Mark's, Bath, 1941–44; Rector of Claverton, 1944–50; Vicar of Chard, 1950–62; Prebendary of Yatton in Wells Cathedral, 1966–71; Archdeacon of Bath, 1962–71; Archdeacon of Taunton, 1971–77; Prebendary of Milverton I, 1971–77. *Address:* The Old Parsonage, Angersleigh, Taunton, Somerset TA3 7SY. *T:* Blagdon Hill 628. *Died 25 Sept.* 1981.

**HOPPER, Prof. Robert John;** Professor of Ancient History, University of Sheffield, 1955–75, later Emeritus; *b* 13 Aug. 1910; *s* of Robert and Alice Hopper, Cardiff, Glamorgan; *m* 1939, Henriette, *d* of Edward and Ella Kiernan, Timperley, Cheshire; no *c*. *Educ:* Mount Radford Sch., Exeter; University of Wales; Gonville and Caius Coll., Cambridge. Served Royal Welch Fusiliers and Intelligence Corps, 1941–45. Macmillan Student of British Sch. at Athens, 1935–37; Fellow of Univ. of Wales (in Athens and Rome), 1936–38; Lectr in Classics, UCW Aberystwyth, 1938–41 and 1945–47; Senior Lecturer in Ancient History, Univ. of Sheffield, 1947–55, Dean of Faculty of Arts, 1967–70. FRNS 1949; FSA 1951. *Publications:* The Acropolis, 1971; The Early Greeks, 1976; Greek Trade and Industry, 1978; articles in classical and archæological periodicals. *Recreations:* numismatics; foreign travel. *Address:* 41 Barholm Road, Sheffield S10 5RR. *T:* Sheffield 302587. *Club:* National Liberal. *Died 3 July* 1987.

**HOPWOOD, Brig. John Adam,** CBE 1958; DSO 1943 (and Bar 1944); *b* 26 Jan. 1910; *s* of Ernest Hopwood and Constance Marion Adam; *m* Cressida Mona Browning, *d* of R. Campbell Browning, Armsworth, Alresford, Hants; no *c*. *Educ:* St David's, Reigate; Eton; RMC Sandhurst. Commissioned Black Watch, 1930; served with 1st Bn in India, 1931–35; ADC to Governor of Bengal, 1935–37; with 1st Bn Black Watch, and BEF in France, 1939–40; Staff Coll., 1940; Bde Major, 154 Inf. Bde, 1941; Second in Comd, 7th Bn Black Watch, N Africa and Sicily, 1942; comd 1st Bn Black Watch, Sicily and NW Europe, 1943–45; comd 154 and 156 Inf. Bdes, Germany, 1946; Mem. Training Mission to Iraq Army, Baghdad, 1946–48; attended jssc, Latimer, 1948; Liaison Appt, RAF Fighter Comd, 1949; comd 44 Parachute Bde (TA) London, 1950–53; Col i/c Admin., Hong Kong, 1953–55; comd 3 Inf. Bde, Canal Zone, UK, Cyprus, 1955–58; Vice-Pres., Regular Commissions Board, 1958–60, retd. Chm., Honiton Div. Cons. Assoc., 1977–80. Awarded Bronze Lion of Netherlands. *Recreations:* ornithology (MBOU), field sports, travel. *Address:* Gilletts Farm, Yarcombe, Honiton, Devon. *T:* Chard 3121. *Club:* Naval and Military. *Died 31 July* 1987.

**HORNBY, Sir Antony;** *see* Hornby, Sir R. A.

**HORNBY, Frank Robert,** CBE 1972 (MBE 1944); Chief Officer and Vice-Chairman, Council for National Academic Awards, 1964–72, retired; *b* 20 Aug. 1911; *yr s* of late Robert Wilson Hornby and Jane Hornby; *m* 1939, Kathleen Margaret, *yr d* of late Dr Sidney Berry and Helen Berry. *Educ:* Heversham Sch., Westmorland; Magdalene Coll., Cambridge. 1st Class Natural Sciences Tripos Pts 1 and 2. Schoolmaster, 1933–41. RAOC, 1941–46 (Lieut-Col). Asst Educn Officer, Nottingham Co. Borough, 1946–56; Sec., Nat. Coun. for Technological Awards, 1956–64. Hon. LLD CNAA, 1972. *Address:* 35 High Firs, Gills Hill, Radlett, Herts WD7 8BH. *T:* Radlett 5083. *Died 8 July* 1987.

**HORNBY, James William,** MA; Secretary, Incorporated Association of Preparatory Schools, since 1982; *b* 14 March 1924; *s* of late Rt Rev. and Mrs Hugh Leycester Hornby; *m* 1957, Clare Hedley Visick; two *s* two *d*. *Educ:* Winchester Coll.; Trinity Coll., Oxford (MA). Asst Master, Bramcote Sch., Scarborough, 1947–57, Headmaster, 1957–67; Headmaster, Clifton Coll. Prep. Sch., Bristol, 1967–82. Chairman: Incorporated Assoc. of Prep. Schs, 1966, 1971 and 1978; ISIS, 1981–82. *Recreations:* fishing, sport generally; interest in educational matters. *Address:* 138 Church Street, Kensington, W8 4BN. *T:* 01-727 2316. *Died 21 Feb.* 1984.

**HORNBY, Michael Charles St John;** retired as Vice-Chairman, W. H. Smith & Son Ltd (1944–65); *b* 2 Jan. 1899; *e s* of C. H. St J. Hornby and Cicely Hornby; *m* 1928, Nicolette Joan, *d* of Hon. Cyril Ward, MVO; two *s* one *d*. *Educ:* Winchester; RMC Sandhurst; New Coll., Oxford. Joined Grenadier Guards, 1918; served in France and Germany. New Coll., Oxford, 1919–21. Entered W. H. Smith & Son, 1921. Prime Warden, Goldsmiths' Company, 1954–55. Chm., National Book League, 1959. *Recreations:* fox-hunting, shooting, cricket, gardening. *Address:* Pusey House, Faringdon, Oxon. *T:* Buckland 222. *Clubs:* White's, MCC. *Died 7 Dec.* 1987.

**HORNBY, Sir (Roger) Antony,** Kt 1960; President, Savoy Hotel Ltd, 1977–81 (Vice-Chairman to Dec. 1976); *b* 5 Feb. 1904; *s* of late C. H. St J. Hornby, Shelley House, Chelsea; *m* 1st, 1931, Lady Veronica Blackwood (marr. diss. 1940); one *d*; 2nd, 1949, Lily Ernst (*d* 1985).

*Educ:* Winchester Coll.; New Coll., Oxford. MA Oxon. Vice-Chm. King's Coll. Hosp., 1959–74. Served War of 1939–45, Grenadier Guards. A Trustee of the Wallace Collection, 1963–77; Chm., Nat. Art Collections Fund, 1970–75. *Recreation:* collecting pictures. *Address:* Claridge's Hotel, W1. *Clubs:* Garrick, MCC.
*Died 20 Dec.* 1987.

**HORNE, Sir Alan Edgar,** 2nd Bt *cr* 1929; MC; *b* 19 Sept. 1889; *s* of Sir Edgar Horne, 1st Bt, and Margery (*d* 1939), *d* of George Anderson May, Elford, Staffs; *S* father, 1941; *m* 1st, 1915, Henriette Kelly (*d* 1918); one *d*; 2nd, 1923, Roslyn (*d* 1961), *d* of John Brian Robinson; (one *s* decd). *Educ:* Eton; University Coll., Oxford. Served European War, 1914–19, in France and Balkans as Capt. Surrey Yeomanry and on Staff (despatches 4 times, MC, French Croix de Guerre); War of 1939–45, Basutoland and MELF, 1940–48, as Lt-Col Royal Pioneer Corps (African and Native Troops). *Heir:* g *s* Alan Gray Antony Horne, *b* 11 July 1948. *Address:* 1 The Paragon (Flat 4), Blackheath, SE3 0NX. *Clubs:* Cavalry and Guards, MCC.
*Died 4 Feb.* 1984.

**HORNER, (Lawrence John) Hallam,** CBE 1973 (OBE 1959); Director, Chamber of Shipping of UK, 1966–72; *b* 14 June 1907; *o s* of late David Aitken Horner and Louise Stuart Black; *m* 1935, Kathleen Joan (*d* 1976), *o d* of late Charles D. Taite, Bowdon, Cheshire; two *d*. *Educ:* Malvern Coll.; Corpus Christi Coll., Oxford (MA). Served War of 1939–45, RSF and 52nd Recce Regt, RAC (despatches). Admitted Solicitor (hons), 1931; Asst Solicitor, Cheshire CC, 1932–34; Rees & Freres, parly agents, 1934–51 (Partner, 1936); Sec., Canal Assoc., 1945–48; Parly Solicitor (later also Sec.), Dock and Harbour Authorities' Assoc., 1946–51; Asst Gen. Man. and Solicitor and Parly Agent, Chamber of Shipping of UK, 1951, Gen. Man., 1959. Sec. Adv. Cttee on New Lighthouse Works, etc, 1951–66; Mem. Adv. Cttee on Oil Pollution of the Sea, 1952–66; Mem., City of London Coll. Shipping Adv. Cttee, 1966–72; Mem., Cttee of Management, British Ship Adoption Soc., 1968–72. Hon. FICS, 1972. Netherlands Bronze Cross, 1945. *Recreation:* watching birds. *Address:* 2 Hamstone Court, Great Gates, Salcombe, South Devon TQ8 8JY. *T:* Salcombe 3420. *Club:* Reform.
*Died 21 Oct.* 1989.

**HORNSBY, Harry Reginald,** MBE 1944; *b* 19 Dec. 1907; *s* of Rev. E. F. Hornsby, Hon. CF; *m* 1946, Mary Elizabeth Whitley; no *c*. *Educ:* Bromsgrove Sch.; Brasenose Coll., Oxford. MA 1936. Asst Master, Christ's Hosp., Horsham, 1929–39; Headmaster, The King's Sch., Peterborough, 1939–51; Headmaster: Christ's Coll., Christchurch, NZ, 1951–63; St Paul's Sch., Hamilton, NZ, 1963–69; St Andrew's School, Nukuálofa, Tonga, 1970–72. Lay Canon of Christchurch Cathedral, 1962–63; Mem. of Council, Univ. of Canterbury, NZ, 1962–63. War Service, 1940–45 (despatches): Gunner RA, 1940; commissioned Worcs Regt, 1941; served 3rd Queen Alexandra's Own Gurkha Rifles, 1941–45. Chm. Independent Schools Assoc. of New Zealand, 1960–63; Member: Outward Bound Trust of New Zealand, 1961–64; Council, Univ. of Waikato, 1965–68. Lay Canon of Waikato Cathedral, 1967, 1968, 1969. *Recreations:* golf, gardening. *Address:* 13 Bay View Road, Nelson, New Zealand.
*Died 1 March* 1983.

**HORNSBY-SMITH, Baroness** *cr* 1974 (Life Peer); of Chislehurst; **Margaret Patricia Hornsby-Smith,** PC 1959; DBE 1961; *b* 17 March 1914; *o d* of F. C. Hornsby-Smith. *Educ:* Richmond. Ministry of Economic Warfare, 1941–45; Barnes Borough Council, 1945–49. MP (C) Kent, Chislehurst, 1950–66 and 1970–Feb. 1974; Parly Sec., Ministry of Health, 1951–57; UK delegate to Assembly of UN, 1958; Jt Parly Under-Sec. of State, Home Office, 1957–59; Jt Parly Sec., Min. of Pensions and Nat. Insurance, 1959–61. Led UK Parliamentary Delegation to Australasia, 1961, Kenya 1972. Vice-Chm., Arthritis and Rheumatism Council for Research, 1974– (Chm., Appeals Cttee, 1966–); Chm., St Edward's Housing Assoc., 1983–. FRSA 1971. *Address:* 31 Stafford Mansions, Stafford Place, SW1E 6NL. *Clubs:* Carlton, Special Forces.
*Died 3 July* 1985.

**HOROWITZ, Vladimir;** pianist; *b* Kieff, Russia, 1 Oct. 1904; *s* of Samuel Horowitz and Sophie Bodik; *m* 1933, Wanda Toscanini; one *d*. *Educ:* Kieff Conservatory; studied under Sergi Tarnowsky and Felix Blumenfeld. European Début, 1925; début with New York Philharmonic Orchestra, 1928. Soloist, New York Symphony Orchestra and other American orchestras. Winner 18 Grammy Awards. Royal Philharmonic Soc. Gold Medal, 1972. US Medal of Freedom, 1986. *Address:* c/o Columbia Artists Management, Inc., 165 West 57th Street, New York, NY 10019, USA.
*Died 5 Nov.* 1989.

**HORROCKS, Lt-Gen. Sir Brian Gwynne,** KCB 1949 (CB 1943); KBE 1945; DSO 1943; MC; Gentleman Usher of the Black Rod, House of Lords, 1949–63; *b* 7 Sept. 1895; *o s* of late Col Sir William Heaton Horrocks, KCMG, CB; *m* 1928, Nancy, *d* of Brook and Hon. Mrs Brook Kitchin; one *d* decd. *Educ:* Uppingham; RMC Sandhurst. 2nd Lieut Middlesex Regt, 1914; served European War, France and Belgium, 1914, Russia, 1919 (wounded, MC); War of 1939–45

(wounded, DSO, CB, KBE); Comd 44 (HC Div.), 9 Armd Div., 13 Corps, 10 Corps in Egypt and Africa, 9 Corps Tunis, 30 Corps in BLA. GOC-in-C Western Comd, 1946; GOC-in-C British Army of the Rhine, 1948; invalided out of Army, 1949. Dir, Bovis Holdings, 1963–77. Hon. LLD (Belfast). *Publications:* A Full Life, 1960, new edn, 1974; Corps Commander, 1977; Editor, Famous Regiments Series. *Address:* The Old School House, Singleton, Chichester, Sussex. *Club:* Naval and Military.
*Died 4 Jan.* 1985.

**HORSBRUGH-PORTER, Sir Andrew (Marshall),** 3rd Bt, *cr* 1902; DSO 1940; Col retired, 1953; *b* 1 June 1907; *s* of Sir John Horsbrugh-Porter, 2nd Bt, and Elaine Maud, *y d* of Thomas Jefferies; *S* father, 1953; *m* 1933, Annette Mary, *d* of late Brig.-Gen. R. C. Browne-Clayton, DSO, Browne's Hill, Carlow; one *s* two *d*. *Educ:* Winchester; RMC, Sandhurst. Subaltern 12th Royal Lancers, 1927. Served War of 1939–45 (DSO and Bar); commanded 27th Lancers, 1941–45; GSO1, Liaison attached to US Army, 1947; commanded 12th Royal Lancers, 1948–52; Military Adviser to UK High Commissioner, New Delhi, 1952. *Recreations:* watching polo and hunting. *Heir:* *s* John Simon Horsbrugh-Porter [*b* 18 Dec. 1938; *m* 1964, Lavinia Rose, *d* of Ralph Turton, Kildale Hall, Whitby, Yorks; one *s* two *d*]. *Address:* Manor Farm House, Salford, Chipping Norton, Oxon. *Club:* Cavalry and Guards.
*Died 5 Feb.* 1986.

**HORSFALL, Geoffrey Jonas,** CBE 1967; Judge of the Grand Court of the Cayman Islands, West Indies, 1965–73, retired; *b* 22 Jan. 1905; *s* of late Major A. H. Horsfall, DSO, TD, Newcastle, NSW, Australia; *m* 1947, Robin, *y d* of late Curwin Maclure, Albury, NSW; one *s* two *d*. *Educ:* The King's Sch., Parramatta, NSW; Cheltenham Coll.; Keble Coll., Oxford. BA 1927; Barrister-at-Law, 1928, Gray's Inn; South-Eastern Circuit. Entered Colonial Legal Service, 1936, as Crown Counsel, Nigeria; Crown Counsel, Sierra Leone, 1943; Senior Magistrate, Fiji, 1947; Judicial Commissioner, British Solomon Islands Protectorate, 1953; Judge of the High Court, Zanzibar, 1958; Chief Justice of Zanzibar, 1964, but office abolished in Zanzibar revolution. *Recreations:* bowls, walking, gardening. *Address:* 78 Hawthorne Avenue, Chatswood, NSW 2067, Australia. *T:* 02–411–3892.
*Died 1 July* 1985.

**HORSFALL TURNER, Harold,** CBE 1974; solicitor in private practice; Partner, Oswald Hickson Collier & Co., since 1974; *b* 1 June 1909; *s* of Stanley Horsfall Turner, Reader in Economics, Aberdeen University; *m* 1937, Eileen Mary Jenkins; two *s*. *Educ:* Rossall; The Queen's Coll., Oxford; Birmingham Univ. BA Oxford 1932, BCL Oxford 1934, LLB Birmingham 1935. Admitted Solicitor (with 1st Class Hons) 1936. Asst Solicitor, Dudley Corporation, 1936; Legal Asst, Inland Revenue, 1937; Sen. Legal Asst, Min. of National Insurance, 1945; The Law Society: Under-Sec., 1947; Second Secretary-Gen., 1964; Sec.-Gen., 1969–74. Chm., Solicitors' European Gp, 1978, 1979. *Recreations:* boating, opera, photography. *Address:* 1 Old Palace Terrace, The Green, Richmond, Surrey. *T:* 01–948 1963. *Club:* Garrick.
*Died 26 Dec.* 1981.

**HORSFIELD, Brig. Herbert Eric,** CBE 1943; MC (2 Bars); *b* 23 Aug. 1895; *s* of H. Horsfield; *m* 1924, Harriet Beatrice Mills; one *s* one *d*. *Educ:* Bradfield Coll., Berks; Royal Military Academy, Woolwich. Commissioned RE 1914; France and Flanders, 1915–19; India, Royal Bombay Sappers and Miners, 1920–30; Military Engineer Services, 1930–36; Aldershot, DCRE 1936–37; India, RB Sappers and Miners, 1937–38; Commandant RB Sappers and Miners, 1938–42; Chief Engineer, Eastern Army, 1942–43; Chief Engineer, 14th Army, 1943–44; Chief Engineer, Southern Army, 1945–46; Commandant RE Depot, 1946; Comdr Engineer Stores Group, Long Marston; retired, 1948. John Mowlem & Co. Ltd, 1948–64. Councillor, Bognor Regis UDC, 1960–67 (Chm., 1964–65 and 1965–66). FRSA 1948–70. *Address:* St Julians, 34 Cross Bush Road, Felpham, Sussex. *T:* Middleton-on-Sea 2057. *Club:* Naval and Military.
*Died 17 Jan.* 1981.

**HORSTEAD, Rt. Rev. James Lawrence Cecil,** CMG 1962; CBE 1956; DD (Hon.) 1956; Canon Emeritus of Leicester Cathedral; *b* 16 Feb. 1898; *s* of James William and Mary Leah Horstead; *m* 1926, Olive Davidson (*d* 1988); no *c*. *Educ:* Christ's Hosp.; University and St John's Coll., Durham (Mathematical Scholar, Lightfoot Scholar). BA 2nd Cl. Maths Hons 1921; Theol. Hons 1923; MA 1924; Deacon, 1923; Priest, 1924; Curate St Margaret's Church, Durham, 1923–26; Sec. for Durham Student Christian Movement, 1923–26; Principal Fourah Bay Coll., 1926–36; Canon Missioner Diocese of Sierra Leone, 1928–36; Sec. Church Missionary Soc., Sierra Leone, 1926–36; Bishop of Sierra Leone, 1936–61; Archbishop of West Africa, 1955–61; Rector of Appleby Magna, 1962–68; Asst Bp, Diocese of Leicester, 1962–76. *Publication:* Co-operation with Africans, International Review of Missions, April 1935.
*Died 9 June* 1989.

**HORTON, Maj.-Gen. Frank Cyril,** CB 1957; OBE 1953; RM; *b* 31 May 1907; *s* of late Lieut-Comdr F. Horton, Royal Navy, and late Emma M. Hopper; *m* 1934, Jennie Ellaline Hammond: one *d*. *Educ:* Sir Roger Manwood's Sch. 2nd Lieut RM 1925; Lieut RM

1928; HMS Cumberland, China Station, 1928–29; HMS Royal Oak, Mediterranean Station, 1929–31; Captain RM, 1936; HMS Ajax, America and West Indies Station, 1936–37; Brevet Major, 1940; psc 1941; Actg Lieut-Col 1942; GSO1, Staff of Chief of Combined Operations, 1942–43; Comdg Officer, 44 (RM) Commando, SE Asia, 1943–44; Directing Staff, Army Staff Coll., 1945–46; Plans Div., Admiralty, 1946–48; Directing Staff, Jt Services Staff Coll., 1948–51; Comdt, Amphibious Sch., RM, 1951–52; idc 1953; Col GS, Staff of Comdt Gen., RM, 1954; Chief of Staff to Commandant Gen. Royal Marines, 1955–58; Maj. 1946; Lieut-Col 1949, Col 1953; Maj.-Gen. 1955; retired, 1958. County Civil Defence Officer, Essex, 1959; Regional Dir of Civil Defence, S Eastern Region, 1961–68. *Address:* Hooks Cottage, Bickington, S Devon. *T:* Bickington 312. *Club:* Royal Naval and Royal Albert Yacht (Portsmouth). *Died 18 July 1989.*

**HOSEGOOD, Philip James;** Under-Secretary, Welsh Office, 1976–80, retired; *b* 9 Sept. 1920; *s* of late George Frank and Madeleine Clarisse Hosegood; *m* 1948, Heather (*née* Roriston); two *d. Educ:* Heanor Grammar Sch.; correspondence courses. Joined Civil Service as Tax Officer, 1937; Exec. Officer, India Office, 1939. Served War, Army, 1941–46. Asst Principal, Min. of Civil Aviation, 1948; Principal, Min. of Civil Aviation, 1951 (later Min. of Transport); Asst Sec., Welsh Office, 1965. Chm., Lower Machen Festival, 1977–86. *Recreations:* music, outdoor activities. *Address:* 16 Rheidol Close, Llanishen, Cardiff CF4 5NQ. *T:* Cardiff 756445. *Died 6 July 1987.*

**HOSKYNS-ABRAHALL, Rt. Rev. Anthony Leigh Egerton;** Honorary Assistant Bishop, diocese of Blackburn, since 1975; *b* 13 Oct. 1903; *s* of Bennet Hoskyns-Abrahall, CBE, and Edith Louise (*née* Tapp); *m* 1937, Margaret Ada Storey; two *s* one *d. Educ:* RNC Osborne and Dartmouth; Westcott House Theological Coll., Cambridge. Left RN, 1929; ordained, 1931; Curate, St Mary's Portsea, 1931–33; Chaplain, Shrewsbury Sch., 1933–36; Curate, St Wilfrid's, Harrogate, 1936–39; Chaplain, Tower of London, 1939; Chaplain, RNVR, 1939–45; Vicar, St Michael's, Aldershot, 1945–54; Rural Dean of Aldershot, 1949–54; Bishop Suffragan of Lancaster, 1955–74. Provost, Northern Chapter of Woodard Schools, 1964–77. *Recreations:* fishing, shooting, cricket. *Address:* 14 Rivermead Drive, Garstang, near Preston, Lancs PR3 1JJ. *T:* Garstang 2300. *Club:* MCC. *Died 1 May 1982.*

**HOTHFIELD, 4th Baron,** *cr* 1881; **Thomas Sackville Tufton;** Bt 1851; *b* 20 July 1916; *s* of Hon. Sackville Philip Tufton (*d* 1936; 2nd *s* of 1st Baron), and Winifred Mary Ripley Dalton (*d* 1970); *S* cousin, 1961. *Educ:* Eton; Cambridge Univ. *Heir: cousin* Lieut-Col George William Anthony Tufton, TD [*b* 28 Oct. 1904; *m* 1936, Evelyn Margarette Mordaunt; two *s* one *d*]. *Address:* House of Lords, SW1. *Died 16 May 1986.*

**HOUCHEN, Harry Owen;** Member of Board, for UK, Commercial Development (Pty) Ltd, Johannesburg; *b* 24 Sept. 1907; *s* of late Henry Houchen and Eliza Katherine, *d* of Burgoyne Owen; *m* 1st, 1935, Beatrix Elizabeth (*née* Ellett) (*d* 1976); one *s* one *d*; 2nd, 1978, Renée Char. *Educ:* Canterbury Coll.; University of New Zealand. BE (Civil) 1932. From 1933 concerned with Transport and Civil Aviation, holding overseas appointments. Dir of Current Ops, BOAC, 1956; Man. Dir, Brookhirst Igranic Ltd, 1958; joined BTC as Gen. Man., BR Workshops, 1962; Member BR Bd for Mech. and Electr. Engrg and Workshops, 1964–69; Industrial Consultant, 1969–; Mem., Bd, Transportation Systems and Market Research Ltd, 1970–72. Order of Merit (1st cl.), Syria, 1956; Gold Medal of Merit, Lebanon, 1956. MRAeS 1936; FIMechE 1968 (MIMechE 1964). *Recreations:* travelling, yachting. *Address:* 21 Kylestrome House, Cundy Street, SW1. *T:* 01–730 4415. *Club:* Naval and Military. *Died 10 March 1981.*

**HOUGH, Prof. Graham Goulder;** Praelector and Fellow of Darwin College, Cambridge, 1964–75, then Emeritus Fellow; Professor of English, 1966–75, then Emeritus, University Reader in English, 1965–66; *b* 14 Feb. 1908; *s* of Joseph and Clara Hough; *m* 1st, 1942, Rosamund Oswell; one *s* one *d*; 2nd, 1952, Ingeborg Neumann. *Educ:* Prescot Grammar Sch.; University of Liverpool; Queens' Coll., Cambridge. Lecturer in English, Raffles Coll., Singapore, 1930. Served War of 1939–45, with Singapore Royal Artillery (Volunteer), 1942–45. Professor of English, University of Malaya, 1946; Visiting Lecturer, Johns Hopkins Univ., 1950; Fellow of Christ's Coll., Cambridge, 1950 (Tutor, 1955–60); Visiting Prof. Cornell University, 1958. Hon. DLitt, Malaya, 1955; LittD, Cambridge, 1961. *Publications:* The Last Romantics, 1949; The Romantic Poets, 1953; The Dark Sun, 1957; Image and Experience, 1960; Legends and Pastorals, 1961; A Preface to the Faerie Queene, 1962; The Dream and the Task, 1963; An Essay on Criticism, 1966; Style and Stylistics, 1969; Selected Essays, 1978; The Mystery Religion of W.B. Yeats, 1984. *Recreation:* travel. *Address:* The White Cottage, Grantchester, Cambridge. *T:* Cambridge (0223) 840227. *Died 2 Sept. 1990.*

**HOUGHTON, Albert Morley;** retired 1972 as Under-Secretary, Department of Trade and Industry; *b* 26 June 1914; *s* of late George Albert and Alice Lucy Houghton; *m* 1939, Lallie Whittington Hughes; no *c*. Entered Civil Service, Administrative class, 1946; Civil Service Selection Board, 1946–49; Ministry of Transport, 1949–65; UK Delegn to NATO 1954–56; Shipping Attaché to Comr Gen. for SE Asia, 1956–60; Hd of Gen. Shipping Policy Div., 1961–62, and Hd of Road Safety Div., 1962–65, Min. of Transport; Under-Sec., and Hd of Electronics and Telecommunications Div., Min. of Technology, 1965–70. *Recreations:* reading, music, gardening. *Address:* High Beeches, North Pickenham, Swaffham, Norfolk. *T:* Holme Hale 440489. *Died 10 Nov. 1987.*

**HOUGHTON, Arthur Amory, Jr;** corporation official; Chairman, Steuben Glass, 1972–78 (President, 1933–72); *b* Corning, New York, USA, 12 Dec. 1906; *s* of Arthur Amory and Mabel Hollister Houghton; *m* 1973, Nina Rodale; one *s* three *d* of a previous marriage. *Educ:* St Paul's Sch., Concord; Harvard Univ. Served War of 1942–45, Capt. to Lt-Col, USAAF. Corning Glass Works: manufg dept, 1929; treasury dept, 1929–30; Asst to Pres., 1930–32; Vice-Pres., 1935–42; now Life Dir. Former Director: NY Life Insce Co.; US Steel Corp.; US Trust Co. of NY. Curator of Rare Books, Library of Congress, 1940–42; Chm., Wye Inst.; Mem. Council on Foreign Relations. Formerly: Dir, Amer. Council of Learned Socs; Chairman: Inst. of Internat. Educn; Metropolitan Mus. of Art; Philharmonic Symphony Soc., NY; Parsons Sch. of Design; Vice-Chairman: Fund for Advancement of Educn (Ford Foundn); Lincoln Center for the Performing Arts; President: E-SU of US; Keats-Shelley Soc. of Amer.; Shakespeare Assoc. of Amer.; Vice-Pres., Pierpont Morgan Liby; Trustee: St John's Coll., Annapolis; Rockefeller Foundn. Hon. Trustee: ICA, Boston; Baltimore Mus. of Art; Hon. Curator, Keats Collection, Harvard Univ. Sen. Fellow, RCA; Sen. FRSA. KStJ. Hon. Phi Beta Kappa, Harvard; 20 hon. doctorates. Michael Friedsam Medal in Industrial Art; Gertrude Vanderbilt Whitney award, Skowhegan Sch. Officier, Légion d'Honneur; Comdr, Ordre des Arts et des Lettres. *Address:* Wye Plantation, Queenstown, Maryland 21658, USA. *Clubs:* Century, Union, Knickerbocker, Harvard, Grolier (New York). *Died 3 April 1990.*

**HOUGHTON, Rev. Canon William Reginald;** Canon Residentiary of Gloucester Cathedral, 1969–78, later Emeritus; *b* 28 Sept. 1910; *s* of late William Houghton and late Elizabeth Houghton; unmarried. *Educ:* St John's Coll., Durham; Westcott House, Cambridge. BA (Durham) 1940; Dipl. in Th. (Durham) 1941; MA (Durham) 1943. Curate, St Clement, Leeds, 1941–43, Leeds Parish Church, 1943–47 (Senior Curate, 1945–47); Vicar of Beeston, Leeds, 1947–54. Surrogate, 1949–54. Public Preacher, Dio. Southwark, 1954–62; Asst Sec. South London Church Fund and Southwark Diocesan Board of Finance, 1954–56, Dep. Sec., 1956–60, Sec., 1960–61; Sec. Southwark Dio. Bd of Dilapidations, 1956–60; Canon Residentiary (Treas.) of Southwark Cathedral, 1959–62. Rector of St Mary de Crypt with St John the Baptist, Gloucester, 1962–69. *Recreations:* travel and reading. *Address:* Church Cottage, Diddlebury, Craven Arms, Shropshire SY7 9DH. *T:* Munslow 208. *Died 31 March 1989.*

**HOULDSWORTH, Sir (Harold) Basil,** 2nd Bt, *cr* 1956; Consultant Anæsthetist, Barnsley and District Hospitals, 1954–87; *b* 21 July 1922; *s* of Sir Hubert Stanley Houldsworth, 1st Bt, QC and (Hilda Frances) Lady Houldsworth (*née* Clegg) (*d* 1978); *S* father, 1956; *m* 1946, Norah Clifford Halmshaw; one *d. Educ:* Heckmondwike Grammar Sch.; Leeds Sch. of Medicine, MRCS, LRCP 1946; FFA RCS 1954; DA Eng. 1951. Junior Registrar Anæsthetist, Leeds Gen. Infirmary, 1946–48; Graded Specialist Anæsthetist, RAMC, 1948–50; Registrar Anæsthetist, Leeds General Infirmary and St James Hospital, Leeds, 1950–53; Senior Registrar, Sheffield City General Hospital, 1953–54. *Recreations:* theatre, ballet and gardening. *Heir:* none. *Address:* Shadwell House, Lundhill Road, Wombwell, near Barnsley, South Yorks. *T:* Barnsley 753191. *Died 24 March 1990 (ext).*

**HOULDSWORTH, Sir Reginald (Douglas Henry),** 4th Bt, *cr* 1887; OBE 1945; TD 1944; DL; landowner; *b* 9 July 1903; *s* of Sir Thomas Houldsworth, 3rd Bt, CBE; *S* father, 1961; *m* 1934, Margaret May, *d* of late Cecil Emilius Laurie; one *s* two *d. Educ:* Shrewsbury Sch.; Cambridge Univ. Hon. Col Ayrshire ECO Yeomanry, 1960–67; Commanded: Ayrshire Yeomanry, 1940–42; 4 Pack Mule Group, 1943–45. DL Ayrshire, 1970–. *Heir:* s Richard Thomas Reginald Houldsworth [*b* 2 Aug. 1947; *m* 1970, Jane (marr. diss. 1983), *o d* of Alistair Orr, Sydehead, Beith; two *s*]. *Address:* Kirkbride, Glenburn, Maybole, Ayrshire. *T:* Crosshill 202. *Clubs:* Cavalry and Guards; Western Meeting (Ayr); Prestwick (Prestwick). *Died 19 Jan. 1989.*

**HOULT, (Eleanor) Norah;** novelist and journalist; *b* Dublin; *d* of Powis Hoult and Margaret O'Shaughnessy. *Educ:* various boarding schools. *Publications:* Poor Women, 1928; Time, Gentlemen! Time!, 1929; Apartments to Let, 1931; Youth Can't be Served, 1933; Holy

Ireland, 1935; Coming From the Fair, 1937; Nine Years is a Long Time, 1938; Four Women Grow Up, 1940; Smilin' on The Vine, 1941; Augusta Steps Out, 1942; Scene for Death, 1943; There Were No Windows, 1944; House Under Mars, 1946; Farewell, Happy Fields, 1948; Cocktail Bar, 1950; Frozen Ground, 1952; Sister Mavis, 1953; Journey into Print, 1954; A Death Occurred, 1954; Father Hone and the Television Set, 1956; Father and Daughter, 1957; Husband and Wife, 1959; Last Days of Miss Jenkinson, 1962; Poet's Pilgrimage, 1966; Only Fools and Horses Work, 1969; Not for Our Sins Alone, 1972; Two Girls in the Big Smoke, 1977. *Address:* Jonquil Cottage, Greystones, Co. Wicklow, Ireland.

*Died 6 April 1984.*

**HOUSE, Harry Wilfred,** DSO 1918; MC; MA; Master of Wellington College, 1941–56; *b* Malvern, 26 Sept. 1895; 2nd *s* of late H. H. House, Acre End, Eynsham, Oxon; *m* 1926, Marjorie Stracey, *yr d* of late Arthur Gibbs, of Bramley, Surrey; two *s* one *d. Educ:* Lockers Park, Hemel Hempstead; Rugby Sch.; Queen's Coll., Oxford. Served in HM Forces on leaving Rugby in 1914; temp. 2nd Lieut 7th East Lancs Regt, Sept. 1914; served in France from July 1915 (wounded July 1916; MC; DSO); relinquished commission with rank of Temp. Major, March, 1919; total service in France 3 years 5 months; temp. appointment Colonial Office, March to Dec. 1919; matriculated Oxford Univ., Jan. 1920; 2nd Class Hon. Mods, March 1921; studied at the University of Paris, 1921–23; Fellow and Lecturer Queen's Coll., Oxford, 1923–41; Laming Resident Fellow, Queen's Coll., Oxford, 1924–41; Junior Proctor, Oxford Univ., 1931–32; Major, Oxford and Bucks Light Infantry, 1939–41; Military Asst to Quarter Master Gen., 1940–41. Supernumerary Fellow, Queen's Coll., Oxford, 1953. *Address:* The Old Rectory, Stutton, near Ipswich, Suffolk. *T:* Holbrook 328205.

*Died 9 Jan. 1987.*

**HOUSE, Prof. John William,** MA; FRGS; Halford Mackinder Professor of Geography, University of Oxford, 1974–83; Fellow of St Peter's College, Oxford, 1974–83, later Emeritus; *b* 15 Sept. 1919; *s* of John Albert House and Eveline (*née* Brunton), Bradford; *m* 1942, Eva (*née* Timm); two *s* two *d. Educ:* Bradford Grammar Sch.; Jesus Coll., Oxford (Open Exhibr). BA 1940, MA 1946, DLitt 1980. HM Forces, 1940–46, Major Intell. Corps; Médaille de la Reconnaissance Française 1944. Univ. of Durham: Lectr in Geography, 1946–58; Sen. Lectr, 1958–61; Reader, 1961–63; Leverhulme Research Fellow, 1957–58; Fulbright Prof., Univ. of Nebraska, 1962–63; Univ. of Newcastle upon Tyne: Reader in Applied Geography, 1963–64; Prof., 1964–66; Prof. and Head of Dept, 1966–74. Mem., Northern Econ. Planning Council, 1966–74; Mem., Northern Pennines Rural Develt Bd, 1967–70. Murchison Award, RGS, 1970. *Publications:* Bellingham and Wark, 1952; Northumbrian Tweedside, 1956; Teesside at Mid Century, 1960; (ed) Northern Geographical Essays, 1966; Industrial Britain: the North East, 1969; (ed) The UK Space, 1974; France: an applied geography, 1978; The Rio Grande Frontier, 1982; US Public Policies, 1983; papers on migration and mobility. *Recreations:* drama, gardening. *Address:* 38 North Street, Islip, Oxon OX5 2SQ.

*Died 1 Feb. 1984.*

**HOUSEHOLD, Geoffrey Edward West,** TD; author; *b* 30 Nov. 1900; *s* of H. W. Household, MA, Barrister-at-Law; *m* 1942, Ilona M. J. Zsoldos-Gutmán; one *s* two *d. Educ:* Clifton Coll.; Magdalen Coll., Oxford. Mostly commerce in foreign capitals. *Publications: novels:* The Third Hour, 1937; Rogue Male, 1939; Arabesque, 1948; The High Place, 1950; A Rough Shoot, 1951; A Time to Kill, 1952; Fellow Passenger, 1955; Watcher in the Shadows, 1960; Thing to Love, 1963; Olura, 1965; The Courtesy of Death, 1967; Dance of the Dwarfs, 1968; Doom's Caravan, 1971; The Three Sentinels, 1972; The Lives and Times of Bernardo Brown, 1973; Red Anger, 1975; Hostage: London, 1977; The Last Two Weeks of Georges Rivac, 1978; The Sending, 1980; Summon the Bright Water, 1981; Rogue Justice, 1982; Arrows of Desire, 1985; Face to the Sun, 1988; *autobiography:* Against the Wind, 1958; *short stories:* The Salvation of Pisco Gabar, 1938; Tales of Adventurers, 1952; The Brides of Solomon, 1958; Sabres on the Sand, 1966; The Cats To Come, 1975; The Europe That Was, 1979; Capricorn and Cancer, 1981; The Days of your Fathers, 1987; *for children:* The Spanish Cave, 1940; Xenophon's Adventure, 1955; Prisoner of the Indies, 1967; Escape into Daylight, 1976. *Recreation:* Atlantic Spain. *Address:* Chatterwell, Charlton, Banbury, Oxon. *Died 4 Oct. 1988.*

**HOUSTOUN-BOSWALL, Sir Thomas,** 7th Bt, *cr* 1836; Chairman: Sir Thomas HB Properties Ltd; Continental Sales Agency Co. Ltd; Director: Housetrend Ltd; Southern Television (Pty) Ltd; *b* 13 Feb. 1919; *s* of Major Sir Gordon Houstoun-Boswall, 6th Bt; *S* father, 1961; *m* 1945, Margaret (marr. diss. 1970), *d* of George Bullen-Smith; one *s* one *d*; *m* 1971, Anne-Lucie, *d* of Pierre Naquet; one *d. Educ:* Windlesham House Sch.; Nautical Coll., Pangbourne. Fighter Pilot, RAFVR, 1939–45 (Middle East and UK). *Heir: s* Thomas Alford Houstoun-Boswall [*b* 23 May 1947; *m* 1971, Eliana, *d* of Dr John Pearse, New York; one *s*]. *Address:* Heath Grange, Lingfield, Surrey. *T:* Lingfield 833809. *Died 16 May 1982.*

**HOVDE, Frederick Lawson;** President's Medal for Merit (USA), 1948; President, Purdue University, 1946–71, later President Emeritus; *b* 7 Feb. 1908; *s* of Martin Rudolph Hovde and Julia Essidora Hovde (*née* Lawson); *m* 1933, Priscilla Louise Boyd; one *s* two *d. Educ:* University of Minnesota; Oxford Univ. Asst Dir Gen. Coll., University of Minnesota, 1932–36; Asst to Pres. and Exec. Sec. of Rochester Prize Scholarships, University of Rochester, 1936–41; Head, London Mission, Office of Scientific Research and Development, 1941–42; Exec. Asst to Chm., Nat. Defense Research Cttee, 1942–43; Chief, Rocket Ordnance Research Div., Nat. Defense Research Cttee, 1943–46. Hon. degrees: DSc: Hanover Coll., 1946; Case Inst. of Technology, 1948; Tri-State College, 1967; DEng Rose Polytechnic Inst., 1948; LLD: Wabash Coll., 1946; North Dakota Agricultural Coll., 1949; New York Univ., 1951; Michigan State Univ., 1955; Minnesota, 1956; Northwestern Univ., 1960; Notre Dame, 1964; Ball State Univ., 1965; Indiana State Univ., 1966; Indiana Univ., 1969; Purdue Univ., 1975; DHL Cincinnati, 1956; DCL Oxford, 1957; Dr *hc* University Rural do Estado de Minas Gerais, Brazil, 1965; DEd Valparaiso Univ., 1967; PdD Findlay Coll., 1961; DHum Northwood Inst., 1969. King's Medal for Service in the Cause of Freedom (Britain), 1948; President's Medal for Merit, USA, 1948; Washington Award, Western Soc. of Engineers, 1967; Gold Medal, Nat. Football Foundn and Hall of Fame, 1967; Theodore Roosevelt Award, Nat. Collegiate Athl. Assoc., 1970; Dist. Public Service Medal, Dept of Defense, 1970. Comdr, Order of the Southern Cross, Brazil, 1968. *Recreation:* golf. *Address:* 1701 Redwood Lane, Lafayette, Indiana 47905, USA. *T:* (office) 317–743 4266; (home) 317–447 0808. *Clubs:* Pauma Valley (Calif); Vincent's (Oxford, England).

*Died 1 March 1983.*

**HOW, Sir Friston (Charles),** Kt 1958; CB 1948; *b* 17 Sept. 1897; *o c* of Charles Friston and Jane Ethel How, Leytonstone; *m* 1932, Ann Stewart (*d* 1985), *e d* of late Alexander Chisholm Hunter, Aberdeen; no *c. Educ:* County High Sch. for Boys, Leyton; London Univ. Joined HAC, 1916; commissioned RM, 1917; served in France, 1917–18; demobilised 1919. Exchequer and Audit Dept, 1920; HM Inspector of Taxes, 1920–37; Air Ministry, 1937–40; MAP, 1940–45; Ministry of Supply, 1946–53; Sec., Atomic Energy Office, 1954–59; retired, 1959; Member: Air Transport Advisory Council, 1960–61; Air Transport Licensing Bd, 1960–70. BSc (War) (London), 1917. Called to Bar, Middle Temple, 1927. *Address:* Praesmohr, Birse, Aboyne, Aberdeenshire AB3 5EP. *T:* Aboyne 2032.

*Died 15 Jan. 1990.*

**HOWARD OF HENDERSKELFE, Baron** *cr* 1983 (Life Peer), of Henderskelfe in the County of North Yorkshire; **George Anthony Geoffrey Howard,** DL; Chairman of the BBC, 1980–83 (a Governor, since 1972); Chairman, Museums and Galleries Commission, since 1984; *b* 22 May 1920; *o surv. s* of late Hon. Geoffrey Howard (5th *s* of 9th Earl of Carlisle); *m* 1949, Lady Cecilia FitzRoy (*d* 1974), *d* of 8th Duke of Grafton; four *s. Educ:* Eton; Balliol Coll., Oxford. Served war of 1939–45: Green Howards, and attached Indian Army (wounded, Burma, 1945), Major 1945. RDC, Malton, 1946–74; CC, North Riding Yorks, 1947–55; Hon. NE Rep. for National Trust, 1948–58; Chm., York Georgian Soc., 1951–71 (Pres. 1971); Mem. Council, Country Landowners' Assoc., 1951 (Chm.; Yorks Br, 1955–65, GP Cttee, 1956–61, Legal and Planning Cttee, 1961–68, Exec. Cttee, 1967–69; Pres. of Assoc., 1969–71). Chm., Meat and Livestock Commn, 1974–77. President: Yorkshire Philosophical Soc., 1969–; Historic Houses Assoc., 1978–82. Member: National Parks Commn/Countryside Commn, 1966–74; Council, Royal Coll. of Art, 1968– (Chm., 1981; Sen. Fellow, RCA, 1974); Central Adv. Water Cttee, 1969–71; Museums and Galleries Commn, 1981–. Mayor of the Company of Merchants of the Staple of England, 1964–65. DL, NR Yorks, 1971; Co-founder Agricultural Forum, 1971. FRAgS 1972. DUniv York, 1980. *Address:* Castle Howard, York; 18 Ennismore Mews, SW7. *Clubs:* White's, Pratt's.

*Died 27 Nov. 1984.*

**HOWARD, Sir Douglas Frederick,** KCMG 1953 (CMG 1944); MC; *b* 15 Feb. 1897; *s* of late John Howard Howard and of late Mrs Howard, Biddenham House, Bedford. *Educ:* Harrow. Served European War, 1915–18, France 1916 and 1918. Entered Diplomatic Service as 3rd Sec. Christiania, 1922; Bucharest, 1924; 2nd Sec., 1925; Rome, 1926; FO 1929. BA 1932. 1st Sec., 1934; Sofia, 1935; FO 1936; Madrid, 1939; Counsellor, FO, 1941; Madrid, 1945, where he was Chargé d'Affaires, Dec. 1946–Nov. 1949; Ambassador to Uruguay, 1949–53; HM Minister to the Holy See, 1953–57, retired. *Address:* Clophill House, Clophill, Bedford. *T:* Silsoe 60285.

*Died 26 Dec. 1987.*

**HOWARD, Lt Comdr Hon. Greville (Reginald),** VRD; RNR; *b* 7 Sept. 1909; 3rd *s* of 19th Earl of Suffolk and Berkshire; *m* 1945, Mary Ridehalgh; one *d. Educ:* Eton; RMC Sandhurst. Commissioned in King's Shropshire LI, 1930–35. London Manager of G. W. Joynson, Cotton Merchants and Brokers, 1935–39. Councillor Westminster City Council, 1937; Naval Service, War of 1939–45; destroyers commanded: HMS Viscount (temp.), 1943; HMS Sabre, 1943–44;

HMS Nith, 1944. Rejoined Westminster City Council, 1945; Mayor of Westminster, 1946–47; Chm. Public Cleansing, Transport, Baths and Contracts Cttee, 1945 and 1947–49; Vice-Chm. Establishments Cttee, 1949; Vice-Chm. Refuse Sub-Cttee, Metropolitan Boroughs Standing Joint Cttee, 1947–49. MP (Nat L and C) St Ives Division of Cornwall 1950–66; retired, 1966. Hon. Overseas Director and European Consultant, Colour Processing Laboratories Ltd, 1969–. Overseas Mem. Cttee of Management and Hon. Vice-Pres., RNLI, 1969–; Pres., Lizard Br., RNLI, 1984–; Vice-President: Kensington and Chelsea Scouts Assoc., 1985–; Sea Rangers Assoc., 1984–; Cdre of the Races, Sail Training Assoc., 1984–; Patron, Discovery Dockland Trust, 1984–. *Recreations:* photography, sailing, bicycling, riding, fishing. *Address:* Redlynch, 14 Mandelbach, 7415 Brouch (Mersch), Grand Duché de Luxembourg. *T:* 63560. *Clubs:* (supernumerary or overseas member of all) White's, Pratt's, Naval, Norwegian; Royal Yacht Squadron, Royal Norwegian Yacht, Royal Naval Sailing Assoc., Royal Cornwall Yacht.

*Died 20 Sept. 1987.*

**HOWARD, Sir John,** Kt 1954; DL; FICE; Founder, 1927, and President, since 1982, John Howard and Co. Plc, Civil Engineering Contractors (founding Chairman and Managing Director, 1927–82); *b* 17 Nov. 1901; *s* of John Golding Howard, Biddenham, Bedford; *m* 1931, Margaret Mary, *d* of Herbert Edward Kemp; three *s* one *d. Educ:* Bedford Sch. Chm., Eastern Area Conservative and Unionist Assoc., 1948–52, Treas. 1954–66, Pres. 1966–69; Chm., Publicity Cttee, Nat. Union of Conservative Assocs, 1954–62, Chm. Central Council 1962. Chm., Harpur Trust, Bedford, 1966–78 (now a Life Governor). Hon. Treasurer, Imperial Soc. of Knights Bachelor, 1968–. Hon. DSc Cranfield, 1971. DL Beds, 1978. *Recreations:* shooting, golf. *Address:* Crossland Fosse, Box End, Bedford. *T:* Bedford 854708. *Clubs:* Carlton, Royal Automobile.

*Died 2 Jan. 1986.*

**HOWARD, John Melbourne;** Chartered Accountant; Director: H. Sichel & Sons Ltd; Epsom Glass Industries Ltd; Gismatic Ltd; a Partner in John Howard & Co. and A. J. Pickard & Co., both firms of Chartered Accountants; *b* 10 Aug. 1913; *er s* of Harry Howard, Warlingham, Surrey; *m* 1948, Maisie Alexandra, *d* of Alexander Bartlett Gilbert. *Educ:* Whitgift Sch. ACA 1935; FCA 1945. Served in Royal Navy, 1941–45; commissioned in RNVR. MP (C) Test Division of Southampton, 1955–64; Parliamentary Private Secretary: to Financial Sec. to the Treasury, 1957–58; to Financial and Parliamentary Sec. to Admiralty and to Civil Lord, 1958–59; to Rt Hon. Edward Heath, MP, as Minister of Labour, 1959–60 and as Lord Privy Seal at the Foreign Office, 1960–63. *Recreation:* sailing. *Address:* 31 Marbello, 83980 Le Lavandou, France.

*Died 10 Aug. 1982.*

**HOWARD, Marghanita, (Mrs John E. Howard);** *see* Laski, M.

**HOWARD, Very Rev. Richard Thomas,** MA; Provost of Coventry Cathedral, 1933–58; Provost Emeritus since 1958; *b* 1884; *m* Ethel Marjorie Corfield (*d* 1977); two *s* three *d. Educ:* Weymouth Coll.; Jesus Coll., Cambridge (Rustat Scholar; 23rd Wrangler, First-Class in the Theological Tripos); Ridley Hall. Ordained, 1908; Chaplain of Jesus Coll., Cambridge, 1908–12; went out to St John's Coll., Agra, under the Church Missionary Soc., 1912; Vice-Principal, St Paul's Divinity Sch., Allahabad, 1913–18; Principal of St Aidan's Coll., Birkenhead, 1919–29; Vicar of Luton, 1929–33; Archdeacon of Coventry, 1941–46. Proctor in Convocation for Diocese of St Albans, 1931, and Coventry Cathedral Chapter, 1933. *Publications:* Ruined and Rebuilt: the story of Coventry Cathedral, 1962; Behold Your God, 1969. *Address:* c/o 1 Munnings Close, Swainsthorpe, Norwich, Norfolk. *Died 1 Nov. 1981.*

**HOWARD, Robin Jared Stanley,** CBE 1976; Director-General, Contemporary Dance Trust Ltd, since 1966; *b* 17 May 1924; *s* of Hon. Sir Arthur Howard, KBE, CVO, DL, and of Lady Lorna Howard. *Educ:* Eton; Trinity Coll., Cambridge (MA). Served War, 1942–45, Lieut, Scots Guards. Called to Bar, Inner Temple. Hon. Dir, Internat. Service Dept, United Nations Assoc., 1956–64. Hon. DLitt Kent, 1987. *Recreation:* sleep. *Address:* 7 Sandwich Street, WC1H 9PL. *Clubs:* Garrick, MCC. *Died 12 June 1989.*

**HOWARD, Trevor Wallace;** actor; *b* 29 Sept. 1913; father English, mother Canadian; *m* 1944, Helen Mary Cherry. *Educ:* Clifton Coll. Shakespeare Festival, Stratford-on-Avon, 1936 and 1939; French Without Tears, Criterion, 1936–38. Served War in Army, 1940–43, 1st Airborne Division. Played in the Recruiting Officer and Anna Christie, 1944; Old Vic Season, 1947–48, Petruchio in The Taming of the Shrew. *Films include:* Brief Encounter, 1945; The Third Man, 1949; An Outcast of the Islands, 1951; The Heart of the Matter, 1953 (Acad. award); Lovers of Lisbon (French); Cockleshell Heroes, 1955; Run for the Sun, 1956; The Key, Heaven of Heaven, 1958; Sons and Lovers, 1960 (Acad. nomination); Mutiny on the Bounty, 1962; Von Ryan's Express, 1965; Father Goose, 1965; The Liquidator, 1966; The Charge of the Light Brigade, 1968; Pretty Polly, 1968; Ryan's Daughter, 1970; Mary Queen of Scots, 1971; Ludwig, 1972; The Offence, 1973; A Doll's House, 1973; The Visitor, 1974; 11

Harrowhouse, 1974; Hennessy, 1975; Conduct Unbecoming, 1975; Count of Monte Cristo, 1976 (Acad. nomination); The Last Remake of Beau Geste, 1977; Slavers, 1978; Stevie, 1978; Superman, 1978; Hurricane, 1980; The Sea Wolves, 1980; Sir Henry at Rawlinson End, 1980; Windwalker, (Cheyenne), 1980; Light Years Away, 1981 (Standard award, 1982); The Missionary, 1983; Gandhi, 1983; Dust, 1986; White Mischief, 1987; The Dawning (released posthumously), 1988; *Plays include:* The Devil's General, 1953; Lopahin in The Cherry Orchard, Lyric, 1954; Two Stars for Comfort, Garrick, 1962; The Father, Piccadilly, 1964; Waltz of the Toreadors, Haymarket, 1974; Scenario, Toronto, 1977. *Television:* Hedda Gabler, 1962; The Invincible Mr Disraeli, 1963 (Acad. Award); Napoleon at St Helena, 1966 (Acad. nom.); Catholics, 1974; Staying On, 1980; Jonathan Swift, 1981; The Deadly Game, 1983; In Search of the Third Reich, 1983; George Washington, 1984; Handel, in God Rot Tunbridge Wells!, 1985; Time after Time, 1985; This Lightning always Strikes Twice, 1985; Shaka Zulu, 1986; Sir Isaac Newton, in Peter the Great, 1986. *Recreations:* cricket, travel. *Address:* Rowley Green, Arkley, Herts. *Club:* MCC. *Died 7 Jan. 1988.*

**HOWARD, William McLaren,** QC 1964; *b* 27 Jan. 1921; 3rd *s* of William George Howard and Frances Jane (*née* McLaren). *Educ:* Merchant Taylors' Sch. Entered RN as Cadet, 1938. Served at sea throughout War of 1939–45; Lieut 1942; resigned commission, 1946. Called to the Bar, Lincoln's Inn, 1947, Bencher, 1972; joined Inner Temple (*ad eundem*), 1960; called to Hong Kong Bar, 1986; Dep. Chm., Norfolk QS, 1967–71; Recorder of Ipswich, 1968–71; a Recorder, 1972–86; Judge Advocate of the Fleet, 1973–86. Mem., Bar Council, 1965–69 (also Mem., Bar Council Special Cttee on Sentencing and Penology). Vice-Pres., Norfolk Assoc. for Care and Resettlement of Offenders. Mem., British Acad. Forensic Sci. Hon. Judge Advocate of US Navy, 1984; Hon. Mem. of the Bar, US Court of Mil. Appeals, 1984. *Address:* The Red House, Holkham, Wells-next-the-Sea, Norfolk; 1201 Prince's Building, Chater Road, Hong Kong. *T:* Hong Kong 5–263585. *Clubs:* Garrick; Hong Kong (Hong Kong); Royal Hong Kong Jockey.

*Died 4 March 1990.*

**HOWARD-JONES, Maj.-Gen. Leonard Hamilton,** CB 1959; CBE 1945 (OBE 1942); *b* 4 April 1905; *s* of late Hubert Stanley Howard-Jones, Maindee Park, Newport, Mon; *m* 1st, 1934, Irene Lucy Gillespie (*d* 1944); 2nd, 1945, Violet, *d* of Sidney Alfred Butler, and widow of Lieut-Col Francis John Leland; one *s* one *d. Educ:* Imperial Service Coll.; Cardiff Univ. (BSc Eng). Served War of 1939–45 (despatches; OBE; CBE). Commandant REME Training Centre, 1953–57; Inspector, Royal Electrical and Mechanical Engineers, War Office, 1957–60. MIMechE; AMIEE. *Address:* Rifle Range Farm, Fleet Road, Hartley Wintney, Hants RG27 8ED. *T:* Hartley Wintney 2358. *Died 15 March 1987.*

**HOWARD-SMITH, Trevor Wallace;** *see* Howard.

**HOWARTH, Thomas Edward Brodie,** MC 1945; TD; *b* 21 Oct. 1914; *e s* of Frank Fielding Howarth; *m* 1943, Margaret Teakle; two *s* one *d* (and one *s* decd). *Educ:* Rugby Sch.; Clare Coll., Cambridge (Scholar, MA, 1st cl. Hons Parts I and II, History Tripos). Asst Master, Winchester Coll., 1938–39, 1946–48; Headmaster King Edward's Sch., Birmingham, 1948–52; Second Master, Winchester Coll., 1952–62; High Master, St Paul's School, 1962–73; Fellow and Sen. Tutor, Magdalene Coll., Cambridge, 1973–80; Headmaster, Campion Sch., Athens, 1980–82. Served War of 1939–45, King's (Liverpool) Regt; Brigade Major, HQ Mersey Garrison; Brigade Major 207 Infantry Bde; NW Europe, June 1944; Personal Liaison Officer to C-in-C 21st Army Group. Trustee, Imperial War Museum, 1964–79. Governor: St John's Sch., Leatherhead; British Sch. of Paris. Mem., Public Schs Commission, 1966. Chm., Headmasters' Conference, 1969. *Publications:* Citizen-King, 1961; Culture, Anarchy and the Public Schools, 1969; Cambridge Between Two Wars, 1978; Prospect and Reality: Great Britain 1945–55, 1985; (ed and contrib.) Monty at Close Quarters, 1985. *Recreation:* golf. *Address:* 112A Elgin Crescent, W11. *T:* 01–221 7549. *Clubs:* Savile, Garrick, Beefsteak, East India. *Died 6 May 1988.*

**HOWE, 6th Earl,** *cr* 1821; **Edward Richard Assheton Penn Curzon,** CBE 1961; DL; JP; Baron Howe, 1788; Baron Curzon, 1794; Viscount Curzon, 1802; Lieutenant-Commander RNVR; President, Chesham and Amersham Conservative Association, since 1972; *b* 7 Aug. 1908; a godson of King Edward VII; *o s* of 5th Earl Howe, PC, CBE, VD; *S* father, 1964; *m* 1st, 1935, Priscilla (whom he divorced, 1942), *o c* of Lieut-Col Sir Archibald Weigall, 1st Bt, KCMG; 2nd, 1946, Gay, *e d* of late Stephen Frederick Wakeling, Durban, South Africa; two *d. Educ:* Eton; Corpus Christi Coll., Cambridge. RNVR, 1928–46; war service in Atlantic and Pacific, 1940–46. Mem. (MR) LCC for South Battersea, 1937–46. Commissioner of Bucks St John Ambulance Bde, 1953–55; President: S Bucks Cons. and Unionist Assoc., 1965–72; St John Ambulance, Bucks; Trustee, King William IV Naval Asylum. JP 1946, DL 1960, Bucks. Alderman, Buckinghamshire, 1958, County Councillor, 1973–, Vice Chm., Bucks County Council, 1976–. President: Brit. Automobile Racing Club; Inst. of Road Safety Officers; Fiat Motor Club (GB);

RAC Steward; Vice-Chm., RAC; Dir, Automobile Proprietary Ltd; Member: RAC Public Policy Cttee; British Motor Sports Council; Motoring Services Ltd; RNLI Cttee of Management. Hon. FIRTE. CStJ. *Recreations:* motoring, cricket, shooting, golf. *Heir: cousin* Frederick Richard Penn Curzon [*b* 29 Jan. 1951; *m* 1983, Elizabeth H. Stuart]. *Address:* Penn House, Amersham, Bucks. *T:* High Wycombe 713366; 20 Pitts Head Mews, W1. *T:* 01-499 4706. *Club:* Naval.                                    *Died 29 May 1984.*

**HOWE, Sir Robert George,** GBE 1949; KCMG 1947 (CMG 1937); *b* Derby, 19 Sept. 1893; *s* of H. Howe; *m* 1919, Loveday Mary Hext (*d* 1970); one *s. Educ:* Derby Sch.; St Catharine's Coll., Cambridge. Third Sec. at Copenhagen, 1920; Second Sec., 1920; Belgrade, 1922; Rio de Janeiro, 1924; First Sec., 1926; Bucharest, 1926; Foreign Office, 1930; Acting Counsellor at Peking, 1934; Counsellor, 1936; Minister in Riga, 1940; Minister in Abyssinia, 1942–45; Asst Under-Sec. of State, Foreign Office, 1945; Governor-Gen. of the Sudan, 1947–55; retired 1955. JP Cornwall, 1955–68. *Recreation:* riding. *Address:* Cowbridge, Lostwithiel, Cornwall.
                                                *Died 22 June 1981.*

**HOWELL, Dorothy,** FRAM; Professor of Harmony and Composition, Royal Academy of Music, 1924–70, retired; *b* Handsworth, Birmingham, 1898. *Educ:* Royal Academy of Music. *Publications:* Symphonic Poem, Lamia; various works for Piano, Violin, etc. *Address:* Perrins House, Moorlands Road, Malvern, Worcs WR14 2TZ.                                          *Died 12 Jan. 1982.*

**HOWELLS, Christopher John;** HM Diplomatic Service; Head of Nationality and Treaty Department, Foreign and Commonwealth Office, 1981–83; *b* 2 March 1933; *s* of late Rev. Brinley Howells; *m* 1959, Jane Hayes; two *s* one *d. Educ:* Oakham Sch.; Merton Coll., Oxford (1st Cl. Hons Mod. Hist.). Joined HM Diplomatic Service, 1958; Hong Kong, 1959; Third Sec., Peking, 1960; Foreign Office, 1962; First Sec., Vienna, 1965; MoD, 1967; Asst Political Adviser, Hong Kong, 1969; Counsellor and Head of Chancery, Warsaw, 1973; FCO, 1975; Hd of Chancery, UK Deleg. to NATO, 1978. *Address:* c/o Foreign and Commonwealth Office, SW1. *Clubs:* Athenæum; Hong Kong (Hong Kong).          *Died 3 June 1984.*

**HOWELLS, Derek William; His Honour Judge Howells;** a Circuit Judge, since 1980; *b* 8 Oct. 1928; *s* of William Howells and Dinnie Maud (*née* Weeks); *m* 1965, Anne Griffiths. *Educ:* Cardiff High Sch.; Univ. of London. Called to the Bar, Lincoln's Inn, 1955. *Recreations:* golf, gardening. *Address:* 63 Owl's Lodge Lane, Mayals, Swansea SA3 5DP. *T:* Swansea 403845. *Club:* Bristol Channel Yacht.                                          *Died 9 Nov. 1987.*

**HOWELLS, Gilbert Haywood,** FRCS; *b* 23 Aug. 1897; *s* of Henry Haywood and Hannah Elizabeth Howells; *m* 1926, Dorothy Mary Jones (*d* 1977); no *c. Educ:* Newport High Sch.; University Coll., Cardiff; St Thomas' Hosp. MB, BS London 1923; FRCS 1928. Consulting Surgeon: Royal National Ear Nose and Throat Hospital; (ENT) St George's Hosp.; (ENT), Moorfields Eye Hosp.; King Edward VII Hosp., Windsor; Upton Hosp., Slough; Fellow Royal Society of Medicine and British Association of Otolaryngologists; Mem. BMA; late Corresp. Mem. Société Française d'Otorhin. *Publications:* sundry articles in medical journals. *Address:* Breydon, South Park Drive, Gerrards Cross, Bucks. *T:* Gerrards Cross 83368.                                          *Died 29 July 1982.*

**HOWELLS, Herbert Norman,** CH 1972; CBE 1953; DMus Oxon; MusDoc *hc* Cantab; Hon. DMus RCM; FRCO; FRCM; Hon. RAM; composer; King Edward Professor of Music, University of London, Emeritus 1962; Professor of Composition at Royal College of Music; Director of Music, St Paul's Girls' School, Brook Green, 1936–62; sometime Editor RCM Magazine; Master, Worshipful Company of Musicians, 1959 (first John Collard Fellow; elected to John Collard Life Fellowship, 1959); *b* 17 Oct. 1892; *y s* of late Oliver Howells and Elizabeth Burgham; *m* 1920, Dorothy (*d* 1975), *y d* of late William Goozee; one *d* one *s* decd). *Educ:* Lydney Grammar Sch.; Gloucester Cathedral; RCM. Became pupil of Sir Herbert Brewer, Gloucester Cathedral, 1905; Open Schol. in Composition at RCM, 1912; studied there under Stanford, Parratt, Parry, Charles Wood, and Walford Davies till 1917; succeeded to the Grove Scholarship, 1915, and became Bruce Scholar, 1916; first work heard in London was the Mass produced by Sir Richard Terry at Westminster Cathedral, 1912; was for short time sub-organist at Salisbury Cathedral. President: RCO, 1958–59; Incorporated Soc. of Musicians, 1952; Plainsong and Mediæval Soc. Hon. MusD Cambridge, 1961; Hon. DMus RCM 1982; Hon. FRSCM, 1963; Hon. Fellow: St John's Coll., Cambridge, 1962; Queen's Coll., Oxford, 1977. *Publications:* Sir Patrick Spens; Sine Nomine (Chorus and Orchestra) Procession; Puck's Minuet; Piano Concerto; Elegy for Strings; Concerto for Strings; Lady Audrey's Suite; Phantasy Quartet; Piano Quartet; Rhapsodic Quintet (Clar. and Str.); First and Third Sonatas for violin and pianoforte; Lambert's Clavichord; In Green Ways, five songs for Soprano and Orchestra; Peacock Pie song-cycle; Sonata for Organ; Hymnus Paradisi for Sopr., Ten., Chor. and Orchestra; Missa Sabrinensis for 4 solo voices, Chorus

and Orchestra; Pageantry (Suite for Brass Band); A Kent Yeoman's Wooing Song for 2 Soli, Choir and Orchestra; Four Organ Rhapsodies; Six Psalm Preludes; Music for a Prince (for HRH Prince Charles); Introit (composed for Coronation Service, 1953); Inheritance (commissioned by The Arts Council of Great Britain for A Garland for the Queen, 1953); An English Mass, 1955 (for Chorus and Orch.); Howell's Clavichord (20 pieces); Missa Aedis Christi (for Christ Church, Oxford); Missa, Collegium Regale (for King's Coll., Cambridge); Three Figures (suite for Brass Band); Sequence for St Michael (commnd by St John's Coll., Cambridge); Coventry Antiphon (Commnd for Coventry Cath.); Stabat Mater for Tenor, Chorus and Orchestra (commnd by the London Bach Choir); The Coventry Mass. *Recreations:* seeking quiet, English literature. *Address:* 3 Beverley Close, Barnes, SW13. *T:* 01-876 5119. *Club:* Savile.                               *Died 23 Feb. 1983.*

**HOWES, Rear-Adm. Peter Norris,** CB 1966; DSC 1941; Private Secretary to Lord Mayor of London, 1968–72; *b* 1 July 1916; *s* of Percy Groom Howes; *m* 1952, Priscilla Hamilton, *d* of Maj.-Gen. G. W. E. Heath, CB, CBE, DSO, MC; three *s* one *d. Educ:* St Peter's Court, Broadstairs; Royal Naval College, Dartmouth. Served in HM Ships Hood, Furious, Fortune, Albury, Aberdeen, Westminster, Adamant, Newcastle, Liverpool; commanded 6th Motor Gunboat Flotilla; HMS Chaplet; HMS Mercury; Dartmouth Training Sqdn; HMS Devonshire; specialised as Communications Officer, 1942; Senior Aide-de-Camp to Viceroy of India, 1947; Naval Asst to First Sea Lord, 1955–58; Flag Officer, Middle East Station, 1964–66. *Publication:* The Viceregal Establishments in India, 1948. *Recreations:* riding, shooting, fishing, photography. *Address:* Sutton Parva House, Heytesbury, Wilts. *T:* Sutton Veny 333.                                       *Died 9 Sept. 1983.*

**HOWIE, Thomas McIntyre;** Principal, Paisley College of Technology, since 1972; *b* 21 April 1926; *m* 1951, Catherine Elizabeth Logan; three *s. Educ:* Paisley Coll. of Technology; Strathclyde Univ. BSc (Eng); CEng, FICE. Civil Engrg Asst, Clyde Navigation Trust, 1947–50; Paisley Coll. of Technology: Lectr in Civil Engrg, 1950–55; Sen. Lectr in Civil Engrg, 1955–58; Head, Dept of Civil Engrg, 1958–72; Vice-Principal, 1970–72. *Recreations:* golf, curling. *Address:* Dunscore, 38 Main Road, Castlehead, Paisley PA2 6AW. *T:* 041-889 5723. *Club:* Caledonian.          *Died 16 Nov. 1986.*

**HOWLAND, Robert Leslie,** MA; Fellow of St John's College, Cambridge, since 1929; *b* 25 March 1905; *s* of Robert and Mary Howland; *m* 1930, Eileen, *d* of Robert Reid Tait; two *s* one *d. Educ:* Shrewsbury Sch.; St John's Coll., Cambridge; 1st Cl. Classical Tripos Part I, 1926, Part II, 1928, Strathcona Student, 1928; Fellow of St John's Coll., 1929, Tutor 1932–65, Senior Tutor, 1956–65, President, 1963–67. University Lectr in Classics, 1934–72; Senior Proctor, 1951–52; Warden of Madingley Hall, 1965–75. Mem., Goldsmiths' Co., 1958. Mem. of Cambridge Univ. Athletic Team, 1925–28; Mem. of British National Athletic Team, 1927–39 (Capt. 1934–35), and British Olympic Team, 1928. Holder of English native record for putting the weight, 1930–48; took part in British Empire Games, 1930, 1934, in British Empire *v* USA Matches, 1930, 1936; Pres., Cambridge Univ. AFC, 1946–76, and Cambs AAA, 1960–75. RAF 1941–46, Fighter Controller (Radar), GB, Mediterranean, SE Asia; France and Italy Star, Burma Star. *Publications:* reviews and articles in classical jls and Oxford Classical Dict. *Address:* Elizabethan Cottage, Littlebury, Saffron Walden, Essex; St John's College, Cambridge. *Clubs:* United Oxford & Cambridge University; Achilles; Hawks (Cambridge).
                                                *Died 7 March 1986.*

**HOWSAM, Air Vice-Marshal George Roberts,** CB 1945; MC 1918; RCAF, retired: also retired from Federal Emergency Measures Organization, 1962 (Coordinator, Alberta Civil Defence, 1950–57) and from business; *b* 29 Jan. 1895; *s* of Mary Ida and George Roberts Howsam, Port Perry, Ont; *m* 1st, 1918, Lillian Isobel (*d* 1970), *d* of Mary and William Somerville, Toronto; one *s*; 2nd, 1972, Marion Isobel Garrett, *d* of Clarence Albert Mitchell and Mary Blanche McCurdy, New Brunswick and Nova Scotia. *Educ:* Port Perry and Toronto. Joined Canadian Expeditionary Force, March 1916 and RFC 70 Sqdn and 43 Sqdn, 1917–18; served as fighter pilot France and Belgium, 1917–18 (wounded twice, MC); with Army of Occupation in Germany; returned to Canada, 1921; RCAF photographic survey, NW Canada; RAF Staff Coll., England, 1930 (psa); Senior Mem., RCAF 1st Aerobatic Team (Siskin) Display, Cleveland, USA, 1929; Staff Mem. CGAO Operations at AFHQ, 1931–32; SASO MD2 Toronto, 1933–36; OC 2 Army Co-operation Sqdn, Ottawa, 1937; Dir of Training for RCAF, Ottawa, 1938–40; England and France, 1940; later in 1940, SASO, No 4 Training Command, Regina; commanded No 11 Service Flying Training Sch., Yorkton, 1941; AOC No 4 Training Command, Calgary, 1942–44, also AOC Air Staging Route to Alaska, 1942–43 (thereby holding double command for two years); Chm. Organisation Cttee, Air Force HQ, Ottawa, 1945; retired 1946. Dominion Dir The Air Cadet League of Canada, 1946–47; Alberta Chm. RCAF Assoc., 1958–59. Canadian Deleg. to

Emergency Measures NATO Assembly, Paris, Oct. 1960. Legion of Merit in Degree of Comdr (US), 1945; Order of White Lion (Czecho-Slovakia), 1946; Commandeur de l'ordre de la Couronne (Belgium), 1948. *Publications:* Rocky Mountain Foothills Offer Great Chance to Gliders (Calgary Daily Herald), 1923; Industrial and Mechanical Development: War (Canadian Defence Qtly Prize Essay), 1931. *Recreations:* gardening, writing, shooting. *Address:* (home) 2040 Pauls Terrace, Victoria, BC V8N 2Z3, Canada; Bank of Montreal, Government Street, Victoria, BC. *Clubs:* Union, Canadian, Victoria Golf (Victoria, BC); Empire (Toronto); Ranchmen's (Calgary).

*Died 16 April* 1988.

**HOYER-MILLAR, Dame (Evelyn Louisa) Elizabeth,** DBE 1960 (OBE 1952); DL; Director, Women's Royal Naval Service, 1958–61; Hon. ADC to the Queen, 1958–61; *b* 17 Dec. 1910; *o d* of late Robert Christian Hoyer Millar, Craig, Angus, Scotland, and Muriel (*née* Foster). *Educ:* privately. VAD 1939–41; joined WRNS, 1942. JP 1968–76, DL 1971, Angus. *Recreations:* needlework, gardening, country pursuits. *Address:* The Croft, Hillside, Angus. *T:* Hillside 304. *Died 26 Feb.* 1984.

**HUBBLE, Prof. Sir Douglas (Vernon),** KBE 1971 (CBE 1966); MD (London); FRCP; Emeritus Professor, University of Birmingham; *b* 25 Dec. 1900; *s* of Harry Edward Hubble and Agnes Kate (*née* Field); *m* 1928, Marie Arnott Bryce (*d* 1981); three *d*. *Educ:* St Bartholomew's Hospital, London. Physician, Derbyshire Children's Hospital, 1932; Physician, Derbyshire Royal Infirmary, 1942; Prof. of Pædiatrics and Child Health, and Dir, Inst. of Child Health, Univ. of Birmingham, 1958–68; Dean, Faculty of Medicine, Univ. of Birmingham, 1963–68; Dean, Faculty of Medicine, Haile Selassie I Univ., 1969–71. Pres., Paediatric Section, Royal Society of Medicine, 1956; Mem., British Pharmocopoeia Commission 1958–68; Lectures: Burns, RFPS(G), 1957; Honeyman Gillespie, Univ. of Edinburgh, 1958; Langdon Brown, RCP, 1960; Felton Bequest Travelling, Royal Children's Hosp., Melbourne, Australia, 1961; Lawson Wilkins Meml, Johns Hopkins Univ., 1965; Lloyd Roberts Meml, Univ. of Manchester, 1966; Tisdall, Canadian Med. Assoc., 1967; Osler, Soc. of Apothecaries of London, 1968; Leonard Parsons Meml, Univ. of Birmingham, 1971; Osler Oration, RCP, 1974. Council Mem., RCP, 1960–62; Public Orator, University of Birmingham, 1962–66; Mem., Clinical Research Board, MRC, 1962–66; Pædiatric Consultant, Josiah Macy, Jr, Foundation, 1968–69; Chm. Council for Investigation of Fertility Control, 1963–68. Hon. Mem. Amer. Pediatric Soc., 1963. Pres. Lichfield Johnson Soc., 1956. Member: Tropical Med. Research Bd, MRC, 1965–69; GMC, 1965–69. Hon. Fellow, RSM, 1972. James Spence Gold Medal, British Paediatric Assoc., 1970; Dawson Williams Prize, BMA, 1972. *Publications:* contrib. to medical and literary journals. *Address:* Yonder Hill, Thirtover, Cold Ash, Newbury, Berks. *T:* Thatcham 64177. *Died 6 Nov.* 1981.

**HUCKER, Ernest George,** CBE 1972; Senior Director, Post Office, 1969–71; *b* Wembdon, Som, 20 March 1908; *s* of Albert Hucker; *m* 1934, Mary Louise Jowett; one *s* one *d*. *Educ:* Hele's Sch., Exeter. Post Office Telephones, 1929; Asst Surveyor of Posts, 1932–39; 2nd Lieut RE, SRO, 1935; served War of 1939–45, Army: France, 1939–40; India, 1942–45 (Lt-Col); London Postal Region, 1946–52; Controller of Ops, 1952; Comdt PO Management Trng Centre, 1952–55; Chief Inspector of Postal Services, 1956–62; Asst Sec. 1962–63; Dep. Dir 1963–65, Dir 1965–69, Midland Region. Freeman, City of London, 1952. *Recreation:* music. *Address:* 6 Ratton Drive, Eastbourne, East Sussex BN20 9BJ. *T:* Eastbourne 501414. *Died 24 Feb.* 1986.

**HUDSON, Rt. Rev. A(rthur) W(illiam) Goodwin,** ThD; Hon. Assistant Bishop, Diocese of Derby, since 1981; *b* 1906; *s* of Alfred and Anne Goodwin Hudson; *m* Dr Elena E. de Wirtz; one *s*. *Educ:* London Univ.; London Coll. of Divinity. Ordained Deacon, 1940; Priest, 1941. Curate of St Paul, Chatham, 1940–42; Hon. CF, 1942–45; Vicar of Good Easter, Essex, 1942–45; Diocesan Missioner, Chelmsford Diocese, 1943–45; Head Master, Windsor Sch., Santiago, 1945–48; Chaplain, Santiago, Chile, 1945–48; Vicar of St Mary Magdalene, Holloway, 1948–55 (with St James, 1953–55); Vicar of All Saints, Woodford Wells, 1955–60; Coadjutor Bishop and Dean of Sydney, 1960–65; Vicar of St Paul's, Portman Square, W1, 1965–79. Hon. Gen. Sec., S Amer. Missionary Soc., 1949–60; Hon. Sec., Spanish and Portuguese Church Aid Soc., 1950–55. Chairman: Jerusalem Garden Tomb Assoc.; Council of Christian Churches. *Recreations:* yachting, tennis; and profession! *Address:* 14 Newton Park, Newton Solney, Derbyshire DE15 0SX. *T:* Burton-on-Trent 702367. *Clubs:* National; Army and Navy.

*Died 18 Sept.* 1985.

**HUDSON, Eric Hamilton,** FRCP; Hon. Consulting Physician: West London Hospital; London Chest Hospital; King Edward VII Hospital, Midhurst; Papworth Village Settlement; retired as: Consultant Physician, Manor House Hospital; Senior Medical Officer, Prudential Assurance Co.; *b* 11 July 1902; *s* of James Arthur and Edith Hudson; *m* 1st, 1940, Jessie Marian MacKenzie (*d* 1968);

two *s* one *d*; 2nd, 1972, Nora Joan Pitman. *Educ:* Radley Coll.; Emmanuel Coll., Cambridge; Guy's Hosp., London. MRCS, LRCP, 1927; MA, MB, BCh Cantab, 1931; MRCP 1933, FRCP 1941. Late Wing Commander RAF, Officer in charge Medical Div., 1941–45. Late Examr in Medicine, RCP; Past Pres., W London Medico-Chirurgical Soc., 1959. *Publications:* Section on diagnosis and treatment of respiratory Tuberculosis, Heaf's Symposium of Tuberculosis, 1957; contrib. to Perry and Holmes Sellors Diseases of the Chest, 1964; contrib. to medical jls on diseases of the lungs. *Recreation:* fishing. *Address:* The Shieling, Highclere, near Newbury, Berks. *T:* Highclere (0635) 253574.

*Died 19 June* 1990.

**HUDSON, Rt. Rev. Wilfrid John,** CBE 1973; AKC; Head of Brotherhood of St Paul since 1961; *b* 12 June 1904; *s* of late John William and late Bertha Mildred Hudson, Worthing, Sussex; unmarried. *Educ:* Brighton Coll.; King's Coll., London. AKC, first Cl. and Jelf Prize, 1931. Deacon 1931, Priest 1932, London. Curate of St Barnabas, Pimlico, 1931–36; Principal of Brotherhood of Good Shepherd, Dubbo, Diocese of Bathurst, and Examining Chaplain to Bishop of Bathurst, 1937–42; Curate of All Saints, Woodham, Surrey, 1942–43; Acting Curate of St Barnabas, Ealing, 1944; Rector of Letchworth, Diocese of St Albans, 1944–50; Bishop of Carpentaria, 1950–60; Bishop Coadjutor of Brisbane, 1961–73. Associate of Inst. of Chartered Accountants, 1928. *Address:* Brotherhood House, Dubbo, NSW 2830, Australia. *T:* 068 82-3620.

*Died 16 Feb.* 1981.

**HUGGETT, Mrs Helen Kemp;** *see* Porter, Prof. H. K.

**HUGHES, Albert Henry,** OBE 1961; HM Diplomatic Service, retired; HM Ambassador to El Salvador, 1975–77; *b* 20 Sept. 1917; *s* of George Albert Hughes; *m* 1939, Nancy Russell; two *s* one *d*. *Educ:* The Judd Sch., Tonbridge, Kent. Appointed to the Foreign Office, 1935. War of 1939–45: Served in HM Forces, 1940–45, HM Vice-Consul, Rouen, France, 1949; HM Consul, Tehran, Iran, 1949–52; HM Consul, Philadelphia, USA, 1953–55; HM Consul, Bilbao, Spain, 1962–64; Counsellor (Administration) and HM Consul-General, Washington, 1964–68; Head of Finance Dept, FCO, and Finance Officer of the Diplomatic Service, 1968–71; HM Consul-General, Amsterdam, 1971–75. *Recreations:* reading, gardening, photography. *Address:* The Cottage, Matfield Green, near Tonbridge, Kent. *T:* Brenchley 2462. *Died 2 May* 1985.

**HUGHES, Major Arthur John,** MC 1945; TD and Clasp 1950; DL; Chairman, Hertfordshire Police Authority, since 1980; *b* 29 June 1914; *s* of Arthur Hubert Hughes and Dorothy Maud Hughes; *m* 1946, Penelope Joan Parker; one *s* one *d*. *Educ:* Highgate Sch. Entered family business, Wm Hughes Ltd, 1931; Chm. and Man. Dir, 1951. Commnd, Mddx Regt, 1936; served War of 1939–45 (Lt-Col 1943) (despatches twice, MC); subst. Major, 1949. Mem., Hatfield RDC, 1955–58 and 1961–64; Herts CC: Councillor, 1958; Alderman, 1966–73; Vice-Chm., 1968–69, 1971–73, 1974–77; Chm., 1973, 1977–80; Conservative Gp Leader, 1974. Chm., Herts Society, 1980–. DL Herts, 1974. *Recreations:* golf, gardening, good food, good wine, grand-children. *Address:* The Vineyards, Welwyn, Herts AL6 9NE. *T:* Welwyn 4242. *Died 25 Oct.* 1984.

**HUGHES, Maj.-Gen. Basil Perronet,** CB 1955; CBE 1944; *b* 13 Jan. 1903; *s* of late Rev. E. B. A. Hughes; *m* 1932, Joan Marion Worthington; two *s*. *Educ:* Eton Coll.; RMA, Woolwich. Commissioned RFA 1923; Staff Coll., 1935–36; Directing Staff, Staff Coll., 1940. Served NW Frontier of India, 1930–31 (medal and clasp); Mohmand, 1933 (clasp); War of 1939–45 (star and despatches). Formerly: Hon. Col 2nd (London) Bn, Mobile Defence Corps; Hon. Colonel 571 LAA Regt (9th Battalion The Middx Regt DCO) RA, TA. ADC to the Queen, 1952–54; GOC 4 Anti-Aircraft Group, 1954; Maj.-Gen. RA (AA), War Office, 1955–58; retired, 1958. Controller, Royal Artillery Instn, 1958–75. Col Comdt RA 1961–68; Hon. Colonel: 5th Bn, The Middx Regt (DCO), TA, 1964–69; 10th Bn, The Queen's Regt (Mddx), T&AVR, 1970–71. *Publications:* British Smooth-Bore Artillery, 1969; The Bengal Horse Artillery 1800–1861, 1971; Firepower, 1974; Honour Titles of the Royal Artillery, 1978; Open Fire, 1983. *Address:* St Nicholas Close, Stour Row, near Shaftesbury, Dorset. *Club:* Leander.

*Died 10 Sept.* 1989.

**HUGHES, Brodie;** *see* Hughes, E. B. C.

**HUGHES, Prof. David Leslie,** CBE 1977; PhD, FRCVS, DipBact; Professor of Veterinary Pathology, University of Liverpool, 1955–78, later Emeritus Professor; *b* 26 Oct. 1912; *s* of John and Eva Hughes; *m* 1st, 1938, Ann Marjorie Sparks (*d* 1971); 2nd, 1974, Jean Mavis, *yr d* of C. B. Saul. *Educ:* Wycliffe Coll., Stonehouse; Royal Veterinary Coll., London (MRCVS). PhD Nottingham, 1959. Agricultural Research Council Studentship in Animal Health, 1934–37 (DipBact London, 1936); Research Officer, Veterinary Laboratory, Min. of Agriculture, 1937–38; Lecturer in Bacteriology, Royal Veterinary College, 1938–40; Second Scientific Asst, Agricultural Research Council's Field Station, Compton, 1940–46;

Head of Veterinary Science Div., Research Dept, Boots Pure Drug Co. Ltd, 1948–55; Dean of Faculty of Veterinary Science, University of Liverpool, 1965–68; Warden, Roscoe Hall, Univ. of Liverpool, 1965–72; Pro-Vice-Chancellor, Univ. of Liverpool, 1975–78. Mem., ARC, 1973–83. FRCVS 1952; Mem. Council, RCVS, 1964–76 (Pres. 1974–75; Sen. Vice Pres., 1975–76); Pres., British Veterinary Assoc., 1963–64. Governor, Howells Sch., Denbigh, 1974–84. *Publications:* scientific articles in Veterinary Record, British Veterinary Journal, Journal of Comparative Pathology, Journal of Hygiene, etc. *Recreations:* gardening, painting and travel. *Address:* Ty Maen, Llwyn-y-Rhos, Llanrhaeadr, Denbigh, Clwyd LL16 4NH. *T:* Llanynys 364.                                             *Died 4 May* 1990.

**HUGHES, Prof. Emmet John;** Professor of Politics, Eagleton Institute, Rutgers University, 1970–82; *b* 26 Dec. 1920; *s* of Judge John L. Hughes, Summit, NJ; *m* 1st (marr. diss.); one *s*; 2nd, 1951, Eileen Lanouette (marr. diss.); two *d*; 3rd, Katherine Nouri; two *d Educ:* Princeton Univ. (AB *summa cum laude*); Columbia Univ. (Graduate Sch.). Press Attaché, American Embassy, Madrid, 1942–46. Chief of Bureau for Time and Life Magazines: Rome, 1947–48, Berlin, 1948, 1949; Articles Editor, for Life Magazine, New York, 1949–53. Administrative Asst to the President of the United States, 1953, Special European Correspondent, Life Magazine, 1953–57; Chief of Foreign Correspondents, Time and Life, 1957–60; Senior Advisor on Public Affairs to the Rockefeller Brothers, 1960–63; Newsweek columnist and editorial consultant, Washington Post Co., 1963–68; Special Asst to Governor of NY State, 1968–70. *Publications:* The Church and the Liberal Society, 1944; Report from Spain, 1947; America the Vincible, 1959; The Ordeal of Power, 1963; The Living Presidency, 1973. *Address:* c/o Eagleton Institute, Rutgers University, New Brunswick, NJ 08903, USA.
*Died 20 Sept.* 1982.

**HUGHES, (Ernest) Brodie (Cobbett),** FRCS; Professor of Neurosurgery, 1948–78, and Dean of the Faculty of Medicine and Dentistry, 1974–78, University of Birmingham; *b* 21 Sept. 1913; *o s* of E. T. C. Hughes, surgeon, and D. K. Cobbett, Richmond, Surrey; *m* 1971, Frances Wendy Alexander. *Educ:* Eastbourne Coll.; University Coll. and Hospital, London. MB, BS London 1937, FRCS 1939, ChM Birmingham 1949; resident appointments, UC Hospital, and at National Hospital for Nervous Diseases, Queen Square, London. After various appointments in neurosurgery was appointed Neurosurgeon, Birmingham United Hospitals, 1947. *Publications:* The Visual Fields, 1955; various publications in medical journals on neurosurgery and on perimetry and visual fields in particular. *Recreations:* playing the oboe, fly-fishing for trout; unsuccessful attempts to paint and draw in oils, water-colour, pen-and-ink and other media. *Address:* Fairfield House South, Saxmundham, Suffolk IP17 1AX. *T:* Saxmundham 2060. *Club:* Athenæum.                                             *Died 23 March* 1989.

**HUGHES, George Ravensworth,** CVO 1943; *b* 16 June 1888; *s* of Thomas McKenny Hughes, formerly Professor of Geology at Cambridge Univ.; *m* 1917, Margaret (*d* 1967), *d* of His Honour Judge Graham; one *s* one *d. Educ:* Eton; Trinity Coll., Cambridge. Clerk of the Worshipful Company of Goldsmiths, 1938–53. *Publications:* The Plate of the Goldsmiths' Co. (with J. B. Carrington), 1926; The Goldsmiths' Company as Patrons of their craft, 1919 to 1953; Articles on Antique and Modern Silverwork. *Recreations:* music, gardening, and golf. *Address:* Plummers, Bishopstone, Seaford, East Sussex. *T:* Seaford 892958. *Club:* Athenæum.                                              *Died 21 Feb.* 1983.

**HUGHES, Brig. Gerald Birdwood V.;** *see* Vaughan-Hughes.

**HUGHES, Rear-Adm. Henry Hugh,** CB 1966; retired, 1968; *b* 9 March 1911; British; *m* 1939, Margaret (*née* Lycett); two *d. Educ:* Clydebank High Sch.; Glasgow Univ. (BSc Hons). English Electric Co. Ltd, Stafford, 1932–42; Electrical Officer, RNVR, 1942–45; transf. to RN as Lieut-Comdr, 1945; Comdr 1947; Capt. 1956; Rear-Adm. 1964. HMS Vanguard, 1947–49; subsequently: various appts in Admty and Dockyards; in comd, HMS Collingwood, 1962–63; Dep. Dir of Electrical Engrg, 1963–64; Dir, Naval Electrical Engrg, 1964; Chief Naval Engineer Officer, 1967–68. *Recreation:* tennis. *Address:* Tigh Failté, Argyll Terrace, Tobermory, Isle of Mull, Scotland. *T:* Tobermory 06882432.
*Died 17 May* 1986.

**HUGHES, Rev. H(enry) Trevor,** MA; *b* 27 Feb. 1910; *s* of late Rev. Dr H. Maldwyn Hughes; *m* 1946, Elizabeth Catherine Williams; one *s* one *d. Educ:* Perse Sch., Cambridge. National Provincial Bank, 1926–31; Wesley House, Cambridge, 1932–35 (2nd Class Hons Theol Tripos, 1935); Chaplain, Culford Sch., Bury St Edmunds, 1935–41; Chaplain, Royal Air Force, 1941–45 (despatches). Asst Minister, Central Hall, Westminster, 1945–46; Vice-Principal and Chaplain, Westminster College of Education, 1946–53, Principal, 1953–69; Minister, Attleborough Methodist Church, 1969–75. Incorporated MA, Oxford Univ. through Lincoln Coll., 1959. First Methodist Select Preacher, University of Oxford, 1965; Methodist representative, British Council of Churches

Preachers' Exchange with the USA, 1964. *Publications:* Prophetic Prayer, 1947; Teaching the Bible to Seniors, 1948; Teaching the Bible to Juniors, 1949; Why We Believe, 1950; The Piety of Jeremy Taylor, 1960; Faith and Life, 1962; Life Worth Living, 1965; A Progress of Pilgrims, 1979; pamphlets: Letters to a Christian, 1947; Teaching the Bible Today, 1957; contributor to London Quarterly Review. *Recreation:* painting. *Address:* 10 Park Close, Hethersett, Norfolk NR9 3EW. *T:* Norwich 811038.
*Died 26 April* 1988.

**HUGHES, Rt. Rev. John Richard Worthington P.;** *see* Poole Hughes.

**HUGHES, Paul Grant; His Honour Judge Paul Hughes;** a Circuit Judge, since 1978; *b* 22 March 1928; *s* of Charles Alban Hughes and Kathleen Gough Hughes; *m* 1985, Anne Dickson. *Educ:* Giggleswick School; King's Coll., Cambridge (MA, LLB). RAF, 1946–48. Called to Bar, Inner Temple, 1952. Housemaster, Merton House, Penmaenmawr, 1953–58; Barrister, Nottingham, 1958–78. Part-time Chm., Mental Health Review Tribunal, 1971–78. *Recreations:* nature conservation (Treasurer, Notts Trust for Nature Conservation, 1972–), walking, gardening, opera. *Address:* 203 Loughborough Road, Ruddington, Nottingham. *T:* Nottingham 212275.                                          *Died 17 June* 1985.

**HUGHES, Sean Francis;** MP (Lab) Knowsley South, since 1983; *b* 8 May 1946; *s* of Francis and Mary Hughes; *m* 1985, Patricia Cunliffe, Rainhill, Merseyside; one *d. Educ:* local primary and grammar schs; Liverpool Univ. (BA); Manchester Univ. (MA). Trainee Personnel Manager, Unilever, 1969; History Teacher, 1970–83, and Head of History Dept, 1972–83, Ruffwood Comprehensive Sch., Kirkby, Merseyside. An Opposition Whip, 1984–87; Opposition spokesman on Defence (Army), 1987–. *Recreations:* soccer, running, reading. *Address:* 150 Tarbock Road, Huyton, Merseyside L36 5TJ.                                           *Died 24 June* 1990.

**HUGHES, Rt. Rev. Thomas Maurice;** Assistant Bishop of Llandaff, 1961–70; *b* 17 April 1895; *s* of David and Jane Hughes, Conwil, Carmarthen; *m* 1926, Margaret, *d* of Rev. D. C. Morris, Vicar of Port Talbot; one *s* one *d. Educ:* St John's Coll., Ystradmeurig; St David's Coll., Lampeter; Keble Coll., Oxford (Hons Theol). Served European War, 1915–17: 29th and 9th RF (wounded). Asst Curate, Port Talbot, 1922; Minor Canon, Llandaff Cathedral, 1928; Vicar of Cadoxton Neath, 1931; Vicar of St Catherine, Cardiff, 1937; Rector and Rural Dean, Merthyr Tydfil, 1942. Canon of Llandaff Cathedral, 1943; Vicar of St John Baptist, Cardiff, 1946–61; Canon and Precentor of Llandaff Cathedral, 1946–61; Rural Dean of Cardiff, 1954–61; Archdeacon of Margam, 1961–65; Archdeacon of Llandaff, 1965–69. *Recreation:* gardening. *Address:* 110 Cardiff Road, Llandaff, Cardiff. *T:* Cardiff 561836.
*Died 4 Oct.* 1981.

**HUGHES, His Honour William Henry;** a Circuit Judge, 1972–83; *b* 6 Jan. 1915; *s* of late William Howard Hamilton Hughes and Helena Brown; *m* 1961, Jenny, *d* of late Theodore Francis Turner, QC; one *d. Educ:* privately; Keble Coll., Oxford. Served War of 1939–45; AA & QMG, BEF, France and Belgium, N Africa, Italy (despatches, Croix de Guerre (France)); Staff Coll.; Lieut-Col 1944. Called to the Bar, Inner Temple, 1949. Deputy Chairman: Isle of Ely QS, 1959–63; Essex QS, 1961–63; London Sessions, 1962–63, 1968–71; a Metropolitan Magistrate, 1963–71. Formerly a Mem., General Council of the Bar. Chm., Cttee of Inquiry into Children's Homes and Hostels, apptd by Sec. of State for NI, 1984–85. Governor: Camden Sch. for Girls, 1977–86; NLCS, 1977–87. *Recreations:* books, wine, shooting, travel. *Address:* Old Wardour House, Tisbury, Wilts SP3 6RP. *T:* Tisbury (0747) 870431. *Clubs:* Beefsteak, Garrick, PEN.                                        *Died 5 May* 1990.

**HUGHES, William Reginald Noel,** FRINA, RCNC; *b* 14 Dec. 1913; *s* of Frank George Hughes and Annie May Hughes (*née* Lock); *m* 1936, Doris Margaret (*née* Attwool); two *s* two *d. Educ:* Prince Edward Sch., Salisbury, Rhodesia; Esplanade House Sch., Southsea, Hants; Royal Dockyard Sch., Portsmouth; RN Coll., Greenwich. Constr Sub Lieut, Chatham, 1933; Constr Sub Lieut and Lieut, RN Coll., Greenwich, 1934; Admty, London, 1937; HM Dockyard, Chatham, 1938; Admty, Bath, 1940; Constr Comdr, Staff of C-in-C Home Fleet, 1944; HM Dockyard, Hong Kong, 1947; Admty, Bath, 1951; Chief Constr, HM Dockyard, Devonport, 1954; Admty, Bath, 1958; Admty Repair Manager, Malta, 1961; Manager, Constructive Dept, Portsmouth, 1964; Dep. Dir of Dockyards, Bath, 1967–70; Gen. Manager, HM Dockyard, Chatham, 1970–73. *Recreations:* sailing, foreign travel, photography. *Address:* Capstan House, Tower Street, Old Portsmouth, Hants. *T:* Portsmouth (0705) 812997. *Clubs:* Little Ship; Royal Naval and Royal Albert Yacht; Royal Naval Sailing Association.                             *Died 10 July* 1990.

**HUGHES HALLETT, Vice-Adm. (retd) Sir (Cecil) Charles,** KCB 1954 (CB 1950); CBE 1942; Chairman: Gas Purification and Chemical Co. Ltd, 1958–60; Edwards High Vacuum International Ltd, 1964–68; Mount Row Holdings Ltd, 1962–68; Director, John Tysack & Partners Ltd, 1960–75; *b* 6 April 1898; *s* of Col W. Hughes

Hallett and Clementina Mary Loch; *m* 1920, Eileen Louise Richardson; two *d* (one *s* one *d* decd); *m* 1944, Joyce Plumer Cobbold; one *s* one *d*. *Educ*: Bedford; RN Colls, Osborne and Dartmouth; Emmanuel Coll., Cambridge. Went to sea as Midshipman in Aug. 1914; present at Dardanelles and Battle of Jutland; specialised in gunnery, 1921, in staff duties, 1933; Comdr 1932; Capt. 1939; Rear-Adm. 1949; Vice-Adm. 1952; retd Feb. 1955. Comdg destroyer 1934–35, anti-aircraft ship, 1940–42, aircraft carrier, 1944–46, during War of 1939–45 (despatches twice, CBE); present at operations against Japanese mainland, 1945. Dir of Administrative Plans and Joint Planning Staff, 1942–44; Dep. Chief of Naval Air Equipment, 1946–48; Admiralty for Special Duty, 1948–50; Chief of Staff to C-in-C Home Fleet, 1950–51; Admiral, British Joint Services Mission, Washington, 1952–54; Personal Asst to Chm., Charterhouse Group, 1955–59. Younger Brother of Trinity House, 1938; Renter Warden, Co. of Glovers, 1967, Master, 1968. Fellow, British Inst. of Management. Legion of Merit, Degree of Officer (USA), 1945. *Address*: 103 Old Deanery, The Close, Salisbury, Wiltshire SP1 2EY. *T*: Salisbury 23400.
*Died 2 Dec. 1985.*

**HUGHES-PARRY, Robert**, MD (London), BS, FRCP, MRCS, DPH; retired; formerly Principal Officer to the medical services of Bristol; formerly Professor of Preventive Medicine, University of Bristol; Past President Society of Medical Officers of Health; President Preventive Medicine Section, BMA (1949); Hon. FAPHA; *b* 3 Nov. 1895; *s* of J. Hughes-Parry, JP, Penllwyn, Pwllheli, and Anne Hughes, Cwmcoryn, Caernarvonshire; *m* Elsie Joan Williams, LRCP, MRCS, two *s* two *d*. *Educ*: Pwllheli (Chairman Scholar); University College of Wales, Aberystwyth; University of London, The Middlesex Hospital (Lyell Scholar and Gold Medallist, Junior Broderip Scholar). Lieut, RAF. MS; Asst to Professor of Experimental Pathology at the Middlesex Cancer Hospital, London, 1922–24; Medical Officer of Health of Bristol, 1930–56; Visiting Prof., Yale Univ., USA, 1956; formerly KHP to King George VI and QHP to the Queen. Medical Consultant, WHO, 1959. Member, Local Government Commission for England, 1959–63. High Sheriff of Caernarvonshire, 1958–59. *Publications*: Under the Cherry Tree (autobiography), 1969; Within Life's Span, 1973; various publications on cancer, health centres and other public health problems. *Recreation*: gardening. *Address*: 7 Gwaen Ganol, Criccieth, Gwynedd LL52 0TB.
*Died 1 May 1986.*

**HUGHES-STANTON, Blair Rowlands;** painter and engraver; Member of The London Group; Member of Society of Wood Engravers; *b* 22 Feb. 1902. *Educ*: Colet Court, London; *m* 1926, Gertrude Anna Bertha Hermes (marr. diss. 1932), OBE, RA, RE; one *s* one *d*. HMS Conway, 1915–18. Studied at Byam Shaw Sch., 1919–21, Royal Academy Schools and Leon Underwood Sch., 1921–24. Hon. Academician, Accademia Delle Arti Del Disegno, Florence, 1963. Made Decorations at Wembley, 1925, and Paris Exhibition, 1926. Produced numerous Books at Gregynog Press, Wales, 1930–33, and Illustrated Books for Golden Cockerel, Cresset Presses; also Allen Press, California. International Prize for Engraving at Venice Biennale, 1938. Represented with Engravings in British Museum, Victoria and Albert Museum, Whitworth Gall. (Manchester); etc. and Galls and Museums in Australia, Canada, New Zealand. *Recreation*: travel. *Address*: North House, Manningtree, Essex. *T*: Manningtree 2717.
*Died 6 June 1981.*

**HULL, Field Marshal Sir Richard (Amyatt),** KG 1980; GCB 1961 (KCB 1956; CB 1945); DSO 1943; Lord-Lieutenant of Devon, 1978–82; *b* 7 May 1907; *s* of Maj.-Gen. Sir Charles Patrick Amyatt Hull, KCB; *m* 1934, Antoinette Mary Labouchère de Rougemont; one *s* two *d*. *Educ*: Charterhouse; Trinity Coll., Cambridge (MA). Joined 17th/21st Lancers, 1928; Commanded 17/21st Lancers, 1941; Commanded 12th Infantry Bde, 1943; Commanded 26 Armd Bde, 1943; Comd 1st Armd Div., 1944; Cmd 5th Infantry Div., 1945; Commandant Staff Coll. Camberley, 1946–48; Dir of Staff Duties, War Office, 1948–50; Chief Army Instructor, Imperial Defence Coll., 1950–52; Chief of Staff, GHQ, MELF, 1953–54; General Officer Commanding, British Troops in Egypt, 1954–56; Dep. Chief of the Imperial Gen. Staff, 1956–58; Comdr-in-Chief, Far East Land Forces, 1958–61; Chief of the Imperial Gen. Staff, 1961–64; ADC Gen. to the Queen, 1961–64; Chief of the Gen. Staff, Ministry of Defence, 1964–65; Chief of the Defence Staff, 1965–67. Constable of the Tower of London, 1970–75. Pres., Army Benevolent Fund, 1968–71; Dir, Whitbread & Co. Ltd, 1967–76. Col Comdt, RAC, 1968–71. Dl Devon 1973; High Sheriff, Devon, 1975. Hon. LLD Exeter, 1965. *Address*: Beacon Downe, Pinhoe, Exeter. *Club*: Cavalry and Guards.
*Died 17 Sept. 1989.*

**HULME, Hon. Sir Alan (Shallcross),** KBE 1971; FCA; grazier; *b* 14 Feb. 1907; *s* of Thomas Shallcross Hulme and Emily Clara (*née* Hynes); *m* 1938, Jean Archibald; two *s* one *d*. *Educ*: North Sydney Boys' High School. Pres., Qld Div. of Liberal Party of Aust., 1946–49, 1962–63. Director: Chandlers (Aust.) Ltd, 1952–58; J. B. Chandler Investment Co. Ltd, 1962–63. Hon. Treas., King's Univ.

Coll., 1944–49. Former Vice-Consul for Portugal in Brisbane. Mem., Commonwealth Parlt, Australia, 1949–72; Minister for Supply, 1958–61; acted as Minister: for Army, May-July 1959; for Air, Dec. 1960; Postmaster-General, 1963–72; Minister for Defence, 1965–66 and on subseq. occasions; Vice-Pres., Exec. Council, 1966–72. Member: House Cttee, 1950–58; Jt Cttee of Public Accounts, 1952–58; Chairman: Commonwealth Cttee on Rates of Depreciation, 1954–55; Commonwealth Immigration Planning Council, 1956–58. *Recreations*: gardening, bowls. *Address*: Alcheringa Droughtmaster Stud, Eudlo, Qld 4554, Australia. *T*: Palmwoods 459267. *Club*: Brisbane (Brisbane).
*Died 9 Oct. 1989.*

**HULME, Alfred Clive,** VC 1941; Transport Contractor, New Zealand, since 1945; *b* 24 Jan. 1911; *s* of Harold Clive Hulme, Civil Servant, and Florence Sarah Hulme; *m* 1934, Rona Marjorie Murcott; one *s* one *d*. *Educ*: Dunedin High Sch. New Zealand Military Forces, War of 1939–45 (VC). Formerly toabcco farming; water and metal divining successfully in New Zealand, Australia, South Africa, and England. *Recreations*: tennis, boating, landscape gardening. *Address*: RD6, Te Puke, Bay of Plenty, New Zealand. *Club*: Returned Services Association.
*Died 3 Sept. 1982.*

**HULTON, Sir Edward (George Warris),** Kt 1957; magazine publisher; writer; *b* 29 Nov. 1906; *s* of late Sir Edward Hulton, former proprietor of Evening Standard; *m* 1st, 1927, Kira (marr. diss. 1932), *d* of General Goudime-Levkovitsch, Imperial Russian Army; no *c*; 2nd, 1941, Princess Nika Yourievitch (marr. diss., 1966), 2nd *d* of Prince Serge Yourievitch, Russian sculptor, and Helene de Lipovatz, *d* of Gen. de Lipovatz; two *s* one *d*. *Educ*: Harrow; Brasenose Coll., Oxford (open scholarship. Contested Leek Div. Staffs, as Unionist, 1929; Harwich Div., 1931. Called to Bar, Inner Temple; practised on South-Eastern Circuit. Founder, Hulton Press, 1938; founder and proprietor, Picture Post, 1938–57; Chm., Hulton Publications Ltd. Pres., European Atlantic Group, 1969–70; Mem., British Atlantic Cttee; Vice-Pres., European League for Economic Co-operation; Mem. Nat. Council, British Council of the European Movement. FRSA. Liveryman and Freeman of Company of Stationers; Freeman of City of London. NATO Peace Medal, 1969. *Publications*: The New Age, 1943; When I Was a Child, 1952; Conflicts, 1966; contrib. various newspapers and books. *Recreation*: reading. *Address*: 5 Carlton Gardens, SW1. *Clubs*: Athenæum, Beefsteak, Carlton, Garrick, Travellers', Buck's.
*Died 8 Oct. 1988.*

**HUME, Major Charles Westley,** OBE 1962; MC; BSc; late Senior Examiner, Patent Office; Founder, Universities Federation for Animal Welfare; Scientific Intelligence Officer (CD), Finchley 1950–61; Fellow of Zoological Society; Hon. Life Member, British Deer Society; *b* 13 Jan. 1886; *s* of Charles William Hume (formerly a Pampas rancher), and Louisa, *d* of Captain Waldron Kelly, 26th Cameronians; *m* 1966, Margaret Pattison, MA. *Educ*: Christ's Coll., Finchley; Strand Sch.; Birkbeck Coll. (University of London). Served in France (Royal Engineers Signals) in European War of 1914–18, and afterwards in 47th Divisional signals, TA; 3rd Signal Training Centre, 1939–41; qualified as Instructor, Fire Control (radar), 1941; Signals Experimental Establishment, 1942; HQ staff for Army Operational Research Group under Controller of Physical Research and Signals Development, 1942–45. Editor to the Physical Society, 1919–40; as Hon. Sec. of the British Science Guild organised the campaign which issued in the Patents Act, 1932; founded (1926) the University of London Animal Welfare Soc. and (1939) Universities Federation for Animal Welfare; campaigned successfully for prohibition (1956) of gin traps. Citoyen d'Honneur de Meurchin, Pas-de-Calais, 1953–; medal 'en témoignage de reconnaissance, la Ville de Meurchin', 1970; Prés. d'Honneur of Meurchin Soc., 1970; Union Nat. des Anciens Combatants; Sòci dóu Felibrige, e de l'Escolo de la Targo, 1958–; Sòci d'Ounour di Cardelin de Maiano. *Publications*: The Status of Animals in the Christian Religion, 1956; Man and Beast, 1962; articles on religion, animal welfare, statistical analysis, patent law, Provence, and rabbit-control. *Address*: 2 Cyprus Gardens, Finchley, N3. *Club*: Athenæum.
*Died 22 Sept. 1981.*

**HUMPHREY, Prof. John Herbert,** CBE 1970; BA; MD; FRS 1963; FRCP 1971; Professor of Immunology, Royal Postgraduate Medical School, London University, 1976–81, then Emeritus Professor; *b* 16 Dec. 1915; *s* of Herbert Alfred Humphrey and Mary Elizabeth Humphrey (*née* Horniblow); *m* 1939, Janet Rumney, *d* of Prof. Archibald Vivian Hill, CH, OBE, FRS, ScD, and late Margaret Neville, *d* of late Dr J. N. Keynes; two *s* three *d*. *Educ*: Winchester Coll.; Trinity Coll., Cambridge (Hon. Fellow, 1986); UCH Med. Sch. Jenner Research Student, Lister Inst., 1941–42; Asst Pathologist, Central Middx Hosp., 1942–46; External Staff, Med. Research Council, 1946–49; Member: Scientific Staff, Nat. Inst. for Med. Research, 1949–76, Dep. Dir, 1961–76, Head of Div. of Immunology and Experimental Biology, 1957–76; Expert Cttee on Biological Standardization, WHO, 1955–70; Expert Cttee on Immunology, WHO, 1962–; Nat. Biol. Standards Bd, 1977–85.

Editor, Advances in Immunology, 1960–67; Asst Editor, Immunology, 1958–68. Mem. Council, Royal Society, 1967–69. Past Pres., Internat. Union of Immunological Socs. Pres., Medical Campaign against Nuclear Weapons; Chm., Soc. for the Protection of Science and Learning Ltd. Foreign Associate, Nat. Acad. of Scis, 1986. Hon. DSc Brunel, 1979. *Publications:* Immunology for Students of Medicine (with Prof. R. G. White), 1963; (with J. Zimian and P. Sieghart) The World of Science and the Rule of Law, 1986; contribs to Jls of immunology, biochemistry, physiology, etc. *Address:* 30 St James Mansions, Hilltop Road, NW6 2AA. *T:* 01–624 9376; Ducklake House, Ashwell, Baldock, Herts SG7 5LL. *T:* Ashwell 2491. *Died 25 Dec.* 1987.

**HUMPHREYS, Prof. Arthur Raleigh;** Professor of English, University of Leicester, 1947–76; *b* 28 March 1911; *s* of William Ernest Humphreys and Lois (*née* Rainforth); *m* 1947, Kathryn Jane, *d* of James and Jessie Currie, Drumadoon, Isle of Arran. *Educ:* Grammar Sch., Wallasey, Ches; St Catharine's Coll., Cambridge; Harvard Univ., USA. Charles Oldham Shakespeare Schol., Cambridge, 1932; BA (Cambridge), 1933, MA 1936; Commonwealth Fund Fellow, Harvard, 1933–35; AM (Harvard), 1935. Supervisor in English, Cambridge Univ., 1935–37; Lectr in English, Liverpool Univ., 1937–46. Served War of 1939–45, RAF Intelligence, 1940–42 (Flying Officer); British Council Lecturer in English, Istanbul Univ., 1942–45. Fellow, Folger Shakespeare Library, Washington, DC, 1960, 1961, 1964; Visiting Fellow: All Souls Coll., Oxford, 1966; Huntington Library, Calif, 1978–79; Visiting Professor: Bogaziçi Univ., Istanbul, 1979–80, 1981–82, 1984; Singapore Univ., 1982–83. *Publications:* William Shenstone, 1937; The Augustan World, 1954; Steele, Addison, and their Periodical Essays, 1959; (ed) Henry IV, Part I, 1960, Part II, 1966; Melville, 1962; (ed) Joseph Andrews, 1962; (ed) Tom Jones, 1962; (ed) Amelia, 1963; (ed) Jonathan Wild, 1964; (ed) Melville's White-Jacket, 1966; Shakespeare, Richard II, 1967; (ed) Henry V, 1968; (ed) Henry VIII, 1971; Shakespeare, Merchant of Venice, 1973; Defoe, Robinson Crusoe, 1980; (ed) Much Ado About Nothing, 1981; (ed) Julius Caesar, 1984; contrib: From Dryden to Johnson (ed B. Ford), 1957; Alexander Pope (ed P. Dixon), 1972; Shakespeare's Art (ed M. Crane), 1973; Shakespeare: Select Bibliographical Guides (ed S. Wells), 1973; A Centre of Excellence (ed R. Druce), 1987; Fanned and Winnowed Opinions: Shakespearean essays (ed J. Mahon), 1987; Dickens and other Victorians: essays in honour of Philip Collins (ed J. Shattock), 1988, and to learned journals. *Recreations:* music, architecture, hill walking. *Address:* Springfield Apts 7, 2 St Mary's Road, Leicester LE2 1XA. *T:* Leicester 705118. *Died 9 Aug.* 1988.

**HUMPHREYS, His Honour Christmas;** *see* Humphreys, His Honour T. C.

**HUMPHREYS, Sir Kenneth (Owens),** Kt 1976; company director, Australia; *b* 22 Aug. 1918; *s* of Arthur Gerald Humphreys and Olive Stephens Humphreys; *m* 1973, Gladys Mary Hill; two *s. Educ:* Sydney Technical High Sch. Accounting profession, then RAAF to 1945. Gen. Manager and Dir, Clyde Industries Ltd, 1948–55; Partner, Irish Young & Outhwaite, 1955–74; Chm., International Pacific Corp. Ltd; Director: Quantas Airways Ltd; Aust. Consolidated Industries Ltd; Aust. Reinsurance Co. Ltd; Commercial Bank of Aust. Ltd. *Recreation:* cattle grazing. *Address:* 2 Cabarita Road, Avalon, NSW 2107, Australia. *T:* 918 2373. *Clubs:* Australian, Union (Sydney); Commonwealth (Canberra). *Died 8 Feb.* 1981.

**HUMPHREYS, His Honour (Travers) Christmas,** QC 1959; an Additional Judge, Central Criminal Court, 1968–76; *b* London, 1901; *o* surv. *s* of late Rt Hon. Sir Travers Humphreys, PC; *m* 1927, Aileen Maude (*d* 1975), *d* of Dr Charles Irvine and Alice Faulkner of Escrick, Yorks and Tunbridge Wells. *Educ:* Malvern Coll.; Trinity Hall, Cambridge (MA, LLB). Called to the Bar, Inner Temple, 1924; Bencher, 1955. Junior Counsel to Treasury for certain Appeals, 1932; Junior Counsel to Treasury at Central Criminal Court, 1934; Recorder of: Deal, 1942–56; Guildford, 1956–68; Deputy Chairman: E Kent QS, 1947–71; Co. of Kent QS, 1962–71. Senior Prosecuting Counsel to the Crown at the Central Criminal Court, 1950–59; a Commissioner, 1962–68. Founding Pres. of Buddhist Lodge, London, 1924 (now Buddhist Society); Past Pres. The Shakespearean Authorship Soc.; Joint Vice-Chm. Royal India, Pakistan and Ceylon Society; a Vice-Pres. Tibet Soc., 1962. *Publications:* The Great Pearl Robbery of 1913, 1928; What is Buddhism?, 1928, and Concentration and Meditation, 1935; The Development of Buddhism in England, 1937; Studies in the Middle Way, 1940; Poems of Peace and War, 1941; Seagulls, and other Poems, 1942; Karma and Rebirth, 1943; Shadows and other Poems, 1945; Walk On, 1947; Via Tokyo, 1948; Zen Buddhism, 1949; Buddhism (Pelican books), 1951; The Way of Action, 1960; Zen Comes West, 1960; The Wisdom of Buddhism, 1960; Poems I Remember, 1960; A Popular Dictionary of Buddhism, 1962; Zen, A Way of Life, 1962; Sixty Years of Buddhism in England, 1968; The Buddhist Way of Life, 1969; Buddhist Poems, 1971; A Western

Approach to Zen, 1972; Exploring Buddhism, 1974; The Search Within, 1977; Both Sides of the Circle (autobiog.), 1978; pamphlets, articles, etc. *Recreations:* music, entertaining; Eastern philosophy and Chinese Art. *Address:* 58 Marlborough Place, NW8 0PL. *T:* 01–624 4987. *Died 13 April* 1983.

**HUMPHREYS-DAVIES, (George) Peter,** CB 1953; Deputy Secretary, Ministry of Agriculture, Fisheries and Food, 1960–67; *b* 23 June 1909; *e s* of late J. W. S. Humphreys-Davies, Southfields, Eastbourne; *m* 1935, Barbara, *d* of late Lieut-Col F. G. Crompton, White Court, Alfriston, Sussex; two *s* one *d. Educ:* Sherborne; New Coll., Oxford. Craven Scholar, 1931. Asst Principal, Admiralty, 1932; HM Treasury, 1934; Private Sec. to Prime Ministers, 1936–38; Under-Sec., HM Treasury, 1949–56; Deputy Sec., Ministry of Supply, 1956–60; Directing Staff, Imperial Defence Coll., 1954. *Address:* Sunnyview Cottage, Tisman's Common, Rudgwick, W Sussex. *T:* Rudgwick 2221. *Died 22 May* 1985.

**HUMPHRIES, George James,** CMG 1965; OBE 1954; *b* 23 April 1900. *Educ:* St James Sch., Tyresham; Magdalen Coll. Sch., Brackley; Reading Univ. Served War, 1939–46, Lieut-Col. Surveyor, Nigeria, 1928; Sen., 1945; Deputy Dir, Overseas Surveys, 1946; Dir and Surveys Adviser, Dept of Technical Co-operation, 1963; Dir and Surveys Adviser to Min. of Overseas Development, 1964. *Address:* Greenacre, Heath House Road, Worplesdon Hill, Woking, Surrey. *Died 19 March* 1981.

**HUMPIDGE, Kenneth Palmer,** CMG 1957; *b* 18 Nov. 1902; *s* of James Dickerson Humpidge, Stroud; *m* 1938, Jill Mary Russell, *d* of Russell Pountney, Bristol; two *d. Educ:* Wycliffe Coll.; Univ. of Bristol. BSc (Engineering). Public Works Dept, Nigeria, 1926; Director of Public Works, Northern Region, Nigeria, 1948–54; Director of Federal Public Works, 1954–57; Min. of Transport, Nottingham and Cheltenham, 1958–69. FICE. *Address:* Corner Walls, Amberley, Stroud, Glos. *T:* Amberley 3212. *Died 23 May* 1987.

**HUNNINGS, Dr Gordon;** Professor and Head of the Department of Philosophy, University of Natal, Pietermaritzburg, since 1977; *b* 8 March 1926; *s* of late William Butters Hunnings and late Ellen Hunnings (*née* Robinson); *m* 1947, Jean Mary Hunnings (*née* Marland); one *s. Educ:* Christie Hospital & Holt Radium Inst., Manchester (MSRT); Univ. of Bristol (BA); University Coll., London (PhD). Radium Curator, Hogarth Radiotherapy Centre, Nottingham, 1948–61; Lectr in Philosophy, Univ. of Khartoum, 1966–69; Sen. Lectr in Philosophy, Univ. of Malawi, 1969–70; Prof. of Philosophy, Univ. of Malawi, 1970–73; Vice-Chancellor, Univ. of Malawi, 1973–77. *Publications:* various papers in sci. and philos. jls. *Recreations:* theology, music, philately. *Address:* Department of Philosophy, University of Natal, PO Box 375, Pietermaritzburg, Republic of South Africa. *T:* 64800. *Died 16 April* 1986.

**HUNT;** *see* Crowther-Hunt.

**HUNT OF FAWLEY,** Baron *cr* 1973 (Life Peer), of Fawley in the County of Buckingham; **John Henderson Hunt,** CBE 1970; MA, DM Oxon, FRCP, FRCS, FRCGP; Hon. Fellow, Green College, Oxford, since 1980; President, Royal College of General Practitioners, 1967–70; Consulting Physician, St Dunstan's, 1948–66; Governor: Charterhouse School; Sutton's Hospital, Old Charterhouse; Royal Marsden Hospital; *b* 3 July 1905; *s* of late Edmund Henderson Hunt, MCh, FRCS, and Laura Mary Buckingham; *m* 1941, Elisabeth Ernestine, *d* of Norman Evill, FRIBA; two *s* two *d* (and one *s* decd). *Educ:* Charterhouse School; Balliol College, Oxford; St Bartholomew's Hospital. Theodore Williams Scholar in Physiology, Oxford Univ., 1926; Radcliffe Scholar in Pharmacology, Oxford, 1928. RAF Medical Service, 1940–45 (Wing Comdr). PMO, Provident Mutual Life Assce Assoc., 1947–80. Hon. Cons. in Gen. Practice, RAF. President: Hunterian Soc., 1953; Gen. Practice Section, Royal Soc. Med., 1956; Harveian Soc., 1970; Chelsea Clinical Soc., 1971; Med. Soc. London, 1973; Soc. of Chiropodists, 1974; Carthusian Soc., 1980; Vice-Pres. Brit. Med. Students' Assoc., 1956; Hon. Sec. Council, Coll. of Gen. Practitioners, 1952–67; Med. Soc. of London, 1964–65; Mem. Council: RCS (co-opted), 1957–61; Med. Protection Soc., 1948–69; St Dunstan's, 1966–83. Member: General Advisory Council, BBC, 1958–66; Med. Services Review Cttee, 1958–61; Med. Commn on Accident Prevention, 1967. Fellow and Gold Medallist, BMA, 1980; Honorary Fellow: RSM; Aust. Coll. Gen. Practitioners; Singapore Coll. of Gen. Practitioners; Hon. Mem. and Victor Johnston Medallist, Coll. of Family Physicians of Canada; Hon. Mem., Amer. Acad. of Family Physicians. Lloyd Roberts Lecturer (Manchester), 1956; Albert Wander Lectr (RSM), 1968; Paul Hopkins Memorial Orator (Brisbane), 1969; James MacKenzie Lectr, 1972. Late House Surgeon, and Chief Assistant Medical Professorial Unit, St Bart's Hosp. and House Physician National Hosp. Queen Square. *Publications:* (ed) Accident Prevention and Life Saving, 1965; various papers in medical journals; chapter on Raynaud's Phenomenon, in British Encyclopædia of Medical Practice, 1938 and 1948; chapter on Peripheral Vascular Disease,

in Early Diagnosis, by Henry Miller, 1959; (ed) History of the Royal College of General Practitioners, 1983. *Recreation:* gardening. *Address:* Seven Steep, Fawley, near Henley-on-Thames, Oxon RG9 6JA. *T:* Henley-on-Thames 575853. *Club:* Royal Air Force.
*Died 28 Dec.* 1987.

**HUNT, Prof. (Jack) Naylor,** DSc, MD; FRCP; Professor of Physiology at Baylor College of Medicine, Houston, Texas, since 1977; *b* 29 April 1917; *s* of Charles Frank Hunt and Mary Anne Moss; *m* 1948, Claire, *d* of Sir William Haley, KCMG; no *c. Educ:* Royal Masonic School, Bushey; Guy's Hospital Medical School. Resident MO, Hertford British Hosp., Paris, 1940. Temp. Surgeon Lieutenant, RNVR, 1940–45. Dept of Physiology, Guy's Hospital Medical School, 1945–76, Prof. of Physiology, 1962–76. Mem. Senate, Univ. of London, 1974–76. Rockefeller Fellow, 1951; Arris and Gale Lecturer, 1951; Gillson Scholar, 1952. Med. Licence, Texas. *Publications:* various papers on the alimentary tract. *Address:* Physiology Department, Baylor College of Medicine, Houston, Texas 77030, USA. *Died 14 April* 1986.

**HUNT, Sir Joseph (Anthony),** Kt 1966; MBE 1951; FBIM; Chairman: The Hymatic Engineering Co. Ltd, since 1960 (General Manager, 1938–65); The Hydrovane Compressor Co. Ltd, since 1968 (Director since 1960); Porvair Ltd, since 1969; The Fairey Company Ltd, 1970–75; Huntleigh Group, 1974–80; *b* 1 April 1900; *s* of Patrick and Florence Anne Hunt; *m* 2nd, 1960, Esme Jeanne, *d* of Albert Edward Langston; two *s* one *d. Educ:* St Gregory's Sch., Farnworth, Lancs; Salford Royal Tech. Coll.; Manchester Coll. of Technology. Dir, Chloride Electrical Storage Co. Ltd., 1965–73, Dep. Man. Dir, 1969–71, Dir in charge Overseas Ops, Chloride Gp, 1966–71; Chm., Kellogg-American Inc., 1976–77; Director: Inmont Corp., USA, 1973–77; Nicholas Mendes and Associates, 1976–; Aston Technical Services, 1976–; Micro Image Technology Ltd, 1976–80; Flowtron Aire Ltd, 1976–; Setpoint Ltd, 1976–. Chairman: Economic Planning Council, West Midlands, 1965–67; Hunt Cttee on Intermediate Areas, 1967–69; Pro-Chancellor, Univ. of Aston in Birmingham, 1965–70, Mem. Council, 1971–81; Member, Redditch Devel. Corp., 1964–76; Central Training Council, 1964–74; National Advisory Council on Education for Industry and Commerce, 1961–75, Chm., 1967–75; W Midlands Adv. Council for Further Education, 1960–; Pres., British Assoc. for Commercial and Industrial Educn, 1971–77 (Chm. Exec. Council, 1960–61, Vice-Pres., 1961–71); Vice-Pres., City and Guilds of London Inst., 1971–77; Mem. Council, Birmingham Chamber of Commerce, 1956–74. Hon. ACT (Birmingham), 1950. Hon. DSc Aston; Hon. LLD Birmingham. *Publications:* contrib. to Technical Press: on Organisation, Management, Education and Training. *Recreations:* reading, architecture, theatre. *Address:* 16A Ampton Road, Edgbaston, Birmingham B15 2UJ. *T:* 021–455 0594.
*Died 11 April* 1982.

**HUNT, Prof. Naylor;** *see* Hunt, J. N.

**HUNT, Gen. Sir Peter (Mervyn),** GCB 1973 (KCB 1969; CB 1965); DSO 1945; OBE 1947; DL; Chief of the General Staff, 1973–76; ADC (General) to the Queen, 1973–76; retired; *b* 11 March 1916; *s* of H. V. Hunt, Barrister-at-law; *m* 1st, 1940, Anne Stopford (*d* 1966), *d* of Vice-Adm. Hon. Arthur Stopford, CMG; one *s* one *d*; 2nd, 1978, Susan, *d* of Captain D. G. Davidson, late Queen's Own Cameron Highlanders. *Educ:* Wellington Coll.; RMC Sandhurst. Commissioned QO Cameron Highlanders, 1936; commanded 7 Seaforth Highlanders, 1944–45; graduated Command and Gen. Staff Coll., Ft Leavenworth, USA. 1948; Instructor, Staff Coll., Camberley, 1952–55; Instructor, Imperial Defence Coll., 1956–57; commanded 1 Camerons, 1957–60; Comdr 152 (H) Infantry Brigade, TA, 1960–62; Chief of Staff, Scottish Command, 1962–64; GOC, 17 Div., also Comdr, Land Forces, Borneo, and Major-Gen., Bde of Gurkhas, 1964–65; Comdt, Royal Military Academy, Sandhurst, 1966–68; Comdr, FARELF, 1968–70; Comdr Northern Army Gp and C-in-C, BAOR, 1970–73. Col Queen's Own Highlanders (Seaforth and Camerons), 1966–75; Col 10th Princess Mary's Own Gurkha Rifles, 1966–75. Constable of the Tower of London, 1980–85. Pres., 1940 Dunkirk Veterans' Assoc., 1976–; Vice-Pres., NRA, 1976–; Pres., NSRA, 1978–87; HM Special Comr, Duke of York's Royal Mil. Sch., Dover, 1977–86; Chm. Council, King Edward VII Hosp., 1978–87. Chm., StJ Council for Cornwall, 1978–87. Hon. Liveryman, Haberdashers' Co., 1981. DL Cornwall, 1982. CBIM (FBIM 1975). CStJ 1987 (OStJ 1978). Chevalier of the Order of Leopold II and Croix de Guerre (Belgium), 1940 (awarded 1945). *Address:* Rose Cottage, Portloe, Truro, Cornwall TR2 5RA. *Club:* Naval and Military. *Died 2 Oct.* 1988.

**HUNT, Ralph Holmes V.;** *see* Vernon-Hunt.

**HUNT, Reginald Heber,** DMus; FRCO; FLCM; Member of Corporation, London College of Music (Director, 1954–64; Chairman, 1954–79); *b* 16 June 1891; *m* 1917, Lilian Blanche Shinton (*d* 1956); one *s* one *d*; *m* 1959, Mary Elizabeth Abbott (*d* 1979). FRCO 1915; DMus London, 1925. Served European War, including France, 1915–19; Dir of Music, Sir Walter St John's Sch.,

Battersea, 1927–45; Lectr in Music, Coll. of St Mark and St John, Chelsea, 1933–39; Organist various London churches, 1919–39; Organist Godalming Parish Church, 1940–50, and Dir Music, County Gram. Sch., 1945–52; composer and arranger, BBC Military Band, 1929–40. Mem. Performing Right Soc., 1929–. Sec. Union of Graduates in Music, 1948–50; Prof. and Examr, London Coll. of Music, 1947–; Mem. Senate, Univ. of London, 1951–64; Moderator in Music, General Certificate of Education, University of London, 1950–63. FLCM (Hon.) 1949; Editor, Boosey's Sch. Orchestra Series, 1928–40. Liveryman, Worshipful Co. of Musicians, 1961. *Publications:* include: The Wondrous Cross (Passion setting), 1956; This Blessed Christmastide (Carol Fantasy), 1964; various church and organ works, incl. Communion Service in G, 1966, Fantasy on *O Quanta Qualia,* Fantasy on a Ground, 1973; Album of Six Organ Pieces, 1977; Piano Sonatina in G, 1961; much Educational Music for Piano, Clarinet, Trumpet, Recorder, Sch. Orch., and many children's songs, incl. Fun with Tunes, 1969; More Fun with Tunes, 1972; *text-books* include: School Music Method, 1957; Elements of Music, 1959; First Harmony Book, 1962; Second Harmony Book, 1966; Elements of Organ Playing, 1966; Extemporization for Music Students, 1968; Transposition for Music Students, 1969; Harmony at the Keyboard, 1970; Three Pieces for Piano, 1981. *Address:* Dulas Court, Dulas, Hereford HR2 0HL.
*Died 13 Sept* 1982.

**HUNT, Vernon Arthur Moore,** CBE 1958; farmer; *b* 27 Dec. 1912; *s* of late Cecil Arthur Hunt, RWS, MA, LLB and late Phyllis Clara Hunt (*née* Lucas); *m* 1949, Betty Yvonne Macduff; two *s* one *d. Educ:* Sherborne; Trinity Coll., Cambridge (BA); Coll. of Aeronautical Engrg (Pilot's Licence). Airline Pilot, 1938; Capt., BOAC, 1939–46; Min. of Civil Aviation: Dep. Dir of Ops, 1947; Dir of Control and Navigation, 1949; Dir of Control (Plans), Nat. Air Traffic Control Service, 1962–68; Chief Inspector of Accidents, DTI (formerly BoT), 1968–73. Mollison Trophy, 1939; George Taylor Gold Medal, RAeS, 1954. CEng; FRAeS 1956; FRIN (FIN 1956). *Publications:* contribs to RAeS and Inst. Navigation Jls. *Recreation:* photography. *Address:* Neadon, Manaton, near Newton Abbot, Devon TQ13 9UY. *T:* Manaton 310. *Clubs:* Naval and Military; Hayling Island Sailing. *Died 3 Feb.* 1983.

**HUNT, William Field,** JP; MA; a Deputy Circuit Judge of the Crown Court, 1973–75; *b* 24 Oct. 1900; *s* of late Edwin James Hunt, JP, The Grange, Bescot, Walsall, and Charlotte Sheldon Field; *m* 1939, Helen Margaret (*d* 1961), *d* of late Dr Henry Malet, Wolverhampton; no *c. Educ:* Edgbaston Preparatory Sch., Birmingham; Rydal, Colwyn Bay; Exeter Coll., Oxford. On leaving school, 1919, went into an accountant's office, 1921 became a Bar Student of Inner Temple, to Oxford, called to Bar 1925, and joined Oxford Circuit. Chm., Court of Referees, 1930–72, and of Nat. Ins. Tribunals, Birmimgham District; Chm., Industrial Tribunal, Birmingham Area, 1968–72; a Dep. Chm., Agric. Land Tribunal, W Midlands Area, 1960–75; Recorder of Bridgnorth, 1941–45, of Newcastle-under-Lyme, 1945–71; a Recorder of the Crown Court, 1972. JP Worcestershire, 1956–72. Freeman of Borough of Newcastle, 1970. *Recreations:* music, travel. *Address:* 53 Ascot Road, Moseley, Birmingham B13 9EN. *T:* 021–449 2929; Windmill Cottage, Holberrow Green, Redditch, Worcs. *T:* Inkberrow 792275.
*Died 22 Feb.* 1981.

**HUNTER, Alastair;** *see* Hunter, M. I. A.

**HUNTER, Sir (Ernest) John,** Kt 1964; CBE 1960; DL; Executive Chairman, Swan Hunter Group Ltd, 1972–79 (Chairman and Managing Director, 1957–72); Chairman, Metro Radio; *b* 3 Nov. 1912; 2nd *s* of George Ernest Hunter and Elsie Hunter (*née* Edwards); *m* 1st, 1937, Joanne Winifred Wilkinson; one *s*; 2nd, 1949, Sybil Malfroy (*née* Gordon); one *s* one step *d. Educ:* Oundle Sch.; Cambridge Univ.; Durham Univ. (BSc). Apprentice, Swan, Hunter and Wigham Richardson Ltd, 1930–31; St John's Coll., Cambridge Univ., 1931–32; Durham Univ. (BSc) 1932–35; Draughtsman, SH and WR Ltd, 1935–37; Asst Manager: Barclay, Curle & Co. 1937–39; SH and WR Dry Docks, 1939–41; Asst Gen. Manager, SH and WR Dry Docks, 1941–43, Gen. Manager, 1943–45; Dir, Swan Hunter and Wigham Richardson Ltd, 1945, Chm., 1957–66. Director: Newcastle & Gateshead Water Co., to 1983; Midland Bank. Chairman: N-E Coast Ship-repairer's Association, 1957–58; Tyne Shipbuilders' Association, 1956–57; Dry Dock Owners' and Repairers' Central Council, 1961–62; President: NEC Institution, 1958–60; Shipbuilding Employers' Fedn, 1956–57; British Employers' Confedn, 1962–64; Shipbuilders' and Repairers' Nat. Assoc., 1968–. Mem. NEDC, 1962–64. First Chm., Central Training Council, 1964–68. Mem. of Cttees connected with shipping and with youth. Liveryman, Company of Shipwrights; Freeman: of City of London (by redemption); of Borough of Wallsend, 1972. DL Northumberland, 1968. Hon. DSc Newcastle, 1968. *Publications:* contrib. to Trans NEC Instn. *Recreations:* golf and gardening. *Address:* Beech Close Farm, Newton, Stocksfield, Northumberland. *T:* Stocksfield 3124. *Clubs:* Garrick; Northern Counties (Newcastle upon Tyne). *Died 19 Dec.* 1983.

**HUNTER, Major Joseph Charles,** CBE 1959; MC 1918; DL; Chairman Leeds Regional Hospital Board, 1955–63; *b* 1 Sept. 1894; *s* of W. S. Hunter, Gilling Castle, Yorks; *m* 1st, 1920, Cicely Longueville Heywood-Jones (marr. diss. 1930); one *s* two *d*; 2nd, 1934, Prudence Josephine Whetstone; two *s*. *Educ:* Harrow. Commissioned Yorkshire Hussars Yeo., 1912. Served European War, 1914–18, Europe; Regular Commission RA 1916; retired, 1920 (Major, R of O); War of 1939–45, in RA. Alderman W Riding of Yorks County Council, 1955–61 (Mem. 1947–55); DL W Riding of Yorks and York, 1959, N Yorkshire, 1974. *Address:* Havikil Lodge, Scotton, Knaresborough, N Yorks. *T:* Harrogate 863400.
*Died* 12 *April* 1983.

**HUNTER, Rt. Rev. Leslie Stannard,** MA; DD Lambeth; Hon. LLD Sheffield; Hon. DCL Dunelm; Hon. DD Toronto, 1954; *b* 1890; *yr s* of late Rev. John Hunter, DD, Minister of the King's Weigh House Church, London, and Trinity Church, Glasgow, and Marion Martin; *m* 1919, Grace Marion (*d* 1975), *yr d* of late Samuel McAulay, JP, of Aylesby, Lincs. *Educ:* Kelvinside Academy; New Coll., Oxford. Pres. of the Oxford University Lawn Tennis Club, 1911–12; Asst Sec. of the Student Christian Movement of Great Britain and Ireland, 1913–20; Curate of St Peter's, Brockley, SE, 1915–18; served with YMCA, BEF, 1916, and the Army of Occupation, 1919; Mem. of the Army and Religion Inquiry Commission, 1917–19; Asst Curate of St Martin-in-the-Fields and Chaplain of Charing Cross Hospital, London, 1921–22; Residentiary Canon of Newcastle on Tyne, 1922–26 and 1931–39; Vicar of Barking, Essex, 1926–30; Archdeacon of Northumberland, 1931–39; Chm., Tyneside Council of Social Service, 1933–39; Chaplain to the King, 1936–39; Bishop of Sheffield, 1939–62; Chm. of Sheffield Hospitals Council, 1940–49. House of Lords, 1944–62. Foundation Mem., British Council of Churches; Select Preacher, Universities of: Oxford, Cambridge, Glasgow, Aberdeen, St Andrews and Edinburgh, various years; Birks Memorial Lecturer, McGill Univ., Montreal, 1951. Hon. Freeman of City of Sheffield, 1962. Comdr Order of the Dannebrog, 1952. *Publications:* John Hunter, DD: A Life, 1921; A Parson's Job: Aspects of Work in the English Church, 1931; Let Us Go Forward, 1944; Church Strategy in a Changing World, 1950; The Seed and the Fruit, 1953; A Mission of the People of God, 1961; (Editor and part author) A Diocesan Service Book, 1965; Scandinavian Churches, 1965; The English Church: a New Look, 1966. *Address:* c/o Williams & Glyn's Bank, Columbia House, 69 Aldwych, WC2.
*Died* 15 *July* 1983.

**HUNTER, Prof. Louis,** PhD, DSc (London); FRSC; retired as Professor of Chemistry and Head of Department of Chemistry, University of Leicester (previously University College) (1946–65); Professor Emeritus, 1966; *b* 4 Dec. 1899; *s* of late George Hunter and Mary Edwards; *m* 1926, Laura Thorpe (decd). *Educ:* East London College (subsequently Queen Mary College), University of London. Assistant Lecturer, University Coll. of North Wales, Bangor, 1920–25; Lecturer and Head of Dept of Chemistry, University Coll., Leicester, 1925, Prof. of Chemistry, 1946, and Vice-Principal, 1952–57, Pro-Vice-Chancellor, University of Leicester, 1957–60. Visiting Professor: Univ. of Ibadan, Nigeria, 1963, and Ahmadu Bello Univ., 1966. Mem. of Council: Chemical Soc., 1944–47, 1950–53, 1956–59; Royal Institute of Chemistry, 1947–50, 1961–64 (Vice-Pres., 1964–66; Chm. E Midlands Section, 1938–40); Sec. Section B (Chemistry), British Assoc. for the Advancement of Science, 1939–51, Recorder, 1951–56, mem. of Council, 1956–60. Hon. Fire Observer, Home Office, 1942–54; Scientific Adviser for Civil Defence, N Midlands, 1951–75; Dep. Chm., 1939, Chm., 1952, Leicester Jt Recruiting Bd. *Publications:* mainly in Jl Chem. Soc. *Address:* Thatched Cottage, Frettenham Road, Hainford, Norwich NR10 3BW. *Died* 19 *Dec.* 1986.

**HUNTER, (Mark Ian) Alastair,** MD, FRCP; Physician, St George's Hospital, SW1, 1946–76, later Emeritus; *b* 18 June 1909; *s* of Mark Oliver Hunter and Diana Rachel (*née* Jones); unmarried. *Educ:* Winchester Coll. (Entrance Exhibition); Trinity Coll., Cambridge. Qualified as Doctor, 1933. MD Cambridge, 1935; FRCP (London), 1947. Dean, St George's Hosp. Med. Sch., 1956–71. Asst Registrar, 1950–57, Censor, 1971–73, Vice-Pres. and Sen. Censor, 1974–75, RCP. Mem., GMC. Dep. Vice-Chancellor, Univ. of London, 1972–73. Medical Awards Administrator, Commonwealth Scholarship Commn, 1974–. Hon. Keeper, 20th Century Painting, Fitzwilliam Museum, Cambridge. *Publications:* medical subjects. *Recreations:* various. *Address:* 42 Festing Road, Putney, SW15. *T:* 01-789 8644. *Clubs:* Royal Automobile, MCC.
*Died* 5 *Dec.* 1983.

**HUNTER BLAIR, Sir James,** 7th Bt, *cr* 1786; *b* 7 May 1889; *s* of Capt. Sir E. Hunter Blair, 6th Bt, and Cecilia (*d* 1951), *d* of late Sir W. Farrer; *S* father, 1945; *m* 1st, 1917, Jean (*d* 1953), *d* of late T. W. McIntyre, Sorn Castle, Ayrshire; two *s*; 2nd, 1954, Mrs Ethel Norah Collins (*d* 1966). *Educ:* Wellington; Balliol Coll., Oxford (1st Hon. Mod., 2nd Greats); Christ's Coll., Cambridge (Forestry). Articled to solicitor, 1911–14; served with Seaforth Highlanders, 1915–19;

District Officer with Forestry Commission, 1920–28. Forestry and Farming at Blairquhan, 1928–. *Publications:* articles on Forestry and cognate subjects in various journals. *Recreation:* collecting pictures. *Heir:* *s* Edward Thomas Hunter Blair [*b* 15 Dec. 1920; *m* 1956, Norma (*d* 1972), *d* of W. S. Harris; one adopted *s* one adopted *d. Educ:* Eton; Balliol Coll., Oxford]. *Address:* Milton, Maybole, Ayrshire. *Clubs:* United Oxford & Cambridge University; New (Edinburgh). *Died* 29 *Nov.* 1985.

**HUNTER BLAIR, Dr Peter,** FBA; Emeritus Reader in Anglo-Saxon History, Cambridge University, since 1979; *b* 22 March 1912; *s* of Charles Henry Hunter Blair and Alice Maude Mary France; *m* 1st, 1937, Joyce Hamilton Thompson; one *s* one *d*; 2nd, 1965, Muriel Thompson; 3rd, 1969, Pauline Hilda Clarke. *Educ:* Durham School; Emmanuel Coll., Cambridge (MA, LittD). Research Fellowship, Emmanuel Coll., Cambridge, 1937. European News Service, BBC, 1939–45. Lecturer in Anglo-Saxon Studies, Cambridge, 1945; Senior Tutor, Emmanuel Coll., 1951–65; Vice-Master, 1969; Reader in Anglo-Saxon History, Cambridge Univ., 1974–78. FBA 1980; FRHistS. *Publications:* An Introduction to Anglo-Saxon England, 1956, 2nd edn 1977; The Moore Bede, 1959; Roman Britain and Early England, 1963; The Coming of Pout, 1966; The World of Bede, 1970; Northumbria in the Days of Bede, 1976; papers on Anglo-Saxon history. *Recreations:* hill-walking, sailing, listening to music. *Address:* Church Farm House, High Street, Bottisham, Cambridge CB5 9BA. *T:* Cambridge 811223.
*Died* 9 *Sept.* 1982.

**HUNTING, Richard Haigh;** Chairman, Hunting Petroleum Services plc, since 1985 (Director, since 1978); *b* 12 Oct. 1927; *s* of late Gerald Lindsay Hunting and Ruth (*née* Pyman); *m* 1955, Isobel, *yr d* of late Cecil and Marjorie Hannay Meredith; one *s* three *d. Educ:* Loretto; Trinity Hall, Cambridge. Royal Engineers, 1945–48, commissioned 1947. E. A. Gibson: joined 1952; Dir, 1957; Man. Dir, 1959; Chm., 1961–; Gibson Petroleum Co., Canada: Dir, 1960; Chm., 1984–; Dir, Hunting Group plc, 1985–; Fretoil S. N. Petrole et Affretements, France: Dir, 1957, Chm., 1981–; Mem., Exec. Cttee, Baltic and Internat. Maritime Conf., 1969–85 (Vice-Chm., 1981–85). *Recreations:* field sports, fine arts. *Address:* Westby Lodge, 90 Old Woking Road, West Byfleet, Weybridge, Surrey. *T:* Weybridge 46463. *Clubs:* City Livery, Arts.
*Died* 13 *Feb.* 1988.

**HUNTINGDON, 15th Earl of,** *cr* 1529; **Francis John Clarence Westenra Plantagenet Hastings,** MA; artist; *b* 30 Jan. 1901; *s* of 14th Earl and Maud Margaret (*d* 1953), 2nd *d* of Sir Samuel Wilson, sometime MP for Portsmouth; *S* father, 1939; *m* 1st, 1925, Cristina (who obtained a divorce, 1943 and *m* 2nd, 1944, Hon. Wogan Philipps, who *S*, 1962, as 2nd Baron Milford; she died 1953), *d* of the Marchese Casati, Rome; one *d*; 2nd, 1944, Margaret Lane, novelist, biographer and journalist; two *d. Educ:* Eton; Christ Church, Oxford. MA Hons, History; Slade School, London Univ. Played Oxford Univ. Polo team. Prof., Sch. of Arts & Crafts, Camberwell, 1938. ARP Officer and Dep. Controller Andover Rural district, 1941–45. Jt Parly Sec., Min. of Agriculture and Fisheries, 1945–50. Prof., Central Sch. of Arts & Crafts, London, 1950. A pupil of Diego Rivera. *Exhibitions:* Paris, London, Chicago, San Francisco; Mural paintings, Evanston, Ill; Monterey, Calif; Hall of Science, World's Fair, Chicago, 1933; Marx House; Buscot Park, Faringdon; Birmingham Univ.; Women's Press Club, London; Casa dello Strozzato, Tuscany; The Priory, Reading; Vineyards, Beaulieu, etc. Chm. of Cttee Soc. of Mural Painters, 1953–57. Pres., Solent Protection Soc., 1958–68. Mem., Wine Trade Art Soc. *Publications:* Commonsense about India; The Golden Octopus. *Heir:* *cousin* William Edward Robin Hood Hastings Bass, *b* 30 Jan. 1948. *Address:* Blackbridge House, Beaulieu, Hants.
*Died* 24 *Aug.* 1990.

**HUNTLY, 12th Marquess of,** *cr* 1599, Earl of, *cr* 1450; **Douglas Charles Lindsey Gordon;** Lord of Gordon before 1408; Earl of Enzie, Lord of Badenoch, 1599; Bt 1625; Baron Aboyne, 1627; Earl of Aboyne, Lord Strathavon and Glenlivet, 1660; Baron Meldrum, 1815; sits under creation of 1815; Premier Marquess of Scotland; Chief of House of Gordon; Gordon Highlanders; *b* 3 Feb. 1908; *s* of late Lieut-Col Douglas Gordon, CVO, DSO, and Violet Ida, *d* of Gerard Streatfeild; *S* great-uncle, 1937; *m* 1st, 1941, Hon. Mary Pamela Berry (marr. diss. 1965), *o d* of 1st Viscount Kemsley; one *s* one *d*; 2nd, 1977, Elizabeth Haworth Leigh, *d* of Lt Cdr F. H. Leigh. *Heir:* *s* Earl of Aboyne. *Address:* Hollybrook, Ewhurst Road, Cranleigh, Surrey. *T:* Cranleigh 71500. *Club:* Army and Navy.
*Died* 26 *Jan.* 1987.

**HURD, Derrick Guy Edmund,** JP; Head of the European School, since 1978; *b* 22 June 1928; *s* of Clifford Rowland Hurd and Viola Beatrice Hurd; *m* 1962, Janet Barton; one *s* two *d. Educ:* Peter Symonds' Sch., Winchester; Culham Coll. (Teacher's Cert., 1948); Birkbeck Coll., Univ. of London (BA Hons History 1952, MA (thesis) 1961). Assistant, Hugh Myddelton Sec. Sch., London EC1, 1948–52; Lecteur, Lycée Chaptal, Paris, 1952–53; Head of History Dept,

Librarian, Hatfield School, 1953–60 (Exchange, Helmholtz Gymnasium, Bielefeld, 1956); Headmaster, John Mason High Sch., Abingdon, 1960–70; Headmaster, Blandford Upper Sch., Dorset, 1970–72; Principal, Easthampstead Park Educational Centre, Wokingham, 1972–78. Vice-Pres., Nat. Soc. of Non-smokers. JP Berkshire, 1967, now Oxfordshire. *Publication:* Sir John Mason (1503–1566), 1975. *Recreations:* walking, philately, music, ecclesiastical architecture, travel. *Address:* Ody Wharf, Wilsham Road, Abingdon, Oxon OX14 5HP. *Died 14 Dec.* 1986.

**HURLEY, Ven. Alfred Vincent,** CBE 1945 (OBE 1944); TD 1944; Archdeacon of Dudley, 1951–68, then Archdeacon Emeritus; Rector of Old Swinford, 1948–64; *b* 12 Jan. 1896; *s* of Alfred Walter and Phoebe Hurley, Reading; *m* 1929, Jenny Drummond, 2nd *d* of Henry John Sansom, Pennsylvania Castle, Portland, Dorset; one *s* three *d*. *Educ:* Queen's Sch., Basingstoke; Keble Coll., Oxford (MA); Cuddesdon Coll. Artists' Rifles, 1915; Royal Flying Corps, 1916–19. Curate, Armley, Leeds, 1922; Chaplain: Leeds Prison, 1923–24; Portland Borstal Instn, 1924; Dep. Gov. Portland Borstal Instn, 1928; Rector of Portland, 1931; Rural Dean of Weymouth, 1937; Canon and Preb. of Salisbury, 1939. Chaplain to Forces, 4th Dorsets, 1939; SCF, 42 East Lancs Div. 1940; Asst Chaplain General, 8th Army, 1944 (despatches); Dep. Chaplain General, South East Asia Allied Land Forces, 1945–46; Hon. Canon of Worcester, 1951–; Exam. Chap. to Bishop of Worcester, 1951–68. *Address:* c/o 55 Belbroughton Road, Halesowen, West Midlands B63 4LS. *T:* 021–550 3575. *Died 24 Feb.* 1986.

**HURLEY, Sir Hugh;** *see* Hurley, Sir W. H.

**HURLEY, Sir John Garling,** Kt 1967; CBE 1959; FAIM; FIDCA; JP; Managing Director, Berlei United Ltd, Sydney, 1948–69; *b* Bondi, NSW, 2 Oct. 1906; *s* of late John Hurley, MLA, and late Annie Elizabeth (*née* Garling); *g g g s* of Frederick Garling (1775–1848), free settler, 1815 and senior of first two solicitors admitted to practice in original Supreme Court of Civil Judicature in NSW; *m* 1st 1929, Alice Edith Saunders (*d* 1975); three *d*; 2nd, 1976, Desolie M. Richardson. *Educ:* Sydney Techn. High Sch. FAIM 1949; FIDCA 1980. With Berlei group of cos, 1922–69, incl. Berlei (UK) Ltd, London, 1931–36; Chm., William Adams Ltd, 1963–74 (Dep. Chm. 1974–76); Director: Manufacturers' Mutual Insurance Ltd, Sydney, 1954–82; Develt Finance Corporation Ltd, 1967–79; Australian Fixed Trusts Ltd, 1970–79; Royal North Shore Hosp. of Sydney, 1969–76. President: Associated Chambers of Manufactures of Austr. 1955–56; Chamber of Manufactures of NSW, 1955–57 (Life Mem.); Member: Inst. of Directors in Australia; Techn. and Further Educn Adv. Council of NSW, 1958–76; Industrial Design Council of Australia, 1958–76 (Dep. Chm., 1970–76); Council, Abbotsleigh Sch., 1960–66; Australian Advertising Standards Adv. Authority, 1974–82; Councillor, Nat. Heart Foundn of Australia (NSW Div.), 1969–. Mem., St Andrew's Cathedral Restoration Appeal Cttee; Patron, St Andrew's Cathedral Sch. Building Fund Appeal, 1977–. Chm., Standing Cttee on Productivity, Ministry of Labour Adv. Coun., 1957; Leader of Austr. Trade Mission to India and Ceylon, 1957. Chm. and Trustee, Museum of Applied Arts and Sciences, NSW, 1958–76. Member: Royal Agricultural Soc.; Nat. Trust of Australia; Life Mem., Australia–Britain Soc. Knighted for distinguished service to Government, industry and the community. *Recreations:* swimming, bowls. *Address:* 12 Locksley Street, Killara, NSW 2071, Australia. *Clubs:* Australian (Sydney); Royal Sydney Yacht Squadron; Australasian Pioneers' (NSW); Killara Probus Inc.; Warrawee Bowling, Killara Bowling. *Died 17 Sept.* 1990.

**HURLEY, Sir (Wilfred) Hugh,** Kt 1963; Chief Justice, High Courts of Northern States of Nigeria, 1967–69; retired, 1969; *b* 16 Oct. 1910; *s* of Henry Hutchings Hurley and Elizabeth Louise (*née* Maguire); *m* 1940, Una Kathleen (*née* Wyllie); one *s* two *d*. *Educ:* St Stephen's Green Sch., Dublin; Trinity Coll., Dublin. Barrister-at-Law (King's Inns, Dublin), 1935; Magistrate, Nigeria, 1940; Chief Registrar, Supreme Court, Nigeria, 1949; Puisne Judge, Supreme Court, Nigeria, 1953–55, Judge, 1955–57, Senior Puisne Judge, 1957–60 and Chief Justice, 1960–67, High Court, Northern Nigeria. Chm., Judicial Service Commn, Northern Nigeria, and Mem., Judicial Service Commission, Federation of Nigeria, 1960–63. Called to the Bar, Gray's Inn, 1976. Hon. LLD Ahmadu Bello Univ., Nigeria, 1968. *Address:* 8 Castle Street, Calne, Wilts. *Died 13 July* 1984.

**HURRELL, Col Geoffrey Taylor,** OBE 1944; Lord-Lieutenant of Cambridgeshire, 1974–75 (of Cambridgeshire and Isle of Ely, 1965–74); *b* 12 March 1900; *s* of Arthur Hurrell and Emily Taylor; *m* 1934, Mary Crossman; one *s* one *d*. *Educ:* Rugby; Sandhurst. Gazetted 17th Lancers, 1918; Lieut-Col comdg 17th/21st Lancers, 1940; Col 1944. High Sheriff, Cambridgeshire and Huntingdonshire, 1963; JP Cambs 1952, DL 1958. KStJ 1972. *Recreations:* hunting, shooting. *Address:* Park House, Harston, near Cambridge. *Club:* Cavalry and Guards. *Died 15 Sept.* 1989.

**HURRELL, Ian Murray,** LVO 1961; HM Diplomatic Service, retired; *b* 14 June 1914; *s* of Capt. L. H. M. Hurrell and Mrs Eva Hurrell; *m* 1939, Helen Marjorie Darwin; no *c*. *Educ:* Dover Coll. Anglo-Iranian Oil Co., 1932–34; Indian Police (United Provinces), 1934–48; entered HM Foreign (subseq. Diplomatic) Service, 1948; Vice-Consul, Shiraz, 1948–51; Consul, Benghazi, 1952; FO, 1952–53; 1st Sec., Quito, 1954 (Chargé d'Affaires, 1955); Bangkok, 1956–60; Tehran, 1960–64; Ankara (UK Delegn to CENTO), 1964–67; Ambassador, Costa Rica, 1968–72. Life FRSA, 1979; Fellow, British Interplanetary Soc., 1981. Imperial Order of the Crown (Iran). *Recreations:* rambling, photography, skin-diving, gardening, chess, etc. *Address:* Quarr House, Sway, Hants. *Club:* Royal Over-Seas League. *Died 21 Sept.* 1989.

**HURST, Leonard Henry,** CBE 1949; *b* Shanghai, 22 April 1889; *y s* of late Richard Willett Hurst, HM Consular Service (China); *m* 1st, 1920, Annie (*d* 1922), *d* of Arthur Liley; 2nd, 1928, Olive Rose Madeline (*d* 1967), widow of Major R. M. F. Patrick. *Educ:* Tonbridge; Pembroke Coll., Cambridge. Entered Levant Consular Service, 1908; Vice-Consul at Sofia, 1914; Consul at Bengasi, 1924, at Port Said, 1926, and at Basra, 1932; Consul-Gen. at Rabat, 1936–40, at Istanbul, 1942–47, at Tunis, 1947–49; retired from HM Foreign Service, Nov. 1949; British Consul, Rhodes, 1953–57; British Consul, Crete, 1957–58. *Recreations:* mountaineering, foreign affairs. *Address:* Brynglas, Llechryd, Cardigan, Dyfed SA43 2QL. *T:* Llechryd 393. *Died 25 Nov.* 1981.

**HURST, Margery,** OBE 1976; Chairman, Brook Street Bureau PLC (Managing Director, 1947–76); *b* 23 May 1913; *d* of late Samuel and Deborah Berney; *m* 1948, Eric Hurst, Barrister-at-law; two *d*. *Educ:* Brondesbury and Kilburn High Sch.; Minerva Coll. RADA. Joined ATS on Direct Commission, 1943 (1939–45 war medal); invalided out of the service, 1944. Commenced business of Brook St Bureau of Mayfair Ltd, 1946; founded Margery Hurst Schs and Colls for administrative and secretarial studies. Co-opted Mem. of LCC Children's Cttee, 1956. Started non-profit making social clubs for secretaries, called Society for International Secretaries, in London, 1960; now in New York; awarded Pimm's Cup for Anglo-American friendship in the business world, 1962. Member: American Cttee, BNEC, 1967–70; Exec. Cttee, Mental Health Research Fund, 1967–72. One of first women elected Underwriting Mem. of Lloyd's, 1970. First Lady Mem., Worshipful Co. of Marketors, 1981–; Freeman, City of London, 1981. *Publication:* No Glass Slipper (autobiog.), 1967. *Recreations:* tennis, swimming, drama, opera. *Address:* Flat J, 80 Eaton Square, SW1W 9AP. *Clubs:* Royal Corinthian Yacht; Royal Southern Yacht. *Died 11 Feb.* 1989.

**HUSBAND, Sir (Henry) Charles,** Kt 1975; CBE 1964; BEng, DSc, FICE, PPIStructE, FIMechE, FAmSCE; Founded Husband & Co., Consulting Engineers, in 1936, retired 1982; *b* 30 Oct. 1908; *s* of Prof. Joseph Husband, DEng, MICE and Ellen Walton Husband; *m* 1932, Eileen Margaret, *d* of late Henry Nowill, Sheffield; two *s* two *d*. *Educ:* King Edward VII Sch., Sheffield; Sheffield Univ. Asst to Sir E. Owen Williams, MICE, 1931–33; Engr and Surveyor to First Nat. Housing Trust Ltd, 1933–36; planning and construction of large housing schemes in England and Scotland; from 1936, designed public works at home and overseas incl. major road and railway bridges, drainage and water supply schemes; Princ. Techn. Officer, Central Register, Min. of Labour and Nat. Service, 1939–40; Asst Dir, Directorate of Aircraft Prodn Factories, Min. of Works, 1943–45; designed first high altitude testing plant for continuous running of complete jet engines, 1946, also research estabs for Brit. Iron and Steel Res. Assoc., Prodn Engrg Res. Assoc. and other industrial organisations; designed and supervised construction of 250 ft diameter radio telescope, Jodrell Bank, and other large radio telescopes at home and abroad incl. steerable aerials for GPO satellite stn, Goonhilly Downs, Cornwall. Chm., Yorks Assoc. ICE, 1949; Pres., Instn Struct. Engrs, 1964–65; Chm., Adv. Cttee on Engrg and Metallurgy, University of Sheffield, 1962–65; Mem. Ct, University of Sheffield; Mem. Cons. Panel in Civil Engrg, Bradford Univ. (formerly Inst. of Technology), 1962–68; Mem., Council of Engrg Instns, 1965–66, Board Mem., 1979–; Chm., Assoc. of Consulting Engineers, 1967. Hon. DSc Manchester Univ., 1964; Hon. DEng Sheffield Univ., 1967. Sir Benjamin Baker Gold Medal, ICE, 1959; (first) Queen's Gold Medal for Applied Science, Royal Society, 1965; Wilhelm Exner Medal for Science and Technology, University of Vienna, 1966; Instn Gold Medal, IStructE, 1974; James Watt Medal, ICE, 1976. *Publications:* contributions to British and foreign engrg jls. *Address:* Okenhold, School Green Lane, Sheffield S10 4GP. *T:* 303395. *Died 7 Oct.* 1983.

**HUSKISSON, Alfred,** OBE 1951; MC 1917, and Bar 1918; Director of S. Simpson and of Simpson (Piccadilly), 1940–74 (Dep. Chm. 1959–64; Managing Director Simpson (Piccadilly), 1940–59, S. Simpson Ltd, 1942–59); *b* 27 June 1892; *s* of Joseph Cliffe and Martha Huskisson; *m* 1st, 1922, Constance (marr. diss.), *d* of late Arthur Frederick Houfton, Nottingham; one *s* one *d*; 2nd, 1972, Sheila Mary Bullen Huskisson. *Educ:* privately. Served European

War, 1914–18 (despatches); granted rank of Major, 1920. Managing Dir William Hollins & Co., Nottingham, 1929–38. Mem. Allies Welcome Cttee, 1943–50. Life Member: Overseas League, 1943; National Playing Fields Assoc. 1952. Hon. Treas. Abbey Div., Westminster Conservative Assoc., 1945–54; No 1 Assoc. Mem. Variety Club of GB, 1950–; Chm. Wholesale Clothing Manufacturers Assoc., 1952; Pres. Appeal Cottage Homes, Linen and Woollen Drapers, 1953; Master of the Worshipful Co. of Woolmen, 1952–53, 1964–65; Past Pres. The Piccadilly and St James's Assoc. (Chm. 1950–53); Vice-Pres. Westminster Philanthropic Soc. (Chm. 1956); Vice-Chm. Machine Gun Corps Officers' Club, 1960; Member: Grand Council of FBI, 1953–65; British Olympic Assoc. Appeals Cttee, 1955–56; British Empire & Commonwealth Games Appeal Cttee, 1958; British Olympic Assoc. Appeals Cttee, 1959–60; Export Council for Europe, 1960–66; Empire & Commonwealth Games UK Industrial Appeal Cttee, 1961; Chm. various Westminster and other appeals in the past. *Address:* 3 Edenhurst, 21 Grosvenor Road, Bournemouth, Dorset BH4 8BQ. *Club:* Lord's Taverners (Pres. 1954, 1955).
*Died* 25 *Nov.* 1984.

**HUSSEIN bin Onn, Datuk,** SPMJ 1972; SPDK 1974; SIMP 1975; PIS 1968; MP for Sri Gading, 1974–81; Prime Minister of Malaysia, 1976–81; *b* Johore Bharu, 12 Feb. 1922; *s* of late Dato' Onn bin Jaafar and of Datin Hajjah Halimah binte Hussein; *m* Datin Suhailah; two *s* four *d. Educ:* English Coll., Johore Bharu; Military Acad., Dehra Dun, India. Called to the Bar, Gray's Inn. Cadet, Johore Mil. Forces, 1940; commnd Indian Army; served Egypt, Syria, Palestine, Persia, Iraq, and GHQ, New Delhi; seconded to Malayan Police Recruiting and Trng Centre, Rawalpindi; returned to Malaya with liberation forces, 1945; Comdt, Police Depot, Johore Bharu; demobilised. Joined Malay Admin. Service; served in Selangor State; Officer i/c Kampong (village) guards, Johore, in Communist emergency, 1948. Entered politics; National Youth Leader and Sec.-Gen., United Malays Nat. Org. (UMNO), 1950; Member: Fed. Legislative Council; Johore Council of State; Johore State Exec. Council; left UMNO when his father Dato' Onn bin Jaafar resigned from the organisation in 1951. Studied law in England; in practice, Kuala Lumpur, 1963. Rejoined UMNO, 1968; MP for Johore Bharu Timor, 1969; Minister of Educn, 1970–73; Dep. Prime Minister, 1973–76; Minister of Trade and Industry, 1973–74; Minister of Finance, and Minister of Coordination and Public Corporations, 1974–76. Chairman: Commonwealth Parly Assoc., Malaysia, 1975–76; Inter Parly Union Malaysia Gp. President: Malayan Assoc. for the Blind; Kelab Golf Negara, Subang. *Recreation:* golf. *Address:* 3 Jalan Kenny, Kuala Lumpur, Malaysia.
*Died* 28 *May* 1990.

**HUSSEY, Very Rev. (John) Walter (Atherton);** Dean of Chichester, 1955–77, Dean Emeritus since 1977; *b* 15 May 1909; *yr s* of Rev. Canon John Rowden and Lilian Mary Hussey. *Educ:* Marlborough Coll.; Keble Coll., Oxford (MA); Cuddesdon Coll., Oxford. Asst Curate, S Mary Abbots, Kensington, 1932–37; Vicar of S Matthew, Northampton, 1937–55; Canon of Peterborough Cathedral, 1949–55; Master of S John's Hosp., Weston Favell, 1948–55; Rural Dean of Northampton, 1950–55. Chm. Diocesan Art Council, 1966–77; Mem., Redundant Churches Fund, 1969–78. Hon. FRIBA. Hon. DLitt Sussex, 1977. *Recreation:* enjoying the arts. *Address:* 5 Trevor Street, SW7. *T:* 01–581 1819.          *Died* 25 *July* 1985.

**HUSTON, John;** film director and writer; *b* Nevada, Missouri, 5 Aug. 1906; *s* of Walter Huston and Rhea Gore; *m* 1st, Dorothy Harvey (marr. diss.); 2nd, Lesley Black (marr. diss.); 3rd, Evelyn Keyes (marr. diss. 1950); 4th 1950, Enrica Soma (*d* 1969); one *s* one *d*; 5th, 1972, Celeste Shane (marr. diss. 1975); additionally one *s* and one adopted *s* one adopted *d*. Became an Irish Citizen, 1964. At beginning of career was reporter, artist, writer and actor at various times. Formerly: Writer for Warner Bros Studios, 1938; Director for Warner Bros 1941; Writer and Dir, Metro-Goldwyn-Mayer, 1949. Dir of several Broadway plays. Films directed or produced include: The Maltese Falcon; Key Largo; The Treasure of Sierra Madre; The Asphalt Jungle; The African Queen; Moulin Rouge; Beat the Devil; Moby Dick; Heaven Knows, Mr Allison; The Barbarian and the Geisha; The Roots of Heaven; The Unforgiven; The Misfits; Freud; The Night of the Iguana; The Bible . . . In the Beginning; Reflections in a Golden Eye; Sinful Davey; A Walk with Love and Death; The Kremlin Letter; Fat City; The Life and Times of Judge Roy Bean; The Mackintosh Man; The Man who would be King; Wise Blood; Phobia; Escape to Victory; Annie; Under the Volcano; Prizzi's Honor (Special Gold Lion, Venice Film Fest., 1985); The Dead, 1987, Mr North, 1988 (released posthumously); acted in Lovesick, Young Giants; Winter Kills. Served US Army 1942–45, Major; filmed documentaries of the War. Fellow, BAFTA, 1980. Hon. LittD Trinity Coll., Dublin, 1970. Special Award, Cannes Fest., 1984. *Publication:* (autobiog.) An Open Book, 1981. *Recreation:* foxhunting. *Address:* c/o Jess S. Morgan & Co. Inc., 6420 Wilshire Boulevard, 19th Floor, Los Angeles, Calif 90048, USA.          *Died* 28 *Aug.* 1987.

**HUTCHINGS, Arthur James Bramwell;** Professor of Music, University of Exeter, 1968–71, later Emeritus; *b* Sunbury on Thames, 14 July 1906; *s* of William Thomas Hutchings, Bideford, N Devon, and Annie Bramwell, Freckleton, Lytham, Lancs; *m* 1940, Marie Constance Haverson; one *d*. Formerly schoolmaster and organist; contributor to musical periodicals, critic and reviewer; served with RAF in SEAC; Prof. of Music, University of Durham, 1947–68, now Emeritus. Mem., Editorial Cttee, The English Hymnal, 1954–. Mem. Bd of Governors of Trinity Coll. of Music, 1947–. Vice-Pres., Friends of Cathedral Music, 1985–. BA, BMus, PhD London; Hon. FTCL, FRSCM, Hon. RAM. Compositions include: works for strings, comic operas and church music. *Publications:* Schubert (Master Musicians Series), 1941, 5th edn 1978; Edmund Rubbra (contribution to Penguin Special, Music of Our Time), 1941; Delius (in French, Paris), 1946; A Companion to Mozart's Concertos, 1947; Delius, 1947; The Invention and Composition of Music, 1954; The Baroque Concerto, 1960, 4th edn 1978; Pelican History of Music, Vol 3 (The 19th Century), 1962; Church Music in the Nineteenth Century, 1967; Mozart (2 vols), 1976. Contributions to: Die Musik in Geschichte und Gegenwart, 1956; The Mozart Companion, 1956; New Oxford History of Music, 1962; The Beethoven Companion, 1970; Grove's Dictionary of Music and Musicians, 6th edn, 1975; Purcell (BBC Music Guides), 1982. *Address:* 6 Bulls Court, Colyton, Devon EX13 6NJ. *T:* Colyton 52542.          *Died* 13 *Nov.* 1989.

**HUTCHINGS, Geoffrey Balfour,** CMG 1946; formerly Senior Partner in Lovell, White & King, Solicitors; *b* 24 Feb. 1904; 2nd *s* of late Charles Graham Hutchings, Seaford, Sussex; *m* 1st, 1928, Dorothy Guest (*d* 1967), *o d* of late Rev. J. Guest Gilbert; one *s* one *d*; 2nd, 1969, Mrs Stella Graham. *Educ:* Giggleswick Sch., Yorks. Served with 1/4 Bn South Lancs Regt, Sept. 1939–41; Principal Dir of Salvage and Recovery, Ministry of Supply, 1941–44; Dir-Gen. of British Ministry of Supply Commission, North West Europe, 1944–45; resumed professional practice, 1945. *Recreation:* golf. *Address:* Dunaverty Lodge, Southend by Cambeltown, Argyll. *T:* Southend 634.          *Died* 27 *Dec.* 1982.

**HUTCHINS, Frank Ernest,** CEng, FIEE; RCNC; retired 1981; consultant engineer, since 1982; *b* 27 Sept. 1922; *s* of Sidney William Hutchins and Eleanor Seager; *m* 1946, Patricia Mary Wakeford-Fullagar; one *d. Educ:* Sir Joseph Williamson's Mathematical Sch., Rochester, Kent; Royal Dockyard Sch., Chatham; Royal Naval Coll., Greenwich. BSc(Eng) 1st cl. Hons London. Asst Electrical Engr, Admiralty, Bath, 1945–49; Asst Staff Electrical Officer, BJSM, Washington DC, USA, 1949–51; Electrical Engr, Admiralty, Bath, 1951–63; Suptg Elec. Engr, Weapon Development and Ship Design, MoD (Navy), Bath, 1963–65; HM Dockyard, Devonport: Dep. Elec. Engrg Manager, 1965–68; Dep. Production Manager, 1968–69; Productivity Manager, 1969–70; attended Senior Officers' War Course, RN War Coll., Greenwich, 1970–71; Asst Director Naval Ship Production (Procurement Executive), MoD (Navy), Bath, 1971–73, Dep. Dir of Electrical Engrng, 1973–78; Chief Electrical Engr, Ship Dept, MoD (Navy), 1978–81. Panel Mem., CS Comr's Interview Selection Bd, 1981–.
*Died* 16 *Dec.* 1988.

**HUTCHINSON, Rev. Canon Archibald Campbell,** MA; Chaplain at Cossham Hospital, Bristol, 1950–63, and at Glenside Hospital, 1950–63; retired; Assistant Priest, St Peter's Church, Henleaze, Bristol, 1964–74; *b* 9 Feb. 1883; *s* of Ven. Archdeacon Arthur Blockey Hutchinson; *m* 1912, Constance Clara Auden Stratton (*d* 1950), Newport, Isle of Wight; no *c*; *m* 1951, Dorothy May White, Sherborne, Dorset. *Educ:* St Lawrence Coll., Ramsgate; Corpus Christi Coll., Cambridge. Ordained, 1906; Curate of St John's, Carisbrooke, IoW; joined the Japan Mission of the CMS, 1909; formerly Lecturer at the Fukuoka Divinity Sch.; Lecturer for one year at The Central Theological Coll., Tokyo; Mem. of the Standing Cttee Diocese of Kyushu; Sec. of the CMS, Japan Mission; Hon. Canon of the Cathedral at Fukuoka in the diocese of Kyushu; left Japan, Dec. 1940; Asst Priest, St Andrew's Church, Halfway Tree, Jamaica, 1941–45; Asst Priest, St James' Church, Bristol, 1945–50. *Address:* 120 Howard Road, Westbury Park, Bristol BS6 7XA. *T:* Bristol 45740.          *Died* 20 *June* 1981.

**HUTCHINSON, Sir Arthur (Sydney),** KBE 1953; CB 1946; CVO 1937; idc; *b* 21 March 1896; 2nd and *o surv. s* of late Sir Sydney Hutchinson, formerly Dir General of Telegraphs in India; *m* 1933, Charis Lyle, *d* of late Christopher Bathgate, Liverpool; no *c. Educ:* St Paul's Sch.; New Coll., Oxford. Army, 1916–18 (wounded); entered Home Office, 1919; Deputy Under-Sec. of State, 1948–57; retired, 1957. *Address:* Fairmead, Warren Road, Crowborough, East Sussex. *T:* Crowborough 61616.          *Died* 18 *Jan.* 1981.

**HUTCHINSON, Rear-Adm. Christopher Haynes,** CB 1961; DSO 1940; OBE 1946; RN retired; *b* 13 March 1906; 2nd *s* of late Rev. Canon Frederick William Hutchinson; *m* 1941, Nancy Marguerite Coppinger. *Educ:* Lydgate House Prep. Sch., Hunstanton; Royal Naval Colleges, Osborne and Dartmouth. Naval Cadet RNC

Osborne, Sept. 1919; served largely in submarines; served War of 1939–45, commanding submarine Truant which sank German cruiser Karlsruhe, 9 April 1940 (DSO); submarine base, Malta, 1942 (despatches); Staff Officer, British Pacific Fleet 1945 (OBE); Qualified RN Staff Coll. (1946) and Joint Services Staff Coll. (Directing Staff); Commanding 3rd Submarine Flotilla, 1950–52; Senior Naval Adviser to UK High Commissioner, Australia, 1952–54; Captain, RN Coll., Greenwich, 1954–56; Commodore, 1st Class, Chief of Staff Far East Station, 1956–59; Director-General of Personal Services and Officer Appointments, 1959–61; retired, 1962. *Address:* Pipits Hill, Avington, near Winchester, Hants SO21 1DE. *T:* Itchen Abbas (096278) 363.                    *Died* 24 *Dec.* 1990.

**HUTCHINSON, Sir Joseph (Burtt),** Kt 1956; CMG 1944; ScD Cantab; FRS 1951; Drapers' Professor of Agriculture, Cambridge, 1957–69, later Emeritus; Fellow, St John's College; *b* 21 March 1902; *s* of L. M. and Edmund Hutchinson; *m* 1930, Martha Leonora Johnson; one *s* one *d. Educ:* Ackworth and Bootham Schs; St John's Coll., Cambridge. Asst Geneticist, Empire Cotton Growing Corporation's Cotton Research Station, Trinidad, 1926–33; Geneticist and Botanist, Institute of Plant Industry, Indore, Central India, 1933–37; Geneticist, Empire Growing Corporation's Cotton Research Station, Trinidad, and Cotton Adviser to the Inspector-General of Agriculture, BWI, 1937–44. Chief Geneticist, Empire Cotton Growing Corp., 1944–49; Dir of its Cotton Research Station, Namulonge, Uganda, 1949–57. Chm. of Council of Makerere Coll., University Coll. of East Africa, 1953–57; Hon. Fellow, Makerere Coll., 1957. Pres., British Assoc., 1965–66; Foreign Fellow, Indian Nat. Science Acad., 1974. Royal Medal, Royal Society, 1967. Hon. DSc: Nottingham, 1966; East Anglia, 1972. *Publications:* The Genetics of Gossypium, 1947; Genetics and the Improvement of Tropical Crops, 1958; Application of Genetics to Cotton Improvement, 1959; Farming and Food Supply, 1972; (ed) Evolutionary Studies in World Crops, 1974; The Challenge of the Third World, 1975; Change and Innovation in Norfolk Farming, 1980; numerous papers on the genetics, taxonomy, and economic botany of cotton. *Address:* Huntingfield, Huntingdon Road, Cambridge CB3 0LH. *T:* Cambridge 276272.

*Died* 16 *Jan.* 1988.

**HUTCHINSON, William James,** TD; Chief Executive, County of Avon, 1974–82 (Town Clerk and Chief Executive Officer, Bristol County Borough, 1969–74); *b* 12 Dec. 1919; *s* of William James Hutchinson and Martha Allan Hutchinson (*née* Downie); *m* 1944, Barbara Olive Benaton; one *s* one *d. Educ:* Brighton Hove and Sussex Grammar School. Admitted Solicitor, 1947. Bury County Borough Council, 1947–49; Bristol CBC, 1949–. *Recreations:* gardening, walking, theatre. *Address:* 32 Woodland Grove, Coombe Dingle, Bristol BS9 2BB. *T:* 683415.                    *Died* 2 *Sept.* 1985.

**HUTCHISON, Hon. Sir Douglas;** *see* Hutchison, Hon. Sir J. D.

**HUTCHISON, Isobel Wylie,** Hon. LLD; FRSGS; JP; *d* of late Thomas Hutchison, Carlowrie, West Lothian, and Jeanie Wylie; unmarried. *Educ:* Rothesay House Sch., Edinburgh; Studley Horticultural Coll. for Women. Plant-collecting in Arctic regions, Greenland, Alaska, and Aleutian Islands for the Royal Horticultural Society, Royal Herbarium of Kew, and the British Museum. *Publications: verse:* Lyrics from West Lothian, The Northern Gate, How Joy was Found, The Calling of Bride; *novel:* Original Companions; *travel:* On Greenland's Closed Shore; North to the Rime-Ringed Sun; Arctic Nights Entertainments; Stepping Stones from Alaska to Asia, 1937, republished 1943 under title The Aleutian Islands. *Recreations:* sketching, walking, botany, etc. *Address:* Carlowrie, Kirkliston, West Lothian. *T:* 031-333 3209.

*Died* 20 *Feb.* 1982.

**HUTCHISON, Hon. Sir (James) Douglas,** Kt 1959; Judge of Supreme Court of New Zealand, 1948–66, retired; *b* 29 Sept. 1894; *s* of Sir James Hutchison; *m* 1st, 1924, Mary Bethea Johnston (*d* 1943); two *s* two *d*; 2nd, 1954, Mary Elizabeth Averill. *Educ:* Otago Boys' High Sch.; Otago Univ.; Victoria University Coll. (later Victoria Univ. of Wellington). Served European War, 1914–18, with 1st NZEF in Gallipoli and France; War of 1939–45, DAAG, Southern Military District, NZ. Practised Carterton, 1920–24, Christchurch, 1924–48. *Recreations:* radio and television sports. *Address:* Flat 2, 2 Grafton Road, Roseneath, Wellington, New Zealand. *Clubs:* Wellington, Canterbury (NZ).                    *Died* 20 *July* 1981.

**HUTCHISON, Prof. James Holmes,** CBE 1971 (OBE 1945); FRCP 1947; FRCPE 1960; FRCPGlas 1962; MD (Hons) 1939 (Glasgow); FRSE 1965; Professor of Paediatrics, University of Hong Kong, 1977–80; *b* 16 April 1912; *s* of Alexander Hutchison and Catherine Holmes; *m* 1940, Agnes T. A. Goodall; one *s* one *d. Educ:* High Sch. of Glasgow; University of Glasgow. Qualified MB, ChB (Glasgow) 1934; Resident Hosp. Posts, 1934–36; Royal Hosp. for Sick Children, Glasgow: McCunn Research Schol., 1936–38; Asst Vis. Phys., 1938–39; Physician in charge of Wards, 1947–61; also Consulting Pædiatrician, Queen Mother's Hospital, Glasgow; Leonard Gow Lectr on Med. Diseases of Infancy and Childhood,

1947–61, Samson Gemmell Prof. of Child Health, 1961–77, Univ. of Glasgow. Dean, Fac. of Medicine, Univ. of Glasgow, 1970–73. President: Royal College of Physicians and Surgeons of Glasgow, Nov. 1966–Nov. 1968. British Paediatric Assoc., 1969–70; Assoc. of Physicians of GB and Ireland, 1973–74; Hong Kong Paediatric Soc., 1979–80. Hon. FACP 1968. RAMC, Major and Lieut-Col, 1939–45. *Publications:* Practical Pædiatric Problems, 1964, 6th edn 1986; Rickets, in British Encyclopædia of Medical Practice, 2nd edn, 1952; Disorders of Storage, Obesity and Endocrine Diseases; chapters 50–57, in Pædiatrics for the Practitioner, 1953 (ed Gaisford and Lightwood); Hypothyroidism, in Recent Advances in Pædiatrics, 1958 (ed Gairdner), 2nd edn 1975; chapter in Emergencies in Medical Practice (ed C. Allan Birch); chapter in Textbook of Medical Treatment (ed Davidson, Dunlop and Alstead); chapter in Endocrine and Genetic Diseases of Childhood (ed L. I. Gardner), 1969, 2nd edn 1976; Thyroid section in Paediatric Endrocrinology (ed D.Hubble), 1969; chapter in Textbook of Pædiatrics (ed J. O. Forfar and G. C. Arneil), 1973, 3rd edn 1984; many contributions to medical journals. *Recreations:* golf, country dancing (Scottish), motoring. *Address:* 3 Kelvin Court, Glasgow G12 0AB. *T:* 041–334 7545. *Club:* Royal Scottish Automobile.

*Died* 27 *Dec.* 1987.

**HUTCHISON, James Seller;** Chairman, The British Oxygen Co. Ltd and Associated Companies, 1950–72 (Director, 1940–72); *b* 15 Oct. 1904; *s* of late R. F. Hutchison, Glasgow; *m* Kathleen, *d* of late William Maude, Leeds; two *d. Educ:* Greenock Academy; Glasgow Univ. Chartered Accountant, 1928. *Recreations:* golf, gardening.

*Died* 1 *April* 1986.

**HUTCHISON, Sir (William) Kenneth,** Kt 1962; CBE 1954; FRS 1966; FEng 1976; FIChemE; Hon. FIGasE; *b* 30 Oct. 1903; *s* of late William Hutchison; *m* 1929, Dorothea Marion Eva (*d* 1985), *d* of late Commander Bertie W. Bluett, Royal Navy; one *d. Educ:* Edinburgh Academy; Corpus Christi Coll., Oxford. Joined staff of Gas, Light and Coke Co. as Research Chemist, 1926; seconded to Air Ministry as Asst Dir of Hydrogen Production, 1940, Dir, 1942; Dir of Compressed Gases, 1943; Controller of By-Products, Gas, Light and Coke Co., 1945, and a Managing Dir of the Company from 1947; Chm., South Eastern Gas Board, 1948–59; Deputy Chm., Gas Council, 1960–66; Chm., International Management and Engineering Group, 1967–69; Dir, Newton Chambers & Co. Ltd, 1967–73. President: Institution of Gas Engineers, 1955–56; British Road Tar Assoc., 1953–55; Inst. of Chem. Engineers, 1959–61; Soc. of British Gas Industries, 1967–68; Nat. Soc. for Clean Air, 1969–71. *Publications:* High Speed Gas (autobiog.), 1987; papers in Proc. Royal Society and other jls, 1926–. *Recreations:* garden, golf. *Address:* 2 Arlington Road, Twickenham, Mddx TW1 2BG. *T:* 01–892 1685. *Clubs:* Athenæum, Royal Cruising.

*Died* 28 *Nov.* 1989.

**HUTT, Prof. William Harold;** Distinguished Professor of Economics, University of Dallas, Texas, 1971–77; Professor of Commerce and Dean of the Faculty of Commerce, University of Cape Town, 1931–64; Professor Emeritus since 1965; *b* 3 Aug. 1899; *s* of William Hutt and Louisa (*née* Fricker); *m* 1946, Margarethe Louise Schonken. *Educ:* LCC Schs; Hackney Downs Sch.; London Sch. of Economics, University of London. Personal Asst to Chm., Benn Bros Ltd, and Manager, Individualist Bookshop Ltd, 1924–28; Senior Lecturer, University of Cape Town, 1928–30. Visiting Professor of Economics at various Univs and Colls in USA, 1966–69; Vis. Research Fellow, Hoover Instn, Stanford Univ., Calif., 1969–71; Distinguished Vis. Prof. of Economics, Calif. State Coll., 1970–71. Founding Mem., Mont Pelerin Soc., 1947 (Roe Senior Fellow, 1984–). Adjunct Schol., Ludwig von Mises Inst., 1987. LLD (*hc*) Cape Town, 1977; DSSc (*hc*) Francisco Marroquin Univ., Guatemala, 1978; DHL (*hc*) Dallas, 1984. *Publications:* The Theory of Collective Bargaining, 1930, 2nd edn, 1975; Economists and the Public, 1936; The Theory of Idle Resources, 1939, 2nd edn 1977; Plan for Reconstruction, 1943; Keynesianism-Retrospect and Prospect, 1963; The Economics of the Colour Bar, 1964; Politically Impossible?, 1971; The Strike-Threat System, 1973; A Rehabilitation of Say's Law, 1975; Individual Freedom: a symposium of articles 1934–75 selected and ed by Klingaman and Pejovich, 1976; The Keynesian Episode, 1980; numerous articles in economic jls and symposia. *Recreations:* travel, listening to symphonies, watching football, ballet and opera. *Address:* c/o Standard Bank Ltd, ABC Branch, Adderley Street, Cape Town, South Africa. *Club:* Civil Service and City (Cape Town).                    *Died* 19 *June* 1988.

**HUTTON, (David) Graham,** OBE 1945; economist, author; *b* 13 April 1904; *er s* of late David James and Lavinia Hutton; *m* 1st, Magdalene Ruth Rudolph, Zürich (marr. diss. 1934); 2nd, 1940, Joyce Muriel Green (marr. diss. 1958); three *d*; 3rd, Marjorie, *d* of late Dr and Mrs David Bremner, Chicago. *Educ:* Christ's Hospital; London Sch. of Economics; French and German Univs. Gladstone Meml Prizeman, London Univ., 1929; Barrister-at-Law, Gray's Inn, 1932; Research Fellowship and teaching staff, LSE, 1929–33, Hon. Fellow 1971; Asst Editor, The Economist, 1933–38; FO and Min. of

Information, 1939–45. *Publications:* Nations and the Economic Crisis, 1932; The Burden of Plenty (as ed. and contributor, 1935); Is it Peace?, 1936; Danubian Destiny, 1939; Midwest at Noon, 1946; English Parish Churches, 1952; We Too Can Prosper, 1953; All Capitalists Now, 1960; Inflation and Society, 1960; Mexican Images, 1963; Planning and Enterprise, 1964; Politics and Economic Growth, 1968; (with Olive Cook) English Parish Churches, 1976; Whatever Happened to Productivity? (Wincott Lecture), 1980. *Recreations:* ecclesiology, music, travel. *Address:* 38 Connaught Square, W2 2HL. *T:* 01–723 4067. *Clubs:* Reform, English-Speaking Union.                                                  *Died* 14 *Oct.* 1988.

HUTTON, Sir Leonard, Kt 1956; professional cricketer, retired 1956; Director, Fenner International (Power Transmission) Ltd; retired from business 1984; *b* Fulneck, near Pudsey, Yorks, 23 June 1916; *s* of Henry Hutton; *m* 1939, Dorothy Mary Dennis, *d* of late G. Dennis, Scarborough; two *s*. First played for Yorks, 1934. First played for England *v* New Zealand, 1937; *v* Australia, 1938 (century on first appearance); *v* South Africa, 1938; *v* West Indies, 1939; *v* India, 1946. Captained England *v* India, 1952; *v* Australia, 1953; *v* Pakistan, 1954; *v* Australia, 1954. Captained MCC *v* West Indies, 1953–54. Made record Test score, 364, *v* Australia at the Oval, 1938; record total in a single month, 1294, in June 1949; made over 100 centuries in first-class cricket. Hon. Mem. of MCC, 1955 (first Professional to be elected). A selector, MCC, 1975–77. Pres., Yorks CCC, 1990–. Served War of 1939–45: in RA and APTC. Hon. MA Bradford, 1982. *Publications:* Cricket is my Life, 1950; Just my Story, 1956; Fifty Years in Cricket, 1984. *Recreation:* golf. *Address:* 1 Coombe Neville, Warren Road, Kingston-on-Thames, Surrey KT2 7HW. *T:* 081–942 0604.                         *Died* 6 *Sept.* 1990.

HUTTON, Maurice, PhD, FIMA; Rector, Sunderland Polytechnic, 1969–76; *b* 4 Nov. 1914; *s* of William and Sarah Hutton; *m* 1939, Barbara Stark; one *s* one *d*. *Educ:* Univ. of Durham (BA, PhD). North Manchester High Sch., 1937–41; Oldham Technical Coll., 1941–44; Sunderland Technical Coll.: Lectr, 1945–53; Head of Dept, 1953–61; Vice-Principal, 1958–61; Principal, 1961–68. Comdr, Royal Norwegian Order of St Olav, 1966. *Publication:* (jtly) Engineering Mathematics, 1959. *Recreations:* gardening, walking, music. *Address:* 17 Newlands Avenue, Sunderland SR3 1XW. *T:* Sunderland 285643.                                      *Died* 21 *Feb.* 1986.

HUTTON, Sir Noël (Kilpatrick), GCB 1966 (KCB 1957; CB 1950); QC 1962; *b* 27 Dec. 1907; *s* of late William Hutton and of late Mrs D. M. Hutton, Whiteacre, Kippington, Sevenoaks; *m* 1936, Virginia Jacomyn, *d* of Sir George Young, 4th Bt, MVO; two *s* two *d*. *Educ:* Fettes Coll. (Scholar); University Coll., Oxford (Scholar, Hon. Fellow, 1973). OUBC crew 1930. Called to the Bar, Lincoln's Inn, 1932; entered Parly Counsel Office, 1938; First Parly Counsel, 1956–68. Governor, Alleyn's College. *Recreations:* music, skiing, motoring. *Address:* Greenacre, Steeple Aston, Oxon OX5 3RT. *T:* Steeple Aston 40386. *Clubs:* Athenæum; Leander.
                                                                  *Died* 14 *June* 1984.

HUTTON, Maj.-Gen. Reginald Antony, CIE 1947; DSO 1944, and Bar 1945; OBE 1942; DL; *b* 18 April 1899; *s* of Charles Antony and Laura Beatrice Hutton, Earls Colne, Essex; *m* 1934, Margaret Isabel (*d* 1967), *d* of Mark Feetham; two *d*. *Educ:* Haileybury and RMC, Sandhurst. Commissioned 1917, 2nd KEO Gurkha Rifles; Staff Coll., Camberley, 1934–35; Bde Major, 1938; GSO1 1940; Deputy Dir Military Intelligence, 1941; Bde Commander, 1944; Chief of Staff, 1 Corps, 1946. Served European War, 1914–18, General Service, 1917–18; 3rd Afghan War, 1919; Mahsud and NWF, 1919–20; Mohmand-Bajaur, 1933; Waziristan and NWF, 1938–40; War of 1939–45: despatches 1940; Western Desert, Crete, Somaliland, Abyssinia, and Eritrea, 1940–42; Burma and Malaya, 1944–46; Chief of the General Staff, Pakistan Army, 1947–51; retired list, 1951. DL, Devon, 1962. *Address:* The Haven, Newton Ferrers, Devon. *T:* Plymouth 872325. *Club:* Naval and Military.
                                                                  *Died* 21 *Dec.* 1983.

HUTTON, Lt-Gen. Sir Thomas Jacomb, KCIE 1944; CB 1941; MC; idc; psc; *b* 27 March 1890; *e s* of W. H. Hutton, JP, Clevedon, Som; *m* 1921, Isabel (CBE 1948; she died 1960), *d* of James Emslie, Edinburgh. *Educ:* Rossall; Royal Military Academy, Woolwich. 2nd Lieut Royal Artillery, 1909; Capt. 1915; Bt Major 1918; Major 1927; Bt Lt-Col 1927; Col 1930; Maj.-Gen. 1938; Lieut-Gen. 1941; served European War, 1914–18 (wounded thrice, despatches four times, Bt Major, Legion of Honour, French and Italian War Crosses, MC and Bar); Palestine, 1936; GSO3, 1918; Bde-Major, 1918–19; Asst Military Sec., 1919–20; DAAG, War Office, 1923–24; GSO2 E Command, 1924–26; Military Asst to CIGS 1927–30; GSO1, Military Operations, 1933–36; GSO1, 1st Division, 1936–38; GOC Western Independent District, India, 1938–40; Deputy Chief of General Staff, Army Headquarters, India, 1940–41; Chief of the General Staff, India, 1941; GOC Burma, 1942; Sec. War Resources and Reconstruction Cttees of Council (India), 1942–44; retired pay, 1944; Officiating Sec., Viceroy's Executive Council; Sec., Planning and Development Dept, 1944–46; Regional Officer, Ministry of

Health, 1947–49; General Manager, Anglo-American Council on Productivity, 1949–53; Dir, British Productivity Council, 1953–57. Chm. Organisation and Methods Training Council, 1957–64. Colonel Commandant RA, 1942–52. *Address:* 5 Spanish Place, W1. *T:* 01–935 8831. *Club:* Army and Navy.            *Died* 17 *Jan.* 1981.

HUTTON, William, CBE 1962; FRSE; Solicitor; retired; Member Council, Law Society of Scotland, 1962–67; *b* 2 Feb. 1902; *e s* of late John Hutton, MPS, Brechin; *m* 1932, Marjorie Elizabeth, MStJ, *d* of late John Philip Gibb, Director of Raimes, Clark & Co. Ltd, Leith; one *s* one *d*. *Educ:* Brechin High Sch.; Edinburgh Univ., MA 1925, LLB (dist.) 1927, Thow Schol. 1927. Legal experience with Tait & Crichton, WS and Davidson & Syme, WS; admitted Solicitor, 1928; Legal Asst to Dept of Health for Scotland and Asst Draftsman to Scottish Office, 1929–32; Town Clerk of Kirkcaldy, 1932–39; Sen. Depute Town Clerk of Edinburgh, 1939–48; Dep. Chm. former SW Scotland Electricity Bd, 1948–55; Deputy Chm. South of Scotland Electricity Board, 1955–63. Comp. IEE, 1949–63. Notary Public, 1958; FRSE 1960; JP (Glasgow), 1960–64. *Address:* 21 Craiglockhart Loan, Edinburgh EH14 1JR. *T:* 031–443 3530.
                                                                  *Died* 30 *March* 1983.

HUXHAM, Henry William Walter, CB 1967; CBE 1960; Legal Staff of Law Commission, 1967–78; *b* 10 Feb. 1908; *s* of late William Henry Huxham; *m* 1st, 1934, Mabel Marion (*d* 1949), *d* of W. T. Swain; 2nd, 1950, Winifred Annie, *d* of G. W. Rogers; one *d*. LLB London, 1930; admitted Solicitor, 1933; joined Solicitor's Dept, Min. of Labour, 1934; Solicitor to Min. of Labour, Aug. 1962–Oct. 1967. Chm., Civil Service Legal Soc., 1952, 1953. *Address:* 21 Holyoake Walk, East Finchley, N2 0JX. *T:* 01–883 3196.
                                                                  *Died* 24 *Sept.* 1982.

HUXLEY, Sir Leonard (George Holden), KBE 1964; MA, DPhil Oxon; PhD Adelaide; FAA; Emeritus Professor, University of Adelaide; Vice-Chancellor, The Australian National University, 1960–67; *b* London, UK, 29 May 1902; *s* of George H. and Lilian S. Huxley; *m* 1929, Ella M. C. (*d* 1981), *d* of F. G. and E. Copeland; one *s* one *d*. *Educ:* The Hutchins Sch., Hobart; University of Tasmania; New Coll., Oxford. Rhodes Scholar, Tas., 1923; Jessie Theresa Rowden Scholar, New Coll., 1927; Scott Scholar, University of Oxford, 1929. Scientific staff, CSIR, Sydney, 1929–31; Head of Dept of Physics, University Coll. Leicester, 1932–40; Principal Scientific Officer, Telecommunications Research Estabt, MAP, 1940–46; Reader in Electromagnetism, University of Birmingham, 1946–49; Elder Prof. of Physics, University Adelaide, 1949–60; Mem. Executive, CSIRO, 1960; Mem. Council, University of Adelaide, 1953–60; Mem. Council, Aust. Nat. Univ., 1956–59; Foundation FAA, 1954 (Sec., Physical Sciences, 1959–62); Chm. Australian Radio Research Board, 1958–64; Chm. National Standards Commission, 1953–65; Chm. Radio Frequency Allocation Cttee, 1960–64; Mem. Nat. Library Council, 1961–72; Mem. Bd, US Educnl Foundn in Austr., 1960–65; Australian Deleg. on Cttee on Space Research, (COSPAR), 1959–60. First President Aust. Inst. of Physics, 1962–65. Mem., Queen Elizabeth II Fellowships Cttee, 1963–66; Chm., Gen. Coun. Encyclopædia Britannica Australia Awards, 1964–74; Chm. Bd, Aust./Amer. Educl Foundn, 1965–69; Trustee, Aust. Humanities Res. Council, 1968–70; Mem. Council, Canberra Coll. of Advanced Educn, 1968–74. Hon DSc: Tasmania, 1962; ANU, 1980. *Publications:* Wave Guides, 1949; (with R. W. Crompton) The Diffusion and Drift of Electrons in Gases, 1974; numerous scientific papers on gaseous Electronics, the ionosphere, upper atmosphere and related subjects. *Address:* Unit 26/6, 6 Jardine Street, Kingston, Canberra, ACT 2604, Australia. *Club:* Commonwealth (Canberra).
                                                                  *Died* 4 *Sept.* 1988.

HUXTABLE, Rev. (William) John (Fairchild), DD; Executive Officer, Churches' Unity Commission, 1975–78; *b* 25 July 1912; *s* of Rev. John Huxtable and Florence Huxtable (*née* Watts); *m* 1939, Joan Lorimer Snow; one *s* two *d*. *Educ:* Barnstaple Gram. Sch.; Western Coll., Bristol; Mansfield and St Catherine's Colls, Oxford. BA Bristol 1933; BA Oxon 1937, MA 1940. Minister: Newton Abbot Congreg. Church, 1937–42; Palmers Green Congreg. Church, 1942–54; Princ., New Coll., University of London, 1953–64. Chm., 1962–63, Sec., 1964–66, Minister Sec., 1966–72, Congregational Union of England and Wales; Jt Gen. Sec., United Reformed Church, 1972–74; Moderator, United Reformed Church, 1972–73. Vice-President: British Coun. of Churches, 1967–71; World Alliance of Reformed Churches, 1970–77; Vice-Moderator, Free Church Federal Council, 1975–76, Moderator, 1976–77; Member: Central Cttee, World Council of Churches, 1968–75; Jt Cttee of Translation of New English Bible, 1948–74. Vice-Pres. Council, St Dunstan's, 1973–84. Hon. Fellow, Mansfield Coll., Oxford, 1987. Hon. DD: Lambeth, 1973; Aberdeen, 1973. *Publications:* The Ministry, 1943; (ed) John Owen's True Nature of a Gospel Church, 1947; (ed jtly) A Book of Public Worship, 1948; The Faith that is in Us, 1953; The Promise of the Father, 1959; Like a Strange People, 1961; Church and State in Education (C. J. Cadoux Meml Lect.), 1962; The Bible Says (Maynard Chapman Lects), 1962; Preaching the Law, (Joseph

Smith Meml Lect.), 1964; The Preacher's Integrity (A. S. Peake Meml Lect.), 1966; Christian Unity: some of the issues (Congreg. Lects), 1966; contribs to symposia: The Churches and Christian Unity, 1962; From Uniformity to Unity, 1962; A Companion to the Bible, 1963; Renewal of Worship, 1965; Outlook for Christianity, 1967; contrib. to Christian Confidence, 1970; A New Hope for Christian Unity, 1977; also contribs to Congreg. Quarterly, Theology, Epworth Review, London Quarterly and Holborn Review, Proc. Internat. Congreg. Council and Theologische Realenzyklopädie. *Recreation:* reading. *Address:* Manor Cottage, East Ogwell, South Devon.                                     *Died 16 Nov.* 1990.

**HYDE, H(arford) Montgomery,** MA Oxon, DLit Belfast, FRHistS; FRSL; MRIA; author and barrister; *b* Belfast, 14 Aug. 1907; *o s* of late James J. Hyde, JP, Belfast, and Isobel Greenfield Montgomery; *m* 1st, 1939, Dorothy Mabel Brayshaw (from whom he obtained a divorce, 1952), *e d* of Dr J. Murray Crofts, CBE, Disley, Cheshire; 2nd, 1955, Mary Eleanor (marr. diss., 1966), *d* of Col L. G. Fischer, IMS; 3rd, 1966, Rosalind Roberts, *y d* of Comdr J. F. W. Dimond, RN. *Educ:* Sedbergh (Scholar); Queen's Univ. Belfast (Emily Lady Pakenham Scholar); 1st Class Hons Modern History, 1928; Magdalen Coll., Oxford (Open History Exhibitioner); 2nd Class Hons Jurisprudence, 1930; Harmsworth Law Scholar, Middle Temple, 1932. Called to Bar, Middle Temple, 1934; joined NE Circuit; Extension Lecturer in History, Oxford Univ., 1934; Private Sec. to Marquess of Londonderry, 1935–39; Asst Censor, Gibraltar, 1940; commissioned in Intelligence Corps, 1940; Military Liaison and Censorship Security Officer, Bermuda, 1940–41; Asst Passport Control Officer, New York, 1941–42; with British Army Staff, USA, 1942–44; Major, 1942; attached Supreme HQ Allied Expeditionary Force, 1944; Allied Commission for Austria, 1944–45; Lt-Col 1945; Asst Editor, Law Reports, 1946–47; Legal Adviser, British Lion Film Corp. Ltd, 1947–49; MP (U) North Belfast, 1950–59; UK Delegate to Council of Europe Consultative Assembly, Strasbourg, 1952–55; Hon. Col Intelligence Corps (TA), NI, 1958–61; Professor of Hist. and Polit. Sci., University of the Punjab, Lahore, 1959–61; RAF Museum Leverhulme Research Fellowship, 1971–75. Active in campaign for abolition of capital punishment; has travelled extensively in Russia, The Far East, West Indies, Mexico, and South America. Hon. DLit QUB, 1984. *Publications:* The Rise of Castlereagh, 1933; The Russian Journals of Martha and Catherine Wilmot (with the Marchioness of Londonderry), 1934; More Letters from Martha Wilmot, Impressions of Vienna (with the Marchioness of Londonderry), 1935; The Empress Catherine and Princess Dashkhov, 1935; Air Defence and the Civil Population (with G. R. Falkiner Nuttall), 1937; Londonderry House and Its Pictures, 1937; Princess Lieven, 1938; Judge Jeffreys, 1940, new edn, 1948; Mexican Empire, 1946; A Victorian Historian, 1947; Privacy and the Press, 1947; John Law, 1948, new edn 1969; The Trials of Oscar Wilde, 1948, 3rd edn 1973; Mr and Mrs Beeton, 1951; Cases that changed the Law, 1951; Carson, 1953; The Trial of Craig and Bentley, 1954; United in Crime, 1955; Mr and Mrs Daventry, a play by Frank Harris, 1957; The Strange Death of Lord Castlereagh, 1959; The Trial of Roger Casement, 1960, 2nd edn 1964; The Life and Cases of Sir Patrick Hastings, 1960; Recent Developments in Historical Method and Interpretation, 1960; Simla and the Simla Hill States under British Protection, 1961; An International Crime Case Book, 1962; The Quiet Canadian, 1962; Oscar Wilde: the Aftermath, 1963; Room 3603, 1964; A History of Pornography, 1964; Norman

Birkett, 1964; Cynthia, 1965; The Story of Lamb House, 1966, 2nd edn 1975; Lord Reading, 1967; Strong for Service: The Life of Lord Nathan of Churt, 1968; Henry James At Home, 1969; The Other Love, 1970; Their Good Names, 1970; Stalin, 1971; Baldwin: the unexpected Prime Minister, 1973; Oscar Wilde, 1975; The Cleveland Street Scandal, 1976; British Air Policy between the Wars, 1976; Neville Chamberlain, 1976; Crime has its Heroes, 1976; Solitary in the Ranks, 1977; The Londonderrys, 1979; The Atom Bomb Spies, 1980; (ed) Oscar Wilde: Three Plays, 1981; Secret Intelligence Agent, 1982; (ed) The Annotated Oscar Wilde, 1982; Lord Alfred Douglas, 1984; A Tangled Web, 1986; George Blake Superspy, 1987; (ed) Oscar Wilde: the complete plays, 1988; (ed) J. F. Bloxam: the priest and the acolyte, 1988; Christopher Millard (Stuart Mason), 1988; Walter Monckton, 1989; chapter 12 (The Congress of Vienna) in the Cambridge History of Poland; contribs to DNB; *posthumous publication:* (ed) The Lady Chatterley's Lover Trial, 1990. *Recreations:* criminology, music. *Address:* Westwell House, Tenterden, Kent. *T:* Tenterden 3189. *Clubs:* Garrick, Beefsteak, Institute of Directors, Aspinall Curzon; Dormy House (Rye); Grolier (New York).                                     *Died 10 Aug.* 1989.

**HYDE, John Bean;** Director, Royal Bank of Scotland Group plc, since 1985; Chairman and Chief Executive, Charterhouse Japhet plc, since 1981; *b* 7 Jan. 1928; *s* of John Bean Hyde and Ivy Howard Hyde (*née* Gannon); *m* 1953, Patricia Gabrielle Mebes Gray; one *d* (and one *s* decd). *Educ:* Shrewsbury Sch.; Magdalen Coll., Oxford (BA PPE 2nd Cl.). AIB 1954; FIB 1972. Vice President, Citibank, 1951–68; Director, Hill Samuel & Co., 1968–70; Chief Executive: London Multinational Bank/Chemical Bank International Ltd, 1970–81. *Recreations:* bridge, music, theatre. *Address:* Chagfords, Burdenshot Hill, Worplesdon, Surrey GU3 3RL. *T:* Worplesdon 232619. *Club:* City of London.                                     *Died 20 Aug.* 1985.

**HYND, Henry;** *b* Perth, Scotland, 4 July 1900; *s* of Henry Hynd; *m*, 1st, 1925, Phyllis Jarman (marr. diss. 1971); one *d*; 2nd, 1971, Mrs Anne Nadine Scott. *Educ:* Perth Academy. Railway Clerk, 1915–20; Trade Union Official, 1920–45; Member Hornsey Borough Council, 1939–52; MP (Lab) for Central Hackney, 1945–50, for Accrington, 1950–66; Parliamentary Private Sec. to First Lord of the Admiralty, Dec. 1945–46 and to Min. of Defence, 1946–50. Hon. Pres., London Perthshire Assoc. JP Middlesex. Commander of Belgian Order of the Crown and Officer of Luxembourg Order of the Oak Crown. *Recreation:* travelling. *Address:* 31 Alford House, Stanhope Road, N6 5AL. *T:* 01–340 3308.                                     *Died 1 Feb.* 1985.

**HYSLOP, Dr James Morton;** Principal and Vice-Chancellor, Rhodes University, 1963–75; *b* Dumbarton, 12 Sept. 1908; *s* of Willian Hyslop; *m* 1935, Helen Margaret, *d* of W. W. Hyslop, Glasgow; one *d*. *Educ:* High Sch. of Glasgow; Univ. of Glasgow (MA, DSc); Christ's Coll., Cambridge (BA, PhD). War Service as Flt-Lt, RAF, mainly in Middle East, 1941–45. Lectr, Univ. of Glasgow, 1933–41 and 1945–47; Prof. of Maths, Univ. of the Witwatersrand, 1947–60; Principal, Royal Coll., Nairobi (now University of Nairobi), 1960–63. Hon. LLD: Glasgow, 1967; Rhodes, 1976. Coronation Medal, 1953. *Publications:* Infinite Series, 1941; Real Variable, 1960; papers in learned jls on mathematical topics. *Recreations:* golf, bowls. *Address:* 36 Grand Street, Port Alfred, South Africa. *Clubs:* Port Elizabeth, Albany (Grahamstown).

*Died 18 May* 1984.

# I

**IGNATIEFF, George,** CC 1973; Chancellor, University of Toronto, 1980–86; Hon. Professor, University of Trinity College, Toronto (Vice-Chancellor and Provost, 1972–79); *b* 16 Dec. 1913; *s* of Count Paul N. Ignatieff and Princess Natalie Mestchersky; *m* 1945, Alison Grant, MVO; two *s*. *Educ*: St Paul's, London; Lower Canada Coll., Montreal; Jarvis Coll., Toronto; Univs of Toronto and Oxford. Rhodes Schol., Ont, 1935; BA Toronto 1935; BA Oxon 1938, MA 1960. Dept of External Affairs, Ottawa, 1940; 3rd Sec., London, 1940–44; Ottawa, 1944–45; Adviser, Canadian Delegn, UN Atomic Energy Commn, 1946; UN Assembly, 1946–47; Alt. Rep., UN Security Council, 1948–49; Councillor, Canadian Embassy, Washington, DC, 1948–53; Imp. Def. Coll., London, 1953–54; Head of Defence Liaison Div., External Affairs, Ottawa, 1954–55; Canadian Ambassador to Yugoslavia, 1956–58; Dep. High Comr, London, 1959–60; Asst Under-Sec. of State for External Affairs, Ottawa, 1960–62; Perm. Rep. and Canadian Ambassador to NATO, 1962–65; Canadian Perm. Rep. and Ambassador to UN: NY, 1965–68; to Cttee on Disarmament, Geneva, 1968–71; to UN and other Internat. Organisations, Geneva, 1970–71. Advr to Govt on Disarmament, 1984–. President: UNA Canada, 1979–; Science for Peace, 1987–88. Chm., Bd of Trustees, Nat. Museums of Canada Corp., 1973–79. Mem., Pugwash Council, 1987–. Hon. Fellow, St John's Coll., Winnipeg, 1973. Hon. LLD: Toronto, 1969; Brock, 1969; Guelph 1970; Saskatchewan, 1973; York, 1975; Hon. DCL Bishop's, 1973; Hon. DLitt, Victoria Coll., Toronto, 1977. Pearson Peace Medal, 1984. *Publication*: The Making of a Peacemonger (memoirs), 1985. *Address*: 18 Palmerston Gardens, Toronto, Ont M6G 1V9, Canada. *Died* 10 *Aug.* 1989.

**IKIN, Rutherford Graham;** Headmaster of Trent College, 1936–68; *b* 22 Jan. 1903; *s* of late Dr A. E. Ikin, formerly Dir of Education, Blackpool; *m* 1936, Elizabeth Mary Mason; two *d*. *Educ*: King Edward VI Sch., Norwich; King's Coll., Cambridge (Choral Scholar). BA 1925; MA 1928; Asst Master at King's Sch., Ely, 1926–29; History Master and House Master, St Bees Sch., 1929–36. *Publications*: A Pageant of World History; The Modern Age; The History of the King's School, Ely. *Address*: Green Eaves, Whatstandwell, Matlock, Derbyshire. *T*: Ambergate 2315. *Club*: East India, Devonshire, Sports and Public Schools. *Died* 11 *Oct.* 1989.

**ILLINGWORTH, Rear-Adm. Philip Holden Crothers,** CB 1969; *b* 29 Nov. 1916; *s* of late Norman Holden Illingworth, Woking; *m* 1944, Dorothy Jean, *d* of George Wells, Southbourne; three *s* three *d*. *Educ*: RN Coll., Dartmouth, RNEC. Joined RN 1930, Rear-Adm. 1967. Dep. Controller of Aircraft, Min. of Technology, 1969, MoD, 1971–72; retd 1973; Vice-Chm., EPS (Western) Ltd, 1980–82. *Address*: Manor House, Marston Magna, Somerset. *T*: Marston Magna 850294. *Died* 11 *March* 1987.

**ILLINGWORTH, Ronald Stanley;** Professor of Child Health, University of Sheffield, 1947–75; *b* 7 Oct. 1909; *s* of late H. E. Illingworth, ARIBA, ARPS; *m* Dr Cynthia Illingworth, MB, BS, FRCP, Consultant in Paediatric Accident and Emergency, Children's Hosp., Sheffield; one *s* two *d*. *Educ*: Clifton House Sch., Harrogate; Bradford Grammar Sch. MB, ChB Leeds, 1934; MRCS, LRCP, 1934; MD Leeds, 1937; MRCP, 1937; DPH Leeds (distinction), 1938; DCH (RCP and S), 1938; FRCP 1947; FRPS, Fellow, Royal Society Medicine; Mem. BMA; Hon. Member: British Paediatric Assoc.; Swedish Pædiatric Assoc.; Finnish Pædiatric Assoc.; Amer. Acad. of Pediatrics; Academy of Pædiatricians of the USSR. West Riding County Major Scholar, 1928; Nuffield Research Studentship, Oxford, 1939–41; Rockefeller Research Fellowship, 1939 and 1946. Formerly Resident Asst, Hospital for Sick Children, Great Ormond Street, London, 1938–39; Medical Specialist and officer in charge of Medical Division (Lt-Col), RAMC, 1941–46. Asst to Prof. of Child Health, Univ. of London, 1946. Freedom, City of Sheffield, 1982. Hon. DSc: Univ. of Baghdad, Iraq, 1975; Leeds, 1982; Hon. MD Sheffield, 1976. Medal, Univ. of Turku, Finland, 1974; Aldrich Award, Amer. Acad. of Pediatrics, 1978; Spence Medal, BPA, 1979; Dawson Williams Prize, BMA, 1981. *Publications*: The Normal Child, 1953, 9th edn 1987 (trans. Greek, Spanish, Japanese, Farsi, French, Italian); (with C. M. Illingworth) Babies and Young Children: Feeding, Management and Care, 1954, 7th edn 1984 (trans. Polish); (ed) Recent Advances in Cerebral Palsy, 1958; Development of Infant and Young Child, Normal and Abnormal, 1960, 9th edn 1987 (trans. Japanese, French, Polish, Spanish, Italian); An Introduction to Developmental Assessment in the First Year, 1962; The Normal Schoolchild: His Problems, Physical and Emotional, 1964; (with C. M. Illingworth) Lessons from Childhood: some aspects of the early life of unusual men and women, 1966 (trans. Japanese); Common Symptoms of Disease in Children, 1967, 9th edn 1988 (trans. Greek, Indonesian, Spanish, Italian, German, Japanese, Portuguese); Treatment of the Child at Home: a guide for family doctors, 1971 (trans. Greek); Basic Developmental Screening, 1973, 4th edn 1988

(trans. Greek, Italian, Japanese, Spanish); The Child at School: a Paediatrician's Manual for Teachers, 1974 (trans. Italian); Your Child's Development in the First Five Years, 1981 (trans. Spanish); Infections and Immunisation of your Child, 1981 (trans. Spanish); various medical and photographic papers. *Recreations*: photography, philately, travel. *Address*: 8 Harley Road, Sheffield S11 9SD. *T*: Sheffield (0742) 362774. *Died* 4 *June* 1990.

**IMBERT-TERRY, Sir Andrew Henry Bouhier,** 4th Bt *cr* 1917; *b* 5 Oct. 1945; *s* of Major Sir Edward Henry Bouhier Imbert-Terry, 3rd Bt, MC, and of Jean (who *m* 1983, 6th Baron Sackville), *d* of late Arthur Stanley Garton; *S* father, 1978; *m* 1972, Sarah Margaret Evans (marr. diss. 1974); *m* 1979, Georgina Anne Massie-Taylor. *Educ*: Eton. Formerly Captain, The Life Guards. *Heir*: *b* Michael Edward Stanley Imbert-Terry [*b* 18 April 1950; *m* 1975, Frances D., *d* of Peter Scott; one *s* two *d*]. *Address*: Mead Meadow House, near Chobham, Surrey. *Died* 5 *Sept.* 1985.

**IMRIE, Sir John Dunlop,** Kt 1950; CBE 1942; JP; Chartered Accountant; *b* 16 Oct. 1891; *s* of late Alexander Imrie, Kinross; *m* 1953, Mary Isobel Rae Rowan. *Educ*: Dollar Academy; Edinburgh Univ. MA Edinburgh 1925; BCom Edinburgh 1923; FRSE 1943; City Chamberlain of Edinburgh, 1926–51; Hon. Financial Officer, Edinburgh Festival Society, 1945–51; Local Government Comr, Trinidad, BWI, 1951–53; Dir, Caledonian Insurance Co. Ltd, until 1965; Chairman: Wm Brown (Booksellers) Ltd; Edinburgh Bookshop Ltd; Scottish Bookshops Ltd; Past-Pres., Inst. Municipal Treasurers and Accountants; Hon. Governor Dollar Acad. Member: Scottish War Savings Cttee, 1940–64; Scottish Housing Advisory Cttee, 1942; Scottish Rating and Valuation Cttee, 1943; Cttee on Water Rating in Scotland, 1944; Cttee on Houses of National Importance, 1949; Hospital Endowments Commission, 1949; Cttee on Scottish Financial and Trade Statistics, 1950; Cttee on Economic and Financial Problems of Provision for Old Age, 1954; Historic Buildings Council for Scotland, 1954–58; South of Scotland Electricity Board, 1955–59; Public Works Loans Commission, 1956–65. *Publications*: Contributions to Local Government Finance, Public Administration, etc. *Address*: Invervar Lodge, Glenlyon, Aberfeldy, Perthshire, Scotland. *T*: Glenlyon 203. *Died* 8 *June* 1981.

**INCE, Brigadier Cecil Edward Ronald,** CB 1950; CBE 1946 (OBE 1941); *b* 5 March 1897; 3rd *s* of late C. H. B. Ince, Barrister-at-Law; *m* 1924, Leslie, *o d* of late Robert Badham, Secretary of Midland & GW Rly, Ireland; two *d*. *Educ*: Sevenoaks. Regular Army; RA 1915, RASC 1919–49. Deputy Dir (Supplies), Middle East, 1940–42; War Office, 1943–47; Commandant RASC Trng Centre, 1947–49. Dir of Enforcement, subseq. Dir of Warehousing, Min. of Food and Agric., 1949–55. *Publications*: various military pamphlets and articles in Service publications. *Recreation*: progressive gardening. *Address*: 76 West Grove, Walton-on-Thames, Surrey. *T*: Walton-on-Thames 225035. *Died* 21 *Jan.* 1988.

**INCHIQUIN, 17th Baron of,** *cr* 1543; **Phaedrig Lucius Ambrose O'Brien;** Bt 1686; *b* 4 April 1900; 2nd *s* of 15th Baron of Inchiquin and Ethel Jane (*d* 1940), *d* of late Johnstone J. Foster, Moor Park, Ludlow; *S* brother, 1968; *m* 1945, Vera Maud, *d* of late Rev. C. S. Winter. *Educ*: Eton; Magdalen Coll., Oxford (MA); Imperial Coll., London Univ. Major (retd) Rifle Brigade; served War, 1940–45, attached E African Intelligence Corps, Somalia, Abyssinia, Madagascar (wounded, despatches). Farming and coffee planting, Kenya, 1922–36; Geologist, Anglo-American Corp., 1936–39 and 1946–54; Colonial Service, Overseas Geological Survey (retd), 1954–59. Consulting Geologist, 1960–67. *Heir*: *nephew* Conor Myles John O'Brien, *b* 17 July 1943. *Address*: Hanway Lodge, Richard's Castle, Ludlow, Salop. *T*: Richard's Castle 210; Thomond House, Co. Clare, Ireland. *Club*: Royal Automobile. *Died* 20 *May* 1982.

**INCHYRA, 1st Baron** *cr* 1961; **Frederick Robert Hoyer Millar,** GCMG 1956 (KCMG 1949; CMG 1939); CVO 1938; *b* 6 June 1900; *s* of late R. Hoyer Millar; *m* 1931, Elizabeth de Marees van Swinderen; two *s* two *d*. *Educ*: Wellington Coll.; New Coll., Oxford. Hon. Attaché, HM Embassy, Brussels, 1922; entered HM Diplomatic Service, 1923; served as Third Sec. at Berlin and Paris, and as Second Sec. at Cairo; Asst Private Sec. to Sec. of State for Foreign Affairs, 1934–38; First Sec. at Washington, 1939; Counsellor, 1941–42; Sec., British Civil Secretariat, Washington, 1943; Counsellor, FO, 1944; Asst Under-Sec. 1947; Minister, British Embassy, Washington, 1948; UK Deputy, North Atlantic Treaty Organisation, 1950; UK Permanent Representative on NATO Council, 1952; UK High Commissioner in Germany, 1953–55; British Ambassador to Bonn, 1955–57; Permanent Under-Sec. of State, Foreign Office, 1957–61. *Recreation*: shooting. *Heir*: *s* Hon. Robert (Charles Reneke) Hoyer Millar, *b* 4 April 1935. *Address*: Inchyra House, Glencarse, Perthshire. *Clubs*: Boodle's, Turf; New (Edinburgh); Metropolitan (Washington). *Died* 16 *Oct.* 1989.

**INCLEDON-WEBBER, Lt-Col Godfrey Sturdy,** TD 1943; DL; MA; *b* 1 July 1904; *er s* of William Beare Incledon-Webber, DL, JP, Buckland, Braunton, N Devon; *m* 1931, Angela Florence, *d* of Sir Pierce Lacy, 1st Bt; three *d. Educ:* Eton (1st classical schol. Radley, 1918); Magdalen Coll., Oxford (BA 1926, MA 1947). Joined Royal Devon Yeomanry Artillery, 1924; served in War of 1939–45 (Lieut-Col Comdg 136 Lt AA Regt RA, 1942–45). Partner, Cutler and Lacy, Stockbrokers, Birmingham, 1933–53; Man. Dir, British Trusts Assoc. Ltd, 1953–73; Director: United Dominions Trust Ltd, 1959–73; English Insurance Co. Ltd, 1955–78; Chm., Incledon Estate Co. Ltd, 1949. Alderman (Ward of Farringdon Within) and JP, City of London, 1963–71; one of HM's Lieutenants of City of London; Sheriff, City of London, 1968–69; Master, Worshipful Co. of Clothworkers, 1975–76 (excused service); Master, Worshipful Co. of Saddlers, 1961–62. Hereditary Freeman of Barnstaple (1925); Lord of the Manor of Croyde and Putsborough, Devon. DL Devon, 1969; High Sheriff, Devon, 1970–71. FRSA 1971. OStJ 1968. *Recreations:* shooting; represented Eton at rackets (Public School Rackets winning pair 1922) and cricket, 1922–23, Oxford Univ. at real tennis and squash rackets, 1925–26; mem. British Squash Rackets Team which toured USA and Canada, 1927, winning Lapham Trophy, USA, Canada and GB competing. *Address:* Buckland Manor, Braunton, N Devon EX33 1HN. *T:* Braunton 812016. *Clubs:* Carlton, City Livery. *Died 28 April 1986.*

**INGERSOLL, Ralph McAllister;** Editor and Publisher, USA; *b* 8 Dec. 1900; *s* of Colin Macrae and Theresa (McAllister) Ingersoll; *m* 1st, 1925, Mary Elizabeth Carden (marr. diss., 1935; she *d* 1965); 2nd, 1945, Elaine Brown Keiffer (*d* 1948); two *s*; 3rd, 1948, Mary Hill Doolittle (marr. diss., 1962; she *d* 1980); one adopted *s*; three step *s* one step *d*; 4th, 1964, Thelma Bradford. *Educ:* Hotchkiss Sch., Lakeville, Connecticut; Yale and Columbia Univs. BS Yale, 1921; student, Columbia, 1922. Mining Engineer; Reporter for The New Yorker (mag.), 1925, Managing Editor, 1926–29; Assoc. Editor, Fortune Magazine, 1930, Managing Editor, 1930–35; Vice-Pres. and General Manager, Time, Inc., publishing Time, Life, Fortune, etc. Publisher of Time Magazine, 1937–39; resigned to organise and finance company subsequently to publish PM (NY daily newspaper); Editor, PM, 1940–46. Enlisted as Private, Engr. Amphibian Command, US Army, 1942; advanced to Lt-Col, Gen. Staff Corps; served overseas, 1943–45; in Africa, England, Italy, France, Belgium, Luxembourg and Germany, on staffs of Gen. Jacob Devers, Field-Marshal Montgomery, and Gen. Omar Bradley. Legion of Merit, Bronze Arrowhead for assault landing in Normandy, and 7 campaign stars; Officer of Order of Crown (Belgium); returned to Editorship of PM; resigned, 1946; Pres., The RJ Company, Inc., 1948–59, investments, principally newspapers; President and Director of numerous newspapers and publishing concerns, in RI, NY, NJ, Pa, Conn, NH, Mich, Ohio, Vt and Mass; Pres., General Publications, Inc. (newspaper management), 1959–75; Pres., Ingersoll Publications Co., 1975–82; Director: Central Home Trust Co., Eliz., NJ, 1963–67; Public Welfare Foundn, Washington DC, 1970–74; Recording for the Blind Foundn, NY, 1973–74. Hon. DHum Boston, 1980. *Publications:* Report on England, 1940; America is Worth Fighting For, 1941; Action on All Fronts, 1941; The Battle is the Pay-Off, 1944; Top Secret, 1946; The Great Ones, 1948; Wine of Violence, 1951; Point of Departure, 1961. *Address:* (home) Cornwall Bridge, Conn 06754, USA. *Club:* The Brook (NYC). *Died 8 March 1985.*

**INGLE, Charles Fiennes;** Barrister-at-law; a Recorder (formerly Recorder of Penzance), 1964–78, retired; *b* 30 April 1908; *s* of F. S. Ingle and M. A. Ingle, Bath; *m* 1933, Mary (*née* Linaker); one *s* one *d. Educ:* Oundle; Jesus Coll., Cambridge (MA). Called to Bar, Inner Temple, 1931; Western Circuit; Dep. Chm., Devon QS, 1963–71. Sqdn Ldr, RAFVR, 1940–45. *Recreations:* yachting, shooting. *Address:* West Soar, Malborough, Devon. *T:* Galmpton 561334. *Died 5 Nov. 1983.*

**INGLEFIELD, Col Sir John (Frederick) C.;** *see* Crompton-Inglefield.

**INGLEFIELD-WATSON, Captain Sir Derrick William Inglefield;** *see* Watson.

**INGLESON, Philip,** CMG 1945; MBE 1926; MC 1918; President, Grampian Furniture Ltd (formerly Revel Industrial Products Ltd), 1973–74 (Chairman, 1958–72); retired; *b* 14 June 1892; *s* of William Frederick and Phoebe H. Ingleson; *m* 1921, Gwendoline, *o d* of Col R. Fulton, 1st KGVO Gurkha Rifles, IA; one *d. Educ:* Rossall Sch.; Queens' Coll., Cambridge (Senior Classical Scholar; MA 1981). Served European War (France), 1914–19, Royal Fusiliers and Staff Captain 198th Infantry Brigade 66 Div. (MC, despatches); joined Sudan Political Service, 1919; Governor Halfa Province 1931; Governor Berber Province, 1932; Governor Bahr-el-Ghazal Province, 1934; Governor Darfur Province, 1935–44; Ministry of Production, 1944; Board of Trade, 1945; UK Trade Commissioner in Queensland, 1949–53, and in Western Australia, 1954–56; Chm., Chair Centre Ltd, 1958–72. Order of the Nile, 4th Class, 1929; Order of the Nile, 3rd Class 1935. *Recreation:* travel. *Address:* 36

Campden Hill Court, W8. *T:* 01–937 8993.
*Died 20 Jan. 1985.*

**INGLEWOOD, 1st Baron,** *cr* 1964; **William Morgan Fletcher-Vane,** TD; DL; *b* 12 April 1909; *s* of late Col Hon. W. L. Vane and Lady Katharine Vane; assumed name of Fletcher-Vane by deed poll, 1931; *m* 1949, Mary (*d* 1982) (late Sen. Comdr ATS (despatches), JP, Mem. LCC, 1949–52, Cumberland CC, 1961–74), *e d* of Major Sir Richard G. Proby, 1st Bt, MC; two *s. Educ:* Charterhouse; Trinity Coll., Cambridge (MA). ARICS. 2nd Lt 6 Bn Durham Light Infantry, 1928; served Overseas: 1940, France, with 50 (N) Div. (despatches); 1941–44, Middle East with Durham LI and on the Staff, Lt-Col, 1943. MP (C) for Westmorland, 1945–64; Parliamentary Private Sec. to Minister of Agriculture, 1951–54, to Joint Under-Sec. of State, Foreign Office, 1954–55, and to Minister of Health, Dec. 1955–July 1956; Joint Parliamentary Secretary: Min. of Pensions and National Insurance, 1958–60; Min. of Agriculture, Oct. 1960–July 1962. DL Westmorland 1946, Cumbria 1974–85; Landowner; Mem. Chartered Surveyors Institution; formerly Mem. of Historic Buildings Council for England; Leader of UK Delegation to World Food Congress (FAO) Washington, June 1963. Chm., Anglo-German Assoc., 1973–84 (Vice-Chm., 1966–73). Order of the Phoenix, Greece; Order of the Cedar, Lebanon; Commander, German Order of Merit, 1977. *Heir: s* Hon. (William) Richard Fletcher-Vane, MA (Cantab) [*b* 31 July 1951; *m* 1986, Cressida, *y d* of late Desmond Pemberton-Pigott and of Mrs Pemberton-Pigott; one *d*. Called to the Bar, Lincoln's Inn, 1975; ARICS]. *Address:* Hutton-in-the-Forest, Penrith, Cumbria CA11 9TH. *T:* Skelton 207; 21 Stack House, Cundy Street, Ebury Street, SW1W 9JS. *T:* 01–730 1559. *Club:* Travellers'.
*Died 22 June 1989.*

**INGLIS, Allan,** CMG 1962; Director of Public Works, Hong Kong, retired; *b* 25 Feb. 1906; *m* 1936, Constance M. Maclachlan; two *d. Educ:* Royal High Sch., Edinburgh; Heriot-Watt Coll., Edinburgh. Chartered Civil Engineer (FICE). Joined Colonial Service, 1930; Engrg Surveyor, Singapore, SS, 1930; Asst Engr, 1935, Exec. Engr, 1939, Malaya. Served War of 1939–45, Major Royal Engineers. Sen. Exec. Engr, 1946, State Engr, 1953, Malaya. *Address:* 26 Cramond Road South, Edinburgh EH4 6AA. *T:* 031-336 1695.
*Died 17 June 1984.*

**INGLIS, Maj.-Gen. Sir (John) Drummond,** KBE 1945 (OBE 1939); CB 1944; MC 1916; *b* 4 May 1895; *s* of late Major Thomas Drummond Inglis, RA, Colchester; *m* 1st, 1919, Monica (*d* 1976), *d* of late Philip Percival Whitcombe, MB, London; one *s* (one *d* decd); 2nd, 1977, Joan Proudlove, *d* of Pieter Johannes Jacobus Vrint. *Educ:* Wellington Coll.; RMA, Woolwich. 2nd Lt RE 1914; served European War, 1914–19 (4th Class Order of White Eagle of Serbia with swords, Bt Major); Palestine, 1937–39 (despatches, OBE); War of 1939–45, France, Belgium, Holland, Germany; Chief Engineer, 21st Army Group, 1943–45 (Officer of the Legion of Honour, Croix de Guerre with palms, Knight Grand Officer of the Order of Orange Nassau with swords); retired pay, 1945; Col Comdt RE, 1955–60. *Address:* Flat 1, Henley House, 8 Devonshire Place, Eastbourne, East Sussex BN21 4AF. *Club:* Army and Navy.
*Died 7 Jan. 1985.*

**INGOLDBY, Eric,** CIE 1943; *b* 7 Jan. 1892; *m* 1925, Zyvee Elizabeth Taylor (*d* 1954); two *s*. Served European War of 1914–18, RGA. Joined Indian State Railways, 1921; Chief Mechanical Engineer, GIP Railway, 1934; Dir Railway Board, India, 1935–40; Chief Controller of Standardisation, Railway Board, Govt of India, 1941–47; retired 1949; mem. firm of Rendel, Palmer and Tritton, consulting engineers, 1947–55. *Address:* 5 Lynne Court, Chesham Road, Guildford, Surrey. *T:* Guildford 570878.
*Died 13 May 1986.*

**INMAN, Peter Donald,** CBE 1977; TD 1946; DL; Chief Executive/Clerk, Lancashire County Council, 1974–76; *b* 21 Oct. 1916; *s* of Robert and Sarah Inman, Bradford; *m* 1947, Beatrice Dallas (*d* 1983); one *s* one *d. Educ:* Bradford Grammar Sch.; Leeds Univ. (LLB). Solicitor. Served War, 1939–45: KOYLI; France, India and Germany (Major). Asst Solicitor, Dewsbury, 1946; Lancashire County Council: Asst Solicitor, 1948; Dep. Clerk, 1951; Clerk, 1973–74. DL Lancs 1974. Clerk of Lieutenancy, Lancs, 1974. Hon. Treasurer, Lancs Youth Clubs Assoc., 1948–68, Vice-Pres. 1968. *Recreations:* golf, gardening. *Address:* 1 Beech Drive, Fulwood, Preston PR2 3NB. *T:* Preston 862361.
*Died 1 May 1987.*

**INMAN, Rt. Rev. Thomas George Vernon;** *b* 1904; *s* of late Capt. William James Inman, RE, Durban; *m* 1st, 1935, Alma Coker (*d* 1970), *d* of late Advocate Duncan Stuart Campbell, Bulawayo, Rhodesia; three *s* (one *d* decd); 2nd, 1971, Gladys Marjory Hannah, MB, ChB (she *m* 1st, 1947, Charles William Lysaght, who *d* 1969), *d* of late David Rees Roberts, Cape Town. *Educ:* Selwyn Coll., Cambridge; St Augustine's Coll., Canterbury, MA 1932. Deacon, 1930; priest, 1931; Asst Missioner, Wellington Coll. Mission, Walworth, 1930–33; Curate of Estcourt, Natal, 1933; Curate of St

Paul, Durban, 1933–37, Vicar, 1937–51; Canon of Natal, 1944–51; Archdeacon of Durban, 1950–51; Bishop of Natal, 1951–74; retired, 1974. Dean, Province of S Africa, 1966–74. Chaplain and Subprelate, Order of St John of Jerusalem, 1953. Hon. DD Univ. of the South, Tenn., USA, 1958. *Address:* PO Box 726, Durban, 4000, South Africa. *Died 4 July* 1989.

**INNES, Sir Berowald;** *see* Innes, Sir R. G. B.

**INNES of Coxton, Sir Charles (Kenneth Gordon),** 11th Bt *cr* 1686; *b* 28 Jan. 1910; *s* of Major Charles Gordon Deverell Innes (*d* 1953), and Ethel Hilda, *d* of George Earle; *S* 1973 to baronetcy of Innes of Coxton, dormant since the death of Sir George Innes, 8th Bt, 1886; *m* 1936, Margaret Colquhoun Lockhart, *d* of F. C. L. Robertson and *g d* of Sir James Colquhoun of Luss, 5th Bt; one *s* one *d*. *Educ:* Haileybury Coll., Herts. War Service, 1939–45, Royal Artillery; Captain, Ayrshire Yeomanry. *Recreations:* photography, music, art, gardening. *Heir: s* David Charles Kenneth Gordon Innes [*b* 17 April 1940; *m* 1969, Marjorie Alison, *d* of E. W. Parker; one *s* one *d*. *Educ:* Haileybury; London Univ. BScEng; ACGI]. *Address:* October Cottage, Haslemere, Surrey GU27 2LF.
*Died 27 Dec.* 1990.

**INNES, Lt-Col Sir (Ronald Gordon) Berowald,** 16th Bt *cr* 1628, of Balvenie; OBE 1943; *b* 24 July 1907; *s* of Captain J. W. G. Innes, CBE, RN (*d* 1939) and Sheila (*d* 1949), *d* of Col J. F. Forbes of Rothiemay; *S* kinsman, Sir Walter James Innes, 15th Bt, 1978; *m* 1st, 1933, Elizabeth Haughton (*d* 1958), *e d* of late Alfred Fayle; two *s* one *d*; 2nd, 1961, Elizabeth Christian, *e d* of late Lt-Col C. H. Watson, DSO, IMS. *Educ:* Harrow; RMC Camberley. Commissioned Seaforth Highlanders, 1927; PSC; served War of 1939–45; France, 1939–40; Middle East, 1941–43 (wounded); Sicily, 1943; Holland and Germany, 1944–45; GSO1 50 (Northumbrian) Div., 1942–43; GSO1 Directing Staff, Staff Coll., 1943–44; in comd 7th Bn, Seaforth Highlanders, 1945; GSO1 (Infantry), War Office, 1946–48; in comd 4th (Uganda) Bn, KAR, and OC Troops, Uganda, 1948–49; retired as Lt-Col, 1949. *Recreation:* needlepoint embroidery. *Heir: s* Peter Alexander Berowald Innes, MICE [*b* 6 Jan. 1937; *m* 1959, Julia Mary, *d* of A. S. Levesley; two *s* one *d*]. *Address:* The Loom House, Aultgowrie, by Muir of Ord, Ross-shire IV6 7XA. *T:* Urray 216. *Club:* Naval and Military.
*Died 26 May* 1988.

**INNESS, Air Cdre William Innes Cosmo,** CB 1962; OBE 1954; DL; *b* 25 March 1916; *y s* of Henry Atkinson Inness; *m* 1942, Margaret Rose Nolan, *er d* of Lt-Col P. E. Nolan, MBE, Royal Signals; two *s*. *Educ:* Richmond Sch., Yorkshire. Commissioned, RAF Coll., 1936; India, 1936–39; Iraq, 1939–41; Bomber Command, Flt, Sqdn and Station Comdr and Group Captain, Plans, 1941–45. Air Ministry Directorate-Gen. of Personnel, Brit. Bombing Survey Unit, and Directorate of Staff Duties, 1946–48; Air Attaché, Teheran, 1948–51; Sen. Personnel Staff Officer, No. 23 Gp, 1951–54; RAF Flying Coll., 1954–55; Station Comdr, St Eval, 1955–57; Dep. Asst Chief of Staff (Plans), HQ Allied Forces, Mediterranean, 1957–59; Air Officer i/c Administration, Coastal Command, 1959–62; AOC Gibraltar, 1962–65; Dir Personal Services (Provost Marshal), RAF, 1965–68, retired 1968. ADC 1966–68. Regional Comdt, London and SE, Air Cadets, 1968–81; Pres., London Wing, ATC, 1981. Liveryman, Basketmakers' Co., 1975. DL Greater London, 1973. Chevalier of the Military Order of Aviz (Portugal), 1956. *Recreation:* flying. *Address:* c/o National Westminster Bank PLC, Portland Square, Sutton-in-Ashfield, Nottingham NG17 1BA. *Clubs:* Royal Air Force, City Livery. *Died 13 April* 1986.

**INVERFORTH, 3rd Baron,** *cr* 1919, of Southgate; **(Andrew Charles) Roy Weir;** Chairman and Governing Director, Andrew Weir & Co. Ltd, since 1971; *b* 6 June 1932; *e s* of 2nd Baron Inverforth and of Iris Beryl, *d* of late Charles Vincent; *S* father, 1975; *m* 1966, (Jill) Elizabeth, *o d* of John W. Thornycroft, CBE, CEng, FIMechE; one *s* one *d*. *Educ:* Malvern College. Chairman: The Bank Line Ltd, 1971–; United Baltic Corporation Ltd, 1974–; Internat. Chamber of Shipping, 1981–; Vice-Chm., Baltic Exchange, 1981–; Director: Gen. Council of British Shipping Ltd, 1975–; London Adv. Board, Bank of New South Wales, 1982–; Anglo-American Securities Corp. PLC, 1976–; North Atlantic Securities Corp. PLC, 1976–; Spink & Son Ltd, 1978–; The City Arts Trust Ltd, 1982–, and of many other cos. Chm., Aldeburgh Festival-Snape Maltings Foundn Ltd, 1981–. Pres., Embroiderers' Guild, 1979–; Governor, St Felix Sch., Southwold, 1981–. *Heir: s* Hon. Andrew Peter Weir, *b* 16 Nov. 1966. *Address:* 27 Hyde Park Street, W2 2JS. *T:* 01-283 1266; Walber House, Walberswick, Southwold, Suffolk IP18 6TS. *T:* Southwold 723110. *Club:* Royal Automobile. *Died 6 June* 1982.

**IRELAND, Frank,** FCA; IPFA; Principal City Officer and Town Clerk, Newcastle upon Tyne, 1969–74; *b* 2 May 1909; *s* of C. A. Ireland, Clitheroe, Lancs; *m* 1935, Elsie Mary (*née* Ashworth); one *s* two *d*. *Educ:* Clitheroe Royal Grammar Sch.; Victoria Univ., Manchester BA (Com). Chartered Accountant, 1931; Hons, IMTA, 1936. Derby County Borough, 1933–37; Newcastle upon Tyne, 1937–74; City Treasurer, 1962–69. *Recreations:* music, photography.

*Address:* 61 Kenton Road, Newcastle upon Tyne NE3 4NJ. *T:* Gosforth 856930. *Died 5 Oct.* 1983.

**IRELAND, Lt-Col Gerald Blakeney De C.;** *see* De Courcy-Ireland.

**IRON, Air Cdre Douglas,** CBE 1944; *b* 1 Aug. 1893; *s* of Captain John Iron, OBE, and Anne Iron; *m* 1917, Dorothy Bentham (from whom he obtained a divorce); one *d*; *m* 1930, Mrs P. V. Sankey (from whom he obtained a divorce). *Educ:* Tudor Hall Sch., Hawkhurst. Prob. Flight Sub.-Lt RNAS Sept. 1914; Flight Lt May 1915; Acting Lt-Col GSO1 (Air) April 1918; permanent commission, RAF, as Flight Lt 1919. Sqdn Leader, 1924; Wing Comdr 1930; attended Royal Naval Staff Coll., 1935; Group Capt. 1937; Air officer i/c Administration, 4 Training Command, RCAF, Canada, with rank of Air Commodore, Dec. 1943; Air Officer Commanding 51 Group RAF, 1944–45; retired, 1945. *Recreation:* fishing. *Club:* Army and Navy. *Died 15 March* 1983.

**IRONMONGER, Sir (Charles) Ronald,** Kt 1970; Personnel Officer, GEC Traction Ltd (formerly AEI) Attercliffe, 1966–79, retired; *b* 20 Jan. 1914; *s* of late Charles and Emily Ironmonger; *m* 1938, Jessie Green (decd); one *s* one *d*. *Educ:* Huntsmans Gardens Elementary Sch., Firth Park Secondary Sch.; Sheffield. Elected Sheffield City Council, Nov. 1945; Chairman, Water Cttee, 1951–66; Leader of City Council and Chairman, Policy Cttee, 1966–74; Chm., S Yorks Local Govt Reorganisation Jt Cttee, 1972; Leader, S Yorkshire CC, 1973–79, Dep. Leader, 1979–82; Chm., Policy Cttee, 1973–79, Vice-Chm., 1979–82. Vice-Chm., AMA, 1977–78. *Recreations:* reading, sport. *Address:* Housteads, 1 Richmond Park Grove, Sheffield 13. *Died 30 Sept.* 1984.

**IRVINE, Rev. Thomas Thurstan;** *b* 19 June 1913; 5th *s* of late William Fergusson Irvine; *m* 1943, Elizabeth Marian, *er d* of late Francis More, CA, Edinburgh; five *d*. *Educ:* Shrewsbury; Magdalen Coll., Oxford. BA 2nd Class History, 1934; Diploma in Theology, 1935; MA 1938. Cuddesdon Coll., 1937; deacon, 1938, priest, 1939, St Albans; Curate, All Saints, Hertford, 1938–40; Precentor, St Ninian's Cathedral, Perth, 1940–43; Priest in charge, Lochgelly, 1943–45; Rector: Bridge of Allan, 1945–47; Callander, 1947–66; St John's, Perth, 1966–83. Examining Chaplain to Bishop of St Andrews, 1950; Dean of United Diocese of St Andrews, Dunkeld and Dunblane, 1959–82. *Recreations:* fishing, walking. *Address:* Mayfield, Gannochy Road, Perth PH2 7EF.
*Died 5 Nov.* 1985.

**IRVINE SMITH, Thomas,** OBE 1945; DL; *b* 27 Oct. 1908; *er s* of late Sir Thomas Smith and of Lady (Elsie) Smith (*née* Ledgard); *m* 1942, Mary Peters (*d* 1981). *Educ:* Fettes Coll., Edinburgh; Oriel Coll., Oxford. MA 1935. War Service, 1941–45: commnd 8th Gurkha Rifles; GHQ, MEF; ME Supply Centre, 1943; Liaison Officer with Govt of India, 1944–45; Lt-Col 1945. Business in Cawnpore, India, 1931–47; Mem. London Stock Exchange, 1949–69. Surrey County Council: Mem., 1955–77; Alderman, 1965–74; Vice-Chm., 1969–72; Chm., 1972–74; 1st Chm. of re-constituted Council, 1973–75; Chm., Surrey Educn Cttee, 1965–72. Member: Court, London Univ., 1967–78; Council, Surrey Univ., 1966–84 (Chm., 1975–79, Vice-Chm., 1980–82); Council, Royal Holloway Coll., 1970–79; Murray Cttee, London Univ., 1970–72; Governor: Ottershaw Sch., 1959–77 (Chm. 1961–72); Gordon Boys' Sch., 1965–85. DL Surrey, 1973; High Sheriff, Surrey, 1976–77. DUniv Surrey, 1984. *Recreation:* gardening. *Address:* Thorney, Onslow Road, Sunningdale, Berks SL5 0HW. *T:* Ascot 22334. *Died 26 Nov.* 1985.

**IRVING OF DARTFORD, Baron** *cr* 1979 (Life Peer), of Dartford in the County of Kent; **Sydney Irving;** PC 1969; DL; *b* 1 July 1918; *s* of Sydney Irving, Newcastle upon Tyne; *m* 1942, Mildred, *d* of Charlton Weedy, Morpeth, Northumberland; one *s* one *d* (and one *s* decd). *Educ:* Pendower Sch., Newcastle upon Tyne; London School of Economics, University of London. BSc (Econ.); DipEd. War Service, 1939–46: West Yorks Regt, Major. Chairman Southern Regional Council of Labour Party, 1965–67. Mem., Dartford Borough Council, 1952– (Chm. 1973–74); Mem. North-West Kent Divisional Executive, Kent Education Cttee, 1952–74. MP (Lab and Co-op) Dartford, 1955–70 and Feb. 1974–1979; Opposition Whip (S and S Western), 1959–64; Treasurer of the Household and Deputy Chief Government Whip, 1964–66; Dep. Chm. of Ways and Means, 1966–68; Chm. of Ways and Means, and Deputy Speaker, 1968–70; Chairman Select Committees: on Procedure, 1974–79; on Direct Elections to EEC, 1976–77; Chm., Manifesto Gp, 1976–77; Member: Cttee of Privileges, 1974–79; Select Cttee on Members' Interests, 1974–79; Select Cttee on the Member for Walsall, 1975; Liaison Cttee, Parly Lab Party, 1976–79. Mem. CPA delegations: to Hong Kong and Ceylon, 1958; to Council of Europe and WEU, 1963–64; to Canada, 1974; Leader All Party Delegn: to Malta, 1965; to Israel, 1975; to Australia, 1978. Mem. Exec. Cttee, Council European Municipalities 1972–77; Vice-Pres.,, IULA/ CEMR, 1977–. Chm., Dartford and Darenth Hosp. Management Cttee, 1972–74; Kent County Jt Cttee Chairman, 1967–77; Pres., Dartford and Dist Chamber of Commerce, 1984–. Vice-Chm., Nat. Assoc. of CAB, 1979–85. Pres., Thames-side Assoc. of Teachers,

NUT, 1955; Mem. Min. of Education's Adv. Cttee on Handicapped Children, 1957–67; a Dep. Pro-Chancellor, Univ. of Kent, 1968–71 (Mem. Council, 1974–); Dir, Foundn Fund, Univ. of Kent, 1971–74. Chm. of Trustees, Industry and Parlt Trust, 1982–. DL Kent, 1976. *Address:* 10 Tynedale Close, Dartford, Kent. *T:* 25105.
*Died 18 Dec.* 1989.

**IRVING, David Blair;** Chairman, London Electricity Board, 1956–68; *b* 9 Nov. 1903; *s* of late Mitchell B. Irving, Sorn, Ayrshire, and Mary Ross, Broadford, Isle of Skye; *m* 1933, Isabel Gibson; one *s. Educ:* Ayr Academy. BSc Hons (London), 1923. British Thomson-Houston Co. Ltd; trained Rugby; subseq. positions in London, Sheffield, Bombay and Calcutta. Joined Central Electricity Bd, 1932, and London Electricity Bd at Vesting Day, 1 April 1948: Chief Engineer, 1949–53; Dep. Chm., 1953–56. MIEE, 1945; FIEE, 1966; Mem. Société des Ingénieurs Civils de France, 1949–70; Mem. Royal Institution, 1957–69. Chm., British Electrical Development Assoc., 1960–61; Chm., Power Division IEE, 1962–63. Governor, Ashridge Management Coll., 1965–68. *Publications:* papers to British and internat. engineering and scientific bodies. *Recreation:* golf. *Address:* Nettlecombe, Poughill, Bude, North Cornwall. *T:* Bude 3496. *Club:* Caledonian.
*Died 9 June* 1986.

**IRVING, Rear-Adm. Sir Edmund (George),** KBE 1966 (OBE 1944); CB 1962; Hydrographer of the Navy, 1960–66, retired; *b* 5 April 1910; *s* of George Clerk Irving, British North Borneo, and Ethel Mary Frances (*née* Poole), Kimberley, SA; *m* 1st, 1936, Margaret Scudamore Edwards (*d* 1974); one *s* one *d*; 2nd, 1979, Esther Rebecca Ellison. *Educ:* St Anthony's, Eastbourne; RN College, Dartmouth. Joined HMS Royal Oak, as Cadet and Midshipman, 1927; Sub-Lieut's Courses, 1930–31; HMS Kellett Surveying Service, Dec. 1931 (various surveying ships); despatches, 1941 (minelaying and surveys, N Atlantic), 1943 (invasion of Sicily and Italy); HMS Franklin, in command, 1944; Hydrographic Dept, 1946; HMS Sharpshooter, in command, 1948; Hydrographic Dept, 1949; HMS Dalrymple, in command, 1950; HMS Vidal, in command, 1953; Hydrographic Dept, Asst Hydrographer, 1954; HMS Vidal, in command, Oct. 1956; Hydrographic Dept, Asst Hydrographer, 1959. Acting Conservator of the River Mersey, 1975–85. ADC, 1960. Trustee, Nat. Maritime Museum, 1972–81. FRGS (Pres., 1969–71); FRICS; FRSA. Patron's Medal, RGS, 1976. *Recreation:* golf. *Address:* Camer Green, Meopham, Kent DA13 0XR. *T:* Meopham (0474) 813253. *Club:* Army and Navy.
*Died 1 Oct.* 1990.

**IRVING, Laurence Henry Forster,** OBE; RDI 1939; *b* 11 April 1897; *s* of late H. B. Irving, actor and author; *m* 1920, Rosalind Woolner (*d* 1978); one *s* one *d. Educ:* by Thomas Pellatt; Royal Academy Schools. Served in RNAS and RAF, 1914–19 (Croix de Guerre, France); rejoined RAF Oct. 1939; served on Staff of British Air Forces in France, 1940 (despatches), and in 2nd Tactical Air Force, France, Belgium, 1943–44. Dir of the Times Publishing Co., 1946–62. Exhibited pictures at Royal Academy; held four exhibitions at the Fine Art Soc., 1925, 1928, 1936, 1950, and at Agnew and Sons, 1957; Art Dir to Douglas Fairbanks, 1928 and 1929, for film productions of The Iron Mask and The Taming of the Shrew; has designed a number of stage and film productions, including Pygmalion, Lean Harvest, The Good Companions, Punchinello, The First Gentleman, Marriage à la Mode, Hamlet (Old Vic), 1950, Man and Superman, 1951; The Happy Marriage, 1952; Pygmalion, 1953; The Wild Duck, 1955; produced and designed film production of Lefanu's Uncle Silas. Master of Faculty, RDI, 1963–65. *Publications:* Windmills and Waterways, 1927; Henry Irving: The Actor and his World, 1951; The Successors, 1967; The Precarious Crust, 1971; Great Interruption, 1983; edited and illustrated: The Maid of Athens; Bligh's narrative of The Mutiny of the Bounty; A Selection of Hakluyt's Voyages; illustrated: Masefield's Philip the King; Conrad's The Mirror of the Sea; St Exupéry's Flight to Arras. *Address:* The Lea, Wittersham, Kent. *Club:* Garrick.
*Died 23 Oct.* 1988.

**IRWIN, Francis (Charles);** QC 1974; a Recorder (formerly Recorder of Folkestone), since 1971; *b* 5 June 1928; *s* of late R. Stanley Irwin; *m* 1955, Rosalind Derry Wykes, *d* of late Canon W. M. Wykes, Sedgefield, Co. Durham; four *s* one *d. Educ:* Glasgow Academy; Queen's Coll., Oxford (Scholar, BA). Served in Army, 1946–48. Called to Bar, Middle Temple, 1953, Bencher, 1984; SE Circuit. Prosecuting Counsel, GPO (SE Circuit), 1964–69; Dep. Chm., W Suffolk QS, 1967–71. Contested (C): Bridgeton Div. of Glasgow, 1950; Small Heath Div. of Birmingham, 1951. *Address:* 9 King's Bench Walk, EC4Y 7DX. *T:* 071–353 7202.
*Died 31 May* 1990.

**IRWIN, Sir James (Campbell),** Kt 1971; OBE 1945; ED 1947; psc; FRIBA, LFRAIA; Partner in Woods, Bagot, Laybourne-Smith & Irwin, Architects, Adelaide, 1930–74; *b* 23 June 1906; *s* of Francis James and Margaret Irwin; *m* 1933, Kathleen Agnes (*d* 1989), *d* of G. W. Orr, Sydney; one *s* one *d. Educ:* Queen's Sch., N Adelaide; St Peter's Coll., Adelaide; St Mark's Coll., Univ. of Adelaide (Hon.

Fellow, 1973); Staff Coll., Haifa. Served War, AIF, on active service in Middle East, New Guinea, Philippine Islands, 1940–46; Lt-Col RAA. Col Comdt, RAA, 1966–71. Mem. Adelaide City Council, 1935–72 (except for war years); Lord Mayor of Adelaide, 1963–66; Mem. Nat. Capital Planning Cttee, Canberra, 1964–70. President: RAIA, 1962–63; Adelaide Festival of Arts, 1964–66 (Chm. 1969–73); SA Sch. of Art, 1966–72; Home for Incurables, 1966–82; Pioneers Assoc. of S Australia, 1968–73. Chm., Co-op. Foundn, 1979–86. *Publication:* The Irwin Family: Junior South Australian Branch, 1977. *Address:* 124 Brougham Place, North Adelaide, SA 5006, Australia. *T:* 2672839, *Fax:* (08) 2672307. *Clubs:* Adelaide, Naval Military and Air Force of SA (Adelaide).
*Died 24 July* 1990.

**ISAAC, Sir Neil,** Kt 1986; QSO 1982; JP; Managing Director, Isaac Group of Companies; *b* 29 Dec. 1915; *s* of Ernest Rupert Isaac and Louisa Isaac; *m* 1946, Jun. Comdr Diana Gilbert, ATS. *Educ:* Prep. Sch.; Timaru Boys' High Sch. Served, 2NZEF, 1941; commnd British Army, 1944; served in Greece, Italy and India, until 1947 (Major). Formed Isaac Construction Group, 1950. Works Comr, Rolleston (New Town), 1972. JP 1970. *Recreation:* salmon farming. *Address:* Clifton, McArthurs Road, Harewood, Christchurch, New Zealand. *T:* (03) 599–145. *Club:* Canterbury (Christchurch, NZ).
*Died 8 May* 1987.

**ISAACS, Evelyn M., (Mrs Nathan Isaacs);** *see* Lawrence, E. M.

**ISHERWOOD, Christopher William Bradshaw-;** author; *b* High Lane, Cheshire, 26 Aug. 1904; *s* of Lt-Col Francis B. Isherwood and Kathleen Machell-Smith. *Educ:* Repton Sch.; Corpus Christi, Cambridge. Private Tutor in London, 1926–27; Medical Student, Kings, London, 1928–29; Teacher of English, Berlin, 1930–33; Journalism, etc. in London, 1934–36; Film-Script work for Gaumont-British; went to China with W. H. Auden, 1938; worked for Metro-Goldwyn-Mayer, 1940, American Friends Service Cttee, 1941–42; editor of Vedanta and the West, 1943. Became a US citizen, 1946; travelled in South America, 1947–48. Elected Mem. US Nat. Inst. of Arts and Letters, 1949. Guest Prof., Los Angeles State Coll., and at University of California, Santa Barbara, 1959–62; Regents' Prof., University of California, 1965–66. Brandeis Medal for Fiction, 1975. *Publications: fiction:* All the Conspirators, 1928; The Memorial, 1932; Mr Norris Changes Trains, 1935; Goodbye to Berlin, 1939 (I Am a Camera, play by John van Druten, perf. US 1951, and Cabaret, musical by Joe Masteroff, John Kander and Fred Ebb, perf. US 1966, both based on stories from Goodbye to Berlin); Prater Violet, 1945; The World in The Evening, 1954; Down There on a Visit, 1962; A Single Man, 1964; A Meeting by the River, 1967 (play, adapted from the novel, by C. I. and Don Bachardy, perf. US, 1972); The Berlin of Sally Bowles, 1975; *biography:* Ramakrishna and his Disciples, 1965; *autobiography:* Lions and Shadows, 1938; Kathleen and Frank, 1971; Christopher and His Kind, 1977; My Guru and His Disciple, 1980; October (with D. Bachardy), 1983; *plays:* The Dog Beneath the Skin (with W. H. Auden), 1935; Ascent of F6 (with W. H. Auden), 1937; On the Frontier (with W. H. Auden), 1938; *travel:* Journey to a War (with W. H. Auden), 1939; The Condor and the Cows, 1949; *miscellaneous:* Exhumations, 1966; People One Ought to Know (nonsense poems), 1982; *translation:* (with Swami Prabhavananda) The Bhagavad-Gita, 1944; (with Swami Prabhavananda) Shankara's Crest-Jewel of Discrimination, 1947; Baudelaire's Intimate Journals, 1947; (with Swami Prabhavananda) How to Know God: the Yoga Aphorisms of Patanjali, 1953. *Recreations:* usual. *Address:* 145 Adelaide Drive, Santa Monica, Calif 90402, USA.
*Died 4 Jan.* 1986.

**ISHERWOOD, Rt. Rev. Harold,** LVO 1955; OBE 1959; Auxiliary Bishop, Diocese of Gibraltar in Europe, since 1977; an Assistant Bishop, Diocese of Canterbury, since 1978; *b* 23 June 1907; *s* of James and Margaret Ellen Isherwood; *m* 1940, Hannah Mary Walters. *Educ:* Selwyn Coll., Cambridge; Ely Theol Coll. BA 1938, MA 1946. Deacon 1939; priest 1940; Curate of Beeston, Notts, 1939–43; Chaplain: Nat. Nautical Sch., Portishead, 1943–51; Helsinki and Moscow, 1951–54; Oslo, 1954–59; Brussels, 1959–70; Vicar General, Dio. Gibraltar and Jurisdiction of North and Central Europe, 1970–75; Canon of Gibraltar, 1971–74; Asst Bishop, Dio. Gibraltar, 1974–77. *Recreations:* music, cricket, Rugby and Association football, tennis. *Address:* 16A Burgate, Canterbury, Kent CT1 2HG. *T:* Canterbury 452790. *Club:* Royal Commonwealth Society.
*Died 19 April* 1989.

**ISMAY, Sir George,** KBE 1947; CB 1939; MM 1918; *b* 1891; *s* of late George Ismay, Carlisle; *m* 1919, Jeanette May, *d* of John Lloyd, Tredegar, Mon; two *d. Educ:* private schools, Carlisle. Entered Treasury, 1911; Asst Sec., 1934; Sec. Macmillan Cttee on Finance and Industry, 1929–31; Comptroller and Accountant General, GPO, 1937; Asst Dir-General, 1942; Deputy Dir-Gen., General Post Office, 1947–52; Dir, Woolwich Equitable Building Society, 1952–72; served European War, 1915–19, in Queen's Westminster Rifles (MM); served in France, Salonika and Palestine campaigns, later in France again, in final advance. *Address:* Newstead, 105 Golden Avenue, Angmering-on-Sea, West Sussex BN16 1QT. *T:* Rustington 2855.                          *Died* 20 *May* 1984.

**ISPAHANI, Mirza Abol Hassan;** *b* 23 Jan. 1902; *s* of late Mirza Mohamed Ispahani and late Sakina Sultan; *m* 1st, 1930, Ameneh Sultan Shushtary; two *s* one *d*; 2nd, 1954, Ghamar Azimi. *Educ:* St John's Coll., Cambridge. Joined family business of M. M. Ispahani, 1925; was Dir of M. M. Ispahani Ltd, and other business undertakings; Pres., Muslim Chamber of Commerce, Calcutta; Leader, Indian Trade Delegation to Middle East, 1947. Elected to Calcutta Corporation, 1933; resigned to work for introduction of separate electorates in Calcutta Corp., 1935, re-elected, 1940, Dep. Mayor, 1941–42; Mem. Bengal Legislative Assembly, 1937–47; Mem. of All India Muslim League Working Cttee until end of 1947; Pakistan Constituent Assembly; represented Muslim League at New York Herald Tribune Forum, 1946; toured US as Personal Representative of Quaid-i-Azam, M. A. Jinnah; Ambassador of Pakistan to USA, 1947–52; Dep. Leader, Pakistan Delegn to UN, 1947; Leader Pakistan Delegn to Havana Conf. on Trade and Employment, 1947; Mem., Pakistan Delegn to UN (Jammu and Kashmir). High Comr for Pakistan in the UK, 1952–54; Minister of Industries and Commerce, 1954–55; Minister of Industries, Jan.–Aug. 1955; resigned and reverted to business; mem., Supreme Council, National Reconstruction Movement of Pakistan; Ambassador to Afghanistan, 1973. Interested in sports, journalism and welfare work. *Publications:* 27 Days in China, 1960; Leningrad to Samarkand, 1961; Quaid-e-Azam Jinnah as I knew him, 2nd rev. edn, 1967; Quaid-e-Azam Mohammad Ali Jinnah—Ispahani Correspondence, 1936–48, 1977. *Recreations:* reading, writing. *Address:* 2 Reay Road, Karachi, Pakistan. *T:* 510665.
                                 *Died* 18 *Nov.* 1981.

**ISSERLIS, Alexander Reginald;** Burford Branch Chairman, West Oxfordshire Conservative Association; *b* 18 May 1922; *y s* of Isaak Isserlis, Ilford, Essex; *m* 1949, Eleanor Mary Ord, *d* of Prof. R. D. Laurie, Aberystwyth; two *d*. *Educ:* Ilford High Sch.; Keble Coll., Oxford. British and Indian Army, 1942–46. Entered Civil Service, 1947. Principal, Min. of Health, 1950; Principal Private Secretary: to Lord President of the Council and Minister for Science, 1960–61; to Minister of Housing and Local Govt, 1962; Asst Sec., Min. of Housing and Local Govt, 1963; Under-Secretary: Cabinet Office, 1969; Min. of Housing and Local Government, 1969–70; Principal Private Secretary to the Prime Minister, 1970; Asst Under-Sec. of State, Home Office, 1970–72; Dir, Centre for Studies in Social Policy, 1972–77; Dir of Investigations, Office of Parly Comr for Administration, 1977–80; Sen. Res. Fellow, Policy Studies Inst., 1980–82. *Publications:* Conversations on Policy, 1984; occasional

articles in Policy Studies. *Recreations:* walking, gardening. *Address:* Rose and Crown Cottage, Upton, Burford, Oxon. *T:* Burford 3434. *Club:* Farmers'.                        *Died* 20 *Dec.* 1986.

**ISSIGONIS, Sir Alec (Arnold Constantine),** Kt 1969; CBE 1964; RDI 1964; FRS 1967; Advanced Design Consultant, British Leyland (Austin-Morris) Ltd, since 1972; *b* Smyrna, 18 Nov. 1906; British citizen. *Educ:* Battersea Polytechnic, London (Engrg Dip.). Draughtsman, Rootes Motors Ltd, 1933–36; Suspension Engineer, Morris Motors Ltd, 1936, subsequently Chief Engineer; Deputy Engineering Co-ordinator and Chief Engineer, British Motor Corporation, 1957–61; Technical Director, 1961; Dir of R&D, BMC later British Leyland (Austin-Morris) Ltd, 1961–72; designs include: Morris Minor, 1948; Mini-Minor and Austin Seven, 1959; Morris 1100, 1962. Leverhulme Medal, Royal Society, 1966.
                                 *Died* 2 *Oct.* 1988.

**IVES, Robert;** a Recorder, 1963–77 (formerly Recorder of Bury St Edmunds); *b* 25 Aug. 1906; *o s* of Robert Ives; *m* 1931, Evelyn Harriet Hairby Alston (*d* 1965), *er d* of Rev. F. S. Alston; two *d*; *m* 1966, Vera Bowack, *widow* of Pilot Officer N. H. Bowack. *Educ:* privately; Gonville and Caius Coll., Cambridge (MA). Called to Bar, Gray's Inn, 1928. War Service, 1940–45: RASC and Judge Advocate General's Dept. Judge of Norwich Guildhall Court of Record, 1952–71; Dep. Chm., Norfolk QS, 1967–71. Chairman: Mental Health Review Tribunal (E Anglia Region), 1960–63; Agricultural Land Tribunal (Eastern Area), 1961–79; Mem. panel of Chairmen of Medical Appeal Tribunals, 1969–78. *Recreations:* garden, photography. *Address:* Erpingham House, Erpingham, Norfolk NR11 7QD.                       *Died* 6 *Sept.* 1985.

**IVINS, Prof. John Derek,** CBE 1983; Professor of Agriculture, University of Nottingham, since 1958; *b* Eccleshall, Staffs, 11 March 1923; *s* of Alfred Ivins and Ann Ivins (*née* Holland); *m* 1952, Janet Alice Whitehead, BSc; one *s* one *d*. *Educ:* Wolstanton County Grammar Sch., Newcastle, Staffs. BSc Reading 1944, MSc 1951; PhD Nottingham 1954. Technical Officer, Seed Production Cttee of Nat. Inst. of Agricultural Botany, 1944–46; Regional Trials Officer, Nat. Inst. of Agricultural Botany, 1946–48; Nottingham University: Lectr in Agriculture, 1948–58; Dean: Faculty of Agriculture and Horticulture, 1962–65; Faculty of Agricl Sci., 1976–79; Deputy Vice-Chancellor, 1969–74. Member: UK Seeds Exec., 1973–(Chm., 1978–); Council, NIAB, 1966–(Chm., 1974–75); UGC sub-cttee, Agriculture and Veterinary Studies, 1975–81. FRAgS 1973. *Publications:* papers in technical and agricultural journals. *Recreations:* shooting, gardening. *Address:* University of Nottingham School of Agriculture, Sutton Bonington, near Loughborough. *T:* Nottingham 506101.
                                 *Died* 22 *April* 1986.

# J

**JACK, Sir Daniel (Thomson),** Kt 1966; CBE 1951; Hon. LLD Glasgow; MA; Chairman, Air Transport Licensing Board, 1961–70; David Dale Professor of Economics, University of Durham, King's College, Newcastle upon Tyne, 1935–61; Sub-Rector, King's College, 1950–55; *b* 18 Aug. 1901; *m* 1st, 1945, Nan (*d* 1949), *widow* of Prof. John Dall, Queen's Univ., Canada; 2nd, 1954, Elizabeth Witter Stewart (*d* 1970), Kingston, Ont. *Educ:* Bellahouston Academy, Glasgow; University of Glasgow. Lecturer in Political Economy, University of Glasgow, 1923–28; Lecturer in Political Economy, University of St Andrews, 1928–35. *Publications:* The Economics of the Gold Standard, 1925; The Restoration of European Currencies, 1927; International Trade, 1931; The Crises of 1931, 1931; Currency and Banking, 1932; Studies in Economic Warfare, 1940; Economic Survey of Sierra Leone, 1958; Report on Industrial Relations in the Sisal Industry, 1959; Report on Wage Fixing Machinery in Tanganyika, 1959; (jtly) Economic Survey of Nyasaland, 1959; articles in various journals.
*Died* 15 Dec. 1984.

**JACK, James,** CBE 1967; JP; General Secretary, Scottish Trades Union Congress, 1963–75; retired; Member: Scottish Postal Board, 1972–79; Board of the Crown Agents, 1975–77; *b* 6 Dec. 1910; *s* of late Andrew M. Jack and late Margaret Reid; *m* 1936; one *s. Educ:* Auchinraith Primary Sch., Blantyre; St John's Gram. Sch., Hamilton. Chm., Glasgow N and E Cttee, Manpower Services Commn, 1975–79; Member: Scottish Economic Council, 1964–76; Scottish Oil Develt Council, 1974–76; Scottish Develt Agency, 1975–78; Lanarkshire Health Bd, 1975–83; Employment Appeal Tribunal, 1976–83. JP Lanark. *Address:* 7 Stonefield Place, Blantyre, Glasgow G72 9TH. *T:* Blantyre 823304.
*Died* 28 Feb. 1987.

**JACKLING, Sir Roger William,** GCMG 1976 (KCMG 1965; CMG 1955); HM Diplomatic Service, retired; *b* 10 May 1913; *s* of P. Jackling, OBE, and Lucy Jackling; *m* 1938, Joan Tustin; two *s* (and one *s* decd). *Educ:* Felsted. DPA, London Univ., 1932; Solicitor, Supreme Court, 1935; Actg Vice-Consul, New York, 1940; Commercial Sec., Quito, 1942; 2nd Sec., Washington, 1943; 1st Sec., 1945; transf. Foreign Office, 1947; seconded to Cabinet Office, 1950 (Asst Sec.); Counsellor (commercial), The Hague, 1951; Economic and Financial Adviser to UK High Commr, Bonn; and UK commercial rep. in Germany, 1953; Minister (Economic), British Embassy, Bonn, 1955; Counsellor, British Embassy, Washington, 1957–59; Asst Under-Sec. of State, FO, 1959–63; Dep. Permanent UK Rep. to United Nations, 1963–67 (with personal rank of Ambassador from 1965); Dep. Under-Sec. of State, FO, 1967–68; Ambassador to Federal Republic of Germany, 1968–72; Leader, UK Delegn to UN Conf. on Law of the Sea, 1973–75. Chm., Bd of Trustees, Anglo-German Foundn for Study of Industrial Society, 1973–77; Mem., Chairmen's Panel, CS Selection Bd, 1974–84. *Recreations:* gardening, golf. *Address:* 37 Boundary Road, St John's Wood, NW8. *Club:* Travellers'.
*Died* 23 Nov. 1986.

**JACKMAN, Frank Downer,** CMG 1964; Chairman, Bitumax Pty Ltd, 1968–72; Commissioner of Highways and Director of Local Government for South Australia, 1958–66; *b* 14 May 1901; *s* of Arthur Joseph and Adela Mary Jackman; *m* 1930, Elaine Jean Nairn; two *d. Educ:* Prince Alfred Coll.; University of Adelaide. BE (Civil Engrg) 1923; FSASM 1923. Joined Engineer-in-Chief's Dept, SA Govt, 1923; transferred to Highways and Local Govt Dept, 1929; Asst Engr, 1929–37; District Engr, 1937–49; Chief Engr, 1949–58. MIE Aust., 1940; FCIT (MInstT), 1963. *Recreations:* fishing, racing. *Address:* 7 Crompton Drive, Wattle Park, S Australia 5066.
*Died* 23 May 1981.

**JACKSON;** *see* Mather-Jackson.

**JACKSON OF LODSWORTH,** Baroness *cr* 1976 (Life Peer), of Lodsworth, W Sussex; **Barbara Mary Jackson,** DBE 1974; author; Chairman, Institute for Environment and Development, since 1980 (President, 1973–80); *b* 23 May 1914; *o d* of Walter and Teresa Ward; *m* 1950, Comdr (later Sir) Robert Jackson, KCVO, CMG, OBE; one *s. Educ:* Convent of Jesus and Mary, Felixstowe; Lycée Molière and the Sorbonne, Paris; die Klause, Jugenheim a/d/B, Germany; Somerville Coll., Oxford (Exhibitioner); Hon. Fellow, 1978. Hons Degree in Philosophy, Politics and Economics, 1935; Univ. Extension Lecturer, 1936–39; joined staff of The Economist, 1939, as an Asst Editor; Visiting Scholar, Harvard Univ., 1957–68; Carnegie Fellow, 1959–67; Schweitzer Prof. of Internat. Economic Develt, Columbia Univ., 1968–73. Governor of Sadler's Wells and the Old Vic., 1944–53; Governor of BBC, 1946–50; Mem., Pontifical Commn for Justice and Peace, 1967–. Pres., Conservation Soc., 1973. Hon. Doctorates: Fordham Univ. and Smith Coll., 1949; Columbia Univ., 1954; Kenyon Coll. and Harvard Univ., 1957; Brandeis Univ., 1961, and others. Hon. Fellow LSE, 1976. Hon. FRIBA, 1975. Jawaharlal Nehru Prize, 1974, 1980; Albert Medal,

RSA, 1980. *Publications:* (as Barbara Ward) The International Share-Out, 1938; Turkey, 1941; The West at Bay, 1948; Policy for the West, 1951; Faith and Freedom, 1954; Interplay of East and West, 1957; Five Ideas that Change the World, 1959; India and the West, 1961; The Rich Nations and the Poor Nations, 1962; Spaceship Earth, 1966; Nationalism and Ideology, 1967; The Lopsided World, 1968; (ed) The Widening Gap, 1971; (with René Dubos) Only One Earth, 1972; The Home of Man, 1976; Progress for a Small Planet, 1980. *Recreations:* music, reading. *Address:* The Pound House, Lodsworth, Sussex GU28 9DE.
*Died* 31 May 1981.

**JACKSON, Maj.-Gen. Arthur James,** BSc; CEng; FIEE; independent consultant; *b* Barrow-upon-Humber, Lincs, 31 March 1923; *e s* of late Comdr A. J. Jackson, RD, RNR, Barrow-upon-Humber; *m* 1948, Joan Marguerite, *d* of late Trevor Lyons Relton, MBE, Whyteleafe, Surrey; two *s* two *d. Educ:* Barton Sch.; RMCS. BSc London, 1951. Joined Royal Signals, 1944; commnd 1946; served Italy and British Embassy, Belgrade, 1946–47; Austria, WO, Staff Coll., Far East, RMCS, BAOR, 1948–64; GSO1, Defence Ops Requirements Staff, MoD, 1965–66; CO 4th Div. Signal Regt, BAOR, 1967–68; psc, ptsc, psc†; Comdr (Brigadier), 12 Signal Bde, 1969–71; Dir of Telecommunications (Army), 1972–73; Dep. Comdt and Sen. Military Dir of Studies, RMCS, 1974–75; Mil. Dep., Head of Defence Sales, MoD, 1975–78, retired. Col Comdt, Royal Signals, 1978–84; Chm., Royal Signals Instn, 1979–84. *Recreations:* golf, shooting, gardening, organ music. *Address:* Roughwood House, Fleet, Hampshire; Tower Lodge, Brampford Speke, Devon. *Club:* Army and Navy.
*Died* 8 April 1987.

**JACKSON, Colin;** *see* Jackson, G. C.

**JACKSON, Prof. Derek Ainslie,** OBE; DFC; AFC; MA Cantab and Oxon; DSc Oxon; FRS 1947; Research Professor, Faculté des Sciences, Centre National de la Recherche Scientifique, Orsay, France; *b* 23 June 1906; *s* of late Sir Charles James Jackson; *m* 1st, Poppet John, *d* of Augustus John; 2nd, 1936, Hon. Pamela Freeman-Mitford (marr. diss. 1951), 2nd *d* of 2nd Baron Redesdale; 3rd, 1951, Janetta (marr. diss. 1956), *d* of Rev. G. H. Woolley, VC, OBE, MC and former wife of Robert Kee; one *d*; 4th, 1957, Consuelo Regina Maria (marr. diss. 1959), *d* of late William S. Eyre and *widow* of Prince Ernst Ratibor zu Hohenlohe Schillingsfürst; 5th, 1966, Barbara (*née* Skelton, former wife of Cyril Connolly, CBE, CLit, and of A. G. (later Lord) Weidenfeld); 6th, 1968, Marie-Christine, *d* of Baron Georges Reille. *Educ:* Rugby; Trinity Coll., Cambridge. Lectr, 1934–47, Prof. of Spectroscopy, 1947–57, University of Oxford. Served War of 1939–45, Observer in RAFVR, 1940–45. Wing Comdr 1943. Officer Legion of Merit (USA); Chevalier, Légion d'Honneur, France. *Publications:* numerous papers in Proc. Royal Soc., Jl de Physique, Phys. Review, Zeitschrift für Physik. *Address:* 20 Avenue des Figuiers, Ouchy, Lausanne, Switzerland; 19 rue Auguste Vacquerie, 75116 Paris; Chalet Mariza, 3780 Gstaad, Switzerland.
*Died* 20 Feb. 1982.

**JACKSON, Sir Donald (Edward),** Kt 1953; *b* 1892; *e s* of late Joseph Waterton Jackson, OBE, JP, MLC; *m* 1937, Amy Beatrice, *e d* of late Walter Augustus Reynolds, British Guiana; one *d. Educ:* The Middle Sch., British Guiana. LLB University of London, 1926. Called to Bar, Middle Temple, 1927; practised at Bar, British Guiana; Acting Asst Attorney-Gen., 1933, 1936, and Senior Magistrate, 1936; Registrar of Deeds, of Supreme Court and of West Indian Court of Appeal, British Guiana, 1944; Actg Puisne Judge, various periods, 1945–49; Puisne Judge, Windward and Leeward Islands, 1949; Chief Justice of Windward and Leeward Islands, and Judge of West Indian Court of Appeal, 1950–57, retired. Speaker, Legislative Council, British Guiana, 1957–61; Justice of Appeal, Federal Supreme Court of the West Indies, 1961–62; Justice of Appeal, British Caribbean Court of Appeal, 1962–66. Mem. of Commission on the Unification of the Public Services in the British Caribbean Area, 1948–49; Chm., Labour Commn of Enquiry, St Lucia, 1950; Chm., Commission of Inquiry into the Nutmeg Industry of Grenada, 1951; Mem. Brit. Guiana Constitutional Commn, 1954; Chm. of Commn of Inquiry into causes of Cessation of Work in Sugar Industry, St Lucia, 1957; Chm. Constitutional Cttee for British Guiana, 1958–59; Chm., Commn to review Salaries and Structure of W Indies Federal Civil Service, and also to enquire into remuneration of Ministers and other members of W Indies Fed. Legislature, 1960; Mem., Mixed Commn on Venezuela-Guyana Border Dispute, 1966–70; Chm. Elections Commn, Guyana, 1966–; Mem. Boundaries Commn, Bermuda, 1967. KStJ 1972. Cacique's Crown of Honour, Guyana, 1970. *Address:* Georgetown, Guyana. *Clubs:* Corona (Life Mem.); The Georgetown.
*Died* 18 Nov. 1981.

**JACKSON, Edward Francis,** MA; Director, Oxford University Institute of Economics and Statistics, and Professorial Fellow of St Antony's College, Oxford, 1959–82; *b* 11 July 1915; *o s* of F. E. Jackson, schoolmaster, and Miriam Eveline (*née* Jevon); *m* 1st, 1942, Anne Katherine Cloake (marr. diss.); 2nd, 1954, Mrs Marion

Marianne Marris (*d* 1972), *o c* of late Arthur Ellinger; two *s*. *Educ:* West Bromwich Grammar Sch.; Univ. of Birmingham; Magdalen Coll., Oxford. BCom Birmingham with 1st cl. hons, 1934; Magdalen Coll., Oxford (Demy): 1st in PPE, 1937; Jun. G. W. Medley Schol., 1935–36; Sen. Demy, 1937; Lecturer in Economics: New Coll., 1938; Magdalen Coll., 1939. Temp. Civil Servant in War Cabinet Offices, 1941–45; established Civil Servant (Central Statistical Office), 1945; Dep. Dir, Res. and Planning Div., UN Econ. Commn for Europe, 1951–56. University Lectr in Economic Statistics, Oxford, and Research Fellow of St Antony's Coll., Oxford, 1956–59. Mem. Transport Adv. Council, 1965. *Publications:* The Nigerian National Accounts, 1950–57 (with P. N. C. Obigbo); 1960; articles in economic journals. *Address:* 62 Park Town, Oxford. *Club:* Reform. *Died 9 Jan. 1989.*

**JACKSON, Sir Geoffrey (Holt Seymour)**, KCMG 1971 (CMG 1963); HM Diplomatic Service, retired; Member, BBC General Advisory Council, 1976–80; *b* 4 March 1915; *s* of Samuel Seymour Jackson and Marie Cecile Dudley Ryder; *m* 1939, Patricia Mary Evelyn Delany; one *s*. *Educ:* Bolton Sch.; Emmanuel Coll., Cambridge. Entered Foreign Service, 1937; Vice-Consul, Beirut, Cairo, Bagdad; Acting Consul-Gen., Basra, 1946; 1st Sec., Bogotá, 1946–50; Berne, 1954–56; Minister, Honduras, 1956, HM Ambassador to Honduras, 1957–60; Consul-Gen., Seattle, 1960–64; Senior British Trade Commissioner in Ontario, Canada, 1964; Minister (Commercial), Toronto, 1965–69; Ambassador to Uruguay, 1969–72; kidnapped by terrorists and held prisoner for 8 months, Jan.-Sept. 1971; Dep. Under-Sec. of State, FCO, 1973. Mem. London Bd, Nat. and Provincial Building Soc. (formerly Burnley Building Soc.), 1976–86. Chm., BBC Adv. Gp on Social Effects of TV, 1975–77. Pres., Assoc. of Lancastrians, 1974. Freeman, City of London, 1976. *Publications:* The Oven-Bird, 1972; People's Prison, 1973; Surviving the Long Night, 1974; Concorde Diplomacy, 1981. *Recreations:* remembering ski-ing, golf, Latin-Americana. *Address:* 63B Cadogan Square, SW1. *Club:* Canning. *Died 1 Oct. 1987.*

**JACKSON, (George) Colin**; Barrister; *b* 6 Dec. 1921; *s* of George Hutton and Agnes Scott Jackson. *Educ:* Tewkesbury Grammar Sch.; St John's Coll., Oxford. Called to the Bar, Gray's Inn, 1950. MP (Lab) Brighouse and Spenborough, 1964–70 and Feb. 1974–1979. Lecturer, writer and broadcaster in Britain, America, throughout Africa and Asia. Former Chm., Parly Lab Party Foreign Affairs Gp. Vice-Chm., Council for Advancement of Arab-British Understanding. *Publication:* The New India (Fabian Soc.). *Recreation:* travel. *Address:* 2 Courtfield Gardens, SW5. *T:* 01-370 1992. *Club:* Savile. *Died 19 April 1981.*

**JACKSON, Most Rev. George Frederic Clarence**; Priest-in-charge, All Saints, Katepwe, since 1984; *b* 5 July 1907; *s* of James Sandiford Jackson; *m* 1939, Eileen de Montfort Wellborne; two *s* two *d*. *Educ:* University of Toronto. Deacon, 1934; Priest, 1935, Diocese of Niagara. Diocese of: Toronto, 1937–38; Chester, 1938–46; Niagara, 1946–58; Qu'Appelle, 1958–77. Hon. Canon, Christ Church Cathedral, Hamilton, Ontario, 1952; Dean of Qu'Appelle, 1958; Bishop of Qu'Appelle, 1960; Archbishop of Qu'Appelle and Metropolitan of Rupert's Land, 1970–77; Bishop-Ordinary to the Canadian Armed Forces, 1977–80. Priest-in-charge, Abernethy-Balcarres, 1980–84. Mayor, Katepwe Beach Village, 1980–85. DD (*hc*) 1959. *Recreations:* cross-country skiing, gardening. *Address:* Box 519, Fort Qu'Appelle, Saskatchewan S0G 1S0, Canada. *Died 24 Dec. 1990.*

**JACKSON, Gordon Cameron**, OBE 1979; actor since 1941; *b* 19 Dec. 1923; *m* 1951, Rona Anderson; two *s*. *Educ:* Hillhead High Sch., Glasgow. Originally an engrg draughtsman. First film, Foreman went to France, 1941; since then has appeared in over 60 films, including: Whisky Galore, 1948; Tunes of Glory, 1960; Mutiny on the Bounty, 1961; The Great Escape, 1962; The Ipcress File, 1964; The Prime of Miss Jean Brodie, 1968; The Shooting Party, 1984; The Whistle Blower, 1986. Theatre work includes: Seagulls over Sorrento, 1951; Moby Dick, 1955; Banquo in Macbeth, 1966; Wise Child, 1967; Horatio in Hamlet, 1969 (Clarence Derwent Award); Tesman in Hedda Gabler, 1970; Veterans, 1972; title role, Noah, and Malvolio in Twelfth Night, 1976; Death Trap, 1981; Cards on the Table, and Mass Appeal, 1982; Hawkins in The Kingfisher, 1987. Television series include: Upstairs, Downstairs, 1970–75 (Royal Television Soc. Award and Variety Club Award, 1975; Emmy Award, USA, 1976); The Professionals, 1977–81; A Town Like Alice, 1980 (Logie Award, Australia, 1982); Shaka Zulu, 1985; My Brother Tom, 1987; Noble House, 1988. *Recreations:* listening to Mozart, gardening. *Address:* c/o ICM Ltd, 388 Oxford Street, W1N 9HE. *T:* 01-629 8080. *Club:* Garrick.
*Died 14 Jan. 1990.*

**JACKSON, Harvey**; Hon. Consulting Surgeon, The National Hospital, Queen Square; Hon. Consulting Neurosurgeon, Westminster Hospital; Hon. Neurological Surgeon, St Thomas' Hospital; Hon. Consulting Surgeon, Acton General Hospital, since 1930; *b* 16 Oct. 1900; *s* of Richard Barlow Jackson and Elizabeth Shepherd; *m*

1930, Freda Mary Frampton; one *s* one *d*. *Educ:* Royal Grammar School, Newcastle upon Tyne; Middlesex Hospital. Hon. Asst Surg., West London Hosp., 1935–38. Past Pres., West London Medico-Chirurgical Soc.; Past Pres., Soc. of Brit. Neurological Surgeons; Fellow of Assoc. of Surgeons; Hunterian Prof. RCS of England, 1947, 1951; Elsberg Lectr, Neurological Soc. of New York, 1960; Visiting Prof. in Neurosurgery, University of Cairo, Guest Lectr, Univ. of Cincinnati, 1959; Lectr, Neurological Soc. of Chicago, 1959; Guest Lectr, Univ. of Santiago de Compostela, Spain, 1969. Past President: Section of Neurology, RSM; Surrey Branch, BMA. *Address:* 56 Fairacres, Roehampton Lane, SW15 5LY.
*Died 19 Sept. 1982.*

**JACKSON, Herbert**, FRIBA; FRTPI; architect and planning consultant; in private practice since 1931; *b* 25 June 1909; *s* of John Herbert Jackson; *m* 1930, Margaret Elizabeth Pearson. *Educ:* Handsworth Grammar Sch.; Birmingham Sch. of Architecture. RIBA Bronze Medal, 1928; RIBA Saxon Snell Prizeman, 1930. Mem. RIBA Council, 1956–58; Vice-Pres. RIBA 1960–62; Chm., RIBA Allied Socs Conf., 1960–62. Gov., Birmingham Coll. of Art; Chm. Birmingham Civic Soc., 1960–65; Pres. Birmingham and Five Counties Architectural Assoc., 1956–58; Pres. Royal Birmingham Society of Artists, 1960–62 (Prof. of Architecture, 1961). *Publications:* (jt) Plans (for Minister of Town and Country Planning): S Wales, 1947; W Midlands and N Staffs, 1948. *Recreations:* travelling, reading. *Address:* 14 Clarendon Square, Leamington Spa, Warwicks. *T:* Leamington 424078.
*Died 24 May 1989.*

**JACKSON, James Barry**; *see* Barry, Michael.

**JACKSON, John Wharton**, JP; *b* 25 May 1902; *s* of John Jackson and Mary Wharton; *m* 1928, Mary Rigg; two *d*. *Educ:* Shrewsbury. Formerly Chm., Jackson's (Hurstead) Ltd, Rochdale. High Sheriff of Radnorshire, 1944–45; JP County of Lancaster, 1952. *Recreation:* golf. *Address:* Brackens, Mottram St Andrew, near Macclesfield, Cheshire. *T:* Prestbury 89277. *Died 14 Oct. 1986.*

**JACKSON, Joseph**; QC 1967; *b* 21 Aug. 1924; *s* of late Samuel Jackson and of Hetty Jackson; *m* 1st, 1952, Marjorie Henrietta (*née* Lyons) (marr. diss. 1982); three *d*; 2nd, 1982, Hon. Dame Margaret Myfanwy Wood Booth, DBE. *Educ:* Queens' Coll., Cambridge; University Coll., London. MA, LLB Cantab, LLM London. Barrister, 1947, Gibraltar Bar; Bencher, Middle Temple, 1980. Chairman: Probate and Divorce Bar Assoc., 1968–69; Family Law Bar Assoc., 1980–84. Member: General Council of the Bar, 1969–73; Senate of the Inns of Court, 1975–78; Bar Cttee, 1980–81. Mem., Matrimonial Causes Rules Cttee, 1969–73 and 1977–81; Special Divorce Comr, 1969–70. Dept of Trade Inspector, Dowgate and General Investments Ltd, 1975–78. Mem. legal aid cttees including: Law Soc. Legal Aid Cttee, 1975–78; Lord Chancellor's Working Party to review legal aid legislation; Council of Law Reporting, 1982–. Lectures: Weir Meml, Alberta, 1981; Opas Meml, NSW, 1982. *Publications:* English Legal History, 1951 (2nd edn 1955); Formation and Annulment of Marriage, 1951, 2nd edn, 1969; Rayden on Divorce, 5th edn (supp.) 1951 to 14th edn 1983; Matrimonial Finance and Taxation, 1972, 4th edn, 1986; (consulting editor) Clarke Hall and Morrison on Children, 9th edn, 1977; contrib. to Halsbury's Laws of England, Encyclopædia Britannica, Atkin's Encyclopædia of Court Forms, Law Quarterly Review, Modern Law Review, Canadian Bar Review, Alberta Law Review, etc. *Recreations:* gardening, painting, ceramics. *Address:* 1 Mitre Court Buildings, Temple, EC4. *T:* 01–353 0434/2277.
*Died 14 May 1987.*

**JACKSON, Col Richard John Laurence**, CBE 1971; DL, JP; FRIBA; DipArch; Architect; *b* 17 Oct. 1908; *s* of John Robert and Kathleen Emma Jackson; *m* 1936, Sara Alexander Wilson; one *s*. *Educ:* Scarborough Coll.; Liverpool Univ. Served War of 1939–45, Green Howards; Middle East, Western Desert, Libya, Tunisia, Sicily and Normandy invasions. Member: North Riding of Yorkshire CC, 1949–74 (Alderman, 1961–74); North Yorks CC, 1974–85 (Chm. 1977–81; Hon. Alderman, 1986). JP 1951; DL North Riding, 1967. *Recreation:* angling. *Address:* Bridgeholme, Egton Bridge, Whitby, North Yorks. *T:* Whitby 85221. *Died 21 April 1989.*

**JACKSON, Prof. Richard Meredith**, FBA 1966; LLD; JP; Downing Professor of the Laws of England, 1966–70; Fellow, St John's College, Cambridge, since 1946; *b* 19 Aug. 1903; *s* of James Jackson, JP, Northampton and Jenny May Jackson (*née* Parnell); *m* 1st, Lydia Jibourtovitch (marr. diss.); 2nd, 1936, Lenli, *d* of Alexander Tie Ten Quee, Kingston, Jamaica; one *d* (and one *s* decd). *Educ:* Sidcot; Leighton Park; St John's Coll., Cambridge. Admitted solicitor, 1928. Cambridge Law Sch., LLD 1939; Home Office, 1941–45; Sec. Royal Commn on JPs, 1946–48; Reader in Public Law and Admin., Cambridge, 1950; Member: Royal Commn on Mental Health Services, 1954–57; Deptl Cttee on Children and Young Persons, 1956–60; Council of the Magistrates' Assoc., 1948–72 (Vice-Pres., 1972–). JP Cambs, 1942. *Publications:* History of Quasi-Contract in English Law, 1936; Machinery of Justice in

England, 1940 (7th edn, 1977); Machinery of Local Government, 1958 (2nd edn, 1965); Enforcing the Law, 1967 (2nd edn, 1972); ed, 3rd edn, Justice of the Peace, by Leo Page, 1967; articles in learned jls. *Recreation:* yacht cruising. *Address:* St John's College, Cambridge. *T:* 61621; 10 Halifax Road, Cambridge CB4 3PX. *T:* 358179. *Club:* Royal Cruising. *Died 8 May 1986.*

**JACOB, Gordon (Percival Septimus),** CBE 1968; DMus; FRCM; Hon. RAM; Composer; Professor of Theory, Composition, and Orchestration, Royal College of Music, retired 1966; Editor of Penguin Musical Scores, 1947–57; *b* 5 July 1895; 7th *s* of late Stephen Jacob, CSI; *m* 1st, 1924, Sidney Wilmot (*d* 1958), *er d* of Rev. A. W. Gray, Ipswich; 2nd, 1959, Margaret Sidney Hannah, *d* of C. A. Gray, Helions Bumpstead and niece of first wife; one *s* one *d. Educ:* Dulwich Coll.; Royal College of Music. Served European War, 1914–18; UPS and Queen's Royal West Surrey Regt (Prisoner of War in Germany, April 1917–Dec. 1918); Studied composition at the Royal College of Music under the late Sir Charles V. Stanford; conducting under Adrian Boult, and theory under Herbert Howells. Pres., British Assoc. of Symphonic Bands and Wind Ensembles. Compositions include Orchestral, Choral and Chamber music, many concertos for various instruments, works for Wind Orchestra and Brass Band, also orchestrations and arrangements. Holder of John Collard Fellowship (Worshipful Company of Musicians), 1943–46; Cobbett Medal for Services to Chamber Music, 1949. *Publications:* Orchestral Technique, a Manual for Students; How to Read a Score; The Composer and his Art; The Elements of Orchestration; most of the works alluded to above; also many other smaller compositions. Contributed to Chambers's Encyclopædia and Groves Dictionary of Music. *Recreations:* cross-words, motoring, reading; interested in all forms of art, and in natural history. *Address:* 1 Audley Road, Saffron Walden, Essex CB11 3HW. *T:* 22406. *Died 8 June 1984.*

**JACOB, Very Rev. William Ungoed;** Dean of Brecon Cathedral, 1967–78; Vicar of St Mary's, Brecon with Battle, 1967–78; *b* 6 Oct. 1910; *s* of Wm and L. M. M. Jacob; *m* 1935, Ivy Matilda Hall; one *d. Educ:* Llanelly Gram. Sch.; Llandovery Coll.; Jesus Coll., Oxford; Wycliffe Hall, Oxford. BA 2nd cl. History, 1932; 2nd cl. Theology, 1933; MA 1937. Ordained deacon, 1934; priest, 1935; Curate of Holy Trinity, Aberystwyth, 1934–36; Lampeter, 1936–40; Vicar of Blaenau Ffestiniog 1940–51; Rector of Hubberston, 1951–55; Vicar of St Peter's, Carmarthen, 1955–67; Canon of St David's Cathedral, 1957–67. Rural Dean of Carmarthen, 1958–60; Archdeacon of Carmarthen, 1960–67. Pres., Council of Churches for Wales 1971–76 (Sec., 1960–65). Mem., Coun. for Wales and Mon, 1963–66. Church in Wales: Gen. Sec., Prov. Council for Mission and Unity, 1967–73; Mem., Standing Liturgical Commn, 1951–71; Chm., Provincial Selection Panel, 1974–78. *Publications:* Meditations on the Seven Words, 1960; Three Hours' Devotions, 1965; A Guide to the Parish Eucharist, 1969. *Address:* 110 Sketty Road, Swansea SA2 0JX. *T:* Swansea (0792) 203475. *Died 18 Dec. 1990.*

**JACOBS, Brig. John Conrad S.;** *see* Saunders-Jacobs.

**JACOBS, Sir Roland (Ellis),** Kt 1963; formerly: Chairman: Executive Trustee & Agency Co. of South Australia Ltd; South Australian Brewing Co. Ltd; Director, Mutual Hospital Association Ltd; *b* Adelaide, 28 Feb. 1891; *s* of late S. J. Jacobs, Adelaide; *m* 1st, 1917, Olga (decd), *d* of late A. M. Hertzbay; one *s* two *d;* 2nd, 1970, Esther Lipman Cook. *Educ:* Geelong Coll., Vic. Past Pres., RSPCA; Pres., Post Graduate Foundation in Medicine; former Mem. Bd of Management: Royal Adelaide Hosp.; Queen Elizabeth Hosp.; ex officio Mem. Council: Adelaide Chamber of Commerce (Pres., 1942–43); Crippled Children's Assoc. of SA (past Pres.); Aust. Adv. Council for Physically Handicapped; President, Meals on Wheels Inc.; Mem., Nat. Council, Aust. Boy Scouts Assoc. Hon. Life Member (formerly Director): Aust. Elizabethan Theatre Trust; Adelaide Festival of Arts. *Recreation:* bowls. *Address:* 2 Tusmore Avenue, Leabrook, SA 5068, Australia. *Club:* Adelaide (Adelaide). *Died 29 June 1981.*

**JACOBS-LARKCOM, Eric Herbert Larkcom,** CBE 1946; *b* 21 Jan. 1895; *s* of Herbert Jacobs, Barrister-at-law; (assumed additional surname of Larkcom by Royal Licence, 1915); *m* 1933, Dorothy Primrose Kerr Tasker; two *d. Educ:* University Coll. Sch. Entered Royal Engineers from RMA, Woolwich, 1916; served European War, 1914–18, France, 1917–18 (wounded); Staff Coll., Camberley, 1930–31; served War of 1939–45, France 1939–40; China, 1942–45; Col, 1942; retired pay, 1946; i/c Harbin Consulate-Gen. (at Changchun), 1947–48; Consul-Gen. Kunming, 1948–49; Consul, Tamsui, Formosa, 1951–53; Consul, Chiengmai, 1954–58, retired. Mentioned in despatches, 1945, Chinese Cloud and Banner, 1945, American Bronze Star, 1946. *Address:* White Lodge, 12 Pedn Moran, St Mawes, Truro, Cornwall. *Clubs:* Naval and Military; Royal Cornwall Yacht. *Died 28 May 1982.*

**JACOBSON, Baron** *cr* 1975 (Life Peer), of St Albans; **Sydney Jacobson,** MC 1944; Editorial Director, International Publishing Corporation Newspapers, 1968–74, Deputy Chairman, 1973–74; *b*

26 Oct. 1908; *m* 1938, Phyllis June Buck; two *s* one *d. Educ:* Strand Sch., London; King's Coll., London. Asst Editor: Statesman, India, 1934–36; Lilliput Magazine, 1936–39. Served in Army, 1939–45. Special Correspondent, Picture Post, 1945–48; Editor, Leader Magazine, 1948–50; Political Editor, Daily Mirror, 1952–62; Editor, Daily Herald, 1962–64; Editor, Sun, 1964–65; Chairman, Odhams Newspapers, 1968. Member Press Council, 1969–75. *Recreations:* walking, reading. *Address:* 6 Avenue Road, St Albans, Herts. *T:* St Albans 53873. *Died 13 Aug. 1988.*

**JACQUOT, Général d'Armée Pierre Elie;** Grand Cross of Legion of Honour, 1961; *b* 16 June 1902; *s* of Aimé Jacquot and Marie (*née* Renault); *m* 1929, Lucie Claire Mamet; one *d* (one *s* killed in action, Algeria, 1962). *Educ:* Saint-Cyr Military Academy, France. Commissioned 30th Chasseur Bn, 1922; Foreign Legion Service, 1925–29; French Ecole de Guerre, 1929–31, Belgian, 1931–33; Capt. 1933; posted to GHQ, Sept. 1939; Comdr 3rd Bn of 109th Inf. Regt, 1940; with André Malraux (alias Col Berger) organised French Resistance in the Corrèze, Dordogne and Lot areas, 1943–44; served in First French Army, 1944–45 (Alsace-Lorraine Bde); Brig.-Gen. 1946; Dep. Chief of Army Staff, 1947; Maj.-Gen. 1950; comd 8th Inf. Div., 1951–54; Lieut-Gen. 1954; High Comr and C-in-C, Indo-China, 1955–56; C-in-C French Forces in Germany, 1956–59; Gen. 1957; Inspector-Gen. of French Land Forces, 1959–61; Commander-in-Chief, Allied Forces Central Europe, 1961–63; Cadre de Réserve, Dec. 1963. *Publications:* Essai de stratégie occidentale, 1953; La Stratégie périphérique devant la bombe atomique, 1954. *Address:* (winter) 15 Avenue de Villars, 75007 Paris, France; (summer) Vrécourt, 88140 Contrexéville, France. *Died 29 June 1984.*

**JAGATSINGH, Hon. Sir Keharsingh, (Hon. Sir Kher),** Kt 1981; Officier, Ordre National Malgache, 1969; MLA (Lab) Montagne Blanche and Grand River South East, Mauritius, since 1976; President, Conseil d'Administration, Institut Africain et Mauricien de Bilinguisme, since 1977; Managing Director, Century Investments Ltd, since 1982; *b* Amritsar, 23 July 1931; *m* Radhika; two *s* two *d. Educ:* Beau Bassin Primary Sch.; privately. Civil servant in Dept of Health, 1950–54; co-founded Mauritius Times, weekly newspaper, 1954; trainee journalist on Times of India, 1956–57; on attachment to Slough Observer and Paddington Times, 1957; joined Labour Party, 1958, Sec.-Gen., 1961–; Chairman: Govt and non-Govt Gen. Workers' Union, 1961–67; Central Housing Auth., 1963–67. MLC for Beau Bassin-Petite Rivière, 1959, for Montagne Blanche and Grand River SE, 1967; Minister: of Health, 1967–71; of Economic Planning and Develt, 1971–76; of Education and Cultural Affairs, 1977–82. Mem. Exec. Bd, UNESCO, 1977–80. Co-founder, The Nation, 1970, now Vice-Chm. Governor for Mauritius, IBRD, Washington; Chairman: Giants Internat. Mauritius Br.; Mauritius Nat. Peace Council. Port Louis correspondent, Bombay Commerce, 1982–. *Publication:* Petals of Dust, 1981. *Address:* c/o Ministry of Education and Cultural Affairs, Port Louis, Mauritius. *T:* (office) 083205; (home) 542215. *Died 18 July 1985.*

**JAKOBSON, Prof. Roman;** Samuel Hazzard Cross Professor of Slavic Languages and Literatures and of General Linguistics, Harvard University, 1949–67, later Emeritus; Institute Professor, Massachusetts Institute of Technology, 1957–67, later Emeritus; *b* Moscow, 11 Oct. 1896; *s* of Osip Jakobson, engineer, and Anna (*née* Wolpert); *m* 1935, Dr Svatava Pirkova; *m* 1962, Dr Krystyna Pomorska; no *c. Educ:* Lazarev Inst. of Oriental Languages, Moscow (AB); Moscow Univ. (AM); Prague Univ. (PhD). Research Assoc., Moscow Univ., 1918–20; Prof. Masaryk University (Brno), 1933–39; Vis. lectr at Univs of Copenhagen, Oslo, Uppsala, 1939–41; Professor: Ecole Libre des Hautes Etudes, New York, 1942–46; Columbia Univ., 1943–49. Visiting Professor: Yale, 1967; Princeton, 1968; Brown, 1969–70; Brandeis, 1970; Louvain, 1972; Collège de France, 1972; New York, 1973; Bergen, 1976; Wellesley, 1980. Hon. doctorates in Letters and Philosophy: Cambridge, 1960; Chicago, 1961; Oslo, 1961; Uppsala, 1963; Mich., 1963; Grenoble, 1966; Nice, 1966; Rome, 1966; Yale, 1967; Prague, 1968; Brno, 1968; Zagreb, 1969; Ohio, 1970; Louvain, 1972; Tel Aviv, 1975; Harvard, 1975; Columbia, 1976; Copenhagen and Liège, 1979; Bochum and Georgetown, 1980; Brandeis and Oxford, 1981; in Sciences: New Mexico, 1966; Clark, 1969. Award of Amer. Council of Learned Socs, 1960; Medal, Slovak Acad. of Sci., 1968; Award of Amer. Assoc. for the Advancement of Slavic Studies, 1970; Bicentennial Medal, Boston Coll., 1976; Internat. Prize Feltrinelli for Philol. and Linguistics, 1980; Internat. Prize, Hegel Soc., Stuttgart, 1982. Fellow, Amer. Acad. of Arts and Scis, 1950. Corresp. Mem., British Acad., 1974 and Mem. eight continental Academies; Hon. Member: Assoc. phonétique internationale, 1952; Finno-Ugric Soc., 1963, Acad. of Aphasia, 1969; Royal Soc. of Letters, Lund, 1972; Philological Soc. (London), 1974; Royal Anthropological Inst., 1974; Societas Scientiarum Fennica, 1977; Modern Languages Assoc., 1978; NY Acad. of Scis, 1978; Pres., Permanent Council for Phonetic Sciences, 1955–61; Linguistic Soc. of America, 1956. Vice-Pres., International Cttee of Slavicists,

1966–76; Internat. Soc. of Phonetic Science, 1970–; Internat. Assoc. for Semiotic Studies, 1969–; Hon. Pres., Tokyo Inst. for Advanced Studies of Language, 1967–. Chevalier, Légion d'Honneur, 1948. *Publications:* Remarques sur l'évolution phonologique du russe comparée à celles des autres langues slaves, 1929; Characteristics of the Eurasian Linguistic Affinity (in Russian), 1931; Beitrag zur allgemeinen Kasuslehre, 1936; Kindersprache, Aphasie und allgemeine Lautgesetze, 1941; (joint) La Geste du Prince Igor, 1948; (joint) Preliminaries to Speech Analysis, 1952; The Kernel of Comparative Slavic Literature, 1953; Studies in Comparative Slavic Metrics, 1952; (joint) Fundamentals of Language, 1956; Morphological Inquiry into Slavic Declension, 1958; Essais de linguistique générale, I, 1963, II, 1973; Studies on Child Language and Aphasia, 1971; Selected Writings, Vol. I (Phonological Studies), 1962, expanded, 1971; Vol. IV (Slavic Epic Studies), 1966; Vol. II (Word and Language), 1971; Vol. V (Verse, its masters and explorers), 1979; Vol. III (Grammar of Poetry), 1980; Vol. VI (Early Slavic Paths and Crossroads), 1982; Questions de poétique, 1973; Main Trends in the Science of Language, 1973; Pushkin and His Sculptural Myth, 1975; Six leçons sur le son et le sens, 1976; Hölderlin, Klee, Brecht, 1976; (jtly) Yeats' 'Sorrow of Love' through the Years, 1977; (jtly) The Sound Shape of Language, 1979; Dialogues, 1980; Framework of Language, 1980; Brain and Language, 1980; *relevant publications:* To Honor Roman Jakobson, 1967; Bibliography of R. Jakobson's Writings, 1971; R. Jakobson: echoes of his scholarship, 1977. *Address:* Boylston Hall 301, Harvard University, Cambridge, Massachusetts 02138, USA. *T:* 8685619.
*Died 18 June 1982.*

**JAMES, David G.;** *see* Guthrie-James.

**JAMES, David Pelham;** *see* Guthrie-James, D.

**JAMES, (Eliot) Antony B.;** *see* Brett-James.

**JAMES, John Wynford George,** OBE 1950; FRAeS; FCIT; Member of Board, BEA, 1964–74; Chairman: BEA Airtours, 1972–74; British Airways Helicopters, 1967–74; Gulf Helicopters Ltd, 1970–76; Deputy Chairman, International Aeradio Ltd, 1971–74 (Board Member, 1956); British Airways Group Air Safety Adviser, 1973–74; retired 1976; *b* 13 Feb. 1911; *s* of William George and Elizabeth James; *m* 1934, Bertha Mildred Joyce Everard; one *s* two *d*. *Educ:* Royal Grammar School, Worcester. FCIT 1954; FRAeS 1963. Joined Imperial Airways as a pilot, 1933; Capt., Imperial Airways/BOAC, 1935–46; BEA Chief Pilot, 1946; Operations Dir, BEA, 1954–68. Dir, International Helicopters Ltd, 1965. Chairman: BALPA, 1943–48; SITA, 1964–66 (Mem., Bd, 1961–66). Governor, College of Air Training, 1959– (Chm. 1959–61, 1963–66, 1968–70). Liveryman, GAPAN, 1960. *Recreations:* golf, gardening, fishing, shooting. *Address:* Wynsfield, Mill Lane, Gerrards Cross, Bucks SL9 8AZ. *T:* Gerrards Cross (0753) 884038.
*Died 17 May 1990.*

**JAMES, Robert Leoline,** CBE 1971; MA, PhD; Head Master of Harrow, 1953–71; *b* 27 Sept. 1905; 2nd *s* of late Very Rev. H. L. James, DD; *m* 1939, Maud Eliot, *o c* of late W. M. Gibbons, OBE, LLD; two *s*. *Educ:* Rossall Sch.; Jesus Coll., Oxford (Scholar). 1st Class Hon. Classical Mods 1926, 1st Class Lit. Hum. 1928; Asst Master St Paul's Sch., 1928; Housemaster and Upper VIIIth classical master; Headmaster of Chigwell Sch., Essex, 1939–46; High Master of St Paul's Sch., 1946–53. Chm. of Council, Heathfield Sch., 1960–79. *Publication:* Cicero and Sulpicius, 1933. *Recreations:* fly-fishing and bird-watching. *Address:* 25 Blenheim Drive, Oxford. *Club:* East India, Devonshire, Sports and Public Schools.
*Died 14 May 1982.*

**JAMES, William Henry E.;** *see* Ewart James.

**JAMES, William Thomas,** OBE 1943; formerly Director of numerous public companies both at home and overseas, mainly associated with British Electric Traction, and also Chairman of many of these; Director, United Transport Co.; *b* 5 June 1892; *s* of Morgan James, JP, and Mary James, Maesycwmmer Hse, Maesycwmmer, Mon; unmarried. *Educ:* Lewis's Sch., Pengam, Glam. London and Provincial Bank, 1909. Joined family business, 1911–14. Served European War, Glam Yeomanry, 1914–18 (Meritorious Service Medal). Rejoined family business, 1919–22; pioneered road passenger transport in Monmouthshire Valleys, 1923; developed passenger road services in S Wales and Mon, 1923–43. Having sold financial interests in 1932 to British Electric Traction Co. Ltd, joined staff of BET in London as Executive Dir, 1943; Dir of BET, 1947. Chm., Public Transport Assoc., 1951, 1952. Mem. Cttee set up by Government to consider Rural Bus Services. FCIT. *Recreation:* farming. *Address:* (private) Uplands, Ty-Gwyn Road, Cardiff. *Clubs:* Naval and Military; Cardiff and County (Cardiff); Chepstow; St Pierre Golf and Country.
*Died 4 Sept. 1982.*

**JAMESON, (Margaret) Storm,** MA; Hon. LittD (Leeds); Writer; *b* Whitby, Yorks, 1891; *d* of William Storm Jameson; *m* Prof. Guy Chapman, OBE, MC (*d* 1972); one *s* of a former marriage. *Educ:* Leeds Univ. Hon. Mem., American Acad. and Inst. of Arts and

Letters. *Publications:* Happy Highways, 1920; Modern Drama in Europe, 1920; The Lovely Ship, 1927; The Voyage Home, 1930; A Richer Dust, 1931; That was Yesterday; A Day Off; No Time Like the Present, 1933; Women Against Men, 1933, repr. 1982; Company Parade, 1934, repr. 1982; Love in Winter, 1935; In the Second Year, 1936; None Turn Back, 1936; Delicate Monster, 1937; Civil Journey, 1939; Farewell Night, Welcome Day, 1939; Europe to Let, 1940; Cousin Honoré, 1940; The Fort, 1941; The End of this War, 1941; Then We Shall Hear Singing, 1942; Cloudless May, 1943; The Journal of Mary Hervey Russell, 1945; The Other Side, 1945; Before the Crossing, 1947; The Black Laurel, 1948; The Moment of Truth, 1949; Writer's Situation, 1950; The Green Man, 1952; The Hidden River, 1955; The Intruder, 1956; A Cup of Tea for Mr Thorgill, 1957; A Ulysses Too Many, 1958; A Day Off and other stories, 1959; Last Score, 1961; Morley Roberts: The Last Eminent Victorian, 1961; The Road from the Monument, 1962; A Month Soon Goes, 1963; The Aristide Case, 1964; The Early Life of Stephen Hind, 1966; The White Crow, 1968; (autobiography) Journey from the North, Vol. I 1969, Vol. II 1970, repr. 1984; Parthian Words, 1970; There will be a Short Interval, 1972; (ed) A Kind of Survivor, autobiog. of Guy Chapman, 1975; Speaking of Stendhal, 1979. *Recreation:* travelling. *Address:* c/o C. C. Storm-Clark Esq., Department of Economics and Related Studies, University of York, York YO1 5DD.
*Died 30 Sept. 1986.*

**JAMESON, Maj-Gen. Thomas Henry,** CBE 1946 (OBE 1937); DSO 1919; RM, retired; *b* 10 Dec. 1894; *s* of Robert W. Jameson, JP, and Katherine Anne Jameson; *m* 1918, Barbara Adèle Bayley (*d* 1958); one *d*. *Educ:* Monkton Combe Sch., near Bath, Somerset. Commission in Royal Marines, 1913; served Belgium, France, Gallipoli (despatches) HMS Resolution, HMS Kent, 1914–18; Siberia, 1919 (DSO). War of 1939–45: staff of C-in-C Home Fleet, 15 RM Battalion, Admiralty; Commandant Plymouth, Jan. 1944 and Depot, Deal, June 1944; Commandant Portsmouth Division RM, 1944–46 (CBE); retired, 1946. *Address:* Little Burrow Farm, Broadclyst, Exeter, Devon. *T:* Exeter 61286.
*Died 28 Feb. 1985.*

**JAMIESON, Hon. Donald Campbell,** PC (Can.) 1968; Canadian High Commissioner to the United Kingdom, 1983–85; *b* St John's, Newfoundland, 30 April 1921; *s* of Charles Jamieson and Isabelle Bennett; *m* 1946, Barbara Elizabeth Oakley; one *s* three *d*. *Educ:* Prince of Wales Coll.; St John's, Newfoundland. Served War with Canadian Naval Special Services and United Service Org. Camp Shows. Regular broadcasts, 1941–46; news broadcasting nightly, 1946; Attaché, Parly Press Gallery, Ottawa, 1948; former Pres., Newfoundland Broadcasting Co. Ltd; also Dir of Broadcast News; Past Chm., Affiliates Sect. Network Advt Cttee, CBC. Pres., Canadian Assoc. of Broadcasters, 1961–65. With Dept of Rural Reconstruction; then Crosbie & Co. Ltd, fishery; Sales Manager, Coca Cola, Newfoundland. MP (Liberal) Burin-Burgeo, St John's, Newfoundland, 1966–79; Minister: of Supply and Services, 1968–69; of Transport, 1969–72; of Regional Economic Expansion, 1972–75; of Industry, Trade and Commerce, Sept. 1975–76; Sec. of State for External Affairs, Canada, 1976–79; MHA (L) Bellevue, Newfoundland, 1979–81; Leader of the Opposition, 1979–80. Past Chm., financial campaign of Canadian Cancer Soc.; Past Director: Canadian Centennial Council; Nat. Theatre School. Hon. LLD: Memorial, 1970; Acadia; St Francis Xavier. *Publication:* The Troubled Air, 1966. *Recreations:* fishing, hunting, boating. *Address:* Over Kilmory, Swift Current, Newfoundland, Canada.
*Died 19 Nov. 1986.*

**JANES, Rev. Maxwell Osborne;** Minister, Crowborough United (Methodist and United Reformed) Church, 1967–77, then Emeritus; *b* 14 May 1902; *s* of Harry Janes; *m* 1927, Mildred Bertha Burgess; one *s*. *Educ:* Kilburn Gram. Sch.; University Coll., London; New Coll., London. BA London; BD London. Ordained Congregational Minister, 1927. Minister at: Rectory Road Congreg. Ch., Stoke Newington, 1927–32; Above Bar Congreg. Ch., Southampton, 1932–45; Moderator of Southern Province, Congreg. Union of England and Wales, 1945–50; Gen. Sec., London Missionary Soc., 1950–66; Pres., Congregational Church in England and Wales, 1966–67; Cons. Sec., Congregational Coun. for World Mission, 1966–67. *Publication:* Servant of the Church, 1952. *Recreations:* gardening, philately. *Address:* 45a Appledore Gardens, Lindfield, Sussex RH16 2EX.
*Died 3 April 1981.*

**JANNER, Baron** *cr* 1970 (Life Peer), of the City of Leicester; **Barnett Janner,** Kt 1961; Solicitor; *b* 20 June 1892; *s* of late Joseph and Gertrude Janner, Barry, Glamorgan; *m* 1927, Elsie Sybil Cohen, CBE; one *s* one *d*. *Educ:* Barry County Sch.; University of S Wales and Mon (Cardiff Coll.) (County Scholarship). BA; Pres. of Students Representative Council; editor of University Magazine; served 1st World War in RGA, France and Belgium (gassed); ARP Warden in London, War of 1939–45. Former President: Board of Deputies of British Jews, 1955–64 (now Mem. Exec. Cttee); Zionist Federation of Gt Britain and Ireland; Pres., Assoc. of Jewish Friendly Socs; Vice-Pres., Parly Anglo-Benelux Gp; Past Chm.,

Inter-Parly Union; Hon. Vice-Pres., British-Israel Parly Gp (former Chm.); Vice-Chm., Lords and Commons Solicitors Gp (former Chm.); Former Vice-Pres. and Mem. Exec. Cttee of Conf. on Jewish Material Claims against Germany Inc.; Member: Executive Cttee of Cttee for Jewish Claims on Austria; Exec., World Zionist Organisation; European Council, World Jewish Congress; Council, Jewish Trust Corp.; Exec., World Jewish Relief; Nat. Council for Soviet Jewry; Vice-President: Assoc. of Jewish ex-Servicemen; Assoc. of Metropolitan Authorities; Patron, Intake (Shelter for homeless people); British Friends of Magen David Adom; Hon. Vice-Pres., British Friends of Israel War Disabled; Former Chairman: Leaseholders' Assoc. of Great Britain; Parliamentary Water Safety Cttee. Contested Cardiff Central, 1929; Whitechapel and St George's, 1930 and 1935; MP (L) Whitechapel and St George's Division of Stepney, 1931–35; joined Labour Party, 1936; MP (Lab), West Leicester, 1945–50, North-West Div. of Leicester, 1950–70; Hon. Pres., NW Leicester Lab. Party; former Mem., House of Commons Panel of Chairmen. Vice-President: World Maccabi Assoc.; British Maccabi. Mem. Society of Labour Lawyers; formerly Hon. Rents Adviser to Labour Party. Pres., Leicester Civic Soc. Life Governor, Cardiff Univ. Governor, Ben Gurion Univ. of the Negev. FRSA; FIPM. Hon. LLD Leeds, 1957. Commander: Order of Leopold II (Belgium), 1963; Order of Orange Nassau of Netherlands, 1970. *Recreation:* reading. *Address:* 45 Morpeth Mansions, Morpeth Terrace, SW1P 1ET. *T:* 01–828 8700; 22 Upper Brook Street, W1Y 2HD. *T:* 01–629 3981; The Jungle, Stone Road, Broadstairs, Kent. *T:* Thanet 61642. *Died 4 May 1982.*

**JARDINE, Christopher Willoughby,** CB 1967; Assistant Secretary, Monopolies and Mergers Commission, 1975–76; *b* 5 Aug. 1911; *e s* of Judge Willoughby Jardine, KC; *m* 1940, Anne Eva Katharine, *er d* of Sir George Duckworth-King, 6th Bart; three *d. Educ:* Eton (Scholar); King's Coll., Cambridge (Scholar; 1st Cl. Hons. History); and in France and Germany. BoT, later DTI: Asst Principal, 1934; Principal, 1939; Asst Sec., 1945; Under-Sec., 1962; Adviser on Commercial Policy, 1962–64; Insurance and Companies Dept, 1964–72; Principal, Monopolies and Mergers Commn, 1972–75. *Address:* 8 St Loo Court, St Loo Avenue, SW3. *T:* 01–352 1246. *Club:* MCC. *Died 3 Nov. 1982.*

**JARDINE, Brig. Sir Ian (Liddell),** 4th Bt *cr* 1916; OBE 1966; MC 1945; *b* 13 Oct. 1923; *o s* of Maj.-Gen. Sir Colin Arthur Jardine, 3rd Bt; *S* father, 1957; *m* 1948, Priscilla Daphne, *d* of Douglas Middleton Parnham Scott-Phillips, Halkshill, Largs, Ayrshire; two *s* two *d. Educ:* Charterhouse. Served War, 1942–45, Coldstream Guards (MC); 2nd Lieut, 1943; Major, 1950; Lt-Col 1964; Col 1968; Brig., 1969; Brig., GS, 1973–75, Brig., Inf., 1975–78, UKLF, retired. ADC to the Queen, 1976–78. *Heir:s* Andrew Colin Douglas Jardine, *b* 30 Nov. 1955. *Address:* Coombe Place, Meonstoke, Southampton. *T:* Droxford 569. *Club:* Brooks's. *Died 25 Nov. 1982.*

**JARDINE, John Frederick James;** Director, Sutton Enterprise Agency Ltd, since 1987; *b* 22 Dec. 1926; *s* of late James Jardine; *m* 1957, Pamela Joyce; four *s* two *d. Educ:* Rock Ferry High Sch., Birkenhead. RAF, 1945–48; Inland Revenue, 1948–55; BoT, 1955–58; British Trade Comr, Karachi, 1958–63; BoT, 1963–66; Midland Regional Controller, 1966–71; DTI, 1971–73; seconded to HM Diplomatic Service (Under-Sec.), 1973; HM Consul-General, Johannesburg, 1973–78; Dept of Trade, 1978–80; Dept of Industry, 1980–83; DTI, 1983–85; Under Sec., Dept of Employment, 1985–86. *Recreations:* golf, bridge. *Address:* 7 Lynwood Avenue, Epsom, Surrey KT17 4LQ. *T:* Epsom (0372) 729156.
*Died 12 March 1990.*

**JARDINE, Michael James,** CB 1976; Deputy Director of Public Prosecutions, 1974–79; *b* 20 Nov. 1915; *s* of Judge James Willoughby Jardine, KC; *m* 1939; two *s* one *d. Educ:* Eton; King's Coll., Cambridge (BA). Called to Bar, Middle Temple, 1937. Served War with Scots Guards, 1940–46: active service in North Africa and Italy. Legal Asst to Director of Public Prosecutions, 1946; Asst Solicitor, 1965; Asst Director of Public Prosecutions, 1969. *Recreation:* bridge. *Died 25 June 1988.*

**JARDINE, Robert Frier,** CMG 1928; OBE 1926; Third Class of the Order of Al Rafidain of Iraq, 1937; *b* 9 June 1894; *s* of late Robert Brown Jardine; *m* 1932, Averil (*d* 1975), *o d* of late H. O. Dickin; twin *s* (both Mems of 1960, 1964, 1968 British Olympic Yachting teams). *Educ:* Downing Coll., Cambridge. Commissioned Sept. 1914 from Cambridge Univ. OTC; served European War in Egypt, Gallipoli and Mesopotamia (despatches); in political charge of districts in Northern Iraq and Kurdistan, 1917–21; repatriated Assyrians to their original homes in Hakkiari, 1922; Political Officer to columns in Kurdistan, 1923; Mem. of HMG Delegation to Turkey and League of Nations upon Turkish frontier question, 1924; HM Assessor on League of Nations' Commission in connection with Turco-Iraq frontier, and upon other Commissions, 1925; Administrative Inspector, Mosul Province, 1925–28; Adviser to British Ambassador in Turkey for Tripartite Treaty, 1926; Frontier Commissioner, 1927; Administrative Inspector, Basra

Province, 1928–33; Pres. of Commission for settlement of titles to land in Iraq, 1933–36; acted in various capacities in Palestine, 1936–48, including Dir of Settlement and Registration of titles to Land, Civil Aviation, Commissioner for Auqaf, Irrigation, Commissioner of Compensation for Rebellion and War Damages, 1945; Land Settlement and Water Commissioner; Advisory Councillor. During War of 1939–45 assisted with political advice as Lt-Col, Gen. Staff, Jerusalem Bureau. *Publications:* Grammar in Bahdinan Kurmanji (Kurdish), 1922; Gazetteer of Place Names in Palestine and Trans-Jordan, 1941. *Recreation:* yachting. *Address:* Walhampton March, Lymington, Hants. *T:* Lymington 72481. *Clubs:* Royal Lymington Yacht, etc. *Died 26 Dec. 1982.*

**JARDINE OF APPLEGIRTH, Col Sir William Edward,** 11th Bt of Nova Scotia, *cr* 1672; OBE 1966; TD; DL; JP; Chief of the Clan Jardine; late The KOSB; *b* 15 April 1917; *s* of Sir Alexander Jardine of Applegirth, 10th Baronet, and Winifred Mary Hamilton (*d* 1954), *d* of Major Young, Lincluden House, Dumfries; *S* father, 1942; *m* 1944, Ann Graham, *yr d* of late Lt-Col Claud Maitland, DSO, Gordon Highlanders, of Dundrennan and Cumstoun, Kirkcudbright; two *s.* Mem. of The Queen's Body Guard for Scotland, The Royal Company of Archers. Commnd KOSB 1939, retd as Major, 1960. Lt-Col Comd 4/5 KOSB (TA), 1963–67, Bt Col 1967. Chm., Dumfriesshire SSAFA, 1965–78; Mem., Lowland T&AVRA, 1970 (Chm., Border Area Cttee, 1977–82). Mem., Dumfries CC, 1960–75, Chm. Roads Cttee, 1970–75; Mem., Annandale and Eskdale DC, 1975–84, Chm., Gen. Purposes Cttee, 1976–84. Chairman: Solway River Purification Bd, 1976–; Scottish River Purification Bds Assoc., 1983–84; Annan Dist Salmon Fishery Bd, 1980–84. JP 1962, DL 1970, co. of Dumfries. *Heir:s* Alexander Maule Jardine, *yr* of Applegirth [*b* 24 Aug. 1947; *m* 1982, Mary Beatrice, *d* of late Hon. John Michael Inigo Cross and of Mrs James Parker-Jervis; one *s*]. *Address:* Denbie, Lockerbie, Dumfriesshire DG11 1DH. *T:* Carrutherstown 631. *Clubs:* Army and Navy; Puffin's (Edinburgh). *Died 19 April 1986.*

**JARDINE PATERSON, Lt-Col Arthur James,** OBE 1958; TD 1945; Lord Lieutenant of Dumfries, since 1982; *b* 14 July 1918; *s* of late R. Jardine Paterson; *m* 1948, Mary Fearne Balfour-Kinnear; one *d. Educ:* Eton; Jesus Coll., Cambridge. TA, 1939; served War of 1939–45, KOSB, NW Europe; comd 5th Bn KOSB, 1955–58. CC Dumfriesshire, 1960; Reg. Council, Dumfries and Galloway, 1974–82. DL 1964, JP 1965, Dumfriesshire. *Recreation:* shooting. *Address:* Skairfield, Lockerbie, Dumfriesshire DG11 1JL. *T:* Lochmaben 201. *Club:* Army and Navy.
*Died 10 Feb. 1988.*

**JARMAN, Air Cdre Lance Michael E.;** *see* Elworthy-Jarman.

**JARRETT, Norman Rowlstone,** CMG 1946; BA Oxon; *b* 23 Aug. 1889; *s* of late Arthur E. Jarrett, Netherby Cottage, Anstye, Cuckfield, Sussex; *m* 1st, Doris Griffith; one *s* one *d*; 2nd, Violet (*d* 1972), *d* of Rev. W. H. Wilkinson, Warminster. *Educ:* Highgate Sch.; Exeter Coll., Oxford (2nd Class Lit Hum 1912). Cadet FMS Civil Service, 1912; various administrative appointments in Malayan Civil Service, 1913–37; British Adviser, Trengganu, 1937; Food Controller, Malaya, 1939–41; Acting British Resident, Selangor, 1941–; interned by Japanese in Singapore, 1942–45; Sec., Assoc. of British Malaya, 1946–53. *Recreations:* gardening, music. *Address:* Anvil Cottage, Lye Green, near Crowborough, East Sussex TN6 1UU. *T:* Crowborough 4466. *Died 21 June 1982.*

**JARVIS, Ven. Alfred Clifford,** MA; Archdeacon of Lindsey, and Canon Residentiary of Lincoln Cathedral, 1960–71, Archdeacon Emeritus since 1971; *b* 6 Feb. 1908; *o s* of late A. W. Jarvis; *m* 1937, Mary Dorothea Chapple. *Educ:* Sudbury Grammar Sch.; Fitzwilliam House, Cambridge; Lichfield Theological Coll. Curate of Brightlingsea, 1931; permission to officiate Diocese of Ely, 1936; Vicar of Horningsea, 1937; Chaplain to Fulbourn Mental Hospital, 1937; Rector of Coddenham, 1944–55; Curate in charge of Hemingstone, 1949–52; Hon. Chaplain to Bishop of St Edmundsbury and Ipswich, 1954; Vicar of Elsfield and Beckley, and Curate in charge of Horton cum Studley, 1955–58; Archdeacon of Lincoln, Canon and Preb. of St Mary Crackpool in Lincoln Cathedral, and Rector of Algarkirk, 1958–60. Chaplain to High Sheriffs of Lincolnshire: Lord Worsley, 1964; Sir Anthony Thorold, Bt, 1968. Proctor in Convocation, 1961; Warden of Lincoln Diocesan Assoc. of Readers, 1960. *Recreations:* shooting and fishing. *Address:* Wykeham Hall, Ludford, Lincoln. *T:* Burgh-on-Bain 771. *Club:* Flyfishers'. *Died 21 Nov. 1981.*

**JARVIS, Mrs Doris Annie,** CBE 1969; Headmistress, Tower Hamlets Comprehensive Girls' School, 1963–74; *b* 18 April 1912; *d* of William George Mabbitt (killed on active service, 1918) and Ada Marie Mabbitt; *m* 1940, George Harry Jarvis; one *s. Educ:* South Hackney Central Sch.; City of London Sch. for Girls; King's Coll., London (BSc); Furzedown Training Coll., London. Commenced teaching in Bethnal Green, E2, Sept. 1935; worked in E London schools and evacuation areas during War period; post-war, taught at Daniel Secondary Sch., E2; Emergency Training College Lecturer,

Camden Trg Coll., 1949–50; Headmistress, Wilmot Secondary Girls' Sch., Bethnal Green, E2, 1950–63. *Recreations:* home affairs, reading, walking, gardening; furthering knowledge of education and social work in E London, generally. *Address:* 1a Tolmers Avenue, Cuffley, Herts. *T:* Cuffley 3780.

**JARVIS, Hon. Eric William George,** CMG 1961; Judge of the High Court, Rhodesia, 1963–77; *b* 22 Nov. 1907; *s* of late William Stokes Jarvis and Edith Mary Jarvis (*née* Langley), both of Essex, England; *m* 1937, Eveline Mavis Smith; one *s* one *d. Educ:* Salisbury Boys High Sch. (now Prince Edward Sch.), Salisbury, R; Rhodes Univ., Grahamstown, SA. BA; LLB; admitted as Advocate High Court of Southern Rhodesia, 1929; appointed Law Officer of Crown, 1934; KC (1949); Solicitor-Gen. for Southern Rhodesia, 1949–55; Attorney-Gen. for Southern Rhodesia, 1955–62. *Recreations:* tennis, golf, bowls. *Address:* c/o S. M. J. Young, 64 Drama Street, Somerset West, 7130, South Africa.
*Died 14 June* 1987.

**JASPER, Cyril Charles;** County Treasurer, Hertfordshire County Council, 1972–81; *b* 16 Oct. 1923; *s* of James Edward Jasper and Daisy (*née* Brown); *m* 1949, Vera Newington; three *s* two *d. Educ:* Brockley County Grammar Sch. DPA London 1950; CIPFA (double Hons) 1959; FBIM. Comptroller's Dept, LCC, 1941–60; Asst County Treas., W Sussex CC, 1961–69; Dep. Co. Treas., Herts CC, 1970–72. Consultant to: Mercury Warburg Investment Management Ltd (formerly Rowan Investment Managers Ltd), 1982–87; Lazard Securities Ltd, 1980–; Dist Treasurer and Mem. Central Finance Bd, Methodist Church, 1983–. Financial Adviser to Educn Cttee, Assoc. of County Councils, 1972–81. Pres., Soc. of County Treasurers, 1978–79. Collins Gold Medal, CIPFA, 1959. *Publications:* contrib. local govt papers. *Recreations:* amateur dramatics, youth work. *Address:* The Spinney, Hertford SG13 7JR.
*Died 1 Dec.* 1987.

**JASPER, Very Rev. Ronald Claud Dudley,** CBE 1981; DD; Dean of York, 1975–84, Dean Emeritus, since 1984; *b* 17 Aug. 1917; *o s* of late Claud Albert and late Florence Lily Jasper; *m* 1943, Ethel, *o d* of David and Edith Wiggins; one *s* one *d. Educ:* Plymouth Coll.; University of Leeds; College of the Resurrection, Mirfield. MA (with distinction), 1940; DD 1961. FRHistS 1954. Curate of Ryhope, 1940–42; St Oswald's, Durham, 1942–43; Esh, 1943–46; Chaplain of University Coll., Durham, 1946–48; Vicar of Stillington, 1948–55; Succentor of Exeter Cathedral, 1955–60; Lecturer in Liturgical Studies: King's Coll., London, 1960–67, Reader, 1967–68; RSCM, 1965–69; Canon of Westminster, 1968–75; Archdeacon, 1974–75. Chm., Church of England Liturgical Commn, 1964–81. Hon. DLitt Susquehanna, 1976. *Publications:* Prayer Book Revision in England, 1800–1900, 1954; Walter Howard Frere: Correspondence and Memoranda on Liturgical Revision and Construction, 1954; Arthur Cayley Headlam, 1960; George Bell: Bishop of Chichester, 1967; A Christian's Prayer Book, 1972; (ed) The Renewal of Worship, 1965; (ed) The Calendar and Lectionary, 1967; (ed) The Daily Office, 1968; (ed) Holy Week Services, 1971; (ed) Initiation and Eucharist, 1972; (ed) The Eucharist Today, 1974; Prayers of the Eucharist, 1975; Pray Every Day, 1976; The Daily Office Revised, 1978; A Companion to the Alternative Service Book, 1986; The Development of the Anglican Liturgy 1662–1980, 1989; Language and the Worship of the Church, 1990; contribs to: A New Dictionary of Christian Theology, 1983; A New Dictionary of Liturgy and Worship, 1986; Church Quarterly Review, Jl of Ecclesiastical History, Church Quarterly, London Quarterly, Expository Times, Ecumenica, Heythrop Jl. *Recreations:* reading, writing, television. *Address:* 3 Westmount Close, Ripon HG4 2HU.
*Died 11 April* 1990.

**JAY, Rev. Canon Eric George;** Professor of Historical Theology, Faculty of Divinity, McGill University, 1958–75, Emeritus, 1977; *b* 1 March 1907; *s* of Henry Jay, Colchester, Essex; *m* 1937, Margaret Hilda, *d* of Rev. Alfred W. Webb; one *s* two *d. Educ:* Colchester High Sch.; Leeds Univ. BA 1st Cl. Hons Classics, 1929; MA 1930; BD (London) 1937; MTh 1940; PhD 1951. Deacon, 1931; priest, 1932; Curate, St Augustine, Stockport, 1931–34; Lecturer in Theology, King's Coll., London, 1934–47; Curate, St Andrew Undershaft, City of London, 1935–40. Served War as Chaplain in RAFVR 1940–45. Rector, St Mary-le-Strand, 1945–47; Dean of Nassau, Bahamas, 1948–51; Senior Chaplain to the Archbishop of Canterbury, 1951–58; Principal, Montreal Diocesan Theological Coll., 1958–64; Dean, Faculty of Divinity, McGill Univ., 1963–70. Fellow of King's Coll., London, 1948; Canon of Montreal, 1960. Hon. DD: Montreal Diocesan Theolog. Coll., 1964; Trinity Coll., Toronto, 1975; United Theol Coll., Montreal, 1976. *Publications:* The Existence of God, 1946; Origen's Treatise on Prayer, 1954; New Testament Greek; an Introductory Grammar, 1958; Son of Man, Son of God, 1965; The Church: its changing image through twenty centuries, 1977. *Recreations:* reading "thrillers"; crossword puzzles, watching ice hockey, cricket and Rugby football. *Address:* 3421 Durocher Street, Apt 406, Montreal PQ, H2X 2C6, Canada.
*Died 7 Feb.* 1989.

**JEANS, Isabel;** actress; *b* London, 16 Sept. 1891; *d* of Frederick George Jeans; *m* 1st, Claud Rains (marr. diss.); 2nd, Gilbert Edward (*d* 1963), *y s* of late Rt Rev. Henry Russell Wakefield, Bishop of Birmingham; no *c. Educ:* London. Made first appearance under Sir Herbert Tree's management at His Majesty's; first acting role was at the Garrick as Peggy in The Greatest Wish; went to United States with Granville Barker's Company, playing Titania in A Midsummer Night's Dream and Fanny in Fanny's First Play; on returning to England appeared in musical comedy and then joined the Everyman Repertory Company, playing Fanny, Raina in Arms and the Man, Hypatia in Misalliance, and Olivia in Twelfth Night, and also appeared in a number of Elizabethan and Restoration revivals by the Phœnix Society including Volpone, The Maid's Tragedy, The Jew of Malta, The Old Bachelor, and as Margery Pinchwife in The Country Wife; went to Holland to play Laura Pasquale in At Mr Beam's, and later played Yasmin in Hassan at His Majesty's and Lydia Languish in The Rivals at the Lyric, Hammersmith; since 1924 has appeared as Zelie in The Rat, Nell Gwynne in Mr Pepys, Lady Dare Bellingham in Conflict, Amytis in The Road to Rome, Estelle in Beauty, Crystal Wetherby in The Man in Possession, subsequently playing the same part in New York, Leslie in Counsel's Opinion, Mrs Jelliwell in Springtime for Henry, Lady Coperario in Spring 1600, Lucy Lockit in The Beggar's Opera, Lola in Full House, La Gambogi in The Happy Hypocrite, Alice Galvoisier in Mademoiselle, Susanna Venables in Second Helping, Lady Utterwood in Heartbreak House, Mrs Erlynne in Lady Windermere's Fan; went to New York, Jan. 1948, to play Lucia in Make Way for Lucia; since returning to London has appeared as Madame Arkadina in The Seagull; The Countess in Ardele; Florence Lancaster in The Vortex; Mrs Allonby in A Woman of No Importance; Lady Elizabeth Mulhammer in The Confidential Clerk (created rôle at Edinburgh Festival, 1953, and appeared in it finally at Paris Festival of Dramatic Art, 1954; made first appearance on Television, in this rôle, 1955); Sophie Faramond in the Gates of Summer. In 1957 created rôle of Aunt Alicia in the film Gigi; Duchess of Berwick in Lady Windermere's Fan, 1966; Mrs Malaprop in The Rivals, 1967; Lady Bracknell in The Importance of Being Earnest, Haymarket, 1968; Mme Desmortes in Ring Round the Moon, Haymarket, 1969; Dear Antoine, Piccadilly, 1971. Films and TV plays in Hollywood, Paris, Rome and Vienna. *Recreation:* reading historical biographies. *Address:* 66/24 John Islip Street, SW1.
*Died 4 Sept.* 1985.

**JEFFERY, George Henry Padget,** CMG 1965; FASA; Auditor General for South Australia, 1959–72; Chairman, Board of Trustees, Savings Bank of South Australia, 1972–76 (Trustee, 1965–76); *b* 6 June 1907; *s* of late George Frederick Jeffery and late Adelaide Jeffery (*née* Padget), Victor Harbour, S Aust.; *m* 1934, Jean Loudon Watt, *d* of late Thomas Watt, Adelaide; two *s. Educ:* Adelaide High Sch.; Victor Harbour High Sch.; University of Adelaide. Associate, University of Adelaide, 1933; Auditor, SA Public Service, 1936–40; Chief Inspector, 1940–51; Sec., Public Buildings Dept, 1951–53; Chief Executive, Radium Hill Uranium Project, 1953–59; Mem., SA Public Service Board, 1956–59. Pres., SA Div., Aust. Soc. of Accountants, 1965–67. Chm., Royal Commission of Enquiry into Grape Growing Industry, 1965. Member: Parly. Salaries Tribunal, 1966–79; Royal Commn on State Transport Services, 1966–67; Cttee of Inquiry into S Australian Racing Industry, 1974–75. Dep. Chm., S Australian Egg Bd, 1973–79. Mem., Bd of Management, Queen Victoria Hosp., 1972–76. FASA 1958. *Recreations:* bowls, cricket. *Address:* 49 Anglesey Avenue, St Georges, SA 5064, Australia. *T:* 79–2929. *Clubs:* Commonwealth, SA Cricket Association, Glenunga Bowling (Adelaide).
*Died 16 April* 1987.

**JEFFERY, Lilian Hamilton,** FBA 1965; FSA 1956; Fellow and Tutor in Ancient History, Lady Margaret Hall, Oxford, 1952–80, then Honorary Fellow; *b* 5 Jan. 1915; 3rd *d* of late Thomas Theophilus Jeffery, MA Cantab, and Lilian Mary (*née* Hamilton). *Educ:* Cheltenham Ladies' Coll.; Newnham Coll., Cambridge. BA (Class. Tripos) 1936; MA 1941; Dipl. in Class. Archæology, 1937; DPhil (Oxon) 1951. Mem. British Sch. of Archæology, Athens, 1937–; Mem. Soc. for Promotion of Hellenic Studies, 1937–. Nurse in Military Hosp., 1940–41; WAAF (Intelligence), 1941–45. First Katherine McBride Vis. Prof., Bryn Mawr Coll., USA, 1971–72. Ed. Annual of British School at Athens, 1955–61. *Publications:* (collab.) Dedications from the Athenian Akropolis, 1948; The Local Scripts of Archaic Greece, 1961; (contrib.) A Companion to Homer, 1962; (contrib.) Perachora ii, 1964; Archaic Greece, 1976; (contrib.) Cambridge Ancient History, Vol. iii, part 3, 1982 and Plates Vol., 1984; articles in Jl of Hellenic Studies, Annual of Brit. Sch. at Athens, Hesperia, Amer. Jl of Philology, Historia, Philologus, etc. *Address:* c/o Lady Margaret Hall, Oxford.
*Died 29 Sept.* 1986.

**JEFFREYS, 2nd Baron,** *cr* 1952, of Burkham; **Mark George Christopher Jeffreys;** Major, Grenadier Guards, retired; *b* 2 Feb. 1932; *er s* of Capt. Christopher John Darell Jeffreys, MVO, Grenadier Guards (*o s* of 1st Baron; killed in action, 1940) and Lady

Rosemary Beatrice Agar (*d* 1984), *y d* of 4th Earl of Normanton; *S* grandfather, 1960; *m* 1st, 1956, Sarah Annabelle Mary (marr. diss., 1967), *o d* of Major Henry Claude Lyon Garnett; two *s* two *d*; 2nd, 1967, Anne Louise, *d* of Sir Shirley Worthington-Evans, 2nd Bt, and of Mrs Joan Parry; one *d*; 3rd, 1981, Suzanne, *d* of James Stead, Goudhurst, Kent. *Educ:* Eton; RMA, Sandhurst. *Heir: s* Hon. Christopher Henry Mark Jeffreys [*b* 22 May 1957; *m* 1985, Anne Elisabeth, *d* of Mrs Derek Johnson, Boden Hall, Scholar Green, Cheshire]. *Address:* House of Lords, SW1A 0PW. *Club:* White's.
*Died 13 Feb. 1986.*

**JEFFREYS, Anthony Henry,** CB 1961; *b* 13 Aug. 1896; *yr s* of late Major-Gen. H. B. Jeffreys, CB, CMG; *m* 1922, Dorothy Bertha (*d* 1983), *d* of late Lieut-Col Edward Tufnell. *Educ:* Eton. Served War of 1914–18 (despatches; wounded); 2nd Lieut RFA, 1915; Lieut 'D' Battery RHA, 1917–19; Staff Captain, GHQ, France, and War Office, 1939–41. Entered Parliament Office, House of Lords, 1919; called to the Bar Inner Temple, 1924. Examiner of Petitions for Private Bills, 1941; Chief Clerk of Cttees and Private Bills and Taxing Officer, 1945; Reading Clerk, House of Lords, 1953; Clerk Asst of the Parliaments, 1959–61, retd. Chm., City of Westminster Boy Scouts' Assoc., 1953–60. *Address:* Doom Bar House, Trebetherick, Wadebridge, Cornwall PL27 6SA. *T:* Trebetherick 3380. *Club:* Lansdowne.
*Died 7 Feb. 1984.*

**JEFFREYS, Sir Harold,** Kt 1953; MA Cambridge; DSc Durham; FRS 1925; Fellow of St John's College, Cambridge, since 1914; Plumian Professor of Astronomy and Experimental Philosophy, 1946–58; *b* 22 April 1891; *o s* of R. H. and E. M. Jeffreys, Birtley, Durham; *m* 1940, Bertha, *d* of late W. A. Swirles and H. Swirles, Northampton. *Educ:* Armstrong Coll., Newcastle upon Tyne; St John's Coll., Cambridge. University Reader in Geophysics, 1931–46. Mathematical Tripos, 1913; Isaac Newton Student, 1914; Smith's Prize, 1915; Adams Prize, 1927; commended, 1923; Buchan Prize of Royal Meteorological Society, 1929. Gold Medal of Royal Astronomical Society, 1937; Murchison Medal of Geological Soc., 1939; Victoria Medal of RGS, 1942; Royal Medal of Royal Society, 1948; Ch. Lagrange Prize, Acad. Royal Sci., Belg., 1948; Bowie Medal, Amer. Geophys. Union, 1952; Copley Medal, Royal Society, 1960; Vetlesen Prize, 1962; Guy Medal, Royal Statistical Society, 1963; Wollaston Medal, Geological Soc., 1964; Medal of Seismological Soc. of Amer., 1979. President: Royal Astronomical Soc., 1955–57; Internat. Seism. Assoc., 1957–60; For. Associate, US Nat. Acad. of Sciences; Accad. dei Lincei, Rome, Acad. Sci. Stockholm, New York Acad. Sci., Amer. Acad. of Arts and Sciences, Acad. Roy. de Belgique; Hon. FRSE; Hon. FRSNZ; Corresp. Member: Amer. Geophys. Union; Geolog. Soc. America; RIA; Hon. Member: Inst. of Mathematics; Seismological Soc. of Amer.; RMetS; Hon. Corresponding-Astronomer, Royal Observatory of Belgium, 1984. Hon. LLD Liverpool, 1953; Hon. ScD Dublin, 1956; Hon. DCL Durham, 1960; Hon. DSc, Southern Methodist Univ., Dallas, 1967; Hon. DPhil Uppsala, 1977. *Publications:* The Earth: Its Origin, History, and Physical Constitution, 1924, 1929, 1952, 1959, 1962, 1970, 1976; Operational Methods in Mathematical Physics, 1927, 1931; The Future of the Earth, 1929; Scientific Inference, 1931, 1937, 1957, 1973; Cartesian Tensors, 1931, 1952, 1969; Earthquakes and Mountains, 1935, 1950; Theory of Probability, 1939, 1948, 1962, 1967, 1983; Methods of Mathematical Physics (with B. Jeffreys), 1946, 1950, 1956, 1962, 1972; Asymptotic Approximations, 1962, 1968; papers on Astronomy, Geophysics, Theory of Scientific Method, and Plant Ecology, republished in Collected Papers of Sir Harold Jeffreys, vols 1–6, 1971–77. *Address:* 160 Huntingdon Road, Cambridge CB3 0LB.
*Died 18 March 1989.*

**JEFFREYS, Montagu Vaughan Castelman,** CBE 1953; MA Oxon; Emeritus Professor, University of Birmingham; *b* 16 Dec. 1900; *s* of late Col F. V. Jeffreys, RE, and Lane Annie Augusta Jeffreys (*née* Barton); *m* 1941, Joan Sheila, *d* of late Col R. D. Marjoribanks and Sheila Balfour Maclean Marjoribanks (*née* Jack); one *s* one *d*. *Educ:* Wellington Coll.; Hertford Coll., Oxford. Asst Master, Oundle Sch., 1924–27; Lecturer in Education, Armstrong Coll., Newcastle upon Tyne, 1927–32; Lecturer in Educ., University of London Institute of Education, 1932–39; Prof. of Educn in University of Durham, 1939–46. Prof. of Educn in University of Birmingham and Dir of University of Birmingham Inst. of Educn, 1946–64. Pres. Inst. of Christian Educn, 1958–63. Does occasional broadcasting. *Publications:* Play Production: for Amateurs and Schools (3 edns), 1933 (with R. W. Stopford); History in Schools: The Study of Development, 1939; Education-Christian or Pagan, 1946; Kingdom of This World, 1950; Glaucon: an Inquiry into the Aims of Education (3 edns and 5 reprints), 1950; Beyond Neutrality, 1955; Mystery of Man, 1957; Revolution in Teacher Training, 1961; Personal Values in the Modern World, 1962 (rev. edns 1966, 1968); The Unity of Education, 1966; The Ministry of Teaching, 1967; John Locke, Prophet of Common Sense, 1967; Religion and Morality, 1967; You and Other People, 1969; Education: its nature and purpose, 1972; articles on educational and religious topics in

various periodicals. *Address:* Lyndwell Cottage, 1 Wellands Road, Lyndhurst, Hants.
*Died 6 Sept. 1985.*

**JEFFRIES, Graham Montague;** *see* Graeme, Bruce.

**JENKIN, Sir William Norman Prentice,** Kt 1947; CSI 1946; CIE 1931; KPM 1924; *b* 11 Aug. 1899; *m* 1924, Ayliffe Wansborough, *d* of Percy Stevens. *Educ:* Scottish Academy. Commnd RFC, 1917; joined Indian Police Service, 1919; Superintendent, 1927; late Deputy Dir, Intelligence Bureau, Home Department, Government of India; Dir of Intelligence, Malaya, 1950–51. *Address:* Seven, Oaks Road, Tenterden, Kent TN30 6RD. *T:* Tenterden 2760.
*Died 28 Dec. 1983.*

**JENKINS, A(rthur) Robert,** CBE 1972; JP; Director: Robert Jenkins & Co. Ltd, Rotherham, since 1934 (Chairman, 1958–83); Robert Jenkins (Holdings) Ltd, since 1968 (Chairman, 1968–83); *b* 20 June 1908; *s* of Edgar Jackson Jenkins and Ethel Mary Bescoby; *m* 1933, Margaret Fitton Jones; one *s* three *d*. *Educ:* Rotherham Grammar Sch.; Sheffield Univ. CEng, FIMechE. Chairman: British Welding Res. Assoc., 1956–68; Tank and Industrial Plant Assoc., 1958–61; of Council, Welding Inst., 1968–71; of Council, Process Plant Assoc., 1971–75 (Vice-Pres., 1975); Pres., Welding Inst., 1951–53 and 1973–75; Vice-Pres., British Mechanical Engrg Confedn, 1972–. Mem. Exec. Bd, BSI, 1974. Hon. FWeldI 1982. JP 1948. *Recreation:* gardening. *Address:* 15 Castle Court, Helmsley, North Yorks.
*Died 29 June 1989.*

**JENKINS, Sir Evan Meredith,** GCIE 1947 (KCIE 1944; CIE 1936); KCSI 1945 (CSI 1941); *b* 2 Feb. 1896; *s* of late Sir John Lewis Jenkins, KCSI. *Educ:* Rugby; Balliol Coll., Oxford. Served European War, 1914–19; joined Indian Civil Service, 1920, and served in Punjab; Chief Commissioner, Delhi, 1937; Sec., Dept of Supply, 1940–43; Private Sec to the Viceroy and Sec. to the Governor-General (Personal), 1943–45; Governor of the Punjab, 1946–47; Director: Eastern Bank Ltd, 1947–67 (Chm., 1950–67); Chartered Bank, 1958–67. *Address:* 24 Ashley Gardens, SW1.
*Died 3 Nov. 1985.*

**JENKINS, Sir Gilmour;** *see* Jenkins, Sir T. G.

**JENKINS, Mrs Inez Mary Mackay,** CBE 1943; *b* 30 Oct 1895; *c* of John Mackay Ferguson; *m* 1923, Frederick Cyril Jenkins; one *s*. *Educ:* Berkhamsted Sch. for Girls; St Hilda's Hall, Oxford. Gen. Sec., National Federation of Women's Institutes, 1919–29; Sec., English Folk Dance and Song Soc., 1931–39; Chief Administrative Officer Women's Land Army (England and Wales), 1939–48; Mem. Central Agricultural Wages Board for England and Wales, 1952–63. *Publication:* History of the Women's Institute Movement of England and Wales, 1953. *Recreations:* gardening, philately. *Address:* White Ends, Rotherfield Greys, Oxon. *T:* Rotherfield Greys 206.
*Died 17 Sept. 1981.*

**JENKINS, Ven. (John) Owen;** *b* 13 June 1906; *m* 1939, Gwladys Margaret Clark Jones, *d* of Ven. D. M. Jones, sometime Archdeacon of Carmarthen. *Educ:* St David's Coll., Lampeter; Jesus Coll., Oxford. Deacon 1929, priest 1930; Curate of: Cwmamman, 1929–33; Llanelly, 1933–39; Vicar of Spittal with Trefgarn, 1939–48; TCF, 1943–46; Vicar of Llangadock, 1948–60; Canon of St David's, 1957–62; Rector of Newport, Pembs, 1960–67; Archdeacon of Cardigan, 1962–67; Archdeacon of Carmarthen and Vicar of Llanfihangel Aberbythick, 1967–74. Editor, St David's Dio. Year Book, 1954–63. *Address:* Gwladys, 77 Heol y Graig, Aberporth, Cardigan SA43 2EN. *T:* Aberporth 810060.
*Died 9 Aug. 1988.*

**JENKINS, Sir (Thomas) Gilmour,** KCB 1948 (CB 1941); KBE 1944; MC; Vice-President, Royal Academy of Music; Member, London Philharmonic Orchestra Council; Vice-President, Marine Society; *b* 18 July 1894; *s* of late Thomas Jenkins; *m* 1916, Evelyne Mary (*d* 1976), *d* of C. H. Nash; one *s* one *d*. *Educ:* Rutlish Sch.; London Univ.; BSc. Served European War, RGA (MC and bar); entered Board of Trade, 1919; Asst Sec., 1934; Government Delegate to Maritime Sessions of International Labour Conference Geneva, 1935 and 1936, and Copenhagen, 1945; Principal Asst Sec., Board of Trade, 1937; Second Sec., Ministry of Shipping, 1939; Dep. Dir-Gen., Ministry of War Transport, 1941–46; Permanent Sec., Control Office for Germany and Austria, 1946–47; Joint Permanent Under-Sec. of State, Foreign Office, during 1947; Permanent Sec. to Ministry of Transport, 1947–53; Permanent Secretary to Ministry of Transport and Civil Aviation, 1953–59; Pres. Inst. of Marine Engineers, 1953–54; Pres. Institute of Transport, 1954–55; Pres., International Conference on Safety of Life at Sea, 1960; Pres., International Conference on Pollution of the Sea by Oil, 1954 and 1962; Pres., International Conference on Load Lines, 1966. Hon. FRAM. Grand Officer, Order of Orange Nassau (Netherlands); Comdr with Star, Order of St Olav (Norway); Knight Comdr, Order of George I (Greece); Comdr, Order of the Crown (Belgium). *Publication:* The Ministry of Transport and Civil Aviation, 1959. *Recreation:* music. *Address:* c/o Highams Chase, Goldhanger, Maldon, Essex. *T:* Maldon 88644.
*Died 9 Sept. 1981.*

**JENKINS, Sir William,** Kt 1966; JP; Agent in London for Government of Northern Ireland, 1966–70; *b* 25 July 1904; *m* 1942, Jessie May Watson, Otago, NZ; no *c. Educ:* Whitehouse Sch.; Belfast Coll. of Technology. Joined W. H. Brady & Co. Ltd, Bombay, 1931; became Sen. Dir; retd 1956. JP Bombay, 1946; Hon. Presidency Magistrate Bombay, 1948. Dir various joint cos in Bombay. Chairman: Gilbert-Ash (NI) Ltd; Old Bushmills Distillery Co. Ltd; Director: Belfast Banking Co.; Arthur Guinness Son & Co. (B) Ltd, 1963–79. Entered Belfast Corp., 1957; JP Belfast, 1958; High Sheriff, Belfast, 1961; Dep. Lord Mayor, 1962; Lord Mayor of Belfast, 1964, 1965, 1966. Mem. Senate of N Ireland, 1963–66; Hon. Treas., Queen's Univ., 1963–66; Hon. Treas., Queen's Univ., 1965; first recipient of "Community Award" by New Ireland Soc. of Queen's Univ. for outstanding services to community during term as Lord Mayor. Mem. Council, 1967–70 (Chm. NI Br., 1967–75), Inst. of Directors. *Recreation:* golf. *Address:* 130 Merville Garden Village, Newtown Abbey, Belfast, N Ireland. *Clubs:* Royal Automobile; Willingdon (Bombay); Ulster Reform (Belfast); Royal Belfast Golf, Fortwilliam Golf. *Died* 23 Jan. 1983.

**JENKINSON, Sir Anthony Banks,** 13th Bt, *cr* 1661; *b* 3 July 1912; *s* of Captain John Banks Jenkinson (killed European War, Sept. 1914) and Joan, *o d* of late Col Joseph Hill, CB (she *m* 2nd, 1920, Maj.-Gen. Algernon Langhorne, CB, DSO, who died 1945); *S* grandfather, 1915; *m* 1943, Frances, *d* of Harry Stremmel; one *s* two *d. Educ:* Eton; Balliol Coll., Oxford (Editor, The Isis, 1933–34). Foreign Correspondent, 1935–40: first British reporter to interview Mao Tse-tung in Yenan, NW China, Daily Sketch, 1938; Mediterranean Snoop Cruise Series, Daily Express, 1939; Caribbean Snoop Cruise, N American Newspaper Alliance & Reader's Digest, 1940; Editor, Allied Labour News Service, London and New York, 1940–46. Managing Director: Cayman Boats Ltd, Cayman Is, 1947–52; Morgan's Harbour Ltd, Port Royal, Jamaica, 1953–73; Director: Port Royal Co. of Merchants Ltd, 1965–72; Spanish Main Investments Ltd, Grand Cayman, 1962–; Caribbean Bank (Cayman) Ltd, 1973–80; Cayman Free Press Ltd, 1974–; Cayman Corporate Services Ltd, 1982–. *Publications:* America Came My Way, 1935; Where Seldom a Gun is Heard, 1937. *Recreations:* sailing, travel. *Heir: s* John Banks Jenkinson, *b* 16 Feb. 1945. *Address:* 491 South Church Street, Grand Cayman, British West Indies. *Clubs:* United Oxford & Cambridge University; MCC; Bembridge Sailing; Cayman Islands Yacht.
*Died* 15 Jan. 1989.

**JENNINGS, (Bernard) Antony;** Legal Adviser, BBC, 1977–89; Director: BBC Enterprises Ltd, 1979; Video Copyright Protection Society Ltd, 1981; Confederation of Information Communication Industries Ltd, 1987; *b* 29 May 1939; *s* of Bernard Joseph Francis Jennings and Constance Nora Jennings (*née* O'Shea). *Educ:* St Bede's Coll., Manchester; Christ's Coll., Cambridge (MA). Articled Clerk, John Gorna & Co., Manchester; admitted Solicitor, 1964; BBC Solicitor's Dept, 1964–74; BBC Head of Copyright, 1974–77. Chm., Legal Cttee, EBU, 1982–. *Publications:* (jtly) Satellite Broadcasting, 1985; articles in copyright and media law jls. *Address:* Broadcasting House, W1A 1AA. *T:* 01–580 4468.
*Died* 10 April 1990.

**JENNINGS, Christopher;** *see* Jennings, R. E. C.

**JENNINGS, (Edgar) Owen,** RWS 1953 (ARWS 1943); RE 1970 (ARE 1944); ARCA London 1925; FRSA; Principal, School of Art, Tunbridge Wells, 1934–65; *b* Cowling, Yorks, 28 Dec. 1899; *s* of Wesley Jennings, JP and Ann Elizabeth Jennings (*née* Hardy); *m* 1929, May (*d* 1977), *d* of Arthur Cullingworth; one *s* one *d. Educ:* Sch. of Art, Skipton; Coll. of Art, Leeds; Royal College of Art, London. Examr in Three Dimensional Design for Ministry of Education. Exhibited: Royal Academy, 1925–79; RWS, RE, NEAC, Paris Salon, New York, Chicago, Antwerp, Vienna. CEMA and Brit. Coun. Exhibns in England, China, Russia, Poland, etc. Works in: British Museum; London Museum; Victoria and Albert Museum; Albertina; Brooklyn Museum, New York; Art Inst., Chicago; Public Collections Leeds, Birmingham, Wakefield. Logan Prize Winner, Chicago International, 1930; Silver Medallist, City and Guilds of London Inst.; ATD 1926. Pres., Royal Water-Colour Society Art Club, 1966–70. *Publications:* contrib. to various art jls (line engravings, wood engravings, watercolours). *Relevant publication:* review by Adrian Bury, with illustrations, in Old Water-Colour Soc's Annual Volume, 1973. *Recreations:* reading, drawing. *Address:* Linton, 26 Wilman Road, Tunbridge Wells, Kent TN4 9AP. *T:* 20581. *Club:* Chelsea Arts. *Died* 23 June 1985.

**JENNINGS, Henry Cecil;** Chairman, Co-operative Wholesale Society Ltd, 1966–72; Chief Executive Officer, North Eastern Co-operative Society Ltd, 1970–72; *b* 2 Jan. 1908; *s* of late Alfred Ernest Jennings and Gertrude Sybil Jennings; *m* 1934, Winifred Evelyn Radford; one *s* decd. *Educ:* Gerard Street Sch., Derby. Inspector of Shops, Derby Co-operative Soc. Ltd, 1947–49; Blackburn Co-operative Soc. Ltd: Grocery Manager and Buyer, 1949–51; Gen. Man., 1951–54; Gen. Man., Darlington Co-operative Soc. Ltd, 1954–70.

Dir of Co-operative Insurance Soc. Ltd, 1968–70; Chm., Associated Co-operative Creameries Ltd, 1968–70; Chm., Birtley Distributive Centre, 1964–70. Pres., Co-operative Congress, 1967. FRSA. *Recreations:* reading, gardening, travel. *Address:* 28 Gladelands Way, Corfe Lodge Park, Broadstone, Dorset BH18 9JB. *T:* Broadstone 696388. *Died* 20 Feb. 1983.

**JENNINGS, John Charles;** *b* 10 Feb. 1903; *m* 1927, Berta Nicholson (*d* 1979); one *s* decd. *Educ:* Bede Coll., Durham; King's Coll., Durham Univ. Headmaster. Contested (C), SE Derbyshire, 1950 and 1951. MP (C) Burton-on-Trent, Staffs, 1955–Feb. 1974; Chm., Cttees of House of Commons, 1964–74. *Recreation:* politics. *Address:* 9 Painshawfield Terrace, Stocksfield, Northumberland.
*Died* 17 June 1990.

**JENNINGS, Owen;** *see* Jennings, E. O.

**JENNINGS, Paul (Francis),** FRSL; writer; *b* 20 June 1918; *s* of William Benedict and Mary Gertrude Jennings; *m* 1952, Celia Blom; three *s* three *d. Educ:* King Henry VIII, Coventry, and Douai. Freelance work in Punch and Spectator began while still in Army (Lt Royal Signals); Script-writer at Central Office of Information, 1946–47; Copy writer at Colman Prentis Varley (advertising), 1947–49; on staff of The Observer, 1949–66. *Publications:* Oddly Enough, 1951; Even Oddlier, 1952; Oddly Bodlikins, 1953; Next to Oddliness, 1955; Model Oddlies, 1956; Gladly Oddly, 1957; Idly Oddly, 1959; I Said Oddly, Diddle I?, 1961; Oodles of Oddlies, 1963; The Jenguin Pennings, 1963; Oddly Ad Lib, 1965; I Was Joking, of Course, 1968; The Living Village, 1968; Just a Few Lines, 1969; It's An Odd Thing, But..., 1971; (ed) The English Difference, 1974; Britain As She Is Visit, 1976; The Book of Nonsense, 1977; I Must Have Imagined It, 1977; Companion to Britain, 1980; (ed) A Feast of Days, 1982; (ed) My Favourite Railway Stories, 1982; Golden Oddlies, 1983; East Anglia, 1986; *novel:* And Now for Something Exactly the Same, 1977; *for children:* The Hopping Basket, 1965; The Great Jelly of London, 1967; The Train to Yesterday, 1974. *Recreations:* madrigal singing and thinking about writing another vast serious book. *Address:* 25 High Street, Orford, Woodbridge, Suffolk.
*Died* 26 Dec. 1989.

**JENNINGS, (Richard Edward) Christopher,** MBE 1941; DL; Editor of The Motor, 1946–60; *b* 8 June 1911; *s* of late Lt-Col E. C. Jennings, CBE, DL; *m* 1937, Margaret, *d* of James A. Allan; one *s. Educ:* Repton. Served with Riley (Coventry) Ltd, 1931–37. Joined Temple Press as Midland Editor of The Motor, 1937–39. War of 1939–45: Lt Ordnance Mechanical Engineer, 1940; Capt. 1942; Major, 1943; Lt-Col, 1944; served in Western Desert (MBE), Greece, Crete, Syria and Northern Europe. High Sheriff of Carmarthenshire, 1957. DL Carmarthenshire, 1960. Gen. Comr of Income Tax, 1965–80; Mem., Dyfed-Carmarthen Adv. Cttee for Gen. Comrs of Income Tax, 1974–. Director: Trust Houses Ltd, 1960–68; Buckley's Brewery Ltd, 1961–77; British Automatic Co. Ltd, 1962–68; Teddington Bellows Ltd, 1965–72. Pres. RNLI, Bury Port. *Publications:* (military) dealing with the fall of Greece and Crete, 1941. *Recreations:* sailing and motoring; interested in preservation of historic ships and vehicles. *Address:* Gelli-deg, Kidwelly, Dyfed SA17 4NA. *T:* Ferryside 201. *Club:* Royal Highland Yacht. *Died* 25 July 1982.

**JEPHCOTT, Hon. Sir Bruce (Reginald),** Kt 1983; CBE 1976; company director; Owner/Manager, Dumpu Pty Ltd, since 1961; Chairman: Livestock Development Corporation, Papua New Guinea, since 1983; Kiunga & Telefomin Transport Co., since 1985; *b* 19 March 1929; *s* of Reginald Francis Jephcott and Thelma Mary (*née* Rogers); *m* 1956, Barbara Aileen Harpham; one *s* two *d. Educ:* King's Coll., Adelaide; Prince Alfred Coll., Adelaide; Adelaide Univ. (BSc 1948). ARACI 1951; MRIC, CChem 1953. Bacteriologist, F. H. Faulding, 1949–50; Chief Vet. Bio-chemist, NT Admin, 1950–59; Manager, Ainora Coffee Plantation, 1959–61; Res. Scholar, Rowett Res. Inst., Scotland, 1953; Minister for Transport, PNG, 1972–78; Dir, Pagini Transport Co., 1985–. Alternate Chm., National Airline Commn, PNG, 1982–. Pres., Polocrosse Assoc., PNG, 1982; Vice-Pres., Polocrosse Internat., 1982–. Independence Medal, PNG, 1975; Silver Jubilee Medal, 1977. *Publications:* contrib. veterinary and chemical jls. *Recreations:* tennis, golf, polocrosse. *Address:* Dumpu, Box 1299, Lae, Papua New Guinea. *T:* 443283. *Clubs:* Papua (Port Moresby, PNG); Warwick (Qld).
*Died* 11 July 1987.

**JEPHSON-JONES, Brig. Robert Llewellyn,** GC 1940; Commandant Central Ordnance Depot, Branston, 1957–60, retired; *b* 7 April 1905; *s* of Rev. J. D. Jones, and Margaret Noble Jones (*née* Jephson); *m* 1934, Irene Sykes (*d* 1985); one *d. Educ:* S Edmund's Sch., Canterbury; RMC, Sandhurst. Commissioned as 2nd Lieut Duke of Wellington's Regt, 1925; served in Singapore and India, 1926–30; served in Royal West African Frontier Force, Adjt, 1930–34; transferred to RAOC, 1936; served War, Malta, Palestine, Egypt, Sudan, Italy, 1939–44 (GC Malta); Col, 1943; Brig., 1954; Deputy Dir of Ordnance Services, Scottish Command, 1954–57.

*Address:* 11 Gorselands Court, Glenmoor Road, Ferndown, Dorset BH22 8QF. *T:* Ferndown 873411. *Club:* Naval and Military.
*Died* 27 Oct. 1985.

**JEPSON, Selwyn;** author and occasional soldier; *b* 25 Nov. 1899; *o s* of late Edgar Jepson; *m* 3rd, Tania (*d* 1980); two *d* of former marriages. *Educ:* St Paul's Sch. War of 1939–45, Major, The Buffs, Military Intelligence and SOE (recruiting secret agents). *Publications: novels:* The Qualified Adventurer, 1921; That Fellow MacArthur, 1922; The King's Red-Haired Girl, 1923; Golden Eyes, 1924; Rogues and Diamonds, 1925; Snaggletooth, 1926; The Death Gong, 1928; Tiger Dawn, 1929; I Met Murder, 1930; Rabbit's Paw, 1932; Keep Murder Quiet, 1940; Man Running, 1948; The Golden Dart, 1949; The Hungry Spider, 1950; Man Dead, 1951; The Black Italian, 1954; The Assassin, 1956; Noise in the Night, 1957; The Laughing Fish, 1960; Fear in the Wind, 1964; The Third Possibility, 1965; Angry Millionaire, 1968; Dead Letters, 1970; Letter to a Dead Girl, 1971; The Gill Interrogators, 1974; *short stories:* (with Michael Joseph) Heads or Tails, 1933; *stage play:* (with Lesley Storm) Dark Horizon, 1933; *screen plays:* Going Gay, 1932; For the Love of You, 1932; Irresistible Marmaduke, 1933; Monday at Ten, 1933; The Love Test, 1934; The Riverside Murders, 1934; White Lilac, Hyde Park Corner (Hackett), 1935; Well Done, Henry, 1936; The Scarab Murder, 1936; Toilers of the Sea (adapted and directed), 1936; Sailing Along, 1937; Carnet de Bal: Double Crime on the Maginot Line (English Version), 1938; *television plays:* Thought to Kill, 1952; Dialogue for Two Faces, 1952; My Name is Jones, 1952; Little Brother, 1953; Last Moment, 1953; Forever my Heart, 1953; Leave it to Eve (serial), 1954; The Interloper, 1955; Noise in the Night (USA), 1958; The Hungry Spider, 1964; The Peppermint Child, 1976; The Angry Millionaire (Tom McFadden), 1984; *radio serial:* The Hungry Spider, 1957; *radio plays:* The Bath that Sang, 1958; Noise in the Night, 1958; Art for Art's Sake, 1959; Small Brother, 1960; Call it Greymail, 1961; Dark Corners, 1963. *Recreations:* book collecting, painting. *Address:* The Far House, Liss, Hants. *Club:* Savile. *Died* 10 *March* 1989.

**JERITZA, Maria;** Opera and Concert Star; *b* Brno, Czechoslovakia, 6 Oct. 1887, as Marie Jedlizka; *m* Irving Seery. *Educ:* Royal Academy of Music, Vienna. Debut, Vienna State Opera, 1918; with Metropolitan Opera Company, New York, and with Vienna State Opera, 1922–49. Recipient of the highest orders and decorations, from: HH the Pope; Republic of Austria (Lady of Grand Cross of Holy Sepulchre); Republic of Italy; and Republic of France. *Publication:* Sunlight and Song. *Address:* 200 Elwood Avenue, Newark, New Jersey 07104, USA. *Died* 10 *July* 1982.

**JERRAM, Maurice William,** CBE 1979; JP; Director, Booker McConnell Food Distribution Division, since 1970 (Chairman, 1976–80); *b* 2 May 1922; *s* of William Oliver Jerram and Esther Jerram; *m* 1st, 1943, Molly Kathleen Green (*d* 1965); two *s*; 2nd, 1965, Jean Frances Thomas; one *d*. *Educ:* Richmond Road Central Sch., Kingston-upon-Thames. Apprentice, Catering, Bentalls, Kingston, 1936–38; managed family grocery store, on death of father, 1938–42. Served Army, East Surrey Regt, seconded to 2nd Batt. Nigeria Regt, W African Frontier Force, 1942–47; demobilised, rank of Major. Asst, Food Hall, Bentalls, Kingston, 1947–48; Shop Supervisor to Sales Manager, Purdy's, Gt Yarmouth, 1948–56; Area Manager to Gen. Manager, Waitrose Ltd (John Lewis Partnership), 1956–67; Booker McConnell: Man. Dir (Budgen), 1967–69, to Chm., Food Distribution Div., 1976–80; Dir, 1978–80. FIGD 1976. JP 1981. *Recreations:* gardening, walking. *Address:* 21 Newcombe Park, Mill Hill, NW7 3QN. *T:* 01-959 6594. *Club:* Army and Navy. *Died* 7 *Sept.* 1981.

**JERRAM, Rear-Adm. Sir Rowland Christopher,** KBE 1945 (CBE 1937); DSO 1920; DL; RN, retired; *b* 20 Feb. 1890; *s* of late C. S. Jerram, Talland, Cornwall; *m* 1919, Christine E. M. (*d* 1961), *d* of late J. Grigg, Port Looe, Looe, Cornwall; two *s*. *Educ:* Hillside, Godalming; King's Sch., Canterbury. Entered RN, 1907; served 1914–18 war in HM Ships Iron Duke, Lion and Queen Elizabeth; Sec. to Adm. Sir Ernle Chatfield (later Lord Chatfield), 1919–40, as 4th Sea Lord; 3rd Sea Lord, C-in-C Home Fleet, C-in-C Med. Fleet; 1st Sea Lord; Chm. Commn on Defence of India; Minister for Co-ordination of Defence. Served in HMS Cleopatra, Med., 1942–43 (in Convoy which raised Siege of Malta, Nov. 1942); Sec. to Combined Ops HQ, 1943; Comptroller HQ SACSEA, 1943–45; Head of Admlty Mission to Med., 1945, retd Dec. 1945. Comr, St John Ambulance Bde, Cornwall, 1949–58. DL Cornwall, 1958. KStJ. *Address:* Clare Park, Farnham, Surrey.
*Died* 23 *April* 1981.

**JERVIS, Charles Walter Lionel;** a Recorder of the Crown Court, 1978–86; Senior Partner, 1962–80, Consultant, 1980–86, Vivian Thomas & Jervis, Solicitors, Penzance; *b* 9 Dec. 1914; *s* of Henry Jervis, MA Oxon, and Elsie Jervis; *m* 1939, Mary Aileen Clarke; two *s* one *d*. *Educ:* Exeter Sch., Exeter. Solicitor of the Supreme Court. Served War, 1942–46; RNVR, in Asdic Ships (Atlantic Star 1944); demobilized, Lieut RNVR, 1946. Articled in IoW; Asst

Solicitor, Penzance, 1939; practised as country solicitor, 1946; Dep. Coroner, Penzance Bor., 1948; Dep. Circuit Judge, 1975–86. Pres., Cornwall Law Soc., 1965–66. Mem., Legal Aid Area Cttee, 1967–78. Dir, Tregarthens Hotel (Scilly) Ltd. *Publications:* contrib. Justice of Peace, Law Jl, and Criminal Law Rev. *Recreations:* gardening, steam locomotion, wearing old clothes. *Address:* 62 Park Road, Kingskerswell, Newton Abbot, Devon TQ12 5BG.
*Died* 8 *Dec.* 1989.

**JERVIS READ, Simon Holcombe;** *see* Read.

**JESSEL, 2nd Baron,** *cr* 1924, of Westminster; **Edward Herbert Jessel,** Bt, *cr* 1917; CBE 1963; a Deputy Speaker, House of Lords, 1963–77; *b* 25 March 1904; *o s* of 1st Baron, CB, CMG, and Maud (*d* 1965), 5th *d* of late Rt Hon. Sir Julian Goldsmid, Bt, MP; *S* father, 1950; *m* 1st, 1935, Lady Helen Maglona Vane-Tempest-Stewart (from whom he obtained a divorce, 1960; she *d* 1986), 3rd *d* of 7th Marquess of Londonderry, KG, PC, MVO; one *d* (and one *s* one *d* decd); 2nd, 1960, Jessica, *d* of late William De Wet and Mrs H. W. Taylor, Cape Town. *Educ:* Eton; Christ Church, Oxford (MA). Called to Bar, Inner Temple, 1926. Formerly Chairman, Associated Leisure Ltd; formerly Director: Textile Machinery Makers Ltd; Truscon Ltd; Westminster Trust. Chm., Assoc. of Indep. Unionist Peers, 1959–64. *Address:* 4 Sloane Terrace Mansions, SW1. *T:* 071–730 7843. *Club:* Garrick. *Died* 13 *June* 1990 (*ext*).

**JESSEL, David Charles George,** FIB; Chairman, Intervention Board for Agricultural Produce, since 1980; Deputy Chairman: Eagle Star Holdings, since 1980; Eagle Star Insurance Company, since 1971; Deputy Chairman and Managing Director, Eagle Star Properties, since 1980; *b* 20 June 1924; *s* of late Sir Richard Hugh Jessel and Margaret Ella Jessel; *m* 1st, 1950, Amelia Grace FitzRoy (marr. diss. 1978), 5th *d* of 2nd Viscount Daventry; one *s* one *d*; 2nd, 1980, Matilda McCormick, Kentucky, USA. *Educ:* Eton. FIB 1964. Served Coldstream Gds, 1942–48 (Captain). Joined Jessel Toynbee & Co. Ltd, 1948; Asst Man. Dir, 1950; Chm. and Man. Dir, 1963–77; Director: Great Portland Estates plc, 1961–77; UDS plc, 1982–83; BAT Industries, 1984–. Chm. and Dep. Chm., London Discount Market Assoc., 1967–71; Chm., Bernard Sunley Investment Trust, 1977–80. *Recreations:* fishing, shooting, sailing. *Address:* 22 Cambridge Road, SW11 4RR. *Club:* Cavalry and Guards. *Died* 20 *Sept.* 1985.

**JESSUP, Frank William,** CBE 1972; Director, Department for External Studies, Oxford University, 1952–76; Librarian of Wolfson College, Oxford, 1974–80 (Fellow, 1965–80, Honorary Fellow, 1980); *b* 26 April 1909; *s* of Frederick William Jessup and Alice Sarah (*née* Cheeseman); *m* 1935, Dorothy Hilda Harris; two *s* one *d*. *Educ:* Gravesend Boys' Grammar Sch.; Univ. of London (BA, LLB); Univ. of Oxford (MA). Called to Bar, Gray's Inn, 1935. Dep. County Educn Officer, Kent, until 1952. Chairman: Library Adv. Council (England), 1965–73; British Library Adv. Council, 1976–81; Oxon Rural Community Council, 1976–82; Vice-Chm., Universities Council for Adult Educn, 1973–76. Pres., Kent Archaeol Soc., 1976–82. Chm. of Governors, Rose Bruford Coll. of Speech and Drama, 1960–72. FSA; Hon. FLA. Hon. DCL Kent 1976. *Publications:* Problems of Local Government, 1949; Introduction to Kent Feet of Fines, 1956; A History of Kent, 1958, repr. 1974; Sir Roger Twysden, 1597–1672, 1965, etc; contrib. to Archaeologia Cantiana, Studies in Adult Educn, Möbius. *Recreations:* reading, music, gardening. *Died* 30 *Aug.* 1990.

**JESSUP, Philip C(aryl);** United States teacher and lawyer; Judge of International Court of Justice, 1961–70; Teacher of International Law, Columbia University, 1925–61; Hamilton Fish Professor of International Law and Diplomacy, 1946–61; *b* 5 Jan. 1897; *s* of Henry Wynans and Mary Hay Stotesbury Jessup; *m* 1921, Lois Walcott Kellogg; one *s*. *Educ:* Hamilton Coll., Clinton, NY (AB 1919); Columbia Univ. (AM 1924, PhD 1927); Yale Univ. (LLB). US Army Exped. Forces, 1918. Asst to Pres., and Asst Cashier, First Nat. Bank of Utica, NY, 1919–21; Parker & Duryea Law Firm, New York, 1927–43. Asst Solicitor, Dept of State, 1924–25; Asst to Elihu Root, Conf. of Jurists, Permanent Court of International Justice, Geneva, 1929; Legal Adviser to American Ambassador to Cuba, 1930; Chief, Div. of Office of Foreign Relief, Dept of State, 1943; Associate Dir, Naval Sch. of Military Government and Administration, 1942–44; Asst Sec. Gen. UNRRA and Bretton Woods Confs, 1943–44; Asst on Judicial Organisation, San Francisco Conf. on UNO, 1945; US Dep. Rep. to Interim Cttee of Gen. Assembly and Security Council, UN, 1948; Deleg. Sessions: UN Gen. Assembly, 3rd, Paris-New York, 1948–49, 4th New York, 1949, 6th, Paris, Nov. 1951–Jan. 1952, 7th New York 1952. Ambassador at Large of USA, 1949–53. Trustee, Woodrow Wilson Foundn, 1948–57, Pres., 1957–58. Storrs Lectr, Yale Univ. Law Sch., 1956; Cooley Lectr, Michigan Univ. Law Sch., 1958; Blaustein Lectr, Columbia Univ., 1970; Sibley Lectr, Univ. of Georgia Law Sch., 1970; first Fowler Harper Fellow, Yale Law Sch., 1966. Institute of Pacific Relations: Chm., Amer. Council, 1939–40; Chm., Pacific Council, 1939–42; Mem. Curatorium, Hague Acad.

of Internat. Law, 1957–68; Trustee: Carnegie Endowment for Internat. Peace, 1937–60; Hamilton Coll., 1949–61; Associate Rockefeller Foundation, 1960–61; Vice-Pres. Institut de droit international, 1959–60, 1974–75. Hon. Mem. Inter-American Institute of International Legal Studies, 1964–. Chairman: Chile-Norway Permanent Conciliation Commn, 1958–; Austro-Swedish Commn for Reconciliation and Arbitration, 1976–; Mem. Governing Council, Inst. for Unification of Private Law, 1964–67, Hon. Mem., 1967–. Hon. President: Amer. Soc. of Internat. Law, 1969–73; Amer. Branch, Internat. Law Assoc., 1970–73. Senior Fellow, Council on Foreign Relations (NYC), 1970–71. Fellow, World Acad. of Art and Sci. Member: Amer. Philosophical Soc.; Amer. Acad. of Arts and Scis. Hon. LLD: Western Reserve Univ., Nat. Univ. of Korea, Rutgers Univ., Middlebury Coll., Yale Univ., St Lawrence Univ., Univ. of Michigan; Johns Hopkins Univ.; Brandeis Univ.; Columbia Univ.; Colby Coll.; Pennsylvania Univ.; Hon. LCD: Colgate Univ., Union Coll.; Hon. JD Oslo; Doc (hc) Univ. of Paris; Hon. LittD, Univ. of Hanoi. Hon. Mem., Academia Mexicana de Derecho International. Hungarian Cross of Merit, Class II; Oficial Ordem Nacional do Cruzeiro do Sul, Brazil; Grand Officer, Order of the Cedars, Lebanon; Manley O. Hudson Gold Medal of the American Soc. of International Law, 1964; Distinguished Service Award, Connecticut Bar Assoc., 1970; Wolfgang G. Friedmann Meml Award, 1975; Columbia Univ. Sch. of Law Alumni Assoc. Medal for Excellence, 1977; Graduate Faculties Alumni of Columbia Univ. Award for Excellence, 1977. *Publications:* The Law of Territorial Waters and Maritime Jurisdiction, 1927; United States and the World Court, 1929; Neutrality, Its History, Economics and Law, Vol. I, The Origins (with F. Deak), 1935; Vol. IV, Today and Tomorrow, 1936, repr. 1976; Elihu Root, 1938, repr. 1964; International Problem of Governing Mankind, 1947; A Modern Law of Nations, 1948 (trans. German, Korean, Thai); Transnational Law, 1956 (trans. Arabic, Portuguese, Spanish, Japanese); The Use of International Law, 1959; Controls for Outer Space (with H. J. Taubenfield), 1959; The Price of International Justice, 1971; The Birth of Nations, 1974. *Address:* Windrow Road, Norfolk, Conn 06058, USA. *Clubs:* Century (New York); Cosmos (Washington).

*Died 31 Jan. 1986.*

**JEWKES, John,** CBE 1943; MA (Oxon); MCom; *b* June 1902; *m* 1929, Sylvia Butterworth; one *d. Educ:* Barrow Grammar Sch.; Manchester Univ. MCom. Asst Sec., Manchester Chamber of Commerce, 1925–26; Lecturer in Economics, University of Manchester, 1926–29; Rockefeller Foundation Fellow, 1929–30; Professor of Social Economics, Manchester 1936–46; Stanley Jevons Prof. of Political Economy, Manchester, 1946–48; Prof. of Economic Organisation, Oxford, and Fellow of Merton College, 1948–69, Emeritus Fellow 1969. Visiting Prof., University of Chicago, 1953–54; Visiting Prof., Princeton Univ., 1961. Dir, Economic Section, War Cabinet Secretariat, 1941; Dir-Gen. of Statistics and Programmes, Ministry of Aircraft Production, 1943; Principal Asst Sec., Office of Minister of Reconstruction, 1944; Mem. of Fuel Advisory Cttee, 1945; Independent Mem. of Cotton Industry Working Party, 1946; Mem. of Royal Commission on Gambling, Betting and Lotteries, 1949. Mem. of Royal Commission on Doctors' and Dentists' Remuneration, 1957–60; Dir, Industrial Policy Gp, 1969–74. Hon. DSc Hull, 1973. *Publications:* An Industrial Survey of Cumberland and Furness (with A. Winterbottom), 1931; Juvenile Unemployment (with A. Winterbottom), 1933; Wages and Labour in the Cotton Spinning Industry (with E. M. Gray), 1935; The Juvenile Labour Market (with Sylvia Jewkes) 1938; Ordeal by Planning, 1948; The Sources of Invention (with David Sawers and Richard Stillerman), 1958; The Genesis of the British National Health Service (with Sylvia Jewkes), 1961; Value for Money in Medicine (with Sylvia Jewkes), 1962; Public and Private Enterprise, 1965; New Ordeal by Planning, 1968; A Return to Free Market Economics?, 1978. *Recreation:* gardening. *Address:* Entwood, Red Copse Lane, Boars Hill, Oxford.

*Died 18 Aug. 1988.*

**JIDDU KRISHNAMURTI;** *see* Krishnamurti, J.

**JILLETT, Dr Raymond Leslie,** TD 1964; AE 1977; Medical Superintendent/Governor, HM Prison, Grendon, Grendon Underwood, since 1975; *b* 24 March 1925; *s* of Leslie George and Ethel Florence Jillett, London; *m* 1955, Mary Patricia (née Lewis); two *d. Educ:* Bec Sch., London; King's Coll., Univ. of London; King's Coll. Hosp. Med. Sch., London. MB, BS London 1949, DPM 1964, MRCPsych 1971; FBIM 1980 (MBIM 1976). Various hosp. appts, 1949–62; Asst Psychiatrist, Exe Vale Hosp., Exeter, 1962–68. TA, 1954–66: various appts to regts and 128 Field Amb., RAuxAF, Sqdn/Ldr Med., 1967–. HM Prison Service: MO, 1968; Sen. MO, Wakefield Prison, 1975. Oxford Postgrad. Fellowship in Psychiatry, 1964. Divl Surg. and Area Staff Officer, St John Amb. Bde, 1955–60; County Staff Officer, Cadets, 1960–68 (Devon); Area Comr, N Bucks, 1969–; County Surgeon, 1977. OStJ 1970. *Publications:* articles in Lancet and Brit. Jl of Psychiatry. *Recreations:* theatre, dramatic and operatic production. *Address:* c/o The Home Office,

89 Eccleston Square, SW1V 1PU; HM Prison, Grendon, Grendon Underwood, Aylesbury. *Club:* Royal Air Force.

*Died 30 April 1983.*

**JINKS, Prof. John Leonard,** CBE 1984; FRS 1970; Professor of Genetics, Birmingham University, since 1985; Secretary and Deputy Chairman, Agricultural and Food Research Council, since 1985; *b* 21 Oct. 1929; *s* of Jack and Beatrice May Jinks; *m* 1955, Diana Mary Williams; one *s* one *d. Educ:* Longton High Sch., Stoke-on-Trent; Univ. of Birmingham. BSc Botany 1950, PhD Genetics 1952, DSc Genetics 1964, Birmingham. ARC Research Student: Univ. of Birmingham, 1950–52; Carlsberg Labs, Copenhagen; Istituto Sieroterapico, Milan, 1952–53; Scientific Officer, ARC Unit of Biometrical Genetics, Univ. of Birmingham, 1953–59; Harkness Fellow, California Inst. of Technology, 1959–60; Principal Scientific Officer, ARC Unit of Biometrical Genetics, 1960–65; Birmingham University: Hon. Lectr, 1960–62; Reader, 1962–65; Head of Dept of Genetics, 1965–85; Dean, Faculty of Sci. and Engrg, 1972–75; Pro-Vice-Chancellor, 1981–85; Vice-Principal, 1984–85. Member: SRC, 1975–79; AFRC (formerly ARC), 1979–85; Chm., Governing Body, Nat. Veg. Research Station, 1979–85. Pres., Genetical Soc. of GB, 1981–84. FIBiol 1968. Editor of Heredity, 1960–75, Acting Editor, 1976–77; Editor, Jl of Agricl Scis, 1981–. *Publications:* Extrachromosomal Inheritance, 1964; (jtly) Biometrical Genetics, 1971, 1981; Cytoplasmic Inheritance, 1976; (jtly) Introduction to Biometrical Genetics, 1977; numerous papers and chapters in books on microbial genetics, biometrical genetics and behavioral genetics. *Recreations:* piano, gardening. *Address:* 81 Witherford Way, Selly Oak, Birmingham B29 4AN. *T:* 021–472 2008.

*Died 6 June 1987.*

**JÖDAHL, Ole Erik,** GCVO (Hon.) 1975; Swedish Ambassador to the Court of St James's, 1972–76; *b* 18 Nov. 1910; *s* of Oscar Jödahl and Elida Rapp; *m* 1934, Karin, *d* of Hadar Rissler and Signe Ouchterlony; two *s* one *d.* Journalist, editor and Foreign Affairs commentator in Swedish social democratic and co-operative periodicals and newspapers, 1933–45. Entered Swedish Foreign Service as Press Attaché, Helsinki, 1945, Moscow, 1945–48; Head, Foreign Min. Press and Information Dept, 1948–53; Envoy, Belgrade, 1953–56 (Mem. Neutral Nations Supervisory Commn Korea, 1954); Ambassador to Bonn, 1956–67; Sec.-Gen., Min. for Foreign Affairs, 1967–72. Grand Cross, Swedish Order of the North Star; Grand Cross, Order of Merit of Federal Republic of Germany; Grand Cross of Yugoslav Flag; Chevalier, French Legion of Honour, etc. *Publication:* contrib. The War 1939–45 (in Swedish), 1945–47. *Recreations:* mountain walking, reading. *Address:* Bastugatan 27, S-117 25 Stockholm, Sweden. *Club:* Travellers'.

*Died 10 Sept. 1982.*

**JOHN, Brynmor Thomas;** MP (Lab) Pontypridd since 1970; *b* 18 April 1934; *s* of William Henry and Sarah Jane John; *m* 1960, Anne Pryce Hughes; one *s* one *d. Educ:* Pontypridd Boys' Grammar Sch.; University Coll., London. LLB Hons 1954. Articled, 1954; admitted Solicitor, 1957; National Service (Officer, Educn Br., RAF), 1958–60; practising Solicitor, Pontypridd, 1960–70. Parly Under-Sec. of State for Defence (RAF), MoD, 1974–76; Minister of State, Home Office, 1976–79; Opposition spokesman on NI, 1979, on defence, 1980–81, on social security, 1981–83, on agriculture, 1984–87. *Recreation:* watching Rugby football. *Address:* House of Commons, SW1A 0AA.

*Died 13 Dec. 1988.*

**JOHN, Admiral of the Fleet Sir Caspar,** GCB 1960 (KCB 1956; CB 1952); Vice-President, Star and Garter Home, since 1973 (Chairman, 1967–72); First Sea Lord and Chief of Naval Staff, 1960–64; *b* 22 March 1903; *s* of late Augustus John, OM, RA; *m* 1944, Mary Vanderpump; one *s* two *d. Educ:* Royal Naval College, Dartmouth. Joined Royal Navy, 1916. Served War of 1939–45, Home and Mediterranean Fleets, Captain, 1941; Rear-Adm., 1951; Flag Officer, Commanding Third Aircraft Carrier Squadron and Heavy Squadron, 1951–52; Deputy Controller Aircraft, 1953–54; Vice-Adm. 1954; Flag Officer, Air, 1955–57; Admiral 1957; Vice-Chief of Naval Staff, 1957–60; Principal Naval ADC to the Queen, 1960–62; Admiral of the Fleet, 1962. Chm., Housing Corp., 1964–68; Mem., Govt Security Commn, 1964–73. *Address:* Trethewey, Mousehole, Penzance, Cornwall TR19 6QQ.

*Died 11 July 1984.*

**JOHN, DeWitt;** authorized teacher of Christian Science, since 1964; *b* 1 Aug. 1915; *s* of Franklin Howard John and Frances DeWitt; *m* 1942, Morley Marshall; one *s* one *d. Educ:* Principia Coll. (BA); University of Chicago (MA); Columbia (MS). Editorial Page Ed., St Petersburg (Fla) Times, 1938–39; Political Writer, Christian Science Monitor (Boston), 1939–42; US Navy, 1942–45 (Bronze Star); Editorial Staff, Christian Science Monitor, 1945–49; associated with Christian Science Cttee on Publication of First Church of Christ, Scientist, Boston, Mass, 1949–64 (Asst Man., 1954–62 and Man. of Cttees on Publication, 1962–64); Editor, The Christian Science Monitor, 1964–70; Dir, First Church of Christ, Scientist, Boston, 1970–80; Editor, Christian Science periodicals,

1981–84. Hon. DHL Principia Coll., Elsah, Illinois. *Publication:* The Christian Science Way of Life, 1962. *Address:* Box 103, Old Concord Road, Lincoln, Mass 01773, USA.
*Died 22 Oct. 1985.*

**JOHNES, Herbert Johnes L.;** *see* Lloyd-Johnes.

**JOHNS, Alun Morris,** MD, FRCOG; Hon. Consulting Gynæcological and Obstetric Surgeon, Queen Charlotte's Hospital, London; *m* 1927, Joyce, *d* of T. Willoughby, Carlton-in-Coverdale, Yorks; one *s* two *d*. *Educ:* Manchester Univ. MB, ChB 1923, MD Manchester (Commend) 1925; FRCOG 1947. Late Consulting Surgeon, Surbiton Hospital and Erith and Dartford Hospitals. Examiner Central Midwives Board; Fellow Royal Society of Medicine; Fellow Manchester Med. Soc.; Fellow Manchester Path. Soc. *Address:* Loosley Row, near Princes Risborough, Bucks HP17 0PE. *T:* Princes Risborough 5298.
*Died 16 April 1990.*

**JOHNS, Peter Magrath,** OBE 1981; Secretary, All England Lawn Tennis Ground Ltd, since 1977; *b* 8 June 1914; *s* of late R. E. F. (Ted) Johns and Gladys Johns (*née* Booth); *m* 1949, Kathleen Joan Whitefield; two *s*. *Educ:* Mill Hill School. Served War of 1939–45; commnd 1940; demobilised 1946 (Captain). Lawn Tennis Association: Asst Sec., 1955–73; Sec., 1973–80. Silver Jubilee Medal, 1977. *Recreations:* lawn tennis, real tennis, bowls. *Address:* 54 The Ridgeway, Friern Barnet, N11 3LJ. *T:* 01-368 4655. *Clubs:* Army and Navy, All England Lawn Tennis, Old Millhillians, Queen's; International Lawn Tennis Club of Great Britain.
*Died 3 Dec. 1983.*

**JOHNSON, Alan Woodworth,** MA, ScD, PhD, ARCS, DIC; FRS 1965, FRSC; Professor of Chemistry and Hon. Director, Agricultural Research Council Unit of Invertebrate Chemistry and Physiology, University of Sussex, 1968–82, later Emeritus Professor; Member, British Technology Group, since 1981; *b* 29 Sept. 1917; *s* of late James William and Jean Johnson, Forest Hall, Newcastle upon Tyne; *m* 1941, Lucy Ida Celia (*née* Bennett); one *s* one *d*. *Educ:* Morpeth Grammar Sch., Northumberland; Rutherford Coll., Newcastle-upon-Tyne; Royal College of Science, London. Chemist, Swan, Hunter & Wigham Richardson, Ltd, 1934; Thos Hedley & Co. Ltd, 1935–36; Royal Schol., Imperial Coll. of Science, 1937; BSc, ARCS; PhD, DIC 1940; Research Asst in Organic Chemistry, RCS, 1940–42; Research Chemist, ICI Dyestuffs Div., 1942–46; University of Cambridge: ICI Fellow, 1946–48; Asst Dir of Research in Organic Chemistry, 1948–53; Lecturer in Organic Chemistry, 1953–55; Sir Jesse Boot Prof. of Organic Chemistry and Head of Dept of Chemistry, University of Nottingham, 1955–68; Fellow and Steward, Christ's Coll., Cambridge, 1951–55. Member: ARC Adv. Cttee on Plants and Soils, 1966–71; SRC Chemistry Cttee, 1976–78; Enzyme Panel, 1976; NRDC, 1976–81. Vis. Professor: University of Melbourne, 1960; University of Calif, Berkeley, 1962. Lectures: Tilden, Chemical Soc., 1953; Reilly, Univ. Notre Dame, Ind, USA, 1962; Simonsen, Chemical Soc., 1967; Pedler, Chemical Soc., 1974; Amer. Chem. Soc. W Coast Lectr, 1976; Wheeler, UC Dublin, 1979; Peboc, UC Bangor, 1979. Member Council: Royal Society, 1966–67, 1971–73 (Vice-Pres., 1982–); Chemical Soc., 1955, 1957, 1970–; Hon. Sec. Chemical Society, 1958–65, Vice-Pres., 1965–68, Pres., 1977–78. Corday-Morgan Lecturer, India and Ceylon, 1963; Trustee, Uppingham Sch., 1961–66, 1970–. Fellow, Imperial Coll. of Science and Technology, 1972. Hon. DSc: Memorial Univ., Newfoundland, 1969; Newcastle upon Tyne, 1978; Liverpool, 1978. Meldola Medallist, RIC, 1946; first award for Synthetic Organic Chemistry, Chem. Soc., 1972; Davy Medal, Royal Soc., 1980. *Publications:* Chemistry of Acetylenic Compounds, Vol. I 1946, Vol. II 1950; numerous papers in chemical and biochemical journals. *Recreations:* tennis, philately. *Address:* School of Chemistry and Molecular Sciences, The University of Sussex, Falmer, Brighton, East Sussex. *T:* Brighton 606755.
*Died 5 Dec. 1982.*

**JOHNSON, Rev. Prof. Aubrey Rodway,** PhD; Emeritus Professor of Semitic Languages, University College of South Wales and Monmouthshire, Cardiff; *b* Leamington Spa, 23 April 1901; *y s* of Frank Johnson, Baptist Minister, and Beatrice Mary Bebb; *m* 1947, Winifred Mary Rowley; two *d*. *Educ:* Newport (Mon) Intermediate Sch.; South Wales Baptist Coll., Cardiff; Universities of Wales (University Coll., Cardiff), London (King's Coll.), Oxford (University Coll.) and Halle-Wittenberg. PhD Wales, 1931; Fellow of the University of Wales, 1931–33; Asst Lecturer and subsequently Lecturer in Semitic Languages, University Coll. of South Wales and Mon, Cardiff, 1934–44, Prof., 1944–66. Dean, Faculty of Theology, University Coll., Cardiff, and Chm. of the Cardiff Sch. of Theology, 1944–65; Dean, Faculty of Theology, University of Wales, 1952–55. Haskell Lectr, Graduate Sch. of Theology, Oberlin, 1951. Pres., Soc. for Old Testament Study, 1956. FBA, 1951. Hon. DD Edinburgh, 1952; Hon. DTheol Marburg, 1963; Hon. teol dr Uppsala, 1968. Burkitt Medal of British Academy, 1961. *Publications:* The One and the Many in the Israelite Conception of God, 1942 (2nd edn, 1961); The Cultic Prophet in Ancient Israel, 1944 (2nd edn revised, 1962);

The Vitality of the Individual in the Thought of Ancient Israel, 1949 (2nd edn revised, 1964); Sacral Kingship in Ancient Israel, 1955 (2nd edn revised, 1967); The Cultic Prophet and Israel's Psalmody, 1979. *Recreation:* gardening. *Address:* Carisbrooke, Rectory Drive, Slimbridge, Glos GL2 7BJ. *T:* Cambridge (Glos) 651.
*Died 29 Sept. 1985.*

**JOHNSON, Dame Celia, (Dame Celia Fleming),** DBE 1981 (CBE 1958); Actress; *b* Richmond, Surrey, 18 Dec. 1908; *d* of John Robert Johnson, MRCS, LRCP, and Ethel Griffiths; *m* 1935, Peter Fleming (*d* 1971); one *s* two *d*. *Educ:* St Paul's Girls' Sch.; abroad. Studied at Royal Academy of Dramatic Art. First appearance on stage as Sarah in Major Barbara, Theatre Royal, Huddersfield, 1928; first London appearance as Currita in A Hundred Years Old, Lyric, Hammersmith; rôles include: Suzette in The Artist and the Shadow, Kingsway, 1930; Loveday Trevelyan in Debonair, Lyric, 1930; Elizabeth in The Circle, Vaudeville, 1931; Phyl in After All, Criterion, 1931. First New York appearance, as Ophelia in Hamlet, Broadhurst, 1931. Betty Findon in Ten Minute Alibi, Embassy and Haymarket, 1933; Anne Hargraves in The Wind and the Rain, St Martin's, 1933; Elizabeth Bennet in Pride and Prejudice, St James's, 1936; Mrs de Winter in Rebecca, Queen's, 1940; Jennifer in The Doctor's Dilemma, Haymarket, 1942; Olga in The Three Sisters, Aldwych, 1951; Laura Hammond in Its Never Too Late, Westminster, 1954; Sheila Broadbent in The Reluctant Debutante, Cambridge Theatre, 1955; Isobel Cherry in Flowering Cherry, Haymarket, 1957; Hilary in The Grass is Greener, St Martin's, 1958; Pamela Puffy-Picq in Chin-Chin, Wyndham's, 1960; Clare Elliot in The Tulip Tree, Haymarket, 1962; Helen Hampster in Out of the Crocodile, Phœnix, 1963; Aline in The Master Builder, National Theatre, 1964; Hay Fever, National Theatre, 1965, Duke of York's, 1968; The Cherry Orchard, Chichester Festival Theatre, 1966; Gertrude in Hamlet, Cambridge Theatre, 1971; The Kingfisher, Lyric, 1977. Played St Joan, Old Vic Season, 1948–49, and Viola on Italian tour with Old Vic, 1950. Has appeared in films, including: A Letter from Home; In Which We Serve; Dear Octopus; This Happy Breed; Brief Encounter; The Astonished Heart; I Believe in You; The Holly and the Ivy; The Captain's Paradise; A Kid for Two Farthings; The Good Companions; The Prime of Miss Jean Brodie. *Address:* Merrimoles House, Nettlebed, Oxon.
*Died 25 April 1982.*

**JOHNSON, Hon. Dame Doris (Louise),** DBE 1979; President of the Senate of the Bahamas, since 1973, Senator, since 1967; Acting Governor General, 1979; *b* 19 June 1921; *d* of John A. and Sarah E. Sands; *m* 1943, Carl Johnson; one *s*. *Educ:* Virginia Union Univ. (BA Hons 1956); Univ. of Toronto (MEd 1959); New York Univ. (EdD Hons 1962). Teacher, 1936–51; Principal, All-age Sch., 1951–53; Lectr, Prince William High Sch., 1962–65; Head, Dept of Social Studies, Southern Univ., Baton Rouge, La, 1965–67; Lectr, Florida Memorial Coll., 1967–69. Cabinet Minister without Portfolio, Govt Leader in the Senate, 1968–69; Minister of Transport, 1969–72. Member: Commonwealth Human Ecology Council, 1979–; Internat. Alliance of Women, 1973–; Caribbean Women's Assoc., 1972–; Caribbean Baptist Women's Union, 1978– (Co-ordinator Bahamas Baptist Nat. Women's Convention, 1968); Delta Sigma Theta Sorority, 1955; Nat. Women's Movement, 1968–; Chm., Nat. Commn for Internat. Women's Year, 1975. Hon. LLD Va Union Univ., 1978. Order of the Eastern Star, 1943. *Publication:* The Quiet Revolution, 1972. *Recreations:* reading, boating. *Address:* PO Box N4646, Nassau, Bahamas. *T:* (office) 32 21565, (home) 32 34824 (area code 809).
*Died 21 June 1983.*

**JOHNSON, Sir Henry (Cecil),** KBE 1972 (CBE 1962); Kt 1968; FCIT; Chairman: MEPC Ltd, 1971–76; Development and Property Associates Ltd, since 1984; *b* 11 Sept. 1906; *s* of William Longland and Alice Mary Johnson, Lavendon, Bucks; *m* 1932, Evelyn Mary Morton; two *d*. *Educ:* Bedford Modern Sch. Traffic Apprentice L & NER, 1923–26; series of posts in Operating Dept; Asst Supt, Southern Area, L & NER, 1942; Chief Operating Supt of Eastern Region, BR, 1955; Asst Gen. Man., Eastern Region, Dec. 1955, Gen. Man., 1958; Gen. Man., London Midland Region, BR, 1962, Chm. and Gen. Man., 1963–67; Chm., BR Bd, 1968–71 (Vice-Chm., 1967). Mem., GB Adv. Bd, Imperial Life of Canada, 1976–; Member: Greater London Regional Bd, Lloyds Bank, 1971–76; Imperial Life (UK) Ltd, 1985–; Trident Life Assurance Co. Ltd, 1985–; Trident Investors Life Assurance Co. Ltd, 1985. *Recreations:* golf, continuing interest in farming. *Address:* Rowans, Harewood Road, Chalfont St Giles, Bucks. *T:* Little Chalfont 2409. *Clubs:* MCC; Royal and Ancient (St Andrews).
*Died 13 March 1988.*

**JOHNSON, Pamela Hansford, (Rt. Hon. Lady Snow),** CBE 1975; writer; *b* London, 29 May 1912; *d* of R. Kenneth and Amy Clotilda Johnson; *m* 1st, 1936, Gordon Stewart; one *s* one *d*; 2nd, 1950, (as Dr Charles Percy Snow), Baron Snow, CBE (*d* 1980); one *s*. *Educ:* Clapham County Secondary Sch. Mem. Société Européenne de Culture; Fellow of Center for Advanced Studies, Wesleyan Univ.,

Conn., 1961; FRSL. Fellow: Timothy Dwight Coll., Yale Univ., Founders Coll., York Univ., Toronto. Hon. DLitt: Temple Univ., Philadelphia; York Univ., Toronto; Widener Coll., Chester, Pa; Hon. DHL Louisville, Kentucky. *Publications: novels:* This Bed Thy Centre, 1935; Too Dear For My Possessing, 1940; An Avenue of Stone, 1947; A Summer to Decide, 1948; Catherine Carter, 1952; An Impossible Marriage, 1954; The Last Resort, 1956; The Unspeakable Skipton, 1959; The Humbler Creation, 1959; An Error of Judgment, 1962; Night and Silence Who is Here?, 1963; Cork Street, Next to the Hatter's, 1965; The Survival of the Fittest, 1968; The Honours Board, 1970; The Holiday Friend, 1972; The Good Listener, 1975; The Good Husband, 1978; A Bonfire, 1981; *criticism:* Thomas Wolfe, 1947; I. Compton-Burnett, 1953; *essays:* Important to Me, 1974; *plays:* Corinth House, 1948 (published 1954); Six Proust Reconstructions, 1958; *translation:* (with Kitty Black) Anouilh's The Rehearsal (Globe Theatre), 1961; *social criticism:* On Iniquity, 1967. *Address:* 85 Eaton Terrace, SW1.
*Died 18 June* 1981.

**JOHNSON, Richard Stringer,** CBE 1968 (MBE 1945); TD 1954; Chairman, North Thames Gas Board, 1964–70; *b* 18 Jan. 1907; *s* of Percy Harry and Josephine Johnson; *m* 1933, Isabel Alice, *d* of J. N. Hezlett, Coleraine, N Ireland; one *s* one *d. Educ:* Stationers' Company's Sch.; Gonville and Caius Coll., Cambridge. Admitted a Solicitor, 1930; joined staff of Gas Light and Coke Company, 1935. Served War, RA (TA), 1939–45. Controller of Services, Gas Light and Coke Co., 1946; Dep. Chm., South Eastern Gas Bd, 1949; Chm., East Midlands Gas Bd, 1956–64. *Address:* Medbourne Manor, near Market Harborough, Leics. *T:* Medbourne Green 224. *Club:* United Oxford & Cambridge University.
*Died 8 Oct.* 1981.

**JOHNSON, Sir Victor Philipse Hill,** 6th Bt, *cr* 1818; *b* 7 May 1905; *s* of late Hugh Walters Beaumont Johnson, Kingsmead, Windsor Forest, and Winifred Mena Johnson (*née* Hill, later W. M. Livingstone), Fern Lea, Southampton; *S* cousin, Sir Henry Allen Beaumont Johnson, 5th Bt, 1965; unmarried. *Educ:* Cheltenham Coll. Ranched in BC, Canada, 1926–38. Served with RAF, 1939–45. *Recreations:* gardening, playing at golf. *Heir: kinsman* Robin Eliot Johnson [*b* 1929; *m* 1954, Barbara Alfreda, *d* of late Alfred T. Brown; one *s* two *d*]. *Address:* Beach House, Sea Lane, Goring-by-Sea, Worthing, West Sussex. *T:* Worthing 43630.
*Died 5 Dec.* 1986.

**JOHNSON, Sir William Clarence,** Kt 1957; CMG 1952; CBE 1945 (OBE 1939); HM Chief Inspector of Constabulary for England and Wales, 1962–63, retired; *b* 8 May 1899; *m* 1918, Louisa Mary Humphreys; no *c. Educ:* Willowfield, Eastbourne. RE, 1914–19; joined Police Service at Portsmouth in 1920 and served in various ranks until 1932 when as Superintendent CID was appointed Chief Constable of Plymouth; Asst Chief Constable of Birmingham, 1936; Chief Constable of Birmingham, 1941–45; one of HM Inspectors of Constabulary, 1945–62; Inspector-Gen. of Colonial Police, 1948–51. Chm., Police Salaries Commission, Malta, 1960. *Address:* Fernbank, 25–27 Gratwicke Road, Worthing BN11 4BN.
*Died 9 March* 1982.

**JOHNSON-MARSHALL, Sir Stirrat Andrew William,** Kt 1971; CBE 1954; BArch, FRIBA; architect and industrial designer; partnership, Robert Matthew, Johnson-Marshall & Partners, 1956 (Architects for York and Bath Universities, etc.); *b* 1912; *s* of Felix William Norman Johnson-Marshall and Kate Jane Little; *m* 1937, Joan Mary Brighouse; two *s* one *d. Educ:* Liverpool Univ. Sch. of Architecture (BArch, 1st Cl. Hons). Served War of 1939–45: Royal Engineers. Dep. County Architect, Herts, 1945–48; Chief Architect, Min. of Education, 1948–56. Formerly: Mem. Council, RIBA. Ex-Mem., Medical Research Council. DUniv York, 1972. *Publications:* papers to Building Research Congress, 1951, National Union of Teachers, 1951, British Architects Conference, 1953. *Recreation:* fishing. *Address:* 42/46 Weymouth Street, W1; 16 Great George Street, Bristol BS1 5RH. *Died 16 Dec.* 1981.

**JOHNSTON, Hon. Lord; Douglas Harold Johnston,** TD; a Senator of the College of Justice in Scotland, 1961–78; *b* 1907; *s* of late Joseph Johnston, Advocate, Aberdeen; *m* 1936, Doris Isobel, *d* of late James Kidd, MP; two *s* two *d. Educ:* Aberdeen Grammar Sch.; St John's Coll., Oxford; Edinburgh Univ. Called to Bar, Inner Temple, 1931; Scottish Bar, 1932; Advocate-Depute, 1945; QC (Scot.) 1947; Solicitor-Gen. for Scotland, 1947–51. MP (Lab) Paisley, 1948–61. Chm., Royal Fine Art Commission for Scotland, 1965–78. Served War of 1939–45. Hon. FRIAS. *Address:* 22 Cammo Crescent, Barnton, Edinburgh. *T:* 031–339 3102. *Died 18 Feb.* 1985.

**JOHNSTON, Archibald Gilchrist,** PhD; CEng, FIMinE; Director of Research and Laboratory Services Division and Head of Safety in Mines Research Establishment, since 1980; *b* 3 June 1931; *s* of late John Johnston and Cecilia Marshall Gilchrist Johnston; *m* 1958, Elizabeth Smith Orr; one *s. Educ:* Wishaw High Sch.; Royal College of Science and Technology (ARCST); Glasgow Univ. (PhD). Strata Control/Mechanisation Engineer, National Coal Board, 1955–57;

Mine Management, NCB, 1957–62; HM Inspectorate of Mines and Quarries, 1962–77; Research Laboratory Director, 1977–80. *Publications:* various, in technical jls, incl. Mining Engr, Colliery Guardian, and others. *Recreations:* gardening, golf. *Address:* Belhaven, Tickhill, Doncaster DN11 9QF. *T:* Doncaster 742994.
*Died 10 July* 1985.

**JOHNSTON, Charles Hampton,** QC (Scotland) 1959; MA, LLB; Sheriff Principal of South Strathclyde, Dumfries and Galloway, since 1977; *b* 10 April 1919; *s* of John Johnston and Johanna Johnston (*née* Hampton), Edinburgh; *m* 1950, Isobel Ross Young; one *s* one *d. Educ:* Royal High School, Edinburgh; University of Edinburgh (MA 1940, LLB 1947; Editor, The Student, 1940). Served War of 1939–45, with 52nd (Lowland) and 51st (Highland) Divs, 1940–46; released with rank of Captain. Advocate, 1947; Chm. Scottish Liberal Party, 1955–56; Standing Junior Counsel, Min. of Works, 1956–59; Sheriff of Glasgow and Strathkelvin (formerly Lanarkshire) at Glasgow, 1962–77. *Publications:* (joint) Agricultural Holdings (Scotland) Acts, 1961, new edn 1970. *Recreation:* pottering about in the country. *Address:* The Grange, 12 Grange Road, Bearsden, Glasgow G61 3PL. *T:* 041–942 0659. *Clubs:* Scottish Arts (Edinburgh); Strathclyde University Staff.
*Died 19 Jan.* 1981.

**JOHNSTON, Sir Charles (Hepburn),** GCMG 1971 (KCMG 1959; CMG 1953); Member of Council of Toynbee Hall, since 1974; Member of Lloyd's since 1962; Registrar, Order of St Michael and St George, since 1981; *b* 11 March 1912; *s* of Ernest Johnston and Emma Hepburn; *m* 1944, Princess Natasha Bagration (*d* 1984); no *c. Educ:* Winchester; Balliol Coll., Oxford (1st Class Hon. Mods, 1932, Lit. Hum., 1934). Entered Diplomatic Service, 1936; 3rd Sec., Tokyo, 1939; 1st Sec., Cairo, 1945, and Madrid, 1948; Counsellor, FO, 1951, and British Embassy, Bonn, 1955; HM Ambassador in Amman, 1956; Gov. and C-in-C, Aden, 1960–63; High Comr for Aden and Protectorate of South Arabia, 1963; Dep. Under-Sec. of State, Foreign Office, 1963–65; High Commissioner, Australia, 1965–71. KStJ 1961. *Publications:* The View from Steamer Point, 1964; Mo and Other Originals, 1971; The Brink of Jordan, 1972; Estuary in Scotland (poems), 1974; trans., Pushkin, Eugene Onegin, 1977; Poems and Journeys, 1979; Rivers and Fireworks, 1980; Talk about the Last Poet, 1981; Choiseul and Talleyrand, 1982; The Irish Lights, 1983; (trans.) Narrative Poems by Pushkin and Lermontov, 1984; Selected Poems, 1985. *Address:* 32 Kingston House South, SW7 1NF. *Club:* White's. *Died 23 April* 1986.

**JOHNSTON, Denis;** *see* Johnston, W. D.

**JOHNSTON, Douglas Harold;** *see* Johnston, Hon. Lord.

**JOHNSTON, Frederick William;** *b* 22 Dec. 1899; *er s* of late Frederick and Janey Johnston, Terenure, Co. Dublin, Eire; *m* 1928, Eileen Milne, Dublin; one *d. Educ:* St Patrick's Cathedral Grammar Sch. and Mountjoy Sch., Dublin; Dublin Univ. Merchant Navy (2nd mate), 1915–21; entered Dublin Univ. and King's Inns, Dublin, 1922; BA, LLB (TCD), 1925; called to Irish Bar, 1925; Colonial Administrative Service, Uganda, 1926–32; Magistrate, Uganda, 1933–42; Judge of the Supreme Court, Gambia, 1942–47; Puisne Judge, Nigeria, 1947–50; retired 1950; called to English Bar (Middle Temple), 1951; re-appointed Puisne Judge, Nigeria, 1952, retired 1955. *Address:* Lagos, Peel Hall Lane, Ashton Chester.
*Died 7 March* 1981.

**JOHNSTON, George Alexander,** MA, DPhil; *b* Jamaica, 11 Nov. 1888; *e s* of Rev. Robert Johnston, BD; *m* 1919, Pauline Violet, *y d* of late Sir George Roche; one *s* one *d. Educ:* University of Glasgow (MA, 1st cl. Hons Classics and Philosophy, 1912; DPhil, 1918); University of Berlin. Lecturer in Moral Philosophy, St Andrews Univ., 1912–14; Lecturer in Moral Philosophy, Glasgow Univ., 1914–19; served in Macedonia, at the War Office, and GHQ, Palestine and Cairo, 1916–19; Ministry of Labour, 1919–20; International Labour Office, 1920–40; Vis. Prof. of Social Legislation; Columbia Univ., New York, 1931–32; Ministry of Labour, 1940–45; Asst Dir, ILO, 1945–48; Treasurer ILO, 1948–53; Chm. UN Joint Staff Pensions Board, 1951; Sec.-Gen., Govt Training Inst., Istanbul, 1954; Mem. UN Economic Mission to Viet-Nam, 1955–56; Dir ILO London Office, 1956–57. Officer of Order of Orange-Nassau (Netherlands). *Publications:* An Introduction to Ethics, 1915; Selections from the Scottish Philosphy of Common Sense, 1915; The Development of Berkeley's Philosophy, 1923; International Social Progress, 1924; Citizenship in the Industrial World, 1928; Berkeley's Commonplace Book, 1930; The International Labour Organisation: its work for social and economic progress, 1970; articles in periodicals and encyclopædias. *Address:* Talbot Lodge, Blackrock, Co. Dublin, Ireland. *Died 9 Aug.* 1983.

**JOHNSTON, Maj.-Gen. James Alexander Deans,** OBE 1945; MC 1937; Director of Medical Services, BAOR, 1969–70, retired; *b* 28 Feb. 1911; *s* of Walter Johnston and I. C. Gilchrist; *m* 1940, Enid O. Eldridge; one *s* two *d. Educ:* Glasgow Univ. MB, ChB Glasgow,

1933. House Surgeon, Taunton and Somerset Hosp., 1933–34. Commnd into RAMC, 1934; served in India, 1935–40 (Quetta Earthquake, 1935; Mohmand Ops, 1935; Waziristan Ops, 1936–37); served in NW Europe, 1944–45; SMO during and after liberation of Belsen Concentration Camp, April 1945; ADMS HQ Malaya Comd, 19 Ind. Div. and 2 Br. Inf. Div. in Far East, 1945–47; ADMS Southern Comd, UK, 1947–49; DDMS HQ MELF, 1949–52; ADMS 2 Div., and DDMS HQ BAOR, 1952–57; OC British Military Hosp., Dhekelia, Cyprus, 1957–61; ADG WO, 1961–64; Comdt, Depot and Training Establishment and HQ AER, RAMC, 1964–66; DMS, FARELF, 1966–69. Major 1943; Lt-Col 1948; Col 1957; Brig. 1964; Maj.-Gen. 1966. QHP 1967–70. *Recreations:* swimming, tennis, country pursuits. *Address:* Park Cottage, Ewhurst Lane, Northiam, East Sussex. *Died 17 May* 1988.

**JOHNSTON, Ninian Rutherford Jamieson,** RSA 1965; architect and town planner in private practice since 1946; *b* 6 March 1912; *s* of John Neill Johnston and Agnes Johnston; *m* 1937, Helen, *d* of Robert Henry Jackson and Jean Patrick Jackson; one *s* two *d. Educ:* Glasgow Sch. of Architecture. BArch 1934; FRIAS 1935; FRTPI (MTPI 1946); FRIBA 1951. *Principal Works:* Pollokshaws Central Redevelopment Area; Woodside Central Redevelopment Area, Glasgow; Central Hospitals at Dumfries, Greenock and Rutherglen; original British IBM factory, Spango Valley, Greenock and extensions. Mem. Roy. Fine Art Commission for Scotland, 1969–76. Pres., Glasgow Inst. of Architects, 1955–58. *Recreations:* music, painting, gardening. *Address:* Tithe Barn, Compton Abdale, Cheltenham, Glos. *T:* 041–332 9184. *Club:* Art (Glasgow). *Died 12 Nov.* 1990.

**JOHNSTON, Patrick Murdoch,** CBE 1963; HM Diplomatic Service, retired; *b* 5 Oct. 1911; *s* of late Claude Errington Longden Johnston, Lt-Col, Royal Artillery, and Beatrix (*née* Peppercorn); *m* 1936, Beatrice Jean Davidson; one *d. Educ:* Wellington Coll.; Peterhouse, Cambridge. Entered HM Consular Service and appointed Probationer Vice-Consul, Paris, Nov. 1934; transferred to Hamburg, Nov. 1935, Valparaiso, 1936; Vice-Consul, Lima, Nov. 1938; Foreign Service Officer Grade 7 and appointed Consul, Ponta Delgada, Azores, 1945; Consul, Bremen, 1947; Head of Commonwealth Liaison Dept, Foreign Office, 1949; Consul, Denver, Colorado, Dec. 1951; Bordeaux, Nov. 1954; Ambassador to the Republic of Cameroun, 1960–61; to Nicaragua, 1962–63; Consul-Gen., Casablanca, 1963–69. *Recreations:* local history and archaeology, stamp collecting. *Address:* Crown Cottage, 52 High Street, Dorchester-on-Thames, Oxon. *T:* Oxford 340080. *Club:* Civil Service. *Died 25 April* 1981.

**JOHNSTON, Peter Hope,** CMG 1966; *b* 31 Oct. 1915; *s* of late Robert Hope Johnston; *m* 1949, Patricia Cullen; one *s* two *d. Educ:* Summerfields; St Paul's Sch.; Magdalen Coll., Oxford (Maj. Exhibnr). BA Oxon. Mem. HMOCS. Joined Tanganyika Govt Service, 1938; District Officer in Provincial Administration, 1938–49; on special duty, African Land Settlement, 1949–51; on special duty, Sec., Special Comr, Constitutional Development, 1952; District Comr, Senior District Officer, 1952–58; Provincial Comr, 1958–62; Courts Integration Adviser, High Court of Tanganyika, 1962–65; retd voluntarily from service of Govt of Tanganyika (Tanzania), 1965. Principal, Min. of Overseas Develt, 1965–76; admin. Officer, Develt Planning Unit, University College London, 1976–80. Editor, Jl of Administration Overseas, 1965–80. *Publications:* (ed jtly) The Rural Base for National Development, 1968; Prospects for Employment Opportunities in the Nineteen Seventies, 1971. *Address:* Wotton Cottage, Westcott, near Dorking, Surrey. *T:* Dorking 889793. *Club:* Surrey County Cricket. *Died 17 Feb.* 1982.

**JOHNSTON, Prof. Ronald Carlyle;** Professor of Romance Philology and Medieval French Literature, Westfield College, London, 1961–74, then Emeritus; *b* 19 May 1907; *er s* of late E. W. Johnston and Mrs A. L. Johnston; *m* 1934, Beryl Marie Clark, Lolworth, Cambs; one *s* three *d. Educ:* Ackworth Sch., Yorks; Bootham Sch., York; Merton Coll., Oxford. Travel in France, Germany and Spain, 1929–30. MA Oxon; 1st Cl. Hons Mediaeval and Modern Languages, French, 1929; Docteur de l'Université de Strasbourg, 1935. Asst Master Uppingham Sch., 1930–35; Lectr in French Philology and Old Fr. Lit., Oxford, 1935–45; Fellow of Jesus Coll., Oxford, 1945–48; Professor of French Language and Literature, University of St Andrews, 1948–61. Examiner, awarder etc in modern langs for Oxford Local Exams Delegacy, 1937–87; sometime external examiner in French, Universities of Oxford, Cambridge, Edinburgh, Aberdeen, and Manchester. Pres., Anglo-Norman Text Soc., 1982–87 (Hon. Treasurer, 1969–82). Officier d'Académie. Chevalier de la Légion d'Honneur. *Publications:* Les Poésies lyriques du troubadour Arnaut de Mareuil (Paris), 1935; The Crusade and Death of Richard I (Anglo-Norman Text Soc.), 1961; The Versification of Jordan Fantosme, 1974; Jordan Fantosme's Chronicle, 1981; Orthographia Gallica, 1989; (with A. Ewert) Selected Fables of Marie de France, 1942; (with D. D. R. Owen) Fabliaux, 1957; (with D. D. R. Owen) Two Old French Gauvain

Romances, part 1, 1972; *translations:* (with Ana Cartianu): Creangă's Povești și Povestiri, 1973; Amintiri din copilărie, etc, 1978; articles and reviews in various journals and festschriften. *Recreations:* rough gardening, travel. *Address:* 5 Rawlinson Road, Oxford OX2 6UE. *T:* Oxford 515481. *Died 4 April* 1990.

**JOHNSTON, Sir Thomas Alexander,** 13th Bt of Caskieben, *cr* 1626; Attorney-at-Law; partner in legal firm of Howell, Johnston and Langford, Alabama, USA; *b* 7 Sept. 1916; *s* of Sir Thomas Alexander Johnston, 12th Bt and of Pauline Burke, *d* of Leslie Bragg Sheldon, Mobile; *S* father, 1959; *m* 1941, Helen Torrey, *d* of Benjamin Franklin Du Bois; one *s* two *d. Educ:* University of Alabama (LLB). Mem., Alabama House of Representatives, 1941–49; Mem., Alabama State Senate, 1949–54; Pres., Mobile Co. Bar Assoc., 1963. Member: Alabama Constitution Revision Cttee, 1970–76; Alabama Judicial Compensation Commn, 1976–. *Recreations:* hunting, fishing. *Heir: s* Thomas Alexander Johnston, *b* 1 Feb. 1956. *Address:* Howell, Johnston and Langford, South Trust Bank Building, Mobile, Alabama, USA. *T:* 205–432–2677. *Clubs:* Athelstan, Country (Mobile). *Died 10 Nov.* 1984.

**JOHNSTON, Rt. Rev. William;** *b* 7 July 1914; *s* of late Dr W. Johnston; *m* 1943, Marguerite Pemberton, 2nd *d* of late H. Macpherson, Headingley Hall, Leeds; no *c. Educ:* Bromsgrove Sch.; Selwyn Coll., Cambridge; Westcott House, Cambridge. Asst Curate, S Michael, Headingley, Leeds, 1939–43; Asst Curate, Knaresborough, 1943–45; Vicar of Stourton, Yorks, 1945–49; Vicar of Armley, Leeds, 1949–56; Vicar of St Chad, Shrewsbury, 1956–64; Archdeacon of Bradford, 1965–77; Bishop Suffragan of Dunwich, 1977–80. *Address:* 40 Shrewsbury Road, Church Stretton, Shropshire SY6 6EU. *T:* Church Stretton 722687. *Died 23 May* 1986.

**JOHNSTON, (William) Denis,** OBE 1946; Broadcaster; *b* Dublin, 18 June 1901; *o s* of late Hon. William John Johnston, Judge of the Supreme Court; *m* 1st, 1928, Shelah Kathleen (marr. diss.), *d* of John William Richards, Dublin; one *s* one *d*; 2nd, 1945, Betty, *d* of John William Chancellor, Dublin; two *s. Educ:* St Andrew's Coll., Dublin; Merchiston, Edinburgh; Christ's Coll., Cambridge (MA, LLM 1926, Pres. of the Union); Harvard Univ., USA (Pugsley Scholar). Barrister Inner Temple and King's Inns, 1925 and Northern Ireland, 1926; Dir, Dublin Gate Theatre, 1931–36; joined British Broadcasting Corporation, 1936; BBC War Correspondent, Middle East, Italy, France and Germany, 1942–45 (despatches); Programme Dir, BBC Television Service, 1945–47. Professor in English Dept, Mount Holyoke Coll., Mass, 1950–60; Guggenheim Fellowship, 1955; Head of Dept of Theatre and Speech, Smith Coll., 1961–66; Visiting Lecturer: Amherst Coll., 1966–67; Univ. of Iowa, 1967–68; Univ. of California, Davis, 1970–71. Berg Prof., New York Univ., 1971–72; Arnold Prof., Whitman Coll., 1972–73. Allied Irish Banks Award for literature, 1977. Hon. DLitt: Ulster, 1979; Mount Holyoke Coll., Mass, 1983. *Publications: plays:* The Old Lady says 'No!', 1929; The Moon in the Yellow River, 1931; A Bride for the Unicorn, 1933; Storm Song, 1934; The Golden Cuckoo, 1939; The Dreaming Dust, 1940; A Fourth for Bridge, 1948; Strange Occurrence on Ireland's Eye, 1956; The Scythe and the Sunset, 1958; operatic version of Six Characters in Search of an Author (comp. Hugo Weisgall), 1959; *autobiography:* Nine Rivers from Jordan, 1953, operatic version (comp. Hugo Weisgall), 1968; The Brazen Horn, 1976; *biographies:* In Search of Swift, 1959; J. M. Synge, 1965. *Address:* 7 Adelaide Road, Glasthule, Co. Dublin. *Club:* Royal Irish Yacht (Dun Laoghaire). *Died 8 Aug.* 1984.

**JOHNSTONE, Prof. Alan Stewart;** Professor of Radiodiagnosis, University of Leeds, 1948–68, then Emeritus; Director of Radiodiagnosis (General Infirmary, Leeds), United Leeds Hospitals, 1939–68; *b* 12 May 1905; *s* of Dr David A. and Margaret E. Johnstone, The Biggin, Waterbeck, Dumfriesshire; *m* 1934, Elizabeth Rowlett; one *s* one *d. Educ:* St Bees Sch.; Edinburgh Univ. Radiologist, Hammersmith Post-Graduate Hospital, 1935; Radiologist, Leicester Royal Infirmary, 1936–39. Baker Travelling Prof. in Radiology, Coll. of Radiologists of Australasia, 1959. Pres. Radiology Sect., Royal Society of Med., 1959–60; Pres. Thoracic Soc. of Great Britain, 1961–62. *Publications:* contributor to A Text Book of X-ray Diagnosis by British Authors; many in Br. Jl of Radiology, Jl of Faculty of Radiologists, Post Graduate Med. Jl, Edinburgh Med. Jl, Jl of Anatomy. *Recreations:* golf, fly fishing, chess. *Address:* Evergreen, Fir Road, Rondebosch 7700, Cape Province, South Africa. *T:* Cape Town 6857404. *Died 5 Oct.* 1990.

**JOHNSTONE, Mrs Dorothy (Christian Liddle),** CBE 1955; Commissioner of Customs and Excise, 1964–76; *b* 5 April 1915; *d* of William Hacket, printer, Peterhead, and Ethel Mary Duncan; *m* 1946, James Arthur Johnstone; one *s. Educ:* Peterhead Acad.; Aberdeen Univ. Dept of Health for Scotland, 1937; Home Office, 1939; HM Treasury, 1943; Asst Sec., HM Customs and Excise, 1957. Gwilym Gibbon Res. Fellow, Nuffield Coll., Oxford, 1973–74; Vis. Fellow, Univ. of Bath, 1980. European Affairs Advr, BAT

Industries Ltd, 1976–77. *Publication:* A Tax Shall Be Charged (CS Studies series), 1975. *Address:* 63 Cottesmore Court, Stanford Road, W8. *T:* 01-937 8726. *Died 24 Feb. 1981.*

**JOHNSTONE, James Arthur;** Commissioner of Inland Revenue, 1964–73; *b* 29 July 1913; *o s* of Arthur James Johnstone, solicitor, Ayr, and Euphemia Tennant (*née* Fullarton); *m* 1946, Dorothy C. L. Hacket, CBE (*d* 1981), *d* of William Hacket; one *s. Educ:* Ayr Academy; Glasgow Univ.; St John's Coll., Cambridge. Entered Inland Revenue Dept, 1936. Sec., Royal Commission on Taxation of Profits and Income, 1952–55; Chm., Hong Kong Inland Revenue Ordinance Rev. Cttee, 1976. *Address:* 63 Cottesmore Court, Stanford Road, W8 5QW. *T:* 01–937 8726. *Club:* Reform.
*Died 25 July 1989.*

**JOHNSTONE, Maj.-Gen. Ralph E.;** *see* Edgeworth-Johnstone.

**JOHNSTONE, Maj.-Gen. Robert Maxwell,** MBE 1954; MC 1942; MA, MD, FRCPE; Assistant Director (Overseas), British Postgraduate Medical Federation, 1970–76; *b* 9 March 1914; *s* of late Prof. Emer. R. W. Johnstone, CBE; *m* 1958, Marjorie Jordan Beattie (*d* 1960). *Educ:* Edinburgh Acad.; Craigflower; Fettes Coll.; Christ's Coll., Cambridge; Univ. of Edinburgh (MD 1954); AM Singapore, 1965; MRCPE 1940; FRCPE 1944; MRCP 1966. Resident House Phys. and Surg., Royal Infirmary, Edinburgh, 1938–39. Sen. Pres., Royal Med. Soc., 1938–39. RMO, 129 Fd Regt RA, 1938–41; Company Comdr, 167 Fd Amb., RAMC, 1941–43; Staff Coll., Haifa, 1943; CO, 3 Fd Amb., 1945–46. Adviser in Medicine: HQ, E Africa Comd, 1950–51; Commonwealth Forces Korea, 1954–55; Officer i/c Med. Division: Cambridge Mil. Hosp., 1955–57; QAMH, Millbank, 1957–59; Prof. of Med., Univ. of Baghdad and Hon. Cons. Phys., Iraqi Army, 1959–63; CO, BMH, Iserlohn, 1963–65; Cons. Phys., HQ, FARELF, 1965–67; Dep. Director of Med. Services: Southern Comd, 1967–68; Army Strategic Comd, 1968–69; retd; Postgrad. Med. Dean, SW Metropolitan Region, 1969–70. CStJ 1969. *Recreation:* music. *Address:* c/o Royal Bank of Scotland, West End Office, 142/144 Princes Street, Edinburgh; 76 Central Road, Rossmoyne, WA 6155, Australia.
*Died 11 March 1990.*

**JOHNSTONE, Prof. Thomas Muir;** Professor of Arabic, University of London, since 1970; *b* 18 Jan. 1924; *s* of Thomas Cunningham Johnstone and Margaret Connolly Johnstone (*née* Muir); *m* 1949, Bernice Jobling; two *s* three *d. Educ:* Grove Academy, Broughty Ferry; School of Economics, Dundee. BCom 1944, BA 1954, PhD 1962, London. ICI, Manchester, 1944–57; Lectr in Arabic, School of Oriental and African Studies, 1957; Reader in Arabic, Univ. of London, 1965. Travelled extensively in Eastern Arabia and Oman; Mem., Middle East Comd Expedn to Socotra, 1967. Hon. Mem., Bd of Trustees, Univ. of Sanaa, Yemen. Member Editorial Board: Cambridge Hist. of Arabic Literature; Jl of Arabic Linguistics. *Publications:* Eastern Arabian Dialect Studies, 1967; Harsusi Lexicon, 1977; Jibbali Lexicon, 1981; articles, mainly on Arabian dialects and folklore and modern South Arabian languages, in Bulletin of School of Oriental and African Studies, Jl of Semitic Studies, Jl of Arabic Linguistics, Mariner's Mirror, Geographical Jl, Jl of Arabic Literature, Arabian Studies and Encyclopaedia of Islam. *Address:* School of Oriental and African Studies, Malet Street, WC1E 7HP. *T:* 01-637 2388, ext. 495.
*Died 11 Jan. 1983.*

**JOHORE, Sultan of,** since 1959; **HH Ismail,** First Class of the Johore Family Order (DK); First Class Order of the Crown of Johore (SPMJ); First Class Order Sri Mangku Negara (SMN); Hon. KBE 1937; Hon. CMG 1926; *b* 28 Oct. 1894; *s* of Maj.-Gen. HH Sir Ibrahim, DK (Darjah Karabat), SPMJ (1st class Order of Crown of Johore), Hon. GCMG, Hon. KBE, Sultan of Johore (*d* 1959); *S* father, 1959; Coronation as Sultan, 1960. *Educ:* in England. Major Johore Military and Volunteer Forces. First Class Order of the Crown of Kelantan; also holds some foreign decorations. *Address:* Istana Bukit Serene, Johore Bahru, Johore, Malaysia.
*Died 10 May 1981.*

**JOINT, Sir (Edgar) James,** KCMG 1958 (CMG 1948); OBE 1941; FRGS; HM Ambassador to Republic of Colombia, 1955–60, retired; *b* 7 May 1902; *m* 1st, 1928, Lottie Kerse (*d* 1929); 2nd, 1937, Holly Enid Morgan; three *s. Educ:* Fairfield, Bristol; London Univ.; Gonville and Caius Coll., Cambridge. Entered HM Foreign Service, 1923; subseq. served at Mexico City, Montevideo, Beira, Milan, Santos, Léopoldville, Guatemala, San Salvador, Brussels, Buenos Aires and Rome, 1951–55. Chm., Anglo-Colombian Soc., 1960–70. Grand Cross of Boyacá, Colombia, 1960. *Address:* St Nicholas, Station Road, Chobham, Surrey. *T:* Chobham 8991.
*Died 25 March 1981.*

**JOLLIFFE, John William,** MA; Bodley's Librarian, since 1982; Fellow, Nuffield College, since 1971; *b* 15 July 1929; *s* of late William Benjamin Jolliffe and of Gwendolen Ada Mary Jolliffe; *m* 1957, Inez Beryl Estelle Bailey; three *d. Educ:* The Grammar Sch., Hastings; University College London (BA). MA Oxon 1970.

Assistant Keeper, Dept of Printed Books, British Museum, 1955–70; Keeper of Catalogues, Bodleian Library, Oxford, 1970–82. Mem., Adv. Cttee to British Library Reference Div., 1984–. *Publications:* (ed) J. Du Bellay: Les Regrets, 1966; Computers and Early Books, 1974; contribs to Bibliothèque d'Humanisme et Renaissance, Jl of Documentation, The Library. *Recreations:* chess, computing, music, reading. *Address:* Bodleian Library, Oxford OX1 3BG. *T:* Oxford 244675. *Club:* Savage.
*Died 30 March 1985.*

**JOLLY, Hugh Reginald,** MA, MD, FRCP, DCH; Physician in charge of Pædiatric Department, 1965–84, Hon. Consulting Pædiatrician, since 1984, Charing Cross Hospital, London; *b* 5 May 1918; *s* of late Rev. Canon R. B. Jolly; *m* 1944, Geraldine Mary Howard; two *s* one *d. Educ:* Marlborough Coll.; Sidney Sussex Coll., Cambridge; The London Hospital. MB, BChir (Cantab), 1942; MA (Cantab), 1943; MRCP 1948; DCH (England), 1949; MD (Cantab), 1951 (Raymond Horton-Smith Prize); FRCP 1965. House posts, London Hosp. and N Middlesex Hosp., 1943; Capt., RAMC (Dermatologist), 1944–47; Hosp. for Sick Children, Great Ormond Street, London, 1948–51; Prof. of Paediatrics, Univ. Coll., Ibadan, Nigeria, 1961–62; Vis. Prof. of Child Health, Ghana Med. Sch., 1965–67; Consultant Pædiatrician: Plymouth, 1951–60; Charing Cross Hosp., 1960–84; British Airways, 1980–; Vis. Consultant, Liverpool Sch. of Tropical Medicine, 1969–. Member: Adv. Bd, Parents' Centres, Aust.; Adv. Panel, Nursing Mothers' Assoc. of Aust.; Adv. Council, British Soc. for Music Therapy; Advr in Paediatrics, Bureau for Overseas Med. Service; Advr, Stillbirth and Neonatal Death Soc. Member: Commonwealth Assoc. for Mental Handicap and Develtmental Disabilities; Kingston Br., Royal Coll. of Midwives; Panel of Assessors, Nat. Health and Med. Res. Council, Aust; Founder Mem., Neonatal Soc.; Hon. Member: British Paediatric Assoc.; RSM (Past Pres., Paed. Section); Guest Mem., Old Achimotan Assoc., Ghana. Vice-Pres., FPA. Patron: Down's Children's Assoc. (Mem., Res. Council); Nat. Assoc. for Hosp. Pay Staff; Inst. for Social Inventions; Sponsor, Exploring Childhood. Medical Journalists Award, 1978; (jtly) Bronze Film Award, BMA, 1978; Meering Award, Nat. Assoc. of Nursery Matrons, 1980. *Publications:* Sexual Precocity, 1955; Diseases of Children, 1964, 5th edn 1985 (trans. Spanish); (with Camilla Jessel) Paul in Hospital, 1972; Common Sense about Babies and Children, 1973, 1983; Book of Child Care, 1975 (trans. into German, Japanese, Danish, Spanish and Dutch), 3rd edn 1981; More Common Sense about Babies and Children, 1978 (trans. Dutch, Japanese); contribs (on pædiatric subjects) to: Lancet, Archives Dis. Childr., BMJ, Jl Pediatrics, etc. *Recreations:* aviculture, giving gardening instructions to my wife. *Address:* The Garden House, Warren Park, Kingston Hill, Surrey. *T:* 01–942 7855.
*Died 4 March 1986.*

**JOLY de LOTBINIÈRE, S.;** *see* de Lotbinière.

**JONES;** *see* Elwyn-Jones.

**JONES;** *see* Lloyd Jones and Lloyd-Jones.

**JONES;** *see* Wynne-Jones.

**JONES, Rt. Hon. Alec;** *see* Jones, Rt Hon. T. A.

**JONES, Allan G.;** *see* Gwynne-Jones.

**JONES, Maj.-Gen. Sir Arthur Guy S.;** *see* Salisbury-Jones.

**JONES, Sir Arthur H.;** *see* Hope-Jones.

**JONES, Benjamin George,** CBE 1979; formerly Partner, Linklaters & Paines, Solicitors; *b* 18 Nov. 1914; *s* of Thomas Jones, Llanarth; *m* 1946, Menna, *d* of Rev. Evelyn Wynn-Jones, Holyhead; one *s* one *d. Educ:* Aberaeron County Sch.; UCW Aberystwyth. Chairman: Council for the Welsh Language, 1973–78; Hon. Soc. of Cymmrodorion, 1973–78 (Dep. Sec., 1960–63, Sec., 1963–73; Pres., 1982–). Contested (L) Merioneth, 1959. Mem. Gen. Adv. Council, BBC, 1970–78. Vice-Pres., UCW Aberystwyth, 1975–86; Mem. Court, Univ. of Wales; Mem. Council, Nat. Library of Wales. Dep. Chm., Agricultural Land Tribunal (SE Area). Hon. LLD Wales, 1983. *Recreations:* walking, music, visiting art galleries. *Address:* 12 Thornton Way, NW11 6RY. *Club:* Reform.
*Died 3 April 1989.*

**JONES, Sir Brynmor,** Kt 1968; PhD Wales and Cantab, ScD Cantab, FRSC; Chairman, Foundation Committee for Engineering Technology, since 1978; Vice-Chancellor, University of Hull, 1956–72; *b* 25 Sept. 1903; *o c* of late W. E. Jones, Rhos, Wrexham; *m* 1933, Dora Jones (*d* 1987). *Educ:* The Grammar School, Ruabon; University Coll. of North Wales, Bangor (Exhibitioner and Research Scholar); St John's Coll., Cambridge (Hon. Fellow, 1970); Sorbonne, Paris; Fellow, Univ. of Wales, 1928–31. Asst Demonstrator, Cambridge, 1930; Lecturer in Organic Chemistry, University of Sheffield, 1931–46; Leverhulme Research Fellowship, 1939; Mem. Extra-Mural Research Team, Min. of Supply, University of Sheffield, 1940–45; G. F. Grant Professor of Chemistry, University Coll. and University of Hull, 1947–56; Dean of Faculty of Science and Dep. Principal, 1949–52, Vice-Principal, 1952–54; Pro-Vice-Chancellor, 1954–56; Chm., Univ's Foundn Cttee for Engineering, 1978–. Sometime Examiner for Univs of St Andrews, London, Leeds, Oxford, Manchester, Edinburgh and the Inst. of Civil Engineers. Dir, Yorkshire TV, 1970–72. Chairman: Nat. Council for Educational Technology, 1967–73; UGC and Min. of Educn's sub-cttee on Audio-Visual Aids (Report, HMSO, 1965); Academic Council, BMA; Univs Council for Adult Educn, 1961–65; Pres., Assoc. for Programmed Learning and Educational Technology, 1969–72; Chairman: Vis. Grants Cttee to Univ. of Basutoland, Bechuanaland Protectorate and Swaziland, 1965; Programme Cttee on Higher Educn, BBC Further Educn Adv. Council, 1967–70, Vice-Chm., 1970–72; Member: Kennedy Memorial Trust, 1964–74; GMC, 1964–74; DSIR Postgraduate Trng Awards Cttee, 1963–65; Univ. Science and Technology Bd (SRC), 1965–68; Brit. Cttee of Selection for Frank Knox Fellowships to Harvard Univ., 1962–72; Inter-Univ. Council (and Exec.) for Higher Educn, Overseas; India Cttee of IUC and British Council, 1972–; Adv. Cttee, Planning Cttee and Council of Open Univ., 1967–72; Royal Commn on Higher Educn in Ceylon, 1969–70; University Council, Nairobi; Provisional Council of Univ. of E Africa and of University Coll., Dar es Salaam, 1961–64; Council of University Coll., Dar es Salaam, 1964–68; Provisional Council, Univ. of Mauritius, 1965–67; General Nursing Council, 1960–66; Acad. Adv. Cttee, Welsh Coll. of Advanced Technology 1964–67; East Riding Educn Cttee, 1956–74; Hull Chamber of Commerce and Shipping; Council of Chemical Soc., 1945–48, and 1953–56; Senior Reporter, Annual Reports of Chemical Soc., 1948; Chm., Humberside Br., British Digestive Foundn, 1978–; President: Hull Civic Soc.; Hull Lit. and Philosoph. Soc., 1955–57; Hull Bach Choir; E Riding Local History Soc. Chm., Beverley Minster Restoration Appeal, 1982– (Vice-Chm., 1977–82). Mem., Court of Universities of Nottingham and Sheffield, 1956–72; Governor: Hymers Coll., 1956–84; Pocklington Sch.; E Riding Coll. of Agriculture, 1977–82. Roscoe Lectr, Univ. of Manchester, 1967. Hon. FCP (Sir Philip Magnus Meml Lectr, 1973). Hon. LLD Wales, 1968, Leeds, 1974; Hon. DLitt Hull, 1972. *Publications:* numerous papers on Physical Organic and on Organic Chemistry, mainly on kinetics and mechanism of organic reactions and on mesomorphism (liquid crystals), in Journal of Chemical Soc. and other scientific periodicals; articles and published addresses on new learning resources and Educational Technology. University of Sheffield Record of War Work, 1939–45. *Recreations:* music, photography and walking. *Address:* 46 Westwood Road, Beverley, North Humberside HU17 8EJ. *T:* Beverley 861125.

*Died 16 July 1989.*

**JONES, General Sir Charles (Phibbs),** GCB 1965 (KCB 1960; CB 1952); CBE 1945; MC 1940; Governor of Royal Hospital, Chelsea, 1969–75; Chief Royal Engineer, 1967–72; *b* 29 June 1906; *s* of late Hume Riversdale Jones and Elizabeth Anne (*née* Phibbs); *m* 1934, Ouida Margaret Wallace; two *s. Educ:* Portora Royal School, Enniskillen, N Ireland; Royal Military Academy, Woolwich; Pembroke Coll., Cambridge. Commissioned in RE, 1925; service with Royal Bombay Sappers and Miners in India, 1928–34; Adjt of 42nd (EL) Divl Engineers (TA), 1934–39; student at Staff Coll., Camberley, 1939. War of 1939–45: service in BEF, France and Belgium, as Bde Major 127 Inf. Bde, 1940; Instructor at Staff Coll., Camberley, 1940–41; GSO1 at GHQ Home Forces, 1941–42; CRE Guards Armoured Div. in UK and in NW Europe, 1943–44; BGS XXX Corps in NW Europe, 1945. Chief of Staff, Malaya Comd, 1945–46; BGS HQ Western Comd, UK, 1946; idc, 1947; Comdr 2nd Inf. Bde, 1948–50; Dir of Plans, War Office, 1950; GOC 7th Armoured Div., BAOR, 1951–53; Comdt, Staff Coll., Camberley, 1954–56; Vice AG, WO, 1957–58; Dir, Combined Military Planning Staff, CENTO, 1959; GOC, 1st Corps 1960–62; GOC-in-C, Northern Comd, 1962–63; Master General of the Ordnance, 1963–66; ADC (General) to the Queen, 1965–67. A Governor, Corps of Commissionaires, 1969–. Nat. Pres., Royal British Legion, 1970–81. Col Comdt, RE, 1961–72; Hon. Col, Engineer and Rly Staffs Corps, RE, T&AVR, 1970–77. Order of Leopold, Croix de Guerre (Belgium), 1945. *Recreations:* golf and fishing. *Address:* 13 Abbey Mews, Amesbury Abbey, Amesbury, Wilts SP4 7EX. *Clubs:* Army and Navy; Dormy House (Rye). *Died 4 Jan. 1988.*

**JONES, Rev. Canon Cheslyn Peter Montague,** MA; Rector of Lowick with Sudborough and Slipton, and Priest-in-charge of Islip, Northants, since 1981; *b* 4 July 1918; *e s* of late Montague William and Gladys Muriel Jones; unmarried. *Educ:* Winchester Coll.; New Coll., Oxford. BA 1st cl. Hons Theology, 1939; Senior Demy, Magdalen Coll., 1940–41. Deacon 1941; Priest 1942. Curate of St Peter, Wallsend, 1941–43; St Barnabas, Northolt Park, 1943–46; at Nashdom Abbey, 1946–51; Chaplain, Wells Theological Coll., 1951–52; Librarian, Pusey House, Oxford, 1952–56; Chaplain, Christ Church Cathedral, Oxford, 1953–56; Principal, Chichester Theological Coll., and Chancellor, Chichester Cathedral, 1956–69, Canon Emeritus, 1971; Principal of Pusey House, Oxford, 1971–81. Select Preacher: Oxford Univ., 1960, 1977, 1978 and 1981; Cambridge Univ., 1962; Sir Henry Stephenson Fellow, Univ. of

Sheffield, 1969–70; Bampton Lectr, Oxford Univ., 1970. *Publications:* (ed) A Manual for Holy Week, 1967; contributions to: Studies in the Gospels, 1955; Studies in Ephesians, 1956; Thirty 20th century hymns, 1960; Christian Believing, 1976; (editor and contributor): For Better For Worse, 1977; The Study of Liturgy, 1978; Pusey, by Leonard Prestige, 1982; The Study of Spirituality, 1986. *Recreations:* travel, music. *Address:* The Rectory, Lowick, Kettering, Northants NN14 3BQ. *T:* Thrapston 3216.

*Died 13 Oct. 1987.*

**JONES, Daniel,** BEM 1945; *b* 26 Sept. 1908; *m* 1932, Phyllis, *d* of John Williams Maesteg, Glam.; two *s* one *d. Educ:* Ynyshir Council Sch.; NCLC. In coal-mines of Rhondda Valley for 12 years, 1920–32; unemployed for 4 years; in engineering as a SR Engineer, 1939–54; Aircraft Industry, 1939–45 (BEM; commended by Russian Embassy, 1945); Aircraft Official, part-time 1940–54, full-time 1954–59, AEU. MP (Lab) Burnley, Oct. 1959–1983. Mem. British Legion and Ex-Servicemen's Clubs, London, Burnley and Rhondda Valley. *Recreations:* music and walking. *Address:* 124 Marsden Road, Burnley. *T:* Burnley 25638. *Died 19 Feb. 1985.*

**JONES, David Jeffreys,** CMG 1969; Puisne Judge, High Court, Uganda, 1960–72; *b* 18 Oct. 1909; *s* of Thomas John and Gwendoline Jones, The Larches, Ystradgynlais, Swansea; unmarried. *Educ:* Maesydderwen Grammar Sch.; Middle Temple. Called to Bar, 1933; practised in London and Wales Circuit to 1938; Sec., Ffynone Estates Co., 1938–43; Asst. Trust Officer, Public Trustee Office, 1943–46; Legal Asst, Control Commission, Germany, 1946–48; Dep. Legal Adviser to Commissioner at Hamburg, 1948–50; Resident Magistrate, Uganda, 1950–55; Sen. Res. Magistrate, Actg Asst Judicial Adviser, and Chm. Traffic Appeals Tribunal, 1955–60; Acting Chief Justice, June–Oct. 1969; Mem., Judicial Service Commn, 1969–; Chm., Judicial Inquiry into two missing Americans, 1971. Awarded Internat. Constantinian Order, 1970. *Recreations:* reading, music, all kinds of sport. *Address:* The Larches, Ystradgynlais, Swansea SA9 1QL. *T:* Glantawe 842298. *Club:* Royal Over-Seas League. *Died 2 Nov. 1981.*

**JONES, D(avid) Prys;** Metropolitan Stipendiary Magistrate, 1969–81; *b* 7 May 1913; *s* of John William and Ethel Banks Jones; *m* 1940, Joan Wiltshire; one *s* two *d. Educ:* Wigan Grammar Sch.; Manchester Univ. LLB (Hons) 1934. Called to Bar, Gray's Inn, 1935; joined Northern Circuit, 1936. Commnd Manchester Regt (TA), 1939; JAG's Dept as Captain, Legal Staff and Major Dep. Judge Advocate, 1944–45. Joined Dir of Public Prosecutions Dept, 1946; Asst Dir of Public Prosecutions, 1966. *Recreations:* music, walking. *Address:* c/o National Westminster Bank, 40 Whitgift Centre, Croydon CR9 3QB. *Died 6 Feb. 1982.*

**JONES, Edmund Angus,** CMG 1963; company director; Managing Director, 1954–65, Chairman, 1962–67, Mobil Oil Australia Ltd; *b* 8 Jan. 1903; *s* of Frederick E. Jones; *m* 1926, Elsie May Townley; two *s* one *d. Educ:* Christchurch Boys' High Sch., NZ; Harvard Business Sch. (Advanced Management Programme). Vacuum Oil Co. Pty Ltd, 1928, Salesman, Christchurch, NZ; Branch Manager, Christchurch, NZ, 1932; Asst Gen. Man., 1935, Gen. Man., 1939, Wellington, NZ; Dir, Melbourne, Australia, 1944; Area Consultant, Standard Vacuum, New York, USA, 1948; Dir, 1951, Man. Dir, 1954, Vacuum Oil Co. Pty Ltd, Melbourne, Australia. Hon. DEd State Coll. of Vic, Melbourne, 1980. *Publications:* various articles on Management. *Recreations:* golf, reading. *Address:* 61/546 Toorak Road, Toorak, Victoria 3142, Australia. *T:* 208181. *Clubs:* Athenæum (Melbourne); Royal Melbourne Golf.

*Died 23 Aug. 1983.*

**JONES, Rt. Rev. Edward Michael G.;** *see* Gresford Jones.

**JONES, Edward Norton,** CMG 1952; OBE 1940; *b* 28 Jan, 1902; *s* of Daniel Norton Jones; *m* 1940, Cecilia Lucy Shaen (*née* Hamersley) (*d* 1976). *Educ:* St Paul's Sch., W Kensington; Corpus Christi Coll., Cambridge (BA). Gold Coast: Asst District Comr, 1925; District Commissioner, 1932; Sec. for Social Services, 1943; Dir of Social Welfare and Housing, 1946; Chief Commissioner, Northern Territories, 1948; Sec. for Development and Chm. of Marketing and Development Corporations, 1950; Permanent Sec. to the Ministry of Defence and External Affairs, Gold Coast, 1952; Mem., Public Service Commission, Ghana, 1955–61. *Recreation:* golf. *Address:* Walden, Innhams Wood, Crowborough, East Sussex.

*Died 24 Aug. 1983.*

**JONES, Elfryn;** Chief Statistician, Royal Commission on the Distribution of Income and Wealth, 1974–79; *b* 9 July 1913; *m* 1940, Vera Anne Owen (*d* 1982); two *s. Educ:* Enfield Grammar Sch.; Institute of Actuaries. FIA 1942. Prudential Assurance Co. Ltd, 1930–42; statistical staff Admiralty, 1942–54; Head of Naval Statistics, 1954–68; Under-Sec. (Statistics), MoD, 1968–74. *Publications:* papers on manpower planning in actuarial and operational research jls and in proceedings of NATO science confs; Estimation of the magnitude of accumulated and inherited wealth (Inst. of Actuaries prize paper), 1978. *Recreations:* chess, statistics, gardening. *Address:* 7 Downside Close, Charmouth, Dorset DT6 6BH. *T:* Charmouth 60737. *Died* 22 *July* 1983.

**JONES, Sir Elwyn;** *see* Jones, Sir W. E. E.

**JONES, Enid, (Lady Jones);** *see* Bagnold, E.

**JONES, Sir Eric (Malcolm),** KCMG 1957; CB 1953; CBE 1946; Director, Government Communications Headquarters, Foreign Office, 1952–60, retired; *b* 27 April 1907; *m* 1929, Edith Mary Taylor; one *s* one *d. Educ:* King's Sch., Macclesfield. Textile Merchant and Agent, 1925–40. RAFVR 1940–46, Civil Servant, 1946–60; Dir, Simon Engineering Ltd, 1966–77. Legion of Merit (US), 1946. *Recreations:* ski-ing, golf. *Died* 24 *Dec.* 1986.

**JONES, Ernest Turner,** CB 1953; OBE 1942; MEng; Hon. FAIAA; FRAeS; *b* 7 Jan. 1897; *m* 1921, Millicent Adie Manning; one *s* one *d. Educ:* University of Liverpool. Pilot and flying instructor, RFC/RAF, 1915–19. Aerodynamics Dept, Royal Aircraft Establishment, 1923–30; Marine Aircraft Experimental Establishment, Felixstowe, 1930–38; Chief Technical Officer, Aeroplane and Armament Experimental Establishment, Martlesham, 1938–39; Chief Supt, Aeroplane and Armament Experimental Establishment, Boscombe Down, 1939–47; Dir of Instrument Research and Development, Ministry of Supply, 1947–49; Principal Dir of Scientific Research (Air), 1949–55, Dir-Gen. Tech. Development (Air), 1955–58, Dep. Controller (Overseas Affairs), 1958–59, Min. of Supply. Pres. Royal Aeronatutical Society, 1956–57. *Publications:* many Research Memoranda published by Aeronautical Research Council. Jl Royal Aeronautical Society (paper in Flight Testing Methods). *Address:* Cross Deep House, 102 Cross Deep, Strawberry Hill, Twickenham, Middx. *T:* 01-892 6208. *Died* 31 *May* 1981.

**JONES, Evan David,** CBE 1965; FSA 1959; FLA 1973; Librarian of the National Library of Wales, 1958–69; *b* 6 Dec. 1903; *e s* of Evan Jones and Jane (*née* Davies), Llangeitho; *m* 1933, Eleanor Anne, *o d* of John Humphrey Lewis, master mariner, Aberystwyth; one *s. Educ:* Llangeitho Primary Sch.; Tregaron County Sch.; University Coll. of Wales, Aberystwyth. BA 1926, Hons Welsh, Class 1, History 2a; Sir John Williams Research Student, 1928–29. Archivist Asst, National Library of Wales, 1929–36; Dep. Keeper of MSS and Records, 1936–38, Keeper, 1938–58. Lecturer in Archive Administration, UCW, 1957–58. President: Cambrian Archæological Assoc., 1962–63; New Wales Union, 1965–67; Welsh Harp Soc., 1965–80; Welsh Bibliographical Soc., 1968–; Cymdeithas Emynau Cymru, 1968–; Cymdeithas Bob Owen, 1976–; Pres., Union of Welsh Independents, 1974–75. Chairman: Governors of Welsh Sch., Aberystwyth, 1946–47; Executive Cttee, Urdd Gobaith Cymru, 1954–57; Cambrian Archæological Assoc., 1954–57; Cardigans. Congregational Quarterly Meeting, 1960; Undeb y Cymdeithasau Llyfrau, 1959–61; Welsh Books Centre, 1966–70; Welsh Books Council, 1968–70; Govs, Coll. of Librarianship, Wales, 1968–74 (Vice-Chm.); Three Counties Congregational Assoc., 1972–73; Sec., Welsh Congregational Church, Aberystwyth, 1938–; Treasurer: New Wales Union, 1970–; Interdenominational Cttee on Welsh Lang., 1970–. Mem. Court of Governors: Nat. Museum of Wales, 1958–69; University of Wales, 1958–71; Member: Council of UCW; Congregational Memorial Coll., Swansea; Bala-Bangor Congregational Coll.; Union of Welsh Independents; Bd of Celtic Studies; Hist. and Law Cttee; Ancient Monuments Bd for Wales, 1970–79; Council of Brit. Records Assoc., 1958–69; Pantyfedwen Trust, 1958–69; Council of Hon. Soc. of Cymmrodorion; National Eisteddfod Council; Broadcasting Council for Wales, 1966–71; Library Advisory Council (Wales), 1965–69; Hon. Mem. of the Gorsedd (also Examr). Hon. FLA 1973. Hon LLD Wales, 1972. Editor: NLW Jl, 1958–69; Jl of Merioneth History and Record Soc.; DWB Supplements. *Publications:* Gwaith Lewis Glyn Cothi, 1953; Victorian and Edwardian Wales, 1972; Gwaith Lewis Glyn Cothi 1837–39, 1973; Ystyriaethau ar Undeb Eglwysig, 1974; Trem ar Ganrif, 1978; Beirdd y Bymthegfed ganrif a'u cefndir, 1982; Lewys Glyn Cothi (Detholiad), 1984; articles in Archæologia Cambrensis, Bulletin of Board of Celtic Studies, and many other journals; contrib. Dictionary of Welsh Biography. *Recreations:* colour photography, walking, gardening. *Address:* Penllerneuadd, North Road, Aberystwyth SY23 2EE. *T:* Aberystwyth 612112. *Died* 7 *March* 1987.

**JONES, Francis Edgar,** MBE 1945; PhD, DSc; FRS 1967; FEng, FIEE, FRAeS; FInstP; Director: Philips Industries, 1973–76; Unitech Ltd, since 1974; *b* 16 Jan. 1914; *s* of Edgar Samuel Jones and Annie Maude Lamb; *m* 1942, Jessie Gladys Hazell (*d* 1985); four *s* one *d. Educ:* Royal Liberty Sch., Romford; King's Coll., London. Demonstrator in Physics, King's Coll., London, 1938–39; at Min. of Aircraft Production Research Estab., finishing as Dep. Chief Scientific Officer, 1940–52; Chief Scientific Officer and Dep. Dir, RAE, Farnborough, 1952–56; Technical Dir, Mullard Ltd, 1956–62, Man. Dir, 1962–72; Chm., Associated Semiconductor Manufacturers Ltd, 1962–72. Chairman: Adv. Council on Road Research, 1966–68; Electronic Components Bd, 1967–69; Radio & Electronic Component Manufacturers Fedn, 1967–69; Electronic

Valve & Semiconductor Manufacturers Assoc., 1968; Member: Inland Transport Research and Develt Council, 1969; Cttee on Manpower Resources for Sciences and Technology (Chm., Working Group on Migration, 1967); Council for Scientific Policy, 1965–70; Central Adv. Council for Science and Technology, 1966–70; Nat. Defence Industries Council, 1969–76; Council, IEE, 1965–69 (Vice-Pres. 1972); Council, Royal Society, 1968, 1979–81; Cttee of Enquiry into Research Assocs; (part-time) Monopolies and Mergers Commn, 1973–81; Chairman: EDC for Mech. Engrg, 1973–76; Rank Prize Fund for Optoelectronics. Pres., Engineering Industries Assoc., 1977–81. Fellow, King's Coll., London, 1968. Mem. Delegacy, KCL, 1976. Vis. Prof. of Electrical Engineering, University Coll., London, 1968–. Trustee: Anglo-German Foundn for the Study of Industrial Soc., 1973–79; Rank Prize Funds, 1977–. Hon. FIERE 1988. Hon. Fellow, Univ. of Manchester Inst. of Science and Technology, 1970. Hon. DSc: Southampton, 1968; Nottingham, 1968; Cranfield, 1976; Heriot-Watt, 1978; DUniv Surrey, 1968; Hon. DTech Brunel, 1969; Duddell Premium, IEE, 1949; Glazebrook Medal and Prize, Inst. of Physics, 1971. *Publications:* (with R. A. Smith and R. P. Chasmar) The Detection and Measurement of Infrared-Radiation, 1956; articles in Proc. Royal Society, RAeS Jl, Jl IEE, Nature. *Address:* Hornby House, 5 Latchmoor Avenue, Gerrards Cross, Bucks SL9 8LJ. *T:* Gerrards Cross 885319. *Died* 10 *April* 1988.

**JONES, Ven. Geoffrey G.;** *see* Gower-Jones.

**JONES, G(wyneth) Ceris;** Chief Nursing Officer, British Red Cross Society, 1962–70, retired; *b* 15 Nov. 1906; 2nd *d* of late W. R. Jones, OBE, JP, Tre Venal, Bangor, N Wales. *Educ:* Bangor County Sch. for Girls. State Registered Nurse; trained at Nightingale Training Sch., St Thomas' Hosp., 1927–31; Sister Tutor's Certificate, Univ. of London; Diploma in Nursing, Univ. of London. Sister Tutor, St Thomas' Hosp., 1936–39; served with QAIMNS Reserve, 1939–41; Sister-in-charge, Leys School Annexe to Addenbrooke's Hospital, Cambridge, 1941–43; Asst Matron, London Hospital, 1943–47; Matron, Westminster Hospital, 1947–51; London Hospital, 1951–61. Florence Nightingale Medal, Internat. Cttee, Red Cross, 1971. *Address:* 7 Menai View Terrace, Bangor, Gwynedd LL57 2HF. *Died* 22 *July* 1987.

**JONES, Harry,** BSc, PhD Leeds, PhD Cantab; FRS 1952; *b* Pudsey, Yorks, 12 April 1905; *m* 1931, Frances Molly O'Neill; one *s* two *d. Educ:* University of Leeds; Trinity Coll., Cambridge. Lecturer at Bristol Univ., 1932–37; Imperial College, London: Reader in Mathematics, 1938–46; Prof. of Mathematics, 1946–72, later Professor Emeritus; Head of Dept, 1955–70; Pro-Rector, 1970–72; Sen. Res. Fellow, 1972–81, Fellow, 1975. *Publications:* (with N. F. Mott) The Theory of the Properties of Metals and Alloys, 1936; Theory of Brillouin Zones and Electronic States in Crystals, 1960; various contributions to scientific journals on Theoretical Physics. *Address:* 41 Berwyn Road, Richmond, Surrey. *T:* 01–876 1931. *Died* 15 *Dec.* 1986.

**JONES, Sir Henry (Frank Harding),** GBE 1972 (KBE 1965; MBE 1943); Kt 1956; MA; FEng, FICE, FIChemE; Hon.FIGasE; Chairman of the Gas Council, 1960–71; Vice-Chairman, International Executive Council, World Energy Conference, 1970–73, Hon. Vice-Chm. since 1973 (Chairman, British National Committee, 1968–71); *b* 13 July 1906; *s* of Frank Harding Jones, Housham Tye, Harlow, Essex; *m* 1934, Elizabeth Angela, *d* of J. Spencer Langton, Little Hadham, Herts; three *s* one *d. Educ:* Harrow; Pembroke Coll., Cambridge (Hon. Fellow 1973). Served War of 1939–45 with Essex Regt and on staff: France and Belgium, 1939–40; India and Burma, 1942–45. Lieut-Col 1943; Col 1945; Brigadier 1945. Before nationalisation of gas industry was: Deputy Chairman, Watford and St Albans Gas Co., Wandsworth and District Gas Co.; Dir of South Metropolitan, South Suburban and other gas companies. Chm. East Midlands Gas Board, 1949–52; Dep. Chm. Gas Council, 1952–60. Chairman: Benzene Marketing Co., 1972–77; Benzole Producers Ltd, 1972–77. Mem., Royal Commn on Standards of Conduct in Public Life, 1974–76. Chm., EDC for Chemical Industry, 1972–75. Liveryman, Clothworkers' Co., 1928, Master 1972–73. Hon. FIGasE (Pres. 1956–57); FEng 1976. FRSA 1964. Hon. LLD Leeds, 1967; Hon. DSc: Leicester, 1970; Salford, 1971. *Recreations:* gardening, reading. *Address:* Pathacres, Weston Turville, Aylesbury, Bucks HP22 5RW. *T:* Stoke Mandeville 2274. *Clubs:* Athenæum, MCC.

*Died* 9 *Oct.* 1987.

**JONES, Humphrey Lloyd,** CMG 1961; Secretary of the Ashmolean Museum, Oxford, 1962–76; *b* 5 April 1910; *s* of Arthur Davis Jones, London; *m* 1938, Edith, *d* of W. H. Tatham, Natal; one *s* two *d. Educ:* Westminster (King's Scholar); Christ Church, Oxford (MA). Colonial Administrative Service, Northern Rhodesia, Cadet, 1932; Dist Officer, 1934; Private Sec. to Gov., 1937; Asst Sec., 1948. In 1952: acted as Economic Sec.; MEC and MLC; Chm. Maize Control Bd; Chm. Cold Storage Control Bd; attended Commonwealth Economic Conf. in London as rep. of Northern

Rhodesia Govt. Seconded to Federal Govt of Rhodesia and Nyasaland as Under-Sec., 1954; Administrative Sec., Govt of Northern Rhodesia, 1956; MLC; Chm. Whitley Council. Acted as Chief Sec. and Deputy for the Governor on a number of occasions. MEC and MLC, 1961; Minister of Labour and Mines and of Local Government and Social Welfare, Northern Rhodesia Govt, 1961; retired 1962. *Recreations:* travel and photography. *Address:* 2B Carlton Road, Oxford. *Died 21 May 1983.*

**JONES, Prof. Huw M.;** *see* Morris-Jones.

**JONES, Ivan Ellis,** CIE 1944; *b* 26 June 1903; *s* of James L. Jones, 9 Castlewood Park, Rathmines, Dublin; *m* 1948, Anna, *d* of Peter MacNeil, Eoligarry, Barra; one *s* one *d. Educ:* The High Sch., Harcourt Street, Dublin; Trinity Coll., Dublin. Entered Indian Civil Service, 1927; Asst Commissioner in Punjab, 1927; Under-Sec. to Punjab Govt 1929; Deputy Commissioner (Shahpur, Hissar, Multan, Amritsar), 1931–39; Registrar, Co-operative Societies, Punjab, 1940; Dir Food Purchases, Punjab, 1944; Sec. to Govt Punjab Civil Supplies Dept, 1945; Comr Jullundur, 1947; retired from ICS, 1947. Asst Classics Master, Royal High School, Edinburgh, 1949; Principal Classics Master, John Watson's Sch., Edinburgh, 1958, retd 1973. *Address:* 13 Forbes Road, Edinburgh EH10 4EG. *T:* 031-229 7819; 28 Eoligarry, Northbay, Barra, Hebrides. *T:* Northbay 363. *Died 6 March 1984.*

**JONES, James Idwal;** Welsh Geographer; retired MP; *b* 30 June 1900; *s* of James and Elizabeth Bowyer Jones; *m* 1931, Catherine Humphreys; one *s* (one *d* decd). *Educ:* Ruabon Grammar Sch.; Normal Coll., Bangor. Certificated Teacher, 1922. BSc Econ., London Univ. (Externally), 1936. Headmaster, Grango Secondary Modern Sch., Rhosllanerchrugog, near Wrexham, 1938. MP (Lab) Wrexham Div. of Denbighshire, 1955–70. Mem., Circle of Bards, Nat. Eisteddfod of Wales. Pastor (non-professional) with Scotch Baptists in Wales, 1924–. *Publications:* A Geography of Wales, 1938; An Atlas of Denbighshire, 1950; Atlas Hanesyddol o Gymru, 1952, new edn 1972 (A Welsh Historical Atlas of Wales); A Geographical Atlas of Wales, 1955; A Historical Atlas of Wales, 1955; A New Geography of Wales, 1960; J. R. Jones (Ramoth), 1967. *Recreations:* photography and landscape painting. *Address:* Maelor, Ponciau, Wrexham, Clwyd, Wales.

*Died 18 Oct. 1982.*

**JONES, John Cyril,** CBE 1951; BSc; MICE, FIMechE; *b* 30 Oct. 1899; *s* of John Jones, Swindon, Wilts; *m* 1928, Doris Anne, *d* of A. Tanner, Swindon, Wilts; one *d. Educ:* The College, Swindon; Loughborough Coll., Leics. Design and Research asst, GWR Co., 1922–31; Head of Dept, Loughborough Coll., 1931–34; Principal: St Helen's Municipal Coll., 1934–37; Cardiff Tech. Coll., 1937–41, Royal Tech. Coll., Salford, 1941–44; Dir of Educn, The Polytechnic, Regent Street, W1, 1944–56; Adviser for Tech. Educn to Colonial Office, 1956–61, Dept of Tech. Co-operation, 1961–64, and Min. of Overseas Development, 1964–67. Hon. Sec. Assoc. of Tech. Instns, 1944–56; Hon. Treas. Assoc. of Tech. Instns, 1956–67; Pres., Assoc. of Prins of Tech. Instns, 1951; Mem. Central Advisory Council for Education (Eng.), 1947–56; RAF Educ. Advisory Cttee, 1948–56; Advisory Cttee on Educ. in Colonies, 1953–56; Council for Overseas Colls of Art, Science and Technology, and Council for Tech. Educ. and Training in Overseas Countries, 1949–69. Member: Fulton Commn on Education in Sierra Leone, 1954; Keir Commn on Technical Education in N Rhodesia, 1960. Mem. Council for External Students, University London, 1954–66. Mem. of Council, RSA, 1960–66. Dir Asian Study Tour of Vocational Educ. and Training in the USSR, 1961, 1963; Technical Educn Consultant, World Bank, 1962–83; Mem. International Commn on Tech. Educ. in Sudan, 1966. Officier d'Académie (France), 1950; elected Hon. Mem. City and Guilds of London Inst., 1964. *Publications:* papers on higher technological education and reports on development of technical education in various overseas countries. *Recreations:* books, music, and foreign travel. *Address:* 26 Grand Marine Court, Durley Gardens, Bournemouth BH2 5HS.

*Died 22 Jan. 1990.*

**JONES, Air Marshal Sir John Humphrey E.;** *see* Edwardes Jones.

**JONES, John Iorwerth,** CBE 1977; retired; Lord Mayor of Cardiff, 1976–77; Member, Cardiff City Council, 1958–83; *b* 22 Oct. 1901; *s* of David Nicholls Jones and Minnie Jones (*née* Rees); single. *Educ:* Carmarthen (public and private). Apprenticed Electrical Engineering, 1918–23. Chm., Cardiff Trades Council, 1960–67. Elected to Cardiff City Council, 1958; on reorganisation elected to new City Council and also to South Glamorgan County Council, May 1974; Dep. Lord Mayor, 1974–75; re-elected to City Council, 1976; re-elected to County Council, 1977. Chm., Cardiff Searchlight Tattoo Cttee, 1979–80 and 1980–82. Governor: WNO, to 1983; Nat. Museum of Wales, to 1983. *Recreations:* Rugby fan; interested in opera, music. *Address:* 11 Anderson Place, Cardiff. *T:* Cardiff 494195. *Club:* Cardiff Athletic (Cardiff).

**JONES, John Morgan,** CB 1964; CBE 1946; Secretary Welsh Department, Ministry of Agriculture, 1944–68; *b* 20 July 1903; *s* of late Richard and Mary Ellen Jones, Pertheirin, Caersws, Montgomeryshire; *m* 1933, Dorothy Morris, *yr d* of late David Morris, and Margaret Anne Wigley, Llanbrynmair, Montgomeryshire; no *c. Educ:* Newtown County Sch.; University Coll. of Wales, Aberystwyth. BA 1922; Hons in Econ. 1923, History 1924; MA 1926. Research Staff Dept of Agric. Economics, University Coll. of Wales, 1924–30; Marketing Officer, Min. of Agric. and Fisheries, 1930–35; Registrar Univ. Coll. of Wales, Aberystwyth, 1936; seconded to Min. of Agric. as Minister's Liaison Officer for mid- and south-west Wales, 1940; Chm. Cardigan War Agric. Exec. Cttee, 1943. Sec./Treas. Aberystwyth and Dist Old People's Housing Soc. Ltd, 1972–76. Life Governor, UCW (Mem. Council, 1950–77). Hon. LLD Wales, 1973. *Publications:* Economeg Amaethyddiaeth, 1930; articles on rural economics, mainly in Welsh Journal of Agriculture. *Address:* Maesnewydd, North Road, Aberystwyth. *T:* Aberystwyth 612507. *Died 15 Nov. 1989.*

**JONES, Air Chief Marshal Sir John Whitworth,** GBE 1954 (CBE 1945); KCB 1949 (CB 1942); psa; retd; *b* 28 Feb. 1896; *s* of Lt-Col Aylmer Jones; *m* 1917, Anne Brown; one *s* decd. *Educ:* Magdalen College Sch., Oxford; St Paul's Sch. Temporary Air Commodore, 1942; Acting Air Vice-Marshal, 1942; Air Cdre, 1943; Air Marshal, 1949; Air Chief Marshal, 1953; Asst Deputy Chief of Staff, SEAC, 1943–45; RAF Dir-Gen of Organisation, Air Ministry, 1945–47; AOC Air Headquarters, Malaya, 1948; Air Officer Commanding-in-Chief Technical Training Command, 1948–52; Mem. for Supply and Organisation, Air Council, 1952–54, retired 1954. Commander, Order of Crown (Belgium). *Address:* 6 Gonville House, Manor Fields, Putney Hill, SW15. *Died 4 Feb. 1981.*

**JONES, Maj.-Gen. Leonard Hamilton H.;** *see* Howard-Jones.

**JONES, Leonard Ivan S.;** *see* Stranger-Jones.

**JONES, Mervyn;** *see* Jones, Thomas Mervyn.

**JONES, Sir Owen (Haddon) W.;** *see* Wansbrough-Jones.

**JONES, Sir Philip (Frederick),** Kt 1971; Director: The Herald and Weekly Times Limited, Melbourne, Australia, since 1957 (Chairman, 1970–81); Vice-Chairman, 1966–70; General Manager, 1953–63, retired); Advertiser Newspapers Ltd, since 1975; *b* 14 Aug. 1912; British; *s* of J. F. Jones, Napier, NZ; *m* 1942, Josephine N., *d* of H. Kirschlager; no *c. Educ:* Barker's Coll., Hornsby, NSW Australia. Dept of Treasury to 1951; Sec., The Herald and Weekly Times Ltd, 1951–53. ACA, AASA. *Recreation:* golf. *Address:* 546 Toorak Road, Victoria 3142, Australia. *Clubs:* Melbourne, Athenæum, Metropolitan Golf, VRC, VATC, Moonee Valley Racing (all in Melbourne). *Died 27 April 1983.*

**JONES, Brig. Robert Llewellyn J.;** *see* Jephson-Jones.

**JONES, Sir Samuel Bankole-,** Kt 1965; legal consultant; Chairman, Sierra Leone Commercial Bank, since 1974; *b* 23 Aug. 1911; *s* of Samuel Theophilus Jones, Freetown, and Bernice Janet Jones; *m* 1942, Mary Alexandrina Stuart; three *s* two *d. Educ:* Methodist Boys' High Sch., Freetown; Fourah Bay Coll.; Durham Univ.; Middle Temple, London. MA, BCL, Diploma in Educn (Durham). Barrister-at-Law, 1938; private practice, 1938–49; Police Magistrate, Actg Solicitor Gen., 1949–58; Actg Puisne Judge, 1958–60; Puisne Judge, 1960–63; Chief Justice, Sierra Leone, 1963–65; Acting Governor Gen., Aug.–Nov., 1965; Pres., Court of Appeal, Sierra Leone, 1965–71. Chm., Fourah Bay Coll. Council, University Coll. of Sierra Leone, 1956–69; Chancellor, Univ. of Sierra Leone, 1969. Member: UNO Commn into death of its late Sec. Gen.; World Habeas Corpus Cttee, World Peace through World Center, 1968. Fellow, Internat. Soc. for Study of Comparative Public Law, 1969. Hon. DCL Durham, 1965. *Recreations:* reading, walking, gardening. *Address:* 8 Kingharman Road, Brookfields, Freetown, Sierra Leone, West Africa. *T:* 5061. *Clubs:* Royal Commonwealth Society (London); Freetown Reform (Freetown).

*Died 8 Sept. 1981.*

**JONES, Sir Samuel (Owen),** Kt 1966; FIREE (Aust.), FIE (Aust.); Chairman, Standard Telephones & Cables Pty Ltd, 1968–76 (Managing Director, 1961–69); Chairman: Concrete Industries (Monier) Ltd, 1969–76; Austral Standard Cables Pty Ltd, 1967–69 and 1972–75; Export Finance and Insurance Corporation, 1975–77; Director, Overseas Corporation (Australia) Ltd, 1969–75; *b* 20 Aug. 1905; *s* of late John Henry Jones and Eliza Jones (*née* Davies); *m* 1932, Jean, *d* of late J. W. Sinclair; two *d. Educ:* Warracknabeal High Sch.; University of Melbourne. Engineering Branch, PMG's Dept, 1927–39. Lt-Col comdg Divisional Signal Unit, AIF abroad, 1939–41; CSO Aust. Home Forces, 1941–42; Dir, Radio and Signal Supplies, Min. of Munitions, 1942–45. Technical Manager, Philips Electrical Industries Pty Ltd, 1945–50, Tech. Dir, 1950–61; Chairman: Telecommunication Co. of Aust., 1956–61; Australian Telecommunications Develt Assoc., 1967–70 (Mem., 1963–75); Consultative Council, Export Payments Insurance Corp, 1970–75;

Director: Television Equipment Pty Ltd, 1960–61; Cannon Electric (Australia) Pty Ltd, 1964–68. National Pres., Aust. Inst. of Management, 1968–70; Councillor, Chamber of Manufactures of NSW, 1968–72; Member: Govt's Electronics and Telecommunications Industry Adv. Cttee, 1955–72; Export Develt Council, 1969–74; Council, Macquarie Univ., 1969–74; Council, Nat. Library of Australia, 1971–74; Australian Univs Commn, 1972–75. *Publications:* several technical articles. *Recreations:* bowls, fishing. *Address:* Apartment 11, 321 Edgecliff Road, Woollahra, NSW 2025, Australia. *Clubs:* Union (Sydney); Naval and Military (Melbourne). *Died 19 July* 1985.

**JONES, Sydney,** CBE 1971; PhD; FEng; Chairman, Conformable Wheel Co., since 1981; independent consultant; Member of Board, British Railways, 1965–76, part-time, 1975–76 (Director of Research, BR Board, 1962–65); Chairman, Computer Systems and Electronics Requirement Board, Department of Industry, 1975–78; *b* 18 June 1911; *s* of John Daniel Jones and Margaret Ann (*née* Evans); *m* 1938, Winifred Mary (*née* Boulton); two *s* one *d*. *Educ:* Cyfarthfa Castle Grammar Sch.; Cardiff Technical Coll.; Cardiff Univ. Coll.; Birmingham Univ. BSc 1st cl. hons (London) 1932; PhD (London) 1951. General Electric Co., Witton, 1933–36; teaching in Birmingham, 1936–40; Scientific Civil Service at HQ, RRE, Malvern, and RAE, Farnborough, 1940–58; Dir of Applications Research, Central Electricity Generating Board, 1958–61; Technical Dir, R. B. Pullin, Ltd, 1961–62. Chm., SIRA Inst. Ltd, 1970–78. Chm., Transport Adv. Cttee, Transport and Road Res. Lab., 1972–77; Independent Consultant, Ground Transport Technology, 1978. FIEE 1960; FIMechE 1965; FCIT 1971; Fellow, Fellowship of Engineering, 1977. Hon. DSc City, 1977. *Publications:* Introductory Applied Science, 1942; papers on automatic control, railways and variable geometry elastic wheels. *Recreations:* gardening, wine, photography, house design. *Address:* Cornerstones, Back Lane, Malvern, Worcs WR14 2HJ. *T:* Malvern 572566. *Club:* Athenæum. *Died 21 Feb.* 1990.

**JONES, Thomas;** *see* Jones, Tom.

**JONES, His Honour Thomas E.;** *see* Elder-Jones.

**JONES, (Thomas) Mervyn,** CBE 1961; Chairman, Civic Trust for Wales, 1964–86; *b* 2 March 1910; *s* of late Rev. Dr Richard Jones and Violet Jones, Llandinam; *m* 1st, 1940, Philippa Windsor Bowen (marr. diss. 1960); one *s* one *d*; 2nd, 1960, Margaret, *d* of Ernest E. Cashmore, Newport; one *s* one *d*. *Educ:* Newtown Co. Sch.; University Coll. of Wales, Aberystwyth (LLB); Trinity Hall, Cambridge (MA, LLM). Pres. Trinity Hall Law Soc., 1950. Asst Solicitor, Newport Corporation, Town Clerk, 1948; Chairman: Wales Gas Bd, 1948–70; Wales Tourist Bd, 1970–76; Wales Cttee, European Architectural Heritage Year (EAHY), 1975; Trustee, Welsh National Opera Company, 1960–88; Member: Ashby Cttee on Adult Education, 1953–54; Tucker Cttee on Proceedings before Examining Justices, 1957–58. Member: Council, University of Wales; Council, UWIST; Bd of Governors, Christ Coll., Brecon, 1958–87. Pres., Industrial Assoc., Wales and Mon, 1959–60. FBIM; Hon. FCSD (Hon. FSIAD). *Publications:* Planning Law and the Use of Property; Requisitioned Land and War Works Act, 1945; Going Public, 1987; various titles and articles in Local Govt books and journals. *Recreations:* reading, writing, helping to keep Wales beautiful. *Address:* Erw Hir, 38 Fairwater Road, Llandaff, Cardiff. *T:* Cardiff 562070. *Clubs:* United Oxford & Cambridge University; Cardiff and County (Cardiff). *Died 28 Feb.* 1989.

**JONES, Tom,** CBE 1974 (OBE 1962); JP; Regional Secretary for Wales, Transport and General Workers' Union, 1969–73, retired (N Wales and Border Counties, 1953); Chairman, Appeals Tribunal North Wales, NHS Staff Commission, 1974–81; Member of Industrial Tribunal for North Wales and North West England, 1975–81; *b* 13 Oct. 1908; Welsh parents, father coalminer; *m* 1942, Rosa Jones (*née* Thomas); two *s* two *d*. *Educ:* Elem. Sch., Rhos, Wrexham; WEA Studies, Summer Schools. Coalminer, 1922–36 (having left sch. aged 14). Soldier, Spanish Republican Army (Internat. Bde), 1937–38 (captured by Franco Forces, 1938; PoW, 1940; sentenced to death by Franco Authorities, sentence commuted to 30 years imprisonment; released following representations by British Govt which secured a Trade Agreement; Knight of Order of Loyalty, Spanish Republic (Spanish Govt in Exile) 1974). Worked in Chem. Industry, 1941–44; became full-time Union Official of T&GWU, 1945; Hon. Sec., RAC of N Wales (TUC) for 20 years, retired. Member: Welsh Economic Council; Welsh Council, to 1979 (former Vice-Chm.); Merseyside and N Wales Electricity Bd, 1976–80; Court of Governors, Univ. of Wales, 1968–73; Prince of Wales Cttee; Treasurer, N Wales WEA; Governor, Coleg Harlech (Vice-Chm., 1980–); Past Member: Welsh Industrial Estates Corp.; Welsh Bd for Industry. JP Flint, 1955. Hon. MA Wales, 1989. Kt, Order of Loyalty (Spain), 1974. *Publication:* (autobiog.) A Most Expensive Prisoner, 1985. *Recreations:* reading, do-it-yourself hobbies, extra-mural activities. *Address:* 2 Blackbrook Avenue,

Hawarden, Deeside, Clwyd CH5 3HJ. *T:* Hawarden (0244) 532365. *Died 21 June* 1990.

**JONES, Tom,** CBE 1984 (OBE 1978); FRICS; JP; Senior Partner/Consultant, Tom Parry & Co., Chartered Surveyors, Portmadoc and Bala, since 1976 (Principal, 1963–76); *b* 4 Sept. 1910; *m* 1934, Ethel Jane Edwards (decd); three *s* two *d*. *Educ:* Bala Grammar Sch. FRICS 1963. Merioneth County Sec., NFU, 1946–53; Gen. Man., Farmers Marts Ltd, 1953–63. Member: Merioneth CC, 1953–74 (Chm., 1965–66); Gwynedd CC, 1974– (Chm., 1975–76). JP Gwynedd, 1953; Chm., Bala Bench of Magistrates, 1972–80. Chm., Welsh Counties Cttee, 1976–78; Pres., Welsh Agric. Organisation Soc., 1978–. President, Godre'r Aran Male Choir (Conductor, 1949–74). Hon. MA Wales, 1978. *Recreation:* music. *Address:* Godre'r Aran, Llanuwchllyn, Bala, Gwynedd LL23 7UB. *T:* Llanuwchllyn 687. *Club:* Farmers'. *Died 30 Sept.* 1985.

**JONES, Rt. Hon. (Trevor) Alec;** PC 1979; MP (Lab) Rhondda, since 1974 (Rhondda West, March 1967–74); *b* 12 Aug. 1924; *m* 1950, Mildred M. Evans; one *s*. *Educ:* Porth County Grammar Sch.; Bangor Normal Training Coll. Schoolteacher from 1949. PPS to Minister of Defence for Equipment, 1968–70, to Minister of State, DHSS, 1974; Parliamentary Under-Secretary of State: DHSS, 1974–75; Welsh Office, 1975–79; Labour Party Front Bench Spokesman on Welsh Affairs, 1979–. Sponsored Divorce Reform Act, 1969. *Address:* 58 Kenry Street, Tonypandy, Rhondda, Wales. *T:* Tonypandy 433472. *Club:* Ystrad Labour (Rhondda). *Died 20 March* 1983.

**JONES, Sir (William) Elwyn (Edwards),** Kt 1978; *b* 1904; *s* of the Rev. Robert William Jones and Elizabeth Jane Jones, Welsh Methodist Minister; *m* 1936, Dydd, *d* of Rev. E. Tegla Davies; one *s* one *d* (and one *d* decd). *Educ:* Bootle Secondary Sch.; Festiniog County Sch.; University of Wales. BA (Wales), LLB (London). Admitted Solicitor, 1927; Clerk to the Justices, Bangor Div., Caernarvonshire, 1934–51. Town Clerk, Bangor, 1939–69. MP (Lab) Conway Div. of Caernarvonshire, 1950–51. Member: Nat. Parks Commn, 1966–68, Countryside Commn, 1968–71. Mem. Council and Court of Governors, 1943–, Treasurer, 1970–, Vice-Pres., 1977–82, University Coll. of N Wales; Mem., Court of Governors, Univ. of Wales, 1975–86. Hon. LLD Wales, 1979. CC Caernarvonshire, 1948–69. *Publications:* Press articles in Welsh and English. *Recreation:* walking. *Address:* 23 Glyngarth Court, Glyngarth, Menai Bridge, Gwynedd, N Wales. *T:* Menai Bridge 713422. *Died 4 July* 1989.

**JONES, William Stephen,** CBE 1965; Chairman: J. M. Jones & Sons (Holdings) Ltd, since 1969; J. M. Jones & Sons Ltd, since 1969; Southern Heating Ltd, since 1957; Berks, Bucks & Oxon Trading Co. Ltd, since 1955; Markham Developments Ltd, since 1969; Markham Developments (Investment) Ltd, since 1971; J. M. Jones Homes Ltd, since 1973; President, Markham Foncière SA, Paris, since 1972; *b* 26 Dec. 1913; *s* of John Markham and Alice Jones; *m* 1938, Joan Constance Reach; two *s*. *Educ:* Maidenhead. Joined J. M. J. Construction Group, 1931; Dir, 1943; Man. Dir, 1949; Chm., 1969. Mem., Housing Corp., 1964–; Chm., Agrément Board, 1978– (Mem., 1965–). Dep. Chm., Ramsbury Building Soc., 1967 (Mem., 1965–). FIOB (Mem. Council, Inst. of Building); Pres., Nat. Fedn of Building Trades Employers, 1963. *Recreations:* reading, gardening. *Address:* Lychen Cottage, Littlewick Green, Berks SL6 3QR. *T:* Littlewick Green 2731. *Club:* Reform. *Died 9 Nov.* 1981.

**JONES, William Tinnion,** MD; FFCM; District Community Physician, Brent Health District; Senior Lecturer in Community Medicine, Middlesex Hospital Medical School, since 1975; *b* Maryport, Cumberland, 30 July 1927; *s* of late Ben and Mary Tinnion Jones; *m* 1950, Jennifer Provost Bland, MB; three *d*. *Educ:* St Bees Sch.; Edinburgh Univ.; London Sch. of Hygiene and Tropical Medicine. MB, ChB Edinburgh, 1950; MD Edinburgh, 1957; DPH London, 1955; FFCM 1977. Surg. Lt, RNZN (UN Forces, Korea), 1951–54; Med. Dir, Nuffield Industrial Health Survey, Tyneside, 1956–57; Asst MOH, Reading, 1955–56; Med. Adv., Birfield Ltd, 1957–63; Hubert Wyers Travelling Fellow, 1961; Med. Dir (founder) W Midlands Industrial Health Service, 1963–69; Tutor and Lectr in Industrial Health, Univ. of Birmingham, and London Sch. of Hygiene and Tropical Med., 1965–69; Dir-Gen., Health Educn Council, 1969–71; Physician i/c, Inf. and Adv. Service, TUC Centenary Inst. of Occupational Health, London Sch. of Hygiene and Tropical Med., 1971–75; Cons. Physician (Occupational Health), Gt Ormond Street Hosp. for Sick Children. *Publications:* articles in several med. jls. *Recreations:* the popular arts in their various forms. *Address:* 9 Millhayes, Marsh Drive, Great Linford, Milton Keynes, Bucks MK14 5EP. *T:* Milton Keynes 605730; Central Middlesex Hospital, Acton Lane, NW10 7NS. *T:* 01-965 5733. *Died 27 Jan.* 1981.

**JOOSTE, Gerhardus Petrus,** DMS 1985; retired; South African Secretary for External Affairs, 1956–66 (Secretary for Foreign

Affairs, 1961); retired, 1966; Special Adviser (part-time) on Foreign Affairs to Prime Minister and Minister of Foreign Affairs, 1966–68; Chairman, State Procurement Board, 1968–71; *b* 5 May 1904; *s* of Nicolaas Jooste and Sofie Jooste (*née* Visser); *m* 1st, 1934, Anna van Zyl van der Merwe (*d* 1974); one *s* one *d*; 2nd, 1981, Jemima Neveling (*née* Steyn). *Educ:* Primary and Secondary Schs, Winburg and Kroonstad; Rondebosch Boys High; Grey Coll., Bloemfontein; Pretoria Univ. Entered Union Public Service, 1924; Priv. Sec. to Hon. N. C. Havenga, Minister of Finance, 1929; Dept of External Affairs, 1934; Legation Sec. and Chargé d'Affaires *ad interim*, Brussels, 1937–40; Chargé d'Affaires to Belgian Government-in-Exile, 1940–41; transf. to Dept of External Affairs, Pretoria, as Head of Economic Div., 1941–46; Head of Political and Diplomatic Div. of the Dept, 1946–48; Ambassador to US and Permanent Delegate to UN, 1948–54; High Commissioner of the Union of South Africa in London, 1954–56. Mem., Commn of Enquiry regarding Water Matters, 1966; Mem. (ex officio), Atomic Energy Bd, 1956–66. Mem., South African Acad. of Science and Arts. *Recreation:* bowls. *Address:* 851 Government Avenue, Arcadia, Pretoria, South Africa. *T:* 435464.                                    *Died June* 1990.

**JORDAN, Most Rev. Anthony,** OMI; *b* Uphall, West Lothian, Scotland, 10 Nov. 1901. Priest, 23 June 1929; consecrated Bishop, 8 Sept. 1945; Vicar Apostolic of Prince Rupert, Canada, and Titular Bishop of Vada, 1945–55; Coadjutor, 1955, translated as Archbishop of Edmonton in 1964; retired, 1973. *Address:* 13101 Churchill Crescent, Edmonton, Alberta T5N 0R9, Canada.
                                    *Died 4 March* 1982.

**JORDAN, Rev. Preb. Hugh;** retired; a Prebendary of St Paul's Cathedral, 1963–69, then Emeritus; *b* 29 Dec. 1906; *m* 1936, Elizabeth Hamilton Lamb, Dublin; two *s* one *d*. *Educ:* Trinity Coll., Dublin; Royal School, Cavan, Eire. School Teacher, 1924–29; Curate, St Kevin's Church, Dublin, 1932–34; Gen. Sec. City of Dublin YMCA, 1934–39; Vicar: St Luke's, Eccleston, St Helens, Lancs, 1939–45; Penn Fields, Wolverhampton, 1945–49; Redland, Bristol (and Lecturer and Tutor, Tyndale Hall, Bristol), 1949–56; Principal, London Coll. of Divinity, 1956–69. *Publication:* Born Under a Lucky Star, 1977. *Recreations:* formerly: hockey, soccer, cricket, tennis, athletics and boxing. *Address:* 3 Hartley Russell Close, Church Way, Iffley, Oxford OX4 4EA. *T:* Oxford 777409.
                                    *Died 4 Sept.* 1984.

**JORISCH, Norah, (Mrs Robert Jorisch);** *see* Lofts, N.

**JOSEPH, Sir Maxwell,** Kt 1981; Chairman, Grand Metropolitan plc, Group President designate, since 1982; Chairman: Norfolk Capital Ltd, since 1969; Truman Ltd, since 1971; *b* 31 May 1910. Director: Watney Mann and Truman Holdings Ltd; Express Dairy Co. Ltd; Mecca Ltd; International Distillers & Vintners Ltd. *Recreations:* philately (Cape of Good Hope Gold Medallist), gardening. *Address:* 1 York Gate, Regent's Park, NW1 4PU.
                                    *Died 22 Sept.* 1982.

**JOSKE, Hon. Sir Percy (Ernest),** Kt 1977; CMG 1967; Judge of the Australian Industrial Court, and of the Supreme Courts of the Australian Capital Territory, the Northern Territory of Australia and Norfolk Island, 1960–77; *b* 5 Oct. 1895; *s* of Ernest and Evalyne Joske; *m* 1928, Mavis Connell (*d* 1968); one *s*; *m* 1969, Dorothy Larcombe. *Educ:* Wesley Coll., Melbourne; Melbourne Univ. (MA, LLM). John Madden Exhibitioner and First Class Final Honourman in Laws. QC (Australia) (KC 1944). Editor, Vic. Law Reports, 1936–56; Registrar: Dental Bd of Vic., 1939–58; Dietitians Registration Bd of Vic., 1942–58; Lecturer in Domestic Relations Law, Melbourne Univ., 1948–51. MHR for Balaclava, Australian Parlt, 1951–60. Mem., Parly Standing Cttee on Foreign Affairs, Constitution Review, Privileges and Standing Orders; Aust. Deleg. to UN, 1955; Mem. Coun., ANU, 1956–60; Chm., Aust. Commonwealth Immigration Planning Coun., 1959–60. Pres., Royal Life Saving Soc., Australia, 1951–79. *Publications:* Remuneration of Commission Agents, 1924 (3rd edn 1957); Marriage and Divorce, 1924 (5th edn 1968); Procedure and Conduct of Meetings, 1936 (6th edn 1976); Insurance Law, 1933 (2nd edn 1948); Sale of Goods and Hire Purchase, 1949 (2nd edn 1961); Partnership, 1957 (2nd edn 1966); Local Government, 1963; Australian Federal Government, 1967 (3rd edn 1976); Commission Agency, 1975; Insurance, 1975; Family Law, 1976; Sir Robert Menzies: an informal memoir, 1978. *Recreations:* writing, gardening. *Address:* 119 The Boulevarde, Strathfield, NSW 2135, Australia. *T:* 642 3156. *Club:* Melbourne Cricket.                                    *Died 25 April* 1981.

**JOSLIN, Ivy Collin,** BSc; late Headmistress, Francis Holland School, Clarence Gate, NW1; *b* 12 April 1900. *Educ:* Skinners' Company's Sch., London; University Coll., London. Science Mistress, Howell's Sch., Denbigh, 1922–24; Physics Mistress, Southend-on-Sea High Sch., 1924–29; Science Mistress, St Stephen's High Sch., Clewer, 1929–30; Mathematics Mistress, Dame Alice Owen's Sch., London, 1930–33; Headmistress, Derby High Sch., 1933–39; Headmistress, Newcastle on Tyne Church High Sch., 1943–45. *Publications:* Everyday Domestic Science (with P. M. Taylor), 1932; General

Science, 1937; The Air Around Us, 1961; Water in the World, 1962; Electricity in Use, 1964. *Recreations:* bridge, chess. *Club:* University Women's.                                    *Died 17 July* 1986.

**JOSLIN, Maj.-Gen. Stanley William,** CB 1951; CBE 1950 (MBE 1936); MA; Chief Inspector of Nuclear Installations, Ministry of Power, 1959–64, retired; *b* 25 March 1899; *m* 1939, Eva Hudson (*d* 1976); one *d*. *Educ:* Hackney Downs Sch.; Royal Military Academy Woolwich; Downing Coll., Cambridge. Commissioned 2nd Lieut, Royal Engineers, 1918; served: Germany, 1918–19; India, 1920–23; Nigeria, 1926–28; Singapore, 1937–39; War of 1939–45; NW Europe, 1944–49; transferred to REME, 1943; Maj.-Gen., 1950; Dir of Mechanical Engineering, War Office, 1950–53; retired, 1954. UK Atomic Energy Authority, 1954–59. *Recreations:* walking, music. *Address:* Barbary, Maresfield Park, Uckfield, East Sussex TN22 2HA. *T:* Uckfield 2933.                                    *Died 6 Oct.* 1984.

**JOWETT, Ronald Edward,** CBE 1969; MD, FRCS; Hon. Consultant Otolaryngologist, Sunderland and Durham Hospital Groups; *b* 5 March 1901; *s* of James and Emma Jowett, Halifax, Yorks; *m* 1929, Lilian Waring, Halifax; one *s* (and one *s* decd). *Educ:* Heath Sch., Halifax; Leeds Univ.; Leeds Med. Sch. MB, ChB (Hons) Leeds, 1922; Scattergood and Hardwick Prizes; MD Leeds, 1923; DLO, RCP&S London, 1925, MRCP 1933; FRCS 1966. Otolaryngologist, Sunderland Hosp. Gp, 1925–71; Surgeon, Newcastle upon Tyne Throat, Nose and Ear Hosp., 1937–50. President: Regional Hospitals' Consultants and Specialists Assoc., 1951–53 and 1964–65; Newcastle upon Tyne and Northern Counties Med. Soc., 1955; N of England Otolaryngological Soc., 1955. Mem., Newcastle Regional Hosp. Bd, 1947–69 (Chm. of its Med. Adv. Cttee, 1953–69; Vice-Chm. of the Bd, 1967–69). FRSM. *Publications:* The Injured Workman (with G. F. Walker), 1933; contribs to: Med. Press and Circular, BMJ, Proc. Roy. Soc. Med., Jl of Mental Science, Jl of Laryngology and Otology, Den Norske Turistforenning. *Recreations:* making music, fishing. *Address:* 18 Brookfield, Westfield, Gosforth, Newcastle upon Tyne NE3 4YB. *T:* Tyneside 2853551.                                    *Died 29 Aug.* 1986.

**JOYCE, Alec Houghton,** CIE 1943; CBE 1952 (OBE 1938); *b* 5 March 1894; *m* 1917, Mary, 2nd *d* of late George Frederick Oates, Roundhay, Leeds; two *s*. Served European War, 1914–19, in France and Russia (Meritorious Service Medal); entered India Office, 1919; Joint Publicity Officer to the India and Burma Round Table Conferences, 1930–32; Personal Asst to the Prime Minister during Monetary and Economic Conference, 1933; on special duty in India and Burma, 1935 and in India, 1936–37. Seconded at various times to No. 10 Downing Street as Actg Chief Press Adviser. Paid official visits to USA and Canada, 1943; to India, 1943; again to India with Cabinet Delegation, 1946; and to USA and all Provs of Canada, 1951; on an official tour of Pakistan, India, and Ceylon, 1951–52; Head of Information Dept Commonwealth Relations Office (Asst Sec.), 1948–Nov. 1954, subseq. employed in charge of branch conducting liaison with UK, Commonwealth, and foreign Press and with BBC; retired, 1957. *Address:* 3 Kaye Moor Road, Sutton, Surrey. *Club:* East India, Devonshire, Sports and Public Schools.
                                    *Died 23 May* 1982.

**JOYCE, John Hall;** retired shipowner; *b* 6 Oct. 1906. Formerly: Chm., Elder Dempster Lines Ltd; Dep. Chm., Coast Lines Ltd; Director: Belgian Line; Nigerian National Shipping Line; Nigerian Airways; Liner Holdings Ltd, and associated cos; Chairman: Liverpool and London Steamship Protection and Indemnity Assoc. Ltd; Liverpool and London War Risks Insurance Assoc. Ltd; Liverpool Steamship Owners' Assoc., 1957; General Council of British Shipping, 1957. *Address:* Top Garden, Leicester Road, Ashby de la Zouch, Leics.
                                    *Died 28 Feb.* 1982.

**JUDD, John Basil Thomas;** HM Consul-General at Zagreb, 1961–65; retired; re-employed in the Foreign Office, 1966–69; *b* 12 May 1909; *s* of John Matthews Judd and Helena Beatrice Jenkins; *m* 1939, Cynthia Margaret Georgina, *yr d* of Sir Henry White-Smith, CBE; two *s* one *d*. *Educ:* The Leys; Downing Coll., Cambridge; Inner Temple (called to the Bar, 1931). Entered Levant Consular Service, 1932; Vice-Consul and 3rd Sec. at Jedda, 1936; Vice-Consul at Casablanca and Tangier, 1939–43; Consul at Tunis and Marseilles, 1943–46; Consul and 1st Sec. at Paris, 1946; Consul at Jerusalem, 1949; Foreign Office, 1951; Consul-Gen. at Valparaiso, 1953; Consul-Gen. and Counsellor, Cairo, 1955–57; Consul-Gen. at Basra, 1957–61. *Recreations:* fishing, theatre and opera. *Address:* 12 Cortiletto, 46 Wied is Sir, Mosta, Malta. *Clubs:* Brooks's; Union, Sports (Malta).                                    *Died 5 Dec.* 1983.

**JUKES, E(rnest) Martin,** CBE 1975; QC 1954; Barrister-at-Law; a Chairman of Industrial Tribunals; Member, National Advisory Council on Employment of Disabled People; *b* 5 Dec. 1909; *s* of Ernest and Hilda Gordon Jukes, Purley, Surrey; *m* 1931, Mary Kinloch (*née* Anderson); two *s* one *d*. *Educ:* Merchant Taylors' Sch.; St John's Coll., Oxford (MA). Called to the Bar, Jan. 1933; Mem. of the Bar Council, 1952–56 and 1964; Master of the Bench, Middle Temple, 1962; Judge of the Courts of Appeal for Guernsey and

Jersey, 1964; Commissioner for Municipal Election Petitions, 1961. Dir-Gen., Engineering Employers Fedn, 1966–75. Member: Engineering Industry Training Bd, 1965–75; Council, CBI, 1965–75; Dep. Chm., Health and Safety Commn, 1974–78. Served War of 1939–45 as Lieut-Col RASC, in UK, France, Germany and Belgium (despatches). *Address:* 1 Essex Court, Temple, EC4. *T:* 01-353 0168; The Brambles, School Lane, Amesbury, Wilts. *T:* Amesbury 22642. *Club:* Flyfishers'. *Died 23 April 1982.*

**JUKES, Richard Starr,** CBE 1969; FCA; Director, BPB Industries Ltd, 1943–76 (Chairman, 1965–73); *b* 6 Dec. 1906; *s* of late Rev. Arthur Starr Jukes and Mrs Annie Florance Jukes; *m* 1935, Ruth Mary Wilmot; one *s* two *d*. *Educ:* St Edmund's, Canterbury. Mem. Inst. of Chartered Accountants, 1929. Gyproc Products Ltd: Sec./Accountant, 1934; Dir, 1939; The British Plaster Board (Holdings) Ltd: Dir, 1943; Jt Man. Dir, 1947; Man. Dir, 1954; Dep. Chm., 1962; Chm., 1965 (since Aug. 1965 the company has been known as BPB Industries). *Recreation:* golf. *Address:* White House, Watford Road, Northwood, Mddx. *T:* Northwood 24125. *Clubs:* Island Sailing; Sandy Lodge Golf; Hillside Golf (Zimbabwe). *Died 2 Jan. 1987.*

**JUMA, Sa'ad;** *b* Tafila, Jordan, 21 March 1916; *s* of Mohammed Juma; *m* 1959, Salwa Ghanem, Beirut; two *s* one *d*. *Educ:* Damascus Univ. (L'Essence in Law). Chief of Protocol, Min. of For. Affairs, 1949; Dir of Press, 1950; Sec. to Prime Minister's Office, 1950–54; Under-Sec., Min. of Interior, 1954–57; Governor of Amman, 1957–58; Under-Sec., Min. of For. Affairs, 1958–59; Ambassador: to Iran, 1959–61; to Syria, 1961–62; to USA, 1962–65; Minister of the Royal Court, 1965–67; Prime Minister, 1967; Ambassador to United Kingdom, 1969–70; Senator, 1970–75. Orders of El Nahda (1st Class) and Star of Jordan (1st Class); decorations from Syria, Lebanon, China, Italy, Libya, Malaysia and Ethiopia. *Publications:*

Conspiracy and the Battle of Destiny, 1968; Hostile Society, 1970; God or Destruction, 1973; Sons of Snakes, 1973. *Recreations:* reading, music, bridge. *Address:* Jebel Amman, 4th Circle, Amman, Jordan. *T:* Amman 44111. *Clubs:* Travellers', Hurlingham.

**JUNGWIRTH, Sir (William) John,** Kt 1957; CMG 1948; AASA; JP; retired as Permanent Head of Premier's Department, Melbourne, Victoria, 1962; *b* Melbourne, 10 Aug. 1897; British; *m* 1st, 1923, Ruth Powell (*d* 1938); one *s* one *d*; 2nd, 1942, Edna Tamblyn; two *s*. *Educ:* Melbourne. Joined Victorian Public Service, 1915; Private Sec. to various Premiers, 1920–32; Permanent Head of Premier's Dept, 1934–62. Past President: YMCA; Methodist Men's Soc. of Victoria; Board of Management, Prince Henry's Hospital; Chm., District Trustees, Independent Order of Rechabites; Chm., Healesville Wild Life Sanctuary, 1962–78; Mem., Victorian Patriotic Funds Council, 1941; Mem., Victorian Documentary Films Council, 1948– (Past Chm.); Chm., T. H. Woodrow Meml Trust. *Recreations:* bowls, reading. *Address:* 31 Bulleen Road, North Balwyn, Victoria 3104, Australia. *Club:* Royal Automobile of Victoria (Melbourne). *Died 25 Jan. 1981.*

**JUPP, Clifford Norman,** CMG 1966; *b* 24 Sept. 1919; *s* of Albert Leonard Jupp and Marguerite Isabel (*née* Day Winter); *m* 1945, Brenda (*née* Babbs); one *s* two *d*. *Educ:* Perse Sch., Cambridge; Trinity Hall, Cambridge. Armed Forces, 1940–46. Mem. of HM Foreign and Diplomatic Service, 1946–70; served in: Foreign Office, 1946; Beirut, 1947–49; New York, 1949–51; Foreign Office, 1951–53; Cairo, 1953–56; Kabul, 1956–59; Foreign Office, 1959–61; Brussels, 1961–63; Belgrade, 1963–66; seconded to BoT and Min. of Technology, 1967–70. With Burton Gp Ltd, 1970–72; Dir, British Textile Confedn, 1972–76. *Address:* Tigh nan Croitean, Kildalton, Isle of Islay, Argyll PA42 7EF. *Died 15 March 1989.*

# K

**KAHN,** Baron, *cr* 1965 (Life Peer), of Hampstead; **Richard Ferdinand Kahn,** CBE 1946; FBA 1960; MA; Professor of Economics, Cambridge University, 1951–72; Fellow of King's College, Cambridge, since 1930; *b* 10 Aug. 1905; *s* of late Augustus Kahn. *Educ:* St Paul's Sch. (Scholar); King's College, Cambridge (Scholar). Temporary Civil Servant in various Govt Depts, 1939–46. *Publications:* Selected Essays on Employment and Growth, 1973; The Making of Keynes' General Theory, 1984; articles on economic subjects. *Address:* King's College, Cambridge CB2 1ST. *T:* Cambridge 350411. *Club:* United Oxford & Cambridge University.                                    *Died* 6 *June* 1989.

**KALDOR,** Baron, *cr* 1974 (Life Peer), of Newnham in the City of Cambridge; **Nicholas Kaldor,** MA; FBA 1963; Professor of Economics in the University of Cambridge, 1966–75, now Emeritus (Reader in Economics, 1952–65); Fellow of King's College, Cambridge, since 1949; *b* Budapest, 12 May 1908; *s* of late Dr Julius Kaldor; *m* 1934, Clarissa Elisabeth Goldschmidt; four *d*. *Educ:* Model Gymnasium, Budapest; London Sch. of Economics. BSc (Econ.), 1st Class hons, 1930. Asst Lecturer, Lecturer and Reader in Economics, London Sch. of Economics, 1932–47; Rockefeller travelling Fellowship in US, 1935–36; Research Associate (part-time), Nat. Inst. of Economic and Social Research, 1943–45; Chief of Economic Planning Staff, US Strategic Bombing Survey, 1945; Dir, Research and Planning Division, Economic Commission for Europe, Geneva, 1947–49; Mem. of UN group of experts on international measures for full employment, 1949; Mem. of Royal Commission on Taxation of Profits and Income, 1951–55; Adviser on tax reform, Government of India, 1956; Economic Adviser, Economic Commission for Latin America, Santiago, Chile, 1956; Fiscal Adviser, Govt of Ceylon, 1958; Ford Visiting Research Prof., University of Calif., 1959–60; Fiscal Adviser, Government of Mexico, 1960; Economic Adviser, Govt of Ghana, 1961; Fiscal Adviser, Govt of British Guiana, 1961, of Turkey, 1962, of Iran, 1966, of Venezuela, 1976; Visiting Economist, Reserve Bank of Australia, Sydney, 1963. Special Adviser to the Chancellor of the Exchequer, 1964–68 and 1974–76. Pres., Section F, British Assoc. for Advancement of Science, 1970. Hon. Member: Amer. Acad. of Arts and Scis; Amer. Econ. Assoc.; Royal Econ. Soc. of Belgium; Hungarian Acad. of Scis, 1979. Hon. Fellow, LSE, 1970. Pres., REconS, 1974–76. Hon. doctorates, Dijon and Frankfurt. *Publications:* Quantitative Aspects of the Full Employment Problem in Britain (in Beveridge's Full Employment in a Free Soc.), 1944; (jointly) Statistical Analysis of Advertising Expenditure and Revenue of the Press, 1948; (part author) National and International Measures for Full Employment, 1950; An Expenditure Tax, 1955; Indian Tax Reform, 1956; Essays in Economic Stability and Growth, Essays in Value and Distribution, 1960; Capital Accumulation and Economic Growth (in The Theory of Capital), 1961; Ensayos sobre Desarrollo Económico (Mexico), 1961; Essays on Economic Policy, Vols I, II, 1964; Causes of the Slow Rate of Growth of the United Kingdom (inaugural lecture), 1966; Conflicts in Policy Objectives, 1971; Further Essays on Economic Theory, 1978; Further Essays on Applied Economics, 1978; Reports on Taxation, Vols I, II, 1980; Origins of the New Monetarism, 1981; The Scourge of Monetarism, 1982, 2nd edn 1986; Limitations of the "General Theory", 1983; The Economic Consequences of Mrs Thatcher, 1983; Keynesian Economics after Fifty Years (in Keynes and the Modern World), 1983; Economics Without Equilibrium, 1985; papers in various economic jls. *Address:* King's College, Cambridge CB2 1ST; 2 Adams Road, Cambridge CB3 9AD. *T:* Cambridge 359282. *Club:* Reform.                     *Died* 30 *Sept.* 1986.

**KANTOROVICH, Prof. Leonid Vitaljevich;** Head of Department, Institute of Systems Research, Moscow, USSR, since 1976; mathematician, economist; *b* Leningrad, 19 Jan. 1912; *m* 1938, Natalja Vladimirovna Iljana; one *s* one *d*. *Educ:* Univ. of Leningrad, 1930 (DrSc 1935). Instructor, Leningrad Inst. of Industrial Construction Engineering, 1930–32; Professor, 1932–39; Instructor, Leningrad Univ., 1932–34; Professor, 1934–41, 1945–60, Mathem. Inst., Acad. of Sciences (Leningrad Filial) (Head of Dept, 1945–60); Dep. Dir, Mathem. Inst., Siberian Branch, Acad. of Sciences of the USSR, 1960–71; Prof., Novosibirsk State Univ., 1960–70; Head of Research Lab., Inst. of Nat. Economy Control, Moscow, 1971–76. Corr. Mem., Acad. of Sciences of the USSR, 1958–64; Mem., 1964–. Foreign Member: Hungarian Acad. of Sciences, 1967; Acad. of Arts and Science, Boston, USA, 1969; Mexican Engrg Acad., 1976; Yugoslavian Acad. of Sciences and Arts, 1979; Internat. Acad. of Management, 1985. Dr *hc*: Glasgow, 1966; Grenoble, 1967; Nice, 1969; Helsinki, 1970; Martin Luther Univ., Halle-Wittenberg, 1974; Sorbonne, Paris, 1975; Vysoka Scola Econ. i Plan., Warsaw, 1975; Cambridge, 1976; Pennsylvania, 1976; Indian Statistical Inst., Calcutta, 1978. State Prize, USSR, 1949; Lenin Prize, USSR, 1965; Nobel Prize for Economics, 1975. Order Sign of Honour, 1944; Order of Labour Red banner, 1949, 1950, 1975; Order of

Lenin, 1967, 1982. *Publications:* Variatsionnoe iscislenie (Calculus of Variations), 1933; Priblizhennye metody vysshego analiza (Approximate Methods of Higher Analysis), 1936; Matematicheskie metody organizatsii i planirvaniya proizvodstva (Mathematical Methods of Organizing and Planning Production), 1939; Funktsional'nyi analiz v poluuporyadochennyh prosranstvah (Functional Analysis in Semiordered Spaces), 1950; Rascet ratsional'nogo raskroya promyschlennyh materialov (Calculation of Rational Cutting of Industrial Materials), 1951; Ekonomichesky rascet nailuchschego ispolzovaniya resursov (Economical Calculation of the Best Use of Resources), 1959; Funktsional'nyi analiz y normirovannyh prostranstvah (Functional Analysis in Normed Spaces), 1959; Optimal'nye rescheniya v ekonomike (Optimal Decisions in Economy), 1972; Essays in Optimal Planning, 1976; Funktsional'nyi Analiz (Functional Analysis), 1977. *Recreations:* swimming, chess. *Address:* Akademia Nauk, Leninsky Prospekt, 14, Moscow, USSR.                     *Died* 7 *April* 1986.

**KAPITZA, Peter Leonidovich,** FRS 1929; PhD Cantab; FInstP; Director of Institute for Physical Problems of Academy of Sciences of the USSR; Editor, Journal of Experimental and Theoretical Physics of Academy of Sciences, USSR; late Royal Society Messel Research Professor; late Director of the Royal Society Mond Laboratory; *b* Kronstadt, Russia, 26 June (old style) 1894; *s* of late Gen. Leonid Kapitza and Olga, *d* of Gen. J. Stebnitsckiy; *m* 1st, Nadejda (decd), *d* of Cyril Tschernosvitoff; 2nd, Anna, *d* of Professor A. N. Kryloff; two *s*. *Educ:* Secondary Sch., Kronstadt; Petrograd Politechnical Inst. (Faculty of Electrical Engrg). Lecturer, Petrograd Politechnical Inst., 1919–21; Clerk Maxwell Student, Cambridge Univ., 1923–26; Fellow, Trinity Coll., 1925 (Hon. Fellow, 1966). Asst Dir of Magnetic Research, Cavendish Laboratory, Cambridge, 1924–32; Cor. Mem. Acad. of Science of USSR, 1929; Mem. Acad. of Science, USSR, 1939; Hon. Member: Société des Naturalistes de Moscou, 1935; European Physical Soc., 1981; Fellow, Amer. Physical Soc., 1937; Hon. MInst. Met., 1943; Hon. Mem. and Franklin Medal of Franklin Inst., USA, 1944; Foreign Member: Council, French Physical Soc., 1935; Royal Acad. of Science, Sweden, 1966; Royal Netherlands Acad. of Sciences, 1969; Serbian Acad. of Sciences and Arts, 1971; Finnish Acad. of Science and Letters, 1974; Czechoslovak Acad. of Sciences, 1980; For. Hon. Mem., Amer. Acad. of Arts and Sciences, 1968. Numerous Hon. Doctorates, Fellowships, etc, 1944–. Rutherford Memorial Lectr, 1969. Medal Liege Univ., 1934; State prize for Physics, 1941 and 1943; Faraday Medal of Electr. Engrs, 1942; Sir Devaprasad Sarbadhikari Gold Medal, Calcutta Univ., 1955; Kothenius Gold Medal of German Acad. of Naturalists, 1959; Lomonosov Gold Medal, Acad. of Sciences, USSR, 1959; Great Gold Medal, Exhibn of Economic Achievements USSR, 1962; International Niels Bohr Gold Medal of Dansk Ingeniørvorening, 1964; Rutherford Medal of Inst. of Physics and Physical Soc., England, 1966; Kamerlingh Onnes Gold Medal of Netherlands Soc. for Refrigeration, 1968; Simon Prize, Inst. Physics, 1973; (jtly) Nobel Prize for Physics, 1978; Helmholtz Medal, Akad. der Wissenschaften, DDR, 1981. Order of Lenin, 1943, 1944, 1945, 1964, 1971, 1974; Moscow Defence Medal, 1944; Hero of Socialist Labour, 1945, 1974; Order of the Red Banner of Labour, 1954; Order of Yugoslav Banner with Ribbon, 1967. *Publications:* Collected Papers, 3 vols, 1964–67; Experiment, Theory, Practice, 1980; various publications on physics, mainly on magnetism, cryogenics and high temperature plasma in scientific journals. *Recreation:* chess. *Address:* The Institute for Physical Problems, ul. Kosygina 2, Moscow GSP1, 117973, USSR.                     *Died* 8 *April* 1984.

**KARAJAN, Herbert von;** *see* von Karajan.

**KARASEK, Dr Franz;** Austrian international administrator; Secretary-General, Council of Europe, 1979–84; *b* 22 April 1924; *m* 1951, Gertrud Hnolik; one *s* one *d*. *Educ:* Vienna Univ. and Paris. Official, Ministry for Foreign Affairs, 1950–52; Private Sec. to Fed. Chancellor, 1952–56; Counsellor, Austrian Embassy, Paris 1956–60 and Moscow 1960–64; Prin. Private Sec. to Fed. Chancellor, 1964–66; Dir-Gen. for Foreign Cultural Relations at Fed. Min. of Educn, 1966–70; Mem. Nat. Council (lower house of Parlt), 1970–79; substitute Mem., Austrian delegn to Parly Assembly of Council of Europe, 1970–72, Rep. in Austrian delegn 1972–79; Vice-Pres., Parly Assembly of CE, 1973–74; Mem. Austrian delegn to UN Gen. Assembly, 1970–79; Austrian Mem., Council of IPU, 1972–79. Grosses Goldenes Ehrenzeichen, Austria; Chevalier, Ordre Léopold II, Belgium; Chevalier, Ordre Couronne de Chêne, Luxembourg; Knight of St Sylvester, Vatican; Commandeur, Ordre de la Couronne Belge; Commander of Order of Nat. Merit, Italy; Commandeur de la Légion d'honneur; Grand Croix de l'Ordre de Francisco de Miranda, Venezuela; Grosskreuz des Liechtensteinischen Verdienstordens. *Publications:* articles in international reviews. *Recreation:* horse-riding. *Address:* Pyrkergasse 36, A-1190 Wien, Austria.
                                    *Died* 11 *March* 1986.

**KARIMJEE, Sir Tayabali Hassanali Alibhoy,** Kt 1955; Brilliant Star of Zanzibar (3rd Class); Jubilee Medal of Sultan of Zanzibar; *b* 7

Nov. 1897; *s* of Hassanali A. Karimjee and Zenubbai H. A. Karimjee; *m* 1917, Sugrabai Mohamedali Karimjee; one *d. Educ:* Zanzibar and Karachi. Pres., Indian National Association, Zanzibar, 1930 and 1942; Pres. Chamber of Commerce, Zanzibar, 1940, 1941, 1942; Mem. Fighter Fund Cttee, 1940–43; Mem. Red Cross Cttee, 1940–45; MLC, Zanzibar, 1933–45. Chm. Board of Directors, Karimjee Jivanjee & Co. Ltd, Karimjee Jivanjee Estates Ltd, Karimjee J. Properties Ltd, International Motor Mart Ltd (Tanganyika); Director, Karimjee Jivanjee & Co. (UK) Ltd, London. King George V Jubilee Medal, 1935; Coronation Medals, 1937 and 1953. *Address:* 60 Clifton, Karachi-0602, Pakistan. *Clubs:* Commonwealth Trust, Royal Over-Seas League; Karachi (Karachi); WIAA (Bombay). *Died 14 July* 1987.

**KARMEL, David,** CBE 1967; QC 1950; JP; *b* 1907; *s* of Joseph Michael Karmel; *m* 1943, Barbara, *d* of late Sir Montague Burton; one *d. Educ:* St Andrews College; Trinity Coll., Dublin. Called to Bar, Gray's Inn, 1928; Mem. of the Northern Circuit; Master of the Bench, Gray's Inn, 1954, Treasurer 1970, Vice-Treasurer, 1971; Mem. Inner Temple; Mem. of the Bar of Northern Rhodesia. Enlisted King's Royal Rifle Corps, 1939; commissioned in 60th Rifles, Dec. 1940; Capt., 1942; Major, 1943; served War of 1939–45 (wounded), in 1st Bn Western Desert, Tunisia and Italy, 1941–44, and in Jugoslavia, with Mil. Mission 1944–45. Recorder of Wigan, 1952–62; Dep. Chm., Glos QS, 1970–71; a Recorder of the Crown Court, 1972–79. Mem. Gen. Council of Bar, 1956–60. Steward, British Boxing Bd of Control. Mem. Industrial Disputes Tribunal; Chairman: Cttees of Investigation under Agric. Marketing Act, 1958; Truck Acts Cttee, 1959; Advisory Cttee on Service Candidates, 1963; Dep. Chm., Central Arbitration Cttee, 1977–. Mem. indep. panel of Industrial Court, Mem. Cttee on Legal Education of Students from Africa, 1960. HQ Referee, NCB. JP County of Glos., 1963. *Recreations:* theatre, travelling. *Address:* 1 Brick Court, EC4. *T:* 01-583 0777; 108 Eaton Place, SW1. *T:* 01-235 6159; Domaine Vigne Groussière, 83880 Méounes-les-Montrieux, France. *T:* 94.48.97.21. *Clubs:* Beefsteak, Buck's, Travellers'; Travellers' (Paris). *Died 31 May* 1982.

**KASSANIS, Basil,** OBE 1977; DSc (London); FRS 1966; retired; Senior Principal Scientific Officer, Department of Plant Pathology, Rothamsted Experimental Station, Harpenden, Herts, 1961–77; *b* 16 Oct. 1911; *s* of Zacharias and Helen Kassanis; *m* 1952, Jean Eleanor Matthews; one *s* one *d. Educ:* University of Thessaloniki, Greece. Came to Rothamsted Experimental Station as British Council scholar, 1938; appointed to staff, 1943. Hon. DSc Aristotelian Univ. of Thessaloniki. Research Medal, Royal Agricultural Soc., 1965. *Publications:* scientific papers in various jls. *Recreation:* sculpture (local exhibns). *Address:* 3 Rosebery Avenue, Harpenden, Herts AL5 2QT. *T:* 5739.

*Died 23 March* 1985.

**KASTLER, Alfred;** French physicist; retired; *b* 3 May 1902; *s* of Frédéric Kastler and Anna (*née* Frey); *m* 1924, Elise Cosset; two *s* one *d. Educ:* Lycée Bartholdi, Colmar; Ecole Normale Supérieure. Taught in Lycées, Mulhouse, Colmar, Bordeaux, 1926–31; Asst at Faculty of Sciences, Bordeaux, 1931–36; Lecturer, Faculty of Science, University of Clermont-Ferrand, 1936–38; Prof., Faculty of Sciences, Bordeaux, 1938–41; Prof. of Physics: Ecole Normale Supérieure, and Univ. of Paris, 1941–68; University of Louvain, Belgium, 1953–54; Dir, Atomic Clock Lab., Centre National de la Recherche Scientifique, 1958–72. Member: Institut de France; Académie Royale Flamande; Polish Acad. of Science; Deutsche Akademie der Wissenschaften zu Berlin; Akademie Leopoldina; Indian Acad. of Science; Royal Acad. of the Netherlands; Hungarian Acad. of Science. Hon. Member: Société Française de Physique; Optical Soc. of America; Polish Soc. of Physics. Hon. Doctorates: Louvain, Pisa, Oxford, Edinburgh, Laval and Sherbrooke (Quebec), Jerusalem, Belgrade, Bucharest, Nottingham, Weizmann Inst., Technion Holweck Medal and Prize, Phys. Soc., 1954; Nobel Prize for Physics, 1966. Grand Officier de la Légion d'Honneur; Grand Officier de l'Ordre National du Mérite. *Address:* 1 Rue du Val-de-Grâce, 75005 Paris, France.

*Died 7 Jan.* 1984.

**KATSINA, Emir of;** *see* Nagogo, Alhaji Hon. Sir Usuman.

**KATZIN, Olga;** journalist; pen-name Sagittarius; *b* London, 9 July 1896; *d* of John and Mathilde Katzin; *m* 1921, Hugh Miller, actor (decd); two *s* one *d. Educ:* Privately. *Publications:* Troubadours, 1925; A Little Pilgrim's Peeps at Parnassus, 1927; Sagittarius Rhyming, 1940; London Watches, 1941; Targets, 1943; Quiver's Choice, 1945; Let Cowards Flinch, 1947; Pipes of Peace, 1949; Up the Poll, 1950; Strasbourg Geese and Other Verses, 1953; Unaida (with Michael Barsley), play, 1957; The Perpetual Pessimist (with Daniel George), 1963. *Address:* 44 Hamilton Terrace, NW8.

*Died 6 Jan.* 1987.

**KAWAMATA, Katsuji;** Counsellor, Nissan Motor Co. Ltd, since 1985 (Chairman, 1973–85); *b* 1 March 1905; *s* of Misao and Kin Kawamata; *m* 1933, Haruko Yahagi; three *s* one *d. Educ:* Tokyo Univ. of Commerce (BComSc). Entered Industrial Bank of Japan Ltd (IBJ), 1929; Manager, Hiroshima Branch, 1946; joined Nissan Motor Co. as Managing Director, 1947; Executive Man. Dir, 1948; President, 1957–73; Dir and Counsellor, Nissan Diesel Motor Co. Ltd, 1977–; Adviser, Nissan Shatai Co. Ltd, 1979–. Supreme Adviser, Japan Automobile Manufacturers Assoc., 1972–; Vice Chairman: Fedn of Economic Organizations (Keidanren), 1972–; Japan Productivity Center, 1975–; Vice Pres., Japan Fedn of Employers' Assocs (Nikkeiren), 1980–; Auditor, Tokyo Chamber of Commerce and Industry, 1965–. Blue Ribbon Medal, 1962; First Order of the Sacred Treasure (Japan), 1975; Education: Minister's Commendation, 1974. *Recreations:* reading, golf. *Address:* 17–1, Ginza 6-chome, Chuo-ku, Tokyo, Japan 104. *T:* (03) 543–5523.

*Died 29 March* 1986.

**KAYE, Danny, (Daniel Kominski);** Actor (Stage, Film, TV, and Radio); Comedian; Baseball Executive; conductor; *b* New York, NY, 18 Jan. 1913; *s* of Jacob Kominski and Clara Nemorovsky; *m* 1940, Sylvia Fine, producer, lyricist and composer; one *d.* Official Permanent Ambassador-at-Large for UNICEF (first award for Internat. Distingushed Service). Scopus Laureate, 1977. Founder, managing limited partner, Seattle Mariners baseball team, 1976. Jean Hersholt Humanitarian Award, 1982; George Foster Peabody Award, 1982; Presidential Medal of Freedom (USA), 1987 (awarded posthumously). *Stage:* Straw Hat Review, Ambassador Theatre, New York City, 1939; Lady in the Dark, 1940; Let's Face It, 1941; appeared London Palladium, also provincial tour, Great Britain, 1949; London Palladium, 1955. *Television:* annual 'Look In' for Children, Metropolitan Opera, NYC (founder), 1975–; Pinocchio, 1976; Skokie, 1981. *Films include:* Up In Arms, 1943; Wonder Man, 1944; Kid from Brooklyn, 1945; The Secret Life of Walter Mitty, 1946; That's Life, 1947; A Song is Born, 1949; The Inspector-General, 1950; On the Riviera, 1951; Hans Christian Andersen, 1952; Knock on Wood, 1954; White Christmas, 1954; The Court Jester, 1956; Merry Andrew, 1957; Me And The Colonel, 1958; Five Pennies, 1959; On the Double, 1960; The Man from The Diner's Club, 1963; The Madwoman of Chaillot, 1969; *Play:* Two by Two, NY, 1970; *Television includes:* weekly show (CBS), 1963–67; The Danny Kaye Show (Special Acad. award, 1954; Emmy award, 1963; George Foster Peabody award, 1963; Best Children's Special award, 1975). *Address:* Box 750, Beverly Hills, Calif, USA.

*Died 3 March* 1987.

**KAYE, Sir John (Christopher Lister) L.;** *see* Lister-Kaye.

**KAYE, Sir Stephen Henry Gordon,** 3rd Bt, *cr* 1923; *b* 24 March 1917; *s* of Sir Henry Gordon Kaye, 2nd Bt and Winifred (*d* 1971), *d* of late Walter H. Scales, Verwood, Bradford; *S* father, 1956. *Educ:* Stowe; Trinity Coll., Cambridge. *Heir: brother* David Alexander Gordon Kaye [*b* 26 July 1919; *m* 1st, 1942, Elizabeth (marr. diss. 1950), *o d* of Capt. Malcolm Hurtley, Baynards Manor, Horsham, Sussex; 2nd, 1955, Adelle, *d* of Denis Thomas, Brisbane, Queensland; two *s* four *d*]. *Address:* Mortimore's, New Buildings, Sandford, near Crediton, Devon EX17 4PP. *Died 12 June* 1983.

**KEARNS, Sir Frederick (Matthias),** KCB 1975 (CB 1970); MC 1944; consultant and policy adviser: to Rank Hovis MacDougall Ltd, since 1981; to S. & W. Berisford plc (formerly British Sugar Corp.), since 1982; *b* 21 Feb. 1921; *er s* of G. H. and Ivy Kearns, Burnley; *m* 1946, Betty Broadbent; one *d. Educ:* Burnley Grammar Sch.; Brasenose Coll., Oxford; RMC Sandhurst. BA (Hons) 1941; MA 1947, Oxon. Commissioned Royal Fusiliers, 1942. Served 8th and 5th Armies, N Africa and Italy, 1942–46; Brigade Major, 167th Inf. Brigade, Trieste, 1946. Asst Principal, Ministry of Agriculture, 1948, Principal 1950; Asst Sec., Min. of Agriculture, Fisheries and Food, 1957; Regional Controller, Northern Region, 1957–60; Head of Finance Division, 1960–63; Head of External Relations Div., 1963–64; Under-Sec., External Relations, 1964–68; Meat and Livestock Group, 1968–69; Deputy Secretary, 1969–73; on special assignment to UK Delegn for EEC Negotiations, 1970–72; Second Permant Sec., MAFF, 1973–78. *Recreations:* fishing, poetry. *Address:* 26 Brookway, Blackheath, SE3. *T:* 01-852 0747. *Club:* Reform. *Died 7 Aug.* 1983.

**KEARNS, Prof. Howard George Henry,** OBE 1954; Professor of Agricultural and Horticultural Science, Bristol University 1957–67, later Emeritus; Dir, Long Ashton Research Station, 1957–67; *b* 13 May 1902; *s* of Henry Kearns and Elizabeth Anne Baker; *m* 1930, Molly Yvonne Cousins. *Educ:* St Paul's Sch., West Kensington; Downing Coll., Cambridge; Wye Coll., University of London. Lecturer in Zoology (Entomology), Bristol Univ., 1926–31; Advisory Entomologist, Long Ashton Research Station, 1931–32; Research Entomologist, 1933–; Reader in Entomology, Bristol Univ., 1950. Particular interests in applied biology, spray techniques and design of spray machinery for temperate and tropical crops. *Publications:* contrib. to: Insecticides and Colonial Agricultural Development, 1954; Science and Fruit, 1953; Modern Commercial Fruitgrowing, 1956; articles in learned jls on various aspects of plant protection. *Recreations:* engineering, natural history, photography. *Address:*

Clive Weare House, Clewer, Wedmore, Som. *T:* Cheddar 742165.
*Died* 15 *July* 1986.

**KEARON, Air Cdre Norman Walter,** CMG 1974; CBE 1967 (OBE
1943); Royal Air Force (retd); General Manager and Chief
Executive, Philips/L. M. Ericsson Joint Venture, Riyadh, since
1978; *b* 27 Dec. 1913. Served War of 1939–45 (OBE). Dept of the
Air Member for Supply and Organisation, 1963; retired as Director,
Directorate of Organisation, Royal Air Force, 1968; Chief Exec.,
British Aircraft Corp., Saudi Arabia, to 1978. *Address:* Philips/L.
M. Ericsson Joint Venture, Box 3412, Riyadh, United Arab
Emirates.
*Died* 1 *May* 1981.

**KEELE, Prof. Cyril Arthur;** Emeritus Professor of Pharmacology,
University of London; *b* 23 Nov. 1905; 2nd *s* of Dr David and Jessie
Keele; *m* 1942, Joan Ainslie, *er d* of Lieut-Col G. A. Kempthorne;
three *s*. *Educ:* Epsom Coll.; Middlesex Hospital Medical Sch.
MRCS, LRCP 1927; MB, BS (London) 1928; MRCP 1929; MD
London 1930; FRCP 1948; FFARCS 1958. Medical Registrar,
Middlesex Hosp., 1930–32; Demonstrator and Lectr in Physiology,
1933–38; Lectr in Pharmacology, 1938–49; Reader in Pharmacology
and Therapeutics, 1949–52, at Middlesex Hospital Medical Sch.;
Prof. of Pharmacology and Therapeutics, Univ. of London, 1952–68;
Dir, Rheumatology Res. Dept, Middlesex Hosp. Med. Sch., 1968–73.
Hon. Mem., Internat. Assoc. for the Study of Pain, 1975.
*Publications:* (with Prof. J. M. Robson) Recent Advances in
Pharmacology, 1956; (with Dr D. Armstrong) Substances Producing
Pain and Itch, 1964; (with Prof. E. Neil and Prof. N. Joels) Samson
Wright's Applied Physiology, 13th edn, 1982; papers in scientific
journals on the control of sweating, analgesic drugs and chemical
factors producing pain. *Address:* 17 Emelson Close, East Dereham,
Norfolk NR19 2ES.
*Died* 22 *Oct.* 1987.

**KEELEY, Thomas Clews,** CBE 1944; MA; physicist; Fellow of
Wadham College, Oxford, 1924–61, now Emeritus Fellow; Sub-
Warden, 1947–61, retired; *b* 16 Feb. 1894; *s* of T. F. Keeley,
Erdington, Birmingham. *Educ:* King Edward's School,
Birmingham; St John's Coll., Cambridge (Scholar). Royal Aircraft
Establishment, 1917–19. Oxford from 1919. Fellow of the Institute
of Physics. *Recreations:* photography, travel. *Address:* Wadham
College, Oxford. *T:* 42564. *Club:* English-Speaking Union.
*Died* 25 *Dec.* 1988.

**KEELY, Eric Philipps,** CBE 1950; Director, National Sulphuric Acid
Association Ltd, 1959–67; *b* 11 Aug. 1899; *s* of late Erasmus
Middleton Keely, Nottingham; *m* 1942, Enid Betty Curtis; two *d*.
*Educ:* Highgate Sch. Served European War, 1917–18, Lancashire
Fusiliers; Ministry of Agriculture and Fisheries, 1930; Food
(Defence Plans) Dept, Board of Trade 1937; Ministry of Food,
1939; seconded to Govt of India, 1943–44; Under-Sec., Ministry of
Food, 1952; Under-Sec., Ministry of Agriculture, Fisheries and
Food, 1955–59. *Address:* Queen's Cottage, Horsham Road, Findon,
West Sussex. *T:* Findon 2677.
*Died* 24 *April* 1988.

**KEEN, Sir Bernard (Augustus),** Kt 1952; FRS 1935; DSc; Fellow of
University College, London; *b* 1890; *m* Elsie Isabelle Cowley (*d*
1956); two *s*. *Educ:* University Coll., London. Andrews Scholar,
1908; Trouton Research Scholar, 1911; Carey Foster Res. Prizeman,
1912; Soil Physicist, Rothamsted, 1913; Suffolk Regt (Gallipoli and
Palestine), 1914–17; Research Dept, Woolwich Arsenal, 1918;
returned to Rothamsted, 1919; Dir, Imperial Institute of Agricultural
Research, India, 1930–31; Pres., Royal Meteorological Soc., 1938
and 1939; Vice-Pres., Institute of Physics, 1941–43; Cantor Lecturer,
Royal Society of Arts, 1942; formerly Asst Dir and Head of Soil
Physics Dept, Rothamsted Experimental Station, 1919–43;
Scientific Adviser Middle East Supply Centre, Cairo, 1943–45;
adviser on rural development, Palestine, 1946; Chm. of UK Govt
Mission to W Africa on production of vegetable oils and oil seeds,
1946; adviser to E African Governments on agricultural policy and
research needs, 1947; mem., Scientific Council for Africa, 1950–54;
Chm. of Governors, E African Tea Research Inst., 1951–54.
Broadcast talks to schools on science of agriculture and gardening,
1928–41; Dir, E African Agriculture and Forestry Research
Organisation, 1947–55; Scientific Adviser, Baird and Tatlock
(London) Ltd, 1955–63; Mem., Scientific Panel Colonial
Development Corp., 1955–63; Mem., Forest Products Res. Bd,
DSIR, 1957–59. Travelled extensively in USA, S Africa, India, E
and W Africa, Middle East, Bulgaria and Australia, to examine and
report on the scientific, technical, and administrative problems in
agriculture. *Publications:* The Physical Properties of the Soil, 1931;
The Agricultural Development of the Middle East, 1946; various
papers in scientific and agricultural journals. *Address:* Suite 5, Hotel
Bristowe, Grange Road, Southbourne, Bournemouth BH6 3NY.
*Club:* Athenæum.
*Died* 5 *Aug.* 1981.

**KEEN, Patrick John,** CMG 1968; MBE 1944; retired; *b* 30 June 1911;
*s* of Brig. P. H. Keen, CB; *m* 1st, 1940, Joyce (*d* 1954), *d* of E. Seth-
Ward; two *s* one *d* (and one *s* decd); 2nd, 1958, Anne Cunitia, *d* of
Capt. J. A. A. Morris, RN. *Educ:* Haileybury Coll.; RMC Sandhurst.

Hampshire Regt, 1931; Indian Political Service, 1936–47; served
with 2/13th FF Rifles, 1939–43; HM Diplomatic Service, 1948–68;
served in Afghanistan, Pakistan, Cyprus and British Guiana; retd,
1968. *Address:* Saxted House, Emsworth, Hants. *T:* Emsworth
2302.
*Died* 8 *March* 1983.

**KEENE, Air Vice-Marshal Allan Lancelot Addison P.;** *see* Perry-
Keene.

**KEENLYSIDE, Francis Hugh;** *b* 7 July 1911; *s* of late Capt. Cecil A.
H. Keenlyside and Gladys Mary (*née* Milne); *m* 1st, 1935, Margaret
Joan (*d* 1987), *d* of late E. L. K. Ellis; two *s* two *d*; 2nd, 1962, Joan
Winifred (*née* Collins); one *d*. *Educ:* Charterhouse; Trinity Coll.,
Oxford. 1st class Hons in Philosophy, Politics and Economics, 1933,
Whitehead Travelling Student. Entered Administrative Class,
Home Civil Service, 1934; Principal Private Sec. to four successive
Ministers of Shipping and War Transport, 1939–43; Asst Sec. in
charge of Shipping Policy Div., 1943; Asst Manager, Union Castle,
1947; Dep. Leader, British delegation to Danube Conf., Belgrade,
1948; Gen. Manager, Union Castle, 1953; Asst Managing Dir,
Union-Castle, 1956–60; Shipping Adviser, Suez Canal Users Assoc.,
1957. Mem., Gen. Council of Chamber of Shipping, 1953–60;
Editor, Alpine Journal, 1953–62. Chevalier (1st Cl.) of Order of St
Olav (Norway), 1948; Officer of Order of George I (Greece), 1950;
King Christian X Liberty Medal (Denmark), 1946. *Publications:*
Peaks and Pioneers, 1975; contrib. to mountaineering jls, etc.
*Recreation:* mountaineering. *Address:* Spring Farm Vineyard,
Moorlinch, Bridgwater, Somerset. *Clubs:* Alpine; Salisbury.
*Died* 14 *June* 1990.

**KEENS, Philip Francis,** CBE 1973 (OBE 1966); Director, TSB Unit
Trust Managers (Channel Islands) Ltd, 1972–83; Chairman, TSB
Gilt Fund Ltd, 1978–83; *b* 18 June 1903; *s* of Sir Thomas Keens; *m*
1st, 1930, Sylvia Irene Robinson (*d* 1970); one *s* one *d*; 2nd, 1974,
Mrs Margaret Faith Warne. *Educ:* Tettenhall Coll., Staffs.
Incorporated Accountant, 1925; Chartered Accountant, 1957.
Partner, Keens, Shay, Keens & Co., London, 1926–67; Trustee,
Luton Trustee Savings Bank, 1934 (Chairman, 1949–64); Dep.
Chm., Trustee Savings Bank Assoc., 1966–76 (Chm. Southern Area,
1967–76); Chm., London South Eastern Trustee Savings Bank,
1964–76 (Vice-Chm., 1958–64); Chairman: Trustee Savings Bank
Trust Co. Ltd, 1967–79; Central Trustee Savings Bank Ltd, 1972–79;
Trustee Savings Bank, South East, 1975–78, Pres., 1978; Mem.
Central Bd and Dep Chm., Trustee Savings Bank, 1976–79. Past
Master, Worshipful Co. of Feltmakers. *Recreation:* golf. *Address:*
15 Links Court, Grouville, Jersey, CI. *T:* Jersey 53719. *Club:*
Victoria (Jersey).
*Died* 5 *Oct.* 1989.

**KEEPING, Charles William James;** artist, book designer and Fine Art
Lecturer since 1952; Visiting Lecturer in Printmaking, Camberwell
School of Arts and Crafts; *b* 22 Sept. 1924; *s* of Charles Keeping
and Eliza Ann Trodd; *m* 1952, Renate Meyer; three *s* one *d*. *Educ:*
Frank Bryant Sch., Kennington; Polytechnic, Regent Street.
Apprenticed to printing trade, 1938; served as telegraphist, RN,
1942–46; studied for Nat. Diploma of Design at Polytechnic,
London, 1946–52; Vis. Lectr in Art, Polytechnic, 1956–63. Illustrated
over 180 books, drawings for wall murals, television and advertising.
Certificate of Merit (for illustrations to The God Beneath the Sea)
1970, Library Assoc.; Certificate, Highly Commended, for Hans
Andersen Medal, Rio de Janeiro, Internat. Bd on Books for Young
People, 1974. *Publications:* Black Dolly, 1966; Shaun and the
Carthorse, 1966; Charley Charlotte and the Golden Canary, 1967
(Kate Greenaway Medal); Alfie and the Ferryboat, 1968; Tinker
Tailor, 1968 (a Francis Williams Meml Bequest prize-winner, 1972);
Joseph's Yard, 1969 (Honour Book award) (also filmed for TV);
Through the Window, 1970 (also filmed for TV); Spider's Web,
1973 (Bratislava cert.); Richard, 1973; Railway Passage, 1974
(Golden Apple, Bienalle Illustration Bratislava, 1975); Wasteground
Circus, 1975; Cockney Ding Dong, 1975; The Wildman, 1976 (a
Francis Williams prize-winner, 1977); Inter-City, 1977; River,
1978; Miss Emily and the Bird of Make-believe, 1978; Willie's Fire-
Engine, 1980; Sammy Streetsinger, 1984; (ed) Book of Classic
Ghost Stories, 1986; (ed) Classic Tales of the Macabre, 1987;
*illustrations for:* The Highwayman, by Alfred Noyes, 1981 (Kate
Greenaway Medal, 1982); The Folio Society's Complete Dickens,
1981–; Beowulf, 1982; The Wedding Ghost, by Leon Garfield,
1985; The Lady of Shalott, by Tennyson, 1986; The Tales of Sir
Gawain, by Neil Phillip, 1987; Jack the Treacle Eater, by Charles
Causley, 1987 (Emil Kurt Maschler Award); Black Beauty, by Anna
Sewell, 1988; *posthumous publication:* Adam and Paradise Island,
1989. *Recreations:* talking, walking. *Address:* 16 Church Road,
Shortlands, Bromley BR2 0HP. *T:* 01–460 7679.
*Died* 16 *May* 1988.

**KEETON, George Williams,** FBA 1964; Barrister-at-law; Principal,
London Institute of World Affairs, 1938–52, President, since 1952;
Leverhulme Fellow, 1971; *b* 22 May 1902; *o s* of John William and
Mary Keeton; *m* 1st, 1924, Gladys Edith Calthorpe; two *s*; 2nd,
Kathleen Marian Willard. *Educ:* Gonville and Caius Coll.,

Cambridge (Foundation Scholar in Law); Gray's Inn (Bacon Scholar). BA, LLB, with first class hons, 1923; MA, LLM, 1927; LLD 1932. Called to Bar, 1928; Editor, The Cambridge Review, 1924; Reader in Law and Politics, Hong Kong Univ., 1924-27; Senior Lecturer in Law, Manchester Univ., 1928-31; University College London: Reader in English Law, 1931-37, Prof. of English Law, 1937-69, Dean, Faculty of Laws, 1939-54, Vice-Provost, 1966-69; Professor of English Law, Univ. of Notre Dame, 1969-71; Professor Associate, Brunel Univ., 1969-77. Distinguished Vis. Prof., Miami Univ., 1971-73. Mem. Exec. Cttee, American Judicature Soc., 1974-77. Hon. LLD: Sheffield 1966; Hong Kong 1972; DUniv Brunel, 1977. *Publications:* The Development of Extraterritoriality in China, 1928; The Austinian Theories of Law and Sovereignty (with R. A. Eastwood, LLD), 1929; The Elementary Principles of Jurisprudence, 1930, 2nd edn 1949; Shakespeare and his Legal Problems, 1930; The Problem of the Moscow Trial, 1933; The Law of Trusts, 1st edn 1934, 10th edn 1974; An Introduction to Equity, 1st edn 1938, 8th edn 1976; National Sovereignty and International Order, 1939; Making International Law Work (with G. Schwarzenberger, PhD), 1st edn 1939, 2nd edn 1946; The Speedy Return (novel), 1938; Mutiny in the Caribbean (novel), 1940; The Case for an International University, 1941; Russia and Her Western Neighbours (with R. Schlesinger), 1942; China, the Far East, and the Future, 1st edn 1942, 2nd edn 1949; A Liberal Attorney-General, 1949; The Passing of Parliament, 1952; Social Change in the Law of Trusts, 1958; Case Book on Equity and Trusts, 1958, 2nd edn 1974; Trial for Treason, 1959; Trial by Tribunal, 1960; Guilty but Insane, 1961; (with L. A. Sheridan) The Modern Law of Charities, 1962, 3rd edn 1983; The Investment and Taxation of Trust Funds, 1964; Lord Chancellor Jeffreys, 1964; The Norman Conquest and the Common Law, 1966; Shakespeare's Legal and Political Background, 1967; (with L. A. Sheridan) Equity, 1970; Government in Action, 1970; Modern Developments in the Law of Trusts, 1971; The Football Revolution, 1972; English Law: the judicial contribution, 1974; (with S. N. Frommel) British Industry and European Law, 1974; Keeping the Peace, 1976; (with L. A. Sheridan) Trusts in the Commonwealth, 1977; Harvey the Hasty, 1978; numerous contributions to periodicals. *Address:* Picts Close, Picts Lane, Princes Risborough, Bucks. *T:* Princes Risborough 5094. *Died* 2 *Oct.* 1989.

**KEGGIN, Air Vice-Marshal Harold,** CB 1967; CBE 1962; LDS; Director of Dental Services, Royal Air Force, 1964-69, retired; *b* 25 Feb. 1909; *y s* of John and Margaret Keggin, Port Erin, Isle of Man; *m* 1935, Margaret Joy (*née* Campbell); one *s* two *d. Educ:* Douglas High Sch.; University of Liverpool. Dental Officer, RAF, commissioned, 1932; Flt Lieut 1934; Sqdn Ldr 1939; Wing Comdr 1942; Gp Capt. 1954; Air Cdre 1958; Air Vice-Marshal 1964. QHDS 1958-69. *Address:* Rosecroft, 7 Cotlands, Sidmouth, Devon EX10 8SP. *T:* Sidmouth 4790. *Died* 19 *March* 1989.

**KEGIE, James,** OBE 1967; FRTPI, FRICS, AIAS; Town Planning Consultant and Chartered Surveyor; retired from local government, 1974; *b* 30 Sept. 1913; *s* of Henry Kegie and Mary Ann (May) Kegie; *m* 1st, 1939, Doreen (*d* 1969), *d* of Rev. Nicholas Martin Cuthbert and Mary Ann Cuthbert; two *s*; 2nd, 1974, Helen Ruth, *d* of Alfred Quinton Barton and Amy Elizabeth Barton. *Educ:* Gateshead-upon-Tyne Grammar Sch.; Coll. of Estate Management. Planning appts in private practice and local govt in Durham, W Sussex, Cheshire and Monmouthshire, 1929-45; County Planning Officer, Monmouthshire CC, 1945-74. Member: Exec. Council, Co. Planning Officers' Soc. 1948-74 (Pres., 1968-69); Bd of Housing Corp., 1974-83; Countryside Commn, 1974-82; Welsh Cttee of Countryside Commn, 1974-82 (Chm., 1981-82); Bd of Welsh Develt Agency, 1976-79; Management Cttee, Sch. of Advanced Urban Studies, Bristol Univ., 1974-80; Consultant to Nat. Trust on Structure Plans in Wales, 1974-; Member: European Architectural Heritage Cttee for Wales, 1972-74; Bi-lingual Signs Cttee, Wales, 1971-72; Working Parties and Research Gps on Town and Country Planning, 1960-77; Bd of Civic Trust for Wales, 1970-; Tech. Unit on Structure Plans (Chm.), Sports Council for Wales, 1977-81. Knight of Mark Twain. *Publications:* County of Monmouth Development Plan, 1953; Minority Report, Bilingual Signs Cttee, 1972; contrib. Jl of RICS. *Recreations:* river and sea fishing, caravanning, motoring, walking, gardening; conservation of the countryside and built environment. *Address:* High Meadow, Christchurch, near Newport, Gwent NP6 1JJ. *T:* Caerleon 422141. *Died* 14 *Dec.* 1984.

**KEIGHLEY, Frank;** Director: The Rank Foundation Ltd; Foundation for Christian Communication Ltd; Fellow of Institute of Bankers; *b* 19 March 1900; *e s* of late Wm L. Keighley; *m* 1926, Mary, *e d* of late J. K. Wilson; one *s. Educ:* Northern Institute, Leeds. Entered Union of London & Smiths Bank (which was amalgamated with National Provincial Bank in 1918) as Junior Clerk, 1915; retired, as Chief General Manager, Dec. 1961, and as Dir, Dec. 1969. *Address:* Little Court, 88 Fulmer Drive, Gerrards Cross, Bucks. *T:* Gerrards Cross 84117. *Died* 30 *May* 1981.

**KEIR, Thelma C.;** *see* Cazalet-Keir.

**KEITH, John Lucien,** CBE 1951 (OBE 1943); *b* 22 May 1895; 2nd *s* of George Keith, Director of Cable Companies and Felicie, *d* of Charles Pierce, stockbroker; unmarried. *Educ:* Ecole Closelet, Lausanne; Hertford Coll., Oxford (MA). British South Africa Co., N Rhodesia, 1918-25; District Officer, Colonial Service, N Rhodesia, 1925-38; Acting Dir of African Education, N Rhodesia, 1930-31; African Research Survey, Chatham House, 1938-39; Colonial Office, 1939; Head of Welfare and Students Dept, Colonial Office, 1941-56; missions to overseas territories, USA and Canada. Adviser on Students' Affairs, W Nigeria Office, London, 1957-62; London Rep. of Univ. of Ife, Nigeria, 1962-72. *Recreations:* travelling, talking books for the blind. *Address:* 49A Sea Road, Bexhill-on-Sea, East Sussex. *T:* Bexhill-on-Sea 215463.
*Died* 28 *Feb.* 1988.

**KEITH, Robert Farquharson,** CB 1973; OBE 1948; Chief Registrar of Trade Unions and Employers' Associations from 1971 until repeal of Industrial Relations Act 1971 in 1974; *b* 22 June 1912; *s* of Dr Robert Donald Keith and Mary Lindsay (*née* Duncan), Turriff, Aberdeenshire; *m* 1958, Jean Abernethy (*née* Fisher); one *s. Educ:* Fettes; Caius Coll., Cambridge (Classical Scholar). Indian Civil Service, 1937-47; Dep. Comr, Upper Sind Frontier, 1945-47; Home Civil Service, Min. of Labour, later Dept of Employment, 1948; Under-Sec., Employment Services and Estabs Divs, 1965-71. *Address:* Parkhead, Auchattie, Banchory, Kincardineshire. *T:* Banchory 2166. *Club:* Caledonian. *Died* 23 *May* 1988.

**KEITH, Trevor;** Charity Commissioner, 1972-81; *b* 3 Sept. 1921; 2nd *s* of George Keith and May Mabel Keith (*née* Newman); *m* 1942, Doris Elizabeth (*née* Burrell); two *s* one *d. Educ:* Isleworth County Grammar School. Called to Bar, Lincoln's Inn, 1951. Entered Civil Service, Air Min., 1938; RAF, 1941-45; Air Min., 1946-48; Inland Revenue, Estate Duty Office, 1948-52; Charity Commn, 1952-81. *Recreations:* cricket, travel, gastronomy. *Address:* 7 Lucastes Road, Haywards Heath, Sussex RH16 1JJ. *Died* 16 *May* 1988.

**KELF-COHEN, Reuben,** CB 1950; Economics writer and consultant; Director and Secretary, Radio Industry Council, 1960-66; *b* Leeds, 29 Sept. 1895; *m* 1922, Edith Florence Kelf (*d* 1964); one *d. Educ:* Manchester Grammar Sch.; Wadham Coll., Oxford (Classical Scholar). Gaisford Greek Verse Prize, 1915; Lothian Historical Essay Prize, 1920; 1st Class Hons (History), 1920; 1st class Hons (Economics) London Univ., 1931. Served European War, 1914-18, Royal Field Artillery (wounded). Entered Bd of Educn, 1920; Tutorial Class Tutor, London Univ., 1924-39; Board of Trade, 1925-41; Petroleum Dept, 1941-42; Principal Asst Sec. (Gas and Electricity), Ministry of Fuel and Power, 1942-45; Under-Sec., Ministry of Fuel and Power, 1946-55; Dir, East Indian Produce Co. 1955-59. Vis. Lecturer: St Andrews Univ., 1970; University Coll., Aberystwyth, 1971. Freeman of the City of London; Liveryman of the Company of Horners. *Publications:* Knights of Malta, 1920; Nationalisation in Britain, 1958; Twenty Years of Nationalisation: The British Experience, 1969; British Nationalisation, 1945-1973, 1974; articles on economic subjects. *Recreations:* bridge, bowls, sea voyages. *Address:* 14 Harold Road, Upper Norwood, SE19. *T:* 01-653 1086. *Club:* Savage. *Died* 7 *March* 1981.

**KELLAR, Alexander James,** CMG 1961; OBE 1948; *b* 26 June 1905; *er s* of James Dodds Ballantyne Kellar and Florence Maud Kellar (*née* Coveney). *Educ:* George Watson's Coll.; Edinburgh Univ. (MA, LLB). Sen. Pres., Students' Representative Council; Pres., Nat. Union of Scottish Students, 1929-30; Commonwealth Fund Fellow, Yale (Mem. Elizabethan Club) and Columbia (AM Internat. Law and Relations); called to Bar, Middle Temple, 1936. Asst Sec., Brit. Employers' Confedn, 1938-41; Employers' (Substitute) Delegate, Governing Body of ILO, 1940. Mem. Army Officers' Emergency Reserve, 1938. Attached War Office, 1941-65; ODM, 1970-73; English Tourist Bd, 1970-73. *Recreations:* riding, travel. *Address:* 5 Sheffield Terrace, W8; Grey Walls, Friston, Sussex. *Club:* Travellers'. *Died* 8 *Nov.* 1982.

**KELLETT, Sir Stanley Everard,** 6th Bt *cr* 1801; *b* 1911; *s* of Francis Stanley Kellett (*d* 1955) (2nd *s* of 3rd Bt); *S* kinsman, Sir Henry de Castres Kellett, 5th Bt, 1966; *m* 1938, Audrey Margaret Phillips; one *s* one *d. Heir: s* Stanley Charles Kellett [*b* 5 March 1940; *m* 1st, 1962, Lorraine May (marr. diss. 1968), *d* of F. Winspear; 2nd, 1968, Margaret Ann, *d* of J. Bofinger]. *Address:* 33 Caroma Avenue, Kyeemagh, New South Wales 2216, Australia.
*Died* 1 *April* 1983.

**KELLEY, Richard;** *b* 24 July 1904; *m* 1924; four *s* three *d. Educ:* Elementary Sch. Councillor, West Riding of Yorks County Council, 1949-59; a Trade Union Secretary for ten years. MP (Lab) Don Valley, W Yorks, 1959-79. Mem. of the National Union of Mineworkers. *Address:* 23 St Lawrence Road, Dunscroft, Doncaster, S Yorks DN7 4AS. *Died* 7 *April* 1984.

**KELLY, Sir Arthur (John),** Kt 1961; CBE 1950; *b* 17 Nov. 1898; *yr s* of John Kelly, Hodge Bower, Shropshire; *m* 1928, Florence Mary

Smyth, yr d of John Smyth, Belfast. *Educ:* Bridgnorth; Shrewsbury. Served European War, 1917–19: RFC 12 Sqdn and RAF Army of Occupation, Germany. Temp. Asst, Min. of Labour, Whitehall, 1919–22; Asst Principal, Min. of Labour, N Ireland, 1922; Principal, Cabinet Offices, N Ireland, 1940; Asst Sec., 1941; seconded as N Ireland Govt Liaison Officer at Home Office, Whitehall, 1943; Permanent Sec., Min. of Labour N Ireland, 1956; Sec. to the Cabinet and Clerk of the Privy Council of Northern Ireland, 1957–63, retd. *Recreation:* golf. *Address:* 6 Cherryhill, Beechlands, Malone Road, Belfast. *Club:* Malone Golf (Belfast).

*Died 27 May 1983.*

**KELLY, Kenneth Linden;** Secretary-General of the Automobile Association, 1954–63; *b* 5 Dec. 1913; *s* of Herbert Linden Kelly and Alice Maud Gray; *m* 1939, Betty Joan Roe; two *d. Educ:* Kingston Grammar School. Served War of 1939–45 in RAOC, Europe and Middle East; Actg Dep. Dir of OS Middle East Forces, 1945 (Col.). Chm., Governors of Kingston Grammar School, 1957–72. FRSA 1955. *Address:* 37 Henly House, Lynwood, Sunninghill, Ascot, Berks. *Clubs:* Kingston Rowing (Vice-Pres.); Remenham (Henley). *Died 2 May 1985.*

**KELLY, Richard Denis Lucien,** MC 1944; a Recorder of the Crown Court, 1972–80; *b* 31 Jan. 1916; *e s* of late Richard Cecil Kelly, OBE and Joan Maisie Kelly, Hyde Manor, Kingston, Sussex; *m* 1945, Anne Marie (marr. diss. 1954), *o d* of late James Stuart Anderson, Hinton House, Christchurch; one *d. Educ:* Marlborough Coll.; Balliol Coll., Oxford. Served Surrey and Sussex Yeomanry, 1939–40; Indian Mountain Artillery, India and Burma, 1941–45; Hon. Major, retd. Called to Bar, in absentia, Middle Temple, 1942; Midland and Oxford Circuit; Bencher, 1976, Emeritus 1987. Blackstone Pupillage Prize, 1947; Harmsworth Law Scholar, 1948. Dep. Chm., Kesteven QS, and Dep. Recorder of Bedford, 1968. Alternate Chm., Burnham Cttee, 1973–. *Publications:* (abridgement) The Second World War, by Sir Winston Churchill, 1959; (with R. MacLeod) The Ironside Diaries 1939–40, 1962. *Recreations:* walking, history. *Address:* 3 Temple Gardens, Temple, EC4Y 9AU. *T:* 01–353 4949. *Club:* Garrick. *Died 17 Feb. 1990.*

**KELSEY, Emanuel;** Solicitor and Parliamentary Officer to the Greater London Council, 1964–70; *b* 16 Feb. 1905; *s* of late Emanuel and Margaret Kelsey, Blyth, Northumberland; *m* 1934, Dorothy, *d* of late Alexander Mitchell-Smith, Bathgate, Scotland; one *s* one *d. Educ:* King Edward VI School, Morpeth. Legal Asst, Min. of Agric. and Fisheries, and Commissioners of Crown Lands, 1929; Sen. Asst, Parly Dept, LCC, 1931; Dep. Solicitor and Parly. Officer, LCC, 1962; Solicitor and Parly Officer, LCC, 1964. Hon. Solicitor to Royal Society for the Prevention of Accidents, 1964–70. *Address:* 26 Clifton Road, Wimbledon, SW19 4QT. *T:* 01–946 2564. *Died 11 Dec. 1985.*

**KELSEY, Joan, (Mrs Denys E. R. Kelsey);** *see* Grant, J.

**KELWAY, Colonel George Trevor,** CBE 1963; TD 1941; DL; JP; District Registrar, HM High Court of Justice in Pembrokeshire and Carmarthenshire, 1940–62; *b* 30 March 1899; *yr s* of late George Stuart Kelway, Milford Haven, Ch. de la Légion d'Honneur, Ch. de l'Ordre de Léopold, &c; *m* 1931, Gwladys (decd), *d* of late Joseph Rolfe, Goodig, Burry Port, Carm., formerly High Sheriff of Carmarthenshire; one *d. Educ:* Warminster; St Edmund Hall, Oxford. Served European War, 1914–18, and War of 1939–45; Comdg Pembrokeshire Hy. Regt RA (TA), 1927–35; formerly Hon. Col. Pembs Coast Regt, 424 and 425 (Pembs.) Regts RA (TA), and The Pembroke Yeomanry, 1943–58; Chm. Pembs T&AFA, 1945–60. Admitted a Solicitor, 1922. Dep. Chm., Pembs QS, 1960–71. Chm. Pembs Conservative Assoc., 1950–60; Pres. Wales & Mon Cons. Party, 1957 and 1961; Mem. Lloyd's, 1942–; an original Mem. Milford Haven Conservancy Bd, 1958–. DL 1948, JP 1957, Pembrokeshire; High Sheriff, 1958. Provincial Grand Master, S Wales (Western Div.). *Recreation:* golf. *Address:* Cottesmore Lodge, near Haverfordwest, Dyfed. *T:* Haverfordwest (0437) 766015. *Club:* Pembrokeshire County (Haverfordwest).

*Died 2 Nov. 1990.*

**KEM,** (pseudonym of Kimon Evan Marengo); Political Cartoonist and Journalist; *b* Zifta, Egypt, 4 Feb. 1906; 2nd *s* of Evangelo Tr. Marengo and Aristea, *d* of Capt. John Raftopoulo, Lemnos; *m* 1954, Una O'Connor (*d* 1979); two *s. Educ:* privately, publicly and personally and from time to time attended such seats of learning as the Ecole des Sciences Politiques, Paris, Exeter Coll., Oxford, etc. Edited and Illustrated Maalèsh, a political weekly published simultaneously in Cairo and Alexandria, 1923–31; in summer of 1928 represented a group of Newspapers at International Press Conference, Cologne; has travelled extensively; a fluent linguist, has command of English, French, Greek, Italian, and Arabic and understands a few other languages. *Publications:* In French: Oua Riglak! 1926; Gare les Pattes! 1929; Alexandrie, Reine de la Méditerranée, 1928. In English: Toy Titans, International politics in verse and pictures, 1937; Lines of Attack, 1944. In Arabic: Adolf and his donkey Benito, 1940; now a free-lance, contributing to

newspapers and periodicals all over the world. *Recreations:* swimming, riding, drawing, and castigating politicians. *Address:* 46 Redcliffe Gardens, SW10 9HB. *T:* 01-351 3160.

*Died 4 Nov. 1988.*

**KEMP, Charles,** CMG 1957; CBE 1951; retired as UK Senior Trade Commissioner and Economic Adviser to UK High Commissioner in South Africa (1953–58); *b* Whitstable, Kent, 25 Oct. 1897; *e s* of late Capt. Alfred and Elizabeth Kemp; *m* 1924, Helen Beatrice Stowe (*d* 1957); one *s. Educ:* Christ's Hospital; London University. HM Office of Works, 1915; served European War (wounded 1917); rejoined HM Office of Works, 1917; Dept of Overseas Trade, 1918; Asst to UK Trade Comr in E Africa, 1920; Trade Comr Grade III, 1931; Winnipeg, 1935; Cape Town, 1937; Trade Comr, Grade II, 1942, Grade I and transferred to Johannesburg, 1946. *Address:* 57 Hedge Row, Brighton Beach, Durban, South Africa. *Clubs:* Royal Commonwealth Society; Durban (Durban).

*Died 10 April 1983.*

**KEMP, Charles Edward;** retired as Headmaster of Reading School; *b* 18 Nov. 1901; *e s* of Frederick Kemp, Salford, Lancs; *m* 1927, Catherine Mildred (*d* 1980), *e d* of W. H. Taggart, IOM; two *s. Educ:* Manchester Grammar School (Foundation Scholar); Corpus Christi Coll., Oxford (open Scholar), Goldsmith Exhibitioner, 1922; 1st Class Maths, 1923. Master, Manchester Grammar Sch., 1923–30; Master, Royal Naval Coll., Dartmouth, 1930–34; Headmaster: Chesterfield Sch., 1934–39; Reading Sch., 1939–66. *Address:* The Coombe House, Streatley, Reading, Berks RG8 9QL.

*Died 10 Nov. 1986.*

**KEMP, Sir Leslie (Charles),** KBE 1957 (CBE 1948); BScEng; FICE, MIEE, ACGI; Vice-Chairman, General Development Corporation, Athens, since 1960; *b* 22 April 1890; *s* of John Charles Kemp, London; *m* 1st, 1918, Millicent Constance (marr. diss., 1959), *d* of late Thomas Maitland; two *s*; 2nd, 1961, Melina Enriquez. *Educ:* Forest Hill House School; London Univ. BScEng 1st Cl. Hons, 1910. Engineer with Fraser and Chalmers, Erith, 1910–14. Served as captain in RGA, France, 1914–19. Contract Engineer, English Electric Co., 1919–23; Technical Adviser, Power and Traction Finance Co., 1923–25; Midlands Branch Manager, English Electric Co., 1924–26; Man. Dir, Athens Piraeus Electricity Co., 1926–41; Manager, Asmara War (land plane repair) base, Asmara, Eritrea, 1942–43; Dep. Regional Dir, Middle East, BOAC, 1943–44; Vice-Chm and Managing Director, Athens Piraeus Electricity Co., 1944–55; Vice-Chm., Société Générale Héllenique, 1957–72. Citizen (Feltmaker) and Freedom of City of London, 1956. Cross of Commander of Royal Order of George I of Greece, 1951. *Recreations:* yachting and golf. *Address:* 4 Herodotou Street, Aghia Varvara, Halandri, Athens, Greece. *Club:* Royal Hellenic Yacht (Greece). *Died 24 Feb. 1988.*

**KENDALL, Sir Maurice (George),** Kt 1974; MA, ScD; FBA 1970; Director, World Fertility Survey, 1972–80; Chairman, Scientific Control Systems (Holdings), 1971–72; Fellow: American Statistical Association; Econometric Society; Institute of Mathematical Statistics; London Graduate School of Business Studies; *b* 6 Sept. 1907; *s* of late John Roughton Kendall and Georgina Kendall; *m* 1st, 1933, Sheila Frances Holland Lester; two *s* one *d*; 2nd, 1947, Kathleen Ruth Audrey Whitfield; one *s. Educ:* Central Sch., Derby; St John's Coll., Cambridge (Wrangler 1929). Entered Administrative Class, Civil Service, 1930; Ministry of Agriculture, 1930–41; Statistician, Chamber of Shipping, 1941–49 and Jt Asst Gen. Manager, 1947–49; Professor of Statistics in the University of London, 1949–61. Chm., Scientific Control Systems Ltd, 1967–71. Fellow, British Computer Soc.; ex-President: Royal Statistical Soc.; Operational Research Soc.; Inst. of Statisticians; Hon. Member: Market Research Soc.; Internat. Statistical Inst., 1979. Hon. Fellow, LSE, 1975. Gold Medal, Royal Statistical Society, 1968; United Nations Peace Medal, 1980. DUniv: Essex, 1968; Lancaster, 1975. *Publications:* (with G. Udny Yule) An Introduction to the Theory of Statistics, 14th edn, 1950; (with Alan Stuart) The Advanced Theory of Statistics, vol. I, 1958, 4th edn 1977; vol. II, 1961, 4th edn 1979; vol. III, 1966, 3rd edn 1975; Contributions to Study of Oscillatory Time-Series, 1947; Rank Correlation Methods, 1948, 4th edn 1970; (ed) The Sources and Nature of the Statistics of the United Kingdom, vol. 1, 1952, vol. 2, 1957; Exercises in Theoretical Statistics, 1954, 3rd edn 1968; (with W. R. Buckland) A Dictionary of Statistical Terms, 1955, 3rd edn 1971; A Course in Multivariate Analysis, 1957; A Course in the Geometry of n Dimensions, 1961; (with Alison G. Doig) A Bibliography of Statistical Literature, vol.1, 1962, vol. 2, 1965, vol. 3, 1968; (with P. A. Moran) Geometrical Probability, 1963; (ed) Mathematical Model Building in Economics and Industry, first series, 1968, second series, 1970; (ed, with E. S. Pearson) Studies in the History of Probability and Statistics, 1970; (ed) Cost-benefit Analysis, 1971; (ed, with Alan Stuart) Selected Papers of George Udny Yule, 1971; Time-Series, 1973; Multivariate Analysis, 1975; (ed, with R. L. Plackett) Second Series of Studies in the History of Probability and Statistics, 1977; various papers on theory of statistics and applications to economics and psychology.

*Recreations:* chess, gardening. *Address:* 1 Frank Dixon Close, SE21. *T:* 01-693 6076.
*Died 29 March 1983.*

**KENDALL-CARPENTER, John MacGregor Kendall,** CBE 1989; Headmaster, Wellington School, 1973–90; *b* 25 Sept. 1925; *s* of late C. E. Kendall-Carpenter and F. F. B. Kendall-Carpenter (*née* Rogers); *m* 1955, Iris Anson; three *s* two *d. Educ:* Truro Sch.; Exeter Coll., Oxford. Fleet Air Arm, Pilot RNVR, 1943–46. Oxford, 1947–51; Asst Master, Clifton Coll., 1951–61, and Housemaster, 1957–61; Headmaster: Cranbrook School, Kent, 1961–70; Eastbourne Coll., 1970–73. Member: Air Cadet Council, 1965–70; Air League Council, 1963–70; Chairman: Boarding Schools Assoc., 1981–83; Rugby World Cup Tournament Cttee, 1985–; President: Rugby Football Union, 1980–81 (Member or Captain: Oxford Univ. Rugby XV, 1948–50, England Rugby XV, 1948–54); RFSU, 1985– (Chm., 1981–83); Cornwall RFU, 1984–; Mem., Internat. Rugby Football Bd, 1984–. Hon. Manager Australasian Team, Rugby Football Schools' Union, 1979. Bard of the Gorsedd of Cornwall, 1981–. *Recreations:* outdoor activities, church architecture. *Address:* 1 Coulson's Terrace, Penzance, Cornwall. *Clubs:* East India, Devonshire, Sports and Public Schools; Vincent's (Oxford).
*Died 23 May 1990.*

**KENDON, Donald Henry,** CBE 1961; FIEE, FIMechE; Chairman Merseyside and North Wales Electricity Board, 1954–62, retired; *b* 9 Aug. 1895; *s* of Samuel and Ellen Susan Kendon; *m* 1923, Katharine Grace Honess (*d* 1978); five *s. Educ:* Goudhurst, Kent; King's Coll., University of London. BSc (Eng.) Hons. Served European War, 1914–19, in RE and RAF. Electrical Engineer with Edmundson's Electricity Corp., Ltd, 1921–34; General Manager: Cornwall Electric Power Co., 1934–39; Shropshire, Worcestershire and Staffordshire Electric Power Co., 1939–48; Dep. Chairman, Midlands Electricity Board, 1948–54; formerly Member: Central Electricity Authority, 1956, 1957; Electricity Council. *Address:* Quedley, Flimwell, via Wadhurst, East Sussex.
*Died 18 Sept. 1985.*

**KENDREW, Maj.-Gen. Sir Douglas (Anthony),** KCMG 1963; CB 1958; CBE 1944; DSO 1943 (Bar 1943, 2nd Bar 1944, 3rd Bar 1953); Governor of Western Australia, 1963–73; *b* 22 July 1910; *er s* of Alexander John Kendrew, MC, MD, Barnstaple, North Devon; *m* 1936, Nora Elizabeth, *d* of John Harvey, Malin Hall, County Donegal; one *s* one *d. Educ:* Uppingham Sch. 2nd Lieut Royal Leicestershire Regt, 1931; Capt. 1939; Major 1941; served War of 1939–45: Bde Major, N Africa, 1942; comd 6th Bn York and Lancaster Regt. N Africa and Italy, 1943; Bde Comd. Italy, Middle East and Greece, 1944–46; Commandant, Sch. of Infantry, Rhine Army, 1946–48; Commandant Army Apprentice Sch., Harrogate, 1948–50; Chief of Staff, NID, 1950–52; Bde Comd. 29 Brit. Inf. Bde, Korea, 1952–53; idc 1954; Brig. Administration HQ Northern Comd, 1955; GOC Cyprus Dist, and Dir of Ops, 1956–58; Dir of Infantry, War Office, 1958–60; Head of British Defence Liaison Staff, Australia, 1961–63. Col, Royal Leicestershire Regt, 1963–64. Hon. Col, SAS Regt, RWAR Australia, 1965. Pres., Knights of the Round Table, 1975–83. Comr, Royal Hospital, Chelsea, 1974–80. Hon. LLD Univ. of WA, 1969. KStJ 1964. *Recreations:* Rugby football (played for England 10 times, Capt. 1935; toured NZ and Australia, 1930; Army XV, 1932–36); golf and fishing. *Address:* The Manor House, Islip, Northants. *T:* Thrapston 2325. *Club:* Army and Navy (Chm., 1982). *Died 28 Feb. 1989.*

**KENNEDY, Archibald E. C.;** *see* Clark-Kennedy.

**KENNEDY, Brig. Archibald Gordon M.;** *see* Mackenzie-Kennedy.

**KENNEDY, Daisy;** violinist (Australian); *b* Burra, South Australia, 1893; *d* of J. A. Kennedy, Headmaster, Norwood, Adelaide; *m* 1924, John Drinkwater, poet and dramatist (*d* 1937); one *d*; two *d* by former marriage to Benno Moiseiwitsch, CBE (who *d* 1963). *Educ:* Elder Scholar, University Conservatorium, Adelaide. Left Adelaide for Prague, 1908; studied with Prof. Sevcik; later entered Meisterschule, Vienna, under same Prof., and held a Scholarship during 2nd year; made début in Vienna, 1911, and in London at Queen's Hall with Prof. Sevcik the same year; played at principal concerts at Queen's Hall, (Royal) Albert Hall, and throughout United Kingdom; has given many recitals at Wigmore Hall, Æolian Hall, and Grotrian Hall since début; toured Australia and New Zealand, 1919–20; début in Æolian Hall, New York, Nov. 1920; second tour, 1925; has given first performances of many violin works in London; appeared in recitals and with orchestra in Prague, Vienna and Budapest, and also played on the Radio several times in each city 1931; formed the Kennedy Trio with Lauri and Dorothy Kennedy, 1932; recital in Egypt, 1933. *Address:* 208 Rivermead Court, Ranelagh Gardens, SW6. *T:* 01-736 4379.
*Died 30 July 1981.*

**KENNEDY, Douglas Neil,** OBE 1952 (MBE); Vice-President, English Folk Dance and Song Society; President, Folk Lore Society, 1964–65; *b* Edinburgh, 1893; *s* of John Henderson Kennedy and Patricia Grieve Thomson, *g s* of David Kennedy the Scottish singer;

*m* 1st, 1914, Helen May Karpeles (decd); one *s* (and one *s* decd); 2nd, 1976, Elizabeth Ann Ogden. *Educ:* George Watson's Coll., Edinburgh; Imperial College of Science. Served London Scottish prior to and during European War, 1914–18, and received his commission in that regiment; MBE for War services, and retired with the rank of Captain; served War of 1939–45, RAF, 1940–45. Demonstrator in the Department of Botany, Imperial Coll., 1919–24; Organising Dir, English Folk Dance Society (on the death of its founder Cecil J. Sharp), 1924–61. *Publications:* England's Dances, 1950; English Folk-dancing Today and Yesterday, 1964; other works relating to traditional dance and song. *Address:* Deck House, Waldringfield, Woodbridge, Suffolk IP12 4QL.
*Died 7 Jan. 1988.*

**KENNEDY, Lt-Col Sir (George) Ronald (Derrick),** 7th Bt *cr* 1836; OBE 1975; Director, Saint Francis Hospice Development Trust; *b* 19 Nov. 1927; *s* of Sir Derrick Edward de Vere Kennedy, 6th Bt, and of Phyllis Victoria Levine, *d* of late Gordon Fowler; *S* father, 1976; *m* 1949, Noelle Mona, *d* of Charles Henry Green; one *s* one *d. Educ:* Clifton College. Regimental service in RA, 1947–58; Staff Coll., Camberley, 1959; staff duties, Aden, 1960–63; regimental duty, 1963–66; staff duties, MoD and HQ BAOR, 1966–71; Defence Attaché, Mexico City, Havana and El Salvador, 1971–74; GSO 1, UK Delegn to Live Oak, SHAPE, 1974–77; HQ Dhekelia Garrison, 1977; retired 1979. *Recreations:* foreign travel, military history. *Heir:* s Michael Edward Kennedy [*b* 12 April 1956; *m* 1984, Helen Christine Jennifer, *d* of Patrick Lancelot Rae]. *Address:* Harraton Square, Church Lane, Exning, near Newmarket, Suffolk.
*Died 21 Jan. 1988.*

**KENNEDY, James Cowie;** *b* 27 Dec. 1914; *e s* of Robert and Elizabeth Kennedy; *m* 1st, 1939, Eleanor Colman (*d* 1970); one *s* one *d*; 2nd, 1972, Joan G. Cooper, Bristol. *Educ:* Bishops Stortford Coll.; Northern Polytechnic, London. Joined LCC, 1947; Chief Officer, GLC Parks Dept, 1970–79. Mem. Council, SPCK, 1980. *Recreations:* enjoying food and drink; working for the Church. *Address:* 174 Clarence Gate Gardens, NW1 6AR.
*Died 11 May 1989.*

**KENNEDY, John Norman;** Forestry Commissioner since 1980; *b* 3 March 1927; *e s* of late James Domoné Kennedy, MBE, and late Margaret Henderson Lawrie; *m* 1953, Margaret Rose Johnston; one *s* one *d. Educ:* Hawick High Sch.; Edinburgh Univ. (BSc 1952). FICFor. Served RAF, 1945–48. Forestry Commission: Dist Officer, 1952; Asst Conservator, 1965; Conservator, N Wales, 1973; Dir, Forest Management Div., 1977. Mem., Soc. of High Constables of Edinburgh. *Recreations:* gardening, photography, music. *Address:* 1 Marchfield Park, Edinburgh EH4 5BW. *Club:* New (Edinburgh).
*Died 3 July 1985.*

**KENNEDY, Sir Ronald;** *see* Kennedy, Sir G. R. D.

**KENNEY, Reginald;** Principal, Harper Adams Agricultural College, 1962–77; *b* 24 Aug. 1912; *m* 1946, Sheila Fay De Sa; two adopted *d. Educ:* King Edward VII School, Lytham St Anne's; Leeds Univ.; West of Scotland Agric. Coll. Warden and Lectr, Staffordshire Farm Inst. (now Staffordshire Coll. of Agriculture), 1937–38; Asst County Agric. Educn Officer, Beds CC, 1938–42 (seconded Beds WAEC, 1939–42); Lectr in Farm Management and Animal Husbandry, University of Reading, 1942–48; Principal, Dorset Farm Inst. (now Dorset Coll. of Agriculture), 1948–62. Hon. FRAgS. *Publication:* Dairy Husbandry, 1957. *Recreations:* travel, golf, mountains. *Address:* 10 Woodridge Close, Edgmond, Newport, Shropshire. *T:* Newport 812514. *Club:* Farmers'.
*Died 17 Aug. 1986.*

**KENNY, Sir Patrick (John),** Kt 1976; FRCS, FRACS; Consultant Emeritus Surgeon, St Vincent's Hospital and Lewisham Hospital, Sydney; *b* 12 Jan. 1914; *s* of Patrick John Kenny and Agnes Margaret Carberry; *m* 1942, Beatrice Ella Hammond; two *s. Educ:* Marcellin Coll., Sydney; Sydney Univ. (MB, BS 1936, MS 1946). FRCS 1940; FRACS 1944. War Service, AIF, UK, ME and SWPA, 1940–46. Hon. Surgeon: St Vincent's Hosp., 1946–79; Lewisham Hosp., Sydney, 1946–76. Anderson Stuart Memorial Res. Fellow, Sydney Univ., 1938, Lectr in Surg. Anat., 1949–55. Royal Australasian Coll. of Surgeons: Councillor, 1959; Vice Pres., 1967–69; Pres., 1969–71; Mem., Ct of Honour, 1979–. Pres., NSW Med. Bd, 1974–79. FRCPS(Hon.) 1970. *Publications:* surgical treatises. *Recreation:* gardening. *Address:* 13 David Street, Mosman, Sydney, NSW 2088, Australia. *T:* 960–2820. *Club:* Australian.
*Died 2 June 1987.*

**KENSINGTON, 7th Baron** *cr* 1776; **William Edwardes;** Baron Kensington (UK) 1886; Lieutenant-Colonel Guides Cavalry, Indian Army; *b* 15 May 1904; *s* of 6th Baron and Mabel Carlisle (*d* 1934), *d* of George Pilkington, Stoneleigh, Woolton; *S* father, 1938. *Educ:* Eton; RMC. *Heir:* n Hugh Ivor Edwardes [*b* 24 Nov. 1933; *m* 1961, Juliet Elizabeth Massy Anderson; two *s* one *d*]. *Address:* Mardan, PO Bromley, Zimbabwe. *Club:* Cavalry and Guards.
*Died 19 Aug. 1981.*

**KENT, Rear-Adm. Derrick George,** CB 1971; retired 1971; *b* May 1920; *s* of Eric William Kent and Doris Elizabeth Osborn; *m* 1943, Estelle Clare Firkins; two *d. Educ:* St Lawrence College, Ramsgate. Joined RN 1938; Midshipman, HMS Cumberland, 1939–40; Submarine Service, 1940; Comdr, HM Submarine Spark, in Far East, 1943–45; Captain, 1960; Commanded: HMS Diana, 1963; HMS Plymouth; 22nd Escort Squadron, Far East, 1963–64; Imperial Defence Coll., 1965; Captain (SM), Third Submarine Sqdn, HMS Maidstone, 1966–67; Comdr, Clyde Submarine Base, and HMS Neptune, 1967–68; Commodore, 1968; Comdr, Clyde, and Supt Clyde Submarine Base, 1968–69; Rear-Adm., 1969; Flag Officer, Malta, and NATO Commander, SE Mediterranean, 1969–71. *Address:* 73 Exeter House, Putney Heath, SW15.
*Died 5 March 1983.*

**KENT, Dorothy Miriam;** Under-Secretary, Department of Employment, 1973–80; *b* 1920; *d* of Donald Roy Thom, CBE, and Elsie Miriam Thom (*née* Rundell); *m* 1948, Eric Nelson Kent; one *s* two *d. Educ:* North London Collegiate Sch.; Somerville Coll., Oxford (Scholar). MA Hons History. Temp. wartime civil service posts, 1941–46; entered Min. of Labour, 1946; Principal, 1950; Asst Sec., 1964; Under-Sec., 1973; retired, 1980. *Publication:* Women and Public Appointments, 1984 (report for Equal Opportunities Commn). *Address:* 45 Lytton Grove, SW15 2HD. *T:* 01–788 0214.
*Died 4 Oct. 1988.*

**KENT, Sir Percy Edward, (Sir Peter Kent),** Kt 1973; DSc, PhD; FRS 1966; FGS; consultant geologist; Member, Natural Environment Research Council, 1973–80 (Chairman, 1973–77); *b* 18 March 1913; *s* of Edward Louis Kent and Annie Kate (*née* Woodward); *m* 1940, Margaret Betty Hood, JP (*d* 1974); two *d*; *m* 1976, Lorna Ogilvie Scott, BA. *Educ:* West Bridgford Gram. Sch.; Nottingham Univ. 1st cl. hons BSc London 1934; PhD 1941; DSc 1959. RAFVR, 1941–46 (despatches, 1944). Legion of Merit (USA), 1946. Geologist to E African Archæological Expedn (L. S. B. Leakey), 1934–35. Joined Anglo Iranian Oil (later BP), 1936; responsible for geological survey work in UK, Iran, E Africa, Papua, Canada and Alaska, for BP, 1946–60; managerial duties in BP, 1960–65; Chief Geologist, BP Co. Ltd, 1966–71, Exploration Manager, 1971–73. Dir, London and Scottish Marine Oil, 1977–83; Chairman: Minworth Ltd, 1983–; Strontian Minerals Ltd, 1983–86. Pres. Yorks Geol Soc., 1964–66; Chm., Petroleum Exploration Soc. of Great Britain, 1966–68; Member: Council, Royal Soc., 1968–70; Council for Science Policy, 1968–72; Adv. Bd for Res. Councils, 1972–77; President: Internat. Trust for Zoological Nomenclature, 1969–84; Geological Soc., 1974–76. Adrian Vis. Fellow, Univ. of Leicester, 1967–70. Hon. DSc: Leicester, 1972; Durham, 1974; Bristol, 1977; Hull, 1981; Birmingham, 1983; Hon. LLD: Glasgow, 1977; Aberdeen, 1978; Hon. ScD Cambridge, 1979. Murchison Medal, Geological Soc. of London, 1969; (jt) MacRobert Award, 1970; Royal Medal, Royal Soc., 1971; Sorby Medal, Yorkshire Geol. Soc., 1973. *Publications:* British Regional Geology, Eastern England, 1980; Minerals from the Marine Environment, 1980; many papers on stratigraphy and structural geology, Britain and abroad. *Recreations:* gardening, landscape painting, choral singing. *Address:* 38 Rodney Road, West Bridgford, Nottingham. *T:* Nottingham 23–13–55. *Club:* Geological Society Club.
*Died 9 July 1986.*

**KENTNER, Louis Philip,** CBE 1978; Concert Pianist and Composer; *b* Silesia, 19 July 1905; *s* of Julius and Gisela Kentner; *m* 1931, Ilona Kabos (marr. diss. 1945); *m* 1946, Griselda Gould, *d* of late Evelyn Suart; no *c. Educ:* Budapest, Royal Academy of Music (at age of 6) under Arnold Szekely, Leo Weiner, Zoltan Kodaly. Concert début Budapest at age of 15; awarded a Chopin prize, Warsaw, a Liszt prize, Budapest. Has given concerts in most European countries; toured South Africa, Far East, New Zealand, Australia, S America; 6 tours of USA; three tours of USSR. First world performance, Bartok 2nd Piano Concerto, Budapest, 1933 (Klemperer conducting), and first European performance, Bartok 3rd Piano Concerto, London, 1946 (Boult conducting); many first performances of Kodaly and Weiner's Piano works; first performance: Rawsthorne's First Piano Concerto, London; Tippett's Piano Concerto, London. Came to England, 1935; naturalised British, 1946; since residence in England played much modern British music. Played numerous troop concerts during War of 1939–45. Has made many gramophone recordings. President: Liszt Society, 1965–; European Piano Teachers Assoc., 1978–. Hon. RAM 1970. *Publications:* Three Sonatinas for Piano, 1939; two essays in Liszt Symposium, 1967; The Piano, 1976. *Recreations:* reading, chess playing. *Address:* 1 Mallord Street, Chelsea, SW3.
*Died 22 Sept. 1987.*

**KENYON, Alec Hindle,** CEng, FIEE; Chairman, East Midlands Electricity Board, 1965–69, retired; *b* 11 June 1905; *s* of late William Kenyon, Accrington, Lancs; *m* 1932, Elizabeth Mary Wollaston; one *s* one *d. Educ:* Bootham Sch., York. Accrington Corp., Northampton Electric Light & Power Co., and North Eastern Electricity Supply Co.; Liaison Officer, North Eastern Electricity Board, 1948–59; Dep. Chm., East Midlands Electricity Board, 1959–64. Chm., North Eastern Centre, Instn of Electrical Engineers, 1955–56. *Recreations:* walking and gardening. *Address:* 8 Oakwood, Hexham, Northumberland.
*Died 16 Oct. 1982.*

**KENYON, Hugh;** *b* 11 Jan. 1910; *s* of Thomas and Emily Kenyon; *m* 1941, Mary Winifred, *d* of Sir Peile Thompson, 4th Bt; one *s* one *d. Educ:* Rossall Sch.; St John's Coll., Oxford (MA). Oxford House, Bethnal Green, 1932–34; Prison Commn, 1934–68: Governor of Prisons, 1947–57; Nuffield Travelling Fellowship for Civil Servants (12 months study of penal system in Scandinavia), 1957; Asst Comr of Prisons, 1958–64; Director of Prison Administration, 1964–68; Inspection and Report on conditions in the prisons of the Bahamas, 1966; nine months lecturing, UN, Asia and Far East Inst., Tokyo, 1968 and 1972; Inspection and Report on prison system in Bermuda, 1970. *Recreations:* gardening, golf, music, philately. *Address:* Yarrowfield, Mayford, Woking, Surrey GU22 0SE. *T:* Woking 62870.
*Died 28 Feb. 1981.*

**KEPPEL-COMPTON, Robert Herbert,** CMG 1953; *b* 11 Dec. 1900; *s* of late J. H. Keppel-Compton, Southampton; *m* 1930, Marjorie, *yr d* of late Rev. W. B. Preston; one *s* one *d. Educ:* Oakham Sch.; Sidney Sussex Coll., Cambridge. BA, LLB Cantab. Entered Colonial Administrative Service, 1923. Dep. Provincial Commissioner, 1945; Development Sec., 1946; Provincial Commissioner, Nyasaland, 1949–55; retired from Colonial Service, 1955. *Address:* Shockerwick House, Shockerwick, Bath BA1 7LL.
*Died 19 Nov. 1989.*

**KER, K(eith) R(eginald) Welbore,** OBE 1964; HM Diplomatic Service, retired; Director, Anglo-German Association, 1971–73; *b* 8 Aug. 1913; *s* of late Reginald Arthur Ker and Morna, *d* of Welbore MacCarthy, sometime Bishop of Grantham; *m* 1954, Marisa (*née* Ummarino), formerly Lo Bianco; three *s* two *d* (one step *s* one step *d*). *Educ:* Malvern Coll. Business, 1932–39. Served in HM Army, 1939–46, Major 1945 (despatches). Apptd British Consul, Bolzano, 1946; Second Sec., Rio de Janeiro, 1948; transf. to Stockholm, 1950; to Singapore, 1951; acting Consul, Hanoi, 1952; First Sec., Belgrade, 1953–55; transf. to Rangoon, 1956; to Saigon, 1957; to FO, 1957; to Hamburg, 1958; to Bonn, 1959; HM Consul-Gen., Hanover, 1961–64; First Sec., 1965–67; Counsellor, 1967–69, Lisbon; Consul-General, Cape Town, 1970–73. *Recreations:* walking, travel, collecting water-colour drawings. *Address:* Beckington Abbey, near Bath, Somerset BA3 6TD. *T:* Frome 830695. *Club:* Army and Navy.
*Died 10 Dec. 1984.*

**KER, Neil Ripley,** CBE 1979; FBA 1958; Reader in Palæography, Oxford University, 1946–68, Reader Emeritus since 1968; Fellow of Magdalen College, 1946–68, Honorary Fellow, since 1975; *b* 28 May 1908; *s* of Robert MacNeil Ker and Lucy Winifred Strickland-Constable; *m* 1938, Jean Frances, *d* of Brig. C. B. Findlay; one *s* three *d. Educ:* Eton Coll.; Magdalen Coll., Oxford. BLitt (Oxon), 1933; Lecturer in Palæography, Oxford, 1936–46; James P. R. Lyell Reader in Bibliography, Oxford, 1952–53; Sandars Reader in Bibliography, Cambridge, 1955. Sir Israel Gollancz Mem. Prize, British Acad., 1959; Edwards Lecturer, Glasgow, 1960; Gold Medallist, Bibliographical Soc., 1975. Hon. DLitt Reading, 1964; Hon. Dr Leyden, 1972; Hon. LittD Cambridge, 1975. Corresp. Fellow, Medieval Acad. of America, 1971; Corresp. Mem., Bayerische Akademie der Wissenschaften, 1977. *Publications:* Medieval Libraries of Great Britain, 1941 (2nd edn 1964); Pastedowns in Oxford Bindings, 1954; Catalogue of Manuscripts containing Anglo-Saxon, 1957; English Manuscripts in the Century after the Norman Conquest, 1960; Medieval Manuscripts in British Libraries: I, London, 1969; II, Abbotsford-Keele, 1977; Records of All Souls College Library 1437–1600, 1971; (ed) The Parochial Libraries of the Church of England, 1959; articles and reviews in Medium Aevum, etc. *Recreation:* hill walking. *Address:* 22 London Street, Edinburgh EH3 6NA.
*Died 23 Aug. 1982.*

**KERANS, Comdr John Simon,** DSO 1949; RN retired; *b* 30 June 1915; *m* 1946, Stephanie Campbell Shires; two *d. Educ:* RN Coll., Dartmouth. Cadet and Midshipman, HMS Rodney, Home Fleet, 1932–33; Midshipman and Sub-Lt HMS Cornwall, 1933–35; RN Coll., Greenwich, 1935–37; China Station, 1937–39. Served War of 1939–45: Staff, Chief of Intelligence Staff, Far East, Hong Kong and Singapore, 1939; HMS Naiad, Home and Medit. Stations, 1940–42; Staff Officer (Intelligence), Staff C-in-C, Medit. and Levant, 1942–43; 1st Lt, HMS Icarus, N Atlantic, 1943–44; Staff, C-in-C, Portsmouth, 1944; i/c HMS Blackmore (Lt-Comdr) 1944; Security Intelligence, Hong Kong, 1947; on loan to Malayan Police, Kuala Lumpur, 1948; Asst Naval Attaché, Nanking, 1949, joined frigate Amethyst after her attack by Communist forces (DSO), 1949; Comdr Dec. 1949; RN Staff Course, Greenwich, 1950; Head Far East Section, Naval Intelligence Admiralty, 1950–52; i/c HMS Rinaldo, 1953–54; Brit. Naval Attaché, Bangkok, Phnom Penh, Vientiane, Saigon and Rangoon, 1954–55; Sen. Officers' Technical Course Portsmouth, 1957; retired RN, 1958. MP (C) The Hartlepools, 1959–64; Civil Servant, Pensions Appeal Tribunals, 1969–80. *Address:* 44 Gordons Way, Oxted, Surrey RH8 0LW. *T:*

Oxted 2751. *Clubs:* Littlehampton Sailing; Oxted Cricket.
*Died 12 Sept.* 1985.

**KERENSKY, Dr Oleg Alexander,** CBE 1964; FRS 1970; FEng; Consultant, Freeman Fox & Partners, Consulting Engineers, since 1975 (Partner, 1955–75); *b* 16 April 1905; *s* of late Alexander F. Kerensky and Olga (*née* Baronovsky); *m* 1928, Nathalie (*d* 1969); one *s*; *m* 1971, Mrs Dorothy Harvey. *Educ:* Russia, later small private sch. in England; Northampton Engrg Coll. (now The City Univ.). FICE; FIStructE; FIHE; FWeldI; Fellow, Fellowship of Engineering 1976. Jun. Asst, Oxford CC, 1926; Dorman Long & Co.: Asst Engr, Bridge Design Office, 1927–30, construction of Lambeth Bridge, 1930–32; Sen. Design Engr, Bridge Dept, 1932–37; Chief Engr and Sub-Agent: on construction of Wandsworth Bridge, Holloway Bros (London) Ltd, 1937–40; on Avonmouth Oil Jetty, 1940–43; Chief Engr, Mulberry Harbours, N Wales, 1943–45; Sen. Designer, Holloway Bros (London) Ltd, 1945–46; Principal Bridge Designer, Freeman Fox & Partners, 1946–55. Chm., Bridge Cttee, BSI; Pres., CIRIA, 1978–. Mem. Council, City Univ. President: IStructE, 1970–71; IHE, 1971–72. Hon. Fellow, Concrete Soc. Hon. Dr of Science, City Univ., 1967. Gold Medal, IStructE, 1977; Internat. Award of Merit in Structural Engrg, Internat. Assoc. for Bridge and Structural Engrg, 1979. *Publications:* numerous papers in learned jls. *Recreations:* bridge, croquet. *Address:* 27 Pont Street, SW1. *T:* 01-235 7173. *Clubs:* Athenæum, Hurlingham.
*Died 25 June* 1984.

**KERMACK, Stuart Grace,** CBE 1955; *b* 11 April 1888; 2nd *s* of Henry Kermack, Advocate; *m* 1922, Nell P., *y d* of Thomas White, SSC; two *s* one *d*. *Educ:* Edinburgh Academy; Fettes Coll.; Edinburgh Univ. MA, LLB, Edinburgh Univ.; Scots Bar, 1911; served European War, RFA (TF) Capt., Gallipoli, Egypt, Palestine; Judge in Sudan, 1918–19; Judicial Service, Palestine, 1920–30; Lecturer in Jurisprudence, Edinburgh Univ., 1933–36; Sheriff-Substitute of Lanarkshire at Glasgow, 1936–55; Sheriff-Substitute of Renfrew and Argyll at Oban, 1955–62. King Haakon VII Liberty Cross, 1948. *Publications:* Criminal Procedure in Palestine, 1927; Law of Scotland: Sources and Juridical Organisation, 1933; contributions to Juridical Review, Stair Society's Sources of Scots Law, etc. *Address:* c/o 15 Denham Green Terrace, Edinburgh EH5 3PG.
*Died 18 Aug.* 1981.

**KERR, Archibald Brown,** CBE 1968 (OBE 1945); TD; Hon. Consulting Surgeon, Western Infirmary, Glasgow (Surgeon, 1954–72); *b* 17 Feb. 1907; *s* of late Robert Kerr and Janet Harvey Brown; *m* 1940, Jean Margaret, *d* of late John Cowan, MBE; one *d* (and one *d* decd). *Educ:* High Sch. and University of Glasgow. BSc 1927; MB, ChB 1929; Hon. LLD, 1973; FRFPSGlas. 1933; FRCSEd 1934; FRCSGlas. 1962. Asst to Prof. Path. Glasgow Univ., 1931–33; Surg. to Out-Patients, West. Infirm. Glasgow, 1932–39. Served in 156 (Lowland) Field Amb. and as Surgical Specialist, Officer in Charge of Surgical Div. and Col Comdg No. 23 (Scottish) Gen. Hosp., 1939–45. Surg. to Royal Alexandra Infirmary, Paisley, 1946–54; Asst Surg., West. Infirm., Glasgow, 1945–54. Lectr in Clinical Surgery, Univ. of Glasgow, 1946–72. Pres. 1951–52, Hon. Mem. 1971, Royal Medico-Chirurgical Society of Glasgow; Pres., Royal College of Physicians and Surgeons of Glasgow, 1964–66. Mem., Western Regional Hosp. Bd. Mem. Court, Univ. of Glasgow, 1974–82. Periods on Council of RCPS Glasgow and RCS Edinburgh. *Publications:* The Western Infirmary 1874–1974, 1974; contribs to Med. and Surg. Jls. *Recreation:* golf. *Address:* 18 St Germains, Bearsden, Glasgow G61 2RS. *T:* 041-942 0424. *Clubs:* College (University of Glasgow), Royal Scottish Automobile.
*Died 24 Aug.* 1990.

**KERR, Russell (Whiston);** Air Charter Executive; *b* 1 Feb. 1921; *s* of Ivo W. and Constance Kerr, Australia; *m* 1st, 1946, Shirley W. N. Huie; one *s* one *d*; 2nd, 1960, Anne P. Clark (*née* Bersey) (*d* 1973); no *c*. *Educ:* Shore Sch., Sydney; University of Sydney. BEcon 1941. RAAF Aircrew, 1942–46; operational service with Bomber Comd Pathfinder Force, flying Lancaster Bombers over Germany (Flying Office/Navigator). Returned to England to live, 1948. MP (Lab) Mddx, Feltham, 1966–74, Hounslow, Feltham and Heston, 1974–83. Contested (Lab): Horsham, Sussex, 1951; Merton and Morden, 1959; Preston North, 1964; Feltham and Heston, 1983. Dir (unpaid), Tribune, 1969–; Chairman: Tribune group of MPs, 1969–70; Labour Aviation Gp, 1974–79. Nat. Exec. Mem., ASTMS, 1964–76 (Chm., Aerospace Cttee, 1970–80); Chm., Select Cttee on nationalised industries, 1974–79. Chm., Internat. Commn on human rights in Iran, 1978. *Publications:* articles in various radical and TU jls. *Recreations:* cricket, golf, walking, talking. *Clubs:* Feltham Ex-Servicemen's, Feltham Labour, Royal Mid-Surrey Golf.
*Died 15 Nov.* 1983.

**KERR-DINEEN, Rev. Canon Frederick George;** Canon Emeritus of Chichester, since 1983; *b* 26 Aug. 1915; second *s* of late Mr and Mrs Henry John Dineen and adopted *s* of late Prebendary Colin Kerr; added Kerr to family name in 1938; *m* 1951, Hermione Iris, *er d* of late Major John Norman MacDonald (KEH) and Mrs MacDonald;

four *s* one *d*. *Educ:* Tyndale Hall, Clifton; St John's Coll., Durham. MA, LTh. Ordained, 1941; Curate: St Paul's, Portman Square, 1941–44; St John's, Weymouth, 1945–46; Vicar: St Michael's, Blackheath Park, 1946–53; Lindfield, 1953–62; Holy Trinity, Eastbourne, 1962–73; Archdeacon of Chichester, and Canon Residentiary of Chichester Cathedral, 1973–75; Proctor in Convocation, 1970–74; Archdeacon of Horsham, 1975–83; Rector of Stopham and Hardham, 1973–87. *Publication:* The Company of Merrymakers, 1987. *Address:* The Old Coach-House, Bell Lane, Cocking, W Sussex GU29 2HU.
*Died 6 July* 1988.

**KERRIN, Very Rev. Richard Elual,** MA; Dean of Aberdeen and Orkney, 1956–69; Rector of St John's Episcopal Church, Aberdeen, 1954–70, retired; *b* 4 July 1898; *s* of Rev. Daniel Kerrin and Margaret Kerrin; *m* 1925, Florence Alexandra, *d* of Captain J. Reid; one *s*. *Educ:* Robert Gordon's Coll., Aberdeen; University of Aberdeen (MA); Edinburgh Theological Coll. (Luscombe Scholar). Ordained deacon, 1922; priest, 1923. Curate, Old St Paul, Edinburgh, 1922–25; Rector, Inverurie, 1925–37; Rector, Holy Trinity, Stirling, 1937–47; Rector, Fraserburgh, 1947–54; Canon of Aberdeen, 1954–56, Hon. Canon, 1969. *Address:* Nazareth House, 34 Claremont Street, Aberdeen AB1 6RA. *T:* Aberdeen 582091.
*Died 4 Nov.* 1988.

**KERSHAW, His Honour Philip Charles Stones;** a Circuit Judge (formerly Deputy Chairman, Lancashire Quarter Sessions), 1961–83, retired; *b* 9 April 1910; *s* of Joseph Harry and Ethel Kershaw; *m* 1935, Michaela Raffael; one *s* one *d*. *Educ:* Stonyhurst Coll.; Merton Coll., Oxford. Called to the Bar, Gray's Inn, 1933; practised Northern Circuit until Aug. 1939. Served in Army, 1939–45 (Major). Resumed practice, 1945–61. *Address:* Fountain House, East Beach, Lytham, Lancs. *T:* Lytham 736072. *Club:* Portico Library (Manchester).
*Died 1 July* 1986.

**KERSHAW, Raymond Newton,** CMG 1947; MC; *b* 3 May 1898; *s* of G. W. Kershaw, Wahroonga, Sydney, Australia; *m* 1925, Hilda Mary, *d* of W. J. Ruegg, JP; two *s* one *d*. *Educ:* Sydney High Sch.; Sydney Univ.; New Coll., Oxford; Sorbonne. Served European War, 1914–18, with AIF in France, 1917–18 (MC); Rhodes Scholar for NSW, 1918; Mem. of Secretariat, League of Nations, Geneva, 1924–29; Adviser to the Governors, Bank of England, 1929–53; Member: E African Currency Bd, 1932–53; W African Currency Bd, 1943–53, Palestine Currency Bd, 1943–52, Burma Currency Board, 1946–52; Adviser to Commonwealth Development Finance Co., 1953–55; a Gen. Comr of Income Tax for City of London, 1956–65; a London Director: Commercial Banking Co. of Sydney, 1956–66 (Chm., London Bd, 1964–66); Bank of NZ, 1955–68 (Chm. London Bd, 1963–68); Australian Mutual Provident Soc., 1955–70. *Address:* Warren Row, near Wargrave, Berks. *T:* Littlewick Green 2708.
*Died 28 March* 1981.

**KESSEL, Prof. Lipmann,** MBE (mil.) 1946; MC 1946; FRCS; Emeritus Professor of Orthopaedics, University of London; Hon. Consultant Surgeon, Royal National Orthopaedic Hospital; Hon. Consultant Orthopaedic Surgeon, Charing Cross Hospital; *b* 19 Dec. 1914; *m* 1st, Mary (*née* Morgan); 2nd, Peggy (*née* Oughton); two *s*; 3rd, Beryl (*née* Tilley); two *d*. *Educ:* Pretoria High Sch.; Univ. of the Witwatersrand; St Mary's Hosp., London (qual. 1938). FRCS 1947. Served war, RAMC: Surgeon i/c 1 Parachute Surg. Team; POW Holland, escaped. Jun. hosp. appts; Sen. Registrar Orthopaedics, St Mary's Hosp., London, 1946; Clin. Res. Asst, Inst. of Orthops, 1947; Cons. Orthopaedic Surgeon: Fulham, St Mary Abbots, and Charing Cross Hosps.; Prof. of Orthopaedics, and Dir of Clinical Studies, Inst. of Orthopaedics, Univ. of London, 1976–80. Samuel Camp Vis. Prof., Harvard Med. Sch., 1967. Codman Lectr, Internat. Shoulder Surg. Conf., Toronto, 1983; Guildal Lectr, Copenhagen, 1983. *Publications:* Surgeon at Arms, 1956 (2nd edn 1977); (contrib.) Clinical Surgery, 1967; (contrib.) Watson-Jones, Fractures and Joint Injuries, 1977; (contrib.) Triumphs of Medicine, 1977; Colour Atlas of Clinical Orthopaedics, 1980; Clinical Disorders of the Shoulder, 1981; Shoulder Surgery, 1982; Rotator Cuff Rupture and Repair, 1986; articles on orthop. surg. in jls; *posthumous publication:* Diagnostic Picture Tests in Orthopaedics, 1986. *Recreations:* theatre, games of chance. *Address:* 36 Menelik Road, NW2 3RH. *T:* 01-794 3221. *Clubs:* Garrick, Sportsman.
*Died 5 June* 1986.

**KESWICK, Sir John (Henry),** KCMG 1972 (CMG 1950); Director: Jardine Matheson & Co. Ltd, Hong Kong (Chm. 1971–72); Matheson & Co. Ltd, London (Chairman, 1966–70); *b* 1906; *s* of late Henry Keswick; *m* 1940, Clare, *d* of late Gervase Elwes and Lady Winefride Elwes; one *d*. *Educ:* Eton; Trinity Coll., Cambridge. Min. of Economic Warfare, 1940; Political Liaison Officer, SE Asia Comd, 1942; British Chamber of Commerce, Shanghai, 1946. Served on Exec. Council, Hong Kong, 1951–56. Pres., China Assoc.; Vice-Pres., Sino-British Trade Council; Vice-Chm., GB-China Centre; Member: China Soc.; Japan Soc. Vice Pres., Scottish Assoc. of Youth Clubs. *Address:* Flat 5, 55/56 Holland Park, W11 3RS; Portrack House, Holywood, Dumfries. *T:* Newbridge 276;

Matheson & Co. Ltd, 3 Lombard Street, EC3V 9AQ. *T:* 01–480 6633. *Clubs:* Boodle's, Buck's, White's.                    *Died* 5 *July* 1982.

**KESWICK, Sir William (Johnston),** Kt 1972; Director, Matheson & Co. Ltd, 1943–75 (Chairman, 1966–72); *b* 6 Dec. 1903; *s* of late Major Henry Keswick of Cowhill Tower, Dumfries, Scotland; *m* 1937, Mary, *d* of late Rt Hon. Sir Francis Lindley, PC, GCMG; three *s* one *d. Educ:* Winchester Coll.; Trinity Coll., Cambridge. Director: Hudson's Bay Co., 1943–72 (Governor 1952–65); Bank of England, 1955–73; British Petroleum Co. Ltd, 1950–73; Jardine, Matheson & Co. Ltd (Hong Kong and Far East); Chm. of various public companies in Far East; Chm., Shanghai Municipal Council of late International Settlement; Mem., Royal Commission on Taxation of Profits and Income; Brigadier Staff Duties 21 Army Gp; Mem., Royal Company of Archers. Trustee, National Gallery 1964–71. *Recreations:* shooting, fishing. *Address:* Theydon Priory, Theydon Bois, Essex. *T:* Theydon Bois 2256; Glenkiln, Shawhead, Dumfries, Scotland. *Club:* White's.                    *Died* 16 *Feb.* 1990.

**KEWISH, John Douglas,** CB 1958; TD 1944; DL; Registrar, Westminster County Court, 1971–73; *b* 4 May 1907; *s* of late John James Kewish, Birkenhead; *m* 1934, Marjorie Phyllis, *d* of late Dr Joseph Harvey, Wimbledon; one *s* one *d. Educ:* Birkenhead Sch. Admitted a Solicitor, 1931. Served TA, 1928–45; served 1939–44, with 4th Bn Cheshire Regt (UK, France and Belgium); commanded 4th Bn, 1940–44; commanded depots, The Cheshire Regt and The Manchester Regt and 24 Machine Gun Training Centre, 1944–45. Hon. Col 4th Bn Cheshire Regt, 1947–62. Chm., Cheshire T & AFA, 1951–59. Head of County Courts Branch in Lord Chancellor's Dept, 1960–71; Mem. Civil Judicial Statistics Cttee, 1966–68. Chm., Liverpool Shipwreck and Humane Soc., 1953–60. DL Cheshire, 1952. *Address:* Malpas Old Hall, Malpas, Cheshire SY14 8NG.
                    *Died* 25 *Feb.* 1989.

**KEY, Maj.-Gen. Berthold Wells,** CB 1947; DSO; MC; psc; IA (retired); *b* 19 Dec. 1895; *s* of late Dr J. M. Key; *m* 1917, Aileen Leslie (*d* 1951), *d* of late Col E. L. Dunsterville, RE; (one *s* killed in action in Italy) two *d. Educ:* Dulwich Coll. Joined 45th Rattrays Sikhs, IA, 1914; European War, 1914–19. Mesopotamia (wounded, MC); Afghanistan, 1919; NWF of India, 1930 (despatches); NWF Waziristan, 1936–37 (despatches, DSO); SE Asia, 1941–45; Comd, 2nd (Royal) Bn The Sikh Regt; Comd, 8 Ind. Bde, 1940–41; Comd 11 Ind. Div. 1942; ADC to the King, 1945–47; Comd, Rawalpindi Dist, 1946; Comd, Lahore Dist, 1947; Col, The Sikh Regt, 1947–62. *Recreation:* golf. *Address:* Naini, St George's Road, Sandwich, Kent.                    *Died* 26 *Sept.* 1986.

**KEY, Rt. Rev. John Maurice,** DD Lambeth, 1960; MA; an Assistant Bishop, Diocese of Exeter, since 1975; *b* 4 June 1905; *s* of late Preb. Frederick John Key, Lichfield, and Winifred Mary Head, Hexham, Northumberland; *m* 1935, Agnes Joan Dence (JP 1946–), *d* of late Rev. A. T. Dence, Abbotskerswell, Devon; three *s* one *d. Educ:* Rossall Sch.; Pembroke Coll., Cambridge; Westcott House, Cambridge. Assistant Curate, S. Mary's, Portsea, 1928–32; Vicar of Aylesbeare, Exeter, 1932–34; Rector of Highweek with S. Mary's, Newton Abbot, 1934–40; Rector of Stoke Damerel with S. Bartholomew's and S. Luke's. Devonport, 1940–47; Rural Dean of the Three Towns (Plymouth), 1944–47; Bishop Suffragan of Sherborne, 1947–59; Bishop of Truro, 1959–73. *Recreations:* music, gardening and country. *Address:* Donkeys, Stover, Newton Abbot, Devon. *T:* Newton Abbot 3997.                    *Died* 21 *Dec.* 1984.

**KEY, Sir Neill C.;** *see* Cooper-Key.

**KEYNES, Lady; (Lydia Lopokova);** *b* Russia, 21 Oct. 1892; *d* of Vassili Lopokoff, Leningrad and Constanzia Douglas; *m* 1925, 1st and last Baron Keynes, CB, FBA (*d* 1946), Fellow and Bursar of King's Coll., Cambridge. *Educ:* Imperial Ballet Sch., St Petersburg. First stage appearance, Marinsky Theatre, St Petersburg, 1901; solo parts in Imperial Russian Ballet; Opera, Paris, 1910; Winter Garden Theatre, New York, 1911; as an actress, several parts in New York, 1914–16; subsequently with Diaghileff's Russian Ballet, New York and London; The Lilac Fairy in Diaghileff's revival of The Sleeping Princess, 1921. Created rôle of Mariuccia in Massine's Les Femmes de Bonne Humeur, 1917, and with Leonide Massine, The Can-Can Dancers in La Boutique Fantasque, 1919; Camargo Society, 1930–32; Vic-Wells Ballet, 1932–33; (Lady) Olivia in Twelfth Night, Old Vic, 1933; Nora Helmer in A Doll's House, 1934; Hilda Wangel in The Master Builder, 1936; Célimène in The Misanthrope, 1937; Mem. of Council, Arts Council of GB, Aug. 1946–49. *Address:* Tilton, Firle, Sussex.                    *Died* 8 *June* 1981.

**KEYNES, Sir Geoffrey (Langdon),** Kt 1955; MA, MD Cantab; Hon. LLD Edinburgh; Hon. DLitt: Oxford; Cambridge; Birmingham; Sheffield; Reading; FRCP, FRCS England, FRCS Canada, FRCOG; Hon. FBA 1980; Hon. Fellow, Pembroke College, Cambridge; Hon. Librarian and late Member of Council, Royal College of Surgeons; Hunterian Trustee, 1958; Consulting Surgeon: St Bartholomew's Hospital; New End Endocrine Clinic and City of London Truss Society; a Trustee of the National Portrait Gallery,

1942–66, Chairman, 1958–66; *b* Cambridge, 25 March 1887; 2nd *s* of late John Neville Keynes; *m* 1917, Margaret Elizabeth (*d* 1974), *d* of late Sir George Darwin, KCB; four *s. Educ:* Rugby Sch.; Pembroke Coll., Cambridge (Foundation Scholar); 1st Class Natural Science Tripos, 1909; Entrance Scholar, St Bartholomew's Hospital, 1910; Brackenbury Surgery Scholar and Willett Medal Operative Surgery, 1913; House Surgeon St Bartholomew's Hospital, 1913; Lieut RAMC, 1914; Major, RAMC; Surgical Specialist, BEF (despatches); Chief Asst St Bartholomew's Hospital, 1920; Hunterian Prof., RCS, 1923, 1929, 1945; Cecil Joll Prize, RCS, 1953; Harveian Orator, RCP, 1958; Fitzpatrick Lectr, RCP, 1966; Wilkins Lectr, Royal Society, 1967; Osler Orator and Gold Medal, 1968. Actg Air Vice-Marshal, Sen. Cons. Surg., RAF, 1939–45. Sir Arthur Sims Commonwealth Travelling Professor, 1956. Hon. Foreign Corresp. Mem. Grolier Club, New York; Hon. Mem., Mod. Lang. Assoc., 1966; formerly Pres. Bibliographical Soc. of London; Hon. Fellow American Association Surgeons; Hon. Freeman, Soc. of Apothecaries, 1964; Hon. Fellow, Royal Society of Medicine, 1966. Hon. Fellow, Darwin Coll., Cambridge, 1976. Hon. Gold Medal, RCS, 1969; Gold Medal, Bibliographical Soc. of London, 1981; de Lancey Award, RSM, 1982. *Publications:* Blood Transfusion, 1922, 1949; Catalogue of the Library of Edward Gibbon, 1940, 1980; The Gates of Memory, 1981; many articles in medical journals; Bibliographies of John Donne, 1914, 1932, 1958, and 1972; William Blake, 1921, 1953; Sir Thomas Browne, 1924 and 1968; William Harvey, 1928 and 1953; Jane Austen, 1929; William Hazlitt, 1931 and 1981; John Evelyn, 1937 and 1968; John Ray, 1950; Rupert Brooke, 1954 and 1959; Robert Hooke, 1960; Siegfried Sassoon, 1962; Sir William Petty, 1971; George Berkeley, Bishop of Cloyne, 1975; Henry King, Bishop of Chichester, 1977; Martin Lister, 1980; edited Writings of William Blake, 1925, 1927, 1957 and 1966 of Sir Thomas Browne, 1928, 1964, 1968, of Izaak Walton, 1929, etc; (ed) Letters of William Blake, 1956, 1968, 1980; Compiled William Blake's Illustrations to the Bible, 1957; Blake Studies 1949 and 1971; Bibliotheca Bibliographici (cat. of his library), 1964; William Blake, Poet, Printer, Prophet, 1964; Life of William Harvey, 1966, 2nd edn 1978 (James Tait Black Memorial Prize); Drawings of William Blake: 92 Pencil Studies, 1971; William Blake's Watercolour Designs for the Poems of Thomas Gray, 1972; William Blake's Laocoön: A Last Testament, 1977; Complete Portraiture of William and Catherine Blake, 1978; William Blake as Mrs Buts's Bird, 1982. *Address:* Lammas House, Brinkley, Newmarket, Suffolk CB8 0SB. *T:* Stetchworth 268. *Club:* Roxburghe.                    *Died* 5 *July* 1982.

**KEYS, William Herbert;** General Secretary, Society of Graphical and Allied Trades 1974–85; Chairman, Trade Union Co-ordinating Committee, since 1985; *b* 1 Jan. 1923; *s* of George William and Jessie Keys; *m* 1941, Enid Gledhill; two *s. Educ:* Grammar Sch., South London. Served Army, 1939–46. National Organiser, Printing, Bookbinding and Paper Workers Union, 1953–61; Secretary, London, 1961–70. Society of Graphical and Allied Trades (SOGAT): General President, 1970–74; Gen. Sec., 1974–82 (on amalgamation with NATSOPA); Gen. Sec., after amalgamation, SOGAT '82, 1982–85. Member, General Council, TUC, 1974–85; Chairman: TUC Printing Industries Committee, 1974–85; TUC Employment Policy and Organisation Cttee (Mem., 1976–85); Member: TUC Media Cttee, 1977–85; Equal Rights Cttee, TUC, 1974–85; Race Relations Cttee, TUC, 1974–85; TUC/Lab Party Liaison Cttee, 1981–85; TUC Economic Cttee, 1982–85; TUC Gen. Purposes Cttee, 1982–85. Member: Central Arbitration Cttee, 1977–; Commission for Racial Equality, 1977–81; Manpower Services Commn, 1979–85; Joint Chairman, Pulp and Paper Division, Internat. Chemical Federation, 1976–85. Member: Inst. of Manpower Studies, 1979–; European Social Fund, 1979–86. *Recreation:* music. *Address:* 242 Maplin Way North, Thorpe Bay, Essex SS1 3NT.                    *Died* 19 *May* 1990.

**KHAN, Vice-Adm. Afzal Rahman,** HQA 1961 (SQA 1958); HPk 1964; HJ 1965; Chairman, ARK International, since 1970; *b* 20 March 1921; *s* of late Abdur Rahman Khan, landlord, Gurdaspur District; *m* 1944, Hameeda Khan; one *s* two *d. Educ:* Baring High Sch., Batala; Govt Coll., Lahore. Joined Indian Mercantile Marine Trng Ship Dufferin, 1936; entered Royal Indian Navy, 1938; Actg Sub-Lieut 1940; Lieut 1942; Lieut-Comdr 1947; Comdr 1950; Captain 1953; Cdre 1958; Rear-Adm. 1959; Vice-Adm. 1961. War of 1939–45: active service, HM Ships in Atlantic, Mediterranean and N Sea and in Royal Indian Navy ships in Indian Ocean and Burma Coast. After Independence in 1947, comd various ships and shore estabs of Pakistan Navy and held other sen. appts; Specialist in Gunnery; psc, jssc; C-in-C, Pakistan Navy, 1959; retd from Navy, 1966. Minister for Defence, and for Home Affairs, Pakistan, 1966–69; Minister in charge of Ports and Shipping, 1967–69. Order of Humayun (Iran), 1961; Legion of Merit (US), 1960 and 1964. *Recreations:* shooting, deep-sea fishing, tennis, golf, study of naval history. *Address:* The Anchorage, 27b South Central Avenue, 8th South Street, Defence Housing Society, Karachi, Pakistan. *T:* 541550. *Clubs:* Sind, Rawalpindi; Golf, Gymkhana (Karachi).
                    *Died* 27 *June* 1983.

**KHAN, Sir Muhammad Zafrulla;** *see* Zafrulla Khan.

**KIDD, Dame Margaret (Henderson);** *see* Macdonald, Dame M. H.

**KIDRON, Abraham;** Ambassador of Israel to Australia, since 1979; *b* 19 Nov. 1919; *m* 1946, Shoshanna; two *d*. *Educ:* Hebrew Univ. of Jerusalem (BA). Captain, Israel Def. Forces, 1948. Min. of Foreign Affairs, 1949–50; Attaché, Embassy of Israel, Rome, 1950–52; Min. of Foreign Affairs, 1953–54; Consul, Cyprus, 1954–56; First Sec. (Press), Embassy of Israel, London, 1957–59; Head of Res. Dept and Spokesman for Min. of Foreign Affairs, 1959–63; Minister, Israel Legation, Yugoslavia, 1963–65; Ambassador to the Phillipines, 1965–67; Asst Dir Gen., Min. of Foreign Affairs, 1969–71, Dep. Dir Gen., 1972–73, Dir Gen., 1973–76; Ambassador: to the Netherlands, 1976–77; to the Court of St James's, 1977–79. *Recreation:* golf. *Address:* c/o Embassy of Israel, Canberra, ACT 2600, Australia. *Died* 7 *Dec.* 1982.

**KIER, Olaf,** CBE 1970; Director of J. L. Kier & Co. Ltd, 1934–76; Life President, French Kier Holdings Ltd; *b* Copenhagen, 4 Sept. 1899; *s* of Hector Kier, Cdre Royal Danish Navy; naturalized British subject, 1947; *m* 1st, 1924 (marr. diss.); two *d* (one *s* decd); 2nd, 1963, Bente Gudrun Tummler; one *s*. *Educ:* Copenhagen Univ. MSc Civil Engrg. FICE 1955. Resident in UK from 1922. Founded J. L. Kier & Co. Ltd, Civil Engrg Contractors, 1932 (became a public company, 1963). Underwriting Member of Lloyd's, 1948. Comdr, Order of Dannebrog, 1966. *Address:* Abbotsbury Manor, Barley, Royston, Herts. *T:* Barkway 427.

*Died* 3 *May* 1986.

**KIESINGER, Kurt Georg;** Member of Bundestag, 1949–58 and 1969–80; Chancellor of the Federal Republic of Germany, 1966–69; *b* 6 April 1904; *m* 1932, Marie-Luise Schneider; one *s* one *d*. *Educ:* Tübingen Univ.; Berlin Univ. Lawyer. Minister-Pres., Baden-Württemberg 1958–66; Pres., Bundesrat, 1962–63. Chm., Christian Democratic Group, 1955–58. Member: Consultative Assembly, Council of Europe, 1950–58 (Vice-Pres.); WEU Assembly, 1958; Central Cttee, Christian Democratic Party (Chm., 1967–71). DIuris *hc:* Univ. of Cologne, 1965; New Delhi, 1967; Maryland, 1968; Coimbra, 1968. Grand Cross, Order of Merit, German Federal Republic; Grand Cross, Order of Merit, Italian Republic; Grand Officier de la Légion d'Honneur, Palmes Académiques. *Address:* Tübingen, Engelfriedshalde 48, West Germany.

*Died* 9 *March* 1988.

**KILBRANDON, Baron** *cr* 1971 (Life Peer), of Kilbrandon, Argyll; **Charles James Dalrymple Shaw,** PC 1971; a Lord of Appeal in Ordinary, 1971–76; *b* 15 Aug. 1906; *s* of James Edward Shaw, DL, County Clerk of Ayrshire, and Gladys Elizabeth Lester; *m* 1937, Ruth Caroline Grant; two *s* three *d*. *Educ:* Charterhouse; Balliol Coll., Oxford; Edinburgh Univ. Admitted to Faculty of Advocates, 1932, Dean of Faculty, 1957; KC (Scot.), 1949; Sheriff of Ayr and Bute, 1954–57; Sheriff of Perth and Angus, 1957; Senator of Coll. of Justice in Scotland and Lord of Session, 1959–71. Chairman: Standing Consultative Council on Youth Service in Scotland, 1960–68; Departmental Cttee on Treatment of Children and Young Persons, 1964; Scottish Law Commn, 1965–71; Commn on the Constitution, 1972–73 (Mem., 1969–72); Bd of Management, Royal Infirmary, Edinburgh, 1960–68. Hon. LLD Aberdeen, 1965; Hon. DSc (Soc. Sci.) Edinburgh, 1970. Hon. Fellow, Balliol Coll., Oxford, 1969, Visitor, 1974–86; Hon. Bencher, Gray's Inn, 1971. *Address:* Kilbrandon House, Balvicar, by Oban. *T:* Balvicar 239. *Clubs:* New, Royal Highland Yacht (Oban). *Died* 10 *Sept.* 1989.

**KILLIAN, James Rhyne,** Jr; Chairman of Corporation, 1959–71, Hon. Chairman of Corporation, 1971–79, Massachusetts Institute of Technology, USA; *b* 24 July 1904; *s* of James R. and Jeannette R. Killian; *m* 1929, Elizabeth Parks; one *s* one *d*. *Educ:* Trinity Coll. (Duke Univ.), Durham, North Carolina; Mass Institute of Technology, Cambridge, Mass (BS). Asst Managing Editor, The Technology Review, MIT, 1926–27; Managing Editor, 1927–30; Editor, 1930–39; Exec. Asst to Pres., MIT, 1939–43; Exec. Vice-Pres., MIT, 1943–45; Vice-Pres., MIT, 1945–48; 10th Pres. of MIT, 1948–59 (on leave 1957–59). Special Asst to Pres. of United States for Science and Technology, 1957–59; Mem., 1957–61, Chm. 1957–59, Consultant-at-large, 1961–73, President's Science Advisory Cttee; Mem., President's Bd of Consultants on Foreign Intelligence Activities, 1956–59 (Chm., 1956–57); Mem. of President's Commission on National Goals, 1960; Chm., President's Foreign Intelligence Advisory Board, 1961–63. Mem., Bd of Trustees, Mitre Corporation, 1960–82; Pres. Bd of Trustees, Atoms for Peace Awards, Inc., 1959–69; Mem., Bd of Visitors, Tulane Univ., 1960–69; Trustee: Institute for Defense Analyses, Inc., 1959–69 (Chm., 1956–57, 1959–61); Mount Holyoke Coll., 1962–72; Alfred P. Sloan Foundn, 1954–77; Boston Museum of Science; Boston Museum of Fine Arts, 1966–79; Chairman: Carnegie Commn on Educl TV, 1965–67; Corp. for Public Broadcasting, 1973–74 (Dir, 1968–75); Director: Polaroid Corp.; former Director: Amer. Tel. & Tel. Co.; Cabot Corp.; General Motors Corp.; IBM; Ingersoll-Rand Co. Fellow Amer. Acad. of Arts and Sciences; Hon. Mem.,

Amer. Soc. for Engrg Educn; Mem., Nat. Acad. of Engineering; Moderator, Amer. Unitarian Assoc., 1960–61; President's Certificate of Merit, 1948; Certificate of Appreciation, 1953, and Exceptional Civilian Service Award, 1957, Dept of the Army; Public Welfare Medal of the Nat. Acad. of Sciences, 1957; Officier Légion d'Honneur (France), 1957. Gold Medal Award, Nat. Inst. of Social Sciences, 1958; World Brotherhood Award, Nat. Conf. of Christians and Jews, 1958; Award of Merit, Amer. Inst. of Cons. Engineers, 1958; Washington Award, Western Soc. of Engineers, 1959; Distinguished Achievement Award, Holland Soc. of NY, 1959; Gold Medal of Internat. Benjamin Franklin Soc., 1960; Good Govt Award, Crosscup-Pishon Post, American Legion, 1960; Hoover Medal, 1963; George Foster Peabody Award, 1968 and 1976; first Marconi Internat. Fellowship, 1975; Sylvanus Thayer Award, 1978; Vannevar Bush Award, Nat. Science Foundn, 1980. Hon. degrees: ScD: Middlebury Coll., 1945; Bates Coll., 1950; University of Havana, 1953; University of Notre Dame, Lowell Technological Inst., 1954; Columbia Univ., Coll. of Wooster, Ohio, Oberlin Coll., 1958; University of Akron, 1959; Worcester Polytechnic Inst., 1960; University of Maine, 1963; DEng: Drexel Inst. of Tech., 1948; University of Ill., 1960; University of Mass., 1961; LLD: Union Coll., 1947; Bowdoin Coll., Northeastern Univ., Duke Univ., 1949; Boston Univ., Harvard Univ., 1950; Williams Coll., Lehigh Univ., University of Pa, 1951; University of Chattanooga, 1954; Tufts Univ., 1955; University of Calif. and Amherst Coll., 1956; College of William and Mary, 1957; Brandeis Univ., 1958; Johns Hopkins Univ., New York Univ., 1959; Providence Coll., Temple Univ. 1960; University of S Carolina, 1961; Meadville Theological Sch., 1962; DAppl Sci., University of Montreal, 1958; EdD, Rhode Island Coll., 1962; HHD, Rollins Coll., 1964; DPS, Detroit Inst. of Technology, 1972. *Publications:* Sputnik, Scientists, and Eisenhower, 1977; Moments of Vision (with Harold E. Edgerton), 1979; (autobiog.) The Education of a College President: a memoir, 1985. *Address:* 77 Massachusetts Avenue, Cambridge, Mass 02139, USA. *Clubs:* St Botolph (Boston); The Century, University (New York). *Died* 29 *Jan.* 1988.

**KILMANY, Baron,** *cr* 1966 (Life Peer), of Kilmany; **William John St Clair Anstruther-Gray;** 1st Bt, *cr* 1956; PC 1962; MC 1943; Lord-Lieutenant of Fife, 1975–80; *b* 5 March 1905; *o s* of late Col W. Anstruther-Gray, MP, DL, JP, of Kilmany; *m* 1934, Monica Helen, OBE 1946, JP, *o c* of late Geoffrey Lambton, 2nd *s* of 4th Earl of Durham; two *d*. *Educ:* Eton; Christ Church, Oxford, MA (Hons). Lieut, Coldstream Guards, 1926–30; served Shanghai Defence Force, 1927–28; rejoined Sept. 1939 and served N Africa, France, Germany, etc with Coldstream Guards and Lothians and Border Horse; Major, 1942; MP (U) for North Lanark, 1931–45; up to Sept. 1939 Parly Private Sec. to Rt Hon. Sir John Colville, MP, Sec. of State for Scotland, and previously to the Financial Sec. to the Treasury, and to Sec. for Overseas Trade; Asst Postmaster-Gen., May-July 1945; Crown nominee for Scotland on Gen. Medical Council, 1952–65. Contested (U) Berwick and East Lothian, Feb. 1950; MP (U) Berwick and East Lothian, 1951–66. Chm. of Ways and Means and Dep. Speaker, House of Commons, 1962–64 (Dep. Chm., 1959–62); Chm. Conservative Members' 1922 Cttee, 1964–66. Elected Mem. National Hunt Cttee, 1948; Mem., Horserace Betting Levy Bd, 1966–74. DL Fife, 1953. *Address:* Kilmany, Cupar, Fife. *T:* Gauldry 247. *Clubs:* Pratt's, Brooks's, Cavalry and Guards, Turf, Jockey; New (Edinburgh); Royal and Ancient (St Andrews).

*Died* 6 *Aug.* 1985.

**KILNER, Cyril;** Assistant Editor, Doncaster Gazette, 1952–75, retired; *b* 5 Sept. 1910; *s* of Bernard Kilner and Edith Annie (*née* Booker); *m* 1949, Joan Siddons; one *s* one *d*. *Educ:* Mexborough Grammar School. Army War Service in Royal Tank Regt, 1940–45. Reporter, Barnsley Independent, 1927–30; Reporter, Sports Editor, Sub-Editor, Barnsley Chronicle, 1931–47; Reporter, Sub-Editor, Yorkshire Evening News (Doncaster edn), 1947–52. Member: The Press Council, 1968–74; Nat. Exec. Council, NUJ, 1958–72 (Pres.), 1969, Mem. of Honour, 1976). Hon. Gen. Treasurer, Internat. Fedn. of Journalists, 1972–76. *Recreations:* watching (sports, TV etc.), reading, motoring, travelling. *Address:* Cranford, 159 Boothferry Road, Goole, N Humberside. *T:* Goole 60192.

*Died* 27 *Oct.* 1985.

**KILPATRICK, Rev. George Dunbar;** Dean Ireland's Professor of Exegesis of Holy Scripture, Oxford, 1949–77; Fellow of the Queen's College, Oxford, 1949–77; Fellow of University College, London, since 1967; *b* Coal Creek, Fernie, BC, Canada, 15 Sept. 1910; *o c* of late Wallace Henry and Bessie Kilpatrick; *m* 1943, Marion, *d* of Harold Laver and Dorothy Madeline Woodhouse; one *s* three *d*. *Educ:* Ellis Sch., BC; St Dunstan's Coll.; University Coll., London; Oriel Coll., Oxford (Scholar); University of London, Granville Scholar, 1931; BA Classics (1st Class), 1932; University of Oxford, BA Lit. Hum. (2nd Class), 1934, Theology (2nd Class), 1936, Junior Greek Testament Prize, 1936, Senior Greek Testament Prize, 1937, Junior Denyer and Johnson Scholarship, 1938, BD 1944; Grinfield Lecturer, 1945–49; DD 1948; Schweich Lecturer, 1951. Deacon 1936; Priest 1937; Asst Curate of Horsell, 1936; Tutor, Queen's

Coll., Birmingham, 1939; Asst Curate of Selly Oak, 1940; Acting Warden of Coll. of the Ascension, Birmingham, 1941; Rector of Wishaw, Warwicks, and Lecturer at Lichfield Theological Coll., 1942; Head of Dept of Theology and Reader in Christian Theology, University Coll., Nottingham, 1946. Vice-Pres., British and Foreign Bible Soc., 1958. *Publications:* The Origins of the Gospel according to St Matthew, 1946; The Trial of Jesus, 1953; (ed) The New Testament in Greek, British and Foreign Bible Society's 2nd edn, 1958; Remaking the Liturgy, 1967; The Eucharist in Bible and Liturgy, 1984; contributions to periodicals. *Recreation:* reading. *Address:* 27 Lathbury Road, Oxford. *T:* Oxford 58909.

*Died 14 Jan.* 1989.

**KILPATRICK, Sir William (John),** AC 1981; KBE 1965 (CBE 1958); Chairman: Mulford Holdings Ltd; Kilpatrick Holdings Ltd; Director, Guardian Assurance Group, 1958–74; *b* 27 Dec. 1906; *s* of late James Park Scott Kilpatrick, Scotland; *m* 1932, Alice Margaret Strachan; one *s* three *d*. *Educ:* Wollongong, NSW. Sqdn Ldr, RAAF, 1942–45. Pastoral interests, Victoria. Mem., Melbourne City Council, 1958–64. Chm. Cancer Service Cttee, Anti-Cancer Coun. of Vic., 1958–79; Dep. Nat. Pres., Nat. Heart Foundn of Aust., 1960–64; Chm., Finance Cttee, Nat. Heart Foundn of Aust., 1960–79; Pres. Aust. Cancer Soc., 1961–64, 1974–80; World Chm., Finance Cttee, Internat. Union Against Cancer, 1961–78; Ldr Aust. Delegn to 8th Internat. Cancer Congr, Moscow, 1962. Nat. Chm. Winston Churchill Mem. Trust, 1965; Chm., Drug Educn Sub-Cttee, Commonwealth Govt, 1970; Chm., Plastic and Reconstructive Surgery Foundn, 1970–79. *Recreations:* golf, swimming. *Clubs:* Victorian Golf, VRC, VATC (all Melbourne); Commonwealth (Canberra). *Died 25 April* 1985.

**KING;** *see* Maybray-King.

**KING, Prof. Basil Charles;** Professor of Geology, Bedford College, University of London, 1956–77, later Emeritus; *b* 1 June 1915; *s* of Charles William Argent King; *m* 1939, Dorothy Margaret Wells (*d* 1983); two *s* one *d* (and one *d* decd). *Educ:* King Edward VI Sch., Bury St Edmunds; Durham Univ.; London Univ. Demonstrator, Bedford Coll., London, 1936–38; Chemist and Petrologist, Geological Survey of Uganda, 1938–46; Mineralogist, Geological Survey of Nigeria, 1946–48; Senior Lecturer, University of Glasgow, 1948–56. FRSE 1950; FRSA 1978. Bigsby Medal, Geological Soc., 1959; André Dumont Medal, Société Géologique de Belgique, 1967; Murchison Medal, Geological Soc., 1971; Clough Medal, Geol Soc. of Edinburgh, 1976. *Publications:* geological publications on E Africa, Nigeria, Botswana and Scotland. *Address:* 1 Catacol, Lochranza, Isle of Arran, Scotland KA27 8HN. *T:* Lochranza 658.

*Died 11 Sept.* 1985.

**KING, Cecil Edward,** CMG 1956; HM Diplomatic Service, retired; *b* 27 March 1912; *s* of John Stuart King and Thérèse (*née* Dubied); *m* 1944, Isabel Haynes; two *s* one *d*. *Educ:* King Edward VII Sch., Sheffield, Charterhouse; Queen's Coll., Oxford. Joined HM Consular Service, 1934; served in Europe, North and South America, W Africa; Asst Under-Sec. of State, FO, 1965–67; Ambassador to the Lebanon, 1967–70; pensioned off 1970. Mem., UN Joint Inspection Unit, Geneva, 1972–77. *Address:* 14 Marlborough Hill, NW8 0NN. *Died 4 July* 1981.

**KING, Cecil (Harmsworth);** *b* 20 Feb. 1901; *e* surv. *s* of Sir Lucas White King, CSI, and Geraldine Adelaide Hamilton, *d* of Alfred Harmsworth, barrister of the Middle Temple; *m* 1st, 1923, Agnes Margaret (marr. diss. 1962; she *d* 1985), *d* of the Rev. Canon G. A. Cooke, DD, Regius Prof. of Hebrew, Oxford, and Canon of Christ Church; one *s* one *d* (and two *s* decd); 2nd, 1962, Dame Ruth Railton, DBE. *Educ:* Winchester; Christ Church, Oxford (2nd class hons history, MA). Dir, Daily Mirror, 1929; Dep. Chm., Sunday Pictorial, 1942; Chairman: Daily Mirror Newspapers Ltd and Sunday Pictorial Newspapers Ltd, 1951–1963; International Publishing Corp., 1963–68; The Reed Paper Group, 1963–68; Wall Paper Manufacturers, 1965–67; British Film Institute, 1948–52; Newspaper Proprietors' Assoc., 1961–68; Nigerian Printing & Publishing Co., 1948–68; Butterworth & Co. Ltd, 1968. Director: Reuters, 1953–59; Bank of England, 1965–68. Part-time Mem., National Coal Board, 1966–69. Mem., National Parks Commn, later Countryside Commn, 1966–69. Gold Badge for services to City of Warsaw; Gold Medal for services to British paper trade. Hon. DLitt Boston, 1974. *Publications:* The Future of the Press, 1967; Strictly Personal, 1969; With Malice Towards None: a war diary, 1970; Without Fear or Favour, 1971; The Cecil King Diary 1965–70, 1972; On Ireland, 1973; The Cecil King Diary 1970–74, 1975; Cecil King's Commonplace Book, 1981. *Recreation:* reading. *Address:* 23 Greenfield Park, Dublin 4, Ireland. *T:* Dublin 695870.

*Died 17 April* 1987.

**KING, Rev. Cuthbert,** CIE 1946; MA Oxon; ICS (retired); *b* 27 Jan. 1889; *s* of Rev. E. G. King, DD, and Mary, *d* of Rt Rev. B. F. Westcott, Durham; *m* 1921, Elsie Vivienne (*née* Harris), MBE 1946, K-i-H (1st Cl.) 1936 (*d* 1960). *Educ:* Sherborne Sch.; Christ Church, Oxford; Göttingen; Trinity Coll., Dublin. Indian Civil Service

(Punjab), 1913–47; last appointments as Commissioner of Multan, Lahore and Rawalpindi Divs. On Military Service, IARO, 1917–20. Mem. of Order of Cloud and Banner (Chinese), 1945. Deacon, 1949; Priest, 1950. *Recreations:* golf, literature, languages, art. *Address:* c/o Lloyds Bank, Richmond, Surrey. *Died 3 July* 1981.

**KING, Frank Gordon,** QC 1970; *b* 10 March 1915; *s* of late Lt-Col Frank King, DSO, OBE; *m* 1937, Monica Beatrice, *d* of late Arthur Collins; two *s* one *d*. *Educ:* Charterhouse, Godalming; Christ's Coll., Cambridge (BA 1936, LLM 1938). Served War of 1939–45; RA 1939–46, Major 1943. Called to the Bar, Gray's Inn, 1946. A Church Commissioner, 1973–81. *Address:* Red Chimneys, Warren Drive, Kingswood, Surrey. *Club:* Walton Heath Golf.

*Died 28 Oct.* 1988.

**KING, Sir Geoffrey Stuart,** KCB 1953 (CB 1943); KBE 1946; MC 1918; Civil Service, retired; *b* 1894; *s* of late Charles James Stuart King, Chardstock, Devon; *m* 1920, Ethel Eileen May, *y d* of late D. C. M. Tuke, Chiswick House; four *s*. Sec., Assistance Bd, 1944–48; Dep. Sec., Ministry of National Insurance, 1949–51; Permanent Sec., Ministry of Pensions and National Insurance, 1953–55 (Ministry of National Insurance, 1951); retired, 1955. *Address:* Oliver's Farm, Ash, near Sevenoaks, Kent TN15 7HT.

*Died 11 Aug.* 1981.

**KING, Prof. Hubert John,** CBE 1976; FEng, FIMinE; *b* 5 May 1915; *s* of Hubert and Emmeline Elizabeth King; *m* 1940, Ceridwen Richards; one *s* two *d*. *Educ:* Porth County Sch.; University Coll., Cardiff (PhD London); Glamorgan Polytechnic. Underground worker, S Wales Coalfield, 1931–36; served HM Forces, 1939–45; successively, Lecturer, Reader and Head of Mining and Mineral Sciences Dept, Univ. of Leeds, 1947–67; Univ. of Nottingham: Professor and Head, Mining Engineering Dept, 1967–77, Emeritus Prof., 1977; Dean, Faculty of Applied Science, 1973–76. President, Instn of Mining Engineers, 1974 (Institution Medal, 1980); Member and Chairman, Safety in Mines Research Adv. Cttee, 1967–79; Mem., Internat. Cttee for World Mining Congresses, 1967–77. *Publications:* various research papers in fields of surveying, rock mechanics and mineral economics. *Recreation:* golf. *Address:* 41 Breary Lane East, Leeds LS16 9EU. *Died 20 June* 1988.

**KING, Ivor Edward,** CB 1961; CBE 1943; CEng, FRINA; Royal Corps of Naval Constructors; Director of Dockyards, Admiralty, 1958–61; *b* 1899; *s* of John and Minnie Elizabeth King, Pembroke Dock; *m* 1923, Doris, *d* of John and Catherine Hill, Lee, SE; three *d*. *Educ:* Royal Naval College, Greenwich. Formerly Manager, HM Dockyards, Portsmouth, Malta, Sheerness and Bermuda. Constructor Capt. to Commander-in-Chief, Mediterranean, 1942–44. Served War, 1942–44 (CBE). Hon. Vice-Pres., Royal Institution of Naval Architects. *Recreation:* golf. *Address:* 10 Combe Park, Bath BA1 3NP. *T:* Bath 23047. *Died 7 April* 1983.

**KING, Sir James Granville Le Neve,** 3rd Bt, *cr* 1888; TD; *b* 17 Sept. 1898; *s* of Sir John Westall King, 2nd Bt, and Frances Rosa (*d* 1942), *d* of John Neve, Oaken, Staffs; *S* father, 1940; *m* 1928, Penelope Charlotte, *d* of late Capt. E. Cooper-Key, CB, MVO, RN; one *s* two *d*. *Educ:* Eton; King's Coll., Cambridge. *Heir:* *s* John Christopher King [*b* 31 March 1933; *m* 1st, 1958, Patricia Monica (marr. diss. 1972), *o d* of late Lt-Col Kingsley Foster and of Mrs Foster, Hampton Court Palace; one *s* one *d*; 2nd, 1984, Mrs Aline Jane Holley, *e d* of late Col D. A. Brett, GC, OBE, MC]. *Address:* Church Farm House, Chilbolton, Hants. *Died 20 Dec.* 1989.

**KING, Laurence (Edward),** OBE 1971; FSA; FSAScot; FRSA; FRIBA; Architect; Senior Partner and Founder of firm of Laurence King and Partners, Chartered Architects; Tutor at Royal College of Art, 1936–39 and 1946–51; Lecturer at Royal College of Art, 1951–58; *b* 28 June 1907; *o s* of late Frederick Ernest King and Flora King (*née* Joyner); unmarried. *Educ:* Brentwood Sch.; University of London. Architectural Education under late Prof. Sir Albert Richardson at University of London, 1924–29; entered private practice in 1933. Served in the Army during 1939–45 War, principally in Middle East; rank, Major. Commenced Architectural practice again in 1946. Architect for the United Westminster Schools and Grey Coat Hospital. Re-built: Grey Coat Hospital, 1955; Wren's Church of St Magnus, London Bridge, 1951; Wren's Church of St Mary-le-Bow (Bow Bells) (completed, 1964); Walsingham Parish Church, rebuilt after destruction by fire in 1961, completed 1964; has designed several churches in New Housing areas. Has undertaken work for the following religious communities: Nashdom Abbey; Malling Abbey; Burnham Abbey; St John's Convent, Clewer; rebuilt St Saviour's Priory, Haggerston (completed 1978). Architect for St James' Church, Marden Ash, completed 1958; St Mary's Church, South Ruislip, completed 1959; St Nicholas, Fleetwood, 1961; Ascension Church, Chelmsford, 1962; St Mary and St Nicholas, Perivale, 1965; St Mary, Hobs Moat, Solihull, 1967; St Michael, Letchworth, 1967; St John's, North Woolwich, 1968; St James, Leigh-on-Sea, 1969; Architect to Blackburn Cathedral, 1962 (consecrated 1978); Consulting Architect for Exeter Cathedral, 1965, and for Cathedral and Dio. of Gibraltar, 1974;

Architect for Worksop Priory (restoration and major extensions completed 1974); for various school buildings at Brentwood Sch., Sutton Valence Sch., Emanuel Sch., Wandsworth, Westminster City School, Queen Anne's School, Caversham, Eastbourne Coll., Framlingham Coll.; architect for the Coopers' Co. and Coborn School, completed 1974; St Davids C of E Comp. Sch., Hornsey (completed 1978); numerous Church interior decoration and furnishing schemes including High Altar and furnishings for Eucharistic Congress, 1958; Architect for restoration of various ancient Churches, particularly in London, Middx, Essex, Suffolk, Norfolk, Herts, Notts, Kent, Devon; Architect in association with late A. B. Knapp-Fisher, FRIBA for extensions to the Queen's Chapel of the Savoy for Royal Victorian Order. Mem. Archbishop's Commn in connection with repair of churches, 1951–52; Hon. Cons. Architect for Historic Churches Preservation Trust; Member: General Synod, 1970–80; Council for Places of Worship; Chm., Worship and Arts Assoc. Freeman, City of London. Liveryman: Worshipful Co. of Barbers; Worshipful Co. of Needlemakers; Chm., Ward of Cordwainer Club, London, 1972–73; Mem., Worshipful Co. of Parish Clerks. *Publications:* Sanctuaries and Sacristies; Essex section, Collin's Guide to English Parish Churches; and various articles and reviews in magazines and periodicals. *Recreations:* the visual arts, the theatre, travel. *Address:* (home) The Wayside, Shenfield Common, Brentwood, Essex. *T:* Brentwood 210438; (office) 5 Bloomsbury Place, WC1A 2QA. *T:* 01-580 6752. *Clubs:* Athenæum, Boodle's, City Livery, Art Workers' Guild.
*Died 9 Dec.* 1981.

**KING, Maj.-Gen. Robert Charles Moss,** CB 1955; DSO 1945; OBE 1944; retired; *b* 6 June 1904; *s* of Robert Henry Curzon Moss King, ICS and Mrs King; *m* 1940, Elizabeth Stuart Mackay (*d* 1966); two *d. Educ:* Clifton Coll.; RMC, Camberley. 2nd Lieut, W Yorks Regt, 1924; Capt. 1935. Served War of 1939–45: India, Malaya, Java, Assam and Burma (despatches). Maj.-Gen. 1955. GOC Home Counties District and 44th (HC) Infantry Division TA, Deputy Constable Dover Castle, 1954–56; Dir of Quartering, War Office, 1957–58. *Recreations:* shooting and fishing. *Address:* c/o Willow Hey Cottage, Ovington, Alresford, Hampshire.
*Died 16 Dec.* 1983.

**KINGDOM, Thomas Doyle,** CB 1959; Controller, Government Social Survey Department, 1967–70, retired; *b* 30 Oct. 1910; *er s* of late Thomas Kingdom; *m* 1937, Elsie Margaret, *d* of late L. C. Scott, MBE, Northwood; two *d. Educ:* Rugby; King's Coll., Cambridge (MA). Entered Civil Service as Asst Principal, Inland Revenue, 1933; transferred to Unemployment Assistance Bd, 1934; seconded to HM Treasury as Dep. Dir, Organisation and Methods, 1945–49; Under Sec., 1955. Chm., Exec. Council, Royal Inst. of Public Administration, 1965–66. Chm. Nat London Suppl. Benefit Appeal Tribunal, 1971–83; Charities' VAT Advr, Nat. Council for Voluntary Orgns, 1972–89. *Address:* 2 Grosvenor Road, Northwood, Mddx HA6 3HJ. *T:* Northwood 22006.
*Died 14 March* 1990.

**KININMONTH, Sir William (Hardie),** Kt 1972; PPRSA, FRIBA, FRIAS; Architectural Consultant, formerly Senior Partner, Sir Rowand Anderson, Kininmonth and Paul, architects, Edinburgh; *b* 8 Nov. 1904; *s* of John Kininmonth and Isabella McLean Hardie; *m* 1934, Caroline Eleanor Newsam Sutherland (*d* 1978); one *d. Educ:* George Watson's Coll., Edinburgh. Architectural training in Edinburgh Coll. of Art, and in offices of Sir Edwin Lutyens, Sir Rowand Anderson and Paul, and Wm N. Thomson; entered partnership Rowand Anderson and Paul, 1933; served War of 1939–45: RE 1940, North Africa, Sicily and Italy; resumed architectural practice, 1945; buildings for Edinburgh Univ., Renfrew Air Port and Naval Air Station, Edinburgh Dental Hospital, Town Hall, churches, banks, hospitals, schools, housing, etc. Saltire and Civic Trust Awards. Appointed: 1955, Adviser to City of Edinburgh, for development of Princes Street; 1964, to design new Festival Theatre and Festival Centre. Pres., Royal Scottish Academy, 1969–73 (formerly Treas. and then Sec.); Pres. Edinburgh Architectural Association, 1951–53; Member: Royal Fine Arts Commn for Scotland, 1952–65; Council RIBA, 1951–53; Council Royal Incorp. of Architects in Scot., 1951–53; Board, Edinburgh Coll. of Art, 1951–, Board Merchant Co. of Edinburgh, 1950–52. Edinburgh Dean of Guild Court, 1953–69. Hon. LLD Dundee, 1975; Hon. RA; Hon. RSW. *Address:* The Lane House, 46a Dick Place, Edinburgh EH9 2JB. *T:* 031–667 2724. *Clubs:* Scottish Arts, New (Edinburgh).
*Died 8 Aug.* 1988.

**KINLOCH, Sir Alexander (Davenport),** 12th Bt of Gilmerton, *cr* 1685; Major Special Reserve Grenadier Guards, retired 1952; *b* 17 Sept. 1902; *s* of Brig.-Gen. Sir David Kinloch, 11th Bt, and Elinor Lucy (*d* 1943), *d* of Col Bromley Davenport of Capesthorne, Cheshire; *S* father, 1944; *m* 1st, 1929, Alexandra (marr. diss. 1945), *d* of Frederick Y. Dalziel, New York; two *d*; 2nd, 1946, Hilda Anna (marr. diss. 1965), *d* of late Thomas Walker, Edinburgh; three *s* three *d*; 3rd, 1965, Ann, *d* of late Group Capt. F. L. White and of Mrs H. R. White, London; one *s. Educ:* Eton. Mem. of Queen's

Body Guard for Scotland (Royal Company of Archers). *Heir: s* David Kinloch, *b* 5 Aug. 1951. *Address:* Gilmerton House, North Berwick, East Lothian. *Clubs:* White's; New (Edinburgh).
*Died 22 Nov.* 1982.

**KINMONTH, Prof. John Bernard;** Honorary Consulting Surgeon, St Thomas' Hospital; Professor of Surgery in the University of London, 1955–81, later Emeritus; *b* 9 May 1916; *s* of Dr George Kinmonth; *m* 1946, Kathleen Margaret, *d* of late Admiral J. H. Godfrey, CB; two *s* two *d. Educ:* Dulwich Coll.; St Thomas's Hosp. Medical Sch. House Surgeon, Resident Asst Surgeon, etc, St Thomas' Hosp., 1938–43. Wing Comdr, Surgical Specialist, RAFVR, 1944–47. Research Asst, St Bartholomew's Hosp., 1947–48; Research Fellow, Harvard Univ., 1948–49; Asst Surgeon, Asst Dir, Surgical Unit and Reader in Surgery, St Bartholomew's Hosp., 1950–54; Dir of Univ. Surgical Unit, St Thomas' Hosp., 1955–81. Arris and Gale Lecturer, 1951, Hunterian Prof., 1954, RCS; Sir Arthur Sim's Commonwealth Travelling Professor, 1962. Visiting Professor: Tehran, 1971; California, 1972; Harvard, 1975. Past Pres., European Soc. Cardiovascular Surgery; Vice-Pres. and Matas Lectr, Internat. Cardiovascular Soc.; Member: University of London Cttee on Colleges Overseas in Special Relations; Surgical Research Soc.; Physiological Soc.; Vascular Surgical Soc. (Pres. 1973); Council, RCS, 1977–. Consultant Adviser in Surgery to Min. of Health; Hon. Consultant in Surgery, RAF, 1958–81. Hon. Prof. Universidad Peruana Cayetano Heredia, 1968. Hon. Member: Brazilian Soc. Angiology; Internat. Soc. Lymphology (Asellius Medal); German Soc. of Lymphology, 1979; Associé Etranger, Académie de Chirurgie; Lombard Soc. Surgery; Soc. for Vascular Surgery, USA, 1975. Mickle Fellow, Univ. of London, 1974. Hon. FRCR, 1975; Hon. FACS, 1976. Danish Surgical Soc. Medal, 1978; Freyer Medal Univ. Coll. Galway, 1978; Gold Medal, Internat. Soc. of Lymphology, 1979. *Publications:* Vascular Surgery, 1962; The Lymphatics: Diseases, Lymphography and Surgery, 1972; The Lymphatics: Lymph and Chyle, 1982; articles on gen. and cardiovascular surgery and physiology in scientific journals and on cruising in sailing journals. *Recreations:* sailing, music, ornithology. *Address:* 70 Ladbroke Road, W11. *T:* 01-727 6045; 199 Westminster Bridge Road, SE1. *T:* 01-928 3013. *Clubs:* Royal Cork Yacht, Royal Cruising, Irish Cruising.
*Died 16 Sept.* 1982.

**KINROSS,** 4th Baron *cr* 1902; **David Andrew Balfour,** OBE 1968; TD; Writer to the Signet, retired 1981; *b* 29 March 1906; second *s* of 2nd Baron Kinross and Caroline Elsie (*d* 1969), *d* of A. H. Johnstone Douglas, DL; *S* brother, 1976; *m* 1st, 1936, Araminta Peel (marr. diss. 1941); one *d*; 2nd, 1948, Helen (*d* 1969), *d* of late A. W. Hog, Edinburgh; one *s*; 3rd, 1972, Ruth Beverley, *d* of late W. H. Mill, SSC, and formerly wife of K. W. B. Middleton. *Educ:* Sherborne; Edinburgh Univ. Qualified Solicitor, 1931; joined WS Society, 1931. Commissioned RA (TA), 1926; served War of 1939–45, Europe and Burma; Lt-Col 78 LAA Regt RA, 1942, 56 Anti-Tank Regt RA, 1944; Hon. Col 278 (Lowland) Field Regt RA (TA), 1964–67. Member Queen's Body Guard for Scotland (Royal Company of Archers). National Chairman, British Legion, Scotland, 1965–68; Chm., Astley Ainslie, Edenhall and Associated Hospitals, Edinburgh, 1957–74. DL Edinburgh, 1966–84. *Recreations:* shooting, gardening and travel. *Heir: s* Hon. Christopher Patrick Balfour [*b* 1 Oct. 1949; *m* 1974, Susan, *d* of I. R. Pitman, WS; two *s*]. *Address:* 58 India Street, Edinburgh EH3 6HD. *T:* 031–225 2651; The Forge Cottage, Humbie, East Lothian. *T:* Humbie 277. *Clubs:* Army and Navy; New (Edinburgh); Hon. Co. of Edinburgh Golfers.
*Died 20 July* 1985.

**KINROSS, John Blythe,** CBE 1967 (OBE 1958); *b* 31 Jan. 1904; *s* of late John Kinross, RSA, architect, and late Mary Louisa Margaret Hall; *m* 1st, 1930; one *s* two *d*; 2nd, 1943, Mary Elizabeth Connon (*d* 1988); one *s* two *d. Educ:* George Watson's Coll., Edinburgh. Manager Issue Dept, Gresham Trust, until 1933 when started business on own account as Cheviot Trust (first Issuing House to undertake small issues). Joined Industrial & Commercial Finance Corp. Ltd at inception, 1945; Gen. Man., 1948; Exec. Dir, 1961; Dep. Chm., 1964–74. Mem. Finance Cttee, Royal College of Surgeons, 1956–79; Hon. Financial Adviser to Royal Scottish Academy, 1950–. Founded Mary Kinross Charitable Trust, 1957 (includes Student Homes Ltd and various med. res. projects). Chairman: Imperial Investments (Grosvenor) Ltd, 1980–86; Estate Duties Investment Trust Ltd, 1973–76; Director: Equity Income Trust Ltd, 1962–82; House of Fraser Ltd, 1966–72; London Atlantic Investment Trust Ltd, 1962–83; Scottish Ontario Investment, 1961–79; Investment Trust of Guernsey Ltd and other companies. Hon. RSA, 1957; Hon. FFARCS, 1961. *Publication:* Fifty Years in the City, 1982. *Recreation:* farming. *Address:* 23 Cumberland Terrace, NW1. *T:* 01–935 8979; (office) 01–928 7822. *Club:* Athenæum.
*Died 19 Aug.* 1989.

**KINSEY, Joseph Ronald,** JP; Chairman, West Midland Traffic Users Consultative Committee, since 1981; *b* 28 Aug. 1921; *s* of Walter and Florence Annie Kinsey; *m* 1953, Joan Elizabeth Walters; one *d. Educ:* Birmingham elementary and C of E schools. Shop management trng; served RAF ground staff, 1940–47; GPO telephone engr, 1947–57; started own business, florists, horticultural and fruit shop, 1957. MP (C) Birmingham, Perry Barr, 1970–Feb. 1974; contested (C) Birmingham, Perry Barr, Oct. 1974, 1979. JP Birmingham, 1962. *Address:* 147 Grange Road, Birmingham B24 0ES. *T:* 021-373 4606. *Died 7 July* 1983.

**KINSLEY, Rev. Prof. James,** MA, PhD, DLitt; FBA 1971; Professor of English Studies and Head of Department of English Studies, University of Nottingham, since 1961; *b* Borthwick, Midlothian, 17 April 1922; *s* of late Louis Morrison Kinsley and of Mary Kinsley, Gorebridge; *m* 1949, Helen, 2nd *d* of late C. C. Dawson, Dewsbury; two *s* one *d. Educ:* Royal High Sch., Edinburgh; Edinburgh Univ.; Oriel Coll., Oxford. MA Edinburgh and James Boswell Scholar, 1943; BA Oxford (1st cl. Hons Sch. of Eng. Lang. and Lit.), 1947; PhD Edinburgh, 1951; MA Oxford, 1952; DLitt Edinburgh, 1959. Served with RA, 1943–45 (Captain). Lectr in English, University Coll. of Wales, 1947–54; Prof. of English Language and Literature in Univ. of Wales (at Swansea), 1954–61; Dean, Faculty of Arts, Univ. of Nottingham, 1967–70. Lectures: William Will Meml, 1960, 1975; Gregynog, Aberystwyth, 1963; Warton, British Acad., 1974. Editor, Renaissance and Modern Studies, Nottingham Miscellany, 1961–68; Gen. Editor: Oxford English Novels, 1967–77; Oxford English Memoirs and Travels, 1969–77; (with Kathleen Tillotson) The Clarendon Dickens, 1977–. Vice-President: Tennyson Soc., 1963–; Scottish Text Soc., 1971–79. Ordained deacon 1962, priest 1963; Public Preacher, Southwell Diocese, 1964; Mem., C of E Liturgical Commn, 1976–80; Assessor, Church in Wales Liturgical Commn, 1982–. FRSL 1959; FRHistS 1961. *Publications:* (ed) Lindsay, Ane Satyre of the Thrie Estaits, 1954; Scottish Poetry: A Critical Survey, 1955; (ed) W. Dunbar: Poems, 1958; (ed) John Dryden: Poems, 4 vols, 1958; (ed) Lindsay, Squyer Meldrum, 1959; (ed) Robert Burns: Poems and Songs, 1959; (ed) Dryden, The Works of Virgil, 1961; (ed with Helen Kinsley) Dryden, Absalom and Achitophel, 1961; (ed) John Dryden: Poetical Works, 1962; (ed) John Dryden: Selected Poems, 1963; (with J. T. Boulton) English Satiric Poetry: Dryden to Byron, 1966; (ed) J. Galt, Annals of the Parish, 1967; (ed) Robert Burns: Poems and Songs, 3 vols, 1968; (ed) The Oxford Book of Ballads, 1969; (textual editor) The Novels of Jane Austen, 5 vols, 1970–71; (ed with George Parfitt) Dryden's Criticism, 1970; (with Helen Kinsley) Dryden: The Critical Heritage, 1971; (ed) Alexander Carlyle of Iveresk: Anecdotes and Characters, 1973; Poems of W. Dunbar, 1979. Contribs to Encyclopædia Britannica, Review of English Studies, Medium Aevum, Modern Language Review, etc. *Recreations:* carpentry, gardening, folk-song. *Address:* 17 Elm Avenue, Beeston, Nottingham NG9 1BU. *T:* Nottingham 257438.
*Died 24 Aug.* 1984.

**KINTORE, 12th Earl of,** *cr* 1677; **James Ian Keith;** Lord Keith of Inverurie, 1677 (Scot.); Bt 1897; Baron 1925; Viscount Stonehaven 1938; CEng; AIStructE; Major, RM, Royal Marine Engineers; Member Royal Company of Archers; *b* 25 July 1908; *er s* of John Lawrence Baird, 1st Viscount Stonehaven, PC, GCMG, DSO, and Lady Ethel Sydney Keith-Falconer (later Countess of Kintore, 11th in line), *e d* of 9th Earl of Kintore; name changed from Baird to Keith, 1967; *S* to Viscountcy of Stonehaven, 1941, and to Earldom of Kintore, 1974; *m* 1935, Delia Virginia, *d* of William Loyd; two *s* one *d. Educ:* Eton; Royal School of Mines, London. UK Delegate to Council of Europe and Western European Union, 1954–64. Councillor, Grampian Region (Chm., Water Services Cttee), 1974–78. DL Kincardineshire, 1959; Vice-Lieut, 1965–76. *Heir: s* Master of Kintore, Lord Inverurie, *b* 22 Feb. 1939. *Address:* Glenton House, Rickarton, near Stonehaven, Kincardineshire. *T:* Stonehaven 63071. *Clubs:* Beefsteak, Caledonian.
*Died 1 Oct.* 1989.

**KIRBY, Sir Arthur (Frank),** GBE 1969 (KBE 1957); CMG 1945; FCIT; *b* Slough, 13 July 1899; *s* of George and Lily Maria Kirby; *m* 1935, Winifred Kate, *d* of Fred Bradley, Waterloo Park, Liverpool; one *d. Educ:* Sir William Borlase's Sch., Marlow; London Sch. of Economics. Entered Service GWR 1917; returned 1919 after serving with London Rifle Brigade and 2nd Rifle Brigade; special training for six years with GWR; entered Colonial Service, Asst Sec., Takoradi Harbour, Gold Coast, 1928; Traffic Manager, Gold Coast Railway, 1936; Asst Supt of the Line, Kenya and Uganda Railways and Harbours, 1938; Gen. Man., Palestine Railways and Ports Authority and Dir Gen. Hejaz Railway, 1942–48; Supt of the Line, E African Railways and Harbours, 1949–50; Asst Comr for Transport, E Africa High Commn, 1951–52; Actg Comr for Transport, 1952–53; Gen. Manager, East African Railways and Harbours, 1953–57; Commissioner for East Africa, London, 1958–63; Chairman: British Transport Docks Board, 1963–67; Nat. Ports Council, 1967–71; Pres., Shipping and Forwarding Agents Inst., 1966. Vice-Pres., Royal Commonwealth Society (Dep. Chm., 1965–68); Dep. Chm., Gt Ormond Street Children's Hosp., 1963–69; Governor, National Hosp. for Nervous Diseases, 1966–69; Mem. Council, Royal Society of Arts, 1966–71. Chm., Palestine Assoc.; Vice-Pres., British Inst. in Eastern Africa. OStJ. Liveryman,

Worshipful Co. of Barber Surgeons, 1977–. *Address:* 6 Baltimore Court, The Drive, Hove, E Sussex BN3 3PR.
*Died 13 Jan.* 1983.

**KIRBY, Jack Howard,** CBE 1972; Chairman, International Tanker Owners Pollution Federation, 1968–73; Chairman, Shell Tankers (UK) Ltd, 1963–72; Managing Director, Shell International Marine Ltd, 1959–72; Director, Shell International Petroleum Co. Ltd, 1969–72; *b* 1 Feb. 1913; *s* of late Group Captain Frank Howard Kirby, VC, CBE and late Kate Kirby; *m* 1940, Emily Colton; one *s. Educ:* Sir Roger Manwood's Sch., Sandwich. Joined Shell, 1930, retired 1972; in USA with Shell, 1937–52, incl. secondment to British Shipping Mission and British Petroleum Mission, Washington, DC, 1940–46. Chm., Lights Adv. Cttee, 1958–78. Pres., Chamber of Shipping of the UK, 1971–72. Chevalier 1st Class, Order of St Olav, 1968. *Recreations:* golf, fishing, gardening, bridge. *Address:* 1 Beaufort House, Hillside Park, Sunningdale, Berks SL5 9RP. *T:* Ascot 21429. *Club:* Berkshire Golf.
*Died 27 Dec.* 1989.

**KIRBY, Walter,** CIE 1945; BSc (Birmingham); retired; *b* 6 Dec 1891; *m* 1st, 1920, Lily Watkins (*d* 1957); two *d*; 2nd, 1961, Violet Eveline Harris. *Educ:* Birmingham Univ. (BSc 1919). Past Pres. Mining Geological and Metallurgical Institute of India. Joined Dept of Mines in India as Junior Inspector of Mines, 1921; Senior Inspector, 1925–38; Chief Inspector of Mines in India, 1938–46; retired, 1946. *Address:* 4 Haddington Street, The Range, Toowoomba, Queensland 4350, Australia. *Died 4 June* 1981.

**KIRCHNER, Bernard Joseph,** CBE 1944; *b* 1894; *er s* of Alexander and Teresa Kirchner; *m* 1st, 1924, Vivienne Mary (*d* 1949), *y d* of late Lt-Col T. P. Ffrench, IA, and step *d* of late Ray Knight, ICS; two *d*; 2nd, 1957, Margaret Jane, *o d* of late T. M. Upton, and widow of G. W. F. Brown. *Educ:* Imperial Coll. of Science, London Univ. European War, 1914–18, France and Flanders, Artists' Rifles, South Staffs Regt and RAF (wounded, 1914 Star, Gen. Service and Victory Medals). Joined The Statesman, Calcutta, 1922; Mgr The Englishman, 1928–30; Man. Editor Delhi office of The Statesman, 1932–41, and 1946–48; Dir, 1940; London Agent, The Statesman, 1948–54; Mem. of Nat. Service Advisory Cttee, Delhi, 1939–41; Chief Press Adviser, Govt of India, 1941–44; Vice-Chm. Ex-Services Assoc., India, 1946; Delhi Corresp., The Times, 1946–47. Mem. Council of Commonwealth Press Union; Pres. London Assoc. of British Empire Newspapers Overseas, 1953–54. Silver Jubilee Medal, 1935. *Address:* 7 Bell Road, East Molesey, Surrey.
*Died 18 Jan.* 1982.

**KIRK, James Balfour,** CMG 1941; MB, ChB; FRCP; DPH; DTM and H; retired; *b* 7 April 1893; *s* of John A. G. Kirk, Falkirk, and Jessie Y. Rintoul, also of Falkirk; *m* 1917, Jane C., *d* of Hume Purdie, LDS, Edinburgh; three *d. Educ:* Falkirk High Sch.; George Watson's Coll., Edinburgh; Edinburgh Univ. (Vans Dunlop Scholar). Private, 9th Bn Royal Scots, Aug.–Dec. 1914; 2nd Lt, RFA 1914–16; Lt RAMC, 1917–20 (1914–15 Star, Victory and General Service Medals); Medical Officer of Health, Port Louis, Mauritius, 1922–26; Acting Dir, Medical and Health Dept, Mauritius, 1926–27; Dir, Medical and Health Dept, Mauritius, 1927–41; Dir of Medical Services, Gold Coast, 1941–44; Dir, Health Div. Greece Mission, UNRRA, 1945; Chief Medical Officer, Central Headquarters, Displaced Persons Operation UNRRA, Germany, Aug. 1945–Feb. 1946; Temp. MO, Min. of Health, 1946–62. *Publications:* Public Health Practice in the Tropics, 1928; Hints on Equipment and Health for Intending Residents in the Tropics, 1926; Practical Tropical Sanitation, 1936; numerous articles on public health and medical subjects. *Recreations:* gardening, photography. *Address:* 16 Brook Lane, Haywards Heath, West Sussex RH16 1SG. *T:* Lindfield 2185.
*Died 26 March* 1984.

**KIRKALDY, Prof. John Francis,** DSc (London); FGS; Emeritus Professor of Geology, University of London, since 1974; *b* 14 May 1908; *o s* of late James and Rose Edith Kirkaldy, Sutton, Surrey; *m* 1935, Dora Muriel (*d* 1990), *e d* of late Grimshaw Heyes Berry, Enfield, Middlesex; four *d. Educ:* Felsted Sch.; King's Coll., London. 1st Cl. Special Hons BSc (Geol.) 1929; MSc 1932; DSc 1946. Demonstrator in Geology, King's Coll., 1929–33; Asst Lectr in Geology, University Coll., London, 1933–36; Lectr in Geology, King's Coll., London, 1936–47. War Service with Meteorological Branch, RAF, Sqdn Ldr, 1939–45. Reader in Geology and Head of Dept, Queen Mary Coll., 1947–62; Prof. of Geology and Head of Dept, QMC, 1962–74. FKC 1970; Fellow, Queen Mary College, 1976. Daniel Pidgeon Fund, Geol. Soc., 1935; Foulerton Award, Geologists' Assoc., 1947. *Publications:* Outline of Historical Geology (with A. K. Wells), 1948 (and subseq. edns); General Principles of Geology, 1954 (and subseq. edns); Rocks and Minerals in Colour, 1963. Papers in Quart. Jl Geol. Soc.; Proc. Geol. Assoc., Geol. Mag., etc. *Recreation:* gardening. *Address:* Stone House, Byfield Road, Chipping Warden, Banbury, Oxon OX17 1LE. *T:* Chipping

Warden (029586) 689. *Club:* Geological Society's.
*Died* 1 *July* 1990.

**KIRKLEY, Sir (Howard) Leslie,** Kt 1977; CBE 1966; Chairman, Public Voice Communications Ltd, since 1979; *b* Manchester, 1911; *m* 1st, Elsie May (*née* Rothwell) (*d* 1956); 2nd, Constance Nina Mary (*née* Bannister-Jones); three *s* two *d*. *Educ:* Manchester Central High Sch. Associate of the Chartered Inst. of Secretaries (ACIS). Worked in local government in Manchester until War of 1939-45 (during which he was engaged in relief work in Europe). Founder and Hon. Sec. of the Leeds and District European Relief Cttee; Gen. Sec., Oxford Cttee for Famine Relief, 1951-61; Dir, Oxfam, 1961-74. Mem., Bd of Crown Agents, 1974-80. Chief Exec., Voluntary and Christian Service Trust, 1979-84; Exec. Chm., Action Aid Internat. 1983-84; Exec. Dir, Overseas Develt Action Aid, 1984-85. Pres., Gen. Conf., Internat. Council of Voluntary Agencies, 1968-71, Chm., Governing Board, 1972-76; Vice-Chm., 1974-77, Chm., 1977-81, Disasters Emergency Cttee. Chairman: Standing Conf. on Refugees, 1974-81 (Vice-Chm., 1969-74); UK Standing Conf. on 2nd UN Develt Decade, 1975-76; Chairperson, British Volunteer Programme, 1981-84; Vice-Chairman: Voluntary Cttee for Overseas Aid and Develt, 1973-76; British Refugee Council, 1981-87. Chairman: Cala Sona Enterprise, 1972-; Voluntary and Christian Service Housing Assoc., 1981-84; Help the Aged Housing Trust, 1982-85. Hon. MA: Oxford, 1969; Leeds, 1970; Bradford, 1974. Fellow, Manchester Polytechnic, 1971. Knight Comdr of the Order of St Sylvester (conferred by HH the Pope), 1963; holds other foreign decorations. *Address:* 25 Capel Close, Oxford OX2 7LA. *T:* Oxford 53167. *Club:* Royal Commonwealth Society.                              *Died* 9 *Jan.* 1989.

**KIRKMAN, Gen. Sir Sidney Chevalier,** GCB 1951 (KCB 1949; CB 1944); KBE 1945 (CBE 1943; OBE 1941); MC; retired; *b* 29 July 1895; *s* of late J. P. Kirkman, Bedford; *m* 1932, Amy Caroline Erskine Clarke; two *s*. *Educ:* Bedford Sch.; RMA, Woolwich. Served European War, 1914-18 (wounded twice, MC, despatches). Staff Coll., Camberley, 1931-32. Served War of 1939-45: Brig. RA, 8th Army, 1942; Comd 50 (N) Div., 1943; Comd British 13th Corps in Italy, 1944; GOC-in-C Southern Comd 1945; Comd 1 Corps BLA, 1945; Dep. Chief of Imperial Gen. Staff, 1945-47; Quartermaster-Gen. to the Forces, 1947-50; Mem. of Army Council, 1945-50; Col Comdt RA, 1947-57; Special Financial Representative in Germany, 1951-52; Dir Gen. of Civil Defence, 1954-60; Chm. Central Fire Brigades Advisory Council for England and Wales, 1957-60. Comdr, Legion of Merit (USA); Officier, Légion d'Honneur, Croix de Guerre (France). *Address:* 8 Courtenay Place, Lymington, Hants SO4 9NQ.            *Died* 5 *Nov.* 1982.

**KIRKWOOD, Sir Robert (Lucien Morrison),** KCMG 1972; Kt 1959; OJ 1974; Chairman, Sugar Manufacturers' Association of Jamaica, 1945-74; Chairman: West Indies Sugar Association, 1946-74; Citrus Growers Association, 1944-60; *b* Yeo, Fairy Cross, N Devon, 9 Jan. 1904; *e s* of late Major John Hendley Morrison Kirkwood, DSO, sometime MP for Southend Div. of Essex, and Gertrude Agnes, *e d* of Sir Robert Park Lyle, 1st and last Bt, Eaton Place, SW1; *m* 1925, Sybil Attenborough (*d* 1977), Hartford House, Nottingham; one *s* two *d*. *Educ:* Wixenford; Harrow; Le Rosey (Switzerland). Joined Tate & Lyle, 1922; Managing Dir, The United Sugar Company, 1929-36; Dir Yorks Sugar Co., 1928-36 and Central Sugar Co. (Peterborough), 1929-36; Joined Board of Tate & Lyle, 1935; Man. Dir, West Indies Sugar Co., Jamaica, 1937; Dir, Caroni Ltd, Trinidad, 1937. MLC Jamaica, 1942-62. Rep. Jamaica on Colonial Sugar Cttee, 1937-. Rep. West Indies at Internat. Sugar Confs, 1953, 1956, 1958, 1961, 1965, 1968, 1973. Pres. Sugar Club of New York, 1965-66; Chm. International Sugar Council, 1966. Mem. various Govt Bds and Cttees in Jamaica. Liveryman, Grocers' Co., 1935-. *Publication:* a Farm Production Policy for Jamaica, 1967. *Recreations:* gardening, golf and good food. *Address:* Three Kings, Sandwich, Kent. *T:* Sandwich 612221. *Clubs:* White's, Queen's, St George's (Sandwich); The Brook (New York).                                           *Died* 6 *May* 1984.

**KIRTON, Robert James,** CBE 1963; MA, FIA; Director, Equity and Law Life Assurance Society, Ltd, 1944-77 (General Manager, 1939-66; Actuary, 1947-66); Chairman, Equity and Law Unit Trust Managers Ltd, 1969-77; *b* 13 July 1901; *er s* of late Albert William Kirton, Ealing, Middlesex; *m* 1931, Isabel Susan, *y d* of late Henry Hosegood, JP, Bristol; two *s* two *d*. *Educ:* Merchant Taylors' Sch.; Peterhouse, Cambridge. Scottish Widows' Fund and Life Assurance Soc., 1923-32; Scottish Amicable Life Assce Soc., 1932-38; Equity and Law Life Assce Soc. Ltd, 1938-77. Chairman: Life Offices' Assoc., 1945-47; Royal UK Beneficent Assoc., 1958-74 (Vice-Pres., 1981-); Nat. Council of Social Service: Hon. Treas., 1962-72; Vice-Pres., 1972-80; Trustee, Charities Official Investment Fund, 1962-77; Governor, London Sch. of Economics, 1963-87; Vice-Chm., St Peter's Hosp., 1967-75; Mem. Council, Bath Univ., 1967-75; Mem., Buitengewoon Lid, Actuarial Genootschap, Holland, 1949. Silver Medal, Institute of Actuaries, 1966. *Publications:* contrib. Jl Inst. Actuaries, Trans. Faculty of Actuaries

(with A. T. Haynes). *Recreations:* walking, ski-ing and squash rackets. *Address:* Byron Cottage, North End Avenue, NW3 7HP. *T:* 01-455 0464. *Club:* Athenæum.          *Died* 7 *March* 1988.

**KIRWAN-TAYLOR, Harold George,** MA, MB, BCh Cantab; FRCS; *b* 14 April 1895; *s* of Alfred George Taylor and Mary Kirwan; *m* 1926, Elizabeth Mary (marr. diss. 1946), *d* of late J. R. J. Neild; one *s* three *d*. *Educ:* Epsom Coll.; Trinity Coll., Cambridge. Hon. Consulting Obstetric and Gynæcological Surgeon: St George's Hospital; War Memorial Hospital, Woolwich; Hon. Consulting Gynæcological Surgeon, Royal National Orthopædic Hospital; Hon. Cons. Surg., The General Lying-in Hospital, Lambeth; late Lectr on Obstetrics and Gynæcology, St George's Hospital; late Obstetric Consultant, Borough of Woolwich and Bexley Heath; late Cons. in Gynaecology, Min. of Pensions. Late Examiner: Univ. of Cambridge; Univ. of Durham; Soc. of Apothecaries; Conjoint Board and Central Midwives Board. Served European War, 1914-18, as Surgeon Probationer RNVR and later as Surgeon Royal Navy. Served 1940-43, MEF (despatches), as Lieut-Col, with short period as Temporary Consulting Surgeon, MEF; 1943-45, service in BNAF and Italy, retiring with rank of Hon. Col AMS. Late Prospective Conservative Candidate E Woolwich and Royal Borough of Kingston. Freeman of City of London. *Publications:* various articles in medical journals. *Recreations:* shooting, fishing, riding, golf, farming. *Address:* Denne, Mersham, near Ashford, Kent. *T:* Aldington 278. *Club:* Boodle's.          *Died* 2 *Dec.* 1981.

**KISSEN, Hon. Lord; Manuel Kissen;** a Senator of the College of Justice in Scotland since 1963; *b* 2 May 1912; *er s* of Lewis and Annie Kissen; *m* 1964, Mrs Victoria Solomons (*d* 1976), widow of Professor Edward Solomons, New York, USA. *Educ:* Hutchesons' Boys' Grammar Sch., Glasgow; Glasgow Univ. (MA, LLB). Solicitor, 1934. Served with RAF, 1940-45 (despatches). Admitted to Faculty of Advocates, 1946; Standing Junior Counsel in Scotland to Min. of Labour and to Min. of Nat. Insurance, 1948-55. QC (Scotland) 1955. Chm. National Health Service Tribunal (Scotland), 1962-63; Chm. Law Reform Cttee for Scotland, 1964-70, Mem., Restrictive Practices Court, 1966-; Chm. Scottish Valuation Adv. Council, 1967-71. Mem., Parole Bd for Scotland, 1975-1980. Hon. LLD Glasgow, 1968. *Address:* 22 Braid Avenue, Edinburgh EH10 6EE. *T:* 031-447 3000. *Club:* Scottish Arts (Edinburgh).
*Died* 28 *May* 1981.

**KISTIAKOWSKY, Prof. Emeritus George Bogdan;** Professor of Chemistry, Harvard University, 1938-71 (Chairman, 1947-50), Emeritus since 1971; Special Assistant to the President of the USA for Science and Technology, 1959-61; Vice-President, National Academy of Sciences, 1965-72; *b* Kiev, Ukraine, 18 Nov. 1900; *s* of Bogdan Kistiakowsky and Mary Berenstam; came to USA, 1926; naturalized citizen, 1933; *m* 1st, 1926, Hildegard Moebius (marr. diss. 1942); one *d*; 2nd, 1945, Irma E. Shuler (marr. diss.1962); 3rd, 1962, Elaine Mahoney. *Educ:* University of Berlin (DPhil). Fellow and Staff Mem. Chem. Dept, Princeton, 1926-30; Asst Prof., 1930-33, Associate Prof., 1933-38, Harvard. On leave from Harvard to: Nat. Defense Research Cttee, 1941-43; Los Alamos Lab., 1944-46. Asst to the President for Sci. and Technol., 1959-61; Member: President's Science Adv. Cttee, 1957-64; Gen. Adv. Cttee to US Arms Control and Disarmament Agency, 1962-68. Mem. National Acad. of Sciences, etc; Hon. Fellow, Chem. Soc., London; Foreign Mem. Royal Society, London, 1959. Hon. DSc: Harvard Univ., 1955; Williams Coll., 1958; Oxford Univ., 1959; University of Pennsylvania, 1960; University of Rochester, 1960; Carnegie Inst. of Technology, 1961; Princeton Univ., 1962; Case Institute, 1962; Columbia Univ., 1967. Medal for Merit, USA, 1946; King's Medal for Services in the Cause of Freedom, 1948; Willard Gibbs Medal, 1960; Medal of Freedom (awarded by Pres. Eisenhower), 1961; George Ledlie Prize, Harvard Univ., 1961; Nat. Medal of Science (awarded by Pres. Johnson), 1967; Peter Debye Award, 1968; Theodore William Richards, 1968; Priestley Medal, 1972, and several other awards. *Publications:* Photochemical Processes, 1929; A Scientist at the White House, 1976; numerous articles. *Address:* 12 Oxford Street, Cambridge, Mass 02138, USA. *T:* University 617-495-4083.                       *Died* 7 *Dec.* 1982.

**KITCHIN, John Leslie Harlow,** CB 1981; DipArch; ARIBA; Chief Architect (Under Secretary), Department of Education and Science, since 1975; *b* 11 Oct. 1924; *o s* of late Eric J. H. Kitchin and Muriel Harper; *m* 1956, Madeleine, *d* of late Fernand and Renée Coutant, Reims; two *s* one *d*. *Educ:* Wolverhampton Grammar Sch.; Worcester Coll., Oxford; Brimingham Sch. of Architecture (1947-52). Served with RAF, Bomber Comd, 1943-47. Joined Min. of Educn Develt Gp as Asst Architect, 1952; designed schools and buildings for handicapped children, youth, community; Dept of Educn and Science, 1964-: Head of Building Productivity Gp, 1965; Asst Chief Architect, 1967. *Publications:* various DES building bulletins; articles in architectural and educnl press. *Recreation:* landscape painting. *Address:* 5A Kensington Mansions, Trebovir Road, SW5.                                       *Died* 24 *Jan.* 1982.

**KITTO, Prof. Humphrey Davy Findley,** FBA 1955; FRSL 1957; Professor of Greek, University of Bristol, 1944–62, Emeritus since 1962; *b* 1897; *s* of late H. D. Kitto, Stroud, Glos; *m* 1928, Ann Kraft (*d* 1981); one *s* one *d*. *Educ:* Crypt Grammar Sch., Glos; St John's Coll., Cambridge. Asst to Professor of Greek and then Lecturer in Greek, University of Glasgow, 1921–44. Visiting Prof., Cornell Univ., 1954; Brandeis Univ., 1959; Sather Professor, University of California, 1960–61; Ziskind Prof., Brandeis Univ., 1962–63; Regents' Professor, University of California (Santa Barbara), 1963–64. Hon. D-ès-lettres Aix-Marseille, 1961; Hon. DLitt Glasgow, 1976. *Publications:* In the Mountains of Greece, 1933; Greek Tragedy, 1939, 3rd edn 1961; The Greeks (Pelican), 1951; Form and Meaning in Drama, 1956; Sophocles: Dramatist and Philospher, 1958; Sophocles' Antigone, Electra and Oedipus Rex (translated into English verse), 1962; Poiesis, 1966; articles and reviews in Classical journals. *Recreations:* music and Greek. *Address:* 9 Southfield Road, Bristol BS6 6AX.
*Died 21 Jan. 1982.*

**KLEFFENS, Eelco Nicolaas van;** Netherlands Minister of State (life), 1950; *b* Heerenveen (Netherlands), 17 Nov. 1894; *m* 1935, Margaret Helen Horstman. *Educ:* University of Leyden. Adjusted shipping questions arising out of European War for Netherlands, 1919; Mem. Secretariat League of Nations, 1919–21; Sec. to directorate of Royal Dutch Petroleum Co., 1921–23; deputy-chief of legal section, Netherlands Ministry for Foreign Affairs, 1923–27; deputy-chief of diplomatic section, 1927–29; chief of diplomatic section, 1929–39; appointed Minister to Switzerland and Netherlands representative with League of Nations, 1939; Minister for Foreign Affairs of the Netherlands, 1939–46; Minister without portfolio and Netherlands representative on Security Council and Economic and Social Council of UN, 1946–47; Netherlands Ambassador to the United States of America, 1947–50; Minister to Portugal, 1950–56; Permanent Representative of Netherlands on NATO Council and OEEC (Paris), 1956–58; Chief Representative in UK of High Authority of European Coal and Steel Community, 1958–67; Pres., IX Session United Nations General Assembly. Pres., Arbitral Tribunal established under Bonn-Paris Agreements, 1952–54, by France, Germany, UK, USA, 1957–70. Holds several hon. degrees; Corresponding Mem., Netherlands and Portuguese Academy of Sciences; Mem. of Curatorium, Hague Academy of International Law, 1947–68; Hon. Member, Amer. Soc. of Internat. Law. Grand Cross: Orange-Nassau (Netherl.); Legion of Honour (France); St Gregory (Holy See); Christ (Portugal), *et al. Publications:* The Relations between the Netherlands and Japan in the Light of International Law, 1605–1919, 1919; The Rape of the Netherlands, 1940; Sovereignty in International Law, 1953; Hispanic Law until the end of the Middle Ages, 1968; Belevenissen (Experiences), vol. I, 1980; articles in periodicals. *Address:* Casal de Santa Filomena, Almoçagême, Colares, Portugal. *Clubs:* Haagsche (The Hague); Eça de Queiroz (Lisbon); Century (New York).
*Died 17 June 1983.*

**KLEINWORT, Sir Alexander Santiago,** 2nd Bt, *cr* 1909; *b* 31 Oct. 1892; *e s* of Sir Alexander D. Kleinwort, 1st Bt; *S* father, 1935; *m* 1938, Yvonne, *d* of late John Bloch. *Educ:* St John's Coll., Oxford. *Heir: nephew* Kenneth Drake Kleinwort [ *b* 28 May 1935; *m* 1st, 1959, Lady Davina Rose Pepys (*d* 1973), *d* of 7th Earl of Cottenham; one *s* one *d*; 2nd, 1973, Madeleine Hamilton, *e d* of Ralph Taylor; two *s* one *d*]. *Address:* 1 Third Avenue, Hove, East Sussex. *T:* Hove 71752.
*Died 26 March 1983.*

**KNEALE, Prof. William Calvert,** FBA 1950; White's Professor of Moral Philosophy, University of Oxford, and Fellow of Corpus Christi College, 1960–66; *b* 22 June 1906; *s* of late William Kneale; *m* 1938, Martha Hurst, Fellow of Lady Margaret Hall, Oxford; one *s* one *d*. *Educ:* Liverpool Institute; Brasenose Coll., Oxford (Classical Scholar). Senior Hulme Scholar, Brasenose Coll., 1927, studied in Freiburg and Paris; Asst in Mental Philosophy, University of Aberdeen, 1929; Asst Lecturer in Philosophy, Armstrong Coll., Newcastle upon Tyne, 1931; Lecturer in Philosophy, Exeter Coll., Oxford, 1932; Fellow, 1933–60; Senior Tutor, 1945–50; Emeritus Fellow, 1960. War of 1939–45, temp. Civil Servant, Ministry of Shipping (later War Transport). Vice-Pres., British Acad., 1971–72. Hon. Fellow, Brasenose Coll., Oxford, 1952, and Corpus Christi Coll., Oxford, 1966. Hon. LLD Aberdeen, 1960; Hon. DLitt: Durham, 1966; St Andrews, 1973. *Publications:* Probability and Induction, 1949; (with M. Kneale) The Development of Logic, 1962; On Having a Mind, 1962; articles in Mind, Proceedings of Aristotelian Society, etc. *Address:* 4 Bridge End, Grassington, near Skipton, North Yorks BD23 5NH. *T:* Grassington (0756) 752710.
*Died 24 June 1990.*

**KNELL, Rt. Rev. Eric Henry,** MA Oxon; *b* 1 April 1903; *s* of Edward Henry and Edith Helen Knell; unmarried. *Educ:* Trinity College, Oxford. Assistant Curate of St Barnabas, Southfields, 1928; Domestic Chaplain to Bishop of Lincoln, 1933; in charge of Trinity College, Oxford, Mission in Stratford, E15, 1936; Vicar of Emmanuel, Forest Gate, 1941; Vicar of Christ Church, Reading,

1945; Archdeacon of Berkshire, 1955–67; Suffragan Bishop of Reading, 1955–72; Assistant Bishop, Diocese of Oxford, 1972–75. *Address:* College of St Barnabas, Lingfield, Surrey.
*Died 5 Jan. 1987.*

**KNIGHT, Prof. Bert Cyril James Gabriel,** DSc London; Professor of Microbiology, University of Reading, 1951–69, Emeritus since 1969; *b* 4 Feb. 1904; *s* of late Cyril Fennel Knight and Kate Knight (*née* Gabriel); *m* 1st, 1929, Doris, *d* of late G. D. Kemp; one *d*; 2nd, 1944, Frideswide, *d* of late Dr H. F. Stewart; two *s* two *d* (and one *s* decd). *Educ:* Reigate Grammar Sch.; University Coll., London. BSc (Chemistry), University Coll., London, 1925; MSc 1927; DSc 1938. Worked on problems of bacterial physiology at London Hosp., 1929–34, and at Middlesex Hosp., 1934–38, in Medical Research Council Unit for Bacterial Chemistry. Halley Stewart Research Fellow, 1934–38; Biochemist, Lister Institute of Preventive Medicine, Serum Dept, Elstree, 1939–43; Wellcome Research Laboratories, Beckenham (Depts of Biochemistry and Bateriology), 1943–50. Joint Editor, Journal of General Microbiology, 1946–70. Visiting Commonwealth Prof., New York Univ. Medical Sch., Nov. 1947–Jan. 1948. *Publications:* Bacterial Nutrition, 1936; Growth Factors in Microbiology, 1945; (trans. with J. Stewart) Stendhal's Life of Henry Brulard, 1959. Papers in: Biochem. Jl, British Journal of Experimental Pathology, Journal Chem. Soc., Jl Gen. Microbiol., Bull. Soc. Chim. biol., etc. Harvey Lecture, NY, 1947; William Henry Welch Lecture, NY, 1948. *Recreations:* 18th–20th century French and English literature, walking. *Address:* 28 Park Parade, Cambridge CB5 8AL. *Died 29 Oct. 1981.*

**KNIGHT, Charles,** RWS 1935 (VPRWS 1961–64; ARWS 1933); ROI 1933; Landscape Painter and Designer; Vice-Principal, Brighton College of Art and Crafts, 1959–67, retired; *b* 27 Aug. 1901; *s* of Charles and Evelyn Mary Knight; *m* 1934, Leonora Vasey (*d* 1970); one *s*. Art training, Brighton Coll. of Art; Royal Academy Schools, London (Turner Gold Medal); works in permanent collections, London, British Museum, Victoria and Albert Museum, Sheffield, Leeds, Hull, Oxford, Brighton, Hove, Eastbourne, Preston, etc; regular exhibitor RA, 1924–65. Illustrated monograph by Michael Brockway, 1952. *Address:* Chettles, 34 Beacon Road, Ditchling, Sussex. *T:* Hassocks 3998. *Died 15 May 1990.*

**KNIGHT, Eric John Percy Crawford L.;** *see* Lombard Knight.

**KNIGHT, Esmond Pennington;** actor; *b* 4 May 1906; 3rd *s* of Francis and Bertha Knight; *m* 1st, 1929, Frances Clare (marr. diss.); one *d*; 2nd, 1946, Nora Swinburne. *Educ:* Willington Prep. Sch.; Westminster. Made first appearance on stage at Pax Robertson's salon in Ibsen's Wild Duck, 1925; Old Vic., 1925–27; Birmingham Repertory Co., 1927–28; Contraband, Prince's Theatre; To What Red Hell, Wyndham's, 1928; The Children's Theatre; Fashion, Kingsway; Maya, Studio des Théâtres des Champs-Elysées, Paris, 1929; Art and Mrs Bottle, Royalty; Hamlet, Queen's, 1930; Salome, Gate; Waltzes from Vienna, Alhambra, 1931; Wild Violets, Drury Lane, 1932; Three Sisters, Drury Lane; Streamline, Palace, 1934; Wise Tomorrow, Lyric; Van Gogh, Arts Theatre Club; Night Must Fall, Cambridge Theatre, 1936; The Insect Play, Little; The King and Mistress Shore, Little, 1937; Crest of the Wave, Tour; Twelfth Night, Phœnix, 1938; in management with Wilson Barrett, King's, Hammersmith and Edinburgh, 1939; Peaceful Inn, Duke of York's; Midsummer Night's Dream, Open Air, 1940. Joined RNVR (HMS King Alfred, Drake, Excellent, Prince of Wales); discharged from Navy as a result of being blinded in HMS Prince of Wales during action with Bismarck, 1941. Returned to stage in Crisis in Heaven, March 1945; shared lead with Evelyn Laye in The Three Waltzes, Princes. Season of plays with travelling Repertory Theatre, King's, Hammersmith, 1946; The Relapse, 1947; Memorial Theatre, Stratford-on-Avon, 1948–49; Caroline (by Maugham), Arts Theatre Club; Old Vic Co., Edinburgh Festival, 1950, in Bartholomew Fair by Ben Jonson; Who is Sylvia, Criterion, 1950; Sir Laurence Olivier's Festival Season, St James's Theatre, 1951; Heloise, Duke of York's; Montserrat, Lyric; Bermuda Festival (Bermuda); Emperor's Clothes (New York); Age of Consent; Bell, Book and Candle, Phœnix, 1955; The Caine Mutiny, Hippodrome, 1956; The Country Wife, Adelphi, 1957; The Russian, Lyric, Hammersmith, 1958; A Piece of Silver (Cheltenham), 1960; The Lady from the Sea, Queen's, 1961; Becket, Taming of the Shrew, Aldwych, 1961; Two Stars for Comfort, Garrick, 1962; last Old Vic Season, 1962–63; Season, Mermaid, 1965; Edinburgh Festival: Winter's Tale, and Trojan Women 1966; Getting Married, Strand, 1967; Greenwich Theatre: Martin Luther King, 1969; Spithead, 1969; The Servants and the Snow, 1970; Mister, Duchess, 1971; Family Reunion, '69 Theatre Co., Manchester, 1973, Vaudeville, 1979; The Cocktail Party, '69 Theatre Co., Manchester, 1975; Loves Old Sweet Song, Greenwich, 1976; Three Sisters, Cambridge, 1976; Henry V and Agincourt, The Archer's Tale, Open Air Theatre, 1976; Crime and Punishment, Royal Exchange, Manchester, and City of Munster Fest., 1978; Family Reunion, Royal Exchange, Manchester, The Round House and Vaudeville, 1979; Hamlet, Young Vic, 1982; Moby Dick, Royal Exchange, Manchester, 1983; The Devils, RSC,

1984. *Films:* Romany Love, 77 Park Lane, The Ringer, Pagliacci, Waltzes from Vienna, Black Roses (Ufa, Berlin), What Men Live By, The Bermondsey Kid, The Blue Squadron, Girls Will Be Boys, Dandy Dick, Someday, Crime Unlimited, Contraband, The Silver Fleet, Half-Way House, King Henry V, A Canterbury Tale, Black Narcissus, Hamlet, Red Shoes, Gone to Earth, The River, 1950, Helen of Troy (Rome), 1954, The Dark Avenger, Ratcliffe in Olivier's Richard III, The Sleeping Prince, On Secret Service, Battle of the V1; Sink the Bismarck; The Spy Who Came in From the Cold; Anne of the Thousand Days; Where's Jack, 1968; The Boy who turned Yellow; The Yellow Dog; Robin and Marian, 1975; The Element of Crime, 1985. Assisted in making several Natural History films. *Television:* has appeared frequently on BBC and Independent Television, notably in Dickens and Ibsen; Dr Finlay's Casebook; Elizabeth I; The Pallisers; Fall of Eagles; History of the English-speaking Peoples; Shades of Greene; Ballet Shoes; Quiller; I Claudius; 1900: Voices from the Past; Kilvert's Diaries; Supernatural; Romeo and Juliet; Rebecca; Nelson; The Borgias; Troilus and Cressida; My Cousin Rachel; Drake's Venture; King Lear; The Grassless Grave; The Invisible Man; Blott on the Landscape; Sleeping Murder. Also tours with his one man show: Agincourt—The Archer's Tale. *Publications:* Seeking the Bubble (Autobiography), 1943; Story in Blackwood's, Jan. 1942; various articles in daily and weekly Press. *Recreation:* painting. *Club:* Savage.                                                      *Died* 23 *Feb.* 1987.

**KNIGHT, Prof. (George Richard) Wilson,** CBE 1968; MA Oxon; FRSL; FIAL; Professor of English Literature, Leeds University, 1956–62, then Emeritus (Reader in English Literature, Leeds University, 1946–56); *b* 19 Sept. 1897; *s* of George Knight and Caroline L. Jackson; brother of late W. F. Jackson Knight; unmarried. *Educ:* Dulwich Coll.; St Edmund Hall, Oxford. Served European War, Middle East; Master at Seaford House, Littlehampton, 1920, and St Peter's, Seaford, 1921; St Edmund Hall, 1922–23; Honour Sch. of English Language and Literature, 1923; Chess, Oxford *v* Cambridge, 1923; Master at Hawtreys, Westgate-on-Sea, 1923–25, and Dean Close Sch., Cheltenham, 1925–31; Chancellors' Prof. of English, Trinity Coll., University of Toronto, 1931–40; Master at Stowe, Buckingham, 1941–46. Stage: Shakespearian productions at Hart House Theatre, Toronto, 1932–40; produced and acted in: Hamlet, Rudolf Steiner Hall, London, 1935; This Sceptred Isle, Westminster Theatre, London, 1941; productions (Agamemnon, Athalie, Timon of Athens) and performances (Timon, Lear, Othello, Shylock) at Leeds Univ., 1946–60; Shakespeare's Dramatic Challenge, Northcott Theatre, Exeter, 1975 and 1976, and various other centres, 1976–82; including World Shakespeare Congress, Washington, 1976, Video-tape Yeovil Coll., 1979, and Indiana Univ., 1982. Lectures and lecture recitals since 1951: Cambridge (Clark Lectures); Nottingham (Byron Foundn Lecture); also Canada, S Africa, USA and W Indies. BBC talks and readings on Shakespeare and Byron, 1963–64 and tape recordings (USA); joint-petitioner, Byron Memorial (Westminster Abbey, 1969); shareholder, Byron Soc. Jl, 1972. Sculpted by Robert Russin, USA, 1975, Kenneth Carter, Exeter, 1975 and Peter Thursby, Exeter, 1980. Mem., Internat. Adv. Cttee, World Shakespeare Congress, Vancouver, 1971; Powys Centenary, Cambridge, 1972. Pres., Devonshire Assoc., 1971; Pres.-elect, SW of England Shakespeare Fest. Trust; Hon. Vice-Pres., Spiritualist Assoc. of Great Britain, 1955; Hon. Life Pres., Dulwich Coll. Literary Soc., 1971; Pres., Powys Soc., 1981; Hon. Pres., Interdiscipline Soc. (USA), 1980. Hon. Fellow St Edmund Hall, Oxford, 1965; Hon. LittD Sheffield, 1966; Hon. DLitt Exon, 1968. Hon. Mem., Mark Twain Soc., 1976–. Hon. Chm., 1980–. *Publications:* Myth and Miracle, 1929; The Wheel of Fire, 1930; The Imperial Theme, 1931; The Shakespearian Tempest, 1932; The Christian Renaissance, 1933; Principles of Shakespearian Production, 1936; Atlantic Crossing, 1936; The Burning Oracle, 1939; This Sceptred Isle, 1940; The Starlit Dome, 1941; Chariot of Wrath, 1942; The Olive and the Sword, 1944; The Dynasty of Stowe, 1945; Hiroshima, 1946; The Crown of Life, 1947; Christ and Nietzsche, 1948; Lord Byron: Christian Virtues, 1952; Laureate of Peace, 1954; The Last of the Incas, 1954 (play, first prod. Sheffield, 1954; BBC 1974); The Mutual Flame, 1955; Lord Byron's Marriage, 1957; The Sovereign Flower, 1958; The Golden Labyrinth, 1962; Ibsen, 1962; Shakespearian Production, 1964; The Saturnian Quest, 1965; Byron and Shakespeare, 1966; Shakespeare and Religion, 1967; Poets of Action, 1967; Gold-Dust, 1968; Neglected Powers, 1971; (ed) W. F. Jackson Knight, Elysion, 1970; Jackson Knight: a biography, 1975; Vergil and Shakespeare, 1977; Shakespeare's Dramatic Challenge, 1977; Symbol of Man, 1979; Shakespearean Dimensions, 1984; Klinton Top (novel), 1984; also contribs to: John Masefield, OM, ed G. Handley-Taylor, 1960; Powys to Knight (letters, ed Robert Blackmore), 1982; Times Literary Supplement, The Yorkshire Post, Review of English Studies, Essays in Criticism, Contemporary Review, etc. *Address:* Caroline House, Streatham Rise, Exeter EX4 4PE.                                     *Died* 20 *March* 1985.

**KNIGHT, Air Vice-Marshal Glen Albyn Martin,** CB 1961; CBE 1956; *b* 10 Sept. 1903; *e s* of Lt-Col G. A. Knight, OBE, VD, Melbourne,

Australia; *m* 1933, Janet Elizabeth Warnock (*d* 1982), *o d* of Peter Crawford, Dargavel, Dumfriesshire; two *d. Educ:* Scotch Coll., Melbourne, Australia; Melbourne Univ. MB, BS, 1927; Diploma in Laryngology and Otology (RCP & S), 1937. House Surgeon and Physician, Alfred and Children's Hospitals, Melbourne; joined Medical Branch, RAF, 1932. War Service: South Africa, Malta (despatches), Italy; PMO Desert Air Force. Principal Medical Officer, 2nd Tactical Air Force, 1956–57; Dep. Dir-Gen. of Medical Services, Royal Air Force, 1958–61, retired, 1961. QHS, 1959–61. *Recreation:* golf.                                               *Died* 2 *Feb.* 1990.

**KNIGHT, Henry Lougher;** DL; HM Lieutenant, Mid-Glamorgan, 1974–82; *b* 7 Aug. 1907; *e s* of Robert Lougher Knight; *m* 1932, Pamela, *d* of E. Colville Lyons; three *s. Educ:* Radley; Exeter Coll., Oxford. Regular Army, RA and RHA, invalided 1934. Chartered Land Agent, 1939; Chartered Surveyor, 1970. Pres., Chartered Land Agents Soc., 1964. JP Glam 1946; DL Glam 1957. *Address:* Tythegston Court, Bridgend, Mid-Glamorgan CF32 0NE. *T:* Porthcawl 3379. *Clubs:* Naval and Military, MCC; Cardiff and County (Cardiff).                                         *Died* 22 *March* 1986.

**KNIGHT, Very Rev. Marcus;** Dean of Exeter, 1960–72; *b* 11 Sept. 1903; *e s* of late Mark Knight, Insurance Manager; *m* 1931, Claire L. Hewett, MA, *o d* of late Charles H. Hewett, Bank Dir; two *s* (two *d* decd). *Educ:* Christ's Hosp.; University of London; Birkbeck Coll. (BA Hons); King's Coll. (BD Hons); Fellow of King's Coll.; Union Theological Seminary, New York; STM 1930. Curacies at Stoke Newington and Ealing; Priest-Vicar of Exeter Cathedral; Vicar of Cockington, 1936–40; Vicar of Nuneaton; RD of Atherstone, 1940–44; Examining Chaplain to Bishop of Coventry, 1944; Canon of St Paul's, 1944–60, Precentor, 1944–54, Chancellor, 1954–60. Hon. Sec. Church of England Council for Education, 1949–58; Chapter Treas., St Paul's, 1950–60; Church Commissioner, 1968–72. Hon. LLD Exeter, 1973. *Publications:* Spiritualism, Reincarnation, and Immortality, 1950; (part author) There's an Answer Somewhere, 1953; many papers and reviews. *Recreations:* reading, TV, walking. *Address:* 1 Execliff, Trefusis Terrace, Exmouth, Devon. *T:* Exmouth 271153.                           *Died* 19 *Dec.* 1988.

**KNIGHT, Wilson;** *see* Knight, G. R. W.

**KNOPF, Alfred A.;** publisher; Founding Chairman, Alfred A. Knopf, Inc., 1957–72, now Chairman Emeritus; *b* 12 Sept. 1892; *s* of Samuel Knopf and Ida Japhe; *m* 1st, 1916, Blanche Wolf (*d* 1966); one *s*; 2nd, 1967, Helen Norcross Hedrick. *Educ:* Mackenzie Sch.; Columbia Coll. AB (Columbia), 1912; Pres., Alfred A. Knopf, Inc., NYC, 1918–57 (Chm. of the Board, 1957, now Emeritus). Fellow, Amer. Acad. of Arts and Scis, 1976. Gold Medal, Amer. Inst. of Graphic Arts, 1950; C. A. Pugsley Gold Medal for conservation and preservation, 1960; Alexander Hamilton Medal, Columbia Coll., 1966; Francis Parkman Silver Medal, Soc. of Amer. Historians, 1974; Distinguished Service Award, Assoc. of Amer. Univ. Presses, 1975; Distinguished Achievement Awards: Drexel Univ. Library Sch. Alumni Assoc., 1975; Nat. Book Awards Cttee, 1975; Notable Achievement Award, Brandeis, 1977; Machado de Assis Medal, Brazilian Acad. of Letters, 1978; Gold Medal, Nat. Cowboy Hall of Fame, 1981; Annual Award for distinguished service to the arts, Amer. Acad. and Inst. of Arts and Letters, 1982; MacDowell Colony Special Award for lifelong support of writers and their work, 1984. Hon. LHD: Yale, 1958; Columbia, 1959; Bucknell, 1959; William and Mary, 1960; Lehigh, 1960; Michigan, 1969; Bates Coll., 1971; Univ. of Arizona, 1979; Hon. LLD (Brandeis), 1963; Hon. DLitt: Adelphi, 1966; Chattanooga, 1966; C. W. Post Center, Long Island Univ., 1973. *Address:* (home) Purchase, NY 10577, USA. *TA:* KSP KNOPF.
                                                        *Died* 11 *Aug.* 1984.

**KNOWLES, Maurice Baxendale,** CBE 1952; late Government Actuary's Department; retired 1953; *b* 6 Nov. 1893; *m* 1919, Lilla Shepherdson (decd); one *s* one *d. Educ:* Bridlington Sch. Served European War, 1914–18, in 3 London Regt and RFC. *Address:* Janvier, Moor Road, Langham, Colchester, Essex CO4 5NR.
                                                        *Died* 3 *June* 1988.

**KNOX, Henry Murray Owen,** OBE 1944; Senior Partner, Oxley, Knox & Co., Stock-jobbers, retired, 1965; *b* 5 March 1909; *yr s* of late Brig.-Gen. and Mrs H. O. Knox; *m* 1932, Violet Isabel (*d* 1962), *yr d* of late Mr and Mrs Frank Weare, The Dell, Tunbridge Wells, Kent; two *s*; *m* 1963, Mrs E. M. Davidson. *Educ:* Charterhouse; Trinity Coll., Oxford (MA Hons Law). Joined Oxley, Knox & Co., 1930; Partner, 1931. Served War of 1939–45, Queen's Own Royal West Kent Regt (despatches, wounded, OBE); various appts. Staff, ending in Col "A" Organisation, HQ 21 Army Group. Master, Skinners' Company, 1951–52 and 1972–73. Stock Exchange Council, 1948–64; Dep. Chm., Stock Exchange, 1958–64, Actg Chm., 1963–64. Governor, Tonbridge Sch.; formerly: Governor, Charterhouse Sch.; Chm. of Govs, Sutton's Hosp. in Charterhouse. *Recreations:* golf, gardening. *Address:* Brooklands, Manwood Road, Sandwich, Kent.                                         *Died* 10 *Dec.* 1986.

**KNOX, His Eminence Cardinal James Robert,** DD, DCL; President of the Pontifical Council for the Family, since 1981; President, Permanent Committee for International Eucharistic Congress, since 1973; *b* 2 March 1914; *s* of John Knox and Emily (*née* Walsh). *Educ:* St Ildephonsus Coll., New Norcia, Australia; Pontifical Urban College de Propadganda Fide, Rome. Priest, 1941; Vice Rector, Pontifical Urban College de Propaganda Fide, Rome, 1945–48; attached to Secretariat of State of HH Pope Pius XII, 1948–50; Sec. of Apostolic Internunciature in Tokyo, Japan, 1950–53; Titular Archbishop of Melitene, 1953; Apostolic Delegate to British East and West Africa, 1953–57; Apostolic Internuncio in India, 1957–67; Archbishop of Melbourne, 1967–74; Prefect of the Sacred Congregation for the discipline of the Sacraments and of the Sacred Congregation for Divine Worship, 1974–75, Prefect of the Sacred Congregation for the Sacraments and Divine Worship, 1975–81. Member Sacred Congregation for: Evangelization of Peoples, 1973–; Oriental Churches, 1974–; Catholic Education, 1974–; Bishops, 1974–; Mem., Council for Public Affairs of the Church, 1974–; Member Pontifical Commission for: Revision of Code of Oriental Canon Law, 1974–; Revision of Code of Canon Law, 1974–; Interpretation of Decrees of 2nd Vatican Council, 1978–. Cardinal, 1973. *Publication:* De Necessitudine Deiparam Inter et Eucharistiam, 1949. *Address:* Vatican City State, Europe.
*Died 26 June 1983.*

**KNOX, Prof. Joseph Alan Cruden;** Professor of Physiology in the University of London, at Queen Elizabeth College, 1954–74, later Emeritus; *b* 23 March 1911; *s* of Dr Joseph Knox; *m* 1945, Elsa Margaret Henry; one *d. Educ:* Aberdeen Grammar Sch.; Glasgow High Sch.; Glasgow Univ. MB, ChB (Glasgow) 1935; MD (Hons) 1948; House Surgeon and Physician, Glasgow Royal Infirmary, 1935–36; Asst to Prof. of Physiology, Glasgow Univ., 1936–40; Lecturer in Physiology: Glasgow Univ., 1940–44; King's Coll., London, 1944–48; Senior Lecturer, King's Coll., 1948–54. Mem. of Physiological Soc., 1941. *Publications:* papers in Jl of Physiology, British Heart Jl, etc. *Recreations:* reading, gramophone, railways. *Address:* 129 Northumberland Road, North Harrow, Harrow, Middlesex HA2 7RB. *T:* 01-866 6778.
*Died 28 March 1984.*

**KNUTSFORD, 5th Viscount** *cr* 1895; **Julian Thurstan Holland-Hibbert,** CBE 1957; Bt 1853; Baron 1888; JP; *b* 3 May 1920; *o s* of 4th Viscount Knutsford, and Viola Mary (*d* 1964), *d* of Thomas Meadows Clutterbuck; *S* father, 1976. *Educ:* Eton; Trinity Coll., Cambridge. Served War of 1939–45, Coldstream Guards. JP Herts, 1953. OStJ. *Heir:* cousin Michael Holland-Hibbert [*b* 27 Dec. 1926; *m* 1951, Hon. Sheila Constance, *er d* of 5th Viscount Portman; two *s* one *d*]. *Address:* Munden, Watford, Herts. *T:* Garston 72002.
*Died 8 March 1986.*

**KODICEK, Egon Hynek,** CBE 1974; MD Prague, PhD Cantab; FRS 1973; FIBiol; Director of Dunn Nutritional Laboratory, Medical Research Council and University of Cambridge, 1963–73; Fellow, Wolfson College, Cambridge, 1973–75, Emeritus Fellow, 1977; *b* 3 Aug. 1908; *s* of Emma and Samuel Kodicek, MD; *m* 1936, Jindriska E. M. Hradecká, MD, DOMS; two *d. Educ:* Charles Univ., Medical Sch., Prague; Trinity Coll., Cambridge. MD Prague 1932; Diploma of Specialist for Internal Diseases and Metabolic Disorders, Prague, 1938; PhD Cantab., 1942. Charles Univ., Prague: clinical and experimental research work in Endocrinology, and Nutrition, 1932–39; Demonstrator, Dept of Internal Medicine, 1932–34; Asst-Physician, 1934–38; Physician-in-Charge, Endocrinological Outpatient Unit, Dept of Internal Medicine, 1938–39. Scholar of Soc. for Protection of Science and Learning, 1939; Mem. Scientific Staff, MRC, 1947–73; Hon. Consultant in Nutrition, United Cambridge Hosps, 1972–. Vis. Lectr, Harvard, Yale, Columbia and University of California, 1952, 1958; Lectr, under Nicolaysen Scheme, University of Oslo, 1964; Sandoz Foundn Lectr in Endocrinology, British Postgrad. Med. Fedn, 1973; Thomas Young Lectr, St George's Hosp., London, 1973. Member: Cttee of Biochemical Soc., 1961–65; Council of Nutrition Soc., 1964–67, 1968–71 (Pres., 1971–74); Hon. Mem., 1974–); Nat. Cttee for Nutritional Sciences, Royal Society, 1967–75; Nat. Cttee for Biochemistry, Royal Society, 1970–75; Chm., Commn V, Internat. Union of Nutritional Sciences, 1973–76. Hon. Mem., Czechoslovakia Med. Soc. of J. E. Purkyné, 1968–; Hon. Mem., Amer. Inst. of Nutrition, 1969–. Gottlieb Duttweiler Prize, 1972; Prix André Lichtwitz, 1972; Brit. Nutrition Foundn Prize, 1973; Sabato Visco Prize, 1973; (with Prof. H. De Luca) Prix Roussel, Paris, 1974; CIBA Medal and Prize, Biochem. Soc., 1974. *Publications:* scientific papers in Biochemical Jl, Jl of General Microbiology, and other British and foreign scientific jls. *Address:* Strangeways Laboratory, Wort's Causeway, Cambridge. *T:* Cambridge 243231; 11 Bulstrode Gardens, Cambridge. *T:* Cambridge 357321.
*Died 27 July 1982.*

**KOESTLER, Arthur,** CBE 1972; CLit 1974; FRSL; FRAS; author; *b* Budapest, Hungary, 5 Sept. 1905; *o s* of Henrik and Adela Koestler; *m* 1935, Dorothy Asher, Zürich; divorced 1950; no *c*; *m* 1950,

Mamaine Paget; divorced 1953; no *c*; *m* 1965, Cynthia Jefferies. *Educ:* University of Vienna. Foreign Correspondent in Middle East, Paris, Berlin, 1926–31; Mem. of Graf Zeppelin Arctic Expedition, 1931; travels in Russia and Soviet Central Asia, 1932–33; covering the Spanish Civil War for News Chronicle, London, 1936–37; imprisoned by General Franco; served 1939–40 in French Foreign Legion and 1941–42 in British Pioneer Corps. Fellow, Centre for Advanced Study in the Behavioural Sciences, Stanford, 1964–65. Hon. Mem., AAIL. Hon. LLD Queen's Univ., Kingston, Ont, 1968; Hon. DLitt Leeds, 1977; Dr *hc* Liège, 1979; Hon. DSc Manchester, 1981. Sonning Prize, 1968. *Publications:* Spanish Testament, 1938; The Gladiators, 1939; Darkness at Noon, 1940; Scum of the Earth, 1941; Arrival and Departure, 1943; The Yogi and the Commissar, 1945; Twilight Bar, 1945; Thieves in the Night, 1946; Insight and Outlook, 1948; The God that Failed (with others), 1949; Promise and Fulfilment, 1949; The Age of Longing, 1950; Arrow in the Blue, 1952; The Invisible Writing, 1954; The Trail of the Dinosaur, 1955; Reflections on Hanging, 1956; The Sleepwalkers, 1959; The Lotus and the Robot, 1960; Suicide of a Nation? (ed), 1963; The Act of Creation, 1964; The Ghost in the Machine, 1967; Drinkers of Infinity, 1968; (ed with J. R. Smythies) Beyond Reductionism—New Perspectives in the Life Sciences: The Alpbach Symposium 1968, 1969; The Case of the Midwife Toad, 1971; The Roots of Coincidence, 1972; The Call-Girls, 1972; (with others) The Challenge of Chance, 1973; The Heel of Achilles, Essays 1968–1973, 1974; The Thirteenth Tribe, 1976; (with others) Life After Death, 1976; Janus: a summing-up, 1978; Bricks to Babel, 1980; Kaleidoscope, 1981; contribs: Encyclopaedia of Philosophy, 1967; Encyclopaedia Britannica, 1974; *posthumous publication:* (with Cynthia Koestler) The Stranger on the Square (autobiog.), 1984; *relevant publications:* Arthur Koestler, by John Atkins, 1956; Arthur Koestler, Das Literarische Werk, by Peter Alfred Huber, Zürich 1962; Arthur Koestler, Cahiers de l'Herne, 1975; Astride the Two Cultures: Arthur Koestler at Seventy, ed Harold Harris, 1975; Arthur Koestler, by Sidney A. Pearson Jr, 1978. *Recreations:* chess, good wine. *Address:* c/o A. D. Peters, 10 Buckingham Street, WC2.
*Died 3 March 1983.*

**KOHLER, Foy David;** Associate, Advanced International Studies Institute; consultant, 1978–85; *b* 15 Feb. 1908; *s* of Leander David Kohler and Myrtle McClure; *m* 1935, Phyllis Penn. *Educ:* Toledo and Ohio State Univs, Ohio. US Foreign Service 1932–67: posts include: Amer. Emb., London, 1944; 1st Sec. Amer. Emb., Moscow, 1947; Counselor, 1948; Minister, Oct. 1948; Chief, Internat. Broadcasting Div., Dept of State, 1949; VOA 1949; Asst Administr, Internat. Information Admin, 1952; Policy Planning Staff, Dept of State, 1952; Counselor, Amer. Emb., Ankara, Turkey, 1953–56; detailed ICA, 1956–58; Deputy Asst Sec. of State for European Affairs, 1958–59; Asst Sec. of State, 1959–62; US Ambassador to USSR, 1962–66; Deputy Under-Sec. of State for Political Affairs, United States, 1966–67; Career Ambassador, USA, 1966. Prof., Univ. of Miami, 1968–80. Editor, Soviet World Outlook, 1976–85. Holds honorary doctorates. *Publications:* Understanding the Russians: a citizen's primer, 1970; (jtly) Soviet Strategy for the Seventies: from Cold War to peaceful coexistence, 1973; (jtly) The Role of Nuclear Forces in Current Soviet Strategy, 1974; (jtly) The Soviet Union: yesterday, today, tomorrow, 1975; Custine's Eternal Russia, 1976; Salt II: how not to negotiate with the Russians, 1979. *Recreations:* golf, swimming. *Address:* Waterford Tower Apt 1102, 605 South US Highway #1, Juno Beach, Fla 33408, USA.
*Died 23 Dec. 1990.*

**KOLBUSZEWSKI, Prof. Janusz,** DSc (Eng), PhD, DIC, Dipl. Ing; FICE; FCIT; FCGI; Professor of Transportation and Environmental Planning and Head of Department, University of Birmingham, 1965–81, later Emeritus Professor (Professor of Highway and Traffic Engineering, 1959–64, of Transportation, 1964–65); *b* 18 Feb. 1915; *s* of Jan Alexander and Bronislawa Kolbuszewski; *m* 1946, Marie-Louise Jasinska; one *s* one *d. Educ:* Technical University of Lwow, Poland (Dipl.Ing); Imperial Coll. of Science and Technology, University of London, PhDEng, London, 1948; DIC 1948; DSc(Eng), London, 1968. Lecturer, Technical Univ. of Lwow, Poland, until 1939. Served War of 1939–45; Polish, French and British Armies. Imperial Coll. Science and Technology, London, 1945–48; Prof., Dir of Studies, Polish University Coll., London, 1948–50; Lecturer, Sen. Lecturer, Reader, in charge of Graduate Schs in Foundation Engrg and in Highway and Traffic Engineering, University of Birmingham, 1951–59. External Examiner for Univs of Bradford, Cambridge, City, Glasgow, Leeds, Manchester, Nottingham, East Anglia, Southampton, Wales, New South Wales, and Imp. College. Lectr of Honour, Inst. Traffic Sci., Japan, 1972; James Forrest Lectr, ICE, 1972. Member: Civil Engrg and Aero Cttee, SRC, 1967; Research Cttee, ICE, 1966; Transport Bd, CNAA, 1974; Chm., Bd of the Inst. of Transportation Safety, USA, 1980–. Governor, Birmingham Coll. of Arts. Hon. Mem., Midlands Soc. for Soil Mechanics and Foundn Engrg. Lister Prize, Midland Branch of IStructE, 1953; Nusey Prize, Soc. of Engineers, London, 1967; Certificate of Merit, Inst. of Highway Engineers,

1977. *Publications:* various scientific papers on Geometry, Perspective, Soil Mechanics, Foundations and Highway Engineering, Transportation and Planning. *Recreations:* travelling, oil painting. *Address:* Passy, All Stretton, Shropshire. *T:* Church Stretton 3149. *Died* 24 *July* 1984.

**KOLHAPUR, Maharaja of; Maj.-Gen. HH Sir Shahaji Chhatrapati,** (adopted these names in lieu of those of Vikramsinharao Puar, on succeeding to Kolhapur Gadi, 1947); GCSI 1947 (KCSI 1941); *b* 4 April 1910; one *s* three *d.* Maharaja of Dewas (Senior Branch), 1937–47. State merged with Bombay, 1949. Appointed Major and Hon. ADC to HM King Emperor George VI, 1946; Hon. Maj.-Gen. Indian Army, 1962. *Address:* New Palace, Kolhapur, Maharashtra, India. *Died* 9 *May* 1983.

**KOMINSKI, Daniel;** *see* Kaye, Danny.

**KONOVALOV, Sergey,** MA Oxon, BLitt Oxon; Professor of Russian in the University of Oxford, 1945–67, then Emeritus; Emeritus Fellow of New College, Oxford; *b* Moscow, 31 Oct. 1899; *s* of Alexander Konovalov, Minister of Trade and Industry in Russian Provisional Government of 1917, and of Nadejda Vtorov; *m* 1949, Janina Ryzowa. *Educ:* Classical Lycée, Moscow; Exeter Coll., Oxford (Diploma in Economics and Political Science 1921, BLitt 1927; MA 1936). Professor of Russian Language and Literature, University of Birmingham, 1929–45; Lecturer in Slavonic Studies, University of Oxford, 1930–45; Hon. Lecturer at University of London (Sch. of Slavonic Studies), 1931–32, 1940–41. Mem. Internat. Cttee of Slavists, 1958–68. Editor, Birmingham Russian Memoranda, 1931–40; Co-editor: Birmingham Polish Monographs, 1936–39; Bibliographies of Research Work in Slavonic Countries, 1932–34; editor and contributor, Blackwell's Russian Texts, and OUP's Russian Readers and Oxford Slavonic Papers, vols I–XIII, 1950–67. *Publications:* Anthology of Contemporary Russian Literature, 1932; Russian Critical Essays, (ed with D. J. Richards), 1971–72; article Soviet Union in Encyclopædia Britannica Year-Book, 1941; Russo-Polish Relations: an Historical Survey (in collaboration), 1945. *Address:* 175 Divinity Road, Oxford. *Died* 12 *Feb.* 1982.

**KOO, Vi Kyuin Wellington;** Judge of International Court of Justice, 1957–67 (Vice-President, 1964–67); Senior Adviser to the President of the Republic of China in USA, since 1975; *b* 1888; *m* Juliana Yen. *Educ:* Columbia Univ. (Doctor of Philosophy). Sec. to Pres. of China; Councillor in Foreign Office; Minister to USA, 1915; attended Peace Conference as China's Plenipotentiary, and later as Head of the Chinese Delegation, 1919; Chinese delegate to the Assembly and China's representative on the Council of the League of Nations at Geneva, 1920–22; Chinese Minister to Great Britain, 1921; Plenipotentiary to Washington Conference, 1921–22; Minister of Foreign Affairs, Peking, 1922–24; Finance Minister, 1926; Prime Minister and Minister of Foreign Affairs, 1926–27; Mem. on the International Court of Arbitration at The Hague, 1927–57; Minister of Foreign Affairs, China, 1931; Chinese Assessor to the Commission of Inquiry of the League of Nations, 1932; Chinese Minister to France, 1932–35; Chinese Ambassador to France, 1936–41, in London, 1941–46; Chinese representative on the Council of the League of Nations at Geneva, 1932–34; Delegate 13th and 14th Assemblies of League of Nations and to the Special Assembly of the League of Nations, 1932–33; Delegate to the World Monetary and Economic Conference, London, 1933; Delegate to Conference for Reduction and Limitation of Armaments, at Geneva, 1933; Chief Delegate to Assemblies of League of Nations, 1935–36 and 1938; Special Envoy to Accession of Leopold to throne of Belgium, 1938; Delegate to sessions of League Coun., 1937–39 (Pres. 96th); Chief Deleg. to Brussels Conference, Nov. 1937; Special Envoy to coronation of His Holiness Pius XII; Ambassador Extraordinary to 800th Anniversary of Foundation of Portugal, 1940; Chief Delegate to Dumbarton Oaks Conf.; Rep. on War Crimes Commn, London; Delegate and Actg Chief Delegate to San Francisco Conf. to draft UN charter; Chinese Ambassador in Washington, 1946–56; Delegate to UNRRA and FAO, 1946–49; Mem., Far Eastern Commn, 1946–49; Senior Advisor to General Chiang Kai-Shek, 1956–57, 1967–74. *Publications:* Status of Aliens in China, 1912; Memorandum presented to Lytton Commission (3 volumes), 1932. Hon. degrees: LLD: Columbia, Yale, St John's, Birmingham, Aberdeen, Manchester; LHD, Rollins Coll.; DCL, Miami. *Recreations:* tennis, golf, fishing, skiing. *Address:* 1185 Park Avenue, New York, NY 10028, USA. *Died* 14 *Nov.* 1985.

**KOOPMANS, Prof. Tjalling Charles;** Alfred Cowles Professor Emeritus of Economics, Yale University (Professor of Economics, Yale, 1955–80, Alfred Cowles Professor, 1967–80); *b* Holland, 28 Aug. 1910; *m* 1936, Truus Wanningen; one *s* two *d. Educ:* Univ. of Utrecht (MA, Phys. and Maths); Univ. of Leiden (PhD, Math. Statistics). Lectr, Netherlands Sch. of Economics, Rotterdam, 1936–38; Economist, Financial Section, League of Nations, Geneva, 1938–40; Special Lectr, Sch. of Business, New York Univ., 1940–41; Research Associate, Princeton Univ., 1940–41; Economist, Penn

Mutual Life Ins. Co., 1941–42; Statistician, Combined Shipping Adjustment Bd, Washington, 1942–44; Research Associate, Cowles Commn for Research in Economics, Univ. of Chicago, 1944–54; Associate Prof. of Economics, 1946–48, Prof. of Economics, 1948–55, Univ. of Chicago; Dir of Research, Cowles Commn, 1948–54; Frank W. Taussig Prof. of Economics, Harvard Univ., 1960–61; Dir, Cowles Foundn, 1961–67. Member: Econometric Soc. (Mem. 1934–, Fellow, 1940–, Vice-Pres. 1949, Pres. 1950, Council Mem. 1949–55, 1966–71, 1973–78); American Economic Assoc., 1941– (Distinguished Fellow, 1971, Pres., 1978); (Corresp.) Royal Netherlands Acad. of Arts and Scis, 1950–; Amer. Math. Soc., 1952–; Inst. of Management Scis, 1954–; Ops Research Soc. of Amer., 1954–; Amer. Acad. of Arts and Scis, 1960–; Nat. Acad. of Scis, 1969–. Nobel Prize for Economics (jt), 1975; Honours and Awards from Belgium, Netherlands and USA. Hon. LLD Cambridge, 1984. *Publications:* Linear Regression Analysis of Economic Time Series (PhD Thesis), 1936; Tanker Freight Rates and Tankship Building, 1939; Three Essays on the State of Economic Science: Allocation of Resources and the Price System, The Construction of Economic Knowledge, The Interaction of Tools and Problems in Economics, 1957; ed and contrib. Cowles Commn Monographs Nos 10 and 13, 1950 and 1951; Co-ed and contrib. No 14, 1953; contrib. Studies in the Economics of Transportation (by Beckmann, McGuire and Winsten), 1956; Selected Scientific Papers, 1934–67, repr. 1970; numerous articles to economic and other professional jls, reviews, annals, proc. confs and papers. *Address:* (office) Cowles Foundation, Box 2125 Yale Station, New Haven, Conn 06520, USA. *T:* (203) 436 2578; (home) 459 Ridge Road, Hamden, Connecticut 06517, USA. *T:* (203) 248 5872. *Died* 26 *Feb.* 1985.

**KRAAY, Colin Mackennal,** DPhil; FSA, FRNS; FBA 1978; Keeper, Heberden Coin Room, Ashmolean Museum, Oxford, since 1975; Fellow of Wolfson College, Oxford, since 1965; *b* 23 March 1918; *s* of Casper Alexander Kraay and Henrietta Agnes (*née* Mackennal); *m* 1945, Margaret Janet Carruthers, *d* of H. Prince, Kimberley, SA; one *s. Educ:* Lancing Coll.; Magdalen Coll., Oxford (Barclay Head Prize for Ancient Numismatics, 1948; Conington Prize, 1951; DPhil 1953). FRNS 1948 (Pres. 1970–74); FSA 1961. Asst Keeper of Coins, 1952–62, Sen. Asst Keeper of Coins, 1962–75, Asmolean Museum; Univ. Lectr in Greek Numismatics, Oxford, 1959–. Sec., Cttee on Sylloge Nummorum Graecorum, British Acad., 1967–; Corresp. Mem., Amer. Numismatic Soc., 1967–; Gray Lectr, Cambridge Univ., 1967–68; Mem., Cttee on *Historia Numorum*, British Acad., 1970–. Pres. Consiglio of Centro Internaz. di Studi Numismatici, Naples, 1974–80. Cecil and Ida Green Vis. Prof., Univ. of British Columbia, Vancouver, 1981. RNS Medallist, 1978; Huntington Medallist, Amer. Numismatic Soc., 1980. *Publications:* The *Aes* Coinage of Galba, 1956; Sylloge Nummorum Graecorum V(iA–iv), 1962–; with M. Hirmer) Greek Coins, 1966; (ed with G. K. Jenkins) Essays in Greek Coinage presented to Stanley Robinson, 1968; Greek Coins and History, 1969; (with N. Davis) The Hellenistic Kingdoms: portrait coins and history, 1973; (with M. Thompson and O. Mørkholm) An Inventory of Greek Coin Hoards, 1973; (with C. H. V. Sutherland) Catalogue of Coins of the Roman Empire in the Ashmolean Museum, Pt I: Augustus, 1975; Archaic and Classical Greek Coins, 1976; (ed with R. A. G. Carson) Scripta Nummaria Romana: essays presented to Humphrey Sutherland, 1978; articles in Numismatic Chronicle, Jl Hellenic Studies, etc. *Recreations:* English water-colours, blue and white transfer ware. *Address:* Steere's Close, Hampton Poyle, Oxford OX5 2QA. *T:* Kidlington 3625. *Died* 27 *Jan.* 1982.

**KRABBÉ, Col Clarence Brehmer,** OBE 1918; DL; *b* 16 Jan. 1886; *s* of Charles Krabbé, Buenos Aires; *m* 1915, Joan Alison (*d* 1968), *d* of Col A. Evans-Gordon, IA; one *s* (killed 1940) one *d. Educ:* Dulwich Coll.; Trinity Coll., Oxford. Served European War, 1914–19, with Berks Yeomanry and RFC, Gallipoli and France (despatches). Col Berks Home Guard, 1943–45. Chm., Royal Berks Hosp., 1942–48; Chm., S Berks Conservative Assoc., 1946–52; Vice-Chm., Berks T & AF Assoc., 1950–54; Mem., Oxford Regional Hosp. Bd, 1947–62 (Vice-Chm. 1951–62). Mem., Board of Governors, Oxford United Hosps, 1953–57; Mem. of Reading and District Hosp. Management Cttee (Chm., 1948–50), 1948–66; Mem. St Birinus Hosp. Management Cttee, 1962–66. DL Berks, 1946. High Sheriff of Berks, 1952–53. *Recreation:* gardening. *Address:* Calcot Green, near Reading, Berks. *T:* Reading 27428. *Died* 5 *Jan.* 1985.

**KREBS, Sir Hans (Adolf),** Kt 1958; FRS 1947; FRCP; MD Hamburg, 1925; MA Cantab, 1934; Research Scientist in the Nuffield Department of Clinical Medicine, Radcliffe Infirmary, Oxford, and Supernumerary Fellow of St Cross College, Oxford, since 1967; Visiting Professor of Biochemistry, Royal Free Hospital School of Medicine, since 1967; *b* 25 Aug. 1900; *e s* of late Georg Krebs, MD, and Alma Davidson, Hildesheim, Germany; *m* 1938, Margaret Cicely, *d* of J. L. Fieldhouse, Wickersley, Yorks; two *s* one *d. Educ:* Universities of Göttingen, Freiburg i. B., Munich, Berlin. Asst Kaiser Wilhelm Institut f. Biologie, Dept of Prof. O. H. Warburg, Berlin-Dahlem, 1926–30; Privatdozent f. int. Medizin, Freiburg,

1932; Rockefeller research student, Cambridge, 1933–34; Demonstrator in Biochemistry, Cambridge, 1934–35; Lecturer in Pharmacology, University of Sheffield, 1935–38; Lecturer i/c Dept of Biochemistry, University of Sheffield, 1938–45; Prof., 1945–54. Whitley Prof. of Biochemistry, and Fellow of Trinity Coll., Oxford, 1954–67. Hon. Degrees from Universities of Chicago, Freiburg, Paris, Glasgow, Sheffield, London, Berlin (Humboldt), Jerusalem, Leicester, Leeds, Granada, Pennsylvania, Wales, Bordeaux, Bristol, Hannover, Valencia, Cambridge, Liverpool, Indiana, Göttingen. Hon. Member: Belgian Royal Academy of Medicine, 1962; Amer. Assoc. of Physicians, 1972; Deutsche Ges. Inn. Med., 1972; Société de Biologie, Paris, 1973. Hon. Fellow, Nat. Inst. of Sciences of India, 1956; Associé étranger, Académie Nationale de Médicine, Paris, 1973; Foreign Hon. Mem., Amer. Acad. of Arts and Sciences, 1957; Mem., Amer. Philosophical Soc., 1960; Foreign Associate, Amer. Nat. Acad. of Science, 1964; Hon. Fellow, Weizmann Inst. Science, 1972. (Jointly) Nobel Prize for Medicine, 1953; Royal Medal, Royal Society, 1954; Gold Medal of Netherlands Soc. for Physics, Medical Science, and Surgery, 1958; Copley Medal of Royal Society, 1961. Gold Medal, RSM, 1965. *Publications:* (with Prof. H. Kornberg) Energy Transformations in Living Matter, 1957; Otto Warburg—Biochemist and Eccentric, 1981; Reminiscences and Reflections (autobiog.), 1981; papers on biochemical subjects in scientific journals. *Address:* Nuffield Department of Clinical Medicine, Radcliffe Infirmary, Oxford; 37 Abberbury Road, Oxford.                              *Died* 22 *Nov.* 1981.

**KREMER, Michael,** MD; FRCP; Emeritus Neurologist, Middlesex Hospital, W1; Honorary Consulting Neurologist, National Hospital, Queen Square, WC1; Hon. Consultant Neurologist to St Dunstan's, since 1966; Hon. Consultant in Neurology to the Army, since 1969; *b* 27 Nov. 1907; *s* of W. and S. Kremer; *m* 1933, Lilian Frances (*née* Washbourn); one *s* two *d*. *Educ:* Middlesex Hosp. Medical Sch. BSc 1927; MD 1932; FRCP 1943. *Recreations:* music, reading, photography. *Address:* 121 Harley Street, W1. *T:* 01–935 4545.
                                                              *Died* 1 *March* 1988.

**KRISHNA, Sri,** CIE 1942; DSc (London), PhD; FRSC, FNA; late Scientific Adviser to High Commission of India and Scientific Liaison Officer, London; Deputy Director, Council of Scientific and Industrial Research, New Delhi, India, 1952; Vice-Pres. and Director of Research, Forest Research Institute, Dehra Dun, UP, India, 1950; Biochemist since 1928; *b* 6 July 1896; *s* of M. Mohan; *m* 1st, 1925, Usha Khanna (*d* 1929); (one *s* decd); 2nd, 1972, Olga Hellerman. *Educ:* Forman Coll., Lahore; Government Coll., Lahore; Queen Mary Coll., London; King's Coll., London. Prof. of Chemistry, University of the Punjab, Lahore, 1925–28. *Publications:* numerous scientific. *Recreations:* tennis, etc. *Address:* 62 Perryn Road, Acton, W3 7LX; 88 Rajpur Road, Dehra Dun, UP, India.
                                                              *Died* 3 *Oct.* 1984.

**KRISHNAMURTI, Jiddu;** philosopher and religious teacher; *b* 12 May 1895; *s* of Jiddu Narianiah and Jiddu Sanjeevamma. *Educ:* privately in England. Adopted by Mrs Annie Besant, 1910; made Head of Order of the Star in the East, an offshoot of Theosophy, 1912 (Order proclaimed the Coming of the World Teacher who would occupy the body of Krishnamurti); dissolved Order, 1929; since then, has travelled the world speaking as a philosopher and religious teacher. *Publications:* The First and Last Freedom, 1954; Education and the Significance of Life, 1955; Commentaries on Living: 1st Series, 1956; 2nd Series, 1959; 3rd Series, 1960; Life Ahead, 1963; This Matter of Culture, 1964; Freedom From The Known, 1969; The Only Revolution, 1970; Penguin Krishnamurti Reader, 1970; The Urgency of Change, 1971; The Impossible Question, 1972; Tradition and Revolution, 1972; Beyond Violence, 1973; The Awakening of Intelligence, 1973; The Second Penguin Krishnamurti Reader, 1973; Krishnamurti on Education, 1974; Beginnings of Learning, 1975; Krishnamurti's Notebook, 1976; Truth & Actuality, 1977; The Wholeness of Life, 1978; Beginnings of Learning, 1978; The Impossible Question, 1978; Exploration into Insight, 1979; Meditations, 1979; Poems and Parables, 1981; Krishnamurti's Letters to the Schools, 1981; Krishnamurti's Journal, 1982; Questions & Answers, 1982; The Flame of Attention, 1984; The Ending of Time, 1985; series of books, mainly of talks, 1933–67; many booklets on education, philosophy and religion, 1910–83. *Address:* Brockwood Park, Bramdean, near Alresford, Hants SO24 0LQ. *T:* Bramdean 228.                          *Died* 17 *Feb.* 1986.

**KRISTENSEN, Prof. Thorkil;** Director, Institute for Development Research, Copenhagen, 1969–72; Secretary-General, Organisation for Economic Co-operation and Development, 1960–69; *b* Denmark, 9 Oct. 1899; *m* 1931, Ellen Christine Nielsen; one *s* one *d*. *Educ:* School of Commerce; People's Coll., Askov; University of Copenhagen (Cand. polit.). Dipl. Polit. and Econ. Sciences, 1927. Lectr in High Sch. of Commerce, Aarhus, and in University of Copenhagen, 1927–38; Prof. of Commercial and Industrial Economics: University of Aarhus, 1938–47; Sch. of Advanced Commercial Studies, Copenhagen, 1947–60. Mem., Danish Parliament, 1945–60; Minister of Finance, 1945–47 and 1950–53;

Mem. Finance Cttee, 1947–49 and 1953–60; Mem. Consultative Assembly of Council of Europe, 1949–50; Mem. Foreign Affairs Cttee, 1953–60; Mem. Nordic Council, 1953–60; Mem. Acad. of Technical Sciences; Pres. Foreign Policy Soc., 1948–60; Pres. Nat. Anti-Unemployment Fedn, 1956–60; Mem. Assurance Council, 1958–60; Mem. Institute of History and Economics. DrSc Pol *hc* (Ankara), 1962. *Publications:* several, on finance, 1930–39; The Food Problem of Developing Countries, 1968. Editor of: De europaeiske markedsplaner (European Markets-Plans and Prospects), 1958; The Economic World Balance, 1960; Development in Rich and Poor Countries, 1974, 2nd edn 1982; Inflation and Unemployment in the Modern Society, 1981, etc. *Address:* Odinsvej 18, 3460 Birkerød, Denmark.                          *Died* 26 *June* 1989.

**KUYPERS, Prof. Henricus Gerardus Jacobus Maria,** FRS 1988; Professor of Anatomy and Head of the Department of Anatomy, University of Cambridge, since 1984; *b* 9 Sept. 1925; *s* of A. Kuypers and C. J. M. Kuypers (*née* Buys); *m* 1955, M. F. Schaap (decd); two *s* four *d*. *Educ:* RC Gymnasium, Rotterdam; Univ. of Leiden, faculty of Medicine (MD, PhD). Resident, Clinical Neurology, University, Groningen, 1954–55; Asst Prof./Associate Prof. of Anatomy, Univ. of Maryland Med. Sch., 1955–62; Associate Prof./ Full Prof. of Anatomy, Western Reserve Med. Sch., Cleveland, Ohio, 1962–66; Prof. of Anatomy/Head of Dept of Anatomy, Erasmus University Med. Sch., Rotterdam, 1966–84. *Publications:* Handbook of the American Physiological Society, 1980; Progress in Brain Research, 1982; regular contributor to Brain, Brain Res., Neuroscience Letters, Experimental Brain Res. *Recreations:* history, pictorial art, swimming, canoeing. *Address:* 2 Southmead, 21 Chaucer Road, Cambridge CB2 2EB. *T:* Cambridge 62696.
                                                              *Died* 26 *Sept.* 1989.

**KUZNETS, Prof. Simon,** MA, PhD; Economist and Statistician, USA; Professor Emeritus of Economics, Harvard University; *b* Kharkov, Ukraine, 30 April 1901; *s* of Abraham Kuznets and Pauline (*née* Friedman); *m* 1929, Edith Handler; one *s* one *d*. *Educ:* Columbia Univ., USA. BA 1923, MA 1924, PhD 1926. Nat. Bureau of Economic Research, New York, 1927– (Mem. staff); Asst Prof. Economics and Statistics, Univ. of Pennsylvania, 1930–54; Associate Dir, Bureau of Planning and Statistics, WPB, Washington, DC, 1942–44; Economic Adviser, Nat. Resources Commn of China, 1946; Adviser, Nat. Income Cttee of India, 1950–51; Prof. of Political Economy, Johns Hopkins Univ., 1954–60; Prof. of Economics, Harvard Univ., 1960–71. Marshall Lectures, Cambridge Univ., delivered 1969; Nobel Prize in Economics, 1971. Hon. Fellow, Royal Statistical Soc. (England); FAAAS; Fell. Amer. Statistical Assoc.; Member: Internat. Statistical Inst.; Amer. Philosophical Soc.; Econometric Soc.; Royal Acad. of Sciences, Sweden, etc. Hon. ScD: Princeton; Pennsylvania; Harvard; Hon. DHL: Columbia; Brandeis, 1975; PhD Hebrew Univ. of Jerusalem. *Publications:* Cyclical Fluctuations in Retail and Wholesale Trade, 1926; Secular Movements in Production and Prices, 1930; Seasonal Variations in Industry and Trade, 1934; Commodity Flow and Capital Formation, 1938; National Income and its Composition (2 vols, 1919–38), 1941; National Product since 1869, 1946; Upper Income Shares, 1953; Economic Change, 1954; Six Lectures on Economic Growth, 1959; Capital in the American Economy, 1961; Modern Economic Growth, 1966; Economic Growth of Nations: Total Output and Production Structure, 1971; Population, Capital and Growth, 1974. *Address:* Department of Economics, Harvard University, Cambridge, Mass 02138, USA; 67 Francis Avenue, Cambridge, Mass 02138, USA.                          *Died* 8 *July* 1985.

**KWAN SAI KHEONG;** Singapore Ambassador to the Philippines, since 1980; *b* 11 Sept. 1920; *s* of F. H. Kwan; *m* 1945, Sim Poh Geok; one *s* one *d*. *Educ:* Raffles Instn, Singapore; Raffles Coll., Singapore; Royal College of Art, London. BA Hons, ARCA. Teacher, 1946–53; various appts in Min. of Educn; Permanent Sec. and Dir of Educn, Singapore, 1966–75; concurrently Chm., Singapore Nat. Commn for UNESCO, 1968–75; Vice-Chancellor, Univ. of Singapore, 1975–80. Hon. DLitt, Singapore, 1973; Hon. DEd, Chulalongkorn Univ., Bangkok, 1977. Public Administration Medal (Gold, Singapore Govt award), 1963; Meritorious Service Medal (Singapore Govt), 1968; L'Ordre des Palmes Académiques (French Govt), 1977. *Recreations:* painting, inventing. *Address:* 34–N Mount Elizabeth, Singapore 0922. *T:* 2351272. *Clubs:* Pyramid, American, Island Country (all in Singapore).
                                                              *Died* 24 *Nov.* 1981.

**KYLE, Elisabeth, (Agnes Mary Robertson Dunlop);** novelist and writer of books for children; *d* of late James Dunlop, Ronaldshaw Park, Ayr; unmarried. *Publications: novels:* The Begonia Bed, 1934; Orangefield, 1938; Broken Glass, 1940; The White Lady, 1941; But We Are Exiles, 1942; The Pleasure Dome, 1943; The Skaters' Waltz, 1944; Carp Country, 1946; Mally Lee, 1947; A Man of Talent, 1948; Douce, 1950; The Tontine Belle, 1951; Conor Sands, 1952; The Regent's Candlesticks, 1954; The Other Miss Evans, 1958; Return to the Alcazar, 1962; Love is for the Living, 1966; High Season, 1968; Queen's Evidence, 1969; Mirror Dance, 1970;

The Scent of Danger, 1971; The Silver Pineapple, 1972; The Heron Tree, 1973; Free as Air, 1974; Down to the Water, 1975; All the Nice Girls, 1976; The Stark Inheritance, 1978; A Summer Scandal, 1979; The Deed Box, 1981; *children's books:* The Mirrors of Versailles, 1939; Visitors from England, 1941; Vanishing Island, 1942; Behind the Waterfall, 1944; The Seven Sapphires, 1944; Holly Hotel, 1945; Lost Karin, 1946; The Mirrors of Castle Doone, 1947; West Wind, 1948; The House on the Hill, 1949; The Provost's Jewel, 1950; The Lintowers, 1951; The Captain's House, 1952; Forgotten as a Dream, 1953; The Reiver's Road, 1953; The House of the Pelican, 1954; Caroline House, 1955; A Stillness in the Air, 1956; Run to Earth, 1957; Queen of Scots, 1957; Maid of Orleans, 1957; The Money Cat, 1958; Oh Say, Can You See?, 1959; The Eagle's Nest, 1961; Girl with a Lantern, 1961; Girl with An Easel, 1963; Girl With A Pen, 1964; Girl With A Song, 1964; Victoria, 1964; Girl with a Destiny, 1965; The Boy who asked for More, 1966; The Song of the Waterfall, 1969; The Stilt Walkers, 1972; The Yellow Coach, 1976; The Key of the Castle, 1976; The Burning Hill, 1977. *Recreations:* music, travel, collecting antiques. *Address:* 10 Carrick Park, Ayr, Scotland. *T:* Ayr 63074.

*Died* 23 *Feb.* 1982.

**KYLE, Air Chief Marshal Sir Wallace (Hart),** GCB 1966 (KCB 1960; CB 1953); KCVO 1977; CBE 1945; DSO 1944; DFC 1941; Governor of Western Australia, 1975-80, retired; *b* 22 Jan. 1910; *s* of A. Kyle, Kalgoorlie, Western Australia; *m* 1941, Molly Rimington (*née* Wilkinson); three *s* one *d. Educ:* Guildford Sch., WA; RAF Coll., Cranwell. 17 Sqdn, 1930-31; Fleet Air Arm, 1931-34; Flying Instructor, 1934-39; served War of 1939-45; Bomber Command, 1940-45; Staff Coll., 1945-47; Middle East, 1948-50; ADC to King George VI, 1949; Asst Commandant, RAF Coll., Cranwell, 1950-52; Dir of Operational Requirements, Air Ministry, 1952-54; AOC Malaya, 1955-57; ACAS (Op. Req.), 1957-59. AOC-in-C Technical Training Command, 1959-62; VCAS, 1962-65; AOC-in-C, Bomber Command, 1965-68, Strike Command, 1968; retired. ADC to the Queen, 1952-56. Air Marshal, 1961; Air Chief Marshal, 1964; Air ADC to the Queen, 1966-68. Pres., Fairbridge Soc., 1980-. Hon. DTech W Australia Inst. of Technology, 1979; Hon. LLD Univ. of Western Australia, 1980. KStJ 1976. *Recreation:* golf. *Address:* Kingswood, Tiptoe, near Lymington, Hants. *Club:* Royal Air Force.                                              *Died* 31 *Jan.* 1988.

**KYNCH, Prof. George James,** ARCS, DIC, PhD (London); CPhys; FIMA; Professor of Mathematics at the Institute of Science and Technology and in the University of Manchester, 1957-78, then Emeritus; Dean, Faculty of Technology, 1973-75; *b* 26 Oct. 1915; *s* of Vincent Kynch; *m* 1944, Eve, *d* of Edward A. Robinson; one *s* two *d. Educ:* Selhurst Grammar Sch.; Imperial Coll. of Science, London. BSc in physics, 1935, and mathematics, 1936; PhD 1939; Sir John Lubbock Memorial Prize, 1936; Hon. MScTech Manchester, 1960. Demonstrator at Imperial Coll., 1937; Lecturer at Birmingham Univ., 1942-52; Prof. of Applied Mathematics, University Coll. of Wales, Aberystwyth, 1952-57. Founder Mem., Council of Inst. of Mathematics and its Applications, 1963-66; Pres., Northenden Civic Soc., 1966-80; Member: Manchester Literary and Philosophical Soc., 1959- (Pres., 1971-73); Manchester Statistical Soc., 1983-. *Publications:* Mathematics for the Chemist, 1955; articles in scientific jls. *Recreations:* lecturing, photography, caravanning, dry stone wall-building. *Address:* Rectory Cottage, Ford Lane, Northenden, Manchester M22 4NQ.

*Died* 26 *Feb.* 1987.

# L

**LABOUISSE, Henry (Richardson);** consultant on organisation and development matters; lawyer, US; *b* New Orleans, La., 11 Feb. 1904; *s* of Henry Richardson Labouisse; *m* 1935, Elizabeth Scriven Clark (*d* 1945); one *d*; *m* 1954, Eve Curie. *Educ:* Princeton Univ. (AB); Harvard Univ. (LLB). Attorney-at-Law, NYC, 1929–41. Joined US State Dept, 1941; Minister Economic Affairs, US Embassy, Paris, 1945; Chief, Special Mission to France of Economic Co-operation Administration, 1951–54; Director, UN Relief and Works Agency for Palestine Refugees, 1954–58; Consultant, International Bank for Reconstruction and Development, 1959–61 (Head of IBRD Mission to Venezuela, 1959); Director, International Co-operation Admin., 1961–62; US Ambassador to Greece, 1962–65; Exec. Dir, United Nations Children's Fund (UNICEF), 1965–79. Hon. LLD: University of Bridgeport, 1961; Princeton Univ., 1965; Lafayette Coll., 1966; Tulane Univ., 1967; Hon. LHD: Brandeis Univ., 1983; Hartwick Coll., 1983. Holds several decorations and hon. awards, incl. Woodrow Wilson Award, Princeton Univ., 1978. *Recreation:* swimming, golf, reading. *Address:* 1 Sutton Place South, New York, NY 10022, USA. *Clubs:* Century Association, River, Princeton (NY); Metropolitan, Chevy Chase (Washington). *Died 25 March* 1987.

**LACEY, Daniel;** *see* Lacey, W. D.

**LACEY, Janet,** CBE 1960; Director, Christian Aid Department, British Council of Churches, 1952–68, retired; *b* 25 Oct. 1903; *d* of Joseph Lacey, Property Agent, and Elizabeth Lacey. *Educ:* various schools, Sunderland; Drama Sch., Durham. YWCA, Kendal, 1926; General Secretary, YMCA/YWCA Community Centre, Dagenham, 1932; YMCA Education Secretary, BAOR, Germany, 1945; Youth Secretary, British Council of Churches, 1947. Dir, Family Welfare Assoc., 1969–73; Consultant to Churches' Council for Health and Healing, 1973–77. Hon. DD Lambeth, 1975. *Publications:* A Cup of Water, 1970; series booklets, Refugees, Aid to Developing Countries, Meeting Human Need with Christian Aid, 1956–64. *Recreations:* theatre, music, reading, crosswords. *Club:* Nikaean. *Died 11 July* 1988.

**LACEY, (William) Daniel,** CB 1978; CBE 1961; Director-General, Design Services, Department of the Environment, Property Services Agency, 1975–83; *b* 8 Jan. 1923; *s* of Ivor Ewart and Mary Lacey; *m* 1946, Julie Ellen (*née* Chandler); no *c*. *Educ:* Bishop Gore's Grammar Sch., Swansea. FRIBA 1967; MRTPI. Assistant Architect, Herts County Council, 1946–55; Assistant County Architect, Notts County Council, 1955–58; County Architect, Notts County Council, 1958–64; Chief Architect, 1964–69, Head of Architects and Building Br., 1969–75, DES. RIBA: Hon. Sec., 1967–69; Vice-Pres., 1971–72. Awarded Gran Premio Con Menzione Speciale at Milan Triennale Exhibition, 1960. *Publications:* various papers in Architectural Journals. *Recreation:* gardening. *Address:* 81 Whitney Drive, Stevenage, Herts SG1 4BL. *Club:* Reform. *Died 14 Nov.* 1985.

**LACK, Victor John Frederick,** FRCP, FRCS; FRCOG; retired; *b* 29 Sept. 1893; *m* Beatrice (*d* 1982); two *s*. *Educ:* London Hospital (MB, BS 1934). FRCS 1921; FRCP 1934; FRCOG 1935. Examiner: Universities of Oxford and Cambridge and Central Midwives' Board; Midwifery and Diseases of Women Conjoint Board, London; late Lectr in Midwifery and Diseases of Women, Birmingham Univ.; Asst Obst. Queen Elizabeth Hosp., Birmingham; Obst. Regist., Ho. Surg. and Ho. Phys. London Hosp.; Consultant Obstetrical and Gynæcological Surgeon, London Hospital, to 1958; Cons. Obstetrician Greenwich Borough Council Maternity Home; Gynæcologist King George's Hosp., Ilford; Obst. and Gyn. Surgeon, Royal Bucks Hosp., Aylesbury. FRSM (Mem. Obst. Sect.); a Vice-Pres., RCOG, 1955–. *Publications:* (jointly) Ten Teachers of Midwifery and Diseases of Women. Contrib. to medical jls. *Address:* 82 Bradwell Road, Loughton, Milton Keynes, Bucks MK8 0AL. *T:* Milton Keynes 666243. *Died 17 March* 1988.

**LA COUR, Leonard Francis,** OBE 1973 (MBE 1952); FRS 1970; Professor, University of East Anglia, 1973–78; *b* 28 July 1907; *o c* of Francis La Cour and Maud (*née* Coomber); *m* 1935, Anne Wilkes; no *c*. *Educ:* Merton Sch., Surrey. John Innes Institute: Sen. Exper. Officer 1948, Chief Exper. Officer 1956, Senior Principal Scientific Officer, 1970, retired 1972. Hon. MSc East Anglia, 1969, DSc, 1977. *Publications:* (with C. D. Darlington) The Handling of Chromosomes, 6th edn 1976; various research articles in scientific jls. *Recreation:* gardening. *Address:* 4 Greencroft, Trinity Place, Eastbourne, E Sussex BN21 3DA. *Died 3 Nov.* 1984.

**LACRETELLE, J. de;** *see* de Lacretelle.

**LAGDEN, Godfrey William;** *b* 12 April 1906; *s* of Augustine William and Annie Lagden; *m* 1935, Dorothy Blanche Wheeler (decd). *Educ:* Richmond Hill Sch., Richmond, Surrey. Sun Insurance Office, London, 1931–34; IBM (United Kingdom) Ltd, 1934–71. MP (C)

Hornchurch, 1955–66. *Recreations:* cricket, water polo, boxing, and dog breeding. *Address:* c/o 112 Squirrels Heath Road, Harold Wood, Essex. *Died 31 Aug.* 1989.

**LAIDLAW, William Allison,** MA, LittD; Professor of Classics in the University of London, Queen Mary College, 1949–64, then Emeritus Professor; *b* 15 July 1898; *s* of James and Sarah A. Laidlaw. *Educ:* Wesley Coll., Dublin; Trinity Coll., University of Dublin. Classical Foundation Scholar, Vice-Chancellor's Medallist in Latin, Vice-Chancellor's Prize for Latin Prose; Senior Moderator in Classics and in Mental and Moral Science, 1922; Lecturer in Classics and Philosophy, University of W. Australia, 1923–28; Student of British Sch., Athens, 1929; Asst Lecturer in Classics, University Coll., Southampton, 1929–31; Lecturer in Latin, University of St Andrews, 1931–46; Reader in Classics, University of London, Queen Mary Coll., 1946–49; Ford Visiting Prof. of Classics, University of Ibadan, 1964–65. *Publications:* A History of Delos, 1933; The Prosody of Terence, 1938; Latin Literature, 1951; contribs to: Oxford Classical Dictionary, 1949; Fifty Years of Classical Scholarship, 1954, Chambers's Encyclopædia: articles, notes, reviews in various classical journals. *Recreation:* reading. *Address:* 4 Inverclyde Court, Nicholas Road, Blundellsands, Liverpool L23 6TS. *T:* 051-924 1279. *Died 3 Feb.* 1983.

**LAING, Ronald David,** MB, ChB, DPM; *b* 7 Oct. 1927; *s* of D. P. M. and Amelia Laing; *m*; five *c*; *m* Jutta; one *s* one *d*. *Educ:* Glasgow Univ. Glasgow and West of Scotland Neurosurgical Unit, 1951; Central Army Psychiatric Unit, Netley, 1951–52; Psychiatric Unit, Mil. Hosp., Catterick, 1952–53; Dept of Psychological Med., Glasgow Univ., 1953–56; Tavistock Clinic, 1956–60; Tavistock Inst. of Human Relations, 1960–; Fellow, Foundns Fund for Research in Psychiatry, 1960–67; Dir, Langham Clinic for Psychotherapy, 1962–65; Fellow, Tavistock Inst. of Med. Psychology, 1963–64; Principal Investigator, Schizophrenia and Family Research Unit, Tavistock Inst. of Human Relations, 1964–67. Chm., Philadelphia Assoc., 1964–82. *Publications:* The Divided Self, 1960 (London and New York) (Pelican edn, 1962, Penguin repr. 1971); The Self and Others, 1961 (London and New York) (rev. edn 1969, Penguin, 1971); (with D. Cooper) Reason and Violence (introd. by J. P. Sartre), 1964 (London and New York) (Pantheon, 1971); (with E. Esterson) Sanity, Madness and the Family, 1965 (London and New York); (with H. Phillipson and A. R. Lee) Interpersonal Perception, 1966 (London and NY); The Politics of Experience and the Bird of Paradise (Penguin), 1967 (London, repr. 1971), (Pantheon, 1967, New York); Knots, 1970 (London), (Pantheon, 1970, New York), (Penguin, 1972); The Politics of the Family, 1971 (London); The Facts of Life, 1976 (Pantheon, New York); Do You Love Me?, 1977 (London); Conversations with Children, 1978 (London); Sonnets, 1979 (London); The Voice of Experience, 1982 (London and NY); Wisdom, Madness and Folly, 1985; Paroles d'Enfants, 1989 (Paris). *Address:* c/o Birkett Wesson, 21 Princes Street, Hanover Square, W1. *Died 23 Aug.* 1989.

**LAITHWAITE, Sir (John) Gilbert,** GCMG 1953 (KCMG 1948); KCB 1956; KCIE 1941 (CIE 1935); CSI 1938; Deputy Chairman Inchcape & Co. Ltd, 1960–64, Director 1964–69; former Chairman: Bedford Life Assurance Co. Ltd; Bedford General Insurance Co. Ltd; UK Committee of Federation of Commonwealth Chambers of Commerce; *b* 5 July 1894; *e s* of late J. G. Laithwaite, formerly of the Post Office Survey. *Educ:* Clongowes; Trinity Coll., Oxford (Scholar). Hon. Fellow, Trinity Coll., Oxford, 1955. Served in France with 10th Lancs Fusiliers, 1917–18 (wounded); appointed to India Office, 1919; Principal, 1924; specially attached to Prime Minister (Mr Ramsay MacDonald) for 2nd Indian Round Table Conference, Sept.-Dec. 1931; Secretary, Indian Franchise (Lothian) Committee, Jan.-June 1932; Secretary, Indian Delimitation Cttee, Aug. 1935–Feb. 1936; Private Secretary to the Viceroy of India (Marquess of Linlithgow), 1936–43, and a Secretary to the Governor-General 1937–43; Assistant Under-Secretary of State for India, 1943; an Under-Secretary (Civil) of the War Cabinet, 1944–45; Deputy Under-Secretary of State for Burma, 1945–47, for India, 1947, for Commonwealth Relations, 1948–49; Ambassador, 1950–51 (United Kingdom Representative, 1949–50) to the Republic of Ireland; High Commissioner for the UK in Pakistan, 1951–54; Permanent Under-Secretary of State for Commonwealth Relations, 1955–59. Vice-Chm., Commonwealth Inst., 1963–66; Governor, Queen Mary Coll., Univ. of London, 1959–; Trustee, Hakluyt Soc., 1958–84 (Pres., 1964–69); former Vice-Pres., Royal Central Asian Soc., (Chm. Council, 1964–67); Vice-Pres., RGS, 1969 (Pres., 1966–69); Mem. Standing Commn on Museums and Galleries, 1959–72. A Freeman of the City of London, 1960. Master, Tallowchandlers' Co., 1972–73. Hon. LLD Dublin, 1957. Kt of Malta, 1960; Kt Templar, 1986. *Publications:* The Laithwaites, Some Records of a Lancashire Family, 1941, rev. edn 1961; Memories of an Infantry Officer, 1971; etc. *Address:* c/o Grindlay's Bank, 13 St James's Square, SW1. *Clubs:* Travellers'; United Oxford & Cambridge University. *Died 21 Dec.* 1986.

**LAL, Shavax Ardeshir,** CIE 1941; Advocate, High Court, Bombay; *b* 12 Nov. 1899; *s* of Ardeshir Edulji Lal, Nasik, Bombay Presidency; *m* 1933, Coomi, *d* of N. N. Master; three *d. Educ:* Fergusson College and Law College, Poona. Practised law, 1926–30; joined Bombay Judicial Service, 1930; transferred to Legal Department, Bombay, 1930; Assistant Secretary to Government of Bombay, Legal Department, 1932–36; nominated member and Secretary of Council of State, 1936–46; Secretary to Government of India, Ministry of Law, 1947–48; Secretary to Governor-General of India, 1948–50; Secretary to President of India, 1950–54. *Address:* Windcliffe, Pedder Road, Bombay, India. *Died 25 Feb.* 1987.

**LAMBART, Julian Harold Legge;** *b* 7 May 1893; *s* of late Brig.-General E. A. Lambart, CB, RA, and late Mary Louisa, *d* of Sir James Walker, 2nd Bt, of Sand Hutton; *m* 1948, Margaret, *widow* of Sir Walford Davies. *Educ:* Eton Coll.; King's Coll., Cambridge. Served European War, 1914–18, as Capt. RFA (Croix de Guerre). Assistant Master at Eton, 1919; Lower Master, 1945–59; Vice-Provost, 1959–67. *Recreations:* travel and architecture. *Address:* Amesbury Abbey, Amesbury, Wilts SP4 7EX. *T:* Amesbury 22258. *Died 11 Oct.* 1982.

**LAMBART, Sir Oliver Francis,** 2nd Bt *cr* 1911; Lieut late RASC; *b* 6 April 1913; *s* of 1st Bt and Kathleen Moore-Brabazon; *S* father, 1926. *Heir:* none. *Address:* Beau Parc, Co. Meath. *Club:* Turf. *Died 16 March* 1986 (*ext*).

**LAMBERT, 2nd Viscount,** *cr* 1945, of South Molton; **George Lambert,** TD; *b* 27 Nov. 1909; *e s* of 1st Viscount Lambert, PC; *S* father, 1958; *m* 1939, Patricia Mary, *d* of J. F. Quinn; one *d* (one *s* decd). *Educ:* Harrow Sch.; New Coll., Oxford. War of 1939–45: TA, Lieut-Colonel 1942. MP (L-Nat) South Molton Division, Devon, July 1945–Feb. 1950. (Nat. L-C) Torrington Division, Devon, 1950–58. Chm., Devon and Exeter Savings Bank, 1958–70. Formerly Chm. Governors, Seale-Hayne Agricultural Coll., Newton Abbot, Devon. Pres., Young Farmers' Club, 1968–70; Life Vice-Pres., National Federation of Young Farmers' Clubs, 1970. DL Devon, 1969–70. *Heir presumptive:* b Hon. Michael John Lambert [*b* 29 Sept. 1912; *m* 1939, Florence Dolores, *d* of late N. L. Macaskie, QC; three *d*]. *Address:* Les Fougères, 1806 St-Légier, Switzerland. *T:* (021) 53 10 63. *Clubs:* Carlton, Army and Navy. *Died 24 May* 1989.

**LAMBERT, Ven. Charles Henry,** MA; Archdeacon of Lancaster, 1959–66, Emeritus, 1966; Vicar of St Cuthbert's, Lytham, 1960–66; Senior Examining Chaplain to Bishop of Blackburn; *b* 13 Jan. 1894; *s* of Henry and Frances Ann Lambert; *m* 1920, Dorothy Ellen Birch; three *s* one *d. Educ:* Primary Schools; privately; Leeds Univ.; Cuddesdon Coll. BA 1916; MA 1932; deacon 1917; priest 1918; Curate of Redcar, 1917–20; of Guisborough, 1920–22; Rector of St Denys with St George, York, 1922–24; Vicar of Royston, Yorks, 1924–28; Rector of St Mary Bishophill Senior with St Clement, York, 1928–34; Warden of Whalley Abbey, 1934–45; Director of Religious Education, diocese of Blackburn, 1934–46; Canon, Blackburn, 1934–46; Archdeacon of Blackburn, 1946–59; Proctor, 1929–34, York, 1935–45, Blackburn. OCF 1941–44; Archbishops' Visitor to RAF, 1944–45; Rural Dean of Whalley, 1942–45. *Publications:* Go Ye, .... Teach, 1939; Whalley Abbey, Yesterday and to-Day, 1948. *Recreations:* reading, walking, keenly interested in all outdoor sports. *Address:* 19 Connaught Mansions, Great Pulteney Street, Bath. *T:* Bath 66429. *Died 12 July* 1983.

**LAMBERT, Sir Greville Foley,** 9th Bt, *cr* 1711; *b* 17 Aug. 1900; *s* of late Lionel Foley Lambert, 4th *s* of 6th Bt; *S* cousin (Sir John Foley Grey), 1938; *m* 1932, Edith Roma, *d* of Richard Batson; three *d. Educ:* Rugby Sch. Chartered Accountant. *Heir:* kinsman, Peter John Biddulph Lambert, archaeologist, Min. of Culture and Recreation and Historical Researches Branch, Govt of Ontario [*b* 5 April 1952. *Educ:* Upper Canada Coll.; Trent Univ.; Univ. of Manitoba. BSc(Hons), MA]. *Died 26 Dec.* 1988.

**LAMBERT, Guy William,** CB 1942; BA; *b* 1 Dec. 1889; 2nd *s* of late Col J. A. Lambert, Brookhill, Claremorris, Co. Mayo, and Grace, *e d* of late W. D. Fane, Fulbeck Hall, Lincs; *m* 1917, Nadine (*d* 1983), *y d* of late Wilson Noble, Park Place, Henley-on-Thames; one *s* two *d. Educ:* Cheltenham Coll.; St John's Coll., Oxford. Higher Div. Clerk, War Office, 1913; Private Secretary to Sir C. Harris, KCB, Assistant Financial Secretary, 1915; Private Secretary to H. W. Forster, Financial Secretary, 1916; Chevalier, Légion d'Honneur, 1920; Principal Private Secretary to successive Secretaries of State for War, Rt Hon. Sir L. Worthington-Evans Bt, GBE, and Rt Hon. T. Shaw, CBE, 1926–29; Assistant Under-Secretary of State for War, 1938–51. President Society for Psychical Research, 1955–58. Fellow, Irish Genealogical Research Soc., 1970. Silver Jubilee Medal, 1935; Coronation Medal, 1937. *Clubs:* Athenæum, Leander, London Rowing. *Died 15 Dec.* 1983.

**LAMBERT, Jack Walter,** CBE 1970; DSC 1944; *b* 21 April 1917; *o s* of Walter and Ethel Lambert; *m* 1940, Catherine Margaret, Hon. RCM, *e d* of Alfred Read, CBE; one *s* two *d. Educ:* Tonbridge Sch. Served with Royal Navy in Atlantic, Arctic, North Sea, Channel (Light Coastal Forces), 1940–46, dispatches 1944 (Ordinary Seaman; Lieut-Commander). Editorial Assistant: The Electrician, 1936–37; The Newspaper World, 1937–38; The Fruit-Grower, Florist, and Market Gardener, 1938 (Editor, 1939–40); joined Sunday Times as Assistant Literary Editor, 1948; Literary and Arts Editor, 1960–76; Associate Editor, 1976–81. Member: Bd of Management, British Drama League, later British Theatre Assoc., 1963–84; Drama Adv. Cttee, British Council, 1963–84 (Chm. 1968–69); Council, RADA, 1972–; Mem., Arts Council of GB, 1968–76: Mem., Drama Panel, 1965–76 (Chm. 1968–76); Theatre Enquiry, 1967–69; Vice-Chm., New Activities Cttee, 1969–70; Chm., Computer Booking Working Party, 1969–72; Cttee, Royal Literary Fund, 1960–; Member: Theatres Adv. Cttee, 1973–75; Council, Soc. of Authors, 1975– (Mem., Cttee of Management, 1960–63); Dir, Theatre Investment Fund, 1972–. Governor, British Inst. of Recorded Sound, 1966–69, 1977–82; Chairman: Old Vic Trust, 1978–79; Dir, Opera 80, 1979– (Chm., 1979–81); Trustee, Phoenix Trust, 1975–86. Officier de l'Ordre des arts et des lettres, 1975; Officier de l'Ordre National du Mérite, 1976. *Publications:* Penguin Guide to Cornwall, 1939; The Bodley Head Saki (ed), 1963; Drama in Britain, 1964–73, 1974; much occasional writing and broadcasting on literature, music and the theatre. *Recreation:* singing. *Address:* 30 Belsize Grove, NW3. *T:* 01–722 1668. *Clubs:* Garrick, Beefsteak.

*Died 3 Aug.* 1986.

**LAMBERT, Richard Stanton,** MA; Supervisor of Educational Broadcasts, Canadian Broadcasting Corporation, 1943–60; *b* 25 Aug, 1894; *s* of late Richard Cornthwaite Lambert and Lilian Lambert, London; *m* 1918, Kate Elinor, *d* of Sydney T. Klein; one *s* one *d*; *m* 1944, Joyce, *d* of Edward Morgan. *Educ:* Repton; Wadham Coll., Oxford (classical scholar). Joined staff of The Economist, 1916; served with the Friends' Ambulance Unit, 1916–18; Lecturer to University Tutorial Classes, Sheffield, 1919; Staff Tutor for Tutorial Classes, University of London, 1924; Head of Adult Education Section, BBC, 1927; Editor, The Listener, 1928–39; Member of Commission on Educational and Cultural Films, 1929–33; of Governing Body of British Film Institute, 1933–40; Vice-Chairman, British Institute of Adult Education, 1936–39; Education Adviser to Canadian Broadcasting Corporation, 1940–43, 1960–61. Couns. to UNESCO on media of mass communication, 1946. *Publications:* The Prince of Pickpockets, 1930; A Historian's Scrapbook, 1932; The Railway King, 1934; When Justice Faltered, 1935; (jointly with Harry Price) The Haunting of Cashen's Gap, 1935; The Innocence of Edmund Galley, 1936; The Universal Provider, 1938; Propaganda, 1938; The Cobbett of the West, 1939; Ariel and all his Quality, 1940; Home Front, 1940; Old Country Mail, 1941; For the Time is at Hand, 1946; The Adventure of Canadian Painting, 1947; Franklin of the Arctic, 1949; The Fortunate Traveller, 1950; North for Adventure, 1953; Exploring the Supernatural, 1955; Redcoat Sailor, 1956; Trailmaker, 1957; The Great Heritage, 1958; The Twentieth Century, 1960; School Broadcasting in Canada, 1962; Mutiny in the Bay, 1963; Renewing Nature's Wealth (Ontario Forests), 1967; Greek and Roman Myths and Legends, 1967, 1971; The Gothic Rectory, 1971. Edited (jointly) Memoirs of the Unemployed, 1933; For Filmgoers Only, 1934; Grand Tour, 1935; Art in England, 1938; translated and printed Vida's Game of Chess, 1921; Walafrid Strabo's Hortulus, 1923, and Plays of Roswitha, 1922–23; ed and printed Sir John Davies' Orchestra or a Poeme of Dancing, 1922. *Recreation:* gardening. *Address:* 2713 Seaview Road, Victoria, BC, Canada.

*Died 27 Nov.* 1981.

**LAMBERT, Surgeon Vice-Adm. Roger John William,** QHP 1980; Medical Director-General (Naval), since 1983; *b* 23 April 1928; *s* of Engr Rear Adm. C. W. Lambert, CB and Muriel Nicholson; *m* 1952, Lois Barbara Kermode; one *s* one *d. Educ:* Oundle Sch.; Trinity Coll., Cambridge (MA 1952; MB, BChir 1953); Guy's Hosp. MRCS, LRCP 1952; DPH London, 1965; DIH 1966; MFOM 1980. Served HMS St Angelo, HMS Dolphin, HMS Dreadnought, HMS Maidstone, and Inst. of Naval Medicine, 1953–74; seconded US Naval Submarine Service, 1959; Dir of Health and Res. (Navy), 1975; MO i/c RN Hosp. Gibraltar, 1977. Surg. Comdr 1966, Surg. Captain 1974; Surgeon Rear Adm. (Inst. of Naval Medicine) and Dean of Naval Medicine, 1980–82; Surgeon Rear-Adm. (Ships and Establishments, later Support Medical Services), 1982–83. FRSM 1957; FFCM 1983; Member: BMA, 1952–; European Undersea Biomed. Soc., 1969–; Soc. of Occupational Medicine, 1976–. CStJ 1984. Erroll-Eldridge Prize, 1970. *Publications:* papers in fields of submarine medicine, submarine toxicology, and physiology of submarine escape. *Recreations:* painting, gardening, diving. *Address:* Ministry of Defence (Navy), First Avenue House, High Holborn, WC1V 6HE. *Club:* Army and Navy.

*Died 1 Nov.* 1984.

**LAMBERT, Dr Royston James;** writer; Director of the Reynolds Gallery, Plymouth; *b* 7 Dec. 1932; *s* of Albert Edward Lambert and Edith Alice Tyler; unmarried. *Educ:* Barking Abbey Sch.; Sidney Sussex Coll., Cambridge; Magdalen Coll., Oxford. Open Exhibitioner, Magdalen Coll., Oxford, 1951; Major Scholar, Sidney

Sussex Coll., Cambridge, 1954; Hentsch Prize, 1954. 1st class Hist. Tripos Pt I (dist), 1954, 1st class Pt II 1955, MA 1959, PhD 1960, Cantab; BA Oxon, 1955. Bachelor Schol., Sidney Sussex Coll., Cambridge, 1956–58, Research Fellow, 1958–61; Nuffield Senior Sociological Schol., LSE, 1961–64; Ehrman Fellow, King's Coll., Cambridge, 1962–69; Headmaster, Dartington Hall Sch., 1969–73; Dir, Dartington Res. Unit, 1969–75; Advisor on Educn to Dartington Hall Trust, 1973–75. Founded and directed Research Unit into Boarding Education, 1964–68; directed research for Public Schools Commn, 1966–68; directed research for Home Office into Approved School system, 1968–. Founded Boarding Schools Assoc., 1966. *Publications*: Sir John Simon and English Social Administration, 1963; Nutrition in Britain 1950–1960, 1964; The State and Boarding Education, 1966; The Hothouse Society, 1968; New Wine in Old Bottles?: Studies in integration in the Public Schools, 1968; Manual to the Sociology of the School, 1970; Alternatives to School (W. B. Curry Meml Lecture), 1971; The Chance of a Lifetime?, 1975; Body and Soul, 1980; Beloved and God: the story of Hadrian and Antinous, 1982; contribs in: The Public Schools (G. Kalton, 1966); Religious Education (ed. P. Jebb, 1968); The Progressive School (ed. M. Ash, 1968); Education in the Seventies, 1971; Appendix to the First Report of the Public Schools Commission; pamphlets on education and articles in learned journals on social and administrative history, art history, sociology and education. *Recreations*: restoring paintings; herbaceous borders; Bavarian Rococo; Victorian Gothic; Irish setters. *Address*: Island House, The Barbican, Plymouth. *T*: Plymouth 663318; 37 Lexham Gardens, W8. *T*: 01-370 2407. *Died 25 Oct. 1982.*

**LAMBERT, Prof. Victor Francis,** MD, ChM, FRCS, FRCSE; Professor of Oto-laryngology, Manchester University, 1947–64; Professor Emeritus, 1964; Director, English Sewing Cotton Co., 1947–68; *b* Chequerbent, Lancs, 12 Aug. 1899; *s* of James and Ann Lambert; *m* 1st, 1930, Myra (*d* 1950), *d* of William and Eva Farnworth, Bolton, Lancs; one *s* one *d*; 2nd, 1954, Margaret, *d* of John and Beatrice Norris, Whalley Range, Manchester; one *d*. *Educ*: Bolton Sch.; Manchester Univ. Inns of Court OTC, Royal Artillery, 1917–19. Formerly: Director of Department of Oto-laryngology, Manchester Royal Infirmary; Christie Hospital and Holt Radium Inst.; Laryngologist, Christie Hospital and Holt Radium Inst.; Consultant to Department of Education of the Deaf, University of Manchester; Cons. Surgeon, Manchester Victoria Memorial Jewish Hospital. Hon. Laryngologist, Royal Manchester College of Music; Pres. Sect. of Laryngology, RSM, 1954–55; Chairman Richard Arkwright Educ. Scholarship; Governor of Bolton School; President, Old Boltonians Association, 1962; Member Manchester Regional Hosp. Board, 1951–60; former Member Court of Examiners, RCS of England and Edinburgh; Examiner, National University of Ireland; President: N of England Oto-laryngological Soc., 1950 (Hon. Life Mem.); Manchester Surgical Society, 1955–56; British Assoc. Oto-laryngologists, 1960–64; Manchester Medical Soc., 1963–64; Semon Lecture, 1959; Guest Lecturer, Canadian Medical Society, British Columbia Div., 1963; Watson Williams Memorial Lecture, University of Bristol, 1964. MB, ChB (Victoria Univ., Manchester), 1923; FRCSEd 1927; FRCS Eng (*ad eund.*) 1949; ChM (Victoria Univ., Manchester) 1932; MD 1940. Jobson Horne Memorial Prize, 1963. *Publications*: papers and articles in Journal of Laryngology and Otology; Proc. Royal Society Med.; Anatomical Society of Great Britain; Medical Press; Manchester Univ. Med. Sch. Gazette; Clinical Journal; BMJ Journal of Anatomy. *Recreations*: golf and music. *Address*: (home) 45 The Downs, Altrincham, Cheshire. *T*: 061–928 4144.
*Died 8 June 1981.*

**LAMBORN, Harry George;** MP (Lab) Southwark, Peckham, since 1974 (Southwark, May 1972–1974); *b* 1 May 1915; *s* of late Cecil Lamborn, Dulwich; *m* 1938, Lilian Ruth Smith; two *s* one *d*. *Educ*: LCC elementary school. Camberwell Borough Council: Mem., 1953–65; Chm. Health Cttee, 1954–63; Mayor of Camberwell, 1963–64. LCC: Mem., 1958–65; Chm. Health Cttee, 1962–65; GLC: Mem., 1964–73; Dep. Chm., 1971–72. PPS to Chancellor of Exchequer, 1974–79. Governor: King's Coll. Hosp., 1965–; Bethlem and Maudsley Hosps, 1966–. Dir, Royal Arsenal Co-operative Soc., 1965–72; Member: Labour Party, 1933–; Union of Shop Distributive and Allied Workers, 1933–; Central Health Services Council, 1963–68. MRSH. Hon. Freeman, Borough of Southwark, 1982. *Recreations*: walking, cricket. *Address*: 53 Farne Close, Hailsham, Sussex. *Died 21 Aug. 1982.*

**LAMBRICK, Hugh Trevor,** CIE 1944; DLitt; Fellow of Oriel College, Oxford, 1947–71, Emeritus Fellow since 1971; *b* 20 April 1904; 2nd *s* of late Rev. C. M. Lambrick; *m* 1948, Gabrielle Margaret (*d* 1968), *yr d* of late H. H. Jennings; two *s*. *Educ*: Rossall; Oriel Coll., Oxford (1st Cl. Hons. Mod. Hist. 1926); DLitt Oxon 1971. Entered ICS 1927; Assistant Commissioner in Sind, 1931; Deputy Commissioner, Upper Sind Frontier, 1934; Collector of Sholapur, 1936; Superintendent of Census, Sind, 1939; Secretary to Governor of Sind, 1941; Civil Adviser to Chief Administrator of Martial Law, Sind, 1942; Special Commissioner for Sind, 1943–46; retired 1947;

Spalding Senior Res. Fellow, Oriel Coll., Oxford, 1947, Treasurer, 1951–55, Res. Fellow and Lectr, 1955–71. Richard Burton Meml Medal, 1978. FSA 1971. *Publications*: Sir Charles Napier and Sind, 1952; John Jacob of Jacobabad, 1960, illustrated edn, 1975; History of Sind, Vol. I, 1964, 2nd edn 1976; The Terrorist, 1972; Sind before the Muslim Conquest, 1973; numerous articles on Historical and Archæological subjects in Journal of Sind Historical Society since 1935 (President, 1940–43); Census of India, 1941, Vol. XII; Sind. *Recreation*: music. *Address*: Pickett's heath, Boars Hill, Oxford. *Club*: East India, Devonshire, Sports and Public Schools.
*Died 31 Aug. 1982.*

**LAMING, Rev. Canon Frank Fairbairn;** *b* 24 Aug. 1908; *s* of William John Laming and Maude Elizabeth (*née* Fairbairn); *m* 1939, Ruth Marion, *d* of Herbert William Pinder and Rose Marion (*née* Price). *Educ*: King Edward VI Sch., Retford; The Theological Coll., Edinburgh. In business, 1925–33; Edinburgh Theological Coll., 1933–36; Luscombe Scholar, 1936; Durham LTh, 1936. Deacon, 1936; Priest, 1937; Assistant Priest, Christ Church, Glasgow, 1936–39; Priest in Charge, St Margaret, Renfrew, 1939–44; Rector, Holy Trinity Church, Motherwell, 1944–53; Rector and Provost of St Mary's Cathedral, Glasgow, 1953–66; Provost of St Andrew's Cathedral, Inverness, 1966–74; Priest-in-Charge, St. Ninian's, Glenurquhart, 1974–84, retired; Hon. Canon, Inverness Cathedral, 1974–. Editor, Year Book and Directory of the Episcopal Church in Scotland, 1976–84. *Recreation*: woodworking. *Address*: 16 South Street, Aberchirder, Huntly, Aberdeenshire AB5 5TR. *T*: Aberchirder 625. *Died 3 June 1989.*

**LAMONT, William Dawson,** MA, DPhil; *b* Prince Edward Island, Canada, 3 Feb. 1901; 4th *s* of Rev. Murdoch Lamont, Rothiemurchus, Inverness-shire, and Euphemia Ann Hume; *m* 1930, Ann Fraser, *d* of Dr David Christie, Glasgow; no *c*. *Educ*: Glasgow Univ. (Edward Caird Medallist; First Class in Moral and Mental Philosophy 1924, Euing Fellow and Ferguson Scholar 1924); Balliol Coll., Oxford. Assistant in Moral Philosphy, University of Glasgow, 1926, and Lecturer, 1929; Professor of Philosophy, University of Cairo, 1942. Principal of Makerere Coll., East Africa, 1946–49. Served with Clyde River Patrol and as Naval Intelligence Liaison Officer, West Scotland, 1939–42. Hon. Secretary Anglo-Egyptian Union, 1944; Vice-Chairman Cairo Group of RIIA, 1944. FSA Scot. 1968. HonDLitt, University of East Africa, 1965. *Publications*: Introduction to Green's Moral Philosophy, 1934; Principles of Moral Judgement, 1946; The Value Judgement, 1955; The Early History of Islay, 1966; Ancient and Mediæval Sculptured Stones of Islay, 1968; Law and the Moral Order, 1981; articles (on philosophical subjects) in Mind, Proceedings of the Aristotelian Society, Philosophy; (on historical subjects) in Scottish Studies, Proceedings of the Royal Irish Academy and Scottish Historical Review. *Recreation*: walking. *Address*: 37 Kirklee Road, Glasgow G12 0SP. *T*: 041-339 5399. *Died 9 Nov. 1982.*

**LAMPLOUGH, Maj.-Gen. Charles Robert Wharram,** CBE 1945; DSC 1918; DL; JP; Royal Marines, retired; *b* 10 June 1896; *s* of late Robert Lamplough and Louisa Lamplough, Scarborough; *m* 1921, Doris Mary Ford; one *d*. *Educ*: Warwick Sch. Served European War, 1914–18: joined Royal Marines, 1914, and served in Mediterranean and in Grand Fleet, Dardanelles and Zeebrugge (DSC). Served, 1919–39, in HM ships in various waters and held instructional and staff appointments at home and in Far East. Served War of 1939–45 on Naval Staff, Admiralty, and in 1943 returned to Far East as Maj.-General on staff of Supreme Allied Commander, SEAC (CBE). ADC to King George VI, 1946; Maj.-General Commanding Plymouth Group, Royal Marines, 1946–49; retired, 1949; Hon. Colonel Comdt, Plymouth Group Royal Marines, 1953–57. DL Devonshire, 1966; JP County of Devon, 1954. *Address*: Falklands, 32 Salterton Road, Exmouth, Devon. *T*: Exmouth 3648. *Died 28 Nov. 1981.*

**LAMPLUGH, Maj.-Gen. Stephen,** CB 1954; CBE 1943; Retired 1955; Past Director of Civil Defence, Northern Region (Newcastle upon Tyne), 1955–64; *b* 25 May 1900; *s* of late George William Lamplugh, FRS, Driffield, Yorks; *m* 1938, Mary Lewis, *d* of A. H. Vesey, Suddon Grange, Wincanton, Somerset; one *s* one *d*. *Educ*: St Albans; RMA, Woolwich. 2nd Lieut RE, 1919; Major, 1938; Lt-Col (temp), 1940; Brigadier (temp.), 1942; Maj.-Gen. (temp.), 1945 and 1952; Colonel, 1945; Brigadier, 1947; Maj-General, 1953. Served Near East, 1922–23; NW Frontier, 1930; France, 1939–40 (despatches); psc 1937. Commander Rhine District, BAOR, 1952–55, retired 1955. Chairman Joint War Office Treasury Cttee, 1955. *Recreations*: normal. *Address*: Amesbury Abbey, Amesbury, Wilts. *Died 26 April 1983.*

**LANCASTER, Sir Osbert,** Kt 1975; CBE 1953; RDI 1979; artist and writer; *b* 4 Aug. 1908; *o s* of late Robert Lancaster and Clare Bracebridge Manger; *m* 1933, Karen (*d* 1964), 2nd *d* of late Sir Austin Harris, KBE; one *s* one *d*; *m* 1967, Anne Scott-James. *Educ*: Charterhouse; Lincoln Coll., Oxford (Hon. Fellow, 1979); Slade Sch. Hon. FRIBA. Cartoonist Daily Express since 1939; Foreign

Office (News Dept), 1940; Attached to HM Embassy, Athens, 1944–46; Sydney Jones Lecturer in Art, Liverpool Univ., 1947. Adviser to GLC Historic Buildings Bd, 1969–. Governor King Edward VII Sch., King's Lynn. Hon. DLitt: Birmingham Univ., 1964; Newcastle-upon-Tyne, 1970; St Andrews, 1974; Oxon, 1975. Fellow, University College, London, 1967. Theatre Décors: Pineapple Poll, Sadler's Wells, 1951; Bonne Bouche, Covent Garden, 1952; Love in a Village, English Opera Group, 1952; High Spirits, Hippodrome, 1953; Rake's Progress, Edinburgh (for Glyndebourne), 1953; All's Well That Ends Well, Old Vic, 1953; Don Pasquale, Sadler's Wells, 1954; Coppélia, Covent Garden, 1954; Napoli, Festival Ballet, 1954; Falstaff, Edinburgh (for Glyndebourne), 1955; Hotel Paradiso, Winter Garden, 1956; Zuleika, Saville, 1957; L'Italiana in Algeri, Glyndebourne, 1957; Tiresias, English Opera Group, 1958; Candide, Saville, 1959; La Fille Mal Gardée, Covent Garden, 1960; She Stoops to Conquer, Old Vic, 1960; La Pietra del Paragone, Glyndebourne, 1964; Peter Grimes, Bulgarian National Opera, Sofia, 1964; L'Heure Espagnole, Glyndebourne, 1966; The Rising of the Moon, Glyndebourne, 1970; The Sorcerer, D'Oyly-Carte, 1971. *Publications:* Progress at Pelvis Bay, 1936; Our Sovereigns, 1936; Pillar to Post, 1938; Homes, Sweet Homes, 1939; Classical Landscape with Figures, 1947; The Saracen's Head, 1948; Drayneflete Revealed, 1949; Façades and Faces, 1950; Private Views, 1956; The Year of the Comet, 1957; Etudes, 1958; Here, of All Places, 1959, reissued as A Cartoon History of Architecture, 1976; Signs of the Times, 1961; All Done From Memory (Autobiog.), 1963; With an Eye to the Future (Autobiog.), 1967; Temporary Diversions, 1968; Sailing to Byzantium, 1969; Recorded Live, 1970; Meaningful Confrontations, 1971; Theatre in the Flat, 1972; The Littlehampton Bequest, 1973; (with Anne Scott-James) The Pleasure Garden, 1977; Scene Changes, 1978; Ominous Cracks, 1979; The Life and Times of Maudie Littlehampton, 1982. *Recreation:* topography. *Address:* 78 Cheyne Court, Royal Hospital Road, SW3. *Clubs:* Pratt's, Beefsteak, Garrick.                    *Died 27 July 1986.*

**LANCELYN GREEN, Roger G.;** *see* Green, R. G. L.

**LANCHESTER, Elsa;** actress; *b* 28 Oct. 1902; *d* of James Sullivan and Edith Lanchester; *m* 1929, Charles Laughton (*d* 1962); became American Citizen, 1950. *Educ:* privately. Started the Children's Theatre, Charlotte Street, Soho, 1918; first appearance on stage, 1922; afterwards played at Lyric, Hammersmith, in The Way of the World, 1924, in The Duenna, 1924 and in Riverside Nights, 1926; first appearance in New York at Lyceum Theatre, 1931; joined Old Vic-Sadler's Wells company, 1933; was Peter Pan, Palladium, 1936; was in They Walk Alone, New York, 1941; 10 years as star of Turnabout Theatre, Los Angeles, California; Turnabout Theatre, nightly continuously, from 1941. Acted in The Party, London, 1958. Has appeared in films including The Constant Nymph, Potiphar's Wife, The Private Life of Henry VIII, David Copperfield, Bride of Frankenstein, Naughty Marietta, The Ghost Goes West, Rembrandt, Vessel of Wrath, Ladies in Retirement, Son of Fury, Passport to Destiny, Lassie Come Home, Spiral Staircase, Razor's Edge, The Big Clock, The Inspector General, The Secret Garden, Come to the Stable, Buccaneer Girl, The Glass Slipper, Witness for the Prosecution, Bell, Book and Candle, Mary Poppins, That Darn Cat, Blackbeard's Ghost, Me Natalie, Rascal, My Dog, The Thief, Willard, Terror in the Wax Museum, Arnold, Murder by Death. Television series, The John Forsythe Show; talk shows: Jack Paar; David Frost; Dick Cavitt; Johnny Carson; Joey Bishop. *Publications:* Charles Laughton and I, 1938; Elsa Lanchester Herself (autobiog.), 1983. *Recreation:* wild flowers.

                                                          *Died 26 Dec. 1986.*

**LAND, Prof. Frank William,** MSc, PhD London; Professor of Education, University of Hull, 1961–77; *b* 9 Jan. 1911; *s* of Charles and Mary Land; *m* 1937, Nora Beatrice Channon; two *s* one *d*. *Educ:* King's Coll., University of London. Assistant Master, The Grammar School, Hampton-on-Thames, 1933–37; Mathematics Lecturer: College of St Mark and St John, Chelsea, 1937–39; Birkbeck Coll., London, 1939–40. Instructor Lieut, Royal Navy, 1940–46. Vice-Principal, College of St Mark and St John, Chelsea, 1946–49; Senior Lecturer, University of Liverpool, 1950–61. Chairman, Association of Teachers in Colleges and Departments of Education, 1956–57. *Publications:* Recruits to Teaching, 1960; The Language of Mathematics, 1961. *Recreation:* gardening. *Address:* Ty'n y Llidiart, Llandegla, Wrexham, Clwyd LL11 3AF.

                                                          *Died 2 June 1990.*

**LAND, Dr Roger Burton,** FRSE 1985; Head, Physiology and Genetics Research Station, Roslin, Agricultural Food Research Council, since 1983; *b* 30 April 1940; *s* of Albert Land and Betty Newton Land (*née* Burton); *m* 1968, Moira Helen Murdoch (*née* Mackay); one *s* two *d*. *Educ:* Bradford Grammar School; Nottingham Univ. (BSc 1962); Edinburgh Univ. (PhD 1965). Joined Animal Breeding Research Organisation, 1966, Dir, 1983–86. *Publication:* (jtly) Food Chains to Biotechnology, 1983; contribs to Jl of Reproduction and Fertility and Animal Production. *Recreations:* family activities,

gardening. *Address:* 15 Ferguson View, West Linton, Peeblesshire. *T:* West Linton 60011.                              *Died 17 April 1988.*

**LANDALE, Russell Talbot;** HM Diplomatic Service, retired 1971; Consul-General, Amsterdam, 1969–71; *b* 25 Oct. 1911; 3rd *s* of late W. H. Landale and Ethel (*née* Talbot); *m* 1938, Margaret Myfanwy George; two *d* (one *s* decd). *Educ:* Berkhamsted Sch.; Wiesbaden Konservatorium; Rackows Kaufmännische Schule, Dresden; Institut de Touraine, Tours. British Tabulating Machine Co. (now ICL), 1933–39; HM Forces, 1940–46; Diplomatic Service, 1946–71. Chevalier de l'Ordre de Méduse, 1974. *Recreations:* viticulture, writing, music (compositions include Song of the Waves, Silver Jubilee Rag, Last Time We Met, Love has almost Gone, Meribel, Tulips of Holland, Let Our People Go, On Poets, Carol's Dance, Petit Nocturne Petite Valse, songs for children). *Address:* Fleur de France, Route de l'Ormée, 06140 Vence, France. *T:* Vence 580369.

                                                          *Died 2 May 1984.*

**LANDER, Frank Patrick Lee,** OBE 1944; MD, FRCP; Principal Medical Officer, Guardian & Royal Exchange Assurance Co., retired; Member, Lord Chancellor's Pensions Appeals Tribunal; Medical Member and Medical Chairman, Pension Appeal Tribunals; *b* 1906; *e s* of Edward Lee and Alice Mary Lander, Morecambelake, Dorset; *m* 1932, Dorothy Briggs; two *s*. *Educ:* Dover Coll.; Middlesex Hospital. Medical Registrar: Middlesex Hospital, 1931; Brompton Hospital, 1934; Consulting Physician: Royal Free Hosp., 1937–71; Brompton Hosp. and Putney Hosp., 1939–71. Lt-Col, RAMC, 1941–45: North Africa, Sicily and Italy (despatches). Examiner in Medicine, University of London, University of Cambridge, University Coll., of the West Indies, and Royal College of Physicians. Formerly Censor, and Senior Censor, Royal College of Physicians. *Publications:* various articles in leading medical journals. *Recreation:* fishing. *Address:* 11 King's Keep, Putney Hill, SW15.                              *Died 12 Jan. 1981.*

**LANDON, Alfred Mossman;** Independent Oil Producer; *b* 9 Sept. 1887; *s* of John Manuel Landon and Anne Mossman; *m* 1915, Margaret Fleming (*d* 1918); one *d*; *m* 1930, Theo Cobb; one *s* one *d*. *Educ:* University of Kansas. Republican State Chm., 1928; Governor of Kansas, 1933–37; Republican nominee for Pres. of United States, 1936; Delegate to Eighth International Conference, Lima, Peru, 1938; Chm. Kansas Delegation Republican Nat. Convention, 1940, 1944, and 1948; Mem. Methodist Church; Member, Kansas Bar; Member, Phi Gamma Delta; Mason, Elks, Odd Fellows. Hon. LHD Kansas State, 1968; Hon. LLD Emporia Coll., 1969. Distinguished Citizenship Award: Washburn Univ., 1967; Baker Univ., 1975. *Recreations:* horseback riding, fishing, bridge. *Address:* 521 Westchester Road, Topeka, Kansas 66606, USA. *T:* 233–4136.                              *Died 12 Oct. 1987.*

**LANE, Dame Elizabeth (Kathleen),** DBE 1965; a Judge of the High Court, Family Division (formerly Probate, Divorce and Admiralty Division), 1965–79; *b* 9 Aug. 1905; *o d* of late Edward Alexander Coulborn and late Kate May Coulborn (*née* Wilkinson); *m* 1926, Henry Jerrold Randall Lane, CBE (*d* 1975); one *s* decd. *Educ:* Malvern Girls Coll. and privately. Barrister, Inner Temple, 1940; Master of the Bench, 1965; QC 1960. Mem. of Home Office Committee on Depositions in Criminal Cases, 1948. An Asst Recorder of Birmingham, 1953–61; Chm. of Birmingham Region Mental Health Review Tribunal, 1960–62; Recorder of Derby, 1961–62; Commissioner of the Crown Court at Manchester, 1961–62; Judge of County Courts, 1962–65; Acting Dep. Chm., London Sessions, 1965. Chm., Cttee on the Working of the Abortion Act, 1971–73. Hon. Fellow, Newnham Coll., Cambridge, 1986. *Publication:* Hear the Other Side, 1985. *Recreations:* gardening, needlework. *Address:* Hillcrest, 60 Chilbolton Avenue, Winchester, Hants SO22 5HQ.                              *Died 17 June 1988.*

**LANE, Rear-Adm. Walter Frederick Boyt,** CB 1960; DSC 1941; FIMechE; MIMarE; Director of Marine Engineering, Admiralty, 1958–61; *b* 7 Feb. 1909; *s* of W. H. Lane, Freshwater, IoW; *m* 1931, Anne Littlecott; one *s*. *Educ:* RN Engineering Coll., Devonport. Eng.-in-Chief, Admiralty, Bath, 1957; Rear-Adm., 1957; retired. Formerly Director, Fairfields (Eng.) Co., Glasgow. *Recreations:* tennis, painting. *Address:* Foxleaze, Limpley Stoke, Wilts. *T:* Limpley Stoke 3225.                              *Died 24 May 1988.*

**LANE-FOX,** Baroness *cr* 1981 (Life Peer), of Bramham in the County of West Yorkshire; **Felicity Lane-Fox,** OBE 1976; Vice-President, Royal Association for Disability and Rehabilitation, since 1963; Chairman of Patients' Association, Phipps Respiratory Unit, St Thomas' Hospital, since 1979; *b* 22 June 1918; *d* of late Edward Lane Fox and Enid Maud Lane Fox, MBE. Adviser to Esmée Fairbairn Charitable Trust on grants for disablement causes. Mem. Nat. Union Exec., Cons. and Unionist Assoc., 1963–66. Mem., Nuffield Orthopaedic Centre House Cttee, Oxford, 1958–66; Vice-President: Yorks Assoc. for Disabled, 1958–80; Action for Dysphasic Adults, 1981–; Patron: Handicapped Adventure Playground Assoc., 1978–; Kensington and Chelsea Action for Disabled, 1982–; Third World Gp for Disabled People, 1983–;

Design and Manufacture for Disability (DEMAND), 1983. Chairman: IBA's London Local Radio Adv. Cttee, 1976–80; Thames Television's Help Trust, 1985–. Member: Prince of Wales' Adv. Gp on Disability, 1982–; Carnegie Council for Arts and Disabled People, 1985–. *Recreations:* drama, documentaries and sport on television, radio; watching racing, cricket and tennis. *Address:* 1 Marlborough Court, Pembroke Road, W8 6DE. *T:* 01–602 3734.                                        *Died* 17 *April* 1988.

**LANE FOX, Col Francis Gordon Ward;** Vice-Lieutenant of West Riding of Yorkshire, 1968–74; Royal Horse Guards, 1919–46, retired; *b* 14 Oct. 1899; *s* of late C. Ward Jackson; assumed surname of Lane Fox in lieu of that of Jackson, by deed poll, 1937; *m* 1929, Hon. Marcia Agnes Mary (*d* 1980), *e d* of 1st and last Baron Bingley, PC (*d* 1947); two *s* one *d*. *Educ:* Eton; RMC, Sandhurst. West Riding of Yorkshire: JP 1948; DL 1952; CC 1949, CA 1955. KStJ 1965. Officer Order of the Crown, with Palm, and Croix de Guerre, with Palm (Belgium), 1946. *Address:* The Little House, Bramham Park, Wetherby, W Yorks LS23 6LS. *T:* Boston Spa 843220. *Club:* Yorkshire (York).                                        *Died* 31 *July* 1989.

**LANG, Rev. Gordon;** Nonconformist Minister, Pen-y-waun Church, Cwmbran, 1956–77; Member of Board, Cwmbran New Town Corporation, 1955–64; *b* Monmouth, 1893; *e s* of T. W. Lang, JP; *m* 1916, Emilie Anne, *d* of J. W. Evans, Leechpool, Chepstow; one *s* one *d*. *Educ:* Monmouth Grammar Sch.; Cheshunt. MP (Lab) Oldham, 1929–31; Stalybridge and Hyde Div. of Ches., 1945–51. Hon. Chaplain to Showmen's Guild of Great Britain and Ireland, 1930–; Associate Mem., CPA, 1945–; Chairman: Parliamentary Federal Group; Proportional Representation Soc., 1947–51; Hon. Sec. United Europe Movement; Vice-Pres. International Youth Bureau, 1946–56; Mem. Council of Hansard Soc., 1948–54; Exec. Mem. Internat. Union of Parliamentarians, 1946–51. Criminologist. *Publications:* Biography of Mr Justice Avory, 1935; Modern Epistles, 1952; Mind Behind Murder, 1960; fiction and many works and papers on Applied Psychology and Criminology. *Address:* 6 Bigstone Grove, Tutshill, Chepstow, Gwent. *T:* Chepstow 2462.
                                        *Died* 20 *June* 1981.

**LANG, Sir John (Gerald),** GCB 1954 (KCB 1947; CB 1946); *b* 20 Dec. 1896; *s* of late George and Rebecca Lang, Woolwich; *m* 1st, 1922, Emilie J. (*d* 1963), *d* of late Henry S. Goddard, Eastbourne; one *d*; 2nd, 1970, Kathleen Winifred, *widow* of C. G. E. Edmeades, and *d* of late Henry S. Goddard. *Educ:* Aske's Harberdashers' Sch., Hatcham. Second Div. Clerk, Admiralty, 1914; Royal Marine Artillery, Lt, 1917–18; Returned to Admiralty: Asst Principal, 1930; Principal, 1935; Asst Sec., 1939; Principal Asst Sec., 1942; Under-Sec., 1946; Sec., Admiralty, SW1, 1947–61. Chm. Bettix Ltd, 1961–70. Principal Adviser on Sport to the Government, 1964–71, and Dep. Chm., Sports Council, 1965–71. Mem. Bd of Govs, Bethlem Royal Hosp. and Maudsley Hosp., 1961–70; Treasurer, 1969–82, Hon. Vice Pres., 1977, RINA; Vice-Pres., Royal Naval Assoc. *Recreation:* gardening. *Address:* 2 Egmont Park House, Walton-on-the-Hill, Tadworth, Surrey. *T:* Tadworth 2200. *Club:* Samuel Pepys (Pres. 1965).                                        *Died* 22 *Sept.* 1984.

**LANG, William Marshall F.;** *see* Farquharson-Lang.

**LANGDON, Alfred Gordon,** CMG 1967; CVO 1966; QPM 1961; retired; Security Advisor, Ministry of Home Affairs, Jamaica, 1970–72; *b* 3 July 1915; *s* of Wilfred James Langdon and Norah (*née* Nixon); *m* 1947, Phyllis Elizabeth Pengelley; one *s* two *d*. *Educ:* Munro Coll., Jamaica. Berkhampstead Sch., Herts. Bank of Nova Scotia, Kingston, Jamaica, 1933–37; Jamaica Infantry Volunteers, 1937–39; Jamaica Constabulary Force, 1939–70: Asst Comr of Police, 1954–62; Dep. Comr, 1962–64; Comr, 1964–70, retd. *Recreations:* fishing, tennis, swimming. *Address:* 2637 Burntfork Drive, Clearwater, Fla 33519, USA. *Clubs:* Kingston Cricket; Countryside Country (Clearwater).                                        *Died* 8 *Aug.* 1988.

**LANGKER, Sir Erik,** Kt 1968; OBE 1959; artist; *b* 3 Nov. 1899; *s* of Christian and Elizabeth Langker; *m* 1928, Alice, *d* of Robert Pollock; one *s* one *d*. *Educ:* Fort St Boys' High Sch.; Julian Ashton Art Sch.; Royal Art Society Sch.; studied under Sir William Ashton. Exhibited widely throughout Commonwealth and America. Assoc. Mem. 1926, Fellow 1928, Pres. 1946–, Royal Art Soc. NSW; President: Art Gall. of NSW, 1961– (Vice-Pres., 1958, Trustee, 1947–); Sydney Arts Foundation, 1969; Captain Cook Trust; La Perouse Trust; Foundation President: Nat. Opera of Australia; Opera Guild of NSW; North Shore Historical Soc. Chairman: Independent Theatre Ltd, 1946–; North Side Arts Festival; Member: Winston Churchill Meml Trust; State Adv. Council for Technical Educn; Trustee, Children's Library and Craft Movement, etc. *Publication:* Australian Art Illustrated, 1947. *Recreations:* music, hiking. *Address:* Lombardy, 8 Eastview Street, Wollstonecraft, NSW 2065, Australia. *T:* 43-1209. *Club:* Savage (NSW).
                                        *Died* 3 *Feb.* 1982.

**LANGLEY, Brig. Charles Ardagh,** CB 1962; CBE 1945; MC 1916 (Bar, 1918); Consultant, Kennedy & Donkin, 1974–81; *b* 23 Aug.

1897; *s* of late John Langley, CBE, Under Sec. of State, Egyptian Govt, 1922; *m* 1st, 1920, V. V. M. Sharp (*d* 1931); one *s* one *d*; 2nd, 1936, M. J. Scott (*d* 1981); two *d*. *Educ:* Cheltenham Coll.; Royal Military Academy, Woolwich. Served European War: commissioned Royal Engineers, 1915; France, 1916, served in field co. and as Adjutant to divisional engineers (MC and Bar; despatches three times). Subseq. took course of higher military engineer training, including one year at Cambridge Univ.; Railway Training Centre, Longmoor, 1922–27; seconded to Great Indian Peninsular Railway, 1927–33, in connection with electrification of Bombay-Poona main line, including construction of power station at Kalyan; Railway Trg Centre, Longmoor, 1933–38; various appointments, including Chief Instructor of Railways, War Office, 1938–40; War of 1939–45: responsible for initial transportation developments in Middle East; later formed Transportation Trg Centre for raising and training Docks and Inland Water Transport troops of Indian Engineers. Dep. Quartermaster-Gen. (Movements and Transportation), Allied Land Forces, South East Asia Command, 1943–45 (despatches, CBE); Commandant, Transportation Trg Centre, Longmoor, 1946. Inspecting Officer of Railways, 1946–58, Chief Inspecting Officer, 1958–63, Min. of Transport. Consultant: British Railways Bd, 1963–66; Transmark, 1972–73; Projects Manager, UKRAS (Consultants) Ltd, 1966–69, Man. Dir, 1969–72. Pres. Junior Institution of Engineers, 1961–62. FCIT. *Publications:* several military text books on transportation. *Recreation:* gardening. *Address:* Beeches, Little Austins, Farnham, Surrey GU9 8JR. *T:* Farnham 723212.                                        *Died* 21 *Nov.* 1987.

**LANGLEY MOORE, Doris;** *see* Moore.

**LANGMAN, Sir John Lyell,** 3rd Bt, *cr* 1906; *b* 9 Sept. 1912; *o s* of Sir Archibald Langman, 2nd Bt, CMG, North Cadbury Court, Somerset, and late Eleanor Katherine, 2nd *d* of 1st Baron Lyell; *S* father, 1949; *m* 1936, Pamela, *o d* of Capt. Spencer Kennard; two *d* (one *d* decd). *Educ:* Eton; Christ Church, Oxford. *Heir:* none. *Address:* Perrotts Brook Farm, near Cirencester, Glos. *T:* North Cerney 283.                                        *Died* 5 *Oct.* 1985 (*ext*).

**LANGTON, Bernard Sydney,** CBE 1966; JP; Trustee, since 1967 and Vice-Chairman, since 1974, Young Volunteer Force Foundation (Chairman, Advisory Council, 1967–71); *b* 1 Aug. 1914; *s* of Leon and Theresa Langton; *m* 1st, 1942, Betty Siroto (marr. diss. 1972); two *d*; 2nd, 1975, Margaret Stephen Tait Davies (*née* Gatt), BSc, LTI. *Educ:* Blackpool Grammar Sch.; Manchester Univ. Manchester City Council, 1945–74, Alderman 1963–74 (past Chm., Watch Cttee, Rivers Cttee, Fire Brigade Cttee); Mem., 1973–81, and Chm. Recreation and Arts Cttee, 1973–77, Greater Manchester CC. Mem., Police Council Great Britain, 1956–67; Governor, Police Coll., 1956–67; Mem., Police Adv. Board, 1957–67; Mem., Race Relations Board, 1966–68; Chm., Manchester Port Health Authority, 1956–74; Nat. Pres., Assoc. of Sea and Air Port Health Authorities of GB, 1972–73; Mem., Gen. Adv. Coun. of ITA, 1969–72; Mem., Countryside Commn, 1975–. Mem., Ct of Governors, Manchester Univ., 1975–. JP Manchester 1961. *Recreations:* gardening, theatre, music. *Address:* The Carrs, Horwich End, Whaley Bridge, near Stockport, Cheshire SK12 7JE. *T:* Whaley Bridge 3443. *Club:* Manchester.
                                        *Died* 21 *Jan.* 1982.

**LANGTON, Thomas Bennett,** MC 1942; Underwriting Member of Lloyd's, since 1946; *b* 6 March 1917; *s* of Leslie P. Langton and Mildred (*née* Holmwood); *m* 1st, 1943, Lucy Barbara Ettrick Welford (*d* 1978); three *d*; 2nd, 1980, Rosamonde Ann Clarke. *Educ:* Radley; Jesus Coll., Cambridge (MA). Called to Bar, Middle Temple, 1939. Served War of 1939–45: commnd Irish Guards, 1940; Special Boat Section (Middle East), 1942; 1st SAS Regt, 1943–45; Major. Chairman: Leslie Langton Holdings Ltd, 1972–77; Leslie Langton & Sons Ltd, 1953–80; Dir, Devitt Langton & Dawnay Day, 1965–80. Mem. Cttee of Lloyd's, 1968–71, 1973–76; Dep. Chm., of Lloyd's, 1973, 1974. Dir, Brendoncare Foundn, 1983–. Mem. Council, Radley Coll., 1958–73; Mem. Bd, Royal Merchant Navy Sch., Bearwood, 1975–84. Mem. Court of Skinners' Co., 1959–, Master 1964–65, 1983–84. Hon. Col 65/39 Signals Regt (V), 1967–75. DL Hants 1982–85. *Recreations:* sport, especially rowing (Steward, Henley Royal Regatta). *Address:* Granfers, Southdown, Chale, Isle of Wight.                                        *Died* 14 *Feb.* 1986.

**LAPOINTE, Col Hon. Hugues,** PC (Canada) 1949; QC; Barrister; *b* Rivière-du-Loup, Quebec, 3 March 1911; *s* of Rt Hon. Ernest Lapointe, PC, QC, Minister of Justice at Ottawa, and Emma Pratte; *m* 1938, Lucette, *d* of Dr and Mrs R. E. Valin, Ottawa. *Educ:* University of Ottawa (BA 1932); Laval Univ., Quebec (LLL 1935). Mem. of Quebec Bar, July 1935; KC 1949. Served War of 1939–45, Overseas, with Regt de la Chaudière. Elected (L) to House of Commons, Lotbinière County Constituency, 1940, 1945, 1949, 1953. Delegate to Gen. Assembly, UN: Paris, Sept. 1948; Lake Success, April 1949; Lake Success, Sept. 1950 (Vice-Chm. Canadian Delegation). Parliamentary Asst to Minister of National Defense, 1945, to Sec. of State for External Affairs, 1949; Solicitor-Gen. of

Canada, 1949; Minister of Veterans Affairs, Aug. 1950; Postmaster Gen., 1955; Agent-Gen. for Quebec in the United Kingdom, 1961–66; Lieut-Governor of Quebec, 1966–78. Hon. Col, Le Régiment de la Chaudière, 1970. Hon. LLD: University of Ottawa, 1954; Royal Military Coll. of Canada, 1967. Croix de Guerre avec palme. KStJ 1966; Kt Grand Cross, SMO, Malta, 1966. Is a Roman Catholic. *Clubs:* Garrison (Quebec); Royal Quebec Golf (Boischatel). *Died* 13 *Nov.* 1982.

**LARDINOIS, Petrus Josephus;** Chairman, Executive Board, Rabobank Nederland, since 1977; *b* Noorbeek, 13 Aug. 1924; *m* Maria Hubertina Gerardine Peeters; two *s* three *d*. *Educ:* Wageningen Agricultural Coll. Various agricultural posts until 1960; Agricultural Attaché, Dutch Embassy, London, 1960–63; Mem., Second Chamber, 1963–73 (Catholic People's Party); Mem., European Parliament, 1963–67; Minister of Agriculture and Fisheries, 1967–72; Comr for Agriculture, Commn of the European Communities, 1973–76. Pres., Brabant Farmers' Union, 1965–67. *Address:* Rabobank Nederland, PO Box 17100, 3500 HG Utrecht, The Netherlands. *Died* 16 *July* 1987.

**LARKCOM, Eric Herbert Larkcom J.;** *see* Jacobs-Larkcom.

**LARKIN, Alfred Sloane,** CIE 1944; *b* 11 June 1894; *s* of late George Larkin, Ballsbridge, Co. Dublin; *m* 1925, Phyllis (*d* 1974), *d* of late Thomas Hodson, Wainfleet, Lincs; one *s*. *Educ:* High Sch., Dublin; Trent Coll., Derbyshire; Trinity Coll., Dublin. Entered Indian Civil Service, 1921; late Additional Member, Board of Revenue, Government of Bengal. *Address:* 3 Ashburnham Road, Eastbourne, E Sussex BN21 2HU. *Died* 3 *Jan.* 1982.

**LARKIN, Philip (Arthur),** CH 1985; CBE 1975; MA; CLit 1978; FRSL; poet and novelist; *b* 9 Aug. 1922; *o s* of late Sydney and Eva Emily Larkin. *Educ:* King Henry VIII Sch., Coventry; St John's Coll., Oxford (Hon. Fellow, 1973). Has held posts in different libraries since 1943. Jazz correspondent for the Daily Telegraph, 1961–71. Vis. Fellow, All Souls Coll., Oxford, 1970–71. Chm., Nat. Manuscript Collection of Contemporary Writers Cttee, 1972–79, Member: Literature Panel, 1980–82, Arts Council of GB; Bd, British Library, 1984–; Chm. Bd of Management, Poetry Book Soc., 1981–84. Foreign Hon. Member, Amer. Acad. of Arts and Sciences, 1975. Hon. DLit: Belfast, 1969; NUU, 1983; Hon. DLitt: Leicester, 1970; Warwick, 1973; St Andrews, 1974; Sussex, 1974; Oxon, 1984. Hon. FLA 1980; FRSA. The Queen's Gold Medal for Poetry, 1965; Loines Award for Poetry, 1974; A. C. Benson Silver Medal, RSL, 1975; Shakespeare Prize, FVS Foundation of Hamburg, 1976; Coventry Award of Merit, 1978. *Publications:* The North Ship (poems), 1945; Jill (novel), 1946 (rev. edn 1964: reissued 1985); A Girl in Winter (novel), 1947; The Less Deceived (poems), 1955; The Whitsun Weddings (poems), 1964; All What Jazz (essays), 1970, 2nd edn 1985; (ed) The Oxford Book of Twentieth Century English Verse, 1973; High Windows (poems), 1974; Required Writing (essays), 1983 (W.H. Smith Literary Award). *Address:* c/o Faber & Faber Ltd, 3 Queen Square, WC1N 3AU.

*Died* 2 *Dec.* 1985.

**LASCELLES, Rt. Hon. Sir Alan Frederick,** PC 1943; GCB 1953 (KCB 1944; CB 1937); GCVO 1947 (KCVO 1939; MVO 1926); CMG 1933; MC; MA; Past Director: The Midland Bank; Royal Academy of Music; Private Secretary to the Queen, 1952–53; Keeper of the Queen's Archives, 1952–53 (of the King's Archives, 1943–52); *b* 11 April 1887; *s* of Hon. F. C. Lascelles; *m* 1920, Hon. Joan Thesiger (*d* 1971), *e d* of 1st Viscount Chelmsford; two *d* (one *s* decd). *Educ:* Marlborough Coll.; Trinity Coll., Oxford (Hon. Fellow, Trinity Coll., Oxford, 1948). Served in France with Bedfordshire Yeomanry, 1914–18; Captain, 1916; ADC to Lord Lloyd, when Governor of Bombay, 1919–20; Assistant Private Secretary to Prince of Wales, 1920–29; Secretary to Governor General of Canada, 1931–35; Assistant Private Secretary to King George V, 1935, and to King George VI, 1936–43, Private Secretary, 1943–52. Chairman: The Pilgrim Trust, 1954–60; Historic Buildings Council for England, 1953–63; LLD (Hon.) Bristol and Durham; Hon. DCL (Oxon), FRAM (Hon.). *Address:* Kensington Palace, W8.

*Died* 10 *Aug.* 1981.

**LASCELLES, Daniel Richard,** CBE 1962; *b* 18 Sept. 1908; 4th *s* of Councillor A. Lascelles, JP, Darlington; *m* 1941, Mildred Joyce Burr; two *s* one *d*. *Educ:* Durham Sch.; St John's Coll., Cambridge. Called to Bar, Inner Temple, 1930; Sarawak Administrative Service, 1932; Circuit Judge, Sarawak, 1948; Colonial Legal Service, 1951; Acting Puisne Judge, 1951; Puisne Judge of Supreme Court of Sarawak, North Borneo and Brunei, 1952–62. Legal Chairman Pensions Appeal Tribunals, 1964–74; Chairman, Medical Appeal Tribunals, 1967–74; Member, Mental Health Review Tribunal, 1967–74. *Recreations:* shooting, gardening, golf, tennis. *Address:* 39 13th Avenue, Edenvale, Johannesburg, 1610 South Africa.

*Died* 1 *March* 1985.

**LASH, Rt. Rev. William Quinlan;** *b* 5 Feb. 1905; *s* of Nicholas Alleyne and Violet Maud Lash. *Educ:* Tonbridge Sch.; Emmanuel Coll.,

Cambridge; Westcott House. BA 1927; MA 1932; Deacon, 1928; Priest, 1929; Curate, S Mary's Church, Portsea, 1928–32; Christa Seva Sangha, Poona, 1932; Acharya, Christa Prema Seva Sangha, Poona, 1934–49, 1953–61; Bishop of Bombay, 1947–61; Asst Bishop of Truro, Hon. Canon of St Mary's Cathedral, Truro, 1962–73; Vicar of St Clement, 1963–73. *Publications:* Approach to Christian Mysticism, 1947; The Temple of God's Wounds, 1951. *Address:* The Friary, Hilfield, Dorchester, Dorset DT2 7BE. *T:* Cerne Abbas 346. *Died* 5 *Oct.* 1986.

**LASKEY, Sir Denis (Seward),** KCMG 1974 (CMG 1957); CVO 1958; HM Diplomatic Service, retired; *b* 18 Jan. 1916; *s* of F. S. Laskey; *m* 1947, Perronnelle Mary Gemma, *d* of late Col Sir Edward Le Breton, MVO; one *s* three *d*. *Educ:* Marlborough Coll.; Corpus Christi Coll., Oxford. 3rd Secretary, Diplomatic Service, 1939; FO, Sept. 1939–June 1940; served in Army, 1940–41; FO, 1941–46; Berlin, 1946–49; Member UK Delegation to UN, New York, 1949–53; FO, 1953–59; Private Secretary to Secretary of State for Foreign Affairs, 1956–59; Minister, HM Embassy, Rome, 1960–64; Under-Secretary, Cabinet Office, 1964–67; Minister, HM Embassy, Bonn, 1967–68; Ambassador to: Rumania, 1969–71; Austria, 1972–75. *Recreations:* ski-ing, fishing, golf. *Address:* Loders Mill, near Bridport, Dorset. *Club:* Leander (Henley-on-Thames).

*Died* 16 *Oct.* 1987.

**LASKI, Marghanita; (Mrs J. E. Howard);** *b* 24 Oct. 1915; *d* of late Neville J. Laski, QC; *m* 1937, John Eldred Howard; one *s* one *d*. *Educ:* Ladybarn House Sch., Manchester; Somerville Coll., Oxford. MA Oxon. Novelist, critic, journalist. Mem., Annan Cttee of Inquiry into Future of Broadcasting, 1974–77; Arts Council of Great Britain: Mem., 1979–86; Vice-Chm., Drama Adv. Panel, 1980–82 (Chm., 1980); Chm., Literature Adv. Panel, 1980–84; Vice-Chm., 1982–86; Vice-Chm., Visiting Arts Unit, 1983–86; Chm., Arts Films Cttees 1984–86. Hon. Fellow, Manchester Polytechnic, 1971. F. D. Maurice Meml Lectures, 1974. Radio and TV programmes. *Publications:* Love on the Supertax (novel), 1944; The Patchwork Book (anthology), 1946; To Bed with Grand Music (pseudonymous novel), 1946; (ed) Stories of Adventure, 1947; (ed) Victorian Tales, 1948; Tory Heaven (novel), 1948; Little Boy Lost (novel), 1949; Mrs Ewing, Mrs Molesworth, Mrs Hodgson Burnett (criticism), 1950; The Village (novel), 1952; The Victorian Chaise-Longue (novel), 1953; The Offshore Island (play), 1959; Ecstasy: A study of some secular and religious experiences, 1961; Domestic Life in Edwardian England, 1964; (ed, with E.G. Battiscombe) A Chaplet for Charlotte Yonge, 1965; The Secular Responsibility (Conway Memorial Lecture), 1967; Jane Austen and her World, 1969; George Eliot and her World, 1973; Kipling's English History, 1974 (radio programmes on Kipling, 1973, 1983); Everyday Ecstasy, 1980; Ferry the Jerusalem Cat (children's novel), 1983; From Palm to Pine, 1987; reviews; *posthumous publication:* Common Ground: an anthology, 1989. *Address:* c/o David Higham Associates, 5–8 Lower John Street, W1R 3PE. *Died* 6 *Feb.* 1988.

**LASKIN, Rt. Hon. Bora,** PC (Can.) 1973; FRSC; Chief Justice of Canada since Dec. 1973; *b* 5 Oct. 1912; *s* of late Max and Bluma Laskin; *m* 1938, Peggy Tenenbaum; one *s* one *d*. *Educ:* Univ. of Toronto (BA, MA, LLB); Osgoode Hall Law Sch.; Harvard Univ. (LLM). Lectr in Law, Univ. of Toronto, 1940–43; Asst Prof., 1943–45; Lectr, Osgoode Hall Law Sch., 1945–49; Prof. of Law, Univ. of Toronto, 1949–65; apptd: Justice, Ontario Court of Appeal, Aug. 1965; Justice, Supreme Court of Canada, March 1970. Hon. Bencher, Lincoln's Inn, 1974. Hon. LLD: Queen's; Edinburgh; Trent; Toronto; Alberta; Manitoba; York; Dalhousie; Law Soc. of Upper Canada; McGill; Ottawa; Simon Fraser; Ontario Inst. for Studies in Educn; Victoria; Carleton; Yeshiva; Harvard; British Columbia; Lakehead; Hon. DCL: New Brunswick; Windsor; W Ontario; NY Univ.; Hon. DPhil Hebrew Univ., Jerusalem; DHuL Hebrew Union Coll., Cincinatti. *Publications:* Canadian Constitutional Law (3rd edn), 1969; The British Tradition in Canadian Law, 1969. *Address:* Supreme Court Building, Wellington Street, Ottawa, Ontario K1A 0J1, Canada. *Club:* Rideau (Ottawa).

*Died* 26 *March* 1984.

**LATHAM, Sir Joseph,** Kt 1960; CBE 1950; Director, George Wimpey plc, 1960–84; *b* 1 July 1905; *s* of John and Edith Latham, Prestwich, Lancs; *m* 1932, Phyllis Mary Fitton; one *s* one *d*. *Educ:* Stand Grammar Sch. Chartered Accountant, 1926; Liaison Officer, Lancashire Associated Collieries, 1935; Director and Secretary, Manchester Collieries Ltd, 1941; Director-General of Finance, National Coal Board, 1946–55; Finance Member, NCB, 1955–56; Deputy Chairman, NCB, 1956–60. Vice-Chm., AEI, 1964–65, Dep. Chm., 1965–68, Man. Dir, 1967–68. Mem., ECGD, Advisory Council, 1964–69; Chm., Economic Development Cttees, Food Processing and Chocolate & Sugar Confectionery Industries, 1965–66. *Publication:* Take-over, 1969. *Address:* 25 Badingham Drive, Leatherhead, Surrey KT22 9EU. *T:* Leatherhead 372433. *Club:* Effingham Golf. *Died* 12 *May* 1988.

**LATTIMORE, Owen;** Professor of Chinese Studies, Leeds University, 1963–70, later Professor Emeritus; Director, Page School of

International Relations, 1938–50 and Lecturer in History to 1963, Johns Hopkins University, USA; *b* Washington, DC, 29 July 1900; *s* of David Lattimore and Margaret Barnes; *m* 1926, Eleanor, (*d* 1970), *d* of Dr T. F. Holgate, Evanston, Ill.; one *s. Educ:* St Bees Sch., Cumberland; Collège Classique Cantonal, Lausanne; Research Student at Harvard Univ., 1929. Early childhood in China; returned to China, 1919; engaged in business in Tientsin and Shanghai, 1920; Journalism in Tientsin, 1921; business in Tientsin and Peking with Arnhold and Co., 1922–25; travelled in Mongolia, 1926; in Chinese Turkestan, 1927; studied in America, 1928, 1929; travelled in Manchuria, as Fellow of Social Science Research Council, 1929–30; Research work in Peking, as Fellow of Harvard-Yenching Institute, 1930–31; Research Fellow, Guggenheim Foundation, Peking, 1931–33; travelled in Mongolia, 1932–33; editor, Pacific Affairs, 1934–41; research work in China and Mongolia, 1934–35, 1937; Political Adviser to Generalissimo Chiang Kai-Shek, 1941–42; Director, Pacific Operations, Office of War Information, San Francisco, 1943; accompanied Vice-President Wallace in Siberia and China, 1944; economic consultant, American Reparations Mission in Japan, 1945; UN Technical Aid Mission, Afghanistan, 1950; Visiting Lecturer: Ecole Pratique des Hautes Etudes, Sorbonne, 1958–59; University of Copenhagen, 1961. Travelled in Soviet Central Asia, 1960, Mongolia, 1961, 1964, 1966, 1969, 1970, 1971, 1972, 1973, 1974, 1975, 1976, 1978, 1979, China, 1972. Chichele Lecturer, Oxford, 1965; Vis. Prof., Rutgers Univ., 1979. Awarded Cuthbert Peek Grant by Royal Geographical Society for travels in Central Asia, 1930; gold medallist, Geographical Society of Philadelphia, 1933; Patron's Medal, Royal Geographical Congress, 1942; Univ. of Indiana Medal, Perm. Internat. Altaistic Congress, 1974. FRGS; Fellow, Royal Asiatic Society; Member: Royal Soc. for Asian Affairs; American Historical Society; American Philosophical Society; For. Member, Academy of Sciences, Mongolian People's Republic; Hon. Member: American Geographical Society, Soc. Csoma Kőrösi, Hungary. Hon. DLitt Glasgow, 1964; Hon. PhD: Copenhagen, 1972; Leeds, 1984; Hon. Dr Law Brown Univ., 1974. Order of Golden Nail (Polar Star) (Mongolian People's Republic), 1979. *Publications:* The Desert Road to Turkestan, 1928; High Tartary, 1930; Manchuria: Cradle of Conflict, 1932; The Mongols of Manchuria, 1934; Inner Asian Frontiers of China, 1940; Mongol Journeys, 1941; Solution in Asia, 1945; China, A Short History (with Eleanor Lattimore), 1947; The Situation in Asia, 1949; Sinkiang, Pivot of Asia, 1950; Ordeal by Slander, 1950; Nationalism and Revolution in Mongolia, 1955; Nomads and Commissars, 1962; Studies in Asian Frontier History, 1962; Silks, Spices and Empire (with Eleanor Lattimore), 1968; contributor to periodicals. *Recreation:* cycling. *Address:* 3 Larchfield, Gough Way, Barton Road, Cambridge CB3 9LR; c/o Department of Chinese Studies, The University, Leeds LS2 9JT.
*Died 31 May 1989.*

**LATTIN, Francis Joseph,** CMG 1953; Barrister-at-law, retired; *b* 23 March 1905; *s* of John Lattin, Morland, Westmorland; *m* 1934, May Sadler (*d* 1984), Harrogate; one *s* (and one *s* decd). *Educ:* Appleby Grammar Sch.; Durham Univ. (MA); Cambridge Univ.; called to Bar, Gray's Inn. Assistant District Officer, Colonial Administrative Service, Uganda, 1930; Deputy Controller of Prices and Military Contracts, Kenya, 1942; Development Comr, Uganda, 1949. MLC 1949, MEC 1951, Uganda; Mem. East African Legislative Assembly, 1951; London Representative, Uganda Electricity Board, 1952. Bursar, Grey Coll., Durham, 1963–68. *Publications:* (jointly) Economic Survey of Western Uganda, 1951; articles on various aspects of colonial development. *Recreation:* interest in all outdoor sports. *Address:* The Green, Tirril, Penrith, Cumbria. *T:* Penrith 62960. *Club:* Royal Commonwealth Society.
*Died 19 April 1986.*

**LATYMER, 7th Baron,** *cr* 1431; **Thomas Burdett Money-Coutts;** Member, 1948–80, Chairman, 1948–75, London Committee of Ottoman Bank; *b* 6 Aug. 1901; *e s* of 6th Baron and Hester Frances, 4th *d* of late Maj.-Gen. John Cecil Russell, CVO; *S* father, 1949; *m* 1925, Patience (*d* 1982), *d* of late W. Courtenay-Thompson and Mrs Herbert Money; one *s* two *d. Educ:* Radley; Trinity Coll., Oxford. Served War of 1939–45. OStJ. *Heir:* *s* Hon. Hugo Neville Money-Coutts [*b* 1 March 1926; *m* 1st, 1951, Penelope Ann Clare (marr. diss., 1965), *er d* of late T. A. Emmet and of Baroness Emmet of Amberley; two *s* one *d;* 2nd, 1965, Jinty, *d* of P. G. Calvert, London; one *s* two *d*]. *Address:* San Rebassa, Moscari, Mallorca. *Club:* MCC.
*Died 24 May 1987.*

**LAUDER, Sir George Andrew Dick-,** 12th Bt, *cr* 1688; *b* 17 Nov. 1917; *s* of Lt-Col Sir John North Dalrymple Dick-Lauder, 11th Bt, and Phyllis (*d* 1976), *d* of late Brig.-Gen. H. A. Iggulden, CIE; *S* father, 1958; *m* 1945, Hester Marguerite, *y d* of late Lt-Col G. C. M. Sorell-Cameron, CBE, Gorthleck House, Gorthleck, Inverness-shire; two *s* two *d. Educ:* Stowe; RMC. 2nd Lt Black Watch, 1937; served War of 1939–45, Palestine, Somaliland, Middle East (52nd Commandos), Sudan, Crete (POW); Major, 1945. GCKLJ 1977; Chancellor, Commandery of Lochore, 1974. *Publications:* Let Soldiers Lust, 1963; Our Man for Ganymede, 1969; A Skull and

Two Crystals, 1972. *Heir:* *s* Piers Robert Dick-Lauder, *b* 3 Oct. 1947. *Address:* Firth Mill House, near Roslin, Midlothian EH25 9QQ. *T:* Penicuick 72107. *Club:* Puffins (Edinburgh).
*Died 11 Aug. 1981.*

**LAUGHTON, Prof. Eric;** Firth Professor of Latin in the University of Sheffield, 1952–76, later Emeritus; *b* 4 Sept. 1911; 2nd *s* of Rev. G. W. Laughton; *m* 1938, Elizabeth Gibbons; one *s* one *d. Educ:* King Edward VII Sch., Sheffield; St John's Coll., Oxford (open classical scholar). Asst in Humanity Dept, University of Edinburgh, 1934–36; University of Sheffield: Asst Lecturer in Classics, 1936; Lecturer in Classics, 1939; Senior Lecturer, 1946; Public Orator, 1955–68; Pro-Vice-Chancellor, 1968–72. Service in Intelligence Corps, South East Asia, 1943–45. *Publications:* verse translation of Papyrus (17th-century Latin poem by J. Imberdis), 1952; The Participle in Cicero, 1964. Articles and reviews in various classical journals. *Recreations:* gentle walking, music. *Address:* Forelane, Deerhurst, Glos. *T:* Tewkesbury 295437.
*Died 7 Sept. 1988.*

**LAURIE, Lt-Col George Halliburton Foster Peel V.;** *see* Vere-Laurie.

**LAURIE, Maj.-Gen. Sir John Emilius,** 6th Bt, *cr* 1834; CBE 1940; DSO 1916; *b* 12 Aug. 1892; *S* father, 1936; *m* 1922, Evelyn Clare, *o d* of late Lt-Col L. J. Richardson-Gardner, 14th Hussars; one *s* two *d.* Served European War, 1914–18 (despatches 5 times, DSO and bar, Chevalier Légion d'Honneur); commanded 6th (Morayshire) Bn Seaforth Highlanders, 1918–19, and 2nd Bn Seaforth Highlanders, 1934–38; Comdr, Tientsin Area, British Troops in China, 1939–40 (despatches); 157 Inf. Bde, France, 1940 (CBE); 52nd (Lowland) Div., 1941–42; Combined Operations Training Centre, Inveraray; retired 1945; Col, Seaforth Highlanders, 1947–57. *Heir:* *s* Robert Bayley Emilius Laurie [ *b* 8 March 1931; *m* 1968, Laurelie, *er d* of late Sir Reginald Williams, 7th Bt, MBE, ED; two *d*]. *Address:* Amesbury Abbey, Amesbury, Wilts. *Clubs:* Army and Navy, Caledonian, MCC.
*Died 10 Jan. 1983.*

**LAURIE, Col Vernon Stewart,** CBE 1964 (OBE 1945); TD; *b* 23 Feb. 1896; *o s* of Lt-Col R. M. Laurie, DSO, TD, DL, late of Ford Place, Stifford, Essex; *m* 1922, Mary, 2nd *d* of Selwyn R. Pryor, late of Plaw Hatch, Bishop's Stortford, Herts; one *s* one *d. Educ:* Eton; Christ Church, Oxford. Served European War, 1914–18; Essex RA (TF); 2 Lt 1914, Lt 1915, Capt. 1918, France, Egypt and Palestine (despatches twice). Served War of 1939–45; Lt-Col comdg 147 Essex Yeomanry, RA, 1939–42; 107 LAA Regt RA, 1942–44; 22 LAA Regt RA, 1944–45; N Africa, Malta and Italy. Hon. Col Essex Yeomanry, 1956–60. Actg Master Essex Union Foxhounds, 1946–48, Jt Master, 1956–57. Master Saddlers Co., 1955 and 1958. Mem. London Stock Exchange, 1921–; Dir, Brit. Empire Securities & General Trust, 1929– (Chm., 1947–72). Pres., Chelmsford Conservative Assoc., 1945–49; Chairman: Romford Constituency Assoc., 1952–55; Billiericay Constituency Assoc., 1955–56 (Pres., 1956–67). DL 1946–80, High Sheriff 1950, Essex. *Recreation:* foxhunting. *Address:* The Old Vicarage, South Weald, Brentwood, Essex. *T:* Brentwood 221358. *Clubs:* United Oxford & Cambridge University, MCC.
*Died 29 Jan. 1981.*

**LAUWERYS, Prof. Joseph Albert;** Director, Atlantic Institute of Education, Nova Scotia, 1970–76, then Emeritus; Professeur Associé, Sorbonne, 1969–74; Professor of Comparative Education in University of London Institute of Education, 1947–70, then Emeritus Professor; *b* 7 Nov. 1902; *s* of Henry and Louise Lauwerys (*née* Nagels); *m* 1931, Waltraut Dorothy Bauermeister; three *s. Educ:* Ratcliffe Coll., Leicester; Bournemouth Sch.; King's Coll., London Univ. BScGen, 1st Cl. Hons 1927; Special BSc 1st Cl., Chemistry, 1928; Associate of Institute of Chemistry, 1928; Fellow, 1942. Special Physics BSc, 1929; Science Master, Stirling House, Bournemouth; Sen. Physics Master, Christ's Hosp., Horsham, 1928–32; Lectr in Methods of Science, Inst. of Educn, 1932–41. Reader in Educn, 1941–46. Joint Editor, World Year Book of Education, 1947–70. Rockefeller Foundation, Consultant in Education, 1937; Visiting Professor: Teachers' Coll., Columbia Univ., 1939 and 1951; Univ. of Indiana, 1952; Univ. of Southern Calif., 1953, 1955, 1957, 1959, 1961; Univ. of Michigan, 1954; Kyushu Univ., Japan, 1956; Univ. of Cape Town and Witwatersrand, 1958; International Christian Univ., Tokyo, 1959; Univ. of Chile, 1962; Univ. of Concepción, 1964 and 1965; Univ. of Bahia, 1966; Univ. of Ankara, 1968. Centennial Prof., American Univ. of Beirut, 1967. Dir Commission of Enquiry, Conference of Allied Ministers of Education, 1945; Consultant to UNESCO, 1946–48. Hon. Prof. Univ. of Ankara. Vice-Chm., Internat. New Educn Fellowship; Chm., UNESCO Good Offices and Conciliation Commn, 1979– (Mem. and UK Rep., 1971–, Vice-Chm., 1977–79); Pres., Assoc. Montessori Internationale; Adviser, Inst. of Moralogy, Japan; Chm., Basic English Foundn. DSc (Ghent), 1946; DLit (London), 1958. Comdr, Ordre des Palmes Académiques, 1961. *Publications:* Education and Biology, 1934; Chemistry, 1938; Film in the School, 1936; Film and Radio as Educational Media, 1939; Educational Problems in the Liberated Countries, 1946; The Roots

of Science, 1947; The Enterprise of Education, 1955; Morals, Democracy and Education, 1958; (with H. C. Barnard) Handbook of British Educational Terms, 1963; Essays in Comparative Education (3 vols), 1969; Man's Impact on Nature, 1971; (ed) Education at Home and Abroad, 1973; The Purposes of Canadian Education, 1973; Science, Morals and Moralogy, 1977; Institutional Leadership for Educational Reform, 1978; numerous textbooks, articles, reviews and papers including contrib. to Chambers's Encyclopædia, Encyclopædia Britannica, etc. *Recreations:* walking, chess. *Address:* Aston House, Blackheath, Guildford, Surrey GU4 8RD. *T:* Guildford 892040. *Club:* Athenæum.
*Died 29 June 1981.*

**LAVER, William Scott,** CBE 1962; HM Diplomatic Service, retired; *b* 7 March 1909; *s* of Robert John Laver, Latchingdon, Essex, and Frances Lucy (*née* Pasmore), Windsor; *m* 1969, Marjorie Joan Hall, Chislehurst, Kent. *Educ:* St Dunstan's Coll., Catford; Downing Coll., Cambridge. Dept of Overseas Trade, 1932; Asst to Commercial Counsellor: Brussels, 1934, Rome, 1936; Commercial Sec., Rio de Janeiro, 1940; Commercial Sec., Cairo, 1946; Foreign Office, 1950–51; Financial Sec., Bahrain, 1951; Political Agent, Bahrain, 1951–52; Counsellor (Economic), Belgrade, 1954; Counsellor (Commercial), Oslo, 1958–62; Ambassador to Congo Republic, Gabon, Republic of Chad, and Central African Republic, 1962–66. *Address:* Flat 30, Mapledene, Kemnal Road, Chislehurst, Kent.
*Died 10 Dec. 1988.*

**LAVINGTON, His Honour Cyril Michael,** MBE 1946; JP; a Circuit Judge (formerly Judge of County Courts), 1971–83; *b* 21 June 1912; *e s* of Cyril Claude Lavington, MB, BS of Bristol and Nora Vernon Lavington; *m* 1950, Frances Anne (marr. diss. 1968), *d* of Colston Wintle, MD, of Bristol; one *s*. Barrister-at-Law, Middle Temple, 1936; Western Circuit, Wilts QS. Joined Army, 1939; Major, DAA and QMG, 1 GRTD, N Africa, 1943; DAAG 37 Mil. Miss. to Yugoslav Army of Nat. Liberation, 1944; DAAG 3 Corps, Greece, 1945 (despatches twice, MBE). Returned to practice, 1946. Recorder of Barnstaple, 1964–71; Honorary Recorder, 1972–; Dep. Chm., Quarter Sessions: Dorset, 1962–71; Wiltshire, 1970–71; Hampshire, 1971. JP Cornwall, 1974. *Recreations:* sailing, gardening. *Address:* 182 St Stephen's Road, Saltash, Cornwall PL12 4NJ. *T:* Saltash (0752) 843204. *Clubs:* Royal Yachting Association; Bar Yacht.
*Died 1 Dec. 1990.*

**LAVOIPIERRE, Jacques Joseph Maurice;** Justice of Seychelles Court of Appeal, 1977–83; *b* 4 April 1909; 3rd *s* of Antoine Lavoipierre and Elisa la Hausse de Lalouvière; *m* 1939, Pauline Koenig; two *s* one *d. Educ:* Royal Coll., Mauritius; King's Coll., London (LLB); Middle Temple. Magistrate, Mauritius, 1944; Civil Comr, 1946; Magistrate, Industrial Court, 1949; Master and Registrar, Supreme Court, 1952; Substitute Procureur and Advocate-Gen., 1954. QC (Mauritius), 1961; Judge of Supreme Court, Mauritius, 1956–60; Attorney-Gen., 1960–64; after new constitution, reverted to private practice, 1965–66; Legal Officer, La Trobe Univ., Aust., 1966–74. Coronation Medal, 1953. *Address:* 34 Hillcrest, Sir Winston Churchill Street, Curepipe, Mauritius. *Clubs:* Mauritius Turf, Grand Sable (Mauritius). *Died 1987.*

**LAVRIN, Prof. Janko (John),** MA; Professor of Slavonic Studies, University of Nottingham, 1923, Emeritus Professor since 1953; *b* 10 Feb. 1887; *s* of John Lavrin and Gertrude (*née* Golobich), both Slovene; *m* 1928, Nora (*née* Fry) (*d* 1985), artist; two *s. Educ:* Austria, Russia, and partly in Scandinavia. Began as journalist in Russia, 1910; Russian war correspondent, 1915–17. During War of 1939–45, attached to BBC (European service) as broadcaster and language superviser. Public lecturer. *Publications:* Aspects of Modernism, 1935; An Introduction to the Russian Novel, 1942 (repr. 1974); Dostoevsky, 1943 (repr. 1968); Tolstoy, 1944 (repr. 1968); Pushkin and Russian Literature, 1947 (repr. 1968); Nietzsche, 1948, new edn 1971; From Pushkin to Mayakovsky, 1948; Ibsen, 1950 (repr. 1968); Nikolai Gogol, 1951 (repr. 1968); Goncharov, 1954 (repr. 1968); Russian Writers, 1954; Lermontov, 1959; Tolstoy (in German), 1961; Dostojevsky (in German), 1963; Literature and the Spirit of the Age (in Slovene), 1968; Russia, Slavdom and the Western World, 1969; Nietzsche, 1971; A Panorama of Russian Literature, 1973 (some of these translated into several languages, incl. Japanese). *Recreation:* travels. *Address:* 28 Lower Addison Gardens, W14. *T:* 01–603 8347. *Club:* PEN.
*Died 13 Aug. 1986.*

**LAW, Alfred Noel,** CMG 1947; MC 1918; retired; *b* 1895; *s* of late Frank Law; *m* 1937, Kathleen, *d* of A. Fishkin, Newcastle upon Tyne; one *d. Educ:* Northampton Sch.; Hertford Coll., Oxford. Served European War, 1914–19, with 4th Battalion Northamptonshire Regiment. Entered Colonial Service (Palestine), 1920; District Commissioner, Haifa, Palestine, 1942–48; Chief Sec., British Administration, Somalia, 1948–50; Dep. Dir of Education (Administration), Uganda, 1950–53; Ministry of Education, Labour and Lands, Nairobi, Kenya, 1954–57. *Address:* 23 The Sheraton, Oak Avenue, Kenilworth, 7700, South Africa.

**LAW, Sir Eric (John Ewan),** Kt 1979; Justice of Appeal, Court of Appeal: Seychelles, 1983–87; Gibraltar, 1986–87; *b* 10 June 1913; *er s* of late Sir Charles Ewan Law; *m* 1948, Patricia Constance Elizabeth, *d* of C. W. S. Seed, CBE; two *s* one *d. Educ:* Wrekin Coll.; St Catharine's Coll., Cambridge (Exhibitioner), MA (Hons). Called to Bar, Middle Temple, 1936. War Service, 1939–42: E Yorks Regt and KAR, Capt. Asst Judicial Adviser to Govt of Ethiopia, 1942–44; Crown Counsel, Nyasaland, 1944–53; Resident Magistrate, Tanganyika, 1953–55; Senior Resident Magistrate, 1955–56; Asst Judge, Zanzibar, 1956–58; Judge, Tanganyika, 1958–64; Justice of Appeal, Court of Appeal for E Africa, 1965–77 (Vice-Pres., 1975–77) and for Kenya, 1977–83. *Address:* 19 Blackfriars Street, Canterbury, Kent CT1 2AP. *T:* Canterbury 453771. *Clubs:* Mombasa, Muthaiga (Kenya).
*Died 16 April 1988.*

**LAW, Frank William,** MA, MD, BChir Cantab, FRCS, LRCP; KStJ; Consulting Ophthalmic Surgeon, Guy's Hospital; Consulting Surgeon, Moorfields Eye Hospital; Hon. Visiting Ophthalmologist, Johns Hopkins Hospital, Baltimore; Past Pres. Ophth. Soc. of UK; late Master Oxford Ophth. Congress; Mem., Chapter General and Ophth. Hosp. Cttee, Order of St John; Mem. Council, European Ophth. Soc.; Life Mem., Irish Ophth. Soc.; Membre d'Honneur, Soc. Belge d'Ophth.; Hon. Mem., Greek Ophth. Soc., Pan-American Medical Assoc. and American Acad. Ophth.; American Medical Assoc.; Canadian Ophth. Soc.; Past Master, Company of Spectacle Makers, and Freeman of the City of London; *b* Isleworth, 1898; *y s* of late Thomas Law and Emma Janet MacRae; *m* 1929, Brenda, *d* of Edwin Thomas; one *s* one *d. Educ:* St Paul's Sch.; St John's Coll., Cambridge; Middlesex Hosp. Served European War, France and Flanders, 1917–19, Royal Field Artillery; Capt. Lady Margaret Boat Club, 1922; Spare Man for Varsity Boat and Trial Cap, 1922; rowed 2 for Cambridge, 1923; Late Consultant to the Army in Ophthalmology and Surgeon to Queen Alexandra Military Hosp., Millbank; late Consulting Ophthalmic Surgeon, King Edward VII Hospital for Officers; Past Pres. and Councillor, Faculty of Ophthalmologists; Sec. Gen., International Ophth. Congress, 1950; Past Mem. International Ophthalmological Council. Hon. FBOA 1957. *Publications:* Ultra-Violet Therapy in Eye Disease, 1934; History of Moorfields Eye Hospital, 1975; History of the Worshipful Company of Spectacle Makers, 1979; History of the Ophthalmic Society of the UK, 1980; articles in Brit. Jl of Ophthalmology, Transactions of Ophthalmological Society, and other Med. Jls. *Address:* Baldersby Cottage, Chipperfield, Herts WD4 9DB. *T:* Kings Langley 62905; Flat 14, 59 Weymouth Street, W1N 3LH. *T:* 01–935 7328. *Clubs:* Athenæum, MCC; Leander.
*Died 26 May 1987.*

**LAW, Harry Davis;** President, Portsmouth Polytechnic, since 1982; *b* 10 Nov. 1930; *s* of late Harold and Edna Betina Law; *m* 1956, Hazel M. Harding; one *s* one *d. Educ:* King Edward VI Sch., Stafford; Keele Univ. (BA); Manchester Univ. (PhD). FRSC. Demonstrator, Keele Univ., 1957–58; Commonwealth Fund Fellow, Cornell Med. Sch., NY, 1958–59; ICI Research Fellow, Liverpool Univ., 1959–60; Head, Chemistry, Miles Labs, Stoke Poges, subseq. Head, Therapeutic Research Labs, 1960–65; Head Chemistry and Biol., Liverpool Reg. Coll. Technology, 1965–69; Head Chemistry and Chm., Faculty of Science, Liverpool Polytechnic, 1969–71; Dep. Dir, Glasgow Coll. of Technology, 1971–73; Dir, Preston Polytechnic, 1973–82. Cttee of Directors of Polytechnics: Vice-Chm., 1983–84; Chm., 1984–86; Chm., Polytechnics Central Admission System, 1984–89. Chm., CNAA Bd of Food, Accommodation and Related Sciences (formerly Instnl and Domestic Science), 1975–81; Member: Lancs Educn Cttee, 1974–82; Hampshire CC Educn Cttee, 1982–; TEC, later BTEC, 1977–84 (Vice-Chm., 1982–83; Chm., Educn Cttee, 1979–83); Cttee for Internat. Co-operation in Higher Educn, British Council, 1981– (Vice-Chm., 1983–86); Sci. Bd, SRC, 1978–81; SERC, 1986–. Hon. Fellow, Lancashire Polytechnic, 1983; Hon. DSc Keele, 1986. *Publications:* The Organic Chemistry of Peptides, 1970; numerous pubns in learned jls. *Recreation:* fishing. *Address:* Town Mount, Hampshire Terrace, Portsmouth PO1 2QG. *T:* Portsmouth 833929. *Died 6 May 1990.*

**LAW, Col Hugh Francis d'Assisi Stuart,** DSO 1940; OBE 1956; MC 1917; TD; DL; *b* 29 Jan. 1897; *s* of late Hugh Alexander Law; *m* 1928, Susan Rosemary Dacre, *e d* of Sir George Clerk, 9th Bt of Penicuik; two *s* one *d. Educ:* Shrewsbury; RMC Sandhurst. 2nd Lt Irish Guards, 1915; with Irish Guards, France and Flanders, 1915–18; Acting Capt., 1916; attached General Headquarters, Intelligence, 1916; Capt., 1918 (wounded, MC); with Irish Guards Army of Occupation of Rhineland; ADC to GOC 22nd Army Corps, 1919; ADC Governor and C-in-C, Malta, 1921; with Irish Guards, Turkey, 1922–24; retired, 1931; Brevet Major, Irish Guards, Regular Army Reserve of Officers; Major 5th Bn Border Regt, 1932; Lt-Col, 1938; Col (Temp.) 1941; Commanding 5th Bn Border Regt, 1938–41; served France and Belgium, 1940 (DSO, despatches 1940) and in Middle East, 1943–45. Comdr Sub-District of South-West Scotland, 1941–43; Comdr Sub-Area of the Lebanon, 1943–45;

Comdr Cyprus, 1945; Sec., Army Cadet Force in Scotland, 1948–65. DL Co. of Midlothian, 1965. *Publication:* A Man at Arms, 1983. *Recreations:* shooting, fishing, riding, gardening. *Address:* The Barony House, Lasswade, Midlothian. *T:* Lasswade 3217.
*Died 31 Dec. 1984.*

**LAWDER, Rear-Adm. Keith Macleod,** CB 1948; OBE 1919; Associate of the Chartered Institute of Secretaries; *b* 1893; *s* of F. E. Lawder; *m* 1918, Joyce Katharine Mary Watson (*d* 1980); two *d* (one *s* decd). *Educ:* Fettes Coll., Edinburgh. Joined Royal Navy, 1910; served European War, 1914–18 and War of 1939–45; retired, 1949. *Address:* Brook Cottage, South Zeal, Okehampton, Devon EX20 2QB. *T:* Whiddon Down 308. *Club:* Climbers'.
*Died 23 Nov. 1986.*

**LAWRENCE, Bernard Edwin,** CBE 1957; Chief Education Officer, County of Essex, 1939–65, retired; Dean of the College of Preceptors, 1958–68, Vice President, 1969–80; *b* 3 Jan. 1901; *s* of late Albert Edward and Emma Lawrence; *m* 1925, Dorothy Rosa Collings (*d* 1987); two *s* one *d*. *Educ:* Sir Joseph Williamson's Sch., Rochester; Worcester Coll., Oxford. BA Oxon double first class Hons 1922; MA 1930; PhD, University Coll. London, 1934. Asst Master: George Green's Sch., 1923–25; Skinners' Sch., 1925–28; Lecturer: Goldsmiths' Coll., 1928–35; Birkbeck Coll., 1930–35; Asst Dir of Education, Essex, 1936–39; Chairman: Educational Commission to Uganda and Kenya, 1961; Nat. Inst. of Adult Educn, 1964–69. Pres. Assoc. of Chief Educn. Officers, 1957–58. Chevalier de la Légion d'Honneur, 1958. *Publications:* The Administration of Education in Britain, 1972; occasional contribs to Educational Jls and to Proceedings of London Mathematical Society and Mathematical Gazette. *Recreation:* gardening. *Address:* White Gable, Felsted, Great Dunmow, Essex.
*Died 2 Oct. 1988.*

**LAWRENCE, Evelyn M., (Mrs Nathan Isaacs);** BSc (Econ) London, PhD; *b* 31 Dec. 1892; *d* of Samuel and Mary Lawrence, Walton-on-Thames; *m* 1950, Nathan Isaacs, OBE (*d* 1966). *Educ:* Tiffins Sch., Kingston-on-Thames; Stockwell Training Coll.; London Sch. of Economics, University of London. Teacher in LCC schs, 1913–24; BSc Econ. 1st cl. Hons 1923; Ratan Tata and Metcalfe scholar, London Sch. of Economics, 1924–26; on staff of Malting House Sch., Cambridge, 1926–28; Commonwealth Fund scholar, USA, 1929; Chief Social Worker, London Child Guidance Clinic, 1929–30; Lecturer in Education, National Training Coll. of Domestic Subjects, 1931–43. Dir, National Froebel Foundation, and Editor, Froebel Foundation Bulletin, 1943–63. Hon. Sec. British Psychological Soc., Education Section, 1931–34; Mem. of Council of Eugenics Soc., 1949–59. *Publications:* The Relation between Intelligence and Inheritance, 1931; (Ed) Friedrich Froebel and English Education, 1952. *Recreations:* walking, gardening, music. *Address:* Grove Cottage, Owletts Lane, Ashurst Wood, East Grinstead, W Sussex. *T:* Forest Row 2728.
*Died 13 April 1987.*

**LAWRENCE, Sir Frederick,** Kt 1963; OBE 1957; JP; *b* 23 Sept. 1889; *s* of Lawrence Isaacs, London; *m* 1921, Gertrude (*d* 1974), *d* of Asher Simons; one *d*. *Educ:* LCC Sch. Founder, Chairman and Managing Director of: Fredk Lawrence Ltd, London, W2 (now retired); B. Maggs & Co., Bristol; Maggs Furniture Industries Ltd; formerly Chm., Croydon Estates Ltd. Served in 1914–18 War with RE (Signals). Mem. LCC, 1946–65; Mem., NW Metropolitan Regional Hosp. Bd, 1950–66; Mem. Bd of Govs, St Mary's Hosp., Paddington, 1948; formerly Pres., Paddington (S) Cons. and Unionist Assoc., 1962; Mem., Paddington Borough Council, 1934–65; Alderman, 1942; Dep. Mayor, 1942–44; Mayor, 1944–45; Dep. Leader, 1945–65; Dep. Chm. LCC, 1953–54; Mem., Bow St Magistrates' Panel, 1954–64; Chm. Paddington Gp Hosp. Management Cttee, 1948–60; Member: House Cttee, St Mary's Hosp.; Council, Wright-Fleming Inst. for Microbiology, 1961; British Post-graduate Medical Fedn, 1953–65; Vice-Pres., Anti-Tuberculosis League of Israel. JP, Co. London, 1943. *Recreations:* Association football, golf; dancing. *Address:* 77 Albion Gate, Hyde Park, W2. *T:* 01-723 6964. *Clubs:* Coombe Hill Golf, Potters Bar Golf.
*Died 5 July 1981.*

**LAWRENCE, Sir Robert (Leslie Edward),** Kt 1980; CBE 1975 (OBE 1944); ERD 1952; FCIT; FRSA; CBIM; Member, British Railways Board, 1971–83 (Vice-Chairman, 1975–81); Chairman: British Rail Property Board, since 1972; NFC Property Group, since 1982; *b* 29 Oct. 1915; *s* of late Robert Riach Lawrence; *m* 1940, Joyce Marjorie (*née* Ricketts); one *s* one *d*. *Educ:* Dulwich Coll. Served War of 1939–45 (despatches, 1942, 1945), RE; 2nd Lt; Col 1945; Hon. Col, 73 Movement Control Regt, RE, 1963–65; Col, Engr and Rly Staff Corps RE (TA); Hon. Col, 275 Rly Sqdn, RCT (TAVR), 1978–82. Traffic Apprentice, LNER, 1934; Headquarters, LNER, 1938; appts in operating depts, 1946–59; London Midland Region: Divisional Man., 1959; Line Manager, 1961; Asst Gen. Manager, 1963–67; Chm. and Gen. Manager, 1968–71; Gen. Manager, Sundries Div., British Railways, 1967–; Chairman: BR Hovercraft Ltd, 1971–72; British Rail Engineering, 1971–76; BRE Metro Ltd, 1971–78; Transmark Ltd, 1972–78; British Transport Hotels Ltd,

1978; Nat. Bus Properties Ltd, 1983–. Mem., 1969–82, Chm., 1979–82, Nat. Freight Corp., later Nat. Freight Co.; Chm., Nat. Freight Consortium, 1982 (Dir, 1982–84); Bd Mem., Nat. Bus Co., 1982–; Dir, Mersey Docks and Harbour Bd, 1971–72. Mem., Energy Commn, 1977–79. Vice-Pres., Inst. of Transport, 1970–72 (Mem., Council, 1959–62); Chm., Centre for Physical Distribution Management, 1980–. Mem., Adv. Council, Science Mus., 1979–84. Governor, Dulwich Coll., 1970, Dep. Chm. Bd, 1973–; Mem. Council, Westfield Coll., 1980–. Past Pres., Rly Students Assoc.; Vice-Chm., Movement Control Officers Club. Vice-Pres., London Cornish Assoc., 1979–. Chm., Railway Benevolent Inst., 1979–. Liveryman, Co. of Loriners. Freeman, City of London. CStJ 1982. Legion of Merit (US), 1945. *Publications:* various papers, Inst. of Transport. *Recreations:* swimming, Rugby football. *Address:* 37 Oakfield Gardens, SE19 1HQ. *T:* 01-670 7649; Clifford Cottage, St Levan, Cornwall. *T:* Sennen 297. *Clubs:* Army and Navy, MCC.
*Died 8 Oct. 1984.*

**LAWRENCE, Sir William,** 4th Bt, *cr* 1867; Sales Consultant, Long and Hambly Ltd (retired); Senior Executive, Wilmot Breeden, Ltd (retired); Major East Surrey Regiment; *b* 14 July 1913; *er s* of Sir William Matthew Trevor Lawrence, 3rd Bt, and Iris Eyre (*d* 1955), *y d* of late Brig.-Gen. E. M. S. Crabbe, CB; *S* father, 1934; *m* 1940, Zoë (marr. diss., 1945), *yr d* of H. S. S. Pether, Stowford, Headington, Oxford; *m* 1945, Pamela, *yr d* of J. E. Gordon, Beechbank, Bromborough, Cheshire; one *s* two *d*. *Educ:* Bradfield Coll. FRHS. Pres., W Warwickshire Scout Council; Vice-Pres., Stratford on Avon and S Warwickshire Cons. Assoc. *Recreation:* gardening. *Heir:* *s* William Fettiplace Lawrence, *b* 23 Aug. 1954. *Address:* The Knoll, Walcote, near Alcester, Warwicks. *T:* Great Alne 303.
*Died 3 Nov. 1986.*

**LAWRENCE-WILSON, Harry Lawrence;** Under-Secretary, Procurement Executive, Ministry of Defence, 1971–72; *b* 18 March 1920; *s* of late H. B. Wilson and of Mrs May Wilson, Biddenden, Kent; *m* 1945, Janet Mary Gillespie; two *s* one *d*. *Educ:* Cranbrook Sch.; Worcester Coll., Oxford. Served Indian Army, 1940–46. Colonial Office, 1946–47; MoD, 1947–66; Cabinet Office, 1967–69. Asst Principal, 1947; Principal, 1948; Assistant Secretary, 1956; Under-Secretary, 1961; Under-Secretary: Min. of Technology, 1969–70; DTI, 1970–71; CSD, 1971. *Address:* 22 Marlborough Crescent, Riverhead, Sevenoaks, Kent.
*Died 22 Dec. 1986.*

**LAWSON, His Honour Charles,** QC 1961; a Circuit Judge, Central Criminal Court, 1972–82; *b* 23 Feb. 1916; 2nd *s* of late Barnet Lawson, London; *m* 1943, Olga Daphne Kay; three *d*. *Educ:* Grocers' Company Sch.; University College, London. LLB 1937. Served War of 1939–45: in Army, 1940–46; Major, Royal Artillery. Recorder: Burton-upon-Trent, 1965–68; Gloucester, 1968–71. Bencher, Inner Temple, 1968. *Recreations:* golf, music. *Address:* Mayes Green Cottage, Ockley, Surrey RH5 5PN.
*Died 23 June 1989.*

**LAWSON, Frederick Henry,** DCL 1947; FBA 1956; Part-time Professor of Law, University of Lancaster, 1964–77, later Emeritus; *b* Leeds, 14 July 1897; *s* of Frederick Henry Lawson and Mary Louisa Austerbery; *m* 1933, Elspeth, *yr d* of late Captain Alexander Webster, Kilmarnock; one *s* two *d* (and one *d* decd). *Educ:* Leeds Grammar Sch. Hastings Exhibitioner in Classics (Hon. Scholar), Queen's Coll., Oxford, 1915; Akroyd Scholar, 1915. Served European War, 1916–18. 1st Class, Final Hon. School of Modern History, 1921; 1st Class, Final Hon. School of Jurisprudence, 1922. Barrister-at-Law, Gray's Inn, 1923; Lecturer in Law, University Coll., Oxford, 1924–25, Christ Church, 1925–26, CCC, 1925–26 and 1927–30; Junior Research Fellow, Merton Coll., Oxford, 1925–30, official Fellow and Tutor in Law, 1930–48. Studied at Göttingen, 1926–27; University Lecturer in Byzantine Law, 1929–31; All Souls Reader in Roman Law, 1931–48; Temp. Principal in Ministry of Supply, 1943–45; Prof. of Comparative Law, and Fellow of Brasenose Coll., Oxford, 1948–64. Visiting Prof., Univ. of California, 1953; Thomas M. Cooley Lectr, Univ. of Michigan Law Sch., 1953; Joint Editor Journal of Comparative Legislation and International Law, 1948–52, of International and Comparative Law Quarterly, 1952–55; Senior Editor, Journal of Society of Public Teachers of Law, 1955–61; Member International Social Science Council, 1952–58; Lecturer in Roman Law, Council of Legal Education, 1954–58 (Reader, 1958–64); Visiting Lecturer, New York University School of Law, 1956, 1959, 1962, 1965; Visiting Professor, University of Pennsylvania Law School, 1959 (Spring Semester); University of Michigan Law School, 1959 (Fall Semester); University of Houston, 1967–68. Mem. Internat. Acad. of Comparative Law, 1958–; Sec.-Gen., Internat. Assoc. of Legal Science, 1964–69. Hon. Doctor: Louvain, 1958; Paris, 1964; Ghent, 1968; Hon. Dr jur. Frankfurt; Hon. LLD: Glasgow, 1960; Lancaster, 1977. *Publications:* (with Sir D. L. Keir) Cases in Constitutional Law, 1st edn 1928, 6th edn (with D. J. Bentley) 1979; Negligence in the Civil Law, 1950; The Rational Strength of English Law (Hamlyn Lectures), 1951; A Common Lawyer looks at the Civil Law (Thomas M. Cooley Lectures), 1955; An Introduction to the Law of Property, 1958;

(with D. J. Bently) Constitutional and Administrative Law, 1961; The Oxford Law School, 1850–1965, 1968; The Roman Law Reader, 1969; The Remedies of English Law, 1972; Selected Essays, 1977; much re-editing, including Buckland and McNair, Roman Law and Common Law, 2nd edn 1952. *Address:* 6 Thirsk Road, Stokesley, Middlesbrough, Cleveland TS9 5BW. *T:* Stokesley 710268.

*Died 15 May 1983.*

**LAWSON, Lt-Col Harold Andrew Balvaird,** CVO 1971 (MVO 1963); Rothesay Herald Extraordinary, since 1981 (Rothesay Herald, 1939–81); Lyon Clerk and Keeper of the Records of the Court of the Lord Lyon, 1929–66; *b* 19 Oct. 1899; 2nd *s* of late Dr Charles Wilfrid Lawson, Edinburgh; *m* 1934, Kathleen Alice (*d* 1980), *o d* of Alexander Banks, of Banks & Co., Printers; one *d. Educ:* George Watson's Coll.; Edinburgh Univ. Joined RFA, 1916; 2nd Lieut, 1919; RA (TA), 1924; Major, 1936; Lieut-Colonel, 1939; Unicorn Pursuivant, 1929–39. OStJ 1968. *Address:* Lyon Office, HM Register House, Edinburgh.

*Died 28 Dec. 1985.*

**LAWSON, Sir William (Howard),** 5th Bt *cr* 1841; DL; *b* 15 July 1907; *s* of Sir Henry Joseph Lawson, 3rd Bt, and Ursula Mary (*d* 1960), *o c* of Philip John Canning Howard, Corby Castle, Carlisle; *S* brother, 1975; *m* 1933, Joan Eleanor (*d* 1989), *d* of late Arthur Cowie Stamer, CBE; three *s* one *d. Educ:* Ampleforth College. DL Cumberland, 1963–84. *Recreations:* field sports. *Heir: s* John Philip Howard [*b* 6 June 1934; assumed surname and arms of Howard by Royal Licence, 1962; *m* 1960, Jean Veronica, *d* of late Col John Evelyn Marsh, DSO, OBE; two *s* one *d*]. *Died 3 June 1990.*

**LAWSON DICK, Clare;** OBE 1975; BBC Controller Radio 4, 1975–76; *b* 13 Oct. 1913; *d* of late John Lawson Dick, MD, FRCS, and Winifred Lawson Dick (*née* Duke). *Educ:* Channing Sch., Highgate; King's Coll., London (Dip. Journalism). Joined BBC, 1935. *Recreations:* enjoying the amenities of London; escaping from London into the country. *Address:* Flat 8, 92 Elm Park Gardens, SW10. *T:* 01–352 8395. *Died 15 June 1987.*

**LAWTON, Frank Dickinson,** CB 1972; FRES; a Consultant, British Institute of Management, since 1980; *b* 14 July 1915; *o s* of F. W. Lawton, CB, OBE, and Elizabeth Mary (*née* Savage); *m* 1943, Margaret Joan, *o d* of Frederick Norman Reed, one *s* two *d. Educ:* Epsom Coll.; Law Society's Sch. of Law. Solicitor (hons), 1937. Entered Solicitor's Dept, Ministry of Labour, 1939; seconded to Treasury, Solicitor's Dept, 1940; returned to Solicitor's Dept, Ministry of Labour, 1947; Assistant Solicitor, 1959; Solicitor, Min. of Labour (now Dept of Employment), 1967–76. Mem. Court of Assts, Scriveners' Co. (Master, 1970–71; Mem. Examination Cttee, 1967–76). *Publications:* occasional contribs about parasitic hymenoptera. *Recreations:* natural history, the arts. *Address:* Riversdale, Tarrant Monkton, Blandford Forum, Dorset. *T:* Tarrant Hinton 203. *Club:* Athenæum. *Died 15 Nov. 1983.*

**LAWTON, Kenneth Keith Fullerton; His Honour Judge Lawton;** a Circuit Judge since 1972; *b* 6 Aug. 1924; *o s* of late John William Lawton, MA, BSc, and Susan Fullerton; *m* 1st, 1959, Muriel Iris (*née* Parry) (*d* 1974); 2nd, 1975, Dorothy, *d* of Harold Rogers, Lancaster. *Educ:* Barrow Grammar Sch.; Trinity Hall, Cambridge (Exhibr, MA). Fleet Air Arm, 1943–45. Called to Bar, Middle Temple, 1947; practised Liverpool Bar, 1948–70; part-time Dep. Chm., Lancs QS, 1969 (full-time 1970). Member: Lancs SW Probation and After-Care Cttee, 1973–74; Parole Bd, 1981–83. Contested (C) Barrow, 1951. JP Lancs, 1969. *Recreations:* gardening, reading. *Address:* 19 St Anne's Road, Liverpool L17 6BN. *T:* 051–427 3339. *Clubs:* United Oxford & Cambridge University; Athenæum, Artists (Liverpool). *Died 28 March 1985.*

**LAYCOCK, Sir Leslie (Ernest),** Kt 1974; CBE 1967 (OBE 1960); JP; Company Director; *b* 14 Sept. 1903; *s* of Ernest Bright Laycock and Margaret Ann Laycock; *m* 1931, Hilda Florence, *d* of Christopher Ralph Carr, two *s. Educ:* Uppingham Sch.; Leeds Univ. (BCom). President: Leeds and District Woollen Manufacturers Assoc., 1937–39; Leeds & Holbeck Buildings Soc., 1969–71 (Vice-Pres. 1967–69), Vice-President, Assoc. of British Chambers of Commerce, 1962– (Past Pres., Leeds Chamber; Past Chm, Assoc. of Yorks Chambers); Chm., WR Br., Inst. of Dirs, 1958–72; Chairman: Governors, Leeds Coll. of Commerce, 1948–69; Advisory Cttee to Leeds Prison, 1961–; Harrogate (White Rose) Theatre Trust Ltd, 1961–65 (Pres., 1965–73); Leeds Regional Hosp. Bd, 1963–74; Member Council, Leeds Univ., 1953–74. Civil Defence Director Operations, W Riding, 1958–68. JP Leeds, 1952–. *Recreations:* tennis, badminton, sailing, bridge. *Address:* The Gables, Rayleigh Road, Harrogate. *T:* Harrogate 66219. *Clubs:* Naval and Military; Leeds (Leeds); Club, Sports (Harrogate).

*Died 24 Aug. 1981.*

**LAYMAN, Captain Herbert Francis Hope,** DSO and Bar, 1940; RN; *b* 23 March 1899; *s* of Major F. H. Layman, 11th Hussars; *m* 1934, Elizabeth, *o d* of Rear-Admiral A. P. Hughes; one *s* one *d. Educ:* Haileybury. Grand Fleet, 1918; Fleet Signal Officer, Home Fleet, 1933–36. Director of Radio Equipment, Admiralty, 1949–51;

Commanded HMS Hotspur, 1939–41; HMS Rajah, 1945–46; Royal Naval Air Station, Culham, Oxon, 1947–48; Chief of Staff to Commander-in-Chief, The Nore, 1951–53; retired, 1953. Vice-Pres., Tennis and Rackets Association. *Publications:* articles on Rackets. *Address:* Shortalls, Bridus Way, Blewbury, Didcot, Oxon OX11 9NW. *Died 21 Dec. 1989.*

**LAYTON, 2nd Baron** *cr* 1947, of Danehill; **Michael John Layton;** Director: Wolff Steel Holdings Ltd, 1977–83; Economist Newspaper Ltd, 1973–85; *b* 28 Sept. 1912; *s* of Walter Thomas, 1st Baron Layton, and Eleanor Dorothea (*d* 1959), *d* of Francis B. P. Osmaston; *S* father, 1966; *m* 1938, Dorothy, *d* of Albert Luther Cross, Rugby; one *s* one *d. Educ:* St Paul's Sch.; Gonville and Caius Coll., Cambridge. BA Mech. Scis Cantab, 1934; CEng, FIMechE, CBIM, MIM, FInstD. Student Apprentice, British Thomson Houston Co. Ltd, Rugby (specialised in Industrial Admin), 1934–37; Student Engr, Goss Printing Co., Chicago, 1937–39; Works Man. and Production Engr, Ibbotson Bros & Co. Ltd, Sheffield, Manufacturing 25–pounder armour piercing shot, 1939–43; Gen. Man., two armoured car production plants, Rootes Ltd, Birmingham, 1943–46; Mem. Control Commn for Germany in Metallurgy Br. and latterly in Econ. Sub-Commn, assisting at formation of OEEC, 1946–48; Head of Internat. Relations Dept of British Iron and Steel Fedn, 1948–55; Sales Controller, 1956, Dir, 1960, Asst Man. Dir, 1965–67, Man. Dir, 1967, The Steel Co. of Wales Ltd; Exec. Board Mem., Commercial, BSC, 1967–77. President: Court, British Shippers Council, 1977–; European Atlantic Gp, 1984–. *Heir: s* Hon. Geoffrey Michael Layton [*b* 18 July 1947; *m* 1969, Viviane (marr. diss. 1970), *y d* of François Cracco, Belgium]. *Address:* 6 Old Palace Terrace, The Green, Richmond, Surrey.

*Died 23 Jan. 1989.*

**LAYTON, Dr (Lt-Col) Basil Douglas Bailey,** CD 1958; Principal Medical Officer, International Health, Department of National Health and Welfare, Canada, 1956–72; *b* 8 Aug. 1907; *s* of David Bailey Layton and Mary Eliza Merrick; *m* 1938, Marion Marie McDonald; three *s* one *d. Educ:* University of Toronto Medical Sch. (MD); Harvard University School of Public Health (MPH). Postgrad. medical study, 1931–36; medical practice, 1936–42. RCAMC, 1942–46: service in Canada, UK, and NW Europe. Dept of National Health and Welfare, 1946–72. Certified Specialist, Public Health, Royal Coll. of Phys and Surgs, Canada, 1951; postgrad. public health studies, Harvard School of Public Health, 1951–52. Canadian Army (Militia), RCAMC, 1949–58; retired Lt-Col, OC No 10 Medical Co., RCAMC(M). Mem. Canadian Delegn to 11th-24th World Health Assemblies, Head of Delegn to 15th, 16th; Pres., 25th World Health Assembly. Alternate to Canadian Mem., 1957–59, Mem. (Canada) 1962–65, 1968–71, Chm., 1963–64, of Exec. Board, WHO. Vice-President American Public Health Assoc., 1962–63; Vice-President, Harvard Public Health Alumni Assoc., 1961–63, President, 1963–64. Delta Omega (Beta Chapter) Hon. PH Fraternity, 1952. Fellow, American Public Health Assoc., 1957. France-Germany Star, Defence, Canada War Services and Victory Medals, 1946. *Publications:* scientific articles in Canadian Medical Assoc. Journal, Canadian Public Health Assoc. Journal, etc. *Address:* 1411 The Highlands, 515 St Laurent Boulevard, Ottawa, Ontario K1K 3X5. *T:* 749–5886.

*Died 9 Feb. 1986.*

**LAYTON, His Honour Paul Henry;** a Circuit Judge (formerly Deputy Chairman, Inner London Quarter Sessions), 1965–79, retired; *b* Walsall, 11 July 1905; *s* of Frank George Layton, MRCS, LRCP, and Dorothea Yonge; *m* 1950, Frances Evelyn Weekes, Ottawa; two *s. Educ:* Epsom Coll.; St John's Coll., Cambridge (MA). Called to Bar, Inner Temple, 1929; Joined Oxford Circuit, 1930; Recorder of Smethwick, 1952–64; Dep. Chm., Staffs QS, 1955–65; Chm., Agricultural Land Tribunal, W Midlands, 1955–65; Mem., Mental Health Review Tribunal, Birmingham Region, 1960–65; Recorder of Walsall, 1964–65. Pres., Medico-Legal Soc., 1983–85. Served War of 1939–45, AAF and RAFVR. *Recreation:* gardening. *Address:* 70A Leopold Road, SW19 7JQ. *T:* 01–946 0865.

*Died 11 July 1989.*

**LAYTON, Thomas Arthur;** writer on wine and food; editor; wine merchant; *b* 31 Dec. 1910; *s* of late T. B. Layton, DSO, FRCS, and Edney Sampson; *m* 1935, Eleanor de P. Marshall; one *s* (one *d* decd). *Educ:* Bradfield Coll., Berks. Vintners' Co. Travelling Schol., 1929. Public Relations Officer, Wine Trade, 1951. Pres., Circle of Wine Tasters, 1936. Contested (Spare the Earth): Hove, 1983; Chesterfield, Mar. 1984; Portsmouth, June 1984. Chevalier, Order of Civil Merit (Spain), 1971. *Publications:* Choose Your Wine, 1940 (rewritten, 1959); Table for Two, 1942; Restaurant Roundabout, 1944; Five to a Feast, 1948; Wine's my Line, 1955; Choose Your Cheese, 1957; Winecraft, 1959; Wines and Castles of Spain, 1959; Wines of Italy, 1961; Vignes et Vins de France (trans.), 1962; Choose Your Vegetables, 1963; Modern Wines, 1964; A Year at The Peacock, 1964; Cheese and Cheese Cookery, 1967; Wines and Chateaux of the Loire, 1967; Cognac and Other Brandies, 1968; Wines and People of Alsace, 1969; The Way of St James, 1976.

Editor: Wine Magazine, 1958–60; Anglo-Spanish Journal (Quarterly), 1960–87; Hispano-British Circle, 1987–. *Recreations:* wine, travelling in Spain. *Address:* c/o Lloyds Bank, 39 Old Bond Street, W1X 4BH. *Died* 18 *May* 1988.

**LAZARUS, Ruth, (Mrs David V. Glass);** *see* Glass, R.

**LAZELL, Henry George Leslie;** Hon. President, Beecham Group Ltd (Chairman, 1958–68; President, 1968–70); Chairman, Beecham Incorporated, 1962–72; *b* 23 May 1903; *e s* of late Henry William Lazell and Ada Louise Pickering; *m* 1928, Doris Beatrice Try; one *s. Educ:* LCC Elementary Sch. Left school at age of 13; various clerical employments until 1930; Accountant, Macleans Ltd, 1930; Secretary, 1930; Director and Secretary, 1936; Secretary, Beecham Group Ltd, 1939; Managing Director, Macleans Ltd, and Director, Beecham Group Ltd, 1940; Managing Director, Beecham Group Ltd, 1951; Director, ICI Ltd, 1966–68. Member of Association of Certified and Corporate Accountants, 1929, Fellow, 1965; Associate, Chartered Institute of Secretaries, 1930, Fellow, 1934. *Publication:* From Pills to Penicillin, 1975. *Recreations:* sailing, theatre-going, reading. *Address:* c/o Appleby, Spurling & Kempe, Reid Street, Bermuda; 3 Whaddon House, Williams Mews, SW1. *Clubs:* Thirty, Royal Bermuda Yacht. *Died* 17 *Nov.* 1982.

**LEA, Sir Frederick (Measham),** Kt 1966; CB 1960; CBE 1952 (OBE 1944); DSc; FRSC; Hon. FRIBA; Hon. FIOB; Hon, FICT; Director of Building Research, Department of Scientific and Industrial Research, 1946–65; *b* 10 Feb. 1900; *s* of late Measham Lea, CIE, OBE; *m* 1938, Eleanor, *d* of Frank James. *Educ:* King Edward VI Sch., Birmingham; Univ. of Birmingham. Admiralty, 1922–25; Building Research Station, 1925–65; Guest Research Associate, Nat. Bureau of Standards, Washington, DC, USA, 1928–29; Mem. of Council, Royal Inst. of Chemistry, 1943–46, 1948–51; Chm., Concrete Cttee, Internat. Commn on Large Dams, 1953–59; Pres., Internat. Council for Building Research, 1955–57, 1959–62; Pres., Internat. Union of Testing and Res. Labs for Materials and Structures, 1957–58. Hon. Mem., Amer. Concrete Inst. Walter C. Voss Award, American Society for Testing and Materials, 1964. *Publications:* Chemistry of Cement and Concrete (3rd edn 1970); Science and Building, 1971; (with J. T. Crennel) Alkaline Accumulators, 1928; many papers in scientific and technical journals. *Address:* Sunnyridge, East Ogwell, Newton Abbot, Devon. *T:* Newton Abbot 3269. *Died* 7 *July* 1984.

**LEA, Lt-Gen. Sir George (Harris),** KCB 1967 (CB 1964); DSO 1957; MBE 1950; Lieutenant, HM Tower of London, 1972–75; *b* 28 Dec. 1912; *s* of late George Percy Lea, Franche, Kidderminster, Worcs; *m* 1948, Pamela Elizabeth, *d* of Brig. Guy Lovett-Tayleur; one *s* two *d. Educ:* Charterhouse; RMC, Sandhurst. Commnd into Lancashire Fusiliers, 1933, and served with Regt in UK, China and India until 1940. Served War of 1939–45 with Lancashire Fusiliers and Parachute Regt in India, N Africa, Italy and NW Europe. Post-war service: Regtl duty and on staff with Parachute Regt, Royal Marine Commando Bde and SAS Regt in UK, China and Malaya. Post-war staff appts in Allied Command Europe (SHAPE) and as Dep. Military Secretary, War Office (despatches, 1956); Comd 2nd Inf. Bde Group, 1957–60; GOC 42 (Lancs) Div. and North-West District, 1962–63; Comdr Forces, Northern Rhodesia and Nyasaland, 1963–64; Director of Borneo Operations and Commander Land Forces, Borneo, 1965–66; Head, British Defence Staff, Washington, 1967–70, retired. Col, The Lancashire Fusiliers, 1965–68; Col, The Royal Regt of Fusiliers, 1974–77 (Dep. Col for Lancashire, 1968–73). A Senior Administrator: Spey Investments Ltd, 1972; Brandt's Ltd, 1973–75; Man. Dir, Martin-Scott & Co. Ltd, 1975–82; Chm., Eagle Star Trust Co., Jersey and Guernsey, 1983–88. Dato Seri Setia, Order of Paduka Stia Negara, Brunei, 1965. *Address:* Les Ruisseaux Lodge, St Brelade, Jersey, Channel Islands. *Died* 27 *Dec.* 1990.

**LEA, Sir Julian;** *see* Lea, Sir T. J.

**LEA, Sir Thomas Claude Harris,** 3rd Bt, *cr* 1892; *b* 13 April 1901; *s* of Sir Sydney Lea, 2nd Bt, and Mary Ophelia, *d* of Robert Woodward, of Arley Castle, Worcs; *S* father, 1946; *m* 1st, 1924, Barbara Katherine (*d* 1945), *d* of Albert Julian Pell, Wilburton Manor, Isle of Ely; one *s* four *d*; 2nd, 1950, Diana, *d* of Howard Thompson, Coton Hall, Bridgnorth, Salop. *Educ:* Lancing Coll.; Clare Coll., Cambridge. Served War of 1939–45: joined RNVR 1940 as Sub-Lieut; Lieut-Commander 1943; Commander, 1945; demobilised, 1946. *Recreations:* fishing, shooting, ornithology. *Heir: s* (Thomas) Julian Lea, [*b* 18 Nov. 1934; *m* 1970, Gerry Valerie, *d* of late Captain Gibson C. Fahnestock and of Mrs David Knightly, Brockenhurst, Hants; three *s* two *d*]. *Address:* Coneybury, Bayton, near Kidderminster, Worcs. *TA:* Bayton, Worcs. *T:* Bayton 323. *Died* 26 *Sept.* 1985.

**LEA, Sir (Thomas) Julian,** 4th Bt *cr* 1892; *b* 18 Nov. 1934; *s* of Sir Thomas Claude Harris Lea, 3rd Bt and Barbara Katherine (*d* 1945), *d* of Albert Julian Pell, Wilburton Manor, Isle of Ely; *S* father, 1985; *m* 1970, Gerry Valerie, *d* of late Captain Gibson C.

Fahnestock, USAF, and of Mrs David Knightly, Brockenhurst, Hants; three *s* one *d* (and one *d* decd). Lieut RN, retired. *Heir: s* Thomas William Lea, *b* 6 Sept. 1973. *Address:* Bachelors Hall, Hundon, Sudbury, Suffolk. *Died* 17 *Oct.* 1990.

**LEACH, Archibald A.;** *see* Grant, Cary.

**LEACH, Prof. Sir Edmund Ronald,** Kt 1975; FBA 1972; MA Cantab, PhD London; Provost of King's College, Cambridge, 1966–79; Professor of Social Anthropology, 1972–78 (University Reader, 1957–72); *b* 7 Nov. 1910; *s* of late William Edmund Leach; *m* 1940, Celia Joyce, *d* of late Henry Stephen Guy Buckmaster; one *s* one *d. Educ:* Marlborough Coll.; Clare Coll., Cambridge (Exhibnr; Hon. Fellow, 1986). Served War of 1939–45, Burma Army. Commercial Asst, Butterfield & Swire, Shanghai, 1932–37; Graduate Student, LSE, 1938–39, 1946–47; Lectr, later Reader, in Social Anthrop., LSE, 1947–53 (Hon. Fellow, 1974); Lectr, Cambridge, 1953–57. Anthropological Field Research: Formosa, 1937; Kurdistan, 1938; Burma, 1939–45; Borneo, 1947; Ceylon, 1954, 1956. Fellow of King's Coll., Cambridge, 1960–66, 1979–; Fellow, Center for Advanced Study in Behavioral Sciences, Stanford, 1961; Sen. Fellow, Eton Coll., 1966–79; Hon. Fellow, SOAS, 1974; Hinkley Vis. Prof., Johns Hopkins Univ., 1976. Hon. degrees: Chicago 1976, Brandeis 1976. Mem., Social Science Research Council, 1968–72; Trustee, British Museum, 1975–80. Royal Anthrop. Institute: Vice-Pres., 1964–66, 1968–70, Pres., 1971–75 (Curl Essay Prize, 1951, 1957; Rivers Medal, 1958; Henry Myers Lectr, 1966); Chm. Assoc. of Social Anthropologists, 1966–70; Pres. British Humanist Assoc., 1970–72; Lectures: Malinowski, 1959; Munro, 1963, 1977; Myers, 1966; Reith, 1967; Morgan, 1975; Radcliffe-Brown, 1976; Marett, 1977; Huxley, 1980; Frazer, 1982. Foreign Hon. Mem., Amer. Acad. of Arts and Sciences, 1968. *Publications:* Social and Economic Organization of the Rowanduz Kurds, 1940; Social Science Research in Sarawak, 1950; Political Systems of Highland Burma, 1954; Pul Eliya: A Village in Ceylon, 1961; Rethinking Anthropology, 1961; A Runaway World?, 1968; Genesis as Myth, 1970; Lévi-Strauss, 1970; Culture and Communication, 1976; Social Anthropology, 1982; (with D. A. Aycock) Structuralist Interpretations of Biblical Myth, 1983; Editor and contributor to various anthrop. symposia; numerous papers in Man, Journal of the Royal Anthropological Institute, American Anthropologist, South Western Journal of Anthropology, Daedalus, European Archives of Sociology, New Society, Current Anthropology, etc.; various articles in Encyclop. Britannica, Internat. Encyclop. of the Social Sciences. *Recreation:* travel. *Address:* 11 West Green, Barrington, Cambs. *T:* Cambridge 870675. *Club:* United Oxford & Cambridge University. *Died* 6 *Jan.* 1989.

**LEADBITTER, Jasper Michael,** OBE 1960; HM Diplomatic Service, retired 1973; Secretary, Royal Humane Society, 1974–78, Committee Member, 1978–83; *b* 25 Sept. 1912; *s* of late Francis John Graham Leadbitter, Warden, Northumberland, and Teresa del Riego Leadbitter; *m* 1942, Anna-Lisa Hahne Johansson, Stockholm, Sweden; one *d. Educ:* Shrewsbury and Dresden. Asst Press Attaché, Stockholm, 1938–45, Press Attaché, 1945–47; established in Diplomatic Service, 1947; Foreign Office, 1947; Panama, 1948; Actg Consul-Gen., Detroit, 1952; First Sec. (Information), Buenos Aires, 1953 and Helsinki, 1956; Foreign Office, 1958; HM Consul and, later, 1st Sec. at Léopoldville, Congo, Dec. 1959 and at Brazzaville, 1961; Dep. Permanent UK Representative to Council of Europe and Consul at Strasbourg, March 1962; HM Consul-Gen., Berlin, Nov. 1963–66; Consul, Palermo, 1966–69; Consul-Gen., Hanover, 1969–73. Committee Member: Anglo-German Assoc.; Anglo-Swedish Soc., 1973–83. *Address:* 48 Chancellor House, Mount Ephraim, Tunbridge Wells, Kent TN4 8BT. *T:* Tunbridge Wells 548481. *Club:* East India, Devonshire, Sports and Public Schools. *Died* 5 *Sept.* 1989.

**LEAN, Air Vice-Marshal Daniel Alexander Ronald,** OBE 1968; QHDS 1977; Director of Royal Air Force Dental Services, since 1980; *b* 25 April 1927; *s* of Daniel Reid Lean and Christina Cameron Lean; *m* 1955, Margaret (Peggy) Gell; one *s* two *d. Educ:* Dunoon Grammar Sch.; Keil Sch., Dumbarton; Glasgow Dental Hosp. LDS RFPS(G) 1952. FBIM 1980 (MBIM 1975). Joined RAF, 1952; served Celle, Hereford, Seletar, St Athan, Ascension Islands, and Scottish Area, 1952–68; Dep. Dir, RAF Dental Services, 1968–72; Principal Dental Officer, HQ RAF Germany, 1972–75; OC Inst. of Dental Health and Trng, Halton, 1975–76; Principal Dental Officer: HQ RAF Strike Comd, 1976–77; HQ RAF Support Comd, 1977–80. CStJ 1979. *Recreations:* gardening, small animal welfare, collecting junk. *Address:* Oaklands, 36 Huntingdon Road, Brampton, Huntingdon, Cambs PE18 8QL. *T:* Huntingdon 54571. *Club:* Royal Air Force. *Died* 24 *Aug.* 1982.

**LEAR, Cyril James;** Editorial Manager, News Group Newspapers Ltd, 1974–76 (Editor, News of the World, 1970–73); *b* 9 Sept. 1911; *s* of R. H. Lear, Plymouth; *m* Marie Chatterton; five *s* one *d. Educ:* Hoe Grammar Sch., Plymouth. Served War of 1939–45: Rifleman, Queen's Westminsters; Major, Royal Berks Regt. Western Morning

News, 1928–32; Torquay Times, 1932–34; Daily Mail, 1934–38; Daily Telegraph, 1938–39; News of the World, 1946–70: Features Editor, Asst Editor, Dep. Editor. *Recreations:* fishing, bridge. *Address:* c/o News International Ltd, 30 Bouverie Street, EC4.
*Died 11 March* 1987.

**LEARMONT, Captain Percy Hewitt,** CIE 1946; RIN retired; *b* 25 June 1894; *s* of late Capt. J. Learmont, OBE, DL, JP, Penrith and Skinburness, Cumberland; *m* 1926, Doris Orynthia, *e d* of E. G. Hartley, Dunoon, Argyll; one *s* one *d. Educ:* HMS Conway. Served European War, HMS Alsatian, 1914–17; HMS Ceres, 1917–19; joined RIN, 1919; Comdr, 1935; Extended Defence Officer, Calcutta, 1939–41; Capt. Superintendent, HMI Dockyard, Bombay, 1941–42; in command HMIS Bahadur, 1942–43; Capt., 1942; Naval Officer-in-Charge, Calcutta, 1943–45; in command HMIS Akbar, 1945; HMIS Kakauri, 1946; retired, 1946. *Address:* Crofters, Curry Rivel, Langport, Somerset. *T:* Langport 251317.
*Died 10 Nov.* 1983.

**LEARY, Leonard Poulter,** CMG 1973; MC 1917; QC (New Zealand) 1952; retired; *b* 24 March 1891; *s* of Richard Leary and Florence Lucy Giesen; *m*; three *s* two *d* (and one *d* decd). *Educ:* Palmerston North High Sch.; Wellington Coll.; Victoria University Coll. and Auckland University Coll. (LLB). Called to the Bar, New Zealand, 1920. Served European War, 1914–18: Samoan Exped. Force (NZR), 1914; Special Reserve RFA Egypt and France, 1914–18 (Captain, MC); served War of 1939–45: NZ Home Forces; Lt-Col RNZA, Actg CRA, 1944. Mem., later Chm., Disciplinary Cttee of NZ Law Soc., 1948–74; Pres., Lake Weed Control Soc., 1985– (Chm., 1970–85). *Publications:* New Zealanders in Samoa, 1918; Tutankhamen (musical play), 1923; Abbess of Whitby (musical play), 1924; Not Entirely Legal (autobiog.), 1977. *Recreations:* music, gardening, fishing. *Address:* RD4 Otaramarae, Rotorua, New Zealand. *T:* Okere Falls 635. *Clubs:* Northern, Officers' (Auckland). *Died 11 April* 1990.

**LEATHEM, John Gaston,** JP; Headmaster of Taunton School, 1945–66; *b* 14 May 1906; *s* of late J. G. Leathem, MA, ScD, Fellow and Senior Bursar of St John's Coll., Cambridge, and Annie Muir (*née* McMullan), Belfast. *Educ:* Marlborough Coll.; St John's Coll., Cambridge. Pres. Cambridge Union, 1929. Housemaster, St Lawrence Coll., Ramsgate, 1929; Asst Master, Marlborough Coll., 1932; Headmaster, King Edward VII Sch., King's Lynn, 1939; Marlborough Town Council, 1938; JP King's Lynn, 1941; Somerset Education Cttee, 1946–55; Somerset County Council, 1952–55. JP Somerset 1953; Chm. Juvenile Bench, 1959–68; Chm., Bench, 1968–76. *Recreations:* foreign travel, walking. *Address:* 8 Parkfield Road, Taunton, Somerset. *T:* Taunton 75385. *Clubs:* Royal Over-Seas League; Somerset County (Taunton); Jesters.
*Died 13 July* 1984.

**LEATHES, Maj.-Gen. Reginald Carteret de Mussenden,** CB 1960; LVO 1947; OBE 1952; *b* 19 Sept. 1909; *s* of late Major Carteret de M. Leathes; *m* 1939, Marjorie Mary Elphinston; three *s* one *d. Educ:* Imperial Service Coll. 2nd Lt, Royal Marines, 1928; HMS Resolution, 1931–33; ADC to Governor of Queensland, 1935–37; 1st Bn Royal Marines, 1940–43; 42 Commando RM, 1943–44; GSO1 HQ, SACSEA, 1944–45; GSO1 HQ, Land Forces Hong Kong, 1945–46; HMS Vanguard, 1947; RN Staff Coll., 1947–49; 45 Commando RM, 1950–52; Comdt Amphibious Sch., RM, 1952–55; Col GS Staff Comdt Gen., RM, 1956; idc 1957, ADC to the Queen, 1957–58. Chief of Staff to Comdt Gen., RM, 1958–60; Maj.-Gen. Commanding Royal Marines, Portsmouth, 1961–62. Retired, 1962. Col Comdt, RM, 1971–74. Ski-ing representative, British Olympic Cttee, 1965–76. Officer Order of Phoenix (Greece), 1933; Chevalier Legion of Honour and Croix de Guerre (France), 1945; Officer Order of Cloud and Banner (China), 1945. *Recreations:* fishing, ski-ing. *Address:* c/o Lloyds Bank PLC, Boltro Road, Haywards Heath, West Sussex RH16 1BY. *Died 20 Oct.* 1987.

**LE BAS, Air Vice-Marshal Michael Henry,** CB 1969; CBE 1966; DSO 1944; AFC 1954; retired; *b* 28 Sept. 1916; *s* of late R. W. O. Le Bas and Florence Marrs; *m* 1945, Moyra Benitz; one *s* one *d. Educ:* St George's Coll., Buenos Aires; Malvern Coll. Joined RAF, 1940; served in Fighter Command, Malta, Western Desert, and Italy, 1941–44; RAF Staff Coll., 1948–51; HQ 2 TAF and RAF Wildenrath, 1951–54; Sch. of Land Air Warfare, 1954–56; Suez, 1956; OC, RAF Coningsby, 1959–61; HQ Bomber Comd, 1961–63; SASO, Air Forces Middle East, 1963–66; AOC No. 1 Group, Bomber Command, 1966–68; AOC No. 1 (Bomber) Gp, Strike Comd, 1968; Dir Gen. of Personal Services (RAF), MoD, 1969–71. *Recreations:* golf, shooting, photography. *Address:* c/o Midland Bank, Oakham, Leicestershire. *Club:* Royal Air Force.
*Died 26 Jan.* 1988.

**LECKONBY, William Douglas,** CBE 1967; Collector of Customs and Excise, London Port, 1963–67, retired; *b* 23 April 1907; *m* 1933; one *d. Educ:* Hymers Coll., Hull. Entered Customs and Excise, 1928; subsequently held various posts in that department. *Address:* Ebor,

Withyham Road, Groombridge, Tunbridge Wells, Kent TN3 9QR. *T:* Langton 864481. *Died 8 May* 1989.

**LECLERC, Maj.-Gen. Pierre Edouard,** CBE 1943; MM; ED; CD; *b* 20 Jan. 1893; *s* of late Pierre Leclerc, Civil Engineer, Montreal; *m* 1st, 1918, Esther (*d* 1956), *d* of Capt. Olsen Norlie, Bergen, and Arundal, Norway; one *d;* 2nd 1958, Germaine, *d* of late Robert Sarra-Bournet, Montreal. *Educ:* Mont St Louis Coll., Montreal; Methodist Institute, Westmount, PQ. Joined Canadian Expeditionary Force, 1915, as Sapper; commissioned, 1916; qualified Canadian Militia Staff Course, 1935; commanded 5th Canadian Infantry Bde, 1940 (overseas); Maj.-General, 1942; GOC 7th Canadian Div., 1942; GOC Canadian and Newfoundland Army Forces, Newfoundland, Oct. 1943; retired from Canadian Army, 1945. Mem., Sir Arthur Currie Branch, Montreal, Quebec, The Royal Canadian Legion, 1945. Hon. Colonel Le Regt de Joliette, 1955–; Hon. President Canadian Corps Association, 1956. *Address:* 2555 Benny Avenue, Apt 1208, Montreal, P Que, H4B 2R6 Canada. *Clubs:* Canadian (Montreal); Royal Commonwealth Society (Montreal Branch). *Died 27 May* 1982.

**LEE OF ASHERIDGE, Baroness** *cr* 1970 (Life Peer), of the City of Westminster; **Janet Bevan, (Jennie Lee),** PC 1966; Director of Tribune; Member of Central Advisory Committee on Housing; Member, National Executive Committee, Labour Party, 1958–70 (Chairman, 1967–68); *b* 3 Nov. 1904; *d* of James Lee, Fifeshire miner; *m* 1934, Rt Hon. Aneurin Bevan, PC, MP (*d* 1960). *Educ:* Edinburgh Univ. MA, LLB. MP (Lab) North Lanark, 1929–31, Cannock, 1945–70. Parly Sec., Ministry of Public Building and Works, 1964–65; Parly Under-Sec. of State, Dept of Education and Science, 1965–67, Minister of State, 1967–70. Hon. Fellow, Royal Acad., 1981. Hon. LLD Cambridge, 1974. *Publications:* Tomorrow is a New Day, 1939; Our Ally, Russia, 1941; This Great Journey, 1963; My Life with Nye, 1980. *Address:* 67 Chester Row, SW1.
*Died 16 Nov.* 1988.

**LEE OF NEWTON, Baron** *cr* 1974 (Life Peer), of Newton, Merseyside; **Frederick Lee,** PC 1964; *b* 3 Aug. 1906; *s* of Joseph Wm and Margaret Lee; *m* 1938, Amelia, (Millie), *d* of William Shay; one *d. Educ:* Langworthy Road Sch. Engineer. Chairman: Works Cttee, Metro-Vickers Ltd, Trafford Park, Manchester; National Cttee, Amal. Engineering Union, 1944–45; formerly Member Salford City Council. MP (Lab): Hulme, Manchester, 1945–50, Newton, Lancs, 1950–Feb. 1974; PPS to Chancellor of Exchequer, 1948; Parly Sec., Min. of Labour and Nat. Service, 1950–51; Minister of Power, 1964–66; Secretary of State for the Colonies, 1966–67; Chancellor of the Duchy of Lancaster, 1967–69. *Address:* Sunnyside, 52 Ashton Road, Newton-le-Willows, Merseyside WA12 0AE. *T:* Newton-le-Willows 5012. *Died 4 Feb.* 1984.

**LEE, His Honour Arthur Michael,** DSC 1941; QC 1961; DL; a Circuit Judge (formerly Judge of County Courts), 1962–77; *b* 22 Aug. 1913; *s* of Edward Cornwall Lee and Katherine Sybil Lee (*née* Wilberforce); *m* 1940, Valerie Burnett Georges Drake-Brockman; two *s. Educ:* Horris Hill Preparatory Sch.; Winchester Coll. (Scholar); Brasenose Coll. (Heath Harrison Schol.), Oxford. Honours Degree in Philosophy, Politics and Economics, 1935, in Law, 1936. Called to Bar, Middle Temple (Harmsworth Scholar), 1937. Served War of 1939–45, RNVR: served in destroyers, Atlantic convoys; Lieut, 1939; Lieut-Commander, 1943; Acting Commander, 1945. Returned to practice at the Bar, Jan. 1946; Recorder of Penzance, 1960–62; Dep. Chm., Hants QS, 1960–71. Chm., Hants Area Probation and After-Care Cttee, 1969–77. Chairman Governors, Horris Hill Sch., Newbury, 1964–70. DL Hants, 1975. *Publications:* ed Shawcross on Motor Insurance, 1947; ed Shaw on Evidence in Criminal Cases, 1950. *Recreation:* fishing. *Address:* The Manor Farm House, Easton, Winchester, Hants. *T:* Itchen Abbas 277.
*Died 14 Jan.* 1983.

**LEE, Charles Guy V.;** *see* Vaughan-Lee.

**LEE, Rev. Donald Rathbone,** MBE 1945; Methodist Minister, retired; an Ecumenical Chaplain, St Albans Cathedral, since 1983; President of the Methodist Conference, 1973; Moderator, Free Church Federal Council, 1975–76; *b* 28 March 1911; *s* of Thomas and Alice Lee, Stockport, Cheshire; *m* 1940, Nora Olive Fothergill, Greenock, Renfrewshire; two *s* three *d. Educ:* Stockport Grammar School; Handsworth College, Birmingham. BD (London). Methodist Circuit appointments in: Greenock, 1935; Runcorn, 1936; Edinburgh, 1937; Perth, 1940; Stockport, 1947; Upminster, 1951; Oxford, Wesley Memorial, 1952; Worcester, 1957; Sutton Coldfield, 1964–68; Chm., Southampton District, 1968–77; Supt, Jersey Methodist Circuit, 1977–82. Religious Adviser (Free Church): Southern Television, 1972–77; Channel Television, 1977–82. Chm., Adv. Cttee, Inter-Church Travel Ltd, 1976–83; Pres., Jersey Council of Churches, 1978–80. Royal Army Chaplains' Dept, 1942–47 (Senior Chaplain, 1st Infantry Div., 1946). *Recreations:* music, gardening, ecumenical travel. *Address:* 12 Marshalswick Lane, St Albans, Herts. *Died 21 March* 1988.

**LEE, Sir (George) Wilton,** Kt 1964; TD 1940; President of Arthur Lee & Sons Ltd and Group of Companies, since 1976 (Chairman, 1949–76, Managing Director, 1949–68, Joint Managing Director, 1968–72); *b* 8 April 1904; *e s* of Percy W. Lee, Tapton Holt, Sheffield; *m* 1934, Bettina Stanley, *e d* of Colonel R. B. Haywood, TD; three *s. Educ:* Uppingham Sch.; Queens' Coll., Cambridge. Member Exec. Cttee, BISF, 1953–67 (Joint Vice-President, 1966–67); Founding Chm., British Independent Steel Producers' Assoc., 1967–69; Chairman: S Yorks Industrialists' Council; S Yorks Board of Eagle Star Insurance Co. Ltd, 1948–74. Master Cutler, 1950–51. Chm. City of Sheffield Cons. and Nat. Lib. Fedn., 1959–70. Town Trustee of the City of Sheffield; JP, 1950–64. *Recreations:* golf, shooting, fishing. *Address:* Thornfield, Lindrick Common, near Worksop, Nottinghamshire. *T:* Dinnington 562810. *Club:* Sheffield (Sheffield). *Died* 15 *Jan.* 1986.

**LEE, Col Tun Sir Henry Hau Shik,** SMN 1959 (Federation of Malaya); KBE 1957 (CBE 1948); JP; Chancellor of the Most Exalted Order of the Realm, Malaysia, since 1978; sole Proprietor, H. S. Lee Tin Mines, Malaya; Chairman: China Press Ltd; On Tai Development Sdn Berhad; Development & Commercial Bank Ltd, 1966–85; *b* 19 Nov. 1901; *e s* of late K. L. Lee; *m* 1st, 1922 (wife *d* 1926); one *s*; 2nd, 1929, Choi Lin (*née* Kwan); three *s* one *d* (and two *s* one *d* decd). *Educ:* Queen's Coll., Hongkong; Univ. of Cambridge. BA (Cantab) 1923. FREconS. War of 1939–45; Chief of Passive Defence Forces, Kuala Lumpur, 1941; Col in Allied Armed Forces, 1942–45. Member: Council of State, Selangor, 1946–47; Fed. Finance Cttee, 1946–56 (Chm., 1956–59); Fed. Legislative Council and Fed. Exec. Council, 1948–57; Dir, Ops Cttee, 1948–55; Minister of Transport, 1953–56, of Finance, 1956–59; Member: Merdeka Mission to London, 1956; Financial Mission to London, 1957; Cabinet, 1957–59. Co-founder, Alliance Party, 1949; Mem., Alliance Exec. Cttee and Nat. Council, 1953–59; Chm., MCA Standing Sub-Cttee, 1957–59. Member: KL Sanitary Bd, 1929–32, 1938–41, 1946–48; Council, FMS Chamber of Mines, 1929–55; War Damage Commn, 1946–56; Chinese Tin Mines Rehabilitation Loan Bd, 1946–59; Malayan Union Adv. Council, 1946–47; Tin Adv. Cttee, 1946–55; Malayan Tin Delegn, Internat. Tin Meetings, 1946–60. President: Selangor Chinese Chamber of Commerce, 1936–55; Kuen Cheng Girls' Sch., 1937–41, 1945–52; Miners Assoc. of Negeri Sembilan, Selangor and Pahang, 1938–55; All Malaya Chinese Mining Assoc., 1946–55; Associated Chinese Chambers of Commerce, 1947–55; United Lee's Assoc., 1949–59; Selangor Malaysian Chinese Assoc., 1949–56; Sen. Golfers Soc. of Malaya, 1957–58, 1960–63; Fedn of Malaya Red Cross Soc., 1957–62; Fedn of Malaya Olympic Council, 1957–59; Malaysian Golf Assoc., 1960–75 (Patron, 1975–); Oxford and Cambridge Soc., 1959–64; Royal Commonwealth Soc., 1969–73 (Vice Patron, 1973–); Selangor Miners Club, 1938–; All Malaya Kochow Assoc., 1949–; Fedn of Kwang Tung Assocs, 1962–; Selangor Kwan Tung Assoc., 1962–; Vice-Pres., Malaysian Zoo. Soc., 1965–. Hon. Pres., Wine and Food Soc., KL, 1970–; Hon. Vice-Pres., Selangor Chinese Recreation Club. Hon. Member, Clubs: KL Rotary, 1963–; KL Lake; Royal Selangor Golf; Selangor; Selangor Turf. JP Kuala Lumpur, 1938. *Recreations:* riding, golf, tennis. *Address:* 22 Jalan Langgak Golf, Kuala Lumpur 01–28, Malaysia. *Clubs:* Oriental, United Oxford & Cambridge University; Chinese (Hongkong); Royal and Ancient Golf (St Andrews); Royal Liverpool Golf (Hoylake); Singapore Island Country. *Died* 22 *June* 1988.

**LEE, Sir Wilton;** *see* Lee, Sir G. W.

**LEE POTTER, Air Marshal Sir Patrick (Brunton),** KBE 1958 (CBE 1953; OBE 1946); MD (Sheffield) 1936; *b* 15 March 1904; *s* of Samuel Lee Potter and Isabella Henrietta Handyside; *m* 1933, Audrey Mary Pollock; two *s. Educ:* Epsom Coll.; Sheffield Univ. MB, ChB 1928. Joined RAF Medical Branch, 1928; DTM & H, 1931; DPH 1934; MD 1936. OC RAF Institute of Pathology, 1938; served War of 1939–45: Middle East and Air Ministry (despatches twice, OBE); OC 21 Mobile Field Hospital, 1940–42; Air Ministry, 1943–45; psa 1947; DMS, RNZAF, 1948–50; Director Hygiene and Research, Air Ministry, 1951–53; PMO, Bomber Command, 1953–55; PMO, MEAF, 1955–57; Director General, RAF Medical Services, 1957–62. Air Vice-Marshal, 1956. QHS 1953–62. KStJ. *Publication:* RAF Handbook of Preventive Medicine, 1947. *Recreation:* golf. *Address:* Whitegates, Wittersham, Kent TN30 7NT. *Club:* Royal Air Force. *Died* 5 *Jan.* 1982.

**LEECH, William Charles,** CBE 1980; Founder, 1932, President (since 1975) and Director (since 1940), William Leech Ltd; *b* 15 July 1900; *s* of Albert William Leech and Lucy Sophia Wright (*née* Slack); *m* 1947, Ellen Richards; two *d. Educ:* Westgate Road Council Sch., Newcastle upon Tyne. Apprentice Engineer, 1916–21; served RFC, 1916–19; window cleaning for eleven years; started building in own name, 1932; created limited company, 1940, public company, 1976. Creator and Pres., Northern Home & Estates Ltd; President: William Leech (Investments) Ltd; William Leech Foundation Ltd; William Leech Charity Ltd; William Leech Property Trust Ltd. Hon. DCL Newcastle upon Tyne, 1975. Hon. Freeman, Borough of

Wallsend, 1972. Order of Distinguished Auxiliary Service, Salvation Army, 1974; Paul Harris Medal, Rotary, 1989. Mason (Doric Lodge). *Recreation:* inside gardening. *Address:* High House, Morpeth NE61 2YU. *T:* Morpeth (0670) 513364. *Club:* Heaton Rotary (Founder Mem. 1943).
*Knight Bachelor, New Year's Honours List, 1991.*
*Died* 23 *Dec.* 1990.

**LEECHMAN, Hon. Lord; James Graham Leechman;** a Senator of the College of Justice in Scotland, 1965–76; *b* 6 Oct. 1906; *s* of late Walter Graham Leechman, solicitor, Glasgow, and late Barbara Louisa Leechman (*née* Neilson); *m* 1935, Margaret Helen Edgar; two *d. Educ:* High Sch. and Univ., Glasgow. MA 1927; BSc 1928; LLB 1930. Admitted to Membership of Faculty of Advocates, 1932; Advocate-Depute, 1947–49; KC 1949; Clerk of Justiciary, 1949–64; Solicitor-Gen. for Scotland, 1964–65. *Recreation:* golf. *Address:* 626 Queensferry Road, Edinburgh EH4 6AT. *T:* 031–339 6513.
*Died* 15 *May* 1986.

**LEECHMAN, Barclay,** CMG 1952; OBE 1941; Executive Director, Tanganyika Sisal Growers' Assoc., 1959–66; Chairman, Transport Licensing Authority, Tanganyika, 1956–59; Member for Social Services, Tanganyika, 1948–55; retired from Colonial Service, 1956; *b* Eastbourne, 28 Sept. 1901; *e s* of late Alleyne Leechman, MA, FLS, FCS, Bexhill, and late of Colonial Civil Service and late Jean Macmaster Leechman; *m* 1933, Grace, 4th *d* of late Frederick William Coller, Cape Town, SA; no *c. Educ:* Oundle Sch. Cadet, Colonial Administrative Service, Tanganyika, 1925; Asst District Officer, 1928; District Officer, 1937; Dep. Provincial Commissioner, 1944; Labour Commissioner, 1946. Seconded as Sec. of East African Economic Council, Nairobi, 1940–41, and Dir of Economic Control, Aden, 1943–45. Pres. Fedn of Tanganyika Employers, 1964–66 (Vice-Pres., 1959–63). Fellow, Ancient Monuments Soc. *Recreations:* books and music. *Address:* c/o Grindlay's Bank, 13 St James's Square, SW1. *Clubs:* Reform; City (Cape Town).
*Died* 13 *Dec.* 1984.

**LEECHMAN, James Graham;** *see* Leechman, Hon. Lord.

**LEEDS, Sir George (Graham Mortimer),** 7th Bt *cr* 1812; *b* 21 Aug. 1927; *s* of Sir Reginald Arthur St John Leeds, 6th Bt, and Winnaretta (*d* 1980), *d* of late Paris Eugene Singer; *S* father, 1970; *m* 1954, Nicola (marr. diss. 1965, she *d* 1972), *d* of Douglas Robertson McBean, MC; three *d. Educ:* Eton. Formerly Captain, Grenadier Guards. Chm., Clive Investments (Jersey), 1977–. *Heir: cousin* Christopher Anthony Leeds [*b* 31 Aug. 1935; *m* 1974, Elaine Joyce, *d* of late Sqdn Ldr C. H. A. Mullins]. *Address:* Le Vivier, St Martin, Jersey. *Died* 24 *Aug.* 1983.

**LEELAND, John Roger;** HM Diplomatic Service; Counsellor (Administration)/Deputy Consul-General, New York, since 1987; *b* 11 April 1930; *s* of H. L. A. Leeland and F. Leeland (*née* Bellamy); *m* 1958, D. M. M. O'Donel; four *d. Educ:* Bournemouth School. Army 1949. Board of Trade, 1951; served Karachi, Lahore, Brisbane, Kampala and FCO, 1956–73; First Sec., 1966; Ankara, 1973; Kaduna, 1977; Rangoon, 1981; Counsellor, Inspectorate, 1984. *Recreation:* walking. *Address:* 1313/845 Third Avenue, New York, NY 10022, USA. *T:* (212) 326–0387. *Club:* Travellers'.
*Died* 21 *Feb.* 1990.

**LEEPER, Richard Kevin;** Life President of The Lep Group plc; *b* 14 July 1894; *s* of late William John Leeper of Leeperstown, Welchtown, Co. Donegal; *m* 1916, Elizabeth Mary Fenton (*d* 1975); two *s. Educ:* Sligo Gram. Sch.; London Univ. Served in Army, European War, 1914–18; Dir of Transport, MAP, 1940–45. Engaged in shipping and forwarding in Yugoslavia, 1920–32; British Vice Consul: Dubrovnik, 1925; Susak, 1926–32; Man. Dir, Lep Transport Ltd, and Chief Exec., Lep Group of Cos, 1932; Chm., The Lep Gp Ltd, 1956–72. FCIT; MIFF; FRSA. KCHS; Order of St Sava (Yugoslavia), 1930. *Address:* Holly Wood House, West Byfleet, Surrey. *T:* Byfleet 42537. *Died* 21 *Feb.* 1987.

**LEES, David,** CBE 1963; Rector, The High School of Glasgow, 1950–76; *b* 12 Aug. 1910; *s* of late David Lees and Margaret W. Lees, Airdrie; *m* 1935, Olive, *d* of Arthur and Alice Willington, Montreal; one *s* two *d. Educ:* Airdrie Academy; Glasgow, McGill and London Univs. MA (Hons) Glasgow, 1930; MA in Education, McGill, 1932; BA (Hons) London, 1945. Principal Teacher of Classics, Campbeltown Gram. Sch., 1933–46; Rector, Elgin Academy, 1946–49; Dir of Education, Roxburghshire, 1949–50. Hon. LLD Glasgow, 1970. *Recreations:* bridge, football (Vice-Chm., Airdrieonians FC). *Address:* Oaklea, 16 Larch Road, Glasgow G41 5DA. *T:* 041–427 0322. *Club:* St Andrew Bridge (Glasgow).
*Died* 18 *Jan.* 1986.

**LEES, Roland James,** CB 1977; Director, Royal Signals and Radar Establishment, Malvern, 1976–77, retired; *b* 3 Dec. 1917; *s* of late Roland John Lees and late Ada Bell (*née* Jeavons), Stourbridge, Worcs; *m* 1948, Esmé Joyce, *d* of late Alfred Thomas Hill, Malvern Link, Worcs; no *c. Educ:* King Edward's Sch., Stourbridge; St John's Coll., Cambridge. BA Cantab 1939; BSc London 1939; MA

Cantab 1942. Dir, Scientific Research Electronics and Guided Weapons, Min. of Supply, 1955–56; Head of Airborne Radar Dept, RRE, 1957–58; Head of Instruments and Electrical Engrg Dept, RAE, 1959–62; Dir, Signals Research and Development Establishment, 1963–65; Dep. Dir (Equipment), RAE, 1966–72; Dir, RRE, 1972–76. Chm., Air Traffic Control Bd, 1978–81; Mem., PO Engineering Adv. Cttee, 1978–81. Assessor to Lord Mountbatten, Inquiry into Prison Security, 1966. *Address:* Fairoaks, 4 Frensham Vale, Lower Bourne, Farnham, Surrey GU10 3HN. *T:* Frensham 3146. *Died* 8 *Nov.* 1985.

**LE FÈVRE, Prof. Raymond James Wood,** PhD, DSc London; FRS 1959; FRSC; FRACI; FAA; Professor of Chemistry, 1946–71, then Emeritus, and Head of the School of Chemistry, 1948–71, in the University of Sydney; *b* 1 April 1905; *s* of Raymond James and Ethel May Le Fèvre; *m* 1931, Catherine Gunn Tideman, DSc; one *d* (one *s* decd). *Educ:* Isleworth County Sch.; Queen Mary Coll., University of London (Fellow 1962). Lecturer in Organic Chemistry, University Coll., London, 1928; Reader, 1939; Chemical Adviser to RAF and RAAF in UK, Far East, and Australia, 1939–44; Asst Dir R & D (Armament Chemistry), Ministry of Aircraft Production, London, 1944; Head, Chem. Dept, RAE Farnborough, 1944–46. Hon. Visiting Professor, Macquarie Univ., NSW, 1971–. Trustee, Mitchell Library, Sydney, 1947; Mem., Development Council NSW University of Technology, 1948–50; Trustee, Museum of Applied Arts and Science, Sydney, 1947–75. Liversidge Lecturer, 1960; Masson Lecturer, ANZAAS, 1967. President: Royal Society NSW, 1961; NSW Br., Royal Aust. Chem. Inst. Foundation FAA, 1953. Hon. DSc Sydney Univ. Smith Medal, Royal Aust. Chem. Inst., 1952; Coronation Medal, 1953; Medal of Royal Soc. of NSW, 1969. *Publications:* Dipole Moments, 3rd edn 1953; Molecular Polarizability and Refractivity, 1965; Establishment of Chemistry within Australian Science, 1968; about 450 papers on chemical research topics, mostly in Jl Chem. Soc., Trans. Faraday Soc., Austr. Jl Chem., etc. *Recreation:* pleasant work. *Address:* 6 Aubrey Road, Northbridge, Sydney, NSW 2063, Australia. *T:* 951018.
*Died* 26 *Aug.* 1986.

**le FLEMING, Sir William Kelland,** 11th Bt *cr* 1705; *b* 27 April 1922; *s* of Sir Frank Thomas le Fleming, 10th Bt, and of Isabel Annie Fraser, *d* of late James Craig, Manaia, NZ; *S* father, 1971; *m* 1948, Noveen Avis, *d* of C. C. Sharpe, Rukuhia, Hamilton, NZ; three *s* four *d. Heir: s* Quentin John le Fleming [*b* 27 June 1949; *m* 1971, Judith Ann, *d* of C. J. Peck, JP; two *s* one *d*]. *Address:* Kopane RD6, Palmerston North, New Zealand. *Died* 1 *Nov.* 1988.

**LE GALLAIS, Sir Richard (Lyle),** Kt 1965; Regional Chairman, Industrial Tribunals (Bristol), since 1972; *b* 15 Nov. 1916; *s* of late William Le Gallais and Mrs Cory; *m* 1947, Juliette, *d* of late Lt-Col P. A. Forsythe, KRRC; two *s. Educ:* Victoria Coll., Jersey; Inns of Court Sch. of Law. Called to Bar, 1939. Served War of 1939–45, W Africa and Burma; Dep. Asst JAG (SEAC) 1945. Pres. War Crimes Tribunal, Singapore, 1946 (Lt-Col). Advocate, Royal Court, Jersey, 1947; Resident Magistrate, Kenya, 1949; Sen. Res. Magistrate and Acting Puisne Judge, N Rhodesia, 1958; Chief Justice, Aden, 1960–67. Mem. Panel of Chairmen, Industrial Tribunals for England and Wales, 1968–72. *Recreations:* gastronomy, music. *Address:* Bainly House, Gillingham, Dorset. *T:* Bourton 840373.
*Died* 29 *April* 1983.

**LEGARD, Captain Sir Thomas (Digby),** 14th Bt, *cr* 1660; Captain Royal Artillery; *b* 16 Oct. 1905; *e s* of Sir D. A. H. Legard, 13th Bt; *S* father, 1961; *m* 1935, Mary Helen, *e d* of late Lt-Col E. G. S. L'Estrange Malone; three *s. Educ:* Lancing; Magdalene Coll., Cambridge. *Heir: s* Charles Thomas Legard [*b* 26 Oct. 1938; *m* 1962, Elizabeth, *d* of John M. Guthrie, High House, East Ayton, Scarborough; two *s* one *d*]. *Address:* Scampston Hall, Malton, North Yorks. *T:* Rillington 224. *Club:* MCC.
*Died* 27 *March* 1984.

**LEGGATE, John Mortimer,** MB, ChB, FRCS; Dean of the Faculty of Medicine, University of Liverpool, 1953–69, retired; *b* 7 April 1904; *s* of late Dr James Leggate, Liverpool; *m* 1936, Grace, *d* of late Rev. John Clark, Newport, Fife; one *s. Educ:* Liverpool Coll.; University of Liverpool. Gladstone Divinity Prize, 1923; Pres., Guild of Undergraduates, University of Liverpool, 1927–28; MB, ChB (Hons) 1929; MRCS, LRCP, 1929; FRCS, 1933; John Rankin Fellow in Anatomy, 1929–30. Resident Surgical Officer and Surgical Tutor, Liverpool Royal Infirmary, 1932; Prof. of Surgery, Moukden Med. Coll. (Manchuria), 1935–41 and 1946–49; Resident Asst Surgeon, David Lewis Northern Hosp., Liverpool, 1941–43. Served War of 1939–45, Major, RAMC, comdg Field Surgical Unit, D Day Landing, 1944 (despatches); OC Surgical Div. of a Gen. Hosp. in India, 1945–46; demobilised, 1946 (Hon. Lt-Col). Sen. Registrar in Neuro-Surgical Unit at Walton Hosp., Liverpool, 1950–51. *Address:* 19 Skipton Avenue, Banks Road, Southport, Merseyside. *T:* Southport 29171. *Died* 1 *Jan.* 1985.

**LEGGE, Prof. (Mary) Dominica,** FBA 1974; Personal Professor of French (Anglo-Norman Studies), University of Edinburgh, 1968–73,

Professor Emeritus, 1973; *b* 26 March 1905; 2nd *d* of late James Granville Legge and Josephine (*née* Makins). *Educ:* Liverpool Coll., Huyton; Somerville Coll., Oxford. BA Hon. Mod. Lang, BLitt, MA, DLitt. Editor, Selden Soc., 1928–34; Mary Somerville Res. Fellow, 1935–37; Asst Lectr, Royal Holloway Coll., 1938–42; Voluntary asst, BoT, 1942; Asst, Dundee Univ. Coll., 1942; Lectr, 1943, Reader, 1953, Univ. of Edinburgh. Hon. Fellow, Somerville Coll., 1968. FSAScot; Corresp. Fellow, Mediaeval Acad. of America. Officier des Palmes Académiques. *Publications:* (with Sir William Holdsworth) Year-Book of 10 Edward II, 1934–35; Anglo-Norman Letters and Petitions, 1941; (with E. Vinaver) Le Roman de Balain, 1942; Anglo-Norman in the Cloisters, 1950; Anglo-Norman Literature and its Background, 1963; (with R. J. Dean) The Rule of St Benedict, 1964; contribs to learned jls and volumes, British and foreign. *Recreations:* music, walking. *Address:* 191a Woodstock Road, Oxford OX2 7AB. *T:* Oxford 56455. *Clubs:* Royal Over-Seas League; University of Edinburgh Staff. *Died* 10 *Dec.* 1986.

**LEGGETT, Sir Frederick William,** KBE 1951; Kt 1941; CB 1933; *b* 23 Dec. 1884; *s* of late F. J. Leggett and Frances Mary, *d* of William Murphy, Huntingdon; *m* 1st, Edith Guinevere (*d* 1949), *d* of Henry Kitson, Woodford; one *s* three *d*; 2nd, Beatrice Melville, *d* of Joseph Roe. *Educ:* City of London and Strand Schs; King's Coll., London. Entered Civil Service, 1904; Private Sec. to Parliamentary Sec., Board of Trade, 1915; to Minister of Labour, 1917; Asst Sec. Ministry of Labour, 1919; Under-Sec., 1939; Chief Industrial Commissioner, 1940–42; Mem. of Government Mission of Inquiry into Industrial Conditions in Canada and United States, 1926. Brit. Govt Member of Governing Body of ILO, 1932–44, Chm., 1937–38; Dep. Sec. Ministry of Labour and National Service, 1942–45. Member: British Reparations Mission, Moscow, 1945; Anglo-American Cttee of Inquiry into Palestine, 1946; Docks Emergency Cttee, 1949; Cttee on London Transport, 1956–57; Chairman: London and S-E Regional Board for Industry, 1947–48; London Docks Disputes Inquiry Cttee, 1950; Building Apprenticeship and Training Council, 1953; Bldg and Civil Engrg Holidays Management Bd, 1946–; Industrial Relations Adviser, Anglo-Iranian Oil Co., 1947–60. Vice-Pres. Royal Coll. of Nursing, 1948–. *Address:* Downside Lodge, Coastal Road, Angmering on Sea, Sussex. *T:* Rustington 6074. *Club:* Reform.
*Died* 28 *June* 1983.

**LEGGO, Sir Jack (Frederick),** Kt 1982; DFC 1942, and Bar 1943; FAIM; company director; Chairman, Duke of Edinburgh's Award Scheme, Queensland, since 1982; *b* 21 April 1916; *s* of Frederick Henry Leggo and Leah Leggo; *m* 1947, Mary Patricia Best; one *s* two *d. Educ:* state schs, Orange and Newcastle, NSW. ABIA 1938; FAIM 1955. Served RAAF, 1940–45 (Dam Buster Raids, 1943). Commonwealth Bank, 1931–39; Managing Director: Hobourn Components (Aus.) Pty Ltd, 1950–62; Penn Elastic (Aus.) Pty Ltd, 1960–66; T. G. Cullum Pty Ltd, 1966–80; Chm., Pioneer Sugar Mills Ltd, 1978– (Dir, 1971–); Dir, ICL Holdings (Aust.) Pty Ltd, 1978–. Dep. Chm., Qld Br., Aust. Mutual Provident Soc., 1978– (Dir, 1968–); Mem. Council, Royal Automobile Club of Qld, 1968– (Pres., 1976–79). *Recreation:* boating. *Address:* 105 The Gardens, Alice Street, Brisbane, Qld 4000, Australia. *T:* 07–312059. *Clubs:* Queensland (Brisbane); Naval and Military (Melbourne); Southport Yacht (Southport, Qld). *Died* 14 *Nov.* 1983.

**LEGH, Major Hon. Sir Francis (Michael),** KCVO 1968 (CVO 1967; MVO 1964); Major (retired), Grenadier Guards; Treasurer since 1962 (Private Secretary, 1959–71), to the Princess Margaret; also Equerry to Queen Elizabeth the Queen Mother, since 1956 (Assistant Private Secretary and Equerry, 1956–59); *b* 2 Aug. 1919; 3rd *s* of 3rd Baron Newton and Hon. Helen Winifred Meysey-Thompson (*d* 1958); *m* 1948, Ruadh Daphne (*d* 1973), *o c* of late Alan Holmes Watson; one *s* one *d. Educ:* Eton; Royal Military College, Sandhurst. Served War of 1939–45 (despatches); Italy, 1943–45; GSO2, Military Mission to Greece. *Recreations:* shooting, golf. *Address:* Orchard House, Littlestone-on-Sea, New Romney, Kent. *T:* New Romney 3167. *Clubs:* White's, Brooks's, Pratt's, Beefsteak, Cavalry and Guards. *Died* 26 *Oct.* 1984.

**LEHMANN, Prof. Hermann,** CBE 1980; MD, PhD, ScD; FRCP; FRS 1972; FRSC, FRCPath (Hon. Fellow 1981); Research Worker, University Department of Biochemistry, Cambridge; Professor of Clinical Biochemistry, Cambridge University, 1967–77, later Emeritus; University Biochemist to Addenbrooke's Hospital, Cambridge, 1963–77, later Hon. Consultant; Fellow of Christ's College, Cambridge, 1965–82, Hon. Fellow, since 1982; *b* 8 July 1910; *s* of Paul Lehmann, Publisher, and Bella Lehmann (*née* Apelt); *m* 1942, Benigna Norman-Butler; one *s* two *d* (and one *s* decd). *Educ:* Kreuzschule, Dresden; Universities of Freiburg-i-B, Frankfurt, Berlin, Heidelberg. MD Basle, 1934; PhD Cantab, 1938. Research Asst, Heidelberg, 1934–36; Research Student: Sch. of Biochem., also Christ's Coll., Cambridge, 1936–38; Beit Memorial Fellow for Med. Res., 1938–42. RAMC 1943–47. Colonial Med. Research Fellow for Malnutrition and Anaemia, Makerere Coll., Uganda, 1947–49; Cons. Pathologist, Pembury Hosp., Kent,

1949–51; Sen. Lectr, (Reader, 1959), Chem. Pathol. St Bart's Hosp., 1951–63 (Hon. Lectr, 1984). Hon. Dir, MRC Abnormal Haemoglobin Unit (WHO Ref. Centre for Abnormal Haemoglobins), 1963–75. Rockefeller Travelling Fellowship to USA, 1954. Pres., British Soc. for Haematology, 1975–76 (Hon. Fellow, 1979). Hon. Prof., University of Freiburg-i-B, 1964–; Praelector in Clinical Biochemistry, Univ. of Dundee, 1977; Vis. Professor: Univ. of Otago, Christchurch, NZ, 1980; Howard Univ., Washington, DC, 1982. Lectures: Ludwig Aschoff Meml, Freiburg Univ., 1964; Sydney Watson Smith, RCPE, 1965; Lord Horder Meml, St Bart's Hosp. and Univ. of Malta, 1971. Mem., WHO Expert Adv. Panel on Human Genetics, 1971–; Chm., WHO Expert Cttee on Haemoglobins and Thalassaemia, 1972–79. President: Biomed. Sect., BAAS, 1978; Cambridge Philosophical Soc., 1985. Mem., Deutsche Akad. der Naturforscher Leopoldina, 1981. Corresp. Mem., Bayerische Akad. der Wissenschaften, 1982. Hon. Member: Haematology Socs of GB, Costa Rica, Europe, Germany, Italy, Netherlands, Switzerland, Turkey, USA, Venezuela; Pathology Soc. of Nigeria; Assoc. of Clinical Biochemists, 1984; Assoc. of Anaesthetists of GB and Ireland, 1984. Dr med hc Johann Wolfgang Goethe Universität, Frankfurt a/M, 1972. Rivers Medal, Royal Anthrop. Inst., 1963; Martin Luther King Prize, Southern Christian Fedn, USA, 1971; Conway Evans Prize, RCP and Royal Soc., 1976; Wellcome Prize, Assoc. of Clinical Biochemists, 1979; Ludwig Heilmeyer Medal, Univ. of Ulm, 1979. Officer, National Order (Ivory Coast), 1981. *Publications:* Man's Haemoglobins (with R. G. Huntsman), 1966, 2nd edn 1974; (ed with R. M. Schmidt and T. H. J. Huisman) The Detection of Hemoglobinopathics, 1974; (with P. A. M. Kynoch) Human Haemoglobin variants and their Characteristics, 1976; articles in sci. jls. *Address:* 22 Newton Road, Cambridge CB2 2AL. *Club:* Athenæum.

*Died 13 July 1985.*

**LEHMANN, John Frederick,** CBE 1964; FRSL; Editor of the London Magazine from its foundation to 1961; Managing Director of John Lehmann Ltd from its foundation to 1952; Founder and Editor of New Writing and of Orpheus; *b* 2 June 1907; *s* of late Rudolph Chambers Lehmann and Alice Marie Davis. *Educ:* Eton (King's Scholar); Trinity Coll., Cambridge. Partner and Gen. Manager, The Hogarth Press, 1938–46; Advisory Editor, The Geographical Magazine, 1940–45. Editor, New Soundings (BBC Third Programme), 1952, The London Magazine, 1954. Chm., Editorial Advisory Panel, British Council, 1952–58; Mem., Anglo-Greek Mixed Commission, 1962–68; Pres., Royal Literary Fund, 1966–76. Vis. Professor: Univ. of Texas, and State Univ. of Calif at San Diego, 1970–72; Univ. of Calif at Berkeley, 1974; Emory Univ., Atlanta, 1977. Pres. Alliance Française in Great Britain, 1955–63. Hon. DLitt Birmingham, 1980. Silver Jubilee Medal, 1977; Officer, Gold Cross, Order of George I (Greece), 1954, Comdr, 1961; Officier Légion d'Honneur, 1958; Grand Officier, Etoile Noire, 1960; Officier, Ordre des Arts et des Lettres, 1965. Prix du Rayonnement Français, 1961. *Publications:* A Garden Revisited, 1931; The Noise of History, 1934; Prometheus and the Bolsheviks, 1937; Evil Was Abroad, 1938; Down River, 1939; New Writing in Europe, 1940; Forty Poems, 1942; The Sphere of Glass, 1944; Shelley in Italy, 1947; The Age of the Dragon, 1951; The Open Night, 1952; Edith Sitwell, 1952; The Whispering Gallery (Autobiography I), 1955; I Am My Brother (Autobiography II), 1960; Ancestors and Friends, 1962; Collected Poems, 1963; Christ the Hunter, 1965; The Ample Proposition (Autobiography III), 1966; A Nest of Tigers, 1968; In My Own Time (condensed one-volume autobiography), 1969 (USA); Holborn, 1970; The Reader at Night and other poems, 1974; Virginia Woolf and Her World, 1975; In the Purely Pagan Sense, 1976; Edward Lear and His World, 1977; Thrown to the Woolfs, 1978; Rupert Brooke: his life and his legend, 1980; English Poets of the First World War, 1981; Three Literary Friendships, 1983; New and Selected Poems, 1985; Editor: Poems from New Writing, 1946, French Stories from New Writing, 1947, The Year's Work in Literature, 1949 and 1950, English Stories from New Writing, 1950, Pleasures of New Writing, 1952; The Chatto Book of Modern Poetry, 1956 (with C. Day Lewis); The Craft of Letters in England, 1956; Modern French Stories, 1956; Coming to London, 1957; Italian Stories of Today, 1959; Selected Poems of Edith Sitwell, 1965; (with Derek Parker) Edith Sitwell: selected letters, 1970; (with Roy Fuller) The Penguin New Writing 1940–50, 1985. *Recreations:* gardening, swimming, reading. *Address:* 85 Cornwall Gardens, SW7. *Clubs:* Naval and Military, Eton Viking.

*Died 7 April 1987.*

**LEHMANN, Rosamond Nina,** CBE 1982; *b* 3 Feb. 1901; 2nd *d* of R. C. Lehmann and Alice Davis; *m* 1923, Hon. Walter Runciman (marr. diss. 1928) (succeeded as 2nd Viscount Runciman of Doxford, 1949; *d* 1989); *m* 1928, Hon. Wogan Philipps (marr. diss. 1944) (succeeded as 2nd Baron Milford, 1962; one *s* (one *d* decd). *Educ:* privately; Girton Coll., Cambridge (scholar; Hon. Fellow, 1986). *Publications:* Dusty Answer, 1927, repr. 1981; A Note in Music, 1930, repr. 1982; Invitation to the Waltz, 1932, repr. 1981; The Weather in the Streets, 1936, repr. 1981 (filmed 1983); The Ballad

and the Source, 1944, repr. 1982; The Gypsy's Baby, 1946, repr. 1973; The Echoing Grove, 1953, repr. 1981; The Swan in the Evening, 1967, repr. 1983; (with W. Tudor Pole) A Man Seen Afar, 1965; (with Cynthia, Baroness Sandys) Letters from Our Daughters, 2 vols, 1971; A Sea-Grape Tree, 1976, repr. 1982; The Awakening Letters, 1978. *Recreations:* reading, music. *Address:* 30 Clareville Grove, SW7 5AS.                                   *Died 12 March 1990.*

**LEIGH, Ralph Alexander,** CBE 1977; FBA 1969; LittD; Professor of French, University of Cambridge, 1973–82, later Emeritus, and Sandars Reader in Bibliography, 1986–87; Professorial Fellow of Trinity College, Cambridge, since 1973 (Fellow since 1952, Prælector since 1967, Senior Research Fellow, 1969–73); *b* London, 6 Jan. 1915; *m* 1945, Edith Helen Kern (*d* 1972); one *s* one *d*. *Educ:* Raine's Sch. for Boys, London; Queen Mary Coll., Univ. of London (Fellow, 1983); Univ. of Paris (Sorbonne). BA London 1st class hons. 1936; Diplôme de l'Université de Paris, 1938. Served War, 1941–46: RASC and Staff; CCG; Lieut (ERE list) 1942; Major, 1944. Lectr, Dept of French, Univ. of Edinburgh, 1946; Lectr, 1952–69, Reader, 1969–73, Cambridge Univ. Vis. Prof., Sorbonne, 1973. Mem., Inst. for Adv. Studies and Fulbright Scholar, Princeton, 1967; Dir and Mem. Cttee, Voltaire Foundn, Oxford, 1983–. Leverhulme Fellow, 1959–60, 1970, 1982–83. LittD (Cambridge) 1968; DUniv Edinburgh, 1986; Docteur (hc): Univ. of Neuchâtel, 1978; Univ. of Geneva, 1983. Médaille d'argent de la Ville de Paris, 1978. Chevalier de la Légion d'Honneur, 1979. *Publications:* Correspondance Complète de Jean Jacques Rousseau, vols I–XLVI, 1965–87 (in progress); Rousseau and the Problem of Tolerance in the XVIIIth Century, 1979; (ed) Rousseau after 200 years, 1982; contribs to Revue de littérature comparée; Annales Rousseau; Revue d'Histoire littéraire; Modern Language Review; French Studies; Studies on Voltaire, etc. *Recreations:* book-collecting, music. *Address:* Trinity College, Cambridge. *Club:* United Oxford & Cambridge University.

*Died 22 Dec. 1987.*

**LEIGH-WOOD, Roger,** DL; *b* 16 Aug. 1906; *s* of Sir James Leigh-Wood, KBE, CB, CMG, and Joanna Elizabeth Turnball; *m* 1936, Norah Elizabeth Holroyde; four *s*. *Educ:* Winchester Coll.; Trinity Coll., Oxford. Lt-Comdr RNVR, 1939–45. Brown Shipley & Co. Ltd, 1930–42; Eastern Bank Ltd, 1945, Chm. 1967–71; Chartered Bank, 1967–72 (Dep. Chm. 1971); Commercial Union Assce Co. Ltd, 1948–71; Dalgety Ltd, 1948–72; Chm., Scott & Bowne Ltd, 1964–78. High Sheriff of Hampshire, 1964–65; DL Hants, 1970. *Recreations:* yachting, gardening; formerly athletics (Pres. Oxford Univ. Athletic Club, 1929; British Olympic Team, 1928; Empire Games Team, 1930). *Address:* Summerley, Bentworth, Alton, Hants. *T:* Alton 62077. *Club:* Royal Yacht Squadron.

*Died 1 March 1987.*

**LEIGHTON, Clare,** RE 1934; *b* 1899; *d* of late Marie Connor Leighton, and late Robert Leighton. *Educ:* privately; Brighton School of Art; Slade School. Elected Member of Society of Wood Engravers, 1928; First prize International Engraving Exhibition, Art Institute of Chicago, 1930; Fellow National Acad. of Design, New York; Member, Society of American Graphic Arts; Member, National Inst. of Arts and Letters, USA, 1951. Prints purchased for permanent collection of British Museum, Victoria and Albert Museum, National Gallery of Canada, Museums of Boston, Baltimore, New York, etc. Designed: 33 stained glass windows for St Paul's Cathedral, Worcester, Mass; 12 plates for Josiah Wedgwood & Sons Ltd. *Publications:* Illustrated with wood engravings the following books: Thomas Hardy's The Return of the Native, 1929; Thornton Wilder's The Bridge of San Luis Rey, 1930; The Sea and the Jungle, 1930; Wuthering Heights, 1931; E. Madox Roberts's The Time of Man, 1943; North Carolina Folk Lore, 1950; Woodcuts: examples of the Work of Clare Leighton, 1930; The Trumpet in the Dust, 1934; Writer: How to do Wood Engraving and Woodcuts, 1932; Wood Engraving of the 1930's, 1936; Tempestuous Petticoat, 1948; written and illustrated: The Musical Box, 1932; The Farmer's Year, 1933; The Wood That Came Back, 1934; Four Hedges, 1935; Country Matters, 1937; Sometime, Never, 1939; Southern Harvest, 1942; Give us this Day, 1943; Where Land meets Sea, 1954. *Address:* Woodbury, Conn 06798, USA.

*Died 3 Nov. 1989.*

**LEIGHTON, Prof. Kenneth,** MA, DMus; LRAM, FRCM; composer, pianist and conductor; Reid Professor of Music, University of Edinburgh, since 1970; *b* 2 Oct. 1929; *s* of Thomas Leighton; *m* 1st, 1953, Lydia Vignapiano; one *s* one *d*; 2nd, 1981, Josephine Ann Prescott. *Educ:* Queen Elizabeth Grammar Sch., Wakefield; Queen's Coll., Oxford (schol.). MA 1955; DMus 1960); Petrassi, Rome. Prof. of Theory, RN Sch. of Music, 1952–53; Gregory Fellow in Music, Leeds Univ., 1953–56; Lectr in Music Composition, Edinburgh Univ., 1956–68; Lectr in Music, Oxford Univ., and Fellow of Worcester Coll., 1968–70. Hon. DMus St Andrews, 1977. *Compositions:* Concertos for: piano (3); violin; cello; viola and two pianos; harpsichord; symphony for string orchestra; three string quartets; piano quintet; sonatas for: violin and piano (2); piano (3); piano duet; partita for cello and piano; clarinet trio; orchestral works; Burlesque, Passacaglia, Chorale and Fugue; three symphonies; The Birds (chorus and strings); The Light Invisible (tenor, chorus and orch.), etc; Fantasia Contrappuntistica (piano); Columba (3 act opera); Columba Mea (chorus, soloists and strings); Veris Gratia (oboe, cello and strings); Laudes Montium (chorus and orch.); Earth, Sweet Earth (song cycle); incidental music for radio and television drama; church, organ, chamber and piano music. *Recreation:* walking. *Address:* Faculty of Music, University of Edinburgh, Alison House, Nicolson Square, Edinburgh EH8 9BH. *Club:* Edinburgh University Staff.                 *Died* 24 *Aug.* 1988.

**LEIGHTON-BOYCE, Guy Gilbert;** Accountant and Comptroller General, HM Customs and Excise, 1973-80; *b* 23 Oct. 1920; *s* of late Charles Edmund Victor and Eleanor Fannie Leighton-Boyce; *m* 1945, Adrienne Jean Elliott Samms; two *s* two *d. Educ:* Dulwich Coll. HM Customs and Excise, 1939. Served War, RAF, 1941-46. Asst Sec., 1960; Under Sec., 1973. *Publications:* Irish Setters, 1973; (with James Iliff) Tephrocactus, 1973; A Survey of Early Setters, 1985; articles in Cactus and Succulent jls. *Recreations:* looking at pictures; dogs, plants. *Address:* 220 Leigham Court Road, Streatham, SW16 2RB. *T:* 01-769 4844. *Club:* Kennel.
                                                         *Died* 31 *March* 1989.

**LEJEUNE, Maj.-Gen. Francis St David Benwell,** CB 1949; CBE 1944; *b* 1 March 1899; 2nd *s* of late J. F. P. Lejeune, Bedford; *m* 1927, Joyce Mary, *d* of late Charles E. Davies, Hampton Court; one *s* one *d. Educ:* Bedford; RMA, Woolwich. 2nd Lieut, RA, 1917; served European War, 1914-18, France and Belgium (despatches); seconded RAF, Somaliland and Iraq Operations, 1920-24; GSO 3 War Office, 1929; Asst Military Attaché, Washington, 1932-34; Special Mission in Spain, 1938-39. War of 1939-45 served in Italy and Burma (despatches); Maj.-General, 1944; Chief of Staff AA Command, Comdr AA Group, 1944; Director Technical Training, War Office, 1946; President Ordnance Board, 1947; retired, 1949; International Staff, NATO, 1952-62; psc; pac. *Address:* 68 South Cliff, Bexhill on Sea, East Sussex. *T:* Bexhill 211971.
                                                         *Died* 1 *June* 1984.

**LELOIR, Luis Federico;** President, Institute of Biochemical Research, Campomar, since 1947; Extraordinary Professor, Faculty of Exact Sciences, University of Buenos Aires, since 1962; *b* Paris, 6 Sept. 1906; *m* Amelie Zuherbuhler de Leloir; one *d. Educ:* Univ. of Buenos Aires. Engaged in research in Gt Britain, Argentina and USA; subseq. at Inst. of Biology and Experimental Med., Buenos Aires, 1946. Chm., Argentine Assoc. for Advancement of Science, 1958-59; Mem. Directorate, Nat. Research Council, 1958-64; Mem., Nat. Acad. of Med., 1961; Foreign Mem: Royal Society, 1972; Nat. Acad. of Sciences, USA; Amer. Acad. of Arts and Sciences; Amer. Philosophical Soc. Holds several hon. doctorates and has won numerous prizes, etc, inc. Nobel Prize for Chemistry, 1970. Légion d'Honneur (France). *Address:* Instituto de Investigaciones Bioquímicas, Fundación Campomar, Antonio Machado 151, (1405) Buenos Aires, Argentina. *T:* 88-4016/19.
                                                         *Died* 3 *Dec.* 1987.

**LEMAIRE, Most Rev. Ishmael Samuel Mills,** DD; Bishop of Accra, 1968-82; Archbishop of West Africa, 1981-82. Priest, Diocese of Accra, 1936-60; Canon of Accra, 1960-63; Archdeacon of Sekondi, 1961-63; Assistant Bishop of Accra, 1963-68. *Address:* c/o Bishopscourt, PO Box 8, Accra, Ghana.            *Died* 9 *July* 1984.

**LE MARCHANT, Sir Denis,** 5th Bt, *cr* 1841; *b* 28 Feb. 1906; *er s* of Brigadier-General Sir Edward Thomas Le Marchant, 4th Bt, KCB, CBE, JP, DL, and Evelyn Brooks (*d* 1957), *er d* of late Robert Millington Knowles, JP, DL, Colston Bassett Hall, Nottinghamshire; *S* father, 1953; *m* 1933, Elizabeth Rowena, *y d* of late Arthur Hovenden Worth; one *s* one *d* (and one *s* decd). *Educ:* Radley. High Sheriff, Lincolnshire, 1958. *Heir:* *s* Francis Arthur Le Marchant, *b* 6 Oct. 1939. *Address:* Hungerton Hall, Grantham, Lincolnshire. *T:* Grantham 870244.            *Died* 20 *Aug.* 1987.

**LE MARCHANT, Sir Spencer,** Kt 1984; Partner, L. Messel & Co., 1961-86; *b* 15 Jan. 1931; *s* of late Alfred Le Marchant and Turdis Le Marchant (*née* Mortensen); *m* 1955, Lucinda Gaye Leveson Gower; two *d. Educ:* Eton. National Service and Territorial Commissions, Sherwood Foresters. Mem., Stock Exchange, 1954. Mem., Westminster City Council, 1956-71; contested (C) Vauxhall, 1966. MP (C) Derbys, High Peak, 1970-83; PPS to Chief Sec., Financial Sec. and Minister of State, Treasury, 1972-74; PPS Dept of Energy, 1974; an Opposition Whip, 1974-79; Comptroller of HM Household and a Govt Whip, 1979-81; PPS to Leader of Commons, 1981-82, to Sec. of State for Foreign and Commonwealth Affairs, 1982. *Address:* 29 Rivermill, Grosvenor Road, SW1; The Saltings, Yarmouth, Isle of Wight. *Clubs:* White's; Royal Yacht Squadron.
                                                         *Died* 7 *Sept.* 1986.

**LEMNITZER, General Lyman L(ouis),** DSM (US Army) (with 3 Oak Leaf Clusters); DSM (US Navy); DSM (US Air Force); Silver Star; Legion of Merit (Officer's Degree); Legion of Merit; Supreme Allied Commander, Europe, 1963-69; Commander-in-Chief, US

European Command, 1962-69; *b* Pennsylvania, 29 Aug. 1899; *s* of late William L. Lemnitzer; *m* 1923, Katherine Mead Tryon; one *s* one *d. Educ:* Honesdale High Sch.; US Military Academy. Duty with troops, Instructor at Army Schools, etc., 1920-40; War Plans Division, War Dept General Staff, 1941; Comdg General, 34th Anti-Aircraft Artillery Bde, and Allied Force HQ England, as Asst Chief of Staff for Plans and Ops, 1942 (2nd in Command, Secret Submarine Mission to contact friendly French Officials in N Africa); served in Europe and N Africa, 1942-45; with Joint Chiefs of Staff, 1945-47; Dep. Comdt National War Coll., 1947-49; Asst to Secretary of Defence, 1949-50; Head of US Delegn to Military Cttee of the Five (Brussels Pact) Powers. London; Student, Basic Airborne Course, Fort Benning, 1950; Comdg General 11th Airborne Div., 1951, 7th Infantry Div. (in Korea), 1951-52; DCS (Plans and Research), 1952-55; Comdg General Far East and 8th US Army, 1955; C-in-C, Far East and UN Commands, and Governor of Ryukyu Is, 1955-57; Vice-Chief of Staff, 1957-59, Chief of Staff, 1959-60, US Army; Chairman Joint Chiefs of Staff, 1960-62. Holds several hon. doctorates. US Presidential Medal of Freedom, 1987. Hon. CB and Hon. CBE (Great Britain); Grand Cross, Legion of Honour (France); Grand Cross, Order of Merit (Germany), 1969; and numerous other foreign Orders and decorations. *Recreations:* golf, fishing, photography, interested in baseball, correspondence with his many friends around the world. *Address:* 3286 Worthington Street, NW, Washington, DC 20015, USA.                                 *Died* 12 *Nov.* 1988.

**LENNON, Most Rev. James Gerard;** Auxiliary Bishop of Armagh, (RC), and titular Bishop of Ceannanus Mor, since 1980; *b* 26 Sept. 1923; *s* of Patrick and Catherine Lennon. *Educ:* St Patrick's College, Armagh; St Patrick's College, Maynooth. Studied Celtic Languages and Sociology. Ordained priest, 1948. Hon. DD National University of Ireland. *Address:* St Peters, Fair Street, Drogheda, Co. Louth, Ireland. *T:* Drogheda 38537.                 *Died* 17 *Oct.* 1989.

**LENNON, Most Rev. Patrick,** DD; *b* Borris, Co. Carlow, 1914. *Educ:* Rockwell Coll., Cashel; St Patrick's Coll., Maynooth. BSc 1934; DD 1940. Prof. of Moral Theology, St Patrick's Coll., Carlow, 1940; Pres., St Patrick's Coll., 1956-66; Auxiliary Bishop and Parish Priest of Mountmellick, 1966-67; Bishop of Kildare and Leighlin, 1967-87. *Address:* Presbytery Annexe, Dublin Road, Carlow, Ireland. *T:* Carlow (0503) 41156.                 *Died* 12 *Jan.* 1990.

**LENNOX;** *see* Gordon Lennox.

**LEONARD,** Baron *cr* 1978 (Life Peer), of the City of Cardiff in the County of S Glamorgan; **John Denis Leonard,** OBE 1976; Chairman, Cardiff Sheet Metal & Engineering Co. Ltd, since 1953; *b* 19 Oct. 1909; *s* of late Denis Leonard and Mary McDermott; *m* 1945, Glenys Evelyn Kenny; one *s* one *d. Educ:* Manorhamilton Boys' School, Republic of Ireland. Member: Cardiff City Council, 1970-76; Glamorgan County Council, 1974-77 (Chairman, 1976-77). A Lord in Waiting (Govt Whip), 1978-79. Mem. Council, Univ. of Wales Inst. of Science and Technology, 1978. *Recreations:* Association football, golf and gardening. *Address:* 19 Queen Anne Square, Cardiff. *T:* Cardiff 387109.                 *Died* 17 *July* 1983.

**LEONARD, Sir Reginald Byron,** Kt 1983; CMG 1972; OBE 1971; Chairman, Queensland Press Ltd and Queensland Newspapers Pty Ltd, 1971-82 (Managing Director, 1970-74); *b* 13 March 1907; *s* of late J. Leonard; *m* 1941, Pat, *d* of late J. Blampied; one *d. Educ:* St Kevin's Coll., Melbourne. Journalist, 1924; Dir, RAAF PR, 1940-41; war corresp., UK and New Guinea; Editor: Guinea Gold, AIF newspaper, 1942-44; Melbourne Herald, 1945-58; Man. Dir, 1958-74, Chm., 1970-82, Telegraph Newspaper Co.; Jt Man. Dir, Queensland Newspapers, 1963-68; Dep. Chm., Queensland Press, 1968-71; Dir, Herald & Weekly Times, 1974-82. Chairman: Brisbane TV Ltd; Cairns Post Pty. *Address:* Unit 15, 104 Station Road, Indooroopilly, Qld 4078, Australia.

                                                         *Died* 12 *March* 1986.

**LEONARD, Sir Walter McEllister,** Kt 1977; DFC; Company Director; *b* Grafton, 22 Feb. 1915; *s* of W. Leonard, Grafton; *m* 1948, Yvonne M., *d* of J. V. Brady; two *s* three *d. Educ:* Cootamundra High Sch. Joined Ampol Petroleum Ltd, 1938; Chief Accountant, 1940; Sec., 1941. Served War, RAAF, Bomber Command, 1942-45 (DFC). Ampol Petroleum Ltd (now Ampol Limited): Asst to Man. Dir, 1946-49; Gen. Manager, 1949-63; Dir, 1958; Man. Dir and Chief Exec., 1963-70; Chm. and Chief Exec., 1970-77; Chm., 1977-81; Ampol Exploration Ltd: Dir, 1954; Man. Dir and Chief Exec., 1967-70; Chm. and Chief Exec., 1970-77; Chm., 1977-81. Director: Australian Industry Develt Corp., 1971-; CRA Ltd, 1977-83; Interscan Australia Pty Ltd, 1978-; Australian Liquid Assets Management Ltd, 1981-. *Address:* 51 Cutler Road, Clontarf, NSW 2093, Australia. *Clubs:* Australian (Sydney); Commonwealth (Canberra); Royal Sydney Yacht Squadron; American National.
                                                         *Died* 17 *Jan.* 1985.

**LE PATOUREL, John Herbert,** FBA 1972; MA, DPhil Oxon; Docteur *hc* Caen; Professor Emeritus, University of Leeds; Archivist to Royal Court of Guernsey since 1946; *b* Guernsey, 29 July 1909; *er s* of late H. A. Le Patourel (HM Attorney-Gen. for Guernsey) and Mary Elizabeth Daw; *m* 1939, Hilda Elizabeth Jean Bird, BA, FSA; three *s* one *d. Educ:* Elizabeth Coll., Guernsey; Jesus Coll., Oxford (King Charles I Scholar); Goldsmiths' Company's Senior Student, 1931–33. Asst Lecturer, Dept of History, University Coll., London, 1933; Lecturer, 1936; Reader in Medieval History, University of London, 1943; Prof. of Medieval History, 1945–70, Research Prof., 1970–74, and Dir, Graduate Centre for Medieval Studies, 1967–70, Univ. of Leeds. Leverhulme Research Fellow, 1950–51. Pres., Leeds Philosophical and Literary Soc., 1966–68; Patron, Thoresby Soc. (Pres. 1949–55); Vice-Pres., Royal Historical Soc., 1968–70; Hon. Vice-Pres., Yorkshire Archæological Soc. (Pres., 1965–69). Hon. Mem., Soc. Guernesiaise. *Publications:* The Medieval Administration of the Channel Islands, 1199–1399, 1937; The Building of Castle Cornet, Guernsey, 1958; The Manor and Borough of Leeds, 1066–1400, 1957; The Norman Empire, 1976; articles, etc, in English and French historical periodicals, publications of Channel Island societies, etc. *Address:* Westcote, Hebers Ghyll Drive, Ilkley, West Yorks. *T:* Ilkley 609502.

*Died 22 July 1981.*

**LERMON, His Honour Norman,** QC 1966; a Circuit Judge (formerly County Court Judge), 1971–87, retired; *b* 12 Dec. 1915; *s* of late Morris and Clara Lermon; *m* 1939, Sheila Veronica Gilks; one *d. Educ:* Clifton Coll.; Trinity Hall, Cambridge. Joined Royal Fusiliers, 1939; commnd into S Wales Borderers, 1940; served in 53 (W) and 11th Armoured Divs; Staff Officer Ops (Air) 8th Corps, France, Holland and Germany; Major, 1945; NW Europe 1946 (despatches). Called to the Bar, 1943. *Recreations:* golf, reading. *Address:* Old Cottage, High Barn Corner, Godalming, Surrey GU8 4AE. *Died 27 Jan. 1989.*

**LERNER, Alan Jay;** playwright; lyricist; *b* NYC, 31 Aug. 1918. *Educ:* Bedales Sch., Hants; Choate Sch., Wallingford, USA; Harvard Univ. Pres., Dramatists' Guild of America, 1958–63; Mem., Songwriter's Hall of Fame, 1971; Bd of Governors: Nat. Hosp. for Speech Disorders; NY Osteopathic Hosp. *Musical plays:* with F. Loewe: What's up, 1943; The Day before Spring, 1945; Brigadoon, 1947 (filmed 1954; NY Drama Critics' Circle Award, 1947; Christopher Award, 1954); Paint your Wagon, 1951 (filmed and produced, 1969); My Fair Lady, 1956 (filmed 1964; NY Drama Critics' Circle Award, Donaldson Award, Antoinette Perry Award, 1956); Camelot, 1960 (filmed 1968); with K. Weill, Love Life, 1948; with B. Lane, On a Clear Day you can see Forever, 1965 (filmed 1970; Grammy Award, 1966); with A. Previn, Coco, 1969; Gigi, 1973 (Antoinette Perry Award, 1973–74); with L. Bernstein, 1600 Pennsylvania Avenue, 1976; with Burton Lane, Carmelina, 1979; with Charles Strouse, Dance a Little Closer, 1983; *films:* Royal Wedding, 1951; An American in Paris, 1951 (Academy Award, Screenwriters' Guild Award, 1951); Gigi, 1958 (two Academy Awards, Screenwriters' Guild Award, 1958); The Little Prince, 1975. *Publications:* The Street Where I Live, 1978; Kennedy Center Honors, 1985; *posthumous publication:* The Musical Theatre: a celebration, 1986. *Address:* c/o Cohen & Grossberg, 635 Madison Avenue–11A, New York, NY 10022, USA. *Clubs:* Players, Lambs, Shaw Soc. *Died 14 June 1986.*

**LESLIE, Mrs D. G.;** *see* Erskine-Lindop, A. B. N.

**LESLIE, Doris, (Lady Fergusson Hannay);** novelist and historian; *b* 9 March 1891; *m* Sir Walter Fergusson Hannay (*d* 1961). *Educ:* London; Brussels; studied art in Florence. Served in Civil Defence, 1941–45. Woman of the Year for Literature (Catholic Women's League), 1970. *Publications: novels:* Full Flavour; Fair Company; Concord in Jeopardy; Another Cynthia; House in the Dust; Folly's End; The Peverills; Peridot Flight; As the Tree Falls; Paragon Street; The Marriage of Martha Todd; A Young Wives' Tale; The Dragon's Head; Call Back Yesterday; *biographical studies:* Royal William (Life of William IV); Polonaise (Life of Chopin); Wreath for Arabella (Life of the Lady Arabella Stuart); That Enchantress (Life of Abigail Hill, Lady Masham); The Great Corinthian (Portrait of the Prince Regent); A Toast to Lady Mary (Life of Lady Mary Wortley Montagu); The Perfect Wife (Life of Mary Anne Disraeli, Viscountess Beaconsfield), 1960; I Return (The Story of François Villon), 1962; This for Caroline (Life of Lady Caroline Lamb), 1964; The Sceptre and the Rose (marriage of Charles II and Catherine of Braganza), 1967; The Rebel Princess (Life of Sophia Dorothea, wife of George I), 1970; The Desert Queen (Life of Lady Hester Stanhope), 1972; The Incredible Duchess (Life of Elizabeth Chudleigh, Duchess of Kingston), 1974; Notorious Lady (Life of Margaret Power, Countess of Blessington), 1976; The Warrior King (Reign of Richard Coeur de Lion and his Crusade), 1977; Crown of Thorns (Life of Richard II), 1979. *Address:* The Grange, Felcourt, near East Grinstead, Sussex. *Died 30 May 1982.*

**LESLIE, Rear-Adm. George Cunningham,** CB 1970; OBE 1944; MA; Domestic Bursar and Fellow of St Edmund Hall, Oxford, 1970–88, retired; *b* 27 Oct. 1920; 4th *s* of Col A. S. Leslie, CMG, WS,

Kininvie, and Mrs M. I. Leslie (*née* Horne); *m* 1953, Margaret Rose Leslie; one *s* three *d. Educ:* Uppingham. Entered RN, 1938; War service in HMS York, Harvester, Volunteer and Cassandra, 1939–45; comd HMS: Wrangler, 1950–51; Wilton, 1951; Surprise, 1954–55; Capt. Fishery Protection Sqdn, 1960–62; Cdre HMS Drake, 1964–65; comd HMS Devonshire, 1966–67; Flag Officer, Admiralty Interview Bd, 1967–68; NATO HQ, Brussels, 1968–70. Comdr 1952; Capt. 1958; Rear-Adm. 1967; retired 1970. *Recreations:* sailing, painting, country pursuits. *Address:* 24 Staverton Road, Oxford OX2 6XJ. *Died 14 Nov. 1988.*

**LESLIE, Ian (William) Murray,** CBE 1971 (OBE 1954); Editor of Building (formerly The Builder), 1948–70; Vice-Chairman, The Builder Ltd, 1970–75; *b* 13 March 1905; 2nd *s* of John Gordon Leslie, MB, CM, Black Isle, Inverness, and Agnes Macrae, Kintail, Wester Ross; *m* 1st, 1929, Josette (marr. diss. 1974), 2nd *d* of late André Délètraz, actor, Paris, and Mme Hachard; one *s*; 2nd, 1974, G. M. Vivian Williams, LLB, barrister, *d* of Evan Hughes, Tintagel, Cornwall. *Educ:* St Paul's (foundation scholar); Crown and Manor Boys' Club, Hoxton. Joined editorial staff of The Builder, 1926; Associate Editor, 1937. Mem. Council, National Assoc. of Boys' Clubs, 1944–54; Chm. London Federation of Boys' Clubs, 1945–50; JP for County of London, 1945–61; Mem., Metropolitan Juvenile Courts Panel, 1947–61 (Chm., Chelsea Children's Court, 1956–61). Founder-Pres., Internat. Assoc. of the Building and Construction Press (UK section), 1970–79; made survey (with J. B. Perks) of Canadian construction industry for The Builder, 1950; organized £1000 house architectural competition for The Builder, 1951; made survey of housing, South Africa and Rhodesia, for The Builder, 1954. Chm., Building Industry Youth Trust, 1975–81. Pres., Invalids Cricket Club, 1974–; Mem., Develt Cttee of MCC, 1974–84; Mem., Medical Sch. Council, St Mary's Hosp., 1974–83. Founder Mem., Sherlock Holmes Soc. of London, and author of "Dr Watson" letters to The Times, 1950. Associate RICS; Hon. Mem. of Art Workers' Guild; Hon. FRIBA; Hon. FCIOB. *Recreations:* watching cricket; sleep. *Address:* 64 Hamilton Terrace, NW8 9UJ. *T:* 01–289 0178. *Clubs:* Savage, Architectural Association (Hon. Mem.), MCC.

*Died 6 June 1987.*

**LESSER, Most Rev. Norman Alfred,** CMG 1971; MA Cantab; ThD 1962; DD Lambeth 1963; *b* 16 March 1902; *s* of Albert Lesser, Liverpool; *m* 1930, Beatrice Barnes, Southport; one *d. Educ:* Liverpool Collegiate Sch.; Fitzwilliam Hall and Ridley Hall, Cambridge. Curate St Simon and St Jude, Anfield, Liverpool, 1925–26; Curate Holy Trinity, Formby, Lancs, 1926–29; Liverpool Cathedral, 1929–31; Vicar St John, Barrow-in-Furness, 1931–39; Rector and Sub-Dean, Nairobi Cathedral, 1939; Provost of Nairobi, 1942; Bishop of Waiapu, 1947–71; Primate and Archbishop of New Zealand, 1961–71. *Recreation:* model-making. *Address:* 4 Sealy Road, Napier, New Zealand. *T:* Napier 53509.

*Died 12 Feb. 1985.*

**LESTANG, Sir (Marie Charles Emmanuel) Clement N. de;** *see* Nageon de Lestang.

**L'ESTRANGE, Laurence Percy Farrer,** OBE 1958; HM Diplomatic Service; retired; company director and consultant; *b* 10 Sept. 1912; *s* of late S. W. L'Estrange and Louie Knights L'Estrange (*née* Farrer); *m* 1933, Anne Catherine (*née* Whiteside) (*d* 1986); two *s. Educ:* Shoreham Grammar Sch., Shoreham, Sussex; Univ. of London. Employed at HM Embassy, Caracas, 1939, and Acting Vice-Consul, 1941 and 1942. Resigned and joined RAF, 1943–46. HM Vice-Consul, Malaga, 1946; Second Sec., San Salvador, 1949; Chargé d'Affaires, 1952; Vice-Consul, Chicago, 1953; First Sec. (Commercial): Manila, 1954; Lima, 1958; Chargé d'Affaires, 1961; seconded to Western Hemisphere Exports Council, in charge of Latin American Div., 1962; HM Consul, Denver, 1963; Counsellor (Commercial), Lagos, 1967; Ambassador to Honduras, 1969–72. FRSA 1973. *Recreations:* golf, riding, sailing, fishing and shooting. *Address:* 154 Frog Grove Lane, Wood Street Village, Guildford, Surrey GU3 3HB. *Died 18 Aug. 1990.*

**LÉVESQUE, Hon. René;** Premier of Province of Québec, Canada, 1976–85; *b* 24 Aug. 1922; *s* of Dominique Lévesque and Diane Dionne; *m* 1st, 1947, Louise L'Heureux (marr. diss. 1978); two *s* one *d*; 2nd, 1979, Corinne Cote. *Educ:* schs in New Carlisle and Gaspé; Québec Univ. (BA); Law Sch., Laval, Québec. Overseas duty as reporter with US Forces (attached to Office of War Information, Europe), 1944–45; reporter and commentator, Canadian Broadcasting Corp., 1946–59. Mem., Québec Nat. Assembly, 1960–70; Minister, Public Works, Natural Resources and Social Welfare, 1960–66; Mem. Opposition, 1966–70; Pres., Parti Québécois, 1968–85. Grand Médaille de Vermeil, 1977. Grand Officer, Legion of Honour, 1977. *Publications:* Option-Québec, 1968; La Passion du Québec, 1978; My Quebec, 1979; Oui, 1980. *Recreations:* tennis, swimming, skiing, reading, movies. *Address:* 91b d'Auteuil Street, Quebec City, PQ, Canada. *Club:* Cercle Universitaire (Québec). *Died 1 Nov. 1987.*

**LEVINGE, Major Sir Richard Vere Henry,** 11th Bt, *cr* 1704; MBE 1941; TD 1977; President, The Salmon and Trout Association; *b* 30 April 1911; *o s* of 10th Bt and Irene Marguerite (who *m* 2nd, 1916, Major R. V. Buxton), *d* of late J. H. C. Pix of Bradford; *S* father, 1914; *m* 1st, 1935, Barbara Mary, 2nd *d* of late George J. Kidston, CMG; two *s* three *d*; 2nd, 1976, Jane Millward. *Educ:* Eton; Balliol Coll., Oxford (Domus Exhibition). Retired, 1976, as Dep. Man. Dir, Arthur Guinness Son & Co. Ltd. Chm. Cttee of Management, Salmon Res. Trust of Ireland, until 1977. War Service, 1939–45, Lovat Scouts and Staff (despatches Burma 1945). *Recreations:* shooting, fishing. *Heir: s* Richard George Robin Levinge [*b* 18 Dec. 1946; *m* 1st, 1969, Hilary Jane, *d* of Dr Derek Mark, Co. Wicklow; 2nd, 1978, Donna Maria d'Ardia Caracciolo, *d* of Prince Frederico Caracciolo, Grange Road, Rathfarnham, Ireland]. *Address:* Spindles, 27 The Grove, Radlett, Herts; Abbey Lodge, Rectory Lane, Itchen Abbas, Winchester, Hants.

*Died 27 Dec. 1984.*

**LÉVIS MIREPOIX, Antoine, Duc de;** Grand d'Espagne; Commandeur de la Légion d'Honneur, Croix de Guerre, Grand Croix de l'Ordre d'Adolphe de Nassau; author; Member of the French Academy since 1953; Mainteneur de l'Académie des Jeux floraux de Toulouse; Commandeur, Ordre des Palmes Académiques; *b* 1 Aug. 1884; *s* of Henri and Henriette de Chabannes La Palice; *m* 1911, Nicole de Chaponay; one *s*. *Educ:* Lycée de Toulouse; Sorbonne (Licencié en philosophie). Lecturer for the Alliance française; Mission Maria Chapdeleine, Canada; President, Cincinnati de France; President, Institut France-Canada. *Publications:* Le Seigneur Inconnu, 1922; Montségur, 1924; François Ier, 1931; Vieilles races et Temps nouveaux, 1934; Les Campagnes ardentes, 1934; Le Coeur secret de Saint-Simon, 1935; Le Siècle de Philippe le Bel, 1936; La Politesse (with M de Vogüé), 1937; Sainte-Jeanne de France, fille de Louis XI, 1943; Les Trois Femmes de Philipe-Auguste, 1947; Les Guerres de religion, 1947; La France de la Renaissance (Grand Prix Gobert de l'Académie française), 1948; La Tragédie des Templiers, 1955; Aventure d'une famille française, 1955; Que signifie 'le Parti de Ducs', 1964; Le roi n'est more qu'une fois, 1965; Le livre d'or des Maréchaux de France, 1970; L'Attentat d'Agnani, 1970; St Louis: Roi de France, 1970; Henri IV, 1971; Grandeur et misère de l'individualisme française, 1973; La France féodale (6 vols); Robespierre, 1978. *Heir: s* Charles Henri, Marquis de Lévis Mirepoix [*b* 4 Jan. 1912; *m* 1962, Mme Françoise Foucault; one *s* one *d*]. *Address:* 27 rue Daru, 75008 Paris, France; Léran, 09600 Laroque-d'Olmes. *Clubs:* Jockey (Vice-President), Union, Interallié (Paris).

*Died 16 July 1981.*

**LEVITT, Walter Montague,** MD, FRCP, FRCR; Barrister-at-Law; Hon. Consulting Radiotherapist, St Bartholomew's Hospital, since 1945; Hon. Life Governor, St Bartholomew's Hospital Medical College; *b* 1900; *e s* of Lewis and Caroline Levitt, Rathmines, Co. Dublin; *m* 1st, 1929, Sonia Esté Nivinsky (*d* 1957), BSc, MRCS, DPH; no *c*; 2nd, 1977, Violet Irene Levitt (*née* Hirschland). *Educ:* High Sch., Dublin; University Coll., Dublin (Med. Schol. and 1st cl. Exhbnr); Cambridge (DMRE); Frankfurt. Called to the Bar, Lincoln's Inn, 1946. Demonstrator of anatomy, 1920–21, of pathology, 1921; formerly: Lectr in X-Ray Therapy for Dip. in Med. Radiol., Univ. Cambridge; Dir, Dept of Radiotherapy, London Clinic; Hon. Physician i/c, Dept of Radiotherapy, St George's Hosp.; MO i/c Radiotherapeutic Dept, St Bartholomew's Hosp. Member: Minister of Labour's Adv. Panel in Radiology; Clinical Res. Cttee, British Empire Cancer Campaign; Dep. Comr, 1967–69, Dep. Chm., 1969–73, Metropolitan Traffic Comrs. Hon. Assoc. Editor, British Jl of Radiology. Hon. Secretary: Section of Radiology, Internat. Cancer Conf., London, 1928; Radiology Section, BMA Centenary Meeting, London, 1932; Deleg. to Internat. Cancer Congress, Atlantic City, 1939. Foundn Fellow, Vice-Pres., Chm., Therapeutic Cttee, Faculty of Radiologists, 1940–43; Fellow, Vice-Pres., and Pres., Section of Radiology, RSM, 1945–46; formerly Hon. Med. Sec., BIR. Freeman, City of London; Liveryman, Apothecaries' Co., 1956. Gold Medallist, Mercers Hosp., 1922. *Publications:* Deep X-Ray Therapy in Malignant Disease (with Introduction by Lord Horder), 1930; completed and edited Knox's Text Book of X-Ray Therapeutics, 1932; Handbook of Radiotherapy for Senior and Post-graduate students, 1952; Short Encyclopædia of Medicine for Lawyers, 1966; Section on Diseases of the Blood in Paterson's Treatment of Malignant Disease by X-Rays and Radium, 1948; Section on X-Ray therapy in Bourne and Williams' Recent Advances in Gynæcology, 1952; Chapter on Reticulosis and Reticulosarcoma (with R. Bodley Scott) in British Practice in Radiotherapy, 1955; various articles on medico-legal subjects. *Address:* 17 Manor Court, Pinehurst, Cambridge CB3 9BE.

*Died 25 Oct. 1983.*

**LEVY, Sir (Enoch) Bruce,** Kt 1953; OBE 1950; retired, 1951; *b* 19 Feb. 1892; *s* of William and Esther Ann Levy; *m* 1925, Phyllis R., *d* of G. H. Mason; no *c*. *Educ:* Primary Sch.; Banks Commercial Coll.; Victoria University College (BSc). Brought up on farm to age 18; appointed Dept Agriculture, 1911; agrostologist to 1937; charge seed-testing station. Ecological studies Grasslands and indigenous

vegetative cover of NZ; transferred to DSIR, 1937, and appointed Director Grasslands Division; Director Green-keeping Research; Chairman NZ Institute for Turf Culture (Life Mem. 1957); Official Rep. International Grassland Conference, Great Britain, 1937, Netherlands, 1949; Lecture tour, Great Britain, 1949–50; Member: Rotary International; Grassland Assoc. (Life Mem. 1951); NZ Animal Production Society (Life Mem. 1961); Manawatu Catchment Board; Central Standing Cttee, Soil Conservation; Trustee, Grassland Memorial Trust (Chm. 1966–68). Life Member NZ Royal Agric. Society, 1956. Hon. Dr of Science, University of NZ; R. B. Bennett Empire Prize, 1951 (Royal Society of Arts, London). *Publications:* Grasslands of New Zealand, 1943 (revised and enlarged, 1951, 1955 and 1970); Construction, Renovation and Care of the Bowling Green, 1949; Construction, Renovation and Care of the Golf Course, 1950; 150 scientific papers in popular and scientific journals in NZ and overseas. *Recreations:* bowling, gardening. *Address:* Main Waihi Road, RDI, Tauranga, New Zealand. *T:* 64–522.

*Died 16 Oct. 1985.*

**LEWIN, Captain (Edgar) Duncan (Goodenough),** CB 1958; CBE 1953; DSO 1941; DSC 1939; Royal Navy, retired; Deputy Chairman, British Aerospace Dynamics Group, 1977–78; *b* 9 Aug. 1912; *s* of Captain G. E. Lewin, RN; *m* 1943, Nancy Emily Hallett, Tintinhull, Somerset; one *s* one *d*. *Educ:* RN Coll., Dartmouth. Cadet, HMS Royal Oak, 1930; specialized in flying, 1935. Served in HMS Ajax, River Plate action, 1939; Comd 808 Squadron in HMS Ark Royal, 1941; served staff of Admiral Vian in Mediterranean and Pacific, 1944–45. Comd HMS Glory, in Korean waters, 1952–53; Director of Air Warfare, Admiralty, 1953–54; Comd HMS Eagle, 1955; Director of Plans, Admiralty, 1956–57; retired from Navy and joined Board of Blackburn's, 1957; Sales Director, Hawker Siddeley Aviation Ltd, 1968–71; Man. Dir, Hawker Siddeley Dynamics, 1971–77, Chm., 1977. *Recreations:* croquet, gardening. *Address:* Hatching Green Lodge, Harpenden, Herts. *T:* Harpenden 62034.

*Died 24 Nov. 1983.*

**LEWIN, (George) Ronald,** CBE 1983; FRSL, FRHistS; military historian; *b* 11 Oct. 1914; *s* of late Frank Lewin, Halifax; *m* 1938, Sylvia Lloyd Sturge; two *s* one *d* (and one *s* decd). *Educ:* Heath Sch., Halifax; The Queen's Coll., Oxford (Hastings Scholar, 1st Class Hon. Mods, 1st Class Lit. Hum., Goldsmiths' Exhibitioner). Editorial Assistant, Jonathan Cape Ltd, Publishers, 1937. Served in Royal Artillery, N Africa and NW Europe (wounded, despatches), 1939–45. Producer, BBC Home Talks Dept, 1946; Chief Asst, Home Service, 1954; Head, 1957; Chief, 1963. Retired 1965. Editor, Hutchinson Publishing Gp, 1966–69. Leverhulme Res. Fellow, 1973. FRSL 1977; FRHistS 1980. Chesney Gold Medal, RUSI, 1982. *Publications:* Rommel as Military Commander, 1968; (ed) Freedom's Battle, vol. 3, The War on Land 1939–45, 1969; Montgomery as Military Commander, 1971; Churchill as War Lord, 1973; Man of Armour: Lieut-General Vyvyan Pope and the development of armoured warfare, 1976; Slim the Standard-Bearer, the biography of Field Marshal the Viscount Slim, 1976 (W. H. Smith Award, 1977); The Life and Death of the Afrika Korps, 1977; Ultra goes to War, 1978; The Chief: Field Marshal Lord Wavell, Commander-in-Chief and Viceroy, 1980; The Other Ultra: codes, ciphers and the defeat of Japan, 1982; Hitler's Mistakes, 1984; sundry introds to Time/Life Histories of the Second World War; numerous articles and reviews on military history. *Address:* Camilla House, Forest Road, East Horsley, Surrey. *T:* East Horsley 3779. *Club:* Army and Navy.

*Died 6 Jan. 1984.*

**LEWIS, Sir Anthony Carey,** Kt 1972; CBE 1967; Principal of the Royal Academy of Music, 1968–82; *b* 2 March 1915; *s* of late Colonel Leonard Carey Lewis, OBE, and Katherine Barbara Lewis; *m* 1959, Lesley, *d* of Mr and Mrs Frank Lisle Smith. *Educ:* Wellington; Peterhouse, Cambridge (Organ Schol.). MA, MusB Cantab. Joined music staff of BBC, 1935; director Foundations of Music and similar programmes; responsible many revivals 16th–18th century music; War of 1939–45, served MEF; planned and supervised music in BBC Third Programme, 1946; Peyton-Barber Prof. of Music, Univ. of Birmingham, 1947–68, and Dean of the Faculty of Arts, 1961–64. Pres. RMA, 1963–69; Chairman: Music Adv. Panel, Arts Council of GB, 1954–65; Music Adv. Cttee, British Council, 1967–73; Founder and Gen. Editor, Musica Britannica; Chairman: Purcell Soc.; Purcell-Handel Festival, 1959; Dir, English Nat. Opera, 1974–78; Governor, Wellington Coll. Hon. RAM; FRCM; FRNCM; Hon. FTCL; Hon. GSM; FRSAMD. Hon. MusD Birmingham. *Compositions include:* Psalm 86 (Cambridge, 1935); A Choral Overture (Queen's Hall, 1937); City Dances for Orchestra (Jerusalem, 1944); Trumpet Concerto (Albert Hall, 1947); Three Invocations (Birmingham, 1949); A Tribute of Praise (Birmingham, 1951); Horn Concerto (London, 1956); Canzona for Orchestra, Homage to Purcell (Birmingham, 1959). Conductor many recordings, especially Purcell and Handel. *Publications:* research: A Restoration Suite (Purcell and others), 1937; Venus and Adonis (Blow), 1939; Matthew Locke, 1948; Libera me (Arne), 1950; Coronation Anthems (Blow), 1953; Apollo and Daphne (Handel), 1956; Odes and Cantatas (Purcell), 1957;

Anthems (3 vols), (Purcell), 1959–62; Fairy Queen (Purcell), 1966; Athalia (Handel), 1967; Imeneo (Handel), 1977; Editor, English Songs Series; numerous contributions on musical subjects to various periodicals. *Address:* High Rising, Holdfast Lane, Haslemere, Surrey.                                                                    *Died 5 June 1983.*

**LEWIS, David John,** JP; retired Architect; Lord Mayor of Liverpool, 1962–63; *b* 29 April 1893; Welsh; *m* 1919, Margaret Elizabeth Stubbs; no *c. Educ:* Aberystwyth Univ.; Faculty of Architecture, Liverpool Univ. Liverpool City Council, 1936–74; Alderman, 1952–74; Hon. Alderman, 1974. Chm. Educn Cttee, 1961–62; Past Chairman: Royal Liverpool Philharmonic Soc.; Liverpool Welsh Choral Union; Merseyside Youth Orchestra; Past Pres., Liverpool Male Voice Soc.; Acting Chm. British Council, Liverpool. JP Liverpool. *Recreations:* music, county cricket, football (Rugby), reading biography. *Address:* 4 Ivyhurst Close, Aigburth, Liverpool L19 3PJ. *T:* 051–427 2911. *Clubs:* Lyceum, Masonic (Liverpool).
*Died 6 May 1982.*

**LEWIS, Eric William Charles,** CB 1971; Member, Civil Service Appeal Board, since 1975; *b* 13 Oct. 1914; *s* of William and May Frances Lewis; *m* 1939, Jessie Davies; two *d. Educ:* Christ's Hospital. LLB London. Joined Estate Duty Office, 1933; Army (Captain, RA), 1942–46; Admin. Staff Coll., 1949; Asst Controller, 1955, Deputy Controller, 1958, Controller, 1964–74, Estate Duty Office, Bd of Inland Revenue. *Publication:* contrib. Capital Taxes Encyclopaedia, 1976. *Address:* 31 Deena Close, Queens Drive, W3 0HR. *T:* 01-992 1752.                                    *Died 31 Dec. 1981.*

**LEWIS, Henry Gethin,** DL, JP; Chairman and Managing Director of private companies; *b* 31 Oct. 1899; *e s* of late Henry Gethin Lewis, LLD, JP, High Sheriff of Glamorgan, 1920–21, Porthkerry, Glamorgan; *m* 1925, Gwendolen Joan, 5th *d* of T. W. David, JP, Ely Rise, Cardiff; one *s* two *d. Educ:* Shrewsbury Sch.; Trinity Coll., Oxford (MA). Served European War 2nd Lt RFC with 48 Sqdn, 1918, BEF France (POW). Called to the Bar, Inner Temple, 1925. RAFVR, 1939–45, Sqdn-Ldr 1943. JP 1957, DL 1961, High Sheriff of Glamorgan, 1958. Chief Comr for Wales, St John Ambulance Bde, 1958–66; KStJ; Mem., Welsh Hosp. Bd, 1958–64, and Mem. Bd of Governors, United Cardiff Hosps, 1958–64. *Address:* Cliffside, Penarth, South Glamorgan. *T:* Penarth 707096. *Clubs:* Royal Air Force; Leander (Henley-on-Thames); Cardiff and County (Cardiff); Penarth Yacht.                                              *Died 20 March 1986.*

**LEWIS, Sir Ian (Malcolm),** Kt 1964; QC (Nigeria) 1961; LLD, MA Cantab, LLM; **His Honour Judge Sir Ian Lewis;** a Circuit Judge, since 1973; *b* 14 Dec. 1925; *s* of late Prof. Malcolm M. Lewis, MC, MA, LLB, and late Eileen (*née* O'Sullivan); *m* 1955, Marjorie, *d* of late W. G. Carrington; one *s. Educ:* Clifton Coll. (Governor, 1972–, Mem. Council, 1975–, Chm. Council, 1981–84); Trinity Hall, Cambridge (Scholar, 1st cl. hons Law Tripos Pt 2, and LLM). Served with RAFVR, 1944–47. Called to Bar, Middle Temple, 1951; pupil of R. W. Goff (the late Rt Hon. Lord Justice Goff), 1951. Western Circuit, 1951; Crown Counsel, Nigeria, 1953; Northern Nigeria: Solicitor-Gen., 1958; Dir of Public Prosecutions, 1962; Attorney-Gen. and Minister in the Government of Northern Nigeria, 1962–66; Chancellor, Diocese of Northern Nigeria, 1964–66; a Justice, Supreme Court of Nigeria, 1966–72; Justice of Appeal, Anguilla, 1972–73; Comr in NI dealing with detention of terrorists, 1972–75; Mem., Detention Appeal Tribunal for NI, 1974–75; Adviser to Sec. of State for NI on Detention, 1975–; Liaison Judge for Wiltshire, 1973–81; Mem., Wilts Probation Cttee, 1973–; Pres., Mental Health Review Tribunal, 1983–. Pres., Bristol Medico-Legal Soc., 1983–85; Hon. Vice-Pres., Magistrates Assoc., Wilts, 1973–. Pro-Chancellor, Univ. of Bristol, 1989– (Mem. Council, 1979–). MEC, N Nigeria, 1962–66; Adv. Coun. on the Prerogative of Mercy, House of Assembly, 1962–66. Mem. of Nigerian Bar Council, 1962–66; Mem. of Nigerian Council of Legal Education, 1962–66; Assoc. Mem. Commonwealth Parly Assoc. Hon. LLD, Ahmadu Bello Univ., Nigeria, 1972. *Recreations:* swimming (Capt. Cambridge Univ. Swimming and Water Polo, 1949); bridge; sailing; trying to find chapels in Wales where Grandfather "Elfed" (late Rev. H. Elvet Lewis, CH, DD) had not preached. *Address:* c/o Courts Administrator, Guildhall, Broad Street, Bristol BS1 2HL. *Clubs:* Commonwealth Trust; Hawks (Cambridge); Bristol, Savages', Commercial Rooms (Bristol).
*Died 16 Feb. 1990.*

**LEWIS, Ven. John Wilfred;** *b* 25 Sept. 1909; *e s* of Fritz and Ethel Mary Lewis; *m* 1938, Winifred Mary Griffin; one *s* two *d. Educ:* privately; Gonville and Caius Coll., Cambridge. History Tripos Pt I Cl. II, 1932; BA 1933; MA 1937; Steel Studentship (University), 1933; Exhibitioner, 1933–34; Westcott House, 1934; Deacon, 1935; Priest, 1936; Asst Dir of London Diocesan Council for Youth, 1935–37; Head of Oxford House, 1937–40; Vicar of Kimbolton, 1940–46; Dir, Hereford Diocesan Council of Educn, 1943–63; Rector of Cradley, 1946–60; Archdeacon of Ludlow, 1960–70; Rector of Wistanstow, 1960–70; Archdeacon of Hereford and Canon Residentiary of Hereford Cathedral, 1970–76; Prebendary

of Colwall in Hereford Cathedral, 1948–76; Archdeacon Emeritus, 1977–. *Recreations:* walking, sailing. *Address:* 9 Claremont Hill, Shrewsbury. *T:* Shrewsbury 65685.                              *Died 4 Jan. 1984.*

**LEWIS, Prof. Norman Bache,** MA, PhD; retired; *b* 8 Nov. 1896; *o s* of G. D. and L. A. Lewis, Newcastle-under-Lyme; *m* 1928, Julia (decd), *o d* of John and Catherine Wood, Riddlesden, Keighley; (one *s* one *d* decd). *Educ:* Boys' High Sch., Newcastle-under-Lyme (foundation scholar); University of Manchester (Jones scholar). Served European War in RFA, 1917–19. Manchester University: Hovell and Shuttleworth Prizes in History, 1919; BA in History Hons Cl. I and graduate scholarship in History, 1921; Research Fellowship in History, 1922. University of Sheffield: Lecturer in Dept of Modern History, 1924; Senior Lecturer in Mediæval History, 1946; Reader in Mediæval History, 1955; Prof. of Mediæval History in the University of Sheffield, 1959–62, Emeritus Prof., 1962. *Publications:* articles in historical journals. *Recreations:* music, reading. *Address:* Sundial House, 79 Old Dover Road, Canterbury CT1 3DB.                                          *Died 30 March 1988.*

**LEWIS, Percival Cecil,** QC; President of the Industrial Court, Antigua, 1976–83, retired; *b* St Vincent, 14 Aug. 1912; *s* of late Philip Owen Lewis; *m* 1936, Gladys Muriel Pool; one *s* one *d. Educ:* St Vincent Intermediate Sch.; St Vincent Gram. Sch. Called to Bar, Middle Temple, 1936. Practised in Uganda and St Vincent, 1936–40; Registrar and Additional Magistrate, St Lucia, 1940–43; Magistrate, Dominica, 1943–45; Crown Attorney, St Vincent, 1945–52; Crown Attorney, St Lucia, 1952–54; Attorney-Gen., Leeward Islands, 1954–56; Puisne Judge of Supreme Court of Windward and Leeward Islands, 1956–67; Justice of Appeal of the WI Assoc. States Supreme Court, 1967–75. *Recreations:* gardening and swimming. *Address:* c/o Mrs A. Jessamy, 15 Riverside Drive, Shorelands, Point Cumana, Trinidad, West Indies.
*Died 22 Sept. 1983.*

**LEWIS, Richard,** (né Thomas Thomas), CBE 1963; FRAM, FRMCM, LRAM; concert and opera singer, tenor; *b* Manchester, of Welsh parents, 10 May 1914; *m* 1st, 1943, Mary Lingard (marr. diss.); one *s;* 2nd, 1963, Elizabeth Robertson; one *s. Educ:* Royal Manchester Coll. of Music (schol.; studied with Norman Allin); RAM. Well known boy soprano in N England. Served in RCS during war. English début in leading rôle of Britten's Opera The Rape of Lucretia at Glyndebourne, where he sang every year, 1947–74; début, Teatro Colono, Buenos Aires, 1963; has sung at Edinburgh Fests, Covent Garden, San Francisco, Chicago, Vienna State Opera and Berlin Opera Houses, and toured America, Australia and NZ; has appeared with leading European and American orchs, incl. NY Philharmonic, Chicago Symphony, San Francisco Symphony and Philadelphia. Recitalist and oratorio singer, particularly of Handel, and in name part of Elgar's The Dream of Gerontius; has created parts: Troilus in Sir William Walton's Opera Troilus and Cressida; Mark in The Midsummer Marriage, and Achilles in King Priam, both operas by Michael Tippett; sang in first perf. of Stravinsky's Canticum Sacrum, under composer's direction, Venice Festival; sang Aaron in first British performance of Schoenberg's opera Moses and Aaron at Covent Garden; leading part in first American presentation of Cherubini's Opera, Medea, San Francisco, USA, 1958. Has made numerous recordings and appearances in films and on radio and television. Pres., ISM, 1975–76. Hon. DMus: St Andrews, 1984; Manchester, 1986. *Recreations:* languages, calligraphy, creative photography. *Address:* Combe House, 22 Church Street, Old Willingdon.                              *Died 13 Nov. 1990.*

**LEWIS, Maj.-Gen. (retd) Robert Stedman,** CB 1946; OBE 1942; late IA; *b* 20 March 1898; *s* of Sidney Cooke Lewis, MInstCE, and Mary Anne Jane Lewis Lloyd; *m* 1925, Margaret Joan Hart (*d* 1980); one *s* one *d. Educ:* Amesbury Sch., Bickley Hall, Kent; Bradfield Coll., Berks; Royal Military Academy, Woolwich. 2nd Lt RFA 1915; Seconded to RFC in 1916 and 1917 and served as a pilot in France in 100 Squadron RFC; served in France with RFA, 1918; proceeded to India with RFA, 1919; Seconded to Indian Army Ordnance Corps, 1922, and permanently transferred to Indian Army, 1925, with promotion to Capt.; Major, 1933; Bt Lt-Col 1937; Lt-Col 1940; Col 1944; employed at General Headquarters, India, 1939; Dir of Ordnance Services (India), 1945; retired, 1948. High Sheriff of Radnorshire, 1951. *Address:* Y Neuadd, Rhayader, Powys. *T:* Rhayader 810227.                                            *Died 3 May 1987.*

**LEWIS, Ronald Howard;** *b* 16 July 1909; *s* of Oliver Lewis, coal miner; *m* 1937, Edna Cooke (*d* 1976); two *s. Educ:* Elementary Sch. and Cliff Methodist Coll. Left school at 14 years of age and worked in coal mines (Somerset; subseq. Derbyshire, 1930–36); then railways (LNER Sheds, Langwith Junction); left that employment on being elected to Parliament. Mem. Bd of Directors, Pleasley Co-operative Soc. Ltd, 1948–70 (Pres. 1952). Mem. NUR. Mem., Blackwell RDC, 1940–73 (twice Chm.); Derbyshire CC, 1949–74. MP (Lab) Carlisle, 1964–87. Vice-Chm., House of Commons Trades Union Gp, 1979–82. Methodist Local Preacher. *Recreations:* walking, football, gardening. *Address:* 22 Alandale Avenue, Langwith

Junction, Mansfield, Notts. *T:* Mansfield (0623) 742460.
*Died 18 June* 1990.

**LEWIS, Saunders,** MA; Welsh writer and dramatist; *b* 15 Oct. 1893; *s* of Rev. Lodwig Lewis and Mary Margaret Thomas; *m* 1924, Margaret Gilcriest; one *d. Educ:* privately; Liverpool Univ. Hon. DLitt, Univ. of Wales, 1983. *Publications: plays:* The Eve of St John, 1921; Gwaed yr Uchelwyr, 1922; Buchedd Garmon, 1937; Amlyn ac Amig, 1940; Blodeuwedd, 1948; Eisteddfod Bodran, 1952; Gan Bwyll, 1952; Siwan a Cherddi Eraill, 1956; Gymerwch Chi Sigaret?, 1956; Brad, 1958; Esther, 1960; Serch Yw'r Doctor (light opera libretto), 1960; Cymru Fydd, 1967; Problemau Prifysgol, 1968; Dwy Briodas Ann, 1973; Dramau'r Parlwr, 1975; Excelsior, 1981; *novels:* Monica, 1930; Merch Gwern Hywel, 1964; *poetry:* Mair Fadlen, 1937; Byd a Betws, 1941; *criticism:* A School of Welsh Augustans, 1924; Williams Pantycelyn, 1927; Ceiriog, 1929; Braslun o Hanes Llenyddiaeth Gymraeg Hyd 1535, 1932; Daniel Owen, 1936; Ysgrifau Dydd Mercher, 1945; Meistri'r Canrifoedd, 1973; *political and economic:* Canlyn Arthur, 1938; also many pamphlets in the Welsh language; *translations:* Molière, Doctor er ei Waethaf, 1924; Beckett, Wrth aros Godot, 1970; (ed with introd.) Ievan Glan Geirionydd, 1931; (ed with introd.) Straeon Glasynys, 1943; (ed) Crefft y Stori Fer (radio broadcasts), 1949. Translations of plays have been presented on stage and television in English, German, and Spanish. *Address:* 158 Westbourne Road, Penarth, South Glam. *Died* 1 *Sept.* 1985.

**LEWIS, Wilfrid Bennett,** CC (Canada) 1967; CBE 1946; FRS 1945; FRSC 1952; MA; PhD; Senior Vice-President, Science, Atomic Energy of Canada Ltd, 1963–73, retired; Distinguished Professor of Science, Queen's University, since 1973; *b* 24 June 1908; *s* of Arthur Wilfrid Lewis and Isoline Maud Steavenson; unmarried. *Educ:* Haileybury Coll., Herts; Gonville and Caius Coll., Cambridge, Hon. Fellow 1971. Cavendish Laboratory, Cambridge, research in Radio-activity and Nuclear Physics, 1930–39; Research Fellowship, Gonville and Caius Coll., 1934–40; University Demonstrator in Physics, 1934; University Lecturer in Physics, 1937; lent to Air Ministry as Senior Scientific Officer, 1939; Chief Superintendent Telecommunications Research Establishment, Ministry of Aircraft Production, 1945–46; Dir of Division of Atomic Energy Research, National Research Council of Canada, 1946–52; Vice-Pres. Research and Development, Atomic Energy of Canada, Ltd, 1952–63. Canadian Representative United Nations Scientific Advisory Cttee, 1955–. Fellow American Nuclear Soc., 1959 (Pres., 1961); For. Associate, Nat. Acad. of Engineering, USA, 1976; Hon. Mem., Alpha Nu Sigma Soc., Iowa State Univ., 1984; Hon. Fellow: IEE, 1974; UMIST, 1974; Silver Jubilee Hon. Fellow, INucE, 1984. Hon. DSc: Queen's Univ., Kingston, Ontario, 1960; Saskatchewan, 1964; McMaster Univ., Hamilton, Ontario, 1965; Dartmouth Coll., New Hampshire, 1967; McGill Univ., Montreal, 1969; Royal Mil. Coll., Kingston, Ont, 1974; Laurentian, 1977; Birmingham, 1977; Univ. of New Brunswick, 1982; Hon. LLD: Dalhousie Univ., Halifax, Nova Scotia, 1960; Carleton Univ., Ottawa, 1962; Trent Univ., Peterborough, Ont, 1969; Toronto, 1972; Victoria, BC, 1975. Amer. Medal of Freedom, with Silver Palms, 1947. First Outstanding Achievement Award, Public Service of Canada, 1966; Atoms for Peace Award (shared), 1967; Can. Assoc. of Physicists 25th anniversary special Gold Medal, 1970; Royal Medal, Royal Soc., 1972; Gen. A. G. L. McNaughton Award and Medal, Canadian Region IEEE, 1981; Enrico Fermi Award and Medal, US Dept of Energy, 1982. *Publications:* Electrical Counting, 1942; (ed jtly) International Arrangements for Nuclear Fuel Reprocessing, 1977; articles in Wireless Engineer, 1929, 1932 and 1936; papers in Proc. Royal Society A. 1931, 1932, 1933, 1934, 1936, 1940; etc. *Recreation:* walking. *Address:* Box 189, 13 Beach Avenue, Deep River, Ontario K0J 1PO. *T:* 613–584–3561. *Died* 10 *Jan.* 1987.

**LEWIS, William Edmund Ames,** OBE 1961; Charity Commissioner, 1962–72; *b* 21 Sept. 1912; *s* of late Ernest W. Lewis, FRCSE, Southport, Lancashire; *m* 1939, Mary Elizabeth, *e d* of late C. R. Ashbee; two *s* one *d. Educ:* Merchant Taylors', Great Crosby; Emmanuel Coll., Cambridge. Barrister-at-law, Inner Temple, 1935. Entered Charity Commission, 1939; Asst Commissioner, 1953–61; Sec., 1961–69. Served in RAF, 1941–46. *Recreations:* music, painting. *Address:* Watermans, Ewhurst Green, Robertsbridge, East Sussex. *T:* Staplecross 523. *Club:* United Oxford & Cambridge University. *Died* 30 *March* 1988.

**LEYLAND, Norman Harrison;** Investment Bursar, since 1965, Bursar, since 1979, Brasenose College, Oxford; *b* 27 Aug. 1921; *m* 1st, J. I. McKillop; one *s* two *d;* 2nd, 1971, E. C. Wiles. *Educ:* Manchester Grammar Sch.; Brasenose Coll., Oxford. Dir, Oxford Centre for Management Studies, 1965–70. Chm., Consumers' Cttee for Great Britain, 1967–70. Fellow: Brasenose Coll., Oxford, 1948–; Oxford Centre for Management Studies. *Address:* Brasenose College, Oxford. *Died* 23 *Nov.* 1981.

**LEYLAND, Sir Vivyan (Edward) N.;** *see* Naylor-Leyland.

**LEYTON, Dr (Robert) Nevil (Arthur);** Consulting Physician, specialising in Migraine, since 1950; *b* 15 June 1910; *s* of Prof. A. S. F. Leyton, MD, DSc, FRCP, and Mrs H. G. Leyton, MD; *m* 1943, Wendy (*d* 1960), *er d* of Tom and Dylis Cooper; one *s. Educ:* private; Gonville and Caius Coll., Cambridge; Westminster Hospital (entrance Schol.). BA (Cantab) Double Hons Natural Sciences Tripos, 1932; MA 1958. MRCP 1953. Ho. Phys. and Surg., Westminster Hospital, 1937. Served with RAF, 1943–46, and with 601 Squadron RAuxAF, 1947–57; retired rank Sqdn Leader. Registrar (Med.), St Stephen's Hospital, 1947–50; Hon. Cons. Physician to Migraine Clinic, Putney Health Centre, 1950–68; Hon. Cons. in migraine to Royal Air Forces Assoc., 1947; Hon. Cons. Physician to Wendy Leyton Memorial Migraine Centre, Harley Street, 1961; Sen. Medical Adviser, International Migraine Foundn, 1961; Consulting Physician to Kingdom of Libya, 1968–69; MO, 1971–72, Chief MO, 1972–73, Gath's Mine Hosp., Mashaba, Rhodesia; Specialist Paediatrician, Estate Group Clinics, Lagos, Nigeria, 1975–76; Consultant Physician, County Hosp., Tralee, Eire, 1976–77. Late Medical Adviser, FA. President, 601 Squadron RAuxAF Old Comrades Assoc., 1963. Air Force Efficiency Medal, 1954. Kt of Mark Twain, 1979. *Publications:* Migraine and Periodic Headache, 1952 (USA, 1954); Headaches, The Reason and the Relief, 1955 (USA); Migraine, 1962; Migraine, Modern Concepts and Preventative Treatment, 1964; contrib.: Lancet, British Medical Journal, Medical World and Journal, Lancet (USA), etc. *Recreations:* travel, riding, horse racing, lawn tennis (Cambridge Univ. Blue, 1933), squash racquets. *Clubs:* Lions (Mashaba and British sections); Hawks (Cambridge). *Died* 1987.

**LIBBERT, Laurence Joseph,** QC 1980; **His Honour Judge Libbert;** a Circuit Judge, since 1985; *b* 22 June 1933; *s* of Arthur and Evelyn Libbert; *m* 1957, Margaret Low-Beer; one *s* one *d. Educ:* King Edward VII Sch., Lytham; Magdalen Coll., Oxford (BA 1st Cl. Hons 1953; BCL 1st Cl. Hons 1954; MA 1957; Vinerian Scholar, 1954). Gray's Inn: Bacon Scholar, 1954; Arden Scholar, 1955; called to the Bar, 1955. Law Lectr, Univ. of BC, Canada, 1957–58; Law Tutor, Christ Church, Oxford, 1958–63; Lectr, Council of Legal Educn, 1963–67. A Recorder, 1983–85. *Recreations:* art history, theatre, tennis. *Address:* 3 Paper Buildings, Temple, EC4Y 7EU. *T:* 01–353 3721; 30 Downshire Hill, NW3 1NT. *T:* 01–435 9286. *Club:* United Oxford & Cambridge University.

*Died* 6 *June* 1985.

**LIDDELL, Edward George Tandy,** FRS 1939; MD, BCh, MA, Oxon; *b* 25 March 1895; *yr s* of Dr John Liddell, Harrogate, and Annie Louisa (*née* Tandy); *m* 1923, Constance Joan Mitford, *y d* of late Dr B. M. H. Rogers; two *s* one *d* (and one *s* decd). *Educ:* Summer Fields; Harrow; Trinity Coll., Oxon; St Thomas' Hospital. 1st class Physiology Finals, Oxford, 1918; Asst Serum Dept, Lister Institute, 1918; Senior Demy, Magdalen Coll., Oxford, 1918; BM Oxon, 1921; Fellow of Trinity Coll., Oxford, 1921–40; University Lecturer in Physiology, Oxford Univ., 1921–40; Waynflete Professor of Physiology, Oxford, 1940–60; Professor Emeritus, 1960; Fellow of Magdalen Coll., 1940–60, Emeritus Fellow, 1970. Formerly: Mem., Hebdomadal Council, Gen. Bd, Bodleian Curators, Oxford Univ.; Chm., Oxford Eye Hosp.; Examr, Oxford, Cambridge, London, Sheffield Univs. Osler Meml Medal, Oxford Univ., 1975. *Publications:* Papers, various since 1923, on physiology of central nervous system, published in Journal Physiol., Brain, Proc. Royal Society, Quarterly Journal of Experimental Physiology; assistant author of Sherrington's Mammalian Physiology, 1929; Reflex Activity of the Spinal Cord, 1932 (jointly); The Discovery of Reflexes, 1960. *Recreation:* FRHS. *Address:* 69 Old High Street, Headington, Oxford OX3 9HT. *Died* 17 *Aug.* 1981.

**LIDDELL, Laurence Ernest,** CBE 1976; ERD, TD; retired; *b* Co. Durham, 27 Oct. 1916; *m* 1940, Alys Chapman, Askrigg, Yorks; two *s* one *d. Educ:* Yorebridge Grammar Sch.; Leeds Univ. (BA); Carnegie Coll. (DipPE). Reserve and Territorial Officer, The Royal Scots, 1939–59; served in France and Belgium (despatches), 1939–40; E Africa, 1944–45; Lectr in Educn, King's Coll., Durham Univ., 1946–59; Lt-Col comdg Univ. OTC, 1955–59; Dir, Dept of Physical Educn, Univ. of Edinburgh, 1959–80. First Pres./Chm., Scottish Orienteering Assoc., 1961–66; Chairman: Adv. Sports Council for Scotland, 1968–71; Main Stadium Cttee for 1970 Commonwealth Games in Edinburgh, 1967–70; Scottish Sports Council, 1971–75; Mem., UK Sports Councils, 1968–75. *Publications:* Batsmanship, 1958; (jtly) Orienteering, 1965. *Recreations:* golf; formerly: cricket (played for Univ., Army, 11 yrs Captain Northumberland, MCC, Captain English Minor Counties XI v NZ, 1958); Association football (played for Univ. and Yorks Amateurs); hockey (played for Northumberland and English Northern Counties). *Address:* 318 Gilmerton Road, Edinburgh EH17 7PR. *T:* 031–664 3710. *Clubs:* Lord's Taverners; Lowland Brigade (Edinburgh). *Died* 7 *Aug.* 1985.

**LIDDLE, Sir Donald (Ross),** Kt 1971; JP; Chairman, Cumbernauld Development Corporation, 1972–78; Vice-Lord-Lieutenant, City of Glasgow, Strathclyde Region, 1978–80; *b* 11 Oct. 1906; *s* of Thomas

Liddle, Bonnington, Edinburgh; *m* 1933, May, *d* of R. Christie, Dennistoun, Glasgow; one *s* two *d*. *Educ:* Allen Glen's School, Glasgow. Served War of 1939–45 with RAOC, Burma and India; Major, 1944. DL, County of Glasgow, 1963; JP 1968; Lord Provost of Glasgow, 1969–72. Chm., Scottish Tourist Consultative Council, 1973–79. CStJ 1970. Hon. LLD Strathclyde, 1971. *Address:* 15 Riddrie Crescent, Riddrie Knowes, Glasgow G33 2QG. *Clubs:* Army and Navy; Conservative (Glasgow).

*Died 12 Nov.* 1989.

**LIFAR, Serge;** Chevalier de la Légion d'Honneur; Dancer, Choreographer, Writer, Painter; Director, later Rector, Université de Danse, since 1958; Professeur de Chorélogie, Sorbonne; Maître de Ballet, Théâtre National de l'Opéra, Paris, 1929–69 (formerly Professeur); *b* Kieff, South Russia, 2 April 1905; *s* of Michel Lifar. Pupil of Bronislava Nijinska, 1921; joined Diaghileff company, Paris, 1923; studied under Cecchetti. Dir, Institut Chorégraphique, 1947–58. First London appearance, in Cimarosiana and Les Fâcheux, Coliseum, 1924. Choreographer (for first time) of Stravinsky's Renard, 1929; produced Prométhée, Opera House, Paris, 1929. Cochran's Revue, London Pavilion, 1930; returned to Paris, produced and danced in Bacchus and Ariadne, Le Spectre de la Rose, Giselle, and L'Après-midi d'un Faune, 1932; Icare, David Triomphant, Le Roi Nu, 1936; Alexandre le Grand, 1937; arranged season of Ballet at the Cambridge, London, 1946; Choreographer of Noces Fantastiques, Romeo et Juliette (Prokofiev), 1955. Paintings exhibited: Paris, 1972–75; Cannes, 1974; Monte Carlo, Florence, Venice, London. Prix de l'Académie Française; Corres. Mem., Institut de France, 1970. Commandeur des Arts et des Lettres, France; Grand Etoile, Yugoslavia; Gold Medal, Vasa, Sweden, 1965; Medal of City of Paris, 1977. *Publications:* Traditional to Modern Ballet, 1938; Diaghilev, a biography, 1940; A History of Russian Ballet from its Origins to the Present Day (trans. 1954); The Three Graces, 1959; Ma Vie, 1965 (in Eng., 1969). *Address:* Villa de Roc, Glion, Switzerland; Beau-Rivage, Ouchy, Lausanne, France. *Died 16 Dec.* 1986.

**LIFFORD, 8th Viscount** *cr* 1781; **Alan William Wingfield Hewitt;** *b* 11 Dec. 1900; 2nd but *o* surv. *s* of Hon. George Wyldbore Hewitt (*d* 1924; 7th *s* of 4th Viscount Lifford) and Elizabeth Mary, *e d* of late Charles Rampini, DL, LLD, Advocate; *S* kinsman, 1954; *m* 1935, Alison Mary Patricia, *d* of T. W. Ashton, The Cottage, Hursley, nr Winchester; one *s* three *d*. *Educ:* Winchester; RMC, Sandhurst. Lieut late Hampshire Regt. *Heir: s* Hon. Edward James Wingfield Hewitt [*b* 27 Jan. 1949; *m* 1976, Alison, *d* of Robert Law; one *s* one *d*]. *Address:* Field House, Hursley, Hants. *T:* Hursley 75203.

*Died 6 Jan.* 1987.

**LIGHTWOOD, Reginald,** MD; FRCP; DPH; Consulting Physician to The Hospital for Sick Children, Great Ormond Street, London, and Consulting Paediatrician to St Mary's Hospital, London, since 1963; *b* 1898; *s* of late John M. Lightwood, Barrister-at-Law, and Gertrude (*née* Clench); *m* 1937, Monica Guise Bicknell, *d* of late Laurance G. Ray; two *s*. *Educ:* Monkton Combe Sch., Bath. Served European War in Royal Artillery, 1917–19. Jelf Medal and Alfred Hughes Memorial Prize, King's Coll., London, 1919; MD (London), 1924, FRCP 1936. Hon. Medical Staff: Westminster Hospital, 1933–39 (resigned); Hospital for Sick Children, Great Ormond Street, London, 1935–63; St Mary's Hospital, London, 1939–63; Prof. of Pediatrics, American University of Beirut, 1964 and 1965; Prof. of Paediatrics and Child Health, University Coll. of Rhodesia, 1966–69. Kenneth Blackfan Memorial Lecturer, Harvard Medical Sch., 1953; Visiting Prof. of Pediatrics: Boston Univ., 1966; Univ. of Calif, Los Angeles, 1969. Cons. Pædiatrician to Internat. Grenfell Assoc., Newfoundland, 1970–71. Pres., British Pædiatric Assoc., 1959–60; FRSM; Hon. Fellow, Amer. Acad. of Pediatrics; Mem., Irish Pædiatric Soc.; Hon. Member: Swedish Pædiatric Soc.; Portuguese Pædiatric Soc.; Mark Twain Soc. of America; corresp. Member: Société de Pédiatrie de Paris; Amer. Pediatric Soc. *Publications:* Textbooks: Pædiatrics for the Practitioner (ed jtly with Prof. W. Gaisford); Sick Children (with Dr F. S. W. Brimblecombe and Dr D. Barltrop); Lectures on the Children in Lappland; Lectures on the Mysterious Maya; scientific papers and political and medical articles. *Address:* 28 Luxford Court, Reigate Heath, Surrey. *Died 26 May* 1985.

**LILEY, Sir (Albert) William,** KCMG 1973 (CMG 1967); PhD; FRSNZ; FRCOG; Professor in Perinatal Physiology, New Zealand Medical Research Council Postgraduate School of Obstetrics and Gynæcology, University of Auckland; *b* 12 March 1929; *s* of Albert Harvey Liley; *m* 1953, Helen Margaret Irwin, *d* of William Irwin Hunt; two *s* three *d*, and one adopted *d*. *Educ:* Auckland Grammar Sch.; University of Auckland; University of Otago; Australian National Univ.; Columbia Univ. BMedSc 1952; MB, ChB (UNZ) 1954; PhD (ANU) 1957; Dip. Obst. (UA) 1962; FRSNZ 1964; FRCOG 1971. Research Schol. in Physiology, ANU, 1955–56. Sandoz Research Fellow in Obstetrics, Postgrad. Sch. of Obstetrics and Gynæcology, 1957–58; NZMRC Research Fellow in Obstetrics, 1959–, United States Public Health Service Internat. Research

Fellowship, 1964–65. Mem., Pontifical Acad. of Scis, 1978. Hon. FACOG, 1975. Hon. DSc Victoria Univ., Wellington, 1971. *Publications:* numerous articles in physiological, obstetric and pædiatric journals. *Recreations:* farming, forestry. *Address:* 19 Pukenui Road, Epsom, Auckland 3, New Zealand. *T:* 656–433.

*Died 15 June* 1983.

**LILIENTHAL, David Eli;** Business Consultant; Author; *b* Morton, Ill, 8 July 1899; *s* of Leo Lilienthal and Minna Rosenak; *m* 1923, Helen Marian Lamb; one *s* one *d*. *Educ:* DePauw Univ. (AB, LLD); LLB Harvard, 1923. Admitted Illinois bar, 1923; practised law, Chicago, 1923–31; Wisconsin Public Service Commn, 1931–33; founding Director, Tennessee Valley Authority, 1933 (Chairman 1941–46); Chairman, State Dept Board of Consultants on international control of atomic energy, 1946; Chairman, US Atomic Energy Commn, 1946–50; Chairman, Development and Resources Corporation, 1955–79; Member of: Delta Upsilon, Delta Sigma Rho, Sigma Delta Chi, Phi Beta Kappa, American Academy of Arts and Sciences; Amer. Philosoph. Soc.; Trustee, The Twentieth Century Fund. Freedom Award, 1949; Public Welfare Medal of National Academy of Science, 1951. Holds Hon. Doctorates from Institutions in USA; also foreign awards; Commendador de la Orden El Sol del Peru, 1964; Order of Rio Blanco, Brazil, 1972. *Publications:* TVA-Democracy on the March, 1944; This I Do Believe, 1949; Big Business: A New Era, 1953; The Multinational Corporation, 1960; Change, Hope and the Bomb, 1963; The Journals of David E. Lilienthal, Vols I and II, 1964; Vol. III, 1966; Vol. IV, 1969; Vol. V, 1971; Vol. VI, 1976; Management: a Humanist Art, 1967; Atomic Energy: a new start, 1980; articles in miscellaneous periodicals. *Recreations:* gardening, small-boat sailing. *Address:* (home) 88 Battle Road, Princeton, NJ 08540, USA; (office) 1230 Avenue of the Americas, New York, NY 10020, USA. *Clubs:* Century Association (New York).

*Died 15 Jan.* 1981.

**LILLIE, Beatrice Gladys, (Lady Peel);** actress; *b* Toronto, 29 May 1894; *d* of John Lillie, Lisburn, Ireland, and Lucie Shaw; *m* 1920, Sir Robert Peel, 5th Bt (*d* 1934); (one *s*, Sir Robert Peel, 6th and last Bt, killed on active service 1942). *Educ:* St Agnes' Coll., Belleville, Ontario. First appearance, Alhambra, 1914; at the Vaudeville, Prince of Wales's etc., 1915–22; in The Nine O'Clock Revue, Little Theatre, 1922; first New York appearance, Times Square Theatre, in André Charlot's Revue, 1924; in Charlot's Revue at Prince of Wales's, 1925; in New York, 1925–26; at The Globe and The Palladium, 1928; This Year of Grace, New York, 1928; Charlot's Masquerade, at the Cambridge, London, 1930; New York; 1931–32; at the Savoy and London Palladium, 1933–34; New York, 1935; Queen's, London, 1939; Big Top, Adelphi, 1940; Troops: England, 1939–42; Africa, Italy, etc, 1942–45; Seven Lively Arts, Ziegfeld, New York, 1945; Better Late, Garrick, London, 1946; appeared in television and radio programmes, England and America, 1946–47; Inside USA, New York, 1948, subs. on tour for one year, USA; returned to London (cabaret), Café de Paris, 1950 and June 1951. Solo artiste at several Royal performances; appeared in NY television, 1951–52; produced one-woman show, Summer Theatre, 1952; subs. on tour and produced show in Broadway, Oct. 1952–June 1953. Radio and TV, London, July-Aug. 1953. Road tour in US of this production, Sept. 1953–June 1954; London, 1954–55. An Evening with Beatrice Lillie, Globe, AEWBL, Florida, Feb and March, 1956; 2nd one-woman show, Beasop's Fables, USA, June-Sept. 1956; Ziegfeld Follies, New York, 1957–58; Auntie Mame, Adelphi, London, 1958–59; High Spirits, Alvin Theatre, NYC, 1964–65. Appeared in films: Exit Smiling, 1927; Are You There, 1933; Doctor Rhythm, 1938; On Approval, 1944; Around the World in Eighty Days, 1956; Thoroughly Modern Millie, 1967. Free French Liberation Medal, N Africa, 1942, also African Star and George VI Medal, Donaldson Award, USA, 1945, also Antoinette Perry Award, New York, 1953, and many others. *Publication:* (with J. Philip and J. Brough) Every Other Inch a Lady (autobiog.), 1973. *Recreation:* painting. *Address:* Peel Fold, Mill Lane, Henley-on-Thames, Oxon. *Died 20 Jan.* 1989.

**LILLIE, Very Rev. Henry Alexander,** MA; Dean of Armagh, and Keeper of Armagh Public Library, 1965–79; *b* 11 May 1911; *s* of David William Lillie and Alicia Lillie (*née* Morris), Carrick-on-Shannon; *m* 1942, Rebecca Isobel, *yr d* of Andrew C. Leitch, Homelea, Omagh, Co. Tyrone; one *d*. *Educ:* Sligo Grammar Sch.; Trinity Coll., Dublin. BA 1935, MA 1942. Junior Master, Grammar Schools: Elphin, 1932; Sligo, 1932–34. Deacon, 1936; Curate Asst, Portadown, 1936–41; Incumbent of: Milltown, 1941–47; Kilmore, 1947–52; Armagh, 1952–65; Armagh Cathedral: Prebendary of Tynan, 1952–60; Treas., 1960–61; Chancellor, 1961; Precentor, 1961–65. *Recreations:* reading, fishing, gardening. *Address:* 104 Drumman More Road, Armagh. *T:* Armagh 524926.

*Died 8 Jan.* 1986.

**LILLIE, John Adam;** QC (Scot.); LLD; *b* 25 July 1884; *e s* of Thomas Lillie and Ellen Harper Tait. *Educ:* Brockley's Acad., Broughty Ferry; Aberdeen Grammar Sch.; University of Aberdeen (MA

1906); University of Edinburgh (LLB 1910). Admitted to Faculty of Advocates, 1912; called to English Bar, 1921; Lecturer on Mercantile Law, University of Edinburgh, 1928–47; KC (Scotland) 1931; Member Royal Commn on Workmen's Compensation, 1938; Sheriff of Fife and Kinross, 1941–71. Chairman for Scotland Board of Referees under Income Tax Acts, 1942–55; Chairman for Scotland and NI of British Motor Trade Assoc. Price Protection Cttee, 1949–52; Legal Commissioner and Dep. Chairman, General Board of Control for Scotland, 1944–62; Convener of the sheriffs, 1960–65; Hon. LLD Aberdeen, 1967. *Publications:* The Mercantile Law of Scotland (6th edn, 1965); Articles in Green's Encyclopædia of the Law of Scotland on Company Law, and Sale of Goods; The Northern Lighthouses Service, 1965; Tradition and Environment in a Time of Change, 1970; An Essay on Speech Literacy, 1974; A Family History, 1976. *Address:* 85 Great King Street, Edinburgh. *T:* 031–556 1862. *Club:* Caledonian (Edinburgh).

*Died 2 June 1983.*

**LIMENTANI, Prof. Uberto;** Professor of Italian, University of Cambridge, 1962–81; Fellow of Magdalene College, Cambridge, 1964–88, Hon. Fellow since 1988; *b* Milan, 15 Dec. 1913; *er s* of Prof. Umberto Limentani and Elisa Levi; *m* 1946, Barbara Hoban (*d* 1984); three *s*. *Educ:* University of Milan (Dr in Giurispr., Dr in Lettere); University of London (PhD); University of Cambridge (MA). Commentator and script-writer Italian Section, BBC European Service, 1939–45. Lector 1945, Assistant Lecturer, 1948, Lecturer, 1952, in Italian, University of Cambridge. Hon. Prof., Dept of Italian, Univ. of Hull, 1981–. Pres., MHRA, 1981. Corresp. Member Accademia Letteraria Ital. dell'Arcadia, 1964. Hon. DLitt Hull, 1985. Commendatore, Ordine al Merito della Repubblica Italiana, 1973. Italian Govt's Gold Medal for services to scholarship, 1982. An Editor, Italian Studies, 1962–82. *Publications:* Stilistica e Metrica, 1936; Poesie e Lettere Inedite di Salvator Rosa, 1950; L'Attività Letteraria di Giuseppe Mazzini, 1950; La Satira nel Seicento, 1961; The Fortunes of Dante in Seventeenth Century Italy, 1964; (ed) The Mind of Dante, 1965; (ed) vol. xii (Scritti vari di critica storica e letteraria) of Edizione Nazionale of Works of U. Foscolo, 1978; (ed) La Fiera, by Michelangelo Buonarroti the Younger (original 1619 version), 1984; Dante's Comedy: introductory readings of selected cantos, 1985; (critical edn, with introduction) Lorenzo Magalotti, traduttore del "Cyder" di John Philips, 1987; co-editor yearly review, Studi Secenteschi (founded 1960); trans. E. R. Vincent's Ugo Foscolo Esule fra gli Inglesi, 1954; several contrib. on Italian Literature to: Encyclopædia Britannica; Cassell's Encyclopædia of Literature; Italian Studies; La Bibliofilia; Giornale Storico della Letteratura Italiana; Amor di Libro; Studi Secenteschi; Il Pensiero Mazziniano; Bollettino della Domus Mazziniana; Il Ponte; Cambridge Review; Modern Language Review; Times Literary Supplement. *Recreation:* walking in the Alps. *Address:* 19A Victoria Street, Cambridge CB1 1JP. *T:* Cambridge 358198. *Died 17 Aug. 1989.*

**LIMERICK, Dowager Countess of,** GBE 1954 (DBE 1946; CBE 1942); CH 1974; DL; **Angela Olivia Pery;** Life Vice-President, British Red Cross Society; *b* 27 Aug. 1897; *yr d* of late Lt-Col Sir Henry Trotter, KCMG, CB; *m* 1926, Hon. Edmund Colquhoun Pery, later 5th Earl of Limerick, GBE, CH, KCB, DSO, TD (*d* 1967); two *s* one *d*. *Educ:* North Foreland Lodge, Broadstairs; London Sch. of Economics. Served as VAD at home and overseas, 1915–19; Poor Law Guardian, 1928–30; on Kensington Borough Council, 1929–35, Chm of Maternity and Child Welfare and Public Health Cttees; Mem. for South Kensington on LCC, 1936–46; Privy Council rep. on Gen. Nursing Council for England and Wales, 1933–50; Mem. of Royal Commn on Equal Pay, and of various Govt Cttees; Dep. Chm. of War Organization BRCS and Order of St John, 1941–47; Vice-Chm., League of Red Cross Societies, 1957–73; Chm., Standing Commn, Internat. Red Cross, 1965–73; Chm., Council, British Red Cross Soc., 1974–76. President: Multiple Sclerosis Soc., 1968–76; Hosp. and Homes of St Giles; Vice-President: Internat. Council of Social Service; Family Welfare Assoc.; Family Planning Assoc.; Star and Garter Home, Richmond; Queen Alexandra Hosp. Home, Worthing. DL West Sussex, 1977. Hon. LLD Manchester Univ., 1945, Leeds Univ., 1951. DStJ, 1952. Commander's Gold Cross, Order of Merit, Republic of Austria, 1959; Prince Carl Medal, Sweden, 1978. Red Cross Decorations and awards from the National Societies of Australia, Austria, Belgium, Canada, Czechoslovakia, Denmark, Ethiopia, Finland, France, Germany, Greece, Iran, Mexico, Netherlands, Philippines, Roumania, South Africa, Sweden, Turkey, USA and Yugoslavia. *Address:* Chiddinglye West Hoathly, East Grinstead, West Sussex RH19 4QT. *T:* Sharpthorne 810214. *Died 25 April 1981.*

**LINCOLN, Air Cdre Philip Lionel,** CB 1945; DSO 1918; MC 1916; late RAF; late Chairman, R. Passmore & Co. Ltd; *b* 20 Jan. 1892; *s* of Philip Passmore Lincoln and Louisa Baxter; *m* 1916, Kathleen Daisy Shepherd (*d* 1965); two *s*. *Educ:* Framlingham Coll. Entered family business R. Passmore & Co., 1910, partner 1913; Pres., Building Industry Distributors, 1948. 2nd Lt Northumberland Fusiliers, 1914; Capt. 1915; Major, 1917; Lt-Col 1918; served

France and Italy (wounded twice, despatches, MC, DSO); demobilised 1919. Flying Officer AAF Balloon Branch; Squadron Leader to Command No 902 Squadron, 1938; Wing Comdr 1939; Group Capt. 1940; Air Commodore, 1941. *Address:* 2 Church Lane, Bearsted, Maidstone, Kent. *T:* Maidstone 37106.

*Died 28 April 1981.*

**LIND-SMITH, His Honour Gerard Gustave;** a Circuit Judge (formerly Judge of County Courts), 1959–75; *b* 1903; *o s* of C. F. Lind-Smith, Liverpool; *m* 1928, Alexandra Eva (*d* 1981) *e d* of Lt-Col J. C. Kirk, CBE, Monmouthshire; three *d*. *Educ:* Wellington Coll.; University Coll., Oxon. Called to Bar, Inner Temple, 1928. JP and Dep. Chm. Ches. QS, 1957, Chm., 1961–68. Recorder of Birkenhead, 1958–59. *Address:* Pitt House, Wellesbourne, Warwick.

*Died 3 Feb. 1982.*

**LINDOP, Audrey Beatrice Noël E.;** *see* Erskine-Lindop, A. B. N.

**LINDSAY, 14th Earl of,** *cr* 1633; **William Tucker Lindsay-Bethune;** Lord Lindsay of The Byres, 1445; Baron Parbroath, 1633; Viscount Garnock; Baron Kilbirny, Kingsburne, and Drumry, 1703; Representative Peer, 1947–59; late Major, Scots Guards; Member of Queen's Body Guard for Scotland, Royal Company of Archers; *b* 28 April 1901; *s* of 13th Earl and Ethel (*d* 1942), *d* of W. Austin Tucker, Boston, USA; assumed addtl surname of Bethune, 1939; *S* father, 1943; *m* 1925, Marjory, DStJ, *d* of late Arthur J. G. Cross and Lady Hawke; two *s*\* two *d*. Served War of 1939–45 (wounded); retd pay, 1947. Hon. Col, Fife and Forfar Yeomanry/Scottish Horse, 1957–62. Zone Comr for Northern Civil Defence Zone of Scotland, 1963–69. Mem., Fife CC, 1956–64. Pres., Shipwrecked Fishermen and Mariners Royal Benevolent Soc., 1966–76. DL Co. of Fife. KStJ. *Heir:* *s* Viscount Garnock. *Address:* Lahill, Upper Largo, Fife KY8 6JE. *T:* Upper Largo 251. *Clubs:* Cavalry and Guards; Leander (Henley). *Died 19 Oct. 1985.*

**LINDSAY, 15th Earl of,** *cr* 1633; **David Lindesay-Bethune;** Lord Lindsay of The Byres, 1445; Lord Parbroath, 1633; Viscount of Garnock, Lord Kilbirny, Kingsburne and Drumry, 1703; *b* 9 Feb. 1926; *er s* of 14th Earl of Lindsay, and Marjory, DStJ (*d* 1988), *d* of late Arthur J. G. Cross and Lady Hawke; *S* father, 1985; *m* 1st, 1953, Hon. Mary Clare Douglas-Scott-Montagu (marr. diss., 1968), *y d* of 2nd Baron Montagu of Beaulieu; one *s* one *d*; 2nd, 1969, Penelope, *er d* of late Anthony Crossley, MP. *Educ:* Eton; Magdalene Coll., Cambridge. Scots Guards, 1943–45. US and Canadian Railroads, 1948–52. Chairman: Severn Valley Railway (Holdings) Ltd, 1972–76 (Pres., 1976–); Romney, Hythe and Dymchurch Light Rly Co., 1976–, Holdings Co., 1976–; Sallingbury Holdings, 1977–83; Sallingbury Ltd, 1977–83; Crossley Karastan Carpet Mills, Canada, 1982–87 (Dir, 1961–); British Property Timeshare Assoc. Ltd, 1981–88; Kilconquhar Castle Estate Ltd, 1980–; Edington PLC, 1986–; Director: John Crossley & Sons, 1957–74; John Crossley Carpet Trades Hldgs, 1960–70; Festiniog Railway Co. Ltd, 1960–; Abbey Life Insurance Co. of Canada, 1964–81; Carpets Internat. Group Services, 1970–85; Interface Flooring Systems Inc. (formerly Carpets International Georgia Inc.), 1972–; Bank of Montreal, 1975–; Manuge Galleries (Nova Scotia), 1976–; International Harvester Co. of GB Ltd, 1976–85; Bain Dawes Ltd (Northern), 1978–81; Bain Dawes (Canada), 1978–82; Riverside Plantation Co., Inc., 1982–84; Coastal Pollution Controls (formerly Associated Marine Industries Offshore Resources Ltd), 1982–86; Debron Investments PLC (formerly Carpets International PLC), 1983–87; Alton Towers Ltd, 1986–; Battersea Leisure Ltd, 1986–; Cole Sherman Inc., 1987–; Alton Group, 1988–. Mem. International Harvester World Adv. Council, 1980–82; Vice-Chm., N American Adv. Gp, BOTB, 1973–87; Chairman: British Carpets Manufrs' Assoc. Export Council, 1976–84; Air Transport Users Cttee, 1983–84; President: Timeshare Developers Assoc., 1988–; Assoc. of Conf. Execs, 1988–; Vice-Pres., Transport Trust, 1973–; Member: BTA, 1976–82; DASA, 1982–. Mem., Queen's Body Guard for Scotland (Royal Company of Archers), 1960. *Recreation:* catching up. *Heir:* *s* Viscount Garnock, *qv. Address:* Combermere Abbey, Whitchurch, Salop SY13 4AJ. *T:* Burleydam 287; Coates House, Upper Largo, Fife. *T:* Upper Largo 249. *Club:* Boodle's.

*Died 1 Aug. 1989.*

**LINDSAY, Maj.-Gen. Edward Stewart,** CB 1956; CBE 1952 (OBE 1944); DSO 1945; Assistant Master General of Ordnance, 1961–64; Deputy Controller, Ministry of Supply, 1957–61; *b* 11 July 1905; *s* of Col M. E. Lindsay, DSO, DL, Craigfoodie, Dairsie, Fife; *m* 1933, Margaret, *d* of late Gen. Sir Norman Macmullen, GCB, CMG, CIE, DSO; two *d* (one *s* decd). *Educ:* Harrow Sch.; Edinburgh Univ. (BSc). 2nd Lt, RA 1926; served War of 1939–45, NW Europe (OBE, DSO); despatches, 1946; Col 1949; Brig. 1953; Maj.-Gen. 1955; Prin. Staff Officer to High Comr, Malaya, 1954–56; retired. Comdr Legion of Merit, USA, 1945. *Address:* Hill Cottage, Eversley, Hants. *T:* Eversley 733107. *Club:* Army and Navy.

*Died 18 March 1990.*

**LINDSAY, Jack;** author, *b* Melbourne, Australia, 1900; *s* of late Norman Lindsay; *m* 1958, Meta Waterdrinker; one *s* one *d*. *Educ:*

Queensland Univ., BA, DLitt. FRSL. Soviet Badge of Honour, 1968. AO 1981. *Publications:* Fauns and Ladies (Poems); Marino Faliero (Verse Drama); Hereward (Verse drama); Helen Comes of Age (Three verse plays); Passionate Neatherd (Poems); William Blake, Creative Will and the Poetic Image, an Essay; Dionysos; The Romans; The Anatomy of Spirt; Mark Antony; John Bunyan; Short History of Culture; Handbook of Freedom; Song of a Falling World; Byzantium into Europe; Life of Dickens; Meredith; The Romans were Here; Arthur and his Times; A World Ahead; Daily Life in Roman Egypt; Leisure and Pleasure in Roman Egypt; Men and Gods on the Roman Nile; Origins of Alchemy; Origins of Astrology; Cleopatra; The Clashing Rocks; Helen of Troy; The Normans; translations of Lysistrata, Women in Parliament (Aristophanes), complete works of Petronius, Love Poems of Propertius, A Homage to Sappho, Theocritos, Herondas, Catullus, Ausonius, Latin Medieval Poets, I am a Roman; Golden Ass; Edited Metamorphosis of Aiax (Sir John Harington, 1956;) Loving Mad Tom (Bedlamite Verses); Parlement of Pratlers (J. Eliot, 1593); Blake's Poetical Sketches; Into Action (Dieppe), a poem; Russian Poetry, 1917–55 (selections and translations); Memoirs of J. Priestley; Blast-Power and Ballistics; Decay and Renewal: critical essays on twentieth century writing; *novels:* Cressida' First Lover; Rome for Sale; Cæsar is Dead, Storm at Sea; Last Days with Cleopatra; Despoiling Venus; The Wanderings of Wenamen; Come Home at Last; Shadow and Flame; Adam of a New World; Sue Verney; 1649; Lost Birthright; Hannibaal Takes a Hand; Brief Light; Light in Italy; The Stormy Violence; We Shall Return; Beyond Terror; Hullo Stranger; The Barriers are Down; Time to Live; The Subtle Knot; Men of Forty-Eight; Fires in Smithfield; Betrayed Spring; Rising Tide; Moment of Choice; The Great Oak; Arthur and His Times; The Revolt of the Sons; The Way the Ball Bounces; All on the Never-Never (filmed as Live Now-Pay Later); Masks and Faces; Choice of Times; Thunder Underground; *history:* 1764; The Writing on the Wall; The Crisis in Marxism, 1981; *autobiography:* Life Rarely Tells; The Roaring Twenties; Fanfrolico and After; Meetings with Poets; *art-criticism:* The Death of the Hero; Life of Turner; Cézanne; Courbet; William Morris; The Troubadours; Hogarth; William Blake; Gainsborough. *Address:* 56 Maids Causeway, Cambridge. *Died* 8 *March* 1990.

**LINDSAY of Dowhill, Sir Martin (Alexander),** 1st Bt *cr* 1962, of Dowhill; CBE 1952; DSO 1945; Representer of Baronial House of Dowhill, 22nd in derivation from Sir William Lindsay, 1st of Dowhill, 1398; *b* 22 Aug. 1905; *s* of late Lt-Col A. B. Lindsay, 2nd KEO Gurkhas; *m* 1st, 1932, Joyce (marr. diss. 1967), *d* of late Major Hon. Robert Lindsay, Royal Scots Greys; two *s* one *d*; 2nd, 1969, Lœlai, Duchess of Westminster, *o d* of 1st Baron Sysonsby, PC, GCB, GCVO, Treasurer to HM King George V. *Educ:* Wellington Coll.; RMC, Sandhurst. 2nd Lt Royal Scots Fusiliers, 1925. Served Army 1925–36 and 1939–45. Active service on staff Norway 1940 (despatches), and commanded 1st Bn The Gordon Highlanders, 51st Highland Div., in 16 operations, July 1944–May 1945 (despatches, wounded, DSO); Lt-Col; seconded 4th Bn Nigeria Regt, 1927; travelled West to East Africa through Ituri Forest, Belgian Congo, 1929; Surveyor to British Arctic Air-Route Expedition to Greenland (King's Polar Medal), 1930–31; Leader British Trans-Greenland Expedition, 1934; Prospective National Unionist Candidate, Brigg Div., 1936–39; MP (C) Solihull Div. of Warwicks, 1945–64. DL for County of Lincoln, 1938–45; Chm., West Midlands Area of Conservative and Unionist Associations, 1949–52; Murchison Grant, Royal Geographical Society; Gold Medallist, French Geographical Soc.; Medallist Royal Belgian Geographical Soc.; André Plaque, Royal Swedish Soc. for Geography and Anthropology; Hon. Member Royal Belgian Geographical Soc.; a Mem. of the Queen's Body Guard for Scotland (Royal Company of Archers); Gold Staff Officer, Coronation, 1953. *Publications:* Those Greenland Days, 1932; The Epic of Captain Scott, 1933; Sledge, 1935; So Few Got Through: the Diary of an Infantry Officer, 1946; Three Got Through: Memoirs of an Arctic Explorer, 1947; The House of Commons (Britain in Pictures), 1947; Shall We Reform "the Lords"?, 1948; The Baronetage, 1977. *Heir:* *s* Ronald Alexander Lindsay [*b* 6 Dec. 1933; *m* 1968, Nicoletta, *yr d* of Capt. Edgar Storich, Italian Navy, retd; three *s* one *d*]. *Address:* The Old Vicarage, Send, near Woking, Surrey. *T:* Guildford 223157. *Died* 5 *May* 1981.

**LINDSAY, Sir William,** Kt 1963; CBE 1956; DL; *b* 22 March 1907; *er s* of late James Robertson Lindsay, Tower of Lethendy, Meikleour, Perthshire, and late Barbara Coupar, *d* of late Sir Charles Barrie; *m* 1936, Anne Diana, *d* of late Arthur Morley, OBE, KC; one *s* two *d*. *Educ:* Trinity Coll., Glenalmond; Christ Church, Oxford. BA 1928, MA 1931; Barrister-at-Law, Inner Temple, 1931. Dir, Royal Caledonian Schs, 1934–; Admin Officer, HM Treas., 1940–45. Member: Cuckfield UD Council, 1946–67 (Chm. 1951–54); Mid-Sussex Water Bd, 1946–60 (Chm. 1952–60); E Sussex CC, 1949– (Ald. 1957, Chm. 1961–64); Nat. Health Exec. Coun. for E Sussex, 1954–66; Hailsham Hospital Management Cttee, 1956–68; National Parks Commn, 1961–68, Countryside Commn, 1968–72; Chairman:

E Grinstead Conservative Assoc., 1948–51 and 1957–59; Sussex Co. Cons. Org., 1951–53 and 1958–59; Vice-Chm., 1951–54 and 1957–60 and Hon. Treas. 1960–69 of SE Area of Nat. Union of Cons. and Unionist Assocs.; Mem. Nat. Exec. Cttee of Conservative Party, 1952–54 and 1957–69. DL West Sussex, 1970–. Dir, Mid Sussex Water Co., 1961–79. *Address:* Mytten Cedars, Broad Street, Cuckfield, West Sussex. *T:* Haywards Heath 450371.
*Died* 16 *Nov.* 1986.

**LINDSAY-FYNN, Sir Basil (Mortimer),** Kt 1982; FCA; Director, Ward White Group Ltd (formerly John White Impregnable Boots Ltd, and Ward White Ltd), 1934–83; President and Founder, Friends of Malta GC, since 1962; *b* 22 Dec. 1901; *s* of Newenham Wight Lindsay-Fynn and Annie Cecilia Victoria (*née* Lindsay); *m* 1932, Marion Audrey Ellen Chapman; two *s* one *d*. *Educ:* Wesley Coll., Dublin; Trinity Coll., Dublin, 1929; London Sch. of Econs and Pol. Science, Univ. of London, 1929–31 (BCom). Chartered Accountant, 1924; FCA 1929. Sen. Partner, Smallfield Lindsay-Fynn & Co., 1929–47; Chairman: Gossard Ltd, 1934–60; Lintafoam Industries Ltd, 1946–66; Crown Estate Paving Commn, 1958–81; Dir, Associated Weavers Ltd and Chm. of its successor, AW Securities Ltd, 1936–77. President: Honiton Cons. Assoc., 1969–72; Holborn & St Pancras (S) Cons. Assoc., 1970–73; St Marylebone Cons. Assoc., 1980–84; Westminster N Cons. Assoc., 1984–85 (Patron, 1985–). *Recreations:* walking, swimming, tennis, ballroom dancing; old paintings, silver, glass, objets d'art and old furniture. *Address:* The Pebbles, Fore Street, Budleigh Salterton, Devon. *T:* Budleigh Salterton 3197. *Club:* Buck's. *Died* 25 *Aug.* 1988.

**LINDSAY-HOGG, Sir William (Lindsay),** 3rd Bt *cr* 1905; *b* 12 Aug. 1930; *s* of Sir Anthony Henry Lindsay-Hogg, 2nd Bt and Frances (*née* Doble; she *d* 1969); *S* father, 1968; *m* 1st, 1961, Victoria Pares (marr. diss. 1968); one *d*; 2nd, 1987, Marie Teresa, *d* of late John Foster. *Educ:* Stowe. Man. Dir, Roebuck Air Charter Ltd, 1967–70, Chm. 1970–74. Hereditary Cavaliere d'Italia. *Recreations:* riding, skiing. *Heir:* *uncle* Edward William Lindsay-Hogg [*b* 23 May 1910; *m* 1st, 1936, Geraldine (marr. diss. 1946), *d* of E. M. Fitzgerald; one *s*; 2nd, 1957, Kathleen Mary, *widow* of Captain Maurice Cadell, MC and *d* of James Cooney]. *Died* 7 *Dec.* 1987.

**LINFOOT, Dr Edward Hubert,** MA, DPhil, DSc (Oxon); ScD (Cantab); John Couch Adams Astronomer in the University of Cambridge and Assistant Director of the University Observatory, 1948–70; *b* 8 June 1905; *s* of late George E. Linfoot; *m* 1935, Joyce, *o d* of James and Ellend Dancer; one *s* one *d*. *Educ:* King Edward VII Sch., Sheffield; Balliol Coll., Oxford. Oxford Junior Mathematical Scholar, 1924; Senior Mathematical Scholar, 1928; Goldsmiths' Senior Student, 1926; J. E. Procter Visiting Fellow, Princeton Univ., USA, 1929; Tutor in Mathmatics, Balliol Coll., 1931; Asst Lecturer in Math., Bristol Univ., 1932, Lecturer, 1935. *Publications:* Recent Advances in Optics, 1955; Qualitätsbewertung optischer Bilder, 1960; Fourier Methods in Optical Image Evaluation, 1964; papers in scientific journals. *Recreations:* music, chess, gardening. *Address:* 7 Sherlock Road, Cambridge. *T:* Cambridge 356513. *Died* 14 *Oct.* 1982.

**LINK, Edwin Albert;** inventor, airman, ocean engineer; Consultant, The Singer Co.; President, Marine Science Center, Florida; Director and Trustee, Harbor Branch Foundation Inc.; *b* 26 July 1904; *s* of Edwin A. Link and Katherine Link; *m* 1931, Marion Clayton; one *s* (and one *s* decd). *Educ:* Binghamton and Lindsley Schools. Aviator, 1927–; President, founder, Link Aviation Inc., 1935–53; President, General Precision Equipment Corp., 1958–59. Director Emeritus, USAir. Inventor Link Aviation Trainers. Founder, Link Foundation, 1953. Awarded Exceptional Service Medal, USAF; Wakefield Medal, RAeS, 1947; Charles A. Lindbergh Fund Award, 1980; also varied awards from American organisations; holds honorary doctorates from Florida, Inst. of Technol., Tufts University, Syracuse Univ. and Hamilton Coll. *Publications:* Simplified Celestial Navigation (with P. V. H. Weems), 1940; articles on diving development and research in National Geographic magazines. *Address:* 10 Avon Road, Binghamton, NY 13905, USA; Link Port, North Old Dixie Highway, Fort Pierce, Fla 33450, USA.
*Died* 7 *Sept.* 1981.

**LINLITHGOW, 3rd Marquess of,** *cr* 1902; **Charles William Frederick Hope,** MC 1945; TD 1973; MA; Earl of Hopetoun, 1703; Viscount Aithrie, Baron Hope, 1703; Baron Hopetoun (UK) 1809; Baron Niddry (UK), 1814; Bt (Scotland), 1698; Captain (retired), 19th (Lothians and Border Horse) Armoured Car Company, Royal Tank Corps (Territorial Army); Director, Eagle Star Insurance Co. Ltd; *b* 7 April 1912; *er s* of 2nd Marquess of Linlithgow, KG, KT, PC and Doreen Maud, CI 1936, Kaisar-i-Hind Medal 1st Class (*d* 1965), 2nd *d* of Rt Hon. Sir F. Milner, 7th Bt; *S* father, 1952; *m* 1st, 1939, Vivien (*d* 1963), *d* of Capt. R. O. R. Kenyon-Slaney, and of Lady Mary Gilmour; one *s* one *d*; 2nd, 1965, Judith, *widow* of Esmond Baring. *Educ:* Eton; Christ Church, Oxford. Lieut, Scots Guards R of O; served War of 1939–45 (prisoner, MC). Lord Lieutenant, West Lothian, 1964–86. *Heir:* *s* Earl of Hopetoun. *Address:* Hopetoun

House, South Queensferry, West Lothian EH30 9SL. *T:* 031-331 1169. *Club:* White's. *Died* 7 *April* 1987.

**LINNELL, Prof. Wilfred Herbert,** MSc, DSc, PhD, FRSC, FPS; retired as Dean of the School of Pharmacy, University of London (1956–62); Professor of Pharmaceutical Chemistry, 1944–62; Professor Emeritus, 1962; Fellow of School of Pharmacy, University of London, 1962; *b* Sandbach, Cheshire, 1894; *s* of John Goodman and Evelyn Pring Linnell; *m* 1927, Margery, *d* of R. H. Hughes, Streetly; one *s. Educ:* Stockport Grammar Sch.; University of Durham; Lincoln Coll., Oxford; Armstrong Coll., Durham Univ., 1919–23; awarded the Earl Grey Memorial Fellowship, which was held at Lincoln Coll., Oxford; Governor, Chelsea College of Science and Technology. Research Chemist at HM Fuel Research Station, 1924–26; Examiner to the Pharmaceutical Society for Statutory Examinations since 1927; Corresp. étranger de l'Acad. Royale de Médecine de Belgique; Corresp. étranger de l'Acad. de Pharmacie de France. *Publications:* original contribs to science, published in the Journal of the Chemical Society, Journal of Society of Chemical Industry, and Journal of Pharmacy and Pharmacology. *Address:* 7 South Drive, Ruislip, Middlesex. *Died* 15 *Oct.* 1983.

**LINSTEAD, Sir Hugh (Nicholas),** Kt 1953; OBE 1937; *b* 3 Feb. 1901; *e s* of late Edward Flatman Linstead and Florence Evelyn Hester; *m* 1928, Alice Winifred Freke (*d* 1978); two *d. Educ:* City of London Sch.; Pharmaceutical Society's Sch. (Jacob Bell Scholar); Birkbeck Coll. Pharmaceutical chemist; barrister, Middle Temple, 1929. MP (C) Putney Div. of Wandsworth, 1942–64. Chm., Macarthys Pharmaceuticals Ltd, 1964–80. Secretary: Pharmaceutical Society of Great Britain, 1926–64; Central Pharmaceutical War Cttee, 1938–46; Pres., Internat. Pharmaceutical Fedn, 1953–65; Member, Medical Research Council, 1956–64; Chairman and Vice-Chairman, Joint Negotiating Cttee (Hospital Staffs), 1946–48; Member Poisons Board (Home Office), 1935–57; Chairman: Wandsworth Group Hospital Cttee, 1948–53; Parliamentary and Scientific Cttee, 1955–57; Library Cttee, House of Commons, 1963–64; Franco-British Parliamentary Relations Cttee, 1955–60. Member: Central Health Services Council (Min. of Health), 1951–66; Departmental Cttee on Homosexual Offences and Prostitution; Departmental Cttee on Experiments on Animals. Parliamentary Charity Comr for England and Wales, 1956–60. First Chm., Farriers' Registration Council, 1976–79. Comr for Training Scout Officers, Boy Scouts' Assoc., 1932–41; Hon. LLD: British Columbia, 1956; Toronto, 1963; Hon. Member American and Canadian Pharmaceutical Assocs, British Dental Assoc. and other societies; Corresponding Member Académie de Médecine de France and Académie de Pharmacie de Paris; Mem. Court, Farriers Co. (Master 1971–72). Commandeur de la Légion d'Honneur; Officier de la Santé Publique (France); Kt Comdr Al Merito Sanitario (Spain). *Address:* 15 Somerville House, Manor Fields, SW15 3LX. *Club:* Athenæum. *Died* 27 *May* 1987.

**LIPMAN, Vivian David,** CVO 1978; DPhil; FRHistS, FSA; Director of Ancient Monuments and Historic Buildings, Department of the Environment, 1972–78; *b* 27 Feb. 1921; *s* of late Samuel N. Lipman, MBE, and Cecelia (*née* Moses); *m* 1964, Sonia Lynette Senslive (*d* 1987); one *s. Educ:* St Paul's Sch.; Magdalen (Classical Demy) and Nuffield Colls, Oxford (MA). Served War, 1942–45, in Royal Signals and Intelligence Corps. Entered Civil Service as Asst Principal, 1947; Principal, 1950; Asst Sec., 1963; Under-Sec., 1972; Crown Estate Paving Commissioner, 1972. Mem., Redundant Churches Fund, 1979–. Hon. Research Fellow, University Coll. London, 1971–. Vice-Pres. (Pres., 1965–67), Jewish Historical Soc. of England, 1967–; Vice-Pres., Ancient Monuments Soc., 1978–; Chm., Conf. on Trng in Architectural Conservation, 1978–. Member Council: Architectural Heritage Fund, 1978– (Chm., Exec. Cttee, 1987–); SPAB, 1978–. Esher Award, SPAB, 1979. Jt Editor, Littman Library, 1981–; British Editorial Co-ordinator, America Holy Land Proj., 1981–. *Publications:* Local Government Areas, 1949; Social History of the Jews in England, 1954; A Century of Social Service, 1959; (ed) Three Centuries of Anglo-Jewish History, 1961; The Jews of Medieval Norwich, 1967; (ed with S. L. Lipman) Jewish Life in Britain 1962–77, 1981; (ed) Sir Moses Montefiore: a symposium, 1983; (with S. L. Lipman) The Century of Moses Montefiore, 1985; Americans and the Holy Land through British Eyes 1820–1917, 1989. *Recreation:* reading detective stories. *Address:* 9 Rotherwick Road, NW11 7DG. *T:* 01–458 9792. *Club:* Athenæum. *Died* 10 *March* 1990.

**LIPMANN, Fritz (Albert),** MD, PhD; Professor of Biochemistry, Rockefeller University, since 1965 (Rockefeller Institute, 1957–65); Head of Biochemical Research Laboratory, Mass. General Hospital, 1941–57; Professor of Biological Chemistry, Harvard Medical School, 1949–57; *b* Koenigsberg, Germany, 12 June 1899; *s* of Leopold Lipmann and Gertrud Lachmanski; *m* 1931, Elfreda M. Hall; one *s. Educ:* Universities of Koenigsberg, Berlin, Munich. MD Berlin, 1924; PhD Koenigsberg, Berlin, 1927. Research Asst, Kaiser Wilhelm Inst., Berlin and Heidelberg, 1927–31; Research Fellow, Rockefeller Inst. for Medical Research, New York, 1931–32;

Research Assoc., Biological Inst. of Carlsberg Foundation, Copenhagen, 1932–39; Res. Assoc., Dept of Biological Chem., Cornell University Med. Sch., NY, 1939–41; Res. Fellow in Surgery, 1941–43, and Associate in Biochemistry, 1943–49, Harvard Medical Sch.; Prof. of Biological Chemistry, Mass. General Hospital, 1949–57. Carl Neuberg Medal, 1948; Mead Johnson and Co. Award, 1948. Hon. MD: Marseilles, 1947; Copenhagen, 1972; Hon. DSc: Chicago, 1953; Sorbonne, 1966; Harvard, 1967; Rockefeller, 1971; Hon. Doc. Humane Letters: Brandeis, 1959; Albert Einstein College of Medicine of Yeshiva Univ., 1964; Nobel Prize in Medicine and Physiology, 1953; National Medal of Science, 1966. Member : National Academy of Sciences, American Association for Advancement of Science, American Chemical Society, Society of Biological Chemists, Harvey Society, Biochem. Society, Society of American Microbiologists; Hon. Life Mem., NY Acad. Scis, 1977; Fellow Danish Royal Academy of Sciences; Hon. Mem., Japanese Biochemical Soc., 1977; Foreign Member Royal Society, 1962. *Publications:* Wanderings of a Biochemist, 1971; articles in German, American and English journals. *Address:* (office) The Rockefeller University, New York, NY 10021, USA; (home) 201 East 17th Street, New York, NY 10003, USA.

*Died* 24 *July* 1986.

**LIPSCOMB, Maj.-Gen. Christopher Godfrey,** CB 1961; DSO and Bar 1945; Chief of Joint Services Liaison Organisation, BAOR, Bonn, 1958–61, retired; *b* 22 Dec. 1907; *s* of Godfrey Lipscomb and Mildred Agnes (*née* Leatham); *m* 1937, Ellen Diana Hayward; two *s. Educ:* Charterhouse; Sandhurst. Commissioned into Somerset Light Infantry, 1928; seconded Nigerian Regt, Royal West African Frontier Force, 1933–39; Commanded 4th Somerset LI, 1944–46; Staff Coll., 1947; AA&QMG, SW District, 1948–50; Comd 19 Inf. Bde, 1950–53; Commandant Senior Officers' Sch., 1954–56; Comd Hanover District, BAOR, 1957–58. *Address:* The Riding, Knook, Warminster, Wilts. *Died* 16 *Jan.* 1982.

**LISLE, Aubrey Edwin O.;** *see* Orchard-Lisle.

**LISSACK, Victor Jack;** a Recorder of the Crown Court, since 1972; solicitor in own practice since 1954; *b* 10 Sept. 1930; *s* of Maurice Solomon Lissack and Anna Lilian Lissack (*née* Falk); *m* 1953, Antoinette Rosalind Mildred Rose; two *s. Educ:* Peterborough Lodge Prep. Sch.; Wyoming High Sch., Ohio; Gresham's Sch., Holt; Law Soc. Sch. of Law. Articled, Hicks Arnold & Co., Solicitors, 1947–52, qual. 1954. Member: Donovan Cttee on Court of Criminal Appeal, 1964–65; James Cttee on Distribution of Criminal Business, 1974–75; Mem. Exec. Cttee, 1966–75, Chm. 1975–, Prisoners' Wives Service; Steward, British Bd of Boxing Control, 1981 (Mem., Southern Area Council, 1964–81); Trustee and Vice-Chm. Bd of Management, London Centre, 1974–; Sec., London Criminal Courts Solicitors' Assoc., 1970–74, Pres., 1974–76; Mem. Exec., Soc. of Conservative Lawyers, 1971–74; Sec., Gardner Cttee on Penal Reform, 1971–72; Sec., Gardner Cttee on Children and Young Persons Act, 1973–. *Recreations:* sporadic sailing, gentle golf, constant car cleaning. *Address:* 52 Wildwood Road, Hampstead, NW11. *T:* 01-455 8766; 8 Bow Street, Covent Garden, WC2E 7AJ. *T:* 01-240 2010. *Clubs:* Carlton, United and Cecil.

*Died* 20 *Dec.* 1981.

**LISTER, Sir (Charles) Percy,** Kt 1947; DL; *b* 15 July 1897; 3rd *s* of late Charles Ashton Lister, CBE; *m* 1st, 1933, Peggy Broom (marr. diss. 1947); one *s*; 2nd, 1953, Mrs Geraldine Bigger (*d* 1982), Portstewart, Ulster. *Educ:* Mill Hill; RMC, Sandhurst. 18th QMO Royal Hussars. Past Chairman and Managing Director: R. A. Lister and Co. Ltd, Dursley; United Kingdom Commercial Corp., 1940–45; Past Director: Sir W. G. Armstrong Whitworth (Engineers) Ltd; Hawker Siddeley Group Ltd. Member: Capital Issues Cttee, 1946–47; Dollar Exports Councils, 1949–64; Iron and Steel Board, 1953–58. DL County of Gloucester, 1960. *Recreations:* hunting, yachting, golf. *Address:* Stinchcombe Hill House, Dursley, Glos. *TA* and *T:* Dursley 2030. *Club:* Cavalry and Guards.

*Died* 7 *March* 1983.

**LISTER, Lt-Col (Bt Col) Harry Laidman,** OBE 1946; TD 1943; JP; retired; Vice Lord-Lieutenant, County of Cleveland, 1974–77; *b* 25 Oct. 1902; *s* of John James Lister, JP, and Margaret Lister; *m* 1st, 1930, Janet McLaren; two *s*; 2nd, 1971, Elizabeth Emmeline Walmsley. *Educ:* Durham School. Coal exporter and shipbroker (AICS), 1927–58; Welfare Officer, South Durham Steel & Iron Co., 1958–69. Joined TA, 1925, 55th (Northumbrian) Medium Bde RA TA; BEF, 1940, France and Belgium with 85th (Tees) HAA Regt RA, TA (despatches 1940); comd 53 City of London HAA Regt, RA TA, 1940; served in London, 1940–41, and India, 1942–45; comd 85 (City of London) Medium Regt, RA, 1944–45; comd 6th Cadet Bn Durham LI, 1945; raised and comd 654 LAA Regt RA, TA, 1946; comd 427 (M) HAA Regt RA, TA, 1948; Bt Col 1952; RofO 1952; comd 18th Bn Home Guard, 1953–56, when disbanded. Mem., Hartlepool Borough Council, 1945–48; Mem. Management Cttee, Hartlepool Gp of Hosps, 1958–74; Mem. T&AFA, Co. Durham, 1947–52 and 1953–68. Freeman, City of London, 1980.

DL Co. Durham, 1956; JP Co. Durham and Hartlepool, 1958. *Recreation:* Rugby football (Captain 1926–27, Pres. 1969, Hartlepool Rovers FC; played for Durham County, 1923–28). *Address:* 10 Cliff Terrace, Hartlepool, Cleveland TS24 0PU. *T:* Hartlepool 66042. *Died* 2 *Nov.* 1982.

**LISTER, John,** CBE 1987; Chairman and Chief Executive, British Shipbuilders, since 1987; *b* 26 Feb. 1931; *s* of Thomas Henry Lister and Florence May Lister; *m* 1955, Catherine Ferguson Mackay; one *s* four *d. Educ:* Sir William Turner's Sch., Redcar; King's Coll., London; Constantine Technical Coll., Middlesbrough. BSc (Hons) Chemistry, London (external); MRSC. Served RAF (FO), 1954–57. ICI, 1957–87: Chm., ICI Fibres, 1978–87. CBIM 1988. Liveryman, Farriers' Co., 1982; Freedom, Shipwrights' Co., 1989. *Recreations:* cricket, wine tasting, motor racing. *Address:* 10 Simon Close, Portobello Road, W11 3DJ. *T:* 01–229 4854. *Clubs:* Royal Air Force; Yorkshire County Cricket. *Died* 31 *July* 1989.

**LISTER, Laurier,** OBE 1976; Theatrical Director and Manager, since 1947; Consultant Director, Yvonne Arnaud Theatre, Guildford; *b* 22 April 1907; *s* of George Daniel Lister and Susie May Kooy. *Educ:* Dulwich Coll. Trained as actor at Royal Academy of Dramatic Art, 1925–26; appeared in Noël Coward's Easy Virtue, 1926; with Bristol Repertory Company, 1926–27; three seasons with Stratford-upon-Avon Festival Company, and also toured Canada and the USA with them, 1927–29; spent a year in S Africa with Olga Lindo's Company, 1930; Death Takes a Holiday, Savoy, 1931; The Lake, Westminster and Piccadilly, 1933; visited Finland with Sir Nigel Playfair's Company, 1933; Hervey House, His Majesty's, 1934; This Desirable Residence, Criterion, 1935; Parnell, New, 1936; People of our Class, New, 1938; The Flashing Stream, Lyric, 1938; also in New York, Biltmore, 1939. Served in RAF, 1940–45. Wrote, with Dorothy Massingham, The Soldier and the Gentlewoman, Vaudeville, 1933; with Hilda Vaughan, She Too Was Young, Wyndham's and New, 1938. Organized Poetry Recitals at the Lyric, Hammersmith, and Globe, 1946–47. Devised, directed and (except for the first two) presented under his own management, the following intimate revues: Tuppence Coloured, Lyric, Hammersmith, and Globe, 1947–48; Oranges and Lemons, Lyric, Hammersmith, and Globe, 1948–49; Penny Plain, St Martin's, 1951–52; Airs on a Shoestring, Royal Court, 1953–55; Joyce Grenfell Requests the Pleasure, Fortune and St Martin's, 1954–55, later, in New York, Bijou, 1955; Fresh Airs, Comedy, 1956. Directed plays in USA, 1957 and 1958; appointed Artistic Director to Sir Laurence Olivier's Company, 1959; Dear Liar (directed and presented) and The Art of Living (directed), Criterion, 1960; J. B., Phœnix, 1961 (directed and presented); Asst to Sir Laurence Olivier at Chichester Festivals, 1962, 1963; Director and Administrator, Yvonne Arnaud Theatre, Guildford, 1964–75. *Publications:* She Too Was Young, 1938; The Apollo Anthology, 1954. *Recreations:* gardening, travelling. *Address:* c/o National Westminster Bank, 57 Aldwych, WC2. *Died* 30 *Sept.* 1986.

**LISTER, Sir Percy;** *see* Lister, Sir C. P.

**LISTER, Thomas Liddell;** Under Secretary, Scottish Development Department, 1977–82, retired; *b* 21 May 1922; *s* of David Lister and Margaret (*née* Liddell); *m* 1949, Isobel Wylie (*née* Winton) (*d* 1984); three *d. Educ:* Allan Glens, Glasgow; Glasgow Univ. DPA. Ministry of Labour, 1939; Scottish Office, 1951; seconded Scottish Council (Development and Industry) as Secretary, Cttee of Inquiry into Scottish Economy, 1959; Regional Development Div., 1961 and 1967; Private Sec. to Minister of State, 1962; Crofting and Estate Management, Dept of Agriculture and Fisheries for Scotland, 1965; Urban Renewal, 1974; Land Use Planning, 1977–82. *Recreations:* hill walking, carpentry, music, dinghy sailing. *Address:* 29 Durham Road, Edinburgh EH15 1PB. *T:* 031–669 2170. *Died* 12 *Nov.* 1985.

**LISTER-KAYE, Sir John (Christopher Lister),** 7th Bt, *cr* 1812; *b* 13 July 1913; *s* of Sir Lister Lister-Kaye, 6th Bt and Emily Mary Lister-Kaye (*d* 1944); *S* father, 1962; *m* 1st, 1942, Audrey Helen Carter (*d* 1979); one *s* one *d*; 2nd, Margaret Isabelle Lovelace, *widow* of Rex Lovelace and *d* of Lt-Col Barnaby Duke, Martinstown. *Educ:* Oundle; Loughborough Coll. *Heir: s* John Phillip Lister Lister-Kaye [*b* 8 May 1946; *m* 1972, Sorrel, *e d* of Count Henry Bentinck; one *s* twin *d*]. *Address:* Glebe House, Piddlehinton, Dorchester DT2 7TE. *T:* Piddletrenthide 229. *Died* 15 *May* 1982.

**LISTON, David Joel,** OBE 1975 (MBE (mil.) 1944); Member of Council and Visiting Professor, European Business School, UK, since 1981; Hon. Education Adviser to British Overseas Trade Board, since 1972; Visiting Fellow, The Management College, Henley, since 1972; Industrial Adviser to Government, 1969–72; *b* 27 March 1914; *s* of Edward Lichtenstein and Hannah Davis, Manchester; *m* Eva Carole Kauffmann (*d* 1987); one *s* two *d. Educ:* Manchester Grammar Sch.; Wadham Coll., Oxford (Open and Philip Wright Exhibr). MA (Lit. Hum.). FSS; FRSA; CIEx. Joined Metal Box Co. 1937. TA, 1938; active service, 1939–46; 2nd in comd 8 Corps Sigs (Major, MBE, despatches). Rejoined Metal Box

as Head, Information and Statistics Div., 1946; Gen. Man., Plastics Group, 1955; Man. Dir, Shorko-Metal Box, 1961; seconded as Asst Dir Manchester Business Sch., 1966. Pro-Rector, Polytechnic of Central London, 1972–79 (Vis. Prof., 1979). Member: Council, British Plastics Fedn, 1956–69; CNAA, Cttee for Arts and Social Studies (Vice-Chm.), 1964–71; Econ. Develt Cttees for Food Manufrg and for Chemical Industries, 1969–72; Bd of Governors, English-Speaking Union, 1973–79 (Mem. Nat. Cttee for England and Wales, 1974–80, Current Affairs Cttee, 1981–). Mem., Liberal Party Industrial Policy Panel, 1975– (Chm., 1975–85); Pres., Winchester City Soc & Lib Dem, 1989–. Series Consultant, Making Your Mark: a language pack for business men, BBC, 1988. Mem., Editl Bd and contributor, Macmillan Internat. Trade Reference Book (formerly Kluwer International Trade Handbook), 1982–. *Publications:* (editor) Hutchinson's Practical Business Management series, 1971; The Purpose and Practice of Management, 1971; Education and Training for Overseas Trade, BOTB, 1973; Liberal Enterprise: a fresh start for British Industry, 1977; Foreign Languages for Overseas Trade (BOTB Working Party), 1979; (with N. Reeves) Business Studies, Languages and Overseas Trade, 1985; The Invisible Economy, 1988. *Recreations:* travel, current affairs. *Address:* 15 Twyford Court, Northlands Drive, Winchester, Hants SO23 7AL. *T:* Winchester 66087. *Clubs:* National Liberal, English-Speaking Union. *Died* 12 *May* 1990.

**LITTERICK, Thomas;** Lecturer, Management Centre, University of Aston in Birmingham, since 1979; *b* 25 May 1929; *s* of late William Litterick; *m* 1957, Jane Ellen, *e d* of Charles Birkenhead; four *d. Educ:* Dundee Sch. of Economics; Queen's Coll., Dundee; Univ. of Warwick. BSc Econ London; MA Industrial Relations Warwick. Sen. Lectr, Management Studies, Lanchester Coll. of Technology, Coventry, 1961–67; Lectr, Industrial Relations, Univ. of Aston, 1967–74. MP (Lab) Birmingham, Selly Oak, Oct. 1974–1979. Chairman: Kenilworth Lab. Party, 1969–70; Warwick and Leamington Constituency Lab. Party, 1970–72 (Political Educn Officer, 1969–70). Mem., Kenilworth UDC, 1970–74. *Died* 6 *Jan.* 1981.

**LITTLE, Prof. Alan Neville,** JP; Lewisham Professor of Social Administration, University of London, Goldsmiths' College, since 1978; *b* 12 July 1934; *s* of Charles Henry and Lilian Little; *m* 1955, Dr Valerie Hopkinson; one *s* two *d. Educ:* Northgate Grammar Sch., Ipswich; London Sch. of Economics (BSc (Sociology), PhD (Econs)); Univ. of Wisconsin. Lectr, LSE, 1959–66; Consultant, OECD, 1966–68; Director: Res. and Stats, ILEA, 1968–73; Community Relations Commn, 1973–78. Dep. Chm., Educn Res. Bd, 1972–74, and Chm., Sociol. and Social Admin Cttee, 1979–82, SSRC; Member: Educnl Adv. Council, IBA; BBC Consultative Cttee on Social Effects of TV; Council Mem., NACRO. Paul Lazarsfeld Lecture, Polytechnic of N London, 1979; The Goldsmiths' March Educn Conf. Lecture, 1980. JP Bromley, 1966–; Chm., Juvenile Panel, 1982–. *Publications:* Development of Secondary Education: trends and implications, 1969 (trans. in French); Strategies of Compensation, 1971 (trans. in French and Japanese); Homelessness and Unemployment, 1974; Urban Deprivation, Racial Inequality and Social Policy, 1977; Multi-Ethnic Education: the way forward, 1981; Loading the Law, 1982; (jtly) Adult Education and the Black Communities (report), 1982; Studies in the Multi-Ethnic Curriculum, 1983; Race and Social Work, 1986; various articles in academic jls. *Address:* 28 West Oak, The Avenue, Beckenham, Kent. *T:* 01–650 3322. *Died* 18 *Oct.* 1986.

**LITTLE, His Honour David John,** QC 1963; *er s* of late Rev. Dr James Little, MP for County Down (*er s* of Francis and Helen Little, Ouley House, Glascar, Co. Down), and Jeanie Graham Hastings, *d* of Rev. Hugh Hastings and Esther Hastings (*née* Larmor); *m* 1939, Nora Eileen Thomson; two *d. Educ:* Royal Belfast Academical Instn; St Andrew's Coll., Dublin; TCD. MA, LLB. Called to Bar 1938 and Inner Bar 1963, N Ireland. Crown Prosecutor for Co. Down and Belfast. MP (U) West Down, Parlt of NI, 1959–65. Recorder of Londonderry, and Judge for the County of Londonderry, 1965–79; Judge for North Antrim Div., 1979; retd 1980. *Recreations:* golf, reading, walking. *Address:* Seaforth, Whitehead, Co. Antrim. *T:* Whitehead 3722. *Club:* Royal Co. Down. *Died* 16 *April* 1984.

**LITTLE, Hon. Sir Douglas (Macfarlan),** Kt 1973; Justice of Supreme Court of Victoria, Australia, 1959–74; *b* 23 July 1904; *s* of John Little and Agnes Little (*née* Macfarlan); *m* 1931, Ida Margaret Chapple; one *d. Educ:* State Sch.; Scotch Coll.; Ormond Coll., Univ. of Melbourne (MA, LLM). QC (Aust.) 1954. Practised profession of the law in Melbourne since admission in 1929. Served War, with RAAF, 1942–45. *Recreations:* golf, lawn bowls. *Address:* 1/74 Serrell Street, East Malvern, Melbourne, Vic 3145, Australia. *Clubs:* Australian (Melbourne); Metropolitan Golf; Glenferrie Hill Recreation. *Died* 30 *Nov.* 1990.

**LITTLE, William Morison,** CBE 1972; BSc; MICE, MIEE, FCIT; Deputy Chairman, Scottish Transport Group, 1969–76, Managing

Director, 1969–75; *b* Leith, 12 Oct. 1909; *s* of Wm J. S. Little and May Morison; *m* 1940, Constance Herries; one *s* one *d. Educ:* Melville Coll.; Edinburgh Univ. Manager of Corporation Transport at: St Helens, 1941; Reading, 1945; Edinburgh, 1948. Subseq. Chm. of Scottish Bus Gp and subsidiary cos, 1963; part-time Mem., Nat. Bus Co., 1968–75. President: Scottish Road Transport Assoc., 1951; Municipal Passenger Transport Assoc., 1963; CIT, 1974–. Mem. Council, Public Road Transport Assoc. (formerly Public Transport Assoc.; Chm. Council, 1965–66, 1966–67). *Publications:* contribs to technical press and Inst. of Transport (Henry Spurrier Memorial Lecture, 1970). *Recreation:* being retired. *Address:* Church Cottage, Ford, Midlothian EH37 5RE. *Died 5 Aug. 1984.*

**LITTLER, Sir Emile,** Kt 1974; Theatrical Impresario, Producer, Author and Company Director; *b* Ramsgate, Kent, 9 Sept. 1903; *s* of F. R. and Agnes Littler; *m* 1933, Cora Goffin (actress); two *d. Educ:* Stratford-on-Avon. Served apprenticeship working on stage of the Theatre; was Asst Manager of Theatre in Southend, 1922; subsequently worked as Asst Stage Manager, Birmingham Rep. Theatre; in US, 1927–31; became Manager and Licensee of Birmingham Rep. Theatre for Sir Barry Jackson, Sept. 1931. Personally started in Management, Sept. 1934; theatrical productions include: Victoria Regina; 1066 and All That; Once in a Lifetime; The Maid of the Mountains, 1942, new production, Palace, 1972; The Night and the Music; Claudia; The Quaker Girl; Lilac Time; Song of Norway; Annie Get Your Gun; Zip Goes a Million; Blue for a Boy; Love from Judy; Affairs of State; Book of the Month; Hot Summer Night; Signpost to Murder; Kill Two Birds; The Right Honourable Gentleman; Latin Quarter; The Impossible Years; 110 in the Shade, Student Prince; Desert Song; Annual Pantomimes in London and big cities of British Isles totalling over 200. Dir, Theatres Mutual Insurance; Chm. and Man. Dir, London Entertainments PLC; controlled Palace Theatre, 1946–83; Pres., Soc. of West End Theatre Managers, 1964–67, 1969–70; formerly Governor, Royal Shakespeare Theatre, Stratford-on-Avon, retd 1973. Prominent play-doctor and race-horse owner. *Publications:* (jointly): Cabbages and Kings; Too Young to Marry; Love Isn't Everything; and 100 Christmas Pantomimes. *Recreations:* tennis, swimming, racing. *Address:* Palace Theatre, Shaftesbury Avenue, W1. *T:* 01–734 9691/2; The Trees, Ditchling, Sussex. *Clubs:* Royal Automobile, Clermont. *Died 23 Jan. 1985.*

**LITTLEWOOD, Rear-Adm. Charles,** CB 1954; OBE 1942; retired; *b* 1 Jan. 1902; *s* of Alfred Littlewood, Croydon, Surrey; *m* 1924, Doris Helen, *d* of William Mackean, London, SW16; no *c. Educ:* Falconbury Sch. (Preparatory), Purley; RN Colls Osborne and Dartmouth. Entered RN 1915; Midshipman, Emperor of India, 1918; Lt (E) RNEC Keyham, 1924; served in Ramillies, Concord, Erebus, Admiralty Experimental Station, 1924–32; Engineer Officer; HMS Ardent, 1932–34; HMS Apollo, 1934–36; Comdr (E) 1936; Flotilla Eng. Officer, HMS Kempenfelt, 1936–38; Manager Engineering Dept, Malta Dockyard, 1938–44; Actg Captain (E) 1942; Captain (E) 1945; Eng. Officer in HMS Howe, Brit. Pacific Fleet, served at Okinawa Operation, 1944–46; Asst Engineer in Chief, 1946–49; Manager Engineering Dept, Rosyth Dockyard, 1949–52; Rear-Admiral, 1952; Asst Dir of Dockyards, 1952–55, retd 1955. *Address:* Saddlers Mead, Sid Road, Sidmouth, Devon. *T:* Sidmouth 5482. *Died 24 Sept. 1984.*

**LIVERMORE, Sir Harry,** Kt 1973; Lord Mayor of Liverpool, 1958–59; *b* 17 Oct. 1908; *m* 1940, Esther Angelman; one *d* (one *s* decd). *Educ:* Royal Grammar Sch., Newcastle upon Tyne; Durham Univ. Solicitor; qualified, 1930; practises in Liverpool. Vice-President: Royal Liverpool Philharmonic Soc.; Liverpool Everyman Theatre, Ltd; Chm., Royal Court Theatre and Arts Trust Ltd. *Recreations:* music, theatre, swimming. *Address:* 18 Burnham Road, Liverpool L18 6JU. *Died 4 Dec. 1989.*

**LIVINGSTON, Air Marshal Sir Philip Clermont,** KBE 1950 (CBE 1946); CB 1948; AFC 1942; retired; FRCS; FRCSE, LRCP, DPH, DOMS; *b* 2 March 1893; *y s* of Clermont Livingston, Cleveland, Vancouver Island, BC, Canada; *m* 1920, Lorna Muriel, *o d* of C. W. Legassicke Crespin, London, Eng.; one *s* (and one *s* decd). *Educ:* Jesus Coll., Cambridge; London Hosp. Served European War, 1914–17, RNVR 4th Destroyer Flotilla, 1915; 10th Cruiser Sqdn, 1916. Qualified Jan. 1919; joined RAF, 1919, as MO; served India, Iraq, Far East; Consultant in Ophthalmology, 1934–46; Dep. Dir RAF Medical Services, 1947; Dir-Gen., 1948–51. Chadwick Prize and Gold Medal for researches in applied physiology, 1938. CStJ. *Publications:* Montgomery, Moynihan, and Chadwick Lectures, 1942–45; *autobiography:* Fringe of the Clouds, 1962; many papers on subjects connected with vision. *Recreation:* rowing (rowed 3 in winning Cambridge Univ. Crew, March 1914). *Address:* Maple Bay, RR1, Duncan, BC, Canada. *Died 13 Feb. 1984.*

**LIVINGSTONE, James Livingstone,** MD, FRCP; Retired; Consulting Physician: King's College Hospital; Brompton Hospital; St Dunstan's; *b* 8 May 1900; *m* 1935, Janet Muriel Rocke; two *s* one *d. Educ:* Worksop Coll., Notts; King's Coll., University of London;

King's Coll. Hospital. MRCS, LRCP, 1922; MB, BS 1923; MRCP 1925; MD London 1925; FRCP 1933. RAF, 1918–19. Fellow of King's Coll., London. Member: Assoc. of Physicians of Gt Britain; Thoracic Soc. *Publications:* Bronchitis and Broncho-pneumonia in Brit. Encyc. of Med. Practice, 2nd edn; Modern Practice in Tuberculosis, 1952; jt editor contributions to medical journals. *Recreations:* golf, fishing. *Address:* 11 Chyngton Road, Seaford, East Sussex. *Club:* Seaford Golf. *Died 21 April 1988.*

**LLEWELLYN, Sir (Frederick) John,** KCMG 1974; Director-General, British Council, 1972–80; *b* 29 April 1915; *er s* of late R. G. Llewellyn, Dursley, Glos.; *m* 1939, Joyce, *d* of late Ernest Barrett, Dursley; one *s* one *d. Educ:* Dursley Gram. Sch.; University of Birmingham. BSc, 1st Cl. Hons Chemistry, 1935; PhD, 1938; DSc, 1951 (Birmingham); FRIC, 1944, FNZIC, 1948; FRSA, 1952; FRSNZ, 1964. Lecturer in Chemistry, Birkbeck Coll., 1939–45; Dir, Min. of Supply Research Team, 1941–46; ICI Research Fellow, 1946–47; Prof. of Chemistry, Auckland Univ. Coll., 1947–55; Vice-Chancellor and Rector, University of Canterbury, Christchurch, NZ, 1956–61; Chairman: University Grants Cttee (NZ), 1961–66; N Zealand Broadcasting Corp., 1962–65; Vice-Chancellor, Exeter Univ., 1966–72. Mem. Senate, University of New Zealand, 1956–60; Mem. Council of Scientific and Industrial Research, 1957–61, 1962; Mem. NZ Atomic Energy Cttee, 1958; Mem. NZ Cttee on Technical Education, 1958–66; Chairman: NZ Council of Adult Educn, 1961–66; NZ Commonwealth Scholarships and Fellowships Cttee, 1961–66; Overall Review of Hong Kong Educn System, 1981–82; Member Council: Royal Society of NZ, 1961–63; Assoc. of Commonwealth Univs, 1967–72; Member: Inter-University Council for Higher Education Overseas, 1967–72; British Council Cttee for Commonwealth Univ. Interchange, 1968–72; Representative of UK Universities on Council of Univ. of Ahmado Bello, Nigeria, 1968–72. Chm., Northcott Theatre Bd of Management, 1966–72. Hon. LLD: Canterbury, 1962; Victoria Univ. of Wellington, 1966; Exeter, 1973; Birmingham, 1975; Hon. DSc Salford, 1975; DUniv Open, 1979. *Publications:* Crystallographic papers in Jl of Chemical Soc., London, and in Acta Crystallographica. *Recreations:* photography, computers. *Address:* 30 Lancaster Road, Wimbledon Village, SW19 5DD. *T:* 01–946 2754. *Club:* Arts. *Died 15 Nov. 1988.*

**LLEWELLYN, Col Sir Godfrey;** *see* Llewellyn, Col Sir R. G.

**LLEWELLYN, Sir John;** *see* Llewellyn, Sir F. J.

**LLEWELLYN, His Honour John Charles,** JP; a Circuit Judge (formerly a Judge of County Courts, and a Deputy Chairman, Inner London Area Sessions), 1965–82; *b* 11 Feb. 1908; *o s* of late J. E. Llewellyn, Letchworth, Herts; *m* 1937, Rae Marguerite Cabell Warrens (*d* 1986), *d* of Lt-Col E. R. C. Warrens, DSO, Froxfield, Hants; one *s* two *d. Educ:* St Christopher Sch., Letchworth; Emmanuel Coll., Cambridge (MA, LLB). Barrister, Inner Temple, 1931; Master of the Bench, Inner Temple, 1963. Common Law Counsel to PO, 1960–65; Recorder of King's Lynn, 1961–65. Mem. Gen. Council of the Bar, 1956–60, and 1961–65; Chm. Jt Advisory Council, Carpet Industry of Gt Brit., 1958–79; Dep. Chm. Agric. Land Tribunal (Eastern Region), 1959–65; JP Greater London, 1965–. *Recreation:* riding. *Address:* Bulford Mill, Braintree, Essex. *T:* Braintree (0376) 20616. *Clubs:* Athenæum, Boodle's. *Died 22 July 1990.*

**LLEWELLYN, Col Sir (Robert) Godfrey,** 1st Bt *cr* 1959; Kt 1953; CB 1950; CBE 1942 (OBE 1927); MC 1918; TD; DL; JP; Chairman Welsh Hospital Board, 1959–65; Director of Companies, including inception of Cambrian Air Services Ltd; Chairman of the Wales and Monmouthshire Conservative and Unionist Council, 1949–56, President, 1958, 1962, 1966, 1967, 1968, 1969; President, National Union of Conservative and Unionist Associations, 1962 (Vice-Chairman 1952–53, Chairman 1954–55); Chairman Glamorgan TA and AFA, 1953–58; *b* 13 May 1893; *y s* of Robert William Llewellyn, DL, JP, Cwrt-Colman, Bridgend and Baglan Hall, Briton-Ferry, Glamorgan; *m* 1920, Frances Doris (*d* 1969), *d* of Rowland S. Kennard, JP, Little Harrow, Christchurch, Hants; one *s* one *d. Educ:* Royal Naval Colls, Osborne and Dartmouth. Joined Royal Navy, 1906; Midshipman, 1910; Sub-Lt 1913; resigned, 1914; served European War, with Montgomeryshire Yeomanry Cavalry to 1917, which became Royal Welch Fusiliers; commanded Brigade Signal Troop 6th Mounted Brigade, 1917–18; Captain 1918; 4th Cavalry Div. Signal Squadron, 1918 (despatches twice, MC); raised and commanded 53rd Div. Signals (TA), 1920–29; Major, 1920; Bt Lt-Col, 1924; Lt-Col 1925; Bt Col 1928; Dep. Chief Signal Officer, Western Command, 1929–37; retired, 1937; Hon. Col 53rd Div. Signals, Royal Corps Signals, 1929–33. Col i/c Administration, Home Guard and Home Guard Adviser, S Wales District, 1940–44; Hon. Col 38th Div. Royal Corps Signals, 1941–49; Col Commandant Glamorgan Army Cadet Force, 1943–49; formerly Hon. Col 16th (Welsh) Battalion The Parachute Regt, TA. JP Neath Borough, 1925. Pres. of the Bath and West Show, 1956; Chm. of Organising Cttee Empire and Commonwealth Games, 1958. DL Glamorgan,

1936–74, Gwent, 1974–; DL Mon, 1960; JP Glamorgan County, 1934; High Sheriff: of Glamorgan, 1947–48, of Monmouth, 1963–64. KStJ 1969. *Recreations:* yachting, shooting, fishing, racing. *Heir: s* Lt-Col Michael Rowland Godfrey Llewellyn. *Address:* Tredilion Park, Abergavenny, Gwent NP7 8BD. *T:* 2178. *Clubs:* Naval and Military, Royal Automobile, Institute of Directors; Royal Thames Yacht; Cardiff and County (Cardiff). *Died* 3 *Oct.* 1986.

**LLEWELYN-DAVIES, Baron,** *cr* 1963 (Life Peer); **Richard Llewelyn-Davies,** MA, FRIBA; FRTPI; Emeritus Professor of Urban Planning, University College London; in private practice as Senior Partner, Llewelyn-Davies Weeks; *b* 24 Dec. 1912; *s* of Crompton Llewelyn Davies and Moya Llewelyn Davies (*née* O'Connor); *m* 1943, Patricia (later Baroness Llewelyn-Davies of Hastoe); three *d*. *Educ:* privately; Trinity Coll., Cambridge; Ecole des Beaux Arts, Paris; Architectural Association. Director: Investigation into Functions and Design of Hospitals; Division of Architectural Studies, Nuffield Foundation, London, 1953–60. Prof. of Architecture, University College London, 1960–69, Prof. of Urban Planning 1969–75. Chm., The Centre for Environmental Studies, 1967–; Mem., Royal Fine Art Commn, 1961–72. Consulting Architect: for rebuilding of London Stock Exchange; for many hosps in the UK and overseas, incl. Res. Labs for Atlantic Richfield, Philadelphia, USA, 1977–. Other projects include: new village at Rushbrooke, Suffolk (West Suffolk Award, 1957); Nuffield diagnostic centre and maternity hosp. at Corby, Northants (RIBA Bronze Medal, 1957); Master Plan for Washington New Town, Co. Durham, 1966; Master Plan for new city of Milton Keynes, 1967–; Master plan for Shahestan Pahlavi, new centre of Tehran, 1976; Master plan for redevelopment of Menninger Campus, Topeka, Kansas, 1977. Hon. Fellow, American Institute of Architects, 1970. Mem., Inst. for Advanced Study, Princeton, 1980. *Publications:* (jointly) Studies in the Functions and Design of Hospitals, 1955; (jointly) Building Elements, 1956; (jointly) The Design of Research Laboratories, 1960; contributions to Nature, Journal of RIBA, Architects' Journal, Architectural Review, Architectural Record, Jl Town Planning Inst., Jl Royal Inst. of Chemistry. *Address:* 36 Parkhill Road, NW3. *T:* 01-485 6576; Brook House, 2–16 Torrington Place, WC1E 7HN. *T:* 01-637 0181. *Club:* Brooks's.

*Died* 27 *Oct.* 1981.

**LLOYD, 2nd Baron,** *cr* 1925, of Dolobran; **Alexander David Frederick Lloyd,** MBE 1945; DL; Captain Welsh Guards (Reserve); Director: Lloyds Bank Ltd, 1957–81; Lloyds Bank International, 1974–78; Lloyds Bank Unit Trust Managers, 1974–81; Beehive Life Insurance, 1974–81; Grindlays Bank Ltd, 1961–74 (Vice-Chairman, 1970–74); Chairman: National Bank of New Zealand, 1970–77 (Deputy Chairman, 1969–70); London Board, National Bank of New Zealand Ltd, 1978–81; *b* 30 Sept. 1912; *o s* of 1st Baron and Hon. Blanche (*d* 1969) (late Maid of Honour to Queen Alexandra), *d* of late Hon. F. C. Lascelles; *S* father, 1941; *m* 1942, Lady Victoria Jean Marjorie Mabel Ogilvy, *e d* of 11th Earl of Airlie; two *d* (one *s* decd). *Educ:* Eton; Cambridge (MA). Served in British Council prior to War of 1939–45; served War of 1939–45 in Palestine, Syria and NW Europe. Pres. Navy League, 1948–51; Mem. LCC, 1949–51. Lord in Waiting to King George VI, Oct. 1951–Feb. 1952, to the Queen until Dec. 1952; Jt Under-Sec. of State for Home Dept with responsibility for Welsh Affairs, Nov. 1952–Oct. 1954; Parliamentary Under-Sec. of State for the Colonies, Oct. 1954–Jan. 1957. Chairman: Grindlays Bank (Uganda), 1969–74; Banque Grindlay Internat. au Zaire, 1970–74; Grindlays Internat. Finance (Kenya), 1970–74; Director: Addis Ababa Bank, 1961–74; Nat. & Grindlays Finance & Develt Corp., 1961–74; Nat. & Grindlays Holdings Ltd, 1969–74. Mem., White Fish Authority and Herring Bd, 1963–69. Pres. Commonwealth and British Empire Chambers of Commerce, 1957–61. Board of Governors, London Sch. of Hygiene and Tropical Medicine. DL Herts 1963. *Recreations:* shooting, fishing, music, reading. *Heir:* none. *Address:* Clouds Hill, Offley, Hitchin, Herts. *T:* Offley 350. *Club:* White's.

*Died* 5 *Nov.* 1985 (*ext*).

**LLOYD, Prof. Arnold de Gorges;** *see* Lloyd, Prof. W. A. de G.

**LLOYD, Bernard Dean,** FRVA; IPFA; City Treasurer, Birmingham, 1980–82; *b* 23 March 1923; *s* of Stanley Lloyd and Eva Mary Lloyd; *m* 1955, Margaret Taylor; one *s* one *d*. *Educ:* Cardiff High Sch. CIPFA 1949; FRVA 1977. Served War, RN, 1942–46. City Treasurer's and Controller's Dept, Cardiff, 1947–48 and 1946–48; Accountancy Asst, Borough Treasurer's Dept, Ipswich, 1948–52; Technical Asst, Treasurer's Dept, Birmingham, 1952–72; Dep. Treasurer, Birmingham, 1972–80. Chm., LAMSAC Computer Panel, 1980–. *Publications:* articles in professional jls. *Recreations:* reading, gardening. *Address:* 39 Queens Court, Alderham Close, Solihull, West Midlands B91 2PR. *T:* 021–705 5431.

*Died* 9 *June* 1987.

**LLOYD, (Charles) Christopher;** author, historian; *b* 2 Sept. 1906; *s* of E. S. Lloyd, CSI, and M. Young; *m* 1938, Katharine Brenda Sturge; one *s* one *d*. *Educ:* Marlborough; Lincoln Coll., Oxford. Lecturer:

Bishop's Univ., Quebec, 1930–34; Royal Naval Coll., Dartmouth, 1934–45; Lectr, 1945–66, Prof. of History, 1962–66, Royal Naval College, Greenwich; retired, 1967. Editor, The Mariner's Mirror, 1970–79. *Publications:* The Navy and the Slave Trade, 1949; The Nation and the Navy, 1961; Medicine and the Navy, 1961; William Dampier, 1966; The British Seaman, 1968; Mr Barrow of the Admiralty, 1970; The Search for the Niger, 1973; The Nile Campaign: Nelson and Napoleon in Egypt, 1973; Nelson and Sea Power, 1973; Atlas of Maritime History, 1976; English Corsairs on the Barbary Coast, 1981, etc. *Address:* Lions Wood, Dern Lane, Heathfield, East Sussex. *T:* Horam Road 2702. *Club:* Travellers'.

*Died* 31 *March* 1986.

**LLOYD, Maj.-Gen. Cyril,** CB 1948; CBE 1944 (OBE 1943); TD 1945 (2 bars); psc; Director-General, City and Guilds of London Institute, 1949–67, Consultant, since 1968; President, Associated Examining Board for General Certificate of Education, since 1976 (Chairman, 1970–76); *b* 14 April 1906; *s* of late Alfred Henry Lloyd; *m* 1931, Winifred Dorothy Moore; one *d*. *Educ:* Brighton Grammar Sch.; London and Cambridge Univs. First Class in Mathematics, Physics, Divinity. Fellow of Institute of Physics; MRST; Lecturer and Teacher; Research Worker in Science; Sussex Territorials (RA), 1929–39; Major, 1939; BEF, 1939–40 (despatches); General Staff, Canadian Army, 1940–42 (despatches, OBE); served various overseas theatres; a Dep Chief of Staff, 21 Army Group, 1943–45; Invasion of Europe (despatches, CBE), 1944–45; Dir-Gen. of Army Education and Training, 1945–49; Member: Council of Boy Scouts Assoc., 1950–70; Council Assoc. of Techn. Institutions, 1961–64; Central Adv. Council for Educn (England) and Adv. Cttee on Educn in Colonies, 1949–53; Adv. Council on Sci. Policy (Jt Enquiry on Technicians, 1962–65); Bd, Internat. Centre for Advanced Technical and Vocational Trg (Turin); Council for Tech. Education and Training for Overseas Countries; Regional Adv. Council for Higher Technological Educn (London), 1950–67; Parly and Scientific Cttee; Nat. Adv. Council for Educn in Industry and Commerce, 1945–68; Southern Regional Council for Further Educn; Council, Instn of Environmental Studies; Vice-Pres. Brit. Assoc. for Commercial and Industrial Educn (Chm. 1955–58); Industrial Trg Council, 1958–64; Central Trg Council and its General Policy Cttee, 1964–68; Chm., Governing Body, National Institute of Agricultural Engineering, 1960–70; Schools Broadcasting Council for the UK, 1962–65; W Sussex Educn Cttee; Council Rural Industries Bureau, 1960–67; Pres., SASLIC, 1970–79; Pres., Soc. for Promotion of Vocational Trng and Educn, 1973; Chm., Cttee on Scientific Library Services; Chm. Governors, Crawley Coll. of Further Educn until 1978; Vice-Pres., Crawley Planning Gp, 1967–; Chief Officer, Commonwealth Tech. Trg Week, 1961; Treas., 1963 Campaign for Educn; Mem. Council for Educl Advance; Trustee: Edward James Foundn; Industrial Trg Foundn; Pres., Roffey Park Management Inst. Governor, Imperial Coll., 1950–70; Mem. Delegacy, City and Guilds Coll., 1950–70; Hon. Exec. Principal, West Dean Coll., 1969–72. Founder Life Mem., Cambridge Soc. Patron, Chalk Pit Museum. Liveryman, Goldsmiths' Co. and Freeman of City of London; FRSA. *Publications:* booklets: British Services Education, 1950; Human Resources and New Systems of Vocational Training and Apprenticeship, 1963; contrib. to jls. *Recreations:* the countryside, sailing, and traditional crafts. *Address:* 1 Normandy Gardens, Horsham, West Sussex RH12 1AS. *Club:* Athenæum.

*Died* 27 *July* 1989.

**LLOYD, Major Sir (Ernest) Guy (Richard),** 1st Bt *cr* 1960; Kt 1953; DSO 1917; DL; late Administrator J. and P. Coats, Ltd, Glasgow (retired 1938); *b* 7 Aug. 1890; *e s* of late Major E. T. Lloyd, late Bengal Civil Service; *m* 1918, Helen Kynaston (*d* 1984), *yr d* of late Col E. W. Greg, CB; one *s* two *d* (and two *d* decd). *Educ:* Rossall; Keble Coll., Oxford, MA. Served European War, 1914–18 (despatches, DSO); War of 1939–45, 1940. MP (U) East Renfrewshire, Scotland, 1940–Sept. 1959. DL, Dunbartonshire, 1953. *Recreations:* fishing and gardening. *Heir: s* Richard Ernest Butler Lloyd. *Address:* Rhu Cottage, Carrick Castle, Lochgoilhead, Argyll. *Died* 22 *Sept.* 1987.

**LLOYD, Air Chief Marshal Sir Hugh Pughe,** GBE 1953 (KBE 1942; CBE 1941); KCB 1951 (CB 1942); MC; DFC; retired; Hon. LLD (Wales); *b* 12 Dec. 1894; *m* Kathleen (*d* 1976), *d* of late Maj. Robert Thornton Meadows, DSO, MD; one *d*. Served European War, 1914–18, with Army and RAF (DFC, MC); War of 1939–45 (CBE, CB, KBE); Air ADC to the King, 1940–41; AOC Malta, 1941–42; Comdr, Allied Coastal Air Forces, Mediterranean, 1943–44; Comdr, Commonwealth Bomber Force, Okinawa, 1944–45; Senior Instructor Imperial Defence Coll., 1946–47; C-in-C, Air Command Far East, 1947–49; AOC-in-C Bomber Command, 1950–53; retired 1953. Master Peshawar Vale Hounds, 1934–36. Order of Legion of Merit (USA), 1944; Officier Légion d'Honneur, 1944. *Publication:* Briefed to Attack, 1949. *Address:* Peterley Manor Farm, Great Missenden, Bucks. *T:* 2959. *Died* 13 *July* 1981.

**LLOYD, His Honour Ifor Bowen,** QC; a County Court Judge, later a Circuit Judge, 1959–76 (Judge of Wandsworth County Court,

1964–76); *b* 9 Sept. 1902; *er s* of late Rev. Thomas Davies Lloyd and Mrs Margaret Lloyd; *m* 1938, Naomi, *y d* of late George Pleydell Bancroft; one *s* one *d*. *Educ:* Winchester (Exhibitioner); Exeter Coll., Oxford (Scholar). BA Oxford (Mod. Hist.), 1924; called to Bar, Inner Temple, 1925, Bencher 1959, Treasurer 1981; Yarborough Anderson scholar, 1926; Midland Circuit; President, Hardwicke Society, 1929; KC 1951. Liberal Candidate, Burton Division of Staffordshire, 1929, Chertsey Division of Surrey, 1931. Member General Council of the Bar, 1950, 1957. *Address:* 1 Harcourt Buildings, Temple, EC4Y 9DA. *T:* 071–353 1484.

*Died 23 July 1990.*

**LLOYD, John Owen,** CBE 1965; HM Diplomatic Service, retired; *b* 7 Feb. 1914; *s* of late George Thomas Lloyd, ICS; *m* 1st, 1940, Ellen Marjorie Howard Andrews; one *s* one *d*; 2nd, 1972, Mrs Barbara Diana Clarke. *Educ:* Marlborough; Clare Coll., Cambridge. Probationer Vice-Consul, Tokyo, 1937; Acting Vice-Consul, Hankow, 1940–41; served at Tokyo, 1941; Vice-Consul, 1943; on staff of HM Special Commission, Singapore, 1946; transferred to Foreign Office, 1948; Foreign Office Representative, Canadian National Defence Coll., 1952; First Secretary (Commercial), Paris, 1953–56; First Secretary, Office of Comr-Gen., Singapore, 1957; Counsellor, Office of the Comissioner-General, Singapore, 1958–60; Foreign Service Inspector, 1960–63; Consul-General: Osaka-Kobe, 1963–67; San Francisco, 1967–70; Ambassador to Laos, 1970–73, retired 1974. *Publication:* A Governor's Sermons (trans. of Governor of Osaka Prefecture Gisen Sato's work), 1967. *Address:* 18 Reynolds Close, NW11. *Died 28 Aug. 1982.*

**LLOYD, Martin,** MA (Cantab); *b* 1908; 2nd *s* of late Thomas Zachary Lloyd, Edgbaston, Birmingham; *m* 1943, Kathleen Rosslyn, *y d* of late Colonel J. J. Robertson, DSO, Wick, Caithness; two *s* two *d*. *Educ:* Marlborough Coll.; Gonville and Caius Coll., Cambridge (1st Class Parts I and II Mod. Languages Tripos). Asst Master, Rugby Sch., 1930–40; on military service, 1940–44. Headmaster of Uppingham Sch., 1944–65; Warden, Missenden Abbey Adult Educn Coll., 1966–74. *Address:* Norton Cottage, Pitchcombe, Stroud, Glos GL6 6LU. *T:* Painswick 812329.

*Died 28 Aug. 1989.*

**LLOYD, Norman,** FRSA, ROI, 1935; Landscape Painter, *b* 16 Oct. 1895; *s* of David Lloyd and Jane Ogilvie; *m* 1923, Edith Eyre-Powell (*d* 1971). *Educ:* Hamilton and Sydney Art School, Australia. Exhibitioner Royal Academy and Royal Institute of Oil Painters; Salon des Artistes Français, Paris; Laureat du Salon Mention Honorable, 1948; Silver Medal, Portrait Salon, Paris, 1956; Palmes, Acad. Française, 1957. Member Société des Artistes Français, Paysagistes; Member Internat. Assoc. of Plastic Arts, 1962. *Recreation:* travel. *Address:* c/o Dr J. A. Farrer, Hall Garth, Clapham, near Lancaster LA2 8DR. *Died 5 March 1983.*

**LLOYD, Richard Dafydd Vivian Llewellyn, (Richard Llewellyn);** author; *b* Wales, Dec. 1906; *m* 1st, 1952, Nona Theresa Sonsteby (marr. diss., 1968), Chicago; 2nd, 1974, Susan Frances Heimann, MA, New York. *Educ:* St David's, Cardiff, London. Coalmining; studied hotel management in Italy; film writing and producing; Captain, The Welsh Guards, 1941–46. *Publications:* (as Richard Llewellyn) How Green Was My Valley, 1939; None But the Lonely Heart, 1943, new completed edn, 1968; A Few Flowers for Shiner, 1950; A Flame for Doubting Thomas, 1954; Sweet Witch, 1955; Mr Hamish Gleave, 1956; The Flame of Hercules, 1957; Warden of the Smoke and Bells, 1958; Chez Pavan, 1959; Up, Into the Singing Mountain, 1963; Sweet Morn of Judas' Day, 1964; A Man in a Mirror, 1964; Down Where the Moon is Small, 1966; The End of the Rug, 1968; But We Didn't Get the Fox, 1970; White Horse to Banbury Cross, 1972; The Night is a Child, 1972; Bride of Israel, My Love, 1973; A Hill of Many Dreams, 1974; Green, Green My Valley Now, 1975; At Sunrise, The Rough Music, 1976; Tell Me Now, and Again, 1977; A Night of Bright Stars, 1979; I Stand on a Quiet Shore, 1982; has also written for the younger reader. *Plays:* Poison Pen, 1937; Noose, 1947; The Scarlet Suit, 1962; Ecce!, 1974; Hat, 1974; Oranges and Lemons, 1980 (for TV). *Recreations:* economics, anthropology, photography. *Address:* c/o Michael Joseph Ltd, 44 Bedford Square, WC1B 3DU. *Club:* Cavalry and Guards.

*Died 30 Nov. 1983.*

**LLOYD, Brigadier Thomas Ifan,** CBE 1957; DSO 1944; MC 1940; retired; *b* 20 March 1903; *s* of late Rev. David Lloyd, Vicar of St Paul's, Weston-super-Mare, Somerset; *m* 1927, Irene Mary, *d* of Andrew Fullerton, CB, CMG, FRCS, of Belfast, N. Ireland; one *s* one *d*. *Educ:* Westminster Sch.; RMA, Woolwich. Commissioned into the Corps of Royal Engineers as Second Lieut, 1923; concluded military career as Dep. Engineer-in-Chief (Brigadier), War Office, 1955–57. Founder, Railway Conversion League, 1958. *Publications:* Twilight of the Railways—What Roads they'll Make!, 1957; Paper, Instn Civil Engineers, 1955. *Recreations:* golf, bridge. *Address:* 24 Grove Road, Merrow, Guildford, Surrey GU1 2HP. *T:* Guildford

75428. *Club:* Royal Commonwealth Society.

*Died 6 Oct. 1981.*

**LLOYD, Prof. (William) Arnold de Gorges;** Professor of Education in the University of Cambridge 1959–71; Fellow of Trinity College, since 1961; Chairman, Cambridge Schools Classics Project, Nuffield Foundation, 1965–71; *b* 20 May 1904; *s* of Jonathan Lloyd and Mary Gorges Lloyd; *m* 1st, 1929, Margaret Elizabeth Manley; three *d*; 2nd, 1952, Daphne Stella Harris; two *s* one *d*. *Educ:* Sidcot Sch., Somerset; Birmingham Univ. (Flounders Scholar); Institut J. J. Rousseau, Geneva; Sorbonne. MA Birmingham 1936; PhD Cambridge, 1946. Schoolmaster in primary, technical and grammar schools, 1926–32 and 1938–44; director of adult education, 1934–38; Lecturer in Education, Selly Oak Colleges, 1933–34; University of Nottingham, 1946–52; Prof. of Education, Dean of the Faculty and Dep. Chairman of the Institute of Social Research, University of Natal, 1952–56; Senior Prof. of Education, University of the Witwatersrand, 1956–59. Travelling fellowship for Universities of Italy, Switzerland and France, 1956; Carnegie fellowship for Universities of USA, 1957; British Council travel grant to visit English universities, 1958; Commissioner to report on technical education in France, 1959. Fellow of Haverford Coll., Pennsylvania, 1959. Consultant, curricula in Education, European University, Council of Europe, 1966–68. Associate editor, Journal of Conflict Resolution, Chicago, 1956–. Editor, Pædagogica Europaea, 1964–. *Publications:* God in the experience of men, 1938; God in the experience of youth, 1940; Quaker Social History, 1950; Creative Learning, 1953; Education and Human Relations, 1957; The Old and the New Schoolmaster, 1959; The Principles and Practice of Education, 1964; (ed) International Dictionary of Educational Terms, vol. I, England and Wales, 1970; Recollected in Tranquillity, 1979; Continuity and Change in Personality, 1982. *Recreations:* Quaker and family history; cabinet-making; book-binding. *Address:* Trinity College, Cambridge; Withersfield House, Withersfield, West Suffolk. *Died 4 July 1982.*

**LLOYD-DAVIES, Oswald Vaughan;** Surgeon Emeritus: Middlesex Hospital (Surgeon, 1950–81); St Mark's Hospital for diseases of the Colon and Rectum (Surgeon, 1935–81); Former Surgeon: Connaught Hospital; Hampstead General Hospital; *b* 13 Jan. 1905; *s* of late Rev. Samuel Lloyd-Davies, BA; *m* 1st, 1939, Menna (*d* 1968), *d* of late Canon D. J. Morgan, MA; one *s* one *d*; 2nd, 1970, Rosamund, *d* of late Rev. E. V. Bond, MA. *Educ:* Caterham Sch.; Middlesex Hospital Medical Sch., London Univ. MRCS, LRCP, 1929; MB, BS (London) 1930; FRCS 1932; MS (London) 1932. Fellow Royal Society of Med. (Past Pres. sect. of proctology); Fellow Assoc. of Surgeons of Great Britain and Ireland; Member, Harveian Society; Hon. Fellow, Amer. Soc. of Colon and Rectal Surgeons. *Publications:* various chapters in British Surgical Practice; articles on colon, rectal and liver surgery. *Recreations:* gardening, fishing. *Address:* Townsend Close, Ashwell, Herts. *T:* Ashwell 2386.

*Died 15 July 1987.*

**LLOYD-JOHNES, Herbert Johnes,** OBE 1973; TD 1950; FSA; *b* 9 Dec. 1900; *e s* of Herbert Thomas Lloyd-Johnes, MC, and Georgina Mary Lloyd-Johnes, Dolaucothy, Co. Carmarthen; *m* 1942, Margaret Ruth Edgar (Lieut, FANY, War of 1939–45); two *d*. *Educ:* St Andrews, Eastbourne; Malvern. Spent much of his time in Poland, 1931–39; Member British Military Mission to Poland, 1939; a Senior British Liaison Officer to Polish Forces, 1940–46. Chairman: Historic Buildings Council for Wales, 1967–77 (Mem. 1955–77); Welsh Folk Museum Cttee, 1953–55; Rural Industries Cttee for Monmouth, Glamorgan and Radnor, 1955–66; Member: Council, Nat. Trust of GB, 1967–74; Court, Nat. Library of Wales, 1948– (Mem. Council, 1948–78); Nat. Museum of Wales, 1949; Court of Governors, University of Wales, 1952–78; Governor, University College of S Wales and Monmouth, Cardiff. Major RA, TA, Pembroke and Cardigan. Hon. LLD Wales, 1973. Cross For Valour (Poland), 1939. *Publications:* (with Sir Leonard Twiston-Davies) Welsh Furniture, 1950, repr. 1971; contributor to several learned journals. *Recreation:* reading. *Address:* Fosse Hill, Coates, near Cirencester, Glos. *T:* Kemble 279. *Club:* Boodle's.

*Died 22 Oct. 1983.*

**LLOYD JONES, Cyril Walter,** CIE 1925; FCGI; FICE; *b* 6 March 1881; *e s* of late Richard Lloyd Jones; *m* 1907, Edith Kathleen, *d* of Frederick Penty; two *s* two *d*. *Educ:* Aske's Sch.; Imperial College of Science. Chief Engineer, HEH Nizam's State Railway Board, 1913; Agent, 1919; Managing Director, 1930; English Agent, 1941; retired. *Address:* Roundhay, Pit Farm Road, Guildford, Surrey.

*Died 10 July 1981.*

**LLOYD-JONES, Sir (Harry) Vincent,** Kt 1960; a Judge of the High Court of Justice, Family Division (formerly Probate, Divorce and Admiralty Division), 1960–72; *b* 16 Oct. 1901; 3rd *s* of late Henry Lloyd-Jones; *m* 1933, Margaret Alwena, *d* of late G. H. Mathias; one *s* one *d*. *Educ:* St Marylebone Grammar Sch. (Old Philological); University Coll., London; Jesus Coll., Oxford. Exhibitioner English Language and Literature, Jesus Coll., Oxford, 1921; BA (Eng. Lang.

and Lit.) 1923; BA (Jurisprudence) 1924; MA 1927. President Oxford Union Society, (Summer Term) 1925. Member Oxford Union Debating Team in USA, 1925. Called to Bar by Inner Temple, 1926, Master of the Bench, 1958; practised Common Law Bar; Wales and Chester Circuit; QC 1949. Recorder of Chester, 1952-58; Recorder of Cardiff, 1958-60. Hon. Fellow: Jesus Coll., Oxford, 1960; University Coll., London, 1962. *Recreations:* reading, walking. *Address:* 24 Vincent Square, SW1P 2NJ. *T:* 01-834 5109.

*Died 23 Sept. 1986.*

**LLOYD PHILLIPS, Ivan,** CBE 1963 (OBE 1959); DPhil Oxon; *b* Cambridge, June 1910; *er s* of late Rev. A. Lloyd Phillips, formerly Vicar of Ware, Herts; *m* 1941, Faith Macleay, *o c* of late Brig.-Gen. G. M. Macarthur Onslow, CMG, DSO, Camden, New South Wales; one *s. Educ:* Worksop Coll.; Selwyn Coll., Cambridge; Balliol Coll., Oxford. Appointed Colonial Administrative Service, 1934; served in: Gold Coast, 1934-38; Palestine, 1938-47; District Commissioner, Gaza-Beersheba, 1946-47; Colonial Office, 1947-48; Cyprus, 1948-51; Commissioner, Nicosia-Kyrenia, 1950-51; Singapore, 1951-53; Commissioner-General's Office, 1951-52; Dep. Secretary for Defence, 1952-53; Malaya, 1953-62; Secretary to Chief Minister and Minister for Home Affairs, 1955-57; Secretary, Ministry of the Interior, 1957-62. Secretary, Oxford Preservation Trust, 1962-65; Inst. of Commonwealth Studies, Oxford Univ., 1965-70. Chairman, Oxfordshire Playing Fields Assoc., 1966-77, Pres., 1977-. Duke of Edinburgh's award for service to Nat. Playing Fields Movement, 1974. Commander, Order of Defender of the Realm (Malaysia), 1958. *Address:* Cranmer Cottage, Dorchester-on-Thames, Oxfordshire. *T:* Oxford 340026. *Clubs:* Travellers', MCC. *Died 14 Jan. 1984.*

**LLOYD-ROBERTS, George Charles,** MChir; FRCS; Consultant Orthopædic Surgeon, St George's Hospital, since 1957; Consultant Orthopædic Surgeon, The Hospital for Sick Children, Great Ormond Street, since 1955; Consultant in Paediatric Orthopaedics to the RAF, since 1970 and RN, since 1972; *b* 23 Nov. 1918; *e s* of Griffith and Gwendoline Lloyd-Roberts; *m* 1st, 1947, Catherine Lansing Ray (marr. diss. 1967), *widow* of Edward Lansing Ray, St Louis, Missouri; one *s* two *d;* 2nd, 1980, Edome Broughton-Adderley. *Educ:* Eton Coll.; Magdalene Coll., Cambridge. BA, MB, BChir (Cantab), 1943, MChir (Cantab), 1966; FRCS, 1949. Graded Surgical Specialist, RAMC, 1944, Surgeon, Yugoslav and Italian Partisan Forces. Late 1st Assistant, Orthopædic Dept, St George's Hospital, 1954; Clinical Research Assistant, Royal National Orthopædic Hospital, 1952; Nuffield Fellow in Orthopædic Surgery, 1952. Mem. Council, RCS, 1976-; President: British Orthopædic Assoc., 1977-78; Orthopædic Section, RSM, 1976-77. Mem. Council, Game Conservancy, 1977-. Robert Jones Gold Medal of British Orthopædic Assoc., 1953. *Publications:* Orthopædics in Infancy and Childhood, 1972; The Hip Joint in Childhood, 1977; (ed) Orthopædic Surgery, 1968; articles on orthopædic subjects in medical journals. *Recreations:* fishing, shooting. *Address:* 9 Cheyne Place, SW3. *T:* 01-352 5622; (Private Consulting Room), Hospital for Sick Children, Great Ormond Street, WC1. *Club:* Boodle's.

*Died 12 Jan. 1986.*

**LLOYD WEBBER, William Southcombe,** CBE 1980; DMus (London) 1938; FRCM 1963; FRCO 1933; FLCM 1963; Hon. RAM 1966; Director, London College of Music, since 1964; Professor of Theory and Composition, Royal College of Music, since 1946; Musical Director, Central Hall, Westminster, since 1958; *b* 11 March 1914; *m* 1942, Jean Hermione Johnstone; two *s. Educ:* Mercers' School; Royal College of Music. Organist: Christ Church, Newgate Street, 1929-32; St Cyprian's, Clarence Gate, 1932-39; All Saints, Margaret Street, 1939-48. Examiner to Associated Board of Royal Schools of Music, 1946-64; Vice-Pres., Incorporated Assoc. of Organists; Past Pres. and Hon. Mem., London Assoc. of Organists; Mem. Council, Royal College of Organists, 1946- (Hon Treas., 1953-64); Mem. Senate, London Univ., 1964-67. Master, Worshipful Co. of Musicians, 1973-74; Guild Master, Civic Guild of Old Mercers, 1977. FRSA 1982. *Publications:* many instrumental, choral and educational works; contrib. to Musical Times, Musical Opinion. *Recreations:* chess, bridge. *Address:* 13A Sussex Mansions, Old Brompton Road, SW7. *T:* 01-589 8614. *Died 29 Oct. 1982.*

**LOCH, 3rd Baron** *cr* 1895, of Drylaw; **George Henry Compton Loch;** Major late 11th Hussars; Director and Proprietor, Lusitano Stud and Equitation Centre (dressage academy), since 1979; *b* 3 Feb. 1916; *s* of 2nd Baron and Lady Margaret Compton (*d* 1970), *o d* of 5th Marquess of Northampton; *S* father, 1942; *m* 1st, 1942, Leila Mary Grace Isabel Hill Mackenzie (marr. diss. 1946); (one *d* decd); 2nd, 1946, Mrs Betty Castillon du Perron (marr. diss. 1952); 3rd, 1952, Joan Dorothy Hawthorn Binns (marr. diss.); 4th, 1975, Sylvia Barbara Beauchamp-Wilson, *o d* of A. G. Beauchamp Cameron; one *d. Educ:* Eton; RMC, Sandhurst. *Heir: b* Hon. Spencer Douglas Loch, MC 1945 [ *b* 1920; *m* 1948, Hon. Rachel (*d* 1976), *yr d* of Group Captain H. L. Cooper, AFC, and of Baroness Lucas and Dingwall (Nan Ino Herbert-Cooper who *d* 1958); one *d* (two *s* decd); *m* 1979, Davina Lady Boughey. *Educ:* Wellington Coll.; Trinity Coll., Cambridge. Major Grenadier Guards; called to Bar, 1948]. *Address:* Green Farm, Stoke-by-Clare, Suffolk. *T:* Clare 277266.

*Died 15 Dec. 1982.*

**LOCK, Air Vice-Marshal Basil Goodhand,** CB 1978; CBE 1969; AFC 1954; security consultant; Director, Assets 2000; *b* 25 June 1923; *s* of J. S. Lock; *m* 1st, 1944, Mona Rita (*d* 1988); one *s;* 2nd, 1988, Sara Horniman. Entered RAF from Durham Univ. Air Sqdn; commnd RAF, 1943; various operational sqdns, 1944-47; Exchange Sqdn posts, USA, 1947-48; Flying Instructor, RAF Coll., Cranwell, 1950-51; OC, HC Exam. Unit, 1951-54; HQ MEAF, 1954-57; Ops (O), Air Min., 1958-61; OC Flying, RAF Leeming, 1961-63; Plans (Cento), 1964-66; OC, RAF West Raynham, 1967-69; SDS (Air), JSSC, 1969-71; Dir of Ops (AS), MoD, 1971-73; Dir of Personal Services, MoD, 1974-75; Air Vice-Marshal 1975; Air Officer Scotland, 1975-77; Dir Gen. of Security (RAF), 1977-79; Security Advr, MPO, later OMCS, 1979-87. CBIM; FRGS. *Recreations:* golf, gardening, music, motoring. *Club:* Royal Air Force.

*Died 13 Nov. 1989.*

**LOCK, (Cecil) Max,** FRIBA (Dist. TP), AADip, FRTPI; Head of Max Lock Group; *b* 29 June 1909; *s* of Cecil William Best Lock and Vivian Cecil Hassell. *Educ:* Berkhamsted Sch. Public Schools' Entrance Scholarship to Architectural Assoc., London, 1926. Entered private practice, 1933; (firm established as Max Lock 1933, Max Lock Group 1944, Max Lock & Associates 1950, Max Lock & Partners 1954); retired 1972, remaining Consultant to partnership (now Max Lock, Easton, Perlston & King); formed Max Lock Group of Planning and Development Consultants, in partnership with Michael Theis, 1972; currently Max Lock Group Nigeria, as consultants to Govt of NE State Nigeria, engaged on surveys and master plans for Maiduguri, Nguru, Potiskum, Bauchi, Gombe, Yola-Jimeta and Mubi; retired 1976. Member Watford Borough Council, 1936-40; on staff of AA School of Architecture, 1937-39; Head of Hull School of Architecture, 1939; Leverhulme Research Schol. (carried out a Civic Diagnosis of Hull). Surveys and plans by Max Lock Group for: Middlesbrough, 1946; The Hartlepools, 1948; Portsmouth District, 1949; Bedford, 1951; by Max Lock and Partners, Surveys and Plans for Amman, Aqaba (Jordan), 1954-55; Town Plans for development of Iraq at Um Qasr, Margil and Basrah, 1954-56; New Towns at El Beida, Libya, 1956, and Sheikh Othman, Aden, 1960. Survey and plan for the Capital City and Territory of Kaduna for Government of Northern Nigeria, 1965-66. British Town Centre redevelopment plans, 1957-71, include: Sevenoaks; Thetford; Sutton Coldfield; Salisbury; Brentford; redevelopment of new central housing communities at Oldham; development of Woodley Airfield, Reading; a plan for Central Area of Beverley, Yorks. Visiting Professor: Dept of City Planning, Harvard Univ., 1957; University of Rio de Janeiro, 1960, 1968; Guest Chairman, 5th Australian National Planning Congress, 1960. Member Council, TPI, 1946-50 and 1961-63. Freeman of the City of London, 1978. *Publications:* The Middlesbrough Survey and Plan, 1946; The Hartlepools Survey and Plan, 1948; The Portsmouth and District Survey and Plan, 1949; Bedford by the River, 1952; The New Basrah, 1956; Kaduna, 1917-1967-2017: A Survey and Plan of the Capital Territory for the Government of Northern Nigeria, 1967; contribs to RIBA Journal, TPI Journal, Town Planning Review, etc. *Recreations:* music, pianist. *Address:* 7 Victoria Square, SW1. *T:* 01-834 7071; Addicroft Mill, Plushabridge, Liskeard, Cornwall. *T:* Liskeard 62510. *Club:* Reform.

*Died 2 April 1988.*

**LOCK, Winifred, (Mrs John Lock);** see Gérin, W.

**LOCKE, Arthur D'Arcy, (Bobby Locke);** professional golfer; Playing Professional at Observatory Golf Club, Johannesburg; *b* Germiston, Transvaal, 20 Nov. 1917; *s* of Charles James Locke; *m* 1943, Lillian, *d* of N. Le Roux, Montagu; one *d; m* 1958, Mary Fenten, USA. *Educ:* Benoni High Sch. Won Open and Amateur South African Championships, 1935; won Irish, Dutch and New Zealand Open Championships, 1938; French Open Championship, 1952-53; British Open Championship, 1949, 1950, 1952, 1957; Canadian Open, 1947; Mexican Open, 1952; Egyptian Open, 1954; German Open, 1954; Swiss Open, 1954; Australian Open, 1955; Member Professional Golfers' Association (London). Served War of 1939-45, Middle East and Italy as Pilot, South African Air Force. *Publication:* Bobby Locke on Golf, 1953. *Died 9 March 1987.*

**LOCKHART;** see Bruce Lockhart.

**LOCKHART, Sir Muir Edward S.;** see Sinclair-Lockhart.

**LOCKHART, Gen. Sir Rob (McGregor Macdonald),** KCB 1946 (CB 1944); CIE 1942; MC; Indian Army (retired); *b* 1893; 3rd *s* of late R. Bruce Lockhart, formerly of Eagle House, Sandhurst, Berks; *m* 1918, Margaret Amy (*d* 1980), *yr d* of late Col Sir R. Neil Campbell, KCMG, CIE, IMS; one *s* three *d. Educ:* Marlborough Coll.; RMC, Sandhurst; Staff Coll., Camberley. Commissioned ULIA, 1913; joined 51st Sikhs FF, March 1914. Acting governor, NWFP (India) June-Aug. 1947. C-in-C IA, Aug.-Dec. 1947; retired 1948. Dir of

Ops, Malaya, Dec. 1951–Feb. 1952; Dep. Dir, Feb. 1952–March 1953. Dep. Chief Scout, Boy Scouts' Association, 1951–61; President: Greater London Central Scout County (Scout Assoc.), 1965–72; Assoc. of British Officers of Indian Army, 1969–75. Order of Star of Nepal (2nd Class), 1946. *Address:* c/o Lloyds Bank Ltd, Cox's & King's branch, 6 Pall Mall, SW1.

*Died* 11 *Sept.* 1981.

**LOCKHART, Prof. Robert Douglas,** MD, ChM; LLD; FSAScot, FRSE; Regius Professor of Anatomy, University of Aberdeen, 1938–65, later Emeritus Professor; concurrently Curator, Anthropological Museum (Hon. Curator, 1939–79, Consultant 1979–80; room in Museum now named The Lockhart Room by the University); *b* 7 Jan. 1894; *s* of William Lockhart and Elizabeth Bogie. *Educ:* Robert Gordon's Coll., Aberdeen; University, Aberdeen (MB, ChB 1918). Ho. Surg. Aberdeen Royal Infirmary; Surgeon-Probationer, RNVR, 1916; Surgeon-Lt, RN 1918; Lecturer in Anatomy, Aberdeen Univ., 1919; Prof. of Anat., Birmingham Univ. 1931; Dean of Faculty of Medicine, Aberdeen, 1959–62. Past Pres., Anatomical Soc. of Great Britain and Ireland. Hon. LLD Aberdeen, 1965. *Publications:* Chapter, Ways of Living, in Man and Nature, 1926; Living Anatomy, Photographic Atlas of Muscles in Action and Surface Contours, 1948, 7th edn 1974; Myology Section in Cunningham's Anatomy, 1964; Anatomy of the Human Body, 1969; contributor to Kodak Med. Film Library, 1933; Structure and Function of Muscle, 1960 (2nd rev. edn, vol. 1, ed Bourne, 1972). *Recreations:* roses and rhododendrons. *Address:* 25 Rubislaw Den North, Aberdeen AB2 4AL. *T:* Aberdeen 37833.

*Died* 26 *Feb.* 1987.

**LOCKHART, Stephen Alexander,** CMG 1960; OBE 1949; HM Diplomatic Service, retired; *b* 19 March 1905; *o s* of late Captain Murray Lockhart, RN, Milton Lockhart, and of Leonora Rynd; *m* 1944, Angela Watson; two *s* two *d*. *Educ:* Harrow; Jesus Coll., Cambridge (BA Hons). Served Lisbon, 1940–43; Ministry of Information, 1943; Press Attaché, Lisbon, 1944, Brussels, 1945; First Sec. (Information), Brussels, 1946–51; Foreign Office, 1951; First Sec., Buenos Aires, 1952–55; UK Rep., Trieste, 1955–57; HM Consul-Gen., Leopoldville, and in French Equatorial Africa, 1957–60; HM Consul-Gen., Zürich, 1960–62; HM Ambassador to Dominican Republic, 1962–65; re-employed in FCO, 1965–70; Hon. Consul, Oporto, 1970–75. *Address:* 10 Shelley Court, Tite Street, SW3 4JB; 4 Clarence Lodge, Englefield Green, Egham TW20 0NO. *Died* 22 *Jan.* 1989.

**LOCKHART-MUMMERY, Sir Hugh (Evelyn),** KCVO 1981; MD, MChir; FRCS; Serjeant-Surgeon to the Queen, 1975–83 (Surgeon to HM Household, 1969–75, to the Queen, 1974–75); *b* 28 April 1918; *s* of John Percy Lockhart-Mummery, FRCS; *m* 1st, 1946, Elizabeth Jean Crerar (*d* 1981), *d* of Sir James Crerar, KCSI, CIE; one *s*; 2nd, 1985, Jean Elizabeth Hoare (*née* Foote). *Educ:* Stowe Sch.; Trinity Coll., Cambridge; Westminster Hosp. Med. Sch. MB, BCh 1942; FRCS 1943; MChir 1950; MD 1956. Served RAF, 1943–46. Consultant Surgeon: King Edward VII's Hosp. for Officers, 1968–86; RAF, 1975–84; Consulting Surgeon: St Mark's Hosp., 1978– (Consultant Surgeon, 1951–78); St Thomas' Hosp., 1982– (Consultant Surgeon, 1960–82). Examr in Surgery, Univ. of London, 1965–75; Pres., Sect. of Proctology, RSM, 1966. Sir Med. Sickness Annuity & Life Assce Soc., 1973– (Chm., 1982–). Hon. Fellow, (French) Académie de Proctologie, 1961; Hon. Fellow, Amer. Soc. of Colon and Rectal Surgeons, 1974. *Publications:* chapters in surgical textbooks; articles on surgery of the colon and rectum in Brit. jls. *Recreations:* golf, fishing. *Address:* Duns House, Hannington, near Basingstoke, Hants RG26 5TX. *T:* Kingsclere 298162. *Club:* Royal Air Force. *Died* 24 *June* 1988.

**LOCKSPEISER, Sir Ben,** KCB 1950; Kt 1946; FRS 1949; FEng, FIMechE, FRAeS; *b* 9 March 1891; *s* of late Leon and Rose Lockspeiser, London; *m* 1920, Elsie Shuttleworth (*d* 1964); one *s* two *d*; *m* 1966, Mary Alice Heywood (*d* 1983). *Educ:* Grocers' Sch.; Sidney Sussex Coll., Cambridge (Hon. Fellow); Royal School of Mines. MA; Hon. DSc Oxford; Hon. DEng Witwatersrand; Hon. DTech, Haifa; Aeronautical Research at Royal Aircraft Establishment, Farnborough, 1920–37; Head of Air Defence Dept, RAE, Farnborough, 1937–39; Asst Dir of Scientific Research, Air Ministry, 1939; Dep. Dir of Scientific Res., Armaments, Min. of Aircraft Production, 1941; Dir of Scientific Research, Ministry of Aircraft Production, 1943; Dir-Gen. of Scientific Research, Ministry of Aircraft Production, 1945; Chief Scientist to Ministry of Supply, 1946–49; Sec. to Cttee of Privy Council for Scientific and Industrial Research, 1949–56; retired 1956. President: Engineering Section of British Association, 1952; Johnson Soc., 1953–54; Council European Organization for Nuclear Research, 1955–57. Hon. Mem., Parly and Scientific Cttee, 1960. Life Fellow, RSA, 1973. Medal of Freedom (Silver Palms), 1946. *Recreations:* music, gardening. *Address:* Birchway, 15 Waverley Road, Farnborough, Hants. *T:* Farnborough (0252) 543021. *Club:* Athenæum.

*Died* 18 *Oct.* 1990.

**LOCKWOOD, Lt-Col John Cutts,** CBE 1960; TD; JP; *b* Dec. 1890; *s* of late Colonel John Lockwood and Mrs Lockwood, Kingham, Oxon. Served European War, 1914–18, in Essex Regt and Coldstream Guards; War of 1939–45, with Essex Territorials; Staff Captain in JAG Dept; later Legal Officer to SHAEF Mission to Denmark, and with them in Copenhagen, 1945. MP (C) Central Hackney, 1931–35; Romford, 1950–55. Barrister, Middle Temple. Freeman of the City of London. Order of Dannebrog (Denmark). *Recreation:* gardening. *Address:* Bishops Hall, Lambourne End, Essex. *T:* 01-500 2016. *Died* 18 *Jan.* 1983.

**LOCKWOOD, Margaret Mary,** CBE 1981; Actress; *b* Karachi, India, 15 Sept. 1916; *m* 1937, Rupert W. Leon (marr. diss.); one *d*. *Educ:* Sydenham Girls' High Sch. Studied for Stage under Italia Conti and at Royal Academy of Dramatic Art. *Films:* Lorna Doone; Case of Gabriel Perry, 1934; Midshipman Easy; Jury's Evidence; Amateur Gentleman, 1935; Irish for Luck; Beloved Vagabond; Street Singer, 1936; Who's Your Lady Friend; Owd Bob; Bank Holiday, 1937; The Lady Vanishes; A Girl Must Live; Stars Look Down; Night Train to Munich, 1939; Quiet Wedding, 1940; Alibi; Man in Grey, 1942; Dear Octopus; Give Us The Moon; Love Story, 1943; Place of One's Own; I'll Be Your Sweetheart, 1944; Wicked Lady; Bedelia, 1945; Hungry Hill; Jassy, 1946; The White Unicorn, 1947; Look Before You Love, 1948; Cardboard Cavalier; Madness of the Heart, 1949; Highly Dangerous, 1950; Laughing Anne, 1952; Trent's Last Case, 1952; Trouble in the Glen, 1954; Cast A Dark Shadow, 1955; The Slipper and the Rose, 1976. Named top money-making Star in Britain by motion Picture Poll; Motion Picture Herald Fame Poll, 1945 and 1946; Winner Daily Mail Film Award, 1945–46, 1946–47 and 1947–48. *Stage:* tour in Private Lives, 1949; Peter Pan, 1949–50, 1950–51 and 1957–58; Pygmalion, 1951; Spider's Web, Savoy, 1954–56; Subway in the Sky, Savoy, 1957; And Suddenly It's Spring, Duke of York's, 1959–60; Signpost to Murder, Cambridge Theatre, 1962–63; Every Other Evening, Phœnix, 1964–65; An Ideal Husband, Strand, 1965 and Garrick, 1966; The Others, Strand, 1967; On a Foggy Day, St Martin's, 1969; Lady Frederick, Vaudeville, 1970; Relative Values (nat. tour), 1972, Westminster, 1973; Double Edge, Vaudeville, 1975–76; Quadrille (nat. tour), 1977; Suite in Two Keys (nat. tour), 1978; Motherdear, Ambassadors, 1980. *Television:* BBC series (with daughter Julia) The Flying Swan, March-Sept. 1965; Yorkshire TV series, Justice, 1971, 1972–73, 1974. *Recreations:* crossword puzzles and swimming. *Died* 15 *July* 1990.

**LOCKWOOD, Walter Sydney Douglas,** CBE 1962 (OBE 1948); CEng; FRAeS; FIProdE; *b* 4 Jan. 1895; *s* of Walter Lockwood, Thetford, Norfolk; *m* 1924, Constance Rose, *d* of T. F. Bayliss, Norwich; one *d*. *Educ:* Thetford Sch.; Bristol Univ. Served European War, 1914–18; Gloucester Regt, France and Belgium (Belgian Croix de Guerre; despatches; wounded). Joined design staff of Sir W. G. Armstrong Whitworth Aircraft Ltd, 1921; transferred to Works Staff, 1940; became Works Manager, 1944; Armstrong Whitworth Aircraft: Works Dir, 1950; Dir and Gen. Man., 1955; Man. Dir, 1960; Man. Dir, Whitworth Gloster Aircraft Ltd (when Armstrong Whitworth Aircraft and Gloster Aircraft Companies merged), 1961–63 (when Co. dissolved); Dir, Hawker Siddeley Aviation Ltd, 1961–64, retired. Mem. Coun., SBAC, 1960. *Address:* Wayside, 101 Abbey Road, Leiston, Suffolk IP16 4TA.

*Died* 10 *Oct.* 1989.

**LODGE, Henry Cabot;** Politician, US; President's Special Representative to the Vatican, 1970; *b* 5 July 1902; *s* of George Cabot Lodge and Mathilda Elizabeth Frelinghuysen Davis; *g s* of late Henry Cabot Lodge, Senator (US); *m* 1926, Emily Sears; two *s*. *Educ:* Middx Sch., Concord, Mass.; Harvard (AB *cum laude*; LLD). Boston Transcript, New York Herald Tribune, 1923–32. Thrice elected US Senator from Massachusetts. Harvard Overseer. Senate author of the Lodge-Brown Act which created Hoover Commission; Chm., resolutions cttee, Republican National Convention, 1948; US Senate Foreign Relations Cttee. Campaign Manager of effort to win Republican nomination for Gen. Eisenhower, 1951–52; Mem. President's Cabinet and US Rep. to UN, 1953–60. Republican nominee for Vice-Pres., USA, 1960. Dir-Gen., Atlantic Inst., Paris, 1961–63; Ambassador to Vietnam, 1963–64, 1965–67, to Federal Republic of Germany, 1968–69. US Representative at Vietnam Peace Talks, Paris, Jan.-Nov. 1969. Had reached grade of reserve Captain when US entered war; served as Major United States Army, with first American tank detachment in Brit. 8th Army, Libya, 1942 (citation); resigned from Senate for further Army service (first Senator to do so since the Civil War); Italy, 1944; Lt-Col S France, Rhine and S Germany, 1944–45 (Bronze Star, US, 1944, Legion of Merit, 1945, Légion d'Honneur and Croix de Guerre with palm, France, 1945). Maj.-Gen., US Army Reserve. Has been awarded numerous Hon. Degrees; Sylvanus Thayer Medal, West Point; Theodore Roosevelt Assoc. Medal; Gold Medal from Pres. Eisenhower, 'for selfless and invaluable service to our nation'. Order of Polonia Restituta; Order of African Redemption, Liberia; Grand Cross of Merit, Order of Malta; National Order, Republic of Viet Nam. *Publications:* The Storm Has Many Eyes, 1973; As It Was,

1976; articles for Atlantic Monthly, Collier's, Life, Reader's Digest, Saturday Evening Post. *Address:* 275 Hale Street, Beverly, Mass 01915, USA. *T:* Beverly 617/922–0404. *Clubs:* Metropolitan, Myopia Hunt, Alfalfa (all Washington); Somerset, Tavern (both Boston).                                    *Died* 27 *Feb.* 1985.

**LODGE, Tom Stewart,** CBE 1967; Director of Research and Statistics, Home Office, 1969–73; retired; *b* 15 Dec. 1909; *s* of George Arthur and Emma Eliza Lodge, Batley, Yorks; *m* 1936, Joan McFadyean (*d* 1961); one *d. Educ:* Batley Grammar Sch.; Merton Coll., Oxford. BA Hons Maths 1931, MA 1934; FIA 1939. Prudential Assurance Co., 1931–43; Min. of Aircraft Production, 1943–46; Admty as Superintending Actuary, 1946–50; Statistical Adviser, Home Office, 1950; Statistical Adviser and Dir of Research, Home Office, 1957. Chm., Criminological Scientific Council, Council of Europe, 1975–77 (Mem., 1970–77). *Publications:* articles in British and French jls. *Address:* 16A The Avenue, Coulsdon, Surrey CR3 2BN. *T:* 01–660 3390. *Club:* Civil Service.                                    *Died* 17 *March* 1987.

**LOEWE, Frederick;** composer; concert pianist; *b* Vienna, 10 June 1901; *s* of Edmund Loewe, actor. Began career as concert pianist playing with leading European orchestras; went to US, 1924; first musical, Salute to Spring, produced in St Louis, 1937; first Broadway production, Great Lady, 1938; began collaboration with Alan Jay Lerner in 1942, since when has written music for: Day Before Spring, 1945; Brigadoon, 1947 (1st musical to win Drama Critics' Award); Paint Your Wagon, 1951 (best score of year); My Fair Lady, 1956 (many awards); Gigi (film), 1958 (Oscar), (stage) 1974; Camelot, 1960; The Little Prince, 1975 (film). DMus *hc* Univ. of Redlands, Calif; Dr of Fine Arts *hc* Univ. of NYC. Kennedy Center Honors Award for Lifetime Achievement in the Arts, 1986. *Address:* c/o ASCAP, One Lincoln Plaza, New York, NY 10023, USA. *Clubs:* Players', Lambs (New York); Palm Springs Racquet.
                                    *Died* 14 *Feb.* 1988.

**LOEWEN, Gen. Sir Charles (Falkland),** GCB 1957 (KCB 1954; CB 1945); KBE 1951 (CBE 1944); DSO 1945; late RA; *b* 17 Sept. 1900; *s* of late Charles J. Loewen, MA, Vancouver, Canada, and Edith Loewen; *m* 1924, Kathleen, *d* of late Maj.-Gen. J. M. Ross; two *s. Educ:* Haileybury Coll.; Royal Military College, Kingston, Canada. 2nd Lt RFA 1918; Capt. 1931; Bt Major, 1937; Major, 1938; Bt Lt-Col 1939; Col 1942; Maj.-Gen. 1944; Lt-Gen. 1950; Gen. 1954. Served War of 1939–45, in Norway (despatches) and in Italy (despatches); comd: 1st Inf. Div., 1944–45; 6th Armd Div., 1946; 1st Armd Div., 1947; Northumb. Dist and 50th (Inf.) Div. (TA), 1948–49; GOC-in-C Anti-Aircraft Command, 1950–53; GOC-in-C, Western Command, April-Sept. 1953; C-in-C Far East Land Forces, 1953–56; Adjutant-Gen. to the Forces, 1956–59; ADC Gen. to the Queen, 1956–59. Col Comdt, RA, 1953–63. Hon. DSc Mil., Roy. Mil. Coll. Canada, 1966. Comdr Legion of Merit (US) 1945. *Recreations:* fishing, gardening. *Address:* Boyne Mills House, Mansfield, Ontario LON 1MO, Canada.
                                    *Died* 17 *Aug.* 1986.

**LOEWENSTEIN-WERTHEIM-FREUDENBERG,**                **Hubertus Friedrich, Prince of,** Dr iur, LittD (*hc*), DPhil (*hc*); Grand Cross with Star of German Order of Merit, 1982 (Commander's Cross, 1968); Special Advisor, German Government, Press and Information Office, 1960–71; Member of Parliament, 1953–57; *b* Schoenwoerth Castle, near Kufstein, Tirol, 14 Oct. 1906; *y s* of Prince Maximilian Loewenstein-Wertheim-Freudenberg and Constance, *y d* of 1st Baron Pirbright, PC; *m* 1929, Helga Maria Mathilde v. d. Schuylenburg; three *d. Educ:* Gymnasium at Gmunden and Klagenfurt, Austria; Universities at Munich, Hamburg, Geneva, and Berlin. Referendar Berlin Kammergericht, 1928, Doctor iuris utriusque, Hamburg, 1931; member of Catholic Centre Party, 1930; leader of Republican Students, and Republican Youth, Berlin, 1930; Prussian delegate to Munich, 1932; left Germany, 1933; returned 1946; Visiting Prof. of Hist. and Gov. to USA and Canada of the Carnegie Endowment for International Peace, 1937–46; Lecturer in History, University of Heidelberg, during 1947. Publisher and editor, Das Reich, Saarbrücken, 1934–35; Founder of American Guild for German Cultural Freedom, 1936; Founder and leader, German Action movement, 1949–. Southern German Editor, Die Zeit, 1952–53; Pres., Free German Authors' Assoc., 1973–. Hon. Mem., Exiles PEN Club, 1982. Hon. DLitt Hamline Univ., 1943; Hon. DPhil Ukrainian Free Univ., Munich, 1983. Grand Cross of Athos, 1966; Commendatore, Order of Merit (Italy), 1970; Saarland Order of Merit, 1980; GCSG, 1982. *Publications:* The Tragedy of a Nation, 1934; After Hitler's Fall, Germany's Coming Reich, 1934; A Catholic in Republican Spain, 1937; Conquest of the Past, autobiography (till 1933), 1938; On Borrowed Peace, autobiography (1933 to 1942), 1942; The Germans in History, 1945; The Child and the Emperor: a Legend, 1945; The Lance of Longinus, 1946; The Eagle and the Cross, 1947; Deutsche Geschichte, 1950, 8th rev. edn, 1983; Stresemann, biography, 1953; Die römischen Tagebücher des Dr von Molitor, 1956; (co-author Volkmar von Zuehlsdorff) Das deutsche Schicksal 1945–1957, 1957; (same co-author) NATO, The

Defence of the West, 1963; Towards The Further Shore (autobiography), 1968; Botschafter ohne Auftrag, 1972; Seneca: Kaiser ohne Purpur, 1975; Tiberius Imperator, 1977; Invitation to Capri, 1979; Rom, Reich ohne Ende, 1979; Trajanus, Optimus Princeps, 1981; Konstantin der Grosse, 1983; Abenteurer der Freiheit, 1983; contributions to (previous to 1933) Berliner Tageblatt, Vossische Zeitung, etc; (after 1933) Spectator, Nineteenth Century Review, Contemporary Review, American Mercury, Atlantic Monthly, New York Herald Tribune, Commonweal, American Scholar, Social Science, Die Tat, Die Zeit, Die Welt, etc. *Recreations:* swimming, riding. *Address:* c/o Mrs Milburne, Weeks Farm, Egerton, Kent; Lahnstrasse 50, 53 Bonn 2–Bad Godesberg, Federal Republic of Germany.
                                    *Died* 28 *Nov.* 1984.

**LOEWY, Raymond Fernand;** Grand Officer, French Legion of Honour, 1980; Industrial Designer; Founder: Raymond Loewy International Inc., consultant designers to US and foreign Corporations; Compagnie de l'Esthétique Industrielle, Paris; Raymond Loewy Co., Lausanne; Lecturer: Massachusetts Institute of Technology; Harvard Graduate School of Business Administration; Institute of Design Technology, Moscow; *b* Paris, 5 Nov. 1893; *s* of Maximillian Loewy and Marie Labalme; naturalized citizen of US 1938; *m* 1948, Viola Erickson; one *d. Educ:* Chaptal Coll., Paris; Paris Univ.; Ecole de Lanneau (grad. eng.). Art Director, Westinghouse Electric Co. 1929; started private organization of Industrial Design, 1929. Served as Capt. Corps of Engineers attached to Gen. Staff, 5th Army, France, 1914–18; Liaison Officer, AEF (Officer Legion of Honour, Croix de Guerre, with 4 citations; Interallied Medal). Hon. RDI 1937; FRSA 1942; Fellow (Past Pres.), American Soc. of Industrial Designers; Lectr, Coll. of Arch., University of Calif. American Design Award, 1938; Indust. Designers Soc. of America Award of Recognition, 1978; Special Award of Recognition, Internat. Cttee of ICSID, Helsinki, 1981. California Design Award, LA, 1979. Hon. Doctor of Fine Arts, University of Cincinnati, 1956; Dr, Calif Coll. of Design, LA. Member: Society of Automotive Engineers; Amer. Soc. Mech. Engrs; Adv. Board on Vocational Educn, Bd of Educn, NYC; Assoc. Mem. Soc. of Naval Arch. and Marine Engrs; Soc. of Space Medicine; Vice-Pres. French Chamber of Commerce of the US, 1958. Included in: Thousand Makers of Twentieth Century, Sunday Times, 1969; US Bicentennial List, 100 Events that shaped America 1776–1976, Smithsonian Institution, Washington. Fellow, Amer. Acad. of Achievement, 1970. Mem., President's Cttee on Employment of the Handicapped, 1965–; Habitability Consultant to NASA Apollo Saturn Application program, 1967–; Skylab and Space Shuttle Orbiter; Design Consultant to Soviet Union State Cttee for Science and Technology, 1973–. Exposition Raymond Loewy Designs, Smithsonian Institution, 1976. Citizen of Honour: France, 1954; New York City, 1966; Palm Springs; Chicago. Knight of Mark Twain. *Publications:* The Locomotive—its Esthetics, 1937; Never Leave Well Enough Alone (autobiography), 1951 (trans. various langs); RL Industrial Design Overlook (illustrated album, published in many countries); Industrial Design, 1980. *Address:* Loewy International Ltd, 117b Fulham Road, Chelsea, SW3 6RL; Fribourg, Switzerland; (home) 2800 Haverill Road North, West Palm Beach, Fla, USA; 20 rue Boissiere, Paris XVI, France; L'Annonciade, Monte Carlo, Monaco. *Club:* NY Athletic.                                    *Died* 14 *July* 1986.

**LOFTS, Norah, (Mrs Robert Jorisch);** *b* 27 Aug. 1904; *d* of Isaac Robinson and Ethel (*née* Garner); *m* 1st, 1931, Geoffrey Lofts (decd); one *s*; 2nd, 1949, Dr Robert Jorisch. *Educ:* West Suffolk County Sch. *Publications:* I Met a Gypsy, 1935; White Hell of Pity, 1937; Out of This Nettle, 1939; Road to Revelation, 1941; Jassy, 1944; Silver Nutmeg, 1947; Women of the Old Testament, 1949; A Calf for Venus, 1949; The Luteplayer, 1951; Bless This House, 1954; Queen in Waiting, 1955; Afternoon of An Autocrat, 1956; Scent of Cloves, 1958; Heaven In Your Hand, 1959; The Town House, 1959; The House at Old Vine, 1961; The House at Sunset, 1963; The Concubine, 1964; How Far to Bethlehem?, 1965; (with M. Weiner) Eternal France, 1969; The Lost Ones, 1969; The King's Pleasure, 1970; Lovers All Untrue, 1970; A Rose For Virtue, 1971; Charlotte, 1972; Nethergate, 1973; Crown of Aloes, 1974; Knights Acre, 1974; The Homecoming, 1975; The Lonely Furrow, 1976; Domestic Life in England, 1976; Queens of Britain, 1977; Gad's Hall, 1977; Haunted House, 1978; Emma Hamilton, 1978; Day of the Butterfly (Georgette Heyer Historical Novel Prize), 1979; Anne Boleyn, 1979; A Wayside Tavern, 1980; The Claw, 1981; *as Peter Curtis:* You're Best Alone, 1939; Dead March in Three Keys, 1940; Lady Living Alone, 1944; The Devil's Own, 1959; *posthumous publication:* Pargeters, 1984. *Address:* Northgate House, Bury St Edmunds, Suffolk. *T:* Bury St Edmunds 2680.
                                    *Died* 10 *Sept.* 1983.

**LOFTUS, Col Ernest Achey,** CBE 1975 (OBE (mil.) 1928); TD 1929; DL; MA, MLitt (TCD), BSc Econ. (London), LCP, FRGS, FRSA, MRST; Member RSL; a pedagogue for 74 years and retired 1975 as the oldest civil servant in the world (in Guinness Book of Records); in service of Zambian Government 1963–75; *b* 11 Jan. 1884; *s* of

Capt. William Loftus, Master Mariner, Kingston-upon-Hull; *m* 1916, Elsie (*d* 1979), *er d* of Allen Charles Cole, West Tilbury, Essex; two *s*. *Educ*: Archbishop Holgate's Gram. Sch., York; Trinity Coll., Dublin. Senior Geography Master, Palmer's Sch., Grays, Essex, 1906–19; Head of Junior Sch., Southend on Sea High Sch. for Boys, 1919–20; Asst Dir of Educn, Southend-on-Sea, 1920–22; Headmaster, Barking Abbey Sch., 1922–49; a select speaker, Conf. of World Educn Assocs, Oxford, 1935; coined term 'Health Science' and drew up first syllabus of work (London Univ.) in that subject, 1937; an Educn Officer in Kenya, 1953–60, in Nyasaland, 1960–63, in Zambia, 1963–75. Formed two Cadet Corps and raised four Territl Units in Co. Essex; served with The Essex Regt 1910–29; European War in Gallipoli 1915, Egypt 1916, France 1918; Staff Officer for Educn 67th Div., Independent Force and Kent Force, 1917; Comdr, first draft of troops (1500 miners) to be demobilised, Dec. 1918; commanded (as Major) 300 troops, Purfleet Garrison, to prevent sabotage on ships in the river or Tilbury Docks and the oil tanks at Purfleet, during the dock strike, 1921; a pioneer officer in what became RAEC; Lt-Col Commanding 6th Essex Regt, 1925–29; Mem. Essex Territorial Army Association 1925–29; Brevet Col, 1929; served in War of 1939—Pioneer Corps, 1939–42, commanding No 13 (Italian) Group in France and No 31 Group in London, etc.; Founder Hon. Sec. Essex County Playing Fields Association, 1925–29; Hon. Organiser or Sec. various Appeals, in Essex. Mem. Standing Cttee Convocation, London Univ., 1944–53, and Bedell of Convocation, 1946–53. A Chm. Nat. Assistance Board, 1949–53; Mem. Exec. Cttee Essex Playing Fields Assoc., 1925–53 (awarded PFA certificate signed by Prince Philip, 1987); Mem. Thurrock UDC 1946–53, Vice-Chm. 1951–52; Controller, Civil Defence, Thurrock area, 1951–53. Former Pres. and Founder Pres., London Br., 1947–49, Archbishop Holgate's Grammar Sch. Old Boys' Assoc. Freeman, City of Kingston-upon-Hull, 1968. For some years a Governor, The Strand Sch. (Brixton), Palmer's Sch. (Grays), etc. A Selborne Lectr. DL Essex 1929–75, now inactive. Mason, 1915–; Rotarian (Pres., Barking, 1935), 1930–. *Publications*: Education and the Citizen; History of a Branch of the Cole Family; Growls and Grumbles; A History of Barking Abbey (with H. F. Chettle); A Visual History of Africa, 1953, 16 reprints, 2nd edn 1974; A Visual History of East Africa; and brochures for the East African Literature Bureau. Contributor of feature articles in London Daily and Weekly Press, etc. on Education; author of 8 scenes of Barking Pageant, 1931, and of Elizabethan scene in Ilford Pageant of Essex, 1932. *Recreations*: historical and genealogical research. *Address*: 149 Enterprise Road, Harare, Zimbabwe. *Club*: Royal Commonwealth Society. *Died 7 July* 1987.

**LOGAN, Sir Douglas (William),** Kt 1959; DPhil, MA, BCL; Principal of the University of London, 1948–75; President, British Universities Sports Board and Federation, 1953–75; Chairman: British Student Sports Federation, 1971–77; Universities Superannuation Scheme Ltd, 1974–77 (Deputy Chairman, 1977–80; Consultant, 1980–86); *b* Liverpool, 27 March 1910; *yr s* of Robert Logan and Euphemia Taylor Stevenson, Edinburgh; *m* 1st, 1940, Vaire Olive Wollaston (from whom he obtained a divorce); two *s*; 2nd, 1947, Christine Peggy Walker; one *s* one *d*. *Educ*: Liverpool Collegiate Sch.; University Coll., Oxford (Open Classical Scholar). First Classes: Hon. Mods 1930, Lit. Hum. 1932, Jurisprudence, 1933; Oxford Univ. Senior Studentship, 1933; Harmsworth Scholar, Middle Temple, 1933 (Hon. Bencher, 1965); Henry Fellowship Harvard Law Sch., 1935–36; Asst Lecturer, LSE, 1936–37; Barstow Scholarship, 1937; called to Bar, Middle Temple, 1937; Fellow of Trinity Coll., Cambridge, 1937–43; Principal, Ministry of Supply, 1940–44; Clerk of the Court, University of London, 1944–47. Rede Lecturer, 1963. Fellow: Wye Coll., 1970; Imperial Coll., 1974; School of Pharmacy, 1975. Vice-Chm., Association of Commonwealth Univs, 1961–67 (Chm. 1962–63; Hon. Treasurer, 1967–74; Dep. Hon. Treasurer, 1974–84); Vice-Chm., Athlone Fellowship Cttee, 1959–71; Member: Commonwealth Scholarships Commn, 1960–86 (Dep. Chm., 1970–86); Marshall Scholarships Commn, 1961–67; Nat. Theatre Bd, 1962–68; a Governor, Old Vic, 1957–80 (Vice-Chm., 1972–80), and Bristol Old Vic; a Trustee, City Parochial Foundation, 1953–67; Member: Anderson Cttee on Grants to Students, 1958–60; Hale Cttee on Superannuation of Univ. Teachers, 1958–60; Northumberland Cttee on Recruitment to the Veterinary Profession, 1962–64; Maddex Working Party on the Superannuation of Univ. Teachers, 1965–68. Mem. British Delegation to 1st, 2nd, 3rd, and 4th Commonwealth Educn Confs, Oxford, 1959, Delhi, 1962, Ottawa, 1964, and Lagos, 1968; Commonwealth Medical Conf. Edinburgh, 1965. Hon. Mem., Pharmaceutical Soc. Hon. Fellow: LSE, 1962; University Coll., Oxford, 1973; University Coll. London, 1975. Hon. DCL Western Ontario; Hon. DLitt Rhodesia; Hon. LLD: Melbourne, Madras, British Columbia, Hong Kong, Liverpool, McGill, CNAA, London; Hon. FDSRCS; Hon. FRIBA. Chevalier de l'Ordre de la Légion d'Honneur. *Publications*: The Birth of a Pension Scheme—a history of the universities superannuation scheme, 1985; annual reports of the Principal of the University of London, 1948–73. *Address*: Restalrig, Mountain Street, Chilham, Canterbury, Kent CT4 8DQ.

*T*: Canterbury 730640. *Club*: Athenæum.
*Died 19 Oct*. 1987.

**LOGAN, Lt-Col John,** TD 1945; Vice-Lieutenant, Stirlingshire, 1965–79; *b* 25 May 1907; *s* of Crawford William Logan and Ada Kathleen Logan (*née* Kidston); *m* 1937, Rosaleen Muriel O'Hara (*d* 1967); one *s* one *d*. *Educ*: Eton Coll., Windsor. British American Tobacco Co. Ltd (China), 1928–32; Imperial Tobacco Co. (of Great Britain and Ireland) Ltd, 1932–39. POW in Germany, 1940–45 (Captain, 7th Argyll and Sutherland Hldrs; C O, 1949–50). Imperial Tobacco Co. (of Great Britain and Ireland) Ltd, 1946–67. DL Stirlingshire, 1956. Hon. MA Stirling, 1983. *Publication*: China Old and New, 1981. *Recreation*: fishing. *Address*: Wester Craigend, Stirling FK7 9PX. *T*: Stirling 75025. *Died 2 Jan*. 1987.

**LOGAN, Thomas Moffat,** CBE 1963; retired as Under-Secretary, National Assistance Board, 1966; *b* 21 June 1904; *s* of late John Logan, builder and contractor, Carluke, Lanarkshire; *m* 1947, Freda Evelyn Andrew; no *c*. *Educ*: Hamilton Academy. Carluke Parish Council 1922; Relieving Officer, Lanark County Council, 1929; National Assistance Board: Area Officer, 1934; Asst Principal, 1942, Principal, 1945; Asst Sec., (Head of Organization and Methods), 1955; Under-Sec., 1964. *Recreations*: gardening, do-it-yourself, dancing. *Address*: Wayside, 52 Seafield Road, Bournemouth BH6 3JF. *T*: Bournemouth 429931.
*Died 14 Jan*. 1981.

**LOGSDON, Geoffrey Edward,** CBE 1962; TD 1950; Clerk to Worshipful Company of Mercers, 1952–74; *b* 24 July 1914; *o s* of late Edward Charles Logsdon; *m* 1st, 1943, Marie Carolinne Dumas (*d* 1957); one *s* one *d*; 2nd, 1958, Barbara Joyce Bird. *Educ*: City of London Sch. Admitted Solicitor, 1937; Legal Asst, Mercers' Company, 1945–52; Commissioned RA (TA), 1938. Served War of 1939–45: Malta, Middle East and UK. Lt-Col Comd 458 (M) HAA Regt (Kent) RA, TA, 1949–52. Formerly Clerk to: Jt Grand Gresham Cttee; The City and Metropolitan Welfare Charity; Mem. City of London Savings Cttee; Chm., Governors, Nat. Corp. for Care of Old People, 1973–78; Governor, Dauntsey's School, 1974–. FRSA 1972. *Address*: Sandford Way, Pound Lane, Burley, Ringwood, Hants BH24 4EF. *T*: Burley 3335.
*Died 11 July* 1982.

**LOMAX, Sir John Garnett,** KBE 1953 (MBE 1928); CMG 1944; MC 1917; HM Diplomatic Service, retired; *b* Liverpool, 27 Aug. 1896; *s* of Rev. Canon Edward Lomax and Bessie Garnett; *m* 1922, Feridah Yvette Krajewski; two *s*. *Educ*: Liverpool Coll.; Liverpool Univ. Served European War, France, Belgium, India, and Egypt; Driver, RFA (West Lancs), 1915, Lt 1916. HM Vice-Consul, New Orleans, 1920, Chicago, 1921; Vice-Consul and 2nd Sec. HM Legation, Bogota, 1926–30; 2nd Commercial Sec. HM Embassy, Rio de Janeiro, 1930; transferred to HM Embassy, Rome, 1935; HM Commercial Agent, Jerusalem, 1938; Commercial Counsellor, HM Embassy, Madrid, 1940; HM Legation, Berne, 1941; Commercial Counsellor at Angora, 1943; Minister (commercial), British Embassy, Buenos Aires, 1946–49; Ambassador to Bolivia, 1949–56. *Publication*: The Diplomatic Smuggler, 1965. *Address*: Tanterfyn, Llaneilian, Anglesey, Gwynedd; 803 Nelson House, Dolphin Square, SW1. *Clubs*: Reform, Royal Automobile.
*Died 23 Dec*. 1987.

**LOMBARD KNIGHT, Eric John Percy Crawford;** Director: Kellock Factors Ltd; Sterling Credit Ltd; Kellock Holdings Ltd; *b* 17 Aug. 1907; *yr s* of late Herbert John Charles and Mary Henrietta Knight; *m* 1933, Peggy Julia (*née* Carter); one *s* one *d*. *Educ*: Ashford Grammar Sch. Served War of 1939–45, RAF. British Mercedes Benz; Bowmaker Ltd; established Lombard Banking, 1947. *Address*: The White House, 18 Limpsfield Road, Sanderstead Village, Surrey. *T*: 01–657 2021. *Died 23 April* 1987.

**LONG, (Adrian) Douglas;** Co-Founder and Chairman, Sunday Newspaper Publishing PLC, since 1988; *b* London, 9 Feb. 1925; *s* of late Harold Edgar Long and Kate Long; *m* 1949, Vera Barbara Wellstead; one *s*. *Educ*: Wandsworth Sch. MBIM. Served Indian Army, 1943–47: Royal Deccan Horse, 43rd Cavalry, Probyns Horse (Captain). Reporter/Feature Writer: Daily Graphic, 1947; Daily Record, Glasgow, 1948–54; Scottish Editor, Daily Herald, 1955–57; Chief News Editor/Features Editor, Daily Herald and Sun newspapers, 1958–68; Gen. Man., Odhams, 1969–71; Mirror Group Newspapers Ltd: Dep. Man. Dir/Dep. Chief Exec., 1972–79; Chief Exec., 1980–84; Group Chief Exec., 1984; Vice Chm., 1984. Chairman: Syndication Internat., 1975–84; Mirrorair Ltd, 1980–84; Director: Odhams Newspapers Ltd, 1976–84; Mirror M&G Management Ltd, 1976–84; Scottish Daily Record & Sunday Mail, 1977–84; Reed Publishing Pension Trustees Ltd, 1980–84; Reed Publishing Holdings Ltd, 1981–85; Mirror Gp Pension Trustees Ltd, 1981–84; Co-Founder and Man. Dir, Newspaper Publishing PLC (The Independent), 1986. Consultant, Surrey Business Enterprise Ltd, 1985–. Mem., Press Council, 1986–89. Member: President's Assoc.; Amer. Management Assoc.; Inst. of Dirs. FRSA 1987. *Recreations*: theatre, cinema, tennis, swimming. *Address*: 3

Garbrand Walk, Ewell Village, Surrey KT17 1UQ. *Clubs:* Royal Automobile, Sandown Park; Presscala; Cuddington Golf.
*Died 7 Feb.* 1990.

**LONG, Ernest,** CBE 1962; Member of Central Electricity Generating Board and of Electricity Council, 1957–62; *b* 15 Aug. 1898; *er s* of late John H. Long, Carlisle; *m* 1st, 1923, Dorothy Phœbe (*d* 1973), *y d* of late John Nichol, Carlisle; one *s*; 2nd, 1975, Cicely, *widow* of A. G. Buck. *Educ:* Carlisle Grammar Sch. Town Clerk's Dept and City Treasurer's Dept, Carlisle Corporation, 1915–25; articled to City Treasurer, Carlisle. Served RFC and RAF, 1917–19. Chief Audit Asst, Croydon Corporation, 1928–30; Dep. City Treasurer, Coventry, 1930–35; Borough Treasurer: Luton, 1935–36, Finchley, 1936–42; City Treasurer, Newcastle upon Tyne, 1942–44; Secretary, Institute of Municipal Treasurers and Accountants, 1944–48 (Hon. Fellow, and Collins Gold Medallist, 1927); Dep. Chief Accountant, British Electricity Authority, 1948–51; Secretary, British (later Central) Electricity Authority, 1951–57. Fellow, Member of Council (1947–75), President 1960, Inst. of Chartered Secretaries and Administrators (formerly Chartered Inst. of Secretaries). Member: Colonial Local Government Advisory Panel, 1948–53; Departmental Cttee on Legal Aid in Criminal Proceedings, 1964–66; Chartered Accountant (Society Gold Medallist, 1924). *Publications:* various articles and lectures on accountancy and public administration. *Recreations:* golf, crosswords. *Address:* 2 Strawberry Bank, Scotby, Carlisle, Cumbria CA4 8BP. *T:* Scotby 267. *Club:* Border (Carlisle). *Died 12 Oct.* 1982.

**LONG, Air Vice-Marshal Francis William,** CB 1946; DL; *b* 10 Oct. 1899; *s* of Rev. F. P. Long, Oxford; *m* 1921, Doreen Langley, *d* of Rev. F. L. Appleford; one *d*. *Educ:* Lancing Coll. Joined RAF 1918; member Schneider Trophy Team, 1931. AOC No. 23 Gp, Flying Training Command, 1952–53; retd, 1953. DL Herts, 1963. *Address:* 2 Cranford Court, Cranford Avenue, Exmouth, Devon. *T:* Exmouth 6320. *Died 25 March* 1983.

**LONG, Sir Ronald,** Kt 1964; Solicitor; *b* 5 Sept. 1902; *s* of Sydney Richard and Kate Long; *m* 1931, Muriel Annie Harper; one *s* two *d*. *Educ:* Earls Colne Grammar Sch.; The School, Stamford, Lincs. President, The Law Society, 1963–64. Chm., Stansted Airport Consultative Cttee, 1969–79. *Recreations:* fishing, gardening. *Address:* Ayletts Farm, Halstead, Essex CO9 1QA. *T:* Halstead 472072. *Died 4 Oct.* 1987.

**LONGBOTHAM, Samuel;** Lord-Lieutenant of the Western Isles, 1975–83; *b* Elgin, Morayshire, 19 March 1908; *s* of George Longbotham and Elizabeth Longbotham (*née* Monks); *m* 1941, Elizabeth Rae, *d* of Donald Davidson, Glasgow; two *s* one *d*. *Educ:* Elgin. Served War, 1940–46: with RA and Intelligence Corps: commissioned, 1944. Major, Lovat Scouts TA (RA), 1952–60; Major, North Highland ACF, 1968–75. DL Ross and Cromarty, 1964. *Recreations:* angling, walking, reading, family life. *Address:* 25 Lewis Street, Stornoway, Isle of Lewis, Scotland. *T:* Stornoway 2519. *Died 22 Nov.* 1988.

**LONGDEN, Maj.-Gen. Harry Leicester,** CB 1947; CBE 1944 (OBE 1940); late The Dorsetshire Regt; psc; *b* 12 Dec. 1900. 2nd Lieut Dorset Regt, 1919; Major, 1938. Served War of 1939–45, France and North-West Europe (despatches, OBE, CBE, CB). Temp. Maj.-Gen., 1946; retired pay, 1948. *Died 13 Dec.* 1981.

**LONGE, Desmond Evelyn,** MC 1944; DL; President, later Chairman, Norwich Union Insurance Group, 1964–81; (Vice-President, 1963); Chairman: Norwich Union Life Insurance Society, 1964–81; Norwich Union Fire Insurance Society Ltd, 1964–81; Maritime Insurance Co. Ltd, 1964–81; Scottish Union and National Insurance Co., 1964–81; East Coast Grain Ltd, 1962–82; Napak Ltd, 1962–82; President, D. E. Longe & Co. 1982 (Chairman, 1962–82); *b* 8 Aug. 1914; *y s* of late Rev. John Charles Longe, MA, Spixworth Park, Norfolk; *m* 1944, Isla (*née* Bell); one *s* one *d*. *Educ:* Woodbridge Sch., Suffolk. Director: Eastern Counties Group Ltd, to 1982; Eastern Counties Newspapers Ltd, 1977–82; Norwich Winterthur Holdings Ltd, 1977–81; Anglia TV Ltd, 1970–82. Member: BR Eastern Region Bd, 1969–70; BR London Midland Region Bd, 1971–74; (and Dep. Chm.) BR London and SE Region Bd, 1975–77; BR Property Bd, 1978–82. Mem., E Anglia Econ. Planning Council, 1965–68. A Church Commissioner, 1970–76. Chm., Royal Norfolk Agric. Assoc. (Pres., 1980). DL Norfolk, 1971; High Sheriff, Norfolk, 1975. Croix de Guerre avec Palme (French), 1944. *Recreations:* travel, hunting, fishing. *Address:* The White House, Upper Olland Street, Bungay, Suffolk. *Clubs:* Special Forces, MCC; Norfolk County (Norwich). *Died 19 Feb.* 1990.

**LONGLAND, Sir David (Walter),** Kt 1977; CMG 1973; Parliamentary Commissioner for Administrative Investigations, Queensland, 1974–79; *b* 1 June 1909; 2nd *s* of David Longland and Mary McGriskin; *m* 1935, Ada Elizabeth Bowness (*d* 1977); one *s* one *d*. *Educ:* Queensland Govt Primary and Secondary Schs. Queensland Educn Dept, High Sch. teaching, 1926. Appointed: to State Treasury Dept, 1938; Premier's Dept, 1939; (re-apptd) Treasury Dept, 1940;

(re-apptd) Premier's Dept, 1942; Officer in Charge of Migration for Qld, 1946; Under-Sec., Dept of Works and Housing, 1957; Chm., Public Service Bd, Qld, 1969. Member: Australian Cerebral Palsy Assoc. (Nat. Pres., 1967–68); Queensland Spastic Welfare League, 1958– (Pres., 1962–); Exec. Dir, Queensland Art Gallery Foundn. FASA, FAIM, FRIPA. Hon. LLD Queensland Univ., 1987. Paul Harris Fellow, Rotary Foundn of Rotary Internat., 1987. *Recreations:* tennis, surfing, reading, gardening. *Address:* Elimbari, Unit 1, 39 Wambool Street, Bulimba Heights, Qld 4171, Australia. *T:* 399–8998. *Club:* Rotary (Brisbane). *Died 17 July* 1988.

**LONGLEY-COOK, Vice-Adm. Eric William,** CB 1950; CBE 1943; DSO 1945; *b* 6 Oct. 1898; *s* of late Herbert William Cook and Alice Longley; *m* 1st, 1920, Helga Mayre Lowles (*d* 1962); one *d*; 2nd, 1965, Elizabeth (*d* 1978), *widow* of Sir Ulick Temple Blake, 16th Baronet. *Educ:* Osborne and Dartmouth. Served at sea European War, 1914–18 (Dardanelles, 1915) and War of 1939–45 (Murmansk, N Africa, Sicily, Salerno, Aegean, E Indies, Okinawa; despatches thrice). Rear-Adm., 1948; Vice-Adm., 1951; Dir of Naval Intelligence, 1948–51; retired, 1951. Formerly: Man. Dir, Fairfield Shipbuilding & Engineering Co., London; Dir, Lithgow Group; Member: Cttee, Lloyd's Register; Amer. Bureau of Ships; a Gen. Comr of Income Tax. Pres., Gallipoli Assoc., 1981 (Vice-Pres., 1975). Légion d'Honneur and Croix de Guerre, 1943. *Address:* Cordwainers, Titchfield, Hants. *Club:* Naval and Military.
*Died 20 April* 1983.

**LONGMORE, William James Maitland,** CBE 1972; Director: Lloyds Bank International Ltd, 1971–75; Bank of London & South America Ltd, 1960–75; *b* 6 May 1919; 2nd *s* of late Air Chief Marshal Sir Arthur Murray Longmore, GCB, DSO; *m* 1941, Jean, *d* of 2nd Baron Forres of Glenogil; three *d*. *Educ:* Eton Coll. Royal Air Force, 1938–46 (Wing Comdr). Balfour, Williamson & Co. Ltd, 1946–75 (Chm., 1967–75). Vice-Chm., 1966–70, Chm., 1970–71, BNEC for Latin America. *Recreations:* shooting, sailing. *Address:* Strete End House, Bishop's Waltham, Hants SO3 1FS. *T:* Bishop's Waltham 2794. *Club:* Royal Yacht Squadron.
*Died 25 Sept.* 1988.

**LOPOKOVA, Lydia;** *see* Keynes, Lady.

**LORAINE, Dr John Alexander,** FRCPEd; FRSE 1978; Senior Lecturer, Department of Community Medicine, University of Edinburgh, since 1979; *b* 14 May 1924; *s* of Lachlan Dempster Loraine and Ruth (*née* Jack); *m* 1974, Alison Blair. *Educ:* George Watson's Boys' Coll., Edinburgh; Univ. of Edinburgh. MB ChB (Hons) 1946, PhD 1949, DSc 1959; FRCPEd 1960; CBiol, FIBiol 1988. House Phys., Royal Infirmary, Edinburgh, under Prof. Sir Stanley Davidson, 1947; Mem., Scientific Staff, MRC Clinical Endocrinology Unit, Edinburgh, 1947–61; Dir of the Unit, 1961–72. Visiting Prof. of Endocrinology, Donner Laboratory and Donner Pavilion, Univ. of Calif., Berkeley, USA, 1964. Hon. Senior Lectr, Dept of Pharmacology, Univ. of Edinburgh, 1965–72; MRC Ext. Sci. Staff, 1972–79; Dir, Centre for Human Ecology, 1978–84. Founder Chm., Doctors and Overpopulation Gp, 1972–; Vice-Chm., Conservation Soc., 1974–87. Member: Internat. Union for Scientific Study of Population, 1977–83; Internat. Epidemiological Assoc., 1985–. FRSA. *Publications:* (co-author) Hormone Assays and their Clinical Application, 1958, (co-editor) 4th edn 1976; (co-author) Recent Research on Gonadotrophic Hormones, 1967; (co-author) Fertility and Contraception in the Human Female, 1968; Sex and the Population Crisis, 1970; The Death of Tomorrow, 1972; (ed) Reproductive Endocrinology and World Population, 1973; (ed) Environmental Medicine, 1973; (ed) Understanding Homosexuality: its biological and psychological bases, 1974; Syndromes of the 'Seventies, 1977; (ed) Here Today: world outlooks from the Centre for Human Ecology, 1979; Global Signposts to the 21st Century, 1979; (ed) Environmental Medicine, 2nd edn, 1980; Energy Policies Around the World, 1982; author and co-author of numerous scientific and general pubns dealing with sex hormones, fertility, contraception, population and related issues, incl. women's rights, mineral resources, nuclear proliferation and environmental medicine. *Recreations:* reading modern history and political biography, music, bridge. *Address:* 20 Buckingham Terrace, Edinburgh EH4 3AD. *T:* 031–332 3698. *Club:* University of Edinburgh Staff. *Died 14 Nov.* 1988.

**LORD, Sir Ackland (Archibald),** Kt 1971; OBE 1970; Director of companies, Australia; Founder and Donor of A. A. Lord Homes for the Aged Inc., Hobart, Tasmania; Past Chairman (Founder): (A.A.) Lords Ltd, Wholesale Hardware and Steel Merchants, 1949–59 (Director to 1969); Lords Holdings Ltd, 1952–59 (Director, 1959–69); Director: Melbourne Builders Lime & Cement Co.; Big Ben Scaffolds Pty Ltd; U-Hire Pty Ltd; Melcann Holdings Ltd; *b* 11 June 1901; *s* of late J. Lord, Tasmania; *m* Ethel Dalton, MBE, *d* of late C. Dalton, Hobart. *Educ:* St Virgil's Coll., Hobart. Has given distinguished services to the community in Victoria and Tasmania. Past Chm. Galvanised Iron Merchants Assoc.; Council Mem., Ryder Cheshire Foundn (Vic.) for Internat. Centre, Dehra Dun,

India; Past Member: Trotting Control Bd; Melbourne & Metropolitan Trotting Assoc. (Chm.); Life Governor: various Melb. Hosps; Royal Victoria Inst. for the Blind, etc. *Address:* Lawrenny, 3 Teringa Place, Toorak, Victoria 3142, Australia. *T:* 24-5283. *Clubs:* Hardware (Melbourne); Victoria Racing; Moonee Valley Racing. *Died June 1982.*

**LORD, Cyril,** LLD (Hon.); Chairman and Managing Director, Cyril Lord Ltd, 1945–68; Director, numerous Companies in Great Britain, Northern Ireland, and South Africa, 1945–68; *b* 12 July 1911; *m* 1st, 1936, Bessie Greenwood (marr. diss. 1959); two *s* two *d*; 2nd, 1960, Shirley Stringer (marr. diss. 1972); 3rd, 1974, Aileen Parnell, *widow* of Val Parnell. *Educ:* Central Sch., Manchester; Manchester Coll. of Technology (Associate), and University. Dir of Hodkin & Lord Ltd, 1939; Technical Adviser to the Cotton Board, England, 1941. Hon. LLD Florida Southern Coll., 1951. *Recreations:* yachting, tennis. *Clubs:* Royal Automobile, Naval and Military; Royal Corinthian (Cowes); Ballyholme Yacht (N Ire.). *Died 29 May 1984.*

**LORD, Maj.-Gen. Wilfrid Austin,** CB 1954; CBE 1952; MEng, CEng; FIMechE; FIEE; REME, retired; *b* 20 Sept. 1902; *s* of late S. Lord, Rochdale and Liverpool; *m* 1937, Mabel (*d* 1973), *d* of late T. Lamb, York and Carlisle; one *s*. *Educ:* Birkenhead Institute; Liverpool Univ. Formerly RAOC, Lt 1927; Capt. 1933; Major 1935; Local Lt-Col 1940, Col 1947; Temp. Brig. 1949; Temp. Maj.-Gen. 1950; Maj.-Gen. 1950; Dir Mechanical Engineers, GHQ, ME Land Forces, 1950–53; Dir, Mechanical Engineering, War Office, 1954–57; retired, 1957. Col Comdt REME, 1957–63. *Address:* c/o Williams & Glyn's Bank Ltd, Lawrie House, Victoria Road, Farnborough, Hants. *Died 10 Jan. 1982.*

**LORENZ, Dr Konrad Zacharias,** MD, DPhil; Director, Research Station for Ethology, Konrad-Lorenz-Institute, Austrian Academy of Sciences, since 1982; *b* 7 Nov. 1903; *s* of Prof. Dr Adolf Lorenz and Emma Lorenz (*née* Lecher); *m* 1927, Dr Margarethe Lorenz (*née* Gebhardt); one *s* two *d*. *Educ:* High Sch., Vienna; Columbia Univ., New York; Univ. of Vienna. Univ. Asst at Anatomical Inst. of University of Vienna (Prof. Hochstetter), 1928–35; Lectr in Comparative Anat. and Animal Psychol., University of Vienna, 1937–40; University Lectr, Vienna, 1940; Prof. of Psychol. and Head of Dept, University of Königsberg, 1940; Head of Research Station for Physiology of Behaviour of the Max-Planck-Inst. for Marine Biol., 1951; Co-Director, Max-Planck-Inst. for Physiology of Behaviour, 1956–73; Dir, Dept for Animal Sociology, Inst. for Comparative Ethology, Austrian Acad. of Scis, 1973–82. Hon. Prof., University of Münster, 1953 and München, 1957. Nobel Prize for Physiology or Medicine (jtly), 1973. Mem., Pour le Mérite for Arts and Science; Hon. Member: Assoc. for Study of Animal Behaviour, 1950; Amer. Ornithol. Union, 1951, etc; For. Mem., Royal Society, 1964. For. Assoc. Nat. Acad. of Sciences, USA, 1966. Hon. degrees: Leeds, 1962; Basel, 1966; Yale, 1967; Oxford, 1968; Chicago, 1970; Durham, 1972; Birmingham, 1974; Vienna, 1980. Gold Medal, Zoological Soc., New York, 1955; City Prize, Vienna, 1959; Gold Boelsche Medal, 1962; Austrian Distinction for Science and Art, 1964; Prix Mondial, Cino del Duca, 1969. Grosses Verdienstkreuz, 1974; Bayerischer Verdienstorden, 1974. *Publications:* King Solomon's Ring, 1952; Man Meets Dog, 1954; Evolution and Modification of Behaviour, 1965; On Aggression, 1966; Studies in Animal and Human Behaviour, 1970; (jtly) Man and Animal, 1972; Civilized Man's Eight Deadly Sins, 1974; Behind the Mirror, 1977; The Year of the Greylag Goose, 1979; The Foundations of Ethology, 1983; The Waning of Humaneness, 1987; articles in Tierpsychologie, Behaviour, etc. *Address:* Adolf-Lorenzgasse 2, A-3422 Altenberg, Austria. *Died 27 Feb. 1989.*

**LORING, James Adrian,** CBE 1979; *b* 22 Nov. 1918; *s* of Francis and Ellen Elizabeth Loring; *m* 1971, Anita Susan (*née* Hunt), JP; one *s* (and one *s* two *d* by previous marr.). *Educ:* Central Foundation Sch., London; London Univ. DipEcon; ACIS. Served War, Royal Air Force, 1940–46; CO No 200 Staging Post, Shanghai, 1946. Secretary, Culpeper House Gp of Companies, 1947–49; John Lewis Partnership, 1949–60: Central Merchandise Advisor Advisor (Food), 1949–55; Gen. Manager, Waitrose Gp, 1955–57; Mem., Central Management (specialising in financial matters), 1958–60. Asst Director, Services to Spastics, Spastics Soc., 1960–67; Director, 1967–80; Dir, Camphill Village Trust, 1981. Pres., Internat. Cerebral Palsy Soc., 1978–84. Vice-Chm., Centre on Environment for the Handicapped, 1976–86 (Hon. Life Mem.); Member: Mental Health Film Council, 1964–86; British Cttee of Rehabilitation Internat., 1980–86. *Publications:* ed, Learning Problems of the Cerebral Palsied, 1964; ed, Teaching the Cerebral Palsied Child, 1965; ed, The Spastic School Child and the Outside World, 1966; ed, The Subnormal Child, 1968; ed, Assessment of the Cerebral Palsied Child for Education, 1968. *Recreation:* country life. *Address:* 19 St Mary's Grove, Chiswick, W4 3LL. *T:* 081–995 5721. *Died 18 May 1990.*

**LOSEY, Joseph;** film director; *b* 14 Jan. 1909; *s* of Joseph Walton Losey and Ina Higbee; *m* ; two *s*. *Educ:* Dartmouth Coll., New Hampshire; Harvard Univ. Writer, producer and editor, radio and documentaries, 1936–43. Resident in England, 1953–74. Directed first Broadway play, 1932; subseq. productions include: (with Charles Laughton) Galileo Galilei, by Bertholt Brecht, NY and Hollywood, 1947; (with Wilfrid Lawson) The Wooden Dish, London, 1954; Boris Godunov, Paris Opera, 1980. Films include: The Boy with Green Hair, 1948; The Dividing Line; The Prowler, 1950; Time Without Pity; Blind Date, 1959; The Criminal, 1960; The Damned, 1960; Eva, 1961; The Servant, 1963; King and Country, 1964; Modesty Blaise, 1965; Accident, 1966; Boom, 1967; Secret Ceremony, 1968; Figures in a Landscape, 1969; The Go-Between (Golden Palm, Cannes Film Festival, 1971), 1970; The Assassination of Trotsky, 1971; A Doll's House, 1973; Galileo, 1974; The Romantic Englishwoman, 1974; Mr Klein, 1976; Les Routes du Sud, 1978; Don Giovanni, 1978; La Truite, 1982; Steaming, 1984. Pres., Cannes Film Festival Jury, 1972. Guest Prof., 1970 and 1975, DLitHum, 1973, Dartmouth Coll., NH; Hon. DLitHum Wisconsin-Madison Univ., 1983. Chevalier de l'Ordre des Arts et des Lettres, 1957. *Recreation:* work. *Address:* c/o Theo Cowan, 45 Poland Street, W1. *Died 22 June 1984.*

**LOSS, Joshua Alexander, (Joe Loss),** LVO 1984; OBE 1978; bandleader; *b* 22 June 1909; *s* of Israel and Ada Loss; *m* 1938, Mildred Blanch Rose; one *s* one *d*. *Educ:* Jewish Free Sch., Spitalfields; Trinity Coll. of Music; London Coll. of Music. Played as silent film accompanist, Coliseum, Ilford and at Tower Ballroom, Blackpool, 1926; formed own orchestra at Astoria Ballroom, Charing Cross Road, 1930; first broadcast, 1934, then broadcast every week; was one of first West End bands to play in provinces in ballrooms and to top bill in variety theatres; toured through war inc. overseas; joined Mecca, 1959; became resident at Hammersmith Palais. Joined Regal Zonophone record co.; hit record, 1936, with Begin the Beguine (gold disc for sales of a million over 25 years); is now joint longest serving artiste on EMI label, has 50-year contract. First record with EMI I Only Have Eyes For You; hit singles inc. Wheels Cha Cha, The Maigret Theme, The Steptoe Theme; gold discs for long-playing albums inc. Joe Loss Plays Glenn Miller and All Time Party Hits. *Television:* Come Dancing, Bid for Fame, Home Town Saturday Night, and Holiday Parade; was featured in This Is Your Life, 1963 and 1980. Awards: 15 Carl Alan Awards; Musical Express Top Big Band Award, 1963, 1964; Weekend Magazine Top Musical Personality Award, 1964; and Music Publishers' Assoc. Award as outstanding personality of 1976. First dance orch. in western world to appear in China, at Dairen, 1979. Has played for dancing on QE2 world cruises, at Buckingham Palace and Windsor Castle for past 30 years, and at pre-wedding balls for Princess Margaret, Princess Alexandra and Princess Anne, for Queen's 50th birthday celebrations and for Queen Mother's 80th birthday; Royal Variety Performance, 1980; 60th anniversary year as bandleader, 1990. Queen's Silver Jubilee Medal, 1978. Freeman, City of London, 1979; Liveryman, Musicians' Co., 1983. *Recreations:* motoring, watching television, collecting watches. *Address:* 89 North Gate, Prince Albert Road, NW8 7EJ. *Clubs:* St James's, Middlesex County Cricket (Life Member). *Died 6 June 1990.*

**LOTH, David;** editor and author; *b* St Louis, Missouri, 7 Dec. 1899; *s* of Albert Loth and Fanny Sunshine. *Educ:* University of Missouri. Staff of New York World, 1920–30; Editor and Publisher The Majorca Sun, 1931–34; Staff, NY Times, 1934–41; US Govt Information Services, 1941–45; Information Dir, Planned Parenthood Federation of America, 1946–51; Acting Nat. Dir, 1951; Information Dir, Columbia Univ. Bicentennial, 1953–54; Assoc. Nieman Fellow, Harvard Univ., 1957–58; Lecturer, Finch Coll., 1961–65. Senior Editor-Writer, High Sch. Geog. Project of Assoc. of Amer. Geographers, 1967–68. Consultant, Psychological Corp., 1969–76. Contributor to various English, American, and Australian publications. *Publications:* The Brownings; Lorenzo the Magnificent; Charles II; Philip II; Public Plunder; Alexander Hamilton; Lafayette; Woodrow Wilson; Chief Justice; A Long Way Forward; Swope of GE; The Erotic in Literature; Pencoyd and the Roberts Family; Crime Lab.: How High is Up; The City Within a City; Crime in Suburbia; The Marriage Counselor; Gold Brick Cassie; Economic Miracle in Israel; The Tertelines: earth movers; Built to Last; Co-author: American Sexual Behaviour and the Kinsey Report; Report on the American Communist; For Better or Worse; Peter Freuchen's Book of the Seven Seas; The Frigid Wife; The Emotional Sex; Ivan Sanderson's Book of Great Jungles; The Taming of Technology; The Colorado Model for Conservation Education. *Address:* 1244 Gillespie Drive, Boulder, Colo 80302, USA.

**LOTT, Air Vice-Marshal Charles George,** CB 1955; CBE 1944; DSO 1940; DFC 1940; Royal Air Force, retired; *b* 28 Oct. 1906; *s* of late Charles Lott, Sandown; *m* 1936, Evelyn Muriel Little; two *s* one *d*. *Educ:* Portsmouth Junior Technical Sch. Joined Royal Air Force as Aircraft Apprentice, 1922; learned to fly at Duxford in No 19 Squadron, 1927–28; Sergeant, 1928; Commissioned 1933 and posted to No 41 Squadron; Iraq, 1935–38; HQ No 11 Gp, 1938–39; Commanded No 43 Squadron, 1939–40 (DFC, wounded, DSO);

Temp. Wing Comdr, 1941; HQ 13 Group, 1940–42; Sector Comdr, Fighter Command, 1952; Acting Group Capt. 1942; Temp. Group Captain 1944; RAF Delegation (USA), 1944–45; Group Captain 1947; Air Commodore, 1954; Air Vice-Marshal, 1956; Dir Air Defence, SHAPE, 1955–57; Commandant, Sch. of Land/Air Warfare, Old Sarum, Wilts, 1957–59. Retd 1959. *Address:* Glen Waverley, Hooke Hill, Freshwater, Isle of Wight PO40 9BG. *Club:* Royal Air Force. *Died* 31 *Dec.* 1989.

**LOTT, Frank Melville,** CBE 1945; DDS, MScD, PhD; retired; formerly Professor and Chairman of the Prosthodontics Department, University of Southern California, USA; *b* 9 Nov. 1896; *s* of Charles Lott, Uxbridge, Ont.; *m* 1933, Mabel Maunder Martin; one *s* one *d. Educ:* Toronto, Ont. Prof., Prosthetic Dentistry, University of Toronto. Dir-Gen. Dental Services, Canadian Forces, 1939–46; Col Comdt Royal Canadian Dental Corps. *Publications:* Bulletins of Canadian Dental Research Foundation and papers to dental congresses and journals. *Recreations:* photography, fishing, hunting. *Address:* 19 Vista Lane, San Luis Obispo, Calif 93401, USA. *Died* 16 *May* 1982.

**LOVEDAY, Rt. Rev. David Goodwin,** MA; Assistant Bishop, Diocese of Oxford, since 1971; *b* 13 April 1896; 6th *s* of late J. E. T. Loveday, JP, of Williamscote, near Banbury, Oxon; unmarried. *Educ:* Shrewsbury Sch. (Careswell Exhibitioner); Magdalene Coll., Cambridge (Sizar), 2nd cl. Class. Tripos, Part I, 2nd cl. Theol. Tripos, Part I. Deacon, 1923; Priest, 1924; Asst Master, Malvern Coll., 1917–19; Asst Master and Chaplain, Aldenham Sch.; 1922–25; Clifton Coll., 1925–31; Headmaster of Cranleigh Sch., 1931–54; Archdeacon of Dorking and Examining Chaplain, Guildford, 1954–57; Suffragan Bishop of Dorchester, 1957–71. Select Preacher: Cambridge 1933 and 1954, Dublin, 1951, Oxford, 1955 and 1957. *Address:* Wardington, Banbury, Oxon. *T:* Cropredy 219. *Died* 7 *April* 1985.

**LOVEDAY, George Arthur,** TD; Partner in Read Hurst-Brown & Co., subsequently Rowe & Pitman, Hurst-Brown, 1948–75, retired; Chairman, The Stock Exchange, 1973–75; *b* 13 May 1909; *s* of late A. F. Loveday, OBE; *m* 1st, 1935, Sylvia Mary Gibbs (*d* 1967); two *s*; 2nd, 1967, Penelope Elton Dugdale (*née* Cunard), *widow* of Brig. N. Dugdale. *Educ:* Winchester Coll.; Magdalen Coll., Oxford. Hons Mod. Langs, MA. Stock Exchange, 1937–39; served RA, 1939–45, Major 1941; Lt-Col comdg Herts Yeomanry, 1954. Mem., Stock Exchange, 1946, Mem. Council, 1961, Dep. Chm., 1971. Mem. Council, Bath Univ., 1975. *Recreation:* golf. *Address:* Bushton Manor, Bushton, Swindon, Wilts. *Club:* Boodle's.
*Died* 25 *Feb.* 1981.

**LOVELACE, Lt-Col. Alec,** CMG 1958; MBE 1941; MC; *b* 1907; *m* 1948, Eleanor, *d* of W. E. Platt. *Educ:* Dorchester Grammar Sch.; University College of the South-West, Exeter; Birkbeck Coll., University of London. Served War of 1939–45 in Army (Lt-Col), Education Officer, Mauritius, 1946; Civil Commissioner, 1949; Administrator, Antigua, 1954; Defence Officer, The West Indies, 1958; Administrator of Dominica, Windward Islands, 1960–64, retired. CStJ. *Address:* North Lane, Guestling Thorn, near Hastings, East Sussex. *T:* Icklesham 317. *Died* 14 *Jan.* 1981.

**LOVELL, Arnold Henry;** Under-Secretary, HM Treasury, 1975–86; *b* 5 Aug. 1926; *s* of Alexander and Anita Lovell; *m* 1950, Joyce Harmer; one *s* one *d. Educ:* Hemsworth Grammar Sch., Yorks; London School of Economics (BScEcon, 1st Cl. Hons). HM Treasury: Asst Principal, 1952; Principal, 1956; Asst Financial Adviser to UK High Commn, New Delhi, India, 1962–65; re-joined HM Treasury, Monetary Policy Div., 1965–70; Asst Sec., 1967; Balance of Payments Div., 1970–75; Under-Sec., Fiscal Policy Div., 1975–80, Industry and Agric. Gp, 1980–86. *Recreations:* walking, Stafford bull terriers. *Address:* 12 Bromley Lane, Chislehurst, Kent BR7 6LE. *T:* 081–467 1116. *Died* 4 *Oct.* 1990.

**LOVELL, Stanley Hains,** CMG 1972; ED; consultant surgeon; *b* 22 Sept. 1906; *er s* of late John Hains Lovell; *m* 1935, Eleanor, *o d* of late Dr Edgar Harold Young; three *d. Educ:* Fort Street Boys' High Sch.; St Andrew's Coll., Univ. of Sydney. MB, BS, MS Sydney; FRACS. Served War of 1939–45, Middle East and Pacific (despatches); Col, RAAMC. Hon. Consultant Surgeon, Royal Prince Alfred, Rachel Forster, Prince Henry, Prince of Wales and Eastern Suburbs Hosps. Fellow, Australian Medical Assoc.; Pres., NSW Medical Defence Union, 1958–. Formerly: Mem. Court of Examrs, and Chm., NSW State Cttee, RACS; Lectr in Clinical Surgery, Sydney Univ.; Examr in Surgery, Sydney Univ.; External Examr, Univ. of Queensland. *Publications:* contrib. various surgical jls. *Recreation:* gardening. *Address:* 229 Macquarie Street, Sydney, NSW 2000, Australia. *T:* 2321060. *Club:* Australian (Sydney).
*Died* 29 *April* 1985.

**LOVERIDGE, Joan Mary,** OBE 1968; Matron and Superintendent of Nursing, St Bartholomew's Hospital, 1949–67; *b* 14 Aug. 1912; *d* of William Ernest Loveridge. *Educ:* Maidenhead, Berkshire. Commenced training, 1930, Royal National Orthopædic Hospital,

W1; St Bartholomew's Hospital, 1933–37; Radcliffe Infirmary, Oxford, Midwifery Training, 1937–38; Night Sister, Ward Sister, Matron's Office Sister, Assistant Matron, St Bartholomew's Hospital. *Address:* 24 Powys, All Saints Road, Sidmouth, Devon.
*Died* 18 *Oct.* 1987.

**LOVETT, Maj.-Gen. Osmond de Turville,** CB 1947; CBE 1945; DSO 1943, and Bar 1944; late 2nd Gurkha Rifles; retired; *b* 1898; *s* of William Edward Turville Lovett, Tamworth, Dunster; *m* 1940, Eleanor Barbara, *d* of late Albert Leslie Wright, late of Butterley Hall, Derbyshire; no *c. Educ:* Blundells, Tiverton; Cadet Coll., Wellington, India. 2nd Lieut, Indian Army, 1917; served European War, 1914–18, India, Mesopotamia; NW Persia, 1919–21 (wounded); transferred 2nd Gurkhas, 1919; Major, 1936; War of 1939–45, 10th Army, transferred to 8th Army, Middle East Forces (wounded); Central Mediterranean Force; Brigadier, 1943; temp. Maj.-General, 1945; retired, 1948. *Recreation:* fishing. *Address:* c/o Standard Bank of South Africa, Mooi River, Natal, South Africa; c/o Lloyds Bank (Cox's and King's Branch), 6 Pall Mall, SW1. *Club:* Naval and Military. *Died* 17 *Oct.* 1982.

**LOVETT, Robert Abercrombie;** Banker, United States; *b* 14 Sept. 1895; *s* of Robert Scott Lovett and Lavinia Chilton (*née* Abercrombie); *m* 1919, Adèle Quartley Brown (*d* 1986); one *s* (one *d* decd). *Educ:* Yale Univ. (BA), 1918; law study, Harvard, 1919–20; course in business administration, Harvard Grad. Schools, 1920–21. Clerk, National Bank of Commerce, NY City, 1921–23; employee, Brown Brothers & Co., later Brown Brothers Harriman & Co., 1923; Partner, 1926–82, Limited Partner, 1983–. Served as Special Asst to Secretary of War, and as Asst Secretary of War for Air in charge of Army Air Program, 1940–45. Under-Secretary of State, 1947–49; Deputy Secretary of Defence, 1950–51; Secretary of Defence, 1951–Jan. 1953. Readmitted Brown Brothers Harriman & Co., March 1953. Director: Union Pacific Railroad Co. and its leased lines, 1921–69 (Chm. Exec. Cttee and Chief Exec. Officer, 1953–67); Union Pacific Corp., 1969–78, retired; New York Life Insurance Co., 1949–68; CBS Inc., 1953–77; Freeport Minerals Co., 1953–70; North American Aviation Inc., 1953–69; Mem., NY Investment Cttee, Royal-Globe Insce Cos, 1953–75. Life Member Emeritus, Corp. of MIT. Holds hon. degrees. Served (pilot to Lieut-Commander) US Naval Air Service, March 1917–Dec. 1918 (Navy Cross, DSM). Grand Cross of the Order of Leopold II (Belgium), 1950; Presidential Medal of Freedom, USA, 1963. *Address:* Locust Valley, Long Island, NY 11560, USA. *Clubs:* Century, Yale, Links (New York); Creek (Locust Valley); Metropolitan (Washington, DC). *Died* 7 *May* 1986.

**LOWE, Arthur,** actor since 1945; *b* 22 Sept. 1915; *s* of Arthur Lowe and Mary Annie Lowe (*née* Ford); *m* 1948, Joan Cooper, actress; one *s. Educ:* Manchester. *Stage:* Various repertory companies, 1945–52; Larger than Life, Duke of York's, 1950; Hassan, Cambridge, 1951; Call Me Madam, Coliseum, 1952–53; Pal Joey, Princes, 1954; The Pajama Game, Coliseum, 1955–57; A Dead Secret, Piccadilly, 1957; The Ring of Truth, Savoy, 1959; Stop It, Whoever You Are, Arts, 1961; various plays, Royal Court, 1963–67; Home and Beauty, Old Vic, 1968; Ann Veronica, Cambridge, 1969; The Tempest, Old Vic, 1974; Bingo, Royal Court, 1974; Dad's Army, Shaftesbury, 1975; Laburnam Grove, Duke of York's, 1977; Hobson's Choice, Lyric Hammersmith, 1981. *Films:* London Belongs to Me, Floodtide, 1948; Kind Hearts and Coronets, Stop Press Girl, Poet's Pub, Spider and the Fly, 1949; Cage of Gold, 1950; The Woman for Joe, Who Done It, 1955; Green Man, 1956; Boy and the Bridge, 1958; Follow that Horse, The Day they Robbed the Bank of England, 1959; Go to Blazes, 1961; This Sporting Life, 1962; You're Joking, of course, The White Bus, 1965; If, Bed Sitting Room, 1968; Spring and Port Wine, Fragment of Fear, Rise and Rise of Michael Rimmer, 1969; Dad's Army, 1970; Ruling Class, 1971; O Lucky Man, Theatre of Blood, Adolf Hitler, my Part in his Downfall, 1972; No Sex Please, We're British, 1973; Man about the House, 1974; Royal Flash, Adventures of Tom Jones, 1975; The Lady Vanishes, 1979; Sweet William, 1979. *Television:* Plays, series etc, inc. Dad's Army, Potter, Bless Me Father, A. J. Wentworth BA; also much radio work. Various nominations and awards. *Address:* Flat C, 2 Maida Avenue, Little Venice, W2 1TF. *T:* 01-262 1782. *Clubs:* BAFTA, BBC. *Died* 15 *April* 1982.

**LOWE, Group Captain Cyril Nelson,** MC, DFC; BA Cambridge; late OC, RAF Station, Amman, Trans Jordan; *b* 7 Oct. 1891; *s* of Rev. C. W. Nelson Lowe, MA; *m* Ethel Mary Watson; one *s* two *d. Educ:* Dulwich Coll.; Pembroke Coll., Cambridge. Rugby Blue at Cambridge, 1911–12–13; first played for England v S. Africa in 1913, and subsequently gained 25 International Caps; Commission Aug. 1914 in ASC, and qualified for 1914 Star; seconded to Royal Flying Corps, 1916; No. 11 Squadron RFC France, 1916–17; 24 Squadron RFC, France, 1918 (MC, DFC). *Address:* Little Brook, Burrow Hill, Chobham, Surrey. *Died* 6 *Feb.* 1983.

**LOWE, Douglas Gordon Arthur,** QC 1964; Barrister-at-Law; a Recorder of the Crown Court, 1972–77 (Recorder of Lincoln,

1964–71); *b* 7 Aug. 1902; *o s* of Arthur John Lowe; *m* 1930, Karen, *e d* of Surgeon Einar Thamsen; one *s*. *Educ:* Highgate Sch.; Pembroke Coll., Cambridge (Exhibitioner, MA). Called to the Bar, Inner Temple, 1928; Bencher, Inner Temple, 1957. Dep. Chm., Warwicks QS, 1965–71. Councillor, Hampstead Borough Council, 1940–44; Governor, Highgate Sch., 1939–76 (Chairman, 1965–76); Chairman, Oxford Mental Health Tribunal, 1962–64. Member, Criminal Injuries Compensation Board, 1965–77. *Publication:* (with Arthur Porritt, now Lord Porritt) Athletics, 1929. *Recreations:* walking, reading, music; formerly athletics, cricket, Association football, Eton fives, lawn tennis and golf. (President Cambridge Univ. Athletic Club; Assoc. Football and Athletics Blue; winner Olympic 800 meters, 1924 and 1928; Hon. Secretary Amateur Athletic Assoc., 1931–38). *Address:* Great Maytham Hall, Rolvenden, Cranbrook, Kent. *Clubs:* Achilles; Hawks (Cambridge). *Died 30 March 1981.*

**LOWE, Sir Francis (Reginald Gordon),** 3rd Bt *cr* 1918; *b* 8 Feb. 1931; *s* of Sir Francis Gordon Lowe, 2nd Bt, and Dorothy Honor, *d* of late Lt-Col H. S. Woolrych; *S* father, 1972; *m* 1st, 1961, Franziska Cornelia Steinkopf (marr. diss. 1971); two *s*; 2nd, 1971, Helen Suzanne, *y d* of late Sandys Stuart Macaskie; one *s*. *Educ:* Stowe; Clare College, Cambridge (BA, LLB). Called to the Bar, Middle Temple, 1959. *Recreation:* wine. *Heir:* *s* Thomas William Gordon Lowe, *b* 14 Aug. 1963. *Address:* Pelham House, 9 Bath Road, Cowes, Isle of Wight. *T:* Cowes 291115; 4 New Square, Lincoln's Inn, WC2A 3RJ. *T:* 01–242 8508. *Died 28 May 1986.*

**LOWRY, Hugh Avant,** CB 1974; retired 1974; Comptroller and Auditor-General for Northern Ireland, 1971–74; *b* 23 May 1913; *s* of late Hugh George Lowry, HM Inspector of Taxes, and late Ellen Louisa Lowry (*née* Avant); *m* 1939, Marjorie Phyllis Mary (*née* Hale); two *d*. *Educ:* Watford Grammar Sch.; Gonville and Caius Coll., Cambridge. 1st Cl. Hons, both parts, Classical Tripos, 1932–35; MA; Apptd Asst Principal, Ministry of Labour for Northern Ireland, 1936. Served War, as Observer in Fleet Air Arm, RNVR, 1943–46. Served in various Ministries of Govt of N Ireland in various grades. Sec. to Nat. Assistance Bd for N Ireland, 1956–57; Second Sec. and Dir of Establishments, Min. of Finance for Northern Ireland, July 1970–June 1971. *Recreations:* bridge, bowls, watching games he used to play—Rugby football, cricket, tennis. *Address:* Woodridings, 7A Greenway Park, Chippenham, Wilts. *T:* Chippenham 3260. *Club:* Civil Service. *Died 14 Dec. 1982.*

**LOWTHER, Captain Hon. Anthony George,** MBE 1954; DL; *b* 23 Sept. 1925; *yr s* of Viscount Lowther (*d* 1949); granted 1954, title, rank and precedence of an earl's son which would have been his had his father survived to succeed to earldom of Lonsdale; *m* 1958, Lavinia, *o c* of late Thomas H. Joyce, San Francisco, California; one *s* three *d*. *Educ:* Eton; RMA, Sandhurst. Joined Army, 1943; 2nd Lieut, 12th Royal Lancers, 1946; served in Egypt, 1946; Palestine, 1946–47; Malaya, 1951–54; Captain, 1952; retired 1954. Director: Lakeland Investments Ltd; Carlisle (New) Racecourse Co. Ltd; Lowther Park Farms Ltd; Lowther Wildlife Park Ltd. Chairman: Cumbria Police Cttee, 1974; CC Westmorland, 1960–74, CC Cumbria, 1973–; Cumberland River Authy, 1963–74; NW Regional Land Drainage Cttee, 1974–; Cumberland Land Drainage Adv. Cttee, 1974–. High Sheriff of Westmorland, 1964; DL Westmorland, 1964–74; DL Cumbria, 1974. Dep. Master 1956, Master 1974, Jt Master 1979, Ullswater Foxhounds. *Address:* Whitbysteads, Askham, Penrith, Cumbria. *T:* Hackthorp 284. *Clubs:* White's, National Sporting; Cumberland County (Carlisle). *Died 24 March 1981.*

**LOWTHER, Lt-Col Sir William (Guy),** 5th Bt, *cr* 1824; OBE 1952; DL; retired; one of HM Body Guard of the Honourable Corps of Gentlemen-at-Arms since 1962; *b* 9 Oct. 1912; *o s* of Lieut-Colonel Sir Charles Bingham Lowther, 4th Bt, CB, DSO, and Marjorie Noel (*d* 1925), *d* of Thomas Fielden, MP, of Grimston, Yorks; *S* father, 1949; *m* 1939, Grania Suzanne Douglas Campbell, OStJ, *y d* of late Major A. J. H. Douglas Campbell, OBE, of Blythswood, and the Hon. Mrs Douglas Campbell; one *s* one *d*. *Educ:* Winchester; RMC, Sandhurst. 2nd Lieut, 8th Hussars, 1932; served Palestine, 1936 (despatches); War of 1939–45, in W. Desert (prisoner); Captain, 1941; Major, 1945; Lieut-Colonel, 1951; Staff Coll., 1947; Staff appointment, 1948 and 1949. Served Korea, 1950–51, Lieut-Colonel comd 8th Hussars (despatches); commanding BAOR, 1952–53; retired Jan. 1954. Comr, St John Ambulance Bde for Clwyd (formerly Denbighshire), 1966; Dep. Chief Comr for N Wales, 1976. High Sheriff 1959, DL 1969, Clwyd. KStJ. *Heir:* *s* Major Charles Douglas Lowther, Queen's Royal Irish Hussars [*b* 22 Jan. 1946; *m* 1st, 1969, Melanie Musgrave (marr. diss. 1975), *d* of late R. C. Musgrave and of Mrs J. S. H. Douglas, Ravensheugh, Selkirk; 2nd, 1975, Florence Rose, *y d* of Col A. J. H. Cramsie; one *s* one *d*]. *Address:* Erbistock Hall, near Wrexham. *T:* Overton 246. *Club:* Cavalry and Guards. *Died 7 May 1982.*

**LOWTHIAN, George Henry,** CBE 1963 (MBE 1949); General Secretary, Amalgamated Union of Building Trade Workers,

1951–73, retired; Part-time Member, British Transport Docks Board, 1963–77; *b* 30 Jan. 1908; *s* of Ernest and Margaret Lowthian; *m* 1933, Florence Hartley; one *s* one *d*. *Educ:* Creighton Sch., Carlisle. Branch Secretary, 1930–45; District Secretary, 1934–45; Exec. Council, 1940–45; Divisional Secretary, 1945–50; TUC General Council, 1951–73, Chairman, 1963–64; Chairman, Industrial Training Council, 1960–62; Chairman, Board of Directors, Industrial Training Service, 1965–. Mem., Workmen's Compensation and Pneumoconiosis, Byssinosis and Miscellaneous Diseases Benefit Bds, 1975–78. *Recreations:* photography, motoring. *Address:* 17 Holly Way, Mitcham, Surrey. *T:* 01–764 2200.
*Died 11 June 1986.*

**LUBBOCK, Sir Alan,** Kt 1963; MA, FSA; *b* 13 Jan. 1897; 6th *s* of Frederic Lubbock, Ide Hill, Kent; *m* 1918, Helen Mary (*d* 1987), *d* of late John Bonham-Carter, Adhurst St Mary, Petersfield; two *s*. *Educ:* Eton; King's Coll., Cambridge. Served in Royal Artillery, 1915–19 and 1939–45. Fellow of King's, 1922–28. Hants County Council, 1932–74 (Alderman 1939, Vice-Chairman 1948, Chairman 1955–67); JP (Hants) 1935; DL; High Sheriff of Hants, 1949–; Member: National Parks Commission, 1954–61; Royal Commission on Common Land, 1955; War Works Commission, 1959–64. Chairman: Council, Southampton Univ., 1957–69 (Pro-Chancellor, 1967–83); County Councils Assoc., 1965–69 (Vice-Chairman 1963); Nat. Foundn for Educnl Research, 1967–73. Hon. LLD Southampton, 1969. *Publication:* The Character of John Dryden, 1925. *Address:* Adhurst St Mary, Petersfield, Hants. *T:* Petersfield 63043. *Clubs:* United Oxford & Cambridge University; Leander.
*Died 17 March 1990.*

**LUBBOCK, Roy;** *b* 1 Oct. 1892; *s* of Frederic Lubbock and Catherine Gurney; *m* 1919, Yvonne Vernham; two *s*. *Educ:* Eton (Scholar); King's Coll., Cambridge (Exhibitioner, scholar); Fellow of Peterhouse, Cambridge and University Lecturer in Engineering, 1919–60; Bursar of Peterhouse, 1929–31 and 1940–45, Tutor, 1934–40. *Address:* Riding Oaks, Hildenborough, Tonbridge, Kent.
*Died 16 July 1985.*

**LUCAS, Colin Anderson,** OBE 1972; BA Cantab; FRIBA; Architect; *b* London, 1906; 2nd *s* of late Ralph Lucas, Engineer, and late Mary Anderson Juler; *m* 1930, Dione Narona Margaris (marr. diss.), *d* of Henry Wilson; two *s*; *m* 1952, Pamela Margaret, *e d* of late Sir Gerald Campbell, GCMG; *Educ:* Cheltenham Coll.; Trinity Coll., Cambridge; Cambridge Univ. Sch. of Architecture. In practice in London, 1928–; Founder Mem. of Mars (Modern Architectural Research Group). *Publications:* works published in England, America and Continent. *Recreations:* sailing, ski-ing, travel. *Address:* 2 Queen's Grove Studios, Queen's Grove, NW8 6EP.
*Died 25 Aug. 1984.*

**LUCAS, Donald William;** Fellow of King's College, Cambridge, 1929, and Director of Studies in Classics, 1935–65; University Lecturer in Classics, 1933–69; P. M. Laurence Reader in Classics, 1952–69; *b* 12 May 1905; *s* of Frank William Lucas and Ada Ruth Blackmur; *m* 1933, Mary Irene Cohen; one *s* one *d*. *Educ:* Colfe's Gram. Sch.; Rugby; King's Coll., Cambridge. War of 1939–45: FO, 1940–44. *Publications:* The Greek Tragic Poets, 1950; Aristotle Poetics, 1968; *translations* (from Euripides): Bacchae, 1930; Medea, 1949; Ion, 1949; Alcestis, 1951; Electra, 1951; Joint Editor, Classical Quarterly, 1953–59; articles and reviews in classical journals and Encyclopædia Britannica. *Recreations:* travel and reading. *Address:* 39 Bridle Way, Grantchester, Cambs. *T:* Cambridge 841108; Pwllymarch, Llanbedr, Gwynedd. *T:* Llanbedr 208. *Died 28 Feb. 1985.*

**LUCAS, Maj.-Gen. Geoffrey,** CB 1957; CBE 1944; *b* 19 Oct. 1904; *s* of Henry Lucas, Mossley Hill, Liverpool; *m* 1927, Mabel Ellen, *d* of Dr George Henry Heald, Leeds; one *s* one *d*. *Educ:* Liverpool Institute; RMC, Sandhurst. Commissioned, 1925, in Royal Tank Corps; Staff Coll., Camberley, 1938; served War of 1939–45 in Italy and Greece; DQMG, BAOR, 1947–50; Dep. Dir Personnel Admin, War Office, 1950–53; Dep. Fortress Comd, Gibraltar, 1953–56; Chief Administrative Officer, Suez Operations, 1956; Maj.-Gen. i/c Admin, FARELF, 1957; retired, Hon. Maj.-Gen., 1958. *Address:* Newbold House, Linkway, Camberley, Surrey. *T:* Camberley 65544. *Died 12 Dec. 1982.*

**LUCAS-TOOTH, Sir Hugh;** *see* Munro-Lucas-Tooth.

**LUCE, Hon. Clare Boothe;** playwright and author since 1933; *b* 10 April 1903; *d* of William F. and Ann Snyder Boothe; *m* 1st, 1923, George Tuttle Brokaw; 2nd, 1935, Henry Robinson Luce (*d* 1967). *Educ:* St Mary's Sch., Garden City, Long Island; The Castle, Tarrytown, New York. Associate Editor Vogue, 1930; Associate Editor Vanity Fair, 1931–32; Managing Editor Vanity Fair, 1933–34. Mem. of Congress from 4th District of Connecticut, 1943–47. United States Ambassador to Italy, 1953–57. Mem., President's Foreign Intelligence Adv. Bd, 1973–77, 1982–. Presidential Medal of Freedom, 1983. Holds hon. doctorates. Dame of Magistral Grace, SMO Malta; Kt Gr. Cross, Order of Merit, Italy. *Publications:* Stuffed Shirts, 1933; Europe in the Spring (in

England, European Spring), 1940; (ed) Saints For Now, 1952; *plays:* Abide with Me, 1935; The Women, 1936; Kiss the Boys Goodbye, 1938; Margin for Error, 1939; Child of the Morning, 1951; Slam the Door Softly, 1970; *screenplay:* Come to the Stable, 1947; articles to magazines. *Address:* 700 New Hampshire Avenue NW, Washington, DC 20037, USA. *Died 9 Oct.* 1987.

**LUCET, Charles (Ernest);** French Ambassador, retired; *b* Paris, 16 April 1910; *s* of Louis Lucet and Madeleine Lucet (*née* Zoegger); *m* 1931, Jacqueline Bardoux; one *s* one *d*. *Educ:* University of Paris. Degree in law, also degree of Ecole Libre des Sciences Politiques. French Embassy, Washington, 1935–Nov. 1942; then joined Free French movement and was apptd to its mission in Washington; attached to Foreign affairs Commissariat in Algiers, 1943; First Sec., Ankara, 1943–45; Asst Dir for Middle Eastern Affairs, Foreign Affairs Min., Paris, 1945–46; First Counsellor: Beirut, 1946; Cairo, 1949; Dept Head of Cultural Relations Div. of Foreign Affairs Min., Paris, 1950–53; rank of Minister Plenipotentiary, 1952; Mem. French Delegn to UN, serving as Dep. Permanent Rep. to UN and to Security Council, 1953–55; Minister Counsellor, French Embassy, Washington, 1955–59; Dir of Political Affairs, Foreign Affairs Min., Paris, 1959–65; Ambassador to USA, 1965–72; Ambassador to Italy, 1972–75. Commandeur de la Légion d'Honneur; Commandeur de l'Ordre National du Mérite; holds foreign decorations. *Address:* 9 rue de Thann, 75017 Paris, France. *T:* (1)4622.56.76.
*Died 25 March* 1990.

**LUCEY, Most Rev. Cornelius;** *b* Windsor, Co. Cork. *Educ:* Maynooth; Innsbruck. Priest, 1927. Co-Founder and Pres., Christus Rex Soc. for priests; Founder and Superior, La Sociedad de Santo Toribio (missionary and welfare organisation for the barriadas of Peru). Bishop of Cork, 1952–80, and Ross, 1954–80. *Address:* Bishop's House, Farranferris, Cork, Eire. *Died 24 Sept.* 1982.

**LUCRAFT, Frederick Hickman,** CBE 1952; *b* 10 May 1894; *s* of late Frederick Thomas Lucraft, Customs and Excise Dept; *m* 1927, June, *d* of John Freeman Wright, Dover; one *s* one *d*. *Educ:* Grocers' Company's Sch. Entered Inland Revenue, 1913. Served European War, King's Own Royal Lancaster Regt, 1914–17. Railway Traffic Establishment, 1917–19; Inter-allied Railway Commn, Cologne SubCommn, 1919–22; demobilised with rank of Capt., 1922. Regional Services Dir, Min. of Fuel and Power, North-Western Region, 1942–45; Dep. Accountant and Comptroller Gen., Inland Revenue, 1945–47; Special Comr of Income Tax, Clerk to the Special Commissioners and Inspector of Foreign Dividends, Inland Revenue, 1947–59; HM Treasury, 1959–60. *Address:* 104 Ashdown, Eaton Road, Hove, East Sussex, BN3 3AR. *T:* Brighton 731805.
*Died 17 July* 1981.

**LUFT, Rev. Canon Hyam Mark,** MA, MLitt; FRHistS; JP; Canon Theologian of Liverpool Cathedral, since 1979; *b* 1913; *s* of I. M. Luft, Liverpool; *m* 1943, Frances, *er d* of F. Pilling, CBE; two *s* one *d*. *Educ:* Liverpool Institute; St John's Coll., University of Durham (Foundation Scholar). BA (1st Cl. Classics) 1934; Dip. TPT 1935; MA 1937; MLitt 1953. Deacon, 1937; Priest, 1938. Asst Priest, Liverpool Diocese, 1937–56; Asst Master, Merchant Taylors' Sch., Crosby, 1941–56; Headmaster, Blackpool Grammar Sch., 1956–64; Headmaster, Merchant Taylors' Sch., Crosby, 1964–79. Pres., Literary and Philosophical Soc. of Liverpool, 1953–54; Mem., Religious Education Commn, 1967–. Fellow-Commoner, Emmanuel Coll., Cambridge, 1968. JP Lancs, 1968–. *Publication:* History of Merchant Taylors' School, Crosby, 1620–1970, 1970. *Recreations:* gardening, foreign travel and lecturing. *Address:* 44 St Michael's Road, Liverpool L23 7UN. *T:* 051–924 6034. *Club:* East India, Devonshire, Sports and Public Schools.
*Died 19 April* 1986.

**LUKE, Eric Howard Manley,** CMG 1950; FRCSE 1922; FRACS 1932; retired; *b* 18 Aug. 1894; *s* of Sir Charles Luke; *m* 1923, Gladys Anne, *d* of Col J. J. Esson, CMG; one *s* two *d*. *Educ:* Wellington Coll.; Otago Univ.; Edinburgh Univ. MB, ChB, Otago Univ., NZ, 1920; senior surgeon, Wellington Hospital, NZ, 1925–50; Thoracic Surgeon, East Coast Hospitals, 1942–54; Chm. of Council, British Medical Association, NZ Branch, 1944–49; President BMA, NZ Branch, 1950. Has a citrus orchard. OStJ 1940. *Recreations:* formerly Rugby; now bowls and gardening. *Address:* Keri Keri, Bay of Islands, NZ. *Club:* Wellington (Wellington, NZ).
*Died 8 Dec.* 1987.

**LUKE, Sir Stephen (Elliot Vyvyan),** KCMG 1953 (CMG 1946); *b* 26 Sept. 1905; *o c* of late Brigadier-General Thomas Mawe Luke, CBE, DSO; *m* 1st, 1929, Helen Margaret, *o c* of late Kenneth A. Reinold, Indian Police; two *s*; 2nd, 1948, Margaret Stych; one *d*. *Educ:* St George's Sch., Harpenden; Wadham Coll., Oxford. Asst Clerk, House of Commons, 1930; Asst Principal, Colonial Office, 1930; Asst Private Sec. to successive Secs of State, 1936–35; seconded to Palestine Administration, 1936–37; Sec., Palestine Partition Commission, 1938; Under-Sec., Cabinet Office, 1947–50; Asst Under-Sec. of State, Colonial Office, 1950–53; Comptroller for Development and Welfare in the West Indies, and British Co-Chm.

of Caribbean Commn, 1953–58; Comr for preparation of WI Federal Organisation, 1956–58; Senior Crown Agent for Oversea Governments and Administrations, 1959–68; Interim Comr for the West Indies, May 1962–68; Mem. Exec. Cttee, W India Cttee, 1969–72. Chm., Board of Governors, St George's Sch., Harpenden, 1963–68. Dir, Pirelli Ltd and other companies, 1968–76. *Address:* Merryfields, Breamore, Fordingbridge, Hants. *T:* Downton 22389. *Club:* United Oxford & Cambridge University.
*Died 27 Feb.* 1988.

**LUKE, William Edgell;** Chairman, 1959–79 (Managing Director, 1949–73), Lindustries Ltd (formerly the Linen Thread Co. Ltd) and associated companies at home and abroad; Director: Powell Duffryn Ltd, 1966–79; Bankers Trust (Holdings) Ltd, 1975–78; *b* 9 June 1909; *s* of George Bingley Luke and Violet Edgell; *m* 1st, 1933, Muriel Aske Haley (marr. diss. 1969); one *s* one *d*; 2nd, 1970, Constance Anne Reid; two *d*. *Educ:* Old Hall, Wellington; Kelvinside Academy, Glasgow. Served War of 1939–45: Major, Intelligence Corps, S Africa and Central America. Mem. Grand Coun., FBI, 1947–73 (Chm. Scottish Council, 1957) (FBI is now CBI); Mem. Council, Aims of Industry, 1958–80; Chm. Industrial Advisers to the Blind Ltd, 1963–67; Pres., UK-S Africa Trade Assoc., 1977–79 (Chm., 1963–77); Mem., Brit. Nat. Export Council, and Chm., BNEC Southern Africa Cttee for Exports to Southern Africa, 1965–68; Mem., BOTB Adv. Council, 1975–78; Trustee, South Africa Foundation. FBIM. Master, Worshipful Company of Makers of Playing Cards, 1958. Mem. Lloyd's. Royal Order, Crown of Yugoslavia, 1944. *Recreations:* golf, music and travel. *Address:* Pickhurst Cottage, High Street Green, Chiddingfold, Surrey GU8 4YB. *Clubs:* Royal Thames Yacht, Travellers'.
*Died 30 Oct.* 1987.

**LUMBY, Sir Henry,** Kt 1973; CBE 1957; DL, JP; Chairman of Lancashire County Council, 1967–73; Chairman, Liverpool Diocesan Board of Finance, 1977–80; *b* 9 Jan. 1909; *m* 1936, Dorothy Pearl Watts; two *s*. *Educ:* Merchant Taylors' Sch., Crosby. Served War of 1939–45 (POW, 1942–45). Mem., Lancs CC, 1946; Alderman, 1956–74; Leader of Conservative Gp, Lancs CC, 1965–74; DL 1963, JP 1951, High Sheriff 1973, Lancashire. *Recreation:* gardening. *Address:* The Dawn, Dark Lane, Ormskirk, Lancs. *T:* Ormskirk 72030. *Died 11 Feb.* 1989.

**LUND, Sir Thomas (George),** Kt 1958; CBE 1948; Consultant, Kidd, Rapinet, Badge & Co. and Yarde & Loader, solicitors, since 1979; *b* 6 Jan. 1906; *s* of late Kenneth Fraser Lund, MA, MB; *m* 1931, Catherine Stirling, *d* of late Arthur John Audsley; one *d*. *Educ:* Westminster Sch. Admitted a Solicitor, 1929; Asst Solicitor, The Law Soc., 1930; Asst Sec., 1937; Secretary-General, 1939–69; Treas., Internat. Bar Assoc., 1950–69; Chm. Board of Management, College of Law, 1962–69; Dir, Solicitors' Benevolent Assoc., 1949–69. Dir-Gen., Internat. Bar Assoc., 1969–78; Sec.-Gen., Internat. Legal Aid Assoc., 1963–79. Honorary Member: Holborn Law Soc.; Kent Law Soc.; Member: The Law Soc.; IBA; West London Law Soc.; Westminster Law Soc.; Union Internationale des Avocats. Past Master, Worshipful Co. of Solicitors of the City of London; Liveryman, Worshipful Co. of Cordwainers. Past Pres., British Academy of Forensic Sciences. Local Dir, Sun Alliance London Gp. Mem. Council of Motability, Eton Fives Assoc. *Publications:* The Solicitors Act, 1941, 1943; A Guide to the Professional Conduct of Solicitors, 1960; Professional Ethics, 1970; ed a section of Halsbury's Laws of England; contributed many articles to English and American legal jls. *Recreations:* foreign travel, motoring, gardening. *Address:* 1/2 Gray's Inn Place, Gray's Inn, WC1R 5DZ; Bryanston Court, George Street, W1. *Club:* Athenæum. *Died 20 April* 1981.

**LUNT, Rt. Rev. Francis Evered;** *b* 15 Oct. 1900; *e s* of late Francis Bryan Lunt; *m* 1938, Helen Patricia, *y d* of late Alfred Bolton; three *d*. *Educ:* University Coll., Durham (LTh 1923); London Coll. of Divinity. Deacon, 1925; Priest, 1927; Curate of St Andrew and St Mary, Maidenhead, 1925–31; St Barnabas, Cambridge, 1931–34; licensed to officiate, Diocese of Ely, 1933–43; Chaplain, Downing Coll., Cambridge and Cambridge Pastorate, 1934–43; Hon. Fellow, Downing Coll., 1966–; MA Cambridge, 1939; Senior Chaplain to Oxford Pastorate and Rector of St Aldate, Oxford, 1943–51; Dean of Bristol, 1951–57; Bishop Suffragan of Stepney, 1957–68. MA Oxford (Oriel Coll.), 1945. Select Preacher, Univ. of Cambridge, 1943 and 1962; Surrogate, 1943; Examining Chaplain to Bishop of Oxford, 1946–51, to Bishop of Portsmouth, 1949–51. Mem. Council, Ridley Hall, Cambridge, 1950–71. *Address:* Ridgeway House, Felpham, Sussex. *Died 27 May* 1982.

**LURGAN, 4th Baron** *cr* 1839; **William George Edward Brownlow;** *b* 22 Feb. 1902; *o s* of 3rd Baron and Lady Emily Julia Cadogan (*d* 1909), *d* of 5th Earl Cadogan, KG; *S* father, 1937; *m* 1979, Florence May Cooper, *widow* of E. W. Cooper, Nottingham. *Educ:* Eton; Oxford. *Heir:* cousin John Desmond Cavendish Brownlow, OBE, *b* 29 June 1911. *Address:* c/o Messrs Lee & Pembertons, 45 Pont Street, SW1X 0BX. *Clubs:* Turf; Ulster (Belfast). *Died 30 Jan.* 1984.

**LUSH, Maurice Stanley,** CB 1944; CBE 1942; MC 1916; *b* 23 Nov. 1896; *s* of late Hubert Stanley Lush; *m* 1930, Diana Ruth, *d* of late Charles Alexander Hill; one *s* two *d. Educ:* Tonbridge Sch.; RMA, Woolwich. European War, RA, 1915–19 (MC and Bar); Egyptian Army, 1919–22; Sudan Political Service from 1919; Secretary HM Legation, Addis Ababa, 1919–22; District Commissioner, Sudan, 1922–26; Assistant Civil Secretary Sudan Government, 1926–29; Private Secretary to Governor-General of Sudan, 1929–30; Dep. Governor, Sudan, 1930–35; Sudan Agent, Cairo, 1935–38; Governor, Northern Province, Sudan, 1938–41. War of 1939–45 recalled from RARO as Brig. (despatches thrice); Chief Political Officer, Ethiopia, 1941–42; Military Administrator, Madagascar, 1942; Chief Civil Affairs Officer British Military Administration, Tripolitania, 1942–43; Executive Commissioner and Vice-President, Allied Commission, Italy, 1943–46; Resident representative for Germany and Austria of Intergovernmental Cttee on Refugees, 1946–47; Chief of Mission in Middle East, IRO, 1947–49; Special Representative for Middle East of IRO, 1949–51; Rep. Anglo-Saxon Petroleum Co. (Shell), Libya, 1952–56; Man. Dir, Pakistan Shell Oil Co. Ltd, 1956–59. Vice-Chm., Enterprise Neptune, Nat. Trust, 1965–68. Vice-Pres., British and Foreign Bible Soc. FRSA. FRGS. Order of the Nile, 3rd Class; Officer, Legion of Merit US, 1945; Comdr Order of Knights of Malta, 1945. *Address:* 3 Carlton Mansions, Holland Park Gardens, W14 8DW. *T:* 071–603 4425. *Club:* Athenæum.                          *Died* 20 May 1990.

**LUSHINGTON, Sir Henry Edmund Castleman,** 7th Bt *cr* 1791; *b* 2 May 1909; *s* of Sir Herbert Castleman Lushington, 6th Bt and Barbara Henrietta (*d* 1927), *d* of late Rev. William Greville Hazlerigg; *S* father, 1968; *m* 1937, Pamela Elizabeth Daphne, *er d* of Major Archer R. Hunter, Wokingham, Berks; one *s* two *d. Educ:* Dauntsey's Sch. Served War of 1939–45, Flt-Lieut, RAFVR. Metropolitan Police, 1935–58; retired as Superintendent. *Recreations:* gardening, golf. *Heir: s* John Richard Castleman Lushington [*b* 28 Aug. 1938; *m* 1966, Bridget Gillian Margaret, *d* of Colonel John Foster Longfield, Saunton, Devon; three *s*]. *Address:* Carfax, Crowthorne, Berkshire. *T:* Crowthorne 772819. *Club:* East Berks Golf.                                    *Died* 6 Sept. 1988.

**LUTYENS, (Agnes) Elisabeth, (Mrs Edward Clark),** CBE 1969; musician, composer; *b* London, 9 July 1906; 3rd *d* of late Sir Edwin Landseer Lutyens, OM, KCIE, PRA, LLD and of late Lady Emily Lutyens; *m* 1st, 1933, Ian Herbert Campbell Glennie (marr. diss.); one *s* twin *d*: 2nd, 1942, Edward Clark (*d* 1962); one *s. Compositions include:* The Pit, a dramatic scene (for tenor, bass, women's chorus, and orchestra); 3 Symphonic Preludes for orchestra; String Quartet No 6; O Saisons, O Châteaux! (Rimbaud) (for soprano and strings); String Trio; Viola Concerto; Four Chamber Concertos; Excerpta Tractatus-Logico Philosophici (Wittgenstein), Motet for unaccompanied chorus, 1952; Valediction for clarinet and piano, 1954; Infidelio, 1954; Four Nocturnes, 1954; 6 Tempi for 10 Instruments, 1957; Music for Orchestra, I, II, III; Quincunx for Orchestra, 1959; Wind Quintet, 1961; Symphonies for Solo Piano, Wind, Harps and Percussion, 1961; The Country of the Stars (cantata), 1963; Hymn of Man, 1965; The Valley of Hatsu-se, 1966; Akapotik Rose, 1966; And Suddenly It's Evening, 1967; The Numbered, opera, 1966; Time Off? Not a ghost of a chance, charade in 4 scenes and 3 interruptions, 1968; Isis and Osiris, lyric drama, 1969; Novenaria (for orchestra), 1969; The Tides of Time, 1969; Essence of our Happinesses (cantata), 1970; Oda a la tormenta (Neruda), 1971; The Tears of Night, 1972; Vision of Youth, 1972; Rape of the Moone, 1973; De Amore (cantata), 1973; The Waiting Game (music-theatre), 1973; Plenum I for solo piano, 1972; Plenum II for solo oboe and thirteen instrumentalists, 1973; Plenum III for string quartet, 1974; Plenum IV (What is the wind, what is it? . . .) for organ duet, 1974; Winter of the World (for orchestras), commissioned by English Bach Festival, 1974; FOS, 1975; The Ring of Bone, 1975; Mare et Minutiae, 1976; Constants, 1976; O Absalom, 1977; Variations: Winter Series-Spring Sowing (song cycle), 1977; Elegy of the Flowers, 1978; Footfalls, 1978; Echoi, 1979; The Great Seas, 1979; Fleur du Silence, 1981; Reme de Gourment; also music for numerous films and radio features. City of London Midsummer Prize, 1969. Hon. DMus York, 1977. *Publication:* A Goldfish Bowl (autobiography), 1972. *Address:* 17 King Henry's Road, NW3. *T:* 01-722 8505; c/o Universal Edition (London) Ltd, 2/3 Fareham Street, Dean Street, W1V 4DU. *T:* 01-437 5203.                                    *Died* 14 April 1983.

**LYLE, Thomas Keith,** CBE 1949; MA, MD, MChir (Cantab); FRCP, FRCS; Consulting Ophthalmic Surgeon: King's College Hospital (Ophthalmic Surgeon, 1938–69); Moorfields Eye Hospital (Ophthalmic Surgeon, 1936–69); National Hospital, Queen Square (Ophthalmic Surgeon, 1936–69); Director, Orthoptic Department, Moorfields Eye Hospital, 1947–69; Dean of Institute of Ophthalmology, British Post-graduate Medical Federation of University of London, 1959–67; Teacher of Ophthalmology, University of London; *b* 26 Dec. 1903; *s* of late Herbert Willoughby Lyle, MD, FRCS, Fircliff, Portishead, Somerset; *m* 1949, Jane Bouverie, *e d* of late Major Nigel Maxwell, RA, and Mrs Maxwell,

Great Davids, Kingwood, Henley-on-Thames; one *s* three *d. Educ:* Dulwich Coll.; Sidney Sussex Coll., Cambridge (Exhib.); King's College Hospital (Burney Yeo Schol.). Todd medal for Clinical Medicine; House Physician, House Surg., Sen. Surg. Registrar; First Asst Neurol. Dept, King's Coll. Hosp., 1929–33; House Surgeon, Royal Westminster Ophth. Hosp., 1934. Civilian Consultant in Ophth., RAF, 1948–; Mem., Flying Personnel Res. Cttee, RAF, Chm., Vision sub-cttee, 1975; Consultant in Ophth. Dept of Civil Aviation, Board of Trade; Hon. Consultant in Ophth., BALPA. Examiner in Ophthalmology: Bristol Univ., 1947–50; RCS, 1949–55; FRCS (Ophthalmology), 1958–66; FRCSE (Ophthalmology), 1960–70; Mem. Council, Faculty of Ophthalmologists, 1946–69, Pres., 1965–68, and Rep. on Council of RCS, 1958–63; Chm., Specialist Adv. Cttee in Ophthalmology, RCS; Past Mem., International Council of Ophthalmology; Mem. Court of Assts, Soc. of Apothecaries, Master, 1962–63. Order of St John: Deputy Hospitaller, 1960–69; Hospitaller, 1969–81; Chm., Hosp. Cttee; Member Council: Med. Protection Soc.; British Council for the Prevention of Blindness; Vice-Chm., Royal London Soc. for the Blind; Pres., St John Ambulance, Henley-on-Thames Div. Past Pres., Internat. Strabismological Assoc.; Member: Cttee of Management, Inst of Opthalmology; Ophth. Soc. UK, Pres. 1968–70; Orthoptists Bd, Council for Professions Supplementary to Medicine; Soc. Franc. d'Opthalmologie; FRSocMed (Vice-Pres. Ophth. Section, Pres. United Services Section, 1964–66); Hon. Mem. Ophth. Socs of Australia, New Zealand and Greece. Chas H. May Memorial Lectr, New York, 1952; Doyne Memorial Lectr, Oxford, 1953; Alexander Welch Lectr, Edinburgh, 1965; Vis. Lectr, Blindness Res. Foundn, Univ. of the Witwatersrand, SA, 1974. Nettleship Medal, 1959; Richardson Cross Medal, 1972. Served RAFVR, 1939–46, Temp. Air Cdre Cons. in Ophth. RAF overseas (despatches). GCStJ 1980 (KStJ 1960; CStJ 1956); Kt, Order of Holy Sepulchre, 1970. *Publications:* (co-ed with Sylvia Jackson) Practical Orthoptics in the Treatment of Squint, 1937, 5th edn (co-ed with K. C. Wybar) 1967; (co-ed with Hon. G. J. O. Bridgeman) Worth's Squint by F. B. Chavasse, 9th edn 1959; (co-ed with A. G. Cross) May and Worth's Diseases of the Eye, 13th edn 1968; (co-ed with late H. Willoughby Lyle) Applied Physiology of the Eye, 1958; articles in British Jl Ophth., Lancet, BMJ, Med. Press and Circular, etc, chapters in Sorsby's Modern Trends in Ophthalmology, 1948, in Stallard's Modern Practice in Ophthalmology, 1949 and in Rob and Rodney Smith's Operative Surgery, 1958. *Recreations:* gardening, riding, ski-ing. *Address:* Kingsley, Crowsley Road, Shiplake, near Henley-on-Thames, Oxon. *T:* Wargrave 2832. *Clubs:* Royal Air Force, Royal Automobile, Sloane, Ski Club of GB.
                                           *Died* 9 May 1987.

**LYMINGTON, Viscount; Oliver Kintzing Wallop;** Lieut RNVR (retired); *b* 14 Jan. 1923; *s* and *heir* of 9th Earl of Portsmouth; *m* 1st, 1952, Maureen (marr. diss. 1954), *o d* of Lt-Col Kenneth B. Stanley; 2nd, 1954, Ruth Violet (marr. diss. 1974; she *d* 1978), *yr d* of late Brig.-General G. C. Sladen, CB, CMG, DSO, MC; one *s* two *d*; 3rd, 1974, Julia Kirwan-Taylor (*née* Ogden), *d* of Graeme Ogden, DSC. *Educ:* Eton. *Address:* 11 Douro Place, W8. *Club:* Royal Automobile.                                    *Died* 5 June 1984.

**LYNCH, Rt. Hon. Sir Phillip (Reginald),** KCMG 1981; PC 1977; Minister for Industry and Commerce, Australia, 1977–82; MHR, 1966–82; *b* 27 July 1933; *m* 1958, Leah; three *s. Educ:* Xavier Coll., Melbourne; Melbourne Univ. (BA, DipEd). Management consultant; co. dir. Victorian State Pres., Young Liberal Movement; Nat. Pres., Aust. Jaycees, 1966. Minister for the Army, 1968–69; Minister for Immigration and Minister assisting the Treasurer, 1969–71: Minister for Labor, 1971–72; Dep. Opposition Leader, 1972–75; Treasurer of Australia, 1975–77, and Minister responsible for Dept of Finance, 1976–77. Dep. Leader, Federal Parly Liberal Party, 1973–82. Vice-Pres., Exec. Cttee of Commonwealth Parly Assoc., 1972–; represented Australia at confs in Geneva, Hong Kong, Jakarta, Manila, Paris, Teheran, Barbados and Washington. Certificate of Merit, Royal Humane Soc., 1953. *Publications:* essays on Australian economy in jls and periodicals throughout Australia over past ten years. *Recreations:* sailing, swimming, reading. *Clubs:* Naval and Military, Australian (Melbourne); Davey's Bay Yacht (Victoria).                                    *Died* 19 June 1984.

**LYNN, Stanley B.;** *see* Balfour-Lynn.

**LYON, (Percy) Hugh (Beverley),** MC; MA; *b* 14 Oct. 1893; *s* of late P. C. Lyon, CSI; *m* 1920, Nancy Elinor (*d* 1970), 3rd *d* of William Richardson, Guisborough and Sandsend; three *d*; *m* 1973, Elizabeth Knight (*née* Beater). *Educ:* Rugby Sch.; Oriel Coll., Oxford. Served with 6th Bn the Durham Light Infantry, 1914–19; Captain, 1917; MC 1917; wounded, 1918; prisoner of war, May 1918. Newdigate Prize Poem, 1919; BA and MA 1919; 1st class Final School Lit. Hum., 1921. Asst Master, Cheltenham Coll., 1921–26; Rector of the Edinburgh Academy, 1926–31; Headmaster of Rugby Sch., 1931–48; Chm., HMC, 1948; Director, Public Schools Appointments Bureau, 1950–61. *Publications:* Songs of Youth and War, 1917; Turn Fortune, 1923; The Discovery of Poetry, 1930.

*Address:* Springhill, Amberley, Stroud, Glos. *T:* Amberley 2275.
*Died* 18 *Jan.* 1986.

**LYON DEAN, Dr William John;** *see* Dean.

**LYONS, Hon. Dame Enid Muriel,** AD 1980; GBE 1937; retired 1962; Member Board of Control, Australian Broadcasting Commission, 1951–62; Hon. Fellow College of Nursing, Australia (FCNA), 1951; an original Vice-President, Australian Elizabethan National Theatre Trust, 1954; *b* Leesville (formerly Duck River), Tasmania, 9 July 1897; *d* of William Charles Burnell; *m* 1915, Rt Hon. Joseph Aloysius Lyons, PC, CH (*d* 1939); five *s* six *d. Educ:* State Sch.; Teachers' Training Coll., Hobart. Vice-Pres. of Executive Council, Australia, 1949–51 (first woman member of Federal Cabinet); MHR for Darwin, Tasmania, 1943–51, retired through ill-health; first woman MHR; re-elected at general elections, 1946, 1949. Newspaper columnist, 1951–54. *Publications:* So We Take Comfort (autobiog.), 1965; The Old Haggis (collection), 1970; Among the Carrion Crows (autobiog.), 1973. *Address:* Home Hill, Middle Road, Devonport, Tasmania. *Died* 2 *Sept.* 1981.

**LYONS, Prof. Francis Stewart Leland,** MA, PhD, LittD Dublin; FRHistS; FBA 1974; FRSL; MRIA; Professor of History in the University of Dublin, since 1981; *b* 11 Nov. 1923; *e s* of Stewart Lyons and Florence May Leland; *m* 1954, Jennifer Ann Stuart McAlister, two *s. Educ:* Dover Coll,; Trinity Coll., Dublin. Lecturer in History, University Coll., Hull, 1947–51; Fellow of Trinity Coll., Dublin, 1951–64, 1981–, Provost, 1974–81; Prof. of Modern History, Univ. of Kent, 1964–74. Master of Eliot Coll., Univ. of Kent, 1969–72. Ford's Lectr in English History, Univ. of Oxford, 1977–78. FRSL 1978. Hon. Fellow, Oriel Coll., Oxford, 1975. Hon. DLitt: Pennsylvania, 1975; Hull, 1978; Kent, 1978; NUU, 1980; Hon. DLit QUB, 1978; Hon. LLD St Andrew's, 1981. Wolfson Literary Award, 1980. *Publications:* The Irish Parliamentary Party, 1951; The Fall of Parnell, 1960; Internationalism in Europe, 1815–1914, 1963; John Dillon: a biography, 1968; Ireland since the Famine, 1971; Charles Stewart Parnell, 1977 (Heinemann award, 1978); Culture and Anarchy in Ireland 1890–1939, 1979 (Ewart-Biggs Meml Prize, 1980); (ed with R. A. J. Hawkins) Ireland under the Union: Varieties of Tension, essays in honour of T. W. Moody, 1980; (ed) Bicentenary Essays: Bank of Ireland 1783–1983, 1983; articles and reviews in various historical jls. *Recreations:* walking, squash rackets. *Address:* Trinity College, Dublin. *T:* Dublin 772941. *Club:* Kildare Street and University (Dublin).
*Died* 21 *Sept.* 1983.

**LYONS, James,** OBE 1964; FDSRCSE; FFDRCSIre; retired as dental surgeon, 1974; Hon. Consultant Dental Surgeon to Northern Ireland Hospitals Authority, 1952; *b* 4 June 1887; *s* of Richard Lyons, Sligo; *m* 1916, Kathleen Arnold, *d* of George Myles, Crieff, Scotland; two *s* one *d. Educ:* Clevedon Sch., Somerset; Royal Coll. of Surgeons, Edinburgh. LDS 1912; FDS 1951, RCS Edinburgh; FFD 1963, RCS, Ireland. Hon. Dental Surgeon to Royal Victoria Hospital, Belfast, 1927–51; Lectr on Dental Materia Medica, at Dental Sch. of Queen's Univ., Belfast, 1935–52. Member: Dental Bd of UK, 1939–56; British Dental Assoc. (Pres. N Ireland Branch, 1939–41); N Ireland Health Services Bd, 1948–66; General Dental Council, 1956–61. Hon MDS QUB, 1971. *Recreations:* photography, motoring. *Address:* High Trees, 4 Kincraig Park, Newtownalley, Co. Antrim, NI. *Died* 5 *Aug.* 1983.

**LYONS, Brig. Richard Clarke,** CIE 1946; MC; *b* 4 June 1893; *m* 1920, Francis Emily Gavin (*d* 1969), *d* of late Col A. L. Lindesay; two *s*

one *d. Educ:* Rugby; RMA Woolwich. Royal Artillery, 1914–27; Indian Army, 1927; Chief Inspector of Armaments, India, 1942; Ordnance Consulting Officer for India (India Office), 1945; retired, 1948. Served European War, 1914–18 (wounded, MC, despatches). *Address:* 32A Apsley Road, Clifton, Bristol BS8 2SS. *T:* Bristol 36909. *Club:* Army and Navy. *Died* 14 *Nov.* 1981.

**LYONS, Thomas;** MP (N Ireland) North Tyrone 1943–69, retired; farmer; *b* 18 Feb. 1896; *s* of late J. J. Lyons, JP, farmer, Newtownstewart, Co. Tyrone, and Elizabeth McFarland, Ballinamallaght, Donemana, Co. Tyrone; *m* 1927, Clarice E. Kiss, Croydon, Sydney, Australia; two *s* one *d. Educ:* Albert Agricultural Coll., Glasnevin, Dublin. Enlisted 1915, in N Irish Horse, served European War, France, with that Regt until transferred, 1917, to Royal Irish Fus. (wounded). Went to Australia, 1922; returned N Ireland, 1939; entered politics as result of by-election, Aug. 1943; Dep. Speaker and Chm. of Ways and Means, House of Commons, N Ireland, 1955–69. JP 1944, High Sheriff 1961, Co. Tyrone. *Address:* Riversdale, Newtownstewart, Co. Tyrone. *T:* Newtownstewart 253. *Club:* Tyrone County (Omagh).
*Died* 16 *May* 1985.

**LYONS, Sir William,** Kt 1956; RDI 1954; President, Jaguar Cars Co. Ltd, since 1972; *b* 4th Sept. 1901, Blackpool; *s* of William Lyons; *m* 1924, Greta, *d* of Alfred Jenour Brown; two *d* (one *s* decd). *Educ:* Arnold Hse, Blackpool. Founded in partnership, Swallow Sidecar Co., 1922, which, after several changes in name, became Jaguar Cars Ltd (Chm. and Chief Exec., until 1972); formerly: Dep. Chm., British Leyland Motor Corp.; Chm. and Chief Exec., Daimler Co. Ltd; Chm., Coventry Climax Engines; Chm., Lanchester Motor Co. Ltd and other subsid. cos; retired 1972. Past President: Soc. of Motor Manufrs and Traders, 1950–51; Motor Industry Research Assoc., 1954; Motor Trades Benevolent Fund, 1954; Fellowship of the Motor Industry (FMI). FRSA 1964; Hon. AMIAE. Hon. DTech Loughborough, 1969. Coventry Award of Merit Gold Medal, 1970; Gold Medal, AA, 1972. *Recreation:* golf. *Address:* Wappenbury Hall, Wappenbury, near Leamington Spa, Warwickshire. *T:* Marton 632209. *Died* 8 *Feb.* 1985.

**LYTTON, 4th Earl of,** *cr* 1880; **Noel Anthony Scawen Lytton,** OBE 1945; Viscount Knebworth, 1880; Baron Lytton, 1866; Baron Wentworth, 1529; Bt 1838; *b* 7 April 1900; *s* of 3rd Earl of Lytton, OBE, and 16th Baroness Wentworth (*d* 1957); *S* father, 1951; *m* 1946, Clarissa Mary, *er d* of late Brig.-Gen C. E. Palmer, CB, CMG, DSO, RA, and of Mrs Palmer, Christchurch, Hants; two *s* three *d. Educ:* Downside; RMC Sandhurst. Lieut, Rifle Bde, 1921, attached King's African Rifles, 1922–27; Administrator, Samburu and Turkhana District, Kenya, 1924–25; Instructor (Economics), Sandhurst, 1931–35; Captain Rifle Bde, 1936; Staff Capt., War Office, 1937; Major, 1938; served War of 1939–45 (temp. Lt-Col) in N Africa, Italy, Greece and Austria; Administrator, Patras District, Greece, 1944; Chief Staff Officer, Mil. Government of Vienna, 1945–46; retd, 1946. Leader, Working Boys' Club, Bermondsey, 1937–39; formerly Member: Youth Adv. Council; Central Adv. Council for Educn (England). Farmer, 1959–; author; a crossbencher, House of Lords. Associated with Lady Lytton in local work for Life, care and housing trust, 1975–. Freeman: Missolonghi, Greece; Kismayu, Somalia. *Publications:* The Desert and the Green (autobiography), 1957; Wilfrid Scawen Blunt (biog.), 1961; Mickla Bendore (novel), 1962; Lucia in Taormina (novel), 1963; The Stolen Desert (history), 1966. *Heir:* *s* Viscount Knebworth. *Address:* House of Lords, SW1A 0PW. *Died* 18 *Jan.* 1985.

# M

**MABBOTT, John David,** CMG 1946; President of St John's College, Oxford, 1963–69; *b* 18 Nov. 1898; *s* of late Walter John and Elizabeth Mabbott; *m* 1934, Doreen Roach (*d* 1975). *Educ:* Berwickshire High Sch.; Edinburgh Univ.; St John's Coll., Oxford. Asst Lectr in Classics, Reading Univ., 1922; Asst Lectr in Philosophy, Univ. Coll. of North Wales, 1923; John Locke Scholar, Univ. of Oxford, 1923; Fellow of St John's Coll., Oxford, 1924–63, Tutor, 1930–56, Sen. Tutor, 1956–63 and Hon. Fellow, 1969. *Publications:* The State and the Citizen, 1948; An Introduction to Ethics, 1966; John Locke, 1973; Oxford Memories, 1986; contribs to Philosophy, Proc. Aristotelian Soc., Classical Quarterly, Mind. *Address:* Wing Cottage, Mill Street, Islip, Oxon. *T:* Kidlington 2360. *Died 26 Jan.* 1988.

**McALLISTER, Sir Reginald (Basil),** Kt 1973; CMG 1966; CVO 1963; FRGSA; JP; retired; Trustee, National Party of Australia, Queensland, since 1966; *b* 8 May 1900; *s* of Basil William and Beatrice Maud McAllister; *m* 1951, Joyce Isabel Roper; no *c. Educ:* Brisbane Primary and Secondary State Schools. Clerk, Railway Dept, Brisbane, 1916; secretarial duties, Parlt House, Brisbane, and Sec. to Speaker, 1924–26; reporter, State Reporting Bureau, Parlt House, 1926–33; Sec. to Premier of Queensland, 1933–37 (accompanied Premier on missions to: UK and Canada, 1934; UK and Europe, 1936; UK Internat. Sugar Conf., 1937); Asst Under-Sec., Premier and Chief Secretary's Dept, 1938; Official Sec., Qld Govt Offices, London, 1943–48 (actg Agent-Gen. on many occasions); resumed former duties in Brisbane, 1948; Clerk of Exec. Council of Qld, 1941–43, 1951–66; Under-Sec., Premier's Dept, and Chm., State Stores Board, 1962–66; acted as Sec. to Cabinet on many occasions; retd 1966; Executive Officer of five Premiers and four Governors, 1933–66. State Director, Royal Visits: HM Queen Elizabeth II and Prince Philip, 1963; TRH Duke and Duchess of Gloucester, 1965; HM King and Queen of Thailand, 1962; assisted with Royal Visits: HRH Duke of Gloucester, 1934; HM the Queen and Prince Philip, 1954; HM Queen Elizabeth the Queen Mother, 1958; HRH Princess Alexandra, 1959. Pres., Qld Br., Royal Commonwealth Soc.; Australian-Asian Soc.; Vice Patron, Australia-Japan Soc. (Pres., 1972); Exec. Cttee, Australian Red Cross Soc; Vice Patron and former Pres. Council, RGSA; Mem. State Council and Executive, Scout Assoc. of Australia. Dep. Chm., Bd of Dirs, Warana Spring Festival, 1965–. Liveryman, Farriers' Co.; Freeman, City of London; JP 1933. *Recreations:* golf, fishing, gardening, politics. *Address:* 34 Scott Road, Herston, Brisbane, Queensland 4006, Australia. *T:* 356 5361. *Clubs:* Queensland Turf, Masonic, Tattersall's, Queensland Lawn Tennis, Royal Automobile, Brisbane Cricket (all Queensland).

**McALPINE OF MOFFAT,** Baron *cr* 1980 (Life Peer), of Medmenham in the County of Buckinghamshire; **Robert Edwin McAlpine;** Bt 1918; Kt 1963; Partner, Sir Robert McAlpine & Sons, since 1928; Chairman, Greycoat London Estates Ltd, since 1978; *b* 23 April 1907; *s* of William Hepburn McAlpine and Margaret Donnison; *S* to baronetcy of brother, Sir Thomas George Bishop McAlpine, 4th Bt, 1983; *m* 1st, 1930, Ella Mary Gardner Garnett (*d* 1987); three *s* one *d*; 2nd, 1988, Nancy, *widow* of Robert Hooper. *Educ:* Oundle. Joined Sir Robert McAlpine & Sons, 1925. Chm. Trustees, Apprentice Sch. Charitable Trust, 1980–; a Vice-Pres., Nat. Children's Home 1986–. Hon. FICE 1986. *Recreations:* breeding race horses, farming, travel, golf, theatre. *Heir* (to baronetcy only): *s* Hon. William Hepburn McAlpine [*b* 12 Jan. 1936; *m* 1959, Jill Benton, *o d* of Lt-Col Sir Peter Fawcett Benton Jones, 3rd Bt, OBE, ACA; one *s* one *d*]. *Address:* Benhams, Fawley Green, Henley-on-Thames, Oxon. *T:* Henley-on-Thames 571246. *Clubs:* Garrick, Buck's, Caledonian, Jockey. *Died 7 Jan.* 1990.

**McALPINE, Douglas,** MD, FRCP; Emeritus Consultant Physician to the Middlesex Hospital; *b* 19 Aug. 1890; *s* of late Sir Robert McAlpine, 1st Bt, and late Florence Palmer; *m* 1917, Elizabeth Meg Sidebottom (*d* 1941); one *s* one *d*; *m* 1945, Diana, *d* of late Bertram Plummer; one *s. Educ:* Cheltenham; Glasgow Univ.: Paris. MB, ChB, Glasgow, 1913; joined RAMC, Aug. 1914; served France till 1915; Aug. 1915, joined Navy as Surgeon Lt, RN; served afloat until 1918 (despatches); elected to staff of several London Hospitals; became Neurologist to Middlesex Hospital, 1924; FRCP 1933. Late Brig. RAMC; Cons. Neurol. MEF, India Comd and SEAC, 1941–45 (despatches). *Publications:* Multiple Sclerosis: a Reappraisal (jointly), 1965, 2nd edn 1972; various papers in medical jls. *Recreations:* fishing, golf. *Address:* Lovells Mill, Marnhull, Dorset. *Died 4 Feb.* 1981.

**McALPINE, Hon. Sir John (Kenneth),** KCMG 1977 (CMG 1970); Chairman, New Zealand Ports Authority, 1968–79; *b* 21 July 1906; *s* of Walter Kenneth and Gwendolin Marion McAlpine; *m* 1934, Lesley Ruth Hay; one *s* two *d. Educ:* Christ's Coll., Christchurch, New Zealand. MP Selwyn, NZ, 1946–66. Mem. Tawera CC, 1927–63; Pres., Canterbury Federated Farmers, 1945–47. Mem.

Bd: Arthur's Pass National Park, 1942–79; Lyttleton Harbour, 1937–54 (Chm., 1942–45); Canterbury Univ., 1950–60; Canterbury Agricultural Univ., 1959–79 (Chm., 1967–73). Minister: Railways, Marine, and Printing, 1954–66; Mines, 1956–58; Transport and Civil Aviation, 1957–66; Labour, 1956–58. Mem., Exec., NZ Holiday Travel, etc, 1966–; Chairman: South Island, NZ, Promotion Bd, 1937–79; Canterbury Progress League, 1937–. *Recreations:* Rugby football, long distance running, gardening, skiing. *Address:* 50 McDougall Avenue, Christchurch 1, New Zealand. *Club:* Christchurch (NZ). *Died 11 Jan.* 1984.

**McALPINE, Sir Thomas (George Bishop),** 4th Bt *cr* 1918; Director of Sir Robert McAlpine & Sons; *b* 23 Oct. 1901; *s* of William Hepburn McAlpine (2nd *s* of 1st Bt) and Margaret Donnison, *d* of T. G. Bishop; *S* kinsman, Sir (Alfred) Robert McAlpine, 3rd Bt, 1968; *m* 1st, 1934, Doris Frew (*d* 1964), *d* of late D. C. Campbell and *widow* of W. E. Woodeson; 2nd, 1965, Kathleen Mary, *d* of late Frederick Best and *widow* of Charles Bantock Blackshaw; no *c. Educ:* Warriston; Rossall Sch. Joined firm of Sir Robert McAlpine on leaving school; eventually became a partner and director; retired from the partnership, 1966. *Recreations:* farming, photography, travel. *Heir: b* Baron McAlpine of Moffat. *Address:* The Manor House, Stanford-in-the-Vale, Faringdon, Oxon. *Club:* Royal Automobile. *Died 5 Aug.* 1983.

**MacANDREW,** 2nd Baron *cr* 1959; **Colin Nevil Glen MacAndrew;** *b* 1 Aug. 1919; *s* of 1st Baron MacAndrew, PC, TD, and of Lilian Cathleen, *d* of James Prendergast Curran, St Andrews; *S* father, 1979; *m* 1943, Ursula Beatrice (*d* 1986), *d* of Captain Joseph Steel; two *s* one *d. Educ:* Eton College; Trinity College, Cambridge. Served War, 1939–45. *Recreations:* hunting, racing, golf. *Heir: s* Hon. Christopher Anthony Colin MacAndrew [*b* 16 Feb. 1945; *m* 1975, Sarah, *o d* of Lt-Col P. H. Brazier; one *s* two *d*]. *Address:* Dilston House, Aldborough St John, Richmond, Yorks. *T:* Piercebridge 272. *Died 9 July* 1989.

**MACARA, Sir (Charles) Douglas,** 3rd Bt *cr* 1911; *b* 19 April 1904; *s* of 2nd Bt and Lillian Mary (*d* 1971), *d* of John Chapman, Boyton Court, East Sutton, Kent; *S* father, 1931; *m* 1926, Quenilda (marr. diss. 1945), *d* of late Herbert Whitworth, St Anne's-on-Sea; two *d* (one *s* decd). *Heir: b* Hugh Kenneth Macara, *b* 17 Jan. 1913. *Died* 1982.

**McARDLE, Michael John Francis,** MB, BS (Hons, London), FRCP; Consulting Physician Emeritus for Nervous Diseases, Guy's Hospital; Consulting Physician Emeritus, The National Hospital, Queen Square, WC1; Hon. Consulting Neurologist, Kingston Hospital and St Teresa's Maternity Hospital, Wimbledon, SW19; *b* 1909; *s* of Andrew McArdle; *m* 1955, Maureen MacClancy (*d* 1978). *Educ:* Wimbledon Coll.; Guy's Hospital; Paris. Entrance Scholarship, Arts, Guy's Hospital. Medical Registrar, Guy's Hospital; Asst Medical Officer, Maudsley Hospital. Rockefeller Travelling Fellow in Neurology, 1938. War of 1939–45, Temp. Lt-Col, RAMC and Adviser in Neurology, 21st Army Group. *Publications:* papers on neurological subjects in medical journals. *Recreation:* golf. *Address:* 3 Kingsdown, 115A The Ridgway, SW19 4RL. *T:* 01–946 4149. *Died 28 Jan.* 1989.

**MacARTHUR, (David) Wilson,** MA; author and freelance journalist; *b* 29 Aug. 1903; *s* of Dr Alex. MacArthur, MB, CM; *m* 1956, Patricia Knox Saunders; two *s. Educ:* The Academy, Ayr; Glasgow Univ. (MA Hons Eng. Lang. and Lit.). Fiction Editor, Daily Mail and Evening News, London, 1935. Travelled widely in Europe, America and Africa, 1929–39 (over 500 short stories and innumerable articles). Served War of 1939–45, RNVR. Overland by car London to S Africa, 1947, and again 1949–50. Settled in S Rhodesia, 1947; engaged in tree-farming as well as writing, broadcasting, etc. Publisher and Editor, the RTA Jl. *Publications:* Yellow Stockings, 1925; Lola of the Isles, 1926; Mystery of the "David M", 1929; Landfall, 1932; Quest of the Stormalong, 1934; Carlyle in Old Age, 1934; They Sailed for Senegal, 1938; Convict Captain, 1939; The Royal Navy, 1940; The North Patrol, 1941; The Road to the Nile, 1941; East India Adventure, 1945; The Young Chevalier, 1947; The River Windrush, 1946; The River Fowey, 1948; The River Conway, 1952; The River Doon, 1952; Auto Nomad in Sweden, 1948; Traders North, 1951; Auto Nomad in Barbary, 1950; Auto Nomad Through Africa, 1951; Auto Nomad in Spain, 1953; The Desert Watches, 1954; Simba Bwana, 1956; The Road from Chilanga, 1957; Zambesi Adventure, 1960; Harry Hogbin, 1961; Death at Slack Water, 1962; The Valley of Hidden Gold, 1962; Guns for the Congo, 1963; A Rhino in the Kitchen, 1964; The Past Dies Hard, 1965; My Highland Love, 1978; We Knew a Duiker, 1978; Escape to Sunshine, 1978; My Name is Arabella, 1980; Touch A Tender Spot, 1981; under pseudonym of David Wilson: The Search for Geoffrey Goring, 1962; Murder in Mozambique, 1963; Witch's Cauldron, 1981. *Address:* Post Restante, Richmond, 3780, South Africa. *Died 13 Nov.* 1981.

**McARTHUR, Col Sir Malcolm Hugh,** Kt 1978; OBE; psc; Chairman of companies; farmer and grazier; Past Chairman, Australian Meat

Board, 1970–77; *b* Armidale, NSW, 13 Dec. 1912; *s* of late Alex C. McArthur, Armidale; *m* 1949, Nancy, *d* of late A. Kellett; three *d*. *Educ:* Royal Military Coll., Duntroon, Aust. Aust. Staff Corps, and AIF, 1933–63. Served War of 1939–45: Australia, India, Middle East, Italy, Pacific Area, Japan (wounded, despatches). Chm., Aust. Egg Bd, 1967–70; Pres., Egg Marketing Authorities of Aust., 1960–70. Chairman: M H & N McArthur & Co. Pty Ltd; T L Kingston Pty Ltd; Russel Armstrong Pty Ltd; Mermargal Holdings Pty Ltd; Dep. Chm., Trans Otway Ltd; Councillor, Royal Agric. Soc. of Vic, 1959–. Breeder of Hereford cattle. Knighthood awarded for services to the meat industry. *Recreations:* racing, hunting, polo. *Address:* Melrose Farm, Wollert, Vic 3750, Australia. *Clubs:* Melbourne, Australian, Naval and Military (Melbourne); Union (Sydney); and all metropolitan racing (Melbourne); (Pres.) Findon Hunt.　　　　　　　　　　　　　　　　*Died* 1 *March* 1985.

**MacARTHUR, Wilson;** *see* MacArthur, D. W.

**MACARTHUR-ONSLOW, Maj.-Gen. Sir Denzil,** Kt 1964; CBE 1951; DSO 1941; ED; *b* 5 March 1904; *s* of late F. A. Macarthur-Onslow; *m* 1st, 1927, Elinor Margaret (marr. diss. 1950), *d* of late Gordon Caldwell; three *s* one *d*; 2nd, 1950, Dorothy, *d* of W. D. Scott; one *s* one *d*. *Educ:* Tudor House Sch., Moss Vale; King's Sch., Parramatta, NSW. Commissioned Australian Field Artillery, 1924. Served War of 1939–45 in Middle East and New Guinea (despatches thrice, DSO). GOC 2nd Div. AMF, 1954–58; Citizen Forces Mem. of Australian Mil. Board, 1958–60. Former Partner, Light Aircraft Pty Ltd. *Address:* Mount Gilead, Campbelltown, NSW 2560, Australia. *Clubs:* Australian, Australasian Pioneers (Sydney, NSW).　　　　　　　　　　　　*Died* 30 *Nov.* 1984.

**MACAULAY, Lt-Col Archibald Duncan Campbell,** OBE 1961; Secretary, All England Lawn Tennis Club, Wimbledon, 1946–63, Vice President, 1978; *b* 27 Sept. 1897; *o s* of late Major and Mrs A. Macaulay; unmarried. *Educ:* King's Sch., Canterbury. Served with The Buffs European War, 1914–18 in France, afterwards transferring to Indian Army, 7th Bn Gurkha Rifles, retiring in 1924. Referee and manager of many lawn tennis tournaments in United Kingdom, 1923–39; served with Royal Army Service Corps, 1939–45. *Publication:* Behind the Scenes at Wimbledon, 1965. *Address:* 804 Frobisher House, Dolphin Square, SW1V 3LX. *T:* 01-828 6657. *Clubs:* Army and Navy; All England Lawn Tennis (Wimbledon).　　　　　　　　　　　　　　　　　*Died* 11 *Oct.* 1982.

**MACAULAY, Sir Hamilton,** Kt 1960; CBE 1956; *b* 1901; *s* of late Hugh Stevenson Macaulay, Glasgow; *m* 1930, Marjorie Slinger, *d* of late Francis Gill, Litton, Yorks. *Educ:* Calder HG Sch., Glasgow. Served War of 1939–45 (despatches), Lt-Col. Pres., Chittagong Chamber of Commerce, 1953–54, 1956–57 and 1959–60; Dep. Pres., Assoc. Chambers of Commerce of Pakistan, 1953–54. Chm., Chittagong Branch UK Assoc. of Pakistan, 1955–56 and 1959–60. *Recreation:* golf. *Address:* The Cottage, Harpers Road, Ash, Hants.　　　　　　　　　　　　　　　　*Died* 19 *Sept.* 1986.

**McAULAY, (John) Roy (Vincent);** QC 1978; a Recorder of the Crown Court, since 1975; Barrister-at-law, practising mainly in London and on Midland and Oxford Circuit; a legal assessor to General Medical Council and General Dental Council, since 1981; *b* Sept. 1933; *er s* of Dr John McAulay and Mrs Marty McAulay (*née* Hüni), West Wickham, Kent; *m* 1970, Ruth Hamilton Smith, Sundridge, Kent; one *s* one *d*. *Educ:* Whitgift Sch. (Victoria Scholar); Queens' Coll., Cambridge (MA Hons). National Service, Intelligence Corps, 1951–53. Called to Bar, Gray's Inn, 1957 (Lord Justice Holker Scholar); Recorder, Midland Circuit, 1965–67; Mem., Gen. Council of Bar, 1967–71. Mem. Council, Medico-Legal Soc, 1984–. *Publications:* contrib. Halsbury's Laws of England, 3rd and 4th edns, and other legal pubns. *Recreations:* walking, swimming, animals, sport. *Address:* 1 Harcourt Buildings, Temple, EC4. *T:* 01-353 0375; 5 Montpelier Row, Blackheath, SE3 0RL. *Clubs:* Caledonian; United Services (Nottingham).

　　　　　　　　　　　　　　　　*Died* 22 *Jan.* 1987.

**McBEAN, Angus Rowland;** photographer; *b* 8 June 1904; *s* of Clement Phillip James McBean and Irene Sarah Thomas; *m* 1925, Helena Wood (decd). *Educ:* Monmouth Grammar School. Bank Clerk, 1921–24; Assistant in Liberty's Antique Dept, 1924–31; left to become an odd-job man for the theatre, making masks and building scenery; gradually became a full-time photographer of the theatre, from 1936; also known for his individual approach to portraiture and the use of surrealism for its fun value. *Exhibitions:* 60th birthday, Kodak Gall., 1964; Royal Festival Hall (over 100 pictures of Vivien Leigh), 1988; *retrospectives:* Impressions Gall., York, 1976; Nat. Theatre, 1977; Michael Parkin Gall., 1985; Parco Gall., Tokyo, 1986; Torch Gall., Düsseldorf, 1987; Cripta del Collegio, Siracusa, 1987. *Publications:* Stratford Shakespeare Theatre annuals, 1947–53; (with Adrian Woodhouse) Angus McBean, 1982; (with Adrian Woodhouse) Masters of Photography: Angus McBean, 1985; Vivien, a love affair in Camera, 1989. *Recreations:* photography, interior decorating. *Address:* High Street, Debenham, Suffolk IP14 6QJ. *T:* Debenham (0728) 860422.　　　　*Died* 9 *June* 1990.

**McBEATH, Rear-Admiral John (Edwin Home),** CB 1957; DSO 1940; DSC 1941; DL; retired, 1958; *b* 27 Sept. 1907; *er s* of late Mr and Mrs J. H. McBeath, Natal, S Africa; *m* 1952, Hon. Janet Mary Blades, *y d* of 1st Baron Ebbisham, GBE; one *s* one *d*. *Educ:* Massachusetts, USA; Hilton Coll., Natal, S Africa. Entered Royal Navy, 1923; Comdr 1941; Captain, 1945; Rear-Admiral, 1955. During War of 1939–45 commanded destroyers in North Sea, Atlantic, Arctic, Mediterranean (despatches). HM Naval Base, Singapore, 1945–48; Comd First Destroyer Flotilla, Mediterranean Fleet, 1948–50; Chief of Staff to Flag Officer Commanding Reserve Fleet, 1950–52; Commodore, Royal Naval Barracks, Devonport, 1953–55; lent to RNZN, 1955; Chief of Naval Staff and First Member Naval Board, RNZN, 1955–58. ADC to the Queen 1955. Hon. Commodore, Sea Cadet Corps, 1958–75. DL Surrey, 1968, High Sheriff, 1973–74. Chevalier, Order of Merit (France), 1939. *Address:* Bracken House, Crooksbury Hill, Farnham, Surrey. *T:* Runfold 2605. *Club:* Army and Navy.

　　　　　　　　　　　　　　　　*Died* 28 *March* 1982.

**McBRIDE, Rt. Hon. Sir Philip Albert Martin,** PC 1959; KCMG 1953; *b* 18 June 1892; *s* of late Albert J. McBride, Adelaide; *m* 1914, Rita I., *d* of late E. W. Crews, Kooringa, South Australia; two *s* (and one *s* decd). *Educ:* Burra Public Sch., South Australia; Prince Alfred Coll. MHR for Grey, South Australia, 1931–34; for Wakefield, S Australia, 1946–; Member of Senate for S Australia, 1937–43; Minister without Portfolio assisting Minister for Commerce, March–Aug. 1940; Minister: for the Army and for Repatriation, Aug.–Oct. 1940; for Supply and Development, Oct. 1940–June 1941; for Munitions, 1940–41; Mem. Australian Advisory War Council, Aug.–Oct. 1941; Mem. Economic Cabinet, 1939–40, and War Cabinet, 1940–41; Dep. Leader of Opposition in Senate, 1941–43; Minister for the Interior, 1949–50; Acting Minister for Defence, April–Oct. 1950; Minister: for Defence, 1950–58; for the Navy and for Air, May–July 1951; Leader of Australian Govt Delegn to Defence Conf., London, 1951; Federal Pres. of Liberal Party, 1960–65. *Address:* 30 Briar Avenue, Medindie, SA 5081, Australia. *Club:* Adelaide (Adelaide).　　*Died* 14 *July* 1982.

**MacBRIDE, Seán;** Senior Counsel, Irish Bar; Assistant Secretary-General, United Nations, and United Nations Commissioner for Namibia, 1973–77; *b* 26 Jan. 1904; *s* of late Major John MacBride and late Maud Gonne; *m* 1926, Catalina Bulfin (decd); one *s* one *d*. *Educ:* St Louis de Gonzaque, Paris; Mount St Benedict, Gorey, Co. Wexford, Ireland. Was active in movement for Irish independence and suffered imprisonment in 1918, 1922 and 1930; was Sec. to Mr de Valera; decorated by Irish Govt for Military services in Ireland, 1938. Was a journalist for a number of years before being called to Irish Bar, 1937; Irish correspondent for Havas and some American and South African papers before War of 1939–45. Called to Bar, 1937; called to Inner Bar, 1943; holds record of having become a Senior Counsel in a shorter period of time than any other living member of the Bar; defended many sensational capital cases and had an extensive practice in High Court and Supreme Court. Founder, 1946, and Leader of political party, Clann na Poblachta (Republican Party). Member of Dail Eireann, 1947–58; Minister for External Affairs, Eire, 1948–51. Pres., Council of Foreign Ministers of Council of Europe, 1950; Vice-Pres., OEEC, 1948–51; declined ministerial portfolio, June 1954, on ground of inadequate parliamentary representation; delegate to Council of Europe from Ireland, 1954. Trustee, Internat. Prisoners of Conscience Fund; Mem. Exec., Pan-European Union; Consultant to late President K. N'Krumah in relation to forming OAU; Mem., European Round Table; Mem., Ghana Bar; International Congress of Jurists, New Delhi, 1958 and Rio de Janeiro, 1962; Chm., Irish Assoc. of Jurists; one of the founders of Amnesty International and Chm. Internat. Exec., 1961–75; President: Internat. Commn of Jurists (Sec.-Gen. of the Commn, 1963–70, Mem., 1971–); Internat. Peace Bureau, Geneva, 1972–85 (Pres. Emeritus, 1985–); Internat. Commn for Study of Communication Problems, 1977. Mem., Tunisian Acad. of Scis, 1983. LLD (hc): Coll. of St Thomas, Minnesota, 1975; Guelph Univ., Canada, 1977; TCD, 1978; Univ. of Cape Coast, 1978; DLitt (hc) Bradford Univ., 1977. Elected to Internat. Gaelic Hall of Fame, 1974; Man of the Year, Irish United Socs, 1975. Nobel Peace Prize (jtly), 1974; Lenin Internat. Prize for Peace, 1977; Amer. Medal of Justice, 1978; Internat. Inst. of Human Rights Medal, 1978; Gold Medal, Arab League Educnl and Cultural Council, Tunis, 1985. Commander, Order of Arts and Letters (France), 1984. *Publications:* Civil Liberty, 1948 (pamphlet); Our People—Our Money, 1951; A Message to the Irish People, 1985. *Recreation:* sailing. *Address:* Roebuck House, Clonskea, Dublin 14. *T:* Dublin 694225; International Peace Bureau, 41 rue de Zurich, CH 1201 Geneva, Switzerland.　　　　　　　　　　*Died* 15 *Jan.* 1988.

**McCABE, Most Rev. Thomas,** DD; *b* 30 June 1902; *s* of John Patrick and Elizabeth McCabe. *Educ:* St Augustine's School, Coffs Harbour, NSW; St Columba's College, Springwood, NSW. St Patrick's College, Manly, NSW; Propaganda College, Rome. Ordained Priest in Rome, 1925; Administrator of St Carthage's Cathedral, Lismore, NSW, 1931–39; Bishop of Port Augusta, 1939–52; Bishop of

Wollongong, 1952–74; retired 1974. *Address:* Polding Villa, 2 Arcadia Avenue, Glebe Point, NSW 2037, Australia.
*Died 15 Sept. 1983.*

**McCALL, Charles James**, DA (Edinburgh); ROI 1949, NEAC 1957; artist-painter; *b* 24 Feb. 1907; *s* of late William McCall, Edinburgh; *m* 1945, Eloise Jerwood, *d* of late F. Ward, Bickley, Kent. *Educ:* Edinburgh Univ.; Edinburgh College of Art. RSA Travelling Schol., 1933; Edinburgh College of Art: Travelling Schol., 1936 (Fellow, 1938). Studied in many art galleries in Europe; also in studios in Paris. Returned to London in 1938, exhibiting RA, NEAC, London Group, etc. Commissioned, RE 1940; at end of war taught drawing and painting at Formation College. Has exhibited regularly in London; one-man shows held at: Leicester Galleries, 1950 and 1953; Victor Waddington Galleries, Dublin, 1951; Duveen Graham Galleries, New York, 1955 and 1957; Crane Galleries, Manchester, 1955; Klinkhoff Gallery, Montreal, 1958 and 1960; Whibley Gallery, London, 1963; Federation of British Artists, 1965; Ash Barn Gallery, Stroud, 1965, 1969, 1973; Eaton's Gallery, Winnipeg, Canada, 1966; Nevill Gallery, Canterbury, 1972; Belgrave Gallery, 1975, 1977; Bath Contemporary Festival, 1982–83; Gerber Gallery, Glasgow, 1984; Bridge St Gall., Newmarket, 1988; W. H. Patterson Gall., London, 1988; retrospective, Addison-Ross Gall., London, 1987; paintings in: Sotheby's Centenary NEAC, 1985; Christie's NEAC Centenary exhibn, 1986. BBC TV Programme on his life and work, 1975; profile in Artist magazine, 1981. Painter of portraits, landscapes, interiors with figures, and of contemporary life. Lord Mayor's Art Award, 1963, 1973, 1977. *Relevant publication:* Interior with Figure, the life and painting of Charles McCall, 1987, by Mitzi McCall. *Recreations:* music, literature, travel. *Address:* 1a Caroline Terrace, SW1W 8JS. *T:* 01–730 8737.
*Died 3 Oct. 1989.*

**McCALL, Kenneth Murray**, DL; Lord Lieutenant of Dumfriesshire, 1970–72; *b* 21 Dec. 1912; *s* of late Major William McCall, DL; *m* 1938, Christina Eve Laurie; two *s* two *d*. *Educ:* Merchiston Castle School. DL Dumfriesshire, 1973. *Recreations:* shooting, golf. *Address:* Caitloch, Moniaive, Thornhill, Dumfriesshire. *T:* Moniaive 211.
*Died 14 Feb. 1987.*

**McCALLUM, Brig. Frank**, CIE 1947; OBE 1936; MC 1923; DL; *b* 11 March 1900; *s* of late Lt-Col D. McCallum, RASC, Edinburgh; *m* 1932, Sybilla Mary de Symons (OBE 1977; County Councillor for Kesteven, Lincs, 1964–74), *d* of late Gen. Sir George Barrow, GCB, KCMG; one *s* (and one *s* decd). *Educ:* George Watson's Coll.; RMC. Commissioned 1918; Brig. 1943. ADC to GOC-in-C Eastern Comd, India, 1928–29; Staff Coll., Quetta, 1934–35; Bde Major, Razmak, 1936–39; GSO2 Meerut Dist, 1940–41; served in Iraq, Persia, Western Desert, and Syria, 1941–46; GSO1, 8 Indian Div., 1941–43; Bde Comd, 1943–46; BGS Northern Comd, India, 1946–47; Dir Staff Duties, Army HQ, Pakistan, 1947. Served 3rd Afghan War, 1919; NWF, 1920–21 and 1923 (MC); NWF, 1936 (OBE) and 1937–39; despatches 7 times, 1936–46; retd 30 May 1948. Asst Regional Food Officer, North Midland Region, 1948–51; Regional Sec. Country Landowners Assoc. for Lincs, Notts, and Derbys, 1951–65; CC Kesteven, Lincolnshire, 1952–74, Alderman, 1964–74. DL Lincolnshire, 1965. Syrian Order of Merit, 1st Class, 1945–46. *Address:* Westborough Grange, near Newark, Notts NG23 5HH. *T:* Lovedon 81285.
*Died 14 July 1983.*

**McCANCE, Sir Andrew**, Kt 1947; DSc; LLD; FRS 1943; DL; *b* 30 March 1889; *yr s* of John McCance; *m* 1936, Joya Harriett Gladys Burford (*d* 1969); two *d*. *Educ:* Morrison's Academy, Crieff; Allan Glen's Sch., Glasgow; Royal School of Mines, London. DSc London, 1916. Asst Armour Manager, W. Beardmore & Co., 1910–19; Founder and Man. Dir, Clyde Alloy Steel Co. Ltd, 1919–30, Pres. 1965–71; Formerly: Chm. and Man. Dir, later Hon. Pres., Colvilles Ltd. Past President: Iron and Steel Inst.; Glasgow and West of Scotland Iron and Steel Inst.; Inst. of Engineers and Shipbuilders in Scotland: President: British Iron and Steel Federation, 1957, 1958; Instn of Works Managers, 1964–67. Chm., Mechanical Engineering Research Board, DSIR, 1952–58. DL Lanarkshire. Hon. DSc Strathclyde, 1965. Bessemer Medallist, 1940. *Publications:* several papers in Technical Society jls. *Address:* Malin Court, Maidens, Girvan, Ayrshire KA26 9PB. *Clubs:* Athenæum; Scottish Automobile (Glasgow).
*Died 11 June 1983.*

**McCANN, Hugh James;** Chairman, Cultural Relations Committee, Irish Department of Foreign Affairs, since 1981; President, Ireland-France Economic Association, since 1981; *b* 8 Feb. 1916; *e s* of late District Justice Hugh Joseph McCann, BL, and Sophie McCann, Dublin; *m* 1950, Mary Virginia Larkin, Washington, DC, USA; four *s* one *d*. *Educ:* Belvedere Coll., Dublin; London Sch. of Economics, Univ. of London. Served in Dept of Lands, Dublin, and in Dept of Industry and Commerce, Dublin; Commercial Sec., London, 1944–46; First Sec., Dept of External Affairs, Dublin, 1946–48; Counsellor, Irish Embassy, Washington, DC, 1948–54; Irish Minister to Switzerland and Austria, 1954–56; Asst Sec., Dept of External Affairs, Dublin, 1956–58; Irish Ambassador to the Court

of St James's, 1958–62; Sec., Dept of Foreign Affairs, Dublin, 1963–74; Irish Ambassador to France, Perm. Rep. to OECD and to UNESCO, 1974–81, and concurrently Ambassador to Morocco, 1975–81. Dir, Independent Newspapers Ltd, 1982–. Chm., Nat. Cttee for Study of Internat. Affairs, RIA, 1984–. Grand Cross, Order of Leopold II, Belgium, 1968; Grand Officer, National Order of Merit, France, 1981. *Recreations:* golf, reading, swimming, and photography. *Address:* Shenandoah, Mart Lane, Foxrock, Co. Dublin. *Clubs:* Royal Dublin Society, Stephen's Green (Dublin), Woodbrook Golf.
*Died 11 Nov. 1986.*

**McCANN, Most Rev. James**, MA; PhD; DD; LLD; *b* Grantham, Lincs, 31 Oct. 1897; *s* of James W. and Agnes McCann; *m* 1924, Violet, *d* of James and Mary Henderson, Ballymena, Ireland; no *c*. *Educ:* Royal Belfast Academical Institution; Queen's University, Belfast (BA; Hon. LLD 1966); Trinity College, Dublin (MA, PhD, DD). Ecclesiastical History Prizeman (1st), 1917; Elrington Theological Prizeman (1st), 1930; ordained 1920; held curacies at Ballymena, Ballyclare, Cavan, Oldcastle; Rector of Donaghpatrick, 1930–36; St Mary's, Drogheda, 1936–45; Canon of St Patrick's Cathedral, Dublin, 1944–45; Bishop of Meath, 1945–59; Archbishop of Armagh and Primate of All Ireland, 1959–69. *Publication:* Asceticism: an historical study, 1944. *Recreations:* music, reading. *Address:* c/o Rev. H. A. McCann, The Rectory, Begbroke, Oxford. *T:* Kidlington 3253. *Club:* Kildare Street and University (Dublin).
*Died 19 July 1983.*

**McCARTHY, John Haydon**, CB 1963; Controller, Central Office, Department of Health and Social Security, Newcastle upon Tyne, 1956–74; *b* 1914; 3rd *s* of late Lt-Comdr Jeremiah and Mrs Margaret McCarthy, Walton-on-Thames; *m* 1947, Mary, *e d* of Ebenezer Barclay, Lanark; three *s*. *Educ:* St Joseph's (de la Salle) Coll., London. Entered GPO, 1931; transferred Home Office, 1936; Min. of Nat. Insce, 1945; Under-Sec., 1956. *Recreation:* sea fishing. *Address:* 3 Front Street, Whitley Bay, Tyne and Wear. *T:* 520206.
*Died 20 March 1984.*

**McCARTHY, Mary, (Mrs James West);** writer; *b* 21 June 1912; *m* 1933, Harold Johnsrud; *m* 1938, Edmund Wilson; one *s*; *m* 1946, Bowden Broadwater; *m* 1961, James Raymond West. *Educ:* Annie Wright Seminary; Vassar Coll. Theatre critic, Partisan Review, 1937–57, Editor, Covici Friede, 1937–38; Instructor, Bard Coll., 1945–46; Instructor, Sarah Lawrence Coll., 1948. Lectures and broadcasts, 1952–65. President's Distinguished Visitor, Vassar, 1982; Stevenson Chair of Lit., Bard Coll., 1986–. Mem., Amer. Acad. of Arts and Letters, 1988. Horizon award, 1948; Guggenheim Fellow, 1949–50, 1959–60; National Academy of Arts and Letters award, 1957; Nat. Medal for Literature, 1984; Edward MacDowell Medal, 1984; First Rochester Literary Award, 1985. Hon. Dr Letters: Syracuse Univ., 1973; Bard, 1976; Hon. DLitt Hull, 1974; Hon. LLD Aberdeen, 1979; Hon. Dr Litt: Bowdoin, 1981; Maine, 1982. *Publications:* The Company She Keeps, 1942; The Oasis, 1949; Cast a Cold Eye, 1950; The Groves of Academe, 1952; A Charmed Life, 1955; Venice Observed, 1956; Sights and Spectacles, 1956; Memories of a Catholic Girlhood, 1957; The Stones of Florence, 1959; On the Contrary, 1962; The Group, 1963 (filmed 1966); Vietnam, 1967; Hanoi, 1968; The Writing on the Wall and Other Literary Essays, 1970; Birds of America, 1971; Medina, 1972; The Seventeenth Degree, 1974; The Mask of State: a gallery of Watergate portraits, 1974; Cannibals and Missionaries, 1979; Ideas and the Novel, 1980; Occasional Prose, 1985; How I Grew, 1987; essays, journalism, short stories and reviews in the New Yorker, Partisan Review, Horizon, The New York Review of Books, The Observer, etc. *Address:* 141 Rue de Rennes, Paris, France.
*Died 25 Oct. 1989.*

**McCAULEY, Air Marshal Sir John Patrick Joseph**, KBE 1955 (CBE 1943); CB 1951; *b* 18 March 1899; *s* of late John and Sophia McCauley; *m* 1925, Murielle Mary, *d* of late John Burke, and of Maude Burke; one *s* two *d*. *Educ:* St Joseph's Coll., Sydney; RMC, Duntroon; Melbourne Univ. (BCom 1936). Grad. RMC 1919; Aust. Staff Corps, 1919–23; RAAF, 1924–; passed RAF Staff Coll., 1933; Flying Instructor's Course, Central Flying Sch., RAF, 1934; Dir Trg, RAAF HQ Melbourne, 1937–38; CO 1 Flying Trg Sch. 1939; CO 1 Eng. Sch., 1940; CO RAAF Stn Sembawang, Malaya, 1941–42; CO RAAF Stn, Palembang 11, Sumatra, 1942; SASO RAAF Darwin, 1942; DCAS, 1942–43; Air Cdre Ops, 2nd TAF France and Germany, 1944–45; DCAS, 1946–47; Chief of Staff, BCOF, Japan, 1947–49; AOC E Area, 1949–53; CAS, RAAF, 1954–57, retd. *Address:* 10 Onslow Gardens, Greenknowe Avenue, Elizabeth Bay, Sydney, NSW 2011, Australia.
*Died 3 Feb. 1989.*

**McCAUSLAND, Lucius Perronet T.;** *see* Thompson-McCausland.

**McCLOY, John Jay**, DSM 1945; Medal of Freedom (US), 1963; Partner, Milbank Tweed, Hadley & McCloy, since 1963; Hon. Chairman and Chairman Executive Committee, Squibb Corporation; Hon. Chairman, Board of the Council on Foreign Relations, Inc.; *b* 31 March 1895; *s* of John Jay McCloy and Anna

May Snader; *m* 1930, Ellen Zinsser (*d* 1986); one *s* one *d*. *Educ*: Amherst Coll. (AB); Harvard Univ. (LLB). Admitted to New York Bar, 1921; mem. of law firm of Cravath, de Gersdorff Swaine & Wood, New York City, 1929–40; expert cons. to Sec. of War, 1940; The Asst Sec. of War, 1941–45; Chm. of The Combined Civil Affairs Cttee of Combined Chiefs of Staff; Mem. of law firm of Milbank, Tweed, Hope, Hadley & McCloy, NY City, 1945–47; Pres. International Bank for Reconstruction and Development, Washington, DC, 1947–49; US Military Governor and US High Comr for Germany, Frankfurt, Germany, 1949–52; Mem. State Dept Cttee on Atomic Energy, 1946–47; Counsel, Milbank, Tweed, Hope & Hadley, 1961; Adviser to President Kennedy on Disarmament, 1961; Chairman: Co-ordinating Cttee of the US on Cuban Crisis, 1962–63; Past Chm., Gen. Adv. Cttee on Arms Control and Disarmament; Mem. Exec. Cttee, The Salk Inst., La Jolla, Calif; Hon. Chairman: Atlantic Institute, 1966–68; Amer. Council on Germany Inc. Mem., President's Commn on the Assassination of President Kennedy; Mem., American and NY Bar Assocs; Mem., Bar Assoc. of City of New York. Director: Dreyfus Corp., NYC; Mercedes-Benz of N America, Inc. Past Chm. and Trustee, Ford Foundation. Chm. Public Oversight Bd, Sec. Practice Section, AICPA, 1978–. Retired Director: The Chase Manhattan Bank (Chm. 1953–60); Metropolitan Life Insurance Co.; Westinghouse Electric Corp.; American Telephone & Telegraph Co; Allied Chemical Corp. Trustee, John M. Olin Foundn. Hon. Trustee: Bd of Trustees, Amherst Coll., Mass (Chm.); Lenox Hill Hosp.; Johns Hopkins Univ.; Trustee, Amer. Sch. of Classical Studies, Athens; Mem., Bd of Overseers to visit Center for Internat. Studies, Harvard Univ. Capt. FA, AEF. Holds numerous hon. degrees both in US and abroad, also Civic Hons. Hon. Citizen of Berlin, 1985. Grand Officer of Legion of Honour (France); Grand Officer of Order of Merit of the Republic (Italy); Grand Cross of Order of Merit (Federal Republic of Germany). *Publication*: The Challenge to American Foreign Policy, 1953. *Recreations*: tennis and fishing. *Address*: 1 Chase Manhattan Plaza, New York, NY 10005, USA. *Clubs*: Brook, Links, University, Century, Anglers, Recess, Ausable, Clove Valley Rod and Gun (NY); Metropolitan (Washington). *Died 11 March 1989.*

**McCLURE, Ivor Herbert,** DSO 1918; 2nd *s* of late Rev. Canon Edmund McClure; *m* 1925, Beatrice Eliott-Drake, *e d* of late Rev. H. M. Eliott-Drake Briscoe, MA, formerly Rector of Burnham Thorpe and Rural Dean of Burnham; one *s* one *d*; *m* 1950, Mabel James Orr, Bow Cottage, Charmouth, Dorset, *y d* of late James Angus, Ochiltree House, Ayrshire. *Educ*: Eton; Harrow; Clare Coll., Cambridge (BA). Served European War, 1914–19 (despatches five times, DSO, 1914 Star). Asst Dir, Cardiff Station, BBC, 1926, Head of Aviation Dept, Automobile Assoc., 1929; Chm., Aviation Section, London Chamber of Commerce, 1934; Operational Adviser, Dir of Civil Aviation, Air Min., 1935; Dir of Operational Services and Intelligence, Dept of Civil Aviation, Air Min., 1937; Asst Sec. Gen. for Air Navigation, Provisional Internat. Civil Aviation Organization (later ICAO), 1945; retd, 1949. *Address*: Sutton, County Brome, Quebec, Canada. *Club*: Royal Automobile. *Died 25 April 1981.*

**McCOMB, James Ellis,** CBE 1964; DFC 1940; DL; General Manager, Cwmbran New Town Development Corporation, 1962–74; *b* 19 April 1909; *er s* of late D. K. McComb, TD, JP; *m* 1939, Sonia, *d* of late Col H. J. Decker, TD; one *d*. *Educ*: Stowe Sch. Served War of 1939–45: comd 611 Fighter Sqdn AAF, 1939–40; RAF Staff Coll., 1942; 8th USAF Liaison, 1942; COSSAC Cover Plan, Invasion Europe, 1943; Air Liaison, C-in-C Allied Navies, 1944; SHAEF, 1944–45. Solicitor, 1932; Allen & Overy, City of London, 1933–36; Lancs CC, 1936–48; Dep. Clerk of Peace, Lancs, 1946–48; Gen. Man., Welwyn Garden City and Hatfield New Towns, 1949–62. DL Gwent, 1975. OStJ 1976. *Recreations*: gardening, painting. *Address*: Wye Cottage, Dixton Road, Monmouth.

*Died 4 Aug. 1982.*

**McCOMBS, Hon. Sir Terence (Henderson),** Kt 1975; OBE 1971; ED 1943; retired; *b* 5 Sept. 1905; *m* 1st, 1935, Beryl Butterick (*d* 1952); three *s* one *d*; 2nd, 1955, Christina Mary Tulloch; one *s*. *Educ*: Christchurch and Waitaki Boys' High Schs, NZ; University of Canterbury, NZ (MSc(Hons)). CChem, MRSC; Hon. FNZIC. Teaching, 1931–35. MP Lyttelton (NZ), 1935–51; Parly Under-Sec. to Minister of Finance, 1945–47; Minister of Education and Sci. and Ind. Research, 1947–49. Teacher, 1951–55; Headmaster, Cashmere High Sch., Christchurch, 1956–72; High Commissioner for NZ in the UK and Ambassador for NZ in Ireland, 1973–75. Member: Christchurch City Council, 1950–57, 1977– (Chm., Finance Cttee, 1951–57; Chm., Town Planning Cttee, 1977–); Lyttelton Harbour Bd, 1938–47; Bd of Governors, Canterbury Agric. Coll.; Chm., Christchurch Milk Co. Senate, Univ. of NZ, 1960–61; Chancellor, Univ. of Canterbury, NZ, 1969–73. Chm., Cttee on Secondary Educn, 1975–76. Trustee for NZ, Commonwealth Foundn (Chm., Conf. and Minor Grants Cttee). Freeman, City of London, 1973; Hon. Freeman, Worshipful Co. of Butchers, 1973. *Publications*: scientific papers in: Jl of Chem. Soc.;

Science and Technology (NZ); NZ Foreign Policy (NZ); World Affairs (NZ). *Address*: 7 Freeman Street, Christchurch 8, New Zealand. *Clubs*: Rotary; University of Canterbury (Christchurch); Rotary (Christchurch South) (Governor, Dist 298, 1967–68).

*Died 6 Nov. 1982.*

**McCONNELL, Gerard Hamilton,** CB 1967; Assistant Under-Secretary of State, Home Office, 1957–74; Principal Finance Officer, 1967–74; *b* 22 Jan. 1913; *s* of late Mr and Mrs J. McConnell; *m* 1939, Dorothy Margaret Drummond Wilson; two *d*. *Educ*: Manchester Grammar Sch.; St John's Coll., Cambridge, Scottish Home Dept, 1936–46 (Royal Air Force, 1942–44); Home Office, 1946; Asst Sec., 1948. *Address*: 2 The Slade, Clophill, Beds. *T*: Silsoe 60392. *Died 2 April 1982.*

**McCONNELL, Comdr Sir Robert Melville Terence,** 3rd Bt, *cr* 1900; VRD; RNVR (retired); *b* 7 Feb. 1902; *s* of Sir Joseph McConnell, 2nd Bt, and Lisa (*d* 1956), *d* of late Jackson McGown; *S* father, 1942; *m* 1st, 1928, Rosamond Mary Elizabeth (marr. diss., 1954), *d* of James Stewart Reade, Clonmore, Lisburn, Co. Antrim; three *s* one *d*; 2nd, 1967, Mrs Alice A. M. Hills. *Educ*: Glenalmond; St John's Coll., Cambridge; College of Estate Management, London. Consultant with R. J. McConnell and Co., estate agents, Belfast. *Heir*: *s* Robert Shean McConnell *b* 23 Nov. 1930. *Address*: Pigeon Hill, Island Road, Killyleagh, Co. Down, N Ireland.

*Died 3 May 1987.*

**McCONNELL, William Samuel,** DA (RCS); FFARCS; Consultant Anaesthetist Emeritus, Guy's Hospital; *b* 22 April 1904; *s* of late James McConnell, BA, MB, BCh; *m* 1932, Olive, *d* of late Capt. L. E. Stannard; two *s*. *Educ*: Emanuel Sch., London; Univ. of London. Guy's Hospital Medical Sch.: MRCS, LRCP, 1927; MB, BS (London), 1929; DA (RCS), 1935; FFA, RCS, 1948. Anaesthetist to Guy's Hospital, 1935. Temp. Lt-Col RAMC: Adviser in Anaesthetics, Southern Army, India Comd, 1942–45. Hon. Visiting Anaesthetist, Johns Hopkins Hosp., Baltimore, Md, 1955. Pres., Section of Anaesthetics, RSM, 1969–70. *Publications*: articles on anaesthesia in professional jls. *Address*: 55 Chartfield Avenue, SW15. *Died 25 Feb. 1982.*

**McCORMACK, Robert John Murray,** FRCSEd; FRCPEd; Consultant Cardiothoracic Surgeon, Royal Infirmary and City Hospital, Edinburgh, since 1961; *b* 20 July 1922; *s* of Robert and Isabella McCormack; *m* 1947, Gwyneth Avarina, *d* of Canon Jenkin Jones; one *s* two *d*. *Educ*: North Berwick High Sch. (Dux 1939); Edinburgh Univ. (MB, ChB Hons 1944). FRCSEd 1948; FRCPEd 1974. Served RAMC, UK and India, 1944–47 (Major). Registrar in Gen. Surgery, Royal Infirm., Edinburgh, 1947–49; Registrar, then Sen. Registrar in Thoracic Surgery, Eastern Gen. Hosp., Edinburgh, 1949–53, Consultant Cardiothoracic Surgeon, 1953–61. Chm., Med. Cttee, Royal Victoria Hosps Bd of Management, 1966–74; Member: Scottish Cttee for Hosp. Med. Services, 1974–; Jt Cttee on Higher Surg. Trng in UK, 1977–; Scottish Council, BMA, 1977–. Pres., Scottish Thoracic Soc., 1976–78; Vice-Pres., RCSE, 1977–80 (Mem. Council, 1973–); Hon. Sec., Assoc. of Thoracic and Cardiovascular Surgeons of GB and Ireland, 1971–76. *Publications*: chapters in books; articles in jls on cardiac and thoracic subjects. *Recreations*: golf, crosswords. *Address*: 14 Russell Place, Edinburgh EH5 3HH. *T*: 031–552 2568. *Clubs*: New, University Staff (Edinburgh).

*Died 20 Sept. 1981.*

*This entry did not appear in Who's Who.*

**McCRAY, Sir Lionel (Joseph),** Kt 1978; FASA, FAIM; ACIS; full-time company director, since 1973; *b* 29 Aug. 1908; *s* of Joseph Burney McCray and Florence Mary McCray; *m* 1942, Phyllis Coralie Burbank; one *s* one *d*. *Educ*: Brisbane Grammar Sch. ACIS 1931; FASA 1930; FAIM 1950. Clerk: Eclipse Windmill Co. Ltd, 1923–24; State Govt Insurance Office, 1924–27; State Treasury, 1927–32; Accountancy Coach, Blennerhassetts Inst. of Accountancy, 1932–35; Sales Manager, Campbell Brothers Ltd, 1935–43, Man. Dir, 1943–56; Gen. Manager: Peters-Arctic Delicacy Co. Ltd, 1956–60; QUF Industries Ltd, 1960–73. Chm., Sedgwick Pty Ltd (Qld Bd); Director: Australian United Foods (formerly Chm.); Crusader Oil NL; QUF Industries Ltd. Dep. Chancellor, Univ. of Qld, 1978–83 (Mem. Senate, 1972–). President: Industrial Management Assoc., 1948–50; Rotary Club of Fortitude Valley, 1949–50; Qld Chamber of Manufactures, 1950–53; Royal Qld Golf Club, 1963–66; Brisbane Club, 1970–71. Vice-President: Aust. Inst. of Management, 1950–56; Associated Chambers of Manufactures of Aust., 1951–53. Chm., State Govt Adv. Cttee on Youth Grants, 1967–81. Member: Manufg Industries Adv. Council, 1967–73; State Council, Inst. of Public Affairs, 1976–; State Cttee, the Queen's Silver Jubilee Appeal for Young Australians, 1977–78. Dist Governor, Rotary Internat. Dist 35, 1955–56. Trustee, Spina Bifida Assoc., 1972–. Hon. LLD Qld, 1982. *Recreations*: golf, astronomy, travel. *Address*: 12 Blair Lane, Ascot, Qld 4007, Australia. *T*: 262 2095. *Clubs*: Brisbane, University of Queensland, Royal Queenland Golf, Royal Queensland Automobile (Brisbane); Rotary of Fortitude Valley. *Died 11 March 1984.*

**McCRINDLE, Susan;** see Ertz, S.

**McCRONE, Robert Watson,** MC 1916; BSc, MICE; ARCST; *b* 6 Feb. 1893; *s* of Edward McCrone, Craigallion, Kilmacolm, Renfrewshire; *m* 1934, Enid Marie, OBE, *d* of B. W. Just, Bristol; three *d. Educ:* Merchiston Castle Sch., Edinburgh; Royal College of Science and Technology, Glasgow; Glasgow Univ. Served European War, 1914–18, in Royal Engineers, 51st Highland Div. (despatches, MC); Croix de Guerre, France, 1918. Founder in 1923 of Metal Industries Group of Companies; Man. Dir and then Chm. until 1955; Dir, British Oxygen Co. Ltd, 1933–63; Chm. or Dir of many other industrial concerns until 1963. Former Mem., Lloyd's. Past Mem. East of Scotland Electricity Board. Formerly: Chm., Dunfermline and West Fife Hosp. Bd; Governor Royal College of Science and Technology, Glasgow. *Recreations:* farming, yachting. *Address:* Pitliver, by Dunfermline, Fife. *T:* Limekilns 872232.
*Died 5 April* 1982.

**McCULLOUGH, Thomas Warburton,** CB 1962; OBE 1954; HM Chief Inspector of Factories, Ministry of Labour, 1958–63; *b* 13 March 1901; *o s* of late Robert McCullough and Emma Warburton, *d* of Thomas Rigby; *m* 1928, Lisette Hunter (*d* 1979), *d* of late Henry George Gannaway; one *s. Educ:* Ballymena Academy; Glasgow Univ.; Middle Temple. BSc 1925. Engineering training, 1917–25; Valuation Dept, Ministry of Finance, Belfast, 1925; joined Factory Dept, Home Office, 1926. Member Joint Advisory Cttee on Conditions in Iron Foundries, 1947; Hon. Adviser Scottish Industrial Groups Advisory Council, 1951–53; Chairman of numerous Joint Standing Cttees, 1950–56. Member: Home Office Inter-Departmental Cttee on Accidents in the Home, 1954–57; National Industrial Safety Cttee, 1954–57, Executive Cttee, 1958–63, Royal Society for Prevention of Accidents; Industrial Grants Cttee, Dept of Scientific and Industrial Research, 1958–63; Nuclear Safety Advisory Cttee, 1960–63; Technical Adviser (Safety), The United Steel Companies Ltd, 1963–67. Hon. Life Member, Royal Society for Prevention of Accidents, 1963; Hon. Fellow, Institution of Industrial Safety Officers, 1964; Hon. Adviser (Safety) British Steel Corp. (formerly British Iron and Steel Fedn), 1964–74; Pres., London Construction Safety Group, 1963–74. Silver Medal, L'Institut National de Sécurité, Paris, 1961; Industrial Safety Award, RoSPA, 1970. *Publications:* sundry contribs to literature of accident prevention in industry. *Address:* c/o Hon. Mr Justice McCullough, Royal Courts of Justice, Strand, WC2.
*Died 28 Dec.* 1989.

**McCUSKER, (James) Harold;** MP (UU) Upper Bann, since 1983 (Armagh, 1974–83) (resigned seat Dec. 1985 in protest against Anglo-Irish Agreement; re-elected Jan. 1986); *b* 7 Feb. 1940; *s* of James Harold McCusker and Lily McCusker; *m* 1965, Jennifer Leslie Mills; three *s. Educ:* Lurgan Coll.; Stranmillis Coll., Belfast. Teacher, 1961–68; Trng Officer, 1968–73; Production Man., 1973–74. Sec. and Whip, Ulster Unionist Party, Westminster, 1975–76. Mem. (UU) Armagh and Dep. Leader, Official Unionist Party, NI Assembly, 1982–86. Chm., NI Gas Employers' Bd, 1977–81. *Address:* 33 Seagoe Road, Portadown, Craigavon BT63 5HW. *T:* Portadown 33876; 25 Vincent Square, SW1. *T:* 01–821 7036.
*Died 12 Feb.* 1990.

**McCUTCHEON, Sir (Walter) Osborn,** Kt 1966; LFRAIA, LFRAPI; Consultant (Partner, 1926–77), Bates, Smart & McCutcheon, Melbourne (Architects, Engineers and Town Planners); *b* 8 April 1899; *s* of W. B. McCutcheon, Solicitor, Melbourne; *m* 1928, Mary, *d* of A. A. Buley; two *s* one *d. Educ:* Wesley Coll., Melbourne; Univ. of Melbourne. Mem. Faculty, Melbourne Univ. School of Architecture; Director, Arch., Melbourne Technical Sch., 1930–39; Member Council, Royal Victorian Inst. of Architects, 1930–45 (Pres., 1940–42; Mem. Board of Arch. Educn, 1933–39, 1940–42, 1953–57); Pres., Building Indust. Congr. of Victoria, 1934–36; Member Council, RAIA, 1941–42; Chief Architect, Engineers HQ, US Army, SW Pacific Area, 1942–44; Controller of Planning etc to Australian Commonwealth Govt, 1944–46; resumed private practice, 1946. Mem. various cttees; assessor of sundry competitions. Mem., National Capital Planning Cttee, Nat. Capital Develt Commn, 1967–73; Chairman: Central City Consultative Cttee, 1976–79; Metropolitan Strategy Consultative Cttee, 1979–83, Min. for Planning. Gold Medal, RAIA, 1965. Hon. LLD, Monash Univ., 1968; DArch *hc* Melbourne, 1983. *Publications:* articles in Architecture in Australia, etc. *Recreations:* sailing, reading. *Address:* (office) 1 Clarendon Street, East Melbourne, Vic 3002, Australia. *T:* Melbourne 417-1444; (home) 139 Baden Powell Drive, Mount Eliza, Vic 3930, Australia. *T:* Melbourne 787-1479. *Clubs:* Melbourne, Savage (Melbourne); Peninsula Country Golf, Davey's Bay Yacht, Mornington Yacht.
*Died 6 May* 1983.

**MacDERMOT, The, (Sir Dermot MacDermot),** KCMG 1962 (CMG 1954); CBE 1947; styled Prince of Coolavin; *b* 14 June 1906; 2nd surv. *s* of late Charles Edward, The MacDermot, Prince of Coolavin; *S* brother, 1979; *m* 1934, Betty Steel; three *s. Educ:* Stonyhurst Coll.; Trinity Coll., Dublin, LLD *jure dignitatis,* 1964. Joined HM Consular Service in 1929 and served in Tokyo, Yokohama, Kobe and Osaka in Japan, Manila (Philippines), Tamsui (Formosa), New Orleans, and in the Foreign Office. Appointed a Counsellor in the Foreign Office, 1947; Inspector, HM Foreign Service, 1951; HM Minister to Roumania, 1954–56; HM Ambassador to Indonesia, 1956–59; Assistant Under-Secretary, Foreign Office, 1959–61; HM Ambassador to Thailand, 1961–65. *Recreation:* golf. *Heir: s* Niall Anthony MacDermot, *b* 25 April 1935. *Address:* Dunlavin, Co. Wicklow, Eire. *Club:* Kildare Street and University (Dublin).
*Died 27 Aug.* 1989.

**McDONALD, Sir Alexander Forbes,** Kt 1972; *b* 14 Aug. 1911; *s* of late Angus McDonald and late Christina Jane Forbes; *m* 1937, Ethel Marjorie, *d* of late Theodore Crawford, MC, and late Sarah Anne Mansfield; two *s* two *d. Educ:* Hillhead Sch.; Glasgow Univ. BL Glasgow 1933. Chartered Accountant, 1934. Chairman: The Distillers Company, 1967–76; Council, Scotch Whisky Assoc., 1967–76. DL, County of City of Edinburgh, 1963. *Address:* 6 Oswald Road, Edinburgh EH9 2HF. *T:* 031-667 4246.
*Died 5 Dec.* 1981.

**MACDONALD, Allan Ronald,** CMG 1953; *b* 21 Dec. 1906; *s* of Major Ronald Macdonald and Elizabeth Blair Macdonald (*née* Coats); *m* 1st, 1937, Katherine May Hodson; two *s*; 2nd, 1954, Dr Mary Shaw (*d* 1956). *Educ:* Fettes Coll., Edinburgh; St John's Coll., Cambridge. Ceylon Civil Service, 1929–48; Establishment Sec., Uganda, 1948–51; Colonial Sec., Sierra Leone, 1951–56; Mem. of Lidbury Commn on Gold Coast Public Service, 1951; Chm., Public Service Commn: Kenya, 1956–64; Fedn of South Arabia, 1965–67. *Address:* c/o Hongkong and Shanghai Banking Corporation, PO Box 199, 99 Bishopsgate, EC2P 2LA. *Club:* United Oxford & Cambridge University.
*Died 21 April* 1984.

**MACDONALD, Archibald James Florence,** JP; *b* 2 May 1904; *s* of late Dr G. B. D. Macdonald, MB, ChM, and late Beatrice B. Macdonald; *m* 1945, Hon. Elspeth Ruth Shaw, *d* of 2nd Baron Craigmyle; two *s. Educ:* Chatswood Grammar Sch., Australia; Royal Australian Naval Coll. Joint Chief Executive, Management Research Groups, London, 1937–40; Secretary, Paint Industry Export Group, 1940–47; Dir and Sec., Wartime Paint Manufacturers' Assoc., 1943–45; Dir, Robert Bowran & Co. Ltd, 1949–53; Vice-Chm., Joseph Freeman Sons & Co. Ltd, 1954–66. MP (L) Roxburgh and Selkirk, 1950–51. Member Bd of Visitors, Wormwood Scrubs and Pentonville Prisons. Councillor: Hampstead Borough Council, 1962–65; Camden Borough Council, 1971–76. JP County of London. *Recreations:* travel, people. *Address:* 22 Heath Drive, Hampstead, NW3 7SB. *T:* 01-435 2317. *Clubs:* Reform, Garrick.
*Died 20 April* 1983.

**MACDONALD, Coll;** Headmaster of Uppingham School, 1975–82; *b* 21 Jan. 1924; *s* of Coll Macdonald and Elizabeth (*née* Murray); *m* 1955, Hilary Constance Mowle; two *s. Educ:* Rugby Sch.; Christ's Coll., Cambridge (MA). Pilot, RAFVR, 1943–46. Lectr in Greek, Univ. of Sydney, 1949; Lectr in Classics, Univ. of Otago, 1950–51; Asst Master, Bradfield Coll., 1952–55; Asst Master, Sherborne Sch., 1955–60; Head Master: Maidenhead Grammar Sch., 1960–65; Portsmouth Grammar Sch., 1965–75. Research Fellow in Classical Philology, Harvard Univ., 1972–73. *Publications:* (jtly) From Pericles to Cleophon, 1954; (jtly) Roman Politics 80–44 BC, 1960, 2nd edn 1965; (ed) Cicero: De Imperio Cn, Pompei, 1966, 2nd edn 1971; (ed) Cicero: Pro Murena, 1969; (ed) Cicero: De Provinciis Consularibus, 1971; (ed) Cicero: In Catilinam I-IV, Pro Murena, Pro Sulla, Pro Flacco (Loeb Classical Library), 1977; contrib. Greece and Rome, Classical Review, Classical Qly. *Recreations:* walking, swimming. *Address:* 11 Marine Court, Southsea, Hampshire PO4 9QU. *T:* Portsmouth 756793.
*Died 20 May* 1983.

**MACDONALD, Prof. Donald Farquhar;** Professor of Modern Social and Economic History, University of Dundee, 1967–76 (University of St Andrews, 1955–67); *b* 3 June 1906; 3rd *s* of Donald Macdonald and Annabella Mackenzie; *m* 1955, Jeannette Eileen Bickle; one *s. Educ:* Dingwall Academy; Aberdeen Univ. (MA 1st cl. Hons Hist.); Balliol Coll., Oxford (DPhil). University Lecturer, Aberdeeen Univ. and University Coll., Exeter, 1934–41; Ministry of Supply and Ministry of Labour and National Service, 1941–43; Secretary (later General Manager), National Assoc. of Port Employers, 1943–55. *Publications:* Scotland's Shifting Population, 1770–1850, 1937; The State and the Trade Unions, 1960, revised edn 1976; The Age of Transition, 1967, etc. *Address:* 11 Arnhall Drive, Dundee.
*Died 14 Oct.* 1988.

**MACDONALD, Donald Hardman,** CMG 1974; *b* 16 May 1908; *s* of Archibald J. H. and Elizabeth Macdonald; *m* 1930, Simone Dumortier (decd); one *s* one *d. Educ:* City of London Sch. Partner, Charles Fulton & Co., London, 1935–39; Bank of England, 1939–49; Chief, Allied Bank Commn, Frankfort, 1949–52; Adviser, Bank of England, 1953–54; Bank for International Settlements, Basle, 1954–73 (Head of Banking Dept, 1972–73). *Recreations:* reading, travel, gardening. *Address:* 18 route de Rossillon, 1226 Thônex, Geneva, Switzerland. *T:* (022) 47.39.32.
*Died 3 Oct.* 1990.

**MACDONALD, Air Vice-Marshal Donald Malcolm Thomas**, CB 1952; RAF retired; *b* 15 Aug. 1909; *s* of late D. P. Macdonald, Tormore, Isle of Skye; *m* 1938, Kathleen Mary de Vere, *d* of late J. T. Hunt, Oxford; one *s* four *d. Educ:* Westminster School. Joined Royal Air Force, 1930. Dir-Gen. of Personal Services, Air Min., 1957–58; Dir-Gen. of Manning, Air Min., 1958–61, retd 1961. Mem. Crofters Commn, 1962–65. Chm., Royal British Legion, Scotland, 1977–81. *Address:* Torbeag, Clachan Seil, by Oban, Argyll. *T:* Balvicar 311.
*Died 26 Oct.* 1988.

**MacDONALD, Douglas George;** Managing Director: John Menzies (Holdings) plc, 1971–84; Receptor International Ltd, since 1985; *b* 5 Aug. 1930; *s* of Colin Douglas MacDonald and Jane Grant Stewart; *m* Alexandra von Tschirschky und Boegendorf; one *s. Educ:* Morgan Acad., Dundee; Univ. of St Andrews (BSc). Queen's Own Cameron Highlanders, 1951–57. Potash Ltd, 1957–66; Man. Dir, Wyman Marshall Ltd, 1966–68. Member: National Freight Corp., 1973–80; Scottish Telecommunications Bd, 1973–76; Chm., East Lothian Conservative and Unionist Assoc., 1970–73; Director: Scottish Investment Trust plc, 1977–83; William Muir (Bond 9) Ltd, 1981–; Robert Moss plc, 1981–83; Scottish Life Assce Co. Ltd, 1982–83; Royal Bank of Scotland plc, 1982–85; Chairman: Advent Technol. plc, 1981–; Clan Donald Lands Trust, 1982–. Chm., Scottish Council, Res. Inst. Ltd, 1975–85. Scottish Nat. Orch. Soc., 1984. *Address:* c/o Royal Bank of Scotland, 36 St Andrew Square, Edinburgh EH2 2YB. *Clubs:* Royal Automobile; New (Edinburgh). *Died 4 July* 1989.

**MacDONALD, George Alan;** a Recorder of the Crown Court, 1972–81; *b* 21 April 1909; *s* of George John MacDonald, FIEE and Mabel Elizabeth Miriam (*née* Davies); *m* 1937, Frances Marguerite Davies; two *s* one *d. Educ:* St Joseph's, Totland Bay; Manor House, Havant; Hartley Univ. Coll., Southampton. Solicitor, 1931. RNVSR, 1938; Temp. Lt-Comdr RNVR, 1944. Pres., Hampshire Law Soc., 1959; Chairman: Southern Rent Tribunal, 1962–74; Mental Health Review Tribunal for Oxford and Wessex, 1968–81; Misuse of Drugs Act Tribunal, 1974–82; Isle of Wight Rent Tribunal, 1974–81; Mem. Council, Law Soc., 1970–79; Clerk of the Peace, Portsmouth, 1971; Pres., Southern Rent Assessment Panel, 1979–81. *Publications:* occasional contrib. Law Society's Gazette. *Recreations:* hockey (Hampshire 1947–49), gardening, moorland walking, canal cruising, sound radio, cricket. *Address:* 8 King Street, Emsworth PO10 7AZ. *T:* Emsworth 374459. *Club:* Royal Naval and Royal Albert Yacht (Portsmouth). *Died 22 July* 1985.

**MACDONALD, Ian Wilson**, MA; DLitt; CA; *b* Old Cumnock, Ayrshire, 28 May 1907; *s* of late Rev. Alexander B. Macdonald, BD, PhD, Dron, Perthshire, and late Dr Mary B. W. Macdonald; *m* 1933, Helen Nicolson, MA; one *s* two *d. Educ:* Perth Academy; Edinburgh Academy. Prof. of Accountancy, Univ. of Glasgow, 1938–50. Partner in Kerr Macleod and Macfarlan, CA, Glasgow, 1933–53. Member: Cttee of Investigation into Port Transport Industry, 1945; Court of Inquiry into Omnibus Industry, 1946, Shipbuilding Industry, 1947, Railwaymen's Wages and Hours of Work, 1947; Arbitrator, Nigerian Railways Labour dispute, 1948; Mem. Gen. Claims Tribunal, 1943–58. Member: Cttee of Inquiry: Fishing Industry, 1957–60; Ports and Harbours, 1961–62; Member: S Scotland Electricity Board, 1956–61; National Ports Council, 1963–67; NRDC, 1959–73; CAA, 1972–75. Chairman: Lloyds and Scottish Ltd, 1959–78; Royal Bank of Scotland Ltd, 1969–72; Dir, Lloyds Bank Ltd, 1961–78; Dep. Chm., National and Commercial Banking Group Ltd, 1969–78. Chm., Scottish Hosps Endowments Res. Trust, 1971–83. *Recreation:* fishing. *Address:* Seton Court, Gullane, East Lothian EH31 2BD. *Club:* Caledonian.
*Died 8 Jan.* 1989.

**McDONALD, Sir James**, KBE 1967 (CBE 1956; OBE 1948); Hon. British Consul, Portland, Oregon USA, 1938–87; Managing Partner: Macdon & Co.; Kermac Investment Co.; Renfrew Associates; *b* 23 July 1899; *s* of late James McDonald, Renfrew, Scotland; *m* 1933, Anne, *d* of late Peter Kerr, Portland, Ore, USA; one *s* two *d. Educ:* Allen Glen's Sch., Glasgow. Lt, RFC (later RAF), 1917–19. Partner McDonald Gattie & Co., 1927–67; President: Norpac Shipping Co., 1940–67; McDonald Dock Co., 1955–72. Trustee: Oregon Historical Soc.; Oregon Parks Foundn. *Recreations:* walking, farming. *Address:* 11626 SW Military Lane, Portland, Ore, USA. *T:* 636–4775; Inchinnan Farm, Wilsonville, Ore, USA. *T:* 625–6914. *Clubs:* Boodle's, Royal Air Force; Arlington, University (Portland, Ore.). *Died 23 Jan.* 1989.

**MacDONALD, Rt. Hon. Malcolm John**, OM 1969; PC 1935; Chancellor of the University of Durham, since 1970; *b* Lossiemouth, Morayshire, 1901; *s* of late J. Ramsay and Margaret MacDonald; *m* 1946, Mrs Audrey Fellowes Rowley; one *d. Educ:* Bedales Sch., Petersfield; Queen's Coll., Oxford. MA. Mem. of LCC, 1927–30. Contested (Lab) Bassetlaw Div., 1923, 1924; MP (Lab) Bassetlaw Div. of Notts, 1929–31 (National Labour), 1931–35; MP (National Government) Ross and Cromarty, 1936–45; Parliamentary Under-Sec., Dominions Office, 1931–35; Sec. of State for Dominion Affairs,

1935–38 and 1938–39; Sec. of State for Colonies, 1935 and 1938–40; Minister of Health, 1940–41; United Kingdom High Comr in Canada, 1941–46; Gov.-Gen. of the Malayan Union and Singapore, May–July 1946; Gov.-Gen. of Malaya, Singapore and British Borneo, 1946–48; Special Ambassador at inauguration of Indonesian Republic, 1949; Comr-Gen. for the UK in South-East Asia, 1948–55; UK Representative on SE Asia Defence Treaty Council, 1955; High Commissioner for the UK in India, 1955–60. Leader of British Delegation and Co-Chm., Internat. Conf. on Laos, 1961–62. Governor and C-in-C, Kenya, 1963; Governor-Gen. Kenya, 1963–64; British High Comr in Kenya, 1964–65; British Special Representative in East and Central Africa, 1966–67; Special Representative of HM Govt in Africa, 1967–69; Special Envoy to Sudan, Nov. 1967, and to Somalia, Dec. 1967. Rhodes Trustee, 1948–57; Chancellor of the University of Malaya, 1949–61; Visitor, University Coll., Kenya, 1963–64; Senior Research Fellow, Univ. of Sussex, 1971–73. President: Royal Commonwealth Soc., 1971–; Great Britain-China Centre, 1972–; Fedn of Commonwealth Chambers of Commerce, 1971–; VSO, 1975–; Caribbean Youth Develt Trust, 1977–; Britain Burma Soc., 1980–. Hon. Fellow, Queen's Coll., Oxford. Doctor of Laws and Doctor of Letters, *hc*, Durham; various North American Univs and Univs of Hanoi, Hong Kong, Singapore and Malaya. Freeman of City of Singapore, 1955; Freeman, Burgh of Lossiemouth, 1969. *Publications:* Down North, 1945; The Birds of Brewery Creek, 1947; Borneo People, 1956; Angkor, 1958; Birds in my Indian Garden, 1961; Birds in the Sun, 1962; Treasure of Kenya, 1965; People and Places, 1969; Titans and Others, 1972; Inside China, 1980. *Recreations:* ornithology, collecting, ski-ing. *Address:* Raspit Hill, Ivy Hatch, Sevenoaks, Kent. *Died 11 Jan.* 1981.

**MACDONALD, Dame Margaret (Henderson), (Dame Margaret Kidd)**, DBE 1975; QC (Scotland), 1948; Sheriff Principal of Perth and Angus, 1966–74 (of Dumfries and Galloway, 1960–66); *b* 14 March 1900; *e d* of James Kidd, Solicitor, Linlithgow (sometime MP (U) for W Lothian, and late J. G. Kidd (*née* Turnbull); *m* 1930, Donald Somerled Macdonald (*d* 1958), WS Edinburgh; one *d. Educ:* Linlithgow Acad.; Edinburgh Univ. Admitted to the Scottish Bar, 1923; contested (U) West Lothian, 1928. Keeper of the Advocates' Library, 1956–69; Editor Court of Session Reports in Scots Law Times, 1942–76; Vice-Pres. British Federation of University Women, Int. Hon. LLD: Dundee, 1982; Edinburgh, 1984. *Address:* Flat 5, 40 Drummond Place, Edinburgh EH3 6NR. *T:* 031–558 1700. *Died 22 March* 1989.

**MACDONALD, Patrick Donald**, CMG 1953; CVO 1963; *b* 21 July 1909; *s* of late Major E. W. Macdonald and Amy Beatrice Cavalier; *m* 1937, Delia Edith (marr. diss.), 5th *d* of Capt. R. W. Travers, RN (retired); twin *d* (and one *s* decd). *Educ:* Marlborough Coll.; St John's Coll., Cambridge. BA 1931. Cadet officer, Gilbert and Ellice Islands Colony, 1932; Administrative Officer, 1936; Sec. to Government, 1935–36 and 1938–39; Asst Sec., Western Pacific High Commission, 1940–42; Asst Colonial Sec., Trinidad and Tobago, 1942–45. Fiji: Administrative Officer, Grade II, 1946, Grade I, 1947; Asst Colonial Sec., 1946–49; Colonial Secretary, Governor's Deputy and Acting Governor: Leeward Islands, 1950–57; Colonial Sec. and Acting Governor, Fiji, 1957–66; Chm., Public and Police Service Commns, 1966–71. Actg Archivist, Western Pacific Archives, 1974, 1976 and 1978. *Recreations:* swimming and deep-sea fishing. *Address:* Flat 34, St Margarets, London Road, Guildford, Surrey GU1 1TJ. *T:* Guildford 575396.
*Died 15 June* 1987.

**MACDONALD Sir Peter (George)**, Kt 1963; DL; Hon. Life President, United Biscuits Ltd (Chairman, 1948–67) and McVitie & Price Ltd (Chairman, 1947–64); former Director: Guardian Assurance Co. Ltd, London; Caledonian Insurance Co. and other companies; Senior Partner, W. & J. Burness, retired 1976, now Consultant; *b* 20 Feb. 1898; *s* of William Macdonald, Darnaway, Forres, and Annie Cameron; *m* 1929, Rachel Irene, *d* of Rev. Dr Robert Forgan; one *s* two *d. Educ:* Forres Academy; Edinburgh Univ. Served European War, 1914–18, with Scottish Horse, Black Watch, RGA, and Lovat Scouts. Served with Home Guard, 1940–45; Regional Deferment Officer, Bd of Trade, Edinburgh and SE Scotland; Mem., Edinburgh and dist local Emergency Reconstruction Panel (chm. Food Section); Staff Officer on Scottish Regional Comr's Staff: former Mem. London Council, Inst. of Directors (formerly Chm., Scottish Br.); WS 1927. JP Edinburgh, 1935. DL Edinburgh, 1966. *Recreations:* fishing, shooting, golf. *Address:* 18 Hermitage Drive, Edinburgh EH10 6BZ. *T:* 031-447 1256. *Clubs:* Caledonian (London); Conservative (Edinburgh). *Died 21 July* 1983.

**MACDONALD, Air Chief Marshal Sir William (Laurence Mary)**, GCB 1965 (KCB 1959; CB 1956); CBE 1946; DFC 1940; *b* 10 Aug. 1908; *s* of William Stephen Macdonald, Co. Cork; *m* 1939, Diana (*d* 1964), *d* of late Nicholas Challacombe; one *s* one *d. Educ:* Castleknock Coll., Eire. Joined RAF 1929; Group Capt., 1942; Air Commodore, 1944; Air Vice-Marshal, 1954; Air Marshal, 1960; Air Chief Marshal, 1963. Served War of 1939–45, France, Belgium,

Holland, Germany (despatches twice, DFC, CBE). Comdt, Central Flying Sch., 1946-48; Exchange Officer with USAF, USA, 1948-50; Dep. Dir of Plans (Jt Planning), Air Min., 1952; AOC, RAF, Singapore, 1952-54; Asst Chief of Air Staff (Intelligence), 1954-58; Comdr-in-Chief, Middle East, Air Force, 1958-62, and Administrator of the Sovereign Base Areas of Akrotiri and Dhekelia, Cyprus, 1960-62; Air Sec., Ministry of Defence (formerly Air Ministry), 1962-66. Air ADC to the Queen, 1965-66. Vice-Pres., Oratory Sch. Chevalier, Legion of Honour; Croix de Guerre; Star of Jordan 1st Class. *Address:* Quarry House, Yateley, Camberley, Surrey. *T:* 873283. *Club:* East India, Devonshire, Sports and Public Schools. *Died 9 Nov. 1984.*

**MACDONALD-BUCHANAN, Major Sir Reginald (Narcissus),** KCVO 1964 (CVO 1952); MBE 1942; MC 1917; *b* May 1898; *m* 1922, Hon. Catherine Buchanan, *o c* of 1st Baron Woolavington, GCVO; two *s* two *d*. Joined Scots Guards from RMC, Sandhurst, 1916. Served European War (MC); retired, 1926. Chairman: James Buchanan & Co. Ltd; W. P. Lowrie & Co. Ltd, 1939-70; Director: Buchanan-Dewar Ltd, 1939-69; Distillers Co. Ltd, 1930-69. Mem. Council, King Edward VII's Hosp. for Officers (Chm., House and Finance Cttee 1947-69, Vice-Pres. and Treasurer, 1969). Mem. Racecourse Betting Control Bd, 1949-59; Steward of Jockey Club, 1950-51-52; Pres. Hunter's Improvement and Nat. Light Horse Breeding Soc., 1950-51, 1951-52, 1965-66. Master, Worshipful Co. of Distillers, 1952. DL Northamptonshire; High Sheriff, Northamptonshire, 1939; Pres. Northamptonshire County Agricultural Soc., 1951. Joint Master, Pytchley Hounds, 1934-39 and 1946-49; Rejoined Scots Guards, 1939; ADC to Field-Marshal Sir John Dill, 1940-43; served BEF, France, 1940; War Office, 1940-41; British Joint Staff Mission, Washington, 1941-43 (MBE); France and Belgium, 1944-45 when demobilised (despatches, US Bronze Star Medal). *Address:* Cottesbrooke Hall, Northampton. *T:* Creaton 732; 5 Kingston House South, Ennismore Gardens, SW7 1NS. *T:* 01-589 1042; Scatwell, Muir of Ord, Ross-shire. *T:* Scatwell 244; Egerton House, Newmarket. *T:* Newmarket 2151. *Clubs:* Turf, Cavalry and Guards; Royal Yacht Squadron (Cowes); Muthaiga (Nairobi). *Died 17 Nov. 1981.*

**McDOUGALL, Archibald,** MA, BCL; Attorney at Law and landowner, USA; *b* Hobart, 5 Aug. 1903; 2nd *s* of late Emeritus Prof. Dugald Gordon McDougall and Helen Ione Atkinson; *m* 1932, Corinne Margaret Cunningham Collins, artist (*d* 1977), Mobile, Alabama, and Washington, DC, USA. *Educ:* Hutchins Sch., Hobart; University of Tasmania; Balliol Coll., Oxford; Columbia Univ., New York. BA Tasmania, and Rhodes Scholar, 1924; 1st Class Final Honour Sch. of Jurisprudence, 1926; Proxime Accessit Vinerian Law Scholarship, 1927; 2nd Class Examination for BCL, 1927; Commonwealth Fund Fellowship, 1927-29; US Senate Legislative Counsel's Office, Washington, DC, 1928; Harmsworth Law Scholarship, 1929; Lecturer in Law, Victoria Univ. of Manchester, 1931-35; called to Bar, Middle Temple, 1932; Mem. of Northern Circuit; practised in Chancery Div. of High Court and in Chancery of County Palatine of Lancaster, 1932-35; Examiner in Law, London Univ., 1934-35; 1936-40 Legal Adviser to Iraqui Ministry for Foreign Affairs, Baghdad, and Prof. of Int. Law at Iraqui Law Sch.; Delegate of Iraq at 17th Assembly of League of Nations, 1936; 1940 travelled extensively through India, Burma, Malaya, NEI, and Australia; Counsel, British Purchasing Commission, New York, 1940-41; Head, Non-Ferrous Metals Div., British Raw Materials Mission, Washington, DC, and UK Staff of Combined Raw Materials Board, 1941-43; Combined Production and Resources Board (UK Staff), Washington, DC, 1944-45; Head of UK Economic Group, US Dept of Commerce and British Embassy, Washington, DC, to Aug. 1946; Legal Counsellor, British Embassy, Cairo, 1946-49; Asst Legal Adviser, Foreign Office, 1949-50. Dep. Comr of Forfeited and Delinquent Lands, 1964-. Pres., Berkeley County Bar Assoc., 1964-65; Member: American Bar Assoc.; W Virginia State Bar; W Virginia Bar Assoc.; Sustaining Mem., Assoc. of Trial Lawyers, USA; admitted US Supreme Court Bar and Fourth Circuit Court of Appeals, 1973. Founder, Trial Lawyers for Public Justice, 1982; Governor, W Va Legal Services Plan, Inc., 1982. Mem. Emeritus, Amer. Soc. Internat. Law, 1978 (Mem., 1928-). Judge, Philip C. Jessup Internat. Law Moot Court Competition, Washington, DC, 1978-. Mem., Historic House Assoc. of America, 1980-, Owners' Gp, 1981-. *Publications:* Modern Conveyancing, 1936; and articles in British Year Book of International Law. *Recreation:* motoring. *Address:* Oban Hall, Gerrardstown, West Virginia 25420, USA. *T:* Area Code 304, 229-5400. *Died 14 Jan. 1984.*

**MacDOUGALL OF MacDOUGALL, Madam;** (Coline Helen Elizabeth); 30th Chief of Clan MacDougall, 1953; *b* 17 Aug. 1904; *e d* of Col Alexander J. MacDougall of MacDougall, 29th Chief, and Mrs Colina Edith MacDougall of MacDougall; *m* 1949, Leslie Grahame-Thomson (who assumed the surname of MacDougall, 1953), RSA, FRIBA, PPRIAS, FSAScot (*d* 1974); resumed surname of MacDougall of MacDougall on succession to Chiefship, 1953. *Educ:* St James's, West Malvern. Served WRNS, 1941-46 (First

Officer). *Address:* Dunollie Castle, Oban, Argyll. *T:* Oban 2012. *Died 5 May 1990.*

**MacDOUGALL, Air Cdre Ian Neil,** CBE 1964; DFC 1942; Galt Composites Ltd (formerly Galt Glass Laminates), since 1977; *b* 11 June 1920; *s* of late Archibald MacDougall, Colonial Service, and Helen Grace (*née* Simpson); *m* 1944, Dorothy Eleanor, *d* of late John Frankland; one *s* one *d*. *Educ:* Morrison's Academy, Crieff; RAF Coll., Cranwell. Commnd Sept. 1939; served in Fighter Sqdns in Battle of Britain, Syrian and Western Desert Campaigns, Malta and in invasions of Sicily and Normandy; War Studies Lectr at RAF Coll., 1948-50 and USAF Academy, Colorado, 1956-58; Asst Air Attaché, Paris, 1950-53; Chief Flying Instructor, RAF Coll., 1953-56; Supt of Flying, Boscombe Down, 1959-62; comd RAF Fighter Stn, Binbrook, 1962-64; SASO 38 Gp, 1964-67; comd Zambian Expedn and Zambian Oil Lift, 1965-66; Air Attaché, Paris, 1967-69; jssc, psc, pfc, cfs; retd Dec. 1969. Mil. Liaison, Rolls Royce and Bristol Composite Materials Ltd, 1970-77. *Recreation:* fishing. *Address:* Swifts Cottage, East Grafton, Marlborough, Wilts SN8 3DB. *T:* Marlborough 810482. *Club:* Royal Air Force. *Died 25 Aug. 1987.*

**MacDOUGALL, Richard Sedgwick,** CBE 1957; FCA; *b* 29 May 1904; *o s* of late R. E. C. McDougall and Evelyn Mary, *d* of Richard Sedgwick; *m* 1929, Margaret Sylvia (*d* 1976), *d* of late John Charles Denmead; two *d*. *Educ:* Haileybury Coll. County Treasurer, Hertfordshire County Council, 1939-57; General Manager, Stevenage Development Corporation, 1957-67. Member: Weeks Cttee on Army Works Services, 1956-57; Colonial Secretary's Advisory Cttee on Local Govt, 1950-; North West Metropolitan Regional Hosp. Bd, 1963-68; Chm., Building Research Station Steering Cttee, 1967-70. For British Govt, visited Sierra Leone, 1950, Nyasaland, 1954, Fiji Islands, 1957, and Kenya, 1967. *Recreation:* painting. *Address:* Firbank, 9 Moorside Road, West Moors, Wimborne, Dorset BH22 0EH. *Died 27 April 1983.*

**McDOWALL, Robert John Stewart,** DSc, MD, MRCP; FRCPE; Professor Emeritus in the University of London since 1959; Professor of Physiology, 1923-59, and Dean of Faculty of Medicine and Fellow of King's College, London; Vice-Chairman Medical Advisory Committee and Founder Member, Asthma Research Council; Formerly Examiner for Universities of London, Leeds, Durham, Manchester, Aberdeen, St Andrews, Edinburgh, Sheffield, Bristol, West Indies, Nigeria, RCP, RCS, in India, Egypt, Australasia, and Eire; *b* 1892; *s* of Robert McDowall, Auchengaillie, Wigtonshire, and Fanny Grace Stewart; *m* 1st, 1921, Jessie (*d* 1963), *yr d* of Alexander Macbeth, JP, Pitlochry, Perthshire; two *d*; 2nd, 1964, Dr Jean Rotherham, *d* of Col Ewan Rotherham, TD, DL (Warwickshire). *Educ:* Watson's Coll., Edinburgh; University of Edinburgh (Gold Medal for MD thesis). Assistant and Lecturer in Physiology, University of Edinburgh, 1919-21; Lectr, Experimental Physiology and Experimental Pharmacology, Univ. of Leeds, 1921-23; Lectr in Applied Physiology, London Sch. of Hygiene, 1927-29. Ellis prizeman, 1920; Parkin prizeman, RCP, Edinburgh, 1930; Gunning Victoria Jubilee Cullen Prize, RCP, Edinburgh, 1938; Arris and Gale Lectr, RCS, 1933; Oliver Sharpey Lectr, RCP, 1941; medal of honour, Univ. of Ghent, 1951; has given 3 lecture tours of America. Hon. Fellow: Amer. Acad. of Allergy, 1953; Soc. Française d'Allergie, 1957; European Acad. of Allergy; Finnish Acad. of Allergy. Pres., 4th European Congress of Allergy, 1959; Hon. Mem., British Soc. of Allergy; Extraordinary Mem., British Cardiac Soc. Has been Resident House Physician, Edinburgh Royal Infirmary, and Clinical Tutor in Medicine, Univ. of Edinburgh; served with RAMC, European War, 1914-18, also 1940-41; became DADMS for British Forces in Palestine, Syria, and Cilicia; President, Physiology Sect. British Assoc., 1936; Chairman Board of Intermediate Medical Studies and of Physiology, University of London. *Publications:* Clinical Physiology; The Science of Signs and Symptoms in relation to Modern Diagnosis and Treatment, 4 editions; Handbook of Physiology, 13 editions; The Control of the Circulation of the Blood, 1938, 1957; The Whiskies of Scotland, 1967, 3rd edn 1975 (Swedish, German, Spanish, Japanese and American edns); Editor, The Mind, by various authors; Sane Psychology, 6 reprints; Anatomy and Physiology for students of Physiotherapy (with Smout) and numerous scientific papers. *Recreations:* chess, curling (1st President, Hampstead Curling Club; 1st President, London Watsonian Curling Club; former Pres. and Hon. Mem., Province of London; skipped England against Scotland, 1966 and 1969); golf (Ex-Captain, Life Mem. and Director, Hampstead Golf Club). *Address:* Lea-Rig, Crede Lane, Bosham, near Chichester, W Sussex PO18 8PD. *T:* Bosham 572482. *Died 12 Jan. 1990.*

**McDOWALL, Robert William,** CBE 1977 (OBE 1966); FSA (Lond.); Secretary, Royal Commission on Historical Monuments (England), 1973-79; *b* 13 May 1914; *yr s* of Rev. C. R. L. McDowall; *m* 1939, Avril Betty Everard Hannaford; three *s* one *d*. *Educ:* Eton; Magdalene Coll., Cambridge (MA). Investigator, Royal Commission on Historical Monuments (England), 1936. Served

War, with Royal Engineers, 1939–45. Vis. Lectr, UCL, 1979. Mem., Ancient Monuments Bd for England, 1973–79; Pres., Surrey Archaeological Soc., 1975–80; Vice-Pres., Royal Archaeol Inst., 1980 (Hon. Vice-Pres., 1986). Trustee, Weald and Downland Open-Air Mus., 1985– (Mem. Exec. Bd, 1985). *Publications:* contributor to: Monuments Threatened or Destroyed, 1963; Peterborough New Town, 1969; Shielings and Bastles, 1970; Recording Old Houses, 1980; County Inventories of RCHM; Archaeologia, Antiquaries Jl (and local archaeological jls). *Address:* Chandlers, Ballsdown, Chiddingfold, Surrey. *T:* Wormley 2995.

*Died 8 June 1987.*

**McDOWELL, Sir Frank (Schofield),** Kt 1967; President, McDowells Holdings Ltd, 1971–72 (Chairman and Managing Director, McDowells Ltd, 1935–67, Chairman 1967); *b* 8 Aug. 1889; *s* of John McDowell; *m* 1912, Ethel Sophia Perrott; six *s* one *d*. *Educ:* Petersham Public School. Grand Master: United Grand Lodge of NSW Freemasons, 1947–49; Mark Master Masons NSW, 1946–48; Inspector General, 33rd Rose Croix SE Central District NSW, 1967–72. *Recreations:* bowls, garden, swimming. *Address:* Melrose, 157 Ewos Parade, Cronulla, Sydney, NSW 2230, Australia. *T:* 523115. *Clubs:* (Hon. Mem.) All Nations, (Patron) Retailers, (Past Pres.) Sydney Rotary (Sydney); (Patron) South Cronulla Bowling.

*Died 1 Nov. 1982.*

**McELDERRY, Samuel Burnside Boyd,** CMG 1935; *b* 7 Oct. 1885; *s* of late Thomas McElderry and late Alice Knox of Ballymoney, Co. Antrim; *m* 1913, Mildred Mary Orme (*d* 1974); three *d*. *Educ:* Campbell Coll., Belfast; Trinity Coll., Dublin. Eastern Cadet, 1909; Hong Kong Administrative Service, 1909–28; Deputy Chief Secretary, Tanganyika, 1929–33; Chief Secretary, Zanzibar, 1933–40; retired 1940; attached to office of High Commissioner for Basutoland, Bechuanaland Protectorate and Swaziland (Pretoria and Cape Town), 1940–45; temporarily employed Colonial Office, 1945–46. Member of Council, Royal Commonwealth Society for Blind, 1951–70; Royal National Institute for Blind, 1958–70; certified blind, 1983. *Address:* Fircroft, 19 Kivernell Road, Milford-on-Sea, Lymington, Hants. *Died 20 Oct. 1984.*

**McELENEY, Most Rev. John,** SJ, DD; PhD, MA; Archbishop of Kingston (Jamaica), 1967–70; *b* 13 Nov. 1895; *s* of Charles McEleney and Bridget McEleney (*née* McGaffigan). *Educ:* Woburn Public Sch.; Weston Coll.; Boston Coll. Entered Soc. of Jesus at Yonkers, New York; classical studies at St Andrew on Hudson, 1920–21; Philosophy, Weston Coll. (MA), 1921–23. Teacher, Ateneo de Manila, 1923–27; Theology, 1927–31; formerly: Rector, Shadowbrook Jesuit Novitiate, Lenox, Mass; Rector, Prep. Sch., Fairfield, Conn; Tutor Ateneo de Manila Jesuit Coll., Manila; Provincial, New England Province Soc. of Jesus, 1944–50. Consecrated Bishop, 1950; Vicar Apostolic of Jamaica, 1950; Bishop of Kingston (Jamaica), 1956–67. Hon. Dr of Laws: Fairfield Univ., 1951; Boston Coll., 1968. *Address:* Boston College, Newton, Massachusetts 02167, USA. *T:* (617) 969–0100.

*Died 5 Oct. 1986.*

**McELHONE, Frank;** JP, DL; MP (Lab) Glasgow, Queen's Park, since 1974 (Glasgow, Gorbals, Oct. 1969–1974); *b* Glasgow, 5 April 1929; *m* 1958, Helen Brown; two *s* two *d*. *Educ:* St Bonaventure's Secondary Sch., Glasgow. Member, Glasgow CC, for Hutchesontown Ward, 1963–; JP Glasgow 1966, Senior Magistrate 1968, Police Judge 1969. PPS to Sec. of State for Industry, 1974–75; Parly Under-Sec. of State, Scottish Office, 1975–79; Deputy Opposition spokesman on overseas develt, 1979–80, Opposition spokesman on overseas develt, 1980–. DL Glasgow, 1979. *Address:* House of Commons, SW1; 22 Windlaw Road, Carmunnock, Glasgow. *Died 22 Sept. 1982.*

**McELLIGOTT, Neil Martin;** Metropolitan Magistrate at Great Marlborough Street Magistrates' Court, 1972–76 (at Old Street Magistrates' Court, 1961–72); *b* 21 March 1915; *s* of Judge E. J. McElligott, KC, Limerick; *m* 1939, Suzanne, *d* of late Air Chief Marshal Sir Arthur Barratt, KCB, CMG, MC, DL; one *d*. *Educ:* Ampleforth. Served in Royal Air Force, 1935–45. Called to Bar, Inner Temple, 1945, South Eastern Circuit, Recorder of King's Lynn, 1961. *Recreations:* hunting, racing, fishing, gardening. *Address:* Stone Cottage, Abthorpe, near Towcester, Northants.

*Died 30 April 1989.*

**MacENTEE, Seán;** Member, Dáil Eireann for Dublin South (East), retired May 1969; Member, Council of State; Tánaiste (Deputy Prime Minister), 1959–65; Minister for Health, 1957–65 (of Social Welfare, 1958–61); a consulting electrical engineer, registered patent agent, company director, etc; *b* 1889; *e s* of James MacEntee, TC, Belfast; *m* Margaret, *d* of late Maurice Browne, of Grange-Mockler, Co. Tipperary; one *s* two *d*. *Educ:* St Malachy's Coll., Belfast; Belfast College of Technology. Participated in Irish insurrection, 1916; tried by General Court-Martial, May 1916, and sentenced to death (sentence afterwards commuted to penal servitude for life); imprisoned in Dartmoor, Lewes and Portland prisons and released under General Amnesty, June 1917; MP (SF)

South Monaghan, Dec. 1918; Member of National Executive Cttee of Irish Volunteers and Irish Republican Army, 1917–21; served with Irish Republican Army, 1916–21; contested County Dublin, Aug. 1923, Dec. 1924; TD (Representative Fianna Fail) Co. Dublin, June 1927; re-elected Sept. 1927, 1932, and 1933; TD Dublin Townships, 1937–48, and Dublin SE, 1948–69; Minister for Finance, Irish Free State, 1932–37, and Eire, 1937–39; Minister for Industry and Commerce, Eire, 1939–41; Minister for Local Government and Public Health, Eire, 1941–46; for Local Government, 1946–48; Minister for Finance, Republic of Ireland, 1951–54. LLD (*hc*) NUI. Kt Grand Cross, Pian Order. *Publications:* Poems (1918); Episode at Easter, 1966. *Address:* Montrose, Trimleston Avenue, Booterstown, Co. Dublin. *T:* 692441. *Died 9 Jan. 1984.*

**McEWEN, Sir James (Francis Lindley),** 4th Bt *cr* 1953; *b* 24 Aug. 1960; *s* of Sir Robert Lindley McEwen, 3rd Bt, of Marchmont and Bardrochat, and of Brigid Cecilia, *d* of late James Laver, CBE, and Veronica Turleigh; *S* father, 1980. *Educ:* Eton. *Recreations:* forestry, shooting, music. *Heir: b* John Roderick Hugh McEwen, *b* 4 Nov. 1965. *Address:* Marchmont, Greenlaw, Berwickshire. *T:* Duns 2321. *Club:* Turf. *Died 18 June 1983.*

**McEWIN, Hon. Sir (Alexander) Lyell,** KBE 1954; *b* 29 May 1897; *s* of late A. L. McEwin; *m* 1921, Dora Winifred, *d* of late Mark Williams, Blyth; four *s* one *d*. *Educ:* State Sch.; Prince Alfred Coll., Adelaide. Engaged in farming at Hart, near Blyth, since 1912; Sec., Blyth Agric. Bureau, 1920–26, Pres., 1927–36; Life Mem. State Advisory Bd of Agric., 1930, Chm., 1935–37; Mem. Agric. Settlement Cttee, 1931; Mem. Debt Adjustment Cttee, 1933; Producers' representative for SA on Federal Advisory Cttee for Export Mutton and Beef, prior to appt of Australian Meat Bd, 1934. Entered Legislative Council of South Australian Parliament as Member for Northern District, 1934; Chief Secretary, Minister of Health, and Minister of Mines, 1939–65; Leader of Opposition in Legislative Council, 1965–67; Pres., Legislative Council, S Australia, 1967–75, retired. Councillor, Hart Ward of Hutt and Hill Rivers' District Council, 1932–35; transferred to Blyth Dist Council, 1935–53; retired. Life Mem., South Australian Rifle Assoc. (Chairman, 1948–83); Mem., Commonwealth Council, State Rifle Assocs, 1952–62 (Chm., 1959–62). Chief, Royal Caledonian Society (SA), 1959–68. *Recreation:* bowls. *Address:* 93 First Avenue, St Peters, SA 5069. *T:* 423698. *Died 23 Sept. 1988.*

**MACEY, John Percival,** CBE 1969; FRICS, FIHM; Chairman, Samuel Lewis Housing Trust, since 1974; Treasurer, Peabody Trust, 1974–81; *b* 3 Dec. 1906; *s* of Edward Macey; *m* 1931, Jill, *d* of Joseph Gyngell; one *s* one *d*. *Educ:* Varndean Grammar Sch., Brighton. Entered LCC service, 1926; Principal Asst, Housing Dept, 1948–51; Dep. Housing Manager, City of Birmingham, 1951–54; Housing Manager, City of Birmingham, 1954–63; Director of Housing to LCC, later GLC, 1964–71. President: Inst. of Housing, 1957 and 1963; Inst. of Housing Managers, 1969; Vice-Pres., Surrey and Sussex Rent Assessment Panel, 1971–79. Served with Royal Engineers, 1939–45 (despatches); retired with rank of Major. *Publications:* Macey on the Housing Finance Act, 1972; The Housing Act, 1974; The Housing Rents and Subsidies Act, 1975; (joint author) Housing Management, 1965, 4th edn (sole author) 1983; papers to professional bodies on housing and allied subjects. *Recreations:* motoring, walking, gardening. *Address:* 7 Bath Court, Kings Esplanade, Hove, East Sussex BN3 2WP. *T:* Brighton 728104. *Died 20 Nov. 1987.*

**McFALL, David (Bernard),** RA 1963 (ARA 1955); Sculptor; Master of Sculpture, City and Guilds of London Art School, Lambeth, 1956–75; *b* 21 Dec. 1919; *s* of David McFall and Elizabeth McEvoy; *m* 1968, Mlle Bernadette Hemmer (marr. diss. 1969); *m* 1972, Alexandra Dane, actress; one *s* one *d*. *Educ:* Art Schools, Birmingham, Lambeth and Royal College of Art. Official Commissions: Unicorns (pair, 12 ft, gilt-bronze) mounted on roof of Bristol New Council House, known as The Bristol Unicorns, 1950; Finials (pair, carved, Portland stone, 10 ft), Zodiac Clock (8 ft, carved stone and cast aluminium), Bronze Portrait Bust (Alderman Frank Sheppard), 1955, same building; Festival of Britain, Boy and Foal (carved stone 5 ft), 1951, now at Missenden Abbey, Bucks; Pocahontas (bronze), 1956; Bust (bronze, Lord Methuen), 1956; Head of Ralph Vaughan Williams, OM (bronze) in Royal Festival Hall, 1957; 8 ft Statues of St Bride and St Paul in St Bride's Church, Fleet Street; Bronze Head of Sir Winston Churchill, in Grocers Hall, 1958; 8 ft 6 ins Bronze Figure of Sir Winston Churchill, 1959 (Woodford Green); Lord Balfour, House of Commons, 1962; Bust (bronze) Lord Brabazon of Tara (Royal Institution); Memorial to Sir Albert Richardson, PPRA, for Crypt of St Paul's Cathedral; Crucifixion (Portland stone), Church of Our Lady of Lourdes, Thames-Ditton; bust (bronze, Lord Ridley) for Univ., Newcastle upon Tyne; The Golden Gazelle, Abu Dhabi, Trucial States; bronze figure of Sir Winston Churchill, trophy for Dame Felicity Peake Essay Prize; The Black Horse for LTB Victoria Line, 1968; stone frieze on Wm Whitfield's extension to Inst. of Chartered Accountants, London, 1969; bust of Sir Thomas

Holmes Sellors, Pres., RCS, 1971; Meml to Sir Gerald Kelly, St Paul's Cathedral Crypt, 1973; busts of: Sir George Godber, for RCP; Prof. George Grenfell Baines, for Building Design Partnership, Preston; late Hugh Stenhouse, Glasgow, 1973–74; Oedipus and Jocasta (stone group), W Norwood Library, 1974; posthumous bust of Josiah Wedgwood, Barlaston, Stoke-on-Trent, 1974–75; portrait head of HRH Prince Charles, Duke of Cornwall, 1974–75; Meml to Lord Fraser of Lonsdale, Westminster Abbey, 1976; The Nazarine (8ft Christ figure), Canterbury Cathedral, 1987–88; Official purchase: The Bullcalf (Chantrey Bequest), 1943. Has exhibited at Royal Academy yearly since 1943. *Recreations:* photography, cycling. *Address:* 10 Fulham Park Gardens, SW6 4JX. *T:* 01–736 6532; Natura, Fairlight Cove, Sussex TN35 4DJ.
*Died 18 Sept. 1988.*

**McFARLAND, Sir Basil (Alexander Talbot)**, 2nd Bt, *cr* 1914; CBE 1954; ERD 1954; HM Lieutenant for the City of Londonderry, 1939–75; *b* 18 Feb. 1898; *o c* of Sir John McFarland, 1st Bt, and Annie, 2nd *d* of late John Talbot, Terryglass, County Tipperary; *S* father, 1926; *m* 1st, 1924, Annie Kathleen (*d* 1952), 2nd *d* of late Andrew Henderson, JP, of Parkville, Whiteabbey, Belfast; one *s* (one *d* decd); 2nd, 1955, Mary Eleanor (*d* 1973), 2nd *d* of late William Dougan, Londonderry. *Educ:* Neuwied-on-Rhine, Germany; Brussels; Bedford Sch. High Sheriff, Londonderry, 1930–38 and 1952; Mayor of Londonderry, 1939 and 1945–50. ADC (Additional) to The King, 1950–52, to The Queen, 1952–60. Member: Northern Ireland Air Advisory Council, 1946–65; Londonderry Port & Harbour Commissioners (Chairman, 1952–67); London Midland Area Board, British Transport Commission, 1955–61; Director, Belfast Banking Co. Ltd, 1930–70; Chairman: Lanes (Derry) Ltd; J. W. Corbett & Sons; A. Thompson & Co. Ltd; Lanes (Fuel Oils) Ltd; Lanes (Business Equipment) Ltd; Lanes (Patent Fuels) Ltd; J. & R. Waterson Ltd; R. C. Malseed & Co. Ltd; Holmes Coal Ltd; Londonderry Gaslight Co., 1931–77; Londonderry and Lough Swilly Railway Co., 1946–81; Trustee of Magee University College, 1962–65. Original Member, NI Unemployment Assistance Board, to 1939. Served War of 1914–18, Artists Rifles, 1918; War of 1939–45, Overseas with 9th Londonderry HAA Regt (despatches); Chm., T&AFA (Co. Londonderry), 1947–62; Hon. Col, 9th Londonderry HAA Regt RA (TA); Pres., NI TA&VR Assoc., 1968–71. Irish Rugby International, 1920–22. Hon. Freeman of City of Londonderry since 1944. CStJ. *Heir: s* John Talbot McFarland [*b* 3 Oct. 1927; *m* 1957, Mary Scott, *er d* of late Dr W. Scott Watson, Londonderry; two *s* two *d*]. *Address:* Aberfoyle, Londonderry. *T:* 62881.
*Died 5 March 1986.*

**MACFARLANE, Robert Gwyn**, CBE 1964; MD; FRCP; FRS 1956; retired; *b* 26 June 1907; *o c* of Robert Gray and Eileen Macfarlane; *m* 1936, Hilary, *o c* of H. A. H. and Maude Carson; four *s* one *d*. *Educ:* Highfield Sch., Liphook, Hants; Cheltenham Coll.; St Bartholomew's Hospital, London. MRCS, LRCP, 1933; MB, BS (London), 1933; MD (London), Gold Medal, 1938; MA (Oxford), 1948; FRCP 1960; FRCPS 1986. Sir Halley Stewart Research Fellow, 1935; Asst Clinical Pathologist, Postgrad. Medical School, London, 1936; Asst Bacteriologist, Wellcome Physiological Research Lab., 1939. Major, RAMC, 1944, attached Mobile Bacteriological Research Unit, Normandy and NW Europe. Director, Medical Research Council Blood Coagulation Research Unit, Churchill Hospital, Oxford, 1959–67; Professor of Clinical Pathology, Oxford Univ., 1964–67, now Emeritus (Reader in Haematology, 1957–64); Fellow, All Souls Coll., Oxford, 1963–70, now Quondam Fellow; Clinical Pathologist, Radcliffe Infirmary, Oxford, 1941–67. Pres., Haemophilia Soc., 1982– (Vice-Pres. 1955–82). Cameron Prize, Univ. of Edinburgh, 1968. *Publications:* (with R. Biggs) Human Blood Coagulation and its Disorders (3rd edn, 1962); Howard Florey: the Making of a Great Scientist, 1979; Alexander Fleming: the Man and the Myth, 1984; papers, chapters in books and encyclopædias on haematological and pathological subjects. *Address:* Mallie's Cottage, Opinan, Laide, Ross-shire.
*Died 26 March 1987.*

**MACFARLANE, Hon. Sir Robert Mafeking**, KCMG 1974 (CMG 1954); Speaker, New Zealand Parliament, 1957–60; *b* Christchurch, NZ, 17 May 1901; *m* 1932, Louisa E., *d* of T. F. Jacobs, Woolston. *Educ:* Christchurch, NZ. Secretary, Christchurch Labour Representation Cttee, 1929; MP (L) (NZ) for Christchurch S, 1936–46, for Christchurch Central, 1946–69; formerly Sen. Opposition Whip. Member Christchurch City Council for many years (Mayor, 1938–41). Chairman Metropolitan Transport Licensing Authority. Served War of 1939–45 with Second New Zealand Expeditionary Force. *Address:* 71 Greenpark Street, Christchurch 2, New Zealand.
*Died 2 Dec. 1981.*

**MacFARQUHAR, Sir Alexander**, KBE 1952; CIE 1945; Director of Personnel, United Nations, 1962–67; *b* 6 Nov. 1903; *s* of Roderick MacFarquhar; *m* 1929, Berenice Whitburn; one *s*. *Educ:* Aberdeen Univ. (MA 1st class Hons Classics); Emmanuel Coll., Cambridge. Entered ICS 1926; Deputy Commissioner, Ferozepore, 1930; Deputy Commissioner, Amritsar, 1933; Settlement Officer,

Amritsar, 1936; Deputy Secretary, Government of India, 1941; Deputy Director-General, Directorate-General of Supply, Government of India, 1943; Dir-Gen. Disposals, India, 1946; Commerce and Education Sec. Govt of Pakistan, 1947–51. Resident Rep. to Pakistan of UN Technical Assistance Board, 1952; Regional Rep. to Far East, of UN Technical Assistance Board, Bangkok, 1955; UN Secretary General's Special Adviser for Civilian Affairs in the Congo, 1960. Chm., Pakistan Soc., 1970–81. Hon. LLD Aberdeen, 1980. HQA, Pakistan, 1981. *Address:* Ottershaw, Beverley Lane, Coombe Hill, Kingston-upon-Thames, Surrey.
*Died 29 July 1987.*

**MacFEELY, Most Rev. Anthony C.;** *b* 4 Feb. 1909. *Educ:* St Columb's Coll., Londonderry; St Patrick's Coll., Maynooth; Irish Coll., Rome. Priest, 1932; Prof., St Columb's Coll., Oct. 1934; Pres., St Columb's Coll., 1950; Parish Priest, Strabane, Co. Tyrone, 1959–65; Bishop of Raphoe, 1965–82. *Recreation:* walking. *Address:* Fernbank, Glebe, Letterkenny, Co. Donegal, Ireland. *T:* Letterkenny 074–21422.
*Died 7 Oct. 1986.*

**McFETRICH, Cecil**, OBE 1950; Director, Sunderland and Shields Building Society, 1964–86; Partner, C. & K. M. McFetrich, since 1977; *b* 17 Jan. 1911; *y s* of Archibald B. and Hannah B. McFetrich; *m* 1937, Kathleen M. Proom; four *s*. *Educ:* Cowan Terrace Sch., Sunderland; Skerry's Coll., Newcastle upon Tyne. Qual. Chartered Accountant, 1933. After varied industrial and professional experience, joined Bartram & Sons Ltd, South Dock, Sunderland, as Sec., 1936; apptd a Dir, 1939; responsible for sales and marketing, 1945, Man. Dir, 1964–72; Jt Man. Dir, Austin & Pickersgill Ltd, 1968–69, Man. Dir 1969–72, Dep. Chm. and Chm., 1972–75; Founder Dir, A. & P. Appledore Internat. Ltd, 1970–74. Man. Dir, Ward & Davidson Ltd, 1946–75 (Chm. 1975–79); Chm., Sunderland Structural Steel Ltd, 1947–79. Mem., Sunderland Town Council, 1942–51 (Chm. Finance Cttee, 1943–44); Mem., River Wear Commn, 1943–45, 1969–72; served on various Nat. Savings Cttees, 1940–63; Chairman: Sunderland Savings Cttee, 1947–63; N Regional Industrial Savings Cttee, 1956–62. Life Governor, Nat. Children's Home, 1953–81 (Mem., Order of St Christopher, 1982); Pres., Bishopwearmouth Choral Soc., Sunderland, 1962–65. Liveryman, Worshipful Co. of Shipwrights. Freeman by redemption, City of London. Lord Mayor of London's Gold Medal for Export Achievement, 1963. *Recreations:* local history, antiques (especially maps and Sunderland pottery), champagne. *Address:* 8 Belle Vue Drive, Sunderland, Tyne and Wear. *T:* Wearside 5226449. *Clubs:* MCC; Sunderland (Sunderland).
*Died 2 Dec. 1988.*

**MACFIE, Maj.-Gen. John Mandeville**, CB 1951; CBE 1946; MC 1917; OStJ 1945; *b* 13 Dec. 1891; *s* of Rev. W. G. Macfie, Mowbray, Cape Town; unmarried. *Educ:* S African College School; Glasgow High Sch.; Glasgow Univ. MB, ChB (with honours) Glasgow, 1915. FRCP Glasgow, 1964. Lieut, RAMC, 1915: Dep. Assistant Director of Pathology, India, 1926–29; Dep. Assistant Director-General of Army Medical Services, War Office, 1932–36; Dep. DGAMS War Office, 1943–46; DDMS, East Africa Command, 1946–48; DDMS, Scottish Command, 1949; Commandant RAM Coll., 1949–50; KHS 1950; Dep. Director of Medical Services, Western Command, UK, 1950–51; retired pay, Jan. 1952; Colonel Commandant RAMC, 1951–56. Commander Order Leopold II of Belgium, 1949. *Recreations:* golf, fishing. *Address:* Erskine Hospital, Bishopton, Renfrewshire PA7 5PU. *Club:* Glasgow Art.
*Died 14 June 1985.*

**McGEE, Prof. James Dwyer**, OBE 1952; FRS 1966; MSc Sydney; PhD, ScD, Cantab; CEng; FIEE; FInstP; FRAS; Hon. ARCS; Professor of Applied Physics, 1954–71, later Emeritus, Senior Research Fellow, 1971–80, and Fellow, 1977, Imperial College of Science and Technology, University of London; *b* Canberra, ACT, 17 Dec. 1903; *s* of Francis and Mary McGee; *m* 1944, Hilda Mary, *d* of George Winstone, Takapuna, Auckland, NZ; no *c*. *Educ:* St Patrick's Coll., Goulburn, NSW; St John's Coll., Sydney Univ. (MSc); Clare Coll., Cambridge (PhD). 1851 Exhibition Scholar from Sydney Univ. to Cambridge. Nuclear physics research, Cavendish Laboratory, Cambridge, 1928–31; Research physicist, Electric and Musical Industries Research Laboratories, Hayes, Middx. Engaged on research on photo-electricity and electronic problems of Television, 1932–39; research on electronic problems in connection with military operations, in particular the use of infra-red light, 1939–45; returned to work on photo-electronic devices for television and other scientific purposes, 1945–54. Rutherford Meml Lecturer, New Zealand, 1982. Awarded Research Fellowship, Carnegie Inst., Washington, 1960; Hon. Research Associate, Carnegie Inst., 1960, 1962, 1966. Hon. Life Mem. IREE(Aust.), 1939. Hon. DSc Salford, 1972; Hon. DTech Brunel, 1978. Awarded prize of Worshipful Company of Instrument Makers, 1968; Callendar Medal, Inst. of Measurement and Control, for contribs to opto-electronics, 1975. *Publications:* chap. on Electronic Generation of Television Signals in Electronics (ed B. Lovell), 1947; ed Vols XII, XVI, XXII, XXVIII, XXXIII, Advances in Electronics: Symposia on Photoelectronic Devices, 1960, 1962, 1966, 1969, 1972;

technical papers in Engineering, Physical and Technical Jls. *Recreations:* gardening, music. *Address:* 3E/10 Hilltop Crescent, Fairlight, NSW 2094, Australia. *T:* 949 3723. *Club:* Athenæum.
*Died 28 Feb.* 1987.

**McGEE, Rt. Rev. Joseph;** *b* 13 Dec. 1904; *s* of Denis McGee and Sarah McGlinchey. *Educ:* St Dominic's Sch. and Morrison's Academy, Crieff; Blair's Coll., Aberdeen; Royal Scots Coll., Valladolid. Formerly Vicar-General and Canon (Penitentiary) of Dunkeld. Bishop of Galloway, 1952–81. *Address:* 32 Mansewell Road, Prestwick, Ayrshire KA9 1BB. *Died 5 March* 1983.

**McGHIE, Maj.-Gen. (retd) John,** CB 1976; MD; FRCPsych; DPM; *b* Larkhall, Scotland, 12 June 1914; *s* of Henry and Agnes McGhie; *m* 1940, Hilda Lilian Owen; two *s*. *Educ:* Hamilton Academy; Glasgow University. Medical Officer: Glasgow Western Infirmary, 1936–37; Bellshill Maternity Hosp., 1937; Captain, RAMC, 1938; MO, British Mil. Hosp. Rawalpindi, 1939; Major, 2nd in Comd Field Ambulance, 1939–43; Lt-Col, OC Field Amb., 1943–45; Comd Psychiatrist: Scottish Comd, 1948; Far East, 1949–52; OC, Royal Victoria Hosp., Netley, 1956–61; Dir of Army Psychiatry, 1961–67; DDMS, Malaya and Western Comd, 1967–70; Dir, Army Psychiatry and Consultant in Psychiatry to Army, 1970–76. *Recreations:* golf, motoring. *Address:* 9 Atwater Court, Faversham Road, Lenham, Kent ME17 2PW. *T:* Maidstone 850039.
*Died 12 Sept.* 1985.

**McGILL, Maj.-Gen. Allan,** CB 1969; CBE 1964 (OBE 1945; MBE 1943); Director of Electrical and Mechanical Engineering (Army), 1966–69; *b* 28 June 1914; *s* of William McGill; *m* 1945, Kathleen German. *Educ:* George Heriot's, Edinburgh; Heriot-Watt Coll. (now Heriot-Watt Univ.). Served War of 1939–45 (despatches, 1943). Dir, Electrical and Mechanical Engineering, British Army of the Rhine, 1965–66. Brig., 1961; Maj.-Gen., 1966. Col Comdt, REME, 1969–74. CEng, MIMechE. *Recreations:* motor rallying, ski-ing. *Address:* Tudor House, Vicarage Gardens, Bray, Berks SL6 2AE. *Club:* Army and Navy. *Died 9 March* 1989.

**McGILLIVRAY, Hon. William Alexander;** Chief Justice of Alberta, Canada, since Dec. 1974; *b* 14 Oct. 1918; *s* of Alexander A. and Margaret L. G. McGillivray; *m* 1950, Kathleen A. Bell; two *s* two *d*. *Educ:* Univ. of Alberta, Edmonton, Alta (BA,LLB). Graduated in Law, 1941; admitted to practice, 1942. Bencher, 1958–69, Pres., 1969–70, Law Society of Alberta. *Recreations:* shooting, fishing, golf, bridge. *Address:* The Court House, 611–4th Street, SW, Calgary, Alberta T2P 1T5, Canada. *T:* 261–7434. *Clubs:* Ranchmen's, Calgary Golf and Country, Glencoe (Calgary).
*Died 16 Dec.* 1984.

**McGRATH, Sir Charles (Gullan),** AC 1981; Kt 1968; OBE 1964; Chairman, Nylex Corporation Ltd, 1970–82; *b* Ballarat, 22 Nov. 1910; *s* of David Charles McGrath and Elizabeth McGrath; *m* 1934, Madge Louise, *d* of Andrew McLaren; one *s* four *d*. *Educ:* Ballarat High Sch. Chairman: Repco Ltd, 1957–80; Petersville Australia Ltd, 1971–81; Premier's Economic Adv. Panel, Victoria, 1978–82. Life Governor, Royal Melbourne Inst. of Technol., 1973. Hon. DEng Monash, 1978. Aust. Manufacturers Export Council Award for outstanding personal contrib. to Australia's export, 1969. *Recreation:* farming. *Address:* 46 Lansell Road, Toorak, Vic. 3142, Australia. *Clubs:* Australian, Athenæum, Melbourne, West Brighton (Melbourne). *Died 18 May* 1984.

**McGRATH, John Cornelius,** CBE 1971; FCA; FCIT 1970; Financial Adviser to British Airports Authority, 1971–73; full-time Board Member and Founder Financial Controller of British Airports Authority, 1966–71; *b* 20 Nov. 1905; *s* of Patrick and Johanna McGrath; bachelor. *Educ:* Jesuit Coll. of St Ignatius; Univ. of London. Schoolmaster, 1925–27; Asst to Public Auditor, 1927–34; Lectr in Accountancy and Finance, 1928–39; appointed Public Auditor by HM Treasury, 1934; qual. as Chartered Accountant, 1938; Dep. Man. of Audit Dept, CWS, 1938–66; Chief Accountant and Financial Adviser to LCS, 1947–66. Bd Mem. for Finance of Post Office, 1968–69. Mem., Worshipful Co. of Inn-holders, 1951; Freeman, City of London, 1951. *Recreations:* music, motor racing, travel, swimming. *Address:* 8 River Court, Surbiton, Surrey. *T:* 01–546 3833. *Clubs:* Reform, Royal Automobile, MCC.
*Died 21 June* 1985.

**McGRATH, Peter William;** Vice Chairman, since 1988 and Chief Operating Officer, since 1987, Emess Plc; Chairman: Marlin Electric, since 1986; Tenby Industries, since 1987; *b* 19 Nov. 1931; *s* of Major W. P. McGrath and Winifred Clara (née Fill); *m* 1954, Margaret Irene Page; one *s* three *d*. *Educ:* Boroughmuir Sch.; Royal Liberty Sch.; Univ. of London (Dip. in Econs). Sen. managerial positions in finance and prodn, Ford of Britain and Ford of Germany, 1962–69; Controller of Corporate Finance, BR Bd, 1969–72; Dir of Finance, NFC, 1972–77; Dir of Finance and Systems, Truck and Bus Div., British Leyland, 1977; Man. Dir, British Leyland Internat., 1977–78; Chm. and Man. Dir, BL Components Ltd, 1978–79; Group Man. Dir, Concord Rotaflex,

1980–82; UK Ops Dir, Stone International, 1982–86. *Recreations:* sailing, military history, opera. *Address:* St Leonard's Forest House, Horsham, West Sussex RH13 6HX. *Club:* Medway Yacht (Rochester). *Died 11 Oct.* 1990.

**MacGREGOR, Air Vice-Marshal Andrew,** CB 1949; CBE 1945; DFC 1918; retired; *b* 25 Oct. 1897; *s* of late Andrew MacGregor, Glen Gyle, Crieff; *m* 1939, Isobel Jane, *d* of Gordon Eadie, Crieff; three *d*. *Educ:* Morrison's Acad., Crieff. Commissioned Argyll and Sutherland Highlanders and attached RFC, 1917. Served in Egypt and Iraq, 1919–27; graduated RAF Staff Coll., 1928; served in Sudan and Palestine, 1932–37; Dep. Directorate Organisation, Air Ministry, 1940; Senior Air Staff Officer, HQ, No. 4 Group, 1940–42; Air Officer Administrative, N Africa, 1942–44; Asst Commandant, Staff Coll., 1944; Air Officer comdg No 28 Group, 1945–46; Air Officer Administrative, HQ Fighter Command, 1946–49. Comdr Legion of Honour, 1944; Comdr Order of Crown of Belgium, 1948; Officer of Legion of Merit (USA), 1944; Croix de Guerre. *Address:* Glen Gyle, Crieff, Perthshire, Scotland. *T:* Crieff 2583.
*Died 24 Oct.* 1983.

**MacGREGOR, Sir Colin (Malcolm),** Kt 1959; Chief Justice of Jamaica, 1957–62, retired; *b* 10 April 1901; *s* of John Malcolm MacGregor, Solicitor, Mandeville, Jamaica, and Ann Katherine (née Muirhead); *m* 1926, Dorothy Constance Scarlett; one *s* one *d*. *Educ:* Munro Coll., Jamaica; Denstone Coll., England. Called to Bar, 1922; Clerk, Resident Magistrates' Court, Jamaica, 1925; Resident Magistrate, Jamaica, 1934; Puisne Judge, Jamaica, 1947; Sen. Puisne Judge, Jamaica, 1954–57. Acted as Chief Justice, Jamaica, May–Nov. 1955. *Publications:* (ed) 5 and 6 Jamaica Law Reports. *Recreations:* golf, bridge, philately. *Address:* Garth, Knockpatrick, Jamaica. *Club:* Manchester (Mandeville, Jamaica).
*Died 6 Sept.* 1982.

**MacGREGOR, Duncan;** Convenor of the Council of Fellows in Dental Surgery, Royal College of Surgeons of Edinburgh, 1965–67; President Odonto-Chirurgical Society of Scotland, 1956–57; President, British Dental Association, 1960–61 (now Vice-President); *b* 17 Feb. 1892; *s* of A. D. MacGregor and Jessie Steel Proudfoot; *m* 1921, Elizabeth Ruth Doig; one *s* one *d*. *Educ:* George Heriot's Sch.; Royal Coll. of Surgeons and Edinburgh Dental Hospital and Sch. LDS, RCS Edinburgh 1916; Surgeon Probationer, RNVR 1915–17; Surg. Lt (D) RNVR 1917–19; Surg. Lt-Comdr (D) RNVR, retd 1937. Hon. Dental Surg., Edinburgh Dental Hosp. and Sch., 1921–48; Consultant Dental Surg., Edinburgh Dental Hosp., 1948–61; Member: Dental Board of the UK 1946–56; Gen. Dental Council, 1956–66. Fellowship in Dental Surgery, Royal Coll. of Surgeons, Edinburgh, 1951. *Publications:* contributions to dental journals. *Recreations:* sketching, gardening. *Address:* 8 Seton Place, Edinburgh EH9 2JT. *T:* 031-667 5071. *Club:* Caledonian (Edinburgh). *Died 12 Oct.* 1984.

**MacGREGOR, Edward Ian Roy,** CMG 1966; HM Diplomatic Service, retired; *b* 4 March 1911; *s* of late John MacGregor and late Georgina Agnes MacGregor (née Barbor); *m* 1944, Lilianne, *d* of William Swindlehurst, Washington, DC, USA; one *s* one *d*. *Educ:* Methodist Coll., Belfast; Queen's Univ., Belfast (MSc). Wing Comdr RAF, 1936–47. Asst Civil Air Attaché, Washington, 1948–52; Ministry of Transport and Civil Aviation, 1952–59; Civil Air Attaché, Washington, 1959–65; Asst Sec., BoT, 1965–67; Counsellor, FO, 1967–68; Consul-Gen., Detroit, 1968–71. *Address:* Spinneys, Brock Way, Virginia Water, Surrey. *T:* Wentworth 3612.
*Died 13 Aug.* 1989.

**McGREGOR, James Reid,** CB 1948; CBE 1945; MC 1916; *b* 8 April 1896; *m* 1933, Dorothy Janet, *d* of Mr and Mrs Comrie, Ayr; one *s* one *d*. *Educ:* Edinburgh Academy, RMC Sandhurst. Served European War, 1914–18, Gordon Highlanders, 1915–19 (despatches, wounded, MC); War of 1939–45, Director of Army contracts, 1940–44; Private Secretary to Sir James Grigg, Secretary of State for War, 1944–45; Director of Finance, War Office, 1945–59. Member, Public Health Laboratory Service Board, 1961–69. *Address:* Torphins, Burntwood Road, Sevenoaks, Kent.
*Died 9 Aug.* 1984.

**McGREGOR, Kenneth,** CB 1963; CMG 1951; retired; *b* 11 Feb. 1903; *o c* of late James McGregor and Eugénie Lydia Johnson; *m* 1930, Dorothy Laura Roope (*d* 1982), *o d* of late Judge R. Roope Reeve, QC; two *s*. *Educ:* Westminster (King's Scholar); New Coll., Oxford (Scholar). 1st class Hons; MA. Called to the Bar (Lincoln's Inn). Ministries of Health, Supply and Production; Board of Trade (Under-Secretary); the Senior British Trade Commissioner in Canada, 1958–62. Member of Quangos, and dir or consultant to Companies and Trade Assocs, 1963–73. Islington Borough Councillor, 1968–71. *Address:* 19 Emden House, Old Headington, Oxford OX3 9JU. *T:* Oxford 64897. *Club:* United Oxford & Cambridge University. *Died 8 Oct.* 1984.

**McGUINNESS, James Henry,** CB 1964; Chairman, Scottish Philharmonic Trust, since 1976; *b* 29 Sept. 1912; *s* of James Henry

McGuinness, Scotstoun; *m* 1939, Annie Eveline Fordyce, Ayr; one *s* two *d*. *Educ*: St Aloysius Coll.; Univ. of Glasgow, 1st Cl. Hons Classics 1932, George Clark Fellow; Trinity Coll., Oxford (schol.), 1st cl. Hons Mods, 1934, 1st cl. Lit. Hum. Under-Secretary, Dept of Health for Scotland, 1959–62; Scottish Development Department, 1962–64; Asst Under-Sec. of State, Scottish Office and Chm., Scottish Economic Planning Bd, 1965–72; Sen. Res. Fellow in Politics, Univ. of Glasgow, 1973–74. Mem., Oil Develt Council for Scotland, 1973–75. Chairman: Scottish Baroque Ensemble, 1973–74; Scottish Philharmonic Society Ltd, 1974–78. Hon. MRTPI, 1978. *Address*: 28 Falkland Street, Glasgow G12 9QY; Kendoon, Dalry, Kirkcudbrightshire. *Club*: Scottish Arts.
*Died 22 May* 1987.

**McGUSTY, Victor William Tighe,** CMG 1942; OBE 1937; OStJ; MB; DTM; *b* 20 June 1887; *m* 1st, 1912, Annie Bayliss; one *s* one *d*; 2nd, 1971, Joyce E. Johnston, Auckland, NZ. *Educ*: Coleraine (Ireland) Academical Institution; Trinity Coll., Dublin. Entered Colonial Medical Service, Fiji, 1912; retired, 1945; Director of Medical Services Colony of Fiji; also Director of Civil Defence and Secretary for Indian Affairs; held various other administrative posts as well as medical in the Colony. After retirement from Colonial Service, N London Postgrad. Med. Sch., 1945–46; GP in North Auckland, 1946–58. *Address*: 32 Horarata Road, Takapuna N2, New Zealand. *Died 16 Feb.* 1981.

**MACHIN, George;** Secretary, Sheffield Trades and Labour Club, since 1981; *b* 30 Dec. 1922; *s* of Edwin and Ada Machin, Sheffield; *m* 1949, Margaret Ena (*née* Heard); one *s*. *Educ*: Marlcliffe Sch., Sheffield. Served RAF, 1943–47. Engineering Inspector. Shop Steward, and Mem., Sheffield District Cttee, AUEW. Sec., Sheffield Heeley Constituency Lab. Party, 1966–73. Mem., Sheffield City Council, 1967–74. MP (Lab) Dundee E, March 1973–Feb. 1974; contested (Lab) Dundee E, Oct. 1974. Governor, Granville Coll. of Further Educn, Sheffield, 1968–73. *Recreations*: swimming, walking. *Address*: 104 Norgreave Way, Sheffield S19 5TN.
*Died 5 Dec.* 1989.

**McINERNEY, Hon. Sir Murray (Vincent),** Kt 1978; Judge of Supreme Court of Victoria, 1965–83; retired; *b* 11 Feb. 1911; *s* of Patrick McInerney and Kathleen Ierne (*née* Murray); *m* 1st, 1939, Manda Alice Franich (*d* 1973); two *s* five *d*; 2nd, 1975, Frances Mary Branagan (*née* O'Gorman). *Educ*: Christian Brothers' Coll., Pretoria; Xavier Coll., Melbourne; Newman Coll., Univ. of Melb. (MA, LLM). Served War, RANVR, 1942–45 (Lieut). Admitted as barrister and solicitor, 1934; practised at Victorian Bar, 1935–65; QC 1957. Sen. Law Tutor, Newman Coll., 1933–41; Lectr, Law of Evidence and Civil Procedure, Melb. Univ., 1949–62. Pres., Aust. Sect. of Lawasia, 1967–69; Vice-Pres., Law Council of Aust., 1964–65; Dep. Pres., Courts Martial Appeals Tribunal, 1958–65. Mem., Victorian Bar Council, 1952–65 (Chm., 1962, 1963). Chm., Council, State Coll. of Vic., 1973–81. Melb. Univ. Full Blue Athletics, and Aust. Univs Blue Athletics, 1933; Pres., Victorian Amateur Athletics Assoc., 1979–82; Mem., Lawn Tennis Assoc. of Vic. *Publications*: contrib. Aust. Law Jl and Melb. Univ. Law Review. *Recreations*: reading, watching cricket, tennis, athletics. *Address*: 7 Chatfield Avenue, Balwyn, Vic 3103, Australia. *T*: 8175051. *Clubs*: Australian, Celtic, Melbourne Cricket, Royal Automobile of Victoria (Melbourne), West Brighton.
*Died 23 Nov.* 1988.

**MacINNES, Helen Clark;** novelist; *b* 7 Oct. 1907; *d* of Donald McInnes and Jessica Cecilia Sutherland McDiarmid; *m* 1932, Prof. Gilbert Highet, DLitt (*d* 1978); one *s*. *Educ*: The Hermitage Sch., Helensburgh; The High School for Girls, Glasgow; Glasgow Univ. (MA); University College, London. *Publications*: Above Suspicion, 1941; Assignment in Brittany, 1942; The Unconquerable, 1944; Horizon, 1945; Friends and Lovers, 1947; Rest and Be Thankful, 1949; Neither Five Nor Three, 1951; I and My True Love, 1953; Pray for a Brave Heart, 1955; North from Rome, 1958; Decision at Delphi, 1961; The Venetian Affair, 1963; Home is the Hunter (play), 1964; The Double Image, 1966; The Salzburg Connection, 1968; Message from Málaga, 1972; The Snare of the Hunter, 1974; Agent in Place, 1976; Prelude to Terror, 1978; The Hidden Target, 1980; Cloak of Darkness, 1982; Ride a Pale Horse, 1985. *Address*: 15 Jefferys Lane, East Hampton, NY 11937, USA.
*Died 30 Sept.* 1985.

**MACINTOSH, Sir Robert (Reynolds),** Kt 1955; MA, DM, FRCSE, DA; FFARCS; Hon. Fellow: Faculties of Anæsthetists of Australasia, 1950, of Ireland, 1964, of England, 1968; Royal Society of Medicine, 1966; Pembroke College, Oxford, 1965; Nuffield Professor of Anæsthetics, Oxford University, 1937–65; War time Consultant in Anæsthetics, Royal Air Force (Air Cdre); *b* Timaru, New Zealand, 17 Oct. 1897; *s* of C. N. Macintosh; *m* 1st, Rosa Henderson (*d* 1956); 2nd, Ann Manning; two step *s*. *Educ*: Waitaki, New Zealand; Guy's Hospital. Served European War (despatches), Spanish Civil War (Order of Military Merit); War of 1939–45 (Order of Liberty, Norway). Hon. FRCOG. Dr *hc* Univs of Buenos

Aires, Aix-Marseilles and Poznan; Hon. DSc: Univ. of Wales; Med. Coll. of Ohio. *Publications*: Textbooks, Essentials of General Anæsthesia, Physics for the Anæsthetist, Lumbar Puncture and Spinal Analgesia, Local Anæsthesia, Brachial Plexus; articles on anæsthesia in medical and dental journals. *Address*: 326 Woodstock Road, Oxford OX2 7NS. *Club*: Royal Air Force.
*Died 28 Aug.* 1989.

**McINTYRE, His Honour F(rederick) Donald (Livingstone),** QC 1955; a Circuit Judge (formerly Judge of County Courts), 1962–77; *b* 8 July 1905; 2nd *s* of William and Marjorie McIntyre; *m* 1972, Mrs Marjorie Joyce Bowman. *Educ*: Cardiff High Sch.; St Olave's; St John's Coll., Cambridge (History Scholar and MacMahon Law Student; BA, LLB). Called to Bar, Gray's Inn, 1928; joined Inner Temple, 1936. Served War, 1941–46; Officer Royal Air Force (POW, Far East, 1942–45). Dep. Chairman Inner London Sessions, 1965–71; JP Surrey, 1960. *Recreations*: cricket and chess. *Address*: 19 Village Road, N3. *Clubs*: Royal Automobile; Union Society (Cambridge). *Died 29 Aug.* 1981.

**McINTYRE, James Gordon;** *see* Sorn, Hon. Lord.

**McINTYRE, Air Commodore Kenneth John,** CB 1958; CBE 1951; JP; DL; RAF retired; *b* 23 July 1908; *s* of late William Seymour McIntyre and Winifred May McIntyre, Clevedon, Somerset; *m* 1936, Betty Aveley, *o d* of late Lt-Col Percie C. Cooper, Dulwich. *Educ*: Blundell's Sch.; RMC Sandhurst. Commissioned Royal Tank Regt, 1928; served UK and India; seconded to RAF 1934; permanent commission RAF, 1945. Served War of 1939–45 in UK, France and Belgium. Dep. Dir of Organisation, Air Ministry, 1945–47; Joint Services Staff Coll., 1947–48; Group Capt. 1947; Group Capt. Operations, HQ MEAF, 1948–50; idc 1951; SHAPE (Paris), 1952–54; Air Commodore, 1955; Dir of Policy (Air Staff), Air Ministry, 1955–58. Mem., Dorset CC, 1967–89 (Chm., 1981–88). JP Poole, 1967 (Supplementary list, 1978); DL Dorset, 1983. *Address*: 9 The Spinnakers, Mount Pleasant Road, Poole, Dorset BH15 1TU. *Club*: Royal Air Force. *Died 14 July* 1989.

**McINTYRE, Sir Laurence Rupert,** AC 1979; Kt 1963; CBE 1960 (OBE 1953); Australian diplomat, retired; Chairman, Uranium Advisory Council; *b* Hobart, Tasmania, 22 June 1912; *s* of late L. T. and Hilda McIntyre; *m* 1938, Judith Mary, *d* of John H. Gould; two *s*. *Educ*: Launceston Grammar Sch.; Tasmania Univ.; Exeter Coll., Oxford (Rhodes Scholar). Served Aust. High Commissioner's Office, London, 1936–40; Dept of External Affairs, Canberra, 1940–42; Aust. Embassy, Washington, 1942–47; Counsellor, Dept of External Affairs, Canberra, 1947–50; Actg Commissioner to Malaya, 1950–51; Asst Sec., Dept of External Affairs, Canberra, 1951–52; Commissioner to Malaya, 1952–54; Sen. External Affairs Officer (Minister), London, 1954–57; Aust. Ambassador to Indonesia, 1957–60, to Japan, 1960–65; Deputy Secretary, Australian Dept of External Affairs, 1965–70; Australian Permanent Rep. to the UN, 1970–75; Dir, Aust. Inst of Internat. Affairs, 1976–79. Hon. LLD Tasmania 1975. *Publication*: contrib. to Some Australians Take Stock, 1938. *Address*: 44 Dominion Circuit, Forrest, Canberra, ACT, Australia. *Clubs*: University (Sydney); Commonwealth (Canberra). *Died 21 Nov.* 1981.

**McINTYRE, Stuart Charles,** MBE; FCIS; *b* 6 Feb. 1912; *s* of James and Eleanor McIntyre; *m* 1938, Edith Irene Walton; two *d*. *Educ*: Dulwich Coll. Served War, RAF, Wing Comdr, 1940–46. Joined Pearl Assurance Co. Ltd, 1930; Dir, 1952, Chm. 1972–77, Pres. 1977–80; Director: Arsenal Football Club Ltd, 1962–; The Charter Trust & Agency Ltd, 1962–82; The Cross Investment Trust Ltd, 1962–82; Property Holding & Investment Trust Ltd, 1965–82; Property Selection & Investment Trust Ltd, 1966–82; Property Selection Finance Ltd, 1966–82. Freeman, City of London; Past Master, Glass Sellers' Company. *Recreation*: Association football. *Address*: Barton, East Close, Middleton-on-Sea, Sussex. *T*: Middleton-on-Sea 3746. *Club*: Royal Air Force.
*Died 26 May* 1989.

**McINTYRE, Surgeon Rear-Adm. William Percival Edwin,** CB 1961; RN retired; *b* 21 Aug. 1903; *s* of George McIntyre, Rathgar, Dublin; *m* 1964, Mrs Eve Robertson-Rodger (*d* 1971), widow of P. J. Robertson-Rodger. *Educ*: St Andrews Coll.; Trinity Coll., Dublin. MB, BCh, BAO 1925; MA, MD 1929. Joined RN as Surg. Lt 1925; Surg.-Comdr 1937; Surg.-Captain 1949. Senior Medical Officer (Medical Sect.), RN Hospital, Chatham, 1950–52 and RN Hospital, Plymouth, 1956–58; Fleet Medical Officer, Home Fleet, 1952–54; Surgeon Rear-Adm. 1958; Dep. Medical Dir-Gen., RN, 1958–62. QHP 1958–62. OStJ 1950; CStJ 1960. *Recreations*: golf, tennis. *Address*: Chasmoor, 68 Terenure Road West, Dublin 6.
*Died 2 March* 1986.

**MACK, Alan Frederick,** JP; Director, Manchester Chamber of Commerce and Industry, 1971–81; *b* 5 Dec. 1920; *s* of late Stanley Mack and late Sarah Elizabeth Mack; *m* 1953, Ailsa Muriel Wells; two *d*. *Educ*: Manchester Grammar School. War Service, Royal Artillery, Middle East, Italy, 1940–46. Secretary, Textile Finishing

Trade Assocs, 1946–68; Commercial Manager, British Textile Employers Assoc., 1968–70. Jt Hon. Sec., NW Industrial Devilt Assoc., 1971–81; Hon. Sec., Manchester Post Office Adv. Cttee, 1971–81; Mem., NW Supplementary Benefits Tribunal, 1977–86; Hon. Sec., Greater Manchester East County Scout Council, 1974–80; Pres., Manchester Jun. Ch. of Commerce, 1956–57. JP Manchester (Inner), 1974. *Recreations:* reading, gardening, historic buildings. *Address:* 22 Appleby Road, Gatley, Cheadle, Cheshire SK8 4QD. *T:* 061–428 6512.                                    *Died* 2 *March* 1989.

**McKAY, Sir Alex, (Sir Alick Benson McKay)**, KBE 1977 (CBE 1965); Director, News International Ltd (Deputy Chairman, 1969–78, Group Managing Director 1976–77); *b* Adelaide, S Australia, 5 Aug. 1909; *s* of George Hugh McKay, Master Mariner; *m* 1st, 1935, Muriel Frieda Searcy (decd); one *s* two *d*; 2nd, 1973, Beverley Hylton, *widow* of Jack Hylton. Joined News Ltd, Adelaide, 1933; Manager, News Ltd, Melbourne, 1939; Manager, News Ltd, Sydney, 1941; Dir and Gen. Man., Argus & Australasian Ltd, 1952; joined Daily Mirror Group, London, 1957, Dir, 1958. Dir, Internat. Publishing Corporation, 1963–69. Trustee, Reuters Ltd, 1975–. Chm. in London, Victorian Economic Devilt Corp., Australia. *Address:* Ellingham, St Clements Road, Westgate-on-Sea, Kent. *Club:* Garrick.                                    *Died* 15 *Jan.* 1983.

**MacKAY, Prof. Donald MacCrimmon**, BSc, PhD, FInstP; Professor Emeritus, University of Keele; Joint Editor, Biological Cybernetics; *b* 9 Aug. 1922; *o s* of Dr Henry MacKay; *m* 1955, Valerie Wood; two *s* three *d*. *Educ:* Wick High Sch.; St Andrews Univ. BSc (St Andrews) 1943; PhD (London) 1951. Radar research, Admiralty, 1943–46; Assistant Lecturer in Physics, 1946–48, Lecturer, 1948–59, Reader, 1959–60, King's Coll., London, FKC 1979; Granada Research Prof. of Communication and Neuroscience, Univ. of Keele, 1960–82. Rockefeller Fellow in USA, 1951. Vis. Prof., Univ. of California, 1969; Lectures: Fleming, 1961; Eddington, 1967; Herter, Johns Hopkins Univ., 1971; Foerster, Univ. of California, 1973; Drummond, Univ. of Stirling, 1975; Fremantle, Balliol Coll. Oxford, 1975; Riddell, Univ. of Newcastle, 1977; Pascal, Univ. of Waterloo, 1979; Kelvin, IEE, 1985; Gifford, Univ. of Glasgow, 1986. Foreign Mem., Royal Netherlands Acad. of Arts and Sciences, 1983. Hon. DSc St Andrews, 1986. *Publications:* (with M. E. Fisher) Analogue Computing at Ultra-High Speed, 1962; (ed) Christianity in a Mechanistic Universe, 1965; Freedom of Action in a Mechanistic Universe, 1967; Information, Mechanism and Meaning, 1969; The Clockwork Image, 1974; Science, Chance and Providence, 1978; Human Science and Human Dignity, 1979; Brains, Machines and Persons, 1980; Science and the Quest for Meaning, 1982; Visual Neuroscience, 1986; *chapters in:* Communication Theory, 1953; Information Theory, 1956, 1961; Sensory Communication, 1961; Man and his Future, 1963; Science in its Context, 1964; Information Processing in the Nervous System, 1964; Brain and Conscious Experience, 1966; Structure and Function of Inhibitory Neuronal Mechanisms, 1968; Evoked Brain Potentials, 1969; The Neurosciences, 1971; Non-Verbal Communication, 1972; Handbook of Sensory Physiology, 1973; Cybernetics and Bionics, 1974; Modifying Man: implications and ethics, 1978; Cerebral Correlates of Conscious Experience, 1978; Motivation, Motor and Sensory Processes of the Brain, 1980; Neural Communication and Control, 1981; Thinking: the expanding frontier, 1983; The Study of Information, 1983; Handbook of Cognitive Neuroscience, 1983; Cognition and Motor Processes, 1984; Models of the Visual Cortex, 1985; scientific papers on electronic computing, information theory, experimental psychology, neurophysiology. *Recreation:* photography. *Address:* The Croft, Keele, Staffs ST5 5AN. *T:* Newcastle (Staffs) 627300.
                                    *Died* 6 *Feb.* 1987.

**McKAY, Hon. Sir Donald Norman**, KCMG 1978; farmer and politician, New Zealand; Chairman, New Zealand Ports Authority; *b* Waipu, NZ, 28 Nov. 1908; *s* of Angus John McKay; *m* 1934, Miriam Hilda, *d* of A. T. Stehr; two *s* one *d*. *Educ:* Whangarei High Sch.; Auckland Univ. MP, Marsden, NZ, 1954–72; Minister of Health and Social Security, and Minister in Charge of Child Welfare Div., 1962–72. Member: Marsden National Party; Waipu Centenary Celebrations Cttee; Caledonian Soc.; District High Sch. Cttee; Northland Harbour Bd (Chm. 1974–). *Recreations:* bowls, golf; rep. Auckland Univ., Rugby football, 1928–30; N Auckland, cricket, 1932–36. *Address:* Waipu, Northland, New Zealand.
                                    *Died* 30 *March* 1988.

**MACKAY, Gillian Helen, (Mrs Walter Tallis)**; Public Relations Consultant; former private pilot; *b* 20 Sept. 1923; *er d* of Stuart Mackay; *m* 1971, Walter John Tallis. *Educ:* Hunmanby Hall. WRNS, 1942–46. Dep. Press Officer, Conservative Central Office, 1947–52; BOAC, 1952–56. Executive Secretary, Guild of Air Pilots and Air Navigators, 1956–68 (Freeman; Liveryman, 1968); Press Officer to Liberal Party Leader, 1968–69; Campaign Manager, Health Education Council, 1969–71; Exec. Dir, Fluoridation Soc., 1971–74. Chm., British Women Pilots' Assoc., 1964–69, 1974–76; Mem., Charles Newton Meml Trust Cttee, 1968–; Gen. Sec., PR

Consultants Assoc., 1974; Sec., Internat. Inst. of Human Nutrition, 1975–76; Member Council, Air League, 1966–71, 1972–76; Membership Sec., The Air League, 1976–79. Hon. Advr, Air Safety Gp, 1968–. Mem., Action Opportunities, 1976–; Oxford area rep., Voluntary Euthanasia Soc., 1981–. Companion, RAeS, 1960. Tissandier Diploma, Fédération Aéronautique Internat., 1966. MIPR 1974–82. *Publications:* various specialist journals. *Recreations:* birdwatching, sailing, gardening. *Address:* The Stable House, Burcot, near Abingdon OX14 3DP.
                                    *Died* 18 *March* 1984.

**MACKAY, Ian Keith**, CMG 1963; Consultant, since 1976; Assistant to Chairman, Papua New Guinea Broadcasting Commission, 1973–75; *b* 19 Oct. 1909; *s* of David and Margaret Mackay; *m* 1960, Lilian Adele Beatty; one *s* one *d*. *Educ:* Nelson Coll., New Zealand. New Zealand Broadcasting Service: Announcer, 1935–36; Sports Announcer, 1937; Station Manager, 1938–43; Senior Executive, Commercial Network, 1943–50; Australia: Asst Manager, Station 2GB, 1950–51; Production Manager, Macquarie Network, 1951–61; Director-General, Nigerian Broadcasting Corporation, 1961–64; Advisor on Mass Media to Minister and NBC Board of Governors, 1964–65; PRO, Papua and New Guinea Administration, 1966–68; Sen. Broadcast Officer, 1969–72, seconded Special Administrative duties in setting up the single broadcasting authority for Papua New Guinea, 1972–73. Member, Royal Society of Literature; Member, Society of Authors. *Publications:* Broadcasting in New Zealand, 1953; Broadcasting in Australia, 1957; Macquarie: The Story of a Network, 1960; Broadcasting in Nigeria, 1964; Presenting Papua and New Guinea, 1967; Broadcasting in Papua New Guinea, 1976; articles on social and historical aspects of broadcasting and articles on broadcasting in developing countries in numerous jls; also papers for UN agencies. *Recreations:* conchology, philately. *Address:* 405A Karori Road, Wellington 5, New Zealand.
                                    *Died* 14 *Nov.* 1985.

**MACKAY, Sir James (Mackerron)**, KBE 1966; CB 1964; *b* 9 Aug. 1907; *o s* of Alexander and Annie Mackay; *m* 1938, Katherine (*d* 1983), *d* of R. C. Hamilton; two *s*. *Educ:* Forres and Hamilton Academies; Glasgow and Oxford Universities. Glasgow Univ.: MA, 1929; Assistant in Greek, 1929–30. Balliol Coll., Oxford, 1930–34; Exhibitioner; Mods. and Greats. Lecturer in Humanity, Glasgow Univ., 1934–40. Entered Secretariat, Admiralty, 1940; Assistant Secretary, 1945; Under-Secretary, 1958; Deputy Secretary, 1961; Deputy Under Sec. of State, Min. of Defence, April 1964; Deputy Sec., Min. of Aviation, 1964–66; Deputy Under-Sec. of State, Home Office, 1966–67. Member: Scottish Tourist Bd, 1967–72; Highlands and Islands Devilt Bd, 1967–72 (Dep. Chm., 1970–72); Countryside Commn for Scotland, 1967–72; Cttee of Enquiry into Future of Broadcasting, 1974–77. *Address:* Cluny, Drumnadrochit, Inverness. *T:* Drumnadrochit 268.                     *Died* 24 *Dec.* 1985.

**MACKAY, John Alexander**, MA, LittD, DD, LLD, LHD; President of Princeton Theological Seminary, 1936–59, President Emeritus, 1959; *b* Inverness, Scotland, 17 May 1889; *s* of Duncan Mackay and Isabella Macdonald; *m* 1916, Jane Logan Wells; one *s* three *d*. *Educ:* University of Aberdeen (MA 1912, 1st Cl. Hons in Philosophy); Princeton Theological Seminary (BD 1915). Studied at the University of Madrid, 1915–16, and University of Bonn, 1930. LittD, University of San Marcos, Lima, 1918; DD Princeton Univ., 1937, Aberdeen Univ., 1939, University of Debrecen, Hungary, 1939; LLD Ohio-Wesleyan, 1937, Lincoln Univ., 1953; LHD Boston, 1939; and Hon. Degrees from several colleges; Hon. Fellow, Leland Stanford Univ., 1941. Principal, Anglo-Peruvian Coll., Lima, Peru, 1916–25; Prof. Philosophy, Univ. of San Marcos, Peru, 1925; Writer and Lecturer, South American Fedn YMCA, 1926–32; Pres. Bd Foreign Missions of Presbyterian Church, USA, 1945–51; Pres., World Presbyterian Alliance, 1954–59; Member: Central Cttee World Council of Churches, 1948–54 (Provl Cttee, 1946–48); Council on Theological Education, Presbyterian Church, USA, 1944–46 (Chairman); International Missionary Council, 1948–58 (Chairman); Joint Cttee World Council of Churches and International Missionary Council, 1949– (Chairman, 1949–54); Advisory Council, Dept of Philosophy, Princeton Univ., 1941–62; American Theological Soc.; Hon. For. Mem., British and Foreign Bible Soc.; Trustee of Mackenzie Univ., São Paulo, Brazil (Pres. Bd of Trustees, 1948). Special Lectr at many Univs and Colleges since 1932. Pres., American Assoc. of Theological Schs, 1948; Moderator, General Assembly of the Presbyterian Church in USA, 1953. Comendador, Palmas Magistrales (Peru), 1964. *Publications:* Mas Yo Os Digo, 1927; El Sentido de la Vida, 1931; The Other Spanish Christ, 1932; That Other America, 1935; A Preface to Christian Theology, 1941; Heritage and Destiny, 1943; Christianity on the Frontier, 1950; God's Order, 1953; The Presbyterian Way of Life, 1960; His Life and Our Life, 1964; Ecumenics: The Science of the Church Universal, 1964; Christian Reality and Appearance, 1969; Realidad e Idolatria, 1970. Editor, Theology Today, 1944–51 (Chairman Editorial Council, Theology Today, 1951–59). *Recreations:* walking and motoring. *Address:* Meadow Lakes,

Apartment 39–09, Hightstown, NJ 08520, USA. *Clubs:* Cosmos (Washington); Nassau (Princeton). *Died 8 June 1983.*

**MACKAY, Sir William (Calder),** Kt 1968; OBE 1957; MC 1918; JP; *b* 5 Aug. 1896; *s* of William Scoular Mackay and Anne Armstrong Henderson; *m* 1920, Constance May Harris (*d* 1989); one *s. Educ:* Hillhead High Sch., Glasgow. Served European War, 1914–18, NZEF (Adjt), France; served War of 1939–45 as Hon. YMCA Comr i/c welfare work in military camps, Air Force stations and naval establishments, Auckland Province. Past Member Board, Auckland Provincial Patriotic Fund; Director, Christchurch YMCA, 1929–33; Director, Auckland YMCA, 1934–45; President, YMCA, 1939–45; Chairman, Campaign Cttee for new Auckland YMCA, 1954; Life Member, YMCA, 1966. Past Member: Council, Auckland Chamber of Commerce; Exec. Cttee, Auckland Provincial Retailers' Assoc.; Auckland City Council, 1948–54; Auckland Harbour Bridge Authority; Council, Auckland, War Memorial Museum (Hon. Life Member, 1962). President, Rotary Club of Auckland, 1944–45; District Gov., Rotary, 1948–49; Member Aims and Objects Cttee, Rotary International, 1949–50. Provincial Comr, Boy Scouts, 1958; Organising Comr for Pan-Pacific Boy Scouts Jamboree, 1959 (Medal of Merit). Patron, Crippled Children Soc. (Mem. Exec., 1935–66, past Vice-Pres., and Pres., 1958–66, Life Mem. 1974, Auckland Branch); Vice-President: NZ Crippled Children Soc., 1964; St John Amb. Assoc. Auckland Centre Trust Bd, 1970; Pres., Nat. Children's Med. Res. Foundn, 1974; Past Area Co-ordinator, Duke of Edinburgh Award for Auckland Province and Mem. NZ Council, 1963. Foundn Mem. Bd, St Andrews Presbyterian Hospital and Hostel for Aged. JP 1940. *Recreations:* fishing, outdoor bowls. *Address:* Remuera Gardens, 57 Richard Farrell Avenue, Auckland 5, New Zealand. *T:* 502 495. *Club:* Northern (Auckland). *Died 1990.*

**MACKAY-TALLACK, Sir Hugh,** Kt 1963; Deputy Chairman, The Standard & Chartered Bank PLC, 1972–83; Director, Fleming Japanese Investment Trust PLC (formerly Capital and National Trust Ltd), since 1965 (Chairman, 1970–83); *b* 1912; *s* of E. H. Tallack and Deborah Lyle Mackay; unmarried. *Educ:* Kelly Coll., Devon; Heidelberg Univ. Served War of 1939–45, with 17th Dogra Regt, in Middle East and Burma; Private Sec. to C-in-C ALFSEA, and Mil. Sec. (Col) to Admiral Mountbatten, Supreme Allied Comdr, SEAC. Formerly: Chm., Macneill & Barry Ltd (Inchcape Gp) Calcutta; Governor of State Bank of India; Director numerous other cos in India; Chm., Indian Tea Assoc., 1954–55; Vice-Chairman, Tea Board of India, 1954–55; Member Government of India Tea Auction Cttee, 1954–55; Chairman, Ross Inst. of India, 1951–64; Pres., Bengal Chamber of Commerce and Industry and Associated Chambers of Commerce of India, 1962–63. Director: Inchcape & Co. Ltd, 1963–82 (Dep. Chm., 1964–77); Assam Investments Ltd, 1965–81 (Chm., 1965–74); London & Holyrood Trust Ltd, 1973–82; London & Provincial Trust Ltd, 1973–82. Mem., Fedn of Commonwealth Chambers of Commerce. Governor: Nehru Meml Trust; Victoria League. *Recreation:* riding. *Address:* 47 South Street, Mayfair, W1. *T:* 01–493 5670. *Clubs:* White's, Oriental, City of London; Bengal, Tollygunge, Turf (all in Calcutta). *Died 29 April 1989.*

**McKEE, Air Marshal Sir Andrew,** KCB 1957 (CB 1951); CBE 1944; DSO 1942; DFC 1941; AFC 1938; *b* 1901; *s* of Samuel Hugh McKee, Eyredale, Oxford, Canterbury, NZ; *m* 1949, Cecelia Tarcille, *er d* of Michael Keating, NZ; two *d. Educ:* Christchurch Boys' High Sch., NZ. Joined RAF, 1927. AOC No 205 Group Mediterranean Allied Air Force, 1945–46; Senior Air Staff Officer, MEAF, 1946–47; Comdt OATS, 1947–49; First Comdt, RAF Flying Coll., 1949–51; Air Vice-Marshal, 1952; AOC No 21 Group, 1951–53; Senior Air Staff Officer, Bomber Command, 1953–55; Air Marshal, 1957; Air Officer Commanding-in-Chief, Transport Command, 1955–59, retired. *Address:* 27 Frederick Street, Palmerston North, New Zealand. *Club:* Royal Air Force. *Died 8 Dec. 1988.*

**McKEE, William Desmond,** CBE 1979; FIOB; Chairman and Managing Director, F. B. McKee & Co. Ltd, since 1955; *b* 17 Sept. 1926; *s* of late Frederick McKee and Eleanor McKee; *m* 1951, Rachel McKibben Gordon, Glenluce, SW Scotland; three *d. Educ:* Mourne Grange Sch., Co. Down; St Columba's Coll., Dublin. FIOB 1965. Joined family bldg business, 1945; became Chm. on father's death, 1955. Pres., Fedn of Bldg and Civil Engrg Contractors, NI, 1976–78; Mem., NI Tourist Bd, 1966–75. Belfast Harbour Comr, 1976–; Trustee, James Mackie & Sons Ltd, 1976; Dir, Northern Bank Ltd, 1981–. Former Irish Rugby Internat., wing and centre three-quarter (12 Caps); Mem., Triple Crown Team, 1947–48 and 1948–49. *Recreations:* shooting in winter, swimming in summer. *Address:* Landscape, 63 Shore Road, Greenisland, Carrickfergus, Co. Antrim, N Ireland. *T:* Whiteabbey 63259. *Clubs:* North of Ireland Cricket and Football, Ulster, Rotary (Belfast). *Died 28 Jan. 1982.*

**McKEEVER, Ronald Fraser,** CBE 1975; HM Diplomatic Service, retired; *b* 20 Aug. 1914; *yr s* of late Frederick Leonard McKeever and of late Elizabeth Moore McKeever (*née* Bucher); *m* 1944, Margaret Lilian (*née* Sabine); one *s. Educ:* George Watson's Coll., Edinburgh; Edinburgh Univ. Served in Indian Police, 1935–47. Joined Foreign Service, 1948; Vice-Consul: Dakar, 1948; Chicago, 1950; Consul, Kansas City, 1953; British Embassy, Bonn, 1954; Consul, Gdynia, 1957; Brazzaville, 1959 (Chargé d'Affaires, 1960); Foreign Office, 1961; Consul, Tamsui (Formosa), 1962–66; Ambassador to Togo and Dahomey, 1967–70; Consul-Gen., Naples, 1971–74. *Recreations:* fishing, bird-watching. *Address:* Bowmillholm, St Mungo, by Lockerbie, Dumfriesshire. *Died 20 Oct. 1981.*

**McKELL, Rt. Hon. Sir William John,** GCMG 1951; PC 1948; *b* Pambula, NSW, 26 Sept. 1891; *m* 1920; one *s* two *d. Educ:* Public Sch., Surry Hills, Sydney. Served apprenticeship as boiler-maker, Morts' Dock and Engineering Co., Sydney; elected Financial Secretary, Boilermakers' Union; elected Member Legislative Assembly, NSW, at 25 years of age; Member, 1917–47; Minister of Justice (1920–22) at age of 28 years; Minister of Justice and Assistant Colonial Treasurer, 1925–27; visited London and New York on financial mission for State of New South Wales, 1927; Minister for Local Government, 1930; Minister of Justice, 1931–32; Leader of the Opposition, 1939–41; Premier and Colonial Treasurer of New South Wales, 1941–47; official visit to United States and Great Britain, 1945; Governor-General of Australia, 1947–53. Member Malayan Constitutional Commission, 1956–57. Barrister of Supreme Court of New South Wales, 1925; QC 1945. Chairman of Sydney Cricket Ground Trust, 1938. Hon. LLD, Sydney. *Recreations:* always active in football and boxing circles; played first-grade football and boxed in amateur championships. *Address:* 42/14 Leura Road, Double Bay, NSW 2028, Australia. *Died 11 Jan. 1985.*

**MACKEN, Frederic Raymond,** CMG 1964; *b* 23 Sept. 1903; *s* of Charles Alfred Macken and Ella (*née* Steadman); *m* 1929, Alma Doris (*née* Keesing); one *d. Educ:* Whangarei High Sch.; Auckland Univ., New Zealand. LLM (with Hons), 1927. Retired as Commissioner of Inland Revenue for New Zealand, 1964. *Recreations:* bowls, golf. *Address:* 9 Harley Grove, Lower Hutt, Wellington, New Zealand. *T:* 695205. *Club:* Civil Service (Wellington, NZ). *Died 1 Feb. 1987.*

**MacKENNA, Sir Bernard Joseph Maxwell, (Sir Brian MacKenna),** Kt 1961; Judge of the High Court of Justice (Queen's Bench Division), 1961–77; *b* 12 Sept. 1905; unmarried. Called to the Bar, Inner Temple, Jan. 1932; Western Circuit; QC 1950; Master of the Bench of the Inner Temple, 1958. *Address:* Flat 9, 36 Sloane Court West, SW3 4TB. *T:* 01–823 6246. *Clubs:* Athenæum, Beefsteak. *Died 20 Oct. 1989.*

**MacKENNA, Robert Merttins Bird,** MA, MD, FRCP; Hon. Colonel RAMC, 1954; Dermatologist, King Edward VII's Hospital for Officers, 1946–72, now Consulting Dermatologist; Hon. Consultant in Dermatology to the British Army, 1946–64; Councillor Royal College of Physicians, 1956–59; President: Dermatological Section, Royal Society of Medicine, 1966–67; British Association of Dermatology, 1966–67; Physician in charge of the Department for Diseases of the Skin, St Bartholomew's Hospital, 1946–68, now Hon. Consultant in Dermatology; Hon. Member, British Association of Dermatologists, 1976; *b* 16 Nov. 1903; *s* of late R. W. MacKenna and Harriet A. S. Bird; *m* 1st, 1927, Helen, *e d* of Thomas Todrick; two *d*; 2nd, 1943, Margaret, *d* of Rev. Christmas Hopkins and Eleanor Hopkins; two *s. Educ:* RN Colleges, Osborne and Dartmouth; Clare Coll., Cambridge Univ.; St Thomas' Hospital. Resigned from the Navy, 1919; studied at Liverpool Univ., 1920–21; Cambridge, 1921–24; BA (Nat. Sci. Tripos), 1924; MRCS, LRCP, 1926; MA, MB, BCh Cambridge, 1928; MRCP, 1928; MD Cambridge 1931; FRCP, 1941. Junior Asst MO Venereal Diseases Dept, and Clinical Asst, Dermatological Dept, St Thomas' Hosp., 1927–28; Clinical Asst, St John's Hosp., for Diseases of the Skin, 1928; Hon. Asst Dermatologist Liverpool Radium Inst., 1929; Hon. Dermatologist, Liverpool Stanley Hosp., 1929–34; Hon. Dermatologist, Royal Liverpool United Hosp., (Royal Southern Hosp.), 1934–46; Dermatologist, Catterick Military Hosp., Oct. 1939; Comd Specialist in Dermatology, Northern Comd, 1940–41; Adviser in Dermatology and Asst Dir, Hygiene (c), War Office, 1941–43; Cons. Dermatologist to British Army, 1943–45. Malcolm Morris Meml Lectr, 1955; Watson Smith Lectr, 1957; Prosser White Orator, 1968. Hon. Fellow: Amer. Med. Assoc.; Canadian Dermatological Assoc. Hon. Member: Dermatological Section, RSM; Dermatological Assoc. of Australia; Soc. for Investigative Dermatology; NY Dermatolog. Soc.; Deutsche Dermatologische Gesellschaft; Sociedad Venezolana de Dermatologia; Alpha Omega Alpha Honor Med. Soc.; Corresp. Member: Amer. Dermatological Assoc.; Nederlandse Vereniging van Dermatologen; Societas Dermatologica Danica; Societas Dermatologica Austriaca; Societas Dermatologica Svecica; La Société Française de Dermatologie et de Syphiligraphie; Israeli Dermatological Soc. OStJ 1954. *Publications:* Aids to Dermatology, 1929, 1939, 1946, 1954, 1956;

Diseases of the Skin, 1932, 1937, 1949 and 1952; Dermatology (jointly with E. L. Cohen), 1964. Joint Editor of The Medical History of Liverpool, 1936; Sections on Dermatology in Medical Annual, 1944–63; editor, Modern Trends in Dermatology, Series I, 1948, Series II, 1953, Series III, 1966; Associate Editor for dermatological subjects British Encyclopædia of Medical Practice, 2nd Edition, 1950; short autobiog. in Jl of Amer. Acad. of Dermatology, vol. 6, 1982; various papers on dermatological subjects in medical journals. *Address:* 22 Hillbrow, Richmond Hill, Richmond, Surrey, TW10 6BH. *T:* 01-940 2204.

*Died 12 Nov.* 1984.

**McKENNA, Siobhán;** actress; *b* Belfast, 24 May 1923; *d* of Prof. Owen McKenna and Margaret O'Reilly; *m* 1946, Denis O'Dea (*d* 1978); one *s. Educ:* St Louis Convent, Monaghan; Galway Univ. BA (1st cl. Hons, French, English and Irish Lit.). Holds 5 hon. doctorates in Literature and the Humanities. Apptd to Council of State, Republic of Ireland, by President Cearbhall Ó Dálaigh, 1975. First stage appearances with Irish trans of plays by Molière, O'Neill, O'Casey, Shaw, Shakespeare, for Irish speaking theatre An Taibhdhearc, Galway, 1940–43; Abbey Theatre, Dublin, 1944–47 (first appearance in Le Bourgeois Gentilhomme). *Plays include:* The White Steed (first London appearance), Embassy and Whitehall, 1947; Fading Mansions (dir, Laurence Olivier), Duchess, 1949; Ghosts, Embassy; Berkeley Square, Queen's; Héloise and Abelard, Duke of York's; Shakespeare season, Stratford-upon-Avon, 1952, with As You Like It, Coriolanus, Macbeth, also Ben Johnson's Volpone; Saint Joan, Arts, 1954, St Martin's, 1955 (first Evening Standard Best Actress Award, 1955), European tour, NY, 1956; The Chalk Garden (first NY appearance), NY, 1955; The Rope-Dancers, NY, 1957; Hamlet (title role), NY, 1957; Shakespeare season, as Viola in Twelfth Night (dir, Tyrone Guthrie), Stratford, Ont., Canada, as Lady Macbeth, Cambridge Shakespeare Fest., USA; Playboy of the Western World, Dublin, Edinburgh and Paris Festivals, then Piccadilly, St Martin's, 1960, European tour (Best Actress, Florence Festival); Captain Brassbound's Conversion, Dublin and Philadelphia, 1961; Saint Joan of the Stockyards, Dublin Festival, 1961, Queen's, 1964; Play with a Tiger, Comedy, 1962; The Cavern, Strand; Laurette, Dublin, 1964; Juno and the Paycock, Gaiety, Dublin, 1966, Toronto, 1973, Abbey, Dublin, 1979; The Loves of Cass Maguire, Abbey, 1967; The Cherry Orchard, Abbey, 1968; On a Foggy Day, St Martin's, 1969; Best of Friends, Strand, 1970; Here are Ladies (one woman show), Criterion, 1970, USA, Canada, Australia, Dublin, 1975; Fallen Angels, Gate, 1975; A Moon for the Misbegotten, Gate, 1976; Plough and the Stars, Abbey, 1977, US tour; Sons of Oedipus, Greenwich, 1977; Sarah Bernhardt in Memoir, Canada and Dublin, 1977, Ambassadors, 1978; Riders to the Sea, Greenwich Fest., 1978; Here are Ladies, Vienna, 1979; The Shadow of a Gunman, Vienna, 1980; Agrippina in Britannicus, Lyric, Hammersmith, 1981; All Joyce, Abbey, 1982. *Plays directed:* St Joan (in Gaelic), Galway, 1943; Daughter from over the Water, Dublin; I must be getting out of this Kip, Dublin, 1968; Tinkers Wedding, Shadow of the Glen, Riders to the Sea, Toronto, 1973; Juno and the Paycock, Mermaid, 1973; Playboy of the Western World, USA, 1967, English tour and Hong Kong, 1977; Rising of the Moon; The Cat and the Moon, Purgatory and A Pot of Broth, Riders to the Sea, Greenwich, 1978; The Shadow of a Gunman, Vienna, 1980; The Midnight Court (in Irish), Peacock, Dublin, 1984. *Films include:* Hungry Hill, Daughter of Darkness, The Lost People (Lejeune Gold Medal), The Adventurers, King of Kings, Doctor Zhivago, Playboy of the Western World, Philadelphia Here I Come, Of Human Bondage, Here are Ladies, Memed. *Television* includes: USA: What Every Woman Knows, The Letter, Cradle Song, The Winslow Boy, Misalliance, Don Juan in Hell, The Rope Dancers, The Last Days of Pompeii; UK: The Aspern Papers, Chez Torpe, The Landlady, Vicious Circle, The Diary of Brigid Hitler, Angels in the Annexe. *Publications:* trans. into Irish: Mary Rose, by J. M. Barrie; Saint Joan, by G. B. Shaw. *Recreations:* reading, walking, theatre-going. *Address:* Highfield Road, Rathgar, Dublin 6, Republic of Ireland. *Died 16 Nov.* 1986.

**MACKENZIE, Dr Alastair Stewart, (Sandy);** Regional Medical Officer, North West Thames Regional Health Authority, 1977–82; *b* 28 April 1930; *s* of late James S. Mackenzie, JP and Anne (*née* Evans); *m* 1984, Maria Christina (*née* Towli). *Educ:* Gyfarthfa Castle Sch., Merthyr Tydfil; Bromsgrove Sch., Worcs; Jesus Coll., Cambridge (MA); University Coll. Hospital. MB, BChir; DMRT, FFCM. Captain and Specialist, RAMC, 1959. Sen. Admin. MO, NE Metrop. Regional Hosp. Bd, 1972; Regional MO, NE Thames RHA, 1974–77. Mem. Council (Section of Epidemiology), RSocMed, 1972–82; Mem. Council, British Cancer Council, 1972–82; a British Rep., Hosp. Cttee of EEC, 1974–82; Mem. Council, Queen's Nursing Inst., 1974–82; Mem. Bd of Governors, St John's Hosp. for Diseases of Skin, 1974–82; Mem. Ct of Governors, and Mem. Bd of Management, London Sch. of Hygiene and Trop. Medicine, 1975–82; Mem. Laboratory Develt Adv. Gp, 1975–82; Mem. Cttee of Management, Inst. of Child Health, 1976–82. Mem., London Health Planning Consortium, 1978–82;

Health Dir designate, Emergency War Planning Region 5 (Gtr London), 1980–82. Medical Advr, British Overseas Exec. Service. FRSocMed. *Publications:* various articles on epidemiology and med. care in med. jls. *Recreations:* music, gardening, Egyptology. *Address:* Flat 5, 21 Nevern Place, SW5. *T:* 01–370 2480; Flat 11c, Sussex Square, Brighton, East Sussex. *T:* Brighton 600308.

*Died 31 Jan.* 1986.

**MACKENZIE, Alexander,** OBE 1964; JP; DL; Lord Provost of Dundee and Lord Lieutenant of the County of the City of Dundee, 1967–70; *b* 12 Dec. 1915; *o s* of of Alex. and Elizabeth Mackenzie; *m* 1940, Edna Margaret, *d* of Fred Holder; one *d. Educ:* Morgan Academy, Dundee. Secretary (Dundee Branch), League of Nations, 1935–38; Secretary (Dundee Branch), UNA, 1946–49. Member, Dundee Town Council, 1947–; Chairman, Tay Road Bridge Joint Board, 1967–70; Chairman, Dundee High Sch. Directors, 1967–70; Vice-Chairman: Governors, Dundee Coll. of Art and Technology, 1967–70; Tayside Economic Planning Consultative Group, 1969 (Chm. Publicity Cttee, 1969–70); Member: Univ. Court of Dundee, 1967–70; Dundee Harbour Trust, 1967–70; Academic Council, Univ. of Dundee. Pres., Dundee Brotherhood, 1948. Assessor, Dundee Repertory Theatre, 1964–70. JP, 1951, DL, 1971, County of the City of Dundee. *Publications:* And Nothing But the Truth, 1976; From a Window in Whitehall, 1978; On Stage-Dundee, 1979. *Recreation:* reading. *Address:* 18 Whitehall Crescent, Dundee. *T:* 25774. *Died 8 May* 1982.

**MACKENZIE, Chalmers Jack,** CC (Canada) 1967; CMG 1943; MC 1918; FRS 1946; FRSC; MEIC; Chancellor, Carleton University, 1954–68; Member Atomic Energy Control Board, 1946–61, and President, 1948–61; President, National Research Council of Canada, 1939–52; Member Defence Research Board, 1946–52; President Atomic Energy of Canada, Limited, 1952–53; Director: Canadian Patents and Development Ltd, 1947–61; Chemcell Ltd and Columbia Cellulose Co., 1954–68; Member, Army Technical Development Board, 1942; Chairman War Technical and Scientific Development Cttee, 1940; Inventions Board, 1940–46; *b* 10 July 1888; *s* of late James Mackenzie, St Stephen, NB; *m* 1st, 1916, Claire Rees (*d* 1922); one *s*; 2nd, 1924, Geraldine Gallon (*d* 1976); two *d. Educ:* St Stephen, NB; Dalhousie Univ. (BE 1909); Harvard Univ. (MCE 1915). Engineering Firm, Maxwell & Mackenzie, 1912–16; Overseas 54th Canadian Infantry Bn, 1916–18 (MC); Prof. Civil Engineering, 1918–39, Dean of College of Engineering, 1921–39, University of Sask., President, Engineering Institute of Canada, 1941; Chairman Saskatoon City Planning Commission, 1928–39; Chairman Saskatoon City Hospital Board, 1937–39. Dir Canadian Geographical Soc., 1937–60. Mem., Canada Council, 1963–69. Hon. LLD: Dalhousie, 1941; Western Ontario, 1943; Queen's, 1944, Saskatchewan, 1944; Carleton, 1969; DEng: Toronto, 1944; Nova Scotia Tech. Coll., 1950; Hon. DSc: McGill, 1941; Laval and Cambridge, 1946; UBC, 1947; Princeton, 1949; McMaster Univ., 1951; Univs of New Brunswick, Montreal, Manitoba, 1953; Ottawa, 1958; RMC, 1964; Hon. DCL Bishop's Univ., 1952. Hon. FRCP(C), 1947; Hon. Mem., Amer. Soc. Civil Engrs, 1952; Hon. FICE, 1968. US Medal for Merit, 1947; Chevalier de la Légion d'Honneur, 1947; Kelvin Medal, InstMechE, 1954; R. B. Bennett Empire Prize, RSA, 1954; Royal Bank Award, 1968. *Publications:* in scientific and technical press. *Recreations:* golf, curling. *Address:* 210 Buena Vista Road, Rockcliffe Park, Ottawa, Ontario K1M 0V7, Canada. *Died 26 Feb.* 1984.

**MACKENZIE, Colin Hercules,** CMG 1946; *b* 5 Oct. 1898; *o s* of late Maj.-Gen. Sir Colin Mackenzie, KCB, and Ethel, *er d* of Hercules Ross, ICS; *m* 1940, Evelyn Clodagh, 2nd *d* of Charles and Lady Aileen Meade; one *d. Educ:* Summerfields; Eton (Schol.); King's Coll., Cambridge (1st Class Hons in Economics. Exhibitioner and Senior Scholar, also Chancellor's Medal for English Verse). Served France with 1st Bn Scots Guards in 1918 (wounded). Served in India and with South-East Asia Command, 1941–45, comd Force 136 (CMG, Officier de la Légion d'Honneur, Dutch Resistance Cross). British Economic Mission to Greece, 1946. Dir, J. and P. Coats Ltd, 1928–65. Chairman: Scottish Council, FBI, 1957–59; Scottish Cttee on Electricity, 1961–62; Scottish Arts Council, 1962–70; Inverness Conservative and Unionist Assoc., 1967–70. Hon. Sheriff Inverness-shire. Hon. LLD St Andrews, 1970. *Address:* Kyle House, Kyleakin, Isle of Skye. *T:* Kyle 4517. *Club:* Special Forces. *Died 21 Dec.* 1986.

**MacKENZIE, David Alexander;** General Secretary, Transport Salaried Staffs' Association, 1973–77; Civil Servant, 1980–86; *b* 22 March 1922; *s* of David MacKenzie and Jeannie Ross; *m* 1945, Doreen Joyce Lucas; two *s* one *d. Educ:* Merkinch Public Sch.; Inverness High Sch. Entered London Midland Railway Service, 1936. Served in Royal Navy, 1941–45. Transport Salaried Staffs Assoc.: Divisional Sec., 1952–66; Sen. Asst Sec., 1966–68; Asst Gen. Sec., 1968. Member: TUC Non-Manual Workers' Cttee, 1969–73; Air Transport and Travel Industry Trng Bd, 1969–73; Hotel and Catering Industry Trng Bd, 1969–80. *Recreations:* golf, reading.

*Address:* 19 Grattons Drive, Pound Hill, Three Bridges, West Sussex. *T:* Crawley 513048. *Died* 31 *Dec.* 1989.

**McKENZIE, John,** CMG 1970; MBE 1947; PhD; HM Diplomatic Service, retired; *b* 30 April 1915; *m* 1943, Sigridur Olafsdóttir; two s one *d. Educ:* Archbishop Holgate's Grammar Sch., York; Leeds Univ. Lectr, Univ. of Iceland, 1938–40; Second Sec. and Vice-Consul, Reykjavik, 1945; Consul, Helsinki, 1948; First Sec., 1949; Foreign Office, 1950; Sofia, 1953 (Chargé d'Affaires, 1954, 1955, 1956); Baghdad, 1956; Foreign Office, 1958; Counsellor, seconded to Cabinet Office, 1962; Helsinki, 1964 (Chargé d'Affaires, 1965, 1966); Dep. High Comr Calcutta, 1967–70; Ambassador to Iceland, 1970–75. *Address:* 60 Dome Hill, Caterham, Surrey CR3 6EB. *T:* Caterham 42546. *Died* 17 *Nov.* 1986.

**MACKENZIE, John Moncrieff Ord;** *b* 1911; *s* of Kenneth Mackenzie, Dolphinton; *m* 1936, Delia Alice, *d* of late Wyndham Damer Clark, DL, JP, London, SW3; one *s* four *d. Educ:* Rugby; Corpus Christi Coll., Cambridge. WS, 1936. Captain, Lanarkshire Yeomanry (TA); served War of 1939–45 (despatches, Bronze Star Medal, US): GHQ, Liaison Regt. JP 1947, DL 1953, Peeblesshire. *Address:* Dolphinton House, Dolphinton, Peeblesshire. *T:* Dolphinton 82286. *Died* 10 *Feb.* 1985.

**MACKENZIE, Keith Roderick Turing,** OBE 1983; MC; Secretary, Royal and Ancient Golf Club of St Andrews, Fife, Scotland, 1967–83; President, Golf Foundation, since 1984; *b* 19 Jan. 1921; *s* of Henry Roderick Turing Mackenzie and Betty Dalzell Mackenzie; *m* 1949, Barbara Kershaw Miles; two *s* two *d. Educ:* Uppingham Sch.; RMC, Sandhurst. Served War: Indian Army, 2/6th Gurkha Rifles, 1940–47 (MC, Italy, 1944). Burmah-Shell Oil Storage and Distributing Co. of India, 1947–65; Shell Company of Rhodesia, 1965–66. *Recreations:* gardening, golf. *Address:* Easter Edenhill, Kennedy Gardens, St Andrews, Fife KY16 9DJ. *T:* St Andrews (0334) 73581. *Clubs:* Royal Cinque Ports Golf (Deal); Royal & Ancient Golf (St Andrews); Royal Porthcawl Golf; Royal St George's Golf; Littlestone Golf; Atlanta Athletic (Georgia); Pine Valley Golf (New Jersey); Royal Calcutta Golf (Calcutta); Royal Harare Golf (Zimbabwe); Lake Noma Golf (Florida). *Died* 7 *Oct.* 1990.

**MacKENZIE, Norman Archibald MacRae,** CC (Canada) 1969; CMG 1946; MM and Bar, 1918; CD 1968; QC; BA, LLB (Dalhousie); LLM (Harvard); FRSC 1943; Hon. LLD (Mount Allison, New Brunswick, Toronto, Dalhousie, Ottawa, Bristol, Alberta, Glasgow, St Francis Xavier, McGill, Sydney, Rochester, Alaska, California, British Columbia, RMC (Cambridge)); DCL (Saskatchewan, Whitman College); DSc Social, Laval; DLitt, Memorial University of Newfoundland; President Emeritus, Hon. Professor of International Law, University of British Columbia, Vancouver, since 1962; President of the University, 1944–62; appointed to The Senate of Canada, 1966, retired 1969; *b* Pugwash, Nova Scotia, Canada, 5 Jan. 1894; *s* of Rev. James A. MacKenzie and Elizabeth MacRae; *m* 1928, Margaret, *d* of A. W. and Helen Thomas; one *s* two *d. Educ:* Pictou Acad.; Dalhousie Univ. (BA 1921, LLB 1923); Harvard (LLM 1924); St John's Coll., Cambridge (Postgrad. Dipl., 1925); Grays' Inn, London. Read Law with McInnes, Jenks and Lovitt; called to Bar of Nova Scotia, 1926; KC 1942; Legal Adviser, ILO, Geneva, 1925–27; Assoc. Prof. of Law, 1927–33, Prof. of International and Canadian Constitutional Law, 1933–40, Toronto Univ.; Pres., University of New Brunswick, 1940–44; Pres., Nat. Conf. of Canadian Universities, 1946–48; Pres., Canadian Club of Toronto, 1939–40; Chm., Research Commission, Canadian Inst. of Internat. Affairs, 1929–40; Founding Mem. and Hon. Chm., National Council CIIA; Chm., Wartime Information Board, Canada, 1943–45; Chm., Reconstruction Commn, Province of New Brunswick, 1941–44; Pres., Toronto Branch, League of Nations Soc., 1932–36; Delegate to Institute of Pacific Relations Conferences, Shanghai 1931, Banff 1933, Yosemite 1936, Virginia Beach 1939, Mont Tremblant 1942; Delegate to British Commonwealth Conferences, Toronto, 1933, Sydney, Australia, 1938; Delegate to 7th Congress on Laws of Aviation, Lyons, France, 1925; War Record: Canadian Inf., 1914–19; 6th Canadian Mounted Rifles' 85th Bn, Nova Scotia Highlanders (MM and Bar); Vice-Pres., National Council of Canadian YMCA's; Chm. Victory Loan Executive Cttee, Fredericton and York, New Brunswick, 1941–44; Mem., University Advisory Board, Dept of Labour; Mem., Advisory Cttee on University Training for Veterans, Dept of Veterans Affairs; Hon. Pres. Save the Children Fund, Canada; Mem., Legal Survey Cttee (Survey of Legal Profession of Canada), 1949–57; Chm., Consultative Cttee on Doukhobor Problems; Mem., Royal Commission on National Development in the Arts, Letters and Sciences, 1949–51; Dir, Bank of Nova Scotia, 1960–69; Mem. Vancouver Advisory Board, Canada Permanent Trust Company, 1962–; East African Commission on University Educn, 1962. Trustee: Teachers Insurance and Annuity Association of America, 1948–; Carnegie Foundation for the Advancement of Teaching, 1951– (Chm. Bd Trustees, 1959); Pres. Canadian Assoc. for Adult Education, 1957–59; Chm., University Grants Cttee, Prov. of NS,

1963–69; Mem. Royal Commission on Higher Educn, Prov. of PEI; Pres., Canadian Centenary Council; Dir, Centennial Commn (Canada); Dir, Fathers of Confedn Memorial Foundn; Pres., Nat. Assoc. of Canadian Clubs. Hon. Fellow: St John's Coll., Cambridge, 1964; LSE, 1980. John E. Read Medal for contributions to International Law, 1975. *Publications:* Legal Status of Aliens in Pacific Countries, 1937; Canada and Law of Nations (with L. H. Laing), 1938; Canada in World Affairs (with F. H. Soward, J. F. Parkinson, T. W. L. MacDermot), 1941; The Challenge to Education, 1953; First Principles, 1954; (with Jacob Austin) A Canadian View of Territorial Seas and Fisheries, 1956, etc. Contributor to: Canadian Bar Review, Law Journals, etc. *Recreations:* fishing, hunting, golf, tennis, badminton, ski-ing. *Address:* 4509 West 4th Avenue, Vancouver, BC V6R 1R4, Canada. *Clubs:* Vancouver, University, Faculty (Vancouver).
*Died* 26 *Jan.* 1986.

**MACKENZIE, Sir Robert Evelyn,** 12th Bt, *cr* 1673; *b* 15 Feb. 1906; *s* of 11th Bt and Evelyn Mary Montgomery (*d* 1908), *d* of Major-Gen. Sir Edward W. Ward; *S* father, 1935; *m* 1st, 1940, Mrs Jane Adams-Beck (*d* 1953); 2nd, 1963, Mrs Elizabeth Campbell. *Educ:* Eton; Trinity Coll., Cambridge. Mem. of Lloyd's, 1932–71. Intelligence Corps, 1939; British Embassy, Paris, 1944; Foreign Office, 1947; Washington, 1948; Foreign Office, 1951. *Heir: kinsman* Peter Douglas Mackenzie, *b* 1949. *Address:* 44 Chester Square, SW1W 9EA. *Club:* Brooks's. *Died* 28 *July* 1990.

**McKENZIE, Prof. Robert Trelford;** Professor of Sociology (with special reference to Politics), London School of Economics and Political Science, since 1964; *b* 11 Sept. 1917; *s* of William Meldrum McKenzie and Frances (*née* Chapman). *Educ:* King Edward High Sch., Vancouver; University of British Columbia (BA); University of London (PhD). Taught at University of British Columbia, 1937–42. Served with Canadian Army, 1943–46. Has taught at London Sch. of Economics and Political Science since 1949. Visiting Lectr on Politics at Harvard and Yale Univs, Sept. 1958–Jan. 1959. Hon. LLD Simon Fraser Univ., 1969. *Publications:* British Political Parties: The Distribution of Power within the Conservative and Labour Parties, 1955, 2nd rev. edn, 1964 (translated into Spanish, German and Japanese); (with Allan Silver) Angels in Marble: Working Class Conservatism in Urban England, 1968 (trans, into Japanese). *Recreation:* broadcasting. *Address:* London School of Economics and Political Science, Houghton Street, Aldwych, WC2. *T:* 01-405 7686. *Died* 12 *Oct.* 1981.

**MACKENZIE, Sir Roderick (Campbell),** 10th Bt *cr* 1703 (Nova Scotia); student in foreign languages, University of Virginia, Charlottesville, Va; *b* 15 Nov. 1954; *s* of Kenneth Roderick Mackenzie (*d* 1960) and of Elizabeth Carrington, *d* of late William Barbee Settle; *S* kinsman, Sir (Lewis) Roderick Kenneth Mackenzie, 9th Bt, 1972. *Educ:* Univ. of Virginia. *Heir: cousin* Roderick Edward François McQuhae Mackenzie, CBE, DSC, Captain RN, retired [*b* 11 Dec. 1894; *m* 1938, Marie Evelyn Campbell, *o d* of late W. E. Parkinson; one *s* two *d*]. *Address:* 120 Church Street, Clifton Forge, Virginia 24422, USA. *T:* (703) 862-1203.
*Died* 31 *May* 1981.

**MACKENZIE, Captain Sir Roderick (Edward François McQuhae),** 11th Bt *cr* 1703, of Scatwell; CBE 1945; DSC 1916; RN retired; *b* 11 Dec. 1894; *s* of John Roderick Kenneth Mackenzie (*d* 1958) and Kathleen Elizabeth (*d* 1974), *d* of Captain Thomas Howard Blennerhasset Coulson, Royal Indian Marine; *S* cousin, 1981; *m* 1938, Marie Evelyn Campbell, *o c* of late William Ernest Parkinson; one *s* two *d. Educ:* RN Colls, Osborne and Dartmouth; RN Staff Coll., Greenwich. Served European War, 1914–18 (despatches): Midshipman, then Sub-Lieut, HMS Iron Duke, 1913–15; HMS Royalist, 1915–18; later served as Fleet Torpedo Officer, China Station, N America, W Indies and Home Fleet; also on staff, HMS Dolphin, as Torpedo Officer, Submarines; in comd HMS Sandwich, 1931–33; Admiralty, 1933–39; War of 1939–45, landings in Sicily, Naples, Anzio (despatches); Naval Officer i/c, Naples and Leghorn. Retired, 1946. American Medal of Freedom with silver palm, 1945. *Recreations:* golf, riding. *Heir: s* Roderick McQuhae Mackenzie, MB, BS, MRCP, DCH [*b* 17 April 1942; *m* 1970, Nadine, *d* of Georges Schlatter; one *s* one *d*]. *Address:* Finborough, 11 Morley Road, Farnham, Surrey. *T:* Farnham 716072. *Club:* Naval and Military. *Died* 7 *Jan.* 1986.

**MACKENZIE, Sandy;** *see* Mackenzie, Dr A. S.

**MACKENZIE-KENNEDY, Brig. Archibald Gordon,** CBE 1952 (OBE 1949); DSO 1945; Brigadier late Royal Scots; *b* 1904; *s* of late Maj.-Gen. Sir Edward Charles William Mackenzie-Kennedy, KBE, CB; *m* 1937, Jean Katherine (*d* 1981), *d* of H. A. Law, Marble Hill, Ballymore, Co. Donegal. *Educ:* Marlborough; Royal Military College, Sandhurst. 2nd Lt Royal Scots, 1924. Served War of 1939–45: Burma, 1941–45 (DSO; despatches 1943); Lt-Col, 1943; Brig., 1947; Comdr Eritrea District, 1950–52; retd 1955. County Comdt, Ulster Special Constabulary, 1955. *Address:* Tarff Old

Manse, Kirkcudbright. *T:* Ringford 219.
*Died* 7 *Nov.* 1987.

**MACKEOWN, John Ainslie,** CIE 1942; Secretary, Arthur Guinness Son & Co. (Dublin) Ltd, 1952–67; retired; *b* 27 Oct. 1902; *s* of late Rev. William Mackeown; *m* 1935, Vivienne (marr. diss.), *d* of J. L. Musgrave, Hayfield House, Cork; two *s. Educ:* Radley; Worcester Coll., Oxford. Joined ICS, 1925; left India, 1947, after holding posts, Jt Sec. to Govt of India and Comr, Ambala Div. *Recreations:* golf, music, reading, bridge, sailing. *Address:* 83 Ardoyne House, Pembroke Park, Dublin 4. *T:* Dublin 601343.
*Died* 21 *Sept.* 1984.

**McKEOWN, Prof. Thomas,** BA British Columbia, PhD McGill, DPhil Oxon, MB, BS London, MD Birmingham, FRCP, FFCM; Professor of Social Medicine, 1945–77, and Pro-Vice-Chancellor, 1974–77, University of Birmingham; *b* 2 Nov. 1912; *s* of William McKeown; *m* 1940, Esmé Joan Bryan Widdowson; one *s* one *d. Educ:* Universities: British Columbia; McGill (National Research Council Schol.); Trinity Coll., Oxford (Rhodes Scholar); London (Guy's Hospital: Poulton Research Scholar). Demonstrator in biochemistry, McGill; demonstrator in physiology, Guy's Hosp. Lectures: Cutter, Harvard Sch. of Public Health, 1960; Lowell, Mass, General Hosp., 1963; British Council, Australia, 1963; De Frees, Univ. of Pennsylvania, 1969; Teale, RCP, 1969; BMA Winchester, 1970; Cecil and Ida Green, Univ. of BC, 1975; Osler, McGill, 1979; Alexander D. Langmuir, Center for Disease Control, Atlanta, 1980; James Seth, Univ. of Edinburgh, 1981. Rock Carling Fellow, Nuffield Provincial Hosps Trust, 1976. Jt Editor, Brit. Jl of Preventive and Social Medicine, 1950–58. Hon. FFCM Ireland, 1980; Hon. FACP, 1982; Hon. DSc McGill, 1981. *Publications:* A Balanced Teaching Hospital (jointly), 1965; Medicine in Modern Society, 1965; Introduction to Social Medicine (jt), 1966; Screening in Medical Care (jointly), 1968; Medical History and Medical Care (ed jtly), 1971; The Modern Rise of Population, 1976; The Role of Medicine, 1976; The Origins of Human Disease, 1988; contributions to scientific journals. *Address:* 23 Hintlesham Avenue, Edgbaston, Birmingham B15 2PH. *T:* 021–454 2810.
*Died* 13 *June* 1988.

**MACKESSACK, Lt-Col Kenneth;** Vice-Lieutenant, Moray, 1964–80; *b* 1902; *s* of late George Ross Mackessack; *m* 1st, 1929, Rose Elizabeth (marr. diss.), *d* of Sir Henry D. Craik, 3rd Bt, GCIE, KCSI; one *s* one *d*; 2nd, 1947, Nora Joyce (*d* 1978), *d* of late Maj.-Gen. C. E. Edward-Collins; one *d. Educ:* Rugby; RMC, Sandhurst. Commissioned Seaforth Highlanders, 1923; Adjt 1935. NW Frontier Ops, 1931; served in Middle East and N Africa, 1940–43 (wounded, despatches); on Gen. Staff and with 51st Highland and 4th Indian Divs; Military Attaché, Washington, 1943–46; retd 1947. Convenor, Moray County Council, 1958–67. Chm. TA Assoc. of Moray, 1954–62. DL Moray, 1954. *Recreations:* shooting, fishing. *Address:* Ardgye, Elgin, Morayshire. *T:* Alves 250.
*Died* 18 *Oct.* 1982.

**MACKEY, Prof. William Arthur,** TD; St Mungo Professor of Surgery, University of Glasgow, 1953–72, now Emeritus; *b* 1 Oct. 1906; *s* of Arthur Edward Mackey, Schoolmaster, and Elizabeth Annie (*née* Carr); *m* 1939, Joan Margaret Sykes; two *s* two *d. Educ:* Ardrossan Academy; Univ. of Glasgow. MB, ChB (hons). Asst to Prof. of Pathology, Univ. of Glasgow, 1928; Asst to Regius Prof. of Surgery, University of Glasgow, 1931. Hon. FACS. *Recreations:* golf, gardening, repenting plans and pottering around bohemia. *Address:* Flat 24, Queens Court, East Clyde Street, Helensburgh, Dunbartonshire G84 7AH. *T:* Helensburgh (0436) 3659. *Clubs:* Royal Scottish Automobile (Glasgow), Glasgow Golf.
*Died* 27 *Nov.* 1990.

**MACKIE, James Richard,** CMG 1941; BSc (Agric); *b* 1896; *s* of J. H. Mackie, JP, Castle Cary, Somerset; *m* 1929, Sylvia M. Miller; one *s. Educ:* Sexey's Sch., Bruton; University Coll., Reading. Army, 1914–18 (despatches, Belgian Croix de Guerre). Superintendent in Agricultural Dept, Nigeria, 1921; Dept. Asst Dir of Agriculture, 1928; Asst Dir of Agrticulture, 1929; Dir of Agriculture, Nigeria, 1936–45. Mem. Executive Council of Nigeria, 1942–45. Member: Colonial Adv. Cttee for Agriculture, Forestry and Animal Health, 1946–49; Scientific Adv. Cttee, Empire Cotton Growing Corp.; Soulbury Commission (investigating sugar industry in West Indies), 1948–49; Governing Body of Imperial Coll. of Tropical Agriculture, Trinidad, 1949–56; SW Regional Hospital Board: Mem., 1954–63, Chm., Mental Health Cttee, 1957–63; General Comr of Income Tax, 1962–67. *Address:* 3 Bec-en-Hent, Bickwell Valley, Sidmouth, Devon. *T:* Sidmouth 2707.
*Died* 10 *July* 1981.

**MACKIE, John Leslie,** FBA 1974; Fellow and Praelector in Philosophy, University College, Oxford, since 1967; Reader in Philosophy, University of Oxford, since 1978; *b* 25 Aug. 1917; *s* of late Alexander Mackie and Annie Burnett Mackie (*née* Duncan); *m* 1947, Joan Armiger Meredith; two *s* three *d. Educ:* Knox Grammar Sch., Sydney; Sydney Univ. (BA); Oriel Coll., Oxford (MA). Served War of 1939–45, RAOC, REME, Captain. Lectr in Moral and

Political Philosophy, Sydney Univ., 1946; Prof. of Philosophy, Univ. of Otago, 1955; Challis Prof. of Philosophy, Sydney Univ., 1959; Prof. of Philosophy, Univ. of York, 1963. *Publications:* Truth, Probability, and Paradox, 1973; The Cement of the Universe, 1974; Problems from Locke, 1976; Ethics: inventing right and wrong, 1977; Hume's Moral Theory, 1980; The Miracle of Theism, 1982; articles in philosophical jls, etc. *Address:* University College, Oxford OX1 4BH. *T:* Oxford 41661; 22 Lathbury Road, Oxford OX2 7AU. *T:* Oxford 58163.
*Died* 12 *Dec.* 1981.

**McKIE, Sir William Neil,** Kt 1953; MVO 1948; MA, Hon. DMus Oxon, Melbourne; FRSCM, FRCM, FRCO, FTCL, Hon. RAM; Hon. Secretary, Royal College of Organists, 1963–67; Hon. Fellow, Worcester College, Oxford, 1954; Organist and Master of the Choristers, Westminster Abbey, 1941–63 (on leave of absence, 1941–45, during war service, RAF, Volunteer Reserve); *b* Melbourne, Australia, 22 May 1901; *s* of Rev. William McKie; *m* 1956, Phyllis Ross (*d* 1983), *widow* of Gerald Walker Birks, OBE, and *d* of John Wardrope Ross, Montreal. *Educ:* Melbourne Grammar Sch.; Royal Coll. of Music; Worcester Coll., Oxford. Organist St Agnes, Kennington Park, 1920–21; organ scholar, Worcester Coll., Oxford, 1921–24; asst music master, Radley Coll., 1923–26; Dir of Music, Clifton Coll., 1926–30; City Organist, Melbourne, 1931–38; Dir of Music, Geelong Grammar Sch., 1934–38; Organist and Instructor in Music, Magdalen Coll., Oxford, 1938–41; Organist at Sheldonian Theatre, 1939–41; Organ prof., Royal Acad. of Music, 1946–62; Hon. Associate Dir, Royal School of Church Music, 1947–52; Dir of Music, Coronation Service, 1953; President: Incorporated Association of Organists, 1950–52; organ scholar, College of Organists, 1956–58; London Soc. of Organists, 1958–59; Incorporated Soc. of Musicians, 1959. Hon. Mem., American Guild of Organists; Hon. Fellow: Westminster Choir Coll., Princeton, NJ, 1965; Royal Canadian Coll. of Organists, 1965. Comdr with Star, Order of St Olav, Norway, 1964. *Address:* 10 Driveway, Ottawa, Ontario K2P 1C7, Canada. *Clubs:* Athenæum; Rideau (Ottawa).
*Died* 1 *Dec.* 1984.

**McKILLOP, Edgar Ravenswood,** CMG 1952; OBE 1942; Company Director; Commissioner of Works and Permanent Head, Ministry of Works, NZ, 1944–55, retired; *b* 26 July 1895; *s* of Alexander McKillop and Jean Cameron; *m* 1930, Marguerita Anne Mary Dennis. *Educ:* Canterbury Univ. Coll., New Zealand. Civil engineer, New Zealand Government engaged on developmental works; railway construction, irrigation and hydro-electric projects. Served 1914–18 with 1st NZEF overseas (twice wounded). Lt-Col NZ Eng. 2nd NZ Exp. Force, in Pacific, 1939–42; Dep. Comr Def. Constr., 1942–44, in NZ and South Pacific. Past mem. Scientific and Industrial Research Council; FICE and past mem. of Council; FNZ Inst. of Engineers and past mem. of Council. *Recreation:* golf. *Address:* PO Box 2071, Raumati Beach, Paraparaumu, New Zealand.
*Died* 13 *Jan.* 1987.

**MACKINNON, Angus,** DSO 1945; MC 1940; TD; Director, Brown Shipley Holdings Ltd, since 1960; *b* 20 Feb. 1911; *s* of late William and Lucy Vere Mackinnon; *m* 1947, Beatrice Marsinah Neison; two *s. Educ:* Eton; Pembroke Coll., Oxford. With Gray Dawes & Co., 1932; Mackinnon Mackenzie & Co, Calcutta, 1933–38. Joined Argyll and Sutherland Highlanders (TA), 1939; served BEF, MEF and BLA (despatches); comd 7th Bn A&SH, 1944–45, 51st Highland Div. Joined Brown Shipley & Co. Ltd, 1946, Chm., 1953–63, retired 1976; Chairman: Agricultural Credit Corp., 1959–75; Accepting Houses Cttee, 1967–70; Australia and New Zealand Banking Gp, 1975–77; Director: Australian Pastoral Co., 1955–71; P&O Steam Navigation Co., 1962–72; Guardian Royal Exchange Assurance, 1968–81; Inchcape & Co. Ltd. Chairman: Royal Nat. Orthopaedic Hosp., 1969–78; Governors, Keil Sch., Dumbarton, 1950–. An Underwriting Member of Lloyd's. *Recreations:* shooting, fishing, golf. *Address:* Hunton Down, Sutton Scotney, Winchester, Hants SO21 3PT. *T:* Sutton Scotney 202. *Clubs:* White's, City.
*Died* 5 *July* 1987.

**MACKINNON, Duncan;** *b* 18 Sept. 1909; *e s* of late Capt. William Mackinnon, Loup, Clachan, Argyll; *m* 1932, Pamela Rachel, 2nd *d* of late Capt. R. B. Brassey; one *s* one *d. Educ:* Eton; Magdalen, Oxford. Served War of 1939–45, Argyll and Sutherland Highlanders. Chm., London Discount Market Assoc., 1959–61. JP Oxfordshire, 1945–56; High Sheriff of Oxfordshire, 1949–50. *Recreations:* fishing, shooting. *Address:* Swinbrook House, Burford, Oxfordshire. *T:* Burford 2216. *Club:* White's.
*Died* 3 *Dec.* 1984.

**McKINNON, Hector Brown,** CC (Canada) 1968; CMG 1944; retired as Chairman, Tariff Board, Canada; *b* Priceville, Grey Co., Ont, 6 Dec. 1890; *s* of Neil McKinnon and Elizabeth Brown; *m* 1929, Phyllis, *d* of Aldham Wilson, Brandon, Man.; two *s. Educ:* Jarvis Coll. Inst., Toronto; Coll. Inst., Owen Sound, Ont; Normal Sch., Toronto. Past Commissioner of Tariff; Chm. Wartime Prices and Trade Board, 1940–41; Pres., Commodity Prices Stabilization Corporation, 1941–46; Mem., Economic Advisory Cttee; Dir, Canadian Commercial Corporation. Prior to 1926, was engaged in newspaper work in various capacities on staff of The Globe; served as agric. editor, western corresp., city editor, Parly corresp. and editorial writer; served in European War, 1914-18, as Adjt 110th Inf. Bn. Seconded in Eng. to RFC (despatches). Presbyterian. *Address:* 146 Roger Road, Ottawa, Ont, Canada.

*Died 2 Feb.* 1981.

**McKINNON, His Honour Neil Nairn,** QC 1957; an Additional Judge, Central Criminal Court, 1968-82; *b* 19 Aug. 1909; *s* of late Neil Somerville and Christina McKinnon, Melbourne; *m* 1937, Janet, *d* of late Michael Lilley, Osterley; three *s* four *d*. *Educ:* Geelong Coll.; Trinity Hall, Cambridge (MA). Squadron Leader, RAFVR, Feb. 1940–Dec. 1945. Called to the Bar, Lincoln's Inn, 1937; Bencher, 1964. Recorder of Maidstone, 1961-68. *Recreation:* cricket. *Club:* Hawks (Cambridge). *Died 17 Nov.* 1988.

**MacKINTOSH, Sir Angus (MacKay),** KCVO 1972; CMG 1958; HM Diplomatic Service, retired; British High Commissioner in Sri Lanka and Ambassador to the Republic of Maldives, 1969–73; *b* 23 July 1915; *s* of Angus MacKintosh, JP, Inverness; *m* 1947, Robina Marigold, *d* of J. A. Cochrane, MC; one *s* two *d* (and one *d* decd). *Educ:* Fettes Coll., Edinburgh; University College, Oxford (MA, BLitt). Agricultural Economics Research Institute, Oxford, 1938–41; Nuffield Colonial Research, Oxford, 1941–42. Served Army, 1942–46: Adjutant, 2nd Bn Queen's Own Cameron Highlanders; Major; despatches. Entered Colonial Office as Principal, 1946; Principal Private Secretary to Secretary of State, 1950; Assistant Secretary, 1952; seconded to Foreign Service as Dep. Commissioner-General for the UK in SE Asia, 1956–60; seconded to Cabinet Office, 1961–63; HM High Comr for Brunei, 1963–64; Asst Sec., Min. of Defence, 1964–65; Asst Under-Sec. of State, 1965–66; Senior Civilian Instructor, Imperial Defence Coll., 1966–68; Asst Under-Sec. of State, FCO, 1968–69. DK (Brunei), 1963; NSAIV (Maldives), 1972. *Address:* 9 Leven Terrace, Edinburgh EH3 9LW. *T:* 031–229 1091; Fenecreich, Gorthleck, Inverness IV1 2YS. *T:* Gorthleck 652. *Club:* Royal Commonwealth Society. *Died 26 Dec.* 1986.

**MACKINTOSH, David Forbes;** Headmaster of Loretto, 1945–60; retired; *b* 7 May 1900; *s* of late Very Rev. Professor H. R. Mackintosh, DD; *m* 1930, Caroline Elisabeth, *o d* of Cyril Meade-King, Clifton, Bristol; three *s* one *d*. *Educ:* Merchiston; Oriel Coll., Oxford (MA); Princeton Univ., NJ (AM). Assistant Master at Clifton Coll., 1924–45; Housemaster, 1930–45. Conroy Fellow, St Paul's Sch., USA, 1960. Chm., Scottish Assoc. of Boys' Clubs, 1962–69. *Recreation:* gardening. *Address:* Bowling Green Cottage, Broadwell, by Lechlade, Glos GL7 3QS. *T:* Filkins 336.

*Died 25 July* 1988.

**MACKINTOSH, (Hugh) Stewart,** CBE 1956; Chairman, Scottish Sports Council, 1966–68; Chief Education Officer, Glasgow, 1944–68; *b* 1903; *s* of William Mackintosh, Helmsdale, Sutherland; *m* 1933, Mary, *d* of James Wilson. *Educ:* Helmsdale, Sutherland; Glasgow Univ. (MA, BSc, MEd); Aberdeen Univ. (PhD). Director of Education: Wigtownshire, 1931–37; Aberdeen, 1937–44; Glasgow, 1944. FEIS 1958; Hon. LLD Glasgow, 1969. *Address:* 16 Rowan Crescent, Killearn, Glasgow G63 9RZ; Bayview, Helmsdale, Sutherland. *Died 28 Aug.* 1989.

**McKISACK, Prof. May;** Emeritus Professor of History, University of London, since 1967; *b* 30 March 1900; *o d* of Audley John McKisack, solicitor, Belfast, and Elizabeth (*née* McCullough). *Educ:* Bedford High Sch.; Somerville Coll., Oxford. Mary Somerville Research Fellow, Somerville Coll., Oxford, 1925–28; Lecturer in Mediæval History, University of Liverpool, 1927–35. Fellow and Tutor, Somerville Coll., 1936–55; University Lecturer, 1945–55; Professor of History, University of London (Westfield Coll.), 1955–67; Hon. Fellow, Somerville Coll., 1956; James Bryce Memorial Lecturer, Somerville Coll., 1959; Member of UGC Cttee on Teaching Methods in Universities, 1961. Visiting Professor, Vassar Coll., USA, 1967–68. FRHistS 1928; FSA 1952. *Publications:* The Parliamentary Representation of the English Boroughs in the Middle Ages, 1932; The Fourteenth Century, 1959; Medieval History in the Tudor Age, 1971; articles, reviews in English Historical Review, Review of English Studies, Medium Aevum, etc. *Address:* Somerville College, Oxford.

*Died 14 March* 1981.

**MACKLEY, Garnet Hercules,** CMG 1938; *b* Port Chalmers, 9 Dec. 1883; *s* of John Charles Mackley and Esther Styles; *m* 1914, Isabel Robertson; one *s*. *Educ:* Grammar Sch., Invercargill. Cadet in clerical division, Traffic Branch, NZ Government Railways Department, 1900; had varied experience in railway work in all parts of Dominion in executive capacity; promoted through various ranks of District Office and Head Office; Chief Clerk, Railways Head Office, Wellington, 1928; Assistant General Manager, 1931; General Manager, 1933–40. MP for Masterton, 1943–46; for Wairarapa, 1946–49; MLC, 1950. Dir, 1940, Man. Dir, 1942, Whakatane Paper Mills Ltd; resigned 1962 as Dir, Whakatane Board Mills and NZ Forest Products Ltd; Chm., A. & G. Price Ltd,

1944; retired as Dir, Cable Price Downer Ltd, 1964. *Recreations:* fishing, racing, golf, swimming, field athletics. *Address:* Hillview Eventide Home, Northern King Country, Te Kuiti, New Zealand.

*Died 24 April* 1986.

**MACKLEY, George Edward,** MBE 1983; Hon. Retired RE 1972 (RE 1961; ARE 1950); *b* Tonbridge, 13 May 1900; *m* 1927, Caroline Toller, Hemingford Grey; no *c*. *Educ:* Judd Sch., Tonbridge. Art master, various schools in Kent and Surrey, 1921–45; Headmaster, Thames Ditton Primary Sch., 1945–53; Headmaster, Sutton East Secondary Sch. and Art Department, 1953–60. Hon. Mem., Soc. of Wood Engravers (Associate, 1946). Mem., 1948; Mem., Art Workers' Guild, 1959. Works in permanent collections: Victoria and Albert Museum; Ashmolean Museum; Fitzwilliam Museum; South London Art Gallery; Nat. Museum of Art, Stockholm; Hunt Botanical Library, Pittsburgh. *Publications:* Wood Engraving, 1948; George Mackley: Wood Engraver, 1982. *Recreations:* lurking by, and drawing, waterways and canal and river craft. *Address:* 7 Higham Lane, Tonbridge, Kent. *T:* Tonbridge 353968.

*Died 4 Feb.* 1983.

**MACKWORTH-YOUNG, (Gerard) William;** Chairman, Morgan Grenfell & Co. Ltd, since 1980 (Director since 1974); *b* 10 Oct. 1926; *s* of late Gerard Mackworth-Young, CIE and Natalie Hely-Hutchinson; *m* 1949, Lady Evelyn Leslie, *d* of 20th Earl of Rothes; four *d*. *Educ:* Eton College. Served Welsh Guards, 1945–48 (Lieut, RARO). Partner, Rowe & Pitman, stockbrokers, 1953–73; Vice-Chm., Morgan Grenfell Holdings Ltd; Dep. Chm. and Chief Exec., Morgan Grenfell & Co. Ltd, 1975–79; Director: Union Discount Co. of London plc; Willis Faber plc; Lasmo plc; Lloyds Bank plc; Charter Consolidated plc. Chairman: Industrial Develt Adv. Bd, 1980–; British Invisible Exports Council (formerly Cttee on Invisible Exports), 1983–. *Recreations:* music, shooting. *Address:* Fisherton Mill, Fisherton de la Mere, Wylye, Wilts. *T:* Wylye 246; Flat 86, 3 Whitehall Court, SW1A 2EL. *T:* 01-930 2623; Barrs Lodge, Taynuilt, Argyll. *Clubs:* Boodle's, Pratt's; Union (Sydney); Links (NY). *Died 18 Oct.* 1984.

**McLACHLAN, Charles,** CBE 1985; QPM 1977; HM Inspector of Constabulary for South East England, since 1987; *b* 12 Dec. 1931; *s* of Charles McLachlan and Ruby (*née* Bywater); *m* 1958, Dorothy (*née* Gardner); three *s*. *Educ:* Liverpool Inst. High Sch.; London Univ. (LLB 1962); Keele Univ. (MA 1968). Army Service, 1950–52 (commd RMP, 1951); joined Liverpool City Police, 1953 (promoted through ranks); Chief Inspector, Warwicks, 1966; Chief Supt, Liverpool and Bootle Constab., 1968; Asst Chief Constable (Ops), Lincs, 1970; Dep. Chief Constable, Lincs, 1973; Chief Constable, Notts, 1976. Pres., Assoc. of Chiefs of Police, 1984–85. *Recreations:* caravanning, watching old films, ski-ing. *Address:* (office) White Rose Court, Oriental Road, Woking, Surrey. *Clubs:* Army and Navy; Nottingham and Notts United Services.

*Died 4 April* 1990.

**MACLAGAN, Noel Francis,** DSc, MD, FRCP, FRSC; retired; formerly Professor of Chemical Pathology in University of London at Westminster Medical School, now Emeritus; Chemical Pathologist, Westminster Hospital, 1947–70; *b* 1904; *y s* of late Oscar Frederick and Ada Maclagan, Newcastle and London; *m* 1933, Annemarie, *d* of Curt and Marie Herzog, London; one *s* one *d*. *Educ:* University Coll. Sch.; University Coll., London (First Cl. Hons BSc Chemistry, 1925); Middlesex Hosp. Medical School (MSc London in Biochemistry, 1933). DSc London, 1946; MD London, 1935; MRCP, 1933; FRIC 1946; FRCP 1952. Asst in Courtauld Inst. of Biochemistry, Middlesex Hosp., 1926–33; House Physician Middlesex Hosp., 1932; whole-time worker for Medical Research Council, 1933–34; Biochemist, Westminster Hosp., 1935–46; Pathologist, EMS, 1939–45; Chemical Pathologist at Westminster Hosp. Medical Sch., 1946–47. Chm., Nuffield Project on Clinical Chemistry Labs, 1976–79. Hon. FRSM 1986. Editor, Annals of Clinical Biochemistry, 1974–76. *Publications:* contributions to medical textbooks on various biochemical subjects and articles in scientific journals on thymol turbidity test, thyroid function, lipid metabolism, etc. *Recreations:* music and chess. *Address:* 40 Temple Fortune Lane, NW11. *T:* 01–458 4032. *Died 16 July* 1987.

**MacLAREN, Sir Hamish (Duncan),** KBE 1951; CB 1946; DFC; Director of Electrical Engineering, Admiralty, 1945–60; *b* 7 April 1898; *s* of Rev. Peter MacLaren, MA, and Constance Hamilton Simpson; *m* 1927, Lorna Cicely, *d* of late Dr R. P. N. B. Bluett, MC, Harrow; one *s* one *d*. *Educ:* Fordyce Academy, Banffshire; Edinburgh Univ. (BSc 1921). Served European war, 1914–18, in RNVR, RNAS and RAF (DFC and Bar, French Croix de Guerre with Palm). After completing degree at Edinburgh Univ. in 1921 joined British Thomson Houston Co., Rugby, as student apprentice. Awarded Bursary by Commission for Exhibition of 1851 for 1921–23; British Thomson Houston Fellowship to spend one year with the GE Co. of Schenectady, USA, 1923–24; on staff of British Thomson Houston, Rugby, 1924–26; joined Admiralty Service as Asst Electrical Engineer, 1926. In Admiralty Service at HM

Dockyards, Chatham, Devonport, at Dir of Dockyards Dept, Admiralty, 1933–37, and in Ceylon, 1931–33; Superintending Electrical Engineer, HM Naval Base, Singapore, 1937–40; Asst Dir, Electrical Engineering Dept, Admiralty, 1940–45. Pres. Instn of Electrical Engineers, 1960–61. Hon. LLD St Andrews, 1954; Hon. DSc Bath, 1970. *Address:* 104 Heath Road, Petersfield, Hants GU31 4EL. *T:* Petersfield (0730) 4562. *Died* 15 *Oct.* 1990.

**McLAREN, Prof. Hugh Cameron;** Professor of Obstetrics and Gynæcology, University of Birmingham, 1951–78, now Emeritus; *b* 25 April 1913; *s* of John and Flora McLaren, Glasgow; *m* 1939, Lois Muirhead, Bridge of Weir, Scotland; one *s* six *d*. *Educ:* High Sch. of Glasgow; Univ. of Glasgow; postgraduate studies Glasgow and Aberdeen. MB, ChB Glasgow 1936; MD (Glasgow). Served RAMC, 1941–46; Surgical Specialist (Lt-Col). Univ. of Birmingham, 1946, Reader, 1949. FRCPGlas; FRCSE; FRCOG. Hon. Fellow, Societas Gynaecologica et Obstetrica Italica, 1979. Hon. Mem., Amer. Medical Assoc., 1969. Officer, Legion of Merit (Rhodesia), 1977. *Publications:* The Prevention of Cervical Cancer, 1963; contribs to Journal of Obstetrics and Gynæcology, Lancet, Brit. Med. Jl, etc. *Recreations:* golf, gardening. *Address:* 26 Ampton Road, Birmingham B15 2UP. *T:* 021–440 3223.

*Died* 8 *June* 1986.

**McLAREN, John Watt,** MA, FRCP, FRCR; Physician in charge of X-Ray Department, St Thomas' Hospital, 1946–73; *b* 26 Nov. 1906; *s* of John McLaren and Florence Mary Atkinson. *Educ:* Cheltenham Coll.; Univ. of Cambridge and St Thomas' Hospital, London. MA (Cantab); FFR 1951; FRCP 1963; FRCPE 1972. Junior appointments at St Thomas' Hosp., 1932–35; Chief Asst, X-Ray Dept, 1935–39. Radiologist, Queen Mary's Hosp., East End, 1935–38. Cons. Radiologist, Metropolitan Police, 1946; Examiner in Radiology, Univs of London and Edinburgh and Faculty of Radiologists; Underwriter at Lloyd's, 1948. *Publications:* (ed) Modern Trends in Diagnostic Radiology, Series 1, 2, 3, 4, 1948, 1953, 1960, 1970; various papers in radiological journals. *Recreations:* motoring, travelling, sailing.

*Died* 28 *Oct.* 1982.

**McLAUGHLAN, Roy James Philip,** CMG 1955; CVO 1956; Inspector-General of Police, Nigeria, retired 1956; *b* 25 July 1898; *s* of late Henry Peter Marius McLaughlan and late Elfrida Greenwood; *m* 1931, Catherine Elizabeth Plaisted, *d* of late Lt-Col Thomas Valentine Plaisted McCammon and Charlotte Amelia Garratt. *Educ:* The English Sch., Cyprus; Stonyhurst Coll., Lancs. Gen. Staff Intelligence, Macedonia, Greece and Turkey, 1917–23. Inspector and Surveyor of Roads, Cyprus, 1925; Nigeria: Asst Supt Police, 1927; Supt, 1944; Asst Comr, 1949; Comr, 1951; Inspector-Gen., 1952. Colonial Police Medal, 1942; King's Police Medal, 1950. OStJ 1955. *Recreation:* bridge. *Address:* 7 Rosemary Park, Belfast, N Ireland. *T:* Belfast 665755. *Died* 15 *April* 1982.

**McLAUGHLIN, George Vincent;** Regional Chairman of Industrial Tribunals (Scotland), since 1985; *b* 29 April 1922; *s* of George and Ann McLaughlin; *m* 1946, Jo McLaughlin; four *s* four *d*. *Educ:* Mount St Mary's Coll.; Glasgow Univ. (BL). Captain, RAC, 1943–46. Solicitor, in private practice, 1948–75; Chm., Industrial Tribunals, 1975–84. *Recreations:* golf, swimming. *Address:* 3 Dalziel Quadrant, Pollokshields, Glasgow G41 4NR. *T:* 041–427 5483.

*Died* 6 *Oct.* 1987.

**MACLEAN, Baron** *cr* 1971 (Life Peer), of Duart and Morvern in the County of Argyll; **Charles Hector Fitzroy Maclean;** Bt 1631; KT 1969; GCVO 1971; KBE 1967; Royal Victorian Chain, 1984; PC 1971; JP; 27th Chief of Clan Maclean; a Permanent Lord in Waiting, since 1984; Scots Guards, Major, retired; Lord Lieutenant of Argyll since 1954; Lord High Commissioner, General Assembly of the Church of Scotland, 1984 and 1985; Chief Steward of Hampton Court Palace, since 1985; Lieutenant, Royal Company of Archers (Queen's Body Guard for Scotland); President, Argyll T&AFA; *b* 5 May 1916; *e* surv. *s* of late Hector F. Maclean and Winifred Joan, *y d* of late J. H. Walford; *g* grandfather, Sir Fitzroy Maclean, 10th Bt, KCB, 1936; *m* 1941, Elizabeth, *er d* of late Frank Mann, Upper Farm House, Milton Lilbourne, Wilts; one *s* one *d*. *Educ:* Canford Sch., Wimborne. Served War of 1939–45 (despatches). Chief Commissioner for Scotland, Boy Scouts Assoc., 1954–59; Chief Scout of the UK and Overseas Branches, 1959–71; Chief Scout of the Commonwealth, 1959–75; Lord Chamberlain of HM Household, 1971–84; Chancellor, Royal Victorian Order, 1971–84. Patron: Coombe Trust Fund; Roland House; Argyll Div., Scottish Br., British Red Cross Soc.; Hon. Patron, Friends of World Scouting; Vice Patron: Argyll & Sutherland Highlanders Regimental Assoc.; President: T&AFA of Argyll; Argyll Br., Forces Help Soc. and Lord Robert's Workshops; Convenor, Standing Council of Scottish Chiefs; Hon. President: Argyll Co. Scout Council; Toc H; Scouts Friendly Soc.; Vice President: Highland Cattle Soc.; Scottish Br., Nat. Playing Fields Assoc.; (ex officio) Nat. Small-Bore Rifle Assoc.; Camping Club of GB; Trefoil Residential Sch. for Physically Handicapped Children; Casualties

Union; Member of Council: Earl Haig Officers Meml Fund; Scottish Naval, Military and Air Forces Veteran Residences; Royal Zoological Soc.; Outward Bound Trust; Life Member: Highland and Agricultural Soc. of Scotland; Highland Cattle Soc.; Scottish Nat. Fatstock Club; Royal Agricultural Soc. of England. JP Argyll, 1955. *Publication:* Only (children's book), 1979. *Recreation:* travelling. *Heir:* (to Baronetcy only): *s* Hon. Lachlan Hector Charles Maclean, Major, Scots Guards, retired [*b* 25 Aug. 1942; *m* 1966, Mary Helen, *e d* of W. G. Gordon; two *s* two *d* (and one *d* decd)]. *Address:* Duart Castle, Isle of Mull. *T:* Craignure 309; Wilderness House, Hampton Court Palace, Surrey. *T:* 01–943 4400. *Clubs:* Cavalry and Guards, Pratt's, Commonwealth Trust (Mem. Council); Royal Highland Yacht (Oban). *Died* 8 *Feb.* 1990.

**MACLEAN, Alistair;** author; *b* Scotland, 1922; *m*; three *s*. *Educ:* Glasgow Univ. *Publications:* HMS Ulysses, 1955; The Guns of Navarone, 1957 (filmed 1959); South by Java Head, 1958 (filmed 1959); The Last Frontier, 1959 (filmed 1960 as The Secret Ways); Night Without End, 1960; Fear is the Key, 1961 (filmed 1972); The Golden Rendezvous, 1962 (filmed 1977); (for children) All About Lawrence of Arabia, 1962; Ice Station Zebra, 1963 (filmed 1968); When Eight Bells Toll, 1966 (filmed 1970); Where Eagles Dare, 1967 (filmed 1968); Force 10 from Navarone, 1968 (filmed 1978); Puppet on a Chain, 1969 (filmed 1970); Bear Island, 1971 (filmed 1979); Captain Cook, 1972; The Way to Dusty Death, 1973; (introd.) Alistair MacLean Introduces Scotland, ed, A. M. Dunnett, 1972; Breakheart Pass, 1974 (filmed 1975); Circus, 1975; The Golden Gate, 1976; Sea Witch, 1977; Goodbye California, 1977; Athabasca, 1980; River of Death, 1981; Partisans, 1982; Floodgate, 1983; San Andreas, 1984; The Lonely Sea (short stories), 1985; Santorini, 1986; *as Ian Stuart:* The Dark Crusader, 1961; The Satan Bug, 1962 (filmed 1965). *Screenplays:* Where Eagles Dare, Caravan to Vaccares, Puppet on a Chain, Breakheart Pass. *Film for TV:* Hostage Tower, 1980. *Address:* c/o Wm Collins Sons & Co. Ltd, 8 Grafton Street, W1. *Died* 2 *Feb.* 1987.

**McLEAN, Dr Andrew Sinclair,** CBE 1975; FRCP; Director, National Radiological Protection Board, since 1971; *b* 26 March 1919; *s* of Andrew McLean and Janet Forret; *m* 1943, Christine, *d* of Col J. A. Mackintosh; two *d*. *Educ:* Forres Acad.; Edinburgh Univ. (MB, ChB). DIH. FRCP 1975; FFOM 1980. House Surg., Royal Northern Infirmary, Inverness, 1943; Captain RAMC, 1943–46; gen. practice, 1946–47; MO, Dept of Atomic Energy, Min. of Supply, Springfields, 1948; SMO, Dept of Atomic Energy, Windscale, 1949–52; UK Atomic Energy Authority: PMO, Industrial Gp, 1952–57; Dir, Health and Safety Br., Industrial Gp, 1957–59; Dir of Health and Safety, 1959–71. Member: Internat. Commn on Radiol Protection, 1969–77; WHO Expert Adv. Panel on Radiation, 1963–; Euratom Gp of Experts resp. for advising on Basic Safety Standards, 1973–; Nuclear Safety Adv. Cttee, 1960–76; Scientific and Technical Cttee, Euratom, 1978–. Hon. MD Edinburgh, 1981. *Publications:* papers on radiological health and safety. *Recreations:* cooking, roses, golf. *Address:* Peterhill, Monument Lane, Chalfont St Peter, Bucks. *T:* Chalfont St Giles 3794. *Clubs:* Athenæum; Beaconsfield Golf.

*Died* 27 *July* 1981.

**MACLEAN, Brig. Gordon Forbes,** CBE 1943; MC; DL; *b* 29 May 1897; *s* of George Buchanan Maclean, Pentreheylin Hall, Maesbrook, Shropshire; *m* 1926, Claire, *d* of John Lehane, Melbourne, Australia; one *s*. *Educ:* Shrewsbury School, Sandhurst, 1914–15; Argyll and Sutherland Highlanders, 1915; Staff Coll., Camberley, 1930–31; Colonel, 1945; retired pay, 1946, with hon. rank of Brigadier. High Sheriff of Shropshire, 1965. DL Shropshire, 1966. *Address:* Pentreheylin Hall, Maesbrook, Salop.

*Died* 6 *May* 1982.

**MACLEAN of Pennycross, Rear-Admiral Iain Gilleasbuig,** CB 1954; OBE 1944; retired; *b* 25 Nov. 1902; *s* of late Norman H. Maclean; *m* 1st, 1931, Evelyn Marjorie, *d* of late R. A. and Mrs Winton Reid; one step *d*; 2nd, 1973, Nancy Margaret, *widow* of E. A. Barnard. *Educ:* Cargilfield; RN Colleges, Osborne and Dartmouth. Joined RN, 1916; Captain, 1945; Rear-Admiral, 1952; Served War of 1939–45: in Combined Operations, HMS Renown and Admiralty. Imperial Defence Coll., 1951; Dep. Engineer in Chief of the Fleet, 1952–55; retired, Nov. 1955. Director, Marine Development, Brush Group, 1956–60. Research Survey for National Ports Council, 1963–64. *Recreations:* fishing, gardening. *Address:* Pear Tree Cottage, Moorlands Drive, Pinkney's Green, Maidenhead, Berks. *T:* Maidenhead 30287. *Died* 17 *April* 1988.

**MACLEAN, Ian Albert Druce;** Director, Halifax Building Society, 1953–76 (Chairman, 1961–74); *b* 23 June 1902; *s* of Alick and Nina Maclean; *m* 1st, 1937, Diana, *d* of John and Gertrude Marsden-Smedley; twin *s*; 2nd, 1979, Heather Scott Thompson, *d* of Ronald and Dorothy Mackenzie. *Educ:* Marlborough; Pembroke Coll., Cambridge. Tobacco Industry, 1924; Cotton Industry, 1926; Carpet Industry, 1937; Halifax Building Society, 1953. Vice-Pres., Building Socs Assoc. Former Dir, Carpets International Ltd. *Recreations:* anything in the open air. *Address:* Bay Trees, 30 River Green,

Hamble, Southampton SO3 5JA. *T:* Southampton 453403. *Clubs:* Lansdowne; Royal Southern Yacht (Southampton); Royal Windermere Yacht. *Died* 31 *Jan.* 1986.

**MACLEAN, Colonel John Francis,** JP; Lord-Lieutenant of Hereford and Worcester, 1974–76 (Lord Lieutenant of Herefordshire, 1960–74); *b* 1 March 1901; *s* of late Montague Francis and Florence Maclean; *m* 1925, Vivienne A. M. Miesegaes (*d* 1969); two *s*. *Educ:* Eton Coll. Started in coal trade with Cannop Coal Co. Ltd, Forest of Dean, 1921; became a Director and Commercial Manager, in 1927, after being employed with United Collieries Ltd, Glasgow. Commnd Herefordshire Regt (TA), 1919–23. Coal Supplies Officer for Forest of Dean, 1939–40; commnd in Grenadier Guards, Sept. 1940, reaching rank of Major. Hon. Colonel, Herefordshire Light Infantry (TA), 1963–67; Pres., West Midland TAVR Assoc., 1970–76. Herefordshire: JP 1946, High Sheriff 1951, DL 1953–60. KStJ 1960. *Recreations:* golf; formerly shooting, lawn tennis and cricket (kept wicket for Worcestershire, 1922–24, and occasionally for Gloucestershire, 1929–30; toured Australia and New Zealand with MCC team, 1922–23). *Address:* Old School House, How Caple, Hereford HR1 4SY. *T:* How Caple 281.

*Died* 9 *March* 1986.

**McLEAN, Lieut-General Sir Kenneth Graeme,** KCB 1954 (CB 1944); KBE 1951; US Legion of Merit, 1945; Officer, Legion of Honour (France); Croix de Guerre (France); *b* 11 Dec. 1896; *s* of late Arthur H. McLean, WS; *m* 1926, Daphne Winifred Ashburner Steele (*d* 1979); two *s*. *Educ:* Edinburgh Academy; RMA Woolwich. Commissioned RE 1918; served, in Ireland, 1919–20, and with KGO Bengal Sappers and Miners in India, 1923–29; Staff Coll., Quetta, 1930–31; on General Staff, AHQ, India, 1932–36; Assistant Secretary Cttee of Imperial Defence, 1938; Student at Imperial Defence Coll., 1939. Served France and Germany, 1944–45; Deputy Adjutant-General, GHQ, Far East, 1945–46; Dep. Adjutant-General, GHQ, Middle East, 1946; Vice-Adjutant-General, War Office, 1947–49; Chief of Staff, CCG, and Deputy Military Governor, British Zone in Germany, 1949; Military Secretary to the Secretary of State for War, 1949–51; Chief Staff Officer, Ministry of Defence, 1951–52; Special Duty, War Office, 1952–54. Retired, 1954. Colonel Comdt RE, 1956–61. *Address:* Greenways, Melrose, Roxburghshire. *Died* 5 *June* 1987.

**McLEAN, Lt-Col Neil Loudon Desmond,** DSO 1943; *b* 28 Nov. 1918; *s* of Neil McLean; *m* 1949, Daška Kennedy (*née* Ivanović-Banac), Dubrovnik, Jugoslavia. *Educ:* Eton; RMC, Sandhurst. Gazetted Royal Scots Greys, 1938; Palestine Campaign, 1939; served War of 1939–45, Middle East and Far East: Ethiopia under 101 Mission, 1941; Head of First Military Mission to Albania, 1942 and 1943; Lieut-Colonel, 1943; Far East, 1944–45. Contested (C) Preston South, 1950 and 1951; MP (C) Inverness, Dec. 1954–Sept. 1964. Member Highland and Islands Advisory Panel, 1955. Member of Queen's Body Guard for Scotland, Royal Company of Archers. Distinguished Military Medal of Haile Selassie I, 1941. *Publications:* contributions to Chatham House, Royal Central Asian Society Reviews. *Recreations:* travel, riding, shooting, under-water fishing. *Address:* 5 Sheridan Court, Barkston Gardens, SW5. *Clubs:* White's, Buck's, Cavalry and Guards, Pratt's; Highland (Inverness).

*Died* 17 *Nov.* 1986.

**McLEAN, Robert Colquhoun,** MA, DSc, FLS; Professor of Botany, University College of South Wales and Monmouthshire, Cardiff, 1919–55; retired Dec. 1955; *b* Kilcreggan, Dunbartonshire, 18 July 1890; *s* of Rev. Robert McLean, MA, Kilcreggan, Dunbartonshire; *m* 1914, Freda Marguerite (*d* 1955), *d* of George Washington Kilner, MA; three *s*. *Educ:* The Leys School, Cambridge; University College, London; St John's Coll., Cambridge. Lecturer in Botany at University Coll., Reading, 1913; has travelled in many parts of the world for botanical purposes and for comparative study of University Systems; General Secretary of International University Conference, founded 1934; President Assoc. of University Teachers, 1940–41; President, International Assoc. of University Professors, 1950; Member: Nature Conservancy, 1949–56; National Parks Commission, 1949–56; Universities Advisory Cttee, British Council, 1953. *Publications:* Plant Science Formulæ, Textbook of Theoretical Botany (4 vols), Text Book of Practical Botany, and Practical Field Ecology (with W. R. I. Cook); numerous articles in scientific periodicals, etc. *Recreation:* sleep. *Address:* Hickley Lodge, Old Cogan, Penarth, S Glam. *Died* 7 *April* 1981.

**McLEAY, Hon. Sir John,** KCMG 1962; MM; retired as Speaker of the House of Representatives, Canberra, Australia (1956–66); Federal Member for Boothby, South Australia, 1949–66; *b* 19 Nov. 1893; *m* 1921, Eileen H. (*d* 1971), *d* of late H. Elden, Geelong; two *s* one *d*. Stretcher Bearer, 13 Field Ambulance, 1st AIF (awarded Military Medal); Life Member, Hindmarsh Ambulance. Formerly: Mayor of City of Unley; Lord Mayor of Adelaide; Member for Unley, House of Assembly, SA; Member Council of Governors, Adelaide Univ. and Scotch Coll., Adelaide. President or Past President various organisations; Hon. Member Town Planning

Institute, SA, etc. *Address:* 7 Brae Road, St Georges, SA 5064, Australia. *Died* 22 *June* 1982.

**MacLEAY, His Honour Oswell Searight,** JP; retired; a Circuit Judge (formerly Deputy Chairman, Inner Division Greater London Sessions), 1965–75; Barrister-at-law; *b* 11 Dec. 1905; *o s* of late Oswell Sullivan MacLeay and Ida Marion MacLeay, 29 Draycott Place, SW1; *m* 1930, Viola Elizabeth Mary French, *o d* of late Frank Austen French, MRCS, LRCP, and Dora Emmeline French, Hollamby House, Herne Bay; two *s*. *Educ:* RN College, Osborne; RN College, Dartmouth; Charterhouse; Magdalen Coll., Oxford. Called to the Bar, Inner Temple, 1932; South Eastern Circuit. Recorder of Maidstone, 1959–61. Dep. Chairman, West Kent Quarter Sessions, 1954–62; Asst Chairman of County of Middlesex Sessions, 1959–60; Dep. Chairman, 1960–61; Dep. Chairman County of London Sessions, 1961–65; Member Mental Health Review Tribunal, 1960–61. Served War, RNVR, 1939–45; Sub-Lieut, 1939; Lieut, 1939; Lieut-Commander, 1941. JP Kent. Member Kent Standing Joint Cttee and Police Authority, 1956–64; Member Malling Rural District Council, 1949–55 (Chairman, 1951–55); Member Visiting Cttee, Maidstone Prison, 1954–58. President Sevenoaks Conservative and Unionist Assoc., 1959–61. *Recreations:* watching and umpiring cricket; naval and military history; travel (particularly by rail). *Address:* The Old Farm House, Wrotham, Kent. *T:* Borough Green 884138. *Clubs:* Naval and Military, MCC; Band of Brothers (Kent).

*Died* 25 *Aug.* 1982.

**MacLEISH, Archibald;** *b* 7 May 1892, *s* of Andrew MacLeish and Martha Hillard; *m* 1916, Ada Hitchcock; one *s* one *d* (and two *s* decd). *Educ:* The Hotchkiss Sch., Lakeville, Connecticut; Yale Univ. (AB); Harvard Univ. (LLB). Hon. MA Tufts, 1932; Hon. LittD: Wesleyan, 1938; Colby, 1938; Yale, 1939; Pennsylvania, 1941; Illinois, 1947; Rockford Coll., 1952; Columbia, 1954; Harvard, 1955; Princeton, 1965; Massachusetts, 1969; York Univ., Toronto, 1971; Hon. LLD: Dartmouth, 1940; Johns Hopkins Univ., 1941; University of California, 1943; Queen's Coll., Canada, 1948; University of Puerto Rico, 1953; Amherst Coll., 1963; Hon. DCL. Union Coll., 1941; Hon. LHD: Williams Coll., 1942; Washington Univ., 1948. Enlisted as private, United States Army, 1917; discharged with rank of Captain, 1919; spent 12 months in American Expeditionary Force, France. An instructor in government at Harvard, 1919–21; practised law in Boston offices of Choate, Hall and Stewart, 1920–23; devoted his time to travel and literature, 1923–30; Editor of Fortune, 1929–38; Librarian of Congress, 1939–44; Director, Office of Facts and Figures, 1941–42; Asst Director, Office of War Information, 1942–43; Asst Secretary of State, 1944–45. Chm., American Delegation to London Conference, UN, to establish a Cultural and Educational Organisation, 1945; American Mem. Exec. Bd of UNESCO, 1946. Boylston Prof., Harvard Univ., 1949–62; Simpson Lectr, Amherst Coll., 1963, 1964, 1965, 1966. Pres., Amer. Acad. of Arts and Letters, 1953–56. Nat. Medal for Literature, 1978; Gold Medal for Poetry, Amer. Acad. and Inst., 1979. Presidential Medal of Freedom (USA), 1977. Commander, Légion d'Honneur (France); Commander, El Sol del Peru. *Publications:* The Happy Marriage (verse), 1924; The Pot of Earth (verse), 1925; Nobodaddy (verse play), 1925; Streets in the Moon (verse), 1926; The Hamlet of A. MacLeish (verse), 1928; New Found Land, 1930; Conquistador (Pulitzer poetry prize), 1932; Frescoes for Mr Rockefeller's City (verse), 1933; Union Pacific-a Ballet, 1934; Panic (verse play), 1935; Public Speech (verse), 1936; The Fall of the City (verse play for radio), 1937; Land of the Free (verse), 1938; Air Raid (verse play for radio), 1938; America was Promises (verse), 1939; The Irresponsibles (prose), 1940; The American Cause (prose), 1941; A Time to Speak (prose), 1941; American Opinion and the War (Rede Lecture at Cambridge Univ., 1942), 1943; A Time to Act (prose), 1943; The American Story (radio broadcasts), 1944; Actfive and Other Poems, 1948; Poetry and Opinion (prose), 1950; Freedom Is The Right To Choose (prose), 1951; Collected Poems, 1952 (Bollingen Prize, National Book Award, Pulitzer poetry prize); This Music Crept By Me Upon The Waters (verse play), 1953; Songs For Eve (verse), 1954; J.B. (verse play), 1958 (produced NY, Dec. 1958; Pulitzer Prize for Drama, 1959); Poetry and Experience (prose), 1961; The Dialogues of Archibald MacLeish and Mark Van Dover, 1964; The Eleanor Roosevelt Story, 1965 (filmed, 1965, Academy Award, 1966); Herakles (verse play), 1967; A Continuing Journey (prose), 1968; The Wild Old Wicked Man and other poems, 1968; Scratch (prose play), 1971; The Human Season (selected poems), 1972; The Great American Fourth of July Parade (verse play for radio), 1975; New and Collected Poems, 1917–1976, 1976; Riders on the Earth (prose), 1978; Six Plays (verse), 1980. *Address:* Conway, Mass 01341, USA. *Clubs:* Century Association (NY); Tavern (Boston). *Died* 20 *April* 1982.

**McLELLAN, David,** CMG 1957; ED 1951; Education Consultant, International Bank for Reconstruction and Development, 1965–69; *b* 23 Dec. 1904; *e s* of David McLellan; *m* 1934, Winifred (*née* Henderson); three *s*. *Educ:* King Edward VII Sch., Lytham; Queen's

Coll., Cambridge. Colonial Education Service: Hong Kong, 1931, Chief Inspector of Schools, 1951; Singapore, Dep. Director of Education, and Mem., Legislative Council, 1953; Director of Education and Permanent Secretary to Min. of Education, 1955; Regional Education Adviser to Comr General for UK in SE Asia, 1959–62; Director, Cultural Relations, SEATO, Bangkok, 1963–65. *Recreation:* golf. *Address:* 6 Grazebrook Close, Bexhill-on-Sea, East Sussex. *T:* Cooden 2650. *Died 5 Oct.* 1982.

**McLELLAN, James Kidd,** CBE 1974; QPM 1966; Senior Assistant Chief Constable, Strathclyde Police, 1975–76; retired; *b* 16 Oct. 1914; *s* of John Young McLellan, MPS, FBOA, Chemist and Optician, and Robina (*née* Kidd); *m* 1942, Margaret A. G. F. Selby; two *s* one *d. Educ:* Lenzie Academy; Glasgow Univ.; Royal Technical Coll. (now Strathclyde Univ.). MA Hons, BSc; ARIC 1948, FRIC 1965. City of Glasgow Police, 1936–65: i/c Police Laboratory, attached to Identification Bureau, 1946–60; Det. Supt (ii) in Ident. Bureau and Scottish Criminal Record Office, 1960; Det. Supt (i) i/c SCRO and IB, 1962; Chief Constable: Motherwell and Wishaw Burgh, 1965; Lanarkshire, 1967. Past Chm. (Scottish Section), Soc. for Analytical Chemistry. *Publications:* articles in Police Jl, Fire Service Jl. *Recreation:* youth work. *Address:* 181 Manse Road, Motherwell, Lanarkshire. *T:* Motherwell 62812. *Died 6 July* 1981.

**MACLENNAN, Sir Ian (Morrison Ross),** KCMG 1957 (CMG 1951); HM Diplomatic Service, retired; *b* 30 Oct. 1909; *s* of late W. Maclennan, Glasgow; *m* 1936, Margherita Lucas, *d* of late F. Lucas Jarratt, Bedford; one *s* one *d. Educ:* Hymers Coll., Hull; Worcester Coll., Oxford. Appointed Colonial Office, 1933; Dominions Office, 1937; UK High Commissioner's Office, Ottawa, 1938; Pretoria, 1945; UK High Commissioner S Rhodesia, 1951–53; Federation of Rhodesia and Nyasaland, 1953–55; Assistant Under-Secretary of State, CRO, 1955–57; UK High Commissioner in Ghana, 1957–59; Ambassador to the Republic of Ireland, 1960–63; High Commissioner in New Zealand, 1964–69. Mem., Gen. Adv. Council, IBA, 1974–82 (Chm., 1979–82). *Address:* 26 Ham Street, Richmond, Surrey. *Club:* Travellers'. *Died 25 Dec.* 1986.

**MacLENNAN, (John) Hugh;** CC (Canada) 1967; Professor, English Literature, McGill University, 1967–79 (Associate Professor, 1951–67), then Professor Emeritus; *b* 20 March 1907; *s* of Dr Samuel John MacLennan and Katherine MacQuarrie; *m* 1st, 1936, Dorothy Duncan (*d* 1957); 2nd, 1959, Frances Aline, *d* of late Frank Earle Walker and Isabella Scott Benson. *Educ:* Dalhousie Univ.; Oriel Coll., Oxford; Graduate Coll., Princeton. Rhodes Schol. (Canada at large), 1928; PhD (Princeton) 1935. Classics Master, Lower Canada Coll., Montreal, 1935–45; writing, 1945–51. FRS Canada, 1953 (Gold Medal, 1951); FRSL, 1959. Governor-General's Award for Fiction, 1945, 1948, 1959; Governor-General's Award for non-fiction, 1949, 1954. Hon. DLitt: Waterloo Lutheran, 1961; Carleton Univ., 1967; Western Ontario, 1953, Manitoba, 1955; Hon. LLD: Dalhousie, 1956, Saskatchewan, 1959; McMaster, 1965; Toronto, 1966; Laurentian, 1966; Sherbrooke, 1967; British Columbia, 1968; St Mary's, 1968; Hon. DCL Bishop's, 1965. *Publications:* Oxyrhynchus: An Economic and Social Study, 1935; Barometer Rising, 1941; Two Solitudes, 1945; The Precipice, 1948; Cross Country (essays), 1949; Each Man's Son, 1951; Thirty and Three (essays), 1954; The Watch That Ends The Night, 1959; Scotchman's Return (essays), 1960; Return of the Sphinx, 1967; Rivers of Canada, 1974; Voices in Time, 1980. *Recreations:* walking, gardening. *Address:* 1535 Summerhill Avenue, Montreal, PQ H3C 1C2, Canada. *T:* 932–0475. *Clubs:* Montreal Amateur Athletic Association, McGill Faculty (Montreal). *Died 7 Nov.* 1990.

**MacLENNAN OF MacLENNAN, Ronald George;** 34th Chief of Clan MacLennan; Chairman, Kintail Museum Company, since 1983; teacher of and lecturer in physical education, 1949–82, retired; *b* 7 Feb. 1925; *s* of George Mitchell MacLennan and Helen Ames Thomson; recognised as Chief of Clan MacLennan, 1978; *m* 1970, Margaret, 2nd *d* of Donald and Jemima MacLennan; one *s* two *d. Educ:* Boroughmuir Secondary Sch., Edinburgh; Univ. of Copenhagen (Dip. in Physical Educn). Served War, 1939–45. Editor, Clan MacLennan Newsletter, 1971–. Mem., Standing Council of Scottish Chiefs, 1978–. FSAScot 1969; FRHistS 1977; FRSA 1982. Hon. Col, Oregon National Guard, 1981–; Hon. Ambassador of Scotland to Poland, London, 1981–; Hon. Brig.-Gen., Polish Armed Forces (in exile), 1982–. Hon. DLitt London, 1984. Kt, Order of St Lazarus of Jerusalem, 1976; Kt Comdr's Cross, Order of Polonia Restituta, 1981; Order of Virtuti Militari (1st cl., 1939–45), Poland, 1982; Count of Holy Roman Empire, 1986; several international knighthoods (including Kt Niadh Nask, 1983 and Kt Grand Cross and Collar, Imperial Constantinian Military Order of St George, 1986), and many other honours, govt and civic receptions, etc, in USA, Canada and Australia. *Publication:* History of the MacLennans, 1978. *Recreations:* history, gardening, kayaking. *Heir:* s Ruairidh Donald George MacLennan, yr of

MacLennan, *b* 22 April 1977. *Address:* The Old Mill, Dores, Inverness. *T:* Dores 228. *Died 7 Nov.* 1989.

**McLEOD, Sir Alan Cumbrae Rose,** KCVO 1966 (CVO 1955); Surgeon Dentist to The Queen, 1952–75 (to King George VI, 1946–52); *b* Brisbane, Queensland, 9 Dec. 1904; *yr s* of late Frederick Rose McLeod and of Mrs Ellen McLeod; *m* 1939, Noreen Egremont King; one *s* two *d. Educ:* Toowoomba Grammar Sch., Queensland. Matric. University of Queensland; DDS University of Pennsylvania, USA, 1928; BSc (Dent) Univ. of Toronto, Canada, 1929; LDS RCS 1930; FDS RCS 1948; Undergraduate and Postgraduate Teaching, 1932–46. East Grinstead Maxillo-Facial Unit, 1939–45. FACD 1959. *Publications:* contributions to dental literature. *Recreation:* woodwork. *Address:* Westbrook, The Batch, Wincanton, Somerset. *T:* Wincanton 32012.

*Died 9 Jan.* 1981.

**MacLEOD, Sir John,** Kt 1963; TD; *b* 23 Feb. 1913; *y s* of late Duncan MacLeod, CBE, Skeabost, Isle of Skye; *m* 1938, Rosemary Theodora Hamilton, *d* of late Frederick Noel Hamilton Wills, Miserden Park, Stroud, Glos; two *s* three *d. Educ:* Fettes Coll., Edinburgh. TA 1935. Served War of 1939–45, 51st Highland Division; France, 1940. MP (Nat. Liberal) Ross and Cromarty Div., 1945–64. *Address:* Bunkers Hill, Farmington, Northleach, Glos. *T:* Northleach 731. *Club:* Highland (Inverness). *Died 3 June* 1984.

**MACLEOD, Joseph Todd Gordon;** author and broadcaster; *b* 24 April 1903; *o surv. s* of late James Gordon Macleod; *m* 1st, 1928, Kate Macgregor (*d* 1953), *d* of late Robert Davis, Uddingston; 2nd, Maria Teresa, *d* of late Ing. Alfredo Foschini, Rome; one *s* one *d. Educ:* Rugby Sch.; Balliol Coll., Oxford. BA 1925; MA 1945; called to Bar, Inner Temple, 1928. Was book-reviewer, private tutor, actor, producer, lecturer on theatre-history. Directed the Festival Theatre, Cambridge, 1933–36; visited theatres in USSR, 1937; Secretary of Huntingdonshire Divisional Labour Party, 1937–38, also Parliamentary Candidate; announcer BBC, 1938–45. Managing Director, Scottish National Film Studios, Glasgow, 1946–47; Convener, Drama, Gœthe Festival Society, 1948–49; produced The Lady from the Sea, Festival of Britain, Aberdeen, 1951; Scottish Episcopal Church chronicle play St Mary's Cathedral, Edinburgh, 1952; toured Holland as guest of Dutch Ministry of Fine Arts, 1946; visited Soviet Union as guest of Moscow and Kiev Cultural Relations Societies, 1947; Silver Medal, Royal Society of Arts for paper on the Theatre in Soviet Culture, 1944. Hon. Member, British Actors' Equity. *Plays performed:* The Suppliants of Aeschylus translated with a verse sequel, 1933; A Woman Turned to Stone, 1934; Overture to Cambridge, 1934; A Miracle for St George, 1935; Leap in September (Arts Council Prize), 1952. *Publications:* Beauty and the Beast, 1927; The Ecliptic (poem), 1930; Foray of Centaurs (poem), 1931; Overture to Cambridge (novel), 1936; The New Soviet Theatre, 1943; Actors Cross the Volga, 1946; A Job at the BBC, 1947; A Soviet Theatre Sketchbook, 1951; The Passage of the Torch (poem), 1951; A Short History of the British Theatre (Italian edn), 1958; People of Florence, 1968; The Sisters D'Aranyi, 1969; An Old Olive Tree, 1971 (Arts Council Award); The Actor's Right to Act, 1981; poetry under *non-de-plume* Adam Drinan: The Cove, 1940; The Men of the Rocks, 1942; The Ghosts of the Strath, 1943; Women of the Happy Island, 1944; Script from Norway, 1953; contribution on Theatre history to Chambers's Encyclopædia. *Music:* The Kid from the City, 1941. *Recreations:* painting, music, bird-watching. *Address:* Via delle Ballodole 9/7, Trespiano, 50139 Firenze, Italy. *T:* Firenze 417056. *Died 22 March* 1984.

**MacLEOD, Maj.-Gen. Minden Whyte-Melville,** CB 1945; CBE 1943; DSO 1918; Commander, US Legion of Merit, 1946; late Royal Artillery; British Advisory Staff, Polish Resettlement Corps, 1946–49; Colonel Commandant Royal Artillery, 1952–61; *b* 1896; *y s* of late M. N. MacLeod, Behar, India; *m* 1926, Violet, *o d* of late Major J. Elsdale Molson and Mrs Molson, of the Pound House, Angmering, Sussex; two *d. Educ:* Rugby; Woolwich; graduated Staff Coll., Dec. 1932; served European War, 1914–18 (DSO, despatches); Iraq, 1920 (medal and clasp); Waziristan, 1921–24 (medal and clasp); North West Frontier of India, 1930 (clasp); War of 1939–45 (despatches, CBE, CB); retired pay, 1949. *Address:* 12 Lower Sloane Street, SW1. *T:* 01-730 2358. *Club:* Naval and Military. *Died 17 Dec.* 1981.

**McLINTOCK, Sir William Traven,** 3rd Bt, *cr* 1934; *b* 4 Jan. 1931; *s* of Sir Thomas McLintock, 2nd Bt and Jean, *d* of R. T. D. Aitken, New Brunswick; *S* father, 1953; *m* 1952, André (marr. diss.), *d* of Richard Lonsdale-Hands; three *s; m* Heather, *d* of Philip Homfray-Davies; one step *s* one step *d. Educ:* Harrow. *Heir:* s Michael William McLintock, *b* 13 Aug. 1958. *Died 26 June* 1987.

**MacLYSAGHT, Edward Anthony,** LLD, DLitt, MRIA; Member, Irish Manuscripts Commission, 1949–73 (Inspector, 1939–43); Chairman, 1956–73); Chief Herald and Genealogical Officer, Office of Arms, Dublin Castle, 1943–49; Keeper of Manuscripts, National Library of Ireland, 1949–55; *b* at sea, 1887 (bapt. Co. Clare); *m* 1st, 1915, Maureen Pattison; one *s* one *d;* 2nd, 1936, Mary Frances

Cunneen; three s. Educ: abroad; Nat. Univ. of Ireland (MA). Engaged in cattle-breeding and forestry since 1909; mem. of Irish Convention, 1917–18, Irish Senate, 1922–25; working in South Africa, 1929–30, 1936–38. Mem. Gov. Body, Sch. of Celtic Studies, Dublin Inst for Advanced Studies, 1942–76. Publications: The Gael, 1919, 2nd edn 1929; Cûrsaí Thomáis, 1927, new edn 1969; Toil Dé, 1933; Short Study of a Transplanted Family, 1935; Irish Life in the Seventeenth Century, 1939, 3rd edn 1969; (ed) The Kenmare Manuscripts, 1942, 2nd edn 1970; (ed) Analecta Hibernica (14 and 15), 1944; An Aifric Theas, 1947, East Clare (1916–21), 1954; Irish Families: Their Names, Arms and Origins, 1957, 4th edn 1985; More Irish Families, 1960, 2nd enlarged edn, inc. Supplement to Irish Families, 1982; The Surnames of Ireland, 1969, 6th edn 1985; (ed) Forth the Banners Go, reminiscences of William O'Brien, 1969; Leathanaigh óm' Dhialann, 1978; Changing Times, 1978. Address: Raheen, Tuamgraney, Co. Clare. Club: United Arts (Dublin).

*Died 3 March 1986.*

**McMAHON, Rt. Hon. Sir William,** GCMG 1977; CH 1972; PC 1966; MP for Lowe, NSW, 1949–82; Prime Minister of Australia, 1971–72; b 23 Feb. 1908; s of William Daniel McMahon; m 1965, Sonia R. Hopkins; one s two d. Educ: Sydney Grammar Sch.; St Paul's Coll., Univ. of Sydney (LLB, BEc with distinction; Frank Albert Prize for proficiency; John D'Arcy Meml Prize for Public Admin). Practised as solicitor until 1939. Australian Army, 1940–45, Major. Elected to House of Representatives for Lowe, NSW, in gen. elections, 1949, 1951, 1954, 1955, 1958, 1961, 1963, 1966, 1969, 1972, 1974, 1975, 1977, 1980; Minister: for Navy, and for Air, 1951–54 (visited Korea and Japan in that capacity, 1952); for Social Services, 1954–56; for Primary Industry, 1956–58; for Labour and National Service, 1958–66; Treasurer, Commonwealth of Australia, 1966–69; Minister for External Affairs, later Foreign Affairs, 1969–71. Vice-Pres., Executive Council, 1964–66; Dep. Leader of Liberal Party, 1966–71, Leader, 1971–72; Acting Minister for Trade, Acting Minister for Labour and Nat. Service, Acting Minister in Charge, CSIRO, Acting Minister for National Development, Acting Minister for Territories, and Acting Attorney-Gen., for short periods, 1956–69; Leader of Aust. Delegation to Commonwealth Parliamentary Conf., New Delhi, Nov. 1957–Jan. 1958; Visiting Minister to ILO Conf., Geneva, June 1960 and June 1964; Pres., ILO Asian Regional Conf., Melbourne, Nov.-Dec., 1962; Mem., Bd of Governors, IMF and World Bank, 1966–69. Chm., Bd of Governors, Asian Development Bank, 1968–69. Led Australian delegns to Bangkok, Djakarta, Wellington, Tokyo, Manila and Saigon, 1970. As Prime Minister officially visited: USA, GB, 1971; Indonesia, Malaysia, Singapore, 1972. Recreations: squash, swimming. Address: 18 Drumalbyn Road, Bellevue Hill, NSW 2023, Australia; Ashleigh Park, Orange, NSW 2800, Australia; 1 Rapallo Avenue, Surfers Paradise, Qld 4127, Australia. Clubs: Union, Australian, Australian Jockey (Sydney); Melbourne (Melbourne). *Died 31 March 1988.*

**McMANUS, Maurice,** CBE 1966; JP; DL; Lord Provost of Dundee and Lord Lieutenant of the County of the City of Dundee, 1960–67; b 17 Jan. 1906; s of Patrick and Ann McManus; m 1931, Lillian, d of James and Isobel Lindsay; three s two d. Educ: West Calder. Tutor at National Council of Labour Coll., 1945–. Chm. Dundee City Labour Party, 1950–56; Councillor, Tayside Region, 1974–. Member: Exec. Cttee, Scottish Council for Development and Industry; Scottish Advisory Cttee for Civil Aviation; Court of St Andrews Univ.; Council of Queen's Coll., Dundee; Dundee Univ., 1967; Chairman: Tayside Region Manpower Cttee, 1975–; Tay Road Bridge Jt Bd; Dundee Coll. of Art and Technology; Dundee & N Fife Local Employment Cttee, 1969. JP 1958, DL 1967, Dundee. Hon. LLD Dundee, 1969. Recreation: gardening. Address: 20 Merton Avenue, Dundee. *Died 15 July 1982.*

**McMEEKAN, Brig. Gilbert Reader,** CB 1955; DSO 1942; OBE 1942; JP, 1956; retired, Regular Army, 1955; b 22 June 1900; s of late Major F. H. F. R. McMeekan, RA; m 1932, Marion Janet, d of late Sir John Percival, KBE; one s two d. Educ: Wellington Coll,; RMA Woolwich. Commissioned RE 1919; BAOR 1922–24; Sudan Defence Force, 1924–31; Aldershot, 1931–37; Malta, 1938–42; o/c Fortress, RE Malta, 1940–42; CRE 10 Armoured Div. (Alamein), 1942–43; Liaison Staff, USA, 1944–45; Chief Superintendent, Military Engineering Experimental Establishment, Christchurch, 1946–50; Comdr, 25 Eng. Group TA, 1950–52; Comdr, RE Ripon, 1952–55. Officer, American Legion of Merit, 1946. Address: Greenacres, Painswick, Glos. T: Painswick 812395.

*Died 25 Aug. 1982.*

**McMEEKIN, Lt-Gen. Sir Terence (Douglas Herbert),** KCB 1973 (CB 1972); OBE 1960; b 27 Sept. 1918; e s of late Herbert William Porter McMeekin, Cogry, Co. Antrim, and Jean McMeekin, Elm Grove, Cirencester; m 1947, Averil Anne Spence Longstaff, 7th d of late Dr Tom Longstaff and Dora Longstaff (née Scott); one s two d. Educ: King William's Coll., IOM; RMA Woolwich. 2nd Lt RA, 1938; served War of 1939–45 (despatches); GSO2 (L) HQ 8th Army, 1943; Staff Coll., Haifa, 1943; GSO2 (Ops), HQ 3 Corps, 1944; Bde Major

RA, 1 Airborne Div., 1945; Battery Comdr, 6 Airborne Div., Palestine, 1945–46; Instructor in Gunnery, 1947–48; GSO2 (Tactics), School of Artillery, Manorbier, 1949–50; DAQMG, HQ 1 (British) Corps, 1952–54; jssc 1955; Battery Comdr, 5 RHA, 1955–57; Bt Lt-Col, 1957; AA & QMG, HQ Land Forces, Hong Kong, 1958–60; comd 29 Field Regt, RA, 1960–62; converted regt to Commando role, 1962; Col 1962; Chief Instructor (Tactics), School of Artillery, Larkhill, 1962–64; comd 28 Commonwealth Inf. Bde Gp, Malaya, 1964–66; Dir of Public Relations (Army), 1967–68; GOC 3rd Div., 1968–70; Comdt, Nat. Defence Coll. (formerly Jt Services Staff Coll.), 1970–72; GOC SE District, 1972–74, retd 1975. Col Comdt, RA, 1972–80; Hon. Col, 289 Commando Battery, RA, TAVR, 1978–83. Lieut, HM Tower of London, 1981–83. President: Army Cricket Assoc., 1969–72; Combined Services Cricket Assoc., 1971–72. Area Appeals Sec., Avon, Glos and Wilts, CRC, 1976–82. Mem., Worshipful Co. of Basketmakers, 1982–. Freeman, City of London, 1982. Recreations: cricket, most field sports. Address: The Old Rectory, Beverston, near Tetbury, Glos. T: Tetbury 52735. Clubs: Army and Navy, MCC, Stragglers of Asia. *Died 3 Aug. 1984.*

**MacMICHAEL, Nicholas Hugh,** FSA; Keeper of the Muniments of Westminster Abbey since 1967; b 2 Feb. 1933; o s of late Canon Arthur William MacMichael and late Elizabeth Helen Royale, o d of Rev. Arthur William Newboult; unmarried. Educ: Eastbourne Coll.; Magdalene Coll., Cambridge. Asst Librarian and Asst Keeper of the Muniments of Westminster Abbey, 1956–66; Hon. Sec., 1961–64, Hon. Editor, 1964–70, Harleian Soc.; Member: Exec. Cttee, Soc. of Genealogists, 1963–67; Council: British Archaeological Assoc., 1960–62; Monumental Brass Soc., 1960–66; Kent Archaeological Soc., 1973–78. FSA 1962; FRHistS 1972; Fellow, Soc. of Genealogists, 1969. Publications: (ed) Westminster Abbey Official Guide, 1977; articles in learned jls. Recreations: genealogical and heraldic research; ecclesiology; watching cricket. Address: 2b Little Cloister, Westminster Abbey, SW1. T: 01–799 6893; Church Cottage, Bethersden, Ashford, Kent. T: Bethersden 359. Club: United Oxford & Cambridge University.

*Died 24 Nov. 1985.*

**MACMILLAN OF OVENDEN, Viscount; Maurice Victor Macmillan;** PC 1972; MP (C) Surrey South West, since 1983 (Farnham, 1966–83); Group Chairman, Macmillan Ltd; Director, Yarrow and Co. Ltd; b 27 Jan. 1921; s and heir of 1st Earl of Stockton, OM, PC, FRS; m 1942, Hon. Katherine Margaret Alice Ormsby-Gore, DBE 1974, 2nd d of 4th Baron Harlech, KG, PC, GCMG; three s one d (and one s decd). Educ: Eton; Baliol Coll., Oxford. Served War of 1939–45 with Sussex Yeomanry, and after as Mil. Asst to Adjt-General. Mem. of Kensington Borough Council, 1949–53. Contested (C) Seaham Harbour, 1945, Lincoln, 1951, Wakefield, by-election, 1954; MP (C) Halifax, 1955–64; Economic Sec. to the Treasury, Oct. 1963–64; Chief Sec. to the Treasury, 1970–72; Sec. of State for Employment, 1972–73; Chief Sec. to the Treasury, 1970–72; Sec. of State for Employment, 1972–73; Paymaster-General, 1973–74. Delegate: to Council of Europe, 1960–63 (Political Cttee rapporteur, 1962–63); to WEU, 1960–63; a Pres., UK Council of European Movement, 1961–63; Treasurer, British Section, European Movement, 1979. Chairman: Macmillan & Co. Ltd, 1967–70; Macmillan Journals Ltd, 1967–70; Macmillan & Cleaver Ltd, 1967–70; Macmillan (Publications) Ltd, 1974–77; Dep. Chm., Macmillan (Holdings) Ltd, 1966–70; formerly also Director: Monotype Corporation Ltd; Yorkshire Television Ltd; and Founder Chm., Wider Share Ownership Council. Heir: s Hon. Alexander Daniel Alan Macmillan [b 10 Oct. 1943; m 1970, Hélène Birgitte, o d of late Alan D. C. Hamilton; one s two d]. Address: 9 Warwick Square, SW1; Birch Grove House, Chelwood Gate, Haywards Heath, Sussex. T: Chelwoodgate 588. Clubs: Turf, Beefsteak, Pratt's, Garrick, Carlton. *Died 10 March 1984.*

**MACMILLAN, Donald,** OBE 1981; TD 1966; JP; MB, ChB; FSAScot 1948; MFCM; FRSH; Director, Nuffield Centre for Health Services Studies, University of Leeds, since 1962; b 10 April 1919; er s of late James Orr Macmillan and Sarah Dunsmore Graham; m 1950, Jean Alison Taylor, MA; two d (and twin s and d decd in infancy). Educ: Hillhead High Sch., Glasgow; Univ. of Glasgow (MB, ChB, 1952). Pres., Student's Rep. Council, 1950–51; Chm., Students' Quincentenary Cttee, 1948–51 (Quincentenary Medal, 1951). FRSH 1970 (MRSH 1968); MFCM 1980; MBIM 1965. Hosp. clinical posts, 1952–56; Med. Supt, Maryfield Teaching Hosp., Dundee, 1956–58; Principal Asst SMO, Birmingham Reg. Hosp. Bd, 1958–62. Warden, Albert Mansbridge Hall, Leeds Univ., 1971–. Served War, HLI, Captain, 1939–47; re-commnd RAMC/TA, Captain, 1954; SMO, Lt-Col, 44 Ind. Para. Bde Gp, TA, 1961–66; Bt-Col 1966; US Army Airborne Wing Dip., 1965. SJAB: Divl Surg., 1965–67; Comr, Leeds Met. Area, 1967–; Mem. Council, S and W Yorks, 1974–; StJ 1975 (OStJ 1965). Member, NHS Cttees: Nat. Nursing Staff, 1965–68; Leeds Area Nursing Trng, 1967–74; Leeds (Western) Community Health Council, 1974–79; Leeds AHA (Teaching), 1979–. Adviser in Health Admin. to Imp. Govts of Iran, 1965–72; Pakistan, 1969; Kuwait, 1977–; Nuffield Trust Fellow to USA, 1965 and 1974; Vis. Prof., Health Planning, NW Univ., USA, 1975–76; Vis. Lectr, numerous US Univ. Health Programmes, 1963–76 (Mem. Assoc. of Univ. Progs in Health Admin., USA, 1976); Founder Mem., European Assoc. of Progs in Health Services Studies, 1963. JP Leeds 1969– (Vice-Chm. Leeds Juv. Panel, 1976–; Member: Bd of Visitors, 1971–, Parole Rev. Cttee, 1973–, HM Prison, Armley, Leeds; Exec. Cttee, Nat. Council of Alcoholism, 1979–; Chm., Leeds Council for Alcoholism, 1979. Freeman Citizen of Glasgow, 1948. *Publications:* numerous contribs to Health Services pubns in UK and USA. *Recreations:* dinghy sailing, parachuting (now watching). *Address:* 71 Clarendon Road, Leeds LS2 9PL. *T:* Leeds 442422. *Clubs:* Royal Over-Seas League, English-Speaking Union, Royal Army Medical Corps (Hon. Mem. HQ Mess).

*Died 10 April 1982.*

**MacMILLAN OF MacMILLAN, Gen. Sir Gordon Holmes Alexander,** of Knap, KCB 1949 (CB 1945); KCVO 1954; CBE 1943; DSO 1943; MC (two bars); Hereditary Chief of the Clan MacMillan; Colonel The Argyll and Sutherland Highlanders, 1945–58; Hon. Colonel The Argyll and Sutherland Highlanders of Canada, 1948–72; 402 (A. and S. H.) Lt Regt RA (TA), 1956–61; *b* 7 Jan. 1897; *s* of D. A. MacMillan and L. W. Allardice; *m* 1929, Marian Blakiston-Houston, OBE, CStJ, four *s* one *d. Educ:* St Edmund's Sch., Canterbury. RMC, Sandhurst, 1915; commissioned in Argyll and Sutherland Highdrs, 1915; served European War in 2nd Bn Argyll and Sutherland Highdrs, France, 1916–18 (MC and two bars); Adjutant, 1917–20; Staff Coll., Camberley, 1928–29; Staff Capt., War Office, 1930–32; GSO3, 1932–34; GSO2 RMC, Kingston, Ont., 1935–37; GSO2 WO and Eastern Command, 1937–40; GSO1, 1940–41; Brig. commanding Infantry Brigade, 1941; BGS UK and N Africa, 1941–43 (CBE); commanding Infantry Brigade, Sicily, 1943 (DSO); commanding 15th Scottish, 49 (WR) and 51st Highland Divs, 1943–45, UK, Normandy, Holland and Germany (CB); DWD War Office, 1945–46; GOC Palestine, 1947–48; Gen. Officer, C-in-C, Scottish Command, and Gov. of Edinburgh Castle, 1949–52; Gov. and C-in-C of Gibraltar, 1952–55, retd 1955. Chairman: Cumbernauld New Town Corporation, 1956–65; Greenock Harbour Trust, 1955–65; Erskine Hospital, 1955–80; Firth of Clyde Dry Dock, 1960–67. DL Renfrewshire, 1950, Vice-Lieutenant, 1955–72. Kt Grand Cross Order of Orange Nassau; KStJ. Mem. of The Queen's Body Guard for Scotland. Hon. LLD (Glasgow), 1964. *Address:* Finlaystone, Langbank, Renfrewshire PA14 6TJ. *T:* Langbank 235. *Club:* Caledonian. *Died 21 Jan. 1986.*

**MacMILLAN, His Honour James;** Judge of County Courts, 1950–65, retired; *b* Schoolhouse, Fisherton, Ayrshire, 18 April 1898; *s* of George Arthur MacMillan, MA, and Catherine, *d* of Alexander McQuiston; *m* 1931, Marjorie J. Triffitt, DSc (*d* 1957); one *d. Educ:* Troon Sch.; Ayr Acad.; Glasgow Univ. (MA, LLB). Royal Artillery, 1917–19, Lt. Called to Bar, Middle Temple, 1925, Midland Circuit; Legal Adviser, Ministry of Pensions, 1939–44. Mem. Bar Council, 1947–50; Mem. Supreme Court Rule Cttee, 1948–50; Dep. Chm. Beds Quarter Sessions, 1949–50; County Court Judge, Circuit 37, April-June 1950, Circuit 38, 1950–55, Circuit 39, 1955–65. *Recreation:* walking. *Address:* Cotswolds, 11 Lillington Avenue, Leamington Spa, Warwickshire CV32 5UL.

*Died 16 March 1985.*

**MACMILLAN, Sir (James) Wilson,** KBE 1976 (CBE 1962, OBE 1951); Governing Director, Macmillan Brothers Ltd; President, British Red Cross and Scout Association; *b* 1906; *m* Beatrice Woods. Served in Legislature for many years; formerly Minister of Education, Health and Housing. British Red Cross Badge of Honour, Class I, 1964. *Address:* 3 St Edward Street, Belize City, Belize. *Died 8 Aug. 1989.*

**McMORRAN, Helen Isabella,** MA; Life Fellow, Girton College, Cambridge; *b* 26 July 1898; *d* of late Thomas McMorran and late Louise Maud White. *Educ:* Sutton High Sch., GPDST; Girton Coll., Cambridge. Assistant Librarian, Bedford Coll., London, 1921–28; Girton Coll., Cambridge: Librarian, 1930–62; Vice-Mistress, 1946–62; Registrar of the Roll, 1947–69. Member of Council, Girls' Public Day School Trust, 1952–69; Trustee, Homerton Coll., Cambridge, 1954–67. *Publications:* Editor, Girton Review, 1932–62; Joint Editor (with K. T. Butler) of Girton College Register, 1869–1946, 1948. *Address:* c/o Girton College, Cambridge. *Died 9 Nov. 1985.*

**McMULLAN, Henry Wallace,** OBE 1967; Member of Independent Broadcasting Authority (formerly Independent Television Authority), 1971–74; *b* 20 Feb. 1909; *s* of William Muir McMullan and Euphemia McMullan; *m* 1934, Roberta Tener Gardiner; three *s. Educ:* King William's Coll., IOM. Worked on Belfast Telegraph and Belfast Newsletter; Producer and Commentator, BBC NI, 1930; Lt-Comdr RNVR, Map Room, Admty, 1939; Head of Programmes, BBC NI, 1945–69. *Recreations:* gardening, watching and listening to people, television and radio. *Address:* 119 Garner

Crescent, Nanaimo, British Columbia, Canada. *Club:* Naval.

*Died 18 May 1988.*

**McMULLEN, Rear-Admiral Morrice Alexander,** CB 1964; OBE 1944; Flag Officer, Admiralty Interview Board, HMS Sultan, Gosport, 1961–64, retired; Director, Civil Defence for London, 1965–68; *b* Hertford, 16 Feb. 1909; *m* 1st, 1946, Pamela (*née* May) (marr. diss. 1967), widow of Lt-Comdr J. Buckley, DSC, RN; two step *s;* 2nd, 1972, Peggy, *widow* of Comdr Richard Dakeyne, RN; two step *s* one step *d. Educ:* Oakley Hall, Cirencester; Cheltenham Coll. Entered Royal Navy, as Paymaster Cadet, HMS Erebus, 1927. Appts prewar included: S Africa Station, 1929–32; China Station, 1933–36; Asst Sec. to Admiral of the Fleet Sir Ernle Chatfield, First Sea Lord, 1936–38; Served War of 1939–45 (despatches, OBE); Atlantic, North Sea, Norwegian waters; served in HMS Prince of Wales (battle with Bismarck, and Atlantic Charter Meeting); HQ, Western Approaches, 1941–43; Member Allied Anti-Submarine Survey Board, 1943; served Mediterranean, 1944–45 (Anzio Landing, re-entry into Greece, invasion of S. France); Sec. to Vice-Adm. Sir John Mansfield, 1941–48. Post-war appointments at home included Dep. Dir Manning (Suez operation), 1956–58, and Captain of Fleet to C-in-C Far East Station, Singapore, 1959–61. Chairman Royal Naval Ski Club, 1955–58. *Recreations:* fishing, sailing, gardening. *Address:* 3 The Crescent, Alverstoke, Hants PO12 2DH. *T:* Gosport 582974. *Clubs:* Naval and Military, Royal Cruising, Royal Naval Sailing Association. *Died 18 March 1990.*

**McMULLIN, Hon. Sir Alister (Maxwell),** KCMG 1957; Chancellor, University of Newcastle, NSW, 1966–77; President of the Australian Senate, 1953–71; *b* Scone, NSW, Australia, 14 July 1900; *s* of W. G. McMullin, Upper Rouchet, NSW; *m* 1945, Thelma Louise (*née* Smith); one *d. Educ:* Public Sch., Australia. Elected to the Australian Senate, 1951, Senator to New South Wales. Chm., Gen. Council, Commonwealth Parly Assoc., 1959–60, 1969–70. Chm., Scott Memorial Hospital, Scone, NSW, 1934–40. Hon. DLitt Newcastle, NSW, 1966. *Address:* St Aubins, Scone, NSW 2337, Australia.

*Died 8 June 1984.*

**McNAIR, 2nd Baron** *cr* 1955, of Gleniffer; **Clement John McNair;** *b* 11 Jan. 1915; *s* of 1st Baron McNair, CBE, QC, and Marjorie (*d* 1971), *yr d* of late Sir Clement Meacher Bailhache; *S* father, 1975; *m* 1941, Vera, *d* of Theodore James Faithfull; two *s* one *d. Educ:* Shrewsbury; Balliol Coll., Oxford. Served War of 1939–45, Major, RA. Substitute Mem., Council of Europe and WEU, 1979–84. Dep. Liberal Whip, H of L, 1985–88; Dep. SLD Whip, H of L, 1988–. *Publications:* Wagonload, 1971; A Place Called Marathon, 1976. *Heir: s* Hon. Duncan James McNair, *b* 26 June 1947. *Address:* House of Lords, SW1. *Died 7 Aug. 1989.*

**McNAIR, Air Vice-Marshal James Jamieson;** Principal Medical Officer, Headquarters Support Command, Royal Air Force, 1974–77, retired; *b* 15 June 1917; *s* of Gordon McNair and Barbara MacNaughton; *m* 1945, Zobell Pyper (*d* 1977). *Educ:* Kirkcudbright Academy; Huntly Gordon Sch.; Aberdeen Univ.; London Sch. of Hygiene and Tropical Medicine; Liverpool Sch. of Tropical Medicine. MB, ChB; FFCM; DPH; DTM&H. Sqdn Med. Officer, UK, N Africa, Sicily, Italy, 1942–45; OC, RAF Sch. of Hygiene at Home and Egypt, 1946–51; SMO, 66, 21 and 25 Gp HQ at Home, 1951–57; SMO Air HQ and OC RAF Hosp. Ceylon, 1957–59; OC RAF Inst. of Hygiene, 1959–62; DGMS Staff, Air Min., 1962–65; OC RAF Hosp. Changi, Singapore, 1965–67; PMO HQ's Fighter Comd, 1967–68; OC Jt Service Med. Rehabilitation Unit, 1968–71; Dir of Health and Research, MoD (Air), 1971–74; Dep. Dir GMS RAF, 1974; QHP 1974–77. CStJ. *Recreations:* golf, gardening, travel. *Address:* Woodstock, Thursley Road, Elstead, Godalming GU8 6EA. *Clubs:* Royal Air Force; Hankley Common Golf.

*Died 9 Oct. 1990.*

**McNAMARA, Most Rev. Kevin,** DD; Archbishop of Dublin and Primate of Ireland, (RC), since 1984; *b* 10 June 1926; *s* of Patrick and Eileen McNamara. *Educ:* St Flannan's Coll., Ennis; St Patrick's Coll., Maynooth (BA, DD); Univ. of Munich; BA NUI. Prof. of Dogmatic Theology 1954–76, Vice-Pres. 1968–76, St Patrick's Coll., Maynooth; Bishop of Kerry, 1976–84. Mem., Internat. Dialogue Commn, Roman Catholics/Disciples of Christ; Chm., Episcopal Commn for Doctrine of Irish Bishops' Conf.; Consultor, Pontifical Council for the Family. Chairman: Bd of Govs and Trustees, St Vincent's Hosp., Fairview; Cttee of Management, Our Lady's Hosp. for Sick Children, Crumlin; Nat. Maternity Hosp., Holles Street; Bd of Management, Mater Hosp.; Mem. Cttee of Management, Jervis St Hosp. *Publications:* (ed and contrib.) Mother of the Redeemer, 1959; (ed and contrib.) Christian Unity, 1962; (jtly) Truth and Life, 1968; (ed. and jt author) Vatican II: Constitution on the Church—A Theological and Pastoral Commentary, 1968; Sacrament of Salvation—Studies in the Mystery of Christ and the Church, 1977; regular contribs to Irish Theolog. Quarterly, Irish Eccles. Record, The Furrow, etc; popular series of booklets on religious subjects. *Recreations:* reading and walking. *Address:*

Archbishop's House, Drumcondra, Dublin 9. *T:* 37 37 32.
*Died* 8 *April* 1987.

**McNEE, Sir John (William),** Kt 1951; DSO 1918; MD; DSc, FRCP (London, Edinburgh and Glasgow); FRS(E); Regius Professor of Practice of Medicine, Glasgow University, 1936–53; Professor Emeritus, 1953; Physician to the Queen in Scotland, 1952–54 (and to King George VI, 1937–52); Consulting Physician to Royal Navy, 1935–55; Consulting Physician to University College Hospital, London, and to the Western Infirmary, Glasgow; *b* 17 Dec. 1887; *o s* of late John McNee, Glasgow and Newcastle upon Tyne; *m* 1923, Geraldine Z. L., MSc (London) (*d* 1975), *o d* of late Cecil H. A. Le Bas, The Charterhouse, London. *Educ:* Royal Grammar Sch., Newcastle upon Tyne; Glasgow, Freiburg, and Johns Hopkins, USA, Universities. MB (Hons), 1909; MD (Hons) and Bellahouston Gold Medal, 1914; DSc 1920. Asst Professor of Medicine and Lecturer in Pathology, Glasgow University; Asst Professor of Medicine, and Associate Physician, Johns Hopkins Univ., USA; Consulting Physician UCH, London, and formerly Holme Lecturer in Clinical Medicine, UCH Medical Sch.; Rockefeller Fellow in Medicine, 1923; Lettsomian Lecturer, Medical Society of London, 1931; Croonian Lecturer, RCP, 1932; Anglo-Batavian Lectr, all Univs of Holland, 1936; Harveian Lecturer, Harveian Society, London, 1952; Vicary Lecturer, RCS, 1958. Examiner in Medicine, Universities of Cambridge, St Andrews, Sheffield, Glasgow, Aberdeen, Edinburgh, Leeds, National University of Ireland, and Conjoint Board; Inspector for GMC of all Univs in Gt Britain and Ireland and of Final Examinations in Medicine, 1954–56. Visiting Prof., Harvard Univ., USA (Brigham Hospital), 1949. President: Royal Medico-Chirurgical Society of Glasgow, 1950–51; Gastro-Enterological Society of Great Britain, 1950–51; Assoc. of Physicians, Great Britain and Ireland, 1951–52; BMA 1954–55. Original Mem., 1942 Club. Editor, Quarterly Journal of Medicine, 1929–48. Master of the Barber-Surgeons' Company of London, 1957–58. Served European War, Major, RAMC, 1914–19 (despatches, DSO; Comdr Military Order Aviz, Portugal; Médaille Militaire, France); served War of 1939–45, Surgeon Rear-Admiral RN, and Consulting Physician to the Navy in Scotland and Western Approaches, 1939–45. Hon. MD (NUI); LLD (Glasgow), LLD (Toronto). *Publications:* Diseases of the Liver-Gall-Bladder and Bile-Ducts (3rd edn, 1929, with Sir Humphrey Rolleston); Textbook of Medical Treatment (with Dunlop and Davidson), 1st edn 1939, and 6th edn 1955; numerous medical papers, especially on diseases of liver and spleen and various war diseases (Trench Fever, Gas Gangrene, War Nephritis, Immersion Foot (RN)), Rescue Ships (RN), New Internat. Med. Code for Ships. *Recreations:* country sports. *Address:* Barton Edge, Worthy Road, Winchester, Hants. *T:* Winchester 65444. *Clubs:* Athenæum, Fly-fishers'.
*Died* 26 *Jan.* 1984.

**McNEIL, Anne,** CBE 1950 (OBE 1946); retired; *b* 1902; *d* of Archibald and Elizabeth McNeil, Thorganby, York. *Educ:* privately. Dist Comr of Girl Guides, E Yorks, 1927–40. Served WRNS, 1940–50; Levant and E Mediterranean, 1945, E Indies Stn, 1946; last appointment, Superintendent (training). Sec., Service Women's Club, 52 Lower Sloane Street, London, 1950–64. *Address:* Birkwood, Thorganby, York YO4 6DH. *Died* 12 *Jan.* 1984.

**McNEILE, Robert Arbuthnot,** MBE 1943; Deputy Chairman, Arthur Guinness Son & Co. Ltd, 1978–81 (Managing Director, 1968–75; Co-Chairman, 1975–78); *b* 14 March 1913; *s* of A. M. McNeile, Housemaster at Eton College; *m* 1944, Pamela Rachel Paton (*née* Pollock); three *s* one *d. Educ:* Eton; King's Coll., Cambridge. Asst Master, Eton Coll., 1935; joined Arthur Guinness Son & Co. Ltd, 1936. Served War of 1939–45 in Royal Engineers, First Airborne Div., HQ 21st Army Group, Control Commn for Germany; Lt-Col. Chm., Brewers' Society, 1976–77 (Vice-Chm., 1974–75). *Recreations:* archaeology, ornithology, Tennis, ski-ing, shooting. *Address:* The Mount, Brancaster, Norfolk. *T:* Brancaster 210227. *Clubs:* Sloane; Hawks (Cambridge).
*Died* 14 *Sept.* 1985.

**McNEILL, Hon. Sir David (Bruce),** Kt 1979; Hon. Mr Justice McNeill; a Judge of the High Court of Justice, Queen's Bench Division, since 1979; Member, Restrictive Practices Court, since 1981; *b* 6 June 1922; *s* of late Ferguson and Elizabeth Bruce McNeill; *m* 1949, Margaret Lewis; one *s* three *d. Educ:* Rydal Sch.; Merton Coll., Oxford. BCL, MA Oxon, 1947. Called to Bar, Lincoln's Inn, 1947 (Cassel Schol.); Bencher, 1974; Northern Circuit, Leader, 1974–78, Presiding Judge, 1980–84. Lecturer in Law, Liverpool Univ., 1948–58. QC 1966; Recorder of Blackburn, 1969–71; Recorder of the Crown Court, 1972–78. Mem., Parole Bd, 1986–88. Member: Bar Council, 1968–72; Senate of the Inns of Court and the Bar, 1975–81 (Vice-Chm., 1976–77; Chm., 1977–78). Hon. Member: American Bar Assoc.; Canadian Bar Assoc. Hon. LLD Liverpool, 1982. Commissioned into Reconnaissance Corps, 1943; served in N Africa, Sicily, Italy, Germany. *Address:* Royal Courts of Justice, Strand, WC2A 2LL. *Died* 26 *Feb.* 1990.

**McNEILL, Sir James (Charles),** Kt 1978; AC 1986; CBE 1972; FASA; FAIM; Chairman, The Broken Hill Proprietary Co. Ltd, 1977–84; *b* 29 July 1916; *s* of Charles Arthur Henry McNeill and Una Beatrice Gould; *m* 1942, Audrey Evelyn Mathieson; one *s. Educ:* Newcastle Boys' High Sch., NSW. Chm., Tubemakers of Aust. Ltd, 1978–86; Dir, ANZ Bank, 1982–86. Member: Internat. Adv. Council, Morgan Guaranty Trust Co. of NY; AT & T (International). Member: Aust. Govt Consultative Cttee on Relations with Japan; Chm., Aust.–Japan Business Forum, 1985–86; Vice-Pres., Aust.–Japan Business Consultative Council, 1977–86. Member: Council, Monash Univ. (Chm., Finance Cttee); Finance Adv. Cttee, Walter & Eliza Hall Inst. for Med. Res. Hon. DSc Newcastle, NSW, 1981; Hon. Dr jur, Monash Univ., 1986. *Recreations:* music, farming, gardening. *Address:* 104 Mont Albert Road, Canterbury, Victoria 3126, Australia. *T:* 836.4924. *Clubs:* Australian (Pres.), Athenæum, Melbourne (all Melbourne); Frankston Golf. *Died* 12 *March* 1987.

**McNICOLL, Vice-Adm. Sir Alan (Wedel Ramsay),** KBE 1966 (CBE 1954); CB 1965; GM 1941; Australian Ambassador to Turkey, 1968–73; *b* 3 April 1908; 2nd *s* of late Brig.-Gen. Sir Walter McNicoll and Lady McNicoll; *m* 1st, 1937, Ruth, *d* of late W. N. Timmins; two *s* one *d*; 2nd, 1957, Frances, *d* of late J. Chadwick. *Educ:* Scotch Coll., Melbourne; Royal Australian Naval Coll. Joined Navy, 1922; Lieut, 1930; Captain, 1949; Rear-Admiral, 1958; Dep. Chief of Naval Staff, 1951–52; Commanded 10th Destroyer Flotilla, 1950; HMAS Australia, 1953–54; IDC, 1955; 2nd Naval Member, Commonwealth Naval Board, 1960–61; Commanded Australian Fleet, 1962–64; Vice-Admiral, 1965; Chief of Naval Staff, Australia, 1965–68. Comdr of Order of Orange Nassau, 1955. *Publications:* Sea Voices (verse), 1931; trans., Odes of Horace, 1979. *Recreations:* music, fly-fishing. *Address:* 6 Hutt Street, Yarralumla, ACT 2600, Australia.
*Died* 11 *Oct.* 1987.

**McPETRIE, James Stuart,** CB 1960; *b* 13 June 1902; *s* of John McPetrie and Mary (*née* Simpson); *m* 1st, 1931, Helen Noreen McGregor (*d* 1974); one *s*; 2nd, 1975, Myra, *widow* of John F. Pullen. *Educ:* Robert Gordon's Coll., Aberdeen; Aberdeen Univ. National Physical Laboratory, 1925–43; Radio Physicist, British Supply Mission, Washington, DC, 1943–44; Research Superintendent, Signals Research and Development Establishment, Ministry of Supply, 1944–50; Head of Radio Dept, Royal Aircraft Establishment, 1950–58; Dir-Gen. of Electronics Research and Development at Ministry of Aviation, 1958–62; Consulting Electronic Engineer, 1962–; Dir, Racal Electronics, 1965–69. *Publications:* series of papers on various aspects of radio research to learned societies. *Address:* 3 Edenhurst Court, Parkhill Road, Torquay, Devon TQ1 2DD. *Died* 4 *Jan.* 1990.

**MACPHERSON, Rt. Rev. Colin;** Bishop of Argyll and the Isles (RC), since 1968; *b* Lochboisdale, South Uist, 5 Aug. 1917; *e s* of Malcolm MacPherson and Mary MacPherson (*née* MacMillan). *Educ:* Lochboisdale School; Daliburgh H.G. School; Blairs Coll., Aberdeen; Pontificium Athenæum Urbanum, Rome. Bachelor of Philosophy, 1936; Bachelor of Theology, 1938; Licentiate of Theology, 1940 (Rome). Asst Priest, St Columba's Cathedral, Oban, 1940–42. Parish Priest: Knoydart, 1942–51; Eriskay, 1951–56; Benbecula, 1956–66; Fort William, 1966–68. Hon. LLD Univ. of St Francis Xavier, Canada, 1974. *Address:* Bishop's House, Esplanade, Oban, Argyll. *T:* Oban 2010. *Died* 24 *March* 1990.

**MACPHERSON, Colin,** MA; CA; Senior Partner, Smith & Williamson, Chartered Accountants, 1973–86 (Partner, 1959); *b* 17 Feb. 1927; *s* of Ian Macpherson and Anna Elizabeth McLean; *m* 1st, 1951, Christian Elizabeth Randolph; two *s* one *d*; 2nd, 1981, Judith Margaret Jackson, *widow* of Brig. Tom Jackson. *Educ:* Eton; Trinity Coll., Cambridge (MA). Director: Sun Life Assce, 1968–; Keystone Investment, 1975–. Dep. Chm., 1976–78, Chm., 1978–82, Commn for New Towns. Mem., Pilcher Cttee on Commercial Property Develt, 1975; Chm., Guide Dogs for the Blind, 1987– (Vice-Chm., 1976–87); Vice-Chm., Regents Coll., 1985–. *Recreations:* skiing, shooting. *Address:* The Mill, Droxford, Hants SO3 1QS. *Clubs:* Oriental, City of London.
*Died* 21 *Feb.* 1988.

**MacPHERSON, Donald,** CIE 1946; *b* 22 March 1894; *s* of D. MacPherson, Edinburgh; *m* 1931, Marie Elizabeth (*d* 1983), *d* of John Nicholson, Sydney, NSW; two *d. Educ:* Royal High Sch. and Univ., Edinburgh. Indian Civil Service; District Magistrate, Bengal, 1928; Commissioner of Excise, 1935; Commissioner of Division, 1944. Retired, 1947. *Address:* 51 Marlborough Mansions, Cannon Hill, NW6 1JS. *T:* 01–435 4358. *Died* 24 *Oct.* 1989.

**MACPHERSON, George Philip Stewart,** CBE 1976 (OBE 1943); TD 1945; Director, Kleinwort Benson Lonsdale, 1960–74; *b* 14 Dec. 1903; *s* of late Sir T. Stewart Macpherson, CIE, LLD, ICS, and Lady (Helen) Macpherson, K-I-H (*née* Cameron); *m* 1939, Elizabeth Margaret Cameron, *d* of late James Cameron Smail, OBE, LLD; three *s. Educ:* Edinburgh Acad.; Fettes Coll. (Schol.); Oriel Coll.,

Oxford (Schol. and Field Schol.; 1st class Classical Mods, 1st class Lit. Hum.; MA 1944), Hon. Fellow, 1973; Yale Univ., USA (Schol.); Edinburgh Univ.; Chartered Accountant (Edinburgh), 1930; partner in Layton-Bennett, Chiene and Tait, CA, 1930–36; Man. Dir, Robert Benson and Co. Ltd, Merchant Bankers, 1936; Chm., Robert Benson Lonsdale & Co. Ltd, 1958–60; Dir, Kleinwort Benson Ltd, 1960–69 (Vice-Chm., 1960–66); Dir Standard Life Assurance Co. Ltd, 1934–76 and of several industrial companies and investment trusts, until 1976 and 1977. Chm., Issuing Houses Association, 1955, 1956; Mem. Exec. Cttee, Investment Trust Assoc., 1955–68. Chairman: Esmée Fairbairn Charitable Trust, 1969–79; English-Speaking Union Finance Cttee, 1969–74; Royal Caledonian Schs Finance Cttee, 1952–73; Mem., Greenwich Hosp. Adv. Panel on financial matters, 1960–76. Governor, Fettes Coll., 1957–76. Hon. DLitt, Heriot Watt, 1971. 7/9 Battalion The Royal Scots, 1927–36; 1st Bn London Scottish, 1939, sc; Brig. 1945, Dir Finance Div. (Brit. Element) Allied Control Commn to Austria, 1945–46. *Publications:* contrib. to Accountants' Magazine. *Recreations:* active outdoor occupations and gardening. Formerly Rugby football and athletics (Oxford XV, 1922–24; Edinburgh Univ. Athletic Blue; Rep. Scotland Long Jump and Hurdles, 1929, and Rugby football, 1922–32; Scottish Rugby Union Cttee, 1934–36). *Address:* The Old Rectory, Aston Sandford, near Aylesbury, Bucks. *T:* Haddenham 291335. *Clubs:* Caledonian, English-Speaking Union; Vincent's (Oxford); New (Edinburgh).
*Died 2 March 1981.*

**MACPHERSON, James;** Administrative Adviser, Scottish Office, 1970–75, retired; *b* 16 Dec. 1911; *s* of late John Campbell Macpherson and Agnes Arkley Mitchell, Auchterarder, Perthshire; *m* 1939, Marion Cooper Cochrane Allison; two *s* one *d. Educ:* George Heriot's Sch. Asst Preventive Officer, subseq. Officer, Customs and Excise, 1932–39; Gunner, TA, 1939; 54th Light AA Regt, RA; service in France, Belgium, Italy, Austria, 1939–46; Brig. 1946; Dir Finance Div. (Br Element), Allied Control Commn to Austria; Princ., Min. of Civil Aviation, 1946–48; Treasury, 1949–53; Asst Sec., Treasury, 1953–63; Scottish Home and Health Dept, 1963–66; Scottish Development Dept, 1966–67; Under-Sec., Scottish Develt Dept, 1967–70. *Recreations:* reading, golf. *Address:* 92 Ravelston Dykes, Edinburgh EH12 6HB. *T:* 031-337 6560. *Clubs:* New (Edinburgh); Hon. Company of Edinburgh Golfers.
*Died 1 March 1982.*

**MACPHERSON-GRANT, Sir Ewan (George),** 6th Bt, *cr* 1838; TD; DL; Member Scottish Faculty of Advocates; Hon. Sheriff Substitute, Counties of Perth and Angus; *b* 29 Sept. 1907; *s* of late George Bertram Macpherson-Grant, OBE (2nd *s* of 3rd Bt) and of Dorothy Eleanor Kellie-MacCallum (*d* 1952); *S* cousin, 1951; *m* 1937, Evelyn Nancy Stopford, *yr d* of late Major Edward Spencer Dickin, Spenford House, Loppington, Salop; one *d. Educ:* Winchester; Christ Church, Oxford. DL, Co. Banff, 1952. Mem. of Royal Company of Archers. *Heir:* none. *Address:* Pitchroy Lodge, Ballindalloch, Banffshire. *T:* Ballindalloch 208; Craigo, by Montrose, Angus. *T:* Hillside 205. *Club:* Army and Navy.
*Died 12 Feb. 1983 (ext).*

**McQUADE, John;** *b* Shankill, Belfast, July 1912; *m* Hanna Williams. *Educ:* public elementary sch., Snugville, Belfast. Served War of 1939–45, with Chindits in Burma. Formerly professional boxer (as Jack Higgins), and docker. Member: Belfast, Woodvale, NI Parlt, 1965–72, resigned, and, later, NI Assembly, 1974–75, resigned; Belfast City Council, Court Ward and later Shankill Ward, to 1972, resigned. Contested (UUUP) Belfast W, Feb. and Oct. 1974; MP (DUP) Belfast N, 1979–83.
*Died 19 Nov. 1984.*

**MACRAE, Christopher,** CBE 1956; MA, DPhil; Vice-President, Ashridge Management College, since 1969 (Principal, 1962–69); *b* 6 Jan. 1910; *s* of John Tait Macrae and Mary (*née* Mackenzie), Kintail, Ross-shire; *m* 1939, Mary Margaret Campbell Greig, *er d* of Robert Elliott, Glasgow; two *s* one *d* (er *d* decd in infancy). *Educ:* Dingwall Acad.; Glasgow Univ. (MA); New Coll., Oxford (DPhil). Civil Servant, 1937–46; Chief Exec. Scottish Council (Develt and Industry), 1946–56; Prof. of Industrial Admin., The Royal Coll. of Science and Technology, Glasgow, and Head of Chesters Residential Management Educn Centre, 1956–62. FBIM. *Publications:* various articles and papers. *Recreations:* reading, music, walking, climbing, sailing. *Address:* 37 Buckingham Terrace, Edinburgh.
*Died 28 March 1990.*

**MacRITCHIE, Prof. Farquhar,** CBE 1968; MA, LLB (Aberdeen); Professor of Conveyancing at Aberdeen University, 1946–74; Consultant, Burnett & Reid, Advocates, Aberdeen, since 1979; *b* 1 Nov. 1902; *s* of Donald MacRitchie, Isle of Lewis; *m* 1941, Isobel, *d* of William Ross, Aberdeen; one *s* decd. *Educ:* Aberdeen Univ. Asst Lecturer in Law, Aberdeen Univ., 1940–45; Lecturer in Mercantile Law, Aberdeen Univ., 1945–46. Hon. Sheriff in Aberdeen. Convener, Legal Education Cttee, Law Soc. of Scotland, 1955–70; Vice-Pres., Law Soc. of Scotland, 1963. Mem. of firm of Morice & Wilson, Advocates, Aberdeen, 1939–79. Hon. LLD

Edinburgh, 1965. *Publication:* (ed) 4th edn, Burns, Conveyancing Practice (Scotland), 1957. *Recreation:* golf. *Address:* 60 Rubislaw Den North, Aberdeen AB24AN. *T:* 315458. *Clubs:* Royal Northern, University (Aberdeen).
*Died 15 April 1988.*

**McROBERT, Brig. Leslie Harrison,** CBE 1943 (OBE 1937); TD 1937; DL; Chartered Accountant; Executive Director, 1945–64, Deputy Chairman, 1951–61, Chairman, 1961–64, Cerebos Ltd and associated cos; Member, North Eastern Railway Board, 1956–64; Member, Local Employment Act, 1960, etc, Advisory Committee, Ministry of Technology (formerly Treasury, later Board of Trade), 1945–70; *b* 22 Aug. 1898; *s* of late James William McRobert, Hartlepool; *m* 1st, 1929, May (*d* 1962), *d* of late W. G. Smith, Alston, Cumberland; two *d;* 2nd, 1963, Dorothy, *widow* of Lt-Col F. Ruddy, MC, DCM. *Educ:* Royal Gram. Sch., Newcastle upon Tyne. European War 1914–18, France and Belgium, RFC and RAF; commanded 55th (Northumbrian) Medium Bde RA and 63rd (Northumbrian) HAA Regt RA and 30, 59 and 28 AA Brigades during 1939–44 War. Chm. TA & AF Assoc., Co. of Durham, 1958–63. Chm. Hartlepools Hosp. Management Cttee, 1950–58; Chm., Friends of the Penrith Hosps, 1971–74. Hon. Colonel: 377 Corps Locating Regt RA (TA), 1955–56; 274 N Field Regt RA (TA), 1956–60; Durham Univ. (now Northumbrian Univs) OTC, 1960–68. DL Durham, 1941; Vice-Lieutenant, 1959–69; High Sheriff of Co. Durham, 1954–55. *Recreations:* fishing, etc. *Address:* 14 Glyn Garth Court, Glyn Garth, Anglesey, Gwynedd LL59 5BP.
*Died 3 Feb. 1981.*

**MACTAGGART, Sir Ian (Auld),** 3rd Bt *cr* 1938; Managing Director The Western Heritable Investment Company and Director of several Property and other Companies; *b* Glasgow, 19 April 1923; *e s* of Sir John (Jack) Mactaggart, 2nd Bt, Nassau, Bahamas; *S* father, 1960; *m* 1946, Rosemary (marr. diss. 1969), *d* of Sir Herbert Williams, 1st Bt, MP; two *s* two *d. Educ:* Oundle; Clare Coll., Cambridge. Served with Royal Engineers in India, 1942–45. Contested (U) Gorbals div. of Glasgow, 1945; contested (C) Fulham, 1970. Mem. (C) London County Council, for Fulham, 1949–51. Chm., Soc. for Individual Freedom. *Heir: s* John Auld Mactaggart [*b* 21 Jan. 1951; *m* 1977, Patricia, *y d* of late Major Harry Alastair Gordon]. *Address:* 2A Westmoreland Terrace, SW1. *T:* 01–834 8062. *Club:* English-Speaking Union.
*Died 27 Jan. 1987.*

**McTAGGART, Robert;** MP (Lab) Glasgow Central, since June 1980; *b* 2 Nov. 1945; *s* of Robert and Mary McTaggart; *m* 1966, Elizabeth Jardine; one *s* two *d. Educ:* St Constantine's, St Bartholomew's and Holyrood. Apprentice Marine Plumber, 1962–67; Trigonometrical Calculator, 1968–72; Pipework Planner, 1972–80. EETPU Shop Steward, 1971–77. Joined Labour Party, 1969; Glasgow Corporation Councillor, 1974–75, District Councillor 1977–80; Parliamentary Election Agent, 1978–80. *Recreations:* watching football, athletics, playing draughts, snooker, reading. *Address:* 61 St Mungo Avenue, Townhead, Glasgow G4 0PL. *T:* 041–552 7346.
*Died 23 March 1989.*

**MacTAGGART, Sir William,** Kt 1962; PPRSA; RA 1973 (ARA 1968); FRSE 1967; RSA 1948 (ARSA 1937); President, Royal Scottish Academy, 1959–69; *b* Loanhead, 15 May 1903; *er s* of late Hugh Holmes MacTaggart, Engineer and Managing Dir of MacTaggart, Scott & Co. Ltd, Loanhead, and *g s* of late William McTaggart, RSA; *m* 1937, Fanny Margaretha Basilier, Kt 1st Cl. Order of St Olav, Norway, *er d* of late Gen. Ivar Aavatsmark, Oslo, Norway. *Educ:* privately; Edinburgh Coll. of Art; abroad. Elected professional mem. Soc. of Scottish Artists, 1922 (Pres., 1934–36); Mem. Soc. of Eight. Has held one-man exhibitions at home and abroad. Works purchased by Tate Gallery, Contemporary Art Soc. and the Arts Council; also represented in public galleries in Glasgow, Edinburgh, Aberdeen and Bradford, and in USA and Australia. Hon. RA 1959; Hon. RSW; Hon. FRIAS 1968. Hon. Burgess of Loanhead, 1965. Hon. LLD Edinburgh, 1961. Chevalier de la Légion d'Honneur, 1968. *Relevant publication:* Sir William MacTaggart, by H. Harvey Wood, 1974. *Address:* 4 Drummond Place, Edinburgh. *T:* 031-556 1657. *Club:* Scottish Arts (Edinburgh).
*Died 9 Jan. 1981.*

**MacTIER, Sir (Reginald) Stewart,** Kt 1961; CBE 1946; Director: The Ocean Steam Ship Co. Ltd, 1955–67; Glen Line Ltd, London, 1939–67; *b* 9 Dec. 1905; *s* of late Major H. C. MacTier, Newton St Loe, Somerset, and of Mary Fitzroy MacTier, *d* of Sir Charles Hobhouse, 3rd Bt; *m* 1941, Maya, *d* of Brig. C. G. Ling, DB, DSO, MC; two *s* one *d. Educ:* Eton; Magdalene Coll., Cambridge. Mansfield & Co. Ltd, Singapore, Shipping Agents, 1928–37; Dep. Dir and subseq. Dir of Port and Transit Control, Min. of War Transport, 1940–45. Chm. Liverpool Steam Ship Owners' Assoc. and Gen. Council of British Shipping, 1960–61; Pres., Inst. Marine Engineers, 1966–67. Comdr Order of Maritime Merit (French); Medal of Victory with silver palm (US). *Address:* Durris, Haulands Gap Road, Flinders Island, Tas 7255, Australia.
*Died 28 Nov. 1984.*

**McTIERNAN, Rt. Hon. Sir Edward (Aloysius),** KBE 1951; PC 1963; Justice of the High Court of Australia, 1930–76; *b* 16 Feb. 1892; *s* of Patrick and Isabella McTiernan; *m* 1948, Kathleen, *d* of Sidney and Ann Lloyd, Melbourne. *Educ:* Marist Brothers' High Sch., Sydney; Sydney Univ. (BA, LLB, 1st cl. Hons). Admitted to Bar, NSW, 1917; Lecturer in Law, Sydney Univ.; NSW Parliament, 1920–27; Attorney-Gen., 1920–22 and 1925–27; NSW Govt Representative in London, 1926; MHR for Parkes, Commonwealth Parl., 1928, Papal Chamberlain, 1927. *Address:* 36 Chilton Parade, Warrawee, Sydney, NSW 2074, Australia. *Club:* Australian (Sydney).
*Died 9 Jan.* 1990.

**McVITTIE, Maj.-Gen. Charles Harold,** CB 1962; CBE 1953; *b* 6 Aug. 1908; *s* of Col R. H. McVittie, CB, CMG, CBE; *m* 1939, Margaret Wark (*d* 1984), *d* of Dr T. Divine, Huddersfield; two *s. Educ:* Haileybury; Brighton Coll.; Sandhurst. 2nd Lt Queen's Own Royal West Kent Regt, 1928; transferred to RAOC, 1935; Served War of 1939–45, ADOS Singapore Fortress, 1941–42; POW, 1942–45; comd Vehicle Organization, 1948–50; DOS, GHQ Farelf, 1951–53; comd Technical Stores Organization, 1953–56; comd RAOC Trg Centre, 1956–60; Comdr Stores Organization, RAOC, 1960–63. Hon. Col AER Units RAOC, 1961–64. Col Commandant, RAOC, 1965–69. *Recreation:* fencing (Blue, Sandhurst, 1928). *Address:* Clovers, Garelochhead, Dunbartonshire. *T:* Garelochhead 810266.
*Died 24 May* 1988.

**McVITTIE, George Cunliffe,** OBE 1946; MA Edinburgh, PhD Cantab; Professor of Astronomy, University of Illinois, 1952–72, Emeritus Professor, 1972; Hon. Professor of Theoretical Astronomy, University of Kent at Canterbury, 1972–85; *b* 5 June 1904; *e s* of Frank S. McVittie; *m* 1934, Mildred Bond (*d* 1985), *d* of Prof. John Strong, CBE; no *c. Educ:* Edinburgh Univ.; Christ's Coll., Cambridge. Asst Lecturer, Leeds Univ., 1930–34; Lecturer in Applied Mathematics, Liverpool Univ., 1934–36; Reader in Mathematics, King's Coll., London, 1936–48; Prof. of Mathematics, Queen Mary Coll., London, 1948–52. War service with Meteorological Office, Air Ministry, and a Dept of the Foreign Office, 1939–45. FRS (Edinburgh), 1943. Mem. Sub-Cttee of Meteorological Research Cttee, 1948–52. Jt Editor of The Observatory, 1938–48. Jt Exec. Editor of Quarterly Journal of Mechanics and Applied Mathematics, 1947–51; Pres., Commn on Galaxies, Internat. Astronomical Union, 1967–70; Sec., American Astronomical Soc., 1961–69. Minor Planet 2417 named "McVittie" by IAU, 1984. Hon. DSc Kent, 1985. *Publications:* Cosmological Theory, 1937; General Relativity and Cosmology, 1956, 2nd edn, 1965; Fact and Theory in Cosmology, 1961; (ed) Problems of Extra-galactic Research, 1962; papers on Relativity and its astronomical applications, classical mechanics, etc., Proc. Royal Soc. and other journals. *Address:* 74 Old Dover Road, Canterbury, Kent CT1 3AY. *Club:* Athenæum. *Died 8 March* 1988.

**McWHINNIE, Donald;** Freelance Director, Stage and Television, since 1960; *b* 16 Oct. 1920; *s* of Herbert McWhinnie and Margaret Elizabeth (*née* Holland). *Educ:* Rotherham Gram. Sch.; Gonville and Caius Coll., Cambridge. MA Cantab 1941. Served War of 1939–45: RAF, 1941–46. Joined BBC, 1947; Asst Head of Drama (Sound), 1953–60, resigned. Theatrical productions include: Krapp's Last Tape, Royal Court, 1958; The Caretaker, Arts and Duchess, 1960, Lyceum, NY, 1961; The Duchess of Malfi, Aldwych, 1960; Three, Arts and Criterion, 1961; The Tenth Man, Comedy, 1961; A Passage to India, Ambassador, NY, 1962; Everything in the Garden, Arts and Duke of York's, 1962; Macbeth, Royal Shakespeare, 1962; Rattle of a Simple Man, Garrick, 1962, Booth, NY, 1963; Doctors of Philosophy, Arts, 1962; The Doctor's Dilemma, Haymarket, 1963; Alfie, Mermaid and Duchess, 1963; Out of the Crocodile, Phœnix, 1963; The Fourth of June, St Martin's, 1964; End Game, Aldwych, 1964; The Creeper, St Martin's, 1965; All in Good Time, Royale, NY, 1965; The Cavern, Strand, 1965; This Winter's Hobby, US Tour, 1966; The Astrakhan Coat, Helen Hayes, NY, 1967; Happy Family, St Martin's, 1967; Tinker's Curse, Nottingham Playhouse, 1968; Vacant Possession, Nottingham Playhouse, 1968; Hamlet, Covent Garden, 1969; No Quarter, Hampstead, 1969; There'll be Some Changes Made, Fortune, 1969; The Apple Cart, Mermaid, 1970; A Hearts and Minds Job, Hampstead, 1971; Meeting at Night, Duke of York's, 1971; Endgame, and Play and Other Plays, Royal Court, 1976; Translations, Hampstead and Nat. Theatre, 1981; Hedda Gabler, Cambridge, 1982; Lovers Dancing, Albery, 1983; also numerous television productions for BBC and ITV. *Publication:* The Art of Radio, 1959. *Address:* 16 Chepstow Place, W2. *T:* 01–229 2120.
*Died 8 Oct.* 1987.

**McWILLIAM, William Nicholson,** CB 1960; *b* 26 Nov. 1897; *er s* of W. N. McWilliam, MD, Banbridge, Co. Down; *m* 1927, V. Maureen (decd), *er d* of H. H. Mussen, Asst Chief Crown Solicitor; one *s* two *d. Educ:* Excelsior Academy, Banbridge; Campbell Coll., Belfast; Trinity Coll., Dublin. Served European War, 1916–18, Lieut, RGA, 1916–18. BA, BAI, 1921. Entered NI Civil Service, 1922; Asst Sec. to Cabinet, NI, 1945–57; Dep. Clerk of the Privy Council, NI,

1945–57; Permanent Sec., Min. of Labour and National Insurance, NI, 1957–62 (retired). Member Boundary Commn for NI, 1963–69. *Address:* Garryard, 34 Massey Avenue, Belfast BT4 2JT. *T:* Belfast 63179. *Died 9 Dec.* 1987.

**MADDEX, Sir George (Henry),** KBE 1948; Government Actuary, 1946–58, retired; *b* 1895; *m* 1921, Emily Macdonald Jeffrey (*d* 1980); one *s* killed on active service, 1943. *Educ:* Owen's Sch. Pres., Inst. of Actuaries, 1948–50. Dep. Govt Actuary, 1944–46. Fellow, Society of Actuaries (US), 1949; Hon. Fellow, Faculty of Actuaries in Scotland, 1956. *Address:* 1 Clairville Court, Reigate, Surrey. *Clubs:* Naval and Military, St Stephen's Constitutional.
*Died 27 March* 1982.

**MADDOCK, Rt. Rev. David Rokeby;** *b* 30 May 1915; *s* of Walter Rokeby Maddock; *m* 1943, Mary Jesse Hoernle, widow of Edward Selwyn Hoernle, ICS and *d* of Rev. Selwyn Charles Freer; one *s* one *d. Educ:* Clifton Coll.; Bristol Univ.; St Catherine's, Oxford; Wycliffe Hall, Oxford. Curate, Chard, Somerset, 1939–43; Vicar, Wilton, Taunton, 1943–47; Rector, Wareham, 1947–61; Rector of Bradford Peverell and Stratton, 1961–66; Rector of West Stafford with Frome Billet, 1966–67. Rural Dean of Purbeck, 1948–61; Canon of Salisbury, 1956–67; Archdeacon of Sherborne, 1961–67; Bishop Suffragan of Dunwich, 1967–76; Archdeacon of Sudbury, 1968–70; Provost of St Edmundsbury, 1976–80. Hon. Chaplain Dorset Constabulary, 1964–67. *Address:* 3 Norfolk Court, East Street, Bridport, Dorset. *T:* Bridport 25338.
*Died 14 Aug.* 1984.

**MADDOCK, Sir Ieuan,** Kt 1975; CB 1968; OBE 1953; FRS 1967; FEng 1975; Chairman: Corporate Consulting Group, since 1979; Enterprise Capital Ltd, since 1983; Amazon Computers Ltd, 1983–87; Deputy Chairman, International General Electric Co. of New York Ltd, 1983–88; Director, Cogent Ltd, since 1982; *b* 29 March 1917; British; *m* 1943, Eurfron May Davies; one *s. Educ:* Gowerton Grammar Sch., Glamorgan; University of Wales, Swansea (Hon. Fellow, 1985). Entered Government service, Explosives Res. and Develt, 1940; Principal Scientific Officer, Armament Res. Dept, Fort Halstead, 1949; Head of Field Experiments Div., Atomic Weapons Research Establishment, 1960; directed UK Research programme for Nuclear Test Ban Treaty, 1957–66; Dep. Controller B, 1965–67, Controller (Industrial Technology) 1967–71, Min. of Technology; Chief Scientist: DTI, 1971–74; DoI, 1974–77; Dir, Nat. Physical Laboratory, 1976–77; Chairman: Sira Inst., 1978–87; Fulmer Res. Inst., 1978–87. Principal of St Edmund Hall, Oxford, 1979–82 (Hon. Fellow, 1982). Director: Prutec, 1980–82; Chubb & Sons Ltd, 1978–84. Sec., BAAS, 1977–81. Vis. Prof., Imperial Coll., London, 1977–79. Member: SRC, 1973–77; NERC, 1973–77; Science Cons. Cttee to BBC, 1969–80 (Chm., 1977–80); ABRC, 1973–77; Adv. Council for Applied R&D, 1977–80; Gen. Adv. Council, BBC, 1977–80; Ct, Brunel Univ., 1979–82; Ct, Cranfield Coll. of Technology, 1969–77; Ct, Surrey Univ., 1974–79; Ct, University Coll. of Swansea, 1981–. President: IERE, 1973–75; IMGTechE, 1976; Dep. Chm., Nat. Electronics Council, 1977–80; Vice-Pres., ASLIB, 1977–. For. Mem., Royal Swedish Acad. of Engrg Science, 1975. Hon. FIQA. Hon. Fellow: Manchester Polytechnic, 1977; Polytechnic of Wales, 1982; IERE, 1983; Hon. Mem., CGLI, 1986. Hon. DSc: Wales, 1970; Bath, 1978; Reading, 1980; Salford, 1980; Hon. DTech CNAA, 1980; DUniv Surrey, 1983. *Publications:* in various scientific and technical jls. *Address:* 13 Darell Road, Caversham, Reading, Berks. *T:* Reading 474096. *Died 29 Dec.* 1988.

**MADDOX, Sir (John) Kempson,** Kt 1964; VRD 1948; Hon. Consulting Physician: Royal Prince Alfred Hospital, Sydney; Royal Hospital for Women, Sydney; *b* Dunedin, NZ, 20 Sept. 1901; *s* of Sidney Harold Maddox and Mabel Kempson; *m* 1940, Madeleine Scott; one *s* one *d. Educ:* N Sydney Boys' High Sch.; Univ. of Sydney. MD, ChM (Sydney) 1924; MRCP 1928; FRACP 1935; FRCP 1958; Hon. FACP 1980. Served War of 1939–45, Surgeon Comdr, RANR. President: BMA (NSW), 1950; Cardiac Soc. of Australia and NZ, 1958; Asian-Pacific Soc. of Cardiology, 1960–64; Internat. Soc. of Cardiology, 1966–70; Vice-Pres., Nat. Heart Foundation of Australia, 1960–64 (Pres. NSW Div.); FACC 1965; FACP 1968; Hon. Pres., Internat. Soc. of Cardiology, 1970–74. Hon. AM (Singapore) 1963. Chevalier de l'Ordre de la Santé Publique, France, 1961; Comendador, Orden Hispolito Unanue (Peru), 1968. *Recreations:* golf, fishing. *Address:* 8 Annandale Street, Darling Point, Sydney, NSW 2027, Australia. *T:* 32–1707. *Clubs:* Australian (Sydney); Royal Sydney Golf. *Died 1990.*

**MADOC, Maj.-Gen. Reginald William,** CB 1959; DSO 1957; OBE 1951; Royal Marines, retired; *b* 15 Aug. 1907; *s* of late Lieut-Colonel H. W. Madoc, CBE, MVO, Garwick, Isle of Man; *m* 1938, Rosemary, *d* of late Dr Cyril Shepherd, Sydney, Australia; one *d. Educ:* King William's Coll., Isle of Man. 2nd Lieut, RM, 1926; HMS Rodney, 1929–31; HMS Royal Oak, 1932–34; ADC to Governor of Madras, 1934–38; HMS Furious, 1938–39; RM Mobile Naval Base Defence Org., UK, Egypt, Crete, 1940–41 (despatches twice, POW, 1941–45). Instructor, Officers' Sch., RM, 1946; Staff Coll., Camberley, 1947; Instructor, School of Combined Ops, 1948; HMS Vanguard, 1948–49; CO, 42 Commando, RM, Malaya, 1950–51 (despatches); CO Commando Sch., RM, 1952–53; Chief Instructor, School of Amphibious Warfare, 1953–55; Commanded 3rd Commando Bde, RM, Malta, Cyprus, Port Said, 1955–57; ADC to the Queen, 1955–57; Maj.-Gen., Plymouth Gp, RM, 1957–59; Maj.-Gen., Portsmouth Gp, RM, 1959–61; retired 1961. Col Comdt, RM, 1967–68; Rep. Col Comdt, RM, 1969–70. *Address:* The Malthouse, Meonstoke, by Southampton, SO3 1NH. *T:* Droxford 877323. *Club:* Army and Navy. *Died 24 May 1986.*

**MAEGRAITH, Brian Gilmore,** CMG 1968; TD (2 bars) 1975; MA, MB, MSc, DPhil; FRCP, FRCPE, FRACP; Alfred Jones and Warrington Yorke Professor of Tropical Medicine, School of Tropical Medicine, Liverpool University, 1944–72, then Professor Emeritus; Hon. Senior Research Fellow, Department of Tropical Paediatrics, since 1978, and Dean, 1946–75, Vice-President, since 1975, Liverpool School of Tropical Medicine; *b* 26 Aug. 1907; *s* of late A. E. R. Maegraith, Adelaide, S Australia; *m* 1934, Lorna Langley, St Peters, Adelaide; one *s. Educ:* St Peter's and St Mark's Colleges, Adelaide University (MB 1930); Magdalen and Exeter Colleges, Oxford (Rhodes Scholar, Rolleston Memorial Prize). Beit Memorial Fellow, 1932–34; Medical Fellow, Exeter Coll., Oxford, 1934–40; University Lecturer and Demonstrator in Pathology, Dean of Faculty of Medicine, Oxford Univ.; War of 1939–45, OC Army Malaria Research Unit. Med. Advisory Cttee ODM, 1963–72. Tropical Med. Research Board, MRC, 1960–65, 1966–69; Cttees on Malaria and Abnormal Haemoglobins, 1960–69; Hon. Consulting Physician, Liverpool Royal Infirmary; Hon. Consultant in Trop. Med., RAF (Consultant 1964–76); Hon. Malariologist, Army, 1967–73; Adviser: Council for Health in Socio-economic Developments, Thailand, 1964–; Faculty Tropical Medicine, Bangkok, 1959–; Reg. Trop. Medicine and Public Health Project, SE Asian Ministers of Educn Orgn. Sec.-Gen., Council of Institutes of Tropical Medicine, Europe and USSR, 1969–72 (Hon. Life Pres., 1972–); Pres., Royal Society Tropical Medicine, 1969–71 (Vice-Pres., 1949–51 and 1957–59; Chalmers Gold Medal, 1951); Vis. Prof., Univ. of Alexandria, 1956; Lecture: Litchfield, Oxford, 1955; Maurice Bloch, Glasgow, 1969; Heath Clark, London, 1970; Craig, US Soc. Trop. Med., 1976; Justus Ström, Stockholm, 1980. Membre d'Honneur: de Soc. Belg. de Méd. Tropicale; Soc. de Pathologie Exotique, Paris; Hon. Member American, Canadian and German Socs of Tropical Medicine and Hygiene. Hon. Fellow: St Mark's Coll., 1956–; London Sch. of Hygiene and Tropical Med., 1980–. Hon. DSc Bangkok, 1966; MD (Emeritus) Athens, 1972. Le Prince Award and Medal, Soc. of Tropical Medicine, USA, 1954; Bernhard Nocht Medal (Hamburg), 1957; Mary Kingsley Medal, Liverpool Sch. of Trop. Med., 1973; Jubilee Medal, Swedish Med. Acad., 1980; Anniv. Plaque, Faculty of Trop. Medicine, Bangkok, 1980. Tritabhorn, Order of the White Elephant, Thailand, 1982. KLJ 1977. *Publications:* Pathological Processes in Malaria and Blackwater Fever, 1948; Clinical Tropical Diseases, 5th edn, 1970, to 8th edn 1984; Tropical Medicine for Nurses (with A. R. D. Adams), 1956, 5th edn (with H. M. Gilles), 1980; (with C. S. Leithead) Clinical Methods in Tropical Medicine, 1962; Exotic Diseases in Practice, 1965; (with H. M. Gilles) Management and Treatment of Diseases in the Tropics, 1970; One World, 1973; papers and articles in technical and scientific journals on various subjects. *Address:* 23 Eaton Road, Cressington Park, Liverpool L19 0PN. *T:* 051–427 1133; Department of Tropical Paediatrics, Liverpool School of Tropical Medicine, Liverpool L3 5QA. *T:* 051–708 9393. *Clubs:* Athenæum; Athenæum (Liverpool). *Died 2 April 1989.*

**MAELOR, Baron,** *cr* 1966 (Life Peer), of Rhosllanerchrugog; **Thomas William Jones;** JP (Chairman Ruabon Bench); *b* 10 Feb. 1898; *s* of James Jones, Wrexham; *m* 1928, Flossy, *d* of Jonathan Thomas, Birkenhead; one *s* one *d. Educ:* Poncian Boys' Sch.; Bangor Normal Coll. Began working life as a miner; became pupil teacher and went to Bangor Coll. Welfare Officer and Education Officer for Merseyside and North Wales Electricity Board in North Wales. MP (Lab) Merioneth, 1951–66; Formerly: Chairman North Wales Labour Federation; Chairman Wrexham Trades Council. *Address:* Ger-y-Llyn, Poncian, Wrexham, Clwyd. *Died 18 Nov. 1984.*

**MAGAREY, Sir (James) Rupert,** Kt 1980; FRCS, FRACS: Senior Visiting Consultant Surgeon, The Queen Elizabeth Hospital, Adelaide, 1979–84; *b* 21 Feb. 1914; *s* of Dr Rupert Eric Magarey and Elsie Emily (*née* Cowell); *m* 1940, (Catherine) Mary Gilbert; one *s* two *d* (and one *d* decd). *Educ:* St Peter's Coll., Adelaide; St Mark's Coll., Univ. of Adelaide (MB, BS 1938; MS 1951). FRCS 1949; FRACS 1950. Served War, RAAMC, 1939–46: despatches, Syria, 1941; Captain, subseq. Major; retd with rank of Lt-Col. Hon. Asst Surgeon, Royal Adelaide Hosp., 1950–58; Hon. Surgeon, 1958–70, and Sen. Vis. Surgeon, 1970–79, Queen Elizabeth Hosp., Adelaide. Pres., AMA, 1976–79 (Pres. SA Br., 1969–70); Mem. Ct of Examrs, RACS, 1960–; Hon. Fellow, Royal Aust. Coll. of Gen. Practitioners, 1978; Hon. Life Governor, Aust. Post-Grad. Fedn in Medicine, 1980. Silver Jubilee Medal, 1977. *Publications:* scientific articles in British Jl of Surgery and in Med. Jl of Australia. *Recreations:* music, the theatre, beef cattle breeding. *Address:* 78 Kingston Terrace, North Adelaide, SA 5006, Australia. *T:* 267 2159. *Clubs:* Adelaide (Adelaide); Royal Adelaide Golf (Seaton, Adelaide). *Died 13 Oct. 1990.*

**MAGEE, Reginald Arthur Edward,** CBE 1989; FRCSI, FRCOG; Consultant Gynaecologist, Belfast; President, Royal College of Surgeons in Ireland, 1986–88 (Vice-President, 1984–86); *b* 18 Aug. 1914; *s* of James and Ellen Magee; *m* 1945, Gwladys Susannah (*née* Chapman); two *d. Educ:* Campbell Coll., Belfast (Sen. Science Prizeman); Queen's Univ., Belfast (MB, BCh, BAO, 1937). FRCSI 1947; FRCOG 1963 (MRCOG 1947). Mem. Students' Rep. Council, QUB; Mem., Univ. Athletic Team; Prizeman, Diseases of Children, Royal Belfast Hosp. for Sick Children. Demonstr in Physiol., QUB; House Surgeon, later Resident Surg. Officer, Royal Victoria Hosp., Belfast; House Surg. and Asst in Plastic Surgery, N Staffs Royal Infirm.; House Surg., Royal Maternity Hosp., Belfast; Jun., later Sen. Tutor in Obs, QUB; Temp. Consultant Gen. Surgery, Belfast City Hosp.; Obstet. and Gynaecologist, Massereene Hosp., and Antrim and Newtownards Dist Hosp.; post-grad. studies, Radium Inst., Stockholm; Clin. Teacher in Obs and Gynae., Clin. Lectr and Examr, QUB; Sen. Obstet., Royal Maternity Hosp., Belfast, and Sen. Gynaecologist, Royal Victoria Hosp., Belfast, and Ulster Hosp., Belfast, 1948–79; Administrative Med. Officer, Royal Gp of Hospitals, Belfast, 1979–84. Vis. Professor: Univ. of Basrah; Univ. of Baghdad; Vis. Lectr, Univ. of Cairo. Mem., NI Council for Post-grad. Med. Educn. Formerly: Chairman: Gp Med. Adv. Cttee, Royal Hosps, Belfast; Computer Cttee, Royal Victoria Hosp.; Member: Council, Jt Nurses and Midwives Council (also Lectr); Management Cttee, Ulster Hosp., Belfast; Royal Maternity Hosp. Cttee; Standing Cttee of Convocation, QUB. NI Hospitals Authority: formerly Chairman: Policy and Planning Cttee; Nurses and Midwives Cttee; Grading Cttee; Grading Appeals Cttee; formerly Mem., Exec. Cttee. Councillor: RCSI, 1974–; RCOG, 1972–78; Mem., Inst. of Obs and Gynae., Royal Coll. of Physicians of Ireland; Fellow, Ulster Med. Soc. (formerly Mem. Council); Mem., Ulster Obstet. and Gynaecol Soc. (formerly Pres.). Chm., Unionist Party of NI; Official Unionist Mem. for S Belfast, NI Assembly, 1973: Mem., Cttee of Privileges, Cttee on Finance, and Cttee on Health and Social Services; Leader of Pro-Assembly Unionist Back Bench Cttee; Mem., Public Accounts Cttee, NI; Advisor, Sunningdale Conf., 1973. Mem. Senate, QUB, 1979–82. Pres., Old Campbellian Soc., 1979. Hon. FRACS, 1988. *Publications:* A Modern Record System of Obstetrics, 1963; A Computerised System of Obstetric Records, 1970; Royal Maternity Hospital Clinical Reports, and Ulster Hospital Clinical Reports, 1963–77; monographs on obstetric and gynaecological subjects; various hospital service reports. *Recreations:* riding, horse breeding, travel, photography. *Address:* Montpelier, 96 Malone Road, Belfast BT9 5HP. *T:* Belfast 666765. *Clubs:* Athenæum, Royal Over-Seas League, English-Speaking Union; Kildare Street and University (Dublin). *Died 16 Dec. 1989.*

**MAGILL, Sir Ivan Whiteside,** KCVO 1960 (CVO 1946); FRCS 1951; FFARCS; MB, BCh, Belfast, 1913; DA 1935; formerly Hon. Consulting Anæsthetist, Westminster, Brompton and St Andrew's, Dollis Hill, Hospitals; *b* Larne, 1888; *s* of Samuel Magill; *m* 1916, Edith (*d* 1973), *d* of Thomas Robinson Banbridge. *Educ:* Larne Grammar Sch.; Queen's Univ., Belfast. Formerly: Consultant Army, Navy, EMS; Senior Anæsthetist, Queen's Hospital, Sidcup; Anæsthetist, Seamens Hospital, Greenwich; Res. MO, Stanley Hospital, Liverpool; Examiner, DA; Robert Campbell Memorial Orator, Belfast, 1939; Bengué Memorial Lecturer, Royal Institute of Public Health, 1950; Hon. Member: Liverpool Medical Institution; American Society of Anæsthesiologists; New York State Society of Anæsthesiologists; British Assoc. of Plastic Surgeons; Canadian Society of Anæsthetists; Hon. Fellow: Royal Society of Medicine, 1956; Faculty of Anæsthetists, Royal College of Surgeons, 1958; Assoc. of Anæsthetists of Great Britain and Ireland, 1958; Hon. FFARCSI, 1961. Henry Hill Hickman Medal, 1938; John Snow Medal, 1958; Canadian Anæsthetists Society Medal, 1963; Medal, American Assoc. of Plastic Surgeons, 1965; Gillies Mem. Lecturer, British Assoc. of Plastic Surgeons, 1965; Ralph M. Waters Prize, Chicago, 1966. Hon. DSc, Belfast, 1945. Frederic Hewitt Lecturer for 1965. *Publications:* contributions and chapters in various medical journals. *Recreation:* trout fishing. *Address:* c/o Royal Bank of Scotland, Holts Branch, Kirkland House, Whitehall, SW1. *Died 25 Nov. 1986.*

**MAGNUS, Hilary Barrow,** TD; QC 1957; Social Security (formerly National Insurance) Commissioner, 1964–82; *b* 3 March 1909; *yr s* of late Laurie Magnus, 34 Cambridge Square, W2; *b* and *heir-pres.* to Sir Philip Magnus-Allcroft, 2nd Bt; *m* 1950, Rosemary, *d* of G. H. Masefield and *widow* of Quentin Hurst; one *s* one *d* and one step *s. Educ:* Westminster; Christ Church, Oxford. Barrister, Lincoln's Inn, 1933 (Bencher, 1963; Treasurer, 1982). Served War of 1939–45, Rifle Brigade TA (Lieut–Colonel). JP (Kent) 1948. *Recreations:*

reading, gardening. *Address:* Cragmore House, Church Street, Wye, Ashford, Kent TN25 5BJ. *T:* Wye 812036; 3 Temple Gardens, EC4. *T:* 01–353 7884. *Clubs:* Garrick, Beefsteak.
*Died 15 Jan.* 1987.

**MAGNUS-ALLCROFT, Sir Philip,** 2nd Bt, *cr* 1917; CBE 1971; MA; FRSL; FRHistS; author; *b* 8 Feb. 1906; *er s* of late Laurie Magnus and Dora, *e d* of late Sir I. Spielman, CMG; *S* grandfather, Sir Philip Magnus, 1st Bt, 1933; *m* 1943, Jewell Allcroft, Stokesay Court, Onibury, Shropshire, *d* of late Herbert Allcroft and of Mrs John Rotton. Formally assumed surname of Allcroft (in addition to that of Magnus), 1951. *Educ:* Westminster Sch.; Wadham Coll., Oxford. Civil Service, 1928–32 and 1946–50. Served War of 1939–45 in Royal Artillery and Intelligence Corps (Iceland and Italy); Major. CC 1952, CA 1968–74, Salop (Chairman, Planning Cttee, 1962–74; formerly: Chm., Records Cttee; Vice-Chm., Educn Cttee); Chairman of Governors, Attingham Coll.; JP Salop, 1953–71 (Chm., Juvenile Ct). Trustee, National Portrait Gall., 1970–77. Mem., Mercia Regional Cttee, Nat. Trust, 1973–81. Governor, Ludlow Grammar Sch., 1952–77. *Publications:* (as Philip Magnus): Life of Edmund Burke, 1939; Selected Prose of Edmund Burke (with Introduction), 1948; Sir Walter Raleigh, 1951 (revised edns, 1956, 1968); Gladstone—A Biography, 1954; Kitchener—Portrait of an Imperialist, 1958 (revised edn, 1968); King Edward the Seventh, 1964. *Recreations:* travel, gardening. *Heir:* nephew Laurence Henry Philip Magnus [*b* 24 Sept. 1955; *m* 1983, Jocelyn, *d* of Robin Stanton; one *s*]. *Address:* Stokesay Court, Onibury, Craven Arms, Shropshire SY7 9BD. *T:* Bromfield 372 and 394. *Clubs:* Brooks's, Pratt's.
*Died 21 Dec.* 1988.

**MAGUINNES, Prof. William Stuart;** Professor of Latin Language and Literature, University of London, King's College, 1946–71, now Emeritus; Senior Research Fellow, 1971–72; Head of Department of Classics, 1952–72; General Editor, Methuen's Classical Texts; Vice-President, Classical Association, Orbilian Society, Virgil Society and London Classical Society; *b* 12 Oct. 1903; *s* of George J. Maguinness, Belfast; *m* 1933, Olive D., *d* of George T. Y. Dickinson, Sheffield; one *d*. *Educ:* Royal Belfast Academical Institution; Trinity Coll., Dublin (Classical Sizarship, Classical Foundation Scholarship; Sen. Moderatorships with Gold Medals in Classics and Modern Literature (French and Italian) and Univ. Studentship in Classics 1926; MA 1929). FKC 1966. Asst Lecturer in Classics, University of Manchester, 1927–30; Lecturer in Classics, University of Sheffield, 1930–46; Administrative Officer, Admiralty, 1941–43; Visiting Lecturer in various Universities in France, Holland, Italy, Brazil, Poland and Greece. Hon. Fellow, Polish Acad. *Publications:* contributions on Classical subjects to the Oxford Classical Dictionary, Encyclopædia Britannica, Proc. Leeds Philosophical Society, Classical Review, Classical Quarterly, Revue de la Franco-ancienne, Wiener humanistische Blätter, Rivista di Cultura classica e medioevale, Phoenix, Aevum, Antiquité classique, Estudios Clásicos, Notes and Queries, Vita Latina, various Actes de Congrès, Hermathena and other journals, 1928–; Edition: of Racine's Bérénice, 1929 (2nd edn, 1956); of Virgil's Aeneid, Book XII, 1953 (3rd edn, 1973); 4th (revised) edn of Stobart's Grandeur that was Rome (in collaboration with H. H. Scullard), 1961; Index to the Speeches of Isaeus (in collaboration with the late W. A. Goligher), 1964; English translation of P. Grimal's La Civilisation romaine, 1963, and F. Chamoux' La Civilisation grecque, 1965; Chapter in volume on Lucretius, 1965. *Address:* 25 Hillway, Highgate, N6. *T:* 01-340 3064.
*Died 17 Nov.* 1982.

**MAGUIRE, Meredith Francis, (Frank Maguire); MP** (Ind) Fermanagh and South Tyrone, since Oct. 1974; publican, Frank's Bar, Lisnaskea; *b* 1929; *m*; three *s* one *d*. *Educ:* St Mary's Marist Brothers Sch., Athlone. Joined uncle in business in Lisnaskea, later forming own company. *Address:* House of Commons, SW1A 0AA.
*Died 5 March* 1981.

**MAHLER, Kurt,** FAA 1965; FRS 1948; PhD, DSc; Professor Emeritus, Australian National University, since 1975; *b* 1903. *Educ:* Univs of Frankfurt and Göttingen. Research work at Univs of Göttingen, Groningen, and Manchester. Asst Lecturer at Manchester Univ., 1937–39, 1941–44; Lecturer, 1944–47; Senior Lecturer, 1948–49; Reader, 1949–52; Prof. of Mathematical Analysis, 1952–63; Prof. of Mathematics, Institute of Advanced Studies, ANU, 1963–68; Prof. of Mathematics, Ohio State Univ., USA, 1968–72. De Morgan Medal, 1971; Thomas Ranken Lyle Medal, 1977. *Publications:* Lectures on Diophantine Approximations, 1961; Introduction to p-adic Numbers and their Functions, 1973, 2nd edn 1980; Lectures on Transcendental Numbers, 1976; papers on different subjects in pure mathematics (Theory and Geometry of Numbers) in various journals, from 1928. *Recreations:* Chinese, photography. *Address:* Mathematics Department, Institute of Advanced Studies, Australian National University, Canberra, PO Box 4, ACT 2601, Australia.
*Died 25 Feb.* 1988.

**MAHON, Sir George Edward John,** 6th Bt, *cr* 1819; *b* 22 June 1911; *s* of 5th Bt and late Hon. Edith Dillon, 2nd *d* of 4th Lord Clonbrock;

*S* father, 1926; *m* 1st, 1938, Audrey Evelyn (*d* 1957), *o c* of late Dr Walter Jagger and late Mrs Maxwell Coote; two *s* one *d*; 2nd, 1958, Suzanne, *d* of late Thomas Donnellan, Pirbright, Surrey, and late Mrs Donnellan; one *d*. *Heir:* s Col William Walter Mahon, Irish Guards [*b* 4 Dec. 1940; *m* 1968, Rosemary Jane, *yr d* of Lt-Col M. E. Melvill, West Linton, Peebles-shire; one *s* two *d*]. *Address:* 7 Waltham Terrace, Blackrock, Co. Dublin. *T:* Dublin 880473.
*Died 16 Dec.* 1987.

**MAHON, Sir Gerald MacMahon,** Kt 1962; Chairman, Medical Appeal Tribunals under Industrial Injuries Acts, 1964–76; *b* 24 July 1904; *o* surv. *s* of late Foster MacMahon Mahon, and of Mrs Lilian Frances Mahon, OBE (*née* Moore), Sheringham, Norfolk; *m* 1938, Roma Irene Maxtone Mailer; two *s*. *Educ:* Alleyn Court Preparatory Sch., Dulwich Coll.; Brasenose Coll., Oxford (BA). Called to the Bar (Inner Temple), 1928. Resident Magistrate, Tanganyika, 1936; Judge, HM High Court of Tanganyika Territory, 1949–59; Chief Justice of Zanzibar, 1959–64, retired. *Address:* The Plough House, Stratton Audley, Bicester, Oxon. *Club:* Vincent's (Oxford).
*Died 6 April* 1982.

**MAHON, Simon;** *b* 1914; *s* of late Alderman Simon Mahon, OBE, JP, Bootle, Liverpool; *m* 1941, Veronica Robertshaw. *Educ:* St James Elementary Sch.; St Joseph's Coll. Served War of 1939–45; commissioned Royal Engineers. Alderman of Bootle Borough Council; Mayor, 1962. MP (Lab) Bootle, 1955–1979; Opposition Whip, 1959–61. Trustee, Far Eastern Prisoners of War Fund. Freeman, Borough of Bootle, 1974. KCSG 1968; KHS 1977. *Address:* Greenrushes, 34 Princes Avenue, Great Crosby, Liverpool.
*Died 19 Oct.* 1986.

**MAHONY, Lt-Col John Keefer,** VC 1944; *b* 30 June 1911; *s* of Joseph Jackson and Louise Mary Mahony; *m* 1950, Bonnie Johnston, Ottawa; two *d*. *Educ:* Duke of Connaught Sch., New Westminster, BC, Canada. On editorial staff of Vancouver Daily Province (newspaper) until outbreak of war of 1939–45; mem. Canadian Militia (equivalent of British Territorials) from 1936 until going on active service in Sept. 1939. Served War of 1939–45 (VC): (Canada, UK, Africa, Italy) Westminster Regt, Canadian Army; Major, 1943. Liaison Officer, US Dept of the Army, Washington, DC, 1954; retd as AA and QMG, Alberta Area, 1963. Exec. Dir, Junior Achievement of London, Inc. *Recreations:* swimming, lacrosse, baseball. *Address:* 657 Santa Monica Road, London, Ontario, Canada.
*Died 15 Dec.* 1990.

**MAHTAB, Maharajadhiraja Bahadur Sir Uday Chand, of Burdwan,** KCIE 1945; *b* 1905; *s* of late Maharajadhiraja Bahadur Sir Bijay Chand Mahtab of Burdwan, GCIE, KCSI, IOM; *m* 1929, Radharani Devi, Amritsar, Punjab; three *s* three *d*. *Educ:* Presidency Coll., Calcutta; Calcutta Univ. (BA 1926). Pres. Non-Muslim block of Bengal Partition meeting, June 1947; Mem., Constituent Assembly. MLA Bengal, 1937–52; is a Zemindar; a Mem. of Damodar Canal Enquiry Cttee, 1938, and of Select Cttee on Calcutta Municipal (amendment) Bill, 1940; Chm. of Burdwan District Flood Relief and Bengal Central Flood Relief Cttees, 1943–44, of Indian Red Cross Appeal (Bengal), 1943–46, of Calcutta War Cttee, 1943–46, and of Damodar Flood Control Enquiry Cttee, 1944; a Mem. of Bengal Tanks Improvement Bill Select Cttee, 1944, of Advisory Cttee to examine cases of Terrorist Convicts in Bengal, 1944, of W Bengal Forest Denudation Enquiry Cttee, 1944, and of Select Cttee on Bengal Agricultural Income Tax Bill, 1944; Pres., British Indian Association; Mem., Central Jute Board, 1951–52; Dir of over 30 business firms and Chm. of several Boards. Mem. of Managing Body of several Government Organisations. Silver Jubilee (1935) and Coronation (1937) medals. *Address:* The Palace, Burdwan, India; Bijay Manzil, Alipore, Calcutta. *Clubs:* Calcutta (Calcutta); Aftab (Burdwan); Gymkhana (Darjeeling).
*Died 10 Oct.* 1984.

**MAIDMENT, Kenneth John,** MA; Emeritus Fellow, Merton College, Oxford; Vice-Chancellor, University of Auckland, 1957–71; *b* 29 Oct. 1910; *s* of Francis George Maidment and Jessie Louisa Taylor; *m* 1937, Isobel Felicity, *d* of Archibald Leitch; one *s* three *d*. *Educ:* Bristol Gram. Sch.; Merton Coll., Oxford. Hertford Scholar, 1929; First Class Classical Hon. Mods, 1930; Craven Scholar, 1930; First Class Litt. Hum., 1932; Junior Research Fellow, Merton Coll., 1932–34; Fellow and Classical Tutor, Jesus Coll. (Oxford), 1934–38; Fellow and Classical Tutor, Merton Coll., 1938–49; Oxford and Bucks Lt Infantry, 1940; seconded War Office, 1941; liaison duties in US, 1942–45, Lt-Col; University Lecturer in Greek Literature, 1947–49; Principal, Auckland Univ. Coll., 1950–57. Governor, Bristol Grammar Sch., 1972–79. Hon. LLD Auckland. *Publications:* critical edition and translation of Antiphon and Andocides (Loeb Library), 1940; contribs to classical journals. *Address:* 9 Highfield Avenue, Headington, Oxford OX3 7LR.
*Died 3 Oct.* 1990.

**MAINGOT, Rodney M. Honor,** TC 1976; FRCS; Surgeon and writer; Consulting Surgeon: Royal Free Hospital, Royal Waterloo Hospital, Southend General Hospital, Royal Prince Alfred Hospital, Sydney; late Regional Consultant in Surgery, Emergency Medical Service;

Fellow, Surgical Section, RSM (late President); Fellow, Association of Surgeons of Great Britain and Ireland; Editor-in-Chief, British Journal of Clinical Practice; *b* Trinidad, BWI, 1893; *m* Rosalind Smeaton (*d* 1957), Brisbane, Australia; *m* 1965, Evelyn Plesch, London. *Educ:* Ushaw Coll., Durham. House Surg. (twice), Surgical Receiving Officer and Chief Asst to a Surgical Unit, St Bartholomew's Hospital; Surgical Registrar, West London Hospital. Visiting Professor in Surgery: Ohio State Univ. Hosp., 1960; Mount Sinai Hosp., Miami, 1963; Maadi Hosp., Cairo, 1967–68. Served War of 1914–18 (Captain RAMC) in Egypt and Palestine (despatches twice). Editor-in-Chief, Brit. Jl of Clinical Practice. Sydney Body Gold Medallist, 1958. *Publications:* Post Graduate Surgery, 1936; Technique of Gastric Operations, 1941; The Surgical Treatment of Gastric and Duodenal Ulcer, 1945; Techniques in British Surgery, 1950; The Management of Abdominal Operations, 2nd edn 1957; Abdominal Operations, 7th edn 1980; The Relationship of Art and Medicine, 1974; contributor to Surgery of the Gallbladder and Bile Ducts, ed Smith and Sherlock, 1964, also in Operative Surgery, 2nd ed Rob and Smith, 1969; Dr Frank H. Lahey Memorial Lecture in Boston, 1963. *Recreations:* painting, art, travelling, writing. *Address:* 8 Ashley Court, Grand Avenue, Hove, Sussex BN3 2NP. *Died 3 Jan. 1982.*

**MAINLAND, Prof. William Faulkner,** MA; Professor of German, University of Sheffield, 1953–70; *b* 31 May 1905; *s* of late George Mainland and of Ada (*née* Froggatt); *m* 1930, Clarice Vowles, *d* of late A. E. Brewer; no *c*. *Educ:* George Heriot's Sch.; Univ. of Edinburgh. 1st Class Hons. Vans Dunlop Schol. in German; Postgrad. studies in London under late Prof. J. G. Robertson, and in Germany. Asst for French and German at London Sch. of Economics, 1929–30; thereafter attached to German Depts of Univs of: Manitoba, 1930; Manchester, 1935; London (UC, 1937, King's Coll., 1938, Birkbeck Coll., 1938); Sheffield, 1946; Leeds, 1947. Voluntary evening tutor in German, HM Prison, Wormwood Scrubs, 1938; Public Orator, Univ. of Sheffield, 1968–70. *Publications:* German for Students of Medicine, 1938; German Lyrics of the Seventeenth Century (with Prof. August Closs), 1941; E. T. A. Hoffmann, Der goldene Topf (Editor), 1942, 2nd edn, 1945; Schiller, Uber naive und sentimentalische Dichtung (Editor), 1951; Schiller and the Changing Past, 1957; Wilhelm Tell in metrical translation with commentary, 1972; chapters on Th. Storm, H. Sudermann, Fr. v. Unruh, H. Kasack, in German Men of Letters, 1961–66; Schiller, Jungfrau v. Orleans (Editor with Prof. E. J. Engel), 1963; Schiller, Wilhelm Tell (Editor), 1968. Reviews and articles on German and Dutch literature. *Recreations:* drawing, painting; Lithuanian language studies. *Address:* Apt 3, 46 Sale Hill, Sheffield S10 5BX. *T:* Sheffield 665759. *Club:* University Staff (Sheffield). *Died 31 March 1988.*

**MAIR, Prof. Lucy Philip;** Professor of Applied Anthropology, London School of Economics, 1963–68; *b* 28 Jan. 1901; *d* of David Beveridge Mair and Jessy Philip. *Educ:* St Paul's Girls' Sch.; Newnham Coll., Cambridge (Hon. Fellow, 1982). London Sch. of Economics: Asst Lectr, 1927; Lectr, 1932; Reader, 1946; Prof., 1963; Hon. Fellow 1975. Australian Land Headquarters Civil Affairs Sch., 1945–46; Lugard Memorial Lectr, Internat. African Inst., 1958; Gildersleeve Visiting Prof. Barnard Coll., Columbia Univ., 1965; Frazer Lecture, Cambridge, 1967; Hon. Prof. of Social Anthropology, Univ. of Kent, 1974–79. Vice-Pres., Royal Anthropological Inst., 1978–79 (Hon. Sec., 1974–78; Wellcome Medal 1936). Hon. DLitt: Durham, 1972; Kent, 1980. *Publications:* An African People in the Twentieth Century, 1934; Native Policies in Africa, 1936; Australia in New Guinea, 1948, 2nd edn 1971; Primitive Government, 1962; New Nations, 1963; An Introduction to Social Anthropology, 1966, 2nd edn 1972; The New Africa, 1967; Witchcraft, 1969; Marriage, 1971; African Societies, 1974; African Kingdoms, 1977; contribs to Africa, Cahiers d'Etudes Africaines, etc. *Address:* 19 Hallgate, Blackheath Park, SE3 9SG. *T:* 01-852 8531.

*Died 1 April 1986.*

**MAITLAND, Air Vice-Marshal Percy Eric,** CB 1945; CBE 1951; MVO 1935; AFC 1918; *b* 26 Oct. 1895; *s* of Surgeon-Captain P. E. Maitland, Royal Navy; *m* 1927, Alison Mary Kettlewell; six *s*. *Educ:* RN Coll., Osborne and Dartmouth. Royal Navy, 1908–18, attached RNAS 1915 for Airships (AFC); transferred to Royal Air Force 1918 as Captain; specialised in Navigation. Served in Egypt and Iraq; Navigator in Far East Flight to Australia, 1928–29; Staff Officer for Royal Review, 1935 (MVO); Singapore, 1937–39, promoted Group Captain; Flying Training Command, 1939–40; Bomber Command, 1940–43; Air Ministry, Director of Operational Training, 1943; AOC No 2 Group, BAOR, 1945; AOC, No 84 Group, BAOR, 1945–47; AOC No 22 Group; Technical Training Command, 1948–50; retired, 1950. JP Somerset, 1952. *Recreation:* fishing. *Address:* 60 Station Road, Wallingford OX10 0JZ. *T:* Wallingford 38921. *Died 22 Aug. 1985.*

**MAITLAND-TITTERTON, Major David Maitland,** TD 1947; Marchmont Herald of Arms to Court of Lord Lyon, since 1982; *b* 8 Aug. 1904; *s* of Rev. Charles Henry Titterton and Anna Louise, *d*

of Rear-Adm. Lewis Maitland; *m* 1929, Mary Etheldritha (*d* 1987), *y d* of Senator Rt Hon. James Graham Leslie, sometime HM Lieutenant, Co. Antrim; two *s*. *Educ:* Queens' Coll., Cambridge (MA). Commissioned, 1924; Ayrshire Yeo., 1926; Asst Dist Officer, Political Service, Nigeria, 1927–32; Instructor, 124 OCTU, Llandrindod Wells, 1939; served War of 1939–45; Major 1942; comd School of Artillery, Nigeria, 1943; Liaison Officer with Polish Army, 1944; Staff Officer with 51 Highland Div., 1954–63. Falkland Pursuivant Extraordinary, 1969–71; Ormond Pursuivant, 1971–84. Grand Juror, Co. of Londonderry, 1939. OStJ. Knight Grand Cross, Order of St Lazarus. *Recreations:* racing, books, print collecting. *Address:* Moberty, Craigton of Airlie, by Kirriemuir, Angus DD8 5NW. *T:* Craigton 249. *Clubs:* Cavalry and Guards (Life Mem.); Puffin's (Edinburgh) (Life Mem.). *Died 5 Dec. 1988.*

**MAKIN, Frank;** Chief Inspector, Department of Education and Science, 1976–79; *b* 29 Oct. 1918; *s* of Tom Kay Makin and Phyllis H. Makin (*née* Taylor); *m* 1949, Marjorie Elizabeth Thomasson; three *d*. *Educ:* Bolton Municipal Secondary Sch.; Corpus Christi Coll., Cambridge (MA). Asst Master, Cheadle Hulme Sch., Burnley Grammar Sch., and Stretford Grammar Sch., 1941–56; Headmaster, South Hunsley Co. Secondary Sch., Yorks, 1956–62; HM Inspector of Schools, 1962–; Divisional Inspector, 1970–76. *Recreations:* languages, gardening. *Address:* 127 Hookfield, Epsom KT19 8JH. *T:* Epsom 40872. *Died 24 Dec. 1984.*

**MAKIN, Hon. Norman John Oswald;** AO 1980; *b* Petersham, NSW, Australia, 31 March 1889; *s* of John Hulme Makin and Elizabeth Makin; *m* 1932, Ruby Florence Jennings; two *s*. *Educ:* Superior Public Sch., Broken Hill. Member Commonwealth Parliament for Hindmarsh, 1919–46; Member Joint Cttee Public Accounts, 1922–26; Member Select Cttee case ex-Gunner Yates; Temp. Chairman of Cttees, 1923–29; Speaker House of Representatives, Commonwealth of Australia, 1929–32; Member Advisory War Council, 1940; Ministry for Navy and Munitions, Australia, 1941–46; Minister for Aircraft Production, 1945–46. Australian Ambassador to United States, 1946–51. MP for Sturt, 1954–Nov. 1955, for Bonython Division, Dec. 1955–Nov. 1963, Commonwealth Parliament; retired. President Labour Party, 1936; Secretary Federal Parliamentary Labour Party, 1931; Member of Delegation to United Kingdom, King George V Jubilee in 1935 and to King George VI Coronation in 1937; 1st President of Security Council, Jan. 1946, and President, 1947; Leader, Australian Delegation to United Nations; Leader, Australian Delegation to ILO Conference, San Francisco. Alternate Governor, International Bank and International Monetary Fund; Member, Far Eastern Commn, 1947–48. Hon. Doctor of Laws, Univ. of Syracuse. *Publications:* A Progressive Democracy; Federal Labour Leaders, 1961. *Address:* Flat 219, 7 Raymond Grove, Glenelg, SA 5045, Australia.

*Died 20 July 1982.*

**MALAMUD, Bernard;** writer; Member, Division of Literature, Bennington College, since 1961; *b* 26 April 1914; *s* of Max and Bertha Malamud; *m* 1945, Ann de Chiara; one *s* one *d*. *Educ:* The City Coll., New York; Columbia Univ. Taught at Oregon State Coll., 1949–61, while writing first four books. Visiting Lecturer, Harvard Univ., 1966–68. Partisan Review Fiction Fellowship, 1956; Ford Foundation Fellowship, Humanities and Arts Program, 1959–60; Member: Amer. Acad. and Institute of Arts and Letters, 1964; American Academy of Arts and Sciences, 1967; Pres., Amer. PEN Center, 1979–81. Governor's Award for Excellence in The Arts, Vermont Council on the Arts, 1979; Creative Arts Award for Fiction, Brandeis Univ.; Gold Medal for Fiction, Amer. Acad. and Inst., 1983. *Publications:* The Natural, 1952; The Assistant, 1957 (Rosenthal Prize, Daroff Memorial Award, 1958); The Magic Barrel (short stories), 1958 (National Book Award, 1959); A New Life, 1961; Idiots First (short stories), 1963; The Fixer, 1966 (National Book Award and Pulitzer Prize for Fiction, 1967); Pictures of Fidelman, 1969; The Tenants, 1971; Rembrandt's Hat (short stories), 1973; Dubin's Lives, 1979; God's Grace, 1982; The Short Stories of Bernard Malamud, 1983; *posthumous publication:* The People and Uncollected Stories, 1990. *Recreations:* the usual. *Address:* c/o Russell and Volkening, 551 Fifth Avenue, New York, NY 10017, USA. *Died 18 March 1986.*

**MALCOLM, Lt-Col Arthur William Alexander,** CVO 1954 (MVO 1949); *b* 31 May 1903; *s* of Major Charles Edward Malcolm, London; *heir-pres.* to cousin, Sir David Malcolm, 11th Bt; *m* 1928, Hester Mary, *d* of S. F. Mann, Lawrenny-Caramut, Victoria, Australia; two *s*. *Educ:* Repton. 2nd Lieut, Welsh Guards, 1924; psc 1938; served War of 1939–45 (POW); Lieut-Colonel, 1945; comd 3rd, 2nd and 1st Bn, Welsh Guards, 1945–49. ADC to Governor of Victoria, Australia, 1926–28. Asst Military Attaché, British Embassy, Paris, 1950–52; retired from Army, 1952. Private Secretary to Governor of South Australia, 1953–55; Queen's Foreign Service Messenger, 1955–68. *Recreation:* golf. *Address:* Faraway, Sandwich Bay, Kent. *T:* Sandwich 612054. *Clubs:* Army and Navy; Royal St George's Golf, Prince's Golf (Sandwich).

*Died 18 March 1989.*

**MALCOLM, Kenneth Robert,** CBE 1964; *b* 17 Dec. 1908; 2nd *s* of Ronald Malcolm, Walton Manor, Walton-on-the-Hill, Surrey; *m* 1950, Iris Lilian Knowles; two *s* one *d*. *Educ:* Eton; New College, Oxford. Indian Civil Service, 1932–47; Home Civil Service (Ministry of National Insurance, subseq. Dept of Health and Social Security), 1947–73; Under-Sec., 1969, retd 1973. *Address:* Ferndale, Dry Arch Road, Sunningdale, Ascot, Berks SL5 0DB. *T:* Ascot 22946. *Club:* Travellers'.
*Died* 3 *Oct.* 1984.

**MALENKOV, Georgi Maximilianovich;** Manager of Ust-Kamenogorsk Hydro-Electric Station, 1957–63, retired; *b* Orenburg, 8 Jan. 1902; *m* 1st (marr. diss.); 2nd, Elena Khrushcheva. *Educ:* Moscow Higher Technical Coll. Member of the Communist Party, 1920–; Member of Organisation Bureau and Sec., Central Cttee of the Communist Party, 1939; Member Cttee for State Defence, 1941; Member Cttee for Economic Rehabilitation of Liberated Districts, 1943; Dep.-Chairman, Council of Ministers, 1946; Dep.-Chairman, Council of Ministers of the Soviet Union, 1955–57 (Dep.-Chairman, 1946, Chairman, 1953–55); Minister of Electric Power Stations, 1955–57. Holds title Hero of Socialist Labour, Hammer and Sickle Gold Medal, Order of Lenin (twice). *Died* 14 *Jan.* 1988.

**MALET, Colonel Sir Edward William St Lo,** 8th Bt, *cr* 1791; OBE 1953; 8th King's Royal Irish Hussars; retired; *b* 27 Nov. 1908; *o s* of Sir Harry Charles Malet, DSO, OBE, 7th Bt and Mildred Laura (*d* 1951), *d* of Captain H. S. Swiney, Gensing House, St Leonards; *S* father, 1931; *m* 1935, Baroness Benedicta Maasburg (*d* 1979), *e d* of Baron William von Maasburg; one *s* two *d*. *Educ:* Dover Coll.; Christ Church, Oxford. BA. Dep.-Chief Civil Affairs Officer, HQ, British Troops, Egypt, 1953–55. President Bridgwater Division, Conservative Assoc., 1959. High Sheriff of Somerset, 1966. *Heir: s* Harry Douglas St Lo Malet, late Lieut, The Queen's Royal Irish Hussars, now Special Reserve [*b* 26 Oct. 1936; *m* 1967, Julia Harper, Perth, WA; one *s*. *Educ:* Downside; Trinity Coll., Oxford]. *Address:* Chargot, Washford, Somerset. *Club:* Cavalry and Guards.
*Died* 9 *Oct.* 1990.

**MALHERBE, Ernst G.,** MA, PhD; Hon. LLD Universities of: Cambridge, Queen's (Kingston, Ont), Melbourne, McGill, Capetown, Rhodes, Natal, Witwatersrand, St Andrews; Principal and Vice-Chancellor, University of Natal, Pietermaritzburg and Durban, 1945–65; *b* OFS, 8 Nov. 1895; *s* of late Rev. E. G. Malherbe, Villiersdorp, Cape Province, French Huguenot descent; *m* Janie A., *d* of Rev. Paul Nel, Moderator of Dutch Reformed Church, Transvaal; three *s* one *d*. *Educ:* Stellenbosch Univ., Stellenbosch, CP (BA, Hons, MA in Philosophy); Columbia Univ., New York (MA and PhD in Education). Union Government Scholarship for 2 years to study Education overseas; Oxford, The Hague, Amsterdam, Germany, etc.; 3 years in succession H. B. Webb Research Scholar for overseas Research in Educational Administration; Fellow of Teachers Coll., Columbia Univ., 1923–34; Chalmers Memorial Prize for Essay on Educational Administration, 1923; invited as special SA representative to Centenary meeting of British Assoc., London, 1931; teacher at Cape Town Training Coll.; Lecturer in Educational Psychology, University of Stellenbosch; Senior Lecturer in Education, University of Cape Town, 5 years; Chief Investigator Education Section Carnegie Poor White Commission of Research, 1928–32; Member of Government Commission to investigate Native Education in South Africa, 1935; Director, National Bureau of Educational and Social Research for SA, 1929–39; Sec. Government Commission on Medical Training in S Africa, 1938. Director of Census and Statistics for Union of South Africa, 1939–40; (Lieut-Col) Director of Military Intelligence, S African Army and Director Army Education Services, 1940–45. Member of Social and Economic Planning Council, 1946–50; of National Council for Social Research, 1945–50; Chairman National War Histories Cttee, 1945–49; President SA Assoc. for the Advancement of Science, 1950–51; President SA Institute of Race Relations, 1966–67; Mem., Govt Commn on Financial Relations between Central Govt and Provinces, 1960–64. Simon Biesheuvel Medal for Study of Man, 1969. *Publications:* Education in S Africa, 1652–1922, 1925; Chapters on S Africa in Year-books of Education, 1932–56; Education and the Poor White, 1929; articles in Chambers's Encyclopædia, Standard Encyclopaedia for Southern Africa; numerous articles in Educational and Scientific Journals; Carnegie Commission's Poor White Report on Education, 1932; Education in a Changing Empire, 1932; Educational Adaptations in a Changing Society (Editor), 1937; Entrance Age of University Students in Relation to Success, 1938; Whither Matric?, 1938; Educational and Social Research in SA, 1939; The Bilingual School, 1943; Race Attitudes and Education, 1946; Our Universities and the Advancement of Science, 1951; The Autonomy of our Universities and Apartheid, 1957; Education for Leadership in Africa, 1960; Problems of School Medium in a Bilingual Country, 1962; Into the 70's: Education and the Development of South Africa's Human Resources, 1966; The Need for Dialogue, 1967; The Nemesis of Docility, 1968; Bantu Manpower and Education, 1969; Differing Values, 1973; Education in South Africa, 1923–1975, 1977; Never a Dull Moment, 1980.

*Recreations:* swimming; Full Blue, Stellenbosch University; Half Blue, Capetown University; captained Hockey Team representing CP at inter-provincial tournament. *Address:* By-die-See, Salt Rock, Umhlali, Natal, South Africa. *Club:* Durban (Durban).
*Died* 27 *Nov.* 1982.

**MALIK, Sardar Hardit Singh,** CIE 1941; OBE 1938; Indian Diplomat, retired, 1957; *b* 23 Nov. 1894; *s* of Malik Mohan Singh and Lajanwanti; *m* 1919, Prakash; one *s* two *d*. *Educ:* Eastbourne Coll.; Balliol Coll., Oxford, England. BA Hons in Mod. Hist., 1915. Served with French Army on Western Front, 1916. Fighter Pilot in RFC, 1917–18 (wounded in air combat over France, 1917); served in RAF, France, Italy and in home defence of UK. Entered ICS; Asst Commissioner, Punjab, 1922–23; Deputy Commissioner, Punjab, 1924–30; Dep. Trade Commissioner, London and Hamburg, 1931–34; Dep. Secretary Government of India, Commerce Dept, 1934–36; Joint Secretary, Government of India, Commerce Dept, 1937; Indian Government Trade Commissioner, New York, 1938; Delegate to International Cotton Conf., Washington, 1939, International Labour Office Conf., New York, 1940, UN Food Conf., Hotsprings, Virginia, 1943, and UN Relief Conf., Atlantic City, USA, 1943. Prime Minister, Patiala, 1944–47. Leader Indian States Industrial Delegation to UK and USA, 1945–46; represented Government of India at First and Second Sessions of Prep. Cttee of UN Conf. on Trade and Employment in London, Nov. 1946, and Geneva, April 1947, respectively. Leader Indian Delegation to UN Conf. on Trade and Employment, Havana, Nov. 1947; High Commissioner for India in Canada, 1947–49; Indian Ambassador to France, 1949–56, also Indian Minister to Norway, 1950–56. President, 3rd General Assembly of International Civil Aviation Organisation, Montreal, 1949; Leader of Indian Delegation to UN General Assembly, Paris, 1952. Grand Officier, Légion d'Honneur, 1954. *Recreations:* golf, cricket and tennis. *Address:* Palam Marg, New Delhi, India. *Clubs:* Imperial Gymkhana (New Delhi); Delhi Golf; Pine Valley Golf (USA). *Died Nov.* 1985.

**MALIM, Comdr David Wentworth,** RN retd; Director, Marconi Space & Defence Systems Ltd, retired 1982; *b* 28 April 1914; *s* of Frederick Blagden Malim and Amy Gertrude Malim; *m* 1939, Theodora Katharine Thackwell Lewis; one *s* two *d*. *Educ:* RNC, Dartmouth; RNEC, Keyham. Engineer Officer: HMS Cumberland, 1936–38; HMS Edinburgh, 1939–40; RNATE Torpoint, 1940–42; Ordnance Engineer Officer: HMS Warspite, 1943–44; HMS Excellent, 1944–46; Staff, BJSM, Washington, 1947–49; Naval Ordnance Dept, Admiralty, 1949–54; retd as Comdr (E) at own request. Laurence Scott & Electromotors Ltd, 1954–59; Manager, Lancashire Dynamo Co., 1959–61; Jt Man. Dir, Elliot Space & Weapon Automation Ltd, 1962–70; Chm., Marconi Space & Defence Systems Ltd, 1970–78. Pres., Electronic Engrg Assoc., 1975–76. *Recreation:* fishing. *Address:* Manor Mead, Great Chesterford, Saffron Walden, Essex CB10 1PL. *T:* Saffron Walden 30363.
*Died* 8 *Jan.* 1985.

**MALLABAR, Sir John (Frederick),** Kt 1969; FCA; Senior Partner, J. F. Mallabar & Co., Chartered Accountants, 1929–80; *b* 19 July 1900; *e s* of Herbert John Mallabar and Gertrude Mallabar, *d* of Hugh Jones, Barrow; *m* 1st, 1931, Henrietta, *d* of George Goodwin-Norris; 2nd, 1949, Annie Emily (Pat), *d* of Charles Mealing, Princes Risborough, and widow of Richard Howard Ford, Bodweni, Merionethshire; no *c*. *Educ:* privately, at Sunbury House Sch. An External Underwriting Member of Lloyd's. Chairman: Ruston & Hornby, 1964–66; Harland and Wolff Ltd, 1966–70; former Chairman: Franco-British Electrical Co.; Villiers Engrg Co.; Agricl Central Trading; NFU Seeds; Combined Telephone Hldgs; Kelvin Bergins; former Director: local Bd, Martins Bank; Plessey Co.; Chubb & Son; S. G. Warburg Finance & Develt; David Brown Corp. etc. Chm., Cttee on Govt Industrial Establishments, 1968–70. *Recreations:* stalking, salmon fishing. *Address:* 39 Arlington House, St James's, SW1. *Clubs:* Carlton, Flyfishers'.
*Died* 20 *Aug.* 1988.

**MALLET, Hooper Pelgué;** Commodore P&OSN Company, 1960–61, retired; *b* 4 June 1901; *s* of Wesley John Mallet and Harriet Anley; *m* 1932, Ethel Margaret Stewart (*d* 1972), Launceston, Tasmania; no *c*. *Educ:* Oxenford House Sch., Jersey; HMS Worcester. Royal Naval Reserve, 1918–19; joined P&OSN Co., 1919. *Recreations:* chess, bowls. *Address:* 9 Selworthy Avenue, Melbourne, Vic 3167, Australia. *Died* 12 *Jan.* 1985.

**MALLET, Sir (William) Ivo,** GBE 1960; KCMG 1951 (CMG 1945); retired as Ambassador to Spain (1954–60); *b* 7 April 1900; *yr s* of late Sir Charles Mallet; *m* 1929, Marie-Angèle (*d* 1985), *d* of Joseph Wierusz-Kowalski; two *s* one *d*. *Educ:* Harrow; Balliol Coll., Oxford. Entered Diplomatic Service, 1925. Served in Constantinople, Angora, London, Berlin, Rome; Asst Private Secretary to Secretary of State for Foreign Affairs, 1938–41; Acting Counsellor in FO, 1941; Counsellor, 1943; Consul-General, Tangier, 1946; Asst Under-Secretary, Foreign Office, 1949; HM Ambassador,

Belgrade, 1951. *Address:* Chalet La Combe, Rossinière, Vaud, Switzerland.
*Died* 7 *Dec.* 1988.

**MALLEY, Cecil Patrick;** late Aural Surgeon St Mary's Hospital for Women and Children, Plaistow, Acton Hospital and Hounslow Hospital; late Surgeon Metropolitan Ear, Nose and Throat Hospital, Fitzroy Square; *b* Castlebar, Co. Mayo, 5 April 1902; *s* of Luke Malley and Marrion Kearney; *m*; two *s* one *d. Educ:* O'Connell's Schools; University College, Dublin. MB, BCh, BAO, 1925; FRCS 1933; FICS. Late Resident Surgical Officer St Mary's Hospital, Plaistow; House Surgeon All Saints Hosp.; Aural Registrar Charing Cross Hosp.; Registrar Golden Square Hosp.; Senior Clinical Asst Metropolitan Ear, Nose and Throat Hospital; late Clinical Assistant Ear, Nose and Throat Dept, West London Hospital. *Publications:* Acute Mastoiditis, Otalgia Charing Cross Journal, Section on Larynx in Pye's Surgical Handicraft. *Recreations:* golf, yachting. *Address:* 4A Edificio Bolera, Ruiz Vertedoor, Fuengerola, Malaga, Spain. *Clubs:* Royal Thames Yacht, National University.
*Died* 21 *June* 1981.

**MALLINSON, Sir Paul;** *see* Mallinson, Sir W. P.

**MALLINSON, Col Sir Stuart Sidney,** Kt 1954; CBE 1938; DSO 1918; MC; DL; Hon. President, William Mallinson & Sons, Ltd, London (Director, 1912–44, Chairman and Managing Director, 1944–62); Hon. President, Mallinson & Denny Mott Ltd; President, Timber Research and Development Association, 1963–73; Director, Eastern Electricity Board, 1954; *b* 1888; *s* of Sir Wm Mallinson, 1st Bt; *m* 1916, Marjorie Gray, CBE 1960 (*d* 1969), *d* of late Rev. Alfred Soothill; two *s* (and one *s* killed in action, 1944, one *d* decd). *Educ:* Ashville Coll., Harrogate; Leys Sch., Cambridge. Entered the firm of Wm Mallinson & Sons, Ltd, 1907; joined HAC Aug. 1914; France, Sept. 1914; commissioned April 1915; MC June 1916; transferred to RE as Captain, Sept. 1916; Major, Dec. 1916; Lt-Col, March 1917; (DSO; despatches three times); Officier du Mérite Agricole, 1918; Hon. Colonel 28th Essex AA, 1937–45; Hon. Colonel 563 Regt (Essex) TA, RA, 1947–55; Hon. Colonel 517 Regt (5th Essex) RA, TA, 1955–57. Governor: Leys Sch., 1920; St Felix Sch., Southwold; Chigwell Sch.; Ashville Coll., Harrogate; Hon. Pres., Town and Country Building Soc.; Pres., Nat. Sunday School Union, 1923–24; Vice-Pres., English-Speaking Union of the Commonwealth; Pres., Commonwealth Forestry Soc. JP Essex; DL, Essex, 1937–66; High Sheriff of Essex, 1939; Chairman, Leyton Employment Exchange, 1931–38, 1951–63; DL Greater London, 1966–76; Sector Commander HG; Chairman Essex National Fitness Cttee; County War Welfare Officer; Chairman Essex Playing Fields Assoc., 1945; President Essex County Football Assoc., 1954; Dep. Pres., Hon. Soc. of Knights of the Round Table. OStJ 1951. *Recreations:* fishing, travel. *Address:* The White House, Woodford Green, Essex. *T:* 01-504 1234. *Clubs:* British Sportsman's, Royal Commonwealth Society, English-Speaking Union.
*Died* 30 *Oct.* 1981.

**MALLINSON, Sir (William) Paul,** 3rd Bt, *cr* 1935; MA, BM, BCh, FRCP; FRCPsych; Hon. Consulting Psychiatrist to St George's Hospital, SW1; Civilian Consultant Emeritus in Psychiatry to Royal Navy; Chairman, Wm Mallinson & Denny Mott Ltd, 1962–73; *b* 6 July 1909; *s* of Sir William Mallinson, 2nd Bt, and Mabel (*d* 1948), *d* of J. W. Rush, Tunbridge Wells; *S* father, 1944; *m* 1st, 1940, Eila Mary (marr. diss. 1968; she *d* 1985), *d* of Roland Graeme Guy, Hastings, NZ; one *s* two *d*; 2nd, 1968, Margaret Cooper Bowden, BA, MB, BS (served in FO during war, 1939–45), *d* of S. A. Bowden, Barnstaple, Devon. *Educ:* Westminster; Christ Church, Oxford; St Thomas's Hospital. Served RNVR, 1940–46, Surgeon Lieut-Commander. First class Order of the Family, Brunei, 1973. *Heir:* s William John Mallinson [*b* 8 Oct. 1942; *m* 1968, Rosalind Angela (marr. diss.), *o d* of Rollo Hoare, Dogmersfield, Hampshire; one *s* one *d*]. *Address:* 25 Wimpole Street, W1. *T:* 01-580 7919; Meadow Lea, Northclose Road, Bembridge, Isle of Wight. *T:* Isle of Wight 872239. *Clubs:* Athenæum, MCC; Royal Thames Yacht.
*Died* 18 *March* 1989.

**MALONE, Denis George Withers,** OBE 1967; retired as Governor, HM Prison, Dartmoor, (1960–66); lately, HM Prison Service; *b* 12 July 1906; *s* of Col William George Malone and Ida Katharine Withers; *m* 1935, Anita Cecilie Sophie Wolfermann. *Educ:* Douai Sch., Woolhampton, Berks. Asst Housemaster, Housemaster, Dep. Gov. (Gov. Cl. IV) and Gov. (Cl. III, II, I) Borstal and Prison Service of England and Wales, 1931–67; Seconded Foreign Office (German Section), Control Officer I and Sen. Control Officer, CCG Legal Div., Penal Branch, 1947–49; Seconded Colonial Office; Asst Commissioner, Prisons Dept, Kenya, 1950–54; Director of Prisons, Prisons Dept, Cyprus, 1958–60 (despatches). Vice-Pres., Kerikeri and Dist Beautifying Soc. *Recreations:* foreign travel and outdoor activities. *Address:* Kerikeri, Bay of Islands, Northland, New Zealand.
*Died* 19 *Oct.* 1983.

**MALVERN, Harry Ladyman,** CBE 1970; Managing Director of Remploy Ltd, 1964–73; *b* 4 June 1980; *s* of late Harry Arthur Malvern, Wirral, Cheshire; *m* 1935, Doreen, *d* of late John James

Peters; one *s* one *d. Educ:* Birkenhead Sch., Cheshire. FCA; FInstD. Joint Man. Dir, Spratts Patent Ltd, 1961–64. Pres., Cookham Soc., 1970–81; Mem. Exec. Cttee, Royal Assoc. for Disability and Rehabilitation, 1977–. *Recreations:* gardening, reading, archaeology. *Address:* Meadow Cottage, Hockett Lane, Cookham Dean, Berks SL6 9UF. *T:* Marlow 2043.
*Died* 11 *May* 1982.

**MAMOULIAN, Rouben;** stage and screen director; producer; author; *b* 8 Oct. 1897; *s* of Zachary Mamoulian and Virginia Kalantarian; *m* Azadia Newman, Washington, DC. *Educ:* Lycée Montaigne, Paris; Gymnasium, Tiflis; Univ., Moscow. First English production, Beating on the Door, at St James's Theatre, London, Nov. 1922; arrived in Rochester, New York, Aug. 1923; from that date to summer of 1926 was Director of Production at the Eastman Theatre, producing Grand Operas, Operettas, Dramas, and stage presentations, among which were the following: Carmen, Faust, Boris Godounoff, Shanewis, Gilbert and Sullivan Operettas, Sister Beatrice, etc; also organised and was Director of the Eastman Theatre Sch.; came to New York at the end of 1926; started there as a Director of the Theatre Guild Sch.; first production of a play on Broadway, 10 Oct. 1927, Porgy, for the Theatre Guild; Porgy was followed by direction of the following plays on Broadway: Marco Millions, Congai, Wings over Europe, These Modern Women, RUR, The Game of Love and Death, A Month in the Country, A Farewell to Arms, and Solid South; also an opera at the Metropolitan Opera House, Hand of Fate, with L. Stokowski and the Philadelphia Orchestra; Opera Porgy and Bess (music by George Gershwin) for Theatre Guild, New York, 1935; in Los Angeles and San Francisco, 1938. Directed following motion pictures: Applause 1928; City Streets and Dr Jekyll and Mr Hyde, 1932; Love Me Tonight, and Song of Songs, 1933; Queen Christina, 1933 and We Live Again, 1934; Becky Sharp (Technicolor), 1935; The Gay Desperado, 1936; High, Wide and Handsome, 1937; Golden Boy, 1939; The Mark of Zorro, 1940; Blood and Sand (Technicolor), 1941; Rings on Her Fingers, 1942; Summer Holiday (technicolor musical, based on Eugene O'Neill's Ah Wilderness), 1947; Silk Stockings (musical film, cinemascope, color) 1957. *Stage productions:* Oklahoma!, 1943; Sadie Thompson, 1944, and Carousel, 1945, St Louis Woman, 1946, musical dramas in New York; Lost In The Stars (musical tragedy), 1949; Arms And The Girl (musical play), 1950, New York; Oklahoma! (for Berlin Arts Festival), 1951; Adolph Zukor's Golden Jubilee Celebration, Hollywood, 1953; Carousel (New Prod.), Los Angeles and San Francisco, 1953; Oklahoma!, new production for Paris, Rome, Milan, Naples and Venice, 1955. Co-Author (with Maxwell Anderson) of musical play The Devil's Hornpipe (made musical film Never Steal Anything Small), 1959. World Première Perf. of Shakespeare's Hamlet, A New Version, Lexington, Ky, 1966. Tributes and retrospective showings: NY, 1967, 1970, 1971; London, 1968; Montreal, Beverly Hills and Washington, 1970; Amer. Inst. for Advanced Studies, San Francisco, Toronto and Univs of Calif. at LA, S Florida and Yale, 1971; Hollywood, 1972; UCLA, Hollywood, Paris, San Sebastian, 1973; Washington DC, 1974; Univ. of California, Univ. of S California, 1975; Calif State Coll., 1976; Amer. Film Inst., 1976, 1977; Hollywood, N Carolina State Univ., 1977. Guest of Honour: Republics of Armenia and Georgia, 1971; Internat. Film Festivals, Moscow 1971, Iran 1974, Australia 1974, San Sebastian 1974, Boston 1976. Lectures, and appears on TV. Award of Excellence, Armenian Amer. Bicentennial Commemoration Cttee Inc., 1976. *Publications:* Abigayil, 1964; Hamlet Revised and Interpreted, 1965; contrib. Scoundrels and Scalawags, 1968; Ararat, 1969; Foreword to Chevalier, 1973. *Recreations:* swimming, horseback riding, and reading detective stories. *Address:* 1112 Schuyler Road, Beverly Hills, Calif 90210, USA.
*Died* 4 *Dec.* 1987.

**MAN, Maj.-Gen. Christopher Mark Morrice,** CB 1968; OBE 1958; MC 1945; retired; *b* 20 April 1914; *s* of late Rev. M. L. Man, MA, and late Evelyn Dora Man, Tenterden, Kent; *m* 1940, Georgina, *d* of late James Marr, Edinburgh; no *c. Educ:* Eastbourne Coll.; Emmanuel Coll., Cambridge. (MA). Lieut, Middlesex Regt, 1936; 1st Bn, The Middlesex Regt, 1937–45. Commanded Army Air Transport Training and Development Centre, 1953–55; GSO 1, WO, 1955–57; comdg Infantry Junior Leaders Battalion, 1957–59; comdg 125 Infantry Bde (TA), 1959–62; Head of Commonwealth Liaison Mission, UN Command, Korea and British Military Attaché, Seoul, 1962–64; GOC 49th Infantry Div. TA and N Midland District, 1964–67; Colonel, The Middlesex Regt, 1965–66; Pres., Regular Army Commn, 1967–69; Dep. Colonel The Queen's Regt, 1967–69, Hon. Colonel, 1970–71. Private, Atholl Highlanders, 1969. *Address:* The Clock Tower Flat, Blair Castle, Blair Atholl, Pitlochry, Perthshire PH18 5TL. *T:* Blair Atholl 452.
*Died* 25 *Oct.* 1989.

**MAN, Morgan Charles Garnet,** CMG 1961; *b* 6 Aug. 1915; *s* of Henry Morgan Stoe Man and Nora Loeck; *m* 1st, 1941, Moira Farquharson Main (marr. diss. 1956); two *d*; 2nd, 1956, Patricia Mary (*née* Talbot) (marr. diss.). *Educ:* Cheltenham Coll.; Queen's Coll., Oxford. Joined HM Consular Service, 1937; Vice-Consul, Beirut,

1937–39; Assistant Oriental Secretary, HM Embassy, Bagdad, 1939; 2nd Secretary, HM Embassy, Jedda, 1943; Consul, Atlanta, Ga, USA, 1946; Consul, Kirkuk, 1948; First Secretary, HM Legation, Damascus, 1949; Oriental Secretary, HM Embassy, Bagdad, 1951; Assistant in American Dept, Foreign Office, Sept. 1953; Head of American Dept, 1954; Counsellor at HM Embassy, Oslo, Nov. 1956; Deputy Political Resident, Bahrain, 1959–62; Minister, HM Embassy, Ankara, 1962–64; HM Ambassador to Saudi Arabia, 1964–68; Senior Civilian Instructor, Imperial Defence Coll., 1968–69; retired, 1970. Director: Metallurgical Plantmakers' Fedn, 1970–80; British Metalworking Plantmakers' Assoc., 1970–80; Ironmaking and Steelmaking Plant Contractors' Assoc., 1970–80. Served in MoD, 1980–82. DL Greater London, 1977–84. *Address:* Sumner Cottage, Preston Candover, near Basingstoke, Hants RG25 9EE. *T:* Preston Candover 522.

*Died 24 Aug.* 1986.

**MANCE, Sir Henry (Stenhouse),** Kt 1971; Deputy Chairman and Treasurer, Lloyd's Register of Shipping, 1979–81; Chairman of Lloyd's, 1969, 1970, 1971, 1972 (Deputy Chairman, 1967, 1968); *b* 5 Feb. 1913; *e s* of late Brig.-Gen. Sir H. O. Mance, KBE, CB, CMG, DSO; *m* 1940, Joan Erica Robertson Baker; one *s* three *d*. *Educ:* Charterhouse; St John's Coll., Cambridge (MA). Entered Lloyd's, 1935; Underwriting Member of Lloyd's, 1940; elected to Cttee of Lloyd's, 1966. Chairman, Lloyd's Underwriters' Assoc., 1965 and 1966; Member, Cttee of Lloyd's Register, 1966–. Min. of War Transport, 1941–46. Director: Lloyds Life Assurance Ltd, 1971–; Willis, Faber & Dumas (Agencies), 1973–; Willis, Faber Ltd, 1973–78; Craigmyle & Co. Ltd, 1973–. President: Insurance Inst. of London, 1975–76; Chartered Insurance Inst., 1977–78. Treasurer, Church Missionary Soc., 1972–81; Trustee of Ridley and Wycliffe Halls. Lloyd's Gold Medal, 1973. *Recreations:* gardening, carpentry, fishing. *Address:* Gatefield Cottage, Okehurst, Billingshurst, W Sussex. *T:* Billingshurst 2155. *Club:* National Liberal.

*Died 15 June* 1981.

**MANCHESTER,** 11th Duke of, *cr* 1719; **Sidney Arthur Robin George Drogo Montagu;** Baron Montagu, Viscount Mandeville, 1620; Earl of Manchester, 1626; *b* 5 Feb. 1929; *er s* of 10th Duke of Manchester, OBE, and Nell Vere (*d* 1966), *d* of Sidney Vere Stead, Melbourne; *S* father, 1977; *m* 1st, 1955, Adrienne Valerie (marr. diss. 1978), *d* of J. K. Christie; 2nd, 1978, Andrea Kent (*née* Joss). *Heir:* b Lord Angus Charles Drogo Montagu [*b* 9 Oct. 1938; *m* 1st, 1961, Mary Eveleen (marr. diss. 1970), *d* of Walter Gillespie McClure; two *s* one *d*; 2nd, 1971, Diane Pauline, *d* of Arthur Plimsaul]. *Address:* PO Box 24667, Karen, Kenya. *Clubs:* St James'; Muthaiga, Mount Kenya Safari (Nairobi); Rift Valley Sports (Nakuru); Jockey Club of Kenya. *Died 3 June* 1985.

**MANCROFT,** 2nd Baron, *cr* 1937, of Mancroft in the City of Norwich; Bt, *cr* 1932; **Stormont Mancroft Samuel Mancroft;** KBE 1959 (MBE 1945); TD 1950; MA; Chairman, British Greyhound Racing Board, 1977–85; *b* 27 July 1914; *s* of 1st Baron and Phœbe (*d* 1969), 2nd *d* of Alfred Chune Fletcher, MRCS; *S* father, 1942; *m* 1951, Mrs Diana Elizabeth Quarry, *o d* of Lieut-Colonel Horace Lloyd; one *s* two *d*. *Educ:* Winchester; Christ Church, Oxford. Called to Bar, Inner Temple, 1938; Member of Bar Council, 1947–51; Member St Marylebone Borough Council, 1947–53; a Lord in Waiting to the Queen, 1952–54; Parliamentary Under-Secretary for Home Dept, Oct. 1954–Jan. 1957; Parliamentary Secretary, Min. of Defence, Jan.-June 1957; Minister without Portfolio, June 1957–Oct. 1958, resigned. Dir, GUS, 1958–66; Dep. Chm., Cunard Line Ltd, 1966–71; Chm., Horserace Totalisator Bd, 1972–76; Mem., Council on Tribunals, 1972–80; President: The Institute of Marketing, 1959–63; St Marylebone Conservative Assoc., 1961–67; London Tourist Board, 1963–73. Served RA (TA), 1939–46; Lieut-Colonel (despatches twice, MBE); commissioned TA, 1938; rejoined TA 1947–55. Hon. Col Comdt, RA, 1970–80. Croix de Guerre. *Publications:* Booking the Cooks (essays from Punch), 1969; A Chinaman in My Bath, 1974; Bees in some Bonnets, 1979. *Heir: s* Hon. Benjamin Lloyd Stormont Mancroft, *b* 16 May 1957. *Address:* 29 Margaretta Terrace, SW3 5NU. *T:* 01–352 7674. *Clubs:* Pratt's; West Ham Boys. *Died 14 Sept.* 1987.

**MANDER, Raymond Josiah Gale;** Joint Founder and Director, The Raymond Mander and Joe Mitchenson Theatre Collection, since 1939 (Theatre Collection Trust, since 1977); *b* 15 July 1911; *s* of Albert Edwin Mander, MSA, LRIBA, FIAAS, and Edith Christina Gale. *Educ:* Battersea Grammar Sch. 1st professional appearance on stage, Bedford, 1934; acted in repertory, on tour and in London, until 1948. With Joe Mitchenson, founded Theatre Collection, 1939; during the War, resp. together for many BBC theatre gramophone progs; toured together in ENSA and in jt management, 1943; management of Collection became full-time occupation as authors and theatrical consultants; Collection subject of Aquarius programme, 1971; many TV appearances on theatrical subjects; many theatrical exhibns, incl. 50 Years of British Stage Design, for British Council, USSR, 1979. Archivist to: Sadler's Wells; Old Vic. Mem., Soc. of West End Theatre Awards Panel, 1976–78.

*Publications:* with Joe Mitchenson: Hamlet Through the Ages, 1952 (2nd rev. edn 1955); Theatrical Companion to Shaw, 1954; Theatrical Companion to Maugham, 1955; The Artist and the Theatre, 1955; Theatrical Companion to Coward, 1957; A Picture History of British Theatre, 1957; (with J. C. Trewin) The Gay Twenties, 1958; (with Philip Hope-Wallace) A Picture History of Opera, 1959; (with J. C. Trewin) The Turbulent Thirties, 1960; The Theatres of London, 1961, illus. by Timothy Birdsall (2nd rev. edn, paperback, 1963; 3rd rev. edn 1975); A Picture History of Gilbert and Sullivan, 1962; British Music Hall: A Story in Pictures, 1965 (rev. and enlarged edn 1974); Lost Theatres of London, 1968 (2nd edn, rev. and enlarged, 1976); Musical Comedy: A Story in Pictures, 1969; Revue: A Story in Pictures, 1971; Pantomime: A Story in Pictures, 1973; The Wagner Companion, 1977; Victorian and Edwardian Entertainment from Old Photographs, 1978; Introd. to Plays, by Noël Coward (4 vols), 1979; Guide to the W. Somerset Maugham Theatrical Paintings, 1980; contribs to and revs in Encyc. Britannica, Theatre Notebook, and Books and Bookmen. *Recreations:* going to the theatre, gardening. *Address:* 5 Venner Road, Sydenham, SE26 5EQ. *T:* 01-778 6730.

*Died 20 Dec.* 1983.

**MANDER, Lady (Rosalie), (R. Glynn Grylls),** MA Oxon; biographer; lecturer; *b* 13 April 1905, Cornish ancestry; *m* 1930, Sir Geoffrey Mander (*d* 1962), sometime MP for East Wolverhampton; one *d* (and one *s* decd). *Educ:* Queen's Coll., Harley Street, London; Lady Margaret Hall, Oxford. Lectures frequently in USA. *Publications:* Mary Shelley, 1936; Trelawny, 1950; Portrait of Rossetti, 1965; Mrs Browning, 1980. *Address:* Wightwick Manor, Wolverhampton, West Midlands; 35 Buckingham Gate, SW1.

*Died 2 Nov.* 1988.

**MANDI, Lt-Col Raja (Sir) Joginder Sen Bahadur of;** KCSI 1931; *b* 20 Aug. 1904; *s* of late Mian Kishan Singh; *m* 1930, *d* of late Kanwar Prithiraj Sinhji, Rajpipla; two *s* two *d*. *Educ:* Queen Mary's Coll. and Aitchison Coll., Lahore. Ascended Gadi, 1913; full ruler, 1925. Visited various countries. Ambassador of Republic of India to Brazil, 1952–56; Member of Lok Sabha, 1957–62. Hon. Lt-Col 3rd/17th Dogra Regt and Bengal Sappers and Miners. *Address:* Bhawani Palace, Mandi, Mandi District (HP) 175001, India.

*Died 16 June* 1986.

**MANN, Frederick George,** FRS 1947; ScD (Cantab), DSc (London), FRSC; Reader Emeritus in Organic Chemistry, Cambridge University, 1964; Fellow of Trinity College, Cambridge; *b* 29 June 1897; *s* of William Clarence Herbert and Elizabeth Ann Mann; *m* 1st, 1930, Margaret Reid (*d* 1950), *d* of William Shackleton, FRAS; two *d*; 2nd, 1951, Barbara, *d* of Percy Thornber; one *d*. *Educ:* London Univ., 1914–17, 1919 (BSc 1919). Served European War, finally as 2nd Lieut Special Bde, RE, BEF, France, 1917–19. Research student, Downing Coll., Cambridge, 1920–23; PhD (Cantab) 1923; Assistant to Professor of Chemistry (Sir William Pope), 1922; DSc (London), 1929; ScD (Cantab) 1932; FRIC 1929. Lecturer in Chemistry, Cambridge Univ., 1930; Reader in Organic Chemistry, Cambridge Univ., 1946; Fellow and Lecturer, Trinity Coll., Cambridge, 1930, Praelector in Chemistry, 1960. Tilden Lectr, 1944; Member Council: Chemical Soc., 1935–38, 1940–43, 1946–49 (Vice-Pres., 1958–61); Royal Institute of Chemistry, 1942–45, 1948–51 (Examnr, 1955–60); Visiting Senior Prof. of Chemistry, University of Hawaii, 1946–47. Transition Metal Chemistry award, 1977. *Publications:* Practical Organic Chemistry, 1936, 4th edn, 1960; Introduction to Practical Organic Chemistry, 1939, 2nd edn, 1964 (both with Dr B. C. Saunders). The Heterocyclic Derivatives of Phosphorus, Arsenic, Antimony, Bismuth, and Silicon, 1950 (2nd edn, 1970); Lord Rutherford on the Golf Course, 1976; numerous papers in Proceedings of the Royal Society, Journal of the Chemical Society, Journal of Society of Chemical Industry, etc. *Recreation:* ornithology. *Address:* 24 Porson Road, Cambridge CB2 2EU. *T:* Cambridge 352704; Trinity College, Cambridge CB2 1TQ. *T:* Cambridge 358201; University Chemical Laboratory, Lensfield Road, Cambridge CB2 1EW. *T:* Cambridge 66499.

*Died 29 March* 1982.

**MANN, Rev. George Albert Douglas;** General Secretary, Free Church Federal Council, 1970–79; *b* 17 April 1914; *er s* of George and Alice Mann; *m* 1940, Mabel Harwood; no *c*. *Educ:* Clifford Road Sch., Ipswich; Manchester Baptist Coll.; Manchester Univ. Minister, Mount Pleasant Baptist Church, Burnley, 1940–42. Chaplain to HM Forces, 1942–45 (now Hon. CF); Sen. Staff Chaplain, ALFSEA, 1945–46. Minister: Park Tabernacle Baptist Church, Great Yarmouth, 1947–52; Union Baptist Church, High Wycombe, 1952–58. Mem. Baptist Union Council, 1948–; Asst Sec., and Sec. of Hosp. Chaplaincy Bd, Free Church Federal Council, 1958–69. *Recreations:* gardening, philately. *Address:* 5 Gresham Close, Eastbourne, E Sussex BN21 1UW. *T:* Eastbourne 32540.

*Died 26 March* 1983.

**MANN, Dame Ida (Caroline),** DBE 1980 (CBE 1950); MA Oxon, DSc London; MB, BS London; FRCS; FRACS; Cons. Surgeon, Royal

London Ophthalmic (Moorfields) Hospital; late Member Expert Committee, WHO; late Cons. Ophthalmologist to Government of Western Australia; *b* London, 1893; *d* of F. W. Mann, MBE, and Ellen Packham; *m* 1944, William Ewart Gye, FRS, MD, FRCP (*d* 1952). *Educ:* University of London. Ophthalmic surgeon and research worker; late Research Student, Institute of Pathology, St Mary's Hospital; Henry George Plimmer Fellow of the Imperial College of Science and Technology; Assistant Surgeon, Central London Ophthalmic Hospital; Ophthalmic Surgeon, Royal Free Hospital and Elizabeth Garrett Anderson Hospital; Pathologist, Central London Ophthalmic Hospital; Senior Surgeon Oxford Eye Hospital; Margaret Ogilvie Reader, University of Oxford, 1941, Professor 1945–47; War Service as Head of Research Team for Ministry of Supply. Hon. MD Western Australia, 1977. Fellow of St Hugh's College; Gifford Edmonds Prize in Ophthalmology, 1926; Arris and Gale Lecturer, 1928; Doyne Memorial Lecturer, 1929; Montgomery Lecturer, 1935; Nettleship Prize, 1930; Mackenzie Memorial Medal, 1935; Howe Memorial Medal, 1958; Bowman Medal, 1961. Member: Ophthalmological Society of UK and other societies. *Publications:* The Development of the Human Eye; Developmental Abnormalities of the Eye; Culture, Race, Climate and Eye Disease; and numerous papers in medical journals. *Recreation:* travel. *Address:* 56 Hobbs Avenue, Nedlands, Western Australia 6009, Australia. *Died 19 Nov.* 1983.

**MANN, Julia de Lacy**, MA; Principal, St Hilda's College, Oxford, 1928–55; *b* Aug. 1891; *o d* of James Saumarez Mann, MA, sometime Fellow of Trinity College, Oxford. *Educ:* Bromley High Sch.; Somerville Coll., Oxford (Hon. Fellow, 1978). Classical Hon. Mods. 1912; Lit. Hum. 1914. Secretarial work, Admiralty and Foreign Office, 1915–19; Vice-Principal, St Hilda's Coll., 1923–28. Hon. Fellow, Merton Coll., Oxford, 1979. Hon. DLitt Oxon, 1973. *Publications:* (with A. P. Wadsworth), The Cotton Trade and Industrial Lancashire, 1600–1780, 1931, Ed. Documents illustrating the Wiltshire Textile Trades in the 18th Century (Wilts Arch. Society, Records Branch, Vol. XIX), 1964; The Cloth Industry in the West of England, 1640–1880, 1971. *Address:* The Cottage, Bower Hill, Melksham, Wilts. *Club:* University Women's. *Died 23 May* 1985.

**MANN, Ronald**; Deputy Chairman, Grindlays Bank Ltd, 1964–77; Director, Grindlays Holdings Ltd, 1969–78; *b* 22 April 1908; *s* of Harry Ainsley Mann and Millicent (*née* Copplestone); *m* 1935, Beatrice Elinor Crüwell Wright; one *s* three *d*. *Educ:* Cranleigh Sch., Surrey. The Eastern Produce and Estates Co. Ltd: Asst, Ceylon, 1930–35; Man., Ceylon, 1935–46; Man. Dir, London, 1947–71; Chm., Eastern Produce Holdings Ltd, 1957–71. *Recreations:* golf, gardening. *Address:* Fernhurst Place, Fernhurst, near Haslemere, Surrey. *T:* Haslemere 52220. *Club:* Oriental. *Died 27 May* 1987.

**MANN, William Somervell**; Radio Broadcaster on music since 1949; Associate Editor, Opera, since 1954; *b* 14 Feb. 1924; *s* of late Gerald and Joyce Mann; *m* 1948, Erika Charlotte Emilie Sohler; four *d*. *Educ:* Winchester Coll.; Magdalene Coll., Cambridge (BA, MusB). Music Critic, Cambridge Review, 1946–48; Asst Music Critic, The Times, 1948–60, Chief Music Critic 1960–82. Artistic Dir, Bath Fest., 1985. Member: Royal Musical Assoc.; The Critics' Circle (Pres., 1963–64). *Publications:* Introduction to the Music of J. S. Bach, 1950; (contrib. to symposium) Benjamin Britten, 1952; (contrib. to): The Concerto, 1952; The Record Guide, 1955; Chamber Music, 1957; The Analytical Concert Guide (English Editor), 1957; (contrib.) Music and Western Man, 1958; Let's Fake an Opera (with F. Reizenstein), 1958; Richard Strauss's Operas, 1964; Wagner's The Ring, Introduction and Translation, 1964; (contrib. to symposium) Michael Tippett, 1965; Wagner's Tristan, Introduction and Translation, 1968; The Operas of Mozart, 1977; (contrib.) Opera on Record, vol. 1 1979, vol. 2 1983, vol. 3 1984; Music in Time, 1982; (contrib.) The Book of the Violin, 1984; trans. W. Schwinger, Penderecki, 1989; contributor: opera guides to Aida, 1982, Arabella, 1985 and La Bohème, 1983; Musical Times, Opera, Opernwelt, The Gramophone, Internat. Concert and Opera Guide. *Recreations:* camping, watching Rugby, destructive gardening, phillumenism, food and drink, foreign languages, crosswords, shove-halfpenny, Mah-Jong, making music. *Address:* The Old Vicarage, Coleford, Bath BA3 5NG. *T:* Mells 812245. *Died 5 Sept.* 1989.

**MANNIN, Ethel**, author; *b* London, 1900; *e d* of Robert Mannin and Edith Gray; *m* 1920, J. A. Porteous (*d* 1954); one *d*; *m* 1938, Reginald Reynolds (*d* 1958). *Educ:* Local Council Sch. Associate-Editor, theatrical paper, The Pelican, 1918; joined ILP 1932. *Publications:* Martha, 1923; Hunger of the Sea, 1924; Sounding Brass, 1925; Pilgrims, 1927; Green Willow, 1928; Crescendo, 1929; Children of the Earth, 1930; Confessions and Impressions, 1930; Ragged Banners, 1931; Commonsense and the Child, 1931; Green Figs (stories), 1931; Linda Shawn, 1932; All Experience (travel sketches), 1932; Venetian Blinds, 1933; Dryad (stories), 1933; Men are Unwise, 1934; Forever Wandering (travel sketches), 1934;

Cactus, 1935; The Falconer's Voice (stories), 1935; The Pure Flame, 1936; South to Samarkand (travel), 1936; Women also Dream, 1937; Commonsense and the Adolescent, 1938; Women and the Revolution, 1938; Rose and Sylvie, 1938; Darkness my Bride, 1939; Privileged Spectator (sequel to Confessions), 1939; Julie, 1940; Rolling in the Dew, 1940; Christianity or Chaos: a Re-Statement of Religion, 1940; Red Rose: a Novel based on the Life of Emma Goldman, 1941; Commonsense and Morality, 1942; Captain Moonlight, 1942; The Blossoming Bough, 1943; No More Mimosa (stories), 1943; Proud Heaven, 1944; Bread and Roses, A Survey of and a Blue-Print for Utopia, 1944; Lucifer and the Child, 1945; The Dark Forest, 1946; Comrade, O Comrade, 1947; Late Have I Loved Thee, 1948; Connemara Journal (memoirs), 1948; German Journey (travel), 1948; Every Man a Stranger, 1949; Jungle Journey (travel), 1950; Bavarian Story, 1950; At Sundown, the Tiger..., 1951; The Fields at Evening, 1952; The Wild Swans (Tales from the Ancient Irish), 1952; This Was a Man (biography), 1952; Moroccan Mosaic (travel), 1953; Lover Under Another Name, 1953; Two Studies in Integrity (biography), 1954; So Tiberius (novella), 1954; Land of the Crested Lion (travel), 1955; The Living Lotus, 1956; Pity the Innocent, 1957; Country of the Sea (travel), 1957; A Scent of Hyacinths, 1958; Ann and Peter in Sweden (Children's book), 1958; Ann and Peter in Japan, 1960; Ann and Peter in Austria, 1961; The Blue-eyed Boy, 1959; Brief Voices (autobiography) 1959; The Flowery Sword (travel), 1960; Sabishisa, 1961; Curfew at Dawn, 1962; With Will Adams through Japan, 1962; A Lance for the Arabs (Travels in the Middle East), 1963; The Road to Beersheba (novel), 1963; Rebels' Ride, the Revolt of the Individual, 1964; Aspects of Egypt, some Travels in the United Arab Republic, 1964; The Burning Bush, 1965; The Lovely Land: the Hashemite Kingdom of Jordan, 1965; The Night and its Homing, 1966; Loneliness, A Study of the Human Condition, 1966; An American Journey, 1967; The Lady and the Mystic, 1967; England for a Change (travel), 1968; Bitter Babylon, 1968; The Saga of Sammy-Cat (children's story), 1969; The Midnight Street (novel), 1969; Practitioners of Love, Some Aspects of the Human Phenomenon, 1969; England at Large (travel), 1970; Free Pass to Nowhere (novel), 1970; Young in the Twenties (autobiography), 1971; My Cat Sammy, 1971; The Curious Adventure of Major Fosdick (novel), 1972; England My Adventure (travel), 1972; Mission to Beirut (novel), 1973; Stories from My Life (autobiog.), 1973; Kildoon (novel), 1974; An Italian Journey (travel), 1974; The Late Miss Guthrie (novel), 1976; Sunset over Dartmoor, A Final Chapter of Autobiography, 1977. *Recreation:* gardening. *Address:* Overhill, Shaldon, Teignmouth, Devon. *Died 5 Dec.* 1984.

**MANNING, Cecil Aubrey Gwynne**; *b* 1892; *s* of Charles Walter Manning; *m* 1915, *d* of William Twitchett; two *s* two *d*; *m* 1940, *d* of William Green; one *s*. Rifleman, 1914–18, Queen's Westminsters and The Rangers (wounded in France, amputation of right arm); ARP and Civil Defence, and Invasion Defence Controller (Camberwell), 1939–44 (Defence Medal). Mem. LCC 1922–32 and 1937–49. Leader of Opposition, 1929–30, Dep. Chm., 1930–31; Member Metropolitan Borough Councils: Wandsworth, 1919–22; Camberwell, 1931–53 (Mayor, 1951–53); Mem., Shepton Mallet UDC, 1954–68 (Chm., 1967–68). MP (Lab) N Camberwell, 1944–50. Formerly Member: Metropolitan Water Bd; London Old Age Pensions Cttee; London Insurance Cttee (Chm.); War Pensions Cttees, Wandsworth, Battersea, Camberwell (Vice-Chm.). JP 1927, DL 1931–82, Greater London (formerly Co. London). Coronation Medal 1953. *Address:* Woodstock, Norville Lane, Cheddar, Somerset. *Died 12 April* 1985.

**MANNING, Frederick Edwin Alfred**, CBE 1954; MC 1919; TD 1937; BSc (Eng.); Hon. MA London; Hon. DEng NSTC; Hon. LLD RMC of Canada; Hon. DSc City; CEng; FIMechE; FIEE; FINucE; DPA (London); retired; *b* 6 April 1897; *s* of late Francis Alfred Manning and late Ellen Lavinia Manning; *m* 1927, Alice Beatrice Wistow, BSc; one *s* one *d* (and one *s* decd.). *Educ:* Christ's Hospital; St Olave's; Univ. of London. Academic Diploma of Mil. Studies, Univ. of London; Certificate in Statistics, Univ. of Vienna. War Service, 1915–20 (Order of St Stanislas, 2nd Class; Order of St Vladimir, 4th Class); RE (TA) 1920–38; Royal Signals (TA), 1938–52. Hon. Col, Univ. of London OTC, 1958–68, retired 1968, retaining rank of Col. Entered GPO 1925; idc 1937; Home Office and Min. of Home Security, 1938–41; GPO, 1941; SHAEF, 1943–45; Asst Sec., Foreign Office (Allied Commission for Austria), 1945–47; GPO, 1947; Dir of the Post Office in Wales and Border Counties, 1950–59; Adviser on Athlone Fellowship Scheme, 1961–72; Chm. Boards for the CS Commn, 1961–68; Hon. Sen. Treas., Univ. of London Union, 1928–52, Chm. of Union Court, 1952–69, Chm., Sports Finance Cttee, 1969–74; Mem. of Senate, Univ. of London, 1952–74 (Chm. Military Educ. Cttee, 1952–55); First Chm. of Convocation, The City Univ., 1967–70; Vice-Pres., Univs in London Catholic Chaplaincy Assoc., 1970–. Metrop. Special Constabulary (Comdt, GPO Div.), 1931–41. Freeman, City of London. KSG 1972. *Recreations:* gardening, philately, Rotary (Pres. Shepperton, 1964–65). *Address:* 1 Range Way, Shepperton,

TW17 9NW. *T:* Walton-on-Thames 223400. *Club:* Royal Commonwealth Society. *Died* 16 *Sept.* 1987.

**MANNING, Air Cdre Frederick John,** CB 1954; CBE 1948; retired, 1967; *b* 5 May 1912; *s* of late Frederick Manning; *m* 1937, Elizabeth Anwyl, *er d* of late Rev. Æ. C. Ruthven-Murray, BA, Bishop Burton, Beverley; four *d* (and one *s* decd). Cadet, P&OSN Co., 1928; Midshipman, RNR, 1929; Actg Sub-Lt, RNR, 1933; Pilot Officer, RAF, 1934; Flt Lt, 269 Squadron, 1938; Actg Group Capt., 1942; Dir of Organisation (Establishments), Air Ministry, 1944–45 (actg Air Commodore); commanding RAF Station Shaibah, Abu Sueir Shallufa, 1945–47 (acting Group Capt.); Group Capt., Organisation, HQ, RAF, Mediterranean and Middle East, 1947–48; Senior Air Adviser, and Dep. Head of Mission, British Services Mission, Burma, 1949–52; Senior Officer i/c Administration HQ Transport Command, 1952; Dep. Dir of Work Study, Air Ministry, 1956–59; Dir of Manning (2) Air Ministry, 1960–63; Air Officer Administration: HQ Near East Air Force, 1963–65; HQ Fighter Comd, 1965–67. *Address:* Myrtle Cottage, Eynsham, Oxford. *Club:* Royal Air Force. *Died* 26 *Nov.* 1988.

**MANSELL, Lt-Col George William,** CBE 1959; DL; RA, retired; Chairman, new Dorset County Council, 1973–77; *b* 25 Dec. 1904; *s* of late Lt-Col Sir John H. Mansell, KBE, DL, RA (retd); *m* 1st, 1934, Joan (*d* 1940), *d* of late Spencer Dawson, Stratton Hall, Levington, Ipswich; one *s* one *d*; 2nd, 1941, Mary Elizabeth, *d* of late Major C. L. Blew, Hafod, Trefnant, Denbigh. *Educ:* Wellington Coll., Berks; RMA Woolwich. Commnd into RA, 1924; wounded N Africa, 1942; invalided as a result, 1947. Dorset CC, 1950–77: Alderman, 1955–74; Vice-Chm., 1966; Chm., 1967–74; Hon. Alderman, 1977. DL Dorset, 1968. *Recreation:* fishing. *Address:* Kit Robins, Lytchett Matravers, Poole, Dorset. *T:* Morden (Dorset) 240. *Died* 23 *May* 1983.

**MANSERGH, Vice-Adm. Sir (Cecil) Aubrey (Lawson),** KBE 1953; CB 1950; DSC 1915; retired; *b* 7 Oct. 1898; *s* of Ernest Lawson Mansergh and Emma Cecilia Fisher Hogg; *m* 1st, 1928, Helen Raynor Scott (*d* 1967); one *s* (and one *s* decd); 2nd, 1969, Dora, *widow* of Comdr L. H. L. Clarke, RN. *Educ:* RN Colleges Osborne and Dartmouth. Served European War, 1914–18; Comdr, 1932; Captain, 1938; Commanded HMNZS Achilles, 1942 and HMNZS Leander, 1943, in Pacific; Commodore 1st Cl., Admiralty, 1944–46; Commanded HMS Implacable, 1946–47; Rear-Adm. 1948; Vice-Controller of Navy and Dir of Naval Equipment, 1948–50; Commanded 2nd Cruiser Squadron, 1950–52; Vice-Adm., 1951. Pres., Royal Naval Coll., Greenwich, 1952–54, retired Dec. 1954. *Address:* 102 High Street, Rottingdean, Sussex BN2 7HF. *T:* Brighton (0273) 302213. *Died* 31 *July* 1990.

**MANT, Sir Cecil (George),** Kt 1964; CBE 1955; consultant and company director; Consultant to Corporation of London, 1972–83; Project Co-ordinator for Barbican Arts Centre, 1972–81; *b* 24 May 1906; *o s* of late George Frederick Mant and Beatrice May Mant; *m* 1940, Hilda Florence (*née* Knowles); three *d*. *Educ:* Trinity County Sch.; Hornsey School of Art; Northern Polytechnic School of Architecture. ARIBA 1929, FRIBA 1944, resigned 1970. Entered HM Office of Works, 1928. Visiting Lecturer in Architecture and Building to Northern Polytechnic, 1930–39; Departmental Liaison Officer to Works and Buildings Priority Cttee, 1939–40. Ministry of Public Building and Works: Deputy Director-General of Works, 1950–60; Director-General of Works, 1960–63; Controller-Gen. of Works, 1963–67. Served as member and chairman of various cttees, to British Standards Institution and Codes of Practice, Departmental Working Parties and Investigating Boards, Civil Service Commission Selection Boards, Joint Min. of Works and PO Study Group on PO Buildings Costs and Procedure, etc. Assessor to Advisory Cttee on Building Research, 1958–67; Member, Architecture Consultative Cttee, Hammersmith College of Art and Building, 1966–75. Mem. Council, London Assoc. for the Blind, 1970–. Mem., Ct of Assts, Guild of Freemen of City of London, 1972–. *Address:* 44 Hamilton Court, Maida Vale, W9 1QR. *T:* 071–286 8719. *Club:* Naval. *Died* 2 *Nov.* 1990.

**MANTLE, Philip Jaques,** CMG 1952; *b* 7 Aug. 1901; 2nd *s* of late Paul Mantle; *m* 1930, Gwendolen, *d* of late John Webb, CMG, CBE, MC; one *s* one *d*. *Educ:* Bancroft's Sch., Woodford; St John's Coll., Oxford (Scholar, Goldsmiths' exhibitioner, 1st class Mod. Hist. Finals). Entered Inland Revenue Dept, 1923 (Taxes); Secretaries' office, 1928; Asst Secretary Min. of Supply, 1940, Board of Trade, 1942; Deputy Head, Administration of Enemy Property Dept, 1949; Controller-General, 1955–57; Companies Dept, 1957–61; with Charity Commission, 1962; retired 1966. *Address:* 10 Lonsdale Road, Cannington, near Bridgwater, Som TA5 2JR. *T:* Combwich 652477. *Died* 2 *July* 1989.

**MANTON, Prof. Irene,** BA, ScD, PhD; FRS 1961; Emeritus Professor of Botany, University of Leeds; retired 1969; *b* 17 April 1904. *Educ:* Girton Coll., Cambridge (Hon. Fellow 1985). BA 1926, PhD 1930, ScD 1940, Cambridge. Made studies with the light and electron microscope on the ultramicroscopic structure of plants, and studies on the cytology and evolution of ferns. Hon. Member: Danish Acad. of Sciences and Letters, 1953; Deutsche Akad. Leopoldina, 1967; Amer. Acad. of Arts and Sciences, 1969. Hon. DSc: McGill Univ., Canada, 1958; Durham Univ., 1966; Lancaster Univ., 1979; Leeds Univ., 1985; Hon. Doctorate, Oslo Univ., 1961. *Publications:* Problems of Cytology and Evolution in the Pteridophyta, 1950; papers in scientific journals. *Address:* 15 Harrowby Crescent, West Park, Leeds LS16 5HP. *Died* 31 *May* 1988.

**MANUEL, Joseph Thomas,** CBE 1970; QPM 1967; one of HM's Inspectors of Constabulary, 1963–74; *b* 10 June 1909; *s* of George and Lucy Manuel; *m* 1933, Millicent Eveline Baker; one *s*. *Educ:* Dorchester Boys' Sch., Dorchester, Dorset. Joined Metropolitan Police, 1929. Served in Allied Military Government, Italy (rank of Captain and Major), 1943–46. Returned Metropolitan Police and promoted: Superintendent, 1954; Chief Superintendent, 1957; Dep. Commander, 1958; Commander 1959. *Recreations:* walking, motoring. *Address:* Cranbrook, Pyrford Road, West Byfleet, Weybridge, Surrey KT14 6RE. *T:* Byfleet 46360.
                                                                            *Died* 14 *Feb.* 1990.

**MANVELL, (Arnold) Roger,** PhD (London), DLitt (Sussex); film historian, biographer; scriptwriter and lecturer; Professor of Film, since 1975, and University Professor, since 1982, Boston University; Director: Rationalist Press Association Ltd; Pemberton Publishing Co. Ltd, etc; *b* 10 Oct. 1909; *s* of Canon A. E. W. Manvell; *m* 1946, Margaret, *d* of P. J. Lee, Bristol; *m* 1956, Louise (marr. diss. 1981), *d* of Charles Luson Cribb, London; *m* 1981, Françoise, *d* of René Nautré, Antibes, France. *Educ:* Wyggeston Sch., Leicester; King's Sch., Peterborough; University College, Leicester; Univ. of London. Schoolmaster and Lecturer in adult education, 1931–37; Lecturer in Literature and Drama, Dept Extramural Studies, University of Bristol, 1937–40; Ministry of Information, specialising in film work, 1940–45; Research Officer, BFI, 1945–47; Dir, British Film Acad., 1947–59; Consultant to BAFTA and Editor of its Jl, 1959–76. Associate Editor, New Humanist (formerly Humanist), 1967–75. Has lectured on film subjects for BFI, British Council and other authorities in Great Britain, US, Canada, Far East, India, Caribbean, W Africa and most European countries; regular broadcaster, 1946–, including BBC's long-established programme The Critics. Visiting Fellow, Sussex Univ.; Bingham Prof. of Humanities, Louisville Univ., 1973. Governor, London Film School, 1966–74; Vice-Chm., Nat. Panel for Film Festivals, 1974–76; Member Cttee of Management, Society of Authors, 1954–57, 1965–68; Chairman: Society of Lecturers, 1959–61; Radiowriters' Assoc., 1962–64; Authors' Club, 1972–75. Hon. DFA New England Coll., USA, 1972; Hon. DLitt: Leicester, 1974; Louisville, 1979. Scholar-Teacher of the Year Award for 1984–85, Boston Univ. Commander of the Order of Merit of the Italian Republic, 1970; Order of Merit (First Class) of German Federal Republic, 1971. *Publications:* Film, 1944, revised 1946 and 1950; A Seat at the Cinema, 1951; On the Air (a study of broadcasting in sound and vision), 1953; The Animated Film, 1954; The Film and the Public, 1955; The Dreamers (novel), 1958; The Passion (novel), 1960; The Living Screen (a study of film and TV), 1961; What is a Film?, 1965; This Age of Communication, 1967; New Cinema in Europe, 1966; The July Plot (television play), 1966; New Cinema in the USA, 1968; Ellen Terry, 1968; New Cinema in Britain, 1969; SS and Gestapo, 1969; Sarah Siddons, 1970; Shakespeare and the Film, 1971; The Conspirators: 20 July 1944, 1971; Goering, 1972; Films and the Second World War, 1974; Charles Chaplin, 1974; Love Goddesses of the Movies, 1975; The Trial of Annie Besant, 1976; Theater and Film, 1979; Ingmar Bergman, 1980; Art and Animation, 1980; Elizabeth Inchbald, England's Leading Woman Dramatist, 1987; (ed and contributed) Experiment in the Film, 1949; (contributed) Twenty Years of British Film, 1947; collaborated: with Rachel Low in The History of the British Film 1896–1906, 1948; with Paul Rotha in revised edn of Movie Parade, 1950; with John Huntley in The Technique of Film Music, 1957; with John Halas in The Technique of Film Animation, 1959, Design in Motion, 1962, and Art in Movement, 1970; with Michael Fleming in Images of Madness: the portrayal of insanity in the feature film, 1985; with Heinrich Fraenkel in: Dr Goebbels, 1959, Hermann Goering, 1962, The July Plot, 1964, Heinrich Himmler, 1965, The Incomparable Crime, 1967, The Canaris Conspiracy, 1969, History of the German Cinema, 1971, Hess, 1971, Inside Adolf Hitler, 1973 (revd as Adolf Hitler, the Man and the Myth, 1977; enlarged UK edn, 1978), The Hundred Days to Hitler, 1974; Editor: Three British Screenplays, 1950; Penguin Film Review, 1946–49; The Cinema, 1950–52; The Year's Work in the Film (for British Council), 1949 and 1950; International Encyclopedia of Film, 1972; Five Plays by Elizabeth Inchbald, 1987; for over thirty years contrib. on Cinema to the Annual Register; contributed to Encyclopædia Britannica, journals at home and overseas concerned with history and art of the film and history of the Nazi régime; Archive of photographs (12,000 historic film stills), book manuscripts and proofs, and editions of all books in English and in many translations deposited in library, Louisville Univ., Kentucky; book collections in English deposited

in Mugar Library, Boston Univ. and Library, Sussex Univ. *Recreation:* travel abroad. *Address:* College of Communication, Boston University, 640 Commonwealth Avenue, Boston, Mass 02215, USA; 15 Above Town, Dartmouth, Devon TQ6 9RG.
*Died 30 Nov.* 1987.

**MARC;** *see* Boxer, C. M. E.

**MARCH, George Frederick,** CMG 1946; MC 1917; *b* 6 July 1893; *o s* of late Frederick J. March, Ockbrook Grange, Derbyshire; *m* 1935, Myrtle Lloyd, Carmarthen; two *s*. *Educ:* Rugby Sch.; Wye Agricultural Coll. (dip. Agric. 1914). Commissioned in Sherwood Foresters, Aug. 1914; France, 1915–19 (wounded thrice); Egypt (Alexandria), 1919–21; demobilised, 1921; Inspector of Agriculture, Sudan Government, 1921; Senior Inspector of Agriculture, 1928; Asst Director, Agriculture and Forests, 1935; Dep. Director, 1942; Director, 1944–47. Chairman, Rural Water Supplies and Soil Conservation Board. Member Governor-General's Council (Sudan). Agricultural Consultant on mission to Swaziland by Colonial Development Corporation, Jan.-April, 1950; Manager and Secretary, Flishinghurst Farms Ltd, 1950–52; now farming on own (hops, fruit, etc.), in Kent. *Recreation:* fishing. *Address:* Swigs Hole, Horsmonden, Tonbridge, Kent TN12 8DE. *T:* Tunbridge Wells 722651. *Died 28 March* 1985.

**MARCH, Henry Arthur,** MA (Oxon); *b* 14 March 1905; *s* of late Edward Gerald March, MD, Reading; *m* 1943, Mary (*d* 1968), *d* of late Rev. P. P. W. Gendall, Launceston; two *s* one *d*. *Educ:* Leighton Park Sch.; St John's Coll., Oxford. Asst Master, Merchant Taylors' Sch., 1929–39; Head of Modern Language side, 1940–54, and Housemaster, 1945–54, Charterhouse; Headmaster, Cranleigh Sch., 1954–59; Temp. Asst Master, Marlborough Coll., 1959–61; Asst Master, 1961–65. Acting Headmaster, Charterhouse, 1964. *Address:* Horsna Parc, St Tudy, Bodmin, Cornwall.
*Died 27 Sept.* 1988.

**MARCHANT, Sir Herbert (Stanley),** KCMG 1963 (CMG 1957); OBE 1946; MA Cantab; *b* 18 May 1906; *s* of E. J. Marchant; *m* 1937, Diana Selway, *d* of C. J. Selway, CVO, CBE; one *s*. *Educ:* Perse Sch.; St John's Coll., Cambridge (MA 1929). Asst Master, Harrow Sch., 1928–39; Foreign Office, 1940–46; Consul, Denver, Colorado, USA, 1946–48; First Secretary, British Legation, Bucharest, 1948–49; Counsellor, British Embassy, Paris, 1950–52; Consul-General, Zagreb, 1952–54; Land Commissioner and Consul-General for North Rhine/Westphalia, 1954–55; Consul-General, Düsseldorf, 1955–57; Consul-General, San Francisco, 1957–60; Ambassador to Cuba, 1960–63; Ambassador to Tunisia, 1963–66. Asst Dir, Inst. of Race Relations, 1966–68; UK Representative, UN Cttee for Elimination of Racial Discrimination, 1969–73. Chm., British-Tunisian Soc., 1970–74. *Publications:* Scratch a Russian, 1936; His Excellency Regrets, 1980. *Address:* 5 Kensington Park Gardens, W11. *Died 8 Aug.* 1990.

**MARENGO, Kimon Evan;** *see* Kem.

**MARETT, Sir Robert (Hugh Kirk),** KCMG 1964 (CMG 1955); OBE 1942; FRAI; Seigneur du Franc Fief, in Jersey; Director, Royal Trust Co. of Canada (CI) Ltd; Deputy, States of Jersey and President, Policy Advisory Committee; *b* 20 April 1907; *s* of late Dr Robert Ranulph Marett, one-time Rector of Exeter Coll., Oxford, and Nora Kirk; *m* 1934, Piedad, *d* of late Vicente Sanchez Gavito, Mexico City; one *d*. *Educ:* Dragon Sch., Oxford; Winchester Coll. Entered business: Norton, Megaw & Co. Ltd, 1926–30; Mexican Railway Co. Ltd, 1931–36; Shell Petroleum Co., 1937–39; Times Correspondent in Mexico, 1932–38; Ministry of Information, London, Mexico, Washington and Ottawa, 1939–46; First Secretary, HM Foreign Service, 1946; New York, 1946–48; Lima, 1948–52; Foreign Office, 1952–55; Secretary, Drogheda Cttee, 1952–53; Counsellor (Head of Information Policy Dept, of FO), 1953–55; HM Consul-General, Boston, 1955–58; Asst Under-Secretary of State, Foreign Office, 1959–63; British Ambassador to Peru, 1963–67; special Ambassador for inauguration of President Allende of Chile, 1970. *Publications:* Archæological Tours from Mexico City, 1932; An Eye-Witness of Mexico, 1939; Through the Back Door, An Inside View of Britain's Overseas Information Services, 1968; Peru, 1969; Mexico, 1971; Latin America: British trade and investment, 1973. *Address:* Mon Plaisir, St Aubin, Jersey, CI. *Club:* Travellers'. *Died 2 Nov.* 1981.

**MARGETSON, Major Sir Philip (Reginald),** KCVO 1953 (CVO 1948); MC 1916; QPM 1956; Assistant Commissioner of Police of the Metropolis, 1946–57, retired; *b* 2 Jan. 1894; *s* of late William Parker Margetson and Ellen Maria Snell; *m* 1918, Diana, *er d* of late Sir John Edward Thornycroft, KBE; one *s* (and *er s* killed on active service in N. Africa, 1943). *Educ:* Marlborough; RMC, Sandhurst. Gazetted to RSF, 1915; European War, 1914–18, served 1914–19 (MC); Adjutant 1st Bn 1923; Captain, 1923; Bt Major, 1933; Staff Captain 54th East Anglian Div. (TA) and East Anglian Area, 1928–32; retired and joined Metropolitan Police, 1933; Chief Constable No 2 District, 1936, No 1 District, Feb.-Nov. 1938, No 3

District, Nov. 1938–Feb. 1940; Dep. Asst Commissioner A Dept, New Scotland Yard, Feb.-Aug. 1940; Dep. Asst Commissioner No 1 District, Aug. 1940–June 1946; Asst Commissioner i/c D Dept, New Scotland Yard, June-Oct. 1946, transferred to A Dept, Oct. 1946. Chairman: Securicor Ltd, 1960–73 (Hon. Pres., 1973); British Security Industry Assoc., 1966–73. CStJ. Officer of the Legion of Honour; Officer of Orange Nassau (Netherlands); Commander Order of the Dannebrog (Denmark); Commander Order of St Olaf (Norway). *Recreation:* gardening. *Address:* Steyne Wood Battery, Bembridge, IoW PO35 5PG. *T:* Bembridge 2424. *Clubs:* Naval and Military, MCC; Bembridge Sailing (Bembridge).
*Died 5 Dec.* 1985.

**MARGETTS, Frederick Chilton,** CBE 1966 (MBE 1943); Consultant, Containerisation; *b* 2 Nov. 1905; *m* 1929, Dorothy Walls; one *d*. *Educ:* Driffield Grammar Sch.; St Martin's Grammar Sch., Scarborough. Asst Operating Supt, LNER Scotland, 1946; BR Scotland, 1949; Chief Operating Supt, BR Scotland, 1955; Chief Traffic Manager, 1958, Asst General Manager, 1959, General Manager, 1961, BR York; Member BR Cttee, 1962; Operating Mem., BR Board, 1962–67. *Publication:* Records of the York Cordwainers Company from circa 1395, 1983. *Recreations:* œnology, history of ancient gilds. *Address:* 9 Riseborough House, York YO3 6NQ. *T:* York 26207. *Died 28 March* 1989.

**MARJOLIN, Robert Ernest;** Commandeur de la Légion d'Honneur, 1978; Officier du Mérite Agricole, 1958; Hon. CBE 1957; economist; Membre de l'Institut (Académie des Sciences Morales et Politiques), 1984; *b* 27 July 1911; *s* of Ernest Marjolin and Elise Vacher; *m* 1944, Dorothy Smith (*d* 1971); one *s* one *d*. *Educ:* Sorbonne and Law Sch., Paris; Yale Univ., New Haven, Conn. Asst to Professor Charles Rist at Institut Scientifique de Recherches Economiques et Sociales, 1934–37; Chief Asst, 1938–39. Joined General de Gaulle in London, 1941; Head of French Supply Mission in USA, 1944; Directeur des Relations Economiques Extérieures, Ministère de l'Economie Nationale, 1945; Commissaire Général Adjoint du Plan de Modernisation et d'Equipement, 1946–48; Secretary General, Organisation for European Economic Co-operation, 1948–55; Professor of Economics, University of Nancy, 1955–58; Vice-President, Commission of European Economic Community (Common Market), 1958–67; Prof. of Economics, Univ. of Paris, 1967–69. Dir, Shell Française. Foreign Hon. Member American Academy of Arts and Sciences, 1963. Hon. LLD: Yale, 1965; Harvard, 1967; University of East Anglia, 1967. American Medal of Freedom, 1947; King's Medal, 1947; Grand-Croix de l'Ordre d'Orange-Nassau (Holland), Cavaliere di Gran Croce nell' Ordine al Merito della Repubblica (Italy). Grand-Croix du Mérite de la République Fédérale d'Allemagne, Grand-Croix de l'Ordre Royal du Phœnix (Greece), 1955, Commandeur de l'Ordre du Drapeau (Yugoslavia), 1956. Grand-Officier de l'Ordre de la Couronne (Belgique); Grand Croix de l'Ordre du Dannebrog (Denmark), 1958; Grand Croix de l'Ordre de Leopold II (Belgique), 1967. *Publications:* L'Evolution du Syndicalisme aux Etats-Unis, de Washington à Roosevelt, 1936; Prix, monnaie, production: Essai sur les mouvements économiques de longue durée, 1945; Europe and the United States in the World Economy, 1953; Europe in Search of its Identity, 1981. *Address:* 9 rue de Valois, 75001 Paris, France. *T:* 261.3758. *Died 15 April* 1986.

**MARKHAM, Rt. Rev. Bernard;** *b* 26 Feb. 1907. *Educ:* Bingley Grammar School; Leeds University (BA Hons History, 1928); College of the Resurrection. Deacon, 1930; Priest 1931. Curate of: Lidget Green, 1930–35; S Francis, N Kensington, 1935–37; Stoke-on-Trent, 1937–39; Vicar of Bierley, 1939–46; Rector of St Benedict, Ardwick, 1946–59; Vicar of St Margaret's, Liverpool, 1959–62; Bishop of Nassau and the Bahamas, 1962–72; Asst Bishop, Dio. of Southwell and Rector of E Bridgford, 1972–77; Asst Bishop, Dio. Southwark, 1977–80. Hon. DD Nashotah House, Wisconsin, 1979. *Address:* 209 London Road, Balderton, Newark, Notts NG24 3HB. *Died 21 June* 1984.

**MARKS, Sir John (Hedley Douglas),** Kt 1972; CBE 1966; FCA; Chairman: Development Finance Corporation Ltd, since inception, 1955 (Managing Director, 1955–75); Development Holdings Ltd; Garratt's Ltd; Reinsurance Co. of Australasia Ltd; Brambles Industries Ltd; Vice-Chairman, Australian Consolidated Industries Ltd; Directorships include: CHEP International Finance SA; CHEP International Investments SA; West Lakes Ltd; Borg-Warner (Aust.) Ltd; Japan Aust. Invest Co. Ltd; Alcan Australia Ltd; *b* 8 May 1916; *s* of late Frederick William Marks, CBE, and late Viva Bessie Meurant Stinson; *m* 1941, Judith Norma Glenwright; two *d*. *Educ:* St Peter's Prep. Sch.; Sydney Church of England Sch. Qualified as Chartered Accountant and Secretary, and commenced practice on own behalf, 1937. Served War of 1939–45: enlisted in 2nd AIF, 1939; commissioned, 1941, and rose to rank of Lt-Col. Founded Development Finance Corp. Ltd, Investment Bankers, 1955. Member: Cttee on Community Health Services (Starr Report), 1968–69; Aust. Manufacturing Council; NSW Electricity Commn, 1966–81; Chm., Cttee of Inquiry into State

Taxation (NSW), 1975–76. Trustee: Shore Foundn; Nat. Parks and Wildlife Foundn, NSW, 1969–81. Mem. Council, Macquarie Univ., 1963–76; Governor, Queenwood Sch.; Chairman Emeritus: The Prince Henry Hosp.; The Prince of Wales Hosp.; Fellow, Internat. Banker Assoc. *Recreations:* yachting, golf, tennis. *Address:* 6b Raglan Street, Mosman, NSW 2088, Australia. *T:* 960 2221. *Clubs:* Australian, Royal Sydney Yacht, Elanora Country, American National, Manly Golf (all in NSW). *Died* 22 *Oct.* 1982.

**MARKS, Kenneth;** *b* 15 June 1920; *s* of Robert P. Marks, electrician and Edith Collins, cotton weaver; *m* 1944, Kathleen Lynch; one *s* one *d. Educ:* Peacock Street Sch., Gorton; Central High Sch., Manchester; Didsbury Coll. of Education. Worked in offices of LNER, 1936–40. Joined ranks, Grenadier Guards, 1940–42; commnd into Cheshire Regt, 1942–46 (Capt.); served in Middle East, Malta, Italy, NW Europe and Germany as Infantry Platoon and Company Comdr. Taught in Manchester schs, 1946–67; Headmaster, Clough Top Sec. Sch. for Boys, 1964–67. MP (Lab) Gorton, Nov. 1967–1983; Parliamentary Private Secretary: to Rt Hon. Anthony Crosland, 1969–70; to Roy Hattersley, 1974–75; to Rt Hon. Harold Wilson, 1975; Opposition Whip, 1971–72; Parly Under-Sec. of State, DoE, 1975–79. Member: House of Commons Select Cttee for Educn and Science, 1968–70; Select Cttee on Expenditure, 1974–75; Exec. Cttee, CPA, 1972–75; Exec. Cttee, UK Br., IPU, 1981–83. Chm., Parly Labour Party Educn Gp, 1972–75, NW Reg. Gp, 1974–83; Mem., N Atlantic Assembly, 1974–75, 1979–83. Vice-Pres., YHA, 1980–. Voluntary worker, CAB, 1983–. *Address:* 50 Boothfields, Knutsford, Cheshire WA16 8JU. *T:* Knutsford 53063. *Died* 13 *Jan.* 1988.

**MARLER, Leslie Sydney,** OBE 1957; TD 1946; Hon. President, Capital & Counties Property Co. Ltd, 1971–73 (Chairman, 1950–71); Director, Norwich Union Insurance Societies, 1972–75, Chairman, London Board, 1974–75 (Deputy Chairman, 1972–73); Chairman, Marler Estates Ltd, 1972–78; *b* 7 July 1900; *e s* of L. T. Marler, Birdham, Sussex; *m* 1926, Doris Marguerite (JP Bucks, 1946), 3rd *d* of late H. E. Swaffer, Brighton; one *s* one *d* (and one *s* decd). *Educ:* St Paul's Sch. Served European War, 1914–18, with HAC, 1917–19; re-employed, 1939, as Captain RA; Major 1941; retd 1945. Chm. Buckingham Div., Conservative Assoc., 1946–56, Pres., 1955–77. Master, Worshipful Co. of Merchant Taylors, 1960. Life Mem., Court of The City University, 1970. High Sheriff, Bucks, 1971–72. *Recreations:* fox-hunting, bloodstock breeding, golf, collecting first editions, travel. *Address:* Bolebec House, Whitchurch, Bucks. *T:* Whitchurch 231. *Club:* Carlton. *Died* 12 *April* 1981.

**MARLEY,** 2nd Baron *cr* 1930, of Marley in the County of Sussex; **Godfrey Pelham Leigh Aman;** *b* 6 Sept. 1913; *s* of 1st Baron Marley and Octable Turquet (*d* 1969), *d* of Sir Hugh Gilzean-Reid, DL, LLD, formerly MP for Aston Manor; *S* father, 1952; *m* 1st, 1938, Lilian Mary (marr. diss. 1948); 2nd, 1956, Catherine Doone Beal. *Educ:* Bedales Sch; Univ. of Grenoble. Royal Marines, 1939–45. *Heir:* none. *Address:* 104 Ebury Mews, SW1. *T:* 01–730 4844; House of Lords, SW1. *Died* 31 *March* 1990 (*ext*).

**MARLOW, Roger Douglas Frederick,** DSC 1943; JP; Deputy Director-General, Institute of Directors, 1975–77; *b* 21 Aug. 1912; *s* of Frederick George Marlow and Mabel Marlow(e), authoress; *m* 1st 1951, Mary (Bernadette Teresa) Savage, actress (*d* 1972); two *s* one *d*; 2nd, 1977, Jean Marian White (*née* Watts); two step *d. Educ:* Christ's Hospital; London School of Economics and Political Science. BScEcon (Hons). Initial trng in merchant banking, 1934–35; Executive, Overseas Sections, London Chamber of Commerce, 1935–39. War service, 1939–46, Lt-Comdr RNVR (Commendation (Naval) 1941, DSC). Dep. Asst Sec., London Chamber of Commerce, 1946–60; concurrently, Chief Executive and Secretary: London Building Acts Cttee; Mica Trade Assoc.; Horological Trade Pool Ltd (incl. import Licence admin for BoT); British Essence Mfrs Assoc.; British Aromatic Compound Mfrs Assoc.; Asst Dir-Gen. and Educn Dir, Inst. of Dirs, 1960–75. Dir, Gardner Arts Centre Ltd, 1985–. Member: Essential Oils Adv. Cttee (Govt and Industry), 1946–51; Adv. Panel, PER, Dept of Employment, 1972–77; Co-ordinating Sec., Sino-British Trade Council, 1954–60; Mem., Negotiating Mission to USSR for Estabt of Reciprocal Trade Fairs, 1959. Mem. Council, Nat. Inst. of Industrial Psychology, 1960–74; Mem. Court and Council, Univ. of Sussex, 1970–; Governor, Christ's Hospital, 1978–. JP E Sussex, Brighton Div., 1965–. *Publications:* Selling to Finland, 1959; Trading with the Soviet Union, 1959; (with R. Earnshaw) Falcon Workshop Business Course for Sixth Formers, 1980; various articles in trade and professional jls. *Recreations:* croquet, swimming, music, painting, bridge. *Address:* 5 Surrenden Crescent, Brighton, Sussex BN1 6WE. *T:* Brighton 503072. *Died* 12 *Feb.* 1986.

**MARLOW, Roy George;** HM Diplomatic Service; Consul General, Karachi, 1985–88; *b* 24 April 1931; *s* of George Henry Marlow and May Marlow (*née* Wright); *m* 1st, 1959, Hilary Ann Charlesworth (marr. diss. 1975); one *s* two *d*; 2nd, 1976, Vali Ceballos; one step *s* one step *d. Educ:* Nottingham High Sch.; Jesus Coll., Cambridge

(BA). United Africa Group (Unilever): Manchester, 1953–56, 1958–59, 1961–65; Nigeria, 1956–58, 1959–61. Joined Foreign and Commonwealth Office, 1966; First Secretary (Commercial): Calcutta, 1967–70; Bogotá, 1971–73; FCO, 1973–76; Head of Chancery, Quito, 1976–79; Counsellor (Commercial), Manila, 1980–83; Ambassador to Dominican Republic, 1983–85. *Recreations:* music, tennis. *Address:* c/o Foreign and Commonwealth Office, SW1; Flat 4, 40 Redcliffe Square, SW10. *T:* 01–370 6005. *Died* 11 *Oct.* 1988.

**MARNAN, His Honour John Fitzgerald,** MBE 1944; QC 1954; a Circuit Judge, lately sitting at Central Criminal Court, 1972–80, retired; *b* 23 Jan. 1908; *s* of late T. G. Marnan, Irish Bar; *m* 1st, 1934, Morwenna (marr. diss., 1958), *d* of late Sir Keith Price; one *s* (and one *s* decd); 2nd, 1958, Mrs Diana Back (marr. diss., 1963), *o d* of late Comdr Charles Crawshay, RN (retd), and late Mrs M. L. Greville; 3rd, 1966, Joanna, *o d* of late Maj.-Gen. W. N. Herbert, CB, CMG, DSO. *Educ:* Ampleforth; Trinity Coll., Oxford. Commnd TA (Oxford Univ. OTC), 1929. Called to Bar, 1931; joined Chester and N Wales Circuit; joined Supplementary Reserve, Irish Guards, 1936; served War of 1939–45 (MBE, despatches); Western Europe with Irish Guards, and on staff of 15th (Scottish) Div.; Major (GSO2), 1944. A Metropolitan Magistrate, 1956–58, resigned. Crown Counsel in the Ministry of Legal Affairs, Kenya Government, 1958–59; Federal Justice of the Federal Supreme Court, the West Indies, 1959–62; subseq. Justice of Appeal of the British Caribbean Court of Appeal. Sat as Commissioner at Crown Courts, at Manchester, 1962–63, at Liverpool, 1963, and at Central Criminal Court, 1964–66; a Dep. Chm., Greater London Sessions, 1966–68; Chm., NE London QS, 1968–71. *Recreation:* field sports. *Address:* Cottrells, Dinton, near Salisbury, Wilts. *T:* Teffont (072276) 315. *Club:* Cavalry and Guards.

*Died* 24 *Nov.* 1990.

**MARNHAM, Harold,** MBE 1945; QC 1965; Barrister-at-Law; Leader of Parliamentary Bar, 1967–74; *b* 14 July 1911; *y s* of late Arthur Henry Marnham and late Janet Elizabeth Marnham; *m* 1947, Hilary, *y d* of late Ernest Jukes; two *s. Educ:* Stellenbosch Boys' High Sch.; Stellenbosch Univ.; Jesus Coll., Cambridge. Called to Bar, Gray's Inn, 1935; Bencher, 1969. Served War 1939–45; BEF, 1939–40; BLA, 1944–45 (despatches); 2nd Lt RA (TA); Capt. 1940; Major 1942; Lt-Col 1945. Dep. Chm., Oxfordshire QS, 1966–71. Chm., Industrial Tribunals, 1975–79. *Address:* Brook House, 7 Quay Street, Halesworth, Suffolk. *T:* Halesworth 2805. *Clubs:* Hawks (Cambridge); Leander (Henley-on-Thames).

*Died* 11 *Nov.* 1987.

**MARNHAM, John Ewart,** CMG 1955; MC 1944; TD 1949; HM Diplomatic Service, retired; *b* Hampstead, 24 Jan. 1916; *er s* of late Col Arthur Ewart Marnham, MC, TD, DL, JP, Foxley Grove, Holyport, Berks, and late Dorothy Clare Morgan; *m* 1944, Susan, *er d* of late Walter Foster (formerly Friedenstein), Vienna and London; two *s. Educ:* Mill Hill; Jesus Coll., Cambridge. Asst Principal, Colonial Office, 1938. Served War, 1939–45: BEF 1939–40; BLA 1944–45 (despatches); 2nd Lt RA (TA) 1938; Major, 1942; Lt-Col, Commanding 353 (London) Medium Regt RA (TA), 1954–57; Brevet Col, 1958. Principal, Colonial Office, 1946; Asst Sec. 1948; Imperial Defence Coll., 1961; Asst Under-Sec. of State: CO, 1964; Foreign Office, 1966–67; Consul-Gen., Johannesburg, 1967–70; British Govt Rep., WI Associated States, 1970–73; Ambassador to Tunisia, 1973–75. Clerk in Cttee Office, House of Commons, 1977–81. *Recreations:* reading, gardening, riding. *Address:* Glebe House, Blake's Lane, Hare Hatch, Berks RG10 9TD. *T:* Wargrave 3469. *Club:* United Oxford & Cambridge University.

*Died* 28 *Dec.* 1985.

**MARNHAM, Sir Ralph,** KCVO 1957; MChir, FRCS; Serjeant Surgeon to the Queen, 1967–71; Consulting Surgeon to: St George's Hospital; King Edward VII's Hospital for Officers; Fellow, Association of Surgeons of Great Britain and Ireland; *b* 7 June 1901; *e s* of Arthur Henry Marnham and late Janet Elizabeth Micklem; *m* 1st, 1927, Muriel, *y d* of Herbert Marnham; one *d*; 2nd, 1942, Helena Mary, *e d* of Patrick Daly; two *s. Educ:* Diocesan Coll., Rondebosch, South Africa; Gonville and Caius Coll., Cambridge; St George's Hospital. Allingham Scholarship Surgery; Sir Francis Laking Research Scholarship; Moynihan Fellow Assoc. of Surgeons of Great Britain and Ireland. War of 1939–45: Officer in Charge Surgical Divs of No. 62 and 6 Gen. Hospitals. Cons. Surgeon, 9th Army, East Africa and Southern Command (despatches twice). Usual House Appointments St George's Hospital; also Asst Curator of Museum, Surgical Registrar, and Resident Asst Surgeon. *Publications:* various in medical journals. *Recreation:* golf. *Address:* 74 Eyre Court, Finchley Road, NW8 9TX. *T:* 01–586 3001. *Club:* Pratt's. *Died* 25 *Nov.* 1984.

**MARR, Allan James,** CBE 1965; Director and Chairman, EGS Co. Ltd; *b* 6 May 1907; *s* of late William Bell Marr and Hilda May Marr; *cousin* and *heir pres.* to Sir Leslie Lynn Marr, 2nd Bt; *m* 1935, Joan de Wolf Ranken; one *s* two *d. Educ:* Oundle; Durham Univ.

Apprenticeship, Joseph L. Thompson & Sons Ltd, 1926–31; joined Sir James Laing & Sons Ltd, 1932. Dir, Doxford and Sunderland Shipbuilding and Eng. Co. Ltd; retd from all shipbldg activities, 1973. Pres. Shipbuilding Conf., 1963–65; Fellow of North-East Coast Inst. of Engineers and Shipbuilders (Pres., 1966–68); Chm., Research Council of British Ship Research Assoc., 1965–73. *Recreation:* photography. *Address:* Dalesford, Thropton, Morpeth, Northumberland NE65 7JE. *Died 20 Sept.* 1989.

**MARRE, Sir Alan (Samuel)**, KCB 1970 (CB 1955); Parliamentary Commissioner for Administration, 1971–76; ex officio Member, Council on Tribunals, 1971–76; *b* 25 Feb. 1914; *s* of late Joseph and late Rebecca Marre; *m* 1943, Romola Mary, CBE, *d* of late Aubrey John Gilling and Romola Marjorie Angier; one *s* one *d*. *Educ:* St Olave's and St Saviour's Grammar Sch., Southwark; Trinity Hall, Cambridge (Major open Schol.) John Stewart of Rannoch Schol. and 1st cl. hons Class. Trip. Parts I and II. Ministry of Health: Asst Principal, 1936; Principal, 1941; Asst Sec., 1946; Under-Sec., 1952–63; Under-Sec., Ministry of Labour, 1963–64; Dep. Sec.: Ministry of Health, 1964–66; Min. of Labour (later Dept of Employment and Productivity), 1966–68; Second Perm. Under-Sec. of State, Dept of Health and Social Security, 1968–71. Health Service Comr for England, Wales and Scotland, 1973–76; ex officio Mem. Commns for Local Admin, 1974–76. Chairman: Age Concern England, 1977–80; Crown Housing Assoc., 1978– ; Rural Dispensing Cttee, 1983–87. Mem., British Nutrition Foundn, 1981– (Chm., 1983–85). Vice-Chm., Adv. Cttee on Distinction Awards for Consultants, 1979–85. Trustee, Whitechapel Art Gall., 1977–83; Pres., The Maccabaeans, 1982–. *Recreations:* reading, walking, travel. *Address:* 44 The Vale, NW11 8SG. *T:* 01–458 1787. *Clubs:* Athenæum, MCC. *Died 20 March* 1990.

**MARRIAGE, John Goodbody**, QC 1971; a Recorder of the Crown Court, since 1972; *b* 17 Aug. 1929; *s* of late Llewellyn Marriage and late Norah (*née* Goodbody); *m* 1955, Caroline June Swainson; two *s* four *d*. *Educ:* Downs Sch., Colwall; Leighton Park Sch., Reading; Trinity Hall, Cambridge (BA). Royal Marines, 1947–49. Called to Bar, Inner Temple, 1953; Bencher, 1979. Dep. Chm., W Suffolk QS, 1965–71. Dep. Chm., Horserace Betting Levy Bd, 1975–83; Chm., Criminal Bar Assoc., 1979–82; Mem., Judicial Studies Bd, 1980–. *Recreation:* horses (for pleasure not profit). *Address:* South End House, Bassingbourn, Cambs. *T:* Royston 42327. *Clubs:* Norfolk (Norwich); Lough Derg Yacht. *Died 16 April* 1984.

**MARRIAN, Guy Frederic**, CBE 1969; FRS 1944; Fellow of University College, London, 1946; Director of Research, Imperial Cancer Research Fund, 1959–68; Professor of Chemistry in Relation to Medicine in the University of Edinburgh, 1939–59; *b* 3 March 1904; *s* of late Frederick York Marrian, AMICE, and Mary Eddington Currie; *m* 1928, Phyllis May Lewis; two *d*. *Educ:* Tollington Sch., London N; University Coll., London. BSc (Hons), 1925; DSc (London), 1930; FRIC 1931; Meldola Medallist, Institute of Chemistry, 1931; William Julius Mickle Fellowship, University of London, 1932; Francis Amory Prize, Amer. Acad. Arts and Sciences, 1948; Beit Memorial Fellowship for Medical Research, 1927–30; Sir Henry Dale Medallist of the Society for Endocrinology, 1966. Lecturer in Dept of Biochemistry, University Coll., London, 1930–33; Assoc. Prof. of Biochemistry, University of Toronto, 1933–36; Prof. of Biochemistry, Univ. of Toronto, 1936–38. Hon. MD Edinburgh, 1975. *Publications:* papers in Biochemical Journal, Journal of Biological Chemistry, etc, mainly on the chemistry of the sex-hormones. *Address:* School Cottage, Ickham, Canterbury, Kent. *T:* Littlebourne 317. *Club:* Athenæum. *Died 24 July* 1981.

**MARRIOTT, Hugh Leslie**, CBE 1946; MD London; FRCP; Physician Emeritus, Middlesex Hospital; formerly: Consulting Physician; Lecturer in Middlesex Hospital Medical School; Hon. Consulting Physician to the Army; Examiner to the Conjoint Board of the Royal Colleges of Physicians and Surgeons and to Oxford, London and Glasgow Universities; Croonian Lecturer, Royal College of Physicians; Editor Quarterly Journal of Medicine; Member Association of Physicians of Great Britain; Fellow and ex-Member of Council Royal Society of Medicine; Fellow Royal Society of Tropical Medicine and Hygiene; *b* 6 Nov. 1900; *s* of Samuel Augustus Marriott; *m* 1930, Vida Cureton; no *c*. Served RAMC 1939–45; Brig. 1942–45; Mission to Middle East for War Office and Medical Research Council, 1941; Consulting Physician to Army and Hon. Consultant to Royal Air Force, India Command, 1942–44; Consulting Physician to Allied Land Forces and Hon. Consultant to Royal Air Force, South-East Asia Command, 1944–45; Burma campaign (CBE). *Publications:* originated (with Alan Kekwick) Continuous Drip Blood Transfusion, Lancet, 1935; various papers in medical journals and articles in medical text-books. *Address:* Shepherd's Down, Ridgeway, Friston, Eastbourne BN20 0EZ. *T:* East Dean 3123. *Died 29 Jan.* 1983.

**MARRIOTT, John Hayes**, CB 1965; OBE 1953; *b* 14 June 1909; *s* of late Sir Hayes Marriott, KBE, CMG, and late Alice (*née* Smith); Malayan Civil Service; *m* 1936, Barbara Rosemary (*née* Salmon);

two *s* two *d*. *Educ:* Uppingham Sch.; King's Coll., Cambridge (MA). Admitted solicitor, 1934; Partner in Deacon & Co., solicitors, 149 Leadenhall Street, EC3, 1936–45. Royal Artillery (HAC), 1939–40; attached MoD, formerly War Office, 1940–69; retd 1969. Royal Order of the Crown, Yugoslavia, 1945. *Address:* 7 Martin's Close, Tenterden, Kent TN30 7AJ. *T:* Tenterden 2497. *Club:* Rye Golf. *Died 1 Sept.* 1982.

**MARRIOTT, Sir Ralph G. C. S.;** *see* Smith-Marriott.

**MARRIOTT, Richard D'Arcy**, CBE 1965; DFC 1944; Assistant Director of Radio (formerly of Sound Broadcasting), BBC, 1957–69; *b* 9 June 1911; *s* of late Sir Hayes Marriott, KBE, CMG, Malayan Civil Service; *m* 1951, Dawn Kingdon; two *d*. *Educ:* Uppingham; Corpus Christi Coll., Cambridge. Joined BBC, 1933; Foreign Liaison Officer, BBC, 1936; started BBC Monitoring Unit, at outbreak of war, 1939; served as navigator in Fighter Command, RAF, 1942–45 (DFC and Bar); attached as Wing Commander to Control Commission for Germany, in charge of German Broadcasting Service in British Zone, 1945–46. Re-joined BBC as Head of European Liaison, 1946; Head of Transcription Service, BBC, 1951–52; Head of Monitoring Service, BBC, 1952–53; Controller, BBC, Northern Ireland, 1953–56. *Address:* 6 Windmill Hill, Hampstead, NW3. *T:* 01–435 4648.
*Died 27 Nov.* 1985.

**MARRIOTT, Brig. Sir Robert Ecklin**, Kt 1943; VD; FInstCE; BSc; with Sir Owen Williams and Partners, on M1 Construction, 1958–68; retired, 1968; *b* 15 Oct. 1887; *m* 1920, Valerie Hoch; four *d*; *m* 1953, Mary Bauer; no *c*. Joined Indian State Railways, 1910; Indian Sappers and Miners (East Africa), 1915–1920; Chief Engineer, 1937, Gen. Man., EI Rly, 1939; Dir Gen. Rlys Calcutta Area, 1944; Dir General Rlys, Control Commission Germany, 1945; Royal Engineers, 1945–47; Col Commandant, East Indian Rly Regt, Aux. Force, India; ADC to the Viceroy. Bursar, Administrative Staff Coll., Henley-on-Thames, 1948–50; Air Ministry Works Department, 1951–57. *Address:* Hartfield, Crick, Northamptonshire NN6 7TT. *T:* Crick 822378.
*Died 22 Feb.* 1984.

**MARRIS, Adam Denzil**, CMG 1944; *b* 11 June 1906; *o s* of late Sir William Marris, KCSI, KCIE; *m* 1934, B. Waterfield; one *s* two *d*. *Educ:* Winchester; Trinity Coll., Oxford. With Lazard Bros & Co. Ltd, 11 Old Broad Street, London, 1929–39; Ministry of Economic Warfare, London, 1939–40; First Sec., HM Embassy, Washington, 1940–41; Counsellor, War Trade Dept, British Embassy, Washington, 1941–45; Secretary-General, Emergency Economic Cttee for Europe, Aug. 1945-Feb. 1946, with temp. rank of Principal Asst Sec., Foreign Office; Deputy Leader of UK Delegn to Marshall Plan Conference, July-Sept. 1947, and to Washington Conf. of Cttee for European Economic Co-operation, Nov.-Dec. 1947. Director: Lazard Bros & Co. Ltd, 1947–73 (Man. Dir, 1947–71); Commercial Union Assce Co. Ltd 1948–78 (Vice-Chm., 1965–78); English Scottish & Australian Bank Ltd, 1951–71; Barclays Bank Ltd, 1953–77; Australia and New Zealand Banking Group Ltd, 1969–76; P&O Steam Navigation Co., 1952–72. *Address:* The Merchants House, 86 High Street, Blakeney, Norfolk. *T:* Cley 740260; 36 King's Court North, SW3. *T:* 01-352 8656; 01-588 2721. *Clubs:* Boodle's; Melbourne (Vic). *Died 15 June* 1983.

**MARSACK, Hon. Sir Charles (Croft)**, KBE 1981 (CBE 1962); Judge, Fiji Court of Appeal, 1957–85, retired; *b* 7 May 1892; *s* of Richard Marsack and Mary Ann Marsack; *m* 1918, Ninette Padiou (*d* 1986); two *s*. *Educ:* Auckland Univ., New Zealand (BA, LLB). Legal practice, New Zealand, 1914–39, except for overseas service with NZ Rifle Brigade, 1915–18; service with 2 NZEF, Middle East and Italy, 1939–45. New Zealand Stipendiary Magistrate, 1945–47; Chief Justice, Western Samoa, 1947–62; Independent Chairman, Fiji Sugar Industry, 1962–70. *Publications:* Samoan Medley, 1961, 2nd edn 1964; Teach Yourself Samoan, 1962, 3rd edn 1973. *Recreation:* gardening. *Address:* PO Box 3751, Samabula, Suva, Fiji. *T:* Suva 383150. *Club:* Returned Servicemen's (Suva).
*Died 3 Oct.* 1987.

**MARSDEN, Allen Gatenby**, CBE 1945; FCIT; Hon. President of International Transport-Users Commission, Paris; *b* 13 Sept. 1893; *s* of late William Allen Marsden, OBE, and Marianne Turvey; *m* 1st, 1918, Mabel Kathleen Buckley (*decd*); one *s* two *d*; 2nd, 1933, Janet Helen Williamson (*d* 1982); one *s*. *Educ:* Wadham House, Hale; Bedford Grammar Sch. Joined staff of London & North-Western Railway as a probationer, 1909; served European War with commission in 8th Bn Manchester Regt, TF, 1914–16, in Egypt, Cyprus and Gallipoli, invalided home with rank of Capt.; under Dir-Gen. of Transportation, France, 1917; Transport and Storage Div., Min. of Food, 1917–18; Traffic Asst, Ministry of Transport, 1920; transport manager of Cadbury Bros Ltd, Bournville, 1921; subsequently transport Supervisor, Cadbury-Fry Joint Transport until 1940; Dir of Transport, Ministry of Food, Aug. 1940–May 1946; Transport Adviser to Bd of Unilever Ltd, 1946–58. On retirement apptd Independent Mem., Scottish

Agricultural Wages Bd, 1959–65. Chairman: Transport Cttee, CBI, 1946–58; British Gen. Transport Cttee, ICC; Vice-Pres., Internat. Container Bureau, Paris, 1948–58; Pres., Internat. Transport Users Commn, Paris, 1948–58. Commerce and industry rep., Central Transport Consultative Cttee for GB, 1946–58; former Mem. Council, CIT (British Transport Commn Award for paper on Traders and the Transport Act, 1949). *Recreations:* golf, fishing. *Address:* 64 Heathfield Road, Audlem, near Crewe, Cheshire. *T:* Audlem 811555. *Died 29 Sept. 1988.*

**MARSDEN, Sir John Denton,** 2nd Bt, *cr* 1924; JP; *b* 25 Aug. 1913; *s* of Sir John Marsden, 1st Bt, and Agnes Mary (*d* 1951), *d* of Thomas Robert Ronald of Little Danson, Welling, Kent; *S* father, 1944; *m* 1939, Hope, *yr d* of late G. E. Llewelyn; two *s* two *d. Educ:* Downside; St John's Coll., Cambridge (BA). Served European War of 1939–45 (prisoner); Lt RA. JP; High Sheriff of Lincs, 1955–56. *Recreations:* shooting, fishing. *Heir: s* Nigel John Denton Marsden [*b* 26 May 1940; *m* 1961, Diana Jean Dunn, *er d* of Air Marshal Sir Patrick H. Dunn, KBE, CB, DFC; three *d*]. *Address:* White Abbey, Linton-in-Craven, Skipton, N Yorks. *Died 22 July 1985.*

**MARSDEN, Leslie Alfred,** CMG 1966; *b* 25 Sept. 1921; *s* of late William Marsden, Stanmore, Middx, and of Kitty Marsden; *m* 1947, Doris Winifred, *d* of late Walter Richard Grant and of Winifred Grant; two *d. Educ:* Kingsbury County Sch. Served War: The Queen's Own Royal West Kent Regt, 1940–42; 14th Punjab Regt, Indian Army, 1942–46; serving in India, Burma and Thailand; retd as Hon. Major. Joined Nigeria Police Force, 1946; Commissioner of Police, 1964; Asst Inspector-General, 1966–68. Associate Director, Sierra Leone Selection Trust, 1969; Security Adviser, Standard Telephones and Cables Ltd, 1970–82; retired 1982. Nigeria Police Medal, 1964; Queen's Police Medal, 1964; Colonial Police Medal, 1958. *Recreations:* walking, reading, public affairs. *Address:* Ashbank, 14 Orchard Rise, Groombridge, Sussex. *T:* Groombridge 486. *Died 28 June 1987.*

**MARSDEN, Dr Terence Barclay,** CEng; FIM; Registrar-Secretary Institution of Metallurgists, since 1976; *b* 31 March 1932; *s* of late Henry Arthur Marsden and Edith Maud Marsden; *m* 1954, Margaret Jean, *o d* of late Percival Charles Davies and Edith Davies; two *s. Educ:* Swansea Grammar Sch.; University Coll. of Swansea (BSc Hons I Metallurgy, Wales, 1952; PhD Wales, 1955). FIM 1970. Technical Officer, ICI Metals Ltd, 1955–60, Develt Officer, 1960–64; Asst Commercial Manager, Imperial Metal Industries Ltd, 1964–67; Tech. Man., CIDEC-Internat. Copper Develt Council, 1967–76. Chm., London Metallurgical Soc., 1974–75. *Publications:* papers in tech. and learned soc. jls on properties and applications of metals and alloys. *Recreations:* bridge, music, swimming, watching cricket. *Address:* Fairmead, 20 Dove Park, Chorleywood, Herts WD3 5NY. *T:* Chorleywood 2229. *Club:* Anglo-Belgian.

*Died 15 Oct. 1981.*

**MARSH, Prof. David Charles;** Professor of Applied Social Science, University of Nottingham, 1954–82, later Emeritus; *b* 9 Jan. 1917; *s* of F. C. Marsh, Aberdare, Glam., S Wales; *m* 1941, Maisie Done; one *s. Educ:* University of Birmingham. Research Scholar University of Birmingham, 1938–39. Military Service, 1940–46, Royal Artillery. Lecturer, University Coll. of Swansea, 1947–49; Professor of Social Science, Victoria Univ. Coll., Wellington, NZ, 1949–54. *Publications:* National Insurance and Assistance in Great Britain, 1949; The Changing Social Structure of England and Wales, 1958, new edn 1967; The Future of the Welfare State, 1964; The Welfare State, 1970. *Recreations:* tennis, badminton. *Address:* 239 Chilwell Lane, Bramcote, Notts. *T:* 25-7567.

*Died 2 July 1983.*

**MARSH, George Fletcher Riley,** CB 1951; *b* 16 Oct. 1895; *s* of late Richard Howard Heywood Marsh, director of Geo. Fletcher & Co. Ltd, Derby; *m* 1927, Phyllis Henderson (*d* 1973), *d* of late Frank Barton, Brasted, Kent; one *s* one *d. Educ:* Bedford Sch. Entered Civil Service (Naval Store Dept, Admiralty), 1914; Deputy Dir of Stores, 1942; Dir of Stores, 1949–55; retired, 1955. *Address:* 14 William Way, Letchworth, Herts. *Died 17 April 1984.*

**MARSH, Michael John Waller,** MC 1942; TD 1954; a Recorder of the Crown Court, since 1974; *b* 12 April 1921; *s* of Arthur Percival Marsh and Gladys Adine Marsh; *m* 1948, Kathleen Harrison; one *s. Educ:* Uppingham; Pembroke Coll., Cambridge (BA). 9th Queen's Royal Lancers, 1942–46; Prince Albert's Own Leics Yeo., 1947–54, retd (Major). Admitted Solicitor, 1949. *Recreations:* shooting; playing around with small boats. *Address:* Park House, Burton Lazars, Melton Mowbray, Leics. *T:* Melton Mowbray 66730. *Died 29 Jan. 1983.*

**MARSH, Dame Ngaio,** DBE 1966 (OBE 1948); FRSA; Novelist and Theatrical Producer, NZ; *b* 23 April 1899; *d* of Henry Edmond and Rose Elizabeth (Seager) Marsh. *Educ:* St Margaret's Coll., NZ; Canterbury Univ. Coll. Sch. of Art, Christchurch, NZ. On stage for two years; to England in 1928; in partnership with Hon. Mrs Tahu Rhodes as house decorator; first novel published in 1934; travelled in Europe, 1937–38; in New Zealand at outbreak of war and joined Red Cross Transport unit. Producer D. D. O'Connor Theatre Management, 1944–; Hon. Lecturer in Drama, Canterbury Univ., 1948. Hon. DLit Canterbury, NZ. *Publications:* A Man Lay Dead, 1934; Enter a Murderer, 1935; Nursing Home Murder (with Henry Jellett), 1936; Death in Ecstasy, 1937; Vintage Murder, 1937; Artists in Crime, 1938; Death in a White Tie, 1938; Overture to Death, 1939; Death at the Bar, 1940; Surfeit of Lampreys, 1941; Death and the Dancing Footman, 1942; Colour Scheme, 1943; Died in the Wool, 1945; Final Curtain, 1947; Swing, Brother, Swing, 1948; Opening Night, 1951; Spinsters in Jeopardy, 1953; Scales of Justice, 1954; Off With His Head, 1957; Singing in the Shrouds, 1959; False Scent, 1960; Hand in Glove, 1962; Dead Water, 1964; Black Beech and Honeydew, 1966; Death at the Dolphin, 1967; Clutch of Constables, 1968; When in Rome, 1970; Tied up in Tinsel, 1972; Black As He's Painted, 1974; Last Ditch, 1977; Grave Mistake, 1978; Photo-finish, 1980; *posthumous publication:* Light Thickens, 1982. *Plays:* A Unicorn for Christmas, 1962 (Libretto to David Farquhar's Opera from this play); Murder Sails at Nidnight, 1973 (adapted from Singing in the Shrouds). *Recreations:* Theatre production, painting, books, travel, gardening. *Address:* c/o Hughes Massie, 31 Southampton Row, WC1B 5HL; (residence) 37 Valley Road, Cashmere, Christchurch, New Zealand. *Club:* PEN.

*Died 18 Feb. 1982.*

**MARSH, William Thomas,** OBE 1944; MA; Headmaster, St Albans School, 1931–64, retd; Commander RNVR (Sp); *b* Birmingham, 18 March 1897; *o s* of W. T. Marsh; *m* 1923, Olive Constance Nightingale; three *s. Educ:* Northampton Sch.; Queens' Coll., Cambridge (Open Classical Scholar). RNVR, 1916–19; First-class Hons Classical Tripos, 1922; VIth Form Classical Master, Brighton Coll., 1923–27; Headmaster Hertford Grammar Sch., 1927–31. Blue for Athletics and Cross Country. *Recreations:* archæology, music. *Address:* Priory Close, Bishops Cleeve, Cheltenham, Glos. *T:* Bishops Cleeve 3171. *Died 28 March 1985.*

**MARSHALL OF LEEDS,** Baron *cr* 1980 (Life Peer), of Shadwell in the City of Leeds; **Frank Shaw Marshall,** Kt 1971; solicitor; Chairman, Municipal Mutual Insurance Group of Companies, since 1978 (Managing Trustee, since 1970); Director, Leeds & Holbeck Building Society, 1962–88 (President, 1967–69 and 1977–79); Chairman, Dartford International Ferry Terminal Ltd, since 1987; Director, Barr & Wallace Arnold Trust PLC, since 1953; director of other companies; *b* Wakefield, 26 Sept. 1915; 4th *s* of Charles William Marshall and Edith Marshall; *g g s* of Charles Marshall (*b* Wakefield, 1827), of New York, Philadelphia and Columbia, Missouri, who fought in American Civil War; *m* 1941, Mary, *e c* of Robert and Edith Barr, Shadwell House, Leeds; two *d. Educ:* Queen Elizabeth's Sch., Wakefield; Downing Coll., Cambridge (scholar); MA, LLM; Associate Fellow, 1986). Served War, 1940–46: Captain RTR; SO JAG's Dept, WO. Leeds City Council: Leader, and Chm. Finance Cttee, 1967–72; Alderman, 1967–73. Chairman: NE Leeds Cons. Assoc., 1962–65; City of Leeds Cons. Assoc., 1967–69; Yorks Provincial Area, Nat. Union of Cons. and Unionist Assocs, 1976–78; Conservative and Unionist Party: Mem., Nat. Exec., 1968–; Mem., Gen. Purposes Cttee, 1969 and 1976–86; Mem., Adv. Cttee on Policy, 1977–86; a Vice-Chm., Nat. Union, 1978–79; a Vice-Chm. of the Cons. Party, 1979–85; Member: Sub-Cttee 'A', House of Lords Select Cttee on Eur. Communities, 1985; Select Cttee, Docklands Light Railway. Special Advr to Govt on Third London Airport Proj., 1972. Chairman: Maplin Develt Authority, 1973–74; Leeds and Bradford Airport, 1968–69; Leeds Grand Theatre and Opera House Ltd, 1969–72; Local Govt Inf. Office of England and Wales, 1968–73; Assoc. of Municipal Corps of England, Wales and NI, 1968–73; Local Authorities Conditions of Service Adv. Bd, 1971–73; Steering Cttee on Local Authority Management Structures, 1972–73; Marshall Inquiry on Govt of Greater London, 1977–78; Yorks Reg. Cttee, RSA, 1972–84; President: Leeds Law Soc., 1975–76; Leeds Philosophical and Literary Soc., 1981–83; Inst. of Transport Admin, 1983–87; Vice-Pres., Building Socs Assoc., 1979–. Member: Yorks and Humberside Econ. Planning Council, 1971–74; Adv. Cttee on Local Govt Audit, 1979–82; Uganda Resettlement Bd, 1972–73; BBC North Regional Council, 1969–72; Leeds Radio Council, BBC, 1969–73; Vice-Pres., AA, 1985– (Mem. Exec. Cttee, 1974–85; a Vice-Chm., 1983–85). Member Court: Leeds Univ., 1965–84 (Mem. Council, 1965–72 and 1975–81); Bradford Univ., 1967–71; Univ. of York, 1981–; Mem., Council of Management, Univ. of Buckingham (formerly University Coll. at Buckingham), 1975–85; Vice-Chm., Bd of Governors, Centre for Environmental Studies, 1971–80. Hon. Freedom, City of Leeds, 1976; Freeman, City of London. FRSA. *Publications:* The Marshall Report on Greater London, 1978; contrib. Local Government and other jls; press articles. *Recreations:* theatre, reading. *Address:* House of Lords, SW1A 0PW.

*Died 1 Nov. 1990.*

**MARSHALL, Arthur;** *see* Marshall, C. A. B.

**MARSHALL, Bruce;** novelist; *b* 24 June 1899; *s* of Claude Niven Marshall, Edinburgh; *m* 1928, Phyllis, *d* of late William Glen Clark,

Edinburgh; one d. *Educ*: Edinburgh Acad.; Trinity Coll., Glenalmond; St Andrews and Edinburgh Univs. Served in Royal Irish Fusiliers, 1914–18 War and in Royal Army Pay Corps and Intelligence in War of 1939–45; MA Edinburgh, 1924; B Com. Edinburgh, 1925; admitted a mem. of the Soc of Accountants in Edinburgh, 1926. *Publications*: Father Malachy's Miracle, 1931; Prayer for the Living, 1934; The Uncertain Glory, 1935; Yellow Tapers for Paris, 1943; All Glorious Within, 1944; George Brown's Schooldays, 1946; The Red Danube, 1947; Every Man a Penny, 1950; The White Rabbit, 1952; The Fair Bride, 1953; Only Fade Away; Thoughts of my Cats, 1954; Girl in May, 1956; The Bank Audit, 1958; A Thread of Scarlet, 1959; The Divided Lady, 1960; A Girl from Lübeck, 1962; The Month of the Falling Leaves, 1963; Father Hilary's Holiday, 1965; The Bishop, 1970; The Black Oxen, 1972; Urban the Ninth, 1973; Operation Iscariot, 1974; Marx the First, 1975; Peter the Second, 1976; The Yellow Streak, 1977; Prayer for a Concubine, 1978; Flutter in the Dovecot, 1986; A Foot in the Grave, 1987; *posthumous publication*: An Account of Capers, 1988. *Address*: c/o Lloyds Bank, 6 Pall Mall, SW1.

*Died 18 June 1987.*

**MARSHALL, (Charles) Arthur (Bertram),** MBE 1944; journalist and author; *b* 10 May 1910; *s* of Charles Frederick Bertram Marshall and Dorothy (*née* Lee). *Educ*: Edinburgh House, Lee-on-Solent, Hampshire; Oundle Sch.; Christ's Coll., Cambridge (MA). Schoolmaster and Housemaster, Oundle Sch., 1931–54; Private Sec. to Lord Rothschild, 1954–58; TV Script Editor for H. M. Tennent Ltd, 1958–64. Has written for New Statesman, 1935–81; regular columnist, 1976–81; broadcaster, in variety and more serious programmes, 1934–. American Bronze Star, 1945. *Publications*: Nineteen to the Dozen, 1953; (ed) New Statesman Competitions, 1955; Salome Dear, NOT in the Fridge, 1968; Girls Will Be Girls, 1974; I SAY!, 1977; I'll Let You Know, 1981; Whimpering in the Rhododendrons, 1982; Smile Please, 1982; Life's Rich Pageant, 1984; Giggling in the Shrubbery, 1985; Sunny Side Up, 1987. *Recreations*: reading, sitting in the sun. *Address*: Pound Cottage, Christow, Exeter, Devon EX6 7LX. *T*: Christow 52236. *Club*: Reform.

*Died 27 Jan. 1989.*

**MARSHALL, Sir Geoffrey,** KCVO 1951; CBE 1951 (OBE 1917); MD, FRCP; retired as Consulting Physician to: Guy's Hospital; King Edward VII Hospital, Midhurst, and Brompton Hospital for Diseases of Chest; Hon. Consulting Physician to Ministry of Pensions; Medical Referee to the Civil Service Commission; Chairman Chemotherapy of Tuberculosis Trials Committee of Medical Research Council; Censor and Harveian Orator, Royal College of Physicians; *b* 1887; *s* of Henry Marshall, Bognor, Sussex; *m* 1918, Belle (*d* 1974), *d* of George Philip, Dundee; (one *s* died on active service, MEF, 1941); *m* 1979, Joan Felicity Wilson-Brown (*d* 1980), *d* of late John Cabourn. *Educ*: St Paul's Sch. Demonstrator of Physiology and Medical Registrar, Guy's Hospital; Gold Medal, London MD; Major RAMC, SR, served with Brit. Exp. Force (despatches twice, OBE); Med. Officer i/c Tuberculosis Dept, Sub-dean of Medical Sch. (Guy's Hospital); Pres. Royal Society of Medicine, 1958–60 (late Pres., Section of Medicine, RSM); Hon. Mem. (Past Pres.) Thoracic Soc.; Hon. FRCPI; Hon. FRSocMed. *Publications*: Papers on Medical Subjects, *eg* Surgical Shock in Wounded Soldiers; and many on Respiratory Disease; (ed) Diseases of the Chest, 1952. *Address*: King Edward VII Hospital, Midhurst, Sussex.

*Died 9 Aug. 1982.*

**MARSHALL, George Wicks,** CMG 1974; MBE 1955; BEM 1946; *b* 6 March 1916; *e s* of G. L. Marshall, Highbury, London, N5; *m* 1946, Mary Cook Kirkland. General Post Office, 1930–48. Served War, Royal Artillery (HAA), 1940–46. Board of Trade, 1948–56; Trade Commn Service, 1956–65; Asst Trade Comr, Nairobi, 1956; Trade Comr: Accra, 1958, Colombo, 1961; Principal Trade Comr, Hong Kong, 1963; Dep. Controller, BoT office for Scotland, 1965; Dep. Dir, Export Services Br., 1967; seconded to HM Diplomatic Service as Counsellor (Commercial) HM Embassy, Copenhagen, 1969–76. Asst Gen. Sec., 1976–78; Gen. Sec., 1978–81, Assoc. of First Div. Civil Servants. Mem. Cttee of Management, 1977–, Vice Chm., 1983–, Civil Service Retirement Fellowship. *Recreations*: theatre, television, working. *Address*: 30 Withdean Avenue, Goring by Sea, West Sussex BN12 4XD. *T*: Worthing 45158. *Clubs*: Civil Service, Royal Commonwealth Society; Hong Kong (Hong Kong).

*Died 23 Dec. 1987.*

**MARSHALL, Hedley Herbert,** CMG 1959; QC (Nigeria) 1955; LLB (London); FRGS; Consultant, Commonwealth Law, British Institute of International and Comparative Law, since 1977; Director, Commonwealth Legal Adv. Service, since 1963; *b* 28 March 1909; *s* of late Herbert Marshall, Sydenham, and Elizabeth, *d* of late Edwin Smith Adams; *m* 1952, Faith, *widow* of Wing-Comdr John Collins Mayhew, RAF; one step-*d*. *Educ*: Dulwich Coll. Prep. Sch.; Dulwich Coll.; London Univ. Admitted Solicitor of Supreme Court, England, 1931; joined Army, 1940; 2nd Lieut 1941; Captain, 1942; Major, 1945; after service at home and overseas, released 1946 and joined Colonial Service; Asst Administrator-Gen.,

Nigeria, 1946; Magistrate Grade I, 1946; called to Bar, Gray's Inn, 1949; Crown Counsel, Nigeria, 1950; Senior Crown Counsel, 1951; Legal Sec., Northern Region of Nigeria, 1952; Chancellor of Diocese of Northern Nigeria, 1953; Attorney-Gen., and Minister in Govt, Northern Nigeria, 1954–62; Dir of Public Prosecutions, Northern Nigeria, 1959–62; Member: House of Assembly, House of Chiefs and Executive Council, Northern Nigeria, 1951–62; Privy Council, Northern Nigeria, 1959–59; Advisory Cttee on the Prerogative of Mercy, Northern Nigeria, 1959–62. Adviser to Government of Northern Nigeria at Nigerian Constitutional Conferences, 1957 and 1958; Mem. Provisional Council of Ahmadu Bello Univ., 1961. Commissioner for Revision of Laws of Northern Nigeria, 1962–63. Asst Dir (Commonwealth), Brit. Inst. Internat. and Comparative Law, 1963–68, Dep. Dir, 1968–77. Founder Mem. and Mem. Council, 1968–, Statute Law Soc. (Chm., 1979–80). *Publications*: Natural Justice, 1959; rev. edn of The Laws of Northern Nigeria, 1963, in 5 Vols (Vols I to III with F. A. O. Schwarz Jr); From Dependence to Statehood: Vol. 1, Southern Africa, 1980; contrib. to International Encyclopaedia of Comparative Law; contribs to legal and other periodicals. *Recreations*: travel, photography. *Address*: The Red House, Bassingbourn, Royston, Herts. *Club*: Royal Commonwealth Society.

*Died 27 April 1982.*

**MARSHALL, Sir Hugo Frank,** KBE 1953; CMG 1950; JP; retired; *b* 1905; *s* of late Henry Mieres Marshall and Cecil Mabel Balfour; *m* 1931, Christine Phyllida, *d* of late Major R. Brinckman, OBE; two *s* one *d*. *Educ*: Malvern Coll.; Exeter Coll., Oxford. Colonial Service, Nigeria, 1928; Administrative Officer, Class I, 1946; Staff Grade, 1947; Administrative Sec., Nigeria, 1947–52; Lt-Governor, Western Region, Nigeria, 1952–54; Chief Sec., Federation of Nigeria, 1954–55. JP Wilts 1958. *Recreation*: ornithology. *Address*: Murrell House, Limpley Stoke, near Bath. *T*: Limpley Stoke 2162.

*Died 10 June 1986.*

**MARSHALL, John Robert Neil,** CMG 1977; MBE 1968; *b* 15 July 1922; *s* of William Gilchrist Marshall and Mabel Marshall. *Educ*: Wisbech Grammar Sch.; Balliol Coll., Oxford (MA). Nigerian Administrative Service, 1950–79 (Adviser, Local Govt Reforms, 1976–79); Ahmadu Bello University (Institute of Administration), Zaria, 1979–81, retired 1981. *Address*: 2 Saxon Lane, Seaford, East Sussex. *T*: Seaford (0323) 895447. *Club*: Commonwealth Trust.

*Died 14 July 1990.*

**MARSHALL, Rt. Hon. Sir John (Ross),** PC 1966; GBE 1974; CH 1973; BA, LLM; Prime Minister of New Zealand, Feb.-Nov. 1972; Leader of the Opposition, 1972–74; Chairman of Directors, National Bank of New Zealand, 1975–83; *b* Wellington, 5 March 1912; *s* of Allan Marshall; *m* 1944, Margaret Livingston; two *s* two *d*. *Educ*: Whangarei High Sch.; Otago Boys' High Sch.; Victoria Univ. Coll. Barrister and Solicitor, 1936; served War, with 2nd NZEF, Pacific Is and Italy, 1941–46 (Inf. Major); MP (Nat.) for Mount Victoria, 1946–54, for Karori, 1954–75; Lectr in Law, Victoria Univ. Coll., 1948–51, Vis. Fellow, 1975–82; Minister, Asst to Prime Minister, in charge of State Advances Corp., Public Trust Office and Census and Statistics Dept, 1949–54; Minister of Health, 1951–54, and Information and Publicity, 1951–57; Attorney-Gen. and Minister of Justice, 1954–57; Dep. Prime Minister, 1957; Dep. Leader of the Opposition, 1957–60; Minister of Customs, 1960–61; Minister of Industries and Commerce, 1960–69; Attorney-General, 1969–71; Dep. Prime Minister, and Minister of Overseas Trade, 1960–72; Minister of Labour and Immigration, 1969–72. NZ Rep. at Colombo Plan Conf., New Delhi, 1953; visited US on Foreign Leader Grant, April 1958; NZ Representative: GATT, 1961, 1963, 1966, and ECAFE, 1962, 1964, 1966, 1968, 1970; Commonwealth Prime Ministers' Conf., 1962; Commonwealth Trade Ministers' Conf., 1963, 1966; Commonwealth Parly Conf., 1965; UN 25th Annual Session, NY, 1970; ILO Conf., Geneva, 1971; EEC Negotiations, 1961–71. Mem., Adv. Council, World Peace through Law. Chairman: NZ Commn for Expo 70; Nat. Develt Council, 1969–72; Cttee of Registration of Teachers, 1976–77. Chairman: Philips Electrical Industries, 1974–84; Contractors Bonding Corp., 1975–; Norwich Winterthur Insurance (NZ) Ltd, 1977–82; DRG (NZ) Ltd, 1975–87; Williams Property Hldgs Ltd, 1983–87; Director: Norwich Union Insurance Soc.; Hallenstein Bros Ltd, 1974–82. Consultant Partner, Buddle Findlay, 1974–86. Pres., Bible Soc. in NZ, 1978–80; World Vice Pres., United Bible Socs, 1982–; Patron, World Vision in NZ; Chm., NZ Internat. Festival of the Arts. Hon. Bencher, Gray's Inn. Hon. LLD Wellington, 1975. *Publications*: The Law of Watercourses, 1957; Memoirs, 1983; *for children*: The Adventures of Dr Duffer, 1978; More Adventures of Dr Duffer, 1979; Dr Duffer and the Treasure Hunt, 1980; Dr Duffer and his Australian Adventures, 1981. *Recreations*: fishing, golf, breeding Connemara ponies. *Address*: 22 Fitzroy Street, Wellington, NZ. *T*: 736.631.

*Died 30 Aug. 1988.*

**MARSHALL, Maj.-Gen. Roy Stuart,** CB 1970; OBE 1960; MC 1945; MM 1940; *b* 28 Oct. 1917; *s* of Andrew Adamson Marshall and Bessie Marshall, Whitley Bay, Northumberland; *m* 1946, Phyllis

Mary Rawlings; two s. Educ: Whitley Bay and Monkseaton High Sch. Joined TA 88 (West Lancs) Field Regt, 1939; commd into RA, 1942; War Service in Europe and Middle East, 1939–45; Staff Coll., Camberley, 1947; GSO 2, 2 Inf. Div., 1948–50; DAA & QMG, 6 Inf. Bde, 1950–51; jssc 1952–53; AA & QMG, 1 (BR) Corps, 1958–60; CO 12th Regt RA, 1960–62; Comdr 7th Artillery Bde, 1962–64; Indian Nat. Def. Coll., 1965; Maj.-Gen. RA, BAOR, 1966–69; Dep. Master-General of the Ordnance, 1969–70, retired; Col Comdt, RA, 1972–77. Dynamics Group, British Aerospace, 1970–82. Recreations: fishing, golf, bridge. Address: Sherford Place East, Taunton. Died 11 Nov. 1987.

**MARSHALL, Sir Stirrat Andrew William J.; see Johnson-Marshall.**

**MARSHALL, Thomas Humphrey,** CMG 1947; MA; Professor Emeritus, University of London; b London, 19 Dec. 1893; s of William C. Marshall, architect, and Margaret d of Archdeacon Lloyd, sometime Archdeacon of Waitemata, New Zealand; m 1st, 1925, Marjorie Tomson (d 1931); 2nd, 1934, Nadine, d of late Mark Hambourg; one s. Educ: Rugby; Trinity Coll., Cambridge. Civilian prisoner in Germany, 1914–18; Fellow of Trinity Coll., Cambridge, 1919–25; Lecturer LSE, 1925; Reader in Sociology, London, 1930; Research Dept of FO, Head of German Section and Dep. Dir, 1939–44; Head of the Social Science Dept, London Sch. of Economics and Political Science, 1944–50; Mem. of Lord Chancellor's Cttee on Practice and Procedure of Supreme Court, 1947–53; Educational Adviser in the British Zone of Germany, 1949–50; Member: UK Cttee for Unesco; UK Delegation to Unesco General Conference, 1952. Martin White Prof. of Sociology, London Sch. of Economics, London Univ., 1954–56; Dir of the Social Sciences Dept, Unesco, 1956–60; Pres., Internat. Sociological Assoc., 1959–62. Hon. DSc Southampton 1969; Hon. DLitt Leicester, 1970; DUniv York, 1971; Hon. LittD Cambridge, 1978. Publications: James Watt, 1925; Class Conflict and Social Stratification (ed), 1938; The Population Problem (ed), 1938; Citizenship and Social Class, 1950; Sociology at the Crossroads and other Essays, 1963; Social Policy, 1965; The Right to Welfare, 1981; numerous articles in Economic Journal, Economic History Review, Sociological Review, etc. Recreation: music. Address: 6 Drosier Road, Cambridge. Died 29 Nov. 1981.

**MARSHALL-CORNWALL, Gen. Sir James (Handyside),** KCB 1940 (CB 1936); CBE 1919; DSO 1917; MC 1916; b 27 May 1887; o s of late Jas Cornwall, Postmaster-Gen. UP, India; m 1921, Marjorie (d 1976), d of late W. Scott Owen, OBE, JP of Cefngwifed, Newtown, Montgomeryshire; one d (and one s killed on active service, 1944). Educ: Cargilfield; Rugby; RMA, Woolwich. Commissioned in Royal Artillery, 1907; served European War in France and Flanders, 1914–18, as Intelligence Officer and Gen. Staff Officer (despatches 5 times, DSO, MC, Bt Major 1916; Bt Lt-Col 1918; Legion of Honour, Belgian Ordre de la Couronne (Croix d'Officier), Belgian Croix de Guerre, American Distinguished Service Medal, Order of the Nile); served on Gen. Staff at War Office, 1918; attended Peace Conference at Paris as mem. of British Delegation, 1919 (CBE); passed Staff Coll., 1919; served in Army of the Black Sea, 1920–23; acted as British Delegate, Thracian Boundary Commission, 1924–25; served in Shanghai Defence Force, 1927; Military Attaché, Berlin, Stockholm, Oslo and Copenhagen, 1928–32; Comdr RA 51st (Highland) Div. TA, 1932–34; Chief of British Military Mission to Egyptian Army, 1937–38; Dir-Gen. Air and Coast Defence, War Office, 1938–39; Special Employment, War Office, 1939–40; III Corps, Comdr, 1940; GOC British Troops in Egypt, 1941; GOC-in-C Western Command, 1941–42 (despatches twice); retd pay, 1943; Amer. Legion of Merit (Comdr), 1946. Editor-in-Chief of Captured German Archives, attached Foreign Office, 1948–51. Pres., Royal Geographical Society, 1954–58 (Hon. Vice-Pres.; Hon. Mem., 1975). Publications: Geographic Disarmament, 1935; Marshal Massena, 1965; Napoleon, 1967; Grant, 1970; Foch, 1972; Haig, 1973; Wars and Rumours of Wars (autobiog.), 1984. Recreation: historical research. Address: Birdsall House, Malton, N Yorks YO17 9NR. T: North Grimston 202. Clubs: Brooks's, Beefsteak, Geographical. Died 25 Dec. 1985.

**MARSHAM, Thomas Nelson,** CBE 1976 (OBE 1964); BSc, PhD; FRS 1986; FEng 1986; MIEE, MInstP; United Kingdom Atomic Energy Authority, retired; non-executive Director, British Nuclear Fuels Ltd, since 1979; consultant, since 1987; b 10 Nov. 1923; s of late Captain Thomas Brabban Marsham, OBE, and Jane Wise Marsham (née Nelson); m 1958, Dr Sheila Margaret Griffin; two s. Educ: Merchant Taylors' Sch., Crosby; Univ. of Liverpool (BSc, PhD). Ocean Steam Ship Co., 1941–46; Oliver Lodge Fellow, Univ. of Liverpool, 1951–53; joined UKAEA, 1953; Reactor Manager, Calder Hall Nuclear Power Station, 1955–57; Dep. Gen. Man., Windscale and Calder Works, 1958–64; Dir, Technical Policy, Reactor Gp, 1964–77; Man. Dir, Northern Div., 1977–87; Mem., UKAEA, 1979–87. Mem., Adv. Council on R&D for Fuel and Power, 1974–. Mem. Council, Univ. of Liverpool, 1980–84. Publications: papers in scientific jls on nuclear physics. Recreations: sailing, Rugby football. Address: Fairfield, Eskdale, Holmrook,

Cumbria CA19 1UA. T: Eskdale 252. Club: East India, Devonshire, Sports and Public Schools. Died 12 Oct. 1989.

**MARSON, Air Vice-Marshal John,** CB 1953; CBE 1950; CEng; RAF (retired); b 24 Aug. 1906; s of late Wing Comdr T. B. Marson, MBE, and late Mrs E. G. Marson, (née Atkins); m 1935, Louise Joy Stephen Paterson; two s. Educ: Oakham Sch. RAF Coll., Cranwell, 1924–26. STSO, HQ, Coastal Command, 1949–50; AOC 42 Group, 1951–54; Pres., Ordnance Board, 1956–57 (Vice-Pres., 1954–56); Dir-Gen. of Technical Services, 1957–58; AOC 24 Group, 1959–61. Recreations: sailing, golf. Address: Marygold, Aldeburgh, Suffolk IP15 5HF. Clubs: Royal Air Force; Royal Cruising; Cruising Association; Aldeburgh Golf. Died 1 May 1988.

**MARTEN, Rt. Hon. Sir (H.) Neil,** Kt 1983; PC 1981; b 3 Dec. 1916; 3rd s of F. W. Marten; m 1944, Joan Olive, d of Vice-Adm. W. J. C. Lake, CBE; one s two d. Educ: Rossall Sch.; Law Soc. Solicitor, 1939. Served War of 1939–45 (despatches); Army, 1940–45, Northants Yeomanry, Special Forces, French Resistance, Norwegian Resistance (Croix de Guerre; Norwegian War Medal). Foreign Office, 1947–57, Egypt, Turkey, Germany. MP (C) Banbury, Oxon, 1959–83; PPS to Pres. of Board of Trade, 1960–62; Parliamentary Sec., Ministry of Aviation, 1962–64; Minister of State, FCO, and Minister for Overseas Develt, 1979–83. Mem., 1922 Exec. Cttee, 1965–79; Chm., British Norwegian Parly Gp, 1964–79; Hon. Treasurer: British-Amer. Parly Gp, 1975–78; CPA, 1976–79; Vice-Pres., Disabled Drivers Assoc. Governor: Inter Amer. Develt Bank; Asian Develt Bank; Caribbean Develt Bank, 1979–83. Chevalier 1st Class, Order of St Olav, Norway. Recreations: tennis, ski-ing. Address: Broad Oak House, Manston, Dorset. Clubs: Special Forces, Carlton. Died 22 Dec. 1985.

**MARTIN, Andrew,** QC 1965; PhD (London); Professor of International and Comparative Law, University of Southampton, 1963–77; Member: Law Commission, 1965–70; Law Reform Committee, since 1970; b 21 April 1906; m 1932, Anna Szekely; one s. Educ: Lutheran Coll., Budapest; Universities of Budapest, Paris, Vienna, Berlin and London. Barrister-at-Law, Middle Temple, 1940, Bencher, 1976. Publications: A Commentary on the Charter of the United Nations (with Norman Bentwich), 1950; Collective Security, 1952; The Changing Charter (with J. B. S. Edwards), 1955; Restrictive Trade Practices and Monopolies, 1957; Law Reform Now (jt editor and part-author), 1963; Legal Aspects of Disarmament, 1963; More Law Reform Now (jt editor and part-author), 1983; numerous papers and articles published by learned socs and jls. Recreations: chamber music and alpine walks. Address: 4 Pump Court, Temple, EC4. T: 01–353 9178. Clubs: Reform, Hurlingham. Died 27 Feb. 1985.

**MARTIN, Rear-Adm. Sir David (James),** KCMG 1988; AO 1985; Governor of New South Wales, 1989–90; b 15 April 1933; s of William Harold Martin (killed in action, March 1942, when Comdr RAN, in HMAS Perth) and late Isla Estelle Martin; m 1957, Suzanne Millear; one s two d. Educ: The Scots Coll., Sydney; RAN Coll. (entered 1947). Served Korean War, 1951; qual. in Gunnery, HMS Excellent, 1958; Staff of Aust. High Commn in London, 1964–65; commanded HM Australian Ships: Queenborough, 1969; Torrens, 1974; Supply, 1978; Melbourne, 1979; RCDS 1980; Chief of Naval Personnel, 1982–83; Flag Officer, Naval Support Comd, 1984–88. Mem., Fellowship of First Fleeters, 1976–. KStJ 1989. Clubs: Australian, Australian Pioneers, Australian Jockey (Sydney). Died 10 Aug. 1990.

**MARTIN, Douglas Whitwell;** Chairman, Gill & Duffus Ltd, 1964–70; President, Gill & Duffus Group PLC, 1973–85; b 17 Feb. 1906; s of Rev. T. H. Martin, MA, and Lily Janet Vaughan Martin; m 1st, 1931, Jessie Milroy Lawrie (d 1965); three s; 2nd, 1967, Margaret Helen Simms, FCIS. Educ: Rossall Sch.; Lausanne University. Member of staff, Export Dept of Lever Brothers Ltd, 1923–27; joined Gill & Duffus Ltd, 1929. Underwriting Member of Lloyd's, 1950–69. Recreations: reading, theatre. Address: 74 Fort George, St Peter Port, Guernsey, CI. T: Guernsey 25381.
Died 7 Jan. 1989.

**MARTIN, Edward H.; see Holland-Martin.**

**MARTIN, Hon. (Fred) Russell (Beauchamp),** MC; Justice of the Supreme Court of Victoria, 1934–57; b 28 May 1887; s of Frederick Martin and Alice Maud Evelyn Wood; m 1915, Ethel Muriel Swinburne; three s. Educ: Wesley Coll., Melbourne; Melbourne Univ. (Queen's Coll.). Called to Victoria Bar, 1911; served in 38th Bn AIF 1915–19 (MC). Recreations: golf, bowls. Address: 15 Berkeley Street, Hawthorn, Victoria 3122, Australia. Clubs: Royal Automobile (Victoria); Peninsula Country Golf.
Died 28 April 1981.

**MARTIN, Frederick George Stephen,** CIE 1941; MC; MIME; b 26 Aug. 1890; s of Frederick Martin, Newcastle-under-Lyme; m 1939, Mrs Herta Portzeba, d of Fritz Loose, Berlin; no c. Served European War, 1914–18 (despatches, MC, wounded twice); entered Indian State Rlys, 1923; Dep. Chief Mechanical Engineer, EI Rly, 1928;

Controller of Stores, EI Rly, 1930; Dep. Dir-Gen., Engineering and Civil Production, Dept of Supply, Govt of India, 1939–42; Addl Dir, Gen. Supply Dept, India, 1942–43; Dir in charge, Tata Aircraft Ltd, 1943–46; Tech. Adviser, Tata Industries and Tata Ltd, 1946–59, retired. *Address:* Golmuri, Cranham, Gloucester GL4 8HB. *T:* Painswick 812061.                                     *Died* 22 *May* 1981.

**MARTIN, Prof. Frederick Morris;** Professor of Social Administration, University of Glasgow, since 1972; Dean of Faculty of Social Sciences, 1976–78; *b* 2 Oct. 1923; *s* of J. and M. Martin; *m* 1947, Cicely Frances Brown; one *s* two *d*. *Educ:* London elem. and secondary schs; Birkbeck Coll., Univ. of London. BA 1949, PhD London 1953. Asst Lectr in Social Psychology, London Sch. of Economics, 1949–52; Lectr in Social Psychology and Sociology, Birkbeck Coll., and Mem. research staff, London Sch. of Hygiene, 1952–55; Lectr, Dept of Social Med., Univ. of Edin., 1956–60, Sen. Lectr, 1960–65, Reader, 1965–67; Asst Dir of Research and Intell., GLC, 1967–69; Head of Social Research and Policy Div., 1969–71. Member: Adv. Council on Social Work, 1974–81; Personal Social Services Council, 1974–80; (Chm.) Cttee on Social Work Statistics, 1975–81; Data Protection Cttee, 1976–78; SSRC Sociology and Social Admin. Cttee, 1971–75; (Chm.) SSRC Panel on North Sea Oil, 1975–82; Central Council for Educn and Trng in Social Work (and Chm., Scottish Cttee), 1973–76 and 1978–84. *Publications:* (with Jean Floud and A. H. Halsey) Social Class and Educational Opportunity, 1956; (with G. F. Rehin) Patterns of Performance in Community Care, 1978; (with Margaret Bone and Bernadette Spain) Plans and Provisions for the Mentally Handicapped, 1972; (ed with Kathleen Murray) Children's Hearings, 1976; (ed) Social Services in Scotland, 1979, 2nd edn 1983; (with S. J. Fox and Kathleen Murray) Children out of Court, 1981; (with Kathleen Murray) The Scottish Juvenile Justice System, 1982; Between the Acts: community mental health services 1959–1983, 1984; Welfare Abroad, 1985; WHO Reports, PEP pamphlets, papers and reviews in social sci. and med. jls. *Recreations:* books, music. *Address:* Department of Social Administration and Social Work, 53–57 Southpark Avenue, Glasgow G12 8LF. *T:* 041–339 8855.
                                              *Died* 1 *Feb.* 1985.

**MARTIN, Air Marshal Sir Harold Brownlow Morgan,** KCB 1971 (CB 1968); DSO 1943 (Bar 1944); DFC 1942 (Bar 1943, 1944); AFC 1948; *b* Edgecliffe, 27 Feb. 1918; *s* of the late J. H. O. M. Martin, MD, and of Colina Elizabeth Dixon; *m* 1944, Wendy Lawrence, *d* of late Grenville Outhwaite, Melbourne; two *d*. *Educ:* Bloomfields; Sydney; Randwick. Served war, 1939–45, Bomber Comd; took part in raid on Möhne dam, 1943. psa 1945; won Britannia Flying Trophy, 1947; Air Attaché, British Embassy, Israel, 1952–55; jssc, 1958; idc, 1965. SASO, Near East Air Force and Jt Services Chief of Staff, 1966–67; Air Vice-Marshal 1967; AOC No 38 Gp, Air Support Command, 1967–70; Air Marshal 1970; C-in-C, RAF Germany, and Commander, NATO 2nd Tactical Air Force, 1970–73; Air Member for Personnel, MoD, 1973–74, retired. ADC to HM the Queen, 1963. Hawker Siddeley International Ltd: Advr, 1974–75, Principal, Beirut, 1975–78, Middle East Future Markets; Market Advr, Hawker Siddeley PE Ltd, 1979–85, retd. Oswald Watt Memorial Medal. *Recreations:* flying, horse racing, tennis, travel. *Clubs:* Royal Air Force, Arts, Hurlingham.
                                              *Died* 3 *Nov.* 1988.

**MARTIN, Sir James,** Kt 1965; CBE 1957 (OBE 1950); DSc; CEng; FIMechE; Managing Director and Chief Designer, Martin-Baker Aircraft Co. Ltd, since formation of Company, 1934; *b* 1893; *s* of Thomas Martin and Sarah (*né* Coulter), Co. Down, NI; *m* 1942, Muriel Haines; two *s* two *d*. *Educ:* privately. Founder, Martin Aircraft Co., 1929. Designed: Martin patent balloon barrage cable cutter; 12 gun nose for Havoc night fighter; Spitfire jettison hood; flat feed for 20 mm Hispano gun; M-B1, 2, 3, and 5 prototype aeroplanes; started work on aircraft ejector seats, 1945; explosive hood jettison gear; rocket ejection seats. Hon. FRAeS; RAeS Wakefield Gold Medal, 1952; Barbour Air Safety Award, 1958; Cumberbatch Air Safety Trophy, 1959; Royal Aero Club Gold Medal, 1964. Hon. Fellow, Manchester Inst. of Science and Technology, 1968. Pioneer and authority on aircraft seat ejection. *Publications:* numerous papers on air-survival (read by learned socs in UK and USA). *Recreation:* design work. *Address:* Southlands Manor, Denham, Bucks. *T:* Denham 2214. *Club:* Naval and Military.                                        *Died* 5 *Jan.* 1981.

**MARTIN, Maj.-Gen. James Mansergh Wentworth,** CB 1953; CBE 1944; late 8th King George V's Own Light Cavalry; *b* 5 Aug. 1902; *er s* of late James Wentworth Martin, Castle Jane, Glanmire, Co. Cork, Ireland, and late Mrs J. Wentworth Martin, Great Meadow, Hambledon, Surrey; *m* 1944, Mrs Jean Lindsay Barnes (*d* 1978), *d* of late Sir Henry Cowan, MP. *Educ:* Charterhouse; Royal Military Academy, Woolwich. Joined RFA 1922; with Royal West African Frontier Force, 1925–27; Private Sec. to Governor of Assam, 1928–29; transferred to Indian Army, 1930. During War of 1939–45, Persia and Iraq, Syria, Tunisia, Sicily, Italy and Burma; Brig., Gen. Staff, 1943–44. Comd 1st Indian Armoured Bde, 1945–47;

transferred to Royal Scots Greys, Jan. 1948; Chief of Staff, British Forces in Trieste, 1948–49; Comd 9th Armoured Brigade, 1949–51; Dep. Chief of Staff Allied Land Forces Central Europe, Fontainebleau, 1951–53; GOC Salisbury Plain District, 1953–56; retired Sept. 1956. Liveryman of the Merchant Taylors' Company. *Address:* Great Meadow, Hambledon, Godalming, Surrey. *T:* Wormley 2665.                                     *Died* 16 *Nov.* 1986.

**MARTIN, James Purdon,** MA, MD, BCh (Belfast), FRCP; Consulting Physician to the National Hospital for Nervous Diseases, Queen Square, WC1; *b* Jordanstown, County Antrim, 1893; *s* of late Samuel Martin, Garmoyle, Bangor, Co. Down; *m* 1st, Marjorie, MB, BS (*d* 1937), *d* of Richard Blandy, Madeira; two *s*; 2nd, Janet Smiles Ferguson, MA (*d* 1978). *Educ:* Royal Academical Institution and Queen's Univ., Belfast; (Medical Schs: Belfast, St Bart's, St Mary's) BA (first class hons in Mathematical subjects), 1915; Purser Studentship; MB, BCh, BAO, 1920; MRCP, 1922; FRCP 1930; Neurologist to British Post-Graduate Medical Sch., 1935–57. Examnr, London Univ. and Conjoint Bd, 1940–49. Dean: Nat. Hosp. Med. Sch., 1944–48; Inst. Neurology, 1948–49. Mem. of the Senate of Queen's Univ. (representative for Students), 1916–17. Neurologist Eastern Command, Home Forces, 1940–44. Vis. Prof. of Neurology, University of Colorado, 1959. Lumleian Lecturer, RCP, 1947; Arris and Gale Lecturer, RCS, 1963. Hon. Member: Assoc. of British Neurologists; Soc. of Brit. Neuropathologists; Neurolog. Sect., RSM; Soc. Française de Neurologie; Amer. Neurolog. Assoc.; Canadian Neurolog. Congress, etc. FRSocMed (Pres. Neurolog. Sect., 1945–46). DSc *hc* QUB, 1982. *Publications:* The Basal Ganglia and Posture, 1967; many papers on neurological subjects in Brain, The Lancet, etc. *Address:* 36 Queen Court, Queen Square, WC1. *T:* 01-278 5426.                       *Died* 7 *May* 1984.

**MARTIN, John Hanbury;** *b* 4 April 1892; *s* of W. A. H. Martin, DL, JP, and Frances Hanbury-Williams; *m* 1st, 1934, Avice Blaneid (marr. diss. 1938), *d* of Herbert Trench; 2nd, 1950, Dorothy Helen, *d* of E. Lloyd-Jones, Plas Mancott, Flints. *Educ:* Wellington; Brasenose Coll., Oxford. Served War of 1914–18; Captain, Queen's Westminster Rifles, 1915–19 (wounded). Labour candidate for Great Yarmouth, 1931; MP (Lab) Central Southwark, 1939–48. Co-founder and Chm., Southwark Housing Assoc., 1930–. Mem., London Insurance Cttee, 1936–45; Sec. Franco-British Parly Assoc., 1943–48. *Publications:* Corner of England; Peace Adventure; Portrait of a King; contrib. to New Survey of London Life and Labour; numerous articles and reviews. *Address:* c/o Barclays Bank Ltd, 68 Lombard Street, EC3. *Club:* Brooks's.
                                              *Died* 3 *Feb.* 1983.

**MARTIN, Leonard Charles James;** Under-Secretary, Overseas Development Administration, FCO (formerly Ministry of Overseas Development), 1968–80, retired; *b* 28 June 1920; *s* of Leonard Howard Martin and Esther Martin (*née* Avis); *m* 1945, Althea Lilian Charles; three *d*. *Educ:* Brighton, Hove and Sussex Grammar Sch.; London Sch. of Economics. Served RAFVR, 1941–45. Min. of Educn, and Dept of Educn and Science, 1946–64; ODM, 1965–80. UK Permanent Delegate to UNESCO, 1965–68; Mem. Exec. Bd, UNESCO, 1974–78 (Chm., 1976–78). *Address:* 87 Downside, Shoreham-by-Sea, West Sussex BN4 6HF.
                                              *Died* 15 *May* 1987.

**MARTIN, Sir Leslie Harold,** Kt 1957; CBE 1954; FRS 1957; FAA; PhD (Cantab); DSc (Australian National University, Melbourne, Qld, NSW, Adelaide); LLD (WA); DLitt (Sydney); Dean of Military Studies, and Professor of Physics, Royal Military College, Duntroon, Canberra, 1967–70; *b* 21 Dec. 1900; *s* of Richard Martin, Melbourne; *m* 1923, Gladys Maude Elaine, *d* of H. J. Bull; one *s* (and one *s* decd). *Educ:* Melbourne High Sch.; Melbourne Univ.; Trinity Coll., Cambridge. Scholar of Exhibn of 1851, 1923; apptd to Natural Philosophy Dept of Melbourne Univ., 1927; Rockefeller Fellow, 1927; Syme Prize, 1934; Associate Professor of Natural Philosophy, University of Melbourne, 1937–45; Professor of Physics, 1945–59; Emeritus Prof., 1960. Defence Scientific Adviser to Aust. Govt, and Chm., Defence Res. and Develt Policy, 1948–67; Comr, Atomic Energy Commn of Aust., 1958–68; Chm., Aust. Univ. Commn, 1959–66. *Address:* 11 Wedge Court, Glen Waverley, Victoria 3150, Australia. *T:* 2321125.                     *Died* 1 *Feb.* 1983.

**MARTIN, Louis Claude,** ARCS, DIC, DSc (London); *b* 16 June 1891; *s* of late Alfred Henry Martin and Eleanor Gertrude Martin, Norwich; *m* 1916, Elsie Maud Lock; one *s* (one *d* decd). *Educ:* King Edward VI Middle Sch., Norwich; Royal College of Science. Lecturer, West Ham Municipal Technical Coll., 1913–14; served European War, Royal Naval Divisional Engineers, 1914–16; Lecturer and Asst Prof. in Technical Optics, Imperial College, 1917–43, Professor of Technical Optics, 1943–51. Visiting Prof., University of Rochester, NY, USA, 1936–37; Chm. Lens Research Sub-Cttee, Min. of Aircraft Prod., 1941–45; Manager Royal Institution, 1947–49 and 1951–52; Chm. of Optical Group, Physical Soc., 1947–50; Vice-Pres., International Optic Commission, 1950–53; Hon. Fellow, Royal Microscopical Soc., 1967. Deacons'

Sec., Beckenham Congregational Church, 1947–49. Reader: Diocese of Norwich, 1958, 1969–71; Diocese of Winchester, 1960. Liveryman, Worshipful Company of Spectacle Makers. *Publications:* (with W. Gamble) Colour and Methods of Colour Reproduction, 1923; Optical Measuring Instruments, 1924; Introduction to Applied Optics, 1930; (with B. K. Johnson) Practical Microscopy, 1931; Technical Optics, 1949; Geometrical Optics, 1955 (with W. T. Welford) Technical Optics, 2nd edn., 1966; Theory of the Microscope, 1966. About forty papers mainly on optical subjects, especially the theory of the microscope. *Recreations:* poetry, sketching. *Address:* Golden Goose Cottage, Wiveton, Holt, Norfolk. *Died 5 Oct.* 1981.

**MARTIN, Most Rev. Pierre,** Officer, Legion of Honour, 1967; President, Episcopal Conference of The Pacific, since 1971; Former Archbishop of Noumea (1966–71); *b* 22 Feb. 1910. *Educ:* Univ. de Lyon; Lyon Séminaire and in Belgium. Priest, 1939. POW, Buchenwald and Dachau Camps, until 1945. Séminaire de Missions d'Océanie, Lyon: Professor, 1945–47; Supérieure, 1947–53; Provincial, Sté de Marie, Paris, 1953–56; Bishop of New Caledonia, 1956. Apostolic Administrator of the Diocese of Port-Vila, 1976–77. *Address:* CEPAC, PO Box 1200, Suva, Fiji.
*Died 8 April* 1987.

**MARTIN, Prof. Nicholas Henry,** TD 1947; FRCP, FRIC, FRCPath; Professor of Chemical Pathology, University of London, 1952–70, now Emeritus; Hon. Consultant to St George's Hospital (Consultant from 1947); Advisor, Wessex Regional Health Authority, since 1969; Member Lister Institute since 1954; *b* 26 Oct. 1906; *s* of late William and Ellen Renfree Martin, Crellow, Cornwall, and Newcastle; *m* 1948, Ursula, 2nd *d* of William Brodie and *widow* of T. H. Worth, Lincs; two *s*. *Educ:* Sedburgh Sch.; Durham, Oxford and Munich Univs. Buckle Travelling Fellow, 1929; Oxford Univ. Scholar, Middlesex Hosp., 1932. Served War of 1939–45: Asst Dir of Pathology, 21st Army Group (despatches twice); Consultant to UNRRA, 1945–46; Fellow, Harvard Univ., 1946–47. Hon. Consultant in Chemical Pathology to the Army, 1963–69. Chm., Association of Clinical Pathologists, 1963–68, Pres., 1969–70; Vice-Pres., College of Pathologists, 1966–69. Mem., Governing Body, Lord Mayor Treloar Homes, 1977–. *Publications:* numerous medical and scientific publications in internat. literature. *Recreations:* sailing, gardening, reading. *Address:* 6 Coastguard Cottages, Helford Passage, near Falmouth, Cornwall. *T:* Mawnan Smith 250442. *Clubs:* Athenæum, Bath. *Died 13 Dec.* 1981.

**MARTIN, Olaus Macleod,** CIE 1937; *b* Stornoway, 1 Feb. 1890; *s* of Rev. Donald John Martin; *m* 1919, Helen Frances Steele (Kaisar-i-Hind Gold Medal, 1943) (*d* 1971); four *s* one *d*. *Educ:* Edinburgh and Oxford Univs. MA (1st Class Hons Classics and Mental Philosophy) 1913; Indian Civil Service, 1913; Magistrate-Collector, 1921; Divisional Comr, 1940; Development Comr, Bengal, 1945; retired from ICS, 1948. British Administration, Eritrea, 1947–51. *Recreations:* riding, tennis, shooting, fishing. *Address:* 32 Drummond Road, Inverness. *T:* Inverness 36035.
*Died 28 Dec.* 1981.

**MARTIN, Rev. Philip Montague;** Canon Residentiary and Chancellor of Wells Cathedral, 1971–79; *b* 8 Aug. 1913; *o s* of Montague Egerton and Ada Martin; *m* 1940, Mollie Elizabeth, *d* of John Mitchell Ainsworth; one *s* one *d*. *Educ:* Whitgift Sch.; Exeter Coll., Oxford. Hasker Scholar and Squire Scholar, Oxford; BA 1936, MA 1939; Teachers' Diploma (London) 1945. Deacon, 1937; Priest, 1938, Southwark. Curate of Limpsfield, 1937–40; Curate of Minehead, 1940–44; Asst Master, Clifton Coll., 1944; Chaplain and Lecturer, St Luke's Coll., Exeter, 1945–48; Canon Residentiary of Newcastle Cathedral and Diocesan Dir of Religious Education, 1948–61; Vicar of St Mary the Virgin (University Church), Oxford, 1961–71, with St Cross (Holywell), 1966–71; Chaplain, Nuffield Coll., Oxford, 1969–71; Fellow, St Cross Coll., Oxford, 1970. Examining Chaplain to Bishop of Newcastle, 1952–73; Rural Dean of Oxford, 1965–68. *Publications:* Mastery and Mercy: a study of two religious poems, 1957; None but He and I and other poems, 1966; Earnest-pennies, 1973; (contrib.) Readings of The Wreck: essays in commemoration of G. M. Hopkins' The Wreck of the Deutschland, 1976. *Address:* 7 Belworth Drive, Cheltenham GL51 6EL. *Died 24 July* 1981.

**MARTIN, Philippa Parry;** Consulting Surgeon: Western Ophthalmic Hospital; St Mary's Hospital Group; Fellow of University College, London; Hunterian Professor, The Royal College of Surgeons of England; *b* 3 April 1897; *d* of late Canon T. St J. P. Pughe, Penn, Bucks; *m* 1923, Edward Kenneth Martin, FRCS; three *d*. *Educ:* Switzerland; St Felix Sch., Southwold; University Coll., and University Coll. Hospital, London. MS, FRCS. Formerly Chm. Editorial Cttee, Med. Women's Fedn. *Publications:* articles in medical journals. *Recreation:* travelling. *Address:* 97 Dorset House, NW1 5AF. *T:* 01-935 6322; Goose Neck, Chinnor Hill, Oxon. *T:* Kingston Blount 51242. *Died 22 Jan.* 1981.

**MARTIN, Hon. Russell;** *see* Martin, Hon. F. R. B.

**MARTINS, (Virgilio) Armando;** Ambassador; Professor, Institute of Oriental Studies, University of Lisbon, since 1980; *b* 1 Sept. 1914; *s* of José Júlio Martins and Elvira Janeiro; *m* 1959, Ingrid Bloser; one *s* one *d*. *Educ:* Coimbra and Lisbon Univs. Degree in Law. Entered Foreign Service, 1939; Attaché, Foreign Min., Lisbon, 1941; Consul: Leopoldville, 1943; Liverpool, 1947; Sydney, 1949; special mission, NZ, 1951; First Sec., Tokyo, 1952; Brussels, 1955; Substitute of Permanent Rep. to NATO, 1956; Minister, 2nd Cl., Foreign Min., Lisbon, 1959; NATO, 1961; Ambassador to: Tokyo, 1964; Rome, 1971; the Court of St James's, 1977–79. *Publications:* Figuras De Silêncio (Portuguese Cultural Tradition in the Japan of Today), 1981; Japão construção de um país moderno (Japan, Construction of a Modern Country), 1985; O Impacto Português sobre a Civilização Japonesa (Portuguese Impact on Japanese Civilization), new edn 1988; books on internat. law, social questions, literary criticism, history, poetry, and the theatre. *Recreations:* oriental studies, reading, writing. *Address:* 40 Avenida de Portugal, 2765 Estoril, Portugal. *Died 19 July* 1988.

**MARTONMERE, 1st Baron,** *cr* 1964; **John Roland Robinson,** PC 1962; GBE 1973; KCMG 1966; Kt 1954; MA, LLB; Governor and C-in-C of Bermuda, 1964–72; *b* 22 Feb. 1907; *e s* of Roland Walkden Robinson, Solicitor, Blackpool; *m* 1930, Maysie, *d* of late Clarence Warren Gasque; one *d* (one *s* decd). *Educ:* Trinity Hall, Cambridge. Barrister-at-law, 1929 (Certificate of Honour and Buchanan Prize Lincoln's Inn, 1928); MP (U) Widnes Division of Lancs, 1931–35, Blackpool, 1935–45, S Blackpool, 1945–64. W/Cdr RAFVR, 1940–45. Pres. Royal Lancs Agricultural Society, 1936; Past Pres. Assoc. of Health and Pleasure Resorts; Past Pres. Residential Hotels Assoc. of Great Britain. Past Chm. Conservative Party Commonwealth Affairs Cttee; Chm. Gen. Council, Commonwealth Parliamentary Assoc., 1961–62. Past Dep. Chm. United Kingdom Branch, Commonwealth Parliamentary Association. Hon. Freeman, Town of St George and City of Hamilton (Bermuda). Officer, Legion of Merit (USA). *Heir: g s* John Stephen Robinson, *b* 10 July 1963. *Address:* Romay House, Tuckers Town, Bermuda; El Mirador, Lyford Cay, PO Box 7776, Nassau, Bahamas. *Clubs:* Carlton; Royal Lytham and St Annes Golf (St Annes); Royal Yacht Squadron (Cowes); Lyford Cay (Bahamas); Hon. Life Member: Royal Bermuda Yacht, Mid-Ocean (Bermuda).
*Died 3 May* 1989.

**MARTYN, Joan,** OBE 1962; Governor Class II, HM Prison Commission; Governor, Bullwood Hall, 1962–64, retired; *b* 9 Aug. 1899; 3rd *d* of George Harold and Eve Martyn. *Educ:* Municipal Coll., Grimsby; Queenwood, Eastbourne; Bedford Physical Training Coll. (diploma). Staff of St Mary's Coll., Lancaster Gate, London, W2, 1919–36; staff of HM Borstal Institution, Aylesbury, 1937 (Governor 1946–59); Governor, HM Borstal, Cardiff, 1959–62. *Address:* 22 Pelham Road, Grimsby, S Humberside.
*Died 30 Dec.* 1989.

**MARWOOD, Sidney Lionel,** CIE 1941; *b* 8 April 1891; *s* of John Marwood, Shipbroker, Liverpool; *m* 1924, Agnes (*d* 1952), *e d* of Adam Rolland Rainy, MP; two *s* one *d*; *m* 1953, Mary, *d* of William Logsdail. *Educ:* St. Paul's Sch.; Hertford Coll., Oxford, MA. Commissioned in West Lancs Divisional Engineers, RE (TF), in 1914; saw service in India and Mesopotamia, 1914–19; reverted to Indian Civil Service, 1920, posted to Bihar Province. Collector, 1924, Commissioner, 1939, Revenue Commissioner, Orissa, 1943; retired 1947. Kaisar-i-Hind Gold Medal (I Class) in 1934 after Bihar earthquake. *Address:* St Audrey's, Church Street, Old Hatfield, Herts. *Died 26 Jan.* 1981.

**MARY REGIS, Sister;** *see* Morant, Dame Mary Maud.

**MASON, Ailsa Mary, (Mrs John Rollit Mason);** *see* Garland, A. M.

**MASON, Alan Kenneth,** ISO 1983; HM Diplomatic Service, retired 1979; *b* 18 May 1920; *s* of Richard Mason and Mary Mason (*née* Williams); *m* 1948, Kathleen Mary Redman (marr. diss.); two *s*; *m* 1979, Marion Basden. *Educ:* Westcliff High School. Served with British and Indian Army, India, Burma, 1940–46. Customs and Excise, 1946–48; Min. of Works, 1949–65 (Sec., Ancient Monuments Bds, 1958–63); Diplomatic Service, 1965: Head of Chancery, Jakarta, 1967–70; Dep. Defence Sec., Hong Kong, 1972–75; Consul-General, Hanover, 1975–78; Dep. Sec. for Security, Hong Kong, 1979–84. *Recreations:* archæology, bird watching, Chinese porcelain, walking, bridge. *Address:* Tregunter, Charlcombe Lane, Lansdown, Bath. *Clubs:* Commonwealth Trust; Hong Kong (Hong Kong).
*Died 8 Jan.* 1990.

**MASON, Brewster;** actor; Associate Artist, Royal Shakespeare Company, since 1965; *b* Kidsgrove, Staffs, 30 Aug. 1922; *s* of Jesse Mason and Constance May Kemp; *m* 1st, 1948, Lorna Whittaker (marr. diss.); one *d*; 2nd, 1966, Kate Meredith. *Educ:* privately; Royal Naval Colls; RADA (Bancroft Gold Medal); Guildhall Sch. of Music and Drama (Hons. Grad.). First appeared as a professional actor at Lyric, Hammersmith, as Flt/Sgt John Nabb in An English Summer, Sept. 1948, followed by London appearances to 1960; took over part of Gen. Allenby in Ross, Haymarket, 1960. First appearance in New York, at Henry Miller Theatre, Sept. 1962, as Sir Lewis Eliot in The Affair. Joined RSC, Aldwych, London, Feb. 1963, to play Kent in King Lear, subseq. appearing at Royal Shakespeare, Stratford, July 1963, as Earl of Warwick in trilogy The Wars of the Roses; since 1963 has appeared in repertory at Stratford and Aldwych, in productions including The Birthday Party, 1964; Hamlet, 1965; Macbeth, All's Well that Ends Well, 1967; Julius Caesar, Merry Wives of Windsor, 1968; Major Barbara, King Henry VIII, 1970; Othello in Othello, 1972; Falstaff in Henry IV and Merry Wives of Windsor, 1975; John of Gaunt in Richard II, 1986; at National Theatre: The Trojan War Will Not Take Place, and You Can't Take It With You, 1983; Undershaft in Major Barbara, 1983; Venice Preserv'd, Wild Honey, 1984. Director, Shakespeare Festivals in New England; lectures on Drama and Acting at Univ. of California (Irvine). *Films include:* The Dam Busters, Private Potter, etc. *TV:* first appeared on television, 1953, subseq. playing leading parts, including: Abel Wharton in The Pallisers, 1974; Mr Voysey in The Voysey Inheritance, 1979. FGSM 1976. *Recreations:* golf, painting. *Address:* c/o ICM, 388–396 Oxford Street, W1. *Clubs:* Garrick, Naval; Stage Golfing; Players (New York). *Died 14 Aug. 1987.*

**MASON, Sir Dan (Hurdis)**, Kt 1961; OBE 1940; ERD 1956; *b* 24 July 1911; *e s* of late Charles Mason; *m* 1933, Joyce Louise, *d* of late Horace Young Nutt, Radlett, Herts; three *s* one *d. Educ:* Blundell's; Germany. Chm., West London Hospital, 1947–48; Governor, West London Hosp. Med. Sch., 1947–62; Chm., West London Hosp. Med. Trust, 1962–; Chm., Horsham Conservative Assoc., 1951–58; Sussex Conservative Council, 1955–58; Chm., SE Area of Conservative Nat. Union, 1957–62; Chm., Nat. Union of Conservative Assocs, 1966; Mem., Nat. Exec. Cttee of Conservative Party, 1956–78; Hon. Treas., Nat. Florence Nightingale Meml Cttee, 1956–66; Dep. Pres. 1966–. Served War of 1939–45, Royal Engineers (Supplementary Reserve) (OBE). *Recreations:* gardening, do-it-yourself, crosswords. *Address:* Chatley House, Norton St Philip, Somerset BA3 6NP. *T:* Beckington 325. *Club:* Naval and Military. *Died 4 Dec. 1982.*

**MASON, Vice-Adm. Sir Frank (Trowbridge)**, KCB 1955 (CB 1953); FEng; Hon. FIMechE; FIMarE; retired; Member of Council for Scientific and Industrial Research, 1958–63 (Vice-Chairman, 1962); *b* 25 April 1900; *s* of late F. J. Mason, MBE, JP; *m* 1924, Dora Margaret Brand; one *s* two *d. Educ:* Ipswich Sch. RNC, Keyham, 1918; HMS Collingwood, 1918; HMS Queen Elizabeth, 1919–21; HMS Tiger, 1921; RN Coll., Greenwich, 1921–22; RN Engineering Coll., Keyham, 1922–23; HMS Malaya, 1923–25; HM Dockyard, Malta, 1925–28; HMS Rodney, 1929 and 1933–34; HMS Galatea, 1937–39; Fleet Gunnery Engineer Officer, Home Fleet, 1943–44; Chief Gunnery Engineer Officer and Dep. Dir of Naval Ordnance, 1947–48; idc 1949; Deputy Engineer-in-Chief of The Fleet, 1950–52; Staff of C-in-C The Nore, 1952–53; Engineer-in-Chief of the Fleet, 1953–57, retired. Commander, 1934; Captain, 1943; Rear-Adm., 1950; Vice-Adm., 1953. Parsons Memorial Lectr, 1956. Chm. Steering Cttee, Nat. Engineering Laboratory, 1958–69, Chm. Adv. Board, 1969, Chm. Adv. Cttee, 1973–75; Mem. Steering Cttee, Nat. Physical Laboratory, 1966–68; Chm., Froude Cttee, 1966. Mem. Council, Institution of Mechanical Engineers, 1953–57, and 1961 (Vice-Pres., 1962, Pres., 1964); Institute of Marine Engineers: Chm., Panel of Jt Nuclear Marine Propulsion, 1957; Mem. Council, 1958–60; Vice-Chm., 1961; Chm., 1962; Pres., 1967. Dep. Chm., Schools Science and Technology Cttee, 1968; Mem. Governing Body: National Council for Technological Awards, 1960–64; Royal Naval Sch., Haslemere, 1953–83; Ipswich Sch., 1961–72; Further Education Staff Coll., 1964–74; Navy League, 1967–75; Hurstpierpoint Coll., 1966–80; Brighton Polytechnic, 1969–73; Mem. Council and Exec. Cttee, City and Guilds of London Inst., 1968–77, Vice Chm., 1970–77, Hon. FCGI 1977. Chm., Standing Conf. on Schools Science and Technology, 1971–75, Vice-Pres., 1975. Founder Fellow, Fellowship of Engineering, 1976. Asst to Court, Worshipful Co. of Shipwrights. Mem. Smeatonian Soc. of Civil Engineers (Pres., 1977); Hon. MIPlantE. High Steward of Ipswich, 1967 (life appointment). *Address:* Townfield House, 114 High Street, Hurstpierpoint, W Sussex BN6 9PX. *T:* Hurstpierpoint 833375. *Clubs:* Naval, MCC. *Died 29 Aug. 1988.*

**MASON, James;** actor; *b* 15 May 1909; *s* of late John Mason and Mabel Gaunt; *m* 1st, 1941, Pamela Kellino (marr. diss. 1965); one *s* one *d;* 2nd, 1971, Clarissa Kaye. *Educ:* Marlborough Coll.; Peterhouse, Cambridge. Début on professional stage in The Rascal, Hippodrome, Aldershot, 1931; Old Vic, 1933–34; Gate Theatre, Dublin, 1934–35. Début in Films, Late Extra, 1935. *Films include:* I Met a Murderer; Thunder Rock; The Man in Grey; Fanny by Gaslight; A Place of One's Own; They were Sisters; The Seventh Veil; The Wicked Lady; Odd Man Out; The Upturned Glass; Caught; The Reckless Moment; Pandora and the Flying Dutchman; Rommel-Desert Fox; Five Fingers; Julius Caesar; The Man Between; A Star is Born; Bigger than Life; North by North-West; Twenty Thousand Leagues under the Sea; Journey to the Center of the Earth; Touch of Larceny; Lolita; Heroes' Island; Tiara Tahiti; The Fall of the Roman Empire; The Pumpkin Eater; Lord Jim; Les Pianos Mécaniques; The Blue Max; Georgy Girl; The Deadly Affair; Duffy; Mayerling; Age of Consent; The Seagull; Spring and Port Wine; Child's Play; Last of Sheila; The Mackintosh Man; Dr Frankenstein; Cold Sweat; 11 Harrowhouse; What Are Friends For; Mandingo; Left Hand of the Law; The Deal; The Schoolteacher and the Devil; Inside Out; Autobiography of a Princess; The Voyage of the Damned; Jesus of Nazareth; The Iron Cross; Fear in the City; Heaven Can Wait; The Passage; The Boys from Brazil; The Water Babies; Murder by Decree; Sidney Sheldon's Bloodline; North Sea Hijack; Evil under the Sun; The Verdict; Yellowbeard; The Shooting Party; *Stage:* The Faith Healer, NY, 1979. *Publications:* (with Pamela Kellino) The Cats in Our Lives, 1949 (US); Before I Forget (autobiog.), 1981. *Recreation:* painting. *Address:* c/o Al Parker Ltd, 50 Mount Street, W1.
*Died 27 July 1984.*

**MASON, Ven. Lancelot**, MBE 1984; MA; Archdeacon of Chichester, 1946–73; Canon Residentiary of Chichester Cathedral, 1949–73, subseq. Canon Emeritus; *b* 22 July 1905; *s* of late Canon A. J. Mason, DD; unmarried. *Educ:* RN Colls Osborne and Dartmouth; Trinity Coll., Cambridge. Deacon, 1928; Priest, 1929; Rector of Plumpton, 1938; Chaplain RNVR, 1939–46 (despatches). Chm., Friends of Rampton Hosp., 1976–88. *Address:* The Stables, Morton Hall, Retford, Notts. *T:* Retford 705477. *Died 9 Feb. 1990.*

**MASON, Michael Henry**, DL; Lieutenant-Commander RNVR, retired; *b* 3 Oct. 1900; *s* of late James Francis and Lady Evelyn Mason, Eynsham Hall, Witney, Oxon; *m* 1st, 1925, Hon. Annette Sydney Baird (*d* 1950); *e d* of 1st Viscount Stonehaven, PC, GCMG, DSO; no *c;* 2nd, 1951, Dorothy Margaret Sturdee, Thames Ditton, Surrey; two *s* one *d. Educ:* Eton; Sandhurst. Has travelled extensively, mostly in wild places. Served in the Royal Navy throughout the war, 1939–45; Atlantic, Mediterranean and Far East. DL 1949, High Sheriff 1951, Oxon. Hon. Director: Royal Agricultural Society of England, 1950–52, and of Oxon Agricultural Soc., 1947–70. CC 1947–61. OStJ 1952. *Publications:* The Arctic Forests, 1924; Deserts Idle, 1928; Trivial Adventures in the Spanish Highlands, 1931; Where Tempests Blow, 1933; Where the River Runs Dry, 1934; The Paradise of Fools, 1936; Spain Untroubled, 1936; The Golden Evening, 1957; The Wild Ass Free, 1959; One Man's War (privately), 1966; In Pursuit of Big Fish, 1968; Willoughby the Immortal, 1969. *Recreations:* wild beasts and birds, sailing. *Address:* Scott's House, Eynsham Park, Witney, Oxon OX8 6PP. *T:* Freeland 881283. *Clubs:* Beefsteak, White's, Turf, Royal Ocean Racing (Cdre, 1937–47), Special Forces; Royal Yacht Squadron (Cowes); Cruising of America (Hon. Life Mem.); Zerzura; Cabo Blanco Fishing (Peru). *Died 18 Oct. 1982.*

**MASON, Robert Whyte**, CMG 1956; *b* Glasgow, 1905; *s* of William Whyte Mason and Jane Miller MacKellar Watt; *m* 1952, Monica (*d* 1975), *d* of late George H. Powell, Truro. *Educ:* Glasgow Academy; Morrison's Academy, Crieff. Served War of 1939–45, in Army, 1940–45; Lt-Col Gen. Staff, Gen. Headquarters, Middle East; seconded to Ministry of Information as Dir of Policy, Middle East Services, 1943. 1st Sec., British Embassy, Baghdad, 1945; Foreign Office, 1947–48; Political Adviser in Eritrea and Somalia, 1948; 1st Sec. and Consul, British Legation, Amman, 1949; Consul-Gen., Brazzaville, 1951, Chicago, 1954–59; Dir of Research, Librarian and Keeper of the Papers at the Foreign Office, 1960–65. *Publications:* Murder to Measure, 1934; The Slaying Squad, 1934; Courage for Sale, 1939; And the Shouting Dies, 1940; Three Cheers for Treason, 1940; Cairo Communiqué, 1942; More News from the Middle East, 1943; Arab Agent, 1944; Tandra, 1945; There is a Green Hill, 1946; Tender Leaves, 1950; No Easy Way Out, 1952; (ed) Anthony Trollope's North America, 1968. *Recreations:* golf, opera; writing thrillers. *Address:* 44 Sussex Square, Brighton BN2 1GE. *T:* 685093. *Club:* Travellers'. *Died 7 Jan. 1984.*

**MASON, Stewart Carlton**, CBE 1968; *b* 28 Feb. 1906; *s* of Carlton Willicomb Mason and Alys Kastor; *m* 1941, Ruth Elizabeth Wise; three *s* (and one *s* decd). *Educ:* Uppingham Sch.; Worcester Coll., Oxford (Exhibr, MA). Asst Master: Berkhamsted Sch., 1930–31; Harrow Sch., 1931–37; HM Inspector of Schools, 1937–39 and 1944–47; seconded to Admty, 1939–44; Dir of Educn for Leics, 1947–71; Curator, Inst. of Contemporary Prints, 1972–76. Mem., Nat. Adv. Council on Art Educn, 1957–71; Chairman: Nat. Council for Diplomas in Art and Design, 1970–74 (Vice-Chm., 1961–70); Art and Design Main Cttee, CNAA, 1974–75; Trustee: Tate Gallery, 1966–73; Nat. Gallery, 1971–73; Mem. Adv. Council, Victoria and Albert Museum, 1961–73; Mem., Standing Commn on Museums and Galleries, 1973–76; Chm. of Visual Arts Panel, E Mids Arts Assoc., 1971–75 and Eastern Arts Assoc., 1972–78; Chm. Management Cttee, The Minories, Colchester, 1976–80; Mem. over many years of Councils of Univs of Leicester, Nottingham, Loughborough and RCA. Hon. DSc Loughborough, 1966; Senior Fellow, RCA (Hon. ARCA 1965). *Publication:* (ed) In Our

Experience, 1970. *Address:* The Orangery, Ufford Place, Woodbridge, Suffolk. *T:* Eyke 322. *Died* 17 *Nov.* 1983.

**MASSEY, Sir Harrie Stewart Wilson,** Kt. 1960; PhD Cantab; LLD Melbourne; FRS 1940; Quain Professor of Physics, University College, London, 1950–75, now Emeritus; *b* 1908; *s* of Harrie and Eleanor Massey, Melbourne, Australia; *m* Jessica, *d* of Alex and Alice Mary Barton Bruce, Western Australia; one *d*. *Educ:* University High Sch., Melbourne; Melbourne Univ. (BA, MSc, Hon. LLD, Hon. DSc); Trinity Coll., Cambridge (PhD); Aitchison Travelling Scholar, Melbourne Univ., 1929–31; Research at Cavendish Laboratory, Cambridge, 1929–33; Exhibition of 1851 Senior Research Student, 1931–33; Independent Lecturer in Mathematical Physics, Queen's Univ., Belfast, 1933–38; Goldsmid Prof. of Mathematics, University of London, University Coll., 1938–50; Vice-Provost, UCL, 1969–73, Hon. Fellow, 1976. Temp. Senior Experimental Officer, Admiralty Research Laboratory, 1940; Dep. Chief Scientist, 1941–43, Chief Scientist, 1943, Mine Design Dept, Admiralty; Technical Officer, DSIR Mission to Berkeley, Calif., 1943–45. Chm., Brit. Nat. Cttee for Space Research, 1959–; Mem. Bureau of Cttee on Space Research, 1959–78; President European Prep. Commn for Space Research, 1960–64; Council ESRO, 1964; Chm. Council for Scientific Policy, 1965–69; Member: Adv. Council, Science Museum, 1959–61; Central Advisory Council for Science and Technology, 1967–69; Royal Commn for Exhbn of 1851, 1972–; Prov. Space Science Adv. Bd for Europe, 1974–78 (Chm. Standing Cttee on Space Research, European Science Foundn); Anglo-Australian Telescope Bd, 1975–; assessor, SRC (now SERC), 1972–. Vice-President: Atomic Scientists Assoc., 1949–53 (Pres., 1953–57); Royal Astronomical Soc., 1950–53; Royal Society, 1969–78 (Council Mem., 1949–51, 1959–60; Phys. Sec. and Vice-Pres., 1969–78); Council Mem., Physical Soc., 1949– (Pres., 1954–56, Hon. Fellow, 1976). Mem., Governing Bd, Nat. Inst. for Res. in Nuclear Sci., 1957–65; Governor: Rugby Sch., 1955–59; Chelsea Polytechnic, 1956–59. Rutherford Meml Lectr, 1967. Corr. Mem., Acad. of Sci., Liège, 1974; Aust. Acad. of Scis, 1976; Mem., Amer. Philosoph. Soc., 1975; Hon. Mem., Royal Met. Soc., 1967–. Hon. DSc: QUB, 1960; Leicester, 1964; Hull, 1968; Western Ontario, 1970; Melbourne 1974; Adelaide, 1974; Heriot-Watt, 1975; Liverpool, 1975; York, 1981; Ontario, 1981; Hon. LLD: Melbourne, 1955; Glasgow, 1962. Hughes Medal, Royal Society, 1955; Royal Medal, Royal Society, 1958; Gold Medal, RAS, 1982. *Publications:* Theory of Atomic Collisions (with N. F. Mott), 1933, 3rd edn, 1965; Negative Ions, 1938, 3rd edn, 1976; Electronic and Ionic Impact Phenomena (with E. H. S. Burhop), 1952, 2nd edn 1969; Atoms and Energy, 1953; The Upper Atmosphere (with R. L. F. Boyd), 1958; Ancillary Mathematics (with H. Kestelman), 1958; New Age in Physics, 1960; Space Physics, 1964; Atomic and Molecular Collisions, 1979; various publications on atomic physics in Proc. of Royal Society and other scientific jls. *Recreations:* cricket, tennis, billiards and snooker, badminton, travel, study of other sciences. *Address:* Kalamunda, 29 Pelhams Walk, Esher, Surrey. *Clubs:* MCC; Explorers' (New York); Melbourne Cricket.
*Died* 27 *Nov.* 1983.

⸜ **MASSEY, Raymond;** Actor and Producer; *b* Toronto, Canada, 30 Aug. 1896; *s* of Chester D. Massey and Anna Vincent; *m* 1st, Margery Fremantle (marr. diss.); one *s*; 2nd, Adrianne Allen (marr. diss.); one *s* one *d*; 3rd, 1939, Dorothy (Ludington) Whitney. *Educ:* Appleby Sch., Ontario; Toronto Univ.; Balliol Coll., Oxford. Hon. DLitt Lafayette Univ. 1939; Hon. LLD Queen's Univ., Kingston, Ontario, 1949; Hon. LittD Hobart Coll., NY, 1953; Hon. Dr Fine Arts: Northwestern Univ., 1959, Ripon Coll., 1962, Wooster Coll., 1966; Hon. Dr Hum., American International Coll., 1960. Served European War, 1915–19 as Lt in Canadian Field Artillery; in France, 1916 (wounded), in USA as Instructor in Field Artillery at Yale and Princeton Univs, 1917 and in Siberia, 1918; staff of Adj.-Gen. Canadian Army, rank of Major, 1942–43; naturalized US Citizen, March 1944. First appearance on professional stage at Everyman Theatre, 1922, in In the Zone, Jonty in The Round Table, played Captain La Hire and Canon D'Estivet in Saint Joan, 1924; in 1926 with Allan Wade and George Carr, entered on management of the Everyman Theatre, producing a number of plays and taking a variety of parts; played James Bebb in At Mrs Beam's, the Khan Aghaba in The Transit of Venus, the Rev. MacMillan in An American Tragedy, Robert in Beyond the Horizon, 1926, and Reuben Manassa in the Golden Calf, 1927; Austin Lowe in The Second Man, Joe Cobb in Spread Eagle, and Lewis Dodd in The Constant Nymph, 1928; Raymond Dabney in The Man in Possession, 1930; Randall in Late Night Final, 1931; Hamlet in the Norman Bel Geddes production at Broadhurst Theatre, New York, 1931; Smith in Never Come Back, 1932; Hugh Sebastian in The Rats of Norway; Von Hagen in the Ace, 1933; David Linden in the Shining Hour: At Booth Theatre, New York, 1934, and at St James' Theatre, 1935; Ethan in Ethan Frome, at the National Theatre, New York, 1936; at Apollo Theatre 1938, presented with Henry Sherek, Idiot's Delight, playing the part of Harry Van; Abraham Lincoln in Abe Lincoln in Illinois, Plymouth Theatre, New York,

1938–39; toured the US in this play, 1939–40; in The Doctor's Dilemma, Candida, Pygmalion, Lovers and Friends, The Father, John Brown's Body, J. B.; I Never Sang for my Father, Duke of York's, 1970; Night of the Iguana, Ahmanson Theatre, LA, 1977. Productions include: The White Chateau, The Crooked Billet, Spread Eagle, The Sacred Flame, The Stag, The Silver Tassie, Symphony in Two Flats, The Man in Possession, Lean Harvest, Late Night Final, Grand Hotel, The Rats of Norway, The Shining Hour, Idiot's Delight. *Films played-in include:* The Scarlet Pimpernel, The Old Dark House, Things to Come, Fire Over England, Under the Red Robe, The Prisoner of Zenda, The Hurricane, The Drum, Abe Lincoln in Illinois, Santa Fé Trail, Reap the Wild Wind, Arsenic and Old Lace, Invaders (49th Parallel), Action in the North Atlantic, The Woman in the Window, God is my Co-Pilot, Hotel Berlin, A Matter of Life and Death, Possessed, Mourning Becomes Electra, Fountainhead, David and Bathsheba, Come Fill the Cup, East of Eden, The Naked and the Dead, The Queen's Guards. Co-star, as "Dr Gillespie" in Television series Dr Kildare. Author of play, The Hanging Judge, produced New Theatre, London, 1952. *Publications:* When I was Young, 1976; A Hundred Different Lives, 1979. *Recreations:* golf, carpentry. *Address:* 913 Beverly Drive, Beverly Hills, California 90210, USA. *Clubs:* Garrick, Century (New York). *Died* 29 *July* 1983.

**MASSIGLI, René,** (Hon.) GCVO 1950; (Hon.) KBE 1938; (Hon.) CH 1954; Grand Cross, Legion of Honour, 1954; *b* 22 March 1888; *s* of late Charles Massigli and late Marguerite Michel; *m* 1932, Odette Boissier; one *d*. *Educ:* Ecole normale supérieure. Mem. of the Ecole Française de Rome, 1910–13; Chargé de cours at the University of Lille, 1913–14; Gen. Sec. at the Conference of Ambassadors, 1920; Maître des Requêtes at the Conseil d'Etat, 1924–28; Ministre plénipotentiaire, Head of the League of Nations' Section at the Ministry of Foreign Affairs, 1928–33; Asst Dir of Political Section at the Ministry of Foreign Affairs, 1933–37, Dir, 1937–38; Ambassador to Turkey, 1939–40; escaped from France, 1943; Commissioner for Foreign Affairs, French Cttee of National Liberation, 1943–44; French Ambassador to Great Britain, Sept. 1944–Jan. 1955; Sec.-Gen. at the Quai d'Orsay, Jan. 1955–June 1956; retired 1956. French Pres., Channel Tunnel Study Gp, 1958–69. *Publications:* Quelques Maladies de l'Etat, 1958; La Turquie devant la guerre, 1964; Une Comédie des Erreurs, 1978. *Address:* 3 avenue Robert Schuman, 75007 Paris, France.
*Died* 3 *Feb.* 1988.

**MASTERMAN, Sir Christopher Hughes,** Kt 1947; CSI 1944; CIE 1939; ICS (retired); *b* 7 Oct. 1889; *s* of late Captain J. Masterman, RN; *m* 1921, Hope Gladys (*d* 1972), *d* of late Henry Gearing; two *s*. *Educ:* Winchester; Trinity Coll., Oxford, MA. Entered Indian Civil Service, 1914; Sec. to Govt Education and Public Health Depts, Madras, 1936–39; Collector and District Magistrate, Vizagapatam, 1939–42; Mem. Board of Revenue, Madras, 1943; Chief Sec. and Adviser to the Governor of Madras, 1946; Deputy High Commissioner for UK, Madras, 1947. *Address:* 1 Derwentwater Road, Wimborne, Dorset. *T:* Wimborne 6534.
*Died* 16 *Feb.* 1982.

**MASTERS, John,** DSO 1944; OBE 1945; author; *b* 26 Oct. 1914; *s* of late John Masters, 16th Rajputs, and Ada (neé Coulthard); *m* Barbara Allcard; one *s* one *d* (one *d* decd). *Educ:* Wellington; RMC, Sandhurst. Commissioned 2nd Lieut, Indian Army, 1934; 2nd Bn, 4th PWO Gurkha Rifles, 1935; Adjutant, 1939; Comdt 3rd Bn, 1944; Bde Major, 114 Ind. Inf. Bde, 1942; 111 Ind. Inf. Bde, 1943; GSO1 19 Ind. Div., 1945; GSO1, MO1, GHQ (I), 1946; GSO2 Staff Coll., Camberley, 1947; retired 1948. Active service: NW Frontier, 1936–37; Iraq, Syria, Persia, 1941; Burma, 1944–45. *Publications:* Nightrunners of Bengal, 1951; The Deceivers, 1952, repr. 1966; The Lotus and the Wind, 1953; Bhowani Junction, 1954; Coromandel, 1955; Far, Far the Mountain Peak, 1957; Fandango Rock, 1959; The Venus of Konpara, 1960; To the Coral Strand, 1962; Trial at Monomoy, 1964; Fourteen Eighteen, 1965; The Breaking Strain, 1967; The Rock, 1969; The Ravi Lancers, 1972; Thunder at Sunset, 1974; The Field-Marshal's Memoirs, 1975; The Himalayan Concerto, 1976; Now, God Be Thanked, 1979; Heart of War, 1980; By the Green of the Spring, 1981; *autobiography:* Bugles and a Tiger, 1956; The Road Past Mandalay, 1961; Pilgrim Son, 1971; *posthumous publication:* Man of War, 1983. *Recreations:* mountains, railways. *Address:* c/o Brandt, 1501 Broadway, New York, NY 10036, USA. *Died* 7 *May* 1983.

**MASTON, Charles James,** CB 1965; CBE 1954; *b* 15 May 1912; *s* of James and Amelia Maston; *m* 1940, Eileen Sybil Stopher; no *c*. *Educ:* Yeadon and Guiseley Secondary Sch.; Bradford Gram. Sch.; St John's Coll., Cambridge. Asst Principal, Min. of Labour, 1934; Asst Private Sec. to Minister, 1937–39; Principal, 1939. Served HM Forces, 1942–44. Asst Sec., Min. of Labour (later Dept of Employment), 1944; Industrial Relations Dept, 1953–56; Under Secretary: Military Recruitment Dept, 1957–60; Employment Dept, 1960–64; Industrial Relations Dept, 1964–65; Safety, Health and Welfare Dept, 1965–68; Employment Services Div., 1968–72.

*Recreation:* philately. *Address:* Flaska, Doggetts Wood Lane, Chalfont St Giles, Bucks. *T:* Little Chalfont 2033.

*Died* 6 *July* 1986.

**MATCHAN, Leonard Joseph;** Hon. Life President, Cope Allman International Ltd; Chairman, Guarantee Trust of Jersey Ltd, to 1979; *b* 26 March 1911; *s* of late George Matchan and Elsie Harriet Greenleaf; *m* 1933, Kathleen Artis; one *s* one *d*. *Educ:* Trinity, Croydon. FACCA; JDipMA; Certified Accountant. Vice President and European General Manager, Max Factor, Hollywood, 1936–49. Practice as accountant, 1950–55. President, Toilet Preparations Assoc., 1940–48. *Recreation:* work. *Address:* Island of Brecqhou, Channel Islands. *T:* Guernsey 25000 and Sark 2222.

*Died* 6 *Oct.* 1987.

**MATHER, Sir Kenneth,** Kt 1979; CBE 1956; FRS 1949; DSc (London), 1940; Professor Emeritus and Hon. Senior Fellow in Genetics, University of Birmingham, since 1984 (Hon. Professor of Genetics, 1971–84); *b* 22 June 1911; *e c* and *o s* of R. W. Mather; *m* 1937, Mona Rhodes (*d* 1987); one *s*. *Educ:* Nantwich and Acton Grammar Sch.; University of Manchester (BSc 1931). Ministry of Agriculture and Fisheries Research Scholar, 1931–34; Lecturer in Galton Laboratory, University Coll., London, 1934–37; Rockefeller Research Fellow, at California Institute of Technology and Harvard University, 1937–38; Head of Genetics Dept, John Innes Horticultural Institution, 1938–48; Professor of Genetics, University of Birmingham, 1948–65; Vice-Chancellor, Univ. of Southampton, 1965–71, now Emeritus Prof. Member: Agricultural Research Council, 1949–54, 1955–60, and 1969–79; Science Research Council, 1965–69; Academic Adv. Cttee of Bath Univ. of Technology, 1967–71; DHSS Cttee on the Irradiation of Food, 1967–74; Cttee on Medical Aspects of Chemicals in Food and the Environment, 1972–74; Genetic Manipulation Adv. Gp, 1976–78; Wessex Regional Hosp. Bd, 1968–71. Hon. LLD Southampton, 1972; Hon. DSc: Bath, 1975; Manchester, 1980; Wales, 1980. *Publications:* The Measurement of Linkage in Heredity, 1938; Statistical Analysis in Biology, 1943; Biometrical Genetics, 1949, 3rd edn (with J. L. Jinks), 1982; Human Diversity, 1964; The Elements of Biometry, 1967; Genetical Structure of Populations, 1973; (jointly): The Elements of Genetics, 1949; Genes, Plants and People, 1950; Introduction to Biometrical Genetics, 1977; many papers on Genetics, Cytology, and Statistics. *Address:* School of Biological Sciences, University of Birmingham, B15 2TT. *T:* 021–414 5884; The White House, 296 Bristol Road, Edgbaston, Birmingham B5 7SN. *T:* 021–472 2093. *Club:* Athenæum.

*Died* 20 *March* 1990.

**MATHER-JACKSON, Sir Anthony (Henry Mather),** 6th Bt *cr* 1869; retired Mining Engineer; *b* 9 Nov. 1899; *y s* of William Birkenhead Mather Jackson (*d* 1934) (2nd *s* of 2nd Bt) and Georgiana Catherine (*d* 1932), *d* of Rev. Brabazon Hallowes, Glapwell Hall, Chesterfield; *S* brother, 1976; *m* 1923, Evelyn Mary, *d* of Sir Henry Kenyon Stephenson, 1st Bt, DSO; three *d*. *Educ:* Harrow. Commission, Grenadier Guards, 1918–20; coal industry, 1921–47; company director, 1947–71. *Recreations:* formerly shooting, golf, hunting, racing. *Heir: cousin* William Jackson [*b* 18 Sept. 1902; *m* 1st, 1927, Lady Ankaret Howard (*d* 1945), 2nd *d* of 10th Earl of Carlisle; one *s* one *d*; 2nd, 1966, Ina, *d* of·late James Leonard Joyce, FRCS]. *Address:* Archway House, Kirklington, Newark, Notts. *Club:* White's.

*Died* 11 *Oct.* 1983.

**MATHER-JACKSON, Sir William,** 7th Bt *cr* 1869; *b* 18 Sept. 1902; *s* of William Jackson (*d* 1951) (*g s* of 1st Bt) and Blanche Whitworth (*d* 1953), *y d* of George Atkin; *S* cousin, Sir Anthony Mather-Jackson, 6th Bt, 1983; *m* 1st, 1927, Lady Ankaret Howard (*d* 1945), 2nd *d* of 10th Earl of Carlisle; one *s* one *d*; 2nd, 1966, Ina, *d* of late James Leonard Joyce, FRCS. *Educ:* Birkenhead; Harrow; Balliol Coll., Oxford. Major RAC (Border Regt) TA; served War of 1939–45. *Heir: s* William Thomas Jackson [*b* 12 Oct. 1927; *m* 1951, Gillian Malise, *er d* of John William Stobart, MBE; three *s*]. *Address:* 8 West View, Brampton, Cumbria CA8 1QC. *T:* Brampton 2207.

*Died* 19 *Jan.* 1985.

**MATHESON, Arthur Alexander,** QC Scotland 1956; MA, LLB; Professor of Scots Law at the University of Dundee (formerly Queen's College in the University of St Andrews), 1949–80, retired; *b* 17 June 1919; *o s* of Charles Matheson, MA, FRSGS, and Edith Margaret Matheson, MA; unmarried. *Educ:* Daniel Stewart's Coll., Edinburgh; Balliol Coll., Oxford (Classical Exhibnr); University of Edinburgh (MA, 1st Cl. Hons in Classics; LLB with distinction; 1st entrance Bursar, 1936; Butcher Meml Prize in Greek; Soc. of Writers to the Signet Prize in Latin; 1st Hardie Prize in Latin Prose; Guthrie Fellowship in Classics; C. B. Black Scholarship in New Testament Greek; Vans Dunlop Scholarship in Public Law). Admitted to Faculty of Advocates, 1944; in practice at Scottish Bar, 1944–49; Jun. Counsel in Scotland, MoT, 1947–49; Queen's College, Dundee: Lectr in Public Internat. Law, 1950–60; Dean of Faculty of Law, 1955–58 and 1963–64; Master, 1958–66; Mem. Court, Univ. of St Andrews, 1954–66. Hon. Sheriff of Tayside Central, and Fife

(formerly Perth and Angus) at Dundee, 1950–. Chancellor, Dio. Brechin, 1958–. A Pres., Speculative Soc., 1948–49; Chm., Robert Louis Stevenson Club, Edinburgh, 1953–56. *Address:* 434 Perth Road, Dundee DD2 1JQ. *T:* Dundee 642677. *Club:* New (Edinburgh).

*Died* 22 *Dec.* 1981.

**MATHEWS, Denis Owen,** CMG 1965; OBE 1959; *b* 21 Feb. 1901; *s* of Albert Edward Mathews and Edith (*née* Benton); *m* Violet Morgan (decd); one *s*. *Educ:* Latymer Sch., London; Varndean, Brighton. Served with RAF, 1918; Royal Engineers, 1940–43. Uganda Survey Dept, 1921–46; East Africa Tourist Travel Assoc., 1948–65; UN Tourist Expert, 1965; Dir of Tourism, and Information and Broadcasting, Seychelles, 1965–66; Gen. Manager, Ker, Downey & Selby Safaris, 1967–70. Hon. Pres., E African Prof. Hunters' Assoc.; Founder Mem., E African Wildlife Soc. Hon. Citizen, Dallas, Texas, USA. *Publications:* technical papers on tourism and wild-life. *Address:* Bungalow 2, Manor House, Hingham, Norfolk NR9 4HP. *T:* Attleborough 850507. *Clubs:* Kiambu (Kenya), Mount Kenya Safari (Nanyuki).

*Died* 24 *Jan.* 1984.

**MATHEWS, Henry Mends,** CIE 1944; CEng, FIEE; *b* 16 Feb 1903; *s* of late Henry Montague Segundo Mathews, CSI, JP, Northam, Devon; *m* 1st, 1928, Dorothy Bertha Gubbins (*d* 1941); one *s*; 2nd, 1943, Christina Adam (*née* Nemchinovich; marr. diss., 1960); one *d*; 3rd, 1971, Margaret Patricia Humphreys, Condobolin, NSW. *Educ:* The Wells House Sch., Malvern Wells, Worcs; Cheltenham Coll. Asst Engineer, City of Winnipeg Hydro-Electric System, 1924–26; on staff of Merz & McLellan, consulting engineers, 1927–41; Electrical Commissioner to Govt of India, 1941–48; Chm., Central Technical Power Board, India, 1945–48; joined English Electric Co. Ltd, London, 1948; Dir of Engineering, 1954–68; Dir, Nuclear Design & Construction Ltd, 1966–68; retd, 1968. *Address:* 4 Tower Court, Dunchideock, Exeter EX6 7YD.

*Died* 5 *April* 1982.

**MATHIESON, William Gordon,** CMG 1963; BEc; FASA; *b* 5 July 1902; *s* of James L. Mathieson; *m* 1934, Margery Macdonald; two *d* (and two *d* decd). *Educ:* Fort Street High Sch.; University of Sydney. Permanent Head, NSW State Treasury, 1959–63; Vice-Pres., Sydney Water Board, 1960–63; Mem., Sydney Harbour Transport Board, 1959–63; Chm., Companies Auditors Board, 1963–67; Auditor General of New South Wales, 1963–67. *Address:* 25 Bell Street, Gordon, NSW 2072, Australia. *T:* 498-1444.

*Died* 3 *Oct.* 1981.

**MATTHEWS, Sir Bryan Harold Cabot,** Kt 1952; CBE 1944; FRS 1940; MA, ScD; Professor of Physiology, University of Cambridge, 1952–73, Professor Emeritus, 1973; Life Fellow of King's College, 1973 (Fellow, 1929–73); *b* 14 June 1906; *s* of Harold Evan Matthews and Ruby Sarah Harrison; *m* 1926; one *s* two *d*; *m* 1970, Audrey, widow of Air Vice-Marshal W. K. Stewart. *Educ:* Clifton Coll.; King's Coll., Cambridge. BA Hons, 1st Class Part II Physiology, 1927; Beit Memorial Fellow for Med. Res., 1928–32; Corresponding Mem. Société Philomatique de Paris; British Mem. of the 1935 International High Altitude Expedition for Physiological Research; Chm. of Flying Personnel Research Cttee, RAF, 1967–78; Consultant to RAF in Applied Physiology; Head of RAF Physiological Research Unit, 1940; Head of RAF Institute of Aviation Medicine, 1944–46. Asst Dir of Physiological Research, Cambridge, 1932–48, Reader, 1948–52. Dir of Studies, King's Coll., 1932–52. Royal Soc. Leverhulme Vis. Prof. to African med. schs, 1974. Oliver-Sharpey Lecturer, RCP, 1945; Kelvin Lecturer, Instn of Electrical Engineers, 1948. Pres. Section I British Association, 1961; Vice-Pres., Royal Society, 1957 and 1958. Hon. Pres., 11th Internat. Congress of Electroencephalography and Clinical Neurology, 1965. *Publications:* Electricity in our Bodies; Essay on Physiological Research in Cambridge University Studies, 1933; Papers on Electrical Instruments and electrical phenomena in the nervous system, etc. in the Journal of Physiology, Proceedings of the Royal Society, etc. *Recreations:* ski-ing, sailing. *Address:* King's College, Cambridge.

*Died* 23 *July* 1986.

**MATTHEWS, Prof. Denis (James),** CBE 1975; Concert Pianist; (first) Professor of Music, University of Newcastle upon Tyne, 1971–84; *b* Coventry, 27 Feb. 1919; *o s* of Arthur and Elsie Randall Matthews; *m* 1st, 1941, Mira Howe (marr. diss., 1960); one *s* three *d*; 2nd, 1963, Brenda McDermott (marr. diss. 1985); one *s* one *d*; 3rd, 1986, Beryl Chempin. *Educ:* Warwick. Thalberg Scholar, 1935, Blumenthal Composition Scholar, 1937, at RAM; studied with Harold Craxton and William Alwyn; Worshipful Co. of Musicians' Medal, 1938; first public appearances in London at Queen's Hall and National Gallery, 1939; has broadcast frequently, made records, given talks on musical subjects; soloist at Royal Philharmonic Society's concerts, May and Nov. 1945; toured USA and visited Potsdam with Royal Air Force Orchestra, 1944–45; Vienna Bach Festival, 1950; Canada, 1951, 1957, 1963; South Africa, 1953, 1954, 1962; Poland, 1956, 1960; Egypt and Far East, 1963; World Tour, 1964; N Africa, 1966; W and E Africa, 1968; Latin America, 1968, 1970; Australia, 1977,

1979. Mem., Arts Council of GB, 1972–73. Favourite composers: Bach, Mozart, Beethoven, Wagner. Hon. DMus: St Andrews, 1973; Hull, 1978; Hon. DLitt Warwick, 1982. Cobbett Medal, Musicians' Co., 1973. *Publications:* piano pieces, works for violin, 'cello; In Pursuit of Music (autobiog.), 1966; Beethoven Piano Sonatas, 1968; Keyboard Music, 1972; Brahms's Three Phases, 1972; Brahms Piano Music, 1978; Toscanini, 1982; Beethoven, 1985. *Recreations:* astronomy, filing-systems, reading aloud. *Address:* 6 Reddings Road, Moseley, Birmingham B13 8LN. *T:* 021–449 0888.
*Died 24 Dec.* 1988.

**MATTHEWS, Ven. Frederick Albert John;** Archdeacon of Plymouth, 1962–78; Archdeacon Emeritus since 1978; Vicar of Plympton St Mary, Devon, 1961–83; Prebendary of Exeter Cathedral, since 1978; *b* 4 Jan. 1913; *s* of Albert and Elizabeth Anne Matthews; *m* 1941, Edna Stacey; one *d. Educ:* Devonport High Sch.; Exeter Coll., Oxford. Curate of Stoke Damerel, Plymouth, 1936–44; Vicar of Pinhoe, Devon, 1944–61; Rural Dean of Aylesbeare, 1957–61; Vicar of Plympton St Mary, 1961–83. *Recreations:* Association football (spectator), walking, photography. *Address:* 183 St Margaret's Road, Plympton, Plymouth PL7 4RG.
*Died 14 May* 1985.

**MATTHEWS, Sir (Harold Lancelot) Roy,** Kt 1967; CBE 1943; *b* 24 April 1901; *s* of Harold Hamilton and Jeanie Matthews; *m* 1927, Violet Mary, *d* of T. L. Wilkinson, Solicitor, Liverpool and Dublin; one *s* one *d. Educ:* Preparatory Sch., Eastbourne; The Leys, Cambridge. Was abroad, 1919–22; articled to Matthews & Goodman, Chartered Surveyors, 1923; qualified, 1925; Partner Matthews & Goodman, 1927. Emergency R of O, 1938. Served War of 1939–45 (temp. Brigadier) (despatches four times); France (BEF), 1939–40; War Office, 1940–42; N Africa, Middle East, Italy, 1942–43; Normandy, 1944; Belgium, Holland, Germany, 1945. Resumed City activities, 1946; Chm., Crosse & Blackwell, 1954–63; Dep. Chm. 1963, Chm. 1964–72, Abbey National Building Soc.; Director: Lloyds Bank, 1948–72; Sun Alliance Insurance Gp, 1948–72 (Chm., IOM Bd); Nestlé Co., 1959–63; Standard Chartered Bank, IOM Bd; Chm., White Fish Authority, 1954–63. Legion of Merit (USA) Degree of Officer, 1945; Order of Orange Nassau (Holland) Degree of Commander, 1945. *Recreation:* gardening. *Address:* Road End, Ramsey, Isle of Man. *T:* Ramsay 812663. *Clubs:* Carlton; Ellan Vannin (Douglas, IoM).
*Died 11 Jan.* 1981.

**MATTHEWS, Sir James (Henry John),** Kt 1966; JP; retired as District Secretary, Workers' Educational Association; *b* 25 March 1887; *s* of James Alfred and Mary Matthews; *m* 1919, Clara Collin; one *d. Educ:* Higher Grade Sch., Portsmouth. Shipbuilding, Portsmouth Dockyard and Admty, 1901–24; Officer of WEA, 1924–52. Mem., Southampton County Council, 1934–67, Alderman, 1945–67. JP Hants, 1942–. Hon. Freeman, City of Southampton, 1958. Hon. MA, Bristol Univ., 1949; Hon. LLD, Southampton Univ., 1962. *Publications:* articles on local government and adult education. *Address:* 56 Ethelburt Avenue, Southampton. *T:* Southampton 557334. *Died 29 Aug.* 1981.

**MATTHEWS, Jessie,** OBE 1970; actress; singer; *b* Soho, London, 11 March 1907; *d* of late George Ernest Matthews and late Jane Townshend; *m* 1st, 1926, Lord Alva Lytton (Henry Lytton Jr) (from who she obt. a div., 1929, and who *d* 1965); 2nd, 1931, John Robert Hale Monro (Sonnie Hale) (from whom she obt. a div., 1944, and who *d* 1959); one *d* (one *s* decd); 3rd, 1945, Brian Lewis (from whom she obt. a div., 1959); one *s* decd. *Educ:* Pulteney St (LCC) Sch. for Girls, Soho. Trained as a classical ballet dancer under Mme Elise Clerc, and Miss Terry Freedman of Terry's Juveniles; first London appearance, in Bluebell in Fairyland, Metropolitan, 1919. Early successes in: The Music Box Review, Palace, 1923; The Charlot Show of 1926, Prince of Wales, 1926. Then (C. B. Cochran contract) starred in (London Pavilion): One Dam Thing After Another, 1927; This Year of Grace, 1928; Wake Up and Dream, 1929; Ever Green, Adelphi, 1930 (during these years she originated songs, incl.: Noel Coward's A Room with a View; Cole Porter's Let's Do It; Harry Woods' Over My Shoulder; Richard Rodgers' My Heart Stood Still and Dancing on the Ceiling). London stage (cont.) in: Hold my Hand, Gaiety, 1931; Sally Who?, Strand, 1933; Come Out to Play, Phœnix, 1940; Wild Rose, Princes, 1942; Maid to Measure, Cambridge, 1948; Sweethearts and Wives, Wyndhams, 1949; Sauce Tartare, Cambridge, 1949–50; Five Finger Exercise, Unity, 1960; A Share in the Sun, Cambridge, 1966; The Water Babies, Royalty, 1973; The Jessie Matthews Show, Shaftesbury, 1976. First New York appearance, in André Charlot's Revue of 1924, Times Square, 1924; then in Wake Up and Dream, Selwyn, 1929–30; The Lady Comes Across, Shubert, 1941; toured: in Larger than Life, Aust. and NZ, 1952–53, S Africa, 1955–56; in Janus, Aust. and NZ, 1956–57. Films (1923–) include: This England, The Beloved Vagabond, Straws in the Wind, Out of the Blue, There Goes the Bride, The Man from Toronto, The Midshipman, The Good Companions, Friday the Thirteenth, Waltzes from Vienna, Evergreen, First a Girl, It's Love Again, Head Over Heels, Gangway, Sailing Along, Climbing High, Forever and a Day (In Hollywood), Candles at Nine, Victory Wedding (as director), Making the Grade, Life is Nothing without Music, Tom Thumb, The Hound of the Baskervilles. Starred in two seasons of cabaret, Society, London, 1964. Tribute to Jessie Matthews, Festival, NY, 1965. Recording star, 1926–, on many labels. Television: many appearances in plays, programmes, etc, UK and Canada, incl. Edward and Mrs Simpson, ITV, 1978. Radio: Mrs Dale in serial, The Dales, 1963–69. *Publication:* Over My Shoulder (autobiog.), 1974; *relevant publication:* Jessie Matthews, by Michael Thornton, 1974. *Recreations:* drawing, gardening, motoring. *Address:* c/o CCA Personal Management Ltd, 29 Dawes Road, SW6 7DT. *T:* 01–381 3551. *Died 19 Aug.* 1981.

**MATTHEWS, L(eonard) Harrison,** FRS 1954, MA, ScD; Scientific Director, Zoological Society of London, 1951–66; *b* 12 June 1901; *s* of Harold Evan Matthews and Ruby Sarah Matthews (*née* Harrison); *m* 1924, Dorothy Hélène Harris; one *s* one *d. Educ:* Bristol Grammar Sch.; King's Coll., Cambridge. BA Hons 1st Class Nat. Sci. Trip., 1922; Vintner Exhibitioner King's Coll., University Frank Smart Prize. Has carried out biological researches in Africa, S America, Arctic and Antarctic, etc. Mem. of scientific staff "Discovery" Expedition, 1924; special lectr in Zoology, Univ. of Bristol, 1935; Radio Officer, Anti-Aircraft Command, 1941; Sen. Scientific Officer, Telecommunications Research Establishment, 1942; Radar liaison duties with RAF, 1943–45; Research Fellow, Univ. of Bristol, 1945. Pres. Section D, British Assoc. for the Advancement of Science, 1959; President: British Academy of Forensic Science, 1962; Ray Soc., 1965; Chm., Seals Sub-Cttee, NERC, 1967–71; Tsetse Fly and Trypanosomiasis Cttee, CO, 1955–63. Member Council: Marine Biological Assoc. of UK, 1944–51; Zoological Soc. of London, 1943–45, 1946–49, 1950–51 (Vice-Pres., 1944–45, 1947–49, 1950–51; Silver Medal, 1986); Inst. of Biology, 1954–57; Linnean Soc., of London, 1953–57; Sec., 1947–48, Pres., 1960, Assoc. of British Zoologists; Chm., World List of Scientific Periodicals, 1959–66; Acad. Mem., Assoc. of British Sci. Writers, 1956. Has made numerous sound and TV broadcasts. *Publications:* South Georgia, the Empire's Subantarctic Outpost, 1931; Wandering Albatross, 1951; British Mammals (New Naturalist), 1952; Amphibia and Reptiles, 1952; Sea Elephant, 1952; Beasts of the Field, 1954; Animals in Colour, 1959; The Senses of Animals (with Maxwell Knight), 1963; (ed) The Whale, 1968; The Life of Mammals, Vol. I, 1969, Vol. II, 1971; Introd., Darwin's Origin of Species, 1972; Introd. and explanatory notes, Waterton's Wanderings in South America, 1973; Man and Wildlife, 1975; Penguin, 1977 (with Foreword by HRH The Duke of Edinburgh); The Life of the Whale, 1978; The Seals and the Scientists, 1979; Mammals in the British Isles, 1982; numerous scientific papers on zoological subjects in jls of learned socs, Discovery Reports, Philosophical Transactions, Encyclopædia Britannica, etc. *Address:* The Old Rectory, Stansfield, via Sudbury, Suffolk CO10 8LT. *Club:* Explorers' (New York).
*Died 27 Nov.* 1986.

**MATTHEWS, Paul Taunton,** CBE 1975; MA, PhD; FRS 1963; Vice-Chancellor, Bath University, 1976–83; *b* 19 Nov. 1919; *s* of Rev. Gordon Matthews and Janet (*née* Viney); *m* 1947, Margit Zohn; two *s* two *d. Educ:* Mill Hill Sch.; Clare Coll., Cambridge. Research Fellow, Inst. for Advanced Study, Princeton, USA, 1950–51; ICI Research Fellow, Cambridge, 1951–52; Lectr, Univ. of Birmingham, 1952–57; Visiting Prof., Univ. of Rochester, USA, 1957; Imperial College, London: Reader in Theoretical Physics, 1957–62; Prof. of Theoretical Physics, 1962–76; Head of Dept of Physics, 1971–76; Dean, RCS, 1972–75. Mem., SRC, 1970–74; Chm., SRC Nuclear Physics Bd, 1972–74; Mem., Scientific Policy Cttee, CERN, Geneva, 1972–78; Chm., Radioactive Waste Management Adv. Cttee, 1983–. Hon. DSc Bath, 1983. Adams Prize, Cambridge, 1958; Rutherford Medal and Prize, IPPS, 1979. *Publications:* Quantum Mechanics, 1963 (USA); Nuclear Apple, 1971; papers on elementary particle physics in Proc. Royal Soc., Phil. Mag., Phys. Review, Nuovo Cimento, Review Mod. Phys., Annals of Physics. *Address:* 64 Highsett, Hills Road, Cambridge.
*Died 26 Feb.* 1987.

**MATTHEWS, Rt. Rev. Ralph Vernon;** Bishop of Waiapu, since 1979; *b* 3 April 1928; *s* of Vernon Arthur F. Matthews and Thelma O. Matthews; *m* 1957, Pauline Cecily Glover; two *s. Educ:* Napier Boys' High School; Univ. of Auckland and S John's Theological Coll. LTh, 1st Cl. Hons. Assistant Agricultural Master and Scinde Housemaster, Napier Boys' High School, 1949. Deacon 1955, priest 1956, Waiapu; Asst Curate, Hastings, 1955–60; Vicar of Waipukurau, 1960–70; Vicar of Taupo, 1970–76; Hon. Canon, Waiapu, 1969, Canon 1970–76; Vicar of Gisborne and Archdeacon of Waiapu, 1976–79; Chairman, Diocesan Council of Christian Education, 1970–76. Territorial Chaplain, 4th Armoured Regt, RNZAC, 1957–63. *Recreations:* tennis, trout-fishing. *Address:* Bishop's House, 8 Cameron Terrace, Napier, NZ. *T:* Napier 57846. *Died 4 March* 1983.

**MATTHEWS, Roy;** *see* Matthews, H. L. R.

**MATTHEWS, Sir Russell**, Kt 1982; OBE 1971; company director; retired civil engineer; *b* 26 July 1896; *s* of Robert and Grace Matthews; *m* 1932, Elizabeth Mary Brodie; two *s* two *d*. *Educ*: New Plymouth Boys' High Sch.; London Sch. of Engineering. Formed Matthews & Kirkby and ran business as Man. Dir, 1936–42, then sole Proprietor, Matthews & Co., at that time the country's leading road sealing contractor; Founder Chm., and Dir, Ivon Watkins Dow, 1944–62; Founder Director: Kaikariki Sand & Gravel Co., 1944–68; R. J. Burkitt, 1956–; Pacific Constructors, 1958–71; Russell Matthews Industries, 1959–80; Taranaki Hldgs, 1959–; Fitzroy Engineering, 1960–80; Maxwell Machines, 1962–71; Technic Industries, 1965–80; Aid Industries, 1967–71; Technic Group, 1969–80; Asphaltic Construction, 1971–80. *Recreation*: gardening. *Address*: Tupare, 487 Mangorei Road, New Plymouth, New Zealand. *T*: 86480. *Died 25 Nov. 1987.*

**MATTURI, Sahr Thomas**, CMG 1967; BSc, PhD; farmer; High Commissioner in London for Sierra Leone, 1978–80; retired from Sierra Leone Foreign Service; *b* 22 Oct. 1925; *s* of Sahr and Konneh Matturi; *m* 1956, Anna Adella Stephens; two *s* one *d*. *Educ*: University Coll., Ibadan; Hull Univ. School Teacher, 1944–47, 1954–55; University Lecturer, 1959–63; Principal, Njala Univ. Coll., 1963–76; Vice-Chancellor, Univ. of Sierra Leone, 1968–70; Acting Vice-Chancellor and Pro Vice-Chancellor, 1972–74, Pro Vice-Chancellor, 1966–68, 1970–72, 1973–75. Ambassador of Sierra Leone to Italy, Austria and Yugoslavia, and Perm. Rep. to UN Specialised Agencies in Rome, Geneva and Vienna, 1977–78. Chm., W African Exams Council, 1971–76. Mem., British Mycol. Soc. FRSA. *Recreations*: cricket, lawn tennis, shooting. *Address*: c/o Jaiama Secondary School, Private Mail Bag, Koidu Town, Sierra Leone. *Died 5 Jan. 1987.*

**MAUCHLINE, Rev. Prof. John**, MA, BD (Glasgow), DD (Edinburgh); Professor of Old Testament Language and Literature, University of Glasgow, 1935–72, and Principal of Trinity College, Glasgow, 1953–72; *b* 5 July 1902; *m* 1930, Helen Brisbane Paterson, MA; three *s*. *Educ*: Hutchesons' Grammar Sch.; Glasgow Univ. (First Class Hons in Semitic Langs); British Sch. of Archæology, American Sch. of Oriental Research, and l'Ecole St Etienne, Jerusalem. Maclean Scholar, 1925; Faulds Fellow, 1926–29; Minister of South Dalziel Church, Motherwell, 1929–34; Prof. of Old Testament Language and Literature, Trinity Coll., Glasgow, 1934. Principal Pollok Lecturer in Pine Hill Divinity Hall, Halifax, Nova Scotia, 1949. *Publications*: God's People Israel; The Balaam–Balak Songs and Saga, in W. B. Stevenson Anniversary Volume; Hosea in The Interpreter's Bible; 1st and 2nd Kings, in Peake's Commentary on The Bible (new and revised edn); Isaiah 1–39 (Torch Bible Commentary); (ed) An Introductory Hebrew Grammar, by A. B. Davidson, 26th edn, 1967; 1 and 2 Samuel (New Century Bible), 1971; articles in periodicals. *Address*: Tigh-na-Drochaidh, Benderloch, near Connel, Argyll *T*: Ledaig 305. *Died 7 Jan. 1984.*

**MAUD**; *see* Redcliffe-Maud.

**MAUDE, His Honour John Cyril**, QC 1942; *b* 3 April 1901; *s* of Cyril Maude and Winifred Emery; *m* 1st, 1927, Rosamond Willing Murray (from whom he obtained a divorce, 1955), *d* of late Dr T. Morris Murray, Boston, Mass, USA; one *d*; *m* 2nd, 1955, Maureen Constance (who *m* 1st, 1930, 4th Marquess of Dufferin and Ava, killed in action, 1945; one *s* two *d*; 2nd, 1948, Major (Harry Alexander) Desmond Buchanan, MC (from whom she obtained a divorce, 1954)), 2nd *d* of late Hon. Arthur Ernest Guinness. *Educ*: Eton; Christ Church, Oxford. Joined Gen. Staff, War Office, temporary civil asst, 1939; Intelligence Corps, actg Major, 1940; offices of War Cabinet, 1942. Barrister, Middle Temple, 1925; KC 1943; Bencher, 1951; Mem., Bar Council, 1952. Counsel to PO at Central Criminal Court, 1935–42; Jun. Counsel to Treasury at Central Criminal Court, 1942–43; Recorder of Devizes, 1939–44, of Plymouth, 1944–54; Additional Judge, Mayor's and City of London Court, 1954–65; Additional Judge, Central Criminal Court, 1965–68. MP (C) Exeter, 1945–51. Chancellor of the Diocese of Bristol, 1948–50. Dir, Old Vic Trust Ltd, 1951–54; Chairman of the British Drama League, 1952–54; Governor, Royal Victoria Hall Foundn, 1953. Chm., Family Service Units, 1954; Mem. Bd, Middlesex Hosp., 1951–62. *Address*: Amesbury Abbey, Amesbury, Wiltshire. *Died 16 Aug. 1986.*

**MAUDE-ROXBY, John Henry**; Chairman: Cameron Choat and Partners, since 1977; Maude-Roxby, Sussman Associates, since 1978; *b* 4 March 1919; *m* 1966, Katherine Jewell; one *s*. *Educ*: Radley Coll.; Hertford Coll., Oxford (BA). ACIS. Regular Army Officer, Royal Artillery, 1939–59. Allied Suppliers Ltd, 1959–73 (Chm. and Man. Dir, 1972–73); Dir, Cavenham Ltd, 1972–73; Dep. Chm. and Man. Dir, Morgan Edwards Ltd, 1973–74; Dir Gen., Inst. of Grocery Distribution, 1974–77. Regional Trading Manager, Mercia Region, Nat. Trust, 1979–84. *Recreations*: shooting, golf, gardening. *Address*: Cedar Cottage, Batch Valley, All Stretton,

Shropshire SY6 6JW. *T*: Church Stretton 722481. *Clubs*: Army and Navy; Vincent's (Oxford). *Died 10 Sept. 1989.*

**MAUDSLAY, Major Sir (James) Rennie**, GCVO 1980 (KCVO 1972; CVO 1967); KCB 1979; MBE 1945; Keeper of the Privy Purse and Treasurer to the Queen, 1971–81 (Assistant Keeper, 1958–71); Extra Equerry to the Queen, since 1973; *b* 13 Aug. 1915; *o s* of late Joseph Maudslay and of Mrs Ruth Maudslay (*née* Partridge), Pinewood Copse, Boundstone, Farnham, Surrey; *m* 1951, (Jane) Ann, *d* of A. V. McCarty, Helena, Arkansas; two *s* one *d*. *Educ*: Harrow Sch. 2nd Lt, KRRC, 1938; served 1938–45 (despatches five times); Hon. Major, 1945. Chm., Mid-Southern Water Co. Mem. of Lloyd's. Pres., Farnham Conservative Assoc., 1954–57; Pres., Maudslay Soc., 1963–65; Hon. Mem., Jun. Instn of Engineers. Employed Lord Chamberlain's Office, 1952–53. Holds Order of: Verdienst (Germany), 1958; Taj (Iran), 1959; Dakshuna Bahu (Nepal), 1960; Legion of Honour (France), 1960; Crown of Thai (Thailand), 1960; Phœnix (Greece), 1963; Al Kawkab (Jordan), 1966; Ordine al Merito della Repubblica (Italy), 1969; Order of Kroonorde (Netherlands), 1972; Order of Merit (Germany), 1972; Order of Star (Afghanistan), 1972; Order of Dannebrog (Denmark), 1974. *Recreations*: shooting, gardening. *Address*: 12 Bradbourne Street, SW6 4RE. *Clubs*: White's, MCC. *Died 8 June 1988.*

**MAUGHAM, 2nd Viscount**, *cr* 1939, of Hartfield; **Robert Cecil Romer Maugham**; author (as Robin Maugham); barrister-at-law; *b* 17 May 1916; *o s* of 1st Viscount Maugham, PC, KC, and Helen Mary (*d* 1950), *d* of Rt Hon. Sir Robert Romer, GCB; *S* father 1958. *Educ*: Eton; Trinity Hall, Cambridge. Served War of 1939–45; Inns of Court Regt, 1939; commissioned Fourth County of London Yeomanry, 1940; Western Desert, 1941–42 (despatches, wounded); Middle East Intelligence Centre, 1943; invalided out, 1944. Called to Bar, Lincoln's Inn, 1945. *Publications*: Come to Dust, 1945; Nomad, 1947; Approach to Palestine, 1947; The Servant, 1948 (dramatised 1963; filmed, 1965); North African Notebook, 1948; Line on Ginger, 1949; Journey to Siwa, 1950; The Rough and the Smooth, 1951; Behind the Mirror, 1955; The Man with Two Shadows, 1958; The Slaves of Timbuktu, 1961; November Reef, 1962; The Joyita Mystery, 1962; Somerset and all the Maughams, 1966; The Green Shade, 1966; The Second Window, 1968; The Link, 1969; The Wrong People, 1970; The Last Encounter, 1972; Escape from the Shadows (autobiog.), 1972; The Barrier, 1973; The Black Tent and other stories, 1973; The Sign, 1974; Search for Nirvana, 1975; Knock on Teak, 1976; Lovers in Exile, 1977; Conversations with Willie: recollections of W. Somerset Maugham, 1978; The Dividing Line, 1979; The Corridor, 1980; *plays*: The Last Hero; Odd Man In (adaptation); Its in the Bag (adaptation); The Lonesome Road (in collaboration with Philip King); The Claimant, 1964; Enemy!, 1969. *Recreations*: reading and travel. *Address*: 5 Clifton Road, Brighton BN1 3HP. *Club*: Garrick. *Died 13 March 1981 (ext).*

**MAVROGORDATO, John George**, CMG 1952; *b* 9 May 1905; 2nd *s* of late George Michel and Irene Mavrogordato. *Educ*: Charterhouse; Christ Church, Oxford (BA 1927). Called to Bar, Gray's Inn, 1932; practised at Chancery Bar, 1932–39. Asst Dir, Ministry of Aircraft Production, 1943. Advocate-Gen., Sudan Government, 1946; Legal Adviser to Governor-Gen. of the Sudan, 1953; Senior Legal Counsel, Ministry of Justice, Sudan, 1958–61; retired, 1961. MBOU. *Publications*: A Hawk for the Bush, 1960; A Falcon in the Field, 1966; Behind the Scenes (autobiog.), 1982. *Recreations*: ornithology, wild life conservation. *Died 14 June 1987.*

**MAWBY, Raymond Llewellyn**; *b* 6 Feb. 1922; *m* 1944, Carrie Aldwinckle; one *d* (one *s* decd). *Educ*: Long Lawford Council Sch., Warwicks. One-time Pres. Rugby branch Electrical Trades Union; one-time mem. of Rugby Borough Council. MP (C) Totnes, 1955–83; Asst Postmaster-Gen., 1963–64. *Address*: 29 Applegarth Avenue, Newton Abbot, S Devon. *Died 22 July 1990.*

**MAWER, Air Cdre Allen Henry**, DFC 1943; *b* 16 Dec. 1921; *s* of Gordon Mawer and Emily Naomi Mawer (*née* Block); *m* 1st, 1947, Pamela Mitchell (*d* 1982), *d* of David Thomas; one *s* one *d*; 2nd, 1982, Elizabeth Mary Stokes. *Educ*: Bancroft's School. Joined RAF, 1940; bomber and special duties ops, 1941–45; psc 1956; Stn Comdr, RAF Scampton, 1965–68; idc 1968; Comdt RAF Coll. of Air Warfare, 1969–71; Air Cdre Plans, HQ Strike Comd, RAF, 1971–73; Air Comdr, Malta, 1973–75, retd. Gen. Manager, Basildon Develt Corp., 1975–78; Man. Dir, Docklands Develt Organisation, 1979–80. Croix de Guerre, France, 1944. *Recreations*: painting, golf, shooting. *Address*: 68 High Street, Burnham-on-Crouch, Essex CM0 8AA. *Clubs*: Royal Air Force; Royal Burnham Yacht. *Died 15 May 1989.*

**MAXWELL, Sir Aymer**, 8th Bt of Monreith, *cr* 1681; Hon. Captain Scots Guards; *b* 7 Dec. 1911; *s* of late Lt-Col Aymer Maxwell, Royal Naval Div., Captain Grenadier Guards and Lovat Scouts, and Lady Mary Percy, 5th *d* of 7th Duke of Northumberland; *S* grandfather, Rt. Hon. Sir Herbert Eustace Maxwell, 7th Bt, KT, PC, FRS, 1937.

*Educ:* Eton; Magdalene Coll., Cambridge. BA (Hons). *Heir: nephew* Michael Eustace George Maxwell, *b* 28 Aug. 1943. *Address:* Monreith, Wigtownshire. *T:* Portwilliam 248; 11 Lansdowne House, Lansdowne Road, W11 3LP. *T:* 01–727 6394.

*Died 8 July* 1987.

**MAXWELL, Maurice William;** President, Associated Book Publishers, 1976–80 (Chairman, 1974–76); *b* 11 March 1910; *s* of William Harold Maxwell and Hilda Maxwell (*née* Cox); *m* 1936, Margaret Lucy Carnahan (marr. diss. 1958); one *d. Educ:* Dean Close, Cheltenham. Joined Sweet & Maxwell, 1928, Man. Dir 1948, Chm. 1952–72; Vice-Chm., Associated Book Publishers, 1963–73; Pres., Carswell Co., Canada, 1958–74. Served in RAFVR, 1940–45 (Sqdn Ldr); RAuxAF, 1947–57 (AEM 1953). *Recreations:* reading, listening to music, motoring, travel. *Address:* 1 Church Road, Seal, Sevenoaks, Kent TN15 0AU. *T:* Sevenoaks 62742; Apt 11K, Le Lavallière, Résidence le Roi Soleil, 06600 Antibes, France. *Clubs:* Reform, Royal Air Force. *Died 13 July* 1982.

**MAXWELL, Sir Patrick Ivor H.;** *see* Heron-Maxwell.

**MAXWELL, William Wayland,** MA (Cantab); FEng, FIMechE; FIEE; FCIT; Consultant, Mott, Hay & Anderson, since 1981; *b* 10 March 1925; *s* of Somerset Maxwell and Molly Cullen; *m* 1963, Eugenie Pamela Cavanagh, *d* of Leslie Crump and Eugenie Thurlow; no *c. Educ:* Bedales Sch.; Trinity Hall, Cambridge (Mech. Scis Tripos). FEng 1980. Entered London Transport, 1947; Development Engr (Victoria Line), 1963; Mechanical Engr, Development: Railways, 1964; Mechanical Engr, Running: Railways, 1969; Chief Operating Manager (Railways), 1970; Bd Mem. for Engrg, LTE, 1973; Man. Dir, Railways, LTE, 1979–80. Dir, Whelpdale, Maxwell & Codd Ltd, piano and harpsichord makers. Chm., Rly Div., IMechE, 1977–78. Pres., ITEME, 1981–83. Hon. FIMechTE. Col, Engr and Transport Staff Corps RE (TA). OStJ 1980. *Publications:* papers in Proc. IMechE and Proc. IEE. *Recreations:* reading, music, theatre and gardening. *Address:* 40 Elm Bank Gardens, Barnes, SW13 0NT. *T:* 01–876 9575. *Club:* Naval and Military. *Died 15 Oct.* 1986.

**MAXWELL SCOTT, Sir Michael Fergus,** 13th Bt *cr* 1642; *b* 23 July 1921; *s* of Rear-Adm. Malcolm Raphael Joseph Maxwell Scott, DSO (*d* 1943), and Fearga Victoria Mary (*d* 1969), *e d* of Rt Hon. Sir Nicholas Roderick O'Conor, PC, GCB, GCMG; *S* to baronetcy of kinsman, Sir Ralph (Raphael) Stanley De Marie Haggerston, 12th Bt, 1972; *m* 1963, Deirdre Moire, *d* of late Alexander McKechnie; two *s* one *d. Educ:* Ampleforth; Trinity College, Cambridge. *Publication:* Stories of Famous Scientists, 1965. *Recreations:* sailing, fishing, gardening. *Heir: s* Dominic James Maxwell Scott, *b* 22 July 1968. *Address:* 130 Ritherdon Road, SW17 8QQ. *T:* 01–673 8442. *Died 29 Nov.* 1989.

**MAYBRAY-KING, Baron** *cr* 1971 (Life Peer), of the City of Southampton; **Horace Maybray Maybray-King,** PC 1965; DL; Deputy Speaker of the House of Lords, since 1971; *b* 25 May 1901; *s* of John William and Margaret Ann King; changed name by deed poll to Maybray-King, 1971; *m* 1st, 1924, Victoria Florence Harris (*d* 1966); one *d*; 2nd, 1967, Una Porter (*d* 1978); 3rd, 1981, Mrs Ivy Duncan Forster (marr. diss. 1985); 4th, 1986, Sheila Catherine Atkinson. *Educ:* Norton Council Sch.; Stockton Secondary Sch.; King's Coll., University of London. BA 1st Class Hons 1922, PhD 1940. Head of English Dept, Taunton's Sch., Southampton, 1930–47; Headmaster, Regent's Park Secondary Sch., 1947–50. MP (Lab): Test Div. of Southampton, 1950–55; Itchen Div. of Southampton, 1955–65 (when elected Speaker); Chairman of Ways and Means and Deputy Speaker, 1964–65; MP Itchen Division of Southampton and Speaker of the House of Commons, 1965–70. Mem., BBC Complaints Commn, 1971–74. Hon. Treasurer, Help the Aged, 1972–; Pres., Spina Bifida Assoc., 1971–. FKC; Hon. FRCP. Hon. DCL Durham, 1968; Hon. LLD: Southampton, 1967; London, 1967; Bath Univ. of Technology, 1969; Hon. DSocSci Ottawa, 1969; Hon. DLitt Loughborough Univ. of Technology, 1971. Hants County Hon. Alderman; Freeman of Southampton and Stockton-on-Tees. DL Hants, 1975. *Publications:* Selections from Macaulay, 1930; Selections from Homer, 1935; (ed) Sherlock Holmes Stories, 1950; Parliament and Freedom, 1953; State Crimes, 1967; Songs in the Night, 1968; Before Hansard, 1968; The Speaker and Parliament, 1973. *Recreations:* music and the entertainment of children. *Address:* 37 Manor Farm Road, Southampton. *T:* Southampton 555884. *Club:* Farmers'. *Died 3 Sept.* 1986.

**MAYCOCK, Sir William d'Auvergne,** Kt 1978; CBE 1970 (MBE 1945); LVO 1961; MD, FRCP, FRCPath; Superintendent, Elstree Laboratories, 1949–73, and Director of Blood Products Laboratory, 1973–78, Lister Institute of Preventive Medicine; retired; *b* 7 Feb. 1911; *s* of William Perren Maycock, MIEE, and Florence Marion, *d* of Alfred Hart; *m* 1940, Muriel Mary, *d* of Duncan Macdonald, Toronto; two *s. Educ:* The King's School, Canterbury; McGill Univ., Montreal. MD McGill, 1935; FRCP, MRCS, FRCPath. Demonstrator in Pathology, McGill Univ., 1935; Leverhulme Scholar, RCS of Eng., 1936–39; Dept of Physiology, St Thomas's

Hosp. Med. Sch., 1939. Served in RAMC, 1939–45: Temp. Col, AMS, 1945. Mem. Staff of Lister Inst., London, 1946–48; Consultant Adviser in Transfusion, Min. of Health (later Dept of Health and Social Security), 1946–78; Hon. Cons. in Transfusion and Resuscitation to War Office (later Min. of Defence), 1946–78. Oliver Memorial Award for Blood Transfusion, 1955; Karl Landsteiner Gold Medal, Netherlands Red Cross Soc., 1978; Guthrie Medal, RAMC, 1979; Pres., Brit. Soc. for Haematology, 1966–67. *Publications:* scientific and other papers. *Recreations:* various. *Address:* 59 Ivinghoe Road, Bushey, Herts. *Club:* Athenæum. *Died 19 Feb.* 1987.

**MAYER, Sir Robert,** CH 1973; KCVO 1979; Kt 1939; FRCM; FTCL (Hon.); Hon. GSM; Hon. RAM; Founder: Robert Mayer Concerts for Children; Transatlantic Foundation Anglo-American Scholarships; Founder, Vice-President, since 1981, and Director, Robert Mayer Trust for Youth and Music (formerly Youth and Music Trust; Co-Chairman, until 1981); Member Council: National Music Council; English Chamber Orchestra; Wind Music Society; Anglo-Israel Association; Live Music; International Music Seminar; *b* Mannheim, 5 June 1879; *s* of Emil Mayer; *m* 1st, 1919, Dorothy Moulton Piper (*d* 1974), *d* of George Piper; two *s* one *d*; 2nd, 1980, Mrs Jacqueline Noble (*née* Norman). *Educ:* Mannheim Conservatoire. Hon. LLD Leeds, 1967; Hon. DSc City University, 1968; Hon. Dr of Music, Cleveland, O, 1970. Albert Medal, RSA, 1979. Grand Cross, Order of Merit (Germany), 1967; Ordre de la Couronne (Belgium), 1969. *Publications:* Young People in Trouble; Crescendo; My First Hundred Years, 1979. *Recreations:* philanthropy, music. *Club:* Athenæum. *Died 9 Jan.* 1985.

**MAYERS, Norman,** CMG 1952; *b* 22 May 1895; 2nd *s* of late S. A. Mayers, Bolton, and Mary Alice, *e d* of late Charles Ditchfield. *Educ:* King's Coll., London; Caius Coll., Cambridge; abroad. Served in India, 1914–19, Middlesex and Hampshire Regts (Territorials). Entered Levant Consular Service, 1922, and served in Lebanon and Saudi Arabia; Asst Oriental Sec. at the Residency, Cairo, 1927–34; Oriental Sec., Addis Ababa, 1935–37; Consul at Alexandria, 1937; Bucharest, 1938; Shiraz and Isfahan, 1941; Mersin, 1941; served at Foreign Office, 1943–44; Chargé d'Affaires at San José, Costa Rica, 1944–45; Minister to El Salvador, 1945–48; Consul-Gen., São Paulo, 1948–51; Ambassador to Ecuador, 1951–55; retired. Consul (Hon.) Palma de Mallorca, 1957–63. *Recreations:* drawing, painting. *Address:* Calle Virgen de la Bonanova 11, Genova, Palma de Mallorca, Spain. *Clubs:* United Oxford & Cambridge University, Travellers'.

*Died 11 Aug.* 1986.

**MAYNEORD, Prof. William Valentine,** CBE 1957; FRS 1965; Emeritus Professor of Physics as Applied to Medicine, University of London; formerly Director of Physics Department, Institute of Cancer Research, Royal Cancer Hospital; *b* 14 Feb. 1902; *s* of late Walter Mayneord; *m* 1963, Audrey Morrell, Kingston-upon-Thames. *Educ:* Prince Henry's Grammar Sch., Evesham; Birmingham Univ. BSc 1921, MSc 1922, DSc 1933. Chairman: Internat. Commn on Radiological Units, 1950–53; MRC Cttee on Protection against Ionising Radiations, 1951–58; Member: Internat. Commn on Radiological Protection, 1950–58; UK Delegn to UN Scientific Cttee on the Effects of Atomic Radiation, 1956–57; MRC Cttee on Hazards to Man of Nuclear and Allied Radiations, 1955–60; President: British Inst. of Radiology, 1942–43; 1st Internat. Conf. on Medical Physics, 1965; Internat. Orgn for Medical Physics, 1965–69; Consultant: UKAEA, 1945–70; CEGB; WHO; Mem. Council and Scientific Cttee, Imp. Cancer Research Fund, 1965–73. A Trustee, National Gallery, 1966–71 (Mem., 1952–81, Chm., 1966–71, Hon. Adv. Scientific Cttee). Many awards and hon. memberships of British and foreign learned societies incl. RSocMed. Coronation Medal, 1953; Gold Medals: Royal Swedish Acad. of Science, 1965; Faculty of Radiologists (now RCR), 1966; Univ. of Arizona, 1974. Sievert Award, Internat. Radiation Protection Assoc., 1977; Beclère Prize and medal, Internat. Soc. of Radiology, 1985. Hon. LLD Aberdeen, 1969; DUniv Surrey, 1978. *Publications:* Physics of X-Ray Therapy, 1929; Some Applications of Nuclear Physics to Medicine, 1950; Radiation and Health, 1964; Carcinogenesis and Radiation Risk, 1975; articles on chemical carcinogenesis, and on applications of physics to medicine and radiation hazards. *Recreation:* Italian Renaissance art and literature, particularly Dante. *Address:* 7 Downs Way Close, Tadworth, Surrey KT20 5DR. *T:* Tadworth 2297. *Died 10 Aug.* 1988.

**MEAD, (Elsie) Stella;** journalist and authoress; *d* of John Mead. *Educ:* Stewkley C of E School; Toulouse University; Deutsches Institut für Ausländer an der Universität Berlin. After two years at Toulouse, went to Paris, did journalism, and attended lectures at the Sorbonne; spent three years in Berlin, studied folklore, contributed to several German papers (children's sections), taught English, and told English stories in German schools; spent two years, 1933–35, travelling in British India, and also in various Native States; contributed to Statesman (Calcutta), Times of India, Illustrated Weekly of India; did series of broadcasts to Bengali children from

Calcutta Broadcasting House in co-operation with late J. C. Bose; occasional contributor to English and American Journals. *Publications:* The Land of Legends and Heroes; The Land of Happy Hours; The Land where Stories Grow; The Land where Tales are Told; The Land where Dreams come True; Princes and Fairies; Great Stories from many Lands; The Land of Never-grow-old; Rama and Sita; The Shining Way; Morning Light; Golden Day; Under the Sun; Traveller's Joy; Magic Journeys. *Recreations:* reading, gardening. *Address:* c/o National Westminster Bank, Wembley Park, Mddx.                                        *Died 30 March 1981.*

**MEAD, (William Howard) Lloyd;** *b* 14 April 1905; *yr s* of late F. J. Mead; *m* 1951, Mary Pattinson, *e d* of late L. Borthwick Greig, Kendrew, S Africa. *Educ:* Marlborough; London Univ. BSc (Econ.) Hons. Industrial and Commercial Law, 1925. Chartered Accountant, 1930; RNVR 1938. Served War of 1939–45: in HMS Orion, 1939–41; Flag Lt to Vice-Adm. at Dover, 1942–45. Lt-Comdr (Sp) RNVR, retired, 1950. Clerk to the Vintners' Co., 1947–69. Dir, Royal Insurance Gp (London Bd), 1967–69. *Address:* 20 Bowen Court, The Drive, Hove, East Sussex BN3 3JF.
                                                            *Died 24 Sept. 1987.*

**MEADE, (Charles Alan) Gerald,** CMG 1951; *b* 9 Aug. 1905; *s* of Charles Austin Meade; *m* 1936, Beatrix Audibert, Paris; one *s* two *d. Educ:* Leighton Park Sch., Reading; St John's Coll., Oxford. Entered Consular Service, 1927; Vice-Consul: Bangkok, 1927; Saigon, 1930; Barcelona, 1932; Chargé d'Affaires, Tegucigulpa, 1935; Consul: Savannah, Ga, 1936; Jacksonville, Florida, 1937; Second Sec., 1941, First Sec., 1943, Lima; First Sec., Buenos Aires, 1946; Counsellor, Washington, 1948; Minister (Economic and Social) to UK Delegation to UN, 1952. Permanent UK Representative to Council of Europe with rank of Minister, and Consul Gen. at Strasbourg, 1955–59; British Ambassador to Ecuador, 1959–62; retired, 1963. *Address:* Casa de d'Alt, Capdepera, Mallorca, Spain. *T:* Capdepera 563295; 55 rue de la Fédération, 75015 Paris, France. *T:* 273 08 81.                            *Died 19 Feb. 1985.*

**MEADEN, Rt. Rev. John Alfred,** DD, MA, LTh; *b* 16 Feb. 1892. *Educ:* Queen's Coll., Newfoundland; University Coll., Durham, England. LTh Durham, 1916, BA 1917, MA 1935. Deacon, 1917, Nova Scotia for Newfoundland; Priest, 1918, Newfoundland. Incumbent of White Bay, 1917–21; Rector of Burin, 1921–29; Pouch Cove, 1929–34; Sec.-treasurer of Executive Cttee of Newfoundland Diocesan Synod, 1934–47; Examining Chaplain to the Bishop of Newfoundland, 1943–47; Canon of St John Baptist's Cathedral, St John's, Newfoundland, 1938–57. Principal of Queen's Coll., St John's, 1947–57. Bishop of Newfoundland, 1956–65. Hon. DCL, Bishop's Univ., Lennoxville, 1957; Hon. DD, Trinity Coll., Toronto, 1959; Hon. LLD, Memorial Univ. of Nfld, 1961. *Address:* Saint Luke's Homes, Topsail Road, St John's, Newfoundland, Canada.                                              *Died 24 June 1987.*

**MEARS, Lady, (Margaret Mary);** *see* Tempest, M. M.

**MEDAWAR, Sir Peter (Brian),** OM 1981; CH 1972; Kt 1965; CBE 1958; MA, DSc (Oxford); FRS 1949; Hon. FBA 1981; medical scientist; President, Royal Postgraduate Medical School, since 1981; Member, Scientific Staff, Medical Research Council, 1962–84; *b* 28 Feb. 1915; *s* of Nicholas Medawar and Edith Muriel Dowling; *m* 1937, Jean Shinglewood, *d* of Dr C. H. S. Taylor; two *s* two *d. Educ:* Marlborough Coll.; Magdalen Coll., Oxford. Christopher Welch Scholar and Senior Demy of Magdalen Coll., 1935; Fellow of Magdalen Coll., 1938–44, 1946–47; Fellow of St John's Coll., 1944 (Hon. Fellow, 1986); Mason Prof. of Zoology, Birmingham Univ., 1947–51; Jodrell Prof. of Zoology and Comparative Anatomy, University Coll., London, 1951–62; Dir, Nat. Inst. for Medical Research, Mill Hill, 1962–71, Dir Emeritus, 1975. Lectures: Croonian, Royal Society, 1958; Reith, 1959; Dunham, Harvard Med. Sch., 1959; Romanes, 1968; Danz, Washington Univ., 1984. Prof. of Experimental Medicine, Royal Institution, 1977–83. Pres., Brit. Assoc. for the Advancement of Science, 1968–69; Member: Agricultural Research Council, 1952–62; University Grants Cttee, 1955–59; Royal Commn on Med. Educn, 1965–68; Bd of Scientific Consultants, Meml Sloan-Kettering Cancer Centre; Inst. of Cellular Pathology, Brussels. Foreign Member: New York Acad. of Sciences, 1957; Amer. Acad. Arts and Sciences, 1959; Amer. Philosophical Soc., 1961; National Acad. of Sciences, 1965; Indian Acad. of Sciences, 1967. Hon. Fellow: St Catherine's Coll., 1960; Magdalen Coll., 1961; University Coll., London, 1971; London Sch. of Economics, 1975; Wolfson Coll., Oxford, 1981; American Coll. of Physicians, 1964; Royal College Physicians and Surgeons, Canada, 1966; RCS, 1967; RSE, 1965; RCPE, 1966; RCPath, 1971; RCP, 1974; Prof. at Large, Cornell Univ., 1965; Royal Medal of Royal Society, 1959, Copley Medal, 1969, Michael Faraday Award, 1987. Nobel Prize for Medicine, 1960; Kalinga Prize (India), 1985. Hon. ScD Cambridge; Hon. D de l'Univ.: Liège; Brussels; Hon. DSc: Aston, Birmingham, Hull, Glasgow, Brazil, Alberta, Dundee, Dalhousie, British Columbia, Chicago, Exeter, Florida, Gustavus Adolphus Coll., Harvard, Southampton, London, Queen's Univ.

Glasgow. *Publications:* The Uniqueness of the Individual, 1957; The Future of Man, 1960; The Art of the Soluble, 1967; Induction and Intuition, 1969; The Hope of Progress, 1972; (with J. S. Medawar) Life Science, 1977; Advice to a Young Scientist, 1979; Pluto's Republic, 1982; (with J. S. Medawar) Aristotle to Zoos, 1983; The Limits of Science, 1984; Memoir of a Thinking Radish, 1986. *Address:* Clinical Research Centre, Watford Road, Harrow, Mddx HA1 3UJ; 25 Downshire Hill, NW3.
                                                             *Died 2 Oct. 1987.*

**MEDLICOTT, Prof. William Norton,** CBE 1983; DLit, MA (London); FRHistS; Stevenson Professor of International History, University of London, 1953–67; Professor Emeritus, 1967; Senior Editor of Documents on British Foreign Policy, 1919–39, since 1965; *b* 11 May 1900; *s* of William Norton Medlicott (Editor, Church Family Newspaper, 1905–11) and Margaret Louisa McMillan; *m* 1936, Dr Dorothy Kathleen Coveney, Univ. Lectr and palaeographer (*d* 1979). *Educ:* Aske's Sch., Hatcham; University College, London; Institute of Historical Research. Gladstone Prizeman, Hester Rothschild Prizeman, UCL; Lindley Student, Univ. of London. Mil. service, Beds Herts Regt, 1918–20. Lecturer, University Coll., Swansea, 1926–45; Visiting Prof., Univ. of Texas, USA, 1931–32; Principal, Board of Trade, 1941–42; official historian, Ministry of Economic Warfare, 1942–58; Prof. of History, University Coll. of the South West, 1946–53; Vice-Principal, 1953. Creighton Lectr, Univ. of London, 1968. Fellow of UCL. Hon. Fellow LSE. Travel and research in US, 1946, 1952, and 1957; Hon. Sec. Historical Association, 1943–46, Pres., 1952–55. Mem. editl bd, Annual Register, 1947–71; Chm. editorial board, International Affairs, 1954–62. Mem. Institute for Advanced Studies, Princeton, 1952, 1957; Chm. British Co-ordinating Cttee for Internat. Studies. Mem. Council, Chatham House, 1955–71. Hon. DLitt: Wales, 1970; Buckingham, 1984; Hon. LittD Leeds, 1977. *Publications:* The Congress of Berlin and After, 1938, new edn 1963; British Foreign Policy since Versailles, 1940, new edn, 1968; The Economic Blockade, vol. i, 1952, vol. ii, 1959; Bismarck, Gladstone, and the Concert of Europe, 1956; The Coming of War in 1939, 1963; Bismarck and Modern Germany, 1965; Contemporary England, 1914–1964, 1967, rev. edn 1976; Britain and Germany: The Search for Agreement, 1930–1937, 1969; (with D. K. Coveney) Bismarck and Europe, 1971; (with D. K. Coveney) The Lion's Tail, 1971; (ed) Documents on British Foreign Policy 1919–1939, 2nd series, vols i–xxi, 1969–84; numerous articles and reviews. *Address:* 172 Watchfield Court, Sutton Court Road, W4 4NE. *T:* 01–995 7287. *Club:* Athenæum.                                        *Died 7 Oct. 1987.*

**MEDLYCOTT, Sir (James) Christopher,** 8th Bt, *cr* 1808; *b* 17 April 1907; *e s* of Sir Hubert Mervyn Medlycott, 7th Bt, and Nellie Adah (*d* 1964), *e d* of late Hector Edmond Monro, Edmondsham, Dorset; *S* father, 1964. *Educ:* Harrow; Magdalene Coll., Cambridge. BA 1930. *Heir: nephew* Mervyn Tregonwell Medlycott, *b* 20 Feb. 1947. *Address:* The Yard House, Milborne Port, near Sherborne, Dorset. *T:* Milborne Port 250312.                             *Died 11 April 1986.*

**MEE, Mrs Ellen Catherine,** CBE 1956; MA; *b* 19 Nov. 1894; *d* of William Henry and Rebecca Catherine Oakden; *m* 1945, Frederick George Mee, MC, BA (*d* 1971). *Educ:* Birmingham Univ. (MA, Arts Fellowship); Somerville Coll., Oxford (Research). Lecturer in English, Goldsmiths' Coll., London Univ., 1921–29; Exchange Lecturer in English, USA, 1924–25; HM Inspector of Schools, 1929; Staff Inspector (Training of Teachers), 1945; Chief Inspector of Schs, Min. of Education, 1952–58. Consultant, Schs Broadcasting Council, BBC, 1962–72. Mem. Advisory Cttee on Educn in the Colonies, Colonial Office, 1938–52. Asst Sec. McNair Cttee on Training of Teachers, 1942–44 (Min. of Education). *Address:* 112 Murray Avenue, Bromley, Kent. *T:* 01–460 0031.
                                                             *Died 31 May 1981.*

**MEERE, Sir Frank, (Francis Anthony),** Kt 1960; CBE 1955; FAIM; Comptroller General of Customs, Canberra, 1952–60; *b* 24 July 1895; *s* of Philip Francis and Harriet Charlotte Meere of Daylesford, Vic; *m* 1st, 1920, Helena Agnes (decd), *d* of late Wm G. Doyle; two *s*; 2nd, 1970, Mary Irene Higgins. *Educ:* Christian Brothers Coll., East St Kilda, Vic. Joined Australian Commonwealth Public Service, 1913; Deputy Dir, Division of Import Procurement, Brisbane, 1942–45; Dir, Division of Import Procurement, Sydney, 1945–47; Asst Comptroller General of Customs, Canberra, 1947–52. *Recreation:* gardening. *Address:* 3 Meehan Gardens, Canberra, ACT 2603, Australia. *Club:* Commonwealth (Canberra).
                                                             *Died 15 April 1985.*

**MEGRAH, Maurice Henry;** QC 1971; *b* 5 Feb. 1896; *e s* of Henry Barnard Megrah and Annie, *d* of H. Jepps; *m* 1917, Jessie Halstead (*d* 1977); one *d. Educ:* London Sch. of Economics. MCom. (London) 1931. Westminster Bank Ltd, 1914. Served European War, 1914–18, London Scottish, 1915; commissioned Royal Field Artillery, 1917. Returned Westminster Bank Ltd, 1919; Secretary, Inst. of Bankers, 1935–59, Hon. Fellow 1959. Called to Bar, Gray's Inn, 1937; Gilbart Lecturer, University of London, 1950, 1951, 1952, 1958, 1959, 1960,

1962, 1963, 1969. *Publications:* Bills of Exchange Act, 1882, 1929; The Banker's Customer, 1932; (ed) Paget's Law of Banking, 9th edn 1982; (ed) Byles on Bills of Exchange, 23rd edn 1972 - 25th edn 1983; Gutteridge and Megrah on Law of Bankers' Commercial Credits, 5th edn 1976–7th edn 1984; contributions to Halsbury's Laws of England, and to law and banking periodicals. *Address:* 5 Paper Buildings, EC4. *T:* 01–353 8494. *Clubs:* Athenæum, Overseas Bankers'. *Died 23 March 1985.*

**MEIGGS, Russell,** MA; FBA 1961; *b* 20 Oct. 1902; *s* of William Herrick Meiggs, London; *m* 1941, Pauline Gregg; two *d. Educ:* Christ's Hospital; Keble Coll., Oxford. Fellow of Keble Coll., 1930–39; Fellow and Tutor in Ancient History, Balliol Coll., Oxford, 1939–70, Hon. Fellow, 1970; Univ. Lectr in Ancient History, 1939–70; Praefectus of Holywell Manor, 1945–69. Vis. Prof., Swarthmore Coll., 1960, 1970–71, 1974, 1977–78; Kipling Fellow, Marlborough Coll., Vermont, 1967. For. Mem., Amer. Philosophical Soc., 1981. DHL Swarthmore Coll., 1971. *Publications:* Home Timber Production, 1939–1945, 1949; (ed jtly) Sources for Greek History between the Persian and Peloponnesian Wars, new edn, 1951; (ed) Bury's History of Greece, 3rd edn, 1951, 4th edn, 1975; Roman Ostia, 1960, 2nd edn, 1974; (ed with David Lewis) Selection of Greek Historical Inscriptions to the end of the 5th century BC, 1969; The Athenian Empire, 1972; Trees and Timber in the Ancient Mediterranean World, 1983. *Recreations:* gardening, America. *Address:* The Malt House, Garsington, Oxford.
*Died 24 June 1989.*

**MEKIE, David Eric Cameron,** OBE 1955; FRCSEd; FRCPEd; FRSE; Conservator, Royal College of Surgeons of Edinburgh, 1955–74; *b* 8 March 1902; *s* of Dr D. C. T. Mekie and Mary Cameron; *m* 1930, Winifred Knott (*d* 1970); two *s* one *d. Educ:* George Watson's Coll., Edinburgh; University of Edinburgh. MB, ChB 1925; FRCSEd 1928; FRSEd 1962; MRCP 1962; FRCPEd, 1966. Tutor, Dept of Clinical Surgery, University of Edinburgh, 1928–33; Ernest Hart Scholar, 1931–33; Professor of Clinical Surgery and Surgery, University of Malaya, 1935–55 (now Prof. Emeritus). Dir, Postgrad. Bd for Medicine, Edinburgh, 1960–71; Postgrad. Dean of Medicine, Edinburgh Univ., 1970–71. Surgeon, Singapore General Hospital and Hon. Surgical Consultant, Far East Command. *Publications:* Handbook of Surgery, 1936; (ed with Sir James Fraser) A Colour Atlas of Demonstrations in Surgical Pathology, 1983; numerous surgical papers. *Recreations:* fishing, gardening. *Address:* 58 Findhorn Place, Edinburgh EH9 2NW. *T:* 031–667 6472.
*Died 17 Nov. 1989.*

**MELLOR, Sir John Francis,** 3rd Bt *cr* 1924, of Culmhead, Somerset; accountant; *b* 9 March 1925; *s* of Sir John Serocold Paget Mellor, 2nd Bt and of Rachel Margaret, *d* of Sir Herbert Frederick Cook, 3rd Bt; *S* father, 1986; *m* 1948, Alix Marie, *d* of late Charles François Villaret. *Educ:* Eton. Served War of 1939–45 with RASC and Intelligence Corps. *Heir:* none. *Died 8 Nov. 1990 (ext).*

**MELLOR, Sir John (Serocold Paget),** 2nd Bt, *cr* 1924; *b* 6 July 1893; *er s* of 1st Bt and Mabel, *d* of G. E. Serocold Pearce-Serocold, of Cherryhinton, Torquay; *S* father, 1929; *m* 1st, 1922, Rachael Margaret (who obtained a divorce, 1937), *d* of Sir Herbert F. Cook, 3rd Bt, of Doughty House, Richmond; one *s*; 2nd, 1937, Mrs Raie Mendes (*d* 1965); 3rd, 1971, Mrs Jessica de Pass, *er d* of late Clarence de Sola, Montreal. *Educ:* Eton; New Coll., Oxford. Barrister, Inner Temple; formerly Capt. Prince Albert's Somerset LI. Served overseas 1914–18 (1914–15 Star, twice wounded, taken prisoner-of-war by Turks at Kut); rejoined Somerset LI, Sept. 1939; contested (C) Workington Division, 1929; adopted Conservative Candidate for Luton Division, 1931, but withdrew in favour of Liberal National Candidate; MP (C) Tamworth Division of Warwicks, 1935–45, Sutton Coldfield Division of Warwicks, 1945–55. Pres., Prudential Assurance Co. Ltd, 1972–77 (Dir, 1946–72; Dep. Chm., 1959–65; Chm., 1965–70). *Heir:* s John Francis Mellor [*b* 9 March 1925; *m* 1948, Alix Marie, *d* of late Charles François Villaret]. *Address:* Binley House, near Andover, Hants. *Club:* Carlton.
*Died 15 July 1986.*

**MELONEY, Rose (Dorothy), (Mrs W. B. Meloney);** *see* Franken, R. D.

**MELVILLE, Alan, (William Melville Caverhill);** revue writer and author; *b* 9 April 1910; *m* 1983, Dorothy Catherine, (Midge), Embery. *Educ:* Edinburgh Academy. BBC features and drama producer and script-writer, 1936–40. Served with RAF, 1940–46. *Publications: revues:* Rise Above It (Comedy), 1940; Sky High (Phoenix), 1941; Sweet and Low, Sweeter and Lower, Sweetest and Lowest (Ambassadors), 1943–46; A La Carte (Savoy), 1948; At the Lyric (Lyric, Hammersmith), 1953; Going to Town (St Martin's), 1954; All Square (Vaudeville), 1963; (jtly) Hulla Baloo (Criterion), 1972; Déjà Revue, 1975; *plays:* Jonathan (Aldwych), 1948; Top Secret (Winter Garden), 1949; Castle in the Air (Adelphi), 1949–50; Dear Charles (New), 1952–53; Simon and Laura, 1954; The Bargain (Ethel Barrymore Theatre, New York), 1953; Mrs Willie, 1955; Change of Tune (Strand), 1959; Devil May Care, 1963; Fuender

Bitte Melden (Stadt Theater, Baden-Baden), 1966; Demandez Vicky (Théatre des Nouveautés, Paris), 1966; Content to Whsiper (adaptation from French) (Theatre Royal, York); Darling You Were Wonderful (Richmond); *musical plays:* Gay's the Word (Saville), 1951; Bet Your Life (Hippodrome), 1952; Marigold (Savoy), 1959; Congress Dances (Continental productions), 1977; Set to Music, 1979; *films:* Derby Day, 1952; Hot Ice, 1952; As Long as They're Happy, 1954; All for Mary, 1955; Simon and Laura, 1955; *novels:* Week-end at Thrackley, 1935; Death of Anton, 1936; Quick Curtain, 1937; The Vicar in Hell, 1938; Warning to Critics, 1939; *war autobiography:* First Tide, 1945; *autobiography:* Myself When Young, 1956; Merely Melville, 1970; Blithe Thou Never Wert, 1983; *gardening book:* Gnomes and Gardens, 1983; *TV series:* A-Z, Merely Melville, Melvillainy, What's My Line?, Parade, Raise Your Glasses, Whitehall Worrier, Before the Fringe, Misleading Cases, The Very Merry Widow, The Brighton Belle; also Titipu, Iolanthe; By the Sword Divided; *radio:* 1972–83: The King's Favourite, The Sun King, Mellers and Sellers, Lovely Morning this Evening, Radio Burps, The Knocker. *Recreations:* tennis, swimming. *Address:* 28 Victoria Street, Brighton BN1 3FQ. *T:* Brighton 26682. *Died 24 Dec. 1983.*

**MELVILLE, Archibald Ralph,** CB 1976; CMG 1964; agricultural consultant; Member, Commonwealth Development Corporation, 1977–81; *b* 24 May 1912; *e s* of late James Melville, MA, Edinburgh, and Mrs K. E. Melville, Lynton, Devon; *m* 1943, Theresa Kelly, SRN, SCM, QAIMNS (*d* 1976); two *d. Educ:* George Heriot's Sch., Edinburgh; University of Edinburgh; Royal College of Science, London; Imperial Coll. of Tropical Agriculture, Trinidad. BSc in Agriculture with Hons Zoology, Edinburgh, 1934; AICTA, Trinidad, 1936. Entomologist, Kenya Dept of Agriculture, 1936; Senior Entomologist, 1947; Chief Research Officer, 1956; Dir of Agriculture, 1960–64, Kenya Government Service; Agricultural Adviser, ODM, 1965–71; Chief Natural Resources Advr, 1971–76, Under Sec., 1972–76, ODM. Pres., Tropical Agriculture Assoc. UK. Served 1939–44 with Kenya Regt and East African Army Medical Corps (Major). *Publications:* contributions to technical journals. *Recreations:* golf, gardening, natural history. *Address:* Spearpoint Cottage, Kennington, Ashford, Kent TN24 9QP. *T:* Ashford 20056. *Club:* Farmers'. *Died 8 Dec. 1982.*

**MELVILLE, Sir Eugene,** KCMG 1965 (CMG 1952); HM Diplomatic Service, retired; Director-General, British Property Federation, 1974–80; *b* 15 Dec. 1911; *s* of George E. Melville; *m* 1937, Elizabeth, *d* of Chas M. Strachan, OBE; two *s* one *d. Educ:* Queen's Park Sch., Glasgow; St Andrews Univ. (Harkness Residential Scholar; 1st cl. Hons Classics; 1st cl. Hons Economics). Appointed to Colonial Office, 1936; Colonies Supply Mission, Washington, 1941–45; PS to Sec. of State for Colonies, 1945–46; Financial Adviser, Control Commission for Germany, 1949–52; Asst Under-Sec. of State, Colonial Office, 1952; Asst Under-Sec. of State, Foreign Office, 1961; Minister (Economic), Bonn, 1962–65; Permanent UK Delegate to EFTA and GATT, 1965; Ambassador and Permanent UK Representative to UN and other Internat. Organisations at Geneva, 1966–71; Special Advr, Channel Tunnel Studies, 1971–73. Sec-Gen., Malta Round Table Conf., 1955; Hon. Treasurer, British Sailors' Soc.; Chm., Aldeburgh Festival, Snape Maltings Foundn, 1976–81, Pres., 1981–86. *Address:* Longcroft, Aldeburgh, Suffolk. *Club:* Reform. *Died 9 Dec. 1986.*

**MELVILLE, Dr James,** CMG 1969; Director, Waite Agricultural Research Institute, University of Adelaide, 1956–73, retired; *b* 10 July 1908; *s* of Andrew Melville, Lovells' Flat, NZ; *m* 1938, Margaret, *d* of Charles Ogilvie, Christchurch, NZ; one *s* two *d* (and one *d* decd). *Educ:* Otago, London & Yale Univs. MSc (NZ) 1930, PhD (London) 1934. Commonwealth Fund Fellow, Yale Univ., 1934–36; Asst Chemist, Wheat Research Inst., NZ, 1936–38; Dir, Plant Chemistry Laboratory, DSIR, NZ, 1939–50. War Service: S and SW Pacific Areas, 1941–45. Dir, Grasslands Div., DSIR, NZ, 1951–55. Mem., CSIRO Exec., 1958–65. Chm., Bushfire Research Cttee, 1959–77; Chm., Aust. Wool Industry Conf., 1964–66. FRACI 1958; FAIAS 1968. *Publications:* contrib. scientific jls (agricultural and chemical). *Address:* 10/47 Eve Road, Bellevue Heights, SA 5050, Australia. *Died 8 Oct. 1984.*

**MELVIN, Air Cdre James Douglas,** CB 1956; OBE 1947; idc 1956; retired; Property Manager, Coutts & Co.; *b* 20 Feb. 1914; *s* of William Adamson Melvin, The Square, Turriff, Aberdeenshire, and Agnes Fyffe, The Hunghar, Kirriemuir; *m* 1946, Mary Wills; one *d* (one *s* decd). *Educ:* Turriff Secondary Sch. Apprentice, Halton, 1930; Cadet, Cranwell, 1933. Dep. Dir Organization, Air Ministry, 1951–53; Group Capt. Organization, MEAF, 1953–55; Dir of Organization, Air Ministry, 1957–61, retd. *Address:* Kyrenia Cottage, Old Bosham, Sussex. *Club:* Royal Air Force.
*Died 7 Nov. 1987.*

**MENAUL, Air Vice-Marshal Stewart William Blacker,** CB 1963; CBE 1957; DFC 1941; AFC 1942; Defence Consultant: Institute for Study of Conflict; Institute for Foreign Policy Analysis, Cambridge,

Mass; *b* 17 July 1915; 2nd *s* of late Captain W. J. Menaul, MC, and Mrs M. Menaul, Co. Armagh, N Ireland; *m* 1943, Hélène Mary, *d* of late F. R. Taylor; one *s* one *d*. *Educ:* Portadown; RAF Coll., Cranwell. Bomber Command Squadrons, 1936–39; on outbreak of war serving with No 21 Sqdn until 1940; Flying Instructor, 1940–41; No 15 Sqdn, 1941–42; Air Staff No 3 Gp, Bomber Command, 1943; Pathfinder Force, 1943–45; RAF Staff Coll., 1946; Air Ministry, 1947–49; Imperial Defence Coll., 1950–51; Air Ministry, Dep. Dir of Operations, 1951–54; Comd British Atomic Trials Task Forces, Monte Bello and Maralinga (Australia), 1955–56; Commanding Officer, Bombing Sch., Lindholme, 1957–58; Air Officer Administration, Aden, 1959–60; Senior Air Staff Officer, Headquarters Bomber Command, 1961–65; Commandant, Joint Services Staff Coll., 1965–67; Dir-Gen., RUSI, 1968–76. *Publications:* Soviet War Machine, 1980; Countdown: Britain's strategic nuclear forces, 1980. *Recreations:* ornithology, painting. *Address:* The Lodge, Frensham Vale, Lower Bourne, Farnham, Surrey. *Club:* Royal Air Force. *Died* 22 *May* 1987.

**MENDÈS FRANCE, Pierre;** Commander of the Legion of Honour; Lawyer; *b* Paris, 11 Jan. 1907; *m* 1933, Lily Cicurel (*d* 1967); two *s*. Prof., Ecole Nationale d'Administration. Under-Sec. for the Treasury, 1938; tried by Vichy Administration, 1940, escaped to serve with Fighting French Air Force. Finance Minister, French Provisional Govt, 1943–44; Head of French Financial Missions, Washington and Breton Woods, 1944; Minister of National Economy, 1944–45; Governor for France of International Bank for Reconstruction and Development and Monetary Fund, 1946–58, resigned. Prime Minister and Minister of Foreign Affairs, France, June 1954–Feb. 1955; Minister of State without portfolio, France, Jan.–May 1956. Mem., Herr Brandt's Commn on Development Issues, 1977–80. Docteur en Droit (*hc*). *Publications:* L'Œuvre financiére du gouvernement Poincaré, 1928; La Banque internationale, 1930, Liberté, liberté chérie . . ., 1942 (trans. Eng. as The Pursuit of Freedom, 1956); Gouverner c'est choisir, 1953; Sept mois, dix-sept jours, 1955; La Science économique et l'action (with Gabriel Ardant), 1954 (trans. Eng. and other langs) (with A. Bevan and P. Nenni) Rencontres, 1959; La Politique et la vérité, 1959; La République Moderne, 1962, trans. Eng. as A Modern French Republic, 1963, new edn, 1965; Pour préparer l'avenir, 1968; Dialogues avec l'Asie, 1972, trans. Eng. as Face to Face with Asia; Science économique et lucidité politique (with Gabriel Ardant), 1973; Choisir, 1974; La Vérité guidait leurs pas, 1975. *Address:* Les Monts, 27400 Louviers, France *Died* 18 *Oct.* 1982.

**MENNELL, Peter,** CMG 1970; MBE 1945; Director, The Thomson Foundation, since 1979; *b* 29 Aug. 1918; *s* of Dr James B. Mennell, London, and Elizabeth Walton Allen, St Louis, Mo.; *m* 1946, Prudence Helen Vansittart; two *s* two *d*. *Educ:* Oundle Sch.; King's Coll., Cambridge (MA). Served 67th Field Regt, RA, 1939–46 (despatches, MBE). HM Diplomatic Service; served in NY, Moscow, Madrid, Cleveland, Ohio, Zaire and FO; Ambassador to Ecuador and High Comr in the Bahamas, retired 1978. Leader, UK Delegn to Econ. Commn for Latin America, 1973, and in Guatemala, 1977. Mem., Pilgrims Soc. Liveryman of Worshipful Company of Grocers, 1954; Col in Hon. Order of Kentucky Colonels, 1961; Visiting Cttee of Bd of Govs, Western Reserve Univ. for Lang. and Lit., 1964. Member: Royal Television Soc.; Internat. Assoc. for Mass Communication Res. Hon. Mem., Quito Br., Internat. Law Assoc. *Recreations:* usual outdoor sports and choral singing. *Address:* 7 Sheen Common Drive, Richmond, Surrey TW10 5BW. *T:* 01–876 6222. *Clubs:* United Oxford & Cambridge University, Royal Commonwealth Society, Press; (Hon. Life Mem.) English-Speaking Union (Cleveland). *Died* 12 *April* 1981.

**MENZIES, Sir Laurence James,** Kt 1962; *b* 23 Dec. 1906; *yr s* of late James Menzies, Coupar Angus, Perthshire; *m* 1935, Agnes Cameron, *yr d* of late John Smart; one *s* one *d*. *Educ:* Wandsworth Sch. Entered Bank of England, 1925; Asst Chief Cashier, 1943; Dep. Chief Cashier, 1952; Adviser to the Governors, 1957–58, 1962–64; Sec. of the Export Credits Guarantee Dept, 1958–61. Pres., Union d'Assureurs des Crédits Internationaux (Berne Union), 1960–61. *Recreation:* golf. *Address:* Timbers, Vincent Close, Esher, Surrey. *T:* Esher 64257. *Clubs:* Overseas Bankers', MCC.
*Died* 22 May 1983.

**MENZIES, Marie Ney;** actress producer; *b* 1895; *d* of William Fix and Agnes Rohan; *m* 1930, T. H. Menzies (marr. diss., 1949; remarried to T. H. Menzies, 1959, he *d* 1962). *Educ:* St Mary's Convent, Wellington, NZ. Stage debut in Melbourne, 1917; played in Australia until 1922, supporting among other visiting stars Marie Tempest; leading lady at the Old Vic 1924–25; parts included Ophelia, Lady Macbeth and Beatrice; visited Cairo 1927 with company invited by the Egyptian Government, parts included Desdemona, Portia and Viola; leading roles in London include Kate Hardcastle in Sir Nigel Playfair's production She Stoops To Conquer, Milady in The Three Musketeers, Miss Janus in John Van Druten's London Wall; leading part in J. B. Priestley's Dangerous Corner; star role in The Lake by Dorothy Massingham and Murray Macdonald; this play was especially written for her; leading role in Touch Wood; played leading role in Mrs Nobby Clark under her own management; Olga, in Anton Tchehov's Three Sisters (Old Vic); lead with Frank Vosper in Love from a Stranger; Mrs Alving in Ghosts; leading part in Sanctity, by Mrs Violet Clifton; leading roles in G. Bernard Shaw's The Millionairess (Dublin and Hull) and Candida (Dutch Tour 1939); Australian Season, Sydney and Melbourne, 1940–41; Ladies in Retirement, No Time for Comedy, Private Lives; Shakespearean Recitals, Australia, Malaya; with South African Broadcasting Corporation, Johannesburg Production, etc, 1942, 1943, 1944; African-Middle-East Tour, Shakespeare's Women, for British Council and ENSA; Italy and Holland, 1945, and performances for Arts Council; Hecuba in Trojan Women for Company of 4, Lyric Theatre; King of Rome, Fish in the Family, Native Son, Bolton's Theatre, SW10, 1947–48; Nurse Braddock in the Gioconda Smile, 1948; Lady Corbel in Rain on the Just, 1948; Sara Cantrey in The Young and Fair, St Martin's 1949; Mrs Cortelyon in The Second Mrs Tanqueray, Haymarket, 1950; Martha in The Other Heart, Old Vic, 1952; Mary in Fotheringhay, Edinburgh Festival, 1953. Played in films including The Wandering Jew; Brief Ecstasy; Jamaica Inn; Uneasy Terms; Conspirators; Romantic Age; Seven Days to Noon; Lavender Hill Mob; Night was our Friend; Simba. Television: The Little Dry Thorn, The Infernal Machine, Family Reunion, The Lake, The Sacred Flame, Time and the Conways, The Wrong Side of the Park, Do you Remember the Germans. *Recreations:* reading, riding, walking, painting. *Address:* 91 Dovehouse Street, SW3 6JZ. *Club:* Lansdowne. *Died* 11 *April* 1981.

**MERCHANT, Vivien;** actress since 1943; *b* 22 July 1929; *d* of William Thomson and Margaret McNaughton; *m* 1956, Harold Pinter (marr. diss. 1980); one *s*. *Educ:* Bury Convent, Manchester. Principal Appearances: Stella in The Collection (TV), 1961; Sarah in The Lover (stage and TV), 1963; Ruth in The Homecoming (stage, London and NY), 1965–67; Natasha Petrovna in A Month in the Country (TV), 1966; Lady Macbeth in Macbeth (Royal Shakespeare Co.), 1967; Mixed Doubles, Comedy, 1969; Flint, Criterion, 1970; The Tea Party, Duchess, 1970; Exiles, Mermaid, 1970, Aldwych 1971; The Man of Mode, Old Times, Aldwych, 1971; The Maids, Greenwich, 1974; Gaslight, Guildford, 1974; The Vortex, Greenwich, 1975; The Lover (TV), 1976; The Father, Greenwich, 1977; Breakaway (TV), 1980; Tale of Two Cities (TV), 1980; Crown Court (TV), 1982. *films:* Alfie, 1966 (nominated for Academy Award); Accident, 1967; Under Milk Wood, 1972; Frenzy, 1972; The Offence, 1973; The Homecoming, 1974; The Maids, 1974; Man in an Iron Mask, 1976. TV Actress of the Year award, 1963. *Recreations:* table tennis, listening to jazz, reading. *Address:* c/o International Creative Management, 22 Grafton Street, W1.
*Died* 3 *Oct.* 1982.

**MERITT, Benjamin Dean;** Visiting Scholar, University of Texas, since 1973; *b* Durham, North Carolina, 31 March 1899; *s* of Arthur Herbert Meritt and Cornelia Frances Dean; *m* 1st, 1923, Mary Elizabeth Kirkland; two *s*; 2nd, 1964, Lucy T. Shoe. *Educ:* Hamilton Coll. (AB 1920, AM 1923, LLD 1937); American Sch. of Class. Studies at Athens. AM Princeton 1923, PhD 1924, LittD 1947; DLitt Oxford, 1936; LLD Glasgow, 1948; LHD: University of Pennsylvania, 1967; Brown Univ., 1974; Dr *hc* Sch. of Philosophy, Univ. of Athens. Instr Greek Univ. of Vermont, 1923–24; Brown Univ., 1924–25; Asst Prof. Greek, Princeton, 1925–26; Asst Dir, Am. Sch. of Class. Studies at Athens, 1926–28; Associate Prof. Greek and Latin, University of Michigan, 1928–29, Prof. 1929–33; Visiting Prof. Am. Sch. Class. Studies at Athens, 1932–33; Dir Athens Coll., 1932–33; Francis White Prof. of Greek, Johns Hopkins, 1933–35; lecturer at Oxford, 1935; Annual Prof. Am Sch. of Class. Studies at Athens, 1936, 1954–55, 1969–70; Eastman Prof., Oxford Univ., 1945–46; Sather Prof., University of California, 1959; Prof. of Greek Epigraphy, Inst. for Advanced Study, Princeton, NJ, 1935–69, Emeritus, 1969–; Vis. Prof., Univ. of Texas, 1972; Member: American Philosophical Soc.; German Archae. Inst.; Fellow American Academy of Arts and Sciences; Corr. fellow British Academy; hon. councillor, Greek Archæ. Soc.; hon. mem. Michigan Acad. of Sciences, Arts and Letters, Society for the Promotion of Hellenic Studies; Assoc. Mem., Royal Flemish Acad.; Foreign Mem., Acad. of Athens; Pres. Amer. Philological Assoc., 1953. Commander: Order of the Phœnix (Greece); Order of George I (Greece). *Publications:* The Athenian Calendar in the Fifth Century, 1928; Supplementum Epigraphicum Graecum, Vol. V (with Allen B. West), 1931; Corinth, Vol. VIII, Part I-Greek Inscriptions, 1931; Athenian Financial Documents, 1932; The Athenian Assessment of 425 BC (with Allen B. West), 1934; Documents on Athenian Tribute, 1937; The Athenian Tribute Lists (with H. T. Wade-Gery and M. F. McGregor), Vol. I, 1939, Vol. II, 1949, Vol. III, 1950, Vol. IV, 1953; Epigraphica Attica, 1940; The Chronology of Hellenistic Athens (with W. K. Pritchett), 1940; The Athenian Year, 1961; The Athenian Agora Vol. XV: The Athenian Councillors (with J. S. Traill), 1974; articles in Hesperia 1933–81, Proceedings of the American Philosophical Soc. and other jls.

*Address:* 712 W 16th Street, Austin, Texas 78701, USA.
*Died 7 July* 1989.

**MERMAGEN, Patrick Hassell Frederick,** TD; MA Cantab; Headmaster, Ipswich School, 1950–72; *b* 8 May 1911; *s* of late L. H. Mermagen, MA, Taunton; *m* 1st, 1934, Neva Sonia (*d* 1953), *d* of late E. Haughton James, Forton House, Chard, Somerset; two *s* one *d* (and one *s* decd); 2nd, 1965, Inge (*née* Schütt), Hamburg; one *s* one *d. Educ:* Sherborne Sch.; Pembroke Coll., Cambridge (Open Scholar in Mathematics). Asst master, Loretto Sch., 1933–39, Radley Coll., 1939–50. Served War of 1939–45, Sept. 1940–Feb. 1946, The Royal Berkshire Regt; Staff Coll., Camberley (sc), 1944; held appointments in NW Europe and in SE Asia. *Recreations:* cricket, golf, gardening. *Address:* The Old Rectory, Otley, Ipswich IP6 9NP. *T:* Helmingham 495. *Club:* MCC.
*Died 20 Dec.* 1984.

**MERRELLS, Thomas Ernest;** Lord Mayor of Cardiff, 1970–71; *b* 5 Aug. 1891; *s* of Thomas Arthur Merrells, OBE, JP, and Kate Merrells, Swansea; *m* 1922, Vera Pughe Charles; one *s* one *d. Educ:* Bishop Gore Grammar Sch., Swansea. Served European War, 1914–18, in France; commissioned in Welsh Regt; seconded to HQ Staff, Royal Engineers, 1917; War of 1939–45: Chm., S Wales Area Nat. Dock Labour Bd; Mem., Exec. Cttee, Regional Port Director of Bristol Channel. Dep. Chm., S Wales Fedn of Port Employers, 1926–47, and Chm., Jt Conciliation Cttee for S Wales Ports. Councillor, City of Cardiff, 1951–74; Alderman, 1966–74. Freeman of City of London, 1971. Chevalier, Order of Mérite Social (France), 1958. *Recreation:* golf. *Address:* 5/11 Conway Road, Cardiff. *T:* Cardiff 398391. *Clubs:* Cardiff Athletic and Rugby; Cardiff Golf.
*Died 13 Nov.* 1987.

**MERRISON, Sir Alexander Walter, (Sir Alec Merrison),** Kt 1976; DL; FRS 1969; Vice-Chancellor, University of Bristol, 1969–84; *b* 20 March 1924; *s* of late Henry Walter and Violet Henrietta Merrison; *m* 1st, 1948, Beryl Glencora Le Marquand (*d* 1968); two *s*; 2nd, 1970, Maureen Michèle Barry; one *s* one *d. Educ:* Enfield Gram. Sch.; King's Coll., London. BSc (London) 1944; PhD (Liverpool) 1957. Res. in Radio Wave Propagation, as Experimental Officer, Signals Research and Development Establishment, Christchurch, 1944–46, Research in Reactor and Nuclear Physics, as Sen. Scientific Officer, AERE, Harwell, 1946–51; Research in Elementary Particle Physics, as Leverhulme Fellow and Lecturer, Liverpool Univ., 1951–57; Physicist, European Organisation for Nuclear Research (CERN) Geneva, 1957–60; Prof. of Experimental Physics, Liverpool Univ., 1960–69, and Dir, Daresbury Nuclear Physics Lab., SRC, 1962–69. Chairman: Cttee of Inquiry into Design and Erection of Steel Box Girder Bridges, 1970–73; Cttee of Inquiry into the Regulation of the Medical Profession, 1972–75; Royal Commn on NHS, 1976–79; Adv. Bd for the Research Councils, 1979–83 (Mem., 1972–73); Cttee of Vice-Chancellors and Principals, 1979–81; ACU, 1982–83; Management Cttee, Univs Superannuation Scheme, 1984–88. Chm., Bristol Regional Bd, Lloyds Bank and Dir, Lloyds Bank UK Management Bd, 1983–86; Director: Bristol Evening Post, 1979–; Western Provident Assoc., 1983– (Chm., 1985–); Bristol Waterworks Co., 1984–; Lloyds Bank PLC, 1986–. Charles Vernon Boys Prizeman of Inst. of Physics and the Physical Soc., 1961, Mem. Council, 1964–66, 1983–, Pres., 1984–86. Member: Council for Scientific Policy, 1967–72; Nuclear Power Adv. Bd, 1973–76; Adv. Council for Applied R&D, 1979–83; Cttee of Inquiry into Academic Validation of Public Sector Higher Educn, 1984–86; Pres. Council, CERN, 1982–85. Governor, Bristol Old Vic Trust, 1969–87, Chm., 1971–87. Mem. Haberdashers' Co., 1982; Freeman, City of London, 1982. FRSA 1970; FKC 1973. DL Avon, 1974, High Sheriff, 1986–87. Hon. FFCM 1980; Hon. FIStructE 1981; Hon. FRCPsych 1983. Hon. LLD Bristol, 1971; Hon. DSc: Ulster, 1976; Bath, 1977; Southampton, 1980; Leeds, 1981; Liverpool 1982. *Publications:* contrib. to scientific jls on nuclear and elementary particle physics. *Address:* The Manor, Hinton Blewett, Bristol BS18 5AN. *Club:* Athenæum.
*Died 19 Feb.* 1989.

**MERTON, Air Chief Marshal Sir Walter (Hugh),** GBE 1963 (OBE 1941); KCB 1959 (CB 1953); *b* 29 Aug. 1905; *s* of late G. R. Merton; *m* 1st, 1930, B. H. B. Kirby (from whom he obtained a divorce, 1932); one *s*; 2nd, 1938, Margaret Ethel Wilson, 2nd *d* of late J. C. Macro Wilson, Cossington Manor, Som. *Educ:* Eastbourne Coll.; RAF Cadet Coll., Cranwell. Commissioned, 1925; Wing Comdr, 1940; served War of 1939–45 (despatches thrice); Middle East, 1940–43: Directing Staff and Asst Comdt, RAF War Staff Coll., 1943–44; Dir of Organization, Air Ministry, 1944–45. Air Attaché, Prague, 1947–48; AOC and Head of RAF Delegation, Greece, 1949–50. AOC No. 63 (Western and Welsh) Group, 1951–52; AOC No. 22 Gp, Tech. Trg Comd, 1952–53; Chief of the Air Staff, Royal NZ Air Force, 1954–56; Air Officer in charge of Administration, Headquarters Bomber Command, RAF High Wycombe, 1956–59; Chief of Staff, Allied Air Forces, Central Europe, 1959–60; Air Mem. for Supply and Organisation, April 1960–Aug. 1963, retd; Inspector General of Civil Defence, 1964–68. Air Cdre, 1949; Air

Vice-Marshal, 1953; Air Marshal, 1959; Air Chief Marshal, 1961. Air ADC to the Queen, 1962–63. Gold Cross, Royal Order of George I, with crossed swords (Greece), 1941; Order of the Phœnix, Class I (Greece), 1963. *Address:* The Coach House, West Street, Wilton, Salisbury, Wilts SP2 0DL. *T:* Salisbury 743429. *Club:* Royal Air Force.
*Died 23 March* 1986.

**MESSER, Malcolm,** CBE 1949; *b* 1901; *s* of late Andrew Messer, MB, ChM; *m* 1943, Mary (*d* 1951), *er d* of G. F. Grigs; one *d. Educ:* Edinburgh Univ. (MA); Oxford Univ. (BA). Research Asst, Agricultural Economics Research Institute, Oxford, 1927–34; Technical Editor, Farmers' Weekly, 1934–38; Editor, Farmers' Weekly, 1938–66, retired editorship, 1 July 1966. Chm., Farm Journals Ltd, 1966–69. *Address:* 66 Tarlton, near Cirencester, Glos.
*Died 31 May* 1984.

**MESSERVY, Professor Albert;** Professor of Veterinary Surgery, University of Bristol, 1953–73, then Emeritus Professor; *b* 8 Feb. 1908; 2nd *s* of late E. P. Messervy, Jersey; *m* May, *d* of late F. E. Luce, Jersey; two *s* one *d. Educ:* Victoria Coll., Jersey; Royal Veterinary Coll., London. Private practice, 1929–40; Lecturer. Dept of Veterinary Surgery, Royal Vet. Coll., 1941–45; private practice, 1945–53. Mem. of Council, RCVS, 1957–65; Pres., Royal Jersey Agric. and Hort. Soc., 1974–77. Hon. MSc, 1964. *Publications:* clinical veterinary. *Recreation:* fishing. *Address:* Ville à L'Eveque, Trinity, Jersey, Channel Islands. *T:* Jersey Central 62588.
*Died 15 Nov.* 1985.

**MESTON, 2nd Baron,** *cr* 1919, of Agra and Dunottar; **Dougall Meston;** *b* 17 Dec. 1984; *s* of 1st Baron and Jeannie, CBE (*d* 1946), *o d* of James M'Donald; *S* father, 1943; *m* 1947, Diana Mary Came, *o d* of late Capt. O. S. Doll, 16 Upper Cheyne Row, Chelsea; two *s. Educ:* Charterhouse; RMA, Woolwich. Served European War, 1914–19; Capt., RA, 1917; N-W Frontier, India (Afghan War, 1919, Waziristan, 1919–20); retired, 1922; Barrister, Lincoln's Inn, 1924. Hon. Mem. Incorporated Association of Architects and Surveyors. President, British Soc. of Commerce. Contested (L) Southend Bye-Election, 1927, and General Election, 1929. *Publications:* Law of Moneylenders; Law of Nuisances, The Restrictive Trade Practices Act, 1956; The Rent Act, 1957; The Rating and Valuation Act, 1961; The Betting, Gaming and Lotteries Act, 1963; The Offices, Shops and Railway Premises Act, 1963; Weights and Measures Act, 1963; Rent Act, 1965; Leasehold Reform Act, 1967; The Gaming Act, 1968; Industrial Relations Act, 1971; Consumer Credit Act, 1974; several works on Gaming, Landlord and Tenant, War Damage, Local Government, Town and Country Planning, Highways, Trade Wastes, Public Health and Housing Acts; Jt Ed. of Mather's Sheriff and Execution Law (3rd edn). *Heir:* *s* Hon. James Meston [*b* 10 Feb. 1950; *m* 1974, Anne, *yr d* of John Carder; one *s* one *d*]. *Address:* Hurst Place, Cookham Dene, Berks; Queen Elizabeth Building, Temple, EC4. *T:* 01–353 3911. *Club:* Reform.
*Died 2 Jan.* 1984.

**METSON, Gilbert Harold,** MC 1940; MSc, PhD, DSc; Consulting Engineer; formerly Director of Research, Post Office; *b* 4 July 1907; British; *m* 1932, Una (*née* Pyke); two *d. Educ:* Mercers' Sch., Queen Elizabeth's Sch., Barnet. BSc (Eng.) London; MSc, PhD and DSc Queen's Univ. of Belfast. Post Office Engineer. Served War, in Royal Signals, 1939–45; comd 11th L of C Signals in N Africa and Italy; GS01, War Office. *Publications:* wide range, mainly concerned with thermionic emission from oxide cathodes. *Recreation:* fly-fishing. *Address:* 38 Wheathampstead Road, Harpenden, Herts AL5 1ND.
*Died 10 Feb.* 1981.

**MEYER, Prof. Alfred,** MD; FRCPsych; Professor of Neuropathology in the University of London, Institute of Psychiatry, 1949–56, retired; *b* 3 Feb. 1895; *m* 1949, Nina Cohen. Assoc. Prof. of Neurology at University of Bonn, 1931; Rockefeller Research Fellow in Pathological Laboratory, Maudlsey Hosp., London, 1933; Neuropathologist in the Pathological Laboratory, Maudsley Hospital, 1943. Honorary Member: German Soc. of Neurology and Psychiatry; French Soc. of Neuro-Surgery; Brit. Soc. of Neuropathology; Internat. Soc. of Neuropathology, 1970. Hon. FRCPsych 1987. *Publications:* (jt) Prefrontal Leucotomy and Related Operations: anatomical aspects, 1954; (jt) Neuropathology, 1958, 2nd edn 1963; Historical Aspects of Cerebral Anatomy, 1971; articles and papers on neuroanatomical and neuropathological subjects. *Address:* 38 Wood Lane, N6 5UB.
*Died 27 Sept.* 1990.

**MEYER, Sir Oscar (Gwynne),** Kt 1979; OBE 1944; ED 1945; FAIM 1959; FIEAust; company chairman and director; *b* 10 Feb. 1910; *s* of Oscar Arthur Meyer and Muriel Meyer; *m* 1938, Marion Bohle; one *s* one *d. Educ:* N Sydney High Sch.; Sydney Tech. Coll. (Dip. in Mech. Engrg); Harvard Business Sch. (Grad., Advanced Management Prog., 1956). CMF, 1932–39; served War, AIF (RAE), 1940–46; ME, New Guinea and Borneo (mentioned in despatches twice); Col; Col Gp Comdr in Vic, CMF (RAE), 1956–59; Col Comdt, Corps in Vic. NSW Railways, 1932–39; Dir of Mech. Engrg, Railways Standardisation Div. of Commonwealth Dept of

Transport, 1946–50; Comr, Victorian Railways, 1950–58 (Dep. Chm., 1956–58); Man. Dir, Australian Carbon Black Pty Ltd, 1958–73, Chm. 1973–75. Chairman: West Gate Bridge Authority; Watts Holdings Ltd; Ashton Mining NL; Mildara Wines Ltd; Director: Colonial Mutual Life Assurance Soc. Ltd; Nylex Corp. Ltd; The Perpetual Executors & Trustees Assoc. of Aust. Ltd; Perpetual Trustees Australia Ltd; Australian Innovation Corp. Ltd; Valvoline (Australia) Pty Ltd; Weeks Petroleum Ltd; Alliance Oil Development. Chm., Adv. Bd, American Internat. Underwriters. John Storey Medal, AIM, 1977. *Publications:* various. *Recreations:* yachting, golf. *Address:* (home) 2 Cross Street, Toorak, Vic 3142, Australia. *T:* 20–5264; (office) Suite 4, 14th Floor, 50 Queen Street, Melbourne, Vic 3000. *T:* 62–6393. *Clubs:* Australian, Naval and Military (Melbourne); Royal Melbourne Golf, Barwon Heads Golf, Royal Sydney Yacht Squadron (Sydney).

*Died 30 Sept. 1981.*

**MEYNELL, Laurence Walter, (Robert Eton);** author; *b* Wolverhampton, 1899; *y s* of late Herbert and Agnes Meynell; *m* 1932, Shirley Ruth (*d* 1955), *e d* of late Taylor Darbyshire; one *d*; *m* 1956, Joan Belfrage (*née* Henley) (*d* 1986). *Educ:* St Edmund's Coll., Old Hall, Ware. After serving in the Honourable Artillery Company became successively schoolmaster, estate agent and finally professional writer; Royal Air Force in War of 1939–45 (despatches). Literary Editor, Time and Tide, 1958–60, Past Pres. Johnson Soc. *Publications:* as *Robert Eton:* The Pattern; The Dividing Air; The Bus Leaves for the Village; Not In Our Stars; The Journey; Palace Pier; The Legacy; The Faithful Years; The Corner of Paradise Place; St Lynn's Advertiser; The Dragon at the Gate; as *Laurence Meynell:* Bluefeather; Paid in Full; The Door in the Wall; The House in the Hills; The Dandy; Third Time Unlucky; His Aunt Came Late; The Creaking Chair; The Dark Square; Strange Landing; The Evil Hour; The Bright Face of Danger; The Echo in the Cave; The Lady on Platform One; Party of Eight; The Man No One Knew; Give me the Knife; Saturday Out; Famous Cricket Grounds; Life of Sir P. Warner; Builder and Dreamer; Smoky Joe; Too Clever by Half; Smoky Joe in Trouble; Rolls, Man of Speed; Young Master Carver; Under the Hollies; Bridge Under the Water; Great Men of Staffordshire; Policeman in the Family; James Brindley; Sonia Back Stage; The Young Architect; District Nurse Carter; The Breaking Point; One Step from Murder; The Abandoned Doll; The House in Marsh Road; The Pit in the Garden; Virgin Luck; Sleep of the Unjust; Airmen on the Run; More Deadly Than the Male; Double Fault; Die by the Book; Week-end in the Scampi Belt; Death of a Philanderer; The Curious Crime of Miss Julia Blossom; The End of the Long Hot Summer; Death by Arrangement; A Little Matter of Arson; A View from the Terrace; The Fatal Flaw; The Thirteen Trumpeters; The Woman in Number Five; The Fortunate Miss East; The Fairly Innocent Little Man; The Footpath; Don't Stop For Hooky Heffernan; Hooky and the Crock of Gold; The Lost Half Hour; Hooky Gets the Wooden Spoon; Affair at Barwold; Parasol in the Park; Quenell's; The Sisters; Hooky and the Prancing Horse; The Secret of the Pit; The Visitor; The Open Door; The Abiding Thing; Hooky Catches a Tartar; Hooky on Loan; The Rivals; Hooky Hooked; as *A. Stephen Tring* (for children): The Old Gang; The Cave By the Sea; Penny Dreadful; Barry's Exciting Year; Penny Triumphant; Penny Penitent; Penny Dramatic; Smoky Joe Goes to School; Penny in Italy; Penny Goodbye. *Recreations:* walking, trying to write a play. *Address:* 79 The Drive, Hove, Sussex BN3 3PG. *Club:* Authors'.                                          *Died 14 April 1989.*

**MEYNER, Robert Baumle;** Lawyer since 1934; Governor, State of New Jersey, USA, 1954–62; *b* 3 July 1908; *s* of late Gustave H. Meyner and Sophia Baumle Meyner; *m* 1957, Helen Day Stevenson. *Educ:* Lafayette Coll. (AB); Columbia Univ. Law Sch. (LLB). State Senator from Warren County, 1948–52; Senate Minority (Democrat) Leader, 1950; Director: Phillipsburg (NJ) National Bank and Trust Co.; NJ State Safety Council; Hon. degrees: Dr of Laws: Rutgers (The State Univ.) 1954; Lafayette Coll., 1954; Princeton Univ., 1956; Long Island Univ., 1958; Fairleigh Dickinson Univ., 1959; Syracuse Univ., 1960; Lincoln Univ., 1960; Colorado Coll., 1961. *Address:* (business) Suite 2500, Gateway 1, Newark, New Jersey 07102, USA; 16 Olden Lane, Princeton, NJ 08540, USA; 372 Lincoln Street, Phillipsburg, NJ 08865, USA. *Clubs:* River, Princeton (New York); Essex, 744 (Newark, NJ); Pomfret (Easton, Pa); Prettybrook Tennis (Princeton).          *Died 27 May 1990.*

**MEYRICK, Lt-Col Sir George David Eliott Tapps Gervis,** 6th Bt, *cr* 1791; MC 1943; *b* 15 April 1915; *o s* of Major Sir George Llewelyn Tapps Gervis Meyrick, 5th Bt, and Marjorie (*née* Hamlin) (*d* 1972); *S* father, 1960; *m* 1940, Ann, *d* of Clive Miller; one *s* one *d*. *Educ:* Eton; Trinity Coll., Cambridge (BA). 2nd Lieut, 9th Queen's Royal Lancers, 1937. Served War of 1939–45 (wounded, MC): BEF, 1940; Middle East, 1941–43; Italy, 1945; Captain, 1940; Lt-Col, 1947; retired, 1952. Dir, Southampton FC, 1953–. High Sheriff, Anglesey, 1962. *Recreations:* shooting, travel. *Heir:* *s* George Christopher Cadafael Tapps Gervis Meyrick [*b* 10 March 1941; *m* 1968, Jean Louise Montagu Douglas Scott, *d* of late Lt-Col Lord William Scott

and of Lady William Scott, Beechwood, Melrose, Scotland; two *s* one *d*]. *Address:* Hinton Admiral, Christchurch, Dorset. *T:* Highcliffe 72887; Bodorgan, Anglesey, Gwynedd. *T:* Bodorgan 840204. *Club:* Cavalry and Guards.          *Died 21 Dec. 1988.*

**MEYRICK, Col Sir Thomas Frederick,** 3rd Bt, *cr* 1880; TD; late 15th/19th Hussars; DL, JP, Pembrokeshire; *b* 28 Nov. 1899; *o s* of Brigadier-General Sir Frederick Charlton Meyrick, 2nd Bt; *S* father, 1932; *m* 1st, 1926, Ivy Frances (*d* 1947), *d* of late Lieut-Col F. C. Pilkington, DSO; three *s* three *d*; 2nd, 1951, Gladice Joyce (*d* 1977), *d* of late Bertram W. Allen, Cilrhiw, Narberth, Pembs; one *s*; 3rd, 1978, Suzannne (*d* 1979), *yr d* of late D. A. Evans. Capt. 15/19 Hussars, 1927; Equitation Instructor, Weedon, 1922–27, and RMC, 1930–34; retd pay, 1934; Captain 102 (Pembroke and Cardigan), Field Brigade RA (TA), 1937; Major, 1939; Hon. Col 302 Pembroke Yeo. Field Regt, RA (TA), 1955–59. Sheriff of Pembrokeshire, 1938; Master Pembrokeshire Foxhounds, 1934–35, South Pembrokeshire, 1936–39; V. W. H., Lord Bathurst's, 1939, Pembrokeshire, 1946–58; President: Royal Welsh Agricultural Soc., 1955; Hunters Improvement Soc., 1972; Chm., Pembs Branch, NFU, 1968. *Heir:* *s* David John Charlton Meyrick [*b* 2 Dec. 1926; *m* 1962, Penelope Anne Marsden-Smedley; three *s*]. *Address:* Gumfreston, Tenby, Dyfed SA70 8RA. *Club:* English-Speaking Union.                                          *Died 23 Dec. 1983.*

**MICHAEL, David Parry Martin,** CBE 1972; MA; Headmaster, Newport High School, Gwent, 1960–76; Secretary (part-time) University College Cardiff Press Board, since 1976; *b* 21 Dec. 1910; *m* 1937, Mary Horner Hayward; one *s*. *Educ:* University Coll., Cardiff (Fellow, 1981). Major, RAOC, combined ops, 1941–46 (despatches). Asst Master, Bassaleg Gram. Sch., Mon., 1935–41 and 1946–50; Headmaster, Cathays High Sch. for Boys, Cardiff, 1950–60. Member: Council, University Coll., Cardiff, 1961–; Governing Body, Church in Wales, 1963–. Governor, Nat. Library of Wales, 1967–; Member: Broadcasting Council for Wales, 1969–73; Exec. Cttee, SE Wales Arts Assoc., 1975–. Pres., Incorporated Assoc. of Headmasters, 1968; Mem., HMC, 1971–76; Pres., Welsh Secondary Schools Assoc., 1973. Editor, Welsh Secondary Schools' Review, 1965–76. *Publications:* The Idea of a Staff College, 1967; Guide to the Sixth Form, 1969; Arthur Machen, 1971; Town Walks, 1977; The Mapping of Monmouthshire, 1985; articles and reviews in educational and other jls. *Recreations:* collecting Victorian Staffordshire portrait figures; setting and solving crosswords (pseudonym, Egma). *Address:* 28 Fields Road, Newport, Gwent. *T:* Newport (Gwent) 62747.          *Died 12 Dec. 1986.*

**MICHELHAM, 2nd Baron,** *cr* 1905, of Hellingly; **Herman Alfred Stern;** Bt, *cr* 1905; a Baron of Portugal; *b* 5 Sept. 1900; *e s* of 1st Baron Michelham; *S* father, 1919; *m* 1919, Berthe Isabella Susanna Flora (*d* 1961), *d* of Arthur Joseph Capel; *m* 1980, Marie-José Dupas. *Educ:* Malvern College.          *Died 19 March 1984 (ext).*

**MICHELL, Alan,** CMG 1966; HM Diplomatic Service, retired; *b* 11 Nov. 1913; *s* of late Pierre William Michell and late Mary Michell; *m* 1st, 1941, Glenys Enid Davies (*d* 1965); one *s* two *d*; 2nd, 1980, Mrs Josephine Thogersen, *yr d* of late William and Iris Price, Farnham, Surrey. *Educ:* Barry School; Jesus Coll., Oxford (Stanhope Univ. Prize, 1934). Served Royal Tank Regt, 1940–46. Asst Master, King's Sch., Canterbury, 1937–40; Foreign Office, 1947; Second Sec., Paris, 1952; Nicosia, 1954; Singapore, 1956; First Sec., Saigon, 1959; FO, later FCO, 1961–72. *Address:* Wyche House, Woodchurch Road, Tenterden, Kent. *T:* Tenterden 2059.

*Died 28 Nov. 1985.*

**MICHELL, Francis Victor,** CMG 1955; *b* 17 Jan. 1908; *s* of late Pierre William Michell and late Mary Michell; *m* 1943, Betty Enid Tempest, *d* of late William Tempest Olver, JP, Tamworth; no *c*. *Educ:* Barry Sch.; Jesus Coll., Oxford. Attaché British Embassy, Rio de Janeiro, 1943–46; First Sec., Istanbul, 1947–51; First Sec., Commissioner-General's Office, Singapore, 1951–53; Foreign Office, 1953–65. *Address:* Nettlesworth Farm, Vines Cross, Heathfield, East Sussex. *T:* Heathfield 2695. *Club:* Travellers'.

*Died 12 Jan. 1985.*

**MICHELMORE, Maj.-Gen. Sir Godwin;** see Michelmore, Maj.-Gen. Sir W. G.

**MICHELMORE, Sir Walter Harold Strachan,** Kt 1958; MBE 1945; Company Director; *b* Chudleigh, Devon, 4 April 1908; 2nd *s* of late Harold G. Michelmore; *m* 1933, Dorothy Walrond (*d* 1964), *o c* of late E. W. Bryant; one *d*; *m* 1967, Mrs Dulcie Mary Scott, *d* of late Leonard Haughton. *Educ:* Sherborne Sch.; Balliol Coll., Oxford. Joined Bird & Co., Calcutta, 1929. Served Indian Army (Staff), 1940–46 (MBE). Chm., Indian Mining Assoc., 1947–48. Managing Dir, Bird & Co. (Pvt) Ltd and F. W. Heilgers & Co. (Pvt) Ltd, Calcutta, 1948–63; Dep. Chm., 1955, Chm. 1961; retired 1963. Pres. Bengal Chamber of Commerce and Industry and Associated Chambers of Commerce of India, 1957. *Recreations:* golf, fishing, gardening. *Address:* Derriwong, 33 Derriwong Road, Round Corner, via Dural, NSW 2158, Australia. *Clubs:* Oriental, Queen's;

Bengal (Calcutta); Australian (Sydney).
*Died* 18 *Feb.* 1988.

**MICHELMORE, Maj.-Gen. Sir (William) Godwin,** KBE 1953; CB 1945; DSO 1919; MC, TD; JP; DL; Solicitor and Notary Public; Deputy Diocesan Registrar, Bishop's Secretary; *b* 14 March 1894; 3rd *s* of late Henry William Michelmore of Exeter; *m* 1st, 1921, Margaret Phœbe (*d* 1965), *d* of late Sir F. G. Newbolt, KC; one *s* two *d*; 2nd, 1971, Maud Winifred, *widow* of Lt-Col William Holderness and *d* of late Rt Rev. Henry Hutchinson Montgomery, KCMG, DD. *Educ:* Rugby; London Univ.; LLB. Served European War, 1914–19 (despatches, MC, DSO); wounded at Passchendaele, 1917; commanded 43rd (Wessex) Div. Signals TA, 1919–29; Dep. Chief Signal Officer, Southern Command, 1929–33; Col 1933; commanded 4th Bn Devonshire Regt, 1936–39; commanded Infantry Brigade, 1939–41, Division Commander, 1941–45; ADC to the King, 1942–47; Mayor of Exeter, 1949–50. Chm. Devon T&AFA, 1948–58; Vice-Chm. Council of T&AFA, 1956–59. Resigned 1975: Chm. Devon Magistrates Courts Cttee; Chm. Govs, St Luke's Coll., Exeter; Governor, Blundell's Sch.; Mem. Coun., University Exeter. DL 1938, JP 1950, Devon. *Address:* 10 St Leonard's Road, Exeter, Devon EX2 4LA. *T:* 59585.
*Died* 25 *Oct.* 1982.

**MICHIE, Charles Watt,** CMG 1960; OBE 1943; Secretary: Scottish Universities Entrance Board, 1967–69 (Assistant to Secretary, 1963–67); Scottish Universities Council on Entrance, 1968–72; *b* 1 Sept. 1907; *s* of late Charles Michie and late Emily (*née* MacGregor); *m* 1935, Janet Leslie Graham Kinloch; two *d*. *Educ:* Aberdeen Gram. Sch.; Aberdeen Univ. Cadet, Colonial Admin. Service, 1930; Cadet, N Region of Nigeria, 1931; Consul for Spanish Territories of Gulf of Guinea and Labour Officer in Nigerian Department of Labour, 1940–42; Labour Officer on Nigerian tin minesfield, 1942; N Regional Secretariat, Kaduna, 1944; Chm. Labour Advisory Bd for Nigerian tin minesfield, 1947; District Administration, 1948; Sen. District Officer, and Asst Sec., Actg Principal, Nigerian Secretariat, 1949; returned to provincial administration and promoted Resident, 1954; Sen. Resident, 1954; Permanent Sec. to N Region Min. of Agriculture in Nigeria, 1957; retired 1960. Asst Teacher, Mod. Langs, Morgan Academy, Dundee, 1960–63. Defence Medal, 1945; Coronation Medal, 1953. *Recreations:* gardening, photography. *Address:* Nethermiln, Blebo Craigs, Cupar, Fife. *T:* Strathkinness 316.
*Died* 20 *March* 1982.

**MIDDLEDITCH, Edward,** MC 1945; RA 1973 (ARA 1968); ARCA 1951; painter; Head of Fine Art Department, Norwich School of Art, since 1964; *b* 23 March 1923; *s* of Charles Henry Middleditch and Esme Buckley; *m* 1947, Jean Kathleen Whitehouse (*d* 1979); one *d*. *Educ:* Mundella School, Nottingham; King Edward VI Grammar Sch., Chelmsford; Royal College of Art. Served Army, 1942–47, France, Germany, India, W Africa; commissioned Middx Regt 1944. Keeper, Royal Academy Schools, 1985–86. Eleven Exhibitions, London, 1954–74; contrib. to mixed exhibitions: Paris; Rome; Venice Biennale, 1956; Six Young Painters, 1957; Pittsburgh Internat., 1958; Whitechapel, 1959; English Landscape Tradition in the 20th Century, 1969; British Painting '74, 1974; 25 Years of British Painting, 1977; The Forgotten Fifties, 1984, etc. Gulbenkian Foundn Scholarship, 1962; Arts Council of GB Bursary, 1964; Arts Council of NI Bursary, 1968. Paintings in private and public collections, including: Tate Gall.; Arts Council; V & A Museum; Contemporary Art Soc.; Manchester City Art Gall.; Ferens Art Gall., Hull; Nat. Gall. of Victoria; Nat. Gall. of S Aust.; Nat. Gall. of Canada; Chrysler Art Museum, Mass; Toledo Museum of Art, Ohio. *Died* 29 *July* 1987.

**MIDDLEMISS, Sir (John) Howard,** Kt 1981; CMG 1968; Professor of Radiodiagnosis, University of Bristol, and Director of Radiology, United Bristol Hospitals, 1949–81; Dean, Faculty of Medicine, Bristol University, 1978–81; *b* 14 May 1916; *s* of Thomas Middlemiss, Monkseaton, Northumberland; *m* 1942, Isobel Mary, *d* of Ivan Pirrie, MC, MD, Maldon, Essex; one *s* two *d*. *Educ:* Repton; Durham Univ. MB, BS 1940; MD 1947; DMRD 1946; FFR 1948; MRCP 1964, FRCP 1972; FRCS 1976. Served with RAMC as Temp. Major and Actg Lieut-Col, 1941–46. Asst Radiologist, Royal Victoria Infirmary, Newcastle upon Tyne, 1946–48. Adviser in Radiology to Governments of: Burma, Iran, Laos, Malaysia, Nigeria, Pakistan, Philippines, South Vietnam, Tanzania, Turkey and Uganda, and to Universities of Ahmadu Bello, Ghana, Ibadan, Makerere, West Indies, for periods between 1953–80. Member: Med. Adv. Cttee, Min. of Overseas Devlt; Inter-Univ. Council, 1969–81; British Deleg. to 13th Internat. Congress of Radiology, 1973 (Chm.); Accident Service Review Cttee; Jt Consultants Cttee, 1972–76; Cons. to WHO; Chm., Internat. Commn on Radiological Educn, 1978–; Past Chm., Bristol Standing Cttee on Disarmament; Examnr, FFR, UK 1958–60 and 1962–63, Aust. and NZ 1969, DM (Rad.) W Indies, 1973–81. Harkness Fellow, US, 1964. Lectures: Long Fox, Bristol, 1962; Mackenzie Davidson, BIR, 1971; Litchfield, Oxford, 1972; Skinner, FR, 1972;

Lindblom, Univ. of Stockholm, 1973; Edelstein, Johannesburg, 1975; Frimann-Dahl, Univ. of Oslo, 1976; Kemp., Univ. of Oxford, 1980. Warden, Faculty of Radiologists, 1966–71, Pres. 1972–75, Pres., Royal Coll. of Radiologists, 1975–76; FRSocMed. Hon. FFR, RCSI, 1969; Hon. FACR, 1972; Mem., BIR (Past Chm. of Med. Cttee); Past Vice-Pres., Section of Radiol, RSM; Hon. Member: Soc. of Radiology, Luxembourg, 1971; W African Assoc. of Radiologists, 1971; Radiol Soc. of N America, 1976; Deutsche Röntgengesellschaft, 1977; Swedish Radiol Soc., 1978; Danish Radiol Soc., 1980; Swiss Radiol Soc., 1982; Hon. Fellow, Royal Aust. Coll. of Radiologists, 1972. *Publications:* Radiology in Surgery, 1960; Tropical Radiology, 1961; Clinical Radiology in the Tropics, 1979; numerous scientific papers in Clinical Radiology, British Jl of Radiology; contrib. Encyclopaedia Britannica. *Recreations:* international relations, arboriculture. *Address:* 48 Pembroke Road, Clifton, Bristol BS8 3DT. *T:* Bristol 738553; White Cottage, Wellington Heath, Ledbury, Herefordshire. *T:* Ledbury 2454. *Club:* English-Speaking Union. *Died* 27 *April* 1983.

**MIDDLEMORE, Sir William Hawkslow,** 2nd Bt, *cr* 1919; *b* 10 April 1908; *s* of 1st Bt and Mary, *d* of late Rev. Thomas Price, Selly Oak, Birmingham; *S* father, 1924; *m* 1934, Violet Constance (*d* 1976), *d* of Andrew Kennagh, Worcester. *Heir:* none.
*Died* 1 *June* 1987 (*ext*).

**MIDDLETON, Drew,** CBE (Hon.) 1986; Military Correspondent of The New York Times, since 1970; *b* 14 Oct. 1914; *o s* of E. T. and Jean Drew Middleton, New York; *m* 1943, Estelle Mansel-Edwards, Dinas Powis, Glamorgan; one *d*. *Educ:* Syracuse Univ., Syracuse, New York. Correspondent: for Associated Press in London, 1939; for Associated Press in France, Belgium, London, Iceland, with the British Army and RAF, 1939–42; for The New York Times with US and British Forces in North Africa, Sicily, Britain, Normandy, Belgium and Germany, 1942–45; Chief Correspondent: in USSR, 1946–47; in Germany, 1948–53; in London, 1953–63; in Paris, 1963–65; UN, 1965–69; European Affairs Correspondent, 1969–70. Correspondent at four meetings of Council of Foreign Ministers, also Potsdam and Casablanca Conferences. Medal of Freedom (US). English-Speaking Union Better Understanding Award, 1955. Doctor of Letters (*hc*) Syracuse Univ., 1963. *Publications:* Our Share of Night, 1946; The Struggle for Germany, 1949; The Defence of Western Europe, 1952; The British, 1957; The Sky Suspended, 1960; The Supreme Choice: Britain and the European Community, 1963; Crisis in the West, 1965; Retreat From Victory, 1973; Where Has Last July Gone?, 1974; Can America Win the Next War?, 1975; Submarine, 1976; Duel of the Giants, 1977; Crossroads of Modern War, 1983; (jtly) This War Called Peace, 1984. *Recreations:* tennis, the theatre. *Address:* The New York Times, 229 W 43rd Street, New York, NY 10036, USA. *Clubs:* Beefsteak, Press, Garrick; Travellers' (Paris); The Brook, Century (New York).
*Died* 10 *Jan.* 1990.

**MIDDLETON, Sir George (Proctor),** KCVO 1962 (CVO 1951; MVO 1941); MB, ChB (Aberdeen); Medical Practitioner, retired 1973; Surgeon Apothecary to HM Household at Balmoral Castle, 1932–73; *b* Schoolhouse, Findhorn, Morayshire, 26 Jan. 1905; *s* of late A. Middleton, FEIS, Kincorth, Elgin; *m* 1931, Margaret Wilson (*d* 1964), *er d* of late A. Silver; one *s* one *d*. *Educ:* Findhorn; Forres Academy; Aberdeen Univ. Entered the Faculty of Medicine, 1921; Graduated, 1926, Bachelor of Medicine and Bachelor of Surgery, Ogston Prize and 1st medallist in Senior Systematic Surgery, 1st Medallist in Operative Surgery, House Surgeon Ward X, and House Physician Ward 4, Aberdeen Royal Infirmary, 1926; went to practice in Sheffield, 1927; Asst to Sir Alexander Hendry, 1928; into partnership, 1929; partnership dissolved, 1931; taken into partnership, Dr James G. Moir, 1948. *Recreations:* golf, Association football, bowling. *Address:* Highland Home, Ballater, Aberdeenshire AB3 5RP. *TA:* Highland Home, Ballater. *T:* Ballater 55478. *Died* 16 *Oct.* 1987.

**MIDDLETON, Lucy Annie;** Vice-President, Trade Union, Labour and Co-operative Democratic History Society, since 1969; Director and Foundation Chairman of War on Want, 1958–68; *b* 9 May 1894; 2nd *d* of late Sydney J. Cox, Keynsham, Somerset; *m* 1936, James S. Middleton (*d* 1962), sometime Sec. of Labour Party. *Educ:* Elementary Sch.; Colston's Girls' High Sch., Bristol; Bristol Univ. Held teaching appts under Gloucester and Bristol Authorities until 1924 when she became Organising Sec. in the Peace Movement; political adviser to Hindu Minorities during sittings of Round Table Conferences; joined staff of Labour Party, 1934. Governor of Chelsea Polytechnic, 1936–57. Certified Advertising Consultant. Attended Inter-Parliamentary Union Confs Brussels, Nice, Rome, Stockholm, presenting Reports on Maternity and Child Welfare, Family Allowances, and Safeguarding of Women in Employment throughout the World; formerly Mem. of House of Commons Estimates Cttee. MP (Labour) Sutton Div. of Plymouth, 1945–50 (re-elected for enlarged Div., 1950–51). Life Pres., Wimbledon Lab. Party, 1978. *Publication:* Women in the Labour Movement, 1977. *Recreations:* cooking, gardening, golf. *Address:* 7 Princes Road,

Wimbledon, SW19 8RQ. *T:* 01–542 2791.
*Died 20 Nov. 1983.*

**MIDLETON**, 11th Viscount *cr* 1717, of Midleton, Ireland; **Trevor Lowther Brodrick;** Baron Brodrick, Midleton, Ireland, 1715; Baron Brodrick, Peper Harow, 1796; *b* 7 March 1903; *s* of William John Henry Brodrick, OBE (*d* 1964) (*g s* of 7th Viscount), and Blanche Sophia Emily (*d* 1944), *e d* of F. A. Hawker; *S* to viscountcy of cousin, 2nd Earl of Midleton, MC, 1979; *m* 1940, Sheila Campbell MacLeod, *d* of Charles Campbell MacLeod. *Educ:* privately. *Recreations:* photography and gardening. *Heir: nephew* Alan Henry Brodrick [*b* 4 Aug. 1949; *m* 1978, Julia Helen, *d* of Michael Pitt; two *s* one *d*]. *Address:* Frogmore Cottage, 105 North Road, Bourne, Lincolnshire PE10 9BU. *Died 30 Oct. 1988.*

**MIERS, Rear-Adm. Sir Anthony (Cecil Capel)**, VC 1942; KBE 1959; CB 1958; DSO 1941; Royal Navy retired; joined National Car Parks as Director for Development Coordination, 1971; *b* 11 Nov. 1906; 2nd *s* of late Capt. D. N. C. C. Miers, Queen's Own Cameron Highlanders (Killed in France, Sept. 1914); *m* 1945, Patricia Mary, *d* of late D. M. Millar, of the Chartered Bank of India, Australia and China; one *s* one *d*. *Educ:* Stubbington House; Edinburgh Academy; Wellington Coll. Special entry cadet RN 1924. Joined submarines, 1929; commanded HM Submarine L54, 1936–37 (Coronation medal at HM's review in 1937); HMS Iron Duke, 1937–38; naval staff course, 1938 (psc); on staff of Admiral of the Fleet Sir Charles Forbes, C-in-C Home Fleet, in HM Ships Nelson, Rodney, and Warspite (despatches), 1939–40; commanded HM Submarine Torbay, 1940–42 (DSO and Bar, VC); Staff of Fleet Adm. C. W. Nimitz, C-in-C US Pacific Fleet, 1943–44 (US Legion of Merit, degree of Officer, 1945); Comdr S/M 8th Submarine Flotilla in HMS Maidstone, 1944–45; Commanded HMS Vernon II (Ramillies and Malaya), 1946; jssc 1947; Comd HMS Blackcap (RN Air Station, Stretton), 1948–50; Comd HMS Forth and Capt. S/M, 1st Submarine Flotilla, 1950–52. Capt. of the RN Coll., Greenwich, 1952–54 (Coronation medal, 1953); Commanded HMS Theseus, 1954–55; Flag Officer, Middle East, 1956–59. With Mills and Allen Ltd, 1962–74, and with London and Provincial Poster Group, 1962–83. Obtained pilot's certificate ("A" License), 1948. Governor, Star and Garter Home, Richmond, 1970–76; Chm., RN Scholarship Fund, 1968–73. Nat. Pres., Submarine Old Comrades Assoc., 1967–81. Chm., Hudsons Offshore Ltd, 1972–73. Burgess and Freeman of Burgh of Inverness, 1955; Mem., Royal Highland Soc., 1966. Councillor, Lawn Tennis Assoc., 1954–78, Hon. Life Councillor 1979; Pres. RN Squash Rackets Assoc., 1960–70; Pres. RN Lawn Tennis Assoc., 1962–78; FInstD 1960. Freeman of the City of London, 1966; Mem., Court of Assistants, 1969, Under Warden, 1982, Upper Warden, 1983, Master, 1984, Worshipful Company of Tin Plate Workers; Hon. Kt, Hon. Soc. of Knights of Round Table, 1967. Silver Jubilee Medal, 1977. *Address:* 8 Highdown Road, Roehampton, SW15 5BU. *T:* 01–788 6863. *Clubs:* Army and Navy, Hurlingham, MCC, British Sportsman's, National Sporting (Patron); London Scottish Football; Royal Navy 1765 and 1785; Hampshire Hog Cricket; Anchorites (President 1968).
*Died 26 June 1985.*

**MIGDALE, Hon. Lord; James Frederick Gordon Thomson**, MA; DL; a Lord Commissioner of Justiciary, Scotland, and a Senator of HM College of Justice in Scotland, 1953–73; Lord Lieutenant of Sutherland, 1962–72; *b* 22 June 1897; *s* of late William Thomson, advocate, and Emmeline E. Gordon; *m* 1938, Louise Carnegie (*d* 1947), *d* of Roswell Miller and Mrs Carnegie Miller, of NY and Skibo Castle, Dornoch; one *s* three *d* (and one *d* decd). *Educ:* Edinburgh Academy and Clayesmore; Edinburgh and Glasgow Univs. Served European War, 1914–19, Royal Scots; War of 1939–45, Lt-Col Home Guard. Mem. Faculty of Advocates, 1924; Advocate-Depute, 1939–40; Standing Counsel to Board of Inland Revenue in Scotland, 1944–45; QC (Scotland) 1945; Sheriff of Ayr and Bute, 1949–52; Home Advocate Depute, 1952–53. Life Trustee, Carnegie UK Trust. DL Sutherlandshire, 1959. *Address:* Ospisdale, Dornoch, Sutherland IV25 3RH. *Clubs:* New (Edinburgh); Hon. Company of Edinburgh Golfers. *Died 30 Dec. 1983.*

**MIKES, George**, LLD (Budapest); Author; *b* Siklós, Hungary, 15 Feb. 1912; *s* of Dr Alfred Mikes and Margit Gál; *m* 1st, 1941, Isobel Gerson (marr. diss.; she *d* 1986); one *s*; 2nd, 1948, Lea Hanak (*d* 1986); one *d*. *Educ:* Cistercian Gymnasium, Pécs; Budapest Univ. Theatrical critic on Budapest newspapers, 1931–38; London correspondent of Budapest papers, 1938–41; working for Hungarian Service of BBC, 1941–51. Pres., PEN in Exile, 1972–80. Governor, London Oratory School, 1978–. *Publications:* How to be an Alien, 1946; How to Scrape Skies, 1948; Wisdom for Others, 1950; Milk and Honey, 1950; Down with Everybody!, 1951; Shakespeare and Myself, 1952; Über Alles, 1953; Eight Humorists, 1954; Little Cabbages, 1955; Italy for Beginners, 1956; The Hungarian Revolution, 1957; East is East, 1958; A Study in Infamy, 1959; How to be Inimitable, 1960; Tango, 1961; Switzerland for Beginners, 1962, new edn 1975; Mortal Passion, 1963; Prison (ed), 1963; How to Unite Nations, 1963; Eureka!, 1965; (with the Duke of Bedford)

Book of Snobs, 1965; How to be Affluent, 1966; Not by Sun Alone, 1967; Boomerang, 1968; The Prophet Motive, 1969; Humour-In Memoriam, 1970; The Land of the Rising Yen, 1970; (with Duke of Bedford) How to run a Stately Home, 1971; Any Souvenirs?, 1971; The Spy Who Died of Boredom, 1973; Charlie, 1976; How to be Decadent, 1977; Tsi-Tsa, 1978; English Humour for Beginners, 1980; How to be Seventy, 1982; The Virgin and the Bull (play), 1982; How to be Poor, 1983; Arthur Koestler, the Story of a Friendship, 1983; How to be a Guru, 1984; How to be a Brit, 1984; How to be God, 1986; The Riches of the Poor, 1987; How to be a Yank, 1987. *Recreations:* tennis, cooking, and not listening to funny stories. *Address:* 1B Dorncliffe Road, SW6. *T:* 01–736 2624. *Clubs:* Garrick, Hurlingham, PEN. *Died 30 Aug. 1987.*

**MILBANK, Major Sir Mark (Vane)**, 4th Bt, *cr* 1882; KCVO 1962; MC 1944; Extra Equerry to the Queen since 1954; Master of HM's Household, 1954–67; *b* 11 Jan. 1907; *e s* of Sir Frederick Milbank, 3rd Bt; *S* father, 1964; *m* 1938, Hon. Verena Aileen (she *m* 1st, 1934, Charles Lambert Crawley who died 1935), *yr d* of 11th Baron Farnham, DSO; two *s*. *Educ:* Eton; RMC, Sandhurst. Coldstream Guards, 1927–36 and 1939–45; ADC to Governor of Bombay, 1933–38; Comptroller to Governor General of Canada, 1946–52; Dir, Norwich Union, London Advisory Board, 1964–74. *Heir: s* Anthony Frederick Milbank [*b* 16 Aug. 1939; *m* 1970, Belinda Beatrice, *yr d* of Brigadier Adrian Gore, Sellindge, Kent; two *s* one *d*]. *Address:* Gate House, Barningham, Richmond, N Yorks. *T:* Teesdale 21269. *Died 4 April 1984.*

**MILBURN, Sir John (Nigel)**, 4th Bt *cr* 1905; *b* 22 April 1918; *s* of Sir Leonard John Milburn, 3rd Bt, and Joan, 2nd *d* of Henry Anson-Horton, Catton Hall, Derbs; *S* father, 1957; *m* 1940, Dorothy Joan, *d* of Leslie Butcher, Dunholme, Lincoln; one *s* decd. *Educ:* Eton; Trinity Coll., Cambridge. Served War of 1939–45 with Northumberland Hussars. *Recreations:* Joint-Master West Percy Foxhounds, 1955–59, 1963–. *Heir: nephew* Anthony Rupert Milburn [*b* 17 April 1947; *m* 1977, Olivia Shirley Catlow; one *s* one *d*. *Educ:* Eton; Royal Agric. Coll., Cirencester]. *Address:* Brainshaugh, Acklington, Northumberland. *T:* Shilbottle 631. *Club:* Northern Counties (Newcastle upon Tyne). *Died 14 July 1985.*

**MILES, Sir (Arnold) Ashley**, Kt 1966; CBE 1953; FRS 1961; MA, MD, FRCP, FRCPath; Professor of Experimental Pathology, University of London, 1952–71, later Emeritus Professor; Director of the Lister Institute of Preventive Medicine, London, 1952–71; Deputy Director, Department of Medical Microbiology, London Hospital Medical College, since 1976 (Fellow, London Hospital Medical College, 1986); Hon. Consultant in Microbiology, London Hospital, 1976; *b* 20 March 1904; *s* of Harry Miles and Kate (*née* Hindley), York; *m* 1930, Ellen Marguerite (*d* 1988), *d* of Harald Dahl, Cardiff; no *c*. *Educ:* Bootham Sch., York; King's Coll., Cambridge, Hon. Fellow, 1971; St Bartholomew's Hosp., London. Demonstrator in Bacteriology, London Sch. of Hygiene and Tropical Medicine, 1929; Demonstrator in Pathol., University of Cambridge, 1931; Reader in Bacteriology, British Postgraduate Medical Sch., London, 1935; Prof. Bacteriology, University of London, 1937–45; Acting Dir Graham Medical Research Laboratories, University Coll. Hosp. Medical Sch., 1943–45; London Sector Pathologist, Emergency Medical Services, 1939–44; Dir, Medical Research Council Wound Infection Unit, Birmingham Accident Hosp., 1942–46; Dep. Dir, 1947–52 and Dir of Dept of Biological Standards, 1946–52, National Institute for Medical Research, London. MRC grant holder, Clinical Res. Centre, 1971–76. Mem., MRC, 1957–61 and 1967–68; Biological Sec. and Vice-Pres., Royal Society, 1963–68. President: Soc. Gen. Microbiology, 1957–59 (Hon. Mem., 1972); Internat. Assoc. Microbiological Socs, 1974–78. Trustee, Beit Memorial Fellowships, 1970–81. For. Corresp., Acad. de Médecine de Belgique, 1972. Hon. Member: Amer. Soc. for Microbiol., 1974; Amer. Assoc. of Pathologists, 1977; Deutsche Gesellschaft für Hygiene und Mikrobiologie, 1978; British Acad. of Forensic Scis, 1978; Path. Soc. of GB, 1980; Fellow, World Acad. Art and Science, 1975; Hon. Fellow: Infectious Diseases Soc. of Amer., 1979; RSocMed, 1981; Hon. FInstBiol, 1975; Consejero de Honor, Consejo Superior de Investigaciones Científicas, Madrid, 1966. Hon. DSc, Newcastle, 1969. *Publications:* (with G. S. Wilson) Topley and Wilson's Principles of Bacteriology, Virology and Immunity, 1945, 7th edn (also with M. T. Parker), 1985; various scientific papers. *Recreations:* various. *Address:* Department of Medical Microbiology, London Hospital Medical College, Turner Street, E1 2AD. *T:* 01–377 7644; 7 Holly Place, Hampstead, NW3 6QU. *T:* 01–435 5811. *Died 11 Feb. 1988.*

**MILES, Basil Raymond**, CBE 1968; Puisne Judge, Kenya, 1957–67, retired; *b* 10 Oct. 1906; *s* of John Thomas Miles and Winifred Miles, Wrexham, Denbighshire; *m* 1944, Margaret Baldwin Neilson; one *s* one *d*. *Educ:* Harrow; Magdalen Coll., Oxford. Barrister, Inner Temple, 1931; appointed Resident Magistrate, Tanganyika, 1946; Judge of the Supreme Court, The Gambia, 1953–57. A part-time Chm. of Industrial Tribunals, 1967–74. *Recreation:* music. *Address:*

Mbeya, Chesham Road, Bovingdon, Herts. *T:* 3187.
*Died* 25 *March* 1984.

**MILES, Adm. Sir Geoffrey John Audley,** KCB 1945 (CB 1942); KCSI 1947; *b* 2 May 1890; 3rd *s* of Audley Charles Miles and Eveline Cradock-Hartopp; *m* 1918, Alison Mary Cadell (*d* 1981); two *s*. *Educ:* Bedford; HMS Britannia. Joined the Royal Navy, served with Submarines and Destroyers during European War, 1914–18; later appointments include: Dep. Dir Staff Coll., Dir Tactical Sch.; Capt. HMS Nelson, 1939–41; Rear-Adm., 1941; Vice-Adm., 1944; Adm., 1948. Head of Mil. Mission in Moscow, 1941–43; Flag Officer Comdg Western Mediterranean, 1944–45; C-in-C, Royal Indian Navy, 1946–47. *Address:* Holyport Lodge, The Green, Holyport, Maidenhead, Berks SL6 2JA. *Club:* Naval and Military.
*Died* 31 *Dec.* 1986.

**MILES, Prof. Herbert William,** MSc (Bristol), DSc (Manchester). Adviser and Lecturer in Entomology, University of Manchester, 1927–42; Advisory Entomologist, University of Bristol (Long Ashton Research Station), 1942–46; Deputy Provincial Director (West Midland Province), National Agricultural Advisory Service, 1946–47; Prof. of Horticulture, Wye Coll., London Univ., 1947–65, now Emeritus. Hon. Consultant in Horticulture to RASE, 1948–75. President: Lincolnshire Naturalists' Union, 1938; Assoc. of Applied Biology, 1956. Officier, Ordre du Mérite Agricole, 1974. *Publications:* (with Mary Miles, MSc) Insect Pests of Glasshouse Crops, revised edn 1947; original papers on Economic Entomology in leading scientific journals; original studies on the biology of British sawflies. *Address:* 2 Wood Broughton, Grange-over-Sands, Cumbria.
*Died* 18 *Feb.* 1987.

**MILES, Maurice Edward;** Conductor; Professor of Conducting, Royal Academy of Music, 1953–84; *b* 1908; *s* of T. S. Miles; *m* 1936, Eileen Spencer Wood (*d* 1977); one *s* two *d*. *Educ:* Wells Cathedral Gram. Sch.; Royal Academy of Music, London. Employed BBC, 1930–36; Conductor of Buxton Municipal Orchestra and of Bath Municipal Orchestra, 1936–39. Served in RAC, 1940–43. Returned to BBC, 1943; Conductor: Yorks Symphony Orchestra, 1947–54; City of Belfast Orchestra and Belfast Philharmonic Society, 1955–66; Ulster Orchestra, 1966–67. FRAM. *Publication:* Are You Beating 2 or 4?, 1977. *Recreations:* walking, reading. *Address:* 32 The Orchard, North Holmwood, Dorking, Surrey.        *Died* 26 *June* 1985.

**MILES, Maxine Frances Mary;** lately Director of F. G. Miles Engineering Ltd, Riverbank Works, Old Shoreham Road, Shoreham, Sussex; *b* 22 Sept. 1901; *d* of late Sir Johnston Forbes-Robertson; *m* 1932, Frederick George Miles, FRAeS, MSAE (decd); one *s* (and one *d* decd). *Address:* Batts, Ashurst, Steyning, W Sussex.
*Died* 6 *April* 1984.

**MILES, Surgeon Rear-Adm. Stanley,** CB 1968; FRCP, FRCS; Vice President, International Trauma Foundation, since 1982 (Chairman, 1978–82); *b* 14 Aug. 1911; *s* of late T. C. Miles, Company Dir, Sheffield; *m* 1939, Frances Mary Rose; one *s* one *d*. *Educ:* King Edward VII Sch.; University of Sheffield. MSc Sheffield, 1934; MB, ChB, 1936; DTM&HEng, 1949; MD, 1955; FRCP 1971, FRCS 1971. Joined RN Medical Service, 1936; served in China, W Africa, Pacific and Mediterranean Fleets. Medical Officer-in-Charge, RN Medical Sch. and Dir of Medical Research, 1961; Consultant in Physiology; Med. Officer-in-Charge, Royal Naval Hosp., Plymouth, 1966–69. Surg. Captain 1960; Surg. Rear-Adm. 1966. Dean, Postgraduate Med. Studies, Univ. of Manchester, 1969–76. Gilbert Blane Medal, RCS, 1957. QHP 1966–69. CStJ 1968. *Publication:* Underwater Medicine, 1962. *Recreations:* tennis, golf. *Address:* 15 Solent Drive, Barton-on-Sea, New Milton, Hants BH25 7AW.
*Died* 9 *July* 1987.

**MILFORD, Rev. Canon Campbell Seymour,** MC 1918; Canon Residentiary of Bristol Cathedral, 1962–67; retired, 1967; *b* 20 July 1896; *s* of Robert Theodore and Elspeth Milford; *m* 1926, Edith Mary (*née* Sandys) (*d* 1974); one *s*. *Educ:* Marlborough; Brasenose, Oxford. Lieut R West Kent Regt, 1915–19. BA 1st Class Lit. Hum., 1921; Lecturer, S Paul's Coll., Calcutta, 1922–25; MA and Diploma in Theology, Oxford, 1926. Deacon 1926, Priest 1927; Curate, Christ Church, Hampstead, 1926–28; Vice-Principal, S Paul's Coll., Calcutta (CMS), 1928–44; Lecturer and Fellow, Calcutta Univ., 1937–44; Canon of Calcutta Cathedral, 1943–44; Sec. for West Asia, CMS, London, 1944–57; Incumbent, Christ Church, Colombo, 1957–62. *Publications:* India Revisited, 1952; Middle East, Bridge or Barrier, 1956. *Recreation:* music. *Address:* 2 Priory Road, Bristol BS8 1TX. *T:* Bristol 38566.        *Died* 5 *Jan.* 1981.

**MILFORD, Rev. Canon Theodore Richard;** Master of the Temple, 1958–68; *b* 10 June 1895; *e s* of Robert Theodore Milford, MA, and Elspeth Barter; *m* 1st, 1932, Nancy Dickens Bourchier Hawksley; two *d*; 2nd, 1937, Margaret Nowell Smith; two *d*. *Educ:* Denstone; Fonthill, East Grinstead; Clifton; Magdalen Coll., Oxford; Westcott House, Cambridge. Served European War, 1914–18, 19th Royal Fusiliers, 1914; Oxford & Bucks LI, 1915–19 (Mesopotamia, 1916–18); Magdalen Coll., Oxford, 1919–21; BA (1st Cl. Lit. Hum),

1921; Union Christian Coll., Alwaye, Travancore, 1921–23; St John's Coll., Agra, 1923–24, 1926–30, 1931–34; Sec. Student Christian Movement, 1924–26 and 1935–38; Westcott House, 1930–31; Deacon, 1931; Priest, 1934 (Lucknow); Curate All Hallows, Lombard Street, 1935–37; Vicar of St Mary the Virgin, Oxford (University Church), 1938–47; Canon and Chancellor of Lincoln, 1947–58; Canon of Norton Episcopi, Lincoln Cathedral, 1947–68, Canon Emeritus, 1968. Chm., Oxfam, 1942–47 and 1960–65, Emeritus 1965. Greek Red Cross (Bronze), 1947. *Publications:* Foolishness to the Greeks, 1953; The Valley of Decision, 1961; Belated Harvest (verse), 1978. *Recreations:* music, chess. *Address:* 1 Kingsman Lane, Shaftesbury, Dorset SP7 8HD. *T:* Shaftesbury 2843.        *Died* 19 *Jan.* 1987.

**MILL, Rear-Adm. Ernest,** CB 1960; OBE 1944; Director General, Aircraft, Admiralty, 1959–62; *b* 12 April 1904; *s* of Charles and Rosina Jane Mill; *m* 1939, Isobel Mary Neilson (*d* 1971). *Educ:* Merchant Venturers Sch. Fleet Engr Officer on staff of C-in-C, Mediterranean, 1957; Rear-Adm., 1958. *Recreations:* sailing, fishing. *Club:* Army and Navy.        *Died* 29 *April* 1988.

**MILL, Laura Margaret Dorothea,** OBE 1962; MB, ChB, DipPsych; Medical Commissioner, Mental Welfare Commission for Scotland, 1962–63, retired; *b* 28 Nov. 1897; *d* of Rev. William Alexander Mill, MA and Isabel Clunas. *Educ:* The Park Sch., Glasgow; Glasgow Univ. House Surg., Samaritan Hosp. for Women, and Royal Maternity Hospital, Glasgow, House Physician, Royal Hospital for Sick Children, and Senior Medical Officer Out-patient Dispensary, Glasgow; Resident Medical Officer, York General Dispensary; Asst Physician, Riccartsbar Mental Hosp., Paisley, and Murray Royal Mental Hosp., Perth; Clinical Medical Officer, Glasgow Public Health Dept. Dep. Medical Commissioner, Gen. Board of Control for Scotland, 1936; Medical Commissioner, Gen. Board of Control for Scotland (later Mental Welfare Commission), 1947, and Senior Medical Officer, Dept of Health for Scotland.
*Died* 10 *March* 1990.

**MILLAND, Raymond Alton, (Ray Milland);** film actor and director, US; *b* Wales, 3 Jan. 1907; *s* of Alfred Milland and Elizabeth Truscott; *m* 1932, Muriel Weber; one *s* one *d*. *Educ:* private schs in Wales and England; Monks Preparatory Sch.; University of Wales. Served with Household Cavalry, 1926–29; became actor in 1930; went to USA, 1930, and became naturalized citizen, 1938. *Films include:* The Flying Scotsman; Payment Deferred; Bolero; Four Hours to Kill; The Glass Key; Ebb Tide; Beau Geste; The Lost Weekend; French Without Tears; So Evil My Love; Circle of Danger; A Man Alone; Lisbon; The Safecracker (also directed); Kitty; Golden Earrings; It Happens Every Spring; Alias Nick Beal; Dial M for Murder; 3 Brave Men; Man Alone; Love Story; The House in Nightmare Park; Gold; The Swiss Conspiracy; The Last Tycoon; Oliver's Story; Starflight One. Received Motion Picture Acad. Award for best actor, for part in The Lost Weekend. Has also appeared on stage and television. *Publication:* Wide-Eyed in Babylon (autobiog.), 1975.        *Died* 10 *March* 1986.

**MILLAR, Dame (Evelyn Louisa) Elizabeth H.;** *see* Hoyer-Millar.

**MILLAR of Orton, Maj.-Gen. Robert Kirkpatrick,** CB 1954; DSO 1944; DL; late Royal Engineers; *b* 29 June 1901; *s* of late Professor John Hepburn Millar and late Margaret Wilhelmina, *e d* of late J. W. Wharton Duff, of Orton, Morayshire; *m* 1934, Frances Rhodes, *yr d* of late Col W. G. Beyts, CBE; two *s* (and one *s* decd). *Educ:* Edinburgh Academy; RMA Woolwich. 2nd Lt Royal Engineers, 1921; served in India and China, 1925–33; served War of 1939–45 (despatches 5 times, 1939–46, DSO); Field Co. 49 (WR) Div. (Norway), 1940; CRE 15 (Scottish) Div. 1942–45 (France and Germany); CE London District, 1949–51; CE Scottish Command, 1951–53; Engineer-in-Chief, Pakistan Army, 1953–57. DL Moray, 1959. *Recreations:* golf, shooting, fishing. *Address:* Darnethills, Orton, By Fochabers, Moray. *T:* Orton 284.
*Died* 17 *April* 1981.

**MILLAR-CRAIG, Hamish,** CMG 1960; OBE 1958; Public Finance Consultant; *b* 25 Sept. 1918; *yr s* of late Captain David Millar-Craig and late Winifred Margaret Cargill; *m* 1953, Rose Ernestine Boohene. *Educ:* Shrewsbury; Keble Coll., Oxford. Served War of 1939–45, 2nd Lt Royal Scots, 1940; Colonial Civil Service, Gold Coast, 1940–57; Ghana Civil Service, 1957–62; Reader in Public Administration (UN Technical Assistance), Ghana Institute of Public Administration, 1962–65; Dir, E African Staff Coll., 1965–69; Adviser, Min. of Finance, Somalia, 1969–71; Bursar, UNITAR, 1972–77; Adviser: St Kitts-Nevis, 1978; Micronesia, 1980; Ghana, 1980–82; Antigua and Barbuda, 1982–84; Belize, 1986. Economic Development Institute, Washington, 1957–58. *Recreation:* philately. *Address:* c/o Lloyds Bank, Taunton, Somerset TA1 1HN.
*Died* 8 *Feb.* 1989.

**MILLBOURN, Sir (Philip) Eric,** Kt 1955; CMG 1950; MIMechE; Adviser on Shipping in Port to Minister of Transport, 1946–63; Chairman Council of Administration, Malta Dockyard, since 1963;

*b* 1 June 1902; *s* of late Philip Millbourn, Brunswick Square, Hove, Sussex; *m* 1931, Ethel Marjorie, *d* of late Joseph E. Sennett; one *s* one *d*. *Educ*: privately; London Univ. Chm., The London Airport Development Cttee. Dep. Chm., Nat. Ports Council, 1964–67. *Address*: Conkwell Grange, Limpley Stoke, near Bath, Avon BA3 6HD. *T*: Limpley Stoke 3102. *Club*: Travellers'.
*Died* 17 *April* 1982.

**MILLER, Rear-Adm. Andrew John;** Assistant General Secretary, Missions to Seamen, since 1981 (London and South East Regional Director, 1977–81); *b* 12 Dec. 1926; *s* of Major A. D. Miller, Baluch Regt, IA; *m* 1954, Elizabeth Rosanne Foster; one *s* two *d*. *Educ*: Craigflower, Fife; RNC Dartmouth. Midshipman 1944; Sub-Lt 1946; Lieut 1948; Lt-Comdr 1956; Comdr 1959; Captain 1965; Rear-Adm. 1972. Commanded ML3513, Asheldham, Grafton, Scorpion, Nubian. Dir Public Relations (Navy), 1970–71; Flag Officer Second Flotilla, 1972–73. *Recreation*: gardening. *Address*: Forge Cottage, Bosham, West Sussex. *T*: Bosham 572144. *Club*: Army and Navy. *Died* 1 *July* 1986.

**MILLER, Desmond Campbell,** TD; QC 1961; *b* 17 Dec. 1914; *y s* of late Robert Miller, DD, sometime Bishop of Cashel and Waterford, and of Mary Miller, *yr d* of Dean Potter of Raphoe; *m* 1948, Ailsa, *y d* of Hon. Allan Victor Maxwell, CMG, and Margaret (*née* Lawless); two *s* one *d*. *Educ*: Manor Sch., Fermoy; Dean Close Sch., Cheltenham; St Columba's Coll., Rathfarnham; Pembroke Coll., Oxford. Called to Bar, Inner Temple, 1939, Gray's Inn (*ad eundem*), 1960; Master of the Bench, Inner Temple, 1968; retired from practice at the Bar, 1976. Served War of 1939–45 (despatches): Middx Yeo.; Northants Yeo.; 2nd, 6th and 11th Armoured Divs; HQ 1 Corps; HQ, ALFSEA; Staff Coll., Camberley, 1942. Lt-Col TA. Chm., Rossminster Group, 1973–78. Mem. General Council of the Bar, 1964–68, 1971–73 (Chm., Taxation and Retirement Benefits Cttees). ACIArb. *Recreations*: golf, flyfishing, reading. *Address*: Aux Cordiers, La Couperderie, St Peter Port, Guernsey, CI. *T*: Guernsey 20322. *Clubs*: Brooks's; MCC, Hurlingham; Royal Mid-Surrey Golf; Royal Guernsey Golf, Royal Channel Islands Yacht.
*Died* 15 *Jan*. 1986.

**MILLER, Lt-Gen. (retired) Sir Euan (Alfred Bews),** KCB 1954 (CB 1949); KBE 1951; DSO 1945; MC 1918; Lieutenant of the Tower of London, 1957–60; *b* 5 July 1897; *s* of Dr A. E. Miller; *m* 1926, Margaret (*d* 1969), *d* of late Captain H. C. R. Brocklebank, CBE; two *d* (and one *s* decd). *Educ*: Wellington Coll.; RMC Sandhurst. 2nd Lieut, KRRC, 1915. Served European War, France and Salonika, 1915–18 (despatches, MC). Staff Coll., 1926–27; Bt Lt-Col, 1936; served War of 1939–45, GSO1, GHQ, BEF, 1939; OC2 KRRC, 1940 (despatches, prisoner of war, DSO). Col, 1945; Brig., 1946; Dep. Mil. Sec., 1946; ADC to the King, 1946–48; Comdr Hanover Dist, 1948; Maj.-Gen., 1948; Chief of Staff, Middle East Land Forces, 1949–51; Lieut-Gen. 1951; Military Sec. to the Sec. of State for War, 1951; retired, 1955. Col Comdt, 1 KRRC, 1954–61. Chm. Kent T&AFA, 1956–61. DL Kent, 1958–81. *Club*: Army and Navy. *Died* 30 *Aug*. 1985.

**MILLER, Brigadier George Patrick Rose-,** DSO 1940; MC; beef farmer; inventor and export salesman; *b* 20 July 1897; 3rd *s* of late John Gardner Miller, Mayfield, Perth; *m* 1929, Millicent Rose Lang-Rose; two *s* two *d*. *Educ*: Trinity Coll., Glenalmond; RMC, Sandhurst. Gazetted to Queen's Own Cameron Highlanders, 1915; served in France and Belgium, 1916–17 (MC, immediate award); served with 1st Bn in India, Burma and Sudan; commanded 1st Bn in France 1940 (DSO); raised and commanded 227 Brigade; commanded 155 Brigade. Invented calf feeder, 1948, and new device for feeding young animals, patented 1978; having bought estate of 4,800 acres, produced new method of breeding out-wintered cattle with self-feed labour saving silage in the hills of Nairnshire (losing none in the very bad winter of 1978–79). *Publications*: articles on agricultural subjects. *Address*: Barevan, Cawdor, Nairnshire. *T*: Croy 218. *Club*: Naval and Military. *Died* 19 *Oct*. 1984.

**MILLER, Gerald Cedar,** MC; MA; Headmaster Forest School, near Snaresbrook, 1936–60; *b* 11 May 1894; *s* of Rev. Ernest George and Emilie Miller; *m* 1st, 1930, Alice Rosemary Taylor (*d* 1957); three *d*; 2nd, 1960, Molly Sherry. *Educ*: University Sch., Victoria, BC; Ardingly Coll., Sussex; Keble Coll., Oxford. Served European War, 1914–19, Commission in Oxon. and Bucks Lt Infty, in France and Salonika; Asst Master Ardingly Coll., 1921–25; Sch. House Master, 1925–28; Second Master and Junior House Master, 1928–35. *Address*: Home Close, Gubblecote, near Tring, Herts. *Club*: East India, Devonshire, Sports and Public Schools.
*Died* 3 *June* 1982.

**MILLER, Sir Holmes;** *see* Miller, Sir J. H.

**MILLER, James,** RSA 1964; RSW 1934; Artist, Painter; *b* 25 Oct. 1893; *s* of William Miller and Margaret Palmer; *m* 1934, Mary MacNeill, MA (*d* 1973); no *c*. *Educ*: Woodside Sch.; Sch. of Art, Glasgow. Teaching, 1917–47. Commissioned by Artists' Adv. Coun. of Min. of Information to make drawings of buildings damaged by

enemy action in Scotland, 1939–41; travelled extensively in Spain looking at buildings and making drawings; made drawings for Pilgrim Trust, 1942. Paintings have been bought by Bradford, Newport, Glasgow, Dundee, Hertford, Paisley, Nat. Gall. of S Australia, Melbourne, Aberdeen, Dumbarton, Perth, Arts Council of GB (Scotland) and Muirhead Bequest, Edinburgh. Has held several one-man shows in Glasgow; retrospective exhibn, Glasgow Art Club, 1986. *Recreations*: listening to gramophone records, reading. *Address*: Tigh-na-bruaich, Dunvegan, Isle of Skye. *Club*: Art (Glasgow). *Died* 4 *March* 1987.

**MILLER, Maj.-Gen. Joseph Esmond,** MC 1943; retired; *b* 22 Sept. 1914; *s* of Col J. F. X. Miller, OBE; *m* 1946, Kathleen Veronica Lochée-Bayne; one *s*. *Educ*: St George's Coll., Weybridge; London Univ. (St Bartholomew's Hosp.). MRCS, LRCP; MRCGP; MFCM; MBIM. Qualified, July 1940. Fellow RoySocMed; Mem., BMA. Served War of 1939–45: commissioned in RAMC, Dec. 1940 (ante-dated Sept. 1940); RAMC Depot, 1940–42; Airborne Forces, 1942–45: N Africa, Sicily, Italy, Holland, Germany. RAMC Depot, 1945–47; Staff Coll., 1948; DADMS, HQ MELF, Egypt, 1949–50; CO, 35 Field Amb., Tripoli and Egypt, 1950–54; SMO, RMA Sandhurst, 1954–57; CO, 4 Field Amb., Germany, 1957–59; CO, 10 Bde Gp Med. Co., Aden, 1959–61; ADMS, Middle East Command, Aden, 1961; Chief Instr, RAMC Depot, 1961–65; CO, BMH Hong Kong, 1965–68; ADMS, 4 Div., Germany, 1968–69; DDMS: HQ BAOR, 1969–71; HQ Scotland (Army), 1971–72; HQ UKLF, 1972–73; DMS, HQ UKLF, 1973–76. QHS 1973–76. CStJ 1975. *Recreations*: golf, gardening. *Address*: The Beechings, Folly Close, Salisbury, Wilts SP2 8BU. *T*: Salisbury 21423.
*Died* 3 *Feb*. 1990.

**MILLER, Sir (Joseph) Holmes,** Kt 1979; OBE 1958; Surveyor, New Zealand; Partner, Spencer, Holmes Miller and Jackson, Wellington, NZ; *b* Waimate, NZ, 12 Feb. 1919; *s* of Samuel Miller; *m* 1947, Marjorie, *d* of Harold Tomlinson; one *s* one *d*. *Educ*: Willowbridge Sch.; Waimate High Sch.; Victoria Univ., Wellington, NZ (BA). DSc 1979. Served War, 2 NZEF, 1940–44; NZ Artillery (wounded, Tunisia, 1943). Surveyor, Lands and Survey Dept, on rehabilitation farms, geodetic survey; consulting surveyor, Masterton, 1952–55; Wellington, 1959–. Fulton Medallion Exploratory Surveys, Fiordland, 1949; Expedition, Antipodes and Bounty Is, 1950; Dep. Leader, NZ Trans-Antarctic Expedn, 1955–58; Leader, NZ Expedn, Oates Land, Antarctica, 1963–64. Member: NZ Antarctic Soc. (Pres. 1960–63); NZ Inst. Surveyors, 1960–68 (Pres. 1969–71); NZ Survey Bd, 1962–71; NZ Geographic Bd, 1966–; Nature Conservation Council, 1972–. NZ Delegate to SCAR, Paris, 1964, Wyoming, 1974. *Publications*: numerous, on Antarctic and surveying literature. *Address*: 95 Amritsar Street, Khandallah, Wellington, New Zealand. *Died Feb*. 1986.

**MILLER, Olga, (Mrs Hugh Miller);** *see* Katzin, O.

**MILLER, Sir Richard Hope,** Kt 1955; Chairman, North West Region, Arthritis and Rheumatism Council, since 1974; *b* 26 July 1904; 2nd *s* of late Hubert James Miller, The Old Court House, Knutsford, Cheshire, and of Elsa Mary Colimann; unmarried. *Educ*: Wellington Coll.; Trinity Hall, Cambridge. BA 1925; MA 1930. Served War of 1939–46: commissioned in 7th Bn (TA) The Manchester Regt; Adjutant 1941; Major 1945; served in Staff appointments (Britain, Ceylon, and Singapore), 1942–46. Hon. Sec., Greater Manchester and Area Br., Inst. of Dirs, 1966–81. President: Tatton Div. Cons. Assoc., 1983–88 (Chm., Knutsford Div., 1975–83); David Lewis Epileptic Centre, 1977–87; Cheshire County Lawn Tennis Assoc., 1981–82. *Recreations*: skiing, tennis. *Address*: 9 Carrwood, Knutsford, Cheshire WA16 8NG. *T*: Knutsford 3422; National Westminster Bank, Knutsford, Cheshire.
*Died* 5 *May* 1989.

**MILLER, Prof. Ronald,** MA, PhD, FRSE, FRSGS; Professor of Geography, Glasgow University, 1953–76; Dean of the Faculty of Science, 1964–67; *b* 21 Aug. 1910; *o c* of late John Robert Miller and Georgina Park; *m* 1940, Constance Mary Phillips, SRN, SCM; one *s* one *d*. *Educ*: North Queensferry; Stromness Acad.; Edinburgh Univ. Silver Medal, Royal Scottish Geographical Soc.; MA 1931; Carnegie Research Fellowship at Marine Laboratory of Scottish Home Dept, Aberdeen, 1931–33; PhD 1933; Asst Lecturer Manchester Univ., 1933–36; Education Officer, Nigeria, 1936–46; Royal West African Frontier Force, 1939–44; Lecturer, Edinburgh Univ., 1947–53. Guest Lecturer: University of Montpellier, 1957; University of Oslo and Handelshlyskole Bergen, 1966; Simon Fraser Univ., 1967; Ife, 1969. Pres., RSGS, 1974–77. *Publications*: (with MacNair) Livingstone's Travels; The Travels of Mungo Park; (with Tivy) ed. The Glasgow Region, 1958; (with Watson) Ogilvie Essays, 1959; Africa, 1967; Orkney, 1976; papers in geographical journals. *Address*: Ruah, 20 South End, Stromness, Orkney KW16 3DJ. *T*: Stromness (0856) 850594. *Died* 10 *Aug*. 1990.

**MILLER, Rudolph Valdemar Thor C.;** *see* Castle-Miller.

**MILLING, Geoffrey;** Chairman, Bowring Steamship Company, 1965–68; Deputy Chairman, Lloyd's Register of Shipping, 1963–72; *b* 1 Sept. 1901; *s* of Henry Milling, Warrington, Lancs; *m* 1928, Dorothy Gordon Baird (*d* 1979), St John's, Newfoundland; one *s* one *d. Educ.:* Radley; Merton Coll., Oxford (MA). In USA, 1923, as Sec. to Sir Wilfred Grenfell; joined Lever Brothers, England, 1924; Hudson's Bay Co., 1926 (2 years in Baffin Land, as Manager of trading post, etc.); Bowring Brothers Ltd, St John's, 1935–48, returning to parent firm, London, 1948. Chm., Royal Alfred Merchant Seamen's Soc., 1951–59; Chm., London General Shipowners' Soc., 1959–60; Mem. Port of London Authority, 1959–67. *Recreation:* golf. *Address:* Cranford, Love Lane, Bembridge, Isle of Wight. *Clubs:* Leander; Swinley Forest Golf.
*Died 21 Jan. 1983.*

**MILLINGTON, Air Commodore Edward Geoffrey Lyall,** CB 1966; CBE 1946; DFC 1943; Manager, Regional Defence Sales, SE Asia, Orient Lloyd Pte Ltd, since 1985; *b* 7 Jan. 1914; *s* of late Edward Turner Millington, Ceylon CS; *m* 1st, 1939, Mary Bonynge (marr. diss. 1956), *d* of W. Heaton Smith, FRCS; 2nd, 1956, Anne Elizabeth, *d* of Robert Brennan. *Educ.:* Nautical Coll., Pangbourne. Served Cameron Highlanders, Palestine, 1936 (despatches); War of 1939–45, RAF, in N Africa, Sicily, Italy (actg Gp Capt.: despatches); Air Cdre, 1960; Comdr, RAF Persian Gulf, 1964–66; Air Commander, Zambia Air Force, 1968–70; Air Defence Adviser, Singapore Air Defence Command, 1970–72. psc; idc; Order Mil. Valour (Poland). *Address:* c/o Royal Bank of Scotland, Holt's Branch, 22 Whitehall, SW1. *Club:* Royal Air Force.
*Died 17 Jan. 1988.*

**MILLINGTON-DRAKE, James Mackay Henry;** Managing Director, Inchcape & Co. Ltd, since 1976 (Director since 1971); Chairman, Gray Mackenzie & Co. Ltd; Director, Commonwealth Development Corporation since 1972; *b* 10 Jan. 1928; *s* of late Sir (John Henry) Eugen Vanstegen Millington-Drake, KCMG and Lady Effie Millington-Drake; *m* 1953, Manon Marie Redvers-Bate; two *s* two *d. Educ.:* Upper Canada Coll., Toronto; RNC Dartmouth. Joined Inchcape Group, London, 1956: Sydney, 1958–65; UK, 1965; subseq. Man. Dir, Inchcape & Co. Ltd. Governor, Reed's Sch., Cobham. Chevalier, Royal Order of Swedish Sword, 1949. *Recreations:* tennis, swimming, ski-ing, water ski-ing. *Address:* Flat 2, 6 Reeves Mews, W1Y 5DG. *Clubs:* City of London, Oriental, All England Lawn Tennis and Croquet; Union (Sydney).
*Died 31 Jan. 1983.*

**MILLIS, Charles Howard Goulden,** DSO 1918; OBE 1946; MC; *b* 1894; *e s* of C. T. Millis; *m* 1919, Violet, *o c* of late Herbert J. Gifford; one *s* one *d. Educ.:* King's Coll. Sch.; Oxford, MA. Served European War, 1914–18, Brevet Major (despatches, DSO, MC and bar, Croix de Guerre with Palm, France); served War of 1939–45 (OBE). Managing Director, Baring Brothers & Co. Ltd, 1933–55; Vice-Chm., BBC, 1937–45; Mem., Nat. Res. Develt Corp., 1955–65; Rhodes Trustee, 1948–61. *Address:* 22 Belvedere Grove, SW19 7RL.
*Died 8 Feb. 1984.*

**MILLIS, Sir Leonard (William Francis),** Kt 1977; CBE 1970 (OBE 1948); JP; Secretary from 1939, subsequently Director and President, 1973, British Waterworks Association; *b* 1 Aug. 1908; *o s* of William John Millis and Jessie Millis, Hackney; *m* 1932, Ethel May, *o c* of John T. W. Willmott, Enfield; two *d* (and one *d* decd). *Educ.:* Grocers' Company Sch., Hackney; London Sch. of Economics (BSc Econ). Called to Bar, Inner Temple, 1936; served with Metropolitan Water Board; Asst Sec., British Waterworks Assoc. Pres., Internat. Water Supply Assoc., 1974 (Sec.-Gen., 1947–72); Chm., North Surrey Water Co., 1956–; Thames Conservator, 1959–74; Chm., Sutton District Water Co., 1971–. Member: Council, Water Companies Assoc. (Vice-Pres.); Nat. Water Council, 1973–80; Water Services Staff Commn, 1973–79; Commn on High Water Charges in Wales, 1974–76. Sec., Public Works and Municipal Services Congress Council, 1965–; Vice-Pres., Freshwater Biological Assoc.; Vice-Chm. of Council, Water Research Assoc.; Master, Plumbers' Co., 1978; Mem., Water Supply Industry Trng Board, 1966–74. Hon. MIWE 1966; Hon. FIPHE 1980; FRSA. Hon. Member: Amer. Water Works Assoc., 1969; Deutsche Verein von Gas- und Wasserfachmannern, 1974. JP Mddx (Barnet Div.). *Publications:* contribs to scientific and technical papers, also other papers about water supply. *Recreations:* reading, gardening, sport. *Address:* 51 Kingwell Road, Hadley Wood, Herts. *T:* 01–449 6164. *Club:* Lansdowne.
*Died 30 July 1986.*

**MILLOTT, Prof. Norman;** Emeritus Professor, University of London, since 1976; Director, 1960–76, Fellow since 1987, University Marine Biological Station, Millport; *b* 24 Oct. 1912; *s* of Reuben Tomlinson Millott and Mary Millott (*née* Thistlethwaite); *m* 1939, Margaret Newns; three *d. Educ.:* The Brunts Sch., Mansfield, Notts; Univs of Sheffield (BSc 1935, MSc 1936, DSc 1961), Manchester, Cambridge (PhD 1944). Demonstrator in Zoology, Manchester Univ., 1935–36; Rouse Ball Student, Trinity Coll., Cambridge, 1936–38; Lectr in Zoology, Manchester Univ., 1938–40 and 1945–47. Commissioned RAFVR Technical Branch, 1940–45. Prof. of Zoology, University Coll. of the West Indies, 1948–55; Prof. of Zoology, Bedford Coll., London Univ., 1955–70. Staff Councillor, 1957–60, and Dean of Faculty of Science, Bedford Coll., 1958–60; Chm. of Board of Studies in Zoology, Univ. of London, 1961–65; Chm. Photobiology Group, UK, 1960–62; Chm. Academic Advisory Board, Kingston-upon-Thames Technical Coll., 1960–66; Vice-Pres., International Congress of Photobiology, 1964; Mem. Council, Scottish Marine Biological Assoc., 1971–76. Royal Society Vis. Prof., Univ. of Malta, 1976–77. Governor, Bedford Coll., London Univ., 1976–82. *Publications:* scientific papers chiefly on invertebrate morphology, histology, physiology, and biochemistry. *Address:* Dunmore House, Millport, Isle of Cumbrae, Scotland.
*Died 24 Feb. 1990.*

**MILLS, 2nd Viscount,** *cr* 1962; **Roger Clinton Mills;** Bt 1953; Baron 1957; management consultant, since 1983; Chairman, Harrogate District Health Authority, since 1984; *b* 14 June 1919; *o s* of 1st Viscount Mills, PC, KBE, and Winifred Mary (*d* 1974), *d* of George Conaty, Birmingham; *S* father, 1968; *m* 1945, Joan Dorothy, *d* of James Shirreff; one *s* two *d. Educ.:* Canford Sch.; Jesus Coll., Cambridge. Served War as Major, RA, 1940–46. Administrative Officer, Colonial Service, Kenya, 1946–63. Barrister, Inner Temple, 1956. *Heir: s* Hon. Christopher Philip Roger Mills [*b* 20 May 1956; *m* 1980, Lesley, *er d* of Alan Bailey, Lichfield, Staffs]. *Address:* Whitecroft, Abbey Road, Knaresborough, N Yorks. *T:* Harrogate 866201.
*Died 6 Dec. 1988.*

**MILLS, (Charles) Ernest,** CBE 1979; consultant; Director, United Heating Services Group, since 1978; Member, British Gas Corporation, 1973–78 (Member for Economic Planning, Gas Council, 1968–72); *b* 9 Dec. 1916; *s* of late Charles and Mary Elizabeth Mills; *m* 1943, Irene Hickman; one *s* one *d. Educ.:* Barnsley and District Holgate Grammar Sch.; Manchester Coll. of Technology. Administrative Staff Coll., Henley, 1958. Inspector of Naval Ordnance, 1939–45. Engrg Asst, Rochdale Corp. Gas Dept, 1945–51; East Midlands Gas Board: Asst Divisional Engr, 1951–54; Divisional Engr, 1954–58; Asst Chief Engr and Production Controller, 1958–61; Chief Engr and Production Controller, 1961–64; Dep. Chm., E. Midlands Gas Bd, 1964–66, Chm., W Midlands Gas Bd, 1966–68. Chm. and Chief Exec., Gas Gathering Pipelines (N Sea) Ltd, 1977–79. Mem., Econ. and Soc. Cttee, EEC, 1978–. *Recreations:* travel, sports. *Address:* Long Rafters, Sheethanger Lane, Felden, Hemel Hempstead, Herts HP3 0BG. *T:* Hemel Hempstead 55220.
*Died 20 June 1983.*

**MILLS, Herbert Horatio,** MC 1944; Rector of the Edinburgh Academy, 1962–77; *b* Jan. 1917; *s* of Edward Charles and Sarah Mills; *m* 1987, Rosalind Henn. *Educ.:* Marling Sch.; St Catharine's Coll., Cambridge (PhD). Commonwealth Fellow, University of Pennsylvania, USA, 1950. Asst Master, Sedbergh Sch., 1953–62. *Recreations:* mountaineering; Cambridge Rugby XV, 1947, 1948. *Clubs:* Alpine; Scottish Mountaineering; Scottish Arts (Edinburgh).
*Died 22 Aug. 1987.*

**MILLS, (John) Vivian G.,** DLitt; *b* 22 Sept. 1887; *s* of late Comdr J. F. Mills, ISO, RN (retd); *m* 1st, 1915, Lilian (*d* 1947), *d* of late A. Brisley; no *c*; 2nd, 1968, Marguerite Mélanie (*d* 1983), *d* of late Jean Hoffman. *Educ.:* privately; Merton Coll., Oxford; Classical Mods and Lit Hum; MA 1946; DLitt 1974. Barrister-at-law, Middle Temple, 1919; Cadet, Malayan Civil Service, 1911; qualified in Chinese, 1914; held various administrative, legal and judicial appointments, 1914–28; Solicitor-Gen., Straits Settlements, 1928–32; acting Attorney-Gen., and Mem. of the Executive and Legislative Councils, 1932; Commissioner of Currency, 1932; Puisne Judge, Straits Settlements, 1933; Judge, Johore, 1934; retired, 1940; Attached to office of Federal Attorney-Gen., Sydney, Australia, 1944–45; Additional Lecturer in Chinese Law, School of Oriental and African Studies, London, 1946–47; Pres. of Malayan Branch, Royal Asiatic Society, 1937; Joint Hon. Sec., 1950–53, Hon. Mem. 1983, Hakluyt Soc. *Publications:* Eredia's Malaca, Meridional India and Cathay, 1930; Malaya in the Wu-pei-chi Charts, 1937; (trans. and ed) Ma Huan: Ying-yai sheng-lan, The Overall Survey of the Ocean's Shores, 1970; various official publications. *Recreations:* Oriental research and watching first-class cricket. *Address:* Bellaria 62, 1814 La Tour de Peilz, Switzerland. *Club:* Athenæum.
*Died 9 Feb. 1987.*

**MILLS, Brig. Stephen Douglas,** CBE 1943; MC; *b* 1892; *s* of late Stephen E. Mills, JP, Longmead, Havant, Hants; *m* 1923, Rosamond, *d* of late W. R. Merk, CSI, CIE, ICS; one *s* one *d. Educ.:* Bradfield coll.; RMC, Sandhurst. Late Beds and Herts Regt, European War 1914–19, in France, Belgium, and Palestine (wounded, MC); Palestine, 1936–39 (despatches); War of 1939–45 in Middle East (despatches, CBE); retired pay, 1946. *Address:* Quidhams, Bowerchalke, near Salisbury, Wilts. *T:* Broadchalke 243.
*Died 11 Jan. 1984.*

**MILLS, Vivian;** *see* Mills, J. V. G.

**MILLS-OWENS, Richard Hugh,** CBE 1972; Puisne Judge, Hong Kong, 1967–71, retired (also 1961–64); Chief Justice, Fiji, 1964–67; *b* Jan. 1910; *s* of George Edward Owens and Jessie Mary Mills; *m* 1935, Elizabeth Ann Hiles (*d* 1968); two *s*. *Educ*: Rhyl Grammar Sch. Admitted Solicitor, 1932; Clifford's Inn Prizeman; Barrister-at-law, 1956, Middle Temple. Practised in Wales (including service with Carmarthenshire County Council) until 1949 when joined Colonial Legal Service as a Registrar of Titles; Principal Registrar, Kenya; Crown Counsel and Legal Draftsman, 1952; Magistrate, 1956, District Judge, 1958, Hong Kong. *Address*: Westwood, Hangersley, Ringwood, Hants.                    *Died* 15 *Aug.* 1987.

**MILMAN, Sir Dermot (Lionel Kennedy),** 8th Bt, *cr* 1800; *b* 24 Oct. 1912; *e s* of Brig.-Gen. Sir Lionel Charles Patrick Milman, 7th Bt, CMG, and Marjorie Aletta (*d* 1980), *d* of Col A. H. Clark-Kennedy, late Indian Civil Service; *S* father, 1962; *m* 1941, Muriel, *o d* of J. E. S. Taylor, King's Lynn; one *d*. *Educ*: Uppingham; Corpus Christi Coll., Cambridge. BA 1934, MA 1938. Served War of 1939–45, Royal Army Service Corps, in France, Belgium and Burma (despatches), Major. Hon. Major, RCT (formerly RARO, RASC). British Council service overseas and home, 1946–76, retired 1976. Chairman: Assoc. for British-Arab Univ. Visits; Phyllis Konstam Meml Trust; India Arise Fund. *Heir*: *b* Lt-Col Derek Milman, MC [*b* 23 June 1918; *m* 1942, Christine, *d* of Alfred Whitehouse; two *s*]. *Address*: 7 Old Westhall Close, Warlingham, Surrey. *T*: Upper Warlingham 4843.                    *Died* 13 *Jan.* 1990.

**MILMO, Sir Helenus (Patrick Joseph),** Kt 1964; DL; Judge of High Court of Justice, Queen's Bench Division, 1964–82; *b* 24 Aug. 1908; 3rd *s* of late Daniel Milmo, Furbough, Co. Galway, Eire; *m* 1st, 1933, Joan Frances (*d* 1978), *d* of late Francis Morley, London; two *s* three *d* (and one *d* decd); 2nd, 1980, Anne (Nan), *widow* of F. B. Brand. *Educ*: Downside; Trinity Coll., Cambridge. Barrister, Middle Temple, 1931; Bencher, 1955; QC 1961; Dep. Treasurer, 1972; Treasurer 1973. Civil Asst, General Staff, War Office, 1940–45. Dep. Chm., West Sussex QS, 1960–64. DL Sussex, 1962. *Recreations*: hunting, fishing, wine. *Address*: Arborfield, Castlegate, West Chiltington, West Sussex RH20 2NJ. *T*: West Chiltington 2398. *Club*: Garrick.                    *Died* 30 *Aug.* 1988.

**MILNE, Alexander George,** CIE 1945; FICE, FIMechE; *b* Skene, Aberdeenshire, 27 July 1891; *s* of Alexander Milne; *m* 1927, Mary Agnes Murphy (*d* 1965), MB, BCh, DTM, *d* of P. J. Murphy, Macroom, Cork; one *d*. *Educ*: Robert Gordon's Coll., Aberdeen. Pupil with late R. Gordon Nicol, OBE, MICE, MIMechE, Harbour Engineer, Aberdeen, 1908–13; in Admiralty Works Dept service HM Dockyard, Rosyth and Cromarty, 1913–18; Resident Engineer and Contractors' Agent various Public Works, England, 1918–23; Senior Asst Engineer and Exec. Engineer, Bombay Port Trust, 1923–27; from 1927 was engaged on opening up and development of Cochin Harbour, S India, as Exec. Engineer and Dep. Chief Engineer; Administrative Officer and Chief Engineer, Cochin Harbour, 1941–48. *Recreation*: golf. *Address*: c/o Bank of Scotland, 501 Union Street, Aberdeen AB1 2DB.                    *Died* 16 *Oct.* 1981.

**MILNE, Edward James;** author and lecturer; *b* 18 Oct. 1915; *s* of Edward James Milne and Isabella Stewart; *m* 1939, Emily Constable; three *d*. *Educ*: George Street and Kittybrewster Primary; Sunnybank Intermediate; Robert Gordon's Coll., Aberdeen (Schol.). Lecturer and Organiser, National Council of Labour Colls, 1942–47; Area Organiser, Union of Shop Distributive and Allied Workers, 1952–61. MP (Lab) Blyth, Nov. 1960–Feb. 1974, MP (Ind Lab) Blyth, Feb.–Sept. 1974; PPS to Sir Frank Soskice, Home Sec., 1964–65; Vice-Chm., Parly Labour Party, 1967–68; Secretary: Anglo-Norwegian Parly Gp, 1967–74; Anglo-Swedish Parly Gp, 1968–74; contested (Ind Lab) Blyth, 1979. Mem., (Seaton Delaval Ward), Blyth Valley DC, 1975–79. Grand Order of Star of Africa (Liberia), 1964. *Publication*: No Shining Armour, 1976. *Recreations*: walking, swimming. *Address*: 3 Scotstoun Park, South Queensferry, West Lothian EH30 9PQ.                    *Died* 23 *March* 1983.

**MILNE, James;** General Secretary, Scottish Trades Union Congress, 1975–86 (Assistant General Secretary, 1969–75); Member, General Council of Scottish TUC; Chairman, Scottish Business Education Council; patternmaker; *b* 1921. Secretary to Aberdeen Trades Council, 1948–69. Joined Young Communist League, 1939. *Address*: Scottish Trades Union Congress, 16 Woodlands Terrace, Glasgow G3 6DF. *T*: 041–332 4946.                    *Died* 14 *April* 1986.

**MILNE-WATSON, Sir (David) Ronald,** 2nd Bt, *cr* 1937; *b* 15 July 1904; *s* of Sir David Milne-Watson, 1st Bt, and Olga Cecily (*d* 1952), *d* of Rev. George Herbert; *S* father, 1945. *Educ*: Trinity Coll., Glenalmond; Balliol Coll., Oxford; Capt. IA, 1942–45. *Recreation*: gardening. *Heir*: *b* Sir Michael Milne-Watson, CBE, *b* 16 Feb. 1910. *Address*: The Stables, Oakfield, Mortimer, Berks; *Club*: Travellers'.                    *Died* 15 *June* 1982.

**MILNER, George (Andrew); His Honour Judge Milner;** a Circuit Judge, since 1974; *b* 11 Jan. 1927; *s* of Charles and Mary Elizabeth Milner; *m* 1952, Eileen Janet Blackett; two *s*. *Educ*: Tadcaster

Grammar Sch.; Selwyn Coll., Cambridge (MA). Instructor Lieut RN, 1947–51. Called to Bar, Lincoln's Inn, 1951; practised in Sheffield from 1951. A Recorder of the Crown Court, 1972–74. *Recreations*: gardening, music, history. *Address*: Greatham House, Greatham, Hartlepool, Cleveland TS25 2ER. *T*: Hartlepool 872216. *Club*: Durham County.                    *Died* 14 *Feb.* 1986.

**MILNER, John Giddings;** Consulting Surgeon, Moorfields Eye Hospital, since 1956; Consulting Ophthalmic Surgeon: Charing Cross Hospital since 1966; St Andrew's Hospital, Dollis Hill, since 1966; *b* 7 Dec. 1900; 2nd *s* of late T. J. Milner, Blythwood, Radlett, and late Carrie, *d* of John Carpenter; *m* 1928, Monica Thrale, *d* of late Henry Mardall, Harpenden; one *s* two *d*. *Educ*: Marlborough Coll.; Trinity Coll., Cambridge; St Bartholomew's Hosp. MRCS, LRCP, 1925; MA, MB, BCh Cantab, 1929; FRCS, 1930. Ophthalmic Surgeon, Hertford County Hosp., 1929–46; Surgeon, Moorfields, Westminster and Central Eye Hosp., 1936–56; Wing Comdr RAFVR Medical Branch, 1940–45; Cons. Ophthalmic Surgeon, Hertford County Hosp., 1947; Surgeon Oculist to the late Queen Mary, 1948–53. Coronation Medal, 1953. *Publications*: Modern Treatment in General Practice (contribution), 1949; Brit. Jl Opth., 1934; Brit. Medical Jl, 1941, 1944. *Recreations*: golf, natural history. *Address*: 17 High Firs, Gills Hill, Radlett, Herts WD7 8BH. *T*: Radlett 5750.                    *Died* 1 *May* 1985.

**MILNES COATES, Sir Robert (Edward James Clive),** 3rd Bt *cr* 1911; DSO 1945; landowner and farmer; *b* 27 Sept. 1907; *s* of Captain Sir (Edward) Clive Milnes Coates, 2nd Bt, OBE and of Lady Celia Hermione, *d* of 1st Marquess of Crewe, KG, PC; *S* father, 1971; *m* 1945, Lady Patricia, *d* of 4th Earl of Listowel and *widow* of Lt-Col Charles Thomas Milnes-Gaskell, Coldstream Guards; one *s* one *d*. *Educ*: Harrow; RMC Camberley; Queens' College, Cambridge (MA). JP N Riding of Yorks, 1960; Patron of two livings. 2nd Lieut Coldstream Guards, 1927; ADC to Commander-in-Chief, India, 1930–33; served with Transjordan Frontier Force, 1937–40 (despatches); Italy, 1944–45 (despatches, DSO); retired, 1947. *Heir*: son. *Address*: Moor House Farm, Helperby, York. *T*: Helperby 662. *Club*: Pratt's.                    *Died* 9 *May* 1982.

**MILNES WALKER, Robert;** *see* Walker, R. M.

**MILSON, Rev. Dr Frederick William;** Methodist Minister, retired; Chairman, Birmingham Young Volunteers, since 1982; *b* 25 Dec. 1912; *m* 1939, Joyce Betty Haggerjudd; one *s* one *d*. *Educ*: Swanwick Hall Sch.; Univ. of London (BD Hons 1950); Univ. of Leeds (MA Sociology, 1957); Univ. of Birmingham (PhD 1966; Hon. Fellow 1964). Methodist Minister i/c central churches, 1936–60; Principal Lectr and Head, Community and Youth Studies Dept, Westhill Coll., Selly Oak, Birmingham, 1960–77; Chm., Radio Birmingham, 1968–73; Res. Fellow, Birmingham Univ. Sch. of Educn, 1974–75. Chairman: Cttee on Youth Service, DES, 1966–69; Govt Working Party on Youth Participation, 1979; National Council for Voluntary Youth Services, 1976–82; Member: Youth Service Develt Council, DES, 1964–70; Youth Service Forum, DES, 1976–79. Consultant on youth affairs, Commonwealth Conf., Kuala Lumpur, 1971; visited, in consultancy role for youth and community work, Jamaica, Hong Kong, Israel, Japan, W Berlin, W Germany, Australia and S Africa; visited, to study youth and community work, E Germany, E Berlin, USA, USSR, Malaysia, India, Holland and China. Broadcasts on BBC Radios 1, 2 and 4; contributor of Reflections, BBC World Service; regular Mem., Round Britain Quiz team, 1974–77. *Publications*: Social Group Method and Christian Education, 1963; Group Methods for Christian Workers, 1965; Growing with the Job, 1968; His Leadership and Ours, 1969; (jtly) Youth Service and Interprofessional Studies, 1970; Youth Work in the 1970s (Fairbairn and Milson Report), 1970; Living and Loving; Sex and a Pastor, 1972; Why I Am a Youth Worker, 1972; Youth in a Changing Society, 1972; An Introduction to Group Work Skill, 1973; An Introduction to Community Work, 1974; Community Work and the Christian Faith, 1975; Coming of Age: present opportunities for voluntary youth organizations, 1979; Political Education: practical guidelines for Christian youth workers, 1980; Youth in the Local Church, 1981; You're More Important than You Think, 1982; contrib. New Soc., Teaching Politics, Social Services Qly, TES, Youth in Soc., Birmingham Evening Mail, Birmingham Post, Guardian, Methodist Recorder, British Weekly, and Baptist Times. *Recreation*: overseas travel. *Address*: 1 Kestrel Grove, Bournville, Birmingham B30 1TQ. *T*: 021–472 8131.

*Died* 2 *Sept.* 1983.

**MILTHORPE, Prof. Frederick Leon,** DSc London, MScAgr, DIC; FInstBiol; FRSA; Professor of Biology, Macquarie University, Sydney, New South Wales, 1967–82, then Emeritus; *b* 24 Sept. 1917; 2nd *s* of S. G. and Annie Milthorpe, Hillston, NSW; *m* 1941, Elma Joan, *o d* of R. K. Hobbs, Sydney; two *s*. *Educ*: McCaughey Memorial High Sch.; Univ. of Sydney; Imperial Coll. of Science, London. Walter and Eliza Hall Agricultural Fellow, 1940–42; Plant Pathologist, NSW Dept of Agriculture, 1942–46; Farrer Memorial Scholar, 1946–48; Leverhulme Research Fellow, 1948–49; Senior

Plant Physiologist, Waite Agricultural Research Inst., University of Adelaide, 1949–54; Prof. of Agricultural Botany, University of Nottingham, 1954–67. Australian Medal of Agricultural Sciences, 1975. *Publications:* An Introduction to Crop Physiology (with J. Moorby), 1974, 2nd edn 1979; chapters, some jtly, on water relations and crop growth; various papers on plant physiology in scientific journals. *Address:* Macquarie University, North Ryde, NSW 2113, Australia. *Died 10 June* 1985.

**MILWARD, Sir Anthony (Horace)**, Kt 1966; CBE 1960 (OBE 1945); FCIT; President, London Tourist Board, 1976–80 (Chairman, 1971–76); *b* 2 March 1905; *s* of Henry T. and Elsie T. Milward, Redditch, Worcs; *m* 1931, Frieda Elizabeth Anne von der Becke; one *s* one *d*. *Educ:* Rugby Sch.; Clare Coll., Cambridge (BA). With Glazebrook, Steel & Co. Ltd, Manchester, 1926–40. Served Fleet Air Arm, RNVR, as Pilot, 1940–45, reaching rank of Lieut-Cdr. With BEA in various capacities, 1946–70, Chm., 1964–70; Mem. Bd, BOAC, 1964–70. Mem., Air Registration Board, 1964–70. *Recreations:* fishing, shooting, walking. *Address:* Dene House, Lower Slaughter, Cheltenham, Glos. *Club:* Royal Automobile.
*Died 12 May* 1981.

**MILWARD, John Frederic;** JP; DL; Stipendiary Magistrate for Metropolitan County of West Midlands, 1974–81 (for Birmingham, 1951–74); *b* 26 June 1908; *s* of late Charles Frederic and Emily Constantia Milward, Alvechurch, Worcs; *m* 1946, Doris Evelyn McMurdo, 2nd *d* of Aston E. McMurdo, Charlottesville, Va; two *s*. *Educ:* Bedales Sch.; Clare Coll., Cambridge. Called to Bar, Middle Temple, 1932. Associate of Oxford Circuit, 1942–51. JP Worcs 1940; Chm. of Worcs QS, 1964–71 (Dep. Chm., 1943–64); a Dep. Circuit Judge, 1972; DL Worcs 1972. A Life Governor of Birmingham Univ., 1952. Liveryman of Needlemakers' Company, Mem. Ct of Assistants, 1972, Senior Warden, 1981. *Address:* Stable Door House, Alvechurch, Birmingham B48 7SA. *T:* 021–445 1218. *Club:* Birmingham. *Died 3 Oct.* 1982.

**MIMPRISS, Trevor Walter**, MS; FRCS; Hon. Consultant; retired, 1970, as: Surgeon to St Thomas' Hospital; Surgeon-in-Charge, Urological Division, St Peter's Hospital, Chertsey, Surrey; *b* 12 May 1905; *s* of late S. T. Mimpriss, Bromley, Kent; *m* 1938, Eleanor Joan, *d* of Gordon Innes; two *s* one *d*. *Educ:* Brighton Coll.; St Thomas' Hospital, London Univ. FRCS 1932; MS London 1935. Cheselden Medal for Surgery, St Thomas' Hospital, 1932; Louis Jenner Research Scholarship, 1936–37. Hunterian Professor of Royal College of Surgeons, 1938. *Publications:* various papers in medical journals. *Recreations:* shooting, fishing, golf. *Address:* Muskoka, Kingsley Green, Haslemere, Surrey.
*Died 31 Aug.* 1989.

**MINIO-PALUELLO, Lorenzo**, FBA 1957; Reader in Medieval Philosophy, University of Oxford, 1956–75 (Senior Lecturer, 1948–56); Professorial Fellow of Oriel College, 1962–75, now Emeritus and (1979) Hon. Fellow; *b* 21 Sept. 1907; *s* of Michelangelo Minio and Ersilia (*née* Bisson); *m* 1938, Magda Ungar; one *s* one *d* (and one *d* decd). *Educ:* Ginnasio-Liceo Foscarini, Venice; Univ. of Padua; Sorbonne and Ecole des Hautes Etudes, Paris. Dr of Philosophy (Padua), 1929; Asst Librarian, University of Padua, 1929–32; Fellow of Warburg Inst., Univ. of London, 1947–48; DPhil Oxon, MA Oxon, 1948; Barlow Lectr, Univ. of London, 1955; Prof. straord. of medieval and humanistic philology, Univ. of Padua, for 1956–57; Hon. Dir of Aristoteles Latinus (Union Acad. Internat.), 1959–72; Mem., Inst. for Advanced Study, Princeton, 1969–70, 1974–76; Corresp. Fellow, Amer. Mediaeval Acad., 1970; Member: Amer. Philosophical Soc., 1971; Unione Accademica Nazionale (Pres., Corpus Philosophorum Medii Aevi), 1971–72; Corresp. Member: Koninklijke Academie voor Wetenschappen, Letteren en Schone Kunsten van België, 1975; Accad. Patavina di Scienze, Lettere ed Arti, 1977; Ist. Veneto di Scienze, Lettere ed Arti, 1980. Medal of the Collège de France, 1975. *Publications:* Education in Fascist Italy, 1946; editions of Aristotle's Categoriae and De intérpretatione (1949, 1957), Plato's Phaedo (Medieval Latin trans., 1950), Aristotle's Categoriae, De interpretatione, Prior and Posterior Analytics, Topics (Ancient and Medieval Latin trans. and paraphrases, 1953, 1954, 1961, 1962, 1965, 1967, 1969), Pseudo-Aristotle's De Mundo (Apuleius', Rinucio's, Sadoleto's trans, 1965), Porphyry's Isagoge (Boethius' trans, 1966); 'Liber VI Principiorum' (1966); co-ed Aristoteles Latinus Codices, vol. ii, and (ed) Supplementa Altera (1955, 1961), and Poetics (Latin trans., 1953, 1968); Twelfth Century Logic, vol. i, 1956, vol. ii, 1958; Opuscula: The Latin Aristotle, 1972; articles in The Classical Quart., Jl of Hellenic Studies, Mediaeval and Renaiss. Studies, Italian Studies, Studi Danteschi, Riv. di Filos. Neoscolastica, Studi Medievali, Rev. Philos. de Louvain, Traditio, Encyclopædia Britannica, Dizion. Biograf. degli Ital., Dictionary of Scientific Biography, etc. *Address:* 22 Polstead Road, Oxford OX2 6TN. *T:* Oxford 57798.
*Died 6 May* 1986.

**MINION, Stephen**, OBE 1954; JP; DL; *b* 2 June 1908; *s* of Stephen and Elizabeth Minion; *m* 1935, Ada, *d* of George and Jane Evans;

no *c*. *Educ:* Liverpool Technical and Commercial Colleges. Formerly Man. Dir, The Lancashire & Cheshire Rubber Co. Ltd, retired 1980. City Councillor 1940, Alderman 1961, Lord Mayor 1969–70, Liverpool. JP Liverpool, 1954; High Sheriff Merseyside, 1976; DL Merseyside, 1976. *Recreations:* outdoor sports, reading, history, theatre and music. *Address:* Glen Cairn, 223 Booker Avenue, Liverpool L18 9TA. *T:* 051–724 2671. *Club:* Athenæum (Liverpool). *Died 13 Oct.* 1990.

**MINOGUE, Hon. Sir John (Patrick)**, Kt 1976; QC; Law Reform Commissioner, Victoria, 1977–82; *b* 15 Sept. 1909; *s* of John Patrick Minogue and Emma Minogue; *m* 1938, Mary Alicia O'Farrell. *Educ:* St Kevin's Coll., Melbourne; Univ. of Melbourne (LLB). Australian Army, 1940–46; GSO1 HQ 1 Aust. Corps and HQ New Guinea Force, 1942–43 (mentioned in despatches); GSO1 Aust. Mil. Mission, Washington, 1945–46. Solicitor, Bendigo, 1937–39; called to the Bar, Melbourne, 1939; QC Victoria 1957, NSW 1958; Papua New Guinea: Judge, Supreme Court, 1962; Chief Justice, 1970–74. Vice-Pres., Aust. Section, Internat. Commn of Jurists, 1965–76. Member: Council and Faculty of Law, Univ. of Papua New Guinea, 1965–74 (Pro-Chancellor, 1972–74); Law Faculty, Melbourne Univ., 1975–79; Law Faculty, Monash Univ., 1977–82. Pres., Graduate Union, Melbourne Univ., 1983–86. Hon. LLD Papua New Guinea, 1974. *Recreations:* reading, conversation, golf. *Address:* 13 Millicent Avenue, Toorak, Vic 3142, Australia. *T:* (03) 240 9034. *Clubs:* Melbourne, Naval and Military, Royal Automobile of Victoria, Melbourne Cricket (Melbourne).
*Died 19 Sept.* 1989.

**MIREPOIX, Duc de L.;** *see* Lévis Mirepoix.

**MIRÓ, Joan;** artist; *b* Barcelona, 20 April 1893; *s* of Miguel and Dolores Miró; *m* 1929, Pilar. *Educ:* Barcelona Academy of Fine Art. Work includes paintings, ceramics, sculptures, engravings, lithographs. Guggenheim Award for ceramic mural in grounds of Unesco Building, Paris, 1958. Foundation Joan Miró, Parc Montjuïc, Barcelona, opened in 1975 with exhibn of 92 paintings and sculptures dated 1917–74. *Exhibitions include:* Galérie Pierre, 1925; Goeman's Gallery, 1928; Galérie Maeght, Paris, 5 exhibns, 1948–70; Pierre Matisse Gallery, New York, 36 exhbns, 1932–80; Tate Gallery, London, 1964; Marlborough Fine Art Gallery, London, 1966; Tokyo, Kyoto, 1966; Barcelona, 1968; Fondation Maeght, St Paul de Vence, 1968, 1979; Munich, 1968; Museum of Modern Art, NY, 1974; Grand Palais, Paris, 1974; Madrid Museum of Contemp. Art, 1978; Hayward Gall., London, 1979; St Louis/Chicago, 1980; Hirshhorn Mus., Washington/Buffalo, 1980; Mexico City, 1980. Grand Cross of Isabel la Católica (Spain), 1978. *Recreation:* walking. *Address:* Pierre Matisse Gallery, 41 East 57th Street, New York, NY 10022, USA; Galérie Maeght, 13 rue de Téhéran, Paris, 8e, France. *Died 25 Dec.* 1983.

**MISSEN, Leslie Robert**, CMG 1956; MC 1918; Research Consultant; *b* 2 May 1897; *e s* of Robert Symonds Missen, Chesterton, Cambs; *m* 1932, Muriel, *o d* of Robert Alstead, OBE, Gathurst, Lancs, formerly MP for Altrincham; two *s*. *Educ:* Perse Sch. and Christ's Coll., Cambridge. Served European War, Capt., 7th Bn N Stafford Regt, Mesopotamia, Persia and Caucasus, 1915–19. Asst Education Officer, Leeds, 1922–26; Dep. Chief Educ. Officer, Middlesbrough, 1926–30; Chief Educ. Officer: Wigan, 1930–36; East Suffolk County Council, 1936–62; Mem., Local Govt Commn for England, 1962–66. Educational Adviser to: Ministry of Education, 1950–57; Ministry of Agriculture, 1944–54; Colonial Sec., 1952–55; Royal Navy, 1958–64; Chairman: Working Party on Educn in Trinidad, BWI, 1954; Trustees of Homerton Coll., Cambridge, 1946–62; President: Assoc. of Education Officers, 1952; Old Persean Soc., 1953–55; Education Section of British Assoc., 1957; County Educn Officers' Soc., 1960; Chairman: Ipswich and District War Pensions Cttee, 1942–70; Suffolk War Pensions Cttee, 1971–. *Publications:* War History of 7th Bn N Stafford Regt, 1920; The Employment of Leisure, 1935; Anecdotes and After Dinner Stories, 1961; Quotable Anecdotes, 1966; Toptable Talk, 1968; contrib. Purnell's History of the First World War, 1971. *Recreations:* gardening, writing, piano. *Address:* 34 Saxmundham Road, Aldeburgh, Suffolk. *T:* Aldeburgh 3163. *Died 27 Aug.* 1983.

**MITCHELL, Lt-Col Brian Granville Blayney**, DSC 1940; RM (Retired); DL; *b* 14 March 1900; *er s* of William Blayney Mitchell, Drumreaske, Co. Monaghan, Eire; *m* 1937, Violet Gwyndolin, *o d* of late Major Sir Charles Price, DL, Haverfordwest, Pembs; two *d*. *Educ:* King's Sch., Bruton, Somerset. Joined Royal Marines, 2nd Lt 1917; Lt 1919; HMS Erin, 1919; Emperor of India, Mediterranean, 1921–22; Hood, Atlantic and Round the World Cruise, 1923–24; Instructor, Sigs Portsmouth, 1925–27; HMS Champion, Home, 1928; Capt. 1928; Queen Elizabeth, Mediterranean, 1929–31; St Vincent (Boys' Training Estab.), 1932–33; Hermes, China, 1934–37; Coronation Review, Spithead, 1937; Supt of Sigs, RM, 1938–40; Major 1937; Actg Lt-Col 1940; Hook of Holland, 1940; The RM Div., 1941–42; Commando Group, Chief Signal Officer, 1943–44; Actg Col 1945; CO Molcab IV, 1945; retired, 1945. DL 1956, High

Sheriff, 1959, County of Pembroke. Order of Orange Nassau with Crossed Swords (Netherlands), 1940. *Address:* Manor House, Wiston, Dyfed SA62 4PN. *T:* Clarbeston 258.

*Died 28 Sept. 1983.*

**MITCHELL, Gladys (Maude Winifred);** Writer; *b* 19 April 1901; *e d* of James Mitchell and Annie Julia Maude Simmonds. *Educ:* The Green Sch., Isleworth; Goldsmiths' and University Colls, University of London. First novel published, 1929; followed by other novels, short stories, BBC short detective plays, BBC excerpts from books, BBC Talks on Home Service. Member: Ancient Monuments Soc.; Soc. of Authors; Crime Writers' Assoc.; Detection Club. *Publications:* Speedy Death, 1929; and subsequently numerous other detective novels, including Dead Men's Morris; My Father Sleeps; Rising of the Moon; Dancing Druids; Tom Brown's Body; Groaning Spinney; The Devil's Elbow; The Echoing Strangers; Merlin's Furlong; Faintley Speaking; Watson's Choice; Twelve Horses and the Hangman's Noose; The Twenty-third Man; Spotted Hemlock; The Man Who Grew Tomatoes; Say It With Flowers, 1960; The Nodding Canaries, 1961; My Bones Will Keep, 1962; Adders on the Heath, 1963; Death of a Delft Blue, 1964; Pageant of Murder, 1965; The Croaking Raven, 1966; Skeleton Island, 1967; Three Quick and Five Dead, 1968; Dance to Your Daddy, 1969; Gory Dew, 1970; Lament for Leto, 1971; A Hearse on May-Day, 1972; The Murder of Busy Lizzie, 1973; A Javelin in for Jonah, 1974; Winking at the Brim, 1974; Convent on Styx, 1975; Late, Late in the Evening, 1976; Noonday and Night, 1977; Fault in the Structure, 1977; Wraiths and Changelings, 1978; Mingled with Venom, 1978; Nest of Vipers, 1979; The Mudflats of the Dead, 1979; Uncoffin'd Clay, 1980; The Whispering Knights, 1980; The Death-Cap Dancers, 1981; Lovers, Make Moan, 1981; Here Lies Gloria Mundy, 1982; Death of a Burrowing Mole, 1982; The Greenstone Griffins, 1983; Cold, Lone and Still, 1983; *as Stephen Hockaby:* Marsh Hay, 1934; Seven Stars and Orion, 1935; Shallow Brown, 1936; Grand Master, 1939; *as Malcolm Torrie:* Heavy As Lead, 1966; Late and Cold, 1967; Your Secret Friend, 1968; Churchyard Salad, 1969; Shades of Darkness, 1970; Bismarck Herrings, 1971; *children's books:* Outlaws of the Border, The Three Fingerprints, Holiday River, 1948; Seven Stones Mystery, 1949; The Malory Secret, 1950; Pam at Storne Castle, 1951; On Your Marks, 1954; Caravan Creek, 1954; The Light-Blue Hills, 1959; *posthumous publications:* No Winding-Sheet, 1984; The Crozier Pharaohs, 1984. *Recreations:* reading, studying architecture, writing poetry. *Address:* 1 Cecil Close, Corfe Mullen, Wimborne, Dorset.

*Died 27 July 1983.*

**MITCHELL, Sir Godfrey Way,** Kt 1948; President, George Wimpey Ltd (Chairman, 1930–73, Executive Director, 1973–79); *b* 31 Oct. 1891; *s* of Christopher Mitchell and Margaret Mitchell (*née* Way); *m* 1929, Doreen Lilian Mitchell (*d* 1953); two *d. Educ:* Aske's Sch., Hatcham. Employed in father's business, Rowe & Mitchell, 1908, until European War, 1914–18; served in France; temp. commission RE; demobilized with rank Captain. Managing Dir of George Wimpey Ltd, 1919. Hon. Fellow, ICE, 1968; Hon. FIOB, 1971. *Address:* Copper Beech, 2 Curzon Avenue, Beaconsfield, Bucks HP9 2NN. *T:* Beaconsfield 3128. *Died 9 Dec. 1982.*

**MITCHELL, Graham Russell,** CB 1957; OBE 1951; attached War Office, 1939–63, retired; *b* 4 Nov. 1905; *s* of late Capt. A. S. Mitchell; *m* 1934, Eleonora Patricia (*née* Robertson); one *s* one *d. Educ:* Winchester; Magdalen Coll., Oxford. *Recreations:* yacht racing, chess. *Address:* 3 Field Close, Sherington, Newport Pagnell, Bucks. *Clubs:* Bembridge Sailing (Bembridge, I of W); Royal Thames Yacht. *Died 19 Nov. 1984.*

**MITCHELL, Sir Hamilton,** KBE 1969; Barrister and Solicitor, in private practice, New Zealand; *b* 24 Feb. 1910; *s* of Ernest Hamilton Mitchell and Catherine Mitchell; *m* 1st, 1938, Marion Frances Norman; two *s* one *d*; 2nd, 1980, Dorothy Good. *Educ:* Auckland Grammar Sch.; New Zealand Univ. (LLM). Practice on own account, 1941–. Served 2nd NZEF, 1943–46 (Captain, Egypt and Italy). President: Disabled Servicemen's Re-establishment League, 1959–63; NZ Returned Services Assoc., 1962–74; Vice-President: World Veterans' Fedn, 1964–66; British Commonwealth Ex-Services League, 1962–74; Judge, Courts Martial Appeal Court, 1962–82; Dep. Chm., Winston Churchill Trust, 1966–76; Chairman: National Art Gallery Management Council, 1967–73; Canteen Fund Bd, 1967–84; NZ Patriotic Fund, 1970–84; Nat. War Meml Council, 1973–; War Pensions Appeal Bd, 1978–83; Dep. Chm., Rehabilitation League, NZ, 1970–86. Pres., Wellington Show Assoc., 1980–85. *Address:* 78 Orangikaupapa Road, Wellington, New Zealand. *T:* 757224. *Clubs:* Wellesley (Wellington); Royal New Zealand Yacht Squadron. *Died 3 June 1989.*

**MITCHELL, Col Sir Harold (Paton),** 1st Bt, *cr* 1945; *b* 21 May 1900; *e s* of late Col Alexander Mitchell, TD, JP, DL, of Tulliallan; *m* 1947, Mary, *d* of late William Pringle; one *d. Educ:* Eton; RMC, Sandhurst; University Coll., Oxford (MA), Hon. Fellow 1972; University of Geneva (Docteur ès Sciences Politiques). Vice-Chm.

of Conservative Party, 1942–45; Contested (C) Clackmannan and East Stirlingshire in 1929; MP (C) Brentford and Chiswick Div. of Middlesex, 1931–45; Parliamentary Private Sec. to Rt Hon. John Colville, MP (Dept of Overseas Trade), 1931–35; Parliamentary Private Sec. to Rt Hon. Ralph Assheton, MP (Ministry of Labour, 1939–41, and Ministry of Supply, 1941); Mem. Departmental Cttee on Education and Training of Overseas Students, 1933–34; Mem. Selection Board for Consular Service, 1934–35; Mem. Company Law Amendment Cttee, 1943–45; Command Welfare Officer, AA Command, 1940–48, and Liaison Officer to Polish Forces (France, Belgium, Holland, 1944). Lectr, Hispanic American Studies, Stanford University 1959–65; Research Prof. of Latin American Studies, Rollins Coll. Hon. Col, 123 LAA Regt (City of London Rifles) TA, 1939–48; Hon. Col of 61st (City of Edinburgh) Signal Regt, TA, 1947–65. Chm. and Chief Exec., Luscar Ltd Group, Edmonton, Alberta; sometime Dir London and North Eastern Railway Co.; Joint Master Lauderdale Foxhounds, 1934–35; sometime Mem. Queen's Body Guard for Scotland. DL Clackmannanshire, 1943–47. Hon. LLD Alberta, Rollins and St Andrews. KStJ; Knight Commander of Polonia Restituta; Polish Cross of Valour. *Publications:* Downhill Ski-Racing, 1930; Into Peace, 1945; In My Stride, 1951; Europe in the Caribbean, 1963; Caribbean Patterns, 1967, 2nd edn 1972; The Spice of Life, 1974. *Recreation:* ski-ing, represented Gt Britain, 1929, 1931 and 1933. *Address:* Haus Gornerwald, 3920 Zermatt, Switzerland; Marshall's Island, Bermuda. *Clubs:* Alpine; Royal Bermuda Yacht.

*Died 8 April 1983 (ext).*

**MITCHELL, James Alexander Hugh;** publisher; Chairman, Mitchell Beazley Ltd, since 1977; Founder Chairman, Mitchell Beazley Television, since 1981; *b* 20 July 1939; *s* of William Moncur Mitchell and Christine Mary Browne; *m* 1962, Janice Page Davison; three *s. Educ:* Winchester; Trinity Coll., Cambridge (BA). Hatchards (bookseller), 1960–61; Constable & Co. (Editor), 1961–67; Editorial Director, Thomas Nelson, 1967–69; Jt Founder of Mitchell Beazley with John Beazley (*d* 1977), 1969. Senior Vice-Pres., Communications Div., American Express Co., 1980–83. Chm. Bd of Trustees, Royal College of Art, 1982–84 (Hon. Fellow, 1983). *Publications:* (ed) The God I Want, 1966; (gen. ed) The Joy of Knowledge Encyclopaedia (also called The Random House Encyclopedia, in USA, l'Univers en couleurs, in France (Larousse)), etc (now 28 editions in 23 languages). *Recreations:* family, fishing, gardening, birds, dogs. *Address:* c/o Mitchell Beazley, Artists House, 14/15 Manette Street, W1V 5LB. *T:* 01–434 3272. *Club:* Garrick.

*Died 12 March 1985.*

**MITCHELL, John Fowler,** CIE 1935; Indian Civil Service, retired; *b* 30 Dec. 1886; *s* of William Mitchell and Jane Woodrow; *m* 1920, Sheila Macbeth, MBE; one *s* two *d. Educ:* Allan Glen's Sch., Glasgow; Royal College of Science, S Kensington; Glasgow Univ,; Merton Coll., Oxford; London Univ. (BSc 1st cl. Hons, Exptl Physics, 1908). Entered Indian Civil Service, 1910; from 1910–19 various posts as Asst Comr Punjab, including Magistrate and Sec. Municipal Cttee, Delhi; Subdivisional Officer, Fazilka; Superintendent Central Jail, Multan; Forest Settlement Officer, Kangra; from 1920–34 various finance and audit posts, including Under Sec. Finance, Punjab; Accountant General Madras, Central Provinces and Central Revenues; Dir of Audit Indian Railways; officiating Dep. Auditor General, India; retired 1937. Military Service, 1940–46; Allied Commission for Austria, 1946–47. *Publications:* (with Sheila Mitchell): Monumental Inscriptions in Kinross-shire, 1967; Monumental Inscriptions (pre-1855) in Clackmannanshire, 1968; similar volumes for West Lothian, 1969; Dunbartonshire, 1969; Renfrewshire, 1970; East Fife, 1971; West Fife, 1972; East Stirlingshire, 1972; West Stirlingshire, 1973; South Perthshire, 1974; North Perthshire, 1975. *Address:* 47 Connaught Mansions, Bath, Avon BA2 4BP. *T:* Bath 60107.

*Died 28 April 1984.*

**MITCHELL, Prof. Joseph Stanley,** CBE 1951; FRS 1952; FRCP; Emeritus Regius Professor of Physic, University of Cambridge, since 1975; engaged on work in the Research Laboratories of the Clinical School, Radiotherapeutic Centre, Addenbrooke's Hospital, Cambridge; Fellow, St John's College, Cambridge, 1936–39, and since 1943; *b* 22 July 1909; *s* of late Joseph Brown Mitchell and Ethel Maud Mary Arnold, Birmingham; *m* 1934, Dr Lilian Mary Buxton, MA, MB, ChB (*d* 1983); one *s* one *d. Educ:* Marlborough Road Council Sch., Birmingham; King Edward's High Sch., Birmingham; Univ. of Birmingham (Nat. Scis Tripos Pt II, Cl. I Physics, 1931); St John's Coll., Cambridge (MB, BChir 1934; MA 1935; PhD 1937; MD 1957). DMR RCS 1943; FFR 1954; MRCP 1956, FRCP 1958. Formerly House Physician, Gen. Hosp., Birmingham; Beit Meml Med. Res. Fellow, Colloid Science Lab., Cambridge, 1934–37; Resident Radiological Officer, Christie Hosp., Manchester, 1937–38; Radiotherapist, EMS, 1939; Univ. of Cambridge: Asst in Res. in Radiotherapy, Dept of Medicine, 1938; Regius Prof. of Physic, 1957–75; Prof. of Radiotherapeutics, 1946–57 and 1975–76; Dir, Radiotherapeutic Centre, Addenbrooke's Hospital, Cambridge, 1943–76; i/c med.

investigations, National Res. Council Lab., Montreal, 1944–45. Chm. 1971–77 and Vice-Chm. 1977–79, Faith Courtauld Unit for Human Studies in Cancer, KCH, London; Leverhulme Emeritus Fellow, Univ. of Cambridge Clinical Sch., Res. Lab, 1976–77; Hon. Consultant, AEA, 1951–. Pres., British Section, Anglo-German Med. Soc., 1959–68; Hon. Mem., German Roentgen Soc., 1967; Foreign Fellow, Indian Natural Science Acad., 1975. Linacre Lectr, St John's Coll., Cambridge, 1970. DSc (*hc*) Birmingham, 1958. Pirogoff Medal, Acad. of Medicine, USSR, 1967. *Publications:* Studies in Radiotherapeutics, 1960; Cancer, if curable why not cured?, 1971; (with M. Cohen) Cobalt 60 Teletherapy: a compendium of international practice, 1984; papers in scientific and med. jls on mechanism of therapeutic action of radiations and on develt of radioactive compounds for treatment of cancer. *Recreations:* walking, modern languages. *Address:* Thorndyke, Huntingdon Road, Girton, Cambridge CB3 0LG. *T:* Cambridge 276102; Research Laboratories, Radiotherapeutic Centre, Addenbrooke's Hospital, Hills Road, Cambridge CB2 2QQ. *T:* Cambridge 243619. *Died 22 Feb. 1987.*

**MITCHELL, Leslie Herbert,** CBE 1955 (OBE 1949); *b* 28 May 1914; *s* of J. W. and A. J. Mitchell; *m* 1937, Margaret Winifred Pellow; three *s. Educ:* Christ's Hospital. Served War of 1939–45 in HM Forces in NW Europe. 2nd Sec., British Embassy, Copenhagen, 1945–50; 1st Sec., British Embassy, Washington, 1953–56; 1st Sec., Bonn, 1956–57; FO, retd 1968. Order of Dannebrog (Denmark), 1947. *Recreations:* music, railways. *Address:* 2 Lakeside Court, East Approach Drive, Cheltenham, Glos. *Club:* New (Cheltenham).
*Died 20 Oct. 1989.*

**MITCHELL, Dr Robert Lyell;** Director, Macaulay Institute for Soil Research, Aberdeen, 1968–75, retired; *b* 3 June 1910; *s* of late David Hay Lyell Mitchell, marine engr, and late Agnes Davidson Brown, Edinburgh. *Educ:* Bathgate Academy; Univs of Edinburgh and Aberdeen. BSc Edinburgh, 1st cl. hons Chem., 1931; PhD Aberdeen, 1934; ETH Zürich; FRIC 1949; FRSE 1955. Macaulay Inst. for Soil Research: Head of Dept of Spectrochemistry, 1937–68; Dep. Dir, 1955–68. Research Medal, RASE, 1963; Gold Medal, Soc. for Analytical Chemistry, 1975. *Publications:* Spectrochemical Analysis of Soils, Plants and Related Materials, 1948; numerous contribs to scientific jls and internat. confs concerned with the soil, agriculture and analytical chemistry. *Recreations:* mountaineering, photography. *Address:* 125 Cranford Road, Aberdeen AB1 7NJ. *T:* Aberdeen 35916. *Clubs:* Alpine; Scottish Mountaineering (Edinburgh). *Died 7 Feb. 1982.*

**MITCHELL, Sir (Seton) Steuart (Crichton),** KBE 1954 (OBE 1941); CB 1951; *b* 9 March 1902; *s* of A. Crichton Mitchell, DSc, FRSE; *m* 1929, Elizabeth (*née* Duke); no *c. Educ:* Edinburgh Acad.; RN Colls, Osborne and Dartmouth. Joined Royal Navy as Cadet, 1916; at sea in HMS Hercules, Grand Fleet, 1918, subsequently served in HM Ships Ramillies, Sportive, Tomahawk, Marlborough; qualified as Gunnery Specialist, 1927–29, subsequently Gunnery Officer of HM Ships Comus and Frobisher; Naval Ordnance Inspection Dept and Asst Supt of Design, 1931–39; War of 1939–45, Inspector of Naval Ordnance, in charge of Admiralty Ordnance contracts in Switzerland, 1939–40, in USA, 1940–44; Chief Engineer and Supt, in charge of Armament Design Establishment, Min. of Supply, 1945; Controller, Guided Weapons and Electronics, Min. of Supply, 1951–56; Controller, Royal Ordnance Factories, 1956–59; Controller, Guided Weapons and Electronics, Ministry of Aviation, 1959–62; Mem., BTC, Feb.-Nov. 1962; Vice-Chm., British Railways Bd, Nov. 1962–64; Chairman: Machine Tool Industry EDC, 1964–; Shipbuilding Industry Trng Bd, 1964–; Mem., Central Trng Council, 1965–; Adviser (part-time) to Min. of Technology, 1965–; Mem. Scottish Economic Planning Council, 1965–67; Mem. Nat. Economic Develt Council, 1968–70. Chm., Carrier Engineering Co., 1968–70; Director: Parkinson Cowan Ltd, 1964–71; Plessey Numerical Controls Ltd, 1970–73. Officer Legion of Merit (USA), 1945. *Recreations:* music, gardening, antiques. *Address:* 9 The Stratford Beaumont, New Street, Stratford on Avon, Warwicks CV37 6BX. *Died 4 March 1990.*

**MITCHELL, William Eric Marcus,** MC; MB; BS London; FRCS; FRCSC; MRCP; DPH; Surgeon, genito-urinary specialist, Consulting Surgeon, Royal Jubilee Hospital, Victoria, BC, retired; *b* 29 April 1897; *e s* of Dr J. F. Mitchell, formerly of Bangor, Co. Down; *m* 1922, Catherine, *d* of W. F. Hamilton, of Ashwick, NZ; one *d*; *m* 1958, Margery, *d* of D. O. Thomas, Victoria, BC. *Educ:* Campbell Coll., Belfast; St Bartholomew's Hosp., University of London. Served as a Lt with the 11th Battalion Royal Irish Rifles in France, 1916 (wounded, MC); various prizes during sch. and Univ. career; House Surg., St Bartholomew's Hosp.; Chief Asst to a Surgical Unit, St Bartholomew's Hosp.; Clinical Asst, St Peter's Hosp., London; Pres., Abernethian Soc., St Bartholomew's Hosp. War of 1939–45, Lt-Col RAMC, Officer in Charge Surgical Div. No 13 Gen. Hosp. MEF. *Publications:* Health, Wealth and Happiness, 1969; numerous papers on surgical subjects published in the Lancet, the Canadian Medical Association Journal, St Bartholomew's

Hospital Journal. *Recreations:* fishing, ski-ing, mountaineering. *Address:* 2171 Granite Street, Oak Bay, Victoria, BC V8S 3G8, Canada. *TA:* Victoria, BC. *Club:* Alpine Club of Canada.
*Died 27 Dec. 1990.*

**MITFORD-SLADE, Col Cecil Townley;** *b* 19 April 1903; *s* of late Col William Kenyon Mitford, CMG, CVO; assumed additional name of Slade by deed poll, 1941; *m* 1931, Phyllis (*d* 1985), *d* of late E. G. Buxton; two *s* one *d. Educ:* Eton; RMC; joined 60th Rifles, 1923; psc† 1938–39; Gen. Staff, GHQ BEF, 1940; Jt planning, WO, 1941; Gibraltar, 1942–43; comd 8th Bn KRRC, 1943–44; Burma, 1944–45; Palestine, 1946–47; 1st Bn KRRC, 1948–50; Comdt, WRAC Staff Coll., 1951; HM Bodyguard of Hon. Corps of Gentlemen-at-Arms, 1952–73. DL, Somerset, 1955–66, 1978; JP, 1953; CC, 1955; High Sheriff, 1963; Vice-Lieut, 1966–68; Lord-Lieutenant, 1968–78; Hon. County Alderman, 1978. County Comr, St John Amb. Bde, 1954–68; Chm., Taunton Race Course Co. KStJ; Order of Mercy. *Recreations:* shooting, fishing. *Address:* Montys Court, Taunton, Somerset. *T:* Bishop's Lydeard 432255. *Club:* Naval and Military.
*Died 13 Aug. 1986.*

**MITMAN, Frederick S(nyder),** CBE 1941; *b* 21 April 1900; *s* of late William and Elizabeth Mitman; *m* 1925, Helen McNary; one *s* one *d. Educ:* Lehigh Univ., USA (Deg. of Engineer of Mines, 1923). Dir of Light Alloys and Magnesium (Sheet and Strip) Control, Ministry of Aircraft Production, 1939–41; Co-ordinator of Aircraft Supplies for Fighter and Naval Aircraft, Ministry of Aircraft Production, 1940–41; Adviser on Light Metals Fabrication, Ministry of Aircraft Production, 1941–42. *Address:* 10 Campden House Close, Kensington, W8. *T:* 01–937 9071. *Died 4 April 1989.*

**MOCATTA, Sir Alan Abraham,** Kt 1961; OBE 1944; Judge of the High Court of Justice (Queen's Bench Division), 1961–81; Member, 1961–81, President, 1970–81, Restrictive Practices Court; *b* 27 June 1907; *s* of Edward L. Mocatta and Flora Gubbay; *m* 1930, Pamela Halford, JP; four *s. Educ:* Clifton Coll.; New Coll., Oxford (exhbnr); 1st cl. History, 1928, 2nd cl. Jurisprudence, 1929; MA. Called to the Bar, Inner Temple, 1930; Bencher, 1960, Treas., 1982; Northern circuit; QC 1951. Served War of 1939–45: 2nd Lieut 12 LAA Regt, RA, TA, 1939; Bde Major, 56 AA Bde, 1940–41; GSO (2) AA HQ BTNI, 1941–42; Lt-Col GS, Army Council Secretariat, War Office, 1942–45. Chm., Council of Jews' Coll., 1945–61; Vice-Pres., Board of Elders, Spanish and Portuguese Jews' Congregation, London, 1961–67, Pres., 1967–82; Chm. Treasury Cttee on Cheque Endorsement, 1955–56. Joint editor, 14th-19th editions of Scrutton on Charter Parties; Editor, 3rd edn Rowlatt on Principal and Surety; Mem., Adv. Panel for 4th edn of Halsbury's Laws of England. *Address:* 18 Hanover House, NW8 7DX. *T:* 071–722 2857. *Club:* MCC. *Died 1 Nov. 1990.*

**MOFFAT, Sir John Smith,** Kt 1955; OBE 1944; MLC Northern Rhodesia, 1951–64; Member Federal Parliament, Salisbury, 1954–62; *b* N Rhodesia, April 1905; *s* of Rev. Malcolm Moffat; *m* 1930, Margaret Prentice; two *d. Educ:* Grey High Sch., Port Elizabeth, South Africa; Glasgow Univ. Cadet Northern Rhodesia Provincial Administration, 1927; District Officer, 1929. Served at Serenje, Fort Jameson, etc. Commissioner for National Development, 1945; retd from CS, 1951. Chm. Federal African Affairs Board, and leader Liberal Party until 1962, when disbanded. Farmer. *Address:* Kulinda, RD3, Whangarei, North Island, New Zealand. *Died 9 June 1985.*

**MOIR, Alan John,** CMG 1971; *b* 19 July 1903; *s* of George Allen Moir and Louise Elvina Moir (*née* Evans); *m* 1929, Eileen Walker; one *s* one *d. Educ:* Scotch Coll., Melbourne; Univ. of Melbourne. Barrister and Solicitor, Supreme Court of Victoria. Partner, Gillott Moir & Ahern, 1929–63, retd. *Recreations:* racing, bowls. *Address:* 27 Hopetoun Road, Toorak, Victoria 3142, Australia. *T:* 20–5267. *Clubs:* Athenæum (Melbourne) (ex-Pres.); Victoria Racing, Victoria Amateur Turf, Moonee Valley Racing (ex-Chm.), Melbourne Cricket. *Died 24 Dec. 1982.*

**MOLESWORTH-ST AUBYN, Sir John,** 14th Bt, *cr* 1689; CBE 1968; *b* 12 Jan. 1899; *s* of Sir Hugh Molesworth-St Aubyn, 13th Bt, and Emma Sybil (*d* 1929), *d* of Admiral Charles Wake; *S* father, 1942; *m* 1926, Celia Marjorie (*d* 1965), *e d* of late Lieut-Col Valentine Vivian, CMG, DSO, MVO; one *s* two *d. Educ:* Eton; Christ Church, Oxford. Flight Lieut, RAFVR, 1941. JP Cornwall, 1942; Sheriff of Cornwall, 1948. *Heir: s* John Arscott Molesworth-St Aubyn, MBE. *Address:* Pencarrow, Washaway, Bodmin, Cornwall.
*Died 15 Nov. 1985.*

**MOLLAN, Maj.-Gen. Francis Robert Henry,** CB 1950; OBE 1943; MC 1918; *b* 20 June 1893; *s* of late Rev. H. J. G. Mollan; *m* 1st, 1921, Violet Samana Desvoeux (*d* 1930); one *s* (and one *s* killed in action, Italy, 1944); 2nd, 1937, Alison Beatrice Hesmondhalgh; two *s* one *d. Educ:* Corrig Sch.; Royal College of Surgeons of Ireland. Served European War, 1915–18, France and Belgium (despatches twice, 1914–15 Star, British War Medal, Victory Medal, MC). Served North-West Frontier of India (Mohmand), 1933 (despatches,

Medal and clasp). War of 1939–45 (despatches thrice, OBE, Africa Star and 8th Army clasp). Comdt and Dir of Studies, Royal Army Medical College, 1950–53; Maj.-Gen., 1951; retired 1953; re-employed as Pres., Standing Medical Boards SW District, 1954–61; Area Medical Officer, Taunton, 1961–68. QHS 1952–53 (KHS 1950–52). *Publications:* Contrib. to Jl of the RAMC. *Address:* 5a Mount Street, Taunton, Som. *T:* 73097. *Died 28 Feb.* 1982.

**MOLLER, Marjorie**, MA; *b* 23 June 1899; *e d* of late C. G. C. Moller. *Educ:* Clapham High Sch.; St Hugh's Coll., Oxford (Honour School of Natural Science). Science mistress City of London Girls' Sch., 1923; Walter Page travelling scholarship, 1930; Head of Science dept, 1928, and House mistress at Wycombe Abbey Sch., 1930; Head Mistress of Headington Sch., Oxford, 1934–59; Warden of Denman Coll. (NFWI), 1959–64. *Address:* 26 Bickerton Road, Headington, Oxford. *Died* 1 *Jan.* 1981.

**MOLLO, Victor**; Bridge Correspondent, The Mail on Sunday, since 1982; Bridge Editor, Methuen, since 1985; Bridge Cruise Director: P&O, 1973–74; Norwegian-America Line, 1975; *b* St Petersburg, 17 Sept. 1909; Russian parents; *m* 1952, Jeanne Victoria Forbes. *Educ:* privately in Paris; Cordwalles, Surrey (Prep. Sch.); Brighton Coll.; London School of Economics, London Univ. Freelance journalism, also reading French and Russian texts for publishers, 1927–40; sub editor and editor, European Services (now External) BBC, 1940 till retirement in Oct. 1969. Bridge Correspondent, The Evening Standard, 1970–75; Bridge Editor: Faber & Faber, 1966–79; Pelham Books, 1980–82. *Publications:* Streamlined Bridge, 1947; Card-Play Technique (in collab. with N. Gardener), 1955; Bridge for Beginners (in collab. with N. Gardener) 1956; Bridge Psychology, 1958; Will You Be My Partner?, 1959; Bridge: Modern Bidding, 1961; Success at Bridge, 1964; Bridge in the Menagerie, 1965; Confessions of an Addict, 1966; The Bridge Immortals, 1967; Victor Mollo's Winning Double, 1968; Bridge: Case for the Defence, 1970; (with E. Jannersten) Best of Bridge, 1972; Bridge in the Fourth Dimension, 1974; Instant Bridge, 1975; (with Aksel J. Nielsen) Defence at Bridge, 1976; Bridge Unlimited, 1976; Bridge Course Complete, 1977; The Finer Arts of Bridge, 1977; Masters and Monsters, 1978; Streamline Your Bidding, 1979; Streamline Your Card Play, 1981; Bridge à la Carte, 1982; Winning Bridge, 1983; You Need Never Lose at Bridge, 1983; I Challenge You, 1984; The Other Side of Bridge, 1984; Tomorrow's Textbook, 1985; The Compleat Bridge Player, 1986; Destiny at Bay, 1987; also Pocket Guides: ACOL: Winning Bidding, 1969 and Winning Defence, Winning Conventions. Contributing Editor to the Official Encyclopaedia of Bridge. Regular contributor to Bridge Magazines in USA, France, Denmark, Norway and Sweden and to Bridge Magazine in Britain. *Recreations:* gastronomy, conversation, bridge. *Address:* 801 Grenville House, Dolphin Square, SW1. *Club:* St James's Bridge. *Died* 24 *Sept.* 1987.

**MOLOTOV, Vyacheslav Mikhailovich**, (*pseudonym* of V. M. Skryabin); Soviet diplomat; *b* Kirov district (Vyatka), 9 March 1890; son of a ship assistant; as mem. of students' Marxist circles in Kazan, took part in first Revolution, 1905; joined Bolshevik section of Russian Social Democratic Labour Party and organised students, 1906; arrested and deported to Vologda; organised Vologda railwaymen; graduated, 1909; organised students, Petrograd; contributed to Zvezda; part-founder with Stalin and sec. of Pravda, 1911; exiled from Petrograd for political activity, 1912; continued Party work from suburbs, organising elections and work of Party deputies in Duma, 1913; reorganised Moscow Bolshevik Party; exiled to Irkutsk, Siberia, 1915; escaped, returned to Petrograd and appointed mem. of Russian Bureau of Bolshevik Central Committee, 1916; mem. of executive of Petrograd Soviet and of military revolutionary cttee, 1917; chm. of People's Economy Council, Northern Region, 1918; chm. Nijegorodsky regional executive, 1919; sec. of Donets Regional Party cttee, 1920; elected mem. and sec. of Central Cttee of Communist Party of Soviet Union and candidate mem. of Political Bureau, 1921; mem. of Political Bureau of CPSU; worked against Zinovievists, Leningrad, 1926; elected mem. of Central Executive Cttee of Russian Soviet Socialist Republic, 1927; sec., Moscow cttee of CPSU; worked against Bukharinists in Moscow, 1928; elected mem. of Presidium of Central Executive Cttee of USSR, 1929; chm. of Council, of People's Commissars of USSR, 1930–41; 1st Dep. Chm., Council of People's Commissars, 1941–46; Dep. Chm., State Defence Cttee, 1941–45; took part in Teheran, Crimean, Potsdam and San Francisco Conferences; Leader of Soviet Delegn to Paris Peace Conf., 1946, to UN Gen. Assemblies, 1945–48; People's Commissar for For. Affairs, 1939–46, For. Min., 1946–49, 1953–56; First Dep. Chm. of USSR Council of Ministers, 1953–57; Min. of State Control, 1956–57; Dep. to Supreme Soviet, 1937–57; Soviet Ambassador to Mongolia, 1957–60; Chief Permanent Representative of the Soviet Union (rank Ambassador) to the International Atomic Energy Agency, Vienna, 1960–62. Hon. Mem. USSR Acad. of Sciences, 1946. Hero of Socialist Labour (and Hammer and Sickle Medal), 1943; Order of Lenin (4 awards). *Publications:* In the Struggle for Socialism, 1934; Articles and Speeches, 1935–36, 1937; Problems of Foreign Policy, 1948. *Address:* c/o Ministry of Social Security, 14 Shabolovka, Moscow, USSR. *Died* 8 *Nov.* 1986.

**MOLYNEUX, John Anthony (Tony)**; HM Diplomatic Service, retired; County Councillor, Oxfordshire, since 1981; *b* 1 Aug. 1923; *s* of late Mr and Mrs E. D. Molyneux; *m* 1958, Patricia Dawson; two *s* one *d* (and one *s* decd). *Educ:* Lancing; Worcester Coll., Oxford (MA). Royal Navy, 1941–46. Joined Commonwealth Relations Office, 1949; 2nd Sec., New Delhi, 1950–52; 1st Sec., Karachi, 1955–59, Canberra, 1959–62; Special Adviser to Governor of N Rhodesia, 1964; Dep. High Comr, Lusaka, 1964–66; Counsellor (Economic/Commercial), Belgrade, 1967–70; seconded to Birmingham Chamber of Commerce and Industry (to help planning of Nat. Exhibn Centre), 1971–72; Commercial Counsellor, The Hague, 1972–74; seconded to Dept of Energy, 1974–76. Governor, N Oxon Tech. Coll., etc. *Recreation:* watching cricket. *Address:* The Old Farmhouse, Wroxton, Banbury, Oxon. *Clubs:* MCC; Delhi Gymkhana; Karachi Yacht. *Died* 12 *Sept.* 1982.

**MOMIGLIANO, Prof. Arnaldo Dante**, Hon. KBE 1974; DLitt (Turin); FBA 1954; Professor of Ancient History in the University of London at University College, 1951–75; Alexander White Visiting Professor, University of Chicago, 1959 and since 1975; *b* 5 Sept. 1908; *s* of late Riccardo Momigliano and late Ilda Levi; *m* 1932, Gemma Segre; one *d*. *Educ:* privately, and at Univs of Turin and Rome. Professore Incaricato di Storia Greca, Univ. of Rome, 1932–36; Professore Titolare di Storia Romana, 1936–38, Professore Ordinario di Storia Romana in soprannumero, 1945–64, Univ. of Turin, *Id*, 1964–, Scuola Normale Superiore of Pisa. Lecturer in Ancient History, 1947–49, Reader in Ancient History, 1949–51, University of Bristol; research work in Oxford, 1939–47. Sather Prof. in Classics, Univ. of California, 1961–62; J. H. Gray Lectr, Univ. of Cambridge, 1963; Wingate Lectr, Hebrew Univ. of Jerusalem, 1964; Vis. Prof. and Lauro de Bosis Lectr, Harvard Univ., 1964–65; C. N. Jackson Lectr, Harvard Univ., 1968; Jerome Lectr, Michigan Univ., 1971–72; Vis. Schol., Harvard, 1972; Trevelyan Lectr, Cambridge Univ., 1973; Flexner Lectr, Bryn Mawr, 1974; Grinfield Lectr on the Septuagint, Oxford, 1978–82; Efroymson Lectr, Hebrew Union Coll., Cincinnati, 1978; Chr. Gauss Lectr, Princeton, 1979; Lurcy Prof., Univ. of Chicago, 1982; Vis. Fellow: Peterhouse, Cambridge, 1983–85; Princeton Univ., 1984; Vis. Prof., Ecole Normale Supérieure, Paris, 1984. Socio Nazionale: Accademia dei Lincei, 1961 (corresp. mem., 1947–61); Arcadia, 1967; Accademia delle Scienze di Torino, 1968; Istituto di Studi Romani, 1970 (corresp. mem., 1954–70); Istituto Studi Etruschi, 1973. Foreign Member: Royal Dutch Academy; Amer. Philosophical Soc.; Amer. Acad. of Arts and Scis; Institut de France; Corresp. Mem., German Archæological Institute, 1935; Hon. Mem., Amer. Hist. Assoc., 1964. Pres., Soc. for Promotion of Roman Studies, 1965–68. Hon. MA Oxford; Hon. DLitt: Bristol, 1959; Edinburgh, 1964; Oxford, 1970; Cambridge, 1971; London, 1975; Chicago, 1976; Leiden, 1977; Urbino, 1978; Marburg, 1986; Hon. DHL: Columbia, 1974; Brandeis, 1977; Hebrew Union Coll., 1980; Bard Coll., 1983; Yale, 1985; Hon. DPhil: Hebrew Univ., 1974; Tel-Aviv Univ., 1981. Hon. Fellow: Warburg Inst., 1975; UCL, 1976; Peterhouse, 1985. Premio Cantoni, Univ. of Florence, 1932; Premio Feltrinelli for historical res. (Accademia dei Lincei award), 1960; Kaplun Prize for historical res., Hebrew Univ., 1975; Gold Medal, Italian Min. of Educn, 1977; Kenyon Medal, British Acad., 1981; Premio Sila per la saggistica, Cosenza Univ., 1985. Co-editor of Rivista Storica Italiana, 1948–. *Publications:* La composizione della Storia di Tucidide, 1930; Prime Linee di storia della tradizione maccabaica, 1931 (2nd edn 1968); Claudius, 1934 (2nd edn 1961); Filippo il Macedone, 1934; La storiografia sull' impero romano, 1936; Contributo alla storia degli studi classici, 1955; Secondo Contributo alla storia degli studi classici, 1960; Terzo Contributo alla storia degli studi classici, 1966; Studies in Historiography, 1966; (ed) Paganism and Christianity in the Fourth Century, 1963 (trans. Italian); Quarto contributo alla storia degli studi classici, 1969; The Development of Greek Biography, 1971 (trans. Italian, Japanese); Introduzione Bibliografica alla Storia Greca fino a Socrate, 1975; Quinto Contributo alla Storia degli studi classici, 1975; Alien Wisdom, the limits of Hellenization, 1975, 2nd edn 1978 (trans. Italian, German, French, Spanish); Essays on Historiography, 1977; Sesto Contributo alla Storia degli Studi Classici, 1981; La Storiografia Greca, 1982 (trans. Spanish, 1984); Problèmes d'historiographie ancienne et moderne, 1983; New Paths of Classicism in the Nineteenth Century, 1983; (ed) Aspetti dell'opera di G. Dumézil, 1983; Sui Fondamenti della Storia Antica, 1984; Settimo Contributo alla Storia degli Studi Classici, 1984; Tra Storiae Storicismo, 1985; Ottavo Contributo alla Storia degli Studi Classici, 1987; contribs to Cambridge Ancient History, Jl of Roman Studies, History and Theory, Jl of Warburg Inst., Daedalus, Enciclopedia Italiana, Encycl. Britannica, Encycl. Judaica, Encycl. of Religion. *Recreation:* walking. *Address:* Department of Classics, University of Chicago, Chicago, Ill 60637, USA. *Died* 1 *Sept.* 1987.

**MONAHAN, James Henry Francis,** CBE 1962; Director, Royal Ballet School, 1977–83; *b* 16 Dec. 1912; *s* of late George John Monahan, Indian Civil Service, and Helen Monahan (*née* Kennedy); *m* 1941, Joan Barker-Mill (*née* Eaden); two *s* three *d*; *m* 1965, Merle Park, ballerina (marr. diss. 1970); one *s*; *m* 1970, Gail Thomas; one *s* one *d*. *Educ:* Stonyhurst Coll.; Christ Church, Oxford. The Manchester Guardian: critic and reporter, London office, 1937–39; film critic, 1945–63; dance critic, 1945–77. Government Service and attached to BBC German Service, 1939–42; Army Service: (despatches); Special Forces and No 10 Commando, 1942–45; Captain, 1944. British Broadcasting Corporation: Asst Head, West European Services, 1946; Head, West European Services, 1946–51; Controller, European Services, 1952–70; Dir of Programmes, External Services, 1971, retired. Part-time cons., Corp. for Public Broadcasting, USA, 1973. *Publications:* Far from the Land (poems), 1944; After Battle (poems), 1947; Fonteyn, 1958; report on Deutsche Welle, West Germany, 1972; The Nature of Ballet, 1976; British Ballet Today, 1980. *Recreation:* lawn tennis. *Address:* 42 Castelnau, SW13. *T:* 01–748 7287. *Club:* Hurlingham.                                    *Died* 23 *Nov.* 1985.

**MONCK, 6th Viscount** *cr* 1800; **Henry Wyndham Stanley Monck,** OBE 1961; JP; DL; Baron Monck, 1797; Baron Monck (UK), 1866; formerly Coldstream Guards; formerly Company Director; Vice-Chairman, National Association of Boys' Clubs, 1938–78; *b* 11 Dec. 1905; *s* of Hon. Charles H. S. Monck (*d* 1914) and Mary Florence (*d* 1918), *d* of Sir W. Portal, 2nd Bt; *S* grandfather, 1927; *m* 1st, 1937, Eva Maria, Baroness Vreto (marr. diss. 1951), 2nd *d* of Prof. Zaunmüller-Freudenthaler, Vienna; 2nd, 1951, Brenda Mildred, *o d* of G. W. Adkins, Bowers Close, Harpenden; three *s*. *Educ:* Eton; RMC, Sandhurst. Member, Southern Gas Board, 1965–72. JP Hants, 1944; DL Hants 1973. *Heir:* *s* Hon. Charles Stanley Monck, BTech, *b* 2 April 1953. *Address:* Hurstbourne Priors House, Whitchurch, Hants RG28 7SB. *T:* Whitchurch, Hants, 2277. *Club:* MCC.                                    *Died* 21 *June* 1982.

**MONCREIFF, Rt. Rev. Francis Hamilton;** *b* North Berwick, 29 Sept. 1906; *s* of late James Hamilton Moncreiff. *Educ:* Shrewsbury Sch.; St John's Coll., Cambridge; Cuddesdon Theological Coll. Ordained, 1931; Curate at St Giles, Cambridge, 1931–35, at St Augustine's, Kilburn, 1935–41; Priest-in-charge, St Salvador's, Edinburgh, 1941, Rector, 1947–51; Chaplain at HM Prison, Edinburgh, 1942–51; Canon of St Mary's Cathedral, Edinburgh, 1950; Diocesan Missioner in diocese of Edinburgh, 1951–52; Bishop of Glasgow and Galloway, 1952–74; Primus of the Episcopal Church in Scotland, 1962–74. Went on a Mission to European parishes in Northern Rhodesia, 1948 and 1951, to Pretoria and Johannesburg, 1953. Hon. DD Glasgow, 1967. *Address:* 19 Eglinton Crescent, Edinburgh EH12 5BY. *T:* 031–337 1523.

*Died* 3 *Sept.* 1984.

**MONCREIFFE OF THAT ILK, Sir (Rupert) Iain (Kay),** 11th Bt, *cr* 1685; CVO 1980; DL; QC (Scot.) 1980; author; *b* 9 April 1919; *s* of late Lt-Comdr Gerald Moncreiffe, Royal Navy, and Hinda (*d* 1960), *d* of late Frank Meredyth, styled Count de Miremont; *S* cousin, Sir David Moncreiffe of that Ilk, Bt, 23rd Laird of Moncreiffe, 1957; *m* 1st, 1946, Countess of Erroll, 23rd in line (marr. diss. 1964; she *d* 1978); two *s* one *d*; 2nd, 1966, Hermione, *d* of late Lt-Col W. D. Faulkner, MC, Irish Guards and of Patricia, Countess of Dundee, *d* of late Lord Herbert Montagu-Douglas-Scott. *Educ:* Stowe; Heidelberg; Christ Church, Oxford (MA); Edinburgh Univ. (LLB, PhD). Capt. late Scots Guards; served 1939–46 (wounded in Italy): ADC to Gen. Sir Andrew Thorne (GOC-in-C Scottish Comd), 1944–45; Military Liaison Officer for Norway to Adm. Sir William Whitworth (C-in-C Rosyth), 1945. Private Sec. to Sir Maurice Peterson (Ambassador to USSR) and attaché at British Embassy in Moscow, 1946. Mem. Queen's Body Guard for Scotland (Royal Company of Archers), 1948–; called to Scottish Bar, 1950; Mem. of Lloyd's, 1952–. Chm., Debrett's Peerage, 1977–81. Mem. Advisory Cttee Scottish Nat. Portrait Gallery, 1957–81. President: Assoc. of Genealogists and Record Agents, 1980–; Scottish Genealogy Soc., 1984; Hon. Pres., Dozenal Soc. of GB, 1966–. Hon. Sheriff of Perth and Angus, 1958–. Albany Herald, 1961; DL Perth, 1961. FSA 1959. KStJ 1982. Cross with Swords, Grand Officer of Merit, SMO Malta, 1980; Gold Medal, Constantinian St George, 1982. *Publications:* (with D. Pottinger) Simple Heraldry, 1953; Simple Custom, 1954; Blood Royal, 1956; Map of Scotland of Old, 1960; (with David Hicks) The Highland Clans, 1967, rev. edn 1982; Royal Highness, 1982; (with Jean Goodman) Royal Scotland, 1983. *Recreation:* travel. *Heir:* *s* Earl of Erroll. *Address:* Easter Moncreiffe, by Perth PH2 8QA. *T:* Bridge of Earn 812338; 117 Ashley Gardens, SW1. *T:* 01–828 8421. *Clubs:* Turf, White's, Pratt's, Beefsteak; Royal and Ancient Golf (St Andrews); (Founder) Puffin's, New (Edinburgh).                                    *Died* 27 *Feb.* 1985.

**MONEY, Col Reginald Angel,** CBE 1943; MC 1917; ED; FRCS; FRACS; MB, ChM (Sydney); RAAMC; *b* Sydney, Australia, 3 March 1897; *s* of late Angel Money, MD, FRCP, Harley Street, W1, and of late Mrs Amy Money, 138 Ocean Street, Edgecliff, Sydney; *m* 1937, Dorothy Jean Wilkinson, Strathfield, NSW; two

*d*. *Educ:* Sydney Grammar Sch.; Univ. of Sydney. Enlisted in AIF and was abroad with Australian Field Artillery, 1916–19 (Lt, MC); CO 2/6 Australian Gen. Hosp., AIF, 1940–44 (Col, CBE); MB, ChM from Medical Sch. of Univ. of Sydney, 1923; House Surgeon, Registrar, and Medical Supt, Royal Prince Alfred Hosp., Sydney, 1923–28, Hon. Asst Surgeon, 1928; Hon. Neuro-Surgeon, 1937–57. FRCS 1932; FRACS 1931; Tutor in Surgery, Sydney Univ., 1929–37; Lecturer in Head and Spinal Injuries, 1935–57; Mem., Bd of Directors, Royal Prince Alfred Hospital, Sydney, 1953. Hon. Consulting Neuro-Surgeon, Royal Prince Alfred Hosp., Royal North Shore Hosp., and St George Hosp., Sydney; Visiting Neuro-Surgeon, NSW Masonic Hosp., Sydney. Postgraduate Professional Tours of Great Britain, Europe, USA, Canada, USSR, Mexico, South America, Japan, S Africa, Asia, Romania, Far East, 1928–81. *Publications:* articles and case reports in med. and surgical jls, etc. *Recreations:* swimming, contract bridge, farming. *Address:* 28 Bathurst Street, Woollahra, Sydney, NSW 2025, Australia. *T:* (02) 387-2165. *Clubs:* Australian, Royal Sydney Golf, Australian Jockey (Sydney).                                    *Died* 16 *Jan.* 1984.

**MONEY, Maj.-Gen. Robert Cotton,** CB 1943; MC; psc; *b* 21 July 1888; *o c* of late Col R. C. Money, CMG, CBE; *m* 1st, 1917, Daphne Dorina (*d* 1968), 2nd *d* of Brig.-Gen. C. W. Gartside Spaight, Derry Castle, Killaloe, Ireland; (one *s* killed in action, 1940) one *d*; 2nd, 1978, Evelyn, 3rd *d* of late E. J. Grosstephan. *Educ:* Arnold House, Llandulas; Wellington Coll.; RMC, Sandhurst. Joined Cameronians (Scottish Rifles), 1909; served with both battalions, European War and India; commanded 1st Bn 1931–34; commanded Lucknow Bde, 1936–39; Commandant Senior Officers' Sch., 1939; comd 15th (Scottish) Div., 1940–41; District Comdr, India, 1942–44; retired pay, 1944. Ministry of Transport, 1944–52; retired, 1952. *Recreation:* gardening. *Address:* Moat House, Cholesbury, Tring, Herts.

*Died* 16 *April* 1985.

**MONKS, Constance Mary,** OBE 1962; *b* 20 May 1911; *d* of Ellis Green and Bessie A. Green (*née* Burwell); *m* 1937, Jack Monks (decd); one *s* (decd). *Educ:* Wheelton County Sch.; Chorley Grammar Sch.; City of Leeds Training Coll. Apptd Asst Teacher, 1931. Started retail business as partner with husband, 1945. Councillor (C), Chorley (N Ward), 1947–67, Alderman, 1967–74; Mayor of Chorley, 1959–60; Mem. Lancs CC, 1961–64. MP (C) Chorley, Lancs, 1970–Feb. 1974. JP Chorley, 1954. *Recreations:* reading, needlework.                                    *Died* 4 *Feb.* 1989.

**MONROE, Elizabeth, (Mrs Humphrey Neame),** CMG 1973; MA Oxon; Fellow of St Antony's College, Oxford, 1963–73, then Emeritus Fellow; Hon. Fellow of St Anne's College; *b* 16 Jan. 1905; *d* of late Canon Horace Monroe, Vicar of Wimbledon; *m* 1938, Humphrey Neame (*d* 1968). *Educ:* Putney High Sch., GPDST; St Anne's Coll., Oxford. Secretariat of League of Nations, Geneva, 1931; staff of Royal Institute of International Affairs, 1933; Rockefeller Travelling Fellowship, held in Middle East and French N Africa, 1936–37; Min. of Information, Dir, Middle East Div., 1940; Diplomatic correspondent, The Observer, 1944. UK rep. on UN Sub-Commn for Prevention of Discrimination and Protection of Minorities, 1947–52; staff of Economist Newspaper, London, 1945–58. Leverhulme Research Fellowship, 1969. T. E. Lawrence Medal, Royal Soc. for Asian Affairs, 1980. *Publications:* (with A. H. M. Jones) A History of Abyssinia, 1935; The Mediterranean in Politics, 1938; Britain's Moment in the Middle East: 1914–1956, 1963, rev. edn 1982; The Changing Balance of Power in the Persian Gulf, 1972; Philby of Arabia, 1973; (with Robert Mabro) Oil Producers and Consumers: conflict or cooperation, 1974. *Address:* Flat 11, Ritchie Court, 380 Banbury Road, Oxford OX2 2PW. *T:* Oxford 53778.                                    *Died* 10 *March* 1986.

**MONROE, Hubert Holmes,** QC 1960; Special Commissioner, since 1973, Presiding Commissioner, since 1977; *b* 2 July 1920; *s* of James Harvey Monroe, KC, late of Dublin; *m* 1946, June Elsie, *d* of Harold Lawson Murphy, KC, late of London; one *s* two *d*. *Educ:* Dragon School; Rugby; Corpus Christi Coll., Oxford. Called to the Bar, Middle Temple, 1948; Bencher, 1965; Hon. Treasurer, Senate of the Inns of Court and the Bar, 1975–77. Hamlyn Lectr, 1981 (Intolerable Inquisition? Reflections on the Law of Tax). Commodore, Island Cruising Club, 1972–78. *Address:* 83 Rennie Court, Upper Ground, SE1 9NZ. *T:* 01-633 0562. *Club:* Garrick.

*Died* 5 *June* 1982.

**MONTAGU, Hon. Ewen Edward Samuel,** CBE 1950 (OBE mil. 1944); QC 1939; The Judge Advocate of the Fleet, 1945–73; Hon. Captain RNR, 1973; *b* 29 March 1901; 2nd *s* of 2nd Baron Swaythling; *m* 1923, Iris Rachel, *d* of late Solomon J. Solomon, RA; one *s* one *d*. *Educ:* Westminster Sch.; Harvard Univ.; Trinity Coll., Cambridge (MA, LLB). Called to Bar, Middle Temple, 1924, Bencher, 1948, Treas., 1968; Western Circuit. Recorder of Devizes, 1944–51, of Southampton, 1951–60; Chairman of Quarter Sessions: Hampshire, 1951–60 (Dep. Chm., 1948–51, and 1960–71)); Middlesex, 1956–65 (Asst Chm., 1951–54; Dep. Chm., 1954–56); Middlesex Area of Gtr London, 1965–69; Judge, 1969; Chm. Central Council of

Magistrates' Courts Cttees, 1963–71 (Vice-Chm., 1954–63). Pres. United Synagogue, 1954–62; Vice-President: Anglo-Jewish Assoc.; Nat. Addiction and Research Inst., 1969; Chm. Gen. Purposes Cttee, RYA, 1960–68; RYA Award, 1972. DL County of Southampton, 1953. RNVR, 1939–45. Order of the Crown, Yugoslavia, 1943. *Publications:* The Man Who Never Was, 1953; The Archer-Shee Case, 1974; Beyond "Top Secret U", 1977. *Recreations:* sailing, fly-fishing, shooting, beagling, golf, painting, grandchildren, great grandchildren. *Address:* 24 Montrose Court, Exhibition Road, SW7 2QQ. *T:* 01–589 9999; Warren Beach, Beaulieu, Hants. *T:* Bucklers Hard 239. *Clubs:* Royal Ocean Racing, Bar Yacht (Hon. Commodore).                    *Died* 19 *July* 1985.

**MONTAGU, (Hon.) Ivor (Goldsmid Samuel);** author; *b* 23 April 1904; 3rd *s* of 2nd Baron Swaythling; *m* 1927, Eileen (*d* 1984), *d* of late Francis Anton Hellstern. *Educ:* Westminster Sch.; Royal Coll. of Science, London; King's Coll., Cambridge. Pres. and/or Chm., (Ping Pong Assoc., then Table Tennis Assoc., then) English Table Tennis Assoc., 1922–33, 1936–66, Life Vice-Pres., 1970–; Pres. and Chm., International Table Tennis Fedn, 1926–67, Life Founder Pres. 1967–; Chm., Film Soc., 1925–39; film critic, editor, director, writer, producer, 1925–. Hon. Member: Assoc. of Cine and Television Technicians, 1970; Writers Guild, 1964; Editorial Staff, Daily Worker, 1932–33 and 1937–47; Mem. Secretariat and Bureau, World Council of Peace, 1948–67, Presidential Cttee, 1969–72; Pres., Soc. for Cultural Relations with USSR, 1973–82. Order of Liberation, 1st Class (Bulgaria), 1952; Lenin Peace Prize, 1959; Order of Pole Star (Mongolia), 1963; Lenin Centenary Commemoration Medal, 1970; Dimitrov Anniv. Medal, 1972; Mongolian Peace Medal, 1973; Dimitrov Centenary Medal, 1983; Star of International Friendship, GDR, 1984. *Publications:* Table Tennis Today, 1924; Table Tennis, 1936; The Traitor Class, 1940; Plot against Peace, 1952; Land of Blue Sky, 1956; Film World, 1964; Germany's New Nazis, 1967; With Eisenstein in Hollywood, 1968; The Youngest Son (Vol. I of memoirs), 1970; numerous scenarios, translations, pamphlets, articles on current affairs, contribs to Proc. Zool. Soc. London. *Recreations:* washing up, pottering about, sleeping through television. *Address:* Old Timbers, Verdure Close, Watford WD2 7NJ. *Clubs:* MCC; Hampshire County Cricket.                    *Died* 5 *Nov.* 1984.

**MONTAGU-POLLOCK, Sir George Seymour;** *see* Pollock.

**MONTAGUE, Leslie Clarence;** Chairman, Johnson Matthey & Co. Ltd, 1966–71; *b* 28 May 1901; *s* of Albert Edward Montague and Clara Amelia Chapman; *m* 1926, Ellen Rose Margaret Keene; no *c. Educ:* Bancroft's School, Woodford. 50 years' service with Johnson Matthey & Co. Ltd; appointed Secretary, 1934, and a Director, 1946. *Recreations:* walking, gardening. *Address:* Firle House, Firle Road, Seaford, East Sussex.                    *Died* 3 *Oct.* 1986.

**MONTAGUE-SMITH, Patrick Wykeham;** Editor of Debrett, 1962–80, Consulting Editor since 1980; *b* 3 Jan. 1920; *o s* of late Major Vernon Milner Montague-Smith, Richmond, Surrey, and Sybil Katherine, *d* of late William Wykeham Frederick Bourne, Kensington, and Fockbury House, Worcs; *m* 1974, Annabelle Christina Calvert, *o d* of late Noël Newton, MA and Isabella Newton, 65 Abbotsbury Close, Kensington, W14. *Educ:* Lynfield, Hunstanton and Mercers' Sch. Served RASC, 8 Corps, 1940–46; in NW Europe, 1944–46. Asst Editor of Debrett, 1946–62. Dir, Debrett's Peerage Ltd, 1976–81. A Vice-Pres., English Genealogical Congress, Cambridge, 1975; Vice-Pres., Assoc. of Genealogists and Record Agents, 1983–; Fellow, Soc. of Genealogists, 1969–; Member: Heraldry Soc.; Soc. of Descendants of Knights of the Garter (Windsor). Freeman of the City of London. *Publications:* Royal Line of Succession, 1953; The Prince of Wales, 1958; Princess Margaret, 1961; Debrett's Correct Form, 1970, new edn 1976; Debrett's Royal Wedding: HRH Princess Anne and Captain Mark Phillips, 1973; The Royal Year, 1974, 1975, 1976, (contribs) 1977–; The Country Life Book of the Royal Silver Jubilee (1977), 1976; (with Charles Kidd) The Royal Betrothal, 1981; (with Hugh Montgomery-Massingberd) The Country Life Book of Royal Palaces, Castles and Homes, 1981; (with Charles Kidd) Debrett's Book of Royal Children, 1982; Queen Elizabeth The Queen Mother, 1985; contribs to Encyclopædia Britannica and various journals and newspapers, principally on genealogy, heraldry, royal and historical subjects, also lectures, television and broadcasts. *Recreations:* genealogy, heraldry, British history, visiting country houses and browsing in bookshops. *Address:* Brereton, 197 Park Road, Kingston upon Thames, Surrey. *T:* 01–546 8807.                    *Died* 26 *Jan.* 1986.

**MONTALE, Eugenio;** Italian poet; Literary and music critic, Corriere della Sera, since 1948; *b* Genoa, 12 Oct. 1896; *s* of Domenico Montale and Giuseppina (*née* Ricci); *m* Drusilla Tanzi (*d* 1963). *Educ:* studied opera singing under Ernesto Sivon; served as Infantry officer, 1917–18; jt founder Primo Tempo, 1922; on staff of Bemporad, Florence, 1927; curator of Gabinetto Vieussex Library, 1928–38; poetry critic, La Fiera Letteraria, 1938–48. Life Mem., Italian Senate, 1967. Feltrinelli Prize, 1963–64; Calouste

Gulbenkian Prize, Paris, 1971; Nobel Prize for Literature, 1975. Hon. degrees from Univs of Milan, Rome and Cambridge. Works trans. into English and other languages. *Publications: poetry:* Ossi di seppia, 1925; La casa dei doganieri, 1932 (Antico Fattore Poetry Prize); Quaterno di traduzione, 1948; Le occasioni, 1948; La bufèra e altro, 1956 (Premio Manzotto); Satura, 1962, Xenia, 1966, published together as Satura, 1971; Diario del '71 e del '72, 1973; Tutte le poesie, 1977; Quaderno di quattro anni, 1978; *prose:* La farfalla di Dinard (autobiog.), 1956; Auto da fé, 1966; Furori di casa, 1969; Sulla poesia, 1978; Selected Essays, 1978; contribs to anthologies and jls. *Recreations:* music and art. *Address:* c/o Corriere della Sera, Milan, Italy; Via Bigli 11, Milan, Italy.
                    *Died* 12 *Sept.* 1981.

**MONTAND, Simone H. C.;** *see* Signoret, Simone.

**MONTEATH, Robert Campbell,** CBE 1964; County Clerk, Treasurer and Local Taxation Officer, Kirkcudbright, 1946–72, and Clerk to the Lieutenancy, since 1966; *b* 15 June 1907; *s* of Gordon Drysdale Monteath, Dumbarton; *m* 1936, Sarah McGregor, *d* of John Fenwick, Dumbarton; two *s* one *d. Educ:* Dumbarton Academy; Glasgow Univ. Dep. County Clerk, Dunbartonshire, 1937–46; Dep. Civil Defence Controller, 1939–46; Hon. Sheriff, Kirkcudbright, 1966–. Past District Governor, Rotary Internat., District 102. *Address:* Gortonbrae, Townhead, Kirkcudbright. *T:* Townhead 251. *Clubs:* Royal Over-Seas League; Royal Scottish Automobile (Glasgow).                    *Died* 14 *Nov.* 1985.

**MONTEITH, Brig. John Cassels,** CBE 1968; MC 1938; JP; Colonel, The Black Watch, 1976–81; *b* 28 Sept. 1915; *s* of Lt-Col John Cassels Monteith (killed in action 1915), Moniaive, Dumfriesshire, and of Mrs Jane Robertson Monteith (*née* Wilson), Dunning, Perthshire; *m* 1st, 1949, Winifred Elisabeth (*d* 1968), *d* of Louis Cecil Breitmeyer, Kettering; one *s* one *d*; 2nd, 1973, Pamela Joan, *d* of Col Francis E. Laughton, MC, TD. *Educ:* Stowe; Trinity Coll., Cambridge (BA). 2nd Lieut Black Watch, 1935; served War 1939–45, ME, Italy and NW Europe; CO 1st Bn Black Watch, 1957–59; Col 1961; Comdr 155 (L) Inf. Bde, TA, 1962–65; Brig. 1963; Defence and Mil. Attaché, Bonn, 1965–68; Comdr Highland Area, 1968–70; retd 1970. Chm., Highland TAVR Assoc., 1971–76. Brig., Queen's Body Guard for Scotland (Royal Company of Archers), 1972. JP Perthshire, 1972. *Recreations:* shooting, gardening. *Address:* Essendy House, Blairgowrie, Perthshire. *T:* Essendy 260. *Clubs:* Army and Navy; Royal Perth.                    *Died* 21 *April* 1983.

**MONTGOMERY of Blessingbourne, Captain Peter Stephen;** Vice-Lieutenant of County Tyrone, Northern Ireland, 1971–79; *b* 13 Aug. 1909; 2nd *s* of late Maj.-Gen. Hugh Maude de Fellenberg Montgomery, CB, CMG, DL, RA, and late Mary, 2nd *d* of Edmund Langton and Mrs Massingberd, Gunby Hall, Lincs. *Educ:* Wellington Coll.; Trinity Coll., Cambridge (MA). Founder, 1927, and Conductor until 1969, of Fivemiletown Choral Soc.; employed with BBC in N Ireland and London, 1931–47; Asst Music Dir and Conductor, BBC Northern Ireland Symphony Orchestra, 1933–38. Served War of 1939–45: Captain, Royal Intelligence Corps, ADC to Viceroy of India (FM Earl Wavell), 1945–46. Mem. BBC Northern Ireland Advisory Council, 1952–71, and BBC Gen. Adv. Council, 1963–71. Hon. ADC to Governor of Northern Ireland (Lord Wakehurst), 1954–64; Member: National Trust Cttee for NI, 1955–75; Bd of Visitors, HM Prison, Belfast (Chm. 1971); Friends of National Collections of Ireland; Bd of Arts Council of NI (Pres., 1964–74). JP 1959, DL 1956, Co. Tyrone; High Sheriff of Co. Tyrone, 1964. Hon. LLD Queen's Univ. Belfast, 1976. Silver Jubilee Medal, 1977. *Address:* Blessingbourne, Fivemiletown, Co. Tyrone, Northern Ireland. *Clubs:* Oriental; Ulster (Belfast); Tyrone County (Omagh).                    *Died* 24 *Feb.* 1988.

**MOODY, Theodore William,** MA, PhD; Hon. DLit; Corr. FBA; Professor of Modern History, Dublin University, and Fellow of Trinity College, Dublin, 1939–77, later Fellow Emeritus; *b* 26 Nov. 1907; *o s* of William J. Moody, Belfast, and Ann I. Dippie; *m* 1935, Margaret C. P. Robertson, LLB, Bristol; one *s* four *d. Educ:* Royal Academical Instn, Belfast; Queen's Univ., Belfast (BA Mediæval and Modern Hist., 1930); Inst. of Historical Research, Univ. of London, 1930–32 (PhD 1934). FRHistS 1934; MRIA 1940. Queen's Univ., Belfast: Asst in History, 1932–35; Lectr in History, 1935–39. Trinity Coll., Dublin: Fellow and Prof., 1939–77; Tutor, 1939–52 (MA 1941); Sen. Tutor, 1952–58; Sen. Lectr, 1958–64; first Dean, Faculty of Arts, 1967–69. Hon. Treasurer, Social Service Co., TCD, 1942–53, Chm. 1953–. Member: Irish MSS Commn, 1943–; Adv. Cttee on Cultural Relations, Ireland, 1949–63; Govt Commn on Higher Educn in Ireland, 1960–67; Comhairle Radio Eireann (Irish Broadcasting Council), 1953–60; Irish Broadcasting Authority, 1960–72. Leverhulme Res. Fellow, 1964–66. Mem., Sch. of Historical Studies, Inst. for Advanced Study, Princeton, 1965; Mem., Acad. Council, Irish Sch. of Ecumenics, 1972– (Exec. Bd, 1978–). Jt Editor, Irish Historical Studies, 1937–77; Editor, Studies in Irish History, 1st series, 1944–56, 2nd series, 1960–75; Chm., Bd of Editors, A New History of Ireland, 1968–. Hon. DLit, Queen's

Univ., Belfast, 1959; Hon. DLit NUI, 1978; Corr. FBA, 1977; Hon. life mem., RDS, 1983. *Publications:* The Londonderry Plantation, 1609–41: the City of London and the plantation in Ulster, 1939; The Irish Parliament under Elizabeth and James I: a general survey (Proc. of RIA, vol xiv, sect C, no 6), 1939; Thomas Davis, 1814–45, 1945; (with J. C. Beckett) Queen's, Belfast, 1845–1949: the history of a university, 1959; The Ulster Question 1603–1973, 1974; Davitt and Irish Revolution, 1846–82, 1981; *Editor and contributor:* (with H. A. Cronne and D. B. Quinn) Essays in British and Irish History in honour of J. E. Todd, 1949; (with J. C. Beckett) Ulster since 1800, 1st series, 1955, 2nd series, 1957; (with F. X. Martin) The Course of Irish History, 1967; Historical Studies vi, 1968; The Fenian Movement, 1968; Irish Historiography 1936–70, 1971; (with F. X. Martin and F. J. Byrne) A New History of Ireland, vol. iii, 1976, vol. viii, 1982, vol. ix, 1983; Nationality and the Pursuit of National Independence, 1978; *Editor:* Ulster Plantation Papers, 1608–13 (Analecta Hibernica, no 8), 1938; An Irish Countryman in the British Navy, 1809–1815: the memoirs of Henry Walsh (The Irish Sword, iv–v, nos 16–21), 1960–62; (with J. G. Simms) The Bishopric of Derry and the Irish Society of London, 1602–1705, 2 vols, 1968, 1983; Michael Davitt's Leaves from a Prison Diary, repr. 1972; various contribs on modern Irish history, the Irish in America, the Irish university question, and on Michael Davitt 1846–1906 (in Irish Historical Studies, Studies, History, Trans of Royal Hist. Soc., Hermathena). *Festschrift:* Ireland under the Union: essays in honour of T. W. Moody (ed F. S. L. Lyons and R. A. J. Hawkins), 1980. *Recreations:* listening to music, walking. *Address:* 25 Trinity College, Dublin. *Died* 11 Feb. 1984.

**MOON, Maj.-Gen. Alan Neilson,** CB 1966; CBE 1961; Director, Army Dental Service, 1963–66; *b* 10 June 1906; *s* of late E. W. Moon, Weston-super-Mare; *m* 1st, 1933, Joyce Beatrix (marr. diss., 1943), *d* of E. E. Searles, Bristol; one *d*; 2nd, 1961, Dorothy Mary, ARRC, *d* of W. H. Wilson, Blairgowrie. *Educ:* Queen's Coll., Taunton; Univ. of Bristol. LDS 1930; commnd Lieut, The Army Dental Corps, 1931; Captain 1934; Major 1941; Lt-Col 1948; Col 1956; Brig. 1959; Maj.-Gen. 1963. Served: India, 1939–45; Middle East, 1950–53; Dep. Dir Dental Service Western Command, 1956, Southern Command, 1957; Asst Dir, War Office, 1958–63. OStJ 1961. *Address:* Fulwood, Torphins, Aberdeenshire AB3 4JS. *T:* Torphins 384. *Died* 2 Feb. 1981.

**MOON, Sir Edward,** 5th Bt *cr* 1887; MC 1944; retired; *b* 23 Feb. 1911; *s* of Jasper Moon (*d* 1975) (*g s* of 1st Bt) and Isabel Moon (*née* Logan) (*d* 1961); *S* cousin, Sir John Arthur Moon, 4th Bt, 1979; *m* 1947, Mary, *d* of late Captain B. D. Conolly, RAMC. *Educ:* Sedbergh. Farming, Kenya, 1934–62. Served 1939–45, King's African Rifles (Major). *Recreations:* gardening, cooking, fishing and all games. *Heir: b* Roger Moon [*b* 17 Nov. 1914; *m* 1950, Meg, *d* of late Arthur Mainwaring Maxwell, DSO, MC; three *d*]. *Address:* c/o Midland Bank, Oswestry, Salop. *Died* 14 Sept. 1988.

**MOON, Sir (Edward) Penderel,** Kt 1962; OBE 1941; *b* 13 Nov. 1905; *s* of Dr R. O. Moon, FRCP; *m* 1966, Pauline Marion (marr. diss.), *d* of Rev. W. E. C. Barns. *Educ:* Winchester; New Coll., Oxford (MA). Fellow of All Souls College, Oxford, 1927–35 and 1965–72. Entered ICS, 1929, resigned, 1944; Sec., Development Board and Planning Advisory Board, Govt of India; Min. of Revenue and Public Works, Bahawalpur State; Chief Comr, Himachal Pradesh; Chief Comr, Manipur; Adviser, Planning Commission. Editor, India Office Records on Transfer of Power, 1972–82. *Publications:* Strangers in India; The Future of India; Warren Hastings and British India; Divide and Quit; Gandhi and Modern India; Disbelief in God; (ed) Wavell: the Viceroy's Journal; *posthumous publication:* The British Conquest and Dominion of India, 1989. *Recreations:* hunting, shooting and singing. *Address:* Manor Farm, Wotton Underwood, Aylesbury, Bucks. *Died* 2 June 1987.

**MOON, Prof. Harold Philip,** MA Cantab; Professor of Zoology, University of Leicester, 1950–70, then Professor Emeritus; *b* 15 Jan. 1910; *er s* of Harold Joseph Moon, LRCP, MRCS, and Beatrice Sarah, *yr d* of George Greenwood; *m* 1939, Ruth Hannah, *er d* of late Capt. E. Rivenhall Goffe, RAOC (Retd); three *s* one *d*. *Educ:* Bootham Sch., York; King's Coll., Cambridge. Asst Naturalist, Freshwater Biological Assoc., 1933–35; Asst Research Officer, Avon Biological Research, University Coll., Southampton, 1936–39 (on leave of absence, Percy Sladen expedn to Lake Titicaca, S America, 1937); Asst Lecturer, Dept of Zoology, Manchester, 1939; Demonstrator, Bedford Coll. for Women, Univ. of London, 1941; Junior Scientific Officer, Operational Research, MAP, 1942; Insect Infestation Branch, MOF, 1943–45; promoted Sen. Inspector, 1944; Lecturer in Charge, Dept of Zoology, University Coll., Leicester, 1945–50. *Publications:* papers on freshwater biology in scientific journals. *Recreation:* walking. *Address:* The Beeches, 48 Elmfield Avenue, Stoneygate, Leicester LE2 1RD. *T:* Leicester 707625. *Died* 26 March 1982.

**MOON, Sir Penderel;** *see* Moon, Sir E. P.

**MOON, Lieut (Hon. Captain) Rupert Vance,** VC 1917; *b* Bacchus Marsh, 1892; *s* of Arthur Moon, of the Nat. Bank of Australasia, Melbourne; *m* 1931, Susan Alison May, *yr d* of Robert Vincent, Prospect House, Geelong; one *s* one *d*. *Educ:* Kyneton Grammar Sch. Served European War (VC). Formerly Accountant, National Bank of Australasia Ltd, Geelong; Gen. Manager, Dennys Lascelles Ltd, retd 1960, and Dir, retd 1975. *Address:* 13 Bostock Avenue, Barwon Heads, Vic 3227, Australia. *Clubs:* Melbourne, Naval and Military, Victorian Racing, Moonee Valley Racing (Melbourne); Geelong, Geelong Racing (Geelong); Victoria Amateur Turf (Caulfield); Barwon Heads Golf. *Died* 28 Feb. 1986.

**MOORE, Maj.-Gen. Denis Grattan,** CB 1960; DL; retired; *b* 15 March 1909; *s* of Col F. G. Moore, CBE and Marian, *d* of Very Rev. W. H. Stone, Dean of Kilmore; *m* 1st, 1932, Alexandra, *d* of W. H. Wann; two *d*; 2nd, 1946, Beatrice Glynn, *d* of W. S. Williamson; one adopted *d*. *Educ:* Wellington Coll.; Royal Military College, Sandhurst (cadet schol., 1928). Commissioned 1929, Royal Inniskilling Fusiliers; RMCS, 1935–37 (pac, sac); Sec., Ordnance Bd, 1938; Staff Coll., Quetta, 1939–40 (psc); GHQ India, 1940; GSO1, HQ Tenth Army, 1941; special duties, N Persia, 1941–42; Asst Dir of Artillery (Weapons), HQ Eighth Army, 1943–44; GSO1, War Office, 1946 (Technical and Scientific Intell.); Parachute Regt, 1948–50; Mil. Security Bd, Berlin, 1950; comd 1 Inniskillings, 1951–52; GSO1 (Col) War Office, 1952–54 (Technical Intell.); comd 47 Infantry Bde, TA, 1954–57; Dep. Comd, RMCS, 1957–58; Dir of Weapons and Development, War Office, 1958–60; Dir of Equipment Policy, War Office, 1960–61; Chief, Jt Services Liaison Staff, BAOR, 1961–63. Col, The Royal Inniskilling Fusiliers, 1960–66. Chm., Ulster Timber Growers Organisation, 1965–81. High Sheriff, Co. Tyrone, 1969; DL Co. Tyrone, 1974. *Publications:* pamphlets and articles on the oceanic forest. *Recreation:* palæontological research (forest and fish). *Address:* 26 Headbourne Worthy House, Winchester SO23 7JG. *T:* Winchester 881631. *Club:* Naval and Military. *Died* 16 Feb. 1987.

**MOORE, Mrs D(oris) Langley,** OBE 1971; FRSL; Founder (1955) and former Adviser, Museum of Costume, Assembly Rooms, Bath; author; *b* 23 July 1902; *m* 1926, Robert Sugden Moore (decd); one *d*. Has done varied literary work in connection with films, television, and ballet, and has specialized in promoting the study of costume by means of exhibns and lectures in England and abroad. Designer of clothes for period films. *Publications: fiction:* A Winter's Passion, 1932; The Unknown Eros, 1935; They Knew Her When . . ., 1938 (subseq. re-published as A Game of Snakes and Ladders); Not at Home, 1948; All Done by Kindness, 1951; My Caravaggio Style, 1959; *non-fiction:* Anacreon: 29 Odes, 1926; The Technique of the Love Affair, 1928; Pandora's Letter Box, A Discourse on Fashionable Life, 1929; E. Nesbit, A Biography, 1933 (rev. 1966); The Vulgar Heart, An Enquiry into the Sentimental Tendencies of Public Opinion, 1945; The Woman in Fashion, 1949; The Child in Fashion, 1953; Pleasure, A Discursive Guide Book, 1953; The Late Lord Byron, 1961; Marie and the Duke of H, The Daydream Love Affair of Marie Bashkirtseff, 1966; Fashion through Fashion Plates, 1771–1970, 1971; Lord Byron: Accounts Rendered, 1974 (Rose Mary Crawshay Prize, awarded by British Academy, 1975); Ada, Countess of Lovelace, 1977; Doris Langley Moore's Book of Scraps, 1984; (with June Langley Moore): Our Loving Duty, 1932; The Pleasure of Your Company, 1933. *Recreation:* Byron research. *Address:* 5 Prince Albert Road, NW1. *Died* 24 Feb. 1989.

**MOORE, the Worshipful Chancellor the Rev. E(velyn) Garth;** barrister-at-law; Chancellor, Vicar-General and Official Principal: of Diocese of Durham, 1954–89, later Chancellor Emeritus; of Diocese of Southwark since 1948; of Diocese of Gloucester since 1957 (and Official Principal of Archdeaconries of Lewisham, Southwark, Kingston-on-Thames and Ely); Vicar, Guild Church of St Mary Abchurch, London, 1972, Priest-in-Charge since 1980; Fellow of Corpus Christi College, Cambridge, since 1947, and formerly Lecturer in Law (Director of Studies in Law, 1947–72); *b* 6 Feb. 1906; *y s* of His Honour the late Judge (Robert Ernest) Moore and late Hilda Mary, *d* of Rev. John Davis Letts; unmarried. *Educ:* The Hall, Belsize Sch.; Durham Sch.; Trinity Coll., Cambridge (MA); Cuddesdon Theol Coll., 1962. Deacon, 1962; Priest, 1962. Called to Bar, Gray's Inn, 1928; SE Circuit. Formerly: Tutor of Gray's Inn; Lector of Trinity Coll., Cambridge; Mem. Gen. Council of Bar and of Professional Conduct Cttee. Commnd 2nd Lt RA, 1940; Major on staff of JAG; served at WO and throughout Great Britain, N Ireland, Paiforce, Middle East (for a time local Lt-Col), Greece, etc. Mem. of Church Assembly (for Dio. Ely), 1955–62; a Church Comr, 1964–77; Mem., Legal Adv. Commn (formerly Legal Bd of C of E), 1956–86 (Chm., 1972–86). High Bailiff of Ely Cathedral, 1961–86. JP and Dep. Chm. of QS, Hunts, 1948–63 and Cambs, 1959–63; Lectr in Criminal Procedure, Council of Legal Educn, 1957–68, Lectr in Evidence, 1952–68. Council, St David's Coll., Lampeter, 1949–65 and Westcott House, 1961–65; Mem. Governing Body, St Chad's Coll., Durham, 1955–78. Legal Assessor to Disciplinary Cttee, RCVS, 1963–68. Pres., Churches' Fellowship for Psychical and Spiritual Studies, 1963–83. Pres., Sion Coll., 1977–78. Vis. Prof.,

Khartoum Univ., 1961. Mere's Preacher, Cambridge Univ., 1965. DCL Lambeth, 1986. *Publications:* An Introduction to English Canon Law, 1966; 8th Edn (with Suppl.) of Kenny's Cases on Criminal Law; (jt) Ecclesiastical Law, in Halsbury's Laws of England (3rd edn); Believe it or Not: Christianity and psychical research, 1977; The Church's Ministry of Healing, 1977; (ed jtly) Macmorran Elphinstone and Moore's A Handbook for Churchwardens and Parochial Church Councillors, 1980; (with Timothy Briden) Moore's Introduction to English Canon Law, 1985; various contribs mainly to legal and theological jls. *Recreations:* travel, architecture, furniture, etc, psychical research. *Address:* Corpus Christi College, Cambridge CB2 1RH. *T:* Cambridge (0223) 338000; 1 Raymond Buildings, Gray's Inn, WC1R 5BH. *T:* 071–242 3734; St Mary Abchurch, EC4N 7BA. *T:* 071–626 0306. *Clubs:* Gresham; Pitt (Cambridge). *Died 5 June 1990.*

**MOORE, Frederick Thomas,** OBE 1943; FRCS, FRCSE; Consulting Plastic Surgeon to King's College Hospital, London, since 1948; Plastic Unit East Grinstead since 1948; *b* 19 Oct. 1913; *s* of Francis Moore and Rose Perry; *m* 1957, Margrethe Johanne Holland (actress, as Greta Gynt); one *d*. *Educ:* St Bartholomew's Hosp. MRCS, LRCP 1936; FRCSE 1939; FRCS 1945. Served War of 1939–45 (OBE): RAF, Plastic Surgeon, 1939–48. Mem. Council, British Assoc. Plastic Surgeons, 1949. Founder Mem., British Hand Club. Legion of Honour, 1948. *Publications:* numerous on surgical problems. *Recreations:* golf, sailing, writing, research (medical). *Address:* L'Annonciade, ave L'Annonciade, Monte-Carlo. *T:* 504600. *Clubs:* Royal Thames Yacht; Monaco Yacht. *Died 21 June 1983.*

**MOORE, Geoffrey Ernest,** CBE 1977; FCIS, FIMI; Director, Vauxhall Motors Ltd, retired 1981 (Chairman, 1979–81); *b* 31 Dec. 1916; *s* of late Charles Frederick Moore and Alice Isobel (*née* Large); *m* 1950, Olive Christine Moore; one *s* one *d*. *Educ:* Dunstable Grammar Sch. FCIS 1975; FIMI 1973. Served War, Armed Forces, 1939–45. Joined Vauxhall Motors, 1933; returned to Vauxhall Motors, Sales Dept, 1946; Asst Sales Manager, 1953; Domestic Sales Manager, 1955; Sales Dir, 1967; Dir of Govt and Public Relations, 1971; Dir of Personnel and Govt and Public Relations, 1974; Chm., Stampings Alliance Ltd (Vauxhall Subsid.), 1974–81; Asst to Man. Dir, 1975. Vice-Pres., Inst. of Motor Industry, 1972–83; Pres., Luton Indust. Coll., 1984– (Vice-Pres., 1973–84); Pres., SMMT, 1981–82; Member: Eastern Reg. Council, CBI, 1975–79; Council, CBI, 1981–84; Exec. Council, Soc. of the Irish Motor Industry, 1981–. Trustee, National Motor Mus., Beaulieu; Hon. Pres., Luton Coll. of Higher Educn. Silver Jubilee Medal, 1977. *Recreations:* golf, gardening. *Address:* Windyridge, Little Gaddesden, Berkhamsted, Herts HP4 1QE. *T:* Little Gaddesden 2431. *Died 13 Sept. 1989.*

**MOORE, Gerald,** CBE 1954; FRCM; pianoforte accompanist; *b* Watford, Herts, 30 July 1899; *e s* of David Frank Moore, Tiverton, Devon; *m* Enid Kathleen, *d* of Montague Richard, Beckenham, Kent. *Educ:* Watford Grammar Sch.; Toronto Univ. Studied piano in Toronto; toured Canada as a boy pianist; returning to England, devoted himself to accompanying and chamber music. Associated with world's leading singers and instrumentalists. Festivals of Edinburgh, Salzburg, Holland, etc. Retired from concert platform, 1967. Ensemble Classes in USA, Tokyo, Stockholm, Helsinki, Dartington Hall, Salzburg Mozarteum, London S Bank Fest. Awarded Cobbett Gold Medal, 1951, for services to Chamber Music; Pres. Incorporated Soc. of Musicians, 1962. FRCM 1980. Hon. RAM 1962. Grand Prix du Disque: Amsterdam, 1968, 1970; Paris, 1970; Granados Medal, Barcelona, 1971; Hugo Wolf Medal, Vienna, 1973. Hon. DLitt Sussex, 1968; Hon. MusD Cambridge, 1973. *Publications:* The Unashamed Accompanist, 1943, rev. edn 1957, enlarged edn 1984; Careers in Music, 1950; Singer and Accompanist, 1953, repr. 1982; Am I Too Loud?, 1962; The Schubert Song Cycles, 1975; Farewell Recital, 1978; Poet's Love and other Schumann Songs, 1981; Furthermoore: interludes in an accompanist's life, 1983; Collected Memoirs, 1986; arrangements of songs and folk songs. *Recreations:* walking, reading, bridge. *Address:* Pond House, Penn, Bucks. *T:* Penn 3038. *Died 13 March 1987.*

**MOORE, Brig. Guy Newton,** CBE 1941; DFC; ED; Chartered Accountant, retired; *b* 13 Jan. 1893; *s* of A. Capper and Alice Eleanor Moore; *m* 1922, Marguerite Thompson; three *d*. *Educ:* Wesley Coll., Melbourne. Served with Royal Flying Corps and Royal Air Force (Capt.), 1916–18; Hon. Sqdn Leader, Citizens Air Force (Australia); Chief Paymaster, AIF. Dir of Finance Administration, Australian Commonwealth Forces, 1939–45, Brigadier. *Recreations:* golf, swimming, bowls. *Address:* 5 Brandon Road, Brighton, Vic 3186, Australia. *Clubs:* Naval and Military, Emerald Country, RACV (Melbourne); Royal Federation of Aero Clubs. *Died Feb. 1984.*

**MOORE, Harry T(hornton);** Research Professor, Southern Illinois University, 1957–78, then Emeritus; *b* Oakland, California, 2 Aug.

1908; *s* of Lt-Col H. T. Moore, US Army; *m* 1st, Winifred Sheehan; one *s* one *d*; 2nd, 1946, Beatrice Walker. *Educ:* Univ. of Chicago (PhB); Northwestern Univ. (MA); Boston Univ. (PhD). Instructor: Ill. Inst. of Techn., 1940–41; Inst., Northwestern Univ., 1941–42. Served USAAF, 2nd World War (Asst Sec. of Air Staff, 1944–45), later Lt-Col USAF Reserve. Chm., Dept of Hist. and Lit., Babson Inst., 1947–57 (subseq. Babson Coll.); Prof. of English, Southern Illinois Univ., 1957–63. Visiting Professor: Univ. of Colorado, 1959 and 1962–63; Columbia Univ. and New York Univ., 1961; Staff Mem., Univ. of Nottingham Lawrence Summer Sch., 1971, 1975. Pres. of Coll. English Assoc., 1961. Co-Editor: series: Crosscurrents/Modern Critiques; Crosscurrents: Modern Fiction; on editorial adv. boards of Virginia Woolf Qly, D. H. Lawrence Rev., and English Language Notes. FRSL 1952–; Guggenheim Fellowships, 1958, 1960. *Publications:* The Novels of John Steinbeck, 1939; The Life and Works of D. H. Lawrence, 1951; The Intelligent Heart, 1955; Poste Restante, 1956; E. M. Forster, 1965; 20th Century French Literature (2 vols), 1966; The Age of the Modern, 1971; The Priest of Love: a life of D. H. Lawrence, 1974 (filmed 1980); Henry James and his World, 1974; Co-author: D. H. Lawrence and his World: a Pictorial Biography, 1966; 20th Century German Literature, 1967; (jtly) 20th Century Russian Literature, 1974; Co-Editor: The Achievement of D. H. Lawrence, 1953; The Human Prospect (by Lewis Mumford), 1956; Phœnix II: Uncollected, Unpublished and other Prose Works by D. H. Lawrence, 1968; The Richard Aldington-Lawrence Durrell Correspondence, 1980; Frieda Lawrence and her Circle, 1980; Co-Translator: Tragedy is Not Enough (by Karl Jaspers); Editor: D. H. Lawrence's Letters to Bertrand Russell, 1948; D. H. Lawrence's Essays on Sex, Literature, and Censorship, 1953; A D. H. Lawrence Miscellany, 1959; Selected Letters of Rainer Maria Rilke, 1960; The World of Lawrence Durrell, 1962; The Collected Letters of D. H. Lawrence, 1962 (2 vols); Contemporary American Novelists, 1964; The Elizabethan Age, 1965; contributed NY Times Book Review; Saturday Review; Kenyon Review; New Republic, etc. *Recreation:* listening to Shakespearean recordings. *Address:* 922 South Division Street, Carterville, Illinois 62918, USA. *T:* 618-985-2014. *Clubs:* Cliff Dwellers (Chicago); PEN. *Died 11 April 1981.*

**MOORE, Henry,** OM 1963; CH 1955; FBA 1966; Hon. FRIBA; sculptor; *b* Castleford, Yorks, 30 July 1898; *s* of Raymond Spencer Moore and Mary Baker; *m* 1929, Irene Radetzky; one *d*. *Educ:* Castleford Grammar Sch. After serving European War, 1917–19, in Army, studied at Leeds Sch. of Art and Royal College of Art. Official War Artist, 1940–42. A Trustee: Tate Gallery, 1941–48 and 1949–56; National Gallery, 1955–63 and 1964–74; Member: Arts Council, 1963–67; Royal Fine Art Commn, 1947–71. Formed Henry Moore Foundation, 1977. *Major exhibitions of his work held:* London 1928, 1931, 1933, 1935, 1936, 1940, 1945, 1946, 1948, 1951, 1953, 1955, 1960, 1961, 1963, 1965, 1967, 1968, 1974, 1975, 1976, 1978, 1983; Leeds, 1941; New York, 1946; Chicago, 1947; San Francisco, 1947; Australia Tour, 1947; Venice Biennale, 1948 (of which he was awarded First Prize for Sculpture); Europe Tour, 1949–51; Cape Town, 1951; Scandinavian Tour, 1952–53; Rotterdam, 1953; Antwerp, 1953; São Paulo, 1953 (of which he was awarded 1st Prize in Foreign Sculpture); Germany Tour, 1953–54; USA Tour, 1955; Basle, 1955; Yugoslavia Tour, 1955; Canada, New Zealand, Australia, RSA Tour, 1955–58; Paris, 1957; Arnhem, 1957; Japan Tour, 1959; Spain and Portugal Tour, 1959; Poland Tour, 1959; Europe Tour, 1960–61; Edinburgh, 1961; USA Tour, 1963; Latin America Tour, 1964–65; USA Tour, 1966–68; East Europe Tour, 1966; Israel Tour, 1966; Canada Tour, 1967–68; Holland and Germany Tour, 1968; Japan Tour, 1969–70; New York, 1970; Iran Tour, 1971; Munich, 1971; Paris, 1971; Florence, 1972; Luxembourg, 1973; Los Angeles, 1973; Toronto, 1974; Scandinavia Tour, 1975–76; Zurich, 1976; Paris, 1977; Madrid, 1981; Hong Kong and Japan, 1986. *Examples of work are in:* the Tate Gallery, British Museum, St Paul's Cathedral, the Museum of Modern Art, New York, the Allbright Knox Art Gallery, Buffalo, and other public galleries in the UK, USA, Germany, Italy, Switzerland, Holland, Sweden, Denmark, Norway, France, Australia, Brazil, Israel, South Africa and Japan. Foreign Corresp. Mem., Acad. Flamande des Sciences; For. Mem., Acad. Lettres et Beaux Arts de Belgique; For. Mem., Swedish Royal Academy of Fine Arts; For. Hon. Mem., Amer. Acad. of Arts and Sciences; Mem. de l'Institut, Acad. des Beaux-Arts, Paris, 1975; Hon. Fellow, Churchill Coll., Cambridge. Hon. Degrees: Dr of Lit: Leeds, London, Reading, Oxford, Hull, York, Durham; Dr of Arts: Yale, Harvard; Dr of Law: Cambridge, St Andrews, Sheffield, Toronto, Manchester; Dr of Letters: Sussex, Warwick, Leicester, York (Toronto), Columbia; Dr of Engineering, Berlin; Hon. Dr, RCA, 1967; Hon. Prof. Emeritus of Sculpture, Carrara Acad. of Fine Arts, 1967. Feltrinelli Foundn Internat. Sculpture Prize, 1963; Erasmus Prize, 1968; Einstein Prize, 1968. Biancoumano Prize, 1973; Goslar Prize, 1975. Order of Merit, West Germany, 1968, Grand Cross, 1980; Order of Merit, Italy, 1972; Commandeur de l'Ordre des Arts et des Lettres, Paris, 1973; Decoration of Honour for Science and Art, Austria, 1978; Order of the Aztec Eagle, Mexico, 1984. *Publications:* Heads,

Figures and Ideas, 1958; Henry Moore on Sculpture (with Philip James), 1966; (with photographs by David Finn) Henry Moore at the British Museum, 1981; Catalogues Raisonné: Sculpture, 4 vols; Graphics, 2 vols; principal monographs by Will Grohmann, John Russell, Robert Melville, Kenneth Clark, (drawings) David Finn, John Hedgecoe, G. C. Argan, Henry Seldis. *Address:* Hoglands, Perry Green, Much Hadham, Herts. *T:* Much Hadham 2566. *Club:* Athenæum. *Died* 31 *Aug.* 1986.

**MOORE, Rear-Adm. Humfrey John Bradley,** CBE 1951; RI 1955; *b* 16 May 1898; *s* of Harry Farr Bradley and Mabel Clara Adelaide Moore; *m* 1925, Doris May Best; one *s* one *d. Educ:* Rugby Sch. Served European War, Grand Fleet, 1916–18. Thereafter various afloat and administrative posts, including Royal Naval Engineering Coll., Devonport staff, Admiralty (Engineer-in-Chief's and Naval Ordnance Depts) and Manager, Engineering Depts at Rosyth and Devonport and Staff of C-in-C, The Nore; retired 1952. *Recreations:* painting, music. *Address:* Prestons Cottage, Ightham, Kent. *T:* Borough Green 882668. *Club:* Arts. *Died* 4 *May* 1985.

**MOORE, Gen. Sir (James Newton) Rodney,** GCVO 1966 (KCVO 1959); KCB 1960 (CB 1955); CBE 1948; DSO 1944; PMN 1961; Chief Steward, Hampton Court Palace, since 1975; *b* 9 June 1905; *s* of late Maj.-Gen. Sir Newton Moore, KCMG, Perth, WA; *m* 1st, 1927, Olive Marion (marr. diss., 1947), *d* of late Lt-Col Sir Thomas Bilbe Robinson, GBE, KCMG; one *s* two *d*; 2nd, 1947, Patricia Margery Lillian, *d* of late James Catty, New York. *Educ:* Harrow; RMC, Sandhurst. Gazetted to Grenadier Guards, 1925, and served with Regt in England until 1933, then served in Egypt until 1936. Returned to England, 1936, and at outbreak of European War was at staff Coll., Camberley. Served War of 1939–45 (despatches, DSO): at GHQ Home Forces, 1940; Bde Major 30th Guards Bde and 6th Guards Armd Bde, 1940–42; GSO1, Guards Armd Div., 1942–44; Comd 2nd Armd Bn Gren. Guards in campaign NW Europe, 1944–45. Brig. comdg 8th Brit. Inf. Bde, Germany, Egypt and Palestine, 1945–46; Comd 1st Guards Bde, Palestine, 1946–47; Chief of Staff, HQ London Dist, 1948–50; idc 1950; Dep. Adjt Gen. HQ BAOR, 1951–53; Chief of Staff, Allied Forces, Northern Europe, 1953–55; GOC, 1st Infantry Div., MELF, 1955; GOC, 10th Armoured Div., 1955–57; Gen. Officer Commanding, London Dist; Maj.-Gen. Commanding Household Brigade, 1957–59; Chief of the Armed Forces Staff and Dir of Border Operations, Federation of Malaya, 1959–64; Defence Services Sec., Min. of Defence, 1964–66, retd. ADC Gen., 1965–66; Gentleman Usher to the Queen, 1966–75, Extra Gentleman Usher, 1975–. Col Comdt, HAC, 1966–76. Officer Order of Crown of Belgium and Belgian Croix de Guerre with Palm, 1944. Panglima Mangku Negara, 1961. *Recreations:* hunting, polo, fishing. *Address:* Hampton Court Palace, East Molesey, Surrey. *Club:* Cavalry and Guards.
*Died* 19 *May* 1985.

**MOORE, Prof. Stanford;** Member and Professor, Rockefeller Institute, since 1952; *b* 4 Sept. 1913; *s* of John Howard and Ruth Fowler Moore. *Educ:* Vanderbilt and Wisconsin Univs. BS Vanderbilt, 1935; PhD Wisconsin, 1938. Rockefeller Inst. for Med. Research: Asst, 1939–42; Associate, 1942–49; Associate Mem., 1949–52. Techn. Aide, Office of Scientific R&D, Nat. Defense Research Cttee, 1942–45. Vis. Prof. (Francqui Chair), Univ. of Brussels, 1950–51; Vis. Investigator, Cambridge, 1950; Vis. Prof., Vanderbilt, 1968. Mem., US Nat. Acad. of Sciences, 1960. (Jtly) Richards Medal, Amer. Chem. Soc., 1972; Linderstrøm-Lang Medal, Copenhagen, 1972; Nobel Prize in Chemistry, 1972. Hon. MD Brussels, 1954; Hon. Dr Paris, 1964; Hon. DSc Wisconsin, 1974. *Publications:* technical articles on chemistry of proteins and carbohydrates. *Address:* The Rockefeller University, 66th Street and York Avenue, New York, NY 10021, USA. *T:* 212-570-8250.
*Died* 23 *Aug.* 1982.

**MOORE, Thomas,** OBE 1968 (MBE 1951); formerly, Chief Constable of City of Nottingham, and Deputy Chief Constable of Nottinghamshire; *b* 16 March 1903; *s* of Alfred and Fanny Moore; *m* 1932, Norah Carruthers; two *s. Educ:* The Hickling Sch., Loughborough. *Recreations:* shooting and fishing. *Address:* Lowcroft, Manvers Grove, Radcliffe-on-Trent, Notts. *T:* Radcliffe 2108. *Died* 12 *Jan.* 1983.

**MOORE-COULSON, Maj.-Gen. Samuel,** CB 1959; ERD 1948; *b* 26 May 1908; *s* of late Samuel Coulson and Laura Elizabeth Moore, Leicestershire; *m* 1936, Joan Hardy, *d* of late J. R. H. Watkiss, London; one *s* two *d. Educ:* Wyggeston, Leicester; University Coll., Nottingham. Commnd Royal Leicestershire Regt (SRO), 1930; Asst Master, Queen Elizabeth Gram. Sch., Barnet, 1932–39; served with 2nd Bn Royal Leicestershire Regt, Palestine, 1939–40; Western Desert, 1940–41; Crete, 1941; Syria, 1941; Staff Officer, Lebanon, 1941–43; Canal Zone, 1944; War Office (AG1), 1945–46; transferred to RAEC, 1946; War Office (AE7/8), 1946–48; Regular Commn, 1948; SO1 Education, Far East, 1949–52; Dep. Dir of Army Education, 1952–55; Chief Education Officer, Eastern Command, 1955–57; Dir of Army Education, 1957–62; Maj.-Gen.,

1957; retired, 1962. Head of Educn and Research Div., FBI, 1962–65; Asst Dir, Educn and Training, CBI, 1965–69; Chief Training and Develt Adviser, Dunlop Co. Ltd, 1969–70. Vice-Chm. Governors, Brit. Soc. for Internat. Understanding, 1964–70; Chm., Internat. Youth Science Fortnight, 1963–65, Vice-Pres., 1967–72. Hon. Fellow, Corporation of Secretaries, 1966; Mem., Adv. Cttee, Duke of Edinburgh Award, 1958–62 and 1968–70. Former Chairman: Army Rugby Referees Soc., Army Chess Soc.; MoD Foreign Language Trng Cttee; Standing Cttee on Educn of Service Children Overseas. Member: Min. of Education Cttee on R&D in Modern Languages; Co-ord. Cttee on Overseas Vol. Service; Comr Duke of York's Royal Mil. Sch.; Governor, Centre for Inf. on Language Teaching, SOAS. *Recreation:* chess. *Address:* 3 Addington Court, Keats Avenue, Milford-on-Sea, Hants SO40WN. *T:* Milford-on-Sea 5883. *Died* 25 *Nov.* 1983.

**MOOREHEAD, Alan McCrae,** CBE 1968 (OBE 1946); AO 1978; *b* 22 July 1910; 2nd *s* of Richard Moorehead, Croydon, Vic., Aust.; *m* 1939, Lucy (*d* 1979), yr *d* of Dr Vincent Milner, Torquay; two *s* one *d. Educ:* Scotch Coll., Melbourne; Melbourne Univ. Editor Melbourne Univ. Magazine, 1929. Worked on various newspapers in Australia and England, mostly as war correspondent, 1930–46, when retired from active journalism to write books. *Publications:* Mediterranean Front, 1941; A Year of Battle, 1943; The End in Africa, 1943; African Trilogy, 1944; Eclipse, 1945; Montgomery, 1946; The Rage of the Vulture, 1948; The Villa Diana, 1951; The Traitors, 1952; Rum Jungle, 1953; A Summer Night, 1954; Gallipoli, 1956 (Sunday Times 1956 Book Prize and Duff Cooper Memorial Award); The Russian Revolution, 1958; No Room in the Ark, 1959; The White Nile, 1960; The Blue Nile, 1962, 2nd edn 1972; Cooper's Creek, 1963 (Royal Society of Literature Award); The Fatal Impact, 1966; Darwin and the Beagle, 1969; A Late Education; episodes in a Life, 1970. *Address:* 10 Egbert Street, NW1.
*Died* 29 *Sept.* 1983.

**MOORMAN, Rt. Rev. John Richard Humpidge,** MA, DD, Cambridge; LittD: Leeds; St Bonaventure, USA; FSA; Hon. Fellow of Emmanuel College; *b* Leeds, 4 June 1905; 2nd *s* of late Professor F. W. Moorman; *m* 1930, Mary Caroline Trevelyan. *Educ:* Gresham's School, Holt; Emmanuel College, Cambridge. Curate of Holbeck, Leeds, 1929–33; of Leighton Buzzard, 1933–35; Rector of Fallowfield, Manchester, 1935–42; Hon. and Examining Chaplain to Bishop of Manchester, 1940–44; Vicar of Lancercost, 1945–46, and Examining Chaplain to Bishop of Carlisle, 1945–59; Principal of Chichester Theological Coll. and Chancellor of Chichester Cathedral, 1946–56; Prebendary of Heathfield in Chichester Cathedral, 1956–59; Bishop of Ripon, 1959–75. Delegate-observer to 2nd Vatican Council, 1962–65. Hale Memorial Lectr, Evanston, USA, 1966. Chairman: Anglican members, Anglican-Roman Catholic Preparatory Commn, 1967–69; Advisory Council for Religious Communities, 1971–80. Member, Jt Internat. Commn of the Roman Catholic Church and the Anglican Communion, 1969–83. Pres., Henry Bradshaw Soc., 1977–. *Publications:* Sources for the Life of S Francis of Assisi, 1940; Church Life in England in the Thirteenth Century, 1945; A New Fioretti, 1946; B. K. Cunningham, a Memoir, 1947; S Francis of Assisi, 1950, 2nd edn 1976; The Grey Friars in Cambridge (Birkbeck Lectures), 1952; A History of the Church in England, 1953; The Curate of Souls, 1958; The Path to Glory, 1960; Vatican Observed, 1967; A History of the Franciscan Order, 1968; The Franciscans in England, 1974; Richest of Poor Men, 1977; The Anglican Spiritual Tradition, 1983; Medieval Franciscan Houses, 1983. *Recreations:* country life, music. *Address:* 22 Springwell Road, Durham. *T:* Durham 3863503.
*Died* 13 *Jan.* 1989.

**MORAN, Prof. Patrick Alfred Pierce,** FRS 1975; FAA; Professor of Statistics, Australian National University, 1952–82, later Emeritus; *b* 14 July 1917; *s* of late Herbert Michael Moran and of Eva Moran; *m* 1946, Jean Mavis Frame; two *s* one *d. Educ:* St Stanislaus Coll., Bathurst, NSW; Univs of Sydney (DSc) and Cambridge (ScD). Exper. Officer, Min. of Supply, 1940–42; Australian Sci. Liaison Officer, London, 1942–45; Baylis Student, Cambridge, 1945–46; Sen. Res. Officer, Oxford Inst. of Statistics, 1946–51; Lectr in Maths, Trinity Coll., Oxford, 1949–51; Univ. Lectr in Maths, Oxford, 1951. Vis. Fellow, Social Psychiatry Res. Unit, ANU, 1983–87. Mem. Council, Australian Acad. of Scis, 1971–74; Vice-Pres., Internat. Statistical Inst., 1971–73, 1975–77. Hon. FSS. Lyle Medal, Australian Acad. of Scis, 1963; Pitman Medal, Statistical Soc. of Aust., 1982. *Publications:* The Theory of Storage, 1960; The Random Processes of Evolutionary Theory, 1962; (with M. G. Kendall) Geometrical Probability, 1963; Introduction to the Theory of Probability, 1968. *Address:* 17 Tennyson Crescent, Forrest, Canberra, ACT 2603, Australia. *T:* Canberra 731140.
*Died* 19 *Sept.* 1988.

**MORAN, Thomas,** CBE 1946; ScD; DSc; Scientific Adviser, Home Grown Cereals Authority, 1966–69; Director of Research, Research Association of British Flour Millers, 1939–66, retired; *b* 1899; *s* of late Thomas Moran; *m* 1st, 1924, Elizabeth Ann Flynn (*d* 1952);

one *s* one *d* (and one *d* decd); 2nd, 1959, June Patricia Martin. *Educ:* St Francis Xavier's Coll., Liverpool; Liverpool Univ.; Gonville and Caius Coll., Cambridge. Sir John Willox Schol., 1920, Univ. Scholar, 1920, Liverpool Univ.; served European War, 1914–18, with Liverpool Scottish (KLR), 1917–19; with DSIR at Low Temperature Station, Cambridge, 1922–39. Mem. Advisory Scientific Cttee, Food Defence Plans Dept, 1938–39; Dir of Research and Dep. Scientific Adviser, Min. of Food, 1940–46; UK delegate, Quadripartite Food Conf., Berlin, Jan. 1946. Mem. Council, British Nutrition Foundation, 1967–70. *Publications:* Bread (with Lord Horder and Sir Charles Dodds), 1954; papers on different aspects of Food Science in scientific and medical journals, 1922–; reports on applied food research published by HM Stationery Office. *Address:* 5 Amhurst Court, Grange Road, Cambridge CB3 9BH. *T:* Cambridge 354548. *Died* 6 *Feb.* 1987.

**MORANT, Dame Mary (Maud),** DBE 1969, **(Sister Mary Regis)** (to be addressed as Sr Mary Regis, DBE); Headmistress, Roman Catholic Schools, 1933–70; voluntary social worker in convents at Battersea, Southwark and Woolton, 1969–81; *b* 21 Dec. 1903; *d* of Stephen Augustus and Mary Morant. *Educ:* Notre Dame High Sch. and Notre Dame Coll. of Educn, Mt Pleasant. Asst, Notre Dame Demonstration Sch., 1924; Asst, St Mary's, Battersea, 1929; Headmistress, St John's, Wigan, 1933; Headmistress, Central Sch., Embakwe Mission, S Rhodesia, 1938; Vice-Pres., Chikuni Trg. Coll., N Rhodesia, 1946; Headmistress: St Peter Claver, Kroonstad, 1948; Lowe House, St Helens, Lancs, 1956; Our Lady's, Eldon St, Liverpool, 1961; Preparatory School, Convent of Notre Dame, Birkdale, 1969–70. Pro Pontifice et Ecclesia Medal, 1969, from HH Pope Paul VI. *Recreations:* drama, music. *Address:* Convent of Notre Dame, 21 Weld Road, Birkdale, Southport, Merseyside PR8 2AZ. *Died* 9 *Aug.* 1985.

**MORAVIA, Alberto;** Italian author; Member of European Parliament, since 1984; *b* 28 Nov. 1907; *s* of Carlo and Teresa de Marsanich; *m* 1941, Elsa Morante (*d* 1985); *m* 1986, Carmen Llera; one step *s*. Commandeur de la Légion d'Honneur, France (Chevalier, 1952). *Publications: novels:* Gli indifferenti, 1929 (Eng. trans.: The Time of Indifference, 1953); Le ambizioni sbagliate, 1935; La mascherata, 1941 (Eng. trans.: The Fancy Dress Party, 1948); Agostino, 1944 (Eng. trans.: Agostino, 1947); La Romana, 1947 (Eng. trans.: The Woman of Rome, 1949); La disubbidienza, 1948 (Eng. trans: Disobedience, 1950); L'amore Coniugale, 1949 (Eng. trans.: Conjugal Love, 1951); Il Conformista, 1951 (Eng. Trans.: The Conformist, 1952); La Ciociara, 1957 (Eng. trans.: Two Women, 1958); La Noia, 1961 (Viareggio Prize) (Eng. trans.: The Empty Canvas, 1961); The Fetish, 1965; L'attenzione, 1965 (Eng. trans.: The Lie, 1966); La vita interiore, 1978 (Eng. trans: Time of Desecration, 1980); 1934, 1983; L'uomo che guarda, 1985 (Eng. trans.: The Voyeur, 1986); Il Viaggio a Roma, 1988; *short stories:* (and selections in Eng.); La bella vita, 1935; L'imbroglio, 1937; I sogni del pigro, 1940; L'amante infelice, 1943; L'epidemia, 1945; Racconti, 1952 (Eng. trans.: Bitter Honeymoon, and the Wayward Wife, 1959); Racconti romani, 1954 (Eng. trans.: Roman Tales, 1956); Nuovi racconti romani, 1959; L'automa, 1964; Una cosa è una cosa, 1966; Il Paradiso, 1970 (Eng. trans.: Paradise, 1971); Io e lui, 1971 (Eng. trans.: The Two of Us, 1971); Un'altra vita, 1973 (Eng. trans.: Lady Godiva and Other Stories, 1975); The Voice of the Sea, 1978; Erotic Tales, 1985; *essays:* L'uomo come fine e altri saggi, 1964 (Eng. trans.: Man as an End, 1966); Impegno Controvoglia, 1980; *plays:* Beatrice Cenci, 1955; Il mondo è quello che è, 1966; Il dio Kurt, 1967; La Vita è Gioco, 1970; L'angelo dell' informazione, 1986; *travel:* Un Mese in URSS, 1958; Un Idea dell' India, 1962; La rivoluzione culturale in Cina, 1967 (Eng. trans: The Red Book and The Great Wall, 1968); Which Tribe Do You Belong To?, 1974; Lettere dal Sahara, 1981; Passeggiate Africane, 1987. *Address:* Lungotevere della Vittoria 1, 00195 Rome, Italy. *T:* 3603698. *Died* 26 *Sept.* 1990.

**MORDECAI, Sir John Stanley,** Kt 1962; CMG 1956; formerly Secretary, Development Planning, University of the West Indies; *b* 21 Oct. 1903; *s* of Segismund T. and Marie A. Mordecai; *m* 1st, 1929, Pearl K. Redmond (*d* 1947); two *s* four *d*; 2nd, 1951, Phyllis M. Walcott; two *s*. *Educ:* Wolmer's Boys' High Sch., Jamaica; Syracuse Univ., New York, USA. MSc (Pub. Adm.). Entered public service as clerical asst in Treasury, Jamaica, 1920; Finance officer, 1942; asst treasurer, 1944; asst sec. in charge of local government secretariat, 1946; trade administrator and sec. trade control board, 1949; principal, seconded to Colonial Office, 1950; Executive Sec. Regional Economic Cttee of the West Indies, British Guiana and British Honduras, with headquarters in Barbados, 1952–56; Federal Sec., West Indies Federation, 1956–60 (Special work on preparatory arrangements for Federation, 1955–58); Dep. Gov.-Gen., WI Fedn, 1960–62; Gen. Manager, Jamaica Industrial Develt Corp., 1962–63. Fellow, Princeton Univ., NJ, 1964–66. Chairman: Jamaica Public Services Commn, 1962; Cttee of Inquiry into Sugar Ind., 1969. *Publication:* The West Indies, 1968. *Recreations:* horse racing, music. *Address:* 34 Mona Road, Kingston 6, Jamaica. *Died* 2 *Aug.* 1986.

**MORE, Sir Jasper,** Kt 1979; JP, DL; *b* 31 July 1907; *s* of Thomas Jasper Mytton More and Lady Norah, *d* of 5th Marquess of Sligo; *m* 1944, Clare Mary Hope-Edwardes, Netley, Shropshire, *d* of Capt. Vincent Coldwell, 4th Indian Cavalry; no *c*. *Educ:* Eton (Schol.); King's Coll., Cambridge. Barrister, Lincoln's Inn, 1930, and Middle Temple, 1931; Harmsworth Law Schol., 1932; in practice, 1930–39. Served War of 1939–45: in Min. of Economic Warfare, MAP and Light Metals Control, 1939–42; commissioned as legal officer in Military Govt, 1943; with Allied Commission (Italy), 8th Army and 5th Army, 1943–45; Legal Adviser, Military Govt, Dodecanese, 1946. MP (C) Ludlow, 1960–79; An Asst Government Whip, Feb.-Oct. 1964; Asst Opposition Whip, 1964–70; Vice-Chamberlain, HM Household, 1970–71. JP Salop, 1950; DL Salop, 1955; CC Salop, 1958–70, 1973–85. *Publications:* The Land of Italy, 1949; The Mediterranean, 1956; A Tale of Two Houses, 1978; The Land of Egypt, 1980; (contrib.) Shell Guide to English Villages, 1980. *Recreations:* travel, landscape gardening. *Address:* Linley Hall, Bishop's Castle, Shropshire. *Clubs:* Travellers', Brooks's, Naval and Military. *Died* 28 *Oct.* 1987.

**MORE, Kenneth (Gilbert),** CBE 1970; actor; *b* Gerrards Cross, Bucks, 20 Sept. 1914; *s* of Charles Gilbert More and Edith Winifred (*née* Watkins); *m* 1st, 1940, Beryl Johnstone (marr. diss.) (she *d* 1969); one *d*; 2nd, 1952, Mabel Edith Barkby (marr. diss.); one *d*; 3rd, 1968, Angela McDonagh Douglas. *Educ:* Victoria Coll., Jersey. First appeared on stage in a revue sketch, Windmill Theatre, 1936. Served War of 1939–45, Lieut RNVR. Returned to stage and took part in Rev. Arthur Platt in revival of And No Birds Sing, Aldwych, Nov. 1946; Eddie, in Power Without Glory, New Lindsey and Fortune, 1947; George Bourne, in Peace In Our Time, Lyric, 1948; John, in The Way Things Go, Phoenix, 1950; Freddie Page, in The Deep Blue Sea, Duchess, 1952; Peter Pounce, in Out of the Crocodile, Phoenix, 1963; Crichton, in Our Man Crichton, Shaftesbury, 1964; Hugh, in The Secretary Bird, Savoy, 1968; Sir Robert Morton in The Winslow Boy, New, 1970; George in Getting On, Queen's, 1971; Andrew Perry in Signs of the Times, Vaudeville, 1973; Duke in On Approval, Vaudeville, 1977. First appeared in films, 1948, in Scott of the Antarctic. Films include: Chance of a Lifetime; Genevieve; Doctor in the House (Brit. Film Acad. Award as best actor, 1954); Raising a Riot; The Deep Blue Sea (Venice Volpi Cup, as best actor, 1955); Reach for the Sky (Picturegoer annual award for best male performance, as Douglas Bader, also Belgian Prix Femina), 1956; The Admirable Crichton, 1957; Next to No Time, 1958; A Night to Remember, 1958; The Sheriff of Fractured Jaw, 1958; The Thirty Nine Steps, 1959; North West Frontier, 1959; Sink the Bismarck!, 1960; Man in the Moon, 1960; The Greengage Summer, 1961; The Longest Day, 1962; Some People, 1962 (For the Duke of Edinburgh's Award Scheme); We Joined the Navy, 1962; The Comedy Man, 1963; Dark of the Sun, 1967; Oh! What A Lovely War, 1968; Battle of Britain, 1969; Scrooge, 1970; The Slipper and the Rose, 1976; Journey to the Centre of the Earth, 1976; Leopard in the Snow, 1977; The Spaceman and King Arthur, 1978. First Eurovision Production by BBC: Heart to Heart, 1963. Played Young Jolyon in The Forstye Saga, BBC TV, 1966–67; Richard Drew in Six Faces, 1973; Father Brown, ATV, 1974; An Englishman's Castle, BBC, 1978. *Publications:* Happy Go Lucky (autobiography), 1959; Kindly Leave the Stage, 1965; More or Less (autobiog.), 1978. *Recreation:* golf. *Address:* 27 Rumbold Road, Fulham, SW6. *Clubs:* Garrick, Green Room. *Died* 12 *July* 1982.

**MORELL, Joan, (Mrs André Morell);** *see* Greenwood, Joan.

**MOREY, Very Rev. Dom Adrian,** MA, DPhil, LittD; FRHistS; Prior, Downside House of Studies, Cambridge; *b* 10 April 1904; *s* of late John Morey and Charlotte Helen Morey (*née* Nelson). *Educ:* Latymer Upper Sch.; Christ's Coll., Cambridge (Schol.); Univ. of Munich. 1st cl. hons Hist. Tripos Pts I and II, Cambridge. Housemaster, Downside Sch., 1934; Bursar, Downside Abbey and Sch., 1940–50; Headmaster, Oratory Sch., Reading, 1953–67; Rector, St Wulstan's, Little Malvern, Worcs, 1967–69. *Publications:* Bartholomew of Exeter, 1937; (with Prof. C. N. Brooke) Gilbert Foliot and His Letters, 1965; The Letters and Charters of Gilbert Foliot, 1967; The Catholic Subjects of Elizabeth I, 1977; David Knowles: a memoir, 1979; articles in English Hist. Review, Jl Eccles. History, Cambridge Hist. Jl. *Address:* Benet House, Mount Pleasant, Cambridge. *T:* Cambridge 354637.

*Died* 3 *Feb.* 1989.

**MORFEE, Air Vice-Marshal Arthur Laurence,** CD; CB 1946; CBE 1943; retired; *b* 27 May 1897; *s* of George Thomas Morfee; *m* Estelle Lillian, *d* of William Edward Hurd of South Carolina, USA; one *s* one *d*. *Educ:* Finchley County Sch. Canadian Army from 1915; served France and Belgium, 19th Can. Inf. (wounded); joined RAF 1918; Air Board (Civil Service), 1921–24; appointed RCAF 1924; psa Andover, Eng., 1933; Air Vice-Marshal, 1945; retd 1949. Dir of Air Cadet League; Vice-Chm., Nova Scotia Div., Corps of Commissionaires. US Legion of Merit (Comdr), 1949. *Address:* 380 St George Street, Annapolis Royal, NS, Canada.

**MORGAN, Alun Michael,** CMG 1957; Member, Committee of Independent Experts, European Social Charter, 1976–80; Under-Secretary, Overseas Division, Department of Employment, 1966–75; UK Government Representative on ILO Governing Body, 1971–75; *b* 31 March 1915; *s* of late Richard Michael Morgan, Rhayader; *m* 1958, Hilary Jane, *d* of late Eric Wilkinson, OBE, Kelsale, Suffolk. *Educ:* St Paul's Sch.; Magdalen Coll., Oxford. Min. of Labour, 1937; Served with Royal Fusiliers, 1940; with Special Forces, 1942–45 (Lieut-Col); Dep. Chief, Manpower Div., CCG, 1946. Asst Sec., Min. of Labour and Nat. Service, 1947; Manpower Counsellor, OEEC, 1948; Counsellor and Labour Attaché, HM Embassy, Washington, 1957–60; Under-Sec., Min. of Labour, 1964. *Address:* Spaniel Cottage, Wentworth Road, Aldeburgh, Suffolk. *Died 3 Dec. 1981.*

**MORGAN, Sir Clifford Naunton,** Kt 1966; MS; FRCS; FRCOG; Hon. FRCSI; Hon. FACS; Commander of the Order of the Star of the North (Sweden); Hon. Consulting Surgeon: St Bartholomew's Hospital; St Mark's Hospital for Diseases of the Rectum and Colon; Hospital for Tropical Diseases; Surgeon, King Edward VII's Hospital for Officers; Consulting Surgeon: RAF; (Colon and Rectum) RN; *b* 20 Dec. 1901; *s* of late Thomas Naunton Morgan, Penygraig; *m* 1930, Ena Muriel Evans; two *s* one *d. Educ:* Royal Masonic Sch.; University Coll., Cardiff; Univ. of London (St Bartholomew's Hosp.). MB 1924; FRCS 1926. Surgeon: Metropolitan Hosp., 1930; Royal Masonic Hosp.; St Bartholomew's Hospital: Demonstrator of Anatomy, Med. Coll., 1929; Chief Asst to a Surgical Unit, 1930; Casualty Surgeon, 1936; Asst Dir of Surgery, Professorial Unit, 1937. Lectr and Examr in Surgery, Univ. of London; Examr in Surgery, Univs of Cambridge, Glasgow, and Edinburgh. Officer i/c Surgical Divs, MEF, 1941–43 (despatches); Cons. Surgeon: Persia-Iraq Force, 1943–45; E Africa Comd, 1945; Hon. Col and late Brig., AMS. Twice Pres., Section of Proctology, Royal Soc. of Medicine; Mem. Council, RCS of England, 1953–68 (Vice-Pres., 1963–65); Past Vice-Chm., Imperial Cancer Research Fund. Sims Commonwealth Travelling Prof., 1963; Bradshaw Lectr, RCS, 1964; Vicary Lectr, 1967. Fellow, Assoc. of Surgeons of Great Britain and Ireland (Pres., 1968); Hon. Fellow: Amer. Surgical Assoc.; Amer. Protologic Soc.; For. Mem., Académie de Chirurgie; Hon. Member: Pennsylvania Proctologic Soc.; Société Nationale Française de Proctologie; Sociedades Argentina, Brasileira and Chilena de Proctologia; Med. Assoc. of Thessaloniki; Burmese Med. Assoc. *Publications:* various chapters in British Surgical Practice and other surgical Text Books. Contributor St Mark's Hosp. Centenary Vol., 1935. Many articles on Surgery of the Colon and Rectum in Brit. and Amer. Jls. *Recreation:* farming. *Address:* Rolfe's Farm, Inkpen, Berks RG15 0PZ. *T:* Inkpen 259. *Club:* Royal Air Force. *Died 24 Feb. 1986.*

**MORGAN, Dennis,** OBE 1972; FEng 1983; Chief Executive, Dowty Group PLC, 1983–86; *b* 25 Oct. 1928; *s* of Thomas Wells and Ellen Morgan; *m* 1953, Hazel Wood; two *s* one *d. Educ:* Durham Univ. (BSc Hons). FIMinE. Asst Undermanager, Linton Colliery, NCB, 1953–54; Undermanager 1954–56, Manager 1956–58, Montague Colliery, NCB; Manager, Weetslade Colliery, NCB, 1958–60; Dowty Mining: Regional Mining Engr, 1960–64; Sen. Mining Engr, 1964–65; Sales Manager, 1965–67; Export Dir, 1967–70; Dep. Man. Dir, 1970–72; Dowty Meco: Man. Dir Designate, 1972–73; Man. Dir, 1973–76; Dowty Group: Div. Man. Dir, Mining Div., 1976–83; Board Mem., 1977; Dep. Chief Exec. (Chief Exec. Designate), 1981. *Recreation:* sailing. *Died 25 Feb. 1987.*

**MORGAN, Graham,** CMG 1954; FICE; Chartered Civil Engineer; *b* 12 July 1903; *m* 1931, Alice Jane Morgan; three *d. Educ:* King Henry VIII Grammar Sch., Abergavenny; University Coll., Cardiff. BSc Civil Engineering, Wales, 1923; Asst Engineer: Newport, Mon., 1924; Devon CC, 1924; Federated Malay States, 1926; Sen. Exec. Engineer, Malayan Public Works Service, 1941; State Engineer, Johore, 1948; Dir of Public Works, Tanganyika, 1950–Sept. 1954, retired. FICE (Mem. of Council, 1953–55). *Address:* 2 Cooper Place, Headington Quarry, Oxford. *Died 29 Aug. 1987.*

**MORGAN, Guy (Leslie Llewellyn),** FRIBA; AIStructE; FRSA; BA; Senior Partner, in architectural practice; *b* 14 June 1902; *s* of late Francis Morgan and Miriam Hanley; *m* 1937, Violet Guy (*d* 1986); one *d* (one *s* decd). *Educ:* Mill Hill; Cambridge; University Coll., London. Andrew Taylor Prizeman, 1923. Lecturer and Year Master, Architectural Assoc., 1931–36. In practice, 1927–; principal works include: large blocks of flats and offices in London and Provinces; aircraft factories and air bases; town planning schemes and housing in England and abroad; agricultural buildings and country houses; ecclesiastical and hospital works; film studios; racing and sports stadia. Past Joint Master, Cowdray Foxhounds. Past Master of Worshipful Company of Woolmen. *Recreations:* foxhunting, sailing, travel; music. *Address:* Lower House Farm, Fernhurst, Haslemere, Surrey. *T:* Haslemere 53022; 12A Eaton Square, SW1. *T:* 01–235 5101. *Club:* Royal Thames Yacht. *Died 25 July 1987.*

**MORGAN, Hilda, (Mrs Charles L. Morgan);** *see* Vaughan, H.

**MORGAN, Hugh Travers,** CMG 1966; HM Diplomatic Service, retired; Ambassador to Austria, 1976–79; *b* 3 Aug. 1919; *s* of Dr Montagu Travers Morgan, CMG, MC; *m* 1959, Alexandra Belinoff; two *s* one *d. Educ:* Winchester Coll.; Magdalene Coll., Cambridge. RAF, 1939–45, prisoner-of-war in Germany, 1941–45. Entered HM Diplomatic Service, 1945, and served: New York, 1946–48; Moscow, 1948–50; Foreign Office, 1950–53; Canadian National Defence Coll., 1953–54; Mexico City, 1954–57; Foreign Office, 1957–58; UK Delegation to Conference on Nuclear Tests, Geneva, 1958–61; Peking (Counsellor), 1961–63; Political Adviser to the British Commandant, Berlin, 1964–67; FCO, 1967–70; Ambassador, Peru, 1970–74; Asst Under-Sec. of State, FCO, 1974–75. Grand Cross, Peruvian Order of Merit, 1985. *Address:* 42 Waldemar Avenue, SW6. *Died 13 June 1988.*

**MORGAN, Irvonwy,** MA, BD Cantab, PhD (London); Secretary, Department of the London Mission of the Methodist Church, since 1951; *b* 11 April 1907; *s* of Rev. Llewelyn Morgan and Alice Anna Davies; *m* 1942, Florence Mary Lewis; two *d* decd. *Educ:* Kingswood Sch.; Wesley House, Cambridge (1st cl. hons Theol., Schofield Univ. Prize). PhD London, 1949; BD Cantab 1957. Asst at Poplar Mission; in charge of Poplar Mission from 1937. Methodist Delegate, World Council of Churches, Evanston, 1954; Guest Preacher, Methodist Church of Australasia, 1959; visited US on behalf of World Coun. of Churches, 1962 and 1966. Pres. of the Methodist Conference, 1967–68; Moderator, Free Church Federal Council, 1972–73. Pres., Bible Lands Soc. Fellow, Internat. PEN. *Publications:* The Nonconformity of Richard Baxter, 1949; Twixt the Mount and Multitude, 1955; Prince Charles' Puritan Chaplain, 1957; The Godly Preachers of the Elizabethan Church, 1965; Puritan Spirituality, 1973; *poems:* A Rent for Love, 1973; Moonflight, 1979. *Recreation:* gardening. *Address:* (home) 12 Heathdene Road, Wallington, Surrey. *T:* Wallington 9418; (office) 1 Central Buildings, Westminster, SW1H 9NH. *T:* 01–930 1453. *Club:* Reform. *Died 24 Sept. 1982.*

**MORGAN, Leslie James Joseph;** a Recorder of the Crown Court, since 1975; *b* Ballina, NSW, 2 June 1922; *er s* of late Bertram Norman Morgan and Margaret Mary Morgan, MA (*née* Meere); *m* 1949, Sheila Doreen Elton Williamson; one *s* one *d. Educ:* Bournemouth Sch.; University Coll., Southampton. LLB (London) 1943. Served, Home Guard, 1940, Radio Security Service, 1941–43. Solicitor (Distinction) 1944; general practice in Bournemouth, 1944–. Chairman: Southern Area Legal Aid Cttee, 1973–74; Bournemouth Exec. Council (NHS), 1962–74; Dorset Family Practitioner Cttee, 1974–77; Law Society's Standing Cttee on Criminal Law, 1979–82 and Contentious Business Cttee, 1982–85; Member: Council, Law Society, 1973–85; Matrimonial Causes Rule Cttee, 1978–82; Crown Court Rule Cttee, 1982–88; Mental Health Review Tribunal, 1982–; President: Bournemouth and Dist Law Soc., 1972–73; Soc. of Family Practitioner Cttees, 1975–76. *Publications:* articles on aspects of radio communication. *Recreations:* music, reading, amateur radio (G2HNO). *Address:* 4 Tree Tops, Martello Park, Canford Cliffs, Poole, Dorset BH13 7BA. *T:* Canford Cliffs 708405. *Died 18 Oct. 1988.*

**MORGAN, Oswald Gayer,** MA, MCh Cantab; FRCS; Consultant Surgeon Emeritus; Past President, Ophthalmological Society of UK; *b* 1889; *m* 1926, Jessie Campbell (*d* 1938), *yr d* of Colin MacDonald, 38 Abbey Road, NW; two *d. Educ:* Epsom Coll.; Clare Coll., Cambridge; Guy's Hosp. Surgeon in charge Duchess of Sutherland's Hosp., France, 1914–18; Ophthalmic House Surg. at Moorfield's Eye Hosp., 1920. Vice-Pres., BMA, 1965. *Publications:* The Wounded in Namur; Some Aspects of the Treatment of Infected War Wounds, British Journal of Surgery, 1916; Ophthalmology in General Practice. *Address:* 6 The Oaks, West Byfleet, Surrey KT14 6RL. *Died 11 Aug. 1984.*

**MORGAN, Rear-Adm. Sir Patrick (John),** KCVO 1970; CB 1967; DSC 1942; Flag Officer, Royal Yachts, 1965–70, retired; *b* 26 Jan. 1917; *s* of late Vice-Adm. Sir Charles Morgan, KCB, DSO; *m* 1944, Mary Hermione Fraser-Tytler, *d* of late Col Neil Fraser-Tytler, DSO, and of Mrs C. H. Fraser-Tytler, CBE, TD; three *s* one *d. Educ:* RN College, Dartmouth. Served War of 1939–45 (despatches, DSC). Naval Attaché, Ankara, 1957–59; Imperial Defence Coll. 1960; Asst Chief of Staff, Northwood, 1961–62; Commanding Officer, Commando Ship, HMS Bulwark, 1963–64. *Recreations:* sports. *Address:* Swallow Barn, Well Road, Crondall, Farnham, Surrey GU10 5PW. *T:* Aldershot 850107.

*Died 20 May 1989.*

**MORGAN, William Stanley,** CMG 1965; Colonial Administrative Service, retired; *b* 29 April 1908; *s* of late J. W. Morgan; *m* 1957, Joan Ruth Dixon Williams; two *s* one *d. Educ:* Rendcomb Coll.; (Open Scholar in History) Queens' Coll., Cambridge (MA). Malayan Education Service, 1931–50; Colonial Administrative Service, 1950–57; Malaya, 1931–47; Sec., Commn on Univ. Educn in Malaya, 1947; Principal, Colonial Office, 1947–50; Sierra Leone,

Ministerial Sec., 1950–57; Asst Adviser to Qatar Govt, 1957–60; Chm., Public and Police Service Commns, Mauritius, 1960–69. *Publication:* Story of Malaya, 1938. *Recreations:* travel and music. *Address:* Old Vicarage, Kirk Maughold, Isle of Man. *T:* Ramsey 812863. *Died 16 June 1986.*

**MORGAN JONES, John;** *see* Jones, J. M.

**MORLEY;** *see* Headlam-Morley.

**MORLEY, Sir Godfrey (William Rowland),** Kt 1971; OBE 1944; TD 1946; *b* 15 June 1909; *o s* of late Arthur Morley, OBE, KC, and late Dorothy Innes Murray Forrest; *m* 1st, 1934, Phyllis Dyce (*d* 1963), *d* of late Sir Edward Duckworth, 2nd Bt; twin *s* two *d*; 2nd, 1967, Sonia Gisèle, *d* of late Thomas Ritchie; two *s*. *Educ:* Westminster; Christ Church, Oxford (MA). Solicitor, 1934; Partner in Allen & Overy, 1936, Senior Partner, 1960–75. Joined Territorial Army, 1937; served War of 1939–45, Rifle Bde and on Staff in Middle East and Italy (despatches); Lt-Col 1944. Law Society: Mem. Council, 1952–73; Vice-Pres., 1969–70; Pres., 1970–71. Member: Lord Chancellor's Law Reform Cttee, 1957–73; Denning Cttee on Legal Educn of Students from Africa, 1960; Cttee of Management, Inst. of Advanced Legal Studies, 1961–77; CBI Company Affairs Cttee, 1972; Law Adv. Panel, British Council, 1974–82; Council, Selden Soc., 1975– (Pres., 1979–82). Dir, Bowater Corp. Ltd, 1968–79. Trustee, Thalidomide Children's Trust, 1980–84. Hon. Mem., Canadian Bar Assoc., 1970. Bronze Star Medal (US), 1945. *Address:* Hunter's Lodge, Warren Drive, Kingswood, Tadworth, Surrey KT20 6PT. *T:* Mogador 832485. *Clubs:* Athenæum, Boodle's. *Died 13 Oct. 1987.*

**MORONY, Gen. Sir Thomas (Lovett),** KCB 1981; OBE 1969; retired; UK Military Representative to NATO, 1983–86; Aide-de-Camp General to the Queen, 1984–86; *b* 23 Sept. 1926; *s* of late Thomas Henry Morony, CSI, CIE, and Evelyn Myra (*née* Lovett); *m* 1961, Elizabeth, *d* of G. W. N. Clark; two *s*. *Educ:* Eton (KS). Commissioned, 1947. BM, King's African Rifles, 1958–61; GSO1 (DS) at Camberley and RMCS, 1963–65; GSO1, HQ Northern Army Gp, 1966–67; commanded 22 Light Air Defence Regt, RA, 1968–69; Comdr, 1st Artillery Bde, 1970–72; Dep. Comdt, Staff Coll., Camberley, 1973–75; Director RA, 1975–78; Comdt, RMCS, 1978–80; Vice Chief of the General Staff, 1980–83. Col Commandant: RA, 1978–; RHA, 1983–; Master Gunner, St James's Park, 1983–88. Vice-Pres., Royal Patriotic Fund Corp., 1988–. Chm., Bd of Governors, Sherborne Sch., 1987–. *Recreations:* gardening, music. *Address:* c/o Bank of Scotland, 8 Morningside Road, Edinburgh EH10 4DD. *Club:* Army and Navy. *Died 27 May 1989.*

**MORRAH, Ruth, (Mrs Dermot Morrah),** JP; Chairman, Metropolitan Juvenile Courts, 1945–64; *b* 21 Aug. 1899; *d* of Willmott Houselander; *m* 1923, Dermot Michael Macgregor Morrah (*d* 1974); two *d*. *Educ:* convent schs; St Anne's Coll., Oxford. JP 1944. Pro Ecclesia et Pontifice, 1964. *Address:* Meadbank Nursing Home, Parkgate Road, SW11. *T:* 071–223 9522. *Died 4 Oct. 1990.*

**MORRELL, William Bowes;** *b* York, 18 Feb. 1913; *s* of J. B. Morrell, LLD, JP and Bertha Morrell (*née* Spence Watson); *m* 1939, Kate Lisa, *d* of Prof. E. and Elisabeth Probst; three *s*. *Educ:* Bootham Sch., York; St John's Coll., Cambridge (MA). Served War of 1939–45 (2 stars, 2 medals), RA; Capt. 1945. Joined Westminster Press Group, 1935; Man., Nottingham Journal Ltd, 1939; Dir and Man., Birmingham Gazette Ltd, 1948, Man. Dir, 1953; Dir and Gen. Man., London Hd Office, Westminster Press Ltd, 1957; Gp Advertisement Dir, 1958; Gp Dep. Man. Dir, 1964; Gp Man. Dir, 1965; Gp Vice-Chm., 1975; Vice-Chm., 1976–78. Chairman: Joseph Rowntree Social Service Trust Ltd; Joseph Rowntree Social Service Trust (Investments) Ltd; Turret Press (Holdings) Ltd; York Conservation Trust Ltd; York Common Good Trust; Trustee: Reuters (Dir, 1970–73); Sir Halley Stewart Trust; Director: Press Assoc., 1966 (Chm., 1970–71); York and County Press; Herald Printers; BPM (Hldgs) Ltd (alternate). Member: Adv. Cttee on Advertising; York Merchant Adventurers Co.; co-opted Mem., York Castle Museum Cttee; Mem., Court of Univ. of York. Liveryman, Co. of Stationers and Newspaper Makers. *Recreation:* swimming. *Address:* 99 South End Road, NW3 2RJ. *T:* 01–435 0785; Flat 1, Ingram House, 90 Bootham, York. *T:* York 23197. *Club:* Lansdowne. *Died 11 Dec. 1981.*

**MORRIS OF GRASMERE, Baron** *cr* 1967 (Life Peer), of Grasmere; **Charles Richard Morris,** KCMG 1963; Kt 1953; MA Oxon; Hon. LLD: Manchester, 1951; Aberdeen, 1963; Leeds, 1964; Malta, 1964; Hull, 1965; Hon. DLitt: Sydney, 1954; Lancaster, 1967; Hon. DTech Bradford, 1970; *b* 25 Jan. 1898; *s* of M. C. Morris, Sutton Valence, Kent; *m* 1923, Mary de Selincourt (*d* 1988); one *s* one *d*. *Educ:* Tonbridge Sch.; Trinity Coll., Oxford. Lt RGA 1916–19; Fellow and Tutor of Balliol Coll., 1921–43; for one year, 1926–27 (while on leave of absence from Balliol), Prof. of Philosophy, Univ. of Michigan, USA; Senior Proctor, 1937–38; Mem. of Council of Girls Public Day Sch. Trust, 1933–38; Oxford City Councillor,

1939–41; Ministry of Supply, 1939–42; Under-Sec., Min. of Production, 1942–43; Head Master, King Edward's Sch., Birmingham, 1941–48; Chm., Cttee of Vice-Chancellors and Principals, 1952–55; Central Joint Adv. Cttee on Tutorial Classes, 1948–58; Commonwealth Univ. Interchange Cttee and Recruitment Sub-Cttee of British Council, 1951; Sch. Broadcasting Council, 1954–64; Inter-Univ. Council for Higher Education Overseas, 1957–64; Independent Chm., Jt Adv. Cttee for Wool Textile Industry, 1952; Pres., Council of Coll. of Preceptors, 1954–63. Vice-Chancellor of Leeds Univ., 1948–63; Pro-Chancellor, Univ. of Bradford, 1966–69. Member: Royal Commn on Local Govt in Greater London, 1957; Cttee of Inquiry on Australian Univs, 1957; Chairman: Adv. Bd Of Univs Quarterly, 1960; Local Govt Training Bd, 1967–75; President: Brit. Student Tuberculosis Foundn, 1960; Assoc. of Teachers in Colls and Depts of Educn, 1961–64. *Publications:* A History of Political Ideas (with Mary Morris), 1924; Locke, Berkeley, Hume, 1931; Idealistic Logic, 1933; In Defence of Democracy (with J. S. Fulton), 1936; British Democracy, 1939; various essays and papers to learned societies. *Recreation:* fell walking. *Address:* Ladywood, White Moss, Ambleside, Cumbria LA22 9SF. *T:* Grasmere (09665) 286. *Club:* Athenæum. *Died 30 May 1990.*

**MORRIS, Prof. Benjamin Stephen;** Professor of Education, University of Bristol, 1956–75, then Emeritus; *b* 25 May 1910; *s* of Rev. B. S. Morris, Sherborne, Dorset, and Annie McNicol Duncan, Rothesay, Bute; *m* 1938, Margaret, *d* of Mr and Mrs Lamont, Glasgow; two *s* one *d*. *Educ:* Rothesay Academy; Glasgow Univ. BSc 1933, MEd 1937 (Glasgow). Trained as teacher, Jordanhill Training Coll., Glasgow; teacher, primary and secondary schs, 1936–39; Lecturer: in Psychology, Logic and Ethics, Jordanhill Trng Coll., 1939–40; in Educn, Univ. of Glasgow, 1940–46. Temp. Civil Servant, Min. of Food, 1941; Army Psychologist, 1942–46; Sen. Psychologist (WOSB), 1945–46; Hon. Lt-Col 1946. Student at Inst. of Psychoanalysis, London, 1946–50; Senior staff, Tavistock Institute of Human Relations, 1946–50 (Chm. Management Cttee, 1947–49); Dir Nat. Foundation for Educl Research in England and Wales, 1950–56. Vis. Prof. of Education, Harvard Univ., 1969–70. *Publications:* Objectives and Perspectives in Education, 1972; Some Aspects of Professional Freedom of Teachers, 1977; contributed to: The Function of Teaching, 1959; How and Why Do We Learn?, 1965; Study of Education, 1966; Higher Education, Demand and Response, 1969; Towards a Policy for the Education of Teachers, 1969; Towards Community Mental Health, 1971; The Sciences, The Humanities and the Technological Threat, 1975; articles in educational and psychological jls. *Recreation:* living in the country. *Address:* 13 Park View, Leyburn, N Yorks DL8 5HN. *T:* Wensleydale (0969) 22603. *Died 8 June 1990.*

**MORRIS, Sir Cedric Lockwood,** 9th Bt, *cr* 1806; of Clasemont, Glamorganshire; painter and horticulturist; Principal of The East Anglian School of Painting and Drawing, Hadleigh, Suffolk; President, South Wales Art Society; *b* Sketty, Glamorganshire, 11 Dec. 1889; *s* of Sir George Lockwood Morris, 8th Bt; *S* father, 1947; unmarried. *Educ:* Charterhouse; on the Continent. In early years worked as a farmer in Canada; studied art in Paris, Berlin, and Rome; works in most public galleries; served in the ranks, 1914–15; later with Remounts; International Exhibitor at Venice, Chicago, Brussels, etc; Exhibitions at Rome, 1922; New York, 1923; London (private), 1923; New York, 1924; Paris, 1925; London, 1928; The Hague, 1928; London, 1931, 1934, 1936, 1940, 1944, and 1952. RCA (Wales), 1930. Lectr in Design, RCA (London), 1950–53. Vice-Pres., Contemporary Art Soc. for Wales, 1967. *Publications:* reproductions of works in art and general periodicals; illustrations to books treating of plant and bird life; articles and poems. *Heir:* *c* Robert Byng Morris [*b* 25 Feb. 1913; *m* 1947, Christine Kathleen, *d* of Archibald Field, Toddington, Glos; one *s* three *d*]. *Address:* Benton End, Hadleigh, Suffolk. *Died 8 Feb. 1982.*

**MORRIS, Charles Alfred,** RWS 1949 (ARWS 1943); RBA 1948; retired as Vice-Principal Brighton College of Art (1952–59); Vice-President, RWS, 1957–60; *b* 5 Sept. 1898; *s* of G. W. Morris and Susan (*née* Lee); *m* 1927, Alice Muriel Drummond, *d* of Rev. Dr. W. H. Drummond; one *s* two *d*. *Educ:* Royal Academy Schs and Brighton Coll. of Art. Served with HAC, 1916–19. Teacher of advanced drawing and painting, Liverpool Coll. of Art, 1926; Senior Asst, County Sch. of Art, Worthing, 1931, Principal, 1942. Examples of work in following public collections: Birkenhead, Blackburn, Brighton, Eastbourne, Hove, Worthing. *Recreation:* gardening. *Address:* Malthouse Barn, Kingsley, Bordon, Hants. *Died 11 Dec. 1983.*

**MORRIS, Prof. Colin John Owen Rhonabwy,** MSc, PhD; Professor of Experimental Biochemistry, London Hospital Medical College, University of London, 1954–78, later Emeritus; *b* 3 May 1910; *s* of John Jenkin Morris and Annie Margaret (*née* Thomas); *m* 1946, Peggy (*née* Clark); two *d* decd. *Educ:* Cowbridge Grammar Sch.; University Coll., Cardiff (MSc Wales). Lister Institute, London,

1932–36 (PhD London); Kaiser Wilhelm Institute, Heidelberg, 1936–37; London Hospital and London Hospital Med. Coll., 1937–78; Reader in Chemical Pathology, 1947. *Publications:* (with Mrs P. Morris) Separation Methods in Biochemistry, 1964, 2nd edn 1976; numerous scientific papers in Journal of Chem. Soc., Biochem. Jl, etc. *Recreation:* sailing. *Address:* 14 Trowlock Avenue, Teddington, Mddx. *T:* 01-977 4853. *Died 7 June* 1981.

**MORRIS, David Edward;** Chief Scientist, Civil Aviation Authority, 1972–78, retired; *b* 23 July 1915; *m* 1950, Heather Anne Court; one *s* two *d*. *Educ:* University Coll. of North Wales, Bangor; Trinity Coll., Cambridge. Aerodynamics Dept, RAE, 1938–56; Chief Supt, A&AEE, 1956–59; Chief Supt, RAE, Bedford, 1959–61; Dir-General, Development (RAF), Min. of Aviation, 1961–65; Dir-Gen., Civil Aircraft and Gen. Services Research and Develt, 1965–69; Scientific Adviser (Civil Aviation), BoT, later DTI, 1969–72. FRAeS 1956. *Publications:* various reports and memoranda. *Recreations:* walking, bridge. *Address:* 38 Days Lane, Biddenham, Bedford. *T:* Bedford (0234) 66644.

*Died 17 July* 1990.

**MORRIS, Air Marshal Sir Douglas (Griffith),** KCB 1962 (CB 1954); CBE 1945; DSO 1945; DFC 1941; AOC-in-C, RAF Fighter Command, 1962–66; *b* 3 Dec. 1908; 2nd *s* of D. G. Morris, late of Natal, South Africa; *m* 1936, Audrey Beryl Heard; one *s* one *d*. *Educ:* St John's Coll., Johannesburg, South Africa. Commissioned RAF, 1930; trained as pilot, 1930–31; No. 40 (B) Sqdn, 1931–32; Fleet Air Arm, 1932–34; qualified as Flying Instructor, Central Flying Sch., 1934; on instructor duties, 1934–40; RAF Staff Coll., 1940; Air Ministry, 1940–41; on night fighting ops, 1941–42; Comdg No. 406 RCAF Sqdn, 1941–42, as Wing Comdr; Comd RAF North Weald, as Group Capt., 1942–43; on staff of Allied Exped. Air HQ, 1943–44; Comd No. 132 (F) Wing, 1944–45, in Normandy, Belgium, Holland; SASO No 84 Gp HQ, as Air Cdre, Feb.-Nov. 1945; in W Africa, Nov. 1945–46; Jt Planning staff, Min. of Defence, 1946–47; Nat. War Coll., Washington, 1947–48; on staff of Brit. Jt Services Mission, Washington, DC, 1948–50; Sector Comdr, Southern Sector, 1950–52; Sector Comdr, Metropolitan Sector, Fighter Comd, 1952–53; idc 1954; Air Vice-Marshal, 1955, and SASO, 2nd TAF; ACAS (Air Defence), Air Ministry, 1957–59; Chief of Staff, Allied Air Forces, Central Europe, 1960–62. Comdr Order of St Olav, 1945; Comdr Order of Orange-Nassau, 1947; ADC to King George VI, 1949–52; ADC to the Queen, 1952. Retired, 1966. Mem. Council, St Dunstan's, 1968–85. *Recreations:* golf, ski-ing. *Address:* Friar's Côte, Northiam, Rye, East Sussex. *Clubs:* Royal Air Force; Rye Golf (Captain, 1975). *Died 26 March* 1990.

**MORRIS, Sir Geoffrey N.;** *see* Newman-Morris.

**MORRIS, Sir Gwilym;** *see* Morris, Sir T. G.

**MORRIS, His Honour Gwyn Rhyse Francis,** QC 1959; a Circuit Judge, Central Criminal Court, 1972–81; *b* 1910; *s* of late Wm John Morris, Co. Pembroke; *m* 1st, 1933, Margaret, *d* of late Ridley Mackenzie, MD; one *s* one *d* (and one *s* decd); 2nd, 1945, Lady Victoria Audrey Beatrice, *d* of Viscount Ingestre and *sister* of 21st Earl of Shrewsbury. *Educ:* New Coll., Oxford. Called to Bar, Middle Temple, 1937. Mem. Gen. Council of the Bar, 1964–67; Master of the Bench, Middle Temple, 1966. Mem., Commn at CCC, 1971. *Address:* Goldsmith Building, Temple, EC4. *T:* 01–353 7881; (residence) Carpmael Building, Temple, EC4. *T:* 01–353 1373.

*Died 18 Jan.* 1982.

**MORRIS, Harry Frank Grave,** CMG 1958; *b* 11 May 1907; *e s* of late Frank Morris; unmarried. *Educ:* Harrow; Balliol Coll., Oxford. MA Oxon 1928. Solicitor, 1931–41. Joined Foreign Service, 1943, Madrid, Lisbon, Budapest, Rome; retired, Dec. 1962. *Address:* 32 Pont Street, SW1. *T:* 01–584 0883. *Club:* Garrick.

*Died 31 May* 1982.

**MORRIS, Maj.-Gen. John Edward Longworth,** CB 1963; CBE 1956; DSO 1945; Director of Recruiting, War Office, 1960–64, retired; *b* 1 June 1909; *s* of Col A. E. Morris and M. E. Stanyon; *m* 1939, Pamela Gresley Ball; two *d*. *Educ:* Cheltenham Coll. Commissioned Regular Army, 1929; served War of 1939–45: India, Middle East and NW Europe, Col Comdt, RA, 1966–74. *Recreations:* sailing, model railways, electronics. *Address:* Garden House, Garden Road, Burley, Hants. *Clubs:* Royal Ocean Racing, Royal Artillery Yacht (Admiral, 1972–78). *Died 6 Aug.* 1988.

**MORRIS, Dr John Humphrey Carlile,** QC 1981; FBA 1966; DCL; LLD; Fellow of Magdalen College, Oxford, 1936–77, Hon. Fellow, 1977; University Reader in Conflict of Laws, 1951–77; *b* 18 Feb. 1910; *e s* of H. W. Morris, Solicitor, and J. M. Morris; *m* 1939, Mercy Jane Kinch; no *c*. *Educ:* Charterhouse; Christ Church, Oxford. DCL Oxford, 1949; LLD Cantab, 1979. Barrister-at-Law, 1934; Fellow and Tutor in Law, Magdalen Coll., Oxford, 1936; All Souls Lecturer in Private Internat. Law, 1939–51; Arthur Goodhart Vis. Prof. of Legal Sci., and Fellow of Gonville and Caius Coll., Cambridge, 1979–80. Hon. Bencher of Gray's Inn, 1980. Lt-Comdr RNVR, 1940–45. Visiting Prof., Harvard Law Sch., 1950–51;

Assoc. Mem. Amer. Acad. of Arts and Sciences, 1960. *Publications:* Cases in Private International Law, 1939, 4th edn, 1968; (with Prof. W. Barton Leach) The Rule against Perpetuities, 1956, 2nd edn 1962; The Conflict of Laws, 1971, 3rd edn 1984; (with Dr. P. M. North) Cases and Materials on Private International Law, 1984; title Conflict of Laws in Halsbury's Laws of England, 4th edn, 1974; Thank You, Wodehouse, 1981; Editor, 9th, 10th and 11th edns of Theobald on Wills, 1939–54; Gen. Editor: Dicey's Conflict of Laws, 6th to 10th edns, 1949–80; Chitty on Contracts, 22nd edn, 1961. *Recreation:* yacht cruising. *Address:* Sparepenny Cottage, Front Street, Orford, Suffolk IP12 2LP. *T:* Orford 664. *Club:* Royal Cruising. *Died 29 Sept.* 1984.

**MORRIS, Rev. (John) Marcus (Harston),** OBE 1983; Editorial Director, 1960–64, Managing Director, 1964–82, Deputy Chairman, 1979–84, The National Magazine Co. Ltd; *b* 25 April 1915; *e s* of late Rev. Canon W. E. H. Morris and Edith (*née* Nield); *m* 1941, Jessica *d* of late John Hamlet Dunning and Alice (*née* Hunt-Jones); three *d* (one *s* decd). *Educ:* Dean Close Sch., Cheltenham; Brasenose Coll., Oxford (Colquitt Exhibnr; BA Lit. Hum. 1937); Wycliffe Hall, Oxford (BA Theol. 1939, MA 1947). Deacon 1939, priest 1940. Curate: St Bartholomew's, Roby, 1939–40; Great Yarmouth, 1940–41; Chaplain, RAFVR, 1941–43; Rector of Weeley, 1943–45; Vicar of St James's, Birkdale, 1945–50; Editor, The Anvil, 1946–50; Founder and Editor, Eagle, Girl, Swift, and Robin, 1950–59; Man. Editor, Housewife, 1954–59. Hon. Chaplain, St Bride's, Fleet Street, 1952–83. *Publications:* Stories of the Old Testament, 1961; Stories of the New Testament, 1961; (ed) The Best of Eagle, 1977. *Recreation:* salmon and trout fishing. *Address:* The Mill House, Midford, near Bath, Avon BA2 7DE. *T:* Combe Down 833939.

*Died 16 March* 1989.

**MORRIS, Sir Keith (Douglas),** Kt 1980; CBE 1972; company director; Chairman: Besser (Qld) Ltd, since 1958; General Publishers Ltd, since 1973; Australian Burglar Alarm Co, since 1974; Deputy Chairman, United Packages, since 1970; *b* W Maitland, NSW, 13 Dec. 1908; *s* of late I. T. W. Morris; *m* 1934, Clarice, *d* of H. M. England; three *s*. *Educ:* Commercial High Sch., W Maitland. Director: Pillar Industries Pty Ltd, 1968–; Univ. of Qld Housing Ltd; Pres., Qld Chapter Aust. Inst. of Bldg, 1958–60, also Nat. Pres., Aust. Inst. of Bldg, 1968–70 (Inst. Medal 1972); Pres., Qld Master Builders Assoc., 1962–64 (Trustee, 1966–); Councillor, Nat. Safety Council of Aust., Qld; Governor: Qld Fest. of Arts Cttee; Boys Town Beaudesert State Cttee; Industrial Design Council of Aust.; Mem., Brisbane Adv. Bd, Salvation Army. Trustee: Qld Overseas Foundn; Spina Bifida Assoc. of Qld. FIOB; FRSH; FAIB; FAIM; FInstD. *Recreations:* reading, motoring, gardening. *Address:* 59 Denham Terrace, Wellers Hill, Queensland 4121, Australia. *T:* 48 2153. *Clubs:* Tattersall's, Brisbane QTC, BATC (Brisbane). *Died 8 March* 1981.

**MORRIS, Rev. Marcus;** *see* Morris, Rev. J. M. H.

**MORRIS, His Honour Sir Owen T.;** *see* Temple-Morris.

**MORRIS, Quentin Mathew;** Director: Globe Investment Trust, since 1984; Granada Group, since 1981; Johnson Matthey, since 1984; Waterford Group, since 1985; UGC (Unipart Group), since 1987; Medical Sickness Annuity & Life Assurance Society, since 1989; *b* 28 March 1930; *s* of John Eric and Annie Morris. *Educ:* St Clement Danes Grammar School; LSE (BSc Econ 1952). FTII 1964. Inland Revenue, 1952–64; British Petroleum, 1964–85 (Director: Group Finance, 1977–85; Africa, 1979–81; Latin America, 1981–84; Scicon International, 1981–84 (Chm.); Mercury Communications, 1984). Financial Adviser, Channel Tunnel Group (later Eurotunnel), 1985–86; Dir, Haden Gp, 1985–87; Chm., British Satellite Broadcasting working group, 1986; Advr to PO on sale of Girobank, 1988–89; Mem., CS Commn Final Selection Bd, 1976–85. Trustee: Whitechapel Art Gallery, 1983–87; Whitechapel Art Gallery Foundn, 1984–88 (Chm., 1984–87); Governor, LSE, 1982–(Standing Cttee, 1985–87; Chm., Inf. Technology Panel, 1985–); Special Trustee, Middlesex Hosp., 1982–; Mem. Council, Middlesex Hosp. Med. Sch., 1982–88 (Chm., Investment Sub-Cttee, 1982–88); Mem., Investment Cttee, UCL, 1987–. *Publications:* articles in newspapers and professional jls. *Recreations:* ski-ing, shooting, modern art, walking in cities. *Address:* Investment Trust, Globe House, 4 Temple Place, WC2R 3HP. *T:* 01–836 7766, *Fax:* 01–240 5599. *Clubs:* City of London, Reform, MCC; British Pottery Manufacturers' Fedn. *Died 6 Sept.* 1989.

**MORRIS, Rex G.;** *see* Goring-Morris.

**MORRIS, Sir (Thomas) Gwilym,** Kt 1979; CBE 1974; QPM 1968; DL; Chief Constable, South Wales Constabulary, 1971–79; *b* 16 Oct. 1913; *m* 1940, Mair Eluned Williams; one *s* one *d*. *Educ:* Swansea Grammar Sch. Certif. of Educn (1st cl.) of Civil Service Commn. Joined Metropolitan Police Force, 1933. Joined HM Forces, 1943; served War: commissioned 2nd Lieut, Suffolk Regt, 1944; Staff Captain G3 and ADC to Governor-Gen. of Jamaica, 1946; Major and Dep. Asst Adjt and QMG, N Caribbean Area,

1946. Rejoined Metropolitan Police, after War; Dist Supt, No 2 Dist HQ, Paddington, 1959; Asst Chief Constable, Cardiff, 1962, Chief Constable, Dec. 1963; Dep. Chief Constable, S Wales Constabulary, 1969. Pres., Vice-Pres., etc, various Socs. Admitted as Druid, Bardic Circle, National Eisteddfod, 1973. DL South Glamorgan 1972. Comr, E Glam Dist, Order of St John; CStJ 1970. *Recreations:* Rugby football, golf. *Address:* Erw Deg, 39 Llantrisant Road, Llandaff, Cardiff CF5 2PU. *T:* Cardiff 551877. *Clubs:* (Hon. Mem.) Cardiff and County (Cardiff); Crawshays'; (Vice-Pres.) Cardiff Athletic; (Vice-Pres.) Glamorgan Wanderers; Bridgend RFC.                                                      *Died* 18 *May* 1982.

**MORRIS, His Honour Sir William (Gerard),** Kt 1972; a Circuit Judge and Honorary Recorder of Manchester, 1972–77; *b* 20 June 1909; *s* of Joseph Thomas and Ellen Morris; *m* 1935, Mollie Broadbent; two *s* (and one *s* decd). *Educ:* Bolton Sch.; Gonville and Caius Coll., Cambridge. Called to Bar, 1931; practised on Northern Circuit till 1961; County Court Judge, 1961–66. Served in RAFVR, 1940–45, rank Sqdn Leader. Asst Recorder of Salford, 1956–61; Recorder of Liverpool, 1966–67; Recorder of Manchester, and Judge of the Crown Court at Manchester, 1967. *Recreation:* golf. *Address:* Kingslea, Chorley New Road, Bolton, Lancs. *T:* Bolton 40900.
                                                      *Died* 13 *Jan.* 1984.

**MORRIS, Sir Willie,** KCMG 1977 (CMG 1963); HM Diplomatic Service, retired; Director, Lloyds Bank International, 1980–82; *b* 3 Dec. 1919; *m* 1959, Ghislaine Margaret Trammell; three *s*. *Educ:* Batley Grammar Sch., Yorks; St John's Coll., Oxford. Served in Royal Navy, 1940–45. Joined Foreign Service, 1947; Third Sec., Middle East Centre for Arab Studies, 1947; Second Sec., Cairo, 1948; First Sec., 1951; transferred to Foreign Office, 1952; attended course at Canadian Defence Coll., 1954; transferred to Washington, 1955; Counsellor, Amman (Chargé d'Affaires, 1960, 1961 and 1962), 1960–63; Head of Eastern Dept, FO, 1963–67; Fellow, Center for Internat. Affairs, Harvard Univ., 1966–67; Ambassador: Jedda, 1968–72; (non-resident) Yemen Arab Republic, 1971; Addis Ababa, 1972–75; Cairo, 1975–79. *Address:* 2 Abberbury Avenue, Iffley, Oxford OX4 4EU. *Club:* Travellers'.        *Died* 13 *April* 1982.

**MORRIS-EYTON, Lt-Col Robert Charles Gilfrid,** TD; farmer; Vice Lord-Lieutenant of Shropshire, since 1987; *b* 8 May 1921; *s* of late Robert Edward Morris-Eyton and Violet Mary, *d* of Sir William Lewthwaite, 1st Bt; *m* 1956, Jean Jocelyn, *d* of Maj-Gen. E. G. Miles, CB, DSO, MC and Lady Marcia Valda, *y d* of 7th Earl of Roden; one *s* one *d*. *Educ:* Bilton Grange; Shrewsbury Sch.; Trinity Coll., Cambridge (BA). Served 75 Shropshire Yeomanry Med. Regt, RA (ME and Italy), 1942–45 (Lieut); Shropshire Yeomanry, TA, 1947–67 (Lt-Col). Farms 600 acres. Member: Telford Develt Corp., 1965–75; Salop CC, 1965–81 (Chm., 1974–77). Chm., W Mercia Police Authy, 1978–79. President: Shropshire Vol. Assoc. for Blind, 1975–; Shropshire Assoc. of Parish and Town Councils, 1977–84; Shropshire Horticultural Soc., 1978; Wrekin Div. Cons. Assoc., 1978–80. Churchwarden, Sambrook, 1946–. Shropshire: DL 1973; High Sheriff, 1980–81. *Recreations:* shooting, conservation. *Address:* Calvington, Newport, Shropshire TF10 8BG. *T:* Sambrook 316. *Club:* Farmers'.                                 *Died* 19 *Feb.* 1990.

**MORRIS JOHNS, Alun;** see Johns.

**MORRIS-JONES, Prof. Huw,** CBE 1983; Professor, University College of North Wales, Bangor, 1966–79; Head of Department of Social Theory and Institutions, University College, 1966–79; *b* 1 May 1912; *s* of William Oliver Jones and Margaret Jones; *m* 1942, Gwladys Evans; one *s* one *d*. *Educ:* Alun Grammar Sch., Mold, Flintshire; University Coll. of North Wales, Bangor; Oriel Coll., Oxford. Educn Officer, S Wales Council of Social Service, 1937–39; Tutor and Lectr, Dept of Extra-Mural Studies, Univ. of Nottingham, 1939–42; Lectr, Sen. Lectr and Prof., Bangor, 1942–79. Member: Aves Cttee of Inquiry into Voluntary Workers in Social Services, 1966–69; Welsh Hosp. Bd, 1967–70; Prince of Wales Cttee for Wales, 1967–70; Welsh Economic Council (Chm., Environmental Panel), 1967–71; Broadcasting Council for Wales, 1957–60; IBA (Chm., Welsh Adv. Cttee), 1976–82; Welsh Fourth TV Channel Auth., 1981–82. Chm., Caernarfon Borough, later Jt Caernarfon-Gwyrfai, Magistrates' Ct, 1949–82; Mem. Council, Magistrates' Assoc., 1950– (Chm., Gwynedd Br., 1952–). *Publications:* Y Gelfyddyd Lenyddol yng Nghymru, 1957; (contrib.) Aesthetics in the Modern World (ed Osborne), 1968; Emile Durkheim, 1983; Philosophy, Jl of Royal Inst. Philosophy, Monist, Efrydiau Athronyddol. *Address:* Ceredigion, Pentraeth Road, Menai Bridge, N Wales. *T:* Menai Bridge 712522. *Club:* United Oxford & Cambridge University.                               *Died* 6 *Jan.* 1989.

**MORRISON, Maj.-Gen. (retd) Albert Edward,** CB 1956; OBE 1942; *b* 17 March 1901; *s* of late Major A. Morrison; *m* 1926, Esther May Lacey (*d* 1988). *Educ:* Dover Coll.; RMA Woolwich. Royal Artillery, 1922–26; Royal Signals, 1926–57. Retired as Chief Signal Officer, AFHQ, March 1957. Col Commandant, Royal Corps of Signals, 1959–. Legion of Merit (US), 1946; Order of Rafidain (Iraq), 1940. *Recreation:* golf. *Address:* Wesley House, 68 Fairways,

Ferndown, Wimborne, Dorset BH22 8BB.
                                                      *Died* 20 *Dec.* 1989.

**MORRISON, Alexander,** CBE 1976; Chairman, Anglian Water Authority, 1978–81; *b* 25 Jan. 1917; *e s* of late Alexander Morrison and Sarah (*née* Drummond); *m* 1941, Jennie (*d* 1978), *o d* of late Henry and Ellen Mason; one *s* one *d*. *Educ:* Boroughmuir Sch., Edinburgh. Tax Officer, Inland Revenue, Edinburgh, 1934–36; Excise Off., Customs and Excise, Edinburgh, 1936; Royal Ordnance Factories: Jun. Exec. Off., Royal Arsenal, Woolwich, 1937–40; Higher Exec. Off.: Wigan, 1940–41; Poole, 1941–43; Sen. Exec. Off., Fazakerley, 1943–49; Chief Exec. Off., London, 1949–50; Overseas Food Corp., E Africa: Stores Controller, 1950–51; Chief Internal Auditor, 1951–52; Chief Accountant, 1952–54; Nat. Coal Board: Stores Controller, London, 1955–58; Purchasing and Stores Controller: W Mids Div., 1958–59; N Eastern Div., 1959–61; Chief Officer of Supplies, LCC, 1961–64; GLC: Dir of Supplies, 1964–67; Exec. Dir, Highways and Transportation, 1967–69; Traffic Comr and Dir of Develt, 1969–70; Controller of Operational Services, 1970–73. Chief Exec., Thames Water Authority, 1973–78. Pres., Purchasing Officers' Assoc., 1966–67; Member: Nat. Council for Quality and Reliability, 1963–71; Accounting Standards Cttee, 1979–81. FCMA (Mem. Council, 1971–, Vice-Pres., 1975, Pres., 1977); FInstPS; FCIT. Swinbank Medal, Inst. of Purchasing and Supply, 1968. *Publications:* Storage and Control of Stock, 1962, rev. edn 1981. *Recreations:* bowls, painting. *Address:* 70 Park Avenue, Bromley, Kent. *T:* 01–464 1460.                      *Died* 18 *May* 1982.

**MORRISON, Prof. James,** OBE 1963; BSc, NDA; Professor of Crop and Animal Husbandry, The Queen's University of Belfast, 1944–65, also Director, Agricultural Research Institute, Hillsborough, NI, 1934–65; retired; *b* 11 Aug. 1900; *m* 1934, Grace F. Stockdale, Clogher, Co. Tyrone; three *d*. *Educ:* Fordyce Academy, Banffshire, Scotland; Marischal Coll., Aberdeen Univ. Instructor in Agriculture, Co. Tyrone and Co. Down, 1925 and 1926; Sec. and Agric. Organiser, Co. Armagh, 1927–30; Inspector, Min. of Agric. for N Ireland, 1931–33; Lectr in Crop and Animal Husbandry, QUB, 1934. *Recreation:* gardening. *Address:* Loxwood, 35 Lisburn Road, Hillsborough, Co. Down BT26 6HW. *T:* Hillsborough (Co. Down) 682208.                                *Died* 12 *Nov.* 1987.

**MORRISON, James Victor,** CB 1979; TD 1950; *b* 13 Sept. 1917; *s* of Frederick Armand Morrison, Mountstewart, Co. Down, and Hannah Maria Snow, Kells, Co. Meath; *m* 1944, Sophie Winifred Ives; one *s* two *d*. *Educ:* Regent House. Entered NICS, 1937; War service, 1939–46: BEF, France; SE Asia; TA Service, 1947–57; comd 245 (Ulster) Light Air Defence Regt. NI Industrial Develt Rep., New York, 1957–60; Chief Administrative Officer, Police Authority for NI, 1970–74; Dep. Sec., NICS, seconded to NI Office, 1974–79. Mem., Police Authy for NI, 1979–85. *Recreations:* gardening, hi-fi, reading, walking. *Address:* 49 Castlehill Road, Belfast BT4 3GP. *T:* Belfast 63344.                    *Died* 26 *Feb.* 1990.

**MORRISON, Sir Nicholas (Godfrey),** KCB 1974 (CB 1967); Chairman, Local Government Boundary Commission for England, since 1978; Permanent Under-Secretary of State, Scottish Office, 1973–78; *b* 31 March 1918; *y s* of late John Wheatley Morrison and Kathleen King, Shotley Bridge, Co. Durham; *m* 1959, Rosemary, widow of E. H. U. de Groot; two step *d*. *Educ:* Cheltenham Coll.; Clare Coll., Cambridge (MA). Entered War Office, 1939; Asst Private Sec. to Sec. of State for War, 1942–44. Served War of 1939–45, in HM Forces, 1944–46. Private Sec. to Minister of Defence, 1952–53; Asst Sec., War Office, 1955; Asst Under-Sec. of State (Dir of Establishments), War Office, 1960; Asst Under-Sec. of State, Min. of Defence, 1964; Under-Secretary: HM Treasury, 1967–68; CSD, 1968–69; Dep. Sec., CSD, 1969–72; Dep. Under-Sec. of State, Scottish Office, 1972–73. Dir, Smith Kline and French Laboratories Ltd, 1981–. A Vice-Pres., RIPA, 1973–. Vice-Chairman Council and Cttee of Management, Inst. of Educn, Univ. of London, 1980–. CBIM; FIPM. *Recreations:* gardening, horseracing. *Address:* Gosse Ford, Clare, Suffolk. *T:* Clare 200. *Club:* Athenæum.                                  *Died* 7 *July* 1981.

**MORRISON, Rear-Adm. Thomas Kenneth,** CB 1967; CBE 1962 (OBE 1941); DSC; Royal Australian Navy, retired; *b* 31 Oct. 1911; *s* of late L. N. Morrison, Sydney, Australia; *m* 1938, Dorothy C. (decd), *d* of late W. M. Hole; one *s* three *d*. *Educ:* Jervis Bay Sch.; Royal Australian Naval College. Served War, 1939–45: Indian Ocean, Red Sea, Pacific (despatches, OBE, DSC). Qualified (Short Staff Course) RNC, Greenwich, 1945. Dir, Training and Staff Requirements, Navy Office, Melbourne, 1946–47; Comdr, Royal Australian Naval Coll., 1948–49; Capt., HMAS Tobruk, on commissioning, 1950–51; Dir of Manning, Navy Office, 1951–52; Dep. Chief of Naval Personnel, 1952–53; Commanding: 1st Frigate Squadron, Royal Australian Navy, 1954–55; HMAS Melbourne, 1959; Royal Australian Naval Air Stn, Nowra, NSW, 1961–62; Dep. Chief of the Naval Staff, Royal Australian Navy, 1962–64; Flag Officer Commanding the Australian Fleet, 1965; Flag Officer-in-Charge, East Australian Area, 1966–68. Australian Comr-Gen.

for Osaka Exposition, 1970. *Recreation:* golf. *Address:* 14 Milton Avenue, Woollahra, NSW 2025, Australia. *Club:* Royal Sydney Golf.                                                        *Died* 20 *April* 1983.

**MORSE, David Abner;** partner, law firm of Jones, Day, Reavis & Pogue (Washington DC, Ohio, California, New York City, Texas, Hong Kong, Geneva, Paris, London and Riyadh), since 1970; *b* New York City, 31 May 1907; *m* 1937, Mildred H. Hockstader. *Educ:* Somerville Public Schs, NJ; Rutgers Coll., NJ; Harvard Law Sch. LittB (Rutgers), 1929, LLB (Harvard), 1932. Admitted to New Jersey Bar, 1932, NY Bar, Washington DC Bar; Chief Counsel Petroleum Labor Policy Bd, Dept of Interior, 1934–35. US Dept of Interior; Special Asst to US Attorney-Gen., 1934–35; Regional Attorney, National Labor Relations Bd (Second Region), 1935–38. Impartial Chm., Milk Industry Metropolitan Area of New York, 1940–42, when entered Army. Lectr on Labor Relations, Labor Law, Administrative Law, various colleges and law schools, 1938–47. Gustav Pollak Lectr on Research in Govt, Harvard Univ., 1955–56. Formerly: Perm. US Govt Mem. on Governing Body of Internat. Labor Office; US Govt Deleg. to Internat. Labor Confs; Statutory Mem. Bd of Foreign Service; Dep. Chm. Interdepartmental Cttee on Internat. Social Policy; Mem., Cttee for Conservation of Manpower in War Industry, State of NJ; served in N Africa, Sicily and Italy, 1943–44 (Chief of Labor Div., Allied Mil. Govt) arrived in England, 1944. Major, 1944; Chief of Labor Section, US Group Control Council for Germany and prepared Labor Policy and Program for Germany; also advised and assisted SHAEF in preparation of Labor Policy and Program for France, Belgium, Holland, etc; Lt-Col and Dir Labor for Mil. Govt Group, 1945; returned to US; Gen. Counsel, Nat. Labor Relations Bd, 1945–46; Asst Sec. of Labor, 1946–47; Under-Sec. of Labor, 1947–48; Actg Sec. of Labor, June-Aug. 1948; Dir-Gen., Internat. Labor Office, Geneva, 1948–70; Adviser to Administrator, UN Develt Programme. Member: Amer. Bar Assoc.; Council on Foreign Relations; World Rehabilitation Fund; Albert and Mary Lasker Foundn; Nat. Council of UN Assoc. of USA; Amer. Arbitration Assoc.; American Legion; Impartial Chm., Coat and Suit Ind. of Metropolitan Area of NY, 1970–. Hon. LLD: Rutgers, 1957; Geneva, 1962; Strasbourg, 1968; Hon. DSc, Laval, Quebec, 1969; Hon. DHL Brandeis Univ., 1971. Sidney Hillman Foundn Award, 1969; Rutgers Univ. Alumni Award, 1970; Internat. League for Rights of Man Award, 1970; Three Bronze Battle Stars; Legion of Merit; Officier de l'Etoile Equatoriale (Gabon); Ordre de la valeur (Cameroon); Order of Merit of Labour (Brazil); Grand Officer, Simon Bolivar, (Columbia), 1970; Grand Officer, Order of Merit (Italy), 1971; Grand Officer, French Legion of Honour, 1971; Orden El Sol (Peru), 1972; Grand Officer, Ordre National du Lion (Senegal), 1978. *Address:* 575 Park Avenue, New York, NY 10021, USA. *Clubs:* Metropolitan (Washington DC); Century Association (New York); Interalliée (Paris).                         *Died* 1 *Dec.* 1990.

**MORTIMER, Chapman;** *see* Chapman-Mortimer, W. C.

**MORTON, Digby;** *see* Morton, H. D.

**MORTON, Rev. Harry Osborne;** Methodist Minister, supernumerary 1981, due to ill-health; *b* 28 June 1925; *s* of John William Morton and Alice Morton (*née* Betteridge); *m* 1954, Patricia Mary McGrath; two *s* two *d* (and one *d* decd). *Educ:* The King's Sch., Pontefract, Yorks; King's Coll., Cambridge (MA Cantab); Hartley Victoria Methodist Theological Coll., Manchester. Marconi's Wireless Telegraph Co. Ltd, 1945; Gen. Sec., Order of Christian Witness, 1947; entered Methodist Ministry, 1949; ordained Deacon, Church of South India, 1954, Presbyter, 1955; Sec. for Scholarships, World Council of Churches, Geneva, 1960; Sec. for East and Central Africa, Methodist Missionary Soc., 1963, Gen. Sec. 1972–73; Gen. Sec., BCC, 1973–80; Superintendent Minister, London Mission (East Ham) Circuit, 1980–81. Pres., Methodist Conf., 1972. Select Preacher, Cambridge Univ., 1972 and 1975. *Recreation:* music. *Address:* 34B Campbell Road, Bow, E3 4DT. *T:* 01–980 9460.
                                                        *Died* 5 *Dec.* 1988.

**MORTON, (Henry) Digby;** consultant designer (independent); *b* 27 Nov. 1906; *e s* of Digby Berkeley Morton, Dublin; *m* 1936, Phyllis May, *d* of James Harwood Panting, London. *Educ:* Dublin. Trained in Art and Architecture, Metropolitan Sch. of Art, Dublin, 1923–29. Opened Couture Establishment in London, 1930; designed WVS uniform for Lady Reading, 1939; worked in USA, 1953–57. Founder Member: Incorporated Soc. of London Fashion Designers, 1939 (Vice-Pres., 1955–56); Visual Arts Soc. of the Cayman Is, for the promotion of art in this Crown Colony. *Recreation:* painting. *Address:* PO Box 191, Grand Cayman, Cayman Islands.
                                                        *Died* 5 *Dec.* 1983.

**MORTON, John Percival,** CMG 1965; OBE 1946; Indian Police Medal for gallantry, 1935, Bar 1940; retired; *b* 15 May 1911; *e s* of late Henry Percy Dee Morton; *m* 1939, Leonora Margaret Sale, *d* of late Hon. Mr Justice S. L. Sale, ICS; one *d* (one *s* decd). *Educ:* Bedford Modern Sch. Indian Police, Punjab, 1930–47 (Dist Supt Police Jullundur; Central Int. Officer, Govt of India, Punjab and

Delhi Provinces; seconded HQ British Troops (Egypt); Senior Supt Police, Lahore Dist.); Principal, War Office, 1947; Civil Asst, Staff of AOC RAF Iraq, 1947–49; Counsellor, Office of Comr-Gen., SE Asia, 1949–52; Dir of Int., Govt of Malaya, 1952–54; Asst Sec., War Office, 1954–59; IDC 1959; Sec. of State's Adv. Staff, Colonial Office, 1961–65; Asst Under-Sec. of State, MoD, 1968–71; retired 1971. Advisory missions for FCO to Jordan, Pakistan, Mauritius, E Caribbean and Sri Lanka, 1972–79, for MoD to N Ireland, 1973; Consultant: The De La Rue Co. Ltd, 1972–75; N. M. Rothschild & Sons Ltd, 1972–76; Panel Chm., Civil Service Commn Selection Bd, 1973–80; Chm., Aviation Industry Security Trng Steering Gp, 1978–79. *Recreations:* golf, music. *Address:* Courtlands Cottage, Green Lane, Pangbourne, Berks. *T:* Pangbourne 3908. *Clubs:* East India, Devonshire, Sports and Public Schools; Huntercombe (Oxon).                                             *Died* 7 *June* 1985.

**MORTON, Sir Ralph (John),** Kt 1960; CMG 1954; OBE 1947; MC 1918; Judge of High Court of Southern Rhodesia, 1949–59; *b* 2 Aug. 1896; *yr s* of John Morton, Wotton-under-Edge, Glos; *m* 1923, Cato Marie van den Berg (*d* 1975); one *d*. *Educ:* Bishop's Stortford; Cambridge Univ. Served European War, RFA, 1915–19. Southern Rhodesia: Solicitor General, 1934; Attorney General, 1944. *Address:* 3 Dundalk Avenue, Parkview, Johannesburg, 2193, South Africa.                                             *Died* 7 *March* 1985.

**MORTON, Sir Wilfred;** *see* Morton, Sir William W.

**MORTON, Prof. William Ernest,** MSc Tech; FTI; Professor Emeritus in the University of Manchester, 1967; Professor of Textile Technology, 1926–57, Arkwright Professor, and Vice-Principal of the University Institute of Science and Technology, 1957–67, Pro-Vice-Chancellor, 1963–65 and Dean of the Faculty of Technology, 1964–66; *b* 1902; *s* of J. Morton, LDS Ed., Penrith; *m* 1927, Elsie Maud, *d* of Charles Harlow, Fallowfield, Manchester; two *s* two *d*. *Educ:* St Bees Sch., Cumbria; Manchester Univ.; MScTech 1923; Research Studentship, British Cotton Industry Research Assoc., 1923; Technical Asst to the Dir BCIRA, 1924; Technical Adviser to Dir of Narrow Fabrics, Min. of Supply, 1941–45. Chm., Heightside Housing Assoc., 1967–75. Hon. Fellow, UMIST, 1977. Textile Inst. Medal, 1952; Warner Medal, 1957. *Publications:* An Introduction to the Study of Spinning, 1938; (with J. W. S. Hearle) Physical Properties of Textile Fibres, 1963; papers read before the Textile Institute, and contribs to technical journals. *Recreation:* bridge. *Address:* Solway, Delahays Drive, Hale, Altrincham, Cheshire WA15 8OP. *T:* 061-980 4520.                *Died* 8 *Oct.* 1981.

**MORTON, Sir (William) Wilfred,** KCB 1966 (CB 1958); Chairman, Board of Customs and Excise, 1965–69; *b* 14 April 1906; *s* of late William Morton; *m* 1939, Jacqueline Harriet, *d* of late H. P. B. Newman, Grenfell, New South Wales. *Educ:* Hutchesons' Grammar Sch.; Glasgow Univ. Entered Inland Revenue, 1927. Consultant to Govt of Bolivia, 1952–54; Comr of Inland Revenue and Dir of Establishments, 1955–58; Third Sec., HM Treasury, 1958–65. *Address:* Brook House, Bagnor, Newbury, Berks. *Club:* Athenæum.                                             *Died* 7 *Jan.* 1981.

**MOSES, Sir Charles (Joseph Alfred),** Kt 1961; CBE 1954; Hon. Councillor, Asian Broadcasting Union, since 1977 (Secretary-General, 1965–77); General Manager, Australian Broadcasting Commission, 1935–65; Company Director; *b* 21 Jan. 1900; *s* of Joseph Moses and Lily (*née* Henderson); *m* 1922, Kathleen, *d* of Patrick O'Sullivan, Bruree, Co. Limerick; one *s* (one *d* decd). *Educ:* Oswestry Grammar Sch.; RMC Sandhurst. Lt 2nd Border Regt, 1918–22, serving in Germany and Ireland; fruitgrower, Bendigo, Australia, 1922–24; in motor business in Melbourne, 1924–30; in radio, ABC: Announcer/Commentator, 1930–32; Talks and Sporting Editor, Sydney, 1933–34; Federal Talks Controller, 1934–35. War of 1939–45 (despatches): AIF in Malaya and Singapore, Major, 1941–42, in New Guinea, Lt-Col, 1942–43. Leader of Austr. Delegn to UNESCO Annual Gen. Conf., Paris, 1952; Chm. Commonwealth Jubilee Arts Cttee, 1951; Vice-President: Royal Agricultural Society of NSW, 1951–; Elizabethan Theatre Trust, 1954–84; Royal NSW Instn for Deaf and Blind Children, 1965–; President: Remembrance Driveway (NSW), 1953–; Aust. Acad. of Broadcast Arts and Sciences, 1986–. Hon. Dir, Postgraduate Med. Foundn (NSW). Mem., Internat. Inst. of Communications, London, 1965–; Vice-Chm., Asian Mass Communications and Inf. Centre, Singapore, 1969–83. Pres., 1944–69, Patron, 1969–, Eastern Suburbs Rugby Club; Pres., Athletic Assoc. of NSW, 1946–67. *Publication:* Diverse Unity: a history of the Asia-Pacific Broadcasting Union 1957–77, 1978. *Recreations:* reading, music. *Address:* 56/28 Curagul Road, North Turramurra, NSW 2074, Australia. *T:* 44 2752. *Clubs:* Australian, Tattersall's, Rugby Union (Sydney).                     *Died* 9 *Feb.* 1988.

**MOSS, Dr Alfred Allinson;** Keeper of Minerals, British Museum (Natural History), 1968–74; *b* 30 Dec. 1912; *o s* of Frank Allinson and Alice Moss; *m* 1938, Sheila Mary, *o d* of Charles H. Sendell; two *d*. *Educ:* Ilfracombe Grammar Sch.; University Coll., Exeter. BSc London; PhD London. Chemist: War Dept, 1936; Govt

Laboratory, 1937–39; Asst Keeper, Brit. Mus., 1939–40; Chemist, Chief Chemical Inspectorate, Min. of Supply, 1940–45; Asst Keeper, Brit. Mus., 1945–49; Principal Scientific Officer: Brit. Mus., 1949–53; Brit. Mus. (Nat. Hist.), 1953–59; Dep. Keeper of Minerals, Brit. Mus. (Nat. Hist.), 1959; Keeper, 1968. Treas., Mineralogical Soc., 1966–73. *Publications:* papers on archaeological and mineralogical subjects in various jls. *Recreations:* horology, chess, photography. *Address:* 12 Somerfields, Lyme Regis, Dorset DT7 3EZ. *T:* Lyme Regis (02974) 3443. *Died* 28 *Oct.* 1990.

**MOSS, Sir Eric (de Vere),** Kt 1952; CIE 1943; late ICS; subsequently posts in Pakistan and lately Northern Rhodesia; *b* 13 April 1896; *s* of F. J. Moss; *m* 1919, Monica Meriton-Reed; one *s* three *d. Educ:* Victoria Coll., Jersey. Served War of 1914–18, 6th (S) Bn Dorsetshire Regt, 2nd Lt; active service in France, inc. Battle of the Somme, 1916; Indian Army, 1916–23: Staff Captain, 6th Indian Inf. Brigade, 1919; fought in 3rd Afghan War. Joined ICS, 1923; District Magistrate and Collector of Gorakhpur, UP, 1940–42; War Production Comr, UP, 1943–46; Commissioner Jhansi Division, UP, 1946; Sec. to Min. of Industries and Commerce, Govt of Pakistan, 1947; Pakistan Refugees Commissioner; Sec. to Ministry of Refugees and Rehabilitation, Govt of Pakistan, 1948–49; Sec. to Ministry of Health and Works, Government of Pakistan, 1950; Road Traffic Commissioner, Government of Northern Rhodesia, 1952–62. *Recreations:* shooting and fishing. *Address:* Bracken Lodge, Brookside Close, Runcton, Chichester, West Sussex PO20 6PY. *T:* Chichester 784521. *Club:* East India, Devonshire, Sports and Public Schools. *Died* 25 *June* 1981.

**MOSS, Sir John Herbert Theodore E.;** *see* Edwards-Moss.

**MOSS, Rosalind Louisa Beaufort,** FSA; Editor of Porter-Moss Topographical Bibliography of Ancient Egyptian Hieroglyphic Texts, Reliefs, and Paintings, 1924–72, retired; *b* 21 Sept. 1890; *d* of Rev. H. W. Moss, Headmaster of Shrewsbury Sch., 1866–1908. *Educ:* Heathfield Sch., Ascot; St Anne's Coll., Oxford. Diploma in Anthropology (distinction), 1917, BSc Oxon 1922. Took up Egyptology, 1917. FSA 1949. Hon. DLitt Oxon, 1961. Hon. Fellow, St Anne's Coll., Oxford, 1967. *Publications:* Life after Death in Oceania, 1925; Topographical Bibliography (see above); articles in Journal of Egyptian Archæology, etc. *Address:* 51 Yew Tree Bottom Road, Epsom, Surrey KT17 3NQ. *Died* 22 *April* 1990.

**MOSTYN, Sir Jeremy (John Anthony),** 14th Bt *cr* 1670; *b* 24 Nov. 1933; *s* of Sir Basil Anthony Trevor Mostyn, 13th Bt and Anita Mary, *d* of late Lt-Col Rowland Charles Feilding, DSO; *S* father, 1956; *m* 1963, Cristina, *o d* of Marchese Orengo, Turin; one *s* two *d. Educ:* Rhodesia and Downside. Contested: Ealing South (L) General Election, 1959; Cities of London and Westminster, LCC Elections, 1960. Green Staff Officer, Investiture of the Prince of Wales, 1969. FRSA; AMRSH. Kt of Honour and Devotion, SMO Malta. *Recreation:* saving and restoring old houses. *Heir: s* William Basil John Mostyn, *b* 15 Oct. 1975. *Address:* Westbrook Court, Dorstone, Hereford HR3 5SY; The Coach House, Lower Heyford, Oxford OX5 3NZ. *Died* 8 *Nov.* 1988.

**MOTT, Norman Gilbert,** CMG 1962; retired, 1969; *b* 7 Sept. 1910; *s* of late Albert Norman Mott and late Ada Emily Kilby; *m* 1941, Betty Mary, *d* of late Sidney Hugh Breeze; two *s. Educ:* Christ's Coll., Finchley. Served in HM Forces (Intelligence Corps), 1940–47. Joined HM Diplomatic Service, 1948; served in Foreign Office and at Trieste. *Recreations:* gardening, photography. *Address:* 34 Ferndale Road, Chichester, West Sussex. *T:* Chichester 527960. *Died* 15 *Feb.* 1987.

**MOTTERSHEAD, Peter Michael Hall,** QC 1979; *b* 15 Nov. 1926; *o s* of late Harry Mottershead and Constance Helen, 7th *d* of Frederick Hall, Macclesfield; *m* All Saints Day 1952, Lorna Eden, *o d* of R. W. and Lily Evans, Manchester; one *s. Educ:* The King's Sch., Macclesfield; Jesus Coll., Cambridge (Exhibnr 1946, BA 1951, MA 1954). National Service, 1946–48: Border Regt and RAOC, commnd 1947. Called to the Bar, Inner Temple, 1952 (Philip Teichman Schol.; Yarborough-Anderson Schol.); in practice, 1952–; admitted *ad eundem*, Lincoln's Inn, 1982; Member: General Council of the Bar and of Senate of the Inns of Court and the Bar, 1971–75. *Recreations:* water colour drawing, walking, modest climbing, compulsory gardening, avoiding people. *Address:* 11 New Square, Lincoln's Inn, WC2A 3QB. *T:* 01-405 1793; Thundridge, Ware, Herts. *Club:* Reform. *Died* 17 *April* 1985.

**MOTZ, Prof. Hans;** Professor of Engineering, University of Oxford, 1972–77, later Emeritus; Emeritus Fellow of St John's College, Oxford and St Catherine's College, Oxford; Honorary Professor, Technical University, Vienna, since 1980; Hon. Consultant, Culham Laboratory, United Kingdom Atomic Energy Authority; *b* 1 Oct. 1909; *s* of Karl and Paula Motz; *m* 1959, Lotte Norwood-Edlis; one *d. Educ:* Technische Hochschule, Vienna; Besançon Univ. (Schol.); Trinity Coll., Dublin (Schol.). Dipl. Ing 1932, Dr Techn. Sc. 1935, MSc TCD, MA Oxon; FInstP. Research Engr, Standard Telephones & Cables, 1939–41; Demonstrator, Dept of Engrg Science, Oxford,

1941; Lectr in Engrg Physics, Sheffield Univ., 1946–48; Research Assoc., Microwave Lab., Stanford Univ., 1949; Donald Pollock Reader in Engrg Science, Oxford, 1954; Professorial Fellow, St Catherine's Coll., Oxford, 1963. Internat. Fellow, Stanford Res. Inst., 1956; Guest Prof., Paris Univ. (Saclay), 1964; Visiting Professor: Brown Univ., 1959; Brooklyn Polytech., 1965; Innsbruck Univ., 1967; Tech. Univ., Vienna, 1979–80 (permanent Hon. Prof., 1980). Ehrenkreuz für Wissenschaft und Kunst, 1st class (Austria), 1980. *Publications:* Problems of Microwave Theory, 1951; The Physics of Laser Fusion, 1979; many papers in sci. jls, including Neuroscience. *Recreations:* ski-ing, yachting, silversmith, and enamel work. *Address:* 16 Bedford Street, Oxford. *T:* Oxford 241895. *Died* 6 *Aug.* 1987.

**MOULE-EVANS, David,** DMus Oxon; Composer; Conductor; Professor of Harmony, Counterpoint and Composition, Royal College of Music, 1945–74; *b* 21 Nov. 1905; *s* of John Evans, MA Cantab, and Emily Blanche Evans (*née* Cookson); *m* 1935, Monica Warden Evans, *d* of Richardson Evans, ICS; no *c. Educ:* The Judd Sch.; Royal College of Music. Mem. of Queen's Coll., Oxford. Open Scholarship in Composition, RCM, 1925 (Senior Composition Scholar); Mendelssohn Scholarship, 1928; DMus Oxford, 1930. Carnegie Publication Award (for Concerto for String Orchestra), 1928. Symphony in G Major awarded £1,000 Prize offered by Australian Govt, 1952. Examiner, Associated Bd, Royal Schs of Music, 1945–74. Many public and broadcast performances of orchestral and other works; has written music for many documentary films, including British Council commissions. *Publications: published orchestral works include:* Overture: The Spirit of London, 1947; Vienna Rhapsody, 1948; The Haunted Place (for String Orchestra), 1949; Old Tupper's Dance, 1951; chamber works: instrumental pieces and songs. *Recreations:* reading and studying subjects other than music. *Address:* Claremont, Rose Hill, Dorking, Surrey. *Died* 18 *May* 1988.

**MOUNT EDGCUMBE,** 7th Earl of, *cr* 1789; **Edward Piers Edgcumbe;** Viscount Mount Edgcumbe and Valletort, 1781; Baron Edgcumbe of Mount Edgcumbe, Co. Cornwall (UK), 1742; *b* 13 July 1903; *s* of George Valletort Edgcumbe (*d* 1947) and Georgina Mildred (*d* 1941), *d* of T. A. Bell; *S* cousin, 1965; *m* 1944, Victoria Effie Warbrick (widow) (*d* 1979), *y d* of late Robert Campbell, N Ireland and NZ. *Heir: nephew* Robert Charles Edgcumbe [*b* 1 June 1939; *m* 1960; five *d*]. *Address:* Mount Edgcumbe, Plymouth. *Died* 9 *Dec.* 1982.

**MOUNTFIELD, Alexander Stuart;** *b* 5 Dec. 1902; *s* of Robert Mountfield and Caroline (*née* Appleyard); *m* 1934, Agnes Elizabeth Gurney; two *s. Educ:* Merchant Taylors' Sch., Crosby. Entered service of Mersey Docks and Harbour Board as Apprentice, 1918; served through clerical grades and in various administrative capacities. Gen. Man. and Sec., Mersey Docks and Harbour Bd, 1957–62; retd 1962. FCIT. *Recreation:* reading. *Address:* Helena House Nursing Home, 20 Albert Road, Southport PR9 0LE. *Club:* Athenæum (Liverpool). *Died* 1 *Dec.* 1984.

**MOWLEM, Rainsford,** FRCS; Emeritus Consulting Plastic Surgeon, Middlesex Hospital; Surgeon i/c Department for Plastic Surgery, Middlesex Hospital, 1939–62, retired; Surgeon i/c North West Regional Centre for Plastic Surgery, Mount Vernon Hospital; Consulting Plastic Surgeon to King Edward VII Hospital, Windsor, Luton and Dunstable Hospital, Birmingham Accident Hospital; *b* 21 Dec. 1902; *s* of Arthur Manwell Mowlem, New Zealand; *m* 1933, Margaret West Harvey; two *d. Educ:* Auckland Grammar Sch.; Univ. of New Zealand. MB, ChB, NZ 1924, FRCS 1929. Asst Med. Officer i/c Plastic Surgery Unit, LCC, 1933–37; Asst Plastic Surgeon, St Andrews Hosp., Dollis Hill, 1937–39; Surgeon i/c NW Centre Plastic Surgery, Hill End Hosp., 1939–53. Hunterian Prof., RCS, 1940. President: British Assoc. of Plastic Surgeons, 1950, 1959 (Mem. Council, 1947–57; Hon. Fellow, 1975); Internat. Congress of Plastic Surgeons, 1959. Sen. Fellow, Assoc. Surgeons of GB and Ireland; Fellow: RSM; Brit. Orthopædic Assoc.; Hon. Fellow, Amer. Assoc. Plastic Surgeons. Sen. Corresp. Mem., Amer. Soc. of Plastic and Reconstructive Surgeons; Hon. Member: Netherlands Soc. of Plastic Surgery; Soc. Italiana di Cirurgia Plastica; Soc. Française de Chirurgie Plastique et Reconstructive; Nordisk Plastikkirurgisk Forening; Soc. Española de Cirurgia Plástica y Reparadora; Internat. Soc. of Aesthetic Plastic Surgery; Inst. of Accident Surgery. Hon. ScD Trinity Coll., Hartford. *Publications:* various on subjects related to plastic surgery. *Address:* La Morena, Apartado 56, Mijas, Málaga, Spain. *Died* 6 *Feb.* 1986.

**MOYNIHAN, Rodrigo,** CBE 1953; RA 1954 (ARA 1944); artist; lately Professor of Painting at the Royal College of Art; *b* 17 Oct. 1910; *s* of Herbert James Moynihan and late Maria de la Puerta; *m* 1931, Elinor Bellingham Smith (marr. diss.; she *d* 1988); one *s; m* 1960, Anne (marr. diss.), *d* of Sir James Hamet Dunn, 1st Bt; one *s. Educ:* UCS, London, and in USA. Slade Sch., 1928–31; Mem. of London Group, 1933; one-man shows at: Redfern Gall., 1940, 1958, 1961; Leicester Gallery, 1946; Hanover Gallery, 1963, 1967; Fischer

Fine Art, 1973, 1982; Royal Academy (major retrospective), 1978; Galerie Claude Bernard, Paris, 1984; New York: Egan Gallery, 1966; Tibor de Nagy, 1968; Robert Miller Gall., 1980, 1983; drawings exhibited at: Karsten Schubertgall., David Grob Gall., 1988. Vis. Prof., Slade Sch., 1980–84. Army Service, 1940–43; Official War Artist, 1943–44. Pictures purchased by Chantrey Bequest, Tate Gallery, Contemporary Art Soc., War Artists' Advisory Cttee, Nat. Portrait Gallery, Hirschhorn Coll., Washington. Hon. Dr RCA 1969; Fellow UCL, 1970–. Editor (jtly with wife), Art and Literature, 1963–68. *Publication:* Goya, 1951. *Address:* c/o Royal Academy, Piccadilly, W1V 0DS. *Club:* Buck's.

*Died 6 Nov.* 1990.

**MUGGERIDGE, Douglas (Thomas);** Managing Director, External Broadcasting, BBC, 1981–85; *b* 2 Dec. 1928; *s* of late Col Harry Douglas Muggeridge, OBE, and Bertha Ursula Rutland; *m* 1953, Diana Marguerite Hakim; two *d. Educ:* Shrewsbury; London Sch. of Economics. Sub-Editor and Leader-Writer, Liverpool Daily Post, 1953; joined BBC as Talks Producer, 1956; Senior Producer, 1959; Chief Publicity Officer, Overseas, 1961; Chief Asst, Publicity, 1964; Head of Overseas Talks and Features, 1965; Controller, Radio 1 and 2, 1969; Dir of Programmes, Radio, 1976; Dep. Man. Dir, BBC Radio, 1978–80. Pres., Radio Industries Club, 1977–78. *Recreations:* music, fishing, book collecting. *Address:* Castle Hill Cottage, Rotherfield, Sussex. *T:* Rotherfield 2770.

*Died 26 Feb.* 1985.

**MUGGERIDGE, (Thomas) Malcolm;** *b* 24 March 1903; *s* of late H. T. Muggeridge; *m* 1927, Katherine, *d* of G. C. Dobbs; two *s* one *d* (and one *s* decd). *Educ:* Selhurst Grammar Sch.; Selwyn Coll., Cambridge. Lecturer at Egyptian Univ., Cairo, 1927–30; Editorial Staff, Manchester Guardian, 1930–32; Manchester Guardian correspondent, Moscow, 1932–33; Asst Editor, Calcutta Statesman, 1934–35; Editorial staff, Evening Standard, 1935–36. Served in War of 1939–45, in East Africa, North Africa, Italy and France, Intelligence Corps, Major (Legion of Hon., Croix de Guerre with Palm, Médaille de la Reconnaissance Française). Daily Telegraph Washington Correspondent, 1946–47; Dep. Editor Daily Telegraph, 1950–52; Editor of Punch, Jan. 1953–Oct. 1957. Rector, Edinburgh Univ., 1967–68. *Television:* Muggeridge Ancient and Modern (series), 1981. *Publications:* Three Flats, produced by the Stage Society, 1931; Autumnal Face, 1931; Winter in Moscow, 1933; The Earnest Atheist, a life of Samuel Butler, 1936; In A Valley of this Restless Mind, 1938, new edn, 1978; The Thirties, 1940; edited English edn Ciano's Diary, 1947; Ciano's Papers, 1948; Affairs of the Heart, 1949; Tread Softly for you Tread on my Jokes, 1966; London à la Mode (with Paul Hogarth), 1966; Muggeridge through the Microphone (Edited by C. Ralling); Jesus Rediscovered, 1969; Something Beautiful for God, 1971; Paul: envoy extraordinary (with A. R. Vidler), 1972; Chronicles of Wasted Time (autobiog.), vol. 1, 1972, vol. 2, 1973; Malcolm's Choice, 1972; Jesus: the man who lives, 1975; A Third Testament, 1977; A Twentieth-Century Testimony, 1979; Like It Was (diaries), 1981; Picture Palace, 1987; My Life in Pictures, 1987; Conversion: A Spiritual Journey, 1988. *Recreation:* walking. *Address:* Park Cottage, Robertsbridge, East Sussex TN32 5ND.　　　*Died 14 Nov.* 1990.

**MUHAMMAD, Valiyaveettil Abdulaziz Seyid,** PhD; barrister; High Commissioner for India in London, 1980–84; *b* Kerala, 29 May 1923; *m* 1958, Sara Beebi; two *s* two *d. Educ:* Aligarh Muslim Univ. (MA, LLB 1st Cl. 1946); Univ. of London (PhD 1955). Called to the Bar, Inner Temple, 1953. Lawyer and Advocate Gen., Kerala State, 1965–67; Sen. Standing Counsel for State of Kerala and Union Govt in the Supreme Court, 1967–75; Mem., Rajya Sabha, 1973–77, Lok Sabha, 1977–80; Minister of State for Law, Justice, and Company Affairs, 1975–77. Sen. Adviser to Indian Delegn to UN, 1971; alternate Mem., Indian Delegn to UN Gen. Assembly, 1975; Chm., Panel on Minorities, Scheduled Castes, Scheduled Tribes and Weaker Sections, 1980. *Publications:* (ed jtly) The Indian Advocate; The Legal Framework of World Trade, 1958; Our Constitution: For Haves or Have-Nots?, 1974. *Recreations:* reading, walking, gardening. *Address:* Bar Association, Supreme Court of India, Tilak Marg, New Delhi 11 00 11, India.

*Died 28 Feb.* 1985.

**MUIL, Maj.-Gen. David John,** CB 1956; OBE 1945; *b* 18 Oct. 1898; *s* of David Muil, Kirkintilloch, Scotland; *m* 1924, Ruth, *d* of Mark Burgess, Alderley Edge, Cheshire; one *d. Educ:* Aston Grammar Sch.; Birmingham Univ. Served European War, 1917–19, with London Scottish, Royal Warwickshire Regt and RFC (France and Belgium). Joined Royal Army Dental Corps, 1923, and served with them War of 1939–45, in India and Far East; Col, 1949. Dir Army Dental Service, 1955–58. QHDS 1955. *Address:* 4 Courtslands, Court Downs Road, Beckenham, Kent. *T:* 01-650 9060.

*Died 25 Dec.* 1982.

**MUIR, Air Commodore Adam,** CB 1967; retired, 1977; *b* 4 Aug. 1908; *s* of George Muir and Mary Gillies Ferguson; *m* 1938, Isobel Janet Arbuckle Turnbull (*d* 1967); one *s* one *d. Educ:* Greenock Acad.;

Glasgow Univ. MA 1929; BSc 1931; MB, ChB (Commend.) 1934; DTM&H (Eng) 1954; MRCPE 1955; FRCPE 1963. Joined RAF Medical Branch, 1937, retd 1967; served War of 1939–45, Iceland and Mediterranean Theatres (despatches twice); Dir of Hygiene and Research, RAF, 1959–63; PMO, RAF Germany, 1963–67; Officer i/c Reception, BMH Rinteln, 1967–70; MO, Army Careers Information Office, Glasgow, 1970–77. CStJ 1966. *Recreation:* music. *Address:* Clachan, Tighnabruaich, Argyll PA21 2DY. *T:* Tighnabruaich 378. *Club:* Royal Air Force.

*Died 20 March* 1986.

**MUIR, (Charles) Augustus (Carlow);** author and journalist; Regimental Historian, The Royal Scots; *b* Carluke, Ontario, Canada, 15 Nov. 1892; *s* of late Rev. Walter Muir and Elizabeth Carlow; *m* Jean Murray Dow Walker (*d* 1972); *m* 1975, Mair Davies. *Educ:* George Heriot's Sch. and Edinburgh Univ.; contributor to various dailies, weeklies, and monthlies; Asst Editor and subsequently Editor, the World; served 1914–19 in Royal Scots, King's Own Scottish Borderers, and on Staff. *Publications:* The Third Warning, 1925; The Black Pavilion, 1926; The Blue Bonnet, 1926; The Shadow on the Left, 1928; The Silent Partner, 1929; Birds of the Night, 1930; Beginning the Adventure, 1932; The House of Lies, 1932; The Green Lantern, 1933; The Riddle of Garth, 1933; Scotland's Road of Romance, 1934; Raphael MD, 1935; The Crimson Crescent, 1935; Satyr Mask, 1936; The Bronze Door, 1936; The Red Carnation, 1937; The Man Who Stole the Crown Jewels, 1937; Castles in the Air, 1938; The Sands of Fear, 1939; The Intimate Thoughts of John Baxter, Bookseller, 1942; Joey and the Greenwings, 1943; Heather-Track and High Road, 1944; (ed jtly) The Saintsbury Memorial Volume, 1945; Scottish Portrait, 1948; (ed jtly) A Last Vintage: Essays by George Saintsbury, 1950; The Story of Jesus, 1953; The Fife Coal Company, 1953; (ed) How to Choose and Enjoy Wine, 1953; The History of the Shotts Iron Company, 1954; Candlelight in Avalon, A Spiritual Pilgrimage, 1954; Nairns of Kirkcaldy, 1956; 75 Years of Progress: The History of Smith's Stamping Works (Coventry) Ltd and Smith-Clayton Forge, Lincoln, 1958; The Life of the Very Rev. Dr John White, CH, 1958; The First of Foot: the History of The Royal Scots (The Royal Regiment), 1961; Andersons of Islington, The History of C. F. Anderson & Son Ltd, 1963; Churchill & Sim Ltd, 1963; Blyth, Greene, Jourdain & Co. Ltd, Merchant Bankers, 1963; The Kenyon Tradition, 1964; The History of Baker Perkins Ltd, 1968; In Blackburne Valley: The History of Bowers Mills, 1969; The History of the British Paper and Board Makers Association, 1972; The Vintner of Nazareth, a study of the early life of Christ, 1972; (with Mair Davies) A Victorian Shipowner: A Portrait of Sir Charles Cayzer Baronet, of Gartmore, 1978. *Address:* 26 Bentfield Road, Stansted-Mountfitchet, Essex CM24 8HW. *T:* Bishops Stortford 812289. *Clubs:* Savage, Saintsbury; Royal Scots (Edinburgh).

*Died 5 May* 1989.

**MUIR, Sir David (John),** Kt 1961; CMG 1959; FCIS, FASA, FAIM, AAUQ; Chairman, Queensland Cultural Centre Trust, since 1976; *b* 20 June 1916; *s* of John Arthur and Grace Elizabeth Muir, Brisbane; *m* 1942, Joan Haworth; one *s* one *d. Educ:* Kangaroo Point State Sch.; State Commercial High Sch., Brisbane. Entered Qld Public Service, 1932, as Clerk in Dept of Public Lands; transf. to Premier's Dept, 1938. Made special study of problems associated with production and marketing of sugar. Permanent Under Sec., Premier and Chief Secretary's Dept, 1948–51; also Clerk of Exec. Council of Qld and Mem. of State Stores Bd. Agent General for Qld in London and Australian Govt Rep. on Internat. Sugar Council, 1951–63 (Chm. 1958); Dir, Industrial Develt, Queensland, and Chm., Industries Assistance Bd, 1964–77; Chm., Qld Public Service Bd, 1977–79; Parly Comr for Administrative Investigations (Ombudsman), 1979–81. Pres., Chartered Institute of Secretaries, 1964. Chairman: Queensland Theatre Co. Bd, 1969–78. James N. Kirby Medal, InstProdE, Australia, 1969. JP. *Recreations:* gardening and golf. *Address:* Box 159 PO, South Brisbane, Qld 4101, Australia; 5/124 Moray Street, New Farm, Brisbane, Qld 4005, Australia.　　　*Died 23 March* 1986.

**MUIR, Gordon;** *see* Muir, W. A. G.

**MUIR, John Cochran,** CMG 1951; OBE 1944; retired; Colonial Agricultural Service; Member for Agriculture and Natural Resources, Tanganyika, 1949; *b* 1902; *m* 1936, Cathey, *d* of Maurice Hincks; one *s* two *d. Educ:* Allan Glen's Sch.; West of Scotland Agricultural Coll.; Univ. of Glasgow. BSc (agric.); National Diploma in Agriculture; National Diploma in Dairying, Asst Superintendent, Agriculture, Gold Coast, 1925; Senior Agricultural Officer, Zanzibar, 1935; Dir of Agriculture, 1941; Trinidad, 1944; Tanganyika, 1948. Order of Brilliant Star, Zanzibar, 1944. *Address:* 100 Lynn Road, Ely, Cambs.　　　*Died 7 July* 1981.

**MUIR, John Gerald Grainger,** CBE 1975; DSC 1944; bee-keeper; *b* 19 Jan. 1918; *s* of George Basil Muir, ICS and Gladys Stack; *m* 1945, Lionella Maria Terni; three *d. Educ:* Rugby Sch.; Corpus Christi Coll., Oxford (MA). Bd of Educn Studentship, 1938. RN,

Norway, Medit., Channel and Germany, 1939–46. British Council: Italy, 1946–49; Asst, Leeds, 1949–50; Asst Rep., Syria, 1950–55; Representative: Arab Gulf, 1955–60; Portugal, 1960–64; Iraq, 1964–67; Dep. Controller, Educn, 1968–72; Rep., Spain, 1972–76; Controller, Overseas Div. (Europe), 1976–78, retired. Mem., Inst. of Advanced Motorists, 1989–. *Publications:* contribs to Mariner's Mirror, Bull. SOAS, and Soc. de Geographia, Lisbon. *Recreations:* music, nautical research, travel, flowers. *Address:* West Wing, Maidenhatch House, Pangbourne, Berks RG8 8HJ. *Club:* Naval.
*Died* 2 *Oct.* 1990.

**MUIR, (William Archibald) Gordon,** FRICS; chartered surveyor; partner in private practice; Member Board, Housing Corporation, from 1981; *b* Glasgow, 4 Feb. 1931; *s* of William J. I. Muir and Isabella H. Muir; *m* 1956, Joanna Margaret Calverley; two *s* two *d*. *Educ:* Glasgow Acad.; Trinity Coll., Glenalmond; St John's Coll., Cambridge (MA). National Service, HLI, 1949–51; TA, 5/6 HLI, 1951–57. Member, Corporation of Glasgow, 1966–72; Magistrate, City of Glasgow, 1969–71. Member: Scottish Housing Adv. Cttee, 1970–80 (Chm. 1978–80); Nat. House-Building Council (Scotland), 1970–; Chairman: Scottish Special Housing Assoc., 1972–78; Scottish Home Ownership Forum, 1978–79. Member, Gen. Practice Divisional Council, RICS, 1974–76; Dir, Nat. Building Agency, 1976–. Dir, Whatlings Ltd, 1978–80. OStJ 1978. *Recreations:* gliding, 'satiable curiosity. *Address:* The White House, Cardross, Dunbartonshire. *T:* Cardross 451. *Clubs:* Caledonian; Royal Scottish Automobile (Glasgow).
*Died* 28 *Sept.* 1981.

**MULHOLLAND, Hon. Mrs John, (Olivia Vernon),** DCVO 1971 (CVO 1958); Extra Woman of the Bedchamber to Queen Elizabeth The Queen Mother since 1983 (Woman of the Bedchamber, 1950–82); Chairman, Elizabeth Garrett Anderson Hospital, 1945–72; Vice-Chairman, Royal Free Hospital Group, 1950–61; Member: North London Group Hospital Management Committee, 1961–72; King Edward's Hospital Fund Management Committee, 1961; *b* 1902; 2nd *d* of 1st Viscount Harcourt and Mary Ethel, Viscountess Harcourt, GBE, *o d* of Walter Haynes Burns, New York and North Mymms Park, Hatfield; *m* 1923, Hon. (Godfrey) John A. M. L. Mulholland (*d* 1948), *y s* of 2nd Baron Dunleath, Ballywalter Park, Co. Down, N Ireland; one *s* two *d*. *Educ:* Notting Hill High Sch.; Lady Margaret Hall, Oxford. *Address:* Orchard House, Mews Lane, Winchester, Hants. *T:* Winchester 53329.
*Died* 2 *Aug.* 1984.

**MULLER, Hon. Dr Hilgard,** DMS (RSA) 1976; director of companies and farmer; Law Consultant with firm of Dyason, Pretoria; MP for Beaufort West, 1964–77; *b* 4 May 1914; *s* of C. J. Muller; *m* 1943, Anita Dyason; one *s*. *Educ:* Pretoria Univ.; Oxford Univ.; DLitt Pretoria, BLitt Oxon., LLB S Africa. Rhodes Scholar, 1937; Oxford Rugby Blue, 1938. Univ. Lecturer, Pretoria, 1941–47. Solicitor, 1947–61; Dir of Companies and farmer. Mayor of Pretoria, 1953–55; MP for Pretoria East, 1958–61; High Commissioner for Union of South Africa in the UK, Jan.-May, 1961; South African Ambassador to the Court of St James's, 1961–63; Minister of Foreign Affairs, South Africa, 1964–77. Hon. Pres., S Africa - Republic of China (Taiwan) Chamber of Economic Co-operation, 1980. Chancellor of the Univ. of Pretoria, 1965–, formerly Pres. of Convocation. DPhil (*hc*) Pretoria; PhD (*hc*) Stellenbosch. Mem. RSA. Grand Cross, Order of Merit (Paraguay), 1966; Grand Cross, Order of Christ (Portugal), 1968; Grand Cross of Order of Infante Dom Henrique (Portugal), 1973; Grand Officer of Order of Merit of Central African Republic, 1976; Grand Officer's Cross of Merit, SMO Malta, 1978; Grand Cordon, Order of the Brilliant Star of the Republic of China, 1982. *Recreations:* golf, farming, reading. *Address:* PO Box 793, Pretoria, South Africa. *Clubs:* various in South Africa.
*Died* 10 *July* 1985.

**MULLIGAN, Col Hugh Waddell,** CMG 1954; MD, DSc; *b* 13 Nov. 1901; *s* of late Rev. J. A. W. Mulligan and Jem Anderson; *m* Rita, *d* of late J. E. Armstrong; two *s* one *d*. *Educ:* Robert Gordon's Coll., Aberdeen; Aberdeen Univ. MB, ChB 1923; MD (Hons) Aberdeen 1930; DSc, 1934, IMS, 1923–47. Served War of 1939–45 (active service, 1940–43). Commonwealth Fund Fellow, Univ. Chicago, 1933–35. Dir Pasteur Inst. of Southern India, 1938–40; Dir, Central Research Inst., Kasauli, 1944–47; Dir, West African Inst. for Trypanosomiasis Research (Colonial Research Service), 1947–54; Dir and Head of Biological Division, Wellcome Research Laboratories, Beckenham, Kent, 1954–66. Vis. Lectr, Dept of Biology, Univ. of Salford, 1967–76. *Publications:* (ed) The African Trypanosomiases, 1970; papers on protozoology, immunology, pathology, etc. *Recreations:* fishing, shooting, gardening. *Address:* 5 Thorngrove Road, Wilmslow, Cheshire. *T:* Wilmslow 522579.
*Died* 26 *July* 1982.

**MULLIKEN, Prof. Robert S(anderson),** PhD; Professor of Physics and Chemistry, University of Chicago, Emeritus, 1983; *b* Newburyport, Mass, 7 June 1896; *s* of Samuel Parsons Mulliken, Prof. of Organic Chemistry, and Katherine (*née* Mulliken); *m* 1929, Mary Helen von Noé (decd); two *d*. *Educ:* Massachusetts Inst. of Technology; Univ. of Chicago. BS (MIT), 1917; PhD (Chicago), 1921. Nat. Research Coun. Fellow, Univ. of Chicago, and Harvard Univ., 1921–25; Guggenheim Fellow, Europe, 1930 and 1932–33; Fulbright Scholar, Oxford Univ., 1952–53; Vis. Fellow, St John's Coll., Oxford, 1952–53. Jun. Chem. Engr, Bureau of Mines, US Dept of Interior, Washington, 1917–18; Chemical Warfare Service, US Army, 1918 (Pte First-Class); Asst in Rubber Research, New Jersey Zinc Co., Penn., 1919; Asst Prof. of Physics, Washington Sq. Coll., New York Univ., 1926–28; Univ. of Chicago: Assoc. Prof. of Physics, 1928–31; Prof. of Physics, 1931–61 and Chemistry, 1961–83; Ernest de Witt Burton Distinguished Service Prof., 1956–61; Distinguished Service Prof. of Physics and Chemistry, 1961–83; Distinguished Research Prof. of Chemical Physics, Florida State Univ., (Jan.-March) 1965–72. Dir, Editorial Work and Information, Plutonium Project, Univ. of Chicago, 1942–45; Scientific Attaché, US Embassy, London, 1955. Baker Lectr, Cornell Univ., 1960; Silliman Lectr, Yale Univ., 1965; Visiting Professor: Bombay, 1962; Kanpur, 1962; Jan van Geuns Vis. Prof., Amsterdam Univ., 1965. Member: Amer. Acad. of Arts and Sciences; Nat. Acad. of Sciences; Amer. Philosophical Soc.; Amer. Chem. Soc.; Fellow: Amer. Physical Soc.; Amer. Acad. for Advancement of Science; Internat. Acad. of Quantum Molecular Science; Hon. Fellow: Chem. Soc. of Gt Britain; Indian Nat. Acad. of Science; Foreign Mem., Royal Soc.; Hon. Member: Soc. de Chimie Physique, Paris; Chem. Soc., Japan; Corresp. Mem., Soc. Royale des Sciences de Liège. Hon. Mem., Royal Irish Acad.; Hon. ScD: Columbia, 1939; Marquette, 1966; Cantab, 1966; Hon. PhD Stockholm, 1960. Nobel Prize for Chemistry, 1966; other medals and awards. *Publications:* (with Willis B. Person) Molecular Complexes, 1969; Selected Papers, 1975; (with Walter C. Ermler) Diatomic Molecules: results of ab initio calculations, 1977; (with Walter C. Ermler) Polyatomic Molecules: results of ab initio calculations, 1981; over 200 contributions (1919–; in recent years dealing extensively with structure and spectra of molecular complexes) to various American and foreign journals including: Jl Am. Chem. Soc.; Jl Chem. Phys.; Rev. Mod. Phys; Phys Rev.; Chem. Rev.; Nature; also contributions: Proc. Nat. Acad. Sci.; Trans Faraday Soc. *Recreations:* driving a car, Oriental rugs, art. *Address:* 4000 North 25th Place, Arlington, Va 22207–5103, USA. *Club:* Cosmos (Washington).
*Died* 31 *Oct.* 1986.

**MULLINS, Brian Percival,** PhD; Director of Research and Laboratory Services and Head of Safety in Mines Research Establishment, Health and Safety Executive, (Under-Secretary), 1975–80; *b* 5 Aug. 1920; *s* of Thomas Percival Mullins and Lillian May Mullins; *m* 1944, Margaret Fiona Howell, MA; one *s* one *d*. *Educ:* Shooters' Hill Sch., London; Woolwich Polytechnic Evening Inst. BSc Nat. Sciences (London), 1940; PhD Fuel Techn. (Extern. London), 1951; BA Modern and Classical Chinese (London) 1984. Clerical Officer, Air Ministry, 1937–40; Research Scientist, Engine Dept, Royal Aircraft Estabt, 1941–42; seconded to Univ. of Cambridge for high vacuum gas analysis research, 1943; fuels, combustion and aero-engine research at Power Jets (R&D) Ltd and at Nat. Gas Turbine Estabt, 1944–60; Head of Chemistry Dept, RAE, 1960–62; Head of Chemistry, Physics and Metallurgy Dept, RAE, 1962–65; idc (seconded), 1966; Head of Structures Dept, RAE, 1967–74. Chm., Combustion Panel, AGARD-NATO, 1954–57; Sen. UK Mem., Structures and Materials Panel, AGARD-NATO, 1967–74. *Publications:* Spontaneous Ignition of Liquid Fuels, 1955; (jtly) Explosions, Detonations, Flammability and Ignition, 1959; numerous scientific research papers. *Recreations:* oriental languages, industrial archaeology. *Address:* 1 St Michael's Road, Farnborough, Hants GU14 8ND. *T:* Farnborough (Hants) 542137.
*Died* 27 *Feb.* 1990.

**MUMFORD, Sir Albert (Henry),** KBE 1963 (OBE 1946); CEng, Hon. FIEE; Engineer-in-Chief, GPO, 1960–65, retd; *b* 16 April 1903; *s* of late George Mumford; *m* 1927, Eileen Berry; two *s* two *d*. *Educ:* Bancroft's Sch.; Queen Mary Coll., Univ. of London. BSc (Eng) 1st Class Hons (London) 1923. Entered GPO Engineering Dept, 1924; Staff Engineer radio branch, 1938; Imperial Defence Coll., 1948; Asst Engineer-in-Chief, 1951; Dep. Engineer-in-Chief, 1954. Treasurer, Instn of Electrical Engineers, 1969–72 (Chm. Radio Section, 1945–46; Vice-Pres. 1958–63; Pres. 1963–64; Hon. Fellow, 1980); Pres. Assoc. Supervising Electrical Engineers, 1964–66; Treas., Instn of Electrical and Electronic Incorporated Engineers, 1967– (Hon. Fellow 1978). Fellow, Queen Mary Coll., 1962; Hon. Fellow, Polytechnic of the South Bank, 1982; Hon. Mem., City and Guilds of London Inst.; Hon. CGIA, 1986. *Publications:* many scientific papers. *Address:* 27 Grendon Gardens, Wembley Park, Mddx. *T:* 01–904 2360.
*Died* 19 *Feb.* 1989.

**MUMFORD, L(awrence) Quincy;** Librarian of Congress, 1954–75, retd; *b* 11 Dec. 1903; *s* of Jacob Edward Mumford and Emma Luvenia (*née* Stocks); *m* 1930, Permelia Catharine Stevens (*d* 1961); one *d*; *m* 1969, Betsy Perrin Fox. *Educ:* Duke Univ. (AB *magna cum laude;* AM); Columbia Univ. (BS). Mem. staff, Duke Univ. Library, 1922–28; Head of Circulation Dept, 1926; Chief of Reference and Circulation, 1927–28; Student Asst, Columbia Univ. Library,

1928–29; Mem. staff, New York Public Library, 1929–45; General Asst in charge of Director's Office, 1932–35; Executive Asst and Chief of Preparation Div., 1936–43; Exec. Asst and Coordinator Gen. Services Divs, 1943–45; on leave from New York Public Library to serve as dir Processing Dept, Library of Congress, 1940–41; Asst Dir, Cleveland Public Library, 1945–50, Dir, 1950–54. Hon. degrees: LittD: Bethany Coll. (WVa), 1954; Rutgers Univ. (NJ), 1956; Duke Univ. (NC), 1957; Belmont Abbey Coll. (NC), 1963; LLD: Union Coll. (NY), 1955, Bucknell Univ. (Pa), 1956; Univ. of Notre Dame (Ind.), 1964; Univ. of Pittsburgh (Pa), 1964; Michigan Univ., 1970; Hon. DrHum King's Coll. (Pa), 1970. President: Ohio Library Assoc., 1947–48; Amer. Library Assoc., 1954–55; Manuscript Soc., 1968–69. Chairman: Federal Library Cttee; Bd of Visitors, Duke Univ. Library. Member: Lincoln Sesquicentennial Commn, 1958–60; Sponsors Cttee, Papers of Woodrow Wilson; Board of Advisors, Dumbarton Oaks Research Library and Collection; US Nat. Book Cttee. Corresponding Mem. for the US of Unesco's Internat. Advisory Cttee on Bibliography, Documentation and Terminology. Benjamin Franklin Fellow, Royal Soc. for Encouragement of Arts, Manufactures and Commerce (London); President's Commn on Libraries, 1966–68. Chm. or Mem. ex officio of various cttees, bds, etc. *Publications:* contributions to library periodicals. *Address:* (home) 3721 49th Street NW, Washington, DC 20016, USA. *Clubs:* Cosmos (Washington); Explorers' (New York). *Died* 15 *Aug.* 1982.

**MUMFORD, Lewis;** writer; *b* 19 Oct. 1895; *s* of Lewis Mack and Elvina Mumford; *m* 1921, Sophia Wittenberg; (one son killed in action 1944) one *d. Educ:* Coll. of the City of New York, Columbia Univ. Radio operator (USN) 1918; Associate editor Fortnightly Dial, 1919; Acting Editor Sociological Review (London), 1920; Co-editor American Caravan, 1927–36. Member: National Inst. of Arts and Letters 1930–; Amer. Academy of Arts and Letters, 1956– (Pres., 1962–65); Amer. Philosophical Soc., Amer. Academy of Arts and Sciences; Bd of Higher Educn, City of New York, 1935–37; Commn on Teacher Educn, Amer. Council on Educn, 1938–44; Prof. of Humanities, Stanford Univ., 1942–44. Hon. LLD Edinburgh 1965; Hon. Dr Arch., Rome, 1967. Hon. Phi Beta Kappa, 1957; Hon. Fellow, Stanford Univ., 1941. Hon. FRIBA (Hon. ARIBA, 1942); Hon. MRTPI (Hon. Mem. TPI, 1946); Hon. Member: Amer. Inst. of Architects, 1951; Town Planning Inst. of Canada, 1960; Amer. Inst. of Planners, 1955; Colegio del Arquitectas del Peru; Prof. of City Planning, Univ. of Pennsylvania, 1951–56; Vis. Prof., MIT, 1957–60; Ford Prof., Univ. of Pennsylvania, 1959–60; Univ. of Calif., 1961; Fellow, Wesleyan Univ. Center for Advanced Studies, 1963; MIT: Vis. Lectr, 1973–74; Charles Abrams Prof., 1975. Co-chairman Wenner-Gren Foundation Conf. on Man's Use of the Earth, 1955. Made six documentary films on City for National Film Board, Canada, 1964. Hon. Fellow, Royal Inst. of Architects of Ireland. Townsend Harris Medal, 1939; Ebenezer Howard Memorial Medal, 1946; Medal of Honour, Fairmount Park Art Assoc., 1953; TPI (later RTPI) Gold Medal, 1957; RIBA Royal Gold Medal for Architecture, 1961; Presidential Medal of Freedom, 1964; Emerson-Thoreau Medal, Amer. Acad. of Arts and Sciences, 1965; Gold Medal, Belles Lettres, Nat. Inst. of Arts and Letters, 1970; Leonardo da Vinci Medal, Soc. for Hist. of Technology, 1969; Hodgkins Medal, Smithsonian Instn, 1971; Thomas Jefferson Meml Foundn Medal, 1972; Nat. Medal for Literature, 1972; Prix Mondial del Duca, 1976; Benjamin Franklin Medal, RSA, 1983; Nat. Medal of Arts, 1986. Hon. KBE 1975. *Publications:* The Story of Utopias, 1922; Sticks and Stones, 1924; The Golden Day, 1926; Herman Melville, 1929; The Brown Decades, 1931; Technics and Civilization, 1934; The Culture of Cities, 1938; Whither Honolulu?, 1938; Men Must Act, 1939; Faith for Living, 1940; The South in Architecture, 1941; The Condition of Man, 1944; City Development, 1945; Values for Survival, 1946 (Programme for Survival (Eng.), 1946); Green Memories: The Story of Geddes Mumford, 1947; The Conduct of Life, 1951; Art and Technics, 1952; In the Name of Sanity, 1954; The Human Prospect, 1955; From the Ground Up, 1956; The Transformations of Man, 1956; The City in History, 1961; Highway and City, 1962; Herman Melville (rev. edn), 1963; The Myth of the Machine, 1967; The Urban Prospect, 1968; The Van Wyck Brooks-Lewis Mumford Letters, 1970; The Pentagon of Power, 1971; The Letters of Lewis Mumford and Frederic J. Osborn, 1971; Interpretations and Forecasts, 1973; Findings and Keepings: analects for an autobiography, 1975; Architecture as a Home for Man, 1975; My Works and Days: a personal chronicle, 1979; Sketches from Life: the early years, 1982. *Address:* Amenia, New York 12501, USA. *Died* 26 *Jan.* 1990.

**MUMMERY, Sir Hugh (Evelyn) L.;** *see* Lockhart Mummery.

**MUNN, Rear-Adm. William James,** CB 1962; DSO 1941; OBE 1946; *b* 15 July 1911; *s* of late Col R. G. Munn, CMG, FRGS, and late Mrs R. G. Munn; *m* 1940, Susan Astle Sperling, Teviot Bank, Hawick, Scotland; two *s. Educ:* Britannia Royal Naval College, Dartmouth. Cadet and Midshipman in HMS Nelson, 1929–31. Flag Lt (Battle Cruiser Sqdn during Spanish Civil War); served War of 1939–45 (despatches, DSO): First Lt Destroyer HMS Mohawk;

Comd Destroyer HMS Hereward (Battle of Matapan, evacuation of Crete), 1941. POW in Italy and Germany, 1941–45. Comd HMS Venus (Mediterranean during Palestine trouble, OBE), 1945–47; Comdr 1946; psc 1949; Exec. Officer, Cruiser HMS Kenya (Far East Station, Korean War, despatches), 1949–51; Capt., 1951; Capt. of the Britannia Royal Naval College, Dartmouth, 1956–58; Capt. of HMS Gambia, Nov. 1958–Dec. 1960; Rear-Adm. 1960; Chief of Staff to the Comdr-in-Chief, Home Fleet, 1961–63, retd. *Recreation:* golf. *Address:* Beechbrook House, Dalham, Newmarket, Suffolk CB8 8TH. *T:* Ousden 425. *Clubs:* Royal Worlington Golf, North Berwick Golf. *Died* 5 *Oct.* 1989.

**MUNRO, Robert Wilson,** CMG 1967; HM Diplomatic Service, retired; *b* 21 Jan. 1915; *yr s* of late J. S. Munro and late Mrs E. G. Munro, Dunedin, NZ; *m* 1946, Annette Kilroy; two *s. Educ:* Otago Boys' High Sch., Univ. of Otago, New Zealand, MSc 1936, and Univ. of London, BSc(Econ), 1950. Research Chemist, NZ Dept of Agriculture, 1938–40. Served with 2 NZEF and UK Forces, 1941–45. Sudan Civil Service, 1945–52; HM Diplomatic Service, 1952–74: served in London, Warsaw, Paris, Baghdad and Khartoum; Inspector, Diplomatic Service, 1967–69; Dep. High Comr, Nairobi, 1969–71; RN College, Greenwich, 1971–72; Dep. High Comr, Wellington, 1972–74. Middle East Advr, NZ Meat Producers' Bd, 1978–80. Order of Nilein, 1965. *Recreations:* camping, shooting. *Address:* 7 Lynmouth Avenue, Karori, Wellington, New Zealand. *Club:* Wellington (Wellington). *Died* 25 *Dec.* 1985.

**MUNRO, Sir (Thomas) Torquil (Alfonso),** 5th Bt, *cr* 1825; JP Angus; *b* 7 Feb. 1901; *e s* of Sir Hugh Thomas Munro, 4th Bt and Selina Dorothea (*d* 1902), *d* of Major-General T. E. Byrne; *S* father, 1919; *m* 1st, 1925, Beatrice (who obtained a divorce, 1932), *d* of late Robert Sanderson Whitaker; one *s*; 2nd, 1934, Averil Moira Katharine (*d* 1982), *d* of Kenneth Owen Hunter; one *s* one *d. Educ:* Winchester. *Heir: s* Alasdair Thomas Ian Munro [*b* 6 July 1927; *m* 1954, Marguerite Lillian, *d* of late Franklin R. Loy, Dayton, Ohio, USA; one *s* one *d*]. *Address:* Lindertis, Kirriemuir, Angus. *TA:* Munro, Lindertis, Kirriemuir, Angus. *T:* Craigton 209.
*Died* 10 *July* 1985.

**MUNRO-LUCAS-TOOTH of Teananich, Sir Hugh (Vere Huntly Duff),** 1st Bt, *cr* 1920; Lieutenant-Colonel Queen's Own Cameron Highlanders; *b* 13 Jan. 1903; *er s* of Major Hugh Munro Warrand of Bught and Beatrice Maud Lucas, *e c* of late Sir Robert Lucas Lucas-Tooth, Bt, of Holme Lacy, Co. Hereford, and *co-heiress* with her sisters in the lordship of the Manor of Holme Lacy; *m* 1925, Laetitia Florence, OBE 1958 (*d* 1978), *er d* of Sir John R. Findlay, 1st Bt; one *s* two *d. Educ:* Eton; Balliol Coll., Oxford. Called to Bar, Lincoln's Inn, 1933; MP (C) Isle of Ely, 1924–29, Hendon South, 1945–70; Parliamentary Under-Sec. of State, Home Office, 1952–55. Mem., Nat. Water Council, 1973–76. Sir Robert Lucas-Tooth, 1st Bt, having died, and all his three sons having lost their lives in France during the European War, HM the King was graciously pleased to grant a re-creation of the baronetcy in favour of Sir Robert's eldest grandson, H. V. H. D. Warrand, who assumed the name and arms of Lucas-Tooth in place of Warrand by Royal Letters Patent; changed name by Deed Poll from Lucas-Tooth to Munro-Lucas-Tooth of Teananich, 1965. *Heir: s* Hugh John Lucas-Tooth [*b* 20 Aug. 1932; *m* 1955, Caroline, *e d* of 1st Baron Poole, CBE, TD, PC; three *d*]. *Address:* Burgate Court, Fordingbridge, Hants. *Club:* Brooks's. *Died* 18 *Nov.* 1985.

**MUNROW, William Davis,** CBE 1963; Chief Inspector of Audit, Ministry of Housing and Local Government, 1965–68; *b* 28 April 1903; 2nd *s* of Alexander Gordon Davis and Charlotte Munrow; *m* 1st, 1927, Constance Caroline Moorcroft (*d* 1977); one *s*; 2nd, 1983, Winifred McLellan, widow. *Educ:* Council Schs; Birkbeck Coll.; and London Sch. of Economics (BSc(Econ)). District Auditor for London, 1950; Dep. Chief Inspector of Audit, 1958. *Recreation:* golf. *Address:* 6 Grazebrook Close, Cooden, Bexhill-on-Sea, East Sussex TN39 4TB. *T:* Cooden 2650. *Died* 15 *Sept.* 1986.

**MUNSTER, 6th Earl of,** *cr* 1831; **Edward Charles FitzClarence;** Viscount FitzClarence, Baron Tewkesbury, 1831; *b* 3 Oct. 1899; *s* of Brig.-Gen. Charles FitzClarence, VC (*g s* of 1st Earl) (killed in action, 1914), and Violet (*d* 1941), *d* of Lord Alfred Spencer-Churchill; *S* cousin, 1975; *m* 1st, 1925, Monica Shiela Harrington (marr. diss. 1930; she *d* 1958), *d* of Lt-Col Sir Henry Mulleneux Grayson, 1st Bt, KBE; one *s* one *d*; 2nd, 1939, Mrs Vivian Schofield, *d* of late Benjamin Schofield, JP, and step *d* of late Judge A. J. Chotzner (MP Upton Div., West Ham, 1931–34). *Educ:* Eton; RMC Sandhurst. Captain Irish Guards, retired. Served 1st Bn Irish Guards, Narvik, Norway, 1940; No 8 Commando, Western Desert, 1941. *Heir: s* Viscount FitzClarence. *Address:* 98 Whitelands House, Cheltenham Terrace, SW3. *Died* 15 *Nov.* 1983.

**MUNTZ, (Frederick) Alan (Irving),** FRAeS; Consultant; *b* 7 June 1899; *s* of Major Irving Muntz and Jessie Challoner; *m* 1st, 1923, Mary Lee (marr diss., 1934), 3rd *d* of Canon W. L. Harnett; one *s* two *d*; 2nd, 1934, Lady Margaret Frances Anne (marr. diss., 1939),

2nd *d* of 7th Marquess of Londonderry; 3rd, 1948, Marjorie Mary Helena, 2nd *d* of Edward Strickland, Ceylon; one *d. Educ:* Winchester; Trinity Coll., Cambridge. (BA Mech. Sciences). Served in France; 2nd Lt 432nd Field Co. RE, 1918; British Petroleum Co., Ltd, 1922–26; Anglo-Iranian Oil Co., Ltd, 1926–28; with Sir Nigel Norman founded Airwork Ltd, and Heston Airport, 1928; with Talaat Harb Pasha, Banque Misr, Cairo, founded Misr Airwork SAE, 1932; with R. E. Grant Govan, Delhi, helped found Indian National Airways Ltd, 1933; founded: Alan Muntz & Co. Ltd to develop Pescara free piston engine system and other inventions, 1937; Alan Muntz Consultants, 1965, retired, 1975. *Recreations:* golf, fishing, travelling. *Address:* The Bothy, Furzedown Lane, Amport, near Andover, Hants. *T:* Weyhill 3254.

*Died 7 March 1985.*

**MUNTZ, (Isabelle) Hope,** FSA; FRHistS; mediaevalist; *b* Toronto, Canada, 8 July 1907; *er d* of late Rupert Gustavus Muntz and 2nd wife, Lucy Elsie Muntz; unmarried. *Educ:* private schs, Bournemouth and Eastbourne. Commercial Art, aircraft engineering; secretarial work and free-lance journalism, to 1931; work and research on novel, 1931–39. ARP, driving, precision-engineering, 1939–45. Spare-time on research and book, 1943–45; novel completed, 1947. FAMS 1958; FSA 1969; FRHistS 1972. *Publications:* The Golden Warrior, England and Commonwealth, 1948, USA, 1949, Sweden, 1950, Norway, 1951, Germany, 1952, Denmark 1954 (also published in Braille and Talking Books); Battles for the Crown, 1966; (ed with Catherine Morton MA, FSA; FRHistS) Carmen de Hastingae Proelio, 1972. Script: The Norman Conquest in the Bayeux Tapestry (film), 1966. Articles, sketches, etc. to journals; contributions to Graya (magazine for members of Gray's Inn). *Recreations:* travel, driving, riding, reading, music, drama. *Address:* c/o Chatto & Windus Ltd, 40/42 William IV Street, WC2. *Club:* University Women's. *Died 25 Sept. 1981.*

**MUNTZ, Thomas Godric Aylett,** CMG 1951; OBE 1948; retired; *b* 31 May 1906; *s* of R. A. Muntz, Tansor Manor, Peterborough; *m* 1st, 1932, Marjorie (*d* 1968), *d* of Sir Charles Statham; two *s*; 2nd, 1969, June Robertson (*d* 1982). *Educ:* Lancing; Pembroke Coll., Oxford. Appointed to Dept of Overseas Trade, 1929; served at office of HM Trade Commissioner, New Zealand, 1931–38; Embassy, Warsaw, 1938–39; Board of Trade, 1939–40; Montreal, 1940–42; Embassy, Rio de Janeiro, 1942–43; Lisbon, 1944–47; Ankara, 1947–50; Head of Economic Relations Dept, Foreign Office, 1950–51; Tangier, 1952–55; Antwerp, 1957–59. *Address:* Kirk's Lodge, King's Cliffe, near Peterborough. *Died 19 June 1986.*

**MURCHISON, Very Rev. Thomas Moffat,** DD; *b* 27 July 1907; *s* of Malcolm Murchison and Ann Moffat; *m* 1940, Mary Black Morton Philp; one *s* two *d. Educ:* Portree High Sch.; University and Trinity Coll., Glasgow. DD Glasgow, 1964. Minister of Glenelg, Invernessshire, 1932–37; St Columba Copland Road Church Glasgow, 1937–66; St Columba Summertown Church, Glasgow, 1966–72. Member: BBC National Broadcasting Council for Scotland, 1952–57; Scottish National Parks Cttee, 1946–47; Panel of Religious Advisers, ITA, 1966–70; Pres., Highland Development League; Convener, Church of Scotland Home Board, 1959–64; Convener, Church of Scotland Adv. Board, 1967–72; Moderator of Gen. Assembly of Church of Scotland, 1969–70. Internat. Pres., Celtic Congress, 1966–71. Chm. Dirs, Scottish Jl of Theology, 1970–74. Crowned Bard of the National Mod, 1958; Chief of Gaelic Society of Inverness, 1961; Bard of the Gorseth of the Bards of Cornwall, 1969. *Publications:* The Plight of the Smallholders, 1935; (Jt Editor) Alba: A Miscellany, 1948; (ed) The Golden Key, 1950; Gaelic Prose Writings of Donald Lamont, 1960; Editor, The Gael, 1946–57; Editor, Gaelic Supplement, Life and Work, 1951–80; numerous English and Gaelic articles and broadcasts. *Recreations:* Gaelic literature, highland history. *Address:* Kylerhea, Isle of Skye, by Kyle, Ross-shire; 10 Mount Stuart Street, Glasgow G41 3YL. *T:* 041-632 4276. *Died 9 Jan. 1984.*

**MURDOCH, Air Marshal Sir Alister Murray,** KBE 1966 (CBE 1946); CB 1960; *b* 9 Dec. 1912; *s* of Brig. T. Murdoch, DSO, Melbourne; *m* 1937, Florence Eilene, *d* of Charles Herbert Miller, Sydney; one *d. Educ:* Caulfield Grammar Sch.; RMC Duntroon, Canberra. Attached to Directorate of Operations and Intelligence, 1938–39. Served War of 1939–45 (CBE). Senior Air Staff Officer, RAAF HQ, 1944; Dir, Air Staff Plans and Policy, 1949–52; AOC RAAF Pt Cook, and Comdt RAAF Coll., Pt Cook, 1952–53; AOC Training Command, 1954–58; Dep. Chief of the Air Staff, 1958–59; RAAF Representative in London, 1959–62; AOC, HQ Operational Command, 1962–65; idc; Chief of the Air Staff, RAAF, 1965–70. *Recreations:* golf and tennis. *Address:* 11 East View Road, Church Point, NSW 2105, Australia. *Clubs:* Imperial Service, Manly Golf (Sydney). *Died 29 Nov. 1984.*

**MURDOCH, Richard Bernard;** actor (stage, films, broadcasting, television); *b* Keston, Kent, 6 April 1907; *s* of late Bernard Murdoch and Amy Florence Scott, both of Tunbridge Wells; *m* 1932, Peggy Rawlings; one *s* two *d. Educ:* Charterhouse; Pembroke Coll.,

Cambridge. Commenced theatrical career in chorus of musical comedies, after which played dancing, light comedy and juvenile rôles in musical comedy and revue. Productions include: The Blue Train; Oh, Kay; That's a Good Girl; The Five O'Clock Girl; C. B. Cochran's 1930 Revue; Stand Up and Sing; Ballyhoo; various Charlot revues; Over She Goes. The advent of broadcasting brought firstly several appearances as an early television star and then the famous partnership with Arthur Askey. At outbreak of War, 1939, was playing in Band Waggon at London Palladium and also making films; these include; The Terror; Over She Goes; Band Waggon; Charlie's Big-Hearted Aunt; The Ghost Train; I Thank You. In Jan. 1941 joined RAF as Pilot-Officer in Admin. and Special Duties Branch; one year at Bomber Command HQ (Intelligence Br.) and subs. Intelligence Officer at various stations all over the country; towards end of War became Sqdn Ldr under Wing-Comdr Kenneth Horne in Directorate of Administrative Plans, Air Ministry. In off-duty hours at Air Ministry during this period Much-Binding-in-the-Marsh was evolved with Kenneth Horne. Released from RAF Oct. 1945; went on tour with George Black's revue, Strike a New Note. Dame in Emile Littler's Pantomime, Little Miss Muffet, London Casino, Dec. 1949. 20 weeks in Australia for ABC recordings, 1954. Other films include: Three Men and a Girl. BBC radio series: Men from the Ministry, 1961–77; A Slight Case of Murdoch, 1986. Season with Shaw Festival of Canada and tour of USA, 1973. TV appearances include: Hazell; The Avengers; Owner Occupied; In the Looking Glass; This is Your Life; Rumpole of the Bailey; Doctor's Daughters; Churchill: The Wilderness Years, etc. *Recreation:* golf. *Address:* 2 Priory Close, Harrow Road West, Dorking, Surrey RH4 3BG. *Clubs:* Royal Automobile; Walton Heath Golf. *Died 9 Oct. 1990.*

**MURISON, Maj.-Gen. Charles Alexander Phipps,** CB 1944; CBE 1940; MC; *b* Grenfell, Sask, Canada, 7 Oct. 1894; *s* of late W. J. H. Murison, Montreal and Vancouver, and Alice Lepel, *d* of late Major C. E. Phipps; *m* 1920, Mary Pope Shirley (*d* 1977), *d* of late Hon. Mr Justice W. H. P. Clement, of Supreme Court of British Columbia; one *d. Educ:* Vancouver High Sch.; Trinity Coll. Sch., Ont.; McGill Univ. 2nd Lt Royal Field Artillery, 1914; Brevet Major, 1932; Major, 1934; Brevet Lt-Col and Lt-Col 1939; Col, 1940; Brig., 1940; Temp. Maj.-Gen. 1943; Maj.-Gen. 1945; pac; psc; various Staff Appointments; served European War, 1914–18 (wounded, despatches, MC); War of 1939–45, France (CBE, CB); retired, 1949. Freedom, Municipality of North Cowichan, 1973. *Publications:* sundry articles in military journals. *Recreations:* riding, shooting, fishing, golf, etc. *Address:* 319/1645 West 14th Avenue, Vancouver, BC V6J 2J4, Canada. *Died 30 Oct. 1981.*

**MURLESS, Sir (Charles Francis) Noel,** Kt 1977; Trainer of racehorses, Newmarket, 1953–76; formerly Owner: Woodditton Stud, Cambridgeshire; Cliff Stud, Yorkshire; *b* 1910; *m* 1940, Gwen Carlow; one *d.* Leading Trainer on the flat for ninth year at end of British flat racing season, 1973 (former years being 1948, 1957, 1959, 1960, 1961, 1967, 1968, 1970); The Queen's trainer until flat racing season of 1969. He made a new record in earnings (£256,899) for his patrons, 1967; over £2,500,000 in winning stakes; has trained the winners of 19 Classic races: Two Thousand Guineas (2); One Thousand Guineas (6); Derby (3) (Crepello, 1957; St Paddy, 1960; Royal Palace, 1967); Oaks (5); St Leger (3); other major races: King George VI and Queen Elizabeth (3); Eclipse (5); Coronation Cup (5); Champion Stakes (3). Mem., Jockey Club, 1977–. *Address:* The Bungalow, Woodditton, Newmarket, Suffolk.

*Died 9 May 1987.*

**MURPHY, Lionel Keith;** Justice of the High Court of Australia, 1975; *b* 31 Aug. 1922; *s* of William and Lily Murphy; *m*; one *d*; *m* 2nd, 1969, Ingrid Gee; two *s. Educ:* Sydney Boys' High Sch.; Univ. of Sydney (BSc, LLB). Admitted to NSW Bar, 1947, to Victoria Bar, 1958; QC, NSW 1960, Vic 1961. Senator in Federal Parlt, 1962–75; Leader of Opposition in Senate, 1967–72; Leader of Govt in Senate, 1972–75; Attorney-General of Australia and Minister for Customs and Excise, 1972–75. Initiated reforms in legislative areas of human rights, family law, anti-trust, consumer protection. Mem. Executive, Australian section, Internat. Commn of Jurists; Delegate to UN Conf. on Human Rights, Teheran, 1968; represented Australia, Nuclear Tests Case, Internat. Court of Justice, 1973–74. Mem. Council, ANU, 1969–73. Humanist of the Year, 1982.

*Died 21 Oct. 1986.*

**MURPHY, Stephen Dunlop;** Chief Assistant (Television), Independent Broadcasting Authority, 1982–85; *b* Glasgow, 28 Aug. 1921; *s* of Stephen Dunlop Murphy and Jean Irwin; *m* 1944, Jean Marian Smith, Burnley; two *s* one *d. Educ:* Royal Grammar Sch., Newcastle upon Tyne; Manchester Grammar Sch.; Balliol Coll., Oxford (BA). Asst Master, Manchester Grammar Sch., 1943; BBC Educn Officer, 1951; BBC Producer, 1955; ITA Regional Officer North, 1961; Senior Programme Officer, ITA, 1966; Secretary, British Bd of Film Censors, 1971–75; Programme Officer, IBA, 1976–82. *Address:* 16 Selwyn Court, Church Road, Richmond, Surrey. *Died 11 April 1990.*

**MURPHY, William Parry,** AB, MD; Lecturer on Medicine, Harvard Medical School, 1948–58, Lecturer Emeritus, 1958; Senior Associate in Medicine, Peter Bent Brigham Hospital, 1935–58, Senior Associate Emeritus in Medicine and Consultant in Hematology since 1958; Consultant Hematologist: Melrose Hospital, Melrose, Mass; Quincy City Hospital, Quincy, Mass; Emerson Hospital, Concord, Mass; Consultant in Internal Medicine, Delaware State Hospital, Farnhurst, Delaware; *b* 6 Feb. 1892; *s* of Thomas Francis Murphy and Rose Anna Parry; *m* 1919, Pearl Harriett Adams; one *s* (one *d* decd). *Educ:* Univ. of Oregon (AB); Harvard Med. Sch. (MD). Army, enlisted Medical Reserve, 1917–18; acted as House Officer at the Rhode Island Hosp., 1920–22; as Asst Resident Physician, 1922–23; Junior Associate in Medicine, 1923–28; Associate in Medicine, 1928–35 at Peter Bent Brigham Hospital; Asst in Medicine, 1923–28; Instructor in Medicine, 1928–35; Associate in Medicine, Harvard Medical Sch., 1935–48; has been engaged in the practice of Medicine since 1923, and carried on research at the Peter Bent Brigham Hospital in Boston; Diplomate in Internal Medicine, 1937. Mem. Bd of Dirs, Cordis Corp., 1960–70. Mem. many American and foreign medical and scientific socs; co-discoverer of the liver treatment for pernicious anemia; Cameron Prize in Medicine, Univ. of Edinburgh Medical Faculty, 1930; Bronze Medal, American Medical Association, 1934; Nobel Prize in Physiology or Medicine, 1934; Paul Harris Fellow Award, Brookline Rotary Club, 1980. Hon. Dr of Science, Gustavus Adolphus Coll., 1963; Hon. Member: Univ. of Oregon Med. Alumni Assoc., 1964; Internat. Soc. for Research on Civilisation Diseases and Vital Substances, 1969. Commander of the first rank, Order of the White Rose, Finland, 1934; gold medal, Mass Humane Soc., 1935; National Order of Merit, Carlos J. Finlay, Official, Havana, Cuba, 1952; Dist. Achievement Award, City of Boston, 1965; Internat. Bicentennial Symposium Award, Boston, 1972; Gold Badge, Mass Med. Soc. 50th Anniv., 1973. *Publications:* Anemia in Practice: Pernicious Anemia, 1939; about 75 papers published in medical journals, especially on diseases of the blood. *Recreation:* collector of rare old firearms. *Address:* 97 Sewall Avenue, Brookline, Mass 02146, USA. *Clubs:* Sigma xi (Harvard); Harvard (Boston); Rotary (Brookline, Mass).                      *Died Oct. 1987.*

**MURRAY, Angus,** MC and Bar; CEng, FIMechE; Chairman: Redman Heenan International plc, since 1972 (Chief Executive, 1971–76); Candover Investments Ltd, since 1980; Deputy Chairman, Fairey Holdings Ltd, since 1981 (Chairman, 1978–80); Director: Sandvik Ltd, since 1971; Doulton & Co. Ltd, since 1980; Barmel Associates Ltd, since 1981; Drake and Scull Holdings Ltd, since 1981; Industrial Adviser, Hambros Bank Ltd, since 1970; *b* 9 March 1919; *e s* of late Dr F. Anderson Murray, MD, and Margaret Murray; *m* 1950, Dorothy Anne (*née* Walker); two *s*. *Educ:* Glasgow High Sch.; Glasgow Univ. (BSc Hons MechEng); Univ. of Strathclyde. CBIM. Served War, Royal Engineers, 1940–46; att. 4th Indian Div., 1943–46. PE Consulting Gp, 1947–56; Managing Director: Expert Tool Gp, 1956–62; Tap & Die Corp., 1963; Chairman and Managing Director: Umbrako Ltd, and Gen. Man., Internat. Div. Standard Pressed Steel Co. (USA), 1964–68; H. H. Robertson Pty (SA) Ltd, and Man. Dir, Metal Sales Co. (Pty) Ltd, 1969–70; Director: Hambros Industrial Management Ltd, 1971–82; Crane Fruehauf Ltd, 1971–77 (Dep. Chm, 1976, Chm. 1977); Dir and Chm., Backer Electric Co. Ltd, 1972–76; Dir, Newman Industries Ltd, 1974–76; Dep. Chm., Newall Machine Tool Co. Ltd, 1976 (Chm. 1976–77). Member: Adv. Panel to Electra Fund Managers Ltd, 1977–; Co. Affairs Cttee, Inst. of Dirs, 1981–; Commercial and Economic Cttee, EEF, 1982–; Cttee of Management, Inst. of Obstetrics and Gynaecology, 1978–; Council of Management, UC at Buckingham, 1981–; a Vice-Pres., Instn of Industrial Managers, 1979–. *Recreations:* golf, music, family. *Address:* Atholl House, Church Lane, Stoke Poges, Bucks SL2 4NZ. *T:* Slough 30477. *Clubs:* Caledonian, MCC, London Scottish Rugby Football; Denham Golf.                           *Died 23 Aug. 1982.*

**MURRAY, Sir (Francis) Ralph (Hay),** KCMG 1962 (CMG 1950); CB 1957; Chairman: SAFT (UK) Ltd; CSM Parliamentary Consultants Ltd; Director, CSM European Consultants Ltd; *b* 3 March 1908; *s* of Rev. Charles Hay Murray and Mabel Umfreville; *m* 1935, Mauricette, *d* of Count Bernhard Kuenburg; three *s* one *d*. *Educ:* Brentwood Sch.; St Edmund Hall, Oxford. BBC, 1934–39; Foreign Office, 1939–45; Allied Commission for Austria, 1945–46; Special Commissioner's Staff, SE Asia, 1946–47; Foreign Office, 1947–51; Counsellor, HM Embassy, Madrid, 1951–54; Minister, HM Embassy, Cairo, 1954–56; Asst Under-Sec. of State, FO, 1957–61; Dep. Under-Sec. of State, FO, 1961–62; Ambassador to Greece, 1962–67. A Governor of the BBC, 1967–73. *Address:* 3 Whaddon Hall Mews, Whaddon, Milton Keynes. *T:* Milton Keynes 501967. *Club:* Travellers'.                                   *Died 11 Sept. 1983.*

**MURRAY, Gen. Sir Horatius,** GCB 1962 (CB 1945); KBE 1956; DSO 1943; Colonel of The Cameronians (Scottish Rifles), 1958–64, now retired; *b* 18 April 1903; *s* of late Charles Murray; *m* 1953, Beatrice (*d* 1983), artist, *y d* of Frederick Cuthbert, Upwood Park. *Educ:* Peter Symonds Sch., Winchester; RMC, Sandhurst. Gazetted to Cameronians, 1923; transferred to Camerons, 1935. Served War of 1939–45, North Africa, Sicily, Italy, France (DSO, CB); GOC 6 Armoured Division, 1944–45; Dir of Personal Services, War Office, 1946–47; GOC 1st Infantry Division, 1947–50; GOC Northumbrian District, 1951–53; Commander, Commonwealth Division in Korea, 1953–54; GOC-in-C, Scottish Command and Governor of Edinburgh Castle, 1955–58; Commander-in-Chief, Allied Forces, Northern Europe, 1958–61, retired. Commander Legion of Merit (US); Knight of the Sword (Sweden). *Recreations:* golf, cricket. *Address:* The Distressed Gentlefolk's Aid Association, Vicarage Gate, W8.                                    *Died 2 July 1989.*

**MURRAY, James Dalton,** CMG 1957; HM Diplomatic Service, retired; *b* Edinburgh, 6 March 1911; *s* of late Dr James Murray, Edinburgh, and late Eleanor (*née* Mortimer); *m* 1st, 1949, Dora Maud (Denny) Carter (*d* 1958); one *s* two *d*; 2nd, 1959, Merriall Rose, 2nd *d* of Sir Timothy Eden, 8th Bart; two *s*. *Educ:* Edinburgh Acad.; Stowe; Magdalene Coll., Cambridge (Exhibitioner). Entered HM Consular Service, 1933; Vice-Consul: San Francisco, 1933, Mexico City, 1936; 2nd Sec., Embassy, Washington, 1939; 1st Sec. and Consul, La Paz, 1943; Foreign Office, 1945; Office of Comr-Gen. for SE Asia, Singapore, 1948; Counsellor, HM Foreign Service, and apptd to FO, 1950; seconded to CRO, 1952; Dep. High Comr for UK, Karachi, 1952; returned FO, 1955; Counsellor, British Embassy, Lisbon, 1959–61; Minister, 1961–63, Ambassador, 1963–65, Rumania; British High Comr, Jamaica, 1965–70, and Ambassador to Haiti (non-resident), 1966–70; retired 1970. Re-employed, 1970–76, as First Secretary and Consul (Chargé d'Affaires) resident in Port-au-Prince, Haiti. *Recreations:* golf, relaxing. *Address:* c/o Foreign and Commonwealth Office, SW1.
                                               *Died 4 June 1984.*

**MURRAY, Prof. James Greig;** Professor of Surgery, University of London, 1964–80, retired; Hon. Consultant Surgeon, King's College Hospital, London; *b* 1 April 1919; *s* of J. A. F. Murray and Christina (*née* Davidson) (*d* 1946, Cecilia (*née* Mitchell Park) (*d* 1987); one *s* one *d*. *Educ:* Peterhead Acad.; Aberdeen Univ. MB, ChB 1942; FRCS Edinburgh 1950; ChM (Aberdeen) 1961; FRCS 1964. Surg.-Lt, RNVR, 1943–46. Lectr in Anatomy Dept, Univ. Coll., London, 1950–54; Clinical Research Fellow, MRC, RCS of England, 1954–56; Sen. Lectr in Surgery, Univ. of Aberdeen, 1958–59. Member: Senate of Univ. of London, 1973–77; SE Thames RHA, 1977–80. Chm., Cancer Res. Campaign Study on Breast Cancer. *Publications:* Scientific Basis of Surgery, 1965; Gastric Secretion: Mechanism and Control, 1965; After Vagotomy, 1969; articles in scientific and clinical jls on composition of vagus nerves, regeneration of nerves, physiology of gastric secretion and treatment of peptic ulceration, cancer of the breast, etc. *Recreations:* fishing, golf. *Address:* Pitearn, Alves by Forres, Moray, Scotland IV36 ORB. *T:* Alves 616.                        *Died 21 Dec. 1987.*

**MURRAY, Keith (Day Pearce),** MC 1917; RDI 1936; FRIBA, 1939; retired; *b* 5 July 1892; *s* of Charles Murray, Auckland, NZ; *m* 1948, Mary Beatrice de Cartaret Hayes, *d* of Lt-Col R. Malet; one *d*. *Educ:* King's Coll., Auckland, NZ; Mill Hill Sch., London. Served RFC and RAF in France, 1915–19 (MC, Croix de Guerre Belge, despatches 5 times); OC No 10 Sqdn, 1917–19; Major. Served in RAF, 1939–41. Studied at Architectural Association School. Commenced practice as partner with C. S. White, 1936. Designed pottery, glass and silver during the thirties; Master of the Faculty of Royal Designers for Industry, 1945–47. Gold Medal, 5th Triennale of Milan, 1933. Principal works: Wedgwood Factory at Barlaston; Hong Kong Air Terminal; BEA Engineering Base at London Airport; various industrial and office buildings. *Recreation:* trout fishing. *Address:* Stephouse, Tarrant Gunville, Blandford, Dorset. *T:* Tarrant Hinton 339.                          *Died 16 May 1981.*

**MURRAY, Sir Ralph;** *see* Murray, Sir F. R. H.

**MURRAY-BROWN, Gilbert Alexander,** CIE 1942; OBE 1918; BSc; FICE; *b* 24 Jan. 1893; *m* 1928, Norah Frances, *e d* of late F. H. Burkitt, CIE; one *s* (and one *s* decd). *Educ:* Glasgow Univ. Joined RE (TF) 1914; served European War, 1914–19; Capt. 1916; Major, AIRO 1928. Joined Indian Service of Engineers, 1919; Chief Engr and Sec. to Govt, PWD, NWFP, India, 1940–46. Pres., Central Bd of Irrigation, India, 1943. *Recreations:* golf, fishing, shooting. *Address:* Kinnelhook, Lockerbie, Dumfriesshire. *T:* Lochmaben 211.                                           *Died 19 May 1981.*

**MUSCHAMP, Rt. Rev. Cecil Emerson Barron,** AM 1982; MA, ThL; *b* Wing, Bucks, England, 16 June 1902; *s* of late Canon E. G. Muschamp, Launceston, Tasmania; *m* 1931, Margaret Warren Crane; two *s* two *d*. *Educ:* Church Grammar Sch., Launceston, Tasmania; Univ. of Tasmania; Univ. of Oxford; St Stephen's House, Oxford. BA Univ. of Tasmania, 1924, Oxon (Hon. Sch. of Theology), 1927; ThL Australian Coll. of Theology, 1925; MA Oxon, 1934. Schoolmaster, 1920–25, Hutchins Sch., Hobart, and St Peter's Coll., Adelaide. Deacon, 1927; Priest, 1928. Curate of St Luke, Bournemouth, 1927–30; in charge of St Albans and St Aidan's, Aldershot, 1930–32; Curate, Withycombe Raleigh (in charge of All Saints, Exmouth), 1932–37; Vicar of St Michael and All Angels, City and Diocese of Christchurch, NZ, 1937–50; Asst Bishop of Perth, 1950–55; Bishop of Kalgoorlie, 1950–67; Dean of Brisbane, 1967–72, Dean Emeritus, 1981–. Retired 1972. Served War of 1939–45: Chaplain in Royal New Zealand Air Force, 1942–45; Sen. Chaplain, 1944, S Pacific Comd. Pres., WCC in WA, 1953–55; Councillor, Royal Flying Doctor Service, Kalgoorlie Base, 1955–67. *Publications:* Table Manners, 1945; Sin and its Remedy, 1961; The Church of England and Roman Catholicism, 1962. *Recreations:* golf, gardening. *Address:* 9 Samson Street, Mosman Park, WA 6012, Australia. *Club:* Rotary (Mosman Park) (Paul Harris Fellow of Rotary, 1982). *Died 28 Sept.* 1984.

**MUSGRAVE, Clifford,** OBE 1958; Director Brighton Public Libraries, Art Gallery, Museums and the Royal Pavilion, 1939–68; *b* 26 July 1904; *s* of William Francis Musgrave, bookseller; *m* 1928 Margaret Esther, *d* of Walter Meakin, journalist; two *s.* Director: Birkenhead Public Libraries and Williamson Art Gallery, 1937–39. Member Council of Museum Association, 1951–54; Pres. South-East Federation of Museums and Art Galleries, 1947–48–49; Mem. Cttee for 18th Century English Taste Exhibition, Royal Academy, 1955–56; Mem. Cttee for Le Siècle de l'Elégance Exhibition, Paris, 1959; Hon. Mem., Georgian Group; Mem. Advisory Council of Victoria and Albert Museum, 1957–69; Vice-Pres., Regency Soc.; FLA; Fellow Museums Assoc. Hon. DLitt Sussex, 1969. *Publications:* Late Georgian Architecture 1760–1810, 1956; Sussex, 1957; Regency Architecture 1810–1830 (The Connoisseur Period Guides, 1956–58), 1958; Royal Pavilion: an episode in the romantic, 1959; Regency Furniture, 1961, 2nd edn 1971; Adam and Hepplewhite Furniture, 1965; Life in Brighton, 1969, 2nd edn 1980; articles and reviews in various jls. *Recreations:* music, travel. *Address:* 9 Buckle Drive, Seaford, Sussex. *T:* Seaford 898059.
*Died 15 Sept.* 1982.

**MUSGRAVE, Sir (Frank) Cyril,** KCB 1955 (CB 1946); retired; *b* 21 June 1900; *s* of late Frank Musgrave; *m* 1st, Elsie Mary, *d* of late Christopher Williams; one *s* one *d*; 2nd, Jean Elsie, *d* of late John Soulsby; two *s. Educ:* St George's Coll., London. Entered Civil Service, 1919; served Inland Revenue, 1920–37; Air Ministry, 1937–40; Ministry of Aircraft Production, 1940–46; Min. of Supply, 1946–59, Permanent Sec., 1956–59. Chm., Iron and Steel Bd, 1959–67; Mem. (part time), BSC, 1967–70; Dir various companies, 1960–76. *Recreations:* music, gardening. *Address:* Needles Eye, Drinkstone, Bury St Edmunds, Suffolk IP30 9TL. *T:* Rattlesden 652. *Died 20 July* 1986.

**MUSKERRY, 8th Baron (Ireland),** *cr* 1781; **Hastings Fitzmaurice Tilson Deane;** 13th Bt (Ireland), *cr* 1710; Radiologist to Regional Health Authority, Limerick, 1961–85; *b* 12 March 1907; 3rd and *o* surv. *s* of 7th Baron Muskerry and Mabel Kathleen Vivienne (*d* 1954), *d* of Charles Henry Robinson, MD, FRCSI; *S* father, 1966; *m* 1944, Betty Fairbridge (*d* 1988), *e d* of George Wilfred Reckless Palmer, South Africa; one *s* one *d. Educ:* Sandford Park Sch., Dublin; Trinity Coll., Dublin; MA, MB, BCh, BAO; DMR London. Served War of 1939–45, S African Army (Western Desert; regtl battle honour, Desert Rat Flash, mentioned in despatches, 1942; seconded RAMC, Italy, Greece). Specialised in Radiology, London Univ., 1946–48; Consultant Radiologist to Transvaal Administration, 1949–57. *Heir: s* Hon. Robert Fitzmaurice Deane, BA, BAI [*b* 26 March 1948; *m* 1975, Rita Brink, Pietermaritzburg. *Educ:* Sandford Park Sch., Dublin; Trinity Coll. Dublin]. *Address:* Springfield House, Drumcollogher, Co. Limerick. *T:* Drumcollogher 83–101. *Died 14 Oct.* 1988.

**MUSKETT, Prof. Arthur Edmund,** OBE 1957; DSc London, ARCS, MRIA; FIBiol; Professor of Plant Pathology and Head of Department of Mycology and Plant Pathology, The Queen's University, Belfast, 1945–65; Professor Emeritus, since 1966; Head of Plant Pathology Division, Ministry of Agriculture, N Ireland, 1938–65; *b* 15 April 1900; *s* of late Arthur Muskett, Wood Farm, Ashwellthorpe, Norwich, Norfolk; *m* 1926, Hilda Elizabeth, *d* of late Henry Smith, Manor Farm, Fundenhall, Norwich; three *s* one *d. Educ:* City of Norwich Sch., Norwich; Imperial Coll. of Science, London. BSc, ARCS (Botany); MSc (London) 1931; MRIA 1933; DSc (London) 1938. RAF Flight Cadet A, 1918–19. Asst in Plant Pathology, Min. of Agr., NI and QUB, 1923–26, Junior Lectr QUB 1926; Dep. Head Plant Pathology Div., Min. of Agric. NI and Lectr QUB, 1931; Dean of Faculty of Agriculture, Queen's Univ., Belfast, 1950–57. Pres. British Mycological Soc., 1948; Vice-Pres., Assoc. Applied Biologists, 1954–55. Chairman: Central Gardens Assoc. for Northern Ireland; Ulster Countryside Cttee, 1965–72; N Ireland Amenity Council; Ulster Tree Cttee. Instrumental in introducing 'Best Kept' competitions for villages, small and large towns, 1957; more recently, Best Kept housing estates, streets and buildings in NI; involved in innovation of Tree Week, NI, leading to similar exercises throughout UK. *Publications:* Diseases of the Flax Plant, 1947; A. A. McGuckian: A Memorial Volume, 1956; Autonomous Dispersal: Plant Pathology (An Advanced Treatise), Vol. III, 1960; Mycology and Plant Pathology in Ireland, 1976; Catalogue of Irish

Fungi, I Gasteromycetes, 1978, II Hymenomycetes, 1980, III Teliomycetes, 1980, IV Ascomycetes, 1983; Ulster Garden Handbook (annually); numerous papers in Annals of Applied Biology, Annals of Botany, Trans Brit. Mycological Soc., etc. *Recreations:* horticulture; extra work. *Address:* The Cottage, 29 Ballynahinch Road, Carryduff, Belfast. *T:* Carryduff 812350.
*Died 22 Oct.* 1984.

**MUSSEN, Surgeon Rear-Adm. Robert Walsh,** CB 1954; CBE 1949; MD; FRCP; retired; *b* 13 May 1900; *s* of Hugh Harper Mussen, JP, Belfast, late Crown Solicitor, N Ireland; *m* 1932, Mary Katherine Annie, *d* of late Surgeon Rear-Adm. H. E. R. Stephens; one *s* two *d* (and one *s* decd). *Educ:* Campbell Coll., Belfast; Queen's Univ., Belfast; Charing Cross Hosp., London. Entered Royal Navy, 1922. Served in ships and Naval hosps at home and abroad; specialized in Clin. Pathology and Internal Medicine. MD (Belfast); MRCP 1935; FRCP 1949. Sqdn MO, 1st Battle Sqdn, 1938; Brit. Naval Med. Liaison Officer with US Navy, 1943–45; Surgeon Capt., 1944; MO i/c and Dir Med. Studies, RN Medical Sch., 1945–48. Surgeon Rear-Adm., 1952; QHP 1952–55; Medical Officer in Charge, RN Hosp., Chatham, and Command MO on staff of Comdr-in-Chief, the Nore, 1952–55; Min. of Health, 1955–65. Chm., Chailey RDC, 1972–74. Comdr Order of St John, 1954. *Publications:* The Story of a Naval Doctor (autobiog.) 1983; various papers on medical subjects and on naval medical history. *Recreations:* walking, reading and writing. *Address:* Cleves, 40 Lewes Road, Ditchling, Sussex BN6 8TU. *T:* Hassocks 2920. *Died 12 Nov.* 1985.

**MUTCH, Nathan,** MA, MD Cantab, FRCP (London); Consulting Physician, Guy's Hospital; formerly Staff Examiner in Applied Pharmacology, London University; Examiner in Therapeutics, Cambridge University; Lecturer in Pharmacology, London University; Director of Department of Pharmacology, Guy's Hospital; originator of medicinal Magnesium Trisilicate; Member of the first Editorial Board, British Journal of Pharmacology and Chemotherapy; Sector Adviser in Medicine, Emergency Medical Service; Consulting Physician to American Red Cross Society in Europe; *b* 22 May 1886; *s* of Nathan Mutch, Rochdale, and Helen Hollinshead; *m* 1913, Eileen Caroline Arbuthnot, 3rd *d* of Sir W. Arbuthnot Lane, 1st Bt, CB; one *d* (one *s* decd). *Educ:* Manchester Grammar Sch. (The King's prize for Chemistry); Emmanuel Coll., Cambridge (Senior Scholar and Research Student); 1st class Parts I and II, Nat. Science Tripos, 1906–07; Guy's Hosp. Medical Sch., (Univ. Scholar). Mem. of Physiological Soc.; founder Mem. of British Pharmacological Soc.; FRSM. *Publications:* articles on pathology and treatment of intestinal disorders, in scientific journals; also on magnesium trisilicate, other medicinal silicates, alumina and clays. *Address:* Pitt-White, Uplyme, Devon. *T:* Lyme Regis 2094. *Died 3 June* 1982.

**MWENDWA, Hon. Maluki Kitili;** MP Kitui West, Kenya, since 1984; Chairman: United Nations Association, Kenya; Chania Enterprises Ltd; ExpoAfrica Ltd; Fad Investments Ltd; Export Promotion Services; Inter Continental Holdings Ltd; Kenya Advertising Corporation Ltd; Kenya Allied Travel Enterprises Ltd; Kenya Pisci-Culture Ltd; Mugie Ltd; Pasha Club Ltd; Housing Finance Company of Kenya; Ranching and Agricultural Consultants Ltd; Research, Editorial and Design Services Ltd; Wendo Ltd; Consultant General, Private Sector; *b* 24 Dec. 1929; *s* of Senior Chief M. Kitavi Mwendwa and Mrs Kathuka Mwendwa; *m* 1964, Winifred Nyiva Mangole (Hon. Mrs Winifred Mwendwa, MP Kitui West; one of first four Kenya women MPs, Oct. 1974); one *s* three *d. Educ:* Alliance High Sch., Kenya; Nabumali High Sch., Uganda; Makerere University Coll.; London Univ.; Exeter Univ.; St Catherine's Coll., Oxford. DipEd 1950; LLB 1955 (Sir Archibald Bodkin Prize for Criminal Law, 1953); DPA 1956; BA 1959, MA 1963. President: Cosmos Soc., 1959; Jowett Soc., 1959; St Catherine's Debating Soc., 1959, Oxford. Called to the Bar, Lincoln's Inn, 1961. Lectr Kagumo Teacher Training Coll., 1951. Asst Sec., Min. of Commerce and Industry, 1962, Min. of Works and Communications, 1962; Sen. Asst Sec., Min. of Tourism, Forests and Wild Life, 1962–63; Perm. Sec., Min. of Social Services, 1963, and Min. of Home Affairs, 1963–64; Solicitor Gen., 1964–68 (acting Attorney Gen., 1967); Chief Justice of Kenya, 1968–71. Leader, Kenya Delegn: Commonwealth and Empire Law Conf., Sydney, 1965; World Peace through Law Conf., Washington, 1965; Conf. on Intellectual Property, Stockholm, 1967 (Vice-Pres. of Conf.); UN Special Cttee on Friendly Relations, Geneva, 1967; Conf. on Law of Treaties, Vienna, 1968; Kenya Rep. on 6th Cttee, 21st Session, and on 2nd and 6th Cttees (Vice-Chm. of 6th Cttee), 22nd Session, UN Gen. Assembly; Ambassador to 22nd Session, UN Gen. Assembly, 1967 (Vice-Chm., Kenya Delegn to April/May 1967 Special Session); Mem., UN Internat. Trade Law Commn, 1967–74; Chm., Business Premises Rent Tribunal, 1983; Mem., Executive Council: African Inst. of Internat. Law, Lagos; Kenya Farmers' Assoc.; Donovan Maule Theatre, Nairobi; Agricultural Soc. of Kenya, Nairobi, 1970–73 (Life Governor, 1978); African Automobile Assoc., Nairobi. Chm., Bd of Governors: Ngara Sch., 1965–73; Parklands Sch., 1967–73; Kitui Sch., 1972–74. *Publication:*

Constitutional Contrasts in the East African Territories, 1965. *Recreations:* hunting, swimming, cycling, walking. *Address:* c/o Gigiri House, Gigiri Crescent, PO Box 40198, Nairobi, Kenya. *T:* Nairobi 23450. *Clubs:* Pasha (Nairobi), Mount Kenya Safari (Nanyuki). *Died* 27 *Sept.* 1985.

**MYDDELTON, Lt-Col Ririd,** MVO 1945; JP; Extra Equerry to The Queen since 1952; Vice-Lieutenant of Denbighshire, 1968–74; *b* 25 Feb. 1902; *e s* of late Col Robert Edward Myddelton, TD, DL, JP, Chirk Castle, and late Lady Violet, *d* of 1st Marquess of Abergavenny; *m* 1931, Margaret Elizabeth Mercer Nairne (later Lady Margaret Elizabeth Myddelton; granted rank as *d* of a Marquess, 1946), *d* of late Lord Charles Mercer Nairne; two *s* one *d. Educ:* Eton; RMC Sandhurst. 2nd Lt Coldstream Guards, 1923; Adjutant, 3rd Bn, 1928–31; Staff Capt., London District, 1934–37; seconded as Dep. Master of the Household to King George VI, 1937–39; DAAG London District, 1939–40; Staff Coll., Camberley, War Course, 1942; Commanded: 1st (Armd) Bn, Coldstream Guards, 1942–44 (Normandy); retired, 1946. JP 1948, DL 1949, High Sheriff, 1951–52, Denbigh. KStJ 1961. *Recreations:* hunting, fishing. *Address:* Chirk Castle, North Wales. *T:* Chirk 772460. *Club:* Turf. *Died* 7 *Feb.* 1988.

**MYER, Dame (Margery) Merlyn Baillieu,** DBE 1960 (OBE 1948); *b* Queenscliff, Vic., 8 Jan. 1900; *d* of George Francis Baillieu and Agnes Sheehan; *m* 1920, Sidney Myer (*d* 1934); two *s* two *d. Educ:* Cromarty Girls' Sch., Victoria; Melbourne Univ. Interest in The Myer Emporium Ltd enterprises throughout Australia and abroad (founded by her late husband, Sidney Myer). Member: Cttee of Management of Royal Melbourne Hospital for 42 years; Victorian Council and Nat. Council of Australian Red Cross Soc. for 10 years; Sidney Myer Music Bowl Trust, which administers Sidney Myer Music Bowl. Collector of Jade, Porcelain and Objects d'Art. *Recreations:* garden lover, agricultural and musical interests, travel. *Address:* Cranlana, 62 Clendon Road, Toorak, Victoria 3142, Australia. *T:* 241-4966. *Died* 3 *Sept.* 1982.

**MYERS, His Honour Mark;** QC 1977; a Circuit Judge, 1984–85; *b* 22 July 1930; *s* of late Lewis Myers and Hannah Myers; *m* 1964, Katherine Ellen Desormeaux Waldram; one *s* one *d. Educ:* King's Sch., Ely; Trinity Coll., Cambridge (Exhibnr; MA). Called to the Bar, Gray's Inn, 1954; Recorder, 1979–84. Sublector in Law, Trinity Coll., Cambridge, 1954–61; Part-time Lectr in Law, Southampton Univ., 1959–61. Mem., Consumers Cttee for England and Wales, and Consumers Cttee for GB, 1974–85. *Publications:* articles in legal jls. *Recreations:* music and country life. *Address:* 73 Cholmeley Crescent, Highgate, N6 5EX. *T:* 081–340 7623.
*Died* 1 *Dec.* 1990.

**MYERSON, Aubrey Selwyn,** QC 1967; a Recorder of the Crown Court, since 1972; *b* Johannesburg, S Africa, 10 Dec. 1926; *o s* of late Michael Colman Myerson, MRCSI, LRCPI, and late Lee Myerson; *m* 1955, Helen Margaret, *d* of late Hedley Lavis, Adelaide, S Austr.; one *s* one *d. Educ:* Cardiff High Sch.; University Coll., Cardiff (Fellow, 1981). Called to Bar, Lincoln's Inn, 1950, Bencher, 1975. Leader, Wales and Chester Circuit, 1981–83. Mem., Criminal Injuries Compensation Bd, 1985–. *Recreations:* competing aggressively at all pursuits. *Address:* 8 Sloane Court East, Chelsea, SW3. *T:* 01–730 4707; 1 Dr Johnson's Buildings, Temple, EC4. *T:* 01–353 9328. *Clubs:* Western (Glasgow); Bristol Channel Yacht.
*Died* 5 *Nov.* 1986.

**MYINT, Prof. Hla;** Professor of Economics, London School of Economics, 1966–85, then Professor Emeritus; *b* Bassein, Burma, 20 March 1920; *m* 1944, Joan (*née* Morris); no *c. Educ:* Rangoon Univ.; London Sch. of Economics. Prof. of Econs, Rangoon Univ., and Econ. Adviser to Govt of Burma, 1946–49; Univ. Lectr in Econs of Underdeveloped Countries, Oxford Univ., 1950–65; Rector of Rangoon Univ., 1958–61. Vis. Prof., Univs of Yale, Cornell and Wisconsin; has served on UN Expert Cttees; Hon. DLitt, Rangoon, 1961. Order of Sithu (Burma), 1961. *Publications:* Theories of Welfare Economics, 1948; The Economics of the Developing Countries, 1964; Economic Theory and the Underdeveloped Countries, 1971; Southeast Asia's Economy: development policies in the 1970s, 1972; many papers in learned jls. *Recreations:* walking, garden watching. *Address:* 12 Willow Drive, Barnet, Herts. *T:* 01–449 3028. *Died* 9 *Jan.* 1989.

**MYNETT, George Kenneth,** QC 1960; JP; **His Honour Judge Mynett;** a Circuit Judge, Oxford Crown Court, since 1972; *b* 16 Nov. 1913; *s* of E. Mynett, Wellington, Salop; *m* 1940, Margaret Verna Bass-Hammonds; two *s. Educ:* Adams Grammar Sch., Newport, Salop; London Univ. Admitted solicitor of Supreme Court, 1937; LLB Hons (London) 1938. Served War of 1939–45, RAF, 1940–46; Dep. Judge Advocate Staff, Dept of JAG, 1945, 1946. Barrister, Middle Temple, 1942, 1st Cl. Hons, Certificate of Honour; after demobilisation practised on Oxford Circuit. Master of the Bench, Middle Temple, 1967. Recorder of Stoke-on-Trent, 1961–71; Honorary Recorder 1972–; JP Stoke-on-Trent, 1961; JP Oxon, 1969–71; Dep. Chm., Oxfordshire QS, 1969–71; Comr of Assize:

SE Circuit, 1970; Oxford Circuit, 1971. UK Representative, Conferences of Judges of Supreme Administrative Courts of EEC Countries in Berlin, Rome, The Hague, Luxembourg etc. Member: Council for the Training of Magistrates, 1967; Gen. Council of the Bar, 1968; Court of Governors, Univ. of Keele, 1961–. *Recreations:* landscape painting, golf, travel. *Address:* Tanglewood House, Boar's Hill, Oxford. *T:* Oxford 730439; 12 King's Bench Walk, Temple, EC4. *T:* 01-353 7008. *Died* 5 *July* 1984.

**MYNORS, Sir Humphrey (Charles Baskerville),** 1st Bt, *cr* 1964; *b* 28 July 1903; 2nd *s* of Rev. A. B. Mynors, Rector of Langley Burrell, Wilts; *m* 1939, Lydia Marian, *d* of late Sir Ellis Minns, LittD, FSA, FBA; one *s* four *d. Educ:* Marlborough; Corpus Christi Coll., Cambridge. Fellow of Corpus Christi Coll., Cambridge, 1926–33; Hon. Fellow, 1953. Entered the service of the Bank of England, 1933; a Dir, 1949–54; Dep. Governor, 1954–64. Chm., Panel on Take-overs and Mergers, 1968–69; Dep. Chm., 1969–70. Hon. DCL Durham. *Heir: s* Richard Baskerville Mynors [*b* 5 May 1947; *m* 1970, Fiona Bridget, *d* of Rt Rev. G. E. Reindorp; three *d*]. *Address:* Treago, St Weonards, Hereford HR2 8QB. *T:* St Weonards 208.
*Died* 25 *May* 1989.

**MYNORS, Sir Roger (Aubrey Baskerville),** Kt 1963; FBA 1944; *b* 28 July 1903; *s* of Rev. A. B. Mynors, Rector of Langley Burrell, Wilts; *m* 1945, Lavinia Sybil, *d* of late Very Rev. C. A. Alington, DD. *Educ:* Eton; Balliol College, Oxford. Fellow and Classical Tutor of Balliol, 1926–44 (Hon. Fellow 1963); Kennedy Prof. of Latin in the Univ. of Cambridge and Fellow of Pembroke Coll., 1944–53 (Hon. Fellow, 1965); Corpus Christi Prof. of Latin Language and Literature, Oxford, 1953–70 (Hon. Fellow, Corpus Christi Coll., 1970). Vis. Lectr, Harvard, 1938. Temp. Principal, HM Treasury, 1940. Longman Vis. Fellow, Leeds Univ., 1974. Pres., Classical Assoc., 1966. Hon. DLitt: Edinburgh; Durham; Hon. LittD: Cambridge; Sheffield; Hon. LLD Toronto. Hon. Fellow, Warburg Inst.; Hon. Member: Amer. Acad. of Arts and Sciences; Amer. Philosophical Soc.; Istituto di Studi Romani. *Publications:* Cassiodori Senatoris Institutiones, 1937; Durham Cathedral MSS before 1200, 1939; Catulli Carmina, 1958; Catalogue of Balliol MSS, 1963; Plinii Epistulae, 1963; Panegyrici Latini, 1964; Vergilii Opera, 1969. *Address:* Treago, St Weonards, Hereford HR2 8QB. *T:* St Weonards 208. *Died* 17 *Oct.* 1989.

**MYRDAL, Alva;** former Swedish Cabinet Minister, diplomatist, sociologist and author; Ambassador at large since 1961; Member of Swedish Parliament, 1962–70; Minister without Portfolio (in charge of disarmament and Church affairs) in Swedish Government, 1967–73; *b* 31 Jan. 1902; *d* of Albert and Lova Reimer; *m* 1924, Dr Gunnar Myrdal; one *s* two *d. Educ:* Stockholm Univ. (AB); Uppsala Univ. (AM); USA; Geneva. Founder 1936, and Dir, 1936–48, Training Coll. for Pre-Sch. Teachers, Stockholm; Principal Dir, UN Dept of Social Affairs, 1949–50; Dir, Unesco Dept of Social Sciences, 1951–55; Minister to India, Burma, Ceylon and Nepal, 1955–56, Ambassador, 1956–61. Delegate to: ILO Conf., Paris, 1945, Geneva, 1947; Unesco Conf., Paris, 1946, New Delhi, 1956; UN General Assemblies, 1962, 1963, 1965–73. Chief Swedish Delegate to UN Disarmament Cttee, Geneva, 1962–73. Fellow, Center for Study of Democratic Instns, Santa Barbara, Calif., 1974. Vis. Professor: MIT 1974, 1975; Wellesley Coll., 1976; Texas Univ., 1978. Chairman: Internat. Inst. for Peace Research, Stockholm, 1965–66; UN Expert Group on South Africa, 1964; Swedish Govt Cttees: on relations between State and Church, 1968–72; on Research on the Future, 1971–72; UN Expert Gp on Disarmament and Development, 1972. World Council on Pre-School Educn, 1947–49. Board Member: Internat. Fedn of Univ. Women; Swedish Organisation for Cultural Relief in Europe; Swedish Fedn of Business and Professional Women (Chm. 1935–38, 1940–42). Hon. LLD: Mount Holyoke Coll., USA, 1950; Edinburgh Univ., 1964; Dr Humane Letters, Columbia Univ., 1965; Temple Univ., 1968; Hon. PhD, Leeds Univ., England, 1956; Hon. DD: Gustavus Adolphus, Miami, 1971; Brandeis, 1974; Gothenburg, 1975; East Anglia, 1976; Helsinki, 1981. West German Peace Prize (with G. Myrdal), 1970; Wateler Peace Prize, Hague Acad., 1973; Royal Inst. of Technology award, Stockholm, 1975; Albert Einstein Peace Award, 1980; People's Peace Prize, Oslo, 1982; (jtly) Nobel Peace Prize, 1982. *Publications:* (with G. Myrdal) Crisis in the Population Problem, 1934; City Children, 1935; Nation and Family, 1941; Postwar Planning, 1944; Are We Too Many?, 1950; (with V. Klein) Women's Two Roles, 1956; Towards Equality, 1970; Game of Disarmament, 1976, etc.; numerous contribs to newspapers, periodicals, books and reports. *Recreations:* travel, theatre, cooking, reading. *Address:* Svalnäs Allé 12B, 18263 Djursholm, Sweden.
*Died* 1 *Feb.* 1986.

**MYRDAL, Prof. (Karl) Gunnar;** Swedish economist; *b* 6 Dec. 1898; *s* of Carl Adolf Pettersson and Anna Sofia Carlsdotter; *m* 1924, Alva Reimer (*d* 1986); one *s* two *d. Educ:* Stockholm Univ. Studied in Germany and Britain, 1925–29; Rockefeller Fellow, US, 1929–30; Assoc. Prof., Post-Grad. Inst. of Internat. Studies, Geneva; Lars Hierta Prof. of Polit. Econ. and Public Finance, Stockholm Univ.,

1933; Mem. Swedish Senate (Social Democrat), 1934; directed study of Amer. Negro problem for Carnegie Corp., NY, 1938; returned to Sweden, 1942, re-elected to Senate, Mem. Bd of Bank of Sweden, Chm. Post-War Planning Commn; Minister of Commerce, 1945–47; Exec. Sec., UN Econ. Commn for Europe, 1947–57; directed study of econ. trends and policies in S Asian countries for Twentieth Century Fund, 1957–67; Prof. of Internat. Econs, Stockholm Univ., 1961; founded Inst. for Internat. Econ. Studies, Stockholm Univ., 1961; past Chm., Bd of Stockholm Internat. Peace Research Inst. (Mem. Bd); Vis. Res. Fellow, Center for Study of Democratic Instns, Santa Barbara, 1973–74; Distinguished Vis. Prof., New York City Univ., 1974–75; Regents' Prof., Univ. of California, Irvine, Spring 1977; Dist. Vis. Prof., Univ. of Madison, Autumn 1977; Jt Slick Prof. of Peace, L. B. Johnson Sch. of Public Affairs, Univ. of Texas, 1978. Member: British Acad.; Amer. Acad. of Arts and Scis; Royal Swedish Acad. of Scis; Hungarian Acad. of Scis; Fellow, Econometric Soc.; Hon. Mem., Amer. Econ. Assoc. Holds numerous hon. degrees and has received many awards, incl. Nitti Prize, 1976; Nobel Prize for Economics (jtly), 1974; Nehru Award, 1982. *Publications:* numerous sci. works, incl: The Cost of Living in Sweden 1830–1930, 1933; Monetary Equilibrium, 1939; An American Dilemma: The Negro Problem and Modern Democracy, 1944; The Political Element in the Development of Economic Theory, 1953; An International Economy: Problems and Prospects, 1956; Economic Theory and Underdeveloped Regions, 1957; Value in Social Theory, 1958; Beyond the Welfare State: Economic Planning and its International Implications, 1960; Challenge to Affluence, 1963; Asian Drama: An Inquiry into the Poverty of Nations, 1968; Objectivity in Social Research, 1969; The Challenge of World Poverty: A World Anti-Poverty Program in Outline, 1970; Against the Stream: Critical Essays on Economics, 1973. *Address:* Svalnäs Allé 12B, 18263 Djursholm, Sweden.

*Died 17 May 1987.*

**MYRES, John Nowell Linton,** CBE 1972; LLD, DLitt, DLit, MA; FBA 1966; FSA; President, Society of Antiquaries, 1970–75 (Vice-President, 1959–63; Director, 1966–70), later Hon. Vice-President; Bodley's Librarian, University of Oxford, 1947–65; Hon. Student of Christ Church, 1971 (Student 1928–70), and Fellow of Winchester College, 1951–77; *b* 27 Dec. 1902; *yr s* of late Emeritus Prof. Sir John Linton Myres, OBE; *m* 1929, Joan Mary Lovell, *o d* of late G. L. Stevens, Jersey; two *s. Educ:* Winchester Coll. (Scholar); New Coll., Oxford (Scholar), Hon. Fellow, 1973. 1st Class Lit Hum., 1924; 1st Class Modern History, 1926; BA 1924; MA 1928; Lecturer, 1926, Student and Tutor, 1928–48, Librarian, 1938–48, of Christ Church; Univ. Lectr in Early English History, 1935–47; served in Min. of Food, 1940–45 (Head of Fruit and Veg. Products Div., 1943–45); mem. of Council of St Hilda's Coll., Oxford, 1937–52; Pres. Oxford Architectural and Historical Soc., 1946–49. Mem. Institute for Advanced Study, Princeton, 1956; Pres. Council for British Archæology, 1959–61; Member: Ancient Monuments Board (England), 1959–76; Royal Commn on Historical Monuments (England), 1969–74; Chm. Standing Conference of National and Univ. Libraries, 1959–61. Pres: Library Assoc., 1963; Soc. for Medieval Archæology, 1963–66. Lectures: Ford's, in English History, 1958–59; O'Donnell, Edinburgh Univ., 1961; Oxford 1966–67; Rhind, Edinburgh, 1964–65; Raleigh, British Acad., 1970. Hon. Mem., Deutsches Archäologisches Institut. Hon. LLD Toronto, 1954; Hon. DLitt: Reading, 1964; Durham, 1983; Hon. DLit Belfast, 1965. Has supervised excavations at Caerleon Amphitheatre, 1926, St Catharine's Hill, Winchester, 1925–28, Colchester, 1930, Butley Priory, 1931–33, Aldborough, 1934–35 and elsewhere. Gold Medal, Soc. of Antiquaries, 1976. Hon. Foreign Corresp. Mem. Grolier Club, New York. *Publications:* part-author: St Catharine's Hill, Winchester, 1930; Anglo-Saxon Pottery and the Settlement of England, 1969; A Corpus of Anglo-Saxon Pottery, 1977; (contrib.) Oxford History of England, Vol. I, (with R. G. Collingwood) Roman Britain and the English Settlements, 1936, pt revd as Vol. IB, The English Settlements, 1986; articles and reviews in learned periodicals. *Recreations:* growing of vegetables and fruit; bibliophily, study of antiquities. *Address:* Manor House, Kennington, Oxford. *T:* Oxford 735353.

*Died 25 July 1989.*

# N

**NAGEON de LESTANG, Sir (Marie Charles Emmanuel) Clement,** Kt 1960; *b* 20 Oct. 1910; *e s* of late M. F. C. Nageon de Lestang, Solicitor and Simone Savy; *m* 1933, Danielle Sauvage; one *s* three *d* (and one *s* decd). *Educ:* St Louis' Coll., Seychelles; King's Coll., London. LLB (Hons) London, 1931. Called to the Bar, Middle Temple, 1931. Private practice, Seychelles, 1932–35; Legal Adviser and Crown Prosecutor to Govt of Seychelles, 1936–39; Actg Chief Justice, Seychelles, 1939–44; Resident Magistrate, Kenya, 1944–47; Puisne Judge, Kenya, 1947–56; Federal Justice, Federal Supreme Court of Nigeria, 1956–58; Chief Justice of the High Court of Lagos, 1958–64, and of the Southern Cameroons, 1958–60; Justice of Appeal, Court of Appeal for Eastern Africa, 1964, Vice-Pres., 1966–69. *Recreations:* yachting, fishing. *Address:* Pennies, Court Drive, Shillingford, Oxon. *Died 11 Nov.* 1986.

**NAGOGO, Alhaji Hon. Sir Usuman;** Emir of Katsina, KBE 1962 (CBE 1948); CMG 1953; President, Council of Chiefs, North-Central State (formerly Minister without Portfolio, Northern Region of Nigeria, and Member, House of Assembly). Hon. DCL Ife Univ., 1973. *Address:* Katsina, Northern Nigeria.
*Died 19 March* 1981.

**NAIPAUL, Shivadhar Srinivasa, (Shiva);** author; *b* 25 Feb. 1945; *s* of Seepersad and Dropatie Naipaul; *m* 1967, Virginia Margaret Stuart; one *s. Educ:* Queen's Royal College and St Mary's College, Trinidad; University College, Oxford. *Publications:* Fireflies, 1970 (Jock Campbell New Statesman Award, John Llewellyn Rees Meml Award, Winifred Holtby Prize); The Chip-Chip Gatherers, 1973 (Whitbread Literary Award); North of South: an African journey, 1978; Black and White, 1980; A Hot Country, 1983; Beyond the Dragon's Mouth: stories and pieces, 1984; *posthumous publication:* An Unfinished Journey, 1986. *Address:* c/o Hamish Hamilton Ltd, 57–59 Long Acre, WC2. *Died 13 Aug.* 1985.

**NAIRAC, Hon. Sir André (Lawrence),** Kt 1963; CBE 1953; QC (Mauritius); *b* 1905. *Educ:* Royal Coll., Mauritius; Balliol Coll., Oxford Univ. Called to the Bar, Middle Temple, 1929. Formerly: Minister of Industry, Commerce and External Communications; Mem. of Legislative Council and Mem. of Executive Council, Mauritius. *Address:* Reunion Road, Vacoas, Mauritius.
*Died 3 July* 1981.

**NAIRN, Sir (Michael) George,** 3rd Bt, *cr* 1904; TD 1948; *b* 30 Jan. 1911; *s* of Sir Michael Nairn, 2nd Bt, and Mildred Margaret, *e d* of G. W. Neish; *S* father 1952; *m* 1936, Helen Louise, *e d* of late Major E. J. W. Bruce, Melbourne, Aust., and late Mrs L. Warre Graham-Clarke; two *s. Educ:* Trinity Coll., Glenalmond. Chairman: Kirkcaldy and Dist Trustee Savings Bank, 1952–71; Michael Nairn & Greenwich Ltd, 1958–62; Nairn Williamson (Holdings) Ltd, 1962–70. Served War of 1939–45, with The Black Watch (wounded); Major, 1939. Mem. of the Queen's Body Guard for Scotland (Royal Company of Archers). *Heir: s* Michael Nairn [*b* 1 July 1938; *m* 1972, Diana (*d* 1982), *er d* of Leonard Bligh; two *s* one *d*]. *Address:* Pitcarmick, Bridge of Cally, Blairgowrie, Perthshire PH10 9NW. *T:* Strath Ardle 214. *Club:* Caledonian.
*Died 2 Sept.* 1984.

**NAISBY, John Vickers,** MC 1918; TD 1935; QC 1947; *b* 1894; *m* 1954, Dorothy Helen (*d* 1977), *d* of late J. H. Fellows. *Educ:* Rossall; Emmanuel Coll., Cambridge. Called to Bar, Inner Temple, 1922. Lt-Col and Brevet Col. *Died 16 May* 1983.

**NAPIER OF MAGDALA,** 5th Baron (UK), *cr* 1868; **Robert John Napier,** OBE 1944; MICE; late Royal Engineers; Brigadier, Chief Engineer, HQ, Scottish Command, retd; *b* 16 June 1904; *o s* of 4th Baron and Florence Martha (*d* 1946), *d* of Gen. John Maxwell Perceval, CB; *S* father, 1948; *m* 1939, Elizabeth Marian, *y d* of E. H. Hunt, FRCS; three *s* two *d. Educ:* Wellington. Served Waziristan, 1936–37 (despatches); War of 1939–45, Sicily (OBE). *Heir: s* Hon. Robert Alan Napier [*b* 6 Sept. 1940; *m* 1964, Frances Clare, *er d* of late A. F. Skinner, Monks Close, Woolpit, Suffolk; one *s* one *d*]. *Address:* 8 Mortonhall Road, Edinburgh EH9 2HW.
*Died 29 Oct.* 1987.

**NAPIER, Sir Joseph William Lennox,** 4th Bt, *cr* 1867; OBE 1944; *b* 1 Aug. 1895; *s* of 3rd Bt and Mabel Edith Geraldine (*d* 1955), *d* of late Rev. Charles Thornton Forster; *S* father (killed in action, Gallipoli), 1915; *m* 1931, Isabel Muriel, *yr d* of late Maj. Siward Surtees, DL, JP, Redworth Hall, Co Durham; two *s. Educ:* Rugby; Jesus College, Cambridge. Served European War, 1914–18, in South Wales Borderers, Gallipoli and Mesopotamia (wounded three times; POW, Turkey). Joined 57 Home Counties Bde RFA (TF), 1920; re-employed 1939, Lt-Col (AQMG (Movt)) HQ Staff, Eastern Command and Italy (OBE mil.). Mem., Lloyds, 1921–73. Former Dir of public companies and Mem., Council of Inst. of Directors. Gold Staff Officer, Coronations 1937 and 1953. *Recreations:* painting, fishing. *Heir: s* Robert Surtees Napier [*b* 5 March 1932; *m* 1971,

Jennifer Beryl, *d* of late H. Warwick Daw; one *s*]. *Address:* 17 Cheyne Gardens, Chelsea, SW3. *Clubs:* Alpine, Hurlingham; Swinley Forest Golf. *Died 13 Oct.* 1986.

**NAPIER, Brigadier Vivian John Lennox,** MC 1918; late S Wales Borderers; Vice-Lieutenant, Brecknock, 1964–74; *b* 13 July 1898; 3rd *s* of Sir William Lennox Napier, 3rd Bt; *m* 1958, Marion Avis, OBE, *d* of late Sir John and Lady Lloyd. *Educ:* Uppingham; RMC. Served European War, 1914–18: France and Belgium (wounded, MC); served War of 1939–45: HQ Cairo Bde and 1 Bn Welch Regt, North Africa (despatches, prisoner). Brig. Comdg Mombasa Area, 1948–49; Dep. Comdr S-W District, UK, 1949–51; retd, 1952. Commissioner, St John Ambulance, Breconshire, 1957–62. DL Brecknock, 1958. Order of Leopold (Belgium), 1925; OStJ 1959. *Recreation:* fishing. *Address:* Ty Nant, Groesffordd, Brecon, Powys. *Died 9 March* 1990.

**NAPIER, Sir William Archibald,** 13th Bt, of Merchiston, *cr* 1627; *b* 19 July 1915; *s* of Sir Robert Archibald Napier, 12th Bt and Violet Payn; *S* father, 1965; *m* 1942, Kathleen Mabel, *d* of late Reginald Greaves, Tafelberg, CP; one *s. Educ:* Cheam School; Stowe. Captain S African Engineers, Middle East, 1939–45. Mechanical Engineer. AM Inst. of (SA) Mech. Engineers; AM Inst. of Cert. Engineers (Works); Fellow, Inst. of Materials Handling. *Recreations:* golf, squash. *Heir: s* John Archibald Lennox Napier [*b* 6 Dec. 1946; *m* 1969, Erica, *d* of late Kurt Kingsfield; one *s* one *d*]. *Address:* Merchiston Croft, PO Box 65177, Benmore, Transvaal, 2010, S Africa. *T:* 7832651. *Clubs:* Rand, Johannesburg Country (Johannesburg). *Died 31 Aug.* 1990.

**NASH, Prof. John Kevin Tyrie Llewellyn;** Professor of Civil Engineering, King's College, University of London; *b* 24 April 1922; *s* of George Llewellyn Nash and Menie Tyrie; *m* 1947, Margaret Elizabeth Littleboy; one *s* three *d. Educ:* Newtown Sch., Waterford; Trinity Coll., Dublin. BA, BAI 1944, MA, MAI 1947, DSc (Eng) London 1975; FKC 1972; FICE, FASCE, FGS. Asst Engrg with K. C. D. Gp on Phoenix Caissons for Mulberry Harbour, 1943–44; Jun. Sci. Officer, Road Res. Lab. in Soil Mechs Div., 1944–46; King's Coll., London: Lectr, 1946–51; Reader, 1951–61; Prof. of Civil Engrg, 1961–; Head of Civil Engrg Dept, 1971–; Asst Principal, 1973–77. Cons. to Nigerian Govt on engrg educn in Nigeria, 1963; soil mechs cons. on Kainji dam, Nigeria, 1961–69 and various earth and rock-fill dams and dykes in Nigeria, Jordan, Israel, Cyprus, Portugal, Greece, Sudan, Britain and Ireland; expert witness for NCB at Aberfan Tribunal, 1966–67 and for BP at Sea Gem enquiry, 1967; cons. for foundns of London Bridge and Humber Bridge. Mem. Council, ICE, 1959–62 and 1963–68; Chm., British Geotechnical Soc., 1959–61; Sec.-Gen., Internat. Soc. for Soil Mechs and Foundn Engrg, 1967–; Chm. Editorial Panel, Géotechnique, 1960–66. Governor, Leighton Park Sch., Reading, 1974– (Chm., 1979–). *Publications:* Elements of Soil Mechanics, 1951; Civil Engineering, 1957; sci. papers on soil mechs in Proc. Int. Soc. Soil Mechs and Foundn Engrg, specialist symposia and confs, Géotechnique, etc. *Recreations:* music, photography, bird-watching. *Address:* King's College, Strand, WC2R 2LS. *T:* 01-836 5454; Shandon, Jordans, Beaconsfield, Bucks HP9 2ST. *T:* Chalfont St. Giles 3295. *Club:* Athenæum. *Died 24 April* 1981.

**NASH, Kenneth Twigg;** Academic Registrar and Secretary, University of Exeter, since 1976; *b* Rotherham, 15 Sept. 1918; *s* of Albert Nash, AIC, AMIChemE, Chemical Engineer, and Marjorie Nora Twigg; *m* 1960, Patricia Mary Kate Batchelor; two *s. Educ:* Rotherham Grammar Sch.; Gonville and Caius Coll., Cambridge. War of 1939–45: 67th (York and Lancs) and 62nd (1st/3rd E Riding) HAA Regts, RA. Admiralty, 1948; Private Sec. to Sir John Lang; Prin. Private Sec. to three First Lords (Cilcennin, Hailsham, Selkirk); service in civil establishments, finance and as a Head of Military Branch of Admiralty. Called to Bar, Inner Temple, 1955. IDC, 1964; Defence Counsellor, British Embassy, Washington, 1965; Asst Under-Sec. (Policy), MoD, 1968; Asst Sec. Gen., NATO, 1969–72; Asst Under-Sec. (Defence Staff), 1972–74; Dep. Under-Sec. of State, MoD (PE), 1974–75. *Address:* West Riding, West Avenue, Exeter. *Died 31 March* 1981.

**NASIR, Rt. Rev. Eric Samuel;** *b* 7 Dec. 1916. *Educ:* St Stephen's College, Delhi (MA); St Xavier's College, Calcutta (BT); Westcott House, Cambridge; Bishop's College, Calcutta. Warden, St Paul's Hostel, Delhi, 1942–45, 1951–52, 1956–62; Principal, Delhi United Christian School, 1956–62. Vicar, St Andrew's Church, Rewari, 1942–47; Chaplain, St Stephen's Coll., Delhi, 1945–47; Vicar: St Mary's Church, Ajmer, 1947–49; St James' Church, Delhi, 1949–51; Holy Trinity Church, Delhi, 1952; St Thomas' Church, New Delhi, 1953–62; Bishop of: Assam, 1962–68; Amritsar, 1968–70; Delhi, 1970–81; Moderator, Church of N India, 1971–81. Member, Central Committee, World Council of Churches, 1968–81. *Address:* c/o Bishop's House, 1 Church Lane, New Delhi 1, India. *T:* 387471.
*Died 12 July* 1987.

**NATALI, Lorenzo;** politician and lawyer, Italy; a Vice-President, Commission of the European Communities, 1977–88; *b* 1 Oct. 1922.

*Educ:* Collegio d'Abruzzo dei Padri Gesuiti; Univ. of Florence. MP (Christian Democrat); Under-Secretary of State: for the Press and Information, 1955–57; Min. of Finance, 1957–59; Treasury, 1960–64; Minister: for Merchant Marine, 1966–68; of Public Works, 1968; of Tourism and Entertainments, 1968–69; of Agriculture, 1970–73. *Recreation:* sport. *Address:* Via Nibby 18, Rome, Italy. *Died* 28 *Aug.* 1989.

**NATHAN, Kandiah Shanmuga;** QC 1987; Part-time Chairman, VAT Tribunals, since 1988; *b* 24 May 1930; *s* of Sanmugam Kandiah and Sundram Murugesu; *m* 1966, Elizabeth Mary Woodwark; two *s* one *d. Educ:* Methodist Boys' Sch., Kuala Lumpur, Malaya; Japanese Sch., Occupied Malaya; Anglo-Chinese Sch., Ipoh, Malaya. LLB London (external). Teacher, Singapore, 1950–52; Labour Officer, Malaya, 1952–57; Asst Personnel Officer, City Council, Singapore, 1957–59; Called to the Bar, Lincoln's Inn, 1963; Industrial Relations Adviser, Malayan Mining Employers' Assoc., 1963–64; Mem., Industrial Tribunal, Malaya, 1964; Advocate and Solicitor, Malaya and Singapore, 1964–69; UK Immigrants' Adv. Service (Immigration Counsellor), 1970–72. *Recreations:* golf, gardening. *Address:* Gray's Inn Chambers, Gray's Inn, WC1R 5JA. *T:* 071–404 1111; 20 The Chine, N21 2EB. *T:* 081–360 5893. *Clubs:* Commonwealth Trust; Commonwealth Golfing Society; Royal Selangor, Royal Selangor Golf. *Died* 20 *Nov.* 1990.

**NATHAN, Sir Maurice (Arnold),** KBE 1963 (CBE 1957); *b* Kew, Vic, 17 July 1914; *s* of late Harold B. Nathan, Melbourne; *m* 1942, Margaret Frances, *d* of David McKay; one *s. Educ:* Geelong C of E Gram. Sch. Served War of 1939–45, Capt. AIF. Formerly Chm. and Man. Dir., Patersons (Australia) Ltd and associated cos; Pres., Victorian Industries Confederation, Furnishers Soc. of Victoria and Aust. Retail Furnishers Assoc., 1951–53; Mem. Melbourne City Council, 1952–72; Lord Mayor of Melbourne, 1961–63; Founder and Chm., Victoria Promotion Cttee; Chm., Olympic Park Cttee of Management; Founder and Chairman, Australian World Exposition Project; Pres., Victorian Football League, 1971–77. *Recreations:* gardening, racing, squash, football, tennis, golf. *Address:* c/o Suite 600, 55 Exhibition Street, Melbourne, Vic 3000, Australia. *T:* 63.9384; 25 St Georges Road, Toorak, Vic 3142. *T:* 2412282. *Clubs:* Victoria Amateur Turf, Victoria Racing, Moonee Valley Racing, Melbourne Cricket, Lawn Tennis Assoc. of Vic., Metropolitan Golf. *Died* 13 *Dec.* 1982.

**NAUNTON MORGAN, Sir Clifford;** *see* Morgan.

**NAYLOR, Arthur Holden,** MSc; FICE; FIMechE; Emeritus Professor; *b* 1897; *er s* of Rev. John and Eunice Naylor; *m* 1925, Edith Riley; one *s* one *d.* RE, 1916–19 and 1940–43; Aeroplane Research under DSIR 1919; engaged on construction of Johore Causeway and Prai Power Station, Malaya, 1921–24; Sir Lawrence Guillemard Service Reservoir, Penang, 1925–29; Severn Barrage Investigation, 1930–31; Lochaber Water Power Scheme, 1931–34; Kenya and Uganda Hydro-Electric Investigations, 1934–35; Research Officer, Institution of Civil Engineers, 1935–38; Professor of Civil Engineering, Queen's University, Belfast, 1938–63; Professor of Civil Engineering, Ahmadu Bello University, Nigeria, 1963–66; Visiting Lecturer, 1966–67, Senior Research Fellow, School of Engineering, 1967–70, University College of Swansea. *Publication:* Siphon Spillways, 1935. *Address:* 2 Hael Lane, Southgate, near Swansea, West Glamorgan.
*Died* 20 *Aug.* 1983.

**NAYLOR, Rev. Canon Charles Basil;** Chancellor and Canon Residentiary of Liverpool Cathedral, 1956–81, retired 1982; Canon Emeritus, Diocese of Liverpool, since 1981; *b* 29 Oct. 1911; *s* of Charles Henry Naylor and Eva Garforth Naylor. *Educ:* Rugby School; Keble College, Oxford. BA 2nd class Lit. Hum., 1934; MA 1939. Deacon, 1939, priest, 1940, Liverpool; Asst Master, Llandovery Coll., 1935–39; Asst Master, Chaplain and Housemaster, Liverpool College, 1939–43; Chaplain RNVR, 1943–46, East Indies Station and Fleet. Curate, St Peter le Bailey Oxford, 1946–56; Chaplain of St Peter's Coll., 1946–56, Dean, 1946–52, Fellow, 1950–56; Tutor in Theology, 1952–56. Examining Chaplain: to Bishop of Blackburn, 1951–; and to Bishop of Liverpool, 1954–; Senior Proctor of Univ. of Oxford, 1952–53. Exchanged duties with Dean of Christchurch, New Zealand, Dec. 1960–April 1961. Dir of Ordination Candidates and Dir of Post-Ordination Training, Liverpool dio., 1956–72; Dir of In-service Trng, Liverpool dio., 1973–81. Librarian, Radcliffe Library, Liverpool Cathedral, 1958–81. Mem., Liturgical Commn, 1962–66. Trustee, St Peter's Coll., Oxford, 1971–. *Publications:* Why Prayer Book Revision at all, 1964; contrib. Theological Collections: The Eucharist Then and Now, 1968; Ground for Hope, 1968; contrib. Arias of J. S. Bach, 1977; (ed) Front Line Praying, 1981. *Recreations:* music, walking. *Address:* 50 Park Road, Rugby, Warwickshire CV21 2QH. *Clubs:* National Liberal; Athenæum (Liverpool). *Died* 13 *March* 1988.

**NAYLOR, (Gordon) Keith,** TD 1973; **His Honour Judge Naylor;** a Circuit Judge, since 1985; *b* 26 Feb. 1933; *yr s* of late Henry and

Elizabeth Naylor, Hoylake; *m* 1962, Anthea Laverock, *d* of late G. E. Shaw and Mrs Elizabeth Douglas; two *s. Educ:* Wallasey Grammar Sch.; Univ. of Liverpool (Grotius Prize, 1953; LLB 1955). Called to the Bar, Gray's Inn, 1957; in practice on Northern Circuit, 1957–85; a Recorder, 1980–85. National Service, Cheshire Regt, 1955–57 (commnd, 1956); served TA, 4th and 4th/7th Bns Cheshire Regt, 1957–70; Lt-Col, comd Liverpool Univ. OTC, 1975–78 (Jubilee Medal); TA Col, HQ NW Dist, 1979–80. *Publications:* book revs and articles in legal pubns. *Address:* Queen Elizabeth II Law Courts, Derby Square, Liverpool L2 1XA; Hantsport, Lightfoot Lane, Gayton, Wirral, Merseyside L60 2TP. *T:* 051–342 6739. *Club:* Border and County (Carlisle).
*Died* 17 *Dec.* 1990.

**NAYLOR-LEYLAND, Sir Vivyan (Edward),** 3rd Bt, *cr* 1895; *b* 5 March 1924; *e s* of Sir Edward Naylor-Leyland, 2nd Bt, and Marguerite Helene (*d* 1945), 2nd *d* of late Baron de Belabre; *S* father, 1952; *m* 1st, 1952, Elizabeth Anne (marr. diss. 1960), *yr d* of 2nd Viscount FitzAlan of Derwent, OBE; one *s*; 2nd, 1967, Starr Anker-Simmons (marr. diss. 1975); one *d*; 3rd, 1980, Jameina F. Reid, *d* of James Freeman Reid, High Park, Co. Offaly, Eire; two *d. Educ:* Eton; Christ Church, Oxford; Royal Agricultural Coll., Cirencester. Grenadier Guards, 1942–47. *Heir: s* Philip Vyvyan Naylor-Leyland [*b* 9 August 1953; *m* 1980, Lady Isabella Lambton, *d* of Viscount Lambton; one *s* one *d*]. *Address:* Le Neuf Chemin, St Saviours, Guernsey, Channel Islands. *T:* Guernsey 65708. *Clubs:* White's (overseas mem.), MCC. *Died* 2 *Sept.* 1987.

**NEAGLE, Dame Anna, (Dame (Florence) Marjorie Wilcox),** DBE 1969 (CBE 1952); Hon. Vice-President, FANY Corps, 1972 (Hon. Ensign 1950); actress, producer; Member: Executive Council, King George VI Memorial Foundation; Council Edith Cavell Homes of Rest for Nurses; Council, King George's Pension Fund for Actors and Actresses; Vice-President: Forces Help Society; Royal Alfred Society for Seafarers; *b* Forest Gate, Essex, 20 Oct. 1904; *d* of late Captain Herbert William Robertson, RNR, and Florence Neagle Robertson; *m* 1943, Herbert Wilcox, CBE (*d* 1977). *Educ:* High School, St Albans, Herts; Wordsworth's Physical Training College. Theatre Royal, Drury Lane, Charlot and Cochran revues, London and New York, 1926–30; Stand up and Sing, with Jack Buchanan, 1931; Open Air Theatre—Rosalind and Olivia, 1934; Peter Pan, 1937; Jane Austen's Emma, 1944–45; *later plays include:* The Glorious Days, Palace Theatre, 1952–53; The More the Merrier, Strand, 1960; Person Unknown, 1964; Charlie Girl, Adelphi, 1965–71, Aust. and NZ presentation 1971–72; No, No, Nanette, Drury Lane, 1973; The Dame of Sark, Duke of York's and O'Keefe Centre, Toronto, 1975; The First Mrs Fraser; Maggie, Shaftesbury, 1977; Most Gracious Lady, 1978; Relative Values, 1978 (Vienna); Nat. tour, My Fair Lady, 1978–79, Adelphi, 1979–81, Toronto 1982; Cinderella, Richmond, 1982, Palladium, 1985. Has appeared in plays on television. *Films:* Good Night, Vienna, 1931; Bitter Sweet, 1933; Nell Gwyn, 1934; Peg of Old Drury, 1935; Victoria The Great, 1937; Sixty Glorious Years, 1938; Hollywood: Edith Cavell, 1939; Irene, No, No, Nanette, Sunny, 1939–40; England: They Flew Alone, 1941; Yellow Canary, 1943; I Live in Grosvenor Square, 1944; Piccadilly Incident, 1946; The Courtneys of Curzon Street, 1947; Spring in Park Lane, Elizabeth of Ladymead, 1948; Maytime in Mayfair, 1949; Odette, 1950; The Lady With The Lamp, 1951; Derby Day, 1951; Lilacs in the Spring, 1954; King's Rhapsody, 1955; My Teenage Daughter, 1956; No Time for Tears, 1957; The Man Who Wouldn't Talk, 1957; The Lady is a Square, 1958. *Produced:* These Dangerous Years, 1957; Wonderful Things, 1958; Heart of a Man, 1959. Has received numerous awards both international and national. Freedom of City of London, 1981. OStJ 1981. *Publication:* There's Always Tomorrow (autobiog.), 1974, rev. edn 1979. *Recreations:* walking, travel, reading. *Address:* c/o H. de Leon, 19 Gloucester Place Mews, W1. *Club:* FANY Regimental.
*Died* 3 *June* 1986.

**NEAME, Captain Douglas Mortimer Lewes,** DSO 1940, Bar 1942; RN retired; *b* Oct. 1901; *s* of late Douglas John Neame; *m* 1937, Elizabeth Ogilvy Carnegy; one *s* two *d. Educ:* RN Colleges, Osborne and Dartmouth. Served European War, 1917–19; Fleet Air Arm, 1927–31; Commander, 1936; Capt. 1940. Commanded HM Ships Carlisle and Vengeance in War of 1939–45; Commodore 2nd Class, 1947–50; retd 1950. Member of Olympic Team, Amsterdam, 1928, British Empire Games, Canada, 1930. Vice-Patron AAA; Vice-Pres. LAC. *Address:* Cradock House, Salisbury, Wilts. *Clubs:* Naval; Milocarian, London Athletic. *Died* 13 *June* 1988.

**NEAME, Elizabeth, (Mrs Humphrey Neame);** *see* Monroe, E.

**NEEDHAM, Dorothy Mary Moyle,** ScD Cantab; FRS 1948; Research Worker, Biochemical Laboratory, Cambridge, 1920–63; Foundation Fellow, Lucy Cavendish Collegiate Society, University of Cambridge, 1965, Emeritus Fellow, 1966; *b* London, 22 Sept. 1896; *d* of John Moyle and Ellen Daves; *m* 1924, Joseph Needham, FRS, FBA; no *c. Educ:* Claremont Coll., Stockport; Girton Coll., Cambridge (Hon. Fellow, 1976). Research for DSIR, 1920–24;

Gamble Prize, 1924; Beit Meml Research Fellow, 1925–28. Specialised in biochemistry of muscle, carbohydrate metabolism and phosphorylations; carried out research and teaching at Cambridge and in laboratories in USA, France, Germany, Belgium, etc., 1928–40; Research Worker for Ministry of Supply (Chemical Defence), 1940–43; Chemical Adviser and Acting Director, Sino-British Science Cooperation Office, Chungking, China, 1944–45; Research Worker for MRC 1946–52; Research grant from Broodbank Fund, Univ. of Cambridge, 1952–55; Research Worker for ARC, 1955–62; Foulerton Gift Donation, Royal Society, 1961–62; Leverhulme Award, 1963. Hon. Fellow, Gonville and Caius Coll., Cambridge, 1979. *Publications:* Biochemistry of Muscle, 1932; Science Outpost (ed jtly), 1948; Machina Carnis: the biochemistry of muscle contraction in its historical development, 1971; Source-Book in the History of Biochemistry 1740 to 1940, 1987; numerous original papers in biochemical journals and Proc. Royal Soc. *Address:* 42 Grange Road, Cambridge CB3 9DG. *T:* Cambridge 352183.                          *Died* 22 *Dec.* 1987.

**NEEDHAM, Prof. John,** MA (Sheffield); FRIBA, DipArch (Leeds); Professor of Architecture, The University, Sheffield, 1957–72, now Professor Emeritus; *b* 2 April 1909; British; *s* of P. Needham; *m* 1934, Bessie Grange; three *d.* *Educ:* Belle Vue Grammar School, Bradford; Leeds School of Architecture. Diploma in Architecture, Leeds, 1931; ARIBA 1931, FRIBA 1948; RIBA; Alfred Bossom Silver Medal, 1937; Alfred Bossom Gold Medal, 1938; Soane Medal, 1938; Athens Bursar, 1949. Head, Dundee School of Architecture, 1938–57. 1st Premium in Open Architectural Competition for new County Buildings, Cupar, Fife, 1947. Mem. Amenity Cttee set up by Sec. of State for Scotland under Hydro Electric (Scotland) Development Acts, 1956–81. Hon. Editor, Quarterly Jl of Royal Incorporation of Architects in Scotland, 1946–50. *Address:* 16 Ferndene Court, Moor Road South, Gosforth, Newcastle upon Tyne NE3 1NN.                      *Died* 14 *Jan.* 1990.

**NEEDHAM, Commissioner John Edward Dunmore;** National Commander of The Salvation Army in the USA, since 1982; *b* 13 July 1917; *s* of Major Walter Needham and Major Miriam Needham; *m* 1935, Florence E. M. Jolly; three *s* one *d.* *Educ:* Alabama, USA. Member: Nat. Assoc. of Social Workers; Acad. of Certified Social Workers. Salvation Army Officer, 1939–, serving in pastoral work, youth work, training work, public relations, senior administrative positions; has had charge of Salvation Army operations in the Caribbean, 1974–77, and in central USA, 1977–80; British Comr, 1980–81. *Address:* The Salvation Army National Headquarters, 799 Bloomfield Avenue, Verona, NJ 07044, USA. *Club:* Rotary.                              *Died* 13 *April* 1983.

**NEEL, Dr Louis Boyd,** OC 1973; CBE 1953; MA (Cantab); Hon. RAM; MRCS, LRCP; international conductor; musical director; Founder and Conductor, Boyd Neel Orchestra; Dean Royal Conservatory of Music of Toronto, Canada, 1953–71; radio speaker on musical subjects; *b* 19 July 1905; *s* of Louis Anthoine Neel and Ruby le Couteur; unmarried. *Educ:* RNC, Osborne and Dartmouth; Caius Coll., Cambridge. Originally destined for Navy, but took up a medical career on leaving Dartmouth; qualified as a doctor, 1930; House Surgeon and Physician, St George's Hospital, London; resident doctor, King Edward VII's Hosp. for Officers, 1931. Founded Boyd Neel Orchestra, 1932, and owing to success of this, forsook medicine for music; conducted the orchestra all over Europe, incl. the Salzburg Festival, 1937, and made many recordings, incl. several important firsts; has also conducted other famous English orchestras on many occasions; conducted first performance at Glyndebourne, 1934, soon after the theatre was built; conducted Robert Mayer Children's Concerts, 1938–39 and 1947–53. On outbreak of war in 1939 returned to medical work, and was engaged in the fitting of artificial limbs. Later in the war, undertook a lecture tour of the Mediterranean area at the request of the Admiralty. Conductor Sadler's Wells Opera Co., 1944–45, and two London seasons D'Oyly Carte Opera Co., 1948–49. In 1947 took his orchestra to Paris, then to Australia and New Zealand under auspices of British Council; entire orchestra, instruments and music transported by air across Atlantic and Pacific, thus making history. In 1948–49 his orchestra toured Holland, Germany and Portugal (2nd time) and gave ten concerts at Edinburgh Festival; in 1950, visited France, Denmark, Norway, Sweden and Finland. In 1951 toured Italy, gave concerts in Berlin, and again appeared at Edinburgh Festival. In 1952, gave two concerts at Aix-en-Provence Festival, and took orchestra on tour in Canada and USA. In 1953 toured France and Switzerland and gave concerts at Strasbourg Festival. Founded Hart House Orchestra of Toronto, 1955; toured with it Canada and USA; brought it to Europe, 1958 (Brussels World Fair), 1966 (Aldeburgh and Bergen Festivals); week of Canadian music, Expo '67, 1967; orchestra has made numerous recordings; in 1977 embarked on recording project by new Direct-to-Disc technique. World tour, 1971; conducted ballet and opera seasons in S Africa. Jury Mem., internat. music competitions. Hon. MusD Toronto, 1979. *Publication:* The Story of an Orchestra, 1950. *Address:* c/o York

Club, 135 St George Street, Toronto, Ontario, Canada.
                                              *Died* 30 *Sept.* 1981.

**NEELY, Air Vice-Marshal John Conrad,** CB 1957; CBE 1952; DM; FRCS; retired; Senior Consultant, 1955, and Consultant in Ophthalmology, RAF Central Medical Establishment, 1950–59; *b* 29 Mar. 1901; *s* of late William Neely; *m* 1st, 1938, Marjorie Monica (*d* 1964), *d* of Dr Ernest Bramley, Eastbourne; 2nd, 1966, Roma, *widow* of Group Capt. Neil McKechnie, GC. *Educ:* Stonyhurst; Oxford Univ.; Guy's Hosp. MRCS, LRCP, 1927; MA, BM, BCh, 1928, DO (Oxon) 1935, DM 1945, Oxford; DOMS London, 1933. Joined RAF 1928; served War of 1939–45; Middle East (despatches); RAF Hosp., Halton. KHS 1951. Wing Comdr, 1940; Air Cdre, 1950; Air Vice-Marshal, 1955; retired, 1959. FRCS 1958. CStJ 1955.                                      *Died* 2 *June* 1989.

**NEGUS, Arthur George,** OBE 1982; Partner, Messrs Bruton, Knowles & Co., Gloucester, since 1972; *b* 29 March 1903; *s* of Arthur George Negus and Amy Julia Worsley; *m* 1926, Irene Amy Hollett; two *d.* *Educ:* Reading Sch. Dealer in Antiques, 1920–40; Police War Reserve, 1941–45; joined Messrs Bruton, Knowles & Co., Fine Art Auctioneers, as Appraiser, 1946. BBC Television, 1966–, and BBC Radio, 1968–. Freeman of the City of London, 1976; Liveryman, Plaisterers' Co., 1977. *Publication:* Going for a Song: English Furniture, 1969, 5th edn 1977; A Life among Antiques, 1982. *Recreations:* watching sport, philately. *Address:* 31 Queens Court, Cheltenham, Glos GL50 2LU. *T:* Cheltenham 45696. *Club:* Lord's Taverners.                                    *Died* 5 *April* 1985.

**NEIL, Prof. Eric;** John Astor Professor of Physiology in the University of London, at the Middlesex Hospital Medical School, 1956–84, now Emeritus Professor; *b* 15 Feb. 1918; *s* of George Neil, MC, and Florence Neil; *m* 1946, Anne Baron, *d* of late T. J. M. B. Parker and of Evelyn Maud Parker; two *d.* *Educ:* Heath Grammar School; University of Leeds. BSc Hons (Physiology) (Leeds), 1939; MB, ChB, 1942; MD (Dist.), 1944 and DSc, 1953 (Leeds); FRCP 1978. Demonstrator and Lecturer in Physiology, Univ. of Leeds, 1942–50; Sen. Lecturer and later Reader in Physiology, Middx Hosp. Med. School., 1950–56. Hon. Treas., Physiological Soc.; Chm., European Editorial Bd of Physiological Reviews, 1960–67; Mem., Brit. Nat. Cttee of Physiological Sciences, 1960–80; Pres., Internat. Union of Physiological Sciences, 1974–77, 1977–84 (Treasurer, 1968–74). Hon. For. Mem., Royal Acad. of Medicine, Belgium, 1978. Examiner in Physiology, Univs of London, Oxford, Cambridge, Birmingham, Trinity Coll., Dublin. Hon. MD Ghent, 1977. Queen's Silver Jubilee Medal, 1977. *Publications:* (with Prof. C. Heymans) Reflexogenic Areas in the Cardiovascular System, 1958; (with Prof. C. A. Keele) Samson Wright's Applied Physiology, 10th edn 1961, 13th edn 1982; (with Prof. B. Folkow) Circulation, 1971; The Mammalian Circulation, 1974, 2nd edn, 1978; The Life and Work of William Harvey, 1975; papers on physiological topics in British and foreign med. scientific jls. *Recreations:* pianoforte, Venetian painting. *Address:* 53 Talbot Road, Highgate, N6. *T:* 081–340 0543.                                     *Died* 8 *May* 1990.

**NEILL, Rt. Rev. Stephen Charles,** FBA 1969; an Assistant Bishop, Diocese of Oxford, since 1979; *b* 31 Dec. 1900; *s* of Rev. Charles Neill, MB, and of Margaret, *d* of late James Monro, CB. *Educ:* Dean Close School; Trinity College, Cambridge (MA 1926, DD 1980). Fellow of Trinity College, Cambridge, 1924–28; Missionary in dioceses of Tinnevelly and Travancore, 1924–30; Warden, Bishop's Theological College, Tirumaraiyur, Nazareth, S India, 1930–38; Bishop of Tinnevelly, 1939–45; Chaplain of Trinity Coll., Cambridge; Univ. Lecturer in Divinity, 1945–47; Co-Director Study Dept of World Council of Churches, 1947–48; Asst Bishop to Archbishop of Canterbury, 1947–50; Associate Gen. Sec. of World Council of Churches, 1948–51; General Editor, World Christian Books, 1952–62, Director, 1962–70; Prof. of Missions and Ecumenical Theology, Univ. of Hamburg, 1962–67; Prof. of Philosophy and Religious Studies, Nairobi Univ., 1969–73. Lectures: Hulsean, Cambridge, 1946–47; Birkbeck, Trinity Coll., Cambridge, 1949–50; Godfrey Day in Missions, TCD, 1950; Earle, Pacific School of Religions, Berkeley, California, 1950; Cody Meml, Toronto, 1956; Carnahan, Faculty of Theology, Buenos Aires, 1958; Duff in Missions, Edinburgh and Glasgow, 1958–59; Moorhouse, Melbourne, 1960; Firth, Nottingham, 1962; Bampton, Oxford, 1964; Ziskind, Dartmouth Coll., NH, 1966; Westcott-Teape, Delhi and Madras, 1972; Livingstone Meml, Blantyre, Malawi, 1973. Visiting Professor: of Missions, Hamburg Univ., 1956–57, 1961; of Theol., Colgate-Rochester Divinity Sch., 1961–62; of Theol., Wycliffe Coll., Toronto, 1962; Drew Univ., NJ, 1967; of Religion, Univ. Coll., Nairobi, 1968; of Science of Religion, Durban-Westville Univ., SA, 1975; of World Christianity, Union Theol. Seminary, NY, 1979. Hon. DD: Trinity Coll., Toronto, 1950; Culver-Stockton, 1953; Glasgow, 1961; Acadia, 1976; Montreal, 1983; Hon. ThD: Hamburg, 1957; Uppsala, 1965; Hon. LittD St Paul's Univ., Tokyo, 1960. *Publications:* Out of Bondage, 1928; Builders of the Indian Church, 1933; Beliefs, 1940; Foundation Beliefs, 1942; The Challenge of Jesus Christ, 1944; Christ, His

Church and His World, 1948; The Cross over Asia, 1948; On the Ministry, 1952; The Christian Society, 1952; Christian Partnership, 1952; Towards Church Union, 1937–1952, 1952; Under Three Flags, 1954; The Christian's God, 1954; Christian Faith To-day, 1955; The Christian Character, 1955; Who is Jesus Christ?, 1956; The Unfinished Task, 1957; Anglicanism, 1958; A Genuinely Human Existence, 1959; Creative Tension, 1959; Christian Holiness, 1960; Men of Unity, 1960; Christian Faith and other Faiths, 1961 (revd edn as Crises of Belief, 1984); The Eternal Dimension, 1963; The Interpretation of the New Testament, 1964; A History of Christian Missions, 1964; Colonialism and Christian Missions, 1966; The Church and Christian Union, 1968; Christianity in India and Pakistan, 1970; Bible Words and Christian Meanings, 1970; What do wwe know of Jesus?, 1970; Bhakti Hindu and Christian, 1974; Salvation Tomorrow, 1976; Jesus Through Many Eyes, 1976; A History of Christianity in India, 1984; The Supremacy of Jesus, 1984. (Editor) Twentieth Century Christianity, 1961; (ed jtly) A History of the Ecumenical Movement, 1517–1948, 1951–54; (ed jtly) The Layman in Christian History, 1963; (ed jtly) The Concise Dictionary of the Christian World Mission, 1970; (contrib) When Will Ye Be Wise?, 1983; contrib. to: Encyclopædia Britannica; Chamber's Encyclopædia; Die Religion in Geschichte und Gegenwart; Evangelisches Kirchenlexikon; Weltkirchenlexicon. *Address:* Wycliffe Hall, Oxford.

*Died 20 July 1984.*

**NEILSON, Hon. William Arthur,** AC 1978; Premier of Tasmania, 1975–77; Agent-General for Tasmania, in London, 1978–81; *b* 27 Aug. 1925; *s* of late Arthur R. Neilson; *m* 1948, Jill, *d* of A. H. Benjamin; one *s* three *d. Educ:* Ogilvie Commercial High Sch., Hobart. When first elected to Tasmanian Parlt in 1946, aged 21, youngest MP in British Commonwealth and youngest member ever elected to any Australian parlt. Re-elected, 1948, 1950, 1955, 1956, 1959, 1964, 1969 and 1972, resigned 1977. Labor Party Whip, Dec. 1946–Feb. 1955; Minister for Tourists and Immigration and Forests, Oct. 1956–Aug. 1958; Attorney-Gen. and Minister for Educn, Aug.-Oct 1958; Minister for Educn, until April 1959, then Treasurer and Minister for Educn, April-May 1959; Minister for Educn, 1959–69 and May 1972–March 1974; Attorney-Gen., also Dep. Premier, Minister for Environment and Minister administering Police Dept and Licensing Act, April 1974–March 1975; Treasurer, 1975–77. *Recreations:* reading, writing, chess, Australian Rules football, amateur theatre. *Address:* 7 Amarina Court, Kingston Beach, Hobart, Tasmania 7051, Australia.                            *Died 1989.*

**NELSON, 8th Earl** *cr* 1805, of Trafalgar and of Merton; **George Joseph Horatio Nelson;** Baron Nelson of the Nile and of Hilborough, Norfolk, 1801; Viscount Merton, 1805; retired; *b* 20 April 1905; 4th *s* of 5th Earl Nelson and Geraldine (*d* 1936), *d* of Henry H Cave, Northampton; *S* brother, 1972; *m* 1945, Winifred Mary, *d* of G. Bevan, Swansea; one *d. Educ:* Ampleforth. FCA (resigned). *Heir: nephew* Peter John Horatio Nelson [*b* 9 Oct. 1941; *m* 1969, Maureen Quinn; one *s* one *d]. Address:* 9 Pwlldu Lane, Bishopston, Swansea SA3 3HA. *T:* Bishopston 2682                            *Died 21 Sept. 1981.*

**NELSON, Bertram,** CBE 1956; FCA; *b* 1905; *s* of W. E. Nelson, Liverpool; *m* 1954, Eleanor Kinsey; one *s* one *d. Educ:* The Leys School, Cambridge. Hon. Sec. Merseyside Civic Soc. 1938–53. Chm. Liverpool Chamber of Commerce, 1951–53, Treas., 1953–60; a Vice-Pres. of Assoc. of British Chambers of Commerce, 1956. Pres. Soc. of Incorporated Accountants, 1954–56; Mem. Council of Inst. of Chartered Accountants, 1957–75 (Chairman of Education Committee, 1961–66). Chm., Liverpool Daily Post and Echo Gp, 1972–76. BBC North Regional Council, 1947–57. Mem. Board of Trade Consultative Cttee on Companies, 1954–73, and of Bd of Trade Treas. Cttee on Export Credit Guarantees Dept., 1958; Part-time Mem., Merseyside and N Wales Electricity Bd 1967–76. Treas. of Liverpool Univ., 1948–57, Vice-Pres., 1957–63, Pres. and Pro-Chancellor, 1963–67, Senior Pro-Chancellor, 1967–73; Chm., Univ. Develt Cttee, 1961–68; Governor: The Leys Sch., Cambridge (Vice-Chm., 1970); Staff Coll. for Further Education; Mem. Mersey Docks and Harbour Bd, 1951–65; Chm. Liverpool Youth Welfare Advisory Cttee, 1952–65; Dir, the Playhouse, Liverpool, 1949–63; Chm. of Appeals Cttee on Gradings and Salaries in Colls of Advanced Technology, 1964–65. Trustee, Civic Trust for NW. JP Liverpool, 1944. Hon. LLD Liverpool, 1972. *Publication:* Tables of Procedure, 1933. *Address:* Maylands, Gayton Lane, Heswall, Wirral, Merseyside. *Clubs:* Reform, Athenæum (Pres. 1962); University Staff House (Liverpool).            *Died 28 April 1984.*

**NELSON, Geoffrey Sheard,** CBE 1970; Director, Leased Hotels Ltd; *b* 1 Jan. 1909; *s* of late William Nelson and Sarah Nelson (*née* Sheard); *m* 1932, Gladys, *d* of late C. W. Brown; two *d. Educ:* Leeds Central High Sch. Chartered Accountant (Incorporated Accountant, 1931). Min. of Supply (Costing Br.), 1942–45. Subseq. with Finance Corp. for Industry Ltd., Gen. Manager, 1948–73. FCA, ACMA. *Recreations:* golf, photography, travel. *Address:* 4 Norman Way, Southgate, N14 6NA. *T:* 01–886 0442.            *Died 30 Nov. 1984.*

**NELSON, Henry Ince,** QC 1945; BA, LLB; Commissioner of National Insurance, 1968–69 (Deputy Commissioner, 1959–68); retired; *b* 29 May 1897; *s* of late Henry Nelson, OBE, and of late Ada Bell Nelson; *m* 1933, Mary Howard Cooper; three *s* one *d. Educ:* Aldenham School; Pembroke Coll., Cambridge. RFA 1915–19, rank Lt (twice wounded); served on Western Front with VI Divisional Artillery. Called to Bar, Inner Temple, 1922; Bencher 1952. Judge of Salford Hundred Court of Record, 1947–48; Judge of Liverpool Court of Passage, 1948–50; Recorder of Liverpool, 1950–54. *Recreations:* gardening and golf. *Address:* Brackendene, Hockering Road, Woking, Surrey. *T:* Woking 61210. *Club:* Golf (Woking).                            *Died 1 Aug. 1981.*

**NEMON, Oscar;** sculptor; *b* 13 March 1906; *s* of Mavro and Eugenia Nemon, Yugoslavia; *m* 1939, Patricia Villiers-Stuart; one *s* two *d. Educ:* Osijek; Brussels; Paris. Exhibitions held in principal capitals of Europe. Examples of his work are in: House of Commons; Windsor Castle; The Guildhall, London; Somerville College and The Union, Oxford. His sitters include: HM The Queen, HM the Queen Mother, Rt Hon. Sir Winston Churchill, Rt Hon. Harold Macmillan, Lord Beaverbrook, Sigmund Freud, Sir Max Beerbohm, Lord Montgomery, President Eisenhower, Rt Hon. Margaret Thatcher, Lord Shinwell; other work: Lord Portal, 1975. Hon. DLitt St Andrews, 1978. *Recreation:* searching for lost opportunities. *Address:* Pleasant Land, Boars Hill, Oxford. *T:* Oxford 735583.

*Died 13 April 1985.*

**NESBITT, Cathleen Mary,** CBE 1978; actress; *b* 24 Nov. 1888; *d* of Captain T. Nesbitt, RN, and Mary Catherine Parry; *m* 1921, Captain C. B. Ramage, MC; one *s* one *d. Educ:* Belfast; Lisieux; Paris. 1st London appearance as Perdita in Granville Barker's production of The Winter's Tale, 1912; subsequently played lead in Quality Street, Justice, Hassan, Spring Cleaning, The Case of the Frightened Lady, Children in Uniform, Our Betters, Medea, The Uninvited Guest, and Goneril in Granville Barker's all star production of Lear, 1940. Later appearances in: The Cocktail Party; Gigi (New York); Sabrina Fair (New York and London); My Fair Lady (New York; US tour, 1980); The Sleeping Prince, NY; Anastasia, NY; The Royal Family; The Aspern Papers, Chichester, etc. *Films:* An Affair to Remember, So Long At The Fair, Three Coins in the Fountain, Separate Tables, The French Connection II, Hitchcock's Family Plot; *Television:* series in Hollywood; Abide With Me (Monte Carlo award). *Publication:* A Little Love and Good Company (autobiog.), 1974. *Address:* c/o ICM, 22 Grafton Street, W1X 3LD.                            *Died 2 Aug. 1982.*

**NETHERTHORPE, 2nd Baron** *cr* 1959, of Anston, W Riding; **James Andrew Turner,** FCA; Deputy Chairman, Dalgety Ltd, since 1978 (Chief Executive, 1978–81); *b* 23 July 1936; *s* of 1st Baron Netherthorpe, and of Margaret Lucy, *d* of James Arthur Mattock; *S* father, 1980; *m* 1960, Belinda Nicholson; two *s* two *d. Educ:* Rugby Sch.; Pembroke Coll., Cambridge. Peat, Marwick, Mitchell & Co., Chartered Accountants, 1958–61; joined Lazard Brothers & Co. Ltd, 1961; seconded to Australian United Corp. Ltd, 1966–67; apptd Head of Lazards' Corporate Finance Dept, 1969; Dir, Lazards, 1971–; Dalgety Ltd: Director; Vice-Chm. and Exec. Dir, 1972–75; Man. Dir, 1975–78; also Director: Dalgety UK Ltd; Dalgety Australia Ltd; Dalgety New Zealand Ltd; Babcock International Ltd, 1971–82. Mem., Council of British Australia Soc. Chairman of Tree Foundation. *Heir: s* Hon. James Frederick Turner, *b* 7 Jan. 1964. *Address:* Boothby Hall, Boothby Pagnell, Grantham, Lincs NG33 4DQ. *T:* Ingoldsby 374.

*Died 4 Nov. 1982.*

**NEVILL, Air Vice-Marshal Sir Arthur de Terrotte,** KBE 1950 (CBE 1941); CB 1946; CEng; FRAeS; Director of Civil Aviation, New Zealand, 1956–65, retired; Royal New Zealand Air Force; *b* 29 April 1899; *s* of late H. G. Nevill; *m* 1927, Mary Seton, *d* of E. T. Norris; two *d. Educ:* Auckland Grammar School; Royal Military College, Duntroon. BSc 1921; MSc 1952. Chief of Air Staff, NZ, 1946–51; Member Air Licensing Authority, 1952; Deputy Director of Civil Aviation, New Zealand, 1952–56, Director, 1956–65. President NZ Div., RAeS, 1949–52. Member: NZ Univ. Grants Cttee, 1955–68 (Dep.-Chm., 1961–68); Research and Scholarships Cttee, UGC, 1968–79; US Educational Foundation in NZ, 1958–70; NZ Architects Educn and Registration Board, 1964–79; engaged in research administration, UGC, until resignation in 1979. President: Air Force Association, 1967–72; Air Cadet League, 1972–76. Hon. D Waikato Univ., 1969. Legion of Merit (USA). *Address:* 27 Colway Street, Ngaio, Wellington 4, New Zealand. *Club:* United Services (Wellington).                            *Died 14 March 1985.*

**NEVILL, Lord Rupert Charles Montacute,** CVO 1978; JP; DL; Member of London Stock Exchange; Treasurer, since 1970, and Private Secretary, since 1975, to the Duke of Edinburgh; *b* 29 Jan. 1923; 2nd *s* of 4th Marquess of Abergavenny; *m* 1944, Lady Anne Camilla Eveline Wallop, *e d* of 9th Earl of Portsmouth; two *s* two *d. Educ:* Eton. JP 1953, DL 1960, Sussex; High Sheriff of Sussex, 1952–53. Captain, Life Guards, ADC to Lt-Gen. Sir Brian Horrocks,

1945–47. Director: Sun Life Assurance Society (a Vice-Chm., 1971–); Owners of Middlesbrough Estates Co.; Australian Estates, 1968–75; Household and General Insurance Co. Ltd, 1965–72; Courier Printing & Publishing Co. Ltd (formerly Kent & Sussex Courier), 1974– (Chm. 1980–); West Cumberland Silk Mills, 1964–72; Daily Mail & General Trust Ltd, 1980–. President: S Eastern Area Building Socs, 1960–72; S Eastern Area Trustee Savings Bank, 1964–72; Vice-Pres., London and SE Trustee Savings Bank, 1972–; Vice-Pres., Building Societies Assoc., 1960. Pres., Metropolitan Union of YMCAs, 1956–71; Mem., World Council of YMCAs, 1956–77; Pres., Nat. Council of YMCAs, 1966–; Pres., British Olympic Assoc., 1977– (Chm., 1966–77); Vice-Pres., Nat. Playing Fields Assoc., 1981– (Vice-Chm., 1963–81); Chairman: Invalid Children's Aid Assoc., 1969–; Sussex Army Cadets, 1951–68; Greater London and SE Regional Sports Council, 1969–76; Greater London and SE Regional Council for Sport and Recreation, 1976–77; Mem., Sports Council, 1971–80; Pres., BSJA, 1973–75; Vice-Pres., Sussex Boy Scouts, 1950–74, Pres., E Sussex Boy Scouts, 1974–; Vice-Pres., Sussex Boys' Clubs; Pres., Sussex St John Ambulance Cadets, 1952–61; Commander, Sussex St John Ambulance Bde, 1969–77 (Pres. 1961–69); Mem., Sussex St John's Council, 1952, Chm., 1966–. Member: E Sussex CC, 1954–67; Uckfield RDC, 1949–67. KStJ 1972. *Address:* Horsted Place, Uckfield, East Sussex. *T:* Isfield 315; 30B St James's Palace, SW1. *T:* 01-839 7206. *Clubs:* White's, Bucks, Beefsteak.

*Died 18 July 1982.*

**NEVILLE, Lt-Col Sir (James) Edmund (Henderson),** 2nd Bt, *cr* 1927; MC 1918; *b* 5 July 1897; *er s* of Sir Reginald James Neville, 1st Bt and Ida (*d* 1913), 4th *d* of Lt-Col Sir Edmund Y. W. Henderson, KCB, RE; *S* father 1950; *m* 1st, 1932, Marie Louise (*d* 1980), *o d* of C. E. Pierson, Flesk, Burnham, Somerset; two *d*; 2nd, 1981, Mrs Betty Cowell. *Educ:* Eton; RMC Sandhurst. Served European War, 1914–19 (wounded, MC); joined 52nd Light Infantry, 1916; with 43rd Light Infantry to North Russia, 1919 (wounded); captain and adjutant, 1923; Regular Reserve of Officers, 1925; served in 12th London Regt (Rangers), 1931–36; Major; Master Worshipful Company of Bowyers, 1936–38; War of 1939–45, recalled, Aug. 1939; in command Light Infantry Training Centre, 1941–44; trooping, 1945–46; retd as Lt-Col, July 1946. Prime Warden, Fishmongers' Co., 1958. *Publication:* History of 43rd Light Infantry, 1914–19. *Heir: half-b* Richard Lionel John Baines Neville [*b* July 1921. *Educ:* Eton; Trinity College, Cambridge (MA). Served Burma, 1943–45, as Captain Oxford and Bucks LI, and West African Frontier Force]. *Address:* Sloley Old Hall, Norwich NR12 8HA. *T:* Swanton Abbott 232. *Clubs:* Army and Navy, Greenjackets, Light Infantry. *Died 24 June 1982.*

**NEVILLE, Maj.-Gen. Sir Robert Arthur Ross,** KCMG 1952; CBE 1948; late RM; *b* 17 Dec. 1896; *s* of late Col William Neville, DSO, Cheshire Regt; *m* 1943, Doris Marie (*d* 1977), *y d* of late Capt. Philip Collen, 14th Sikh Regiment; one *s* one *d. Educ:* Cheltenham College. Joined Royal Marines, 1914, served European War, 1914–18, Grand Fleet and France (despatches); Lt-Col, 1940; served War of 1939–45, Admlty, as Asst Dir of Naval Intelligence, Combined Ops, and in Mediterranean; Colonel, 1945; ADC to the King, 1946–48; Maj.-Gen., 1948. Governor and C-in-C, Bahamas, 1950–Dec. 1953. Dir, Epsylon Industries Ltd, 1954–61; Chm., Vectron Electronics, 1961–66. *Address:* Townsend Wood, Sutton Mandeville, Salisbury, Wiltshire. *Club:* White's.

*Died 12 June 1987.*

**NEWBURGH, 11th Earl of,** *cr* 1660; **Don Giulio Cesare Taddeo Cosimo Maria Rospigliosi;** Viscount Kynnaird, Baron Levingston, 1660; 10th Prince Rospigliosi (Holy Roman Empire), 10th Duke of Zagarolo, 13th Prince of Castiglione, Marquis of Giuliana, Count of Chiusa, Baron of La Miraglia and Valcorrente, Lord of Aidione, Burgio, Contessa and Trappeto, and Conscript Roman Noble, Patrician of Venice, Genoa and Pistoia; *b* 26 Oct. 1907; *s* of Prince Giambattista Rospigliosi (*d* 1956) and Ethel (*d* 1924), *d* of Isaac Bronson; *S* cousin, 1977; *m* 1940, Donna Giulia, *d* of Don Guido Carlo dei Duchi Visconti di Mondrone, Count of Lonate Pozzolo; two *s. Educ:* Corpus Christi College, Cambridge (Engineering Tripos, MA). *Heir: s* Viscount Kynnaird. *Address:* Via Corridoni 3, 20. 122 Milan, Italy. *Died 18 April 1986.*

**NEWCASTLE, 9th Duke of,** *cr* 1756; **Henry Edward Hugh Pelham-Clinton-Hope,** OBE 1945; Earl of Lincoln, 1572; Wing Comdr, retd; *b* 8 April 1907; *o s* of 8th Duke and Olive Muriel (*d* 1912), *d* of George Horatio Thompson, banker, Melbourne, formerly wife of Richard Owen; *S* father, 1941; *m* 1st, 1931, Jean (from whom he obtained a divorce, 1940), *d* of D. Banks, Park Avenue, New York; 2nd, 1946, Lady Mary Diana Montagu-Stuart-Wortley (marr. diss. 1959), 2nd *d* of 3rd Earl of Wharncliffe; two *d*; 3rd, 1959, Mrs Sally Ann Wemyss Hope (Jamal), *d* of Brig. John Henry Anstice, DSO. *Educ:* Eton; Cambridge. Sqdn Ldr Comdg No 616 Sqdn, 1938–39; served War of 1939–45 in RAF at home and overseas. *Heir: cousin* Edward Charles Pelham-Clinton, *b* 18 Aug. 1920. *Address:* 5 Quay Hill, Lymington, Hants SO4 9AB. *Died 4 Nov. 1988.*

**NEWCASTLE, 10th Duke of,** *cr* 1756; **Edward Charles Pelham-Clinton;** Earl of Lincoln 1572; *b* 18 Aug. 1920; *s* of Captain Guy Edward Pelham-Clinton, MC (*d* 1934) (*g g s* of 4th Duke) and Hermione Edith Agnes, *d* of Arthur Frederick Churchill Tollemache; *S* cousin, 1988. *Educ:* Eton; Trinity Coll., Cambridge. Served War of 1939–45 (despatches), Captain RA. Entomologist, authority on Lepidoptera; former Deputy Keeper, Royal Scottish Museum, Edinburgh. *Heir* (to earldom only): *kinsman* Edward Horace Fiennes-Clinton [*b* 23 Feb. 1913; *m* 1st, 1940, Leila Ruth Millen (*d* 1947); one *s* one *d*; 2nd, 1953, Linda Alice O'Brien].

*Died 25 Dec. 1988 (ext).*

*This entry did not appear in Who's Who.*

**NEWE, Rt. Hon. Gerard Benedict,** PC (N Ireland) 1971; CBE 1977 (OBE 1961); Chairman, Personal Social Services Advisory Committee for Northern Ireland, 1974–81; *b* 5 Feb. 1907; *s* of Patrick Newe and Catherine Newe (*née* McCanny); unmarried. *Educ:* St Malachy's Coll., Belfast; Belcamp Coll., Dublin. Editor, The Ulster Farmer, 1931–67. Area Admin. Officer, Min. of Health and Local Govt, NI, 1941–48; Regional Officer and Dir, NI Council of Social Service, 1948–72. First Roman Catholic Minister of State, Govt of NI, 1971–72. Last Minister to be appointed to HM Privy Council in Northern Ireland. Chief Welfare Officer, Civil Defence, Belfast, 1951–68; Member: BBC's NI Adv. Cttee, 1954–58; BBC's NI Appeals Adv. Cttee, 1956–59; ITA NI Cttee, 1960–66; Nat. Trust Cttee for NI, 1962–71; NI Indust. Trng Council, 1964–73 (Chm., Res. Cttee); NI Cttee, Nuffield Provincial Hosps Trust, 1954–63; First Bd of Governors, Rupert Stanley Coll. of Further Educn, Belfast, 1964–72; NI Legal Aid Adv. Cttee, 1967–75; NI Adv. Cttee, Council for Trng in Social Work, 1966–70; N Area Health and Social Services Bd, 1973–77 (Chm., Personal Social Services Cttee); Founder Member: Ulster Folklife Soc. (Vice-Pres.); PACE (and co-Patron); NIACRO (a Vice-Pres.); The Assissi Fellowship (Chm.). Council of Europe Fellow, 1970. Hon. MA The Queen's Univ. of Belfast, 1967; Hon. DLitt New Univ. of Ulster, Coleraine, 1971. *Publications:* The Catholic in the Community, 1958, 2nd edn 1965; The Story of the Northern Ireland Council of Social Service, 1963; contribs to Tablet, The Furrow, Christus Rex, Aquarius. *Recreations:* reading, trying to be lazy. *Address:* Prospect House, 28 Coast Road, Cushendall, Ballymena, Co. Antrim BT44 0RY. *Died 25 Nov. 1982.*

**NEWELL, Prof. Kenneth Wyatt,** MD; Middlemass Hunt Professor of Tropical Community Health and Head of Department of International Community Health, Liverpool School of Tropical Medicine, since 1984; *b* 7 Nov. 1925; *s* of Herbert William and Mary Irene Newell; *m* 1977, Priscilla Jane Watts; four *s. Educ:* Univ. of New Zealand; MB, ChB; DPH (distinction) London, MD Tulane, USA, MCCM (NZ), FFCM. Epidemiologist, PHLS, Colindale, 1954–56; Lectr, Social and Preventive Medicine, QUB, 1956–58; WHO Epidemiologist, Indonesia, 1958–60; Field Dir, ICMRT Cali, Colombia, 1960–67; William Hamilton Watkins Professor of Epidemiology, Tulane Univ., USA, 1960–67; Dir, WHO, Geneva, 1967–77; Prof. of Community Health, Univ. of Otago, NZ, 1977–83. *Publication:* (ed) Health by the People, 1975. *Recreations:* fishing, gardening, opera. *Address:* Five Oaks, Street Hey Lane, Willaston, South Wirral, Cheshire L64 1SS. *T:* 051-327 4057. *Died 18 March 1990.*

**NEWELL, Philip Staniforth,** CB 1961; *b* 1903; *m* 1927, Sylvia May Webb (*d* 1982); two *s* one *d. Educ:* Uppingham; Emmanuel College, Cambridge (Scholar). First Class Part I, Mathematical Tripos, First Class Mechanical Sciences Tripos; Assistant Master at Uppingham; Chief Mathematical Master, Repton; Headmaster of Gresham's School, Holt, 1935–44; Admiralty, 1944–64; Imperial Defence College, 1955; Under-Secretary, 1956; Principal Finance Officer, 1961–64. Director, Greenwich Hosp., 1964–69; a Maths Master, Pierrepont Sch., Surrey, 1969–72. *Publications:* Greenwich Hospital, a Royal Foundation 1692–1983, 1984; Gresham's in Wartime, 1988. *Address:* Dawson's, Tilford, Surrey. *T:* Frensham (025125) 2787. *Club:* Athenæum. *Died 10 July 1990.*

**NEWMAN, Charles Edward Kingsley,** CBE 1965; MD (Cantab); FRCP; retired; Emeritus Dean, Postgraduate Medical School (later Royal Postgraduate Medical School); Harveian Librarian, 1962–79, Royal College of Physicians; *b* 16 March 1900; *s* of Charles Arnold Newman and Kate Beck; *m* 1st, 1952, Phyllis (*d* 1965), *d* of I. Bloomfield; 2nd, 1971, Anne (*d* 1982), *d* of F. W. Stallard. *Educ:* Shrewsbury Sch.; Magdalene Coll., Cambridge (Scholar); King's College Hospital (Scholar; Fellow of Med. School, 1980). Murchison Scholar RCP, 1926; FRCP 1932; FKC 1982. Volunteer Asst to Prof. Aschoff, Univ. of Freiburg i B. 1930; Hon. Treas., RSocMed, 1946–50; Fellow Medical Society of London (Orator, 1961); Hon. Member Assoc. of Physicians, 1965. Hon. Secretary, 1942–47. Hon. Treasurer, 1948–58; Mem., British Gastro-enterological Soc. (Pres., 1964); Governor, St Clement Dane's Sch., 1955–76, Vice-Chm., 1958–76; Mem. Cttee of Management of Conjoint Board in England, 1958–68 (Chm., 1965–68). Goulstonian Lectr, 1933; FitzPatrick Lectr, 1954, 1955 and 1968; Linacre Fellow, 1966; Harveian Orator, 1973; Assistant Registrar, RCP, 1933–38; Sub-Editor, EMS, Official

Medical History of the War, 1942–47; late Physician, Medical Tutor and Vice-Dean, King's College Hospital and Asst Physician, Belgrave Hospital for Children. *Publications:* Medical Emergencies, 1932, 3rd edn 1946, repr. 1948; Evolution of Medical Education in the Nineteenth Century, 1957; articles in medical text-books and encyclopædias; papers on diseases of the liver and gall-bladder, medical history and education. *Address:* Woodstock Grange, 99 Bessborough Road, Harrow on the Hill, Middlesex HA1 3BD. *Club:* Athenæum. *Died 22 Aug.* 1989.

**NEWMAN, Sir Gerard (Robert Henry Sigismund)**, 3rd Bt, *cr* 1912; *b* 19 July 1927; *s* of Sir Cecil Gustavus Jacques Newman, 2nd Bt, and Joan Florence Mary, CBE (*d* 1969), *e d* of late Rev. Canon Hon. Robert Grimston; *S* father, 1955; *m* 1960, Caroline Philippa, *d* of late Brig. Alfred Geoffrey Neville, CBE, MC; three *s* one *d. Educ:* Eton; Jesus Coll., Oxford (BA 1951). Dir, APL Engineering Ltd, 1951–53; Asst to Man. Dir, Enfield Rolling Mills Ltd, 1953–56; Director: Enfield Zinc Products Ltd, 1953–56; The Rom River Co. Ltd, 1954–72 (Chm., 1955); Galloway (Mechanical Services) Ltd, Dundee, 1973– (Chm., 1980); Chairman: Seven Seas Engineering Ltd, Glasgow, 1975–78; Woodcote Grove Estate Ltd, 1975–. Dep. Traffic Comr for the Metropolitan Area, 1972–85. Governor, Wellesley House & St Peter's Court Schs Trust, 1963–86; Pres., Friends of Royston and District Hosp., 1975–; Chm., Cambridge Symphony Orchestra Trust, 1982– (Trustee, 1979–). Farmer, 1969–; Pres., Herts Agricl Soc., 1983. High Sheriff, Herts, 1981–82. *Recreations:* travel and pursuits of the countryside. *Heir:* s Francis Hugh Cecil Newman, *b* 12 June 1963. *Address:* Burloes, Royston, Herts. *T:* Royston 42150; 27 Bloomfield Terrace, SW1. *T:* 01–730 7540. *Club:* Boodle's. *Died 15 Aug.* 1987.

**NEWMAN, Maxwell Herman Alexander**, MA, FRS 1939; Professor Emeritus, University of Manchester; *b* 7 Feb. 1897; *m* 1st, 1934, Lyn (*d* 1973), *d* of Rev. J. A. Irvine; two *s*; 2nd, 1973, Margaret, widow of Prof. L. S. Penrose, FRS. *Educ:* City of London School; St John's College, Cambridge; Vienna Univ., 1922–23. MA 1924; Fellow of St John's College, Cambridge, 1923–45 (Hon. Fellow, 1973); Rockefeller Research Fellow at Princeton, 1928–29; University Lecturer in Mathematics, Cambridge University, 1927–45; Fielden Professor of Mathematics, Manchester Univ., 1945–64; Visiting Professor in Australian National Univ., 1964–65 and 1967; in Univ. of Wisconsin and Rice Univ., 1965–66. Royal Soc. Council, 1946–47; Pres., London Mathematical Soc., 1950–51; Pres. Mathematical Assoc., 1959. Hon. DSc Hull, 1968. Sylvester Medal of Royal Society, 1959; De Morgan Medal, 1962. *Publications:* Topology of Plane Sets of Points, 1939, 2nd edn 1951; papers on Mathematics in various journals. *Address:* Cross Farm, Comberton, Cambridge. *Died 22 Feb.* 1984

**NEWMAN, Ronald William**; HM Diplomatic Service, retired; *b* 6 April 1921; *s* of William James Newman and Louisa Ellen Taylor; *m* 1943, Victoria Brady; three *d. Educ:* Wandsworth Sch. Served War, RAF, 1940–46. Min. of Agriculture and Fisheries, later MAFF, 1946–58; Statistical Org. Adviser to Central Bureau of Statistics, Jerusalem, 1958; O&M Adviser to Basutoland, Bechuanaland and Swaziland, 1959–61; MAFF, 1962–65; CRO, 1965–67; First Secretary: (Econs), Accra, 1967; (Capital Aid), Nairobi, 1968–72; (Econs), Islamabad, 1973–75; Counsellor, Khartoum, 1975–76; Consul General, Casablanca, 1977. *Recreations:* squash, swimming, diving, flying. *Address:* 20 Cranley Close, Guildford, Surrey GU1 2JN. *T:* Guildford 576728. *Died 16 March* 1987.

**NEWMAN-MORRIS, Sir Geoffrey**, Kt 1969; ED 1946; *b* 14 May 1909; *s* of John and Eleanor Annie Newman-Morris; *m* 1945, Sheila, *d* of Martin Brown; two *s* one *d. Educ:* Melbourne Church of England Grammar Sch.; Trinity Coll., Univ. of Melbourne. MB BS Melbourne 1932, MS Melbourne 1936, FRCS 1937, FRACS 1938. Lt-Col, RAAMC (Ret.); served 1939–45, Mid. East and New Guinea (despatches 1944). Hon. Cons. Surg. Prince Henry's Hosp., Melbourne. Pres., 5th Aust. Med. Congress, 1974. Mem., Standing Commn, Internat. Red Cross, 1965–73 (Chm., 1973–77); Vice-Chm., League of Red Cross Socs, 1969–73; Pres., Confedn Medical Assocs of Asia and Oceania, 1975–77; Vice-Pres., Aust. Red Cross Soc., 1978–81 (Chm., 1958–78). Henry Dunant Medal, Internat. Red Cross, 1979. KStJ 1964. *Publications:* contrib. med. jls. *Recreation:* bowls. *Address:* Denby Dale, 9/424 Glenferrie Road, Kooyong, Victoria 3144, Australia. *T:* 205072. *Clubs:* Melbourne, Melbourne Cricket (Australia). *Died 20 Oct.* 1981.

**NEWNS, George Henry**, MD, FRCP; Physician, The Hospital for Sick Children, Great Ormond Street, WC1, 1946–73, Hon. Consulting Physician since 1974; Dean, Institute of Child Health, University of London, 1949–73, Emeritus Dean, 1974; Chairman, Leukaemia Research Fund, 1963–84; *b* 27 July 1908; *s* of late George Newns, Dartford, Kent; *m* 1936, Deirdre, *d* of late Lawrence Kenny, Clonmel, Tipperary, Eire; one *s* one *d. Educ:* Whitgift School; King's Coll., and King's Coll. Hosp., London. MB, BS (London) 1931; MRCP 1932; MD (London), 1933; FRCP 1951.

Registrar: Roy. Northern Hosp., 1933–34; to Children's Dept, King's Coll. Hosp., 1934–35; Med. Registrar and Pathologist, Hosp. for Sick Children, Gt Ormond St, 1935–38; Physician: Bolingbroke Hosp., London, 1938–45; Queen Elizabeth Hosp. for Children, 1939–46; Pædiatrician to Barnet Gen. Hosp., 1946–67; Civilian Pædiatric Consultant to Admiralty, 1962–74; Hon. Consultant in Pædiatrics to Army, 1966–74. Mem., British Pædiatric Assoc., 1945–; Pres., Pædiatric Section, RSM, 1966–67. *Publications:* contributor to Medical Annual, 1953–61; (with Dr Donald Paterson) Modern Methods of Feeding in Infancy and Childhood, 10th edn, 1955; contrib. to Pædiatric Urology (ed D. I. Williams), 1968; Urology in Childhood, 1974; numerous contributions to med. journals. *Recreations:* reading and looking at paintings. *Address:* 12 Milborne Grove, SW10 9SN. *T:* 01–373 2011; 34 Great Ormond Street, WC1N 3JH. *T:* 01–405 1306. *Died 20 Jan.* 1985.

**NEWSAM, Richard William**, CVO 1961; HM Diplomatic Service, retired; *b* 23 June 1918; *s* of late W. O. Newsam, ICS; *m* 1952, Joan Rostgard; one *s. Educ:* St Paul's; Trinity Coll., Oxford. Commnd RASC; served War of 1939–45: with East African Forces, Kenya, Abyssinia, Ceylon and Burma. Temporary Administrative Assistant, Colonial Office, 1946; Assistant Principal, Colonial Office, 1947; Principal, 1948; Nigeria secondment, 1952–53; joined Commonwealth Relations Office, 1957; served in: Ceylon, 1958; Pakistan, 1960; Dept of Technical Co-operation, 1963; Ministry of Overseas Development, 1964; Deputy High Commissioner, Dar es Salaam, 1965; Accra, 1967–69. *Recreations:* reading, bowling. *Address:* 2 Clarendon Road, St Heliers, Auckland, New Zealand. *Clubs:* Auckland Racing, St Heliers Bowling.

*Died 23 July* 1983.

**NEWTH, Prof. David Richmond**; Regius Professor of Zoology, University of Glasgow, 1965–81; *b* 10 Oct. 1921; *s* of late Herbert Greenway Newth and Annie Munroe (*née* Fraser); *m* 1946, Jean Winifred (*née* Haddon); two *s* one *d. Educ:* King Edward VI High Sch., Birmingham. Entered University Coll., London, 1938; graduated in Zoology, 1942. Served War of 1939–45, REME, commnd 1943. Asst Lectr in Zoology at University Coll., London, 1947; Lectr, 1949; Prof. of Biology as Applied to Medicine in the Univ. of London, at the Middlesex Hospital Medical Sch., 1960–65. Mem., Nature Conservancy Council, 1978–81. President: Scottish Marine Biol. Assoc., 1973–79; British Soc. for Developmental Biology, 1979–83. FRSE 1966. Editor, Journal of Embryology and Experimental Morphology, 1960–69. *Publications:* Animal Growth and Development, 1970; original articles in scientific journals, translations, and contrib. (popular) scientific works. *Recreation:* resting. *Address:* Monevechadan, Lochgoilhead, Cairndow, Argyll PA24 8AN. *T:* Lochgoilhead 287. *Died 5 June* 1988.

**NEWTON, Sir Hubert**, Kt 1968; President, Britannia Building Society, since 1985 (Chairman, 1976–85); *b* 2 Sept. 1904; *s* of Joe Newton and Gertrude Eliza Newton; *m* 1931, Elsie (*née* Wilson); one *d. Educ:* Burnley Gram. School. Burnley Building Soc., 1918–23; Mortgage Dept Controller, Northampton Town Building Soc., 1923–26; Controller of Investment Dept, Leeds Perm. Building Soc., 1926–30; Asst Sec., Bristol & West Building Soc., 1930–33; Leek and Moorlands Building Soc.: Sec., 1933–40; Gen. Man., 1940–63; Chm. and Man. Dir, 1963–66, when Leek and Moorlands amalgamated with Westbourne Park Building Soc. to form Leek and Westbourne Building Soc.; Man. Dir, 1966–69, Chm., 1966–74, Leek and Westbourne Building Soc.; on further amalgamation, Jt Dep. Chm., Leek Westbourne and Eastern Counties Building Soc. (name changed to Britannia Building Soc., 1975), 1974–76, 1978–84. Local Dir, N Staffs, Royal Insce Co. Ltd. Former Member Council: Building Socs Assoc. of Gt Britain (Chm., 1952–54); and Mem., Exec. Cttee, Internat. Union of Building Socs and Savings Assocs (Dep. Pres., Washington Congress, 1962; Pres., London Congress, 1965); Vice-President: Chartered Building Socs Inst., 1962; Building Socs Assoc. of Jamaica Ltd, 1967; President: Midland Assoc. of Building Socs, 1979; N Staffs Chamber of Commerce, 1964–65. Former Mem., Skelmersdale Develt Corp. Past Mem., Central Housing Adv. Cttee; Mem. Council, Nat. House-Building Council (Vice-Pres.). Founder Pres., Rotary Club, Leek, 1937; Pres., Stoke City FC, 1983–. Liveryman, Gold and Silver Wyre Drawers' Company. Hon. MA Keele, 1971. Coronation Medal, 1953. *Publications:* contribs to Building Socs Gazette. *Recreations:* golf, travel. *Address:* Birchall, Leek, Staffs ST13 5RA. *T:* Leek 382397. *Club:* English-Speaking Union. *Died 9 March* 1989.

**NEWTON, Ivor**, CBE 1973; FRCM; Pianoforte Accompanist; *b* London, 15 Dec. 1892; *s* of William and Gertrude Newton. Studied the piano with Arthur Barclay (Dir of Music, Brompton Oratory), York Bowen, and Isidore Snook (Amsterdam); studied Art of Accompanying and Repertoire with Raimund von zur Muhlen and Coenraad Bos (Berlin). Associated as accompanist with Kirsten Flagstad, Melba, Clara Butt, Tetrazzini, Conchita Supervia, Lily Pons, Lotte Lehmann, Elizabeth Schumann, Victoria de los Angeles, Joan Hammond, Kathleen Ferrier, Chaliapine, Gigli, Tito Schipa, John McCormack, Jussi Björling, Tito Gobbi, Ysaye, Yehudi

Menuhin, Milstein, Casals, Piatigorsky, Suggia, di Stefano and Maria Callas. Toured extensively in Europe, United States, Canada, Africa, Australia, New Zealand and the Orient. Salzburg, Edinburgh and Aldeburgh Festivals. Organised first concert in aid of British War Relief in United States at British Embassy, Washington, 1940; toured Egypt, Irak, and the Persian Gulf giving concerts to forces, 1943; concerts to Royal Navy and Soviet Fleet in Scapa Flow, 1944; toured Germany and Austria with Grace Moore on invitation of American C-in-C, 1946; British Council Tours, Scandinavia with Henry Holst, 1946; France with Maggie Teyte, 1947, Persia, Turkey and Austria with Leon Goossens, 1955. Adviser on music for HM Prisons. Cobbett Gold Medal (Worshipful Co. of Musicians) for services to Chamber Music, 1977. *Publication:* At the Piano—Ivor Newton (autobiog.), 1966. *Address:* Kirsten House, Kinnerton Street, Belgrave Square SW1. *T:* 01-235 2882. *Clubs:* Garrick, Chelsea Arts; Royal Naval and Royal Albert Yacht (Portsmouth).
*Died 21 April* 1981.

**NEWTON, John Mordaunt,** CB 1964; retired from Post Office Central HQ, 1973; *b* 24 April 1913; *o s* of late Wallis and Mabel Newton; *m* 1939, Pamela Frances, *e d* of late Sir E. John Maude, KCB, KBE; five *d. Educ:* Manchester Gram. Sch.; CCC, Cambridge (Scholar). BA 1st Cl. History Tripos, 1935. Assistant Principal, Post Office, 1936; Principal: Ministry of Home Security, 1941; Home Office, 1943; Treasury, 1945–47; Post Office 1947–73: Assistant Secretary, 1949; Under Secretary, 1957; Director of Personnel, GPO, 1957–67; Dir, Management Develt, 1967–73. Mem., London Diocesan Synod, 1979–82. Hon. Secretary, Abbeyfield Chiswick Soc., 1965–77. *Recreations:* reading, bookbinding, historic buildings. *Address:* Thames Bank, Chiswick Mall, W4 2PR. *T:* 01–994 1803.
*Died 7 March* 1986.

**NEWTON, Prof. Lily,** DSc, PhD; Professor of Botany, University College of Wales, Aberystwyth, 1930–58, Prof. Emeritus since 1959; Vice-Principal, 1951–52; Acting Principal, May 1952–Sept. 1953; *b* 26 Jan. 1893; *d* of George Batten and Melinda Batten (*née* Casling); *m* 1925, William Charles Frank Newton (*d* 1927). *Educ:* Colston's Girls' School, Bristol; University of Bristol. Assistant Lecturer in Botany, University of Bristol, 1919–20; Lecturer in Botany, Birkbeck Coll., Univ. of London, 1920–23; research worker, Imperial College of Science and British Museum, Natural History, 1923–25; Lecturer in Botany, University College of Wales, Aberystwyth, 1928–30. President: Section K, British Association, 1949; British Phycological Soc., 1955–57; UK Fedn for Educn in Home Economics, 1957–63. Hon. LLD Wales, 1973. *Publications:* Handbook of British Seaweeds, 1931; Plant distribution in the Aberystwyth district, 1935; (jointly) A Study of certain British Seaweeds and their utilisation in the preparation of agar, 1949; Utilisation of Seaweeds, 1951. Papers in Jl of Linnean Soc., Jl of Ecology, Annals of Applied Biology, Vistas in Botany and others. *Recreations:* cookery, needlework, gardening. *Address:* Maes-y-Wern, 20 Upper Heathfield Road, Pontardawe, Swansea SA8 4LE.
*Died 26 March* 1981.

**NEWTON, Robert,** CMG 1953; retired as Colonial Secretary, Mauritius, 1961; *b* Newcastle upon Tyne, 12 Oct. 1908; *m* 1933, Muriel Winifred, *d* of late Mr and Mrs R. P. Chinneck; one *s* two *d. Educ:* Aysgarth School; Malvern College; Pembroke College, Cambridge. Joined Colonial Administrative Service as Administrative Officer (Cadet), Nigeria, 1931; served there as an Assistant District Officer until 1937; served Palestine until 1946; IDC 1947; seconded for duty in Colonial Office, 1948; Financial Secretary, Jamaica, 1949. Member, British Ornithologists Union. PhD (Exon) 1966. FRSA 1972. *Publications:* Tarnished Brocade, 1937; Swords of Bronze, 1939; Victorian Exeter, 1968; The Northumberland Landscape, 1972. *Recreations:* ornithology, walking. *Address:* 14 Howell Road, Exeter, Devon. *Club:* United Oxford & Cambridge University.
*Died 10 Dec.* 1983.

**NICHOLAS, Sir Alfred James,** Kt 1967; CBE 1960 (OBE 1954); Chairman: Aberdare Holdings Ltd, 1963–70; South Wales Switchgear Ltd, 1965–70; *b* 1900; *s* of George and Harriet Nicholas; *m* 1927, Ethel (*d* 1978), *d* of Thomas Platt; one *s. Educ:* Bishop's Castle Sch.; Wellington Sch., Salop; Manchester Coll. of Technology. With Metropolitan Vickers Ltd, and Ferguson-Pailin Ltd until 1941. Formerly Chm. and Man. Director: Aberdare Cables Ltd; Aberdare Engineering Ltd; Erskine Heap & Co. Ltd; South Wales Group (Pty) Ltd South Africa; South Wales Electric (Pvt) Ltd Rhodesia; South Wales Electric Australia (Pty) Ltd; South Wales Electric Zambia Ltd. Founder Mem. and former Chm., Develt Corp. for Wales, President, 1971–; founder Mem. and former Pres., Industrial Assoc. of Wales and Monmouthshire; a Vice-Chm., Welsh Economic Council, 1966–68; Vice-Pres., Welsh Council, 1968–71; Past President: Electrical Res. Assoc.; Cardiff Chamber of Commerce and Industry. Member, Court of Governors: University Coll., Cardiff, 1952–82; UWIST; Governor, Christ Coll., Brecon, 1965–81. Assoc. Mem. Manchester Coll. of Technology; FIEE; MIEEE (USA); CEng; FBIM. Freeman of the City of London; Liveryman, Worshipful Co. of Tin Plate Workers.

Hon. LLD Wales. CStJ (Pres., East Mon area). *Recreations:* photography, gardening. *Address:* Bovil House, Machen, Gwent NP1 8SN.
*Died 5 March* 1984.

**NICHOLAS, Reginald Owen Mercer,** CB 1956; retired as Commissioner of Inland Revenue and Secretary, Board of Inland Revenue (1954–65); *b* 20 June 1903; *e s* of Reginald John Nicholas, mining engineer, Gold Coast, and Margaret Mary (*née* Trice); *m* 1929, Joan Estelle, *d* of E. S. Friend, Uplyme, Devon; two *s* one *d. Educ:* Royal Masonic Sch.; Gonville and Caius Coll., Cambridge (Scholar). Entered Inland Revenue Dept, 1925. Mem. War Damage Commn, 1962–64. *Address:* Thornton Cottage, Higher Metcombe, Ottery-St-Mary, Devon.
*Died 18 April* 1981.

**NICHOLETTS, Air Marshal Sir Gilbert (Edward),** KBE 1956; CB 1949; AFC 1931 and Bar, 1933; retired; *b* 9 Nov. 1902; *s* of Edward Cornewall Nicholetts and Ellen Fanny Hollond; *m* 1956, Nora Beswick, *d* of Francis John Butt, MB, Chester. *Educ:* RN Colleges, Osborne and Dartmouth. Cranwell Cadet Coll., 1921–22; Calshot, Lee-on-Solent, 1922–24; HMS Eagle (Med. Fleet), 1924–26; Far East Flight and 205 Sqdn, 1927–30; 209 Sqdn, 1931–32; long distance flight (World Record, 5309 miles non-stop), 1933; Air Staff, 23 Group HQ, 1934; Staff Coll., 1935; Air Staff, AHQ Iraq, 1936–38; Air Ministry organization, 1938–39; War of 1939–45, OC 228 Sqdn, 1939–41; Haifa, Shallufa, 1941; POW Far East, 1942–45; AOC Central Photographic Establishment, 1946–48; Dir of Organization, Air Ministry, 1948–51; SASO Coastal Command, 1951; AOC No 21 Group, Flying Training Command, 1953; AOC-in-C Flying Training Command, Sept.–Dec. 1955; AOC Malta, and Dep. C-in-C (Air), Allied Forces, Mediterranean, Jan. 1956–Dec. 1957; Inspector-Gen., Royal Air Force, Jan. 1958–June 1959; retired, 1959. *Address:* Stoborough Croft, Wareham, Dorset. *T:* Wareham 2992. *Club:* Royal Air Force.
*Died 7 Sept.* 1983.

**NICHOLLS, Pastor Sir Douglas (Ralph),** KCVO 1977; Kt 1972; OBE 1968; Governor of South Australia, 1976–77; *b* Cummeragunja, NSW, 9 Dec. 1906; *s* of H. Nicholls, Cummeragunja; *m* 1942, Gladys (*d* 1981), *d* of M. Bux; one *s* one *d. Educ:* at Cummeragunja. Formerly one of the best-known aborigines of Australia in the field of athletics and football; Pastor, Churches of Christ Aborigines' Mission, Fitzroy, Victoria; Dir, Aborigines Advancement League, 1969–76. KStJ 1977. *Publications:* contribs AAL quarterly magazines. *Recreations:* formerly running (won Nyah Gift and Warracknabeal Gift, 4th Melbourne Thousand, 1929); football (rep. Vic. in interstate matches).
*Died 4 June* 1988.

**NICHOLS, Beverley;** author and composer; *b* 9 Sept. 1898; *y s* of late John Nichols, Solicitor, of Bristol; unmarried. *Educ:* Marlborough Coll.; Balliol Coll., Oxford (Pres. of the Union, Editor of the Isis, Founder and Editor of the Oxford Outlook). *Publications:* Prelude (a public school novel), 1920; Patchwork, 1921; Self, 1922; Twenty-Five (an autobiography), 1926; Crazy Pavements, 1927; Are They the Same at Home?, 1927; The Star Spangled Manner, 1928; Women and Children Last, 1931; Evensong, 1932; Down the Garden Path, 1932; For Adults Only, 1932; Failures, 1933; Cry Havoc, 1933; A Thatched Roof, 1933; A Village in a Valley, 1934; The Fool Hath Said, 1936; No Place Like Home, 1936; News of England, 1938; Revue, 1939; Green Grows the City, 1939; Men do not Weep, 1941; Verdict on India, 1944; The Tree that Sat Down, 1945; The Stream that Stood Still, 1948; All I Could Never Be, 1949; Uncle Samson, 1950; The Mountain of Magic, 1950; Merry Hall, 1951; A Pilgrim's Progress, 1952; Laughter on the Stairs, 1953; No Man's Street, 1954; The Moonflower, 1955; Death to Slow Music, 1956; Sunlight on the Lawn, 1956; The Rich Die Hard, 1957; The Sweet and Twenties, 1958; Murder by Request, 1960; Beverley Nichols' Cats ABC, 1960; Beverley Nichols' Cats XYZ, 1961; Garden Open Today, 1963; Forty Favourite Flowers, 1964; Powers That Be, 1966; A Case of Human Bondage, 1966; The Art of Flower Arrangement, 1967; Garden Open Tomorrow, 1968; The Sun in My Eyes, 1969; The Wickedest Witch in the World, 1971; Father Figure (autobiog.), 1972; Down the Kitchen Sink, 1978; The Unforgiving Minute (autobiog.), 1978; *poems:* Twilight: First and probably Last poems, 1982; *plays:* (Musical and otherwise): The Stag, 1929; Cochran's 1930 Revue, 1930; Avalanche, 1931; Evensong, 1932; When The Crash Comes, 1933; Dr Mesmer, 1934; Floodlight, 1937; Song on the Wind (Operette), 1948; Shadow of the Vine, 1949; Lady's Guide, 1950. *Address:* Sudbrook Cottage, Ham Common, Surrey. *Club:* Garrick.
*Died 15 Sept.* 1983.

**NICHOLS, Peter,** OBE 1982; Rome Correspondent of The Times, 1957–87; *b* 15 Feb. 1928; *s* of Walter and Beatrice Nichols; *m* 1st, 1949, Marie Pamela Foulkes (marr. diss.); two *s* two *d*; 2nd, 1974, Paola Rosi; one *s. Educ:* Portsmouth Grammar Sch.; Oxford Univ. BA (Mod. Hist.). Asst. Correspondent, The Times, Bonn, 1954–57. Peripheral activities include BBC TV documentaries, radio and television programmes for Italian broadcasting corporation. Internat. prize for journalism, Città di Roma, 1973. Commendatore, Italian Republic, 1988. *Publications:* Piedmont and the English, 1967; Politics of the Vatican, 1968; Italia, Italia, 1973 (Book of the

Year Prize, 1976, for Italian edn); Italian Decision, 1977; Ruffo in Calabria, 1977; The Pope's Divisions, The Roman Catholic Church Today, 1981; contrib. Foreign Affairs, etc. *Recreation:* relaxing. *Address:* 45 Via degli Spagnoli, Rome, Italy. *T:* Rome 6541076.
*Died 11 Jan.* 1989.

**NICHOLSON, Sir Arthur (William),** Kt 1968; OBE 1962; Mayor of City of Ballarat, 1952–53, 1960–61, 1967–68, and 1974–75; Chairman of Ballarat Water Commissioners and Ballarat Sewerage Authority, 1956–76; Councillor, City of Ballarat, 1946–76; *b* 1 June 1903; *s* of A. H. Nicholson; *m* 1932, Jessie Beryl, *d* of H. A. Campbell; one *s. Educ:* Ballarat High School and School of Mines. Master Builder-family business. Hon. Life Mem. Master Builders' Assoc. (twice Pres.). Foundation Member: Western Moorabool Water Board; Water Resources Council of Victoria; Chairman: Provincial Sewerage Authorities Assoc. of Victoria, 1959–68; Waterworks Trusts Assoc. of Victoria, Pres., Ballarat YMCA for 16 yrs; Nat. Pres., YMCA of Australia, 1970–73, Hon. Life Mem., 1977. Pres., Ballarat Area Boy Scouts Assoc.; former Chm., State Library Services Div., Queen Elizabeth Geriatric Hosp. Mem. Council, Ballarat School of Mines and Industries; Govt Nominee on Ballarat Coll. of Advanced Education Council. Dir of Ballarat Television Station. First Pres., Ballarat Begonia Festival. Mem. Trust Corp., Presbyterian Church of Victoria. *Recreations:* bowls, photography. *Address:* 103 Wendouree Parade, Ballarat, Victoria 3350, Australia. *T:* Ballarat 311375. *Club:* Old Colonists (Ballarat).
*Died 5 Nov.* 1981.

**NICHOLSON, Ben,** OM 1968; painter; *b* 10 April 1894; *s* of late Sir William and Mabel Nicholson; *m* 1st, Winifred Roberts, painter and writer (marr. diss.; she *d* 1981); two *s* one *d;* 2nd, 1931, Barbara Hepworth (marr. diss.) (Dame Barbara Hepworth, DBE, *d* 1975); one *s* two *d;* 3rd, 1957, Dr Felicitas Vogler. *Educ:* Heddon Court, Cockfosters; Gresham Sch. (one term); Slade School of Art (one term); Tours: Milan. Awarded 1st prize Carnegie International, Pittsburgh, 1952; Ulissi prize, Venice Biennale, 1954; Governor of Tokyo prize at 3rd International Exhibition, Japan, 1955; Grand Prix at 4th Lugano International, 1956; 1st Guggenheim Foundation Award, 1957; 1st Internat. Prize, 4th S Paulo Biennial, 1957; Rembrandt Prize, 1974. Works included in following public collections: Tate Gallery; British Council; Arts Council; Contemporary Art Society; Victoria and Albert Museum, London; City Art Galleries: Leeds; Manchester; Birmingham; Bristol; Glasgow; Nottingham City Museum; Bedford Museum; Museum of Modern Art, New York; Guggenheim Museum, New York; Carnegie Institute, Pittsburgh; Walker Art Centre, Minneapolis; Allbright Museum, Buffalo; San Francisco Art Museum; Philadelphia Museum; Phillips Gallery and American University, Washington; Kunstmuseum, Zürich; Kunstmuseum, Berne; Wintherthur, Kunstmuseum; Kunsthalle, Hamburg; Musée des Beaux Arts, Antwerp; Museum of Fine Arts, Rotterdam; Palais des Beaux Arts, Brussels; Australian National Gallery; Canadian National Gallery; Museum of Fine Arts, Tel-Aviv, Israel; Museo de Arte Moderno, Rio de Janeiro; Museo Nacional de Buenos Aires; Centre National d'Art Moderne; Ohara Museum, Japan, etc. Retrospective one-man exhibitions include: Venice Biennale, 1954; Stedilijk Museum, Amsterdam, 1954; Musée Nationale d'Art Moderne, Paris, 1955; Palais des Beaux Arts, Brussels, 1955; Kunsthalle, Zürich, 1955; Tate Gallery, London, 1955, 1956, 1969, 1970; in German Cities, 1959; Kunsthalle, Bern, 1961; Marlborough New London Gallery, 1967; Crane Kalman Gall., 1968; Galerie Beyeler, Basle, 1968; Marlborough Gall., 1971; Waddington and Tooth Gall., 1978. *Publications:* (co-editor) Circle international survey of constructive art, 1937, repr. 1971; monographs: Ben Nicholson (introduction Sir John Summerson), Penguin, 1948; Notes on Abstract Art (by Ben Nicholson), included in Ben Nicholson (introduction Sir Herbert Read), Lund Humphries, vol. 1, 1911–1948, Vol. 2, Work from 1948–1955. Ben Nicholson, The Meaning of His Art (introd. Dr J. P. Hodin), 1957; Ben Nicholson (introd. Sir Herbert Read), 1962; Ben Nicholson (introd. D. Baxandall), 1962; Ben Nicholson (introd. Ronald Alley), 1962; Ben Nicholson: Drawings, Paintings and Reliefs, 1911–1968 (introd. John Russell), 1969; Ben Nicholson (ed Maurice de Sausmarez), 1969. *Recreations:* painting, tennis, golf, table tennis, etc. *Address:* c/o Banca della Svizzera, Locarno, Ticino, Switzerland.
*Died 6 Feb.* 1982.

**NICHOLSON, (Frank) Douglas,** TD; MA Cantab; JP; DL; President, Vaux Breweries Ltd and subsidiary cos (Chairman, 1953–76; Joint Managing Director, 1937–52; Director 1928–77); Vice-President, The Brewers' Society (Chairman 1970–71); *b* 30 July 1905; *o s* of late Sir Frank Nicholson, CBE; *m* 1937, Pauline, *y d* of late Sir Thomas Lawson Tancred, 9th Bt, Borobridge; five *s. Educ:* Harrow; Clare Coll., Cambridge. Scottish Horse (TA), 1928; served in Scottish Horse and RA, War of 1939–45, in charge of British and American Supply Mission to Saudi Arabia, 1944. Contested (C) Spennymoor, at 1945 Election. Chm., Durham Police Authority, 1955–64. Pres. and Treasurer, Durham Co. Assoc. of Boys' Clubs, 1952–78. High Sheriff Durham County, 1948–49; DL 1948; JP 1949.

British Team Winner, World Driving Championship, Munster, W Germany, 1972. *Recreations:* farming, etc. *Address:* Southill Hall, near Chester-le-Street, Co. Durham DH3 4EQ. *T:* Chester-le-Street 882286.
*Died 28 Dec.* 1984.

**NICHOLSON, Sir John (Charles),** 3rd Bt, *cr* 1859; TD 1954; FRCS 1934; BM, BCh; Consulting Surgeon; Senior Surgeon, Bethnal Green, St Leonard's and St Matthew's Hospitals, London, retired 1969; *b* 10 Jan. 1904; *s* of Sir Charles Nicholson, 2nd Bt, and Evelyn Louise (*d* 1927), *d* of Rev. H. Olivier; *S* father, 1949; *m* 1928, Caroline Elizabeth (*d* 1981), *d* of late Rt Rev. John Frederick McNeice, Bishop of Down; no *c. Educ:* Brighton Coll.; New Coll., Oxford; St Bartholomew's Hospital. Major, RAMC, TA (commissioned 1932); Temp. Lieut-Colonel, RAMC, 1942; Hon. Lieut-Colonel 1945. Late Surgical Registrar, Royal National Orthopædic Hospital, etc.; Clinical Fellow in Surgery, Harvard Univ., 1947–48. Qualified 1929; BM, BCh, Oxford, 1929. *Publications:* various on professional subjects in British Medical Journal and other periodicals. *Recreation:* yachting. *Heir:* none. *Address:* Thames Cottage, Thames Street, Sunbury-on-Thames. *T:* Sunbury 82148.
*Died 16 March* 1986 *(ext).*

**NICHOLSON, (John) Leonard,** DSc(Econ); formerly Chief Economic Adviser to Department of Health and Social Security; *b* 18 Feb. 1916; *er s* of late Percy Merwyn Nicholson (clan, Macleod of Macleod) and late Jane Winifred Nicholson (née Morris). *Educ:* Stowe; Institute of Actuaries; London School of Economics. MSc (Econ), DSc (Econ), London (Bowley and Frances Wood Meml Prizes). With Oxford University Inst. of Statistics, 1940–47; Ministry of Home Security, 1943–44; Central Statistical Office, 1947–68; Simon Research Fellow, Manchester Univ., 1962–63; Chief Economic Advr to DHSS and to successive Secretaries of State for Social Services, 1968–76; Assoc. Prof. of Quantitative Econs, Brunel Univ., 1972–74; Sen. Leverhulme Fellowship, 1977; Sen. Fellow, PSI, 1977–83; Rockefeller Fellowship, 1984. Chm., Cabinet Office Br., First Div. Assoc., 1952–62. FSS (formerly Mem. Council). *Publications:* The Beveridge Plan for Social Security (jtly), 1943; Variations in Working Class Family Expenditure, 1949; The Interim Index of Industrial Production, 1949; Redistribution of Income in the United Kingdom, 1965; contrib. to: D. Wedderburn, Poverty, Inequality and Class Structure, 1974; A. B. Atkinson, The Personal Distribution of Incomes, 1976; V. Halberstadt and A. J. Culyer, Public Economics and Human Resources, 1977; DHSS Definition and Measurement of Poverty, 1979; P. Streeten and H. Maier, Human Resources, Employment and Development, vol. 2, 1983; various articles concerned with national income, economic welfare and statistical methods in academic journals. *Recreations:* music, painting, real tennis, golf. *Address:* 53 Frognal, NW3 6YA. *T:* 071–435 8015. *Clubs:* Savile, MCC, Queen's.
*Died 4 Dec.* 1990.

**NICHOLSON, Rev. John Malcolm;** *b* 26 May 1908; 2nd *s* of John and Madeleine Nicholson; *m* 1939, Dorothy Lisle Preston; one *s* two *d. Educ:* Whitgift Sch.; King's Coll., Cambridge; Cuddesdon Theological Coll. Asst Curate, St John's, Newcastle upon Tyne, 1932–36; Vicar, St Mary's, Monkseaton, 1936–38; Vicar, Sugley, 1938–46; Vicar, St George's, Cullercoats, 1946–55; Archdeacon of Doncaster, 1955–59; Vicar of High Melton, 1955–59; Headmaster, The King's School, Tynemouth, 1959–70. Examining Chaplain: to Bishop of Newcastle, 1944–55; to Bishop of Sheffield, 1955–59; Select Preacher, Cambridge Univ., 1959. *Address:* 12 Carrsfield, Corbridge NE45 5LJ.
*Died 2 Dec.* 1983.

**NICHOLSON, Hon. John Paton;** Hon. Chief Justice Nicholson; Chief Justice, Supreme Court of Prince Edward Island, Canada, since 1977; *b* 16 Nov. 1922; *s* of Robert H. Nicholson and Beatrice Paton; *m* 1950, Grace Diamond; one *s* two *d. Educ:* Prince of Wales Coll., Charlottetown, PEI; Dalhousie Univ., Halifax, NS (LLB). Called to Bar of PEI, 1948; private law practice, 1948–70; QC 1966; apptd Judge, Supreme Court, PEI, 1970. *Recreations:* sailing, sport fishing. *Address:* Law Courts Building, Charlottetown, PEI C1A 7K4, Canada. *T:* (area code) 902–892–9131. *Clubs:* Canadian, United Services Officers' (Hon.) (PEI).
*Died 24 May* 1985.

**NICHOLSON, Leonard;** *see* Nicholson, J. L.

**NICHOLSON, Norman Cornthwaite,** OBE 1981; poet and critic; *b* Millom, Cumberland, 8 Jan. 1914; *s* of Joseph and Edith Nicholson; *m* 1956, Yvonne Edith Gardner (*d* 1982). *Educ:* local schools. Literary criticism in weekly press. FRSL 1945; Hon. Fellow, Manchester Polytechnic, 1979. MA (Hon.): Manchester Univ., 1959; Open Univ., 1975; Hon. DLitt Liverpool, 1980; Hon. LittD Lancaster, 1984. Cholmondley Award for Poetry, 1967; Soc. of Authors Travelling Award, 1972; Queen's Medal for Poetry, 1977. *Publications: poetry:* Five Rivers, 1944 (Heinemann Prize, 1945); Rock Face, 1948; The Pot Geranium, 1954; Selected Poems, 1966; A Local Habitation, 1973; Sea to the West, 1981; Selected Poems 1940–1982, 1982; *verse drama:* The Old Man of the Mountains (produced Mercury Theatre), 1946; A Match for the Devil, 1955;

Birth by Drowning, 1960; *criticism:* Man and Literature, 1943; William Cowper, 1951; *topography:* Cumberland and Westmorland, 1949; The Lakers, 1955; Provincial Pleasures, 1959; Portrait of the Lakes, 1963; Greater Lakeland, 1969; *autobiography:* Wednesday Early Closing, 1975; *anthology:* The Pelican Anthology of Modern Religious Verse, 1943; A Choice of Cowper's Verse, 1975; The Lake District, 1977. *Address:* 14 St George's Terrace, Millom, Cumbria. *T:* Millom 2024. *Died 30 May 1987.*

NICHOLSON, William Ewart, CBE 1941; BA, FRAI; *b* 29 Dec. 1890; *s* of Robert Francis Nicholson, Leeds; *m* 1920, Alice Elgie, *d* of W. E. Cork; one *d. Educ:* Leeds Grammar Sch.; Jesus Coll., Oxford. Education Dept, N Nigeria, 1914; Lieut, Nigeria Regt, 1917; Principal, Katsina Coll., 1934; Director of Education, Sierra Leone, 1935–45; Member Fourah Bay College Commission, 1938; Member of Exec. Council, JP, Sierra Leone; Educational Adviser to Government of The Gambia, 1944–45; Secretary Commission of Enquiry into the system of Education of the Jewish Community in Palestine, 1945–46; Director of Training, Ministry of Food, 1946–48. Hon. Keeper of Ethnography, Leeds City Museum, 1959–74. *Address:* 2 Washington Road, P/Bag 7633, Chinhoyi, Zimbabwe. *Died 28 July 1983.*

NICOL, Claude Scott, CBE 1977; TD; Hon. Physician, Genitourinary Medicine Department, St Thomas' Hospital, London; Hon. Consultant to the Army; late Adviser in Genitourinary Medicine to Department of Health and Social Security; *b* 1914; *s* of late Dr C. G. Nicol, barrister-at-law (Lincoln's Inn); *m* 1939, Janet Wickham Bosworth Smith; one *s* two *d. Educ:* Harrow Sch.; St Mary's Hospital; St John's Coll., Oxford. MRCS, LRCP, 1936; MB, BS, 1938; MD 1946; MRCP, 1946; FRCP, 1962. Formerly: Physician in charge of Venereal Diseases Dept, St Bartholomew's Hosp., London; Physician, Whitechapel Clinic, London Hospital; Fellow in Medicine, Johns Hopkins Hospital, Baltimore; House Physician, St Mary's Hosp., London. Former Asst Dist Surgeon, St John Amb. Assoc. and Brigade. Ex-Pres., Medical Soc. for Study of Venereal Diseases; FRSM. QHP 1967–69. *Publications:* contributions to medical textbooks and journals. *Recreations:* squash racquets, tennis. *Address:* 40 Ferncroft Avenue, NW3 7PE. *T:* 01–435 1310; The Albert Embankment Consulting Rooms, 199 Westminster Bridge Road, SE1 7EH. *T:* 01-928 5485.
*Died 17 Feb. 1984.*

NICOL, Prof. Thomas, MD, DSc (Glasgow and London); FRCS; FRCSE; FRSE; FKC; Emeritus Professor of Anatomy, University of London; Professor of Anatomy and Head of Anatomical Department, King's College, University of London, 1936–67 (Senior Professor in all Faculties, since Oct. 1966); Director of Department of Clinical Anatomy, Institute of Laryngology and Otology; Member: New York Academy of Sciences; Anatomical Society of Great Britain and Ireland; American Assoc. of Anatomists; International Reticulo-Endothelial Society; Society of Endocrinology; Fellow, Medical Society of London; Hon. Member, Mark Twain Society, in succession to Sir Alexander Fleming; *b* 4 Aug. 1900; *s* of Wm Nicol and Mary Wilson Gilmour; *m* 1927, Evelyn Bertha (*d* 1966), *d* of Thomas Keeling, MICE, Engineer-in-Chief late Glasgow and South Western Railway; one *s* one *d. Educ:* University of Glasgow. Honours and Bellahouston Gold Medal for MD Thesis, University of Glasgow, 1935; Struthers Gold Medal and Prize, University of Glasgow, 1935. Sen. House Surgeon to Sir William Macewen, FRS (the discoverer of asepsis), Western Infirmary, Glasgow, 1921; Demonstrator of Anatomy, 1922–27, Senior Lecturer in Anatomy, 1927–35, University of Glasgow. Pioneer of experimental stimulation of phagocytes as suggested by Bernard Shaw in The Doctor's Dilemma; succeeded in doing this with oestrogen in late twenties; later discovered that body defence is under hormone control and that 17β-oestradiol is the principal stimulant in both sexes. Lately: Dean of Faculty of Medicine, King's Coll., Univ. of London; Chm., Board of Studies in Human Anatomy and Morphology, Univ. of London; Examiner, Univs of London, Birmingham, Durham, Glasgow, and St Andrews, RCS England, Edinburgh and Ireland, and RCP; John Hunter Lectr in Applied Anatomy, St George's Hosp. Med. Sch.; Malcolm McHardy Lectr, Royal Eye Hosp. Lord of the Manor of Heveningham, Suffolk. *Publications:* research articles on raising body defence against infection and cancer, in British Jl of Surgery, Jl of Obstetrics and Gynaec. of British Empire, Jl of Anatomy, Trans. and Proc. Royal Society of Edinburgh, BMJ, Nature, Jl of Endocrinology, Jl of Reticuloendothelial Soc. *Recreations:* music, golf, swimming. *Address:* 18 Penn House, Moor Park, Northwood, Mddx. *T:* Northwood 25081. *Died 7 Feb. 1983.*

NICOL, William Allardyce, CA, FCIS; Chairman, Kitchin Engineering Group Ltd, since 1987; *b* 20 March 1909; *s* of William Nicol and Mary Wilson Gilmour; *m* 1st, 1933, Elizabeth (*d* 1967), *d* of James Miller; one *s* one *d*; 2nd, 1970, Sally Philippa, *d* of Robert Patrick Vernon Brettell; one *s* one *d. Educ:* Glasgow University. Guest, Keen & Nettlefolds: Asst to Man. Dir, 1939–48; Group Sec., 1948–60; Dir, 1958–77; full-time Exec. Admin. Dir, 1960–68;

Deputy Chairman: Eagle Star Insurance Co. Ltd, 1968–75; Eagle Star (Internat. Life), 1982–88; Director: Eagle Star Insurance Co. Ltd (Isle of Man), 1975–88; Powell Duffryn Ltd, 1968–75; Barclays Bank Ltd (Birmingham Bd), 1961–75; Stait Carding Gp Ltd (Chm., 1973–75); Chm., John Stait Gp, 1972–75. Chm., Assoc. Scottish Chartered Accountants in Midlands, 1953–68; Mem. Grand Council, CBI, 1965–67. *Recreations:* golf, fishing, music. *Address:* Longmead, Ballakillowey, Colby, Isle of Man. *T:* Port Erin 832005. *Died 12 Nov. 1989.*

NICOLL, Sir John (Fearns), KCMG 1953 (CMG 1946); *b* 26 April 1899; *s* of late John Nicoll; *m* 1939, Irene, *d* of Major J. D. Lenagan, MBE; one *s. Educ:* Carlisle Grammar Sch.; Pembroke Coll., Oxford. S Lancs Regt, 1918–19; Administrative Officer, British N Borneo, 1921–25; Administrative Officer, Tanganyika Territory, 1925–37; Dep. Colonial Sec., Trinidad, 1937–44; Colonial Sec., Fiji, 1944–49; Colonial Sec., Hong-Kong, 1949–52; Governor and Comdr-in-Chief, Singapore, 1952–55, retired. KStJ. *Club:* East India, Devonshire, Sports and Public Schools.
*Died 12 Jan. 1981.*

NIDDITCH, Prof. Peter Harold; Professor and Head of Department of Philosophy, University of Sheffield, since 1969; *b* 15 Sept. 1928; *o s* of Lazarus Nidditch and Matilda Nidditch (*née* Freeman); *m* 1951, Bridget Veronica McDonnell; no *c. Educ:* Clifton Coll.; Birkbeck Coll., Univ. of London (BA (External) 1949, MA 1951, PhD 1953, DLit 1980). Asst, Birkbeck Coll., 1953–54; Asst Lectr, Queen's Univ., Belfast, 1954–56; Lectr, Univ. of Liverpool, 1956–59; Univ. of Bristol, 1959–63; Univ. of Sussex: Sen. Lectr, 1963–64; Reader in Phil. and History of Science, and Chm. of Logic, History, and Policy of Science Div., Sch. of Math. and Phys. Scis, 1964–70; Editor, official pubns of Univ. of Sussex, 1965–69. Univ. of Sheffield: Dean, Faculty of Arts, 1977–79; Chm., Library Cttee, 1979–82; Chm., Academic Staffing Cttee, 1980–. Gen. Editor, Clarendon Edn of Works of John Locke (30 vols), in progress. *Publications:* Introductory Formal Logic of Mathematics, 1957; Elementary Logic of Science and Mathematics, 1960; Propositional Calculus, 1962; Russian Reader in Pure and Applied Mathematics, 1962; The Development of Mathematical Logic (in C. K. Ogden's Basic English), 1962 (Spanish edn 1978); (ed) Philosophy of Science, 1968 (Spanish edn 1978); The Intellectual Virtues, 1970; A Bibliographical and Text-Historical Study of the Early Printings of Locke's Some Thoughts concerning Education, 1972; critical edn, Locke's Essay concerning Human Understanding, 1975, revd edn 1979; (ed) Hume's Enquiries, 1975; An Apparatus of Variant Readings for Hume's Treatise of Human Nature, 1976; critical edn, Hume's Treatise of Human Nature, 1978; Preface to the Grammar of Postulates (Proc. Aristotelian Soc. supp. vol.), 1979; The Earliest Extant Autograph Version (Draft A) of Locke's Essay, transcribed with critical apparatus, 1980; Index to J. L. Austin, How To Do Things With Words, 1980; (ed) Draft B of Locke's Essay, 1982; chapters in several other books; contribs to learned jls. *Address:* Sparlands, Grindleford, Derbyshire S30 1HQ. *T:* Hope Valley 30670. *Died 12 Feb. 1983.*

NIEMÖLLER, Rev. Dr (Friedrich Gustav Emil) Martin; a President of the World Council of Churches, 1961–68; Church President of Evangelical Church in Hesse and Nassau, Germany, 1947–64, retired; *b* Lippstadt, Westphalia, 14 Jan. 1892; *s* of Pastor Heinrich Niemoeller; *m* 1st, 1919, Else (*née* Bremer) (*d* 1961); three *s* two *d* (and one *s* one *d* decd); 2nd, 1971, Sibylle (*née* von Sell). *Educ:* Gymnasium, Elberfeld. Midshipman in German Navy, 1910; retd 1919, as Kapitänleutnant; studied Theology, Münster, Westfalen; Pastor, 1924; Pastor of Berlin-Dahlem, 1931; creator of Pastors' Union and Confessing Church; prisoner in concentration camps at Sachsenhausen and Dachau, 1937–45; Pres. Office of Foreign Affairs of Evangelical Church in Germany, 1945–56. Holds Hon. DD of Univ. of Göttingen (Germany), and several foreign hon. doctorates. *Publications:* Vom U-Boot zu Kanzel (Berlin), 1934; ... Dass wir an Ihm bleiben: Sechzehn Dahlemer Predigten (Berlin), 1935; Alles und in allem Christus; Fünfzehn Dahlemer Predigten (Berlin), 1935; Fran U-Bat till Predikstol (trans.) (Stockholm), 1936; Dennoch getrost: Die letzten 28 Predigten (Switzerland), 1939; Ach Gott vom Himmel sieh darein: Sechs Predigten (Munich), 1946; ... Zu verkündigen ein Gnädiges: Jahr des Herrn: Sechs Dachauer Predigten (1944–45), (Munich), 1946; Herr ist Jesus Christus: Die letzten 28 Predigten (Gütersloh), 1946; Herr, wohin sollen win gehen? Ausgewählte Predigten (Munich), 1956; some hundred articles about theological, cultural and political themes. *Address:* Brentanostrasse 3, Wiesbaden, Germany.
*Died 6 March 1984.*

NIGHTINGALE, Percy Herbert, CMG 1957; *b* 22 Dec. 1907; *s* of late Rev. S. J. Nightingale and late Mrs Nightingale; *m* 1935, Doris Aileen Butcher; one *s* one *d. Educ:* St Michael's, Limpsfield, Surrey; Monkton Combe Sch., near Bath; Christ's Coll., Cambridge. BA Cantab, 1928. Colonial Administrative Service, Fiji, 1930–52; District Commissioner, 1940; Asst Colonial Sec., 1947; Financial Sec., Zanzibar, 1952–60. Appeal Organiser, Monkton Combe Sch.,

1960–64; Lay Asst to Bishop of Salisbury, 1964–73; Coronation Medal, 1953; Order of Brilliant Star, Zanzibar (2nd Class), 1960. *Address:* 17 Grange Mansions, Kingston Road, Ewell, Surrey.
*Died 26 Nov. 1981.*

**NIVEN, (James) David (Graham);** Actor-producer (international); author; *b* 1 March 1910; *s* of late William Graham Niven and late Lady Comyn-Platt, Carswell Manor, Abingdon, Berks; *m* 1st, Primula (*d* 1946), *d* of Hon. William and Lady Kathleen Rollo; two *s*; 2nd, Hjördis Tersmeden, Stockholm; two *d*. *Educ:* Stowe; RMC Sandhurst. Commissioned HLI, 1929, Malta and Home Service; resigned commission, 1932; roamed Canada, USA, West Indies and Cuba till 1935. Journalist; Whisky Salesman; indoor pony-racing promoter; delivery of laundry; etc. Arrived California; became "extra" in films in Hollywood, 1935 ("English Type No 2008"); played bits and small parts; first starring rôle, Bachelor Mother, 1938, with Ginger Rogers. Returned to England at outbreak of War of 1939–45; rejoined Army; commissioned Rifle Brigade, later to Phantom Reconnaissance Regt; served Normandy, Belgium, Holland, Germany (usual campaign decorations, American Legion of Merit). Important films: Wuthering Heights, Dawn Patrol, Raffles, The First of the Few, The Way Ahead, A Matter of Life and Death, The Bishop's Wife, Bonnie Prince Charlie, The Elusive Pimpernel, Enchantment, Soldiers Three, Happy Go Lovely, The Moon is Blue, The Love Lottery, Happy Ever After, Carrington VC, Around the World in 80 Days, The Birds and the Bees, Silken Affair, The Little Hut, Oh, Men, Oh, Women, Bonjour Tristesse, My Man Godfrey, Separate Tables, Ask Any Girl, Please don't eat the Daisies, The Guns of Navarone, The Best of Enemies, Guns of Darkness, 55 Days at Peking, The Pink Panther, The King of the Mountain, Bedtime Story, Lady L., Where the Spies Are, Eye of the Devil, Casino Royale, Extraordinary Seaman, Prudence and the Pill, The Impossible Years, Before Winter Comes, The Brain, The Statue; King, Queen, Knave; Vampira, Paper Tiger, No Deposit No Return, Murder by Death, Candleshoe, Death on the Nile, Escape to Athena, A Man Called Intrepid, A Nightingale Sang in Berkeley Square, Rough Cut, Sea Wolves, Ménage à Trois, Trail of the Pink Panther, Curse of the Pink Panther. Formed Four Star Television, 1952, which has since produced over 2000 films for TV. Winner Academy Award, 1959; New York Critics' Award, 1960. *Publications:* Round the Rugged Rocks, 1951; The Moon's a Ballon (autobiog.), 1971; Bring on the Empty Horses, 1975; Go Slowly, Come Back Quickly, 1981. *Recreations:* ski-ing, skin diving, oil painting. *Address:* c/o Coutts & Co., 440 Strand, WC2. *Club:* White's. *Died 29 July 1983.*

**NIVEN, Col Thomas Murray,** CB 1964; TD 1941; FICE (retired); FIMechE (retired); *b* 20 Aug. 1900; *s* of Thomas Ogilvie Niven, Civil Engineer, Glasgow. *Educ:* Glasgow Academy; Glasgow Univ. Served War of 1939–45 with Royal Signals: comdg 52 (Lowland) Div. Signals, 1938–40; Dep. Chief Signal Officer, Northern Command, 1941–43; Dep. Chief Signal Officer, Northern Command, 1944. Comdg 6 Glasgow Home Guard Bn, 1952–56; Hon. Col 52 (Lowland) Signal Regt (TA), 1950–66; Chm., Glasgow T & AFA, 1959–62. Formerly Dir of Mechans Ltd, Engineers, Scotstoun Iron Works, Glasgow. DL Glasgow, 1949–75. *Recreation:* walking. *Clubs:* Naval and Military; Royal Channel Islands Yacht (Guernsey). *Died 24 Nov. 1987.*

**NIXON, Rear-Adm. Harry Desmond,** CB 1973; LVO 1958; DL; *b* 6 May 1920; *s* of Harry Earle Nixon and Ethel Maude Nixon; *m* 1946, Elizabeth June Witherington; one *s* two *d*. *Educ:* Brigg. CEng, FIMechE. Joined RN as Cadet, 1938; RNEC, 1939–42; HMS: Suffolk, 1942; Indomitable, 1943–45; HM Dockyard, Malta, 1954–55; HM Yacht Britannia, 1956–58; Ship Dept, Admty, Bath, 1958–60; RNEC, 1960–62; Naval District Engr Overseer Midlands, 1962–64; CO, HMS Sultan, 1964–66; idc 1967; Dir of Fleet Maintenance, 1968–71; Vice-Pres. (Naval), 1971–73, Pres., 1973–74, Ordnance Board. Comdr 1953; Captain 1962; Rear-Adm. 1971. Mem., Public Inquiries Panel for Dept of Transport, 1974–82. Chm., 1974–77, Vice-Chm., 1977–79, Wilts Assocs of Boys' Clubs and Youth Clubs. DL Wilts 1978. *Address:* Ashley Cottage, Ashley, Box, Corsham, Wilts SN14 9AJ. *Club:* Army and Navy.
*Died 6 Oct. 1986.*

**NIXON, Howard Millar,** OBE 1983; FSA; Librarian, Westminster Abbey, since 1974; *b* 3 Sept. 1909; *s* of Rev. Leigh H. Nixon, MVO, and Harrie (*née* Millar); *m* 1951, Enid Dorothy Bromley; three *s*. *Educ:* Marlborough; Keble Coll., Oxford. BA 1931; MA 1974. Served in Army, 1939–46 (Major, RA). Asst Cataloguer, Dept of Printed Books, British Museum, 1936; Asst Keeper, 1946, Dep. Keeper, 1959–74. Lectr in Bibliography, Sch. of Library Studies, University Coll., London, 1959–76; Sandars Reader in Bibliography, Univ. of Cambridge, 1967–68; Lyell Lecturer in Bibliography, Oxford, 1978–79. Pres., Bibliographical Soc., 1972–74. Editor, British Library Jl, 1974–77. Chm., Panel for allocation of Printed Books received in lieu of Death Duties, 1976–. Hon. Fellow: Keble Coll., Oxford; Pierpont Morgan Library, NY. Gold Medal, Bibliographical Soc., 1978. Officier, Ordre de la Couronne (Belgium),

1979. *Publications:* Twelve Books in Fine Bindings, 1953; Broxbourne Library, 1956; Bookbindings from the Library of Jean Grolier, 1965; Sixteenth-century Gold-tooled Bookbindings in the Pierpont Morgan Library, 1971; English Restoration Bookbindings, 1974; Five Centuries of English Bookbinding, 1978; British Bookbindings presented by Kenneth H. Oldaker to the Chapter Library of Westminster Abbey, 1982; articles in The Library, Book Collector, etc. *Recreation:* golf. *Address:* 4A Little Cloister, Westminster Abbey, SW1P 3PL. *T:* 01-222 6428. *Club:* Grolier (New York). *Died 18 Feb. 1983.*

**NOAKES, Col Geoffrey William,** OBE 1958; TD 1948; JP; DL; Past Managing Director, William Timpson Ltd, Footwear Retailers; Member, Industrial Tribunals, Manchester, since 1975; *b* Manor House, Basingstoke, Hants, 19 Nov. 1913; *s* of Charles William Noakes; *m* 1936, Annie, *d* of Albert Hough, Peel Green; two *s* two *d*. *Educ:* Wyggeston Sch. Commissioned RA, 1936. Served War: in France, 1940; Burma, 1940–46 (despatches); Staff Coll., Quetta, 1944; AQMG, Fourteenth Army, 1944–45. In command 252 Field Regt RA, 1951–57; DCRA, 42 Div., 1957–62. Past Pres., Multiple Shoe Retailers' Assoc.; Past Pres. and Chm., Footwear Distributors' Fedn; Past Leader and Sec., Employer's side, Boot and Shoe Repairing Wages Council; Past Pres., Nat. Assoc. of Shoe Repair Factories. Past Chm., Publicity and Recruiting Cttee, and Vice-Chm., NW of England and IOM TAVR Assoc.; Pres., Burma Star Assoc., Altrincham; Past Mem., Bd of Examiners, Sch. of Business Studies, Manchester Polytechnic; Mem. Exec. Cttee, Manchester and Dist Boys' Clubs; Governor, Manchester Univ.; formerly Rep. Col Comdt, RA Uniformed Staff; Vice-President: Cholmondeley Cons. Assoc.; Cholmondeley FC; Chm., Border Castles Driving Club. JP Manchester, 1963; DL Lancs 1974. FBIM, FIWM, MIPM, ABSI. *Recreations:* hunting, shooting, fishing (Pres. Altrincham Angling Club), golf. *Address:* The Mill House, Bickley, near Malpas, Cheshire SY14 8EG. *T:* Hampton Heath 309. *Club:* Army and Navy. *Died 5 Feb. 1989.*

**NOBLE, Comdr Rt. Hon. Sir Allan (Herbert Percy),** KCMG 1959; DSO 1943; DSC 1941; PC 1956; DL; a Member of Lloyd's; *b* 2 May 1908; *s* of late Admiral Sir Percy Noble, GBE, KCB, CVO, and Diamantina Campbell; *m* 1938, Barbara Janet Margaret, *o d* of late Brigadier Kenneth Gabbett. *Educ:* Radley College. Entered Royal Navy, 1927; ADC to Viceroy of India (Lord Linlithgow), 1936–38; commanded HM Destroyers Newport, Fernie and Quentin, 1940–42; Commander, 1943. Attended Quebec and Yalta Conferences. Served War of 1939–45 (despatches, DSC, DSO); retired list, 1945. MP (C) for Chelsea, 1945–59, retired; Government Observer, Bikini Atomic Bomb Tests, 1946; PPS to Mr Anthony Eden, 1947–51; Parly and Financial Sec., Admiralty, 1951–55; Parly Under-Sec. of State for Commonwealth Relations, 1955–56; Minister of State for Foreign Affairs, 1956–59; Leader, UK Delegation: to UN Gen. Assembly, 1957–58; to UN Disarmament Sub-Cttee, 1957; Special Ambassador, Ivory Coast Independence, 1961; Mem., Adv. Cttee on Service Parly candidates, 1963–74. Dir and Chm., Tollemache & Cobbold Breweries Ltd, 1960–73; Dir, Colonial Mutual Life Assurance Soc. Ltd (UK Br.), 1960–76. Member Cttee of Management, Inst. of Cancer Research, Royal Cancer Hosp., 1959–67. President: Chelsea Cons. Assoc., 1962–66; Cambridgeshire Cons. Assoc., 1967–72; a Mem. of Radley Coll. Council, 1947–63; Chm., National Trainers' Assoc., 1963–66. Hon. Freeman: Chelsea, 1963; Royal Borough of Kensington and Chelsea, 1965. DL Suffolk, 1973. Inter Services Athletics (Hurdles), 1931. *Address:* Troston Cottage, Bury St Edmunds, Suffolk IP31 1EX. *T:* Honington 250. *Club:* White's. *Died 17 Nov. 1982.*

**NOBLE, Sir Andrew Napier,** 2nd Bt, *cr* 1923; KCMG 1954 (CMG 1947); *b* 16 Sept. 1904; *s* of Sir John Henry Brunel Noble, 1st Bt, and Amie (*d* 1973), *d* of S. A. Walker Waters; *S* father, 1938; *m* 1934, Sigrid, 2nd *d* of M. Michelet, of Royal Norwegian Diplomatic Service; two *s* one *d*. *Educ:* Eton; Balliol Coll., Oxford. Counsellor of the British Embassy, Buenos Aires, 1945–47; Assistant Under-Secretary of State, Foreign Office, 1949; HM Minister at Helsinki, 1951–54; HM Ambassador: Warsaw, 1954–56; Mexico, 1956–60; Netherlands, 1960–64, retired. *Publications:* (jt author) Centenary History, OURFC, 1969; History of the Nobles of Ardmore and of Ardkinglas, 1971. *Heir:* *s* Iain Andrew Noble, *b* 8 Sept. 1935. *Address:* 11 Cedar House, Marloes Road, W8 5LA. *T:* 01–937 7952. *Club:* Boodle's. *Died 30 April 1987.*

**NOBLE, Col Sir Arthur,** KBE 1972; CB 1965; DSO 1943; TD; DL; Deputy Chairman, W. & C. French Ltd, 1966–68 (Director, 1953–68); President, Harlow and District Sports Trust, 1976 (Chairman, 1957–76); *b* 13 Sept. 1908; *s* of F. M. Noble, Chipping Ongar, Essex; *m* 1935, Irene Susan, OBE 1970, JP, *d* of J. D. Taylor, Wimbledon; three *s* two *d*. *Educ:* Felsted School. Chartered Quantity Surveyor, 1934; joined W. & C. French Ltd, 1945. Essex Regt (Territorial Army), 1927; Served Middle East and Italy, 1939–45; Commanded 4th Essex, 1941–44 and 1947–51; Chief Instructor, Sch. of Infantry, 1944–45. Hon. Col, TA and T&AVR Bn, The Essex Regt, 1955–71; a Dep. Hon. Col, The Royal Anglian Regt

(Essex), T&AVR, 1971–73. Chm. Essex County Playing Fields Assoc., 1956–61; Chm., County of Essex T&AF Assoc., 1958–66; Vice-Chm., Council of TA&VRA, 1966–72. Mem. of Council, Federation of Civil Engineering Contractors, 1963–68. Mem., Eastern Sports Council, 1966–72; Vice-Pres., Nat. Playing Fields Assoc., 1977; Pres., Essex County AAA, 1981. Governor, Chigwell Sch. DL (Essex) 1946. *Recreations:* many. *Address:* Marchings, Chigwell, Essex IG7 6DQ. *Club:* Army and Navy.

*Died 26 Feb.* 1982.

**NOBLE, Michael Alfred, (Mike);** *b* 10 March 1935; *s* of Alfred and Olive Noble; *m* 1956, Brenda Kathleen Peak; one *s* two *d. Educ:* Hull Grammar Sch.; Sheffield Univ. (BA); Hull Univ. (DipEd). Secondary Sch. Teacher, Hull, 1959–63; WEA Tutor in Industrial Relations, 1963–73; Consultant in Industrial Relations and Trng, 1973–74. MP (Lab) Rossendale, Oct. 1974–1979; PPS to Sec. for Prices and Consumer Protection, 1976–79. *Recreations:* golf, fishing, reading. *Address:* 10 Kingsway, Hapton, Burnley, Lancs. *T:* Padiham 74416. *Club:* Workingmen's (Ramsbottom).

*Died 12 March* 1983.

**NOBLE, Sir Peter (Scott),** Kt 1967; Principal of King's College, University of London, 1952–July 1968; *b* 17 Oct. 1899; *s* of Andrew Noble and Margaret Trail; *m* 1928, Mary Stephen (*d* 1983); two *s* one *d. Educ:* Aberdeen Univ.; St John's Coll., Cambridge. First Bursar at Aberdeen Univ., 1916, MA, with 1st Class Honours in Classics 1921, Simpson Prize and Robbie Gold Medal in Greek, Seafield Medal and Dr Black prize in Latin, Jenkyns Prize in Comparative Philology, Liddell Prize in Greek Verse, Fullerton Scholarship in Classics, 1921, Croom Robertson Fellow (1923–26); Scholar of St John's Coll., Cambridge; 1st class Classical Tripos Part I (1922) Part II (1923), 1st Class Oriental Langs Tripos Part I (1924) Part II (1925), Bendall Sanskrit Exhibition (1924), (1925), Hutchison Student (1925); Lecturer in Latin at Liverpool Univ., 1926–30; Professor of Latin Language and Literature in the University of Leeds, 1930–37; Fellow of St John's Coll., Cambridge, 1928–31; Regius Professor of Humanity, University of Aberdeen, 1938–52; Member of University Grants Cttee, 1943–53; Vice-Chancellor, University of London, 1961–64; Member of General Dental Council, 1955; Member of Educational Trust, English-Speaking Union, 1958; Governor of St Thomas' Hospital, 1960. Hon. LLD Aberdeen, 1955. *Publications:* Joint editor of Kharosthi Inscriptions Vol. III; reviews, etc, classical journals. *Address:* 17 Glenorchy Terrace, Edinburgh EH9 2DQ.

*Died 12 May* 1987.

**NOBLE, Robert More Hilary;** a Recorder of the Crown Court 1972–82; Chairman: National Health Service Tribunal for England and Wales, 1970–83; West Sussex Supplementary Benefits Appeal Tribunal, 1970–82; Industrial Tribunals, 1975–82 (part-time); *b* 23 Aug. 1909; *s* of late Mr Justice Noble, KCSG, Colonial Legal Service, and of late Mrs Robert Noble; *m* 1936, Faith (*née* Varley); two *s* three *d* (and one *d* decd). *Educ:* Beaumont Coll.; Balliol Coll. (BA Hons). Admitted Solicitor, 1934. Served War, 1939–45: Commissioned RAFVR, Air Force Dept of Judge Advocate General's Office, France and Middle East, also Accidents Investigation Br., 1940–41, ranks Sqdn Ldr, Actg Wing Comdr. Partner: Underwood & Co., 1946–59; Vernor Miles & Noble, 1959–70 (both of London). Trustee of a number of Charitable Trusts (concerned with educn and the disabled); Chm., Possum Controls Ltd. *Address:* 15 Warwick Gardens, W14 8PH.

*Died 4 Jan.* 1984.

**NOCK, Rt. Rev. Frank Foley,** DD; *b* 27 Feb. 1916; *s* of David Nock and Esther Maddams; *m* 1942, Elizabeth Hope Adams; one *s* one *d. Educ:* Trinity Coll., Toronto (BA, BD). Curate, St Matthew's, Toronto, 1940–42; Incumbent, Christ Church, Korah, Sault Ste Marie, 1942–45; Rector: Bracebridge, St Thomas', 1945–48; Church of the Epiphany, Sudbury, 1948–57; St Luke's Cathedral, 1957–74; Dean of Algoma, 1957–74; Bishop of Algoma, 1975–83; Priest in Charge, St John the Divine, Arva, Ont, 1983–86. Chancellor, Thorneloe Univ., Sudbury, 1974–83; Director: Sault Ste Marie & Dist Gp Health Assoc.; Community Concerts Assoc.; Mem., Sault Ste Marie Rotary Club. Hon. DD Toronto, 1957; Hon. STD Thorneloe, 1980. *Recreations:* music, golfing, cross country skiing. *Address:* 1220 Royal York Road, Unit 45, London, Ont N6H 3Z9, Canada. *Died 17 Aug.* 1989.

**NOCK, Sir Norman (Lindfield),** Kt 1939; Director, Nock & Kirby Holdings Ltd, Sydney (Chairman, 1926–79); *b* 11 April 1899; *s* of Thomas Nock, Stanhope Road, Killara, Sydney; *m* 1927, Ethel Evelina Bradford; one *s. Educ:* Sydney Church of England Grammar Sch. Alderman for Gipps Ward, City of Sydney, 1933–41; Lord Mayor of Sydney, 1938–39; Chairman, Federal Australian Comforts Fund, 1939–43; Chairman, Australian Comforts Fund, NSW Division, 1939–45; President of the National Roads and Motorists Association, 1954–69; Chairman Royal North Shore Hospital of Sydney, 1940–69; Member National Health and Medical Research Council, 1946–69. JP for New South Wales. *Recreations:* golf, sailing

and motoring. *Address:* Keera, Cullens Road, Kincumber, NSW 2250, Australia. *Club:* Royal Sydney Golf (Sydney).

*Died June* 1990.

**NOCKOLDS, Stephen Robert,** FRS 1959; PhD; Reader in Geochemistry in the University of Cambridge, 1957–72, now Emeritus Reader; *b* 10 May 1909; *s* of Dr Stephen and Hilda May Nockolds; *m* 1st, 1932, Hilda Jackson (*d* 1976); 2nd, 1978, Patricia, *d* of late Flying Officer F. Horsley; one step *s* two step *d. Educ:* Felsted; University of Manchester (BSc); University of Cambridge (PhD). Fellow of Trinity Coll. and formerly Lectr in Petrology, Univ. of Cambridge. Murchison Medal, Geol Soc., 1972. Hon. Fellow, Geol. Soc. of India. *Publications:* (jtly) Petrology for Students, 1978; various papers in mineralogical and geological journals. *Recreation:* gardening. *Address:* Elm Lodge, Station Road, Keyingham, North Humberside HU12 9TB.

*Died 7 Feb.* 1990.

**NOËL, Sir (Martial Ernest) Claude,** Kt 1976; CMG 1973; Director and Chairman of sugar and other companies; *b* 1 Feb. 1912; *m* 1937, Hélène Fromet de Rosnay; three *s* three *d. Educ:* College du St Esprit, Mauritius. Maths teacher, 1930; joined sugar industry, 1931; Manager sugar estate, 1939–. Chairman: Central Cttee of Estate Managers on several occasions; Mauritius Sugar Producers; Mauritius Employers Fedn, 1962–63. Membre d'Honneur, Mauritius Chamber of Agriculture, 1980 (Chm., 1971–72, Pres., 1974–). Citoyen d'Honneur Escalier Village. *Address:* Floréal, Mauritius. *T:* Curepipe 2235. *Clubs:* Dodo, Mauritius Turf (Mauritius). *Died 17 Oct.* 1985.

**NOEL-BAKER,** Baron *cr* 1977 (Life Peer), of the City of Derby; **Philip John Noel-Baker,** PC 1945; *b* Nov. 1889; *s* of late J. Allen Baker, MP; *m* 1915, Irene (*d* 1956), *o d* of Frank Noel, British landowner, of Achmetaga, Greece; one *s. Educ:* Bootham School, York; Haverford Coll., Pa; King's Coll., Cambridge, MA. Historical Tripos, Part I, Class II, 1910; Economics Tripos, Part II, Class I, 1912; University Whewell Scholar, 1911 (continued, 1913); President CUAC, 1910–12; President Cambridge Union Society, 1912; Vice-Principal, Ruskin Coll., Oxford, 1914; First Commandant Friend's Ambulance Unit, Aug. 1914–July 1915; Officer First British Ambulance Unit for Italy, 1915–18; Mons Star; Silver Medal for Military Valour (Italy), 1917; Croce di Guerra, 1918; League of Nations Section of British Delegation during Peace Conference, 1919; League of Nations Secretariat till 1922; contested (Lab) Handsworth Division of Birmingham, 1924; MP (Lab), for Coventry, 1929–31, for Derby, 1936–50, for Derby South, 1950–70; PPS to the Sec. of State for Foreign Affairs, 1929–31; Parly Sec. to Min. of War Transport, 1942–45; Minister of State, FO, 1945–46; Sec. of State for Air, 1946–47; Sec. of State for Commonwealth Relations, 1947–50; Minister of Fuel and Power, 1050–51. Chairman, Foreign Affairs Group, Parly Labour Party, 1964–70. Late Fellow, King's Coll., Cambridge; Hon. Fellow, 1961–; Sir Ernest Cassel Prof. of International Relations in the Univ. of London, 1924–29; Member of British Delegation to the 10th Assembly of the League of Nations, 1929 and 1930; Principal Asst to the Pres. of the Disarmament Conference at Geneva, 1932–33; British Delegate to UN Preparatory Commn, 1945; Mem., British Delegn to Gen. Assembly of UN, 1946–47; Delegate to Colombo Conf. on Economic Aid, 1950. Pres., Internat Council on Sport and Physical Recreation, UNESCO, 1960–76. Dodge Lectr, Yale Univ., 1934; Howland Prize for distinguished work in the sphere of Government, Yale Univ., 1934; Nobel Peace Prize, 1959; Albert Schweitzer Book Prize, 1960; Olympia Diploma of Merit, 1975. Officer, Legion of Honour, 1976; Papal Knight, Order of St Sylvester, 1977. Hon. Degrees: Birmingham Univ.; Nottingham Univ.; Manchester Univ.; Univ. of Colombo; Queen's Univ., Ontario; Haverford Coll., USA; Brandeis Univ., USA; Loughborough Univ. *Publications:* The Geneva Protocol, 1925; Disarmament, 1926; The League of Nations at Work, 1926; Disarmament and the Coolidge Conference, 1927; J. Allen Baker, MP, a Memoir (with E. B. Baker); The Juridical Status of the British Dominions in International Law 1929; The Private Manufacture of Armaments, Vol I, 1936; The Arms Race: A Programme for World Disarmament, 1958; pamphlets and articles. *Address:* 16 South Eaton Place, SW1. *T:* 01–730 5377.

*Died 8 Oct.* 1982.

**NOONE, Dr Paul;** Consultant Medical Microbiologist, Royal Free Hospital, NW3, since 1972; *b* 4 March 1939; *s* of Michael John Noone and Florence Miriam Noone (*née* Knox); *m* 1st, 1963, Ahilya Nehaul (marr. diss.); two *s;* 2nd, 1982, Malila Perera (*née* Tambimuttu); one step *s* three step *d. Educ:* Darlington Grammar Sch.; Christ Church, Oxford (BA, 1st Class Hons Animal Physiology, 1960; BM BCh, 1965); Middlesex Hosp. Med. Sch. FRCPath 1983 (MRCPath 1971). Various house officer jobs in London; Lectr in Pathology, Bland Sutton Inst. of Pathology, 1967; Sen. Registrar in Bacteriology, Central Middx Hosp., 1969; Lectr in Bacteriology, Middx Hosp., 1970. Specialises in diagnosis and management of infection, especially treatment of life-threatening hospital-acquired infection; lectures extensively on various aspects of antibiotics and infection throughout Britain, also Europe, USA, Saudi Arabia, Sri Lanka, Thailand, Malaysia, Indonesia, Turkey, Australia and Hong Kong. Engaged in junior hospital doctors' campaign for improved conditions and trng; Mem., ASTMS delegn to TUC Annual Congress, 1971 and 1972. Founder, 1977, and Chm. 1978–88, NHS Consultants Assoc. *Publications:* A Clinician's Guide to Antibiotic Therapy, 1977, 2nd edn 1979 (also Italian edn 1978, Spanish 1983); Some Poems: 1958–1982, 1983; over 120 articles in Lancet, BMJ and many other specialist medical jls on antibiotics, infections and related subjects. *Recreations:* spending time with family and friends. *Address:* 39 Wykeham Hill, Wembley, Middx HA9 9RY.                                                    *Died 19 Feb.* 1989.

**NORDMEYER, Hon. Sir Arnold (Henry),** ONZ 1987; KCMG 1975 (CMG 1970); JP; Leader of the Opposition (Labour), New Zealand, 1963–65; *b* Dunedin, New Zealand, 7 Feb. 1901; *s* of Arnold and Martha Nordmeyer; *m* 1931, Frances Maria Kernahan; one *s* one *d. Educ:* Waitaki Boys' High Sch.; Otago Univ. (BA, DipSocSci.). Presbyterian Minister for 10 years. Entered New Zealand Parliament, 1935; MP for Oamaru, 1935–49, for Brooklyn, 1951–54, for Island Bay, 1954–69; Minister of: Health, 1941–47; Industries and Commerce, 1947–49; Finance, 1957–60. JP 1970. Hon. LLD Otago, 1970. *Recreations:* shooting, fishing. *Address:* 53 Milne Terrace, Wellington, New Zealand.                                *Died 2 Feb.* 1989.

**NÖRLUND, Niels Erik,** PhD (Copenhagen), Hon. DSc (London), Hon. DEng (Darmstadt); Hon. PhD (Lund); Hon. DSc (Dijon); Hon. PhD (Oslo); Hon. DASc (Copenhagen); Formerly Professor of Mathematics in University of Copenhagen; Director Danish Geodetic Institute; Editor Acta Mathematica; *b* Slagelse, Denmark, 26 Oct. 1885; *m* 1912, Agnete Weaver (*d* 1959); two *d. Educ:* University of Copenhagen, Paris and Cambridge. Formerly Pres., International Council of Scientific Unions; Formerly Pres. Rask-Örsted Foundation; lately Pres., Royal Danish Academy of Science; formerly Pres. Baltic Geodetic Commission; formerly Rector of Univ. of Copenhagen; Foreign Mem. Royal Soc., Royal Astronomical Soc., Acad. Science Paris, Rome, Stockholm, Oslo, Helsingfors, Uppsala and Naples; Hon. Member Royal Institution, London. *Publications:* Vorlesungen über Differenzenrechnung (Berlin), 1924; Leçons sur les Séries d'interpolation (Paris), 1926; Sur la somme d'une fonction (Paris), 1927; Leçons sur les équations aux différences finies (Paris), 1929; The map of Iceland (Copenhagen) 1944. *Address:* Copenhagen, Breeltvej 1, 2970 Hörsholm, Denmark.                                        *Died 4 July* 1981.

**NORMAN, Sir Edward (James),** Kt 1958; Chief Inspector of Taxes, 1956–64, retired; *b* Bridport, Dorset, 8 Jan. 1900; *s* of Edward Robert Norman; *m* 1923, Lilian May Sly (*d* 1974); three *d. Educ:* Weymouth Grammar Sch. Entered Inland Revenue Department, 1917; Assistant Inspector of Taxes, 1920; Principal Inspector, Somerset House, 1947; Assistant Secretary, Board of Inland Revenue, 1948; Dep. Chief Inspector of Taxes, 1950–55. Member, and later Dep. Chm., Housing Corporation, 1964–69. Financial Advr, 1964–72, Indep. Chm., Building & Civil Engineering Holidays Scheme Management Ltd, 1972–78, Benefits Scheme Trustee Ltd, 1975–78. *Address:* Bourn Cottage, Westhumble, Dorking, Surrey.
                                                                        *Died 28 June* 1983.

**NORMAN, Rt. Rev. Edward Kinsella,** KBE 1984; DSO 1945; MC 1943; Assistant Bishop, Diocese of Lichfield, since 1986; *b* 1916; *m* 1941, Margaret Edith Wilson; four *d. Educ:* Univ. of New Zealand (BA 1939); St John's Coll., Auckland; Westcott House, Cambridge. Served War of 1939–45 (despatches, MC, DSO). Deacon 1947, priest 1948, Newcastle upon Tyne; Curate of Berwick-on-Tweed, 1947–49; Vicar of Waiwhetu, 1949–52; Levin, 1952–59; Tauranga, 1959–65; Karori, 1965–73; Chaplain to Samuel Marsden Coll. Sch., 1965–73; Chaplain to RNZNVR, 1966–73; Archdeacon of Wellington, 1969–73; Bishop of Wellington, 1973–86; Senior Anglican Chaplain to NZ Forces, 1979–86. Legion of Merit (US), 1945. *Address:* 14 The Close, Lichfield, Staffs WS13 7LD. *Clubs:* Wellington, United Services Officers' (Wellington).
                                                                        *Died 8 March* 1987.

**NORMAN-WALKER, Sir Hugh (Selby),** KCMG 1966 (CMG 1964); OBE 1961; *b* 17 Dec. 1916; *s* of late Colonel J. N. Norman-Walker, CIE; *m* 1948, Janet Baldock; no *c. Educ:* Sherborne; Corpus Christi Coll., Cambridge. MA. Indian Civil Service, 1938–48; Colonial Administrative Service, 1949; Development Secretary, Nyasaland, 1954; Secretary to the Treasury, Nyasaland, 1960–64, Malawi, 1964–65; HM Commissioner, Bechuanaland, 1965–66; Governor and C-in-C, Seychelles, and Comr, British Indian Ocean Territory, 1967–69; Colonial Sec., Hong Kong, 1969–74. KStJ 1967. *Recreations:* sailing, shooting, bridge. *Address:* Houndwood, Farley, Wilts SP5 1AN. *Clubs:* East India, Devonshire, Sports and Public Schools, etc.                                        *Died 28 Aug.* 1985.

**NORMAND, Sir Charles William Blyth,** Kt 1945; CIE 1938; MA, DSc; *b* 10 Sept. 1889; *m* 1920, Alison MacLennan (*d* 1953); one *s* (and one *s* decd). *Educ:* Royal High School and University,

Edinburgh. Research Scholar at Edinburgh, 1911–13; Imperial Meteorologist, Simla, India, 1913–15 and 1919–27; joined IARO and served in Mesopotamia, 1916–19 (despatches 1917); Director-General of Observatories in India, 1927–44; Pres., Maths Phys Sect., Indian Sci. Congress, 1931, 1938; on special duty with Govt of India, 1944–45. Member, Met. Research Cttee, Air Ministry, 1945–58, Chairman, 1955–58; Secretary International Ozone Commn, 1948–59. Royal Meteorological Society: Hon. Fellow; Pres., 1951–53; Symons Gold Medal, 1944; Founder Fellow, Indian Nat. Sci. Acad., 1935; Hon. Mem., Amer. Met. Soc. *Publications:* articles, mainly on meteorological subjects, in scientific journals. *Address:* 23 St Thomas' Street, Winchester, Hants. *T:* Winchester 2550.                                                    *Died 25 Oct.* 1982.

**NORRINGTON, Sir Arthur (Lionel Pugh),** Kt 1968; MA; JP; President of Trinity College, Oxford, 1954–70; Vice-Chancellor, Oxford University, 1960–62; Warden of Winchester College, 1970–74; *b* 27 Oct. 1899; *o s* of late Arthur James Norrington; *m* 1st, 1928, Edith Joyce (*d* 1964), *d* of William Moberly Carver; two *s* two *d*; 2nd, 1969, Mrs Ruth Margaret Waterlow, *widow* of Rupert Waterlow, and *y d* of Edmund Cude. *Educ:* Winchester; Trinity Coll., Oxford (Scholar). Served in RFA, 1918. Joined Oxford University Press, 1923. Secretary to Delegates of Oxford University Press, 1948–54. Chm., Adv. Cttee on the Selection of Low-priced Books for Overseas, 1960–. JP City of Oxford. Hon. Fellow, Trinity, St Cross and Wolfson Colleges. Officier de la Légion d'Honneur, 1962. *Publication:* (with H. F. Lowry and F. L. Mulhauser), The Poems of A. H. Clough, 1951. *Recreations:* music, gardening. *Address:* Grenville Manor, Haddenham, Bucks; 3 Beach Cottages, Fishguard. *Club:* United Oxford & Cambridge University.
                                                                        *Died 21 May* 1982.

**NORRIS, Dame Ada (May),** DBE 1976 (OBE 1954); CMG 1969; *b* 28 July 1901; *d* of Allan Herbert Bickford and Alice Hannah (*née* Baggs); *m* 1929, Hon. Sir John Gerald Norris, ED; two *d. Educ:* Melbourne High Sch.; Melbourne Univ. (MA, DipEd). Teacher, 1925–29. Vice-Chm., Victorian Council on the Ageing, 1951–80; Member-at-Large, Aust. Council on the Ageing; Vice-Pres., Victorian Soc. for Crippled Children and Adults, 1951–; President: Australian Adv. Council for the Physically Handicapped, 1955–57; Children's Book Council of Victoria, 1954–60, of Aust., 1960; Member: Commonwealth Immigration Adv. Council, 1950–71 (Dep. Chm., 1968–71); Exec. Cttee, Internat. Council of Women, 1950–79; Life-Vice-Pres., Nat. Council of Women of Australia (Pres., 1967–70); Chairman: Nat. Cttee for Internat. Women's Year, 1974–76; UNAA Nat. Cttee for Status of Women and Decade for Women, 1976–; Mem. Exec. Cttee, Melbourne Internat. Centenary Exhbn 1980, 1979–. Australian Rep., UN Commn on Status of Women, 1961–63. Chm., Appeal Cttee, Hall of Residence for Women Students, Univ. of Papua New Guinea, 1969–73. Hon. LLD Melbourne, 1980. UN Peace Medal, 1975. *Publications:* The Society: history of the Victorian Society for Crippled Children and Adults, 1974; Champions of the Impossible, 1978; papers on status of women and social welfare matters. *Recreations:* gardening, travel. *Address:* 10 Winifred Crescent, Toorak, Vic 3142, Australia. *T:* Melbourne (03) 2415166.                                *Died 10 July* 1989.

**NORRIS, Alan Hedley;** Chairman, North Eastern Electricity Board, 1969–77 (Deputy Chairman, 1968–69); *b* 15 July 1913; *s* of Hedley Faithfull Norris, Solicitor; *m* 1941, Rachel Mary Earle; one *s* two *d. Educ:* Bradfield; Clare Coll., Cambridge. Served with RAF, 1940–45. HM Inspector of Factories, 1937–46; Min. of Power: Asst Principal, 1946–48; Principal, 1948–52; Asst Secretary, 1952–65; Under Secretary, 1965–68. *Recreation:* fishing. *Address:* Ednam East Mill, Kelso, Roxburghshire. *T:* Kelso 2000. *Club:* Flyfishers'.
                                                                        *Died 8 Jan.* 1981.

**NORRIS, Sir Alfred (Henry),** KBE 1961 (OBE 1950; MBE 1938); *b* 27 April 1894; *s* of late Alfred James Norris, Hornchurch, Essex, and Charlotte Norris; *m* 1925, Betty K. R. Davidson (decd); *m* 1936, Winifred Gladys, *d* of late Archibald Henry Butler; three *s. Educ:* Cranbrook Sch., Kent. Served War of 1914–18, King's Own Royal (Lancaster) Regt. Retired Company Director and Chartered Accountant; formerly of Brazil. *Recreations:* social work, gardening. *Address:* 11 Abbey Close, Elmbridge, Cranleigh, Surrey. *Clubs:* Canning; Royal British (Lisbon).                        *Died 2 Aug.* 1989.

**NORRIS, Vice-Adm. Sir Charles (Fred Wivell),** KBE 1956; CB 1952; DSO 1944; *b* 16 Dec. 1900; *s* of Charles H. Norris and Gertrude Norris; *m* 1924, Violet Cremer (*d* 1987); one *s. Educ:* RNC Osborne and Dartmouth. Comdr, 1934; RN Staff Course, 1935; commanded HMS Aberdeen, 1936–39; Captain, 1941; commanded HMS Bellona, 1943–45; commanded HMS Dryad (Navigation and Direction School), 1945–46; Imperial Defence Coll., 1947; Captain of the Fleet, Home Fleet, 1948–50; Rear-Admiral, 1950; Director of Naval Training, and Deputy Chief of Naval Personnel, 1950–52; Vice-Admiral, 1953; Flag Officer (Flotilla), Mediterranean, 1953–54. Commander-in-Chief, East Indies Station, 1954–56, retired, 1956. Director of the British Productivity Council, 1957–65.

*Address:* Clouds, 56 Shepherds Way, Liphook, Hants GU30 7HH. *T:* Liphook 722456. *Died* 17 Dec. 1989.

**NORRIS, Maj.-Gen. Sir (Frank) Kingsley,** KBE 1957 (CBE 1943); CB 1953; DSO; ED; MD; Hon. Consultant Pædiatrician, Alfred Hospital, Melbourne, since 1948; *b* 25 June 1893; *s* of Dr W. Perrin Norris; *m* 1920, Dorothy Leonard Stevenson; two *d*. *Educ:* Melbourne Church of England Grammar Sch.; Trinity Coll., Melbourne Univ. Served War of 1914–18, Australian Imperial Forces, ME; CO 1 CCS, AIF, 1939; ADMS 7 Australian Div. AIF, 1940–43; DDMS 1 Australian Corps AIF, 1943; Service in Middle East, Libya, 1940; Palestine 1941; Syria, 1941; Java, 1942; New Guinea, 1942–44; Korea, 1951–53. DGMS Commonwealth Military Forces, 1948–55; President: Royal Empire Soc., Vic. Br., 1948–54; BMA, Vic. Br., 1947; Good Neighbour Council, Vic., 1958–63; Alcoholic Foundn of Vic., 1961–68. Comr St John's Ambulance Bde, 1956, Chief Comr, 1963–; Chief Comr, Priory of St John Ambulance in Australia. Medical Adviser, Civil Defence, Australia, 1956–61. KStJ 1961 CStJ 1959). KHP 1948; QPH 1953–55. *Publications:* The Syrian Campaign, 1944; The New Guinea Campaign, 1946; Major-General Sir Neville Howse, VC, 1965; No Memory for Pain (autobiography), 1970; various papers to medical journals. *Recreations:* bridge, chess, golf, model-ship building, cooking. *Address:* 69 Broadway, Camberwell, Victoria 3124, Australia. *Clubs:* MCC; Beefsteak, Melbourne, Naval and Military (Melbourne). *Died* 4 May 1984.

**NORRIS, Hon. Sir John (Gerald),** Kt 1982; ED 1945; Judge of the Supreme Court of Victoria, 1972–75, retired; *b* 12 June 1903; *s* of John Alexander Norris, CMG and Mary Ellen (*née* Heffernan); *m* 1929, Ada May Bickford (Dame Ada Norris, DBE, CMG) (*d* 1989); two *d*. *Educ:* Camberwell State Sch.; Melbourne High Sch.; Univ. of Melbourne (LLM; (jtly) Supreme Court Prize, 1924). Called to the Victorian Bar, 1925; KC 1950. Served War, 1939–45: Australia and New Guinea; Lt-Col. Actg County Court Judge, 1950; County Court Judge, 1955–72; Actg Supreme Court Judge for periods during 1968–72. Royal Comr on admin of law relating to prostitution in WA, 1975–76; Chm., Victorian Govt Cttee to consider recommendations of Bd of Inquiry into allegations against Victorian Police, 1976–78; reviewed law relating to coroners for Victorian Govt, 1979–80; conducted inquiry into concentration of ownership and control of press in Vic, 1980–81. Univ. of Melbourne: Lectr in Commercial Law, 1932–52; Mem., Standing Cttee of Convocation, 1952–62; Warden of Convocation, 1962–65; Mem. Council, 1965–81. Chm., Sir Edmund Herring Meml Cttee, 1983–87. Pres., Baden Powell Scout Guild of Australia, 1979–81. Hon. Col, 4th/19th Prince of Wales's Light Horse, 1964–72; Patron, Vic Br., Royal Aust. Armoured Corps Assoc., 1975–. Hon. LLD Melb., 1980. *Publications:* The Financial Emergency Acts, 1932; articles in legal jls. *Recreations:* gardening, walking, reading. *Address:* 459 The Boulevard, East Ivanhoe, Vic 3079, Australia. *Clubs:* Australian, Royal Automobile of Victoria (Melbourne); Toorak Services. *Died* 21 May 1990.

**NORRIS, Maj.-Gen. Sir Kingsley;** *see* Norris, Maj.-Gen. Sir F. K.

**NORSTAD, Gen. Lauris,** DSM (US) with Oak Leaf Cluster and Silver Star; Legion of Merit (US) with Cluster; Air Medal; United States Air Forces, retired; Hon. Chairman (formerly Chairman and Chief Executive Officer, 1967–72), Owens-Corning Fiberglas Corporation (President, Owens-Corning Fiberglas International, January-December 1963); *b* Minneapolis, USA, 24 March 1907; *s* of Martin Norstad; *m* 1935, Isabelle Helen Jenkins; one *d*. *Educ:* US Military Academy (BS). 2nd Lieut, Cavalry, 1930; graduated, Air Corps Sch., 1931. Served in various branches of Air Force; duty at GHQ Air Force, Langley Field, Va., 1940; Assistant Chief of Staff for Operations, 12th Air Force, 1942, served with 12th Air Force, England and Algiers; Director of Operations, Allied Air Forces, Mediterranean, Dec. 1943; Chief of Staff, 20th Air Force, Washington, 1944; Asst Chief of Staff for Plans, Army Air Force HQ, 1945; Director of Plans and Operations Div., War Dept, Washington, 1946; Dep. Chief of Staff for Operations, USAF, 1947; Acting Vice Chief of Staff, Air Force, May 1950; C-in-C US Air Forces in Europe and C-in-C Allied Air Forces Central Europe, 1951; Deputy (Air) to Supreme Allied Commander, Europe, 1953; C-in-C, US European Comd, 1956–62, and Supreme Allied Commander, Europe, 1956–62; retired, 1963. Has several hon. degrees. Hon. CBE (GB). Holds other foreign orders. *Address:* (business) 717 Fifth Avenue, New York, NY 10022, USA. *Died* 12 Sept. 1988.

**NORTH, Rt. Hon. Sir Alfred Kingsley,** PC 1966; KBE 1964; Kt 1959; Judge of the Court of Appeal, New Zealand, 1957–72 (President of the Court, 1963–72); first Chairman, New Zealand Press Council, 1972–78; *b* 17 Dec. 1900; *s* of late Rev. J. J. North, DD; *m* 1924, Thelma Grace Dawson; two *s* one *d*. *Educ:* Canterbury Coll., Christchurch, New Zealand (LLM). Was, for many years, in the legal firm of Earl Kent and Co., Auckland, New Zealand. One of HM Counsel (KC 1947); Judge of the Supreme Court of New Zealand, 1951–57. Past President Auckland Rotary Club; Past Chairman Auckland Branch of Crippled Children's Society, etc. Hon. Bencher, Gray's Inn. *Recreation:* trout-fishing. *Address:* 28 Mahoe Avenue, Remuera, Auckland, NZ. *Club:* Northern (Auckland, NZ). *Died* 22 June 1981.

**NORTH, Roger,** JP; a Recorder of the Crown Court, 1971–73; Chairman West Norfolk Valuation Panel, since 1949; *b* 10 Dec. 1901; *s* of F. K. North, Rougham Hall, King's Lynn, and Grace, *d* of Gen. Sir Percy Feilding; *m* 1934, Pamela Susan, *d* of Rev. H. W. L. O'Rorke, North Litchfield, Hants; one *s* three *d*. *Educ:* Eton; Trinity Coll., Cambridge. Called to the Bar, 1925. Began farming at Rougham, Norfolk, 1932. Dep. Chm., Norfolk QS, 1962–69 (apptd by Royal Warrant); Chm., King's Lynn QS, 1942–71. Late Chm. Tractor Users' Assoc. and Oxford Farming Conf. Cttee; Council Mem. Instn of Agricultural Engineers, 1954–58; Chm., Norfolk Br., Mathematical Assoc. JP Norfolk, 1941. *Publication:* The Art of Algebra, 1965. *Recreations:* veteran motor cars and mathematics. *Address:* Rougham Hall, Rougham, King's Lynn, Norfolk. *T:* Weasenham St Peter 230. *Clubs:* Royal Institution; Norfolk. *Died* 15 Dec. 1985.

**NORTHBOURNE, 4th Baron,** *cr* 1884; **Walter Ernest Christopher James,** Bt, 1791; *b* 1896; *o* surv. *s* of 3rd Baron and Laura Gwenllian (who *m* 2nd, 1935, William Curtis Green, RA; he *d* 1960), *d* of late Admiral Sir Ernest Rice, KCB; *S* father, 1932; *m* 1925, Katherine Nickerson (*d* 1980), *d* of Hon. Lady Hood, and late George A. Nickerson, Boston, Mass; one *s* four *d*. *Educ:* Eton; Magdalen Coll., Oxford. Chairman, Kent Agricultural Executive Cttee, 1946–57. Fellow, Wye Coll., 1967. *Publications:* Look to the Land, 1940; Religion in The Modern World, 1963; Looking Back on Progress, 1970. *Heir: s* Hon. Christopher George Walter James [*b* 18 Feb. 1926; *m* 1959, Marie Sygne, *e d* of M and Mme Henri Claudel; three *s* one *d*]. *Address:* Northbourne Court, Deal, Kent. *T:* Deal 4617. *Club:* Leander. *Died* 17 June 1982.

**NORTHBROOK, 5th Baron,** *cr* 1866; **Francis John Baring,** Bt 1793; DL; Chairman, Winchester District Health Authority, 1981–88; *b* 31 May 1915; *s* of 4th Baron Northbrook and Evelyn Gladys Isabel (*d* 1919), *d* of J. G. Charles; *S* father, 1947; *m* 1951, Rowena Margaret, 2nd *d* of late Brig-General Sir William Manning, and of Lady Manning, Hampton Court Palace; one *s* three *d*. *Educ:* Winchester; Trinity Coll., Oxford. Chm., Hants AHA, 1978–81. JP 1955, DL 1972, Hants. *Heir: s* Hon. Francis Thomas Baring [*b* 21 Feb. 1954; *m* 1987, Amelia, *er d* of Dr Reginald Taylor; one *d*]. *Address:* East Stratton House, East Stratton, Winchester, Hants. *Died* 4 Dec. 1990.

**NORTHCHURCH, Baroness** (Life Peer); *see under* Davidson, Dowager Viscountess.

**NORTHCOTE-GREEN, Roger James,** MC 1944; TD 1950 (Bar 1952); JP; Headmaster, Worksop College, Notts, 1952–70; *b* 25 July 1912; *s* of Rev. Edward Joseph Northcote-Green and Mary Louisa Catt; *m* 1947, Joan, *d* of Ernest Greswell and Grace Lillian (*née* Egerton); three *s* one *d*. *Educ:* St Edward's Sch. and The Queen's Coll., Oxford (MA). Served with Oxford and Bucks Light Infantry, 1939–44, in India and Burma; Staff Coll., Quetta, 1944–45; Bde Major, 53rd Ind. Inf. Bde, Malaya, 1945. Assistant Master, St Edward's Sch., 1936–39, 1946–52; Housemaster, 1947. Representative OURFC on RU Cttee, 1946–52. S Western Sec., Independent Schs Careers Orgn, 1970–77. JP Nottinghamshire, 1964. *Recreations:* gardening, poultry. *Address:* Manor Cottage, Woolston, Williton, Som. *T:* Williton 32445. *Clubs:* East India, Devonshire, Sports and Public Schools, MCC; Vincent's (Oxford). *Died* 19 Jan. 1990.

**NORTHCOTT, Rev. (William) Cecil,** MA; PhD; Churches Correspondent, Daily Telegraph, 1967–79; Editorial Secretary United Society for Christian Literature and Editor, Lutterworth Press, 1952–72; Editor-at-large, Christian Century of USA, 1945–70; *b* Buckfast, Devon, 5 April 1902; *s* of William Ashplant Northcott; *m* 1930, Jessie Morton, MA, 2nd *d* of J. L. Morton, MD, Hampstead and Colyford, Devon; one *s* one *d*. *Educ:* Hele's Sch., Exeter; Fitzwilliam Coll., and Cheshunt Coll., Cambridge. PhD London Univ. (School of Oriental and African Studies), 1961. Three years social work East End of London; Member Cambridge delegation to League of Nations, Geneva, 1926; Joint Proprietor and Editor The Granta, 1927–28; Congregational Church, St Helens, 1929–32; Minister Duckworth Street Congregational Church, Darwen, Lancs, 1932–35; Home Secretary and Literary Superintendent London Missionary Society, 1935–50; General Secretary and Editor United Council for Missionary Education (Edinburgh House Press), 1950–52; Chairman, London Missionary Society, 1954–55 (World Conferences, Amsterdam, 1948, Willingen, 1952, Evanston, 1954, New Delhi, 1961, Uppsala, 1968, Nairobi, 1975). Member, World Council of Churches Information Cttee, 1954–61; Member, British Council of Churches Christian Aid Cttee, 1946–64. Select Preacher, Cambridge, 1958; Danforth Foundation Lecturer, USA, 1961; Visiting Lecturer, Garrett Theological Seminary, USA, 1965, 1967,

1969, 1971. British Information Services, USA, 1944; editor, Congregational Monthly, 1953–58. Leverhulme Research Award, 1958. *Publications:* Time to Spare (Collab. BBC Talks), 1935; Southward Ho!, 1936; Guinea Gold, 1937; Who Claims the World?, 1938; John Williams Sails On, 1939; Change Here for Britain, 1942; Glorious Company, 1945; Whose Dominion?, 1946; Religious Liberty, 1948; Venturers of Faith, 1950; Voice Out of Africa, 1952; Robert Moffat: Pioneer in Africa, 1961; Christianity in Africa, 1963; David Livingstone: his triumph, decline and fall, 1973; Slavery's Martyr, 1976; ed Encyclopedia of the Bible for Children, 1964; People of the Bible, 1967. *Recreation:* old books. *Club:* Royal Commonwealth Society. *Died* 10 *Nov.* 1987.

**NORTHEDGE, Prof. Frederick Samuel;** Professor of International Relations, London School of Economics and Political Science, University of London, since 1968; *b* 16 Oct. 1918; *s* of William and Alice Northedge; *m* 1939, Betty Cynthia Earnshaw (*d* 1984); two *s* one *d*; *m* 1984, Muriel Grove. *Educ:* Bemrose Sch., Derby; Merton Coll., Oxford; Univ. of Nottingham; LSE. BSc (Econ) 1st class, PhD, DSc (Econ), London. London School of Economics: Asst Lectr in Internat. Relations, 1949–52; Lectr, 1952–60; Reader, 1960–68; Convener, Dept of Internat. Relations, 1969–72, 1975–78 and 1981–84. Vis. Prof., Makerere Univ., Uganda, 1965. *Publications:* British Foreign Policy: the process of readjustment, 1945–1961, 1962; The Troubled Giant: Britain among the Great Powers, 1916–1939, 1966; (ed) The Foreign Policies of the Powers, 1968, 2nd edn, 1974; (jtly) A Hundred Years of International Relations, 1971; (jtly) International Disputes: the Political Aspects, 1971; Order and the System of International Relations, 1971; Freedom and Necessity in British Foreign Policy, 1972; East-West Relations: Détente and After, 1973; Descent from Power: British foreign policy, 1945–1973, 1974; (ed) The Use of Force in International Relations, 1974; The International Political System, 1976; Britain and Soviet Communism, 1982; articles and reviews in acad. jls on politics and internat. affairs. *Recreations:* talking, music, drinking wine. *Address:* 21 Marlborough Road, Chiswick, W4. *T:* 01–995 3171. *Died* 3 *March* 1985.

**NORTHROP, John Howard;** Member Rockefeller University (formerly Institute), 1924, Emeritus 1962; Visiting Professor of Bacteriology, University of California, 1949, Emeritus, 1959; Professor Biophysics, 1958, Emeritus 1959; Research Biophysicist, Donner Laboratory, 1958; *b* Yonkers, NY, 5 July 1891; *s* of Dr John I. Northrop, of Department of Zoology, Columbia Univ., and Alice Rich Northrop, of Dept of Botany, Hunter Coll., NY City; *m* 1917, Louise Walker, NY City; one *s* one *d*. *Educ:* Columbia Univ. BS 1912; AM 1913; PhD 1915; W. B. Cutting Travelling Fellow, Columbia Univ. (year in Jacques Loeb's laboratory at Rockefeller Inst.), 1915; on staff of Rockefeller Inst. 1916; Member, 1924; Stevens prize, Coll. of Physicians and Surgeons, Columbia Univ., 1931; Captain, Chemical Warfare Service, 1917–18; discovered and worked on fermentation process for manufacturing acetone; ScD Harvard 1936, Columbia 1937, Yale 1937, Princeton 1940, Rutgers 1941; LLD, University of California, 1939; Chandler Medal, Columbia Univ., 1937; DeLamar Lectr, Sch. of Hygiene and Public Health, Johns Hopkins, 1937; Jesup Lectr, Columbia Univ., 1938; Hitchcock Lectr, Univ. of California, 1939; Thayer Lectr, Johns Hopkins, 1940; Daniel Giraud Elliot Medal for 1939 of National Acad. of Science, 1944; Consultant, OSRD, 1941–45. Shared Nobel Prize in Chemistry, 1946. Certificate of Merit, USA, 1948. Alex. Hamilton Medal, Columbia Univ., 1961. Member: Sons of the American Revolution; Delta Kappa Epsilon fraternity, Sigma Xi, Phi Lambda Upsilon; American Society of Biological Chemists; National Acad. of Sciences, Halle Akademie der Naturforscher; Société Philomathique (Paris); American Philosophical Society; Society of General Physiologists; Chemical Society (Hon. Fellow); Fellow World Academy; Benjamin Franklin Fellow, RSA. *Publications:* Crystalline Enzymes, 1939; numerous papers on physical chemistry of proteins, agglutination of bacteria, kinetics of enzyme reactions, and isolation and chemical nature of enzymes; editorial board of Journal of General Physiology, Experimental Biology Monographs; Contrib. Editor, Funk & Wagnell's Encyclopedia. *Recreations:* field shooting, salmon fishing. *Address:* PO Box 1387, Wickenburg, Arizona 85358, USA. *Club:* Century Association (New York). *Died* 27 *May* 1987.

**NORTHUMBERLAND, 10th Duke of,** *cr* 1766; **Hugh Algernon Percy,** KG 1959; GCVO 1981; TD 1961; PC 1973; JP; FRS 1970; Earl of Northumberland, Baron Warkworth, 1749; Earl Percy, 1776; Earl of Beverly, 1790; Lord Lovaine, Baron of Alnwick, 1784; Bt, *cr* 1660; Baron Percy (by writ), 1722; Lord Steward of HM Household, since 1973; Lord-Lieutenant and Custos Rotulorum of Northumberland 1956–84; Chancellor of University of Newcastle since 1964; *b* 6 April 1914; 2nd *s* of 8th Duke of Northumberland, KG, CBE, MVO (*d* 1930), and Lady Helen Gordon-Lennox (Helen, Dowager Duchess of Northumberland, who *d* 1965), *y d* of 7th Duke of Richmond and Gordon; *S* brother (killed in action), 1940; *m* 1946, Lady Elizabeth Diana Montagu-Douglas-Scott, *er d* of 8th Duke of Buccleuch and Queensberry, KT, PC, GCVO; three *s* three

*d. Educ:* Eton; Oxford. Lieut, Northumberland Hussars, 1936; RA, 1940; Captain, 1941; Captain, Northumberland Hussars, 1947; TARO, 1949–64; Chm., T&AFA, 1950–56; Pres., Northumberland T&AFA, 1956–68; Pres., TA&VR Assoc. for North of England, 1968–71; Hon. Colonel: 7th Bn, Royal Northumberland Fusiliers, 1948–70; The Northumbrian Volunteers, 1971–75; 6th (V) Bn, Royal Regt of Fusiliers, T&AVR, 1975–. A Lord in Waiting, May-July 1945. Mem., Northumberland CC, 1944–55, Alderman, 1955–67. President: Northern Area, British Legion; Northumberland Boy Scouts' Assoc., 1946–; Northumb. Assoc. of Boys' Clubs, 1942–; British Horse Soc., 1950; North of England Shipowners' Assoc., 1952–78; Hunters Improvement and Light Horse Breeding Soc., 1954; Royal Agricultural Soc. of England, 1956, 1962; BSJA, 1959; The Wildfowl Trust, 1968–72. Chairman: Departmental Cttee on Slaughter of Horses, 1952; Court of Durham Univ., 1956–64; Border Forest Park Cttee, 1956–68; ARC, 1958–68; Departmental Cttee for Recruitment of Veterinary Surgeons, 1964; Cttee of Enquiry on Foot-and-Mouth Disease, 1968–69; MRC, 1969–77; Agricultural EDC, 1971–78. Member: Agricultural Improvement Council, 1953–62; National Forestry Cttee for England and Wales, 1954–60; Hill Farming Advisory Cttee for England and Wales, 1946–60; County Agricultural Exec. Cttee, 1948–59; Royal Commn on Historical Manuscripts, 1973–. Chm. Council, RASE, 1971–74. Hon. Treasurer, RNLI; Associate, RCVS, 1967. Master of Percy Foxhounds, 1940–. KStJ 1957. Hon. DCL Durham, 1958. *Heir: s* Earl Percy. *Address:* Alnwick Castle, Northumberland NE66 1NG. *T:* Alnwick 602456; Syon House, Brentford, Middx TW8 8JF. *T:* 01–560 2353; Clive Lodge, Albury, Guildford. *T:* Shere 2695. *Clubs:* Boodle's, Northern Counties, Turf. *Died* 11 *Oct.* 1988.

**NORTON, Sir Clifford John,** KCMG 1946 (CMG 1933); CVO 1937; *b* 17 July 1891; *o surv. s* of late Rev. George Norton and Clara, *d* of late John Dewey; *m* 1927, Noel Evelyn (*d* 1972), *d* of late Sir Walter Charleton Hughes, CIE, MInstCE; no *c. Educ:* Rugby Sch.; Queen's Coll., Oxford, MA 1915. Suffolk Regt, 1914, Gallipoli, Palestine; Captain, General Staff EEF, 1917; Political Officer, Damascus, Deraa, Haifa, 1919–20; entered Diplomatic Service, 1921; Private Secretary to the Permanent Under-Secretary of State for Foreign Affairs, 1930–37; First Secretary, 1933; Counsellor British Embassy, Warsaw, 1937–39; Foreign Office, 1939–42; Minister, Berne, 1942–46; HM Ambassador in Athens, 1946–51; retired, 1951; Hon. Citizen of Athens, 1951. UK Delegate (alternate) to United Nations Assembly, 1952 and 1953. Past President, Anglo-Swiss Society. Hon. Fellow, Queen's Coll., Oxford, 1963. *Address:* 21a Carlyle Square, SW3. *Died* 6 *Dec.* 1990.

**NORTON, Maj.-Gen. Cyril Henry,** CB 1952; CBE 1945; DSO 1943; Colonel Commandant RA, 1958–63; *b* 4 Nov. 1898; *s* of late F. H. Norton, Tilehurst, Caterham, Surrey; *m* 1934, Ethel, *d* of Kapten R. E. G. Lindberg, Stockholm, Sweden; one *s* one *d. Educ:* Rugby Sch.; RMA, Woolwich. 2nd Lieut, RFA, 1916; Captain, 1929; Major, 1938; Lieut-Colonel, 1945; Colonel, 1946. Brig., 1950; Maj.-Gen., 1951; GOC 5th Anti-Aircraft Group, 1950–53; retired Nov. 1953. Served Great War, 1914–19 (Salonika); Palestine, 1937–39 (despatches); War of 1939–45: in Middle East, Sicily and NW Europe. *Address:* Dunn House, Long Melford, Sudbury, Suffolk. *Club:* Army and Navy. *Died* 11 *May* 1983.

**NORTON-GRIFFITHS, Sir Peter,** 2nd Bt, *cr* 1922; Barrister-at-Law, Inner Temple, 1931; *b* 3 May 1905; *e s* of late Sir John Norton-Griffiths, 1st Bt, KCB, DSO; *S* father, 1930; *m* 1935, Kathryn (*d* 1980), *e d* of late George F. Schrafft, Boston, Massachusetts, USA; two *s* one *d. Educ:* Eton; Magdalen Coll., Oxford. Asst to President, Shell Union Oil Corporation, NY, 1936–39; enlisted Intelligence Corps, 1940; Asst Military Attaché, British Embassy, Madrid (GSO2) 1941–42; Instructor School of Military Intelligence, GSO3, 1943–44; GSO3, Intelligence Staff, SHAEF, 1944–45. Asst to General manager, Deutsche Shell AG, 1948–50; General Manager, Shell Co. of Portugal Ltd, 1950–53; Managing Director, Belgian Shell Co., SA, 1953–60; retired from business. Officier de l'Ordre de la Couronne (Belgium); Officier de l'Ordre de la Couronne de Chêne (Luxembourg). *Recreations:* music, sight-seeing. *Heir: s* John Norton-Griffiths [*b* 4 Oct. 1938; *m* 1964, Marilyn Margaret, *er d* of Norman Grimley]. *Address:* Apartado 4, Santo António (Oeiras), 2780 Oeiras, Portugal. *Clubs:* Boodle's; Eça de Queiroz (Lisbon). *Died* 13 *Oct.* 1983.

**NORWICH, Diana, Viscountess;** *see* Cooper, Lady Diana.

**NOSER, Most Rev. Adolf;** *b* Belleville, Ill, 4 July 1900. *Educ:* Angelicum Univ., Rome. Ordained Priest, 1925. Seminary Professor, US, 1927–34; Seminary Rector, US, 1934–39; Superior of Accra, Ghana, 1939–47; Bishop of Accra, 1947; transferred to Alexishafen, 1953; Archbishop of Madang, 1966–76, retired. Dr of Sacred Theology, 1927. *Publications:* pamphlets and magazine articles. *Address:* PO Alexishafen, via Madang, Papua New Guinea. *Died* 15 *April* 1981.

**NOSWORTHY, Sir John (Reeve),** Kt 1988; CBE 1973; Chairman, Campbell Brothers Ltd, since 1980; *b* 2 Aug. 1915; *s* of John Frederick Wills Nosworthy and Madeline Maud Reeve; *m* 1940, Kathleen Griffith; four *d. Educ:* Brisbane Grammar Sch. Solicitors' Bd Law Exams. Admitted Solicitor, 1936. Aust. Mil. Forces, 1939–45. Partner, Morris Fletcher & Cross, 1947–81 (Sen. Partner, 1969–81), Consultant, 1981–. Notary Public, 1967. Pres., Qld Law Soc., 1970–72; former Vice Pres., Law Council of Australia. Chairman: Queensland Trustees Ltd, 1976–87; Bank of Queensland, 1984–87. Mem., Nat. Cos and Securities Commn, 1980–. *Recreations:* golf, bowls. *Address:* Unit 83A, Highpoint, 32 Swann Road, Taringa, Brisbane, Qld 4008, Australia. *T:* (07) 371–4788. *Clubs:* Queensland, United Service, Tattersall's (Brisbane).
*Died 17 March* 1990.

**NOTT, Very Rev. Michael John,** BD; FKC; Provost of Portsmouth, 1972–82; Hon. Officiating Chaplain, Royal Navy, since 1978; *b* 9 Nov. 1916; *s* of Frank and Ann Nott; *m* 1942, Elisabeth Margaret Edwards; one *s* one *d. Educ:* St Paul's; King's Coll., London, FKC 1972; Lincoln Theological Coll. Curate of: Abington, Northampton, 1939–45; St Mary, Reading, 1945–46; Vicar of St Andrew, Kettering, 1946–54; Rural Dean of Kettering, 1952–54; Warden and Chaplain, Heritage Craft Sch. and Hospital, Chailey; Vicar of Seaford, 1957–64; Rural Dean of Seaford, 1961–64; Senior Chaplain to Archbishop of Canterbury, 1964–65; Archdeacon of Maidstone, 1965–67; Archdeacon of Canterbury, 1967–72; Canon Residentiary of Canterbury Cathedral, 1965–72. *Recreations:* reading, walking, travel. *Address:* 9 Clarence Parade, Southsea, Hants. *Club:* Royal Naval (Portsmouth).
*Died 3 Feb.* 1988.

**NUGENT of Bellême, David James Douglas,** (Prince HSH, title of Austrian Empire, *cr* 1816; also 7th Baron Nugent, Austrian title *cr* 1859 and confirmed by Royal Warrant of Edward VII, 1908); *b* 24 Nov. 1917; 2nd *s* of Albert Beauchamp Cecil Nugent (HSH Prince Nugent, and 5th Baron) and Frances Every Douglas, niece of 3rd Baron Blythswood, KCB, CVO; *S* brother, 1944; *m* 1958, Rosemary (marr. diss. 1960), *o d* of W. F. Edwards and Mrs Lennox Edwards; *m* 1968, Mary Louise (*d* 1975), *er d* of William Henry Wroth, Bigbury Court, Devonshire; *m* 1979, Evelyn Diana, *er d* of late Lt-Col Francis Noel, OBE, and *widow* of Sir Hector Lethbridge, 6th Bt. *Educ:* Lancing Coll. Director, Book Guild, Lewes, Sussex. *Recreation:* historical research. *Address:* Gresham Hall Cottage, Gresham Hall, Gresham, near Norwich NR11 8RW. *Club:* Norfolk (Norwich).
*Died 31 May* 1988.

**NUGENT, Sir Hugh Charles,** 6th Bt, *cr* 1795; Count of the Holy Roman Empire; *b* 26 May 1904; *s* of late Charles Hugh Nugent, *o s* of 5th Bt and Anna Maria (she *m* 2nd, Edwin John King, Danemore Park, Speldhurst, Kent), *d* of Edwin Adams; *S* grandfather, 1927; *m* 1931, Margaret Mary Lavallin, *er d* of late Rev. H. L. Puxley, The White House, Chaddleworth, Newbury, Berks; two *s. Educ:* Stonyhurst Coll. Knight of Malta. *Heir: s* John Edwin Lavallin Nugent [*b* 16 March 1933; *m* 1959, Penelope Ann, *d* of late Brig. R. N. Hanbury, of Braughing, Hertfordshire; one *s* one *d. Educ:* Eton]. *Address:* Ballinlough Castle, Clonmellon, Co. Westmeath, Ireland. *T:* Trim 33135.
*Died 30 Oct.* 1983.

**NUNN, Jean Josephine,** CB 1971; CBE 1966; Deputy Secretary, Cabinet Office, 1966–70; *b* 21 July 1916; *d* of late Major John Henry Nunn, RHA, and Mrs Doris Josephine Nunn (*née* Gregory); unmarried. *Educ:* The Royal School for Daughters of Officers of the Army, Bath; Girton Coll., Cambridge, Hon. Fellow 1971. Entered Home Office, 1938; Secretary, Royal Commission on the Press, 1947–49; Private Secretary to the Secretary of State, 1949–51; Assistant Secretary, 1952; Assistant Under-Secretary of State, 1961–63; Under-Secretary, Cabinet Office, 1963–66. *Recreations:* gardening, bird-watching, reading. *Address:* Garden Cottage, School Lane, Washington, Pulborough, West Sussex. *T:* Ashington 892280. *Club:* Royal Commonwealth Society.
*Died 24 Nov.* 1982.

**NURSE, Ven. Charles Euston,** MA; Archdeacon of Carlisle, 1958–70, later Archdeacon Emeritus; Canon Residentiary of Carlisle Cathedral, 1958–73; *b* 12 June 1909; *s* of Rev. Canon Euston John Nurse, MA, and Mrs Edith Jane Robins Nurse, Windermere Rectory. *Educ:* Windermere Grammar Sch.; Gonville and Caius Coll., Cambridge. Assistant Curate, Holy Trinity, Carlisle, 1932; Vicar of St Nicholas, Whitehaven, 1937; Vicar of St George, Barrow-in-Furness, 1948; Rural Dean of Dalton, 1949; Hon. Canon of Carlisle Cathedral, 1950–58. Examining Chaplain to the Bishop of Carlisle, 1959–. *Recreations:* fell-walking, fishing, entomology.
*Died 14 Oct.* 1981.

**NUTTALL, Major William Francis D.;** *see* Dixon-Nuttall.

# O

**OAKELEY, Sir (Edward) Atholl,** 7th Bt *cr* 1790; author; *b* 31 May 1900; *s* of late Major E. F. Oakeley, South Lancashire Regiment, and late Everilde A. Oakeley, *d* of Henry Beaumont; *S* cousin, Sir Charles Richard Andrew Oakeley, 6th Bt, 1959; *m* 1st, 1922, Ethyl Felice O'Coffey (marr. diss. 1929); 2nd, 1930, (Patricia) Mabel Mary (*née* Birtchnell) (marr. diss. 1951); one *s*; 3rd, 1952, Doreen (*née* Wells) (marr. diss. 1960); 4th, 1960, Shirley Church; one *d. Educ:* Clifton and Sandhurst. Lieutenant, Oxfordshire and Buckinghamshire Light Infantry, 1919–23; then Chief Contact to late Sir Charles Higham in Advertising; Captain, Amateur International Wrestling Team, 1928–29; Heavyweight Wrestling Champion of Europe, 1932; Heavyweight Wrestling Champion of Gt Britain, 1930–35; Manager to World Heavyweight Wrestling Champion, Jack Sherry, 1935–39; Promoter of Championship Wrestling, Harringay Arena, 1949–54. Hon. Mem., Mark Twain Soc. of America, 1977; Hon. Chm., Anglo-American Lorna Doone Soc.,1985. *Publications:* The Facts on which R. D. Blackmore based Lorna Doone, 1969; Blue Blood on the Mat, 1971. *Recreations:* cricket; hunting; athletics; sailing; wrestling; boxing; weight-lifting. *Heir: s* John Digby Atholl Oakeley [*b* 27 Nov. 1932; *m* 1958, Maureen, *d* of John and Helen Cox, Hamble, Hants; one *s* one *d*]. *Address:* Nomad, Lynton, Devon.                    *Died* 7 *Jan.* 1987.

**OAKESHOTT, Michael Joseph,** FBA 1966; MA; Professor Emeritus, University of London, 1969; Fellow of Gonville and Caius College, Cambridge, since 1925; *b* 11 Dec. 1901; *s* of Joseph Francis Oakeshott and Frances Maude Hellicar. *Educ:* St George's School, Harpenden; Gonville and Caius College, Cambridge. Fellow, Nuffield College, Oxford, 1949–50; University Prof. of Political Science at LSE, Univ. of London, 1951–69. Served in British Army, 1940–45. Muirhead Lecturer, Univ. of Birmingham, 1953. *Publications:* Experience and its Modes, 1933, repr. 1986; A Guide to the Classics (with G. T. Griffith), 1936, 1947; Social and Political Doctrines of Contemporary Europe, 1939; Hobbes's Leviathan, 1946; The Voice of Poetry in the Conversation of Mankind, 1959; Rationalism in Politics and other Essays, 1962; Hobbes on Civil Association, 1975; On Human Conduct, 1975, 1990; On History, 1983; The Voice of Liberal Learning, 1989. *Address:* Victoria Cottage, Acton, Langton Matravers, Swanage, Dorset BH19 3JS.
*Died* 18 *Dec.* 1990.

**OAKESHOTT, Sir Walter (Fraser),** Kt 1980; MA; FBA 1971; FSA; Hon. LLD (St Andrews); Hon. DLitt (East Anglia); Rector of Lincoln College, Oxford, 1953–72, Hon. Fellow, 1972; *b* 11 Nov. 1903; *s* of Walter Field Oakeshott, MD, and Kathleen Fraser; *m* 1928, Noël Rose (*d* 1976), *d* of R. O. Moon, MD, FRCP; twin *s* two *d. Educ:* Tonbridge; Balliol Coll., Oxford. Class. Mods 1924; Lit. Hum. 1926; Hon. Fellow, 1974. Assistant Master, Bec School, SW17, 1926–27; Assistant Master Merchant Taylors', 1927–30; Kent Education Office, 1930–31; Assistant Master Winchester College, 1931–38; released for 15 months (1936–37) for membership of Pilgrim Trust Unemployment Enquiry; High Master of St Paul's School, 1939–46; Headmaster of Winchester College, 1946–54. Vice-Chancellor, Oxford University, 1962–64; Pro-Vice-Chancellor, 1964–66. President, Bibliographical Society, 1966–68. Trustee, Pilgrim Trust, 1949–76. Rhind Lecturer, Edinburgh Univ., 1956. Master, Skinners' Co., 1960–61. *Publications:* Men Without Work (joint), 1938; The Artists of the Winchester Bible, 1945; The Mosaics of Rome, Fourth to Fourteenth Centuries, 1967; Sigena Wall Paintings, 1972; The Two Winchester Bibles, 1981; various semi-popular books on literature and medieval art. *Recreations:* pictures, books. *Address:* The Old School House, Eynsham, Oxford. *Club:* Roxburghe.                              *Died* 13 *Oct.* 1987.

**OAKLEY, Kenneth (Page),** FBA; Deputy Keeper (Anthropology) British Museum (Natural History), 1959–69, retired; *b* 7 April 1911; *s* of Tom Page Oakley, BSc, LCP, and Dorothy Louise Oakley (*née* Thomas); *m* 1941, Edith Margaret Martin; two *s. Educ:* Challoner's Grammar School, Amersham; University College School, Hampstead; University College, London. BSc in Geology (1st cl. Hons), 1933; PhD 1938, DSc 1955. Geologist in Geological Survey, GB, 1934–35; Asst Keeper Dept of Geology (Palæontology), Brit. Mus. (Nat. Hist.), 1935 (seconded to Geological Survey for war-time service); Principal Scientific Officer, 1947–55; Senior Principal, 1955–69; head of Anthropology Sub-Dept, 1959–69. Rosa Morison Memorial Medal, University Coll., London, 1933; Wollaston Fund, 1941; Prestwick Medal, Geological Soc. of London, 1963; Henry Stopes Memorial Medal, Geologists' Assoc., 1952. Sec. Geol. Soc. Lond., 1946–49. Pres., Anthropological Section, British Assoc. for Advancement of Science, 1961. Collecting and research expeditions to East Africa, 1947, and South Africa, 1953. Viking Fund (Wenner–Gren Foundn) Lectures, New York, 1950, 1952; Royal Institution Discourse, 1953; Visiting Professor in Anthropology, University of Chicago, 1956. Corresponding Member, Istituto Italiano di Paleontologia Umana, 1955; Hon. Mem., British Acad. of Forensic Sciences, 1959; Hon. Life Mem., Quaternary Res.

Assoc., 1981; Hon. Research Fellow in Dept of Anthropology, UCL, 1979–82; FSA 1953; FBA 1957; Fellow of University Coll., London, 1958. Fellow, Explorers Club, NY, 1979. *Publications:* Man the Tool-maker, Brit. Mus. Nat. Hist., 1949 (6th edn 1972; repr. Chicago, 1957, 1976; Japanese edn 1971); The Fluorine-dating Method (in Year-book of Physical Anthropology for 1949), 1951; (part-author) The Solution of the Piltdown Problem (Bull. Brit. Mus. Nat. Hist.), 1953; Frameworks for Dating Fossil Man, 1964 (3rd edn 1969; Cronologia del hombre fósil, 1968; Die Datierung menschlicher Fossilien, 1971); The Problem of Man's Antiquity (Brit. Mus. Nat. Hist.), 1964; (Co-ed) Catalogue of Fossil Hominids (Brit. Mus. Nat. Hist.), part 1, Africa, 1967, rev. repr. 1977, part 2, Europe, 1971, part 3, Americas, Asia, Australasia, 1975; Decorative and Symbolic Uses of Vertebrate Fossils (Pitt Rivers Mus.), 1975; Relative Dating of the Fossil Hominids of Europe (Brit. Mus. Nat. Hist.), 1980; contrib. chapter, Skill as a Human Possession, in A History of Technology, vol. I (ed Singer et al), 1954, rev. version in Festschrift, Perspectives on Human Evolution, 2 (ed Washburn and Dolhinow), 1972; contrib. paper, Emergence of Higher Thought 3.0–0.2 Ma BP, in The Emergence of Man, 1981. *Recreations:* listening to music, art, pursuit of the unusual. *Address:* 2 Islip Place, Summertown, Oxford OX2 7SR. *T:* Oxford 56524; 2 Chestnut Close, Amersham, Bucks.                        *Died* 2 *Nov.* 1981.

**OATES, John Claud Trewinard,** FBA 1976; Emeritus Reader in Historical Bibliography, University of Cambridge; Emeritus Fellow of Darwin College, Cambridge; *b* 24 June 1912; *s* of Claud Albert Oates and Clarissa Alberta Wakeham; *m* 1960, Helen Cooke (*née* Lister). *Educ:* Crypt Sch., Gloucester; Trinity Coll., Cambridge (BA 1935, MA 1938). Sch. of Tank Technol., Mil. Coll. of Science, 1941–46. Univ. of Cambridge: Walston Student, 1935; Asst Under-Librarian, 1936, Under-Librarian, 1949, Dep. Librarian, 1975, Acting Librarian, 1979–80, Univ. Library; Sandars Reader in Bibliography, 1952, 1965. Pres., Bibliograph. Soc., 1970–72; Pres., Cambridge Bibliograph. Soc., 1978–81; Trustee, Laurence Sterne Trust, 1968–. Editor, The Library (Trans Bibliograph. Soc.), 1953–60. *Publications:* A Catalogue of the Fifteenth-Century Printed Books in the University Library, Cambridge, 1954; (contrib.) The English Library before 1700 (ed F. Wormald and C. E. Wright), 1958; Shandyism and Sentiment 1760–1800 (bicentenary lecture), 1968; Cambridge University Library: a history from the beginnings to the Copyright Act of Queen Anne, 1986; contrib. bibliograph. jls. *Recreation:* walking the dog. *Address:* 144 Thornton Road, Cambridge CB3 0ND. *T:* Cambridge (0223) 276653.
*Died* 11 *June* 1990.

**Ó BRIAIN, Hon. Barra,** MSM; President of the Circuit Court and, *ex officio,* Judge of High Court in Ireland 1959–73 (seconded as President of the High Court of Justice, Cyprus, 1960–62); *b* 19 September 1901; *s* of Dr Christopher Michael and Mary Theresa Ó Briain, Merrion Square, Dublin; *m* 1928, Anna Flood, Terenure, Dublin (*d* 1968); three *s* eight *d. Educ:* Belvedere College; University Coll., Dublin; Paris University. Served in IRA in Irish War of Independence, 1920–21; National Army, 1922–27; Mil. Sec. to Chief of Staff, 1926–27. Called to Irish Bar, 1926; Hon. Bencher, King's Inns, 1974. Sen. Counsel, 1940; Circuit Judge, 1943 (S Western Circuit). Mem., Cttee of Inquiry into operation of Courts in Ireland, 1962; Chm., Cttee to recommend safeguards for persons in police custody, 1977. *Publication:* The Irish Constitution, 1927. *Recreations:* fishing, gardening, walking. *Address:* Dún Ard, Islington Avenue, Sandycove, Co. Dublin.
*Died* 19 *June* 1988.

**O'BRIEN, Sir David (Edmond),** 6th Bt *cr* 1849; *b* 19 Feb. 1902; *s* of Edmond Lyons O'Brien (*y b* of 3rd Bt) and Audrey Townshend, *d* of late David Crawford, New York; *S* brother, 1969; *m* 1927, Mary Alice (*d* 1974), *y d* of Sir Henry Foley Grey, 7th Bt; one *s* one *d* (and one *s* decd). *Educ:* Oratory School. *Recreations:* fishing, gardening. *Heir: g s* Timothy John O'Brien, *b* 6 July 1958. *Club:* Kildare Street and University (Dublin).                        *Died* 26 *Nov.* 1982.

**O'BRIEN, Owen;** Joint General Secretary, Society of Graphical and Allied Trades 1982 (SOGAT 82), 1982–83; *b* February, 22 June 1920; *m*; two *s* two *d. Educ:* Tower Hill Sch., E1. Entered printing industry, 1934. Served War: Merchant Navy, 1939–41; RAF, 1941–46. Elected: Asst Sec., London Machine Br. of NATSOPA, Dec. 1951; (unopposed) Sec. of Br., Nov. 1952; Sec. of Union's London Jt Branches, 1952–63; Nat. Asst Sec., 1964–75; Gen. Sec., 1975–82. Mem., Employment Appeal Tribunal, 1984–. Past Mem., local Labour Party and London Labour Party; Mem., Stepney Borough Council, 1947–50. Contested (Lab) Darlington, 1987. Chm., Printing and Publishing Industry Training Board, 1977– (Mem. Exec. Cttee and Chm., Levy and Grant Cttee from Bd's constitution, 1968–77); Mem. Council, Industrial Soc. Governor, London Coll. of Printing, 1964– (Chm., Governors, 1969, 1977). *Recreations:* walking, reading, swimming. *Address:* 58 Hurst Road, Sidcup, Kent DA15 9AA.                        *Died* 2 *Nov.* 1987.

**O'COLLINS, Most Rev. Sir James (Patrick),** KBE 1980; DD 1930; *b* Melbourne, Australia, 31 March 1892. *Educ:* St Columba's,

Springwood; St Patrick's, Sydney; Urban Coll., Rome. Ordained Priest, Rome, 1922 for the Diocese of Melbourne; RC Bishop of Geraldton, 1930–41; Bishop of Ballarat, 1942–71. Nominated Asst Bishop at the Papal Throne, 1955. *Address:* 1444 Sturt Street, Ballarat, Victoria 3350, Australia. *Died 25 Nov.* 1983.

**O'CONNELL, Sir Bernard Thomas,** Kt 1972; Deputy Chairman, New Zealand Breweries Ltd, since 1970; *b* 31 Dec. 1909; *s* of Bernard O'Connell and Mary Walker, Yorkshire, England; *m* 1939, Margaret Mary Collins; three *s. Educ:* Christian Brothers Schools in Australia and New Zealand. New Zealand Breweries Ltd, Wellington, New Zealand: Sec. 1939; Gen. Manager, 1946; Man. Dir, 1958; Dep. Chm., 1970. FCA. *Recreations:* golf, racing. *Address:* 7 Wai-te-ata Road, Wellington, New Zealand. *T:* Wellington 726–704. *Clubs:* Wellesley, Wellington Golf, Wellington Racing (all in Wellington, NZ). *Died 11 Jan.* 1981.

**O'CONNELL, Sir Morgan (Donal Conail),** 6th Bt, *cr* 1869; *b* 29 Jan. 1923; *o s* of Captain Sir Maurice James Arthur O'Connell, 5th Bt, KM, MC, and Margaret Mary, *d* of late Matthew J. Purcell, Burton Park, Buttevant; *S* father, 1949; *m* 1953, Elizabeth, *o d* of late Major and Mrs John MacCarthy O'Leary, Lavenders, West Malling, Kent; two *s* four *d. Educ:* The Abbey School, Fort Augustus, Scotland. Served War of 1939–45, in Royal Corps of Signals, 1943–46; BLA, 1944–46. *Recreations:* fishing and shooting. *Heir: s* Maurice James Donagh MacCarthy O'Connell, *b* 10 June 1958. *Address:* Lakeview, Killarney, Co. Kerry. *T:* 31845. *Died 25 July* 1989.

**O'CONNOR, Lt-Gen. Sir Denis (Stuart Scott),** KBE 1963 (CBE 1949; OBE 1946); CB 1959; DL; *b* Simla, 2 July 1907; *s* of Lieut-Colonel Malcolm Scott O'Connor and Edith Annie (*née* Rees); *m* 1936, Martha Neill Algie (*née* Johnston), Donaghadee, Co. Down; two *s* one *d. Educ:* Glengorse, Eastbourne; Harrow School; RMA Woolwich. Commnd 2nd Lieut, Royal Artillery, 1927; India, 1929–35; France, 1939, Captain; Student Staff Coll., 1940; Major Instructor, Staff Coll., 1941, Lieut-Colonel GSO 1, 11th Armoured Division, 1942–44; N.W. Europe, CO Artillery Regt, 1944 (despatches); Colonel, 14th Army, 1945; Brigadier, Director of Plans, Supreme Allied Commander, South East Asia, 1945–46; Middle East, BGS, 1946–49; Student, IDC 1950; School of Artillery, 1951–52; CRA, 11th Armoured Division, BAOR, 1953–54; Director of Plans, War Office, 1955–56; Maj.-General, Commander, 6th Armoured Division, BAOR, 1957–58; Chief Army Instructor, Imperial Defence Coll., London, 1958–60; GOC, Aldershot District, 1960–62; Vice Chief of Defence Staff, Ministry of Defence, 1962–64; Commander British Forces, Hong Kong, 1964–66, retired. Colonel Commandant, RA, 1963–72. Member of Administrative Board of Governors, Corps of Commissionaires, 1964–75, Life Governor, 1975. HQ Staff, Army Benevolent Fund, 1967–75. DL Surrey, 1968. *Recreations:* shooting, fishing, golf. *Address:* Springfield Lodge, Camberley, Surrey. *Died 18 Jan.* 1988.

**O'CONNOR, Sir Kenneth Kennedy,** KBE 1961; Kt 1952; MC 1918; QC (Kenya) 1950; *b* 21 Dec. 1896; *s* of Rev. William O'Connor and Emma Louisa O'Connor; *m* 1928, Margaret Helen (*née* Wise); two *s. Educ:* Abbey Sch., Beckenham; St Columba's Coll., near Dublin. Indian Army, 14th (KGO) Sikhs, 1915–18 (despatches, MC). Pol. Dept, Mesopotamia, 1919. Foreign and Pol. Dept, Government of India, 1920–22; resigned, 1922. Called to Bar, Gray's Inn, 1924; practised at Bar, London and Singapore, 1924–41. President, Straits Settlements Assoc., 1938, 1939, 1940. Colonial Legal Service, 1943; Acting Attorney-General, Nyasaland, 1944; Colonel, 1945; Attorney-General, Malaya, 1946–48; Attorney-General, Kenya, 1948–51; Chief Justice, Jamaica, 1951–54; Chief Justice of Kenya, 1954; President, Court of Appeal for Eastern Africa, 1957–62, retired. *Publications:* Index Guide to the Law of Property Act, 1925, 1926. Editor Straits Settlements Law Reports. Contributions to legal journals. *Recreations:* cricket, lawn tennis, golf. *Address:* 7 Westfield Close, Wimborne, Dorset. *Club:* Royal Over-Seas League. *Died 13 Jan.* 1985.

**O'CONNOR, General Sir Richard Nugent,** KT 1971; GCB 1947 (KCB 1941; CB 1940); (Scottish Rifles) DSO 1917; MC; *b* 1889; *s* of Major Maurice Nugent O'Connor, Royal Irish Fusiliers; *m* 1st, 1935, Jean (*d* 1959), *d* of Sir Walter Ross, KBE, of Cromarty; 2nd, 1963, Dorothy, *widow* of Brigadier Hugh Russell, DSO. *Educ:* Wellington Coll.; Royal Military Coll., Sandhurst. Served European War, 1914–18 (despatches 9 times, DSO, bar, MC, Italian Silver medal for valour); GSO 2nd Grade, War Office, 1932–34; Imperial Defence College Course, 1935; Commander Peshawar Brigade, India, 1936–38; Military Governor of Jerusalem, 1938–39; served War of 1939–45; commanded Western Desert Corps in successful Libyan Campaign, 1940–41 (prisoner, escaped Dec. 1943); a Corps Commander in France, 1944 (despatches, 1939–45 Star, France and Germany Star, Legion of Honour, Commander, Croix de Guerre with palm); GOC-in-C Eastern Command, India, Jan. 1945; GOC-in-C N. Western Army, India, 1945; General, 1945; Adjutant-General to the Forces, 1946–47; ADC General to the King, 1946; retired, 1948. Commandant Army Cadet Force, Scotland, 1948–59;

Colonel, The Cameronians (Scottish Rifles), 1951–54. Lord Lieutenant County of Ross and Cromarty, 1955–64. Lord High Commissioner, Church of Scotland General Assembly, 1964. JP Ross and Cromarty, 1952. *Address:* Flat 3, 28 Lennox Gardens, SW1. *Died 17 June* 1981.

**O'DEA, William Thomas,** FIEE; FMA; formerly founder Director-General, Ontario Science Centre, 1966–70; *b* 27 Jan. 1905; *s* of late William O'Dea, MBE; *m* 1933, Kathleen Alice Busby; no *c. Educ:* Manchester University (BSc). Entered Science Museum from industry, 1930, as Assistant Keeper; transferred 1939, to Air Ministry (later MAP); Asst Director, Engine Accessories Production, 1940; Acting Director, Propeller Production, 1941; Dep. Regional Controller, London and SE England, Ministry of Production, 1942–44; Dep. Controller of Storage, Board of Trade, 1944–46. Keeper, Dept of Aeronautics, and Sailing Ships, Science Museum, SW7, 1948–66. Unesco adviser to Governments of Ceylon and India on establishment of Science Museums, 1956–60; Adviser to Government of UAR (Egypt), 1962. Chairman, Cttee for Museum of Science and Technology, International Council of Museums, 1966–71. Hon. Citizen, Quincy, Mass, 1965. *Publications:* The Meaning of Engineering, 1961; The Social History of Lighting, 1958; Science Museum Handbooks on Electric Power, 1933, Radio Communications, 1934, Illumination, 1936, 1948 and 1959; papers in Journals of IEE and IMechE; contributor, Festival Lectures, Royal Society of Arts, 1951, and to various societies on history of engineering and illumination. *Address:* Pippins, Lower Farm Road, Effingham, Surrey KT24 5JL. *Died 9 Nov.* 1981.

**ODELL, Prof. Noel Ewart;** geological research worker, since retirement from last professorship in 1962; *b* 25 Dec. 1890; *s* of Rev. R. W. Odell and M. M. Odell (*née* Ewart); *m* 1917, Gwladys Jones (*d* 1977); one *s. Educ:* Brighton College; Imperial Coll. of Science and Technology (ARSM); Clare Coll., Cambridge (PhD); Hon. Fellow, 1983). MIMM, FGS, FRSE, FRGS. Served RE: 1915–19 (wounded three times); 1940–42, British and Indian Armies (Major, Bengal Sappers and Miners). Staff Lectr, Council for Adult Educn in Forces, 1942–47. Geologist, Anglo Persian Oil Co. Ltd, 1922–25; cons. geologist and mining engineer, Canada, 1927–30; Univ. Lectr in Geology and Tutor, Harvard Univ., 1928–30; Research Student and Univ. Lectr, Cambridge, 1931–40 (Fellow Commoner and Supervisor of Studies, Clare Coll.); Leverhulme Fellowships, 1934 and 1938; Lectr, McGill Univ. and Vis. Prof., Univ. of BC, Canada, 1948–49; Prof. of Geology and Head of Dept, Univ. of Otago, NZ, 1950–56, Peshawar Univ., Pakistan, 1960–62. British Council Lectr, Scandinavian univs 1946, 1959, Swiss univs 1947; Vis. Lectr, Göttingen Univ., Germany, 1985. Foreign expeditions: geologist to Oxford Univ. Spitsbergen expedn, 1921; geologist and leader, Merton Coll. Arctic expedn, 1923; Mt Everest 1924 (geologist, to 27,500 ft without oxygen, search for Mallory and Irvine) (private audience of HM King George V at Buckingham Palace, Nov. 1924); Mt Everest 1938, to 25,000 ft; Norway 1929 and British Columbia 1930, geological research; mountaineering and exploration in Canadian Rockies, 1927–47; Nanda Devi, 26,640 ft, first ascent with H. W. Tilman, 1936 (for 14 years highest peak climbed to summit); geol exploration in N Labrador, 1931; NE Greenland, 1933; Lloyd George Mts, Rockies, 1947; St Elias Mts, Yukon, Alaska, 1949 and 1977. Star in constellation Lyra named after N. E. Odell, Internat. Star Register, 1925. *Publications:* chapters in: Norton: The Fight for Everest, 1925; Tilman: Everest, 1938; Granites of Himalaya, Karakorum and Hindu Kush, ed Prof. F. A. Shams; contribs to journals, scientific *et al. Recreations:* fell-walking, watching Rugby football, listening to music. *Address:* Clare College, Cambridge CB2 1TL; 5 Dean Court, Cambridge. *T:* Cambridge 247701. *Clubs:* (Hon. Mem.) Alpine, Himalayan, and many foreign alpine and mountaineering clubs in Canada, NZ, SA, USA, Switzerland, Norway, Japan, inc. Arctic (former Pres.), and Arctic Inst. of N America. *Died 21 Feb.* 1987.

**ODEY, George William,** CBE 1945; DL; Honorary President, Barrow, Hepburn Group Ltd, since 1974 (Chairman, 1937–74); *b* 21 April 1900; *s* of late George William Odey; *m* 1st, 1926, Dorothy Christian (*d* 1975), *d* of late James Moir; one *s*; 2nd, 1976, Mrs Doris Harrison-Broadley (*d* 1981); 3rd, 1981, Denise (*d* 1985), *widow* of Sir Richard Barwick, 3rd Bt. *Educ:* Faversham Grammar Sch.; University College, London. President Union Society, UCL, 1921–22. University of London Union Society, 1922. Fellow, UCL 1953; Assistant Secretary, University of London Appointments Board, 1922–25. Joined firm of Barrow, Hepburn & Gale, Ltd, 1925; Board of Barrow, Hepburn & Gale, Ltd, 1929, Managing Director, 1933. Representative Ministry of Supply in Washington for negotiations in connection with joint purchase of hides between UK and USA, 1941; Member joint UK and USA Mission on Hides and Leather to S. America, 1943; Chairman: Board of Governors, National Leathersellers Coll., 1951–77; United Tanners' Federation, 1951. MP (C) Howdenshire Division of E Yorks, Nov. 1947–Feb. 1950, Beverley Division of the East Riding of Yorkshire, 1950–55; CC East Riding, Yorkshire, 1964–74. Leathersellers' Company Livery, 1939. Hon. Air Commodore (RAuxAF), retired. Commodore House of Commons Yacht Club, 1954. President: International Tanners' Council, 1954–67; British Leather Manufacturers Research Assoc., 1964; British Leather Federation, 1965; Federation of Gelatine and Glue Manufacturers, 1955–57; British Gelatine and Glue Research Assoc., 1950–. Member: Western Hemisphere Export Council, 1960–64; Cttee for Exports to the US, 1964; Member of Lloyd's. Hon. Freeman of Beverley, 1977. DL Humberside, 1977. *Recreations:* farming, yachting. *Address:* Keldgate Manor, Beverley, North Humberside. *T:* Beverley 882418. *Clubs:* Royal Automobile; Royal Yorkshire Yacht; Lloyds Yacht; Scarborough Yacht; House of Commons Yacht. *Died 16 Oct. 1985.*

**ODGERS, James Rowland,** CB 1980; CBE 1968; *b* 9 Aug. 1914; *s* of Matthew John Odgers and Lilian Odgers; *m* 1939, Helen Jean Horner; two *s* one *d*. *Educ:* South Australian public schools. Parliamentary officer, 1937–79; Clerk of the Australian Senate, 1965–79; retired 1979. *Publication:* Australian Senate Practice, 1954, 5th edn 1976. *Recreations:* bowls, writing. *Address:* 30 Barnett Close, Swinger Hill, Canberra, ACT 2606, Australia. *T:* 864224. *Died 30 July 1985.*

**ODLUM, Dr Doris Maude;** Consultant Psychiatrist, since 1928; formerly Senior Physician for Psychological Medicine, Elizabeth Garrett Anderson (Royal Free) Hospital, London; Consultant Emeritus, Marylebone Hospital for Psychiatry and Child Guidance, London; Consultant Emeritus, Bournemouth and East Dorset Hospital Group; Fellow, British Medical Association, 1959; *b* 26 June 1890; *d* of Walter Edward and Maude Gough Odlum. *Educ:* Talbot Heath, Bournemouth; St Hilda's Coll., Oxford (Hon. Fellow 1981); St Mary's Hospital and London School of Medicine for Women. MA Oxon; BA London; MRCS; LRCP, Foundn Fellow, Royal Coll. Psychiatrists, 1971; DPM; DipEd. Hon. Consultant Phys., Lady Chichester Hospital for Nervous Diseases, Hove, 1928–48; Hon. Phys. for Psychiatry, Royal Victoria and W. Hants Hospital, Bournemouth, 1928–48; President, British Med. Women's Federation, 1950–53; President, European League for Mental Hygiene, 1953–56; Vice-President, International Med. Women's Assoc., 1950–54; Vice-President, National Assoc. for Mental Health, 1946–; Member Exec. World Federation for Mental Health, 1948–51; Hon. Cons. Psychiatrist to the Samaritans Inc., 1961–, Life Pres., 1973–. Corresponding Member Swiss Psychiatric Assoc., 1946–; Member Home Office Cttee on Adoption, 1954. *Publications:* You and Your Children, 1948; Psychology, the Nurse and the Patient (3rd edn 1959, US edn 1960); Journey Through Adolescence, 1957 (2nd edn, 1965, 3rd edn 1977); The Mind of Your Child, 1959; L'Età Difficile, 1962 (2nd edn 1968); Puber Puberteit, 1965; The Male Predicament, 1975; Understanding Your Child, 1976; Adolescence, 1978; articles in British Medical Journal, Lancet, Practitioner, etc. *Recreations:* painting, golf, swimming, travel. *Address:* 11 Golden Gates, Ferry Way, Sandbanks, Poole, Dorset BH13 7QH. *T:* Canford Cliffs 707915. *Club:* Naval and Military. *Died 14 Oct. 1985.*

**O'DONNELL, Peadar;** Member Irish Academy of Letters; *b* 1893. *Educ:* St Patrick's, Dublin. *Publications:* Storm; Islanders, 1925; Adrigoole, 1928; The Knife, 1930; The Gates Flew Open; On The Edge of the Stream, 1934; Salud; An Irishman in Spain, 1937; The Big Windows, 1955; Proud Island, 1976. *Address:* c/o O'Brien Press, 11 Clare Street, Dublin 2, Ireland. *Died 13 May 1986.*

**OFFICER, Maj.-Gen. William James,** CB 1962; CBE 1959 (OBE 1945); MB, ChB; late RAMC; *b* 24 August 1903; *s* of John Liddell Officer, OBE, WS, Edinburgh; *m* 1934, Doris, *d* of William Charles Mattinson, Keswick, Cumberland; three *d*. *Educ:* Edinburgh Acad.; Durham School; Edinburgh University. MB, ChB, Edin., 1927. Commissioned 7/9 (Highland) Bn, The Royal Scots (TA), 1920; joined RAMC, 1929; Major, 1939; Commanding Officer British Military Hosp., Deolali, and Officer-in-Charge RAMC Records, India and Burma, 1939–41; Served War of 1939–45 (despatches twice); in Burma, 1941–45; ADMS, 17th Indian Division and 2nd British Division; DDMS, Chindits Special Force and 33rd Indian Corps. Lt-Col, 1946; Asst Commandant, RAMC Depot and Training Establishment; Commanding Officer, British Military Hospital, Fayid (T/Col), 1949; Col 1951; ADMS, Hannover Dist, 1952; ADMS, N Midland Dist, 1954; DDMS (Actg Brig.), 2 (Br) Corps (Suez), 1956; Brig., 1957; Dir of Medical Services (temp. Maj.-Gen.), Middle East Land Forces, 1957–60; Maj.-Gen., 1960; Dir of Medical Services, Far East Land Forces, 1960–63; QHS 1961–63, retired 1963. *Address:* c/o Royal Bank of Scotland, Kirkland House, SW1. *Club:* Naval and Military. *Died 24 Feb. 1989.*

**OFFICER BROWN, Sir (Charles) James;** *see* Brown.

**O'FIAICH, His Eminence Cardinal Tomás Séamus,** MRIA 1977; Archbishop of Armagh and Primate of All Ireland (RC), since 1977; *b* Crossmaglen, 3 Nov. 1923; *s* of Patrick Fee and Annie Fee (*née* Caraher). *Educ:* Cregganduff Public Elem. School; St Patrick's Coll., Armagh; St Patrick's Coll., Maynooth; St Peter's Coll., Wexford; University Coll., Dublin; Catholic Univ. of Louvain. BA

(Celtic Studies) 1943, MA (Early Irish History) 1950 (NUI); LicScHist 1952 (Louvain). Ordained, Wexford, 1948; Curate, Moy, Co. Tyrone, 1952–53; St Patrick's College, Maynooth: Lectr in Modern History, 1953–59; Prof. of Modern History, 1959–74; Pres., 1974–77. Cardinal, 1979. Chairman: Govt Commn on Restoration of the Irish Language, 1959–63; Irish Language Advisory Council, 1965–68; Pres., Soc. of Irish-speaking Priests, 1955–67; Treas., Catholic Record Soc. of Ireland, 1954–74; Pres., Irish Episcopal Conf., 1977–; Member: Congregation for Catholic Education and Congregation for the Clergy, and Secretariate for Christian Unity, Vatican, 1979–; Congregation for the Evangelisation of Peoples, 1984–89; Congregation for Bishops, 1984–; Council for Public Affairs of the Church, 1984–. Editor, Jl of Armagh Historical Soc. and other jls. Hon. Doctorates: St Mary's, Notre Dame, Indiana and Thiel Coll., Greenville, Pa, 1979; Boston Coll. and College of St Thomas, St Paul, Minn, USA, 1981; NUI, 1984. *Publications:* Gaelscrínte i gCéin, 1960; Irish Cultural Influence in Europe, 1967; Imeacht na nIarlaí, 1972; Má Nuad, 1972; Art MacCumhaigh, 1973; St Columbanus in his own words, 1974; Oliver Plunkett: Ireland's New Saint, 1975; Aifreann Ceolta Tíre, 1977; Art Mac Bionaid, 1979; Gaelscrínte San Eoraip, 1986. *Address:* Ara Coeli, Armagh, Ireland. *T:* Armagh (0861) 522045.
*Died 8 May 1990.*

**O'FLAHERTY, Liam;** novelist; *b* Aran Islands, Co. Galway, 28 Aug. 1896. *Educ:* Rockwell College; Blackrock College; University College, Dublin. Hon. DLitt Nat. Univ. of Ireland, 1974. Allied Irish Bank-Irish Academy of Letters Literary Award, 1979. *Publications:* Thy Neighbour's Wife, a novel; The Black Soul, a novel; Spring Sowing, short stories; The Informer, a novel; The Tent, and other stories, 1926; Mr Gilhooley, 1926; The Life of Tim Healy, 1927; The Assassin, 1928; Return of the Brute, 1929; The Mountain Tavern, and other stories, 1929; A Tourist's Guide to Ireland, 1929; The House of Gold, 1929; Two Years, 1930; I went to Russia, 1931; The Puritan, 1932; Skerrett, 1932, repr. 1977; The Martyr, 1933; Shame the Devil, 1934; Hollywood Cemetery, 1935; Famine, 1937; Short Stories of Liam O'Flaherty, 1937; Land, 1946; Two Lovely Beasts, short stories, 1948; Insurrection, 1950; The Short Stories of Liam O'Flaherty, 1956; The Pedlar's Revenge and other stories, 1976; The Wilderness, 1978. *Address:* c/o A. D. Peters, 10 Buckingham Street, Adelphi, WC2. *Died 7 Sept. 1984.*

**O'FLYNN, Brigadier (Retd) Dennis John Edwin,** CBE 1960 (MBE 1937); DSO 1945; Army Officer retired; *b* 2 Aug. 1907; *s* of late Patrick Horace George O'Flynn and of Katie Alice (*née* Pye); *m* 1936, Winifred Madge Cairn Hogbin; (one *s* and one *d* decd). *Educ:* St Paul's School; RMC Sandhurst. Commissioned 2nd Lieut, Royal Tank Corps, 1928; served in Trans-Jordan Frontier Force, 1932–36; commanded: Westminster Dragoons (2nd Co. Lond. Yeo.), 1947–48; 3rd Royal Tank Regiment, 1948–50. Brigade Commander, 1953–60; retired 1960. Area Comr, St John Ambulance Brigade, 1966–69. OStJ 1967. *Recreations:* golf, gardening, photography. *Address:* High Copse, Pinemount Road, Camberley, Surrey. *T:* Camberley 63736. *Club:* Army and Navy.
*Died 19 Jan. 1985.*

**OGDEN, Sir Alwyne (George Neville),** KBE 1948 (OBE 1927); CMG 1946; retired; *b* Simla, India, 29 June 1889; *s* of William Ogden, Indian Government Railways, and Emily Mary Stowell; *m* 1922, Jessie Vera (*d* 1969), *d* of Albert Bridge (Adviser to Chinese Government); one *s* one *d*. *Educ:* Dulwich College; Corpus Christi College, Cambridge (Scholar, BA (Hons) in Classics and History). Student-Interpreter in China Consular Service, 1912; special service (War Office) with Chinese Labour Corps, 1917–18, and on Tibetan Frontier, 1922; Actg Consul-General at Chengtu 1922–23, and Tientsin, 1929–30; Consul (Grade I) 1929, (Grade I), 1934. Served at Peking, Tientsin, Tsinanfu, Chengtu, Hankow, Changsha, Kiukiang, Chefoo, Wei-Hai-Wei, Nanking, Shanghai; Consul-General at Tientsin, 1941, Kunming, 1942–45, Shanghai, 1945–48; retired from Foreign Service, 1948. Acting Judge of HBM Supreme Court for China, 1942–43. FRSA 1952. *Address:* Kingsbury, 51 Ridgway Road, Farnham, Surrey. *T:* Farnham 715461. *Club:* Carlton. *Died 17 Sept. 1981.*

**OGDEN, Frank Collinge,** CBE 1956; *b* 30 Mar. 1907; *s* of Paul and Nora Ogden; *m* 1944, Margaret, *o d* of Fred and Elizabeth Greenwood; one *s* two *d* (and one *d* decd). *Educ:* Manchester Grammar School; King's College, Cambridge. Entered Levant Consular Service, 1930; served in Cairo, Alexandria, Bagdad and Damascus; served War, 1941–42; Min. of Information, 1942; Tabriz, 1942; 1st Sec., Bogotá, 1944, Chargé d'Affaires, 1945; Consul, Shiraz, 1947; transferred to Seattle, 1949; Consul-General, Seattle, 1952; Basra, 1953; Gothenburg, 1955; Couns., Brit. Emb. in Libya, 1958; Chargé d'Affaires, 1958, 1959; Counsellor and Consul-General, Brit. Emb., Buenos Aires, 1960–65; retired. *Recreations:* swimming, motoring. *Address:* Yellow Sands, Thorney Drive, Selsey, Chichester, West Sussex. *Club:* Royal Automobile.
*Died 5 June 1989.*

**OGDEN, Sir George (Chester),** Kt 1973; CBE 1966; DL; Chief Executive, Greater Manchester Metropolitan County Council, 1973–76; *b* 7 June 1913; *s* of late Harry and Florence A. Ogden, Burnley, Lancs; *m* 1942, Nina Marion (*née* Lewis); one *s* two *d*. *Educ*: Burnley Gram. Sch.; Giggleswick Sch.; Corpus Christi Coll., Oxford (MA). Asst Solicitor, Middlesbrough Corp., 1940. Served in Royal Marines, Middle East, Sicily and NW Europe, 1941–45 (Major). Dep. Town Clerk: Middlesbrough, 1947–53; Leicester, 1953–54; Town Clerk, Leicester, 1955–66; Town Clerk, Manchester, 1966–73. Dep. Chm., Police Complaints Bd, 1977–83. DL Greater Manchester (formerly Co. Palatine of Lancaster), 1971. FBIM, Hon. LLD Manchester, 1976. *Recreations*: golf, fell walking. *Address*: Wood Lea, Twemlow, Holmes Chapel, Crewe. *T*: Holmes Chapel 33362. *Club*: National Liberal.                    *Died* 12 *April* 1983.

**OGDON, John (Andrew Howard);** pianist, composer; *b* Mansfield Woodhouse, Notts, 27 Jan. 1937; *m* 1960, Brenda Mary Lucas; one *s* one *d*. *Educ*: Manchester Gram. Sch.; Royal Manchester Coll. of Music. Concert Appearances include: Michelangeli Festival, Brescia, 1966; Festivals of Spoleto, Edinburgh, Prague Spring, Zagreb Biennale, Cheltenham. Founded Cardiff Festival (with Alun Hoddinott), 1967. Two-piano recitals with Brenda Lucas; concert appearances, USA, USSR, Australia, Far East, European capitals. Prof. in Music Dept, Univ. of Indiana, Bloomington, 1977–80. Awards: Liverpool, 1959; Liszt Prize, 1961; Tchaikovsky Prize (*ex aequo* with Vladimir Ashkenazy), Moscow, 1962; Harriet Cohen International Award. *Compositions*: large and small, mainly for piano. *Recreations*: history, literature, especially P. G. Wodehouse. *Address*: c/o Basil Douglas Ltd, 8 St George's Terrace, Regent's Park Road, NW1 8XJ.
                                                            *Died* 1 *Aug*. 1989.

**OGILVIE, Lady, (Mary Helen)** Principal of St Anne's College, Oxford, 1953–66, retired; *b* 22 March 1900; *e d* of late Rev. Professor A. B. Macaulay, DD, of Glasgow; *m* 1922, (Sir) Frederick Wolff Ogilvie, LLD (*d* 1949), Principal of Jesus College, Oxford, 1945–49; one *s* (and two *s* decd). *Educ*: St George's, Edinburgh; Somerville College, Oxford (Hon. Fellow, 1978). BA Hon. Sch. of Mod. Hist., Oxford, 1922, MA 1937. Member: Royal Commission on Population, 1944–49; Archbp's Commn on Church and State, 1967–70. Tutor of Women Students, University of Leeds, 1949–53. Member of Arts Council of Great Britain, 1953–58; on Governing Board of Cheltenham Ladies' College, 1951–75; Governing Board of Clifton College, 1960–72. Hon. LLD: Wilson College, Pa, 1956, QUB 1960; Leeds Univ., 1962; Trent Univ., Ont, 1972; Hon. DCL Stirling, 1973. Hon. Fellow: St Anne's College, Oxford, 1966; Lucy Cavendish Collegiate Soc., 1971.                    *Died* 10 *Nov*. 1990.

**OGILVIE, Prof. Robert Maxwell,** FBA 1972; MA, DLitt; Professor of Humanity, University of St Andrews, since 1975; *b* 5 June 1932; *y s* of late Sir Frederick Ogilvie and of Lady Ogilvie; *m* 1959, Jennifer Margaret, *d* of D. W. Roberts, Lymington; two *s* one *d*. *Educ*: Rugby; Balliol College, Oxford. First class Hon. Mods, 1952; first class, Lit. Hum., 1954; Harmsworth Sen. Schol. Merton Coll., 1954–55; Fellow and Dir of Studies in Classics, Clare Coll., Cambridge, 1955–57; Fellow of Balliol, 1957–70; Sen. Tutor, 1966–70; Mem., Gen. Board of the Faculties, 1967–70; Mem., Hart Cttee on Relations with Junior Members, 1968; Headmaster, Tonbridge Sch., 1970–75. Visiting Special Lecturer, University Coll., Toronto, 1965–66; Vis. Prof., Yale Univ., 1969; Hofmeyr Vis. Fellow, Wits Univ., 1969. Vice-Pres., Soc. for Roman Studies, 1976. Chm., Council, Trinity Coll., Glenalmond, 1976–. Mem. Scottish Council, Queen's Silver Jubilee Appeal. Editor, Classical Qly, 1977–. DLitt Oxon, 1967; FSA 1968; FSAScot 1972; FRSE 1979. *Publications*: Latin and Greek: a history of the influence of the classics on English life, 1964; A Commentary on Livy, 1–5, 1965; Tacitus, *Agricola* (with Sir Ian Richmond), 1967; The Ancient World (Oxford Children's Reference Library), 1969; The Romans and Their Gods, 1970; Livy 1–5 (Oxford Classical Texts), 1974; Early Rome and the Etruscans, 1975; The Library of Lactantius, 1978; Roman Literature and Society, 1980. *Recreations*: music, climbing, golf. *Address*: Department of Humanity, University of St Andrews, St Andrews, Fife KY16 9AJ; Errachd, By Fort William, Inverness-shire. *Club*: Royal and Ancient Golf.
                                                            *Died* 7 *Nov*. 1981.

**O'HARA, Rear-Adm. Derek,** CB 1983; consultant; Director, Post Design (Ships), Ministry of Defence, 1980–83, retired; *b* 5 March 1927; *s* of William and Hilda O'Hara; *m* 1953, Irene Margaret (*née* Pirie); one *s* one *d*. *Educ*: Tadcaster Grammar Sch., W Hartlepool; RNEC Keyham and Manadon; RNC Greenwich. FIMechE (Mem. Council, 1983–). Entered RN, 1944; served in HM Ships Berwick, Indomitable, Liverpool, Newcastle, Ocean and Cardigan Bay; various MoD appointments, 1958–67; HMS Bulwark, 1967–69; Gibraltar Dockyard, 1969–72; Dir, Naval Officer Appointments (E), 1976–78; Rear-Adm. 1978; Chief Staff Officer (E), Fleet, 1978–80. ADC to HM the Queen, 1978. *Recreations*: cabinet making, gardening, British Sailors Society (Bath Chm.). *Address*: c/o Barclays Bank, Milsom Road, Bath.                    *Died* 1 *Feb*. 1986.

**O'HARA, Frank,** MA, CEng, FRAeS; Senior Research Fellow, Glasgow University, since 1978; *b* 1 Oct. 1917; *s* of Francis O'Hara and Lily Mary O'Hara (*née* Slaven); *m* 1943, Mhuire Wheldon Hattle; one *s* three *d*. *Educ*: Alloa Academy; Edinburgh Univ.; Christ's Coll., Cambridge. MA Hons Maths and Nat. Phil., Edinburgh, 1938; BA Hons Maths 1940, MA Cantab 1944. Marine Aircraft Experimental Estab., 1940; Airborne Forces Exper. Estab., 1942; Aircraft and Armament Exper. Estab., 1950; RAE Bedford, 1954; Head, 3' Supersonic Tunnel, 1956; Head, Aero Flight, 1959; Chief Supt and Head Flight Group, 1966. Dir-Gen. Civil Aircraft, MoD, 1970–73; Dir-Gen. Equipment, MoD (PE), 1972–77. FRAES 1966. Alston Medal for Flight Testing, 1970; Busk Prize, 1965. *Publications*: papers in Reports and Memoranda of ARC, and various jls. *Recreations*: literature and the arts, gardening. *Address*: 11 Glasgow Street, Helensburgh, Dunbartonshire. *T*: Helensburgh 3412.                    *Died* 15 *May* 1985.

**OHLSON, Sir Eric James,** 2nd Bt, *cr* 1920; *b* 16 March 1911; *s* of Sir Erik Ohlson, 1st Bt, and Jennie (*d* 1952), *d* of J. Blakeley; *S* father 1934; *m* 1935, Marjorie Joan, *d* of late C. H. Roosmale-Cocq, Dorking, Surrey; two *s* one *d*. *Heir*: *s* Brian Eric Christopher Ohlson, *b* 27 July 1936. *Address*: 9 Park Edge, Harrogate HG2 8JU.
                                                            *Died* 5 *March* 1983.

**O'KEEFFE, Georgia;** artist; *b* Sun Prairie, Wisconsin, USA, 15 Nov. 1887; *d* of Francis O'Keeffe and Ida Totto; *m* 1924, Alfred Stieglitz. *Educ*: Sacred Heart Acad., Madison, Wis; Chatham (Va) Episcopal Inst.; Art Inst., Chicago; Art Students' League, NY; Univ. of Va; Columbia Univ. Head of Art Dept, West Texas State Normal Coll., Canyon, 1916–18. Painting, only, 1918–; annual one-man shows, 1923–46, in Stieglitz galls. Retrospective exhibitions: Brooklyn Museum, 1927; Art Inst. of Chicago, 1943; Museum of Modern Art (New York), 1946; Worcester Art Museum, USA, 1960; Whitney Mus. of Mod. Art, 1970; Art Inst. of Chicago, 1971; San Francisco Mus. of Art, 1971. Paintings in permanent collections of many museums and galleries in USA. Member National Institute of Arts and Letters; Benjamin Franklin Fellow, Royal Soc. for Encouragement of Arts, Manufactures and Commerce, 1969. Holds many hon. degrees. Creative Arts Award, Brandeis Univ., 1963; Wisconsin Governor's Award, 1966; Gold Medal, Nat. Inst. of Arts and Letters, 1970; M. Carey Thomas Award, Bryn Mawr Coll., 1971; Nat. Assoc. of Schs of Art award, 1971; Skowhegan Sch. of Painting and Sculpture award, 1973. Film, Georgia O'Keeffe (Public Broadcasting Service, dir. P. M. Adato), 1977. Presidential Medal of Freedom, 1976. *Publications*: Georgia O'Keeffe (portfolio of 12 reproductions with text), 1937; Georgia O'Keeffe Drawings, 1968; Georgia O'Keeffe (autobiog.), 1976. *Address*: Abiquiu, Rio Arriba County, New Mexico 87510, USA.                    *Died* 6 *March* 1986.

**OKEOVER, Col Sir Ian Peter Andrew Monro W.;** *see* Walker-Okeover.

**OLDFIELD, Sir Maurice,** GCMG 1978 (KCMG 1975; CMG 1964); CBE 1956 (MBE 1946); HM Diplomatic Service, retired; *b* 16 Nov. 1915; *e s* of late Joseph and Ada Annie Oldfield, Over Haddon. *Educ*: Lady Manners School, Bakewell; Manchester Univ. 1st Cl. Hons History; MA 1938. Served War of 1939–45, Intelligence Corps, Middle East, 1941–46 (Lt-Col; MBE). Jones Fellow in History and Tutor, Hulme Hall, Manchester, 1938–39. Attached to Foreign Office, 1947–49; Office of Commissioner-General for UK in South East Asia, Singapore, 1950–52; Foreign Office 1953–55; First Secretary, Singapore, 1956–58; Foreign Office, 1958–59; Counsellor: Washington, 1960–64; FO, subseq. FCO, 1965–77; Security Co-ordinator, NI, 1979–80. Foundn Governor, Lady Manners Sch., Bakewell. Vis. Fellow, All Souls Coll., Oxford, 1978–79. *Recreation*: farming. *Clubs*: Athenæum, Royal Commonwealth Society, Royal Over-Seas League.
                                                            *Died* 11 *March* 1981.

**OLDFIELD-DAVIES, Alun Bennett,** CBE 1955; MA; Controller, Wales, British Broadcasting Corporation, 1945–67; *b* 18 April 1905; *s* of Rev. J. Oldfield-Davies, Wallasey, Cheshire; *m* 1931, Lilian M. Lewis, BA (decd). *Educ*: Porth County Sch., Rhondda; University College, Aberystwyth. Schoolmaster and Lecturer to University Extension Classes in Ammanford, Carmarthenshire, and Cardiff, 1926–37. British Broadcasting Corporation: Schools Asst, 1937–40; Welsh Executive, 1940–44; Overseas Services Establishment Officer, 1944–45. Mem., Court, Univ. of Wales; Vice-Pres., University Coll., Cardiff; President: Nat. Museum of Wales, 1972–77; Welsh Council for Education in World Citizenship. Formerly Warden, University of Wales Guild of Graduates. Hon. LLD, Univ. of Wales, 1967. *Address*: Ty Gwyn, Llantrisant Road, Llandaff, Cardiff. *T*: 565920.                    *Died* 1 *Dec*. 1988.

**OLDMAN, Col Sir Hugh (Richard Deare),** KBE 1974 (OBE 1960); MC 1942; retired; *b* 24 June 1914; *s* of late Maj.-Gen. R. D. F. Oldman, CB, CMG, DSO, and Mrs Helen Marie Oldman (*née* Pigot); *m* 1947, Agnes Fielding Murray Oldman (*née* Bayles) (*d* 1978); *m* 1979, Susan V. Oldman (*née* Vance). *Educ*: Wellington Coll.; RMC Sandhurst. CO 8th Bn Durham LI, 1944–45; psc 1945;

Chief Instructor, Quetta Staff Coll.; comd Bn, Aden Protectorate Levies, 1957–60; comd Sultan's Armed Forces, Oman, 1961–64; Staff, HQ Allied Forces Southern Europe (NATO), 1965–67; retd from Army, 1967; subseq. Sec. for Defence, Sultanate of Oman. Croix de Guerre (Palme), 1944; Order of Merit 1st cl., Oman, 1972. *Address:* PO Box 73, White Marsh, Va 23183, USA. *Clubs:* Liphook Golf; Ware River Yacht (Gloucester Co., Va); Muthaiga Country (Kenya). *Died 26 Nov.* 1988.

**OLDROYD, Prof. James Gardner,** MA, PhD, ScD (Cantab); Professor of Applied Mathematics since 1965 and Head of Department of Applied Mathematics and Theoretical Physics since 1973, University of Liverpool; *b* 25 April 1921; *o s* of late H. and R. Oldroyd; *m* 1946, Marged Katryn, *e d* of late Rev. J. D. Evans; three *s. Educ:* Bradford Grammar Sch.; Trinity Coll., Cambridge (Schol.). Min. of Supply (PDE), 1942–45; Fundamental Research Lab., Courtaulds Ltd, Maidenhead, 1945–53; Fellow, Trinity Coll., Cambridge, 1947–51; Prof. of Applied Maths, UC Swansea, Univ. of Wales, 1953–65; Dean, Faculty of Science, UC Swansea, 1957–59. Pres., Brit. Soc. of Rheology, 1955–57 (Gold Medal 1980). Adams Prize, Cambridge Univ., 1963–64. *Publications:* papers on mathematical theory of deformation and flow in Proc. Royal Soc., Proc. Cambridge Phil. Soc., etc. *Address:* Department of Applied Mathematics and Theoretical Physics, University of Liverpool, Liverpool L69 3BX. *T:* 051-709 6022; Ardenmohr, Graham Road, West Kirby, Wirral, Merseyside L48 5DN. *T:* 051-632 2684. *Died 22 Nov.* 1982.

**O'LEARY, Patrick;** *see* Guerisse, A. M. E.

**OLIVER, George Harold,** QC 1949; *b* 24 Nov. 1888; *m* 1910, Christina Bennett; one *s.* Barrister, Middle Temple, 1927. MP (Lab) Ilkeston Division of Derbys, 1922–31 and 1935–64; Parliamentary Under-Secretary of State, Home Office, 1945–47. *Address:* c/o 79 Bedford Road, Little Houghton, Northampton. *Died 22 Sept.* 1984.

**OLIVER, Brig. James Alexander,** CB 1957; CBE 1945; DSO 1942 (and Bar to DSO 1943); TD; DL; solicitor; Vice-Lieutenant, County of Angus, 1967–81; *b* 19 March 1906; *s* of Adam Oliver, Arbroath, Angus; *m* 1932, Margaret Whytock Scott; no *c. Educ:* Trinity Coll., Glenalmond. Commanded: 7th Black Watch, 1942; 152 Infantry Bde (Highland Div.), 1943; 154 Infantry Bde (Highland Div.), 1944; served War of 1939–45 with 51st Highland Div. in N Africa, Sicily and NW Europe (despatches). ADC to the Queen, 1953–63; Hon. Colonel, 6/7th Black Watch, 1960–67; Hon. Colonel, 51st Highland Volunteers, 1967–70. Member, Angus and Dundee T&AFA, 1938–59 (Chairman, 1945–59). Chm., 1972–73, Vice-Pres., 1973, The Earl Haig Fund, Scotland. Hon. LLD Dundee, 1967. DL Angus, 1948. *Address:* West Newton, Arbroath, Angus DD11 5RQ. *T:* Arbroath (0241) 72579. *Club:* Naval and Military. *Died 4 Oct.* 1990.

**OLIVER, Leslie Claremont,** FRCS; FACS; Consulting Neurosurgeon: Charing Cross Hospital; Westminster Hospital; West London Hospital; Royal Northern Hospital; Founder, Neurosurgical Centre, Oldchurch Hospital, Romford; *b* 5 Feb. 1909; *m* 1st, Irene Ferguson; two *s*; 2nd, Regine de Quidt; one *s* one *d. Educ:* Latymer Sch.; Guy's Hospital. LRCP, MRCS, 1933; MB, BS, London, 1953; FRCS England, 1935; FACS 1957. Formerly: 1st Assistant and Registrar, Dept of Neurosurgery, London Hospital; Resident Asst Surgeon, W London Hospital; Surgical Registrar and Teacher in Surgery, Bristol General Hospital. Member Society British Neurological Surgeons; Corr. Member Soc. de Neurochirurgie de Langue Française. Formerly Chm. Court of Examiners, RCS. *Publications:* Essentials of Neurosurgery, 1952; Parkinson's Disease and its Surgical Treatment, 1953; (ed and contrib.) Basic Surgery, 1958; Parkinson's Disease, 1967; Removable Intracranical Tumours, 1969; Le Français Pratique. *Recreation:* travel. *Address:* 157 Rivermead Court, SW6 3SF. *T:* 071–731 0466. *Clubs:* Royal Society of Medicine, Hurlingham. *Died 4 Aug.* 1990.

**OLIVER, Martin Hugh,** PhD, CEng; Director General, Research Electronics, Procurement Executive, Ministry of Defence, 1972–76; *b* 9 July 1916; *s* of late Thomas Frederick Oliver and late Jessie Oliver (*née* Gibson), Peterborough; *m* 1963, Barbara Rivcah, *d* of late Richard Burgis Blakeley, Worcester; one *d. Educ:* King's Sch., Peterborough; Imperial Coll. (City and Guilds Coll.), Univ. of London. BSc (Eng) 1937, PhD (Eng) 1939; ACGI, DIC, MIEE. Metropolitan Vickers Electrical Co. Ltd, Manchester, 1938–41; National Physical Laboratory, Teddington, 1941–43; RRE, Malvern, 1943–65; Head of Radio Dept, RAE, Farnborough, 1965–68; Dir, Services Electronics Res. Lab., MoD, 1968–72. *Died 27 Nov.* 1987.

**OLIVER, Lt-Gen. Sir William (Pasfield),** GBE 1965 (OBE 1945); KCB 1956 (CB 1947); KCMG 1962; DL; late Infantry; *b* 8 Sept. 1901; *e s* of late Captain P. V. Oliver, Royal Navy; *m* 1938, Elizabeth Margaret, *o d* of late General Sir J. E. S. Brind, KCB, KBE, CMG, DSO; one *s* one *d. Educ:* Radley Coll.; RMC, Sandhurst. Chief of General Staff, GHQ, ME (Maj.-Gen.), 1945–46;

Maj.-Gen., 1949; Chief Army Instructor, Imperial Defence Coll., 1949–50; Chief of Staff, Eastern Command, Jan. 1951–Dec. 1952; Principal Staff Officer to High Commissioner, Federation of Malaya, 1953–54; General Officer Commanding Berlin (British Sector), 1954–55; Vice-Chief of Imperial General Staff, 1955–57, retired; Principal Staff Officer to Secretary of State for Commonwealth Relations, 1957–59; British High Commissioner in the Commonwealth of Australia, 1959–65; UK Commissioner General for 1967 Exhibition, Montreal, Canada, 1965–67. Dir, Viyella International Ltd, 1968–69. Mem., Adv. Cttee on Rhodesian Travel Restrictions. Colonel, The Queen's Own Royal W. Kent Regt, 1949–59. DL Kent. Governor, Corps of Commissionaires. Hon. DCL, Bishop's Univ., Quebec Province. Commander Legion of Merit (USA), 1946; Knight Grand Cross Royal Order Phoenix (Greece) 1949. *Address:* Little Crofts, Sweethaws, Crowborough, East Sussex. *Died 26 Feb.* 1981.

**OLIVIER,** Baron *cr* 1970 (Life Peer), of Brighton; **Laurence Kerr Olivier,** OM 1981; Kt 1947; Actor; Director, 1962–73, Associate Director, 1973–74, National Theatre; Member, South Bank Theatre Board, since 1967 (South Bank Theatre and Opera House Board, 1962–67; Olivier Theatre opened, 1976, in presence of the Queen); *b* 22 May 1907; *s* of late Rev. G. K. Olivier and Agnes Louise Crookenden; *m* 1st, 1930, Jill Esmond (marr. diss., 1940); one *s*; 2nd, 1940, Vivien Leigh (marr. diss., 1961; she *d* 1967); 3rd, 1961, Joan Plowright, CBE; one *s* two *d. Educ:* St Edward's Sch., Oxford. MA Hon. Tufts, Mass, 1946; Hon. DLitt: Oxon, 1957; Manchester, 1968; Sussex, 1978; Hon. LLD Edinburgh 1964; Hon. DLitt London, 1968; Fellow, BAFTA, 1976. Sonning Prize, Denmark, 1966; Gold Medallion, Swedish Acad. of Literature, 1968; Special Award for directorship of Nat. Theatre, Evening Standard, 1973; Albert Medal, RSA, 1976; Hon. Oscar, 1979, for lifetime's contrib. to films; SWET Awards renamed Laurence Olivier Awards, 1984. Commander, Order Dannebrog, 1949; Officier Legion d'Honneur, 1953; Grande Ufficiale dell' Ordino al Merito della Repubblica (Italian), 1953; Order of Yugoslav Flag with Golden Wreath, 1971. First appeared in 1922 at Shakespeare Festival, Stratford-on-Avon special boys' performance, as Katherine in Taming of the Shrew; played in Byron, King Henry IV, toured in sketch Unfailing Instinct, with Ruby Miller, Season with Lena Ashwell, King Henry VIII, 1924–25; under management of Dame Sybil Thorndike, played with Birmingham Repertory Company till 1928; Stanhope in Journey's End, for Stage Society; Beau Geste; Circle of Chalk, Paris Bound, The Stranger Within; went to America, 1929; returned 1930 and played in The Last Enemy, After All and in Private Lives; New York, 1931, played Private Lives, 1933; Rats of Norway, London; Green Bay Tree, New York; returned London, 1934, Biography, Queen of Scots, Theatre Royal; Ringmaster under his own management, Golden Arrow, Romeo and Juliet, 1935; Bees on the Boat Deck and Hamlet at Old Vic, 1936; Sir Toby Belch in Twelfth Night, and Henry V, Hamlet at Kronborg, Elsinore, Denmark, 1937; Macbeth, 1937; Iago in Othello, King of Nowhere, and Coriolanus, 1938; No Time for Comedy, New York, 1939; under his own management produced and played Romeo and Juliet with Vivien Leigh. Lieut (A) RNVR until released from Fleet Air Arm, 1944, to co-direct The Old Vic Theatre Company with Joan Burrell and Ralph Richardson, at New Theatre; played in Old Vic, 1944–45 Season; Peer Gynt, Arms and the Man, Richard III, Uncle Vanya; toured Continent in May 1945 with Peer Gynt, Arms and the Man, Richard III; Old Vic Season, 1945–46; Henry IV, Parts I and II, Oedipus, The Critic, Uncle Vanya, Arms and the Man; six weeks' season in New York with Henry IV, Parts I and II, Oedipus, The Critic and Uncle Vanya; Old Vic, 1946–47 Season, produced and played King Lear. Made a tour of Australia and New Zealand, 1948, with Old Vic Company, in Richard III, School for Scandal, Skin of our Teeth, Old Vic, 1949 Season, Richard III, The School for Scandal, Antigone. Directed A Street Car Named Desire, Aldwych, 1949; St James's, 1950–51; produced and acted in Venus Observed, under own management, produced Captain Carvallo, 1950, Antony in Antony and Cleopatra, Caesar in Caeser and Cleopatra, 1951; also in US, 1951–52; The Sleeping Prince, Phoenix, 1953; Stratford Season, 1955; Macbeth, Malvolio in Twelfth Night, Titus in Titus Andronicus; Archie Rice in The Entertainer, Royal Court Theatre, 1957; presented The Summer of the Seventeenth Doll, 1957; toured Europe in Titus Andronicus, 1957; Titus in Titus Andronicus, Stoll, 1957; Archie Rice in The Entertainer (revival), Palace Theatre, 1957, and New York, 1958; Coriolanus in Coriolanus, Stratford, 1959; directed The Tumbler, New York; Berenger in Rhinoceros, Royal Court Theatre and Strand Theatre, 1960; Becket in Becket, New York, 1960; Henry II in Becket, US Tour and New York, 1961; Fred Midway in Semi-Detached, Saville Theatre, 1962. Apptd Dir of National Theatre (first, as Old Vic): 1963: (produced) Hamlet; 1963–64; acted in Uncle Vanya and in The Recruiting Officer, 1964; acted in Othello and in The Master Builder, 1964–65. Chichester Festival: first Director, also acted, 1962 (Uncle Vanya; The Broken Heart; also Director, The Chances), 1963 (Uncle Vanya, also Director); National Theatre (produced) The Crucible; in Love for Love, Moscow and London, 1965;

Othello, Moscow and London, 1965; Othello, Love for Love, (dir.) Juno and the Paycock, 1966; Edgar in The Dance of Death, Othello, Love for Love (dir.) Three Sisters, National Theatre, 1967; A Flea in Her Ear, 1968; Home and Beauty, Three Sisters (directed and played Chebutikin), 1968-69; Shylock in Merchant of Venice, 1970, Long Day's Journey into Night, 1971, 1972; Saturday, Sunday, Monday, 1973; The Party, 1974; (dir.) Eden End, 1974; (appearance on film as Akash) Time, Dominion, 1986; *films:* Potiphar's Wife, The Yellow Passport, Perfect Understanding, No Funny Business, Moscow Nights, Fire Over England, As You Like It, The First and the Last, Divorce of Lady X, Wuthering Heights, Rebecca, Pride and Prejudice, Lady Hamilton, 49th Parallel, Demi-Paradise; produced, directed, played Henry V; produced, directed, played Hamlet (International Grand Prix, 1948, Oscar award, 1949); Carrie (Hollywood), 1950; Macheath in film The Beggar's Opera, 1953; produced, directed, played Richard III (British Film Academy's Award), 1956; produced, directed and played in The Prince and the Showgirl, 1957; General Burgoyne in The Devil's Disciple, 1959; The Entertainer; Spartacus; Term of Trial; Bunny Lake is Missing; Othello; Khartoum; The Power and The Glory, 1961, (TV) USA; Dance of Death; Shoes of the Fisherman; Oh! What a Lovely War; Battle of Britain; David Copperfield; directed and played Chebutikin in Three Sisters; Nicholas and Alexandra; Lady Caroline Lamb; Sleuth (NY Film Critics Award, Best Actor, 1972); Seven-per-cent Solution; Marathon Man (Variety Club of GB Award, 1977); A Bridge Too Far; The Betsy; Boys from Brazil; A Little Romance; Dracula; Clash of the Titans; Inchon; The Jazz Singer; The Jigsaw Man; The Bounty; Wild Geese II; Peter the Great; War Requiem; *television:* John Gabriel Borkmann, 1959; Long Day's Journey Into Night, 1972 (Emmy Award, 1973); The Merchant of Venice, 1973; Love Among The Ruins, USA, 1974 (Emmy Award, 1975); Jesus of Nazareth, 1976; The Collection, 1976; Cat on a Hot Tin Roof, 1976; Hindle Wakes, 1976; Come Back Little Sheba, Daphne Laureola, Saturday Sunday Monday, 1977; Brideshead Revisited, 1981; A Voyage Round My Father, 1982; King Lear, 1983; The Ebony Tower, 1984. Narrated World at War (TV), 1963. *Publications:* Confessions of an Actor (autobiog.), 1982; On Acting, 1986. *Recreations:* tennis, swimming, motoring, flying, gardening. *Address:* c/o Write on Cue, 10 Garrick Street, WC2E 9BH. *Clubs:* Garrick, Green Room, MCC.
*Died 11 July 1989.*

**OLUWASANMI, Hezekiah Adedunmola**, MA, PhD Harvard; Vice-Chancellor, University of Ife, Nigeria, 1966-75; *b* 12 Nov. 1919; *s* of late John Oluwasanmi and Jane Ola Oluwasanmi; *m* 1959, Edwina Marie Clarke (decd); one *s* two *d*. *Educ:* Morehouse Coll. (BA); Harvard University. Secondary School Teacher, 1940-41; Meteorological Observer, 1941-44; Clerk, Shell Oil Co., 1944-47; Student, 1948-55; Lectr, Sen. Lectr, and Prof. of Agricultural Economics, Univ. of Ibadan, 1955-66, Dean, Faculty of Agriculture, 1963-66. Member: W Nigeria Economic Planning Cttee, 1961-62; W Nigeria Economic Adv. Cttee, 1966-71. Chairman: Cttee of Vice-Chancellors of Nigerian Univs, 1970-72; Univ. of Zambia Grants Cttee; Member: Council, Univ. of Ghana; Assoc. of Commonwealth Univs; Bd of Governors, Internat. Develt Res. Centre, Ottawa; Bd of Trustees, Internat. Inst. of Tropical Agriculture, 1970-72. Member: Nigerian Econ. Soc.; Agricultural Soc., Nigeria; Internat. Assoc. Agricultural Economists. Hon. DSc, Univ. of Nigeria, Nsukka, 1971; Hon. LLD: Univ. of Wisconsin, 1974; Univ. of Ife, Nigeria, 1980; Hon. LHD, Morehouse Coll., Georgia, USA, 1974. *Publications:* Agriculture and Nigerian Economic Development, 1966; (jt author) Uboma, a socio-economic and nutritional survey of a rural community in Eastern Nigeria, 1966; various reports, contribs to symposia and papers in learned jls. *Recreations:* reading, walking, listening to music. *Address:* 19 Osuntokun Avenue, Bodija, UIPO Box 4162, Ibadan, Oyo State, Nigeria.
*Died 15 Aug. 1983.*

**OMAN, Charles Chichele;** *b* 5 June 1901; *s* of late Sir Charles Oman, KBE; *m* 1929, Joan Trevelyan (*d* 1973); one *s* one *d*. *Educ:* Winchester; New Coll., Oxford; British School at Rome. Entered Victoria and Albert Museum, 1924; lent to Ministry of War Transport, 1939-44; Keeper of Department of Metalwork, Victoria and Albert Museum, 1945-66. Hon. Vice-Pres., Royal Archaeological Inst. Hon. FSA, 1980; Hon. Mem., Hispanic Soc. of America. Liveryman of Company of Goldsmiths, 1946. *Publications:* English Domestic Silver, 1934; English Church Plate, 1957; English Silver in the Kremlin, 1961; Golden Age of Hispanic Silver, 1968; Caroline Silver 1625-1688, 1971; British Rings 800-1914, 1974; English Engraved Silver, 1978. *Address:* 13 Woodborough Road, Putney, SW15. *T:* 01-788 2744.
*Died 26 Jan. 1982.*

**O'NEILL OF THE MAINE,** Baron *cr* 1970 (Life Peer), of Ahoghill, Co. Antrim; **Terence Marne O'Neill,** PC (N Ireland) 1956; DL; *b* 10 Sept. 1914; *s* of Capt. Hon. Arthur O'Neill, MP (killed in action, 1914; *s* of 2nd Baron O'Neill, Shane's Castle, Antrim) and of late Lady Annabel Crewe-Milnes, *e d* of 1st and last Marquis of Crewe, KG; *m* 1944, Katherine Jean, *y d* of late W. I. Whitaker, Pylewell Park, Lymington, Hants; one *s* one *d*. *Educ:* Eton. Served, 1939-45,

Irish Guards. MP (Unionist) Bannside, Parlt of N Ireland, 1946-70; Parly Sec., Min. of Health, 1948; Deputy Speaker and Chairman of Ways and Means, 1953; Joint Parly Sec., Home Affairs and Health, 1955; Minister: Home Affairs, 1956; Finance, 1956; Prime Minister of N Ireland, 1963-69. Mem., Hansard Soc. Commn on Electoral Reform, 1975-76. Director: Warburg International Holdings Ltd, 1970-83; Phoenix Assurance, 1969-84. Trustee, Winston Churchill Meml Trust; Governor, Nat. Gall. of Ireland. DL Co. Antrim, 1948; High Sheriff County Antrim, 1953. Hon. LLD, Queen's Univ., Belfast, 1967. *Publications:* Ulster at the Crossroads, 1969; The Autobiography of Terence O'Neill, 1972. *Address:* Lisle Court, Lymington, Hants. *Club:* Brooks's.
*Died 12 June 1990.*

**O'NEILL, Hon. Sir Con (Douglas Walter),** GCMG 1972 (KCMG 1962; CMG 1953); *b* 3 June 1912; 2nd *s* of 1st Baron Rathcavan, PC and late Sylvia, *d* of Walter A. Sandeman, Morden House, Royston; *m* 1st, 1940, Rosemary (marriage dissolved 1954), *d* of late H. Pritchard, MD; one *s* one *d*; 2nd, 1954, Baroness Mady Marschall von Bieberstein (*d* 1960), *d* of late Baron von Holzing-Berstett; 3rd, 1961, Mrs Anne-Marie Lindberg, Helsinki. *Educ:* Eton College; Balliol Coll., Oxford (History Scholar). BA 1934 (1st Class, English), MA 1937; Fellow, All Souls College, Oxford, 1935-46; called to Bar, Inner Temple, 1936; entered Diplomatic Service, 1936; Third Secretary, Berlin, 1938; resigned from Service, 1939. Served War of 1939-45 in Army (Intelligence Corps), 1940-Nov. 1943; temp. employed in Foreign Office, 1943-46; Leader-writer on staff of Times, 1946-47; returned to Foreign Office, 1947; re-established in Foreign Service, 1948; served in Frankfurt and Bonn, 1948-53; Counsellor, HM Foreign Service, 1951; Imperial Defence College, 1953; Head of News Department, Foreign Office, 1954-55; Chargé d'Affaires, Peking, 1955-57; Asst Under-Sec., FO, 1957-60; Ambassador to Finland, 1961-63; Ambassador to the European Communities in Brussels, 1963-65; Dep. Under-Sec. of State, FO, 1965-68; Dir, Hill, Samuel & Co. Ltd, 1968-69; Dep. Under-Sec. of State, FCO, and Leader at official level of British delegn to negotiate entry to EEC, 1969-72; Chm., Intervention Bd for Agricl Produce, 1972-74; Dir, Unigate Ltd, 1974-83. Dir, Britain in Europe Campaign, 1974-75. *Publication:* Our European Future, 1972 (Stamp Meml Lecture). *Address:* 37 Flood Street, SW3.
*Died 11 Jan. 1988.*

**O'NEILL, Denis Edmund,** CB 1957; formerly Under-Secretary, Ministry of Transport, retired 1968; *b* 26 Feb. 1908; *e* surv. *s* of late Very Rev. F. W. S. O'Neill, DD and Mrs O'Neill, Belfast and Manchuria; *m* 1st, 1930, Pamela (marr. diss. 1936), *d* of John Walter; one *s*; 2nd, 1944, Barbara (*d* 1980), *d* of Mrs W. E. Norton; one adopted *d*. *Educ:* Royal Academical Institution, Belfast; Oriel Coll., Oxford (scholar). Entered Ministry of Transport, Oct. 1931; successively Private Secretary to following Ministers of Transport: Rt Hon. Leslie (later Lord) Hore-Belisha, MP, 1935-37; Leslie Burgin, MP, 1937-39; Euan Wallace, MP, 1939-40; Sir John (Lord) Reith, MP, 1940; Lt-Col J. T. C. Moore-Brabazon, MP (later Lord Brabazan of Tara), 1940-41, and (with F. H. Keenlyside) Lord Leathers (Minister of War Transport), Asst Sec., 1943; Under-Sec., Min. of Transport, 1951. *Recreations:* reading, football, bridge. *Address:* Twyford Abbey Nursing Home, Twyford Abbey Road, Park Royal, NW10.
*Died 22 Dec. 1981.*

**O'NEILL, Most Rev. Michael Cornelius,** OBE 1945; MM 1918; *b* 15 Feb. 1898; Irish Canadian. *Educ:* St Michael's College, University of Toronto; St Augustine's Seminary, Toronto. Overseas Service, Signaller, CFA, European War, 1916-19. St Joseph's Seminary, Edmonton; Professor, 1928-39; Rector, 1930-39. Overseas Service, Canadian Chaplain Services, War of 1939-45; Principal Chaplain (Army) Overseas, (RC), 1941-45; Principal Chaplain (Army), (RC), 1945-46. Archbishop of Regina, 1948-73. Hon. Chaplain, Saskatchewan Comd, Royal Canadian Legion, 1973. Nat. Lutheran Merit Award, 1974. Hon. LLD: Toronto, 1952; Univ. of Saskatchewan (Regina Campus), 1974; Hon. DD Univ. of St Michael's Coll., Toronto, 1977. *Address:* 67 Hudson Drive, Regina, Sask, Canada. *Club:* East India, Devonshire, Sports and Public Schools.
*Died 10 June 1983.*

**ONIANS, Richard Broxton,** MA (Liverpool), PhD (Cantab); Hildred Carlile Professor of Latin in University of London, 1936-66, later Emeritus; *b* 11 January 1899; *s* of late Richard Henry Onians, Liverpool; *m* 1937, Rosalind, *d* of late Lt-Col Ernest Browning Lathbury, OBE, MD, RAMC, Chipperfield, Herts; two *s* four *d*. *Educ:* Liverpool Inst.; Liverpool Univ. (1st Class Hons Classics); Trinity Coll. Cambridge (Senior Scholarship Examination, Open Research Studentship, Hooper English Oration Prize); Craven Grant for archæological research in Greece, and Hare Prize (Univ. of Cambridge). Member Council Assoc. of Univ. Teachers, 1945-53; Exec. Cttee 1946-51; Chm. London Consultative Cttee (AUT), 1946-48; Chm., Nat. Campaign Cttee for Expansion of Higher Educ., 1947-Feb. 1948 and June 1948-53; Chm. Joint Standing Cttee and Conf. on Library Cooperation, 1948-60; Mem. Exec. Cttee and Finance Committee of National Central Library, 1947-53. Formerly 4th South Lancs and RAF (1917-18); Lecturer in Latin,

Univ. of Liverpool, 1925–33; Professor of Classics, Univ. of Wales (Swansea), 1933–35. *Publications:* The Origins of European Thought about the Body, the Mind, the Soul, the World, Time, and Fate: new interpretations of Greek, Roman, and kindred evidence, also of some basic Jewish and Christian beliefs, 1951, enlarged edn 1954; articles and reviews in Classical Journals. *Recreation:* walking. *Address:* Stokesay, 21 Luard Road, Cambridge. *T:* Cambridge 244250.                                   *Died* 21 *May* 1986.

**ONION, Francis Leo,** CMG 1968; JP; Director, NZ Co-operative Dairy Co. Ltd (Chairman, 1961–69); Chairman, NZ Dairy Board, 1968–76 (Deputy Chairman, 1964–68); *b* 10 July 1903; *s* of Edwin Joseph Onion, Blenheim, NZ; *m* 1931, *d* of D. Ross, Otorohanga, NZ; two *s* one *d*. *Educ:* Hamilton High School. Farmer and Company Director; Chairman: Waipa County Council, NZ, 1947–61; New Zealand Counties Ward, 1947–61; Central Waikato Electric Power Board, 1947–61; Maramurua Coalfields Ltd, 1961–69; Auckland Farm Products Ltd, 1967–; New Zealand Dairy Exporter Newspaper, 1963–; Mem. Bd, NZ Meat Producers, 1969–75. JP Hamilton, 1961. Coronation Medal, 1953. *Recreations:* shooting and bowls. *Address:* Te-Kowhai, RD8, Frankton, New Zealand. *T:* HOT 832 NZ. *Club:* National (Hamilton, NZ).
                                                     *Died* 26 *Aug.* 1983.

**ONSLOW, Maj.-Gen. Sir Denzil M.;** *see* Macarthur-Onslow.

**ONSLOW, William George,** CB 1970; Chairman Yorkshire and Humberside Economic Planning Board, 1965–71; *b* 12 June 1908; *s* of Albert Edward and Ann Onslow; *m* Joyce Elizabeth Robson; two *s* one *d*. *Educ:* Medway Technical College; London University. Board of Trade: Patent Examiner, 1930–39; Principal, 1942–46; Assistant Secretary, 1946–65; Under Secretary, Department of Economic Affairs, 1965, Min. of Housing and Local Govt, 1969, DoE, 1970–71. *Recreation:* golf. *Address:* 9 Elmete Avenue, Leeds, West Yorkshire. *T:* Leeds 659706.                *Died* 1 *Sept.* 1983.

**OPENSHAW, William Harrison,** DL; **His Honour Judge Openshaw;** a Circuit Judge (formerly Chairman Lancashire Quarter Sessions), since 1958; *b* 11 Dec. 1912; *s* of late Sir James Openshaw, OBE, JP, DL; *m* 1945, Joyce Lawford; two *s* one *d*. *Educ:* Harrow; St Catharine's, Cambridge. Called to Bar, Inner Temple, 1936; practised on Northern Circuit; Recorder of Preston, 1958–71, Hon. Recorder, 1971–; Judge and Assessor of the Borough Court of Pleas, Preston, 1958–72. DL Lancs, 1968. *Address:* Park House, Broughton, Lancs.                                              *Died* 12 *May* 1981.

**OPHER, William David,** CBE 1963; CEng, FIMechE; Joint Managing Director, Vickers Limited, 1967–68, retired; Pro-Chancellor, Lancaster University, 1978–80; *b* 30 May 1903; *s* of William Thomas Opher, London, and Margaret Mary Carson, Belfast; *m* 1930, Marie Dorothy, 3rd *d* of William Fane; one *s*. *Educ:* Borough Polytechnic, London. Apprenticed Arnold Goodwin & Son, Bankside; joined Vickers, 1928; Director: Vickers Ltd, Shipbuilding Group, 1955; Vickers Ltd, 1959; Rolls-Royce & Associates Ltd, 1959; Vickers & Bookers Ltd, 1959; British Hovercraft Corporation, 1966; Chairman Vickers, Ltd, Engineering Group, 1962–67. Mem. Council, Lancaster Univ., 1968; Governor, Polytechnic of the South bank (formerly Borough Polytechnic), 1969–73. Freeman, City of London, 1949. Hon. LLD Lancaster, 1980. Serving Brother, Order of St John, 1962, Officer Brother, 1973. *Recreations:* golfing, fishing, shooting. *Address:* 1 Dunkeld, The Esplanade, Grange-over-Sands, Cumbria LA11 7HH *T:* (home) Grange-over-Sands 3151. *Club:* Bexleyheath Golf.                                             *Died* 9 *June* 1983.

**OPIE, Evelyn Arnold;** Matron, King's College Hospital, SE5, 1947–60; *b* 21 Aug. 1905; twin *d* of George and Annie Opie. *Educ:* Wentworth School for Girls, Bournemouth. Westminster Sick Children's Hosp., 1924–26 (sick children's trng); Guy's Hosp., SE1, 1926–29; SRN Oct. 1929. Midwifery Trng SCM, 1930, Sister, 1930–32, Guy's Hosp.; private nursing, Bournemouth, 1932–33; Sister (Radium Dept and Children's Ward), 1933–39, Administrative Sister, Asst Matron, Dep. Matron, 1939–47, Guy's Hosp. Diploma in Nursing of London Univ., 1935. *Recreations:* music, gardening. *Address:* Sundial Cottage Rest Home, Fawley, Southampton SO4 1BW. *T:* Southampton (0703) 899011.                       *Died* 12 *May* 1990.

**OPIE, Peter Mason;** author; *b* 25 Nov. 1918; *o s* of late Major Philip Adams Opie, RAMC and Margaret Collett-Mason; *m* 1943, Iona Margaret Balfour Opie; two *s* one *d*. *Educ:* Eton. Served Royal Fusiliers, 1939; commnd Royal Sussex Regt, 1940, invalided 1941. Engaged in research with wife from 1944. Pres. Anthropology Section, British Assoc., 1962–63; Pres., Folklore Soc., 1963–64. Silver Medal, RSA, 1953; Coote-Lake Medal (jtly with wife), 1960. Hon. MA Oxon, 1962. *Publications:* I Want to Be, 1939; Having Held the Nettle, 1945; The Case of Being a Young Man, 1946 (joint-winner Chosen Book Competition); works on child life and literature (with Iona Opie): I Saw Esau, 1947; The Oxford Dictionary of Nursery Rhymes, 1951; The Oxford Nursery Rhyme Book, 1955; Christmas Party Games, 1957; The Lore and Language of Schoolchildren, 1959; Puffin Book of Nursery Rhymes 1963

(European Prize City of Caorle); Children's Games in Street and Playground, 1969 (Chicago Folklore Prize); The Oxford Book of Children's Verse, 1973; Three Centuries of Nusery Rhymes and Poetry for Children (exhibition catalogue), 1973, enl. edn 1977; The Classic Fairy Tales, 1974; A Nursery Companion, 1980; contrib. Encycl. Britannica, Chambers Encycl., New Cambridge Bibliog. of English Lit., etc. *Recreations:* book collecting, blackberry picking. *Address:* Westerfield House, West Liss, Hants.
                                                     *Died* 5 *Feb.* 1982.

**OPIE, Redvers,** CMG 1944; MA (Oxon and Harvard); PhD (Harvard); Director: Business International (New York), since 1954; Fomentadora Rural SA (Mexico); Mexico–US Chamber of Commerce, since 1979; Chairman: Amparo Servicios Turisticos SA, since 1979; Amparo Travel Services Inc., Washington DC, since 1982; ECANAL SA de CV, publisher of reports on Mexico, since 1978; *b* 20 January 1900; *s* of late James Reid and Bessie Hockaday Opie; naturalised US citizen, 1948, Mexican citizen, 1978; *m* 1st, 1929, Catharine Crombie Taussig (marr. diss., 1948), Cambridge, Mass; one *s* one *d*; 2nd, 1971, Blanca Bolaños Aceves, México, DF. *Educ:* Rutherford Coll.; Univ. of Durham. Lectr in Economics, Univ. of Durham, 1919–23, Wellesley Coll. (USA), 1923–24, Harvard Univ. 1924–30; Fellow of Magdalen College, Oxford, 1931–45, Home Bursar, 1935–40 (on leave of absence for National Service from Sept. 1939); University Lecturer in Economic Science, 1936–39; Counsellor and Economic Adviser to British Embassy, Washington, DC (resigned 1946). Adviser, UK Delegation, International Food Conference, 1943; UK Delegate, International Monetary and Financial Conference, 1944; Member US Govt Mission, on Private Foreign Investment, to Turkey, 1953; Senior Staff Mem., Brookings Institution, Washington, DC, 1947–53. Economic Counsellor, Amer. Chamber of Commerce, Mexico City, 1966–78. President, American Ligurian Company Inc., New York, 1947–54. Gen. Editor, Oxford Economic Papers, 1938–39. Hon. Vis. Prof., City Univ. Business Sch., 1983–84. Dhc: City Univ.; Universidad de las Americas. *Publications:* (joint) Major Problems of US Foreign Policy, annually, 1947–52; Anglo-American Economic Relations, 1950; Current Issues in Foreign Economic Assistance, 1951; The Search For Peace Settlements, 1951; American Foreign Assistance, 1953; Selected papers on the Mexican and International Economies, 1966–68, 1968. *Recreations:* tennis and music. *Address:* Rio Lerma 156, 06500 Mexico, DF. *T:* 5145373. *Clubs:* Harvard (New York); Metropolitan (Washington, DC); Churubusco, University (Mexico).
                                                     *Died* 10 *Feb.* 1984.

**OPPENHEIMER, Raymond Harry,** CBE 1959; *b* 13 Nov. 1905; *s* of Louis Oppenheimer and Charlotte Emily Pollak. *Educ:* Harrow; Christ Church, Oxford. Served in RAFVR, 1940–45 (Fighter Controller). *Recreations:* golf, dog breeding (bull terriers). *Address:* White Waltham Place, Berkshire. *T:* Maidenhead 27103. *Clubs:* Royal and Ancient; Royal Lytham, etc.
                                                     *Died* 12 *Aug.* 1984.

**ORCHARD-LISLE, Aubrey Edwin,** CBE 1973; Consultant Partner, Healey & Baker, Surveyors, London, Amsterdam, Paris, New York and Brussels (Senior Partner until 1973); *b* 12 March 1908; *s* of late Edwin Orchard-Lisle and late Lucy Ellen Lock; *m* 1934, Phyllis Muriel Viall (*d* 1981); one *s* one *d*. *Educ:* West Buckland Sch., N Devon; Coll. of Estate Management. FRICS. Joined Healey & Baker, 1926. Governor, Guy's Hosp. 1953–74; Vice-Chm. of Bd, 1963–74; Governor, Guy's Hosp. Med. Sch., 1964–84; Chm., Special Trustees, Guy's Hosp., 1974–84; Mem., Lambeth, Southwark, Lewisham, AHA (Teaching), 1974–79; Property Consultant, NCB Superannuation Schemes, 1953–; Mem. Bd, Gen. Practice Finance Corp., 1966–80; Chm., Adv. Panel for Institutional Finance in New Towns, 1969–80. National Bus Company: part-time Mem., 1971–77; Mem., Property Cttee, 1971–83; Mem., Investment Adv. Cttee, Pension Schemes (Best (Estates) Ltd), 1974–86; Mem., Property Div., 1987–88 (Dir, National Bus Properties Ltd, 1983–87). *Recreations:* work, gardens. *Address:* 30 Mount Row, Grosvenor Square, W1Y 5DA. *T:* 01–499 6470; White Walls, Quarry Wood Road, Marlow, Bucks. *T:* Marlow 2573. *Clubs:* St Stephen's Constitutional, Naval and Military, Buck's, Lansdowne, MCC.
                                                     *Died* 5 *Aug.* 1989.

**ORGANE, Sir Geoffrey (Stephen William),** Kt 1968; MD, FFARCS; FRCS; Emeritus Professor of Anæsthetics, University of London, Westminster Medical School; formerly: Civilian Consultant in Anæsthetics to Royal Navy; Consultant Adviser in Anæsthetics, Ministry of Health; *b* Madras, 25 Dec. 1908; *er s* of Rev. William Edward Hartland Organe, K-i-H, and Alice (*née* Williams); *m* 1935, Margaret Mary Bailey, *e d* of Rev. David Bailey Davies, MC; one *s* two *d*. *Educ:* Taunton Sch.; Christ's Coll., Cambridge; Westminster Med. Sch. MRCS, LRCP, 1933; DA, RCP&S, 1937; MA, MD Cantab 1941; FFARCS 1948; FRCS 1965. Various resident appointments and first Anæsthetic Registrar (1938–39), Westminster Hospital; two years in general practice. Hon. Secretary, Medical Research Council's Anæsthetics Sub-Committee of

Committee on Traumatic Shock, 1941–47; formerly Hon. Sec. Anæsthetics Cttee, Cttee on Analgesia in Midwifery; Vice-Pres., BMA Sect. Anæsthetics, Harrogate, 1949, Toronto, 1955; Pres., World Fedn of Socs. of Anæsthesiologists, 1964–68 (Sec.-Treas., 1955–64); Mem. Coun., RCS, 1958–61, Joseph Clover Lectr, Fac. of Anæsthetics; Royal Society of Medicine: Mem. Council; Hon. Sec. 1953–58; Hon. Fellow, 1974; Pres. Sect. of Anæsthetics, 1949–50 (Hon. Mem.); Assoc. of Anæsthetists of Gt Brit. and Ire.: Hon. Sec. 1949–53; Vice-Pres. 1953–54; Mem. Council, 1957–59; Pres. 1954–57; Hon. Mem., 1974; John Snow Silver Medal, 1972; Mem. Cttee of Anæsthetists' Group of BMA (Chm. 1955–58); Pres. SW Metropolitan Soc. of Anæsthetists, 1957–59; Dean, Faculty of Anæsthetists, 1958–61; Examr in Anæsthetics, Conjoint Bd; Examiner for FFARCS. Visited Italy, Turkey, Greece, Syria, Lebanon for Brit. Council; Denmark, Norway for WHO; also Portugal, France, Switzerland, Spain, Belgium, Netherlands, Germany, Finland, USA, Canada, Argentina, Australia, Venezuela, Mexico, Uganda, Peru, Japan, Hong Kong, Philippines, Brazil, Ceylon, Egypt, India, Iran, Israel, Malaysia, Uruguay, Austria, Sweden, Poland, USSR, Bulgaria, Czechoslovakia, Malta. Hon. or Corr. Mem., Danish, Argentine, Australian, Austrian, Brazilian, Canadian, Greek, Portuguese, French, German, Italian, Philippine, Spanish, Venezuelan Societies of Anæsthetists; Hon. FFARACS 1957; Hon. FFARCS 1975. *Publications:* various articles and chapters in medical journals and textbooks. *Recreations:* travel, gardening, photography, competitive sports; (formerly Pres., Vice-Pres., Hon. Treas., Capt. 1933) United Hospitals Athletic Club. *Address:* March Hares, The Street, Cherhill, Calne, Wilts SN11 8XP. *Died* 7 *Jan.* 1989.

**ORIGO, Marchesa Iris,** DBE 1977; FRSL; author; *b* Birdlip, Glos, 15 August 1902; *o d* of W. Bayard Cutting, Westbrook, Long Island, USA, and Lady Sybil Cuffe; *m* 1924, Marchese Antonio Origo (*d* 1976); two *d. Educ:* privately, mostly in Florence. Holds honorary doctorates from Smith College and Wheaton College, USA; Isabella d'Este medal for essays and historical studies, Mantua, Italy, 1966. Gold Medal, Italian Red Cross, 1944 (for relief work in villages destroyed during Second World War); DBE (for work for partisans and escaped British POWs during Second World War). *Publications:* Leopardi, a biography, 1935 (revised 1953); Allegra, 1935; Tribune of Rome, 1938; War in Val d'Orcia, 1947; Giovanna and Jane, 1948; The Last Attachment, 1949; The Merchant of Prato, 1957; A Measure of Love, 1957; The World of San Bernardino, 1963; Images and Shadows, Part of a Life, 1970; The Vagabond Path: an anthology, 1972; A Need to Testify, 1983; Un'amica: rittrato di Elsa Dallolio, 1988; articles in Speculum, History Today, Atlantic Monthly, TLS. *Recreations:* travel, gardening. *Address:* La Foce, Chianciano Terme, 53042 Siena, Italy. *Died* 28 *June* 1988.

**ORMANDY, Eugene,** KBE (Hon.) 1976; MusD; Conductor and Music Director of Philadelphia Orchestra, 1936–80, then Conductor Laureate; *b* 18 Nov. 1899; Hungarian; *s* of Benjamin and Rosalie Ormandy; *m* 1st, 1922, Steffy Goldner (marr. diss. 1947; decd), harpist, NY Philharmonic Orchestra; no *c*; 2nd, 1950, Margaret Frances Hitsch. *Educ:* Royal State Acad. of Music, BA 1914; state diploma for art of violin playing, 1916, and as prof., 1917; Grad. Gymnasium; student Univ. of Budapest, 1917–20. Hon. MusD: Hamline Univ., St Paul, 1934; Univ. of Pennsylvania, 1937; Philadelphia Academy of Music, 1939; Curtis Inst. of Music, 1946; Temple Univ., 1949; Univ. of Michigan, 1952; Lehigh Univ., 1953; Villanova Univ., 1968; Rensselaer Polytechnic Inst., 1968; Peabody Inst., 1968; Univ. of Illinois, 1969; Doctor of Letters: Clark Univ., 1956, Miami Univ., 1959, Rutgers Univ., 1960, Long Island Univ., 1965; Lafayette Coll., 1966; Jefferson Medical Coll., 1973; Moravian Coll., 1976; holds many other hon. degrees. Toured Hungary as child prodigy; Head of master classes, State Conservatorium of Music, Budapest, at age of 20; arrived in United States, 1921, naturalised 1927; substituted for Toscanini as Conductor Philadelphia Orchestra; Conductor Minneapolis Symphony Orch., 1931–36; toured Australia, 1944, S America, 1946, Europe, 1950, 1951, 1952, 1953, 1954, 1955, 1957, 1958, 1975, Japan, 1967, 1972, 1978. Appeared Edinburgh Festival, 1955, 1957. Caballero, Order of Merit of Juan Pablo Duarte, Dominican Republic, 1945; Commandeur, French Legion of Honour, 1958; Knight, Order of Dannebrog, 1st cl., 1952; Knight 1st cl., Order of the White Rose, Finland, 1955; Comdr, Order of Lion of Finland, 1966; Honor Cross for Arts and Sciences, Austria, 1967; Golden Medallion, Vienna Philharmonic Orch., 1967; Freedom Medal, USA, 1970; Commendatore, Italy, 1972; Gold Baton Award, Amer. Symph. Orch. League, 1979. *Address:* 1420 Locust Street, Philadelphia, Pa 19102, USA. *Died* 12 *March* 1985.

**ORMATHWAITE, 6th Baron,** *cr* 1868; **John Arthur Charles Walsh,** Bt 1804; Farming since 1950; *b* 25 December 1912; *s* of 5th Baron Ormathwaite and Lady Margaret Jane Douglas-Home (*d* 1955), 3rd *d* of 12th Earl of Home; *S* father, 1944; unmarried. *Educ:* Eton College; Trinity College, Cambridge. *Heir:* none. *Address:* Pen-y-Bont Hall, Llandrindod Wells, Powys. *T:* Pen-y-Bont 228.
*Died* 8 *March* 1984 (*ext*).

**ORME, John Samuel,** CB 1963; OBE (mil.) 1945; *b* 7 May 1916; *s* of late Sidney Wilkinson Orme, solicitor, and Evelyn Orme; *m* 1940, Jean, *d* of G. H. Harris; three *s* one *d. Educ:* The High School, Newcastle under Lyme; St John's College, Oxford; Ecole des Sciences Politiques, Paris. BA 1937, 1st Cl. Hons, Sch. of Mod. Hist.; MA 1957. Air Ministry, 1938; served RAF, 1941–45; Wing Comdr, 1944 (despatches, OBE); Air Ministry, 1945; Internat. Staff of NATO, Paris, 1954–57; Assistant Under Secretary of State, Air Ministry, 1957–58, and again 1960–64; Under-Secretary: Cabinet Office, 1958–60; Min. of Transport, 1964–66; Assistant Under-Secretary of State: Welsh Office, 1966–70; DHSS, 1970–75. LSE, 1976–77. Cleveland, USA, Foundation Fellow, 1977. *Address:* Third House, Manor Crescent, Seer Green, Bucks HP9 2QX. *T:* Beaconsfield 5920. *Club:* Reform. *Died* 20 *Jan.* 1984.

**ORMEROD, Major Sir (Cyril) Berkeley,** KBE 1960 (CBE 1954, OBE 1946); Director, Public Relations, British Information Services, New York, 1945–62 (Financial Adviser, British Press Service, 1940–45); formerly Chairman, Director and Trustee of public companies and trusts, now retired; *b* London, 3 Oct. 1897; *s* of late Ernest Berkeley Ormerod, Ashton-under-Lyne, Lancs, and late Alice Heys; *m* 1962, Beatrice (*d* 1981), *widow* of Frederick Sigrist, Nassau, Bahamas. *Educ:* Colet Court; St Paul's Sch.; Royal Military Academy. Royal Regt of Artillery, 1916–26; European War, active service in France and Belgium, 1917–18. London Stock Exchange (Foster and Braithwaite), 1929–39. Regular contributor to Financial Times, Investor's Chronicle, Barron's (New York), 1934–39. Member UK Delegation, UN organizational Conference, San Francisco, 1945; Public Relations Adviser to Secretary of State (late Ernest Bevin), Foreign Ministers' Conference, New York, 1946. Specially attached to the Ambassador's Staff as Press Adviser to the Royal Party during American visit of the Queen and the Duke of Edinburgh, Oct. 1957; Press Advisor to the Governor of the Bahamas during Nassau talks between Prime Minister Macmillan and late President Kennedy, Dec. 1962. Member of The Pilgrims; RIIA (Chatham House); FIPR; Hon. Life Mem., Assoc. of Radio and TV News Analysts, USA. *Publication:* Dow Theory Applied to the London Stock Exchange, 1937. *Recreations:* cricket (Oxfordshire, The Army, RA, MCC, I Zingari, Free Foresters, etc), golf (won Army Championship, 1924), bridge. *Address:* PO Box N 969, Nassau, Bahamas. *Clubs:* Cavalry and Guards, Boodle's, MCC; Royal and Ancient (St Andrews); Berkshire Golf; Knickerbocker, Lotos, Dutch Treat (New York); Travellers' (Paris); Lyford Cay (Nassau). *Died* 1 *Nov.* 1983.

**ORMEROD, Richard Caton;** HM Diplomatic Service, retired; *b* 22 Jan. 1915; *s* of late Prof. Henry Arderne Ormerod and Mildred Robina Ormerod (*née* Caton); *m* 1947, Elizabeth Muriel, *yr d* of late Sheriff J. W. More, St Andrews; two *s* one *d* (and one *d* decd). *Educ:* Winchester Coll.; New Coll., Oxford (BA). India Office, 1938. War Service, 1941–45: Indian Army, 7th Light Cavalry; active service in Imphal and Burma (wounded). Asst Private Secretary to Secretary of State for India and Burma, 1945–46; Principal, Burma Office, 1946; CRO, 1948; First Secretary, British High Commn: Bombay, 1951–53; Wellington, 1956–59; Asst Secretary, 1960; Counsellor, British High Commn, Calcutta, 1962–65; Ministry of Overseas Development, 1965; Consul-Gen., Marseilles, 1967–71. *Publication:* Ferns in the Waste, 1943. *Recreations:* music, gardening, archaeology. *Address:* Chequers, 44 The Street, Marden, Devizes, Wilts SN10 3RQ; La Gourguette, 84750 Viens, France.
*Died* 17 *May* 1981.

**OROWAN, Egon,** DrIng; FRS 1947; Professor of Mechanical Engineering, Massachusetts Institute of Technology, Cambridge, Massachusetts, USA, 1950–67, now Emeritus; Senior Lecturer, MIT, 1967–73; *b* Budapest, 2 Aug. 1902; *s* of Berthold Orowan and Josephine Ságvári; *m* 1941, Yolande Schonfeld; one *d. Educ:* University of Vienna; Technical Univ., Berlin-Charlottenburg. Demonstrator Technical Univ., Berlin-Charlottenburg, 1928; i/c Krypton Works, United Incandescent Lamp and Electrical Co. Ltd, Ujpest, Hungary, 1936; Research in Physics of Metals, Physics Dept, University of Birmingham, 1937, and Cavendish Laboratory, Cambridge, 1939; Reader in the Physics of Metals, University of Cambridge. Alcoa Vis. Prof., Univ. of Pittsburgh, 1972–73. Mem., Nat. Acad. of Sciences; Corresp. Mem., Akademie der Wissenschaften, Göttingen. Thomas Hawksley Gold Medal, MechE, 1944; Bingham Medal, Society of Rheology, 1959; Carl Friedrich Gauss Medal, Braunschweigische Wissenschaftliche Gesellschaft, 1968; Vincent Bendix Gold Medal, Amer. Soc. of Engrg Educn, 1971; Paul Bergsøe Medal, Dansk Metallurgisk Selskab, 1973; Acta Metallurgica Gold Medal, 1985; Heyn Medal, Deutsche Gesellschaft für Metallkunde, 1986. DrIng (*hc*) Technische Universität, Berlin, 1965. *Publications:* Papers in scientific and engineering journals. *Address:* 44 Payson Terrace, Belmont, Mass 02178, USA. *Died* 3 *Aug.* 1989.

**ORR, Prof. John Washington;** Professor of Pathology and Director of Cancer Research, University of Birmingham, and Hon. Pathologist, United Birmingham Hospitals, 1948–66; Professor Emeritus, 1967;

*b* 5 Aug. 1901; *er s* of Frederick William and Elizabeth Orr, Belfast; *m* 1932, Nora Margaret (*d* 1965), 2nd *d* of David James and Margaret Carmichael; one *s* one *d*. *Educ:* Royal Academical Institution, Belfast; Queen's University of Belfast. MB, BCh, BAO, Belfast, 1923; BSc (1st class Hons) Belfast, 1924, DPH 1924; MD (Gold Medal) Belfast, 1926; MRCP London, 1940; MD Birmingham, 1948; FRCP London, 1950. Hon. MD Perugia, 1961. Riddell Demonstrator of Pathology, Belfast, 1924; Musgrave student in Pathology, Belfast, 1925; First Assistant Pathologist and Asst Curator of the Museum, St Mary's Hospital, W2, 1926; Lecturer in Exp. Pathology and Asst Director of Cancer Research, University of Leeds, 1932; Reader in Exp. Pathology, 1937; President of Leeds Pathological Club, 1946–47. Senior Research Pathologist, Detroit Institute of Cancer Research, 1966–67; Research Pathologist, Royal Victoria Hosp., Bournemouth, 1967–69. Served War of 1939–45 as Pathologist in EMS and Battalion MO, Home Guard. *Publications:* articles on medical subjects in Journal of Pathology and Bacteriology, British Journal of Exp. Pathology, British Journal of Cancer, Lancet, American Journal of Cancer, etc, especially papers on experimental cancer research. *Address:* c/o Lloyds Bank, 359 Bristol Road, Birmingham BS 7SS.                                    *Died* 17 *June* 1984.

**ORR, Captain Lawrence Percy Story;** Director, Associated Leisure Ltd, 1972–84; *b* 16 Sept. 1918; *s* of late Very Rev. W. R. M. Orr, MA, LLD, sometime Dean of Dromore; *m* 1939, Jean Mary (separated 1952; marr. diss. 1976), *d* of F. C. Hughes; four *s* (one *d* decd). *Educ:* Campbell Coll., Belfast; Trinity Coll., Dublin. Served with East Lancashire Regt, Royal Armoured Corps, and Life Guards, 1939–46. MP (UU) South Down, 1950–Sept. 1974. Mem. Exec., British Chamber of Commerce, 1951–56. Dir, Pye (Scottish) Telecommunications, 1952–62. Vice-Chairman, Conservative Broadcasting Cttee, 1959–62; Leader, Ulster Unionist Parly Party, 1964–74; Vice-Pres., Ulster Unionist Council. Imperial Grand Master, Orange Order, 1964–73. *Recreations:* fishing, painting, chess. *Address:* The Lodge, Honeywood House, Lydiard Millicent, Swindon, Wilts.                                        *Died* 11 *July* 1990.

**OSBORN, Sir Danvers (Lionel Rouse),** 8th Bt, *cr* 1662; *b* 31 Jan. 1916; *s* of Sir Algernon K. B. Osborn, 7th Bt, JP and Beatrice Elliot Kennard, *d* of William Bunce Greenfield, JP, DL; *S* father, 1948; *m* 1943, Constance Violette, JP, SSStJ, *d* of late Major Leonard Frank Rooke, KOSB; one *s* one *d* (one *s* and one *d* decd). *Educ:* Eton; Magdalene Coll., Cambridge. Employed as Civil Assistant in Intelligence Dept of War Office, 1940–45. Joined Spicers Ltd, 1955. Director of two Picture Galleries. *Recreations:* golf, tennis, bridge. *Heir: s* Richard Henry Danvers Osborn, *b* 12 Aug. 1958. *Address:* The Dower House, Moor Park, Farnham, Surrey. *Club:* MCC.
                                                      *Died* 19 *July* 1983.

**OSBORN, Margaret,** MA; High Mistress of St Paul's Girls' School, Hammersmith, 1948–63, retired; *b* 23 April 1906; *d* of Rev. G. S. Osborn, late Rector of Milton, Cambridge. *Educ:* St Leonard's Sch., St Andrews, Fife; St Hugh's Coll., Oxford. Graduated 1929; MA Hons Lit.Hum. Oxon. Pelham Student at British School at Rome, 1931; Headmistress of St George's School for Girls, Edinburgh, 1943–48. *Publication:* A Latin Epithet, article in Mnemosyne (Leyden Journal), 1932. *Recreations:* music and reading. *Address:* Woodstock House, Woodstock, Oxford OX7 1UG.
                                                     *Died* 29 *April* 1985.

**OSBORNE, Sir Basil,** Kt 1967; CBE 1962; Lord Mayor of Hobart, Tasmania, 1959–70, Alderman, 1952–76; Chairman, Metropolitan Transport Trust, 1971–78; business consultant; *b* 19 April 1907; *s* of late Alderman W. W. Osborne, MBE; *m* 1934, Esma (*d* 1983), *d* of late T. Green; one *s*. *Educ:* Metropolitan Business Coll. Mem. Gen. Cttee, Savings Bank of Tas, 1969–85. Dir, Australian Brain Foundn (formerly Aust. Neurol Foundn), 1970–. Chm., Board of Management, Royal Hobart Hospital, 1968–81 (Vice-Chairman, 1952–68); President: St John's Ambulance Assoc., 1960–76; Asia-Pacific Life Saving Council, 1984–86; Australian Pres., RLSS, 1979–87 (Life Governor, Commonwealth Vice Pres., 1982–, Commonwealth Council). Life Member: City of Hobart Eisteddfod Soc., 1972; (first), Asthma Foundn, 1984; Hon. Life Member: Hobart Orpheus Club, 1977; Hospital Public Relns Officers' Assoc. of Australia, 1977. Hon. Fellow: Australian Marketing Inst., 1967; Inst. of Ambulance Officers (Aust.), 1975. OStJ 1972. *Recreations:* music, sport. *Address:* 6 Myella Drive, Chigwell, Tasmania 7011, Australia. *Club:* Royal Autocar (Tasmania).
                                                     *Died* 11 *Nov.* 1987.

**OSBORNE, Prof. John;** (First) Professor of Dental Prosthetics, University of Birmingham, 1948–73; *b* 6 April 1911; *s* of John W. and Gertrude Osborne; *m* 1937, Virginia Preston, *d* of W. H. Fruish; one *s* one *d*. *Educ:* Bishop Vesey Grammar Sch.; Birmingham Univ. LDS Birmingham, 1933; PhD Sheffield, 1945; MDS 1948; FDS, RCS, 1948; FFD, RCSI, 1964; House Surgeon and junior staff appointments at Birmingham Dental Hospital, 1933–37; also private practice during same period; Lectr in Dental Prosthetics, Univ. of Sheffield, 1937, Univ. of Birmingham, 1946; Dir of Dental Studies,

Univ. of Birmingham, 1965–69 (Dep. Dir, 1953–65). Visiting Professor: NW University, Chicago, 1956–57; Univ. of Adelaide, 1971; Univ. of Malaya, 1973–74. Guest lecturer, Australian Dental Assoc., 1962. External Examiner to Universities of Malaya, Liverpool, Durham, London, Manchester, Glasgow, Dundee, Bristol, Edinburgh, Sheffield, Belfast, Lagos, Singapore, and to RCS and RCSI. President: British Dental Students Assoc., 1956–58; Central Counties Branch, British Dental Assoc., 1958–59, Hospitals Group, 1968–69. Queen's Silver Jubilee Medal, 1977; Tomes Medal, British Dental Assoc., 1981. *Publications:* Dental Mechanics for Students, 1939, 6th edn 1970; Acrylic Resins in Dentistry, 1942, 3rd edn 1948; Partial Dentures (with Dr G. A. Lammie), 1954, 4th edn, 1974; Dental Technology and Materials (with H. J. Wilson and M. Mansfield), 1978; scientific papers in leading dental journals. *Recreations:* philately, gardening. *Address:* Vesey Cottage, Warlands Lane, Shalfleet, Isle of Wight. *T:* Calbourne 384. *Club:* Island Sailing (Cowes).                                    *Died* 16 *Nov.* 1984.

**OSBORNE, Surgeon Rear-Admiral (D) Leslie Bartlet,** CB 1956; *b* 16 Sept. 1900; *s* of late Rev. Joseph Osborne, MA, and of Miriam Duke James; *m* 1929 (marr. diss. 1953); two *s* one *d*; *m* 1955, Joan Mary Williams (*née* Parnell). *Educ:* Caterham Sch.; Guy's Hospital. LDS, RCS England 1923; FDS, RCS (Edinburgh) 1955. Dental House Surgeon, Guy's Hospital, 1923. Entered Royal Navy, Surgeon Lieutenant (D), 1923; Surgeon Commander (D), 1936; Surgeon Captain (D), 1948; Surgeon Rear-Admiral (D), 1954; Deputy Director-General for Dental Services in the Royal Navy, 1954–57, retired. Served War of 1939–45. KHDS 1951; QHDS 1953–58. *Recreations:* Rugby Football (rep. RN, Sussex and Devonport Services; Hon. Manager British Isles Rugby Union Team to New Zealand and Australia, 1950; Chairman Rugby Football Union Selection Cttee, 1949–51; President, Rugby Football Union, 1956); gardening. *Address:* 4 Westbourne Court, Cooden Drive, Cooden Beach, Bexhill-on-Sea, East Sussex TN39 3AA. *T:* Cooden 4431.
                                                     *Died* 26 *Feb.* 1989.

**O'SHEA, Alexander Paterson,** CMG 1962; North American Director, New Zealand Meat Producers' Board, USA, 1964–68, retired, 1968; *b* 29 Dec. 1902; *s* of John O'Shea; *m* 1935; one *d*. *Educ:* Otago Boys' High Sch.; Victoria University College (now Victoria Univ. of Wellington) (BCom). Farming, 1919–27. Wellington City Corporation, 1928–35; Secretary, Farmers' Union, 1935–46 (later Federated Farmers of NZ Inc.); General Secretary, Federated Farmers of New Zealand Inc., Wellington, NZ, 1946–64. Fellow (Chartered Accountant) New Zealand Society of Accountants. *Publication:* The Public Be Damned, 1946. *Recreation:* onlooker, Rugby football. *Club:* Civil Service (Wellington, NZ).
                                                     *Died* 24 *Dec.* 1990.

**OSLEY, Arthur Sidney,** PhD; Consultant to Engineering Council, since 1983; *b* 21 Jan. 1917; *s* of Sidney Charles Osley and Emily Elizabeth Osley (*née* Fearn); *m* 1st, 1941, Betty Doreen Laird; two *s*; 2nd, 1955, Sheila Patricia Branigan. *Educ:* Peter Symonds School, Winchester; University College London (BA 1st Cl. Hons Classics 1938; DipEd 1940; PhD 1943). Admiralty, 1940–66; IDC 1961; MoD, 1966–74; Under Sec., Price Commn, 1976–78; Council of Engineering Instns, 1978–83. Set up Glade Press, 1969. Member: Art Workers' Guild; Double Crown Club. Hon. Mem., Vereniging Mercator, Holland. Editor, Jl of Soc. for Italic Handwriting, 1962–. *Publications:* Calligraphy and Palaeography: essays presented to Alfred Fairbank (ed), 1965; Mercator, 1969; Luminario: an introduction to the Italian Writing-Books of the sixteenth and seventeenth centuries, 1972; Scribes and Sources: handbook of the Chancery hand in the sixteenth century, 1980; contribs to learned jls. *Recreation:* printing, bookbinding, research into handwriting and calligraphy, chess, gardening, reading. *Address:* The Glade, Brook Road, Wormley, Godalming GU8 5UR. *T:* Wormley 2474.
                                                     *Died* 20 *March* 1987.

**OSMOND, Thomas Edward,** BA (hons), MB Cantab; MRCS, LRCP; late Hon. Consulting Venereologist to the British Army; *b* Thorpe-le-Soken, 7 Oct. 1884; *s* of Edward Osmond, JP; *m* 1920, Daisy Stewart Mathews (*d* 1963); one *s* one *d*. *Educ:* King's Sch., Rochester; Emmanuel Coll., Cambridge; St Bart.'s Hospital. MB Cantab 1912; joined RAMC; service in India and Mesopotamia, 1914–18 (despatches); transferred to RARO 1920 and appointed Pathologist VD Dept St Thomas' Hospital; recalled to Army 1 Sept. 1939; served in France; late Brig. RAMC; adviser in venereology to the Army, 1939, Consultant 1943–45; late MO i/c Male VD Dept and Marlborough Path. Lab., Royal Free Hospital, London; late Pres. Med. Society for the Study of Venereal Diseases; Fellow Med. Society of London; President Middlesex Partial County Committee and Ashford (Middlesex) Branch British Legion. *Publications:* Article, Venereal Disease, Encyclopædia Britannica, Book of the Year, 1939; Aids to the diagnosis and treatment of Venereal Diseases, 1946; articles, Venereal Disease and Social Implications of Venereal Disease, Chambers's Encyclopædia, 1947; Venereal Disease in Peace and War, British Journal of Venereal Diseases, 1949; contributions to British Medical Journal, The Practitioner,

etc. *Recreations:* gardening, bridge. *Address:* Lavender Cottage, Passage Hill, Mylor Bridge, near Falmouth, Cornwall.
*Died 30 June 1985.*

**OSMOND-CLARKE, Sir Henry,** KCVO 1969; CBE 1947; FRCS; Consulting Orthopædic Surgeon: London Hospital, E1 (Orthopædic Surgeon, 1946–70); Robert Jones and Agnes Hunt Orthopædic Hospital, Oswestry (Senior Visiting Surgeon, 1930–70); Hon. Civilian Consultant in Orthopædics, RAF, since 1946; Orthopædic Surgeon to the Queen, 1965–73; *b* 8 Feb. 1905; *e s* of W. J. Clarke, Brookeborough, Co. Fermanagh, NI; *m* 1936, Freda, *e d* of Richard Hutchinson, Bury, Lancs; two *d. Educ:* Clones High School; Trinity College, Dublin University; Vienna, Bologna, New York, Boston, London. BA 1925; MB, BCh (stip. cand.) 1926; FRCSIre 1930; FRCS 1932; Surgical Travelling Prize, TCD 1930. Consultant Orthopædic Surgeon, Oldchurch, Black Notley, Tilbury and East Grinstead Hosps; Orthopædic Surgeon, King Edward VII Hosp. for Officers, London; Cons. King Edward VII Convalescent Home for Officers, Osborne; Hunterian Prof. RCS, 1936. Service Cons. in Orthop. Surg., Air Cdre, RAF, 1941–46; Mayo Clinic Foundation Lecturer, 1948; Orthop. Mem. WHO Mission to Israel, 1951, to India, 1953, to Persia, 1957. Past President, British Orthop. Assoc. (former Editorial Sec. and Acting Sec.); FRSocMed and several Brit. Med. Socs. Formerly: Clinical Tutor in Orthop. Surg., Manchester Roy. Infirmary and Lecturer in Surg. Pathology (Orthop.), Univ. of Manchester; Orthop. Surg., Crumpsall Hosp., Manchester, and Biddulph Grange Orthop. Hosp., Stoke-on-Trent; Sen. Ho. Surg. and Orthop. Ho. Surg. Ancoats Hosp., Manchester, and Royal Nat. Orthop. Hospital, London. Mem. Council, RCS, 1959–75, Vice-Pres. 1970–72. Chm. Accident Services Review Cttee of Great Britain and Ireland, 1960. Hon. Member: American Orthop. Assoc.; American Acad. of Orthopædic Surgery; Australian, New Zealand and Canadian Orthopædic Assocs; Corresp. Mem., French Orthopædic Society and Surg. Soc. of Lyon; Mem. International Soc. of Orthopædics and Traumatology. *Publications:* papers on surgical and orthopædic subjects in leading surgical text-books and med. jls, including Half a Century of Orthopædic Progress in Great Britain, 1951. *Recreations:* travel, reading, fishing. *Address:* 46 Harley House, Marylebone Road, NW1 5HJ. *T:* 01–486 9975. *Club:* Royal Air Force.
*Died 24 Oct. 1986.*

**OSWALD, Thomas;** *b* 1 May 1904; *s* of John Oswald and Agnes Love, Leith; *m* 1933, Colina MacAskill, *d* of Archibald MacAlpin and Margaret MacAskill, Ballachulish, Argyllshire; three *s* one *d. Educ:* Yardheads and Bonnington Elementary Schools. Shipyard worker, transport worker. Official of Transport and General Workers' Union; Scottish Regional Trade Group Secretary, 1941–69. Contested (Lab) West Aberdeenshire, 1950. MP (Lab) Edinburgh Central, 1951–Feb. 1974; PPS to Secretary of State for Scotland, 1967–70. Sec. Treasurer, Scottish Parly Lab. Group, 1953–64; Sec., Members' Parly Cttee, 1956–66. Dir, St Andrew Animal Fund; Mem. Cttee, Scottish Soc. for Prevention of Vivisection; Nat. Pres., Scottish Old Age Pensions Assoc. *Recreations:* student economic and industrial history; swimming, camping, etc. *Address:* 46 Seaview Crescent, Joppa, Edinburgh EH15 2HD. *T:* 031–669 5569.
*Died 23 Oct. 1990.*

**OTTER, Rt. Rev. Anthony,** MA; an Assistant Bishop, Diocese of Lincoln, since 1965; *b* 8 Sept. 1896; *s* of Robert Charles and Marianne Eva Otter; *m* 1929, Dorothy Margaret Ramsbotham (*d* 1979); no *c. Educ:* Repton; Trinity College, Cambridge. Served European War, 1914–18, in RNVR, 1914–19. BA (2nd cl. History Tripos), 1920; MA 1925. Cambridge Mission to Delhi, 1921–24; Westcott House, Cambridge, 1924–25; Deacon, 1925; Priest, 1926; Curate of Holy Trinity, St Marylebone, 1925–31; London Secretary of SCM, 1926–31; Vicar of Lowdham with Gunthorpe, Dio. of Southwell, 1931–49; Chaplain of Lowdham Grange Borstal Institution, 1931–45; Ed. of Southwell Diocesan Magazine, 1941–46; Hon. Canon of Southwell Cathedral, 1942–49; Rural Dean of Gedling, 1946–49; Bishop Suffragan of Grantham, 1949–65; Dean of Stamford, 1949–71. *Publications:* William Temple and the Universal Church, 1949; Beginning with Atoms, 1971, rev. edn, From Atoms to Infinity, 1977. *Recreations:* country, birds; maintenance of domestic machinery. *Address:* The Old Rectory, Belton, Grantham, Lincs. *T:* Grantham 62061.
*Died 9 March 1986.*

**OTTLEY, Agnes May;** retired as Principal, S Katharine's College, Tottenham, N17, Dec. 1959; *b* 29 June 1899; *d* of late Rev. Canon Robert Lawrence Ottley, Professor of Moral and Pastoral Theology, Oxford. *Educ:* privately; Society of Oxford Home Students. Final Honours School of Modern History, Oxford, 1921; MA Oxon; Assistant Mistress at S Felix School, Southwold, 1925; Lecturer in History, Avery Hill Training College, 1927.
*Died 10 Nov. 1990.*

**OUTERBRIDGE, Col Hon. Sir Leonard Cecil,** Kt 1946; CC (Canada) 1967; CBE 1926; DSO 1919; CD 1954; Director, Harvey & Co.,

Ltd, and other Cos, St John's, Newfoundland; *b* 1888; *s* of late Sir Joseph Outerbridge; *m* 1915, Dorothy Winifred (*d* 1972), *d* of late John Alexander Strathy, Barrie, Ontario. *Educ:* Marlborough; Toronto Univ. (BA, LLB; Hon. LLD, 1950); Hon. LLD: Laval Univ., 1952; Memorial Univ. of Newfoundland, 1961. Solicitor and Barrister, Ontario, 1914; President, Newfoundland Board of Trade, 1923–24; Chairman, Newfoundland Committee arranging Exhibits at British Empire Exhibition (1924 and 1925) (CBE); served European War, 1914–19 (despatches twice, DSO). Hon. Private Sec. to the Governor of Newfoundland, 1931–44; Director of Civil Defence, 1942–45; Lieutenant-Governor of Newfoundland, 1949–57. Hon. Col, Royal Newfoundland Regt, 1950–75. KStJ 1951. *Address:* Littlefield, 3 Pringle Place, St John's, Newfoundland, Canada.
*Died Sept. 1986.*

**OVEREND, Douglas,** CB 1965; Assistant Under-Secretary of State, Department of Health and Social Security, 1968–75; *b* 22 Nov. 1914; *s* of Simeon and Frances Overend, Rodley, Leeds. *Educ:* Leeds Grammar School; Queen's College (Hastings Scholar, Taberdar), Oxford. 1st cl. Classical Mods. 1936; Greats 1938. Army Service, 1939–46. Entered Min. of Nat. Insce as Principal, 1946; Asst Sec., 1953; Under-Sec., 1959; Min. of Pensions and Nat. Insce, 1959–66; Min. of Social Security, 1966–68. *Recreation:* golf. *Address:* 2 The Orchard, Tayles Hill, Ewell, Surrey. *T:* 01-394 0094.
*Died 8 Oct. 1981.*

**OWEN, Dr David Elystan,** CBE 1972; Director, Manchester Museum, 1957–76; *b* 27 Feb. 1912; *s* of Dr John Griffith Owen, Kingston-on-Thames, and Mrs Gertrude Owen (*née* Heaton); *m* 1936, Pearl Jennings, Leicester; one *s* one *d. Educ:* The Leys Sch., Cambridge; King's Coll., London Univ. 1st cl. hons BSc 1933, PhD 1935. Keeper, Dept of Geology, Liverpool Museum, 1935–47; War Service, 1939–45 in Artillery (Major, RA); Dir, Leeds City Museums, 1947–57. Treas. 1956–61, Pres. 1968–69, Museums Assoc. *Publications:* The Story of Mersey and Deeside Rocks, 1939; A History of Kirkstall Abbey, 1955; Water Highways, 1967; Water Rallies, 1969; Water Byways, 1973; Canals to Manchester, 1977; Cheshire Waterways, 1979; The Manchester Ship Canal, 1982; Exploring England by Canal, 1986; Staffordshire Waterways, 1986; numerous palaeontological papers in Palaeontology, Geological Jl, etc. *Recreation:* cruising the British canal and river system. *Address:* 9 Carleton Road, Higher Poynton, Cheshire. *T:* Poynton 872924.
*Died 9 April 1987.*

**OWEN, Sir Dudley (Herbert) C.;** *see* Cunliffe-Owen.

**OWEN, Eric Hamilton;** retired; *b* 4 Aug. 1903; *s* of Harold Edwin Owen and Hilda Guernsey; *m* 1937, Margaret Jeannie Slipper. Served Artists' Rifles, 1921–39; RASC, 8th Army, 1940–45 (despatches); 21st SAS Regt (Artists), 1946–48. Formerly: Chm., Charterhouse Investment Trust; Dep. Chm., Charterhouse Gp Ltd and Grindlays Bank Ltd. Dir, Gabbitas-Thring Educational Trust Ltd. Member Board of Trade Mission to Ghana, 1959. CBIM. *Recreations:* photography, travel. *Address:* 11 Broom Hall, Oxshott, Surrey.
*Died 2 Jan. 1989.*

**OWEN, Prof. Gwilym Ellis Lane,** FBA 1969; Laurence Professor of Ancient Philosophy, University of Cambridge, since 1973; Fellow of King's College, Cambridge, since 1973; *b* 18 May 1922; *o s* of Ellis William Owen, Portsmouth; *m* 1947, Sally Lila Ann Clothier; two *s. Educ:* Portsmouth Grammar Sch.; Corpus Christi Coll., Oxford. MA (Oxon) 1949; BPhil 1950; MA (Cantab) 1973. Res. Fellow in Arts, Univ. of Durham, 1950; Univ. Lectr in Ancient Philosophy, Univ. of Oxford, 1953; Reader in Ancient Philosophy, 1957; Fellow of Corpus Christi Coll., 1958; Prof. of Ancient Philosophy, 1963; Victor S. Thomas Prof. of Philosophy and the Classics, Harvard Univ., 1966–73. Visiting Professor of Philosophy: Pennsylvania, 1956; Harvard, 1959; California, 1964; Princeton, 1975; Sather Lectr, Berkeley, 1979. Fellow, Amer. Acad. of Arts and Sciences, 1967; For. Mem., Finnish Acad. of Arts and Letters, 1976. Hon. DLit Durham, 1978. *Publications:* (ed. with I. Düring) Aristotle and Plato in the Mid-Fourth Century, 1960; (ed) Aristotle on Dialectic, 1968; (ed with G. E. R. Lloyd) Aristotle on Mind and the Senses, 1978. *Address:* King's College, Cambridge; The Beeches, Lower Heyford, Oxford. *T:* Steeple Aston 40467.
*Died 10 July 1982.*

**OWEN, Col John Edward,** CBE 1989; Deputy Receiver, Metropolitan Police, since 1986; *b* 21 Aug. 1928; *s* of John and Mary Owen; *m* 1951, Jean Pendlebury; one *s* two *d. Educ:* Aberdare Grammar Sch.; Woolwich Polytechnic. CEng, FIEE, FIERE; FMS; FBIM; CDipAF. Commnd, REME, 1950; OC 6 Infantry Workshop, 1964–66; Commander: REME Sch. of Artillery, 1966–69; REME 1st Div., BAOR, 1969–71; Asst Dir, HQ DEME, 1971–72; Metropolitan Police: Dep. Chief Engr, 1972–76; Dir, Management Services, 1976; Chief Engr, 1976–86. *Recreations:* gardening, reading. *Address:* 9 St Catherine's Drive, Guildford GU2 5HE.
*Died 26 Feb. 1989.*

**OWEN, Prof. Paul Robert,** CBE 1974; FRS 1971; FEng; Zaharoff Professor of Aviation, London University, at Imperial College of Science and Technology, 1963–84, then Emeritus Professor; *b* 24 Jan. 1920; *s* of Joseph and Deborah Owen; *m* 1958, Margaret Ann, *d* of Herbert and Dr Lily Baron; two *s* two *d*. *Educ:* Queen Mary Coll., London Univ. BSc (London) 1940, MSc (Manchester), FRAeS, FRMetS. Aerodynamics Dept, RAE, Farnborough, 1941–53; Reader and Director of Fluid Motion Laboratory, Manchester Univ., 1953–56; Professor of the Mechanics of Fluids and Director of the Laboratory, Manchester Univ., 1956–62. Vis. Prof., Univ. of Colorado, 1985–86. Member: ARC, 1964–67, 1969–80 (Chm., 1971–79); Safety in Mines Research Adv. Bd, 1956–73; Environmental Design Res. Cttee, DoE (Chm., 1973–); British Nat. Cttee for Theoretical and Applied Mechanics, 1971–78 (Chm., 1973–78); Construction and Housing Res. Adv. Council, 1976–80; Anglo-French Mixed Commn on Cultural Exchange, 1976–; Anglo-Italian Mixed Commn on Cultural Exchange, 1983–. Fellow, Queen Mary Coll., 1967. Founder Fellow, Fellowship of Engineering, 1976; Hon. FCGI 1983. Hon. Dr Aix-Marseille, 1976. *Publications:* papers on Aerodynamics in R & M series of Aeronautical Research Council, Journal of Fluid Mechanics, etc. *Recreations:* music, theatre. *Address:* 1 Stanley Lodge, 25 Stanley Crescent, W11 2NA. *T:* 071–229 5111.          *Died* 11 *Nov.* 1990.

**OWEN, Peter Granville,** CMG 1965; QPM 1964; CPM 1960; Deputy Director, Fund Raising, Save the Children Fund, 1978–84; *b* 28 Oct. 1918; *s* of Walter Lincoln Owen, Highgate, and Ethel Belton, London, N6; *m* 1943, Mercia Louvaine Palmer; one *s* one *d*. *Educ:* Grove House Sch., Highgate; City of Norwich Sch. Great Yarmouth Borough Police, 1938–42; RAF, F/O, 1942–46; Public Prosecutor, Somalia Gendarmerie, 1946; Resident Magistrate, Mogadishu, Somalia, 1948; District Commissioner: Somalia, 1949–50; Eritrea, 1950; Tanganyika Police: Cadet, Asst Superintendent and Dep. Superintendent of Police, 1950; Somaliland Police: Superintendent and Senior Superintendent of Police, 1956; Commissioner of Police: Gibraltar, 1960; British Guiana, 1962; Aden, 1965; UN Police Adviser, Govt of Somali Republic, 1968. Adjudication Officer, Cadastral Surveys, British Virgin Is, 1971, Cayman Is, 1973, Blantyre, Malawi, 1976. OStJ 1960. *Recreations:* cricket, swimming, walking. *Address:* Commoners, Low Common, Swardeston, Norwich, Norfolk NR14 8LG. *T:* Mulbarton 70928. *Clubs:* Royal Commonwealth Society, MCC.          *Died* 25 *May* 1986.

**OWEN, Robert Davies,** CBE 1962; FRCS; FRCSE; Senior Ear and Throat Surgeon, Cardiff Royal Infirmary, 1928–64, retired; Lecturer in Oto-Laryngology, Welsh National School of Medicine, 1929–64, retired; *b* 8 May 1898; 2nd *s* of late Capt. Griffith Owen and Mrs Jane Owen; *m* 1928, Janet Miles, Llantrisant; two *d*. *Educ:* Towyn Grammar Sch. Cadet, Harrison Line, Liverpool, 1916–18; University College, Cardiff, 1918–21; Guy's Hospital, London, 1921–27. BSc (Wales) 1921. MRCS, LRCP 1923; FRCS 1930; FRCSEd 1926. *Publications:* contrib. BMJ, Lancet, Proc. Royal Society of Medicine. *Recreations:* shooting, fishing. *Address:* 1 The Mount, Cardiff Road, Llandaff, Cardiff. *T:* Cardiff 568739. *Club:* Cardiff and County.          *Died* 15 *Oct.* 1988.

**OWEN, Ronald Allan;** Under Secretary, Health and Social Work Department, Welsh Office, 1978–80; *b* 3 Dec. 1920; *s* of David Owen and Eugenie Louise (*née* Trapagna); *m* 1948, Joan Elizabeth Carter; one *s* two *d*. *Educ:* Nantwich and Acton Grammar School. Executive Officer, Min. of War Pensions, 1939; war service, RAF, 1940–46; transf. to Min. of Health as Sen. Exec. Officer, 1953; Asst Sec., 1964; transf. to Welsh Office, 1970. *Recreations:* reading, walking, gardening. *Address:* Beili Bychan, Hundred House, Llandrindod Wells, Wales. *T:* Hundred House 346.
          *Died* 29 *April* 1982.

**OWEN, Sir Ronald (Hugh),** Kt 1980; Director, Prudential Assurance Co. Ltd, 1974–80 (Chairman, 1975–80); President, Prudential Corporation plc, since 1985 (Director, 1978–85; Chairman, 1978–80); *b* 2 June 1910; *er s* of late Owen Hugh Owen and late Jane Tegwedd Owen; *m* 1939, Claire May Tully; one *s*. *Educ:* King's College Sch., Wimbledon. FIA 1936. Served War of 1939–45: 52 Field Regt, RA (Major); Bde Major RA, 8 Ind. Division, Middle East and Italy. Joined Prudential, 1929: India, 1936–39; Dep. General Manager, 1959–67; Chief General Manager, 1968–73. Dep.

Chm., British Insurance Assoc., 1971–72. Member, Governing Body, King's College Sch., Wimbledon (Chm., Finance Cttee, 1966–85). *Recreation:* golf. *Club:* MCC.
          *Died* 26 *June* 1988.

**OWEN, Thomas Joseph,** DL; Town Clerk, Nottingham, 1951–66; *b* 3 Nov. 1903; *s* of late Richard Owen, Sarn, Caernarvonshire; *m* 1935, Marjorie Ethel Tilbury (*d* 1985). Articled to late Sir Hugh Vincent, 1921–26; admitted a Solicitor, 1926; Asst Solicitor with Town Clerk, Stoke-on-Trent, 1926–27; Asst Solicitor, Leeds, 1927–30; Asst Solicitor, Brighton, 1930–36; Deputy Town Clerk, Nottingham, 1936–50. President: Nottinghamshire Law Society, 1957–58; Commn of Income Tax for Nottingham Dist. Trustee: Nottingham Roosevelt Travelling Scholarship Fund; Holbrook Trust (Painting and Sculpture). DL Notts, 1966. *Recreations:* watching Rugby football and cricket; travel abroad, reading. *Address:* Woodlands, Sherwood, Nottingham. *T:* Nottingham 61767. *Club:* United Services (Nottingham).          *Died* 23 *Dec.* 1986.

**OWEN, William James;** *b* 18 Feb. 1901; *m* 1930, Ann Smith; one *s* one *d*. *Educ:* Elementary Sch., Blaina, Mon; Central Labour Coll. Miner, 1914–20; College Student, 1921–23; Tutor-Organiser, National Council Labour Colleges, 1923–30; Urban District Councillor, Blaina, Mon, 1927–30; ILP Secretary, Leicester, 1930–35; City Councillor, Leicester, 1933–38; Education Secretary: Co-operative Society, Burslem, Staffs, 1937–40; London Co-op. Society, 1940–44; Bristol Co-op. Society, 1944–48; Community Welfare Officer, National Coal Board, 1948–51; contested (Lab and Co-op) Dover, 1950 and 1951; MP (Lab and Co-op) Morpeth Div. of Northumberland, 1954–70, retired. Chm., Sutton and Carshalton Constituency Labour Party, 1974–. Gen. Secretary, Assoc. of Clothing Contractors, 1960–70; Mem. Exec. Cttee, Sutton Br., RNIB. Class teacher and lecturer, adult education, 1970–. *Recreations:* walking, gardening, writing, painting. *Address:* 18a Woodstock Road, Carshalton, Surrey.          *Died* 3 *April* 1981.

**OWENS, Ernest Stanley,** CBE 1979 (OBE 1971); FCA; chartered accountant and company director, since 1947; Chairman, Enterprise Australia, since 1976; Director, Bank of New South Wales, since 1978; *b* 22 Sept. 1916; *s* of Rev. William James Owens, MA Oxon, and Juanita (*née* Stanley); *m* 1943, Margaret Clara Brown, Killara; one *s* one *d*. *Educ:* The King's Sch., Parramatta, NSW. Accountants' Clerk, 1935–39; war service, Trooper to Lt.-Col 1946 (despatches); own practice as chartered accountant, 1956–69; Chairman: Monier Group Ltd, 1967; Hill Samuel Aust. Ltd, 1969; Simon Engrg (Aust.) Pty Ltd, 1971; Coates Brothers Aust. Pty Ltd, 1977; Internat. Computers Aust. Pty Ltd, 1979; AUSSAT Pty Ltd, 1981; Director: Standard Telephones & Cables Pty Ltd, 1964; Byrne & Davidson Industries Ltd, 1975; Renison Goldfields Consolidated Ltd, 1977; Bank of New South Wales, 1978; Australian National Industries Ltd, 1982. Dir, Royal Prince Alfred Hosp., 1975–. Governor, Thalidomide Foundn Ltd. Freeman of City of London. *Publication:* Annual Reports of Companies (with R. K. Yorston), 1958. *Recreations:* surfing, bowls. *Address:* 11/576 Pacific Highway, Killara, NSW 2071, Australia. *T:* 498.8990; 50 Bridge Street, Sydney, NSW 2000, Australia. *Clubs:* Australian, American National (Sydney); Elanora Country, Killara Golf.
          *Died* 3 *June* 1983.

**OWENS, Richard Hugh M.;** *see* Mills-Owens.

**OXFUIRD, 12th Viscount of,** *cr* 1651; **(John) Donald (Alexander Arthur) Makgill;** Bt 1627; Lord Macgill of Cousland 1651; late Lt Coldstream Guards; RARO; *b* 31 Dec. 1899; *e s* of Sir George Makgill, 11th Bt (*de jure* 11th Viscount) and Frances Elizabeth (*d* 1947), *e d* of Alexander Innes Grant, of Merchiston, Otago, NZ; *S* father, 1926; claim to Viscountcy admitted by Committee for Privileges, House of Lords, 1977; *m* 1927, Esther Lilian (marr. diss. 1943), *y d* of late Sir Robert Bromley, 6th Bt; one *d*; *m* 1955, Mrs Maureen Gillington, *y d* of late Lt-Col A. T. S. Magan, CMG. *Educ:* Eton; RMC. *Recreation:* fishing. *Heir: nephew* George Hubbard Makgill [*b* 7 Jan. 1934; *m* 1967, Alison Campbell (marr. diss. 1977), *d* of late Neils Max Jensen, Randers, Denmark; three *s* (inc. twin *s*); *m* 1980, Valerie Steward, *d* of Major Steward, late 9th Lancers; one *s*]. *Address:* The Flat, Blairquhan, Maybole, Ayrshire. *T:* Straiton 278. *Clubs:* Royal Over-Seas League; New (Edinburgh).
          *Died* 24 *Jan.* 1986.

# P

**PÄCHT, Otto Ernst,** MA, DPhil; FBA 1956; Professor in the History of Art, and Director of the Kunsthistorisches Institut, Vienna University, 1963–72, then Professor Emeritus; *b* Vienna, 7 Sept. 1902; *s* of David and Josephine Pächt; *m* 1940, Jeanne Michalopulo (*d* 1971); one *s. Educ:* Vienna and Berlin Universities. Lecturer in History of Art: Heidelberg Univ., 1933; Oriel Coll., Oxford, 1945. Senior Lecturer in Medieval Art, 1952, Reader, 1962, Oxford Univ. Lyell Reader, Oxford, 1971. Membre de la Société Archéologique française. Wirkl. Mitgl. Oesterr. Akad. d. Wissenschaft, 1967. Hon. DLitt Oxon, 1971. *Publications:* Oesterreichische Tafelmalerei der Gotik, 1929; Master of Mary of Burgundy, 1948; The St Albans Psalter, 1960; The Rise of Pictorial Narrative in Twelfth-century England, 1962; Vita Sancti Simperti, 1964; (ed with J. J. G. Alexander) Illuminated Manuscripts in the Bodleian Library, 1973; (ed with D. Thoss) Illuminated Manuscripts in the Austrian National Library, French School, 1974–77; (ed with U. Jenni) Illuminated Manuscripts in the Austrian National Library, Dutch School, 1975; Methodisches zur kunsthistorischen Praxis, 1977; (ed with U. Jenni and D. Thoss) Illuminated Manuscripts in the Austrian National Library, Flemish School I, 1983; contribs to Kritische Berichte, Kunstwissenschaftliche Forschungen, Burlington Magazine, Journal of the Warburg Institute, Revue des Arts, Jahrbuch der Kunsthistorischen Sammlungen Wien, Pantheon, Revue de l'Art, Gazette des Beaux-Arts. *Address:* Pötzleinsdorferstrasse 66, 1180 Vienna, Austria.

*Died April 1988.*

**PADLEY, Walter Ernest;** Member National Executive Committee of Labour Party, 1956–79 (Chairman, Labour Party, 1965–66; Chairman, Overseas Cttee, 1963–71); *b* 24 July 1916; *s* of Ernest and Mildred Padley; *m* 1942, Sylvia Elsie Wilson; one *s* one *d. Educ:* Chipping Norton Grammar Sch.; Ruskin Coll., Oxford. Active in distributive workers' trade union, 1933–; President, Union of Shop, Distributive and Allied Workers, 1948–64. Member of National Council of Independent Labour Party, 1940–46. MP (Lab) Ogmore, Mid-Glam, 1950–79; Minister of State for Foreign Affairs, 1964–67. *Publications:* The Economic Problem of the Peace, 1944; Am I My Brother's Keeper?, 1945; Britain: Pawn or Power?, 1947; USSR: Empire or Free Union?, 1948. *Address:* 73 Priory Gardens, Highgate, N6. *T:* 01-340 2969. *Died 15 April 1984.*

**PAGAN, Brig. Sir John (Ernest),** Kt 1971; CMG 1969; MBE (Mil.) 1944; ED; Chairman: P. Rowe Holdings Pty Ltd, since 1958; Associated National Insurance Co. Ltd, since 1973; Medicine Journal Pty Ltd; Nationale-Nederlanden (Aust.) Ltd; Deputy Chairman: NSW Permanent Building Society Ltd; Mercantile Mutual Holdings Ltd (Group); Director: Angus & Coote (Holdings) Ltd; H. M. Bates Pty Ltd; Rowetex Pty Ltd; *b* 13 May 1914; *s* of late D. C. Pagan, Hay, NSW; *m* 1948, Marjorie Hoskins, *d* of late Sir Cecil Hoskins; one *s* two *d. Educ:* St Peter's Coll., Adelaide. Served RAA, AIF, Middle East, Papua/New Guinea, 1939–45, 2/1st AA Regt; 2/4th LAA Regt 9 Div. Finschhafen 1943; Citizen Military Forces, E Command; Lt-Col 1948, Brig. 1958; Hon. Col, Corps of School Cadets, 1970–72; Representative Col Comdt in Australia, Royal Regt of Australian Artillery, 1974–78. Hon. ADC to Governor of NSW, 1950–55; Member: Council, Scout Assoc. of Austr., 1975– (Dist Comr 1950, Area Pres. 1955); NSW Council, Girl Guides Assoc., 1969; Board, NSW Soc. for Crippled Children, 1967–; Council, Big Brother Movement, 1947 (Chm., 1965, Pres., 1981); Mem. Board, Anglican Retirement Villages, 1961–; Federal Vice-Pres., Aust. Brain Foundn, 1977–; Dir, James McGrath Foundn (Odessey Drug Prevention and Cure); Hon. Treas., Australiana Fund, NSW, 1978–; Federal Dep. Chm, Cttee for Employer Support for Reserve Forces of Aust.; Mem. Nat. Cttee, Sir Robert Menzies Meml Trust, 1978–; Trustee, World Wildlife Fund, 1978–. Mem., Commonwealth Immigration Adv. Council, 1959–70. Mem. Exec. Council, Nat. Parks and Wildlife Foundn, 1970–. Governor, Frensham Sch., 1968–70; Councillor, Nat. Heart Foundn, 1969–; Chm., Red Shield Appeal, 1975; Trustee, Salvation Army Darwin Relief Fund, 1974–78; Member: Bd, Royal Prince Alfred Hospital, 1974–; NSW Exec., Inst. of Public Affairs, 1975–80. Liberal Party of Australia: State Pres., NSW, 1963–66; Federal Pres., 1966–70; Agent-General for NSW in London, 1970–72. Freeman, City of London, 1973. KStJ 1985 (CStJ 1972). FRGS, 1981. *Address:* 2 Lincoln Place, Edgecliff, NSW 2027, Australia; Kennerton Green, Mittagong, NSW 2575, Australia. *Clubs:* White's, MCC (London); Imperial Service, Union, Royal Sydney Golf (Sydney); Melbourne (Melbourne). *Died 26 June 1986.*

**PAGE, Ven. Alfred Charles;** Archdeacon of Leeds, 1969–81, later Archdeacon Emeritus; *b* 24 Dec. 1912; *s* of late Henry Page, Homersfield, Suffolk; *m* 1944, Margaret Stevenson, *d* of late Surtees Foster Dodd, Sunderland, Co. Durham. *Educ:* Bungay Grammar Sch.; Corpus Christi Coll., Cambridge (MA); Wycliffe Hall, Oxford. Curate: Wortley-de-Leeds, 1936; Leeds Parish Church, 1940 (Sen.

Curate and Priest-in-charge of S Mary, Quarry Hill, 1941); Vicar: St Mark, Woodhouse, Leeds, 1944; Rothwell, Yorks, 1955. Rural Dean of Whitkirk, 1961–69; Surrogate, 1963; Hon. Canon of Ripon, 1966; Vicar of Arthington, 1969–73. *Recreation:* photography. *Address:* 602 King Lane, Alwoodley Park, Leeds LS17 7AN. *T:* Leeds 696458. *Died 5 Feb. 1988.*

**PAGE, Col Alfred John,** CB 1964; TD 1945; DL; Chairman, TA&VR Association for Greater London, 1968–71 (Chairman, County of London T&AFA, 1957–68); *b* 3 January 1912; *s* of Harry Gould Page, Surbiton, Surrey; *m* 1941, Sheila Margaret Aileen (marr. diss. 1966), *d* of Charles Skinner Wilson, Ugley, Essex; one *s* two *d*; *m* 1969, Margaret Mary Juliet Driver (*d* 1985), *widow* of Harold Driver. *Educ:* Westminster School. 2nd Lt 19th London Regt (TA), 1931. Served 1939–45 with RA in AA Comd. Brevet Colonel 1952; ADC (TA) to the Queen, 1961–66; Hon. Col, Greater London Regt RA (Territorials), 1967–71; Dep. Hon. Col, 6th Bn, Queen's Regt, T&AVR, 1971–72. Master, Worshipful Co. of Pattenmakers, 1973–74. DL Co. of London, 1951; DL Greater London, 1965. *Address:* 66 Iverna Court, W8. *T:* 01–937 2590. *Club:* Army and Navy. *Died 7 Oct. 1987.*

**PAGE, (Charles) James,** CBE 1978; QPM 1971; HM Inspector of Constabulary, since 1977; *b* 31 May 1925; *s* of Charles Page and Mabel Cowan; *m* 1st, 1947, Margaret Dobson; two *s* one *d*; 2nd, 1971, Shirley Marina Woodward. *Educ:* Sloane Grammar Sch., Chelsea. Served War, RAF, 1943–47. Blackpool Police, 1947–57; Metropolitan Police, 1957–67; City of London Police, 1967–77; apptd Asst Commissioner, 1969; Comr, 1971–77. Dir, Police Extended Interviews, 1975–77. Vice Pres., Police Athletic Assoc., 1977. CBIM. CStJ 1974. Officer of Légion d'Honneur, 1976, and other foreign decorations. *Recreations:* fell walking, photography. *Address:* Mitre House, Church Street, Lancaster. *Club:* Royal Commonwealth Society. *Died 5 Oct. 1981.*

**PAGE, Rt. Hon. Sir Graham;** see Page, Rt Hon. Sir R. G.

**PAGE, Sir Harry (Robertson),** Kt 1968; Chairman: National Transport Tokens Ltd, since 1973; Butler, Laing Cruickshank Ltd, since 1982; *b* 14 Apr. 1911; *s* of late Henry Page and Dora (*née* Robertson); *m* 1937, Elsie Dixon; two *s. Educ:* Manchester Grammar Sch.; Manchester University. BA (Admin) 1932; MA (Admin) 1934. IPFA 1938 (Pres. 1968). Appointed City Treasurer's Dept, Manchester, 1927, Dep. Treasurer, 1952; Treasurer, 1957–71. Consultant, Butler Till Ltd, 1971–81. Sen. Hon. Financial Adviser to Assoc. of Municipal Corps, 1962–71; Chm., Chancellor's Cttee to review Nat. Savings, 1971–73. Hon. Fellow, Manchester Polytechnic, 1970. Hon. Simon Res. Fellow, Manchester Univ., 1974–. Freeman, City of London, 1976. Haldane Medal (RIPA), 1933. *Publications:* Co-ordination and Planning in the Local Authority, 1936; Councillor's Handbook, 1945; Local Government up-to-date, 1946; contrib. to symposium of papers given to British Assoc., Leeds, 1968; contribs to Local Govt Finance, Bank Reviews, financial jls, etc. *Recreation:* collecting Victorian and other nineteenth century ephemera; ex libris; heraldry. *Address:* 205 Old Hall Lane, Fallowfield, Manchester M14 6HJ. *T:* 061–224 2891. *Died 1 Jan. 1985.*

**PAGE, James;** see Page, C. J.

**PAGE, Norman John,** OBE 1981; MC 1945; FCCA; Secretary-General, Institute of Actuaries, 1977–83; *b* 11 June 1920; *s* of John Francis Page and Ellen Catherine (*née* Fox); *m* 1949, Valerie Gascoine; two *d. Educ:* Harrow County Grammar Sch. for Boys. Fellow: Inst. of Chartered Secs and Administrators, 1955; Assoc. of Certified Accountants, 1970. Served War, RAF, 1941–46: commnd RAF regt; active service in UK, NW Europe, India, Singapore and Sumatra; Flt Lieut. Prudential Assurance Co. Ltd, 1937–41, and 1946–52; Asst Sec., Inst. of Actuaries, 1952–62, Sec. 1962–77. Liveryman, Chartered Secretaries and Administrators' Co., 1980; Hon. Freeman, Actuaries' Co., 1983. *Recreations:* gardening, travel, bridge, most sports. *Address:* Trehaven, 17 Grange Road, Bushey, Watford, Herts WD2 2LQ. *T:* Watford 34177. *Club:* Royal Air Force. *Died 13 Oct. 1985.*

**PAGE, Rt. Hon. Sir (Rodney) Graham,** Kt 1980; MBE 1944; PC 1972; LLB (London); MP (C) Crosby since Nov. 1953; solicitor (admitted 1934); Privy Council Appeal Agent; *b* 30 June 1911; *s* of Lt-Col Frank Page, DSO and bar, and Margaret Payne Farley; *m* 1934, Hilda Agatha Dixon; one *s* one *d. Educ:* Magdalen College School, Oxford; London University (External). Served War of 1939–45: Flt-Lt, RAFVR. Chm., Select Cttee on Statutory Instruments, 1964–70, 1974–79; an Opposition Front Bench spokesman on Housing and Land, 1965–70; Minister of State, Min. of Housing and Local Govt, June–Oct. 1970; Minister for Local Govt and Develt, DoE, 1970–74. Chm., Select Cttee on Home Affairs, 1979–; Sec., Parly All-Party Solicitors Gp. Promoter: (Private Member's Bills) Cheques Act, 1957, Wages Bill, 1958, Pawnbrokers Act, 1960; Road Safety Bills 1960, 1964, 1965; Stock Transfer Act, 1963; National Sweepstakes Bill, 1966; Lotteries Bill, 1974. Dir, United Real Property Trust Ltd.

Formerly: A Governor of St Thomas' Hosp., London; Treas., Pedestrians' Assoc. for Road Safety. Hon. FCIS; Hon. FIPA; Hon. FIWSP; Hon. FFB. *Publications:* Law Relating to Flats, 1934; Road Traffic Courts, 1938; Rent Acts, 1966; contributions to legal journals. *Address:* 21 Cholmeley Lodge, Cholmeley Park, N6 5EN. *T:* 01–340 3579. *Died* 1 *Oct.* 1981.

**PAGE, Russell,** OBE 1951; garden designer; *b* 1 Nov. 1906. *Educ:* Charterhouse; Slade Sch.; University College London. Resident in France, 1945–62. Battersea Festival Gardens, 1951; designed gardens in UK, Belgium, Egypt, France, Germany, Italy, Portugal, Spain, Switzerland, W Indies and USA. French Academy of Architecture Medal, 1977. *Publication:* The Education of a Gardener, 1962. *Died* 4 *Jan.* 1985.

**PAGET OF NORTHAMPTON,** Baron *cr* 1974 (Life Peer), of Lubenham, Leics; **Reginald Thomas Paget,** QC 1947; *b* 2 Sept. 1908; *m* 1931. *Educ:* Eton; Trinity College, Cambridge. Barrister, 1934. Lt RNVR, 1940–43 (invalided). Contested Northampton, 1935; MP (Lab) Northampton, 1945–Feb. 1974. Hon. Sec., UK Council of European Movement, 1954. Master, Pytchley Hounds, 1968–71. *Publications:* Manstein-Campaigns and Trial, 1951; (with late S. S. Silverman, MP) Hanged—and Innocent?, 1958; The Human Journey, 1979. *Address:* 9 Grosvenor Cottages, SW1. *T:* 01–730 4034. *Died* 2 *Jan.* 1990.

**PAGET, Paul Edward,** CVO 1971; FSA, FRIBA; Chairman, Norwich Diocesan Advisory Committee, 1973–76; Master, Art Workers Guild, 1971; Member: Redundant Churches Fund, 1969–76; Crafts Advisory Committee, 1971–75; Surveyor to the Fabric of St Paul's Cathedral, 1963–69; Senior Partner in Firm of Seely & Paget, Chartered Architects, 1963–69 (from death of late Lord Mottistone, OBE, FSA, FRIBA, in Jan. 1963); Architect to St George's Chapel, Windsor, and Portsmouth Cathedral, 1950–69; *b* 24 Jan. 1901; 2nd and *o* surv *s* of Bishop Henry Luke Paget and Elma Katie (*née* Hoare); *m* 1971, Verily, *d* of late Rev. F. R. C. Bruce, DD, and *widow* of Captain Donald Anderson. *Educ:* Winchester; Trinity Coll., Cambridge. Asst Private Sec. to 1st Viscount Templewood, PC, GCSI, GBE, CMG, 1924–26. Flight Lieutenant, RAuxAF, 1939–44. Asst Director, Emergency Works, 1941–44; Common Councilman, Corporation of London, 1949–55. CStJ 1962. *Principal Works:* Restorations: Eltham Palace; Lambeth Palace; Upper Sch., Eton Coll.; London Charterhouse, Deanery and Little Cloister, Westminster Abbey; Churches: Lee-on-Solent, Six Mile Bottom, All Hallows-by-the-Tower, City Temple, Stevenage New Town; Colleges of Education: Oxford, Norwich, Bristol, Culham. *Address:* Templewood, Northrepps, near Cromer, Norfolk. *T:* Overstrand 243. *Club:* Norfolk (Norwich). *Died* 13 *Aug.* 1985.

**PAISH, Frank Walter,** MC 1918; MA; Professor Emeritus, University of London; *b* 15 January 1898; *e s* of late Sir George Paish; *m* 1927, Beatrice Marie, *d* of late G. C. Eckhard; two *s* one *d*. *Educ:* Winchester College; Trinity College, Cambridge. Served European War (RFA), 1916–19. Employed by Standard Bank of South Africa, Ltd, in London and South Africa, 1921–32. Lecturer, London School of Economics, 1932–38; Reader, 1938–49; Professor of Economics (with special reference to Business Finance), 1949–65; Hon. Fellow, 1970. Secretary, London and Cambridge Economic Service, 1932–41 and 1945–49; Editor, 1947–49. Deputy-Director of Programmes, Ministry of Aircraft Production, 1941–45. Consultant on Economic Affairs, Lloyds Bank Ltd, 1965–70. *Publications:* (with G. L. Schwartz) Insurance Funds and their Investment, 1934; The Post-War Financial Problem and Other Essays, 1950; Business Finance, 1953; Studies in an Inflationary Economy, 1962; Long-term and Short-term Interest Rates in the United Kingdom, 1966; (ed) Benham's Economics, 8th edn, 1967, (with A. J. Culyer) 9th edn, 1973; How the Economy Works and Other Essays, 1970; The Rise and Fall of Incomes Policy, 1969; articles in The Economic Journal, Economica, London and Cambridge Bulletin, etc. *Address:* The Old Rectory Cottage, Kentchurch, Hereford.

*Died* 23 *May* 1988.

**PAISLEY, John Lawrence,** CB 1970; MBE 1946; Consultant with L. G. Mouchel & Partners, Consulting Engineers, 1971–82, retired; *b* Manchester, 4 Sept. 1909; *e s* of J. R. and Mrs E. W. Paisley; *m* 1937, Angela Dorothy Catliff; three *d*. *Educ:* King George V Sch., Southport; Univ. of Liverpool. BEng 1930, MEng 1935. Asst Engineer: Siemens Bros & Co. Ltd, North Delta Transmission Lines, Egypt, 1930–34; Howard Humphreys & Sons, Cons. Engrs, Tunnels and Viaduct on A55, in N Wales, 1934–35; W Sussex CC, 1935–37; Asst Engr in Scotland, Min. of Transport, 1937–39. War Service with Royal Engineers, 1939–46: took part in Dunkirk evacuation and finally as Major, RE (now Hon. Major), commanded 804 Road Construction Co. in UK, France and Germany (MBE). Ministry of Transport: Engr in Scotland, 1946–52; Senr Engr in HQ, London, 1952–60; Divl Rd Engr, NW Div. at Manchester, 1960–64; Dep. Chief Engr, HQ, London, 1964–66; Chief Highway Engr, Min. of Transport, 1966–70. Hon. Vice-Pres., Permanent Internat. Assoc. of Road Congresses. FICE, FInstHE. *Publications:*

contribs Proc. Instn of Civil Engrs, Proc. Instn of Highway Engrs. *Recreation:* fell walking. *Address:* Weybrook, Warren Road, Guildford, Surrey. *T:* Guildford 62798. *Clubs:* Civil Service, Victory; Rucksack (Manchester). *Died* 14 *Jan.* 1987.

**PAKES, Ernest John,** CBE 1954; Under-writing Member of Lloyd's, since 1956; *b* 28 Jan. 1899; *s* of Ernest William Pakes; *m* 1st, 1928, Emilie Pickering (*d* 1981); one *s*; 2nd, 1984, Mrs Margarita Eileen Gilmore. *Educ:* Hampton Gram. Sch. Served with London Scottish Regt, 1917–19; Ceylon Defence Force, 1940–44; Min. of War Transport, Karachi, 1945–46. Employed in shipping industry, P&O Group, 1916–62 including: Mackinnon Mackenzie & Co., India, Ceylon etc., 1921–54 (Chm., 1951–54); British India Steam Navigation Co. Ltd, 1954–62 (Chm., 1960–62); Director: Allahabad Bank, India, 1947–54 (Chm., 1951–54); Chartered Bank, London, 1958–62. Chm., Karachi Chamber of Commerce, 1946–47; Pres., Bengal Chamber of Commerce and Assocd Chambers of Commerce of India, 1953–54. Liveryman, Worshipful Co. of Shipwrights. *Recreation:* golf. *Address:* Staneway, Tyrrells Wood, Leatherhead, Surrey. *T:* Leatherhead 373243. *Clubs:* Oriental; Walton Heath.

*Died* 30 *June* 1988.

**PAL, Dr Benjamin Peary,** Padma Shri 1958; Padma Bhushan 1968; FRS 1972; Chairman, National Committee on Environmental Planning and Coordination, 1977–81; *b* 26 May 1906; *s* of Dr R. R. Pal; unmarried. *Educ:* Rangoon Univ.; Downing Coll., Cambridge University. MSc hons, PhD Cantab. 2nd Economic Botanist, Imperial Agric. Research Inst., 1933; Imperial Economic Botanist, 1937; Dir, Indian Agric. Res. Inst., 1950; Dir-Gen., Indian Council of Agric. Research, 1965–72, Scientist Emeritus 1972. Hon. DSc: Punjab Agric. Univ.; Sardar Patel Univ.; UP Agric. Univ.; Haryana Agric. Univ.; Orissa Agric. Univ.; Foreign Mem., All Union Lenin Acad. of Agric. Sciences; Hon. Member: Japan Acad.; Acad. d'Agriculture de France; Fellow: Linnean Soc. of London; Indian Nat. Science Acad. (Pres., 1975–76). *Publications:* Beautiful Climbers of India, 1960; Wheat, 1966; Charophyta, The Rose in India, 1966; Flowering Shrubs, 1967; All About Roses, 1973; Bougainvilleas, 1974. *Recreations:* rose gardening, painting. *Address:* P11, Hauz Khas Enclave, New Delhi 110016, India. *T:* 660245. *Died Sept.* 1989.

**PALAMOUNTAIN, Edgar William Irwin;** Chairman, Wider Share Ownership Council, since 1971; *b* 24 Dec. 1917; *s* of William Bennett and Eveleigh Mary Palamountain; *m* 1948, Eleanor, *d* of Maj.-Gen. Sir Richard Lewis, KCMG, CB, GBE; one *s* two *d*. *Educ:* Charterhouse; St John's Coll., Oxford (MA). Served War of 1939–45, RHA and staff (mentioned in despatches) Major 1945, Actg Lt-Col 1946; Allied Commn for Austria, 1945–47. Anglo-Iranian Oil Co., London and Tehran, 1948–51; Tootal Ltd, 1952–56; M & G Group, 1957–79: Exec. Dir, 1962; Man. Dir, 1968; Chm., 1977. Dir of various cos. Chairman: Unit Trust Assoc., 1977–79; Institutional Shareholders Cttee, 1978–79; Pres., Money Management Council, 1987– (Chm., 1985–87). Trustee: Nat. Assoc. of Almshouses, 1963–80; Esmée Fairbairn Trust, 1966–80, 1988– (Dir, 1980–88); Thames Help Trust, 1980; Social Affairs Unit, 1982–; Prospect Trust, 1988–. Patron, Inst. of Economic Affairs, 1972–; Governor: NIESR, 1981–; Ditchley Foundn, 1986–; Mem. Bd, Adam Smith Inst., 1982–; Mem. Council, Univ. of Buckingham (formerly UC, Buckingham), 1975–(Chm., 1979–84). Mem. Cttee, London Voluntary Service Council, 1969–. FRSA 1984. DUniv Buckingham, 1985. *Publication:* Taurus Pursuant: a history of the Eleventh Armoured Division, 1945. *Recreations:* lawn tennis, golf, stalking. *Address:* Duns Tew Manor, Oxford; 35 Chelsea Towers, SW3. *Clubs:* Boodle's, City of London, MCC.

*Died* 5 *June* 1990.

**PALME, (Sven) Olof (Joachim);** MP (SDP of Sweden), Stockholm, since 1958; Prime Minister of Sweden, 1969–76 and since 1982; *b* Stockholm, 30 Jan. 1927; *m* 1956, Lisbeth Beck-Friis; three *s*. *Educ:* Kenyon Coll., Ohio; Univ. of Stockholm. Special Counsel to Swedish Prime Minister, 1953–63; Minister without Portfolio, 1963–65; Minister of: Communications, 1965–67; Education and Culture, 1967–69. Mem. Exec. Bd, 1964–, Chm., 1969–, Swedish SDP. Mem., Indep. Commn on Internat. Develt Issues, 1977–; Chm., Indep. Commn on Disarmament and Security Issues, 1980–; UN Secretary General's Special Representative in the conflict between Iran and Iraq, 1980–. *Address:* Statsrådsberedningen, S-103 33 Stockholm, Sweden. *T:* (468) 7631000.

*Died* 28 *Feb.* 1986.

**PALMER,** 3rd Baron, *cr* 1933, of Reading; **Raymond Cecil Palmer,** OBE 1968; Bt *cr* 1916; former Director, Associated Biscuit Manufacturers Ltd, retired 1980; Chairman: Huntley & Palmers Ltd, 1969–80; Huntley Boorne & Stevens Ltd, Reading, 1956–80 (Deputy Chairman, 1948); *b* 24 June 1916; *er s* of 2nd Baron Palmer and Marguerite (*d* 1959), *d* of William McKinley Osborne, USA, Consul-General to Great Britain; *S* father, 1950; *m* 1941, Victoria Ellen, (CBE 1984), *o c* of late Captain J. A. R. Weston-Stevens, Maidenhead; two *d* (and one *d* decd). *Educ:* Harrow; University

Coll., Oxford. Joined Huntley & Palmers Ltd, 1938, Dep. Chm., 1966–69, Man. Dir, 1967–69. Served War of 1939–45 in Grenadier Guards as Lieut, in UK and North Africa, 1940–43 (invalided). Mem., Southern Electricity Bd, 1965–77. Pres., Berks CCC. *Recreations:* music, gardening. *Heir: nephew* Adrian Bailie Nottage Palmer [*b* 8 Oct. 1951; *m* 1977, Cornelia Dorothy Katharine, *d* of Rohan Wadham, DFC; two *s* one *d*]. *Address:* Farley Hill House, Farley Hill, Reading, Berkshire. *T:* Eversley (0734) 732260. *Club:* Cavalry and Guards. *Died* 26 *June* 1990.

**PALMER, Charles Alan Salier,** CBE 1969; DSO 1945; Chairman, Associated Biscuit Manufacturers Ltd, 1969–72 (Vice-Chm., 1963); *b* 23 Oct. 1913; *s* of late Sir (Charles) Eric Palmer, Shinfield Grange, near Reading; *m* 1939, Auriol Mary, *d* of late Brig.-Gen. Cyril R. Harbord, CB, CMG, DSO. *Educ:* Harrow; Exeter Coll., Oxford. Joined Huntley & Palmer's, 1934 (Bd, 1938; Dep.-Chm. 1955; Chm., Huntley & Palmer's, 1963). Served War of 1939–45: with Berks Yeo., Adjt, 1939–41; GSO3, HQ 61 Div., 1941–42; GSO2, HQ III Corps, 1942–43; Lt-Col; commanded SOE mission, Albania, 1943–45 (despatches). Pres., Reading Conservative Assoc., 1946–86. Chm., Cake & Biscuit Alliance, 1967–70; Mem. Council, CBI 1967–70; Mem. British Productivity Council, 1970–73. *Recreations:* shooting, fishing, tropical agriculture. *Address:* Forest Edge, Farley Hill, Reading, Berks. *T:* Arborfield Cross (0734) 760223.
*Died* 13 *Sept.* 1990.

**PALMER, Gerald Eustace Howell,** Hon. DLitt Reading, 1957; farmer, forester and iconographer; *b* 9 June 1904; *s* of late Eustace Exall Palmer, Chairman of Huntley and Palmers Ltd, and Madeline Mary Howell. *Educ:* Winchester; New College, Oxford (Scholar). MP (Nat. C) for Winchester Division of Hampshire, 1935–45. Served RA, Captain (despatches). President of the Council, Univ. of Reading, 1966–69; A Verderer of the New Forest, 1957–66; Chm., Forestry Commission Regional Adv. Cttee for South-East England, 1954–63; A Forestry Commissioner, 1963–65; Chm., Forestry Commn Nat. Cttee for England, 1964–65. Hon. Fellow, Soc. of Foresters of GB. *Publications:* following translations (in collab. with E. Kadloubovsky): Writings from the Philokalia, 1951; Unseen Warfare, 1952; The Meaning of Icons, by Lossky and Ouspensky, 1952; Early Fathers, from the Philokalia, 1954; (with Philip Shevrard and Father Kallistos Ware) The Philokalia, vol. I, 1979, vol. II, 1981. *Address:* Bussock Mayne, Newbury, Berks. *T:* Chieveley 265. *Club:* Brooks's. *Died* 7 *Feb.* 1984.

**PALMER, Col Hon. Sir Gordon William Nottage,** KCVO 1989; OBE 1957 (MBE 1944); TD 1950; Lord-Lieutenant of Berkshire, 1978–89; *b* 18 July 1918; *yr s* of 2nd Baron Palmer and Marguerite Osborne, USA; *heir-pres.* to 3rd Baron Palmer, OBE; *m* 1950, Lorna Eveline Hope, *d* of Major C. W. H. Bailie; two *s*. *Educ:* Eton Coll.; Christ Church, Oxford. Served War of 1939–45, with Berks Yeo., 1939–41; staff Capt. RA, HQ 61 Div., 1941; DAQMG, Malta, 1942: GSO2, Ops, GHQ Middle East, 1943–44; GSO2, HQ 5 Div., 1944–45; Lt-Col, Instructor Staff College, Camberley, 1945; Comd Berkshire Yeo., TA, 1954–56. Hon. Colonel: Berkshire and Westminster Dragoons, 1966–67; Royal Yeomanry, 1972–75; 2nd Bn The Wessex Regt (V), 1983–85. Dir, Huntley, Boorne & Stevens Ltd, 1948–69; Chm. Cake and Biscuit Alliance, 1957–59; Man. Dir, Huntley & Palmer Ltd, 1959–65; Chm. and Man. Dir, Associated Biscuits Ltd, 1978–83; Chm., Huntley & Palmer Foods plc (formerly Associated Biscuit Manufacturers), 1978–83. Vice-Chm., Morlands Brewery (Abingdon). Mem., British National Export Council, 1966–69. Dir, Thames Valley S Midlands Regional Bd, Lloyds Bank Ltd, 1976–89. Pres., Council, Reading Univ., 1973–75 (Mem. 1954–, Treas., 1955–59, Vice-Pres., 1966–73; Hon. LLD, 1975); Chm. Council, Royal Coll. of Music, 1973–88; FRCM 1965; FRAM 1983; Mem. Council, Bradfield College (Warden, 1984–89); DL Berks, 1960; JP 1956; High Sheriff, 1965; Vice Lord-Lieutenant, 1976; Chairman, Berkshire T&AFA, 1961–68. KStJ. *Recreation:* gardening. *Address:* Harris House, Mortimer, Berkshire. *T:* Mortimer 332317; Edrom Newton, Duns, Berwickshire. *T:* Chirnside 292. *Club:* Cavalry and Guards. *Died* 3 *July* 1989.

**PALMER, Leonard Robert;** Professor of Comparative Philology, University of Oxford, and Fellow of Worcester College, 1952–71, Emeritus Professor, 1971, Emeritus Fellow, 1972; *b* 5 June 1906; *m*; one *d*. *Educ:* High School, Canton, Cardiff; University College of South Wales and Monmouthshire; Trinity College, Cambridge; University of Vienna. BA Wales 1927; PhD Vienna 1931; PhD Cambridge 1936; MA Oxford 1952. Fellow of Univ. of Wales, 1930–31; Assistant Lecturer in Classics, 1931–35, Lecturer in Classics, 1935–41, Victoria University of Manchester; temp. Civil Servant in Foreign Office, 1941–45; Professor of Greek and Head of Dept of Classics at King's Coll., London, 1945–52. Hon. Secretary Philological Society, 1947–51, President, 1957–61. Corresponding Member Deutsches Archäologisches Institut, 1958. Dr Phil *hc* Innsbruck, 1981. *Publications:* Translation of E. Zeller: Outlines of the History of Greek Philosophy, 14th edn, 1931; Introduction to Modern Linguistics, 1936; A Grammar of the Post-Ptolemaic Papyri, Vol. I (Publications of the Philological Society), 1945; The

Latin Language, 1954 (as Introducción al Latin, rev. Spanish edn, 1974; as La Lingua Latina, Italian edn, 1977); Mycenaeans and Minoans, 1961, 2nd edn 1965 (trans. as De Aegeische Wereld, 1963, Knossosoch Mykene, 1963, Minoici e Micenei, 1970); The Language of Homer (in A Companion to Homer), 1962; The Interpretation of Mycenaean Greek Texts, 1963, rev. edn 1969; The Find Places of the Knossos Tablets, 1963; A New Guide to the Palace of Knossos, 1969; The Penultimate Palace at Knossos, 1969; Descriptive and Comparative Linguistics: a critical introduction, 1972 (Spanish edn, Introduccion critica a la linguistica descriptiva y comparada, 1975, rev. Italian edn, Linguistica descrittiva e comparativa, 1979, rev. Japanese edn 1979); The Greek Language, 1981; Studies in Aegean Chronology, 1984; various articles in English and foreign learned journals. *Festschrift:* Studies in Greek, Italic, and Indo-European Linguistics, offered to Leonard R. Palmer on the occasion of his seventieth birthday, ed Anna M. Davies and W. Meid, 1976. *Address:* Church Hill, Pitney, Langport TA10 9PE. *T:* Langport 250683. *Died* 26 *Aug.* 1984.

**PALMER, Brig. Sir Otho (Leslie) P.;** *see* Prior-Palmer.

**PALUELLO, Lorenzo M.;** *see* Minio-Paluello.

**PANCKRIDGE, Surg. Vice-Adm. Sir (William) Robert (Silvester),** KBE 1962; CB 1960; Medical Director-General of the Navy, 1960–63, retired; *b* 11 Sept. 1901; *s* of W. P. Panckridge, OBE, MB, MRCS, LRCP, and Mrs Panckridge; *m* 1932, Edith Muriel, *d* of Sir John and Lady Crosbie, St John, Newfoundland; one *d*. *Educ:* Tonbridge School; Middlesex Hospital. FRSM 1955; QHP 1958. PMO, RN Coll., Dartmouth, 1948; Medical Officer-in-Charge; RN Hosp., Hong Kong, 1952; RN Hosp., Chatham, 1958; Surgeon Captain, 1952; Surgeon Rear-Admiral, 1958; Surgeon Vice-Admiral, 1960. QHP, 1958–63. CStJ 1959. *Recreations:* shooting, fishing, gardening. *Address:* Waterfall Lodge, Oughterard, Co. Galway. *T:* Galway 82168. *Died* 30 *June* 1990.

**PANDIT, Vijaya Lakshmi, (Mrs Ranjit S. Pandit);** Padma Vibhusan, India, 1962; *b* 18 August 1900; *d* of Motilal Nehru and Sarup Rani Nehru; *m* 1921, Ranjit S. Pandit (*d* 1944); three *d*. *Educ:* privately. Member Municipal Board, Allahabad, and Chm. Education Cttee, 1935; MLA, UP, and Minister of Local Govt and Health in Congress Cabinet of UP, 1937–39, and 1946–47. Leader India delegation to UN General Assembly, 1946, 1947, 1948; Ambassador to Moscow, 1947–49; Ambassador of India to the USA and Mexico, 1949–51; Member of Indian Parliament, 1952–54; High Commissioner for India in London, and Indian Ambassador to Ireland, 1954–61, concurrently Indian Ambassador to Spain, 1958–61; Governor of Maharashtra, 1962–64; MP, Phulpur, UP, 1964–69. Imprisoned three times for participation in national movement, 1932, 1941, 1942. President of the United Nations Assembly, 1953–54, Mem. Indian Delegn to UN, 1963. Trustee, Mountbatten Meml Trust, 1980–. Hon. DCL, Oxford, 1964, and numerous other Hon. degrees from Universities and Colleges. *Publications:* The Evolution of India (Whidden Lectures), 1958; The Scope of Happiness: a personal memoir, 1979. *Address:* 181B Rajpur Road, Dehra Dun, Uttar Pradesh, India.
*Died* 1 *Dec.* 1990.

**PANET, Brig. Henri de Lotbinière,** CBE 1943 (OBE 1941); *b* 21 Apr. 1896; *s* of late Brig.-Gen. A. E. Panet, CB, CMG, DSO; *m* 1931, Truda Buchanan Hope; one *d*. *Educ:* Loyola Coll., Montreal; Royal Military Coll., Canada. Served European War, 1915–18. Royal Engineers, France and Salonica (wounded, despatches); Indian State Railways, 1920–34; served Egypt and Palestine, 1935–36 (despatches); Hong Kong, 1938–41 (OBE); Iraq and Persia, 1941–43 (CBE); BLA, 1944–45 (despatches); Director of Fortifications and Works, War Office, 1947–49; retired, 1949. *Recreation:* fishing. *Address:* 161 Wilton Road, Salisbury, Wilts. *T:* Salisbury 3615.
*Died* 30 *Oct.* 1985.

**PANTCHEFF, Theodore Xenophon Henry,** CMG 1977; HM Diplomatic Service, retired; *b* 29 Dec. 1920; *s* of Sophocles Xenophon Pantcheff and Ella Jessie, *d* of Dr S. H. Ramsbotham, Leeds; *m* 1954, Patricia Mary Tully; two *s*. *Educ:* Merchant Taylors' Sch.; Gonville and Caius Coll., Cambridge (MA). HM Forces, 1941–47; Control Commn for Germany, 1948–51; joined Foreign Office, 1951; Vice-Consul, Munich, 1954–56; 1st Sec., Lagos, 1958–60; 1st Sec., Leopoldville, 1961–63; seconded MoD, 1969–71; Counsellor, FCO, 1971–77. Jurat of the Court of Alderney, 1979. *Publications:* Alderney: fortress island, 1981; The Emsland Executioner, 1987. *Recreations:* reading and conversation. *Address:* Butes Cottage, Alderney. *Clubs:* Carlton; Alderney Society (Alderney); Société Guernesiaise (Guernsey).
*Died* 28 *Nov.* 1989.

**PAPE, Hon. Sir George (Augustus),** Kt 1968; Judge of Supreme Court of Victoria, 1957–75, retired; *b* 29 Jan. 1903; *s* of George Frederick Pape and Minnie Maud Pape (*née* Bryan); *m* 1952, Mabel (*d* 1983), *d* of Alfred Lloyd; no *c*. *Educ:* All Saints Grammar Sch., St Kilda; University of Melbourne (LLB). QC 1955. RAAF, 1940–46.

*Recreation:* golf. *Address:* 146 Kooyong Road, Toorak, Victoria 3142, Australia. *T:* 20–6158. *Club:* Australian (Melbourne).
*Died June* 1987.

**PARBURY, George Mark,** CB 1980; Chief Registrar of the High Court of Justice in Bankruptcy, 1975–80; *b* 27 April 1908; *s* of late Norman Cecil Parbury and Ellen Parbury; *m* 1942, Roma Constance, *d* of late James Robert Raw, JP, New Zealand, and Clare Raw. *Educ:* Geelong, Australia; Jesus Coll., Cambridge. Called to Bar, Lincoln's Inn, 1934. Practised at Chancery Bar, 1934–39. Served War of 1939–45, 1940–45, Temp. Lt-Col, 1944; AAG, AG3e War Office, Mil. Govt 21 Army Group. Again practised at Chancery Bar, 1946–65; Mem. Bar Council, 1961–62. Registrar, High Court of Justice in Bankruptcy, 1965–75. *Recreations:* walking on the Downs; gardening. *Died* 25 *Dec.* 1988.

**PARENT, Most Rev. Charles Eugène,** ThD; former Archbishop of Rimouski, from 1970; Titular Archbishop of Vassinassa, 1967–70; *b* Les Trois-Pistoles, Qué, 22 April 1902; *s* of Louis Parent and Marie Lavoie. *Educ:* Rimouski Seminary; Laval University of Quebec; Institutum Angelicum, Rome. ThD 1929. Professor of Theology at Rimouski Seminary and Chaplain at St Joseph's Hospital of Rimouski, 1931–41; Rector of Saint Germain's Cathedral, 1941–45; Auxiliary Bishop at Rimouski, 1944–50; Capitulaire Vicaire, 1950–51; Archbishop of Rimouski, 1951–67. *Publication:* Mandements et circulaires au clergé et au peuple de l'archidiocèse de Rimouski, 3 vols, 1951–67. *Address:* Archevêché, PO Box 730, Rimouski, Québec G5L 7C7, Canada.
*Died* 2 *June* 1982.

**PARFITT, Rt. Rev. Thomas Richards;** Assistant Bishop, diocese of Derby, since 1962; *b* 24 May 1911; *s* of Charles Henry John and Maud Sarah Parfitt. *Educ:* S John Baptist Coll., Oxford. BA Oxon 1933 (2nd class Lit. Hum., 1933; 2nd class Theology, 1934); MA 1936. Cuddesdon Coll., 1934–35. Deacon, 1935; Priest, 1936; Asst Curate of New Mills, 1935–39; Curate of Rugby (in charge of Holy Trinity), 1939–43; Chaplain RNVR, 1943–46; Vicar of S Andrew, Derby, 1946–52; Rural Dean of Derby, 1951–52; Bishop in Madagascar, 1952–61; Rector of Matlock with Tansley, 1962–80. *Address:* St Paul's Vicarage, Old Chester Road, Derby DE1 3SA.
*Died* 10 *Dec.* 1984.

**PARGITER, Baron,** *cr* 1966 (Life Peer) of Southall; **George Albert Pargiter,** CBE 1961; *b* 16 March 1897; *s* of William Pargiter, Greens Norton; *m* 1919, Dorothy Woods; two *s* one *d. Educ:* Towcester Grammar Sch. Engineer by profession. Served 1914–16 Army, at Gallipoli. MP (Lab) Spelthorne Division of Middlesex, 1945–50, Southall, 1950–66; Member Middlesex County Council, 1934–65, County Alderman, 1946 (Chairman, 1959–60). Member several public bodies. Mayor of Southall, 1938–40 (three years); DL Middlesex 1953; DL County of London, later Greater London, 1965–76. *Address:* 190 Whyteleafe Road, Caterham, Surrey CR3 5ED. *T:* Caterham 45588. *Died* 16 *Jan.* 1982.

**PARGITER, Maj.-Gen. Robert Beverley,** CB 1942; CBE 1945; *b* 11 July 1889; *s* of late F. E. Pargiter, ICS; *m* 1st, 1917, Muriel Huxley (*d* 1971); one *s* two *d*; 2nd, 1973, Elaine Ilma, *widow* of Colin C. Gulliland. *Educ:* Rugby; RMA, Woolwich. Commissioned RA 1909; served with RA, European War, 1914–18, on NWF, India, France, and Belgium (severely wounded, despatches); Military Mission to Baltic States, 1919–21 (Brevet of Major); psc Camberley, 1924; Instructor Staff Coll., Quetta, 1930–33; idc 1934; GSO 1 Operations, WO, 1936–38; War Service, 1939–45; Commander 1st AA Brigade; 4th, 7th and 5th AA Divisions; 3rd AA Group; Maj.-Gen. Anti-Aircraft, Allied Force HQ, N. Africa and Central Mediterranean Forces (despatches, CBE, Commander of Legion of Merit); retired, 1945; Commissioner, British Red Cross and St John's War Organisation, Middle East, 1945, Malaya, 1946. Colonel Comdt RA, 1951–54. *Publication:* (with late Colonel H. Eady) The Army and Sea Power, 1927. *Recreations:* fishing, gardening, braille. *Address:* The Dye House, Biddenden, Kent.
*Died* 2 *Sept.* 1984.

**PARIKIAN, Manoug;** violinist; Professor of Violin, Royal Academy of Music, since 1959; *b* Mersin, Turkey, 15 Sept. 1920, of Armenian parentage; *s* of late Stepan Parikian and Vanouhi (*née* Bedelian); *m* 1957, Diana Margaret (*née* Carbutt); two *s. Educ:* Trinity College of Music, London (Fellow). Leader: Liverpool Philharmonic Orchestra, 1947–48; Philharmonia Orchestra, London, 1949, until resignation, 1957; has appeared in all European countries as solo violinist. Introduced Shostakovitch Violin Concerto to Scandinavia (Stockholm), 1956; first public performance of works by Iain Hamilton, Rawsthorne, Musgrave, Alexander Goehr, Elizabeth Maconchy, Gordon Crosse and Hugh Wood. Toured: USSR, April-May 1961, and Nov. 1965; Latin America, July-Aug. 1974. Dir, Yorkshire Sinfonia, 1976–78; Musical Dir, Manchester Camerata, 1980–84; Artistic Dir, Giggleswick Summer Music Fest., 1981. Formed trio with Amaryllis Fleming ('cello) and Bernard Roberts (piano), 1977 (Roberts replaced by Hamish Milne, 1984). Sir Robert Mayer Vis. Lectr, Leeds Univ., 1974–75. Member Jury: Tchaikovsky Violin Competition, Moscow, 1970; Carl Flesch Internat. Competition, 1984. Hon. RAM, 1963. *Recreations:* collecting early printed books in Armenian; backgammon. *Address:* The Old Rectory, Waterstock, Oxford. *T:* Ickford 603.
*Died* 24 *Dec.* 1987.

**PARIS, Sir Edward (Talbot),** Kt 1954; CB 1947; DSc (London), FInstP; *b* 23 Jan. 1889; *s* of late Edward and Eliza Paris; *m* 1925, Eveline Amy (*d* 1968), *d* of late J. W. Shortt, MD; three *d. Educ:* Dean Close Sch., Cheltenham; Imperial College of Science; University College, London. Fellow University College, London, 1921; served European War, 1914–18, RA, 1915–18; seconded to Ministry of Munitions, 1918; Signals Experimental Establishment, War Dept, 1919; Experimental Officer in Air Defence Experimental Establishment, 1923; Dep. Director of Scientific Research, WO, 1938; transferred Ministry of Supply, 1939; Controller of Physical Research, 1941; Controller of Physical Research and Signals Development, 1942; Principal Director of Scientific Research (Defence), Ministry of Supply, 1946; Chief Scientific Adviser, Home Office, 1948–54. US Medal of Freedom with Bronze Palm, 1947. *Publications:* various papers in scientific journals. *Address:* Apartado 57, San Vicente de la Barquera, Santander, Spain.
*Died* 26 *Aug.* 1985.

**PARIS, John;** Director, National Army Museum, 1967–69; *b* Hove, 2 May 1912; *s* of Herbert Henry Paris, Comptroller of Telegraphs and Postmaster, Durban, during Boer War; *m* 1940, Beryl Maria Thomson; no *c. Educ:* Brighton Coll.; Brighton College of Art; Worcester Coll., Oxford. BA (English) 1936; MA 1938; MLitt 1938. Commissioned into RA, 1940; SO Fixed Defences Scottish Command, 1942; Major. Dep. Director, Walker Art Gallery, Liverpool, 1938–49; Director, National Gallery of S Africa, Cape Town, 1949–62. Hon. Life Vice-President, Friends of Italy; Past President, S African Museums Assoc.; Kolbe Memorial Lecturer, University of Cape Town, 1961. Has made broadcasts. *Publications:* English Water-Colour Painters, 1945; William Gilpin and the Cult of the Picturesque; introductions, catalogues and articles in learned journals; occasional poems, etc. *Address:* 5 Brook House, Ardingly, Sussex. *T:* Ardingly 892274. *Died* 14 *June* 1985.

**PARISH, Alan Raymond,** FEng 1983; Deputy Chairman, since 1975, and Chief Executive, since 1978, W. S. Atkins Group Consultants, since 1975; *b* 14 Oct. 1925; *s* of Benjamin Wilkin Parish and Constance Isabel (*née* Ashford); *m* 1950, Norma Beryl Butlin; two *s. Educ:* Westcliff High Sch.; Bromley County Sch.; King's Coll., London Univ. (BSc Eng). FICE 1968; FIMechE 1965; FIEE 1962; FIPENZ 1966; CBIM 1978. English Electric Co. Ltd: Graduate Apprentice, 1945–47; Engr, 1947–50; Liaison Engr, USA, 1950–52; Sen. Engr, 1952–58; W. S. Atkins Group: Dep. Chief Engr, 1958–60; Proj. Man., 1960–65; Proj. Dir, NZ, 1965–67; Director: W. S. Atkins & Partners, 1967–; W. S. Atkins International, 1973–; W. S. Atkins International Operations Ltd, 1976–; W. S. Atkins (Services) Ltd, 1983–; President: W. S. Atkins Inc., USA, 1979–; Atkins SA, Mexico, 1978–. *Publications:* articles on aspects of engrg management. *Recreation:* gardening. *Address:* The Gables, Coulsdon Lane, Chipstead, Coulsdon, Surrey CR3 3QG. *T:* Downland 55488. *Died* 5 *April* 1985.

**PARK, William,** OBE 1967; Keeper of Manuscripts, National Library of Scotland, 1946–72; *b* 14 April 1909; *s* of John Park and Isabella Stephenson Berridge; *m* 1935, Mary Allan (decd), *d* of Robert Wilson; two *d. Educ:* Hawick High Sch.; Edinburgh Univ. (MA); School of Librarianship, University College, London. Assistant, National Library of Scotland, 1932–46; seconded to Scottish Home Department, 1940–46. *Address:* c/o A. C. Bennett & Fairweather, WS, 54 Queen Street, Edinburgh EH2 3NX.
*Died* 2 *March* 1982.

**PARKE, Herbert William,** MA (Oxon), LittD (Dublin); Fellow Emeritus of Trinity College, Dublin, since 1973, Fellow, 1929–73; Professor of Ancient History, 1934–73, Vice-Provost, 1952–73, Librarian 1947–65, Curator, 1965–73; *b* Moneymore, Co. Londonderry, 7 Sept. 1903; *o s* of William and Bertha Blair Parke; *m* 1930, Nancy Bankart (*d* 1980), *y d* of Arthur R. Gurney, Cracoe, Yorks; one *d. Educ:* Coleraine Academical Institution; Bradford Grammar Sch.; Wadham Coll., Oxford (Scholar). 1st Class Hon. Mods, 1924; 1st Class Lit. Hum. 1926; A. M. P. Read Scholar, 1927; Craven Fellow, 1928; Cromer Essay Prize, 1928; Member of Royal Irish Academy, 1933; L. C. Purser Lect. in Archæology, 1934; Temp. Principal, Board of Trade, 1942–44; FRNS, 1947. Member Institute for Advanced Study, Princeton, USA, 1960; Vis. Schol., Arts Faculty, Southampton Univ., 1979. Hon. Fellow Durham Univ., 1982; Hon. DLit QUB, 1974; Hon. LittD NUU, 1978. *Publications:* Greek Mercenary Soldiers, 1933; Delphic Oracle, 1939 (2nd edition with Professor D. E. W. Wormell, 1956); Oracles of Zeus, 1967; Greek Oracles, 1967; Festivals of the Athenians, 1977; Oracles of Apollo in Asia Minor, 1985; contrib. to Journal of Hellenic Studies, Hermathena, etc., articles on Greek History and Mythology in Chambers's Encyclopædia, Encyclopædia Britannica, and Oxford Classical Dictionary; *posthumous publication:* (ed Dr Brian McGing) Sibyls and Sibylline Prophecy in Classical Antiquity, 1988. *Address:* 275 West Dyke Road, Redcar, Cleveland TS10 4JU. *Died 20 Jan. 1986.*

**PARKE, Dr Mary,** FRS 1972; Senior Phycologist, Marine Biological Association, Plymouth, 1947–73, retired; *b* 23 March 1908. *Educ:* Notre Dame Convent, Everton Valley; Univ. of Liverpool. DSc, PhD; FLS, FIBiol. Isaac Roberts Research Schol. in Biology, 1929; Phycologist, Marine Biological Stn, Port Erin, IoM, 1930–40; research on algae for Develt Commn and Min. of Supply, 1941–46. Corresp. Mem., Royal Botanical Soc. of Netherlands, 1970; Mem., Norwegian Acad. of Science and Letters, 1971. Hon. DSc Liverpool, 1986. *Publications:* (with M. Knight) Manx Algae, 1931; papers in Jl of Marine Biol Assoc., Plymouth, etc. *Address:* 6 Alfred Street, Plymouth PL1 2RP. *T:* Plymouth 668609.
*Died 17 July 1989.*

**PARKER, Sir Alan;** *see* Parker, Sir W. A.

**PARKER, Prof. Alexander Augustine,** MA, LittD; Professor of Spanish Literature, University of Texas at Austin, 1970–78, then Emeritus; *b* Montevideo, 1908; *er s* of Arthur Parker and Laura Bustamante; *m* 1941, Frances Ludwig; two *s* two *d*. *Educ:* Hawkesyard School (later Blackfriars School, Laxton); Gonville and Caius Coll., Cambridge (Exhibn. and scholar; 1st Class Mod. and Medieval Langs Tripos, Part I 1928, Part II 1930; Gibson Schol., 1931; LittD 1968). Fellow of Gonville and Caius Coll., 1933–39, Hon. Fellow 1985. Lecturer and Head of Dept of Spanish, University of Aberdeen, 1939–49; Reader in Spanish, University of Aberdeen, 1949–53; Cervantes Professor of Spanish, University of London (King's Coll.), 1953–63; Prof. of Hispanic Studies, Univ. of Edinburgh, 1963–69. Seconded to University College of the West Indies as Prof. of Modern Languages, 1960–61; Andrew Mellon Visiting Prof., University of Pittsburgh, 1964, 1968, 1969–70. Corresponding Member: Royal Acad. of Letters of Seville, 1958; Hispanic Society of America, 1960 (Member, 1976); Royal Spanish Academy, 1964. Hon. DLitt: Durham, 1975; St Andrews, 1978; Hon. LittD Liverpool, 1978. Commander of the Order of Isabel la Católica, 1956. *Publications:* The Allegorical Drama of Calderón, An Introduction to the Autos Sacramentales, 1943; (ed) No hay más Fortuna que Dios, by Calderón, 1949; Literature and the Delinquent: the Picaresque Novel in Spain and Europe (1599–1753), 1967; Luis de Góngora, Fable of Polyphemus and Galatea: a study of a baroque poem, 1977; The Philosophy of Love in Spanish Literature (1480–1680), 1985; The Mind and Art of Calderón: essays on the Comedias, 1988; papers and articles in literary and academic journals. *Recreations:* opera, horticulture and lepidoptera. *Address:* 9 West Castle Road, Edinburgh EH10 5AT. *T:* 031–229 1632.
*Died 23 Nov. 1989.*

**PARKER, Sir Douglas William Leigh,** Kt 1966; OBE 1954; retired as Director of Orthopædic Services, Tasmanian Government Health Dept, 1966; *b* 12 July 1900; *m* 1933, Hilary Secretan; two *s* one *d*. *Educ:* University of Sydney; University of Liverpool. MB, ChM (Sydney), 1923; FRCSEd 1925; MChOrth (Liverpool), 1930; FRACS, 1935. War of 1939–45: Surgeon, 2/9 AGH, 1940–42, 111 AGH, 1942–46. Senior Orthopædic Surgeon, Royal Hobart Hospital. Comr St John Ambulance Bde, Tasmania. Member Legacy, Hobart. OStJ. *Address:* 30 Fisher's Avenue, Lower Sandy Bay, Hobart, Tasmania 7005, Australia. *Clubs:* Tasmanian, Naval and Military and Air Force (Hobart). *Died Feb. 1988.*

**PARKER, Sir Edmund;** *see* Parker, Sir W. E.

**PARKER, Eric;** *see* Parker, R. E.

**PARKER, Geoffrey,** CB 1966; Under-Secretary, Department of Industry, formerly Department of Trade and Industry, 1970–76; *b* 17 Jan. 1917; *o s* of James and Florence Parker; *m* 1942, Janet Crawford Chidley (decd), 2nd *d* of Edgar Blackford Chidley; two *s* one *d*. *Educ:* Hulme Grammar Sch., Oldham; New Coll., Oxford; Queen's Coll., Oxford; Universities of Berlin and Berne, MA, DPhil (Oxon). Entered Board of Trade as temp. Assistant Principal, May 1940; established as Principal, 1946. Counsellor (Commercial), HM Embassy, Washington, DC, 1952–55; Under-Sec., 1961; Principal Establishment and Organisation Officer, 1965–70. *Recreations:* reading, languages. *Address:* 5 Hove Court, Raymond Road, Wimbledon SW19 4AG. *T:* 01–946 9300.
*Died 27 Sept. 1985.*

**PARKER, John,** CBE 1965; President, Fabian Society, since 1980 (Vice-President, 1972–80); *b* 15 July 1906; *s* of H. A. M. Parker, schoolmaster and N. P. Parker; *m* 1943, Zena Mimardiere; one *s*. *Educ:* Marlborough; St John's College, Oxford. Chm., Oxford Univ. Labour Club, 1928; Asst to Director, Social Survey of Merseyside (Liverpool Univ.), 1929–32; Gen. Sec., New Fabian Res. Bureau, 1933–39; Fabian Society: Gen. Sec., 1939–45; Vice-Chm., 1946–50; Chm., 1950–53. Contested (Lab) Holland with Boston, 1931; MP (Lab): Romford, Essex, 1935–45; Dagenham, 1945–83; PPS to Miss Ellen Wilkinson, Min. of Home Security, 1940–42; Parly Under-

Sec. of State, Dominions Office, 1945–46; Member: Speaker's Conferences, 1944, 1965–67, 1973–74; Procedure Cttee, 1966–73; Parly Delegation to USSR, 1945; National Executive Labour Party, 1943–44; Executive London Labour Party, 1942–47; Select Cttee Parliamentary Disqualifications, 1956; Parly Delegations to Italy, 1957, Ethiopia, 1964, Forestry Delegation, Yugoslavia, 1971; Leader, Delegation to Windward Islands, 1965; Chm., British-Yugoslav Parly Gp, 1960–83; Father of the House of Commons, 1979–83; Chairman: History of Parlt Trust, 1979–83; H of C Pensions Fund, 1969–83. Hon. Sec., Webb Trustees; Governor, LSE, 1949–81; Member: Court, Essex Univ., 1968–; Exec. Cttee, Nat. Trust, 1969–81; Historic Buildings Council, 1974–84; Inland Waterways Amenity Council, 1968–83. Mem., TGWU. Yugoslav Red Star, 1975. *Publications:* The Independent Worker and Small Family Business, 1931; Public Enterprise (Forestry Commission), 1937; Democratic Sweden (Political Parties); Modern Turkey, 1940; 42 Days in the Soviet Union, 1946; Labour Marches On, 1947; Newfoundland, 1950; (ed) Modern Yugoslav Novels (English edn), 1958–64; (comp. and ed) biographies, inc. Harold Wilson and Willy Brandt, 1964; Father of the House: 50 Years in Politics, 1982. *Recreations:* architecture and gardening. *Address:* 4 Essex Court, Temple, EC4. *T:* 01–353 8521. *Died 24 Nov. 1987.*

**PARKER, Sir John (Edward),** Kt 1975; BCE; Hon. FIEAust; retired; *b* 28 Sept. 1904; *s* of late Matthew Parker and Edith Florence Parker; *m* 1932, Winifred Mary Becher; two *s* one *d*. *Educ:* Wesley Coll., Melbourne, Vic; Queen's Coll., Melbourne Univ. (BCE). Served War: RAE, AIF, in SW Pacific Area, rank Major, 1942–45. Dep. Dir of Works, Public Works Dept, Perth, WA, 1953–62; Dir of Engineering, PWD, Perth, WA, 1962–69. Chm., State Electricity Commn of WA, 1969–74. *Recreations:* golf, fishing, gardening. *Address:* 11 Hopetoun Street, South Perth, WA 6151, Australia. *T:* Perth 67 1272. *Clubs:* Weld (Perth, WA); Royal Perth Golf.
*Died 1985.*

**PARKER, (Richard) Eric,** PhD (London), CChem, FRSC; Registrar and Secretary for Public Affairs, Royal Society of Chemistry, since 1980; *b* 6 May 1925; *s* of late Leonard Parker and of Louisa Mary Parker (*née* Frearson); *m* 1st, 1949, Audrey Smith; 2nd, 1964, Jane Norris; no *c*; 3rd 1969, Elizabeth Howgego; one *s* two step *d*. *Educ:* Wyggeston Sch., Leicester; University Coll., Leicester. Tutorial Student, King's Coll., London, 1946; Asst Lectr, 1947, and Lectr in Organic Chemistry, 1950–62, Univ. of Southampton; Sec. and Registrar, Royal Inst. of Chemistry, 1962–80 (Mem. Council, 1959–62). Hon. Treas., 1966–69, and Jt Hon. Sec., 1973–76, Parly and Scientific Cttee; Chm., European Communities Chemistry Cttee, 1973–; Mem. Exec. Cttee, Fedn of European Chemical Socs, 1977– (Jt Hon. Sec., 1970–76); Mem., UK Nat. Commn for UNESCO, 1981–. FRSA 1970. *Publications:* papers and articles on physical organic chemistry, mainly in Jl Chem. Soc. *Recreations:* bridge, travel, swimming, Rugby football. *Address:* Royal Society of Chemistry, 30 Russell Square, WC1B 5DT. *T:* 01-631 1355; 6 Woodside House, Woodside, SW19 7QN. *T:* 01-947 9904. *Club:* Savage. *Died 1 April 1982.*

**PARKER, Rear-Adm. Robert William,** CBE 1954; JP; *b* 1902; *s* of Colonel W. F. Parker, Delamore, Cornwood, Devon; *m* 1935, Noemi Vyvian, *d* of C. V. Espeut; no *c*. *Educ:* Royal Naval Colleges Osborne and Dartmouth. Midshipman, 1918; served in Grand Fleet; specialised Engineering, 1922–24; served as Engineer Officer: HMS Rodney, 1942–44; HMS Indomitable (British Pacific Fleet), 1944–46; comd HMS Caledonia, RN Apprentices Training Establishment, Rosyth, 1949–52; Rear-Adm. (E), 1952, on staff of C-in-C, Plymouth; Deputy Engineer-in-Chief of the Fleet, 1953–55; retired 1955. JP Somerset, 1961. *Recreation:* model engineering. *Address:* The Hermitage, Freshford, near Bath, Avon BA3 6DA. *T:* Limpley Stoke 3220. *Died 15 May 1985.*

**PARKER, Rev. Thomas Maynard,** DD; Fellow and Praelector in Theology and Modern History, University College, Oxford, 1952–73; then Emeritus Fellow; *b* 7 March 1906; *s* of late Thomas Maynard and Emily Mary Parker; unmarried. *Educ:* King Edward VI School, Stratford-upon-Avon; Exeter College, Oxford (Scholar). 1st Class Hon. School of Modern History, 1927; BA 1927; 1st Cl. Hon. Sch. of Theology, 1929; Liddon Student, 1928–30; MA 1931; BD, DD 1956. St Stephen's House, Oxford, 1927–29. Liveryman of Butchers' Company, 1927 (Mem. Ct of Assistants, 1955–57, 1963–65; Warden, 1957–61; Providitor, 1960–61; Renter Asst, 1961–62; Master, 1962–63; Past Master, 1963–); Freeman of City of London, 1927. Deacon, 1930; Priest, 1931; Librarian and Tutor, Chichester Theological College, 1930–32; Curate of St Mary's, Somers Town, London, NW1, 1932–35; Librarian of Pusey House, Oxford, 1935–52; Custodian of the Pusey Memorial Library, 1946–52; University of Oxford: Mem., Faculty of Modern History, 1935–81; Faculty of Theology, 1935–73; Univ. Lectr in Theology, 1950–73; Bampton Lecturer, 1950; Acting Chaplain and Lecturer in Medieval History and Political Science, Pembroke College, 1951–52; Assistant Chaplain, Exeter College, 1946–52; Chaplain, University Coll., 1952–70; Lecturer in Theology, Pembroke Coll., 1952–61; Chairman: Faculty of Theology, 1963–65; Board of Faculty of

Theology, 1964–65; Examiner in: Honour School of Theology, 1963–65; Honour School of Mod. Hist., 1953–55. Select Preacher: Cambridge Univ., 1955; Oxford Univ., 1960–61. Examining Chaplain to Bishop of Bradford, 1943–55; Birkbeck Lecturer, Trinity College, Cambridge, 1956–57. External Examr, QUB, 1964–66; External Examr in Church History for BD, St David's Coll., Lampeter, 1968–70; Examr for BPhil in European History, Oxford Univ., 1972–74. Member Central Advisory Council for Training of Ministry, 1948–55; Member Faith and Order Department of Brit. Council of Churches, 1949–55. FRHistS, 1956 (Mem. Council 1964–68); FSA, 1962. *Publications:* The Re-Creation of Man, 1940; The English Reformation to 1558, 1950 (2nd edn 1966); Christianity and the State in the Light of History (Bampton Lectures), 1955. Contributor to: Union of Christendom, 1938; The Apostolic Ministry, 1946; Ideas and Beliefs of the Victorians (Broadcast Talks), 1949, new edn 1966; Augustinus Magister, 1955; Oxford Dictionary of the Christian Church, 1957, 2nd edn, 1974; Miscellanea Historiæ Ecclesiasticæ, Congrès de Stockholm, 1960; Studies in Church History, vol. I, 1964; Trends in Mediæval Political Thought, 1965; Essays in Modern English Church History in Memory of Norman Sykes, 1966; Anglican Initiatives in Christian Unity, 1967; The Rediscovery of Newman, 1967; The New Cambridge Modern History, Vol. III, 1968; Encyclopædia Britannica, Chambers's Encycl., Journal Theol. Studies, English Historical Review, Journal of Eccles. Hist., Speculum, Medium Aevum, Church Quarterly Review, Time and Tide, Oxford Magazine, Proc. of British Academy. *Recreation:* study of railways. *Address:* Flat 2, Ritchie Court, 380 Banbury Road, Oxford OX2 7PW. *T:* Oxford 65504. *Club:* Athenæum.

*Died 16 June 1985.*

**PARKER, Sir (Walter) Edmund,** Kt 1974; CBE 1946; Partner in Price Waterhouse & Co., Chartered Accountants, 1944–71; *b* 24 June 1908; *er s* of late Col Frederic James Parker, CB, and Emily Margaret Joan Parker (*née* Bullock); *m* 1934, Elizabeth Mary Butterfield; one *s. Educ:* Winchester. Joined Price Waterhouse & Co., 1926; admitted Mem. Inst. of Chartered Accountants in England and Wales, 1931. 2nd Lieut 1/5 Essex Regt (TA), 1939. Bd of Trade: Chief Accountant, 1940; Asst Sec., 1941–45. Various Govt Cttees, 1946–50; Mem., Industrial Develt Adv. Bd, 1972–74. Mem. Council, Inst. of Chartered Accountants, 1957–69 (President, 1967); Chairman, Cinematograph Films Council, 1964–66. Auditor, Duchy of Cornwall, 1956–71; Chm., Local Employment Acts Financial Adv. Cttee, 1971–73. *Recreations:* garden and countryside. *Address:* Stable Cottage, Manuden, near Bishop's Stortford, Herts CM23 1DH. *T:* Bishop's Stortford 812273.

*Died 21 March 1981.*

**PARKER, Sir (William) Alan,** 4th Bt *cr* 1844; *b* 20 March 1916; *er s* of Sir William Lorenzo Parker, 3rd Bt, OBE, and late Lady Parker; *S* father, 1971; *m* 1946, Sheelagh Mary, *o d* of late Dr Sinclair Stevenson; one *s* one *d. Educ:* Eton; New College, Oxford. Served War of 1939–45, RE (Captain); Middle East, 1941–45. *Heir: s* William Peter Brian Parker, FCA [*b* 30 Nov. 1950; *m* 1976, Patricia Ann, *d* of R. Filtness; one *s* one *d*]. *Address:* Apricot Hall, Sutton-cum-Beckingham, Lincoln LN5 0RE. *T:* Fenton Claypole (0636) 626322.

*Died 22 Nov. 1990.*

**PARKER, Rt. Rev. William Alonzo;** *b* 31 Jan. 1897; *s* of late W. H. Parker, Alkrington, Lancs; *m* 1930, Ellen, *d* of Rev. Robert Hodgson, Hooton Roberts, Yorks; one *s. Educ:* Manchester University (MA). Royal Tank Corps, 1916–24; served European War (despatches); Ordained, 1929; Curate of Sheffield Cathedral; Chaplain of St George's Cathedral, Jerusalem, 1931–37; Vicar of St Matthew, Gosport, 1937–42; Vicar of St Chad, Shrewsbury, 1942–45; Rector of Stafford, 1945–55; Archdeacon of Stafford, 1945–59; Bishop Suffragan of Shrewsbury, 1959–69; Prebendary of Tachbrook, 1947–55; Canon Residentiary, Treasurer, and Prebendary of Offley in Lichfield Cathedral, 1955–59, Hon. Canon, 1968–. Prebendary of Freeford, 1959–68; Provost of Denstone, 1960–67. SCF, 1939–40. Pres., Shropshire and W Midland Agric. Soc., 1966–. Sub-Prelate OStJ. *Recreation:* fishing. *Address:* 104 Stretton Farm Road, Church Stretton, Salop SY6 6DX.

*Died 28 April 1982.*

**PARKER BOWLES, Dame Ann,** DCVO 1977; CBE 1972; Chief Commissioner, Girl Guides, 1966–75; *b* 14 July 1918; *d* of Sir Humphrey de Trafford, 4th Bt, MC; *m* 1939, Derek Henry Parker Bowles (*d* 1977); three *s* one *d*. County Comr, Girl Guides (Berkshire), 1959–64; Dep. Chief Comr, Girl Guides, 1962–66. *Recreation:* horse racing. *Address:* Forty Hill, Highclere, Newbury, Berkshire. *T:* Highclere 253735.

*Died 22 Jan. 1987.*

**PARKES, Sir Alan (Sterling),** Kt 1968; CBE 1956; FRS 1933; MA, PhD, DSc, ScD; Fellow of Christ's College, Cambridge, 1961–69, Hon. Fellow 1970; Fellow of University College, London; Chairman, Galton Foundation, 1969–85; *b* 10 Sept. 1900; *y s* of E. T. Parkes, Purley; *m* 1933, Ruth, *d* of Edward Deanesly, FRCS, Cheltenham; one *s* two *d. Educ:* Willaston School; Christ's College,

Cambridge; BA Cantab, 1921, ScD 1931; PhD Manchester, 1923; Sharpey Scholar, University College, London, 1923–24; Beit Memorial Research Fellow, 1924–30; MA Cantab 1925; Schäfer Prize in Physiology, 1926; DSc London 1927; Julius Mickle Fellowship, University of London, 1929; Hon. Lecturer, University College, London, 1929–31; Member of the Staff of the National Institute for Medical Research, London, 1932–61; Mary Marshall Prof. of the Physiology of Reproduction, Univ. of Cambridge, 1961–67, Professor Emeritus 1968. Consultant, Cayman Turtle Farm Ltd, Grand Cayman, BWI, 1973–80. Foulerton Student of the Royal Society, 1930–34. Mem., Biol. and Med. Cttee, Royal Commn on Population, 1944–46. Lectures: Sidney Ringer, University College Hospital, 1934; Ingleby, Univ. of Birmingham, 1940; Galton, Eugenics Society, 1950; Addison, Guy's Hospital, 1957; Darwin, Inst. of Biology; Robert J. Terry, Washington Univ., Sch. of Medicine, 1963; Ayerst, Amer. Fertility Soc., 1965; Dale, Soc. for Endocrinology, 1965; Dick, Univ. of Edinburgh, 1969; Cosgrave, Amer. Coll. of Obstetricians and Gynaecologists, 1970; Tracy and Ruth Storer, Univ. of Calif, Davis, 1973. President: Section of Endocrinology, Roy. Soc. Med., 1949–50, Section of Comparative Medicine, 1962–63; Section D Brit. Assoc. for the Advancement of Science, 1958; Eugenics Soc., 1968–70; Inst. of Biology, 1959–61; Assoc. of Scientific Workers, 1960–62. Chairman: Soc. for Endocrinology, 1944–51; Soc. for Study of Fertility, 1950–52, 1963–66; Nuffield Unit of Tropical Animal Ecology, 1966–69; Breeding Policy Cttee, Zool Soc. of London, 1960–67; Scientific Adv. Cttee, Brit. Egg Mkting Bd, 1961–70. Mem. Adv. Cttee on Med. Research of the WHO, 1968–71. Executive Editor, Jl Biosocial Science, 1969–78; Sec., Jls of Reproduction & Fertility Ltd, 1960–76. Consultant, IPPF, 1969–79. Cameron Prize, 1962; Sir Henry Dale Medal, Soc. for Endocrinology, 1965; John Scott Award (jtly with Dr A. U. Smith and Dr C. Polge), City of Philadelphia, 1969; Marshall Medal, Soc. Stud. Fert., 1970; Oliver Bird Medal, FPA, 1970. *Publications:* The Internal Secretions of the Ovary, 1929; Sex, Science and Society, 1966; Patterns of Sexuality and Reproduction, 1976; Off-beat Biologist, 1985; Biologist at Large, 1988; papers on the Physiology of Reproduction, on Endocrinology and on the behaviour of living cells at low temperatures in Jl of Physiology, Proc. Royal Society, and other scientific jls. Ed. Marshall's Physiology of Reproduction, 3rd edn, 1952, consultant 4th edn (in preparation). *Address:* 1 The Bramleys, Shepreth, Royston, Hertfordshire SG8 6PY.

*Died 17 July 1990.*

**PARKES, Geoffrey,** CMG 1947; FTI 1942; Deputy Chairman, National Westminster Bank Ltd, North Region, 1969–72; *b* 24 April 1902; *er s* of late Harry Clement Parkes, JP, and late Edith Newton; *m* 1st, 1925, Marjorie Syddall (*d* 1976); no *c*; 2nd, 1979, Bertha Livesley. *Educ:* Clifton College; L'Institut Technique, Roubaix. Director: Small & Parkes Ltd, 1927–64; Geigy (UK) Ltd, 1943–66; Director of Narrow Fabrics, Ministry of Supply, and Hon. Adviser to Board of Trade, 1939–44; Director-General Textiles & Light Industries Branch, CCG, 1944–46; Dep. Director (Exec.) Trade and Industry Div., CCG, 1946. Director: District Bank Ltd, 1949–69; National Provincial Bank Ltd, 1963–69. Mem. Court, Manchester Univ., 1949–69. MA (*hc*) Manchester Univ., 1966. FRSA 1952. JP Manchester, 1949–65. *Recreation:* gardening. *Address:* Berth-y-Coed, Walshaw Avenue, Colwyn Bay, North Wales. *T:* Colwyn Bay 30377.

*Died 21 Nov. 1982.*

**PARKES, Rev. James William,** MA, DPhil; Hon. DLitt; Hon. DHL; *b* 22 Dec. 1896; *s* of late Henry Parkes, and Annie Katharine Bell; *m* 1942, Dorothy E., *d* of F. Iden Wickings, Hildenborough. *Educ:* Elizabeth College, Guernsey; Hertford Coll., Oxford, Open Classical Scholar. Private, Artists Rifles, 1916; 2nd Lieut, Queen's Royal West Surrey Regt, 1917; Captain and Adj., 19th Queen's 1918; BA (Aegrotat) Theology, 1923; MA 1926; Post-Graduate Schol. Exeter College, 1930; DPhil 1934; Internat. Study Sec. Student Christian Movement, 1923–26; Warden, Student Movement House, London, 1926–28; Study Sec. Internat. Student Service, Geneva, 1928–34; Chairman Nat. Com. Common Wealth, 1942–43, Vice-Pres. 1943; Charles William Eliot lecturer, Jewish Inst. of Religion, NY, 1946–47; Pres. Jewish Historical Soc. of England, 1949–51; Director, The Parkes Library, 1956–64; Deacon, 1925; Priest, 1926. Hon. Fellow, Hebrew Univ. of Jerusalem, 1970. Buber-Rosenzweig Medal, 1979. *Publications:* The Jew and His Neighbour, 1930, 2nd and revised edn 1938; International Conferences, 1933; The Conflict of the Church and the Synagogue, 1934; Jesus, Paul and the Jews, 1936; The Jew in the Medieval Community, 1938; The Jewish Problem in the Modern World, 1939, 2nd (American) edn 1946, 3rd (German) edn 1948, 4th (Italian) edn, 1953; Oxford Pamphlets on World Affairs; Palestine, 1940; The Jewish Question, 1941; An Enemy of the People: Antisemitism, 1945, 2nd (German) edn 1948; The Emergence of the Jewish Problem, 1878–1939, 1946; Judaism and Christianity, 1948; A History of Palestine from 135 AD to Modern Times, 1949; The Story of Jerusalem, 1949; God at work, 1952; End of an Exile, 1954; The Foundations of Judaism and Christianity, 1960; A History of the Jewish People, 1962 (German, Dutch, Italian and Spanish trans.); Antisemitism, 1963 (German and Spanish trans.); Prelude to Dialogue, 1969; Voyage of Discoveries: an autobiography, 1969; Whose Land? The Peoples of Palestine, 1970; (as John Hadham) Good God, 1940 (US edn 1965, rev. edn 1966); God in a World at War, 1940; Between God and Man, 1942; God and Human Progress, 1944; Common Sense About Religion, 1961. *Relevant Publication:* A Bibliography of the Printed Works of James Parkes with selected quotations, by Sidney Sugarman and Diana Bailey, 1977. *Recreations:* architecture and gardening. *Address:* 12 Homeleigh House, 52 Wellington Road, Bournemouth BH8 8LF. *Club:* Athenæum.

*Died 6 Aug. 1981.*

**PARKINSON, Sir Kenneth Wade,** Kt 1957; MA; DL; *b* 1908; *e s* of late Bertram Parkinson, JP, Creskeld Hall, Arthington; *m* 1937, Hon. Dorothy Lane-Fox, OBE, (*d* 1980), *d* of 1st and last Baron Bingley, PC; one *d* (and one *d* decd). *Educ:* Uppingham; Clare College, Cambridge. Director: B. Parkinson and Co. Ltd; Yorkshire Post Newspapers Ltd; United Newspapers Ltd. High Sheriff of Yorkshire, 1963; DL West Yorks (formerly WR Yorks), 1967. *Address:* (business) 268 Thornton Road, Bradford; (home) Aketon Close, Follifoot, North Yorks. *T:* Spofforth 222.

*Died 20 June 1981.*

**PARKINSON, Norman,** CBE 1981; photographer; *b* 21 April 1913; *m* 1945, Wenda (*née* Rogerson) (*d* 1987); one *s*. *Educ:* Westminster School. Always a photographer of people old and young, horses, birds, still-life, active life, fashion, reportage and travel. Photographed, together and separately, all members of the Royal Family (in particular 21st Birthday and Engagement pictures of HRH The Princess Anne, and official 80th and 85th Birthday photographs of Queen Elizabeth, the Queen Mother, incl. the stamp issued to mark the 80th birthday occasion). Retrospective Exhibn, Fifty Years of Portraits and Fashion, National Portrait Gall., 1981; comprehensive exhibn of photographs, Sotheby Parke Bernet Gall., NY, 1983. Hon. FRPS; Hon. FIIP. Lifetime Achievement Award, Amer. Magazine Photographers Assoc., 1983. *Publications:* Life, Look Magazines, (USA) continually contributing to all the Vogues; his photographs have appeared in almost all the world's periodicals, in particular Town and Country, 1977–; Sisters Under the Skin (photographs, with text by leading authors), 1978; Photographs by Norman Parkinson, 1981; Lifework (collected works), 1983 (Fifty Years of Style and Fashion, US, 1983); Would You Let Your Daughter . . .?, 1985. *Recreations:* pig farming (manufactures the famous Porkinson banger in Tobago); sun worshipping, bird watching, breeding Creole racehorses. *Address:* Tobago, West Indies. *T:* none fortunately. *Clubs:* Annabel's; Union (Trinidad); Turf (Tobago). *Died 15 Feb. 1990.*

**PARKS, Sir Alan (Guyatt),** Kt 1977; MD; FRCP, FRCPE, FRCS; Consultant Surgeon to the London Hospital and St Mark's Hospital, since 1959; *b* 19 Dec. 1920; *s* of Harry Parks and Grace Parks; *m* 1956, Caroline Jean Cranston; three *s* one *d*. *Educ:* Epsom Coll.; Brasenose Coll., Oxford (Exhibnr; MA, MCh); Johns Hopkins Univ. Med. Sch. (Rockefeller Student; MD); Guy's Hosp. Med. Sch. FRCS 1948; FRCP 1976; FRCPE 1981. Captain, RAMC, 1950–52. Med. Internship, Johns Hopkins Hosp., 1945–46; house appts, Guy's Hosp., 1946, registrar appts, 1952–59. Hon. Consultant in Colon and Rectal Surgery to the Army, 1974–. Hunterian Prof., RCS, 1965. Pres., Sect. Proctol., RSocMed. 1974–75, Chm., Jt Consultants Cttee, 1974–79. Mem. Council, RCS, 1971– (Pres., 1980–); Chm., Conference of Medical Royal Colls, 1982; Lectures: Howard M. Frykman Meml, Minnesota, 1978; Fleming, RCPGlas, 1979; Sir Arthur Hurst, British Soc. of Gastroenterology, 1980; William Mitchell Banks Meml, Univ. of Liverpool, 1982. Pres., Assoc. Européenne et Méditerranéenne de Colo-Proctologie, 1979–81. Hon. FRCSEd 1981; Hon. FRCSGlas 1981; Hon. Fellow: Amer. Soc. of Colon and Rectal Surgeons, 1975–; Amer. Coll. of Surgeons, 1981; RACS, 1982; Royal Coll. of Physicians and Surgeons of Canada, 1982; Corresp. Mem., Deutsche Gesell. für Chirurgie, 1980. Ernst Jung Prize for Medicine, 1980; Cecil Joll Prize, RCS, 1981; Nessim Habif Prize, Univ. of Geneva, 1981. *Publications:* articles on various aspects of intestinal surgery in med. jls. *Recreations:* natural history; formerly Rugby and athletics for Oxford University. *Address:* 33 Alwyne Road, N1 2HW. *T:* 01-226 8045. *Club:* Athenæum. *Died 3 Nov. 1982.*

**PARR, Martin Willoughby,** CBE 1944 (OBE 1929); Foundation Committee, Gordon Boys' School, Woking; *b* 22 Nov. 1892; *s* of Rev. Willoughby Chase Parr and Laura, *d* of Colonel Francklyn, Speen Hill Lodge, Newbury; unmarried. *Educ:* Winchester (Scholar); BNC Oxford (Scholar). Commissioned HLI (SR), 1914; served France 1914–15, Palestine 1917–18, France 1918 (wounded); Sudan Political Service, 1919; Private Secretary to Governor-General, 1927–33; Deputy Civil Secretary, 1933–34; Governor Upper Nile, 1934–36; Governor Equatoria, 1936–42; retired, 1942. Member: NABC Council, 1944; Vice-President: B&FBS, CMS and NABC; Alderman, LCC, 1954–61. *Recreations:* rifle-shooting; played Rugby football for Oxford 1913–14, half-blue rifle shooting, 1913–14. Shot for Sudan and for England in Elcho Shield at Bisley

on several occasions. *Address:* Delves House, 31 Queen's Gate Terrace, SW7. *T:* 01-584 8639, 01-584 1334. *Clubs:* Royal Commonwealth Society; Vincent's (Oxford).

*Died 15 June 1985.*

**PARR, Stanley,** CBE 1975; QPM 1968; Chief Constable of Lancashire, 1972–78; *b* 14 July 1917; *s* of Thomas Walmsley and Ada Parr; *m* 1943, Charlotte Lilian Wilson, St Helens; three *s*. *Educ:* St Helens, Lancashire. Joined Lancashire Constabulary, 1937. Served War: commissioned RNVR, 1942–46, landing craft D day, Normandy, minesweeping in Far East. Dep. Chief Constable, Blackpool, 1958; Chief Constable, Blackpool, 1962; Dep. Chief Constable, Lancashire, 1967. DL Lancs, 1976–78. OStJ 1970. *Address:* 2 Holly Road, Blackpool FY1 2SF. *Died 17 Feb. 1985.*

**PARRINGTON, Francis Rex,** ScD; FRS 1962; Reader in Vertebrate Zoology, Cambridge, 1963–70, then Emeritus; Director, University Museum of Zoology, 1938–70; *b* 20 Feb. 1905; 2nd *s* of late Frank Harding Parrington and Bessie May Parrington (*née* Harding); *m* 1946, Margaret Aileen Knox Johnson (marr. diss., 1963); one *s* one *d*. *Educ:* Liverpool Coll.; Sidney Sussex Coll., Cambridge. BA 1927; ScD 1958. Asst Director, Museum of Zoology, 1927; Strickland Curator, 1928; Balfour Student, 1933; Demonstrator in Zoology, 1935; Lecturer in Zoology, 1938–63. Palæontological expeditions, East Africa, 1930, 1933. Served Royal Artillery, 1939–45, Major. Deputy Chairman, John Joule & Sons, Stone, Staffs, 1962–64 (Director, 1945–64). *Publications:* various on comparative anatomy and palæontology, Proc. Zoological Society, London, etc. *Recreation:* fly-fishing. *Address:* Clare House, 36 Hersham Road, Walton-on-Thames, Surrey KT12 1JJ. *T:* Walton-on-Thames 44004.

*Died 17 April 1981.*

**PARRISH, Alfred Sherwen;** Chief Constable, Derbyshire, 1981–85; *b* 21 Feb. 1931; *s* of Claude Tunstall Parrish and Georgena Parrish (*née* Sherwen); *m* 1953, Amy Johnston; one *s* one *d*. *Educ:* Whitehaven (West Cumberland) Grammar School. FBIM. Joined Cumberland and Westmorland Constabulary, 1953; Police Constable, Traffic, CID; Det/Sgt 1964; transf. to E Riding of Yorkshire, Det/Inspector 1966; Head of CID, 1967; York and NE Yorks Police, 1968, Supt; West Mercia Police, 1973, Chief Supt; Director, Police Staff Coll., Bramshill, Hants, 1976; Asst Chief Constable (Operations), N Yorkshire Police, 1976–79; Dep. Chief Constable, Derbyshire, 1979. FBIM. OStJ 1984. *Recreations:* music, photography, golf. *Address:* c/o Police Headquarters, Butterley Hall, Ripley, Derbyshire DE5 3RS. *Club:* Special Forces.

*Died 1 Oct. 1990.*

**PARROTT, Sir Cecil (Cuthbert),** KCMG 1964 (CMG 1953); OBE 1947; MA; FRSL 1979; Hon. FIL; Professor Emeritus in Central and South-Eastern European Studies, University of Lancaster; Founder, and Hon. Pres., Comenius Centre, University of Lancaster (Director, 1968–76); *b* 29 Jan. 1909; *s* of Engineer Captain Jasper W. A. Parrott, RN, and Grace Edith West; *m* 1935, Ellen Julie, *d* of Hermann and Marie Matzow, Trondhjem, Norway; three *s*. *Educ:* Berkhamsted Sch.; Peterhouse, Cambridge. Asst Master at Christ's Hospital and at Edinburgh Acad., 1931–34. Tutor to King Peter of Yugoslavia, at Belgrade, 1934–39; HM Legation, Oslo, 1939–40; Stockholm, 1940–45; HM Embassy, Prague, 1945–48; Foreign Office, 1948–50; Head of UN Political Dept, 1950–52; Principal Political Adviser to UK Delegation to the United Nations, 1951–52; Counsellor, HM Embassy, Brussels, 1952–54; HM Minister, Moscow, 1954–57; Director of Research, Librarian and Keeper of the Papers, at the Foreign Office, 1957–60; Ambassador to Czechoslovakia, 1960–66; Univ. of Lancaster: Prof. of Russian and Soviet Studies, 1966–71; Prof. of Central and SE Europ. Studies, 1971–76. *Publications:* The Good Soldier Švejk (first complete English trans.), 1973; The Tightrope (memoirs), 1975; The Serpent and The Nightingale (memoirs), 1977; The Bad Bohemian Hašek, 1977; trans. The Red Commissar and Other Tales, short stories of J. Hašek, 1981; Hašek, a study of Švejk and the short stories, 1982; various articles and broadcast talks on Slavonic history, music, art and literature. *Recreations:* music, theatre, literature, languages. *Address:* The Old Vicarage, Abbeystead, Lancaster LA2 9BG.

*Died 23 June 1984.*

**PARRY, Prof. Clive,** LLD (Cantab); LLD (Birmingham); Professor of International Law, University of Cambridge, since 1969; Fellow of Downing College; *b* 13 July 1917; 2nd *s* of Frank Parry, LRCPI, and Katharine Haughton Billington; *m* 1945, Luba Poole; one *s* one *d*. Barrister, Gray's Inn. Tagore Law Prof., Univ. of Calcutta, 1972. Associé de l'Institut de Droit International; Pres. Grotian Soc.; Member, Carlyle Club. *Publications:* Nationality and Citizenship Laws of the Commonwealth and of the Republic of Ireland, vol. 1 1957, vol. 2 1960; The Sources and Evidences of International Law, 1965; (ed) British Digest of International Law, 1965–; (ed) British International Law Cases, 1964–; (ed) Consolidated Treaty Series, 1969–80. *Address:* Downing College, Cambridge; 5 The Cenacle, Cambridge. *T:* Cambridge 356187; 13 Old Square, Lincoln's Inn, WC2. *T:* 01-405 5441. *Died 10 Sept. 1982.*

**PARRY, Prof. John Horace,** CMG 1960; MBE 1942; Professor of Oceanic History and Affairs, Harvard University, since 1965; *b* 26 April 1914; *s* of late Walter Austin Parry and Ethel Parry; *m* 1939, Joyce, *d* of Rev. H. C. and Mabel Carter; one *s* three *d. Educ:* King Edward's Sch., Birmingham; Clare Coll., Cambridge; Harvard University. Fellow of Clare Coll., Cambridge, 1938; served in RN, 1940–45. Asst Tutor, Clare Coll., Cambridge, and University Lecturer in History, 1945–49; Prof. of Modern History in University College of the West Indies, 1949–56; Principal of University College, Ibadan, Nigeria, 1956–60; Principal of University College, Swansea, 1960–65; Vice-Chancellor, University of Wales, 1963–65. Commander, Order of Alfonso X (Spain), 1976. *Publications:* The Spanish Theory of Empire, 1940; The Audiencia of New Galicia, 1948; Europe and a Wider World, 1949; The Sale of Public Office in the Spanish Indies, 1953; A Short History of the West Indies, 1956; The Age of Reconnaissance, 1963; The Spanish Seaborne Empire, 1966; Ed., The European Reconnaissance, 1968; Trade and Dominion, 1971; The Discovery of the Sea, 1974; The Discovery of South America, 1979. Contributor to historical journals. *Recreations:* sailing, fishing, mountain walking, ornithology. *Address:* Widener 45, Cambridge, Mass 02138, USA. *Clubs:* Athenæum, United Oxford & Cambridge University; Harvard (New York). *Died* 25 *Aug.* 1982.

**PARRY, Robert H.;** *see* Hughes Parry.

**PARRY, Sir Thomas,** Kt 1978; MA, DLitt (Wales); FBA 1959; President, National Library of Wales, 1969–77; Principal of the University College of Wales, Aberystwyth, 1958–69; *b* 14 Aug. 1904; *e s* of Richard and Jane Parry, Carmel, Caernarvonshire; *m* 1936, Enid, *o d* of Picton Davies, Cardiff. *Educ:* Pen-y-groes Grammar Sch.; University College of North Wales, Bangor. Assistant Lecturer in Welsh and Latin, University College, Cardiff, 1926–29; Lecturer in Welsh, University College, Bangor, 1929–47; Prof. of Welsh, 1947–53; Librarian of National Library of Wales, Aberystwyth, 1953–58; Vice-Chancellor, University of Wales, 1961–63, 1967–69; Chairman, UGC Cttee on Libraries, 1963–67. Pres., Hon. Soc. of Cymmrodorion, 1978–82 (Cymmrodorion Medal, 1976). Hon. Professorial Fellow, University Coll. of Wales, 1971–80. Hon. DLitt Celt. NUI; Hon. LLD Wales. *Publications:* Peniarth 49, 1929; Theater du Mond, 1930; Awdl "Mam", 1932; Saint Greal, 1933; Baledi'r Ddeunawfed Ganrif, 1935; Mynegai i Weithiau Ifor Williams, 1939; Hanes Llenyddiaeth Gymraeg, 1945; Llenyddiaeth Gymraeg, 1900–45, 1945; Hanes ein Llên, 1946; Lladd wrth yr Allor (translation of T. S. Eliot's Murder in the Cathedral), 1949; Gwaith Dafydd ap Gwilym, 1952; Llywelyn Fawr (a play), 1954; (ed) Oxford Book of Welsh Verse, 1962; (ed jtly) Llyfryddiaeth Llenyddiaeth Gymraeg, 1976; articles in Bulletin of Board of Celtic Studies, Trans. Hon. Society of Cymmrodorion, Y Traethodydd, Yr Athro. Welsh Review Celtic Studies. *Address:* Gwyndy, 2 Victoria Avenue, Bangor, Gwynedd LL57 2EP. *T:* Bangor 364460.
*Died* 22 *April* 1985.

**PARS, Dr Leopold Alexander,** MA, ScD Cantab; Fellow, formerly President, of Jesus College, Cambridge; *b* 2 Jan. 1896; *o s* of late Albertus Maclean Pars and Emma Laura Pars (*née* Unwin). *Educ:* Latymer Upper School; Jesus Coll., Cambridge. Smith's Prizeman, 1921; Fellow of Jesus Coll., 1921–. University Lectr in Mathematics, Cambridge, 1926–61. Visiting Professor: Univ. of California, Berkeley, 1949; Florida Atlantic Univ., 1964; Univ. of Sydney, 1965. *Publications:* Introduction to Dynamics, 1953; Calculus of Variations, 1962; A Treatise on Analytical Dynamics, 1965. Papers on Mathematics in scientific jls. *Recreations:* rock climbing, travel, theatre. *Address:* Jesus College, Cambridge. *T:* Cambridge 68611. *Clubs:* Athenæum, United Oxford & Cambridge University.
*Died* 28 *Jan.* 1985.

**PARSHALL, Horace Field,** TD 1947; Receiver-General, Venerable Order of St John of Jerusalem, 1968–72 (Chancellor, 1961–66); *b* 16 June 1903; *o s* of late Horace Field Parshall, DSc, and Annie Matilda Rogers; *m* 1st, 1929, Hon. Ursula Mary Bathurst (marr. diss. 1942, she *d* 1976), *o d* of 1st Viscount Bledisloe; one *s* decd; 2nd, 1953, Margaret Savage, MB, BS, DPH (*d* 1961), *d* of late Captain Philip Alcock, DL, JP, Wilton Castle, Enniscorthy, and Overton Lodge, Ludlow; one *s* two *d*; 3rd, 1965, Lady (Phyllis Gabrielle) Gore, *o d* of M. von den Porten, New York. *Educ:* Eton Coll.; New Coll., Oxford (MA). Barrister-at-Law, Inner Temple. Served War of 1939–45, with Oxford and Bucks Light Inf.; Hon. Major, TARO. Dep. Commissioner-in-Chief, St John Ambulance Brigade, 1950; Director-General, St John Ambulance Assoc., 1951–60; Vice-Chancellor, Order of St John, 1960. Member Court of Assistants, Merchant Taylors' Company (Master, 1958–59); Director, Pyrene Co. Ltd, 1947–68 (Dep.-Chairman, 1962–68). GCStJ 1960. *Recreation:* reading. *Address:* Flat 2, 55 Onslow Square, SW7. *T:* 01–589 3371. *Club:* Garrick.
*Died* 18 *Feb.* 1986.

**PARSLOE, Charles Guy,** MA; Secretary, Institute of Welding, 1943–67, Hon. Fellow, 1968; Vice-President, International Institute of Welding, 1966–69 (Secretary-General, 1948–66); *b* London, 5 Nov. 1900; *o* surv. *s* of Henry Edward Parsloe; *m* 1929, Mary Zirphie Munro, *e d* of J. G. Faiers, Putney; one *s* one *d* (and one *s* decd). *Educ:* Stationers' Company's School and University College, London. First Class hons History, 1921; Franks student in Archæology, 1922; Secretary and Librarian, Institute of Historical Research, 1927–43; Assistant in History, University Coll., 1925–27. Secretary OEEC Welding Mission to USA, 1953; organised Commonwealth Welding Conferences, 1957, 1965; President, Junior Institution of Engineers, 1967. Hon. Freeman, Founders' Company, 1964. Pres., John Evelyn Soc. for Wimbledon, 1975–81. Wheatley Medal, Library Association, 1965; Edstrom Medal, Internat. Inst. of Welding, 1971. *Publications:* The English Country Town, 1932; The Minute Book of the Corporation of Bedford, 1647–64, 1949; some 400 bibliographies in the Cambridge Bibliography of English Literature, 1940; Wimbledon Village Club and Lecture Hall, 1858–1958, 1958; Wardens' Accounts of the Worshipful Company of Founders of the City of London, 1497–1681, 1964; (jtly) A Present from Seaview, 1979; papers on historical and bibliographical subjects. *Recreation:* historical research. *Address:* 1 Leopold Avenue, SW19 7ET. *T:* 01–946 0764. *Club:* Athenæum.
*Died* 8 *March* 1985.

**PART, Sir Antony (Alexander),** GCB 1974 (KCB 1966; CB 1959); MBE (mil.) 1943; Chairman, Orion Insurance Company, 1976–87; *b* 28 June 1916; *s* of late Alexander Francis Part and late Una Margaret Reynolds (*née* Snowdon); *m* 1940, Isabella Bennett; no *c. Educ:* Wellesley House, Broadstairs; Harrow; Trinity Coll., Cambridge. First Class Hons Modern and Mediæval Langs Tripos. Entered Board of Education, 1937; Asst Secretary to successive Ministers of Supply, 1939–40. Served War of 1939–45 (despatches); Army Service, 1940–44; Lt-Col GS(1) HQ 21 Army Group, 1944. Principal Private Secretary to successive Ministers of Education, 1945–46; Home Civil Service Commonwealth Fund Fellow to USA, 1950–51; Under-Secretary, Ministry of Education, 1954–60; Deputy Secretary: Ministry of Education, 1960–63; MPBW, 1963–65; Permanent Secretary: MPBW, 1965–68; BoT, 1968–70; DTI, 1970–74; DoI, 1974–76. Director: Debenhams, 1976–80; EMI, 1976–80; Metal Box, 1976–86; Life Assoc. of Scotland, 1976–87; Lucas Industries, 1976–86; Savoy Hotel Group, 1976–87. Chairman: Cttee on N Sea Oil Taxation, 1981; Govt Adv. Panel on tech. transmission standards for UK services of direct broadcasting by satellite, 1982; Mem. Council, Regular Forces Employment Assoc., 1982–86. Governor, Administrative Staff Coll., 1968–87; Governor, LSE, 1968– (Vice-Chm. of Governors, 1979–84). Hon. Fellow, LSE, 1984. Hon DTech Brunel, 1966; Hon. DSc: Aston, 1974; Cranfield, 1976. CBIM. *Posthumous publication:* (autobiog.) The Making of a Mandarin, 1990. *Recreation:* travel. *Address:* Flat 5, 71 Elm Park Gardens, SW10 9QE. *T:* 01–352 2950. *Clubs:* MCC, United Oxford & Cambridge University.
*Died* 11 *Jan.* 1990.

**PARTRIDGE, Sir (Ernest) John,** KBE 1971; Chairman, Imperial Group Ltd (formerly Imperial Tobacco Group Ltd), 1964–75; *b* 18 July 1908; *s* of William Henry and Alice Mary Partridge; *m* 1st, 1934, Madeline Fabian (*d* 1944); one *s* one *d*; 2nd, 1949, Joan Johnson, MBE; one *s* one *d. Educ:* Queen Elizabeth's Hospital, Bristol. Joined Imperial Tobacco Co., 1923; Asst Secretary, 1944; Secretary, 1946; Dep. Chairman, 1960. Director: British-American Tobacco Co. Ltd, 1963–75; Tobacco Securities Trust Ltd, 1964–75; National Westminster Bank, 1968–78; Dunlop Holdings Ltd, 1973–81; Delta Metal Co. Ltd, 1973–81; General Accident Fire & Life Assurance Corporation Ltd, 1973–79; Finance for Industry, 1975–78; Member: Tobacco Advisory Cttee, 1945–58; Cheque Endorsement Cttee, 1955–56; NEDC, 1967–75; BNEC, 1968–71; Internat. Adv. Bd, Chemical Bank, NY, 1972–78; Internat. Adv. Bd, Amax Inc., NY, 1980–; Chairman: Tobacco Manufacturers' Standing Cttee, 1960–62; Industrial Management Research Assoc., 1964–67; Council of Industry for Management Education, 1967–71; Pres., CBI, 1970–72 (Dep. Pres., 1969–70, Vice-Pres., 1972–76; Chm., Educn Foundn, 1976–81); President: Foundn for Management Educn, 1972–; Nat. Council of Voluntary Organisations, 1973–80. Vice-President: Industrial Participation Assoc., 1966–; Soc. of Business Economists, 1976–. Governor, Clifton Coll. (Pres., 1980–); Badminton Sch.; Ashridge Management Coll., 1963–73; Chm. Governors, United World College of the Atlantic, 1979–; Member: Governing Body, London Graduate School of Business Studies, 1967–75; Court of Patrons, RCS, 1971–; The Queen's Silver Jubilee Appeal Council, 1976–78. CBIM (FBIM 1963). Hon. LLD Bristol, 1972; Hon. DSc Cranfield Inst. of Technology, 1974. *Recreations:* walking, gardening, listening to music. *Address:* Wildwood, Haslemere, Surrey. *T:* Haslemere 51002. *Club:* Athenæum. *Died* 4 *June* 1982.

**PARTRIDGE, Harry Cowderoy;** Chairman, Caviapen Investments Ltd, since 1985 (Non-executive Chairman, 1983–85); *b* 29 Aug. 1925; *y s* of late Harry Ewart Partridge and Edith Cowderoy; *m* 1st, 1950, Margaret Neill Cadzow (*d* 1967), *o d* of Charles J. M. Cadzow, OBE; two *s* one *d*; 2nd, 1973, Jeanne Margaret Henderson; one *s* one d. *Educ:* George Watson's Coll., Edinburgh; Edinburgh Univ. CA. Air-gunner, RAF, 1943–47. Company Accountant, McGrouther Ltd, 1955–59; Plant Controller, IBM UK Ltd, 1959–63; Sec., George Kent Ltd, 1963, Financial Dir 1965–71; Civil Aviation Authority: Controller of Finance and Planning, 1972; Mem. Bd, 1974–85; Gp Dir, Finance and Central Services, 1977. Director: Charterhouse Japhet Venture Fund Management Ltd, 1984–; German Smaller Cos Investment Trust PLC, 1985–; Automated Microbiology Systems Inc., San Diego, Calif. *Recreations:* house and garden. *Address:* Rushey Ford House, Box End, Kempston, Beds. *T:* Bedford (0234) 851594. *Club:* Savile.

*Died 3 Oct.* 1990.

**PASLEY, Sir Rodney (Marshall Sabine),** 4th Bt, *cr* 1794; retired as Headmaster, Central Grammar School, Birmingham (1943–59); *b* 22 Feb. 1899; *s* of late Captain Malcolm Sabine Pasley, RN, and late Nona Marion Paine; *S* uncle, 1947; *m* 1922, Aldyth Werge Hamber; one *s* one *d. Educ:* Sherborne School; University Coll., Oxford. Served European War, 1914–18, 2nd Lt RFA. BA 1921, MA 1925; Asst Master, Alleyn's School, 1921–25; Vice-Principal, Rajkumar Coll., Rajkot, India, 1926–28; Asst Master, Alleyn's School, 1931–36; Headmaster, Barnstaple Grammar School, 1936–43. *Publication:* Private Sea Journals, 1778–1782, kept by Admiral Sir Thomas Pasley, 1931. *Heir: s* John Malcolm Sabine Pasley, Fellow of Magdalen Coll., Oxford [*b* 5 April 1926; *m* 1965, Virginia Killigrew Wait; two *s*]. *Address:* c/o J. M. S. Pasley, Esq., 25 Lathbury Road, Oxford. *Died 25 July* 1982.

**PATCH, Air Chief Marshal Sir Hubert (Leonard),** KCB 1957 (CB 1952); CBE 1942; *b* 16 Dec. 1904; *s* of late Captain Leonard W. Patch, RN (retd), St Margarets-on-Thames; *m* Marjorie (*d* 1958), *d* of Harold Greenhalgh, Woodhey, Moor Park; *m* 1960, Claude Renée, *d* of Major Jean-Marie Botéculet (Légion d'Honneur, Croix de Guerre, Médaille Militaire, MC (British), killed in action in Morocco, 1925). *Educ:* Stonyhurst; RAF Coll., Cranwell, Lincs. Joined RAF, 1925; Acting Group Captain, 1942; Group Captain, 1946; Air Cdre, 1947; Air Vice-Marshal, 1951. Served 1939–44 (despatches, CBE). Senior Air Staff Officer, HQ Far East Air Force, 1952–53; AOC No 11 Gp, Fighter Comd, Nov. 1953–Jan. 1956; Air Officer Commanding-in-Chief (Temp.), Fighter Command, Jan.-Aug. 1956; Commander-in-Chief, Middle East Air Force, 1956–58; Air Member for Personnel April-Sept. 1959; Commander-in-Chief, British Forces, Arabian Peninsula, October 1959–May 1960; Acting Air Marshal, 1956; Air Marshal, 1957; Air Chief Marshal, 1959. Retired from Royal Air Force, 1961. Representative of British Aircraft Corporation to the NATO countries, 1961–63. *Address:* Apartado 27, Marbella, Málaga, Spain; c/o Barclays Bank, Colchester, Essex. *Club:* Royal Air Force.

*Died 18 Nov.* 1987.

**PATEL, Ambalal Bhailalbhai,** CMG 1949; *b* 1 May 1898; *e s* of late Bhailalbhai Dharamdas Patel, Changa, Gujarat; *m* Gangalaxmi Patel (decd); three *s* one *d* (and one *s* decd). *Educ:* Petlad High School; Baroda Coll. (BA); Bombay University (LLB). Barrister-at-Law, Lincoln's Inn, 1923. Advocate, Supreme Court of Kenya, 1924; as Kenya Indian Deleg. gave evidence before Joint Parl. Committee on Closer Union, London, 1931. Pres. E African Indian National Congress, 1938–42, and 1945–46; Pres. Kenya Indian Conf., 1942; Mem. standing and exec. Cttees of EAIN Congress, 1924–56; Chm. Indian Elected Members Organization, 1941–48; Hon. Sec. Coast Elected Members Organization, 1949–56; Mem. Makerere Coll. Assembly, 1938–48. Chm. Central Indian Advisory Man-Power Cttee and Indian E Dist Man-Power Cttee during War of 1939–45. Chm. Indian and Arab Land Settlement Bd, 1946–54; attended African Conf. in London, 1948; Mem. E African Central Legislative Assembly, 1948–52; Minister without Portfolio, Govt of Kenya, 1954–56, retired. MLC 1938–56, MEC Kenya, 1941–56. Mem. Royal Technical College Council, Nairobi, and Makerere University Coll. Council, 1954–56. Gen. Sec. and Treasurer, World Union, 1964–; Member: Emergency Council for World Govt, World Union Movement (Hesbjerg, Denmark), 1974–83; World Federal Authority Cttee (Geneva), 1975–81; Co-pres., World Constitution and Parliament Assoc., 1977–83, Hon. Pres., 1983; First signatory, Constitution for Fedn of Earth, 1977; elected Speaker, 1st Provisional World Parliament, Brighton, Sept. 1982. Pres. or trustee various political, social and cultural institutions at different times. Coronation Medal, 1953. *Publications:* Toward a New World Order, 1974; Earth an Evolutionary Planet, 1986. *Address:* c/o Sri Aurobindo Ashram, Pondicherry-605002 (via Madras), India. *T:* 4834. *Died 18 May* 1987.

**PATER, John Edward,** CB 1953; PhD; Under Secretary, Ministry of Health and Department of Health and Social Security, 1947–73 (retired); *b* 15 March 1911; *s* of Edward Rhodes and Lilian Pater; *m* 1938, Margaret Anderson, *yr d* of M. C. Furtado; two *s* one *d. Educ:* King Edward VI School, Retford; Queens' College, Cambridge. Foundation Scholar, Queens' College; BA 1933, MA 1935, PhD 1982. Assistant Principal, Ministry of Health, 1933; Principal, 1938; Assistant Secretary, 1943; Principal Assistant

Secretary, 1945; Director of Establishments and Organisation, 1960–65. Treasurer: Methodist Church Dept of Connexional Funds and Finance Bd, 1959–73; Div. of Finance, 1973–84; Central Finance Bd, 1968–74. Governor, Kingswood Sch., 1973–85. *Publication:* The Making of the National Health Service, 1981. *Recreations:* reading, archæology, walking (preferably on hills). *Address:* Ginko, 1B Croham Mount, South Croydon CR2 0BR. *T:* 01–651 1601. *Died 27 Oct.* 1989.

**PATERSON, Lt-Col Arthur James J.;** *see* Jardine Paterson.

**PATERSON, Arthur Spencer,** MA (Oxon); MD; FRCPE, MRCP; FRCPsych; Consultant Psychiatrist; Physician in Charge, Department of Psychiatry, and Director Psychiatric Laboratory, West London Hospital, 1946–66; *b* 22 Feb. 1900; 4th *s* of late Professor W. P. Paterson, Edinburgh Univ., and Jane Sanderson; *m* 1933, Antoinette, *d* of late Chas Baxter, WS; two *s* one *d. Educ:* Edinburgh Academy; Fettes (Scholar); 2nd Lt RHA 1919. Oriel, Oxford (Hon. Mods and Lit. Hum.; BA 1923); Edinburgh Univ. (MB, ChB 1928). Ho. Phys to Prof. of Medicine, Roy. Infirmary, Edinburgh, 1928–29; Asst Phys., Glasgow Royal Mental Hospital, 1929–30; Rockefeller Fellow, 1930–31; Pinsent-Darwin Research Student in Mental Pathology, Cambridge University, 1931–33; held research posts at: Johns Hopkins Univ., Baltimore, Md, USA, Research Inst. of Psychiatry, Munich; Maudsley Hosp., London. Asst Phys., Cassel Hosp., Penshurst, 1933–36; First Asst, Dept of Psychiatry, Middlesex Hosp., 1936–45, Psychiatrist, Sector V. EMS Metrop. Area, 1939–45. Honeyman-Gillespie Lectr, Edin. Univ., 1948. Membre d'honneur Soc. Méd. Ment. Belge, 1969; Membre Etranger, Soc. Méd.-Psychol., Paris, 1969; Corr. Member: American Psychiat. Association; American Pavlovian Soc. Hon. Secretary, Internat. Soc. for Experimental and Clin. Hypnosis, 1968–73. Herman Goldman Lectr, NY Coll., Med., 1964. Foundation FRCPsych, 1971; FRSM (Pres. Sect., Hypnosis, 1981); FBPsS. *Publications:* Electrical and Drug Treatments in Psychiatry, 1963; Control of the Autonomic Nervous Functions by Conditioning and Hypnosis, in Hypnosis and Behaviour Therapy, ed E. Dengrove, 1975; numerous articles on psychiatric and allied subjects in British and foreign scientific periodicals. *Recreations:* travel, golf, chess. *Address:* 5 Cranley Mews, SW7 3BX. *T:* 01-373 0773. *Club:* Athenæum. *Died 27 Dec.* 1983.

**PATERSON, Prof. James Ralston Kennedy,** CBE 1949; MC 1917; MD (Edinburgh); FRCSEd; FRCS; FFR; Professor Emeritus of Radiotherapeutics, University of Manchester, since 1960; Director of Radiotherapy, Christie Hospital and Holt Radium Institute, 1931–62; *b* 21 May 1897; *s* of Rev. David Paterson; *m* 1930, Edith Isabel Myfanwy Irvine-Jones; two *s* one *d. Educ:* George Heriot's School, Edinburgh; Edinburgh University. Fellow in Radiology, Mayo Clinic, America, 1926. Acting Director, Radiological Department, Edinburgh, 1930. *Publication:* Treatment of Malignant Disease by Radium and X-rays, 1962. *Recreations:* various. *Address:* Stenrieshill, Moffat, Scotland. *T:* Johnstone Bridge 221.

*Died 31 Aug.* 1981.

**PATERSON, Noel Kennedy,** CIE 1947; OBE 1943; lately United Kingdom Trade Commissioner, Dublin; *b* 25 Dec. 1905; *s* of Rev. David Paterson, BD, Edinburgh; *m* 1934, Margaret Winifred Schreiber (*d* 1981); two *s* two *d; m* 1983, Joyce Margaret Burnard. *Educ:* George Heriot's School, Edinburgh; Edinburgh University; St John's College, Cambridge. Entered Indian Civil Service, 1929; Asst Comr, 1929–34; Under Sec. to Govt of Central Provinces, 1934–36; Deputy Comr, 1936–37 and 1939–45; Under Sec. to Govt of India, 1937–38; Chief Comr, Andaman and Nicobar Islands, 1945–47. *Recreation:* travel. *Address:* Chestnut Cottage, Gabriels Farm, Park Lane, Twyford, Hants. *T:* Twyford 713116.

*Died 19 Dec.* 1984.

**PATON, Alan (Stewart);** writer; was National President of the South African Liberal Party until it was made an illegal organisation in 1968; living at Botha's Hill, Natal; *b* Pietermaritzburg, 11 Jan. 1903; *s* of James Paton; *m* 1st, 1928, Doris Olive (*d* 1967), *d* of George Francis; two *s;* 2nd, 1969, Anne Hopkins. *Educ:* Natal Univ. (BSc, BEd). Formerly Principal Diepkloof Reformatory, 1935–48. Chubb Fellow, Yale Univ., 1973. Hon. LHD: Yale, 1954; La Salle, 1986; Hon. DLitt: Kenyon Coll., 1962; Univ. of Natal, 1968; Trent Univ., 1971; Harvard, 1971; Rhodes, 1972; Williamette Univ., 1974; Michigan, 1977; Univ. of Durban-Westville, 1986; Hon. DD Edinburgh, 1971; Hon. LLB Univ. of Witwatersrand, 1975. Freedom House Award (USA), 1960. *Publications:* Cry, the Beloved Country, 1948; Too Late the Phalarope, 1953; Land and People of South Africa, 1955; South Africa in Transition (with Dan Weiner), 1956; Debbie Go Home (short stories), 1961; Hofmeyr (biography), 1965; Instrument of Thy Peace, 1968; The Long View, 1969; Kontakion For You Departed, 1969; Apartheid and the Archbishop, 1973; Knocking on the Door, 1975; Towards the Mountain (autobiog.), 1980; Ah, But Your Land is Beautiful, 1981; *posthumous publication:* Journey Continued (autobiog.), 1988.

*Address:* PO Box 530, Botha's Hill, Natal, 3660, South Africa.
*Died 12 April 1988.*

**PATON, Col Alexander,** DSO 1937; MC; RA, retired; *b* 13 Jan. 1897; *s* of Alexander Paton, Glasgow; *m* 1923, Sybil (*d* 1983), *er d* of late Sir Grimwood Mears, KCIE; two *s. Educ:* Marlborough Coll.; RMA, Woolwich. Commissioned, 1915; served European War, France, 1916–19; Staff Captain, 1918; 15th Corps (despatches twice, MC and bar, General Service and Victory Medals); India, 1919–25; Staff Captain RA, Afghan War, 1919 (1908, General Service Medal, India, and clasp, 1919); Staff Officer RA, Simla, 1921–22; Chitral, NWF India, 1922–24; Home Service, 1925–36; Terr. Adj. 13th (Highland) Brigade, TA, Argyllshire, 1926–30; Company Officer at Royal Military Academy, Woolwich, 1932–34; Adjutant, 3rd Medium Brigade RA, Shoeburyness, 1934–36; India, NWF, 1937 (wounded, despatches, DSO, Medal and clasp); Burma, 1938–40; Comd 21 Mtn Regt NWF, 1940; Comdt MATC Ambala, Punjab, 1941–42; Comdt FATC Muttra, UP, 1942–44; Col 1943–44; Recruiting Staff, Rawalpindi, Punjab, 1944–45. Defence Medal, 1939–45, and War Medal (1939–45). Retd pay, 1947. *Recreation:* philately. *Address:* Willow Cottage, 33 Crofton Lane, Hillhead, Fareham, Hants. *T:* Stubbington 2116. *Died 13 July 1985.*

**PATON, George Campbell Henderson,** QC (Scotland) 1967; LLD Edin 1969; Reader in Scots Law, Edinburgh University, 1967–75; *b* 6 Aug. 1905; *s* of George Grieve Paton, MA, LLB, Solicitor, Glasgow and Mary Campbell Sclanders; *m* 1950, Eva French, *d* of David French Cranston, Edinburgh; two *d. Educ:* Glasgow Academy; Glasgow University. MA 1927; LLB (Distinction) 1930. Solicitor 1931; Advocate 1951. Served Admiralty, 1942–46. Faulds Fellow in Law, Glasgow Univ., 1931–34; Asst to Professor of Law, Glasgow, 1934–46. Lectr in History of Scots Law, Glasgow, 1951–59; Senior Lectr, Dept of Scots Law, Edinburgh, 1959–67. Literary Dir, Stair Soc., 1954–60. *Publications:* Ed., Baron Hume's Lectures (Stair Soc.), 1939–57; Ed. and Contrib., Introductory History of Scots Law (Stair Soc.), 1958; Asst Ed., A Source Book and History of Administrative Law in Scotland, 1956; (with J. G. S. Cameron) Law of Landlord and Tenant in Scotland, 1967; articles in various legal periodicals. *Recreations:* golf, tennis, walking. *Address:* 163 Colinton Road, Edinburgh EH14 1BE. *T:* 031–443 1660.
*Died 5 July 1984.*

**PATON, Sir George Whitecross,** Kt 1957; Vice-Chancellor, University of Melbourne, 1951–68; *b* 16 August 1902; *s* of Rev. Frank H. L. Paton; *m* 1931, Alice Watson, CBE; one *s* three *d. Educ:* Scotch Coll., Melbourne; University of Melbourne; Magdalen College, University of Oxford. MA (Melb.), 1926; BA (Oxon), 1928; BCL (Oxon), 1929. Barrister-at-Law, Gray's Inn, 1929. Asst Lecturer, LSE, 1930; Professor of Jurisprudence, Univ. of Melbourne, 1931–51; Dean of Faculty of Law, 1946–51. Chairman Royal Commission on Television (Australia, 1953–54). LLD (Hon.): Glasgow, 1953; Sydney, 1955; Queensland, 1960; Tasmania, 1963; London, 1963; Monash, 1968; Melbourne, 1971; DCL (Hon.), Western Ontario, 1958. *Publications:* A Text Book of Jurisprudence, 1946, 4th edn 1972; Bailment in the Common Law, 1952; (with Barry and Sawer), Criminal Law in Australia, 1948. *Recreations:* tennis, walking, gardening. *Address:* 7 Dunraven Avenue, Toorak, Victoria 3142, Australia. *T:* 240 1034. *Club:* Melbourne (Victoria, Aust.). *Died 16 June 1985.*

**PATON, His Honour Harold William,** DSC 1943; Judge of County Courts, Circuit No 54 (Bristol, etc) 1950–71; Chairman, Somerset Quarter Sessions, 1965–71; *b* 6 Oct. 1900; *s* of late Clifford James Paton; *m* 1947, Joan Orby, *d* of late Lt-Col Cecil Gascoigne, DSO, Seaforth Hldrs; one *d. Educ:* Winchester College; Christ Church, Oxford. Called to the Bar (Inner Temple), 1923 and practised at Common Law Bar. Served War of 1939–45 in RNVR (Coastal Forces); Lt-Comdr, 1944. *Recreations:* fishing, gardening. *Address:* Heronsbrook, Foulis, Evanton, Ross-shire.
*Died 16 March 1986.*

**PATON, Sir Leonard (Cecil),** Kt 1946; CBE 1944; MC 1915; MA; Director, Harrisons & Crosfield Ltd (Chairman, 1957–62); *b* 7 May 1892; 4th *s* of John Paton, Dunfermline, Fife, Headmaster; *m* 1917, Muriel, *yr d* of William Searles, Maidstone; one *s* one *d. Educ:* George Watson's Coll.; Edinburgh University (MA, 1st Class Hons Classics, 1914); Christ Church, Oxford (Exhibitioner). European War, 1914–18, Captain Cameronians (MC, despatches). *Address:* 52 Wilbury Road, Hove, Sussex. *Died 18 Jan. 1986.*

**PATON, Sir Stuart (Henry),** KCVO 1965; CBE 1945; Captain RN, retired; *b* 9 July 1900; *s* of William Henry Paton and Winifred Powell, Norwood; *m* 1925, Dorothy Morgan (*d* 1984) (Shrewsbury); two *s* two *d. Educ:* Hillside, Godalming; RN Colleges, Osborne and Dartmouth. Served European War: Midshipman, HMS Marlborough, Grand Fleet, 1916; Sub-Lt, HMS Orcadia, English Channel, 1918. Specialised as Torpedo Officer; posts Lieut to Commander: Mediterranean and Home Fleets, Admiralty Plans Division, and New Zealand. War of 1939–45: HMS Vernon, Captain, 1940; Admiralty, Joint Intelligence Staff, 1941; Comd

HMS Curacoa, E. Coast Convoys, 1942; Comd HMS Nigeria, Home Fleet and Eastern Fleet, 1942–44 (despatches Malta Convoy); Admiralty and served as a Dep.-Director, Admin. Planning, 1945–46; student, IDC, 1947; Comd HMS Newcastle, Mediterranean Fleet, 1948–49; Appointed ADC to King George VI, 1949; retired, 1950; General Secretary to King George's Fund for Sailors, 1950–65. *Recreations:* gardening, photography. *Address:* Bernard Sunley Nursing Home, College Road, Maybury Hill, Woking, Surrey GU22 8BT. *T:* Woking 24964.
*Died 14 July 1987.*

**PATRICK, Brig. John,** MC; *b* 10 June 1898; *s* of Lt-Col John Patrick, DL, and Florence Annie Rutherford; *m;* two *s; m* 1949, Nancy (marr. diss.), *er d* of A. White, Woolverstone House, Suffolk. *Educ:* Harrow-on-the-Hill; RMA, Woolwich. 2nd Lieut, RFA, 1916; Chestnut Troop, RHA, 1919–28; Captain, 15/19th The King's Royal Hussars, 1928–38; psc 1934; retired, 1938; Lt-Col RA (SR), 1939; Brigadier, 1940–45; MP for Mid Antrim in Northern Ireland House of Commons, 1938–45. *Address:* Slemish, Preston, Hitchin, Herts. *T:* 32776. *Died 28 Oct. 1985.*

**PATRICK, Nigel Dennis Wemyss;** Actor; *b* 2 May 1913; *s* of Charles Wemyss (Actor) and Dorothy Turner (Actress); *m* 1951, Beatrice Josephine Campbell (*d* 1979); one *s* one *d. Educ:* privately. Started career as actor, Jan. 1932; first appeared West End stage, Oct. 1934, at Whitehall Theatre; played many parts in West End including Dudley in George and Margaret, Wyndham's, until 1939. Joined KRRC as Rifleman, 1939; discharged HM Forces, 1946, with rank of Lt-Col. Resumed career as actor, March 1946; *appeared in:* Tomorrow's Child, Lyric, Hammersmith, 1946; Noose, Saville, 1947; Who Goes There, Vaudeville, 1951; Escapade, St James's, 1953; The Remarkable Mr Pennypacker, New, 1955; The Egg, Saville, 1958; The Schoolmistress, Savoy, 1964; Reunion in Vienna, Chichester Festival, 1971, Piccadilly, 1972; *directed:* Not in the Book, Criterion, 1958; Relatively Speaking, Duke of Yorks, 1967; The Others, Strand, 1967; Avanti, Booth Theatre, New York, 1968; Out of the Question, St Martin's, 1968; Blithe Spirit, Globe, 1970; Finishing Touches, Apollo, 1973; Night Must Fall, Shaw, 1975; The Last of Mrs Cheyney, Cambridge Theatre, 1980; *directed and appeared in:* The Pleasure of His Company, Haymarket, 1959; Settled Out of Court, Strand, 1960; Present Laughter, Queen's, 1965; Best of Friends, Strand, 1970; The Pay Off, Comedy, 1974; Dear Daddy, Ambassadors, 1976, S Africa 1978; Peter Pan, Shaftesbury, 1978; *films include:* Morning Departure, Trio, The Browning Version, Pandora and the Flying Dutchman, Sound Barrier, Pickwick Papers, Raintree County, Sapphire, League of Gentlemen, The Trials of Oscar Wilde, Johnny Nobody, The Informers, The Battle of Britain, The Virgin Soldiers, The Executioner, The Great Waltz, The Macintosh Man. *Recreations:* working, reading and travelling. *Address:* 54 Ovington Street, Chelsea, SW3. *T:* 01-589 4385. *Club:* Garrick.
*Died 21 Sept. 1981.*

**PATRON, Sir Joseph,** Kt 1961; OBE 1945; MC 1917; JP; Speaker of the Legislative Council, Gibraltar, 1958–64; *b* 19 Jan. 1896; *s* of late Joseph Armand Patron, CMG, OBE; *m* 1924, Emily Isham, *d* of John Maxwell Vaughan. *Educ:* Harrow. Served European War, 1914–18, Major; Yeomanry and Machine-Gun Corps (wounded, MC). Managing Director, Saccone and Speed, 1927–45; Company Director and Trustee, John Mackintosh Charitable Trust, Gibraltar; Member, Interdepartmental Cttee to Look After Evacuees, 1940–44. MEC Gibraltar, 1944–47; MLC 1950–58. JP Gibraltar, 1948. *Recreations:* golf, bridge, gardening. *Address:* 10 Calle Avila, Sotogrande, Prov. de Cadiz, Spain. *Clubs:* Boodle's; Royal Gibraltar Yacht. *Died 4 Feb. 1981.*

**PATTERSON, Geoffrey Crosbie,** OBE 1975; Partner, Scott-Moncrieff, Thomson & Shiells, Chartered Accountants, 1936–79 (Senior Partner, 1966–79); *b* 24 Sept. 1912; *s* of late John George and late Elizabeth Louise Patterson; *m* 1939, Fay Mary (*d* 1983), *d* of late James Wilson, solicitor; two *s. Educ:* Edinburgh Academy. Served War of 1939–45, Major, RA (Despatches). Qualified as Chartered Accountant, 1935; Chm., Anderson Brown Ltd, steel stock holders, Edinburgh, retd 1981; Chm., William Muir (Bond 9) Ltd, whisky bottlers and blenders, Edinburgh, 1979–82. Pres., Inst. of Chartered Accountants of Scotland, 1971–72. Hon. Nat. Treasurer, The Royal British Legion, Scotland, 1958–77; Sec. and Treasurer, Scottish National War Memorial, retd 1979. *Recreations:* shooting, golf. *Address:* Bankhead, Humbie, East Lothian EH36 5PD. *Club:* New (Edinburgh). *Died 21 Aug. 1984.*

**PAUL, Rt. Rev. Geoffrey John;** Bishop of Bradford, since 1981; *b* 4 March 1921; *s* of Robert John Paul and Ethel Mary (*née* Arthur); *m* 1951, Pamela Maisie Watts; five *d. Educ:* Rutlish School, Merton; Queens' Coll., Cambridge (MA); King's Coll., London (MTh, AKC). Deacon 1948; Curate of Little Ilford, E12; priest 1949; Church of S India, from Oct. 1950. Chaplain, St John's Coll., Palayamkotta, 1950–52; Kerala United Theological Seminary, 1952–65 (Principal, 1962–65); Church Missionary Society, 1965–66;

Residentiary Canon, Bristol Cathedral, (Director of Ordination Training, Examining Chaplain), 1966–71; Hon. Canon of Bristol, 1971–77; Warden, Lee Abbey, 1971–77; Bishop Suffragan of Hull, 1977–81. Chm., Bd for Mission and Unity, 1983–. Hon. DD Hull, 1982. *Publications:* The Gospel according to St Mark, 1957, and St John's Gospel, 1965, both published by Christian Students' Library in India; *posthumous publication:* A Pattern of Faith, 1986. *Address:* Bishopscroft, Ashwell Road, Bradford, W Yorks BD9 4AU.
*Died 10 July* 1983.

**PAUL, Leslie (Allen);** MA; DLitt (Lambeth); FRSL; author; Writer-in-Residence, St Paul and St Mary College, Cheltenham, since 1981; *b* Dublin, 1905. *Educ:* at a London Central School. Entered Fleet Street at age of 17; founded The Woodcraft Folk, a youth organisation, when 20; first Book (poems) when 21. Headed a delegation, on co-operation, to USSR, 1931; Editor, Plan, 1934–39; worked on Continent (refugees and underground movement); Tutor, WEA and LCC, 1933–40; called up, infantry, 1941; Middle East (AEC); Staff Tutor, Mount Carmel Coll. (MEF). Atlantic Award in Literature, 1946. Asst Director of Studies, Ashridge College of Citizenship, 1947–48; Director of Studies, at Brasted Place, Brasted, 1953–57. Leverhulme Research Fellow, 1957–59. Member Departmental Cttee on the Youth Service, 1958–60; Research Fellow, King George's Jubilee Trust and Industrial Welfare Society, 1960–61; Research Director, Central Advisory Council for the Ministry, for Church Assembly Enquiry into Deployment and Payment of the Clergy, 1962–64. Resident Fellow, Kenyon Coll., Ohio, 1964; Selwyn Lectr, St John's Coll., NZ, 1969; Lectr in Ethics and Social Studies, Queen's Coll., Birmingham, 1965–70; Scholar-in-Residence, Eastern Baptist Coll., Pa, USA, 1970. Mem., Gen. Synod of Church of England, 1970–75; Vice-Pres., Philosophical Soc., 1973–; Chm., Diocesan Council of Social Action (Hereford), 1972–78. Hale Meml Lectr, and Hon. DCL, Seabury-Western, USA, 1970; DLitt *hc. Publications:* (chief books, 1944–): Annihilation of Man, 1944; The Living Hedge, 1946; The Meaning of Human Existence, 1949; Angry Young Man, 1951; The English Philosophers, 1953; Sir Thomas More, 1953; The Boy Down Kitchener Street, 1957; Nature into History, 1957; Persons and Perception, 1961; Son of Man, 1961; The Transition from School to Work, 1962; Traveller on Sacred Ground, 1963; The Deployment and Payment of the Clergy, 1964; Alternatives to Christian Belief, 1967; The Death and Resurrection of the Church, 1968; Coming to Terms with Sex, 1969; Eros Rediscovered, 1970; Journey to Connemara and other poems, 1972; A Church by Daylight, 1973; The Waters and the Wild, 1975; First Love, 1977; The Bulgarian Horse, 1979; The Springs of Good and Evil, 1979; Early Days of the Woodcraft Folk, 1980; Pioneers O Pioneers! The Mississippi Cantos, 1983; The Secret War Against Hitler, 1984. *Recreations:* bird-watching, photography, making lawns. *Address:* 73 Shurdington Road, Cheltenham, Glos GL53 0JQ. *T:* Cheltenham 511762. *Club:* Royal Commonwealth Society.
*Died 8 July* 1985.

**PAULL, Sir Gilbert (James),** Kt 1957; Judge of High Court of Justice, Queen's Bench Division, 1957–71; *b* 18 April 1896; *s* of Alan Paull, FSI, JP; *m* 1922, Maud Winifred (*d* 1978), *d* of Charles Harris, Streatham; one *s* one *d. Educ:* St Paul's Sch.; Trinity Coll., Cambridge. Called to Bar, Inner Temple, 1920; QC, 1939; Bencher of Inner Temple 1946, Reader 1969, Treasurer 1970; Member of the Council of Legal Education, 1947–65; Recorder of Leicester, 1944–57.
*Died 13 Nov.* 1984.

**PAULSON, Godfrey Martin Ellis,** CB 1966; CMG 1959; OBE (mil.) 1945; HM Diplomatic Service, retired 1970; *b* 6 July 1908; *s* of late Lt-Col P. Z. Paulson, OBE, Manchester Regt and Royal Signals, and late Mrs M. G. Paulson, *d* of late Dr W. H. Ellis, Shipley Hall, Bradford, Yorkshire; *m* 1936, Patricia Emma, *d* of late Sir Hugh Murray, KCIE, CBE, and late Lady Murray, Englefield Green House, Surrey; one *s* one *d. Educ:* Westminster and Peterhouse, Cambridge. BA (Hons), 1930, MA 1940. Colonial Service; Assistant District Commissioner, Gold Coast Colony, 1930–32. Admitted Solicitor, 1936; practised in City of London until outbreak of war, 1939. Served 1939–45, Manchester Regt and on General Staff in Africa, UK, and North West Europe, including Military Mission to Free French; Lt-Col, 1945 (OBE 1945). Control Commn for Germany, 1945, for Austria, 1946. Joined Foreign Service, 1946, and served in Venice, Stockholm, Far East (Singapore), Beirut, Rome, Nice and Foreign Office. Member: British Sect., Franco-British Council, 1978–88; Exec. Cttee, Franco-British Sect., 1972–85. Officer, Order of St Charles, Monaco, 1981. *Address:* Yew Tree Cottage, Church Street, Hampstead Norreys, near Newbury, Berks RG16 0TD. *T:* Hermitage (0635) 201572. *Clubs:* United Oxford & Cambridge University, Garrick, Special Forces, MCC.
*Died 31 July* 1990.

**PAVITT, Laurence Anstice;** *b* 1 Feb. 1914; *s* of George Anstice Pavitt and May (*née* Brooshooft); *m* 1937, Rosina (*née* Walton); one *s* one *d. Educ:* Elementary and Central Sch., West Ham. National Organising Secretary, British Fedn of Young Co-operators, 1942–46;

Gen. Secretary, Anglo Chinese Development Soc., 1946–52; Regional Education Officer, Co-operative Union, 1947–52; UN Technical Assistance Programme, Asian Co-operative Field Mission, 1952–55; National Organiser, Medical Practitioners' Union, 1956–59. MP (Lab and Co-op): Willesden West, 1959–74; Brent South, 1974–87. PPS to: Secretary for Education and Science, 1964–65; Secretary of State for Foreign Affairs, 1965–66; Secretary of State for Economic Affairs, 1966–67; an Asst Govt Whip, 1974–76. Vice-Chairman: Parly Labour Party's Health Gp, 1977–80 (Chm., 1964–77); British China All Party Gp, 1978–87 (Chm., 1974–78); Chm., All Party Gp on Action on Smoking and Health, 1974–78; Member: Select Cttee on Overseas Aid, 1969–71; Exec. Cttee, Inter-Parly Union, 1967–81, 1984–87; Exec. Cttee, Commonwealth Parly Assoc., 1969–82; UK Delegn to Council of Europe, 1980–84; UK Delegn to WEU, 1980–84; Nat. Exec., Cooperative Party (Chm. Parly Gp), 1980–81. Vice-President: Brit. Assoc. for the Hard of Hearing; Royal Coll. of Nursing; Member: Hearing Aid Council, 1968–74; MRC, 1969–72. *Recreations:* reading, walking.
*Died 14 Dec.* 1989.

**PAWLEY, Ven. Bernard Clinton;** Archdeacon of Canterbury and Canon Residentiary of Canterbury Cathedral, 1972–81; Archdeacon Emeritus, since 1981; *b* 24 Jan. 1911; *s* of late Lt-Comdr S. G. Pawley, RN; *m* 1958, Margaret Grozier, *d* of late J. J. W. Herbertson, MVO, OBE; one *s* one *d. Educ:* Portsmouth Grammar School; Wadham College, Oxford; Wells Theological College. MA (Oxon), 1933. Deacon 1934, Priest 1936; Curate: Stoke on Trent Parish Church, 1934; Leeds Parish Church, 1937. CF (Emergency Commn), 1940–45 (despatches, 1945). Rector of Elland (dio. Wakefield), 1945–55; Diocesan Sec., Ely, 1955–59; Canon Residentiary, Vice-Dean and Treasurer, Ely, 1959–70; Canon Residentiary and Chancellor of St Paul's Cathedral, 1970–72. Proctor in Convocation, York, 1949–55, Canterbury, 1955–81; Member: Church Assembly, 1949–70; General Synod, 1972–81; Archbishops' Liaison with Vatican Secretariat for Unity, 1960–65; Vice-Chairman, Archbishops' Commission for RC Relations, 1966. Church Commissioner, 1963–78. Mem., British Council of Churches, 1966–78; Delegate, World Council of Churches, 1968 and 1975. *Publications:* Looking at the Vatican Council, 1962; Anglican-Roman Relations, 1964; (ed) The Second Vatican Council, 1967; (with M. G. Pawley) Rome and Canterbury through Four Centuries, 1975. *Recreations:* music, foreign languages. *Address:* Forge Cottage, Warehorne, near Ashford, Kent. *T:* Ham Street 2408.
*Died 15 Nov.* 1981.

**PAWSON, Albert Guy,** CMG 1935; Secretary General, International Rubber Study Group, 1948–60 (Secretary, 1944–48); *b* 30 May 1888; *s* of Albert Henry and Alice Sarah Pawson; *m* 1917, Helen Humphrey Lawson (*d* 1980); two *s. Educ:* Winchester College; Christ Church, Oxford. 2nd Class Honours School of History; joined Sudan Political Service, 1911; Governor, White Nile Province, 1927–31; Governor, Upper Nile Province, 1931–34; Sec., Internat. Rubber Regulation Cttee, 1934–42; Colonial Office, 1942–44. *Recreations:* fishing, cricket, tennis, Oxford Cricket Blue, 1908, 1909, 1910 and 1911, Captain 1910. *Address:* c/o P. H. C. Pawson, MBE, Lower Grenofen, Tavistock, Devon PL19 9ES.
*Died 25 Feb.* 1986.

**PAYNE, Anson;** *see* Payne, J. A.

**PAYNE, Prof. Jack Marsh;** Director, AFRC Institute for Research on Animal Diseases, 1973–86; *b* 9 March 1929; *m* 1952, Sylvia Bryant; two *s* two *d. Educ:* Royal Veterinary Coll., London; University Coll. Hosp. Med. Sch., London. PhD, BSc; MRCVS; FIBiol. Res. Fellowship under Sir Roy Cameron, FRS, 1952–57; apptd, 1957, to staff of IRAD, Compton, Newbury, Berks, where principal res. has involved investigation of metabolic disorders of dairy cattle; esp. interest has centred around the concept of prodn disease and the develt of the Compton Metabolic Profile Test; recent esp. interest in zoonoses. Head of Dept of Functional Pathology, IRAD, 1961–73. Member: British Veterinary Assoc.; Assoc. of Veterinary Teachers and Res. Workers; Pathological Soc. Chm., VETEC (round table of experts on vet. science in EEC), 1976. WHO adviser; Veterinary Advr, British Council, 1977. FRSA. G. Norman Hall Gold Medal, 1972; RASE: Res. Gold Medal, 1972; Bledisloe Trophy and Medal, 1981; Victory Medal, Central Vet. Assoc. London, 1984. Editor: British Veterinary Jl, 1984–; Zoonosis Data Base, 1984–. *Publications:* Metabolic Disorders in Farm Animals, 1977; Metabolic Profile Test, 1987; numerous references in sci. jls, esp. on subject of metabolic disorders. *Recreations:* fell walking, music (especially collecting rare operas), painting. *Address:* University of Reading Department of Agriculture, PO Box 236, Reading, Berks RG6 2AT. *T:* Reading 875123. *Club:* Athenæum.
*Died 19 March* 1988.

**PAYNE, (John) Anson,** OBE 1945; Chairman, FMC, 1974–75 (Executive Vice-Chairman, 1972–74); formerly Director: FMC (Meat); C. & T. Harris (Calne); Marsh and Baxter, and other cos; *b* 19 May 1917; *yr s* of late Major R. L. Payne, DSO and of Mrs L. M.

Payne (née Duncan); m 1949, Deirdre Kelly; one s one d. Educ: St Lawrence Coll., Ramsgate; Trinity Hall, Cambridge (MA). Entered Civil Service as Assistant Principal, 1939. Served War of 1939–45 (despatches twice, OBE): RAFVR, 1940–45; Wing Commander, 1943. Principal Private Secretary to Minister of Agriculture and Fisheries, 1947–51; Asst Secretary, 1951; seconded to Treasury, 1953–54; Under-Secretary, Min. of Agriculture, 1960–68. *Address:* Sandpit Cottage, 4 High Street, Ditchling, Sussex BN6 8TA. *T:* Hassocks 2310. *Died 31 July 1987.*

**PAYNE, Sir Robert (Frederick),** Kt 1970; President, The Law Society, 1969–70; Principal in Payne & Payne, Solicitors, Hull, until 1985, then Consultant; *b* 22 Jan. 1908; *s* of late Frederick Charles Payne and of Edith Constance Payne (née Carlton); *m* 1st, 1937, Alice Marguerite, *d* of William Sydney Cussons, one s one d; 2nd, 1951, Maureen Ruth, *d* of William Charles Walsh; one s. *Educ:* Hymers Coll., Hull. Solicitor, 1931. Served in RAF (Fighter Command), 1940–44, Sqdn Ldr, 2nd TAF. Chm., Cttee of Inquiry into Whittingham Hosp., 1971–72; Mem., Home Office Cttee on Liquor Licensing, 1971–72. Pres., Hull Incorporated Law Soc., 1954–55. Founder Mem., British Acad. of Forensic Sciences, 1959. Sheriff of Kingston-upon-Hull, 1957. Hon. Fellow, Victoria Coll. of Music, 1978. *Recreations:* golf, music. *Address:* Long View, 26 Swanland Hill, North Ferriby, Humberside HU14 3JJ. *T:* Hull 631533. *Club:* Royal Yorkshire Yacht (Life Member). *Died 18 Aug. 1985.*

**PAYNTER, (Thomas) William;** Secretary, National Union of Mineworkers, 1959–68; Member, Arbitration Panel for the Advisory Arbitration and Conciliation Service (formerly the TUC-CBI Conciliation Panel), since 1972; *b* 6 Dec. 1903; *s* of a Miner; *m* 1st, 1937; two s (twins); 2nd, 1943; five s (one set of twins). *Educ:* Whitchurch (Cardiff) and Porth Elementary Schools. Left school at age of 13 to work on a farm, 1917; commenced work in Rhondda Pits; elected Checkweigher at Cymmer Colliery, Porth, 1929; removed by Court injunction, 1931. Took part in hunger marches, 1931, 1932, 1936. Elected to Executive Committee, South Wales Miners' Federation for Rhondda, 1936; joined International Brigade, 1937; Miners' agent for Rhymney Area, 1939; President South Wales Miners, 1951. Mem., Commn on Industrial Relations, 1969–70. Chm., London Region, Nat. Fedn of Pension Assocs; Sec., London Jt Council for Senior Citizens. *Publications:* British Trade Unions and the Problem of Change, 1970; My Generation (autobiog.), 1972. *Recreations:* reading and gardening. *Address:* 32 Glengall Road, Edgware, Mddx. *Died 11 Dec. 1984.*

**PAYTON, Rev. Wilfred Ernest Granville,** CB 1965; Vicar of Abingdon, 1969–79; Rural Dean of Abingdon, 1976–79; *b* 27 Dec. 1913; *s* of Wilfred Richard Daniel Payton and Alice Payton (née Lewin); *m* 1946, Nita Mary Barber; one s one d. *Educ:* Nottingham High School; Emmanuel College, Cambridge (MA); Ridley Hall, Cambridge. Ordained, 1938; Chaplain, RAF, 1941; Asst Chaplain-in-Chief, 1959; Chaplain-in-Chief, 1965–69; Archdeacon, Prebendary and Canon of St Botolph, Lincoln Cathedral, 1965–69. Hon. Chaplain to the Queen, 1965–69. *Recreations:* cricket (Cambridge Univ. 1937), hockey (Notts 1938–39), tennis. *Address:* Westwood, Nailsworth, Gloucester GL6 0AW. *Clubs:* MCC; Hawks (Cambridge). *Died 4 Sept. 1989.*

**PEACOCK, (John) Roydon;** retired as Consultant Surgeon, Ear, Nose and Throat Department, St George's Hospital, SW1; *b* 5 Sept. 1902; *s* of late Ralph Peacock; *m* Olive Joan (d 1977), *d* of late Sir Arthur Blake, KBE. *Educ:* Westminster Sch.; Trinity Coll., Cambridge; St George's Hospital, University Entrance Schol.; Brackenbury Prize, Allingham Scholar. FRCS; BCh Cantab; MRCS, LRCP; 1st Class Hons Natural Sciences Tripos, Cambridge; late Hon. Asst Surgeon Throat, Nose and Ear Hospital, Golden Square, W1; late Hon. Surgeon in charge of Ear, Nose and Throat Dept, Metropolitan Hospital, Kingsland Road; late Hon. Aural Surgeon to Maida Vale Hospital for nervous diseases; late Hon. Laryngologist, King Edward's Memorial Hospital, Ealing; late Hon. Surgeon Royal National Throat, Nose and Ear Hospital; late Surgeon to Ear, Nose and Throat Dept, Canadian Red Cross Memorial Hospital, Taplow, Bucks; late Surgeon, Ear, Nose and Throat Dept, St George's Hospital, SW1; late recog. teacher in Otolaryngology, University of London. *Publications:* Alcoholic Labyrinthine Injection through the oval window in the treatment of aural vertigo, Lancet, Feb. 1938; Meniere's Syndrome, an observation, Lancet, Dec. 1938. *Address:* Windrush, Bicknoller, Taunton, Somerset TA4 4EE. *T:* Stogumber 265. *Died 28 March 1982.*

**PEAKE, Sir Francis (Harold),** Kt 1951; *b* 31 Jan. 1889; *s* of late John Henry Hill Peake, Chingford, Essex; *m* 1914, Winifred Marie, *d* of late Thomas McKinnon Clark, Wood Green; two d. *Educ:* Tottenham Grammar Sch. Entered Civil Service, 1907. Called to Bar, Lincoln's Inn, 1915. Controller of Death Duties, Aug. 1948–31 July 1951. *Address:* 5 Churchfield House, Guessens Road, Welwyn Garden City, Herts. *T:* Welwyn Garden 20456. *Died 27 Aug. 1984.*

**PEARCE, Baron** (Life Peer) cr 1962, of Sweethaws; **Edward Holroyd Pearce,** PC 1957; Kt 1948; RBA 1940; Chairman of the Press Council, 1969–74; Chairman, Appeals Committee, Take-over Panel, 1969–76; *b* 9 Feb. 1901; *s* of late John W. E. Pearce and Irene, *d* of Holroyd Chaplin; *m* 1927, Erica (*d* 1985), *d* of late Bertram Priestman, RA; two s decd. *Educ:* Charterhouse; Corpus Christi Coll., Oxford. Hon. Fellow, Corpus Christi Coll., 1950. Called to Bar, 1925; QC 1945; Bencher, Hon. Society of Lincoln's Inn, 1948; Treasurer, 1966. Deputy Chairman, East Sussex Quarter Sessions, 1947–48; Judge of High Court of Justice, Probate, Divorce and Admiralty Division, 1948–54, Queen's Bench Division, 1954–57; a Lord Justice of Appeal, 1957–62; a Lord of Appeal in Ordinary, 1962–69. Chairman, Cttee on Shipbuilding Costs, 1947–49; Mem., Royal Commission on Marriage and Divorce, 1951; Chairman: Commn to test Rhodesian approval of proposed British-Rhodesian settlements, 1971–72; Cttee on the organisation of Bar and Inns of Court, 1971–73 (Hon. Mem. Senate, Four Inns of Court, 1974); Indep. Chm., Press discussions on Charter of Press Freedom, 1976–77. Mem., Governing Body, Charterhouse Sch., 1943–64; Governor: Tonbridge Sch., 1945–78; Sutton's Hospital in Charterhouse; Fedn of British Artists, 1970–73. Prof. of Law, Royal Acad. of Arts, 1971–. Past Master and past Member of Court of Company of Skinners; President, Artists League of GB, 1950–74; Trustee, Chantrey Bequest; Hon. FRBS. One-man show of landscapes at The Mall Galleries, 1971 and (with wife) 1973, 1976; also in provinces; one-man show of Alpine landscapes at Chur, Switzerland, 1977 and at Alpine Gall., London, 1983. Publisher (as Sweethaws Press) of The Permissive Garden by Erica, Lady Pearce, 1987. *Recreations:* painting and pictures. *Address:* House of Lords, SW1; Sweethaws, Crowborough. *T:* (0892) 61520. *Club:* Athenæum. *Died 26 Nov. 1990.*

**PEARCE, Clifford James,** CB 1974; Under Secretary (Local Government), Department of the Environment (formerly Ministry of Housing and Local Government), 1968–76; *b* 14 Aug. 1916; *s* of late Samuel Lightfoot Pearce and Maude Evelyn Neville; *m* 1946, Elaine Hilda (née Baggley); one s one d. *Educ:* Strand Sch.; King's Coll., London; London Sch. of Economics. Entered Inland Revenue, 1935; served in RN, 1941–46 (Lieut, RNVR); entered Min. of Health, 1946; Asst Sec., Min. of Housing and Local Govt, 1957; Under Sec. 1968. Hon. Res. Fellow, Birmingham Univ., 1976–78. *Publication:* The Machinery of Change in Local Government 1888–1974, 1980. *Recreation:* bookbinding. *Address:* Elm Cottage, The Street, Boxgrove, Chichester. *Died 6 March 1985.*

**PEARCE, Hon. James Edward Holroyd,** QC 1979; *b* 18 March 1934; *s* of Baron Pearce, RBA, and Erica, *d* of late Bertram Priestman, RA; *m* 1969, Julia, *yr d* of late C. D. Hill; two s two d. *Educ:* Charterhouse; Corpus Christi Coll., Oxford (1st Cl. Hons Jurisprudence, MA). Military service, RE, 2nd Lieut, 1953–54. Teaching Associate, Northwestern Univ. Law Sch., Chicago, 1959; called to Bar: Middle Temple, 1960, NI, 1974. Hon. Legal Adviser to National Skating Assoc., 1970–. Mem. Council, Artists' General Benevolent Instn, 1978–. *Address:* Turf Lodge, Sheep Plain, Crowborough, Sussex TN6 3ST. *T:* Crowborough 5505. *Club:* Athenæum. *Died 11 June 1985.*

**PEARCE, Kenneth Leslie;** retired as Chairman, East Midlands Gas Region (formerly East Midlands Gas Board), 1968–74; *b* 2 May 1910; *s* of late George Benjamin Pearce and Eliza Jane Pearce; *m* 1940, Evlyn Sarah Preedy (d 1957); two s. *Educ:* Dudley Grammar Sch.; Birmingham Central Techn. Coll. Engr and Man., Bilston Gas Light & Coke Co., 1939–48; Engr and Man., City of Leicester Gas Dept, 1948–49; East Midlands Gas Board: Divisional Gen. Man., Leicester and Northants, 1949–50; Divisional Gen. Man., Notts and Derby, 1950–62; Chief Distribution Engr, 1962–67; Dep. Chairman, 1967–68. *Recreations:* fishing, gardening. *Address:* Stoneridge, Coppice Lane, The Wergs, Wolverhampton WV6 9BS. *T:* Wolverhampton 755260. *Died 3 April 1988.*

**PEARCE, Hon. Richard Bruce Holroyd;** QC 1969; **His Honour Judge Pearce;** a Circuit Judge, since 1982; *b* 12 May 1930; *s* of Baron Pearce, RBA, and Erica, *d* of late Bertram Priestman, RA; *m* 1958, Dornie Smith-Pert; one s one d; *m* 1987, Christine Westwood. *Educ:* Charterhouse; Corpus Christi Coll., Oxford (MA). Served HM Forces, 1949–56: RE and E African Engrs, 1949–50; 119 Field Engr Regt RE, TA, 1950–56. Called to Bar, Lincoln's Inn, 1955, Bencher, 1977; ad eund. Mem., Middle Temple, 1958; a Recorder of the Crown Court, 1972–82. A Legal Assessor to GMC, 1974–82, GDC, 1974–82, GNC, 1975–82. Master, Skinner's Co., 1976–77. Governor, Tonbridge School. *Club:* Beefsteak. *Died 3 Sept. 1987.*

**PEARCE, William Harvey,** CBE 1977 (OBE 1968); HM Chief Inspector of Prisons for England and Wales, since 1981; *b* 8 April 1920; *s* of late William Charles Pearce and of Agnes Jane Pearce; *m* 1941, Agnes Prescott; one d. *Educ:* Arnot School. Probation Officer, Southampton, London and Berkshire, 1944–52; Chief Probation Officer: Durham County, 1952–70; Inner London, 1970–80; Chm.

of Conf. of Chief Probation Officers, 1964–67; Member: Parole Board, 1967–71; Adv. Council for Probation and After-Care, 1967–72. Associate Teacher of Social Work, Univ. of Newcastle, 1954–70; Mem. Council, Univ. of Durham, 1967–70. Lecturer and Consultant: to UN Inst. for Prevention of Crime and Treatment of Offenders, Japan, 1972–79; for British Council in Thailand, Singapore, Philippines, Malaysia, Israel, 1976–80; lecture tours in USA and Canada, 1966–80. Churchill Fellowship, 1966. *Publications:* articles in internat. periodicals on crime and delinquency. *Recreations:* oriental travel, art, music; golf, Southampton FC, Larry Gatlin (Texas). *Address:* 16 Lingwood Close, Bassett, Southampton, Hants SO1 7GJ. *T:* Southampton 768575. *Club:* Naval. *Died 3 Jan.* 1982.

**PEARCE-HIGGINS, Rev. Canon John Denis;** Hon. Chaplain to the Forces; Residentiary Canon and Vice-Provost of Southwark, 1963–71, later Emeritus; *b* 1 June 1905; 2nd *s* of late Prof. Alexander Pearce Higgins and Mina MacLennan; *m* 1938, Margaret Edna, 2nd *d* of Harry and Marguerite Hodge, Kettering; two *s* three *d*. *Educ:* St Faith's Sch., Cambridge; Rugby Sch. (scholar); Gonville and Caius Coll., Cambridge (schol. and prizeman). Charles Winter Warr Research Schol. in Ancient Philosophy, 1928; 1st class hons Parts I and II Class. Tripos; Research at Vienna Univ., 1928–29; Ripon Hall Theological Coll., 1934–37. Priest, 1937; Curate: St Agnes, Cotteridge; Priory Church, Malvern, 1940. Chaplain in RAChD, Oct. 1940–Nov. 1945 (invalided; Overseas, Africa Star, Italy, Defence and Victory medals). Vicar of Hanley Castle, Worcs, 1945–53; OCF; Chaplain and Sen. Divinity Lecturer, City of Worcester Training Coll., 1946–53; Vicar of Putney, St Mary with St John and All Saints, Surrogate, 1953–63. Chairman, Modern Churchmen's Union, 1958–68. Vice-Chairman, Churches' Fellowship for Psychical and Spiritual Studies, 1961–. Member Society for Psychical Research. *Publications:* Resurrection, 1959; (ed) Life, Death and Psychical Research, 1973; articles in: Modern Churchman, Journal of SPR. *Recreations:* music, painting, swimming. *Address:* 13 Abbotstone Road, Putney, SW15 1QR. *T:* 01–788 4573. *Died 24 Jan.* 1985.

**PEARKES, Maj.-Gen. Hon. George Randolph,** VC 1918; CC (Canada) 1967; PC (Canada) 1957; CB 1943; DSO 1919; MC; Legion of Merit (US); Lieutenant-Governor, British Columbia, 1960–68, retired; *b* Watford, Herts, 26 Feb. 1888; *m* Constance Blytha, *o d* of W. F. U. Copeman, Sidney, BC; one *s*. *Educ:* Berkhamsted Sch. Went to Canada; farmed for three years; joined Royal N-W Mounted Police, 1909; enlisted in Canadian Expeditionary Force, 1914; arrived in France, Sept. 1915; Bombing Sgt, Dec. 1915; Lieut on the field, March 1916; Battalion Bombing Officer; Brigade Bombing Officer; Captain, Oct. 1916; Major, Nov. 1917; took command of Battalion, Dec. 1917 (VC, MC, despatches, wounded several times); passed Staff Coll., Camberley, 1919; served on the General Staff of Permanent Force of Canada as GSO at Calgary, Winnipeg, Esquimalt and Kingston; DMT and SD; at Imperial Defence Coll., 1937; DOC, MD 13, Calgary, 1938–40; GOC First Canadian Division, 1940; GOC-in-C Pacific Command, Canada, 1942–45; retired April, 1945. Minister of National Defence, 1957–60. Hon. LLD, University of British Columbia. *Address:* 1268 Tattersall Drive, Victoria, BC V8P 1Z3, Canada. *Club:* Union (Victoria). *Died 30 May* 1984.

**PEARS, Harold Snowden; His Honour Judge Pears;** a Circuit Judge (formerly Judge of County Courts), since 1971; *b* 21 April 1926; *s* of late Harold Pears and Florence Elizabeth (*née* Snowden); *m* 1960, Inge Haumann, *d* of late Heinrich Elvensø, and Agnes Elvensø, Denmark; no *c*. *Educ:* Dauntsey's Sch.; Emmanuel Coll., Cambridge (MA). Called to the Bar, Inner Temple, 1948; North Eastern Circuit, 1948–71. Dep. Chm., W Riding QS, 1967–71; Recorder of Doncaster, 1968–71, Hon. Recorder of Doncaster, 1972–75; Hon. Recorder of Sheffield, 1976. Legal Mem., Mental Health Review Tribunal, 1964–71. Pres., S Yorks Br., Magistrates' Assoc., 1980. *Recreations:* boats, travel, fishing. *T:* Sheffield 366244. *Club:* Sheffield (Sheffield). *Died 14 June* 1982.

**PEARS, Sir Peter,** Kt 1978; CBE 1957; Tenor; *b* 22 June 1910; *s* of Arthur and Jessie Pears. *Educ:* Lancing; Oxford; Royal College of Music. BBC Singers, 1934–37; New English Singers, 1936–38; began American and European tours with Benjamin Britten, 1939, with Julian Bream, 1956, with Osian Ellis, 1972. Sadler's Wells Opera, 1943–46; Peter Grimes in Peter Grimes 1945 and 1960; Aschenbach in Death in Venice, NY Met., 1974; Vere in Billy Budd, NY Met., 1978. Co-Founder of English Opera Gp, 1947; Covent Garden Opera, 1948; Co-Founder of Aldeburgh Festival, 1948; Founder and Dir of Singing, Britten-Pears Sch. of Advanced Musical Studies, 1972–. Pres., Incorporated Soc. of Musicians, 1970. First performed many new works by Britten, Tippett, Berkeley, etc. Cramb Lectr, Univ. of Glasgow, 1961. FRCM; Hon. RAM; Hon. RSAMD; Hon. RNCM; Hon. Fellow, Keble Coll., Oxford, 1978; DUniv York, 1969; Hon. DLitt Sussex, 1971; Hon. MusD Cantab, 1972; Hon. DMus Evansville (Indiana), 1976; Hon. DMus Edinburgh, 1976; Hon. DMus East Anglia, 1980; Hon. DMus

Oxon, 1981; DUniv Essex, 1981. Musician of the Year, ISM, 1978; Queen's Jubilee Medal, 1977; Royal Opera House Long Service Medal, 1979. *Publications:* (with Benjamin Britten) Purcell Edition; occasional articles. *Address:* The Red House, Aldeburgh, Suffolk IP15 5PZ. *Died 3 April* 1986.

**PEARSON, Bertram Lamb,** CB 1947; DSO 1917; MC; *b* 1893; *y s* of late William Pearson of Wakefield, Yorkshire, and late Mary Ann Pearson; *m* 1920, Gladys Mary (*d* 1980), *er d* of John Stewart of Yapham Hall, Pocklington, East Yorkshire. *Educ:* Bedford Grammar Sch.; Wakefield Grammar Sch.; The Queen's Coll., Oxford; 1st Hastings Exhibitioner and Honorary Scholar; 1st Class Honour (Classical) Moderations, 1913; 1st Class Literæ Humaniores, 1919. Served European War, 1914–19, as Captain, The Green Howards (wounded twice, despatches, MC, DSO); tutor, The Queen's Coll., Oxford, 1919–20; Private Sec. to Permanent Sec., Bd of Educn, 1924–28; Principal Private Sec. to President, Board of Educn, 1937; Accountant-General to Min. of Educn, 1944–55; Under-Secretary, 1946–55. Member Council: Central Council of Physical Recreation, 1956–; Girls' Public Day School Trust, 1958–69. *Recreations:* cricket, bowls, reading. *Address:* Astley Nursing Home, 1 Lypiatt Lawn, Lypiatt Road, Cheltenham, Glos GL50 2SY. *Died 17 Aug.* 1984.

**PEARSON, David Morris,** OBE 1969 (MBE 1945); HM Diplomatic Service, retired; Ambassador to the Republic of Honduras, 1972–75; *b* 21 July 1915; *s* of late Isaac Bedlington Pearson and late Margaret Elizabeth Williams; *m* 1945, Camille Henriette Etey; no *c*. *Educ:* Kelvinside Academy, Glasgow; Sedbergh Sch.; Glasgow University. HM Forces, 1939–46 (Intell. Corps, then SOE in France, leading Pedagogue Mission). Personnel Manager, Gold Coast Main Reef Ltd, 1946–50; Sierra Leone Administrative Service, 1950–59; seconded to Foreign Service, in Consulate-General, Dakar, Senegal, 1954–59; entered Foreign Service, 1959; FO, 1960–62; Head of Chancery, Brazzaville, 1962–65; Rio de Janeiro, 1965–67; Kinshasa, 1967–69; Consul-Gen., Casablanca, 1969–72. French Croix de Guerre (with star), 1945. *Recreations:* music, reading, foreign travel. *Address:* 32 Les Trompettes Hautes, Montesquieu, 66740 St Génis-des-Fontaines, Pyrénées-Orientales, France. *Club:* Atalanta (Glasgow). *Died 19 May* 1985.

**PEARSON, Denise, (Mrs R. O'Neill Pearson);** *see* Robins, D.

**PEARSON, Sir (James) Reginald,** Kt 1959; OBE 1950; retired in Nov. 1962 as Deputy Chairman (1958) and Executive Assistant to Managing Director (1953), Vauxhall Motors Ltd, Luton, Beds; *b* 17 Nov. 1897; *s* of George Henry Pearson and Annie Pearson (*née* Stringer); *m* 1925, Nellie Rose Vittery (*d* 1977); one *d*. *Educ:* Dudley, Worcestershire. Apprenticed at Bullers Ltd, Tipton; National Projectile Factory, Dudley; Vauxhall Motors Ltd (1919); Craftsman, Journeyman, Foreman, Area Manager, Production Manager, Factory Manager, Director (1946). Chairman, Dawley Development Corporation, 1962–68 (now Telford). Vice-President, Royal Society for the Prevention of Accidents. High Sheriff of Bedfordshire, 1964; DL Beds, 1968–78. FIMechE; MIProdE. *Recreations:* golf, gardening; interested in all forms of sport; Hon. Life President, Vauxhall Motors Recreation Club. *Address:* 45 Bloomfield Road, Harpenden, Herts. *T:* Harpenden 3052. *Died 17 March* 1984.

**PEARSON, Sir Neville (Arthur),** 2nd Bt *cr* 1916; *b* 13 Feb. 1898; *s* of 1st Bt, and Ethel Lady Pearson, DBE; *S* father, 1921; *m* 1st, 1922, Mary Angela (marr. diss. 1928, she *m* 1928, C. Willoughby Hordern and *d* 1937), 2nd *d* of 1st Baron Melchett; one *d* (one *s* decd); 2nd, 1928, Gladys Cooper (later Dame Gladys Cooper, DBE) (*d* 1971), (marr. diss. 1937; she *m* 1937, Philip Merivale); one *d*; 3rd, 1943, Mrs Anne Davis Elebash (*d* 1981), New York. *Educ:* Eton.RFA, European War, 1917–18; subsequently entered firm of C. Arthur Pearson, Ltd, publishers; retired from all directorships, 1968. President, St Dunstan's, 1947–77; President, Fresh Air Fund. AA Artillery, War of 1939–45. *Heir:* none. *Address:* c/o Wyndham L. Gary, 37 Highland Avenue, Fair Haven, NJ 07701, USA. *Died 6 Nov.* 1982 (*ext*).

**PEARSON, Sir Reginald;** *see* Pearson, Sir J. R.

**PEARSON, Rt. Rev. Thomas Bernard;** Bishop Auxiliary in the Diocese of Lancaster, 1952–62 and 1965–83; Episcopal Vicar for Cumbria (formerly Cumberland, Westmorland and Furness), 1967–83; *b* Preston, Lancs, 18 January 1907; *s* of Joseph Pearson and Alice (*née* Cartmell). *Educ:* Upholland College; Ven. English College, Rome. Pontifical Gregorian University, Rome; PhD 1930; Bachelor of Canon Law, Licent. Sacred Theology, 1933. Priest, 1933; Assistant Priest, 1934–44; Parish Priest, St Cuthbert's, Blackpool, 1944–67; Titular Bishop of Sinda, 1949. Mem., Order of Discalced Carmelites, 1974. *Recreation:* mountaineering. *Address:* Howard Lodge, 90 Warwick Road, Carlisle CA1 1JU. *T:* Carlisle 24952. *Clubs:* Alpine, Fell and Rock, English Lake District; Achille Ratti Climbing (Founder President). *Died 17 Nov.* 1987.

**PEARSON, William Thomas Shipston;** retired from Civil Service, 1980; *b* 21 Aug. 1917; *s* of William Pearson and Alice (*née* Shipston); *m* 1948, Pauline Daphne Scott (*née* Wilkinson); one *s* two *d*. *Educ:* High Pavement Sch., Nottingham; University Coll., Nottingham (BSc). MRAeS, CEng. Appts at RAE, 1939–45; Hon. Commn, Flying Officer, RAFVR, 1944; Blind Landing Experimental Unit, Martlesham Heath, 1945–47; RAF Transport Comd Develt Unit, 1947–50; TRE, 1950–52; seconded to Australian Scientific Service, Long Range Weapons Estab., 1952–56; RAE, Farnborough, 1956–62; Asst Dir, Air Armaments, Min. of Aviation, 1962–65; Div. Head, Weapons Dept, RAE (concerned with various projs), 1965–76; seconded to FCO, as Counsellor (Defence Res.), British High Commn, Canberra, and Head of British Defence Res. and Supply Staffs, Australia, 1977–79. *Publications:* official reports. *Recreation:* photography. *Address:* 17 Woodland Way, New Milton, Hants BH25 5RT. *Club:* Royal Air Force.

*Died 14 Feb. 1990.*

**PEART, Baron** *cr* 1976 (Life Peer), of Workington; **(Thomas) Frederick Peart,** PC 1964; Leader of the Opposition in the House of Lords, 1979–82; *b* 30 Apr. 1914; *m* 1945, Sarah Elizabeth Lewis; one *s*. *Educ:* Crook Council; Wolsingham Grammar; Henry Smith Secondary, Hartlepool; Bede Coll., Durham Univ. (BSc); Inner Temple, Inns of Court. Pres. Durham University Union Soc. Councillor Easington RDC, 1937–40. Became a Schoolmaster. Served War of 1939–45, commissioned Royal Artillery, served in North Africa and Italy. MP (Lab) Workington Div. of Cumberland, 1945–76; PPS to Minister of Agriculture, 1945–51; Minister of Agriculture, Fisheries and Food, 1964–68 and 1974–76; Leader of the House of Commons, 1968–70; Lord Privy Seal, April–Oct. 1968; Lord President of the Council, Oct. 1968–1970; Opposition Spokesman; House of Commons Matters, 1970–71; Agriculture, 1971–72; Defence, 1972–74; Lord Privy Seal and Leader of the House of Lords, 1976–79; British Delegate to Council of Europe, 1952–55 (Rep. Agriculture Cttee and Cttee for Culture and Science (Vice-Pres.)); Leader, Labour delegn, and Vice-Pres., Council of Europe, 1973–74. Privy Council Rep. on Council of RCVS, Dir, FMC, 1971–74. Chairman: Adv. Council for Applied R&D, 1976–80; Retail Consortium, 1979–81. Pres., Durham Univ. Soc., 1975–. Freeman, City of London, 1968. Hon. FRCVS 1969. Hon. DSc Cranfield, 1977. *Address:* House of Lords, SW1.

*Died 26 Aug. 1988.*

**PEART, Donald Richard,** MA, BMus Oxon, FRCM; composer, conductor, violinist; First Professor of Music, University of Sydney, New South Wales, 1948–74, Professor Emeritus, 1975; founder and President of Pro Musica Society, Sydney University; *b* Fovant, Wilts, 9 Jan. 1909; *s* of Herbert and Dorothy Peart, Welling Hill, Haslemere, Surrey; *m* Ellen Lilian, *d* of W. H. Germon; one *s* one *d*. *Educ:* Cheltenham College (Scholar); Queen's College, Oxford (Bible Clerk). Osgood Memorial Prizeman, University of Oxford, 1932; studied at Royal College of Music, 1932–35; Librarian, 1935–39. War service, 1939–46; commissioned into The Gloucestershire Regt, 1940; served in W Africa, Burma, and India, 1942–46. Mem., Australian UNESCO Cttee for Music, 1956–68, Chm., 1965–68; Founder-Pres., Internat. Soc. for Contemp. Music (Australian Section) and of Musicological Society of Australia. Works include: two symphonies; cantata Red Night; string quartets, etc. Hon. DMus Sydney, 1980. *Recreations:* travelling, mountain climbing, etc. *Address:* 14 Windward Avenue, Mosman, NSW 2088, Australia. *T:* 9694308.

*Died 26 Nov. 1981.*

**PEART, Ernest Grafford,** CD 1978; High Commissioner for Jamaica in London, 1978–81; *b* 11 May 1918; *s* of Cyril and Sarah Peart; *m* 1947, Dorothy; three *s* one *d*. *Educ:* New Green Primary Sch., Jamaica; Manchester High Sch., Jamaica; RAF Coll.; Letchworth Tech. High Sch., UK; Yatesbury No 9 Radar Sch., UK. Mem. House of Representatives (PNP), Western Manchester, 1959–; Mem., Parly Public Accounts Cttee; Minister of Labour, 1972; Minister of Works, 1976. Pres., New Green JAS Branch; Jamaica Legion: Parish Chm. (Manchester), 1963; Area Chm., 1970–78; Chm., Mandeville Branch, and Mem., Island Council; Member: Manchester Secondary Sch. Trust, 1956; Manchester Sch. Bd; Bd of Governors, Manchester Nursing Home; Bd of Visitors, Mandeville Hosp.; Local Management Cttee, Curphey Home; Exec. Cttee, Manchester Boy Scouts Assoc. Mem., Manchester Parish Council, 1956–59 (Vice-Chm., 1958, 1959). *Recreations:* cricket, football, table tennis, reading. *Address:* c/o Ministry of Foreign Affairs, Kingston, Jamaica. *Clubs:* MCC, Travellers'; Lucas Cricket (Jamaica).

*Died 23 April 1982.*

**PEATE, Dr Iorwerth Cyfeiliog,** FSA; Curator, Welsh Folk Museum, 1948–71; *b* 1901; *y s* of George Howard Peate and Elizabeth Peate, Llanbryn-Mair, Mont.; *m* 1929, Nansi, *d* of David and Rachel Davies, Eglwys-fach, Card.; one *s*. *Educ:* Llanbryn-Mair Sch.; Machynlleth Intermed. Sch.; Univ. Coll. of Wales, Aberystwyth. MA 1924; DSc 1941. Staff Tutor, Univ. Coll. of Wales, Aberystwyth, 1924–27; Nat. Mus. of Wales, Cardiff: Asst Keeper, Dept of Archæology, 1927–32; Asst Keeper i/c Sub-Dept of Folk Culture

and Industries, 1932–36; Keeper, Dept of Folk Life, 1936–48. Ellis Gruffydd Prizeman, Univ. Wales, 1943; G. T. Clark Prizeman, Cambrian Archæol. Assoc., 1946; Pres., Sect. H (Anthrop.), Brit. Assoc. for Advancement of Science, 1958; Mem. Coun., British Assoc., 1961–66, 1970–74; Ed. of Gwerin, Internat. Jl of Folk Life, 1956–62; Pres., Soc. of Folk-Life Studies, 1961–66; a Vice-Pres., Hon. Soc. of Cymmrodorion, 1964– (Cymmrodorion Medal, 1978). Hon. DLitt Celt., Nat. Univ. of Ireland, 1960; Hon. DLitt Wales, 1970. *Publications:* Y Cawg Aur, 1928; Welsh Bygones, 1929; Cymru a'i Phobl, 1931; Y Crefftwr yng Nghymru, 1933; Plu'r Gweunydd, 1933; Welsh Folk Crafts and Industries, 1935; Sylfeini, 1938; The Welsh House, 1940; Diwylliant Gwerin Cymru, 1942; Clock and Watch Makers in Wales, 1945; Y Deyrnas Goll, 1947; Ym Mhob Pen, 1948; Folk Museums, 1948; Canu Chwarter Canrif, 1957; Syniadau, 1969; Tradition and Folk Life, 1972; Rhwng Dau Fyd, 1976; *edited:* Studies in Regional Consciousness and Environment, 1930; Hen Gapel Llanbryn-Mair, 1939; Ysgrifau John Breese Davies, 1949; Cilhaul ac Ysgrifau eraill gan Samuel Roberts, 1961; John Cowper Powys: Letters 1937–54, 1974. *Address:* Maes-y-coed, St Nicholas, Cardiff, S Glam. *T:* Peterston-super-Ely 760574.

*Died 19 Oct. 1982.*

**PECHELL, Sir Ronald (Horace),** 9th Bt *cr* 1797; *b* 4 June 1918; *o s* of Major Hugh Charles Pechell (and *g g s* of Commander Charles Pechell, *b* of 5th Bt), and Caroline Charlotte, *d* of G. A. Strickland; *S* kinsman, Sir Paul Pechell, 8th Bt, 1972; *m* 1949, Dora Constance, *d* of late John Crampthorne. *Educ:* St Paul's Sch.; HMS Worcester. Naval Cadet, Royal Air Force (Marine Craft Section) and Civil Aviation. Served War of 1939–45; Air-Sea Rescue five medals. Royal Humane Society Medal, 1950. *Recreations:* sailing and overseas travel. *Heir:* none. *Address:* c/o Child & Co., 1 Fleet Street, EC4.

*Died 29 Jan. 1984 (ext).*

**PECK, Antony Dilwyn,** CB 1965; MBE 1945; Deputy Secretary, Department of Trade and Industry, 1970–73; retired; *b* 10 April 1914; *s* of late Sir James Peck, CB, and late Lady Peck; *m* 1st, 1939, Joan de Burgh Whyte (*d* 1955); one *s* one *d*; 2nd, 1956, Sylvia Glenister; one *s* two *d*. *Educ:* Eton; Trinity College, Oxford. Fellow of Trinity College, 1938–45. Served War of 1939–45, Army, 1940–46 (Major). Joined Treasury as Principal, 1946; Asst Secretary, 1950; Under-Secretary, 1959; Dep. Under-Sec. of State, MoD, 1963–68; Second Sec., BoT, 1968–70. *Recreation:* bridge. *Address:* Holly Tree House, Compton, Chichester, W Sussex PO18 9HD.

*Died 10 Nov. 1987.*

**PEDDIE, Maj.-Gen. Graham,** CB 1959; DSO 1945; MBE 1941; *b* 15 Oct. 1905; *s* of late Graham Peddie and of Mrs Peddie; *m* 1937, Dorothy Mary Humfress (decd); one *s* one *d*; *m* 1959, Alexandra Mavrojani. *Educ:* Sherborne School, Royal Military Academy, Woolwich. Commissioned into RA, 1926; served in UK, 1926–30, in Egypt and Sudan, 1930–36; Instructor, RMA, Woolwich, 1937–39. War of 1939–45, in UK and NW Europe; 1st AA Group (Dep. Comd), 1948–50; idc, 1950–51. BAOR 1953–56; Director of Manpower Planning, War Office, 1957–60; retired, 1960. *Address:* 19 Mullings Court, Dugdale Road, Cirencester, Glos GL7 2AW. *T:* Cirencester 3087.

*Died 16 Aug. 1987.*

**PEDDIE, Ronald,** CBE 1971; JP; *b* 24 May 1905; *s* of Rev. James Peddie, BA and Elsie Mary, *d* of John Edward Corby; *m* 1931, Vera (*d* 1981), *d* of W. G. Nicklin, Guildford; three *s* one *d*. *Educ:* Glasgow Academy; Leys Sch., Cambridge; St John's Coll., Cambridge (MA). CA 1930; Jt Dipl. Management Accounting, 1967. McClelland Ker & Co., CA, Glasgow, 1926–31; Accountant and Asst Sec., C. & J. Clark Ltd, Street, Som, 1931–43; The United Steel Cos Ltd, 1943–67 (Sec. from 1946, later Dir Finance and Admin); British Steel Corp.: Dir, Finance and Admin, Midland Group, 1967–69; Man. Dir, Administration, 1969–71, retd. Dir, Iron Trades Employers' Insurance Assoc. Ltd, 1970–75. Sec., Trevelyan Scholarships, 1958–81; Governor, Ashorne Hill Management Coll., 1967–71. Past Mem., Cambridge and Leeds Univs Appt Bds. JP Sheffield, 1964. *Publications:* The United Steel Companies, 1918–1968: a History, 1968; The Trevelyan Scholarships, 1975; articles in Accountants Magazine and Accountancy. *Recreations:* gardening, reading, all games (now as a spectator). *Address:* Springwater Farm, Mudgley, Wedmore, Somerset BS28 4TY. *T:* Wedmore 713065.

*Died 24 Nov. 1986.*

**PEDERSEN, Charles John;** Du Pont Research Scientist, 1927–69, retired; *b* 10 March 1904; *s* of Brede Pedersen and Takino Yasui; *m* 1947, Susan Ault; two *d*. *Educ:* Univ. of Dayton (BScChemEng 1926); Massachusetts Inst. of Technology (MScOrgChem 1927). Du Pont Company: Research Chemist, Jackson Lab., 1927; Research Associate, 1947. Hon. MSc Glassboro State Coll., NJ, 1988. Delaware Sect. of ACS Award, 1968; (jtly) Nobel Prize for Chemistry, 1987. *Publications:* 25 papers in sci. jls, notably two landmark papers in Jl of ACS, 1967. *Recreations:* fishing, gardening, bird study, poetry. *Address:* 57 Market Street, Salem, NJ 08079, USA. *T:* 609/935–1724.

*Died 26 Oct. 1989.*

**PEDLEY, Prof. Robin;** Professor Emeritus, University of Southampton, since 1979; *b* 11 Aug. 1914; *s* of Edward and Martha Jane Pedley; *m* 1951, Jeanne Lesley Hitching, BA; one *s* one *d. Educ:* Richmond Sch., Yorks; Durham Univ. (MA, PhD, Teaching Dip.; Gibson Prize in Archaeology, Gladstone Meml Prize in Mod. Hist.). Research Fellow, Durham Univ., 1936–38; Teacher, Friends' Sch., Great Ayton, 1938–42, and Crossley and Porter Schs, Halifax, 1943–46. Lecturer: Coll. of St Mark and St John, Chelsea, 1946–47; Leicester Univ. Dept of Educn, 1947–63. Dir, Exeter Univ. Inst. of Educn, 1963–71; University of Southampton: Head of Sch. of Educn and Dean, Faculty of Educn, 1971–75; Head, Dept of Educn, 1976–79. *Publications:* Comprehensive Schools Today, 1955; Comprehensive Education: a new approach, 1956; The Comprehensive School, 1963, 3rd edn 1978; The Comprehensive School (with J. Orring, publ. in Hebrew, Jerusalem), 1966; Towards the Comprehensive University, 1977; many articles various educational jls. *Recreations:* sport, reading. *Address:* Annerley, Waters Green, Brockenhurst, Hants, SO4 7RG. *T:* Lymington 23001. *Died* 20 *Nov.* 1988.

**PEEL, Beatrice Gladys, (Lady Peel);** see Lillie, B. G.

**PEEL, The Lady Delia, (Adelaide Margaret),** DCVO 1950 (CVO 1947); *b* 1889; *d* of 6th Earl Spencer, KG; *m* 1914, Col Hon. Sir Sidney Cornwallis Peel, 1st and last Bt, CB, DSO, TD (*d* 1938). A Woman of the Bedchamber, 1939–50; an Extra Woman of the Bedchamber, 1950, to the Queen; to Queen Elizabeth the Queen Mother, 1952. *Address:* Barton Turf, Norwich NR12 8AU. *Died* 16 *Jan.* 1981.

**PEEL, Prof. Ronald Francis Edward Waite,** MBE 1945; MA (Cambridge) 1937; Professor of Geography, University of Bristol, 1957–77, later Emeritus; Dean of Science, 1968–70; *b* 22 Aug. 1912; *s* of late Albert Edward Peel, Bridgnorth, Shropshire, and Matilda Mary Peel (*née* Anderson), Helensburgh, Dunbartonshire; *m* 1938, Mary Annette Preston, MA Cantab, *o d* of H. Preston, Northampton; one *d. Educ:* Northampton Gram. Sch.; St Catharine's Coll., Cambridge (scholar). Lecturer in Geography, King's College, University of Durham, 1935–39; accompanied Brig. R. A. Bagnold, OBE, FRS, on exploring expedition in Libyan Desert, 1938. Served War of 1939–45, with RE; France, 1939–40; UK (staff appts), 1940–44; N Africa and Italy, 1944–45; UK, 1945. King's College, Newcastle, 1945–46; Department of Geography, Cambridge University, 1946, Lecturer in Geography, 1949; Prof. of Geography, University of Leeds, 1951–57, Head of Dept, 1953–57. Fellow of St Catharine's Coll., Cambridge, 1949. Cuthbert Peake Award of RGS, 1950; Livingstone Gold Medal, RSGS, 1979. Expeditions to Ruwenzori Mountains, 1952; W and C Sahara, 1961. President: Inst. British Geographers, 1965; Section E, British Assoc., 1967; Colston Research Soc., Bristol, 1973–76. FRGS, FRMetSoc. Editor, Geographical Jl, 1978–80. *Publications:* Physical Geography, 1951; (ed) Processes in Physical and Human Geography, 1975; (ed) Remote Sensing of Terrestrial Environment, 1976; articles on geographical subjects to technical jls, British and foreign. *Recreation:* travel. *Address:* 18 Porson Road, Cambridge. *Club:* Hawks (Cambridge). *Died* 21 *Sept.* 1985.

**PEILE, Vice-Admiral Sir Lancelot Arthur Babington,** KBE 1960; CB 1957; DSO 1941; LVO 1947; DL; retired; *b* 22 Jan. 1905; *s* of late Basil Wilson Peile and Katharine Rosamond (*née* Taylor); *m* 1928, Gertrude Margaret (*née* Tolcher); two *s. Educ:* RN Colleges, Osborne and Dartmouth. Commander (E) 1939; Captain (E), 1947; Rear-Admiral, 1955; Vice-Admiral, 1958. Asst Engineer-in-Chief, 1948; Command of RN Engineering College, 1951; idc 1954. Asst Director of Dockyards, 1955–57; Admiral Superintendent, Devonport Dockyard, 1957–60; retired, 1960. DL Devon, 1969. *Address:* Strawberry How, Thurlestone, Kingsbridge, Devon. *T:* Kingsbridge 560209. *Died* 7 *July* 1989.

**PEIRIS, Dr Mahapitage Velin Peter,** OBE 1956; *b* 28 July 1898; *s* of M. A. Peiris and H. D. Selestina, Panadura, Ceylon; *m* 1945, Edith Doreen Idona Carey, Negombo, Ceylon; three *s* one *d. Educ:* St John's Coll., Panadura; St Joseph's Coll., Colombo; Ceylon Medical Coll., Colombo. LMS Ceylon, 1926; MB, BS London, 1936; FRCS 1930; FICS 1957; FACS 1959. Served in Ceylon Army Med. Corps, 1930–45: Surg. to Mil. Hosps, Ceylon, 1940–45. Vis. Surgeon: Gen. Hosp., 1936–60; Children's Hosp., Colombo, 1951–60; Surg. to Orthop. Clinic, 1950–60; Cons. Orthop. Surg., Gen. Hosp., Colombo; Medico-Legal Adviser to Crown; Prof. of Surgery, Univ. of Ceylon, 1952–60. Senator, Ceylon Parlt, 1954–68: Minister of Health, 1960; Leader of Senate, and Minister of Commerce and Trade, 1965–68. Ambassador of Ceylon to USSR, 1968–69; High Comr for Ceylon in the UK, 1969–70. Mem. Coun., Univ. of Ceylon, 1960; President: Ceylon Med. Assoc., 1954; University Teachers' Assoc.; UNA of Ceylon, 1966–68. *Publications:* contribs to Indian and Ceylon medical jls. *Recreations:* swimming, photography. *Address:* 19 Beverley Court, Wellesley Road, W4 4LQ. *Died* 26 *April* 1988.

**PELHAM, Sir (George) Clinton,** KBE 1957; CMG 1949; FRGS; HM Ambassador to Czechoslovakia, 1955–57, retired; *b* 20 May 1898; *s* of George Pelham; *m* 1930, Jeanie Adelina Morton; two *d. Educ:* privately. Served European War, 1915–18. Foreign Office, 1920; China Consular Service, 1923; HM Trade Commissioner and Commercial Secretary for South China, 1933; Acting Consul-General, Madagascar, 1943; First Secretary (Commercial), Bagdad, 1945; Counsellor (Commercial), Bagdad, 1946; Counsellor (Commercial), Madrid, 1948–51; HM Ambassador to Saudi Arabia, 1951–55. County Councillor, West Sussex, 1963–70. *Recreations:* music, painting, travel. *Address:* Belcroute, Boughton Hall Avenue, Send, Surrey GU23 7DF. *Club:* Carlton.
*Died* 17 *June* 1984.

**PELLETIER, Wilfrid,** CC (Canada) 1967; CMG 1946; DM; *b* 20 June 1896; *m* 1936, Rose Bampton; two *s. Educ:* Montreal; Paris (France). Prix d'Europe, 1914; Assistant-conductor with Pierre Monteux, Albert Wolff and Louis Hasselmans at Metropolitan Opera House, New York City, 1916–19, Conductor, French and Italian Opera, to 1950; Ministère des Affaires Culturelles de la Province de Québec, 1942–70; Director Founder, Conservatoire de la Province de Québec, 1942–61. *Publication:* Une symphonie inachevée (autobiog.), 1972. *Recreations:* farm, collecting music manuscripts, autographs. *Address:* 322 East 57th Street, New York City, NY 10022, USA. *Cable:* Tierpelle Newyork. *Club:* Dutch Treat (New York City). *Died* 9 *April* 1982.

**PELLOE, Rev. Canon John Parker;** a Chaplain to the Queen, 1964–75; Hon. Canon of Ely Cathedral, 1952–53, and 1965–79; then Canon Emeritus; *b* 31 May 1905; *e s* of late Rev. E. P. Pelloe; *m* 1945, Kathleen, *d* of late Arthur Bland. *Educ:* Charterhouse; Queen's Coll., Oxford (MA); Cuddesdon Theological Coll. In business, 1922–32. Ordained 1936; Curate: St Columba, Sunderland, 1936–39; St Cuthbert, Kensington, 1939–42; Domestic Chaplain to Bishop of Ely, 1942–46; Vicar of Wisbech, 1946–60 (Rural Dean, 1946–53); Vicar of Stuntney, 1960–68; Archdeacon of Wisbech, 1953–64. *Recreation:* walking. *Address:* 14 Lynn Road, Ely, Cambs. *T:* Ely 2232. *Died* 23 *March* 1983.

**PELLY, Major Sir Alwyne;** see Pelly, Major Sir H. A.

**PELLY, Cornelius James,** CMG 1952; OBE 1944; *b* 8 April 1908; *e s* of Hyacinth Albert and Charity Mary Pelly, Benmore, Rushbrooke, Co. Cork, Eire; *m* 1949, Una O'Shea, *y d* of Patrick Seaborn O'Shea, Lismore, Co. Waterford; one *s* one *d. Educ:* Clongowes Wood Coll., Co. Kildare; Trinity Coll., Dublin. Entered Indian Civil Service by competitive examination, 1930; appointed to Punjab, 1931; Under-Secretary Punjab Government, 1935–36; transferred to Indian Political Service, 1936; Colonization Officer, Bahawalpur State, 1936–39; Political Agent and HM's Consul, Muscat, 1941–44; Consul, Bushire, 1946–47; Political Agent, Bahrain, 1947–51; Political Agent, Kuwait, 1951–55; Acting Political Resident, Persian Gulf, 1950 and 1952; Secretary for Financial Affairs, Sultanate of Muscat and Oman, 1968–70. *Address:* 12 Stokewater House, Beaminster, Dorset DT8 3LW. *Died* 26 *March* 1985.

**PELLY, Major Sir (Harold) Alwyne,** 5th Bt, *cr* 1840; MC 1918; 7th Hussars, retired; *b* 27 Aug. 1893; *e s* of Sir Harold Pelly, 4th Bt, and Anna (*d* 1939), *d* of Robert Poore, Old Lodge, Salisbury; *S* father, 1950; *m* 1917, Carol (*d* 1976), *d* of late R. Heywood-Jones of Badsworth Hall, Yorkshire; three *s* one *d* (and one *s* decd). *Educ:* Wellington Coll.; Merton Coll., Oxford. Served European War, France and Mesopotamia (MC); Instructor Cavalry Sch., Netheravon, and Equitation Sch., Weedon, 1920–24; Adjutant, Leicestershire Yeomanry, 1927–31; retired, 1935. *Heir:* *s* Major John Alwyne Pelly, Coldstream Guards [*b* 11 Sept. 1918; *m* 1950, Elsie May, *d* of late L. Thomas Dechow, Rhodesia; one *d*. Served War of 1939–45 (prisoner of war); DL, JP and High Sheriff (1970–71), Hants]. *Address:* Preshaw House, Upham, Southampton SO3 1HP. *T:* Bishops Waltham 2531. *Club:* Cavalry and Guards.
*Died* 22 *June* 1981.

**PENDRED, Air Marshal Sir Lawrence Fleming,** KBE 1954 (MBE 1933); CB 1947; DFC; DL; *b* 5 May 1899; *s* of Dr B. F. and Eleanor Pendred; *m* 1923, Nina Chour (*d* 1986); two *s. Educ:* Epsom Coll. Served European War, 1914–18, with RNAS and RAF in France, 1918; Permanent Commission RAF, 1920; served in Egypt and Turkey (208 Squadron), 1920–23; Flying Instructor, including 4 years at Central Flying School, 1924–30; Staff Officer Intelligence, Transjordan and Palestine, 1930–34; psa Andover, 1935; Sqdn Leader, 1935; Chief Flying Instructor, Montrose, 1936–37; Air Ministry, 1937–40; Wing Comdr, 1938; Bomber Station Commander, 1940–41, Group Captain; Chief Intelligence Officer, Bomber Command, 1942; Director of Intelligence, Air Ministry, 1943; Air Commodore, Chief Intelligence Officer, AEAF, 1944; Asst Comdt RAF, Staff Coll., 1944–45; AOC 227 Group, India, 1945; Director of Intelligence to Supreme Commander, South East Asia, 1946; acting Air Vice-Marshal, Dec. 1945; Air Vice-Marshal, 1948; Assistant Chief of Air Staff (Intelligence), 1947–49; Commandant, School of Land-Air Warfare, 1950–52; Air Officer

Commanding-in-Chief, Flying Training Command, 1952–55; retired, 1955. Regional Director Civil Defence (Midland), 1955–63. DL Warwickshire, 1959. Grand Officer Polonia Restituta; Commander, Legion of Merit. *Address:* 13 Lansdowne Circus, Leamington Spa, Warwicks. *T:* Leamington Spa 23559.
*Died 19 Sept.* 1986.

**PENGELLY, William Lister;** Master of Supreme Court of Judicature, Chancery Division, 1950–64; *b* 21 Dec. 1892; *s* of Frederick Charles Goldsworthy Pengelly; *m* 1919, Gwendolyn Emélie; two *d. Educ:* Varndean, Brighton; Culham Coll., Culham, Oxfordshire. Lady Aubrey Fletcher Exhib. for violin, Brighton School of Music, 1908. Solicitor, 1921; Senior Partner in Pengelly & Co., 8 New Court, Lincoln's Inn, WC2, solicitors, until 1950. Served European War, 1914–18; 2nd Lieut, 2/5 Devon Regt, 1914; Lieut, 1915; in Egypt, 1915–16; in Mesopotamia, 1916 and 1917 with 4th Devon Regt (wounded); Asst Adjutant with 4th (R) Devon Regt, 1918–19; Captain, 1919. War of 1939–45, Major and Supervising Military Liaison Officer (Z Sector), Home Guard. Chairman of The Comedy Club, 1932–59; Captain London Solicitors Golfing Society, 1950–51; Founder Royal Courts of Justice Music Club, 1953. Member Worshipful Company of Musicians; Freeman of the City of London. *Recreations:* music, bridge, croquet. *Address:* 11 West Hill Court, Budleigh Salterton, Devon. *Clubs:* Budleigh Salterton Bridge and Croquet. *Died 23 Nov.* 1983.

**PENHALIGON, David Charles;** MP (L) Truro since Oct. 1974; *b* 6 June 1944; *s* of late Robert Charles Penhaligon and of Sadie Jewell; *m* 1968, Annette Lidgey; one *s* one *d. Educ:* Truro Sch.; Cornwall Techn. College. CEng, MIMechE. R&D Engr, Holman Bros, Camborne, 1962–74. Liberal Party spokesman on employment, 1976–81, 1983–, on energy, 1979–82, on industry, 1981–83, and on the treasury, 1985–; Pres., Liberal Party, 1985–86. *Address:* 54 Daniell Road, Truro, Cornwall. *T:* Truro 70977. *Club:* National Liberal. *Died 22 Dec.* 1986.

**PENMAN, Most Rev. David John;** Archbishop of Melbourne and Metropolitan of the Province of Victoria, since 1984; *b* 8 Aug. 1936; *s* of John James and Irene May Penman; *m* 1962, Jean Frances (*née* Newson); one *s* three *d. Educ:* Keith St School, Wanganui, NZ; Intermediate School, Wanganui and Hutt Valley High Sch., NZ; Teachers' Coll., Wellington; Univ. of New Zealand (BA 1962); Christchurch Theol Coll. (LTh 1964); Univ. of Karachi, Pakistan (MA 1970, PhD 1977, Sociology and Islam). Teacher in Hutt Valley and Palmerston North, NZ, 1957–59; Asst Curate, Christ Church Anglican Church, Wanganui, 1961–64; Missionary work with NZ Church Missionary Soc. in W Asia and Middle East, 1965–75; Principal, St Andrew's Hall, CMS Federal Training Coll., Melbourne, Aust., 1976–79; Vicar of All Saints' Anglican Church, Palmerston North, NZ, 1979–82; a Bishop Coadjutor, Dio. Melbourne, 1982–84. President: Aust. Council of Churches; CCJ; Vice President: United Bible Socs; Aust. Fellowship of Evangelical Students. Trustee, AIDS Trust of Australia. Patron: Life Educn Centre; SCF; Overseas Service Bureau; Family Life; Parkinson's Disease Assoc. *Recreations:* sport, music, stamp collecting and reading. *Address:* Bishopscourt, 120 Clarendon Street, East Melbourne, Victoria 3002, Australia. *Died 1 Oct.* 1989.

**PENMAN, Gerard Giles,** MA, MD (Cantab), FRCS; Hon. Consulting Ophthalmic Surgeon, St Thomas' Hospital; Hon. Consulting Surgeon, Moorfields Eye Hospital; Consulting Ophthalmic Surgeon, Royal Hospital for Incurables, Putney; Fellow, Royal Society of Medicine and Hunterian Society; Member Opthalmological Society of the UK and Oxford Opthalmological Congress; *b* Port Elizabeth, 7 March 1899; *s* of late J. C. Penman and Grace Penman, Salisbury, Rhodesia, and Sherborne, Dorset; *m* 1928, Janet (*d* 1979), *d* of late Dr J. Walter Carr, CBE; three *s. Educ:* Sherborne Sch.; Pembroke Coll., Cambridge; St Thomas' Hospital. Royal Field Artillery, 1917–19; Ophthalmic Surgeon, Royal Northern Hospital, 1926–31; Ophthalmic Surgeon, Hospital for Sick Children, Great Ormond Street, 1931–36; Examiner in Ophthalmology, RCP, 1962–65. Vice-President: Dorset County Assoc. for the Blind; Sherborne Historical Soc. *Publications:* The Projection of the Retina in the Lateral Geniculate Body (with W. E. le Gros Clark) (Proceedings of the Royal Society, 1934); The Position occupied by the Peripheral Retinal Fibres at the Nerve Head (with E. Wolff) (Internat. Ophthalmological Congress, 1950), etc. *Recreations:* archaeology, philately. *Address:* c/o National Westminster Bank, 50 Cheap Street, Sherborne, Dorset DT9 3BH. *Died 21 Nov.* 1982.

**PENMAN, Dr Howard Latimer,** OBE 1962; FRS 1962; Head of Physics Department, Rothamsted Experimental Station, 1955–74; *b* 10 April 1909. Doctorate, Durham Univ., 1937. Has made physical studies of agricultural and botanical problems, particularly on transpiration and the irrigation of crops. Hon. FRMetS, 1978. *Publications:* Humidity (Monographs for Students, Inst. of Physics), 1955; Vegetation and Hydrology (Comm. Agric. Bur.), 1963. *Recreations:* music, golf. *Address:* 11A Kirkwick Avenue,

Harpenden, Herts AL5 2QU. *T:* Harpenden 3366.
*Died 13 Oct.* 1984.

**PENNELL, Montague Mattinson,** CBE 1970; FRS 1980; Deputy Chairman, 1975–79 and Managing Director, 1972–79, British Petroleum Co. Ltd; *b* 20 March 1916; *s* of F. M. S. Pennell; *m* 1945, Helen, *d* of Very Rev. Canon B. Williams, Dean of Grahamstown, S Africa, and Provost of Portsmouth; one *s* two *d. Educ:* Liverpool Univ. (BSc). Royal Corps of Signals, 1939–46; British Petroleum Co. Ltd, 1946–79, Iran, E Africa, Sicily, USA, Libya and London. Member: Adv. Council for R&D in Fuel and Power, 1972–78; Adv. Council for Applied R&D, 1976–79. Director: Standard Oil (Ohio), 1970–; BP Canada Inc., 1972–; Cadbury-Schweppes Ltd, 1979–; Brown Bros Corp. Ltd, 1980–. Pres., Welding Inst., 1979–. Hon. DSc Liverpool, 1980. *Address:* 52 Onslow Square, SW7 3NX; Rushdens Farm, Stanford Dingley, Berks. *Club:* MCC.
*Died 30 Dec.* 1981.

**PENNINGTON, Prof. Anne Elizabeth,** DPhil; Professor of Comparative Slavonic Philology, University of Oxford, since 1980; *b* 31 March 1934; *d* of Alan Mather Pennington and Janet Winifred Aitken, MA NZ. *Educ:* Simon Langton Girls' Grammar Sch.; Lady Margaret Hall, Oxford (MA, DPhil, Dip. in Slavonic Studies). Fellow and Tutor in Slavonic Languages, Lady Margaret Hall, Oxford, 1959–80. *Publications:* Vasko Popa, Collected Poems 1943–76 (trans.), 1978; Grigorij Kotošixin 'O Rossii v Carstvovanie Alekseja Mixajloviča', 1980; contrib. Oxford Slavonic Papers, Slavonic and E Eur. Rev., and Mod. Langs Rev. *Recreation:* Balkan dancing. *Address:* Lady Margaret Hall, Oxford OX2 6QA. *T:* Oxford 54353. *Died 27 May* 1981.

**PENNINGTON-RAMSDEN, Major Sir (Geoffrey) William,** 7th Bt, *cr* 1689; Major, Life Guards, retired; *b* 28 Aug. 1904; *yr* (but *o* surv.) *s* of Sir John Frecheville Ramsden, 6th Bt and Joan (*d* 1974), *d* of late G. F. Buxton, CB, Hoveton Hall; *S* father, 1958; assumed by deed poll, 1925, surname of Pennington in lieu of Ramsden; resumed surname of Ramsden after that of Pennington by deed poll, 1958; *m* 1927, Veronica Prudence Betty, *o d* of F. W. Morley, formerly of Biddestone Manor, Chippenham, Wilts; three *d. Educ:* Ludgrove; Eton; Jesus Coll., Cambridge (BA). Joined 11th Hussars, 1925; transferred Life Guards, 1927–38; served War of 1939–45; seconded to Provost Branch; APM 9th Armd Div. and APM 14th Army; Major, 1942. High Sheriff, Cumberland, 1962–63. *Heir: kinsman* Caryl Oliver Imbert Ramsden, CMG, CVO, *b* 4 April 1915. Address: Versions Farm, Brackley, Northants. *T:* Brackley 702412; Ardverikie, Newtonmore, Scotland; (seat) Muncaster Castle, Ravenglass, Cumbria. *T:* Ravenglass 203. *Club:* Lansdowne.
*Died 13 Jan.* 1986.

**PENNYBACKER, Joseph Buford,** CBE 1967; Director, Department of Neurological Surgery, Radcliffe Infirmary, Oxford, 1954–71; *b* 23 Aug. 1907; *s* of Claude Martin Pennybacker and Katherine Miller Mershon; *m* 1941, Winifrid Dean (*d* 1980); one *s. Educ:* Universities of Tennessee and Edinburgh. BA (Tennessee) 1926; MB, ChB (Edinburgh) 1930; FRCS 1935; MA (Oxon) 1938; MD Edinburgh 1941. Resident appointments: Royal Infirmary, Edinburgh; Grimsby District Hospital; National Hospital, Queen Square; First Asst, Neurosurgical Dept, London Hospital; First Asst to Nuffield Prof. of Surgery, University of Oxford. Cross of Royal Order of George I, Greece, 1966. *Publications:* papers in neurological and surgical journals. *Recreations:* history, horticulture. *Address:* Creagandarraich, Tighnabruaich, Argyll. *T:* Tighnabruaich 260. *Club:* Athenæum. *Died 27 March* 1983.

**PENNYCUICK, Rt. Hon. Sir John,** PC 1974; Kt 1960; Judge of High Court of Justice, Chancery Division, 1960–74, Vice-Chancellor, 1970–74; *b* 6 Nov. 1899; *s* of late Colonel John Pennycuick, CSI, and Georgiana Grace Pennycuick; *m* 1930, Lucy Johnstone (*d* 1972); one *s* one *d. Educ:* Winchester; New Coll., Oxford. 2nd Lieut, Coldstream Guards, 1919; BA Oxford, 1922; Barrister, Inner Temple, 1925; KC 1947; Bencher, 1954; Treasurer, 1978. *Address:* 2 Harcourt Buildings, Temple, EC4. *T:* 01-583 1815. *Clubs:* Garrick; All England Lawn Tennis (Wimbledon).
*Died 14 Jan.* 1982.

**PENROSE, Sir Roland (Algernon),** Kt 1966; CBE 1961; Chairman, Institute of Contemporary Arts, 1947–69, President, 1969–76 and 1980–83; *b* 14 Oct. 1900; *s* of James Doyle Penrose and Hon. Elizabeth Josephine Peckover; *m* 1st, 1925, Valentine Andrée Boué (*d* 1978); 2nd, 1947, Lee Miller (*d* 1977); one *s. Educ:* Leighton Park School, Reading; Queen's College, Cambridge. BA Cantab 1922; lived in France, studied and painted, 1922–35; returned to London, organised Internat. Surrealist Exhibition, 1936; painted and exhibited in London and Paris with Surrealist Group, 1936–39. Served War, 1940–45, WO Lecturer to Home Guard, 1940–42; commissioned Army, Gen. List, Capt. 1943–45. Founder, Inst. of Contemporary Arts; Fine Arts Officer, British Council, Paris, 1956–59; Member Fine Arts Panel: Brit. Council, 1955–79; Arts Coun., 1959–67; Trustee, Tate Gall., 1959–66; organised Exhibitions at Tate Gallery for Arts Council: Picasso, 1960; Max Ernst, 1962;

Miró, 1964; Picasso (sculpture), 1967. *Publications:* The Road is Wider than Long, 1939, rev. edn 1980; In the Service of the People, 1945; Picasso his Life and Work, 1958, 3rd rev. edn 1980; Portrait of Picasso, 1958, 2nd rev. edn 1980; Miró, 1970; (ed with John Golding) Picasso 1881–1973, 1973; Man Ray, 1975; Tàpies, 1978; Scrapbook 1900–1981, 1981. *Recreation:* gardening. *Address:* Farley Farm, Chiddingly, nr Lewes, E Sussex. *T:* Chiddingly 308. *Club:* Garrick. *Died* 23 April 1984.

**PENRUDDOCK, Sir Clement (Frederick),** Kt 1973; CBE 1954; Consultant with Lawrance, Messer & Co., Solicitors (Senior Partner, 1947–81); *b* 30 Jan. 1905; *s* of Rev. Frederick Fitzpatrick Penruddock and Edith Florence Smith; *m* 1945, Philippa Mary Tolhurst; one *s* two *d* (and one *d* decd). *Educ:* Marlborough Coll.; Keble Coll., Oxford. BA 1927. Admitted Solicitor, 1931. Sec., Chequers Trust, 1941–72. Chairman: Channel Islands & Internat. Investment Trust Ltd, 1960–; Granville Investment Trust Ltd, 1963–; Paten & Co. (Peterborough) Ltd, 1967–; Director: Save & Prosper Group Ltd, 1947–80; The Steetley Co. Ltd, 1951–75; Ocean Wilsons (Holdings) Ltd, 1955–; Lancashire & London Investment Trust Ltd, 1963–; The Scottish & Mercantile PLC, 1978–. Scottish Cities Investment Trust PLC, 1982–; *Recreations:* golf, ski-ing. *Address:* Venars, Nutfield, Redhill, Surrey RH1 4HS. *T:* Nutfield Ridge 2218, (office) 01–606 7691. *Clubs:* City, United Oxford & Cambridge University. *Died* 18 June 1988.

**PENTLAND, 2nd Baron,** *cr* 1909, of Lyth, Caithness; **Henry John Sinclair,** BA; Member American IEE, MICE, MIEE; Director: American British Electric Corporation (New York); Hunting Surveys Inc. (New York); *b* 6 June 1907; *o s* of 1st Baron and Lady Marjorie Gordon, DBE, JP (d 1970), *o d* of 1st Marquis of Aberdeen and *sister* of 2nd Marquis; *S* father, 1925; *m* 1941, Lucy Elisabeth, 3rd *d* of late Sir Henry Babington Smith, GBE, KCB, CH; one *d*. *Educ:* Cargilfield; Wellington; Trinity College, Cambridge; President, Cambridge Union Society, 1929; Asst Secretary Ministry of Production, and CPRB, Washington, 1944–45. *Address:* 131 East 66th Street, New York, NY 10021, USA.

*Died* 14 Feb. 1984 (*ext*).

**PENTNEY, Richard George;** Administrator, Legat School, Mark Cross, 1986–87; *b* 17 Aug. 1922; *s* of late Rev. A. F. Pentney, MC; *m* 1953, Elisabeth, *d* of Sir Eric Berthoud, KCMG; four *d*. *Educ:* Kingswood School, Bath; St John's Coll., Cambridge. Mem., Univ. Cricket and Hockey XIs. RNVR (Lieut), 1942–46. Asst Master, Sedbergh School, 1947–58; Headmaster, St Andrew's Coll., Minaki, Tanzania, 1958–64; Asst Master, Oundle School, 1964–65; Headmaster, King's Coll., Taunton, 1965–69; Sec. for Appeals, St Christopher's Fellowship, 1969–70; Commoner Fellow, St John's Coll., Cambridge, 1970; Dir, Attlee House, Toynbee Hall, 1970–73; employed by Kent Social Services Cttee, 1981–86. *Recreations:* cooking, water-colour painting. *Address:* Kessnock House, Battle, E Sussex TN33 0LY. *Died* 19 May 1990.

**PENTREATH, Rev. Canon Arthur Godolphin Guy Carleton,** MA (Cantab); Residentiary Canon, Rochester Cathedral, 1959–65, Emeritus, 1965; Headmaster of Cheltenham College, 1952–59, retired; *b* 30 March 1902; *s* of late Reverend Dr A. G. Pentreath, Royal Army Chaplains' Department, and Helen Guy Carleton, County Cork; *m* 1927, Margaret Lesley Cadman (*d* 1980); two *s* one *d*. *Educ:* Haileybury College; Magdalene College, Cambridge. (Classical Scholar), 1st class Hon. with distinction in Classical Archæology, Class. Tripos Part II. Westcott House, Cambridge, 1925–26. Master at Oundle School, 1927; Deacon, 1928; Priest, 1929; Chaplain and Master at Michaelhouse School, Natal, 1928–30; Master of the King's Scholars, Westminster School, 1930–34; Headmaster St Peter's College, Adelaide, S Australia, 1934–43; Headmaster of Wrekin College, 1944–51. Hon. Sec., Hellenic Travellers' Club, 1958–82, retd. *Publication:* Hellenic Traveller, 1964. *Address:* Wooden Walls, Dock Lane, Beaulieu, Hants. *T:* Beaulieu 612348. *Died* 30 Oct. 1985.

**PEPPER, Claude Denson;** Member of United States House of Representatives, former United States Senator (Democrat); *b* Dudleyville, Alabama, USA, 8 Sept. 1900; *s* of Joseph Wheeler Pepper and Lena (*née* Talbot); *m* 1936, Irene Mildred Webster (*d* 1979), St Petersburg, Fla; no *c*. *Educ:* University of Alabama (AB); Harvard Law School (JD, Phi Beta Kappa). Served with Armed Forces, 1918. Instr in Law, Univ. of Arkansas, 1924–25. Admitted to Alabama Bar, 1924; Florida Bar, 1925; practised law at Perry, Fla, 1925–30; House Mem. Fla State Legislature, 1929; practised law, Tallahassee, Fla, 1930–37; Mem. State Bd of: Public Welfare, 1931–32; Law Examiners, 1933–34; US Senator from Fla, 1936–51; Mem., various cttees; Chm., Middle East Sub-Cttee of Senate Foreign Relations Cttee (12 yrs) etc.; Chm. Fla Delegation to Dem. Nat. Convention, 1940–44; subseq. alternate Delegate, 1948, 1952, 1956, 1960, 1964, Delegate, 1968 and five succeeding Conventions. Elected to: 88th Congress, 1962; 89th Congress, 1964; 90th Congress, 1966 (without opposition); 91st Congress, 1968; 92nd Congress, 1970; 93rd Congress, 1972; 94th Congress, 1974; 95th Congress,

1976; 96th Congress, 1978; 97th Congress, 1980; 98th Congress, 1982; 99th Congress, 1984; 100th Congress, 1986; 101st Congress, 1988; Member: (88th Congress) House Cttee on Banking and Currency, and sub cttees on Domestic Finance, Internat. Trade, and Internat. Finance; (89th–101st Congresses) House Rules Cttee (Chm., 98th–101st Congresses); 1st Chm. (91st and 92nd Congress) House Select Cttee on Crime, Cttee on Internal Security; Chm. (95th, 96th and 97th Congress) House Select Cttee on Aging; Chm. (94th–101st Congresses) Sub-Cttee on Health and Long Term Care. Member: American Bar Assoc.; International Bar Association, etc. Counsel, Mershon, Sawyer, Johnston, Dunwody & Cole, Miami, Fla; Mary and Albert Lasker Public Service Award, 1967; various other awards. Holds 16 hon. degrees. Member, American Legion; Baptist; Mason; Shriner; Elk; Moose, Kiwanian. *Publications:* Pepper: Eyewitness to a Century; contributor to periodicals. *Recreations:* hunting, golf, swimming. *Address:* (home) 2121 North Bayshore Drive, Miami, Florida 33137, USA; 4201 Cathedral Avenue, NW, Washington, DC 20016, USA; (offices) 2239 Rayburn House Office Building, Washington, DC 20515. *Clubs:* Harvard, Jefferson Island, Army-Navy, Columbia Country, Burning Tree, etc (Washington); Miami, Bankers (Miami); various country (Florida). *Died* 30 May 1989.

**PEPPER, Brig. Ernest Cecil,** CMG 1967; CBE 1943 (OBE 1940); DSO 1944; *b* 3 Oct. 1899; *s* of W. E. Pepper, The Manor House, Nocton, Lincs; *m* 1929, Margaret, *d* of A. W. Allan, MD, Seacroft, Lincs; two *s*. *Educ:* Royal Military College, Sandhurst. Worcestershire Regt, Aug. 1918; India, 1925; ADC to Governor of UP, 1925–26; China, 1928; promoted Bedfordshire Regt, 1930; Adj. 1931; Staff College, 1935–36; Bde Major, Chatham, 1937–39; GSO2, France, 1939–40; GSO1, War Office, 1940–41; Bn Comdr, 1941–42; BGS Africa, 1942–43; BGS Washington, 1943–44; Brigade-Commander, Normandy, 1944–45; Comdt, School of Infantry, 1945; retd pay at own request, 1946. Warden, Dominion Students Hall Trust, 1945–70. Bd of Governors: Church of England Children's Society (Waifs and Strays); Victoria League. DL County of London, later Greater London, 1948–76. *Publication:* A Place to Remember, 1970. *Recreations:* cricket, golf. *Address:* Flat 1, Nutcombe Height, Portsmouth Road, Hindhead, Surrey. *T:* Hindhead 4644. *Died* 3 Aug. 1981.

**PEPPERCORN, Trevor Edward,** BA Oxon; *b* 4 June 1904; *s* of late William and Kate Peppercorn; *m* 1st, 1935, Sheila (*d* 1972), *d* of F. W. Ayre, St John's Newfoundland; one *s*; 2nd, 1977, Mary Gertrude (*née* Cumming), widow of L. G. Williamson. *Educ:* Beaumont College; Balliol College, Oxford. Dunlop Rubber Co. Ltd, 1928; Dunlop Rubber Co. (India) Ltd, 1929; Dunlop South Africa Ltd, 1940 (Managing Director, 1943–52); Director, Dunlop Rubber Co. Ltd, 1957–76; Dir, Triplex Holdings, 1966–77 (Chm., 1966–75); Chairman: Weldall Engineering Ltd, 1971–77; Fibreglass-Pilkington Ltd, Bombay, 1972–77. Chm., Overseas Develt Inst., 1967–72. *Recreations:* gardening, shooting. *Address:* The Grange, Yattendon, Newbury, Berks. *Died* 15 Jan. 1984.

**PEPPIATT, Sir Kenneth Oswald,** KBE 1941; MC; *b* 25 March 1893; *s* of late W. R. Peppiatt; *m* 1929, Pamela, *d* of late Captain E. W. Carter, MC; two *s* one *d*. *Educ:* Bancrofts. Entered service of Bank of England, 1911; Principal of Discount Office, 1928–34; Chief Cashier, 1934–49; Exec. Dir, 1949–57. Dir, Coutts and Co., 1958–69. Fellow, Inst. of Bankers. Hon. Treasurer, Army Benevolent Fund, 1949–64. Served European War 1914–18, retd rank Major (despatches, MC and Bar, twice wounded). *Recreations:* racing, fishing. *Address:* 7 Harvey Orchard, Beaconsfield, Bucks. *T:* Beaconsfield 3158. *Died* 12 May 1983.

**PERCIVAL, Edgar Wikner,** CEng, FRAeS, FIMechE, FIMarE, MSAE, MIAeE, AFIAeS, FRSA; formerly engaged on Research and Design for national purposes; Founder, Percival Aircraft Ltd, Aircraft Manufacturers (formerly Chairman, Managing Director and Chief Designer); formerly Director: Valbank Ltd; Percival Power Units Ltd; *b* Albury, New South Wales, 23 Feb. 1897; *s* of late William and Hilda Percival, Clarendon Park, Richmond, NSW; unmarried. *Educ:* Sydney Tech. Coll.; Sydney Univ. Served 7th Australian Light Horse, 60 Sqdn RFC and founder member 111 Sqdn RFC, RAF, 1914–18; RAFO, 1929–39; RAFVR, 1939–45; formerly Air Ministry approved test pilot on flying boats, seaplanes and land planes; is the first to have produced low-wing cantilever monoplanes in British Commonwealth; winner of numerous Air races and trophies, both national and international; won Melbourne Herald Air Race, Melbourne-Geelong-Melbourne, 1923; has flown fastest time in King's Cup Air Races for 5 years; holds record for fastest time ever flown in King's Cup; designed, built and flew man-carrying gliders, Richmond, Aust., 1910–11; designed and built: King's Cup Air Race winners for the 3 consecutive years prior to world war II, and winners for 3 years since War; Saro-Percival Mail Plane, 1930; Percival Gull, 1931–32; Percival Mew Gull (first civil aircraft in British Commonwealth to have a speed of over 200 m.p.h.), 1933; Vega Gull, Q6 and Proctor; first aeroplane in British Empire to carry 1000 pounds load for 1000 miles range; a group of lakes discovered in Australia in 1934 was named Percival Lakes in his honour; first person to have flown to Africa and back in a day (1935); winner of Johnstone Memorial Trophy and of Oswald Watt Memorial Gold Medal; three times winner of International Speed Trophy. By enactment in 1948 of US Senate Bill specifically for him, he became a permanent resident of US; this was in recognition of his valuable research work in US on high-altitude flying; he is allowed the exceptional privilege of unlimited periods of stay, at his option, outside US. Founder Mem. Guild of Air Pilots and Air Navigators; formerly Mem., Institute of Directors. Mem., Lloyd's of London, 1944–83. *Address:* Coker Wood Cottage, Pendomer, near Yeovil, Som BA22 9PD. *T:* Corscombe 328.

*Died 21 Jan. 1984.*

**PERCIVAL, George Hector,** MD, PhD, FRCPE, DPH; Professor Emeritus of Dermatology, University of Edinburgh (Grant Professor, 1946); *b* 1901; *s* of late E. J. Percival, Kirkcaldy; *m* 1937, Kathleen, *d* of late John Dawson, MD, Buckhaven; one *s* one *d*. *Educ:* George Watson's Coll., Edinburgh; Univs of Edinburgh and Paris. Physician to the Skin Dept, Edinburgh Royal Infirmary, 1936. *Publications:* An Introduction to Dermatology; The Histopathology of the Skin; scientific articles in British Med. Journ., Lancet, etc., Encyclopædia of Med., System of Bacteriology (Med. Res. Council). *Recreations:* golf, fishing. *Address:* Woodcroft, Barnton Avenue, Edinburgh EH4 6JJ. *T:* 031-336 2438.

*Died 3 April 1983.*

**PERCY, Lord Richard Charles;** Lecturer, Department of Zoology, in the University of Newcastle upon Tyne, 1951–86; *b* 11 February 1921; *s* of 8th Duke of Northumberland and Lady Helen Gordon-Lennox (who *d* 1965, as Dowager Duchess of Northumberland, GCVO, CBE); *m* 1st, 1966, Sarah Jane Elizabeth Norton (*d* 1978), *o d* of Mr and Mrs Petre Norton, La Charca, Coin, Malaga, Spain; two *s*; 2nd, 1979, Hon. Mrs Clayre Ridley, 2nd *d* of 4th Baron Stratheden and Campbell, CBE. *Educ:* Eton; Christ Church, Oxford; Durham University. BSc. Lieut-Colonel Comdg Northumberland Hussars, TA, 1959–61; late Capt. Gren. Guards. Served War, 1941–45. DL Northumberland, 1968. *Address:* Lesbury House, Alnwick, Northumberland NE66 3PT. *T:* Alnmouth 830330; 212 Lambeth Road, SE1. *T:* 01–928 3441. *Clubs:* Turf; Northern Counties (Newcastle upon Tyne).

*Died 20 Dec. 1989.*

**PEREIRA, Marguerite Scott,** MD; Consultant, Fundação Oswaldo Cruz, Rio de Janeiro; *b* 29 July 1921; *d* of Dr William McDonald Scott and Alice Clotilde Mollard Scott; *m* 1946, Dr Helio Gelli Pereira, FRS; one *s* one *d* (and one *d* decd). *Educ:* James Allens Girls' Sch., Dulwich; Univ. of Aberdeen (MB, ChB, MD). Bacteriologist, Univ. of Manchester, 1944–46; Clinical Pathologist, Rio de Janeiro, 1947–49; Dir, Public Health Laboratory, Salisbury, 1954–57; Sen. Bacteriologist, Virus Reference Lab., and Dir, WHO Nat. Influenza Centre for England and Wales, 1957–69; Co-Dir, WHO Collaborating Centre for Reference and Research on Influenza, 1975–86; Dir, Virus Reference Lab., PHLS, 1970–86. *Publications:* mostly on medical virology and epidemiology, espec. influenza and respiratory disease. *Recreation:* reading. *Address:* 3 Ducks Walk, Twickenham, Mddx. *T:* 01–892 4511.

*Died 17 Aug. 1987.*

**PERHAM, Dame Margery,** DCMG 1965; CBE 1948; FBA 1961; DLitt Oxon; Hon. Fellow of Nuffield College since 1963; *b* 6 Sept. 1895. *Educ:* St Stephens Coll., Windsor; St Anne's Sch., Abbots Bromley; St Hugh's College, Oxford, Modern History. Assistant Lecturer in History, Sheffield University; in Somaliland, 1922–23; Fellow and Tutor in Modern History and Modern Greats, St Hugh's College, Oxford, 1924–29; Rhodes Travelling Fellowship for travel and study of administration of coloured races in N America, Polynesia, Australia, Africa, 1929–31, and in West Africa, 1931–32; Research Fellow St Hugh's College, Oxford, 1930–39; Official Fellow, Nuffield College, 1939–63; Reader in Colonial Administration in the University of Oxford, 1939–48; Director of Oxford Univ. Institute of Colonial Studies, 1945–48. Rockefeller Travelling Fellowship of Int. Inst. of African Languages and Culture for travel and study in E Africa and Sudan, 1932; Research Lecturer in Colonial Administration, Oxford, 1935–39; Vice-Chairman, Oxford University Summer School of Colonial Administration, 1937–38; Member: Advisory Committee on Education in the Colonies, 1939–45; Higher Education Commission and West Indies Higher Education Cttee, 1944; Exec. Cttee of Inter-University Council on Higher Education Overseas, 1946–67; Colonial Social Science Research Council, 1947–61. Editor, Colonial and Comparative Studies, 1946–. Chairman, Oxford University Colonial Records Project, 1963–73. Reith Lecturer, BBC 1961; President, Universities' Mission to Central Africa, 1963–64. Mem., Amer. Acad. of Arts and Sciences, 1969. Hon. Fellow: St Hugh's College, Oxford, 1962; Makerere College, Uganda, 1963; School of Oriental and African Studies, 1964; Hon. LLD St Andrews Univ., 1952; Hon. DLitt: Southampton University, 1962; London University, 1964; Birmingham, 1969; Hon. LittD, Cambridge, 1966. Gold Wellcome Medal (Royal Africa Soc.). *Publications:* Major Dane's

Garden, 1924; Josie Vine, 1925, new edn 1970; The Protectorates of South Africa (with Lionel Curtis), 1935; Ten Africans (ed), 1936; Native Administration in Nigeria, 1937; Africans and British Rule, 1941; African Discovery (with J. Simmons), 1943; Race and Politics in Kenya (with E. Huxley), 1944; The Government of Ethiopia, 1948, rev. edn 1969; Lugard—The Years of Adventure, 1956; The Diaries of Lord Lugard, 1889–1892 (ed with Mary Bull), 1959; Lugard—The Years of Authority, 1960; The Colonial Reckoning, The Reith Lectures for 1961, 1962; Colonial Sequence, Vol. I, 1967, Vol. II, 1970; African Apprenticeship, 1974; East African Journey, 1976; also articles in The Times, Africa, etc. *Relevant publication:* Essays in Imperial Government presented to Margery Perham, 1963. *Died 19 Feb. 1982.*

**PERKINS, Dexter;** Professor Emeritus, University of Rochester, USA, also of Cornell University; President, Salzburg Seminar in American Studies, 1950–62; Prof. of History from 1922 and Chairman, Department of History, 1925–54, University of Rochester; John L. Senior Prof. of American Civilization, Cornell University, 1954–59; City Historian of City of Rochester, 1936–48; *b* 20 June 1889; *s* of Herbert William Perkins and Cora Farmer, Boston, Mass; *m* 1918, Wilma Lois Lord, Rochester, NY; two *s*. *Educ:* Boston Latin School and Sanford School, Redding Ridge, Conn; Harvard University (AB 1909, PhD 1914). Instructor in history, Univ. of Cincinnati, 1914–15; instructor and asst prof. history, Univ. of Rochester, 1915–22; lecturer on Commonwealth Fund at University College, London, 1937; secretary of American Historical Assoc., 1928–39. Served as 1st lieut, later captain, inf. USA, 1918; attached to historical section, GHQ, Chaumont, France, Oct. 1918–Feb. 1919; work connected with the Peace Conf., Feb.–June 1919; gave Albert Shaw Lectures on Diplomatic History at Johns Hopkins Univ., 1932 and 1937; Professor of American History and Institutions, Cambridge Univ., 1945–46, MA Camb. 1946. Official historian for Overseas Branch of Office of War Information for San Francisco Conf. Lectures, Nat. War College, US, 1946–; Lectures, British Universities and RIIA, 1948 and 1952; Visiting Professor, University of Uppsala 1949; Chm. Council, Harvard Foundation for Advanced Study and Research, Harvard Univ., 1951–56. LLD, Union Coll., 1951, LittD, Harvard, 1953. Moderator of Unitarian Churches of US and Canada, 1952–54; Pres., Amer. Hist. Assoc., 1955–56. Pres., Salzburg Seminar in Amer. Studies, 1950–62. Member of Phi Beta Kappa. *Publications:* John Quincy Adams as Secretary of State; The Monroe Doctrine, 1823–26, 1927; The Monroe Doctrine, 1826–67, 1933; The Monroe Doctrine, 1867–1907, 1938; Hands Off! A History of the Monroe Doctrine, 1823–1940, 1941; America and Two Wars, 1944; The United States and the Caribbean, 1947; The Evolution of American Foreign Policy, 1948; The American Approach to Foreign Policy, 1952; The History of The Monroe Doctrine (revised edn, 1955); Charles Evans-Hughes and American Democratic Statesmanship, 1956; Short Biography of Charles Evans Hughes; The New Age of Franklin Roosevelt, 1957; The American Way, 1957; The American Quest for Peace, 1960; The United States and Latin America, 1960; The United States of America: A History (with G. G. Van Deusen), 1962; The American Democracy: its rise to power, 1964; The Yield of the Years, 1969. *Recreations:* bridge and Russian Bank. *Address:* The Brightonian, 1919 Elmwood Avenue, Rochester, NY 14620, USA. *Died 12 May 1984.*

**PERKINS, (George) Dudley (Gwynne),** MA; Director-General of the Port of London Authority, 1964–71; *b* 19 March 1911; *s* of Gwynne Oliver Perkins and Sarah Perkins; *m* 1st, 1939, Enid Prys-Jones (*d* 1943); one *d*; 2nd, 1946, Pamela Marigo Blake (*d* 1980); one *d*. *Educ:* Clifton College (Scholar); King's College, Cambridge (Choral Scholar; 1st cl. hons Eng. Lit.). Solicitor, 1937; Asst Legal Adviser, BBC, 1945–48; Asst Legal Adviser, National Coal Board, 1948–51; Chief Solicitor, PLA, 1955–62; Jt Dep. General Manager, PLA, 1962–64. Member: Council of Law Society, 1954–62; Central Transport Consultative Cttee, 1962–69; SE/ Economic Planning Council, 1966–71; Performing Right Tribunal, 1974–. Governor, Clifton Coll., 1969–. FCIT; FBIM. Regular broadcaster in Can I Help You and other broadcasts on law and current affairs, 1950–62. *Publications:* Can I Help You, 1959; Family Lawyer, 1962. *Recreations:* music, walking. *Address:* 4 Victoria Court, Durdham Park, Clifton, Bristol BS6 6XS. *T:* Bristol 732504. *Clubs:* Garrick, MCC. *Died 15 April 1986.*

**PERKINS, John Bryan W.;** *see* Ward-Perkins.

**PERKINS, Air Vice-Marshal Maxwell Edmund Massy,** CB 1962; CBE 1957; Director of Engineering, Aviation Division, Smiths Industries Ltd, retired; *b* Portsmouth, Hants, 22 Aug. 1907; *s* of late Donald Maxwell Perkins; *m* 1st, 1934, Helena Joan Penelope (*d* 1973), *d* of Herbert John Newberry, Hitchin; one *s* two *d*; 2nd, 1974, Sylvia Mary, *widow* of Willson Gatward, Hitchin, Herts. *Educ:* Portsmouth College; London University (BA). Entered RAF, 1929; 13 Sqdn, 1930–32; India, 1934–38. Served War of 1939–45, Bomber Command and Burma; America, 1952–54; STSO Fighter Command, 1954–56; Commandant, St Athan, 1956–58; Senior

Technical Staff Officer, Bomber Command, 1958–61; Dir-Gen. of Engineering, Air Min., 1961–64, retired. Air Cdre, 1957; Air Vice-Marshal, 1961. CEng 1966, FIMechE (MIMechE 1957); FRAeS 1960. Co. Councillor, Herts, 1977–81. *Recreations:* sailing, golf. *Address:* Little Court, London Road, Hitchin, Herts. *Clubs:* Royal Air Force; Letchworth Golf. *Died 9 Aug.* 1985.

**PERKINS, Sir (Walter) Robert (Dempster),** Kt 1954; *b* 1903; *s* of late W. Frank Perkins; *m* 1944, Lady Norman (*d* 1987), *widow* of Sir Nigel Norman, 2nd Bt. *Educ:* Eton; Trinity Coll., Cambridge, MA. Mechanical Engineer. MP (C) Stroud (by-election May), 1931–45; MP (C) Stroud and Thornbury Division of Gloucestershire, 1950–55; Parliamentary Secretary, Ministry of Civil Aviation, 1945. Vice-Pres., BALPA, 1937–73, Pres. 1973–76. *Recreations:* aviation and fishing. *Address:* The Manor House, Downton, Salisbury, Wilts SP5 3PU. *Died 8 Dec.* 1988.

**PEROWNE, Maj.-Gen. Lancelot Edgar Connop Mervyn,** CB 1953; CBE 1945; Royal Engineers, retired; Company Director, retired; *b* 11 June 1902; 2nd and *o* surv. *s* of late Colonel Woolrych Perowne; *m* 1927, Gertrude Jenny Johanna Stein, Cologne, Germany; one *d.* *Educ:* Wellington Coll.; RMA, Woolwich. 2nd Lieut, RE, 1923; Temp. Brig., 1942; Col, 1945; Brig., 1951; Temp. Maj.-Gen., 1951; Maj.-Gen., 1952. Served France, 1940 (despatches); comd 69 and 37 AA Bdes, AA Comd, 1942–43; 23 Inf. Bde, India and Burma, 1943–45 (despatches, CBE); Penang Sub-Area and 74 Indian Inf. Bde, SE Asia, 1945–46 (despatches); 72 Inf. Bde, India, 1946–47; Comdt School of Combined Operations, 1947–48; comd 151 Northumberland and Durham Inf. Bde, TA, 1949–51; Commander British Military Mission to Greece, 1951–52; South Malaya District, 17th Gurkha Division, 1952–55 (despatches); Maj.-Gen., The Brigade of Gurkhas, 1952–55, retired 1955. Colonel, The Gurkha Engineers, 1957–66. CEng; MIEE; KJStJ 1945; Star of Nepal (2nd Class), 1954. *Address:* Benfleet Hall, Green Lane, Cobham, Surrey KT11 2NN. *Died 24 March* 1982.

**PEROWNE, Stewart Henry,** OBE 1944; KStJ 1956; FSA; FRSA; Orientalist and Historian; Colonial Administrative Service (retired); *b* 17 June 1901; 3rd *s* of late Arthur William Thomson Perowne, DD, Bishop of Worcester, and late Helena Frances Oldnall-Russell; *m* 1947, Freya Madeline Stark (later Dame Freya Stark, DBE) (marr. diss. 1952). *Educ:* Haileybury Coll. (champion sprinter); Corpus Christi Coll., Cambridge (Hon. Fellow, 1981); Harvard Univ., USA. BA 1923, MA 1931, Cambridge. Joined Palestine Government Education Service, 1927; Administrative Service, 1930 (Press Officer 1931); Asst District Commissioner, Galilee, 1934; Asst Secretary Malta, 1934 (pioneered Pasteurization); Political Officer, Aden Prot., 1937; recovered inscriptions and sculpture from Imadia and Beihan; Arabic Programme Organiser, BBC, 1938 (pioneered programme, English by Radio); Information Officer, Aden, 1939; Public Relations Attaché, British Embassy, Baghdad, 1941; Oriental Counsellor, 1944; Colonial Secretary, Barbados, 1947–51; seconded as Principal Adviser (Interior), Cyrenaica, 1950–51; retired 1951. Discovered ancient city of Aziris, 1951. Adviser, UK delegation to UN Assembly, Paris, Nov. 1951. Helped design stamps for Malta, 1936, Aden, 1938, Barbados, 1949, Libya, 1951; currency notes for W. Indies Federation, 1949, and Libya, 1951; Assistant to the Bishop in Jerusalem for Refugee work, 1952; designer and supervisor of Refugee model villages. FSA 1957. Coronation Medal, 1937; Iraq Coronation Medal, 1953; Metropolitan Police Mounted Officers certificate. Member, C. of E. Foreign Relations Council. *Publications:* The One Remains, 1954; Herod the Great, 1956; The Later Herods, 1958; Hadrian, 1960; Cæsars and Saints, 1962; The Pilgrim's Companion in Jerusalem and Bethlehem, 1964; The Pilgrim's Companion in Roman Rome, 1964; The Pilgrim's Companion in Athens, 1964; Jerusalem, 1965; The End of the Roman World, 1966; The Death of the Roman Republic: from 146 BC to the birth of the Roman Empire, 1969; Roman Mythology, 1968, rev. edn 1983; (contrib.) Ancient Cities of the Middle East, 1970; The Siege within the Walls: Malta 1940–43, 1970; Rome, 1971; The Journeys of St Paul, 1973; The Caesars' Wives, 1974; The Archaeology of Greece and the Aegean, 1974; Holy Places of Christendom, 1976; articles in Encyclopædia Britannica, The Times, History Today, etc. *Recreations:* horses, the arts, archæology. *Address:* Vicarage Gate House, Vicarage Gate, W8 4AQ. *T:* 01–229 1907. *Clubs:* Travellers'; Casino (1852) Malta; Savannah (Bridgetown); Phoenix-SK (Harvard).
*Died 10 May* 1989.

**PERRIN, Sir Michael (Willcox),** Kt 1967; CBE 1952 (OBE 1946); FRSC; Chairman, The Wellcome Foundation Ltd, 1953–70; Director: Inveresk Research International, 1961–74 (Chairman, 1971–73); Radiochemical Centre Ltd, 1971–75; *b* 13 Sept. 1905; *s* of late Bishop W. W. Perrin; *m* 1934, Nancy May, *d* of late Bishop C. E. Curzon; one *s* one *d. Educ:* Winchester; New Coll., Oxford (BA, BSc). Post-graduate research, Toronto Univ. (MA), 1928–29; Amsterdam Univ., 1929–33; ICI (Alkali) Research Dept, Northwich, 1933–38; Asst Director, Tube Alloys (Atomic Energy), DSIR, 1941–46; Dep. Controller, Atomic Energy (Technical Policy),

Ministry of Supply, 1946–51; Research Adviser, ICI, 1951–52. Chm. (Treasurer) Bd of Governors, St Bartholomew's Hosp. and Pres., Med. Coll. of St Bartholomew's Hosp., 1960–69; Member: Council, Royal Veterinary Coll., London Univ., 1967–76 (Chm. 1967–72); Council, Sch. of Pharmacy, London Univ., 1963–76; Central Adv. Council for Science and Technology, 1969–70; Governing Body, British Postgrad. Med. Fedn, 1970–77 (Chm., 1972–77). Trustee, British Museum (Natural History), 1974–83. Chm. Council, Roedean Sch., 1974–79. Hon. DSc Univ. of British Columbia, 1969. *Publications:* papers in scientific and technical journals. *Address:* 14 Christchurch Hill, Hampstead, NW3 1LB. *T:* 01–794 3064. *Club:* Athenæum. *Died 18 Aug.* 1988.

**PERRINS, Wesley,** MBE 1952; former official of Municipal and General Workers' Union, Birmingham District Secretary; Member, Worcestershire County Council until 1974 (formerly Alderman); formerly Member, West Midlands Economic Planning Council; *b* 21 Sept. 1905; *s* of Councillor Amos Perrins, Stourbridge; *m* 1932, Mary, *d* of Charles Evans; one *s* one *d. Educ:* Wollescote Council Sch.; Upper Standard Sch., Lye. MP (Lab) Yardley Division of Birmingham, 1945–50. Member of: Lye & Wollescote UDC, 1928–31; Stourbridge Borough Council, 1931–46, 1971. Mem., Court of Governors, Birmingham Univ., 1967–74. Hon. Alderman, Dudley MBC, 1982. *Address:* Cromlech Cottage, 19 Walker Avenue, Wollescote, Stourbridge, West Midlands DY9 9EB. *T:* Stourbridge (0384) 394640. *Died 12 Jan.* 1990.

**PERROTT, Sir Donald (Cyril Vincent),** KBE 1949; *b* 12 April 1902; *s* of late Frederick John Perrott and of Alice Perrott, Southampton; *m* 1st, 1925, Marjorie May (*d* 1969), *d* of late William Holway, Taunton; one *s*; 2nd, 1969, Mrs L. L. Byre. *Educ:* Tauntons' Sch., Southampton; University College, Southampton. Inland Revenue Dept, 1920; Ministry of Aircraft Production, 1941; Ministry of Supply, 1942; Dep. Secretary Ministry of Food, 1947–49; Deputy Chairman, Overseas Food Corporation, 1949–51; Chairman: Queensland British Food Corporation, 1950–53; British Ministry of Supply, European Purchasing Commission, 1951–52; Interdepartmental Cttee, Woolwich Arsenal, 1953; Secretary, Department of Atomic Energy, 1954 and Member for Finance and Administration of Atomic Energy Authority, 1954–60; Member, Governing Board of National Institute for Research in Nuclear Science, 1957–60. *Recreations:* golf and bridge. *Address:* 5 Plane Tree House, Duchess of Bedford's Walk, W8 7QT.
*Died 13 June* 1985.

**PERRY, Hon. Sir (Alan) Clifford,** Kt 1976; Senior Puisne Judge, Supreme Court of New Zealand, 1976–79 (Judge, 1962); *b* 10 July 1907; *s* of George Perry and Agnes Mary Jenkins; *m* 1943, Barbara Jean Head; two *s* one *d. Educ:* Hornby Primary Sch.; Christ's Coll., Christchurch; Canterbury University Coll., Univ. of NZ (LLM, 2nd Cl. Hons). Admitted barrister and solicitor, 1928; Partner, Wilding & Acland (legal firm), 1935–62; part-time Lectr in Commercial Law, Canterbury University Coll., 1939–47. Chairman Court of Enquiry: into fire on M. V. Holmburn, 1959; into loss of M. V. Holmglen, 1960. Pres., Canterbury Dist Law Soc., 1950; Chm., Council of Legal Educn, 1975–79 (Mem., 1954–62 and 1964–79); Mem., Disciplin. Cttee, NZ Law Soc., 1952–62. Silver Jubilee Medal, 1977. Royal Danish Consul for S Island, NZ, 1948–62. Chevalier, Royal Order of Dannebrog, 1955. *Recreations:* reading; cottage in Arthur's Pass National Park. *Address:* 54 Mountain Road, Epsom, Auckland 3, New Zealand. *T:* 601-035. *Clubs:* Northern (Auckland); Canterbury (Christchurch).
*Died 1 May* 1983.

**PERRY, Kenneth Murray Allan,** MA, MD (Cantab); FRCP; Consulting Physician to: The London Hospital (Physician, 1946–72); the Royal Masonic Hospital (Physician, 1949–72); Medical Advisor to Central Advisory Council for Training for the Ministry of the Church of England, 1958–70; *b* 1 Feb. 1909; *s* of Major H. Perry, Ware, Herts; *m* 1938, Winifred, *d* of F. P. Grassi; no *c. Educ:* Christ's Hospital; Queen's Coll., Cambridge. Kitchener Scholar, 1927; Price University Entrance Scholarship, 1930; Medical Registrar, London Hospital, 1935–38; Dorothy Temple Cross Fellowship, Mass. General Hospital, Boston, 1938–39; Research Fellow, Harvard, 1939. Member of Scientific Staff, Medical Research Council, 1942–46. Ernestine Henry Lecturer, Royal College of Physicians, 1955. Visiting Physician, Papworth Village Settlement, 1946–72; Consulting Physician, Brentwood District and Warley Hospitals, 1947–72. Examiner in Medicine, Universities of Cambridge, London, Liverpool and Hong Kong; Royal College of Physicians, London; Society of Apothecaries of London. UK representative, International Society of Internal Medicine, 1969–72. Member: Assoc. of Physicians of Great Britain and Ireland, 1946–72; Thoracic Society, 1946–72. Miembro Correspondiente Extranjeo de Academia Nacional de Medicina de Buenos Aires. *Publications:* (with Sir Geoffrey Marshall) Diseases of the Chest, 1952; Pulmonary Œdema, in British Encyclopædia of Medical Practice, 1948; Industrial Medicine in Chambers's Encyclopædia, 1948; (with Sir Thomas Holmes Sellors) Chest

Diseases, 1963. *Recreations:* travel, photography. *Address:* One Tower House, Old Portsmouth PO1 2JR. *T:* Portsmouth 821446. *Clubs:* Royal Over-Seas League; Royal Naval and Royal Albert Yacht (Portsmouth).                                        *Died 4 Sept.* 1984.

**PERRY, Lt-Col Robert Stanley Grosvenor,** DSO 1943; DL; *b* 4 May 1909; *s* of late Robert Grosvenor Perry, CBE, Barton House, Moreton-in-Marsh, Glos; *m* 1937, Margaret Louisa Elphinstone, *o c* of Horace Czarnikow; one *s. Educ:* Harrow; RMC, Sandhurst. 2nd Lieut, 9th Lancers, 1929, Major, 1941; Adjutant, Cheshire Yeomanry, 1938–40; Commanding: 2nd Lothians and Border Yeomanry, 1943; 9th Lancers, 1944–45; served War of 1939–45, Palestine, Western Desert, N Africa, Italy (despatches, wounded twice); Commandant, RACOCTU, 1945–48. One of HM Bodyguard of Hon. Corps of Gentlemen at Arms, 1959–79. High Sheriff of Dorset, 1961. DL Dorset, 1962. Member British Olympic Yachting Team, Helsinki, 1952, Melbourne (Silver Medal), 1956; Winner: Cup of Italy with Vision (5.5 Metre), 1956; One Ton Cup with Royal Thames (6 Metre), 1958. *Recreations:* yacht racing, foxhunting, National Hunt racing. *Address:* Crendle Court, Purse Caundle, Sherborne, Dorset. *T:* Milborne Port 250364. *Clubs:* Cavalry and Guards, Royal Yacht Squadron.
*Died 3 April* 1987.

**PERRY-KEENE, Air Vice-Marshal Allan Lancelot Addison,** CB 1947; OBE 1940; RAF (retired); *b* 10 Nov. 1898; *s* of late L. H. A. and M. Perry-Keene; *m* 1923, K. L., *d* of late C. A. S. Silberrad, ICS; two *d. Educ:* Wolverley; King Edward's, Birmingham. Served European War, 1914–18; joined RFC, 1917; France, 1918–19; transferred RAF, 1918; Iraq, 1927–29; India, 1935–41; Burma and India, 1942; Director of Ground Training and Training Plans, Air Ministry, 1943–45; AOC 227 Group, India, and 3 (Indian) Group, 1946; Air Officer i/c Administration, Air HQ, India, 1946; Air Commander, Royal Pakistan Air Force, 1947–49. *Address:* Millway House, Weyhill, Andover, Hants SP11 8DE.                    *Died 16 March* 1987.

**PERT, Maj.-Gen. Claude Ernest,** CB 1947; CVO 1976; DSO 1945; retired; *b* 26 Sept. 1898; *s* of F. J. Pert, late ICS; *m* 1922, Lilian Katherine Nicolls (*d* 1980). *Educ:* Royal Naval Coll., Osborne; Clifton Coll. Commissioned into Indian Army, 1917, and joined 15th Lancers; Comd Probyn's Horse, 1940–42; Comd 255 Indian Tank Bde in 14th Army, Burma; Comd 1st Indian Armoured Div., 1945–48; retired 1948. *Recreations:* polo and fishing. *Address:* 3 Cumberland Lodge Mews, Windsor Great Park, Windsor, Berks. *T:* Egham 31063. *Club:* Buck's.                    *Died 14 March* 1982.

**PETCH, Sir Louis,** KCB 1968 (CB 1964); Chairman, Wine Standards Board of Vintners' Company, since 1973; *b* 16 Aug. 1913; *s* of William and Rhoda Petch, Preston, Lancs; *m* 1939, Gwendoline Bolton; one *s* one *d. Educ:* Preston Grammar Sch.; Peterhouse, Cambridge. Entered Administrative Class of Home Civil Service, 1937; Secretaries' Office, Customs and Excise, 1937–40; Home Defence Executive, 1940–45; Treasury, 1945–68; Private Secretary to successive Chancellors of the Exchequer, 1953–56; Third Secretary and Treasury Officer of Accounts, 1962–66; Second Secretary, 1966–68; Second Permanent Sec., Civil Service Dept, 1968–69; Chairman: Bd of Customs and Excise, 1969–73; Civil Service Benevolent Fund, 1969–73; Civil Service Sports Council, 1973–77; Civil Service and PO Life-Boat Fund, 1972–77; Parole Board, 1974–79. Freeman, City of London, 1976; Hon. Freeman, Vintners' Co., 1979. *Address:* 15 Cole Park Road, Twickenham, Middlesex. *T:* 01-892 2089. *Club:* United Oxford & Cambridge University.                    *Died 29 March* 1981.

**PETERKIN, Ishbel Allan;** *b* 2 March 1903; *d* of late J. Ramsay MacDonald and late Margaret Ethel Gladstone; *m* 1st, 1938, Norman Ridgley (*d* 1950); 2nd, 1953, James Peterkin (*d* 1955). *Educ:* City of London Sch.; North London Collegiate. Member of London County Council, 1928–34. Licensee at Plough Inn, Speen, 1936–53. *Address:* Hillocks, Moray Street, Lossiemouth, Moray IV31 6HX. *T:* Lossiemouth 3076.                    *Died 14 June* 1982.

**PETERS, John,** CB 1988; Assistant Under Secretary of State (Material Navy), Ministry of Defence, since 1984; *b* 5 Dec. 1929; *s* of Dr G. F. Peters and Mrs C. P. Peters; *m* 1955, Jane Catherine Mary Sheldon; one *s* two *d. Educ:* Downside Sch.; Balliol Coll., Oxford (MA). HM Forces, 1948–49. Pres., Oxford Union Soc., 1953. Entered Administrative Class, Home Civil Service, Admiralty, 1953; PS to Civil Lord, 1956–59; PS to Navy Minister, 1964–67; PS to Minister of Defence (Equipment), 1967–68; Dir of Naval Sales, 1968–72; Cabinet Office, 1974–75; Defence Counsellor, UK Delegn to NATO, Brussels, 1975–78; Asst Under Sec. of State (Air Staff), MoD, 1979–84. *Publication:* A Family from Flanders, 1985. *Address:* 60 Scotts Lane, Bromley, Kent. *T:* 01–650 0063. *Club:* United Oxford & Cambridge University.                    *Died 6 June* 1988.

**PETERS, Sir Rudolph (Albert),** Kt 1952; MC 1917 (Bar); FRS 1935; FRCP 1952; *b* 13 April 1889; *s* of Albert Edward Peters, MRCS, LRCP, and Agnes Malvina Watts; *m* 1917, Frances W. Vérel; two *s. Educ:* Warden House, Deal; Wellington Coll., Berks; King's

Coll., London; Gonville and Caius Coll., Cambridge. MA Cantab, 1914; MD 1919, St Bartholomew's Hospital; MA Oxon (by decree), 1923; Hon. MD (Liège), 1950; Doctor *hc* (Paris), 1952; Hon. DSc (Cincinnati), 1953; Hon. MD (Amsterdam), 1954; Hon. DSc: London, 1954; Leeds, 1959; Australian National University, 1961; Hon. LLD (Glasgow), 1963; Hon. FRSE, 1957; late Drosier Fellow and Tutor Gonville and Caius Coll., Cambridge; Hon. Fellow Gonville and Caius Coll., Cambridge, 1951; Hon. Fellow Trinity Coll., Oxford, 1958; Thruston Medal, 1918; Royal Medal of Royal Society, 1949; Cameron Prize, Edinburgh, 1949; Hopkins Memorial Medal, 1959; British Nutrition Foundn Prize, 1972. Benn W. Levy Student of Biochemistry, Cambridge, 1912–13; formerly, Dunn Lecturer and Senior Demonstrator Biochemistry, Cambridge; Whitley Professor of Biochemistry, University of Oxford, 1923–54; Fellow Trinity Coll., Oxford, 1925–54; Scientific Staff, Agricultural Research Council, 1954–59. Mem., Biochemical and Physiological Societies, BMA. Assoc. Sci. Nat., Acad. Roy. Belg. For. Member Royal Nether. Acad. Sci. and Letters and Accademia Nazionale dei Lincei, Rome; For. Hon. Member American Academy of Art and Sciences; Hon. Member: Finnish Biochem. Soc.; Assoc. Clin. Biochemists; Assoc. of Physicians; Biochemical Soc., Celer et Audax Club; Nutrition Soc.; Royal Acad. of Medicine, Belgium; American Inst. of Nutrition; Hon. Fellow: RSM; American Soc. Biological Chemists; Physiological Soc. Lectures: Croonian, Royal Society; Dixon Meml, RSM, 1948; Louis Abrahams, RCP, 1952; Dunham, Harvard, 1946–47; Herman Leo Loeb, St Louis Univ., 1947; Christian Herter, New York Univ., 1947; Dohme, Johns Hopkins Univ., 1954; Linacre, Cambridge, 1962. Visiting Professor, Canadian MRC, Dalhousie Univ., Halifax, Nova Scotia, 1963. Member: MRC, 1946–50; Military College of Science Advisory Council, 1947–50; Sci. Adv. Council, Ministry of Supply, 1950–53. President, International Council of Scientific Unions, 1958–61. President, Cambridge Philosophical Society, 1965–67. RAMC (SR) 1915–18 (MC and bar, Brevet-Major, despatches). Hon. FCPath, 1967. Medal of Freedom with silver palm (USA), 1947. *Publications:* Biochemical Lesions and Lethal Synthesis, 1963; contributions to scientific journals. *Address:* 3 Newnham Walk, Cambridge. *T:* Cambridge 50819.                    *Died 29 Jan.* 1982.

**PETERSON, Alexander Duncan Campbell,** OBE 1946; Vice-President, International Council of United World Colleges, since 1980; *b* 13 Sept. 1908; 2nd *s* of late J. C. K. Peterson, CIE; *m* 1946, Corinna May, *d* of late Sir Arthur Cochrane, KCVO; two *s* one *d. Educ:* Radley; Balliol Coll., Oxford. Assistant master, Shrewsbury Sch., 1932–40; commissioned in MOI (SP), 1940; Deputy Director of Psychological Warfare, SEAC, 1944–46; Headmaster, Adams' Grammar Sch., 1946–52; Director-General of Information Services, Federation of Malaya, 1952–54; Headmaster, Dover College, 1954–57; Director: Dept of Educn, Oxford Univ., 1958–73; Internat. Baccalaureate Office, 1968–77. Contested (L) Oxford City, 1966. Chm., Army Educn Adv. Bd, 1959–66. Chairman: Farmington Trust, 1963–71; Internat. Council of United World Colls, 1978–80. Hon. DPed Univ. of Trieste, 1985. *Publications:* The Far East, 1948; 100 Years of Education, 1952; Educating our Rulers, 1957; The Techniques of Teaching (ed), 1965; The Future of Education, 1968; International Baccalaureate, 1972; The Future of the Sixth Form, 1973; Schools across Frontiers, 1987. *Address:* 107A Hamilton Terrace, NW8. *T:* 01–286 3995. *Clubs:* Travellers', Special Forces.
*Died 17 Oct.* 1988.

**PETERSON, Sir Arthur (William),** KCB 1973 (CB 1963); LVO 1953; Chairman, British Refugee Council, since 1981; *b* 22 May 1916; *s* of J. C. K. Peterson and F. Campbell; *m* 1940, Mary Isabel Maples; one *s* two *d. Educ:* Shrewsbury; Merton College, Oxford. Asst Principal, Home Office, 1938; Principal Private Secretary to Home Secretary, 1946–49; Secretary, Royal Commission on Betting and Lotteries, 1949–51; Asst Secretary, Home Office, 1951–56; Personal Assistant to Lord Privy Seal, 1957; Dep. Chm., Prison Commission, 1957–60, Chm., 1960–63; Asst Under-Sec. of State, Prison Dept, Home Office, 1963–64; Dep. Sec., DEA, 1964–68; Dir-Gen. and Clerk to GLC, 1968–72; Permanent Under-Sec. of State, Home Office, 1972–77; Chairman: Mersey Docks & Harbour Co., 1977–80; Nat. Ports Council, 1980–81; Family Service Units, 1978–84. Mem., Royal Commn on Criminal Procedure, 1978–80. Chm., Jt Cttee on Refugees from Vietnam, 1979–82. Hon. Fellow, Inst. of Local Government Studies, Birmingham Univ. *Address:* Norton Mill House, Nortonbury Lane, Baldock, Herts. *T:* Baldock 892353. *Club:* Travellers'.                    *Died 8 May* 1986.

**PETHERICK, Maurice,** MA; *b* 5 Oct. 1894; *s* of George Tallack and Edith Petherick. *Educ:* St Peter's Court, Broadstairs; Marlborough College; Trinity College, Cambridge. 2nd Lieutenant Royal 1st Devon Yeomanry 1914; invalided out, 1915; served in Foreign Office, 1916–17; recommissioned Royal Scots Greys, 1917; served in France, 1918; recommissioned General List Army, Oct. 1939. Captain, Temp. Major. Contested (C) Penryn and Falmouth Division, 1929 and 1945; MP (C) Penryn and Falmouth, 1931–45; Financial Secretary, War Office, May-July, 1945; High Sheriff of Cornwall, 1957. Director, Prudential Assurance Co. Ltd, 1953–71.

*Publications:* Captain Culverin, 1932; Victoire, 1943; Restoration Rogues, 1950. *Recreations:* racing, gardening. *Address:* Porthpean House, St Austell, Cornwall. *Club:* United Oxford & Cambridge University.
*Died 4 Aug.* 1985.

**PETHYBRIDGE, Frank,** CBE 1977; Regional Administrator, North Western Regional Health Authority, 1973–82, retired; Chairman, Lancashire Family Practitioner Committee, since 1985; *b* 19 Jan. 1924; *s* of Frank and Margaret Pethybridge; *m* 1947, Jean Ewing; one *s* one *d. Educ:* William Hulme's Grammar Sch., Manchester; Univ. of Manchester (BA Admin). FHSM, FRSH. Served with RAF, 1942–47 (Flt-Lt). Town Clerk's Dept, Manchester CBC, 1940–42 and 1947–62; Manchester Regional Hosp. Bd, 1962–73. *Recreations:* woodwork, walking, swimming. *Address:* 12 The Leylands, West Beach, Lytham St Annes FY8 5QS. *T:* Lytham 739854.
*Died 14 March* 1989.

**PETIT, Sir Dinshaw Manockjee,** 3rd Bt, *cr* 1890; *b* 24 June 1901; *s* of Sir Dinshaw Manockjee Petit, 2nd Bt, and Dinbai, *d* of Sir J. Jejeebhoy, 3rd Bt; *S* father, 1933; *m* 1928, Sylla (*d* 1963), *d* of late R. D. Tata; one *s* one *d. Educ:* St Xavier's, Bombay; Trinity Hall, Cambridge. Called to Bar, Inner Temple, 1925. President: SPCA, Bombay; Petit Boys Sch., Poona; Petit Girls' Sch., Pali Hill, Bombay; Petit Sanatorium, Cumballa Hill, Bombay; Trustee: V.J.T. Technical Inst., Bombay; Parsee Gen. Hosp., Bombay. Pres., Northbrook Soc., London; Life Gov., Royal Hosp. for Incurables; Hon. Life Mem., RSPCA. Vice-Pres., British Assoc. of Riviera. Citizen of Honour of France. *Heir: s* Nasserwanjee Dinshaw Petit [*b* 13 Aug. 1934; *m* 1964, Nirmala Nanavatty; two *s*]. *Address:* Petit Hall, 66 Nepean Sea Road, Bombay, India; Savaric, 06 Eze-Village, France; 8 Mount Row, W1.
*Died 24 Sept.* 1983.

**PETRE,** 17th Baron, *cr* 1603; **Joseph William Lionel Petre;** Captain Essex Regiment; *b* 5 June 1914; *s* of 16th Baron and Catherine (who *m* 2nd, 1921, Sir Frederic Carne Rasch, 2nd Bt, TD; he *d* 1963), *d* of late Hon. John and late Lady Margaret Boscawen, Tregye, Falmouth, Cornwall; *S* father, 1915; *m* 1941, Marguerite, *d* of late Ion Wentworth Hamilton, Westwood, Nettlebed, Oxfordshire; one *s. Heir: s* Hon. John Patrick Lionel Petre [*b* 4 Aug. 1942; *m* 1965, Marcia Gwendolyn, *o d* of Alfred Plumpton; two *s* one *d*]. *Address:* Ingatestone Hall, Essex.
*Died 1 Jan.* 1989.

**PETRIE, Cecilia, (Lady Petrie);** *b* 15 July 1901; *d* of late F. J. G. Mason, Kensington; *m* 1926, Sir Charles Petrie, 3rd Bt, CBE, FRHistS (*d* 1977); one *s.* Mem. Kensington Borough Council (Queen's Gate Ward), 1946–62; Alderman, 1965–71; Freeman, 1971; Mayor of the Royal Borough of Kensington, 1954–56. Member: (C) LCC, for S Kensington, 1949–65; Fulham & Kensington Hospital Management Committee, 1948–59 (Chairman, 1955–59); Chelsea and Kensington Hospital Management Cttee, 1959–72; Board of Governors, Charing Cross Hospital, 1959–68; Member Board of Governors of Hospital for Diseases of the Chest, 1951–73; Mem. Central Health Services Council, 1955–61; Dep.-Chm. of the London County Council, 1958–59; UK Delegate to United Nations Assembly, 14th Session, 1959; Member: SW Metropolitan Regional Hospital Board, 1959–65; London Exec. Council, Nat. Health Service, 1965–74; Family Practitioner Service, 1974–78; Whitley Council Committee C, 1949–71. *Recreation:* reading detective stories. *Address:* 31 Queen's Gate Terrace, SW7 5PP. *T:* 01–581 0112.
*Died 8 Jan.* 1987.

**PETRIE, Sir (Charles) Richard (Borthwick),** 4th Bt *cr* 1918; TD; MA(Oxon); Director, Richard Petrie Ltd Audio-Visual Programme Production; *b* 19 Oct. 1921; *s* of Sir Charles Alexander Petrie, 3rd Bt, CBE, and Ursula Gabrielle Borthwick (*d* 1962), *d* of late Judge Harold Chaloner Dowdall, QC; *S* father, 1977; *m* 1962, Jessie Ariana Borthwick, *d* of late Comdr Patrick Straton Campbell, RN. *Educ:* Radley College; Heidelberg Univ.; New Coll., Oxford. Served REME, 1942–47 and again (TA), 1949–67, Lt-Col; Commander REME, 43rd (Wessex) Inf. Div., TA, 1962–65. Member of Exec. Cttee, Assoc. of Professional Recording Studios, 1968–75. *Publications:* Ghana: Portrait of a West African State, 1974; (contrib.) Sound Recording Practice, 1976. *Recreations:* music, shrub gardening. *Heir: half-b* Peter Charles Petrie, CMG, *b* 7 March 1932. *Address:* 3 Northmoor Road, Oxford. *T:* Oxford 56081.
*Died 8 March* 1988.

**PETRIE, Edward James,** CMG 1955; retired from HM Treasury, Nairobi; *b* 1907; *m* Winifred Hewitt Wilkie (*d* 1960); two *s* one *d.* Assistant Revenue Officer, Kenya, 1933; Assistant Treasurer, 1934; Senior Accountant, 1943; Assistant Financial Secretary, 1946; Financial Secretary, Barbados, 1948; Accountant-General, Kenya, 1951; Sec. to Treasury, Kenya, 1953–56; retd 1956. *Address:* 19 Stirling Road, Edinburgh EH5 3JA.
*Died 4 March* 1983.

**PETRIE, (Jessie) Cecilia, (Lady Petrie);** *see* Petrie, C.

**PETRIE, Sir Richard;** *see* Petrie, Sir C. R. B.

**PETTINGELL, Sir William (Walter),** Kt 1972; CBE 1965 (OBE 1959); Deputy Chairman, The Australian Gas Light Co. (General Manager, 1952–74); *b* Corrimal, NSW, 4 Sept. 1914; *s* of H. G. W. Pettingell, Cootamundra, NSW; *m* 1942, Thora M., *d* of J. Stokes; one *s* two *d. Educ:* Wollongong High Sch.; Univ. of Sydney. BSc (Sydney) 1st cl. hons, 1934. The Australian Gas Light Co.: Research Chemist, 1936; Production Engr, 1948; Works Manager, 1950; Asst Gen. Manager (Technical), 1951; Gen. Manager, 1952–74; Dir, 1974–. Chairman: Leighton Holdings Ltd; Indosuez Australia Ltd; Blackwood Hodge Ltd. Deputy Chairman: Australian Consolidated Industries; Sun Alliance Insurance; Director: Howard Smith Ltd; Coal and Allied Industries Ltd; Santos Ltd. FAIM, FIAM, FInstF, MInstGasE. *Recreation:* yachting (sails a 43 foot ocean racer and has taken part in annual Sydney to Hobart and other ocean yacht races). *Address:* 54 Linden Way, Castlecrag, NSW 2068, Australia. *T:* 95 1976. *Clubs:* Union, American, Royal Prince Alfred Yacht, Royal Sydney Yacht Squadron, Elanora Golf (all in NSW).
*Died 27 Jan.* 1987.

**PETTY, Hon. Sir Horace (Rostill),** Kt 1964; BCom, FASA; Agent-General for State of Victoria, in London, 1964–69; *b* 29 March 1904; *m* 1st, 1930 (marr. diss.); two *s* two *d*; 2nd, 1959, Beryl Anne Hoelter. *Educ:* South Yarra School; University High School; Melbourne University. Accountant and auditor (managerial appts in retail business field, etc.) from mid-twenties to 1939. Australian Army, 1940–44; Infty, Aust. Armd Div. and AHQ in North, rank Major. Mem. Municipal Council, City of Prahran, 1949–64 (Mayor, 1951–52). MLA for Toorak (Liberal) in Victorian Parl., 1952–64. (Victorian Govt) Minister of: Housing, July 1955–July 1961; Immigration, July 1956–Dec. 1961; Public Works, Victorian State Government, July 1961–Apr. 1964. Mem., RSSAILA. *Recreations:* golf, racing, motoring. *Address:* 593 Toorak Road, Toorak, Victoria 3142, Australia. *Clubs:* Naval and Military (Melbourne), Melbourne Cricket, Victoria Racing, RAC of Victoria.
*Died 16 Feb.* 1982.

**PEVSNER, Sir Nikolaus (Bernhard Leon),** Kt 1969; CBE 1953; FBA 1965; MA Cantab; MA Oxon; PhD; FSA; Hon. FRIBA; Hon. ARCA; Hon. FNZIA; Hon. Academician, Accademia di Belle Arti, Venice; Hon. Fellow, Royal Scottish Academy; Hon. Member, American Academy of Arts and Sciences; Hon. Fellow, Akademie der Wissenschaften Göttingen; Emeritus Professor of History of Art, Birkbeck College, University of London; *b* 30 Jan. 1902; *s* of late Hugo Pevsner; *m* 1923, Karola Kurlbaum (*d* 1963); two *s* one *d. Educ:* St Thomas's Sch., Leipzig; Univs of Leipzig, Munich, Berlin and Frankfort. PhD History of Art and Architecture, 1924; Asst Keeper, Dresden Gallery, 1924–28; Lectr, History of Art and Architecture, Goettingen Univ., 1929–33; Slade Prof. of Fine Art, Univ. of Cambridge, 1949–55; Fellow, St John's Coll., Cambridge, 1950–55, Hon. Fellow, 1967–; Slade Prof. of Fine Art, Univ. of Oxford, 1968–69. Former Chm., Victorian Soc. (to 1976); Member: Historic Buildings Council, 1966–79; Council, Wm Morris Soc.; (formerly) Adv. Bd for Redundant Churches (to 1977). Reith Lectr, BBC, 1955. Royal Gold Medal for Architecture (RIBA), 1967; Albert Medal, RSA, 1976; other medals: Howland, Yale, 1963; Hitchcock, London, 1966; Thomas Jefferson, Univ. of Virginia, 1975; German Prize, Nat. Cttee for Monumental Preservation, 1982. Hon. Doctorates: Leicester, York, Leeds, Oxford, Cambridge, E Anglia, Zagreb, Keele, Open Univ., Heriot-Watt Univ., Edinburgh, Univ. of Pennsylvania; Hon. DLitt Cantab. 1979. Grand Cross of Merit, Fed. Rep. of Germany. *Publications:* The Baroque Architecture of Leipzig, 1928; Italian Painting from the end of the Renaissance to the end of the Rococo (a vol. of the Handbuch der Kunstwissenschaft), 1927–30; Pioneers of the Modern Movement, from William Morris to Walter Gropius, 1936 (revised edn: Pioneers of Modern Design, Museum of Modern Art, New York, 1949; new edn 1972; also foreign edns); An Enquiry into Industrial Art in England, 1937; German Baroque Sculpture (with S. Sitwell and A. Ayscough), 1938; Academies of Art, Past and Present, 1940; An Outline of European Architecture, Pelican Books, 1942, most recent edn, 1973 (also edns in numerous foreign langs); High Victorian Design, 1951; The Buildings of England (46 vols), 1951–74; The Planning of the Elizabethan Country House, 1961; The Englishness of English Art, 1956; Sir Christopher Wren (in Italian), 1958; Sources of Modern Art, 1962 (re-issued as The Sources of Modern Architecture and Design, 1968); Dictionary of Architecture (with John Fleming and Hugh Honour), 1966; Studies in Art, Architecture and Design (2 vols), 1968; (with J. M. Richards) The Anti-Rationalists, 1973; Some Architectural Writers of the Nineteenth Century, 1973; A History of Building Types, 1976 (Wolfson Literary Award). *Address:* 2 Wildwood Terrace, North End, NW3.
*Died 18 Aug.* 1983.

**PEYTON, Sidney Augustus,** PhD; Librarian of Sheffield University, 1941–56; *b* 1891; *e s* of late Sidney Peyton, Newbury; *m* Muriel Kathleen Pearse (*d* 1980). *Educ:* University Coll., Reading. Lectr, University Coll., Reading, 1919; Univ. Librarian, Reading, 1922–41. Hon. LittD Sheffield. *Publications:* Oxfordshire Peculiars (Oxford Record Society); Kesteven Quarter Sessions Minutes (Lincoln Record Society); Kettering Vestry Minutes (Northamptonshire Record Society); Northamptonshire QS

Records, Introduction; various historical papers. *Recreation:* music. *Address:* 14 Brincliffe Court, Nether Edge Road, Sheffield S7 1RX. *T:* Sheffield 52767. *Died 19 Dec.* 1982.

**PFEIFFER, Alois;** Member, Commission of the European Communities, since 1985; *b* 25 Sept. 1924. *Educ.:* evening classes; Labour Acad., Frankfurt. Served War of 1939–45; PoW 1942–45. Horticultural, Agricultural and Forestry Workers' Union: Regl Dir, S Hessen, 1949–54; Land Dir, N Rhine-Westphalia, 1954–60; Mem. Nat. Exec., 1966–67; Dep. Pres., 1967–69; Pres., 1969–75. Member: Fed. Exec., Deutscher Gewerkschaftsbund, 1975–84; Exec., ETUC; Pres., European Fedn of Agricl Workers. *Address:* 200 rue de la Loi, 1049 Brussels, Belgium. *Died 1 Aug.* 1987.

**PHALP, Geoffrey Anderson,** CBE 1968; TD; Secretary, King Edward's Hospital Fund for London, 1968–80; *b* 8 July 1915; *s* of late Charles Anderson Phalp and late Sara Gertrude Phalp (*née* Wilkie); *m* 1946, Jeanne Margaret, OBE, JP, *d* of late Emeritus Prof. G. R. Goldsborough, CBE, FRS; one *s* one *d.* *Educ.:* Durham Sch.; Univ. of Durham (BCom). Served with RA (despatches), 1939–46. Asst Registrar, Med. Sch., King's Coll., Newcastle upon Tyne, 1946–49; Dep. House Governor and Sec., United Newcastle upon Tyne Hosps, 1949–51; Sec. and Principal Admin. Officer, United Birmingham Hosps, 1951–68. Trustee, Child Accident Prevention Trust, 1982– (Chm. 1983). W. K. Kellogg Foundn Citation for contribn to develt of health admin, 1980. *Recreations:* fly fishing, gardening, music. *Address:* 19 Norfolk Road, Edgbaston, Birmingham B15 3PZ. *T:* 021–454 2616. *Club:* Savile.
*Died 26 Dec.* 1986.

**PHEMISTER, James,** MA, DSc, FRSE, FGS; FMSA; *b* 3 April 1893; 2nd *s* of John Clark Phemister and Elizabeth G. Crawford; *m* 1921, Margaret Clark, MA (*d* 1982); two *s* one *d.* *Educ.:* Govan High Sch.; Glasgow Univ. Served European War, RE and RGA; disabled 1917, and placed on retired list, 1918; teacher of Mathematics and Science, 1918–21; appointed Geological Survey, 1921; Petrographer, 1935–45; Curator, Museum of Practical Geology, 1945–46; Asst Dir Specialist Services, 1946–53; Pres. Mineralogical Soc., 1951–54; Pres. Glasgow Geol. Soc., 1961–64. Editor, Mineralogical Abstracts, 1959–66. *Publications:* papers on Petrological and Geophysical subjects. *Recreation:* swimming. *Address:* 39A Fountainhall Road, Edinburgh EH9 2LN. *T:* 031–667 4700.
*Died 18 May* 1986.

**PHEMISTER, Prof. Thomas Crawford,** MSc (Chicago), PhD (Cantab), DSc (Glasgow); FRSE, FGS; Dr de l'Univ. de Rennes (hon. causa); Professor and Head of Department of Geology and Mineralogy, Aberdeen University, 1937–72, then Professor Emeritus; *b* 25 May 1902; 4th *s* of John Clark Phemister and Elizabeth G. Crawford; *m* 1926, Mary Wood Reid, MA; three *d.* *Educ.:* Allan Glen's School and University of Glasgow; St John's College, Cambridge; Chicago University. Assoc. Prof. of Geology and Mineralogy, Univ. of British Columbia, 1926–33; Field Officer, Geological Survey of Canada, 1928–30; University Demonstrator in Mineralogy and Petrology, Cambridge Univ., 1933–37. Served in Royal Engineers, War of 1939–45. Dean of Faculty of Science, 1945–48, Vice-Principal, 1963–66, Aberdeen University. Chm., Macaulay Inst. for Soil Research, 1958–. Chm., Robert Gordon's Colleges, 1971–82. *Publications:* papers on mineralogical and petrological subjects. *Address:* Department of Geology and Mineralogy, University of Aberdeen, Aberdeen AB9 1AS. *T:* Aberdeen 36489. *Died 30 Dec.* 1982.

**PHILIPPS, Hon. James Perrott,** TD; *b* 25 Nov. 1905; 3rd *s* of 1st Baron and *b* of 2nd Baron Milford; *m* 1930, Hon. Elizabeth Joan, *d* of 1st Baron Kindersley; one *s* two *d.* *Educ.:* Eton; Christ Church, Oxford. Chm., Dalham Farms Ltd. Mem., Jockey Club. Served War of 1939–45; Leicestershire Yeomanry and Shropshire Yeomanry (despatches). Major TA Reserve. High Sheriff of Suffolk, 1955–56. *Recreations:* breeding, racing. *Address:* Dalham Hall, Newmarket, Suffolk. *T:* Ousden 242. *Club:* Jockey.
*Died 22 Sept.* 1984.

**PHILIPSON, Oliphant James;** *b* 9 Sept. 1905; 2nd *s* of late Hylton Philipson; *m* 1946, Helen Mabel (*d* 1976), *d* of David Fell. *Educ.:* Eton. Served War of 1939–45, RNVR. *Address:* Manor House, Everton, near Lymington, Hampshire SO41 0HE. *Clubs:* Carlton; Royal Yacht Squadron. *Died 16 Aug.* 1987.

**PHILIPSON-STOW, Sir Edmond (Cecil),** 4th Bt *cr* 1907; MBE (mil.) 1946; retired; *b* 25 Aug. 1912; second *s* of Sir Elliot Philipson Philipson-Stow, 2nd Bt and Edith (*d* 1943), *y d* of late E. H. Pery-Knox-Gore, DL, JP; *S* brother, 1976. *Educ.:* Malvern College; Royal Military College, Sandhurst. Served in The Duke of Cornwall's Light Infantry, 1932–52; Major (retd). *Heir:* cousin Christopher Philipson-Stow, DFC [*b* 13 Sept. 1920; *m* 1952, Elizabeth Nairn, *d* of late James Dixon Trees; two *s*]. *Address:* Cloonaghmore, Crossmolina, Co. Mayo. *Died 14 June* 1982.

**PHILLIMORE,** 3rd Baron, *cr* 1918, of Shiplake in County of Oxford; **Robert Godfrey Phillimore,** Bt, *cr* 1881; *b* 24 Sept. 1939; *s* of Capt.

Hon. Anthony Francis Phillimore, 9th Queen's Royal Lancers (*e s* of 2nd Baron) and Anne, 2nd *d* of Maj.-Gen. Sir Cecil Pereira, KCB; *S* grandfather, 1947; *m* 1st, 1974, Amanda (marr. diss. 1982), *d* of Carlo Hugo Gonzales-Castillo; 2nd, 1983, Maria, *d* of Ilya Slonim, *g d* of Maxim Litvinov, Soviet diplomat. *Heir: u* Major Hon. Claud Stephen Phillimore [*b* 15 Jan. 1911; *m* 1944, Anne Elizabeth, *e d* of Maj. Arthur Algernon Dorrien-Smith, DSO; one *s* one *d*]. *Address:* Crumplehorn Barn, Corks Farm, Dunsden Green, near Reading, Berks. *Died 26 Feb.* 1990.

**PHILLIPS, Maj.-Gen. Charles George,** CB 1944; DSO 1919, Bar 1940; MC; *b* 7 July 1889; *s* of Major George Edward Phillips, DSO, RE (killed in action Somaliland Expedition, 1902), and L. V. C. Alluaud; *m* 1924, Norah Butler; three *d.* *Educ.:* Repton; RMC, Sandhurst. 2nd Lt West Yorkshire Regiment, 1909; Lieut 1910; seconded for service Merehan Somali Expedition, Jubaland, Kenya, 1912–14; European War, served in German East Africa; Captain, 1914; temp. Lt-Col, 1916–19; commanded 3/2 KAR; commanded Column, Philcol, Portuguese East Africa, 1918; wounded, Njangao, 1917 (German East Africa); temp. Major, 1919; temp. Lt-Col, 1919–23; commanded 1st Batt. 1st King's African Rifles and OC Troops in Nyasaland; Major, 1924; Lt-Col 1933; commanded 1st Battalion The West Yorkshire Regt (Prince of Wales Own), 1933–37; Bt Col, 1935; Commander 146th (1st West Riding) Infantry Brigade TA, 1938; (Medals, AGS, DSO, MC, 1914–15 Star, General Service Medal, Allied Victory Medal, French Croix de Guerre (avec palme), Officer Military Order of Aviz); War of 1939–45 (3 medals, Bar to DSO); Comdr British Troops, Namsos, Norway, 1940; Northern Iceland, 1940–41; Gambia and Sierra Leone areas, 1942–44; Maj.-Gen. 1942; retired pay, 1944. *Address:* PO Box 42370, Nairobi, Kenya. *Club:* Naval and Military.
*Died 1 May* 1982.

**PHILLIPS, Douglas Herbert Charles;** HM Diplomatic Service, retired; Deputy High Commissioner, Sri Lanka, and Counsellor, Maldives, 1978–81; *b* 4 Nov. 1924; *s* of late Herbert Henry Phillips and Aida Phillips (*née* Gervasi); *m* 1st, 1950, Olwen Laverick (*d* 1971); one *d*; 2nd, 1972, Noreen Evelyn Mendelsohn; one step *s* one step *d.* *Educ.:* Vaughan Sch., Kensington. RN, 1943–46; Min. of Civil Aviation, 1947; joined Commonwealth Service, 1948; served in Pakistan (Karachi and Peshawar), 1950–53; Second Sec., Calcutta, 1954–57; First Sec., Bombay, 1959–62; CRO, 1963–64; Diplomatic Service Admin., 1965–67; First Sec. (Commercial), Melbourne, 1967–72; FCO, 1972–75; First Sec. (Commercial), Singapore, 1975–78. *Address:* 7 Talbots Drive, Maidenhead, Berks. *T:* Maidenhead 35240. *Clubs:* Royal Colombo Golf; Gymkhana (Bombay). *Died 10 March* 1990.

**PHILLIPS, Frank Coles,** MA, PhD, FGS; Professor of Mineralogy and Petrology, University of Bristol, 1964–67, retired 1967; then Emeritus; *b* 19 March 1902; *s* of Nicholas Phillips and Kate Salmon; *m* 1929, Seonee Barker; one *s* one *d.* *Educ.:* Plymouth Coll.; Corpus Christi Coll., Cambridge. 1st class, Natural Sciences Tripos, Part II (Geology), 1924; Amy Mary Preston Read Studentship, 1925; Fellow of Corpus Christi Coll., Cambridge, 1927–30; University Demonstrator in Mineralogy, 1928–32; Assistant Director of Studies in Natural Sciences, Corpus Christi College, 1931–46; University Lecturer in Mineralogy and Petrology, Cambridge, 1932–46; Lecturer in Mineralogy, Trinity Coll., 1945–46; Lecturer in Geology, University of Bristol, 1948–50; Reader in Petrology, 1950–64. Sedgwick Prize, 1937; Murchison Fund, Geological Society of London, 1937; Bolitho Gold Medal, Royal Geological Society of Cornwall, 1962. *Publications:* An Introduction to Crystallography, 1947 (4th edn 1971); The Use of Stereographic Projection in Structural Geology, 1954 (3rd edn 1971); revised (14th) edition of G. F. Herbert Smith's Gemstones, 1972; (with G. Windsor) trans. B. Sander, Einführung in die Gefügekunde der geologischen Körper, 1970. Papers on petrology and mineralogy communicated to scientific periodicals. *Recreations:* gardening, carpentry and mechanics. *Address:* Wains Way, Butt's Lawn, Brockenhurst, Hants. *T:* Lymington 23000. *Died 11 Sept.* 1982.

**PHILLIPS, Rev. Gordon Lewis;** Gresham Professor of Divinity, 1971–73; Chaplain to the English-Speaking Church in Luxembourg, 1972–74; *b* 27 June 1911; *s* of Herbert Lewis and Margaret Gertrude Phillips. *Educ.:* Cathedral Sch., Llandaff; Dean Close Sch., Cheltenham; Brasenose Coll., Oxford (scholar; exhibitioner; BA 1st cl. Lit. Hum., 1933; 3rd cl. Theology, 1935; MA 1937); Kelham Theological Coll. Deacon 1937; Priest 1938; Curate, St Julian, Newport, Mon, 1937–40; Rector: Northolt, Mddx, 1940–55; Bloomsbury, Diocese of London, 1956–68; Anglican Chaplain, London Univ., 1955–68; Examg Chaplain to Bishop of St Albans, 1957; Prebendary of Hoxton in St Paul's Cathedral, 1960–68; Proctor, Convocation of London, 1960–65; Dean of Llandaff, 1968–71. Mem., Standing Cttee on Anglican and Roman Catholic Relations; Select Preacher: Univ. of Oxford, 1942, 1964; Univ. of Cambridge, 1963. Hon. Fellow, University Coll., Cardiff, 1970. *Publications:* Seeing and Believing, 1953; Flame in the Mind, 1957;

contrib. to Studies in the Fourth Gospel, 1957. *Address:* Tŷ Cornel, Cilycwm, Llandovery, Dyfed. *Died 5 Dec.* 1982.

**PHILLIPS, Herbert Moore,** CMG 1949; MA; *b* 7 Feb. 1908; *s* of Herbert Phillips and Beatrice Moore; *m* 1934, Martha Löffler (marr. diss.); one *d*; *m* 1952, Doris Rushbrooke. *Educ:* St Olave's; Wadham Coll., Oxford (MA (Hons) Oxon 1931). Entered Min. of Labour, 1934; Asst Sec., Manpower Dept, 1942–45, Overseas Dept 1946; FO, 1946–49, as Counsellor for Econ. and Soc. Affairs in UK Delegn at seat of UN, Alternate UK Delegate to ECOSOC and Delegate to ECLA; Consultant, ECLA, 1950–51; UNESCO, 1952–68, as Head of Div. of Applied Social Sciences and Dir Analysis Office. Consultant, 1968–: OECD; UNESCO, UN, UNICEF, World Bank; Leader of World Bank Missions to Ethiopia, Taiwan and Turkey for preparation of educn loans; Mem., UN Family Planning Mission to Iran. *Publications:* Literacy and Development, 1970; Basic Education, a World Challenge, 1975; Educational Cooperation between Developed and Developing Countries, 1976. *Address:* Hameau du Plan, Plan de la Tour, 83120 Ste Maxime, France. *Died 2 Sept.* 1987.

**PHILLIPS, Ivan L.;** *see* Lloyd Phillips.

**PHILLIPS, Rev. Canon John Bertram,** MA (Cantab) 1933; DD (Lambeth), 1966; writer and broadcaster since 1955; *b* 16 Sept. 1906; *e s* of late Philip William Phillips, OBE, and late Emily Maud Powell; *m* 1939, Vera May, *o d* of William Ernest and May Jones; one *d*. *Educ:* Emanuel Sch., London; Emmanuel Coll. and Ridley Hall, Cambridge. Asst Master, Sherborne Prep. School for boys, 1927–28; Curate, St John's, Penge, London, 1930–33; freelance journalist and Editorial Secretary, Pathfinder Press, 1934–36; Curate, St Margaret's, Lee, London, 1936–40; Vicar of Good Shepherd, Lee, London, 1940–44; Vicar of St John's, Redhill, Surrey, 1945–55; Wiccamical Prebendary of Exceit in Chichester Cathedral, 1957–60. Canon of Salisbury Cathedral, 1964–69, later Canon Emeritus. Hon. DLitt, Exeter, 1970. *Publications:* Letters to Young Churches, 1947; Your God is too Small, 1952; The Gospels in Modern English, 1952; Making Men Whole, 1952; Plain Christianity, 1954; When God was Man, 1954; Appointment with God, 1954; The Young Church in Action, 1955; New Testament Christianity, 1956; The Church under the Cross, 1956; St Luke's Life of Christ, 1956; The Book of Revelation, 1957; Is God at Home?, 1957; The New Testament in Modern English, 1958; A Man Called Jesus, 1959; God our Contemporary, 1960; Good News, 1963; Four Prophets, 1963; Ring of Truth, 1967; Through the Year with J. B. Phillips (ed Denis Duncan), 1974; Peter's Portrait of Jesus, 1976. *Recreations:* painting, photography, music, reading. *Address:* Golden Cap, 17 Gannetts Park, Swanage, Dorset. *T:* 3122. *Died 21 July* 1982.

**PHILLIPS, John George Crispin,** QC 1980; *b* 27 Oct. 1938; *s* of late G. Godfrey Phillips, CBE, and of Betty Phillips. *Educ:* Harrow; Trinity Coll., Cambridge (BA). National Service, Scots Guards, 1956–58. Called to the Bar, Gray's Inn, 1962. *Recreations:* croquet, golf, chess. *Address:* 1 Brick Court, Temple, EC4Y 9BY. *Club:* White's. *Died Sept.* 1982.

**PHILLIPS, Sir John (Grant),** KBE 1972 (CBE 1968); Governor and Chairman of Board, Reserve Bank of Australia, 1968–75; *b* 13 March 1911; *s* of Oswald and Ethel Phillips, Sydney; *m* 1935, Mary W. Debenham; two *s* two *d*. *Educ:* C of E Grammar Sch., Sydney; University of Sydney (BEc). Research Officer, NSW Retail Traders' Assoc., 1932–35; Econ. Asst, Royal Commn Monetary and Banking Systems, 1936–37; Econ. Dept, Commonwealth Bank of Australia, 1937–51; Investment Adviser, Commonwealth Bank, 1954–60; Dep. Governor and Dep. Chairman of Board, Reserve Bank of Australia, 1960–68. Leader, Australian Delegation to 6th Conf. GATT, Geneva, 1951; Member: Council, Macquarie Univ., 1967–79; Bd, Howard Florey Inst. of Experimental Physiology and Medicine, 1971–; Adv. Cttee, The Australian Birthright Movement, Sydney Br., 1971–; Dir, Lend Lease Corp. Ltd, 1976–81. Chm., Aust. Stats Adv. Council, 1976–81. *Recreations:* lawn bowls, contract bridge. *Address:* 2/25 Marshall Street, Manly, NSW 2095, Australia. *Died Oct.* 1986.

**PHILLIPS, Prof. John Guest,** PhD, DSc; FRS 1981; Vice-Chancellor and Hon. Professor, Loughborough University of Technology, since 1986; *b* 13 June 1933; *s* of Owen Gwynne Phillips and Dorothy Constance Phillips; *m* 1961, Jacqueline Ann Myles-White; two *s*. *Educ:* Llanelli Grammar Sch. (County Major Scholar); Univ. of Liverpool (State Scholar, Univ. Studentship; ARC Studentship). BSc 1954, PhD 1957, Liverpool; DSc Hong Kong 1967; FIBiol; CBiol; FRSocMed. Vis. Scientist: Collège de France, 1955; CIBA Ag, Basel, 1956; Commonwealth Fund Fellow, Yale Univ., 1957–59; Fellow, Davenport Coll., Yale Univ., 1957–59; Lectr in Zoology, Univ. of Sheffield, 1959–62; Vis. Asst Prof., Univ. of BC, 1959; Milton Res. Assoc., Harvard Univ., 1960; Prof. of Zoology, Univ. of Hong Kong, 1962–67; Dir, Nuffield Unit, Univ. of Hong Kong, 1963–67; Dean of Faculty of Science, Hong Kong, 1965–66, acting Vice-Chancellor, 1966; Vis. Scientist, US Navy Namru 2, Manilla,

1963; University of Hull: Prof. and Head of Dept of Zoology, 1967–79; Dir, Wolfson Lab. for Res. in Gerontology, 1975–79; Dean, Faculty of Science, 1978–80; Wolfson Professor and Dir Wolfson Inst., 1979–85; Public Orator, 1970, 1972, 1976, 1979–81, 1983; Sen. Fellow, SERC (formerly SRC), 1979–83. Visiting Professor: Biology, Univ. of California, 1975; Pharmacology and Therapeutics, Univ. of Texas, 1979; Bengurion Univ., Israel, 1980; McKenzie Vis. Prof., Univ. of Alberta, 1986. Distinguished Visitor, La Trobe Univ., 1983; Vis. Fellow, Commonwealth Scholarship and Fellowship Plan to Australia, 1984. Member: Commonwealth Scholarships Commn, 1968–; Royal Commn for Exhibition of 1851, 1986–; Council, Marine Biological Assoc. of UK, 1969–71; Biology Cttee, SRC, 1975–78; Cttee of Soc. for Endocrinology, 1971–84; Treasurer, Soc. for Endocrinology, 1975–81, Chm., 1981–84; Chm., British Endocrine Socs, 1981–84. Chm., Hull DHA, 1981–84; Member: Humberside AHA, 1974–81 (Vice-Chm., 1979–81); Humberside Area Nurse Educn Adv. Cttee (Chm., 1976–82); Internat. Cttee for Comparative Endocrinology, 1974–; Humber Adv. Gp, 1975–80; Internat. Cttee for Endocrinology, 1976–84; Commonwealth Human Ecology Council, 1976–80; Exec. Cttee, British Soc. for Res. in Ageing, 1976– (Treas., 1980–83; Chm., 1983–87); Institute of Biology: Vice-Pres., 1983–84; Pres. Yorkshire Br., 1969–72; Mem. Council, 1979–84, Sec., 1982–84, Zool Soc. of London; Vice Pres., Soc. for Wildlife Art of the Nation. Chm., Editl Bd, Jl of Endocrinology, 1982–84 (Mem. 1971–84, Chm. 1981–84, Council of Management); Associate Editor, Procs of Royal Soc., 1982–; Mem., Editl Bd, Age and Ageing, 1983–. Fellow, Acad. of Zoology of India, 1966–. Trustee: Hull and E Riding Cardiac Trust, 1983–; Ferens Educnl Trust, 1983–; Chm. Bd of Trustees, Post Grad. Med. Educn Centre, Hull, 1983–. Governor: Endsleigh Coll. of Educn, Hull, 1967–77; St Anne's Special Sch., Hull, 1975–81 (Vice-Chm., 1978–81); Bridgeview Special Sch., 1977–81; Wold Special Sch., 1983–; Loughborough Endowed Schools. Assessor: Univ. of Malaya, 1979–; Univ. of Singapore, 1981–; British Council Visitor, Hungary, 1968, Singapore, 1982. Mem., Academic Adv. Council, 1978–84, Patron, 1984–, Univ. of Buckingham (formerly University Coll. of Buckingham). Annual Lecture, Biological Council, 1982; Colin Roscoe Lectr, Univ. of Manchester, 1984. Zoological Soc. of London Scientific Medal, 1970; Medal of Soc. for Endocrinology, 1971. *Publications:* Hormones and the Environment, 1971; Environmental Physiology, 1975; Physiological Strategies in Avian Biology, 1985; numerous papers in zoological, endocrinological and physiological jls. *Recreations:* gardening, music, travel. *Address:* Vice-Chancellor's Office, Loughborough University of Technology, Loughborough, Leics LE11 3TU. *T:* Loughborough 263171. *Club:* Royal Commonwealth Society.
*Died 14 March* 1987.

**PHILLIPS, Rt. Rev. John Henry Lawrence;** *b* 2 Feb. 1910; *s* of Rev. H. L. Phillips, Wimborne, Dorset; *m* 1936, Morna, *d* of E. H. W. Winfield-King, OBE; one *s* three *d*. *Educ:* Weymouth Coll., Trinity Hall, Cambridge, BA 1932; MA 1937; Ridley Hall, Cambridge, 1932–34. Deacon, 1934; priest, 1935. Curate of Christ Church, Harrogate, 1934–35; Curate of Methley, 1935–38; Rector of Farnley, Leeds, 1938–45; Surrogate, 1939–45; Chaplain RNVR, 1942–45; Director of Service Ordination Candidates, 1945–47; General Secretary Central Advisory Council of Training for the Ministry, 1947–49; Vicar of Radcliffe-on-Trent and of Shelford, 1949–57; Archdeacon of Nottingham, 1949–60; Rector of Clifton with Glapton, 1958–60; Bishop of Portsmouth, 1960–75; Priest-in-charge, West with East Lulworth, 1975–78. Chaplain to the Queen, 1959–60. Provincial Grand Master, Masonic Order, Hampshire and Isle of Wight, 1975–79. *Recreations:* cricket, golf, Rugby football, etc. *Address:* Highlands, Harkstead, Ipswich. *T:* Holbrook 328261. *Club:* Naval. *Died 1 Nov.* 1985.

**PHILLIPS, Hon. Sir (John) Raymond,** Kt 1971; MC 1945; **Hon. Mr Justice Phillips;** a Justice of the High Court, Queen's Bench Division, since 1971; *b* 20 Nov. 1915; *o surv. s* of David Rupert and Amy Isabel Phillips, Radyr, Glam; *m* 1951, Hazel Bradbury Evans, *o d* of T. John Evans, Cyncoed, Cardiff; two *s*. *Educ:* Rugby; Balliol Coll., Oxford (MA, BCL). Barrister, Gray's Inn, 1939; Arden Scholar; Bencher, 1965; QC 1968. Served 3rd Medium Regt, RA, 1940–45 (despatches). Practised at Bar, 1946–71; Wales and Chester Circuit, 1939 (Presiding Judge, 1980–81); Jun. Counsel, Inland Revenue (Rating Valuation), 1958–63; Jun. Counsel, Inland Revenue (Common Law), 1963–68. Dep. Chm., Glamorgan QS, 1964–71. Mem., Parole Bd, 1975–77, Vice-Chm., 1976; Pres., Employment Appeal Tribunal, 1976–78. Pres., San Gimignano and London Fountain Soc. *Publications:* (ed) The Belsen Trial, 1949; Halsbury's Laws, 4th edn, vol. 23 on Income Taxation. *Address:* The Elms, Park Road, Teddington, Middx. *T:* 01–977 1584; Royal Courts of Justice, WC2A 2LL. *Club:* United Oxford & Cambridge University. *Died 2 Aug.* 1982.

**PHILLIPS, Sir Leslie (Walter),** Kt 1962; CBE 1947; Chairman, Baltic Exchange, 1963–65 (Vice-Chairman 1961–63); *b* 12 Aug. 1894; 2nd *s* of late Charles Phillips; *m* 1915, Mary (*d* 1971), *d* of late John Corby; one *s*; *m* 1972, Patricia, *d* of late Claude Palmer. Chm., T.

A. Jones Co. Ltd, Grain Brokers, 1943–70. President National Federation of Corn Trade Associations, 1949–52; President, London Corn Trade Assoc., 1959–60; Vice-Chairman, Sugar Board, 1966–68. Director of Freight, Ministry of Food, 1941–45; Controller of Freight and Warehousing, 1946–47. *Address:* 18 The Village, Meads, Eastbourne, E Sussex. *T:* Eastbourne 37624.

*Died 22 Feb.* 1983.

**PHILLIPS, Air Cdre Manfred Norman;** retired, RAF Medical Branch; Consultant Radiologist, RAF Hospital, Ely, 1968–77; *b* 6 Nov. 1912; *s* of Lewis and Norah Phillips, Portsmouth; *m* 1942, Dorothy Ellen (*née* Green); two *s*. *Educ:* Liverpool Coll.; Liverpool Univ. Med. Sch.; Middlesex Hospital. MB, ChB 1936; DMRD 1954. *Publications:* articles in Brit. Jl Clinical Practice and Brit. Jl Radiology. *Recreations:* gardening, golf, walking. *Address:* Quaney, 83C Cambridge Road, Ely, Cambs. *T:* Ely 3539.

*Died 29 Nov.* 1986.

**PHILLIPS, Prof. Owen Hood,** DCL, MA, Oxon; MA, LLB, Dublin; LLM Birmingham; QC 1970; JP; *b* 30 Sept. 1907; *yr s* of late Surgeon-Captain J. E. Hood Phillips, RN, Portsmouth; *m* 1949, Lucy Mary Carden, 3rd *d* of late Arnold Philip, and formerly Lecturer in Physical Educn, Univ. of Birmingham. *Educ:* Weymouth Coll.; Merton Coll., Oxford. Asst Lecturer in Laws, King's Coll., London, 1931–35; Lectr in General Jurisprudence, Univ. of Dublin (Trinity Coll.), 1935–37; Reader in English Law, Univ. of London, 1937–46; Vice-Dean of Faculty of Laws, King's Coll., London, 1937–40; University of Birmingham: Barber Prof. of Jurisprudence, 1946–74; Dean, Faculty of Law, and Dir Legal Studies, 1949–68, Public Orator, 1950–62, Vice-Principal and Pro-Vice-Chancellor, 1971–74. Vis. Prof. in English Law, University Coll. at Buckingham, 1974–78, Mem., Acad. Adv. Council, 1978–84; Patron, Univ. of Buckingham, 1984–. Min. of Labour and National Service, 1940; Min. of Aircraft Production, 1940–45; adviser to Singapore Constitutional Commn, 1953–54; delegate to Malta Round Table Conf., 1955, to Malta Constitutional Conf., 1958. Governor King Edward VI Schs, Birmingham, 1951–76 (Bailiff, 1958–59); President: Soc. of Public Teachers of Law, 1963–64; British and Irish Assoc. of Law Librarians, 1972–76; Hon. Mem., Midland and Oxford Circuit Bar Mess. *Publications:* Principles of English Law and the Constitution, 1939; A First Book of English Law, 1948, 7th edn (with A. H. Hudson), 1977; Consitutional and Administrative Law, 1952, 7th edn (with P. Jackson), 1987 (published posthumously); Leading Cases in Constitutional and Administrative Law, 1952, 5th edn 1979; Reform of the Constitution, 1970; Shakespeare and the Lawyers, 1972; contributions to various legal periodicals. *Address:* 24 Heaton Drive, Edgbaston, Birmingham B15 3LW. *T:* 021–454 2042.

*Died 25 May* 1986.

**PHILLIPS, Hon. Sir Raymond;** *see* Phillips, Hon. Sir J. R.

**PHILLIPS, Reginald Arthur,** CMG 1965; OBE 1951; Deputy Director-General, British Council, 1966–73, retired; *b* 31 Jan. 1913; *y s* of late James and Catherine Ann Phillips, Tredegar, Mon; *m* 1939, Doris Tate, *d* of William and Angelina Tate, São Paulo, Brazil; one *s* two *d*. *Educ:* Tredegar Grammar Sch.; Balliol Coll., Oxford (MA). Asst Master, St Paul's School, Brazil, 1936; Lecturer, Anglo-Brazilian Cultural Society, 1937–39. War of 1939–45: Intelligence Corps (Major), 1940–46. British Council: Latin America Dept, 1947; Home Div., 1948–54; Colonies Dept, 1954–57; Controller, Commonwealth Div., 1957–59; Controller, Finance Div., 1959–62; Assistant Director-General, 1962–66. *Recreations:* golf, walking, television, gardening. *Address:* 76 Chiltley Way, Liphook, Hants GU30 7HE. *T:* Liphook 722610. *Club:* Athenæum.

*Died 7 Feb.* 1988.

**PHILLPOTTS, Christopher Louis George,** CMG 1957; HM Diplomatic Service, retired; Adviser to Employment Conditions Abroad Ltd, 1972–82; *b* 23 April 1915; *s* of Admiral Edward Montgomery Phillpotts, CB, and Violet Selina (*née* Cockburn); *m* 1942, Vivien Chanter-Bowden; one *s* one *d*. *Educ:* Royal Naval Coll., Dartmouth. Served in Royal Navy, 1932–43; War service, HMS Ilex, HMS Quorn, SO 9th MTB Flotilla (despatches twice). Joined Foreign Office, Nov. 1943; 3rd, later 2nd, Secretary, Copenhagen, 1947–51; FO, 1951; 1st Secretary, Athens, 1953; Counsellor: Paris, 1957–62; Washington, 1964–66; FCO, 1966–70, retired. *Recreation:* theatre. *Address:* Flat E, 6 Eastern Terrace, Brighton, Sussex BN2 1DJ. *T:* Brighton 673270. *Club:* White's.

*Died 6 March* 1985.

**PHILPOTT, Air Vice-Marshal Peter Theodore,** CB 1966; CBE 1954 (OBE 1945); Director of Service Intelligence, Ministry of Defence, 1968–70, retired; *b* 20 March 1915; *s* of late Rev. and Mrs R. G. K. F. Philpott, Worcester; *m* 1942, Marie, *d* of Charles Griffin, Malvern; two *d*. *Educ:* Malvern Coll.; RAF Coll., Cranwell, 1933; No. 31 Sqn, India, 1936–41; Staff Coll., Quetta, 1941; Directorate of Op. Trg., Air Ministry, 1942–44; OC, RAF, Horsham St Faith, 1945–46; JSSC, 1947; HQ, Fighter Command, 1948–51; OC, RAF Deversoir, 1952–54; DD Policy, Air Ministry, 1954–56; IDC Student, 1957; Director of Policy and Plans, Air Ministry, 1958–61;

Senior RAF Directing Staff, Imperial Defence Coll., 1961–63; AOC No. 23 Group, Flying Training Comd, 1963–65; Head of British Defence Liaison Staff, Canberra, 1965–68. *Address:* c/o Lloyds Bank, 19 Obelisk Way, Camberley, Surrey GU15 3SE. *Club:* Royal Air Force.

*Died 13 July* 1988.

**PHIPPS, John Constantine;** Metropolitan Magistrate, 1959–75; *b* 19 Jan. 1910; *er s* of Sir Edmund Phipps, CB, and Margaret Percy, *d* of late Dame Jessie Phipps, DBE; *m* 1st, 1945, Priscilla Russell Cooke (*d* 1947); 2nd, 1949, Sheila (formerly Dilke; *née* Seeds) (from whom he obtained a divorce 1965); two *d*; 3rd, 1965, Hermione Deedes. *Educ:* Winchester Coll.; Trinity Coll., Oxford. Called to Bar, Middle Temple, 1933. RE (TA) 1938; War Office, 1940; Intelligence Corps, Captain, 1941, Major, 1943; Personal Asst to Lord Justice Lawrence (later 1st Baron Oaksey), President of International Military Tribunal, Nuremburg, 1945–46. County of London Sessions: Prosecuting Counsel to Post Office, 1951–53, Junior Counsel to the Crown in Appeals, 1953–59, Prosecuting Counsel to the Crown, 1958–59; Recorder of Gravesend, 1957–59. *Address:* St Giles, Burwash, Etchingham, East Sussex TN19 7HT. *T:* Burwash 882031. *Club:* Army and Navy.

*Died 30 July* 1986.

**PHIPPS, Vice-Adm. Sir Peter,** KBE 1964 (CBE 1962); DSC 1941 (Bar 1943); VRD 1945; retired, 1965; *b* 7 June 1909; *m* 1937, Jean Hutton; two *s* one *d*. *Educ:* Sumner Primary School; Christchurch Boys' High School. Joined staff of National Bank of NZ Ltd, 1927. Joined RNZNVR as Ord. Seaman, 1928; Sub-Lieut, 1930; Lieut, 1933. Served War of 1939–45 (American Navy Cross, 1943). Transferred to RNZN as Commander, 1945; Captain, 1952; Rear-Admiral, 1960. Chief of Naval Staff, NZ Naval Board, 1960–63; Chief of Defence Staff, New Zealand, 1963–65; Vice-Adm. 1964, retired 1965. *Recreations:* yachting, fishing, herpetology. *Address:* Picton, New Zealand. *Club:* Wellington (Wellington, NZ).

*Died* 1989.

**PICKARD, Rt. Rev. Stanley Chapman,** CBE 1968; retired; *b* 4 July 1910; *s* of John Chapman and Louisa Mary Pickard, Gloucester; unmarried. *Educ:* Grammar Sch., Birmingham. Studied pharmacy, 1928–32. Dorchester Theological College, 1933–36; Deacon, 1937; Priest, 1938; Curate St Catherine's, New Cross, SE14, 1937–39; joined UMCA, 1939; Kota Kota, Nyasaland, 1939–40; Likoma Island, Nyasaland, 1940–48; Archdeacon of Msumba, Portuguese East Africa, 1949–58; Bishop of Lebombo, 1958–68; Provincial Exec. Officer, Province of S Africa, 1968–71; Asst Bishop of Johannesburg, 1968–83; Rector of St John's, Belgravia, dio. Johannesburg, 1972–83; Chaplain to Anglicans of Jeppe Boys High School, 1972–83. *Recreations:* walking, bridge. *Address:* The Beauchamp Community, Newland, Malvern, Worcs WR13 5AX.

*Died 31 March* 1988.

**PICKERILL, Dame Cecily (Mary Wise),** DBE 1977 (OBE 1958); Retired Surgeon; *b* 9 Feb. 1903; *d* of Rev. Percy Wise Clarkson and Margaret Ann Clarkson; *m* 1934, Henry Percy Pickerill, CBE, MD, MDS (*d* 1956); one *d*. *Educ:* Diocesan High School for Girls, Auckland, NZ; Otago Univ. Medical School, Dunedin, NZ (MB, ChB). House Surg., Dunedin Hosp., 1926; Asst Plastic Surgeon in Sydney, Aust., 1927–35; Specialist Plastic Surgeon, Wellington, NZ, 1935–68; retired, 1968. Licencee, with late husband, and owner of Bassam Hosp., Lower Hutt, NZ—a "Rooming-In" hospital for mother nursing of infants and small children with congenital defects requiring plastic surgery. *Publications:* contribs to medical and nursing jls and NZ Education Jl, 1980. *Recreations:* travel, gardening, camping, nature conservation, great involvement with NZ Anglican Church. *Address:* Beech Dale, 50 Blue Mountains Road, Silverstream, New Zealand. *T:* Wellington 284542.

**PICKERING, Frederick Derwent, (Derek Pickering),** CBE 1974; DL; Chairman, Local Authorities Mutual Investment Trust, 1975–81; Member, Conference of Local and Regional Authorities of Europe, 1977–81; County Councillor, Berkshire, 1961–81; *b* 28 Nov. 1909; *s* of Frederick Owen Pickering and Emma Pickering; *m* 1935, Marjorie Champion (*née* Shotter) (*d* 1980), JP; one *s*. *Educ:* Bedford House Sch., Oxford. Employed in industry, 1927–43; Sudan CS, 1943–55; company dir, 1955–63. County Alderman, Berks, 1967–74; Chm., Berks CC, 1973–77; Vice-Chm., Exec. Council, ACC, 1976–78; Chm., Local Authorities Management Services and Computer Cttee, 1980–81. DL Berks, 1978. Hon. DLitt Reading, 1976. *Recreations:* cricket (now as spectator), politics (sometime Pres., Reading South, Windsor and Maidenhead Conservative Assocs). *Address:* Grimston Court, Hull Road, Dunnington, York YO1 5LE. *T:* York 489343.

*Died 15 March* 1989.

**PICKERING, Frederick Pickering,** PhD (Breslau); Professor of German, University of Reading, 1953–74, later Emeritus; *b* Bradford, Yorkshire, 10 March 1909; *s* of late F. W. Pickering and Martha (*née* Pickering); *m* 1939, Florence Joan Anderson. *Educ:* Grange High School, Bradford; Leeds University (BA). Gilchrist Travelling Studentship; Germanic languages and literature at Breslau University (PhD). Lektor in English, 1931–32; Asst Lectr and Lectr in German, Univ. of Manchester, 1932–41. Bletchley

Park (Hut 3), 1941–45. Head of German Dept, Univ. of Sheffield, 1945–53; Dean of the Faculty of Letters, Univ. of Reading, 1957–60. Goethe Medal, Goethe Inst., Munich, 1975. *Publications:* Medieval language, literature and art: Christi Leiden in einer Vision geschaut, 1952, an edn; Augustinus oder Boethius?, 2 vols, 1967, 1976; University German, 1968; Literatur und darstellende Kunst im Mittelalter, 1968 (trans. as Literature and Art in the Middle Ages, 1970); The Anglo-Norman Text of the Holkham Bible Picture Book, 1971; Essays on Medieval German Literature and Iconography, 1980; articles and reviews in English and German learned journals. *Recreations:* anything but reading. *Address:* 1 Arborfield Court, Arborfield Cross, Berks RG2 9JS. *T:* Reading 760350.
*Died 17 April 1981.*

**PICKERING, Ian George Walker,** VRD (with clasp) 1952; MD; FRCP 1972; Consultant in forensic psychiatry, special hospitals, Department of Health and Social Security, since 1976; *b* 24 Nov. 1915; *e s* of Geo. W. Pickering, Bradford, Yorks; *m* 1948, Jean (*d* 1975), 2nd *d* of John Bell Lowthian, MC and Bar; one *s* one *d*. *Educ:* Bradford Grammar Sch.; Leeds Univ. MB, ChB 1939; MD 1947; MRCP 1966; FRCPsych 1971; FFCM 1972. Various hosp. appts, 1939 and 1946–47. RNVR, 1939–46: at sea and appts RN Hosps, Plymouth and Sydney, NSW. Surgeon Lt-Comdr RNR, retd list, 1965. HM Prison Service, 1947; Senior MO, HM Prison and Borstal, Durham, 1955–63. Nuffield Travelling Fellow, 1961–62. Dir, Prison Med. Services and Inspector of Retreats for Inebriates, 1963–76; Mem. Prisons Bd, Home Office, 1967–76. Hon. Clinical Lectr in Psychiatry, Univ. of Sheffield, 1977–. Pres., British Acad. of Forensic Sciences, 1969–70; Vice-President: 2nd Internat. Congress of Social Psychiatry, London, 1969; British Assoc. of Social Psychiatry; Oxford Postgrad. Fellowship in Psychiatry, 1966–76; Chm., Dukeries Div., BMA, 1980–81; Vice-Chm., Soc. for Study of Addiction, 1967–74; Member, Executive Councils: Med. Council on Alcoholism, 1967–76; N of England Medico-Legal Soc., Newcastle upon Tyne, 1960–63. Officier de Jurade and Vigneron (*hc*), St Emilion, Aquitaine; Hon. Mem., Prichard Soc., Bristol. *Publications:* articles in professional journals. *Recreations:* travel, music, wine. *Address:* Rampton Hospital, Retford, Notts DN22 0PD. *T:* Retford 84321; (home) Drift House, Ockham Road North, East Horsley, Surrey KT24 6NU. *Clubs:* Royal Automobile, Naval.
*Died 18 Jan. 1984.*

**PICKFORD, Frank;** Under-Secretary, General Manpower Division, Department of Employment, 1970–72, retired; *b* 26 Oct. 1917; *s* of late Edwin Pickford, Bulwell, Nottingham; *m* 1944, May Talbot; two *s*. *Educ:* Nottingham High Sch.; St John's Coll., Cambridge. Entered Min. of Labour, 1939; Asst Private Sec. to Minister of Labour, 1941–43; Dir, London Office, Internat. Labour Office, 1951–56; Sec., NEDC, 1962–64; Under-Sec., Ministry of Labour, 1964; Asst Under-Sec. of State, Dept of Employment and Productivity, 1968–70. *Address:* 64 Westbere Road, NW2. *T:* 01–435 1207.
*Died 28 April 1984.*

**PICKFORD, Prof. Ralph William;** Professor of Psychology in the University of Glasgow, 1955–73, later Emeritus; *b* 11 Feb. 1903; *s* of William Pickford and Evelyn May Flower; *m* 1st, 1933, Alexis Susan Macquisten (*d* 1971); 2nd, 1971, Laura Ruth Bowyer. *Educ:* Bournemouth School and Municipal Coll.; Emmanuel Coll., Cambridge. Emmanuel College: Exhibitioner, 1924, Sen. Schol. and Internal Research Student, 1927; BA 1927, MA 1930, PhD 1932. Goldsmiths' Company's Exhibitioner, 1925; Moral Sciences Tripos, First Class, 1927. Lecturer in Psychology and Acting Head of Dept, Aberdeen Univ., 1929. Asst in Psychology Dept, 1930, Lectr, 1935, Sen. Lectr and Acting Head of Psychology Dept 1947, Glasgow Univ. DLitt (Glasgow) 1947. Hon. Psychotherapist Notre Dame Child Guidance Clinic, 1942–80, and Davidson Clinic, Glasgow, 1952–80. First Pres., Experimental Psychology Group; Chm. and then Hon. Sec. Scottish Br. British Psychological Soc.; Pres. Sect. J Brit. Assoc., 1958. Vice-Pres., Internat. Assoc. of Empirical Aesthetics; Hon. Mem. Soc. Française d'Esthétique; Mem., Council of Soc. Internat. de Psychopathologie de l'Expression; Hon. Pres., Scottish Assoc. for Art and Psychopathology. FBPsS. *Publications:* Individual Differences in Colour Vision, 1951; The Analysis of an Obsessional, 1954; (with R. Kherumian), Hérédité et Fréquence des Dyschromatopsies, 1959; (with G. M. Wyburn and R. J. Hirst), The Human Senses and Perception, 1963; Pickford Projective Pictures, 1963; Studies in Psychiatric Art, 1967; Psychology and Visual Aesthetics, 1972; Monograph: The Psychology of Cultural Change in Painting, 1943; many articles on Experimental, Social and Clinical Psychology, and the Psychology of Art. *Recreations:* painting, gardening, music. *Address:* 34 Morven Road, Bearsden, Glasgow G61 3BX. *T:* 041–942 5386.
*Died 7 June 1986.*

**PICOT, Jacques Marie Charles G.;** *see* Georges-Picot.

**PIERCE-GOULDING, Lt-Col Terence Leslie Crawford,** MBE 1943; CD; Director, Commonwealth Press Union, since 1984 (Secretary, 1970–84); *b* 2 March 1918; *o s* of late Rev. Edward Pierce-Goulding and Christina; *m* 1964, Catherine Yvonne, *d* of John Welsh,

Dunedin, NZ; one *s* one *d*. *Educ:* public and private schs, Edmonton, Alta. Enlisted British Army, 1940, 2nd Lieut Mddx Regt (DCO); Capt. Loyal Edmonton Regt, 1941–42; Staff Coll., 1943; GS03 (Ops), Canadian Planning Staff and HQ 1st Canadian Army, 1943–44; GSO2 (PR), HQ 21 Army Gp and BAOR, 1945–46; Sen. PRO, Central Comd HQ, 1947–48; Adviser to Perm. Canadian Delegn to UN, 1948–50; regtl and staff appts, Royal Canadian Regt and Army HQ, 1950–60; Chief Logistics Officer, UN Emergency Force (Middle East), 1962–63; Dir of Sen. Appts (Army), Canadian Forces HQ, 1963–66; Sen. Admin. Officer, Canadian Defence Liaison Staff (London), 1966–69, retd 1969. Canadian Internat. Development Agency, 1969–70. *Recreations:* golf, travel, photography, literature. *Address:* 20 Hill Rise, NW11. *T:* 01–455 2306. *Club:* Pathfinders.
*Died 16 Jan. 1987.*

**PIERCY,** 2nd Baron, *cr* 1945, of Burford; **Nicholas Pelham Piercy;** *b* 23 June 1918; *s* of 1st Baron Piercy, CBE; *S* father, 1966; *m* 1944, Oonagh Lavinia Baylay; two *s* three *d*. *Educ:* Eton; King's Coll., Cambridge (BA 1940, MA 1944). Lieut (A) RNVR (Fleet Air Arm), 1940; retd 1946. *Heir: s* Hon. James William Piercy, *b* 19 Jan. 1946. *Address:* The Old Rectory, Elford, Tamworth, Staffs. *T:* Harlaston 233. *Club:* United Oxford & Cambridge University.
*Died 22 March 1981.*

**PIERRE, Sir (Joseph) Henry,** Kt 1957; CMT; FRCS; Consultant Surgeon, General Hospital, Port of Spain, Trinidad, WI, 1950–83; Hon. Surgeon, Caura Tuberculosis Sanatorium, Trinidad; Hon. Surgeon, Mental Hospital, Trinidad; *b* 28 Oct. 1904; *s* of Charles Henry and Carmen M. Pierre; *m* 1939, Lilian Brontlett Withers, Monmouthshire; one *s*; *m* 1962, Marjorie Boös; one *s*. *Educ:* Queen's Royal College, Trinidad. WI; St Bartholomew's Hosp., London; London Univ.; Royal Coll. of Surgeons, Edinburgh. Qualified in medicine, 1931; Casualty House Physician, St Bartholomew's Hosp., 1931; junior MO, Trinidad Medical Service, 1932; FRCSE 1939; FRCS 1959; Medical Officer, Grade A, 1945; Sen. Officer Surgeon, Gen. Hosp., San Fernando, 1945; Pres., Trinidad and Tobago Red Cross Soc.; Fellow Internat. Coll. of Surgeons, USA. Navy Meritorious Public Service Citation from US Govt, 1957; Chaconia Medal, Trinidad, 1976; Scroll of Honour, Surgery, Trinidad and Tobago Medical Assoc., 1982. Coronation Medal, 1953. *Recreations:* photography, golf, yachting, tennis, horticulture. *Address:* St Florian, Fishery Road, Bray, near Maidenhead, Berks SL6 1UN. *Clubs:* Royal Commonwealth Society (West Indian); Yacht, Union, Country, St Andrew's Golf, (Hon. mem.) Pointe-a-Pierre (Trinidad, WI).
*Died 28 Dec. 1984.*

**PIGOT, Maj.-Gen. Sir Robert (Anthony),** 7th Bt *cr* 1764; CB 1964; OBE 1959; DL; *b* 6 July 1915; *s* of George Douglas Hugh Pigot (*d* 1959) (2nd *s* of 5th Bt) and Hersey Elizabeth Pigot (*née* Maltby) (*d* 1970); *S* uncle, 1977; *m* 1942, Honor (*d* 1966), *d* of late Capt. Wilfred St Martin Gibbon; one *s* one *d*; *m* 1968, Sarah Anne Colville, *e d* of late David Colville and of Lady Joan Colville, The Old Vicarage, Dorton; one *s* one *d*. *Educ:* Stowe Sch. Commissioned into the Royal Marines, 1934; served War of 1939–45 (despatches): Regimental service in RM Div. and Special Service Group; Staff appts in 3rd Commando Brigade in SE Asia; psc 1943–44; Directing Staff, Staff Coll., Camberley, 1946–47; Min. of Defence, 1953–54; Standing Group, NATO, Washington, 1954–57; Dep. Standing Gp Rep. with North Atlantic Council, Paris, 1958–59; Chief of Staff, Royal Marines, 1960–64; retd, Dec. 1964. Man. Director, Bone Brothers Ltd, 1964–66; Director: John Brown Plastics Machinery Ltd, 1965–66; Executive Appointments Ltd, 1968–70. Pres. and Mem. Cttee of Management, RNLI; Pres., Union Jack Club. High Sheriff, DL, Isle of Wight, 1978. *Recreations:* field sports and yachting. *Heir: s* George Hugh Pigot [*b* 28 Nov. 1946; *m* 1st, 1967, Judith (marr. diss. 1973), *er d* of late Major John Hele Sandeman-Allen, RA; one *d*; 2nd, 1980, Lucinda Jane, *yr d* of Donald Charles Spandler; two *s*]. *Address:* Yew Tree Lodge, Bembridge, Isle of Wight. *Clubs:* Royal Yacht Squadron; Bembridge Sailing; Royal Naval Sailing Association; Solent Cruising and Racing Association.
*Died 30 Nov. 1986.*

**PIGOTT, Major Sir Berkeley,** 4th Bt, *cr* 1808; *b* 29 May 1894; *s* of Charles Berkeley, *e s* of 3rd Bt and Fanny Ada, *d* of Rev. W. P. Pigott; *S* grandfather, 1911; *m* 1919, Christabel (*d* 1974), *d* of late Rev. F. H. Bowden-Smith, of Careys, Brockenhurst, Hants; one *s* two *d*. Served European War, 1914–18; Adjutant Ceylon Mounted Rifles and Ceylon Planters' Rifle Corps, 1924–28; retired pay, 1930; President, The National Pony Society, 1948; Chairman County Polo Association, 1948; Verderer of the New Forest, 1955–68; Chairman National Pony Society, 1961–62. *Heir: s* Berkeley Henry Sebastian Pigott [*b* 24 June 1925; *m* 1954, Jean, *d* of J. W. Balls, Surlingham, Norfolk; two *s* one *d*]. *Address:* 86 Admirals Walk, Bournemouth.
*Died 9 May 1982.*

**PIGOTT, Air Vice-Marshal Michael Joseph,** CBE 1956; Director of Dental Services, RAF, 1954–58; retired, 1958; *b* 16 May 1904; *m* 1938, Ethel Norah, *d* of Alfred Sutherland Blackman; one *d*. *Educ:* Blackrock College, Dublin; Nat. Univ. of Ireland; Nat. Dental

Hosp. of Ireland. BDS 1925; FDSRCS 1948. Joined RAF 1930. Served War of 1939–45, Bomber Command; Inspecting Dental Officer: MEAF, 1945–48, Flying Trng Comd, 1948–49, Tech. Trng Comd, 1949–50; Principal Dental Officer, Home Comd 1950–54; Air Vice-Marshal, 1955. QHDS, 1950–58. *Address:* 18 Duck Street, Cerne Abbas, Dorchester, Dorset DT2 7LA. *T:* Cerne Abbas 538.
*Died 26 Jan.* 1990.

**PIKE, Andrew Hamilton,** CMG 1956; OBE 1945; Minister for Lands and Mineral Resources, Tanganyika, 1957–59, retired; *b* 26 August 1903; *s* of late Canon William Pike, Thurles, Co. Tipperary; *m* 1951, Catherine Provan Cathcart, *y d* of late Prof. E. P. Cathcart, CBE; four *s*. *Educ:* The Abbey, Tipperary; Trinity College, Dublin; University College, Oxford. Tanganyika: Administrative Officer (Cadet), 1927; Asst Dist Officer, 1930; Dist Officer, 1938; Dep. Provincial Comr, 1947; Provincial Comr, 1948; Senior Provincial Comr, 1951; Member for Lands and Mines, 1953. President Tanganyika Society, 1954–57; Member Editorial Board of "Tanganyika Notes and Records", until 1959. *Recreation:* historical research. *Address:* Blatchfeld, Blackheath, Guildford, Surrey GU4 8QY. *T:* Guildford 892358. *Died 13 Jan.* 1984.

**PIKE, Sir Theodore (Ouseley),** KCMG 1956 (CMG 1953); Chairman, Tricolor International, since 1984; *b* 1904; 3rd *s* of late Canon W. Pike, Thurles, Co. Tipperary; *m* 1934, Violet F., *d* of late Sir William Robinson, DL, JP; two *s* one *d*. *Educ:* The Abbey, Tipperary; Trinity Coll., Dublin; University Coll., Oxford. Irish Rugby International (8 caps), 1927–28. Colonial Administrative Service, Tanganyika, 1928–53. Governor, Somaliland Protectorate, 1953; Governor and Commander-in-Chief, Somaliland Protectorate, 1954–59. Hon. LLD (Dublin). *Address:* c/o Grindlay's Bank, 13 St James's Square, SW1. *Club:* Lansdowne (Hon. Mem.).
*Died 27 Dec.* 1987.

**PIKE, Marshal of the Royal Air Force Sir Thomas (Geoffrey),** GCB 1961 (KCB 1955; CB 1946); CBE 1944; DFC 1942 and Bar, 1942; Deputy Supreme Allied Commander, Europe, 1964–67; *b* 29 June 1906; *s* of late Capt. S. R. Pike, RA; *m* 1930, Kathleen Althea, *e d* of Maj. H. Elwell; one *s* two *d*. *Educ:* Bedford School; RAF Coll., Cranwell. Joined RAF, 1923. Served War of 1939–45, Directorate of Organisation, Air Ministry; commanded a Fighter Squadron, 1941; Desert Air Force, 1943–45; AOC No 11 Group Fighter Command, 1950–51; DCS, HQ Air Forces Central Europe, 1951–53; Deputy Chief of the Air Staff, Dec. 1953–July 1956; Air Officer Commanding-in-Chief, Fighter Command, July 1956–Dec. 1959; Chief of the Air Staff, 1960–63. Squadron Leader, 1937; Group Captain, 1941; Air Commodore, 1944; Air Vice-Marshal, 1950; Air Marshal, 1955; Air Chief Marshal, 1957; Marshal of the RAF, 1962. DL Essex, 1973–81. Officer Legion of Merit (USA). *Address:* Little Wynters, Hastingwood, Harlow, Essex.
*Died 1 June* 1983.

**PIKE, Rt. Rev. Victor Joseph,** CB 1953; CBE 1950 (OBE 1944); DD (*hc*) 1955; *b* 1 July 1907; *s* of late Canon William Pike, Thurles, Co. Tipperary, and Mrs William Pike (*née* Surridge); *m* 1937, Dorothea Elizabeth Frend, *d* of late Capt. W. R. Frend, Sherwood Foresters; one *s* two *d*. *Educ:* Bishop Foy School, Waterford; Trinity College, Dublin, BA 1930; MA 1935 (Hon. DD 1955). Curate, Dundrum, Co. Dublin, 1930–32; CF 4th Class, Aldershot, Gibraltar, RMA Woolwich, 1932–39; Senior Chaplain, 43rd Div., 11th Armoured Div., 1940–42; DACG, 5th Corps, CMF, 1942–44 (despatches 1943); ACG, 8th Army, 1945 (despatches); DCG, MELF, 1946; ACG, Western Command, 1947–49; ACG, BAOR, 1950–51; Chaplain-General to the Forces, 1951–60 (with title of Archdeacon, 1958–60); Prebend of Fordington with Writhlington in Salisbury Cathedral, 1960; Bishop Suffragan of Sherborne, 1960–76. Hon. Canon of Canterbury, 1951–60; QHC, 1948; Chaplain to the Queen, Nov. 1953–June 1960. *Recreation:* Rugby. *Address:* 53 The Close, Salisbury, Wilts. *T:* Salisbury 5766. *Club:* Cavalry and Guards. *Died 25 Feb.* 1986.

**PILCHER, Sir John (Arthur),** GCMG 1973 (KCMG 1966; CMG 1957); HM Diplomatic Service, retired; *b* 16 May 1912; *s* of late Lt-Col A. J. Pilcher; *m* 1942, Delia Margaret Taylor; one *d*. *Educ:* Shrewsbury; Clare Coll., Cambridge; France, Austria and Italy. Served in Japan, 1936–39; China, 1939–41; Ministry of Information and Foreign Office, 1941–48; Italy, 1948–51; Foreign Office, 1951–54; Spain (Counsellor, Madrid), 1954–59; Philippines (Ambassador), 1959–63; Assistant Under-Secretary, Foreign Office, 1963–65; Ambassador to: Austria, 1965–67; Japan, 1967–72. Dir, Foreign & Colonial Investment Trust, 1973–82; Chairman: Brazil Fund, 1975–82; Fleming Japan Fund, SA, 1976–85; Advisor on Far Eastern Affairs, Robert Fleming & Co., 1973–85. Member: Museums and Galleries Commn (formerly Standing Commission on Museums and Galleries), 1973–83; Cttee, Soc. for Protection of Ancient Buildings, 1974–82; Treasure Trove Reviewing Cttee, 1977–. Pres., Inst. of Linguists, 1982–84. Grand Cross (Gold) Austrian Decoration of Honour, 1966; Order of the Rising Sun, First Class, Japan, 1971; Grand Official of Order of Merit of the Italian Republic, 1977. *Address:* 33 The Terrace, SW13. *T:* 01–876 9710. *Club:* Brooks's. *Died 10 Feb.* 1990.

**PILE, Sir John (Devereux),** Kt 1978; Chairman, Imperial Group Ltd, 1975–80 (Group Chief Executive, 1973–75; Member, Group Policy Committee, 1971–80; Director, 1967–80); *b* 5 June 1918; 2nd *s* of Gen. Sir Frederick A. Pile, 2nd Bt, GCB, DSO, MC, and Lady Ferguson; *m* 1946, Katharine Mary Shafe; two *s* two *d*. *Educ:* Weymouth Coll., Dorset; Trinity Coll., Cambridge (MA). Service with RA, 1939–46 (Major). Joined Imperial Tobacco Group, 1946; Manager, W. D. & H. O. Wills and Wm Clarke & Son, Dublin, 1956–59; Chairman: Robert Sinclair Ltd, 1960–64; Churchmans, 1964–67; Chm. and Man. Dir, W. D. & H. O. Wills, 1968–71; Dep. Chm., Imperial Tobacco Gp Ltd, 1971–73; Dir, Nat. West. Bank, 1977–81. Member: Council, CBI, 1975–80; Council, Industry for Management Educn, 1975–80. FBIM 1973–80. Governor, London Graduate Sch. of Business Studies, 1976–80. Freeman of City of London. *Address:* Munstead, Godalming, Surrey. *T:* Godalming 4716. *Died 13 Dec.* 1982.

**PILKINGTON, Baron,** *cr* 1968 (Life Peer), of St Helens; **Harry (William Henry) Pilkington,** Kt 1953; DL; Hon. Life President, Pilkington Brothers Ltd (Chairman, 1949–73); *b* 19 April 1905; *e s* of Richard Austin Pilkington and Hon.Hope (*née* Cozens-Hardy); *m* 1930, Rosamond Margaret Rowan (*d* 1953); one *s* one *d* (and one *d* decd); *m* 1961, Mrs Mavis Wilding. *Educ:* Rugby; Magdalene Coll., Cambridge. Joined Pilkington Brothers Ltd, 1927; Dir, 1934–80; Director of the Bank of England, 1955–72. President: Federation of British Industries, 1953–55; Council of European Industrial Federations, 1954–57; Court of British Shippers' Council, 1971–74; Chairman: Royal Commn to consider pay of Doctors and Dentists, 1957–60; Cttee on Broadcasting, 1960–62; National Advisory Council for Education for Industry and Commerce, 1956–66; Econ. Develt Cttee for the Chemical Industry, 1967–72; NW Management Centre, 1974–76; NW Regional Sports and Recreations Council, 1976–82; Mem. Council Manchester Business Sch., 1964–72; President: Assoc. of Technical Institutions, 1966–68; British Plastics Fedn, 1972–74. Chancellor, Loughborough Univ. of Technology, 1966–80. DL Merseyside (formerly Lancs), 1968; Vice Lord-Lieutenant, 1974–80. Hon. FIOB 1974. Hon. LLD: Manchester, 1959; Liverpool, 1963; Hon. DSc Loughborough, 1966; Hon. DCL Kent, 1968. Freeman, St Helens, 1968. *Recreations:* walking, gardening, tennis, cycling. *Address:* Windle Hall, St Helens, Lancs. *T:* 23423. *Club:* United Oxford & Cambridge University. *Died 22 Dec.* 1983.

**PILKINGTON, Charles Vere;** retired as Chairman, Sotheby & Co.; *b* 11 Jan. 1905; *e s* of Charles Carlisle Pilkington and Emilia (*née* Lloyd); *m* 1936, Honor Chedworth (*d* 1961), *y d* of first and last Baron Kylsant; one *s*. *Educ:* Eton; Christ Church, Oxford, (MA). Dir, Sotheby & Co., Fine Art Auctioneers, 1927–58, Chm. 1953–58. Member of Council, Royal Musical Assoc., 1952–58; Member Business Cttee Musica Britannica. *Recreation:* music (harpsichord). *Address:* Casal da Nora, Colares, Sintra 2710, Portugal. *T:* 2990.253. *Clubs:* Travellers'; Eça de Queiroz. *Died 21 June* 1983.

**PILKINGTON, Rev. Canon Evan Matthias,** MA; Canon Residentiary of St Paul's Cathedral, 1976–82, later Canon Emeritus; *b* 27 Dec. 1916; *s* of Rev. Matthias Pilkington; *m* 1946, Elsie (*née* Lashley); four *s*. *Educ:* Worksop Coll.; Keble Coll., Oxford; Cuddesdon Theol. College. Curate of: Bottesford and Ashby, Scunthorpe, 1940; Holy Trinity, Southall, 1942; St John the Divine, Kennington, 1944; Vicar of: East Kirkby and Miningsby, Lincs, 1946; Holy Trinity, Upper Tooting, 1952; Kingston upon Thames, 1961; Canon Residentiary, Bristol Cathedral, 1968–76. Chaplain to the Queen, 1969–86. *Publications:* Learning to Pray, 1986; Learning to Live, 1987. *Recreations:* walking, lettering. *Address:* 14 Park Close, Bladon, Oxford OX7 1RN. *T:* Woodstock 811122.
*Died 8 Oct.* 1987.

**PIM, Captain Sir Richard (Pike),** KBE 1960; Kt 1945; VRD; DL; Inspector-General, Royal Ulster Constabulary, retired; National Governor for Northern Ireland, BBC, 1962–67; Member of Council, Winston Churchill Memorial Trust, 1965–69; Member, Ulster Transport Authority, 1962–64, retired; *b* Dunmurry, Co. Antrim, 1900; *yr s* of late Cecil Pim; *m* 1925, Marjorie Angel (*d* 1986), 3rd *d* of late John ff. Young, Dungiven, Londonderry; two *s*. *Educ:* Lancing Coll., Sussex; Trinity College, Dublin. Served in RNVR in European War, 1914–18; Royal Irish Constabulary, 1921. Appointed to Civil Service, N Ireland, 1922; Asst Secretary, Ministry of Home Affairs (N Ireland), 1935; Staff of Prime Minister, Northern Ireland, 1938; in charge of Mr Churchill's War Room at Admiralty, 1939, and later of Map Room at Downing St; Capt. RNVR. North African Campaign (despatches). DL City of Belfast, 1957. Order of Crown of Yugoslavia; Legion of Merit, USA. *Address:* Mullagh, Killyleagh, Co. Down, Northern Ireland.
*Died 26 June* 1987.

**PINCKNEY, Charles Percy,** FRCP; retired; Hon. Consulting Physician to: Pædiatric Department, St George's Hospital, SW1;

Heritage Craft Schools and Hospitals, Chailey, Sussex; Windsor Group Hospitals, Windsor, Berks; *b* 28 April 1901; *er s* of late W. P. Pinckney, Dir of Rubber Cos; *m* 1934, Norah Manisty Boucher; one *s* one *d*. *Educ*: Radley College; Clare College, Cambridge (MA, MB, BCH). Qualified St George's Hospital, SW1. MRCS, LRCP 1925; FRCP 1941. Held various resident appointments St George's Hospital. Physician to King George Hospital, Ilford, 1931–59. *Publications*: articles in BMJ, Archives of Diseases in Children, and Medical Press, 1940–50. *Recreations*: tennis and ski-ing. *Address*: Park House, Watersplash Lane, Cheapside, Ascot, Berks SL5 7QP. *T*: Ascot 26466. *Club*: Hurlingham.                    *Died* 20 *Feb*. 1982.

**PINE, John Bradley;** *b* 2 Dec. 1913; *yr s* of late Percival William Pine and late Maud Mary Pine (*née* Bradley); *m* 1st, 1945, Elizabeth Mary (Jayne) Hallett (*d* 1948); one *s*; 2nd, 1952, Ann Carney (*d* 1984); one *s*. *Educ*: Douai School. Asst Solicitor, GWR, Eng., 1935–39; Mil. Service, Captain 3rd Dragoon Guards, 1939–45; a Sen. Prosecutor, CCG, 1945–47; Resident Magistrate and Crown Counsel, N Rhodesia, 1947–49; Called to Bar, 1950; Asst Attorney Gen., Gibraltar, 1949–54; QC (Bermuda), 1955; Attorney Gen., Bermuda, 1955–57; Actg Governor of Bermuda, 1956; QC (Nyasaland), 1958; Solicitor Gen., Nyasaland, 1958–60; Minister of Justice and Attorney Gen., Nyasaland, 1960–62, when replaced by an Elected Minister under self-governing Constitution; Legal Adviser to Governor of Nyasaland, July 1963, until Independence, July 1964; Parly Draftsman, Govt of N Ireland, 1965–66; Sec., Ulster Tourist Develt Assoc., 1967; antique business, 1968–70. *Address*: 8 Hanover Court, Blackfriars, Sudbury, Suffolk CO10 6AQ. *T*: Sudbury 72314.                       *Died* 1 *Aug*. 1989.

**PINE, Leslie Gilbert;** author and lecturer; Consultant, Burke's Peerage Ltd, since 1984; Editor, The National Message, 1977–80 (Assistant Editor, 1975–77); Chairman, Covenant Publishing Co. Ltd, 1978–79; *b* 22 Dec. 1907; *s* of Henry Moorshead Pine, Bristol, and Lilian Grace (*née* Beswetherick); *m* 1948, Grace V. Griffin; one *s*. *Educ*: Tellisford House Sch., Bristol; South-West London Coll., Barnes; London Univ. (BA). Asst Editor, Burke's Landed Gentry, 1935; subseq. Editor of Burke's Peerage and Landed Gentry and other reference books and then Managing Editor, The Shooting Times, 1960–64, and Shooting Times Library, 1962–64 (resigned as unable to agree with blood sports); Director L. & G. Pine & Co. Ltd, 1964–69; Man. Ed., Internat. Who's Who of the Arab World, 1975–76. Censorship Air Min., 1940; Min. of Labour, 1941; RAF 1942; Sqn Ldr 1945–46; served in N Africa, Italy, Greece and India (Intel. Branch). Barrister-at-Law, Inner Temple, 1953; Freeman, City of London, Liveryman of the Glaziers' Company, 1954. Prospective Parly Candidate (C) Bristol Central, 1956; contested seat, 1959; re-adopted, 1960; resigned and joined Liberal Party, 1962; Prospective Parly Candidate (L), S Croydon, 1963, resigned candidature, June 1964, disagreeing profoundly with Liberalism. Dioc. Lay Reader, London, 1939, Canterbury, 1961, St Edmundsbury and Ipswich, 1975; received into Catholic Church, 1964; reconciled to C of E, 1971. Corr. Mem. Inst. Internacional de Genealogica y Heraldica (Madrid) and of Gen. Socs in Belgium, Chile and Brazil; Gov., St And. Sch., S Croydon, 1960–64. FSA Scot., 1940; MJI, 1947 (Mem. Council, 1953–61); FJI 1957; Associate, Zool. Soc., London, 1961; FRSA 1961; FRGS 1969; FRAS 1970; Fellow: Augustan Soc., 1967; Octavian Soc., 1982; Distinguished Fellow, Amer. Coll. of Heraldry, 1983. Member: RUSI; Royal Soc. St George. DLitt Central School of Religion, 1985. Has given over 1,000 lectures in Gt Britain, Ireland, Europe, Africa, etc, also series of tutorial lectures under WEA and Further Educn; Cambridge Univ. extra-mural lectures, 1986. Trustee and Reg. Org. Sec., Prayer Book Soc., 1976–. *Publications*: The Stuarts of Traquair, 1940; The House of Wavell, 1948; The Middle Sea, 1950, new edn, 1972; The Story of Heraldry, 1952 (4th edn 1968, Japan, USA); Trace Your Ancestors, 1953; The Golden Book of the Coronation, 1953; They Came with The Conqueror, 1954; The Story of the Peerage, 1956; Tales of the British Aristocracy, 1956; The House of Constantine, 1957; Teach Yourself Heraldry and Genealogy, 1957, 4th (enlarged) edn 1975; The Twilight of Monarchy, 1958; A Guide to Titles, 1959; Princes of Wales, 1959, new edn, 1970; American Origins, 1960, 1968; Your Family Tree, 1962; Ramshackledom, A Critical Appraisal of the Establishment, 1962; Heirs of the Conqueror, 1965; Heraldry, Ancestry and Titles, Questions and Answers, 1965; The Story of Surnames, 1965; After Their Blood, 1966; Tradition and Custom in Modern Britain, 1967; The Genealogist's Encyclopedia (USA and UK), 1969; The Story of Titles, 1969; International Heraldry, 1970; The Highland Clans, 1972; Sons of the Conqueror, 1972; The New Extinct Peerage, 1972; The History of Hunting, 1973; (contrib. to) World-wide Family Historian, 1982; A Dictionary of Mottoes, 1983; A Dictionary of Nicknames, 1984; Teach Yourself to Trace Family History, 1984; A Genealogy Workbook, 1986; contrib. Encyclopedia Britannica, 1974; Contributing Editor, The Augustan (USA). *Recreations*: reading, walking, gardening, travel, lecturing, contributing articles to press. *Address*: Hall Lodge Cottage, Brettenham, Ipswich, Suffolk IP7 7QP. *T*: Rattlesden 402. *Clubs*: City Livery, Press, Wig and Pen.                                         *Died* 15 *May* 1987.

**PINK, Ralph Bonner,** CBE 1961; VRD 1951; JP; MP (C) Portsmouth South since 1966; *b* 30 Sept. 1912; *s* of Frank Pink and Helen Mary (*née* Mumby); *m* 1939, Marguerite Nora Bannar-Martin; one *s* one *d*. *Educ*: Oundle School. Portsmouth City Council, 1948–; Lord Mayor of Portsmouth, 1961–62; JP for City of Portsmouth, 1950. Knight of Order of Dannebrog (Denmark). *Recreation*: yachting. *Address*: House of Commons, SW1A 0AA. *Club*: Royal Naval and Royal Albert Yacht (Portsmouth).                     *Died* 6 *May* 1984.

**PINKERTON, John Macpherson,** QC (Scot.) 1984; FSAScot; *b* 18 April 1941; *s* of John Cassels Pinkerton, CBE, MC, JP, BL, PPRICS and Mary Banks Macpherson, OBE, JP. *Educ*: Rugby School; Oxford Univ. (BA); Edinburgh Univ. (LLB). Advocate, 1966; Clerk of the Faculty of Advocates, 1971–77; Standing Junior Counsel: to Countryside Commn for Scotland; to HM Commissioners of Customs and Excise. Mem., Scottish Valuation Adv. Council. Trustee, Nat. Library of Scotland. Chairman: Cockburn Assoc.; Dunimarle Instn Adv. Cttee. *Publications*: (ed) Faculty of Advocates Minute Books, Vol. I, 1976, Vol. II, 1980; contrib to Macmillan Dictionary of Art, Stair Encyclopaedia of Scots Law. *Recreations*: conservation and collecting. *Address*: Arthur Lodge, 60 Dalkeith Road, Edinburgh EH16 5AD. *T*: 031–667 5163. *Club*: New (Edinburgh).                                       *Died* 28 *Sept*. 1988.

**PIPER, Sir David (Towry),** Kt 1983; CBE 1969; MA, FSA; FRSL; Director, Ashmolean Museum, Oxford, 1973–85; Fellow of Worcester College, Oxford, 1973–85, now Emeritus; *b* 21 July 1918; *s* of late Prof. S. H. Piper; *m* 1945, Anne Horatia Richmond; one *s* three *d*. *Educ*: Clifton Coll.; St Catharine's Coll., Cambridge. Served War of 1939–45: Indian Army (9th Jat Regt); Japanese prisoner-of-war, 1942–45. National Portrait Gallery: Asst-Keeper, 1946–64; Dir, Keeper and Sec., 1964–67; Dir and Marlay Curator, Fitzwilliam Museum, Cambridge, 1967–73; Fellow, Christ's College, Cambridge, 1967–73. Slade Prof. of Fine Art, Oxford, 1966–67. Clark Lectr, Cambridge, 1977–78; Rede Lectr, Cambridge, 1983. Mem., Royal Fine Art Commn, 1970–86. Trustee: Watts Gall., 1966–88; Paul Mellon Foundn for British Art, 1969–70; Pilgrim Trust, 1973–90; Leeds Castle Foundn, 1981–88. Sen. Fellow, RCA, 1985; Hon. Fellow, Royal Acad., 1985. Hon. DLitt Bristol, 1984. *Publications*: The English Face, 1957, 3rd edn 1989; Catalogue of the 17th Century Portraits in the National Portrait Gallery, 1963; The Royal College of Physicians; Portraits (ed G. Wolstenholme), 1964; (ed) Enjoying Paintings, 1964; The Companion Guide to London, 1964, 6th edn 1977; Shades, 1970; London, 1971; (ed) The Genius of British Painting, 1975; The Treasures of Oxford, 1977; Kings and Queens of England and Scotland, 1980; (ed) Mitchell Beazley Library of Art, 1981; Artists' London, 1982; The Image of the Poet, 1982; (ed) Treasures of the Ashmolean Museum, 1985; *novels* (as Peter Towry) include: It's Warm Inside, 1953; Trial by Battle, 1959, 3rd edn (under own name) 1987. *Address*: Overford Farm, Wytham, Oxford OX2 8QN. *T*: Oxford (0865) 247736. *Club*: United Oxford & Cambridge University.
                                                         *Died* 29 *Dec*. 1990.

**PIRBHAI, Diwan Sir Eboo;** *see* Eboo Pirbhai.

**PIRIE, Anne Gillespie, (Mrs J. H. Pirie);** *see* Shaw, A. G.

**PITCHFORD, Denys James W.;** *see* Watkins-Pitchford.

**PITCHFORTH, (Roland) Vivian,** RA 1953 (ARA 1942); RWS; ARCA (London); *b* 23 April 1895; *s* of Joseph Pitchforth, Wakefield; *m* 1932, Brenda Matthews (*d* 1977). *Educ*: Wakefield Grammar Sch. Studied art at Wakefield and Leeds Schools of Art and Royal College of Art. Pictures in Public Collections: Tate Gallery, Aberdeen, Southport, Stoke, Preston, Rochdale, Salford, Bradford, Wakefield, Leeds, Liverpool, Manchester, Helsinki, Sydney Art Gallery, Australia, Hamilton Art Gallery, NZ; Night Transport in possession of Tate Gallery bought by Chantrey Bequest. One man exhibitions: Coolings, Lefevre, Redfern, Leicester and Wildenstein's Galleries, also in S Africa, 1946. Exhibited at New York Fair, Pittsburgh, Chicago, Canada, Australia, Warsaw, Brussels, Paris, Sweden, and most provincial Galleries in England. Official War Artist to Ministry of Information and later to the Admiralty. *Address*: Flat 17, 7 Elm Park Gardens, SW10. *Club*: Chelsea Arts.                                  *Died* 6 *Aug*. 1982.

**PITMAN, Sir Hubert,** Kt 1961; OBE 1953; Member of Lloyd's since 1926; Chairman, H. Pitman Ltd, London, EC; *b* 19 Aug. 1901; *yr s* of W. H. Pitman, JP, sometime one of HM's Lieutenants for the City of London; unmarried. *Educ*: Repton. Member, Corporation of London, 1929–54; one of HM's Lieutenants for City of London, 1950–; Member LCC (Cities of London and Westminster), 1955–58; Alderman, 1954–63 (Sheriff, 1959–60) City of London. Senior Past Master, Painter Stainers' Co. OStJ. Comdr Etoile Noire, France. *Recreation*: country. *Address*: 57 Porchester Terrace, W2. *T*: 01–262 6593; Danemore Park, Speldhurst, Kent. *T*: Langton (089–286) 2829; 11 Blomfield Street, EC2. *T*: 01–588 1852. *Club*: Carlton.
                                                       *Died* 19 *March* 1986.

**PITMAN, Sir (Isaac) James,** KBE 1961; MA; Vice-President: British and Foreign School Society; British Association for Commercial and Industrial Education; Member, National Union of Teachers; Proponent of Initial Teaching Alphabet, and its designer, for the easier learning of literacy, oracy and the language in English; *b* London, 14 Aug. 1901; *e s* of late Ernest Pitman; *g s* of late Sir Isaac Pitman; *m* 1927, Hon. Margaret Beaufort Lawson-Johnston (Order of Mercy) (*d* 1983), 2nd *d* of 1st Baron Luke of Pavenham; three *s* one *d*. *Educ:* Eton; Christ Church, Oxford, 2nd Class Hons Mod. Hist. Played Rugby football for Oxford v Cambridge, 1921, for England v Scotland, 1922; ran for Oxford v Cambridge, 1922; skied for Oxford v Cambridge, 1922; won Middle Weight Public Schools Boxing, 1919. Bursar, Duke of York's and King's Camp, 1933–39. Chairman, Sir Isaac Pitman and Sons Ltd, 1934–66. RAF 1940–43, Acting Sqdn Leader; Director of Bank of England, 1941–45; HM Treasury, Director of Organisation and Methods, 1943–45. MP (C) Bath, 1945–64. Formerly Chm., Royal Soc. of Teachers; Chm. of Council, Initial Teaching Alphabet Foundn and Nat. Centre for Cued Speech (for the deaf child); Life Pres., UK Fedn of ita Schs; Mem. Cttee, Nat. Foundn for Educational Res. (which conducted comparative researches into reasons for reading failure in earliest stages of learning); Mem., Cttee advising Public Trustee under Will of late George Bernard Shaw in carrying out his wishes for design and publication of a proposed British alphabet. Formerly Charter Pro-Chancellor, Bath Univ. Hon. Pres., Parly Group for World Govt; Vice-Pres., Inst. of Administrative Management, 1965–69. Hon. DLittHum Hofstra, NY; Hon. DLitt: Strathclyde and Bath. *Address:* 58 Chelsea Park Gardens, SW3 6AE. *T:* 01–352 7004. *Clubs:* Harlequins, Achilles.                *Died* 1 *Sept.* 1985.

**PITT, Terence John;** Member (Lab) Midlands West, European Parliament, since 1984; *b* Willenhall, Staffs, 2 March 1937. *Educ:* Queen Mary's Sch., Walsall; Univ. of Aston, Birmingham. Head of Labour Party Research Department, 1965–74; Special Adviser to Lord President of the Council, 1974. Freelance writer and consultant on govt affairs, 1975–78; Founding Dir, Inst. of Nat. Affairs, PNG, 1978–81; Sen. Adviser on Economic Develt, W Midlands CC, 1981–84. *Publications:* contrib.: Nuclear Power Technology (ed Pearson), 1963; People and Parliament (ed McIntosh), 1978. *Address:* 6 Templefield Square, Wheeley's Road, Birmingham B15 2LJ. *T:* 021–440 8471.                *Died* 3 *Oct.* 1986.

**PITT, William Augustus Fitzgerald Lane F.;** *see* Fox-Pitt.

**PITT-RIVERS, Dr Rosalind Venetia,** FRS 1954; *b* 4 March 1907; *d* of late Hon. Anthony Morton Henley, CMG, DSO, and late Hon. Sylvia Laura Henley, OBE (*née* Stanley); *m* 1931, Captain George Henry Lane Fox Pitt-Rivers (*d* 1966); one *s*. *Educ:* Notting Hill High Sch.; Bedford Coll., University of London. MSc London 1931; PhD London, 1939. Head, Chemistry Division, Nat. Inst. for Medical Research, 1969–72. Hon. FRCP 1986. *Publications:* The Thyroid Hormones, 1959; The Chemistry of Thyroid Diseases, 1960; (with W. R. Trotter) The Thyroid Gland, 1964. *Address:* The Old Estate Office, Hinton St Mary, Sturminster Newton, Dorset DT10 1NA.                *Died* 14 *Jan.* 1990.

**PITTOM, L(ois) Audrey,** CB 1979; retired; Under Secretary, Health and Safety Executive, Department of Employment, 1975–78; *b* 4 July 1918; *d* of Thomas Pittom and Hylda (*née* Ashby). *Educ:* Laurels Sch., Wroxall Abbey, Warwick; St Anne's Coll., Oxford (BA Hons). Inspector of Factories, 1945; Superintending Inspector, Nottingham, 1967; Dep. Chief Inspector of Factories, 1970. *Recreations:* gardening, sight-seeing in Europe. *Address:* 1 Rectory Lane, Barby, Rugby, Warwicks. *T:* Rugby 890424.
                                                *Died* 5 *April* 1990.

**PLANT, Baron** *cr* 1978 (Life Peer), of Benenden in the County of Kent; **Cyril Thomas Howe Plant,** CBE 1975 (OBE 1965); *b* Leek, Staffs, 27 Aug. 1910; *s* of late Sidney Plant and late Rose Edna Plant; *m* 1931, Gladys Mayers; two *s* one *d*. *Educ:* Leek High School. Entered Post Office, 1927; Inland Revenue, 1934; Inland Revenue Staff Federation: Asst Sec., 1944; Gen. Sec., 1960–76; Chm. of Post Office and Civil Service Sanatorium Soc., 1950–75; Mem. General Council TUC, 1964–76 (Mem. Economic, Internat. Cttees TUC, Adviser to UK Workers' Deleg. ILO, 1965–); Chm., TUC, 1976; Mem. Exec. Cttee, Public Service International, 1960–77; UK Workers' Mem. of ILO Governing Body, Nov. 1969–77. Member: NE Metrop. Hosp. Bd, 1965–68; Community Relations Commn, 1974–77; Monopolies and Mergers Commn, 1975–78; Race Relations Bd, 1976–77; Southern Water Bd, 1977–80; Chm., NI Standing Adv. Commn on Human Rights, 1976–80; Mem., Police Pay and Structure Cttee, 1977–79; Vice-Chm., British Waterways Bd, 1977–80. Chm. of Governors, Ruskin Coll., Oxford, 1967–79; Treas., London Trades Council, 1952–74; Member: Civil Service Nat. Whitley Council, 1948–76; Inland Revenue Departmental Whitley Council, 1938–76 (Chm. 1958–76); Chm. British Productivity Council, 1972–77; Vice Pres., WEA, 1981–85 (Treasurer, 1969–81). A Dir, LOB, 1977–80. Trustee, Brighton and Hove Engineerium, 1980–. *Recreations:* horse racing, international

activity. *Address:* Longridge, 19 Montacute Road, Lewes, East Sussex. *T:* Lewes 472556. *Club:* English-Speaking Union.
                                                *Died* 9 *Aug.* 1986.

**PLATT, Prof. (Desmond) Christopher (Martin);** Professor of the History of Latin America, University of Oxford, since 1972; Fellow, since 1972, Senior Tutor, 1979–85, St Antony's College, Oxford; *b* 11 Nov. 1934; twin *s* of late J. W. Platt, CBE; *m* 1st, 1958, Sarah Elizabeth Russell (marr. diss.); no *c*; 2nd, 1984, Sylvia Haanel Matthew. *Educ:* Collyer's Sch., Horsham; Balliol Coll., Oxford; Stanford Univ.; St Antony's Coll., Oxford. BA 1st cl. Hist. 1958, MA, DPhil 1962, Oxon; FRHistS. Asst Principal, Min. of Aviation, 1960–61; Asst Lectr, Edinburgh Univ., 1961–62; Lectr, Exeter Univ., 1962–68; Fellow, Queens' Coll., Cambridge and Univ. Lectr in Latin American History, 1969–72; Director: Centre of Latin Amer. Studies, Univ. of Cambridge, 1971–72; Latin American Centre, Univ. of Oxford, 1972–83. Chm., Soc. for Latin American Studies, 1973–75. *Publications:* Finance, Trade and Politics in British Foreign Policy 1815–1914, 1968; The Cinderella Service: British Consuls since 1825, 1971; Latin America and British Trade 1806–1914, 1972; (ed) Business Imperialism: an inquiry based on British experience in Latin America before 1930, 1977; Foreign Finance in Continental Europe and the USA 1815–1870, 1984; (ed) Argentina, Australia and Canada: studies in comparative development 1870–1965, 1985; (ed) The Political Economy of Argentina 1880–1946, 1986; Britain's Investment Overseas on the Eve of the First World War: the use and abuse of numbers, 1986; The Most Obliging Man in Europe: life and times of the Oxford Scout, 1986; Mickey Mouse Numbers in World History: the short view, 1989. *Address:* 23 Park Town, Oxford OX2 6SN. *T:* Oxford 54908.                *Died* 15 *Aug.* 1989.

**PLATT, Sir Harry,** 1st Bt, *cr* 1958; Kt 1948; MD (Victoria), MS (London), FRCS; Hon. FACS; Hon. FRCS (Canada); Hon. FRCSE; Hon. FDS; Professor of Orthopædic Surgery, University of Manchester, 1939–51, then Emeritus Professor; President, National Fund for Research into Crippling Diseases, since 1970; Hon. President: International Federation of Surgical Colleges (Pres., 1958–66); Société Internationale de Chirurgie Orthopédique et de Traumatologie; *b* Thornham, Lancashire, 7 Oct. 1886; *e s* of Ernest Platt; *m* 1916, Gertrude Sarah (*d* 1980), 2nd *d* of Richard Turney; one *s* four *d*. *Educ:* Victoria Univ. of Manchester. University Gold Medal. MB, BS (London), 1909; Gold Medal for thesis MD (Vic), 1921; Hunterian Prof. of Surgery and Pathology, RCS, 1921; post-graduate study in USA, 1913–14 (Boston, New York, etc). Captain RAMC (TF), 1915–19. Surgeon in charge of Special Military Surgical Centre (Orthopædic Hospital), Manchester. Consultant Adviser: Ministry of Health, 1940–63; Ministry of Labour, 1952–64. President: British Orthopædic Assoc., 1934–35; RCS, 1954–57; Central Council for the Disabled, 1969; Mem., Central Health Services Council, 1948–57. Hon. Degrees: DM Berne, 1954; Dr, Univ. of Paris, 1966; LLD: Univs of Manchester, 1955, Liverpool, 1955, Belfast, 1955, Leeds, 1965. KStJ 1972. *Publications:* monographs and articles on orthopædic surgery, medical education, hospital organisation, etc. *Recreations:* music, travel. *Heir:* *s* F(rank) Lindsey Platt, Barrister-at-Law [*b* 16 Jan. 1919; *m* 1951, Johanna Laenger]. *Address:* 14 Rusholme Gardens, Platt Lane, Manchester M14 5LS. *T:* 061–224 2427. *Clubs:* Travellers' (Life Mem.); St James's (Manchester).
                                                *Died* 20 *Dec.* 1986.

**PLATT, Kenneth Harry,** CBE 1966 (MBE 1944); Secretary, Institution of Mechanical Engineers, 1961–76, Secretary Emeritus, 1977; *b* 14 March 1909; *m* 1956, Janet Heather Walters; one *d*. *Educ:* Shrewsbury School; Glasgow Univ. (BSc in Mech. Eng.). Lecturer, School of Mines, Treforest, 1936–38; Prof. of Mech. Engineering, Benares, India, 1938–39. War Service, RAOC and REME (Major), 1939–45. HM Inspectorate of Schools, 1946–48; Educn and Personnel Manager, Brush Elec. Eng. Co. Ltd, 1949–52; Instn of Mechanical Engineers, 1952–76; Dep. Secretary, 1955. *Address:* 3 Eaton Close, Avonlea, Leamington Spa, CV32 6HR.
                                                *Died* 9 *Nov.* 1985.

**PLATZER, Dr Wilfried,** Gold Cross of Commander, Order of Merit (Austria), 1968; Hon. GCVO 1969; Ambassador of Austria to the Court of St James's, 1970–74; *b* 5 April 1909; *s* of Karl Platzer and Paula (*née* Rochelt); *m* 1939, Edith von Donat; one *s* one *d*. *Educ:* Univ. of Vienna; Foreign Service College. Dr of Law. Attaché, Austr. Legation, Berlin, 1933–34; Austr. Min. for Foreign Affairs, Economic Section: Attaché, 1935–38; Counsellor, 1946–49; Counsellor, Austr. Embassy, Washington, 1950–54; Minister, and Head of Economic Section, Austr. Min. for Foreign Affairs, 1954–58; Ambassador, Washington, 1958–65; Head of Econ. Section, Min. for For. Affairs, 1965–67; Sec.-Gen. for For. Affairs, 1967–70. Grand Cross of: German Order of Merit, 1969; Cedar of Lebanon, 1968; Grand Officer's Cross: Order of St Olav, Norway, 1967; Order of White Elephant, Thailand, 1967; Menelik Order of Ethiopia, 1954; Comdr, Legion d'Honneur, 1957. *Recreation:* reading. *Club:* Wiener Rennverein (Vienna).
                                                *Died* 12 *Nov.* 1981.

**PLAYFORD, Hon. Sir Thomas,** GCMG 1957; Premier, Treasurer and Minister of Immigration of S Australia, Nov. 1938–March 1965; Minister of Industry and Employment, 1946–53; Leader of the Opposition, 1965–66; MP, South Australia, 1933–66; *b* 5 July 1896; *o s* of T. Playford, Norton's Summit, SA; *gs* of late Hon. T. Playford, sometime Premier of S Australia; *m* 1928, Lorna Beaman, *e d* of F. S. Clark; one *s* two *d*. *Educ:* Norton Summit Public School. Engaged in primary production (fruit grower); served European War 27th Bn AIF obtaining a Commission; entered SA Parliament, 1933, as one of representatives for District of Murray; representative for Gumeracha District, 1938–68; Member of Liberal Country Party; Commissioner of Crown Lands, Minister of Repatriation and Irrigation, March 1938; succeeded Hon. R. L. Butler as Leader of Liberal Country Party, 1938. *Recreation:* horticulture. *Address:* Norton Summit, SA 5136, Australia.                      *Died 16 June* 1981.

**PLEASS, Sir Clement (John),** KCMG 1955 (CMG 1950); KCVO 1956; KBE 1953; MA; retired as Governor; *b* 19 November 1901; *s* of J. W. A. Pleass, Tiverton, Devon; *m* 1927, Sybil, *d* of Alwyn Child, Gerrard's Cross; one *s*. *Educ:* Royal Masonic School; Selwyn College, Cambridge. Joined Colonial Administrative Service, Jan. 1924; served in Nigeria, 1924–56. Lieut-Governor, 1952–54, Governor, 1954–56, Eastern Region of Nigeria. Formerly Mem., Colonial Development Corporation. *Recreation:* golf. *Address:* Higher Barton, Malborough, near Kingsbridge, S Devon. *Club:* Royal Commonwealth Society.                        *Died 27 Oct.* 1988.

**PLIMMER, Sir Clifford (Ulric),** KBE 1967; *b* 25 July 1905; *s* of late Arthur Bloomfield Plimmer and Jessie Elizabeth (*née* Townsend); *m* 1935, Letha May (*née* Port); three *s* (and one *s* decd). *Educ:* Scots Coll., Wellington; Victoria Univ. of Wellington. Office Junior, 1922, Wright, Stephenson & Co. Ltd (stock and station agents, woolbrokers, gen. merchants, manufrs, car dealers, insurance agents, etc), retired as Chm. and Man. Dir, 1970. Director: McKechnie Bros. (NZ) Ltd; James Smith Ltd; Tradespan NZ Ltd; owns and operates a number of sheep and cattle farms in New Zealand. Nat. Patron, Intellectually Handicapped Children's Soc. Inc.; Member: Dr Barnardos in NZ; Wellington Med. Res. Foundn. *Address:* PO Box 10218, Wellington, New Zealand. *Clubs:* Wellington; Northern, (Auckland); Hutt (Lower Hutt, NZ).              *Died 14 Dec.* 1988.

**PLIMSOLL, Sir James,** AC 1978; Kt 1962; CBE 1956; Governor of Tasmania, since 1982; *b* Sydney, New South Wales, 25 April 1917; *s* of late James E. and Jessie Plimsoll; unmarried. *Educ:* Sydney High School; University of Sydney. Economic Department, Bank of New South Wales, 1938–42; Australian Army, 1942–47. Australian Delegation, Far Eastern Commission, 1945–48; Australian Representative, United Nations Commission for the Unification and Rehabilitation of Korea, 1950–52; Assistant Secretary, Department of External Affairs, Canberra, 1953–59; Australian Permanent Representative at the United Nations, 1959–63; Australian High Commissioner to India and Ambassador to Nepal, 1963–65; Secretary of Dept of External Affairs, Australia, 1965–70; Australian Ambassador to USA, 1970–74, to the USSR and Mongolia, 1974–77, to Belgium, Luxembourg, and the European Communities, 1977–80; High Commissioner for Australia in UK, 1980–81; Australian Ambassador to Japan, 1981–82. Hon. DScEcon Sydney, 1984; Hon. LLD Tasmania, 1987. KStJ 1982. *Address:* Government House, Hobart, Tasmania 7000, Australia.
*Died 8 May* 1987.

**PLOMLEY, (Francis) Roy,** OBE 1975; writer and broadcaster; *s* of Francis John Plomley, MPS, and Ellinor Maud Wigg; *m* Diana Beatrice Wong; one *d*. *Educ:* King's Coll. Sch. Announcer and Producer with Internat. Broadcasting Co. (Radio Normandy, Poste Parisien, Radio Internat.), 1936–40; devised: Desert Island Discs, BBC, 1941; Hurrah for Hollywood, 1942; To Town on Two Pianos, 1944; Gala Night at the Rhubarb Room, 1948; Chairman: We Beg to Differ, 1949 (television, 1951); One Minute, Please, 1951; These Foolish Things, 1956; Round Britain Quiz, 1961; Many a Slip, 1964; produced Dinner Date with Death, first film made in UK esp. for television, 1949. Chairman: Exec. Cttee, Radio and Television Writers Assoc., 1957–59; Exec. Cttee, Radiowriters Assoc., 1960–62. Variety Club Award as BBC Radio Personality of the Year, 1979; Radio Programme of the Year Award, Television and Radio Industries Club, 1981; Broadcasting Press Guild Radio Award, 1981. *Plays:* All Expenses Paid, 1951; Devil's Highway, 1952; Half Seas Over, 1953; We'll All Be Millionaires, 1956; (with Arthur Swinson) Lock, Stock and Barrel, 1957; (with Archie Menzies) Tax Free, 1960; The First Time I Saw Paris, 1960; The Best Hotel in Boulogne, 1961; The Shiny Surface, 1963; Everybody's Making Money—Except Shakespeare, 1964; Home and Dry, 1964; (with John Allegro) The Lively Oracles, 1965; Moonlight Behind You, 1967; You're Welcome to My Wife (from the French), 1971; Just Plain Murder, 1972; Murder for Two (from the French), 1973. *Publications:* Desert Island Discs, 1975; French Dressing (novel), 1977; Desert Island Book, 1979; Days Seemed Longer, 1980; Plomley's Pick, 1982; *posthumous publication:* Desert Island Lists, 1985. *Recreations:* English history, French travels, painting,

swimming, playing boules. *Address:* 91 Deodar Road, Putney, SW15 2NU. *Clubs:* Garrick, Savage.              *Died 28 May* 1985.

**PLOW, Maj.-Gen. the Hon. Edward Chester,** CBE 1945; DSO 1944; CD 1950; DCL; DScMil; Canadian Army (Retired); *b* St Albans, Vermont, 28 September 1904; *s* of late John Plow and Hortense Harlow Plow (*née* Locklin); *m* 1937, Mary Nichols, *d* of late Thomas E. G. Lynch and M. Edith Lynch (*née* Nichols), Digby, NS; one *d*. *Educ:* Montreal schools; RMC Kingston. Commnd in RCHA, 1925; served in Canada and UK until 1939. Served War of 1939–45 (despatches twice): Italy and NW Europe; Artillery Staff Officer and Comdr; during latter part of War was Senior Artillery Officer, Canadian Army. Following the War served in various appts in Germany, Canada and the UK, and was GOC Eastern Command, Canada, 1950–58. Lieut-Governor of the Province of Nova Scotia, 1958–63. Dir, Canadian Imperial Bank of Commerce, 1963–74. Member Board of Governors: Izaak Walton Killam Hosp. for Children, Halifax; Canadian Corps of Commissionaires. Life Mem., Royal Canadian Artillery Assoc. Patron, St John Ambulance Assoc. KStJ; Comdr, Order of Orange Nassau (Netherlands). Anglican. *Address:* Locklands, RR1, Brockville, Ont, Canada. *Club:* Brockville Country.                         *Died 25 April* 1988.

**PLUGGE, Capt. Leonard Frank,** BSc; Politician, Scientist, Writer, Inventor, Painter and Sculptor; Hon. Colonel RE 29th (Kent) Cadet Bn; *b* London, 21 Sept. 1889; *o s* of Frank Plugge, Brighton; *m* Gertrude Ann, *o d* of Frederick Rowland Muckleston, Kensington, and Muckleston, Shropshire; one *s* (one *s* and one *d* decd). *Educ:* at Dulwich; University Coll., London (BSc); Univ. of Brussels (Ingénieur des Mines). Mem., Accademia di Belle Arti, Rome and Academy of Sciences, NY. FRAeS 1921. Served European War; Lieut RNVR, 1917; Capt. RAF, 1918; Inter-Allied Aeronautical Commission of Control in Berlin, 1919–20; Aeronautical Delegate Spa Conference, 1919–20; Commission of Aeronautical Control, Paris, 1920–21; National Physical Laboratory, Teddington, 1917; Owens College, Manchester, 1917; Royal Aircraft Establishment, Farnborough, 1918; Imperial College of Science, South Kensington, 1918; Department of Scientific Research of Air Ministry, 1918–19; with Underground Railways Group of Companies, 1923–30. MP (C) Chatham division of Rochester, 1935–45; Chairman Parliamentary Science Committee, 1939–43; Hon. Sec. Inter-Parliamentary Union, 1937–43; President International Broadcasting Club; Chairman, International Broadcasting Co., London, Imperial Broadcasting Corp., New York, and International Broadcasting Co., Toronto, Canada; created Army network, Radio International, first Radio programme for the British Expeditionary Forces in France. Delivered speech The Aether as the Twentieth Century Battlefront (printed Hansard, July 1941, re-printed Cdn Hansard). Partly owned and operated many Continental Broadcasting Stations. General Committee Radio Society of Great Britain, 1923–25; invented Radio two-way Telephone in Car, Television Glasses, Stereoscopic Cinematograph, Plugge Patent Auto Circuit; Member, Société Astronomique de France, 1910–. Balletomane. Chevalier of the Légion d'Honneur; Commander of Dragon of Annam. *Publications:* Royal Aeronautical Society's Glossary of Aeronautical Terms (French Translation) 1921; contributions on Travel and Radio to publications all over the world. *Recreations:* ice skating (champion), yachting (yacht, My Lennyann, Cannes), golf, tennis, backgammon. *Address:* 1919 North Argyle Avenue, Hollywood, Calif 90068, USA.
*Died 19 Feb.* 1981.

**PLUMTREE, Air Vice-Marshal Eric,** CB 1974; OBE 1946; DFC 1940; Co-ordinator of Anglo-American Relations, Ministry of Defence (Air), 1977–84; *b* 9 March 1919; *s* of William Plumtree, Plumbley Farm, Mosborough, Derbys, and Minnie Plumtree (*née* Wheatley); *m* 1942, Dorothy Patricia (*née* Lyall); two *s* (and one *s* decd). *Educ:* Eckington Grammar Sch. Served War of 1939–45: No 53 Army Co-op. Sqdn, 1940–41; No 241 FR Sqdn, 1942; OC No 169 FR Sqdn, 1943; Chief Instr, No 41, OTU, 1944; HQ, Fighter Command, 1945; Staff Coll., Haifa, 1946; Personal Staff Officer to C-in-C, MEAF, 1947–49; OC, No 54 (F) Sqdn, 1949–52; PSO to Chief of Air Staff, 1953–56; OC Flying Wing, Oldenburg, 1957–58; OC, Admin. Wing, Jever, 1958; JSSC, Latimer, 1959; OC, RAF Leuchars, 1959–61; Dep. Dir, Joint Planning Staff, 1962–63; IDC, 1964; Air Adviser to UK High Comr and Head of BDLS (Air), Ottawa, 1965–67; Air Cdre 1966; Dir, Air Plans, MoD (Air), 1968–69; AOC 22 Group RAF, 1970–71; Air Vice-Marshal 1971; Comdr, Southern Maritime Air Region, 1971–73; Economy Project Officer (RAF), MoD, 1973–74. Mem. Council, Ardingly Coll., 1976–86. *Recreations:* gardening, most sports. *Address:* Wings Cottage, Ditchling, Sussex. *T:* Hassocks (07918) 5539. *Club:* Royal Air Force.                                          *Died 11 June* 1990.

**PLUNKETT, Brig. James Joseph,** CBE 1945; Colonel Commandant, Royal Army Veterinary Corps, 1953–59; *b* 1893; *m* 1951, Mrs Rachel Kelly, *d* of Eustace H. Bent, Lelant, Cornwall. *Educ:* Royal Dick Veterinary College. Commissioned, 1914; continuous military service; mentioned in despatches: War of 1914–18 (twice);

Waziristan Campaign (once); War of 1939–45 (twice). Director Army Veterinary and Remount Services, 1947–51; retired pay, 1951. *Address:* Templeshanbo, near Enniscorthy, Co. Wexford, Eire. *Club:* Naval and Military. *Died 30 June 1990.*

**POCHIN, Sir Edward (Eric),** Kt 1975; CBE 1959; MA, MD, FRCP; *b* 22 Sept. 1909; *s* of Charles Davenport Pochin; *m* 1940, Constance Margaret Julia (*d* 1971), *d* of T. H. Tilly; one *s* one *d*. *Educ:* Repton; St John's Coll., Cambridge. Natural Science Tripos, Part I, 1st 1930, Part II (Physiology) 1st, 1931; Michael Foster Student, Strathcona Student, 1931–32; MA 1935; MD 1945 (Horton Smith Prize); FRCP 1946. Mem. of Scientific Staff of MRC, 1941; Dir, Dept of Clinical Research, UCH Med. Sch., 1946–74. Lectures: Oliver Sharpey, London, 1950; Robert Campbell Oration, Belfast, 1953; Mackenzie Davidson, London, 1959; Skinner, London, 1966; Ringer, London, 1968; Hevesy, 1970; Lauriston Taylor, Washington, 1978; Douglas Lee, Bristol, 1979; Antoine Béclère, Paris, 1979; Sievert, IRPA, W Berlin, 1984. Mem., International Commn on Radiological Protection, 1959, Chm., 1962–69, Emeritus Mem., 1977; Member: Nat. Radiological Protection Bd, 1971–82; Physiological Soc., Assoc. of Physicians, Internat. Radiation Protection Assoc.; British Inst. of Radiology; Medical Research Soc.; Hon. Fellow: Royal Coll. of Radiologists; Hon. Member: British Radiological Protection Assoc.; Nippon Soc. Radiologica; British Nuclear Med. Soc.; Hospital Physicists' Assoc.; Amer. Thyroid Assoc. UK Representative, UN Scientific Cttee on Effects of Atomic Radiation, 1956–82. Gifford-Edmunds Prize, Ophthalmol Soc., 1940. *Publications:* Nuclear Radiation: risks and benefits, 1984; articles on thyroid disease, radiation protection and risk estimation in scientific journals. *Recreations:* trivial painting, fell walking. *Address:* c/o National Radiological Protection Board, Chilton, Didcot, Oxon. *Clubs:* Athenæum, Oriental.
*Died 29 Jan. 1990.*

**POCOCK, Hugh Shellshear;** formerly: Director, Associated Iliffe Press Ltd; Chairman of Iliffe Electrical Publications Ltd; Managing Editor, The Electrical Review; (formerly Editor) of The Wireless World; retired Dec. 1962; *b* 6 May 1894; 3rd *s* of late Lexden Lewis Pocock, artist; *m* 1920, Mayda, *d* of late Serab Sévian. *Educ:* Privately. Served European War, 1914–18: commissioned RE, 1915; served in Egypt, Mesopotamia, Persia, on wireless and intelligence work with rank of Capt. (despatches). Assisted in organisation of first short wave amateur transatlantic tests, 1921–22; organised first transatlantic broadcasting trials, 1923; proposed Empire Broadcasting on short wave in 1926, and urged its adoption in face of BBC opposition. Promoted and organised the National Wireless Register of technical personnel 1938, under Service auspices; CEng, FIEE; Life Senior Member of the Institute of Electrical and Electronics Engineers. Hon. Mem., British Record Soc.; Member of Honour, Union Internationale de la Presse Radiotechnique et Electronique. *Publications:* numerous articles relating to radio and electrical progress, technical and general. *Recreations:* genealogy and local history research. *Address:* 103 Boydell Court, St Johns Wood, NW8 6NH. *Clubs:* 25, Dynamicables. *Died 16 March 1987.*

**POCOCK, Most Rev. Philip F(rancis),** LLD; retired 1978; *b* 2 July 1906. *Educ:* Univ. of Western Ontario; St Peter's Seminary, London, Can.; Catholic University of America, Washington, DC; Angelicum University, Rome. Ordination to Priesthood, 1930; Angelicum University, Rome, JCD, 1934; Professor of Moral Theology, St Peter's Seminary, 1934; consecrated Bishop of Saskatoon, 1944; Apostolic Administrator of Winnipeg, June 1951; Titular Archbishop of Apro and Coadjutor Archbishop of Winnipeg, Aug. 1951; Archbishop of Winnipeg, 1952–61; Coadjutor Archbishop of Toronto, 1961–71; Archbishop of Toronto, 1971–78. Hon. LLD: Univ. of Western Ontario, 1955; Univ. of Ottawa, 1958; Univ. of Manitoba, 1958; Assumption Univ. of Windsor, Ont., 1961; St Francis Xavier Univ., Antigonish, 1963; Hon. DD: Huron Coll., London, Ont., 1967. *Address:* 3 Woodbrook Drive, Brampton, Ont L6W 3P2, Canada. *Died 6 Sept. 1984.*

**POLAND, Rear-Admiral Allan,** CBE 1943; DSO 1918; RN, retired; *b* 1888; *s* of William Poland, Blackheath; *m* 1912, Phyllis (*d* 1968), *d* of Dr R. A. Weston, Portsmouth; one *d* (and one *s* lost in HMS Thetis, 1939). Entered Navy, 1903; served in submarines and in command of submarine flotillas, 1910–37; Senior Naval Officer, Persian Gulf, 1937–39; Commodore Commanding East Indies Station, 1938 and 1939; ADC to the King, 1939; Commodore Commanding 9th Cruiser Squadron, 1939–40; Chief of Staff to Commander-in-Chief America and West Indies, 1940–42; Senior British Naval Officer Western Atlantic (Acting Vice-Admiral), 1942; Rear-Admiral, Alexandria, 1942–45; Naval Assistant to Director of Sea Transport, 1945–47. Grand Officer, Order of Humayun (Persia); Kt Comdr Order of Phœnix (Greece). *Address:* 35 Chiltley Way, Liphook, Hants. *T:* Liphook 722359.
*Died 6 Feb. 1984.*

**POLLARD, Sir (Charles) Herbert,** Kt 1962; CBE 1957 (OBE 1946; MBE 1943); retired as City Treasurer, Kingston upon Hull, 1961; *b* 23 Oct. 1898; *s* of Charles Pollard; *m* 1922, Elsie (*d* 1970), *d* of Charles Crain; one *d*; *m* 1971, Hilda M. Levitch. *Educ:* Blackpool. City Treasurer, Kingston upon Hull, 1929–61; formerly held appointments in Finance Depts of Blackpool and Wallasey. Fellow, Inst. of Chartered Accountants; Member Council, Inst. of Municipal Treasurers and Accountants, 1944–61 (President Inst. 1952–53); Financial Adviser to Assoc. of Municipal Corporations, 1951–61; Member several cttees and working parties arranged by government departments on various aspects of education, housing, police and local authority finance; Hon. Manager, Savings Bank, Hull Area, 1943–78. Trustee: C. C. Grundy Trust; Chamberlain Trust for over 25 yrs. Life Vice-Pres., Hanover Housing Assoc.; Mem., Nat. Savings Cttee, 1946–51; Official delegate at International Confs on aspects of local government finance (including Education) in Rome and Geneva, held under auspices of International Union of Local Authorities (prepared British paper for this) and UNESCO. Licentiate, London College of Music. Hon. Treas. and Member Council, General Assembly of Unitarian and Free Christian Churches, 1959–70 (President, 1956–57); Hon. Treas., British and Foreign Unitarian Assoc. Inc., 1964–79; Member, St John Council for Lancs, 1962–72. OStJ 1962. *Publications:* contrib. to: Local Government Finance and to other local government journals. *Recreations:* music, theatre; membership of voluntary service organisations. *Address:* St Peter's Court, St Peter's Grove, York YO3 6AQ. *Clubs:* Yorkshire (York); Rotary (Past Pres., Hull and St Annes-on-Sea). *Died 5 March 1990.*

**POLLARD, Geoffrey Samuel,** IPFA, FCA; Director of Finance, West Yorkshire Metropolitan County Council, since 1973; *b* 5 March 1926; *s* of Reginald Samuel Pollard and Kezia Mary (*née* Piper); *m* 1949, Estelle Mercia (*née* Smith); one *s* one *d*. *Educ:* Eastbourne Grammar School. Clerical Asst, E Sussex CC, 1941–44; Accountancy Asst, Brighton Co. Borough Council, 1944–48; Techn. Asst, Tunbridge Wells Borough Council, 1948–50; Coventry County Borough Council: Sectional Accountant, 1950–52; Chief Accountant, 1952–55; Asst City Treas., 1955–57; Dep. Borough Treas., West Ham Co. Borough Council, 1957–62; Borough Treas., Swansea Co. Borough Council, 1962–68; Treas., W Glamorgan Water Bd, 1966–68; City Treas. and Jt Co-ordinator, Bradford Co. Borough Council, 1968–74. President: CIPFA, 1975 (Mem. Council, 1965–83; Hon. Treasurer, 1978–83); Soc. of Co. Borough Treasurers, 1972–73 (Mem. Exec. Cttee, 1969–74); Soc. of County Treasurers, 1984–85 (Mem. Exec. Cttee, 1974–); Soc. of Metropolitan Treasurers, 1979–80; Chm., CIPFA Jt Cttee of Students Socs, 1972–73; Mem. Students Soc. Exec. Cttee, 1951–; Pres., NE Students Soc., CIPFA, 1974–75; Financial Adviser, Assoc. of Metrop. Authorities, 1974–; Mem., DoE Steering Gp on Regional Water Authorities Econ. and Financial Objectives (Jukes Cttee), 1972–74; Hon. Treas., Royal National Eisteddfod of Wales, 1964; Yorks Arts Assoc.: Hon. Treas., 1969–73; Hon. Auditor, 1973–83; Hon. Treas., Bradford Arts Festival, 1969–73. Hon. Editor, Telescope (Jl of CIPFA Students), 1959–71 (Sir Harry Page Merit Award 1970). Sowerby Award, CIPFA, 1983. *Publications:* contrib. various financial jls. *Recreations:* classical music, cricket, football, photography. *Address:* Department of Finance, West Yorkshire Metropolitan County Council, County Hall, Wakefield, W Yorks WF1 2QN. *T:* Wakefield 367111. *Died 1 Sept. 1985.*

**POLLARD, Sir Herbert;** see Pollard, Sir C. H.

**POLLEY, Denis William;** computer consultant; Under Secretary, Management Support and Computers Division, Department of Health and Social Security, 1978–81, retired; *b* 11 Feb. 1921; *s* of William Henry Polley and Laura Emily (*née* Eyre); *m* 1943, Joyce Stopford; two *d*. *Educ:* Baines Grammar Sch., Poulton le Fylde; Lancashire Indep. Coll., Manchester. Served War, Army, RASC (Captain), 1942–47. Entered Civil Service, 1947; Asst Comr, Nat. Savings Cttee, 1947–48; HEO, Min. of Nat. Insce, 1948; Asst Sec., Computers Div., 1969; Central Computer Agency, Civil Service Dept, 1972–75; Family Support Div., DHSS, 1975–76; Under Sec., Contributions Div., DHSS, 1977–78. *Recreations:* horticulture, exploring countryside. *Address:* Inniscarra, 19 Springfarm Road, Camelsdale, Haslemere, Surrey GU27 3RH. *T:* Haslemere 2481.
*Died Jan. 1983.*

**POLLOCK, Sir George Seymour Montagu-;** 4th Bt, *cr* 1872; Lieutenant-Commander, RN (retired); *b* 14 Sept. 1900; *s* of Sir Montagu Frederick Montagu-Pollock, 3rd Bt, and Margaret Angela (*d* 1959), *d* of late W. A. Bell, Pendell Court, Blechingley; *S* father, 1938; *m* 1927, Karen-Sofie, *o c* of Hans Ludvig Dedekam, of Oslo; one *s* one *d*. *Educ:* Royal Naval Colleges, Osborne and Dartmouth. Entered RN, 1913; retired, 1920; With Unilever, 1920–64. Served in RN, War of 1939–45. *Heir: s* Giles Hampden Montagu-Pollock [*b* 19 Oct. 1928; *m* 1963, Caroline Veronica, *yr d* of Richard Russell; one *s* one *d*]. *Address:* 6 Amesbury Abbey Mews, Amesbury, Wilts. *T:* Amesbury 23632. *Died 21 Feb. 1985.*

**POLLOCK, James Huey Hamill,** CMG 1946; OBE 1939; *b* 6 Aug. 1893; *s* of late William Charles Pollock; *m* 1919, Margaret Doris,

OStJ (d 1962), d of late P. B. Kearns; two s. Educ: Royal School, Armagh. Served in Royal Irish Rifles, London Regt and Staff, 1914–20 (wounded, despatches); Dep. Governor, Ramallah, Palestine, 1920; Administrative Officer, Nigeria, 1923; Assistant Secretary, Nigerian Secretariat, Lagos, 1927; Administrative Officer, Palestine, 1930; District Commissioner, Haifa, 1939, Galilee, 1942, Jerusalem, 1944–48; Mem., Adv. Council, Palestine, 1939–48, and Exec. Council, 1945–48; Chief Civil Adviser to GOC British Troops in Palestine, 15 May 1948 till final withdrawal 30 June 1948. Colonial Office, 1949–52. Member, Senate of Northern Ireland, 1954–57; Deputy Speaker, 1956–57. Member Management Cttee, South Tyrone and Drumglass Hospitals, 1960–64. Lieutenant of Commandery of Ards, 1952–61. High Sheriff, Co. Tyrone, 1963. KJStJ. Commander of Order of George I of Greece, 1948. Address: 6 Crescent Road, Wokingham, Berkshire.

Died 14 March 1982.

**POLSON, Prof. Cyril John;** Professor of Forensic Medicine, University of Leeds, 1947–69, then Emeritus Professor; b 9 Nov. 1901; s of William Polson, MB, CM, and A. D., d of Thomas Parker, JP, MInstCE, FRSE; m 1932, Mary Watkinson Tordoff (d 1961); one d; m 1963, G. Mary Pullan (BSc, MB, ChB, MFCM, DObst, RCOG). Educ: Wrekin Coll.; Birmingham Univ. MB, ChB and MRCS, LRCP, 1924; MRCP 1926; FRCP, 1941; FRCPath, 1964; MD 1929, Birmingham. Called to the Bar, Inner Temple, 1940. Assistant Lecturer, Univ. of Manchester, 1927; Univ. of Leeds: Lecturer in Pathology, 1928; Senior Lecturer in Pathology, and Pathologist to St J. Hospital, Leeds, 1945; Hon. Member, N England Laryngological Society, 1948. Corr. Member la Société de Médecine Légale de France, 1950. Vice-President 2nd International Meeting in Forensic Medicine, NY, 1960; President: British Association in Forensic Medicine, 1962–65; British Acad. of Forensic Sciences, 1974–75; Mem., Leeds and West Riding Medico-Legal Society, 1963 (Pres. 1966); Hon. Mem., Leeds and West Riding Medico-Chirurgical Soc., 1970. A. G. Marshall Lectr, Midland Inst. of Forensic Medicine and Bd of Grad. Studies, Birmingham Univ., 1979. Publications: Clinical Toxicology (with M. A. Green and M. R. Lee), 2nd edn, 1969, 3rd edn, 1983; The Scientific Aspects of Forensic Medicine, 1969, Swedish trans., 1973; The Essentials of Forensic Medicine, 3rd edn (with D. J. Gee), 1973, 4th edn (with D. J. Gee and Bernard Knight), 1984; The Disposal of the Dead (with T. K. Marshall), 3rd edn, 1975; papers in scientific journals devoted to pathology and forensic medicine. Recreations: gardening, photography. Address: 16 Tewit Well Road, Harrogate HG2 8JE. T: Harrogate 503434.

Died 31 Dec. 1986.

**POLUNIN, Oleg;** Assistant Master, Charterhouse School, 1938–72; b 28 Nov. 1914; Russian father, British mother; m 1943, Lorna Mary Venning; one s one d. Educ: St Paul's Sch.; Magdalen Coll., Oxford. Served War of 1939–45, Intelligence Corps. Botanical Exploration and collecting, Nepal, 1949–52; Turkey, 1954–56; Karakoram, Pakistan, 1960; Kashmir; Iraq; Lebanon; Lecturer and Guide on Hellenic cruises and other tours, often off the beaten track. Founder member, past Chairman, and Secretary, Surrey Naturalists' Trust. H. H. Bloomer Award, Linnean Soc., 1983. Publications: (with A. J. Huxley) Flowers of the Mediterranean, 1965; Flowers of Europe, 1969; Concise Flowers of Europe, 1972; (with B. E. Smythies) Flowers of South West Europe, 1973; (with B. Everard) Trees and Bushes of Europe, 1976; Flowers of Greece and the Balkans, 1980; (with J. D. A. Stainton) Flowers of the Himalaya, 1984; (with Martin Walters) Guide to the Vegetation of Britain and Europe, 1985; posthumous publications: Wild Flowers of Britain and Northern Ireland, 1988; (with Adam Stainton) Concise Flowers of the Himalaya, 1988. Recreations: travel, plant photography and collecting, pottery. Address: 2 Lockwood Court, Knoll Road, Godalming, Surrey.

Died 2 July 1985.

**POMFRET, Surgeon Rear-Adm. Arnold Ashworth,** CB 1957; OBE 1941; retired, 1957; b 1 June 1900; s of John and Eleanor Pomfret; m 1928, Carlene Blundstone; one s two d. Educ: Manchester Univ. Postgraduate at London, Capetown and Oxford. MB, ChB (Manchester), 1922; DO (Oxon) 1934; DOMS (RCS&PEng), 1934. Senior Ophthalmic Specialist, RN. Last MO i/c Wei-Hai-Wei, 1940. Formerly Asst to MDG, 1944–45 and 1952–54. MO i/c RN Hospitals: Simonstown, 1946; Portland, 1948; Bermuda, 1950; MO i/c RN Hospital, Plymouth, and Command MO Plymouth, 1954–57. Gilbert Blane Medallist, 1934. Surgeon Comdr, 1934; Surgeon Captain, 1944; Surgeon Rear-Adm., 1954. QHS, 1954–57. CStJ 1957. Recreations: cricket, Association football. Address: Passlands, Forton, Chard, Somerset.

Died 3 April 1984.

**POND, Sir Desmond (Arthur),** Kt 1981; MA, MD, FRCP, FRCPsych; Chief Scientist, Department of Health and Social Security, 1982–85, retired; b 2 Sept. 1919; o s of Thomas Arthur and Ada Celia Pond; m 1945, Margaret Helen (née Jordan), MD; three d. Educ: John Lyon's, Harrow; St Olave's, SE1; Clare Coll., Cambridge; University College Hospital. Rockefeller Scholar, Duke Med. Sch., N Carolina, 1942–44; Sen. Lectr, Dept of Clin. Neurophysiology,

Maudsley Hosp., and Cons. Psychiatrist, UCH, 1952–66; Prof. of Psychiatry, Univ. of London at London Hosp. Medical Coll., E1, 1966–82. Goulstonian Lectr, RCP, 1961; Founder Mem., Inst. of Religion and Med., 1964; Mem., Archbishop's Gp on Divorce Law ('Putting Asunder'), 1964–66; Mem., MRC, 1968–72, 1982–85; H. B. Williams Vis. Prof., Australian and New Zealand Coll. of Psychiatrists, 1968; Riddell Memorial Lectr, Univ. of Newcastle, 1971. Pres., RCPsych, 1978–81. Hon. Mem., British Paediatric Assoc., 1982; Hon. FBPsS, 1980; Hon. FRCGP, 1981; Hon. FRSM, 1985. Publications: Counselling in Religion and Psychiatry, 1973; various, on psychiatry and electroencephalography. Recreations: making music, gardens. Address: Welcombe, Bridford, Exeter EX6 7JA. T: Christow 52645.

Died 29 June 1986.

**PONSFORD, Brian David;** Under Secretary (Director of HM Inspectorate of Pollution), Department of the Environment, since 1987; b 23 Dec. 1938; s of Herbert E. Ponsford and Kathleen W. C. (née Parish); m 1966, Erica Neumark; one s. Educ: City of London Sch.; Corpus Christi Coll., Oxford (1st Cl. Classical Mods 1958, 1st Cl. Lit. Hum. 1960). Teacher, Westminster Sch., 1960–61; Asst Principal, Min. of Housing and Local Govt, 1961–67; Asst Private Sec. to Minister, 1964–66; Private Sec. to Minister of State, 1966–67; Principal, 1967–69; Principal, Cabinet Office, 1969–71, DoE, 1971–73; Asst Sec., DoE, 1973; Counsellor, Office of UK Perm. Representative to European Communities, 1975–78; Under Sec., DoE, 1981–; Dir, Local Govt Finance Policy, 1981–84, Housing, 1984–85, Waste Disposal, 1985–87. Dir, Medical Systems Gp, Smiths Industries, 1985–. Recreations: music, books, films. Address: Department of the Environment, Marsham Street, SW1.

Died 4 Dec. 1989.

**PONSONBY OF SHULBREDE,** 3rd Baron cr 1930, of Shulbrede; **Thomas Arthur Ponsonby;** Chief Opposition Whip, House of Lords, since 1982; b 23 Oct. 1930; o surv. s of 2nd Baron Ponsonby of Shulbrede, and Hon. Elizabeth Bigham (d 1985), o d of 2nd Viscount Mersey, PC, CMG, CBE; S father, 1976; m 1st, 1956, Ursula Mary (marr. diss. 1973), yr d of Comdr Thomas Stanley Lane Fox-Pitt, OBE, RN; one s two d (and one d decd); 2nd, 1973, Maureen Estelle Campbell-Tiech, d of Alfred William Windsor, Reigate, Surrey. Educ: St Ronan's Sch.; Bryanston; Hertford Coll., Oxford (Pres., Hertford Soc., 1989–). Royal Borough of Kensington and Chelsea (formerly Royal Borough of Kensington): Councillor, 1956–65; Alderman, 1964–74; Leader, Labour Gp, 1968–73. GLC: Alderman, 1970–77; Chm. Covent Garden Cttee, 1973–75; Chm., Central Area Bd (Transport and Planning Cttees), 1973–76; Chm. of Council, 1976–77. An Opposition Whip, 1979–81, Dep. Chief Opposition Whip, 1981–82, House of Lords. Chairman: Local Govt Trng Bd, 1981–; London Tourist Bd, 1976–80; Greater London Citizens Advice Bureaux Service Ltd, 1977–79; Age Concern Greater London, 1977–78; London Convention Bureau, 1977–85; Lord Chancellor's Adv. Cttee on Appt of Magistrates for Inner London, 1987–; Football Pools Panel, 1987–; Tourism Soc., 1980–83 (Pres., 1984–); Bd of Trustees, Community Projects Foundn, 1978–82; Galleon Trust, 1981– (Pres., Galleon World Travel Assoc. Ltd, 1977–81); Rona-Naïve Artists Ltd, 1978–83. Contested (Lab) Heston and Isleworth, general election, 1959. Fabian Society: Asst Gen. Sec., 1961–64; Gen. Sec., 1964–76. President: British Handball Assoc., 1981–; Hotel Industry Mkty Gp, 1983–; Fedn of Industrial Develt Authorities, 1983–. Governor, London Sch. of Economics, 1970–. Patron: New Mozart Orch., 1978–88; Guild of Guide Lectrs, 1987–. Recreations: eating, drinking, gardening. Heir: s Hon. Frederick Matthew Thomas Ponsonby, b 27 Oct. 1958. Address: House of Lords, SW1A 0PW.

Died 13 June 1990.

**POOLE, Rev. Canon Joseph Weston;** Canon Emeritus of Coventry Cathedral, since 1977; b 25 March 1909; s of Rev. S. J. Poole and Mrs Poole (née Weston); m 1945, Esmé Beatrice Mounsey; three s two d. Educ: St George's School, Windsor; King's School, Canterbury; Jesus Coll., Cambridge (Organ Schol. and Class. Exhibnr); Westcott House, Cambridge. Curate of St Mary-at-the-Walls, Colchester, 1933; Sub-Warden of Student Movement House, 1935; Minor Canon and Sacrist of Canterbury, 1936; Precentor of Canterbury, 1937; Rector of Merstham, Surrey, 1949; Hon. Canon of Coventry, 1958, Precentor, 1958–77; Canon Residentiary, 1963–77. ChStJ, 1974. FRSCM 1977. Recreations: music, literature, typography. Address: The Coventry Beaumont, 56 Kenilworth Road, Coventry CV4 7AH.

Died 7 July 1989.

**POOLE HUGHES, Rt. Rev. John Richard Worthington;** b 8 Aug. 1916; s of late Canon W. W. Poole Hughes, Warden of Llandovery College and late Bertha Cecil (née Rhys). Educ: Uppingham School; Hertford College, Oxford; Wells Theological College. BA (Lit. Hum.) 1939, MA 1945. Royal Artillery, 1939–45. Deacon, 1947; Priest, 1948; Curate, St Michael and All Angels, Aberystwyth, 1947–50; UMCA Missionary, 1950–57; Staff, St Michael's College, Llandaff, 1957–59; Home Secretary, Universities' Mission to Central Africa, 1959–62; Bishop of South-West Tanganyika, 1962–74; Asst Bishop of Llandaff and Asst Curate, Llantwit Major, 1975; Bishop of Llandaff, 1976–85. Publication: Asomaye na Afahamu (SPCK),

1959. *Recreation:* writing. *Address:* St Ethelbert's House, Castle Hill, Hereford HR1 2NJ.                    *Died* 25 Oct. 1988.

**POORE, Roger Dennistoun, (Dennis);** Executive Chairman: Manganese Bronze Holdings plc (Chairman, since 1963; Director, since 1961); Federated Trust Corporation Ltd, since 1967; Chairman, The Scottish & Mercantile Investment plc, since 1971 (Director, since 1965); Member Lloyd's, since 1950; *b* 19 Aug. 1916; *s* of Lt-Col Roger Alvin Poore, DSO, and Lorne Margery, *d* of Major R. J. W. Dennistoun; *m* 1949, Mrs Peta Farley; one *d. Educ:* Eton; King's College, Cambridge (MA). Served War, Royal Air Force, 1939–46 (Wing Comdr 1944). Motor racing successes, 1947–55 (British Hill Climb Champion, 1950). *Recreations:* tennis, golf, bridge. *Address:* 33 Phillimore Gardens, W8. *T:* 01–937 1384.
                                                              *Died* 12 Feb. 1987.

**POPE, Sir Barton;** *see* Pope, Sir S. B.

**POPE, Sir George (Reginald),** Kt 1967; General Manager of The Times, 1965–67; Director: Times Newspapers Ltd, 1967–76 (Deputy General Manager during 1967); Kingsway Press Ltd; *b* 25 Mar. 1902; *s* of G. J. Pope; *m* 1930, Susie A. Hendy; one *s. Educ:* Clapham Parochial Sch. The Morning Post, 1916–37; The Daily Telegraph, 1937; The Times, 1937–. Pres. of the Advertising Assoc., 1962–63. Mackintosh Medal, 1953; Publicity Club of London Cup, 1961. *Recreation:* bowls. *Address:* 57 West Drive, Cheam, Surrey. *T:* 01-642 4754.                            *Died* 17 Dec. 1982.

**POPE, Rev. (John) Russell;** President of Methodist Conference, 1974–75; *b* 15 Aug. 1909; 3rd *s* of George and Rhoda Pope; *m* 1939, Doreen Minette Foulkes; one *s* one *d. Educ:* Canton High Sch., and Technical Coll., Cardiff; Handsworth Theological Coll., Birmingham. Manchester and Salford Mission, 1936–39; Liverpool South Circuit, 1939–44; Manchester and Salford Mission, 1944–48; Bristol Mission, 1948–57; Nottingham Mission, 1957–59; Chm., Plymouth and Exeter Methodist District, 1959–76, retired; Second Minister, Ilfracombe Circuit, 1976–79. Preaching tours: S Africa, 1953; NSW, 1959; Bahamas, 1962; New England, 1966; two visits to Holy Land, 1964 and 1969 (second visit being Jt Leadership of Ecumenical Pilgrimage to Rome and Holy Land with Bp of Bath and Wells, and Bishop of Clifton); audience with the Pope. *Recreations:* gardening, travel. *Address:* 11 Lime Grove, Exmouth, Devon. *T:* Exmouth 278438. *Club:* National Liberal.
                                                              *Died* 5 July 1985.

**POPE, Sir (Sidney) Barton,** Kt 1959; *b* 18 Feb. 1905; *s* of Henry Pope, Northam, W Australia; *m* 1944, Ada Lilian, *d* of late J. B. Hawkins; two *s* two *d. Educ:* Pulteney Grammar School, S Australia. President S Aust. Chamber of Manufacturers, 1947–49. Patron: SA Assoc. for Mental Health; Aust. Council of Elders. *Address:* 8/4 Chisholm Avenue, Burnside, SA 5066, Australia.        *Died* 2 Sept. 1983.

**POPHAM, Margaret Evelyn,** CBE 1953; Principal, Ladies' College, Cheltenham, Jan. 1937–July 1953; now nearly blind; *b* 5 Sept. 1894; *d* of Rev. B. G. Popham. *Educ:* Blackheath High School; Westfield College, London Univ., BA Hons Classics; Camb. Teachers Dip.; Ont. Teachers Certif. Classical Mistress Co. Sch., Chatham, 1919–23; Classical and Senior Mistress, Havergal College, Toronto, Canada, 1923–30; Headmistress: Ladies' College, Jersey, CI, 1930–32; Westonbirt School, 1932–37. Vice-Chm., Gabbitas-Thring Educational Trust, 1960–74; Member: Westfield College Council, 1935–66; Independent Television Authority, 1954–56; ITA Children's Committee, 1956–60; Individual Freedom Society (Executive), 1954–68 (now Vice-Pres.); Commonwealth Migration Council (Exec.), 1956–66; Conservative Commonwealth Coun., and Conservative Women's National Advisory Committee, 1954–57, and 1960–61; Canning House, 1955–65. South Kensington Conservative (Executive), 1958–62; European Union of Women (Executive), 1960–75; National Broadcasting Development Committee, 1961–63; formerly Mem., Governing Body of Girls' Sch. Exec. *Publication:* (memoirs) Boring—Never!, 1968. *Recreations:* literature and travelling; politics and Commonwealth questions. *Address:* 60 Stafford Court, W8 7DN. *T:* 01-937 2717.
                                                              *Died* 25 April 1982.

**POPPLEWELL, Patrick John Lyon;** HM Diplomatic Service; retired; *b* 2 April 1937; *s* of Geoffrey Douglas Popplewell and late Marjorie Helen (*née* Macdonald). *Educ:* Haileybury and Imperial Service Coll.; Brasenose Coll., Oxford (Hons degree Law). HM Armed Forces, 1955–57. Appointed Foreign Office, 1960; 3rd and 2nd Sec., Tokyo, 1960–65; Resident Clerk, CRO and FO, 1965–67; 1st (Press) Sec., Cairo, 1968–70; Tokyo, 1970–74; Foreign and Commonwealth Office: Trade Relations and Export Dept, 1974–76; Far Eastern Dept, 1976–77; Counsellor, Peking, 1977–78; FCO, 1978–80. *Recreation:* all aspects of Japanese Art. *Address:* Clouds Hill, Shillingstone, near Blandford Forum, Dorset. *T:* Child Okeford 263. *Club:* United Oxford & Cambridge University.
                                                              *Died* 3 Jan. 1983.

**PORBANDAR, Maharaja of, Lt-Col HH Maharaja Rana Saheb, Shri Sir Natwarsinhji Bhavsinhji,** KCSI 1929; *b* 30 June 1901; *s* of HH the Rana Saheb Shri Bhavsinhji Bahadur of Porbandar; *m* 1st, 1920, Princess Rupaliba, MBE (*d* 1943), *d* of late Thakore Saheb of Limbdi, KCSI, KCIE; 2nd, 1954, Anantkunver. *Educ:* Rajkumar College, Rajkot; stood first in the Diploma Examination of the Chiefs' Colleges in 1918. Officially received by HH the Pope, at the Vatican, 1922. Captained first All-India Cricket Team which toured England 1932. Orchestral works published: 42 compositions (as N. Porbandar). *Publications:* Introspect, 1950; Values Reviewed, 1952; Three Essays, 1954; From the Flow of Life, 1967; India's Problems, 1970; International Solidarity, 1975. *Recreations:* music, painting and writing.                              *Died* 4 Oct. 1982.

**PORTAL OF HUNGERFORD, Baroness** (2nd in line), *cr* 1945; **Rosemary Ann Portal;** *b* 12 May 1923; *d* of 1st Viscount Portal of Hungerford, KG, GCB, OM, DSO, MC, and Joan Margaret, *y d* of Sir Charles Glynne Earle Welby, 5th Bt; *S* to barony of father, 1971. Formerly Section Officer, WAAF. *Heir:* none. *Address:* West Ashling House, Chichester, West Sussex PO18 8DN.
                                                              *Died* 29 Sept. 1990 (*ext*).

**PORTAL, Sir Francis Spencer,** 5th Bt, *cr* 1901; DL; President, Portals Holdings Ltd; *b* 27 June 1903; *s* of 4th Bt and late Mary, *d* of late Colonel William Mure, Caldwell, Ayrshire; *S* father, 1955; *m* 1st, 1930, Rowena (*d* 1948), *d* of late Paul Selby, Johannesburg; two *d*; 2nd, 1950, Jane Mary, *d* of late Albert Henry Williams, OBE, Flint House, Langston, Havant, Hants, and of Mrs E. G. Selwyn, Priors Barton Cottage, Kingsgate Road, Winchester; two *s* one *d. Educ:* Winchester; Christ Church, Oxford; McGill Univ., Montreal. Served War of 1939–45, Captain, late Welsh Guards, Guards Armoured Division (Croix de Guerre, 2nd Class Belgium). Chm., YMCA Nat. Commn, 1968. Master, Worshipful Co. of Clothworkers, 1970. High Sheriff of Hampshire, 1963, DL Hants, 1967–. *Recreations:* miscellaneous. *Heir:* *s* Jonathan Francis Portal [*b* 13 Jan. 1953; *m* 1982, Louisa Caroline, *er d* of F. J. C. G. Hervey-Bathurst, Somborne Park, near Stockbridge, Hants]. *Address:* Burley Wood, Ashe, near Basingstoke, Hants RG25 3AG. *T:* Basingstoke 770269.                            *Died* 11 Nov. 1984.

**PORTAL, Admiral Sir Reginald Henry,** KCB 1949 (CB 1946); DSC 1916; *b* 6 Sept. 1894; *s* of late Edward Robert Portal, JP; DL; *m* 1926, Helen (*d* 1983), *d* of late Frederick Anderson; two *s* two *d*. Served European War, 1914–19, with RN and RNAS (DSC); War of 1939–45 (despatches, CB); comd HMS York, 1939–41; HMS Royal Sovereign, 1941–42; Asst Chief of Naval Staff (Air), 1943–44; ADC to the King, 1943; Flag Officer Naval Air Stations (Australia), 1945; Naval representative on Joint Chiefs of Staff Cttee (Australia), 1946–47; Flag Officer, Air (Home), 1947–51; retired, 1951. *Address:* Overton House, Queen Camel, Yeovil, Somerset.
                                                              *Died* 18 June 1983.

**PORTEOUS, Alexander James Dow,** MA; Sydney Jones Professor of Education, University of Liverpool, 1954–63 (Professor of Education, 1938–54); retired Sept. 1963, later Professor Emeritus; Temporary Professor of Moral Philosophy, University of Edinburgh, 1963–64; *b* 22 July 1896; *s* of late John Dow Porteous, MA, former Rector of Knox Memorial Institute, Haddington, and Agnes Paton Walker; *m* 1926, Eliza Murray Dalziel (*d* 1972), MA (Hons Edinburgh), *e d* of late George Ross, Solicitor, Inverness; three *s* two *d* (and one *s* decd). *Educ:* Knox Memorial Institute, Haddington; Universities of Edinburgh and Oxford (Bible Clerk, Oriel College); Moray House Provincial Training College for Teachers, Edinburgh. Served in Army 1916–19, first with the Royal Scots; gazetted 2nd Lieut to the Royal Scots Fusiliers June 1918 and spent seven months on active service in France with the 11th Battalion; MA (Edinburgh) with First Class Honours in Classics, 1921 (Rhind Classical Scholarship, 1920, Guthrie Classical Fellowship, 1922); Ferguson Scholar in Classics, 1922; First Class in Literae Humaniores, Oxford, 1923; MA 1928; First Class Honours in Mental Philosophy (after Graduation) at Edinburgh University, and Diploma in Education, 1924; Shaw Fellow in Mental Philosophy in the University of Edinburgh, 1924–29; Assistant Lecturer in the Department of Logic and Metaphysics, Edinburgh University, 1924–26; Professor of Philosophy at Smith College, Northampton, Mass., USA, 1926–30; Associate Professor of Moral Philosophy, McGill University, Montreal, Canada, 1930–31; Professor, 1931–32; Lecturer in Ancient Philosophy, Edinburgh University, 1932–37; Reader, 1937–38. *Publications:* reviews and papers in philosophical journals. *Address:* Kinross, 8 Well Lane, Gayton, Heswall, Wirral, Merseyside L60 8NE. *T:* 051-342 1713.
                                                              *Died* 2 Aug. 1981.

**PORTER, Alfred Ernest,** CSI 1947; CIE 1942; *b* 2 Nov. 1896; *s* of F. L. Porter; *m* 1929, Nancy Florence (decd), *d* of late E. L. Melly; two *s. Educ:* Manchester Grammar Sch.; Corpus Christi Coll., Oxford. Manchester Regt, 1915; Machine Gun Corps, 1916; Indian Civil Service, 1922–48. *Address:* The Old Hall, Chawleigh, Chulmleigh, Devon EX18 7HH. *T:* Chulmleigh 80280.
                                                              *Died* 24 Feb. 1987.

**PORTER, Sir Andrew Marshall H.;** *see* Horsbrugh-Porter.

**PORTER, Prof. Helen Kemp,** FRS 1956; DSc; FRSC; Emeritus Professor, University of London; Scientific Adviser to the Secretary, Agricultural Research Council, 1971–72 (Second Secretary, 1969–71); Fellow, Imperial College of Science and Technology, 1966; *b* 10 Nov. 1899; *d* of George Kemp Archbold and Caroline E. B. Archbold (*née* Whitehead); *m* 1937, William George Porter, MD, MRCP (decd); *m* 1962, Arthur St George Huggett, FRS, DSc, MB, BS (*d* 1968). *Educ:* Clifton High School for Girls, Bristol; University of London, Research Assistant, Food Investigation Board, 1922–32; DSc London, 1932. On staff of Research Institute of Plant Physiology, Imperial Coll., 1932–59; Reader in Enzymology, University of London, Imperial College of Science and Technology, 1957–59; Prof. of Plant Physiology, Imperial Coll. of Science and Technology, London Univ., 1959–64; Dir, ARC Unit of Plant Physiology, 1959–64. Hon. ARCS 1964. *Publications:* contributions to Annals of Botany, Biochemical Journal, Journal of Experimental Botany, etc. *Recreation:* needlework. *Address:* 49e Beaumont Street, W1N 1RE. *T:* 01–935 5862. *Died* 7 Dec. 1987.

**PORTER, Prof. Joseph William Geoffrey,** PhD; Director, National Institute for Research in Dairying, since 1978; *b* 22 May 1920; *s* of Joseph Henry Porter and Alice Porter; *m* 1944, Brenda Mary Matthews; one *s* one *d*. *Educ:* Repton Sch.; Emmanuel Coll., Cambridge (MA, PhD; Sen. Scholar, 1941). Res. Worker, Organic Chemistry Dept, Cambridge, 1942–46; Nat. Inst. for Research in Dairying: Scientific Officer, Nutrition Dept, 1946–65; Head of Nutrition Dept, 1965–77. *Publications:* Milk and Dairy Foods, 1975; papers in scientific jls on nutrition. *Recreation:* gardening. *Address:* National Institute for Research in Dairying, Shinfield, Reading, Berks RG2 9AT. *T:* Reading 883103. *Died* 17 Nov. 1983.

**PORTER, Raymond Alfred James,** OBE 1988; *b* 14 Oct. 1896; *o s* of Philip and Alice Porter; *m* 1922, Nellie (*d* 1979), *er d* of George Edward Loveland; no *c*. *Educ:* Reigate Grammar Sch. Entered Lloyd's, 1912, Under-writing Member, 1934. Served European War, 1914–19, in Queen's Royal (West Surrey) Regt. Member, Cttee of Lloyd's, 1950–53, 1955–58, 1960–63 (Deputy Chairman of Lloyd's, 1961); Member, Cttee, Lloyd's Underwriters' Assoc., 1945–65 (Chairman, 1949–54, 1962); Chairman Joint Hull Cttee, 1958 and 1959. Member: Local Govt Management Cttee, 1964–67; Godstone RDC, 1946–60 and 1962–69 (Chairman, 1952–54); Surrey CC, 1955–58. Silver Medal for Services to Lloyd's, 1978. *Address:* Mashobra, Limpsfield, Oxted, Surrey. *T:* Oxted 712509.
*Died* 3 June 1988.

**PORTER, Sir Robert (Evelyn),** Kt 1978; Partner, F. W. Porter & Co. (Member of the Stock Exchange of Adelaide), since 1937; *b* 10 July 1913; *s* of Frederick Windmill Porter and Clara Francis Niall Porter; *m* 1942, June Leah Perry, *d* of late Stanley W. Perry, OBE, Perth, WA. *Educ:* St Peter's Collegiate Sch., Adelaide, SA; Univ. of Adelaide. Served War, 2/10 Bn AIF, 1939–45, enlisted as private, 1939; commnd, 1940; Major, 1942 (mentioned in despatches); personal staff C-in-C Field Marshal Sir Thomas Blamey and Lord Casey, Governor of Bengal, 1945–46. Director: Standard Chartered Australia Ltd; Castalloy Ltd; Freeman Motors Ltd. Lord Mayor of Adelaide, 1968–71. President: Good Neighbour Council of SA, 1971–74; RSPCA, SA, 1956–. Past Pres. and Vice Patron: SA Polo Assoc.; (captain SA team, Australian Polo Championships, 1952–65); SA Rugby Union (Mem. Australian team, Ceylon tour, 1938). Chm., Rothman Nat. Sports Foundn. Governor: Anti-Cancer Foundn, Univ. of Adelaide; Adelaide Festival of Arts. Consul of Belgium for SA and Northern Territory, 1949–. Chevalier, Order of the Crown, Belgium, 1959; Kt, Order of Leopold, 1969; Officer, Order of Leopold II, 1973. *Recreation:* golf. *Address:* 1 Edwin Terrace, Gilberton, SA 5081, Australia. *T:* 44 1455. *Clubs:* Adelaide, Royal Adelaide Golf (Adelaide); Melbourne (Melbourne); Union (Sydney); Royal and Ancient Golf (Scotland).
*Died* 23 July 1983.

**PORTER, Prof. Rodney Robert,** CH 1985; FRS 1964; Whitley Professor of Biochemistry, 1967–85, Fellow, Trinity College, since 1967, University of Oxford; Hon. Director, Medical Research Council Immunochemistry Unit, Oxford, since 1967; *b* 8 Oct. 1917; *s* of Joseph L. and Isobel M. Porter; *m* 1948, Julia Frances New; two *s* three *d*. *Educ:* Grammar Sch., Ashton-in-Makerfield; Liverpool Univ.; Pembroke Coll., Cambridge (Hon. Fellow, 1983). Scientific Staff at Nat. Inst. for Medical Research, Mill Hill, NW7, 1949–60; Pfizer Prof. of Immunology, St Mary's Hospital Medical Sch., London Univ., 1960–67. Mem., MRC, 1970–74. Linacre Lectr, Cambridge Univ., 1975; Gowland Hopkins Meml Lectr, Biochem. Soc., 1977. Award of Merit, Gairdner Foundn, 1966; Ciba Medal, Biochemical Soc., 1967; Karl Landsteiner Meml Award, Amer. Assoc. of Blood Banks, 1968; (jtly) Nobel Prize for Medicine or Physiology, 1972; Royal Medal, Royal Soc., 1973; Copley Medal, Royal Soc., 1983. Hon. Member: Amer. Soc. of Biological Chemists, 1968; Amer. Assoc. of Immunologists, 1973; Société Française d'Immunologie, 1978; Hon. Foreign Mem., Amer. Acad. of Arts and Sciences, 1968; Foreign Associate, Amer. Nat. Acad. of Scis, 1972. Hon. FRCP, 1974; Hon. FRSE, 1976; Hon. FIBiol, 1977.

Hon. DSc: Liverpool, 1973; Hull, 1974; St Andrews, 1976; Manchester, 1979; London, 1983; Dr *hc* Vrije Univ., Brussels, 1974. *Publications:* papers in Biochemical Journal and other learned journals. *Recreation:* walking. *Address:* Downhill Farm, Witney, Oxon. *Died* 6 Sept. 1985.

**PORTLAND, 9th Duke of,** *cr* 1716; **Victor Frederick William Cavendish-Bentinck,** CMG 1942; Earl of Portland, Viscount Woodstock, Baron Cirencester, 1689; Marquess of Titchfield, 1716; *b* 18 June 1897; *s* of (William George) Frederick Cavendish-Bentinck (*d* 1948) (*ggs* of 3rd Duke) and Ruth Mary St Maur (*d* 1953); granted, 1977, the same title and precedence that would have been due to him if his father had succeeded to the Dukedom of Portland; *S* brother, 1980; *m* 1st, 1924 (marr. diss.); one *d* (one *s* decd); 2nd, 1948, Kathleen Elsie, *yr d* of Arthur Barry, Montreal. *Educ:* Wellington Coll., Berks. Attaché HM Legation, Oslo, 1915; 2nd Lieut, Grenadier Guards, 1918; 3rd Sec., HM Legation, Warsaw, 1919; transferred to Foreign Office, 1922; attended Lausanne Conference, 1922–23; 2nd Sec., HM Embassy, Paris, 1923; HM Legation, The Hague, 1924; transferred to Foreign Office, 1925; attended Locarno Conference, 1925; 1st Sec., HM Embassy, Paris, 1928; HM Legation, Athens, 1932; HM Embassy, Santiago, 1934; transferred to Foreign Office, 1937; Asst Under-Sec. of State, 1944; Chm. Jt Intelligence Cttee of Chiefs of Staff, 1939–45, also Foreign Office Adviser to Directors of Plans, 1942–45; Ambassador to Poland, 1945–47; retired from Diplomatic Service, 1947. Chm., Bayer (UK) Ltd, 1968–86. Hon. Life Pres., British Nuclear Forum. (Pres. Council, 1969–84). Grosses Verdienstkreuz (Germany). *Recreations:* travelling and antiques. *Heir* (to earldom only): *kinsman* Henry Noel Bentinck, Count of the Holy Roman Empire [*b* 2 Oct. 1919; *m* 1st, 1940, Pauline Ursula (*d* 1967), *y d* of late Frederick William Mellowes; one *s* two *d*; 2nd, 1974, Jenifer, *d* of late Reginald Hopkins]. *Address:* 21 Carlyle Square, SW3. *T:* 071–352 1258. *Clubs:* Turf, Beefsteak. *Died* 30 July 1990 (*ext*).

**PORTLOCK, Rear-Admiral Ronald Etridge,** CB 1961; OBE 1947; DL; retired; *b* London, 28 June 1908; *o s* of late Henry and Doris Portlock; *m* 1939, Angela, *d* of late Gerard Kirke Smith; no *c*. *Educ:* Royal Naval Coll., Dartmouth. Naval Cadet, 1922; Midshipman, 1926; Lieut-Commander, 1938; Commander, 1943; Captain, 1949; Rear-Admiral 1959. Served War of 1939–45 in HMS Ark Royal and King George V as Lieut-Commander; Admiralty as Commander. Post-war Mine Clearance in Far East, 1946–47; Captain, HM Underwater Detection Establishment, 1950–52; Chief of Staff to C-in-C, The Nore, 1953–54; in comd HMS Newfoundland, and Flag Captain to Flag Officer; Second in Command Far East Station, 1955–56; Director of Underwater Weapons, Admiralty, 1957–58; Chief of Staff to the Commander-in-Chief, Far East Station, 1959–61, retired, 1961. ADC to the Queen, 1958. Chairman, Assoc. of Retired Naval Officers, 1965–67. DL Greater London, 1967–83. Royal Swedish Order of the Swords, 1954. *Address:* 1 Swan Court, Chelsea, SW3. *T:* 01-352 4390. *Died* 6 Nov. 1983.

**PORTSMOUTH, 9th Earl of,** *cr* 1743; **Gerard Vernon Wallop;** Viscount Lymington, Baron Wallop, 1720; Hereditary Bailiff of Burley, New Forest; Vice-Chairman, East Africa Natural Resources Research Council, since 1963; *b* 16 May 1898; *e s* of 8th Earl and Marguerite (*d* 1938), *d* of S. J. Walker, Kentucky; *S* father 1943; *m* 1st, 1920, Mary Lawrence (who obtained a divorce, 1936, and *m* 2nd, 1938, E. J. B. How), *d* of W. K. Post, Bayport, Long Island; one *d* (one *s* decd); 2nd, 1936, Bridget (*d* 1979), *o d* of late Captain P. B. Crohan, Royal Navy, Owlpen Manor, Glos; one *s* two *d*. Served European War, 1916–19; MP (U) Basingstoke Division of Hants, 1929–34; Member of the Milk Marketing Board, July 1933; Vice-Chairman Hampshire War Agric. Cttee, 1939–47; Vice-President and Chairman Country Landowners Assoc., 1947–48. President, Electors Union, Kenya, 1953–55; MLC Kenya (Corporate Member for Agric.), 1957–60; Vice-Chairman, East African Natural Resources Research Council, 1963–. *Publications:* Git le Cœur, 1928; Ich Dien; The Tory Path, 1931; Horn, Hoof and Corn, 1932; Famine in England, 1938; Alternative to Death, 1943; British Farm Stock, 1950; A Knot of Roots (autobiog.), 1965. *Heir:* *g s* Viscount Lymington. *Address:* c/o Farleigh Wallop, Basingstoke, Hants. *Club:* Buck's. *Died* 28 Sept. 1984.

**POSKITT, Frederick Richard,** CBE 1962; *b* 15 Aug. 1900; *s* of Frederick Hardy Poskitt and Kate Penlington Spencer; *m* 1936, Margaret Embree, *e d* of Cecil E. Turner, Woolton, Liverpool; two *s* one *d*. *Educ:* Kilburn Grammar Sch.; Downing Coll., Cambridge. Asst Master, Colchester Royal Grammar Sch., 1921–25; Head of History Dept, Manchester Grammar Sch., 1926–33; Headmaster, Bolton Sch., 1933–66; Dir, Nat. Teachers' Coll., Kampala, Uganda, 1966–71. Former Member: Cttee, Headmasters' Conf.; Council, IAHM. Founder Mem., Fifty-One Soc. (BBC), 1951–60; Mem., Chief Scout's Adv. Panel, 1943–49; Chairman: SE Lancs County Scout Council, 1943–60; Bolton Lads Club, 1944–53; Oxford Br., Save the Children Fund, 1976–81; Pres., Bolton Br., Historical Assoc., 1933–66. *Recreation:* travel. *Address:* 11 Hedge End, Hensington Gate, Woodstock, Oxon OX7 1NP. *T:* Woodstock

811590. *Club:* Royal Commonwealth Society (Mem. Cttee, Oxford Br., 1974–). *Died 20 Feb. 1983.*

**POSTAN, Sir Michael (Moïssey),** Kt 1980; FBA 1959; Professor of Economic History, 1938–65 (later Emeritus) and Fellow of Peterhouse, 1935–65 (later Hon. Fellow), Cambridge; *b* Sept. 1899; *s* of Efim and Elena Postan, Tighina, Bessarabia; *m* 1937, Eileen Power (*d* 1940); *m* 1944, Lady Cynthia Rosalie Keppel, 2nd *d* of 9th Earl of Albemarle, MC; two *s.* Lecturer in History in University College (University of London), 1927–31; Lecturer in Economic History at London School of Economics, 1931–35, Hon. Fellow, 1974; Lecturer in Economic History in University of Cambridge, 1935–38. Head of Section in MEW, 1939–42; Official Historian of Munitions at Offices of War Cabinet, 1942. Hon. President, Internat. Economic History Assoc. Hon. DLitt Birmingham; Hon. LittD York; Hon. DSc Edinburgh; Dr *hc* Sorbonne. *Publications:* (with Eileen Power) Studies in English Trade in the Fifteenth Century, 1933, new edn 1951; Historical Method in Social Science, 1939; British War Production, 1952; The Famulus, 1954; (with D. Hay and J. D. Scott) Design and Development of Weapons: studies in government and organisation, 1964; An Economic History of Western Europe, 1945–64, 1967; Fact and Relevance: essays in historical method, 1971; The Medieval Economy and Society, 1973; Essays on Medieval Agriculture and the Medieval Economy, 1973; Medieval Trade and Finance, 1973; General Editor, Cambridge Economic History of Europe; edited: vol. 1, The Agrarian Life of the Middle Ages, 2nd edn 1966; (with E. E. Rich) vol. 2, Trade and Industry in the Middle Ages, 1952; (with E. E. Rich and E. Miller) vol. 3, Economic Organisation and Policies in the Middle Ages, 1963; (with H. J. Habakkuk) vol. 6, The Industrial Revolutions and After, 1965; (with P. Mathias) vol. 7, The Industrial Economies, 1978; also numerous articles and essays in learned publications. *Address:* 2 Sylvester Road, Cambridge; Penrallt Goch, Ffestiniog, Gwynedd. *Club:* United Oxford & Cambridge University.
*Died 12 Dec. 1981.*

**POTT, Sir Leslie,** KBE 1962 (CBE 1957); *b* 4 July 1903; *s* of Charles Groves Pott; *m* 1937, Norma (*d* 1978), *d* of Captain Kynaston Lyons-Montgomery, Jersey; one *s. Educ:* Manchester Grammar Sch.; Gonville and Caius Coll., Cambridge (Open Scholar). Entered Levant Consular Service, 1924; served at Casablanca, Damascus and Beirut, 1926–29; Moscow and Leningrad, 1930–35; Foreign Office, 1936–37; Piraeus and Athens, 1938–40; Consul at Baghdad, 1940–43; Foreign Office, 1943–45; Consul at Alexandria, 1946–47. Consul-General at Tabriz, 1947–50; Deputy High Commissioner for the UK at Bombay, 1950–52; Consul-General at Istanbul, 1952–55; at Marseilles, 1955–61, also to Monaco, 1957–61. Retired from HM Diplomatic Service, 1962. *Address:* Becking Spring, Hudnall Common, near Berkhamsted, Herts HP4 1QJ. *T:* Little Gaddesden 3409. *Died 16 Jan. 1985.*

**POTTER, His Honour Douglas Charles Loftus;** a Circuit Judge (formerly Judge of County Courts), 1959–78; *b* 17 Dec. 1903; *s* of John Charles Potter, solicitor, Putney, and Caroline Annette Tidy Potter (*née* Onslow); *m* 1st, 1934, Margaret Isabel (*d* 1979), *d* of Dr William Savile Henderson, Liverpool; one *d*; 2nd, 1980, Nicole, *d* of Dr Eugene Charles Joseph Kayser, Versailles. *Educ:* Radley; Trinity Coll., Oxford (MA). Rowed in winning crew, Ladies' Plate, Henley Regatta, 1923; Half-blue, OUAC, 3 miles, 1925. Barrister, Inner Temple, 1928; SE Circuit, Herts and Essex Sessions. Served War of 1939–45 in RAFVR, 1940–45. Judge of County Courts, 1959–71, Willesden, Croydon and Kingston upon Thames. *Publications:* The Law Relating to Garages and Car Parks, 1939; The National Insurance Act, 1946, 1946. *Recreations:* walking, travel, reading, music, gardening. *Address:* 4 Longdown Road, Epsom, Surrey; 32 avenue de Saint-Cloud, 78000 Versailles, France. *Club:* Royal Automobile. *Died 14 Jan. 1983.*

**POTTER, George Richard,** CBE 1977; MA, PhD (Cambridge), FRHistS, FSA; retired as Professor of Medieval History, University of Sheffield, 1965; Emeritus Professor, since 1965; Hon. Research Fellow, 1973–75; Temporary Professor, University of Warwick, 1968–69; *b* 6 Aug. 1900; *e s* of George Potter, Norwich; *m* 1927, Rachel, *y d* of M. Leon, Salisbury, Rhodesia; one *s* one *d. Educ:* King Edward VI Sch., Norwich; St John's Coll., Cambridge; Head of Department of History, University College, Leicester, 1925–27; Lecturer in Medieval History, Queen's Univ. of Belfast, 1927–31; Prof. of Modern History, Univ. of Sheffield, 1931; Dean of the Faculty of Arts, 1939–42; External examiner for a number of Universities; Member Royal Commission on Historical Manuscripts; Vice-Chairman Universities Council for Adult Education, 1938–64; President, Historical Association, 1961–64. Cultural Attaché, British Embassy, Bonn, 1955–57. H. C. Lea Visiting Prof., University of Pennsylvania, 1966–67, 1967–68. Fellow, Newberry Lib., Chicago, 1974; Professorial Fellow, Univ. of Wales, 1976. Served with Royal Naval Volunteer Reserve, 1918–19. *Publications:* Sir Thomas More, 1925; The Autobiography of Ousâma, 1929; (with Bonjour and Offler) Short History of Switzerland, 1952; Zwingli, 1976; contribution to Cambridge

Medieval History; advisory editor and contributor to Chambers's Encyclopædia; editor of New Cambridge Modern History, Vol. I, Renaissance; various articles. *Recreations:* walking, travel. *Address:* 11 Derwent Lane, Hathersage, Sheffield S30 1AS. *T:* Hope Valley 50428. *Died 17 May 1981.*

**POTTER, Marian Anderson, (Mary),** OBE 1979; artist; *b* 9 April 1900; *d* of John Arthur and Kathleen Mary Attenborough; *m* 1927, Stephen Potter, (marr. diss. 1955; he *d* 1969); two *s. Educ:* Private Sch.; Slade Sch. (Scholar). Paintings exhibited in London and provinces since 1921. One-man shows: Bloomsbury Gallery, 1931; Redfern Gallery, 1934 and 1949; Tooth's Gallery, 1939 and 1946; Leicester Gallery, 1951, 1953, 1954, 1957, 1961, 1963; New Art Centre, 1967, 1969, 1972, 1974, 1976, 1978, 1980. Retrospective Exhibitions: Whitechapel Art Gallery, 1964; Serpentine Gall., 1981. Pictures bought by the Tate Gallery, Arts Council, Manchester City Art Gallery, Contemporary Art Society, etc; and galleries in New York and Canada, and Australia. *Address:* Red Studio, Aldeburgh, Suffolk. *T:* Aldeburgh 2081.
*Died 14 Sept. 1981.*

**POTTER, Air Marshal Sir Patrick (Brunton) L.;** *see* Lee Potter.

**POTTINGER, John Inglis Drever, (Don Pottinger),** LVO 1984; Islay Herald of Arms, Lyon Clerk and Keeper of the Records in the Court of the Lord Lyon, 1981–86; *b* 25 March 1919; *s* of Rev. William Pottinger and Janet Woodcock; *m* 1943, Agnes Fay Keeling. *Educ:* Edinburgh Coll. of Art (schol. 1937; Dip. in Drawing and Painting 1948); Edinburgh Univ. (MA Hons in Fine Art 1951). Commnd RA (Field Br.), 1939; served N Africa, Italy and Palestine, 1939–46; Captain. Falkland Pursuivant Extraordinary, 1953; Linlithgow Pursuivant Extraordinary, 1958; Unicorn Pursuivant of Arms, 1961. Freelance artist and portrait painter; many mural decorations in UK and elsewhere. Chalmers Prize, RSA, 1947. *Publications:* (with Sir Iain Moncreiffe of that Ilk): Simple Heraldry, 1952, revd edn 1978; Simple Custom, 1954; Blood Royal, 1956; Scotland of Old, 1961; (with Michael Grant): Greeks, 1958; Romans, 1960; (with A. V. Norman) Warrior to Soldier, 1966; (with P. Belbin) New History Atlas, 1969; (jtly) The Kings and Queens of Great Britain, 1970; (with John Stewart of Ardvorlich) Clan Cameron Map, 1971; (with I. Nicolson) Simple Astronomy, 1973; (with G. Cousins) An Atlas of Golf, 1974; (with J. Munro) Robert the Bruce Maps, 1974; (with J. T. Dunbar) The Official Tartan Map, 1976; The Clan Headquarters Flags Chart, 1977; The Official Chart of the Tower of London, 1978; World of Flags, 1981; and illustrations to many others. *Recreations:* etcetera. *Address:* 11 Ainslie Place, Edinburgh EH3 6AS. *T:* 031–225 6146. *Club:* New (Edinburgh).
*Died 14 June 1986.*

**POTTLE, Frederick Albert,** BA Colby, MA, PhD Yale, Hon. LittD Colby, Rutgers, Hon. LHD Northwestern; Hon. LLD Glasgow; Sterling Professor of English, Yale University, 1944–66, then Professor Emeritus; Fellow Emeritus of Davenport College, Yale University; Public Orator, Yale University, 1942 and 1946; *b* Lovell, Maine, 3 Aug. 1897; *y s* of late Fred Leroy Pottle and Annette Wardwell Kemp; *m* 1920, Marion Isabel Starbird, Oxford, Maine; one *s* (and one *s* decd). *Educ:* Colby Coll. (*summa cum laude*); Yale (John Addison Porter Prize). Served as private in Evacuation Hospital No 8, AEF, 1918–19; formerly Assistant Professor of English, University of New Hampshire; Editor of the Private Papers of James Boswell (succeeding the late Geoffrey Scott); Hon. member of Johnson Club; Vice-Pres., Johnson Soc., London; Pres., Johnson Soc., Lichfield, 1974; Trustee: General Theological Seminary, 1947–68; Colby Coll., 1932–59, 1966–78, Hon. Life Trustee, 1978; Messenger Lecturer, Cornell Univ., 1941; Member of Joint Commission on Holy Matrimony of the Episcopal Church, 1940–46; Guggenheim Fellow, 1945–46, 1952–53; Chancellor Academy of American Poets, 1951–71; Chairman of Editorial Cttee of Yale Editions of Private Papers of James Boswell, 1949–79; Member Provinciaal Utrechtsch Genootschap van Kunsten en Wetenschappen, 1953–; Member American Academy of Arts and Sciences, 1957–; FIAL, 1958–; Member, American Philosophical Society, 1960. Wilbur Lucius Cross Medal, Yale, 1967; William Clyde DeVane Medal, Yale, 1969; Lewis Prize, Amer. Philosophical Soc., 1975; Dist. Alumnus Award, Colby, 1977. *Publications:* Shelley and Browning, 1923; A New Portrait of James Boswell (with Chauncey B. Tinker), 1927; The Literary Career of James Boswell, 1929; Stretchers, the Story of a Hospital on the Western Front, 1929; The Private Papers of James Boswell: A Catalogue (with Marion S. Pottle), 1931; Vols 7–18 of The Private Papers of James Boswell, 1930–34; Boswell's Journal of a Tour to the Hebrides, from the Original Manuscript (with Charles H. Bennett), 1936, revised edition, 1963; Index to the Private Papers of James Boswell (with Joseph Foladare, John P. Kirby and others), 1937; Boswell and the Girl from Botany Bay, 1937; The Idiom of Poetry, 1941, revised and enlarged edition, 1946; James Boswell, the Earlier Years, 1966; Pride and Negligence, A History of the Boswell Papers, 1982; *editions of Boswell's journals:* Boswell's London Journal (1762–63), 1950; Boswell in Holland (1763–64), 1952; Boswell on the Grand

Tour: Germany and Switzerland (1764), 1953; Boswell on the Grand Tour: Italy, Corsica and France, 1765 (with Frank Brady), 1955; Boswell in Search of a Wife, 1766–1769 (with Frank Brady), 1956; Boswell for the Defence, 1769–1774 (with William K. Wimsatt), 1959; Boswell: The Ominous Years, 1774–1776 (with Charles Ryskamp), 1963; Boswell in Extremes, 1776–1778 (with Charles McC. Weis), 1970; Boswell, Laird of Auchinleck, 1778–1782 (with Joseph W. Reed), 1977; Boswell, the Applause of the Jury, 1981; Boswell, the English Experiment, 1785–1789 (with Irma S. Lustig), 1987; various articles. *Recreation:* gardening. *Address:* Edgehill Road, New Haven, Conn 06511, USA. *Clubs:* Elizabethan (New Haven); Grolier, Ends of the Earth (New York).

*Died 16 May 1987.*

**POTTS, Prof. Edward Logan Johnston,** MSc; FEng; Professor of Mining, Department of Mining Engineering, University of Newcastle upon Tyne, 1951–80, then Professor Emeritus; *b* Niddrie, Midlothian, 22 Jan. 1915; *s* of Samuel Potts; *m* 1940, Edith Mary, *d* of A. Hayton, Scarborough; one *s* one *d. Educ:* Coatbridge Grammar Sch., Lanarkshire; Gosforth Grammar Sch., Newcastle upon Tyne; King's Coll., University of Durham. BSc (dist.) 1939, 1st Class Hons (Dunelm) 1940; 1st Class Colliery Manager's Certif., 1941; MSc (Dunelm) 1945. FEng 1980. Apprentice Mine Surveyor, Hazlerigg & Burradon Coal Co., Ltd, 1931–34. Asst to Chief Surveyor, Charlaw & Sacriston Collieries Co. Ltd, 1934–36; Certificated Mine Surveyor, 1936; Apprentice Mining Engineer, Wallsend & Hebburn Coal Co. Ltd, 1936–40; Cons. Mining Engineer, Northumberland, Durham, N Staffs; Surveyor to Northern "A" Regional cttee; prepared report on Northumberland and Cumberland Reserves and output, 1944; Reader in Mining, King's Coll., University of Durham, 1947; Mining Adviser: Northumberland Coal Owners' Assoc., 1947; Mickley Associated Collieries, 1949–51; Peterlee Development Corp. on mining subsidence, 1947–72; Adviser to Kolar Gold Fields, S India, rock bursts in deep mining, 1955–70; Mem., Coal Res. Commn, EEC, 1972–. President, N of England Inst. Mining and Mech. Engineering, 1957–58. Consultant, Rock Mechanics, ICI Mond Div., Cleveland Potash Ltd, etc. Research on rock mechanics, etc; co-designer Dunelm circular fluorescent mine lighting unit, hydraulic coal plough. *Publications:* (jointly) Horizon Mining, 1953; papers on ventilation, mine lighting, strata control in Trans. Inst. Mining Eng., British Assoc. and other journals. *Recreations:* athletics, motoring. *Address:* 4 Montagu Avenue, Gosforth, Newcastle upon Tyne NE3 4HX. *T:* Newcastle 3852171. *Died 29 March 1984.*

**POTTS, Kenneth Hampson;** Chief Executive, Leeds City Council, 1973–79; *b* 29 Sept. 1921; *s* of late James Potts and Martha Ann Potts; *m* 1945, Joan Daphne Wilson; two *s. Educ:* Manchester Grammar Sch.; Liverpool Univ. (LLB Hons). Solicitor. Captain, RA, 1942–46. Deputy Town Clerk, Leeds, 1965; Chief Management and Legal Officer, Leeds, 1969. Member: Yorks and Humberside Economic Planning Council, 1974–79; Data Protection Cttee, 1976–79. *Recreations:* Dandie Dinmonts, gardening, theatre, music, reading. *Address:* 8 Burlyn Road, Hunmanby, Filey, N Yorks YO14 0QA. *T:* Scarborough (0723) 891100. *Died 20 March 1990.*

**POULTON, Rev. Canon John Frederick;** Residentiary Canon, Norwich Cathedral, 1979–86, Canon Emeritus since 1986; *b* 15 June 1925; *m* 1946, Iris Joan Knighton; two *s* two *d. Educ:* King's Coll., London (BA Hons); Ridley Hall, Cambridge. Tutor, 1955–60, and Actg Principal, 1960–61, Bishop Tucker Coll., Mukono, Uganda; Dir, Church of Uganda Literature and Radio Centre, 1962–66; Res. Sec., World Assoc. of Christian Communication, 1966–68; Exec. Sec., Archbishops' Council on Evangelism, 1968–78. *Publications:* A Today Sort of Evangelism, 1972; People under Pressure, 1973; Jesus in Focus, 1975; Dear Archbishop, 1976; The Feast of Life, 1982; Fresh Air: a vision for the rural church, 1985; (contrib.) David Watson, a portrait by his friends, 1985; (contrib.) My Call to Preach, 1986. *Address:* 22 St Michael-at-Pleas, Norwich NR3 1EP. *T:* Norwich 618755. *Died 7 Jan. 1987.*

**POUNCEY, Philip Michael Rivers,** CBE 1987; MA; FBA 1975; Consultant, since 1983, a Director, 1966–83, Sotheby's; Hon. Keeper of Italian Drawings, Fitzwilliam Museum, since 1975; *b* 15 Feb. 1910; *s* of Rev. George Ernest Pouncey and Madeline Mary Roberts; *m* 1937, Myril Gros; two *d. Educ:* Marlborough; Queens' Coll., Cambridge (MA). Hon. Attaché, Fitzwilliam Museum, 1931–33; Assistant, National Gall., London, 1934–45; Asst Keeper, 1945–54, Dep. Keeper, 1954–66, British Museum; Visiting Professor: Columbia Univ., NY, 1958; Inst. of Fine Arts, New York Univ., 1965. *Publications:* Catalogues of Italian Drawings in the British Museum: (with A. E. Popham) XIV-XV Centuries, 1950; (with J. A. Gere) Raphael and his Circle, 1962; Lotto disegnatore, 1965; (with J. A. Gere) Italian Artists Working in Rome *c* 1550–*c* 1640, 1983; articles in Burlington Magazine, etc. *Recreation:* travel in Italy and France. *Address:* 5 Lower Addison Gardens, W14 8BG. *Died 12 Nov. 1990.*

**POWELL, Arthur Geoffrey;** retired; Director, Strategic Plan for the South East, 1976 (Under-Secretary, Department of the Environment, 1975–76); *b* 22 Dec. 1915; *s* of late Dudley and Emma Powell; *m* 1947, Albertine Susan Muller; one *s* one *d. Educ:* Mundella, Nottingham; University Coll., Nottingham. BA London (External) 1937. Demonstrator, Dept of Geography, University Coll., Nottingham, 1938–40. Served with Royal Engineers, Intelligence Corps and Army Educn Corps, Middle East, 1940–46 (despatches). Research Dept, Min. of Town and Country Planning, et seq, 1946–61; Principal Technical Officer, Local Govt Commn for England, 1961–65; Principal Planner, Min. of Housing and Local Govt, 1965–68; Asst Chief Planner, Min. of Housing and Local Govt and DoE, 1968–74; Dep. Chief Planner, DoE, 1974–75; Under-Secretary (Regional Dir, Eastern), DoE, 1975–76. *Recreations:* travel, fell walking, photography, music. *Address:* 114 Lincoln Road, Branston, Lincoln, Lincs.

*Died 4 May 1982.*

**POWELL, Edward,** CBE 1973; *b* 10 June 1907; *s* of Edward Churton Powell and Margaret Nesfield; *m* 1941, Patricia Florence (*née* Harris); one *s* one *d. Educ:* Shrewsbury School. Captain, Royal Marines, 1941–45. Solicitor in private practice until 1941; joined Chloride Electrical Storage Co. Ltd (now Chloride Group Ltd), 1941; Man. Dir, 1962–72; Chm., 1965–74; Hon. Pres., 1974–80. Pres., British Electrical and Allied Manufacturers' Assoc. Ltd, 1973–75. *Recreations:* landscape gardening, fishing. *Address:* Little Orchard, Mayfield, East Sussex. *T:* Mayfield 873441.

*Died 16 Nov. 1982.*

**POWELL, Prof. Gillian Margot;** Professor, since 1983 and Head of Department of Biochemistry, since 1986, Deputy Principal, since 1989, University of Wales College of Cardiff; *b* 20 April 1934; *d* of Hugh Garfield Powell and Elizabeth Sibyl Powell. *Educ:* Brecon Girls Grammar Sch.; University Coll. Cardiff (BSc Cl. 1; PhD 1959). MRC Res. Fellow, 1959–61; University College Cardiff: Lectr in Biochemistry, 1961–69; Sen. Lectr, 1969–77; Reader in Biochemistry, Univ. of Wales, 1977–83. Vis. Scientist, Vermont, USA 1969–70. Mem., Equal Opportunities Commn, 1986–. FRSA 1986. *Publications:* over 80 scientific contribs to learned jls and books. *Recreations:* reading Jane Austen and P. G. Wodehouse, gardening. *Address:* 32 Forsythia Drive, Cyncoed, Cardiff CF2 7HP. *T:* Cardiff 732212; (office) Cardiff 874290.

*Died 28 Aug. 1989.*

**POWELL, Michael Latham,** FRGS; film director; *b* Bekesbourne, near Canterbury, Kent, 30 Sept. 1905; *s* of Thomas William Powell and Mabel, *d* of Frederick Corbett, Worcester; *m* 1st, Frances (*d* 1983), *d* of Dr J. J. Reidy, JP, MD; two *s*; 2nd, 1984, Thelma Schoonmaker, *d* of Bertram Schoonmaker. *Educ:* King's Sch., Canterbury; Dulwich Coll. Hon. DLitt: East Anglia, 1978; Kent, 1984; Hon. Dr RCA, 1987. BFI Special Award (with Emeric Pressburger), 1978; Fellow: BAFTA, 1981; BFI, 1983. Golden Lion of Venice Award, 1982. Joined National Provincial Bank, 1922; Metro-Goldwyn-Mayer film co., 1925, making Mare Nostrum, in the Mediterranean, with Rex Ingram as Dir; various capacities on 2 subseq. Ingram films: Somerset Maugham's The Magician and Robert Hichens' The Garden of Allah; was brought to Elstree, 1928, by the painter and film director, Harry Lachman; worked on 3 Hitchcock silent films, incl. script of Blackmail (later made into talking film). Travelled in Albania; wrote scripts for films of Caste and 77 Park Lane; given chance to direct by Jerry Jackson, 1931; dir Two Crowded Hours and Rynox (both melodramas of 40 mins); went on to make a dozen short features, incl. 4 for Michael Balcon at Shepherd's Bush Studios, incl. The Fire Raisers and The Red Ensign (both orig. stories by Jackson and Powell); wrote and dir The Edge of the World, on Foula, Shetland, 1936 (prod. Joe Rock); given a contract by Alexander Korda, 1938, travelled in Burma, up the Chindwin; met Emeric Pressburger, together wrote and then dir The Spy in Black, and Contraband; co-dir, Thief of Bagdad and The Lion has Wings; prod. and dir 49th Parallel (from orig. story by Pressburger); formed The Archers Company and together with Pressburger wrote, prod. and dir 16 films, incl. Colonel Blimp, I Know Where I'm Going, A Matter of Life and Death, Black Narcissus, The Red Shoes, all for J. Arthur Rank; returned to Korda, 1948, to make 4 films, incl. The Small Back Room and Tales of Hoffman; returned to Rank for The Battle of the River Plate (The Archers' second Royal Perf. film) and Ill Met By Moonlight; also made Rosalinda (film of Fledermaus) at Elstree; The Archers Company then broke up; since then has dir Honeymoon, Peeping Tom, The Queen's Guards, Bluebeard's Castle (Bartók opera); The Sorcerer's Apprentice (ballet film); film (for Children's Film Foundn) from a story and script by Pressburger; The Boy Who Turned Yellow; They're a Weird Mob (Aust.); Age of Consent (Aust.); Return to the Edge of the World, 1978; lectured on film, Dartmouth Coll., New Hampshire, 1980; joined F. Coppola as Sen. Dir in Res., Zoetrope Studios, 1981; supervisor for Pavlova (Anglo-USSR prod.), 1983–85. *In the theatre:* prod. and dir (Hemingway's) The Fifth Column, 1945; (Jan de Hartog's) The Skipper Next to God, 1947; (James Forsyth's) Heloise, 1951; (Raymond Massey's) Hanging Judge, 1955. TV Series (several episodes): Espionage and The Defenders, for Herbert Brodkin. *Publications:* 200,000 Feet on

Foula, 1937; Graf Spee, 1957; A Waiting Game, 1975; (with Emeric Pressburger) The Red Shoes, 1978; A Life in Movies (autobiog.), 1986. *Recreation:* leaning on gates. *Address:* Lee Cottages, Avening, Tetbury, Glos. *Clubs:* Savile, Royal Automobile.
*Died 19 Feb.* 1990.

**POWELL, Roger**, OBE 1976; bookbinder, retired; *b* 17 May 1896; *er s* of late Oswald Byrom Powell and Winifred Marion Powell (*née* Cobb); *m* 1924, Rita Glanville (*d* 1988), *y d* of late Frank and Katherine F. Harvey; one *s* twin *d*. *Educ:* Bedales Sch. Served European War, 1914–18: Hampshire Regt, Palestine, 1917; Flt Lt, RAF, Egypt, 1918. Poultry farming, 1921–30; studied bookbinding at LCC Central Sch., 1930–31; joined Douglas Cockerell & Son, bookbinders, 1935; Partner, 1936; opened own bindery at Froxfield, 1947. Member: Art Workers' Guild; Double Crown Club; Red Rose Guild. Has repaired and bound many early manuscripts, incunabula and other early printed books including: for Winchester (both Coll. and Cathedral); for TCD, The Book of Kells, 1953; The Book of Durrow, The Book of Armagh, The Book of Dimma (in accommod. Brit. Mus.), 1954–57; for Lichfield Cath., The St Chad Gospels, 1961–62; for RIA, The Book of Lecan, Lebor na hUidre, Leabhar Breac, The Book of Fermoy, The Cathach of St Columba, 1968–81; for Durham Cathedral, The A. II. 17 Gospels, 1976. Tooled Memorial Bindings, incl: WVS Roll of Honour, Civilian War Dead, 1939–45, in Westminster Abbey. Rolls of Honour: for RMA Sandhurst and Woolwich; Coastal Command, RAF; S Africa, India, Pakistan. Other tooled bindings, in: Brit. Mus., Victoria and Albert Mus.; in Libraries: (Bodleian, Oxford; Pierpont Morgan; Syracuse Univ.; Grolier Club, New York; Newberry, Chicago), and in private collections in Britain, Ireland and USA. Visited, to advise on book-conservation: Iceland, 1965; Florence, 1966; Portugal, 1967. Hon. For. Corresp. Mem., Grolier Club, NY. Hon. MA Dublin, 1961. *Publications:* various contribs to The Library; Scriptorium, Brussels; Ériu, Dublin, 1956–69. *Recreations:* cricket, singing, 'finding out', photography, amateur operatics and dramatics, organic cultivations, bee-keeping, golf. *Address:* The Slade, Froxfield, Petersfield, Hants GU32 1EB. *T:* Hawkley (073084) 229. *Died 16 Oct.* 1990.

**POWER, Vice-Adm. Sir Arthur (Mackenzie)**, KCB 1974; MBE 1952; Secretary to the Senate of the Inns of Court and the Bar, since 1975; *b* 18 June 1921; *s* of Admiral of the Fleet Sir Arthur Power, GCB, GBE, CVO; *m* 1949, Marcia Helen Gell; two *s* one *d*. *Educ:* Rugby. Royal Navy, 1938; served War of 1939–45 and Korean War; specialised in gunnery; Captain, 1959; ADC to the Queen, 1968; Rear-Admiral, 1968; Adm. Supt, Portsmouth, 1968–71; Flag Officer, Spithead, 1969–71; Vice-Adm., 1971; Flag Officer Flotillas, Western Fleet, 1971–72; Flag Officer, First Flotilla, 1972–73; Flag Officer Plymouth, Port Adm. Devonport, Cmdr Central Sub Area, E Atlantic, and Cmdr Plymouth Sub Area, Channel, 1973–75. *Address:* Gunnsmead, South Road, Liphook, Hants. *Club:* Army and Navy.
*Died 17 Nov.* 1984.

**POWER, Sir John (Patrick McLannahan)**, 3rd Bt, *cr* 1924, of Newlands Manor; Chairman, Arthur Beale Ltd, London; *b* 16 March 1928; *s* of Sir Ivan McLannahan Cecil Power, 2nd Baronet, and Nancy Hilary, *d* of late Reverend J. W. Griffiths, Wentworth, Virginia Water; *m* 1st, 1957, Melanie (marr. diss. 1967), *d* of Hon. Alastair Erskine, Glenfintaig House, Spean Bridge, Inverness-shire; two *s* one *d*; 2nd, 1970, Tracey (marr. diss. 1974), *d* of George Cooper, Amberley Place, Amberley, Sussex. *Educ:* Pangbourne Coll. Served RN, 1946–48, The Cunard Steamship Co. Ltd, London, 1945–58. *Recreations:* sailing, painting. *Heir:* *s* Alastair John Cecil Power, *b* 15 Aug. 1958. *Address:* Ashwick House, Dulverton, Somerset. *T:* Dulverton 488. *Clubs:* Arts, Royal Ocean Racing, Royal London Yacht; Royal Naval Sailing Association; Island Sailing. *Died 24 May* 1984.

**POWER, Adm. (retd) Sir Manley (Laurence)**, KCB 1958 (CB 1955); CBE 1943 (OBE 1940); DSO 1944, Bar 1945; DL; *b* 10 Jan. 1904; *s* of Adm. Sir Laurence E. Power, KCB, CVO; *m* 1930, Barbara Alice Mary Topham; one *d* (one *s* decd). *Educ:* RN Colleges, Osborne and Dartmouth. Naval Cadet, 1917; Midshipman, 1921; Sub-Lt 1924; Lt 1926; Lt-Comdr 1934; Comdr 1939; Capt. 1943; Rear-Adm. 1953; Vice-Adm. 1956; Admiral, 1960. Deputy Chief of Naval Staff, and Fifth Sea Lord, 1957–59; Commander-in-Chief, Portsmouth, Allied C-in-C, Channel, and C-in-C, Home Station (Designate), 1959–61; retired, 1961. CC, Isle of Wight, 1964–74. DL, Hampshire, 1965–74, Isle of Wight, 1974. Officer of Legion of Merit (US); Croix de Guerre avec Palme (France). *Address:* Norton Cottage, Yarmouth, Isle of Wight. *T:* Yarmouth 760401.
*Died 17 May* 1981.

**POWIS, 6th Earl of**, *cr* 1804; **Christian Victor Charles Herbert**; Baron Clive (Ire.), 1762; Baron Clive, 1794; Viscount Clive, Baron Herbert, Baron Powis, 1804; *b* 28 May 1904; 2nd *s* of Colonel Edward William Herbert, CB (*d* 1924) (*g s* of 2nd Earl of Powis) and Beatrice Anne (*d* 1928), *d* of Sir Hedworth Williamson, 8th Bt; *S* brother, 1974. *Educ:* Oundle; Trinity Coll., Cambridge (BA);

University Coll., London. Barrister, Inner Temple, 1932; Private Secretary to: Governor and C-in-C, British Honduras, 1947–55; Governor of British Guiana, 1955–64. Served War of 1939–45 with RAOC, UK and India; Major, 1943. *Heir:* cousin George William Herbert [*b* 4 June 1925; *m* 1949, Hon. Katharine Odeyne de Grey, *d* of 8th Baron Walsingham, DSO, OBE; four *s* two adopted *d*]. *Address:* Powis Castle, Welshpool, N Wales. *T:* 3360. *Clubs:* Brooks's, MCC. *Died 7 Oct.* 1988.

**POWLETT, Vice-Admiral Sir Peveril Barton Reibey Wallop W.;** *see* William-Powlett.

**PRAIN, Alexander Moncur**, CBE 1964; Sheriff: of Perth and Angus at Perth, 1946–71; of Lanarkshire at Airdrie, 1943–46; *b* Longforgan, Perthshire, 19 Feb. 1908; 2nd *s* of A. M. Prain, JP, and Mary Stuart Whytock; *m* 1936, Florence Margaret Robertson; one *s*. *Educ:* Merchiston Castle; Edinburgh Academy; Edinburgh Univ. Called to Scottish Bar, 1932; Army, 1940–43, Major, RAC. *Recreations:* fishing, reading. *Address:* Castellar, Crieff, Perthshire.
*Died 13 Oct.* 1989.

**PRAIN, John Murray**, DSO 1940; OBE 1956; TD 1943 (two Bars); DL; *b* 17 Dec. 1902; *e s* of late James Prain, Hon. LLD St Andrews University, of Kincaple by St Andrews, Fife, and late Victoria Eleanor Murray; *m* 1934, Lorina Helen Elspeth, *o d* of late Colonel P. G. M. Skene, OBE, DL, of Halyards and Pitlour, Fife; one *s* one *d*. *Educ:* Charterhouse; Clare Coll., Cambridge, BA 1924. Chm., James Prain & Sons Ltd, Dundee, 1945–56; Vice-Chm., Caird (Dundee) Ltd, 1956–64; Director: Alliance Trust Co. Ltd, 1946–73; 2nd Alliance Trust Co. Ltd, 1946–73; Tayside Floorcloth Co. Ltd, 1946–69; The Scottish Life Assurance Co. Ltd, 1949–72; Royal Bank of Scotland, 1955–71; William Halley & Sons Ltd; Member Scottish Committee, Industrial and Commercial Finance Corporation, 1946–55; Chairman: Jute Importers Association, 1947–49; Assoc. of Jute Spinners and Manufacturers, 1950–52; Dundee District Cttee, Scottish Board for Industry, 1948–62. Member, Jute Working Party, 1946–48; part-time Member Scottish Gas Board, 1952–56; Member Employers' Panel Industrial Disputes Tribunal, 1952–59. Member: Employers' Panel, Industrial Court, 1959–71; Industrial Arbitration Bd, 1971–72. DL for County of Fife, 1958; Served in War of 1939–45, Fife and Forfar Yeomanry (wounded, despatches, DSO); GSO(2), 1943–44; Lt-Col (AQ) RAC, OCTU, RMC Sandhurst, 1944–45; Member Queen's Body Guard for Scotland, Royal Company of Archers; Hon. President, Fife and Kinross Area Council, Royal British Legion (Scotland). *Address:* Long Rigg, Hepburn Gardens, St Andrews, Fife KY16 9LT. *T:* St Andrews 73205. *Club:* Royal and Ancient (St Andrews).
*Died 22 May* 1985.

**PRAIN, Vyvyen Alice:** retired as Principal, Princess Helena College, Temple Dinsley, Herts, 1935–58; *b* 11 Oct 1895; *d* of Hunter Douglas Prain and Ellen Flora Davis. *Educ:* Edinburgh Ladies' Coll.; Edinburgh Univ. Graduated MA (Hons) in History (second class) in 1918, having gained the Gladstone Memorial Prize for History and Political Economy, and three class medals; Trained for teaching at Cambridge Training Coll., and gained a First Class Teacher's Certificate in 1919; History Mistress at Princess Helena Coll., Ealing, 1919–24; History and Economics at Wycombe Abbey Sch., 1924–29; Principal of the Ladies' Coll., Guernsey, 1929–35. *Recreations:* needlework, reading, travelling. *Address:* Halesworth, Suffolk. *Died 31 March* 1983.

**PRATT, Rev. Ronald Arthur Frederick;** *b* 27 Aug. 1886; *s* of Charles Robert and Florence Maria Pratt; *m* 1925, Margaret Elam; no *c*. *Educ:* Tonbridge Sch.; Gonville and Caius Coll., Cambridge. Curate of Emmanuel, West Hampstead, 1910–13; of St Matthew's, Bethnal Green, E2, 1913–21; Chaplain RN (temp.), 1917–19; Vicar of Ossington, Newark on Trent, 1921–23; Vicar of St John, Long Eaton, Derbyshire, 1923–32; Vicar of St Barnabas, Derby, 1932–35; Archdeacon of Belize, British Honduras, CA, 1935–46; Licentiate to Officiate Dio. Canterbury, 1947–62. Missionary work in the Diocese of British Honduras, 1930–31. *Address:* Barham House Nursing Home, The Street, Barham, Canterbury, Kent.
*Died 10 Dec.* 1983.

**PRAZ, Mario**, KBE (Hon.) 1962; Grand'Ufficiale della Repubblica italiana 1972; LittD Florence , Dr Juris Rome; Hon. LittD Cambridge University, 1957; Professor of English Language and Literature, University of Rome, 1934–66, Professor Emerito, 1966; British Academy Gold Medallist for Anglo-Italian Studies, 1935; Italian Gold Medal, for cultural merits, 1958; national member of the Accademia dei Lincei; Hon. Member, Modern Language Association of America, 1954; *b* Rome 1896; *s* of Luciano Praz and Giulia Testa Di Marsciano; *m* 1934, Vivyan (marr. diss. 1947), *d* of late Leonora Eyles, and *step-d* of late D. L. Murray; one *d*. *Educ:* Rome; Florence. Came to England in 1923 to qualify for the title of *libero docente* in English Literature, which eventually he obtained in 1925; worked in the British Museum, 1923; Senior Lecturer in Italian at Liverpool Univ., 1924–32; Professor of Italian Studies at Manchester Univ., 1932–34; co-editor of La Cultura; editor of

English Miscellany (Rome). Hon. LittD: Aix-Marseille Univ., 1964; Paris Univ. (Sorbonne), 1967; Uppsala Univ., 1977. *Publications:* I Saggi di Elia di Carlo Lamb, 1924; La Fortuna di Byron in Inghilterra, 1925; Poeti inglesi dell' Ottocento, 1925; Secentismo e Marinismo in Inghilterra, 1925; Machiavelli and the Elizabethans (British Academy Annual Italian Lecture), 1928; Penisola Pentagonale, 1928 (translated into English with the title Unromantic Spain, 1929); The Italian Element in English, 1929; La Carne, la Morte e il Diavolo nella Letteratura Romantica, 1930 (translated into English with the title The Romantic Agony, 1933); Studi sul concettismo, 1934 (translated into English as Studies in Seventeenth-century Imagery, 1939, 2nd vol., 1948; revised enlarged edition in one vol., 1964; Part II Addenda et Corrigenda, 1975); Antologia della letteratura inglese, 1936; Storia della letteratura inglese, 1937 (new rev. enlarged edition, 1960); Studi e svaghi inglesi, 1937; Gusto neoclassico, 1940 (3rd edn, 1974; translated into English as On Neoclassicism, 1968); Machiavelli in Inghilterra ed altri saggi, 1942 (rev. enlarged edition, 1962); Viaggio in Grecia, 1943; Fiori freschi, 1943; Ricerche anglo-italiane, 1944; La filosofia dell' arredamento, 1945 (rev. enlarged edition, 1964, in English as An Illustrated History of Interior Decoration, 1964); Motivi e figure, 1945; Prospettiva della letteratura inglese, 1947; Antologia delle letterature straniere, 1947; Cronache letterarie anglo-sassoni, Vols. I, II, 1951, III, IV, 1966; Il Libro della poesia inglese, 1951; La Casa della Fama, Saggi di letteratura e d'arte, 1952; Lettrice notturna, 1952; La crisi dell'eroe nel romanzo vittoriano, 1952 (translated into English with the title The Hero in Eclipse in Victorian Fiction, 1956); Viaggi in Occidente, 1955; The Flaming Heart, Essays on Crashaw, Machiavelli, and other studies of the relations between Italian and English Literature, 1958; La Casa della Vita, 1958, 2nd enlarged edn 1979 (translated into English as The House of Life, 1964); Bellezza e bizzarria, 1960; I Volti del tempo, 1964; Panopticon Romano, 1967; Caleidoscopio shakespeariano, 1969; Mnemosyne: the parallel between literature and the visual arts, 1970; Scene di conversazione, 1970 (translated into English as Conversation Pieces: a survey of the intimate group portrait in Europe and America, 1971); Il patto col serpente, paralipomeni a La Carne, La Morte e il Diavolo nella Lett. Romantica, 1972; Il giardino dei sensi, studi sul manierismo e il barocco, 1975; Introduction to G. B. Piranesi, Le Carceri, 1975; Panopticon Romano Secondo, 1978; Perseo e la Medusa, dal romanticismo all'avanguardia, 1979; Voce dietro la scena: una antologia personale, 1980; translations of Shakespeare's Measure for Measure and Troilus and Cressida, 1939, and of other works (by W. Pater, J. Austen, etc); general editor of standard Italian prose translation of Shakespeare's plays, 1943–47 and of Teatro elisabettiano, 1948; editor: works of Lorenzo Magalotti, 1945; D'Annunzio's selected works, 1966; contributions to literary and philological periodicals, both Italian and English. *Recreations:* travelling, Empire furniture. *Address:* Via Zanardelli 1, Rome, Italy. *Died 23 March 1982.*

**PREMINGER, Otto (Ludwig);** Producer-Director since 1928; *b* 5 Dec. 1906; *m* 1960, Hope Preminger (*née* Bryce); two *s* one *d* (one *s* one *d* are twins). *Educ:* University of Vienna (LLD). Associate Professor, Yale Univ., 1938–41. *Films:* Margin for Error, 1942; A Royal Scandal, 1944; Laura, 1944; Fallen Angel, 1945; Centennial Summer, 1945; Forever Amber, 1947; Daisy Kenyon, 1948; That Lady in Ermine, 1948; The Fan, 1949; Whirlpool, 1949; Where the Sidewalk Ends, 1950; The 13th Letter, 1950; Angel Face, 1952; The Moon is Blue, 1953; The River of No Return, 1953; Carmen Jones, 1954; Court Martial of Billy Mitchell, 1955; The Man with the Golden Arm, 1955; Saint Joan, 1957; Bonjour Tristesse, 1958; Porgy and Bess, 1959; Anatomy of a Murder, 1959; Exodus, 1960; Advise and Consent, 1961; The Cardinal, 1963; In Harm's Way, 1965; Bunny Lake is Missing, 1965; Hurry Sundown, 1967; Skidoo, 1968; Tell Me that You Love Me, Julie Moon, 1970; Such Good Friends, 1972; Rosebud, 1974; The Human Factor, 1979; *plays include:* (director) Libel, Broadway, 1936; (prod. and dir) Outward Bound, Broadway, 1938; (leading rôle and director) Margin for Error, Broadway, 1939; (prod. and dir) My Dear Children, 1940; Beverley Hills, 1940; Cue for Passion, 1940; The More the Merrier, 1941; In Time to Come, 1941; Four Twelves are 48, 1951; A Modern Primitive, 1951; (prod. and dir) The Moon is Blue, Broadway, 1951; The Trial, 1953; This is Goggle, 1958; (prod. and dir) Critic's Choice, Broadway, 1960; Full Circle, Broadway, 1973. *Publication:* Preminger: an autobiography, 1977. *Recreation:* art collector. *Address:* 129 East 64th Street, New York, NY 10021, USA. *T:* (212) 535 6001. *Died 23 April 1986.*

**PRESCOTT, James Arthur,** CBE 1947; DSc; FRS 1951; FAA; retired; Director, Waite Agricultural Research Institute, 1938–55; Professor of Agricultural Chemistry, University of Adelaide, 1924–55, Emeritus Professor since 1956; *b* 7 Oct. 1890; *e s* of Joseph Arthur Prescott, Bolton, Lancs; *m* 1915, Elsie Mason, Accrington, Lancs; one *s*. *Educ:* Ecole Littré, Lille; Accrington Grammar Sch.; Manchester Univ.; Leipzig Univ. Rothamsted Experimental Station; Chief Chemist and Superintendent of Field Experiments, Bahtim Experimental Station, Sultanic Agricultural Society of

Egypt, 1916–24; Chief, Division of Soils, Commonwealth Council for Scientific and Industrial Research, 1929–47. Mem. Council and Scientific Adviser, Australian Wine Research Inst., 1954–69. Hon. DAgSc Melbourne, 1956. Hon. Member: Internat. Society of Soil Science, 1964; All-Union (Soviet) Soc. of Soil Science, 1977. (Foundn) FAA 1954. *Publications:* various scientific, chiefly on soils, climatology and principles of crop production. *Address:* 6 Kinross Lodge, 2 Netherby Avenue, Netherby, SA 5062, Australia.
*Died 6 Feb. 1987.*

**PRESS, Dr Robert,** CB 1972; CBE 1962; Deputy Secretary, Science and Technology, Cabinet Office, 1974–76, retired; Adviser in the Cabinet Office since 1976; *b* 22 Feb. 1915; *s* of William J. Press; *m* 1946, Honor Elizabeth Tapp; no *c. Educ:* Regent House Secondary Sch., Co. Down; Queen's Univ., Belfast; Trinity Coll., Dublin Univ. BSc 1936, MSc 1937 QUB; PhD 1949 Dublin. Res. Physicist, TCD, 1938–40; Physics Master, Dungannon Royal Sch., NI, 1940–41; Physicist: War Dept Research, UK, 1941–43, and in India, 1944–46; on Staff of Scientific Adviser, Army Council, 1946–48; in Dept of Atomic Energy, Min. of Supply, 1948–51. Attaché at HM Embassy, Washington, 1951–55; Head of Technical Res. Unit, MoD, 1955–59; Mem. British Delegn to Conf. for Discontinuance of Nuclear Tests, 1958–59. Dep. Chief Scientific Officer, MoD, 1960–62, Chief Scientific Officer, 1962; Asst Chief Scientific Adviser (Nuclear), MoD, 1963–66; Chief Scientific Officer, Cabinet Office, 1967–71; Dep. Sec., Cabinet Office, 1971–74; Dep. to Chief Scientific Adviser to HM Govt, 1971–74. Mem., Internat. Consultative Gp on Nuclear Energy, 1979–80. Hon. Sec., Inst. of Physics, 1966–76; Foundn Mem., Council of European Physical Soc., 1969–72; Chm., Council of Science and Technology Insts, 1978–80 (Mem. Council, 1976–). FPhysS 1950, FInstP 1961, FRSA 1967 (Mem. Council, 1971–76). Hon. DSc QUB, 1983. *Publications:* papers in: Nature, and Proc. Royal Soc., 1938, 1941; Scientific Proc. Royal Dublin Soc., 1939; Irish Jl of Med. Science, 1941; Internat. Consultative Gp on Nuclear Energy (series), 1978–80. *Address:* 8 Ardross Avenue, Northwood, Mddx HA6 3DS. *T:* Northwood 23707. *Club:* Army and Navy.
*Died 30 Aug. 1984.*

**PRESSBURGER, Emeric;** author, film producer; *b* 5 Dec. 1902; one *d. Educ:* Universities of Prague and Stuttgart. Journalist in Hungary and Germany, author and writer of films in Berlin and Paris; came to England in 1935; formed jointly with Michael Powell, The Archers Film Producing Company, and Vega Productions Ltd, and made the following films: Spy in Black, 1938; 49th Parallel, 1940 (USA Academy Award 1942, under American title, The Original Story of The Invaders); One of our Aircraft is Missing, 1941; Colonel Blimp, 1942; I Know Where I'm Going, 1944; A Matter of Life and Death, 1945; Black Narcissus, 1946; The Red Shoes, 1947; Small Back Room, 1948; Gone to Earth, 1949; The Tales of Hoffmann, 1951; Oh Rosalinda!!, 1955; The Battle of the River Plate, 1956; Ill Met by Moonlight, 1956. Wrote, produced, and directed first film Twice Upon a Time, 1952; wrote and produced Miracle in Soho, 1957; wrote The Boy who Turned Yellow (film). British Film Institute Special Award (with Michael Powell), 1978; Fellow: BAFTA, 1981; BFI, 1983. *Publications:* Killing a Mouse on Sunday (novel), 1961; The Glass Pearls (novel), 1966; (with Michael Powell) The Red Shoes, 1978. *Recreations:* music, travel, and sports. *Address:* Shoemaker's Cottage, Aspall, Stowmarket, Suffolk. *Club:* Savile. *Died 5 Feb. 1988.*

**PREST, Prof. Alan Richmond;** Professor of Economics (with special reference to the Public Sector), London School of Economics, 1970–84, then Emeritus; *b* 1 March 1919; *s* of F. and E. A. Prest; *m* 1945, Pauline Chasey Noble; two *s* one *d. Educ:* Archbishop Holgate's Sch., York; Clare Coll., Cambridge; Christ's Coll., Cambridge. Res. Worker, Dept of Applied Economics, Cambridge, 1946–48; Rockefeller Fellow, USA, 1948–49; University Lecturer, Cambridge, 1949–64; Fellow, Christ's Coll., Cambridge, 1950–64; Tutor, 1954–55, Bursar, 1955–64, Christ's Coll.; Prof. of Economics and Public Finance, 1964–68, and Stanley Jevons Prof. of Political Economy, 1968–70, University of Manchester. Visiting Professor: Columbia Univ., New York, 1961–62; Univ. of Pittsburgh, 1969; ANU, 1971; Vis. Fellow, ANU, 1977, 1978, 1983; Leverhulme Emeritus Fellow, 1984. Member: Departmental Cttee on Liquor Licensing, 1971–72; Royal Commn on Civil Liability and Compensation for Personal Injury, 1973–78; Monopolies and Mergers Commn, 1983–. Pres., Section F, British Assoc., 1967. Treasurer, Royal Economic Soc., 1971–75. *Publications:* War Economics of Primary Producing Countries, 1948; The National Income of Nigeria, 1950–51, (with I. G. Stewart), 1953; Consumers' Expenditure in the UK, 1900–19, 1954; Fiscal Survey of the British Caribbean, 1957; Public Finance in Theory and Practice, 1960; Public Finance in Under-Developed Countries, 1962; (ed) The UK Economy, 1966; (ed) Public Sector Economics, 1968; Transport Economics in Developing Countries, 1969; (with N. A. Barr and S. R. James) Self-Assessment for Income Tax, 1977; Intergovernmental Financial Relations in the UK, 1978; The Taxation of Urban Land, 1981; papers in various professional journals. *Address:* 21 Leeward Gardens, Wimbledon Hill, SW19. *T:* 01–947 4492. *Club:* United Oxford & Cambridge University. *Died 22 Dec.* 1984.

**PRESTIE, Janet Miriam Taylor;** *see* Caldwell, Taylor.

**PRESTON, Alan;** Director of Fisheries Research, Ministry of Agriculture, Fisheries and Food, since 1980; *b* 23 May 1929; *s* of Ivor Gordon Preston and Lottie May Preston (*née* Bentley); *m* 1952, Beatrice Patricia Smith; two *s* two *d*. *Educ:* Newcastle High Sch., Staffs; Univ. of Reading (BSc (Gen.) 1950, BSc Hons Marine Zoology 1951). Nat. Service, RCS, 1953–55; 2nd Lieut 1954. Joined Fisheries Lab., Lowestoft, 1951: Head, Fisheries Radiobiol Lab., 1965–72; Dep. Dir, Fisheries Res., 1972–80; Co-ordinator, Fisheries Res. and Develt for GB, 1983–85. Buckland Foundation Professor, 1981 (Chm., Buckland Foundn Trustees, 1983–); Hon. Prof., Univ. of East Anglia, 1980–. Founder Mem., Soc. for Radiological Protection (Council Mem., 1969–73, 1981–84: Pres., 1982–83); Governor and Council Mem., Marine Biol Assoc. of the UK, 1981–. Delegate, 1981–, Vice-Pres., 1985–, Internat. Council for Exploration of the Sea. FRSA 1983. *Publications:* papers in learned jls. *Recreations:* gardening, haute cuisine, American history. *Address:* The Hall, Oulton, Lowestoft, Suffolk. *T:* Lowestoft 65115. *Club:* Rotary (Lowestoft South). *Died 10 Jan.* 1988.

**PRESTON, Hon. Mrs Angela C.;** *see* Campbell-Preston.

**PRESTON, Aston Zachariah,** JP; Vice-Chancellor, University of the West Indies, since 1974; *b* 16 April 1925; *s* of Zachariah and Caroline Preston; *m* 1954, Barbara Marie (*née* Mordecai); two *s* one *d*. *Educ:* Univ. of London (LLB); FCA, FCCA, FCIS, FREconS. University of the West Indies: Bursar, 1956; Pro-Vice-Chancellor, 1969. Mem., Bd of Governors, Univ. of Guyana, 1967; Financial Adviser to E Africa, S Africa, Zambia and S Pacific Govts on univ. financing and develt, 1968; Chm., Shortwood Teachers' Coll., Jamaica, 1970–77; Mem., Council, ACU, 1975–79, Chm. 1981–82; Mem., Adv. Cttee, Unesco Reg. Centre for Higher Educn in Latin America and the Caribbean, 1978–; Chm., Caribbean Exams Council, 1979–. Chairman: Public Passenger Transport Bd of Control, Jamaica, 1972–74; Jamaica Omnibus Services Ltd, 1974–77, 1979–80; Jamaica State Trading Corp. Ltd, 1979–; Inst. of Internat. Relations, Trinidad, 1974; PAHO Caribbean Epidemiology Centre, Trinidad, 1975–; Bd of Directors, Workers' Savings & Loan Bank, Jamaica, 1978; Finance Cttee, Port Authority, 1980–; Finance Cttee, Air Jamaica, 1981–; Income Tax Reform Cttee, Jamaica, 1985–; Sole Comr of Enquiries into two railway accidents, 1973; Pres., Public Accounting Bd, Jamaica, 1975; Mem., Industrial Disputes Tribunal, 1977. Member: Council, Univ. of Zambia, 1979–; Adv. Bd, Centre for Caribbean Studies, Univ. of Warwick, 1985–. Trustee: Caribbean News Agency; Centro Internacional de Agricultura, Colombia. JP Jamaica, 1957. Hon. LLD Hull, 1983. *Recreations:* reading, music, bridge. *Address:* Vice-Chancellor's House, University of the West Indies, Mona, Kingston 7, Jamaica. *T:* 92–70736. *Died 24 June* 1986.

**PRESTON, Prof. Joseph Henry;** Professor of Fluid Mechanics, University of Liverpool, 1955–76, later Emeritus; Fellow, Queen Mary College, London, since Dec. 1959; *b* 1 March 1911; *s* of William and Jean Preston, Penruddock, Cumberland; *m* 1938, Ethel Noble, Bampton, Westmorland; one *s* one *d*. *Educ:* Queen Elizabeth Grammar Sch., Penrith, Cumberland; Queen Mary Coll., University of London. BSc Eng London 1932; 1851 Industrial Bursary, for practical training at Short Bros Ltd, Rochester, 1932–34; PhD (Aeronautics) London 1936; Asst Lecturer, Imperial Coll., 1936–38; Officer, Aero Division, National Physical Laboratory, Teddington, 1938–46; Lecturer in Aeronautics, Cambridge Univ., 1946–54 (MA Cantab); Reader in Engineering, at Cambridge, 1955. FRAeS. *Publications:* contributor to Phil. Mag.; Journal Royal Aero. Society; Engineer; Engineering; Aero. Engineer; Aero. Quarterly; Journal of Mechanics and Applied Maths; Reports and Memoranda of the Stationery Office. *Recreation:* mountaineering. *Address:* 2 Croome Drive, West Kirby, Wirral L48 8AH. *Club:* Wayfarers (Liverpool). *Died 28 July* 1985.

**PRESTON, Col Rupert Lionel,** CBE 1945; Vice-Chairman, Royal Aero Club, 1970; Secretary-General, Royal Aero Club of the United Kingdom, 1945–63; *b* 1 Nov. 1902; *s* of late Admiral Sir Lionel Preston, KCB; *m* 1st, 1932, Jean Mary (*d* 1976), *d* of late F. B. Pitcairn and of Mrs Pitcairn; 2nd, 1978, Mrs Lona Margit Chambers. *Educ:* Cheltenham College. Coldstream Guards, 1924–45. Assistant Provost Marshal, London, 1938–40; 11 Group RAF Defence Officer, 1940–43; comd RAF Regt 83 Group RAF, 1943–45 (despatches, 1945). Mem. Council Air Registration Boards, 1946–65; Vice-Pres. Fédération Aeronautique Internationale, 1961–64; AFRAeS; Vice-Patron, Guards Flying Club; Hon. Member Soc. of Licensed Aeronautical Engineers. Silver Medal of Royal Aero Club, 1964. Specialist in 17th century Seascape paintings of the Netherlands. *Publications:* How to Become an Airline Pilot, 1930; 17th Century Seascape: paintings of the Netherlands, 1974. *Address:* 1 St Olaves Court, St Petersburgh Place, W2 4JY. *T:* 01–727 9878. *Clubs:* Naval

and Military, Cavalry and Guards; Aero Club de France, Wings (New York). *Died 2 Nov.* 1982.

**PRETYMAN, Sir Walter (Frederick),** KBE 1972; President, Usina Santa Cruz; *b* 17 Oct. 1901; *s* of Rt Hon. E. G. Pretyman and Lady Beatrice Pretyman; *m* 1st, 1929, Margaret Cunningham (*d* 1942); one *d*; 2nd, 1947, Vera de Sa Sotto Maior (*d* 1986); two *s*; 3rd, 1986, Marie Therese de Castro Brandão. *Educ:* Eton; Magdalen Coll., Oxford. From 1923 onwards, industrial and agricultural activities in Brasil. Served War, with RAFVR, 1943–45; despatches, 1946; retd with rank of Sqdn Ldr. *Address:* (office) 90 Rua Mexico, Rio de Janeiro, Brazil. *T:* 232–8179. *Clubs:* Gavea Golf and Country, Jockey (Rio de Janeiro). *Died 4 Dec.* 1988.

**PREVOST, Captain Sir George James Augustine,** 5th Bt, *cr* 1805; *b* 16 Jan. 1910; *s* of Sir Charles Thomas Keble Prevost, 4th Bart, and Beatrice Mary (*d* 1973), *o d* of Rev. J. A. Burrow of Tunstall, Kirkby Lonsdale; *S* father, 1939; *m* 1st, 1935, Muriel Emily (*d* 1939), *d* of late Lewis William Oram; one *s* one *d*; 2nd, 1940, Phyllis Catherine Mattock (from whom he obtained a divorce, 1949); 3rd, 1952, Patricia Betty Porter, Harpenden, Herts; two *s*. *Educ:* Repton. *Heir:* *s* Christopher Gerald Prevost [*b* 25 July 1935; *m* 1964, Dolores Nelly, *o d* of Dezo Hoffman; one *s* one *d*]. *Address:* St Mary's, Little Petherick, Cornwall. *Died 18 Nov.* 1985.

**PRICE, Arnold Justin,** QC 1976; a Recorder of the Crown Court, since 1972; *b* 16 Aug. 1919; *s* of late Sydney Walter Price, LLB, Solicitor, and Sophia Price (*née* Marks); *m* 1948, Ruth Corinne, *d* of Ralph and Dorothy Marks; four *d*. *Educ:* St Christopher's Sch., Liverpool; Kingsmead Sch., Meols; Liverpool Coll.; Liverpool Univ. Bd of Legal Studies. Served War, Royal Engrs, 42nd Inf. Div. TA (invalided), later 2nd Lieut Royal Corps Mil. Police, 42nd Inf. Div. TA. Called to Bar, Middle Temple, 1952; practised Wales and Chester Circuit; Resident Magistrate, Nyasaland, 1955; Magistrate, N Nigeria, 1957; Actg Chief Magistrate and Judge, High Court N Nigeria, 1957–60; returned to practice, Wales and Chester Circuit, 1960; Northern Circuit, 1969. CC Chester, 1963–68. *Publications:* articles on politics, agriculture and legal subjects. *Recreations:* fishing, the countryside, beekeeping. *Address:* Thicket Ford, Thornton Hough, Wirral. *T:* 051–336 4444; Peel House, Harrington Street, Liverpool. *T:* 051–236 5072, 051–227 5661; 2 Pump Court, Temple, EC4. *T:* 01–353 3106. *Club:* Athenæum (Liverpool). *Died 25 March* 1987.

**PRICE, Byron,** KBE (Hon.) 1948; Medal for Merit, US, 1946; *b* Topeka, Indiana, 25 March 1891; *s* of John Price and Emaline Barnes; *m* 1920, Priscilla Alden (*d* 1978); no *c*. *Educ:* Wabash College (AB). In newspaper work, 1909; exec. news editor Associated Press, 1937–41, actg gen. man., 1939; US Dir of Censorship, Dec. 1941–Nov. 1945; on special mission to Germany as personal rep. of President Truman, 1945. Vice-Pres. Motion Picture Assoc. of America; Chm. Bd Assoc. Motion Picture Producers; Pres. Central Casting Corp.; 1st Vice-Pres. Educnl Film Research Inst.; Dir Hollywood Coordinating Cttee, 1946–47; Assistant Secretary-Gen., Administrative and Financial Services, United Nations, 1947–54; retired 1954. Served as 1st Lt, later Capt., Inf., US Army, 1917–19. Special Pulitzer citation for creation and administration of press and broadcasting censorship codes, 1944; Director General, Press Congress of the World, Columbia, Mo., 1959. Mem., Indiana Acad., 1976. Holds several hon. degrees. *Address:* Box 994, Carolina Village,,, Hendersonville, NC 28739, USA. *Clubs:* National Press, Gridiron (Washington). *Died 6 Aug.* 1981.

**PRICE, Maj.-Gen. Cedric Rhys,** CB 1951; CBE 1945 (OBE 1943); Principal Staff Officer to Secretary of State for Commonwealth Relations, 1959–64; ADC to the Queen, 1954–57; *b* 13 June 1905; *o s* of late Colonel Sir Rhys H. Price, KBE, CMG, Highlands, Purley Downs; *m* 1935, Rosamund, *e d* of late Arthur W. Clifford, Dursley, Glos; two *d*. *Educ:* Wellington College; RMA Woolwich; Trinity College, Cambridge. Commissioned Royal Engineers, 1925; served in India, 1932–38; Staff College, 1938–39; Military Assistant Secretary, offices of War Cabinet, 1940–46; Secretary, British Joint Services Mission, Washington, USA, 1946–48; Secretary, Chiefs of Staff Cttee, Ministry of Defence, 1948–50; student, Imperial Defence College, SW1, 1951; Chief of Staff to Chairman of British Joint Services Mission, Washington, 1952–54; Brigadier, General Staff, Eastern Command, 1955–56; Director of Military Intelligence, War Office, 1956–59. *Recreations:* golf, tennis, riding. *Address:* Furze Field Cottage, Hoe Lane, Peaslake, Guildford, Surrey. *T:* Dorking 730586. *Club:* Army and Navy. *Died 16 July* 1987.

**PRICE, David William T.;** *see* Tudor Price.

**PRICE, Gwilym Ivor;** Chairman and Managing Director, Unigate Ltd, 1960–70; Chairman and Managing Director, United Dairies Ltd, 1959–70; *b* 2 Oct. 1899; *er s* of late Sir William Price; *m* 1st, 1927, Nancye Freeman (*d* 1957); two *s*; 2nd, 1958, Margaret Ryrie Greaves. *Educ:* St Paul's School; Magdalene College, Cambridge. Served European War, 1914–18 in Army; commissioned. Director of United Dairies Ltd, 1931; Managing Director, 1936. *Address:* Ryrie Cottage, Coleshill, Bucks.      *Died 26 Nov.* 1981.

**PRICE, Prof. Harold Louis;** Professor of Mathematics for Applied Science, University of Leeds, 1968–82, later Emeritus Professor; *b* 3 Sept. 1917; *s* of Reuben Price and Annie Boltsa; *m* 1941, Gertrude Halpern; two *d. Educ:* Manchester Grammar Sch.; Sidney Sussex Coll., Cambridge; Univ. of Leeds. MA Cantab; MSc (distinction), PhD Leeds; FRAeS; FIMA. Mathematician, Rotol Airscrews Ltd, 1939–40; Aerodynamicist, Blackburn Aircraft, 1940–45; Research Mathematician, Sperry Gyroscope Co., 1945–46; Univ. of Leeds: Lectr in Applied Maths, 1946–60; Sen. Lectr, 1960–64; Prof. of Maths, 1964–68; Chm., Sch. of Mathematics, 1970–73. *Publications:* research papers on aircraft dynamics, etc. *Address:* 11 West Park Place, Leeds LS8 2EY. *T:* Leeds 664212.

                                 *Died 11 Nov.* 1986.

**PRICE, Henry Alfred,** CBE 1962; Managing Director, Grove Paper Co. Ltd; *b* 3 Jan. 1911; *s* of James Wm and Louisa Rebecca Price; *m* 1938, Ivy May Trimmer; one *s* one *d. Educ:* Holloway County School. Joined paper trade, 1927. Member LCC, 1946–52; MP (C) West Lewisham, 1950–64. *Recreations:* music and sport. *Address:* 22 Cator Road, Sydenham, SE26. *T:* 01-778 3838.

                                  *Died 4 Dec.* 1982.

**PRICE, Henry Habberley,** FBA 1943; MA, BSc; Professor Emeritus, University of Oxford, and Honorary Fellow of New College; *b* 1899; *s* of H. H. Price; unmarried. *Educ:* Winchester College; New College, Oxford (Scholar). Served in Royal Air Force, 1917–19; 1st Class in Lit. Hum. 1921; Fellow of Magdalen College, 1922–24; Assistant lecturer at Liverpool University, 1922–23; Fellow and Lecturer in Philosophy at Trin. Coll., 1924–35; Univ. Lectr in Philosophy, 1932–35; Wykeham Prof. of Logic, and Fell. New Coll., 1935–59. Pres. of Soc. for Psychical Research, 1939–40 and 1960–61. Visiting Professor at Princeton University, USA, 1948; Gifford Lecturer, Aberdeen University, 1959–60; Flint Visiting Prof., Univ. of California, Los Angeles, 1962; Boutwood Lecturer, Cambridge, 1965; Sarum Lectr, Oxford, 1970–71. Hon. DLitt, Dublin, 1953; Hon. LLD, St Andrews, 1954; Hon DLitt, Univ. of Wales, 1964. *Publications:* Perception, 1932, repr. 1973; Hume's Theory of the External World, 1940; Thinking and Experience, 1953; Belief (Gifford Lectures), 1969; Essays in the Philosophy of Religion, 1972; articles in Proc. Aristotelian Society and other philosophical periodicals. *Recreations:* aviation, painting and ornithology. Founder-member of Oxford University and City Gliding Club. *Address:* 69 Jack Straw's Lane, Oxford. *T:* Oxford 68945.                             *Died 26 Nov.* 1984.

**PRICE, Captain Henry Ryan,** MC; racehorse trainer, 1937–82, retired; *b* 16 Aug. 1912; *m* 1946, Dorothy Audrey Dale; two *s* one *d.* Served War of 1939–45, 6th Commandos (N Staffs) (MC). Big races won include: Grand National, Champion Hurdle, Schweppes Gold Trophy (four times), Oaks Stakes, St Leger Stakes. *Recreations:* shooting, fishing, work. *Address:* Soldiers Field, Findon, Sussex BN14 0SH. *T:* Findon 2388.              *Died 16 Aug.* 1986.

**PRICE, Comdr Hugh Perceval,** DSO 1940; OBE 1945; RN retired; Hydrographic Surveyor; *b* 19 May 1901; *s* of late Lt-Col Ivon Henry Price, DSO, LLD, Asst Insp.-Gen., Royal Irish Constabulary, and May Emily Kinahan; *m* 1925, Annie Grant Berry; one *s* one *d. Educ:* Monkstown Park School, Co. Dublin; Chesterfield School, Birr; RN Colleges, Osborne and Dartmouth. Entered RNC Osborne, 1915; HMS King George V, 1917; joined Surveying Service in 1925; employed on escort work and Hydrographic duties during war of 1939–45; retired list, 1946. *Recreation:* fishing. *Address:* c/o Mrs A. M. Thornton, 62 Manor Way, Onslow Village, Guildford, Surrey. *T:* Guildford 67637.                  *Died 19 July* 1983.

**PRICE, John Playfair;** *b* 4 July 1905; *s* of William Arthur Price and Edith Octavia Playfair; *m* 1932, Alice Elizabeth Kendall, Boston, Mass; two *d. Educ:* Gresham School; New College, Oxford. Hon. Exhib., New Coll., Oxford; Pres. Oxford Union Society. Diplomatic and Consular posts at Peking, Nanking, Tientsin, Canton, Chinkiang, Harbin (Manchuria), Katmandu (Nepal), Gangtok (Sikkim), Los Angeles, Kansas City, Tunis, Tangier, Lisbon, Santiago (Chile), and Geneva. Additional Judge, China, 1933–37; Foreign Office, 1938; 1st Secretary of Embassy, 1943; Consul-General for Khorasan, Sistan and Persian Baluchistan, 1948; retired from Diplomatic Service, 1950. Civil Service and Foreign Service Selection and Final Selection Boards, 1950; Dir and Chm. of Exec., Central African Rhodes Centenary Exhibition, 1951–52; British Council, 1959–61. *Address:* 3 rue Pasteur, 74200 Thonon, France. *T:* (50) 26.63.96.                    *Died 5 May* 1988.

**PRICE, Norman Stewart,** CMG 1959; OBE 1946; *b* 9 Aug. 1907; *s* of late Lt-Col Ivon Henry Price, DSO, LLD, Asst Inspr-Gen., RIC, and May Emily (*née* Kinahan), Greystones, Ireland; *m* 1933, Rosalind Evelyn Noelle (*née* Ormsby) (*d* 1973); two *d. Educ:* Portora Royal School, Enniskillen; Exeter Sch.; Trinity Coll., Dublin; Queens Coll., Oxford. LLB 1929, BA Hons 1930. Cadet, Northern

Rhodesia, 1930, District Officer, 1932, Provincial Comr, Northern Rhodesia, 1951–59; retired, 1959. Coronation Medal, 1953. *Recreations:* gardening; Captain Dublin University Harriers and Athletic Club, 1928–29; Half-Blue Oxford University Cross Country, 1929. *Address:* 24 Halcombe, Chard, Somerset TA20 2DS. *T:* Chard 61688.                         *Died 16 Jan.* 1988.

**PRICE, Robert;** *see* Price, W. R.

**PRICE, Very Rev. Robert Peel;** Chaplain to the Queen, 1957–61; *b* 18 Sept. 1905. *Educ:* Dover College; Wadham College, Oxford (MA); Wells Theological College. Deacon, 1930; Priest, 1931; Curate of: Wimbledon, 1930–34; St Martin, Knowle, 1934–40; Cheam (in charge of St Oswald's), 1940–42; St Peter's, Bournemouth, 1942–45; Vicar of Christchurch with Mudeford, Diocese of Winchester, 1945–61; Hon. Canon of Winchester, 1950–61; Dean of Hereford, 1961–68, now Emeritus; Priest-in-charge, St Swithun's, Bournemouth, 1968–71. *Address:* c/o Lloyds Bank Ltd, Lansdowne, Bournemouth, Dorset.                 *Died 26 Dec.* 1981.

**PRICE, Walter Robert;** Executive Director: Latin American and South African Operations, General Motors, since 1984; Overseas Assembly, North American Vehicles, since 1982; Joint Ventures and African Operations, General Motors, since 1981; Managing Director, GM de Venezuela, since 1983; *b* 26 Feb. 1926; *m* 1951, Mary Alice Hubbard; one *s* three *d. Educ:* Wesleyan Univ., Middletown, Conn, USA (BA). Managing Director: General Motors Suisse, Bienne, Switzerland, 1967; General Motors Continental, Antwerp, Belgium, 1970; General Motors South African (Pty) Ltd, Port Elizabeth, S Africa, 1971; Chm. and Man. Dir, Vauxhall Motors Ltd, Luton, 1974–79; Vice Pres., General Motors Corp., 1978–. Vice Pres., SMMT, 1978–79. *Recreations:* tennis, squash, golf. *Address:* General Motors Corporation, General Motors Building, 3044 West Grand Boulevard, Detroit, Mich 48202, USA.

                                  *Died 10 Oct.* 1987.

**PRICE, Willard De Mille;** explorer, naturalist, author; *b* Peterboro, Ontario, Canada, 28 July 1887; *s* of Albert Melancthon Price, and Estella Martin; *m* 1st, 1914, Eugenia Reeve (*d* 1929), Willoughby, Ohio; one *s*; 2nd, 1932, Mary Selden, New York. To United States, 1901; BA, Western Reserve Univ., Cleveland, Ohio, 1909; studied New York School of Philanthropy, 1911–12; MA, Columbia University, 1914; studied Journalism New York Univ. and Columbia; editorial staff, The Survey, New York, 1912–13; editorial secretary Board of Foreign Missions, Methodist Episcopal Church, 1915–19; editor World Outlook; manager of publication of Everyland and La Nueva Democracia; director periodical department of Interchurch World Movement and supervising editor various class and travel publications; travel in 148 countries, particularly on expeditions for National Geographic Society and American Museum of Natural History, 1920–67. *Publications: books:* Ancient Peoples at New Tasks; The Negro Around the World; Study of American Influence in the Orient; Pacific Adventure; Rip Tide in the South Seas; Where Are You Going, Japan?; Children of the Rising Sun; Japan Reaches Out; Barbarian (a novel); Japan Rides the Tiger; Japan's Islands of Mystery; The Son of Heaven; Key to Japan; Roving South; Tropic Adventure; Amazon Adventure; I Cannot Rest from Travel; The Amazing Amazon; Journey by Junk; Underwater Adventure; Adventures in Paradise; Volcano Adventure; Innocents in Britain; Whale Adventure; Incredible Africa; African Adventure; The Amazing Mississippi; Elephant Adventure; Rivers I Have Known; America's Paradise Lost; Safari Adventure; Lion Adventure; Gorilla Adventure; Odd Way Round the World; Diving Adventure; The Japanese Miracle; Cannibal Adventure; Tiger Adventure; Arctic Adventure; My Own Life of Adventure; contrib. to Spectator, Daily Telegraph, Saturday Evening Post, Encyc. Brit., etc. *Address:* 814-N Via Alhambra, Laguna Hills, Calif 92653, USA.

                                *Died 14 Oct.* 1983.

**PRICE, William Thomas,** CBE 1960; MC 1917; BSc; Principal, Harper Adams Agricultural College, Shropshire, 1946–62, retired 1962; *b* 15 Nov. 1895; *m* 1923, Fanny Louise (*d* 1964), *d* of Philip T. Dale, Stafford; no *c*; *m* 1965, Mrs Beryl E. Drew, *d* of T. W. Tayler, Northleach, Glos. *Educ:* Christ Coll., London; Reading Univ. Served European War, 1915–18, Royal Warwickshire Regt, RFC and RAF with rank of Captain. Lecturer in Dairy Husbandry, Staffordshire Farm Institute, 1920–22; Lecturer in Estate Management, Harper Adams Agricultural Coll., 1922–24; Wiltshire County Council: Lecturer in Agriculture, 1924–26; Organiser of Agricultural Education, 1926–46. Chief Exec. Officer, Wilts WAEC, 1939–46. President Shropshire and W Midland Agric. Society, 1963. David Black Award, 1961 (for greatest contrib. to British pig industry). Lecturer and broadcaster on agriculture. *Publications:* Wiltshire Agricultural Advisory Reports, 1939; The Housing of the Pig, 1953. Editor, The Pig, 1961; various articles on agricultural subjects. *Recreations:* fishing and travel. *Address:* Eversleigh, 2 Clarendon Place, Leamington Spa, Warwicks.

                                *Died 17 Jan.* 1982.

**PRICE HOLMES, Eric Montagu;** *see* Holmes.

**PRIESTLEY, John Boynton,** OM 1977; MA, LittD; LLD; DLitt; Author; *b* Bradford, 13 Sept, 1894; *s* of Jonathan Priestley, schoolmaster; *m* Jacquetta Hawkes, OBE; one *s* four *d* by previous marriages. *Educ:* Bradford; Trinity Hall, Cambridge (Hon. Fellow, 1978). Served with Duke of Wellington's and Devon Regts, 1914–19. UK Delegate to UNESCO Conferences, 1946–47; Chairman of International Theatre Conf.: Paris, 1947, Prague, 1948; Chairman British Theatre Conf., 1948; President International Theatre Institute, 1949; Member of the National Theatre Board, 1966–67. Freeman, City of Bradford, 1973. *Publications:* Brief Diversions, 1922; Papers from Lilliput, 1922; I for One, 1923; Figures in Modern Literature, 1924; The English Comic Characters, 1925; George Meredith (English Men of Letters), 1926; Talking, 1926; Adam in Moonshine, 1927; Open House, 1927; Peacock (English Men of Letters), 1927; Benighted, 1927; The English Novel, 1927; Apes and Angels, 1928; English Humour, 1928; The Good Companions, 1929 (dramatised with E. Knoblock, 1931); The Balconinny, 1929; Town Major of Miraucourt; Angel Pavement, 1930; Self-Selected Essays, 1932; Dangerous Corner, play, 1932; Faraway, 1932; Wonder Hero, 1933, The Roundabout, play, 1933; Laburnum Grove, play, 1933; English Journey, 1934, repr. 1984; Eden End, 1934; Duet in Floodlight, play, 1935; Cornelius, play, 1935; Bees on the Boat Deck, play, 1936; They Walk in the City, 1936; Midnight on the Desert, 1937; Time and the Conways, play, 1937; I Have Been Here Before, play, 1937; People at Sea, play, 1937; The Doomsday Men, 1938; Music at Night, play, 1938; When We Are Married, play, 1938; Johnson Over Jordan, play, 1939; Rain upon Godshill, 1939; Let the People Sing, 1939; The Long Mirror, play, 1940; Postscripts, 1940; Out of the People, 1941; Goodnight, Children, play, 1942; Black-Out in Gretley, 1942; The Foreman went to France, film screenplay, 1942; They Came to a City, play, 1943; Daylight on Saturday, 1943; The Man-Power Story, 1943; British Women go to War, 1943; Desert Highway, play, 1943; How Are They At Home?, play, 1944; Three Men in New Suits, 1945; An Inspector Calls, Ever Since Paradise, plays, 1946; The Secret Dream; Bright Day, 1946; Arts under Socialism; Theatre Outlook; Jenny Villiers; The Linden Tree, play, 1947; Home is Tomorrow, play, 1948; Summer Day's Dream, play, 1949; libretto, The Olympians, opera, 1948; Delight (essays), 1949; libretto, Last Holiday (film), 1950; Festival at Farbridge, 1951; (with Jacquetta Hawkes) Dragon's Mouth, play, 1952; The Other Place, 1953; The Magicians; Low Notes on a High Level, 1954; Mr Kettle and Mrs Moon, play, 1955; Journey Down a Rainbow (with Jacquetta Hawkes), 1955; The Glass Cage, play, 1957; Thoughts in the Wilderness, 1957; The Art of the Dramatist, 1957; Topside or the Future of England, 1958; Literature and Western Man, 1960; Saturn Over The Water, 1961; The Thirty-First of June, 1961; Charles Dickens: A Pictorial Biography, 1961; The Shapes of Sleep, 1962; Margin Released, 1962; A Severed Head (with Iris Murdoch), play, 1963; Sir Michael and Sir George, 1964; Man and Time, 1964; Lost Empires, 1965; The Moment—And Other Pieces (essays), 1966; Salt is Leaving, 1966; It's an Old Country, 1967; Trumpets Over the Sea, 1968; The Image Men, Vol. I, Out of Town, 1968, Vol. II, London End, 1968; Essays of Five Decades, ed Susan Cooper, 1969; The Prince of Pleasure and his Regency, 1969; The Edwardians, 1970; Snoggle, 1971; Victoria's Heyday, 1972; Over the Long High Wall, 1972; The English, 1973; Outcries and Asides (essays), 1974; A Visit to New Zealand, 1974; The Carfitt Crisis, 1975; Particular Pleasures, 1975; Found, Lost, Found, or the English Way of Life, 1976; The Happy Dream, 1976; English Humour, 1976; Instead of the Trees (autobiog.), 1977. *Relevant publications:* J. B. Priestley: An Informal Study of His Work, by David Hughes, 1959; J. B. Priestley: the Dramatist, by Gareth Lloyd Evans, 1964; J. B. Priestley: portrait of an author, by Susan Cooper, 1970; J. B. Priestley, by John Braine, 1978; J. B. Priestley: the last of the sages, by John Atkins, 1980, etc. *Address:* Alveston, Stratford-upon-Avon, Warwickshire. *Died 14 Aug. 1984.*

**PRIME, Derek Arthur,** RDI 1982; FCSD; Managing Director, J. C. B. Research, since 1973; *b* 16 July 1932; *s* of Thomas Beasley Prime and Lucy Prime; *m* 1963, Pamela Dix; one *s* one *d*. *Educ:* Alleynes Grammar Sch., N Staffs Technical Coll. (HNC Mech. Engrg). MIED 1964; REngDes, 1986; FCSD (FSIAD 1979); FRSA 1983. Engrg Apprentice, Thomas Bolton & Sons Ltd, 1948–52; Designer, J. C. Bamford Excavators Ltd, 1952–59; J. C. B. Research: Asst Chief Designer, 1959; Chief Designer, 1964; Technical Dir, 1970. Queen's Award for Technical Innovation, 1973; Design Council Awards, 1973, 1975 and 1984; RSA Award for Design Management, 1979. Listed as inventor on 22 patents in field of construction machinery. *Recreations:* gardening, photography, equestrian events as a spectator. *Address:* Bladon House, Lodge Hill, Tutbury, Burton on Trent, Staffs DE13 9HF. *T:* Burton on Trent (0283) 813839. *Died 16 June 1990.*

**PRIMROSE, Sir Alasdair Neil,** 4th Bt *cr* 1903, of Redholme, Dumbreck, Govan; Senior Master, St Andrews Scots School, Olivos, Buenos Aires; *b* 11 Dec. 1935; *s* of Sir John Ure Primrose, 3rd Bt and of Enid, *d* of James Evans Sladen, British Columbia; *S* father, 1984; *m* 1958, Elaine Noreen, *d* of Edmund Cecil Lowndes, Buenos Aires; two *s* two *d*. *Educ:* St George's College, Buenos Aires. *Heir: s* John Ure Primrose [*b* 28 May 1960; *m* 1983, Marion Cecilia, *d* of Hans Otto Altgelt; two *d*]. *Address:* Ada Elflein 3155, 1609 Boulogne, Provincia Buenos Aires, Argentina. *Died 15 June 1986.*

**PRIMROSE, Sir John Ure,** 3rd Bt, *cr* 1903, of Redholme; retired farmer; *b* 15 April 1908; *er s* of Sir William Louis Primrose, 2nd Bt, and Elizabeth Caroline (*d* 1951), *d* of Hugh Dunsmuir, Glasgow; *S* father, 1953; *m* Enid, *d* of James Evans Sladen, British Columbia; one *s*. *Educ:* Rugby; Sandhurst. Lieut, QO Cameron Highlanders, 1928–33. *Heir: s* Alasdair Neil Primrose [*b* 11 Dec. 1935; *m* 1958, Elaine Noreen, *d* of E. C. Lowndes, Buenos Aires; two *s* two *d*. *Educ:* St George's College, Buenos Aires]. *Address:* Ada Elflein 3155, 1609 Boulogne, Provincia Buenos Aires, Argentina. *Died 2 Aug. 1984.*

**PRIMROSE, William,** CBE 1952; FGSM (Hon.); Viola Soloist; *b* 23 Aug. 1904; *s* of late John Primrose and of Margaret Primrose, both of Glasgow; *m* 1st, 1928, Dorothy (*d* 1951), *d* of John Friend of Exeter; two *d*; 2nd, 1952, Alice Virginia French, Davenport, Iowa; 3rd, Hiroko, *d* of Isao F. Sawa, Osaka, Japan. *Educ:* Guildhall School of Music, London; privately with Eugen Ysaye, Brussels. Violist with London String Quartet, 1930–35; First Violist with NBC Orchestra, New York, under Toscanini, 1937–42; since then exclusively as soloist. Professor, Viola and Chamber Music, Curtis Institute of Music, Philadelphia, 1940–50; taught at: Juilliard Sch. of Music, NY; Univ. of Southern Calif; LA special classes with Heifetz and Piatigorski; Indiana Univ.; Tokyo Univ. of Fine Arts; Banff Centre of Fine Arts, Canada. Has toured extensively in US, Canada, Central and S America, Great Britain, Western Europe and Israel. *Publication:* Walk on the North Side (memoirs) 1978. *Recreations:* chess, cricket and reading. *Club:* Savage. *Died 1 May 1982.*

**PRINCE, Leslie Barnett,** CBE 1973; MA; FCA; FCIArb; *b* 27 May 1901; *s* of Sir Alexander William Prince, KBE, and Lady Prince (*née* Edith Jonas); *m* 1st, 1924, Norah Millie (*d* 1979), *d* of Eliot Lewis, JP; one *s* two *d*; 2nd, 1980, Gerwin Sylvia Delacour Davis, MB ChB, DPM (Univ. of Cape Town), MRCPsych, *d* of Harold Delacour Davis, South Africa. *Educ:* Clifton Coll.; Magdalene Coll., Cambridge (MA). FCA 1930. Chartered Accountant; Dir, Hand in Hand Assce Co. (Commercial Union), 1934–84 (Chm., 1974–82); Dep. Chm., 1982–84). London Chest Hospital Board, 1937–48; Hospital for Diseases of the Chest, Board of Management, 1948–61. Joint Chairman of Jewish Refugees Cttee, 1939–43; Hon. Director of Accounts, ROF, Ministry of Supply, 1944–46. Member Court of Common Council, City of London, 1950–; Chairman: Rates Finance Cttee, 1957–65; Coal and Corn and Finance Cttee, Corporation of London, 1967; Coal, Corn and Rates Finance Cttee, 1968–70; Real Estate Cttee, 1970–; Chief Commoner, City Lands and Bridge House Estates Cttee, 1971. Sheriff of City of London, 1954–55; Chm., London Court of Arbitration, 1974–77. Member Council: Metropolitan Hospital Sunday Fund, 1951–; Royal Veterinary Coll., 1971–. Deputy of Ward of Bishopsgate, 1970–83. Master, Worshipful Co. of Farriers, 1955–56. President: United Wards Club, 1957; Bishopsgate Ward Club, 1958. Chm., City of London Br., Royal Soc. of St George, 1959. Pres., Old Cliftonian Soc., 1973–75 (Hon. Treas., 1934–73). Companion of Star of Ethiopia, 1954; Commandeur Léopold II, 1963; Order of Sacred Treasure (Japan), 1972; Order of Stor (Afghanistan), 1972. *Publication:* The Farrier and his Craft, 1980. *Recreation:* knitting. *Address:* 21 Cadogan Gardens, SW3. *T:* 01–730 0515. *Clubs:* Gresham, City Livery (Treasurer, 1966–72, and 1974–78, Pres., 1973–74), Samuel Pepys (Treasurer, 1982–). *Died 17 Aug. 1985.*

**PRINGLE, John William Sutton,** MBE 1945; FRS 1954; ScD 1955; Linacre Professor of Zoology, Oxford, and Fellow of Merton College, Oxford, 1961–79; later Professor Emeritus; *b* 22 July 1912; *e s* of late John Pringle, MD, Manchester, and of Dorothy Emily (*née* Beney); *m* 1946, Beatrice Laura Wilson (*née* Gilbert-Carter); one *s* two *d*. *Educ:* Winchester Coll.; King's Coll., Cambridge (MA). University Demonstrator in Zoology, 1937–39; University Lecturer, 1945–59; Fellow of King's Coll., Cambridge, 1938–45; Telecommunications Research Establishment, 1939–44; Ministry of War Transport, 1944–45; Fellow of Peterhouse, Cambridge, 1945–61, Emeritus Fellow, 1961, Hon. Fellow, 1982–. Senior Tutor, 1948–57; Senior Bursar, 1957–59; Librarian, 1959–61; Reader in Experimental Cytology, Cambridge, 1959–61. Pres., Soc. for Experimental Biol., 1977–. American Medal of Freedom, 1945. *Publications:* Insect Flight, 1957; (ed) Biology and the Human Sciences, 1972; papers in Journal of Experimental Biology, Journal of Physiology, Philos. Trans. Royal Society. *Recreation:* bee-keeping. *Address:* 437 Banbury Road, Oxford OX2 8ED. *T:* 58470. *Died 2 Nov. 1982.*

**PRINGLE, Dr Mia Lilly Kellmer,** CBE 1975; Founder, and Director, National Children's Bureau, 1963–81, Vice-President, since 1982; *b*

20 June 1920; *d* of late Samuel and Sophie Kellmer; *m* 1946, William Joseph Sommerville Pringle, BSc (*d* 1962); *m* 1969, William Leonard Hooper, MA Oxon (*d* 1980). *Educ:* schools in Vienna; Birkbeck Coll., University of London (Hon. Fellow, 1980). BA (Hons) 1944; Dip. Educ. Psychol. 1945; Fellowship, London Child Guidance Training Centre, 1945; PhD (Psych.) 1950. Teaching in Primary Schools, Middx and Herts, 1940–44; Educ. and Clin. Psychologist, Herts Child Guidance Service, 1945–50; University of Birmingham: Lecturer in Educ. Psych., 1950–54; Dep. Head, Dept of Child Study, 1954–63; Senior Lecturer in Educ. Psych., 1960–63. Member: Birmingham Educ. Cttee, 1957–63; Home Sec.'s Adv. Council on Child Care, 1966–72; Consultative Panel for Social Develt, ODM, 1968–71; Sec. of State's Adv. Cttee on Handicapped Children, 1971–; Bd of Governors, Hosp. for Sick Children, Gt Ormond Street, 1969–81; Research Consultant: on play needs, to Min. of Housing and Local Govt, 1968–73; UN Research Inst. for Social Develt, 1967–69; co-opted Mem., Islington Social Services Cttee, 1972–78; Personal Social Services Council, 1973–80 (Chm. Study Gp on A Future for Intermediate Treatment, report published 1977); Chm., Assoc. of Social Res Orgns, 1977–81; Vice-Chairman: UK Assoc. for Internat. Year of the Child, 1978–80; Children's Cttee (apptd by Sec. of State for Health and Social Security), 1978–81; Consultant to Unicef (Europe), 1982–; Pres., Pre-school Playgroups Assoc., 1982–. Hon. DSc: Bradford, 1972; Aston, 1979; Hull, 1982, Hon. Fellow, Manchester Polytechnic; Hon. FCP. Hon. Mem., British Paediatric Assoc. FBPsS; FRSocMed; FRSA. *Publications:* The Emotional and Social Adjustment of Physically Handicapped Children, 1964; Deprivation and Education, 1965; Investment in Children (ed), 1965; Social Learning and its Measurement, 1966; Adoption—Facts and Fallacies, 1966; Caring for Children (ed), 1968; Able Misfits, 1970; The Needs of Children, 1974, 2nd edn 1980; co-author: 11,000 Seven-Year-Olds, 1966; Four Years On, 1967; Residential Child Care—Facts and Fallacies, 1967; Foster Care—Facts and Fallacies, 1967; The Community's Children, 1967; Directory of National, Voluntary Children's Organisations, 1968; The Challenge of Thalidomide, 1970; Living with Handicap, 1970; Born Illegitimate, 1971; Growing Up Adopted, 1972; Advances in Educational Psychology, vol. 2, 1973; Early Child Care and Education, 1975; Controversial Issues in Child Development, 1978; Preparation for Parenthood, 1980; Psychological Approaches to Child Abuse, 1980; A Fairer Future, 1980; papers in journals of psychology, education and child care. *Recreations:* swimming, music, theatre-going, cooking. *Address:* 68 Wimpole Street, W1. *T:* 01-935 3144. *Club:* Royal Over-Seas League.
*Died 21 Feb. 1983.*

**PRINZ, Gerhard,** Dr jur; Chairman of the Executive Board, since 1980, and Director, since 1974, Daimler-Benz AG; *b* Solingen, 5 April 1929; *s* of Albert Prinz; *m* Renate Ebner. Joined Volkswagen, 1967; Mem., Bd of Management, Volkswagenwerk AG, 1969–73; Chm., Bd of Management, Audi-NSU, 1972–73; Director: Carl Prinz AG, Solingen; Agrippina-Vers. AG, Köln; Bertelsmann AG; Beirat Deutsche Bank AG, Braunschweig. *Address:* Daimler-Benz AG, Mercedesstrasse 136, 7000 Stuttgart 60, Federal Republic of Germany.
*Died 30 Oct. 1983.*

**PRIOR-PALMER, Brig. Sir Otho (Leslie),** Kt 1959; DSO 1945; *b* 28 Oct. 1897; *s* of late Spunner Prior-Palmer, County Sligo, Ireland, and Merrion Square, Dublin, and Anne Leslie Gason. Kilteelagh, Co. Tipperary; *m* 1940, Sheila Mary Weller Poley (OBE 1958), Boxted Hall, Bury St Edmunds; one *s* two *d* (and one *d* by previous marr.); *m* 1964, Elizabeth, *d* of late Harold Henderson; two *s*. *Educ:* Wellington; RMC, Sandhurst. Commissioned 9th Lancers, 1916; commanded 2nd Northamptonshire Yeo., 1940–42; comd 30th Armoured Brigade, Mar.–Aug. 1942; 29th Armoured Brigade, 1942–43; 7th Armoured Brigade, 1943–45 (DSO); commanded latter during Italian Campaign; retd pay 1946, hon. rank of Brig. MP (C) Worthing Div. W Sussex, 1945–50, Worthing, 1950–64. Vice-Chm. Conservative Members' Defence Cttee, 1958–59; Past Chm. NATO Parliamentarians Defence Cttee. *Recreations:* ski-ing, sailing, all field sports, fishing. *Address:* Grange, Honiton, Devon. *T:* Broadhembury 377. *Clubs:* Royal Yacht Squadron (Cowes); Pratt's.
*Died 29 Jan. 1986.*

**PRITCHARD, Sir Asa Hubert,** Kt 1965; Merchant, retired; President, Asa H. Pritchard Ltd, Nassau; *b* 1 Aug. 1891; *s* of William Edward Pritchard, Bahamas; *m* 1915, Maud Pauline Pyfrom (*d* 1978); two *s* two *d*. *Educ:* Queen's College, Bahamas. MHA, Bahamas, 1925–62; Deputy Speaker, 1942–46; Speaker, 1946–62. Member: Board of Education, 1930–35; Electricity Board, 1940–46; Chm., Bahamas Develt Bd, 1946. *Address:* Breezy Ridge, PO Box 6218 ES, Nassau, Bahamas.
*Died 18 March 1990.*

**PRITCHARD, Sir Fred Eills,** Kt 1947; MBE 1942; Director, Inns of Court School of Law, 1958–68; *b* 23 June 1899; *s* of late Fred Pritchard, Liverpool; *m* 1931, Mabel Celia, *d* of late F. W. Gaskin, Liverpool; one *d*. *Educ:* Shrewsbury Sch.; Liverpool Univ. (LLM); Middle Temple; called to Bar, Middle Temple, 1923; practised on Northern Circuit in Liverpool, 1923–37; KC 1937; commission in

RMA, 1917–19; commission in Royal Artillery, 1939; Major, and Deputy Judge Advocate, 1939–42; Lt-Col and Assistant Judge Advocate-General, 1942–45; Judge of the Salford Hundred Court of Record, 1944–47; Judge of Queen's Bench Division of High Court of Justice, 1947–53, resigned; Master of the Bench of the Middle Temple since 1946, Treasurer, 1964; Hon. Bencher, Gray's Inn, 1965–; Churchwarden St John's, St John's Wood, 1945–73; Mem. of House of Laity in National Assembly of Church of England, 1955–60; Mem. Bd, Church Army, 1956–76; Chairman Appellate Tribunal for Conscientious Objectors under Nat. Service Act 1948, 1956–71; Chm. Cttee on the Rating of Charities, 1958–59; Chm. Special Grants Cttee, 1960–72; Chm. (apptd by LCJ), Governing Body Shrewsbury School, 1960–68. A Church Commissioner, 1959–68; a Comr apptd by Min. of Aviation, Civil Aviation (Licensing) Regulations, 1960. Pres., Bar Musical Soc., 1977–. Hon. LLD Liverpool, 1956. *Publication:* The Common Calendar: a notebook on Criminal Law for Circuiteers; Rigby: a memoir of Mr Justice Swift. *Address:* Tye Cottage, Mill Road, Slindon, West Sussex. *T:* Slindon 404. *Clubs:* Middlesex County Cricket, Arundel Cricket.
*Died 10 Aug. 1982.*

**PRITCHARD, Frederick Hugh Dalzel,** CBE 1961; Secretary-General, British Red Cross Society, 1951–70; *b* 26 Aug. 1905; *e s* of Gerald William and Alice Bayes Pritchard (*née* Dalzel), Richmond, Surrey; *m* 1935, Rosamond Wright Marshall; two *d*. *Educ:* Charterhouse School; Oriel College, Oxford. Admitted Solicitor, 1931. Partner in Pritchard Sons Partington & Holland, solicitors, London, 1933. Legal Adviser, War Organisation of British Red Cross Soc. and Order of St John, 1940. Exec. Asst to Vice-Chm., British Red Cross Soc., 1948. OStJ 1942. *Address:* Denver, Bulstrode Way, Gerrards Cross, Bucks. *T:* Gerrards Cross 883483.
*Died 12 Aug. 1983.*

**PRITCHARD, Sir John (Michael),** Kt 1983; CBE 1962; Music Director, San Francisco Opera, since 1986; Chief Guest Conductor, Cologne Opera, since 1989 (Chief Conductor, 1978–89); *b* 5 Feb. 1921; *s* of Albert Edward Pritchard and Amy Edith Shaylor. *Educ:* Sir George Monoux School, London; privately. Conductor: Derby String Orchestra, 1943–51; Music Staff, Glyndebourne Opera, 1947, Chorus master, 1949; Conductor, Jacques Orchestra, 1950–52; Asst to Fritz Busch, Vittorio Gui, 1950–51; Conductor Glyndebourne Festivals, 1952–77; Conductor and Musical Director, Royal Liverpool Philharmonic Orchestra, 1957–63; Musical Director, London Philharmonic Orchestra, 1962–66; Principal Conductor, 1967–77, and Musical Director, 1969–77, Glyndebourne Opera; Music Dir, Belgian Nat. Opera, 1981–87; Chief Conductor, BBC Symphony Orchestra, 1982–89; Guest Conductor: Vienna State Opera, 1952–53, 1964–65; Covent Garden Opera, 1952–77; Edinburgh Internat. Festivals, opera and symphony concerts 1951–55, 1960–63, 1979–81; Aix-en-Provence Festival, 1963, 1981; Frankfurt Radio Orchestra, 1953; Cologne Radio Orchestra, 1953; Vienna Symphony Orchestra, 1953–55; Berlin Festival, 1954, 1964; Zürich Radio Orchestra, 1955, 1961; Santa Cecilia Orchestra, Rome, 1958, 1972, 1979; Orchestre Nationale, Brussels, 1958, 1965–67; Cracow Philharmonic Orch., 1961; Basel, Winterthur Orch., 1961, 1969; RIAS Orchestra, Berlin, 1961, 1966; Royal Philharmonic Soc., London, 1959, 1961, 1963, 1964, 1965, 1966, 1970, 1974, 1979–83, 1985; Wexford Festival, 1959, 1961; Oslo Philharmonic Orch., 1960, 1961, 1966, 1975; Pittsburgh Symphony Orch., 1963, 1964, and San Francisco Symphony, 1964; BBC Promenade Concerts, 1960–77, 1979–85; tour of Switzerland, 1962, 1966, 1985; of Australia, 1962; of Germany, 1963, 1966; with BBC Symph. Orch., 1968, 1982; tour of Jugoslavia, 1968; Georges Enesco Festival, Bucharest, 1964; Lausanne Festival, 1964; Berlin Philharmonic, 1964; New York Opera Assoc., 1964; Société Philharmonic, Brussels, 1965, 1967; Helsinki Philharmonic, 1966; Salzburg Festival, 1966, 1989; Teatro Colon, Buenos Aires, 1966; RAI Symphony Orch., Turin, 1967; Sjaellands Symphony Orch., Copenhagen, 1967–70; SABC Orchestra, Johannesburg, 1967–70; Scandinavian Tour, Glyndebourne Opera, 1967; Teatro San Carlo, Naples, 1969–70; Danish Radio Symph., 1968; Palermo Sinfonia, 1968; Munich State Opera, 1968–69, 1983; Athens Festival, 1968–70; Leipzig Gewandhaus, 1968–70; Dresden Staatskapelle, 1968–70, 1972; Berlin Radio, 1968–70, 1972; Chicago Lyric Opera, 1969, 1975, 1977, 1978, 1984; Florence Maggio Musicale, 1977, 1978, 1979, 1989; Zürich Tonhalle, 1977–78, 1979; London Philharmonic Tours: Far East, 1969; USA, 1971; Hong Kong and China, 1973; New Philharmonia Orch., Osaka, Tokyo, 1970; San Francisco Opera, 1970, 1973–74, 1976, 1977, 1979, 1985–; Geneva Opera, 1971, 1974; Metropolitan Opera, NY, 1971, 1973–74, 1977–79, 1983–84; Yomiuri Nippon Orch., Tokyo, 1972; English Chamber Orch. Tour, Latin America, 1972; Australian Opera, Sydney, 1974, 1977; Cologne Opera, 1975–; Philadelphia Orch., 1975, 1976, 1978; Opera Orch., Monte Carlo, 1976–78, 1984; Houston Grand Opera, 1976, 1978, 1979; Vancouver Symphony, 1978; Paris Opéra, 1979, 1981, 1988–. Shakespeare Prize, Hamburg, 1975. *Recreations:* good food and wine, theatre. *Address:* c/o Johannes Adams, Kreishausgalerie, Magnusstrasse 3, D-5000

Cologne 1, Federal Republic of Germany. *T:* 49–221–242778.
*Died 5 Dec.* 1989.

**PRITTIE, Hon. Terence Cornelius Farmer,** MBE 1945; Editor, Britain and Israel, since 1970; *b* 15 Dec. 1913; *yr s* of 5th Baron Dunalley, DSO; *m* 1946, Laura Dundas; two *s. Educ:* Cheam Sch.; Stowe; Christ Church, Oxford (MA). Butler Exhibn for Modern History, 1934. Served Rifle Bde, 1938–45 (despatches, Calais, 1940); POW, Germany, escaped 6 times (MBE). Staff, Manchester Guardian, 1945–70: Cricket Corresp., 1946; Chief Corresp. in Germany, 1946–63; Diplomatic Corresp., 1963–70. Federal Cross of Merit of West Germany, 1971. *Publications:* South to Freedom, 1946; Mainly Middlesex, 1947; (with John Kay) Second Innings, 1947; Lancashire Hot-Pot, 1948; A History of Middlesex Cricket, 1951; Germany Divided, 1960; Germany (Life Magazine World Series), 1963; Germans Against Hitler, 1964; Israel: Miracle in the Desert, 1967; Eshkol, the Man and the Nation, 1969; Adenauer: A Study in Fortitude, 1972; (with Otto Loeb) Wines of the Moselle, 1972; Willy Brandt, 1974; Through Irish Eyes, 1977; The Economic War against the Jews, 1977; The Velvet Chancellors: the history of post-war Germany, 1979; Whose Jerusalem?, 1981; My Germans: 1933–1983, 1983. *Recreations:* cricket, real tennis, lawn tennis. *Address:* 9 Blithfield Street, W8 6RH. *Clubs:* Travellers', MCC, Greenjackets.                                            *Died 28 May* 1985.

**PROCTOR, Sir Dennis;** *see* Proctor, Sir P. D.

**PROCTOR, Sir (George) Philip,** KBE 1971 (CBE 1961); retired; *b* 8 June 1902; *s* of late C. A. Proctor; *m* 1st, 1926, Mary Turney (*d* 1939), *d* of late K. W. Monsarrat; one *s* two *d*; 2nd, 1939, Hilary Frances, *d* of late F. S. Clark; one *s* two *d. Educ:* Cheltenham Coll., Liverpool Univ. (BEng). Joined Dunlop Gp, 1927; Manager, Dunlop (NZ) Ltd, 1936–41 (Chm. and Man. Dir, 1945–65). Chm., NZ Industrial Design Council, 1968–79; Mem., Prison Parole Bd, 1964–78; Chm., NZ Heart Foundn, 1968–78; Nat. Co-ordinator and Chm., Duke of Edinburgh Award in NZ, 1963–69. Hon. FRACP. KStJ 1976. *Recreation:* fly-fishing. *Address:* Flat 5, Landscape Apartments, 123 Austin Street, Wellington 1, New Zealand. *Club:* Wellington (New Zealand).
*Died 22 June* 1986.

**PROCTOR, Sir (Philip) Dennis,** KCB 1959 (CB 1946); *b* 1 Sept. 1905; *s* of late Sir Philip Proctor, KBE; *m* 1st, 1936, Dorothy Varda (*d* 1951); no *c*; 2nd, 1953, Barbara, *d* of Sir Ronald Adam, 2nd Bt, GCB, DSO, OBE; two *s* one *d. Educ:* Falconbury; Harrow; King's Coll., Cambridge. MA, 1929; entered Min. of Health, 1929; transferred to Treasury, 1930; Third Secretary, HM Treasury, 1948–50; resigned from Civil Service; joined the firm of A. P. Moller, Copenhagen, 1950; Man. Dir, The Maersk Company Ltd, 1951–53; re-entered Civil Service, 1953; Dep. Sec., Min. of Transport and Civil Aviation, 1953–58; Permanent Sec., Min. of Power, 1958–65. Dir, William Hudson Ltd, 1966–71. Trustee of Tate Gallery, 1952; Chairman of the Tate Gallery, 1953–59. Hon. Fellow, King's Coll., Cambridge, 1968. *Publications:* Hannibal's March in History, 1971; Autobiography of G. Lowes Dickinson, 1973; The Experience of Thucydides, 1980. *Address:* 102 High Street, Lewes, Sussex.                                   *Died 30 Aug.* 1983.

**PROKOSCH, Frederic;** writer; *b* 17 May 1906; *s* of Eduard (Professor of Linguistics, Yale University) and Mathilde Prokosch. *Educ:* Yale University (PhD, 1933); King's College, Cambridge. Educated as a child in Wisconsin, Texas, Munich, Austria; travelled extensively all his life; research work in Chaucerian MSS, 1933–38 (PhD Dissertation: The Chaucerian Apocrypha). *Publications:* The Asiatics (novel), 1935; The Assassins (poems), 1936; The Seven Who Fled (novel), 1937; The Carnival (poems), 1938; Night of The Poor (novel), 1939; Death at Sea (poems), 1940; The Skies of Europe (novel), 1942; The Conspirators (novel), 1943; Some Poems of Hölderlin, 1943; Chosen Poems, 1944; Age of Thunder (novel), 1945; The Idols of the Cave (novel), 1946; The Medea of Euripides, 1947; The Sonnets of Louise Labé, 1947; Storm and Echo (novel), 1948; Nine Days to Mukalla (novel), 1953; A Tale for Midnight (novel), 1955; A Ballad of Love (novel), 1960; The Seven Sisters (novel), 1962; The Dark Dancer (novel), 1964; The Wreck of the Cassandra (novel), 1966; The Missolonghi Manuscript (novel), 1968; America, My Wilderness (novel), 1972; Voices (a memoir), 1983. *Recreations:* squash racquets (Champion of France, 1938, 1939, Champion of Sweden, 1944), lawn tennis (Champion of Mallorca). *Address:* Ma Trouvaille, 06 Plan de Grasse, France. *Clubs:* Pitt (Cambridge); Yale (New York); France-Amérique (Paris).                                                        *Died June* 1989.

**PROSSER, (Albert) Russell (Garness),** CMG 1967; MBE 1953; Senior Adviser (formerly Adviser), Social Development, Overseas Development Administration, 1967–80; *b* 8 April 1915; *s* of late Thomas Prosser; *m* 1957, Ruth Avalon Moore; one *s* (and one *s* decd). *Educ:* Godlys Sch.; London Sch. of Economics. Principal, Sch. of Social Welfare, Accra, 1947; Dep. Sec., Uganda, 1959; Permanent Secretary, Uganda, 1962; Adviser, Social Development, Kenya, 1963. Alternate UK delegate, UN Social Develt Commn,

1965–72, UK delegate, 1973–80. Associate Mem., Inst. of Develt Studies, Univ. of Sussex; External Examr Rural Develt, Univ. of Reading. Editor, Clare Market Review, 1939–40. FRSA 1974. La Belgique Reconnaissante, Belgian Govt, 1962. *Recreations:* angling, gardening. *Address:* 18b Wray Park Road, Reigate, Surrey. *T:* Reigate 42792.                                                *Died 12 Sept.* 1988.

**PROSSER, Thomas Vivian,** CBE 1963; chartered builder, retired; *b* 25 April 1908; *er s* of T. V. Prosser, Liverpool; *m* 1935, Florence Minnie (Billie), 2nd *d* of W. J. Boulton, Highworth, Wilts; one *s* one *d. Educ:* Old Swan Technical Institute (now West Derby High School); College of Technology, Liverpool. Pupil of A. E. Cuddy, LRIBA, Architect, 1924. Joined Wm Thornton & Sons Ltd, Contractors of Liverpool, 1925, Man. Dir, 1945–64; Founder, Chm. and Man. Dir, Nat. Building Agency, 1964–67; Chm., T. V. Prosser & Son (Estates) Ltd, 1968–76. Formerly: President, Liverpool Regional Fedn of Building Trades Employers, 1956; Pres., Nat. Fedn of Building Trades Employers, 1959–60. *Recreations:* gardening, reading. *Address:* Priory Cottage, 1 Mill Street, Steventon, near Abingdon, Oxon OX13 6SP. *T:* Abingdon 831219. *Club:* Lyceum.                                                *Died 1 Dec.* 1987.

**PROUDFOOT, William,** FFA; Director, since 1977, and Chief General Manager and Actuary, 1969–90, Scottish Amicable Life Assurance Society; *b* 4 April 1932; *s* of William Proudfoot and Mary Proudfoot (*née* Stewart); *m* 1st, 1955, Joan Elizabeth Rowland (marr. diss. 1989); two *d*; 2nd, 1989, Moira Whyte (*née* McCallum). *Educ:* Rutherglen Acad.; Rutherglen, Lanarkshire. FFA 1955. Joined Scottish Amicable, 1948; National Service, 1954–56, 2nd Lieut RASC; Asst Actuary, 1957; Actuary and Sec. for Australia, 1959; Man. and Actuary for Aust., 1961; Asst Gen. Man., 1968; Gen. Man. and Actuary, 1969 (title altered to Chief Gen. Man., 1982). Chm., Associated Scottish Life Offices, 1978–80; Member: DTI Panel of Insce Advrs, 1981–; Marketing of Investments Bd Organising Cttee, 1985–86; Dir, Securities and Investments Bd, 1986–89. Dir, Scottish Opera, 1982– (Dep. Chm., 1986). *Recreations:* golf, music. *Address:* 46B Whitehouse Road, Edinburgh EH4 6PH. *T:* 031–312 8187. *Club:* Pollok Golf (Glasgow).
*Died 19 Dec.* 1990.

**PRYOR, Norman Selwyn;** *b* 1896; *s* of Selwyn Robert Pryor, Plaw Hatch, Bishop's Stortford, Hertfordshire; *m* 1927, Nancy Mary, *d* of Kingsmill Henry Power, Sandpit Hall, Chobham, Surrey; two *d* (and one *d* decd). *Educ:* Eton; Trinity Coll., Cambridge. Served European War, 1914–19; Lieut, RFA (TF), 1916; Captain, 1918. DL 1956–68, JP, 1932–68, Essex; High Sheriff of Essex for 1957. *Address:* Manuden House, Manuden, Bishop's Stortford, Herts. *T:* Bishop's Stortford 813282. *Club:* Oriental.
*Died 29 July* 1982.

**PRYS JONES, David;** *see* Jones.

**PUCKEY, Sir Walter (Charles),** Kt 1954; FEng; *b* Fowey, 28 Dec. 1899; *s* of Thomas Edward Puckey; *m* 1926, Alice Rebecca, *d* of Frederick Richards; no *c. Educ:* Bristol. Apprenticed Cosmos Engineering Co., Bristol, 1920; Dir and Gen. Works Manager, Hoover; Dep. Controller of Supplies (Aircraft Prodn), Min. of Supply, 1951–53; Pres., IProdE, 1953–55 (Hon. FIProdE); Co-founder, Management Selection Ltd (later MSL), 1957. *Publications:* What is this Management?, 1944; So You're Going to a Meeting?, 1954; Management Principles, 1962; Organization in Business Management, 1963; The Board Room—a guide to the role and function of directors, 1969. *Address:* Silverdale, Beech Drive, Kingswood, Surrey.                                    *Died 6 Oct.* 1983.

**PUGH, Rt. Rev. Edward;** *see* Pugh, Rt Rev. W. E. A.

**PUGH, Prof. Leslie Penrhys,** CBE 1962; MA (Cantab); BSc (London); FRCVS; Emeritus Professor, Cambridge University; Professor of Veterinary Clinical Studies, Cambridge, 1951–63; Life Fellow of Magdalene Coll., Cambridge; Member, Agricultural Research Council, 1952–57; President, Royal College of Veterinary Surgeons, 1956; *b* 19 Dec. 1895; *s* of David Pugh and Emily Epton Hornby; *m* 1st, 1918, Paula Storie (*d* 1930); one *s* two *d*; 2nd, 1933, Betty Chandley; one *s* one *d. Educ:* Tonbridge; Royal Veterinary Coll.; London Univ. MRCVS 1917, BSc (London) 1917; FRCVS, 1923 (Hon. FRCVS, 1979). General Practitioner in West Kent, 1919–50; Deputy Assistant Director of Veterinary Services (44th Home Counties Division TA), 1927; Major, 1927; Divisional Commandant Kent Special Constabulary (Sevenoaks Division), 1949. *Publication:* From Farriery to Veterinary Medicine, 1962. *Recreation:* gardening. *Address:* 69 South Cliff, Bexhill-on-Sea, East Sussex. *T:* Bexhill 212047.                                                *Died 18 July* 1983.

**PUGH, Maj.-Gen. Lewis (Owain),** CB 1957; CBE 1952; DSO 1945 (2 Bars, 1945, 1946); Indian Police Medal, 1940; JP; Colonel, 2 King Edward VII's Own Goorkhas (The Sirmoor Rifles), 1956–69; Representative Colonel Brigade of Gurkhas, 1958–69; Hon. Colonel: 4th Battalion, 1961–71, 3rd (Volunteer) Battalion, 1971–72, The Royal Welch Fusiliers; Vice-Lieutenant, Cardiganshire, 1961–72; *b* 18 May 1907; *s* of late Major H. O. Pugh, DSO, DL; *m*

1941, Wanda, *d* of F. F. Kendzior, Kington Langley, Wilts; two *d*. *Educ*: Wellington Coll.; RMA, Woolwich. Commissioned RA, 1927; RHA 1934; Royal Indian Artillery, 1940; seconded Indian Police, 1936; Staff Coll., Quetta, 1940; North West Frontier, India, 1933. Served War of 1939–45: North West Frontier, India, 1940; Burma, 1942–45 (Special Service Forces, 1942–43) (despatches); Netherlands East Indies, 1946; Malaya, 1950–52 (despatches), and 1956–57. Commander: 33 Indian Inf. Bde, 1945; 49 Indian Inf. Bde, 1946; 26th Gurkha Inf. Bde, 1949–52; Dep. Director, Military Operations, WO, 1953; IDC, 1955; Chief of Staff, GHQ, Far East, 1956–57; GOC 53 Welsh Inf. Div. (TA), and Mid West District, 1958–61; retired, 1961. Col, 1951; Brig., 1955; Maj.-Gen., 1957. MFH, RA Salisbury Plain, 1947–48. Pres., Burma Star Assoc., Mid-Wales, 1974. Vice-Pres., Council for Protection of Rural Wales; President, ACF Recreational Cttee, Wales Area, 1958; Mem., Cymmrodorion Soc., 1957; Fellow, Ancient Monuments Soc., 1958; formerly member: Council, Nat. Library of Wales; Council, Nat. Museum of Wales; Governing Body of the Church in Wales; Welsh Programme Advisory Cttee, ITA. Chairman: Merioneth and Montgomery Bi-County Cttee, 1961–72; N Wales Sub-Assoc., T&AVR; Vice-Chm., T&AVR Assoc., Wales and Monmouth, 1969–72. Vice-Pres., Royal British Legion, Cardiganshire, 1959–77. Chm., Cons. and Unionist Assoc., Cardigan, 1975–77. KStJ; Seneschal of Priory of Hosp. of St John in Wales. Dato, The Most Blessed Order of Stia Negara (1st class), Brunei. JP 1961, DL 1961, High Sheriff 1964, Cardiganshire. *Recreations*: all country pursuits. *Address*: Wonastow House, Wonastow, Monmouth, Gwent NP5 4DN. *T*: Dingestow 215. *Club*: Naval and Military.
*Died 10 March 1981.*

**PUGH, Prof. Ralph Bernard,** MA Oxon; DLit London; FSA; Professor of English History in the University of London, 1968–77, later Emeritus; Emeritus Fellow of St Edmund Hall, Oxford, since 1977 (Supernumerary Fellow, 1959–77; Lecturer in Administrative History, 1952–59); *b* 1 Aug. 1910; *o c* of Bernard Carr and Mabel Elizabeth Pugh, Sutton, Surrey; unmarried. *Educ*: St Paul's Sch.; Queen's Coll., Oxford. 1st Class Hons, Modern History, 1932 (BA). Asst Keeper of Public Records, 2nd Cl. 1934, 1st Cl. 1946; Dominions Office, 1940–46, Acting Principal, 1941–46. Member, Institute for Advanced Study, Princeton, NJ, 1963–64, 1969–70; Raleigh Lectr, British Acad., 1973; Fellow, Folger Shakespeare Lib., Washington, DC, 1973; British Acad. Fellow, Newberry Lib., Chicago, 1978. Wiltshire Archaeological and Nat. History Society: President, 1950–51, 1953–55; Vice-President, 1955–; Wiltshire Record Society (until 1967 Records Br. of Wilts Archaeological and Nat. History Society): Hon. Secretary and Editor, 1937–53; Chairman, 1953–67; President, 1967–; Vice-President: Seldon Society, 1966–69; Nat. Trust Council, 1967–75. Editor, Victoria History of Counties of England, 1949–77. *Publications*: (ed) Abstracts of Feet of Fines for Wiltshire, Edw. I and II, 1929; (ed) Calendar of Antrobus Deeds, 1947; How to Write a Parish History, 1954; The Crown Estate, 1960; Records of the Colonial and Dominions Offices (PRO Handbooks), 1964; Itinerant Justices in English History, 1967; Imprisonment in Medieval England, 1968; (ed) Court Rolls of the Wiltshire Manors of Adam de Stratton, 1970; (ed) Calendar of London Trailbaston Trials, 1976 for 1975; (ed) Wiltshire Gaol Delivery and Trailbaston Trials, 1978; articles in Victoria County History, Cambridge History of the British Empire and in learned periodicals. *Recreation*: sight-seeing. *Address*: 67 Southwood Park, N6 5SQ. *T*: 01-340 5661. *Club*: Reform.
*Died 3 Dec. 1982.*

**PUGH, Rt. Rev. William Edward Augustus,** MA, LRAM (Singing); Hon. Assistant Bishop, diocese of Carlisle; *b* 22 July 1909; *s* of William Arthur Augustus and Margaret Caroline Pugh; *m* 1937, Freda Mary (*d* 1985), *er d* of Charles Frederick and Susannah Merishaw; no *c*. *Educ*: Leeds Univ.; College of the Resurrection, Mirfield. Assistant Curate: Staveley, Derbys, 1934–37; Edwinstowe, Notts, 1937–38; Rector of Bestwood Park, Notts, 1938–44; Vicar of Sutton-in-Ashfield, Notts, 1944–55; Hon. Canon of Southwell, 1954; Vicar of East Retford, Notts, 1955–59; Rector of Harrington, 1959–62; Vicar of Cockermouth, 1962–70, and Archdeacon of West Cumberland, 1959–70; Bishop Suffragan of Penrith, 1970–79. *Recreations*: fishing, music. *Address*: 25 Brigham Road, Cockermouth, Cumbria CA13 0AX.    *Died 4 Jan. 1986.*

**PUGSLEY, Rear-Admiral Anthony Follett,** CB 1944; DSO 1943; retired; *b* 7 Dec. 1901; *e s* of late J. Follett Pugsley, Whitefield, Wiveliscombe, Somerset; *m* 1931, Barbara (*d* 1989), *d* of late J. Byam Shaw; one *s*. *Educ*: RN Colleges, Osborne and Dartmouth. Midshipman, 1918; Commander, 1936; Captain, 1942; Rear-Admiral, 1952; retired, 1954. Served European War from May 1918; on Upper Yangtse, 1925–27, and in command HM Ships P.40, Antelope and Westcott, 1933–36; during War of 1939–45, in command HM Ships Javelin, Fearless, Paladin; Captain (D) 14th Flotilla, Jervis (despatches thrice, DSO and bar, Greek War Cross); Assault Gp Comdr, Normandy landing, 1944 (2nd bar to DSO); Naval Force Commander in assault on Walcheren, 1944 (CB); Captain (D) 19th Flotilla (Far East), 1945–46; Directing Staff,

Senior Officers War Course, 1947–48; Naval Officer in charge, Londonderry and Director (RN) Joint Anti-Submarine School, 1948–50; in command HMS Warrior, 1951; Flag Officer, Malayan Area, Dec. 1951–Nov. 1953. *Publication*: Destroyer Man, 1957. *Address*: Javelin, Milverton, Taunton, Somerset TA4 1QU. *T*: Milverton (0823) 400355.    *Died 17 July 1990.*

**PULAY, George;** Chairman: Charles Barker CBC Ltd (formerly Charles Barker City Ltd), since 1977 (Founder Director, 1968); Charles Barker Lyons Ltd, since 1977; Director, Charles Barker Group Ltd (formerly Charles Barker ABH International Ltd), since 1972; *b* 5 March 1923; *s* of late Dr Erwin Pulay and Ida Barbara Pulay; *m* 1st, 1953, Lilette Anna (*d* 1962), *o d* of late George and Anna Callil, Melbourne; 2nd, 1965, Katharine Frances Goddard, *o d* of Rt Hon. Sir Eric Sachs, MBE, TD, and of Hon. Margaret, 2nd *d* of Baron Goddard of Aldbourne, GCB; two *d*. *Educ*: Continent; Manchester Grammar Sch.; London Univ. Served War, Army, Intelligence Corps, 1943–47. Editorial Staff, Daily Telegraph, 1950–55, Asst City Editor, 1956–59; Deputy City Editor: News Chronicle, 1959–60; The Times, 1962–66; City Editor, The Times, 1966–68. *Publications*: The World's Money (with William M. Clarke), 1970; The Bridge Builders (with James Derriman), 1980; contrib. Director's Handbook, 1969, 2nd edn 1977; frequent contrib. to Economist, Statist, BBC and overseas jls, 1950–70. *Recreations*: skiing, tennis, music. *Address*: 83 Dovehouse Street, SW3 6JZ. *T*: 01-351 1342. *Clubs*: City of London, Hurlingham.
*Died 27 Sept. 1981.*

**PULLAR, Hubert Norman,** CBE 1964; MA; HM Diplomatic Service, retired; *b* 26 Dec. 1914; *y s* of late William Laurence and Christine Ellen Pullar, formerly of Uplands, Bridge-of-Allan, Stirlingshire; *m* 1943, Helen Alice La Fontaine; one *s* one *d*. *Educ*: Trin. Coll., Glenalmond; Trin. Coll., Oxford. Entered HM Consular Service, 1938. Served in Turkey, 1938–42; USA, 1943–46; Persia, 1946–48; Morocco, 1949–52; Foreign Office, 1952–54; Finland, 1954–56; Syria, 1956; Iraq, 1957–59; Consul-Gen., Antwerp, 1960–64; HM Consul-General, Jerusalem, 1964–67; Foreign Office, 1967–68; Consul-General, Durban, 1968–71. Order of Ouissam Alouite, Morocco, 1952. CStJ 1966. Coronation Medal, 1953. *Recreations*: golf, motoring, travel. *Address*: Camelot, Ringles Cross, Uckfield, East Sussex. *T*: Uckfield 2159.    *Died 14 June 1988.*

**PULLICINO, Dr Anthony Alfred;** *b* 14 March 1917; *s* of late Sir Philip Pullicino; *m* 1944, Edith Baker; three *s* two *d*. *Educ*: St Aloysius Coll., Malta; Royal Univ. of Malta; Melbourne University. BA 1939, LLD 1943, Malta; LLB Melbourne 1963. Served in Royal Malta Artillery, 1944–45 (Lieut). MLA Malta, 1951–55 (Speaker, 1951–52). Mem. Council, CPA, attending sessions in London 1952, Nairobi 1953. Practised as Solicitor, Melbourne, 1963–65; High Comr for Malta in Canberra, 1965–69; High Comr in London and Ambassador of Malta to USSR, 1970–71. *Recreation*: golf. *Address*: 191/4 Tower Road, Sliema, Malta. *Club*: Casino Maltese (Malta).
*Died 9 March 1986.*

**PULLING, Martin John Langley,** CBE 1958 (OBE 1954); *b* 30 May 1906; *o s* of late Rev. Augustine J. Pulling and Dorothea Fremlin Key; *m* 1939, Yvonne Limborgh, Antwerp, Belgium; no *c*. *Educ*: Marlborough College; King's College, Cambridge (Scholar). Mech. Scis Tripos, BA 1928; MA 1943. Various posts in radio industry, 1929–34; joined BBC Engrg Div., 1934; retired as Dep. Dir of Engrg, 1967. Was Chm. of Technical Cttee (of European Broadcasting Union) responsible for development of "Eurovision" from its inception in 1952 until 1962. Chairman: The Ferrograph Co., 1968–72; Rendar Instruments Ltd, 1968–72; Dir, Compagnie Générale d'Electricité Internationale (UK) Ltd, 1971–76. FIEE 1967 (MIEE 1945, AMIEE 1935); Chm., Electronics and Communications Section, IEE, 1959–60; Mem. Council, IEE, 1963–66; MITE 1966; Hon. FBKS. *Address*: 6 Cadogan House, 93 Sloane Street, SW1X 9PD. *T*: 01–235 1739. *Clubs*: Hurlingham, MCC, Anglo-Belgian; Phyllis Court (Henley-on-Thames).
*Died 22 April 1988.*

**PULVERTAFT, Prof. Robert James Valentine,** OBE 1944; MD Cantab; FRCP; FRCPath; Emeritus Professor of Clinical Pathology, University of London (Professor, 1950–62); Visiting Professor of Pathology, Makerere University College; Visiting Professor of Pathology, University of Ibadan, W Nigeria; President Association of Clinical Pathologists, 1953; Director of Laboratories, Westminster Hospital, until 1962; Lieutenant-Colonel RAMC, 1943, serving Middle East Forces; subsequently Assistant Director of Pathology, Northern Command and MEF; lately Hon. Consultant in Pathology to the Army at Home; *b* 14 Feb. 1897; *s* of Rev. T. J. Pulvertaft and B. C. Denroche; *m* E. L. M. Costello (*d* 1985); one *s* two *d*. *Educ*: Westminster School; Trinity College, Cambridge (Classical Scholar); St Thomas' Hosp. Lt 3rd Royal Sussex 1915–19; served with 4th Royal Sussex (Palestine); seconded to RFC as observer (Palestine) and pilot in 205 Squadron RAF (France); Senior Exhibitioner and Scholar, Nat. Science, Trinity College Cantab. 2nd class Part II Tripos Nat. Science (Physiology);

Entrance University Scholar St Thomas' Hospital; Asst Bacteriologist, VD Dept St Thomas' Hospital; Pathologist to Units, St Thomas' Hosp., 1923–32; Plimmer Research Fellow in Pathology, 1929–32; EMS Sept.-Nov. 1939; National Institute Medical Research, 1939–40. Examiner in Pathology, Univs of Cambridge, Oxford, London, Trinity College, Dublin, National University of Ireland, Liverpool University; also for the Conjoint Board and Royal Army Medical Coll. Hon. FRSM 1972. *Publications:* Studies on Malignant Disease in Nigeria by Tissue Culture; various papers on bacteriology and pathology, particularly in relation to the study of living cells by cinemicrography. *Address:* 31 Izaak Walton Way, Chesterton, Cambridge.                    *Died 30 March* 1990.

**PURCELL, (John) Denis;** Metropolitan Magistrate, Clerkenwell Magistrates' Court, 1963–86; *b* 7 Dec. 1913; *s* of John Poyntz Purcell and Dorothy Branston, Newark; *m* 1951, Pauline Mary, *e d* of Rev. Hiram Craven, Painswick, Glos; two *s*. *Educ:* Marlborough; Wadham College, Oxford. Called to Bar, Gray's Inn, 1938; SE Circuit; Sussex QS. Served War of 1939–45: commnd from HAC, 1939, to Shropshire Yeo., 1940; ADC to GOC-in-C, Western Command, 1941; Staff Capt., Western Command; GSO3, Italy; DAAG, HQ British Troops, Palestine. Actg Dep. Chm., London QS, 1962. *Recreations:* back-yard gardening, racing. *Address:* 1 Cheltenham Terrace, SW3 4RD. *T:* 071–730 2896.
*Died* 1 *Oct.* 1990.

**PURDIE, Cora Gwendolyn Jean C., (Wendy);** *see* Campbell-Purdie.

**PURDY, Prof. Richard Little;** *b* 21 April 1904; *s* of Leander Crawford Purdy and Louisa Canfield Purdy. *Educ:* Yale Univ. (BA 1925, PhD 1930). Associate Professor and Fellow of Berkeley Coll., Yale Univ., 1928–70, retired. *Publications:* The Larpent MS of The Rivals, 1935; Thomas Hardy, a Bibliographical Study, 1954, 1978; (ed with Prof. Michael Millgate) The Collected Letters of Thomas Hardy: Vols I-VII, 1978–88. *Clubs:* Athenæum, Bibliographical Society; Elizabethan (New Haven, Connecticut).
*Died* 7 *Aug.* 1990.

**PURNELL, Anthony Guy,** QC 1984; a Recorder of the Crown Court, since 1982; *b* 7 Sept. 1944; *s* of Peter A. Medcraft; *m* 1973, Christina

Elizabeth, *d* of Comdr T. D. Handley, RN; one *s* two *d*. *Educ:* Stancliffe Hall; Haileybury; Univ. of Sheffield (LLB Hons). Called to the Bar, Inner Temple, 1967; Member, North Eastern Circuit, 1968. *Recreations:* biblical research, music. *Address:* 11 King's Bench Walk, Temple, EC4Y 7EQ. *T:* 01–353 3337. *Club:* Royal Automobile.                    *Died* 17 *Sept.* 1989.

**PURVES, James Grant,** CMG 1971; HM Diplomatic Service, retired; *b* 15 May 1911; *s* of Alexander Murray and Elizabeth Purves; *m* 1947, Mary Tinsley; three *s* one *d*. *Educ:* Universities of St Andrews and Freiburg-im-Breisgau. Rsearch, 1933–35; Market Research, 1935–36; Secretary, Central Council for Health Education, 1936–39; German Section, BBC, 1939–45. 1st Secretary, Foreign Service: in Berne, Waraw, Tel Aviv, Bangkok; Consul in Luanda, Lille, Johannesburg; Counsellor, HM Embassy, Berne, 1965–67; HM Consul-General, Hamburg, 1967–71. *Recreations:* books, grandchildren. *Address:* Lorne Cottage, Lorne Road, Southwold, Suffolk. *T:* Southwold 723054. *Clubs:* Royal Automobile; Anglo-German (Hamburg); Grande Société (Berne).
*Died* 17 *Sept.* 1984.

**PYKE, Sir Louis (Frederick),** Kt 1978; ED 1946; FAIB; FAIM; Chairman and Managing Director, Costain (Aust.) Pty Ltd, 1971–77 (Managing Director, 1965–73); Chairman (Victoria), Haden Engineering Pty Ltd; consultant to Meldrum Burrows & Partners, architects; *b* 21 Nov. 1907; *m* 1936, Sierlah, *d* of H. J. Cohen; two *s* one *d*. *Educ:* Melbourne C of E Grammar Sch. Served War of 1939–45, AASC, Lt-Col. Director: Pyke Simmie, Master Builders, 1947; Union Assce, 1963–74; Costain Investments (Aust.) Pty Ltd, 1977–; Steel Deck Industries Pty Ltd, 1978–; Davis Vindin Pty Ltd, 1978–. Mem., United Services Inst., 1936. Member Council: S Melbourne Tech. Sch., 1963–73; Master Builders Assoc., Vic, 1972–. Mem., Melbourne South Rotary, 1962–; Pres., Multiple Sclerosis Soc. of Vic, 1975–82; Dep. Nat. Chm., Business Adv. Bd, Multiple Sclerosis Soc. of Aust., 1979–. Hon. Life Fellow, Aust. Inst. of Bldg. *Recreation:* farming. *Address:* 419 Wattletree Road, East Malvern, Victoria 3145, Australia. *T:* 25 6961. *Clubs:* Naval and Military, Melbourne Cricket, Victoria Racing (Melbourne).
*Died* 19 *Jan.* 1988.

# Q

**QUARRELL, Prof. Arthur George**, ARCS, DSc, PhD (London); Professor of Metallurgy, Sheffield University, 1950–76, later Emeritus; *b* 30 Oct. 1910; *m* 1934, Rose Amy Atkins; one *s* (and two *s* decd). *Educ:* College Secondary School, Swindon; Imperial College of Science and Technology. FInstP 1938; FIM 1946 (Pres., 1970–72; Hon. FIM, 1979). University of Sheffield, Department of Metallurgy: Assistant Lecturer, 1937–39; Lecturer, 1940–45. British Non-Ferrous Metals Research Association: Senior Metallurgist, Oct. 1945–March 1946; Research Manager March 1946–Sept. 1950; Prof. of Physical Metallurgy, Sheffield Univ., 1950–55; Dean of the Faculty of Metallurgy, 1950–55, 1962–64. Pro-Vice-Chancellor of Sheffield Univ., 1958–62. Warden of Sorby Hall, Sheffield Univ., 1963–71. Hatfield Meml Lectr, 1963; Bessemer Gold Medal, 1970; Hon. Fellow, Sheffield City Polytechnic, 1970; Hon. DMet Sheffield, 1980. *Publications:* Physical Examination of Metals, 1940, 2nd edn 1961; Papers in Proc. Roy. Soc., Proc. Phys Soc., Jl Inst. Metals, Jl Iron and Steel Inst. *Recreations:* gardening and other manual activities. *Address:* 1 The Glade, Endcliffe Vale Road, Sheffield S10 3FQ. *T:* 665857. *Died* 10 *Sept.* 1983.

**QUASTEL, Judah Hirsch**, CC 1970; DSc London; PhD Cantab; ARCS London; FRS 1940; FRSC; Hon. FRSE; Professor of Neurochemistry, University of British Columbia, Canada, 1966–83, then Emeritus; *b* 2 Oct. 1899; *e s* of late Jonas and Flora Quastel, Sheffield, Yorks; *m* 1st, 1931, Henrietta Jungman, MA (*d* 1973); two *s* one *d*; 2nd, 1975, Susan Ricardo. *Educ:* Central Secondary School, Sheffield; Imperial College of Science, London University; Trinity College, Cambridge. Commenced research in biochemistry in Cambridge University, Oct. 1921; awarded Senior Studentship by Royal Commissioners for Exhibition of 1851, 1923; Demonstrator and lecturer in biochemistry, Cambridge Univ. 1923; Fellow of Trinity College, Cambridge, 1924; Meldola Medallist 1927; Beit Memorial Research Fellow, 1928; Director of Research, Cardiff City Mental Hospital, 1929–41; Rockefeller Foundation Fellow, 1936; Director of ARC Unit of Soil Metabolism, 1941–47; Prof. of Biochemistry, McGill Univ., Montreal, 1947–66; Director: McGill-Montreal Gen. Hosp. Research Inst., 1947–65; McGill Unit of Cell Metabolism, 1965–66. Member of Council of Royal Institute of Chemistry, 1944–47; Member: Water Pollution Research Board, 1944–47; Bd of Governors, Hebrew Univ., Jerusalem, 1950; Pres., Montreal Physiological Soc., 1950; Pres. Canadian Biochemical Soc., 1963; Canadian Microbiological Soc. Award, 1965; Flavelle Medal, RSC, 1974; Gairdner Internat. Award for Med. Res., 1974. Member, British, Can. and Amer. scientific societies; Consultant, Montreal General Hosp. Leeuwenhoek Lectr, Royal Society, 1954; Bryan Priestman Lectr, Univ. New Brunswick, 1956; Kearney Foundation Lectr, Univ. Calif, 1958; Seventh Jubilee Lectr, Biochemical Soc. UK, 1974; Royal Society Leverhulme Visiting Professor, in India, 1965–66; Vis. Prof., Nat. Hospital for Nervous Diseases (Neurology Dept), London, 1976–77. Hon. Pres., Internat. Congress of Biochem., 1979. Fellow: NY Academy of Science, 1954; Amer. Assoc. for Advancement of Science, 1964. Hon. Fellow: Japanese Pharmacological Soc., 1963; Canadian Microbiological Soc., 1965; N Pacific Soc. of Neurology and Psychiatry, 1966. Hon. Mem., Biochemical Soc. UK, 1973. Hon. DSc McGill, 1969; Hon. PhD Jerusalem, 1970. *Publications:* since 1923 mainly on subjects of biochemical interest; author and co-editor: Neurochemistry, 1955– (1963); Methods in Medical Research, Vol. 9, 1961; Chemistry of Brain Metabolism, 1962; Metabolic Inhibitors, vol. 1, 1963, vol. 2, 1964, vol. 3, 1972, vol. 4, 1973. *Address:* 4585 Langara Avenue, Vancouver, BC V6R 1C9, Canada. *Died* 15 *Oct.* 1987.

**QUAYLE, Sir Anthony;** *see* Quayle, Sir J. A.

**QUAYLE, Bronte Clucas**, CB 1980; OBE 1969; QC 1978; *b* 24 Oct. 1919; *s* of late Alfred Clucas Quayle and Edith Anne Quayle; *m* 1944, Joan Proctor Strickland; two *s*. *Educ:* St Peter's Coll., Adelaide; Adelaide Univ. (LLB). AIF, 1940–45. Admitted Barrister and Solicitor, Adelaide, 1948; Office of Parliamentary Counsel, Canberra, 1950–82, First Parly Counsel, 1977–81. Consulting Draftsman, Pakistan Constitution, 1962. Sitara-i-Pakistan 1962. *Recreations:* yachting, motor sport, music, reading. *Address:* 68 Stradbroke Street, Deakin, ACT 2600, Australia. *Clubs:* Canberra Yacht, Canberra Sporting Car, Canberra Wine and Food, University House, ANU (Canberra). *Died* Oct. 1986.

**QUAYLE, Sir (John) Anthony**, Kt 1985; CBE 1952; Actor; *b* 7 September 1913; *s* of Arthur Quayle and Esther Quayle (*née* Overton); *m* Hermione Hannen (marr. diss.; she *d* 1983); *m* 1947, Dorothy Hyson; one *s* two *d*. *Educ:* Rugby. Hon. DLitt Hull, 1987. First appeared on stage, 1931; acted in various London productions between then and 1939, including several appearances at Old Vic; also acted in New York. Served War of 1939–45, Royal Artillery. After 1945 became play-producer as well as actor; produced: Crime and Punishment; The Relapse; Harvey; Who is Sylvia. Director,

Shakespeare Memorial Theatre, 1948–56; *productions:* The Winter's Tale, Troilus and Cressida, Macbeth, Julius Caesar, King Lear (with John Gielgud), Richard II, Henry IV, Part I (with John Kidd), Henry V, Othello and Measure for Measure. *Stratford rôles include:* The Bastard, Petruchio, Claudius, Iago, Hector in Troilus and Cressida; Henry VIII, 1949; Antony and Henry VIII, 1950; Falstaff in Henry IV, Parts I and II, 1951; Coriolanus; Mosca in Volpone, 1952; Othello, Bottom in a Midsummer Night's Dream, Pandarus in Troilus and Cressida, 1954; Falstaff in The Merry Wives of Windsor; Aaron in Titus Andronicus, 1955. Took Shakespeare Memorial Theatre Company to Australia, 1949, 1953. *Other appearances include:* Tamburlaine, NY, 1956; A View from the Bridge, Comedy Theatre, 1956; Titus Andronicus, European tour, 1957; (also dir) The Firstborn, NY, 1958; Long Day's Journey into Night, Edinburgh Festival and London, 1958; Look After Lulu!, Royal Court, 1959; Chin-Chin, Wyndham's, 1960; The Right Honourable Gentleman, Her Majesty's, 1964; Incident at Vichy, Phœnix, 1966; Galileo, NY, 1967; Halfway Up The Tree, NY 1967; Sleuth, St Martin's, 1970, NY, 1970–71; The Idiot, National Theatre, 1970; The Headhunters, Washington, 1974; Old World, RSC, 1976–77; Do You Turn Somersaults, USA, 1977; Heartbreak House, Lord Arthur Saville's Crime, Malvern Festival, 1980; Hobson's Choice, A Coat of Varnish, Haymarket, 1982; (also dir) The Clandestine Marriage, Albery, 1984; After the Ball is Over, Old Vic, 1985. Prospect Theatre at Old Vic: (also co-prod.) The Rivals, 1978; King Lear (as Lear), 1978; (also prod.) The Clandestine Marriage, Albery and UK tour, 1984; (also dir) The Tempest, Brighton, 1985; Lear in King Lear, tour, 1987. *Directed:* Lady Windermere's Fan, 1967; Tiger at the Gates, New York, 1968; Harvey, Prince of Wales, 1975; Rip Van Winkle, Washington, 1976; The Old Country, Queen's, 1978; The Rules of the Game, Haymarket, 1982. Founded Compass Theatre, 1983. *Films:* Saraband for Dead Lovers, Hamlet, Oh Rosalinda, Battle of the River Plate, The Wrong Man, Woman in a Dressing Gown, The Man Who Wouldn't Talk, Ice Cold in Alex, Serious Charge, Tarzan's Greatest Adventure, The Challenge, The Guns of Navarone, HMS Defiant, Lawrence of Arabia, The Fall of the Roman Empire, Operation Crossbow, A Study in Terror, Incompreso, MacKenna's Gold, Before Winter Comes, Anne of the Thousand Days, Bequest to the Nation, The Tamarind Seed, Moses the Lawgiver, Great Expectations, 21 Hours in Munich, The Eagle has Landed, The Antagonists, Masada, Dial M for Murder, Last Days of Pompeii. Hon. DLitt St Andrews, 1989. *Publications:* Eight Hours from England, 1945; On Such a Night, 1947. *Club:* Special Forces. *Died* 20 *Oct.* 1989.

**QUEEN, Ellery;** *see* Dannay, Frederic.

**QUÉNET, Hon. Sir Vincent (Ernest)**, Kt 1962; Judge President of Appellate Division, High Court of Rhodesia, 1964–70, retired; *b* 14 Dec. 1906; *y s* of George Alfred Quénet, Worcester, CP, SA; *m* 1938, Gabrielle, *d* of Hon. Norman Price; three *s*. *Educ:* Worcester High Sch.; University of Cape Town. Advocate of Supreme Court of SA and Barrister-at-law, Middle Temple. Practised at Johannesburg Bar, QC; Judge of: High Court of S Rhodesia, 1952–61; Fed. Supreme Court, Federation of Rhodesia and Nyasaland, 1961–64. *Address:* Tiger Valley, Borrowdale, Harare, Zimbabwe. *T:* 8872813. *Clubs:* Rand (Johannesburg); Salisbury (Zimbabwe). *Died* 3 *Feb.* 1983.

**QUICK-SMITH, George William**, CBE 1959; Chief Executive, latterly Vice-Chairman, and Member of National Freight Corporation, 1968–71; *b* 23 Aug. 1905; *s* of George Windsor Smith and Maud Edith (*née* Quick); *m* 1934, Ida Muriel Tinkler; no *c*. *Educ:* Univ. of London (LLB). Barrister-at-law, Inner Temple. FCIS; FCIT (past Vice-Pres.). Various positions in shipping, 1922–35; Sec. of various assocs and Mem. of joint negotiating and other bodies connected with road transport; British employers deleg. to various internat. confs including ILO, 1935–48; First Legal Adviser and Sec. and later Mem. of Board of British Road Services, 1948–59; Adviser on Special Projects, British Transport Commn, 1959–62; Chief Sec. and Chief Exec. of Transport Holding Co., 1962–71. Dir various road haulage and bus cos; Mem., Transport Tribunal, 1973–77; Trustee various transport benevolent funds; Master of Carmen's Co., 1967–68; Freeman of City of London. Churchwarden, All Saints Margaret Street, London, 1960–77. Mem. Governing Body, SPCK, 1967–75 (Vice-Pres., 1976–). Hon. Mem., Road Haulage Assoc., 1971. *Publications:* various books and papers on road transport and road transport law; Commentary on Transport Act 1947. *Recreations:* reading, writing, and the arts. *Address:* 6 Martello Towers, Canford Cliffs, Poole, Dorset BH13 7HX. *T:* Canford Cliffs 708127. *Club:* Royal Motor Yacht (Poole).

*Died* 15 *July* 1986.

**QUILL, Colonel Raymond Humphrey**, CBE 1947; DSO 1947; LVO 1934; Colonel (retired), Royal Marines; *b* 4 May 1897; *s* of late Maj.-General Richard Henry Quill, CB, MD; unmarried. *Educ:* Wellington Coll.; Cheltenham. Joined Royal Marines, 1914. Served European War, 1914–19. Major, RM, 1934; Lieut-Colonel, 1943;

Colonel, 1944. Served War of 1939–45. ADC to the King, 1948–50; retired, 1950. Legion of Merit, USA, 1948. Fellow, British Horological Institute, 1954–; Master, Worshipful Co. of Clockmakers, 1967. *Publication:* John Harrison: the man who found Longitude, 1967. *Recreations:* athletics, fishing, horology. *Clubs:* Boodle's, Royal Thames Yacht, Royal Automobile.

*Died* 7 *Dec.* 1987.

**QUIN, Rt. Rev. George Alderson;** *b* 22 Jan. 1914; *m* Norah; two *s* one *d. Educ:* Trinity College, Dublin (MA). Deacon, 1937, priest 1938, Down; Curate of St Jude, Ballynafeigh, Belfast, 1937–39; Dean's Vicar of St Anne's Cathedral, Belfast, 1939–41; Holywood, 1941–43; Incumbent of Magheralin, 1943–51; Vicar of Ballymacarrett, 1951–58; Canon of St Anne's Cathedral, Belfast, 1955–56; Archdeacon of Down, 1956–70; Exam. Chaplain to Bishop of Down and Dromore, 1957–70; Rector of Bangor, Dio. Down, 1958–70; Bishop of Down and Dromore, 1970–80. *Address:* 20 Kensington Park, Bangor, Co. Down, N Ireland.    *Died* 5 *Aug.* 1990.

**QUIN, Captain Hon. Valentine Maurice W.;** *see* Wyndham-Quin.

**QUINNELL, Air Commodore John Charles,** CB 1943; DFC 1918; *b* 7 Jan. 1891; *er s* of late John B. Quinnell, Edenburn, Gortatlea, Co. Kerry, Ireland; *m* 1923, Atwell (*d* 1945), *d* of late James McFarlane, Fifeshire, Scotland; no *c*; *m* 1948, Mildred Joan (*d* 1976), *widow* of Major Cyril Drummond, Cadland Fawley, Southampton, and *d* of late Horace Humphreys. *Educ:* Royal Sch., Dungannon, Co. Tyrone. Commissioned RA 1914; seconded RFC 1915; transferred RAF, 1918. Served European War, 1914–19 (despatches, DFC); RAF Staff Coll., 1924; Imperial Defence Coll., 1929; Air HQ Staff, Bagdad, 1931; AOC No 6 Auxiliary Group, 1935–38, and of No 6 Group 1939; Senior Air Staff Officer, Advanced Air Striking Force, 1939–40 (despatches); AOC a Group, RAF, 1942; retired, 1945. Pres., Solent Cruising and Racing Assoc., 1947–79, Hon. Life Pres., 1979; Chm., Solent Area Sailing Adv. Cttee. *Recreations:* shooting, yachting. *Address:* Nelson's Place, Fawley, Southampton, Hants. *T:* Fawley, Hants 891002. *Clubs:* Turf, Royal Thames Yacht; Royal Yacht Squadron.    *Died* 3 *Jan.* 1983.

**QVIST, Dame Frances;** *see* Gardner, Dame Frances.

**QVIST, George,** FRCS; Surgeon, Royal Free Hospital, since 1946, Willesden General Hospital, since 1956, Royal National Throat, Nose and Ear Hospital, since 1950; *b* 13 April 1910; *s* of Emil and Emily Qvist; *m* 1958, Dame Frances Gardner. *Educ:* Quintin Sch.; Univ. Coll. Hosp. MB, BS Lond., 1933; FRCS 1934. Surgical Registrar, Royal Free Hospital, 1939–41; Surgeon Emergency Medical Service, 1941–44; Surgical Specialist and O/C Surgical Division, Lieutenant-Colonel RAMC, 1944–46. Member of Council, RCS; Member of Court of Examiners, RCS, 1951–57; Past President, Hunterian Society. Fellow, UCL, 1975. *Publications:* Surgical Diagnosis, 1977; various papers on surgical subjects. *Address:* 72 Harley Street, W1. *T:* 01-580 5265; Fitzroy Lodge, Fitzroy Park, Highgate, N6. *T:* 01-340 5873.

*Died* 28 *July* 1981.

# R

**RABI, Prof. Isidor Isaac,** PhD; University Professor Emeritus, Columbia University, NY; Member: Naval Research Advisory Committee, since 1952; (US Member) Science Committee of United Nations, since 1954; (US Member) Science Committee of NATO, since 1958; General Advisory Committee, Arms Control and Disarmament Agency since 1962; Consultant: to General Advisory Committee, Atomic Energy Commission, since 1956 (Chairman, 1952–56, Member, since 1946); to Department of State, since 1958; etc; *b* Rymanov, Austria, 29 July 1898; *s* of David and Scheindel Rabi; *m* 1926, Helen Newmark; two *d. Educ:* Cornell University (BChem 1919); Columbia University (PhD, 1927). Lecturer, Physics, Columbia University, New York, 1929; then various posts, there, 1930–50, when Higgins Professor of Physics until 1964, University Professor, 1964–67. Associate Director, Radiation Laboratory, Massachusetts Institute of Technology, Cambridge, Mass, 1940–45. Mem., National Academy of Sciences; Fellow, American Physics Soc. (Pres., 1950–51). Holds numerous honorary doctorates; awarded medals and prizes, 1939 onwards, including: Nobel prize in physics, 1944; Atoms for Peace Award (jointly), 1967; Franklin Delano Roosevelt Freedom Medal, 1985; Vannevar Bush Award, 1986. *Publications:* My Life and Times as a Physicist, 1960; communications to The Physical Review, 1927–; contrib. to scientific jls on magnetism, quantum mechanics, nuclear physics, and molecular beams. *Recreations:* the theatre, travel, walking. *Address:* 450 Riverside Drive, New York City, NY 10027, USA. *Clubs:* Athenæum (London); Cosmos (Washington); Century Association (New York). *Died* 11 *Jan.* 1988.

**RABORN, Vice-Adm. William Francis, Jr,** DSM 1960; President, W. F. Raborn Company Inc., McLean, Virginia, since 1966; Director: Curtiss Wright Corporation; Avemco; E-Sys Inc.; S.A.I. Corporation; Wackenhut Corporation; *b* Decatur, Texas, 8 June 1905; *s* of William Francis, Sr, and Mrs Cornelia V. Raborn (*née* Moore); *m* 1955, Mildred T. Terrill; one *s* one *d. Educ:* US Naval Acad., Annapolis, Md (BS); Naval War Coll., Newport, RI. Ensign, USN, 1928; Naval Aviator, 1934; Sea duty, 1928–40; Aviation Gunnery Sch., 1940–42; Exec. Off., USS Hancock, 1943–45; Chief Staff Comdr Task Force 77, W Pacific, 1945–47; Ops Off. Comdr for Air W Coast, 1947–49; R & D Guided Missiles, 1949–50; Guided Missile Div., Office of Naval Ops, 1952–54; CO, USS Bennington, 1954–55; Asst Chief of Staff to C-in-C, Atlantic Fleet, 1955; Dir, Office of Special Projects, Polaris program, 1955; Dep. Chief, Naval Ops (Develt), 1962; retd from USN, 1963; Vice-Pres., Program management Aerojet Gen. Corp., Azusa, Calif, 1963–65; Director of Central Intelligence, USA, 1965–66; Industrial Consultant, Aerojet Gen. Corp. Silver Star, 1945; Bronze Star Medal, 1951; Commendation Medal, 1954; National Security Medal, 1966. *Address:* (home and business) 1606 Crestwood Lane, McLean, Virginia 22101, USA. *Clubs:* Army-Navy, Metropolitan (Washington, DC); Burning Tree (Bethesda, Md); Fair Oaks Golf and Country (San Antonio, Texas). *Died* 7 *March* 1990.

**RABY, Sir Victor Harry,** KBE 1956; CB 1948; MC; Deputy Under-Secretary of State, Department of the Permanent Under-Secretary of State for Air, 1946–57, retired December 1957; *b* 1897; *s* of Harry Raby, Menheniot, Cornwall; *m* 1921, Dorothy Alys, *d* of Rodney Buzzard, Ditchling, Sussex; one *s. Educ:* Grey College, Bloemfontein, S Africa. Served European War, 1914–19, with London Regt (MC). *Address:* New Way, Forder Lane, Bishopsteignton, Devon. *Died* 7 *Dec.* 1990.

**RACE, Robert Russell,** CBE 1970; PhD Cantab, MRCS, FRCP; FRCPath; FRS 1952; Director, Medical Research Council Blood Group Unit, Lister Institute, SW1, 1946–73; *b* 28 Nov. 1907; *e s* of late Joseph Dawson Race and late May Race (*née* Tweddle), Kensington; *m* 1st, 1938, Margaret Monica (*d* 1955), *d* of late J. R. C. Rotton, MVO; three *d*; 2nd, 1956, Dr Ruth Ann Sanger, FRS. *Educ:* St Paul's School; St Bartholomew's Hosp.; Trinity Hall, Cambridge. Asst Pathologist, Hosp. for Consumption and Diseases of the Chest, Brompton, 1935–37; Asst Serologist, Galton Laboratory, UCL, 1937–39; Asst Dir then Dir, Galton Laboratory Serum Unit, at Dept of Pathology, Cambridge, 1939–46. Mem., Deutsche Akademie der Naturforscher Leopoldina, 1973. Hon. MD: Univ. of Paris, 1965; Univ. of Turku, 1970. Oliver Memorial Award for Blood Transfusion, 1948; Carlos J. Finlay Medal, Republic of Cuba, 1955; Landsteiner Memorial Award, USA, jtly with Ruth Sanger, 1957; Oehlecker Medal, Deutsche Gesellschaft für Bluttransfusion, 1970; Philip Levine Award, USA. jtly with Ruth Sanger, 1970; Conway Evans Prize, Royal Soc. and RCP, 1972; Gairdner Foundn Award, Canada, jtly with Ruth Sanger, 1972. Hon. Fellow, RSM, 1974. Kruis van Verdienst, Netherlands Red Cross, 1959. *Publications:* (with Ruth Sanger) Blood Groups in Man, 1950, 6th edn, 1975; many papers in genetical and medical journals. *Address:* 22 Vicarage Road, East Sheen, SW14 8RU. *T:* 01-876 1508. *Died* 15 *April* 1984.

**RADFORD, Air Cdre Dudley Spencer,** CB 1957; DSO 1944; DFC 1940; AFC 1943; *b* 21 Sept. 1910; *s* of late John Francis Radford and of Alice Radford; *m* 1943, Pamela Biddulph Corr (*née* Padley); two *d. Educ:* Bedford School. Pilot training, 1932; No III Fighter Sqdn, 1933–35; flying instructor, 1936–38; Asst Adjt No 600 City of London Sqdn, 1938; Adjutant No 616 S Riding Sqdn, 1939; OC No 8 Sqdn, Aden, 1940–41; Chief Instructor: No 1 Flying Instructors' School, 1942; No 3 Advanced Flying Unit, 1943; OC No 10 Bomber Sqdn, 1944; RN Staff College course, 1944–45; Group Capt. Trng, HQ Transport Comd, 1945–46; Officer Comdg: RAF Spitalgate, 1947; RAF Wittering, 1948; RAF Liaison Officer, S Rhodesian Govt, 1949–50; Dep. Dir Postings, Air Ministry, 1951–53; idc 1954; Dir of Tactical and Air Transport Ops, 1955–56; Commandant, Central Reconnaissance Establishment, 1957–59; retired 1959. Gen. Services Manager, H. S. A. Ltd, 1960–75, retired. Officer, Order of Leopold (Belgium), 1947. *Address:* New Road Cottage, Prestbury, Cheshire. *Died* 20 *Nov.* 1984.

**RADICE, Fulke Rosavo,** CBE 1959; MA; late Vice-Director International Bureau of Universal Postal Union (1946–58); *b* Naples, 8 Feb. 1888; British subject; *s* of Albert Hampden Radice, Thistleborough, NI and Adelaide Anna Teresa (*née* Visetti); *m* 1917, Katharine Stella Mary Speck (*d* 1974) *d* of late Canon J. H. Speck and Mrs Speck (*née* Dalrymple); two *s* (and one *s* killed fighting in French Maquis, 1944). *Educ:* Bedford School (Scholar); Brasenose Coll., Oxford (open scholarship in History; 2nd Cl. Hons Mods (classical), 1909; 1st Cl. Mod. History, 1911). Home Civil Service, 1911; Secretary's Office, Gen. Post Office, 1911–46. Head of Brit. Secretariat of Universal Postal Union Congress, 1929, Head of Congress Secretariat at UPU Congresses, 1947, 1952, 1957. Served European War, 1914–18, in France, Salonica, Egypt, Italy; War of 1939–45 in Home Guard. *Publications:* The Radice Family, 1979; Rootlings, 1982; articles in Nineteenth Century and After, and in History. *Recreations:* rifle shooting (Oxford half blue, Oxford long range; English XX, 1909, 1910; King's Prize at Bisley, gold and silver medals, 1910; record score); Rugby football; ski-ing; freemasonry; historical studies. *Address:* 32 Jersey Avenue, Cheltenham, Glos GL52 2SZ; c/o Coutts & Co., 440 Strand, WC2. *Died* 18 *Jan.* 1987.

**RADO, Prof. Richard,** FRS 1978; Professor of Pure Mathematics, University of Reading, 1954–71, Emeritus since 1971; Canadian Commonwealth Fellow, University of Waterloo, Ontario, 1971–72; *b* 28 April 1906; 2nd *s* of Leopold Rado, Berlin; *m* 1933, Luise, *e d* of Hermann Zadek, Berlin; one *s. Educ:* University of Berlin (DPhil); University of Göttingen; Fitzwilliam Coll., Cambridge (PhD; Hon. Fellow, 1987). Lecturer, Sheffield Univ., 1936–47; Reader, King's College, Univ. of London, 1947–54. Vis. Prof., Calgary, Alberta, 1973. London Mathematical Society: Mem. of Council, 1948–57; Hon. Sec., 1953–54; Vice-President, 1954–56. Chm., British Combinatorial Cttee, 1977–83. Richard Rado Lecture instituted at British Combinatorial Conf., 1985. FIMA. Dr rer. nat. hc Freie Univ., Berlin, 1981; Hon. DMath Univ. of Waterloo, Canada, 1986. Sen. Berwick Prize, London Mathematical Soc., 1972. *Publications:* (with P. Erdös, A. Hajnal and A. Máté) Combinatorial Set Theory: partition relations for cardinals, 1984; articles in various journals on topics in pure mathematics; Mem. Editorial Bds of *Aequationes mathematicae,* Discrete Mathematics, Jl Combinatorial Theory, Combinatorica, Graphs and Combinatorics (Asian Jl); *relevant publication:* Festschrift: Studies in Pure Mathematics, ed Prof. L. Mirsky, 1971. *Recreations:* music, reading, walking. *Address:* 14 Glebe Road, Reading RG2 7AG. *T:* 871281. *Died* 23 *Dec.* 1989.

**RAE, Charles Robert Angus;** *b* 20 Feb. 1922; *s* of Charles E. L. Rae and Gladys M. Horsfall; *m* 1948, Philippa Neild (*d* 1987); one *s* two *d. Educ:* Eton Coll.; Trinity Coll., Cambridge; London Sch. of Slavonic Studies. BA (Hons History) Cantab, 1945, MA 1948. War service in N Russia, RNVR, 1943–45. Foreign Office, 1947, service in Rome, 1950–54, Mexico City, 1957–59, Moscow, 1959–60; Private Sec. to Parly Under-Sec., 1954–57; seconded to Dept of Technical Co-operation on its formation, 1961; transf. to ODM as Asst Sec., 1964; Under Sec., 1975–79. Mem., Bd of Exec. Dirs, Inter-American Development Bank, 1979–82. Chm., Chelsham and Farleigh Parish Council, 1974–79. *Recreations:* walking, gardening. *Address:* The Limes, Shabbington, near Aylesbury, Bucks HP18 9HB. *T:* Long Crendon (0844) 201139. *Died* 28 *Nov.* 1990.

**RAHMAN PUTRA, Tunku (Prince) Abdul;** *see* Abdul Rahman Putra.

**RAIKES, Sir (Henry) Victor (Alpin MacKinnon),** KBE 1953; *b* 19 Jan. 1901; *s* of late H. St John Raikes, CBE, KC; *m* 1940, Audrey Elizabeth Joyce, *o d* of A. P. Wilson, Repton; two *d. Educ:* Westminster School; Trinity Coll., Cambridge (BA). Called to Bar, Inner Temple, 1924; contested (C) Ilkeston Division of Derbyshire, 1924 and 1929; MP (C) SE Essex, 1931–45; MP (C) Wavertree Division of Liverpool, 1945–50, Garston Division of Liverpool, 1950–57 (Ind C 1957). Chm., Monday Club, 1975–78. Flight Lieut

RAFVR, 1940–42. JP Derbyshire, 1927. Kt of Malta, Order of St John of Jerusalem, 1970. *Address:* 8 Gledhow Gardens, SW5. *Club:* Carlton.                                                                              *Died* 18 *April* 1986.

**RAINBIRD, George Meadus;** Director, Thomson Publications Ltd, 1966–77 (Deputy Chairman, 1973–77); author and publisher; *b* 22 May 1905; *s* of Leonard Rainbird and Sarah (*née* Meadus); *m* 1st, 1926, Eva Warner (marr. diss.); one *s* two *d*; 2nd, 1939, Joyce Trinder (*d* 1970); two *s* one *d*; 3rd, 1972, Lena Wickman. *Educ:* local grammar school. Founded publishing house, George Rainbird Ltd, 1951; acquired Zaehnsdorf Ltd and Wigmore Bindery Ltd, 1954–56; merged with Thomson Organization, 1965. Chairman: Thos Nelson & Sons Ltd, 1970–75; George Rainbird Ltd, 1970–75; Rainbird Reference Books Ltd, 1970–75; Sphere Books Ltd, 1970–75; Michael Joseph Ltd, 1970–75; Westerham Press Ltd, 1972–75; Acanthus Press Ltd, 1979–; Dir, Hamish Hamilton Ltd. Chm., International Wine and Food Soc., 1964–72. *Publications:* Escape to Sunshine, 1952; A Pocket Book of Wine, 1963, (with Ronald Searle) repr. as The Subtle Alchemist, 1973; Sherry and the Wines of Spain, 1966; An Illustrated Guide to Wine, 1983; The Rainbird Archive, 1985. *Recreations:* books, gardens and wine. *Address:* The Old Parsonage, Church Street, Moreton-in-Marsh, Glos. *T:* Moreton-in-Marsh 50492; 45 Bramerton Street, SW3. *T:* 01–352 0712. *Clubs:* Brooks's, Saintsbury.
                                                                              *Died* 20 *Aug.* 1986.

**RAINEY, Dr Reginald Charles,** OBE 1979; FRS 1975; Consultant, tropical pest management, since 1960; *b* 18 June 1913; *s* of Charles Albert Rainey and Ethel May Rainey; *m* 1943, Margaret Tasman; three *s* (one *d* decd). *Educ:* Purbrook Park County High Sch., Hants; Imperial Coll. of Science and Technology (ARCS); London Sch. of Hygiene and Trop. Med. DSc London; FIBiol. Res. biologist, Empire Cotton Growing Corp., Transvaal, 1938–40 and 1946–49; Meteorological Officer, S African Air Force, S and E Africa and ME, 1940–46; Sen. Entomologist, Desert Locust Survey, E Africa High Commn (res. and develt work on use of meteorology and aircraft in forecasting and control of desert locust invasions), 1949–58; SPSO, Centre for Overseas Pest Research, ODM (formerly Anti-Locust Research Centre), 1958–78; i/c FAO Desert Locust Inf. Service (desert locust forecasting, with co-operation and support of countries concerned, in Africa and Asia), 1960–67; res. and develt work on use of meteorology and aircraft in forecasting and control of other insect pests, with co-operation and support of E African Agric. and Forestry Res. Org., Sudan Gezira Bd, Canadian Forestry Service, Agricl Aviation Res. Unit (Ciba-Geigy Ltd), Cranfield Coll. of Aeronautics, Univ. of New Brunswick, FAO, Acad. Sinica, 1967–. Pres., Royal Entomological Soc., 1979–81. Fitzroy Prize, Royal Meteorological Soc., 1971. *Publications:* Meteorology and the Migration of Desert Locusts, 1963; (ed) Insect Flight, 1975; (ed with D. L. Gunn) Migrant Pests, 1979; Migration and Meteorology: flight behaviour and the atmospheric environment of migrant pests, 1989; papers in sci. jls. *Recreations:* as above. *Address:* Elmslea, Old Risborough Road, Stoke Mandeville, Bucks. *T:* Stoke Mandeville 2493.                                                                  *Died* 18 *Jan.* 1990.

**RAINWATER, Prof. (Leo) James;** Professor of Physics, Columbia University, New York, since 1952; *b* 9 Dec. 1917; *s* of Leo Jasper Rainwater and Edna Eliza (*née* Teague); *m* 1942, Emma Louise Smith; three *s*. *Educ:* California Inst. of Technol.; Columbia Univ., NY (BS, MA, PhD). Asst in Physics, 1939–42, Instr 1946–47, Asst Prof. 1947–49, Assoc. Prof., 1949–52, Columbia Univ.; Scientist, OSRD and Manhattan Project, 1942–46; Dir, Nevis Cyclotron Lab., 1951–53 and 1956–61; scientific research contracts with US naval research, Atomic Energy Commn and Nat. Science Foundn, 1947–. Fellow: Amer. Phys. Soc.; AAAS; IEEE; NY Acad. of Science; Optical Soc. of Amer.; Mem., Nat Acad. of Sciences. Hon. Mem., Royal Swedish Acad., 1982. Ernest Orlando Lawrence Physics Award, US Atomic Energy Commn, 1963; (jtly) Nobel Prize for Physics, 1975. *Recreations:* classical music, environmental problems, astronomy. *Publications:* numerous articles in Phys. Review, 1946–, and other professional jls. *Address:* Physics Department, Columbia University, New York, NY 10027, USA. *T:* 212–280–3345; (home) 342 Mt Hope Boulevard, Hastings-on-Hudson, NY 10706, USA. *T:* 914–GR8–1368.
                                                                              *Died* 31 *May* 1986.

**RALEIGH, Nigel Hugh C.;** *see* Curtis-Raleigh.

**RALPH, Ronald Seton,** MRCS, LRCP, DPH; retired; late Consultant Pathologist Battersea and Putney Group of Hospitals; Hon. Pathologist, Eltham and Mottingham Cottage Hospital; *b* Saugor, India, 22 July 1895; *s* of late Col A. C. Ralph, DSO; *m* 1918, Marjorie, *d* of late Dr Joseph Bott, Richmond, Surrey; one *s*. *Educ:* Dover College; Guy's Hospital. Late Director of Clinical Research Assoc. Laboratories; late Clinical Pathologist, St John's Hospital, Lewisham, SE13; late Assistant Bacteriologist, Guy's Hospital, and late Physician in Charge of Diseases of the Skin, St John's Hospital, SE13. *Publications:* various on medical subjects in Lancet, Medical

World, and Journal of Clinical Research. *Address:* Les Champs des Cailles, Trinity, Jersey.                                          *Died* 23 *May* 1985.

**RAM, Jagjivan;** Member, Lok Sabha, 1952–79 and since 1980; President, All Indian Congress Committee, since 1981; *b* Arrah, Bihar, 5 April 1908; *s* of late Shri Shobhi Ram; *m* 1935, Indrani Devi; one *s* one *d*. *Educ:* Patna Univ.; Banaras Hindu Univ.; Calcutta Univ. BSc 1930. Appeared before Hammond Commn, 1936; started Agricl Lab. Movement in Bihar and formed Bihar Provincial Khet Mazdoor (Agricl Lab.) Sabha, 1937; Mem., Bihar LC, 1936–37, Bihar LA, 1937–40; Parly Sec., Bihar Govt, 1937–39; jailed in 1940 and 1942 and released in Oct. 1943 on med. grounds; Vice-Pres., Bihar Br. of All India TUC, 1940–46; Sec., Bihar Provincial Congress Cttee, 1940–46; Labour Minister of interim Govt, Sept. 1946–May 1952; appeared before Cabinet Mission, 1946, as accredited leader of Scheduled Castes and rep. their case. Mem., Constituent Assembly, Central Legislative Assembly, and Provisional Parlt, 1946–52. Leader, Indian Delegn to ILO Conf., Geneva, 1947; Chm., Preparatory Asia Regional Conf. of ILO, Oct.-Nov. 1947; Leader, Indian Delegn to 33rd Session of ILO Conf. 1950 (Chm. Conf.); Communication Minister, Govt of India, 1952–56; Minister for: Transport and Railway, Dec. 1956–Apr. 1957; Railways, 1957–62; Transport and Communications, 1962–63; Labour, Employment and Rehabilitation, 1966–67 (AN); Leader, Indian Delegn to Asian Labour Ministers' Conf., Manila, 1966; Minister of Food, Agriculture, Community Develt and Co-op., 1967–70 (also charge Min. of Labour, Employment and Rehabilitation, Nov. 1969–Feb. 1970); Minister of Defence, 1970–74, 1977–79; Minister of Agriculture and Irrigation, 1974–77; Dep. Prime Minister (Defence), 1979; Leader of the Opposition, 1979–80. Leader, Indian Delegns: FAO Conf., Rome, 1967, 1974; World Food Congress, The Hague, 1970, Khartoum, 1974. Mem. Exec. Cttee, Hindustan Mazdoor Sewak Sangh, 1947–; Pres., All India Congress Cttee, 1969–71 (Mem. Cttee, 1940–77, and of its Central Parly Bd, 1950–77); Chm., Reception Cttee, 67th Session, Indian Nat. Congress, Patna, 1962; Member: Disciplinary Action Cttee of Congress Working Cttee (since constituted, to 1977); All India Congress Working Cttee, 1948–77; Central Election Cttee, 1951–56, 1961; Gen. Body, AICC, 1973–77; Gandhi Smarak Nidhi; Chairman: Central Campaign Cttee, AICC, 1974–77; Panchayati Raj Cell, AICC, 1974–77. Formed Congress for Democracy Party, Feb. 1977; Leader, Janata Party, and Leader of the Opposition, 1979–80; Congress (U), 1980; rejoined Indian Nat. Congress, 1981. Chm., Indian Inst. of Public Admin, 1974–75; Mem. Governing Bodies, several colls and educnl instns. Trustee, Nehru Memorial Trust, etc. Past Pres. of several Trades Unions. Hon. Dr of Sciences, Univs of Vikraim, Udaipur, Agra, and others. *Publications:* a collection of speeches on labour problem; Caste Challenge in India. *Recreations:* reading, gardening, chess whenever possible. *Address:* 6 Krishna Menon Marg, New Delhi 110 011, India. *T:* 376555.
                                                                              *Died* 6 *July* 1986.

**RAM CHANDRA,** CIE 1933; MBE 1919; MA (Punjab); MA (Cantab); a Trustee of The Tribune (English daily newspaper in Chandigarh), 1949–76, President of Board of Trustees, 1967–76; *b* 1 March 1889; *m* 1917; one *s* one *d*. *Educ:* Government College, Lahore (Fuller Exhibitioner); Panjab Univ. (MA English 1907; MA 1st class, Mathematics, 1908); Trinity College, Cambridge (Senior Scholar, Mathematical Tripos and Wrangler, b star, 1913); Govt of India Bd of Examrs Cert. of High Proficiency in Persian, 1915; Degree of Honour in Urdu, 1921. Assistant Professor of Mathematics, Government College, Lahore, 1908–10; joined ICS, 1913; served in Punjab as Assistant Commissioner in various districts; Colonisation Officer, 1915; Under-Secretary, 1919–21; Settlement Officer, 1921–25; Director of Land Records, 1924; Deputy Commissioner, 1925; Secretary to Punjab Government, Transferred Department, 1926–27; Home Secretary to Punjab Government, 1928; Deputy Secretary to Govt of India, Department of Education, Health, and Lands, 1928; Joint Secretary, 1932; Secretary, 1935; Member Council of State, 1935; Member, Punjab Legislative Council, 1936; Finance Secretary to Punjab Govt, 1936–37; Commissioner, 1938–39; Sec. to Punjab Govt, Medical and Local Govt Depts, 1939–41; Chief Controller of Imports, India, 1941–44; Leader of Indian Delegation to Egypt for Cotton Conference, 1943; Secretary to Government of India, Commerce Dept, 1944–45; Secretary to Govt of India, Defence Dept, 1945–46; Financial Comr, Punjab, 1946–48; Chairman, Punjab (India) Public Service Commission, 1948–53; Mem., Punjab Legislative Council (elected by Graduates' Constituency), 1954–60; Fellow of Panjab Univ., Chandigarh, 1947–68, Syndic, 1949–64; Syndic and Fellow, Punjabi Univ., Patiala, 1962–72. Chief Comr, Scouts and Guides, Punjab, 1955–68. *Recreation:* gardening. *Address:* Forest Hill, Simla 2, India. *T:* 2129.                                              *Died* 9 *Aug.* 1987.

**RAMAGE, Captain Cecil Beresford,** MC; *b* 17 Jan. 1895; *o s* of John Walker Ramage, Edinburgh; *m* 1921, Cathleen Nesbitt, CBE (*d* 1982); one *s* one *d*. *Educ:* Edinburgh Academy; Pembroke College, Oxford (open Classical Scholar); President Oxford Union Society. Commissioned in the Royal Scots, 1914; served Gallipoli, Egypt,

Palestine, until 1919 (despatches, Order of the Nile). Contested Newcastle upon Tyne, General Election, 1922; MP (L) Newcastle upon Tyne (West Division), 1923–24; contested Southport, 1929. Barrister-at-Law, Middle Temple, 1921; subseq. Oxford Circuit. *Recreation:* golf. *Address:* Flat 2, 11 Dean Park Road, Bournemouth, Dorset. *Died 22 Feb.* 1988.

**RAMBERT, Dame Marie, (Dame Marie Dukes),** DBE 1962 (CBE 1953); Founder and Director of Ballet Rambert; Director, Mercury Theatre Trust Ltd; lecturer and teacher; *b* Warsaw, 20 Feb. 1888; British; *m* 1918, Ashley Dukes, playwright (*d* 1959); two *d. Educ:* Warsaw, Paris. Studied with Jaques Dalcroze and Enrico Cecchetti; Member of Diaghilev's Ballets Russes, 1912–13; opened Rambert School of Ballet, 1920; Founder and Director of Ballet Rambert, 1926, reformed as Modern Dance Company 1966; produced first ballet, Tragedy of Fashion, by Frederick Ashton, 1926; first season of Ballet Rambert (guest artist, Tamara Karsavina) at Lyric Theatre, Hammersmith, 1930; Ballet Club at Mercury Theatre founded 1930; 50th Birthday performance, Sadler's Wells, 15th June 1976. Fellow, Royal Acad. of Dancing, Vice-Pres. 1972. Member: Grand Council, Imperial Soc. of Teachers of Dancing; Inst. of Dirs. Recording, On Ballet (with Karsavina), 1960. Radio and Television personality. Queen Elizabeth Coronation Award, Royal Acad. of Dancing, 1956; Diploma of Associateship, College of Art, Manchester, 1960; FRSA 1963; Hon. DLitt Univ. of Sussex, 1964. Jubilee Medal, 1977; Composers' Guild of GB Award, 1978. Légion d'Honneur, 1957; Gold Medal, Order of Merit, Polish People's Republic, 1979. *Publications:* (trans.) Ulanova: Her Childhood and Schooldays, 1962; Quicksilver: an autobiography—Marie Rambert, 1972, Polish edn 1978; *relevant publications:* Sixteen Years of Ballet Rambert, by Lionel Bradley, 1946; Dancers of Mercury: The Story of Ballet Rambert, by Mary Clarke, 1962; 50 years of Ballet Rambert, 1926–76, ed Anya Sainsbury, Clement Crisp, Peter Williams, 1976. *Address:* Mercury Theatre Trust Ltd, 94 Chiswick High Road, W4 1SH. *T:* 01-995 4246. *Died 12 June* 1982.

**RAMGOOLAM, Dr Rt. Hon. Sir Seewoosagur,** GCMG 1978; Kt 1965; PC 1971; LRCP, MRCS; Governor-General and Commander in Chief of Mauritius, since 1984; *b* Belle Rive, 1900; *m;* one *s* one *d. Educ:* Royal Coll., Curepipe; University Coll. (Fellow, 1971) and University Coll. Hosp., London. Municipal Councillor, 1940–53, 1956–60; Deputy Mayor of Port Louis, 1956; Mayor of Port Louis, 1958; entered Legislative Council, 1940; MLC, Pamplemousse-Rivière du Rempart, 1948, re-elected 1953; Mem., Executive Council, 1948–; Liaison Officer for Education, 1951–56; Ministerial Secretary to the Treasury, 1958–60; MLA (Lab) Pamplemousses-Triolet, 1959–82; Leader of the House, 1960–82; Chief Minister, 1961–65, and Minister of Finance, 1960–72; Prime Minister, 1965–82; Minister for External Affairs, 1968–76; Minister for Defence and Internal Security and Information and Broadcasting, 1969–82. Chm., Organisation of African Unity 1976–77; Président d'Honneur des Parlements africains, 1977; Vice-Pres., Afro-Arab Summit, 1977. Chm., Bd of Dirs, Advance. Founder and Pres., Mauritius Soc. for Prevention of Cruelty to Animals; 1st Patron, World Fedn for Protection of Animals, 1974; Richard Martin Award, RSPCA, 1981. Pres., Indian Cultural Assoc.; Hon. Fellow, All-India Inst. of Med. Scis, New Delhi, 1979; Editor, Indian Cultural Review. Hon. Citizen: Port Louis, 1969; Quatre Bonnes, 1973; Pamplemousses, 1973. Grand Croix de l'Ordre National de la République Malagasy, 1969; Médaille de l'Assemblée Nationale française, 1971; Grand Croix, Ordre National de Lion (Senegal), 1973; Grand Croix de l'Ordre du Mérite (Central African Republic), 1973; Grand Croix National de Benin (Togo), 1973; Grand Officier de la Légion d'honneur (France), 1973; Médaille de la Francophonie, 1975; Grand Croix de l'Ordre du Mérite, République Fédérale d'Allemagne, 1978. UN Prize for Outstanding Achievements in the field of Human Rights, 1973; Prix International des Relations Diplomatiques, Inst. of Diplomatic Relations, Brussels, 1980. Dr in Law *hc,* New Delhi; Hon. DCL Mauritius, 1974; Dr *hc* Aix-en-Provence, 1978. 1st Hon. Mem., African Psychiatric Assoc., 1979. *Recreations:* art and literature. *Address:* 85 Desforges Street, Port Louis, Mauritius. *T:* 20460. *Died 15 Dec.* 1985.

**RAMSAY, J(ames) Arthur,** MBE 1945; FRS 1955; Fellow of Queens' College, Cambridge, 1934–76, later Hon. Fellow; Professor of Comparative Physiology, University of Cambridge, 1969–76, later Emeritus Professor (Reader, 1959); *b* 6 Sept. 1909; *s* of late David Ramsay and Isabella Rae Ramsay (*née* Garvie); *m* 1939, Helen Amelie, *d* of late Oscar Dickson, Stockholm; one *s* one *d. Educ:* Fettes College; Gonville and Caius College, Cambridge. University Demonstrator and Fellow of Queens', 1934. Major RA Coast and Anti-Aircraft Defence Experimental Establishment, 1939–45. Joint Editor, Journal of Experimental Biology, 1952–74. *Publications:* Physiological Approach to the Lower Animals, 1952; The Experimental Basis of Modern Biology, 1965; A Guide to Thermodynamics, 1972; papers in Jl of Experimental Biology. *Recreations:* mountaineering, ski-ing. *Address:* The Boxer's Croft, Achbuie 3, Abriachan, Inverness-shire. *T:* Dochgarroch 269. *Died 5 Feb.* 1988.

**RAMSAY, Cdre Sir James (Maxwell),** KCMG 1978; KCVO 1982; Kt 1976; CBE 1966; DSC 1952; Governor of Queensland, 1977–85; *b* 27 Aug. 1916; *s* of William Ramsay and Mary Ramsay; *m* 1945, Janet Burley; one *s* three *d. Educ:* Hutchins Sch., Hobart; RAN Coll., Jervis Bay. RAN, 1930–72: Naval Representative, London, 1964–65; NOIC, Western Australia, 1968–72; Lieut-Governor of Western Australia, 1974–77. KStJ 1977. Legion of Merit, US, 1952. *Recreations:* golf, yachting, fishing. *Address:* 17 Cedar Place, Cypress Garden, Broadbeach, Qld 4218, Australia. *Club:* Weld.
*Died 1 May* 1986.

**RAMSAY, Sir Neis Alexander,** 12th Bt of Bamff, *cr* 1666; Farmer since 1953; Landowner and Farmer since 1959; *b* 4 Oct. 1909; *s* of Sir James Douglas Ramsay, 11th Bt, MVO, TD, JP; *S* father 1959; *m* 1st, 1940, Edith Alix Ross Hayes (marr. diss. 1950; she *d* 1979), *d* of C. F. Hayes, Linksfield, Johannesburg; 2nd, 1952, Rachel Leanore Beatrice Drummond (*d* 1982), *d* of late Colonel E. B. Urmston, CB, Glenmorven; no *c. Educ:* Winchester; Trinity College, Cambridge. 2nd Lt Gordon Highlanders, 1933–34; British South African Police, 1934–35; Lieutenant, South African Engineer Corps, 1939–45; Mining in South Africa, 1936–50; Returned to UK, 1950. *Recreations:* shooting and golf. *Heir* (*to feudal barony of Bamff*): Paul Robert Warner Ramsay, yr of Bamff [*b* 30 Oct. 1945; *s* of Sir Edward Redston Warner, KCMG, OBE; assumed name of Ramsay, 1975; *m* 1979, Helen Louise Gibbon, *d* of late Lt-Col Aubrey Wynter Gibbon, OBE, Argyll and Sutherland Highlanders; two *s* one *d. Educ:* Eton; Edinburgh Univ.; UCL]. *Address:* Bamff, Alyth, Perthshire. *T:* Alyth 2382. *Club:* New (Edinburgh).
*Died 7 March* 1986.

**RAMSBOTHAM, Rt. Rev. John Alexander;** *b* 25 Feb. 1906; *s* of late Rev. Alexander Ramsbotham and of late Margaret Emily Ramsbotham; *m* 1933, Eirian Morgan Owen (*d* 1988); three *s* two *d. Educ:* Haileybury College; Corpus Christi College, Cambridge; Wells Theological College. Travelling Secretary, 1929–30, Missionary Secretary, 1930–33, Student Christian Movement; Chaplain, 1933–34. Vice-Principal, 1934–36, Wells Theol. Coll.; Priest-Vicar Wells Cathedral, 1933–36; Warden, College of the Ascension, Selly Oak, 1936–40; Rector of Ordsall, Notts, 1941–42; Vicar of St George's, Jesmond, Newcastle on Tyne, 1942–50; Bishop Suffragan of Jarrow, 1950–58, also Archdeacon of Auckland and Canon of Durham; Bishop of Wakefield, 1958–67; Asst Bishop, Dio. Newcastle, 1968–76. *Publication:* Belief in Christ and the Christian Community, 1949. *Recreation:* music. *Address:* West Lindeth Home, Silverdale, Lancs LA5 0TA.
*Died 16 Dec.* 1989.

**RAMSDEN, Sir Caryl (Oliver Imbert),** 8th Bt *cr* 1689, of Byram, Yorks; CMG 1965; CVO 1966; *b* 4 April 1915; *s* of Lt-Col Josslyn Vere Ramsden, CMG, DSO (*d* 1952) (*g g s* of 4th Bt) and Olive Clotilde Bouhier (*d* 1977), *d* of Frederic William Imbert-Terry; *S* kinsman, Sir Geoffrey William Pennington-Ramsden, 7th Bt, 1986; *m* 1945, Anne, *d* of late Sir Charles Wickham, KCMG, KBE, DSO; one *s. Educ:* Eton; New Coll., Oxford. Served in Royal Regiment of Artillery, 1937–49; Assistant Military Attaché, Bucharest, 1947–49. Entered HM Foreign Service, 1949, retired 1967; Private Secretary to Prime Minister, 1957; Consul-General, Hanover, 1957–59; Counsellor, Rio de Janeiro, 1959; acted as Chargé d'Affaires, 1960; Counsellor, Brussels 1962. Pro-Principal (Admin), University College at Buckingham, 1975–79. Commander of the Star of Ethiopia, 1954; Commander, Order of Leopold, 1966. *Heir:* *s* John Charles Josslyn Ramsden [*b* 19 Aug. 1950; *m* 1985, Jane Jennifer Bevan]. *Address:* The Old Brewery, Helperby, York YO6 2NS. *Club:* Cavalry and Guards. *Died 27 March* 1987.

**RAMSDEN, Sir Geoffrey Charles Frescheville,** Kt 1948; CIE 1942; *b* 21 April 1893; *s* of Colonel H. F. S. Ramsden, CBE, and Hon. Edwyna Fiennes, *d* of 17th Lord Saye and Sele, DL, JP, CC; *m* 1930, Margaret Lovell (*d* 1976), *d* of late Rev. J. Robinson; no *c. Educ:* Haileybury College; Sidney Sussex Coll., Cambridge (MA). Served in the Army, 1914–19; Capt. 1st Bn Royal Sussex Regt, NW Frontier (India) 1915–19; joined ICS 1920; Secretary Indian Tariff Board, 1923–25; Deputy Commissioner of Jubbulpore, 1926 and 1931–34, and of various other Districts; Commissioner, Jubbulpore Div., 1936 and 1941–44, and Chhatisgarh Div., 1937–40; Development Adviser to Governor, 1945; Financial Comr CP and Berar, 1941–45 and 1946–47; retd, 1948. *Recreations:* travel, photography, tennis and fishing. *Club:* Royal Over-Seas League.
*Died 14 Feb.* 1990.

**RAMSDEN, Sir Geoffrey William P.;** *see* Pennington-Ramsden.

**RAMSEY OF CANTERBURY, Baron** *cr* 1974 (Life Peer), of Canterbury; **Rt. Rev. and Rt. Hon. Arthur Michael Ramsey,** PC 1956; Royal Victorian Chain, 1974; MA, BD; Hon. Fellow: Magdalene College, Cambridge, since 1952; Merton College, Oxford, since 1974; Keble College, Oxford, since 1975; St Cross College, Oxford, since 1981; Selwyn College, Cambridge, since 1983; *b* 14 Nov. 1904; *s* of late Arthur Stanley Ramsey, Fellow and sometime President of Magdalene Coll., Cambridge; *m* 1942, Joan, *d* of Lieut-Colonel F. A. C. Hamilton. *Educ:* Repton; Magdalene Coll., Cambridge (Scholar); Cuddesdon. 2nd Class, Classical Tripos, 1925; 1st Class, Theological Tripos, 1927; President of Cambridge Union, 1926; ordained, 1928; curate of Liverpool Parish Church, 1928–30; subwarden of Lincoln Theological Coll., 1930–36; Lecturer of Boston Parish Church, 1936–38; Vicar of S Benedict, Cambridge, 1939–40; Canon of Durham Cathedral and Professor of Divinity in Univ. of Durham, 1940–50, Emeritus Prof., 1977, Hon. Fellow, St Chad's Coll., 1980; Regius Professor of Divinity, Univ. of Cambridge, and Fellow of Magdalene Coll., 1950–52; Canon and Prebendary in Lincoln Cathedral, 1951–52; Bishop of Durham, 1952–56; Archbishop of York, 1956–61; Archbishop of Canterbury, 1961–74. Examining Chaplain to Bishop of Chester, 1932–39, to Bishop of Durham, 1940–50, and to Bishop of Lincoln, 1951–52; Select Preacher, Cambridge 1934, 1940, 1948, 1959, 1964, Oxford, 1945–46; Hulsean Preacher, Cambridge, 1969–70. Hon. Master of the Bench, Inner Temple, 1962. A President of World Council of Churches, 1961–68. Trustee, British Museum, 1963–69. Hon. FBA 1983. Hon. degrees include: Hon. DD: Durham, 1951; Leeds, Edinburgh, Cambridge, Hull, 1957; Manchester, 1961; London, 1962; Hon. DCL: Oxford, 1960; Kent, 1966; Hon. DLitt Keele, 1967, and a number from universities overseas. *Publications:* The Gospel and the Catholic Church, 1936; The Resurrection of Christ, 1945; The Glory of God and the Transfiguration of Christ, 1949; F. D. Maurice and the Conflicts of Modern Theology, 1951; Durham Essays and Addresses, 1956; From Gore to Temple, 1960; Introducing the Christian Faith, 1961; Canterbury Essays and Addresses, 1964; Sacred and Secular, 1965; God, Christ and the World, 1969; (with Cardinal Suenens) The Future of the Christian Church, 1971; The Christian Priest Today, 1972; Canterbury Pilgrim, 1974; Holy Spirit, 1977; Jesus and the Living Past, 1980; Be Still and Know, 1982. *Recreation:* walking. *Address:* St John's Home, St Mary's Road, Oxford OX4 1QE.

*Died 23 April 1988.*

**RAMSEY, Rt. Rev. Kenneth Venner;** an Assistant Bishop, Diocese of Manchester, since 1975; *b* 26 Jan. 1909; *s* of James Ernest and Laura Rebecca Ramsey, Southsea, Hants; unmarried. *Educ:* Portsmouth Grammar Sch.; University Coll., Oxford; Manchester Univ. Curate of St Matthew, Stretford, 1933–35; Vice-Prin., Egerton Hall, Manchester, and Lectr in Christian Ethics, Manchester Univ., 1935–38; Vice-Prin., Bishop Wilson Coll., Isle of Man, 1938–39; Prin., Egerton Hall, Manchester, 1939–41; Vicar of St Paul, Peel, Little Hulton, Lancs, 1941–48; Rector of Emmanuel Church, Didsbury, Manchester, 1948–55; Hon. Canon, Manchester Cathedral, 1950–55; Proctor in Convocation and mem. Church Assembly, 1950–55; Rural Dean of Heaton, 1950–53; Bishop Suffragan of Hulme, 1953–75. *Address:* 41 Bradwell Drive, Heald Green, Cheadle, Cheshire SK8 3BX. *T:* 061–437 8612.

*Died 21 June 1990.*

**RAMSEY, Leonard Gerald Gwynne;** Editor of The Connoisseur, 1951–72; *b* 17 March 1913; *s* of late L. B. Ramsey, London Stock Exchange; *m* 1941, Dorothy Elizabeth, *y d* of late W. J. McMillan, Belfast; one *s* one *d. Educ:* Radley College. Commissioned Oxfordshire and Buckinghamshire Light Infantry (T), 1938; invalided out of Army, 1944; on General Staff, War Office, 1941–44, and other staff appointments. Public Relations Officer, The National Trust, 1946–49; Press Officer at Board of Trade and Colonial Office, 1950–51. Member of several Committees associated with ecclesiastical art and charitable matters. FSA 1949. *Publications:* (ed) The Connoisseur Encyclopædia of Antiques, 5 vols, 1954–60; (ed with Ralph Edwards) The Connoisseur Period Guides, 6 vols, 1956–59; Montague Dawson, marine artist, a biography, 1967; (ed with Helen Comstock) The Connoisseur's Guide to Antique Furniture, 1969. *Recreations:* historic buildings, works of art, gardening. *Address:* 28 Morley Avenue, Woodbridge, Suffolk IP12 4AZ. *Club:* Light Infantry.

*Died 14 May 1990.*

**RAMSEY, Robert John,** CBE 1977; President, Institute of Personnel Management, 1981–83; *b* 16 Aug. 1921; *m* 1949, Arlette Ikor; one *s* one *d. Educ:* Royal Liberty Sch., Romford. Joined Ford Motor Co. Ltd, as student, 1937. Served War of 1939–45: RAF Air Crew, Flt-Lt, 1942–46; POW, 1944–45. Rejoined Ford Motor Co. Ltd, 1946; Industrial Relations Manager, 1958; Dir of Labour Relations, 1969–73; Dir of Indust. Relations, 1973–81. Non-Exec. Dir, Yorkshire Television, 1982–. Member: CRE, 1977–82; Council, Industrial Soc., 1977–81; Employment Policy Cttee, CBI, 1975–81; Megaw Inquiry into Civil Service Pay, 1981–82; (non-exec.) Anglian Water Authority, 1983–; Chairman: Essex Area Manpower Bd, 1983–; Nat. Advisory Council on Employment of Disabled People, 1984–. FRSA 1979; CIPM 1977. *Recreations:* reading, theatre, walking, boating. *Address:* 47 Eastwood Road, Leigh-on-Sea, Essex. *T:* Southend-on-Sea 72884. *Club:* Royal Air Force.

*Died 7 May 1986.*

**RANDALL, Sir John (Turton),** Kt 1962; FRS 1946; FInstP; DSc (Manchester); Honorary Professor in the University of Edinburgh; Emeritus Professor of Biophysics in the University of London,

King's College; FKC 1960; *b* 23 March 1905; *o s* of late Sidney and Hannah Cawley Randall; *m* 1928, Doris Duckworth; one *s. Educ:* Univ. of Manchester (Graduate Res. Schol. and Prizeman, 1925; MSc 1926, DSc 1938). Res. physicist, Res. Lab of GEC Ltd, 1926–37; Warren Res. Fellow of Royal Soc. 1937–43; Hon. Mem. of the staff, Univ. of Birmingham, 1940–43; res. in Univ. of Birmingham for Admiralty, 1939–43, jt inventor (with H. A. H. Boot) of cavity magnetron; Temp. Lectr in Cavendish Laboratory, Cambridge, 1943–44; Prof. of Natural Philosophy, United Coll. of St Salvator and St Leonard, Univ. of St Andrews, 1944–46; Wheatstone Prof. of Physics, 1946–61, Prof. of Biophysics, 1961–70, Univ. of London (King's Coll.); Dir, MRC Biophysics Research Unit, 1947–70; Chm., Sch. of Biological Sciences, KCL, 1963–69. Lectr, Rockefeller Inst. for Med. Res., NY, 1956–67; Gregynog Lectr, UCW Aberystwyth, 1958; Vis. Prof. of Biophysics, Yale Univ., 1960. Awarded (with H. A. H. Boot) Thomas Gray Meml Prize of Royal Soc. of Arts (1943) for discovery of the cavity magnetron. Duddell Medallist, Physical Soc. of London, 1945; Hughes Medallist, Royal Soc. 1946; John Price Wetherill Medal of Franklin Inst. of State of Pennsylvania, 1958; John Scott Award, City of Philadelphia, 1959. FRSE 1972. *Publications:* The Diffraction of X-rays by Amorphous Solids, Liquids and Gases, 1934; (Editor) The Nature and Structure of Collagen, 1953; (Jt Editor) Progress in Biophysics, 1950–55; papers in various scientific journals on structure in gasses and liquids, the luminescence of solids, the cavity magnetron; since 1946, the biophysics of connective tissues, problems of fine structure, the morphogenesis of cellular organelles; and, since 1975, the scattering of neutrons, synchrotron radiation and light by various biological systems. *Address:* Department of Zoology, University of Edinburgh, West Mains Road, Edinburgh EH9 3JT; 1/16 Sunbury Place, Dean Village, Edinburgh EH4 3BY. *Club:* Athenæum.

*Died 16 June 1984.*

**RANDALL, Sir Richard (John),** Kt 1964; BEcon; ACIS; Secretary to the Treasury, Commonwealth of Australia, 1966–71; *b* 13 Oct. 1906; *s* of G. Randall, Birkdale, Queensland; *m* 1945, Nora Barry, *d* of T. J. Clyne; two *s* one *d. Educ:* Wynnum High School; University of Sydney (BEcon, 1st cl. hons). Carnegie Research Scholar, Sydney University, 1937; Research Officer, Premier's Office, Sydney, 1937–39; Commonwealth Treasury, 1940. Served with AIF, 1941–45. *Recreations:* golf, fishing. *Address:* 5 Throsby Crescent, Narrabundah, Canberra, ACT 2604, Australia. *Clubs:* Royal Canberra Golf, Commonwealth (Canberra).

*Died 15 Nov. 1982.*

**RANDELL, John Bulmer;** Physician for Psychological Medicine, Charing Cross Hospital, since 1949; *b* 25 Aug. 1918; 2nd *s* of Percy G. Randell and Katie E. Bulmer; *m* 1944, Margaret Davies; one *d. Educ:* The College, Penarth; Welsh Nat. School of Medicine. BSc (Wales) 1938; MB, BCh (Wales) 1941; MD 1960. MO, Cefn Coed Hosp., 1941; MO, Sully Hosp., 1941–42; Temp. Surg. Lieut, RNVR, 1942–46; DPM 1945. First Asst MO, York Clinic, Guy's Hosp., 1946–48; MRCP 1947; FRCP 1964; FRCPsych 1971; Psychotherapist, St George's Hosp., 1948–51; Asst Psychiatrist, St Thomas' Hosp., 1949–59. *Publication:* Sexual Variations, 1973. *Recreations:* photography, cooking, gardening. *Address:* 118 Harley Street, W1. *T:* 01-486 2494. *Club:*

*Died 30 April 1982.*

**RANDOLPH, Cyril George;** *b* 26 June 1899; *s* of late Felton Randolph; *m* 1927, Betty Dixey (*d* 1983); one *d. Educ:* Christ's Hospital. A Man. Dir, Glyn, Mills & Co., 1941–64; Chairman: Sun Life Assurance Society, 1953–71 (Director, 1943–71); General Funds Investment Trust, 1965–73 (Director, 1964–73); Household & General Insurance Co. Ltd, 1965–71. Almoner, Christ's Hospital. *Recreation:* golf. *Address:* c/o Brent House, N Warnborough, Basingstoke. *Club:* New Zealand Golf (West Byfleet).

*Died 19 June 1985.*

**RANDOLPH, Ven. Thomas Berkeley;** Archdeacon of Hereford, 1959–70, Archdeacon Emeritus, since 1970; Canon Residentiary of Hereford Cathedral, 1961–70; *b* 15 March 1904; *s* of Felton George Randolph, Barrister-at-law, and Emily Margaret Randolph, Chichester, Sx; *m* 1935, Margaret, *d* of Rev. H. C. R. F. Jenner, Vennwood, Hereford and Wenvoe, Glam; two *s* one *d. Educ:* Christ's Hospital; Queen's College, Oxford (Scholar). BA (2nd Class Theology) 1927; MA 1932; Cuddesdon. Curate of St Mary's, Portsea, 1928–33; Chaplain (Eccles. Est.) St Paul's Cathedral, Calcutta, 1934–37; Vicar of Eastleigh, 1938–46; Vicar of St Mary the Virgin with All Saints, St Saviour's, St Mark's and St Matthew's, Reading, 1946–59. Proctor in Convocation for the Diocese of Oxford, 1950–55; Hon. Canon of Christ Church, Oxford, 1957–59; Vicar of Wellington, Hereford, 1959–61. *Address:* 14 Heatherwood, Midhurst, West Sussex. *T:* Midhurst 2765.

*Died 31 May 1987.*

**RANDRUP, Michael;** retired; *b* 20 April 1913; *s* of Soeren Revsgaard and Alexandra Randrup, Skive, Denmark; *m* 1941, Betty Perry (*d* 1949); one *s* one *d; m* 1954, Florence May Dryden. *Educ:* King's School, Canterbury; Chelsea College of Aeronautics. Learned to fly,

1934; RAF, 1940–46; OC Engine Research Flight RAE, 1945; Chief Test Pilot, D. Napier & Son Ltd, 1946–60; Manager, British Aircraft Corporation, Saudi Arabia, 1966–73. Aircraft Altitude World Record, 1957; Britannia Trophy, 1958; Derry Richards Meml Trophy, 1958. *Address:* 10 Fairlawn Road, Lytham, Lancs.
*Died Jan.* 1984.

**RANFURLY,** 6th Earl of, *cr* 1831; **Thomas Daniel Knox,** KCMG 1955; Baron Welles, 1781; Viscount Northland, 1791; Baron Ranfurly (UK) 1826; Chairman, Inchcape Insurance Holdings Ltd, 1966–83; Director: Inchcape & Co. Ltd, 1966–83; a Member of Lloyd's, since 1947; *b* 29 May 1913; *s* of late Viscount Northland (killed in action, 1915) and Hilda, *d* of late Sir Daniel Cooper, 2nd Bt; *S* grandfather, 1933; *m* 1939, Hermione, *e d* of late G. R. P. Llewellyn, Baglan Hall, Monmouth Road, Abergavenny, Mon; one *d. Educ:* Eton; Trinity Coll., Cambridge. ADC to Gov.-Gen. of Australia, 1936–38; served European War of 1939–45 (prisoner). Governor and C-in-C, Bahamas, 1953–56. Colonial Mutual Life Assurance Soc. Ltd (London Bd), 1966–82. Chairman London Scout Council, 1957–65; Chief Scout's Commissioner, Greater London, 1965–79. President, Shaftesbury Homes and "Arethusa" Training Ship, 1959–83; Chairman: Madame Tussauds Ltd, 1971–80; Bd of Governors, London Clinic, 1973–84; Ranfurly Library Service Ltd. Steward, Jockey Club, 1973–75. *Heir: kinsman* Gerald François Needham Knox [*b* 4 Jan. 1929; *m* 1955, Rosemary, *o d* of late Air Vice-Marshal Felton Vesey Holt, CMG, DSO; two *s* two *d*]. *Address:* Great Pednor, Chesham, Bucks. *T:* Gt Missenden 2155. *Clubs:* White's; Jockey (Newmarket). *Died* 6 *Nov.* 1988.

**RANKIN, Dame Annabelle (Jane Mary),** DBE 1957; Australian High Commissioner, New Zealand, 1971–74; *b* Brisbane; *d* of Mrs A. Rankin, Brisbane, and late Col C. D. W. Rankin, former Qld MLA for many years and sometime Minister for Railways; unmarried. *Educ:* Childers and Howard State Schools, Queensland; Glennie Memorial School, Toowoomba, Queensland. Clerk in Trustee Company; State Sec., Queensland Girl Guides' Assoc. War Service: YWCA Assistant Commissioner for Queensland, attached to Australian Women's Services, 1943–46. Appointed Organiser, Junior Red Cross, Queensland, 1946. First Queensland woman to enter Federal Parliament; Senator for Queensland, 1946–71; Mem., of Public Works Cttee, 1950; Govt Whip, Senate, 1951–66; Minister of Housing, 1966–71. Mem., Parly Standing Cttee on Broadcasting, 1947; Whip of Senate Opposition, 1947; Vice-Pres, Liberal Party of Australia, Queensland Div., 1949; Mem., Australian delegn to Commonwealth Parly Assoc. Conf., Ottawa, 1952. Represented Austr. Govt at Independence Celebrations, Mauritius, 1968. *Recreations:* motoring, reading. *Address:* 79 Captain Cook Parade, Deception Bay, Qld, Australia. *Clubs:* Moreton, Lyceum (Brisbane). *Died* 30 *Aug.* 1986.

**RANKIN, Sir Hugh (Charles Rhys),** 3rd Bt, *cr* 1898; FSAScot 1948; Member, Standing Council of the Baronetage, since 1979; Representative to District Council Perth CC (Eastern District), 1949, Perth CC 1950; Councillor for Boro' of Rattray and Blairgowrie, 1949; joined RASC as 2nd Lieut, May 1940, at age of 41 years; Captain 1940–45, India; sheep farmer and a judge of sheep at prominent shows; formerly Senior Vice-President of the Western Islamic Association; a former Vice-President of Scottish National Liberal Association; lived during the reigns of six sovereigns; *b* 8 Aug. 1899; *er s* of Sir Reginald Rankin, 2nd Bt, and Hon. Nest Rice (*d* 1943), 2nd *d* of 6th Baron Dynevor; changed his names by Scotch law in July 1946 to above; *S* father, 1931; *m* 1932, Helen Margaret (*d* 1945), *e d* of Sir Charles Stewart, KBE, 1st Public Trustee, and widow of Capt. Colin Campbell, Scots Guards; *m* 1946, Robina Kelly, FSA (Scot.), SRN, Cordon Bleu (Edin.), Crieff, Perthshire. *Educ:* Harrow. Served in 1st Royal Dragoon Guards in Sinn Feinn Campaign, 1920–22 (oldest surviving mem.); ex-Pres. Clun Forest Sheep Breeders Assoc., 1928, and their representative to National Sheep Breeders Association that year; whole-time 'piece-work' shearer, in W Australia, covering area between Bunbury and Broome, 1929–31; in 1938 was a representative on committee of British sheep breeders in London appointed to petition Government *re* sheep industry. Runner-up All Britain Sheep Judging Competition (6,000 entrants), 1962. A writer on agricultural stock; expert on Highland problems; was Brit. Rep., 1937, to 1st all European Muslim Congress at Geneva; a practising Non-Theistic Theravada Buddhist since 1944, and performed Holy Buddhist Pilgrimage, Nov. 1944, the 2nd Britisher to do so; Vice-Pres. World's Buddhist Assoc., 1945. Joined Labour Party 1939 and held extreme political views; sometime Dominion Home Ruler for Scotland, member Scottish National Party; joined Scottish Communist Party, 1945, resigned 1980; Welsh Republican Nationalist and Welsh speaker; left-side Labour; also zealous SNP who desired an independent Red Republic of all Scotland, exc. Orkneys and Shetlands. Made archaeological discoveries in Dumfries, 1977–. Mem. Roy. Inst. and Roy. Soc. of Arts; Hereditary Piper of the Clan Maclaine. News of the World K t of the Road (for courtesy in motor driving). Broadsword Champion of British Army (Cavalry), 1921. *Publications:* articles in agricultural publications, etc. *Recreations:* golf (held an amateur

record amongst golfers of Gt Britain in having played on 382 separate courses of UK and Eire), shooting, coarse fishing, hunting, motoring, cycling on mountain tracks to tops of British mountains (Pres. Rough Stuff Cycling Assoc., 1956); study of ancient track ways; bowls, tennis, archæology (wife and himself the only persons to have crawled under dwarf fir forest for last ½ mile of most northerly known section of any Roman road in Europe, terminating opposite end of Kirriemuir Golf Course), study of domestic animals, speaking on politics, especially *re* Scottish Home Rule and Highland problems. *Heir: nephew* Ian Niall Rankin [*b* 19 Dec. 1932; *s* of Arthur Niall Talbot Rankin and of Lady Jean Rankin, DCVO; *m* 1st, 1959, Alexandra, *o d* of Adm. Sir Laurence Durlacher, KCB, OBE, DSC; one *s* one *d*; 2nd, 1980, Mrs June Norman, *d* of late Captain Thomas Marsham-Townshend; one *s*]. *Address:* Bracken Cottage, Kindallachan, Pitlochry, Perthshire PH9 0NW. *T:* Ballinluig 472. *Clubs:* Royal and Ancient Golf (St Andrews), Burns (Dumfries). *Died* 25 *April* 1988.

**RANKINE, Sir John (Dalzell),** KCMG 1954 (CMG 1947); KCVO 1956; *b* 8 June 1907; *o s* of late Sir Richard Rankine, KCMG; *m* 1939, Janet Grace (*d* 1976), *d* of Major R. L. Austin, Clifton, Bristol; one *d. Educ:* Christ's College, Christchurch, New Zealand; Exeter College, Oxford. BA 1930; entered Colonial Administration Service as Cadet, Uganda, 1931; Asst Sec. East African Governor's Conference, 1939; First Asst Sec., 1942; Asst Colonial Sec., Fiji, 1942; Colonial Sec., Barbados, 1945; Chief Secretary, Kenya, 1947–51; Chairman, Development and Reconstruction Authority. British Resident, Zanzibar, 1952–54; administered Govts of Barbados and Kenya on various occasions; Governor, Western Region, Nigeria, 1954–60. KStJ 1958. Brilliant Star of Zanzibar (1st Class), 1954. *Recreations:* tennis, squash, golf. *Address:* 12A Crittles Court, Townsland Road, Wadhurst, East Sussex TN5 6BY. *T:* Wadhurst 3642. *Clubs:* Athenæum, MCC, Queen's.
*Died* 19 *Feb.* 1987.

**RANSOM, Charles Frederick George,** CMG 1956; OBE 1950; an Historian, Historical Section of Cabinet Office, since 1972; Director of the Centre for Contemporary European Studies, University of Sussex, 1973–74, Fellow of the Centre, 1968–80; *b* 9 July 1911; *s* of late Charles Edward Ransom and Elizabeth Ransom, Harrow, Middlesex; *m* 1943, Eileen Mary Emily, *d* of late Rt Rev. A. I. Greaves, Bishop Suffragan of Grimsby, DD; two *s* one *d. Educ:* Harrow CGS; University College, London (Ricardo Scholar, 1933–35). Schoolmaster and Univ. Extra-Mural Lecturer, 1936–40. Served in UK and Italy, York and Lancaster Regt (Major), 1940–46. FO 1946; First Sec., HM Embassy, Rome, 1958–61; FO Supernumerary Fellow, St Antony's Coll., Oxford, 1966–67. *Publications:* The European Community and Eastern Europe, 1973; (jtly) British Intelligence in the Second World War, vol. I, 1979, vol. II, 1981, vol. III, Part 1, 1984; articles on European affairs. *Recreations:* music, literature, gardening. *Address:* Ladyfield, Etchingham, East Sussex TN19 7AG. *T:* 216.
*Died* 20 *July* 1986.

**RANSOME, Maj.-Gen. Robert St George Tyldesley,** CB 1946; CBE 1944; MC 1940; *b* 22 June 1903; *s* of Dr A. S. Ransome; *m* 1947, Kathleen, *widow* of Brig. C. Leslie-Smith, IA. *Educ:* Winchester Coll.; Royal Military College, Sandhurst. Joined Royal Fusiliers, 1924; Instructor, Royal Military College, Sandhurst, 1935–37; Staff College, 1938–39; BEF 1939–40 (despatches, MC); Instructor, Senior Staff College, 1940; served in Mediterranean, Middle East, 1941–43; commanded 11th Battalion Royal Fusiliers, 1942. Visited Middle East, Quebec, S Africa, Yalta, Potsdam, Italy, France, etc, 1943–45; Vice-QMG to the Forces (Maj.-Gen.), 1946; idc 1947; BGS, GHQ Far East, 1948; Comdr Scottish Beach Bde (TA), 1950; Malaya, 1950 (despatches); Services Adviser, UK High Commission, Germany, 1954–55; Chief (Maj.-Gen), Jt Services Liaison Organisation, BAOR, 1955–58, retd. Deputy Colonel, Royal Fusiliers, 1962–63. Chm., Royal Fusiliers' Old Comrades Assoc., 1960–76. *Recreations:* gardening, shooting, military history. *Address:* Wilford Cottage, Melton, Suffolk. *Clubs:* Army and Navy, MCC. *Died* 5 *Nov.* 1982.

**RAPALLO, Rt. Rev. Edward,** DCnL; Bishop of Gibraltar (RC), since 1973; *b* 19 March 1914; *s* of Edward and Anne Rapallo. *Educ:* Pontifical Univ. of Salamanca, Spain; Lateran Univ., Rome (DCnL). Priest, 1937; Port Chaplain, Gibraltar, 1939–45; Cathedral Choir Master, 1945–54; Diocesan Chancellor, 1955–67; Cathedral Administrator, 1956–72; Vicar General, 1967–72; Vicar Capitular 1973. Chaplain of HH The Pope, 1960; Hon. Prelate of HH The Pope, 1967. *Recreations:* reading, music. *Address:* Bishop's House, 4A Engineer Road, Gibraltar. *T:* 74995 and 4688.
*Died* 6 *Feb.* 1984.

**RAPER, Vice-Adm. Sir (Robert) George,** KCB 1971 (CB 1968); FEng; Director-General, Ships, 1968–74; Chief Naval Engineer Officer, 1968–74; *b* 27 Aug. 1915; *s* of Major Robert George Raper and Ida Jean (*née* MacAdam Smith); *m* 1940, Frances Joan St John (*née* Phillips); one *s* two *d. Educ:* RNC Dartmouth; RN Engineering

College, Keyham; Advanced Engineering Course RNC Greenwich. Sen. Engineer, HMS Edinburgh, 1940 until ship was sunk, 1942 (despatches); Turbine Research Section, Admiralty, 1942–45; Engineer Officer, HMS Broadsword, Battleaxe, Crossbow, 1945–47; Comdr, 1947; Engineer-in-Chief's Dept, Admiralty, 1948–51; Engr Officer, HMS Birmingham, 1952–54; lent to RCN, 1954; Technical Sec. to Engineer-in-Chief of the Fleet, 1955–57; Capt. 1957; IDC 1958; in command HMS Caledonia, 1959–61; Dep. Dir of Marine Engineering, Admiralty, 1961–63; CSO (T) to Flag Officer Sea Training, 1963–65; Dir, Marine Engineering, MoD (Navy Dept), 1966–67. FEng 1976; FRINA; FIMechE; FIMarE (Pres. 1972); FRSA. *Address:* Oast Cottage, Chitcombe, Broad Oak, E Sussex TN31 6EX. *T:* Brightling (0424) 882908. *Died 30 Nov.* 1990.

**RAPP, Sir Thomas (Cecil),** KBE 1950; CMG 1945; MC; *b* Saltburn-by-the-Sea, 1893; *m* 1922, Dorothy, *d* of John Clarke; one *d* (and one *d* decd). *Educ:* Coatham School; Sidney Sussex College, Cambridge. Served European War (Duke of Wellington's Regiment TF), 1914–18, retiring with rank of Major; an assistant in Levant Consular Service, 1919; Acting Vice-Consul, Port Said, 1920; Vice-Consul, Cairo, 1922; Rabat, 1927; Consul, Sofia, 1931; Moscow, 1932; Zagreb, 1936; Consul-General at Zagreb, Jugoslavia, 1939–41. Captured by German armed forces and interned in Germany, 1941–43; Consul-General, Tabriz, 1943–44; Salonica, 1944–45; Minister to Albania (did not proceed), 1946; Deputy head and subsequently head of British Economic Mission to Greece, 1946–47; Ambassador to Mexico, 1947–50; Head of British Middle East Office, Cairo, 1950–53. *Recreation:* walking. *Address:* York Cottage, Sandgate, Kent. *T:* Folkestone 38594. *Died 22 Dec.* 1984.

**RASH, Mrs Doreen E. A.;** *see* Wallace, D.

**RASHLEIGH, Sir Harry (Evelyn Battie),** 5th Bt, *cr* 1831; *b* 17 May 1923; *er s* of late Captain Harry Rashleigh, JP (3rd *s* of 3rd Bt) and Jane Henrietta, *d* of late E. W. Rashleigh, Stoketon, Saltash, Cornwall; *S* kinsman 1951; *m* 1954, Honora Elizabeth Sneyd, *d* of G. S. Sneyd, The Watch House, Downderry, Cornwall; one *s* three *d. Educ:* Wellington Sch., Som. Served War of 1939–45, Westminster Dragoons, 1941–45; 79th Armoured Div. Experimental Wing, 1945–46. Mechanical Engineer with John Mowlem & Co. Ltd, UK, 1947–48; John Mowlem & Co. Ltd, Tanganyika, East Africa, 1948–50; Earth Moving & Construction Ltd, Tanganyika, East Africa, 1948–51; Engineer, UK, 1951–54; farming, Kampi-ya-Moto, Kenya, 1954–65; farming, Holdstrong Farm, Coryton, 1965–71, retired. *Recreations:* shooting, sailing. *Heir:* s Richard Harry Rashleigh, *b* 8 July 1958. *Address:* Stowford Grange, Lewdown, near Okehampton, Devon. *T:* Lewdown 237. *Club:* Royal Fowey Yacht. *Died 6 Sept.*1984.

**RASMUSSEN, Prof. Steen Eiler;** architect; Professor of Architecture, Royal Academy of Fine Arts, Copenhagen, 1938–68; *b* Copenhagen, 9 Feb. 1898; *s* of General Eiler Rasmussen; *m* 1934, Karen Margrete Schrøder (*d* 1985); two *d. Educ:* Metropolitanskolen; Royal Academy of Fine Arts, Copenhagen. Three first prizes in town planning competitions, 1919. Mem. Danish Roy. Acad. of Fine Arts, 1922; Lecturer at Architectural Sch. of the Academy, 1924; Architect to Municipal Town Planning Office, Copenhagen, 1932–38. Pres. Copenhagen Regional Planning Cttee, 1945–58. Visiting Professor in USA: Massachusetts Inst. of Technology, 1953, Yale, 1954, Philadelphia, 1958, Berkeley, 1959. Lethaby Professor, Roy. College of Art, London, 1958. Designed: Tingbjerg Housing Estate, Copenhagen, 1953–68; Schools, Town Hall. Hon. Corr. Member: RIBA London, Bavarian Acad. of Fine Arts, 1958; American Institute of Architects, 1962; Hon. Royal Designer for Industry, London, 1947; Hon. Dr: Technische Hochschule Munich; Univ. of Lund. *Publications:* London, the Unique City, 1937; Towns and Buildings, 1951; Experiencing Architecture, 1959. *Recreation:* to doze in a chair thinking of future books. *Address:* Dreyersvej 9, 2960 Rungsted Kyst, Denmark. *T:* 4286 3510.
*Died 20 June* 1990.

**RASUL, Syed Alay;** Hon. Chairman, Federation of Bangladesh Associations, UK and Europe, since 1974; consultant, Ethnic Advice and Information, since 1983; *b* 1 Feb. 1931; *s* of late Syed Ahmed Rasul and Khodeja Rasul; *m* 1956, Kamrunnessa Rasul; three *s* one *d* (and one *d* decd). *Educ:* Univ. of Aligarh, India (BA 1950); Univ. of Dacca, Bangladesh (MA 1953); Univ. of Manchester (Dipls: Adult Educn and Community Development 1963, Social Admin. 1964; Pres., Pakistan Students Soc., 1963–64); High Wycombe Coll. of Technology. NEBSS Cert., 1974; UN and Govt of Pakistan Cert. of Merit in Community Develt, 1956. Manpower Survey Officer, Pakistan Govt, 1955; E Pakistan Government: Social Welfare Organiser, 1956–60; Divl Welfare Organiser, 1960–62; Exec. Sec., Pakistan Welfare and Inf. Centre, Manchester, 1964–67; Sen. Community Relations Officer, Sheffield, 1967–82. Gen. Sec., E Pakistan Conf. of Social Work, 1956–57; Hon. Sec. Gen., Standing Conf. of Asian Organisations, UK, 1970–82; EC Mem., UK Immigrants Advisory Service, 1977– (Hon. Vice-Chm. 1975); Convenor, EEC Migrant Workers Forum, 1975–; founder

Mem., Bangladesh Immigration and Adv. Service, 1978–; Chm., Campaign for Increases in Pensions Paid Abroad, 1980–81. Member: BBC Adv. Council for Asian Unit, 1965–70; Electricity Consumer Council, 1977–; presenter and broadcaster, Asian programme, Radio Sheffield, 1966–76. Governor, Waltheaf Comp. Sch., Sheffield, 1978–; Gen. Sec., Aligarh Muslim Univ. Old Boys' Assoc., UK, 1983– (Pres., 1981–83). *Publications:* 6 special brochures; weekly column on immigration and race relations in Janomot. *Recreations:* billiards, music; visiting places and meeting people. *Address:* 47 Blenheim Gardens, Wembley, Mddx HA9 7NP. *T:* 01–904 6007. *Died 2 Feb.* 1987.

**RATCLIFFE, John Ashworth,** CB 1965; CBE 1959 (OBE 1947); FRS 1951; FEng; MA; Director of Radio and Space Research Station, Slough, Oct. 1960–Feb. 1966; *b* 12 Dec. 1902; *s* of H. H. Ratcliffe, Rawtenstall, Lancs; *m* 1930, Nora Disley (decd); one *d* (and one *d* decd). *Educ:* Giggleswick School; Sidney Sussex College, Cambridge. Taught Physics at Cambridge and Research in Radio Wave Propagation, 1924–60 (War Service with Telecommunications Res. Est., Malvern); Reader in Physics, Cambridge University, 1947–60; Fellow of Sidney Sussex College, 1927–60, Hon. Fellow 1962. President: Physical Society, 1959–60; Section A, British Association, 1964; Chairman, Electronics Board, IEE, 1962–63; Vice-Pres., IEE, 1963–66, Pres., 1966. Hon. Pres., URSI; Foreign Fellow, Indian Nat. Sci. Acad. FEng 1976; FIEEE. Hon. FInstP; Hon. FIEE; Hon. DSc Kent, 1979. Faraday Medal (IEE), 1966; Royal Medal (Roy. Soc.), 1966; Guthrie Medal (Inst. Physics), 1971; Gold Medal (RAS), 1976. *Publications:* numerous papers in scientific journals on Radio Wave Propagation. *Address:* 193 Huntingdon Road, Cambridge CB3 0DL.
*Died 25 Oct.* 1987.

**RATCLIFFE, Reginald,** CB 1959; MBE 1943; Chief Executive, Machine Tool Division, Staveley Industries, 1965–68, retired; *b* 8 Jan. 1908; *s* of Elias Ratcliffe, Birkenhead; *m* 1933, Vera George; one *s* one *d. Educ:* Liverpool Univ. BEng 1930; MEng 1933; Carlton Stitt Medallist, 1930. Entered Royal Arsenal, Woolwich, as Technical Assistant, 1930; Royal Ordnance Factory, Nottingham, 1938; Dir of Instrument Production, Min. of Supply, 1954; Royal Ordnance Factories: Dep. Controller 1956–59; Controller 1959–64; Deputy Master General of the Ordnance (Production) 1964. President, Institution of Production Engineers, 1963–65. *Publications:* various contributions to technical journals. *Recreations:* tennis, swimming. *Address:* 43 Martins Drive, Ferndown, Dorset BH22 9SG. *T:* Ferndown 4081.
*Died 4 March* 1982.

**RATHBONE, Philip Richardson;** Secretary, Royal Town Planning Institute, 1960–75; *b* 21 May 1913; *s* of Herbert R. Rathbone, sometime Lord Mayor of Liverpool, and Winifred Richardson Evans, Wimbledon; *m* 1940, Angela, *d* of Captain A. B. de Beer, Liverpool; one *s* two *d. Educ:* Clifton Coll., Bristol; University Coll., Oxford. BA Hons Mod. History 1934. Sec., Housing Centre, London, 1935–39. Army, King's Regt, Liverpool; Personnel Selection, WO, 1939–45 (Major). Principal, Min. of Town and Country Planning, 1945–53; Sec., Royal Instn of Chartered Surveyors (Scotland), 1953–60. Hon. MRTPI, 1975. *Publications:* Paradise Merton: The Story of Nelson and the Hamiltons at Merton Place, 1973; The Angel and the Flame: the two marriages of Sir William Hamilton, 1978; A Wheelchair for all Seasons, 1981. *Recreations:* writing, Lady Hamilton. *Address:* 19 Raymond Road, SW19 4AD. *T:* 01–946 2478. *Died 31 Dec.* 1988.

**RATHCAVAN, 1st Baron,** *cr* 1953, of The Braid, Co. Antrim; **(Robert William) Hugh O'Neill,** Bt, *cr* 1929; PC (Ireland 1921, Northern Ireland 1922, Gt Brit. 1937); Hon. LLD, Queen's University Belfast; HM Lieutenant for County Antrim, 1949–59; *b* 8 June 1883; *o surv. s* of 2nd Baron O'Neill; *m* 1909, Sylvia (*d* 1972), *d* of Walter A. Sandeman of Morden House, Royston; two *s* (and one *s* decd). *Educ:* Eton; New Coll., Oxford, BA. Bar, Inner Temple, 1909; contested Stockport, 1906; MP (UU) Mid-Antrim, 1915–22, Co. Antrim, 1922–50, North Antrim, 1950–52; MP for County Antrim in the Parliament of Northern Ireland, 1921–29; first Speaker of the House of Commons of Northern Ireland, 1921–29; Chairman Cons Private Members' (1922) Committee, 1935–39; Parl. Under-Sec. of State for India and Burma, 1939–40; late Lt North of Ireland Imperial Yeomanry; late Captain Royal Irish Rifles and Major (general list); served in European War, 1915–18, France and Palestine. *Recreations:* shooting, fishing. *Heir:* s Rt Hon. Phelim Robert Hugh O'Neill, *b* 2 Nov. 1909. *Address:* Cleggan Lodge, Ballymena, Co. Antrim. *T:* Aughafatten 209; 28 Queen's Gate Gardens, SW7. *T:* 01-584 0358. *Clubs:* Carlton; Ulster (Belfast).
*Died 28 Nov.* 1982.

**RATHCREEDAN, 2nd Baron,** *cr* 1916; **Charles Patrick Norton,** TD; *b* 26 Nov. 1905; *er s* of 1st Baron and Marguerite Macel (*d* 1955), *d* of Sir Charles Huntington, 1st Bt, MP; *S* father, 1930; *m* 1946, Ann Pauline, *er d* of late Surgeon Capt. William Bastian, RN; two *s* one *d. Educ:* Wellington Coll.; Lincoln Coll., Oxford, MA. Called to

Bar, Inner Temple, 1931; admitted Solicitor, 1936; Major 4th Battalion Oxford and Buckinghamshire Light Inf., TA; served France, 1940; prisoner of war, 1940–45. Master, Founders' Co., 1970. *Recreation:* gardening. *Heir: s* Hon. Christopher John Norton [*b* 3 June 1949; *m* 1978, Lavinia, *d* of A. G. R. Ormiston, Coln Orchard, Arlington, Bibury, Glos; two *d*]. *Address:* Church Field, Fawley, Henley-on-Thames, Oxon RG9 6HZ. *T:* Henley (0491) 574160. *Died* 15 *May* 1990.

RATTER, John, CBE 1945 (OBE 1944); ERD 1953; retired; Railway Adviser, World Bank, Washington DC, 1970–74; *b* 15 May 1908; *s* of George Dempster Ratter, South Shields; *m* 1937, Eileen Cail, Knaresborough, Yorkshire; two *s* one *d*. *Educ:* St Peters School, York; Durham University. BSc; MICE. Various appointments as civil engineer with London and North Eastern Railway and London Passenger Transport Board, 1929–39; War of 1939–45: served with Royal Engineers, France, Africa and Italy, and in War Office; Deputy Director of Transportation, CMF, with rank of Colonel. Various appointments with LNE Railway and LPTB and Railway Exec., 1945–53; Chief Civil Engineer, British Transport Commission, 1953–54; Technical Adviser, BTC, 1954–58; Member: BTC, 1958–62. British Railways Board, 1963–70. Pres., Internat. Union of Railways, 1960–62. Legion of Merit (USA), 1944; Légion d'Honneur (France), 1963; Order of Merit, German Federal Republic, 1968; Comdr, Order of Leopold II, Belgium, 1969. *Address:* 7 Chester Close, Queens Ride, Barnes, SW13.
*Died* 25 *Dec.* 1985.

RAVEN, Rear-Adm. John Stanley, CB 1964; BSc, FIEE; *b* 5 Oct. 1910; *s* of Frederick William Raven; *m* 1935, Nancy, *d* of William Harold Murdoch; three *s*. *Educ:* Huddersfield College; Leeds University (BSc). Temp. RNVR Commission, 1939; transferred to RN, 1946; retired, 1965. *Recreation:* painting. *Address:* East Garth, School Lane, Collingham, Yorks. *Died* 15 *June* 1987.

RAVENSDALE, Thomas Corney, CMG 1951; retired; *b* 17 Feb. 1905; *s* of late Henry Ravensdale and late Lilian (*née* Corney); *m* (marriage dissolved); two *s*; *m* 1965, Mme Antoine Watteau (*née* Ricard). *Educ:* Royal Masonic Sch., Bushey, Herts; St Catharine's Coll., Cambridge. Acting Vice-Consul, Smyrna, 1928; 3rd Secretary, British Embassy, Ankara, 1929–34; 2nd Asst Oriental Sec., The Residency, Cairo, 1934–37; Vice-Consul, Bagdad, 1937–42; 1st Asst Oriental Sec., Brit. Embassy, Cairo, 1942–47; Oriental Counsellor, Cairo, 1948–51; Political Adviser, British Residency, Benghazi, 1951; Couns., Brit. Embassy in Libya, 1952–55; Ambassador to Dominican Republic, 1955–58; Insp. Foreign Service Establishments, 1958–60; Ambassador to the Republics of Dahomey, Niger, Upper Volta and the Ivory Coast, 1960–63. *Recreation:* gardening. *Address:* The Cottage, 13 rue de Penthièvre, Petit Andely, 27700 Les Andelys, France. *T:* (32) 54–16–38. *Club:* Athenæum. *Died* 26 *Dec.* 1990.

RAW, Rupert George, CMG 1979; UK Director, European Investment Bank, 1973–81; *b* 5 April 1912; *s* of late Captain Rupert George Raw, DSO, and late Winifred Melville (*née* Francis), later Lady Stuart-Menteth; *m* 1936, Joan Persica, *d* of Sir Alban Young, 9th Bt, KCMG, MVO; one *s* two *d*. *Educ:* Eton; Oxford (BA Hons History). Supplementary Reserve Scots Guards, Lt-Col; parachuted Yugoslavia. CCG, 1946–48; joined OEEC; Finance Director, 1952–55; Bank of England, 1955; Adviser to Governor, 1962–72, retired; Director of Banque Belge, 1973, resigned, 1977; Dep. Chm., Italian Internat. Bank, 1973–76, Chm. 1976–79, retired 1980. *Recreations:* tennis, skiing. *Address:* 23 Warwick Square, SW1.
*Died* 6 *Jan.* 1988.

RAWDEN-SMITH, Rupert Rawden; Metropolitan Stipendiary Magistrate, 1967–78, retired; *b* 24 Sept. 1912; *s* of late Dr Hoyland Smith; *m* 1941, Mollie Snow; one *s* one *d*. *Educ:* Rossall School; King's College, London University (LLB). Barrister, Middle Temple, 1939; Recorder of Sunderland, 1961–67. *Recreations:* gardening, travel. *Address:* 97 Church Road, Wimbledon, SW19 5AL. *T:* 01–946 4325. *Died* 31 *Jan.* 1985.

RAWLINSON, Sir Anthony (Keith), KCB 1978 (CB 1975); Chairman, Gaming Board for Great Britain, since 1985; *b* 5 March 1926; *s* of late Alfred Edward John Rawlinson, Bishop of Derby 1936–59, and Mildred Ansley Rawlinson (*née* Ellis); *m* 1956, Mary Hill; three *s*. *Educ:* Maidwell Hall; Eton; Christ Church, Oxford. Eton: King's Sch., 1939, Newcastle Schol., 1944, Captain of Sch. 1944; Christ Church, Open Schol. (classics), 1944. Gren. Gds (Lieut), 1944–47. Oxford: 1st Cl. Honour Mods (classics), 1949, 2nd Cl. Lit. Hum., 1951. Entered Civil Service by open competition as Asst Principal, 1951; Min. of Labour and Nat. Service, 1951–53; transferred to Treasury, 1953; Principal, 1955; seconded to Atomic Energy Authority as Private Sec. to Chairman, 1958–60; returned to Treasury, 1960: Asst Sec., 1963; Under-Sec., 1968; Dep. Sec., 1972; Econ. Minister and Head of UK Treasury and Supply Delegn, Washington, and UK Exec. Dir, IMF and IBRD, 1972–75; Department of Industry: Dep. Sec., 1975–76; Second Permanent Sec., 1976–77; Second Permanent Sec., HM Treasury, 1977–83;

Permanent Sec., Dept of Trade, 1983; Jt Permanent Sec., DTI, 1983–85. Chm., Mount Everest Foundn, 1970–71; Consultant, Drivers Jonas, 1985–; Dir, Fleming Universal Investment Trust, 1985–. Mem., C of E Central Bd of Finance, 1981–. Governor, Trent Coll., 1983. *Publications:* articles and reviews in mountaineering jls. Editor, Climbers' Club Jl, 1955–59. *Recreation:* mountaineering (Pres. OU Mountaineering Club, 1949–50). *Address:* 105 Corringham Road, NW11 7DL. *T:* 01–458 3402. *Clubs:* United Oxford & Cambridge University, Alpine (Hon. Sec., 1963–66, Vice-Pres., 1972–73). *Died* 22 *Feb.* 1986.

RAWSON, Elizabeth Donata, FBA 1988; Fellow and Tutor, Corpus Christi College, Oxford, since 1980; *b* 13 April 1934; *d* of Graham Stanhope Rawson and Ivy Marion Enthoven. *Educ:* St Paul's Girls' Sch.; Somerville Coll., Oxford (1st cl. Lit Hum). Craven Fellow, Oxford Univ., 1957; Leverhulme Res. Fellow, New Hall, Cambridge, 1959; Fellow and Coll. Lectr, New Hall, Cambridge, 1967. Visiting Lecturer: Pennsylvania State Univ., 1973; Princeton Univ., 1979; Vis. Prof., Nankai Univ., Tianjin, 1988. Hon. Sec., Soc. for the Promotion of Roman Studies, 1985–. *Publications:* The Spartan Tradition in European Thought, 1969; Cicero: a portrait, 1975; Intellectual Life in the Late Roman Republic, 1985; articles and reviews in learned jls. *Recreation:* the arts. *Address:* Corpus Christi College, Oxford OX1 4JF. *T:* Oxford 276756.
*Died* 10 *Dec.* 1988.

RAY, Rt. Rev. Chandu; Senior Lecturer at Haggai Institute for Advanced Leadership Training for men and women in the third world, since 1977, and co-ordinating Officer for Asian Evangelism since 1969; *b* 14 April 1912; Pakistani parentage; *m* Anita Joy (*née* Meggitt); two *s* three *d*. *Educ:* D. J. Sind Coll., Karachi; Bishop's Coll., Calcutta. Bursar, Bishop Cotton Sch., Simla. Deacon, 1943; Priest, 1943. Vicar, St Philip's Church, Hyderabad, 1944; Sec., British and Foreign Bible Soc. in Pakistan, 1948; Canon of Lahore Cathedral, 1954; Archdeacon of Karachi, 1956; Asst Bishop of Lahore and Bishop in Karachi, 1957; first Bishop of Karachi, 1963–69. Hon. Dr of Sacred Theology, Wycliff, Toronto; Hon. Dr of Divinity, Huron, London. Gutenberg Award, 1978. *Publications:* (trans) Old Testament in Sindhi Language, 1954; (revised 2nd edn) New Testament in Sindhi, 1955. *Recreations:* hockey, cricket, tennis. *Address:* 4 Callington Avenue, City Beach, Perth, WA 6015, Australia. *T:* 385 8753.

RAY, Frederick Ivor, CB 1958; CBE 1953; BSc (Eng); FIEE; Telecommunications Consultant; *b* 18 Jan. 1899; *s* of Frederick Pedder Ray; *m* 1923, Katherine (*d* 1968), *d* of Hubert Abdy Fellowes, Newbury; two *s*. *Educ:* Royal British Orphan Sch.; Bournemouth School; Faraday House Electrical Engineering College. Served European War, 1917–19, RE. Entered GPO Engineering Dept, 1922; Sectional Engineer, 1932–35; Telephone Manager, Scotland West, 1935–39; Telecommunications Controller, NW Region, 1939; Controller Telephones, London, 1940–44; Assistant Secretary, 1944–48; Regional Director, London, 1948–56; Director of Inland Telecommunications, 1956–61; CPU Advr on Telecommunications, 1963–67; Dir, Internat. Press Telecommunications Council, 1965–67. *Recreations:* fishing, caravanning, golf. *Address:* 22A Edward Road, Bromley, Kent. *T:* 01-464 3859. *Died* 18 *Oct.* 1983.

RAY, Gordon Norton; President of the John Simon Guggenheim Memorial Foundation, 1963–85; *b* New York City, 8 Sept. 1915; *s* of Jesse Gordon and Jessie Norton Ray; unmarried. *Educ:* University of Indiana (AM); Harvard Univ. (AM, PhD). Instructor in English, Harvard, 1940–42; Guggenheim Fellow, 1941–42, 1946, 1956–57. Lt, US Navy, serving aboard aircraft carriers Belleau Wood and Boxer, Pacific, 1942–46; Professor of English, 1946–60, Head of Dept, 1950–57, Vice-President and Provost, 1957–60, University of Illinois. Associate Secretary General, Guggenheim Foundn, 1960–61; Sec.-Gen., 1961–63. Rockefeller Fellow, 1948–49; Member US Educational Commn in UK, which established Fulbright program, 1948–49. Lowell Lectures, Boston, 1950; Walls Lectures, Pierpont Morgan Lib., 1982; Berg Professor, New York Univ. 1952–53; Professor of English, 1962–80, now Emeritus Professor; Lyell Reader in Bibliography, Oxford Univ., 1984–85. Advisor in literature, Houghton Mifflin Co., 1953–71. Member Commission on Trends in Education, Mod. Lang. Assoc., 1953–59, Trustee 1966–; Mem. Council, Smithsonian Instn, 1968–, Chm. 1970–; Dir and Treasurer, Amer. Council of Learned Socs, 1973–. Advisory Bd, Guggenheim Foundation, 1959–60, Trustee, 1963–; Trustee: Pierpont Morgan Library, 1970–; Rosenbach Foundn, 1972–81; New York Public Library, 1975–84 (Hon. Trustee, 1984–); Columbia Univ. Press, 1977–82; Winterthur Museum, 1977–; American Trust for the British Library, 1979–. Dir, Yaddo, 1979–. Hon. LittD: Monmouth Coll., 1959; Syracuse, 1961; Duke, 1965; Illinois, 1968; Northwestern, 1974; Maryland, 1982; Hon. LLD: New York, 1961; Tulane, 1963; California, 1968; Columbia, 1969; Southern California, 1974; Pennsylvania, 1978; Hon. LHD, Indiana, 1964. FRSL 1948. Fellow, Amer. Acad. of Arts and Sciences, 1962; Mem., Amer. Philosophical Soc., 1977. Joseph

Henry Medal, Smithsonian Instn, 1980. *Publications:* Letters and Private Papers of Thackeray, 4 vols, 1945–46; The Buried Life, 1952; Thackeray: The Uses of Adversity, 1955; Henry James and H. G. Wells, 1958; Thackeray: The Age of Wisdom, 1958; H. G. Wells and Rebecca West, 1974; The Illustrator and the Book in England from 1790 to 1914, 1976; The Art of the French Illustrated Book 1700–1914, 2 vols, 1982, etc; contrib. to magazines and learned jls. *Recreations:* book-collecting, travel. *Address:* (business) 90 Park Avenue, New York, NY 10016; (home) 25 Sutton Place South, New York, NY 10022, USA. *Clubs:* Athenæum, Roxburghe (London); Harvard, Grolier (President, 1965–69), Century (New York).
*Died 15 Dec.* 1986.

**RAYLEIGH, 5th Baron** *cr* 1821; **John Arthur Strutt;** *b* 12 April 1908; *e s* of 4th Baron Rayleigh, FRS, and late Mary Hilda, 2nd *d* of 4th Earl of Leitrim; *S* father, 1947; *m* 1934, Ursula May (*d* 1982), *o d* of Lieut-Colonel R. H. R. Brocklebank, DSO and Charlotte Carissima, *o d* of General Sir Bindon Blood, GCB, GCVO. *Educ:* Eton; Trinity College, Cambridge. *Heir: nephew* John Gerald Strutt, *b* 4 June 1960. *Address:* Terling Place, Chelmsford, Essex. *T:* Terling 235; 01–453 3235. *Died 21 April* 1988.

**RAYMOND, Sir Stanley (Edward),** Kt 1967; FCIT; FBIM; *b* 10 Aug. 1913; *s* of late Frederick George and Lilian Grace Raymond; *m* 1st, 1938, Enid (*d* 1979), *d* of Capt. S. A. Buley, Polruan-by-Fowey; one *s*; 2nd, 1981, Mrs Constance Clarke. *Educ:* Orphanage; Grammar Sch., Hampton, Mx. Entered Civil Service, 1930. Asst Sec., Soc. of Civil Servants, 1939–45. War service in Royal Artillery, 1942–45; Lieutenant-Colonel on demobilisation. London Passenger Transport Board, 1946; British Road Services, 1947; BTC, 1955; Director of Establishment and Staff, 1956; Chief Commercial Manager, Scottish Region, British Railways, 1957 and Asst Gen. Manager, 1959; Traffic Adviser, BTC, 1961; Chm. Western Railway Board, and General Manager, Western Region, British Railways, 1962–63; Member, 1963, a Vice-Chm., 1964–65, and Chm., 1965–67, British Railways Bd. Chairman: Horserace Betting Levy Bd, 1972–74; Gaming Bd for GB, 1968–77. *Recreations:* walking, travelling the world. *Address:* 12 Fairlawns, 159 Kingsway, Hove, Sussex BN3 4FZ. *Died 3 May* 1988.

**RAYNER, Neville,** JP, FRSA; Underwriting Member of Lloyd's, since 1963; General Commissioner of Income Tax, since 1965; property consultant, since 1936; *b* 1914; *m* 1941, Elsie Mary (*née* Lindley); two adopted *s. Educ:* Emanuel Sch., SW11. Commd RAFVR(T), 1941–45. Mem., Court of Common Council, City of London, 1960–81; Sheriff of London, 1971–72. Former Mem., LCC and Wandsworth Borough Council. Director, Bedford Building Soc. Parish Clerk, Priory Church of St Bartholomew-the-Great, Smithfield; Mem., Honourable Artillery Co.; Liveryman: Painter Stainers Co.; Basketmakers Co. (Prime Warden, 1980–81); Glovers' Co. (Master, 1982–83); Playing Card Makers Co.; Mem. Ct of Assts, Worshipful Co. of Parish Clerks. JP, Inner London, 1959; Dep. Chm., Greater London (SW) Valuation Appeals Court, 1950–86; Pres., Greater London Br., Royal British Legion, 1962– (Gold Badge, 1979); Vice-Pres., Nat. Union of Ratepayers. FRVA, FSVA, FCIArb, FInstD, F Land Inst. Past Pres., Farringdon Ward Club. Member: Magistrates Assoc.; British Olympic Assoc.; Magic Circle; Council, Gardeners' Royal Benevolent Soc.; Royal Soc. St George (Vice-Pres., City of London Br.); Luxembourg Soc.; Netherlands Soc.; Sheriff's Soc.; Court, Nene Coll., Northampton; Chm., Rayner Court and Red Oaks Sheltered Housing, Henfield. OStJ. Order of Sacred Treasure (Japan), 1972; Star of Afghanistan, 1972; Comdr, Order of Orange-Nassau (Holland), 1972; Couronne de Chêne (Luxembourg), 1972; Comendador de la Orden del Merito Civil (Spain), 1975. *Recreations:* magic, travel, carpentry. *Address:* Old Selsfield, Turners Hill, West Sussex RH10 4PS. *T:* Copthorne 715203; 1 Montpelier Mews, SW7 1HB. *T:* 01–589 3939. *Clubs:* Guildhall, United Wards (Past Pres.), City Livery, Pilgrims, Press, Anglo-Spanish, Wig and Pen, Belfry, St Stephen's Constitutional.
*Died 21 April* 1988.

**RAYNOR, Prof. Geoffrey Vincent,** MA, DPhil, DSc Oxon; FRS 1959; Professor of Physical Metallurgy, University of Birmingham, 1954–81, later Emeritus; *b* 2 Oct. 1913; *y s* of late Alfred Ernest Raynor, Nottingham; *m* 1943, Emily Jean, *er d* of late Dr Geo. F. Brockless, London; three *s. Educ:* Nottingham High School; Keble Coll., Oxford, 1st cl. Hons, School of Natural Science (Chemistry), 1936, Hon. Fellow, 1972. Research Assistant, Oxford University, 1936; Departmental Demonstrator in Inorganic Chemistry, 1937–45; DSIR Senior Research Award, 1938–41. Metallurgical research for Ministry of Supply and Ministry of Aircraft Production, 1939–45; University of Birmingham: ICI Research Fellow, 1945–47; Beilby Memorial Award, 1947; Reader in Theoretical Metallurgy, 1947–49; Prof. of Metal Physics, 1949–54; Feeney Prof. of Physical Metallurgy, and Head of Dept of Physical Metallurgy and Science of Materials, 1955–69; Dean, Faculty of Science and Engineering, 1966–69; Dep. Principal, 1969–73. Vis. Prof. of Metallurgy, Chicago Univ., 1951–52; Battelle Vis. Prof., Ohio State Univ., 1962; Royal Soc. Leverhulme Vis. Prof., Witwatersrand

Univ., 1974; Vis. Prof., Univ. of NSW, 1975; Canadian Commonwealth Vis. Fellowship, Queen's Univ., 1979; Leverhulme Emeritus Fellow, 1981–83. Vice-President: Inst. of Metals, 1953–56; Instn of Metallurgists, 1963–66, 1977–80; President: Birmingham Metallurgical Assoc., 1965–66; Keble Assoc., 1974. Fellow, New York Acad. of Science, 1961; Member several metallurgical research committees. Walter Rosenhain Medal, Inst. of Metals, 1951; Heyn Medal, Deutsche Gesellschaft für Metallkunde, 1956; Hume-Rothery Prize, Metals Soc., 1981. *Publications:* Introduction to the Electron Theory of Metals, Inst. of Metals monograph and report series, No 4, 1947; contrib. to Butterworth's scientific publications: Progress in Metal Physics, 1949, and Metals Reference Book, 1949; The Structure of Metals and Alloys (with W. Hume-Rothery), 1954; The Physical Metallurgy of Magnesium and its Alloys, 1959; scientific papers on theory of metals and alloys in Proc. Royal Soc., Philosophical Mag., Trans. Faraday Soc., and metallurgical journals. *Recreations:* rowing and sculling. *Address:* 94 Gillhurst Road, Harborne, Birmingham B17 8PA. *T:* 021–429 3176. *Club:* Athenæum. *Died 20 Oct.* 1983.

**REA, 2nd Baron,** *cr* 1937, of Eskdale; **Philip Russell Rea,** PC 1962; OBE 1946; MA; DL; JP; 2nd Bt, *cr* 1935; Underwriter at Lloyd's; *b* London, 7 Feb. 1900; *e s* of 1st Baron Rea of Eskdale and Evelyn (*d* 1930), *d* of J. J. Muirhead; *S* father, 1948; *m* 1922, Lorna Smith (*d* 1978), writer; one *d* (one *s* decd). *Educ:* Westminster; Christ Church, Oxford (exhbnr); Grenoble Univ. Grenadier Guards, 1918–19; served War of 1939–45: KRRC, attached Special Forces in Britain, France, N Africa, Malta, Egypt and Italy, 1940–46 (Lt-Col; despatches; OBE). Founded (with Basil Herbert) Oxford Univ. Liberal Club, 1919. Prospective Parly Candidate (L) for Darwen, 1938–42; FO, 1946–50; Chief Liberal Whip, House of Lords, 1950–55; Dep. Lord Chm. of Cttees, 1950–60; Dep. Lord Speaker, 1950–77; Liberal Leader, House of Lords, 1955–67; Pres., Liberal Party, 1955. Leader, British Parly Delegn to Burma and Indonesia, 1954; UK Deleg. to Council of Europe, Strasbourg, 1957; Mem. Parly Delegn to USA, and to Hong Kong and Ceylon, 1958. Member: Cumberland Develt Council, 1950–60; BBC Adv. Council, 1957–62; Political Honours Scrutiny Cttee, 1962–77; Lord Chancellor's Adv. Cttee, Inner London, 1965–76; Outward Bound Trust Council. President: Fell Dales Assoc., 1950–60; Elizabethan Club, 1965–66; Noblemen and Gentlemen's Catch Club, 1967–74. Pres., Nat. Liberal Club, 1966–. Governor, Westminster Sch., 1955–78. DL Cumberland, 1955, Greater London, 1966–76; JP Cumberland, 1950–66; JP London, 1966–. Officer, Order of Crown (Belgium); Chevalier, Legion of Honour, and Croix de Guerre with palm (France); Grand Commandeur, Ordre de Mérite (France). Hon. Adm. Louisiana, USA. *Heir: n* John Nicolas Rea, MD [*b* 6 June 1928; *m* 1951, Elizabeth Anne, *d* of late W. H. Robinson; four *s*]. *Address:* 5 St John's House, 30 Smith Square, SW1. *T:* 01-222 4040. *Clubs:* Garrick, Grillions, Special Forces (Pres. 1955–77), National Liberal (Pres.). *Died 22 April* 1981.

**READ, Cyril Norman, (Charles),** CBE 1983; Chairman, Confederation of Information Communication Industries, since 1984; *b* 5 Feb. 1925; *s* of Ernest Archibald Read and Rosa Read; *m* 1950, Patricia Edna May King; one *s* two *d. Educ:* Chatham House Grammar Sch., Ramsgate; London Sch. of Econs and Pol. Science (BSc Econ 1951). Served War, Royal Corps of Signals, 1943–47. ITT Gp, 1951–56; Philips Electrical Industries, 1956–64; Scicon, 1964–67; Logica, 1967–68; Director: IBRO, 1968–83; IT, PO, 1983–86. Chm., Prime Minister's IT Adv. Panel, 1981–86; Member: Computers System and Electronics Requirements Bd, Dept of Industry, 1973–78; Lindop Cttee on Data Protection, 1977–78; Alvey Cttee on 5th Generation Computing Res., 1983; ACARD, 1986–. *Publications:* articles in jls and conf. papers on information technology and on payment systems and banking. *Recreations:* walking, classical music and opera, art, crafts, DIY.
*Died 14 July* 1987.

**READ, Lt-Gen. Sir John (Hugh Sherlock),** KCB 1972; OBE 1944; retired; Adviser, West Africa Committee, since 1975; *b* 6 Sept. 1917; *s* of late Group Captain John Victor Read, Blunham, Bedfordshire, and Chacewater, Cornwall, and Elizabeth Hannah (*née* Link); *m* 1942, Mary Monica Wulfhilde Curtis (*d* 1985), *d* of late Henry Curtis, Spofforth, Yorks, and Harrogate; two *s* one *d. Educ:* Bedford School; RMA Woolwich; Magdalene Coll., Cambridge. BA (Cantab.) 1939. MA (Cantab.) 1944. Commissioned 2nd Lt RE, 1937. Served UK, France, Belgium, Egypt, Palestine, Greece, Austria at regimental duty and on staff, 1939–45, and UK, Austria, Germany, Hong Kong, 1945–57; GSO1, Singapore Base Dist, 1957; CO, Training Regt, RE, 1959; IDC, 1962; Min. of Defence (War Office), 1963; Comdr, Training Bde, RE, 1963; Asst Comdt, RMA, 1966–68; Director of Military Operations, MoD, 1968–70; ACDS (Policy), MoD, 1970–71; Dir, Internat. Mil. Staff, HQ, NATO, Brussels, 1971–75. Col Comdt, Corps of Royal Engineers, 1972–77. *Recreations:* fishing, shooting, gardening. *Address:* Bathealton Court, Bathealton, Taunton, Som TA4 2AJ. *T:* Wivelscombe 24134. *Club:* Oriental.
*Died 5 March* 1987.

**READ, Simon Holcombe Jervis,** CBE 1977; MC 1944; HM Diplomatic Service, retired 1977; Secretary, Game Farmers' Association, since 1977; *b* 7 Feb. 1922; *s* of John Dale Read and Evelyn Constance Read (*née* Bowen); *m* 1st, 1946, Bridget Elizabeth Dawson (marr. diss. 1959); two *s* one *d*; 2nd, 1960, Coelestine von der Marwitz. *Educ:* Winchester Coll. Served War: Private soldier, Essex Regt, 1940; commissioned 10th Baluch Regt, 1941; SOE and Detachment 101 (US Army), 1942, in Burma; service in Burma, Malaya, Thailand, Cambodia, Indo-China, China. Joined FCO, 1946; 3rd/2nd Sec., Singapore, Thailand, 1946–50; 1st Secretary: Hongkong, 1952–54; Iran, 1954–59; Berlin, 1959–64; UK, 1964–77. *Publication:* provisional check list of Birds of Iran (Teheran Univ.), 1958. *Recreations:* ornithology, shooting, gardening. *Address:* The Cottage, Little Chart, near Ashford, Kent. *T:* Pluckley 610. *Club:* Special Forces. *Died* 3 *Nov.* 1989.

**READER, Dame Audrey Tattie Hinchcliff,** DBE 1978 (OBE 1966); voluntary worker in several community organizations and in politics; *b* 9 Dec. 1903; *d* of William Henry Nicholls and Mabel Tattie Brimacombe Nicholls (*née* Mallett); *m* 1928, Reginald John Reader; one *d*. *Educ:* Macedon Primary Sch., Victoria; Malvern Coll., Melbourne. Housewife. Member: Victoria League for Commonwealth Friendship, Melbourne, to 1986; Royal Soc. of St George. Patron, Victorian Br., Freedom Coalition. *Recreations:* reading, writing, gardening. *Address:* 68 Millewa Avenue, Chadstone, Victoria 3148, Australia. *T:* 5688716. *Died* 6 *March* 1989.

**READER, (William Henry) Ralph,** CBE 1957 (MBE 1942); theatrical producer, author, composer and actor; Producer, Scout Gang Show, 1942–74; *b* 25 May 1903; *s* of William Henry and Emma Reader, Crewkerne, Somerset. *Educ:* Crewkerne; Cardiff. Started as clerk in office in Sussex; went to Ireland with same firm; returned to England; went to America to study for the stage; appeared in numerous productions, then took up producing; after 6 years returned to London to produce shows there; in 1928 appeared in Good News at Carlton Theatre, Haymarket; has produced nine Drury Lane productions, including Jack and the Beanstalk 1936, Rise and Shine 1937, three Ivor Novello shows, also about six shows at the London Hippodrome including Yes Madam and Please Teacher; starred in The Gang Show Film, also in Limelight with Anna Neagle; appeared with The Gang at the London Palladium in the Royal Command Variety Performance, produced Daily Express Pageant, Albert Hall, London, Battle for Freedom; Hearts of Oak Naval Pageant for Daily Express, 1945; British Legion Festival of Remembrance, annually, 1944–; RAF Pageant, Per Ardua Ad Astra, 1945, all at Albert Hall, London; produced Wings for Air Council, 1947; produced Out of the Blue, June 1947, season show, Grand, Blackpool; appeared in The Gang Show, Stoll Theatre. Produced (with all star cast) Pilgrim's Progress, Covent Garden, 1948, also in 1969. Was Officer in charge of RAF Gang Shows (official RAF entertainment units). Instituted Nat. Light Opera Company, 1950. Appeared in film Derby Day; took first entertainment to the Troops in Malaya; appeared in Meet the Gang. Produced Coronation Pageant, Royal Albert Hall, Pageant of Nursing, Royal Festival Hall, Centenary Rally of YMCA Sports de Paris, Rotary Pageant, Royal Albert Hall; produced Wild Grows the Heather, London Hippodrome, 1956; produced Voyage of the Venturer, Youth Festival, English Ranger Pageant, Royal Albert hall, 1956; appeared Royal Command Performance, 1957; prod. 1st Amer. Gang Show, Chicago, 1958; prod. Lord Mayor's Show, 1958; wrote music, book and lyrics of Summer Holiday, musical play, prod. Scarborough Open Air Theatre, 1960; Produced Gang Show in US, 1958, 1959, 1960, 1961; prod. World Refugee Finale, Albert Hall, 1960; wrote play, The Hill, prod. 1960; appd in Here Comes the Gang, touring Gt Britain, 1961; appeared in: Royal Command Perf., London Palladium, 1937, 1957, 1964; The Story of Mike, 1961; wrote and produced 4 One-Act Plays (We Present), 1962; staged ensembles for film, The Lonely Stage, 1962; prod. Burma Reunion, also The Voyage of the Venturer (wrote book and music), Royal Albert Hall, 1962; prod. Flying High for ITV 1962; wrote and appd in All for the Boys, London, 1963; prod. El Alamein Re-union, Royal Albert Hall, 1963; wrote play, Happy Family, also played lead, 1964; prod. and appd in Babes in the Wood, 1968; carol concert for SOS, Festival Hall, 1974; prod. and appd in Cinderella, 1973; produced at Royal Albert Hall: Dr Barnardo Centenary, 1966; The Old Contemptibles; Leclerc Reunion, 1972; 30th annual Festival of Remembrance, 1972; Jewish Lads Brigade Display, 1972 (140th perf. at RAH); Burmah Reunion, 1974; A Night with the Stars, 1974; personal appearance tour, NZ, Singapore and Hong Kong, 1976. Writer and producer: yearly editions of the Gang Show; The Pathfinders, Toronto, 1965; musical play, You Can't go wrong if you're right, 1967; Next Door, 1971; Look Wide, Look Wider, Nat. Conf., LA, 1972; Holme from Holme, 1974. Toured with Ralph Reader and The Stars of Tomorrow, 1972. Appears on BBC TV, Radio, ITV, US and Canadian TV. Compéred Radio Series "Startime", also, for Overseas BBC, "A Star Remembers". Subject of This Is Your Life, 1967. Illuminated

Address from State of Illinois, for Services to Boyhood throughout the World, 1964. Life Member, Boy Scouts of America. Universal Declaration of Human Rights Medal, 1975; Bronze Wolf, World Scouting highest award, 1976. *Publications:* Good Turns; The Road to Where; Gang Show Music and Sketches; Music and Book of Boy Scout, performed at Albert Hall; More Sketches: Great Oaks, Oh Scouting is a Boy, The Wingate Patrol; We'll Live Forever; The Story of Mike; Leave it to Pete; The Gang Show Story; All for the Boys; *autobiography:* It's been terrific: Ralph Reader Remembers, 1974. *Recreations:* motoring, writing, football. *Address:* Round Corners, Hedsor Road, Bourne End, Bucks. *T:* Bourne End 25586. *Died* 13 *May* 1982.

**READHEAD, James (Templeman),** 3rd Bt, *cr* 1922 (but discontinued style of Sir and the use of his title, 1965); Lieutenant late King's Own Yorkshire Light Infantry, TA; *b* 12 Feb. 1910; *s* of late Stanley Readhead, Stanhope House, Westoe, South Shields, and late Hilda Maud, *d* of Thomas John Templeman, Weymouth, Dorset; *S* uncle, 1940; *m* 1946, Hilda Rosemary, *o d* of George Henry Hudson, The Manor, Hatfield, nr Doncaster, Yorks; one *d*. *Educ:* Repton School. Electrical Engineer, retired. *Recreations:* various. *Died* 7 *Aug.* 1988 (*ext*).

**REASON, Dr Richard Edmund,** OBE 1967; FRS 1971; Consultant, Rank Taylor-Hobson; *b* 21 Dec. 1903; *m* Jane Eve; two step *s* one step *d*. *Educ:* Tonbridge Sch.; Royal Coll. of Science. Joined Taylor, Taylor & Hobson (later Rank Taylor Hobson) to design instruments for lens manufacture and testing; invented Talysurf, Talyrond and Talystep instruments; holder of some 85 British patents. *Address:* 5 Manor Road, Great Bowden, Leicestershire LE16 7HE. *T:* Market Harborough 63219. *Died* 20 *March* 1987.

**REAY, (Stanley) Basil,** OBE 1957; Secretary, Lawn Tennis Association, 1948–73; *b* 2 Feb. 1909; *s* of Robert and Maud Reay (*née* Cox), Stockton on Tees; *m* 1935, Beatrice Levene; one *s* one *d*. *Educ:* Queen Elizabeth Grammar School, Hexham; St John's College. Schoolmaster in England, 1929–32; Min. of Education, Egypt, 1932–39. Chairman Inter-Services Language Training Cttee, 1945–47. Served RAF, 1939–47, chiefly in ME (Wing Comdr, 1944). Wing Comdr, RAFVR. Sec. Gen., Internat. Lawn Tennis Fedn and Davis Cup Competition, 1973–76 (Hon. Sec., 1948–73; Hon. Life Counsellor, 1976–). Chm., British Schs LTA, 1980–84. Commandeur, Ordre de Merite Sportif (France), 1960; Gold Medal of Jerusalem (Israel); sports decorations from Yugoslavia, Brazil and others. *Recreations:* travel and sports. *Address:* Molende, Molember Road, East Molesey, Surrey. *Clubs:* Royal Automobile, Queen's; All England (Wimbledon); International Lawn Tennis Clubs of Great Britain, USA, France, Italy and several other countries. *Died* 7 *Nov.* 1987.

**REBBECK, Rear-Admiral Sir (Leopold) Edward,** KBE 1956; CB 1954; retired; *b* 26 July 1901; *s* of Edward Wise Rebbeck, Bournemouth; *m* Clara Margaret Allen, *e d* of R. G. Coombe, Ceylon; two *s* two *d*. *Educ:* Pembroke Lodge; Royal Naval Colls Osborne and Dartmouth. Served European War in HMS Erin; HM Yacht Victoria and Albert, 1932–35; War of 1939–45; HMS Birmingham, and as Assistant Naval Attaché, USA. Commanding Officer, RN Air Station Anthorn, 1946; Fleet Engineer Officer to C in C Mediterranean, 1949. ADC to King George VI, 1951–52; ADC to the Queen, 1952; Rear-Admiral Reserve Aircraft, 1952–55, retired. Vickers Group, 1956–66. Mem., Soc. Naval Architects and Marine Engineers (New York). *Recreations:* golf, motoring. *Address:* Stubb Hill House, Iping, near Midhurst, West Sussex GU29 0PQ. *T:* Milland 238. *Clubs:* Army and Navy, Royal Automobile. *Died* 23 *May* 1983.

**REDCLIFFE-MAUD, Baron** *cr* 1967 (Life Peer), of City and County of Bristol; **John Primatt Redcliffe Redcliffe-Maud,** GCB 1955 (KCB 1946); CBE 1942; Master of University College, Oxford, 1963–76; *b* 3 Feb. 1906; *yr s* of late John Primatt Maud, Bishop of Kensington, and late Elizabeth Diana Furse; *m* 1932, Jean, *yr d* of late J. B. Hamilton, Melrose; one *s* two *d* (and one *d* decd). *Educ:* Eton (King's Scholar); New College, Oxford (Open Classical Scholar); Harvard College, USA. Henry P. Davison Scholar from Oxford Univ. to Harvard College, 1928–29; AB Harvard, 1929; Junior Research Fellow, 1929, University College, Oxford; Fellow and Dean, 1932–39; Rhodes Travelling Fellowship to Africa, 1932; University Lecturer in Politics, 1938–39; Councillor Oxford City, 1930–36; invited by Johannesburg City Council to write municipal history of city; Tutor to Colonial Administrative Services Course, Oxford, 1937–39; Master of Birkbeck College, University of London, 1939–43; Deputy Secretary, later Second Secretary, Ministry of Food, 1941–44; Second Secretary, Office of the Minister of Reconstruction, 1944–45; Secretary, Office of Lord President of the Council, 1945; Permanent Secretary, Ministry of Education, 1945–52; Mem. Economic Planning Board, 1952–58; Permanent Secretary, Ministry of Fuel and Power, 1952–59; British Ambassador in South Africa, 1961–63 (High Commissioner, 1959–61), and High Commissioner for Basutoland, Bechuanaland Protectorate and

Swaziland, 1959–63. High Bailiff of Westminster, 1967–. UK deleg. to Confs on Food and Agric., Hot Springs, 1943, UNRRA, Atlantic City, 1943, and UNESCO, 1946, 1947, 1948, 1949, 1950 (President Executive Board, 1949–50). Chm., Council, Royal Coll. of Music, 1965–73. Chairman: Local Govt Management Cttee, 1964–67; Royal Commn on Local Govt in England, 1966–69; Prime Minister's Cttee on Local Govt Rules of Conduct, 1973–74. President: RIPA, 1969–79; British Diabetic Assoc., 1977–. Hon. Fellow: New Coll., Oxford, 1964; University Coll., Oxford, 1976; Fellow, Eton Coll., 1964–76. For. Associate, Venezuelan Acad. of Scis, 1973. Hon. LLD: Witwatersrand, 1960; Natal, 1963; Leeds, 1967; Nottingham, 1968; Hon. DSocSc Birmingham, 1968. Sen. Fell., RCA, 1961; FRCM, 1964; Associate Fellow, Jonathan Edwards Coll., Yale, 1968. *Publications:* English Local Government, 1932; City Government: The Johannesburg Experiment, 1938; Chapter in Oxford and the Groups, 1934; Chapter in Personal Ethics, 1935; Johannesburg and the Art of Self-Government, 1937; Chapter in Education in a Changing World, 1951; English Local Government Reformed, 1974; Support for the Arts in England and Wales, 1976; Experiences of an Optimist (memoirs), 1981. *Address:* 221 Woodstock Road, Oxford. *T:* Oxford 55354. *Clubs:* Savile; Eton Ramblers.                                        *Died* 20 *Nov.* 1982.

**REDDAWAY, (Arthur Frederick) John,** CMG 1959; OBE 1957; Deputy Commissioner-General, United Nations Relief and Works Agency, 1960–68; *b* 12 April 1916; *s* of Arthur Joseph Reddaway, Chartered Accountant, and Thirza May King; *m* 1945, Anthoula, *d* of Dr Christodoulos Papaioannou, Nicosia; two *s*. *Educ:* County High School, Ilford; University of Reading. Colonial Administrative Service, Cyprus, 1938; Imperial Defence College, 1954; Administrative Sec., Cyprus, 1957–60. Dir-Gen., Arab-British Centre, London, 1970–80. *Publication:* Burdened with Cyprus, 1987. *Address:* 19 Woodsyre, Sydenham Hill, SE26. *Club:* Commonwealth Trust.                                        *Died* 25 *June* 1990.

**REDFEARN, Sir Herbert,** Kt 1973; JP; DL; wire and wire goods manufacturer; Chairman, John Brown (Brighouse) Ltd, since 1949; *b* 26 Sept. 1915; *s* of Harry Reginald and Annie Elizabeth Redfearn; *m* 1942, Doris Vickerman, *y d* of Joseph Vickerman and Sarah Elizabeth Vickerman; one *s* one *d*. *Educ:* local council and technical schs. Brighouse: Borough Council, 1943–74; Alderman of Borough, 1953–74; Mayor, 1967. Chm., Brighouse and Spenborough Conservative Constituency Assoc., 1961–66, Pres., 1966–83; Treas., Yorks Provincial Area Council of Conservative and Unionist Assoc., 1966–70, Chm., 1971–76. Member: Conservative Party Bd of Finance, 1966–70; Nat. Union Exec. Cttee, 1966–83; Vice Chm., Nat. Union of Cons. and Unionist Assocs, 1977–77, Chm. 1978; Hon. Patron, Calder Valley Cons. Assoc., 1986. JP W Yorks, 1956; DL W Yorks, 1977. *Recreations:* freemasonry, gardening. *Address:* Ash Lea, Woodhouse Lane, Brighouse, West Yorkshire. *Club:* Carlton.                                        *Died* 23 *Aug.* 1988.

**REDFERN, Sir (Arthur) Shuldham,** KCVO 1939; CMG 1945; *b* 13 June 1895; *er s* of Dr J. J. Redfern; *m* 1925, Ruth Marion Grimshaw (*d* 1972); one *s*. *Educ:* Winchester; Trinity College, Cambridge. Served European War, 1914–19, Major Royal Flying Corps and RAF, 1918; joined Sudan Political Service, 1920; successively Assistant District Commissioner in Provinces of Khartoum, Darfur, Blue Nile; Dep. Governor of Blue Nile Province, 1927; Assistant Civil Secretary, Khartoum, 1929; Commissioner Port Sudan, 1932; Governor Kassala Province, 1934; Secretary to Governor-General of Canada, 1935–45; British Council, 1947–51. Pres., English Chamber Orch. and Music Soc., 1982–. CStJ; Officer of Order of the Nile, 1925. *Publications:* articles in Canadian papers. *Recreations:* music, painting. *Address:* 32 Sheffield Terrace, W8. *T:* 01–229 1323. *Club:* Athenæum.                        *Died* 18 *Feb.* 1985.

**REDGRAVE, Sir Michael (Scudamore),** Kt 1959; CBE 1952; actor; *b* 20 March 1908; *s* of G. E. ("Roy") Redgrave, actor, and Margaret Scudamore, actress; *m* 1935, Rachel Kempson; one *s* two *d*. *Educ:* Clifton Coll.; Magdalene Coll., Cambridge. MA; formerly modern language master Cranleigh Sch. Liverpool Repertory Theatre, 1934–36; Country Wife, As You Like It, Hamlet, etc, Old Vic Season, 1936–37; Richard II, School for Scandal, Three Sisters, Queen's Theatre, 1937–38; White Guard, Twelfth Night, Phœnix Theatre, 1938–39; Family Reunion, Westminster Theatre, 1939; Beggar's Opera, Haymarket Theatre, 1940; Thunder Rock, Globe Theatre, 1940; The Duke in Darkness, St James's Theatre, 1942; A Month in the Country, Parisienne, St James's Theatre, 1943; Uncle Harry, Garrick Theatre, 1944; Jacobowsky and the Colonel, Piccadilly, 1945; Macbeth, Aldwych, 1947; Macbeth, National Theatre, New York, 1948; The Father, Embassy, 1948, and Duchess, 1949; A Woman in Love, Embassy, 1949; Love's Labour's Lost, She Stoops to Conquer, A Month in the Country, Hamlet, with Old Vic Theatre Co., New, 1949–50; played Hamlet at Switzerland and Holland Festivals, also at Kronborg Castle, Elsinore, 1950; Richard II, Henry IV Parts 1 and 2, Henry V, The Tempest, Memorial Theatre, Stratford-on-Avon, 1951; solo performance of Shakespeare, Holland Festival, 1951; Winter Journey, St James's, 1952; Rockefeller Foundation Lecturer, Bristol Univ., 1952; Shylock, Antony and King Lear, Stratford-on-Avon, 1953; Antony, Princes, 1953, and Amsterdam, Brussels and Paris, 1954; Tiger at the Gates, Apollo, 1955, and Plymouth, New York, 1955; Theodore Spencer Memorial Lecturer, Harvard Univ., 1956; The Sleeping Prince, Coronet, New York, 1956; A Touch of the Sun, Saville, 1958; Hamlet and Benedick, Stratford-on-Avon, 1958; played Hamlet with Shakespeare Memorial Theatre Co., in Russia, 1958; The Aspern Papers, Queen's, 1959; The Tiger and the Horse, Queen's, 1960; solo performances of Shakespeare and of Hans Andersen, Bath Festival, 1961; The Complaisant Lover, Barrymore, NY, 1961; Uncle Vanya, Chichester Festival, 1962; Out of Bounds, Wyndham's, 1962; Uncle Vanya, Chichester Festival, 1963; joined National Theatre, 1963 (first production, Oct. 1963); Claudius in Hamlet; Uncle Vanya, Hobson's Choice, The Master Builder; A Month in the Country, Y. Arnaud and Cambridge Theatres, also Samson Agonistes (YA), 1965; The Old Boys, Mermaid, 1971; A Voyage Round My Father, Haymarket, Canada and Australia, 1972–73; The Hollow Crown, and Pleasure and Repentance, US 1973, 1974, World Tour, 1975; Shakespeare's People, S African tour, 1975; South America and Eastern Canada Tour, 1976; Denmark, British Columbia, NZ, US tours, 1977; Close of Play, Nat. Theatre, 1979; *films:* The Lady Vanishes, The Stars Look Down, Kipps, Jeannie, Thunder Rock, The Way to the Stars, Dead of Night, The Captive Heart, The Man Within, Fame is the Spur, Mourning Becomes Electra, The Browning Version, The Importance of being Earnest, The Green Scarf, Dam Busters, The Night My Number Came Up, Confidential Report, 1984, Time without Pity, The Happy Road, The Quiet American, Shake Hands with the Devil, Wreck of the Mary Deare; No, My Darling Daughter!, The Innocents, The Loneliness of the Long-Distance Runner, Young Cassidy, The Hill, The Heroes of Telemark, Oh What a Lovely War!, The Battle of Britain, Goodbye Mr Chips, Connecting Rooms, The Go-Between, Nicholas and Alexandra. Producer: Werther, Glyndebourne, 1966, 1969; La Bohème, Glyndebourne, 1967. Joined Royal Navy, 1941; discharged on medical grounds, 1942. President, English-Speaking Board; President, Questors Theatre; Director of Festival, Yvonne Arnaud Theatre, Guildford, 1965. FRSA; Hon. DLitt (Bristol), 1966. Commander Order of Dannebrog, 1955. *Publications:* The Seventh Man (play), 1936; Actor's Ways and Means, 1953; Mask or Face, 1958; The Aspern Papers (play), 1959; The Mountebank's Tale (novel), 1959; Circus Boy (play), 1963; In My Mind's Eye (autobiog.) (USA as In My Mind's I), 1983. *Relevant Publication:* Michael Redgrave, Actor, by Richard Findlater, 1956. *Address:* c/o Hutton Management Ltd, 200 Fulham Road, SW10 9PN.                        *Died* 21 *March* 1985.

**REDGRAVE, William Archibald;** sculptor, painter and poet; *b* 7 Dec. 1903; *s* of Joseph Ernest Redgrave and Rose Mabel (*née* Bradley); *m* 1st, 1925 Renée Marshall (later Renée Lady Truscott) (decd); one *d*; 2nd, 1949, Mary Crinkley; one *s* one *d*; 3rd, 1973, Elizabeth Eleanor Holbrook (solo violist); one *s* two *d*. *Educ:* Christchurch Rd Sch., Ilford; Central Sch. of Arts and Crafts; West Clapham Sch. of Art; The Old Vic, The National Gallery, The Tate Gallery. Junior clerk, insurance office, 1917; Pay-roll clerk, London Transport, 1919–40; Asst, later Music Asst, Recorded Programmes, BBC, 1940–47; long illness (TB), 1947–52; founded St Peter's Loft School of Art, St Ives, Cornwall (partnered with Peter Lanyon); returned to London, 1960; commissions in painting and sculpture; altarpiece, St Antony, Hayes, Middx; sculpture, Luminastra, Bristol; financial help from Sir Eric Truscott, Bt, to construct bronze triptych, The Event, now on loan to ILEA. *Bronze portraiture includes:* Sir Adrian Boult (Festival Hall and BBC Concert Hall), Lord Olivier (Nat. Theatre), Francis Bacon, Diana Rigg, Paul Tortelier, Henry Cooper, Margaret Barbieri, Bevis Hillier, Robert Hanson, Sydney Cowan; (statue) Call of the Sea, Lowestoft; (trophy) Young Cricketer, Lord's Taverners. *Publications:* Tread and Rise, Tread and Fall, (illust. poems), 1975; Collected Poems (illust.), 1976; Residua (poems), 1980. *Recreations:* violin, viola, snooker. *Address:* 23 Hungate Street, Aylsham, Norfolk. *T:* Aylsham 733487. *Clubs:* Chelsea Arts; Aylsham Ex-Service Men's.                        *Died* 20 *June* 1986.

**REDINGTON, Frank Mitchell,** MA, FIA; Chief Actuary, Prudential Assurance Co. Ltd, 1950–68, Director 1968–81; *b* 10 May 1906; *e s* of late William David and Lily Redington; *m* 1938, Katie Marianne Rosenfeld; one *s* one *d*. *Educ:* Liverpool Institute; Magdalene College, Cambridge (MA). Entered Prudential, 1928; FIA 1934; Chairman, Life Offices Association, 1956–57; President, Institute of Actuaries, 1958–60 (Gold Medal of Inst., 1968). *Publications:* contributions to Jl of Inst. of Actuaries and foreign actuarial journals. *Address:* 10 Rose Walk, St Albans, Herts. *T:* St Albans 54722.                                        *Died* 23 *May* 1984.

**REDMAN, Lt-Gen. Sir Harold,** KCB 1953 (CB 1947); CBE 1944; *b* 25 August 1899; *s* of late A. E. Redman, Shawford, Winchester; *m* 1st, 1947, Patricia Mary (*d* 1951), *d* of late Brig. John Leslie Weston, CBE, DSO; one *d*; 2nd, 1953, Barbara Ann, *d* of late J. R. Wharton, Haffield, nr Ledbury; one *s* one *d*. *Educ:* Farnham Grammar Sch.; RMA, Woolwich. Commissioned into R Artillery, 1917; served in

France and Germany, 1918 (BWM, VM); Waziristan, 1923–24 (NWF medal); Staff College, Camberley, 1929–30; transferred to KOYLI 1929; GSO 3 War Office, 1932–34; Bt Major, 1935; Brigade Major (3rd Division), 1934–36; GSO 2 Senior Officer School, 1937–38; GSO 2 Staff College, 1938–39; Bt Lt-Col 1939; War Cabinet Secretariat, 1939–40; Col 1942; Comd 7 Bn KOYLI 1940–41; Comd 151 (DLI) Infantry Bde Feb.-Dec. 1941; BGS Eighth Army, 1941–42; Comd 10 Ind. Motor Bde 1942–43; Secretary Combined Chiefs of Staff (Brig.), 1943–44; Deputy Commander French Forces of the Interior (Maj.-Gen.), Aug.-Sept. 1944; SHAEF Mission to French High Command, 1944–45; Head British Military Mission (France), 1945–46; CGS, ALFSEA, 1946–48; Director of Military Operations, War Office, 1948–51; Principal Staff Officer to Deputy Supreme Allied Commander, Europe, 1951–52; Vice-Chief of the Imperial General Staff, 1952–55; Governor and Commander-in-Chief, Gibraltar, 1955–58, retired. Director and Secretary The Wolfson Foundation, 1958–67. Col KOYLI, 1950–60. *Address:* Stair House, West Lulworth, Dorset. *T:* West Lulworth 257.

*Died 24 Aug.* 1986.

**REDMAYNE,** Baron *cr* 1966 (Life Peer), of Rushcliffe; **Martin Redmayne;** Bt *cr* 1964; PC 1959; DSO 1944; DL; Deputy Chairman, House of Fraser Ltd, 1972–78; Director, The Boots Co., 1969–80; Chairman, Retail Consortium, 1971–76; *b* 16 Nov. 1910; *s* of Leonard Redmayne; *m* 1933, Anne Griffiths (*d* 1982); one *s*. *Educ:* Radley. Commanded 14th Bn The Sherwood Foresters, Italy, 1943; formed and commanded 66 Inf. Bde, 1944–45; Hon. Brig., 1945. MP (C) Rushcliffe Div. of Notts, 1950–66. A Govt Whip, 1951; A Lord Comr of the Treasury, 1953–59; Dep. Govt Chief Whip, 1955–59; Parly Sec. to Treasury and Govt Chief Whip, Oct. 1959–64; Opposition Chief Whip, Oct.-Nov. 1964. Chm., N American Adv. Gp, BOTB, 1972–76. JP Nottingham, 1946–66; DL Notts, 1954. *Recreations:* golf, fishing. *Heir:* (to Baronetcy only): *s* Hon. Nicholas Redmayne [*b* 1Feb. 1938; *m* 1st, 1963, Ann Saunders (marr. diss. 1976); one *s* one *d*; 2nd, 1978, Mrs Christine Hewitt]. *Address:* Flat 1, 18 Hans Place, SW1X 0EP. *T:* 01-584 1525. *Club:* Buck's. *Died 28 April* 1983.

**REDSHAW, Sir Leonard,** Kt 1972; FEng 1976; FRINA; industrial consultant; Member, Safety Committee, Pacific Nuclear Transport Ltd (BNFL), 1978–88; *b* 15 April 1911; *s* of late Joseph Stanley Redshaw, Naval Architect; *m* 1939, Joan Mary, *d* of Wm White, London; one *s* one *d*. *Educ:* Barrow Grammar Sch.; Univ. of Liverpool. 1st cl. Hons degree in naval architecture; 1851 Exhibn Royal Comr's post grad. Schol. (welding research), Master's degree. Joined the Management Staff of Vickers-Armstrongs, 1936; Asst to Shipbuilding Manager, 1950; Special Dir, 1953; when Vickers-Armstrongs (Shipbuilders) Ltd was formed he was apptd Shipbuilding Gen. Man. of Yards at Barrow-in-Furness and Newcastle, 1955; Dir, Vickers-Armstrongs (Shipbuilders) Ltd, 1956, Deputy Managing Director, 1961; Builders' Chief Polaris Exec., 1963; Man. Dir, Vickers Ltd Shipbuilding Group, 1964; Special Dir, Vickers Ltd, 1965; Dir, 1967, Asst Man. Dir, 1967–76; Chairman: Vickers Ltd Shipbuilding Group, 1967–76; Vickers Oceanics Ltd, 1972–78; Vickers Offshore Engineering Group, 1975–78; Slingsby Sailplanes, 1969–77; Brown Brothers & Co. Ltd, 1973–77; Director: Rolls Royce & Associates, Ltd, 1966–77; Shipbuilding Corp. Ltd, 1970–77; Brown Bros & Co. Ltd, 1970–77; Cockatoo Docks & Eng. Co. Pty Ltd, 1972–76; Fillite (Runcorn) Ltd, 1971–85; Silica Fillers Ltd, 1971–85. Jt Chm., Technical Cttee, Lloyd's Register of Shipping, 1972–81; Mem., Lloyd's Gen. Cttee, 1972–81. Mem., Nat. Defence Industries Council, 1971–76; Chairman: Assoc. W European Shipbuilders, 1972–73; Warshipbuilders Cttee; President: Shipbuilders and Repairers Nat. Assoc., 1971–72; Inst. of Welding, 1963–65 (Mem. Council); Welding Institute, 1977–79. Hon. FWeldI. John Smeaton Medal, CEI, 1977; William Froude Medal, RINA, 1977. *Publications:* British Shipbuilding-Welding, 1947; Application of Welding to Ship Construction, 1962. *Recreations:* gliding, fishing, farming. *Address:* Netherclose, Ireleth, Askam-in-Furness, Cumbria LA16 7EZ. *T:* Dalton-in-Furness 62529. *Died 29 April* 1989.

**REECE, Sir Alan;** *see* Reece, Sir L. A.

**REECE, Courtenay Walton;** Puisne Judge, Hong Kong, 1952–61, retired; *b* 4 Dec. 1899; 3rd *s* of H. Walter Reece, KC (Barbados); *m* 1927, Rosa U. E. Parker (*d* 1956); two *d*. *Educ:* Harrison College and Codrington College, Barbados; Jesus College, Oxford (BA). Called to Bar, Middle Temple, 1925; Police Magistrate, Barbados, 1926; Registrar, Barbados, 1931; Magistrate, Nigeria, 1938; Crown Counsel, Nigeria, 1939; Senior Crown Counsel, Nigeria, 1946; Puisne Judge, Nigeria, 1949. *Recreations:* motor-boating, swimming, carpentry, fishing. *Died 16 April* 1984.

**REECE, Sir Gerald,** KCMG 1950; CBE 1943 (OBE 1937); DL; Chairman of Managers, Loaningdale Approved School, 1968–76; *b* 10 Jan. 1897; *s* of Edward Mackintosh Reece; *m* 1936, Alys Isabel Wingfield (MBE 1978, JP), *d* of Dr H. E. H. Tracy; one *s* two *d* (and one *s* decd). *Educ:* Rugby School. Commissioned Sherwood

Foresters, 1915; served France and Belgium (wounded thrice); served London Scottish (Territorial) Regt, 1920–25 (non-commnd). Solicitor Sup. Court, England, 1921; entered Kenya Administrative Service, 1925; seconded as HBM's Consul for Southern Ethiopia, 1934; Senior Political Officer, Borana Province of Ethiopia, 1941; Officer in Charge, Northern Frontier of Kenya, 1939–45; Provincial Commissioner, Kenya, 1945–48; Military Governor, British Somaliland, 1948; Governor and Commander-in-Chief, Somaliland Protectorate, 1948–53. Patron, Anglo-Somali Soc., 1978–. Scottish Chm., Howard League for Penal Reform, 1961–73. Chairman: Scottish Soc. for Prevention of Vivisection, 1973–83; St Andrew Animal Fund, 1974–83. Hon. Sheriff, E Lothian, 1962–73; DL, E Lothian, 1971–. *Publications:* sundry papers on Somalia. *Address:* Bolton Old Manse, near Haddington, East Lothian. *T:* Gifford 351. *Died 14 Oct.* 1985.

**REECE, Sir (Louis) Alan,** TC 1977; Kt 1964; CMG 1963; *b* 1906; *s* of Claud Austin Reece; *m* 1941, Erna Irmgard Meyer. *Educ:* Queen's Royal Coll., Trinidad. Secretary to the Cabinet and Permanent Secretary to the Prime Minister, Trinidad and Tobago, 1961–63, retd. Chm., Elections and Boundaries Commn; former Chairman: Trinidad and Tobago Electricity Commn; Industrial Develt Corp. *Address:* c/o 4 Hayes Street, St Clair, Port of Spain, Trinidad.

*Died 23 June* 1984.

**REED, Henry;** poet, radio-dramatist, translator; *b* 22 Feb. 1914; *s* of late Henry Reed and late Mary Ann Ball; unmarried. *Educ:* King Edward VI Sch., Aston, Birmingham; Birmingham Univ. (BA 1st cl. Hons Lang. and Lit., 1934; Charles Grant Robertson Scholar, 1934; MA 1936). From then on, verse and journalism. Taught for a year before call-up in 1941; served (or rather *studied*) in Army, 1941–42; transf. to Naval Intelligence, FO, 1942–45; released VJ day, 1945; recalled to Army, 1945; did not go, 1945; matter silently dropped, 1945. During war continued to write and publish verse and book-reviews; began occasional broadcasting; began writing radio-plays, 1946 (Premio della Radio Italiana, 1953), and doing much translation from Italian and French. Academic appts at Univ. of Washington, Seattle: Vis. Prof. of Poetry, winter quarter 1964; Asst Prof. of English, 1965–66; Vis. Prof. of Poetry, winter quarter 1967. Pye gold award (Soc. of Authors), 1979. *Publications:* A Map of Verona (poems), 1946, enl. edn NY 1948; Moby Dick (radio-version in prose and verse of Melville's novel), 1947; The Novel since 1939 (British Council booklet), 1947; The Lessons of the War (poems), 1970; Hilda Tablet and others, 1971; The Streets of Pompeii and other plays for radio, 1971. Numerous published translations include: Paride Rombi: Perdu and his Father (novel), 1954; Ugo Betti: Three Plays (with foreword), 1956, NY 1958; Ugo Betti: Crime on Goat Island, 1961 (staged NY 1960); Dino Buzzati: Larger than Life (novel), 1962; Balzac: Père Goriot, NY 1962; Balzac: Eugénie Grandet, NY 1964; Natalia Ginzburg: The Advertisement (play), 1969 (Nat. Theatre 1969). *Address:* c/o Messrs Jonathan Cape Ltd, 32 Bedford Square, WC1. *Club:* Savile.

*Died 8 Dec.* 1986.

**REED, Michael,** CB 1962; *b* 7 July 1912; *s* of late Richard and Winifred Reed; *m* 1st, 1939, Marcia Jackson; two *d*; 2nd, 1950, Hermione Jeanne, *d* of late Dr P. Roux, Kimberley, SA; one *s* one *d*. *Educ:* Christ's Hospital; Jesus College, Cambridge. Entered Ministry of Health, 1935; Private Secretary to Minister, 1942–45; Under-Secretary, Ministry of Health, 1956–58, Cabinet Office, 1958–61, Ministry of Health, 1961–63; Registrar General, 1963–72 and Dir, Office of Population Censuses and Surveys, 1970–72. *Address:* 16 Bisham Gardens, Highgate, N6 6DD.

*Died 4 Dec.* 1985.

**REED, Philip Dunham;** Corporation Director; *b* Milwaukee, Wisconsin, 16 Nov. 1899; *s* of William Dennis Reed and Virginia Brandreth Dunham; *m* 1921, Mabel Mayhew Smith (*d* 1984); one *s* one *d*. *Educ:* University of Wisconsin (BS in Electrical Engineering); Fordham Univ. (LLB). Hon. LLD, Union Coll. and Brooklyn Poly. Inst., Hon. DEng Rensslaer Poly. Inst.; Hon. Dr of Commercial Science, New York Univ. 1950; Hon. Dr of Laws, Univ. of Wisconsin, 1950. Swarthmore Coll., 1954. With General Electric Co. (Law Dept), 1926–; Asst to Pres. and Dir, 1937–39; Chm. of Bd, 1940; resigned Chairmanship Dec. 1942 to continue war work in England; re-elected Chm. of Bd, 1945–58; Chm., Finance Cttee, General Electric Co., NY, 1945–59, Director Emeritus, 1968–. Chm. of Board: of Internat. General Electric Company, 1945 until merger with parent co., 1952; Federal Reserve Bank of NY, 1960–65. Director: American Express Co.; American Express Internat. Banking Corp., 1958–72; US Financial, 1970–72; Otis Elevator Company, 1958–72; Kraftco Corp., 1958–70; Scott Paper Co., 1958–66; Metropolitan Life Insurance Co., 1940–73; Tiffany & Co., 1956–81; Bigelow-Sanford Inc., 1959–74; Bankers Trust Co., 1939–58 and 1966–72; Cowles Communications Inc., 1972–83; Cowles Broadcasting Inc., 1983–85; Metropolitan Opera Assoc. Inc., 1945–53; Mem. Business Advisory Council for Dept of Commerce, 1940– (Vice-Chm. 1951–52); US Adv. Commn on Information, 1948–61; Member: Executive Commn, Payroll Savings

Adv. Cttee for US Treasury Dept, 1946–56; Dir, Council on Foreign Relations, 1946–69; Trustee: Carnegie Endowment for Internat. Peace, 1945–53; Cttee for Economic Development (and Member Research and Policy Cttee); Member of the Visiting Cttee, Graduate School of Business Admin., Harvard Univ., 1940–60; Director, Ford Foundation Fund for Advancement of Education, 1951–53; Consultant to US Deleg., San Francisco Conf. on World Organization; Chm. US Associates (now US Council), Internat. Chamber of Commerce, 1945–Jan. 1948; mem. Exec. Cttee, US Council, ICC; Hon. Pres. Internat. Chamber of Commerce (Pres., 1949–51); Chm. US Side of Anglo-American Productivity Council, 1948–52; Vice-Chm. Eisenhower Exchange Fellowships, 1953–74; Chm. Finance Cttee, 1955–56. Mem. President's Cttee on Information Activities Abroad, 1960; Mem. Cttee on the Univ. and World Affairs (Ford Foundn), 1960; Trustee of Kress Foundn, 1960–65. Entered War work, 1941, with Office of Production Management, Washington, and its successor the War Production Board (Chief of Bureau of Industry Branches responsible for organising and converting peacetime industries to war production). Went to London, July 1942, as Deputy Chief of Economic Mission headed by W. Averell Harriman; Chief of Mission for Economic Affairs, London, with rank of Minister, Oct. 1943–31 Dec. 1944. Special Ambassador to Mexico, 1958. President's Certificate of Merit Award, 1947; Comdr Légion d'Honneur (France), 1951 (Officer, 1947). *Address:* 375 Park Avenue, New York, NY 10022, USA; (home) Rye, NY. *Clubs:* University, The Links (NY City); Apawamis (Rye, NY); Blind Brook (Purchase, NY); Bohemian (San Francisco); Mill Reef (Antigua, WI).
*Died 10 March 1989.*

**REED, Sir Reginald Charles,** Kt 1971; CBE 1967; Managing Director, Patrick Operations Pty Ltd; Chairman: Glebe Island Terminals Pty Ltd; Opal Maritime Agencies Pty, Ltd; Director: J. Meloy Ltd; Universal Shipbrokers Pty Ltd; Howard Smith Ltd; Scottish Ship Management Ltd; *b* 26 Sept. 1909; *s* of Reginald Paul and Emily Christina Reed; *m* 1934, May Moore; one *s*. *Educ:* Greenwich Public Sch., Australia. Associated with James Patrick & Co. Pty Ltd, and Patrick Stevedoring Co., 1930–; Commonwealth Govt appt, Australian Stevedoring Industry Authority, 1949–56. *Recreations:* surfing, reading, riding. *Address:* 11 Montah Avenue, Killara, NSW 2071, Australia. *T:* 498-2734. *Clubs:* Australian, American National, Royal Sydney Yacht Squadron, Tattersall's (all in Sydney). *Died 17 Aug. 1982.*

**REES, Dame Dorothy (Mary),** DBE 1975 (CBE 1964); Member, Central Training Council, 1964–67; *b* 1898; widow. *Educ:* Elementary and Secondary Schools. Formerly: school teacher; Member of Barry Borough Council. Alderman of Glamorgan CC; former Mem. Nat. Advisory Committee for National Insurance; Member: Joint Education Committee for Wales (Chm., Technical Educn Sub-Cttee); Welsh Teaching Hospitals Board. Liaison Officer, Ministry of Food, during War of 1939–45. MP (Lab) Barry Division of Glamorganshire, 1950–51; formerly Parliamentary Private Secretary to the Minister of National Insurance. *Address:* Mor-Hafren, 341 Barry Road, Barry, S Glam.

**REES, Prof. Garnet;** Professor of French, 1957–79, later Emeritus Professor, University of Hull; Pro-Vice-Chancellor, 1972–74; *b* 15 March 1912; *o s* of William Garnet and Mabel Rees; *m* 1941, Dilys, *o d* of Robert and Ellen Hughes; two *d. Educ:* Pontardawe Grammar School; University College of Wales, Aberystwyth; University of Paris. BA (Wales), 1934; MA (Wales), 1937; Docteur de l'Université de Paris, 1940; Fellow of Univ. of Wales, 1937–39; Asst Lecturer in French, Univ. Coll., Aberystwyth, 1939–40. Served War of 1939–45, in Roy. Regt of Artillery (Captain, Instructor in Gunnery), 1940–45. Lecturer in French, Univ. of Southampton, 1945–46; Sen. Lecturer in French, Univ. Coll., Swansea, 1946–57. Hon. DLitt Hull, 1979. Officier des Palmes Académiques (France), 1961. Chevalier de la Légion d'Honneur, 1967. *Publications:* Remy de Gourmont, 1940; Guillaume Apollinaire, Alcools, 1975; Baudelaire, Sartre and Camus: lectures and commentaries, 1976; articles on modern French literature and bibliography in learned journals. *Recreations:* gardening and motoring. *Address:* 45 Exeter Gardens, Stamford, Lincs PE9 2RN. *T:* Stamford (0780) 63672.
*Died 20 Oct. 1990.*

**REES, His Honour Richard Geraint;** a Circuit Judge (formerly Deputy Chairman, Inner London Sessions), 1971–81; Judge, Central Criminal Court, Old Bailey, 1971–81; *b* 5 May 1907; *s* of Rev. Richard Jenkyn Rees, MA, and Apphia Mary Rees, Aberystwyth; *m* 1st, 1938, Mary Davies; one *s*; 2nd, 1950, Margaret Grotrian; one *d. Educ:* Cardiff High School; University College of Wales, Aberystwyth; St John's College, Cambridge. LLB 1st Cl. Hons, University Coll. of Wales, 1929, BA 1st Cl. Parts I and II Law Tripos, 1930 and 1931; Barrister, Inner Temple, 1932 (Certificate of Honour). Practised on S Wales Circuit, 1934–39. Commissioned Welsh Guards, Nov. 1939; DAAG London Dist, 1943–44; Assistant Director Army Welfare Services, Lt-Col, British Army Staff, Paris, 1944–45; Despatches, Bronze Star (USA), 1946. Practised in London

and on Wales and Chester Circuit, 1946–56; Metropolitan Stipendiary Magistrate, 1956–71. *Recreations:* gardening, fishing. *Address:* Fellside, 23 Heath Road, Weybridge, Surrey KT13 8TH. *T:* Weybridge 42230. *Died 27 March 1986.*

**REES-REYNOLDS, Col Alan Randall,** CBE 1945; TD; DL; company director; *b* 24 Feb. 1909; *yr s* of Charles and Adelaide Rees-Reynolds, Woking; *m* 1936, Ruth, *y d* of late Frederick and Anne Hardy, Fittleworth; one *d* (and one *s* decd). *Educ:* Sherborne. Solicitor, 1931. HAC, 1928–31, rejoined 1938; commnd 2nd Lieut 2/5 Queens Royal Regt TA, 1939; Middle East, Western Desert, Libya, Egypt and Italy, 1940–45; Lt-Col 1942; Col 1944; Dep. Provost Marshal British Troops in Egypt, 1942–43; Provost Marshal Allied Armies in Italy, 1943–44 and Central Mediterranean Forces, 1944–45 (despatches 1944). Partner, Joynson-Hicks & Co., until 1965; Exec. Dep. Chm., Pollard Bearings Ltd, 1965–70. Mem., City and Industrial Liaison Council. Mem. Court, Univ. of Surrey. Deputy and Under Sheriff of Surrey, 1956–66, High Sheriff 1970; DL Surrey, 1970. Hon. Deputy Sheriff Middlesex County, Massachusetts, 1969–. Governor, St Catherine's Sch., Bramley; Mem. Council, Cranleigh and Bramley Schs. *Recreations:* people, working for the tax gatherer, shooting, fishing. *Address:* Priors Gate, Priorsfield Road, Godalming, Surrey. *T:* Guildford 810391. *Clubs:* Boodle's, Garrick. *Died 13 April 1982.*

**REEVE, Rt. Rev. (Arthur) Stretton,** DD (Lambeth), 1953; DD (Leeds), 1956; *b* 11 June 1907; *s* of Rev. Arthur and Mrs Violet Inez Reeve; *m* 1936, Flora Montgomerie (née McNeill); one *s* two *d. Educ:* Brighton Coll. (Exhibitioner); Selwyn Coll., Cambridge (Scholar); Westcott House, Cambridge, 1st class Theological Tripos, 1928, 2nd class Theological Tripos, 1929; BA 1929, MA 1933; rowed in Cambridge Univ. crew, 1930. Curate of Putney, 1930–32; Domestic Chaplain to Bishop of Winchester and Joint Hon. Secretary, Winchester Diocesan Council of Youth, 1932–36; Vicar of Highfield, Southampton, 1936–43; Vicar of Leeds, 1943–53; Rural Dean of Leeds, 1943–53; Proctor in Convocation for Diocese of Ripon, 1945–53; Hon. Canon of Ripon Cathedral, 1947–53; Chaplain to the Queen, 1952–53 (to King George VI, 1945–52); Bishop of Lichfield, 1953–74. Hon. Fellow, Selwyn Coll., Cambridge, 1955–; Hon. DLitt Keele, 1975. *Address:* 25 Huntington Green, Ashford Carbonell, Ludlow, Salop SY8 4DN. *T:* Richards Castle 209. *Club:* Leander (Henley on Thames). *Died 27 Jan. 1981.*

**REEVE, Major-General John Talbot Wentworth,** CB 1946; CBE 1941; DSO 1919; *e s* of Charles Sydney Wentworth Reeve; *m* 1st, 1919, Sybil Alice (*d* 1949), 4th *d* of Sir George Agnew, 2nd Bt; one *d* (one *s* killed in North Africa, June 1942); 2nd, 1950, Mrs Marjorie Frances Wagstaff, CBE, TD. *Educ:* Eton; Royal Military College, Sandhurst. Served European War, 1914–19 (despatches, DSO); commanded 1st Bn The Rifle Brigade, 1936–38; Commander Hong Kong Infantry Brigade, 1938–41; DAG Home Forces, 1942–43; Commander Sussex District, 1943–44; DAG, MEF, 1944–46; retd pay, 1946. *Address:* Livermere Lodge, near Bury St Edmunds, Suffolk. *T:* Honington 376. *Club:* Army and Navy.
*Died 25 June 1983.*

**REEVE, Rt. Rev. Stretton;** *see* Reeve, Rt Rev. A. S.

**REICHENBACH, Henry-Béat de F.;** *see* de Fischer-Reichenbach.

**REID, Charles William,** BSc (Econ); ASAA; *b* 29 May 1895; *s* of Charles and Ada Reid; *m* 1924, Gladys Ellen Edith Dudley; two *d. Educ:* Latymer Upper School; Holloway County School; University of London. War Office, 1914; Queen's Westminster Rifles, 1915–19 (served overseas, wounded twice). Exchequer and Audit Department, 1919–38; Exports Credit Guarantee Dept, 1938–39; Ministry of Supply, 1939–40; Ministry of Supply Mission, USA, 1940–46, Director of Requirements and Secretary-General; Ministry of Supply, Overseas Disposals, 1946–48; Dep. Financial Adviser, Control Commn, Germany, 1948–50; Min. of Works, Comptroller of Accounts, 1950–54; Under-Secretary for Finance, 1954–56; retired, 1956. Incorporated Accountant, 1926. Medal of Freedom (USA), 1947. *Recreations:* travel and sports. Athletics purple, Univ. of London; represented Great Britain in first athletics match with France, 1921. *Address:* Pynes, Edington, Bridgwater TA7 9LD. *T:* Chilton Polden 772320. *Died 11 Feb. 1983.*

**REID, Desmond Arthur;** *b* 6 Feb. 1918; *s* of late Col Percy Lester Reid, CBE, DL, and Mrs Katharine Marjorie Elizabeth Reid; *m* 1939, Anne, *d* of late Major J. B. Paget and Mrs J. B. Paget, London SW7; one *s. Educ:* Eton. Joined Lloyd's, 1936, Member 1939. SRO, Irish Guards, 1939 (wounded in Normandy, 1944; Major). Returned Lloyd's, 1946. Chairman: R. K. Harrison & Co. Ltd, 1947–; Yeoman Investment Trust Ltd, 1956–; Young Companies Investment Trust Ltd, 1972–; Prudential Portfolio Management Ltd, 1975–81; Prudential Pensions Ltd, 1975– (Dir, 1970); Director: Prudential Assurance Co. Ltd, 1960–81; Drayton Premier Investment Trust Ltd, 1972–; Edger Investments Ltd, 1965–; Estate Duties Investment Trust Ltd, 1971–; General Consolidated Investment Trust Ltd, 1964– (Dep. Chm., 1978–); London & St

Lawrence Investment Co. Ltd, 1956–; Moorgate Investment Co. Ltd, 1960– (Dep. Chm., 1978–); Practical Investment Co. Ltd, 1948–; Prudential Corp. Ltd, 1979–; Selection Croissance, 1970–; Pan Holding SA, 1975–; Managing Trustee, Irish Guards Common Investment Fund, 1970–. Member: Lloyd's Investment Cttee, 1971– (Chm. 1974–); Cttee of Ottoman Bank, London, 1979– (Chm. 1982–). Governor: Royal Ballet, 1973–; Royal Ballet School, 1974–. Councillor, Chelsea Bor. Council, 1945–52 (Chm. Finance Cttee, 1950–52). Chm., Inst. of Obstetrics and Gynæcology; Vice-Pres., Insurance Inst. of London; Mem., The Livery of Merchant Taylors. *Recreations*: shooting, gardening, ballet. *Address*: 3 Belgrave Place, SW1. *T*: 01-235 6507; Burmans, Ripe, Sussex. *T*: Ripe 271. *Clubs*: White's, City of London (Chm., 1977), MCC; Travellers' (Paris).
*Died 23 April* 1983.

**REID, Francis Alexander;** QC (NI) 1956; Social Security Commissioner, 1970–85; retired; *b* 2 March 1915; *s* of Frank Reid and Annie Stevenson; *m* 1940, Barbara Colville Welsh; one *d*. *Educ*: Trinity Public Elementary Sch., Bangor, Co. Down; Bangor Grammar Sch.; The Queen's Univ., Belfast (BA). Called to Bar of N Ireland, 1939; Bencher of Inn of Court, NI, 1965; admitted Advocate and Solicitor, FMS, 1939. War service in FMS Volunteer Force, 1939–45. Sen. Crown Prosecutor, successively, Armagh, Londonderry, Antrim and Belfast, 1954–67. Member, National Arbitration Tribunal (NI), 1947–56; Chm., War Pensions Appeal Tribunal (NI), 1956–61; President of Industrial Tribunals, 1970. Chm., Bar Council, NI, 1967–69. *Recreation*: reading. *Address*: Flat D, Newfaan Isle House, 65 Abbotsford Road, Galashiels TD1 3HN. *T*: Galashiels 4635. *Club*: New (Edinburgh).
*Died 25 April* 1987.

**REID, George Smith;** retired; Sheriff (formerly Sheriff-Substitute) of Ayr and Bute, later South Strathclyde, Dumfries and Galloway, at Ayr, 1948–76; *b* 29 Feb. 1904; *yr s* of John Mitchell Reid, manufacturer, Glasgow; *m* 1935, Marion Liddell Boyd; two *s* two *d*. *Educ*: Hutchesons' Grammar School, Glasgow; Glasgow University. MA 1925, LLB 1927. Called to Scottish Bar, 1935. *Recreation*: swimming. *Address*: 10 Wheatfield Road, Ayr. *T*: 267858.
*Died 20 Dec.* 1985.

**REID, Very Rev. George Thomson Henderson,** MC 1945; Chaplain to the Queen in Scotland, 1969–80, Extra Chaplain since 1980; *b* 31 March 1910; *s* of Rev. David Reid, DD; *m* 1938, Anne Guilland Watt, *d* of late Principal Very Rev. Hugh Watt, DD, Edinburgh; three *s* one *d*. *Educ*: George Watson's Boys' Coll.; Univ. of Edinburgh. MA 1932, BD 1935, Edinburgh. Served as Chaplain to 3rd Bn Scots Guards, 1940–45, Sen. Chaplain to 15th (S) Div., 1945. Minister at: Port Seton, E Lothian, 1935–38; Juniper Green, Edinburgh, 1938–49; Claremont Church, Glasgow, 1949–55; West Church of St Andrew, Aberdeen, 1955–75. Moderator of the General Assembly of the Church of Scotland, 1973–74. Hon. DD Aberdeen, 1969. *Publication*: Meaning the Lord's Prayer, 1988. *Recreations*: golf, bird-watching, painting. *Address*: 33 Westgarth Avenue, Colinton, Edinburgh.
*Died 5 Dec.* 1990.

**REID, Prof. Gordon Stanley,** AC 1986; Governor of Western Australia, since 1984; Professor Emeritus, University of Western Australia; *b* 22 Sept. 1923; *s* of Emily Matilda Reid (*née* Hewitt) and Stanley Archibald James Reid; *m* 1945, Ruth Amelia Fish; two *s* two *d*. *Educ*: Univ. of Melbourne (BCom 1953); London Sch. of Economics (PhD 1957; Hon. Fellow, 1984). FASSA; Fellow, Royal Aust. Inst. of Public Admin. Flying Officer, RAAF, Europe, RAF Sqdns Nos 83 and 106, 1942–46. Serjeant-at-Arms, House of Representatives, Canberra, 1955–58; Senior Lectr, then Reader, in Politics, Univ. of Adelaide, 1958–66; Prof. of Politics, Univ. of Western Australia, 1966–71, 1974–78, 1983–84 (Dep. Vice-Chancellor, 1978–83); Prof. of Political Science, ANU, 1971–74. Hon. DLitt Murdoch, 1987; Hon. LLD W Australia, 1988. *Publications*: The Politics of Financial Control, 1966; (with C. J. Lloyd), Out of the Wilderness: the return of Labour, 1974; (with M. Oliver) The Premiers of Western Australia, 1983; (with M. Forrest) Australia's Commonwealth Parliament 1901–88, 1989. *Recreation*: tennis. *Address*: Government House, Perth, WA 6000, Australia. *T*: 325 3222; 69 Tyrell Street, Nedlands, WA 6009, Australia. *Clubs*: University House (Canberra); Western Australian Cricket.
*Died 27 Oct.* 1989.

**REID, John,** CB 1967; Chief Veterinary Officer, Ministry of Agriculture, Fisheries and Food, 1965–70; *b* 14 May 1906; *s* of late John and Jessie Jamieson Reid, Callander, Perthshire; *m* 1933, Molly Russell (*d* 1989); one *d*. *Educ*: McLaren High Sch., Callander; Royal (Dick) Veterinary Coll., Edinburgh. FRCVS 1971; DVSM 1931. Asst Veterinary Officer, Midlothian County Council, 1931; Asst Veterinary Officer, Cumberland County Council, 1932; Ministry of Agriculture and Fisheries: Divisional Veterinary Officer, 1938; Superintending Veterinary Officer, 1952; Ministry of Agriculture, Fisheries and Food: Regional Veterinary Officer, 1958; Deputy Chief Veterinary Officer, 1960; Director of Veterinary Field Services, 1963. Mem. ARC, 1965–70. Vice-Chm., FAO European

Commn for Control of Foot-and-Mouth Disease, 1967–70; Member: Cttee of Inquiry into Veterinary Profession, 1971–75; Scientific Authority for Animals, DoE, 1976–77. *Recreations*: gardening, bird watching. *Address*: Owl's Green Cottage, Dennington, Woodbridge, Suffolk IP13 8BY. *T*: Badingham 205.
*Died 24 Jan.* 1990.

**REID, Sir John (Thyne),** Kt 1974; CMG 1971; *b* 15 Oct. 1903; *s* of Andrew Reid and Margaret (*née* Thyne), both born in Scotland; *m* 1929, Gladys Violet Boyd Scott, Glasgow; one *s* three *d*. *Educ*: King's Sch., Parramatta, NSW; Edinburgh Academy, Scotland. Mem., 1961–72, Vice-Chm., 1968–72, Australian Broadcasting Commn. Formerly Mem. Council, Victorian Coll. of the Arts. Hon. LLD Melbourne, 1977; Hon. DASc VIC, 1977. *Address*: 4 St George's Court, 290 Cotham Road, Kew, Vic 3101, Australia. *T*: 80 4759. *Clubs*: Melbourne; Australian (Melbourne and Sydney); Rotary (Melbourne).
*Died 31 Dec.* 1984.

**REID, Louis Arnaud,** MA, PhD, DLitt; Professor Emeritus of Philosophy of Education, Institute of Education, London University (Professor 1947–62); *b* Ellon, Aberdeenshire, 18 Feb. 1895; *s* of late Rev. A. H. Reid and late Margaret C. Miller; *m* 1920, Gladys Kate, *y d* of late W. H. Bignold; two *s*; *m* 1957, Frances Mary Holt, *d* of Denys Horton; two step *d*. *Educ*: Aberdeen Grammar School; Leys Sch., Camb.; University of Edinburgh. Studied engineering, 1913; RE 1914; discharged, 1915; 1st Cl. Hons in Mental Philosophy, 1919; medallist, English Essays; University verse prizeman; Cousin prizeman in Fine Art; medallist in Moral Philosophy; Bruce of Grangehill and Falkland prizeman in Advanced Metaphysics; Vans Dunlop scholar in Moral Philosophy; Lord Rector's prizeman; Hamilton Philosophical Fellow; Mrs Foster Watson Memorial Prizeman; Lecturer in Philosophy in University College, Aberystwyth, 1919–26; Visiting Professor Stanford University, California, 1927; Independent Lecturer in Philosophy University of Liverpool, 1926–32; Prof. of Philosophy Armstrong Coll. (now Univ. of Newcastle upon Tyne), 1932–47. Visiting Prof., Univ. of British Columbia, 1951; Vis. Prof. of Philosophy, Univ. of Oregon, 1962–63; Vis. Prof., Chinese Univ. of Hong Kong, 1966–67. Ext. Examiner, Univs of Liverpool, Sheffield, Leeds, Edinburgh, Aberdeen, Glasgow, London, Warwick, Leicester, W Indies, Hong Kong. Pres., Philosophy of Educn Soc. of GB. Fellow, Nat. Soc. of Art Educn. *Publications*: Knowledge and Truth, An Epistemological Essay, 1923; A Study in Aesthetics, 1931; Creative Morality, 1936; Preface to Faith, 1939; The Rediscovery of Belief, 1945; Ways of Knowledge and Experience, 1960; Philosophy and Education, 1961; Meaning in the Arts, 1970; Ways of Understanding and Education, 1986; articles in Mind, Hibbert, Procs of Aristotelian Soc., Philosophy, British Jl of Aesthetics, Amer. Jl of Aesthetics Educn, TES, etc. *Address*: 50 Rotherwick Road, NW11. *T*: 01–455 6850. *Club*: Royal Commonwealth Society.
*Died 26 Jan.* 1986.

**REID, Patrick Robert,** MBE 1940; MC 1943; Managing Director, Kem Estates Ltd; *b* 13 Nov. 1910; *s* of John Reid, CIE, ICS, and Alice Mabel Daniell; *m* 1943, Jane Cabot (marr. diss. 1966); three *s* two *d*; *m* 1977, Mrs Mary Stewart Cunliffe-Lister (*d* 1978); *m* 1982, Mrs Nicandra Hood. *Educ*: Clongowes Wood College, Co. Kildare; Wimbledon College; King's College, London University. BSc (London) 1932; AMICE, 1936; Pupilage, Sir Alex Gibb & Partners, 1934–37. Served War of 1939–45, BEF, France, Capt. RASC 2nd Div., Ammunition Officer, 1939–40; POW Germany, 1940–42; Asst Mil. Attaché, Berne, 1943–46; First Sec. (Commercial), British Embassy, Ankara, 1946–49; Chief Administrator, OEEC, Paris, 1949–52. Prospective Parly Candidate (C) Dartford and Erith, 1953–55. Director, Richard Costain (Projects) Ltd, 1959–62; Dir, Richard Costain (Middle East) Ltd, 1959–62. W. S. Atkins & Partners, Consulting Engineers, 1962–63. *Publications*: The Colditz Story, 1953; The Latter Days, 1955 (omnibus edn of the two, as Colditz, 1962, televised as The Colditz Story, BBC, 1973–74); (with Sir Olaf Caroe and Sir Thomas Rapp) From Nile to Indus, 1960; Winged Diplomat, 1962; Economic Survey Northern Nigeria, 1962; My Favourite Escape Stories, 1975; Prisoner of War, 1983; Colditz: the full story, 1984. *Recreations*: ski-ing, yachting, gardening. *Address*: Picket House, Avening, Glos GL8 8LS. *Club*: Lansdowne.
*Died 22 May* 1990.

**REID, Dr Robert Douglas;** *b* 6 Sept. 1898; *s* of John and Maud Helen Reid; unmarried. *Educ*: Wells Cathedral School; St John's College, Oxford (DPhil); Bristol University (BSc). Army 1917–19, Somerset Light Infantry in Flanders and Ireland; Assistant Master at Downside School, 1923–24; Canford School, 1924–28; Housemaster at Worksop College, 1928–33; Headmaster Kings School, Taunton, 1933–37. Somerset County Council, 1958–66; High Constable and Dep. Mayor, City of Wells. *Publications*: Cathedral Church of St Andrew at Wells; Diary of Mary Yeoman; Notes on Practical Chemistry; A Concise General Science, 1949; Houses of Mendip, 1979. *Recreations*: archæology, lawn tennis. *Address*: 8 Chamberlain Street, Wells, Somerset. *T*: 72494.
*Died 27 Dec.* 1983.

**REID, Thomas Bertram Wallace,** MA (Oxon), MA, LLB (Dublin), MA (Manchester), L ès L (Montpellier); Officier des Palmes académiques; Professor Emeritus, University of Oxford, and Emeritus Fellow of Trinity College, Oxford; *b* 10 July 1901; *e s* of late Thomas E. Reid, MBE, JP, Little Castledillon, Armagh; *m* 1942, Joyce M. H. Smalley; one *s*. *Educ:* Armagh Royal School; Trinity Coll., Dublin. Foundation Scholar, Hutchinson Stewart Literary Scholar, First Senior Moderator in Modern Literature, Prizeman in Old French and Provençal, Irish, and Law. Lecteur d'Anglais, Univ. of Montpellier, 1924–26; Asst Master, Frome County School, 1926–29; Assistant Lecturer in French, University of Manchester, 1929–35; Lecturer, 1935–45; Prof. of Romance Philology, 1945–58; Dean of the Faculty of Arts, 1950–51; Pro-Vice-Chancellor, 1957–58; Prof. of the Romance Languages, Univ. of Oxford, and Fellow, Trinity Coll., Oxford, 1958–68. Vis. Prof., Univ. of Toronto, 1969–70. Sometime Mem. Council or Executive: AUT; Modern Language Assoc.; Modern Humanities Res. Assoc. (Hon. Treasurer, 1952–58); Philological Soc.; Anglo-Norman Text Soc. (Pres., 1962–); Anglo-Normal Text Soc. (Pres., 1962–); Soc. for Study of Mediæval Lang. and Lit. (Vice-Pres., 1980–). *Publications:* (ed) The Yvain of Chrestien de Troyes, 1942; (ed) Twelve Fabliaux, 1958; Historical Philology and Linguistic Science, 1960; The Romance of Horn by Thomas, ed. M. K. Pope, Vol. II (revised and completed), 1964; The Tristran of Beroul: a textual commentary, 1972; articles and reviews on linguistic subjects in Modern Lang. Review, Medium Aevum, French Studies, etc. *Address:* 37 Blandford Avenue, Oxford. *T:* Oxford 58112.

*Died 30 Aug. 1981.*

**REID, Sir William,** Kt 1972; CBE 1962; PhD, DSc; FRSE 1952; FEng 1977; Chairman, Northern Economic Planning Council, 1970–73; *b* 20 June 1906; *o s* of late Sir Charles Carlow Reid; *m* 1935, Sheila Janette Christiana Davidson; one *s* one *d*. *Educ:* Dollar Acad.; Dunfermline High School. Early underground practical experience in coal mining attached to The Fife Coal Co. Ltd, and in the Ruhr and US. BSc (Mining and Metallurgy) 1929, and PhD (Mining) 1933, Univ. of Edinburgh. Held various mining appointments with The Fife Coal Co. Ltd, 1922–42; apptd Gen. Works Manager and Dir, 1942. Leader of Ministry of Fuel and Power Technical Mission to the Ruhr Coalfield, 1945; apptd in the Scottish Div. Nat. Coal Board, Prod. Dir, 1947, Deputy Chairman, 1950, Chairman, 1952; Board Member for Production, NCB, 1955–57; Chm., Durham Div., NCB, 1957–63; Chm., Northumberland and Durham Div., NCB, 1964–67, Regional Chm., 1967–69. Leader of NCB Technical Mission to coalfields of Soviet Union, 1956. Chm., Northern Regional Marketing Cttee, 1966. Mem., N Reg. Econ. Planning Council, 1965. Chairman: Northern Brick Co., 1968–71; Associated Heat Services (N) Ltd, 1968–71; Victor Products (Wallsend) Ltd, 1972–77; Council, Univ. of Durham, 1971–78 (Mem., 1963–82); Northern Region, Anchor Housing Assoc., 1980–83. President: Mining Inst. of Scotland, 1951–52; IMinE, 1956–57. Hon. DSc Heriot Watt, 1967; Hon. DCL Durham, 1970. *Publications:* numerous papers related to industry, particularly coal mining. *Address:* Norwood, Picktree Village, Washington, Tyne and Wear. *T:* Chester-le-Street 882260.

*Died 2 Oct. 1985.*

**REID-ADAM, Randle,** CBE 1953 (OBE 1947); *b* 16 Jan. 1912; *s* of late James and of Helen Reid-Adam; *m* 1942, Rita Audrey Carty; two *d*. *Educ:* Oundle; Trinity Hall, Cambridge. Appointed to Department of Overseas Trade, 1933. Commercial Secretary, British Embassy, Washington, 1940. Served in Foreign Service posts at Cairo, New York, Cologne, Stockholm, San Francisco and Panama; retired 1964. *Address:* Thuya, Draycott, near Moreton-in-Marsh, Glos. *Died 14 March 1982.*

**REILLY,** Baron *cr* 1978 (Life Peer), of Brompton in the Royal Borough of Kensington and Chelsea; **Paul Reilly;** Kt 1967; Director: Conran Design Group; The Building Trades Exhibition Ltd; Director, Design Council (formerly Council of Industrial Design), 1960–77; *b* 29 May 1912; *s* of late Prof. Sir Charles Reilly, formerly Head of Liverpool Sch. of Architecture; *m* 1st, 1939, Pamela Wentworth Foster; one *d*; 2nd, 1952, Annette Stockwell, *d* of Brig-Gen. C. I. Stockwell, CB, CMG, DSO. *Educ:* Winchester; Hertford College, Oxford; London School of Economics. Salesman and Sales Manager, Venesta Ltd, 1934–36; Leader Page Editor and Features Editor, News Chronicle, 1936–40. RAC, 1940; RNVR 1941–45. Editorial Staff, Modern Plastics, New York, 1946; Co-Editor, British Plastics Encyclopædia, 1947; Chief Information Officer, Council of Industrial Design, 1948; Deputy Director, 1954. Member: Council, Royal Society of Arts, 1959–62, 1963–70; Council, BTA, 1960–70; Council, RCA, 1963–81; BBC General Advisory Council, 1964–70; BNEC, 1966–70; British Railways Bd Design Panel, 1966–88, Environment Panel, 1977–84; GLC Historic Buildings Cttee, 1967–82; Post Office Stamp Adv. Cttee, 1967–; Design Adv. Cttee, 1970–84; British Telecom Design Cttee, 1981–83; British Council Fine Arts Adv. Cttee, 1970–80; Conseil Supérieur de la Création Esthétique Industrielle (France), 1971–73; Adv. Council of Science Policy Foundn, 1971–; British Crafts Centre Bd, 1972–77; Nat. Theatre Design Adv. Cttee, 1974–; Royal Fine Art Commn, 1976–81; Crafts Advisory Cttee, 1977–81 (Chief Exec., 1971–77). Chairman:

Trustees, Building Conservation Trust, 1977–82; Conran Foundn, 1981–86 (Trustee, 1986–). President: Soc. of Designer-Craftsmen, 1976–84; Assoc. of Art Institutions, 1977–80; World Crafts Council, 1978–80; Vice-President: ICSID, 1963–67; Modular Soc., 1968–77; London Soc., 1977–; ICA, 1979–; Rye Conservation Soc., 1980–. Governor: Hammersmith Coll. of Art and Building, 1948–67; Central Sch. of Art and Design, 1953–74; Camberwell Sch. of Art and Design, 1967–77; City of Birmingham Polytechnic, 1970–77. Mem., Ct of Governors, LSE, 1975–80. Hon. FSIA, 1959; Hon. FRIBA, 1965; Sen. Fellow, RCA, 1972; Hon. Assoc. Manchester Coll. of Art, 1963; Hon. Member: Art Workers Guild, 1961; Ornamo, Finland, 1981; Hon. Corresponding Mem., Svenskaslöjdforeningen, 1956; Hon. Comr, Japan Design Foundn, 1983. Hon. Liveryman, Furniture Makers' Co., 1980. Hon. DSc: Loughborough, 1977; Aston, 1981; Cranfield, 1983; Hon. Dr RCA, 1978. Comdr, Royal Order of Vasa (Sweden), 1961. Bicentenary Medal, RSA, 1963. *Publications:* An Introduction to Regency Architecture, 1948; An Eye on Design (autobiog.), 1987. *Recreation:* looking at buildings. *Address:* 3 Alexander Place, SW7 2SG. *T:* 071–589 4031. *Club:* Arts. *Died 11 Oct. 1990.*

**REILLY, Brian Thomas;** Chairman, Panasonic UK Ltd (formerly National Panasonic (UK) Ltd), since 1979; *b* 9 Dec. 1924; *s* of Thomas Joseph and Eugene Reilly; *m* 1952, Jean Cynthia Gilbey; one *s* four *d*. *Educ:* Mount St Mary's Coll., Spinkhill, near Sheffield. Captain, KRRC, 1943–47. Various pursuits, 1947–51; Dist Sales Man., Thomas Hedley & Co. Ltd (now Proctor & Gamble Ltd), 1951–60; Sales Dir, Man. Dir and Dep. Chm., Radio & Allied Industries Ltd (wholly owned subsid. of GEC Co. Ltd), 1960–79; Associate Dir, GEC Co. Ltd, 1976–79. *Address:* (office) 300–306 Bath Road, Slough, Berks SL1 6JB. *T:* Slough 34522; Nutfield, 25 The Fair Mile, Henley-on-Thames, Oxon. *Clubs:* Annabel's, St James's. *Died 23 Nov. 1988.*

**REINDORP, Rt. Rev. George Edmund,** DD; an Assistant Bishop, Diocese of London, since 1982; *b* 19 Dec. 1911; *s* of Rev. Hector William Reindorp and Dora Lucy (*née* George), Goodmayes, Essex; *m* 1943, Alix Violet Edington, MB, ChB (*d* 1987), *d* of Alexander Edington, MD, and Helen Edington, Durban, Natal; three *s* one *d* (and one *d* decd); *m* 1988, Bridget, *widow* of Sir William Mullens, DSO, TD. *Educ:* Felsted Sch.; Trinity Coll., Cambridge; Westcott House, Cambridge. MA Cantab. 1939. Deacon, 1937; Priest, 1938; Curate, S Mary Abbots, Kensington, 1937–39; Chaplain RNVR, 1938–46; Vicar, St Stephen with St John, Westminster, 1946–57; Provost of Southwark and Rector of St Saviour with All Hallows, Southwark, 1957–61; Bishop of Guildford, 1961–73; Bishop of Salisbury, 1973–81. Mem., House of Lords, 1970. With BBC Radio Religious Dept, arranging and performing Daily Service and arranging and producing Morning Service and other programmes, 1982–83. Chaplain, RCGP, 1965. Hon. DD Lambeth, 1961; DUniv Surrey, 1971. *Publications:* What about You?, 1956; No Common Task, 1957; Putting it Over: ten points for preachers, 1961; Over to You, 1964; Preaching Through the Christian Year, 1973. *Recreations:* ski-ing, radio and television; avoiding committees. *Address:* 17 Vincent Square, Westminster, SW1P 2NA. *Clubs:* Ski Club of Great Britain, Kandahar. *Died 20 April 1990.*

**REISS, Sir John (Anthony Ewart),** Kt 1967; BEM 1941; Chairman of Associated Portland Cement Manufacturers Ltd (later Blue Circle Industries), 1957–74; *b* 8 April 1909; *m* 1st, 1938, Marie Ambrosine Phillpotts; one *s* one *d*; 2nd, 1951, Elizabeth Booth-Jones (*née* MacEwan); two *d*. *Educ:* Eton. Cotton, Banking, Insurance, 1928–34. Joined Associated Portland Cement Manufacturers, 1934; Dir, 1946. President: Foundn for Business Responsibilities; Aims of Industry, 1978– (Hon. Treasurer, 1967–78); Vice-Chm., CRC. *Recreations:* shooting, cricket. *Address:* Barrow House, Barrow, Oakham, Leics. *Died 22 Nov. 1989.*

**RENAULT, Mary,** (pseudonym of **Mary Challans**); *b* 4 Sept. 1905; *er d* of late Dr Frank Challans, and of Clementine Mary Newsome Challans (*née* Baxter). *Educ:* Clifton High School, Bristol; St Hugh's Coll. Oxford (MA; Hon. Fellow, 1982). Radcliffe Infirmary, Oxford. Completed nursing training in 1937; returned to nursing, 1939, until end of War. FRSL 1959. *Publications:* Purposes of Love, 1939; Kind are Her Answers, 1940; The Friendly Young Ladies, 1944; Return to Night, 1946; North Face, 1948; The Charioteer, 1953; The Last of the Wine, 1956; The King Must Die, 1958; The Bull from the Sea, 1962; The Lion in the Gateway (for children), 1964; The Mask of Apollo, 1966; Fire from Heaven, 1970 (Silver Pen Award 1971); The Persian Boy, 1972; The Nature of Alexander (biography), 1975; The Praise Singer, 1979; Funeral Games, 1981; contrib. TLS, London Rev. of Books and New York Rev. of Books. *Recreations:* conversation and dogs. *Address:* 3 Atholl Road, Camps Bay, Cape Town 8001, South Africa. *Died 13 Dec. 1983.*

**RENDALL, Archibald,** OBE 1967; HM Diplomatic Service, retired; Consul General, Lille, France, 1977–81; *b* 10 Aug. 1921; *s* of late James Henry Rendall; *m* 1951, Sheila Catherine (*née* Martin); one *d*. *Educ:* Broughton Sch., Edinburgh. Inland Revenue Dept, 1938;

served in RN, 1941–46; joined Foreign (subseq. Diplomatic) Service, 1948; Vice-Consul, Monrovia, 1948–49; Vice-Consul and 2nd Sec., Baghdad, 1950–54; FO, 1954–57; 1st Sec. (Commercial), Beirut, 1957–60; Consul (Commercial), New York, 1960–65; 1st Sec. (Commercial), Bucharest, 1965–68; FCO, 1969–72; Consul-Gen., St Louis, 1972–77. *Address:* 37 Albany Villas, Hove, Sussex BN3 2RT. *T:* Brighton 772968. *Died* 13 *Dec.* 1989.

**RENDALL, Philip Stanley,** MBE 1964; DL; retired as Managing Director of Courtaulds Ltd (1943–61), and as Deputy Chairman (1949–61); *b* 7 July 1895; *s* of late Dr Stanley Rendall and Claire Louise Rendall; *m* 1923, Louise Gwendoline, 2nd *d* of James Calcott; two *d. Educ:* Shrewsbury. Served European War, 1914–18, in France. Joined Courtaulds Ltd, 1920; Director, 1937. Chairman, Lustre Fibres Limited, 1946–57; formerly Chairman, British Nylon Spinners Ltd, Chairman, British Celanese Ltd, 1960–61 (Vice-Chm., 1957–60). High Sheriff of Warwickshire, 1949–50. Commandant, Warwickshire Special Constabulary, retired. DL Co. Warwick, 1967. Chevalier de la Légion d'Honneur, 1957. *Recreations:* golf, tennis. *Address:* 47 Kenilworth Road, Leamington Spa. *T:* Leamington Spa 24682. *Club:* Leamington Tennis Court (Leamington). *Died* 15 *July* 1983.

**RENNIE, Sir Alfred (Baillie),** Kt 1960; formerly a Federal Justice of the West Indies Federation (1958–62); *b* 18 March 1896; *s* of James Malcolm and Mary Jane Rennie; *m* 1925, Patricia Margaret O'Gorman; one *s* two *d. Educ:* Wolmer's School, Kingston, Jamaica; King's College, London. Lieut, British West Indies Regt, 1916–19. Called to the Bar, 1922; practised in Jamaica and Bermuda, 1922–29; Clerk of the Courts, Jamaica, 1929–33; Resident Magistrate, 1933–34; Crown Solicitor, 1934–49; Judge of Supreme Court of Jamaica, 1949–58. *Recreation:* shooting. *Address:* 65 Friary Park, Ballabeg, Isle of Man. *Died* 13 *Oct.* 1987.

**RENNIE, Compton Alexander,** CMG 1969; Nuclear Energy Consultant since 1968; *b* 12 Dec. 1915; *s* of George Malcolm Rennie, Southampton; *m* 1941, Marjorie Dorothy Pearson; no *c. Educ:* Sutton Valence Sch., Kent; Sidney Sussex Coll., Cambridge. Radar Officer, TRE, Malvern, 1940–45. Atomic Energy Research Estabt, Harwell, 1945–59: Overseas Liaison Officer, 1955; Dep. Head, Reactor Div., 1957; Head, High Temperature Reactor Div., 1958; Atomic Energy Estabt, Winfrith, Dorset, and Chief Exec. of OECD High Temperature Reactor Project (Dragon Project), 1959–68; Dir, Nuclear Power and Reactors Div., Internat. Atomic Energy Agency, Vienna, 1970–72. Ford Foundn Atoms for Peace Award, 1969. *Recreation:* gardening. *Address:* 43 East Street, Wareham, Dorset BH20 4NW. *T:* Wareham 2671. *Died* 13 *Feb.* 1987.

**RENNIE, Sir Gilbert (McCall),** GBE 1954; KCMG 1949 (CMG 1941); Kt 1946; MC; MA, Hon. LLD (Glasgow); *b* 24 Sept. 1895; *yr s* of late John Rennie; *m* 1929, Jean Marcella Huggins; two *s* one *d. Educ:* Stirling High School; Glasgow Univ. Served European War, 1915–19, KOSB, Capt.; Ceylon Civil Service, 1920–37; Financial Sec., Gold Coast, 1937–39; Chief Secretary, Kenya, 1939–47; Governor and C-in-C Northern Rhodesia, 1948–54; High Comr in UK for Fedn of Rhodesia and Nyasaland, 1954–61. Chm., Commonwealth Econ. Cttee, 1957 and 1958; Chm., UK Cttee for Freedom from Hunger Campaign, 1965–78; Joint Treasurer, Royal Society of Arts, 1965–70. KStJ. *Recreations:* gardening, fishing, golf. *Address:* 7 Beech Hill, Hadley Wood, Barnet, Herts EN4 0JN. *Club:* Royal Commonwealth Society. *Died* 12 *Nov.* 1981.

**RENNIE, Sir John (Ogilvy),** KCMG 1967 (CMG 1956); Deputy Under-Secretary of State, Foreign and Commonwealth Office, 1967–74; *b* 13 Jan. 1914; *o s* of late Charles Ogilvy Rennie and Agnes Annette Paton; *m* 1938, Anne-Marie Celine Monica Godat (*d* 1964); one *s*; *m* 1966, Mrs Jennifer Margaret Rycroft; two *s. Educ:* Wellington College; Balliol College, Oxford. Kenyon & Eckhardt Inc., New York, 1935–39; Vice-Consul, Baltimore, 1940; British Press Service, New York, 1941; British Information Services, 1942–46; Foreign Office, 1946–49; First Secretary (Commercial) HM Embassy, Washington, 1949–51; First Secretary HM Embassy, Warsaw, 1951–53; Counsellor, Foreign Office, 1953; Head of Information Research Dept, FO, 1953–58; Minister (Commercial), British Embassy: Buenos Aires, 1958–60; Washington, 1960–63; Asst Under Sec. of State, FO, 1964–65; on loan to Civil Service Commission during 1966. *Recreations:* electronics, painting (Exhibitor RA, 1930, 1931; Paris Salon, 1932). *Club:* Brooks's. *Died* 30 *Sept.* 1981.

**RENSHAW, Hon. John Brophy,** AC 1979; Agent-General for New South Wales in London, 1980–83; *b* 8 Aug. 1909; *s* of late J. I. Renshaw; *m* 1st, 1943 (she *d* 1964); one *s*; 2nd, 1966, Mrs M. McKay. *Educ:* Ryde Sch. Mem., Coonabarabran Shire Council, 1937–40 (Pres., 1939–40); MLA, Castlereagh, NSW, 1941–80; Assistant Minister: for Lands, 1950; for Local Govt, 1952; Minister: for Public Works, 1952, and for Local Govt, 1953–56; for Local Govt and Highways, 1956–59; Treasurer, 1959–65; Dep. Premier and Minister for Industrial Develt and Decentralisation, 1962–64;

Premier of NSW, 1964–65; Leader of the Opposition, 1965–68 (resigned); Treasurer, 1976–80. *Died* 28 *July* 1987.

**RENTON, Lady; Claire Cicely Renton;** President, Greater London Association for Disabled People, since 1981; *b* 23 Sept. 1923; *d* of late Walter Duncan; *m* 1947, David Lockhart-Mure Renton (later Baron Renton, KBE, TD, QC); three *d. Educ:* Longstowe Hall, Cambridge, and privately. Served as VAD Nurse, 1941–45; Pres., Huntingdonshire County Red Cross, 1953–63; First Chm., Demand (Design and Manufacture for Disability), 1980–. *Recreations:* gardening and tennis. *Address:* Moat House, Abbots Ripton, Huntingdon, Cambs. *T:* Abbots Ripton 227; 22 Old Buildings, Lincoln's Inn, WC2. *Died* 24 *April* 1986.

**RENWICK, George Russell,** MA; Headmaster, Dover College, 1934–54, retired; *b* 7 Aug. 1901; *s* of George Edward Renwick and Helen Isabella Russell; *m* 1927, Isabella Alice Watkins; one *s* three *d. Educ:* Charterhouse; New College, Oxford. Assistant Master, Stowe School, 1924–25; Charterhouse, 1926–34; OUAC 1923, 1924; British Olympic Team, 1924. Councillor, Dover Borough Council, 1946–50. *Address:* The Old Parsonage, Sidlesham, near Chichester. *Club:* (former Commodore) Royal Cinque Ports Yacht (Dover). *Died* 25 *July* 1984.

**RENWICK, Sir John,** Kt 1968; JP; Consultant with Renwick & Co., Solicitors, Eckington; *b* 16 Nov. 1901; *s* of James David and Mary Beatrice Renwick; *m* 1933, Margaret Rachel, *d* of Alfred Stanley and Rachel Fawcett; one *s* one *d. Educ:* King Edward VII School, Sheffield; Sidney Sussex College, Cambridge (MA, LLB). Admitted a Solicitor, 1927, practising, since, at Eckington, near Sheffield. Mem. Council, Law Society, 1949–72 (Pres. 1967–68); Chm., Trustee Savings Banks Inspection Cttee, 1954–76; Trustee, Sheffield Savings Bank, 1948– (Chm., 1972); Sheffield Town Trustee, 1971. Hon. LLD Sheffield, 1968. *Address:* Saint Cross, Ridgeway, Sheffield S12 3YA. *T:* Eckington (Derbyshire) 433114.
*Died* 24 *April* 1983.

**REVANS, Sir John,** Kt 1977; CBE 1967 (MBE 1943); retired; *b* 7 June 1911; *s* of Thomas William Revans, MINA and Ethel Amelia Revans; *m* 1936, Eileen Parkhurst Mitchell; two *d. Educ:* Middlesex Hosp. Med. Sch. (Broderip Schol. in Med., Surgery and Path.; Forensic Medicine Prize, 1935); Royal Army Med. Coll. (Montefiore Prize in Surgery, 1936). London Univ. DCH 1946; FRCP 1969. Served War of 1939–45 (despatches 1941): Col Indian Med. Service, 1936–47, retd. Sen. Admin. MO, Wessex RHB, 1959–73; Regional MO, Wessex RHA, 1973–76. Adviser on hosps and health services to Royal Commn on Health, Newfoundland and Labrador, 1965–66; Member: Med. Cons. Cttee, Nuffield Provincial Hosps Trust, 1961–76; Standing Nursing Adv. Cttee, Central Health Services Council; Cttee on Gen. Practice of CHSC; Cttee on Senior Nursing Staff Structure in Hosp. Service; Cttee on Rehabilitation; Cttee on Hosp. Complaints; Central Midwives Bd, 1963–67. Vis. Prof. of Health Service Admin, Univ. of London, 1969. Mem. Council, Univ. of Southampton, 1978. Hon. LLD Southampton, 1970. Hon. FRCGP 1974. OStJ 1946. *Recreation:* sailing (RYA/DTI Yachtmaster (Offshore)). *Club:* Little Ship.
*Died* 4 *Nov.* 1988.

**REVIE, Donald,** OBE; formerly professional footballer, then football manager; retired; *b* 10 July 1927; *m* 1949, Elsie May Leonard Duncan; one *s* one *d. Educ:* Archibald Secondary Modern Sch., Middlesbrough, Yorks. Professional footballer with Leicester, Hull, Manchester City, Sunderland, and Leeds United, 1945–61; Player-Manager, then Manager, Leeds United Football Club, 1961–74; Manager of England Team, FA, 1974–77; National Team Coach, UAE FA, 1977–80; Manager: Al Nasr Football Club, 1980; National Football Club, Cairo, 1984. *Publication:* Soccer's Happy Wanderer, 1955. *Recreations:* golf, reading.
*Died* 26 *May* 1989.

**REVINGTON, Air Commodore Arthur Pethick,** CB 1950; CBE 1945 (OBE 1940); retired; *b* 24 June 1901; *s* of late Cdr G. A. Revington, RN; *m* 1946, Joan (*d* 1981), *widow* of Cuthbert William Prideaux Selby. *Educ:* Plymouth College; RAF College, Cranwell. Served War of 1939–45 (despatches thrice); AOC No 4 Gp, 1946–47; AOC No 47 Gp, 1948–50; Sen. Air Liaison Officer, United Kingdom Service Liaison Staff, Canada, 1950–53; retired 1954. *Club:* Royal Air Force. *Died* 21 *April* 1986.

**REY, Jean;** Leader, Parti réformateur-libéral de Wallonie, since 1976; Member, European Parliament, 1979–80; *b* Liège, 15 July 1902; *s* of Arnold Rey, Protestant Pastor; *m*; four *c. Educ:* Athénée and Univ. of Liège (Dr of Law). Advocate, Court of Appeal, Liège, 1926–58; Served War of 1939–45 (Croix de Guerre, Commem. Medal); POW, Germany, 1940–45. Councillor, Liège, 1935–58; Mem. for Liège, Chamber of Deputies, 1939–58; founder Mem., Entente Libérale Wallone; Minister of Reconstruction, 1949–50; Minister of Economic Affairs, 1954–58; Mem. EEC, 1958–67, Pres. 1967–70. Delegate: 3rd Gen. Assembly, UN, Paris, 1948; 1st Assembly, 1949 and 5th Assembly, 1953, Council of Europe; Mem.,

Commn to study European Problems, 1952. President: Court of Arbitration, Internat. Chamber of Commerce, 1972–77; Internat. European Movement, 1974–78. Dir, Philips Electrical Gp, 1970–73; President: Sofina, 1971–79; Papeteries de Belgique, 1973–80. Hon. DCL Oxon, 1968; Dr *hc:* Harvard; Pace Univ., NY; Drew Univ., NJ. Grand Cross, Order of the Crown; Grand Officer, Order of Leopold; Grand Cross, Order of Orange Nassau; Grand Cordon, Order of Lion of Finland; Comdr, Order of Crown of Oak; Comdr, Legion of Honour, and many other high national distinctions. *Address:* 16 rue Hovade, 4040 Tilff, Belgium.

*Died 19 May 1983.*

**REYNOLDS, Col Alan Randall R.;** *see* Rees-Reynolds.

**REYNOLDS, Doris Livesey, (Mrs Arthur Holmes),** DSc, FRSE, FGS; Honorary Research Fellow, Bedford College, since 1962; *b* 1 July 1899; *d* of Alfred Reynolds and Louisa Margaret Livesey; *m* 1939, Arthur Holmes, FRS (*d* 1965). *Educ:* Palmer's School, Grays, Essex; Bedford College, London University. Assistant in Geology, Queen's Univ., Belfast, 1921–26; Dem. in Geology, Bedford Coll., London Univ., 1927–31; Lectr in Petrology, University Coll., London Univ., 1931–33; Lectr in Petrology, Durham Colls, Durham Univ., 1933–43. Hon. Research Fellow of the University of Edinburgh, 1943–62. Leverhulme Fellowship to investigate the geology of the Slieve Gullion volcano, 1946–48. Lyell Medallist, Geological Soc., London, 1960. *Publications:* Elements of Physical Geology, 1969; Revision for 3rd edn of Holmes Principles of Physical Geology, 1978; on the origin of granite and allied subjects in Quart. Journ. Geol Soc., Proc. Roy. Irish Acad., Roy. Soc. of Edin., Geological Magazine, etc. *Address:* 7 Tandridge Road, Hove, E Sussex.

*Died 10 Nov. 1985.*

**REYNOLDS, John Arthur,** JP; Member (Lab), since 1973, and Leader, 1982–83 and since 1987, Cardiff City Council; *b* 28 Oct. 1925; *s* of William Thomas and Elsie Mary Reynolds; *m* 1955, Dorothy Grace Leigh; one *s* one *d. Educ:* London Univ. (BSc Econ); Trinity Coll., Carmarthen (CertEd). Teacher, 1954–64; Technical Coll. Lectr, 1965–87; Principal Lectr, South Glam Inst. of Higher Educn, 1979–88. Member: Regional Cttee, S Wales, CRS Ltd, 1962–; Cardiff Bay Develt Corp.; Local Govt Training Bd, 1979–88. Cardiff City Council: Chairman: Policy (Finance) Cttee, 1973–76, 1979–82; Policy Cttee, 1982–83, 1987–; Opposition Leader, 1983–87. JP Cardiff, 1977. *Recreations:* reading, TV, theatre, music. *Address:* 46 Richmond Road, Cardiff CF2 3AT. *T:* Cardiff 482183. *Club:* Victory Services. *Died 10 April 1990.*

**REYNOLDS, Major-General Roger Clayton,** CB 1944; OBE 1941; MC 1916; *b* 26 Jan. 1895; *s* of late Lewis William Reynolds and Fanny Matilda Clayton; *m* 1st, 1918, Marjorie Grace McVeagh (*d* 1938); one *s* one *d;* 2nd, 1952, Mrs August Oddleifson, Rochester, New York, USA. *Educ:* Bradfield College; RMA, Woolwich. 1st Commission RA, Aug. 1914; served European War, 1914–18 (MC, 1914 Star); Staff College, Camberley, 1928–29; Staff Captain Delhi Independent Brigade, 1931; DAAG, AHQ, India, 1932–36; GSO 1 War Office, 1939–40; AA Brigade Comd 1941–42; comd 3rd AA Group, Bristol, 1942–44; Comd 1 AA Group London, 1944–47; retired pay, 1948. *Recreations:* Bradfield College 1st XI Soccer, cricket; RMA, 1st XI Soccer; Staff College 1st team hockey, tennis. *Address:* The Old Orchard, Avon, New York State 14414, USA. *Club:* Army and Navy. *Died 12 Nov. 1983.*

**REYNOLDS, Seymour John Romer,** MA, MB, BChir (Cambridge) 1936; MRCS, LRCP, 1935; DMRE 1938; Physician to Radiological Department, Charing Cross Hospital, 1945–76; Consultant Radiologist: Kingston Hospital Group, 1948–73; New Victoria Hospital, Kingston-upon-Thames; *b* 26 April 1911; *s* of late Russell J. Reynolds, CBE, FRCP; *m* 1939, Margaret Stuart McCombie; one *s. Educ:* Westminster School; Trinity Coll., Cambridge; Charing Cross Hosp. Med. School. Formerly: House Surgeon, House Physician and Clin. Asst at Charing Cross Hosp.; Univ. Demonstrator in Anatomy, Cambridge Univ., 1937; Radiologist: Victoria Hosp., Kingston-upon-Thames, 1939; Prince of Wales Gen. Hosp., Tottenham, 1939; Highlands Hosp.; Hackney Hosp.; Epsom Hosp. 1943; Queen Mary's Hosp., Roehampton, 1946. Dean of Charing Cross Hosp. Med. Sch., 1962–76. Mem. Bd of Governors, Charing Cross Hosp., 1962–74; Mem., Ealing, Hammersmith and Hounslow AHA, 1974–76. *Recreations:* gardening, visiting art galleries. *Address:* Camelot, Renfrew Road, Kingston Hill, Surrey. *T:* 01–942 3808. *Died 1 March 1987.*

**REYNOLDS, William Vaughan;** Principal, St Marylebone Literary Institute, 1965–70, retired; *b* 10 May 1908; *yr s* of late William Reynolds, MBE, editor of The Midland Daily Telegraph; *m* 1932, Gertrude Mabel, *yr d* of late Arthur Charles Flint; four *s. Educ:* King Henry VIII School, Coventry; St Edmund Hall, Oxford. First class in Final Hons School of Eng. Lang. and Lit., 1930; BLitt, 1931; MA 1934; Senior Exhibitioner, St Edmund Hall, 1930–31. Assistant Lecturer in English Literature, University of Sheffield, 1931–34; Lecturer, 1934–41. Deputy Regional Officer, Ministry of Information (NE Region), 1941–45; Sec., East and West Ridings Industrial Publicity Cttee, 1943–45. Joined staff of The Birmingham Post as Leader-writer and Editorial Asst, 1945; served in London office, 1949; Editor, 1950–64, retired. Mem. British Cttee, Internat. Press Inst., 1952–64; Pres., Rotary Club of Birmingham, 1962–63; Mem., Church Information Adv. Cttee, 1966–72. *Publications:* Selections from Johnson, 1935; articles contributed to The Review of English Studies and to Notes and Queries; literary and dramatic reviews in various periodicals and newspapers. Has broadcast frequently in Gt Britain and US. *Recreations:* motoring, cats, theatre going, and reading. *Address:* Flat 3, Kingsley Court, Kingsley Road, Westward Ho!, Bideford, North Devon.

*Died 26 Aug. 1988.*

**RHIND, Donald,** CMG 1962; OBE 1947; retired 1970; *b* 26 Sept. 1899; *er s* of late Thomas Rhind, MRCS, LRCP; *m* 1939, Annemarie Eugenia Ludovica von Ferrari und Brunnerfeld; one *s* one *d. Educ:* Aldenham School; Bristol University (BSc). Economic Botanist, Burma, 1923–45; Civil Affairs Service, Burma (Lieutenant-Colonel), 1945; Senior Economic Botanist, Burma, 1946–47; Director of Agriculture, Ceylon, 1947–50; Secretary for Agriculture and Forestry Research, West Africa, 1951–53; Secretary for Colonial Agricultural Research, 1953–61; Adviser on Agricultural Research, Department of Technical Co-operation, 1961–64, Min. of Overseas Development, 1964–67; Agricultural Research Coordinator, SEATO, 1968–69. FLS, FIBiol. *Publications:* The Grasses of Burma, 1945; numerous scientific papers on tropical agriculture. *Address:* 1 The Briars, Upper Richmond Road, Putney, SW15. *T:* 01-788 9512.

*Died 15 Dec. 1982.*

**RHODES,** Baron *cr* 1964, of Saddleworth (Life Peer); **Hervey Rhodes,** KG 1972; PC 1969; DFC and Bar; DL; *b* 12 August 1895; *s* of John Eastwood and Eliza Ann Rhodes; *m* 1925, Ann Bradbury (*d* 1983); two *d. Educ:* Greenfield, St Mary's Elementary Sch.; Huddersfield Technical College; evening classes. Woollen worker pre-1914; joined King's Own Royal Lancs, 1914, commissioned, seconded to Flying Corps (wounded, DFC and Bar). Discharged from Hospital, 1921. Commenced business as woollen manufacturer. Served on Local Authority. Chairman of Urban District Council, 1944–45. Chairman, Saddleworth War Charities. Commanded 36th West Riding Bn Home Guard. MP (Lab) Ashton-under-Lyne, 1945–64; PPS, Min. of Pensions, 1948–51; Parliamentary Secretary, Board of Trade, 1950–51, 1964–67. Led all-party Parly delegns to China, 1978, 1979, 1981 and 1983. President: SELCARE, 1971–; North West Arts, 1972–; Saddleworth Fest. of the Arts, 1957–. Lord Lieutenant of Lancashire, 1968–71; DL Lancs, 1971. Freedom of Borough of Ashton-under-Lyne, 1965, and of Saddleworth, Yorks, 1966. KStJ 1968. Hon. Fellow: Huddersfield Polytechnic, 1976; UMIST, 1987; Hon. Mem., RNCM, 1982. Hon. DTech Bradford, 1966; Hon LLD Manchester, 1971. *Address:* Cribbstones, Delph, Oldham, Lancs OL3 5BZ. *T:* Saddleworth 4500.

*Died 11 Sept. 1987.*

**RHODES, Rev. Canon Cecil;** Canon Residentiary of St Edmundsbury Cathedral, 1964–80, later Emeritus; Founder and Editor, Church News, 1946–89; *b* Preston, Lancs, 5 Oct. 1910; *s* of James Rhodes; *m* 1940, Gladys, *d* of H. B. Farlie; one *s* two *d. Educ:* Preston Gram. Sch.; St Peter's Hall, Oxford; Wycliffe Hall, Oxford (MA). Deacon, 1936; Priest, 1937. Curate, St Stephen, Selly Hill, Birmingham, 1936–38; Asst Editor and Youth Sec., The Pathfinder, 1938–40; Jt Editor, Light and Life Publications, 1941–44; Diocesan Chaplain-in-charge, St Mary, Pype Hayes, Birmingham, 1940–44; Vicar: St Luke, Tunbridge Wells, 1944–49; St Augustine, Edgbaston, Birmingham, 1949–64; Birmingham Diocesan Adviser for Stewardship, 1960–64; Hon. Canon of Birmingham, 1961–64. Diocesan Dir of Lay Training, Diocese of St Edmundsbury and Ipswich, 1968–74; Chm., Diocesan Information Cttee, 1968–76. Jt Editor, The Pilgrim, C of E youth magazine, 1949–50; regular contributor to The Birmingham Post, 1950–64; East Anglian Daily Times, 1970–78. *Recreations:* writing, books, travel. *Address:* College Gate House, Bury St Edmunds, Suffolk. *T:* Bury St Edmunds (0284) 753530. *Died 21 Nov. 1990.*

**RHODES, Rev. Clifford Oswald,** MA Oxon; *b* 12 April 1911; *s* of Rev. Edward Rhodes; *m* 1941, Irene Betty, *e d* of H. R. Bowden; one *s* three *d. Educ:* The Grange Grammar Sch., Bradford; St Peter's Coll., Oxford. Journalism, 1934–37; Wycliffe Hall, Oxford, 1937–38; Curate, St Luke's Church, Wythenshawe, Manchester, 1938–40; CF 1940–45; Editor of the Record, 1946–49. Hon. Chaplain, St Bride's, Fleet Street, 1952–; Lectr, St Margaret's, Lothbury, EC2, 1954–. Licence to preach, from Oxford Univ., 1957; Rector of Somerton, 1958–81, also Priest-in-charge, Upper Heyford, Lower Heyford and Rousham, 1976–81, retired. Editor of the Church of England Newspaper, 1949–59; Director and Secretary, the Modern Churchmen's Union, 1954–60; Editor of Business, 1960–63; Account Executive, Gilbert McAllister and Partners Ltd, public relations consultants, 1963–65. Editorial Director, Harcourt Kitchin and Partners Ltd, 1964–72. *Publications:* The New Church in the New Age, 1958; Musical Instruments and the Orchestra, 1968; The Awful Boss's Book, 1968; (ed) Authority in a Changing Society,

1969; The Necessity for Love: the history of interpersonal relations, 1972; contrib. to many newspapers and periodicals and learned jls. *Recreations:* the arts and country life. *Address:* 233 Balmoral Avenue, Banbury, Oxfordshire OX16 0BB. *T:* Banbury 3425.
*Died* 3 *Nov.* 1985.

**RHODES, Stephen,** OBE 1969; solicitor; Secretary, Association of District Councils, 1973–81; *b* 19 Jan. 1918; *s* of late Edward Hugh Rhodes, CBE, and Helen Edith Laurie Patricia Rhodes; *m* 1958, Jane, *d* of late Norman S. Bradley, Sydney, Aust.; one *s* two *d*. *Educ:* St Paul's Sch.; Law Society's Sch. of Law. LLB (London). Articled to Sir Cecil Oakes, CBE, Clerk of East Suffolk CC; admitted solicitor, 1941. Served RAF, 1939–46: commnd 1941; Sqdn-Ldr, 1944 (despatches). Asst Solicitor, East Suffolk CC, 1946–47; Sen. Asst Solicitor, Norfolk CC, 1947–49; Asst Sec., County Councils Assoc., 1949–59; Secretary, Rural District Councils Assoc., 1959–73; Jt Sec., Internat. Union of Local Authorities, 1975–81. Mem., Health Educn Council, 1968–74; Jt Sec., Standing Adv. Cttee on Local Authorities and the Theatre, 1975–81; Sec., Local Authorities Management Services and Computer Cttee, 1980–81. Vice-Chm., London Region, Royal Soc. for Mentally Handicapped Children and Adults, 1978–85. *Recreation:* wine making. *Address:* 14 Hale Avenue, New Milton, Hants BH25 6EZ. *T:* New Milton 611225. *Clubs:* National Liberal, English-Speaking Union.
*Died* 11 *Feb.* 1989.

**RHYL, Baron** *cr* 1970 (Life Peer), of Holywell, Southampton; **(Evelyn) Nigel (Chetwode) Birch,** PC 1955; OBE 1945; *b* 1906; *s* of late Gen. Sir Noel Birch, GBE, KCB, KCMG, 11 Kensington Gore, SW7; *m* 1950, Hon. Esmé Glyn, *d* of 4th Baron Wolverton. *Educ:* Eton. Partner in Cohen Laming Hoare until May 1939 when retired to study politics. Territorial Army officer before the war. Served War of 1939–45 in KRRC and on Gen. Staff; Lt-Col 1944; served in Great Britain and Italy. MP (C) Flintshire, 1945–50, West Flint, 1950–70; Parly Under-Sec. of State, Air Ministry, 1951–52; Parliamentary Sec., Ministry of Defence, 1952–54; Minister of Works, Oct. 1954–Dec. 1955; Sec. of State for Air, Dec. 1955–17 Jan. 1957; Economic Sec. to the Treasury, 1957–58, resigned. Pres., Johnson Soc., Lichfield, 1966. *Publication:* The Conservative Party, 1949. *Recreations:* reading history; gardening; shooting; fishing. *Address:* 73 Ashley Gardens, SW1; Holywell House, Swanmore, Hants. *Clubs:* Pratt's, White's.
*Died* 8 *March* 1981.

**RHYS, Keidrych;** poet and writer; proprietor, Druid Books, Antiquarian and Out-of-print Booksellers, Heath Street, Hampstead; editor (founder) of magazine Wales, 1937–60; *b* Bethlehem, Llandilo, 26 Dec. 1915; *m* 1st, 1939, Lynette Roberts (marr. diss. 1950), poet and novelist, of Buenos Aires; one *s* one *d*; 2nd, 1956, Eva Smith; one *s*. *Educ:* Bethlehem; Llangadog; Llandovery Grammar Sch., etc. Literary and other journalism, London, etc, 1935. Served in Army (London Welsh AA) (1939–45 medals); with Ministry of Information, London, 1943–44; War Correspondent Europe, 1944–45. Public Relations Consultant, various charities and organisations, 1950–54; Welsh columnist and correspondent, The People, 1954–60; London Editor, Poetry London-New York, 1956–60. Arts Council Award in Literature, 1969–70. Vice-President International Musical Festival and Eisteddfod; Executive Committee (writers' group); Chairman Friends of Wales Soc.; Vice-Pres. Carmarthen Arts Club; Carmarthenshire County Drama Cttee and Rural Community Council. *Publications:* The Van Pool and other poems, 1941; Poems from the Forces, 1942; More Poems from the Forces, 1943; Modern Welsh Poetry, 1945; Angry Prayers, 1952; Poems; Contributor to: Wales, Times Lit. Supp., New Statesman, anthologies, and to European and American jls. *Recreations:* Welsh National affairs, lecturing, theatre. *Address:* 40 Heath Street, NW3 6TE. *T:* 01–794 2970.
*Died* 22 *May* 1987.

**RHYS WILLIAMS, Sir Brandon (Meredith),** 2nd Bt, *cr* 1918; MP (C) Kensington, since 1974 (Kensington South, March 1968–1974); *b* 14 Nov. 1927; *s* of Sir Rhys Rhys Williams, 1st Bt, DSO, QC, and Lady (Juliet) Rhys Williams, DBE (*d* 1964); *S* father, 1955; *m* 1961, Caroline Susan, *e d* of L. A. Foster, Greatham Manor, Pulborough, Sussex; one *s* two *d*. *Educ:* Eton. Served in Welsh Guards, 1946–48 (Lt). Contested (C) Pontypridd Div., 1959, and Ebbw Vale Div., 1960 and 1964. Consultant, Management Selection Ltd, 1963–71; formerly with ICI Ltd. Asst Dir, Spastics Soc., 1962–63. Mem. (ED) European Parlt, 1973–84 (elected Mem. for London SE, 1979–84); Vice-Chm., European Parlt Economic and Monetary Affairs Cttee, 1973–79. *Publications:* The New Social Contract, 1967; More Power to the Shareholder?, 1969; Redistributing Income in a Free Society, 1969. *Heir:* *s* Arthur Gareth Ludovic Emrys Rhys Williams, *b* 9 Nov. 1961. *Address:* 32 Rawlings Street, SW3. *T:* 01–584 0636; Gadairwen, Groes Faen, near Pontyclun, Mid-Glamorgan. *Clubs:* White's, Pratt's; Cardiff and County (Cardiff).
*Died* 18 *May* 1988.

**RIALL, Air Cdre Arthur Bookey,** CBE 1956 (OBE 1953); RAF Regiment, retired; General Secretary, National Rifle Association,

1968–80; *b* 7 Dec. 1911; *o s* of late Major M. B. Riall, OBE, and Mrs S. M. Riall (*née* Lefroy); *m* 1950, Pamela Patricia Hewitt; five *s* one *d*. *Educ:* Charterhouse; RMC, Sandhurst. Commissioned E Yorks Regt, 1932; served in India with 1st Bn until 1939 when posted as Instr to Small Arms Sch.; Staff Coll., 1941; staff appts until Home posting, 1944; served 2nd Bn NW Europe (wounded, despatches); seconded to RAF in Iraq, for service with Iraq Levies, 1947; transf. RAF Regt, 1948; Chief Instr, RAF Regt Depot, 1951–53; commanded RAF Levies, until their disbandment, 1953–55 and RAF Regt Depot, Catterick, 1955–59; Staff appts in UK and Cyprus, 1959–62; Air Cdre, 1963; apptd Dir of Ground Defence, RAF, 1962; retd Dec. 1966, and joined staff of NRA, 1967. *Recreations:* hunting (Master, Royal Exodus Hunt, Iraq, until disbandment in 1955), target rifle shooting (rep. GB, Ireland and RAF), match rifle (Captain of Ireland, 1982–), ornithology (Vice-Pres., RAF Ornith. Soc.). *Address:* Hill House, Ewshot, Farnham, Surrey. *Club:* Naval and Military.
*Died* 4 *Oct.* 1984.

**RICE, George Ritchie,** CMG 1947; OBE 1927; *b* 31 July 1881; *s* of late John Norman Rice; *m* 1911, Elvina, *d* of late Charles Moore, Messing, Essex; one *d*; *m* 1956, Helen Woodman, Bexhill. *Educ:* Wilson's School; King's College, London. Civil Service; War Office, 1899; trans. to Army Accounts Dept, 1905; Chief Accountant, 1926; Financial Adviser, GOC China, 1927–29; GOC Egypt, 1934–35; GOC Palestine, 1936; joined Ministry of Supply, 1939; Director of Clothing and Textiles, 1939–43; Dep. Director-Gen. Equipment and Stores, 1943–45; Director-Gen. Disposals Mission, Middle East, 1945–46; Ministry of Supply, Special Representative for S Africa, 1946–47; Ministry of Supply, Director of Sales, Hamburg, 1947–50; retired from Civil Service, 1950. *Address:* 4 Chiltern Court, Sutherland Avenue, Bexhill-on-Sea, East Sussex. *T:* Bexhill-on-Sea 210489. *Club:* National.
*Died* 14 *Feb.* 1982.

**RICE, Roderick Alexander;** Executive Director, Cable & Wireless Ltd, 1965–81; *b* 7 April 1922; *s* of Samuel Richard Rice and Katrine Alice Rice; *m* 1965, Monica McClean; three *s*. *Educ:* Brockley County Grammar Sch. Cable & Wireless Ltd: Asst Chief Accountant, 1959; Dep. Chief Accountant, 1961; Chief Accountant, 1962; Executive Director, 1965. Jordan Star of Independence, 1965. *Recreations:* bowls, cricket, gardening. *Address:* Flat 7, 5 Manor Road, Ashford, Mddx. *Clubs:* Royal Commonwealth Institute, English-Speaking Union, MCC; (Chairman) Exiles (Richmond).
*Died* 16 *March* 1984.

**RICH, Sir Almeric (Frederic Conness),** 6th Bt, *cr* 1791; *b* 9 Feb. 1897; *o s* of Sir Almeric E. F. Rich, 5th Bt, and Louise (*d* 1932), *d* of Hon. John Conness, Mattapan, Mass, USA; *S* father 1948. Lt RGA, 1914–19. HM Borstal Service, 1932–61. *Address:* c/o National Westminster Bank Ltd, 1 St James's Square, SW1.
*Died* 29 *June* 1983.

**RICH, Jacob Morris,** MA, LLB; Hon. Consultant, South African Jewish Board of Deputies (Secretary 1939–74); *b* Longton, Stoke-on-Trent, 4 March 1897; *m* 1940, Sylvia Linken; two *d*. *Educ:* Hanley High School; Fitzwilliam Hall, Cambridge. Served in Palestine with Jewish Battalions of the Royal Fusiliers during European War; Secretary to the Board of Deputies of British Jews, 1926–31; Secretary of the Joint Foreign Committee of the Board of Deputies of British Jews and the Anglo-Jewish Association, 1930–31; Hon. Secretary Jewish Historical Society of England, 1924–31; Editor, The Jewish Chronicle, 1931–36. *Address:* 17 Campbell Road, Parktown West, Johannesburg, 2193, S Africa.
*Died* 26 *Oct.* 1987.

**RICH, Rowland William;** retired; Principal, City of Leeds Training College, 1933–63; *b* 1901; *s* of William Henry Rich of Weston-super-Mare; *m* 1926, Phyllis Mary, *e d* of Charles Linstead Chambers of Southgate; one *s* one *d*. *Educ:* Brighton Grammar School; University College, London; London Day Training College, BA (Hons English), 1921, Teachers' Diploma, 1922, MA (Education), 1925; PhD 1934; English master and housemaster, Newport (Essex) Grammar School, 1922–25; Lecturer in Education, University of Durham (Durham Division), 1925–30; Professor of Education, University College, Hull, 1930–33; Tutor to extra-mural tutorial classes (WEA) in English Literature, Social History and Psychology; Vice-Chairman, Association of Tutors in Adult Education, 1931–33; President Training College Association, 1938; Chairman, Association of Teachers in Colleges and Departments of Education, 1946; Member National Advisory Council on Training and Supply of Teachers, 1950–56. *Publications:* The Training of Teachers in the Nineteenth Century, 1933; The Teacher in a Planned Society, 1949; contributor to Adult Education in Practice, 1934, Britain Today, 1943, Education in Britain, 1944. *Address:* 65 Cheriton Road, Winchester, Hants. *T:* Winchester 3654.
*Died* 4 *June* 1981.

**RICHARDS, Audrey Isabel,** CBE 1955; FBA 1967; Hon. Fellow, Newnham College, Cambridge (Fellow, 1956); Smuts Reader in Anthropology, Cambridge University, 1961–67; *b* 1899. *Educ:* Downe House Sch.; Newnham Coll., Cambridge (MA); PhD

(Lond.). Field work: in Northern Rhodesia (now Zambia), 1930–31, 1933–34, 1957; in Northern Transvaal, 1939–40; in Uganda, 1950–55. Lecturer in Social Anthropology, London School of Economics, 1931–33, 1935–37; Sen. Lectr in Social Anthropology, Univ. of Witwatersrand, 1939–41; Principal, Colonial Office, 1942–45; Reader in Social Anthropology, London Univ. 1946–50; Director, East African Institute of Social Research, Makerere College, Kampala, Uganda, 1950–56; Dir, Centre for African Studies, Cambridge University, 1956–67. Member: Colonial Res. Cttee, 1944–47; Colonial Social Science Res. Council, 1944–50 and 1956–62; Committee for scientific research in Africa South of Sahara, 1954–56. President: Royal Anthropological Institute, 1959–61; African Studies Assoc., 1964–65. Overseas Fellow, American Acad. of Arts and Sciences, 1974. *Publications:* Hunger and Work in a Savage Tribe, 1932; Land, Labour and Diet in N Rhodesia, 1939; (ed) Economic Development and Tribal Change, 1954 (2nd edn, 1975); Chisungu, a study of girls' initiation ceremonies in N Rhodesia, 1956; (ed) East African Chiefs, 1960; The Changing Structure of a Ganda Village, 1966; The Multi-Cultural States of East Africa, 1969; (with A. Kuper) Councils in Action, 1971; (ed) Subsistence to Commercial Farming in Buganda, 1973; (with Jean Robin) Some Elmdon Families, 1974; papers in Africa, African Studies and African Affairs. *Address:* 11 Highsett, Hills Road, Cambridge. *Died 29 June 1984.*

**RICHARDS, Rev. Daniel;** Priest-in-charge of Merthyr Mawr and Ewenny, 1968–77; *b* 13 February 1892; *s* of John and Elizabeth Richards; *m* 1st, 1919, Hilda Roberts (*d* 1972); (one *s* decd and one *s* killed 1944); 2nd, 1973, Mrs Muriel Woodliffe (*née* Snook). *Educ:* St David's College, Lampeter, Cards. LD 1915, Mathews Scholar, 1928–29, BA and BD 1929; Curate of St Mary's Church, Court Henry, Carms, 1915–18; Curate of St Mary's Church, Burry Port, Carms, 1918–24; Rector of Llangeitho, Cards, 1924–31; Vicar of: Llangynwyd with Maesteg, 1931–66; Grouped Parish of Troedyrhiw Garth, Maesteg, 1950–60; Canon of Llandaff Cathedral, 1949–61, Precentor, 1961–67; RD of Margam, 1941–66. SPCK Hon. Group Secretary for Dioceses of St David's, Swansea and Brecon, Llandaff and Monmouth, 1966–. Fellow of Philosophical Society of England, 1942. MTh 1980, PhD 1984, ThD 1987, Geneva Theol Coll.; STh Lambeth Diploma of Student in Theology, 1981. *Publications:* Honest to Self (autobiog.), 1971; History of the Lampeter Society, 1972, revd edn 1982; Honest Memories (autobiog.), 1985; Honest Stewardship, 1988. *Address:* Llandre, 26 Brynteg Avenue, Bridgend, Mid Glamorgan. *T:* Bridgend 5117. *Died 3 June 1989.*

**RICHARDS, Edgar Lynton, (Tony Richards),** CBE 1971 (MBE 1954); MC 1944, Bar 1945; TD 1953; formerly partner, Moy, Vandervell & Co.; *b* 21 April 1912; *s* of late Thomas Edgar Richards, ARIBA, MICE, and Enid Marie (*née* Thomas); *m* 1937, Barbara Lebus; three *s* one *d*. *Educ:* Harrow. Served War, 1939–45. Member: Stock Exchange, 1939–; Stock Exchange Council, 1955–68. Mem., 1965–79, Dep. Chm., 1974–79, Monopolies, later Monopolies and Mergers, Commn. Former Chm. Trustees, Amer. Museums in Britain. *Died 31 May 1983.*

**RICHARDS, Sir Gordon,** Kt 1953; Racing Manager, since 1970 (Jockey, retired 1954, then Trainer, 1955–70); *b* 5 May 1904; *s* of Nathan Richards; *m* Marjery (*d* 1982); two *s*. Started life as a clerk; went as a stable apprentice to Mr Martin G. Hartigan, 1919; has headed the list of winning jockeys, 1925, 1927–29, 1931–33, 1938–40, 1942; 259 winners in 1933, breaking Fred Archer's record; passed Archer's record total of 2,749 winners, 24 April 1943; passed own record with 269 winners, 1947; rode 4000th winner 4 May 1950; broke world record with 4,500 winners 17 July 1952; final total, 4,870. Won the 1953 Derby on Pinza. Hon. Member, Jockey Club, 1970. *Publication:* My Story, 1955. *Recreations:* shooting, watching football. *Address:* Duff House, Kintbury, Berks. *Died 10 Nov. 1986.*

**RICHARDS, Brigadier Hugh Upton,** CBE 1943; DSO 1944; *b* 1894; *s* of J. Richards; *m* Florence Matilda (*d* 1964), *d* of J. McLeod; one *s*; *m* 1966, Mrs Irene Mary Olver, widow of Cecil Paul Olver. Served European War, 1914–19, with Worcestershire Regiment; Lieutenant, 1917; Captain, 1931; Bt Major, 1934; Major, 1936; transfd West Yorkshire Regt, 1936; Lt-Col 1939; Col 1942; Brig. 1940; commanded 4 Bn Nigeria Regt 1933–34, Sierra Leone Bn 1939, and 3 (West African) Inf. Bde, 1940–44; commanded Siege of Kohima, March–April 1944. Campaign Palestine, 1936 and 1938 and Burma. *Address:* Cotheridge Court, Cotheridge, Worcestershire. *Club:* Army and Navy. *Died 16 Dec. 1983.*

**RICHARDS, Rt. Rev. John Richards,** DD (Lambeth); President, St David's University College, Lampeter, 1971–77; *b* 3 March 1901; *s* of Thomas and Elizabeth Richards, Llanbadarn Fawr, Aberystwyth; *m* 1929, Katherine Mary (*d* 1980), *d* of W. E. and M. Hodgkinson, Inglewood, St Michael's, Tenterden; one *s* one *d*. *Educ:* Ardwyn School, Aberystwyth; Univ. College of Wales; St Michael's College Llandaff. BA 1922 (2nd Cl. Hons Mod. Langs); MA 1955; DD 1956. Deacon, 1924; priest, 1925; Curate of Pembrey w Burry Port,

1924–27; CMS missionary in Iran, 1927–45, at Shiraz, 1927–36, at Yezd, 1938–42, at Isfahan, 1942–45; Archdeacon in Iran, 1937–45. Mem. of Near East Christian Council, 1932–38; Hon. CF, Painting 1942–45; Vicar of Skewen, 1945–52, Vicar of St Catherine, Pontypridd, 1952–54; Canon of St Andrew in Llandaff Cathedral, 1949–54; Dean of Bangor, 1955–56; Vicar of St James', Bangor, and Canon of Bangor Cathedral, 1954–55; Bishop of St David's, 1956–March 1971. Pantyfedwen Lectr, UC Swansea, 1972. Mem. of Governing Body of the Church in Wales, 1948–71. Chaplain and Sub-Prelate, Order of St John, 1961. Hon. LLD Wales, 1971. *Publications:* The Religion of the Baha'is, 1932; The Open Road in Persia, 1932; Baha'ism, 1965; Under His Banner, 1973; Jesus: Son of God and Son of Man, 1974. *Address:* Lluest Wen, Llanbadarn Road, Aberystwyth SY23 1EY. *Died 10 March 1990.*

**RICHARDS, Prof. Owain Westmacott,** FRS 1959; MA, DSc (Oxford); Professor of Zoology and Applied Entomology, Imperial College, London, 1953–67, then Emeritus; Fellow of Imperial College, 1969–80; *b* 31 Dec. 1901; 2nd *s* of H. M. Richards, MD; *m* 1st, 1931, Maud Jessie (*d* 1970), *d* of Eng. Capt. C. M. Norris, RN; two *d*; 2nd, 1972, Joyce Elinor Benson (*née* McLuckie). *Educ:* Hereford Cathedral School; Brasenose College, Oxford. Exhibitioner, 1920, and Senior Hulme Schol., Brasenose Coll.; Christopher Welch Schol., Oxford Univ., 1924. Research Asst, Dept of Entomology, Imperial College, 1927; Lecturer, 1930; Reader, 1937. Hon. Mem. Société Entomologique d'Egypte; Hon. Fellow, Royal Entomological Soc. of London; Hon. Member: Nederlandsche Entomologische Vereeniging; British Ecological Soc.; Accademia Nazionale Italiana di Entomologia. *Publications:* The Variations of Animals in Nature (with G. C. Robson), 1936; The Social Insects, 1953; Imms' General Textbook of Entomology, 10th edn (with R. G. Davies), 1977; The Social Wasps of the Americas, 1978. *Recreation:* entomology. *Died 9 Nov. 1984.*

**RICHARDS, Tony;** *see* Richards, E. L.

**RICHARDSON, Alexander Stewart,** CBE 1943; BSc; *b* 17 May 1897; *e s* of late Alexander Stewart Richardson and James Hamilton Horsburgh; *m* 1931, Kathleen Margaret, *o d* of late Angus McColl, Inverness; one *s* one *d*. *Educ:* Edinburgh University. Military Service, 1916–19; Agricultural Officer, Tanganyika Territory, 1924; Senior Agricultural Officer, 1930; Deputy Director of Agriculture, Uganda, 1937; Director of Agriculture, Nyasaland, 1940–44; MLC 1940; Chairman Supply Board and Controller of Essential Supplies and Prices, 1941 and 1942; Controller of Production and Food, 1943. Member of Executive and Legislative Councils; Officer in general charge of Supplies, Prices and Distribution of Commodities; Uganda Govt Rep. on East African Production and Supply Council; Leader of East African Cotton deleg. to New Delhi, India, 1946; retired, 1947; Director of Agriculture, Uganda, 1944–47. *Recreations:* golf, shooting, fishing. *Address:* 24 Drummond Road, Inverness IV2 4NF. *T:* Inverness 233497.
*Died 19 Sept. 1989.*

**RICHARDSON, Sir Earl;** *see* Richardson, Sir L. E. G.

**RICHARDSON, Sir Frank;** *see* Richardson, Sir H. F.

**RICHARDSON, Prof. Frederick Denys,** PhD, DSc; FRS 1968; FEng 1976; FIMM; FIChemE; Professor Emeritus and Senior Research Fellow, Department of Metallurgy, Imperial College of Science and Technology, London University, since 1976; *b* 17 Sept. 1913; *y s* of late Charles Willerton Richardson, Bombay; *m* 1942, Irene Mary, *o d* of late George E. Austin, Birkdale; two *s*. *Educ:* privately; University College, London (Fellow, 1971); Princeton University, USA. Commonwealth Fund Fellow, 1937–39; RNVR 1939–46; Commander, 1942; Deputy Director Miscellaneous Weapon Development, Admiralty, 1943–46; Superintending Chemist, British Iron and Steel Research Association, 1946–50; Nuffield Fellow and Director Nuffield Research Group, Imperial College, 1950–57; Prof. of Extraction Metallurgy, Imperial Coll., 1957–76. Member: Council, Iron and Steel Inst., 1962–74; InstnMM, 1961– (Pres., 1975–76); Metals Soc., 1974–; Charter Fellow, Metallurgical Soc.; American Inst. of Mining and Metallurgical Engineers, 1963. Sir George Beilby Memorial Award for researches on the thermodynamics of high temperature systems, 1956; Bessemer Gold Medal of Iron and Steel Inst. for contribs to kinetics and thermodynamics of metallurgical processes, 1968. Howe, Hatfield, May, Wernher and AIME Extractive Metallurgy and Yukawa Lectures, 1964–73. Hon. Member: Japanese Iron and Steel Inst.; Ingénieurs de Liège; Japan Inst. of Metals; Foreign Associate, Nat. Acad. of Engrg, USA, 1976. Hon. DIng, Technische Hochschule, Aachen; Hon. Dr, Liège. Gold Medal, InstnMM, 1973; Gold Medal, Amer. Soc. of Metals, 1975; Tunner Medal, Verein Eisenhütte Österreich, 1976; Grande Medaille, Soc. Française de Métallurgie, 1977; Carl-Lueg Medal, Verein Deutscher Eisenhüttenleute, 1978; Kelvin Medal, 1983. *Publications:* The Physical Chemistry of Melts in Metallurgy, 1974; papers on chemical and metallurgical research in scientific jls. *Recreations:* riding, fishing, gardening. *Address:* Imperial College, Prince

Consort Road, SW7. *Club:* Royal Automobile.

*Died 8 Sept.* 1983.

**RICHARDSON, Sir George Wigham,** 3rd Bt *cr* 1929; Underwriting Member of Lloyd's; President, Wigham Poland Ltd, and Director of other companies; *b* 12 April 1895; 2nd *s* of Sir Philip Wigham Richardson, 1st Bt; *S* brother, 1973; *m* 1st, 1923, Adela Nancy (marr. diss., 1937), *d* of late A. O. Davies; 2nd, 1944, Barbara, *d* of late Harry Clements Ansell, Sutton Coldfield; three *d. Educ:* Rugby School. Served European War in Flanders and France, 1915–18, and with Army of Occupation in Germany, 1918–19 (despatches). Prime Warden of Worshipful Company of Shipwrights, 1943. *Address:* H3 Albany, W1. *T:* 01-734 1861; Old Manor House, Benenden, Kent. *T:* Benenden 570. *Clubs:* Carlton, Constitutional, City of London. *Died 15 April* 1981 (*ext*).

**RICHARDSON, Prof. Harold Owen Wilson,** DSc, PhD; FRSE; Hildred Carlile Professor of Physics, Bedford College, University of London, 1956–73, now Emeritus; *b* 1907; *e s* of late Sir Owen Richardson; *m* 1st, 1930, Jean Rosemary Campbell (marr. diss., 1940); one *d*; 2nd, 1955, Sylvia Camroux Topsfield. *Educ:* University College School; King's College, London. BSc (London); PhD (Cantab); DSc (Edinburgh). Research student, Cavendish Lab., Cambridge (Trinity Coll.), 1928–30; part-time Demonstrator at King's Coll., London, 1930–31; Demonstrator, Bedford Coll., London, 1931–35; Asst Lectr, Univ. of Leeds, 1935–36; Asst Lecturer and Lecturer, Univ. of Liverpool, 1936–46; Experimental Officer, Projectile Development Establishment, Min. of Supply, 1940–42; Lecturer in Natural Philosophy, Univ. of Edinburgh, 1946–51, Reader, 1951–52; Prof. of Physics, Univ. of Exeter, 1952–56. Warden of Reed Hall, Univ. Coll. of the South-West, 1953–55. Regional Scientific Adviser to the Home Office, 1953–56. *Publications:* papers on radioactivity, the magnetic focusing of electrons and the design of magnets. *Address:* 57 Dartmouth Park Hill, NW5. *Died 4 March* 1982.

**RICHARDSON, Sir (Horace) Frank,** Kt 1953; *b* 15 Oct. 1901; *s* of William Thomas and Louisa Jane Richardson; *m* 1949, Marjorie Amy Hislop; four *s* two *d. Educ:* All Saints Gram. Sch., St Kilda, Vict.; Univ. of Tasmania, Australia. Deputy Chairman: Business Board, Defence Department, Commonwealth of Australia, 1941–47; Commonwealth Disposals Commission, Australia, 1944–49. Past Chairman of various Department Stores, etc., in Australia; now Director of Proprietary companies. Life Governor, Retail Traders Assoc. of Victoria. Mem. Council, The Australian National University, 1953–76. *Recreations:* tennis, golf. *Club:* Athenæum (Melbourne, Australia). *Died 23 Feb.* 1983.

**RICHARDSON, Sir Leslie Lewis,** 2nd Bt, *cr* 1924; Director of Companies; *b* 14 August 1915; *s* of Sir Lewis Richardson, 1st Bart, CBE, head of the firm of L. Richardson & Co. of London, Port Elizabeth, New York and Boston, and Phoebe, *o d* of Isaac Isaacs; *S* father 1934; *m* 1946, Joy Patricia, twin *d* of P. J. Rillstone, Johannesburg; two *s* one *d. Educ:* Harrow, Served with South African Artillery, 1940–44, in the Union and North Africa. *Heir: s* Anthony Lewis Richardson, *b* 5 Aug. 1950. *Address:* Old Vineyard, Constantia, Cape Town, 7800, South Africa. *T:* Cape Town 741176. *Died 20 July* 1985.

**RICHARDSON, Sir (Lionel) Earl (George),** Kt 1986; JP; Chairman, IVth Commonwealth Games Ltd, Auckland, New Zealand, 1987–90; *b* 24 Nov. 1921; *s* of Lionel Harcourt Richardson and Doris Evelyn Richardson; *m* 1st, 1942, June Cecil Stretton (*d* 1984); two *d*; 2nd, 1985, Alison Valerie Langford. *Educ:* Seddon Memorial Coll.; Auckland Univ. FCA; FNZIM. Served War: NZ Army (Lieut) 1939–43; RNZN (Sub Lieut), on loan to RN, 1943–46. Dep. Man. Dir, Holeproof (NZ) Ltd, 1946–73; Director: Ceramco Ltd; MacJays Ltd; Garman Holdings Ltd; First City Finance Ltd. President: Textile and Garment Fedn, 1973–76 (Life Mem.); NZ Manufrs' Fedn, 1982–85. Life Mem., Lions Internat. Service Club, 1988; Foundn Pres., Papatoetoe RSA; Life Mem., Papatoetoe and Dist RSA; Chm., Auckland Maritime Foundn; Founder, Half Moon Bay Marina, 1968. *Recreations:* golf, yachting. *Address:* 5 Shore Road, Remuera, Auckland 5, New Zealand. *T:* 5205701. *Club:* Royal New Zealand Yacht Squadron (Auckland).

*Died 10 Sept.* 1990.

**RICHARDSON, Sir Ralph David,** Kt 1947; Actor; *b* Cheltenham, Glos, 19 Dec. 1902; *s* of Arthur Richardson and Lydia Russell; *m* 1st, 1924, Muriel Hewitt (*d* 1942); no *c*; 2nd, 1944, Meriel Forbes-Robertson; one *s. Educ:* Xaverian Coll., Brighton; privately. Made his first appearance on the stage at Brighton, 1921; toured in the Provinces in Shakespeare Repertory for four years; joined the Birmingham Repertory Theatre in 1925; first London appearance in 1926 at the Haymarket Theatre as Arthur Varwell in Yellow Sands; season of plays at the Court Theatre in 1928; toured in South Africa in 1929; from 1930 to 1932 played two seasons at the Old Vic and two seasons at the Malvern summer theatre; Too True To Be Good at the New Theatre and For Services Rendered at the Queen's in 1933, followed by Wild Decembers and Sheppey; Eden End and

Cornelius at the Duchess Theatre in 1935, and played Mercutio in Romeo and Juliet in the USA in 1936; Promise, Bees on the Boatdeck and The Amazing Dr Clitterhouse, until 1937; in 1938, The Midsummer Night's Dream and Othello at the Old Vic; Johnson over Jordan, Sept. 1939; joined Fleet Air Arm as Sub/Lieut RNVR; Lieut (A) RNVR 1940; Lt-Comdr RNVR 1941. Released from Naval Service, June 1944, to act for and direct Drama of Old Vic Theatre Company; Old Vic 1st Season, 1944–45: played Peer Gynt, Bluntschli in Arms and the Man, Uncle Vanya, Henry VII in Richard the Third, toured Germany and visited Comédie Française in Paris. Old Vic 2nd season, 1945–46: played Falstaff in Henry IV, parts 1 and 2, Bluntschli in Arms and the Man, Tiresias in Oedipus Rex, Lord Burleigh in The Critic. Visited New York for six weeks' season. Old Vic 3rd Season, 1946–47: played Cyrano in Cyrano de Bergerac, the Inspector in An Inspector Calls, Face in The Alchemist, produced Richard II (playing Gaunt); Dr Sloper in The Heiress, Haymarket, 1949; David Preston in Home at Seven, Wyndham's 1950; Vershinin in Three Sisters, Aldwych, 1951; Stratford-on-Avon Season, 1952: Macbeth, Volpone, The Tempest; The White Carnation (playing John Greenwood), Globe, 1953; A Day by the Sea, Haymarket, 1954; Sleeping Prince and Separate Tables, Australian and New Zealand Tour, 1955; The Waltz of the Toreadors (New York), 1957; Flowering Cherry, Haymarket, 1958; The Complaisant Lover, Globe, 1959; The Last Joke, 1960; The School for Scandal, Haymarket and US Tour, 1962; Six Characters in search of an Author, May Fair, 1963; The Merchant of Venice and A Midsummer Night's Dream, South American and European Tour, 1964; Carving a Statue, Haymarket, 1964; You Never Can Tell, 1966; The Rivals, 1966, 1967; Merchant of Venice, 1967; What the Butler Saw, 1969; Home, London, 1970 (Evening Standard Best Actor Award), NY, 1971; West of Suez, 1971; Lloyd George Knew My Father, 1972–73 (Austr. tour 1973); John Gabriel Borkman, National, 1975; No Man's Land, National, 1975, NY 1976; The Kingfisher, Lyric, 1977; The Cherry Orchard, National, 1978; Alice's Boys, Savoy, 1978; The Double Dealer, National, 1978; Fruits of Enlightenment, The Wild Duck, National, 1979; Early Days, National, 1980, then Comedy, 1981, tour, USA and Canada, 1981; The Understanding, Strand, 1982; Inner Voices, National, 1983; *films:* made his first film, The Ghoul, in 1933; other films include: Things to Come; The Man Who Could Work Miracles; Bulldog Drummond; South Riding; Divorce of Lady X; The Citadel; Four Feathers; Q Planes; Night of the Fire; The Silver Fleet; The Volunteer; School for Secrets; Anna Karenina, The Fallen Idol, The Heiress (Hollywood); Outcast of the Islands; Home at Seven; The Holly and the Ivy; The Sound Barrier; The Passionate Stranger; Oscar Wilde; Exodus; Spartacus; Long Day's Journey into Night; Woman of Straw; Dr Zhivago, 1965; The Wrong Box, 1966; Gordon of Khartoum, 1966; Twelfth Night, 1968; Battle of Britain, 1968; Oh! What a Lovely War, 1968; The Bed-Sitting Room, 1968; The Looking-Glass War, 1968; Mr Micawber in David Copperfield, 1969; A Run on Gold, 1969; Gingerbread House, 1971; Lady Caroline Lamb, 1972; Alice's Adventures in Wonderland, 1972; Eagle in a Cage, 1973; A Doll's House, 1973; O Lucky Man, 1973; Rollerball, 1975; Dragonslayer, 1980; Time Bandits, 1981; Invitation to the Wedding, 1982; Greystoke, 1983; Wagner, 1983; My Regards to Broad Street, 1983. Pres., Nat. Youth Theatre, 1959–83. Hon. DLitt Oxon, 1969. SWET Special Award, 1981. Order of St Olaf (Norway), 1950. *Publications:* articles in magazines and newspapers; *relevant publication:* Ralph Richardson, by Robert Tanitch, 1983. *Recreations:* drawing, tennis. *Address:* 1 Chester Terrace, Regent's Park, NW1. *Clubs:* Athenæum, Beefsteak, Savile; Greenroom (Life Mem.).

*Died 10 Oct.* 1983.

**RICHARDSON, Rev. Canon Robert Douglas,** DD, MLitt, MA; *b* 26 February 1893; *er s* of late Frederick Richardson; *m* 1929, Professor Linetta P. de Castelvecchio (*d* 1975). *Educ:* Hertford College and Ripon Hall, Oxford. Served European War, 1914–18, in RN; Curate of Stourport-on-Severn; Succentor of Birmingham Cathedral; Vicar of Four Oaks and Vicar of Harborne; Select Preacher, Cambridge University; Lectr, Univ. of Oxford; sometime External Lectr in Biblical Studies to Univ. of Birmingham; Examining Chaplain to Bishop of Birmingham, 1932–53; Canon Emeritus of Birmingham Cathedral; Principal of Ripon Hall, Oxford, 1948–52; Rector of Boyton with Sherrington, 1952–67. *Publications:* The Conflict of Ideals in the Church of England, 1923; The Gospel of Modernism, 1933; Sectional Editor of Webster's Dictionary (1934 edn); A Revised Order of Holy Communion, 1936; Christian Belief and Practice, 1940; The Psalms as Christian Prayers and Praises, 1960; article on Luke and the Eucharistic Tradition, in Studia Evangelica, 1957, in The Gospels Reconsidered, 1960; Studies in the Origins of the Liturgy (publ. with Lietzmann's Studies in the History of the Liturgy in Mass and Lord's Supper), 1979; Christianity for Today, 1987; contrib. to various theological jls. *Address:* Corton Parva, Warminster, Wilts. *T:* Warminster 50286.

*Died 30 March* 1989.

**RICHARDSON, Sir William (Robert),** Kt 1967; Chief Executive Officer, Cooperative Press Ltd, 1967–74; *b* 16 Jan. 1909; *s* of Thomas and Constance Margaret Richardson; *m* 1932, Gladys Gillians; one *s* two *d*. *Educ:* various public elem. schs, Newcastle upon Tyne; evening classes; Cooperative College. Editor, Cooperative News, 1938; Editor, Reynolds News, later changed name to Sunday Citizen, 1942–67, when paper closed. Mem. Post Office Users' Nat. Council, 1969–79. *Publications:* The CWS in War and Peace 1938–1976, 1977; A Union of Many Trades: the history of USDAW, 1979; The People's Business: a history of Brighton Co-op., 1984. *Recreation:* reading. *Address:* Flat 9, Linton Court, Linton Road, Hastings, E Sussex TN34 1TP. *T:* Hastings 716154.

*Died 16 Jan.* 1986.

**RICHES, Sir Eric (William),** Kt 1958; MC; MS (London), FRCS; Emeritus Surgeon and Urologist to Middlesex Hospital; Hon. Consultant Urologist to Hospital of St John and St Elizabeth; formerly Consulting Urologist to the Army and to Ministry of Pensions Spinal Injury Centre; lately Urologist, St Andrew's Hospital, Dollis Hill; lately Urologist, Royal Masonic Hospital; Hon. Curator, Historical Surgical Instruments Collection, Royal College of Surgeons, 1962; *b* Alford, Lincolnshire, 29 July 1897; *s* of William Riches; *m* 1st, 1927, Annie M. S. (*d* 1952), *d* of late Dr A. T. Brand, Driffield, E Yorks; two *d*; 2nd, 1954, Susan Elizabeth Ann, *d* of late Lt-Col L. H. Kitton, MBE, MC; one *d*. *Educ:* Christ's Hospital; Middlesex Hospital. Served European War, 10th Lincoln and 11th Suffolk Regt, Capt. and Adjutant (MC); Senior Broderip Scholar and Lyell Gold Medallist, Middlesex Hospital, 1925. Past Vice-President, Royal College of Surgeons, Member of Court of Examiners, 1940–46; Hunterian Professor 1938 and 1942, Jacksonian Prizeman, 1942; Bradshaw Lecturer, 1962; Gordon-Taylor Lecturer, 1967. Hon. Fellow Royal Society of Medicine, 1966, lately Hon. Librarian, ex-President Clinical Section, Section of Urology, and Section of Surgery. Past-President Medical Society of London; Lettsomian Lecturer, 1958, Orator, 1970; Senior Fellow Association of Surgeons of Great Britain and Ireland; Past President Hunterian Society, Orator, 1967; Vice-President, Internat. Soc. of Urology (Pres. XIII Congress, 1964); Hon. Fellow and Past Pres. of British Assoc. of Urological Surgeons; St Peters medallist, 1964; Member Association Française d'Urologie; Honorary Member: Urological Society of Australasia; Canadian Urological Assoc.; Swedish Urological Soc.; American Urological Assoc.; American Assoc. of Genito-Urinary Surgeons; Ramon Guitéras Lectr, 1963; Hon. Associate Mem. French Academy of Surgery, 1961; Emeritus Mem. Internat. Soc. of Surgery; Past Treas. British Journal of Surgery; Past Chm., Ed. Cttee, British Jl of Urology; Mem. of Biological and Medical Cttee, Royal Commission on Population. Visiting Professor, Urol.; University of Texas and State University of New York, 1965; Visiting Professor and Balfour Lecturer, University of Toronto, 1966. Treasurer, Christ's Hospital, and Chm., Council of Almoners, 1970–76. *Publications:* Modern Trends in Urology, Series 1, 1953, Series 2, 1960, Series 3, 1969; Tumours of the Kidney and Ureter, 1964; various articles on Surgery and Urology in Scientific journals; contributor to Text Book of Urology, British Surgical Practice, and to Encyclopædia of Urology. *Recreations:* golf, music, photography. *Address:* 23 Eresby House, Rutland Gate, SW7 1BG. *T:* 01–589 7129.

*Died 8 Nov.* 1987.

**RICHMOND, 9th Duke of,** *cr* 1675, **AND GORDON, 4th Duke of,** *cr* 1876; **Frederick Charles Gordon-Lennox;** Earl of March, Baron Settrington, Duke of Lennox, Earl of Darnley, Baron Methuen, 1675; Earl of Kinrara, 1876; Duke d'Aubigny (France), 1683–84; Hereditary Constable of Inverness Castle; Flight Lieut, RAFVR; *b* 5 Feb. 1904; *o surv. s* of 8th Duke and Hilda, DBE, *d* of late Henry Arthur Brassey, Preston Hall, Kent; *S* father, 1935; *m* 1927, Elizabeth Grace, *y d* of late Rev. T. W. Hudson; two *s*. *Educ:* Eton; Christ Church, Oxford. *Heir: s* Earl of March, *b* 19 Sept. 1929. *Address:* Carne's Seat, Goodwood, Chichester, W Sussex; 29 Hyde Park Street, W2. *Died 2 Nov.* 1989.

**RICHMOND, Sir John (Christopher Blake),** KCMG 1963 (CMG 1959); retired; *b* 7 September 1909; *s* of E. T. Richmond, FRIBA, and M. M. Richmond (*née* Lubbock); *m* 1939, D. M. L. Galbraith; one *s* three *d* (and one *s* decd). *Educ:* Lancing College; Hertford College, Oxford; University College, London. Various archaeological expeditions, 1931–36; HM Office of Works, 1937–39; served War, Middle East, 1939–46; Dept of Antiquities, Palestine Govt, 1946–47; HM Diplomatic Service, Baghdad, 1947; Foreign Office, 1951; Counsellor, British Embassy, Amman, 1953–55; HM Consul-General, Houston, Texas, 1955–58; Foreign Office, 1958–59; Counsellor, British Property Commission, Cairo, 1959; HM Ambassador to Kuwait, 1961–63 (Political Agent, Kuwait, 1959–61); Supernumerary Fellow of St Antony's College, Oxford, 1963–64; Ambassador to Sudan, 1965–66; Lectr, Modern Near East History, Sch. of Oriental Studies, Univ. of Durham, 1966–74. *Publication:* Egypt 1798–1952, 1977. *Address:* 21 The Avenue, Durham City DH1 4ED. *Died 6 July* 1990.

**RICHMOND, Vice-Adm. Sir Maxwell,** KBE 1957 (OBE 1940); CB 1954; DSO 1942; RN retired; *b* 19 Oct. 1900; *e s* of Robert Richardson Richmond and Bernadette Richmond (*née* Farrell); *m* 1929, Jessie Messervy Craig (*d* 1985); one *s* three *d* (and one *s* decd). *Educ:* New Zealand State Schools; Westminster. Cadet Royal Navy 1918; Lieutenant 1922; specialised navigation; held various (N) posts, 1926–36. Comdr 1936; HMS Hostile in Comd, 1936–38; Staff Coll., 1939; HMS Basilisk in Comd, 1939–40; Dover Patrol, Norway and Dunkirk; Operations, Admty, 1940–41; HMS Bulldog as Sen. Officer Escort Gp, 1942, Atlantic and Russian Convoys; Capt. 1942; Chief Staff Officer to Cdre, Londonderry, 1943; HMS Milne as Capt. (D) 3rd Dest. Flot., 1944–46; Home Fleet, Russian Convoys and Flank Force, Mediterranean; Asst Chief of Supplies, Admty, 1946–48; Naval Liaison Officer, Wellington, NZ, 1948–50; Sen. Naval Officer, N Ire., 1951; Rear-Adm. 1952; Deputy Chief of Naval Personnel (Training), 1952–55; Flag Officer (Air), Mediterranean, and Flag Officer Second-in-Command, Mediterranean Fleet, 1955–Oct. 1956. Order of the Red Banner (Russian) 1942; Croix de Guerre (French) 1945. *Recreations:* sailing and tramping. *Address:* Little Merton, York Bay, Wellington, New Zealand; No 4 Rural Delivery, Whangarei, New Zealand. *Club:* Naval and Military. *Died 15 May* 1986.

**RICKARDS, Oscar Stanley Norman,** CBE 1945; Grand Officer in the Order of Orange-Nassau, 1947; Haakon VII Liberty Cross, 1947; Director of Victualling, Admiralty, 1941–58; *b* 14 Nov. 1893; *s* of Thomas Rickards and Laura Rose Short; *m* 1925, Sylvia Annie Dean; one *d*. *Educ:* University College School, Hampstead. Joined Admiralty, 1913. *Died 9 Jan.* 1986.

**RICKFORD, Richard Braithwaite Keevil,** MD (London), BS, FRCS, FRCOG; Consulting Physician, Obstetric Department, St Thomas' Hospital, London, 1979–85 (Physician, 1946–79); Consulting Surgeon, Chelsea Hospital for Women, 1979–85 (Surgeon, 1950–79); Gynæcologist, Oxted Hospitals, 1952–82; formerly Dean, Institute of Obstetrics and Gynaecology; *b* 1 June 1914; *e s* of late L. T. R. Rickford; *m* 1939, Dorothy, *d* of late Thomas Lathan; three *s* (and one *s* decd). *Educ:* Weymouth College; University of London. Various surgical, obstetric and gynæcological appointments at Norfolk and Norwich Hospital and St Thomas' Hospital. Examiner to: Universities of London, Cambridge and Glasgow; Royal Coll. of Obstetricians and Gynæcologists; Conjoint Board; Central Midwives Board. Mem. Council, RCOG, 1976–79. *Publications:* contributions to medical journals. *Recreations:* gardening, sailing. *Address:* Kingswear Lodge, Kingswear, Devon TQ6 0BS. *T:* Kingswear 361. *Clubs:* Royal Society of Medicine; Royal Dart Yacht (Kingswear, Devon). *Died 18 March* 1990.

**RIDDELL, Roland William, (Ronald),** MD; FRCP, FRCPE, FRCPath, FZS, FRGS; consultant clinical pathologist; Hon. Consulting Clinical Microbiologist to St John's Hospital for Diseases of the Skin, London, since 1968, and to the National Heart and Chest Hospitals, since 1980; *b* 9 Nov. 1913; *e s* of late William Henry Riddell and Ada (*née* Chamberlin) Highgate, London; *m* 2nd, 1976, Margaret Ann, *e d* of late John Geoffrey Strutt Lewis and of Mercy Eileen (*née* Mennell); two *s* from previous marriage. *Educ:* William Ellis Sch.; St Mary's Hosp. Med. Sch., Univ. of London (BS, DipBact 1947; MD 1948). MRCS 1939; FRCPE 1951; FRCPath 1964; FRCP 1972; FZS (Science) 1960; FRGS 1980. Served War, 1939–45: Staff Scottish Comd, Pathol. Trng Unit, Edinburgh Castle Mil. Hosp. and Edin. Univ. Med. Sch., 1940; Specialist in Pathol. (attached RN), Orkney and Shetland Defences, 1942, and 112 Gen. Hosp. (21st Army Gp), Kent, 1943; Asst Dir of Pathol., AFHQ, Central Medit., 1944–45; Lt-Col RAMC. House Surg. and Casualty Off., Grimsby and Dist Hosp., Lincs, 1939; Registrar in Pathol., Royal Hosp., Montrose, Angus, 1939; Sen. Lectr and Dir, Dept of Med. Mycol., London Sch. of Hygiene and Trop. Medicine, 1946; Travelling Fellow in Microbiol., Commonwealth (Harkness) Fund of New York, Duke Univ., NC, and Columbia Univ., NY, 1948–49; Sen. Lectr, Dept of Med. Mycol., Inst. of Dermatol., 1949–68; Mem. Bd of Governors and Dir, Dept of Microbiol., St John's Hosp. for Diseases of Skin, 1950–65; Consultant Clin. Microbiologist and Chm. Inf. Cttees: Brompton Hosp., 1951–80; London Chest Hosp., 1970–80; Nat. Heart Hosp., 1972–80; Consulting Microbiologist (Mycobact.), Armed Forces of Indonesia, 1978–; Sen. Lectr in Professorial Dept of Medicine, Cardiothoracic Inst., Univ. of London, 1968–80; sometime Lectr, Royal Postgrad. Med. Sch., London, and British Council; Recog. Teacher and Examr in Bact. and Med. Mycol., Univ. of London, 1956–. Vis. Guest: Med. Council of India, 1959 (lectured at Sch. of Trop. Medicine, Calcutta, and in Madras, Bombay and Delhi); Govt of Hong Kong, 1966. Hon. Mem., Cttee on Bact. and Immun., Internat. Union Against Tuberculosis: meetings in Amsterdam, Ankara, Paris, Moscow (Chm.), Munich, New York, 1966–73. Lectured, Dept. Infect. Dis., Presbyt. Hosp., Columbia Univ., NY, 1980. Chm., Clin. Trials Org., Brit. Tuberculosis Assoc., 1958–61; Pres., London Chest Hosp. Assoc., 1981; Member: Cttee of Management, Inst. of Diseases of Chest, 1963; Leprosy Study Centre, London, 1960–80; Edit. Bd, Antimicrobial Agents and Chemotherapy, USA, 1971–74; Assoc. of Clin. Pathologists (Hon. Mem., 1983–); Sen. Mem., Thoracic

Soc. Mitchell Lectr, and Citation for Weber-Parkes Prize, RCP, 1974. *Publications:* (ed and contrib.) Fungus Diseases and their Treatment, 1958; (contrib.) Butterworths Medical Dictionary, 2nd edn 1978; *chapters in:* British Encyclopaedia of Medical Practice, 1951–52; Recent Advances in Clinical Pathology, 1951; Diseases of the Chest, 1952; Leprosy in Theory and Practice, 1959, 2nd edn 1964; Nomenclature of Disease, RCP, 8th edn 1959; Chest Diseases, 1963; Price's Textbook of Medicine, 1966, 1973, 1978 (10th-12th edns); Third Symposium on Advanced Medicine, 1967; Side Effects of Drugs VII, 1972; Modern Chemotherapy of Tuberculosis, 1975; contrib. British, USA, French and Indian jls. *Recreations:* music, travel, history and conservation of Royal Borough of Kensington and Chelsea. *Address:* 38 Devonshire Street, W1N 1LD; 58 Brompton Square, SW3 2AG. *T:* 01–589 1187.
*Died 21 Nov.* 1984.

**RIDEALGH, Mrs Mabel;** General Secretary of Women's Co-operative Guild, 1953–63; Member, Women's Advisory Committee, British Standards Institute, 1953–63; *b* 11 Aug. 1898; *d* of M. A. Jewitt, Wallsend-on-Tyne, Northumberland; *m* 1919, Leonard, *s* of W. R. Ridealgh, Sunderland, Durham; one *s* one *d.* National Pres. Women's Co-op. Guild, 1941–42; Hon. Regional Organiser Bd of Trade (Make-do and Mend), 1942–44; MP (Lab) Ilford North, 1945–50. *Address:* 2 Eastwood Road, Goodmayes, Ilford, Essex. *T:* 01–599 8960.
*Died 20 June* 1989.

**RIDING, George Albert,** MA; Headmaster, Aldenham School, 1933–49; *b* 1 April 1888; *s* of Daniel A. Riding and Anne Deighton; *m* Aideen Maud, *d* of T. W. Rolleston, *g d* of late Rev. Stopford Brooke; two *s. Educ:* Manchester Grammar School (Scholar); University of Manchester (MA Hons English Language and Literature); New College, Oxford, 1st Class Honours, Modern Languages (French and German), 1921, Heath Harrison Travelling Scholarship, 1920; President, Oxford University French Club, 1920; Assistant Master: Penarth County Sch., 1909–14; Mill Hill School, 1914–15; Rugby School, 1921–28 (Sixth Form Master); served with Northumberland Fusiliers (wounded); Registrar, King's Lancashire Military Convalescent Hospital, 1917–18; Captain in Rugby School OTC; Headmaster, Warwick School, 1928–33. Member of House of Laity, Church Assembly, 1944. Member of Council, Inc. Assoc. of Head Masters, 1942–44. Foundation Member of Hispanic Council. Member School Broadcasting Council, 1947–58; Chairman Secondary Programmes Committee, 1947–54. Chairman: Cornwall Modern Churchmen's Union, 1950; Truro Divisional Liberal Association, 1950–51; Cornwall Liberal Council, 1950; Minack Theatre Society, 1960–66; E Cornwall Society for the Mentally Handicapped, 1960–66. Carried out (with headmaster of Fettes Coll.) survey of pre-service education in Pakistan, 1951. *Publications:* Blackie's Longer French Texts; Les Trois Mousquetaires; La Bête dans les Neiges; Moral Foundations of Citizenship; contrib. to Naval Review, Spectator. *Address:* Colona, Port Mellon, Mevagissey, St Austell, Cornwall PL26 6PH. *T:* Mevagissey 3440.
*Died 3 Feb.* 1982.

**RIDLEY, Arnold,** OBE 1982; dramatic author, actor, and producer; *b* Bath, 7 Jan. 1896; *s* of late William Robert Ridley and Rosa Morrish; *m* Althea Parker; one *s. Educ:* Bristol University. Formerly a schoolmaster; enlisted, 1915; served in ranks; was severely wounded, Somme, 1916, and discharged 1917; rejoined HM Forces Oct. 1939, served on PR Staff with acting rank of Major BEF, France, 1939–40; joined Birmingham Repertory Company, 1918, and played various parts for several seasons; later with: Plymouth Repertory Company; White Rose Players, Harrogate; Oxford Repertory Theatre Company; original Walter Gabriel in stage version of The Archers; frequent appearances on Television (Harry Crane in BBC series Starr and Co.; The Vicar in Crossroads; Private Godfrey in Dad's Army); also radio: Doughy Hood in The Archers; author of the following produced plays: The Brass God, 1921; The Ghost Train, 1925, revived 1976; The Burnett Mystery, 1926; The God o' Mud, 1926; The Wrecker (with Bernard Merivale), 1927; Keepers of Youth, 1929; The Flying Fool (with Merivale), 1929; Third Time Lucky, 1929; Recipe for Murder, 1932; Headline, 1934; Half-a-Crown (with Douglas Furber), 1934; Glory Be, 1934; Needs Must, 1938; Out Goes She (with Merivale), 1939; Peril at End House (with Agatha Christie), 1940; Happy Holiday (with Eric Maschwitz), 1954; Tabitha (with Mary Cathcart Borer), 1955; The Running Man (with Anthony Armstrong), 1955; Murder Happens, 1945; Easy Money, 1947; Trifles Light as Air (with St Vincent Troubridge), 1949; East of Ludgate Hill, 1950; The Dark Corridor (with Richard Reich), 1950; Beggar My Neighbour, 1951; You, My Guests!, 1956; Shadows on the Sand (with Borer), 1956; Geranium, 1957; Bellamy (with Anthony Armstrong), 1959; Crocks, 1960; High Fidelity (with Cedric Wallis), 1964; Festive Board, 1970; The Tides of Chance, 1970; prod the following plays: Sunshine House, Little Theatre, 1933; Rude Awakening, Shilling Theatre, 1934; Flood Tide, Phœnix Theatre, 1938; Producer, Malvern Company, 1942–44. Wrote and directed film Royal Eagle, 1935; other films include: East of Ludgate Hill, 1935; Blind Justice, 1935; The Last Chance, 1936; The Seven Sinners, 1936. *Publications:* Keepers of

Youth, 1929; various short stories and articles. *Recreations:* Rugby football and cricket; takes active interest in Bath Rugby Club, served as hon. match sec. several years and elected President 1950–52, and Life Member, 1963. *Address:* c/o Hughes Massie & Co., 31 Southampton Row, WC1. *Clubs:* Savage, Dramatists'.
*Died 12 March* 1984.

**RIGBY, Herbert Cecil,** DFC 1943, and Bar 1944; **His Honour Judge Rigby;** a Circuit Judge since 1980; Senior Partner, H. P. & H. C. Rigby, Solicitors, Sandbach, Cheshire; *b* 2 April 1917; *s* of Captain Herbert Parrot Rigby, TD; *m* 1st, 1939, Ethel Muriel Horton; two *d;* 2nd, 1949, Florence Rita Scotts; one *s. Educ:* Sandbach Sch.; Ellesmere Coll.; Liverpool Univ. (Law Faculty). Articled R. S. Rigby, Winsford. Commissioned, 7th Cheshire Regt, 1937. Served War: Expeditionary Force, France, 1939; evacuated, Dunkirk, 1940; transfer to RAF, 1941; Wings, 11 Gp, Hornchurch (Spitfires), 1942; Landing, N Africa, 1942; commanded 222 Sqdn, Invasion of France, 1944–45 (Bt Militaire de Pilote D'Avion, 1945); demobilised, 1946. Commanded 610 City of Chester Auxiliary Sqdn, 1947–49. Law Final, and admitted solicitor, 1947; partner, H. P. & H. C. Rigby, Sandbach, Cheshire, 1947–; a Recorder of the Crown Court, Wales and Chester Circuit, 1972–80. Member: Cheshire Brine Compensation Bd, 1952–74 (Chm., 1969–74); Cheshire CC, 1955–69; Runcorn Develt Corp., 1964–80 (Dep. Chm., 1974–80). *Recreations:* fishing, golf, boating, gardening. *Address:* Shelbourre, New Platt Lane, Cranage, *via* Crewe, Cheshire.
*Died 30 Oct.* 1986.

**RIGBY, Sir Ivo (Charles Clayton),** Kt 1964; a Metropolitan Stipendiary Magistrate, 1976–83; a Recorder of the Crown Court, 1975–83, retired; *b* 2 June 1911; *s* of late James Philip Clayton Rigby and late Elisabeth Mary Corbett; *m* 1st, 1938, Agnes Bothway (marr. diss.); 2nd, Kathleen Nancy, *d* of late Dr W. E. Jones, CMG; no *c. Educ:* Magdalen College School, Oxford. Called to the Bar (Inner Temple), 1932; Magistrate, Gambia, 1935–38; Chief Magistrate, Crown Counsel, and President of a District Court, Palestine, 1938–48; Assistant Judge, Nyasaland, 1948–54; President of Sessions Court, Malaya, 1954–55; Puisne Judge, Malaya, 1956–61; Senior Puisne Judge, Hong Kong, 1961–70; Chief Justice of Hong Kong and of Brunei, 1970–73; Pres., Court of Appeal, Brunei, 1973–79. *Publications:* The Law Reports of Nyasaland, 1934–1952. *Recreations:* cricket and bridge. *Address:* 1 Dalmeny House, Thurloe Place, SW7 2RY. *T:* 01–589 0267. *Clubs:* Naval and Military, Hurlingham, East India, Devonshire, Sports and Public Schools, MCC.
*Died 19 April* 1987.

**RILEY, Harry Lister,** DSc, ARCS, DIC, FRSC; *b* 7 Sept. 1899; *s* of late Arthur Riley, Keighley, Yorks; *m* 1924, Marion, *o c* of David Belfield; two *s* one *d. Educ:* The Grammar School, Keighley; Imperial College of Science and Technology (Royal College of Science). Served with 9th Bn KOYLI, 1917–19. Beit Scientific Research Fellow, 1921–23; Demonstrator, and later Lecturer in Chemistry at the Royal College of Science, South Kensington, SW7, 1923–32; Professor of Inorganic and Physical Chemistry, King's Coll. (Univ. of Durham), Newcastle on Tyne, 1932–47; Hon. Secretary and Dir of Research to the Northern Coke Research Committee; Jubilee Memorial Lecturer, Society of Chemical Industry, 1938–39; Director of Chemical Research and Development, United Steel Companies Ltd, 1947–64; Dir of carbonization research, Nat. Coal Board, 1947. *Publications:* various research publications in The Journal of the Chemical Society, the Philosophical Magazine, the Geological Magazine, and the Proceedings of the Royal Society, etc. *Recreation:* golf. *Address:* 3a Haldane Terrace, Jesmond, Newcastle upon Tyne NE2 3AN.
*Died 25 March* 1986.

**RINK, George Arnold,** QC 1956; *b* 21 April 1902; *m* 1949, Dr Margaret Joan Suttill. *Educ:* Charterhouse; University College, Oxford. 1st Cl. Hon. Mods, and Lit. Hum.; BCL; MA; half-blue for fencing. Called to Bar, 1926, and practised at the Chancery Bar from then until 1980 except for war-time service in Trading with the Enemy Br. and Mins of Food and Production; Bencher of Lincoln's Inn, 1962– (Treasurer 1978). Chm., Licensed Dealers' Tribunal, 1968–76. Mem., Senate, Inns of Court, 1973–74. Trustee of Charterhouse in Southwark, 1948–66. Board of Governors, Royal Free Hospital, 1955–64, Middlesex Hospital, 1964–70. Advisory Council, Science Policy Foundation, 1966–. Vice-Pres., Bar Musical Soc., 1977–. *Publications:* articles in professional journals. *Recreations:* reading, listening to music, walking, swimming. *Address:* 173 Oakwood Court, W14. *T:* 01-602 2143. *Club:* Athenæum.
*Died 6 April* 1983.

**RINTOUL, Andrew,** CBE 1965; AE; CA; Chairman: Trustee Savings Banks Central Board, 1976–80; Central Trustee Savings Bank, 1979–80; *b* 21 June 1908; *s* of Peter Rintoul, CA, and Margaret MacDonald Tulloch; *m* 1936, Margaret Bell; one *s* one *d. Educ:* Merchiston Castle Sch., Edinburgh; St John's Coll., Cambridge (BA). Chartered Accountant. Partner, Grahams, Rintoul & Co., 1936. Chm., Scottish National Trust Co. Ltd, 1938–79; Chm.,

Glasgow Stockholders Trust Ltd, 1938–79. Chm., Scottish Adv. Bd, Legal & General Assurance Society, 1967–78; Mem., Invest. Adv. Cttee, TSB Unit Trust, 1969–79. Trustee Savings Banks Association: Mem. Exec. Cttee, 1958–67; Dep. Chm., 1961–67; Vice-Pres., 1968–76. Hon. Pres., West of Scotland TSB, 1980–83. *Recreations:* fishing, gardening, golf, shooting. *Address:* Bargaly House, Newton Stewart, Wigtownshire. *T:* Newton Stewart 2392. *Club:* Royal Air Force. *Died* 29 *Nov.* 1984.

**RISK, (Charles) John,** CBE 1984; Secretary, Coats Patons PLC, since 1970; *b* 20 Jan. 1926; *s* of late Ralph Risk, CBE, MC and Margaret Nelson Robertson. *Educ:* Kelvinside Acad., Glasgow; Trinity Coll., Glenalmond; Univ. of Glasgow. LLB. Served Royal Marines, 1944–47. Sec., J. & P. Coats Ltd, 1966. Dir, Scottish Mutual Assce Soc., 1977–. Confederation of British Industry: Mem. Council, 1980–; Mem., Scottish Council, 1980– (Chm., 1983–85); Dir, 1968–, Pres., 1976–78, Glasgow Chamber of Commerce; Mem., Nat. Council, Assoc. of British Chambers of Commerce, 1976– (Chm., 1982–84). Lay Mem., Restrictive Practices Court, 1980–. Trustee: Scottish Civic Trust; Nat. Galls of Scotland. *Recreations:* enjoyment of countryside, wild life. *Address:* Dunselma, Strone, Argyll PA23 8RU. *Died* 30 *May* 1985.
*This entry did not appear in Who's Who.*

**RITCHIE, Sir Douglas;** *see* Ritchie, Sir J. D.

**RITCHIE, Henry Parker, (Harry),** CMG 1966; Fiscal Adviser to Government of Falkland Islands, since 1978; *b* 3 June 1919; *s* of W. S. Ritchie; *m* 1949, Mary Grace, *née* Foster; two *s. Educ:* Royal Belfast Academical Institution; Queen's University, Belfast. Served War of 1939–45 (Captain). Administrative Cadet, Bechuanaland Protectorate, 1946; Swaziland, 1948; District Officer, 1953; seconded to Office of High Commissioner, as Assistant Secretary, 1954; Deputy Financial Secretary, Fiji, 1957, Financial Secretary, 1962–67, Minister of Finance, 1967–70; Secretary for Finance, Papua New Guinea, 1971–74. Financial and Econ. Consultant to Papua New Guinea Govt, 1974–75; Consultant on Civil Service Salaries to Govt of Tonga (report pubd 1976), to Govt of Seychelles (report pubd 1977), to Govt of Falkland Islands (reports pubd 1977, 1981); to Govt of St Helena (report pubd 1980). *Recreations:* gardening, reading. *Address:* 6 Mill Rise, Mill Lane, Bourton, Dorset. *Died* 5 *Oct.* 1988.

**RITCHIE, John,** MBE 1944; Senior Master of the Supreme Court of Judicature (Queen's Bench Division), and Queen's Remembrancer, 1980–82 (Master, 1960); *b* 7 Feb. 1913; *e s* of W. Tod Ritchie, JP, Rector of Hutchesons' Grammar School, Glasgow; *m* 1936, Nora Gwendolen Margaret, *yr d* of Sir Frederic G. Kenyon, GBE, KCB, FBA; one *s* two *d. Educ:* Glasgow Academy; Magdalen College, Oxford. BA 1935; MA 1948. Called to the Bar, Middle Temple, 1935; practised in London and on South-Eastern Circuit, 1935–60; Recorder of King's Lynn, 1956–58. Served War of 1939–45 (MBE, Belgian Croix de Guerre, despatches twice): BEF 1940; BLA 1944–45; private, Royal Fusiliers, 1939; commissioned Queen's Own Cameron Highlanders, 1940; Major, 1942. Belgian Croix de Guerre, 1944. *Recreations:* reading, painting, rose-growing. *Address:* 4 Millwood Rise, Overton-on-Dee, near Wrexham, Clwyd LL13 0EL. *T:* Overton-on-Dee 485. *Died* 21 *March* 1988.

**RITCHIE, Sir (John) Douglas,** Kt 1941; MC; *b* 28 Nov. 1885; *s* of John Walker Ritchie, Collieston, Aberdeenshire, and Mary Southern; *m* 1913, Margaret Stephen, OBE 1946, JP, Officer of the Order of Orange-Nassau (*d* 1976), *d* of James Allan, Methlick, Aberdeenshire; one *s. Educ:* Manchester Grammar School; Manchester Univ. Served European War in France in 4th Gordon Highlanders and Tank Corps (MC); Town Clerk of Burnley, 1920–23; Solicitor to the Port of London Authority, 1923–26; Solicitor and Secretary to the Port of London Authority, 1927–38; Deputy General Manager, 1938; Gen. Manager, 1938–46; Vice-Chm., Port of London Authority, 1946–55. Mem. Aberdeen County Council, 1955–65; Pres., Dock and Harbour Authorities Assoc., 1954–56; Pres. of Burns Club of London, 1934–35; Chief Executive of London Port Emergency Cttee, 1939–46; Member of Inland Transport War Council; Col. Engineer and Railway Staff Corps RE (TA). *Recreations:* sailing, fishing. *Address:* Collieston, Aberdeenshire. *T:* Collieston 216. *Died* 12 *Feb.* 1983.

**RITCHIE, Gen. Sir Neil Methuen,** GBE 1951 (KBE 1945; CBE 1940); KCB 1947 (CB 1944); DSO 1917; MC 1918; retired; Director, Tanqueray Gordon & Co. (Can.) Ltd; *b* 29 July 1897; 2nd *s* of late Dugald Ritchie of Restholme, Liss, Hants; *m* 1937, Catherine, *d* of James A. Minnes, Kingston, Ontario; one *s* one *d. Educ:* Lancing; RMC, Sandhurst. 2nd Lieut The Black Watch, 1914; Lieutenant 1915; Capt. 1917; Bt Major, 1933; Major, 1934; Bt Lt-Col 1936; Lt-Col The King's Own Royal Regt 1938; Col 1939; Brigadier 1939; Acting Maj.-General 1940; Temp. Major-General 1941; Maj.-Gen. 1943; Temp. Lt-Gen. 1944; Lt-Gen. 1945; General 1947; served European War, 1914–19; France, 1915; Mesopotamia, 1916–17; Palestine, 1918 (despatches, DSO, MC); Palestine, 1938–39 (despatches); Gen. Staff Officer, 3rd Grade, War Office, 1923–27;

Staff College, Camberley, 1929–30; GSO2, Northern Command, India, 1933–37; GSO1, 1939; Brigadier, General Staff, 1939; Comdr 51st Highland Division, 1940–41; Deputy Chief of Staff Middle East, 1941; Commander of 8th Army, Libya, acting rank of Lieut-General, 1941; Comd 52nd Lowland Division, 1942–43; Comd 12 Corps BLA, 1944–45; GOC-in-C Scottish Command and Governor of Edinburgh Castle, 1945–47; C-in-C, Far East Land Forces, 1947–49; Commander British Army Staff, Washington, and Military Member of Joint Services Mission, 1950–51; ADC General to the King, 1948–51; retired pay, 1951. Colonel, The Black Watch (Royal Highland Regiment), 1950–52. Queen's Body Guard for Scotland. Dir Emeritus, Mercantile & General Re-insurance Co. of Canada Ltd. Virtuti Militari (Poland), 1942; Comdr Legion of Honour, Croix de Guerre (France), 1945; Kt Comdr Orange Nassau (Holland), 1945; Comdr Order of Merit (USA), 1945. KStJ 1963. *Address:* 355 St Clair Avenue West, Apartment 1406, Toronto, Ontario, Canada M5P 1N9. *T:* (416)960 6209. *Clubs:* Caledonian, I Zingari, Free Foresters; York (Toronto). *Died* 11 *Dec.* 1983.

**RITCHIE, Major-General Walter Henry Dennison,** CB 1953; CBE 1944 (OBE 1940); Life President, Earls Court & Olympia Ltd, 1974 (Chairman, Earls Court Ltd, 1967, Earls Court & Olympia Ltd, 1973); *b* 28 April 1901; *s* of Henry Montague Ritchie, Perth; *m* 1930, Gladys Stella, *d* of William Craven, Southsea; one *s* one *d. Educ:* St John's Coll., Southsea. 2nd Lieut RASC, 1925; served War of 1939–45, in France, Italy; Maj. 1939; 15 Army Group (Brig.), 1943; DQMG to Field Marshal Alexander, Oct. 1943–Dec. 1944, to Gen. Mark Clark, Dec. 1944–May 1945; Maj.-Gen. 1953; Director of Quartering, War Office, 1953–54; Director of Supplies and Transport, War Office, 1954–57; retired. Col Comdt, RASC, 1959–64; Hon. Col 101 AER Regt, RCT, 1965–67. Freeman, City of London, 1962. Officer Legion of Merit, USA 1945. *Club:* Army and Navy. *Died* 3 *Oct.* 1984.

**RITCHIE-CALDER,** Baron, *cr* 1966, of Balmashannar (Life Peer); Peter Ritchie Ritchie-Calder, CBE 1945; MA (Edinburgh) 1961; author and journalist; Senior Fellow, Center for the Study of Democratic Institutions, Santa Barbara, California, 1972–75; *b* 1 July 1906; *s* of David Lindsay Calder and Georgina Ritchie, Forfar, Angus; *m* 1927, Mabel Jane Forbes, *d* of Dr David McKail, Glasgow; three *s* two *d. Educ:* Forfar Academy. Police court reporter, Dundee Courier (1922), D. C. Thomson Press (London office, 1924, Glasgow, 1925), Daily News (1926–30), Daily Chronicle (1930), Daily Herald (1930–41). Author, scientific, social and political journalist and broadcaster (radio and television). Science Editor, News Chronicle, 1945–56. Dept of FO, 1941–45; Editorial Staff, New Statesman, 1945–58; Montague Burton Professor of International Relations, Edinburgh University, 1961–67. Chm., Metrication Bd, 1969–72. Vis Prof., Heriot-Watt Univ., 1973–; Charles Beard lectr, Ruskin College, Oxford, 1957; Bentwich Lectr, Hebrew Univ., 1973; Brodetsky Lectr, Leeds Univ. 1973. Member Council British Association, Pres. Section X, 1955; Fell. Amer. Assoc. for Advancement of Science; Fabian Executive; Secretary of H. G. Wells' Debate, and Viscount Sankey Cttee, on New Declaration of the Rights of Man, 1940; Mem. British delegn to Unesco (Paris, 1946, Mexico City, 1947, 1966, 1968); special adviser at FAO Famine Conf. (Washington, 1946); Desert survey for Unesco, 1950; chief, special UN Mission to SE Asia, 1951; Mission (UN auspices) to Arctic, 1955; Member UN Secretariat, at Peaceful Uses of Atomic Energy Confs, 1955 and 1958, and Member WHO group on mental aspects of Atomic Energy, 1957; Consultant-Editor, UN Science and Technology Conference, Geneva, 1963; Chm. Chicago University study group on Radiation in the Environment, 1960; Special UN Mission to Congo, 1960; 2nd UN Mission to SE Asia, 1962. Chairman Association of British Science Writers, 1949–55. President: Mental Health Film Council; National Peace Council; British Sub-Aqua Club, 1971–74; Danforth Foundation Lecturer, USA, 1965. UK Commn for WHO; UK Commn for Unesco; Cons., OXFAM; Vice-Pres. Workers' Educational Assoc., 1958–68; Member: Gen. Council, Open Univ., 1969–81; Community Relations Commn, 1968–70; Council, Internat. Ocean Inst., 1970–; House of Lords Select Cttee on Sci. and Technology, 1980–; Chm., Adv. Cttee on Pollution of the Sea, 1977–; Consultant, US Librarian of Congress, 1976. Fellow, World Acad. of Arts and Science; DUniv Open, 1975; DSc York, Ont, 1976. Kalinga Internat. Award for science writing, 1960; Victor Gollanz Award for service to humanity, 1969; New York Library Jubilee Medal, 1961; WHO Med. Soc. Medal, 1974. *Publications:* Birth of the Future, 1934; Conquest of Suffering, 1935; Roving Commission, 1935; Lesson of London, 1941; Carry on, London, 1941; Start Planning Britain Now, 1941; Men against the Desert, 1951; Profile of Science, 1951; The Lamp is Lit, 1951; Men against Ignorance, 1953 (UNESCO); Men Against the Jungle, 1954; Science in Our Lives, 1954 (USA); Science Makes Sense, 1955; Men against the Frozen North, 1957; Magic to Medicine, 1958; Medicine and Man, 1958; Ten Steps Forward: The Story of WHO, 1958; The Hand of Life: The Story of the Weizmann Institute, 1959; The

Inheritors, 1960; Agony of the Congo, 1961; Life-Savers, 1961; Common Sense about a Starving World, 1962; Living with the Atom, 1962; World of Opportunity (for United Nations), 1963; Two-Way Passage, 1964; The Evolution of the Machine, 1968; Man and the Cosmos, 1968; Leonardo and the Age of the Eye, 1970; How Long have we got?, 1972; The Pollution of the Mediterranean, 1972; Understanding Energy, 1979. *Recreation:* carpentry. *Address:* Philipstoun House, Linlithgow, W Lothian EH49 7NB. *T:* Philpstoun 187. *Clubs:* Savile; Scottish Arts, University Staff (Edinburgh); Century (New York). *Died 31 Jan.* 1982.

**RITSON, Sir Edward Herbert,** KBE 1950; CB 1945; LLB; *b* 1892; *s* of late Edward E. Ritson, Liverpool; *m* 1922, Norah, *d* of David Halley, Broughty Ferry; one *s*. *Educ:* Liverpool Institute; London Univ. Entered Civil Service, 1910; Deputy Chairman, Board of Inland Revenue, 1949–57. *Address:* The Small House, Dinton, Salisbury, Wilts. *T:* Teffont 209. *Died 31 May* 1981.

**RIVERS, Georgia;** *see* Clark, Marjorie.

**RIVERS, Rosalind Venetia P.;** *see* Pitt-Rivers.

**ROBARTS, David John;** Director of Robert Fleming & Co. Ltd, 1944–76; Director of other companies; Chairman, Committee of London Clearing Bankers and President, British Bankers' Association, 1956–60 and 1968–70; *b* 1906; *e s* of Capt. Gerald Robarts; *m* 1951, Pauline Mary, *d* of Colonel Francis Follett, and widow of Clive Stoddart; three *s* one *d*. *Educ:* Eton; Magdalen College, Oxford. Dir, National Westminster Bank Ltd, to 1976 (Chm., 1969–71; Chm., National Provincial Bank Ltd, 1954–68). Church Commissioner, 1957–65. High Sheriff of Buckinghamshire, 1963. *Address:* 7 Smith Square, Westminster, SW1. *T:* 01–222 2428; Lillingstone House, Buckingham. *T:* Lillingstone Dayrell 202. *Club:* Pratt's. *Died 26 Aug.* 1989.

**ROBATHAN, Rev. Canon Frederick Norman,** OBE 1945; MA; Hon. CF (1st Cl.); Canon Emeritus of Ely Cathedral, since 1960; *b* 4 Jan. 1896; *s* of Reverend Thomas Frederick and Edith Jane Robathan, St Andrew's College, Gorakpur, India; *m* 1st, 1922, Renée Wells (*d* 1972) (JP 1947–53); one *s* (and one *s* decd); 2nd, 1972, Ruth Elizabeth Emma Corfe (*d* 1984), 3rd *d* of late Canon E. C. Corfe and Mrs Emma Corfe. *Educ:* King's School, Chester; Dean Close Sch., Cheltenham; St Edmund Hall, Oxford (MA); Wycliffe Hall, Oxford. Served as Commissioned Officer, European War, 1914–19 (campaign medals), France, 1915–16. Ordained, 1921; Curate, Quarry Bank, Staffs, 1921; Priest Vicar, Truro Cathedral, 1923–25; Priest Vicar, Lincoln Cathedral, 1925–28; Chaplain HM Prison, Lincoln, 1926–28; Minor Canon and Sacrist and Junior Cardinal, St Paul's Cathedral, 1928–34; Chaplain Guy's Hosp., 1932–33; Minor Canon, Westminster Abbey, 1934–37, and Chaplain, Westminster Hospital; Rector of Hackney, 1937–45, and Chaplain East London Hospital, CF, RARO, 1923. War of 1939–45 (campaign medals); BEF 1940; Evacuation, Dunkirk, 1940; Sen. Chaplain 43 Div., 1941; Army Technical Sch., Arborfield, 1941; Sen. Chaplain Royal Garrison Church, Aldershot, 1942; Dep. Asst Chaplain-Gen. 12th Corps, 1943; Asst Chaplain-Gen. 21 Army Grp., 1944; Normandy Landings, 1944 (despatches). Vicar of Brighton, Sussex and Canon and Prebendary of Waltham in Chichester Cathedral, 1945–53; Canon Residentiary and Treasurer, Ely Cathedral, 1953–59; Vicar of Cardington, Bedford, 1959. Sen. Chaplain Army Cadet Force, Cambs, 1954–59. Councillor, Bedford RDC, 1960. Chaplain to High Sheriff of Beds., 1962; Rector of Charleton with Buckland tout Saints, Kingsbridge, S Devon, 1962–66. Hon. Priest Vicar, Truro Cathedral, 1967. Coronation Medal, 1937. *Recreations:* rowing, hockey, cricket, antiquaries. *Address:* Myrtle Court, Mevagissey, Cornwall. *T:* Mevagissey 842233.
*Died 26 Dec.* 1986.

**ROBB, William,** NDA, FRSE; *b* 1885; *e s* of late William Robb, Rochsolloch, Airdrie; *m* 1924, Agnes Logan, *e d* of late Archibald Steel, Prestwick, Ayrshire; two *d*. *Educ:* Airdrie Academy; West of Scotland Agricultural College, Glasgow. Assist, Agriculture Department, The University of St Andrews, 1913–16 and 1919–20; War Service, Royal Engineers, 1916–19; Assistant Director, Scottish Society for Research in Plant Breeding, 1921–25; Director of Research, 1925–50, retired. *Recreation:* gardening. *Address:* c/o 7 Kaimes Road, Edinburgh EH12 6JR. *Died 18 Dec.* 1982.

**ROBBINS, Baron** *cr* 1959 (Life Peer), of Clare Market; **Lionel Charles Robbins,** CH 1968; CB 1944; FBA 1942; MA Oxon, BSc (Econ.); First Chancellor of Stirling University, 1968–78; *b* 22 Nov. 1898; *e s* of late Rowland Richard Robbins, CBE; *m* 1924, Iris Elizabeth, *d* of late A. G. Gardiner; one *s* one *d*. *Educ:* Southall County Sch.; Univ. Coll., London; London School of Economics. Served European War, 1916–19 (RFA); Lecturer New College, Oxford, 1924; Lecturer London School of Economics, 1925–27; Fellow and Lecturer New College, Oxford, 1927–29; Professor of Economics in the University of London, at London School of Economics, 1929–61; Chm., Financial Times, 1961–70. Chm., Cttee on Higher Education, 1961–64; Mem., Court of Governors, London School of Economics,

(Chm., 1968–74). Director of the Economic Section of Offices of the War Cabinet, 1941–45; President of Royal Economic Society, 1954–55. Trustee: National Gallery, 1952–59, 1960–67, 1967–74; Tate Gall., 1953–59, 1962–67; Dir Royal Opera House, Covent Garden, 1955–81; Mem. Planning Board for Univ. of York; President British Academy, 1962–67. Member: Accademia dei Lincei, Rome; American Philosophical Society; American Acad. of Arts and Sciences; Foreign Associate, National Acad. of Education, America; Corr. Fellow, Academia Nacional de Ciencias Economicas, Argentina. Hon. DLitt (Dunelm, Exeter, Strathclyde, Sheffield, Heriot-Watt); Hon. LHD (Columbia); Hon. LLD (Cantab, Leicester, Strasbourg, CNAA); Hon. Dr of Laws, Calif; Hon. Doutor en Ciências Econòmicas e Financeiras Universidade Técnica de Lisboa; Hon. DSc (Econ.) London; Hon. DUniv: York; Stirling; Hon. Dr, RCA; Hon. DHL Pennsylvania; Hon. Fellow: Univ. Coll. London; Manchester Coll. of Science and Technology; LSE; London Grad. Sch. of Business Studies; Courtauld Inst. *Publications:* An Essay on the Nature and Significance of Economic Science; The Great Depression; Economic Planning and International Order; The Economic Basis of Class Conflict and other Essays in Political Economy; The Economic Causes of War; The Economic Problem in Peace and War, 1947; The Theory of Economic Policy in English Classical Political Economy, 1952; The Economist in the Twentieth Century and other Lectures in Political Economy, 1954; Robert Torrens and the Evolution of Classical Economics; Politics and Economics, 1963; The University in the Modern World, 1966; The Theory of Economic Development in the History of Economic Thought, 1968; The Evolution of Modern Economic Theory, 1970; Autobiography of an Economist, 1971; Money, Trade and International Relations, 1971; Political Economy Past and Present: a review of leading theories of economic policy, 1976; Against Inflation: speeches in the Second Chamber 1965–77, 1979; Higher Education Revisited, 1980; articles in Economic Jl, Economica, Lloyds Bank Review, etc. *Address:* 10 Southwood Hall, N6. *Died 15 May* 1984.

**ROBBINS, Dennis;** *see* Robbins, J. D.

**ROBBINS, Edgar Carmichael,** CBE 1957; Legal Adviser to The British Broadcasting Corporation, 1959–74; *b* 22 March 1911; *s* of John Haldeman Robbins; *m* 1936, Alice Eugenia, *d* of Rev. Herbert Norman Nash; two *s* two *d*. *Educ:* Westminster Sch.; London Univ. (LLB). Admitted a solicitor, 1933. Employed by The British Broadcasting Corporation, 1934–74, Solicitor to the BBC 1945–59. Clerk, City of London Solicitors' Company, 1976–84; Hon. Archivist, Cutlers' Co., 1986–. *Publications:* William Paston, Justice, 1932; The Cursed Norfolk Justice, 1936. *Address:* 9 Pensioners' Court, The Charterhouse, EC1. *T:* 01–250 0555. *Club:* Athenæum. *Died 1 Sept.* 1988.

**ROBBINS, John Dennis,** OBE 1945; TD 1950; FCA; *b* 28 July 1915; *s* of Duncan Ross Robbins and Harriette Winifred Robbins (*née* Goodyear); *m* 1942, Joan Mary Mason; one *s* two *d*. *Educ:* Aldenham School. Commnd Mddx Regt (DCO), 2nd Lieut 1939, Captain 1940, Major 1941, Lt-Col 1944; served N Africa, Italy, Palestine (OBE, despatches twice); retd as Lt-Col 1946. Partner, Kay Keeping & Co., Chartered Accountants, 1946–49; joined British Metal Corp. Ltd, 1950; Dir and Gen. Man., 1952; a Man. Dir, 1963. Amalgamated Metal Corp. Ltd: Dir 1965; Chief Exec. 1971; Exec. Dep. Chm., 1972, Chm., 1975–77; Dir, Smith & Nephew Associated Cos, 1958–85. Mem., Worshipful Co. of Chartered Accountants. Freeman, City of London. *Recreations:* gardening, shooting, fly-fishing. *Address:* Orpen's Hill House, Birch, Colchester, Essex CO2 0LY. *T:* Colchester 330797. *Club:* Gresham. *Died 30 Oct.* 1986.

**ROBBINS, Brig. (Hon.) Thomas,** CB 1945; CBE 1945; MC 1918; Croix de Guerre (France) 1918; *b* 4 Feb. 1893; *m* 1955, Clare, *widow* of Lt-Col Malcolm Gordon Douglas, OBE, DSO, MC, HAC. Served European War, 1914–19, with Liverpool Scottish, BEF, 1914, and 6(T) Bn Lancashire Fusiliers; seconded to Intelligence Corps. Intelligence Officer 62 (WR) Division, France and Germany, 1917–19 (despatches thrice); Captain RARO, 1919; War of 1939–45, asst Comdt Intelligence Training Centre and Politico-Military Course, Cambridge; British Army Staff, Washington, DC, and Military Intelligence Training Centre, US Army, Camp Ritchie, Md (Col GSOI), 1942; First Comdt Civil Affairs Staff Centre, Wimbledon; Brigadier, 1943; Chief Staff Officer for Civil Affairs, HQ 21 Army Group, 1943–45; served in NW Europe, 1944–45; retired, 1945. British Commercial Commissioner and 2nd Commercial Secretary, HBM Embassy, Berlin, 1919–20. Freeman and Vintner, City of London, 1946. Officer Legion of Merit (USA); Officier Légion d'Honneur (France); Commander Order of the Cross, Leopold II (Belgium); Citoyen d'Honneur de la Commune de Cornac, Lot, 1966; and, with his wife Clare, enrolled Citoyens d'Honneur de la Commune de Loubressac, 1976. *Address:* 4 Meadow Drive, Bembridge, Isle of Wight PO35 5YA.
*Died 28 April* 1981.

**ROBERTHALL,** Baron *cr* 1969 (Life Peer), of Silverspur, Queensland, and Trenance, Cornwall; **Robert Lowe Roberthall,** KCMG 1954; CB 1950; MA; Principal Hertford College, Oxford, 1964–67, Hon. Fellow since 1969; Member of Economic Planning Board, 1947–61; *b* New South Wales, 6 March 1901; *s* of late Edgar Hall and Rose Helen, *d* of A. K. Cullen; changed surname to Roberthall by deed poll, 1969; *m* 1932, Laura Margaret (marr. diss. 1968), *d* of G. E. Linfoot; two *d*; *m* 1968, Perilla Thyme, *d* of late Sir Richard Southwell, FRS. *Educ:* Ipswich, Qld; Univ. of Queensland; Magdalen College, Oxford. BEng, Queensland, 1922; Rhodes Scholar, 1923–26 (First in Modern Greats, 1926); Lecturer in Economics, Trinity College, 1926–47; Fellow, 1927–50; Hon. Fellow, 1958; Junior Dean, 1927; Dean, 1933–38; Bursar, 1938–39; Proproctor, 1933; Ministry of Supply, 1939–46; British Raw Materials Mission, Washington, 1942–44; Adviser, Board of Trade, 1946–47; Director Economic Section, Cabinet Office, 1947–53; Economic Adviser to HM Government, 1953–61; Advisory Dir, Unilever, 1961–71; advr to Tube Investments, 1961–76. Fellow of Nuffield College, 1938–47, Visiting Fellow, 1961–64. Mem. of Economic and Employment Commn UN, 1946–49; Chm., OEEC Gp of Economic Experts, 1955–61; UK Mem., Commonwealth Economic Cttee, 1961–67; Mem., (Franks) Commn of Inquiry into Oxford Univ., 1964–66; Chm. Exec. Cttee, NIESR, 1962–70; Chm. Select Cttee on Commodity Prices, 1976–77. Royal Economic Society: Hon. Sec., 1948–58; Pres., 1958–60; Vice-Pres., 1960–86; Pres., Soc. of Business Economists, 1968–73, Hon. Fellow, 1973. Rede Lecturer, Cambridge University, 1962. Hon. DSc, University of Queensland. Joined SDP, 1981. *Publications:* Earning and Spending, 1934; The Economic System in a Socialist State, 1936; various articles, etc on economics. *Recreations:* walking, gardening. *Address:* Quarry, Trenance, Newquay, Cornwall. *T:* St Mawgan 860456. *Died 17 Sept. 1988.*

**ROBERTS, Allan;** MP (Lab) Bootle, since 1979; *b* 28 Oct. 1943; *s* of Ernest and Anne Roberts. *Educ:* Droylesden, Little Moss Boys' County Sec. Sch.; Didsbury Coll. of Education (Teachers' Cert.); Manchester Univ. Extra-Mural Dept (CQSW). School teacher, 1967–70; at Manchester Univ., 1970–72; Social Worker and Sen. Social Worker, 1972–74; Training Officer, City of Salford Social Services Dept, 1974–76; Principal Officer (Child Care) with Salford Social Services Dept, 1976–79. Opposition front bench spokesman on environmental protection and development. Mem., CND. *Publications:* contribs to Tribune; regular columnist, Labour Herald. *Recreations:* reading, films, eating, drinking, theatre. *Address:* House of Commons, SW1A 0AA. *Clubs:* Litherland Trades & Labour; Seaforth Socialist. *Died 21 March 1990.*

**ROBERTS, Brian Richard;** Editor, The Sunday Telegraph, 1966–76 (Managing Editor, 1961–66); *b* 16 Sept. 1906; *e s* of late Robert Lewis Roberts, CBE; *m* 1935, Elisabeth Franziska Dora, *er d* of late Dr Leo Zuntz, Berlin; one adopted *s. Educ:* Merchant Taylors' Sch.; St John's Coll., Oxford (MA); Hon. Fellow 1975. Editorial staff, Oxford Mail, 1930–33; Daily Mail, 1933–38 (Night Editor, 1936–38); Joined The Daily Telegraph, 1939 (Night Editor, 1944–57, Chief Asst Editor 1957–60). Pres., Inst. of Journalists, 1954–55; Pres., Guild of Agricultural Journalists, 1976; Mem. Governing Body, Northern Polytechnic, London, 1946–71 (Chm. 1956–71); Polytechnic of North London: Chm., Formation Cttee, 1970–71; Mem. Ct of Governors, 1971–79, Chm., 1971–74; Hon. Fellow 1981; Chm. of Council, Assoc. of Colls for Further and Higher Educn (formerly Assoc. of Technical Instns), 1964–65, Hon. Treasurer, 1967–77. Gold Medal, Inst. of Journalists, 1971; special award, National Press Awards, 1974; Silver Jubilee Medal, 1977. *Recreation:* agriculture. *Address:* Old Foxhunt Manor, Waldron, near Heathfield, Sussex TN21 0RU. *T:* Horam Road 2618. *Died 2 June 1988.*

**ROBERTS, Charles Stuart,** CMG 1975; HM Diplomatic Service, retired; High Commissioner in Barbados, 1973–78; *b* 24 May 1918; *s* of late Charles William Roberts and Dorothy Roberts; *m* 1946, Margaret Ethel Jones (decd); one *s* two *d. Educ:* Merchant Taylors' School. Entered Colonial Office, 1936. Naval Service (Lieut RNVR), 1940–46. Economic and Financial Adviser, Leeward Is, 1955–57; transferred to HM Diplomatic Service (Counsellor), 1966; British Govt Representative, W Indies Associated States, 1967–70; Head of Caribbean Dept, FCO, 1970–73. *Recreations:* chess, crosswords. *Address:* 4 Grange Gardens, Taunton, Somerset. *T:* Taunton 274559. *Clubs:* MCC; Royal Commonwealth Society (West Indian). *Died 30 Jan. 1989.*

**ROBERTS, Colin Henderson,** CBE 1973; Secretary to Delegates of Oxford University Press, 1954–74; Fellow of St John's College, Oxford, 1934–76, Hon. Fellow, 1976; *b* 8 June 1909; *s* of late Robert Lewis Roberts, CBE; *m* 1947, Alison Muriel, *d* of Reginald Haynes and Phyllis Irene Barrow; one *d. Educ:* Merchant Taylors' School; St John's College, Oxford (MA). 1st Cl., Hon. Class. Mods, 1929; 1st Cl., Lit. Hum. 1931; Sen. Schol., St John's Coll., 1931–34; Craven Univ. Fellow, 1932–34. Studied Berlin Univ., 1932; Univ. of Michigan, Near East Research (Egypt), 1932–34; Dept of Foreign

Office, 1939–45. Lecturer in Classics, St John's College, Oxford, 1939–53; tutor, 1946–53; University Lecturer in Papyrology, 1937–48; Reader, 1948–53. Delegate of Oxford Univ. Press, 1946–53; FBA 1947–80; Visiting Mem. of Inst. for Advanced Study, Princeton, NJ, 1951–52; Sandars Reader in Bibliography, University of Cambridge, 1960–61. Schweich Lectr, British Acad., 1977. Hon. DLitt Oxon, 1975. *Publications:* An Unpublished Fragment of the Fourth Gospel, 1935; Catalogue of the Greek Papyri in the Rylands Library, Manchester, Vol. III, 1938, Vol. IV (with E. G. Turner), 1952; part editor of the Oxyrhynchus Papyri, Parts XVIII-XX, 1941–52 and XXII, 1954; The Antinoopolis Papyri, 1950; The Merton Papyri (with H. I. Bell), 1948; The Codex, 1955; The Greek Bookhand, 1955; Manuscript, Society and Belief in Early Christian Egypt, 1979; (with T. C. Skeat) The Birth of the Codex, 1983. *Address:* Hursey House, Broadwindsor, near Beaminster, Dorset DT8 3LN. *T:* Broadwindsor 68281. *Died 11 Feb. 1990.*

**ROBERTS, Cyril Alfred,** CBE 1947 (MBE 1944); DL; *b* 4 June 1908; *s* of late A. W. Roberts; *m* 1932, Christine Annabel Kitson, *d* of late Hon. E. C. Kitson, Leeds; three *s* one *d. Educ:* Eton; Trinity Coll., Oxford. Called to the Bar, 1932, and practised until 1939. Served War of 1939–45, HM Forces, 1939–46; France, 1940; Western Desert, 1941–42; Instructor, Staff Coll., Haifa, 1943; War Office, Army Council Secretariat, 1943–45; Brigadier AG Co-ordination, 1945–46. Asst Sec., NCB, 1946–47, Under-Sec. 1947–51, Sec., 1951–59; Member of the Board, 1960–67. Dir, later Dep. Chm., Woodall-Duckham Gp Ltd, 1968–73. Chm., Inst. of Cardiology, 1967–72; Mem. Bd of Governors, Brompton Hosp., Chm. House Cttee, Nat. Heart Hosp., 1973–76. Adviser to Minister of Defence on Resettlement from the Forces, 1968–70; Mem., Armed Forces Pay Review Bd, 1971–79. Vice-Pres., Coronary Artery Disease Res. Assoc., 1987– (Chm., 1979–81); Chm., League of Friends, Nat. Heart Hosp., 1984–86. Chm., Chichester District Council, 1981–83. DL West Sussex, 1982. *Address:* Bury Gate House, Pulborough, West Sussex RH20 1HA. *T:* Bury 831440. *Died 8 Oct. 1988.*

**ROBERTS, Sir David (Arthur),** KBE 1983; CMG 1975; CVO 1979; HM Diplomatic Service, retired; Chairman, Herefordshire District Health Authority, since 1986; *b* 8 Aug. 1924; *s* of late Rev. T. A. and Mrs Roberts; *m* 1st, 1951, Nicole Marie Fay (*d* 1965); two *d*; 2nd, 1968, Hazel Faith Arnot. *Educ:* Hereford Cathedral Sch.; Jesus Coll., Oxford (Scholar; BA). Served Royal Armoured Corps, 1943–46. HM Foreign Service, Dec. 1947. Served: Baghdad, 1948–49; Tokyo, 1949–51; FO, 1951–53; Alexandria, 1953–55; Khartoum, 1955–58; FO, 1958–60; Dakar, 1960–61 (Chargé d'Affairs at Bamako and at Lomé during same period); FO, 1962–63; Damascus, 1963–66; Political Agent in the Trucial States, Dubai, 1966–68; Head of Accommodation Dept, FCO, 1968–71; High Comr in Barbados, 1971–73; Ambassador to Syria, 1973–76; High Comr in Sierra Leone, 1976–77; Ambassador to the United Arab Emirates, 1977–81; Lebanon, 1981–83. Dir-Gen., Middle East Assoc., 1983–85; Chm., British Lebanese Assoc., 1984–. Hon. Fellow, Centre for Middle Eastern and Islamic Studies, Durham Univ., 1985. *Publications:* The Ba'th and the Creation of Modern Syria, 1987; lectures and contribs to symposia, etc. *Club:* Reform. *Died 7 June 1987.*

**ROBERTS, Dr (Edward Frederick) Denis,** CBE 1989; FRSE 1980; Librarian, National Library of Scotland, since 1970; *b* 16 June 1927; *s* of Herbert Roberts and Jane Spottiswoode Roberts (*née* Wilkinson); *m* 1954, Irene Mary Beatrice (*née* Richardson); one *s* one *d. Educ:* Royal Belfast Academical Institution; Queen's University of Belfast. BA (1st cl. Hons Modern History) 1951; PhD 1955. Research Assistant, Dept of History, Queen's Univ. of Belfast, 1951–55; National Library of Scotland: Asst Keeper, Dept of Manuscripts, 1955–66; Secretary of the Library, 1966–67; Librarian, Trinity College Dublin, 1967–70; Hon. Prof., Univ. of Edinburgh, 1975. Hon. FLA 1983. *Publication:* (with W. G. H. Quigley) Registrum Iohannis Mey: The Register of John Mey, Archbishop of Armagh, 1443–1456, 1972. *Address:* 6 Oswald Court, Edinburgh EH9 2HY. *T:* 031–667 9473. *Club:* New (Edinburgh). *Died 14 Feb. 1990.*

**ROBERTS, Emrys Owain,** CBE 1976 (MBE 1946); *b* 22 Sept. 1910; *s* of late Owen Owens Roberts and of Mary Grace Williams, both of Caernarfon; *m* 1948, Anna Elisabeth Tudor; one *d* (one *s* decd). *Educ:* Caernarfon; Aberystwyth; Gonville and Caius Coll., Cambridge; Geneva. MA (Cantab); LLB (Wales); 1st Class, Parts I and II, Law Tripos, Cambridge, 1933; 1st Class Hons, University of Wales, 1931, S. T. Evans Prize; Solicitor, 1936, 1st Class Hons, Clements Inn Prize. Squadron Leader RAF, 1941–45. Barrister, Gray's Inn, 1944. MP (L) for Merioneth, 1945–51; Member of Parliamentary Delegations to Yugoslavia, Germany, Rumania, and Sweden; Representative at Council of Europe, 1950 and 1951. Director: Tootal Broadhurst Lee Co. Ltd, English Sewing Ltd, English Calico Ltd and Tootal Ltd, 1958–75; Cambrian & General Securities Ltd, 1974–81. Chairman: Mid-Wales Develt Corp.,

1968–77; Develt Bd for Rural Wales, 1977–81; Mem., Welsh Develt Agency, 1977–81; Dir, Develt Corp. of Wales, 1978–81. Mem. Court and Council, Univ. Coll. of Wales, Aberystwyth, 1972–85; Chm. of Council, Nat. Eisteddfod of Wales, 1964–67, and Hon. Counsel, 1957–74; Vice-Pres. Hon. Soc. of Cymmrodorion. *Publication:* (jointly) The Law of Restrictive Trade Practices and Monopolies. *Address:* 8 Kent House, 62 Holland Park Avenue, W11 3RA. *T:* 071–243 1421; 24 Glyn Garth Court, Menai Bridge, Gwynedd LL59 5PB. *T:* Menai Bridge (0248) 713665.

*Died 29 Oct. 1990.*

**ROBERTS, Major-General Frank Crowther,** VC 1918; DSO 1915; OBE 1921; MC 1917; *b* 2 June 1891; *s* of Rev. Frank Roberts, Vicar of St John, Southall; *m* 1932, Winifred Margaret (*d* 1980), *y d* of John Downing Wragg. *Educ:* St Lawrence College; RMC. Commissioned Worcestershire Regt, 1911, Lieut 1914, Captain 1915; served with 1st Bn Worcs Regt, War of 1914–18, in France and Belgium; wounded three times, despatches five times, VC, DSO, MC: OC 1st Bn, 1917–18 (acting Lt-Col); attached Egyptian Army, Sudan, 1919–20 (Brevet Major 1919; despatches; Gold Medal of order of Mohammed Ali; Sudan Medal and Clasp, Aliab Dinka); psc, Camberley, 1921; Egypt, 1923–24; Brigade Major, Rhine Army, 1925–26; GSO2 South China, 1926–28; transf. to Royal Warwickshire Regt, 1927, Major; Iraq, 1930–32 (GSO1; Brevet Lt-Col, Brevet Col; Iraq Medal); GSO2 N Ireland Dist., 1935–36; Lt-Col 1936; Local Brig., S Command, India, 1937; Brigade Comdr, Poona, 1938–May 1939; Maj.-Gen. 1939; Comdr, 48th (S Midland) Div., TA, June–Oct. 1939, retired Dec. 1939. *Address:* Four Winds, Bretby, near Burton-on-Trent DE15 0QF. *T:* Burton-on-Trent 217358. *Died 12 Jan. 1982.*

**ROBERTS, George Charles L.;** *see* Lloyd-Roberts.

**ROBERTS, Captain Gilbert Howland,** CBE 1944; RD 1964; Royal Navy (retired); *b* 11 Oct. 1900; *s* of Colonel Sir Howland Roberts, 12th Baronet, and Elizabeth Marie La Roche; *m* 1930 (marriage dissolved); one *s* one *d*; *m* 1947, Jean Winifred Warren; one *d*. *Educ:* Westminster; Royal Naval Colleges, Osborne and Dartmouth. Served European War, 1916–18; specialised in gunnery, 1922; Medal of Royal Humane Society, 1922; Submarine X One, 1926; Commander, 1935; Staff of HM Tactical School, 1935–36; command HMS Fearless, 1937–38; invalided, 1938; rejoined Royal Navy, 1940; served since in HMS Excellent and on Staff of C-in-C Western Approaches as Director Tactical School (CBE, Comdr Order of Polonia Restituta); Captain, 1942. Commodore Royal Norwegian Navy, Naval Assistant to Norwegian Naval C-in-C, 1946–47 (1st class Comdr, Order of St Olaf; Officer, Legion of Honour); lent Royal Canadian Navy for duty and lecture tour, 1955; Comd HMS Vivid, RNR, 1956–64 (RD 1964). Lees-Knowles Lecturer, Military History, Cambridge Univ., 1951. CC Devon, 1957; Alderman, Torbay County Borough, 1967–74. *Relevant publication:* Captain Gilbert Roberts RN and the Anti-U-Boat School, by Mark Williams, 1979. *Recreation:* gardening. *Address:* Little Priors, Watcome, Torquay. *T:* 38919.

*Died 22 Jan. 1986.*

**ROBERTS, Air Vice-Marshal Glynn S.;** *see* Silyn-Roberts.

**ROBERTS, Rev. Harold,** PhD (Cambridge); Principal, Richmond College, Surrey (University of London), 1955–68; Chair of Systematic Theology and Philosophy of Religion, Richmond College, 1940–68; President of the Methodist Conference, 1957; *b* Ashley, Cheshire, 20 Sept. 1896; *y* of E. J. and A. Roberts; *m* 1st, 1926, Edna Tydvil Thomas, BA (*d* 1964); 2nd, 1972, Myra Stevenson Johnson, BA. *Educ:* Hulme Grammar Sch., Manchester; Univ. Coll., Bangor; Wesley House and Jesus College, Cambridge. BA 1st Class Hons Philosophy 1920, MA 1921, Univ. Coll., Bangor. Asst Tutor, Wesley House, Camb., 1924–26; Minister: Liverpool (Waterloo), 1926–29; Oxford, 1929–34; Chair of Systematic Theology and Philosophy of Religion, Wesley College, Headingley, 1934–40; Minister, Ipswich (Museum St), 1941–45. Univ. of London: Member of Senate, 1951–59, Dean of Faculty of Theology, 1953–56; Examiner in Theology, Univ. of London, Queen's Univ. Belfast, Univ. of Wales, etc. Cato Lecturer, Australia, 1950; Fernley-Hartley Lecturer, 1954; Tipple Lecturer, Drew Univ., USA, 1956. Member of Central Cttee World Council of Churches, 1954–62; Pres. of World Methodist Coun., 1956–61; Jt Chm., Anglican-Methodist Unity Commn, 1967; Slect Preacher, Univ. of Cambridge, 1958. Hon. DD Trinity College, Dublin, 1961. *Publications:* part-author: The Doctrine of the Holy Spirit, 1938; The Message and Mission of Methodism (Ed.), 1945; Jesus and the Kingdom of God, 1955; Anglican-Methodist Conversations, 1963. *Address:* Wincote, 32 Byng Road, Tunbridge Wells, Kent. *T:* 21945. *Died 4 Oct. 1982.*

**ROBERTS, Sir Harold (Charles West),** Kt 1953; CBE 1948; MC 1916; *b* 23 May 1892; *s* of T. B. and Elizabeth Roberts, Stoke-on-Trent; *m* Alice May (*d* 1979), *d* of A. T. Bourne, Trentham, Staffs; no *c*. *Educ:* Newcastle School; Birmingham University. Trained as a mining engineer in North Staffordshire. Served European War, in

France and Italy, Middlesex Regiment, 1916–18; in India, Indian Army, 1918–19. BSc 1921. HM Inspector of Mines, 1922; senior Inspector, 1936; Chief Inspector of Training, Ministry of Fuel and Power, 1943; Deputy Chief Inspector of Mines, 1945; HM Chief Inspector of Mines, 1951–58, retired. *Recreations:* golf and walking. *Address:* 30 Greys Close, Cavendish, Suffolk.

*Died 27 Jan. 1983.*

**ROBERTS, Dame Jean,** DBE 1962; JP; DL; *m* 1922, Cameron Roberts (decd), Headmaster of Albert Senior Secondary Sch., Springburn; one *d*. *Educ:* Albert Sch.; Whitehill Sch. Taught at Bishopstreet School and later in a special school for handicapped children. Representative of Kingston Ward in Corp. of City of Glasgow from Nov. 1929–May 1966; DL 1964, JP 1934, Glasgow; Sen. Magistrate; held the following posts as first woman to do so: Convener of Electrical Cttee; Dep. Chm. of Corporation; Leader of the Labour Group; City Treasurer; Lord Provost of the City of Glasgow and Lord Lieut of the county of the City of Glasgow, 1960–63. Chm., Cumbernauld Develt Corp., 1965–72. Chm., Scottish National Orchestra Society, 1970–75; Member: Scottish Arts Council, 1963; Arts Council of Gt Britain, 1965–68. Since 1930: apptd by Secretary of State for Scotland to serve on many Advisory Cttees dealing with Local Govt, Social and Economic matters in Scotland. Hon. LLD Glasgow, 1977. Order of St Olav, 1962. *Recreations:* music and public service. *Address:* 35 Beechwood Drive, Glasgow G11 7ET. *T:* 041–334 1930.

*Died 26 March 1988.*

**ROBERTS, Dame Joan (Howard),** DBE 1978; President, Yooralla Society of Victoria, 1977–78; *b* 27 June 1907; *d* of Charles A. Norris and Rose M. A. Norris; *m* 1937, Allan Edwin Tainsh Roberts; two *s* one *d*. *Educ:* Presbyterian Ladies' Coll., Melbourne, Australia; Univ. of Melb. (MSc). Res. Biochemist, Dept of Pathology, Univ. of Melb., 1930–34; Biochemist, Prince Henry's Hosp., Melb., 1935–37. Yooralla Hosp. Sch. for Crippled Children: Mem. Cttee, 1948–68; Pres., 1968–77. Member: Council, Presbyterian Ladies' Coll., Melb., 1948–80; Council of Management, Arthritis Foundn of Victoria (formerly Rheumatism and Arthritis Assoc. of Victoria), 1979–87. *Recreations:* travel, reading, classical music. *Address:* 2 Prowse Avenue, Balwyn, Vic 3103, Australia. *T:* 836–1258.

*Died 22 June 1990.*

**ROBERTS, John Alexander Fraser,** CBE 1965; FRS 1963; MA Cantab; MD, DSc (Edinburgh); FRCP; FRCPsych; *b* 8 Sept. 1899; *er s* of late Robert Henry Roberts, Foxhall, Denbigh, and late Elizabeth Mary; *m* 1st, 1941, Doris, *y d* of late Herbert and Kate Hare; two *d*; 2nd, 1975, Margaret, *d* of late Sydney and Dorothy Ralph. *Educ:* Denbigh Gram. Sch.; privately; Gonville and Caius Coll., Cambridge; Univs of Edinburgh, Wales and Bristol. 2nd Lieut Royal Welch Fusiliers, 1918–19; War of 1939–45: Surgeon-Comdr RNVR and Cons. in Med. Statistics, RN, 1942–46. Research Asst, Inst. of Animal Genetics, Univ. of Edinburgh, 1922–28; Biologist, Wool Industries Research Assoc., 1928–31; Macaulay Research Fellow, Univ. of Edinburgh, 1931–33; Dir, Burden Mental Research Dept, Stoke Park Colony, Bristol, 1933–57; Lectr in Med. Genetics, London School of Hygiene and Trop. Med., 1946–57; Consultant in Medical Genetics, Royal Eastern Counties Hosp., Colchester, 1946–80; Dir, Clinical Genetics Research Unit (MRC), Inst. of Child Health, Univ. of London, and Hon. Consultant in Med. Genetics, The Hospital for Sick Children, Gt Ormond St, 1957–64; Geneticist, Paediatric Res. Unit, Guy's Hosp. Med. Sch. and Hon. Clinical Geneticist, Guy's Hosp., 1964–81. President: Royal Anthropological Inst. of Gt Britain and Ire., 1957–59; Biometric Society (British Region), 1960–62; Section of Epidemiology and Preventive Medicine, RSM, 1960–62, Lectures: Charles West, RCP, 1961; Leonard Parsons, Univ. of Birmingham, 1963; Donald Paterson, Univ. of British Columbia (and Vis. Prof.), 1967; Lumleian, RCP, 1971. Ballantyne Prize, RCPE 1976. *Publications:* An Introduction to Medical Genetics, 1940, 7th edn 1978; papers in medical, biological and genetical journals. *Recreation:* country walks. *Address:* 10 Aspley Road, Wandsworth, SW18 2DB. *T:* 01–874 4826. *Club:* Athenæum.

*Died 15 Jan. 1987.*

**ROBERTS, Michael (Hilary Arthur);** MP (C) Cardiff North West, since 1974 (Cardiff North, 1970–74); Parliamentary Under Secretary of State, Welsh Office, since 1979; *b* 1927; *s* of late Rev. T. A. Roberts (formerly Rector of Neath); *m* 1952, Eileen Jean Evans; two *s* (and one *d* decd). *Educ:* Neath Grammar School; Cardiff University College. First Headmaster of the Bishop of Llandaff High School, 1963–70. An Opposition Whip, 1974–79. President: Cons. Trade Unionists, 1977–79; Assoc. of Cons. Clubs, 1980–. *Address:* Ashgrove Farm, Whitchurch, Cardiff. *Club:* Cardiff and County. *Died 10 Feb. 1983.*

**ROBERTS, Gen. Sir Ouvry Lindfield,** GCB 1953 (KCB 1952; CB 1946); KBE 1950 (CBE 1944); DSO 1941; President of Grosvenor Laing (BC) Limited (Canada), 1955–60; formerly Director: Grosvenor/Laing (BC) Ltd; Grosvenor/Laing (Langley Park) Ltd;

Grosvenor International Ltd; Redhill Investment Corporation Ltd; Macdonald Buchanan Properties Ltd; *b* 3 April 1898; *m* 1924, Elsie Nora Eileen Webster (*d* 1955); one *s* (and one *s* decd); *m* 1955, Joyce Mary Segar, *yr d* of Eric W. Scorer, OBE, Coombe Hurst, Lincoln; two *s* one *d*. *Educ*: Cheltenham College; Royal Military Academy, Woolwich; King's Coll., Cambridge (MA). RE, commissioned 1917; Comdg 23 Ind. Div., 1943–45; Comdg 34 Ind. Corps, 1945; Vice-Adjutant-Gen. War Office, 1945–47; GOC Northern Ireland District, 1948–49; GOC-in-C Southern Command, 1949–52; Quarter-master-General to the Forces, 1952–55; ADC General to the Queen, 1952–55; Colonel Commandant, Corps of Royal Engineers, 1952–62. Administrative Officer, Univ. of BC, 1961–68. *Recreations*: cricket (Army, Quidnunc); hockey (Cambridge, Army, Wales). *Address*: Upper Field House, 105 Church Way, Iffley Village, Oxford. *T*: Oxford 779351. *Clubs*: Oriental, MCC.

*Died 16 March 1986.*

**ROBERTS, Sir Peter Geoffrey**, 3rd Bt, *cr* 1919; *b* 23 June 1912; *yr* and *o* surv. *s* of Sir Samuel Roberts, 2nd Bt and Gladys Mary (*d* 1966), *d* of W. E. Dring, MD, Tenterden, Kent; *S* father, 1955; *m* 1939, Judith Randell Hempson; one *s* four *d*. *Educ*: Harrow; Trinity College, Cambridge. Barr.-at-Law, Inner Temple, 1935. Maj. Coldstream Guards. MP (C) Ecclesall Div. of Sheffield, 1945–50; (C-L) Heeley Div. of Sheffield, 1950–66. Chairman: Newton Chambers & Co., Ltd, 1954–72; The Wombwell Management Co. Ltd, 1952–82; Hadfields Ltd, 1961–67; Sterling Silverware, 1978–81; Wellman Engineering Corp. 1952–72; Hill Woolgar plc, 1981–84; Director: Guardian Royal Exchange Assurance Ltd, 1960–82; Royal Bank of Scotland, 1978–82; Williams & Glyn's Bank Ltd, 1964–82. Past Chm., Conservative Members' Committee on Fuel and Power; Past Pres., Soc. of British Gas Industries (Pres., 1963). Master Cutler, Sheffield, 1957. High Sheriff of Hallamshire, 1970–71. Hon. Freeman, 1970, Town Collector, 1971–74, Sheffield. *Publication*: Coal Act, 1938. *Heir*: *s* Samuel Roberts [*b* 16 April 1948; *m* 1977, Georgina, *yr d* of David Cory; two *d*]. *Address*: Cockley Cley Hall, Swaffham, Norfolk PE37 8AG. *T*: Swaffham 21308. *Clubs*: Carlton, Brooks's; Sheffield (Sheffield).

*Died 22 July 1985.*

**ROBERTS, Rev. Roger Lewis**, CVO 1973; MA Oxon; Chaplain, the Queen's Chapel of the Savoy, and Chaplain of the Royal Victorian Order, 1961–73; Chaplain to the Queen, 1969–81; *b* 3 Aug. 1911; 3rd *s* of late Robert Lewis Roberts, CBE; *m* 1935, Katie Agnes Mary Perryman (*d* 1989); (one *s* decd). *Educ*: Highgate School; Exeter College, Oxford. 1st Class Hon. Mods, 1931; 1st Class Lit. Hum., 1933; Charles Oldham Prize, 1933; BA 1933; MA 1938; Sixth Form Master, The Liverpool Institute, 1933–34; Sixth Form Master, Rugby School, 1934–40; enlisted RRA, 1940; Army Educational Corps, 1941–43 (Major). Headmaster, Blundell's Sch., 1943–47; Deacon, Exeter, 1946; Priest, St Albans, 1948; Assistant Priest, Cathedral and Abbey Church of St Alban, 1948–49. Vicar of Sharnbrook, Bedfordshire, 1949–54. Vicar of the Guild Church of All Hallows, London Wall, 1954–58, of St Botolph without Aldersgate, 1958–61. Warden, The Church of England Men's Society, 1957–61 (Gen. Sec. 1954–57, Vice-Pres. 1962–). Member of editorial staff, The Church Times, 1950–76 (Editor, 1960–68). Chaplain: Instn of Electrical Engineers, 1961–73; Worshipful Co. of Glaziers, 1967–77. *Address*: Thorn Farm Cottage, Chagford, Devon. *T*: Chagford 2493.

*Died 16 May 1990.*

**ROBERTS, Stuart**; *see* Roberts, C. S.

**ROBERTS, Thomas Arnold**, OBE 1962; TD 1947; FRICS; Chartered Surveyor; former Senior Partner, Richard Ellis, Chartered Surveyors, London, EC3; *b* 5 Nov. 1911; *s* of Sidney Herbert Roberts, Liverpool; *m* Kathleen Audrey Robertshaw. *Educ*: Bedford Sch. Joined Westminster Dragoons, 1932; transf. to Royal Signals, 1938. Served War, in N Africa and Italy, 1942–44. Partnership in Richard Ellis & Son, Chartered Surveyors, 1946. Surrey TA Assoc., 1950–72 (Chm., 1956–60); Hon. Col: 381 Lt Regt (TA), 1957–61; Surrey Yeomanry, 1961–68. Property Adviser to Electricity Council, 1957–73. A Church Commissioner, 1973–81. A Governor of Cranleigh Sch., 1960–73 (Chm., 1965–72). DL Surrey, 1958–75. *Recreations*: vintage and sporting motor vehicles, travel. *Address*: Purslow Hall, Clunbury, Craven Arms, Shropshire. *Clubs*: Athenæum, Naval and Military.

*Died 12 March 1990.*

**ROBERTS-WRAY, Sir Kenneth Owen**, GCMG 1960 (KCMG 1949; CMG 1946); QC 1959; Legal Adviser, Commonwealth Relations Office (Dominions Office until 1947) and Colonial Office, 1945–60, retired; *b* 6 June 1899; *s* of late Captain Thomas Henry Roberts-Wray, CB, OBE, VD, RNVR, sometime ADC to King George V, and late Florence Grace Roberts-Wray; *m* 1st, 1927, Joan Tremayne Waring (*d* 1961); three *s*; 2nd, 1965, Lady (Mary Howard) Williams, *widow* of Sir Ernest Williams, JP. *Educ*: University Tutorial Coll.; RMA, Woolwich; Merton College, Oxford (1st Class Hons School of Jurisprudence). 2/Lt RA 1918; Lieutenant, 1919; retired on account of wounds, 1920. Called to Bar 1924 (Certificate of Honour); Professional Legal Clerk, Min. of Health, 1926, Asst Chief Clerk,

1929; 2nd Asst Legal Adviser, Dominions Office and Colonial Office, 1931; Asst Legal Adviser, 1943. Chairman: Law Officers Conf., WI, 1944; Judicial Advisers Confs, Uganda, 1953, Nigeria, 1956. Acting Attorney-Gen., Gibraltar, Jan.–June 1969. DCL Oxon, 1967; Hon. LLD Birmingham, 1968. *Publications*: part author of The Law of Collisions on Land, 1925; (Contrib.) Changing Law in Developing Countries (ed Anderson), 1963; Commonwealth and Colonial Law, 1966; articles on Colonial Law in legal publications. *Recreations*: golf, cinematography. *Address*: The Old Golf House, Forest Row, Sussex. *T*: Forest Row 2588; 5 King's Bench Walk, Temple, EC4. *T*: 01-353 2882/2884. *Clubs*: United Oxford & Cambridge University; Royal Ashdown Forest Golf.

*Died 29 Aug. 1983.*

**ROBERTSON, Alan**, OBE 1965; FRS 1964; FRSE 1966; BA; DSc; Deputy Chief Scientific Officer, ARC Unit of Animal Genetics, Edinburgh, 1966–85, retired; *b* 21 Feb. 1920; *s* of late John Mouat Robertson and Annie Grace; *m* 1947, Margaret Sidney, *y d* of late Maurice Bernheim; two *s* one *d*. *Educ*: Liverpool Institute; Gonville and Caius College, Cambridge. Operational Research Section, Coastal Command, RAF, 1943–46. ARC Unit of Animal Genetics, Edinburgh, 1947–85. Hon. Prof., Edinburgh Univ., 1967. For. Assoc., Nat. Acad. of Sci., USA, 1979. Hon. Dr rer nat Univ. of Hohenheim, 1968; Hon. DAgrSc: Norway, 1984; Agricl Univ., Denmark, 1986; Hon. Dr, Fac. of Vet. Med., State Univ., Liège, 1986. Gold Medal, Royal Agric. Soc., 1958. Order of Isabel la Católica (Spain), 1974. *Publications*: papers in scientific jls. *Recreations*: gardening, tennis. *Address*: 47 Braid Road, Edinburgh EH10 6AW. *T*: 031–447 4239. *Club*: Farmers'.

*Died 25 April 1989.*

**ROBERTSON, Alan Murray**; Director, Motherwell Bridge Holdings Ltd; formerly Managing Director, BP Oil Ltd, and a Director, BP Trading Ltd; *b* 19 Dec. 1914; *s* of late Dr James R. Robertson; *m* 1st; one *s* two *d*; 2nd, Judith-Anne, *d* of late Robert Russell, Glasgow; one step *s*. *Educ*: St Anselm's, Bakewell; Malvern; Pembroke Coll., Cambridge (MA). Joined Anglo-Iranian Oil Co., 1937 in Paris; served 1939–46 in RTR and RASC, Middle East and Italian Campaigns (despatches, Major); Anglo-Iranian representative in France, 1949–53; Gen. Man., Scottish Oils & Shell-Mex Ltd, 1955–56; Man. Dir, National Benzole Co. Ltd, 1957–63; Exec. Vice-Pres., BP Oil Corp., New York, 1968–70. Mem. Council, CBI, 1972–76. *Recreations*: travel, fishing, gardening. *Address*: Shepherds Cottage, Shipton-under-Wychwood, Oxon. *Club*: Caledonian.

*Died 2 Nov. 1984.*

**ROBERTSON, Prof. Sir Alexander**, Kt 1970; CBE 1963; Professor of Tropical Animal Health, University of Edinburgh, 1971–78, then Emeritus Professor; Director: Veterinary Field Station, 1968–78; Centre for Tropical Veterinary Medicine, Edinburgh University, 1971–78; *b* 3 Feb. 1908; *m* 1936, Janet McKinlay (*d* 1988); two *d*. *Educ*: Stonehaven Mackie Acad.; Aberdeen University; and Royal (Dick) Veterinary College, Edinburgh. MA Aberdeen, 1929; BSc Aberdeen, 1930; PhD Edinburgh, 1940; MRCVS, 1934. Demonstrator in Anatomy, Royal (Dick) Veterinary College, Edinburgh, 1934; Vet. Inspector, Min. of Agriculture, 1935–37; Sen. Lectr in Physiology, 1938–44, Prof. of Vet. Hygiene, 1944–53, William Dick Prof. of Animal Health, 1953–71, Director, 1957–63, Royal (Dick) School of Veterinary Studies, Univ. of Edinburgh; Dean of Faculty of Vet. Medicine, Univ. of Edinburgh, 1964–70. Exec. Officer for Scotland, Farm Livestock Emergency Service, 1942–47. FRSE, 1945; FRIC, 1946; FRSH, 1950; FRZSScot, 1952; Mem. Departmental Cttee on Foot and Mouth Disease, 1952–54; Pres. Brit. Vet. Assoc., 1954–55; Vice-Pres. Roy. Zoological Soc. of Scotland, 1959– (and Hon. Fellow); Mem. Governing Body, Animal Virus Research Inst., Pirbright, 1954–62; Member: Council Royal Coll. of Veterinary Surgeons, 1957–78 (Treasurer, 1964–67; Vice-Pres., 1967–68, 1969–70; Pres., 1968–69); Artificial Insemination Adv. Cttee for Scotland, 1958–65; ARC Tech. Adv. Cttee on Nutrient Requirements, 1959–78; Departmental Cttee of Inquiry into Fowl Pest, 1960–61; Governing Body Rowett Research Institute, 1962–77; ARC Adv. Cttee on Meat Research, 1968–73; Trustee, Internat. Laboratory for Res. in Animal Diseases, 1973–82 (Chm., 1980–81); Chairman: Sci. Adv. Panel, Pig Industry Develt Authority, 1962–68; Research Adv. Cttee, Meat and Livestock Commn, 1969–73; Vet. Adv. Panel, British Council, 1971–78; Member: FAO/WHO Expert Panel on Veterinary Educn, 1962–78; East African Natural Resources Research Council, 1963–78; Cttee of Inquiry into Veterinary Profession, 1971–75; Council, RSE, 1963–65, Vice-Pres., 1969–72; Inter Univ. Council, 1973–75. Editor, Jl of Tropical Animal Health and Production. Hon. FRCVS, 1970. Hon. Mem., World Veterinary Assoc., 1975. Hon. LLD Aberdeen, 1971; Hon. DVSc Melbourne, 1973. *Publications*: (ed) International Encyclopædia of Veterinary Medicine; numerous articles in veterinary and other scientific journals. *Recreations*: gardening, motoring, hill climbing. *Address*: 205 Mayfield Road, Edinburgh EH9 3BD. *T*: 031–667 1242. *Club*: New (Edinburgh).

*Died 5 Sept. 1990.*

**ROBERTSON, Alexander Thomas Parke Anthony Cecil, (Alec Robertson),** MBE 1972; FRAM, 1945; *b* 3 June 1892; *s* of J. R. S. Robertson, MD, and Elizabeth Macrory. *Educ:* Bradfield College, Berks; Royal Academy of Music. Began professional career as organist of Frensham Parish Church, 1914; Farnham Parish Church, 1914. Served European War, 1914–18, commissioned Hampshire Regt 1914; went to India, 1914, Palestine, for active service, 1917. Joined The Gramophone Co. (His Master's Voice) in 1920 to develop educational use of the gramophone by means of lectures, building up repertoire, etc.; head of this Education Dept, 1925. Went to Rome to study theology, church music, etc., at Collegio Beda, 1930. Joined BBC in Gramophone Dept, 1940, Music Dept, 1941, finally Talks Dept, 1944; Specialist Talks Producer (Music), British Broadcasting Corporation, 1944–53; retired, 1953; besides organising output of music talks, became well known as a broadcaster. An authority on plainchant and early church music; writer, lecturer, and adjudicator. *Publications:* The Interpretation of Plainchant, 1937; Dvořák, 1945; Contrasts, Arts and Religion, 1947; Sacred Music, 1950; More than Music (autobiography), 1961; Catholic Church Music, 1961; Schubert's Songs (in symposium), 1946; (ed) Chamber Music (Pelican), 1956; Jt Ed., Pelican History of Music in 3 vols, 1961–66; Requiem, 1967; Church Cantatas of J. S. Bach, 1972; contrib. to Chambers's Encyc., Grove's Dictionary of Music and Musicians (1954 edn), and to musical and other journals. *Address:* The Platt, Apsley Farm, Pulborough, West Sussex. *T:* Coolham 359.

*Died 18 Jan.* 1982.

**ROBERTSON, Catherine Christian,** MA; Headmistress of George Watson's Ladies' College, 1926–45; *b* 10 Dec. 1886; *d* of late Alexander Robertson, Perth, and Mary Macfarlane Duncan, Edinburgh. *Educ:* privately; Perth Academy; University of Edinburgh. Graduated in Arts, with Hons in English Literature and Language, Class II, 1910; Cherwell Hall, Oxford; Diploma of Education, 1911; George Scott Travelling Scholar, 1911. Head of the English Department, Edinburgh Ladies' Coll., 1919–26; travel in America as Chautauqua Scholar of the English-Speaking Union (first Scotswoman to hold this award), 1925. President, Association of Headmistresses, Scottish Branch, 1941–42; Vice-Chairman of Council, Girls' Training Corps, Scotland, 1942. *Recreation:* music.

*Died 4 Dec.* 1985.

**ROBERTSON, Eric Desmond,** OBE 1964; Controller, English Services, BBC External Services, and Deputy Managing Director, External Broadcasting, 1973–74; *b* 5 Oct. 1914; *s* of late Major Frank George Watt Robertson, Indian Army, and Amy Robertson (*née* Davidson); *m* 1943, Aileen Margaret Broadhead; two *s.* *Educ:* Aberdeen Grammar Sch.; Univ. of Aberdeen. BSc (Forestry) 1934, BSc 1936, Hunter Meml Prize, 1936. Scientific Adviser, Guthrie & Co. Ltd, Malaya, 1938–39; Malayan Forest Service, Asst Conservator, 1939–40. War of 1939–45: Malaya Command, on special duty, 1940–41. Producer, Malaya Broadcasting Corp., 1941–42; Special Officer, Far Eastern Broadcasting, All India Radio, 1942–45; Malay Editor, BBC, 1945–46; Far Eastern Service Organiser, BBC, 1946–49; Asst Head of Far Eastern Service, BBC, 1949–52; Head of Far Eastern Service, BBC, 1952–58; Head of Asian Services, BBC, 1958–64; Asst Controller, Overseas Services, BBC, 1964–70; Controller, Overseas Services, BBC, 1970–73. *Publication:* The Japanese File, 1979. *Address:* B2 Albany, Piccadilly, W1. *T:* 01–734 3355. *Club:* Naval and Military.

*Died 22 April* 1987.

**ROBERTSON, George Paterson;** Executive Director, National and Commercial Banking Group Ltd, 1969–73; *b* 28 March 1911; 2nd *s* of Alexander Paterson Robertson and Helen Allan Guthrie; *m* 1941, Mary Martin Crichton; one *d* (one *s* decd). *Educ:* Allan Glen's Sch., Glasgow. Commissioned RAF Accountant Branch, 1940–46; Cashier and Gen. Manager, The Royal Bank of Scotland, 1965–68; Director: The Royal Bank of Scotland, 1967–68; Glyn Mills & Co., 1965–68; Williams Deacon's Bank Ltd, 1965–68; Scottish Agricultural Securities Corp. Ltd, 1965–68. Pres., Inst. of Bankers in Scotland, 1967–69; Vice-Pres., British Bankers' Assoc., 1968–69; Past Hon. Treasurer: Earl Haig Fund (Scotland), 1965–68; Officers' Assoc. (Scottish Br.), 1965–68; Scottish Veterans' Garden City Assoc. Inc., 1965–68. *Address:* 3 Kings Court, Beckenham, Kent. *T:* 01-650 5414.

*Died 4 Jan.* 1982.

**ROBERTSON, Ian (Gow),** MA Oxon; Keeper of Western Art, Ashmolean Museum, Oxford, and of Hope Collection of Engraved Portraits, and Fellow of Worcester College, Oxford, 1962–68; *b* Killearn, Stirlingshire, 20 Sept. 1910; *er s* of John Gow Robertson and Margaret Stewart. *Educ:* The King's School, Canterbury. Studied art at continental centres, in US and in public and private collections in UK. Assistant Keeper in Dept of Fine Art, Ashmolean Museum, 1931. Ministry of Home Security, 1939–41; served in Royal Navy, 1941–46. Senior Assistant Keeper, Ashmolean Museum, 1949. *Recreations:* gardening, listening to music. *Address:* Flat 3, 15 Gledhow Gardens, SW5.

*Died 7 Oct.* 1983.

**ROBERTSON, Sir James (Anderson),** Kt 1968; CBE 1963 (OBE 1949; MBE 1942); QPM 1961; *b* Glasgow, 8 April 1906; *s* of James Robertson, East Haugh, Pitlochry, Perthshire and later of Glasgow, and Mary Rankin Anderson, Glasgow; *m* 1942, Janet Lorraine Gilfillan Macfarlane, Largs, Ayrshire; two *s* one *d.* *Educ:* Provanside Sch., Glasgow and Glasgow Univ. BL 1936. Chief Constable of Glasgow, 1960–71. Chm., Glasgow Standing Conf. of Voluntary Youth Organisations; Hon. President: Glasgow Bn Boys' Brigade. OStJ 1964. *Recreations:* golf and gardening. *Address:* 3 Kirklee Road, Glasgow G12 0RL. *T:* 041–339 4400.

*Died 3 May* 1990.

**ROBERTSON, Maj.-Gen. James Howden,** CB 1974; Director, Army Dental Service, 1970–74; *b* 16 Oct. 1915; *s* of John and Marion Robertson, Glasgow and Creetown; *m* 1942, Muriel Edna, *d* of Alfred Jefferies, Elgin; two *s* one *d.* *Educ:* White Hill Sch., Glasgow; Glasgow Dental Hospital. LDS, RFPS(G) 1939; FDS, RCSE 1957. Lieut, Army Dental Corps, 1939; Captain 1940; Major 1943; Lt-Col 1954; Col 1962; Brig. 1967; Maj.-Gen. 1970. Served in UK and Norway, 1939–44, Europe, 1944–50; Senior Specialist in Dental Surgery, 1957; Middle East, 1958–61; Consultant, CMH Aldershot, 1962–67; Consulting Dental Surgeon to the Army, 1967–70. Col Comdt, RADC, 1975–80. QHDS, 1967–74. Pres., Oral Surgery Club of GB, 1975–76. OStJ 1969. *Publications:* various articles in medical and dental jls on oral and maxillo-facial surgery. *Recreations:* wildfowling, fishing, gardening. *Address:* Struan, Hethfelton Hollow, East Stoke, Dorset. *T:* Bindon Abbey 462272.

*Died 11 Feb.* 1987.

**ROBERTSON, Sir James (Wilson),** KT 1965; GCMG 1957 (KCMG 1953); GCVO 1956; KBE 1948 (MBE 1931); *b* 27 Oct. 1899; *e s* of late James Robertson, Broughty Ferry, Angus and Edinburgh, and late Mrs Robertson, Glenlyon, Spylaw Bank Road, Colinton, Midlothian; *m* 1926, Nancy, *er d* of H. S. Walker, Huddersfield; one *s* one *d.* *Educ:* Merchiston Castle School, Edinburgh; Balliol College, Oxford. BA 1922, MA 1930; Honorary Fellow of Balliol, 1953. Oxford University Rugby XV, 1921. Officer Cadet, 1918–19; 2nd Lieutenant, Black Watch, 1919; entered Sudan Political Service, 1922; Assistant Dist Commissioner and Dist Comr, 1922–36. Jebel Aulia compensation commission, 1936. Sub-Governor White Nile Province, 1937; Dep. Governor Gezira Province, 1939; actg Governor Gezira Province, 1940–41. Asst Civil Secretary, 1941; Deputy Civil Secretary, 1942; Civil Secretary Sudan Government, 1945–53; Chairman British Guiana Constitutional Commission, 1953–54; Director, Uganda Co. Ltd, 1954–55 and 1961–69; Governor-General and Commander-in-Chief of Federation of Nigeria, 1955–60 (first Governor-General and Commander-in-Chief of the Independent Federation of Nigeria, Oct.–Nov. 1960). Comr to examine the question of Kenya Coastal Strip, Oct. 1961. Dir, Barclays Bank DCO, 1961–71. Chairman: Commonwealth Inst., 1961–68; Central Coun. Roy. Over-Seas League, 1962–67; Sudan British Pensioners' Assoc., 1961–67; Coun. for Aid to African Students, 1961–76; Pres. Overseas Service Pensioners' Assoc., 1961–71; Pres. Britain–Nigeria Assoc., 1961–81; a Governor, Queen Mary Coll., Univ. of London, 1961–74; Mem. Council, Royal Commonwealth Society for the Blind; Deputy Chairman, Nat. Cttee for Commonwealth Immigrants, 1965–68. Hon. LLD Leeds University, 1961. FRSA 1964. Wellcome Medal, Royal African Society, 1961. Order of the Nile, 4th Class, 1934. KStJ 1955. *Publication:* Transition in Africa—Memoirs, 1974. *Address:* The Old Bakehouse, Cholsey, near Wallingford, Oxon. *T:* Cholsey 651234. *Club:* Athenæum.

*Died 23 Sept.* 1983.

**ROBERTSON, John;** *b* 3 Feb. 1913; *s* of William Robertson; *m* 1st, 1939 (marr. diss. 1977); two *s* three *d*; 2nd, 1977, June Robertson (*d* 1978); 3rd, 1979, Mrs Sheena Lynch. *Educ:* elementary and secondary schools. Formerly District Secretary and Assistant Divisional Organizer of the Amalgamated Engineering Union, West of Scotland. Mem., Lanarkshire County Council, Motherwell and Wishaw Town Council, 1946–52. Member of Labour Party, 1943–; contested (Lab) Scotstoun Division of Glasgow, General Election, Oct. 1951; MP Paisley, (Lab) Apr. 1961–76, (SLP) 1976–79. Among the founders of the Scottish Labour Party, Jan. 1976. *Recreations:* politics, painting, bowling and Trade Union. *Address:* 28 Davidson Place, Ayr. *T:* Ayr 261849.

*Died 16 May* 1987.

**ROBERTSON, John Monteath,** CBE 1962; FRS 1945; FRSC, FInstP, FRSE; MA, PhD, DSc (Glasgow); Gardiner Professor of Chemistry, University of Glasgow, 1942–70, later Professor Emeritus; Director of Laboratories, 1955–70; *b* 24 July 1900; *s* of William Robertson and Jane Monteath, of Nether Fordun, Auchterarder; *m* 1930, Stella Kennard Nairn, MA; two *s* one *d.* *Educ:* Perth Academy; Glasgow University. Commonwealth Fellow, USA, 1928; Member staff of Davy Faraday Laboratory of Royal Institution, 1930; Senior Lecturer in Physical Chemistry, University of Sheffield, 1939; Scientific Adviser (Chemical) to Bomber Command, 1941; Hon. Scientific Adviser to RAF, 1942. George Fisher Baker Lecturer, Cornell Univ., USA, 1951; Visiting Prof., Univ. of California,

Berkeley, USA, 1958. Member, University Grants Committee, 1960–65; President, Chemical Society, 1962–64. Corresp. Member Turin Academy of Sciences, 1962. Hon. LLD Aberdeen, 1963; Hon. DSc Strathclyde, 1970. Davy Medal, Royal Soc., 1960; Longstaff Medal, Chemical Soc., 1966; Paracelsus Medal, Swiss Chem. Soc., 1971; Gregori Aminoff Medal, Royal Swedish Acad., 1983. *Publications:* Organic Crystals and Molecules, 1953; papers and articles on chemical, physical, and X-ray diffraction subjects in Proc. Royal Soc., Jl of Chem. Soc., etc. *Address:* 11a Eriskay Road, Inverness IV2 3LX. *T:* Inverness 225561. *Club:* Athenæum.
*Died 27 Dec.* 1989.

**ROBERTSON, William Walter Samuel,** CBE 1957 (OBE 1950); *b* 3 July 1906; *s* of W. H. A. and A. M. Robertson (*née* Lane); *m* 1935, Kathleen Elizabeth Chawner East; one *s* two *d*. *Educ:* Bedford School; King's College, London. BSc (Eng.) First Class Hons, 1926. Apprenticeship to W. H. A. Robertson & Co. Ltd (Director, 1929) and to Torrington Mfg Co., USA, 1926–28. Regional Controller and Chm. of North Midland Regional Bd for Production, 1943–45; Chairman, Eastern Regional Bd for Industry, 1949–64 (Vice-Chm., 1945–49); Member Advisory Committee, Revolving Fund for Industry, 1955–58. MIMechE, 1943. High Sheriff of Bedfordshire, 1963. Governor, St Felix School, Southwold. *Recreations:* rowing, golf. *Address:* The Dale, Pavenham, Beds. *T:* Oakley 2895. *Clubs:* Caledonian; Leander (Henley-on-Thames).
*Died 6 May* 1989.

**ROBEY, Edward George Haydon,** BA, LLB; Barrister-at-Law; a Metropolitan Magistrate, 1954–72; *b* 26 March 1899; *s* of late Sir George Robey, CBE, and his first wife, the late Ethel Haydon; *m* 1942, Denise (*d* 1981), *d* of late Denis Williams, Virginia Water. *Educ:* Westminster School; Jesus Coll., Cambridge. Called to Bar, Inner Temple, 1925; professional staff of Director of Public Prosecutions, 1932–50; apptd to Attorney-General's Executive for prosecution of the Major War Criminals at Nuremberg, 1945. *Publications:* The Jester and the Court, 1976. *Recreation:* music. *Address:* 11 Shrewsbury House, Cheyne Walk, SW3. *T:* 01-352 2403. *Club:* Garrick. *Died 5 March* 1983.

**ROBINS, Daniel Gerard;** QC 1986; *b* 12 March 1942; *o s* of W. A. and H. M. Robins; *m* 1968, Elizabeth Mary Gerran, *e d* of Baron Lloyd of Kilgerran, CBE, QC; three *d*. *Educ:* City of London School; London School of Economics (BSc, LLB). FRAI. Called to the Bar, Lincoln's Inn, 1966; Hardwicke Scholar 1963, Mansfield Scholar 1966. Trustee: Education Trust Ltd; Brantwood (John Ruskin) Trust. *Recreations:* ornithology, squash, golf. *Address:* 2 Harcourt Buildings, Temple, EC4. *T:* 01–353 8415. *Clubs:* Savile; Royal Wimbledon Golf; Royal Naval (Portsmouth).
*Died 4 Oct.* 1989.

**ROBINS, Mrs Denise (Naomi);** *b* Whitehall Court, SW1, 1 Feb. 1897; *d* of Herman Klein; *m* 1st, 1918; three *d*; 2nd, 1939, Lt-Col R. O'Neill Pearson. *Educ:* Staten Island, USA; Convent, Upper Norwood, SE. Entered Dundee Courier Office, Dundee, 1914; became a Free Lance writer, and published numerous serials and short stories; first novel published in 1924. *Publications:* 169 books including House of the 7th Cross, The Noble One, Khamsin, Dark Corridor, etc; *historical novels:* Gold for the Gay Masters, Dance in the Dust, etc; *autobiography:* Stranger Than Fiction. *Recreations:* music, books, travel. *Address:* 6 Kipling Court, Winnals Park, Haywards Heath, West Sussex RH16 1EX. *T:* Haywards Heath 413452. *Died 1 May* 1985.

**ROBINSON, Arnold;** *see* Robinson, F. A.

**ROBINSON, Rt. Rev. Christopher James Gossage,** MA; *b* 10 June 1903; *s* of late Canon Albert Gossage Robinson; unmarried. *Educ:* Marlborough, Christ's Coll., Cambridge. Lecturer at St Stephen's Coll., Delhi, 1926–29; Deacon, 1929; Priest, 1930; Curate St Mary's, Portsea, 1929–31; Asst Priest, St James, Delhi, 1931–32; Vicar of St James, and Chaplain of Delhi, 1932–42; Vicar of St Thomas, New Delhi, 1942–45; Hon. Canon of Lahore Cathedral, 1944–47; Bishop of Lucknow, 1947–62; Bishop of Bombay, 1962–70. Member, Brotherhood of the Ascended Christ (formerly Cambridge Brotherhood of the Ascension), Delhi, since 1931. *Address:* Brotherhood House, 7 Court Lane, Delhi 110–054, India. *Club:* Royal Commonwealth Society. *Died 24 Feb.* 1988.

**ROBINSON, Sir David,** Kt 1985; *b* Cambridge, 13 April 1904; *s* of Herbert Robinson; *m* Mabel Alice; one *d* (one *s* decd). *Educ:* Cambridgeshire High School for Boys. Started in business, 1930; Robinson Rentals, Bedford, 1954–68. Former race-horse owner; won 997 races, 1960–75. Founder, Robinson Trust; Robinson Coll., Cambridge, opened 1981. *Died 10 Jan.* 1987.

**ROBINSON, Sir Dove-Myer,** Kt 1970; JP; MRSH; Mayor of Auckland, New Zealand, 1959–65 and 1968–80; *b* Sheffield, 15 June 1901; 6th *c* of Moss Robinson and Ida Robinson (*née* Brown); of Jewish race; *m* 1st, Bettine Williams; 2nd, Thelma Ruth Thompson; one *s* five *d*. *Educ:* primary schools in Sheffield, Manchester, London and Devonport (Auckland, NZ). Mem., Auckland City Council,

1952–59; Chm., Auckland Metropolitan Drainage Bd, 1953–55; Chm., Auckland Airport Cttee, 1959–61; Mem., Auckland Univ. Council, 1952–80; Chm., Auckland Regional Authority, 1963–65, Mem., 1963–80 (Chm. Rapid Transit Cttee, 1968–74); Sen. Vice-Pres., NZ Municipal Assoc., 1959–65 and 1968–80; President: Auckland Rugby League, 1964–; Auckland Festival Soc., 1959–65 and 1968–80. Fellow, NZ Inst. of Management, 1948, Hon. Fellow, 1974; Patron, NZ Pure Water Assoc., 1954–; Hon. Mem., Inst. Water Pollution Control. CStJ 1979. *Publications:* Utilization of Town and Country Wastes, Garbage and Sewage, 1946; Soil, Food and Health, 1947; Passenger Transport in Auckland, 1969; numerous leaflets and pubns on Pollution, Conservation, Fluoridation, Nutrition, Local and Regional Govt, Town Planning, Rapid Transit, etc. *Recreations:* golf, fishing, boating, photography, motoring, local government. *Address:* 17/57 Richard Farrell Avenue, Remuera, Auckland, New Zealand. *Clubs:* Remuera Golf, Rugby League (Auckland). *Died 14 Aug.* 1989.

**ROBINSON, Forbes;** *see* Robinson, P. F.

**ROBINSON, Frank Arnold,** CBE 1980; DSc, CChem, FRSC; Director of Twyford Laboratories Ltd & Twyford Pharmaceutical Services Ltd, retired; *b* 3 Dec. 1907; *s* of Frank Robinson and Edith Robinson (*née* Jagger); *m* 1st, 1930, Margaret Olive Jones; two *s*; 2nd, 1958, Beth Clarence Smith. *Educ:* Elland Grammar Sch.; Univ. of Manchester (James Gaskill Scholar; Hon. Fellow, UMIST, 1981); BSc Tech (Hons) 1929, MSc Tech 1930, DSc 1958; Univ. of London LLB (Hons.) 1940. Laboratory of Govt Chemist, 1930–33; Research Chemist, Glaxo Laboratories Ltd, Greenford, 1933–45; Manager, Distillers Co. Research Labs, Epsom, 1945–48; Dir of Research, Allen & Hanburys Ltd, Ware, 1948–60. FRIC 1940 (now FRSC). Hon. Professorial Fellow, University Coll., Cardiff, 1967–72; Hon. DSc: Bath, 1968; Salford, 1972. Chm., Biochemical Soc., 1946, and Treas., 1952–62; Pres., Section I (Biomedical) of BAAS, 1972–73; Mem., British National Cttee for Biochemistry, 1973–78; President: Royal Inst. Chem., 1972–74 (Vice-Pres., 1961–63, 1970–72); Chemical Soc., 1975–76; 12th Congress of Assoc. Internat. d'Expertise Chimique, Cambridge, 1972; Mem., UNESCO Cttee on status of scientific researchers, 1974; Chairman: Council, Science and Technology Insts Ltd, 1975–76; Council for Environmental Science and Engineering, 1975–81; Vice-Pres., Parly and Scientific Cttee, 1978–81. Assessor, Sci. Board, SRC, 1978–81. First medal awarded by Royal Soc. of Chem. for service to the Soc., 1983. *Publications:* Principles and Practice of Chromatography, 1941; The Vitamin B Complex, 1951; Antibiotics, 1951; Vitamin Co-Factors of Enzyme Systems, 1966; Chemists and the Law, 1967; research papers and reviews in scientific jls. *Recreations:* gardening, archæology. *Address:* 40 Barnside Court, Welwyn Garden City, Herts AL8 6TL. *T:* Welwyn Garden City 333830.
*Died 18 May* 1988.

**ROBINSON, Sir George (Gilmour),** Kt 1955; *b* 30 Aug. 1894; *s* of George Thomas Robinson and Ada Violet Gallier; *m* 1942, Muriel Alice Fry. *Educ:* Repton; Trinity College, Oxford. (MA). Served European War, 1914–19. Called to Bar, 1924, and practised. Resident Magistrate, Kenya, 1930–38; Puisne Judge, Northern Rhodesia, 1938–46; Puisne Judge, Nigeria, 1947–52; Chief Justice, Zanzibar, 1952–55; retired 1955. *Recreations:* shooting, golf. *Address:* The Old House, Southwold, Suffolk. *T:* 722374.
*Died 19 Oct.* 1985.

**ROBINSON, Prof. Joan Violet;** Professor of Economics, University of Cambridge, 1965–71, retired 1971; *b* Camberley, Surrey, 31 Oct. 1903; *d* of late Major-General Sir Frederick Maurice, KCMG, CB; *m* 1926, Sir E. Austin G. Robinson, CMG, OBE, FBA; two *d*. *Educ:* St Paul's Girls' School, London; Girton Coll., Cambridge. Economics Tripos, 1925; Faculty Asst Lectr in Economics, Cambridge Univ., 1931; Univ. Lectr, 1937; Reader, 1949. FBA 1958–71. *Publications:* Economics of Imperfect Competition, 1933; Essays in the Theory of Employment, 1937; Introduction to the Theory of Employment, 1937; Essay on Marxian Economics, 1942; Collected Economic Papers, Vol. I, 1951; The Rate of Interest and Other Essays, 1952; The Accumulation of Capital, 1956; Collected Economic Papers, Vol. II, 1960; Essays in The Theory of Economic Growth, 1963; Economic Philosophy, 1963; Collected Economic Papers, Vol. III, 1965; Economics: An Awkward Corner, 1966; The Cultural Revolution in China, 1969; Freedom and Necessity, 1970; Economic Heresies, 1971; (ed) After Keynes, 1973; (with John Eatwell) Introduction to Modern Economics, 1973; Collected Economic Papers, Vol. IV, 1973, Vol. V, 1979; contrib. Modern Economics, 1978; articles, etc in Economic Journal, etc. *Address:* 62 Grange Road, Cambridge. *T:* 57548. *Died 5 Aug.* 1983.

**ROBINSON, Rt. Rev. John Arthur Thomas,** MA, BD, DD, PhD; Lecturer in Theology, Trinity College, Cambridge, since 1969; Fellow, and Dean of Chapel, Trinity College, since 1969; *b* 15 June 1919; *s* of Reverend Canon Arthur William Robinson, DD and Mary Beatrice Robinson; *m* 1947, Ruth (*née* Grace); one *s* three *d*. *Educ:* Marlborough College; Jesus and Trinity Colleges,

Cambridge; Westcott House, Cambridge. BA 1942 (1st class Theology); MA 1945; PhD 1946; BD 1962; DD 1968. Curate of St Matthew, Moorfields, Bristol, 1945–48; Chaplain, Wells Theological College, 1948–51; Fellow and Dean, Clare College, Cambridge, 1951–59; Assistant Lecturer in Divinity, Cambridge University, 1953–54; Lecturer in Divinity, 1954–59; Bishop Suffragan of Woolwich, 1959–69. Examining Chaplain to Archbishop of Canterbury, 1953–59; Six Preacher, Canterbury Cathedral, 1958–68; Proctor in Convocation, 1960–70; Assistant Bishop: Diocese of Southwark, 1969–80; Diocese of Bradford, 1981–. Vis. Prof. and Noble Lectr, Harvard, 1955; Vis. Prof.: Union Theological Seminary, Richmond, VA, 1958; Univ. of South Africa, Pretoria, 1975; Univ. of Witwatersrand, 1977; McMaster Univ., Hamilton, Ont, 1982. Lectures: Reinicker, Va Seminary, 1958; Purdy, Hartford Seminary, Conn, 1964; Thorp, Cornell University, 1964; Lilley, Wabash Coll., Indiana, 1966; West, Stanford Univ., 1966; Hulsean, Cambridge, 1970; Nelson, Lancaster Univ., 1971; Owen Evans, University Coll. of Aberystwyth, 1971; Carnahan, Union Theological Seminary, Buenos Aires, 1971; Teape, Delhi, Madras and Calcutta, 1977–78; Selwyn, St John's Coll., Auckland, 1979; Bampton Lectr-elect, Oxford Univ., 1984. Hon. LCD Univ. of Southern California, 1980. *Publications:* In the End God, 1950, rev. edn 1968; The Body, 1952; Jesus and His Coming, 1957, rev. edn 1979; On Being the Church in the World, 1960, rev. edn 1977; Christ Comes In, 1960; Liturgy Coming to Life, 1960; Twelve New Testament Studies, 1962; Honest to God, 1963; Christian Morals Today, 1964; The New Reformation?, 1965; But That I Can't Believe!, 1967; Exploration into God, 1967, rev. edn 1977; Christian Freedom in a Permissive Society, 1970; The Difference in Being a Christian Today, 1972; The Human Face of God, 1973; Redating the New Testament, 1976; Can We Trust the New Testament?, 1977; Wrestling with Romans, 1979; Truth is Two-Eyed, 1979; The Roots of a Radical, 1980; Joseph Barber Lightfoot, 1981; *contrib. to:* Christian Faith and Communist Faith, 1953; Becoming a Christian, 1954; The Historic Episcopate, 1954; Jesus Christ, History, Interpretation and Faith, 1956; New Ways with the Ministry, 1960; Bishops, 1961; The Interpreter's Dictionary of the Bible (article: Resurrection in the NT), 1962; Layman's Church, 1963; The Roads Converge, 1963; The Honest to God Debate, 1963; The Authorship and Integrity of the New Testament, 1965; The Restless Church, 1966; Theologians of our Time, 1966; Theological Freedom and Social Responsibility, 1967; Sermons from Great St Mary's, 1968; The Christian Priesthood, 1970; More Sermons from Great St Mary's, 1971; Theological Crossings, 1971; Christ, Faith and History, 1972; To God be the Glory, 1973; Christ and Spirit in the New Testament, 1973; Face to Face with the Turin Shroud, 1978; Twentieth Century Pulpit, vol. 2, 1981; Debate on Disarmament, 1982; Christological Perspectives, 1982; articles in learned journals, mainly on New Testament subjects; *posthumous publication:* The Priority of John, 1985. *Address:* Trinity College, Cambridge CB2 1TQ. *T:* Cambridge 358201.

*Died 5 Dec. 1983.*

**ROBINSON, Sir John Beverley,** 7th Bt, *cr* 1854; *b* 3 Oct. 1913; *s* of Sir John Beverley Robinson, 6th Bt, and Constance Marie (*d* 1977), *d* of Robert W. Pentecost; *S* father 1954. *Heir: kinsman* Christopher Philipse Robinson [*b* 10 Nov. 1938; *m* 1962, Barbara Judith, *d* of Richard Duncan; two *s* (and one *s* decd)].                    *Died 1988.*

**ROBINSON, John Foster,** CBE 1968; TD; DL; Honorary President, DRG plc, since 1974; *b* 2 Feb. 1909; *s* of late Sir Foster Gotch Robinson; *m* 1st, 1935, Margaret Eve Hannah Paterson (*d* 1977); two *s* two *d*; 2nd, 1979, Mrs Joan De Moraville. *Educ:* Harrow; Christ Church, Oxford. Dir, E. S. & A. Robinson Ltd, 1943, Jt Man. Dir 1948; Chm., E. S. & A. Robinson (Holdings) Ltd, 1961; Dep. Chm., The Dickinson Robinson Group Ltd, 1966, Chm., 1968–74. DL Glos 1972; High Sheriff, Avon, 1975. *Recreations:* shooting, fishing, golf. *Address:* Honor Farm, Failand Lane, Portbury, Bristol BS20 9SR. *T:* Pill 2108. *Clubs:* Clifton, Bristol (Bristol).

*Died 28 Sept. 1988.*

**ROBINSON, Kenneth Dean,** MA Oxon; Administrator, Advertising Code, British Herbal Medicine Association, since 1978 (General Secretary, 1979–86); *b* 9 March 1909; *s* of late Rev. Arthur Edward and late Mary Edith Robinson; *m* 1936, Marjorie Belle Carter, Bradford, Yorks; two *s* two *d*. *Educ:* Bradford Grammar Sch.; Corpus Christi Coll., Oxford (Scholar). Classical Honour Mods Class I, Litt Hum. Class II. Sixth Form Classical Master, St Edmund's, Canterbury, 1932–34; Head of Classical Dept, Wellington College, Berks, 1934–41; Intelligence Corps, 1941–45; Asst to Director of Education, Shire Hall, Reading, Berks, 1945–46; Headmaster: Birkenhead Sch., Cheshire, 1946–63 (Hon. Pres., Old Birkonian Soc., 1986–); Bradford Grammar Sch., 1963–74. Classics panel Secondary Sch. Examinations Council, 1948–50; Pres. Liverpool Br., Class. Assoc., 1958; Council, IAHM, 1949–53; HMC Cttee, 1956–60; Chm. NW Div., HMC, 1958–59; Chm. Direct Grant Cttee, HMC, 1958–59, Mem., 1967–70; Chm., NE Div., HMC, 1971–72; Chm. Op. Res. Sect. Div. XII, IAHM, 1952–60; Chm. Div. XII, IAHM, 1961–62; Mem. Council, 1962–63; Chm.,

1975–79, Hon. Pres., 1979, Leeds/Bradford Branch, Nat. Assoc. for Gifted Children. Governor, Giggleswick Sch., 1974–84. *Publications:* (with R. L. Chambers) Septimus: a First Latin Reader, 1936; The Latin Way, 1947. *Recreations:* gardening, chess, painting, canals, country. *Address:* Lane House, Cowling, near Keighley, West Yorks BD22 0LX. *T:* Crosshills 34487.

*Died 7 March 1987.*

**ROBINSON, Nigel Francis Maltby;** Metropolitan Stipendiary Magistrate, 1962–78; *b* 5 Nov. 1906; *s* of Francis George Robinson, OBE, Ilkeston, Derbyshire; *m* 1933, Flora, *d* of John McKay, Sutton, Surrey. *Educ:* Lancing; Hertford College, Oxford (MA, BCL). Called to Bar, Middle Temple, 1928; Practised Midland Circuit, 1928–62. Served Royal Artillery, 1940–45. JP and Dep. Chairman, Quarter Sessions for Derbyshire, 1958–64; JP and Dep. Chm., Nottinghamshire Quarter Sessions, 1961–66. *Address:* 42 Parkside, Vanbrugh Fields, SE3 7QG. *Clubs:* Flyfishers'; Nottingham and Nottinghamshire United Services.

*Died 3 Sept. 1985.*

**ROBINSON, (Peter) Forbes;** Principal Artist (Bass), Royal Opera House, Covent Garden, 1954–83; *b* Macclesfield, 21 May 1926; *s* of Wilfred and Gertrude Robinson; *m* 1952, Marion Stubbs; two *d*. *Educ:* King's Sch., Macclesfield. St Paul's Coll., Cheltenham (teacher's trg), 1943–45. Capt. in RAEC, 1946–48. Loughborough Coll. (Hons Dipl., Phys. Educn), 1949–50; La Scuola di Canto (Scala, Milan), 1952–53. Promenade Debut, 1957. Guest artist with Dublin, Handel, Sadler's Wells, Opera North, London Savoyards, Scottish and Welsh National Opera Cos. Has sung at Festivals at Aldeburgh, Barcelona, Edinburgh, Holland, Leeds, Lucerne, Ottawa, Portugal and Schwetzingen. Has also sung in Argentina, Belgium, Canada, Denmark, France, Germany, Luxembourg, Sweden, USA, South Korea, Japan and South Africa. First British singer to sing Don Giovanni at Royal Opera House, Covent Garden, for 100 years. Hon. DLitt Loughborough, 1979. Awarded Opera Medal for 1963, for creating King Priam (Tippett). Several recordings, inc. 4 solo albums and 2 TV videos. *Recreations:* walking, talking, gardening, croquet, jazz. *Address:* 225 Princes Gardens, W3. *T:* 01–992 5498. *Club:* Savage.                    *Died 13 May 1987.*

**ROBINSON, Stanford,** OBE 1972; Orchestral, Choral and Opera Conductor; Lecturer on conducting and kindred musical subjects; *b* Leeds, 5 July 1904; *s* of James Percy and Carrie Robinson; *m* 1934, Lorely Dyer; one *d*. *Educ:* Stationers' Company's School; Royal College of Music, London, and abroad. British Broadcasting Corporation, 1924–66; Chorus Master until 1932, during which time formed the BBC choral activities in London, including the BBC Singers, the Choral Society, and the BBC Chorus; during the period also conducted the Wireless Orchestra extensively in all kinds of programmes, symphonic and otherwise; Conductor of BBC Theatre Orchestra, 1932–46; Music Dir Variety Dept, 1932–36; Dir Music Productions, producing and conducting all studio performances of opera besides operetta and other musical feature programmes, 1936–46; Opera Director and Associate Conductor of the BBC Symphony Orchestra, 1946–49; Conductor Opera Orch. and Opera Organiser, BBC, 1949–52. Toured Australia and New Zealand, conducting ABC and NZBC orchestras in numerous cities, 1966–67; Chief Conductor, Queensland Symphony Orchestra, 1968–69. Hon. ARCM; Hon. GSM; Emeritus FGSM, 1980. *Publications:* Orchestral Music, Brass Band Music, part songs, choral arrangements and songs. *Recreations:* gardening, photography. *Address:* Ivor Newton House, 10–12 Edward Road, Sundridge Park, Bromley, Kent BR1 3NQ; Flat 3, Belmont Court, Belmont, Dyke Road, Brighton, Sussex BN1 3TX. *T:* Brighton 202272.

*Died 25 Oct. 1984.*

**ROBINSON, Ursula Harvey, (Mrs Gower Robinson);** *see* Bloom, U. H.

**ROBINSON, Maj.-Gen. William Arthur,** CB 1964; OBE 1944; MA; MD; retired; *b* 2 March 1908; *s* of late Sir William Robinson, DL, JP; *m* 1934, Sheela, *d* of J. R. Yarr, Newbury, Berks; two *s*. *Educ:* Wesley College and Trinity College, Dublin. MA, MD, 1934. MRCGP 1961. Commissioned RAMC, 1931; served in Egypt and Sudan, 1932–37; Instructor and MO Army Gas School, 1938–41; Adviser in Chemical Warfare, 1941–43; Comd 200 Fd Ambulance (Egypt, Sicily and NW Europe), 1943–44; ADMS: 3 (Brit.) Inf. Div., NW Europe, 1945–46; Lt-Col Assistant Director-General Army Medical Dept (AMD1) War Office, 1946–49; jssc 1949; OC Hospital, E Africa, 1950–51; ADMS HQ Cyrenaica Dist (Colonel, ADMS 1 Bn Div., 1951–52, ADG (AMD1) War Office, 1952–54; DDMS Malta, 1954–57; Commandant, Depot and TE RAMC, 1958–60; Major-General, 1960; Deputy Director-General, Army Medical Services, 1960–61; DDMS Southern Command, 1961; DMS, Far East Land Forces, 1963–65; QHS, 1960–65. Col Comdt, RAMC, 1966–. *Recreations:* cross-country running (sen. colours); sailing, hockey, golf. *Address:* Lechlade, Horton Heath, Eastleigh, Hants.                    *Died 29 Nov. 1982.*

**ROBSON, His Honour Denis Hicks,** QC 1955; a County Court Judge, later a Circuit Judge, 1957–72; *b* 7 Jan. 1904; *s* of late Robert Robson, ISO, and Helen Julia, *d* of late James J. Hicks, KCSG; *m* 1931, Mary Grace (*d* 1947), *e d* of late Sir William Orpen, KBE; one *s* one *d*; *m* 1960, Hon. Elizabeth (*widow* of John Cockburn Millar), *d* of late Lord Atkin, PC. *Educ:* Douai School; Trinity Hall, Cambridge. Called to the Bar, Inner Temple, 1927; North Eastern Circuit. War of 1939–45, commissioned in RASC, 1940; Military Department of Judge Advocate General's Office, 1942–45; Major, 1944; Recorder of Doncaster, 1950–53; Recorder of Middlesbrough, 1953–57; Chm., Northamptonshire QS, 1970–71, Vice-Chm., 1960–70. *Died* 26 Sept. 1983.

**ROBSON, Dame Flora,** DBE 1960 (CBE 1952); *b* South Shields, 28 March 1902; *d* of David Mather Robson and Eliza McKenzie. Royal Academy of Dramatic Art (Bronze medal). Hon. DLitt: Oxon, 1974, Durham, Wales; Sussex, 1982; Hon. DLitt London, 1971; Hon. Fellow: St Anne's Coll., Oxford, 1975; Sunderland Polytechnic, 1975; Order of Finland's White Rose and Finland's Lion. First appearance on stage, 1921; in All God's Chillun, 1933; Old Vic Season, 1934; Touchwood and Mary Read, Dragoon and Pirate; Close Quarters, 1935; Mary Tudor, 1936; Lady Brooke in Autumn, St Martin's Theatre; Thérèse Raquin in Guilty, Lyric Theatre, Hammersmith, 1944; Man about the House, Piccadilly; Message from Margaret, Duchess; Lady Macbeth, New York, 1948; Captain Brassbound's Conversion (Shaw), Lyric Hammersmith, 1948; Alicia Christie in Black Chiffon, Westminster, 1949; Paulina in The Winter's Tale, Phœnix, 1951; Miss Giddens in The Innocents, Her Majesty's, 1952; Sister Agatha in The Return, Duchess, 1953; Rachel in No Escape; Sarah in A Kind of Folly, Duchess, 1955; Mrs Smith in Suspect, Royal Court, 1955; Janet Holt in The House by the Lake, Duke of York's, 1956–58; Mrs Alving in Ghosts, Old Vic, 1958; Miss Tina in The Aspern Papers, Queen's, 1959; and tour, S Africa, 1960; Grace Rouarte in Time and Yellow Roses, St Martin's, 1961; Miss Moffat in The Corn is Green, in S Africa, S Rhodesia and at Flora Robson Playhouse, Newcastle upon Tyne, 1962; tour, Close Quarters, 1963; Mrs Borkman in John Gabriel Borkman, Duchess, 1962; The Trojan Women, Edinburgh Festival, 1966; tour, Brother and Sister; Miss Prism in The Importance of Being Earnest, Haymarket, 1968; Ring Round The Moon, 1969; The Old Ladies, 1969. *Films:* Empress Elizabeth of Russia in Catherine the Great, 1933; Queen Elizabeth in Fire Over England; Mrs Blair in Farewell Again; Ellen Dean in Wuthering Heights; Mary Rider in Poison Pen; Ftata Teeta in Cæsar and Cleopatra; Sister Phillippa in Black Narcissus; Nell Dawson, MP, in Frieda; Countess Von Platen in Saraband for Dead Lovers; Mary Rackham in Tall Headlines; Melita in Malta Story; The Nurse in Romeo and Juliet; Donna McKenzie in High Tide at Noon; Mrs Haggard in The Gipsy and the Gentleman; Olivia in Innocent Sinners; The Empress of China in 55 Days at Peking; Miss Gilchrist in Murder at the Gallop; Young Cassidy; Guns at Batasi; Those Magnificent Men in their Flying Machines; Seven Women; The Shuttered Room; Cry in the Wind; Eye of the Devil; Fragment of Fear; The Cellar; The Beloved; Alice in Wonderland; Dominique; Clash of the Titans. BBC TV series: Heidi, 1974; A Legacy, 1975; Mr Lollipop, 1976; The Shrimp and the Anemone, 1977; Eustace and Hilda, 1979; TV films: The Oresteia of Aeschylus, 1978; A Man called Intrepid, 1978, Les Misérables, 1978; Tale of Two Cities, 1980. *Publication:* (contrib.) My Drama School, 1977; *relevant publications:* Flora Robson by Janet Dunbar, 1960; Flora by Kenneth H. Barrow, 1981. *Address:* 7 Wykeham Terrace, Brighton, E Sussex BN1 3FF. *Died* 7 July 1984.

**ROBSON, Vice-Adm. Sir Geoffrey;** *see* Robson, Vice-Adm. Sir W. G. A.

**ROBSON, Professor Emeritus James,** MA, DLitt (Glasgow), DD (Hon. St Andrews); MA (Hon. Manchester); *b* 1890; *s* of Rev. Charles Robson; *m* 1919, Annie, *d* of John Cunningham, Dunblane; one *s* one *d*. *Educ:* Inverness Royal Adac.; Stirling High School; Glasgow University; Trinity College, Glasgow. Assistant to Hebrew Professor, Glasgow Univ., 1915–16. Served with YMCA in Mesopotamia and India, 1916–18. Lecturer in English, Forman Christian College, Lahore, 1918–19; Missionary at Sheikh Othman, Aden, 1919–26; Minister at Shandon, Dunbartonshire, 1926–28; Lecturer in Arabic, 1928–48, Reader in Arabic, 1948–49, Glasgow Univ.; Prof. of Arabic, the Univ. of Manchester, 1949–58; Recording Secretary, Glasgow University Oriental Soc., 1931–49; Secretary, 1959–68. External Examiner for Hons Degree: Manchester, 1933–36, 1942–45, 1961–64; Edinburgh, 1945–47, 1952–54, 1961–63; St Andrews, 1957–60; Aberdeen, 1960–62; Glasgow, 1960, 1962; London, 1955–66; and for PhD on occasion at Cambridge, Melbourne, etc. Hon. Fellow, British Soc. for Middle Eastern Studies. *Publications:* Ion Keith-Falconer of Arabia, 1923; Christ in Islam, 1929; Tracts on listening to Music, 1938; Ancient Arabian Musical Instruments, 1938; An introduction to the science of Tradition, 1953; Mishkāt al-maṣābīḥ (trans and notes), 4 vols, 1963–65; ed and wrote Islam section in A Dictionary of Comparative Religion, 1970; articles in learned journals. *Recreation:* gardening.

*Address:* 17 Woodlands Drive, Glasgow G4 9EQ. *T:* 041-332 4088.
*Died* 9 Jan. 1981.

**ROBSON, James Jeavons,** CBE 1972; FICE; MIStructE; FIArb; Secretary for the Environment, Hong Kong, 1973–76; Member of Legislative Council, Hong Kong, 1969–76; in private practice, since 1976; *b* 4 July 1918; *m* 1945, Avis Metcalfe; one *s*. *Educ:* Constantine Coll., Middlesbrough. MICE 1948, FICE 1958; MIStructE 1960; FIArb 1969. War Service, RM, 1942–46 (Captain). Engrg Trng, Messrs Dorman Long & Co. and ICI, 1936–41; joined Colonial Engrg Service and posted to PWD, Hong Kong, 1946; Dir of Public Works, 1969. Mem. Council, ICE, 1967; Telford Premium (for paper, Overall Planning in Hong Kong), ICE, 1971. *Publications:* articles on civil engineering in Jl ICE. *Recreations:* golf, racing, gardening. *Address:* Labéjan, 32300 Mirande, France. *Clubs:* Oriental; Hong Kong, Royal Hong Kong Jockey, Royal Hong Kong Golf. *Died* 17 May 1989.

**ROBSON, Prof. John Michael;** Professor of Pharmacology, Guy's Hospital Medical School, London University, 1950–68, then Emeritus; *b* 13 Dec. 1900; *m* 1930, Sarah Benjamin. *Educ:* Leeds Central High School; Leeds University. Qualified MB, ChB, 1925; MD, 1930; DSc, 1932. Lecturer in Pharmacology, Edinburgh University, 1934; Reader in Pharmacology, Guy's Hospital Medical School, 1946. *Publications:* Recent Advances in Sex and Reproductive Physiology, 1934 (2nd edn 1940, 3rd edn 1947); Chapter in Endocrine in Theory and Practice, 1937; Chapter in The Practice of Endocrinology, 1948; (with C. A. Keele) Recent Advances in Pharmacology, 1950, 2nd edn 1956, 3rd edn (with S. Stacey) 1962, 4th edn, 1968; papers in British Journal of Pharmacol., Journal Physiol., Lancet, British Medical Journal, etc. *Recreations:* bridge, detective stories. *Address:* 2 Brunel House, Cheyne Walk, SW10. *T:* 01-352 8473. *Died* 18 Feb. 1982.

**ROBSON, Sir Lawrence (William),** Kt 1982; FCA, FCMA, JDipMA; Senior Partner, Robson, Rhodes & Co., 186 City Road, EC1, 1927–75; *b* 8 Aug. 1904; *e s* of late Michael William Robson and of Jane Robson, Norton-on-Tees, Co. Durham; *m* 1940, Inga-Stina Arvidsson (Baroness Robson of Kiddington); one *s* two *d*. *Educ:* Stockton Grammar School; Royal Acad. of Music. Financial Adviser, UNRRA, 1944–46, and IRO, 1946; Chm. of several engineering cos; Member: Lloyd's; London Transport Executive, 1969–75; Council, Inst. of Chartered Accountants in England and Wales, 1949–69; Anglo-Amer. Productivity Team, 1949; Liberal Party Organisation (Pres., 1953–54); Herbert Cttee of Inquiry into efficiency and organisation of elect. supply industry, 1954–56; Economic Policy Cttee, FBI 1956–62; Britain in Europe Cttee (Chm. 1958–64); Adv. Cttee on Censuses of Production, 1961–67; British Nat. Cttee of Internat. Council on Combustion Engines (Chm., 1966–); Council, BIM, 1961–71; Council, Inst. Fiscal Studies, 1970–; Anglo-Swedish Soc. (Chm.); European Atlantic Gp (Vice-Pres., 1969–); Council of European Movement, 1969–. Pres., Inst. Cost and Works Accountants, 1950–51. Master, Painter-Stainers' Co., 1979–80; Liveryman: Farmers' Co.; Shipwrights' Co. Fellow, Woodard Foundn. Knight Commander, Royal Order of the North Star, Sweden, 1981. *Publications:* papers on accountancy, management, political and economic subjects. *Recreations:* ski-ing, cricket, sailing and shooting. *Address:* Kiddington Hall, Woodstock, Oxon. *T:* Enstone 398. *Club:* Boodle's. *Died* 24 Aug. 1982.

**ROBSON, Vice-Adm. Sir (William) Geoffrey (Arthur),** KBE 1956; CB 1953; DSO 1940 (Bar 1941); DSC 1941; Lieutenant-Governor and Commander-in-Chief of Guernsey, 1958–64; *b* 10 March 1902; *s* of Major John Robson; *m* 1st, 1925, Sylvia Margaret Forrester (*d* 1968); one *s*; 2nd, 1969, Elizabeth Kathleen, *widow* of Lt-Col V. H. Holt. *Educ:* RN Colleges, Osborne and Dartmouth. Midshipman, HMS Malaya, 1918; served in Destroyers, 1922–37. Commanded Rowena, 1934; Wren, 1935–36; RN Staff Course, 1937; RAF Staff Course, 1938. Served War of 1939–45 (despatches thrice, DSO and Bar, DSC): Comd HMS Kandahar, 1939–41; Combined Operations, 1942–43; Commanded the 26th Destroyer Flotilla, 1944, in HMS Hardy; Captain of Coastal Forces (Nore), 1945; HMS Superb in command, 1945–47; Comd HMS Ganges, 1948–50; President of Admiralty Interview Board, 1950–51; Flag Officer (Flotillas), Home Fleet, 1951–53; Flag Officer, Scotland, 1952–56; Commander-in-Chief, South Atlantic, 1956–58; retd, 1958. Commander of the Order of St Olav (Norway). *Recreations:* shooting, fishing. *Address:* Amat, Ardgay, Ross-shire; Le Paradou, Forest, Guernsey. *Club:* Army and Navy. *Died* 25 Dec. 1989.

**ROCHFORD, James Donald Henry;** Admiralty Registrar of the Supreme Court, since 1973; Barrister-at-Law; *b* 8 July 1921; *e s* of Leonard Henry Rochford, DSC, DFC; *m* 1953, Elizabeth Mary Beverley Robinson, *d* of late Lt-Col B. B. Robinson, DSO; two *s* one *d*. *Educ:* Douai Sch., Woolhampton, Berks. Served War: Royal Navy and RNVR, 1940–47. Called to Bar, Inner Temple, 1951. *Recreation:* messing about in boats. *Address:* Studland, Stockcroft Road, Balcombe, West Sussex. *Died* 21 April 1986.

**ROCHFORT, Sir Cecil (Charles) B.;** *see* Boyd-Rochfort.

**RODDAN, Gilbert McMicking,** CMG 1957; Deputy Agricultural Adviser, Department of Technical Co-operation, 1961 (to Secretary of State for Colonies, 1956); retired 1965; *b* 13 May 1906; *m* 1934, Olive Mary Wetherill; two *d*. *Educ:* Dumfries Academy; Glasgow and Oxford Universities; Imperial College of Tropical Agriculture, Trinidad. Colonial Service, 1930–56. *Address:* Wayland, Edinburgh Road, Peebles. *Club:* Commonwealth Trust.

*Died* 15 Dec. 1990.

**RODGER, Prof. Alec, (Thomas Alexander),** MA Cantab, FBPsS; Professor of Occupational Psychology, University of London, at Birkbeck College, 1960–75 (Reader in Psychology, 1948–60); later Emeritus Professor; Council Member, Independent Schools Careers Organisation, since 1971; Chairman, The T. Ritchie Rodger Research Fund, since 1976; *b* 22 Nov. 1907; *e s* of late T. Ritchie Rodger, OBE; unmarried. *Educ:* Scarborough College; Gonville and Caius College, Cambridge (Yatman Exhibitioner). Nat. Inst. Industrial Psychology, 1929–47 (Head of Vocational Guidance Dept. 1936–47; concurrently Psychologist, WO, 1940–41, and Senior Psychologist to the Admlty, 1941–47). Established as Sen. Principal Psychologist to Admlty, 1947–48, and first Member of Civil Service Psychologist Class. Mem. Psychology Cttee, MRC, 1946–56; Mem. Human Factors Panel, Govt Cttee on Industrial Productivity, 1948–51; Editor, Occupational Psychology, 1948–68; Adviser, Min. of Labour, 1948–68; Consultant: ODM (W and E Africa and Fiji), 1960–64; OECD, 1968–71; Chm., Audience Res. Adv. Panel of Psychologists, BBC, 1949–63; Mem., Min. of Health's Adv. Cttee for Management Efficiency in the NHS, 1964–66. Vis. Lectr, Dept of Engrg Prodn, Univ. of Birmingham, 1951–68. First Chm., Psychology Bd, CNAA, 1968–73; sometime External Examr for Univ. of Cambridge and twenty other univs. Chm., MoD Working Party on Personnel Selection Methods, 1950–51. Gen. Sec., British Psychological Soc., 1948–54, Pres. 1957–58; Pres. Section J. British Association, 1955; Founder-Dir, MSL Group, 1956–70; Founder-Dir, Manpower Analysis and Planning Ltd, 1971–78. Nuffield Res. Fellow, 1974–75. Hon. Fellow, Inst. of Careers Officers, 1960. Fellow, Amer. Psychological Association, 1968. *Publications:* A Borstal Experiment in Vocational Guidance, 1937; Occupational Versatility and Planned Procrastination, 1961; Seventh C. S. Myers Memorial Lecture, 1970; (with P. Cavanagh) OECD Report on Occupational Guidance, 1970; (with T. Morgan and D. Guest) The Industrial Training Officer, 1971; contrib. to Chambers's Encyclopædia; The Study of Society; Current Trends in British Psychology; Society, Problems and Methods of Study; Educational and Occupational Selection in West Africa; Readings in Psychology; Recruitment Handbook; and to various periodicals. *Recreations:* music, gardening, motoring abroad. *Address:* 3 Prior Bolton Street, N1. *Clubs:* Arts Theatre, Royal Society of Medicine.

*Died* 15 Feb. 1982.

**RODGER, Sir William (Glendinning),** Kt 1978; OBE 1957; FCA (NZ), FCIS; JP; chartered accountant; *b* Glasgow, 5 June 1912; *s* of William Rodger, Eaglesham; *m* 1937, Dulcie Elizabeth, *d* of Frank Bray, Auckland, NZ; one *s* one *d*. *Educ:* Univ. of Auckland; Victoria Univ. of Wellington. BCom. FCA (NZ) 1935; FCIS 1936; FCAI 1937; FIANZ 1946; FNZIM 1947. Commercial appts, 1927–41; with public accountancy firm, 1945–54. Victoria Univ. of Wellington: Mem. Professorial Bd, 1951–61; Dean, Faculty of Commerce, 1953–54, 1957, and 1959–60; Sen. Lectr in Accountancy, Univ. of Auckland, 1967–77. Vis. Prof. of Business Admin (Fulbright Award), Univ. of Calif at LA, 1957–58; Vis. Prof. of Commerce, Sch. of Business, Queen's Univ., Ont, 1962–63; Vis. Lectr in Farm Management Accounting, Wye Coll., Univ. of London, 1965–66; Agricl Economist, Min. of Agriculture, 1965–66; Vis. Fellow: Centre for Continuing Educn, Univ. of Auckland, 1978–; Mitchell Coll. of Advanced Educn, Bathurst, NSW, 1978–79. Founder Mem., NZ Admin. Staff Coll., 1950–65 (Course Dir, 1953–59). Dir, Civic Trust, Auckland, 1978. President: NZ Inst. of Cost Accountants, 1955 (Maxwell Award, 1956); NZ Inst. of Management, 1957. Member: NZ Govt Co. Law Cttee, 1951–55; Jamaican Govt Sugar Industry Commn, 1966–67; Nat. Res. Cttee, NZ Soc. of Accts, 1951–66; Nat. Exec., NZ Statistical Assoc., 1952–54; NZ Div., Chartered Inst. of Secs, 1945–66 (Nat. Pres., 1958; Wellington Pres., 1960); Wellington Br., Econ. Soc. of Aust. and NZ, 1946–52. Hon. Member: NZ Inst. of Valuers, 1952; NZ Libraries Assoc., 1978; NZ Council Mem., Royal Commonwealth Soc., 1979–; founded Auckland Exec. Management Club 1968 (Pres., 1969–72). Pres., NZ Br. of Heraldry Soc., 1980–. Hon. Treas., Boy Scout Assoc., 1937–58. JP Auckland, 1946. Editor: The New Zealand Accountants Journal, 1945–47; Contemporary Commercial Practice, 1946; Management Review, 1948–53; Farm Accounting Research Reports, 1961 and 1966. *Publications:* Balance Sheet Significance, Preparation and Interpretation, 1949; (jtly) Auditing, 1950 (3rd edn 1962); Valuation of Unquoted Shares in New Zealand, 1953; Interpretation of Financial Data and Company Reports, 1955 (2nd edn 1960); Bibliography of Accountancy, 1955; (rev. edn) Yorston's Advanced Accounting, 3 vols, 1956; Private Companies in NZ, 1956; NZ Company Secretary, 1956, 2nd edn 1960; An Introduction to Accounting Theory, 1957; Company Accounts in NZ, 1962; A Study Guide to Auditing, 1963; Estate Planning, 1964; An Introduction to Cost and Management Accounting, 1965; The Management Audit, 1966; Business Administration in Pharmacy, 1969; Management in the Modern Medical Practice, 1975; Introduction to Genealogy and Heraldry in New Zealand, 1980; The Arms of the New Zealand Society of Accountants, 1980; The Heraldry of the Anglican Church in New Zealand, 1982; Case Studies on Heraldry in New Zealand, 1983; reports; contrib. prof. jls. *Address:* 61 Speight Road, St Heliers Bay, Auckland, New Zealand. *T:* 555 947. *Died* 1990.

**RODGERS, Gerald Fleming;** HM Diplomatic Service, retired; *b* 22 Sept. 1917; *s* of Thomas Fleming Rodgers and Mary Elizabeth (*née* Gillespie); *m* 1965, Helen Lucy, *y d* of late Dr Wall, Coleshill; two *s*. *Educ:* Rugby; Queens' Coll., Cambridge. Served War of 1939–45, Army, 1939–46. Foreign (subseq. Diplomatic) Service, 1947; served at: Jedda, 1947–49; British Middle East Office, Cairo and Fayid, 1949–53; FO, 1953–59; Peking, 1959–61; UK Delegation to OECD, 1961–64; Djakarta, 1964–65; Counsellor, Paris, 1965–67. *Address:* Laurelcroft, North Street, Kilsby, Rugby, Warwickshire CV23 8XU. *T:* Crick 822314. *Died* 1 March 1990.

**ROE, Frederic Gordon,** FSA, FRHistS; *b* 24 Sept. 1894; *s* of late Fred Roe, RI, RBC, and Letitia Mabel, *e d* of Sydney W. Lee; *m* 1921, Eleanor Beatrice, *o d* of late Cecil Reginald Grundy; one *d*. *Educ:* Westminster School; in Art under his father, and at the Chelsea School of Art. Joined The Connoisseur, 1913; Art Critic, 1919; Assistant Editor, 1921–32; Acting-Editor, March-June 1926; Editor, 1933; Director, Connoisseur Ltd, 1931–34; Gunner, 1212 Battery, RFA, 1917–19; Art Critic, Daily Mail, 1920 (resigned 1921); Member, Junior Art Workers' Guild, 1920–23; restored to Westminster Abbey Muniments Wren's Original designs for the restoration of the Abbey, 1927; Hon. Member Society of Pewter Collectors, 1933–; Art Critic, The Artist, 1935–36; ARP Warden (and higher grades), 1940–45; Odhams Press Book Dept, 1943–44. FRSA 1968. *Publications:* Henry Bright of the Norwich School, 1920; Charles Bentley, 1921; Dictator of the Royal Academy (Joseph Farington, RA), 1921; David Cox, 1924–original MS of this book is in the National Museum of Wales, Cardiff; Sporting Prints of the 18th and early 19th centuries, 1927; The Life and Times of King Edward the Eighth, 1937; Coronation Cavalcade, 1937; Catalogue of Paintings in the Nettlefold Collection (with C. R. Grundy), 1937–38; Etty and the Nude (with W. Gaunt), 1943; The Nude from Cranach to Etty and beyond, 1944; The Bronze Cross, 1945; Cox the Master, 1946; English Period Furniture, 1946; Rowlandson, 1947; Sea Painters of Britain, 1947–48; Old English Furniture, 1948; Clarence below the Basement (for children), 1948; English Cottage Furniture, 1949, 2nd edn, 1950, rev. edn., 1961; Britain's Birthright, 1950; Victorian Furniture, 1952; Windsor Chairs, 1953; The Victorian Child, 1959; The Georgian Child, 1961; The British Museum's Pictures (with J. R. F. Thompson), 1961; Home Furnishing with Antiques, 1965; Victorian Corners, 1968; Women in Profile: a study in Silhouette, 1970; The Hillingford Saga, 1975; Fred Roe, RI, his life and art (with a catalogue), 1978; much work in over 70 vols of The Connoisseur; also British Racehorse, Concise Encyclopædia of Antiques, etc. *Recreations:* walking, viewing, genealogical research. *Address:* 19 Vallance Road, Alexandra Park, N22 4UD. *T:* 01–888 4029.

*Died* 6 Jan. 1985.

**ROGAN, Rev. William Henry;** an Extra Chaplain to the Queen, since 1978 (Chaplain to the Queen, 1966–78); *b* 1908; *s* of late Rev. John Rogan and Christian Ann McGhie; *m* 1940, Norah Violet Henderson, Helensburgh; one *s* two *d*. *Educ:* Royal High Sch. of Edinburgh; Univ. of Edinburgh. MA 1928; BD 1931. Asst, St Cuthbert's Parish Church, Edinburgh, 1930–32; Minister: Whithorn Parish, 1932; St Bride's Parish, Helensburgh, 1936–50; Paisley Abbey, 1950–69; Humbie, East Lothian, 1969–74. Supt, Church of Scotland Huts and Canteens in Orkney and Shetland, 1941–42; Army Chaplain, 1943–46. Select Preacher: Glasgow Univ., 1960–65; Aberdeen Univ., 1959–66; St Andrews Univ., 1959; Convener, Church of Scotland Youth Cttee, 1965–70. Founder and formerly Chm., Soc. of Friends of Paisley Abbey. Pres., Scottish Church Soc., 1977–78. Hon. DD Edinburgh, 1963. *Recreation:* angling. *Address:* Westwood, Edinburgh Road, Lauder, Berwickshire TD2 6PA. *T:* Lauder 415.

*Died* 11 June 1987.

**ROGERS, Ven. Evan James Gwyn;** Archdeacon of Doncaster, 1967–79; Archdeacon Emeritus since 1979; *b* 14 Jan. 1914; *s* of John Morgan Rogers and Margaret Rogers; *m* 1943, Eleanor Mabel, *d* of Capt. J. H. Evans; one *s* one *d*. *Educ:* St David's, Lampeter; Wycliffe Hall, Oxford. Vicar: Hamer, 1943; St Catharine's, Wigan, 1947; Diocesan Missioner, Dio. Liverpool, 1953; Hon. Chaplain to Bp of Liverpool, 1953; Hon. Canon, Liverpool Cathedral, 1957; Vicar of Coniston Cold, 1960; Dir of Educn, Dio. Bradford, 1960; Exam. Chaplain to Bp of Sheffield, 1963; Vice-Chm. Standing Conf., WR Educn Cttee, 1963; Hon. Canon of Bradford, 1964.

*Publications:* Do This in Remembrance, 1950; Dr Barnardo, 1951; (with Canon F. L. M. Bennett) A Communion Book, 1951; contrib. to West Riding New Agreed Syllabus, 1966. *Address:* St David's, 1a Spring Lane, Sprotborough, Doncaster. *T:* Doncaster 854005.
*Died 30 March* 1982.

**ROGERS, George Henry Roland,** CBE 1965; *b* 1906; *m*; one *s* one *d*. *Educ:* Willesden Elementary School; Middlesex CC Schools. A railway clerk. Member Wembley Borough Council, 1937–41. Served War of 1939–45, Royal Corps of Signals, 1942. MP (Lab) North Kensington, 1945–70; Chairman, London Group of Labour Members, 1949–54; Opposition London Whip, 1954–64; a Lord Commissioner of the Treasury, October 1964–January 1966. To Min. of Supply, 1947–49 and to Minister of State for Foreign Affairs, 1950; Delegate to UN Assembly 1950; Delegate to Council of Europe and Western European Union, 1961–63. Hon. Sec. Parliamentary Painting Group, 1950–70. *Address:* 111 Kingswell Road, Ensbury Park, Bournemouth, Dorset BH10 5DG.
*Died 19 Feb.* 1983.

**ROGERS, Prof. Howard John,** FRCP; Professor of Clinical Pharmacology, United Medical and Dental Schools, and Physician, Guy's Hospital, since 1984; *b* 18 June 1943; *er s* of George Howard Rogers and Vivienne Rogers; *m* 1968, Moira O'Boyle; three *d*. *Educ:* Chislehurst and Sidcup Grammar School; Downing College, Cambridge (Open Major Scholar 1962; MA, MB, BChir); Guy's Hosp. Med. Sch. (Open Scholar 1965, Governors' Research Scholar 1969; PhD). Registrar, Guy's Hosp., 1973; MRC Research Fellow, Johns Hopkins Med. Sch., USA, 1974; Lectr, Sen. Lectr, Reader in Clinical Pharmacology, Guy's Hosp. Med. Sch., 1975–84. *Publications:* jointly: An Introduction to Mechanisms in Pharmacology and Therapeutics, 1976; Aids to Pharmacology, 1980, 2nd edn 1986; Aids to Clinical Pharmacology, 1984; Psychiatry: common drug treatments, 1984; A Textbook of Clinical Pharmacology, 1981, 2nd edn 1986; papers on clinical pharmacology and oncology. *Recreations:* music, reading, Ireland. *Address:* 5 Grovebury Close, Erith, Kent DA8 3DJ. *T:* Dartford 341976.
*Died 30 March* 1987.

**ROGERS, Prof. Neville William,** DLit London; FRSL; Professor of English, Ohio University, 1964–78, now Emeritus; *b* 5 Jan. 1908; *s* of Leonard George and Carrie Elizabeth Rogers (*née* Jennings). *Educ:* Rossall Sch.; Birkbeck Coll., London; studied French, Italian, Spanish and German privately abroad. BA Gen. 1932, BA Hons cl. II Classics, 1934, London; Phi Beta Kappa, Lambda Chapter of Ohio, 1974. Intell. Officer, RAF, Middle East and Italy, 1942–46. Asst Master, various prep. schs, 1927–32; Headmaster, Wellesley Sch., Croydon, 1932–34; Asst Master: King Edward VI Sch., Stafford, 1935–39; St Marylebone Grammar Sch., 1939–52; Leverhulme Fellow at Oxford, working on Shelley MSS, 1952–55; Sen. Res. Fellow and Lectr, Univ. of Birmingham, 1956–62; Vis. Professor: Michigan, 1959; Washington, St Louis, UCLA, 1960; Brandeis, 1962–64; Grant-in-Aid, American Council of Learned Socs for Res. in England, 1974; has lectured at many US and French univs. Has broadcast in English, Italian and French. Mem., Kennedy Scott's Philharmonic Choir, 1933–39; Founder Mem., London Philharmonic Choir (Vice-Chm. 1947–48); Mem. Cttee: British-Italian Soc., 1947–; Keats Shelley Memorial Assoc., 1946–. *Publications:* Keats, Shelley and Rome, 1949 (4th edn 1970); Shelley at Work, 1956 (2nd edn 1968); (ed with Archibald Colquhoun) Italian Regional Tales of the Nineteenth Century, 1961; (ed) The Esdaile Poems, 1966; (ed and annotated) Selected Poetry of Shelley, 1968; (ed) Complete Poetical Works of Percy Bysshe Shelley (Oxford English Texts, 5 vols), Vol I, 1802–1813, 1972, Vol. II, 1814–1817, 1975; contribs to Encycl. Britannica, Times Lit. Supp., Times Educnl Supp., Times, Daily Telegraph, Twentieth Century, Review of English Studies, Mod. Lang. Review, Keats-Shelley Memorial Bulletin, Keats-Shelley Jl, Book Collector, Ulisse, Il Ponte, Ohio Review. *Recreations:* literature, languages, music, travel. *Address:* Vallombrosa, 45 Mound Street, Athens, Ohio 45701, USA. *Clubs:* National Liberal, Authors'.
*Died 22 Dec.* 1985.

**ROGERS, Maj.-Gen. Norman Annesley C.;** *see* Coxwell-Rogers.

**ROGERS, Sir Philip,** GCB 1975 (KCB 1970; CB 1965); CMG 1952; Chairman, Universities Superannuation Scheme, 1977–84; Director: Glaxo Ltd, 1978–84; Greater London Regional Board, Lloyds Bank, 1980–85; *b* 19 Aug. 1914; *s* of William Edward and Sarah Jane Rogers; *m* 1940, Heather Mavis Gordon; one *s* one *d*. *Educ:* William Hulme's Grammar School, Manchester; Emmanuel Coll., Cambridge. Apptd to administrative class of Home Civil Service, as an Asst Principal in Colonial Office, 1936; seconded to be Private Secretary to Governor of Jamaica, Jan.-Dec. 1939; Asst Secretary, Colonial Office, 1946–53; Assistant Under-Secretary of State, Colonial Office, 1953–61; Under-Secretary, Department of Technical Co-operation, 1961–64; Dep. Sec. of Cabinet, 1964–67; Third Secretary, Treasury, 1967–68; Dep. Secretary, 1968–69, Second Permanent Secretary, 1969–70, Civil Service Dept; Permanent Secretary, DHSS, 1970–75. Chm., Bd of Management,

London Sch. of Hygiene and Trop. Medicine, 1977–82; Member: SHA, Hammersmith Hosp., 1982–85; Court, London Univ., 1978–85; Council, Reading Univ., 1978–87 (Pres., 1980–86). Outward Bound Trust: Mem. Council, 1976–82; Chm., 1976–80; Vice-Pres., 1982–. *Recreation:* gardening. *Address:* 96 King's Road, Henley-on-Thames, Oxon RG9 2DQ. *T:* Henley-on-Thames (0491) 575228. *Club:* Phyllis Court (Henley-on-Thames).
*Died 24 May* 1990.

**ROGERSON, John;** Part-time Inspector, Department of the Environment, 1973–75; *b* 9 March 1917; *s* of late Walter John Lancashire Rogerson and Anne Marion Rogerson; *m* 1972, Audrey, *d* of late Adrian and Dorothy Maitland-Heriot. *Educ:* Tonbridge Sch.; St John's Coll., Oxford (BA). Served War, 2nd Lieut, later Captain, Royal Norfolk Regt, 1940–46. Principal: Min. of Town and Country Planning, 1947–49; HM Treasury, 1949–51; Min. of Housing and Local Govt (later Dept of the Environment), 1951–73; Asst Sec., 1955; Under-Sec., 1963; retd 1973. *Recreation:* improving his personal Good Pub Guide. *Address:* 95 Ridgmount Gardens, WC1E 7AZ. *T:* 01–636 0433.
*Died 16 March* 1990.

**ROME, Maj.-Gen. Francis David,** CB 1955; CMG 1959; CBE 1949; DSO 1944; retired; *b* 11 Sept. 1905; *er s* of late Francis James Rome; *m* 1st, 1936, Sybil Parry (*d* 1979), 2nd *d* of late Lieut-Colonel Henry Carden, DCLI; no *c*; 2nd, 1980, Mrs Francesca Finlay. *Educ:* Cheltenham Coll.; RMC, Sandhurst. Commander: 111 Indian Infantry Brigade, Special Force, SEAC, 1944–45 (DSO); 3rd Parachute Bde, 1946–47; 1st Parachute Bde, 1947–48 (CBE). Served War of 1939–45, France, 1939–40, SEAC, 1943–45; Palestine, 1946–48; Malaya, 1950–51; General Officer Commanding, 16th Airborne Division (Territorial Army), 1953–56; General Officer Commanding, Berlin (British Sector), 1956–59. Colonel, The Royal Fusiliers, 1954–59. *Address:* Ferne Down, Ham, Marlborough, Wilts SN8 3RB. *T:* Inkpen 341. *Club:* Army and Navy.
*Died 7 Feb.* 1985.

**ROMILLY, 4th Baron,** *cr* 1865; **William Gaspard Guy Romilly,** Hon. MA Oxon 1943; *b* 8 March 1899; *o c* of 3rd Baron and Violet Edith, *o sister* of Sir Philip H. B. Grey Egerton, 12th Bt, and *niece* of Lord Londesborough; *S* father, 1905; *m* 1st, 1929, Hon. Diana Joan Sackville-West (marriage dissolved, 1944), *o d* of 4th Baron Sackville, KBE; 2nd, 1944, Dora (*d* 1960), *d* of late Reginald Morris; 3rd, 1966, Elizabeth, *widow* of Capt. Lionel Cecil, and *er d* of late Charles M. Clover. *Educ:* Eton; Sandhurst. Coldstream Guards, 1917–23; served in France in European War; Reserve of Officers, 1923. Rejoined Coldstream Guards, September 1939; served until 1945 and granted honorary rank of Major. Member of Malborough and Ramsbury Rural District Council, 1949–74 (Chairman, 1964–67). *Heir:* none. *Address:* Bridge House, Chilton Foliat, near Hungerford, Berks. *T:* Hungerford 2328.
*Died 29 June* 1983 (*ext*).

**ROOK, Dr John Allan Fynes,** CBE 1985; FRSE, FRSC, FIBiol; Second Secretary, Agricultural and Food Research Council (formerly Agricultural Research Council), London, 1981–86; Visiting Professor in Animal Nutrition, Wye College, University of London, 1981–86; *b* 1 May 1926; *s* of Edward Fynes Rook and Annie Rook; *m* 1952, Marion Horsburgh Millar; two *s* one *d*. *Educ:* Scarborough Boys' High Sch.; University College of Wales, Aberystwyth. BSc, DSc (Wales); PhD (Glasgow). National Institute for Research in Dairying, Shinfield, Berks, 1954–65; Prof. of Agricultural Chemistry, Univ. of Leeds, 1965–70; Dir, Hannah Res. Inst., Ayr, and Hannah Prof. of Animal Nutrition, Univ. of Glasgow, 1971–80. *Publications:* (ed jtly) Nutritional Physiology of Farm Animals, 1983; numerous articles in British Jl of Nutrition, Jl of Dairy Research, etc. *Recreations:* gardening, golf; shutting doors and switching off lights after other members of the family. *Address:* Corbiestow, Mill Lane, Rathmell, near Settle, North Yorks BD24 0LA. *Club:* Farmers'.
*Died 6 Jan.* 1987.

**ROOM, Thomas Gerald,** FRS 1941; Professor of Mathematics, Sydney University, 1935–68, later Emeritus; *b* 10 Nov. 1902; 2nd *s* of E. W. Room, OBE, JP; *m* 1937, Jessie, *d* of C. F. Bannerman; one *s* two *d*. *Educ:* Alleyn's School; St John's Coll., Cambridge (ScD). Asst Lectr, Liverpool University, 1925; Fellow of St John's College, Cambridge, 1927–29; Lecturer in Mathematics, Cambridge University, 1929–34; Visiting Prof. of Mathematics: Univ. of Washington, 1948; Univ. of Tennessee, 1949; Univ. of Sussex, 1966; Westfield Coll., Univ. of London, 1969–70; Open Univ., 1971–73. Fellow Sydney University Senate and Dean of Faculty of Science, 1952–56, 1960–65. Member Inst. for Advanced Study, Princeton, NJ, 1949 and 1957–58; Vis. Lectr, Univ. of Princeton, 1958. Pres., Austr. Mathematical Soc., 1960–62. *Publications:* Geometry of Determinantal Loci, 1939; The Sorting Process, 1966; A Background to Geometry, 1967; Miniquaternion Geometry, 1970. *Address:* High Walden, 100 Rosedale Road, St Ives, NSW 2075, Australia. *T:* (Sydney) 449–5743.
*Died 2 April* 1986.

**ROOME, Rear-Admiral Henry Stewart,** CBE 1949; *b* 7 May 1896; *s* of late Eng. Rear-Adm. G. W. Roome, CBE; *m* 1921, Aileen D. M. L., *d* of Comdr C. T. Scott, RIM; two *s* one *d*. *Educ:* RN Colleges;

Osborne, Dartmouth, Keyham. Midshipman, HMS Bellerophon, 1913; acting Sub-Lt 1915. Served European War in Grand Fleet Destroyers, 1916–18 (despatches); Lieut, 1917; RN Coll., Keyham, 1918; Lieut (E) 1919; Comdr (E), 1928; Capt. (E), 1940. ADC to the King, 1946–47; Rear-Adm. (E), 1947. Served War of 1939–45, HM Dockyards, Devonport and Sheerness; and at Admiralty; Manager Engineering Department, HM Dockyard, Portsmouth, 1945–50; retired, 1950. *Address:* c/o P. G. H. Roome, Pencelli, near Brecon, Powys. *Died 21 Dec. 1981.*

**ROOT, Frederick James,** CB 1952; Deputy Secretary, Ministry of Public Building and Works (previously Ministry of Works), 1959–66; *b* 2 July 1906; *s* of late Alan and Elizabeth A. Root; *m* 1941, Margaret Eleanor Barbour, *d* of late Dr G. F. Barbour Simpson, Edinburgh; two *d. Educ:* Christ's Hosp.; Merton Coll., Oxford (Open Exhibnr). Entered Civil Service, 1928; Private Secretary to successive First Commissioners of Works, 1933–37, and to successive Ministers of Works, 1940–43. *Address:* Halland, Pathfields Close, Haslemere, Surrey GU27 2BL. *T:* Haslemere 3750. *Club:* Athenæum. *Died 2 Nov. 1982.*

**ROOTHAM, Jasper St John,** MA; *b* 21 Nov. 1910; *s* of Dr Cyril Bradley and Rosamond Margaret Rootham; *m* 1944, Joan McClelland; one *s* one *d. Educ:* Tonbridge Sch. (Judd Schol.); St John's Coll., Cambridge (Maj. Schol.). 1st cl. Class. Tripos Pts I and II. Entered Civil Service, 1933; Min. of Agric., 1933–34; CO, 1934–36; Treasury, 1936–38; Pte Sec. to Prime Minister, 1938–39; Treasury, 1939–40; resigned to join Army, 1940; served Middle East, Balkans, Germany (despatches); demobilized, 1946 (Col); entered Bank of England as Actg Asst Adviser, 1946; Adviser to Governor, 1957; Chief of Overseas Dept, 1962; Asst to Governor, 1964; retd, 1967. Man. Dir, Lazard Bros & Co. Ltd, 1967–75; Dir, Agricultural Mortgage Corp., 1967–77 (Dep. Chm., 1973–77); Director: British Sugar Corp., 1968–80; Stanley Miller Holdings, Newcastle, 1977–84. *Publications:* Miss Fire, 1946; Demi-Paradise, 1960; Verses 1928–72, 1972; The Celestial City and Other Poems, 1975; Reflections from a Crag, 1978; Selected Poems, 1980; Stand Fixed in Steadfast Gaze, 1981; Affirmation, 1982; Lament for a dead Sculptor and other poems, 1985. *Recreations:* music, country life. *Address:* 30 West Street, Wimborne Minster, Dorset BH21 1JS. *T:* Wimborne 888121. *Club:* United Oxford & Cambridge University. *Died 30 May 1990.*

**ROPER, Captain Edward Gregson,** CBE 1959; DSO 1942; DSC; Capt. RN retd; *b* 12 April 1910; *s* of late John Gregson Roper, OBE; *m* 1933, Sylvia, *d* of E. F. L. Hopkins; one *d. Educ:* Oundle. Joined Royal Navy, 1928; served War of 1939–45 (DSC, DSO): Comd HMS Velox, 1940–42; Impulsive, 1942–43; Comdr, 1943; Comd 18th Destroyer Flotilla, 1944–45. Captain, 1950; Comd HMS Ocean, 1955–56; Royal Naval College, Greenwich, 1956–59; retired, 1959. *Address:* Polmayne, Rock, Cornwall. *Died 13 Feb. 1983.*

**ROPER, Maj.-Gen. Henry Ernest,** CB 1976; BSc(Eng), CEng, FIERE; with the Plessey Co. Ltd, since 1979; *b* 6 April 1923; *s* of late Ernest Roper and Lydia (née Hayward); *m* 1950, Beryl Claire (née Jennings); one *s* one *d. Educ:* Queen Mary's Grammar Sch., Walsall; Worcester Coll., Oxford; RMCS, Shrivenham. Commnd Royal Signals, 1942; served War: UK, NW Europe, SEAC, 1941–45; FE, UK, BAOR, 1946–58; ptsc 1952; HQ 51 Independ. Inf. Bde, Cyprus, 1958–59; DS, RMCS, 1959–62; 7th Signal Regt, BAOR, 1962–64; Comd, 30th Signal Regt, 1964–66; Asst Mil. Sec., MoD, 1966–67; Col, GS Army Signals Equipment, 1967–68; Dir, Proj. Mallard, Min. of Tech., 1968–71; RCDS, 1971–72; CSO, BAOR, 1972–75; Asst Chief of Gen. Staff (Operational Requirements), MoD, 1975–78. Col Comdt, Royal Signals, 1975–80; Representative Col Comdt, 1979. With STC Ltd, 1978. FBIM; CDipAF. *Recreations:* various. *Address:* c/o Midland Bank Ltd, The Bridge, Walsall, Staffs WS1 1LN. *Club:* Army and Navy. *Died 13 July 1982.*

**ROSCOE, (Edward) John (Townsend);** Director, Willis Faber & Dumas Ltd, 1957–73 (Chairman, 1967–71); *b* 21 March 1913; *o s* of late Edward Gawne Roscoe and Mary Frances Roscoe, Clifton Manor, Warwicks; *m* 1st, 1940, Jean Mary Todd; one *s* two *d;* 2nd, 1974, Jennifer Helen, *yr d* of J. R. Fawcus; three *s. Educ:* West Downs, Winchester; Marlborough Coll.; Trinity Coll., Oxford. BA, PPE. Joined Sedgwick Collins & Co., Lloyds Brokers, 1934; War Service, 1939–46; joined Willis Faber & Dumas Ltd, 1949; Underwriting Member of Lloyds, 1945. *Recreations:* foxhunting, tennis, swimming. *Address:* West Penthouse, Parkside, Knightsbridge, SW1. *T:* 01-235 8899. *Clubs:* Boodle's, City of London. *Died 24 Sept. 1984.*

**ROSCOE, Air Cdre Peter Henry,** CB 1967; FCA; *b* 28 May 1912. Dept of Air Member for Personnel, 1963–67; Dir of Personnel (Ground) Min. of Defence (RAF), 1966; retired 1967. *Address:* Fairhaven, Tan-y-Bryn Road, Holyhead, Gwynedd LL65 1AR. *Died 11 Dec. 1987.*

**ROSE, Captain Arthur Martin Thomas,** MC 1944; solicitor; a Recorder of the Crown Court, since 1979; *b* 22 Nov. 1918; *s* of Stanley Arthur

Rose and Hilda Mary Martin Rose (née Hayward); *m* 1952, Patricia Cameron (*d* 1978); two *s. Educ:* Perse Sch.; Uppingham; Trinity Hall, Cambridge (MA, LLM). Served War: commnd Royal Artillery, 1941–46 (MC, twice wounded). Partner in firm of Few & Kester, solicitors, 1949–82, Senior Partner, 1981–82. *Recreations:* sport, freemasonry. *Address:* 10 Marlborough Court, Grange Road, Cambridge CB3 9BQ. *T:* Cambridge 312726. *Clubs:* Camden Cricket; Gog Magog Golf. *Died 5 Sept. 1987.*

**ROSE, Clifford Alan,** CBE 1983; FCIT, MIPM; Member for Operations and Deputy Chief Executive British Railways Board, since 1983 (Railways); *b* 31 Aug. 1929; *s* of Francis William and Edith May Rose; *m* 1953, Maureen (née Wallen); one *d. Educ:* Royal Grammar Sch., High Wycombe. Joined GWR as booking clerk, 1944; served in London area, West Country and S Wales; Divl Movements Manager, Cardiff, 1966; Asst Divl Manager, 1968. Movements Manager, Southern Region, 1968; Divl Manager, first of S Western, then S Eastern Div., 1970; Chief Personnel Officer of Southern Region, 1972; Exec. Dir, Personnel, 1975–77, Mem. for Personnel, BRB, 1977–83. Member: Advisory, Conciliation and Arbitration Service Council, 1978–; Business Educn Council, 1979–. CBIM. OStJ 1975. *Recreations:* cricket, Rugby (watching, now), gardening, walking. *Address:* 45 Durleston Park Drive, Great Bookham, Surrey KT23 4AJ. *T:* Bookham 52705. *Club:* MCC. *Died 20 July 1983.*

**ROSE, (Edward) Michael,** CMG 1955; HM Diplomatic Service, retired; *b* 18 Oct. 1913; *s* of Frank Atcherley Rose and Marian Elizabeth Darling Harris; unmarried. *Educ:* Rugby; St John's College, Cambridge. Entered Diplomatic Service, 1937; served Oslo 1940, Algiers, 1944, Copenhagen 1945–48; Deputy to GOC British Sector of Berlin, 1952–55; Counsellor, Foreign Office, 1955–60; Minister, Bonn, 1960–63; Ambassador to the Congo (Leopoldville), 1963–65; Asst Under-Sec., Foreign Office, 1965–67; Dep. Sec., Cabinet Office, 1967–68. Dir, E Africa and Mauritius Assoc., 1969–80. Chm. Internat. Div., BCC, 1974–84. Fellow, Center for Internat. Affairs, Harvard Univ., 1958–59. *Recreations:* golf, gardening. *Address:* 2 Godfrey Street, SW3; Ovington Grange, Clare, Suffolk. *Club:* National Liberal. *Died 25 March 1986.*

**ROSE, Francis Leslie,** CBE 1978 (OBE 1949); PhD, DSc; FRS 1957; FRSC; Consultant, Imperial Chemical Industries Ltd, since 1974; *b* 27 June 1909; *s* of late Frederick William and Elizabeth Ann Rose, Lincoln; *m* 1935, Ailsa Buckley; one *s. Educ:* City Sch., Lincoln; Univ. Coll. of Nottingham. BSc (Hons Chemistry) London, 1930; PhD London 1934; DSc Nottingham 1950. Research Chemist, ICI Ltd, 1932; Res. Manager, Pharmaceutical Div., ICI, 1954–71, Res. Fellow, 1971–74. Hon. Reader in Organic Chem., UMIST, 1959–72, Hon Fellow, 1972. Mem., later Consultant, Home Office Forensic Science Cttee, 1965–78. Former Mem., Court of Governors, Manchester University and Court of Governors, Univ. of Manchester Inst. of Science and Technology. Hon. Fellow, Manchester Polytechnic. Hon. DSc Loughborough, 1982. Gold Medal, Soc. of Apothecaries, 1948; Tilden Lecture and Medal, Chem. Soc., 1951; Medal, Soc. of Chem. Industry, 1975; Leverhulme Medal, Royal Soc., 1975. *Publications:* numerous scientific papers on chemotherapeutic themes, mainly in Jl of Chem. Soc., Brit. Jl of Pharmacol., Biochem. Jl, etc. *Recreations:* music, in particular the organ; sailing. *Address:* 27 Green Hall Mews, Parkway, Wilmslow, Cheshire SK9 1LP. *T:* Wilmslow 530499; ICI Ltd, Alderley Park, Macclesfield, Cheshire. *Club:* Athenæum.

*Died 3 March 1988.*

**ROSE, Dame Hilda Nora,** DBE 1951; Emeritus Professor of Obstetrics and Gynæcology at Queen Elizabeth Hospital and University of Birmingham; Senior Surgeon, Women's Hospital and Maternity Hospital, Birmingham; *b* 11 Aug. 1891; *d* of John Shufflebotham and Emma Jenkins; *m* 1930, Bertram A. Lloyd (*d* 1948); no *c; m* 1949, Baron Rose, FRCS (*d* 1978). *Educ:* King Edward's High School for Girls, Birmingham; University of Birmingham (BSc 1914, MB, ChB 1916); London Hospital. MRCS, LRCP 1918; FRCS 1920; FRCOG 1936; FRSM; President RCOG, 1949–52; Member Med. Women's Federation, retired, 1954. *Recreations:* mountaineering, gardening. *Address:* Broome House, Clent, Worcestershire. *Club:* VAD Ladies. *Died 18 July 1982.*

**ROSE, Michael;** see Rose, E. M.

**ROSE, Captain Sir Philip (Humphrey Vivian),** 3rd Bt, *cr* 1874; RA, enlisted 1939; *b* 16 March 1903; *g s* of Sir Philip Rose, Rayners, Penn, 2nd Bt (whom he succeeded in 1919), and *s* of late Capt. Philip Vivian Rose, 3rd Batt. Oxfords. Light Infantry, and Maude Winifred, 2nd *d* of William Gillilan, 6 Palace Gate, W8; *m* 1927, Joan, *yr d* of late Dr Martin Richardson; (one *s* killed in aircraft accident at Downside on 15 May 1943) two *d. Heir: cousin,* David Lancaster Rose [*b* 17 Feb. 1934; *m* 1965, Dorothy Whitehead; one *s.*] *Address:* Rayners Cottage, 67 High Street, Prestwood, Great Missenden, Bucks. *T:* Great Missenden 3401.

*Died 14 March 1982.*

**ROSE-MILLER, Brig. George Patrick;** *see* Miller.

**ROSENHEAD, Prof. Louis,** CBE 1954; FRS 1946; DSc (Leeds); PhD (Cantab.); Professor of Applied Mathematics, The University, Liverpool, 1933–73, later Professor Emeritus; formerly Fellow of St John's College, Cambridge; *b* 1 Jan. 1906; *s* of Abraham Rosenhead and Helen Nelson; *m* 1932, Esther Brostoff; two *s. Educ:* Leeds Central High School; The University of Leeds; St John's College, Cambridge (Strathcona Research Student); The University of Göttingen. BSc (Leeds 1st Class Hons); PhD (Leeds); Senior Research Student of the Dept of Scientific and Industrial Research, 1929; PhD (Cantab) 1930; DSc (Leeds) 1935; Senior Research Student of Royal Exhibition of 1851; Lecturer, Applied Mathematics at the University College of Swansea, 1931–33. Temporarily attached Min. of Supply, 1940–45. Mem. of various Govt Scientific Cttees, 1939–75. Pro-Vice-Chancellor, 1961–65, Public Orator, 1968–72, University of Liverpool. *Publications:* Index of Mathematical Tables, 2nd edn 1962 (part-author); Compressible Airflow: Tables, 1952 (part-author); Compressible Airflow: Graphs, 1954 (part-author); Laminar Boundary Layers, 1963 (editor); Scientific Publications in the Proceedings of the Royal Society, Proceedings of the Cambridge Philosophical Society, Monthly Notices of the Royal Astronomical Society, etc. *Address:* 19 Keswick Road, Liverpool L18 9UH. *T:* 051-724 3370.
*Died 10 Nov. 1984.*

**ROSENTHAL, Harold David,** OBE 1983; Editor of Opera, 1953–86, then Editor Emeritus; Lecturer and Broadcaster since 1950; *b* 30 Sept. 1917; *s* of Israel Victor Rosenthal and Leah Samuels; *m* 1944, Lillah Phyllis Weiner; one *s* one *d. Educ:* City of London School; University College, London (BA); Inst. of Education, London. Asst Editor, Opera, 1950–53; Archivist, Royal Opera House, Covent Garden, 1950–56. Member: Arts Council Patrons of Music Fund Cttee, 1960–70; Council, Friends of Covent Garden, 1962–; Chairman, Music Section, Critics' Circle of Gt Britain, 1965–67. Cavaliere Ufficiale, Order of Merit of the Republic (Italy), 1977. *Publications:* Sopranos of Today, 1956; Two Centuries of Opera at Covent Garden, 1958; A Concise Oxford Dictionary of Opera (with John Warrack), 1964, paperback edn, 1972, rev. and enl. edn, 1979; Great Singers of Today, 1966; Mapleson Memoires (ed and annotated), 1966; The Opera Bedside Book, 1965; Opera at Covent Garden, 1967; Covent Garden, 1976; (ed) Loewenberg's Annals of Opera 1597–1940, 3rd edn, 1979; My Mad World of Opera, 1982; Annals of Opera 1940–80, 1986. *Recreations:* travel, food; collecting playbills, prints, programmes, etc. *Address:* 6 Woodland Rise, N10 3UH. *T:* 01-883 4415. *Died 19 March 1987.*

**ROSEVEARE, Sir Martin (Pearson),** Kt 1946; Hon. Fellow of St John's College, Cambridge, since 1952; *b* 24 April 1898; *s* of late Canon R. P. Roseveare, late Vicar of Lewisham; *m* 1921, Edith Mary Pearse (marr. diss., 1958; she *d* 1975); one *s* three *d* (and one *d* decd); *m* 1958, Olivia Margaret Montgomery. *Educ:* Marlborough College; St John's College, Cambridge (scholar). Maths Tripos, Part I, Class 1, 1919; Part II wrangler (b), 1921; Schoolmaster, Repton School, 1921–23; Haileybury College, 1923–26; Board of Education, HM Inspector of Schools, 1927; Staff Inspector of Mathematics, 1939. Lent to Ministry of Information, 1939, Ministry of Food, 1939–44 and 1946 (acting Assistant Sec., 1940, acting Principal Assistant Sec. 1942); Senior Chief Inspector, Ministry of Education, 1944–57, retired; Headmaster Mzuzu School, Nyasaland, 1957–63; Principal, Soche Hill College, Malawi, 1964–67; Schoolmaster, Marymount School, Mzuzu, Malawi, 1967–70. Served European War, RFA, Lt 1916–19, France, Belgium, Italy (wounded, despatches). *Recreations:* hockey, camping. *Address:* Box 29, Mzuzu, Malaŵi. *Died 30 March 1985.*

**ROSKILL, Captain Stephen Wentworth,** CBE 1971; DSC 1944; MA Cantab; LittD Cantab 1971; FBA 1971; FRHistS; late RN; Fellow of Churchill College, Cambridge, 1961, Life Fellow, 1970; *b* 1 Aug. 1903; *s* of John Henry Roskill, KC, and Sybil Mary Dilke, *d* of Ashton Wentworth Dilke, MP; *m* 1930, Elizabeth, *d* of Henry Van den Bergh; four *s* three *d. Educ:* RN Colleges, Osborne and Dartmouth. RN, 1917–48; Gunnery Specialist, 1928; Commander, 1938; Captain, 1944. Served at sea as Commander HMS Warspite, 1939; Naval Staff, 1939–41; Commander and Captain, HMNZS Leander, 1941–44; Senior Observer, Bikini Atomic Bomb Trials, 1946; Dep. Director of Naval Intelligence, 1946–48; invalided, 1948; Cabinet Office, Official Naval Historian, 1949–60. Officer Legion of Merit (USA). Lees Knowles Lecturer, Cambridge, 1961; Distinguished Visitor Lecturer, US Naval Academy, Annapolis, 1965; Richmond Lecturer, Cambridge, 1967; Leverhulme Res. Fellow, National Maritime Museum, 1974. Navy Records Society: Councillor, 1956–66, and 1968–70; Vice-Pres., 1966–68, 1970, Hon. Life Vice-Pres., 1976. Pres. Cambridge Br., RN Assoc., 1976. Hon. LittD Leeds, 1975; Hon. DLitt Oxon, 1980. Chesney Gold Medal, RUSI, 1975. *Publications:* The War at Sea (official history), Vol. I, 1954, Vol. II, 1957; HMS Warspite, 1957; The Secret Capture, 1959; The War at Sea, Vol. III, Part I, 1960; The Navy at War, 1960; The War at Sea, Vol. III, Part II, 1961; The Strategy of Sea Power, 1962; A Merchant Fleet in War, 1962; The Art of Leadership, 1964; Naval Policy between the Wars, Vol. I, 1968, Vol. II, 1976; Documents relating to the Naval Air Service 1908–1918, 1969; Hankey, Man of Secrets, Vol. 1, 1877–1918, 1970, Vol. 2, 1919–1931, 1972; Vol. 3, 1931–63, 1974; Churchill and the Admirals, 1977; Admiral of the Fleet Earl Beatty, 1980; numerous contribs to learned jls. *Recreations:* all country pursuits, painting. *Address:* Frostlake Cottage, Malting Lane, Cambridge. *T:* 354705. *Club:* Travellers'.
*Died 4 Nov. 1982.*

**ROSS OF MARNOCK, Baron** *cr* 1979 (Life Peer), of Kilmarnock in the District of Kilmarnock and Loudoun; **William Ross;** PC 1964; MBE (mil.) 1945; MA; Lord High Commissioner, General Assembly of Church of Scotland, 1978–80; *b* 7 April 1911; *s* of W. Ross, Ayr; *m* 1948, Elizabeth Jane Elma Aitkenhead, Ayr; two *d. Educ:* Ayr Academy; Glasgow University. MA 1932; Schoolmaster. Served War of 1939–45, HLI, R Signals, Major; India, SACSEA. Contested Ayr Burgh, General Election, 1945; MP (Lab) Kilmarnock, Ayr and Bute, 1946–79; Secretary of State for Scotland, 1964–70, 1974–76; Opposition spokesman on Scottish Affairs, 1970–74; Mem., Labour Parly Cttee, 1970–79. Hon. Pres., Scottish Football Assoc., 1978. FEIS 1971. Hon. LLD: St Andrews, 1967; Strathclyde, 1969; Glasgow, 1978. *Recreation:* golf. *Address:* 10 Chapelpark Road, Ayr. *T:* Ayr 265673. *Died 10 June 1988.*

**ROSS, Prof. Allan Dawson,** BSc, PhD (Edinburgh), CEng, FICE, FRSE; Consulting Engineer, advising, in particular, on concrete structures for nuclear power stations; Professor of Civil Engineering at University of London, King's College, 1946–71, Professor Emeritus since 1971; *b* 22 Feb. 1909; 4th *s* of Robert and Anne Ross, Dublin; *m* 1935, Isabel Goodburn; one *d. Educ:* Peebles High School; University of Edinburgh. Bursar of The Royal Commission for the Exhibition of 1851. Held civil engineering appointments in road and railway construction, 1929–32; Assistant to late Prof. Sir T. Hudson Beare, Univ. of Edinburgh, 1932–34; Education Officer, Air Ministry, 1934–35; Lecturer in Civil and Mechanical Engineering, University of London, King's College, 1935–46. *Publications:* numerous papers published in journals of learned and technical institutions. *Address:* 7 Old Farm Avenue, Colinton, Edinburgh EH13 0QQ. *Died 6 Sept. 1982.*

**ROSS, Hon. Sir (Dudley) Bruce,** Kt 1962; retired; *b* 21 May 1892; *s* of William Alexander Ross and Annie Isabella Ross, Adelaide, S Australia; *m* 1st, 1920, Margaret Eleanor Waterhouse (decd); one *s* three *d*; 2nd, 1954, Agnes Jessie Linklater (decd). *Educ:* Queen's School, St Peter's College and University of Adelaide, S Australia. LLB (Adelaide) 1914. KC 1945. Judge of Supreme Court of S Australia, 1952–62. Pres. Law Society of S Australia, 1948–49; Vice-Pres., Law Council of Australia, 1948–49; Chancellor, Diocese of Adelaide and Willochra, 1944–69; Grand Master, Grand Lodge of SA, 1959–64; Member Council of Governors, St Peter's Coll., Adelaide, 1948–60; Pres. Church of England Boys' Home, 1943–73; Pres., Kindergarten Union of SA, 1962–73. Served European War, 1914–18, with 5th Division, AIF. *Recreation:* bowls. *Address:* 19 Sherbourne Road, Medindie Gardens, SA 5081, Australia. *T:* 442178. *Club:* Adelaide. *Died 19 Nov. 1984.*

**ROSS, Col. Walter John Macdonald,** CB 1958; OBE 1955; MC 1946; TD 1946 and 2 Bars; JP; Landed Proprietor and Farmer; Lord-Lieutenant, Dumfries and Galloway Region, District of Stewartry, since 1977; *b* 1914; *s* of late Major Robert Ross of Ledgowan, Ross-shire, and Marion, *d* of late Walter Macfarlane, DL, JP; *m* 1940, Josephine May, 2nd *d* of late Malcolm Cross, and of late Evelyn Cross of Earlston House, Borgue; two *s* one *d. Educ:* Loretto. Commissioned RA (TA), 1935. Served War of 1939–45, UK and NW Europe. Comd 5 KOSB (TA), 1951–55; Deputy Comd 157 (L) Inf. Bde, 1955–59. Underwriting Member of Lloyd's. JP 1958, Stewartry of Kirkcudbright. Royal Humane Society Parchment for Saving Life, 1963. Member of Royal Company of Archers, Queen's Body Guard for Scotland. Formerly County Councillor (Vice-Convener), Stewartry of Kirkcudbright. Hon. FEIS, 1974. *Recreations:* shooting, fishing. *Address:* Netherhall, Bridge-of-Dee, Kirkcudbrightshire DG7 2AA. *T:* Bridge-of-Dee 208. *Clubs:* New (Edinburgh); Western (Glasgow). *Died 29 July 1982.*

**ROSS TAYLOR, Walter;** Assistant Public Trustee, 1971–73; *b* 5 Aug. 1912; *er s* of late Walter and Frances Ross Taylor; *m* 1939, Vera Julia, *y d* of Col Mackenzie Churchill, Cheltenham; two *s* one *d. Educ:* Repton Sch.; Trinity Coll., Oxford (BA). Called to Bar, 1934. Enlisted Princess Louise's Kensington Regt TA, 1938; served War of 1939–45 (despatches, 1945; Captain): commnd Suffolk Regt, 1940; transf. to RAC, 1941; served with 142 Regt RAC in N Africa, and subseq. on staff of Special Ops (Mediterranean). Entered Public Trustee Office, 1938: Chief Administrative Officer, 1966. *Recreations:* travelling, walking. *Address:* Little Court, 13 Courtmoor Avenue, Fleet, Hants. *Died 23 March 1983.*

**ROSSETTI, Harold Ford,** CB 1959; *b* 19 Feb. 1909; *s* of Gabriel Arthur Madox Rossetti and Dora Brandreth Lewis; *m* 1933, Joan, *er d* of Rev. G. H. Holley; two *s* one *d. Educ:* Bolton School;

Gonville and Caius College, Cambridge. Administrative Civil Servant, 1932–69; Customs and Excise Dept, 1932–34; Min. of Labour, 1934–51; OEEC, Paris, 1951–55; Min. of Labour, 1955–63; Dept of Educn and Science, 1963–69; Director, London Office, ILO, 1970–75. *Publication:* The Darkling Plain (novel), 1936. *Address:* 30 Castle Street, Framlingham, Suffolk. *T:* Framlingham 723586.
*Died 3 July 1983.*

**ROSSITER, Hon. Sir John Frederick,** KBE 1978; Agent-General for Victoria, in London, 1976–79; *b* 17 Dec. 1913; *s* of James and Sarah Rossiter; *m* 1st, 1939, Joan Durrant Stewart (*d* 1979); one *s* one *d* (and one *d* decd); 2nd, 1981, Heather Steer; one step *s* one step *d*. *Educ:* Melbourne Univ. (BA 1937). Senior Lecturer in English, Royal Melbourne Inst. of Technology, 1946–55; MLA (Lib.), Brighton, Vic., 1955; Minister of Labour and Industry; Minister of Health; Chief Secretary, 1964–76. *Recreation:* golf. *Address:* 14 Pretoria Avenue, Balmoral, Sydney, NSW 2088, Australia. *Clubs:* Wig and Pen, United Oxford & Cambridge University, Les Ambassadeurs; Naval and Military (Melbourne), Melbourne CC; Elenora Golf, Sydney CC; Hon. Company of Edinburgh Golfers (Muirfield).
*Died 18 Jan. 1988.*

**ROSSITER, Leonard;** actor; *b* 21 Oct. 1926; *s* of John Rossiter and Elizabeth Rossiter; *m* 1972, Gillian Raine; one *d*. *Educ:* Liverpool Collegiate Secondary Sch. Entered theatre, 1954; 1st London appearance, Free As Air, Savoy, 1958; Broadway début, Semi-Detached, 1963. London appearances include: Volpone, Garrick, 1967; (title rôle) The Resistible Rise of Arturo Ui, Saville, 1969 (Edinburgh Festival, 1968; London Critics' Best Actor Award and Variety Club's Best Actor Award, 1969); The Heretic, Duke of York's, 1970; The Caretaker, Mermaid, 1972; The Banana Box, Hampstead Theatre Club and Apollo, 1973; Frontiers of Farce, Old Vic, 1976; Tartuffe (title rôle), Greenwich, 1976; The Immortal Haydon, one-man show, Mermaid, 1977, Greenwich, 1978; Semi Detached, Greenwich, 1979; Make and Break, Haymarket, 1980; Rules of the Game, Haymarket, 1982; Loot, Ambassadors, 1984. Films: This Sporting Life; Billy Liar; The Whisperers; King Rat; More Deadly Than the Male; Oliver; 2001 Space Odyssey; Barry Lyndon; Voyage of the Damned; Rising Damp; Hotel Paradiso; Deadfall; The Wrong Box; Luther; Otley; Britannia Hospital. Television appearances. *Publications:* The Devil's Bedside Book, 1980; The Lowest Form of Wit, 1981. *Recreations:* squash, wine. *Club:* Hurlingham.
*Died 5 Oct. 1984.*

**ROTHA, Paul,** FRSA; Film Producer and Director; Author; Journalist; Managing Director, Paul Rotha Productions Ltd, since 1941; *b* London, 3 June 1907. *Educ:* Highgate School; Slade School of Art, London. Painter and designer; Art Critic to The Connoisseur, 1927–28; specialised in the production of documentary films, starting with Empire Marketing Board; has made documentary films for Unesco, The Times, Shell-Mex, Imperial Airways, Manchester Corporation, Scottish Office, National Council of Social Service, Gas Industry, Royal National Life-Boat Institution, Central Electricity Board, National Book Council, Vickers-Armstrong, Orient Line, etc, Gold Medals for Films at Venice Film Festival (1934), Brussels Film Festival (1935) and Leipsig Film Festival (1962); British Film Academy Awards, 1947 and 1952. Visited US under auspices of Rockefeller Foundation, 1937–38, to lecture on documentary films, 1953–54; Simon Senior Research Fellow, Univ. of Manchester, 1967–68; Head of Documentary at BBC Television; Arts Council Grant, 1970. Tribute to Rotha Films and Books, Nat. Film Theatre, 1979. Producer and/or Director: The Silent Raid (feature), Life of Adolf Hitler, World Without End (co-dir), Cradle of Genius, Cat and Mouse (feature), No Resting Place (feature), The World is Rich, The Challenge of Television (BBC), A City Speaks, Total War in Britain, Land of Promise, Children of the City, World of Plenty, Contact, To-Day We Live, Cover to Cover, The Future's in the Air, The Face of Britain, New Worlds for Old, The Fourth Estate, etc. *Publications:* The Film Till Now, 1930, new edns 1949, 1960, 1967; Celluloid; The Film To-Day, 1931; Documentary Film, 1936, new edns 1939, 1952, 1970; (with Roger Manvell) Movie Parade, 1936, new edn, 1950; (with E. Anstey and others) Shots in the Dark, 1951; (ed) Portrait of a Flying Yorkshireman, 1952; Television in the Making, 1956; Rotha on the Film, 1958; (with Basil Wright and A. Calder-Marshall) The Innocent Eye: a biography of Robert Flaherty, 1963; Documentary Diary, 1973; Richard Winnington: Film Criticism and Caricatures, 1975. *Address:* c/o John Farquharson Ltd, 162–168 Regent Street, W1R 5TB.
*Died 7 March 1984.*

**ROTHSCHILD,** 3rd Baron, *cr* 1885; **Nathaniel Mayer Victor Rothschild;** Bt 1847; GBE 1975; GM 1944; PhD; ScD; FRS 1953; Director: Rothschilds Continuation Ltd (Chairman, 1976–88); N. M. Rothschild & Sons (Chairman, 1975–76); *b* 31 Oct. 1910; *s* of late Hon. (Nathaniel) Charles Rothschild, 2nd *s* of 1st Baron Rothschild; *S* uncle, 1937; *m* 1st, 1933, Barbara (marr. diss. 1945; she *d* 1989; *o d* of late St John Hutchinson, KC; one *s* two *d*; 2nd, 1946, Teresa, MBE, MA, JP, *d* of late R. J. G. Mayor, CB; one *s* two *d* (and one *s* decd). *Educ:* Harrow, Trinity Coll., Cambridge.

Prize-Fellow of Trinity Coll., Cambridge, 1935–39, Hon. Fellow, 1961. War of 1939–45: Military Intelligence (despatches, American Legion of Merit, American Bronze Star). Director, BOAC, 1946–58; Chm., Agricultural Res. Council, 1948–58; Assistant Dir of Research, Dept of Zoology, Cambridge, 1950–70; Vice-Chm., Shell Research Ltd, 1961–63, Chm., 1963–70; Chm., Shell Research NV, 1967–70; Director: Shell Internationale Research Mij, 1965–70; Shell Chemicals UK Ltd, 1963–70; Shell International Gas, 1969–70; Research Co-ordinator, Royal Dutch Shell Group, 1965–70; Dir Gen. and First Perm. Under-Sec., Central Policy Review Staff, Cabinet Office, 1971–74; Dir, Rothschild Inc., 1976–85; Chm., Rothschilds Continuation Hldgs AG, 1982–88. Chm., Biotechnology Investments Ltd, 1981–89. Chairman: Royal Commn on Gambling, 1976–78; Enquiry into SSRC, 1982; Member: BBC General Advisory Council, 1952–56; Council for Scientific Policy, 1965–67; Central Adv. Council for Science and Technology, 1969. 4th Royal Soc. Technol. Lect., 1970; Trueman Wood Lect., RSA, 1972; Dimbleby Lecture, 1978. FSS 1984; Hon. Fellow: Bellairs Research Inst. of McGill Univ., Barbados, 1960; Weizmann Inst. of Science, Rehovoth, 1962; Wolfson Coll., Cambridge, 1966; Inst. of Biol., 1971; Imperial Coll., 1975; RSE, 1986. Hon. DSc: Newcastle, 1964; Manchester, 1966; Technion, Haifa, 1968; City Univ., 1972; Bath, 1978; Hon. PhD: Tel Aviv, 1971; Hebrew Univ., Jerusalem, 1975; Bar-Ilan, Israel, 1980; Hon. LLD London, 1977; DUniv York, 1980. KStJ 1948. Melchett Medal, 1971; RSA Medal, 1972. *Publications:* The History of Tom Jones, a Changeling, 1951; The Rothschild Library, 1954, new edn, 1969; Fertilization, 1956; A Classification of Living Animals, 1961, 1965; A Framework for Government Research and Development, 1971; The Rothschild Family Tree, 1973, new edn 1981; Meditations of a Broomstick, 1977; 'You Have It, Madam', 1980; The Shadow of a Great Man, 1982; Random Variables, 1984; (with N. Logothetis) Probability Distributions, 1986; scientific papers. *Heir:* *s* Hon. (Nathaniel Charles) Jacob Rothschild, *b* 29 April 1936. *Club:* Pratt's.
*Died 20 March 1990.*

**ROUS, Sir Stanley (Ford),** Kt 1949; CBE 1943; JP; Secretary of the Football Association, 1934–61 (now Hon. Vice-President); President, Fédération Internationale de Football Associations, 1961–74 (now Hon. President); *b* 25 April 1895; *s* of George Samuel and Alice Rous; *m* 1924, Adrienne Gacon (*d* 1950). *Educ:* Sir John Leman School, Beccles; St Luke's College, Exeter. Served European War, 1914–18, in France and Palestine, 272nd Brigade RFA (East Anglian); Assistant Master, Watford Grammar School, 1921–34; Member Paddington Borough Council, 1943–47; Past Pres. Paddington and Marylebone Rotary Club; Hon. Vice-Pres., Central Council for Physical Recreation, 1973– (Chm., 1945–73). JP Paddington Div., 1950. Mem. King George's Jubilee Trust, King George VI Foundation. Vice-Pres., Arts Educn Trust; Governor, St Luke's Coll., Exeter, 1964–78. Liveryman Worshipful Co. of Loriners. Chevalier de l'Ordre Grand-Ducal de la Couronne de Chêne de Luxembourg; Chevalier de la Légion d'Honneur; Commendatore, Ordine Al Merito della Repubblica Italiana; Commander, Order of Ouissam Alaouite (Morocco), 1968; Grosses Verdienstkreuz des Verdienstordens der Bundesrepublik Deutschland, 1974; Olympic Diploma of Merit, IOC, 1974. Hon. Mem., UEFA, 1976. *Publications:* (jtly) The Football Association Coaching Manual, 1942; Recreative Physical Exercises and Activities for Association Football and other Games Players, 1942; A History of the Laws of Association Football, 1974; Football Worlds: a lifetime in sport (autobiog.), 1978. *Recreation:* watching a variety of sport. *Address:* 115 Ladbroke Road, W11. *T:* 01–727 4113. *Clubs:* MCC; All England Lawn Tennis and Croquet, Hurlingham.
*Died 18 July 1986.*

**ROUSE, Arthur Frederick,** CMG 1949; *b* 25 Sept. 1910; *s* of late G. A. Rouse, Reading; *m* 1937, Helena, *y d* of late Rev. L. Klamborowski, Clare, Suffolk. *Educ:* Reading School; St John's College, Oxford. White Scholar of St John's, 1928; 1st Cl. Hons Classical Moderations, 1929; 2nd Cl. Literae Humaniores, 1932. Assistant Master Edinburgh Academy, 1932; entered Home Civil Service by competitive exam. starting as Asst Principal in Ministry of Labour, 1933; Private Sec. to Parl. Secretary, 1936–38; accompanied British Delegation to Internat. Labour Conf., 1936–37; Principal, Ministry of Labour, 1938, Asst Secretary, 1944; Dep. Chief, Manpower Division, CCG (British Element), 1945–46; UK Govt Rep. on various Internat. Cttees, 1946–49, including OEEC Manpower Cttee, Chairman of ILO European Manpower Cttee; Special Asst on Manpower to Dir-Gen. of ILO, 1949–50; Head of Latin American Immigration Field Office of ILO, 1950–51; Chairman of Beatrice Intensive Conservative Area Cttee, 1956; Senior Research Fellow, Univ. Coll. of Rhodesia and Nyasaland, 1957–62; Chairman, Wages Advisory Board for Nyasaland, 1960–62. Public administration and industrial consultant. *Recreations:* farming and travel. *Address:* Alicedale Farm, Beatrice, Zimbabwe.
*Died 15 Oct. 1984.*

**ROUTH, Augustus Crosbie;** *b* 7 Aug. 1892; *s* of late Augustus Routh, Manager of Imperial Ottoman Bank, Salonica; *m* 1917, Ethel

Madeleine Martin (d 1973), The Steyne, Worthing; one d (and one s killed in action, 1941, one d decd). *Educ:* abroad; Edinburgh; LSE, London. Shipping Clerk, Consulate-General, Smyrna, 1910, Chief Clerk, 1920; General Consular Service, 1920; Acting Consul-General, Marseilles, Strasbourg, Milan, Genoa, and Monrovia at various dates: Consul at Istanbul, 1934; Actg Consul-Gen., Tripoli, 1935; Consul at Benghazi, 1936; Actg Consul-General, Marseilles, 1937; re-appointed Consul at Istanbul, 1938; Acting Consul-General, Antwerp, 1940; Chargé d'Affaires and Consul-General, Monrovia, Liberia, 1941; promoted Consul-General at Nice, France, 1944; HM Minister, Haiti, 1946–50; retired, 1950. Coronation Medal, 1937. *Address:* 16 Hailsham Road, Worthing, W Sussex. *T:* Worthing 49250.                           *Died 15 July 1982.*

**ROUTLEDGE, Rev. Canon (Kenneth) Graham;** Canon Residentiary and Treasurer of St Paul's Cathedral, since 1982; Chancellor, Diocese of Ely since 1973, of Peterborough since 1976, and of Lichfield since 1976; *b* 21 Sept. 1927; *s* of Edgar Routledge and late Catherine (*née* Perry); *m* 1960, Muriel, *d* of late Robert Shallcross. *Educ:* Birkenhead Sch.; Liverpool Univ. (LLB 1st Cl. Hons 1951); Fitzwilliam Coll., Cambridge (BA 1965 Theol Tripos Pt II, MA 1969); Westcott House, Cambridge. Deacon, 1966; priest, 1967. Called to the Bar, Middle Temple, 1952 (Blackstone Entrance Scholar, Harmsworth Law Scholar, Campbell Foster Prize). HM Forces, RE and RAEC, 1945–48. Practice at Chancery Bar, Liverpool, and on Northern Circuit, 1952–63; Tutor and Lectr in Law, Liverpool Univ., 1952–63; Curate, St George's, Stockport, 1966–69; Lectr in Law, Manchester Univ., 1966–69; Corpus Christi Coll., Cambridge: Dean of Chapel, 1969–77; Lectr and Dir of Studies in Law, 1972–77; Fellow, 1969–83; Canon Residentiary and Treasurer of Peterborough Cathedral, 1977–82. Chm., Ecclesiastical Law Soc., 1987–. Mem., Birkenhead Bor. Council, 1960–63. Contested Birkenhead (Conservative), Gen. Election, 1959. Life Governor, Haileybury and Imperial Service Coll., 1976–; Chm. Council, Westwood House Sch., Peterborough, 1985–89 (Mem. Council, 1979–89); Fellow, Woodard Schools, 1979–89. *Recreations:* Rugby, cricket, golf, bird watching, reading. *Address:* 3 Amen Court, EC4M 7BU. *T:* 01–236 4532. *Clubs:* Royal Commonwealth Society, MCC.                                     *Died 18 May 1989.*

**ROUTLEY, Rev. Erik Reginald;** Professor of Church Music, since 1975 and Director of Chapel, since 1978, Westminster Choir College, Princeton; *b* 31 Oct. 1917; *s* of John and Eleanor Routley; *m* 1944, Margaret Scott; two *s* one *d*. *Educ:* Lancing Coll.; Magdalen and Mansfield Colls, Oxford. BA 1940; MA 1943; BD 1946; DPhil 1952. FRSCM 1965. Ordained, 1943; Minister: Trinity Congl Church, Wednesbury, 1943–45; Dartford Congl Church, 1945–48; Mansfield Coll., Oxford: Tutor in Church History, 1948–56; Mackennal Lectr in Church History, 1956–59; Chaplain, 1949–59; Librarian and Dir of Music, 1948–59; Minister, Augustine-Bristo Congl Church, Edinburgh, 1959–67; Minister, St James's URC, Newcastle upon Tyne, 1967–74. Vis. Dir of Music, Princeton Theol Seminary, 1975. Pres., Congregational Church in England and Wales, 1970–71. Editor: Bulletin of Hymn Soc., 1948–74; Studies in Church Music, 1964–70. *Publications:* The Church and Music, 1950, new edn, 1967; I'll Praise my Maker, 1951; Hymns and Human Life, 1952; (with K. L. Parry) Companion to Congregational Praise, 1953; Hymns and the Faith, 1955; The Wisdom of the Fathers, 1957; The Gift of Conversion, 1957; The Organist's Guide to Congregational Praise, 1957; The Music of Christian Hymnody, 1957; The English Carol, 1958; Church Music and Theology, 1959; What is Conversion?, 1959; English Religious Dissent, 1960; Music, Sacred and Profane, 1960; The Story of Congregationalism, 1961; Creeds and Confessions, 1962; Ascent to the Cross, 1962; Beginning the Old Testament, 1962; Into a Far Country, 1962; Congregationalists and Unity, 1962; Twentieth Century Church Music, 1964; The Man for Others, 1964; Hymns Today and Tomorrow, 1964; Music Leadership in the Church (USA), 1966; Words, Music and the Church, 1967; The Musical Wesleys, 1969; Saul Among the Prophets, 1971; The Puritan Pleasures of the Detective Story, 1972; Exploring the Psalms, 1975; (ed) Westminster Praise, 1976; A Short History of English Church Music, 1977; Victory of Life (play), 1978; Church Music and the Christian Faith, 1978; An English-Speaking Hymnal Guide, 1979; A Panorama of Christian Hymnody, 1979; The Music of Christian Hymns, 1981; 15 Church Anthems (pubd USA). *Recreation:* music. *Address:* 929, Route 518, RD1, Skillman, NJ 08558, USA. *T:* (609) 921 7806.
                                                           *Died 8 Oct. 1982.*

**ROW, Commander Sir Philip (John),** KCVO 1969 (CVO 1965; MVO 1958); OBE 1944; RN Retired; an Extra Equerry to the Queen since 1969; Deputy Treasurer to the Queen, 1958–68. *Address:* Warren Lodge, Warren Lane, Finchampstead, Berks RG11 4HR.
                                                           *Died 28 Nov. 1990.*

**ROWE, Eric George,** CMG 1955; *b* 30 June 1904; *s* of late Ernest Kruse Rowe; *m* 1st, 1931, Gladys Ethel (*d* 1985), *d* of late Charles Horace Rogers, ARCA; 2nd, 1985, Margaret Alison, *d* of late Arthur John Howe. *Educ:* Chatham House School, Ramsgate; St

Edmund Hall Oxford. Assistant Master, Queen Mary's Grammar School, Walsall, 1926–27. Entered Colonial Service, Tanganyika; Administrative Officer (Cadet), 1928; Asst District Officer, 1930; District Officer, 1940; Provincial Commissioner, 1948; Senior Provincial Commissioner, 1952; Minister for Local Government and Administration, Tanganyika, 1958; Supervisor, Overseas Services Courses, Oxford, 1959–69. *Publication:* paper in Ibis. *Recreation:* ornithology. *Address:* Merlin Cottage, 3 Snuggs Lane, East Hanney, near Wantage, Oxon OX12 0HU. *T:* West Hanney 229. *Club:* Royal Commonwealth Society.
                                                           *Died 7 March 1987.*

**ROWE, Norman Francis;** one of the Special Commissioners of Income Tax, 1950–73; Commissioner of Income Tax, St Marylebone Division, 1974–83, retired; *b* 18 May 1908; *o s* of late Frank Rowe and Eva Eveline (*née* Metcalfe), Watford; *m* 1941, Suzanne Marian (marr. diss., 1964), *o d* of D. S. Richardson; one *s*; *m* 1965, Vittoria, *yr d* of P. Cav. Tondi; one *s*. *Educ:* Sherborne. Chartered Accountant, 1931–37, retired; re-admitted, 1977; FCA. Called to Bar, Lincoln's Inn, 1940; Mem. of Western Circuit. Served War of 1939–45 (despatches); RAF, 1940–45, serving in UK, Middle East, India, Burma and Ceylon; demobilised with rank of Squadron Leader. Freeman, City of London; Liveryman, Worshipful Co. of Glaziers and Painters of Glass. *Publications:* author of Schedule C and Profits Tax sections of Simon's Income Tax, 1st edn. *Recreations:* fishing, yachting. *Address:* 2 Pearl Court, Devonshire Place, Eastbourne, East Sussex BN21 4AB. *T:* Eastbourne 38568; Via Leonardo da Vinci 286, 55049 Viareggio, Italy. *T:* Viareggio 961848. *Clubs:* Naval and Military, Bar Yacht, Little Ship; Island Cruising.
                                                           *Died 4 April 1990.*

**ROWELL, Sir (Herbert Babington) Robin,** Kt 1952; CBE 1948; AFC 1918; late of R. & W. Hawthorn, Leslie & Co. Ltd, Hebburn-on-Tyne, (Director 1929, Chairman, 1943–65); *b* 28 May 1894; *s* of late Sir Herbert Babington Rowell, KBE, The Manor House, Newcastle on Tyne, and late Lady Mary Dobree Rowell, Redesmouth House, Bellingham, Northumberland; *m* 1924, Hilda, *d* of Oswald Dobell, Neston, Cheshire; two *d*. *Educ:* Repton. Served European War, 1914–18, with RE, RFC and RAF, 1914–19; Capt. 1916; retd 1920. Chm. of Council, British Shipbuilding Research Assoc., 1951–52; Vice-President Institution of Naval Architects; President: Shipbuilding Conference, 1948; Shipbuilding Employers' Federation, 1941–42; North East Coast Institution of Engineers and Shipbuilders, 1946–48; Chairman Tyne Shipbuilders Association, 1942–47. DL Co. Durham, 1944. Hon. DSc Dunelm. *Recreations:* shooting, golf. *Address:* Wylam Cottage, Wylam, Northumberland. *T:* Wylam 2207.                      *Died 19 Dec. 1981.*

**ROWETT, Geoffrey Charles;** Deputy Chairman, The Charterhouse Group plc, 1981–83 (Managing Director, 1974–82; Group Chief Executive, 1976–82); retired; *b* 1 Aug. 1925; *s* of Frederick Charles and Nell Rowett; *m* 1951, Joyce Eddiford; two *s*. *Educ:* Roundhay Sch., Leeds. Articled to Blackburns, Robson Coates & Co., Leeds and London. FCA, FCMA, JDipMA, FIMC, CBIM, FIAM. Midland Bank Executor & Trustee Co. Ltd, 1941; Royal Navy, 1943–46; Blackburns, Robson Coates & Co., 1947; Deloitte, Plender Griffiths Annan & Co., 1952; Production-Engineering SA (Pty) Ltd, 1954; P-E Consulting Group, 1964; Thomson Newspapers Ltd, 1965; Man. Dir, Sunday Times, 1965–72; Dir and Gen. Manager, Times Newspapers Ltd, 1967–72; Man. Dir, Corporate Finance, British Steel Corp., 1973. Member: Bd of Governors, St Mary's Hosp. Gp, 1970–74; Council, ICMA, 1974–82 (Vice-Pres., 1976; Pres., 1978); Council, Henley Centre for Forecasting. *Address:* 2 Eton Hall, Eton College Road, NW3 2DW. *T:* 01–586 8215; 13 Cork Terrace, Bath BA1 3BE. *T:* Bath 21269. *Clubs:* Bath and County (Bath); Tracey Park (Wick).               *Died 19 June 1986.*

**ROWLAND, Deborah Molly; Her Honour Judge Rowland;** a Circuit Judge (formerly a County Court Judge) since 1971; *b* 7 Aug. 1913; *d* of Samuel and Hilda Rowland. *Educ:* Slade Sch. of Art; Bartlett Sch. of Architecture; Courtauld Inst of Fine Art. Diploma in Fine Art and Architecture. Called to the Bar, Lincoln's Inn, June 1950. *Publication:* Guide to Security of Tenure for Business and Professional Tenants, 1956. *Recreations:* music (Founder, Bar Musical Soc.), painting, sculpture. *Address:* Lincoln's Inn, WC2.
                                                           *Died 26 Dec. 1986.*

**ROWLANDSON, Sir (Stanley) Graham,** Kt 1956; MBE 1943; JP 1944; FCA; Chairman, Rowlandson Organisation; Senior Partner, S. Graham Rowlandson & Co., Chartered Accountants; Chairman, The Finance & Industrial Trust Ltd; *b* 25 Aug. 1908; *s* of late H. Stanley Rowlandson, Claremont, Enfield, Middx; *m* 1938, Vera Elworthy, *d* of late Ernest Alfred Lane, Woodside Pk, N; two *s* one *d*. *Educ:* Mill Hill Sch.; Blois, France. Chm., Fitch Lowell, 1954–59. Member, Enfield UDC, 1934–46 (Chm., 1940–42; Chm. Finance Cttee, 1937–45; Leader, Cons. Group and Council, 1937–40, 1942–45); Middlesex CC, 1942–46, 1947–51, 1959–65, CA, 1951–58, High Sheriff 1958 (Vice-Chm. Establishment Cttee 1949–51, Chm. 1951–55; Chm. Finance Cttee 1949–51, Vice-Chm. 1951–55; Dep.

Leader, 1951, 1964–65; Leader, 1951–54; Vice-Chm. CC 1954–55, Chm. 1955–56; Chm. Health Cttee, 1956–58, 1961–65; Mem., Standing Jt Cttee, 1951–58, 1961–65); Mem. for Enfield, GLC, 1964–73; Chairman: Finance Cttee, GLC, 1969–73; Establishment Cttee, 1967–69; Member: Gen. Purposes Cttee, Supplies Cttee (Leader of Opposition), of GLC, 1964–67; Rep. on Local Govt Training Bd of GLC, 1967–70, Chm. Finance Cttee, 1967–70; Member: Local Govt Computer Centre, 1967–70; Exec. Coun. CCs Assoc., 1955–58; Local Authorities Management Services and Computer Cttee, 1969–70; Jt Hon. Treas., Middx Assoc., 1965–69, Vice-Pres., 1969–76, Pres., 1976–78; Pres., Middx County Assoc., 1972–74; Vice-Chm., Home Counties N Local Govt Adv. Cttee, 1959–64; Greater London Area Local Govt Adv. Cttee, 1964–72, Dep. Chm., 1964–72; Mem., Nat. Local Govt Adv. Cttee, 1960–72; Common Councilman, City of London, for Coleman St Ward, 1961–; Chm., Port and City of London Health and Welfare Cttees, 1964–67; Vice-Chm., Establishment Cttee, 1977–79, 1981–82, Chm., 1979–81; Mem., Lord Mayor and Sheriffs Cttee, 1971; Representative of Corp. on Disablement in the City Exec., 1976– and Greater London Assoc. for the Disabled, 1978–84. Contested (C) N Tottenham, 1937 and 1938; Chairman: Enfield W Cons. Assoc., 1949–52; Enfield Bor. Cons. Assoc., 1952–64 (Pres. 1964–72); Pres., Enfield Town Cons. Club, 1970–; Hon. Life Pres., N Enfield Cons. Assoc., 1972–; Nat. Union of Cons. and Unionist Assocs: Vice-Chm. Home Counties N Prov. Area, 1953–54, 1961–64; Mem. Nat. Exec. Cttee, 1964–78; Mem., GP Cttee, 1972–75; Mem., Cons. Commonwealth and Overseas Council, 1972–84 (Hon. Treas., 1978–84); Jt Hon. Treas., Cons. Foreign and Commonwealth Council, 1984–; Mem. Finance and GP Cttee, Greater London Area, 1964–78 (Dep. Chm., 1964–69, and 1970–71, Chm., 1972–75); Hon. Vice-Pres., 1976–; Chm. Middx Parly and Local Govt Gps, 1953–54; Mem. Middx Exec. Council, 1951–53, 1962–63; Hon. Treasurer, Primrose League, 1975–85; Mem., Eur. Atlantic Gp, 1977– (Hon. Treas., 1985–). Chm., Enfield Savings, 1940–45; Mem., Nat. Savings London Reg. Adv. Cttee, 1942–46; Mem., Admin. Council, Lord Mayor's Nat. Air Raid Distress Fund, 1940–54. Governor: Royal Nat. Órthopædic Hosp., 1948–52; Med. Coll., St Bartholomew's Hosp., 1966–; Chm., Chairmen of Reg. Hosp. Bds, 1971–74; Member: Gen. Council, King Edward's Hosp. Fund for London, 1956–; NE Met. Reg. Hosp. Bd, 1952–74 (Chm., 1956–74); Ct of Govs, London Sch. of Hygiene and Tropical Med., 1957–58; Bd of Governors: St Bartholomew's Hosp., 1957–74, London Hosp., 1960–74, Hammersmith and St Mark's Hosps, 1960–74, Moorfields Eye Hosp., 1961–79; Eastman Dental Hosp., 1974–78; Vice-Chm., Enfield Gp Hosp. Man. Cttees, 1948–53; Chairman: Appeals Cttee, St Antony's Hosp., Cheam, 1974; Funding Cttee, Inst. for the Study of Drug Dependence, 1976–80; Member: Whitley Council for Health Services, 1957–64; Nat. Cons. Council on Recruitment of Nurses and Midwives, 1963–74; Inner London Exec. Council, 1971–74; Family Practitioner Cttee, City and E London Area Health Authority, 1974–85 (Chm. Dental Services Cttee, 1979–85); Council of Fed. Superannuation Scheme for Nurses and Hospital Officers, 1965–74; Nat. Old People's Welfare Council, 1959–74; Adv. Council on Overseas Services Resettlement Bureau, 1968–79; Finance Cttee Internat. Soc. for Rehabilitation of Disabled, 1958–67 (Chm., 1964–67; Vice-Chm., 1963–73, Chm., 1973–75; Brit. Cttee; Mem. Brit. Cttee, Royal Assoc. for Disability and Rehabilitation, 1977–); Nat. Baby Welfare Council, 1961–63; Exec. Cttee, Nat. Assoc. for Maternal and Child Welfare, 1977–81; Vice-Chm., Council for Professions supp. to Medicine, 1961–79 (Chm. Finance Cttee); Vice Pres., 1981–82, Chm. Exec. Cttee 1982–83, Age Concern Kensington and Chelsea; Hon. Treasurer: Infantile Paralysis Fellowship, 1949–52 (Chm. 1952–57); Hand Crafts Adv. Assoc. for the Disabled, 1975–83; Vice-Pres., Edmonton and Enfield Br., British Diabetic Assoc., 1960; Trustee: City Parochial Foundn, 1968–74, 1977–83; Westminster Philanthropic Soc., 1960–75. Vice Pres., UNA, 1965–. Mem., Two Cities Dining Club. Mem., Management Cttee, Bridgehead Housing Assoc. Ltd, 1974–75; Mem. Council, Stonham Housing Assoc. Ltd, 1975–; Trustee, Stonham Meml Trust, 1978–; Chm., Roma Housing Assoc. Ltd, 1975–79; Member: Court, Univ. of Essex, 1965–74; SE Circuit Cttee, 1972–; Governor: Mill Hill Sch., 1952–58, 1961–83; London Festival Ballet Trust, 1971–73; Vice-Pres., Internat. Cultural Exchange, 1964–; Mem. Council RSA, 1966–76 (Hon. Treasurer, 1971–76); Pres., Boy Scouts Assoc., Enfield Br., 1958–77; Vice-President: London Scout Council, 1956–65; Co. of Greater London N Scout Council, 1965–71 (Pres., 1971–80); Pres., Middx Table Tennis Assoc., 1957–; Vice-Pres., Basildon Jikishin Judo Centre, 1980–83; Mem. Council, Royal Warrant Holders' Assoc., 1958–59. Liveryman, Worshipful Co. of Masons (Mem. Ct of Assts; Renter Warden, 1962; Upper Warden, 1963; Master, 1964); Liveryman, Paviors' Co. (Mem., Ct of Assts, 1973–; Renter Warden, 1977; Upper Warden, 1978; Master, 1979). Coleman St Ward Club: Vice-Chm., 1965; Chm., 1966. Recreations: work, entertaining, racing. Address: Boundary House, 91–93 Charterhouse Street, EC1. T: 01–253 0101; 47 Lowndes Square, SW1X 9JJ. T: 01–235 2288. Clubs: United and Cecil (Mem. Cttee,

1972–84); Old Millhillians (Pres. 1965–66).

Died 29 Jan. 1986.

ROWLEY, John Hewitt, CBE 1968; Controller, BBC, Wales, 1967–74; b 1917. Educ: University Coll. of N Wales, Bangor (BA); Jesus Coll., Oxford. ICS, 1939–47. Joined BBC, 1949; Asst Head, Central Estabt, 1949–53; Staff Admin. Officer (II), 1953–55; Staff Admin. Officer, 1955–56; Asst Controller, Staff Admin, 1956–60, Controller, 1960–67. CIPM 1967. Address: 21 Lakeside, The Knap, Barry CF6 8ST. Died 6 July 1986.

ROWSON, Lionel Edward Aston, OBE 1955; MA Cantab 1977; ScD Cantab; FRS 1973; FRCVS; Director, Cambridge and District Cattle Breeders (AI Centre), 1942–84 (part-time, 1979–84); Officer in Charge, Agricultural Research Council Animal Research Station, Cambridge, 1976–79; Fellow of Wolfson College, Cambridge, since 1973; b 28 May 1914; s of L. F. Rowson, LDS, and M. A. Rowson (née Aston); m 1942, Audrey Kathleen Foster; two s two d. Educ: King Edward VIth Sch., Stafford; Royal Veterinary Coll., London. MRCVS, FRCVS 1972; FRVC 1975; ScD Cantab 1986. Engaged in general practice, 1939–42. Dep. Dir, ARC Unit of Reproductive Physiology and Biochemistry, 1955–76. Life Hon. Pres., Internat. Embryo Transfer Soc.; Mem., Acad. Royale de Médecine de Belgique, 1977. Hon. MA Cantab, 1977. Thomas Baxter Prize, 1956; Wooldridge Meml Lecture and Medal, 1974; Dalrymple-Champneys Cup and Medal, 1975; Bledisloe Veterinary Medal, 1978. Publication: (jointly) Reproduction in Domestic Animals (ed H. H. Cole and P. T. Cupps). Recreations: shooting, cricket, thoroughbred breeding. Address: The Grove, Water Lane, Histon, Cambridge. T: Histon 2534. Died 26 July 1989.

ROXBURGH, Air Vice-Marshal Henry Lindsay, CBE 1966; FRCP, FRCPE; Commandant, RAF Institute of Aviation Medicine, 1969–73; retired; b 5 Dec. 1909; s of John Roxburgh, Galston, Ayrshire and Cape Town, and Edith Mary Roxburgh (née Smithers), Kenilworth, Cape; m 1944, Hermione Babington (née Collard); one s two d. Educ: George Watson's College, Edinburgh; Edinburgh University. BSc 1932; PhD 1934; MB, ChB 1940; FRCPE 1966; FRCP 1972. Medical Branch, Royal Air Force, 1941–73. Service mainly at RAF Inst. of Aviation Med.: research undertaken in various aspects of aviation physiology and related subjects; apptd Prof. in Aviation Medicine, 1966. Chairman, Aero-Space Medical Panel of Advisory Gp of Aero-Space Research and Development, Paris, 1965–67. Mem., Internat. Acad. of Aviation and Space Medicine. QHS 1971–73. FRAeS 1965. Publications: papers in field of aviation medicine. Recreation: gardening. Address: 6 Steppes Hill, Langton Matravers, Swanage, Dorset BH19 3ET. Club: Royal Air Force. Died 28 Jan. 1989.

ROXBURGH, Sir Ronald Francis, Kt 1946; Judge of High Court of Justice, Chancery Division, 1946–60, retired; b 19 Nov. 1889; o s of Francis Roxburgh and Annie Gertrude Mortlock; m 1st, 1935, Jane Minney (d 1960), yr d of Archibald H. and Lady Frances Gordon-Duff; one d; 2nd, 1966, Mrs Dorothea Mary Hodge. Educ: Harrow; Trinity College, Cambridge. Classical Tripos Part I, Class I, Division II, 1911. Whewell International Law Scholar, 1912; called to Bar, Middle Temple, 1914; KC 1933; Bencher of Lincoln's Inn, 1937, Treasurer, 1957. Publications: Prisoners of War Information Bureau in London, 1915; International Conventions and Third States, 1917; The Origins of Lincoln's Inn, 1963; (ed) The Black Books of Lincoln's Inn, vol. v, 1968; edited Oppenheim's International Law (3rd edn), 1920–21. Recreation: walking. Address: 8 Old Square, Lincoln's Inn, WC2. T: 01–242 4748; Holman's House, Stone-in-Oxney, Tenterden, Kent. T: Wittersham 321.

Died 19 Aug. 1981.

ROXBY, John Henry M.; see Maude-Roxby.

ROY, Sir Asoka Kumar, Kt 1937; b 9 Sept. 1886; s of late Akshoy Kumar Roy Chaudhury of Taki and late Shoroshi Bala Roy Chaudhurani; m 1908, Charu Hashini, 4th d of late Taraprasad Roy Chaudhury; one s one d. Educ: Doveton College, Presidency College and Ripon College, Calcutta. MA, BL (Calcutta); Vakil, Calcutta High Court, 1908; called to Bar, Middle Temple, 1912 (First Class Honoursman at the Final Bar Examination); Standing Counsel, Bengal, 1929; twice acted as a Judge of the High Court of Calcutta; Advocate-General of Bengal, 1934–43; Law Member, Governor-General's Council, India, 1943–46. Director, Jardine Henderson Ltd and other big companies, 1950–70. Recreations: gardening and walking. Address: 3 Upper Wood Street, Calcutta, India. Clubs: Calcutta, Royal Calcutta Turf (Calcutta).

Died 27 May 1982.

ROY, His Eminence Cardinal Maurice, CC (Canada) 1971; DD (Laval), DPh (Inst. Angelicum); Archbishop of Quebec, 1947–81; Primate of Canada, 1956–81; elevated to the Sacred College of Cardinals and given titular church of Our Lady of the Blessed Sacrament and the Holy Canadian Martyrs, 1965; b 25 Jan. 1905; s of late Ferdinand Roy. Educ: Seminary of Quebec and Laval Univ., Quebec; Collegium Angelicum, Rome; Institut catholique and

Sorbonne, Paris. Priest, 1927; Professor of: Dogmatic Theology, 1930–35; Apologeticx, 1935–36; Sacramentary Theology, 1936–39; Students' Chaplain, 1936–37. Hon. Capt.-Chaplain Royal 22nd Regt 1939; Hon. Major and Chief Chaplain Canadian Base Units at Aldershot, 1941; Hon. Lt-Col, Chaplain HQ First Cdn Corps (England and Italy), 1941; Sicily and Italy Campaigns, 1943; Hon. Col, Asst Prin. Chaplain 1st Cdn Army, 1944; France, Belgium, Germany, Holland campaigns, 1944–45 (despatches). Rector Grand Seminary of Quebec, 1945; Bishop of Three-Rivers, 1946; Bishop Ordinary to Cdn Armed Forces (Military Vicar), 1946. Central Commission preparatory to Council Vatican II, June 1962; Council Vatican II Commission on Sacred Theology, Dec. 1962; Sacred Congregations of the Council and of Seminaries and Universities, 1965; Chairman: Concilium De Laicis; Pontifical Commission, Justitia et Pax, Rome, OBE, 1945; Chevalier of the Legion of Honour, 1947; Commander of the Order of Leopold and Croix de Guerre with palm, 1948; Commander of the Order of Orange Nassau, Holland, 1949; Knight Grand Cross, Equestrian Order to the Holy Sepulchre of Jerusalem, 1965; Bailiff Grand Cross of Honour and Devotion, Sovereign Order of Malta, 1965. *Address:* c/o Archevêché de Québec, Case postale 459, Québec G1R 4R6, Canada.                                *Died* 24 *Oct.* 1985.

**ROY, Maurice Paul Mary;** Grand Officier, Légion d'Honneur; Professor at Ecole Polytechnique, Paris, 1947–69; President: Committee on Space Research; International Union of Theoretical and Applied Mechanics; *b* 7 Nov. 1899; *m* 1932, Maritchu Nebout; one *s. Educ:* Ecole Polytechnique; Ecole Nat. Sup. des Mines. Ingénieur Général des Mines (retd); Contrôle Technique des Chemins de Fer, 1922–35; Director General: Mechanical Industry, 1935–40; Office Nat. de la Recherche Aéronautique, 1949–62; Professor successively at French Nat. Engineering Schs (Ponts et Chaussées, Génie Rural, Aéronautique), and at Ecole Polytechnique. Membre de l'Institut (Académie des Sciences), 1949 (Pres. 1966). Foreign Member: US Nat. Acad. of Sci.; Austrian Acad. of Sci.; Hon. FRAeS. Dr *hc* Bruxelles, Aachen, Saarbrucken, Québec, Oxford. Médaille d'Or Lomonossov, USSR Acad. of Sci., 1976. *Publications:* books on Thermodynamics, Mechanics, Aviation and Propulsion; scientific and technical papers. *Recreations:* literature, golf. *Address:* 86 Avenue Niel, 75017 Paris, France. *T:* 763–01–02.

**ROYLE, Elizabeth Jean, (Mrs J. A. C. Royle);** *see* Harwood, E. J.

**ROYLE, Prof. Joseph Kenneth;** Professor and Head of Department of Mechanical Engineering, University of Sheffield, 1964–84; *b* 3 April 1924; *s* of J. Royle, Accrington, Lancs; *m* 1955, P. R. Wallwork; one *s* two *d. Educ:* Manchester University. Royal Aircraft Estabt, 1944–48; Manchester Univ., 1949–61; Vis. Assoc. Prof., MIT, 1961–62; Sen. Lectr, Univ. of Manchester Inst. of Science and Technology, 1962–64. *Publications:* contribs to Proc. IMechE, etc. *Recreations:* gardening, music. *Address:* Anselm, Over Lane, Baslow, Derbyshire. *T:* Baslow 3149.                                *Died* 12 *March* 1990.

**RUBBRA, Arthur Alexander,** CBE 1961; RDI 1977; *b* 29 Oct. 1903; *s* of Edmund James Rubbra and Mary Jane Rubbra; *m* 1930, Lilian Agnes Webster (*d* 1979); one *s. Educ:* Northampton Sch.; Bristol Univ. (BSc 1st Cl. Hons). FIMechE; FEng 1980. Rolls Royce Ltd: Chief Designer, 1940; Asst Chief Engineer, 1944; Dep. Chief Engr, 1951; Technical Dir, 1954; retd 1968. FRSA 1977; Hon. FRAeS 1977. *Recreations:* music, old buildings. *Address:* 100 Belper Road, Derby DE1 3EQ. *T:* Derby 43107.                                *Died* 24 *Nov.* 1982.

**RUBBRA, Edmund,** CBE 1960; MA Oxon; MRAM 1970; FGSM 1968; composer, pianist; Professor of Composition at Guildhall School of Music, 1961–74; Senior Lecturer in Music, Oxford University, 1947–68; Fellow, Worcester College, Oxford, 1963; *b* Northampton, 23 May 1901; *s* of Edmund James and Mary Jane Rubbra; *m* 1933, Antoinette Chaplin, French violinist; two *s*; *m* 1975, Colette Yardley. *Educ:* Northampton; University of Reading; Royal College of Music. Hon. LLD Leicester, 1959; Hon. DMus Durham, 1949; Hon. DLitt Reading, 1978. *Compositions include: orchestral works:* eleven symphonies; two overtures; Sinfonia Concertante for piano and orchestra; Concertos for piano, violin, and viola; Soliloquy for cello and small orchestra; Improvisation for Violin and orchestra; Improvisations on Virginal Pieces by Giles Farnaby; Variations for Brass Band; Brahms-Handel Variations scored for full orchestra; Nocturne for strings; Sinfonietta for string orch. Opera, The Shadow; *chamber works:* Sonatas for violin and piano, cello and piano, oboe and piano; duo for cor anglais and piano; 2 Piano Trios; four string quartets; Lyric Movement for piano and string quartet; Phantasy for two violins and piano; Introduction and Fugue for piano; Eight Preludes for piano; Prelude and Fugue on a Theme by Cyril Scott for piano; Fantasy Fugue for piano; Pezzo Ostinato for harp solo; Transformations for solo harp; Discourse for harp and 'cello; The Buddha Suite for flute, oboe and string trio; Meditazioni for recorder and harpsichord; Fantasia on a Theme of Machaut for recorder and string quartet; Notturno for four recorders; Passacaglia sopra Plusieurs Regrets for recorder and

harpsichord; Sonatina for recorder and harpsichord; Fantasia on a Chord, for recorder, harpsichord and gamba; 3 works for unaccomp. violin, viola and cello. *vocal works:* 9 Motets; 7 Madrigals; Festival Gloria for double choir; 2 4–part Masses; 3–part Mass; Missa Brevis for 3–part treble choir and organ; Missa Cantuariensis for double choir; The Morning Watch for choir and orchestra; The Dark Night of the Soul for Choir and orchestra; Song of the Soul for choir, strings, harp and timpani; In die et nocte canticum for choir and orchestra; Inscape for choir, strings and harp; Veni, Creator Spiritus, for Choir and Brass; 3 Psalms for low voice and piano; Advent Cantata for baritone, choir and small orchestra; Amoretti for tenor and string quartet; 5 Spenser Sonnets for tenor and string orchestra; 4 Medieval Latin Lyrics for baritone and string orchestra; The Jade Mountain, five songs for harp and voice; Magnificat and Nunc Dimittis for choir and organ; Te Deum for choir, solo, and orchestra; Cantata, in Honorem Mariae Matris Dei, for choir, boys' voices, soprano and alto soli, and orchestra; Ode to the Queen for Voice and orchestra; Tenebrae settings for unaccompanied choir; Two Sonnets by William Alabaster for voice, viola and piano; Cantata Pastorale for voice, recorder, harpsichord and cello; Autumn for 3–part female choir and piano; The Beatitudes for 3–part female choir unaccompanied; *anthems:* Up O my soul; And when the Builders; Lord, with what care; This Spiritual House Almighty God shall inhabit; Blessed is He; Prayer for the Queen; motet, How shall my tongue express?; 3 Greek folk songs; The Givers for 4–part unaccompanied choir; Cantata di camera Crucifixus pro nobis; Te Deum for 8–part unaccompanied choir; Lauda Sion, for unaccompanied double choir; Agnus Dei, for 4–part unaccompanied choir; Creature-Songs to Heaven, for 3–part treble voices, piano and strings; numerous songs. MS collection of works to British Library, 1983. *Publications:* Counterpoint: A Survey; Holst: A monograph; ed Casella, The Evolution of Music, rev. and enl. edn; Collected Essays on Gustav Holst. *Address:* Lindens, Bull Lane, Gerrards Cross, Bucks SL9 8RU. *T:* Gerrards Cross 884560.
                                *Died* 16 *Feb.* 1986.

**RUBINSTEIN, Arthur,** Hon. KBE 1977; pianist; *b* Lodz, Poland, 28 January 1887; *m* 1932, Aniela Mlynarska; two *s* two *d. Educ:* under Joachim, Prof. Heinrich Barth, Robert Kahn and Max Bruch. Gave many concerts in Russia, Poland, Germany, Austria; made first appearance in Spain in 1915, followed by 120 concerts in Spain alone; later in Latin America, where made 13 tours; since 1924 has toured Europe extensively; again in US, 1937, and became American Citizen. Toured Far East. Since 1945, every year, has made tours in US and all Western Europe (but refused to play in Germany, 1914–). In 1961 gave 10 recitals at Carnegie Hall, New York, in 4 weeks' time, all for 10 different charities. Appeared Festival Hall, London, 1954, 1955, 1956, 1957, 1960, 1962, 1963, 1965, 1968, 1969, 1970, 1972. US Medal of Freedom, 1976; holds several foreign Orders. Doctor *hc:* Yale Univ.; Brown Univ.; North-western Univ.; Hon. Member: Acad. Santa Cecilia, Rome; Acad. of Brazil; Gold Medal, Beethoven, Roy. Phil. Society. *Publications:* My Young Years, 1973; My Many Years, 1980. *Address:* 22 square de l'avenue Foch, 75116 Paris, France.                                *Died* 20 *Dec.* 1982.

**RUDGARD, Ven. Richard Cuthbert,** OBE 1944; TD 1950; Rector of Ellisfield and Farleigh Wallop, Basingstoke, 1960–74, and of Dumme, 1968–74; Archdeacon of Basingstoke and Canon of Winchester, 1958–71, later Archdeacon Emeritus; *b* 28 Dec. 1901; *e s* of Canon R. W. and Mrs E. M. Rudgard; *m* 1st, 1933, Mary M. McLean (decd); one *s*; 2nd, 1939, Maisie M. Cooke. *Educ:* Radley College; St Augustine's College, Canterbury. With Melanesian Mission, 1922–33. Assistant Priest, Heene, Worthing, 1934; Rector of Newbold Pacey with Moreton Morrell, 1936–45; Rector of Eversley, 1946–60; Rural Dean of Odiham, 1953–59. War of 1939–45 (despatches thrice); Chaplain to the Forces, TA, 1939; SCF 1st Armoured Division, 1942, N Africa; DACG 13 Corps, 1943, Sicily and Italy; Personal Chaplain to Chaplain General, 1944–46. DACG (TA) Southern Command, 1947–56. Hon. Chaplain to the Queen, 1954–56. *Address:* Clevedale Cottage, 22 Christchurch Road, Winchester SO23 9SS. *T:* Winchester 61419.
                                *Died* 19 *April* 1985.

**RUEGGER, Paul J.;** Swiss diplomat and jurist; *b* 14 August 1897; *s* of Prof. J. Ruegger; *m* 1st, 1932, Countess Isabella Salazar y Munatones (*d* 1969); 2nd, 1971, Marquise Isabella Francesca Fossi. *Educ:* College Lucerne; Univs of Lausanne, Munich, and Zürich (Doctor of Law). Attaché at Swiss Foreign Office and Sec. Swiss Advisory Cttee for League of Nations and post-war problems, 1918; Secretary of the Swiss Delegation to the League of Nations, 1920–25 (technical adviser, 1923–25); Sec. Swiss Delegation to Internat. Econ. Conf. of Genoa, 1922; Asst Prof. of Internat. Law, Univ. of Geneva, 1922–24; Legal Adviser to Swiss Delegation Conference for control of trade of arms, etc., 1925; Deputy Registrar Permanent Court of International Justice, 1926–28; Counsellor Swiss Legation in Rome, 1929–31; Head of Political Office Foreign Affairs Dept in Berne, 1931–33; 1st Counsellor of the Swiss Legation in Paris, 1933–36; Swiss Minister in Rome, 1936–42; Swiss Minister to Great Britain, 1944–48. Head of the Swiss Delegation for establishment of a

Convention between Switzerland and UN on diplomatic privileges and immunities of UNO establishments in Switzerland; member of Swiss Deleg. to last League of Nations Assembly, Geneva, 1946; President Internat. Committee of Red Cross, 1948–55, Chm. 1968–; Chm. ILO Committee on Forced Labour, 1956–60. Prof. of Human Rights, Univ. of Strasbourg, 1964. Member of: Perm. Court of Arbitration, 1948–; Curatorium of Acad. of Internat. Law, at The Hague (Hon. Mem., 1985–); Inst. of Internat. Law, 1967–69 (1st Vice-Pres., 1967–69; Hon. Mem., 1979); Commissions of Conciliation: between Switzerland and USA; between Switzerland and Spain; between France and the Netherlands; between Sweden and Denmark (Chm.); UN Nansen Medal Award Cttee, UN High Commn for Refugees, 1958–78. Ambassador, 1957; Chm. Swiss Deleg. to UN Conf. on Law of the Sea, Geneva, 1958 and 1960, and to UN Confs on Diplomatic Relations and Immunities, Vienna, 1961; on Consular Relations and Immunities, Vienna, 1963; on Law of Treaties, Vienna, 1968 and 1969; Chm. Cttee of UN Atomic Energy Agency, Vienna, on Civil Liability and Internat. Responsibility for Nuclear Hazards, 1959–62; Chm. ILO Arbitral Commn, Ghana-Portugal, 1961–62; Pres., prep. UN Conf., 1964, and of conf. of plenipotentiaries, New York, on transit trade of land-locked countries, 1965; Chm., Study Gp on Labour and Trade Union Situation in Spain, 1968–69. Hon. Pres., Acad. Mondiale pour la Paix, Nice, 1978. Gold Medal, Red Cross Internat. Cttee, and other Red Cross awards; Grand Cross of Merit, SMO Malta, 1949. *Publications:* The Nationality of Corporations in International Law, 1918; Terms of Civil Law in International Law, 1920; The Responsibility of States for Crimes committed on their Territory, 1923; The Practice of International Conciliation Committees, 1929; Foreign Administration as Institutional Function of Intercourse between States, 1934; The Economic Foundations of International Law, 1931; Switzerland's Economy and the British Empire, 1946; The Juridical Aspects of the Organisation of the International Red Cross, 1953; Swiss Neutrality and European Integration, 1953; Notes of the International Responsibility of States for Nuclear Hazards, in Mélanges Séféréades, 1961; Introduction to Max Huber's Denkwürdigkeiten, and book on Max Huber, 1974; Le Rôle Actuel et Futur des Commissions Internationales d'Enquête, 1980; L'aspiration à la paix et la vie internationale, 1986; (contrib.) Nouvelles réflexions sur la rôle des procédures internationales d'enquête, 1987. *Address:* Villa il Pino, 267 Via Bolognese, Florence, Italy; Palazzo Fossi, 16 Via de'Benci, Florence, Italy. *Club:* Circolo dell' Unione (Florence).                                    *Died 9 Aug. 1988.*

**RUETE, Dr jur. Hans Hellmuth;** Ambassador of the Federal Republic of Germany at the Court of St James's, 1977–79; *b* 21 Dec. 1914; *s* of Prof. Dr med. Alfred E. Ruete and Margarita (*née* Bohnstedt); *m* 1948, Ruth (*née* Arfsten); one *s* two *d. Educ:* Univs of Kiel, Lausanne, Marburg, Tokyo (Political Science and Law). Doctor's Degree in Law. Judge at Ministry of Justice in Hesse, 1949–50; then at Federal Min. of Justice; Federal Foreign Office, 1952–80; Tokyo, 1952–56; Bonn, 1956–60 (Head of Russian Desk); Center for International Affairs, Harvard Univ., 1960–61; Consul-Gen., Calcutta, 1961–64; Dept for Eastern Affairs, Bonn, 1964–70; Ambassador: Paris, 1970–72; Warsaw, 1972–77. *Publication:* Der Einfluss des abendländischen Rechts auf die Rechtsentwicklung in China und Japan, 1940. *Recreations:* music, literature, theatre. *Address:* Petersbergstrasse 64, 5300 Bonn-Bad Godesberg, Federal Republic of Germany.                                    *Died 19 June 1987.*

**RUGBY, 2nd Baron,** *cr* 1947, of Rugby; **Alan Loader Maffey;** farmer and inventor; *b* 16 April 1913; *s* of 1st Baron Rugby, GCMG, KCB, KCVO, CSI, CIE, and Dorothy Gladys, OBE 1919 (*d* 1973), *d* of late Charles Lang Huggins, JP, Hadlow Grange, Buxted; *S* father, 1969; *m* 1947, Margaret, *d* of late Harold Bindley; three *s* two *d* (and one *s* decd). *Educ:* Stowe. Joined Whitehall Securities, 1930; joined staff of British Airways, 1935 (also 604 (F) Sqn AAF, 1933); farmer, Trans Nzoia, Kenya, 1937; Flying Instructor, RAF, 1940–46; Fisheries Officer, Kenya Game Dept, 1946–47; Dairy and Mixed Farming, UK, 1947–; invented Landlog Distance Measurer (RASE Highly Commended) for calibration in agriculture, later developed for Marshall Report Highways Standardisation; invented and successfully demonstrated Foldgate Herd Handler for improved cattle handling technique (RASE Silver Medal, 1974). Active instigator and campaigner for removal of opticians' monopoly of spectacles. Mem., Sub Cttee on Environmental Studies, EEC, 1985–. Past Master, Saddlers' Co. *Heir:* s Hon. Robert Charles Maffey [*b* 4 May 1951; *m* 1974, Anne Penelope, *yr d* of late David Hale; two *s*]. *Address:* Grove Farm, Frankton, near Rugby, Warwicks.                                    *Died 12 Jan. 1990.*

**RUGG, Sir (Edward) Percy,** Kt 1959; JP; Councillor for Royal Borough of Kensington and Chelsea, Greater London Council, 1964–70; Leader of Conservative Party, on the Council, 1964–66; Chairman of Council, 1967–68; Councillor for Chelsea, LCC (Alderman, 1958–61; Leader of Conservative Party, on the LCC 1959–65); *b* 14 Jan. 1906; *s* of Albert Henry and Louise Rugg; *m* 1933, Elizabeth Frances Symes; two *s* one *d. Educ:* Leys Sch. Solicitor, 1929. Hertfordshire County Council, 1940–45. Chairman:

Hertford Division Conservative Association, 1948–52; Ware Rural District Council, 1949–54; Junior Carlton Club Political Council, 1954–57; Commercial Law and International Arbitration Committee of British National Committee of International Chamber of Commerce, 1957–; Gen. Purposes Cttee, GLC, 1969–70; Heathrow Airport Consultative Cttee, 1969–70; President: East Herts Conservative Assoc., 1961–81; Chelsea Conservative Assoc., 1974–83. Member: London Tourist Bd, 1968–69; BTA, 1969–. Vice-Pres. and Fellow, Game Conservancy, 1977–. JP, Herts, 1949–; DL Greater London, 1967–82. Dep. Kt Pres., Hon. Soc. of Knights of Round Table; Friend, RCP, 1973–. OStJ 1980. *Recreation:* fishing. *Address:* 703 Hawkins House, Dolphin Square, SW1V 3LX. *T:* 01–821 7620; The Black Horse, Sandwich, Kent. *T:* Sandwich 612184. *Clubs:* City Livery; Royal St George's (Sandwich).                                    *Died 7 Sept. 1986.*

**RUMBOLD, Sir (Horace) Anthony (Claude),** 10th Bt, *cr* 1779; KCMG 1962 (CMG 1953); KCVO 1969; CB 1955; HM Diplomatic Service, retired; *b* 7 March 1911; *s* of Right Hon. Sir Horace Rumbold, 9th Bt, GCB, GCMG, MVO, and Etheldred, Lady Rumbold, CBE (*d* 1964), 2nd *d* of Sir Edmund Fane, KCMG; *m* 1st, 1937, Felicity Ann (marr. diss. 1974) (*d* 1984), *yr d* of late Lt-Col F. G. Bailey and late Lady Janet Bailey, Lake House, Salisbury, Wilts; one *s* three *d*; 2nd, 1974, Mrs Pauline Graham, *d* of late Hon. David Tennant and of Hermione Baddeley. *Educ:* Eton; Magdalen College, Oxford (BA). Fellow, Queen's Coll., Oxford, 1933. Third Sec. in the Foreign Office, 1935; transferred to Washington, 1937; Second Secretary, 1940; transferred to Foreign Office, 1942; served on staff of Resident Minister, Mediterranean, 1944; First Sec., 1945; transferred Prague, 1947; transferred to Foreign Office as Counsellor, 1949; transferred to Paris as Counsellor, 1951; appointed Principal Private Secretary to Foreign Secretary, 1954; Assistant Under-Secretary of State, Foreign Office, 1957; British Minister in Paris, 1960–63; Ambassador to Thailand and UK Representative on the Council of SEATO, 1965–67; Ambassador to Austria, 1967–70. Commander of the Order of St Olaf, 1955; Grand Cross of Order of Merit, Austria, 1969. *Heir:* s Henry John Sebastian Rumbold [ *b* 24 Dec. 1947; *m* 1978, Mrs Holly Berry, *d* of late Dr A. Whitfield Hawkes and of Mrs Alistair Cooke]. *Address:* Var House, Stinsford, Dorchester, Dorset. *T:* Dorchester 62644. *Club:* Travellers'.                                    *Died 4 Dec. 1983.*

**RUNCIMAN OF DOXFORD, 2nd Viscount,** *cr* 1937; **Walter Leslie Runciman,** OBE 1946; AFC; AE; DL; Bt 1906; Baron Runciman, 1933, of Shoreston; *b* 26 Aug. 1900; *er s* of 1st Viscount Runciman of Doxford, PC, and Hilda (*d* 1956), MP (L) St Ives, 1928–29, *d* of J. C. Stevenson; *S* father, 1949; *m* 1st, 1923, Rosamond Nina (marr. diss. 1928), *d* of late Rudolph Chambers Lehmann, Fieldhead, Bourne End, Bucks; 2nd, 1932, Katherine Schuyler, *y d* of late Wm R. Garrison, New York; one *s. Educ:* Eton (King's Scholar); Trinity College, Cambridge (Scholar). Director, 1932, Dep. Chm., 1962–71, Lloyds Bank Ltd. Chm., North of England Shipowners Association, 1931–32 and 1970–71; Chairman of Council, Armstrong College, University of Durham, 1935–37; Director-General of British Overseas Airways Corporation, 1940–43; Air Commodore and Air Attaché, Tehran, 1943–46. Pres. Chamber of Shipping of the UK, and Chm. General Council of British Shipping, 1952; Mem. Air Transport Advisory Council, 1946–54, Vice-Chm., 1951–54; President, RINA, 1951–61; Mem. Shipping Advisory Panel, 1962. Chairman: Cttee on Horticultural Marketing, 1955–56; Trustees, Nat. Maritime Museum, 1962–72; Adv. Cttee on Historic Wreck Sites, 1973–86; British Hallmarking Council, 1974–82. Cdre, RYS, 1968–74. President: Marine Soc., 1974–89; Iran Soc., 1979–. Hon. Elder Brother of Trinity House. Hon. Mem., Hon. Co. of Master Mariners. DL Northumberland, 1961. Hon. DCL, Durham. *Recreations:* sailing, shooting. *Heir:* s Hon. Walter Garrison Runciman, *b* 10 Nov. 1934. *Address:* 46 Abbey Lodge, Park Road, NW8; Doxford, Chathill, Northumberland. *Clubs:* Brooks's; Royal Yacht Squadron.                                    *Died 1 Sept. 1989.*

**RUNDALL, Sir Francis (Brian Anthony),** GCMG 1968 (KCMG 1956; CMG 1951); OBE 1944; Ambassador to Japan, 1963–67; *b* 11 Sept. 1908; *s* of late Lieutenant-Colonel Charles Frank Rundall, CMG, DSO; *m* 1935, Mary, *d* of late Frank Syrett, MD; one *s* one *d. Educ:* Marlborough College; Peterhouse, Cambridge. Entered General Consular Service, 1930; served in Antwerp, Colon, Panama, Boston, Barcelona, Piraeus; Consul, New York, 1944; transferred Foreign Office, 1946; HM Inspector of Foreign Service Establishments, 1949–53. Chief Administrative Officer, UK High Commission in Germany during 1953; Consul-General in New York, 1953–57; Ambassador to Israel, 1957–59; Deputy Under-Secretary of State, Foreign Office, 1959–63. *Address:* Osborne House, East Cowes, Isle of Wight. *Club:* Travellers'.                                    *Died 7 July 1987.*

**RUNDLE, David John,** OBE 1986; Director, British Institute of Florence, since 1981; *b* 21 July 1938; *s* of Richard Norman Rundle and Ivy Evelyn Rundle (*née* Cole); *m* 1963, Charlotte Fallenius (marr. diss. 1979); two *s*; *m* 1987, Teresa Leiferman. *Educ:* Tavistock Sch., Devon; Jesus Coll., Cambridge (BA, MA); Univ. of Leeds

(DipEd, MTEFL 1965). Lektor for British Centre, Sweden, 1961–63; Tutor, English Language Centre, Hove, 1963–64; joined British Council career service, 1965; seconded to Zambian Min. of Educn, Lusaka, 1965–67; Education Officer, Amman, Jordan, 1967–70; Director of Studies, Milan, 1970–75; Regional Director: E Midlands, 1975–79; Munich, 1979–81; on leave of absence, 1981–. Senatore Accademico dell' Accademia Internazionale Medicea, Florence, 1984–. *Publications:* An English Medium Course for Zambia, 1967; articles on cultural diplomacy and teaching of English. *Recreations:* theatre, window-boxing, travel. *Address:* Via Santo Spirito 15, Florence, Italy. *T:* (055) 291978. *Club:* Circolo dell' Unione (Florence). *Died* 1 *May* 1987.

**RUOFF, Theodore Burton Fox,** CB 1970; CBE 1962; Chief Land Registrar, 1963–75; *b* 12 April 1910; *s* of late Percy Ruoff and late Edith Crane; *m* 1947, Marjorie Alice (*d* 1990), *er d* of late George Mawson, Worthing; no *c*. *Educ:* Clarence School, Weston-super-Mare; King Edward VI School, Bury St Edmunds. Admitted as a solicitor, 1933; 2nd class Hons; Hertfordshire Law Society prizeman; Nuffield Fellowship in Australia and New Zealand, 1951–52; Senior Land Registrar of HM Land Registry, 1958. Founder Mem., 1974, and first Hon. Mem., 1982, Soc. for Computers and Law (Mem. Council, 1974–80); Consultant, Oyez Computers Ltd, 1975–85; Consultant, Law Society's Wkg Party on Law Office Management and Technology (formerly Special Cttee on Computer Services), 1985–87 (Mem., 1976–85); Special Adviser on Conveyancing to Royal Commn on Legal Services, 1976–79. Editor, Computers and Law, 1978–82. *Publications:* An Englishman Looks at the Torrens System, 1957; Curtis and Ruoff's The Law and Practice of Registered Conveyancing, 1958, 2nd edn 1965; Concise Land Registration Practice, 1959, 3rd edn (with C. West), 1982; Rentcharges in Registered Conveyancing, 1961; Land Registration Forms, 1962, 3rd edn (with C. West), 1983; (with R. B. Roper and others) Ruoff and Roper's Registered Conveyancing, 1972, 5th edn 1986; Searching without Tears: The Land Charges Computer, 1974; The Solicitor and the Silicon Chip, 1981; (Gen. Ed.) Fourmat Legal Directory, 1981; The Solicitor and the Automated Office, 1984; Legal Legends and Other True Stories, 1988; (with E. J. Pryer) Ruoff's Land Registration Handbook, 1990; regular contribs to Australian Law Jl, Victoria Law Inst. Jl, Newsletter of the Law Soc. of ACT, Law Soc.'s Gazette, Solicitors' Jl. *Recreations:* sketching, indifferent golf, gardening, making talking cassettes for the blind. *Address:* Flat One, 83 South Hill Park, Hampstead, NW3 2SS. *T:* 071–435 8014. *Clubs:* Travellers', MCC. *Died* 6 *Nov.* 1990.

**RUPP, Rev. Prof. (Ernest) Gordon,** MA, DD; FBA 1970; Dixie Professor of Ecclesiastical History, University of Cambridge, 1968–77, then Emeritus Professor; Fellow of Emmanuel College, Cambridge, 1968–77, Hon. Fellow 1983; Principal, Wesley House, Cambridge, 1967–74; *b* 7 Jan. 1910; *m* 1938, Marjorie Hibbard; one *s*. *Educ:* Owen's School, EC; King's College, London (BA); Wesley House, Cambridge (MA, BD 1946, DD Cantab 1955); Universities of Strasbourg and Basel. Methodist Minister, Chislehurst, Kent, 1938–46; Wesley House, Cambridge, 1946–47; Richmond College, Surrey, 1947–52; Birkbeck Lectr, Trinity Coll., Cambridge, 1947; Lecturer in Divinity, Cambridge Univ., 1952–56; Prof. of Ecclesiastical History, Univ. of Manchester, 1956–67. President of the Methodist Conference, 1968–69; Mem., Central Cttee of World Council of Churches, 1969. Hon. Fellow: Fitzwilliam College, 1969; King's Coll., London, 1969. Hon. DD: Aberdeen; Manchester, 1979; Hon. Dr Théol, Paris. *Publications:* Studies in the English Protestant Tradition, 1947; Luther's Progress to the Diet of Worms, 1951; The Righteousness of God (Luther studies), 1953; Some Makers of English Religion, 1957; The Old Reformation and the New, 1967; Patterns of Reformation, 1969; Just Men, 1977; Thomas More, 1978; Religion in England 1688–1791, 1986. *Address:* 42 Malcolm Place, King Street, Cambridge. *Died* 19 *Dec.* 1986.

**RUSBY, Norman Lloyd,** MA, DM Oxon, FRCP; Consulting Physician: London Hospital since 1970 (Physician, 1946–70); London Chest Hospital since 1970 (Physician, 1936–70); Benenden Chest Hospital (Civil Service); Emeritus Consultant, King Edward VII Hospital, Midhurst; Emeritus Civil Consultant in Diseases of the Chest to the Royal Navy; *b* 26 October 1905; *s* of Dr Edward L. M. Rusby, Streatham and Katharine Helen Rusby (*née* Wright); *m* 1941 Elizabeth, *e d* of F. A. Broadhead, FRIBA, Nottingham; three *s*. *Educ:* Lancing College; St John's College, Oxford; St Thomas's Hospital. BA (Hons) Oxon, 1928, MA 1931; DM 1941; BM, BCh 1931. Res. appts, St Thomas' Hosp.; Res. MO and Registrar, London Chest Hosp., 1934–36; Medical Registrar and Tutor, British Postgraduate Medical School, Hammersmith, 1937–39. Member Standing Advisory Committee on Tuberculosis to Min. of Health, 1940–44; Editor of Tubercle, 1938–44; Physician, EMS, 1939; RAMC Med. specialist, 21 Army Gp, 1944–45; Officer i/c Med. Div., ME Chest Unit, 1945–46; Local Brigadier, Consulting Physician Middle East Land Forces, 1946. Nuffield visitor to East Africa, 1950, 1953. Lecturer for British Council: Poland, 1959; Malta, 1966; Nepal, India and Afghanistan, 1973. Examiner in

Medicine: Univ. of London, 1951–56; Univ. of Cambridge, 1957–60; Univ. of W Indies, 1967; RCP, 1962–68. Councillor, RCP, 1964–66; Mitchell Lecturer, RCP, 1967. Member: Attendance Allowance Bd and Med. Appeal Tribunal, 1970–77; Council, Chest, Heart and Stroke Assoc. (Vice-Chm., 1957–77); Council, British Heart Foundn; Council, Metropolitan Hosp. Sunday Fund, 1973–75; Assoc. of Physicians of Gt Britain and Ireland; Hon. Mem., Brit. Thoracic Soc. Mem., Board of Governors: Hospitals for Diseases of the Chest, 1962–67; London Hospital, 1967–70. *Publications:* (jtly) Recent Advances in Respiratory Tuberculosis, 4th and 5th edns, (ed jtly) 6th edn 1968; contributions to various journals, chiefly on diseases of the chest. *Recreations:* history, English literature, entomology. *Address:* 21 Windmill Hill, Hampstead, NW3. *T:* 01–794 6889. *Clubs:* United Oxford & Cambridge University, MCC. *Died* 22 *Nov.* 1988.

**RUSH, His Honour (Edward Antisell) Michael (Stanistreet);** a Circuit Judge, 1980–84; *b* 27 March 1933; *s* of Edward Antisell Evans Rush and Karen (*née* Kröyer Copenhagen). *Educ:* St John's Sch., Leatherhead; Queen's Univ., Belfast; Inns of Court Sch. of Law. Pres., Inns of Court Students' Union, 1958; called to the Bar, Lincoln's Inn, 1958 (Sir Thomas More Scholar). Commissioned, Grenadier Guards, 1958–61. Oxford Circuit, 1961–71 (Junior, 1966); Midland and Oxford Circuit, 1972–80. A Recorder of the Crown Court, 1978–80. Mem., Council on Tribunals, 1986–. *Address:* 2 Harcourt Buildings, Temple, EC4Y 9DB. *Died* 28 *Feb.* 1988.

**RUSHTON, Frederick Alan;** formerly Chief General Manager and Director, District Bank Ltd, Manchester; *b* 15 Feb. 1905; *s* of Frederick and Elizabeth Rushton; *m* 1st, 1931, Eirene Williams (*d* 1982); two *s*; 2nd, 1982, Ethna Lawton Riley. *Educ:* University Sch., Southport, Lancs. Mem. Court, Univ. of Manchester. FIB. *Recreations:* foreign travel, gardening. *Address:* Briarfield, Moss Road, Alderley Edge, Cheshire SK9 7JB. *T:* Alderley Edge 583311. *Died* 25 *Sept.* 1982.

**RUSKA, Dr Ernst August Friedrich;** Director, Fritz Haber Institute, Max Planck Society for Advancement of Science, Berlin, 1957–74, now Director Emeritus; *b* Heidelberg, 25 Dec. 1906; *s* of Dr Julius Ruska and Elisabeth Ruska (*née* Merx); *m* 1937, Irmel Geigis; two *s* one *d*. *Educ:* Heidelberg Gymnasium; Tech. Hochschcule, Munich; Tech. Hochscule, Berlin (DrIng 1934, DrIng habil 1944). Research work on high voltage and vacuum techniques; development work on high performance cathode ray oscillographs; pioneered first electron microscope; with Fernseh AG Berlin, 1933–37, Siemens Halske AG Berlin, 1937–55; joined German Acad. of Science, 1947, later Fritz Haber Inst., Director, 1957. Lecturer: Tech. Univ. Berlin, 1949–71 (Extraord. Prof., 1959); Freie Univ. Berlin, 1949–71 (Hon. Prof. 1949). Hon. degrees from German and foreign univs. Senckenberg Prize, Univ. Frankfurt am-M., 1939; (with J. Hillier) Albert Lasker Prize, APHA, San Francisco, 1960; Diesel Gold Medal, Nürnberg, 1968; (with brother, Dr Helmut Ruska) Paul Ehrlich Prize, 1970; Duddel Medal, Inst. Physics, London, 1975; Cothenius Medal, Leopoldina, 1975; Albrecht von Gräfe Medal, Berlin Med. Soc., 1983; Dist. Scientist Award, Electron Micr. Soc., USA, 1985; Robert Koch Gold Medal, 1986; Nobel Prize for Physics (jointly), 1986. *Publications:* Der frühe Entwicklung der Elektronenlinsen und der Elektronenmikroskopie, 1979 (The Early Development of Electron Lenses and Electron Microscopy, 1980); numerous papers in learned journals. *Recreations:* classical music, literature, history, politics. *Address:* Max-Eyth-Strasse 20, D1000 Berlin 33, Federal Republic of Germany. *T:* 0049–030–8328770. *Died* 27 *May* 1988.

**RUSSELL,** 4th Earl *cr* 1861; **John Conrad Russell;** Viscount Amberley, 1861; *b* 16 Nov. 1921; *er s* of 3rd Earl Russell, OM, FRS, and Dora Winifred, MBE (*d* 1986), *d* of late Sir Frederick Black, KCB; *S* father, 1970; *m* 1946, Susan Doniphan (marr. diss. 1954), *d* of late Vachel Lindsay; one *d* (and one *d* decd). *Educ:* Beacon Hill Sch., 1927–34; Dartington Hall Sch., 1934–39; University of California, Los Angeles, 1939–41; Harvard University, 1941–43. Served War of 1939–45, in RNVR, 1943–46; Temp. Admin. Asst, FAO of the United Nations, Washington, DC, 1946–47; temp. Admin. Asst, HM Treasury, 1947–49. Took his seat in the House of Lords, 12 May 1976. *Heir: half-brother* Hon. Conrad Sebastian Robert Russell. *Address:* Carn Voel, Porthcurno, near Penzance, Cornwall. *Died* 16 *Dec.* 1987.

**RUSSELL OF KILLOWEN,** Baron *cr* 1975 (Life Peer), of Killowen, Co. Down; **Charles Ritchie Russell,** PC 1962; Kt 1960; a Lord of Appeal in Ordinary, 1975–82; *b* 12 Jan. 1908; *s* of Francis Xavier, Baron Russell of Killowen, Lord of Appeal in Ordinary (*s* of Charles, Baron Russell of Killowen, Lord Chief Justice of England) and Mary Emily Ritchie (*d* of 1st Baron Ritchie of Dundee, former Chancellor of Exchequer); *m* 1933, Joan Elisabeth (*d* 1976), *d* of late Dr J. A. Torrens, MD, FRCP; two *s* one *d*; *m* 1979, Elizabeth Cecilia, *widow* of His Honour Judge Laughton-Scott, QC. *Educ:* Beaumont; Oriel College, Oxford. Called to Bar, Lincoln's Inn,

1931; QC 1948; Bencher, 1952; Treasurer, 1972. Army, 1939–45; RA (Airborne) (despatches, French Croix de Guerre with star). Attorney-General to the Duchy of Cornwall, 1951–60; Judge of Chancery Division, High Court of Justice, 1960–62; a Lord Justice of Appeal, 1962–75. President, Restrictive Practices Court, 1961–62 (Member, 1960–62). *Recreation:* golf. *Address:* Orchard House, Sheepdown, Petworth, West Sussex. *T:* Petworth 42657. *Club:* Garrick. *Died 23 June 1986.*

**RUSSELL OF LIVERPOOL, 2nd Baron,** *cr* 1919; **Brig. Edward Frederick Langley Russell,** CBE 1945 (OBE 1943); MC; Barrister-at-Law, Gray's Inn, 1931; *b* 10 April 1895; *o s* of Richard Henry Langley Russell and Mabel Younge; *S* grandfather, 1920; *m* 1st, 1920, Constance Claudine (marr. diss. 1933), *yr d* of late Col Philip Cecil Harcourt Gordon, CMG; one *d* (one *s* decd); 2nd, 1933, Joan Betty (marr. diss. 1946), *d* of late Dr David Ewart, OBE, MD, FRCS, Chichester; one *d*; 3rd, 1946, Alix (*d* 1971), *o d* of Marquis de Bréviaire d'Alaincourt, and *widow* of Comte Bernard de Richard d'Ivry; 4th, 1972, Mrs A. W. Brayley (*d* 1977). *Educ:* Liverpool Coll.; St John's Coll., Oxford. Served European War, 1914–18 (MC and two bars); War of 1939–45 (despatches, OBE, CBE); Brig. (retd) ADJAG, BEF, 1939–40; DJAG, HQ First Army, 1942–43; Allied Force HQ, 1943–45; GHQ Middle East Forces, 1945–46; HQ BAOR, 1946–47, 1948–51; Assistant Judge Advocate General, 1951–54. Officier de la Légion d'Honneur, 1960. *Publications:* The Scourge of the Swastika, 1954; Though the Heavens Fall, 1956; The Knights of Bushido, 1958; That Reminds Me, 1959; If I forget Thee, 1960; The Royal Conscience, 1961; The Trial of Adolf Eichmann, 1962; The Tragedy of the Congo, 1962; South Africa Today-and Tomorrow?, 1963; The Knight of the Sword, 1964; Deadman's Hill, 1965; Caroline the Unhappy Queen, 1967; Return of the Swastika?, 1968; Henry of Navarre, 1969; The French Corsairs, 1970. *Heir: g s* Simon Gordon Jared Russell, *b* 30 Aug. 1952. *Address:* 9 Eversfield Place, St Leonards-on-Sea, East Sussex. *Died 8 April 1981.*

**RUSSELL, Alan;** *b* 5 Dec. 1910; *s* of late Hon. Cyril Russell; *m* 1st, 1937, Grace Evelyn Moore (decd); one *d*; 2nd, 1944, Jean Patricia, *widow* of Wing Comdr J. R. Cridland, AAF, and *d* of late Stafford Croom Johnson, JP; one step *s* one *s*. *Educ:* Beaumont. Joined Helbert Wagg & Co. Ltd, 1929. Served War of 1939–45, in Army, London Scottish, Lt-Col, attached US Army, Europe, 1941–45. Director: Helbert Wagg & Co. Ltd, 1946–62; District Bank Ltd, 1948–70; Alexanders Discount Co. Ltd, 1948–79; IBM United Kingdom Ltd, 1956–79; Legal & General Assurance Society Ltd, 1958–76; J. Henry Schroder & Co. Ltd, 1960–62; United Molasses Co. Ltd, 1962–66; J. Henry Schroder Wagg & Co. Ltd, 1962–70; Turner & Newall Ltd, 1962–75; Schroders Ltd, 1963–70; Yorkshire Bank Ltd, 1965–79; National Westminster Bank Ltd, 1968–79. *Address:* 23 Park Lane, Aldeburgh, Suffolk. *Died 27 Oct. 1986.*

**RUSSELL, Audrey;** *see* Russell, M. A.

**RUSSELL, Dorothy Stuart,** MD (London); MA (Oxon); ScD (Cantab); LLD (Glasgow); DSc (McGill); FRCP; retired 1960; Director of Bernhard Baron Institute of Pathology, London Hospital; Professor of Morbid Anatomy in University of London, 1946–60, Emeritus Professor, 1960; Hon. Fellow: Girton College, Cambridge; St Hugh's College, Oxford; *b* 27 June 1895; 2nd *d* of late Philip Stuart Russell, Sydney, NSW, and Alice Louisa, *d* of William Cave. *Educ:* Perse High School for Girls, Cambridge; Girton College, Cambridge; London Hospital. Natural Sciences Tripos, Part I, Class I, 1918; Gilchrist Studentship, Girton College, 1918; Sutton Prize in Pathology and Clinical Obstetrics and Gynæcology Prize, London Hospital, 1921; Junior Beit Fellow, 1923–26, attached to Bernhard Baron Institute of Pathology, London Hospital, and subsequently with grants from Medical Research Council; Rockefeller Travelling Fellow, 1928–29, at Boston, Mass, and Montreal; Medical Research Council, Scientific Staff, 1933–46. Attached to Nuffield Dept of Surgery, Oxford, 1940–44; returned to London Hospital, Oct. 1944. John Hunter Medal and Triennial Prize, Royal College of Surgeons, 1934, for work on the kidney and the brain; Oliver-Sharpey Prize, RCP, 1968, for research. Hon. FRCPath 1973. *Publications:* Tumours of the Nervous System; papers in pathology to various journals. *Address:* Holcombe End, Westcott, Dorking, Surrey. *Died 19 Oct. 1983.*

**RUSSELL, Sir (Edward) Lionel,** Kt 1962; CBE 1953; *b* 8 May 1903; *s* of Edward and Kate Russell, Bristol. *Educ:* Clifton College; Christ's College, Cambridge. Lecturer in English, Univ. of Lund, Sweden, 1925–31; Assistant Master, Charterhouse, 1932–35; Asst Director of Education, Liverpool, 1935–38; Asst Education Officer, Birmingham, 1938–46; Chief Education Officer, Birmingham, 1946–68. Member: Univ. Grants Cttee, 1954–63; Council for Nat. Academic Awards, 1964–70; Nat. Cttee for Commonwealth Immigrants, 1965–68; Chairman: Inquiry into Adult Educn in England and Wales, 1969–73; Centre for Educnl Develt Overseas, 1970–74; Nat. Adv. Council on Educn for Industry and Commerce,

1975–77; Youth Employment Service Training Bd, 1970–75. Pres., Assoc. of Chief Education Officers, 1955–57. Chm., Bristol Folk House, 1977–80. Hon. ACT Birmingham, 1962; Hon. DEd CNAA, 1969; Hon. DLitt Warwick, 1974; Hon. LLD Birmingham, 1975. *Address:* 24 Tyndall's Park Road, Bristol BS8 1PY. *T:* Bristol 37121. *Club:* Athenæum. *Died 26 Dec. 1983.*

**RUSSELL, Sir Frederick (Stratten),** Kt 1965; CBE 1955; DSC, DFC; FRS 1938; BA Cantab; Secretary to Marine Biological Association of the United Kingdom and Director of the Plymouth Laboratory, 1945–65, retd; *b* Bridport, 3 Nov. 1897; *y s* of late William Russell, MA Oxon, Newquay, and late Lucy Binfield, *d* of Henry Newman, Liverpool; *m* 1923, Gweneth, MBE (*d* 1979), *d* of late John and late Mary Barnhouse Moy Evans; one *s*. *Educ:* Oundle School; Gonville and Caius College, Cambridge (Hon. Fellow 1965). Served European War, RNAS and RAF, 1916–18 (DSC, DFC, French Croix de Guerre avec Palme); Interallied Belgian Coast Defence Committee, 1919; Assistant Director of Fisheries Research to Government of Egypt, 1922–23; on scientific staff of Marine Biological Association's Laboratory, Plymouth, Devon, 1924–65; Great Barrier Reef Expedition, 1928–29; served War of 1939–45 as Wing Comdr on Air Staff Intelligence, 1940–45. Colonial Fisheries Advisory Cttee, 1945–61; Min. Overseas Devlt Fisheries Advisory Panel, 1961–; National Oceanographic Council, 1950–65; Chairman, Advisory Panel on biological research to Central Electricity Generating Board, 1962–75; Trustee, Nat. Maritime Museum, 1965–72; Pres. Devonshire Association, 1953. Editor: Journal of Marine Biological Association, 1945–65; Advances in Marine Biology, 1962–. Hon. FIBiol. 1981. Hon. LLD Glasgow, 1957; Hon. DSc: Exeter, 1960; Birmingham, 1966; Bristol, 1972. Coronation Medal. Linnean Soc. Gold Medal, 1961. For. Mem. Roy. Danish Acad.; Hon. Member: Physiological Soc.; Challenger Soc.; Fisheries Soc. of British Isles. *Publications:* The Seas (with C. M. Yonge), 1928; The Medusae of the British Isles, 1953, vol II, 1970; The Eggs and Planktonic Stages of British Marine Fishes, 1976; numerous scientific publications on biology of marine plankton invertebrates and fishes, in scientific journals, and on marine biology in Britannica Book of The Year, 1949–70. *Recreations:* once golf, angling, sketching; later painting only. *Address:* Thames Bank, Thames Road, Goring-on-Thames, Reading RG8 9AH. *T:* Goring 873848. *Died 5 June 1984.*

**RUSSELL, His Honour Henry Stanway;** a Circuit Judge (formerly County Court Judge), 1965–80; *b* 27 April 1910; *s* of William Stanway Russell and late Dorothy Sophia Taylor; *m* 1937, Norah Patricia Knight Tapson; two *d*. *Educ:* Haileybury College; Merton College, Oxford. Called to Bar Inner Temple, 1934; Western Circuit, 1934. 1st Derbyshire Yeomanry RAC (Lieut). Served Tunisia and Italy, 1942–44. Capt., Judge Advocate General's Dept., 1945; Dep. Chm., Cornwall QS, 1963–71. *Address:* Field Farm House, Bibury, Cirencester, Glos. *Died 9 Aug. 1985.*

**RUSSELL, Sir John (Wriothesley),** GCVO 1968 (KCVO 1965); CMG 1958; HM Diplomatic Service, retired; Chairman, Elf Aquitaine UK (Holdings), since 1981; *b* 22 Aug. 1914; *s* of late Sir Thomas Russell Pasha, KBE, CMG; *m* 1945, Aliki Diplarakos, Athens, Greece; one *s* one *d*. *Educ:* Eton; Trinity Coll., Cambridge (MA). Entered HM Diplomatic Service, 1937; 3rd Sec.: Foreign Office, 1937, Vienna, 1937, Foreign Office, 1938, Moscow, 1939; 2nd Sec., Washington, 1942; 1st Sec.: Warsaw, 1945, Foreign Office, 1948; First Dir-Gen., Brussels Treaty Orgn, London, 1948. Rome, 1950; Counsellor, 1953, and Dir Gen. British Information Services, New York; Counsellor, HM Embassy, Teheran, 1956–59; Foreign Office Spokesman (Head of News Dept, Foreign Office) 1959–62; Ambassador: to Ethiopia, 1962–66; to Brazil, 1966–69; to Spain, 1969–74. Foreign Affairs Adviser, Rolls Royce Ltd, 1974–79. Montagu Burton Vis. Prof. of International Relations, Univ. of Edinburgh, 1980. Chm., Anglo-Spanish Soc., 1980. Joint Master, West Street Foxhounds, 1959–84. Coronation Medal, 1953. Order of the Throne, Iran; Order of the Star of Ethiopia; Order of the Southern Cross, Brazil. *Address:* 80 Chester Square, SW1W 9DU. *T:* 01-730 3355; The Vine Farm, Northbourne, Kent. *T:* Deal 4794. *Clubs:* Beefsteak, White's, Garrick. *Died 3 Aug. 1984.*

**RUSSELL, Hon. Leopold Oliver,** CBE 1970 (OBE 1944); TD; Chairman, Cement Makers' Federation, 1979–86; *b* 26 Jan. 1907; 4th *s* of 2nd Baron Ampthill, GCSI, GCIE; *m* 1st, 1935, Rosemary Wintour (marr. diss. 1954); no *c*; 2nd, 1987, Joanna Christina Gleeson. *Educ:* Eton. Weekly newspaper publishing company, 1925–38; served War of 1939–45, 5th Battalion Beds and Herts Regiment TA; Gen. Staff appts HQ 18th Div., Eastern Command, South-Eastern Command, GHQ Home Forces, HQ 21st Army Group, and CCG; released with rank of Brigadier; Asst Sec. to Board of Trade, 1946–47; Dir, British Institute of Management, 1947–56. Dir-Gen., Cement and Concrete Assoc., 1958–77, Chm. 1976–80. Chm., E Anglian RHA, 1973–78; Member: Bd of Governors, Nat. Hosps for Nervous Diseases, 1963–76; E Anglian Regional Hosp. Bd, 1972–73. *Address:* 17 Onslow Square, SW7. *T:* 01–589 0891; The Old Rectory, Kettlebaston, Ipswich, Suffolk. *T:*

Bildeston 740314. *Clubs:* Brooks's, Buck's, Beefsteak, Pratt's.
*Died* 25 Jan. 1989.

**RUSSELL, Sir Lionel;** *see* Russell, Sir E. L.

**RUSSELL, (Muriel) Audrey,** MVO 1976; broadcaster, radio and television; *o d* of late John Strangman Russell and Muriel Russell (*née* Metcalfe), Co Dublin; *b* 29 June 1906; unmarried. *Educ:* privately, in England, and France. Trained Central School of Speech and Drama. First stage appearance in London in Victoria Regina, Lyric, 1937. National Fire Service, 1939–42; joined war-time staff, BBC, 1942; accredited BBC war correspondent overseas, 1944–45; news reporter, BBC 1946–51. Commentaries on State occasions have included: Funeral of King George VI at Windsor; the Coronation of Queen Elizabeth II in Westminster Abbey; Royal weddings: Princess Elizabeth; Princess Margaret; Princess Alexandra; Duke of Kent; Princess Anne; Prince Charles, Prince of Wales (for CBC); Funeral of Sir Winston Churchill in St Paul's; Royal Silver Wedding, 1972; Silver Jubilee, 1977; opening of Humber Bridge, 1981. BBC Commentator, 1953–: on Commonwealth Tours of the Queen and Duke of Edinburgh to Bermuda, NZ, Australia, Uganda, Malta, Canada, Nigeria, India, Pakistan, Ghana, Sierra Leone, Tanganyika; visits of Queen Elizabeth the Queen Mother to Central and E Africa; State Visits include: Oslo, 1955; Stockholm, 1956; Lisbon, Paris, Copenhagen, USA, 1957; Amsterdam, 1958; Nepal, Iran, Italy, 1961; W Germany, 1965; Austria, 1969; France, 1972. Royal Maundy Distribution broadcasts, 1952–78; numerous TV appearances in connection with history, art, and Royal occasions. FRSA. Freeman of City of London, 1967. *Publication:* A Certain Voice (autobiog.), 1984. *Recreations:* painting in oils, and visiting art galleries. *Address:* c/o F. R. A. Holman Esq., Roche Hardcastles, 29 Bedford Row, WC1R 4HE. *Died* 8 Aug. 1989.

**RUSSELL, Richard Drew,** RDI 1944; Professor of Furniture Design, Royal College of Art, 1948–64; Professor Emeritus, 1964; Consultant Industrial Designer; *b* 21 Dec. 1903; *s* of Sydney Bolton Russell and Elizabeth Russell (*née* Shefford); *m* 1933, Marian Pepler; two *s* one *d*. *Educ:* Dean Close School, Cheltenham. Trained at Architectural Association School; joined Gordon Russell Ltd, 1929, eventually becoming Director in charge of design; joined Murphy Radio Ltd as staff industrial designer, 1934; set up in private practice in London as consultant industrial designer, 1936; joined RNVR to work on camouflage of ships, 1942; resumed private practice in London as designer, 1946. FSIA, 1946; Master of Faculty, RDI, 1957–59. *Recreation:* gardens. *Address:* Falcon Cottage, Falcon Lane, Ditchingham, Bungay, Suffolk NR35 2JG.
*Died* 16 Oct. 1981.

**RUSSELL-SMITH, Dame Enid (Mary Russell),** DBE 1953; MA; Principal of St Aidan's College, Durham University, 1963–70; Hon. part-time Lecturer in Politics, 1964–86, retired; *b* 3 March 1903; *d* of late Arthur Russell-Smith, of Hartfield, Sussex. *Educ:* St Felix Sch., Southwold, Suffolk; Newnham Coll., Cambridge. Modern Languages Tripos (French and German). Entered Civil Service as Assistant Principal in Ministry of Health, 1925. Deputy Secretary, Ministry of Health, 1956–63. Co-opted Mem., Teesside (later Cleveland) Educn Cttee, 1968–75; Chairman: Sunderland Church Commn., 1971; Durham County Conservation Trust, 1973–75; St Paul's Jarrow Develt Trust, 1975–80. Associate Fellow, Newnham College, 1956–72, Hon. Fellow, 1974. Hon. DCL Durham, 1985. *Publication:* Modern Bureaucracy: the Home Civil Service, 1974. *Address:* 3 Pimlico, Durham DH1 4QW. *Club:* University Women's. *Died* 12 July 1989.

**RUSSO, Sir Peter (George),** Kt 1964; CBE 1953 (OBE 1939); JP; Barrister-at-Law; Minister of Housing and Economic Development, Gibraltar Council, 1964–68; *b* 1899; *s* of George Russo; *m* 1926, Margot, *d* of late John A. Imossi, Gibraltar; one *d*. Mem. various Govt bodies and cttees; Dir of several local cos; Trustee, John Mackintosh Foundation; past Chm. City Council, former Mem. Exec. Council, Gibraltar. JP Gibraltar, 1947–. *Address:* 2 Red Sands Road, Gibraltar. *T:* Gibraltar 5622. *Club:* Royal Gibraltar Yacht (past Cdre).

**RUSTON, Rev. Canon (Cuthbert) Mark;** Vicar, Holy Sepulchre with All Saints (The Round Church), Cambridge, 1955–87, retired; Chaplain to The Queen, 1980–86; *b* 23 Aug. 1916; *s* of Samuel Montague Ruston and Florence Mary Ruston, MBE. *Educ:* Tonbridge Sch.; Jesus Coll., Cambridge (Lady Kaye Schol. 1937; BA 1939, MA 1940); Ridley Hall, Cambridge. Curate, St John's, Woking, 1940–42; Chaplain: Cheltenham Coll., 1942–51; Jesus Coll., Cambridge, 1951–53; Emmanuel Coll., Cambridge, 1953–54. *Recreation:* inland waters cruising. *Address:* 12 Beaufort Place, Thompson's Lane, Cambridge CB5 8AG. *T:* Cambridge 357931. *Club:* Commonwealth Trust. *Died* 3 Jan. 1990.

**RUTHVEN OF FREELAND, Lady,** 11th in line, Scot. *cr* 1651; **Bridget Helen Monckton, (The Dowager Viscountess Monckton of Brenchley),** CBE 1947; *b* 27 July 1896; *e d* of 10th Lord Ruthven,

CB, CMG, DSO and Jean Leslie (*d* 1952), *d* of Norman George Lampson; *S* father 1956; *m* 1st, 1918, 11th Earl of Carlisle (marr. diss., 1947; he *d* 1963); one *s* one *d*; 2nd, 1947 (as Sir Walter Monckton), 1st Viscount Monckton of Brenchley, PC, GCVO, KCMG, MC, QC (*d* 1965). Joined ATS, 1938, as Sen. Comdr; promoted Controller, 1941; Dir Women's Auxilliary Corps (India), 1944–46, with rank of Sen. Controller. Governor, St George's Hosp., 1952–69; Mem. SE Metropolitan Regional Hosp. Board, 1953–71; Governor, Bethlem Royal Hosp. and the Maudsley Hosp., 1957–71; Member: St Francis and Lady Chichester Hosp. Management Cttees, 1959–68; Mid-Sussex Hosp. Management Cttee, 1965–68; Hellingley Hosp., Hailsham, 1970–71; Chm. Nat. Assoc. of Leagues of Hosp. Friends, 1962. Formerly Mem. Court, Sussex Univ. Victory Medal, 1946. *Heir:* s Earl of Carlisle. *Address:* c/o The Earl of Carlisle, Naworth Castle, Brampton, Cumbria.
*Died* 17 April 1982.

**RYAN, Arthur James,** CBE 1953; Regional Director, London Postal Region, 1949–60, retired; *b* 10 Oct. 1900; *e s* of late Stephen James Ryan, Little Common, Bexhill on Sea, Sx; *m* 1926, Marjorie (decd), *y d* of late George James Dee; two *d*. *Educ:* City of London College and privately. Clerk, Headquarters, GPO London, 1918; Asst Surveyor, GPO, Class II, 1926, Class I, 1935; served in N Wales, Eastern Counties, South Western District; Chief Superintendent, then Assistant Controller, 1936, Controller (Mails and Transport), 1941, London Postal Region; Assistant Secretary, Min. of Fuel and Power (on loan), 1941; Dep. Regional Director, London Postal Region, 1944; Member of Post Office Board, 1950. Freeman, City of London. *Recreations:* golf, gardening. *Address:* Lindon House, 2 Pound Avenue, Old Stevenage, Herts SG1 3JA. *T:* Stevenage 318513. *Died* 12 Jan. 1990.

**RYAN, Sir Derek Gerald,** 3rd Bt, *cr* 1919; *b* 9 July 1922; *s* of Sir Gerald Ellis Ryan, 2nd Bt, and Hylda Winifryde Herapath; *S* father 1947; *m* 1st, 1947, Penelope Anne Hawkings (marr. diss. 1971); one *s* three *d*; 2nd, 1972, Katja, *d* of Ernst Best. *Educ:* Harrow. Served War of 1939–45. Lieut Grenadier Guards, 1941–45. *Heir:* s Derek Gerald Ryan, Junior, *b* 25 March 1954. *Address:* 6228 Eltville, Scharfensteinstrasse 36, W Germany. *T:* 06123–5333.
*Died* 1 March 1990.

**RYAN, Most Rev. Dermot;** Pro-Prefect of the Sacred Congregation for the Evangelisation of Peoples, Vatican City, since 1984; Archbishop of Dublin and Primate of Ireland, (RC), 1972–84; *b* 27 June 1924; *s* of Dr Andrew Ryan and Theresa (*née* McKenna). *Educ:* Belvedere Coll.; Holy Cross Coll., Clonliffe; UC Dublin (BA 1945); St Patrick's Maynooth; St John Lateran Univ. (BD 1948); Gregorian Univ., Rome (LST 1952); Pontifical Biblical Inst., Rome (LSS 1954); MA NUI 1954. Priest, 1950; Chaplain: Mount Anville Convent, Dublin, 1950; Mater Hosp., Dublin, 1954–55; Prof. of Fundamental Dogmatic Theology 1955–57, and Visiting Prof. of OT Studies 1967–72, Holy Cross Coll., Clonliffe; Prof. (part-time) of Eastern Languages, UC Dublin, 1957; Prof. of Semitic Languages, UC Dublin, 1969. Vice-Pres. Irish Episcopal Conf. (Mem. Standing Cttee); Member: Episcopal Commn for Univs; Jt Commn of Bishops and Major Religious Superiors; Steering Cttee, Ballymascanlon; Working Party, Church Scripture Authority, Ballymascanlon; Maynooth Trustees and Maynooth Visitors; Chairman: Trustees of Chester Beatty Library, 1978–; Bd of Management, Mater Misericordiae Hosp., 1972; Exec. Cttee and Bd of Governors, Nat. Maternity Hosp., 1972–; Our Lady's Hosp. for Sick Children, 1972–; Governor: St Vincent's Hosp., Fairview, 1972–; Jervis Street Hosp., 1972–. Irish Hierarchy rep. at Synod of Bishops, 1974, 1977, 1980, 1983. *Publications:* Mother of the Redeemer, 1959; Sacraments Foreshadowed, 1964; The Mass in Christian Life, 1965; Commentaries on the Old Testament Books of Hosea, Amos, Micah and Zachariah, for the Catholic Commentary on Holy Scripture (2nd edn), 1969. *Recreations:* golf, squash. *Address:* Sacred Congregation for the Evangelisation of Peoples, Palazzo di Propaganda Fide, Piazza di Spagna 48, 00187 Rome, Italy. *Died* 21 Feb. 1985.

**RYAN, (James) Stewart;** Principal Assistant Solicitor, Department of the Environment, 1975–78; *b* 9 Sept 1913; *o s* of late Philip F. Ryan and Bridget Ryan; *m* 1939, Rachel Alleyn; two *s* four *d*. *Educ:* Beaumont Coll.; Balliol Coll., Oxford (BA). Called to Bar, Inner Temple, 1939. Served in Army, 1939–46 (Major). Joined Govt Legal Service, 1946; Asst Solicitor, Min. of Housing and Local Govt, 1957, later DoE. *Address:* 28 Manor Road, Henley-on-Thames RG9 1LU. *T:* Henley-on-Thames (0491) 573345. *Club:* Leander (Henley). *Died* 28 July 1990.

**RYAN, Rt. Rev. Joseph Francis,** DD, JCD; *b* Dundas, Ontario, 1 March 1897; *s* of Wm Ryan and Ellen Manion. *Educ:* St Mary's Sch., Hamilton; St Jerome's Coll., Kitchener; St Augustine's Seminary, Toronto; Appolinaris Univ., Rome, Italy. Ordained 1921; Asst Priest, St Mary's Cathedral, Hamilton, 1921–25; Rector, 1925; First Rector of new Cathedral of Christ the King, Hamilton, 1933; Administrator of diocese after serving several years as

Chancellor; Bishop of Hamilton, 1937–73. *Address:* St Joseph's Motherhouse, PO Box 155, Hamilton, Ontario L8N 3A2, Canada.
*Died 22 March* 1990.

**RYAN, Stewart;** *see* Ryan, J. S.

**RYAN, Thomas;** County Councillor, South Yorkshire, 1973–86 (Chairman, 1977–78); *b* 26 Sept. 1911; *s* of John Ryan and Bridget (*née* Griffin); *m* 1939, Phoebe (*née* Taylor); two *s*. *Educ:* Netherfield Lane Council Sch.; WEA (adult educn); Sheffield Univ. (2 days per week part-time). Coal miner, Aldwarke Main Colliery, at age of 14; life-long NUM Mem.; NUM Sec., Aldwarke Main Colliery, 1955–62, when Colliery closed; transf. to Denaby Main Colliery, 1962; NUM Pres., 1962; resigned, then elected NUM Sec., 1963–68, when Colliery closed and merged with Cadeby Colliery; underground worker, Cadeby, 1968–71; NUM Sec., Cadeby, 1971–73; elected Sec. again but took redundancy, 1973; retd. Councillor, Rawmarsh UDC, 1960–74 (Chm., 1969); County Councillor, W Riding, 1972–73. Silver Jubilee Medal, 1977. *Recreation:* country walks. *Address:* 24 Hawke Close, Manor Farm Estate, Rawmarsh, Rotherham, S Yorks. *T:* Rawmarsh 2581. *Clubs:* Rawmarsh Trades, Rawmarsh Labour.

**RYAN PRICE, Henry;** *see* Price, H. R.

**RYCROFT, Charlotte Susanna, (Mrs W. N. Wenban-Smith);** HM Diplomatic Service; Head of West African Department, Foreign and Commonwealth Office, and Ambassador (non-resident) to Chad, since 1989; *b* 14 June 1941; *d* of late Col David Hugh Rycroft, OBE and Cicely Phoebe Susanna Rycroft (*née* Otter-Barry); *m* 1976, William Nigel Wenban-Smith; two *s*, and two step *s* two step *d*. *Educ:* Malvern Girls' Coll.; Girton Coll., Cambridge (BA 1964). Joined FCO, 1964; Havana, 1965; Second Sec., Sofia, 1968–71; First Sec., FCO, 1971–76; Mem., UK Representation to EC, Brussels, 1976–80; FCO, 1980–81; Counsellor, 1981; Advr, CPRS, Cabinet Office, 1981–83; RCDS, 1984; Counsellor (Economic and Commercial), Ottawa, 1985–89. *Recreations:* hillwalking, reading, ski touring, tennis. *Address:* c/o Foreign and Commonwealth Office, King Charles Street, SW1.                             *Died 12 Aug.* 1990.

**RYDER, Captain Robert Edward Dudley,** VC 1942; RN (retired); *b* 16 Feb. 1908; *s* of late Col C. H. D. Ryder, CB, CIE, DSO; *m* 1941, Hilare Myfanwy Green-Wilkinson (*d* 1982); one *s* one *d*. *Educ:* Hazelhurst, Frant; Cheltenham College. Entered RN 1926; commanded Yacht Tai Mo Shan, 1933–34, on passage from Hong-Kong to Dartmouth; a member of British Graham Land Expedition to the Antarctic, 1934–37, in command of the Research Yacht Penola (Polar Medal with Clasp); commanded Naval forces in attack on St Nazaire, March 1942 (VC); took part in attack on Dieppe, Aug. 1942 (despatches); retd list, 1950. MP (C) Merton and Morden, 1950–55. *Publications:* The Attack on St Nazaire, 1947; Coverplan, 1953. *Address:* c/o Lloyds Bank, Cox's & King's Branch, 6 Pall Mall, SW1.                            *Died 29 June* 1986.

**RYLAND, Sir (Albert) William (Cecil),** Kt 1973; CB 1965; Chairman, Post Office Corporation, 1971–77; *b* 10 Nov. 1913; *s* of late A. E. Ryland, OBE; *m* 1946, Sybil, *d* of late H. C. Wookey; one *s* one *d*. *Educ:* Gosforth County Grammar School. Joined GPO, 1932; Assistant Traffic Superintendent, GPO, 1934; Asst Surveyor, GPO, 1938. Served War of 1939–45 in Royal Engineers (Postal Section), Middle East and Central Mediterranean, Col. Principal, GPO, 1949; Principal Private Secretary to PMG, 1954; Asst Secretary, GPO, 1955; Director of Establishments and Organisation, GPO, 1958; Director of Inland Telecommunications, GPO, 1961–65; Dep. Director-General, 1965–67; Man. Dir, Telecommunications, GPO, 1967–69; PO Corporation: Jt Dep. Chm. and Chief Exec., 1969–70; Acting Chm., 1970–71. Adviser: to Republic of Ireland Posts and Telegraphs Review Gp, 1978–79; to Deloitte, Haskins and Sells, 1981–. Mem., Standing Cttee on Pay Comparability, 1979–80. CompIEE; FBIM; Hon. CGIA. *Address:* 13 Mill View Gardens, Croydon CR0 5HW. *T:* 01–656 4224. *Clubs:* Reform, City Livery, MCC.                                           *Died 20 Feb.* 1988.

**RYLAND, Sir Charles Mortimer Tollemache S.;** *see* Smith-Ryland.

**RYLAND, Sir William;** *see* Ryland, Sir A. W. C.

**RYLE, Sir Martin,** Kt 1966; FRS 1952; FEng 1976; Professor of Radio Astronomy, Cambridge, 1959–82, then Emeritus; Director, Mullard Radio–Astronomy Observatory, Cambridge, 1957–82; Astronomer Royal, 1972–82; *b* 27 Sept. 1918; *s* of late Prof. J. A. Ryle, MD, FRCP, and Mrs Miriam Ryle (*née* Scully); *m* 1947, Ella Rowena Palmer; one *s* two *d*. *Educ:* Bradfield Coll.; Christ Church, Oxford. Telecommunications Research Establishment, 1939–45; ICI Fellowship, Cavendish Laboratory, Cambridge, 1945–48; University Lecturer in Physics, Cambridge, 1948–58, Reader, 1958–59; Fellow, Trinity Coll., Cambridge, 1949–. Foreign Member: Royal Danish Acad. of Scis and Letters, 1968; Russian Academy of Sciences, 1971; For. Associate, US Nat. Acad. of Scis, 1975; Hon. Life Mem., NY Acad. of Scis, 1975; Mem., Pontifical Acad. of Scis, Vatican, 1975. Hon. DSc: Strathclyde, 1968; Oxford, 1969; Hon. Dr Nicholas Copernicus Univ., Poland, 1973. Hughes Medal, 1954, Royal Medal, 1973, Royal Soc.; Gold Medal, Royal Astronomical Soc., 1964; Henry Draper Medal, Nat. Academy of Sciences (US), 1965; Nobel Prize for Physics (jtly), 1974. *Publications:* papers in: Proc. Roy. Soc., Proc. Physical Soc., Monthly Notices of Roy. Astronomical Soc. *Address:* 5a Herschel Road, Cambridge. *T:* 356670.             *Died 14 Oct.* 1984.

**RYLEY, Air Vice-Marshal Douglas William Robert,** CB 1956; CBE 1944; retired, 1962; *b* 11 November 1905; *y s* of late Lachlan Macpherson Ryley, OBE, Ichapur, India and Palta, Bournemouth; *m* 1932, Madeline Doreen, *d* of late William Lloyd-Evans, Postlip, Glos; one *d*. *Educ:* Bedford School; RAF College, Cranwell. Commissioned in RAF 1925; India, 1929–34; Air Armament School, 1935; HQ RAF Far East, 1937; Woolwich Arsenal, 1939; UK Tech. Mission, USA, 1941; UK Tech. Mission, Canada, 1943; Ordnance Board, 1944; Superintendent EE Pendine, 1945; OC 10 S of TT, 1947; STSO No 3 Group, 1948; AOC and Comdt, RAF Tech. Coll., Henlow, 1949; STSO HQ Coastal Comd, 1952; Dir of Armament Engineering, Air Min., 1954; Dir of Guided Weapons Engineering, Air Min., 1957; AOA, HQ Maintenance Command, 1958. *Recreations:* golf and shooting. *Address:* Foresters, Over Wallop, Stockbridge, Hants.             *Died 25 Dec.* 1985.

**RYMAN, Prof. Brenda Edith, (Mrs Harry Barkley),** MA, PhD; FRSC; FRCPath; Mistress of Girton College, Cambridge, since 1976; *b* 6 Dec. 1922; *d* of William Henry Ryman and Edith Florence Terry; *m* 1948, Dr Harry Barkley, BSc, FRCP,FRCPath (*d* 1978); one *s* one *d*. *Educ:* Colston Girls' Sch., Bristol; Cambridge Univ. (BA, MA); Birmingham Univ. (PhD). Royal Free Hospital Medical School: Asst Lectr in Biochemistry, 1948–51; Lectr, 1952–61; Sen. Lectr, 1961–69; Reader, 1970–72; Prof. of Biochemistry, Charing Cross Hosp. Med. Sch., Univ. of London, 1972–83. *Publications:* many scientific, in jls such as Biochem. Jl, European Jl of Biochem., FEBS Letters, Biochim. et Biophys. Acta, Advances in Enzymology, Jl of Clin. Path., Nature. *Recreations:* foreign travel, athletic pursuits, gardening. *Address:* Girton College, Cambridge; 54 Primrose Gardens, Hampstead, NW3 4TP. *T:* 01-722 1627.
*Died 20 Nov.* 1983.

**RYMILL, Hon. Sir Arthur (Campbell),** Kt 1954; MLC, South Australia, 1956–75; Chairman, Advertiser Newspapers Ltd, 1980–83; Director, The Bank of Adelaide, 1953–80 (Chairman, 1953–79); Member of Principal Board, Australian Mutual Provident Society, 1964–80; formerly Director of public companies in South Australia; *b* 8 Dec. 1907; *s* of late Arthur Graham Rymill, North Adelaide; *m* 1934, Margaret Earle, *d* of Roland Cudmore; two *d*. *Educ:* Queen's Sch. and St Peter's Coll., Adelaide; Univ. of Adelaide. Barrister and Solicitor, 1930. Mem. Adelaide City Council, 1933–38, 1946–64; Lord Mayor of Adelaide, 1950–54. Pres., S Australian Liberal and Country League, 1953–55; First Pres., Nat. Trust of S Australia; Vice-Pres., Aust. Elizabethan Theatre Trust, 1954–63; Mem., Found. Bd of Govs, Adelaide Festival of Arts; Vice-Pres., Adelaide Children's Hosp, 1957–84. Won Australasian Unlimited Speedboat Championship, 1933; rep. S Austr. in Australasian Polo Championships, 1938 and 1951. Served War of 1939–45, 2nd AIF: enlisted Private, 2/7th Field Regt, later commissioned. *Recreations:* farming, violin playing, golf. *Address:* 39 Jeffcott Street, North Adelaide, SA 5006, Australia. *T:* 267 2477. *Clubs:* Adelaide (Adelaide); Melbourne (Melbourne); Royal Adelaide Golf, Royal SA Yacht Squadron.
*Died 27 March* 1989.

# S

**SABITI, Most Rev. Erica;** *b* 1903; *m* 1934, Geraldine Kamuhigi; four *s* three *d*. *Educ:* Mbarara High Sch.; King's Coll., Budo; Makerere Coll. Teacher, 1920–25 and 1929–30; training in education, 1925–29; training for Ministry, 1931–32; ordained, 1933; Bishop of Ruwenzori, 1960–72; Bishop of Kampala, 1972–74; Archbishop of Uganda, Rwanda, Burundi and Boga Zaire, 1966–74. *Address:* PO Box 134, Mbarara, Uganda.     *Died* 15 *May* 1988.

**SACHER, Michael Moses;** Vice-Chairman, Marks and Spencer plc, 1972–84 (Joint Vice-Chairman, 1982–84); *b* 17 Oct. 1917; *e s* of late Harry and Miriam Sacher; *m* 1938, Audrey Glucksman (*d* 1984); three *s* two *d*; *m* 1986, Janice Puddephatt. *Educ:* St Paul's Sch.; New Coll., Oxford (MA). RASC, 1940–46: served Western Desert; psc Haifa 1943; Liaison Gen. Leclerc's HQ Free French, N Africa; Allied Armies in Italy. Marks & Spencer, 1938–39 and 1946–84: Alt. Dir, 1954–62; full Dir, 1962–84; Asst Man. Dir, 1967–71; Jt Man. Dir, 1971–83. Former Director: St Michael Finance Ltd; Marks & Spencer Pension Trust Ltd. Mem. and Governor of Jewish Agency, 1971–; Jt Nat. Pres., Jt Israel Appeal (UK); Dir and Mem. Council, Weizmann Inst. Foundn; Vice Pres., Jewish Colonization Assoc.; Governor: Hebrew Univ. of Jerusalem; Weizmann Inst.; Reali Sch., Haifa; Vice-Pres. and Mem. Admin. Cttee, Jewish Nat. Fund for Gt Britain and Ireland (Past Pres.); Chairman: Keren Hayesod Discretionary Trust; Brit Olim Soc. Ltd, Israel; Dir and Mem. Bd of Management, Jewish Nat. Fund Charitable Trust. Hon. Vice-Pres., Zionist Fedn of GB. Trustee, Nat. Gall., 1982–. FRSA; FRPSL. *Publications:* various philatelic monographs. *Recreation:* philately. *Address:* Michael House, Baker Street, W1A 1DN. *T:* 01–935 4422.     *Died* 29 *July* 1986.

**SADAT, Mohamed Anwar E.;** *see* El-Sadat.

**SAGITTARIUS;** *see* Katzin, Olga.

**SAINT, Sir (Sidney) John,** Kt 1950; CMG 1946; OBE 1942; BSc, PhD (London); MSc (Reading); CChem; FRSC; Director, Sugar Technological Laboratory, Barbados, 1949–63, retd; *b* 16 Sept. 1897; *m* 1923, Constance Elizabeth Hole; two *s* one *d*. *Educ:* Beaminster Grammar School; Reading University. Served with RFC and RAF, 1916–19; Salter's Research Fellow, 1920–22; Lecturer in Agricultural Chemistry, Leeds University, 1922–27; Chemist, Department of Agriculture, Barbados, 1927–37; Director of Agriculture Barbados, 1937–49; Chm., BWI Sugar Cane Breeding Station, 1937–49; Competent Authority and Controller of Supplies, Barbados, 1939–46; Pres., Barbados Technologists Assoc., 1939–42, 1950–63; Gen. Chm., Internat. Soc. of Sugar Cane Technologists, 1950–53; Chairman: Barbados Public Service Commn, 1952–57; Barbados Development Bd, 1956–59; Interim Federal Public Service Commn, 1956–59. Pres. Museum and Hist. Soc., 1946–59. MEC, 1947–61; PC (Barbados), 1961–63. Hon. Freeman, City of Bridgetown, Barbados, 1963. *Publications:* numerous papers on soils, manuring of tropical crops and sugar technology. *Address:* Selwyn, St George's Lane, Hurstpierpoint, Sussex. *T:* Hurstpierpoint 832335.     *Died* 15 *June* 1987.

**SAINT, Dr Stafford Eric,** CVO 1956; Medical Practitioner, 1931–70; *b* 13 April 1904; *s* of late Sir Wakelin Saint; *m* 1931, Isabel Mary Saint (*née* Fulford); two *s* one *d*. *Educ:* King's School, Ely; The London Hospital. MRCS Eng., LRCP Lond., 1926. *Address:* 28 The Uplands, Gerrard's Cross, Bucks SL9 7JG.
    *Died* 1 *Dec.* 1988.

**ST ALBANS, 13th Duke of,** *cr* 1684; **Charles Frederic Aubrey de Vere Beauclerk,** OBE 1945; Earl of Burford and Baron of Heddington, 1676; Baron Vere of Hanworth, 1750: Hereditary Grand Falconer of England; Hereditary Registrar, Court of Chancery; Chairman, Amalgamated Developers Group; *b* 16 Aug. 1915; *s* of Aubrey Topham Beauclerk and Gwendolen, *d* of late Sir Frederic Hughes; *S* kinsman, 1964; *m* 1st, Nathalie Chatham (who obtained a divorce, 1947; she *d* 1985), *d* of late P. F. Walker; one *s*; 2nd, 1947, Suzanne Marie Adele, *d* of late Emile William Fesq, Mas Mistral, Vence, AM, France; three *s* one *d*. *Educ:* Eton; Magdalene Coll., Cambridge (MA). Served War of 1939–45 in Infantry, Military Intelligence and Psychological Warfare; Col, Intelligence Corps. Controller Inf. Services, Allied Commn for Austria, 1946–50. Central Office of Information: Chief Books Editor, 1951–58; Chief Films Production Officer, 1958–60; Dir, Films Div., 1960–64. Pres., Fedn of Industrial Develt Assocs; Vice-Pres., Ancient Monuments Soc.; Governor General, Royal Stuart Soc.; Hon. Pres., De Vere Soc., 1986–; Patron, Shakespearian Authorship Trust. *Heir: s* Earl of Burford. *Address:* 207 Park Palace, Monte Carlo, Monaco. *Club:* Brooks's.
    *Died* 8 *Oct.* 1988.

**ST AUBYN, Sir John M.;** *see* Molesworth-St Aubyn.

**SAINT BRIDES, Baron** *cr* 1977 (Life Peer), of Hasguard, Dyfed; **John Morrice Cairns James,** PC 1968; GCMG 1975 (KCMG 1962; CMG 1957); CVO 1961; MBE 1944; *b* 30 April 1916; *s* of late Lewis Cairns James and Catherine, *d* of John Maitland Marshall; *m* 1st, 1948, Elizabeth Margaret Roper Piesse (*d* 1966); one *s* two *d*; 2nd, 1968, Mme Geneviève Sarasin. *Educ:* Bradfield; Balliol Coll., Oxford. Dominions Office, 1939; served Royal Navy and Royal Marines, 1940–45; released as Lieut-Col. Asst Sec., Office of UK High Comr in S Africa, 1946–47; Head of Defence Dept, Commonwealth Relations Office, 1949–51, and of Establishment Dept, 1951–52; Dep. High Comr for the UK, Lahore, 1952–53; attended Imperial Defence Coll., 1954; Dep. High Comr for UK in Pakistan, 1955–56; Asst Under-Sec. of State, Commonwealth Relations Office, 1957. Dep. High Comr for UK in India, 1958–61; British High Comr in Pakistan, 1961–66; Dep. Under Sec. of State, CO, 1966–68; Permanent Under-Sec. of State, CO, March-Oct. 1968; British High Commissioner: in India, 1968–71; in Australia, 1971–76. King of Arms, Most Distinguished Order of St Michael and St George, 1975–86. Vis. Scholar, Univ. of Chicago, 1978–79; Fellow, Center for Internat. Affairs, Harvard Univ., 1979–80; Distinguished Diplomat-in-Residence, For. Policy Res. Inst., Philadelphia, 1980–81 (took part, as mem. FPRI team, with the Lady Saint Brides, in talks at Zvinigorod with Soviet Inst. for the USA and Canada, Dec. 1981, at Valley Forge, Pa, Nov. 1982 and in Moscow, July 1984); Vis. Scholar, Univ. of Texas at Austin, 1982–83; Dist. Vis. Prof. of Internat. Studies, Rhodes Coll., at Memphis, 1983–84; Mem., Center for Internat. Security and Arms Control, Stanford Univ., 1984–. Visited Beijing with delegn from Stanford Univ. for talks with Chinese scholars on security in Asia and the Pacific, 1985; attended CISAC—Soviet Inst. for FE Studies confs, 1986 (Stanford), 1988 (Alma Ata, Kazakstan). Lectured for E-SU, Council on World Affairs and Council for For. Relns in 35 US cities, 1979–88. *Publications:* articles on internat. affairs in learned US jls incl. Internat. Security, and Orbis. *Recreation:* meeting new and intelligent people. *Address:* Cap Saint-Pierre, 83990 Saint-Tropez, France. *T:* 94–97–14–75. *Clubs:* Oriental; Harvard (NY).     *Died* 26 *Nov.* 1989.

**ST CLAIR-FORD, Maj.-Gen. Sir Peter,** KBE 1961 (CBE 1953); CB 1954; DSO 1943 and Bar 1944; idc; psc; General Secretary of the Officers' Association, 1963–66; *b* 25 Nov. 1905; *s* of late Anson St Clair-Ford and Elsie (*née* Adams); unmarried. *Educ:* Dover College; Royal Military College, Sandhurst. Commissioned into KOYLI, 1925; Somaliland Camel Corps, 1932–39; France, 1939; Staff College, Camberley, 1940 (psc); various Staff appts UK, 1940–43; Comd 1 Bn KOYLI, 1943–44, Italy and Palestine; Comd 3 Inf. Bde, 1944–46, Italy and Palestine; Comd 129 Inf. Bde (TA), 1947–48; BGS Southern Command (UK), 1948–49; Imperial Defence College (idc), 1950; BGS, FARELF, 1951–52; Training Adviser to Pakistan Army, 1952–54; Commander 1 Federal Division, Malaya, 1954–57; Deputy Chief of Staff, Headquarters Allied Land Forces Central Europe, 1958–60; retd, 1960. *Recreations:* golf, racing. *Address:* Cotswold Lodge, Littlestone, New Romney, Kent. *T:* New Romney 62368. *Club:* East India.     *Died* 14 *May* 1989.

**ST GEORGE, Sir Denis Howard,** 8th Bt *cr* 1766; priest in Holy Orders; *b* 6 Sept. 1902; *s* of Sir Theophilus John St George, 6th Bt, and Florence Emma, *d* of John Vanderplank, Natal; *S* brother, 1983. *Educ:* St Charles Coll., Pietermaritzburg; Rand Univ. (BSc Eng). *Publication:* Failure and Vindication: The Unedited Journal of Bishop Allard, OMI, indexed and fully annotated, 1981. *Heir: b* George Bligh St George [*b* 23 Sept. 1908; *m* 1935, Mary Somerville, *d* of John Francis Fearly Sutcliffe; two *s* three *d*]. *Address:* Eastwood, 30 Springfield Crescent, Durban, 4001, South Africa.
    *Died* 28 *April* 1989.

**ST GEORGE, Air Vice-Marshal Douglas Fitzclarence,** CB 1974; CBE 1971; DFC; AFC; RNZAF, retd; *b* Nelson, NZ, 7 Sept. 1919; *s* of D. St George; *m* 1953, Patrine, *d* of J. Darrow; two *s*. *Educ:* Auckland Grammar Sch., NZ. Served War, Royal New Zealand Air Force, 1938–45. Comdg Flying Wing, RNZAF, Ohakea, 1953–56; exchange duty, RAAF, Aust., 1956–58; Comdg Ohakea, 1958–60; Dir ops, RNZAF, 1961–63; Rep. of NZ Mil. Advisers, HQ of SEATO, Bangkok, 1963–65; AOC comdg Training Gp, 1966–67; IDC, 1968; Air Mem. for Personnel, HQ of RNZAF, 1969–70; Dep. Chief of the Air Staff, NZ, 1970–71; Chief of the Air Staff, NZ, 1971–74. *Address:* 84 Barton Road, Heretaunga, New Zealand.     *Died* 25 *Oct.* 1985.

**ST GEORGE, Sir Robert Alan,** 7th Bt, *cr* 1766; Religious Lay Brother; *b* 20 March 1900; *s* of Sir Theophilus John St George, 6th Bt, and Florence Emma, *d* of late John Venderplank, Natal; *S* father, 1943. *Educ:* St Charles Coll., Maritzburg. Served RAF, 1918; War of 1939–45, Middle East (prisoner). *Heir: b* Rev. Denis Howard St George, *b* 6 Sept. 1902. *Address:* Nazareth House, 82 South Ridge Road, Durban, Natal, South Africa.     *Died* 21 *April* 1983.

**ST GERMANS, 9th Earl of,** *cr* 1815; **Nicholas Richard Michael Eliot;** Baron Eliot, 1784; Major, Duke of Cornwall's Light Infantry; *b* 26 Jan. 1914; *er s* of 8th Earl of St Germans, KCVO, OBE, and of Helen Agnes Post (*d* 1962) (*d* of Lady Barrymore and late Arthur Post, New York, USA); *S* father, 1960; *m* 1st, 1939, Helen Mary (marr. diss., 1947; she *d* 1951), *d* of late Lt-Col Charles Walter Villiers, CBE, DSO, and late Lady Kathleen Villiers; one *s* one *d*; 2nd, 1948, Mrs Margaret Eleanor Eyston (marr. diss., 1959), *o d* of late Lt-Col William Francis George Wyndham, MVO; 3rd, 1965, Mrs Mary Bridget Lotinga, *d* of late Sir Shenton Thomas and of Lady Thomas, SW7. *Educ*: Eton. Joined Duke of Cornwall's Light Infantry, 1937. Served War of 1939–45: attached Royal Armoured Corps. *Heir*: *s* Lord Eliot. *Address*: Les Arcs, Chemin du Signal, 1807, Blonay, Vaud, Switzerland. *Died* 11 *March* 1988.

**ST JOHNSTON, Sir (Thomas) Eric,** Kt 1967; CBE 1952 (OBE 1945); QPM 1958; MA Cantab; Member of Lloyd's; Director, Group 4 Total Security; security consultant; *b* 7 Jan. 1911; *o s* of late T. G. St Johnston, Edgbaston, Warwicks; *m* 1st, 1937, Joan Wharton (marr. diss. 1969; she *d* 1974); one *s* two *d*; 2nd, 1969, M. E. Jameson Till (marr. diss. 1979); 3rd, 1980, Elizabeth Condy (*née* Thomas). *Educ*: Bromsgrove School, Worcestershire; Corpus Christi, Cambridge. Late RA (TA), 1929–35; employed in rank of Colonel for special duties, War Office, 1943, and as Head of Public Safety Section, G5 Div., SHAEF, 1944; member staff of King's Camp, 1932 *et seq*; employed on civil staff at New Scotland Yard, 1932–35; Barrister, Middle Temple, 1934; Metropolitan Police College, 1935 (winner of Baton of Honour); Inspector, Metropolitan Police, 1936–40; Chief Constable of Oxfordshire, 1940–44, of Durham County, 1944–50, of Lancashire, 1950–67; HM Chief Inspector of Constabulary for England and Wales, 1967–70. Visited USA as guest of US Government, 1953; Visiting Lecturer, Univ. of California, 1953; Visiting Lectr to Israeli Police, 1955; British Council Lecturer in Australia and New Zealand, 1966; idc, 1957; invited by Govt of Victoria, Australia to examine and report on efficiency of Police Force in the State, 1970–71. Dir of Admin, Spencer Stuart & Associates Ltd, 1971–75. Freeman of City of London; Liveryman: Vintners' Company, 1956; Gunmakers' Co., 1979; Chevalier de Tastevin, 1965. Chairman, Christian Police Trust Corp. Ltd, 1954–67. Dep. Chm., Sail Training Assoc., 1968–73. Pres., 1978–83, and Endowment Trustee, Bromsgrove School. Pres., Assoc. of Lancastrians in London, 1982–83. Hon. Col 33rd (Lancs and Cheshire) Signal Regt (V), 1967–70. Hon. MA Manchester, 1961. Mem., Chapter Gen., Order of St John, 1968–69; KStJ 1966 (CStJ, 1960). Legion of Honour and Croix de Guerre (France). *Publications*: One Policeman's Story, 1978; contrib. to Police periodicals in UK, and USA. *Recreations*: shooting, fishing and sailing. *Address*: Old Swan House, Great Rissington, Glos. *T*: Cotswold 20776. *Clubs*: Buck's, Naval and Military, MCC.
*Died* 17 *March* 1986.

**ST JUST,** 2nd Baron, *cr* 1935, of St Just in Penwith; **Peter George Grenfell;** *b* 22 July 1922; *s* of 1st Baron and Florence (*d* 1971), *e d* of late George W. Henderson; *S* father, 1941; *m* 1st, 1949, Leslie (marriage dissolved, 1955), *d* of late Condé Nast, New York; one *d*; 2nd, 1956, Maria Britneva; two *d*. *Educ*: Harrow. Served War, 1941–46, 60th Rifles. *Address*: 9 Gerald Road, SW1. *T*: 01-730 7621; Wilbury Park, Newton Tony, near Salisbury, Wilts. *T*: Cholderton 664. *Club*: White's. *Died* 14 *Oct*. 1984.

**ST LEONARDS,** 4th Baron *cr* 1852; **John Gerard Sugden;** *b* 3 Feb. 1950; *s* of Arthur Herbert Sugden (*g g s* of 1st Baron) (*d* 1958) and of Julia Sheila, *d* of late Philip Wyatt; *S* kinsman, 1972.
*Died* 1 *June* 1985 (*ext*).

**ST OSWALD,** 4th Baron, *cr* 1885; **Rowland Denys Guy Winn,** MC 1951; DL; Vice-Chairman of Central and Eastern European Commission of the European Movement; Chairman, Crabtree Denims Ltd; *b* 19 Sept. 1916; *s* of 3rd Baron St Oswald and Eva (*d* 1976), *d* of Charles Greene; *S* father 1957; *m* 1st, 1952, Laurian (from whom he obtained a divorce, 1955), *o d* of Sir Roderick Jones, KBE; 2nd, 1955, Marie Wanda (*d* 1981), *y d* of late Sigismund Jaxa-Chamiec, Zorawia, Warsaw; no *c*. *Educ*: Stowe Sch.; Universities of Bonn and Freiburg. Reuter's Corresp. for Spain, 1935; Daily Telegraph Corresp. and War Corresp., 1936 (condemned to death, Sept. 1936); Corresp. in Middle East, 1938, in Balkans 1939. Enlisted Army, 1939; served Middle East (8th King's Royal Hussars, 1941–44; Far East, 1945 (despatches). Resided Spain, 1946–50. Volunteered to serve in Korea, 1950; 8th King's Roy. Irish Hussars, 1950–51. Contested (C) Dearne Valley Div., 1955; adopted as Conservative candidate, Pudsey Div., 1957; Mem., European Parlt, 1973–79; contested (C) Yorkshire West, European Parlt, 1979. A Lord-in-Waiting to the Queen, 1959–62; Jt Parly Sec. to Min. of Agriculture, Fisheries and Food, 1962–64. Chairman, Mid-Yorkshire Conservative Assoc., 1965; President: W Riding of Yorks Playing Fields Assoc., 1970–; British Assoc. Industrial Editors, 1964–70; Yorks Region Nat. Soc. Mentally Handicapped Children; Yorkshire Area Young Conservatives; Ackworth, Upton, Hemsworth and Wrangbrooke Branches, British Legion; Vice-President: W Riding British Legion; Anglo-Polish Soc., 1969. Trustee and Pres., Northern Cttee of Cheshire Foundn Homes for the Sick. Pres., Soc. of Yorkshiremen in London, 1960–61; Pres. Huddersfield Branch, Coldstreamers' Assoc.; Patron of Wakefield Trinity Football Club; Pres., Yorkshire Agric. Soc., 1968. Hon. Col

150 (Northumbrian) Regt RCT (V), 1967–84. DL West Riding, Yorks, 1962. Croix de Guerre and Order of Leopold (Belgium), 1951; Légion d'Honneur and Croix de Guerre (France), 1945; Grand Cross, Order of Polonia Restituta, 1977; Grand Cross of Isabel la Católica (Spain), 1980. *Publications*: Lord Highport Dropped at Dawn, 1949; My Dear, it's Heaven, 1950; Carmela, 1954 (USA 1955). *Recreations*: talking and writing to friends. *Heir*: *b* Capt. Hon. Derek Edward Anthony Winn [*b* 9 July 1919; *m* 1954, Denise Eileen Charlotte, *o d* of Wilfrid Haig Loyd; one *s* one *d*]. *Address*: Nostell Priory, Wakefield, W Yorks. *T*: Wakefield 862394; 24 Charles Street, W1. *T*: 01–491 7857. *Clubs*: Cavalry and Guards, Garrick, Press, Special Forces, Beefsteak, Pratt's.
*Died* 19 *Dec*. 1984.

**SAKHAROV, Dr Andrei Dimitrievich;** Deputy, Congress of People's Deputies, USSR, since 1989; Member of Presidium, Academy of Sciences of USSR, since 1988 (Member of the Academy, since 1953); *b* 21 May 1921; *m* 2nd, 1971, Elena Bonner; one *s* one *d*. *Educ*: Moscow State Univ. Joined P. N. Lebedev Physics Inst. as physicist, 1945; worked with Dr Igor Tamm on nuclear fusion. Member: Amer. Acad. of Arts and Sciences, 1969–; Nat. Acad. of Sciences, 1972–; Foreign Associate, Acad. des Sciences, 1981–. Hon. ScD Oxford, 1989. Eleanor Roosevelt Peace Award, 1973; Cino del Duca Prize, 1974; Reinhold Niebuhr Prize, Chicago Univ., 1974; Nobel Peace Prize, 1975; Fritt Ord Prize, 1980. *Publications*: Progress, Peaceful Co-existence and Intellectual Freedom, 1968; Sakharov Speaks, 1974; My Country and the World, 1975; Alarm and Hope, 1979; scientific works, etc.; *posthumous publication*: Memoirs, 1990. *Address*: Academy of Sciences of USSR, Leninsky prospekt 14, Moscow, USSR; 48b Chkalov Street, Moscow, USSR.
*Died* 14 *Dec*. 1989.

**SALAS, Rafael Montinola;** Executive Director (with rank of Under-Secretary-General), United Nations Fund for Population Activities, since 1971 (Sen. Consultant to Administrator of UNDP, 1969; Director UNFPA, 1969); Secretary-General, 1984 International Conference on Population; *b* Bago, Negros Occidental, Philippines, 7 Aug. 1928; *s* of Ernesto Salas and Isabel Montinola; *m* 1967, Carmelita J. Rodriguez; two *s*. *Educ*: Coll. of Liberal Arts, Univ. of the Philippines (Associate in Arts (AA) with high honours, 1950; AB *magna cum laude*, 1953); Coll. of Law, Univ. of the Philippines (LLB *cum laude* 1953); Littauer Center of Public Admin. (MPA), Harvard Univ., 1955. Mem., Philippine Bar, 1953. Professorial Lectr in: Polit. Sci. and Economics, Univ. of the Philippines, 1955–59; Economics, Grad. Sch., Far Eastern Univ., 1960–61; Law, Univ. of the Philippines, 1963–66 (Asst. Vice-Pres., 1962–63; Mem., Board of Regents, 1966–69, of the Univ.). Philippine positions: Nat. Economic Council: Exec. Officer (with Cabinet rank), 1960–61; Exec. Dir (with Cabinet rank), 1961; Actg Chm., 1966, 1968. Gen. Manager, the Manila Chronicle, 1963–65; Asst to the President, Meralco Securities Corp., 1963–65. Action Officer, Nat. Rice and Corn Sufficiency Programme, 1967–69 (of vital importance to "Green Revolution"); Nat. Projects Overall Co-ordinator and Action Officer, 1966–69; Exec. Sec. of Republic of the Philippines, 1966–69 (office 2nd to President in executive powers). Holds numerous hon. degrees. Holds foreign orders. *Publications*: People: an international choice, 1976; International Population Assistance: the first decade, 1979; Reflections on Population, 1984, expanded edn, 1985; More Than the Grains: participatory management in the Philippine Rice Sufficiency Program 1967–1969, 1985; Fifty-Six Stones: a collection of poems, 1985. *Recreation*: reading. *Address*: United Nations, New York 10017, USA.
*Died* 4 *March* 1987.

**SALE, Geoffrey Stead;** Director of Studies, RMA, Sandhurst, Camberley, 1967–71; *b* 6 Aug. 1907; *s* of Frederic W. R. Sale, Solicitor, Carlisle, and Ivy I. Davidson; *m* 1938, Olivia Jean Bell-Scott (*d* 1950), Edinburgh; one *s* three *d*. *Educ*: Berkhamsted School; Lincoln College, Oxford (MA). Diploma in Education; Assistant Master and Housemaster, Fettes College, Edinburgh, 1931–46; Headmaster, King's School, Bruton, 1946–57; Headmaster, Rossall School, 1957–67. Captain TA (General List). Member, House of Laity, Church Assembly, 1960–70. FRSA 1953. *Publications*: Four Hundred Years a School (History of King's School), 1950; History of Casterton School 1823–1983, 1983. *Recreations*: walking, photography, writing. *Address*: 1 Penny's Lane, Wilton, Salisbury, SP2 0BE. *T*: Salisbury 743432. *Died* 26 *March* 1987.

**SALE, Richard;** Headmaster of Brentwood School, 1966–81; *b* 4 Oct. 1919; *e s* of late Richard and Rachel Sale; *m* 1943, Elizabeth Thérèse Bauer; four *s* one *d*. *Educ*: Repton Sch. (Schol.); Oriel Coll., Oxford. Commissioned, KSLI, 1940; served War of 1939–45: Canada and Normandy; demobilised, rank of Major, 1946. Asst Master, Repton Sch., 1946–61; Housemaster of The Priory, 1953–61; Headmaster, Oswestry School, Shropshire, 1962–66. Pres., Arthur Dunn Cup; Life Vice-Pres., Essex Co. Football Assoc. President: Old Brentwoods Soc., 1980; Old Reptonian Soc., 1982. FRSA 1969. *Recreations*: cricket (Oxford Blue; Warwickshire, 1939, 1946, 1947; Derbyshire, 1949–54), golf, fives (Oxford Blue), and other games.

*Address:* Whitegates, Homefield Paddock, Beccles, Suffolk. *T:* Beccles 714486. *Clubs:* MCC; Vincent's (Oxford).

*Died* 3 *Feb.* 1987.

**SALISBURY-JONES, Maj.-Gen. Sir (Arthur) Guy**, GCVO 1961 (KCVO 1953); CMG 1949; CBE 1945; MC; DL; Extra Equerry to the Queen since 1962; *b* 4 July 1896; *s* of late Arthur Thomas Salisbury-Jones; *m* Hilda, *widow* of Maj. Guy Yerburgh, Irish Guards, and *d* of Rt Hon. Sir Maurice de Bunsen, Bt, PC, GCMG, GCVO, CB; one *s* one *d. Educ:* Eton. Joined Coldstream Guards, 1915; served European War, 1914–18 (twice wounded, MC and Bar); student at Ecole Spéciale Militaire, St Cyr, 1920–21; Liaison Officer in Syria, 1924–26; Jebel Druze Campaign, 1925–26 (French Croix de Guerre); China, 1927; Staff College, 1932–34; Staff London District, 1935–38; commanded 3rd Battalion Coldstream Guards, in Palestine, 1938–39 (despatches); served in Syria, Italian Somaliland, Greece and Crete, 1939–41 (despatches); was Head of Military Mission to South Africa, 1941–44; Supreme HQ Allied Exped. Force, 1944–45; Head of British Military Mission to France and Military Attaché, Paris, 1946–49; ADC to the King, 1948–49; retired, 1949; HM Marshal of the Diplomatic Corps, 1950–61. Chm., Franco-British Soc., 1963–67. Wine Grower; Pres., English Vineyards Assoc., 1967–81. DL Hampshire, 1965. Order of Red Banner USSR, Order of White Lion Czechoslovakia, Grand Officier Legion of Honour, Croix de Guerre. *Publication:* So Full a Glory-A Life of Marshal de Lattre de Tassigny, 1964. *Address:* Mill Down, Hambledon, Hants. *T:* Hambledon 475. *Clubs:* Cavalry and Guards, Pratt's, Leander. *Died* 8 *Feb.* 1985.

**SALMON, Cyril**, QC 1970; **His Honour Judge Salmon;** a Circuit Judge, since 1976; *b* 27 Aug. 1924; *s* of Jack and Freda Salmon; *m* 1948, Patrice Ruth Tanchan; one *s* one *d. Educ:* Northampton Sch.; Trinity Hall, Cambridge. Chm. Debates, Cambridge Union Soc., 1944. Called to Bar, Middle Temple, 1947. A Recorder of the Crown Court, 1972–76. *Recreations:* reading history and literature. *Address:* 1 Hare Court, Temple, EC4. *T:* 01-353 5324.

*Died* 22 *May* 1981.

**SALMON, Air Vice-Marshal Sir Cyril John Roderic;** *see* Salmon, Air Vice-Marshal Sir Roderic.

**SALMON, Geoffrey Isidore Hamilton,** CBE 1954; President, J. Lyons & Co. Ltd, 1972–77 (Chairman, 1968–72); *b* 14 Jan. 1908; *s* of Harry Salmon and Lena (*née* Gluckstein); *m* 1936, Peggy Rica (*née* Jacobs) (*d* 1989); two *s* one *d. Educ:* Malvern Coll.; Jesus Coll., Cambridge (BA). Hon. Catering Adviser to the Army, 1959–71. *Address:* 10 Stavordale Lodge, Melbury Road, W14 8LW. *T:* 01–602 3425.

*Died* 29 *April* 1990.

**SALMON, Neil Lawson;** consultant; Member, Monopolies and Mergers Commission, since 1980; *b* 17 Feb. 1921; *s* of Julius and Mimi Salmon; *m* 1944, Yvonne Hélène Isaacs; one *s* one *d. Educ:* Malvern Coll., Malvern; Institut Minerva, Zürich. Trainee, J. Lyons & Co. Ltd, 1938–41. Served War (Army), 1941–46. Gen. Manager, J. Lyons & Co., 1947; Chm., Glacier Foods Ltd, 1962; Dir, J. Lyons & Co., 1965; Jt Managing Dir, 1967; Gp Managing Dir, 1969; Dep. Chm. and Man. Dir, 1972; Chm., 1977–78; Dep. Chm., 1978–81. Director: Allied Breweries (now Allied-Lyons), 1978–81; Glaxo Trustees Ltd, 1982–. Mem., Restrictive Practices Court, 1971–. CBIM (Mem. Council, 1974–88; Chm., Professional Standards Cttee, 1982–88). *Recreations:* opera, ballet, theatre, wine. *Address:* c/o Eldon House, 1 Dorset Street, W1H 3FB. *T:* 01–581 4501. *Club:* Savile. *Died* 8 *Aug.* 1989.

**SALMON, Air Vice-Marshal Sir Roderic,** KBE 1968 (CBE 1945); CB 1959; RAF; *b* 21 Aug. 1911; *s* of Edmund Frederick and Edna Salmon; *m* 1939, Hilda (*née* Mitchell); one *s* two adopted *d. Educ:* Howard Gardens High School, Cardiff; City of Cardiff Technical College. Commissioned in Royal Air Force, 1935; No 2 Squadron, 1936; No 70 Squadron, 1936–38; Air Ministry, Directorate of Movements, 1939–43; Second Tactical Air Force (Senior Movements Staff Officer), 1944–46 (despatches); RAF Staff College (Student), 1946; CO No 33 Maintenance Unit, 1947; No 57 Maintenance Unit, 1947–49; Member of the Directing Staff, Joint Services Staff College, 1949–51; Head of Logistics Planning, HQ Allied Air Forces, Central Europe, 1951–53; CO No 16 Maintenance Unit, 1953–54; Imperial Defence College, 1955; HQ No 40 Group (Operations Staff), 1956–59; Director of Equipment (A), Air Ministry, 1959–62; Senior Air Staff Officer, HQ Maintenance Command, 1962–64; Dir-Gen. of Equipment (RAF), MoD, 1964–68; retd, 1968. Sec., Dio. of St Edmundsbury and Ipswich, 1968–80. *Recreations:* gardening, fishing. *Address:* Damer House, Fonnereau Road, Ipswich IP1 3JP. *T:* Ipswich 58105.

*Died* 8 *April* 1985.

**SALOMON, Sir Walter (Hans),** Kt 1982; President, Rea Brothers Plc, Merchant Bank, since 1984 (Chairman, 1950–84); Director, Canal-Randolph Corporation; *b* 16 April 1906; *s* of Henry Salomon and Rena (*née* Oppenheimer); *m* 1935; one *s* one *d. Educ:* Oberreal, Eppendorf, Hamburg; Hamburg Univ. FIB 1964. Member of

Lloyd's, 1958; Member of Baltic Exchange, 1957; Life President, Young Enterprise (Founder, 1963); Vice-Pres., Cambridge Settlement; Freeman, City of London; Master, Pattenmakers' Co., 1977–78; Member: Luso-Brazilian Council; Anglo-Portuguese Soc.; Hudson Institute, 1976; 1001 Club (World Wildlife), 1973. Has lectured widely on economic and financial matters. Comdr, Southern Cross of Brazil, 1971. Officer's Cross (1 Cl.) of the Order of Merit of the Federal Republic of Germany, 1979. *Publications:* One Man's View, 1973; Fair Warning, 1983; numerous newspaper articles. *Recreations:* yachting, ski-ing, art, bridge, snooker. *Address:* Castlemaine House, 21–22 St James's Place, SW1A 1NH. *T:* 01–493 1273. *Clubs:* Reform, City Livery, Canning House 1001, Royal Automobile, Hurlingham; Wentworth Golf; Norddeutscher Regatta-Verein Hamburg; Poole Harbour and Royal Torbay Yacht. *Died* 16 *June* 1987.

**SALT, Mrs Emmaline Juanita,** CBE 1975; JP; *b* 22 Jan. 1910; *d* of Willie Southcombe Propert and Edith Mary (*née* Bacon); *m* 1934, William Edwar Salt (*d* 1982); two *d. Educ:* Colston's Girls' Sch.; Bristol Univ. (MA Econ). Bristol City Councillor, 1938–41; Member: Central Council of Probation and After-Care Cttees, 1960– (Chm., 1968–71, Vice-Pres., 1979–); Home Secretary's Adv. Council for Probation and After-Care, 1961–77; Chm., Avon Probation and After-Care Cttee, 1974–77. Dep. Sec., SW Regional Cttee for Educn in HM Forces, 1941–45; sometime lecturer for WEA. JP Bristol, 1946–. *Recreations:* grandchildren, walking, opera, history. *Address:* 1 Heathercliffe, Goodeve Road, Sneyd Park, Bristol BS9 1PN. *T:* Bristol 681208. *Died* *Feb.* 1986.

**SALTER, Vice-Admiral Jocelyn Stuart Cambridge,** CB 1954; DSO 1942 (Bar 1951); OBE 1942; *b* 24 Nov. 1901; *s* of late Henry Stuart Salter, of Messrs Lee, Bolton & Lee (Solicitors); *m* 1935, Joan (*d* 1971), *d* of late Rev. C. E. C. de Coetlogon, of the Indian Ecclesiastical Establishment; one *s* one *d. Educ:* Royal Naval Colleges, Osborne and Dartmouth. Joined Royal Navy, 1915; Midshipman, 1917; served European War in HMS Ramillies, Grand Fleet, 1917–19; Lieut 1923; Comdr 1937; Comd HMS Foresight in Force H, and in Home Fleet, 1941–42; Capt. 1942. Comd 16th Dest. Flotilla, 1944–45; Comd RN Air Station, Sembawang, Singapore, 1945–47; Comd HMS Jamaica, 1950–51 (served with UN Fleet in Korean waters); served on staff of SHAPE, 1951; ADC, 1951; Rear-Admiral, 1952; Vice-Admiral, 1954; Flag Officer, Malta, and Admiral Superintendent HM Dockyard, Malta, 1952–54; Admiral Superintendent HM Dockyard, Portsmouth, 1954–57; retired, 1957. Mem., Court of Assistants, Haberdashers' Company, Warden, 1958, 1963, 1968, Master, 1970. Norwegian Haakon VII Liberty Cross, 1946; United States Bronze Star medal, 1950. *Address:* Folly House, Hambledon, Hampshire. *T:* Hambledon 732. *Died* 27 *May* 1989.

**SAMUEL OF WYCH CROSS,** Baron *cr* 1972 (Life Peer), of Wych Cross, Sussex; **Harold Samuel,** Kt 1963; FRICS; Hon. Fellow: Magdalene College, Cambridge, 1961; University College, London, 1968; Chairman, Land Securities PLC; President, The Central London Housing Trust for the Aged; *b* London, 23 April 1912; *s* of late Vivian and Ada Samuel; *m* 1936, Edna Nedas; two *d* (and one *d* decd). *Educ:* Mill Hill School; College of Estate Management. Dir, Railway Sites Ltd (British Rail), 1962–65. Member: Covent Garden Market Authority, 1961–74; Special (Rebuilding) Cttee, RICS, 1962–76; Land Commn, 1967–70; Reserve Pension Bd, 1974; Crown Estate Comrs Regent St Cttee. Member: Court of The City Univ.; Court of Univ. of Sussex; Court of Univ. Coll. of Swansea; Court of Patrons, RCS; a Vice-Pres., British Heart Foundation; Trustee, Mill Hill Sch. *Recreations:* swimming, horticulture. *Address:* 75 Avenue Road, Regent's Park, NW8 6JD; Wych Cross Place, Forest Row, East Sussex RH18 5JJ. *Club:* East India, Devonshire, Sports and Public Schools.

*Died* 28 *Aug.* 1987.

**SAMUEL, Herbert Dawkin;** Director of Greenwich Hospital, Admiralty, 1959–64, retired; *b* 21 Jan. 1904; *o s* of Alfred Samuel, Llanelly; *m* 1936, Evelyn Mary, *d* of Col H. J. Barton, RE; two *s. Educ:* Clifton Coll.; Merton Coll., Oxford; Heidelberg University. 1st cl. Hons, Mod. Langs; Laming Fellow, Queen's Coll., Oxford, 1925–27. Entered Consular Service, 1927; Actg Vice-consul, Genoa, 1927, Paris, 1929. Asst Master: Repton School, 1930; Harrow School, 1931; Dist. Inspector, Bd of Education, 1938. Entered Admiralty as Principal, 1939; Under-Secretary, 1956. Coronation Medal, 1953. *Address:* Great Cliff Hotel, Marine Parade, Dawlish, Devon EX7 9DL. *T:* Dawlish 866342. *Died* 1 *Aug.* 1984.

**SAMUELS, Albert Edward,** LLB; JP; Legal Member, London Rent Assessment Panel, 1965–73; *b* 12 May 1900; *er s* of John Samuels and Esther Stella Samuels; *m* 1934, Sadie Beatrice, BSc (Econ.); one *s. Educ:* Sir Walter St John's School; University of London (King's College). Admitted a Solicitor, 1921. Elected to Battersea Borough Council, 1922; Councillor, 1922–25; Alderman, 1925–31; contested LCC Election, 1925; Mem. of LCC, 1928–31, 1934–37, 1946–49 and 1952–65 (for Bermondsey); Chairman: Public Control Cttee,

1934–37, 1946–48 and 1952–55; Establishment Cttee, 1955–58, 1960–65; Jt Cttee of Members and Staff 1955–58; Interim Staff Panel, 1960–65; Chairman, LCC, 1958–59; Mem., GLC, 1964–67 (Chm. Public Health Services Cttee). Vice-Chm. Jt Cttee of LCC and QS 1934–36, 1947–48. Mem., Metropolitan Water Bd, 1925–28, 1941–46; Chm., Redhill and Netherne Gp HMC, 1968–74. Pres. Sir Walter St John's Old Boys' Assoc., 1956–57. JP (County of London) 1933. Comdr Order of Merit of Italian Republic, 1958; Kt Comdr of the Order of Merit of the Federal Republic of Germany, 1958. *Publication:* DNB article on 1st Baron Latham. *Recreation:* reading. *Address:* The Chantry, Cronks Hill, Reigate, Surrey. *T:* 43717. *Club:* Athenæum.                              *Died 19 June 1982.*

**SAMUELS, Sir Alexander,** Kt 1963; CBE 1956; JP, FRSA, FCIT, MIMechE; Member, (part-time) British Waterways Board, 1966–75, and Covent Garden Market Authority, 1961–75; *b* 15 Sept. 1905; *m* 1930, Abigail Solomons; one *d. Educ:* Elementary Sch. Mem., Shoreditch Borough Council, 1945–61; Chairman: London and Home Counties Traffic Advisory Cttee, 1946–61; Special Enquiry into London Traffic Congestion, 1951; Working Party for Car Parking, 1953; Cttee for Speed limit Enquiry, 1954; Special Survey Cttee on use of Parking Meters, 1956; London Travel Cttee, 1958; Operations Group of the Transport Co-ordinating Council for London, 1966; Dep. Chm., Nat. Road Safety Advisory Council, 1965–66; Vice-Pres., London Accident Prevention Council, 1956; Mem., Departmental Cttee on Road Safety, 1957–64; Adviser to the Minister of Transport on London Traffic Management, 1961–65, on Road Traffic, 1965–66. *Recreation:* golf. *Address:* Redcroft, 19 Hartsbourne Avenue, Bushey Heath, Herts. *T:* 01–950 1162. *Club:* Reform.                              *Died 18 June 1986.*

**SAMUELSON, Sir Francis Henry Bernard,** 4th Bt, *cr* 1884; *b* 22 Feb. 1890; *s* of late Sir Francis (Arthur Edward) Samuelson, 3rd Bt, and Fanny Isabel (*d* 1897), *e d* of William Merritt Wright, St John, New Brunswick, Canada; *S* father, 1946; *m* 1913, Margaret Kendall (*d* 1980), *d* of late H. Kendall Barnes; three *s* one *d* (and one *d* decd). *Educ:* Eton; Trinity College, Cambridge. *Heir: s* (Bernard) Michael (Francis) Samuelson [*b* 17 Jan. 1917; *m* 1952, Janet Amy, *yr d* of Lt-Comdr L. G. Elkington, Chelsea; two *s* two *d*]. *Address:* Midway House, Partridge Green, Sussex.                              *Died 8 Jan. 1981.*

**SANDARS, George Edward Russell,** CMG 1951; MBE 1933; *b* 19 Oct. 1901; *s* of Rev. Canon George Russell Sandars and Mary Lambart Wyld; *m* 1937, Vera Margaret Molyneux-Seel; no *c. Educ:* Winchester; New College, Oxford. Joined Sudan Political Service, 1924; Private Secretary to Governor General, 1933–37; Sudan Agent in Cairo, 1941–45; Governor of Blue Nile Province, 1948–51. Sec., Inst. of Brewing, 1951–64. *Address:* Red Cottages, Dogmersfield, Basingstoke, Hants. *T:* Fleet 4801. *Club:* Athenæum.                              *Died 17 Nov. 1985.*

**SANDERS, Sir Harold (George),** Kt 1963; MA, PhD; Deputy Chairman, University Grants Committee, 1964–67 (Member, 1949–55); *b* 9 Oct. 1898; *s* of W. O. Sanders, JP, Wollaston, nr Wellingborough; *m* 1923, Kathleen Penson Plunkett (*d* 1973); one *s* one *d. Educ:* Wellingborough School; St John's College, Cambridge. Assistant (Physiology), Animal Nutrition Inst., School of Agriculture, Cambridge, 1922–29; University Lecturer (Agriculture), Cambridge, 1929–44; Fellow, St John's College, Cambridge, 1938–44; Executive Officer, Herts War Agricultural Executive Committee, 1941–44; Prof. of Agriculture, Reading Univ., 1945–54; Chief Scientific Adviser (Agriculture) to Ministry of Agriculture, Fisheries and Food, 1955–64. Served European War, 1917–19, 2nd Lt RFA (France). *Publications:* An Outline of British Crop Husbandry, 1939, 3rd edn, 1958; (with G. Eley) Farms of Britain, 1946. *Address:* The Court Home for the Elderly, Wotton-under-Edge, near Dursley, Glos. *Club:* Farmers'.
                              *Died 7 Oct. 1985.*

**SANDERS, Terence Robert Beaumont,** CB 1950; TD; DL; *b* 2 June 1901; *yr s* of late Robert Massy Dawson Sanders, Charleville Park, Co. Cork, and Hilda Beaumont, Buckland Court, Surrey; *m* 1st, 1931, Marion (*d* 1961), *er d* of late Colonel A. W. Macdonald, DSO, Spean Bridge; four *s* (and one *s* decd); 2nd, 1965, Deborah, *y d* of late Daniel C. Donoghue of Philadelphia. *Educ:* Eton; Trinity Coll. Cambridge. Fellow of CCC, Cambridge, 1924, Estates Bursar, 1935, Life Fellow, 1945; sometime Univ. Lectr in Engineering, Cambridge Univ. Commissioned TA, 1923, RA; Capt. 1928, Maj. 1939; Herts Yeo. 1939–42. Min. of Supply, 1944; Asst Chief Engineer, Armament Design and later Principal Dir of Tech. Development (Defence); demobilised, 1945, with rank of Colonel. Entered Scientific Civil Service, 1946, retd 1951. Engrg Advr to BSI, 1952–72, closely associated with work of Internat. Orgn for Standardization; Chm., ISO/STACO, 1964–72. Mem., S-E Gas Bd, 1961–69. Chm., Buckland Sand and Silica Co. Ltd, 1951–78; Dir, GHP Gp, 1962–76. Rowed in Univ. Boat Race, 1922; won Henley Stewards' Cup, 1922, 1923, 1924; Grand, 1929; Olympic IVs, 1924; Hon. Treas., CUBC, 1928–39. FICE, FIMechE, FInstW. High Sheriff, Surrey, 1967; DL Surrey, 1967. *Publication:* Centenary History of Boat Race.

*Recreations:* rowing, shooting, farming. *Address:* Slough House, Buckland, Surrey. *Clubs:* Naval and Military; Leander.
                              *Died 6 April 1985.*

**SANDERSON, John Ellerslie,** CB 1980; Adviser to the Department of Transport on appointments in the ports industry, 1982; *b* 19 March 1922; *yr s* of late Joseph Sanderson and Daisy (*née* Beeman); *m* 1941, Joan Ethel, *y d* of late H. H. Mitchell, Bromley, Kent; three *s. Educ:* Portsmouth Grammar Sch. Entered Civil Service in 1947 and joined Min. of Transport, 1952. On loan to Intergovernmental Maritime Consultative Organisation, 1959–61; Asst Sec., Min. of Transport, 1963; Under-Sec., Ports Directorate, DoE, 1971–76, and Dept of Transport, 1976–82. *Recreation:* music. *Address:* 54 Victoria Street, Englefield Green, Egham, Surrey TW20 0QX. *T:* Egham 33359.                              *Died 12 Sept. 1985.*

**SANDERSON, Captain Lancelot,** CIE 1942; RIN, retired; Captain, RN Emergency List; *b* 1889; *s* of late Herbert Elsworth Sanderson; *m* 1919, Anna St John (*d* 1984), *d* of late William Sloane; two *d. Educ:* HMS Worcester. Joined RIN 1911; served European War, 1914–19; Surveyor-in-Charge, Marine Survey of India, 1935–39; Naval Officer-in-Charge, Calcutta, 1939–43; Chief of Personnel, Naval Headquarters, New Delhi, 1944–45; retired 1946. *Address:* 19 Elm Grove, Saffron Walden CB10 1NA. *T:* Saffron Walden 23405.                              *Died 29 Sept. 1984.*

**SANDERSON, Rt. Rev. Wilfrid Guy;** *b* 17 Aug. 1905; *s* of late Wilfrid E. Sanderson; *m* 1934, Cecily Julia Mary Garratt (*d* 1982); one *s* two *d. Educ:* Malvern College; Merton College, Oxford (MA). Ordained, 1931; Curate at S Farnborough, Hants, till 1934; Priest-in-charge of St Aidan's, Aldershot, 1934–37; Vicar of All Saints, Woodham, Surrey, 1937–46; Vicar of All Saints, Alton, Hants, 1946–54; Rector of Silverton, Devon, 1954–59; Archdeacon of Barnstaple, 1958–62; Rector of Shirwell, 1959–62; Suffragan Bishop of Plymouth, 1962–72. *Address:* Huish House, Huish Episcopi, Langport, Somerset TA10 9OP. *T:* Langport 252544.
                              *Died 22 July 1988.*

**SANDFORD, Sir Folliott Herbert,** KBE 1949; CMG 1944; Registrar of Oxford University, and Fellow, New College, Oxford, 1958–72; *b* 28 Oct. 1906; *s* of late W. C. Sandford, Barrister-at-Law; *m* 1st, 1935, Gwendoline Alexander Masters (*d* 1977); 2nd, 1982, Mrs Peggy Young (*née* Odgear) (*d* 1984). *Educ:* Winchester; New Coll., Oxford (1st Class Greats, 1st Class Law); Geneva. Entered Air Ministry, 1930; Principal Private Secretary to successive Secretaries of State (Viscount Swinton, Sir Kingsley Wood, Sir Samuel Hoare, and Sir Archibald Sinclair), 1937–40; attached to RAF Ferry Command, Montreal, 1941–42; Secretary, Office of Resident Minister, West Africa, 1942–44; Assistant Under-Secretary of State, Air Ministry, 1944–47; Deputy Under-Secretary of State, Air Ministry, 1947–58. Master, Skinners' Company, 1975–76. Hon. Fellow, New Coll. and Wolfson Coll., Oxford, 1972. Hon. DCL Oxon, 1973. *Address:* Resthaven, Pitchcombe, Glos.
                              *Died 5 July 1986.*

**SANDOVER, Sir (Alfred) Eric,** Kt 1967; MC 1916; Chairman, Swan Portland Cement, 1956–77, retired; *b* 11 Feb. 1897; *s* of Alfred Sandover, MBE, and Rosalind Sandover; *m* 1923, Kathleen Barber, OBE, *d* of Maj.-Gen. G. W. Barber, CMG, DSO; two *s.* one *d. Educ:* St Peter's Coll., Adelaide. Served European War, 1914–19: E Surrey Regt; 6th Sherwood Foresters, Somme, 1916; served War of 1939–45: 44 Bn AIF and on Staff, Land HQ, Australian Army. Mem. Cttee, Employers' Fedn of Australia, 1950–; Mem. Cttee, Chamber of Commerce of Australia, 1935–; Past Pres., Hardware Assoc. of Australia; Patron, Mentally Incurable Children Assoc.; Business Adviser, Ngala Mothercraft Home, etc. Mem. Shire Coun. of Peppermint Grove for 25 years. *Recreations:* riding horses (formerly MFH West Australian Hunt Club); golf, swimming, deep-sea fishing, etc. *Address:* 29 Leake Street, Peppermint Grove, West Australia 6011. *T:* 3–2101. *Clubs:* Weld, (Past Pres.) Naval, Military and Air Force, Karrinyup Golf, West Australian Turf, WA Hunt, etc (Perth).                              *Died 27 Dec. 1983.*

**SANDREY, John Gordon,** FRCS; Consultant Surgeon, St Peter's Hospital for Stone; Consultant Urologist to the Royal Navy, etc; *b* 20 May 1903; *m* 1932, Eulie Barbara Johnston; one *d. Educ:* Sydney, Australia; MB, ChM Sydney, 1926; MRCS, LRCP, 1929; FRCS 1930. Temporary Surgeon-Captain RNVR, 1940–46. Mem. de la Soc. Internat. d'Urol.; FRSocMed. Formerly Surgical Registrar, Royal Prince Alfred Hospital, Sydney, and Resident Surgical Officer, St Mark's and St Peter's Hospital. *Publications:* contributions to medical journals from 1943. *Address:* 134 Walton Street, SW3.
                              *Died 28 Feb. 1988.*

**SANDYS;** *see* Duncan-Sandys.

**SANGER, Gerald Fountaine,** CBE 1954; JP; Director: Daily Mail and General Trust Ltd; British Movietonews Ltd; *b* 23 May 1898; *s* of late William Sanger, CB; *m* 1922, Margaret Hope, *d* of late G. H. Munroe, of Chessington Place, Surrey; two *s* one *d. Educ:* Shrewsbury School; Keble College, Oxford, MA. Lieut Royal

Marine Artillery, 1917–19; Private Secretary to Hon. Esmond Harmsworth, 1921–29; Editor of British Movietone News, 1929–54; Admin. Dir Associated Newspapers Ltd, 1954–63. Capt. The Queen's Royal Regt, 1939; Hon. Sec., Old Salopian Club, 1942–55, Chm., 1955–57, Pres., 1963–64; Hon. Production Adviser, Conservative and Unionist Films Assoc., 1948–59; Chm., Dorking Division of Surrey Conservative and Unionist Association, 1949–52, President, 1958–63. JP Surrey, 1949. Surrey CC (Horsleys Division), 1965–74. *Recreations:* photography, study of prosody. *Address:* Willingham Cottage, Send, Surrey. *T:* Guildford 222142. *Club:* Garrick.                                                    *Died* 7 *Oct.* 1981.

**SANSOM, Lt-Gen. Ernest William,** CB 1943; DSO 1919; CD; *b* 18 Dec. 1890; *m* 1st, 1917, Eileen Curzon-Smith (*d* 1927); two *d*; 2nd, 1930, Lucy Aymor Waddell (*d* 1974); one *d*. *Educ:* Public schools, New Brunswick; Commercial Coll., Fredericton, NB; Univ. of Toronto; Staff Coll., Camberley, Surrey. Joined 71st York Regt, Canadian Militia, 1906; Lieut, 1907; Canadian Expeditionary Force during European War, 1914–19; Commanded 16th Canadian Machine Gun Company, 2nd Bn and 1st Bn Canadian Machine Gun Corps; Permanent Active Militia, from 1920; Organised and Commanded Royal Canadian Machine Gun Brigade until 1923; Army Staff College, Camberley, 1924–25; GSO2, Halifax, NS, 1926–27; GSO2, Defence HQ, Ottawa, 1928–30; AA and QMG, Military District No 12, 1931–34; GS01, Military District No 4, Montreal, 1935–36; Director of Military Training for Canada, 1937–39; proceeded overseas 1939 with 1st Canadian Division as AA and QMG; Commanded 2nd Inf. Bde and served as DAG at Canadian Military HQ, London, July-Nov., 1940; Commanded 3rd Canadian Div., 1940–41; 5th Canadian Armoured Division, 1941–43; 2nd Canadian Corps, 1943–44; returned to Canada, Feb. 1944, on sick leave; Inspector-General Canadian Army Overseas, Jan. 1945; retired, May 1945. Hon. ADC to Governor-General of Canada, 1948. Progressive-Conservative candidate York-Sunbury general election, June 1945 (defeated), also by-election 1947. Past President: Fredericton Soc. of St Andrew; Fredericton Br., Royal Canadian Legion; Life Mem., Canadian Rehabilitation Council for Disabled; Dir, St John Ambulance Assoc.; Hon. Vice Pres., United Empire Loyalists Assoc. of Canada. KStJ 1978. *Recreations:* fishing, shooting and gardening. *Address:* Fredericton, New Brunswick E3B 4X3, Canada. *Club:* Fredericton Garrison (Hon. Pres.).

**SANTA CRUZ, Marqués de,** *cr* 1569; **José Fernandez Villaverde y Roca de Togores;** Marqués de Pozo Rubio; Grandee of Spain; Grand Cross of Carlos III; Grand Cross of Isabel la Católica; Grand Cross of Merito Naval; Knight of Calatrava; Spanish Ambassador to Court of St James's, 1958–72; Permanent Counsellor of State, since 1972; *b* 4 April 1902; *s* of Raimundo F. Villaverde, Marqués de Pozo Rubio and Angela, Marquesa de Pozo Rubio, Grandee of Spain; *m* 1942, Casilda de Silva y Fernandez de Henestrosa, Marquesa de Santa Cruz, Duquesa de San Carlos; three *s* one *d. Educ:* privately in Madrid; University of Madrid; New College, Oxford. Entered Diplomatic Service, 1921; Attaché: London, 1921, Rome, 1923; Secretary Legation: Vienna, 1927, Stockholm, 1933, London, 1934; Minister-Counsellor Embassy, London, 1944; Minister: Copenhagen, 1948, The Hague, 1950. Chm. Spanish Delegn, 7th Session The Hague Conf. on Private Internat. Law, 1951; Ambassador to Cairo, 1953; Under Secretary of State for Foreign Affairs, 1955. Representative of Spain on Exec. Council of Latin Union, 1955; Spanish Deleg. to 11th and 12th Gen. Assembly of UN, 1956 and 1957; Chm. of Spanish Delegn to XLVI Conf. of Inter-Parly Union, 1957. Hon. Fellow, New College, Oxford 1959. Holds several foreign decorations. *Recreations:* riding, shooting, golf. *Heir:* *s* Alvaro Villaverde, Marqués del Viso; *b* 3 Nov. 1943. *Address:* San Bernardino 14, Madrid 8, Spain. *Clubs:* Beefsteak, White's; Nuevo (Madrid).                     *Died* 15 *June* 1988.

**SANTA CRUZ, Victor (Rafael Andrés),** GCVO (Hon.) 1965; Ambassador of Chile to the Court of St James's, 1959–70; *b* 7 May 1913; *s* of Don Gregorio Santa Cruz and Doña Matilde Serrano; *m* 1937, Doña Adriana Sutil Alcalde; two *s* two *d. Educ:* Stonyhurst; Instituto Nacional, Chile. Law degree, Chile, 1937; Prof. of Civil Law, in Chile, 1941; elected MP, Chilean Parliament, 1945. *Recreation:* golf. *Address:* Zapallar, V Region, Chile. *Club:* Beefsteak.                                                    *Died* 8 *Sept.* 1990.

**SAPPER, Laurence Joseph;** legal author and broadcaster; part-time Chairman, Social Security Appeal Tribunals, since 1984; General Secretary, Association of University Teachers, 1969–83; *b* 15 Sept. 1922; *s* of late Max and Kate Sapper; *m* 1951, Rita Jeski; one *d. Educ:* Univ. of London (External Student). LLB. Called to Bar, Lincoln's Inn, 1966. Churchill Fellow, 1966. Min. of Agric. and Fisheries, 1939–41 and 1946–51; Educn Instructor, RAF, 1941–46; Private Sec. to Minister of Agriculture, 1948–50; Asst Sec., Instn of Professional Civil Servants, 1951–56; Dep. Gen. Sec., Post Office Engrg Union, 1956–69. Mem. Council, Brunel Univ., 1964–; Mem., NW Met. Regional Hosp. Board, 1965–71. *Publications:* Your Job and the Law, 1969; (with G. Socrates) SI Units and Metrication, 1969; papers, articles, broadcasts. *Recreations:* astronomy, writing,

law reform. *Address:* 35 Waldeck Road, W13 8LY. *T:* 01–997 1251.                                                    *Died* 26 *Aug.* 1989.

**SARAGAT, Giuseppe;** President of the Italian Republic, 1964–71; a Life Senator; President, Social Democratic Party, 1975–76, and since 1976; *b* 19 Sept. 1898; *s* of Giovanni Saragat and Ernestina Stratta; *m* 1922, Giuseppina Bollani (*d* 1961); one *s* one *d. Educ:* University of Economic and Commercial Science, Turin. Served European War, 1915–18 (Lieut); joined Italian Socialist Party, 1924; Member, Exec. Office, Italian Socialist Party, 1925; left Italy for Vienna, Paris and south of France during fascist period, 1926–43; imprisoned by Nazi occupation authorities in Rome, escaped, 1943; Minister without portfolio, 1944; Italian Ambassador in Paris, 1945–46; Pres., Constituent Assembly, 1946; founded Italian Workers Socialist Party (later called Social Democratic Party), 1947; Deputy Prime Minister, 1947–48; Member of Parliament, 1948–64; Deputy Prime Minister and Minister of Merchant Marine, 1948; Deputy Prime Minister, 1954–57; Chm., Standing Cttee for Foreign Affairs, Chamber of Deputies, 1963; Minister of Foreign Affairs, 1963–64. Secretary, Social Democratic Party, 1949–54, 1957–64, and in 1976. *Publications:* L'umanesimo marxista, 1944; Socialismo e libertà, 1944; Per la difesa delle classi lavoratrici, 1951; Il problema della pace, 1951; L'unità socialista, 1956; Per una politica di centrosinistra, 1960; Quaranta anni di lotta per la democrazia, 1965. *Address:* c/o Partito Socialista Democratico, Via Santa Maria in Via 12, 00187 Rome, Italy.

*Died* 11 *June* 1988.

**SARGANT, Thomas,** OBE 1966; JP; Founder Secretary, Justice (British Section of International Commission of Jurists), 1957–82; *b* 17 Aug. 1905; *s* of Norman Thomas Carr Sargant and Alice Rose Walters; *m* 1st, 1929, Marie Hlouskova; two *d*; 2nd, 1942, Dorothy Lattimer; one *s. Educ:* Highgate School. Founder Mem., Nat. Cttee of Common Wealth, 1941–45. Pioneered campaign for Parliamentary Commissioner. Mem. Council, NACRO, 1966–81. Chm. of Governors, Sydenham Sch., 1956–60. Hon. LLM, QUB, 1977. *Publications:* These Things Shall Be, 1941, 2nd edn 1942; (jtly) More Rough Justice, 1985; (jtly) Criminal Trials: the search for truth, 1986; articles in legal jls. *Recreations:* playing the piano, travel, helping prisoners. *Address:* 88 Priory Gardens, N6. *T:* 01–348 7530.                                                    *Died* 26 *June* 1988.

**SARGANT, William Walters,** MA, MB Cantab, FRCP, Hon. FRCPsych, DPM; Hon. Consulting Psychiatrist, St Thomas' Hospital; Physician in charge of Department of Psychological Medicine, St Thomas' Hospital, London, 1948–72; *b* 1907; *s* of Norman T. C. Sargant, Highgate; *m* 1940, Margaret Heriot Glen. *Educ:* Leys School; St John's College, Cambridge. Geraldine Harmsworth Schol., St Mary's Hosp., 1928; Asst to Medical Professorial Unit, St Mary's Hosp., 1932–34; MO and Phys., Maudsley Hosp., 1935–49; Rockefeller Travelling Fellowship and Research Fellow, Harvard Medical Sch., USA, 1938–39; Asst Clinical Dir Sutton Emergency Hosp., 1939–47; Visiting Prof. of Neuropsychiatry, Duke Univ. Med. Sch., USA, 1947–48; Registrar Royal Medico-Psychological Assoc., 1951–71; Actg Dean, Royal Coll. of Psychiatrists, 1971; Pres., Section of Psychiatry, Royal Society of Medicine, 1956–57; Examiner in Psychological Medicine, Conjoint Board of England, 1960–63; Associate Secretary, World Psychiatric Assoc., 1961–66 (Hon. Mem., 1972). Hon. Mem., Canadian, and Hon. Corres. Mem., Indian and Portuguese Psychiatric Assocs. Lectures: Ernest Parsons Memorial, Amer. Soc. of Biological Psychiatry, 1964; Herman Goldham Internat., New York Coll. of Med., 1964; Watson Smith, RCP, 1966; Maudsley, RMPA, 1968; Belisle Memorial, Michigan, 1968. Taylor Manor Hosp. Award, 1971; Starkey Meml Prize, Royal Soc. of Health, 1973. *Publications:* Physical Methods of Treatment in Psychiatry, 1944, 5th edn, 1972; Battle for the Mind, 1957; The Unquiet Mind, 1967; The Mind Possessed, 1973; Various papers on psychiatric topics, in medical jls. *Recreation:* (formerly) Barbarians RFC, St Mary's Hosp. RFC (Capt.) and Middlesex Co. RFC. *Address:* Cobley House, East Woodyates, near Salisbury SP5 5RA. *Club:* Savage.                                                    *Died* 27 *Aug.* 1988.

**SARGENT, Rev. Canon Alexander,** MA; Archdeacon of Canterbury, 1942–68, and Canon Residentiary of Canterbury Cathedral, 1939–68; Hon. Canon, 1968, Canon Emeritus, 1974; *b* 9 May 1895; *s* of Frederick George Sargent and Florence Crundall. *Educ:* King's School, Canterbury; St Edmund Hall, Oxford; Cuddesdon Theological Coll. Deacon, 1919; Priest, 1920; Curate of St Margarets-at-Cliffe, 1919; of All Saints, Maidstone, 1921; Chaplain of Cuddesdon Theological College, 1923; Sub-Warden of St Paul's College, Grahamstown, 1927; Resident Chaplain to the Archbishop of Canterbury, 1929–39; Archdeacon of Maidstone, 1939–42; Commissary to the Bishop of Grahamstown, 1931; Six Preacher in Canterbury Cathedral, 1933; Select Preacher, Univ. of Oxford, 1949–51. *Address:* Starr's House, The Precincts, Canterbury, Kent. *T:* Canterbury 65960.                                    *Died* 5 *Jan.* 1989.

**SARGENT, Sir (Sidney) Donald,** KBE 1961; CB 1951; Chairman; Civil Service Retirement Fellowship, 1968–74; Society of Pension

Consultants, 1970—81; Vice-Chairman, Hospital Saving Association, since 1970; *b* 11 Dec. 1906; *s* of late S. G. Sargent; *m* 1944, Dorothy Mary, *d* of late E. Raven, CB; one *s. Educ:* King Edward's School, Birmingham; Trinity College, Cambridge. BA (Classical Tripos, 1st Cl.), 1928. Asst Principal, GPO, 1929; Private Sec. to Director General, 1935–37; Principal, 1937; Home Office, ARP Dept, 1938–41; Principal Private Secretary to PMG, 1941–44; Asst Sec., GPO, 1944; Dep. Chief Administrative Officer, CCG, 1946–47; idc, 1948; Director of Personnel and Accommodation, GPO 1949–53; Director of Postal Services, 1953–55; Deputy Director General, 1955–59; Secretary, National Assistance Bd, 1959–66; Sec., Supplementary Benefits Commn, and Dep. Sec., Min. of Social Security, 1966–68. Dir, Abbeyfield Soc., 1968–70. *Recreations:* mountaineering, sailing, music. *Address:* 1 Croham Valley Road, Croydon, Surrey. *T:* 01–657 4023. *Clubs:* United Oxford & Cambridge University; MCC.

*Died 15 April* 1984.

**SARGISON, Phillip Harold,** MBE 1946; Director-General of Royal Ordnance Factories (Finance and Procurement), Ministry of Defence, 1977–80; *b* 4 Feb. 1920; *s* of Ernest and Ethel Sargison; *m* 1945, Doreen (*née* Rowley); one *s* one *d. Educ:* De La Salle Coll., Salford. Apptd to War Office, 1938. Served War of 1939–45, HM Forces, 1940–47 (attained rank of Major). Various War Office appts in UK and British Army of the Rhine, 1947–64; Dep. Dir, Civil Service Pay Research Unit, 1964–67; Ministry of Defence: Dir of Accounts, 1967–73; Dep. Dir Gen. of Defence Accounts, 1974–76. *Recreations:* music, literature. *Address:* 2 Reynard Close, Bickley, Kent BR1 2AB. *T:* 01–467 1477. *Club:* East India.

*Died 4 June* 1989.

**SARILA, HH Maharaja Mahipal Singh,** ju Deo, Maharaja of, CSI 1939; *b* 11 Sept. 1898; *m* 1919, *d* of Landlord of Basela, UP; five *s* three *d. Educ:* Daly Coll., Indore. Invested with Ruling Powers, 1919; State Delegate to the First and Second Indian Round Table Conferences, London 1931 and 1932. Late Secretary, General Council and Working Committee, Daly College, Indore. 2nd *s* succeeded, 1942, as HH Maharajadhiraja of Charkhari, UP. *Recreations:* is a keen sportsman and good tennis player and has won tournaments. *Heir:* *s* Raja Bahadur Narendra Singh ju deo, [Indian Ambassador to Switzerland. *Educ:* Mayo Coll., Ajmer, India; Magdalene Coll., Cambridge]. *Address:* Mahipal Niwas Palace, Sarila State, Bundel Khand, UP, India. *TA:* Maharaja Sarila State, India. *Clubs:* National Liberal; Delhi Gymkhana (New Delhi). *Died* 1983.

**SAROYAN, William;** writer; *b* Fresno, California, 31 Aug. 1908; *s* of Armenak Saroyan (*d* 1911) and Takoohi Saroyan (*d* 1950), of Bitlis, Armenia, who emigrated to America in 1905 and 1907; *m* 1943, Carol Marcus (marriage dissolved 1949); one *s* one *d. Educ:* Fresno public schools until fifteen years of age; public libraries; movie and vaudeville theatres; streets. Began selling newspapers when seven; from that year until his twenty-second year worked at a variety of jobs; since twenty-second year has done very little but loaf and write; began to write when nine years old; writing was constantly interrupted or delayed by work; this displeased him, so he stopped working; has no intention of ever working again, as it bores him. *Religion:* living. *Party:* William Saroyan. *Publications:* The Daring Young Man on the Flying Trapeze, 1934; Inhale and Exhale, 1936; Three Times Three, 1936 (US only); The Gay and Melancholy Flux, 1936 (England only); Little Children, 1937; Love, Here Is My Hat, 1938; The Trouble with Tigers, 1938; Peace, It's Wonderful, 1939; My Heart's in the Highlands (play), 1939; The Time of Your Life (play), 1939; Love's Old Sweet Song (play), 1939; My Name is Aram, 1940; Saroyan's Fables (US only), 1941; The Beautiful People (play), 1941; Sweeney in the Trees (play), 1941; Across the Board on Tomorrow Morning (play), 1941; The Human Comedy (novel), 1943; Get Away Old Man (play), 1943; Dear Baby (stories), 1944; The Adventures of Wesley Jackson (novel), 1946; Jim Dandy, Fat Man in a Famine (play), 1947; Don't Go Away Mad (play), 1949; Sam Ego's House (play), 1949; A Decent Birth, A Happy Funeral (play), 1949; The Twin Adventures, 1950, A Novel and a Diary (US only); The Assyrian (short stories), 1950; Rock Wagram (novel), 1951; Tracy's Tiger (novel), 1952; The Laughing Matter (novel), 1953; The Bicycle Rider in Beverly Hills (memoir), 1952; Mama I Love You, 1957; The Whole Voyald (short stories), 1957; Papa You're Crazy, 1958; The Cave Dwellers (play), 1959; Sam, the Highest Jumper of Them All (play, written and directed for Theatre Workshop), 1960; Talking To You (one act play, Duke of York's), 1962; Short Drive, Sweet Chariot (autobiographical), 1964; One Day in the Afternoon of the World (novel), 1965; Not Dying, 1966; (with A. Rothstein) Look At Us, 1967; I Used to Believe I Had Forever, Now I'm Not So Sure (Short Stories), 1968; Letters from 74 Rue Taitbout, or Don't Go, But If You Must, Say Hello to Everybody, 1969; Days of Life and Death and Escape to the Moon, 1971; Places Where I've Done Time, 1973; The Tooth and My Father, 1974. *Recreation:* everything. *Address:* 2729 W Griffith Way, Fresno, Calif 93705, USA. *Died 18 May* 1981.

**SATTERLY, Air Vice-Marshal Harold Vivian,** CB 1949; CBE 1943; DFC 1941; RAF retired; *b* 24 May 1907; *s* of late Ernest Satterly, Exmouth, Devon; *m* 1935, Mary Gavin, *d* of late Col A. L. Lindesay, St Andrews, Fife; one *s* two *d. Educ:* Hele's School, Exeter; Exmouth; RAF Halton, Air Officer Comdg, 205 Group, Middle East Air Forces, 1952–54; ACAS (Operational Requirements), Air Ministry, 1954–57; Air Officer Commanding 64 (Northern) Group, 1957–59. Air Commodore, 1948; Air Vice-Marshal, 1952. Retired, 1959. *Recreations:* various. *Died 28 April* 1982.

**SAUNDERS, Henry George Boulton;** Organist and Choirmaster to the Hon. Society of Benchers at Gray's Inn, 1935–82; Organist and Master of the Choir to the Household Division, 1963–82; Area Inspector of Schools, Surrey County Council, 1962–78; *b* Devonport, Feb. 1914; *m* 1943, Kathleen Mary, *d* of Major S. Brandle, MC, London; one *s* two *d. Educ:* Grammar Sch., Kilburn; Royal Acad. of Music (Thomas Threlfall Organ Scholar). DMus Durham; BMus Durham and London; Grad. Royal Schs of Music, London, 1935; FRCO (La Fontaine prize, 1935) FRAM; Worshipful Company of Musicians Silver Medal, 1937; Organist and Choirmaster at St Saviour's Hampstead, 1934–35; Music Master Trinity County Sch., Wood Green, 1935–46; Inspector of Secondary Schs, City of Leicester, 1946–62. *Publication:* Read and Sing, 1959. *Recreation:* gardening. *Address:* Court Farm, Pebworth, Stratford-upon-Avon, Warwicks CV37 8XW. *T:* Stratford 720428.

*Died 27 Sept.* 1984.

**SAUNDERS, Air Chief Marshal Sir Hugh (William Lumsden),** GCB 1953 (KCB 1950; CB 1943); KBE 1945 (CBE 1941); MC, DFC; MM; *b* 1894; *s* of Frederick William Saunders, Transvaal; *m* 1923, Phyllis Margaret (*d* 1980), *d* of Major P. W. Mabbett, Bidborough, Kent; one *s* (and one *s* decd). *Educ:* Marist Brothers' School, Johannesburg. Served European War, 1914–19, with Witwatersrand Rifles and South African Horse; transf. RFC 1917; Group Capt. 1939; Air Commodore, 1941; temp. Air Vice-Marshal, 1942; Air Marshal, 1947; Air Chief Marshal, 1950; Chief of Air Staff, New Zealand, 1939–41; AOC, No. 11 Group, Fighter Command, 1942–44; Director-General of Postings, Air Ministry, 1944–45; Air Marshal Commanding RAF Burma, 1945–46; AOC-in-C, Bomber Command, 1947; Air Council Member for Personnel, 1947–49; Inspector-General of the RAF, 1949–50; Commander-in-Chief Air Forces Western Europe, Jan.-April 1951. Air Deputy to Supreme Allied Commander Europe, 1951–53; Special Air Adviser to Royal Danish Air Force, 1954–56; Chief Co-ordinator of Anglo-American hospitality activities in UK, 1956–59. A Vice-Chm., Nat. Savings Cttee, 1956–70. Order of Polonia Restituta, 2nd Class (Poland); Commander Order of Merit (US); Officier Légion d'Honneur (France); Grand Cross of Dannebrog (Denmark). *Address:* c/o Barclays Bank PLC, 68 Knightsbridge, SW1X 7LW. *Club:* Royal Air Force. *Died 8 May* 1987.

**SAUNDERS-JACOBS, Brig. John Conrad,** CBE 1945; DSO 1944; Indian Army, retired; *b* 12 Nov. 1900; *s* of George Saunders-Jacobs; *m* 1930, Sylvia (*d* 1985), *e d* of Col H. Drury Shaw, DSO; one *d. Educ:* University College, London; RMC, Sandhurst. Joined Royal Garhwal Rifles in India, 1921; Co. comd, RMC, Sandhurst, 1937–38; Bt Major, 1938; War of 1939–45: GSO1, NWF, India, 1941–42; bn, bde and actg div. comdr, Middle East, Italy and Greece, 1942–46. Staff Coll., Quetta, 1934–35; Imperial Defence Coll., London, 1946; Asst Comdt, Staff Coll., Quetta, 1947; GHQ India, Dir of Mil. Operations, Delhi, 1947; retired Indian Army, 1948. FO UK delegate to UN Special Cttee on the Balkans, 1948; Official mil. historian, Cabinet Office, 1949–50; export agent, London, 1950–53; RO II, War Office, 1954; landscape gardener, 1955–57; govt service in Mins of Defence, Aviation and Technology, 1958–71. *Address:* 10 Winsley Road, Cotham, Bristol.

*Died 28 Dec.* 1986.

**SAVAGE, Anthony,** CB 1980; Chief Executive, Intervention Board for Agricultural Produce, 1972–80; *b* 23 Aug. 1920; *s* of late Edmund Savage and Dorothy Mary (*née* Gray); *m* 1945, Heather Mary (*née* Templeman); one *s* three *d. Educ:* Johnston Sch., Durham. Entered Min. of Agriculture, 1937. War Service, Royal Artillery, 1939–46: Middle East, Italy and NW Europe, 1940–46; commnd 1943; despatches 1945. Asst Principal, MAFF, 1947; Principal, 1951; Cabinet Office, 1951–53; Asst Sec., 1961; Regional Controller, E Midland Region, 1964–69; Head of Land Drainage Div., 1969–71; Under-Sec., 1972. *Address:* 2A Thoresby Road, Bramcote, Nottingham NG9 6SF. *T:* Nottingham 229204.

*Died 17 Nov.* 1989.

**SAVAGE, Sir (Edward) Graham,** Kt 1947; CB 1935; *b* 31 Aug. 1886; *s* of Edward Graham Savage and Mary Matilda Dewey; *m* 1911; two *s* one *d. Educ:* Upper Sheringham School; King Edward VI Middle School, Norwich; Downing College, Cambridge. Tutor Bede College, Durham; Assistant Master, St Andrew's College, Toronto; Tewfikieh School, Cairo; Lecturer, Khedivial Training College, Egypt; served R W Kent Regt Gallipoli and France, 1914–19; Assistant Master, Eton College; District Inspector, Board of

Education, 1919–27; Staff Inspector for Science, 1927; Divisional Inspector NW Division, 1931–32; Chief Inspector, of Technical Schools and Colleges, 1932; Senior Chief Inspector, 1933–40. Education Officer to the LCC, 1940–51, retired. Chm. League of the Empire, 1947–62; Chm. Simplified Spelling Society, 1949–68; President Science Masters' Assoc., 1952–53, Chief Assessor to Industrial Fund for Advancement of Science Teaching in Schools, 1956; Chm., Board of Building Education, 1956–66; Mem. Council and Exec. Cttee, City and Guilds of London Institute, 1963 (Vice-Chairman, 1967–71, Vice-President, 1967–74). Hon. Fellow, Inst. of Builders, 1966. *Publication:* The Planning and Equipment of School Science Blocks, 1964. *Recreations:* walking, gardening. *Address:* Cheverells, Markyate, St Albans, Herts.

*Died 18 May* 1981.

**SAVAGE, Rt. Rev. Gordon David,** MA; *b* 14 April 1915; *s* of Augustus Johnson Savage and Louisa Hannah Atkinson; *m* 1st, 1938, Eva Louise, *y d* of H. J. Jessen, Copenhagen; one *s* two *d*; 2nd, Ammanda Lovejoy; one *s. Educ:* Reading Sch.; Tyndale Hall, Bristol; St Catherine's, Oxford. MA Oxon, 1949. Was a Librarian before ordination, 1932–37; deacon, 1940, priest, 1941; Chaplain, Lecturer and Tutor, Tyndale Hall, Bristol, 1940–44; General Secretary Church Society, London, 1945–52; Curate-in-Charge of the City Church, Oxford, 1948–52; Proctor in Convocation, 1951–61; Vicar of Marston, Oxford, 1952–57; Archdeacon of Buckingham and Vicar of Whitchurch, Bucks, 1957–61; Suffragan Bishop of Buckingham, 1960–64; Bishop of Southwell, 1964–70. *Address:* 11 Ranelagh Street, White Cross, Hereford HR4 0DT.

*Died 9 June* 1990.

**SAVAGE, Sir Graham;** *see* Savage, Sir E. G.

**SAVILLE, (Leonard) Malcolm;** author; Editor of General Books, George Newnes Ltd and C. Arthur Pearson Ltd, 1957–66; *b* 21 February 1901; *s* of Ernest Vivian Saville and Fanny Ethel Hayes; *m* 1926, Dorothy May McCoy; two *s* two *d. Educ:* Private Schools. Wrote original stories for Children's Film Foundation; seven stories adapted as serials for BBC. *Publications:* books for children (as Malcolm Saville): King of Kings; Jane's Country Year; Adventure of the Lifeboat Service; Country Scrapbook for Boys and Girls; Open Air Scrapbook for Boys and Girls; Seaside Scrapbook for Boys and Girls; Coronation Gift Book; Mystery at Witchend; Seven White Gates; The Gay Dolphin Adventure; The Secret of Grey Walls; Lone Pine Five; The Elusive Grasshopper; The Neglected Mountain; Saucers Over the Moor; Wings Over Witchend; Lone Pine London; The Secret of the Gorge; Mystery Mine; Sea Witch Comes Home; Not Scarlet but Gold; Treasure at Amorys; Man with Three Fingers; Rye Royal; Strangers at Witchend; Where's My Girl?; Home to Witchend; All Summer Through; Christmas at Nettleford; Spring Comes to Nettleford; The Secret of Buzzard Scar; Redshank's Warning; Two Fair Plaits; The Sign of the Alpine Rose; The Luck of Sallowby; Strangers at Snowfell; The Ambermere Treasure; The Master of Maryknoll; The Buckinghams at Ravenswyke; The Long Passage; A Palace for the Buckinghams; The Secret of the Villa Rosa; Diamond in the Sky; Trouble at Townsend; The Riddle of the Painted Box; The Flying Fish Adventure; The Secret of the Hidden Pool; Young Johnnie Bimbo; The Fourth Key; Susan, Bill and the Wolfdog; Susan, Bill and the Ivy-clad Oak; Susan, Bill and the Vanishing Boy; Susan, Bill and the Golden Clock; Susan, Bill and the Dark Stranger; Susan, Bill and the Saucy Kate; Susan, Bill and the Brightstar Circus; Susan, Bill and the Pirates Bold; Treasure at the Mill; Four and Twenty Blackbirds (repr. as The Secret of Galleybird Pit); The Thin Grey Man; Malcolm Saville's Country Book; Malcolm Saville's Seaside Book; Three Towers in Tuscany; The Purple Valley; Dark Danger; White Fire; Power of Three; The Dagger and the Flame; Marston, Master Spy; Come to London; Strange Story; Come to Devon; Come to Cornwall; Come to Somerset; See How It Grows; Good Dog Dandy; The Roman Treasure Mystery; Eat What You Grow; Portrait of Rye; Exploring a Wood; Exploring the Seashore; Countryside Quiz; Wild Flowers through the Year; Seashore Quiz; Words for all Seasons (anthology). *Recreations:* walking, watching cricket, reading. *Address:* 9 Delves Way, Ringmer, Lewes, East Sussex BN8 5JU. *T:* Ringmer 812835. *Club:* Savage.

*Died 30 June* 1982.

**SAVIN, Lewis Herbert,** MD, MS, London (University Medal in Ophthalmology), MRCP, FRCS; retired; Fellow, King's College, London, 1953; Hunterian Professor Royal College of Surgeons of England, 1943; FRSM (Member Council Ophthalmic Section, 1943; Vice-President 1955); *b* 1901; *e s* of late Lewis Savin, MRCS, Yunnan and of late Kate C. Savin; *m* 1931, Mary Helen (*d* 1983), *e d* of late Walter Griffith, Wimbledon; two *s* one *d. Educ:* Christ's Hosp.; King's Coll., London; King's Coll. Hosp. (Warneford Entrance Scholarship, Warneford and Barry Prizes). House Physician and House Surg. to the City of London Hosp. for Diseases of Heart and Lungs, 1924; 1st Assistant Medical Officer to St Marylebone Hospital, 1927; Medical Superintendent Seamen's Hospital, Greenwich, 1928; House Surgeon to Royal Eye Hospital,

1923; afterwards clinical assistant, pathologist, assistant Surgeon, Surgeon, Senior Surgeon, Royal Eye Hospital, SE1, resigning 1956. Ophthalmic Surgeon, Metropolitan Hospital, 1929–34; Consulting Ophthalmic Surgeon, Maudsley Hospital, 1937–39; Consulting Ophthalmic Surgeon to the LCC General Hospitals, 1936–48, and to Whipps Cross Hospital, 1931–47; Ophthalmologist to Horton War Hospital (Ministry of Health Emergency Medical Service), 1939–47; Consulting Ophthalmic Surgeon, King's College Hospital, 1966 (Asst Ophthalmic Surgeon, 1931; Senior Ophthalmic Surgeon, 1945–66). Hon. Secretary Ophthalmological Soc. of UK, 1937–39 (Member Council, 1939–42; Vice-President, 1957); Emeritus Lecturer in Ophthalmology, King's Coll. Hosp. Med. Sch.; Examr under Conjoint Examining Bd for DOMS Part I, 1941–46; Examiner in DO, 1949; Staff Examiner in Ophthalmology, Univ. of London, 1952. Vice-Pres. sect. of ophth, Roy. Soc. Med., 1956–57; President Faculty of Ophthalmologists, 1957. *Publications:* Medical and Ophthalmic contributions to Lancet, British Journal of Ophthalmology (The Effect of Aluminium and its Alloys on the Eye: a Report presented to Vision Committee of Medical Research Council, 1947), and Transactions of Ophthalmological Society of the United Kingdom. *Address:* 149 Eastcote Road, Pinner, Middx HA5 1EX. *T:* 01-866 1581.

*Died 11 July* 1983.

**SAVORY, Sir Reginald (Charles Frank),** Kt 1972; CBE 1965; Chairman of Directors, Savory Holdings Ltd, Building Contractors, since 1933; *b* 27 May 1908; *s* of Frank and Margaret Savory, Auckland, NZ; *m* 1935, Fai-Ola, *o c* of Ernest Vaile, Auckland; two *d. Educ:* Auckland Grammar Sch. Past Chm., Bd of Governors, Council of Auckland Technical Institutes; Member: Auckland Harbour Bd (Chm., 1961–71); Auckland City Council, 1953–62, Drainage Bd, 1956–62, and Chamber of Commerce, 1961–71. Pres., NZ Harbours Assoc., 1963–67; Past Pres., NZ Technical Assoc.; Life Mem. (Past Pres.) NZ Builders' Fedn; FIOB (Gt Britain) 1959. *Recreations:* boating, fishing, golf, bowls; watching Rugby football. *Address:* Northbridge Residential Home, Akoranga Drive, Northcote, Auckland 9, New Zealand. *T:* 462–942. *Clubs:* Auckland (Auckland); NZ Royal Yacht Squadron; Newmarket Rotary.

*Died 31 Oct.* 1989.

**SAW, Prof. Ruth Lydia;** Professor Emeritus in Aesthetics, University of London, 1964; *b* 1 August 1901; *d* of Samuel James and Matilda Louisa Saw (*née* Horner). *Educ:* County School for Girls, Wallington, Surrey; Bedford College, University of London. Lecturer in Philosophy, Smith Coll., Northampton, Mass., USA, 1927–34; Lecturer in Philosophy: Bedford College, 1939–44; Birkbeck College, 1939–46, Reader in Philosophy, 1946–61; Prof. of Aesthetics in Univ. of London, 1961–64, and Head of Dept of Philosophy, Birkbeck Coll. British Society of Aesthetics: Founder Mem. and Chm. Council, 1960; Vice-Pres., 1963; Pres., 1969; Pres., Aristotelian Soc., 1965. *Publications:* The Vindication of Metaphysics, 1951; Leibniz, 1954; Aesthetics, 1970; sections (William of Ockham, Leibniz), in A Critical History of Western Philosophy. Contrib. to Proc. Aristotelian Soc., Philosophy, Brit. Jl of Aesthetics. *Recreations:* gardening, the theatre; interested in illuminated manuscripts, early gardening and botany books. *Address:* 72 Grosvenor Avenue, Carshalton, Surrey. *T:* 01–647 8898. *Club:* Women's Farm and Garden.

*Died 23 March* 1986.

**SAWBRIDGE, Henry Raywood,** CBE 1960; retired from HM Foreign Service, 1964; Deputy Director, Centre of Japanese Studies, University of Sheffield, 1964–66; *b* 1 Nov. 1907; 2nd *s* of Rev. John Edward Bridgman Sawbridge; *m* 1947, Lilian, *d* of late William Herbert Wood; one *s* one *d. Educ:* Eton; Trinity Coll., Oxford. Entered HM Consular Service, 1931, and served in Japan, Korea and at FO; served with Australian Forces, 1943; HM Consul-General, Yokohama, 1949; Chargé d'Affaires, Korea, 1950; HM Consul-General, Geneva, 1953; Counsellor at Foreign Office, 1960. Coronation Medal, 1953. *Recreations:* shooting, fishing. *Address:* The Moorings, Kingsgate, Kent. *Club:* Travellers'.

*Died 10 Jan.* 1990.

**SAWERS, Maj.-Gen. James Maxwell,** CB 1974; MBE 1953; Managing Director, Services Kinema Corporation, 1975–81; *b* 14 May 1920; *s* of late Lt-Col James Sawers, Woking, Surrey; *m* 1945, Grace, *d* of Joseph William Walker, Tynemouth; two *s* one *d. Educ:* Rugby; RMA Woolwich. 2nd Lieut, Royal Signals, 1939. Served War of 1939–45 in W Africa and Burma. Lt-Col, 1960; Brig., 1966; BGS, MoD, 1966–68; Comd Corps Royal Signals, 1st British Corps, 1968–69; attended IDC, 1970; Signal Officer in Chief, 1971–74. Col Comdt, Royal Signals, 1974–79; Hon. Col, 71 (Yeomanry) Signal Regt, 1977–83. psc, jssc, idc. CBIM. Managing Trustee: Soldiers' Widows Fund; Single Soldiers' Dependants Fund. *Recreations:* sailing, skiing, gardening, golf, photography. *Address:* Monk's Lantern, Fairfield Close, Lymington, Hants SO41 9NP. *T:* Lymington 73392. *Clubs:* Army and Navy; Royal Lymington Yacht.

*Died 29 Sept.* 1988.

**SAWICKI, Roman Mieczyslaw,** FRS 1987; Senior Principal Scientific Officer, Rothamsted Experimental Station, 1976–90; *b* 20 April

1930; *m* Micheline Dascher; two *d. Educ:* Chelsea College of Science and Technology, Univ. of London (BSc Gen.; BSc Zoology (Class 1); PhD). Research Asst, Chelsea Coll. of Science and Technology, 1954–56; Entomologist, Dept of Insecticides and Fungicides, Rothamsted Experimental Station, 1956–90; leader of unit working on insecticide resistance, 1970–90. *Publications:* numerous, in scientific jls. *Address:* 4 Greenway, Harpenden, Herts AL5 1JQ. *T:* Harpenden (05827) 60716.

*Died 22 July* 1990.

**SAWISTOWSKI, Prof. Henryk,** PhD; FEng 1980; Professor of Chemical Engineering, Imperial College of Science and Technology, University of London, since 1976; *b* 11 Feb. 1925; *s* of Gustaw Sawistowski and Marta (*née* Murawska); *m* 1952, Malgorzata Helena Dzierzanowska; two *d* (one *s* decd). *Educ:* Polish University Coll.; Imperial Coll. of Science and Technol., Univ. of London (BSc Eng 1952, PhD 1955, DIC 1955). FIChemE 1966; FCGI 1980. Imperial Coll. of Science and Technology, London: Lectr, 1955; Sen. Lectr, 1961; Reader in Chem. Engrg, 1966; Dean, City and Guilds College, 1982–84. Rockefeller Vis. Prof., Univ. of Toronto, 1965–66. Chm., EFCE Working Party on Chem. Engrg Educn, 1982–83; Sec., Engrg Professors' Conf., 1977–78; Member: Council, IChemE, 1971–74 and 1981–84 (Vice-Pres., 1981–83); Bd, CSTI, 1982–84. Arnold Greene Medal, IChemE, 1983. *Publications:* Mass Transfer Process Calculations, 1963 (Spanish edn 1967, Czech edn 1969); papers to Chem. Engrg Science, IChemE pubns and to foreign societies. *Recreations:* reading, classical music. *Address:* 5 Beaufort Gardens, Green Lane, SW16 3BP. *T:* 01–764 9355.

*Died 19 Dec.* 1984.

**SAWYERR, Rev. Prof. Canon Harry Alphonso Ebun,** CBE 1963 (MBE 1954); Grand Commander, Order of the Star of Africa (Liberia), 1971; Emeritus Professor of Theology, University of Sierra Leone, since 1980; Warden, Sierra Leone Theological Hall and Church Training Centre, Freetown, since 1982; *b* 16 Oct. 1909; *s* of Rev. Obrien Alphonso Dandeson Sawyerr and Mrs Cleopatra Florence Omodele Sawyerr; *m* 1935, Edith Kehinde Lavinia Edwin; one *d. Educ:* Prince of Wales Sch.; Fourah Bay Coll.; St John's Coll., Durham. BA 1933; MA 1936; MEd 1940. Fourah Bay Coll.: Tutor 1933–45; Lectr 1948–52; Chaplain 1948–56; Sen. Lectr 1952–62; Vice-Principal 1956–58 and 1964–68; Prof. of Theology, 1962–74; Principal, 1968–74; Sen. Lectr in Theology, 1981–82; part-time Lectr, 1982–. Univ. of Sierra Leone: Acting Vice-Chancellor, 1968; Pro-Vice-Chancellor, 1968–70; Vice-Chancellor, 1970–72. Codrington Coll.: Tutor, 1974–80; Vice-Principal, 1975–80; Acting Principal, 1979–80. Sec., Theological Advisers Board, Province of W Africa, 1952–58; Member: World Council of Churches Commn on Faith and Order, 1962–75; Permanent Cttee, Assoc. Internationale pour Etude des Religions Préhistoriques et Ethnologiques, 1976–. Chairman: W African Assoc. of Theol Instns, 1983–85; Conf. of African Theol Instns, 1983–86. Select Preacher, UC Ibadan, 1961; Chm., Board of Teacher Trng, 1960–63; Pres., Milton Margai Trng (now Teachers) Coll., 1960–69; Leader, Sierra Leone Delegn to 3rd Commonwealth Educn Conf., 1964; Mem., Public Service Commn, 1968–69. Editor: Aureol Pamphlets, 1957–74; Sierra Leone Bulletin of Religion, 1962–68; Select Preacher: Fourah Bay Coll., UC Sierra Leone, 1964; Service of Re-interment of Bishop Adjayi Crowther (*ob* 1891), Christ Church Cathedral, Lagos, 1971; Univ. of Ghana, 1974; Service commemorating 150th Anniversary of Landing of 1st Bishop of Barbados, William Hart Coleridge, DD, St Michael's Cath., Barbados, 1975; Lectr, Provincial Clergy Sch., Church of the Province of WI, 1975; Leader of week of prayer for Christian Unity, Trinidad and Tobago, 1975; Conductor of Clergy Retreats, Diocese of Trinidad and Tobago, 1976 and 1977, Dio. of Guyana, 1978, Dio. of Antigua, 1979; Leader of Laity Seminar on Evangelism, Trinidad, 1978; Vis. Lectr on W African Indigenous Religious Thought Forms, Utd Theol Coll. of WI, Kingston, Jamaica and St John's Vianney, RC Seminary, Tunapuna, Trinidad, 1975–81. Consultant: Second Assembly Caribbean Conf. of Churches, 1977; Methodist Consultation on Evangelism in a Pluralist Society, 1980; Mem., Arts and Gen. Studies Faculty Cttee, Univ. of W Indies, 1978. 1st Prize, Thomas Cochrane Essay Comp., 1960. Sierra Leone Independence Medal, 1961. Hon. DD Dunelm, 1970; Hon. DLitt Sierra Leone, 1980. Knight of Mark Twain, 1978. *Publications:* Creative Evangelism, 1968; (with W. T. Harris) The Springs of Mende Belief and Conduct, 1968; God: Ancestor or Creator?, 1970; (contrib.) Biblical Revelation and Traditional Beliefs (ed K. Dickson and P. Ellingworth), 1969; (contrib.) Religion in a Pluralist Society (ed J. Pobee), 1976; articles in Scottish Jl of Theology, Church Quarterly, East Asia Jl of Theology, Internat. Review of Missions, Numen, Sierra Leone Bulletin of Religion, W African Jl of Educn, African Theological Jl, Caribbean Jl of Religious Studies, Caribbean Jl of African Studies. *Recreations:* motor driving, walking, gardening. *Address:* c/o Fourah Bay College, Mount Aureol, Freetown, Sierra Leone. *Died* 1986.

**SAYER, Vice-Adm. Sir Guy (Bourchier),** KBE 1959; CB 1956; DSC 1943; retired as Flag Officer Commanding Reserve Fleet (1958–59);

*b* 2 January 1903; 3rd *s* of late William Feetham and late Edith Alexandra Sayer, E Finchley, London, N; *m* 1925, Sylvia Rosalind Pleadwell, *d* of late Maj.-Gen. R. C. Munday, CB, RAF, and late Mrs Olive Munday, Hartley, Plymouth, Devon; twin *s. Educ:* Cholmeley House, Highgate; RN Colleges Osborne and Dartmouth. Naval Cadet, 1916; Midshipman, 1920; Sub-Lieut, 1923; Lieut-Comdr, 1933; Comdr Dec. 1937; Capt. 1944; Rear-Adm., 1953. Vice-Controller of the Navy and Director of Naval Equipment, Admiralty, 1953–56; Flag Officer, Home Fleet Training Squadron, 1956–57; Vice-Adm. 1957; retired, 1959. *Publication:* The History of HMS Vernon, 1929. *Recreations:* estate maintenance, walking. *Address:* Old Middle Cator, Widecombe-in-the-Moor, Devon. *T:* Widecombe 228. *Died 15 Oct.* 1985.

**SAYERS, Sir Edward (George),** Kt 1965; CMG 1956; MD, Hon. DSc, FRCP, FRACP, Hon. FACP, Hon. FRCPE, FRS (NZ); DTM&H; Formerly Dean of the Medical Faculty and Professor of Therapeutics, University of Otago, New Zealand, 1959–67; *b* 10 Sept. 1902; *s* of Henry Hind Sayers; *m* 1st, 1928, Jane Lumsden, *d* of Wm Grove, MD; two *s* four *d*; 2nd, Patricia Dorothy, *d* of Gordon Coleman. *Educ:* Christ's College, Christchurch; Otago University; Otago Medical School, 1920–24; MB, ChB (NZ), 1924. House Physician, Wellington Hospital, 1925; Student and House Physician, London Sch. of Tropical Medicine, DTM&H 1926; Medical Missionary, British Solomon Is, 1927–34; MRCP 1935. Consulting Physician, Auckland (NZ), 1935–39; FRACP 1938. Served War of 1939–45, Middle East and Pacific, 1939–44; OC Medical Div. 1st NZ Gen. Hosp., Egypt and Greece; Cons. Physician NZ Forces in Pacific; OC 4 New Zealand Gen. Hosp. (Colonel); Cons. Physician, Auckland, NZ, 1945–59; Pres. RACP, 1956–58. Chm. NZ Med. Council, 1956–64; Mem. NZ Med. Research Council, 1959–67; Chm., Scientific Cttee, Nat. Heart Foundn of NZ, 1968–79. Col Comdt, Royal NZMC, 1963–67. Pres., NZ Branch, BMA, 1963; Fellow Christ's College (NZ); Mem. Council, Univ. of Otago, 1959–67. FRCP 1949; Hon. FACP, 1957; Hon. FRCPE, 1960; FRS (NZ), 1961; Hon. DSc Otago, 1975. Cilento Medal for distinguished work in Pacific, 1940. Legion of Merit (USA), 1944, KStJ. *Publications:* articles in med. jls. *Recreation:* fishing. *Address:* 27A Henry Street, Maori Hill, Dunedin, New Zealand. *Club:* Fernhill (Dunedin).

*Died 12 May* 1985.

**SAYERS, Richard Sidney,** FBA 1957; Emeritus Professor of Economics with special reference to Money and Banking, University of London (Cassel Professor of Economics, 1947–68); *b* 11 July 1908; *s* of S. J. Sayers; *m* 1930, Millicent Hodson; one *s* one *d. Educ:* St Catharine's Coll., Cambridge. Asst Lectr in Economics, London Sch. of Economics, 1931–35; Lectr in Economics, Exeter, Corpus Christi and Pembroke Colleges, Oxford, 1935–45; Fellow of Pembroke College, Oxford, 1939–45; Ministry of Supply, 1940–45; Economic Adviser, Cabinet Office, 1945–47. Member: Radcliffe Committee on the Working of the Monetary System, 1957–59; OECD Cttee on Fiscal Measures, 1966–68; Monopolies Commission, 1968. Pres. Section F, Brit. Assoc., 1960; Vice-Pres., Brit. Academy, 1966–67; Pres., Economic Hist. Soc., 1972–74; Vice-Pres., Royal Econ. Soc., 1973–. Hon. Fellow: St Catharine's Coll., Cambridge; LSE; Inst. of Bankers. Hon. DLitt Warwick, 1967; Hon. DCL Kent, 1967. *Publications:* Bank of England Operations, 1890–1914, 1936; Modern Banking, 1938 (7th edn 1967); American Banking System, 1948; (ed) Banking in the British Commonwealth, 1952; (jt editor with T. S. Ashton) Papers in English Monetary History, 1953; Financial Policy, 1939–45, 1956; Central Banking after Bagehot, 1957; Lloyds Bank in the History of English Banking, 1957; (ed) Banking in Western Europe, 1962; (ed) Economic Writings of James Pennington, 1963; A History of Economic Change in England, 1880–1939, 1967; Gilletts in the London Money Market, 1867–1967, 1968; The Bank of England 1891–1944, 1976. *Died 25 Feb.* 1989.

**SCARBOROUGH, Prof. Harold,** CBE 1976; Professor, Department of Medicine, and Provost, College of Medical Sciences, University of Maiduguri, Nigeria, and Chief Medical Director, University of Maiduguri Teaching Hospital, 1979–84, retired; *b* 27 March 1909; British; unmarried. *Educ:* Bridlington School, Yorks; Edinburgh University; St Mary's Hospital Medical School; Harvard University. Clinical Tutor, Royal Infirmary of Edinburgh and Assistant, Dept of Therapeutics, Edinburgh Univ., 1933–38; Beit Memorial Research Fellow and Demonstrator in Pharmacology, Edinburgh Univ., 1938–39; Beit Memorial Research Fellow, Medical Unit, St Mary's Hosp., London, 1945–47; Rockefeller Travelling Fellow at Harvard Medical School, 1947–48; Reader in Medicine, University of Birmingham, 1949–50; Prof. of Medicine in Welsh Nat. Sch. of Medicine, Univ. of Wales, 1950–70; formerly: Dir, Med. Unit, Cardiff Royal Infirmary; Chm., Div. of Medicine, United Cardiff Hosps; Prof. of Medicine and Dean of the Faculty of Medicine, Ahmadu Bello Univ., Zaria, Nigeria, 1970–76; Visiting Professor of Medicine: Garyounis Univ., Libya, 1978–; Faculty of Health Sciences, Univ. of Ilorin, Nigeria, 1978–79. Hon. Fellow, Univ. of Wales Coll. of Medicine, 1986. *Publications:* (part author)

Textbook of Physiology and Biochemistry, 1950; papers in BMJ, Lancet, Quart. Jl Med., and other medical and scientific journals. *Recreations:* gardening, the theatre. *Address:* c/o Barclays Bank, 170 Whitchurch Road, Cardiff CF4 3YG.
*Died 23 Aug.* 1988.

**SCARFE, Prof. Francis Harold,** CBE 1972 (OBE 1965); MA, DLit; FRSL; author; Director, British Institute in Paris, 1959–78, and Professor of French in the University of London, 1965–78, later Professor Emeritus; *b* 18 September 1911; *s* of John James Scarfe and Margaret Ingham Dobson; *m* 1938, Margarete M. Geisler; one *s*. *Educ:* Universities of Durham, Cambridge and Paris. RAOC and RAEC, 1941–46; Lt-Col, 1945. Supervisor of Studies and Secretary, Extension Lectures Committee, University of Oxford, 1946–47; Senior Lecturer in French, University of Glasgow, 1947–59. Chevalier des Arts et Lettres. Prix de l'Ile St Louis, 1967. Chevalier de la Légion d'Honneur, 1978. *Publications: poetry:* Inscapes, 1940; Poems and Ballads, 1941; Underworlds, 1950; Grounds for Conceit, 1984; *criticism:* Auden and After, 1942; W. H. Auden, 1949 (Monaco); The Art of Paul Valéry, 1954; La vie et l'œuvre de T. S. Eliot, 1964 (Paris); *editions:* Baudelaire, 1961; Chénier, 1961; André Chénier, his Life and Work, 1965; (ed and trans.) Baudelaire, Complete Verse, vol. 1, 1985, vol. 2, Poems in Prose,1987 (published posthumously); *novels:* Promises, 1950; Single Blessedness, 1951; Unfinished Woman, 1954; various translations. *Address:* 433 Banbury Road, Oxford OX2 8ED. *T:* Oxford 58127.
*Died 13 March* 1986.

**SCARLETT, Sir Peter (William Shelley Yorke),** KCMG 1958 (CMG 1949); KCVO 1955; *b* 30 March 1905; *s* of late William James Yorke Scarlett, Fyfield House, Andover; *m* 1934, Elisabeth, *d* of late Sir John Dearman Birchall, TD, MP, Cotswold Farm, Cirencester; one *s* three *d*. *Educ:* Eton; Christ Church, Oxford. Apptd to Foreign Office as a Third Secretary, 1929; Cairo, 1930; Bagdad, 1932; Lisbon, 1934; promoted a Second Secretary, 1934; acted as Chargé d'Affaires, Riga, 1937 and 1938. Attached to representative of Latvia at coronation of King George VI, 1937; Brussels, 1938; promoted actg First Sec., 1940; captured by enemy forces, 1940; returned to UK and resumed duties at Foreign Office, 1941; Paris, 1944; Allied Forces Headquarters, Caserta, 1946; Counsellor, Foreign Office, 1947; Inspector of HM Diplomatic Service Establishments, 1950; British Permanent Representative on the Council of Europe, Strasbourg, 1952; HM Ambassador to Norway, 1955; HM Minister to the Holy See, 1960–65, retired. Chairman, Cathedrals Advisory Committee, 1967–81. *Address:* 35 Tivoli Road, Cheltenham, Glos. *Club:* Carlton. *Died 28 Dec.* 1987.

**SCARR, John Geoffrey Fearnley;** *b* 12 July 1910; 2nd *s* of late William Harcourt Scarr and Lydia (*née* Harrop); *m* 1945, Dorothy Edna Terry; two *d*. *Educ:* King's School, Ely; Trinity College, Cambridge (MA Hons, LLB). Called to the Bar, Lincoln's Inn, 1935; practised Northern Circuit and Lancashire Palatine Court. Served throughout War of 1939–45: Far East and War Office; major. Colonial Service; Resident Magistrate and Coroner, N Rhodesia, 1953; Chief Judicial Comr, Western Pacific High Commn Territories, 1959; Judge of the Supreme Court, Nassau and Bahamas, 1961–65; Acting Chief Justice on several occasions; Chancellor Dio. Nassau and the Bahamas, 1962–64; Deputy Chairman, Bahamas Constituencies Commn, 1964; Legal Staff of Law Commn, 1965–66, and of Foreign Compensation Commn, 1970–75; Mem., Oxford Dio. Pastoral Cttee, 1978–. Mem., South Oxfordshire DC, 1978–. *Publications:* The Law and Practice of Land Registration, Northern Rhodesia Law Reports, 1949–54; contrib. to legal journals. *Recreations:* golf, music, sailing, painting. *Address:* Littlegate, Shiplake, Henley-on-Thames, Oxon. *T:* Wargrave 2201. *Club:* Royal Nassau Sailing. *Died 11 Nov.* 1982.

**SCHAEFFER, Prof. Claude Frederic Armand;** Officier Légion d'Honneur, 1947; Hon. Professor, Collège de France; Member of French Academy; General Director of Archæological Expeditions of Ras Shamra Ugarit (Syria) and Enkomi Alasia (Cyprus); Member of National Council of Scientific Research; Member Higher Council of Archaeological Research, Ministry of Cultural Affairs; *b* Strasbourg, Alsace, 6 March 1898; *s* of Henri Schaeffer, industrialist, and Mme Schaeffer (*née* Wiernsberger); *m* 1924, Odile, *d* of Prof. Robert Forrer, archæologist and collector; one *s* two *d*. *Educ:* Univ. Strasbourg. Keeper: Archæological Museum, Strasbourg, 1924–33; Coin Cabinet, Univ. Strasbourg, 1926–33; Museum of Nat. Antiquities, Château de St-Germain-en-Laye, 1933–56; Fellow of St John's Coll., Oxford, 1941–45; Hon. Fellow, 1955–. Captain of Corvette, Free French Naval Forces, England, 1943–45. Director of Research, Nat. Centre of Scientific Research, 1946–54; Prof. of European Pre-history and Nat. Archæology, Ecole de Louvre, 1951–54. Vice-Pres., Commn des Fouilles et Missions Archéologiques, Min. of Foreign Affairs, 1952–69. Life Mem., Cttee of Honour, Internat. Union of Prehistoric and Protohistoric Sciences, 1964. Member or Hon. Mem. of a number of socs. DrLit *hc* Oxford, 1942; Dr of Law *hc* Glasgow, 1948; Gold Medal: Soc. of Antiquaries of London, 1958; Soc. of Sciences, Famagusta, 1965.

Foreign Member, Royal Academy of Denmark. Hon. Citizen: Famagusta, 1970; Latakia, 1950. Holder of foreign awards. *Publications:* Les Haches néolithiques du Musée de Haguenau, 1924; Les Tertres funéraires préhistoriques dans la forêt de Haguenau, Vol. I, Les Tumulus de l'Age du Bronze, 1926; Un Dépôt d'outils et un trésor de bronze de l'époque galloromaine, découverts à Seltz, 1927; Les Tertres funéraires préhistoriques dans la forêt de Haguenau, Vol. II, Les Tumulus de l'Age du Fer, 1930; Le Casque romain de Drusenheim, 1932; Missions en Chypre, 1936; The Cuneiform Texts of Ras Shamra-Ugarit, 1939; Ugaritica, I, 1939; Stratigraphie comparée et chronologie de l'Asie Occidentale, vol. I, 1948; Ugaritica, II, 1949; Enkomi-Alasia, I, 1952; Ugaritica, III, 1956; IV, 1962; V, 1968; VI, 1969; VII, 1978; Alasia, I, 1970; also very numerous contributions to learned journals, etc. *Recreations:* travel, exploration, mountains. *Address:* Le Castel Blanc, 16 rue Turgot, 78100 St Germain-en-Laye, France. *T:* 451.42.25; La Chaumière, Fréland, 68240 Kaysersberg, France. *T:* 47.17.50; L'Escale, 83420 La Croix-Valmer, BP16, France. *T:* 79.62.14.
*Died 25 Aug.* 1982.

**SCHAPIRO, Prof. Leonard Bertram,** CBE 1980; LLB; FBA 1971; Professor of Political Science, with Special Reference to Russian Studies, London School of Economics and Political Science, University of London, 1963–75, later Emeritus; Honorary Fellow, 1980; *b* Glasgow, 22 April 1908; *s* of Max Schapiro and Leah (*née* Levine); *m* 1st, 1943, Isabel Margaret (marr. diss. 1976), *d* of late Don Salvador de Madariaga; no *c*; 2nd, 1976, Roma Thewes, *d* of late Dr C. Sherris. *Educ:* St Paul's Sch.; University Coll., London (Fellow, 1973). Called to Bar, Gray's Inn, 1932; practised at Bar, London and Western Circuit, 1932–39; BBC Monitoring Service, 1940–42; War Office, 1942–45; Intell. Div., German Control Commn, 1945–46 (Maj.); practised at Bar, 1946–55; Dept of Politics, LSE, 1955–75. Member: Res. Bd, Inst. of Jewish Affairs; Council, Keston Coll. Chairman, Editorial Board: Government and Opposition; Soviet Jewish Affairs; Mem., Editorial Board, Soviet Survey; Vice-Pres., Nat. Council for One Parent Families, 1976–. For. Hon. Mem., Amer. Acad. of Arts and Sciences, 1967. *Publications:* The Origin of the Communist Autocracy, 1955, 2nd edn 1976; The Communist Party of the Soviet Union, 1960, 2nd edn 1970; The Government and Politics of Soviet Russia, 1965, 7th edn 1977; Rationalism and Nationalism in Russian Nineteenth Century Political Thought, 1967; trans. (with critical essay) Turgenev's Spring Torrents, 1972; Totalitarianism, 1972; Turgenev: his life and times, 1979; (ed jtly) The Soviet Worker, 1981; 1917: The Russian Revolutionaries and the Origins of Modern Communism, 1984; numerous contribs to learned jls, symposia, Encyclopædia Britannica, etc. *Recreations:* music, looking at paintings. *Address:* c/o London School of Economics and Political Science, Houghton Street, WC2. *Club:* Reform. *Died 2 Nov.* 1983.

**SCHERGER, Air Chief Marshal Sir Frederick (Rudolph Williams),** KBE 1958 (CBE 1950); CB 1954; DSO 1944; AFC 1940; *b* 18 May 1904; *o s* of Frederick H. Scherger and Sarah (*née* Chamberlain), Ararat, Victoria, Australia; *m* 1st, 1929, Thelma Lilian Harricks (*d* 1974); one *d*; 2nd, 1975, Mrs J. Robertson. *Educ:* Ararat High School; Royal Military College, Australia. Grad. Dec. 1924; seconded to RAAF Jan. 1925; completed flying course, Dec. 1925. Various flying training and squadron appts, 1926–35; RAF Staff Coll. Course, 1935; RAF attachments, 1936; Director of Training, RAAF, 1937–40; AOC No 10 Group, RAAF, 1943–44; AOC 1st TAF, RAAF, 1945–46; idc, 1946; Deputy Chief of Air Staff, RAAF, 1947–51; Head Australian Joint Services Staff, Washington, 1951–52; Air Officer Commanding, RAF, Malaya, 1953–54; Air Member for Personnel, RAAF, 1955–57; CAS, RAAF, 1957–61; Chairman, Chiefs of Staff, 1961–66. Chairman: Australian Nat. Airlines Commn, 1966–75; Commonwealth Aircraft Corp. Pty Ltd, 1968–74; Mono Pumps (Aust.), 1970–82; Pipe Line Engrg Aust. Ltd; Director: Associated Broadcasting Services, 1973–80; Plessey (Pacific) Ltd, 1966–81; International Computers Ltd, 1969–81. *Recreations:* golf, shooting, motoring. *Address:* 45 Stephens Street, North Balwyn, Vic 3104, Australia. *Clubs:* Melbourne, Naval and Military (Melbourne). *Died 17 Jan.* 1984.

**SCHILD, Heinz Otto,** FRS 1966; MD, PhD, DSc; FIBiol; Professor of Pharmacology, University of London, at University College, 1961–73, Emeritus Professor, 1973; *b* Fiume, 18 May 1906; *s* of Hermann Schild and Thekla (*née* Spiegel); *m* 1938, Mireille Madeleine Haquin; three *d*. *Educ:* Universities of Munich, Berlin and Edinburgh. MD Munich, 1931; PhD Edinburgh, 1935; DSc London, 1950. Assistant, Pharmacology Dept, Univ. of Edinburgh, 1936; Demonstrator, 1937, Lecturer, 1942, Reader, 1945, Dept of Pharmacology, University Coll., London; Dean, Faculty of Med. Sciences, University Coll., 1964–67; Hon. Fellow UCL, 1982. Vis. Prof., NY State Univ., 1968. Mem., WHO Visiting Team of Medical Scientists to SE Asia, 1952. Examiner, Univs of Leeds, Liverpool, Oxford, Edinburgh, West Africa, West Indies, Makerere College. Schmiedeberg Plakette Deutsche Pharmak. Ges., 1977; Hon. Mem., British Pharmacol Soc.; Sen. Mem., British Immunol. Soc.; Hon. Mem., European Histamine Res. Soc. Wellcome Gold Medal,

British Pharmacol Soc., 1981. *Publications:* Applied Pharmacology, 1980; papers in Journal of Physiology, British Journal of Pharmacology, Immunology, Lancet, Nature. *Recreation:* walking slowly. *Address:* Mole Ridge, St Mary's Road, Leatherhead, Surrey. *T:* Leatherhead 373773. *Died* 15 *June* 1984.

**SCHLESINGER, Bernard Edward,** OBE 1946; MA, MD, FRCP; Consulting Physician to University College Hospital, Hospital for Sick Children, Great Ormond Street, and Royal Northern Hospital; originally Consulting Paediatrician to the Army; retired; *b* 23 Nov. 1896; *s* of late Richard Schlesinger; *m* 1925, Winifred Henrietta, *d* of late H. Regensburg, London; two *s* one *d* (and two *d* decd). *Educ:* Uppingham; Emmanuel Coll., Cambridge. Served European War, 1914–18 as a Private, and in War of 1939–45, as Brigadier, Consulting Physician, NW Army and Central Command, India Command. Fell. of Assoc. of Physicians, Brit. Pædiatric Assoc. (Pres., 1953–54); Fell., Roy. Soc. of Med. (Pres., Pædiatric Sect, 1960–61). Milroy Lectr, 1938. Dawson Williams Prize, 1961. *Publications:* numerous articles and books on diseases of children, researches on rheumatism, and comparative aspects of medicine in the two world wars. *Recreation:* gardening. *Address:* Oliver's Cottage, Boxford, near Newbury, Berks. *T:* Boxford 206. *Club:* Sloane. *Died* 25 *Jan.* 1984.

**SCHMITTHOFF, Clive Macmillan,** Dr jur, LLD; barrister; *b* 24 March 1903; *s* of Hermann and Anna Schmitthoff; *m* 1940, Twinkie (Ilse) (*née* Auerbach). *Educ:* Univs of Berlin and London. Dr jur Berlin 1927; LLM 1936, LLD 1953, London. Called to Bar, Gray's Inn, 1936. Served HM Army, 1940–45: Normandy, War Office, CCG, Warrant Officer (France and Germany Star, Def. and War medals). Lectr, 1948–58, Sen. Lectr, 1958–63, Principal Lectr, 1963–71, Prof. Emeritus, 1982, City of London Polytechnic. Legal Advr to UN, 1966. Visiting Professor: City Univ., 1971–87 (Hon. Vis. Prof., 1988–); Louisiana State Univ., 1964, 1965; Univ. of Manitoba Law Sch., 1965, 1969, 1971, 1978; Univ. of Kent, 1971–84; Gresham Prof. in Law, 1976–86. Jt Vice-Chm., Centre for Commercial Law Studies, QMC, Univ. of London, 1985–. Vice-President: Assoc. of Law Teachers, 1965–; Inst. of Export, 1979–; Mansfield Law Club, 1985– (Founder 1948); Founder and Gen. Editor, Journal of Business Law, 1957–89, Consulting Gen. Editor, 1989–. Hon. Professor of Law: Ruhr Univ., Bochum, 1968; Univ. of Kent, 1978. Hon. Djur: Marburg and Berne, 1977; Bielefeld, 1983; Hon. DLitt Heriot-Watt, 1978; Hon. LLD: Kent, 1982; CNAA, 1986. FIEx 1974. Grand Cross of Merit, German Fed. Republic, 1974. *Publications:* The English Conflict of Laws, 1945, 3rd edn 1954; Schmitthoff's Export Trade, 1948, 9th edn 1990; The Sale of Goods, 1951, 2nd edn 1966; ed, Palmer's Company Law, 1959–, 24th edn 1987; jt ed, Charlesworth's Mercantile Law, 1960–, 14th edn; (ed jtly) International Commercial Arbitration, 1976, 3rd edn 1985; Commercial Law in a Changing Economic Climate, 1977, 2nd edn 1981; Extrajudicial Dispute Settlement, Forum Internationale No 6, 1985; Clive M. Schmitthoff's Select Essays on International Trade Law, ed Chia-Jui Cheng, 1988; contrib. many legal jls, UK and abroad; *relevant publications:* Law and International Trade, ed Fritz Fabricius, 1973; Essays for Clive Schmitthoff, ed John Adams, 1983. *Recreations:* history, literature, music, modern art. *Address:* 29 Blenheim Road, Bedford Park, W4 1ET. *Died* 30 *Sept.* 1990.

**SCHMOLLER, Hans Peter,** RDI 1976; typographer; *b* 9 April 1916; *o c* of Dr Hans Schmoller and Marie (*née* Behrend); *m* 1st, 1947, Dorothée Wachsmuth (*d* 1948); one *d*; 2nd, 1950, Tatyana Kent; one *s*. *Educ:* Berlin. Left sch. after Hitler came to power; served apprenticeship as compositor, 1933–37; Morija Printing Works, Morija, Basutoland (now Lesotho), 1938–46; Curwen Press, London, 1947–49; joined Penguin Books Ltd as Typographer, 1949; Head of Production, 1956–76; Dir, 1960–76; Consultant, 1976–80. Has served on book design juries in Britain, Germany and USA; lectured in England and abroad; participated in internat. book design projects. Mem. Council, RSA, 1979–84 (FRSA, 1977). Various book design awards and medals. Corresp. Mem., Bund Deutscher Buchkünstler (Fed. Germany), 1965. *Publications:* Mr Gladstone's Washi, 1984; (contrib.) Essays in the History of Publishing: Longman 1724–1974, 1974 (ed Asa Briggs); (ed) The Officina Bodoni 1923–1977, (German edn 1979, English and Italian edns 1980); contribs to The Times, TLS, Penrose Annual, Signature, Imprimatur, Philobiblon, Matrix. *Recreations:* book-collecting, paper-chasing, peregrinating. *Address:* Steading, Down Place, Windsor, Berks SL4 5UG. *T:* Maidenhead 23565. *Clubs:* Arts; Double Crown (Pres. 1968–69). *Died* 25 *Sept.* 1985.

**SCHOFIELD, Vice-Adm. Brian Betham,** CB 1949; CBE 1943; *b* 11 Oct. 1895; *s* of Thomas Dodgshon Schofield and Margaret Annie Bradley; *m* 1st, 1922, Doris Sibyl Ambrose (marr. diss., 1941); one *s* (and one *s* decd); 2nd, 1941, Norah Kathleen Handley (*née* Beatty) (*d* 1946); 3rd, 1946, Grace Mildred Seale; two *d*. *Educ:* RN Colleges, Osborne and Dartmouth. Midshipman, 1913 (Dogger Bank action); Lieut-Comdr 1925; Comdr 1931; Capt., 1938; Rear-Admiral, 1947; Vice-Adm., 1950; Naval Attaché at The Hague and Brussels,

1939–40; commanded HMS King George V, 1945–46; despatches, 1946. Retired list, 1950. King George VI Coronation medal. Officer of Legion of Merit (USA). *Publications:* The Royal Navy Today, 1960; The Russian Convoys, 1964; British Seapower, 1967; The Rescue Ships (with L. F. Martyn), 1968; The Loss of the Bismarck, 1972; The Attack on Taranto, 1973; Operation Neptune, 1974; The Arctic Convoys, 1977; Navigation and Direction, 1977. *Address:* Holme, Lower Shiplake, Henley-on-Thames, Oxon. *T:* Wargrave 2809. *Died* 8 *Nov.* 1984.

**SCHOFIELD, (Edward) Guy;** FJI; Journalist; *b* 10 July 1902; *s* of Frank Garside Schofield and Fanny Atkinson; *m* 1st, Norah Ellett (*d* 1935); one *d*; 2nd, Ellen Clark (*d* 1977). *Educ:* Leeds Modern School. Leeds Mercury, 1918–25; Daily Dispatch, Manchester, 1925–27; Evening Chronicle, Manchester, 1929–30; Chief Sub-Editor, Evening Standard, London, 1931–38; Editor: Yorkshire Evening News, 1938–42; The Evening News, London, 1942–50; Daily Mail, London, 1950–55; Director: Associated Newspapers Ltd, 1947–55; United Newspapers Ltd, 1960–79; Sheffield Newspapers Ltd, 1963–79; Yorkshire Post Newspapers Ltd, 1969–82. Member of Press Council, 1953–55; Chairman British Committee, International Press Institute, 1953–55; Director of Publicity, Conservative Party Headquarters, 1955–57. *Publications:* The Purple and the Scarlet, 1959; Crime Before Calvary, 1960; In the Year 62, 1962; Why Was He Killed?, 1965; The Men that Carry the News, 1975. *Address:* Pear Tree Cottage, Sinnington, York YO6 6RZ. *Died* 14 *Feb.* 1990.

**SCHOLES, Joseph,** CB 1945; OBE 1918; *b* 4 Sept. 1889; *s* of John Scholes, Radcliffe, Lancs; *m* 1915, Edna Horrocks (*d* 1981). *Educ:* Manchester Grammar School; Trinity College, Cambridge. Wrangler, Mathematical Tripos, 1911; entered GPO through Higher Division, 1912; Assistant Director of Vegetable Supplies, Ministry of Food, 1916–20; Postmaster-Surveyor, Glasgow, 1936; Regional Director, GPO 1939; Principal Officer to Regional Commissioner, Ministry of Home Security, 1940–43; Assistant Director-General (Personnel) GPO, 1946–49; retired. *Address:* Church Orchard, North Newton, Bridgwater, Somerset. *T:* North Petherton 662338. *Died* 8 *April* 1983.

**SCHOLTE, Lieut-Col Frederick Lewellen,** OBE (mil.) 1919; FIMechE; late RFC; retired Consulting Engineer; *b* 1890; *m* Hilda May (*d* 1969), *d* of James Gardner, Skelmorlie, Ayrshire; one *s* two *d*. *Educ:* Highgate School. *Address:* c/o Captain O. N. G. Scholte, Littlecourt, Kingston, Canterbury, Kent CT4 6HY. *Clubs:* Royal Automobile, Royal Air Force. *Died* 31 *July* 1984.

**SCHOTZ, Benno,** RSA 1937; RGI 1977; artist-sculptor; Queen's Sculptor in Ordinary for Scotland, since 1963; *b* 1891; *s* of Jacob Schotz; *m* 1927, Milly Stelmach; one *s* one *d*. *Educ:* Pärnu, Estonia; Glasgow. BSc 1965. Head of Sculpture and Ceramics Departments, Glasgow School of Art, 1938–61. Originally studied engineering at Darmstadt and Glasgow Royal Technical Coll.; then took up sculpture; at Glasgow Art School; first one-man show in 1926 at Reid and Lefèvre's in Glasgow; second 1929; first London one-man show at the Lefèvre Galleries, 1930; one-man show in Dundee, 1935, Edinburgh, 1945, Jerusalem and Haifa Municipal Galleries, 1954–55; Edinburgh Festival, 1955; Royal Fine Art Institute Rooms, Glasgow, 1957; Exhibitions: by Arts Council of Great Britain (Scottish Cttee) in Edinburgh, Aberdeen, Dundee, Perth, Stirling, 1962; Glasgow, 1963; New Charing Cross Gall., 1968; by Scottish Arts Council, Edinburgh and Aberdeen, 1971; represented in Public Galleries in Glasgow, Edinburgh, Aberdeen, Perth, Dundee, Paisley, Stoke-on-Trent, Belfast, Jerusalem, Tel-Aviv and New Zealand; modelled many personalities in the arts and politics; Bust of Keir Hardie in House of Commons, 1956. Has a number of carvings on buildings in Glasgow and elsewhere; sculpture groups in churches and schools; 23 foot high Group Town Centre piece in Glenrothes; statue of Rob Roy, Stirling, 1975, etc. Freedom, City of Glasgow, 1981. Hon. FRIAS 1969; Hon. President: Glasgow Group, 1970; Royal Glasgow Inst. of Fine Arts, 1973. Hon. Mem., RBS, 1980. Hon. LLD Strathclyde, 1969. *Address:* 2 Kirklee Road, Glasgow G12 0TN. *T:* 041-339 9963. *Club:* Glasgow Art (Glasgow). *Died* 11 *Oct.* 1984.

**SCHRAM, Emil;** Chairman of Board, Peru Trust Co.; *b* Peru, Indiana, 23 November 1893; *s* of Emil Alexander Schram and Katharine Graf; *m* 1914, Mabel Miller (decd); three *s*; *m* 1971, Margaret Beauchamp Percy. *Educ:* Peru High School. Book-keeper, J. O. Cole, Peru, Ind., 1910–15; manager Hartwell Land Trust, Hillview, Ill., 1915–33; Chairman National Drainage Assoc., 1931–33; chief, drainage, levee and irrigation div., Reconstruction Finance Corp., 1933–36; Director, 1936–41; Chm., 1939–41; President, New York Stock Exchange, 1941–51; Director: Cities Service Co.; Associates Investment Co.; Home Insce Co.; Indiana National Bank; CTS Corp. Valley Farms, Inc.; Hon. Mem. Business Council. Hon. degrees: Dr of Law: New York Univ.; Univ. of Vermont; Franklin College; Indiana Univ. *Recreations:* golf and fishing. *Address:*

Hillcrest, RR1, Peru, Ind 46970, USA. *T:* 473 9100. *Club:* Columbia (Indianapolis). *Died* 18 *Sept.* 1987.

**SCHULTZ, Prof. Donald Lorimer,** OBE 1984; Professor of Mechanical Engineering, and Fellow of St Hugh's College, Oxford, since 1984; *b* 20 Dec. 1926; *s* of William Alexander and Olga Schultz; *m* 1954, June (*née* Matheson); three *s* one *d. Educ:* Canterbury University College, NZ (BE (Hons) Elec.); Oriel College, Oxford (MA 1961, DPhil 1954). National Physical Laboratory, 1955–61; Tutor and Fellow, St Catherine's College, Oxford, 1961–84; Donald Pollock Reader in Engineering Sci., Oxford, 1973–84. *Publications:* contribs to Jl Fluid Mech., ASME; papers on physiological fluid dynamics. *Recreation:* carpentry. *Address:* The Bakehouse, Stanton St John, Oxford. *T:* Stanton St John 396. *Died* 27 *April* 1987.

**SCHUSTER, Sir George Ernest,** KCSI 1931; KCMG 1926; CBE 1918; MC; Vice-President, International Council, United World Colleges; *b* 25 April 1881; *s* of late Ernest Schuster, KC; *m* 1908, Hon. Gwendolen (*d* 1981), *d* of Lord Parker of Waddington; one *s* (and one killed in action, 1941). *Educ:* Charterhouse (Scholar); New College, Oxford (Classical Exhibitioner), 1st Class in Greats, 1903. Barrister-at-Law, 1905; partner in Schuster Son & Co.; and Director of numerous companies, 1906–14; served European War, 1914–18, with QO Oxfordshire Hussars and on Staff in France; North Russia, 1919, AA and QMG, Murmansk Force, Lt-Col TF Reserve (despatches four times, MC, CBE); travelled Central Europe to report on economic conditions for Anglo-Danubian Assoc. Ltd, 1920; Chief Assist to Organiser of International Credits under League of Nations, 1921; Member of Advisory Committee to Treasury under Trade Facilities Act, 1921–22; Financial Secretary Sudan Government, 1922–27; Chairman of Advisory Committee to Colonial Secretary on East African Loans, 1926–28; Economic and Financial Adviser, Colonial Office, 1927–28; Member of East African Commission on Closer Union, 1928; Finance Mem. of Executive Council of Viceroy of India, 1928–34; Chairman of Joint Committee of Inquiry into the Anglo Argentine Meat Trade, 1935–38; Mem. of Colonial Development Advisory Cttee, 1936–38; MP (L Nat) Walsall, 1938–45; Member of Select Committee on National Expenditure, 1939–45. Member of Govt Cttee on Industrial Productivity and Chairman of Cttee's Panel on Human Relations, 1947–51; Mem. and Treas. of Medical Research Council, 1947–51; visited Malta at request of Malta Govt to advise on economic and financial policy, 1950 and 1956–57. Chm., Oxford Regional Hosp. Bd, 1951–63; Chm. Bd of Governors, United World Coll. of Atlantic, 1963–73. Mem., Oxon CC, 1952–74. Hon. DCL Oxford. *Publications:* India and Democracy, 1941; Christianity and Human Relations in Industry, 1951; Private Work and Public Causes, 1979. *Recreations:* all country sports. *Address:* Nether Worton House, Middle Barton, Oxon OX5 4AT. *Clubs:* Athenæum, Brooks's.
*Died* 5 *June* 1982.

**SCHWARTZ, George Leopold,** BA, BSc (Econ.); Deputy City Editor Sunday Times, Economic Adviser Kemsley Newspapers, 1944–61; writer of Sunday Times economics column, 1961–71; *b* 10 Feb. 1891; *s* of late Adolph George Schwartz, Philadelphia; *m* 1927, Rhoda Lomax (*d* 1966). *Educ:* Varndean Sch.; St Paul's Coll., Cheltenham; London School of Economics. Teacher, LCC, 1913; Secretary London Cambridge Economic Service, 1923; Cassel Lecturer in University of London, 1929. Editor Bankers' Magazine, 1945–54. Hon. Fellow, London School of Economics. *Publications:* (with F. W. Paish) Insurance Funds and their Investment, 1934; Bread and Circuses, 1959; articles and pamphlets. *Recreation:* detesting government. *Address:* 28 Spencer Drive, N2. *T:* 01-455 7423. *Club:* Reform. *Died* 2 *April* 1983.

**SCICLUNA, Sir Hannibal Publius,** Kt 1955; MBE 1935; MA (*hc* Oxon, 1938); LLD (*hc* Malta, 1966); FSA (London, 1946, Scotland 1959); *b* 15 February 1880; *s* of late Joseph Scicluna and Carmen (*née* Galdes); *m* 1st, 1903, Amalia (*née* Lanfranco) (*d* 1947); two *s* (and one *s* decd) three *d*; 2nd, 1959, Margaret Helen Jarvis (*née* Cadzow) (*d* 1977). *Educ:* St Ignatius College; Royal Malta University. Entered Malta Civil Service, 1902; Solicitor, 1905; Secretary and Registrar of Malta University, 1913–20; Solicitor and Clerk, Crown Advocate's Office and Min. of Justice, 1916–23; Secretary to Legal Sec., Malta Imp. Govt, 1921–23; Rep. of Malta Govt Emigration Cttee in Devastated Regions, France, 1920 (Officier d'Académie, France); Mem. Antiquities Cttee, Malta, 1922; Librarian of Roy. Malta Library, 1923; Malta Rep. Internat. Cttee of Hist. Sciences, 1931; Dir Malta Museum, 1937; Dep. Comr BRCOStJ Joint War Organisation, 1940; Pres. Malta Cttee BRCS, 1952; Archivist and Librarian, Sov. Mil. Order of Malta, 1955 (Rome). Frequent delegate for Malta at internat. congresses, etc. Mem. Council, Imp. Soc. of Kts Bachelor, 1956. Hon. Life Pres., Chamber of Legal Procurators, Malta, 1972. King's Jubilee Medal, 1935; Coronation Medals, 1937 and 1953; Officer of the Legion of Honour, 1950; KStJ 1938; Dist. Service Medal, Order of St John; Kt Grand Cross of Danish Order of St John of Jerusalem, 1966; Kt Grand Cross of Merit of Order of Malta, 1956; Kt Grand Cross of Magistral Grace with Riband, Orders of St John of Jerusalem and

of Malta, 1959; KCSG 1956; Kt of Honour, Order of House of Lippe, 1962; Grand Cross with Riband of Constantinian Order of St George, 1963; Kt Grand Cross Hospitaller and Military Order of St Lazarus of Jerusalem, 1967; Grand Cross, Order of St Maurice and St Lazarus, 1973; Volunteer Medical Service Medal, BRCS, 1970. *Publications:* The Archives of the SM Order of Malta, 1912; The French Occupation of Malta (1798–1800), 1923; The Order of St John of Jerusalem, 1929; The Book of Deliberations of the Venerable Tongue of England, 1949; The Church of St John in Valletta, 1955; The Order of St John of Jerusalem and Places of Interest in Malta and Gozo, 1969; Actes et Documents relatifs à l'Occupation Française de Malte 1798–1800, 1979; numerous historical and documentary. *Recreations:* travel; formerly football (Association), riding, tennis, swimming, boating. *Address:* Villa St Martin, San Martin, Malta, GC. *T:* St Paul's 73428; The Cloisters, 27 Mrabat Street, Sliema, Malta, GC. *T:* Sliema 30493. *Clubs:* Casino Maltese (Valletta); Malta Union (Sliema, Malta, GC).
*Died* 21 *Dec.* 1981.

**SCORGIE, Mervyn Nelson,** OBE 1980; Member of Greater London Council for City of London and Westminster South, 1973–81; Chairman, Industry and Employment Committee, Greater London Council, 1977–81; *b* 21 Oct. 1915; 2nd *s* of late Robert Lind Scorgie and Elsie Ida Mary Scorgie. *Educ:* King Edward VI Sch., Southampton; LSE (BScEcon Hons 1946). Qual. pharmaceutical chemist, 1938. Called to the Bar, Middle Temple, 1948. Abbott Labs, Queenborough, Kent, 1949–64: Man. Dir, 1954–64. Mem. GLC, for Cities of London and Westminster, 1970–73; Opposition spokesman, ILEA Finance Sub-Cttee, 1970–81. Vice-Chm., SE Area Provincial Council, Conservative Party, 1965–71; Chm., SE Area Cons. Polit. Centre, 1967–70; National Chm., Cons. Polit. Centre, 1972–75 (Vice-Chm., 1969–72); Pres., Faversham Cons. Assoc., 1975– (Chm., 1967–70); Vice-Chm., Cities of London and Westminster Cons. Assoc., 1972–75. Cons. Parly Candidate, Neath, 1964. Governor: Parliament Hill Sch., 1971–79; Pimlico Sch., 1973–; William Ellis Sch., 1975–. Governor, Royal Festival Ballet, 1980–. ILEA Rep., Sir William Boreman's Foundn of Drapers Co.; Liveryman, Fletchers Co. Freeman, City of London, 1974. *Recreations:* reading, theatre, bridge, racing. *Clubs:* Carlton (Mem., Political Cttee, 1969–79), St Stephen's Constitutional.
*Died* 30 *March* 1986.

**SCORRER, Aileen Mona,** CBE 1953; Chief Inspector, Children's Department, Home Office, 1950–65; *b* 26 Feb. 1905; *d* of late G. H. Scorrer, Sussex, and late Mina Scorrer (*née* Drury). *Educ:* Huyton College, Liverpool; Royal Holloway College, London. *Address:* The Glade, Mead Road, Chislehurst, Kent BR7 6AD. *T:* 01-467 5370.
*Died* 20 *Oct.* 1984.

**SCOTLAND, James,** CBE 1975; MA, LLB, MEd, FEIS; FRSA; Principal, Aberdeen College of Education, since 1961; *b* 1917; *s* of Duncan Anderson Scotland and Mary Emmerson; *m* 1944, Jean Cowan; two *s. Educ:* Whitehill Sch., Glasgow; Glasgow Univ. MA 1939; BL 1940; LLB 1943; MEd 1949. Served RA, N Africa and Italy, 1940–46. Commandant, Arts and Modern Studies Wing, Formation College, Central Mediterranean Forces, 1945–46. Lectr in History, Jordanhill Coll. of Educn, 1949–50; Principal Lectr in Educn, 1950–61. Member: Scottish Council for Research in Educn, 1951–55; Scottish Certificate of Education Examination Board, 1964–73; General Teaching Council for Scotland, 1965–83 (Chm., 1976–79); Consultative Cttee on Curriculum, 1965–71; Police Advisory Council for Scotland, 1965–; Senatus, Univ. of Aberdeen, 1965–83; Schools Broadcasting Council for Scotland, 1965–79; Pres., Scottish Community Drama Assoc., 1964–69; Governor, Scottish Police College, 1965–; Hon. Sec., Standing Conf. on Studies in Educn, 1967–82; Chm., Cttee of Principals in Scottish Colleges of Educn, 1965–67, 1971–73, 1981–83; Vice Chm. Jt Cttee of Colleges of Educn in Scotland, 1971–73, 1981–83; Member: Scottish Consultative Cttee, CRE, 1982–; Drama Cttee, Scottish Arts Council, 1982–. *Publications:* Modern Scotland, 1953; Our Law, 1955; The History of Scottish Education, two vols, 1970; (jtly) The Management of Innovation, 1970; Doctrines of the Great Educators, 1979; chapters in: Scottish Education Looks Ahead, 1969; The Education of Teachers, 1973; Education in Europe, 1974; various articles in professional jls; author of many plays on stage, radio and television. *Recreation:* theatre. *Address:* 1 Woodburn Avenue, Aberdeen AB1 8JQ. *Club:* Royal Scots (Edinburgh).
*Died* 15 *Aug.* 1983.

**SCOTT, Audrey;** *see* Scott, M. A.

**SCOTT, Sir Bernard (Francis William),** Kt 1979; CBE 1974; TD; FIMechE; FEng; Deputy Chairman, 1969–73, Managing Director, 1972–74, and Chairman, 1974–80, Lucas Industries Ltd; Deputy Chairman: Lloyds Bank, 1980–85 (Director, 1975–85); Lloyds Bank UK Management, 1980–85; Vice-Chairman, Lloyds Bank International, 1980–85 (Director, 1978–85); *b* Kings Norton, 19 Nov. 1914; *s* of Francis William Robert Scott and Agnes Edith Kett; *m* 1st, 1942, Charlotte Kathleen (marr. diss. 1980), *d* of

Charles and Charlotte Laidlow, Monkseaton; one *s* two *d*; 2nd, 1980, Nicole Henriette, *d* of Gustave and Sophy Douchet, Douai. *Educ:* Bishop Vesey's Grammar Sch.; Epsom College. FRSA. Served War of 1939–45 (despatches, 1944): mobilised as TA Officer in 45th Bn Royal Warwicks Regt, 1939; Major, RA, 1946. Joined Joseph Lucas Ltd as apprentice, 1931; Personal Asst to Oliver Lucas, 1936; Sales Dir, Joseph Lucas (Electrical) Ltd, 1947; Vice-Chm. and Gen. Man., CAV Ltd and dir of various Lucas subsids at home and abroad, 1959; Dir, Joseph Lucas (Industries) Ltd, 1968; Vice-Chm., Boots Co., 1983–85 (Dir, 1976–85); Director: Thomas Tilling Ltd, 1979–83; Grindlays Bank, 1981–83. Mem., Export Council for Europe, 1966–71; Chm., European Components Service (BNEC), 1967–71; President: Birmingham Chamber of Commerce, 1972–73 (Vice-Pres. 1970); Motor Industry Res. Assoc. Council, 1975–77; Engineering Industries Council, 1975–81; Fellowship of the Motor Industry, 1984–86; Vice-President: ABCC; Instn of Motor Industry, 1976; EEF, 1976–80; Member: Council, CBI, 1974–80; British Overseas Trade Bd, 1973–77; British Overseas Trade Adv. Council, 1975–77; Nat. Defence Industries Council, 1976–80; Council, SMM&T, 1971 (Exec. Cttee, 1974, Vice-Pres., 1976–80; Pres., 1980–81); Council on Internat. Development, 1977–79. Trustee: Anglo-German Foundn for Study of Industrial Society, 1978–; Duke of Edinburgh Award Scheme, 1980–; Globe Theatre Trust, 1981–; Trustee, Salisbury Cathedral Spire Appeal, 1988–; Chm., Berks Council Boys' Clubs, 1950–70; Vice-Chm., Nat. Assoc. of Boys' Clubs, 1974; Pres., Birmingham Fedn of Boys' Clubs, 1977–81. Hon. LLD Birmingham, 1977; Hon. DSc Aston in Birmingham, 1979. Belgian Croix de Guerre, 1945; Chevalier, Order of Leopold with palm, 1945. *Recreations:* sailing, gardening. *Address:* Grove Corner, Grove Road, Lymington, Hants. *T:* Lymington 78154. *Clubs:* Boodle's, Royal Automobile, Royal Cruising; Royal Yacht Squadron, Royal Lymington Yacht; Cercle de l'Union Interalliée. *Died 25 Dec.* 1987.

**SCOTT, Ven. Claud Syms;** Archdeacon of Suffolk, 1962–70, Archdeacon Emeritus, 1970; Vicar of Hoxne with Denham St John, 1962–70; *b* 31 Aug. 1901; *s* of Claud Syms and Margaret Elizabeth Scott; *m* 1930, Grace Maud Savery. *Educ:* Brentwood Sch.; Trinity Coll., Oxf. BA 1923, MA 1927. Deacon, 1926; Priest, 1927; Asst Curate, St Luke, Bedminster, 1926–30; Curate-in-charge, All Hallows Conventional District, Ipswich, 1930–38; Vicar of Exning with Landwade, 1938–54; Rural Dean of Newmarket, 1946–54; Hon. Canon of St Edmundsbury, 1953; Rector of Stradbroke with Horham and Athelington, 1954–58; Rector of St Mary Stoke, Ipswich, 1958–62; Rural Dean of Ipswich, 1958–Dec. 1961. Master, Worshipful Company of Armourers and Brasiers, 1951. *Address:* 68 Lowestoft Road, Reydon, Southwold, Suffolk. *T:* Southwold 723485. *Died 14 Oct.* 1983.

**SCOTT, Sir David John Montagu Douglas,** KCMG 1941 (CMG 1935); OBE 1919; *b* 7 March 1887; *s* of Adm. Lord Charles Scott, GCB; *m* 1918, Dorothy Charlotte Drummond (*d* 1965); one *s* (killed during the War, 1941); *m* 1970, Valerie Finnis, VMH, *d* of late Comdr Steriker Finnis. *Educ:* Eton; Christ Church, Oxford. Joined 3rd Batt. the Royal Scots, 1906; entered the Foreign Office, 1911; served in France, Flanders and Salonika, 1914–18 (wounded, despatches, Legion of Honour, OBE); re-joined Foreign Office, 1919; Assistant Under-Secretary of State for Foreign Affairs, 1938–44; Deputy Under-Secretary of State in the Foreign Office, 1944; retired, 1947. *Recreations:* gardening, reading, looking at works of art. *Address:* The Dower House, Boughton House, Kettering, Northants NN14 1BJ. *T:* Kettering 82279. *Died 22 Aug.* 1986.

**SCOTT, Douglas,** RDI 1974; FCSD; Profesor Titular, Universidad Nacional Autonoma de Mexico, 1977–80; Profesor and Presidente de la Carrera, Universidad Anahuac, Mexico, 1977–80; *b* 4 April 1913; *s* of Edward Scott and Lilian Scott; *m* 1939, Kathleen Tierney; one *s* one *d*. *Educ:* Central Sch. of Art and Design, London (trained as silversmith and jeweller). Joined Osler & Faraday, 1929, and subseq. other lighting cos, as designer and illuminating engr; Raymond Loewy's London Office, 1936–39; opened own office, 1946; MSIAD 1946, elected FSIAD 1960. Lectr, Central Sch. of Art and Design, 1945: founded Industrial Design course, first in UK, 1946; started postgrad. course: trained Mexican designers from Universidad Nacional Autonoma de Mexico, and helped set up course. Designed for many clients in UK (incl. Routemaster bus for London Transport), Europe and USA. Profesor Honorario, Universitario Autonoma de Guadalajara, Mexico, 1977. Wash basin designed for Ideal Standard, Italy, on perm. exhibn in Museum of Modern Art, New York. Gold Medal for Design, Instituto Mexicano de Comercio Exterior, Mexico, 1973; three Design Council awards; Medal for Design, SIAD, 1983; 2nd Internat. Design Award, Osaka, Japan, 1985. *Publications:* (with James Pilditch) The Business of Product Design, 1964; articles in periodicals. *Recreations:* listening to music, gardening, walking, photography. *Address:* 12 Lentune Way, Lymington, Hants SO41 9PF. *T:* Lymington (0590) 677311. *Died 2 Oct.* 1990.

**SCOTT, Col Sir Douglas Winchester,** 2nd Bt *cr* 1913; *b* 4 Feb. 1907; *s* of Admiral Sir Percy Scott, KCB, KCVO, LLD, 1st Bt, and Roma,

*e d* of Sir Frederic Dixon Hartland, 1st Bt; *S* father, 1924; *m* 1933, Elizabeth Joyce, 2nd *d* of W. N. C. Grant, Lyne Place, Virginia Water, Surrey; two *s* one *d*. *Educ:* Harrow; RMC Sandhurst. Comd 3rd Hussars, 1944; Comd 9th Lancers, 1947; Hon. Col 3rd Hussars, 1955–58; Col Queen's Own Hussars, 1962–65. Treasurer Thomas Coram Foundation, 1958, Vice-Pres. 1970. *Heir: s* Anthony Percy Scott [*b* 1 May 1937; *m* 1962, Caroline Teresa Anne, *er d* of Edward Bacon; two *s* one *d*]. *Address:* Pine Trees, West Strand, West Wittering, Chichester, Sussex. *Club:* Cavalry and Guards.
*Died 10 April* 1984.

**SCOTT, Sir Eric,** Kt 1965; OBE 1958; Federal President, The Pharmacy Guild of Australia (formerly Federated Pharmaceutical Service Guild of Australia), 1947–71; *b* 11 Dec. 1891; *s* of W. G. Scott, Hawthorn, Victoria, Aust.; *m* 1914, Eva Caroline (*d* 1968), *d* of R. J. Poulton; one *s* two *d*; *m* 1971, Peggy Vane, *d* of C. V. Lansell. *Educ:* Wesley College, Melbourne, Victoria. Pharmaceutical Chemist, 1927. State President, Federated Pharmaceutical Service Guild of Australia (Victorian Branch), 1931–47; President, Pharmaceutical Society of Victoria, 1955–60; Chm., Drug Res. Appeal Cttee, 1972; Mem., Commonwealth and State Pharmaceutical Benefits Committees under National Health Act, 1954–. Hon. Mem., Pharmaceutical Society of Great Britain, 1970. *Recreations:* golf, gardening, cooking. *Address:* Woorak, 64 Heyington Place, Toorak, Victoria 3142, Australia. *T:* 20–4883. *Clubs:* Commonwealth (Canberra); Royal Automobile of Victoria, Athenæum (Melbourne). *Died 8 Aug.* 1982.

**SCOTT, Ethleen Mary,** MA; retired as Principal of St Aidan's College, University of Durham, (1961–63); *b* 25 Nov. 1896; *d* of Rev. H. R. Scott, MA, DD, and Jennie Hill Scott. *Educ:* Walthamstow Hall, Sevenoaks, Kent; Royal Holloway College, University of London. BA Hons in French, Cl. I 1919; MA (with dist.) 1923; LRAM 1919; ARCM 1942. French Mistress, Queen Elizabeth's Girls' Grammar School, Barnet, 1921–25; Lecturer in French, Royal Holloway College, 1925–28; Lecturer in French, Durham Colleges in the University of Durham, 1928–47; Principal of St Aidan's College, 1947–61. *Recreations:* music, gardening. *Address:* Whitegates, Westbere, Canterbury, Kent. *Died 27 Sept.* 1985.

**SCOTT, Frank, (Francis Reginald),** CC 1967; QC (Quebec) 1961; FRSC 1947; Emeritus Professor of Law and Poet; *b* Quebec, PQ, 1 Aug. 1899; *s* of Archdeacon Frederick George and Amy Scott; *m* 1928, Marian Mildred Dale; one *s*. *Educ:* Quebec High School; Bishop's College, Lennoxville, PQ (BA 1919); Magdalen College, Oxford (Rhodes Scholar, BA 1922, BLitt 1923); McGill University, Montreal (BCL 1927). Practised law one year, then became full-time teacher, McGill Faculty of Law, 1928; Dean of Faculty, 1961–64. Vis. Professor: Toronto 1953; Michigan State Univ., 1957; French Canada Studies Program, McGill, 1967–71; Dalhousie, 1969–71. Co-founder and past-Pres., League for Social Reconstruction; Mem., Nat. Exec., Canadian Inst. of Internat. Affairs, 1935–50; Nat. Chm., Co-operative Commonwealth Fedn Party, 1942–50; Chm., Legal Research Cttee, Canadian Bar Assoc., 1954–56; Mem., Royal Commn on Bilingualism and Biculturalism, 1963–71. Delegate to British Commonwealth Labour Parties Conferences, London 1944 and Toronto 1947; adviser to Govt of Saskatchewan at Constitutional Confs, 1950 and 1960; UN Technical Assistance Resident Rep. to Burma, 1952. Chm., Canadian Writers' Conf., 1955. Co-editor: McGill Fortnightly Review, 1925–27; The Canadian Mercury, 1928; Canadian Forum, 1936–39; Preview, 1942–45; Northern Review, 1945–47. Counsel in several civil liberties cases, Supreme Court of Canada, 1956–64. Corresp. Fellow, British Acad., 1978. Hon. For. Mem., Amer. Acad. of Arts and Sciences, 1967; Guggenheim Fellowship, 1940. Hon. degrees: Dalhousie; Manitoba; Queen's; British Columbia; Saskatchewan; Osgoode Hall; Sir George Williams; Montreal; Toronto; McGill; Laval; Windsor; Bishop's; York; Carleton; Simon Fraser. Guarantor's Prize for Poetry, Chicago, 1944; Lorne Pierce Medal, Royal Soc. of Canada, 1964; Molson Award, Canada Council, 1967. *Publications:* (poetry): Overture, 1945; Events and Signals, 1954; The Eye of the Needle, 1957; (trans.) Poems of Garneau and Hébert, 1962; Signature, 1964; Selected Poems, 1966; Trouvailles, 1967; The Dance is One, 1973; (trans.) Poems of French Canada, 1977 (Canada Council Award for Translation, 1978); Collected Poems (Governor General's Award for Poetry), 1982; (ed, with A. J. M. Smith): New Provinces: poems of several authors, 1936; The Blasted Pine: an anthology of satire, irreverent and disrespectful verse, 1957, rev. edn 1967; (prose): (jtly) Social Planning for Canada, 1935; Canada Today, Her National Interests and National Policy, 1938; (jtly) Democracy Needs Socialism, 1938; (jtly) Make This Your Canada, 1943; (jtly) Canada after the War, 1943; Civil Liberties and Canadian Federalism, 1959; (jtly) Quebec States Her Case, 1964; Essays on the Constitution: aspects of Canadian law and politics, 1977 (Governor-General's Award for Non-fiction, 1978). *Address:* 451 Clarke Avenue, Westmount, Quebec H3Y 3C5, Canada. *Clubs:* McGill Faculty, University, International PEN (all Montreal). *Died 31 Jan.* 1985.

**SCOTT, George Barclay;** energy policy and general management consultant; Chairman, North Western Region, British Gas Corporation, 1982–85; *b* 10 Aug. 1928; *s* of late Joseph Scott and Margaret Gardner Crawford Barclay Scott; *m* 1955, Janette Margaret Forrester Lindsay (decd); one *s* one *d* (twins). *Educ:* Whitehill Senior Secondary School, Glasgow; Univ. of Strathclyde. BSc (Hons) Mech. Eng. Scottish Gas Board: Distribution Engineer, 1962–70; Member of Board, 1970–72; Dir of Distribution and Service, 1970–73; British Gas Corporation: Commercial Dir, Scottish Region, 1973–74; Dep. Chairman, 1974–82. Pres., Instn of Gas Engineers, 1982–83. Mem. Regl Bd, BIM, 1981–. Mem. Council, Univ. of Salford, 1983–. *Recreations:* gardening, golf, walking, music. *Address:* The Belfry, Chapel Drive, Hale Barns, Altrincham, Cheshire WA15 0BL. *Died 31 Oct. 1990.*

**SCOTT, Sir George (Edward),** Kt 1967; CBE 1963 (OBE 1941); KPM; Chief Constable of the West Riding Constabulary, 1959–68, and of the West Yorkshire Constabulary, 1968–69, retired; *b* 6 June 1903; *s* of late Frederick William Scott; *m* 1926, Lilian, *d* of Matthew Brown, Norwich; one *s* one *d*. *Educ:* City of Norwich School. Joined Norwich City Police, as Cadet, 1918; Dep. Chief Constable, Norwich, 1933–36; Chief Constable: Luton, 1936–44; Newcastle upon Tyne, 1944–48; Sheffield, 1948–59. Vice-President: Royal Life Saving Soc.; RoSPA. King's Police Medal, 1949; KStJ 1966 (CStJ 1957). *Address:* White Lodge, 5 Barham Close, Weybridge, Surrey. *Died 27 Oct. 1989.*

**SCOTT, George Edwin;** author, television commentator, broadcaster, journalist; Special Adviser, Commission of the European Communities, since 1987; Visiting Fellow, City University, since 1987; *b* 22 June 1925; *s* of late George Benjamin Scott and Florence Hilda Scott; *m* 1947, Shelagh Maud Isobel Maw; two *s* (one *d* decd). *Educ:* Middlesbrough High School; New College, Oxford. Northern Echo, 1941–42; Yorkshire Post, 1942–43; RNVR, 1943–46; New College, Oxford, 1946–48 (Founder and Editor of Oxford Viewpoint); Daily Express, 1948–53; Truth, 1953–57 (Deputy Editor, 1954; Editor, 1954–57, when ceased publication); The Economist, 1970–74; Editor, The Listener, 1974–79; Head of UK Offices, EEC, 1979–87. Contested (L): Middlesbrough East, March 1962; Middlesbrough West, June 1962; Wimbledon, 1964; Surrey South West, 1983. Chm., Political Div., Liberal Party, 1962–63. Mem., Panorama team, 1958–59; Chairman/Interviewer: TWW, 1959–67; Rediffusion, 1966–68; Tyne-Tees, 1970–74; Presenter, The Editors, BBC, 1976–79. *Publications:* Time and Place (autobiographical), 1956; The RCs, 1967; Reporter Anonymous, 1968; Rise and Fall of the League of Nations, 1973; contrib. column, Liberal View, Daily Mirror, 1962–64; contribs to Punch and other jls. *Recreations:* theatre, cricket and watching others gardening. *Address:* 26 Vineyard Hill Road, SW19 7JH. *Club:* Reform. *Died 2 Nov. 1988.*

**SCOTT, Prof. George Ian,** CBE 1968; FRCSE; FRCPE; FRSE; Surgeon Oculist to the Queen in Scotland, 1965–78; Professor of Ophthalmology, University of Edinburgh, 1954–72, then Emeritus Professor; Ophthalmic Surgeon, Royal Infirmary, Edinburgh, 1953–72, then Hon. Ophthalmic Surgeon; *b* 15 March 1907; *s* of late George John Scott; *m* 1946, Maxine, *d* of late A. D. Vandamm; one *s*. *Educ:* Edinburgh Acad.; Univ. of Edinburgh. MA 1929; MB, ChB 1933; FRCS Edin. 1937; FRS Edin. 1954. Served War of 1939–45, RAMC; Command Ophthalmologist, Scottish Command, 1939; Mem. Advisory Ophthalmic Panel, Ministry of Supply, 1941; Consultant Ophthalmologist, MEF, 1942; Brig. RAMC, 1942. Asst Ophthalmic Surgeon, Royal Infirmary, Edinburgh, 1946; Mem. Vision Cttee, MRC, 1946; Visiting Consultant, Western General and Bangour Hosps, 1949; Consultant in Neuro-Ophthalmology to Department of Neuro-Surgery, Edinburgh, 1954. Member, International Council of Ophthalmology, 1963–70; Past President: Faculty of Ophthalmologists; RCSE; Ophthalmological Soc. of UK; Member Association of British Neurologists; FRSoc.Med. (former Vice-President Section of Ophthalmology); Hon. Col RAMC. *Publications:* papers in British Journal of Ophthalmology, Nature, Lancet, British Medical Journal, British Journal of Radiology, Proc. Roy. Soc. Med., Trans. Ophthalmological Soc., United Kingdom, and The American Journal of Ophthalmology. *Address:* 4 Moray Place, Edinburgh EH3 6DS. *T:* 031–225 6943. *Club:* New (Edinburgh). *Died 22 May 1989.*

**SCOTT, Rev. G(uthrie) Michael;** Anglican priest, Diocese of Chichester, since 1950; *b* 30 July 1907; *s* of Rev. Perceval Caleb Scott and Ethel Maud (*née* Burn); unmarried. *Educ:* King's College, Taunton; St Paul's College, Grahamstown, S Africa; Chichester Theological College. Ordained, 1930; Curate St Mary, Slaugham, Sussex, 1930–32; St Stephen's, Gloucester Rd, S Kensington, 1932–34. Domestic Chaplain to Bishop of Bombay, 1935–37; Chaplain, St Paul's Cathedral, Calcutta, 1937–38; Kasauli, 1938–39. Enlisted RAF 1940, invalided 1941. Returned to S Africa, 1943; St Alban's Coloured Mission and Chaplain St Joseph's Orphanage, Johannesburg, 1943–46; General License: Diocese of Johannesburg, 1946–50, Chichester, 1950–. In 1947 appealed to United Nations on behalf of two tribes of SW African Mandated Territory; attended sessions of General Assembly at Chiefs' request and was granted hearing by Fourth Cttee 1949, 1950 and 1955; Question referred to International Court of Justice. Took part in formation of Africa Bureau, 1952. Nagaland Peace Mission, 1964–66. Hon. Canon, St George's Cathedral, Windhoek, Namibia, 1975. Grand Companion, Order of Freedom (Zambia), 1968. Hon. STD General Theological Seminary, NY, 1972. *Publications:* Shadow over Africa, 1950; Attitude to Africa (Penguin), 1951; African Episode, 1954; Orphans' Heritage, 1958; A Time to Speak (autobiography), 1958; The Nagas in Search of Peace, 1966; Voices for Life (UN World Population Year), 1974; A Search for Peace and Justice (biog.), 1980; No Faith without Doubt, 1981. *Recreations:* walking, reading, sailing, theatre, etc. *Address:* c/o Lloyds Bank, 6 Pall Mall, SW1. *Died 14 Sept. 1983.*

**SCOTT, J(ames) M(aurice),** OBE 1945; MA; author and explorer; *b* 13 Dec. 1906; *m* 1933, Pamela Watkins (marr. diss. 1958); *m* 1959, Adriana Rinaldi. *Educ:* Fettes College; Clare College, Cambridge. *Publications:* Gino Watkins, 1935; Land of Seals, 1949; Bright Eyes of Danger, 1950; Hudson of Hudson's Bay, 1950; Other Side of the Moon, 1950; Snowstone, 1950; Vineyards of France, 1950; Captain Smith and Pocahontas, 1953; Man Who Made Wine, 1953; Heather Mary, 1953; Sea-wyf and Biscuit, 1955; White Magic, 1955; Choice of Heaven, 1959; The Tea Story, 1964; The Book of Pall Mall, 1965; Dingo, 1966; The Devil You Don't, 1967; In a Beautiful Pea-Green Boat, 1968; The White Poppy, 1968; From Sea to Ocean, 1969; A Walk Along the Appenines, 1973; Boadicea, 1975; Icebound, 1977; Red Hair and Moonwater: Arctic short stories, 1980; The Private Life of Polar Exploration, 1982. *Recreations:* gardening, writing. *Address:* Thatched Cottage, Yelling, Huntingdon, Cambs. *Died 12 March 1986.*

**SCOTT, Sir John Arthur G.;** *see* Guillum Scott.

**SCOTT, Laurence Prestwich;** Chairman of the Manchester Guardian & Evening News Ltd, 1949–73; *b* 10 June 1909; *s* of John Russell and Alice Olga Scott; *m* 1939, Constance Mary Black (*d* 1969); two *s* one *d*; *m* 1970, Jessica Mary Crowther Thompson; one *s*. *Educ:* Rugby; Trinity College, Cambridge. Director, Anglia Television Group Ltd, 1958–80; Dir, Press Assoc. and Reuters, 1948–55, 1956–60. Mem., Council of Manchester University, 1946–70 (Dep. Chm., 1957–70). *Address:* Redes House, Siddington, Macclesfield, Cheshire. *Died 2 Sept. 1983.*

**SCOTT, (Margaret) Audrey;** Headmistress of the Perse School for Girls, Cambridge, 1947–67, retired; *b* 22 Oct. 1904; *d* of late Lieutenant-Colonel C. E. Scott, solicitor, and Mrs M. E. M. Scott, Bradford. *Educ:* Queen Margaret's School, Scarborough (now at Escrick); Newnham College, Cambridge. Teaching at Benenden School, Kent, 1926–29; Atherley School, Southampton, 1929–31; Edgbaston Church College, 1931–40; Thornbury Grammar School, Glos, 1941–43; Headmistress, Yeovil High School, Jan. 1944–Aug. 1947. Association of Headmistresses: Exec. Cttee, 1956–62; Chm., Foreign and Commonwealth Education Cttee, 1960–62; Pres., Six Counties Branch, 1959–61. *Publication:* The First Hundred Years 1881–1981: a history of the Perse School for Girls, 1981. *Address:* 24 Gretton Court, Girton, Cambridge CB3 0QN. *T:* Cambridge 276646. *Died 28 Jan. 1990.*

**SCOTT, Sir Michael Fergus M.;** *see* Maxwell Scott.

**SCOTT, Most Rev. Moses Nathanael Christopher Omobiala,** Commander of the Rokel, 1974; CBE 1970; Hon. DD Durham; *b* 18 Aug. 1911; *s* of late Christopher Columbus Scott, Hastings Village, Sierra Leone, and Cleopatra Eliza Scott, York Village; *m* 1941, Cordelia Elizabeth Deborah Maddy (decd), Gloucester Village; three *s* two *d*. *Educ:* CMS Grammar School and Fourah Bay Coll., Freetown, Sierra Leone. Deacon 1943; Priest, 1946. Curate of: Lunsar, 1943–44; Yongro, Bullom, 1944–46; Missionary-in-charge of Makeni, 1946–48, of Bo, 1948–50; studied at London College of Divinity for DipTheol, 1950–51; Curate of Grappenhall, Cheshire, 1951–53; returned to Bo, 1954; Priest in charge, Bo District, 1954–57 (Educn Sec. to the Diocese, 1955–61); Archdeacon of Missions, Sierra Leone, 1957–59; Archdeacon of Bonthe and Bo, 1959–61; Bishop of Sierra Leone, 1961–81; Archbishop of West Africa, 1969–81. Hon. DD Durham, 1962. *Recreations:* playwriting, croquet. *Address:* c/o PO Box 128, Freetown, Sierra Leone. *Died 9 May 1988.*

**SCOTT, Sir Peter (Markham),** CH 1987; Kt 1973; CBE 1953 (MBE 1942); DSC 1943; FRS 1987; Artist; Ornithologist; Hon. Chairman of Council, World Wildlife Fund International, since 1985 (Chairman, 1961–82; Chairman of Council, 1983–85); Hon. Director: Wildfowl and Wetlands Trust; Survival Anglia Ltd; Lt-Comdr RNVR, retired; *b* 14 Sept. 1909; *s* of Captain Robert Falcon Scott, CVO, RN, and Kathleen Bruce (she *m* 2nd, 1922, Edward Hilton Young, later 1st Baron Kennet, PC, GBE, DSO, DSC, who *d* 1960; she *d* 1947); *m* 1st, 1942, Elizabeth Jane (marr. diss. 1951), *d* of David Howard; one *d*; 2nd, 1951, Philippa, *d* of late Comdr F.

W. Talbot-Ponsonby, RN; one *s* one *d*. *Educ:* Oundle; Trinity College, Cambridge (MA); Munich State Academy; Royal Academy Schools, London. Exhibited paintings Royal Acad. since 1933; held Exhibitions of 6il paintings at Ackermann's Galleries, Bond Street, also New York; specialises in bird-painting and portraits; lectures and nature feature programmes on television. Won international 14–foot Dinghy Championship for Prince of Wales Cup, 1937, 1938, and 1946. Represented Great Britain at Olympic Games, 1936 in single-handed sailing (bronze medal). Served in destroyers in Battle of Atlantic, and Light Coastal Forces in Channel, 1939–45 (despatches thrice, MBE, DSC and Bar). President: Soc. of Wildlife Artists, 1964–78; Fauna and Flora Preservation Soc., 1981–; Glos Assoc. of Youth Clubs; Internat. Yacht Racing Union, 1955–69; The Otter Trust; Glos Trust for Nature Conservation; British Butterfly Conservation Soc.; Vice-President: British Gliding Assoc.; Inland Waterways Assoc.; Camping Club of Great Britain; Bristol Gliding Club; Chairman: Survival Service Commn, IUCN, 1962–81 (now Chm. Emeritus); Falkland Islands Foundn, 1979–; Trustee Emeritus, WWF UK. Chm., Olympic Yachting Cttee, 1947–48; Internat. Jury for Yachting, Olympic Games: 1956, Melbourne; 1960, Naples; 1964, Tokyo. Member Council: Boy Scout Assoc., 1945–73; Winston Churchill Meml Trust. Rector, Aberdeen Univ., 1960–63; Chancellor, Birmingham Univ., 1974–83. Admiral, Manx Herring Fleet, 1962–65. Explored unmapped Perry River area in Canadian Arctic, May-August 1949; Leader of ornithological expeditions to Central Highlands, Iceland, to mark wild geese, 1951, 1953; Expeditions to Australasia Galapagos Is, Seychelles and Antarctic (thrice). Gliding: International Gold Badge, 1958; International Diamond badge, 1963; National Gliding Champion, 1963; Chm., British Gliding Assoc., 1968–70. Hon. Fellow, UMIST, 1974. Hon. LLD: Exeter, 1963; Aberdeen, 1963; Birmingham, 1974; Bristol, 1974; Liverpool, 1984; Hon. DSc: Bath, 1979; Guelph, 1981; Ulster, 1987. Cherry Kearton Medal, 1967, Founder's Medal, 1983, RGS; Albert Medal, RSA, 1970; Bernard Tucker Medal, BOU, 1970; Arthur Allen Medal, Cornell Univ., 1971; Gold Medal, NY Zoological Soc., 1975; IUCN John Phillips Medal, 1981; World Wildlife Fund Twentieth Anniversary Special Award, 1981; Gold Medal, Philadelphia Acad. of Natural Scis, 1983; RSPB Gold Award, 1986; J. P. Getty Prize, 1986; WWF Gold Medal, 1986. Icelandic Order of the Falcon, 1969; Commander, Dutch Order of Golden Ark, 1976; Internat. Pahlavi Environment Prize (UN), 1977. *Publications:* Morning Flight, 1935; Wild Chorus, 1938; The Battle of the Narrow Seas, 1945; Portrait Drawings, 1949; Key to Wildfowl of the World, 1949 (Coloured Key, 1958); Wild Geese and Eskimos, 1951; (with James Fisher) A Thousand Geese, 1953; (with Hugh Boyd) Wildfowl of the British Isles, 1957; The Eye of the Wind (autobiography), 1961; (with Philippa Scott) Animals in Africa, 1962; (with the Wildfowl Trust) The Swans, 1972; Fishwatchers' Guide to West Atlantic Coral Reefs, 1972; Observations of Wildlife, 1980; Travel Diaries of a Naturalist, vol. I, 1983, vol. II, 1985, vol. III, 1987; illustrated: Lord Kennet's A Bird in the Bush, Michael Bratby's Grey Goose and Through the Air, Paul Gallico's The Snow Goose, Adventures Among Birds, Handbook of British Birds, Vol. III, Jean Delacour's Waterfowl of the world, Birds of the Western Palearctic, vol. 1, Malcolm Ogilvie's The Wildfowl of Britain and Europe. *Recreations:* exploring, bird-watching, fish-watching, scuba diving. *Address:* New Grounds, Slimbridge, Glos GL2 7BT. *Clubs:* Royal Thames Yacht; Explorers (New York) (Hon. Mem.). *Died 29 Aug. 1989.*

**SCOTT, Prof. Richard;** Professor of General Practice, University of Edinburgh, 1963–79, now Emeritus; *b* 11 May 1914; *s* of Richard Scott and Beatrice Scott (*née* Aitken); *m* 1938, Mary Ellen Maclachlan; three *s* two *d*. *Educ:* Beath High Sch.; Edinburgh Univ. MB, ChB 1936; MD (with commendation) 1938; Lewis Cameron Postgrad. Prize, 1938; DPH Edin. 1946 (class medal); FRCGP 1967; MRCPE 1971; MCFP (Can) 1972. General Practice, 1936–39. War Service, 1939–46 (Lieutenant-Colonel RAMC). Lecturer in Public Health and Social Medicine, Edin. Univ., 1946; Sen. Lectr and Dir General Practice Teaching Unit, 1951; subseq. Reader in General Practice. Mem. Foundn Steering Cttee, Coll. of GPs 1951; James Mackenzie Lectr, 1964; Albert Warder Lectr, RSM, 1967. Hon. Sec. Scottish Council, RCGP, 1952–68. Consultant and Technical Advisor, WHO. FRCPE 1979. *Publications:* Contrib. to scientific and medical jls. *Address:* 24 Fountainhall Road, Edinburgh EH9 2LW. *T:* 031-667 4244.

*Died 28 Nov. 1983.*

**SCOTT, Sir Robert (Heatlie),** GCMG 1958 (KCMG 1954; CMG 1950); CBE 1946; JP; Lord-Lieutenant of Tweeddale (formerly of Peeblesshire), 1968–80, retired; Permanent Secretary, Ministry of Defence, 1961–63, retired; *b* Peterhead, Scotland, 20 September 1905; *s* of T. H. Scott, OBE, MInstCE; *m* 1933, Rosamond Dewar Durie; one *d*. *Educ:* Queen's Royal College, Trinidad; New College, Oxford. Called to the Bar, Gray's Inn, 1927. Joined HM Consular Service in China, 1927; served in Peking, Shanghai, Canton, Hong Kong, Singapore; Assistant Under-Secretary of State, Foreign Office, 1950–53; Minister British Embassy, Washington, 1953–55;

Commissioner-General for the UK in South-East Asia, 1955–59; Commandant, Imperial Defence College, 1960–61. JP 1968. Hon. LLD Dundee, 1972. *Address:* Lyne Station House, by Peebles, Tweeddale EH45 8NP. *Died 26 Feb. 1982.*

**SCOTT, Sir Ronald B.;** *see* Bodley Scott.

**SCOTT, Group Captain Roy Charles Edwin,** CBE 1965; MVO 1954; AFC 1944 and Bar, 1946; Principal, College of Air Training, Hamble, 1971–81; *b* 11 Jan. 1918; *s* of late John Ellis Scott, Wellington, NZ; *m* 1942, Monica, *d* of Lt-Col F. A. B. Nicoll, OBE, HM Colonial Service; two *s* one *d*. *Educ:* Wellington Coll., NZ; Victoria University. RNZAF, 1939 (Reserve, 1938); RAF, 1940–68: Nos 207 and 103 Sqdns, Bomber Comd, 1940–41; Flying Trng Comd, 1942; Transport Comd, 1943; RAF Staff Coll.; OC Transport Comd Examining Unit, 1946–49; OC The Queen's Flight, 1950–53; Air Attaché, Berne, 1953–56; Dep. Dir of Air Transport Ops, MoD, 1961–64; Dep. Air Comdr, Borneo, 1964–65; retd from RAF, 1968. Dept of the Environment, 1968–71. *Recreations:* tennis, swimming, photography. *Address:* 39 St. Andrews Road, Henley on Thames, Oxfordshire RG9 1HZ. *Club:* Royal Air Force.

*Died 2 July 1982.*

**SCOTT, Sheila (Christine),** OBE 1968; aviator; lecturer; actress; writer; *b* 27 April 1927; *d* of Harold R. Hopkins, Worcester, and Edith Hopkins (*née* Kenward); *m* 1945, Rupert Leaman Bellamy (marr. diss. 1950). *Educ:* Alice Ottley School, Worcs. VAD, RN, 1945; acting, 1946–59, with Repertory Companies at Watford, Aldershot and Windsor; small parts in films, TV and West End Stage. Started flying, 1959; obtained British and USA commercial licences; Racing Pilot: first race won 1960 national air races (De Havilland Trophy, etc); Holder of 100 World Class Records (Aviation), incl. Round the World in class CIc and in open feminine classes; London to Capetown and Capetown to London; N Atlantic (western and eastern crossings direct); S Atlantic, Brazil to W Africa; has flown solo three times round world, including first world flight via North Pole in a light aircraft, 1971; winner of many air races; won female Light Aircraft prize, Transatlantic Air Race London-New York May 1969; won Ford Woman's Prize, London-Sydney Air Race, Dec. 1969. Founder and 1st Gov., Brit. Section, Ninety Nines Inc., 1964. Founder British Balloon and Airships Club. Life Mem. and Hon. Diploma, Academia Romana vel Sodalitis Quirinale. Silver Award of Merit, Brit. Guild of Air Pilots and Navigators, 1966, Liveryman, 1968; Isabella D'Este Award (Italy), 1966; Silver Medal, Royal Aero Club, 1967, Gold Medal, 1972; Harmon Trophy, USA, 1967; Britannia Trophy, 1968. *Publications:* I Must Fly, 1968; On Top of the World, 1973; Barefoot in the Sky, 1974. *Recreation:* sailing. *Address:* c/o Ravenscroft, Highcliffe Lane, Turnditch, Derbyshire DE5 2EA. *T:* Ripley 89362; 01–821 0889. *Club:* Naval and Military.

*Died 20 Oct. 1988.*

**SCOTT, Sir Walter,** Kt 1965; AC; CMG 1960; Director, W. D. Scott and Co. Pty Ltd, since 1938; *b* 10 Nov. 1903; *s* of Alexander and Selina Scott; *m* 1931, Dorothy Ada Ransom; two *s*. *Educ:* Modern School, Perth, WA. Chm., Austr. Decimal Curr. Bd, 1963–69; Industr. Design Coun., 1961–67; Productivity Coun., 1964–68. Member: Secondary Industries Commn, 1944–50; Aust. Aluminium Production Commn, 1944–52; Roy. Commn on Collinsville, 1954–55; Chairman: Motor Car Production Adv. Cttee, 1945–50; Cttee of Investigation, NSW Coal Prices, 1954; Decimal Currency Cttee, 1959–60; Australian Decimal Currency Bd, 1963–69; Australian Pharmaceutical Benefits Pricing Cttee, 1964–; Secondary Sch. Educn Standards, NSW, 1969; Australian Govt Procurement Enquiry, 1973–74. World Pres., Internat. Cttee for Scientific Management (CIOS), 1958–60. Pres., Federated Commonwealth Chamber of Commerce, 1968–70. Wallace Clark Award (for services to Internat. Management) (USA), 1957; Henry Robinson Towne Lectr, 1961; John Storey Award, 1962; Frank and Lillian Gilbreth Award, 1963; Chancellor, Internat. Acad. of Management, 1969 (Vice-Chancellor, 1965); Fellow International Academy of Management, 1961. Gold Medal, Conseil Internat. pour l'Organisation Scientifique, 1966; Leffingwell Award, 1969. *Publications:* Budgetary Control, 1937; Cost Accounting, 1944; Greater Production, 1950; Australia and the Challenge of Change, 1957. *Address:* The Anchorage, 5 Milson Road, Cremorne Point, NSW 2090, Australia. *T:* 90-7569. *Clubs:* Union, Royal Sydney Yacht Squadron, American National, Rotary (Sydney, NSW).

*Died 12 Feb. 1981.*

**SCOTT, William (George),** CBE 1966; RA 1984 (ARA 1977); painter; *b* 15 Feb. 1913; *e s* of William John and Agnes Scott; *m* 1937, Hilda Mary Lucas; two *s*. *Educ:* Enniskillen; Belfast Sch. of Art; Roy. Acad. Schools, London. Hon. Dr RCA, 1975; Hon. DLit: Belfast, 1976; Dublin, 1977. *Exhibitions:* Leger Gall., 1942, 1944, 1946; Leicester Gall., 1948, 1951; Hanover Gall., 1953, 1956, 1961, 1963, 1965, 1967; Martha Jackson Gall., NY, 1954, 1958, 1973; Venice Biennale, 1958; VIth Sao Paulo Biennial, 1953 and 1961, Brazil; Tate Gall., 1972, 1986; Gimpel Fils Gall., 1974, 1980, 1985, 1987;

Martha Jackson Gall., NY, 1974; Moos Gall., Toronto, 1975, 1982; Kasahara Gall., Japan, 1976; Arts Council, Ulster (retrospectives), 1979, 1986; War Paintings 1942–46, Imperial War Mus., 1981; Gimpel Weidenhofer Gall., NY, 1983; Nat. Galleries of Scotland (retrospective), 1986; CCA Gall., 1988; in British Council Exhibns in Europe; *works exhibited in:* Tate Gall.; Victoria and Albert Museum; Paris; New York; Toledo, USA; S Africa; Canada; Australia; S America; Museum of Modern Art, St-Etienne, 1987. Appeared in feature film, Every Picture Tells a Story C4, 1985. Major prizewinner: RA Summer exhibns, 1985, 1986. *Address:* 13 Edith Terrace, Chelsea, SW10. *T:* 01–352 8044.
*Died 28 Dec.* 1989.

**SCOTT BLAIR, George William**, MA (Oxon), DSc (London); FRSC; FInstP; *b* 23 July 1902; *s* of late James and Jessie Scott Blair; *m* 1927, Margaret Florence Riddelsdell; no *c*. *Educ:* Charterhouse; Trinity College, Oxford. Ten years on Research Staff at Rothamsted Experimental Station; sometime Fellow on Rockefeller Foundation at University of Cornell; Head of Chemistry, later Physics Department National Institute for Research in Dairying, University of Reading, 1937–67; retired. Herbert Freundlich Medal, Deutsche Rheol. Ges., 1954; Poiseuille Gold Medal, Internat. Soc. of Biorheology, 1969; Gold Medal, Brit. Soc. of Rheology, 1970. Membre d'honneur, Groupe français de Rhéologie, 1970. *Publications:* An Introduction to Industrial Rheology, 1938; A Survey of General and Applied Rheology, 1943, 2nd edn 1949; Measurements of Mind and Matter, 1950; (ed) Foodstuffs: their Plasticity, Fluidity, and Consistency, 1953; (with Prof. M. Reiner) Agricultural Rheology, 1957; Elementary Rheology, 1969; An Introduction to Biorheology, 1974; many papers in various scientific journals, 1925–82. *Recreations:* music, modern languages, philosophy of science. *Address:* Grist Cottage, Iffley, Oxford. *T:* Oxford 777462.
*Died 30 Sept.* 1987.

**SCOTT-BROWN, Walter Graham**, CVO 1945; BA (Hon. Nat. Sci. Tripos), MD, BCh Cambridge; FRCS, FRCSE; Consulting Surgeon, Throat, Nose and Ear Department, Royal Free Hospital, and late Surgeon and Lecturer Royal National Throat, Nose and Ear Hospital; late Consulting Aurist and Laryngologist at East Grinstead Cottage Hospital and at the Maxillo-facial unit; and Lecturer to University of London; Fellow Royal Society Medicine and Member Otological and Laryngological Section; Fellow Medical Society of London; formerly engaged in consulting practice in London as oto-rhino-laryngologist; *e s* of late George A. Brown; *m* 1926, Margaret Affleck, *d* of G. K. Bannerman, High Wycombe; one *s* three *d*. *Educ:* Whitgift Sch.; Corpus Christi College, Cambridge; St Bartholomew's Hospital, London. Served European War, 1916–18 (despatches, wounded); France and Italy T Battery RHA and Captain and Adjutant 14th Brigade RHA 1918; Exhibitioner Corpus Christi College, Cambridge, 1919; Shuter Scholar St Bartholomew's Hospital, 1922; House Surgeon and Clinical Assistant in Ear, Nose and Throat Dept St Barts; Copeman Medallist for Scientific Research, Cambridge, 1932; Dorothy Temple Cross Research Fellowship (travelling), 1932, Berlin, Vienna, Stockholm, Copenhagen, etc. Mem., Pastel Soc. (former Hon. Sec.); exhibitions of paintings in London, Edinburgh and abroad; work in many private collections. *Publications:* Allergic affections of the Nose, 1945; (ed and contrib.) Diseases of the Ear, Nose and Throat, 2nd edn 1965; Methods of Examination in Ear, Nose and Throat, 1953; Broncho-oesophageal fistula, Cavernous sinus thrombosis: a fatal complication of minor facial sepsis, and other scientific and clinical publications. *Recreations:* fishing, painting. *Address:* Little Down, Monkwood, near Alresford, Hants SO24 0HB. *T:* Ropley 2314.
*Died 12 July* 1987.

**SCOTT FOX, Sir (Robert) David (John)**, KCMG 1963 (CMG 1956); HM Diplomatic Service, retired; *b* 20 June 1910; *yr s* of late Judge John Scott Fox, KC, and late Agnes Maria Theresa, *d* of Hermann Hammer; *m* 1951, Brigitte, *d* of Pierre Taton; three *d*. *Educ:* Eton; Christ Church, Oxford; Fellow Queen's College. Entered HM Diplomatic Service, 1934. Served Berlin, 1937; Prague, 1937–39; Rio de Janeiro, 1940–44; Foreign Office, 1944–49; Counsellor at Jedda, 1949–51; Chargé d'Affaires there in 1949 and 1950; transferred to Ankara, Counsellor, 1951; Chargé d'Affaires there, 1951, 1952, 1953 and 1954; Minister (Economic and Social Affairs) to UK Delegation to UN, 1955–58; Minister to Roumania, 1959–61; Ambassador to Chile, 1961–66; Ambassador to Finland, 1966–69. Special Rep. of the Sec. of State for Foreign and Commonwealth Affairs, 1970–75. Grand Cross, Chilean Order of Merit, 1965; Order of the Finnish Lion, 1969. *Publications:* Mediterranean Heritage, 1978; St George, The Saint with Three Faces, 1983. *Address:* 47 Eaton Terrace, SW1. *T:* 01–730 5505. *Club:* Anglo-Belgian.
*Died 25 Jan.* 1985.

**SCOTTER, Gen. Sir William (Norman Roy)**, KCB 1975; OBE 1965; MC 1945; Deputy Supreme Allied Commander, Europe, designate; Aide-de-Camp General to the Queen, since 1980; *b* 9 Feb. 1922; *s* of late Claude Norman Scotter, Carlisle, and of Hilda Marie (*née* Turner); *m* 1947, Jean, *d* of Rev. D. S. Stiven, MC, DD; one *s* two

*d. Educ:* St Bees Sch., Cumberland. Scots Guards, 1941–42; RMA Dehra Dun, 1942; commnd 7th Gurkha Rifles, 1942; served in Burma, 1944–45, 1/7th Gurkha Rifles (MC); 2nd Bn Border Regt, 1946–47, 1/2 Goorkhas, Malaya, 1948–51; psc 1951; NATO Northern Flank, 1952–54; 1st Bn Border Regt, 1954–56; HQ 6 Bde, 1956–58; jssc 1959; Instructor Camberley, 1960–63; MoD, 1963–65; CO 1 King's Own Royal Border Regt, 1965–67; Comdr 19 Inf. Bde, 1967–69; ndc 1969–70; Chief of Staff, Southern Command, 1970–72, HQ UK Land Forces, 1972; Dir, Mil. Ops, MoD, 1972–75; Vice-Chief of the General Staff, 1975–78; C-in-C BAOR and Comdr, Northern Army Gp, 1978–80. Col, King's Own Royal Border Regt, 1971–; Col Comdt, APTC, 1976–. MBIM. *Recreations:* ball games (Pres., Army Rugby Union, 1972–); sawing logs. *Address:* c/o Midland Bank Ltd, Court Square, Carlisle, Cumbria. *Club:* Army and Navy.
*Died 5 Feb.* 1981.

**SCRAGG, Air Vice-Marshal Sir Colin**, KBE 1963 (CBE 1953; MBE 1940); CB 1960; AFC 1942, Bar to AFC 1949; retired; *b* 8 Sept. 1908; *s* of late Lt A. Scragg, KRRC; *m* 1932, Phyllis Kathleen Rayner, Southampton; one *s* two *d*. *Educ:* King Edward VI School, Southampton. No 1 (Fighter) Squadron, 1931–34; served in a succession of flying training schools, including 34 FTS Canada, until 1943; War of 1939–45, Comd No 166 (Bomber) Squadron, 1944–45 (PoW, Germany). Transport Command Development Unit, 1946–49; Dep. Director, Operational Requirements, Air Min., 1950–53, Director, 1955–58; idc 1954; AOC No 23 Training Group, 1958–60; Deputy Controller Aircraft (RAF), Ministry of Aviation, 1960–64. Order of Orange Nassau (Netherlands), 1945. *Address:* Wedgwood, Pine Walk, Chilworth, Southampton. *T:* Southampton 769110.
*Died 6 April* 1989.

**SCRIMGEOUR, James**, CMG 1959; OBE (mil.)1944; *b* 8 June 1903; *s* of late Alexander Carron Scrimgeour and Helen May Scrimgeour (*née* Bird); *m* 1928, Winifred (*d* 1984), *d* of late Stephen Ward Giles; one *s*. *Educ:* Loretto School; Clare College, Cambridge. Member of Stock Exchange, 1929–69 (Mem. Council, 1951–52). Auxiliary Air Force, 1938–45; Air staff, Air Ministry, 1942–45. Senior Partner, J. & A. Scrimgeour, 1949–69; Chm., Hume Holdings Ltd, 1953–75; Dir, MEPC Ltd, 1946–69 (Vice Chm., 1965–69). Orig. Mem., Council of White Ensign Assoc., 1958–75. *Address:* c/o Royal Bank of Scotland, Burlington Gardens, W1. *Club:* Hawks (Cambridge).
*Died 6 Aug.* 1987.

**SCULLARD, Howard Hayes**, FBA 1955; FSA; Professor Emeritus of Ancient History in the University of London; *b* 9 Feb. 1903; *s* of late Rev. Professor Herbert H. Scullard and Barbara Louise Scullard (*née* Dodds). *Educ:* Highgate School; St John's Coll., Cambridge (Scholar). First Class Classical Tripos Part II, 1926; Thirlwall Prize, Cambridge, 1929; MA Cambridge, PhD London, 1930. Classical Tutor, New College, London, 1926–35; Reader, 1935–59, Professor of Ancient History, 1959–70, King's College, London. A Governor of New College, London, 1930–80; Vice-Pres., Soc. for the Promotion of Roman Studies; former Mem. Council, British Acad. and of Royal Numismatic Soc.; Actg Dir, Inst. of Classical Studies, London, 1964. FKC, 1970. *Publications:* Scipio Africanus in the Second Punic War, 1930; A History of the Roman World from 753 to 146 BC, 1935, 4th edn 1980; (edited with H. E. Butler) Livy book XXX, 1939, 6th edn 1953; (Joint Editor of and contrib. to) The Oxford Classical Dictionary, 1949, Editor (with N. G. L. Hammond) of new edn, 1970; Roman Politics, 220–150 BC, 1951, 2nd edn 1973; (rev.) F. B. Marsh, A History of the Roman World from 146 to 30 BC, 1953, 3rd edn 1962; From the Gracchi to Nero, 1959, 5th edn 1982; (rev. jtly) J. C. Stobbart: The Grandeur that was Rome, 1961; (ed) Atlas of the Classical World, 1959 and Shorter Atlas of the Classical World, 1962 (Dutch, French and Spanish translations); The Etruscan Cities and Rome, 1967 (Italian translation, 1969, 2nd edn, 1977); Scipio Africanus: Soldier and Politician, 1970; The Elephant in the Greek and Roman World, 1974; A History of Rome (rev. and rewritten edn of Prof. M. Cary's book, 1935), 1975; Roman Britain: Outpost of the Empire, 1979; Festivals and Ceremonies of the Roman Republic, 1981; (Gen. Editor of series) Aspects of Greek and Roman Life, over 40 Vols to date; Annual Survey of Roman history in The Year's Work in Classical Studies, 1937–48, and of ancient history in The Year's Work in Classical Studies, 1937–48, and of ancient history in Annual Bulletin of Historical Literature, 1949–73; articles and reviews in Journal of Roman Studies, Classical Review, Encyclopædia Britannica, etc. *Recreation:* golf. *Address:* 6 Foscote Road, Hendon, NW4. *Club:* Athenæum.
*Died 31 March* 1983.

**SCUPHAM, John**, OBE 1961; retired as Controller of Educational Broadcasting, British Broadcasting Corporation, 1963–65; *b* 7 Sept. 1904; *s* of Roger Scupham and Kate Whittingham; *m* 1932, Dorothy Lacey Clark (*d* 1987); one *s* one *d*. *Educ:* Market Rasen Gram. Sch.; Emmanuel Coll., Cambridge (Scholar). BA 1st Cl., History, 1926, 1st Cl. English, 1927 (Cantab). Various teaching posts, 1927–46. Joined staff of BBC as Educn Officer, 1946; Head of Educational Broadcasting, 1954. Member, Central Advisory Council for Education (England), 1961–63; Member, Church of England Board of Education, 1960–72. President, Educational Section of British Association, 1965–66. Mem. Council, Open Univ., 1969–78. DUniv, Open Univ., 1975. *Publications:* Broadcasting and the Community, 1967; The Revolution in Communications, 1970; Open Learning, 1976. *Recreations:* reading, gardening. *Address:* 9 Hillside Road, Thorpe St Andrew, Norwich. *T:* Norwich 35834.

*Died 10 Jan. 1990.*

**SEABROOK, John,** CMG 1970; AFC 1918; ED 1947; JP; Founder Chairman, Seabrook Fowlds Ltd, Auckland, NZ, 1919–70; Chairman, Amalgamated Pacific Industries Ltd, 1970–73; *b* 6 Jan. 1896; *e s* of Albert David Seabrook and Marion May Seabrook; *m* 1926, Doreen Mary Alexina Carr, *d* of Charles Edward and Rose Louise McKenzie Carr, Auckland; one *s* one *d*. *Educ:* Auckland Grammar School. Served RFC, France, 1916–17; RAF, Middle East, 1918 (Captain). Returned to NZ, 1919, and founded Seabrook Fowlds Ltd. Served RNZAF, 1940–44 (Group Captain). Mem. Board of Trustees, NZ Inst. for Blind for 24 years; Dir, NZ National Airways, 1952–61; Dep. Chm., Blinded Servicemen's Trust Board; Mem., Nature Conservation Council, Wellington; Mem., Hauraki Gulf Maritime Park Board; Pres., Auckland Inst. and Museum, 1961–63. Charter Mem., Rotary Club of Auckland, 1921. *Recreations:* yachting, gardening. *Address:* 146 Orakei Road, Remuera, Auckland 5, NZ. *T:* 52735. *Club:* Royal Air Force.

*Died 8 Jan. 1985.*

**SEAGER, Ven. Edward Leslie;** Archdeacon of Dorset, 1955–74, Archdeacon Emeritus of Salisbury Cathedral since 1975; *b* 5 Oct. 1904; *s* of William Seager, Chaddesley Corbett, Worcs; unmarried. *Educ:* Bromsgrove Sch.; Hatfield College, Durham. Foundation Scholar, Hatfield College, 1923; BA, Jenkyn's Scholar, 1926; Diploma in Theology, 1928; MA, 1931. Deacon, 1928, priest, 1929, Newcastle upon Tyne; Chaplain, Wellington School, 1931–39. War of 1939–45, CF, 1937–46; SCF, 1942–45; DACG, 1945–46; HCF, 1946–. Vicar of Gillingham, Dorset, 1946–79, and of Fifehead Magdalen, 1966–79; Team Vicar in Gillingham Team Ministry, 1979; Rural Dean of Shaftesbury, 1951–56; Canon and Prebendary of Shipton in Salisbury Cathedral, 1954–68; Examining Chaplain to Bishop of Salisbury, 1968; Canon and Prebendary of Gillingham Major, 1968–79, Canon Emeritus, 1979–; RD of Blackmore Vale, 1975–79. Governor of Milton Abbey School, 1966–; Chairman of Governors, Gillingham School, 1959–. *Publication:* Day unto Day, 1932. *Recreations:* scouting, golf. *Club:* East India, Devonshire, Sports and Public Schools. *Died 2 Nov. 1983.*

**SEAMAN, Edwin de Grey;** Chairman, Edwin Seaman Farms Ltd; *b* 27 Aug. 1908; *s* of Edwin de Grey Seaman and Catherine Anne Farrow (*née* Sayer); *m* 1940, Eileen Purdy (*d* 1980); two *d*. *Educ:* Glebe House Sch., Hunstanton; Cheltenham Coll., Glos. Started farming 90 acres in Norfolk, 1929; marketing Fatstock for Norfolk Farmers, 1933, and extended to importing from Canada and Ireland; imported 300 pedigree Holstein Friesian cattle from Canada and founded Canadian Holstein Friesian Association, 1946. Joined NFU, 1944; became Delegate to Nat. Council, 1949. Chm., Working Party which produced a scheme for Fatstock Scheme, 1952; (with Lord Netherthorpe) founded Fatstock Marketing Corp., 1953 (which became FMC Ltd, 1963) (Vice-Chm. 1972, Dep. Chm., 1974–75). Founded Seaman's Cream Dairies Ltd, 1963; extended to five counties and sold to Milk Marketing Bd, 1963. During War of 1939–45 was Member: Agricl Exec. Cttee; Milk Production Cttee; Special Police Auxiliary and Home Guard, also Air Training Corps (ATC). Member: Royal Agricultural Soc. of England; Royal Norfolk Agricultural Soc. Freeman, City of London, 1962. *Recreations:* farming (3000 acres), fishing, shooting, and his work. *Address:* Rising Lodge, South Wootton, King's Lynn, Norfolk PE30 3PD. *T:* Kings Lynn 671079. *Clubs:* Farmers', Smithfield; Refley Society (King's Lynn). *Died 31 Jan. 1983.*

**SEARCY, Philip Roy,** OBE 1966; Australian Consul-General, Los Angeles, 1971–75; *b* Adelaide, South Australia, 15 April 1914; *s* of Herbert Leslie Searcy and Mary Ellen MacGregor; *m* 1946, Mary Elizabeth Gavan Duffy; four *d*. *Educ:* Collegiate School of St Peter, Adelaide; Adelaide University. Royal Australian Air Force, 1940; Air Operations, Europe, 1941; Prisoner of War, Germany, Nov. 1941–45. Joined Australian Govt Trade Commissioner Service, 1955; Australian Govt Trade Commissioner, Calcutta, 1956; Commercial Counsellor, Singapore, 1957; Australian Govt Senior Trade Commissioner: London, 1958–62; Tokyo, 1962–65; Hong Kong, 1966–70. *Address:* The Bridge, Gundaroo, NSW 2620, Australia. *Clubs:* Naval and Military (Melbourne); Tokyo; Shek O, Hong Kong. *Died 5 Oct. 1983.*

**SEARLE, Humphrey,** CBE 1968; Composer; *b* Oxford, 26 Aug. 1915; *e s* of late Humphrey Frederic Searle and Charlotte Mathilde Mary (*née* Schlich); *m* 1st, 1949, Margaret (Lesley) Gillen Gray (*d* 1957); 2nd, 1960, Fiona Elizabeth Anne Nicholson. *Educ:* Winchester Coll.; New Coll., Oxford. Composition study at RCM, Vienna Conservatorium, and privately with Dr Anton Webern, 1937–38. Member, BBC Music Department, 1938–40. Served Gloucestershire

Regiment, Intelligence Corps and General List, 1940–46. Programme producer, BBC Music Dept, 1946–48. General Secretary, International Soc. for Contemporary Music, 1947–49. Hon. Secretary, Liszt Society, 1950–62. Member Sadler's Wells Ballet Advisory Panel, 1951–57; Resident Composer, Stanford University, California, 1964–65; Prof. of Composition, Royal Coll. of Music, 1965–; Guest composer, Aspen Music Festival, Colorado, 1967; Guest Prof., Staatliche Hochschule für Musik, Karlsruhe, 1968–72; Vis. Prof., Univ. of Southern California, Los Angeles, 1976–77. Hon. Professorial Fellow, Univ. Coll. of Wales, Aberystwyth, 1977. Hon. ARCM, 1966, FRCM 1969. *Principal Compositions:* Gold Coast Customs (Edith Sitwell), 1949; Poem for 22 Strings, 1950; The Riverrun (James Joyce), 1951; Piano sonata, 1951; The Shadow of Cain (Edith Sitwell), 1952; Symphony No 1, 1953; Piano Concerto No 2, 1955; Noctambules, ballet, 1956; Symphony No 2, 1958; The Great Peacock, ballet, 1958; The Diary of a Madman, opera, 1958; Symphony No 3, 1960; Symphony No 4, 1962; Dualities, ballet, 1963; The Photo of the Colonel, Opera, 1964; Song of the Birds, Song of the Sun, 1964; Symphony No 5, 1964; Scherzi for Orchestra, 1964; The Canticle of the Rose (Edith Sitwell) 1965; Oxus, scena, 1967; Hamlet, opera, 1968; Sinfonietta, 1968–69; Jerusalem (Blake), choral work, 1970; Zodiac Variations, 1970; Labyrinth, 1971; Cello Fantasia, 1972; Les Fleurs du mal, song cycle, 1972; Fantasy-Toccata for organ, 1973; Kubla Khan, cantata, 1974; Five for guitar, 1974; Nocturnall (Donne), 1974; Il Penseroso e L'Allegro, 1974; Contemplations, 1975; Fantasia on British Airs, 1976; Dr Faustus, cantata, 1977; The Serpent Son (Oresteia), 1978; Tamesis, 1979; Three Pieces for Four Horns, 1979; Two Sitwell Songs, 1980; A Winchester Overture, 1981; Cyprus Dances for organ, 1981; Three Ages for orchestra, 1981; also chamber music, theatre, radio, television, and film scores. Orchestration of Liszt, Sonata in B minor, 1962. *Publications:* The Music of Liszt, 1954 (rev. edn, 1967); Twentieth Century Counterpoint, 1954; Ballet Music, an Introduction, 1958 (rev. edn 1973); 20th Century Composers, Vol 3 (Britain and Holland), 1972; (ed) Arnold Schoenberg, Structural Functions of Harmony, 1954; (ed) Hector Berlioz: Selected Letters, 1966; *translated:* Josef Rufer, Composition with Twelve Notes, 1954; H. H. Stuckenschmidt, Arnold Schoenberg, 1959; Friedrich Wildgans, Anton Webern, 1966; Walter Kolneder, Anton Webern, 1967; H. H. Stuckenschmidt, Schoenberg, 1975; has made contributions to: Encyclopædia Britannica; Dictionary of National Biography; Grove's Dictionary of Music and Musicians; Chambers's Encyclopædia; Proceedings of the Royal Musical Association; and to various other musical publications. *Recreation:* travel. *Address:* 44 Ordnance Hill, NW8 6PU. *T:* 01-722 5182. *Club:* Savage.

*Died 12 May 1982.*

**SEBASTIAN, Rear-Admiral (Retired) Brian Leonard Geoffrey,** CB 1948; *b* 7 Feb. 1891; *s* of late Lewis Boyd Sebastian, Barrister-at-Law, and late Harriet M. Lennartson, Karlstad, Sweden; *m* 1927, Cicely Grace, *e d* of Dr F. W. Andrew, Hendon; one *d*. *Educ:* Osborne, Dartmouth and Greenwich Colleges; RN Engineering College, Keyham. Joined RN Coll., Osborne, with first term of new scheme, 1903; various appts at sea as junior officer; qualified in Engineering, 1914. Served in various ships during European War; Comdr (E) 1925; various appointments till 1936; Capt. (E) 1937; Squadron EO Home Fleet, in charge of RN Aircraft Training establishment, Newcastle-under-Lyme, and RN Eng. Coll., Keyham; Rear-Adm. (E) 1944; Deputy Head of British Admiralty Technical Mission, Ottawa; Staffs of C-in-C Rosyth and Plymouth, 1948; retired, 1948. *Address:* Flat 3, Weyside, Farnham, Surrey GU9 7RH. *T:* Farnham 722705. *Died 11 Jan. 1983.*

**SEBRIGHT, Sir Hugo Giles Edmund,** 14th Bt, *cr* 1626; *b* 2 March 1931; *s* of Lt-Col Sir Giles Edward Sebright, 13th Bt, CBE, and of Margery Hilda, *d* of late Admiral Sir Sydney Robert Fremantle, GCB, MVO; *S* father, 1954; *m* 1st, 1952, Deirdre Ann (marr. diss. 1964), *d* of Major Vivian Lionel Slingsby Bethell, late Royal Artillery; one *s*; 2nd, 1965, Mrs Sheila Mary Howard Hervey (marr. diss. 1984); 3rd, 1984, Mrs Victoria Rosamond Ashton-Bostock, *er d* of Captain R. T. White, DSO, RN retired. *Heir: s* Peter Giles Vivian Sebright [*b* 2 Aug. 1953; *m* 1977, Regina Maria, *d* of Francis Steven Clarebrough, Melbourne; one *s*].

*Died 16 April 1985.*

**SEDGWICK, Patrick Cardinall Mason,** CMG 1965; *b* 8 March 1911; 2nd *s* of late William Francis Mason Sedgwick, Goudhurst, Kent; *m* 1943, Beth Mannering, Thompson, *e d* of late Frederick Mannering Thompson, St Kilda, Victoria, Australia; three *s* one *d*. *Educ:* St Lawrence Coll., Ramsgate; Brasenose Coll., Oxford (BA Hons); Queens' College, Cambridge. Colonial Admin. Service: Cadet Officer, Hong Kong, 1935; seconded Malayan Civil Service, Dec. 1941–Feb. 1942; Attaché, British Embassy, Chungking, 1942–43; Hong Kong Planning Unit, CO, London, 1944–45; various Govt Posts in Hong Kong, including Principal Assistant Colonial Secretary, Estabt Officer, Chm. Urban Council, and Dir of Commerce and Industry; Comr of Labour and Mines, 1955–65; MEC and MLC, of Hong Kong up to June 1965; Dir, Hong Kong

Govt Office, London, 1965–69; Salaries Commissioner: St Helena, 1971; Falkland Islands and Mauritius, 1972. *Recreations:* sailing, gardening. *Address:* Ringden Wood, Flimwell, Sussex. *T:* Flimwell 431. *Clubs:* Bewl Valley Sailing; Hong Kong, Royal Hong Kong Yacht (Hong Kong). *Died 22 Jan.* 1985.

**SEEBOHM,** Baron *cr* 1972 (Life Peer), of Hertford; **Frederic Seebohm,** Kt 1970; TD; psc; Lt-Col (Retd); *b* 18 Jan. 1909; *s* of late H. E. Seebohm, Poynders End, Hitchin, Herts; *m* 1932, Evangeline, *d* of late Sir Gerald Hurst, QC; one *s* two *d*. *Educ:* Leighton Park School; Trinity Coll., Cambridge. Joined Staff of Barclays Bank Ltd, 1929; Director: Barclays Bank Ltd, 1947–79 (Dep. Chm., 1968–74); Barclays Bank International Ltd, 1951–79 (formerly Barclays Bank DCO) (Vice-Chm., 1955–59, Dep. Chm., 1959–65, Chm., 1965–72; Vice-Chm., Barclays Bank SA, 1968–73); Friends' Provident Life Office, 1952–79 (Chm., 1962–68); ICFC, 1969–80 (Chm., 1974–79); Finance for Industry Ltd, 1974–80 (Chm., 1974–79); Finance Corp. for Industry Ltd, 1974–80 (Chm., 1974–79). Chairman: Joseph Rowntree Memorial Trust, 1966–81; London House, 1970–83; Seebohm Cttee on Local Authority and Allied Personal Social Services, 1965–68; Export Guarantees Adv. Council, 1967–72; President: Nat. Inst. for Social Work, 1966–87; Age Concern, 1970–89; Royal African Soc., 1978–84 (Hon. Vice Pres., 1984–); Project Fullemploy, 1982–; Vice Chm., Volunteer Centre, 1983–. Mem., Overseas Develt Inst. (Chm., 1972–77). Governor: London School of Economics, 1965–87; Haileybury Imperial Service Coll., 1970–87. Fellow, Chartered Inst. of Bankers (Pres., 1966–68). Served with Royal Artillery, 1939–45 (despatches). High Sheriff, Herts, 1970–71. Hon. LLD Nottingham, 1970; Hon. DSc Aston, 1976. Bronze Star of America, 1945. *Recreations:* gardening, painting. *Address:* 28 Marsham Court, Marsham Street, SW1. *T:* 071–828 2168. *Clubs:* Carlton, Commonwealth Trust; Hurlingham.

*Died 15 Dec.* 1990.

**SEEFRIED, Irmgard Maria Theresia;** Austrian opera and concert singer; Kammersängerin at Vienna State Opera since 1943; *b* Koengetried, Bavaria, 9 Oct. 1919; *m* 1948, Wolfgang Schneiderhan; two *d*. *Educ:* Augsburg Conservatory, Germany. First engagement under von Karajan, at Aachen, Germany, 1940. Concert tours all over the world; appeared: Metropolitan Opera, New York; Covent Garden, London; La Scala, Milan; also festivals at Salzburg, Lucerne, Edinburgh, San Francisco. Honorary Member: Boston Symphony Orch.; Vienna Philharmonic Orch. Hon. Mem., Austrian-German Culture Soc., 1980. Recipient various Mozart Medals; Lilly-Lehmann Medal; Golden Cross of merit for Culture and Science; Decoration of Chevalier I, Denmark; Grosses Verdienstkreuz des Verdienstordens der Bundesrepublik Deutschland, 1963; Schubert Medal; Hugo Wolf Medal; Culture Prize, Luxemburg; Gold Medal of Honour, Vienna, 1979; Werner Egg Prize, 1979; Silver Decoration of merit, Austria, 1979; Gold Burgher Medal, Bad Wörishofen, 1980. *Publications:* articles on Mozart, Bartók, Hindemith, Hugo Wolf. *Address:* Vienna State Opera, Austria. *Died 24 Nov.* 1988.

**SEERS, Dudley,** CMG 1975; Fellow, Institute of Development Studies, University of Sussex, since 1972 (Director, 1967–72, Director MPhil course, 1975–77); *b* 11 April 1920; *s* of late George Clarence Seers and of Mabel Edith Seers (*née* Hallett); *m* 1943, Patricia Hindell; one *s* three *d*. *Educ:* Rugby Sch.; Pembroke Coll., Cambridge. Served Royal Navy, 1941–45. PM's Office, New Zealand Govt, 1945–46; Res. Off. (later Lectr and Sen. Lectr in Economic Statistics) Oxford Univ., 1946–53 and 1954–55; Mem. Min. of Health Cttee on Housebuilding Costs, 1949–50; Economist, UN Headqrs, 1953–54; Statistical Adviser to Barbados, Leeward and Windward Isles, 1955–57; Chief, Survey Section, UN Econ. Commn for Latin America, 1957–61; Vis. Prof., Yale Univ., 1961–63; Dir, Economic Develt Div., UN Econ. Commn for Africa, 1963–64; Leader, UN Economic Mission to Zambia, 1964; Director-General, Economic Planning Staff, Ministry of Overseas Development, 1964–67. Also consultant for Govts of Burma, Fiji, Ghana, Jamaica, Kenya, Malaysia, Malta, Portugal, Sri Lanka, Trinidad, Uganda, for World Bank, ILO, OECD, and UN. Member: Editorial Bd, Jl of Develt Studies; World Development; SSRC panel on N Sea Oil, 1975; OECD team on Japan's social science policy, 1975; Council, Royal Econ. Soc., 1975–78; Chm., WUS Chile Awards Cttee, 1974–78; Pres., European Assoc. of Develt Insts, 1975–78. Leader: ILO Missions to Colombia, 1970, Sri Lanka, 1971, 1978, Nigeria, 1979; Commonwealth Team on Rehabilitation of Uganda, 1979. Order of Boyacá, Colombia, 1970. *Publications:* (ed) Cuba: The Economic and Social Revolution, 1964; (ed) Development in a Divided World, 1971; (ed) Crisis in Planning, 1972; (ed) Underdeveloped Europe: Studies in Core-Periphery Relations, 1979; (ed) European Studies in Development, 1979; (ed) Integration and Unequal Development: the Experience of Western Europe, 1980; Dependency Theory: a critical re-assessment, 1981; (ed) The Second Enlargement of the EEC: Integration of Unequal Partners, 1982; (ed) The Crisis of the European Regions, 1982; contribs to: The Theory and Design of Economic Development (ed Adelman and Thorbecke), 1966; The Teaching of Development

Economics (ed Martin and Knapp), 1967; Crisis in the Civil Service (ed Thomas), 1968; Africa and the World, 1969; Unfashionable Economics: Essays in Honour of Lord Balogh (ed Streeten), 1970; The Labour Government's Economic Record (ed Beckerman), 1972; Redistribution with Growth (ed Chenery), 1974; Employment, Income Dsitribution and Development Strategy: Essays in Honour of Hans Singer (ed Cairncross), 1975; Population and its Problems (ed Parry), 1976; Statistical Needs for Development, 1977; North Sea Oil: The Application of Development Theories, 1977; Transnational Capitalism and National Development, 1979; Development and Change—special issue in honour of Kurt Martin, 1979; The Relevance of Economic Theories to Present-Day Society (ed Feinstein), 1980; Econ. Jl; Oxford Econ. Papers; Social and Econ. Studies; Jl of Development Studies; Bulletin of IDS. *Recreations:* skiing, teasing bureaucrats. *Address:* Broadacres Farm, Chiddingly, near Lewes, East Sussex. *T:* Chiddingly 617, (office) Brighton 606261. *Died 21 March* 1983.

**SEGAL,** Baron *cr* 1964, of Wytham (Life Peer); **Samuel Segal,** MRCS, LRCP; MA Oxon; Deputy Speaker, and Deputy Chairman of Committees, House of Lords, 1973–82; *b* 2 April 1902; *e s* of late Professor M. H. Segal, MA; *m* 1934, Molly, *o d* of Robert J. Rolo, OBE, Alexandria, Egypt; two *d* (one *s* decd). *Educ:* Royal Grammar Sch., Newcastle upon Tyne (Scholar); Jesus Coll., Oxford (Exhibitioner); Westminster Hosp. (Scholar). Casualty Surgeon and HP Westminster Hospital; Senior Clinical Assistant, Great Ormond Street Children's Hospital. Served on several LCC Hospital Committees. Contested (Lab) Tynemouth, 1935, Aston (Birmingham) By-Election, May 1939. Joined RAFVR Medical Branch, Oct. 1939; served in Aden 1940, Western Desert 1941, Syrian Campaign 1941; attached Greek Air Force, 1941; Squadron Leader, 1942; Sen. Med. Officer RAF Naval Co-operation Group in Mediterranean, 1942; on Headquarters Staff Middle East, 1943–44; on Air Min. Med. Staff, 1944–45; travelled extensively on RAF Medical duties throughout North and East Africa, Iraq, Persian Gulf, India, etc.; Regional MO, Min. of Health, 1951–62. MP (Lab) for Preston, 1945–50; Member Parly Delegations: to Austria, 1946; to Nigeria, Cameroons, Gold Coast, Sierra Leone and Gambia, 1947; to Egypt, 1947; Hungary, 1965; Cyprus, 1965; Bahrain, Aden, 1966; Malawi, 1966 (Leader); Hong Kong, Singapore and S Vietnam, 1968; Antigua, Dominica and St Lucia, 1974 (Leader); UK delegate, Inter-Parly Union Conf., Tokyo 1974, London 1975. Mem. FO Mission to Persia, 1947. Chairman: British Assoc. for the Retarded; Council, Anglo-Israel Assoc., 1968–80; Dolphin Square Tenants Assoc., 1973–77; Oxford Soc. in London, 1976–; Anglo-Israel Archaeological Assoc., 1976–; Jesus Coll. Assoc., London Branch, 1976–80; London Old Novocastrian Assoc., 1981–82; Hon. Treasurer: Anglo-Iranian Parly Gp, 1970–; Royal Soc. for Mentally Handicapped Children, 1978– (Chm., 1965–78); Member: Home Office Adv. Cttee on Service Parly Candidates; Council, Oxford Society; President: NI Region, Royal Soc. for Mentally Handicapped Children, 1977–; Oxford-Paddington Passenger Assoc., 1966–83; The Haven Foundn; Trustee, Celebrities' Guild of GB, 1980–84; Vice-Pres., Music Therapy Charity Ltd; Patron, Oxford Diocesan Assoc. for the Deaf. Life Governor, Manchester Coll., Oxford, Visitor 1972–; Governor, Carmel Coll. Hon. Fellow, Jesus College, Oxford, 1966. *Recreation:* getting lost. *Address:* 2 Park Town, Oxford OX2 6TB. *T:* Oxford 513322; 208 Frobisher House, Dolphin Square, SW1V 3LL. *T:* 01–828 7172. *Died 4 June* 1985.

**SEGOVIA TORRES, Andrés;** Marquis of Salobreña, 1981; Grand Cross: Order of Alfonso X el Sabio, 1953; Order of Isabel la Católica, 1958; Spanish concert-guitarist; *b* Linares, Spain, 21 Feb. 1893; *m* 1962, Emilia; one *s* (and one *s* one *d* by former marr.). Brought up in Granada; has been playing the guitar since the age of ten; gave first recital, Granada, 1909; since 1919 has performed in Europe, USA, Japan, Russia, Australia and Canada; first came to England in 1926; has often returned on concert tours since 1952; has had many pupils and has taught at Santiago de Compostela and Academia Musicale Chigiana, Siena, and other schools; has adapted works of Bach, Haydn, Mozart and other classical composers for the guitar; has had many works composed especially for him by Casella, Castelnuovo-Tedesco, Falla, Moreno Torroba, Ponce, Roussel, Tansman, Turina, Villa-Lobos and others. Mem., Spanish Royal Acad. of Fine Arts, 1978. Hon. DMus Oxon, 1972. Gold Medal for Meritorious Work (Spain), 1967; Albert Schweitzer Award, 1981; Ernst Von Siemens Prize, 1985; Gold Medal, Royal Philharmonic Soc., 1986. Order of Rising Sun (Japan), 1985. *Publications:* Segovia: an autobiography of the years 1893–1920, trans. W. F. O'Brien, 1977; (with George Mendoza) Segovia: My Book of the Guitar, 1979. *Address:* c/o Ibbs & Tillett, 450–452 Edgware Road, W2 1EG. *Died 2 June* 1987.

**SEGRÈ, Prof. Emilio;** Grande Ufficiale, Merito della Repubblica (Italy); Professor of Physics, University of California, Berkeley, 1946–72, now Emeritus; *b* 1 Feb. 1905; *s* of Giuseppe Segrè and Amelia Treves-Segrè; *m* 1936, Elfriede Spiro (*d* 1970); one *s* two *d*; *m* 1972, Rosa Mines Segrè. *Educ:* University of Rome, Italy. Asst

Prof. of Physics, Rome, 1929–35; Dir, Physics Inst., Univ. of Palermo, Italy, 1936–38; Research Associate and Lectr, Univ. of Calif., Berkeley, 1938–42; Group Leader, Los Alamos Scientific Lab., 1942–46. Hon. Prof. S Marcos Univ., Lima, 1954; Prof. of Nuclear Physics, Univ. of Rome, 1974–75. Codiscoverer of: slow neutrons, 1934; (chemical elements) technetium, 1937, astatine, 1940, plutonium, 1941; the antiproton, 1955. Hon. DSc Palermo, 1958; Hon. Dr Tel Aviv Univ., 1972. Nobel laureate (joint) for physics, 1959. Member: Nat. Acad. Sciences, USA, 1952; Accad. Nazionale Lincei, Roma, 1959; Accad. Nationale de XL, Roma; Heidelberg Akad. der Wissenschaften; Amer. Phil. Soc.; Amer. Acad. of Arts and Sciences; Indian Acad. of Sciences. *Publications:* Nuclei and Particles, 1964, new edn 1977; Enrico Fermi, Physicist, 1970, 2nd edn 1987; From X-rays to Quarks: modern physicists and their discoveries, 1980; From Falling Bodies to Radio Waves: classical physicists and their discoveries, 1984; contrib. to Physical Review, Proc. Roy. Soc. London, Nature, Nuovo Cimento. *Recreation:* hiking. *Address:* 3802 Quail Ridge Road, Lafayette, Calif 94549, USA. *T:* (415) 2830556; Department of Physics, University of California, Berkeley, Calif 94720. *Club:* University of California Faculty (Berkeley). *Died* 22 *April* 1989.

**SEIFERT, Jaroslav;** poet; *b* 23 Sept. 1901; *m* 1928, Marie Ulrichová; one *s* one *d. Educ:* secondary school, Prague. Writer and journalist, Prague papers and periodicals; co-founder, Devěstil Art Assoc., 1920; Editor, Rovnost, Brno, 1922, Sršatec, 1922–25; Editor-in-Chief, Nová scéna, 1930; Editor: Pestré Květy, 1931–33; Ranninoviny, 1933–39; Národní práce, 1939–45, Práce, 1945–49. Acting Chm., Union of Czechoslovak Writers, 1968–69, Chm., 1969–70. State Prizes, 1936, 1955, 1968; National Artist, 1966; Nobel Prize for Literature, 1984. *Publications:* Ruce Venušiny (Venus' Hands), 1936; Maminka (Mother), 1954; Koncert na ostrově (Concert at the Island), 1968; Odléváni zvonů, Halleyova kometa, Světlem oděná, Mozart in Prague, 1970; Morový sloup (Pests Column), 1978, Deštník z Piccadilly, 1978 (Umbrella from Piccadilly, 1983); Všechny krásy světa (All Beauty of the World), 1978; Býti básníkem (To be a poet), 1983. *Address:* Břevnov U Ladronky 23/1338, Prague 6, Czechoslovakia. *T:* 35–78–71.
*Died* 10 *Jan.* 1986.

**SELBY, Harry;** *b* 18 May 1913; *s* of Max Soldberg and Annie (*née* Saltman); *m* 1937, Jeannie KcKean Reid; one *s. Educ:* Queen's Park Secondary, Glasgow. Served War of 1939–45: Private, Highland Light Infantry, June 1940; Royal Corps of Signals, March 1941; released Dec. 1945. Lectured through Nat. Council of Labour College. Mem., Glasgow Corp., 1972–74. MP (Lab) Glasgow, Govan, Feb. 1974–79. *Address:* House 5, 70 Kennishead Avenue, Glasgow GL6 8RJ. *T:* 041–649 7169. *Died* 8 *Jan.* 1984.

**SELDON TRUSS, Leslie;** author; *b* 21 Aug. 1892; *s* of George Marquand Truss and Ann Blanche, *d* of Samuel Seldon, CB; *m* 1st, 1918, Gwendolen, *d* of Charles Kershaw, Cooden Mount, Sussex; one *d*; 2nd, 1925, Kathleen Mary (*d* 1981), *d* of Charles Hornung, of Oaklands, Hookwood, Surrey; one *s* one *d.* Scenario Editor, Gaumont Co., 1914. Lieut Scots Guards, Special Reserve, 1915–19, Flanders and the Somme; Major Home Guard, 1940–44. *Publications:* Gallows Bait, 1928; The Stolen Millionaire, 1929; The Man Without Pity, 1930; The Hunterstone Outrage, 1931; Turmoil at Brede, 1932; Mr Coroner Presides, 1932; They Came by Night, 1933; The Daughters of Belial, 1934; Murder Paves the Way, Escort to Danger, 1935; Draw the Blinds, Rooksmiths, 1936; The Man who Played Patience, She Could Take Care, Footsteps Behind Them, 1937; Foreign Bodies, 1938; The Disappearance of Julie Hints, 1940; Sweeter for his Going, Where's Mr Chumley?, 1949; Ladies Always Talk, 1950; Never Fight a Lady, 1951; Death of No Lady, 1952; Always Ask a Policeman, 1953; Put Out The Light, The High Wall, 1954; The Long Night, The Barberton Intrigue, 1956; The Truth About Claire Veryan, 1957; In Secret Places, 1958; The Hidden Men, 1959; One Man's Death, 1960; Seven Years Dead, 1961; A Time to Hate, 1962; Technique for Treachery, 1963; Walk a Crooked Mile, 1964; The Town That Went Sick, 1965; Eyes at the Window, 1966; The Bride That Got Away, 1967; The Hands of the Shadow, 1968; The Corpse That Got Away, 1969; under *pseudonym* of George Selmark, Murder in Silence, 1939; various short stories and serials; novels translated in 18 countries. *Recreations:* anything but writing. *Address:* Dale Hill House, Ticehurst, Sussex. *T:* Ticehurst 251. *Died* 5 *Feb.* 1990.

**SELLORS, Sir Thomas Holmes,** Kt 1963; DM, MCh; FRCP; FRCS; Consultant Surgeon, London Chest Hospital, since 1934; Emeritus Thoracic Surgeon, Middlesex Hospital, since 1947; Consultant Surgeon, National Heart and Harefield Hospitals, since 1957; Consulting Surgeon, Aylesbury Group of Hospitals; *b* 7 April 1902; *s* of Dr T. B. Sellors; *m* 1st, Brenda Lyell (*d* 1928); 2nd, 1932, Dorothy Elizabeth Chesshire (*d* 1953); one *s* one *d*; 3rd, 1955, Marie Hobson (*d* 1986). *Educ:* Loretto School; Oriel Coll., Oxford, Hon. Fellow 1973. BA Oxon 1923, MA 1927; MRCS, LRCP 1926; BM, BCh Oxon 1926; G. H. Hunt Travelling Scholarship, Univ. of Oxford, 1928; MCh 1931, DM 1933. Held various appts in London

hosps; FRCS 1930; Member of Council, RCS, 1957–73, Vice-Pres., 1968–69, President 1969–72; FRCP 1963; Chairman of Joint Consultants Committee, 1958–67; President: Thoracic Society, 1960; Soc. of Thoracic Surgeons of Great Britain and Ireland, 1961–62; BMA, 1972; Royal Med. Benevolent Fund; Pres., Internat. Soc. Surg., 1977–79, Pres. Congress 1977; Chm. Council, British Heart Foundn. Surgeon to Royal Waterloo and Queen Mary's Hospitals; Regional Adviser in Thoracic Surgery, 1940–45. Hunterian Prof. RCS, 1944; Chm., Hunterian Trustees, 1981– (Trustee, 1978). Lectures: Carey Coombs, Univ. of Bristol, 1956; G. A. Gibson, RCPE, 1959; Strickland Goodall, Society Apothecaries, 1960; Entwhistle Meml and W. W. Hamburger, Chicago, 1961; St Cyre's, 1965; Grey-Turner, Internat. Soc. Surg., 1967; Gordon-Taylor, RCS, 1968; Tudor Edwards Meml, RCS, 1968; Bradshaw, RCS, 1969; Colles, RCSI, 1975. Hunterian Orator, RCS, 1973. Examiner in Surgery, Univ. of Oxford. Member: Acad. of Medicine, Rome; Royal Acad. of Medicine, Belgium; Membre d'Honneur, Europe Cardiol. Soc.; Hon. Fellow: Amer. Coll. Surgeons, 1971; Coll. of Med., S Africa; RCSE, 1972; RCSI; Faculty of Dental Surgeons, RCS, 1974. MD (*hc*) Groningen, 1964; Hon. DSc Liverpool, 1970; Hon. MS Southampton, 1972; BMA Gold Medal, 1979; Médaille de la Reconnaissance Française. Officer of the Order of Carlos Finlay, Cuba. *Publications:* Surgery of the Thorax, 1933. Editor and contributor in current text books. Articles in English and foreign medical publications. *Recreations:* water-colour painting, gardening. *Address:* Spring Coppice Farm, Speen, Aylesbury, Bucks. *T:* Hampden Row 379.
*Died* 13 *Sept.* 1987.

**SELWAY, Air Marshal Sir Anthony (Dunkerton),** KCB 1961 (CB 1952); DFC 1940; Registrar and Secretary of the Order of the Bath, 1968–79 (Gentleman Usher of the Scarlet Rod, 1964–68); *b* 20 Feb. 1909; *s* of C. J. Selway, CVO, CBE, TD; *m* 1936, Patricia Graham, *d* of Col. P. C. MacFarlane, Ballagan, Strathblane, Stirlingshire; one *s* one *d. Educ:* Highgate School; Cranwell. No 1 Squadron, Tangmere, 1929; Central Flying School, 1932–34; Middle East Command, 1936–42 (despatches); Flying Trg Comd, 1942–44; Fighter Comd, 1944–45; Burma and Far East, 1945–48; Joint Services Staff Coll., 1948; Air Ministry, 1948–51; Commandant, Central Flying School, 1951–53; Air Attaché, Paris, 1953–Nov. 1955; Comdr, RAF Staff, British Joint Services Mission (USA), 1955–58; AOC No 18 Group Coastal Command, and Air Officer, Scotland 1958–60; C-in-C FEAF, 1960–62; AOC-in-C, RAF Coastal Command, 1962–65; Group Capt., 1942; Air Cdre, 1951; Air Vice-Marshal, 1955; Air Marshal, 1961; retired, 1965. *Address:* c/o Williams & Glyn's Bank Ltd, 22 Whitehall, SW1. *Clubs:* Royal Air Force, White's. *Died* 19 *June* 1984.

**SEMENOV, Prof. Nikolai Nikolaevich;** Orders of Lenin; State awards; Director, Institute of Chemical Physics of the USSR Academy of Sciences since 1931; Professor, Moscow State University; *b* 16 April 1896; *s* of a state employee; *m* Lidiya Grigorievna Scherbakova; one *s* one *d. Educ:* Leningrad State University. Chief of Electronic Phenomena Laboratory of Physico-Technical Institute in Leningrad, 1920; Assistant Professor and then Professor, Leningrad Polytechnic Institute, 1920–41. (Jointly) Nobel Prize for Chemistry, 1956. Foreign Member: Royal Society, 1958; Acad. of Sciences of French Inst., 1978–; Member: USSR Academy of Sciences, 1932–; Chem. Soc. of England, 1949–; Naturalists' Soc., Leopoldina (Halle DDR), 1959; Polish Acad. of Scis, 1974; Amer. Chem. Soc., 1976; Hon. Fellow: Indian Academy of Sciences, 1959; Hungarian Academy of Sciences, 1961; New York Academy of Sciences, 1962; Roumanian Acad. Sci., 1965; Czechoslovakian Acad. Sci., 1965; Roy. Soc. of Edinburgh, 1966; For. Associate, Nat. Acad. of Sciences (USA), 1963; Corresp. Member: Akademie der Wissenschaften, Berlin, DDR, 1966; Bulgarian Acad. of Sciences, 1969; Hon. DSc: Oxford, 1960; Bruxelles, 1962; London, 1965; Hon. DrSci: Milan, 1964; Prague, 1965; Budapest, 1965; Humboldt-Universität zu Berlin, 1973; Vroclav Univ., 1976. *Publications:* several textbooks and scientific monographs, notably: Chain reactions, 1934 (Russia), 1935 (Oxford); Some Problems on Chemical Kinetics and Reactivity, 1954 (Russia), enlarged 2nd edn 1958 (Russia), (Eng. trans. 1959); Science and Community, 1973, 2nd edn 1981 (Russia); Science et société, 1981 (France); numerous articles in the field of chemical physics. *Address:* Kosygin str. 4, Institute of Chemical Physics, USSR Academy of Sciences, Moscow 117977, USSR.
*Died* 25 *Sept.* 1986.

**SEMPER, Dudley Henry;** Puisne Judge, Jamaica, 1954–63, retired; *b* St Kitts, BWI, 14 Nov. 1905; *s* of late D. H. Semper, ISO, and Helen Semper; *m* 1937, Aileen Malone; one *d. Educ:* Antigua Grammar School; West Buckland School, North Devon. Called to Bar, Gray's Inn, 1927; practised at Bar of Leeward Islands, 1928–32; Colonial Service, 1933; Actg District Magistrate, Registrar Supreme Court, St Kitts-Nevis, 1933; District Magistrate, St Kitts-Nevis, 1935; Crown Attorney, St Kitts-Nevis, 1939; Actg Attorney General, Leeward Islands, 1943–44; Officer administering Govt of St Kitts-Nevis, intermittently 1943–44; Resident Magistrate, Jamaica, 1944. *Recreations:* shooting, fishing. *Address:* Bracebridge, 50 Cliff Road,

Worlebury, Weston-super-Mare, Avon. *Club:* Royal Commonwealth Society. *Died* 17 *Dec.* 1982.

SEMPLE, John Greenlees, MA, PhD, MRIA; University Professor of Mathematics, King's College, London, 1936–69, now Emeritus; *b* 10 June 1904; *s* of James Semple, 240 Ravenhill Road, Belfast; *m* 1936, Daphne Caroline, *d* of Professor F. H. Hummel, Queen's University, Belfast; one *s* one *d. Educ:* Royal Belfast Academical Institution; Queen's University, Belfast, MA; St John's College, Cambridge (Philip Bayliss Student); Wrangler b star, Rayleigh Prize, 1929, Fellowship of St John's College, 1931; lecturer Edinburgh University, 1929; Professor of Pure Mathematics at Queen's University, Belfast, 1930–36. *Publications:* (with L. Roth) Introduction to Algebraic Geometry, 1949; (with G. T. Kneebone) Algebraic Projective Geometry, 1952; Algebraic Curves, 1959; (with J. A. Tyrrell) Generalized Clifford Parallelism, 1971; various papers in Cambridge Philosophical Society, London Mathematical Society, Royal Irish Academy, Royal Society, London, etc. *Recreations:* reading, gardening, golf. *Address:* 3 Elm Road, Redhill, Surrey. *T:* Redhill 61142. *Died* 23 *Oct.* 1985.

SEMPLE, Professor William Hugh, MA (Belfast and Manchester), PhD (Cambridge); Professor Emeritus, University of Manchester, since 1967; Governor of Sedbergh School, 1943–75; *b* 25 Feb. 1900; *s* of late James Semple, Belfast, Northern Ireland; *m* 1932, Hilda Madeline (*d* 1978), *d* of late E. H. Wood, Malvern, Worcs; one *s. Educ:* Royal Belfast Academical Institution; Queen's University, Belfast; St John's College, Cambridge. Queen's University, Belfast: Assistant in Department of Greek, 1921–22; Senior Assistant in Department of English Literature, 1922–25; Research in Classics, St John's College, Cambridge, 1925–27. University of Reading: Lecturer in Classics, 1927–31; Reader in Latin, 1931–37; Univ. of Manchester, Professor of Latin, 1937–67. *Publications:* various articles in Classical Review; Classical Quarterly; Transactions of Cambridge Philological Soc.; Bulletin of John Rylands Library; Jl of Ecclesiastical History; (with Prof. C. R. Cheney) Selected Letters of Pope Innocent III concerning England. *Recreations:* walking, gardening. *Address:* 3 Linden Road, Didsbury, Manchester M20 8QJ. *T:* 061–445 2558. *Died* 10 *March* 1981.

SEN, K. Chandra; late Indian CS; *b* 5 Oct. 1888; *s* of Durgadas Sen and Mokshada Sundari Devi; *m* 1916, Lilavati Das-Gupta; one *s* two *d. Educ:* Hindu Sch., Calcutta; Presidency College, Calcutta; Trinity Hall, Cambridge (BA in Moral Sciences Tripos, 1913). Joined Indian Civil Service, 1913; Assistant Collector, Bombay Presidency, 1913–21; service in Judicial department of Government of Bombay since 1921; acted as a puisne judge of Bombay High Court, various times 1934–38; Secretary to Government of Bombay, Legal Department and Remembrancer of Legal Affairs, 1935–37; Additional Judge of High Court, 1939–41; Judge, High Court of Bombay, 1941–47; Pres. Industrial Court, Bombay, 1947–53; Pres. Bombay Co-op, Revenue, and Sales Tax Tribunals, between 1953 and 1959; Constitutional Adviser to Govt of West Bengal and Chm., State Law Commn, 1959–64; Chm., Police Commn, W Bengal, and Mem. Hindu Religious Endowments Commn, 1960–62. *Address:* A-12, Sea Face Park, Bombay 26, India. *T:* 82–4368. *Died* 20 *Oct.* 1981.

SENDER, Ramón José; Medal of Morocco, 1924; Spanish Military Cross of Merit, 1924; writer; *b* Alcolea de Cinca, Spain, 3 Feb. 1902; *s* of José Sender and Andrea Garcés Sender; *m* 1st, 1934, Amparo Barayón (*d* 1936); one *s* one *d*; 2nd, 1943, Florence Hall (marr. diss., 1963). *Educ:* Colegio de la Sagrada Familia, Reus (Catalonia); Inst. de Zaragoza; Inst. de Teruel; Univ. of Madrid. Infantry Officer, Morocco, 1923–24; Editor El Sol, Madrid, 1924–31; free-lance writer, 1931–36. Major on General Staff, Spanish Republican Army, 1936–39. Prof. Spanish Lit., Amherst Coll., Mass, 1943–44; Denver Univ., 1944; Prof. of Spanish Lit., Univ. of New Mexico, 1947 (Emer. 1963). Mem. Bd of Advs, Hispanic Soc. of America; Spanish Nat. Prize of Lit., 1935; Guggenheim Fell., 1942. Speaking tour as rep. Spanish Republic, 1938; member: Ateneo governing board, sec. Ibero-American section, 1926–34; Nat. Council of Culture, Spain, 1936–39; Alliance of Intellectuals for Defense of Democracy, Spain, 1936–39. Visiting Prof., Ohio State Univ., summer 1951; Writers' Workshop, Inter Amer. Univ., San Germán, Puerto Rico, summer 1961; Vis. Prof., Univ. of Calif in Los Angeles, semester II, 1961–62; Prof., Univ. of S Calif in Los Angeles, 1964. Life FIAL, Switzerland. Hon. DLitt Univ. of New Mexico, 1968; Hon. LLD Univ. of Southern California. Hon. Citizen of Los Angeles, 1968. *Publications:* Pro Patria, 1934; Seven Red Sundays, 1935; Mr Witt among the Rebels, 1936; Counter-Attack in Spain, 1938; A Man's Place, 1940; Epitalamio del Prieto Trinidad, 1942; Dark Wedding, 1943; Chronicle of Dawn, 1944; The King and the Queen, 1948; The Sphere, 1949; The Affable Hangman, 1954; Before Noon, 1957; Los Laureles de Anselmo, 1958; Requiem for a Spanish Peasant, 1960; The Exemplary Novels of Cibola, 1963; Carolus Rex, 1963; El Bandido Adolescente, 1965; Tres Novelas Teresianas, 1967; Comedia de Diantre y Otras Dos, 1969; Tres Ejemplos de Amor y Una Teoría, 1969; Aventura equinoccial de Lope de Aguirre, 1970; Ensayos del Otro Mundo, 1970; Nocturno de los 14, 1970; Tanit, 1970; Relatos Fronterizos, 1970; El Angel Anfibio, 1971; Las criaturas saturnianas, 1971; Don Juan en la Mancebía, 1972; La luna de los perros, 1972; En la vida de Ignacio Morel, 1972; El Extraño Señor Photynos, 1973; La antesala, 1973; El fugitivo, 1973; Tupac Amaru, 1973; Una Virgen Llama a Tu Puerta, 1973; Jubileo en el Zocalo, 1974; Las Tres Sorores, 1974; Arlene y la Gaya Ciencia, 1976; Iman, 1976; contrib. to literary and popular journals. *Recreations:* chess, tennis. *Address:* Editorial Destino, 425 Consejo de Ciento, Barcelona 9, Spain. *Died* 15 *Jan.* 1982.

SENIOR, Derek; free-lance writer; *b* 4 May 1912; *s* of Oliver and Sally G. Senior; *m* 1st, 1942, Edith Frances Bentley; one *s* two *d*; 2nd, 1959, Helen Elizabeth Mair; one *d. Educ:* six elementary schools; Manchester Grammar Sch.; Balliol Coll., Oxford (BA). Joined editorial staff of Manchester Guardian, 1937; turned free-lance, 1960. Member, Royal Commission on Local Government in England, 1966–69. Mem., Basildon Develt Corp., 1975–79. Hon. MRTPI (Hon. AMTPI 1956). *Publications:* Guide to the Cambridge Plan, 1956; Your Architect, 1964; The Regional City, 1966; Memorandum of Dissent from Redcliffe-Maud Report, 1969; Skopje Resurgent, 1971; numerous planning publications. *Recreation:* gardening. *Address:* Birling House, Birling, Maidstone, Kent. *T:* West Malling 842229. *Died* 6 *Dec.* 1988.

SENIOR, Ronald Henry, DSO 1940, Bar 1943; TD; *b* 3 July 1904; *e s* of Lawrence Henry Senior and Emmadonna Shuttleworth, *d* of Reverend J. S. Holden, Aston-on-Trent, Derbyshire; *m* 1932, Hon. Norah Marguerite Joicey (*d* 1987), *e d* of 2nd Baron Joicey; two *d. Educ:* Cheltenham College. Chairman, Nat. Assoc. of Port Employers, 1954–59. Joined TA 1924; served France, 1940; Middle East; Sicily, NW Europe. Hon. Rank Brigadier. *Recreation:* golf. *Address:* 36 Sloane Court West, SW3. *Club:* Carlton. *Died* 2 *March* 1988.

SENIOR, William Hirst, CB 1964; Deputy Secretary (Agriculture), Dept of Agriculture and Fisheries for Scotland, 1958–66; *b* 24 August 1904; *o s* of Capt. Arthur Senior and Sarah G. G. Binns, Batley, Yorks; *m* 1930, Olive Kathleen (*d* 1978), *e d* of William Henry Killick, Shawford, Hampshire; two *s* three *d. Educ:* Bradford Grammar School; Reading University. BSc London 1926; MSc Reading 1929. Research Scholar, Reading Univ., 1926–28. Joined Dept of Agriculture for Scotland, 1929; Advisory Officer on Farm Economics, 1933; Principal, 1941; Secretary of Balfour of Burleigh Cttee on Hill Sheep Farming in Scotland, 1941–44; Asst Secretary, 1946; FRSE 1947; Under-Secretary, 1958. Mem., Agricultural Research Council, 1959–66. Chairman, Scottish Agricultural Improvement Council, 1960–66. Mem., Small Industries Council for Scotland. Pres., Agricl Econs Soc., 1963–64. Governor, Rannoch Sch. *Recreations:* varied. *Address:* Manse Wood, Innerwick, Dunbar, East Lothian. *Club:* Royal Commonwealth Society. *Died* 11 *Oct.* 1984.

SEPEKU, Rt Rev. John; Bishop of Dar-es-Salaam, since 1965. *Educ:* Hegongo Theological College, Deacon, 1938; priest, 1940; Curate, Diocese of Zanzibar, 1938–55; Priest-in-charge, 1955–60; Canon of Zanzibar, 1957–60; Archdeacon of magila, 1960–63; Vicar-General of Zanzibar, 1963–65; Assistant Bishop of Zanzibar, 1963–65; Archbishop of Tanzania, 1970–78. *Address:* PO Box 25016, Ilala, Dar-es-Salaam, Tanzania, E Africa. *Died* 1983.

SEPHTON, Ven. Arthur; Archdeacon of Craven, 1956–72; Archdeacon Emeritus, since 1972; *b* 25 March 1894; *s* of Thomas G. and Laura Sephton, Newport Pagnell; *m* 1924, Unita Catherine, *d* of E. Brookhouse Richards, JP; one *d. Educ:* Christ Church, Oxford (MA); Cuddesdon Theological College. Assistant Curate: St Mary Redcliffe, Bristol, 1921; St John, Hove, 1924; Christ Church, Harrogate, 1928; Vicar: Holmfirth, Yorks, 1929; Kirkburton, Yorks, 1933; Rector and Rural Dean of Skipton, 1943–64; Hon. Canon of Bradford, 1944. Proctor in Convocation, 1945–56. *Address:* 17 Riversway, Gargrave, Skipton, N Yorks. *T:* Gargrave 266. *Died* 22 *March* 1982.

SERGEANT, (Herbert) Howard, MBE 1978; Founder, and Editor, Outposts (quarterly poetry magazine), since 1943; *b* 6 May 1914; *s* of Edwin Sergeant and Edith Alice Sergeant (*née* Crowther); *m* 1954, Jean Crabtree; one *s* three *d. Educ:* Hull Grammar Sch.; Hull Coll. of Commerce, and privately. FCCA, FCIS, MBIM, FSCA. Dist Chief Accountant, Broadcast Relay Services, 1935–41; Travelling Accountant, Air Min., 1941–48; Co. Sec. and Accountant, Jordan & Sons Ltd, 1949–54; Co. Sec. and Gp Accountant, E. Austin & Sons (London) Ltd, 1954–63; Lectr, Norwood Tech. Coll., 1963–65; Sen. Lectr, Wandsworth Tech. Coll., 1965–68; Sen. Lectr, 1969–72, Head of Sch. of Management, 1972–78, Brooklands Tech. Coll., Weybridge; Creative Writing Fellow, Queen Mary's Coll., Basingstoke, 1978–79. Dorothy Tutin Award, 1980; Henry Shore Award, 1980. *Publications: poetry:* The Leavening Air, 1946; The Headlands, 1954; Selected Poems, 1980; Travelling Without a Valid Ticket, 1982; Fairground Familiars,

1985; A Question of Respect, 1986; *criticism:* The Cumberland Wordsworth, 1950; Tradition in the Making of Modern Poetry, 1952; A Critical Survey of South African Poetry (Cape Town), 1958; compiled selections from the poetry of Milton, 1953, and from Milton and Wordsworth, 1970; *ed anthologies of poetry:* For Those Who Are Alive, 1946; An Anthology of Contemporary Northern Poetry, 1947; These Years (for schools), 1950; (jtly) New Poems, a PEN anthology, 1953; (jtly) Mavericks, 1957; Commonwealth Poems of Today, 1967; New Voices of the Commonwealth, 1968; Poems from Hospital, 1968; Universities' Poetry 8, 1968; Poetry from Africa, 1968; Poetry from Australia, 1969; The Swinging Rainbow, for children, 1969; Poetry from India, 1970; Poetry of the 1940s, 1970; Happy Landings, for children, 1971; Evans Book of Children's Verse, 1972; African Voices, 1973; For Today and Tomorrow, 1974; Poetry South East I, 1976; New Poems 1976/77, a PEN anthology, 1976; Two Continents Book of Children's Verse, 1977; Candles and Lamps, 1979; Poems from The Medical World, 1979; How Strong the Roots, 1981; (jtly) The Gregory Awards Anthology 1980, 1981; (jtly) The Gregory Awards Anthology 1981–82, 1982; Independent Voices (Public School Verse), 1983; Independent Voices, 2, 1984; A Package of Poems, 1984; (jtly) Gregory Awards Anthology 1983–84, 1985; Independent Voices, 3, 1985; (jtly) annual Borestone Mountain Poetry Award anthologies, Best Poems of 1949–78. *Recreations:* walking, writing, poetry workshops. *Address:* 72 Burwood Road, Walton-on-Thames, Surrey KT12 4AL. *T:* Walton-on-Thames 240712. *Clubs:* PEN, Society of Authors, Poetry Society; Ver Poets (St Albans) (Vice Pres.); Kent & Sussex Poetry Society (Vice Pres.).                         *Died 26 Feb.* 1987.

**SERGENT, René Edmond,** Hon. KBE 1973; Officier de la Légion d'Honneur, 1952; *b* 16 January 1904; *s* of Charles Sergent and Emma Duvernet; *m* 1931, Monique Schweisguth; three *s* three *d*. *Educ:* Lycée Janson-de-Sailly, Paris, France; Ecole Polytechnique. Sub-Lieut, Artillery, 1925; Assistant, Inspection Générale des Finances, 1929; Financial Controller, Nat. Socs of Aeronautical Construction, 1937; Direction du Commerce Extérieur, 1940; Pres., French Economic and Financial Deleg. to Control Commission, Berlin, 1945; Financial Attaché, French Embassy, London, 1947; Asst Sec.-Gen. for Economics and Finance, NATO, 1952; Secretary-Gen. of OEEC, Paris, 1955; Vice-Prés. Délégué, Syndicat Général de la Construction Electrique, 1960; Président, Groupement des Industries de la Construction Electrique, 1969–75. *Address:* 1 Boulevard de Beauséjour, 75016 Paris, France. *T:* 288 3031.
*Died 30 June* 1984.

**SETH, Prof. George;** Professor of Psychology, 1958–71, Head of Department of Psychology, 1946–71, The Queen's University, Belfast; later Professor Emeritus; *b* 23 April 1905; *s* of George Seth and Jane Steven Loudon; *m* 1936, May, *er d* of John Dods, Edinburgh, and late Lily Anderson; three *s* one *d*. *Educ:* Royal High School and University of Edinburgh. MA (Edin.) 1928; BEd (Edin.) 1930; PhD (Edin.) 1933. Assistant in Psychology, Edinburgh University and University Psychological Clinic, 1930–34; Research Fellow, Yale Univ., USA, 1934–35; Lecturer in Education, University College, Cardiff, and Psychologist, Cardiff Child Guidance Clinic, 1935–46; Senior Psychologist, Welsh Board of Health, (Evacuation Service), 1941–45; Founder Lectr in Psychology, QUB, 1945. Vans Dunlop Scholar (Psychology), Edinburgh, 1930–33; Rockefeller Fellow, USA, 1935–36. Fellow, British Psychological Soc., President, 1967, Vice-Pres., 1968; President, Psychology Section, British Association, 1961. Member: Psychology Bd, CNAA, 1968–75; N Ireland Council for Educnl Research. Fellow, Psychological Soc. of Ireland, 1970 (Lecture, 1975). *Publications:* (with Douglas Guthrie) Speech in Childhood, 1934; articles in various psychological and educational jls. *Address:* 7 Castleton Court, Osborne Park, Belfast BT9 6HA.
*Died 28 July* 1990.

**SETON, Anya, (Anya Seton Chase);** author; *b* as British subject, New York City, USA; *d* of late Ernest Thompson Seton and late Grace Gallatin Thompson Seton; *m* 1st (marr. diss.); three *c*; 2nd, Hamilton Mercer Chase (marr. diss.). *Educ:* private tutors in England. *Publications:* (in USA, UK and 20 foreign countries) My Theodosia, 1941; Dragonwyck, 1944; The Turquoise, 1946; The Hearth and the Eagle, 1948; Foxfire, 1951; Katherine, 1954; The Mistletoe and Sword (juvenile), 1956; The Winthrop Woman, 1958; Washington Irving (juvenile), 1960; Devil Water, 1962; Avalon, 1966; Green Darkness, 1972; Smouldering Fires (juvenile), 1975. *Recreations:* swimming, croquet, bridge, cooking. *Address:* Binney Lane, Old Greenwich, Conn 06870, USA. *Clubs:* (Hon.) Pen and Brush (New York); PEN.                         *Died 8 Nov.* 1990.

**SETON, Sir (Christopher) Bruce,** 12th Bt *cr* 1663, of Abercorn; farmer; *b* 3 Oct. 1909; *s* of Charles Henry Seton (*d* 1917), and Mrs V. A. Neilson (*d* 1973), Greys, Kelvedon, Essex; *S* cousin, 1969; *m* 1939, Joyce Vivien, *e d* of late O. G. Barnard, Stowmarket; two *s* two *d*. *Educ:* Marlborough; Univ. of Cambridge (BA Agric. 1931). Farming since 1931. *Heir: s* Iain Bruce Seton [*b* 27 Aug. 1942; *m* 1963, Margaret Ann, *o d* of Walter Charles Faulkner; one *s* one *d*].

*Address:* Bay Laurel, 3 Larkfield Road, Great Bentley, Colchester, Essex. *T:* Colchester 250723.                         *Died 17 Jan.* 1988.

**SETON, Sir Claud Ramsay Wilmot,** Kt 1944; MC; *b* 1888; *e s* of Rev. Andrew Ramsay Wilmot Seton and Emily Georgina, *e d* of Rev. George Edmund Walker; *m* 1933, Mary Eleanor (*d* 1965), *yr d* of Sir Francis Bennett; no *c. Educ:* Framlingham Coll.; Laleham, Margate; University College, London. Solicitor, 1910; Member of firm of Shelton and Co. London and Wolverhampton until outbreak of War; served European War, 1914–20 (wounded, despatches twice, MC); President of District Court, Jaffa, Palestine, 1920–26; Judicial Adviser Transjordan, 1926–31 (Order of Istiqlal second class); President District Court of Haifa, Palestine, 1931–35; Puisne Judge, Jamaica, 1935–41; Chief Justice, Nyasaland, 1941–45; Chief Justice of Fiji and Chief Judicial Commissioner for the Western Pacific, 1945–49; retired from Colonial Service, 1950. Various part-time appointments in Kenya, 1950–60. Called to Bar, Gray's Inn, 1928. *Publication:* Legislation of Transjordan, 1918–30. *Address:* Bilney Hall, East Bilney, Dereham, Norfolk. *T:* Gressenhall 246.
*Died 3 Sept.* 1982.

**SETON-WATSON, Prof. (George) Hugh (Nicholas),** CBE 1981; DLitt; FBA 1969; Professor of Russian History, School of Slavonic and East European Studies, University of London, 1951–83, then Emeritus; *b* 15 Feb. 1916; *er s* of late Prof. Robert William Seton-Watson; *m* 1947, Mary Hope, *d* of late G. D. Rokeling, lately of Ministry of Education; three *d. Educ:* Winchester; New College, Oxford. DLitt Oxon, 1974. Was attached to British Legations in Roumania and Yugoslavia, 1940–41; served Special Forces GHQ, Middle East, 1941–44. Fellow and Praelector in Politics, University Coll., Oxford, 1946–51. Mem. Council, RIIA, 1952–84. Vis. Prof., Columbia Univ., 1957–58; Fellow, Center for Advanced Study in the Behavioural Sciences, Stanford, Calif., 1963–64; Vis. Fellow, ANU, Canberra, 1964; Visiting Professor: Indiana Univ., 1973; Washington Univ., Seattle, 1973. Mem. Res. Council, Center for Strategic and Internat. Studies, Georgetown Univ., 1975–79, 1982–. DU Essex, 1983. *Publications:* Eastern Europe between the Wars, 1945; The East European Revolution, 1950; The Decline of Imperial Russia, 1952; The Pattern of Communist Revolution, 1953; Neither War Nor Peace, 1960; The New Imperialism, 1961; Nationalism and Communism (Essays, 1946–63); The Russian Empire, 1801–1917, 1967; The "Sick Heart" of Modern Europe, 1976; Nations and States, 1977; The Imperialist Revolutionaries, 1978; (ed jtly with C. Seton-Watson, L. Boban, M. Gross, B. Krizman, D. Šepić) R. W. Seton-Watson and the Yugoslavs: correspondence 1906–1941 (2 vols), 1976; (with C. Seton-Watson) The Making of a New Europe: R. W. Seton-Watson and the last years of Austria-Hungary, 1981. *Recreations:* travel, ornithology. *Address:* 8 Burghley Road, Wimbledon Common, SW19. *T:* 01–946 0861. *Club:* Athenæum.                         *Died 19 Dec.* 1984.

**SEUFFERT, Stanislaus,** QC 1965; Special Divorce Commissioner and Deputy Judge, 1967–75; Barrister-at-Law, retired 1975; *b* Johannesburg, 17 May 1899; *e s* of late Philip Seuffert and Marie Winefride Seuffert (*née* Brennan); *m* 1st, Alice, *widow* of George Jackson (*née* McCarthy); 2nd, Norma (*née* Klerck), *widow* of Maj.-Gen. Pienaar, CB, DSO; one *s* one *d. Educ:* Marist Brothers, Johannesburg; Stonyhurst Coll., Lancashire. Served World War, Middx Regt, 1917. Barrister, Middle Temple, 1925, Bencher, 1970. Mem. Senate, Four Inns of Court, 1970–74. First Chm., Guild of Catholic Artists, 1929; Chm. Catholic Prisoners' Aid Soc., 1938–60; Hon. Treas. and Sec., Soc. of Our Lady of Good Counsel, 1935–58. Contested (Lab) East Grinstead, 1935; Borough Councillor, Fulham, 1934–49; Dep. Civil Def. Controller, Fulham, and Leader of Council, 1939–44; Chm. Fulham Food Control Committee, 1939–46; Mayor of Fulham 1944–45. KHS Grand Cross, 1955; Kt of Order of St Gregory (Papal), 1962. *Publications:* annotations: Matrimonial Causes Act, 1937; Local Govt Act, 1949; Adoption Act, 1950. Handbook of Matrimonial Causes. *Recreations:* playgoing, reading. *Address:* 2 Gaywood Court, 42 Hawthorne Road, Bickley, Bromley BR1 2TL. *T:* 01–467 6427.
*Died 22 Sept.* 1986.

**SEWARD, Sir Eric (John),** KBE 1960 (CBE 1954); retired; *b* 18 May 1899; *s* of William Edwards Seward and Florence Lloyd; *m* 1924, Ella Maud, *d* of Frederick L'Estrange Wallace and Gwendoline Gilling-Lax; three *s. Educ:* Parkstone Sch. Served European War 1914–18 with 5th Cavalry Reserve Regt in UK. Chm. British Chamber of Commerce in the Argentine Republic, 1951–62, now Hon. Vice-President. Liveryman Worshipful Company of Butchers. *Address:* Dr G. Rawson 2420, 1636 Olivos, Prov. de Buenos Aires, Argentina.                         *Died 30 Nov.* 1981.

**SEYLER, Athene,** CBE 1959; actress on the London stage; *b* London, 31 May 1889; *d* of Clara Thies and Clarence H. Seyler; *m* 1st, 1914, James Bury Sterndale-Bennett (*d* 1941); one *d*; 2nd, 1960, Nicholas James Hannen, OBE (mil.) (*d* 1972). *Educ:* Coombe Hill School; Bedford College. Gold Medallist, Royal Academy of Dramatic Art, 1908; first appearance on the stage at Kingsway Theatre, 1909;

specialised in comedy acting; served on the Drama Panel of CEMA, 1943 and subsequently of the Arts Council of Great Britain. Pres. of RADA, 1950; Pres. of Theatrical Ladies Guild. Principal successes as Madame Ranevska in The Cherry Orchard, Fanny Farrelli in Watch on the Rhine, the Duchess of Berwick in Lady Windermere's Fan, Vita Louise in Harvey, Mrs Malaprop in The Rivals, The Nurse in Romeo and Juliet. Has appeared in films, 1932–. Hon. Treasurer of British Actors Equity Association, 1944, repr. 1990. *Publication:* The Craft of Comedy, 1944. *Recreations:* walking, talking. *Address:* Coach House, 26 Upper Mall, Hammersmith, W6 9TR.
*Died 12 Sept. 1990.*

**SEYMOUR, Derek Robert Gurth,** MA; Headmaster of Bloxham School, 1965–82; *b* 4 Sept. 1917; *s* of G. Haco Seymour; *m* 1940, Betty, *d* of late Lt-Col S. H. Little; two *s*. *Educ:* Trinity Coll., Cambridge. BA 1939; MA 1943. Head of Chemistry, Junior Housemaster, St John's School, Leatherhead, 1939–44; Asst Master, Head of Science, i/c RAF Section, CCF; Housemaster, Marlborough College, 1944–65. Seconded as Head of Chemistry and House Tutor, Cranbrook Sch., Sydney, 1951–52. Examr and Chief Examr in A and S Level Chemistry, Southern Univs Jt Bd, 1955–63. Hon. Sec., HMC Exchange of Schoolmasters Scheme, 1982–; Chm., Arc, Poole and Bournemouth, 1984–. *Address:* 16 Salterns Point, Salterns Way, Lilliput, Poole, Dorset BH14 8LN. *T:* Canford Cliffs 700476.
*Died 5 Feb. 1986.*

**SEYMOUR, Lady Katharine,** DCVO 1961 (CVO 1939); Extra Woman of the Bedchamber to Queen Elizabeth the Queen Mother since 1960 (Woman of the Bedchamber to the Queen (now Queen Elizabeth the Queen Mother), 1937–60); First Woman of the Bedchamber to Queen Mary, 1927–30 (on marriage became Extra Woman of the Bedchamber, 1930–53); *b* 25 Feb. 1900; 3rd *d* of 3rd Duke of Abercorn; *m* 1930, Sir R. H. Seymour, KCVO (*d* 1938); one *s* one *d* (and one *d* decd). *Address:* 25 Regnum Court, North Walls, Chichester, West Sussex. *T:* Chichester 784871.
*Died 28 April 1985.*

**SEYMOUR, Richard,** CMG 1966; CBE 1946; *b* 16 Sept. 1903; *s* of late Richard Seymour and Edith, *d* of William Hales; *m* 1940, Charlotte, *d* of Ernest Leigh; two *d*. *Educ:* Highgate Sch.; Christ Church, Oxford (Scholar, MA). Admitted a Solicitor, 1927; partner in firm of Rhys Roberts & Co. until 1940. Secretary, Books Commission of Conference of Allied Ministers of Education, 1942–45. Deputy Secretary-General, British Council, 1940–47, Secretary, 1947–53; Controller, Commonwealth Div., 1953–57, European Div., 1957–59; Representative in Germany, 1959–66. *Address:* The Old Manse, Staplecross, Robertsbridge, East Sussex.
*Died 3 June 1982.*

**SEYMOUR, Air Commodore Roland George,** CB 1961; CBE 1945; RAF, retired; *b* 16 May 1905; *s* of William and Jeannie Seymour; *m* 1942, Dorothy Beatrice Hutchings (*d* 1980); two *s*. *Educ:* Christ's Hospital. Pilot Officer, RAF, Jan. 1929, psc 1942; Actg Air Commodore, 1945, as Dep. to Air Officer i/c Administration, Mediterranean Allied Air Forces; Air Commodore, 1958; served in: Iraq, 1930–32; N Africa and Italy, 1942–45; Singapore, 1952–54; Deputy Assistant Chief of Staff (Logistics), Supreme HQ Allied Powers Europe, 1961–63. Legion of Merit (USA), 1946. *Address:* c/o Williams & Glyn's Bank Ltd, Lawrie House, Victoria Road, Farnborough GU15 7PA.
*Died 22 July 1983.*

**SEYMOUR, Rosalind;** *see* Wade, R. H.

**SEZNEC, Prof. Jean Joseph,** FBA 1960; Marshal Foch Professor of French Literature, Oxford, 1950–72 and Fellow, All Souls College, now Emeritus; *b* 18 March 1905; *s* of Jean Seznec and Pauline Le Férec; *m* 1st (marr. diss. 1946); one *s*; 2nd, 1954, Mrs Simone Lee. *Educ:* Ecole Normale Supérieure, Paris. Fellow, French School of Archaeology, Rome, 1929–31; Univ. Lecturer, Cambridge, 1931–33; Prof. Lycée of Marseilles, 1933–34; Prof., French Inst., Florence, 1934–39, Asst Director, 1939; Assoc. Professor, Harvard University, 1941–46, Professor, 1946, Smith Professor of the French and Spanish Languages, 1947–50. Mary Flexner Lecturer, Bryn Mawr, 1955; Lord Northcliffe Lecturer, London, 1958; Dillon Visiting Prof., Harvard University, 1958. Mem., Adv. Council, V&A Museum, 1970–. Hon. DLitt: Harvard, 1961; St Andrews, 1972. Officier de la Légion d'Honneur, 1957; Comdr de l'Ordre National du Mérite, 1973. *Publications:* La Survivance des Dieux Antiques, 1940; L'Episode des Dieux dans la Tentation de Saint Antoine, 1940; Nouvelles Etudes sur la Tentation de Saint Antoine, 1949; Essais sur Diderot et l'Antiquité, 1958; John Martin en France, 1964; Un tableau de Paris au milieu du XVIIIe siècle, 1974; (joint) Fragonard, Drawings for Ariosto, 1945; Diderot, Salons, Vol. I, 1957, 2nd edn 1975; Vol. II, 1960, 2nd edn 1979; Vol. III, 1963, 2nd edn 1983; Vol. IV, 1967; contributions to: French Studies, Jl of Warburg and Courtauld Institutes, Romanic Review, Gazette des Beaux Arts, etc. *Address:* 1 Stanton Harcourt, Oxford.
*Died 21 Nov. 1983.*

**SHACKLETON, Robert,** CBE 1986; MA, DLitt; FSA, FRSL; FBA 1966; Bodley's Librarian, 1966–79, Marshal Foch Professor of French Literature, and Fellow of All Souls College, 1979–86, Oxford University, then Emeritus Fellow; *b* 25 Nov. 1919; *e s* of Albert Shackleton and Emily (*née* Sunderland); unmarried. *Educ:* Todmorden Grammar School; Oriel College, Oxford (Scholar). 1st class, Hon. School of Modern Languages, 1940; DLitt 1966. Military Service, Royal Signals, 1940–45. Candidate (L), Blackburn, Gen. Elec., 1945. Oxford University: Lectr, Trinity Coll., 1946–49; Fellow, Brasenose Coll., 1946–79, now Emeritus Fellow (Librarian, 1948–66, Sen. Dean, 1954–61, Vice-Principal, 1963–66); Lectr in French, 1949–65; Reader in French literature, 1965–66; Chm., Cttee on Oxford Univ. Libraries, 1965–66; Lyell Reader in Bibliography, 1983–84. Visiting Professor: Dept of French and Italian, Univ. of Wisconsin, 1968; Folger Inst., Washington, 1981; Istituto Italiano per gli studi filosofici, Naples, 1985; Vis. Fellow, Humanities Res. Centre, ANU, 1980. Lectures: Zaharoff, Oxford Univ., 1970; Foundation, Birkbeck Coll., 1971; Tredegar, RSL, 1972; Lew David Feldman, Univ. of Texas, 1972; Moses Tyson Meml, Manchester Univ., 1976. Delegate, Oxford Univ. Press, 1972–81. Trustee, St Deiniol's Library, Hawarden, 1980–. Chm., Adv. Cttee for Brotherton Coll., Leeds Univ., 1970–; Chm. of Cttee and Dir, Voltaire Foundn, 1983–. Corresp. Member: Acad. de Bordeaux, 1954; Acad. Montesquieu (Bordeaux), 1956 (Prix Montesquieu, 1956); Acad. de Béarn, 1982; President, Society for French Studies, 1959–60; Member, Editorial Board: French Studies, 1960– (Gen. Ed., 1965–67); Archives internationales d'histoire des idées, 1962–; Clarendon Edition of Locke, 1974–; Nouvelles de la République des Lettres, 1981–. Pres., Internat. Comparative Lit. Assoc., 1964–67; Pres., Internat. Soc. for 18th Century Studies, 1975–79. Hon. Member: Soc. d'Histoire Littéraire de la France; Assoc. Internat. de Bibliophilie; Australasian and Pacific Soc. for 18th Century Studies; Soc. Univ. Studi di Lingua e Letteratura Francese; Hungarian Acad. of Sciences, 1979; For. Hon. Mem., Amer. Acad. of Arts and Sciences; Hon. For. Corresp. Mem., Grolier Club, NY. Hon. Fellow, Oriel Coll., Oxford, 1971; Hon. Professorial Fellow, UCW, 1972–81; Assoc. Fellow, Silliman Coll., Yale Univ., 1972. Hon. Dr Univ. Bordeaux, 1966; Hon. LittD: Univ. of Dublin, 1967; Manchester, 1980; Leeds, 1985. Médaille de la Ville de Paris, 1978; Medal, Univ. of Pisa, 1979; John Brademas Inaugural Award, NY Univ., 1981; Medal, President of Italian Republic, 1985; Marc Fitch Medal for Bibliography, Leeds Univ., 1986. Chevalier de la Légion d'Honneur, 1982. *Publications:* Editor: Fontenelle, Entretiens sur la pluralité des mondes, 1955; Montesquieu, a critical biography, 1961 (French translation, 1976); The Encyclopédie and the Clerks (Zaharoff lect.), 1970; (ed jtly) The Artist and Writer in France, 1975; articles in learned jls, Encyclopædia Britannica, etc. *Recreations:* book-collecting, foreign travel. *Address:* 12 Norham Gardens, Oxford OX2 6QB. *T:* Oxford 513594. *Clubs:* Athenæum, United Oxford & Cambridge University; Grolier (New York); Elizabethan (Yale).
*Died 9 Sept. 1986.*

**SHACKMAN, Prof. Ralph;** Professor of Urology, University of London, at Royal Post-graduate Medical School, 1961–75; *b* 29 March 1910; *s* of David and Sophia Shackman; *m* 1940, Ida Mary Seal; no *c*. *Educ:* Grocers' Company School; St Bartholomew's Hospital Medical School. MB, BS (London) 1934; FRCS 1936. Resident Surgical Officer, Royal Infirmary, Sheffield, 1937. Served War of 1939–45, Wing-Commander Surgical Specialist, RAF. Brit. Post-Grad. Travelling Fellowship in USA, 1947–48. Sen. Lectr, Post-grad. Med. Sch., 1949; Reader in Surgery, Univ. of London, 1955; Mem. Court of Examiners, RCS, England, 1962; Member of Council: Experimental Med. and Therapeutics, Roy. Soc. Med., 1962; Sect. of Urology, Roy. Soc. Med., 1963; Brit. Assoc. of Urological Surgeons, 1964; Brit. Assoc. of Surgeons, 1965; Member, International Society of Urology, 1964. *Publications:* contrib. to medical and scientific jls. *Recreations:* gardening, carpentry. *Address:* Motts Farmhouse, Chilton Street, Clare, Suffolk. *T:* Clare 7835.
*Died 5 June 1981.*

**SHAFTESLEY, John Maurice,** OBE 1956; Editor of publications, Jewish Historical Society of England, a Vice-President, 1974; a Director of The Jewish Chronicle, London, 1958–60; *b* 25 June 1901; *s* of late David Shaftesley and Nellie Rosenblum; *m* 1926, Evelyn Adler; one *d*. *Educ:* Salford Grammar Sch.; Manchester Sch. of Art; London University (BA Hons). Allied Newspapers, technical staff, 1924–26; Manchester Guardian staff, 1926–36; Lecturer, Department of Printing Technology, Manchester College of Technology, 1933–36; Assistant Editor, The Jewish Chronicle, 1937–46 (Editor 1946–58). Fellow Royal Society of Arts, 1938; President, Wingate Services Club, High Wycombe, War of 1939–45; Mem. Council, Friends of the Hebrew Univ. of Jerusalem; Chm., Zangwill Centenary Cttee, 1964, and of Israel Zangwill Fellowship; Hon. Sec., Soc. of Indexers, 1967–68, Chm., 1973–76. A Departmental Editor and contributor, Encyclopædia Judaica, 1966–72. Works include: Cumulative Index to the *Jewish Chronicle* 1841–1880, 1881–90; Cumulative Index to the *Voice of Jacob*

1841–1846; Remember the Days (ed and contributor), 1966; Lodge of Israel No 205: A History 1793–1968, 1968, etc. *Address:* 33 The Grove, Edgware, Middx HA8 9QA. *T:* 01-958 9006. *Clubs:* Reform, Press.
*Died* 11 *Aug.* 1981.

**SHAKERLEY, Sir Geoffrey (Peter)**, Kt 1972; CBE 1964; MC 1945; TD; DL; Vice-Lieutenant of Gloucestershire, 1969–81; *b* 11 April 1906; *s* of Lieutenant-Colonel G. C. Shakerley, DSO (killed in action, 1915) and of late Mrs G. C. Shakerley (*née* Harvey); *m* 1932, Barbara Storrs Howard; two *s* two *d. Educ:* Wellington College; Christ Church, Oxford (MA). Served War of 1939–45, with KRRC (TA), UK, Egypt, Italy; comdg R Gloucestershire Hussars (TA), 1951–53; Dep. Comdr, 129 Inf. Bde (TA), 1954–55. Chm., Gloucestershire CC, 1955–67; Vice-Chm., County Councils Assoc., 1965, Chm. 1969. DL Glos 1953; High Sheriff of Gloucestershire, 1961. *Recreation:* golf. *Address:* The Old Barn, Sevenhampton, near Cheltenham, Glos GL54 5SW. *T:* Andoversford 402.
*Died* 6 *March* 1982.

**SHANKLAND, Sir Thomas (Murray)**, Kt 1960; CMG 1955; JP; Deputy-Governor, Western Region, Nigeria, 1954–57; retired; Chairman, London Board of Public Service Commission, Western Region, Nigeria, 1957–61; *b* 25 Aug. 1905; *y s* of late W. C. Shankland, MBE, Barrister-at-Law, and late E. B. Shankland; *m* 1931, Margaret Crawford Goudie; one *d. Educ:* Felsted School; Queens' College, Cambridge (MA). Administrative Officer, Class IV, Nigeria, 1929; Food and Price Controller, Nigeria, 1944–45; Director of Supplies, Nigeria, 1946–47; Secretary, Western Provinces, Nigeria, 1949; Civil Secretary, Western Region, Nigeria, 1951; Chairman, Constituency Delimitation Commn, WR Nigeria, 1959. Mem. Jt CC, Moray and Nairn, 1958–70. JP Morayshire 1960. *Address:* Ardlarig, Grantown-on-Spey, Morayshire. *T:* Grantown-on-Spey 2160. *Clubs:* East India, Devonshire, Sports and Public Schools, MCC.
*Died* 13 *Oct.* 1986.

**SHANKS, Michael James;** Director: BOC International, since 1976; Henley Centre for Forecasting, Environmental Resources, since 1977; P-E International, since 1977; Chairman, George Bassett (Holdings), since 1982 (Director, since 1977); Chairman, National Consumer Council, since 1977; *b* 12 April 1927; *s* of Alan James Shanks and Margaret Lee; *m* 1st, 1953, Elizabeth Juliet Richardson (*d* 1972); three *s* one *d*; 2nd, 1973, Patricia Jaffé (*née* Aspin). *Educ:* Blundell's Sch.; Balliol Coll., Oxford (MA). Lectr in Econs, Williams Coll., Mass, 1950–51; Labour Corresp., Financial Times, 1954–57; Industrial Editor, Financial Times, 1957–64; Economic Corresp., Sunday Times, 1964–65; Industrial Adviser, DEA, 1965–66; Industrial Policy Coordinator, DEA, 1966–67; Economic Adviser, Leyland Motors, 1967–68; Dir of Marketing Services and Economic Planning, British Leyland Motor Corp., 1968–71; Chief Executive, Finance & Planning, British Oxygen, 1971–72, Dir, Group Strategy, Jan.–June 1973; Dir Gen. for Social Affairs, EEC, 1973–76. Dir, Royal Ordnance Factories, 1977–80; Chm., Datastream, 1977–82. Vis. Prof., Brunel Univ., 1973–; Vis. Fellow, Univ. of Lancaster, 1969–. Hon. Treas., Fabian Soc., 1964–65; Member: Cttee of Management, Science Policy Foundn, 1968–73; Adv. Council, Business Graduates Assoc., 1968–73; Editorial Bd, Times Management Library, 1968–73; Exec. Cttee, Warwick Univ. Centre of Industrial and Business Studies, 1968–73; Wilton Park Academic Council, 1967–; Council, Soc. of Business Economists, 1968–73; Electrical Engrg EDC, 1965–73; Employment Appeal Tribunal, 1976–; NEDC, 1977–81; Council, Soc. for Long-Range Planning, 1971–73; Council, Foundn for Management Educn, 1971–; Council, Centre for Studies in Soc. Policy, 1974–78; Council, Inst. of Directors, 1976–77; European Adv. Council, Tenneco Inc., 1980–. FBIM 1972. *Publications:* The Stagnant Society, 1961; (with John Lambert) Britain and the New Europe, 1962; (ed) The Lessons of Public Enterprise, 1963; The Innovators, 1967; The Quest for Growth, 1973; European Social Policy, To-day and To-morrow, 1977; Planning and Politics, 1978; What's Wrong with the Modern World, 1978; pamphlets, contribs to symposia, learned jls, etc. *Recreations:* reading, gardening, travelling. *Address:* Clapton Revel, Wooburn Moor, High Wycombe, Bucks.
*Died* 4 *Jan.* 1984.

**SHANN, Sir Keith (Charles Owen)**, Kt 1980; CBE 1964; retired Australian public servant and diplomat; *b* 22 Nov. 1917; *s* of late F. Shann, Melbourne; *m* 1944, Betty, *d* of late C. L. Evans; two *s* one *d. Educ:* Trinity Grammar Sch., Kew, Vic; Trinity Coll., Melbourne Univ. (BA). Commonwealth Treasury Dept, 1939; Dept of Labour and Nat. Service, 1940; joined Dept of External Affairs: 2nd Sec., UN Div., 1946; 1st Sec., Acting Counsellor i/c UN Div., 1948; Aust. Mission to UN, New York, 1949–52; Head, UN Branch, 1952–55; Head, Americas and Pacific Branch, 1955; Minister, later Ambassador, to the Philippines, 1955–59; External Affairs Officer, London, 1959–62; Ambassador to Indonesia, 1962–66; First Asst Sec., 1966–70, Dep. Sec., 1970–74, Dept of External (later Foreign) Affairs; Ambassador to Japan, 1974–77; Chm., Aust. Public Service Board, 1977–78. Dir, Mount Isa Mines Ltd, 1978–88; Chm., Burns Philp Trustee Co. (Canberra), 1982–. Mem. Delegns to UN Gen. Assembly, Paris, 1948, 1951, NY 1949, 1950, 1952, 1953, 1957,

1967, 1974; Aust. Observer Bandoeng Conf., 1955; *Rapporteur*, UN Special Cttee on Hungary, 1957; Leader, Aust. Delegn to Develt Assistance Cttee of OECD, 1966–67, 1968–69; Commonwealth Observer, Zimbabwe Elections, 1980. Grand Cordon, Order of Sacred Treasure (Japan), 1988. *Recreations:* golf, gardening, music. *Address:* 11 Grey Street, Deakin, Canberra 2600, Australia. *Clubs:* Commonwealth (Canberra); Melbourne Cricket, Royal Canberra Golf.
*Died* 4 *Aug.* 1988.

**SHANNON, Alastair;** journalist; Foreign News department, Daily Telegraph and Morning Post, 1937–71; *b* Hawick, 1894; *o s* of late Rev. J. W. Shannon and Agnes, *d* of Rev. Alexander Renton; *m* 1920, Betty, *d* of Rev. A. Russell; one *s* one *d. Educ:* George Watson's College and University, Edinburgh. Served Flanders, 1915; Commission, Nov. 1915; Mesopotamia Relieving Force; Prisoner of War in Turkey, Apr. 1916 to Nov. 1918; joined Staff of Morning Post, 1919; Editor Madras Mail, 1921–23; rejoined Morning Post, 1924; Foreign Editor, Morning Post, 1928–37. *Publications:* Morning Knowledge, 1920; The Black Scorpion, 1926. *Address:* 1 Highpoint, Lyonsdown Road, New Barnet, Herts. *T:* 01-440 3593.
*Died* 26 *Dec.* 1982.

**SHANNON, Godfrey Eccleston Boyd**, CMG 19f51; Assistant Under-Secretary of State, in the Commonwealth Office, 1956–68, retired 1968; *b* 14 Dec. 1907; *s* of late W. B. Shannon. *Educ:* Wellington; St John's College, Cambridge. Appointed to Dominions Office, 1930; visited Australia and New Zealand, as Private Sec., with 10th Duke of Devonshire, 1936; Official Sec., UK High Commissioner's Office, New Zealand, 1939–41; served on UK Delegation to various international conferences in London, Geneva, New York, Chicago and Moscow, 1944–48, to UNCTAD, 1964, and to Commonwealth Finance Ministers' meetings, Jamaica, Montreal and Trinidad, 1965–67; Deputy United Kingdom High Commissioner in Canada, 1948–50, in Calcutta, 1952–56. Member, Cttee for Exports: to Canada, 1964–68; to Australia, 1965–68. Renter Warden, Dyers' Co., 1967–68, Prime Warden, 1968–69. *Address:* 18 Lamont Road, SW10 0JE. *T:* 01–351 1585. *Club:* Travellers'.
*Died* 16 *Sept.* 1989.

**SHARMAN, Thomas Charles**, OBE 1960; HM Diplomatic Service, retired; *b* 12 April 1912; *s* of Thomas Sharman and Mary Ward; *m* 1935, Paulette Elisabeth Padioleau; one *d. Educ:* Long Eaton County Secondary Sch.; Clare Coll., Cambridge. HM Consular Service, 1934; Paris, 1935; Saigon, 1937; Milan, 1939; British Embassy, Lisbon, 1940, and Moscow, 1945; HM Foreign Service, 1945; Batavia, 1946; São Paulo, 1947; Superintending Trade Consul, New Orleans, 1949; HM Consul, Luanda, 1952; Consul (Commercial) Hamburg, 1953; Counsellor (Commercial) Lisbon, 1960; Consul-General, Atlanta, Georgia, USA, 1965–68; Consul-General, Oporto, 1968–70. *Address:* 103 Résidence Jeanne Hachette, 60000 Beauvais, France.
*Died* 1 *Aug.* 1990.

**SHARP, Baroness** (Life Peer) *cr* 1966, of Hornsey; **Evelyn (Adelaide) Sharp**, GBE 1961 (DBE 1948); President, London and Quadrant Housing Trust, since 1977 (Chairman, 1973–77); *b* 25 May 1903; *d* of Reverend Charles James Sharp, Vicar of Ealing, Middlesex, to 1935. *Educ:* St Paul's Girls' School; Somerville College, Oxford. Entered Administrative Class of Home Civil Service, 1926. Perm. Sec., Min. of Housing and Local Govt, 1955–66. Mem., Independent Broadcasting Authority (formerly ITA), 1966–73. Hon. DCL Oxon, 1960; Hon. LLD: Cantab, 1962; Manchester, 1967; Sussex, 1969. *Recreation:* pottering. *Address:* The Old Post Office, Lavenham, Sudbury, Suffolk.
*Died* 1 *Sept.* 1985.

**SHARP, Sir Edward Herbert**, 3rd Bt *cr* 1922; *b* 3 Dec. 1927; *s* of Sir Herbert Edward Sharp, 2nd Bt, and Ray Alice Mary (*d* 1985), *d* of Frederick George Bloomfield, Ealing; *S* father 1936; *m* 1949, Beryl Kathleen, *d* of L. Simmons-Green, Shirley, Warwicks; two *s* one *d. Educ:* Haileybury. *Heir: s* Adrian Sharp [*b* 17 Sept. 1951; *m* 1976, Hazel Patricia Bothwell (*née* Wallace)]. *Address:* PO Box 749, Manzini, Swaziland.
*Died* 4 *Nov.* 1985.

**SHARP, Henry Sutcliffe**, FRCS; Honorary Consulting Surgeon, Ear, Nose and Throat Department; Hospital for Sick Children, Great Ormond Street; Charing Cross Hospital; Putney Hospital; *b* 23 June 1910; *s* of late Alexander Sharp, CB, CMG; *m* 1st, 1948, Muiriel Oliver; two *s*; 2nd, 1964, Elizabeth Plant; one *s. Educ:* Haileybury College; Caius Coll., Cambridge; St Thomas's Hosp. BA, MB, ChB (Cantab); FRCS 1939. House Surgeon and Chief Asst, Ear, Nose and Throat Dept, St Thomas's Hosp., 1935. Major RAMC, 1940–45. FRSocMed; Member and past Hon. Sec. of Sections of Laryngology and Otology; Corresp. Mem., Excerpta Medica, Amsterdam. *Publications:* various articles concerning otolaryngology in Jl of Laryngology, Lancet, and Brit. Jl of Surgery. *Recreations:* golf, squash rackets. *Address:* 82 Wildwood Road, NW11. *T:* 01-458 3937.
*Died* 17 *Nov.* 1984.

**SHARP, Brig. Mainwaring Cato Ensor**, CBE 1945; *b* 1 March 1897; *s* of late Rev. Cato Ensor Sharp; *m* 1949, Betty Yolande Constance, *o d* of late Col M. H. Knaggs, CMG. *Educ:* Trinity College School,

Port Hope; RMC, Kingston, Canada. Commissioned, 1915, 5th RI Lancers; transfd Leinster Regt 1916; S Lanc. Regt 1922. Staff College, Camberley, 1928–29; retired, 1935; Insurance Broker, 1937–39; rejoined, 1939; Lt-Col 1941; Brig. 1944. Served European War and War of 1939–45 (despatches twice). Director of Maintenance, Control Commission, Germany, 1946–51; employed by War Office, 1951–58. Croix de Guerre (France); Officer, Legion of Merit (USA). *Recreations:* golf, ornithology. *Address:* 11 Maple Road, Walberton, Arundel, West Sussex BN18 0PN. *T:* Yapton (0243) 551563.                                        *Died* 13 *Dec.* 1990.

**SHARP, Rear-Adm. Philip Graham,** CB 1967; DSC 1942; *b* 23 Nov. 1913; *e s* of late Rev. Douglas Simmonds Sharp and Mrs Sharp; *m* 1940, Dilys Mary Aldwyth, *er d* of late David Roberts and Mrs Roberts, Welford-on-Avon, Warwicks; one *s. Educ:* Northampton Sch.; Tynemouth High Sch. Sub-Lt, RNVR, 1937: War Service in destroyers (despatches 1943); Capt. 1956; comdg HMS Defender, 1956–58; NATO, 1958–60; Capt. of Fleet, Home Fleet, 1960–62; comdg HMS Centaur 1962–63; Cdre RN Barracks, Portsmouth, 1963–65; Rear-Adm. 1965; Flag Officer Sea Training, Portland, 1965–67; retired 1967. ADC to the Queen, 1965. Dir Gen., Internat. Union of Air Pollution Prevention Assocs, 1978–86, now Emeritus. County Pres. for Sussex, Royal British Legion, 1983–; Past President: Inter-Allied Confedn of Reserve Officers; Reserve Forces Assoc. Freeman, City of London, 1978. Silver Medal, City of Paris, 1983. *Recreations:* golf, fishing, music, model-making. *Address:* Dolphin House, Old Shoreham Road, Hove, East Sussex. *T:* Brighton 736545. *Clubs:* Naval and Military; Brighton and Hove Golf; Sussex County Cricket.                     *Died* 10 *Feb.* 1988.

**SHARP, Ven. Richard Lloyd;** Archdeacon of Dorset, 1975–82, then Emeritus; *b* 30 Nov. 1916; *s* of Tom and Anne Lloyd Sharp; *m* 1942, Joan Elizabeth Rhodes; two *s. Educ:* Brighton and Hove Grammar Sch.; St Edmund Hall, Oxford (MA). Curate, Holy Trinity, Weymouth, 1940–44; Vicar: St John, Portland, 1944–49; Wootton Bassett, 1949–55; St Mark, Salisbury, 1955–64; Holy Trinity, Weymouth, 1964–74; Canon of Salisbury Cathedral, 1968–. *Recreations:* local history, photography. *Address:* 269 Verity Crescent, Canford Heath, Poole, Dorset BH17 7UB.
                                                    *Died* 4 *July* 1982.

**SHARPE, Sir Frank (Victor),** Kt 1978; CMG 1972; OBE (mil.) 1943; ED 1942; Australian representative, Bell Helicopter Company, Fort Worth, USA, 1955–72; Helicopter Consultant to Bell Helicopter Australia Pty Ltd, Brisbane International Airport, 1972–74; Avocado consultant and farm adviser since 1946; Director of several companies; *b* 21 Jan. 1903; *s* of Frederick Robert Sharpe, Avening, Glos, and Elizabeth Matilda Glassop, Sydney (third generation); *m* 1947, Millicent Adelaide Gardner; one *s* one *d. Educ:* Rudd's Clayfield Coll.; Queensland Univ. Became dir. family merchant tool business, 1923 (Chm. and Man. Dir and sole proprietor, 1946–). Commissioned Aust. Army, 1921 (Militia); served War of 1939–45, AIF, Australia and SW Pacific; Lt-Col, retd 1955. Built and operated first commercial broadcasting station in Queensland, 1925. FAIM; Fellow, Australian Inst. Dirs. JP Brisbane 1947. *Recreations:* flying, farming, amateur radio. *Address:* 138 Adelaide Street, Clayfield, Brisbane, Qld 4011, Australia. *T:* 262.4842. *Clubs:* Athenæum (Melbourne); Queensland, Brisbane, United Service, Royal Queensland Yacht Squadron, Royal Queensland Aero, Queensland Turf, Tattersalls (Brisbane).                     *Died* 9 *July* 1988.

**SHARROCK, Prof. Roger Ian;** Professor of English Language and Literature, University of London, King's College, 1968–81, later Emeritus; *b* Robin Hood's Bay, 23 Aug. 1919; *s* of Arthur and Iva France Sharrock; *m* 1940, Gertrude Elizabeth Adams, *d* of Edgar Leenie Adams, Bradford; one *s* two *d. Educ:* Queen Elizabeth's Sch., Wakefield; St John's Coll., Oxford (Open Exhibr). 1st cl. Hon. Sch. of Eng. Lang. and Lit., 1943; BLitt 1947. Served with King's Own Yorks LI, 1939–41; Nat. Buildings Record, 1942–44; Asst Master, Rugby Sch., 1944–46; Lectr, Univ. of Southampton, 1946; Reader, 1962; Prof. of English, Univ. of Durham, 1963. Editor, Durham Univ. Jl, 1964–68; Fulbright Vis. Prof., Univ. of Virginia, 1972; Warton Lectr of British Academy, 1972; Trustee, Dove Cottage Trust, 1968–; Dir, Shakespeare Globe Centre, 1970–; Chm., English Assoc., 1972–79. Gen. Editor, Oxford Bunyan. *Publications:* Songs and Comments, 1946; John Bunyan, 1954; (ed) Selected Poems of Wordsworth, 1958; (ed) Bunyan, The Pilgrim's Progress, 1960; (ed) Bunyan, Grace Abounding, 1962; (ed) Selected Poems of Dryden, 1963; (ed) Keats, Selected Poems and Letters, 1964; The Pilgrim's Progress, 1966; (ed) Oxford Standard Authors Bunyan, 1966; Solitude and Community in Wordsworth's Poetry, 1969; (ed) Pelican Book of English Prose, 1970; (ed) Casebook on Pilgrim's Progress, 1976; (ed) English Short Stories of Today, 1976; (ed) The Holy War, 1980; Saints, Sinners and Comedians: the novels of Graham Greene, 1984; (ed) Bunyan, The Life and Death of Mr Badman, 1988; contrib. Encycl. Britannica, Essays in Criticism, Mod. Lang. Review, Review of English Studies, Tablet, etc. *Recreations:* walking, chess. *Address:* 12 Plough Lane, Purley,

Surrey CR8 3QA. *T:* 081–660 3248. *Club:* United Oxford & Cambridge University.                             *Died* 27 *Dec.* 1990.

**SHARWOOD-SMITH, Sir Bryan (Evers),** KCMG 1955 (CMG 1950); KCVO 1956; KBE 1953; ED; Governor, Northern Nigeria, 1954–57 (Lieut-Governor, and President Northern House of Chiefs, 1952–54); retd 1957; *b* 5 Jan. 1899; *s* of late Edward Sharwood Smith; *m* 1st, 1926; one *d*; 2nd, 1939, Winifred Joan, *d* of late Thomas and Winifred Mitchell; two *s* one *d. Educ:* Newbury School; Aldenham School, Herts (Platt Schol.). Elected to Open Classical Schol., Emmanuel College, Cambridge, 1916, but entered army (RFC), 1917; served France, Rhine and North West Frontier India, 1917–20. Assistant Master St Cuthbert's Preparatory School, Malvern, 1920. Entered Colonial Administrative Service, 1920; served in British Cameroons, 1920–27, Nigeria, 1927–57. Military Service, 1940–42; Resident, 1942; Resident, Kano, Nigeria, 1950–52; and President of Northern Region House of Assembly, 1950–52. Acting Chief Commissioner, Northern Provinces, Sept.–Dec. 1950. *Publication:* But Always as Friends, 1969. *Address:* 47 Cooden Drive, Bexhill, East Sussex. *Club:* Royal Air Force.
                                                    *Died* 10 *Oct.* 1983.

**SHATTOCK, Rear-Adm. Ernest Henry,** CB 1955; OBE 1943; Consultant for Manufacturing Licences; Director, Filtration Specialists Ltd; *b* 22 October 1904; *s* of late Ernest Mark Shattock and Evelyn Mabel (*née* Byrde); *m* 1934, Madeline Anne Radcliffe, *d* of late Donald Hatt Noble Graham; one *s* three *d*; *m* 1958, Oz Armstrong. *Educ:* Osborne; Dartmouth. Entered Osborne, 1918; specialised in flying, 1927; Commander, 1938; Captain, 1943; Rear-Admiral, 1953. Served War of 1939–45; Chief of Staff to Flag Officer Naval Air Pacific, 1944–46; Director Naval Air Warfare Division, 1946–49; commanded HMS Glory, 1949–50. Directing Captain, Senior Officers' War College, 1951; Flag Officer, Malaya, Nov. 1953–April 1956; retired list, 1956. Naval ADC to the Queen, 1953. *Publications:* An Experiment in Mindfulness, 1958; Mind Your Body, 1978; A Manual of Self-Healing, 1982; Power Thinking, 1983. *Recreations:* music, magic. *Address:* The Mill House, Newark, Ripley, Surrey. *T:* Guildford 225020.               *Died* 5 *June* 1985.

**SHATWELL, Prof. Kenneth Owen;** Emeritus Professor in the University of Sydney; New South Wales Liaison Officer (Recruitment) for Government of Hong Kong, since 1962; *b* 16 Oct. 1909; *m* 1936, Betty, *d* of Thomas Rae Hogarth, Tasmania; one *s* one *d* (and one *d* decd). *Educ:* Lincoln College, Oxford. Served War of 1939–45: Lieut RANVR, on active service in Atlantic and Pacific. Prof. of Law and Dean of the Faculty of Law, Univ. of Tasmania, 1934–47; Challis Prof. of Law, Univ. of Sydney, 1947–74; Dean of the Faculty of Law, Univ. of Sydney, 1947–73; Dir, Inst. of Criminology, Sydney Univ., 1962–74. Vis. Prof., The Queen's Univ., Belfast, 1951; Australian Comr, S Pacific Commn, 1950–52; Sen. Research Fellow, Yale Univ., 1958–59, 1962; Visiting Professor: New York Univ. Law School Summer Workshop on Contracts, 1962; Temple Univ. Law School, 1968. Aust. Mem., Permanent Court of Arbitration under the Hague Convention, 1960–84; Ministerial Cnsltnt to NSW Dept of Corrective Services, and Mem., NSW Corrective Services Adv. Council, 1972–79. FASSA. *Publications:* various articles in legal jls. *Recreation:* criminology. *Address:* 36 Chilton Parade, Turramurra, NSW 2074, Australia. *T:* Sydney 489–1189. *Clubs:* Athenæum; Tasmanian (Hobart).                                         *Died* 24 *March* 1988.

**SHAW, Alan Frederick,** CBE 1977; JP; Chairman, Intervention Board for Agricultural Produce, 1974–80; farmer since 1946; *b* 5 March 1910; *s* of Walter Frederick and Bessie Florence Shaw; *m* 1946, Angela Dearden (*née* Burges); one step *s. Educ:* Dulwich College. J. & J. Colman, Norwich, 1927–31; own business, gravel extraction, 1931–39. War Service: BEF, 1939–40; Middle East, 8th Army, 1941–43; 2nd Army, 1944–45; Lt-Col, RE. Vice-Pres. and Dep. Pres., NFU, 1968–70; Mem. Barker Cttee on Contract Farming, 1971–72; Mem. Intervention Bd, 1972–74; Dir, Nat. Seed Develt Organisation Ltd, 1971–80; Mem., UK Seeds Exec., 1972–78; Mem. Council, Nat. Inst. Agric. Botany, 1971–80. JP Lincs, 1963. *Recreations:* golf; music (especially opera). *Address:* The Old Vicarage, Horbling, near Sleaford, Lincs. *T:* Sleaford 240563. *Clubs:* Farmers', Royal Automobile.               *Died* 9 *April* 1984.

**SHAW, Anne Gillespie, (Mrs J. H. Pirie),** CBE 1954; Life President, The Anne Shaw Organisation Ltd (Chairman, 1945–79, Managing Director, 1945–74); Director, Wescot Ltd, 1964–79; *b* Uddingston, Scotland, 28 May 1904; *d* of late Major David P. Shaw, Cameronians (killed in action, 1915), and late Mrs Helen B. Shaw; *m* 1937, John Henderson Pirie; one *s* two *d. Educ:* St Leonards School, St Andrews, Fife; Edinburgh University; Bryn Mawr College, Philadelphia, USA. MA (Edinburgh) 1927; Post-Graduate Diploma, Social Economy (Bryn Mawr), 1928. Metropolitan-Vickers Electrical Co. Ltd, 1930–45; Production Efficiency Board, advising Sir Stafford Cripps at MAP, 1942–45; Independent Member of Cotton Working Party, 1945–46. Member: National Advisory Council on Education for Industry and Commerce,

1948-60; Cttee of Enquiry on Training of Teachers for Technical Colleges; Milk Marketing Bd, 1964-73; NEDC for Post Office, 1963; Ct of Inquiry into Ford dispute, 1968; Robens Cttee on Safety and Health at Work, 1970-72. Chm. Management Consultants Assoc., 1967-68. Fellow, Inst. of Personnel Management (Pres. 1949-51); FBIM (Mem. Council, 1968-); CEng; FIProdE. Gilbreth Medal for contribution to scientific management (Soc. for Advancement of Management), 1948. *Publications:* Introduction to the Theory and Application of Motion Study, 1944; Purpose and Practice of Motion Study, 1952. *Recreations:* cine-photography, skiing, camping, gardening. *Address:* Coachman's Cottage, Macclesfield Road, Alderley Edge, Cheshire. *T:* Alderley Edge 583492. *Clubs:* University Women's; Royal Scottish Automobile (Glasgow). *Died 4 Feb. 1982.*

**SHAW, Arnold John;** *b* 12 July 1909; *s* of Solomon and Rachel Shaw; *m* 1935, Elizabeth Salomons; one *d*. *Educ:* Trafalgar Sq. (LCC) Primary Sch.; Coopers' Company's Sch.; Univ. of Southampton. BA (Hons) London, 1930. Entered teaching profession, 1932. Member: Stepney Borough Coun., 1934-48; Ilford Borough Coun., 1952-64 (Alderman, 1963-64); Redbridge, London Borough Coun., 1964-68, 1971-74. Contested (Lab) Ilford South, 1964; MP (Lab) Ilford South, 1966-70, Redbridge, Ilford South, Feb. 1974-1979; PPS to Minister for Housing and Construction, 1977-79. Chm., Age Concern, Ilford; Vice Chm., Newlon Housing Trust. *Recreation:* gardening. *Address:* 2a Claybury Broadway, Ilford, Essex. *Died 27 June 1984.*

**SHAW, Rev. Arthur;** *see* Shaw, Rev. B. A.

**SHAW, Benjamin,** CBE 1986; Councillor (Lab), Liverpool City Council, 1957-74, Merseyside County Council, 1974-86 (Chairman, 1984-85); *b* 3 Oct. 1906; *s* of Nathan and Esther Shaw; *m* 1946, Paulette Weinstein; three *s* one *d*. *Educ:* Liverpool. Served in Royal Engineers, 1940-46. Textile wholesaler, now retired. Mem. Cttee, Royal Liverpool Philharmonic Society, 1967-84 (Chm., 1974-77 and 1981-84; Vice-Pres., 1984-); First Chm., Liverpool Heritage Bureau, 1972; Founder, Chm., 1973-79, Pres., 1981-, Friends of Merseyside Museums and Art Galleries; Mem. Cttee, Playhouse Theatre, 1974-84; Chm., Merseyside Arts and Culture Cttee, 1974-77 and 1981-83; Vice-Chm., King David High Sch., Liverpool, 1976-; Member: Merseyside Maritime Trust, 1979-; Merseyside Enterprise Forum, 1984-; Chm., Nat. Cttee, Area Services for Museums and Chm., NW Museum and Art Gallery Service, 1981-; Vice-Pres., Museums' Assoc. of GB, 1981; Chm., Empire Theatre Trust (Liverpool), 1981-83. *Recreations:* reading, music, watching sports. *Address:* 63 Childwall Priory Road, Liverpool L16 7PD. *T:* 051-722 6333. *Died 27 Dec. 1986.*

**SHAW, Rev. (Bernard) Arthur;** Chairman of the Chester and Stoke on Trent District of the Methodist Church, 1962-80; President of the Methodist Conference, 1977-78; *b* 12 Sept. 1914; *s* of John and Lillie Shaw; *m* 1st, 1944, Alma Kirk (*d* 1977); two *s* one *d*; 2nd, 1985, Jean Timperley. *Educ:* Queen Elizabeth Grammar Sch., Wakefield; Lancaster Royal Grammar Sch.; Richmond Coll. (Theological: London Univ.), Surrey. Filton, Bristol, 1941-43; RAF Chaplain, 1943-46; Stoke on Trent, 1946-51; Hinde Street Methodist Church, London Univ. Methodist Chaplaincy, 1951-57; Leeds Mission, 1957-62. DUniv Keele, 1977. *Recreations:* gardening, reading, walking. *Address:* 10 Rope Bank Avenue, Wistaston, Crewe, Cheshire CW2 6RZ. *T:* Crewe 68255. *Died 6 Nov. 1988.*

**SHAW, Sir Bernard (Vidal),** Kt 1957; *b* 28 April 1891; *s* of late Bernard Vidal Shaw; *m* 1929, Katharine Ceceley, *d* of Arthur Stanley Colls. *Educ:* St Paul's School. Indian Police, 1910-23; called to Bar, Gray's Inn, 1925; entered Colonial Service (Kenya), 1925; Resident Magistrate, 1928; Relieving President, District Court, Palestine, 1936; President, 1941; Chairman, Awqaf Commission, 1939-40; Puisne Judge, Supreme Court of Palestine, 1945-48. Chairman, North Midland District Valuation Board, 1950-55; Chm., Medical Appeal Tribunals, 1952-64; Sen. Puisne Judge, Cyprus, 1955-57. *Publications:* Kenya Law Reports, 1927-30 (Collator and Editor), and 1931-32 (Editor). *Recreation:* tennis. *Address:* 45 Rivermead Court, SW6 3RX. *T:* 01-736 1644. *Clubs:* Athenæum; Hurlingham. *Died 26 May 1984.*

**SHAW, Very Rev. Charles Allan;** Rector of Alcester with Arrow, Diocese of Coventry, since 1984; *b* 16 Feb. 1927; *s* of Henry and Anne Shaw. *Educ:* Bolton School; Christ's Coll., Cambridge (MA 1952); Westcott House, Cambridge. Assistant Master, Tonbridge School, 1949; ordained, 1951; Curate of Swinton, Manchester, 1951-54; Chaplain and Asst Master, Malvern Coll., 1954-58; Vicar of St Ambrose, Pendleton, 1958-62; Domestic Chaplain to Bishop of Birmingham and Succentor of Birmingham Cathedral, 1962-67; Dean of Bulawayo, 1967-75, Dean Emeritus, 1975-; Archdeacon of Bulawayo, 1969-75; Vicar General of Matabeleland, 1972-75; Commissary to Bp of Matabeleland, 1975-; Residentiary Canon, Prebendary de Warham and Precentor of Hereford Cathedral, 1975-82; Dean of Ely, 1982-84. *Recreations:* theatre, music and

people. *Address:* The Rectory, Alcester, Warwickshire B49 5AL. *T:* Alcester 764261; 3 The Parks, Burwarton, Shropshire. *T:* Burwarton 622. *Club:* Junior Carlton. *Died 16 July 1989.*

**SHAW, Frank Howard,** MBE 1945; TD; MA; JP; Headmaster, King's College School, Wimbledon, 1960-75; *b* 13 June 1913; *s* of E. H. Shaw; *m* 1950, Harriette Alice, *d* of late His Honour Robert Peel; one *s* two *d*. *Educ:* Altrincham Grammar School; Hertford College, Oxford. Asst master: King's Coll. School, 1935-39; Marlborough College (and Housemaster), 1939-52; first Headmaster of Pakistan Air Force Public School, Murree Hills, 1952-58; Principal, Aden Coll., Aden, 1958-60. Chm., HMC, 1972. Served War of 1939-45 in Devonshire Regt; Jt Planning Staff, 1943-45. Col. JP, SW London, 1966-76. *Publications:* textbooks for teaching of English in Pakistan. *Recreation:* golf. *Address:* Medstead House, Medstead, near Alton, Hants. *T:* Alton (0420) 62195. *Clubs:* East India, Devonshire, Sports and Public Schools, MCC. *Died 13 Sept. 1990.*

**SHAW, George Anthony Theodore,** CBE 1965; *b* 25 Oct. 1917; *s* of late G. E. Shaw, CMG, OBE, LLB; *m* 1st, Suzanne Alexandra Barber (marr. diss.), *d* of late H. C. Barber; one *s* one *d*; 2nd, Joan Margaret (*d* 1984), *d* of late Rev. N. M. Livingstone, DCL, RN; two *d*; 3rd, 1985, Mrs Hilary Aileen Reynolds, *d* of late R. H. Parker. *Educ:* Marlborough Coll.; Clare Coll., Cambridge (MA). Intell. Corps, Army, 1941-46, Indian Civil Service, 1944-45; HM Overseas Civil Service, 1940-67: Malaya, Singapore, Sarawak, Brunei, Malaysia; State Sec., Sarawak, 1963-67; Milton Keynes Develt Corp., 1967-74; Severn Trent Water Auth., 1974-79. Order of Star of Sarawak (PNBS), 1966. *Recreations:* wide. *Address:* Fircroft, Kivernell Road, Milford-on-Sea, Lymington, Hants SO41 0PP. *Clubs:* East India; Royal Lymington Yacht. *Died 25 May 1990.*

**SHAW, Irwin;** writer (US); *b* New York, 27 Feb. 1913; *s* of William Shaw and Rose (*née* Tompkins); *m* 1939, Marian Edwards (marr. diss.; one *s*. *Educ:* Brooklyn College (AB). Served War of 1939-45 in US Army. *Publications:* plays; Bury the Dead, 1936; The Gentle People, 1939; Quiet City, 1939; Retreat to Pleasure, 1941; Sons and Soldiers, 1943; The Assassin, 1945; Children From Their Games, 1963; *short stories:* Sailor Off the Bremen, 1940; Welcome to the City, 1942; Act of Faith, 1946; Mixed Company, 1952; Tip on a Dead Jockey, 1957; Love on a Dark Street, 1965; Whispers in Bedlam, 1972; God was Here, But He Left Early, 1973; Collected Stories, (in US, Five Decades), 1978; *novels:* The Young Lions, 1948; The Troubled Air, 1951; Lucy Crown, 1956; Two Weeks in Another Town, 1960; Voices of a Summer Day, 1965; Rich Man, Poor Man, 1970; Evening in Byzantium, 1973; Nightwork, 1975; Beggarman, Thief, 1977; The Top of the Hill, 1979; Bread upon the Waters, 1981; Acceptable Losses, 1982; *travel:* In the Company of Dolphins, 1962; Paris!, Paris!, 1976. *Address:* c/o Hope Leresche & Sayle, 11 Jubilee Place, SW3 3TE. *Died 16 May 1984.*

**SHAW, John Dennis Bolton,** MVO 1961; HM Diplomatic Service, retired; *b* 5 July 1920; *er s* of William Bolton Shaw and Margaret Bolton Shaw, Manchester; *m* 1955, Isabel Loewy (decd); two *s*. *Educ:* Manchester Grammar Sch.; Balliol Coll., Oxford (MA). Served War: in North Africa, Italy and India, Lieut RA and RWAFF, 1940-46. Colonial Office, 1948-55; District Comr and Dep. Financial Sec., Sierra Leone, 1955-57; Commonwealth Relations Office, 1957-58 and 1962-65; Karachi, 1958-61; Washington, 1961-62; apptd Counsellor, 1962; Nairobi, 1965-67; Counsellor for Trusteeship Affairs, UK Mission to the UN, 1967-71; Head of Gibraltar and General Dept, FCO, 1971-73; Ambassador to Somali Democratic Republic, 1973-76; Dep. High Comr, Kuala Lumpur, 1976-77. *Recreations:* travel, archaeology, music. *Address:* West Beeches, Ashurst Wood, W Sussex RH19 3RQ. *Died 4 July 1989.*

**SHAW, Sir John (James Kenward) B.;** *see* Best-Shaw.

**SHAW, Sir John Valentine Wistar,** KCMG 1947 (CMG 1942); Kt 1946; *b* 1894; *m* 1926, Josephine Mary, *yr d* of Joseph Simpson, Horsehay, Shropshire; two *s*. *Educ:* Repton School. Served with Royal Engineers, 1914-19, in France and Palestine (despatches). Colonial Administrative Service, Gold Coast, 1921-35; Palestine, 1935-40; Colonial Sec. Cyprus, 1940-43 (despatches, CMG); Chief Sec. Palestine, 1943-46; Governor and C-in-C Trinidad and Tobago, 1947-50; retired, 1950. Attached War Office, 1950-54; Chairman, Commission of Inquiry into Industrial dispute and riots, Sierra Leone, 1955. *Address:* 2 White Close, Winchelsea, Sussex. *T:* Winchelsea 283. *Died 24 Dec. 1982.*

**SHAW, Rt. Hon. Sir Sebag,** Kt 1968; PC 1975; a Lord Justice of Appeal, 1975-81; *b* 28 Dec. 1906; 2nd *s* of Henry and Marie Shaw; *m* 1928, Sally (*d* 1982), *d* of Oscar and Bertha Baumgart; one *s*. Called to Bar, Gray's Inn, 1931, Bencher 1967. QC 1962. Acting Deputy Chairman, County of London Sessions, 1949; Recorder of Ipswich, 1958-68; Prosecuting Counsel, Board of Trade, 1959-62; Leader, SE Circuit, 1967-68; Judge of Queen's Bench Division,

High Court of Justice, 1968–75. Member: Interdepartmental Cttee on Court of Criminal Appeal, 1964–65; Bar Council, 1964–68; Parole Bd, 1971–74, Vice-Chm., 1973–74. Fellow UCL, 1970–. *Publication:* Law of Meetings, 1947. *Address:* 69 Wynnstay Gardens, W8. *T:* 01–937 4907. *Died* 27 *Dec.* 1982.

**SHAW, Sinclair,** QC (Scotland) 1950; Sheriff Principal of Edinburgh, the Lothians and Peeblesshire and Sheriff of Chancery, 1966–73; *b* South Africa, 14 March 1905; *m* 1948, Denise Fanny (Mem. French Resistance, 1941–45, Médaille de la Résistance; Croix de Guerre avec Palme; Chevalier Légion d'Honneur), *e d* of Dr Charles Mantoux and Dr Dora Mantoux; no *c*. *Educ:* Stewart College; Edinburgh Univ. Called to Scots Bar, 1936. Chairman Scottish Council of Labour Party, 1947. Member New Towns Committee (Chm. Lord Reith) apptd by Govt to work out principles to be followed in building new towns, 1945–46. Contested (Lab): Moray and Nairn, 1945, S Aberdeen, 1951. Advocate-Depute, 1945–51; Sheriff Substitute of Fife, 1959–66. *Address:* 5 Randolph Cliff, Edinburgh EH3 7TZ. *T:* 031–225 4445; La Diane, 32 Rue des Eveuses, 78120 Rambouillet, France. *T:* 041.76.06.
*Died* 11 *June* 1985.

**SHAW, Thomas Richard,** CMG 1960; HM Diplomatic Service, retired; *b* 5 Sept. 1912; *s* of Colin R. and Ida L. Shaw, Bolton, Lancs; *m* 1939, Evelyn Frances Young (*d* 1987); four *s*. *Educ:* Repton; Clare Coll., Cambridge. Appointed probationer vice-consul at Istanbul, Nov. 1934; transferred to Bushire, December 1937; acting Consul, Grade 2, Tientsin, 1938–39; transferred to Trieste, Jan. 1940, to Leopoldville, Oct. 1940, to Elisabethville, 1942; served at Casablanca, 1943; vice-consul, Rabat, Dec. 1943; appointed one of HM vice-consuls serving in Foreign Office, 1944; promoted to consul, 1945; transferred to Bremen as consul, 1949; Deputy Consul-General, New York, 1953; actg Consul-General, 1953; Consul-General, Izmir, 1955; Inspector of Foreign Service Establishments, 1957, Senior Inspector, 1961; Ambassador to the Republics of Niger, Upper Volta and the Ivory Coast, 1964–67 (also to the Republic of Dahomey, 1964–65); Minister, Tokyo, 1967–69; Ambassador to Morocco, 1969–71. *Address:* Upton, Harrow Road West, Dorking, Surrey. *Died* 25 *March* 1989.

**SHAWYER, Robert Cort,** MA, PhD; *b* 9 Oct. 1913; *e s* of late Arthur Frederic Shawyer, sometime Gen. Manager, Martins Bank; *m* 1939, Isabel Jessie Rogers (*d* 1986); two *d*. *Educ:* Charterhouse; Corpus Christi Coll., Oxford; Birkbeck Coll., Univ. of London. Bank of England, 1935–37. Commissioned RAEC, 1938 (Lt-Col 1945). Princ., Min. of Nat. Insce, 1948; Admty, 1951; Asst Sec., 1957; seconded to NATO, 1960; Nat. Def. Coll., Canada, 1961–62; Commonwealth Office, 1967; Consul-Gen., Buenos Aires, 1967–70; FCO, Cultural Relations Dept, 1970–72; retired. FRGS. *Publications:* articles in professional, etc, jls. *Recreation:* archaeology. *Address:* Southfield, 3 South Road, Taunton, Somerset. *Clubs:* Army and Navy; Royal Commonwealth Society (Bristol).
*Died* 28 *June* 1989.

**SHEA, Patrick,** CB 1972; OBE 1961; *b* 1908; *s* of Patrick Shea and Mary Catherine Shea (*née* McLaughlin); *m* 1941, Eithne, *d* of Michael and Mary J. MacHugh, Balmoral, Belfast; two *s* one *d*. *Educ:* High Sch., Clones; Abbey Sch., Newry. Entered Northern Ireland Civil Service, 1926; Asst Sec., Min. of Finance, 1963; Perm. Sec., Min. of Education for N Ireland, 1969–73. Chm., Enterprise Ulster, 1973–79. Mem. Senate, QUB, 1971–. Hon. Mem., Royal Soc. of Ulster Architects, 1971. FRSA 1977. *Publications:* (play) Waiting Night (prod. Abbey Theatre, Dublin), 1957; Voices and the Sound of Drums (autobiog.), 1981. *Recreation:* occasional writer. *Address:* 1A Adelaide Park, Belfast BT9 6FX. *T:* Belfast 665609. *Club:* (Pres. 1961–62) Ulster Arts (Belfast).
*Died* 31 *May* 1986.

**SHEALS, Dr John Gordon;** Keeper of Zoology, British Museum (Natural History), 1971–85; *b* 19 Dec. 1923; *o s* of late John Joseph Sheals and Anne (*née* Ffoulkes); *m* 1945, Blodwen M. Davies (*d* 1972); one *s* (and one *s* decd). *Educ:* Caernarvon County Sch.; UC North Wales; Glasgow Univ. BSc, PhD, FIBiol. Asst Lectr, West of Scotland Agricultural Coll., Glasgow, 1948–56; Asst Advisory Entomologist, Min. of Agric., Fisheries and Food, 1956–58; Asst Keeper, 1958–68, and Dep. Keeper, 1968–71, Dept of Zoology, British Museum (Natural History). Mem. Council, Freshwater Biological Assoc., 1976–85; Trustee, Percy Sladen Meml Fund, 1978–85. *Publications:* (with G. O. Evans and D. Macfarlane) The Terrestrial Acari of the British Isles: Introduction and Biology, 1961; papers on taxonomy and ecology of mites in scientific jls. *Recreation:* music. *Address:* 49 Broadriding Road, Shevington, Lancs WN6 8EX. *T:* Appley Bridge 3481.
*Died* 17 *Nov.* 1989.

**SHEARER, Rev. W(illiam) Russell;** *b* 12 Oct. 1898; *s* of Henry S. and Jessie A. Shearer; *m* 1934, Phyllis Mary Wigfield (*d* 1986). *Educ:* Harrogate Grammar School; Leeds University; Wesley House, Cambridge. Served European War, 1914–18, in Tank Corps. Since 1923 has been Methodist Minister at: Tunstall, Staffs; Manchester;

Muswell Hill; Sutton, Surrey; Hanley. Chairman, Stoke-on-Trent Methodist District, 1943–50; Chairman, Birmingham Methodist District, 1950–63. Pres. of Methodist Conference, 1954–55; Moderator, National Free Church Federal Council, 1959–60. Pres. UK Bd, Hope Union, 1960–74. *Address:* 32 Layton Lane, Shaftesbury, Dorset SP7 8EY. *T:* Shaftesbury 2678. *Club:* National Liberal. *Died* 26 *Jan.* 1987.

**SHEARMAN, Sir Harold (Charles),** Kt 1965; MA; Chairman, Greater London Council, 1964–66; Member for Lewisham, 1964–67; Chairman: Inner London Education Cttee, 1964–65; Further and Higher Educn Sub-Cttee, 1964–67; *b* 14 March 1896; *e s* of late Rev. C. E. P. Shearman and late Mary Charlotte Shearman; *m* 1924, Frances Mary (*d* 1982), *d* of late Henry Jameson, Hamsterley, Co. Durham; one *s*. *Educ:* Sulgrave National School; Magdalen College School, Brackley; Wolsingham Grammar School; St Edmund Hall, Oxford (1st Class, Modern History, 1922). Elementary Teacher, Durham, 1912–15. Served European War, 1914–18, Private RAMC, and Flying Officer (Observer) RAF, 1916–19. Contested (Lab) Isle of Wight, 1922. Tutor-organiser in Bedfordshire, WEA and Cambridge Extra Mural Board, 1927–35; Education Officer, WEA, 1935–45; Academic Adviser Tutorial Classes, Univ. of London, 1946–61. Member (Deptford) LCC 1946–65 (Chairman Education Cttee, 1955–61); Chairman: LCC, 1961–62; SE Gas Consultative Council, 1963–66; Member: UK delegation, UNESCO Conf., New Delhi, 1956; Committee on Higher Education (1961–63) and other Govt and Educational Cttees; Mem., Commonwealth Scholarships Commn, 1964–68; Pres. School Journey Assoc. of London, 1962–71. Chairman: Metropolitan Exam. Bd (Cert. of Sec. Educn), 1963–72; South Bank Polytechnic, 1970–75 (Hon. Fellow, 1976); Gov. Body, Kidbrooke Sch.; Southfields Sch.; Coombe Lodge Further Educn Coll., 1960–; Rachel Macmillan Coll. of Educn; Garnett College; Member: Court, Brunel Univ.; Univ. of London: Senate, 1966–70; King's College Delegacy; Sch. of Pharmacy, 1960–. DL Greater London, 1967–76. *Address:* 109 Blagdon Road, New Malden, Surrey. *Died* 24 *March* 1984.

**SHEEHAN, Harold Leeming,** MD, DSc, FRCP, FRCOG, FRCPath; Professor of Pathology, University of Liverpool, 1946–65 (Professor Emeritus since 1965); *b* 4 Aug. 1900; *s* of Dr P. Sheehan, Carlisle; *m* 1934, E. S. G. Potter (*d* 1986); no *c*. *Educ:* University of Manchester. Demonstrator and Lecturer in Pathology, University of Manchester, 1927–34; Rockefeller Medical Fellow in USA, 1934–35; Director of Research, Glasgow Royal Maternity Hosp., 1935–46; Hon. Lecturer in Pathology, Univ. of Glasgow, 1943–46. Served in RAMC, 1939–45; Colonel, Deputy Director of Pathology, AFHQ, Italy, 1945 (despatches, TD). Hon. Member: Fac. Med., Univ. of Chile; Fac. Med., Univ. of Concepcion; Soc. Roy. Belge Gyn. Obst.; Soc. Chil. Obst. Gyn.; Soc. Argent. Neurol.; Soc. Med. Hop. Paris; Socs Endocrinology: Chile, Argentine, Roumania, Hungary; Hon. Fellow, Amer. Assoc. Obst. Gyn.; Foreign Associate, Académie Nationale de Médecine, Paris; Foreign Corresp., Acad. Nat. Méd., France. Hon. MD Szeged (Hungary), 1982. *Publications:* papers on pathology, endocrinology and renal physiology in various med. jls. *Address:* 18 Knowsley Road, Liverpool L19 0PG. *T:* 051–427 2936. *Died* 25 *Oct.* 1988.

**SHEFFIELD, Maj.-Gen. John,** CB 1967; CBE 1961; Commandant of the Star and Garter Home, Richmond, 1975–77, a Governor, since 1977; *b* 28 April 1910; *s* of late Major W. G. F. Sheffield, DSO, and Mrs C. G. A. Sheffield (*née* Wing); *m* 1936, Mary Patience Vere (*née* Nicoll); one *s* one *d* (and one *s* decd). *Educ:* Winchester; RMA, Woolwich. Commd, 1930; served RA and RHA; transferred RAOC, 1939. Served War of 1939–45: BEF, 1939–40; MEF, 1944–48. Egypt, 1954–56; Cyprus, 1959–62; Comdr Base Organization, RAOC, 1964–67. Col Comdt, RAOC, 1970–74. *Recreations:* athletics (British Olympic Team, 1936), golf, sailing, numismatics. *Address:* Tuns Arch House, Odiham, Hants. *T:* Odiham 2436. *Club:* Royal Automobile.
*Died* 30 *July* 1987.

**SHELDON, Sir Wilfrid (Percy Henry),** KCVO 1959 (CVO 1954); Physician-Pædiatrician to the Queen, 1952–71; Consulting Pædiatrician, King's College Hospital; Consulting Physician, Hospital for Sick Children, Great Ormond Street; Hon. Fellow of Royal Society of Medicine; *b* 23 Nov. 1901; *s* of John Joseph Sheldon, FLS; *m* 1927, Mabel Winifred Netherway; three *d*. *Educ:* King's College, London; King's College Hospital. MB, BS (Honours Anatomy and Medicine), 1921; MD London 1925. FRCP 1933; FAAP 1966; FRCOG 1972; MMSA 1972. *Publications:* Acute Rheumatism following Tonsillitis, 1931; Amyoplasia Congenita, 1932; Congenital Pancreatic Lipase Deficiency, 1964; Text Book of Diseases of Infancy and Childhood, 8th edn, 1962. *Recreations:* golf, gardening. *Address:* Little Coombe, Warren Cutting, Kingston, Surrey. *T:* 01-942 0252. *Died* 9 *Sept.* 1983.

**SHEPHEARD, Sir Victor (George),** KCB 1954 (CB 1950); FEng 1976; Director: William Denny & Brothers Ltd, Shipbuilders and Engineers, Dumbarton, 1959–63; Marinite Ltd, 1961–73; Director of Research, British Ship Research Association, 1959–63; *b* 21 March 1893; *e s* of late V. G. Shepheard, Shortlands, Kent; *m* 1924, Florence (*d* 1984), *d* of late Capt. James Wood, Bridgwater. *Educ:* HM Dockyard School, Devonport; Royal Naval Coll., Greenwich. Royal Corps of Naval Constructors, 1915; Constructor Lieut, Grand Fleet, 1915–17; present at Battle of Jutland. Professor of Naval Architecture, RN College, Greenwich, 1934–39; Chief Constructor, 1939–42; Asst Director of Naval Construction, 1942–47; Deputy Director 1947–51; Director of Naval Construction, Admiralty, and Head of RCNC, 1951–58. Member Council Royal Inst. of Naval Architects, 1944–, Vice-Pres. 1952–, Hon. Vice-Pres., 1961, Treasurer, 1960–69. Hon. Vice-Pres., Soc. for Nautical Research; Member: Admty Adv. Cttee on Structural Steel; Cttee on application of Nuclear Power to Marine Purposes, 1961–63; HMS Victory Advisory Technical Cttee. Hon. Fell., NEC Inst.; Mem., Smeatonian Soc. of Civil Engineers, Pres., 1976; Liveryman of Worshipful Company of Shipwrights, Prime Warden, 1968; Board of Governors Cutty Sark Society; formerly Trustee, Nat. Maritime Museum. Froude Gold Medal for services to Naval Architecture and Shipbuilding, 1963. Chev. de la Légion d'Honneur, 1947. *Publications:* various papers to Professional Institutions. *Recreations:* gardening, music. *Address:* Manor Place, Manor Park, Chislehurst, Kent. *T:* 01–467 5455.                     *Died* 8 *Dec.* 1989.

**SHEPHERD, Dame Margaret (Alice),** DBE 1964 (CBE 1962); Chairman, Haigh Engineering Co. Ltd, Ross-on-Wye; *b* 1910; *d* of Percy S. Turner, Redcourt, Pyrford; *m* 1935, Thomas Cropper Ryley Shepherd (*d* 1975); three *s* one *d*. *Educ:* Wimbledon, Lausanne and London Univ. Chairman: Conservative and Unionist Women's National Advisory Cttee, 1960–63; Conservative Political Centre National Advisory Cttee, 1966–69; Chm., 1963–64, Pres., 1972–73, Nat. Union of Conservative and Unionist Assocs. Mem. House of Laity, Gen. Synod of C of E, 1980–85. *Recreations:* swimming, gardening. *Address:* 2 Green Court, Wilton, Ross-on-Wye, Herefordshire. *T:* Ross-on-Wye 62370.            *Died* 13 *Feb.* 1990.

**SHEPHERD, Air Vice-Marshal Melvin Clifford Seymour,** CB 1975; OBE 1953; Chief Executive, Wine and Spirit Trades Benevolent Society, since 1980; *b* 22 Oct. 1922; *s* of Clifford Charles Golding Shepherd and Isabella Davidson Shepherd (*née* Kemp); *m* 1949, Patricia Mary Large; one *s*. *Educ:* in South Africa. Commnd SAAF 1942; war service N Africa, Sicily, Burma, 1942–45; joined RAF, 1947; comd No 73 (F) Sqdn Malta, 1950–53 psa 1952; Chief Ops Officer, Western Sector UK, 1954–57; Comdr No 15 MU Wroughton, 1957–60; Air Min. Air Plans, 1960–63; Dirg Staff, Jt Services Staff Coll., 1963–65; Chief Ops Officer, Far East Comd, 1966; ACOS (Intell.) 2ATAF, 1967–69; comd RAF Binbrook, 1969–72; SASO No 38 Gp, 1972–74; Dir of Ops (Air Defence and Overseas), 1974–75; AOA Strike Command, 1976–78. *Recreations:* golf, shooting, fishing, reading. *Club:* Royal Air Force.
                                                                  *Died* 15 *Feb.* 1989.

**SHEPHERD, Prof. William Morgan,** DSc (London); Professor of Theoretical Mechanics in Faculty of Engineering, University of Bristol, 1959–71, Emeritus, 1971; *b* 19 Dec. 1905; *s* of Charles Henry and Elizabeth Shepherd; *m* 1932, Brenda Coulson (*d* 1982); two *d*. *Educ:* Wellington School; University College of the South West, Exeter; University College, London. Asst lecturer and lecturer in mathematics, University College of North Wales, Bangor, 1928–35; Lecturer in mathematics in Faculty of Engineering, University of Bristol, 1935–44; Reader in Elasticity, University of Bristol, 1944–59; Head of Department of Theoretical Mechanics, 1951–71. *Publications:* various publications, mainly on applied mathematics, in Proceedings of the Royal Society and other scientific journals. *Recreations:* gardening, cricket. *Address:* 1 Thorpe Lodge, Cotham Side, Bristol BS6 5TJ. *T:* Bristol 426284.

                                                                  *Died* 24 *Nov.* 1987.

**SHEPPARD, Leslie Alfred,** MA; FSA; Deputy Keeper of Printed Books, British Museum, 1945–53; *b* 9 Jan. 1890; *o s* of late Alfred Sheppard, Keynsham; *m* 1918, Dorothy (*d* 1979), *y d* of late Rev. H. Ewbank, St John's, Ryde; two *s*. *Educ:* Merrywood School, Bristol; St Catharine's College, Cambridge. Served with 1st British Red Cross Unit attached to Italian Army, 1915–19; entered British Museum, 1919; worked on Catalogue of books printed in XVth cent., now in BM, vols vi, viii-x; catalogued incunabula of Bodleian Library, Oxford, 1955–70. Member of Council of Bibliographical Society, 1936–46. *Publications:* articles and reviews in Transactions of Bibliographical Society, Gutenberg Jahrbuch, and elsewhere. Translated Memoirs of Lorenzo da Ponte, 1929. *Address:* The Bishops House, 55 New Street, Henley-on-Thames, Oxon RG9 2BP. *T:* Henley 4658.                                    *Died* 3 *Dec.* 1985.

**SHEPPARD, Sir Richard (Herbert),** Kt 1981; CBE 1964; RA 1972 (ARA 1966); FRIBA 1944 (ARIBA 1936); Founder and now Consultant to Sheppard Robson, Architects, whose work includes universities, schools and technical colleges, industrial and commerical buildings; *b* 2 July 1910; *e s* of William Sheppard and Hilda (*née* Kirby-Evans); *m* 1st, 1938, Jean Shufflebotham, ARIBA,

MRTPI (*d* 1974); one *s* one *d*; 2nd, 1976, Marjorie Head. *Educ:* Bristol Grammar School; Architectural Association School of Architecture, Bedford Square. Hons Diploma, Architectural Assoc. 1935; foreign travel, 1935–37. Principal commissions include: City Univ., London; Brunel Univ., Uxbridge; Churchhill College, Cambridge (competition), 1959; Collingwood College, Univ. of Durham; Campus West, Welwyn Garden City; Manchester Polytechnic; and other educnl and commercial bldgs. Vice-Pres. RIBA, 1969–70. Hon. DTech Brunel, 1972. *Publications:* Building for the People, 1945; Prefabrication and Building, 1946, etc; also technical articles. *Recreation:* looking at the work of others. *Address:* 6 Robin's Nest Hill, Little Berkhamsted, Herts. *T:* Cuffley 5066.
                                                                  *Died* 18 *Dec.* 1982.

**SHEPPARD, William Vincent,** CBE 1963; Deputy Chairman, National Coal Board, 1971–75 (Member, 1967–76); Chairman, PD/NCB (Consultants) Ltd, 1975; *b* 15 Nov. 1909; *s* of late Dr H. P. Sheppard; *m* 1938, Nancy F. Watson; two *s* one *d*. *Educ:* Cheltenham College; Birmingham University (BSc (Hons) Min.). Mining Student with Bolsover Colliery Co. Ltd, 1931–35, Safety Officer to Co., 1935–37; Under Manager, Creswell Colliery, 1937; Manager, Rufford Colliery, 1938; Mining Devel. Engr, No 4 Area, East Midlands Div., NCB, 1947; Area Gen. Man., No 1 Area, East Midlands Div., NCB, 1948; Dir-Gen. of Reconstruction, NCB, 1957–60; Dir-Gen. of Production, NCB, 1960–67. Dir, Wide Range Engineering Services Ltd, 1976–. Past-Pres., Southern Counties Inst. of Instn of Mining Engineers; Hon. FIMinE. CStJ 1957. *Recreations:* gardening, model-making, Rugby football (County Cap, Glos).                                   *Died* 25 *April* 1985.

**SHEPPARD FIDLER, Alwyn Gwilym,** CBE 1963; MA, BArch, DipCD, FRIBA, FRTPI; architect and town planning consultant; *b* 8 May 1909; *e s* of late W. E. Sheppard Fidler and Phoebe M. Williams; *m* 1936, Margaret (*d* 1977), *d* of Capt. J. R. Kidner, Newcastle upon Tyne; one *s*. *Educ:* Holywell Gram. Sch.; University of Liverpool; British Sch. at Rome. Tite Finalist, 1930; studied in USA, 1931; Victory Schol., 1933; Rome Schol. in Architecture, 1933–35. Chief Architect: Land Settlement Assoc., 1937; Barclays Bank Ltd, 1938; Sen. Tech. Intelligence Officer, Min. of Home Security, 1940–46; Chief Archt, Crawley New Town, 1947–52 (Housing Medals of Min. of Housing and Local Govt in 1951, 1952 and 1954); first City Archt of Birmingham, 1952–64 (Distinction in Town Planning, 1955, for work at Crawley and Birmingham Redevelopment Areas); private practice, 1964–74. Council Mem., 1953–62, 1963–75, Vice-Pres., 1958–60, Chm. Practice Cttee, 1958–62, Treasurer, 1974–75, External Examr in Architecture, 1958–75, RIBA. Pres. City and Borough Architects Soc., 1956–58; Chm., British Sch. at Rome, 1972–87 (Chm., Fac. of Architecture, 1958–72; Hon. Fellow, 1988). Mem., Royal Commn for the Exhibn of 1851. Chm. ARC of UK, 1960–63; Mem. Jt Consultative Cttee of Architects, Quantity Surveyors and Builders, 1958–61; Mem. Birmingham and Five Counties Architectural Assoc. (Mem. Council, 1956–64, Vice-Pres., 1960–62, Pres., 1962–64); Chm. Assoc. of Building Centres, 1964–72; Member Council: Building Centre Gp, 1971–81; Royal Albert Hall, 1974–; Gov., Coll. of Estate Management, 1965–72; Mem. SE Regional Adv. Cttee to Land Commn, 1967–70. Mem. or past Mem., of many other councils and cttees. *Publications:* contrib. to professional jls. *Recreations:* travel, reading. *Address:* 1 Burnham Drive, Reigate, Surrey RH2 9HD. *T:* Reigate 243849.                                  *Died* 4 *Jan.* 1990.

**SHERBORNE, 7th Baron,** *cr* 1784; **Charles Dutton;** *b* 13 May 1911; *e s* of 6th Baron, DSO and Ethel Mary (*d* 1969), *e d* of late William Baird; *S* father, 1949; *m* 1943, Joan Molesworth (*d* 1982), *d* of Sir James Dunn, 1st Bt, and *widow* of John Anthony Jenkinson. *Educ:* Stowe. Finance Dept, Hosp. Saving Assoc., mid-Thirties; Prize Dept, Min. of Economic Warfare, 1939–40; Ferry Pilot, ATA, 1940–45. Member: Northleach RDC, 1947–57; Glos CC, 1955–64. *Heir: cousin* Ralph Stawell Dutton, *b* 25 Aug. 1898. *Address:* Lodge Park, Aldsworth, Cheltenham, Glos. *T:* Windrush 296. *Club:* White's.                                          *Died* 25 *Dec.* 1982.

**SHERBORNE, 8th Baron** *cr* 1784; **Ralph Stawell Dutton,** FSA; *b* 25 Aug. 1898; *s* of Henry John Dutton (*d* 1935) (*g s* of 2nd Baron) and Blanche Eleanor (*d* 1946), *d* of Laurence Trent Cave; *S* cousin, 1982. *Educ:* Eton; Christ Church, Oxford. Employed in the Foreign Office, 1939–45. High Sheriff of Hants, 1944. A Trustee of the Wallace Collection, 1948–69. Member: Cttees of Nat. Trust, 1955–73; Historic Buildings Council, 1963–72. *Publications:* The English Country House, 1935; The English Garden, 1937; The Land of France (with Lord Holden), 1939; The English Interior, 1948; Wessex, 1950; The Age of Wren, 1951; London Homes, 1952; Normandy and Brittany, 1953; The Victorian Home, 1954; The Châteaux of France, 1957; English Court Life, 1963; Hinton Ampner, A Hampshire Manor, 1968; Hampshire, 1970. *Heir:* none. *Address:* Hinton Ampner House, Alresford, Hants. *T:* Bramdean 222; 95N Eaton Square, SW1. *T:* 01–235 2950. *Club:* Brooks's.
                                                                  *Died* 20 *April* 1985 (*ext*).

**SHERBROOKE-WALKER, Col Ronald Draycott**, CBE 1961; TD 1945; TA (retired); Director of Securicor (Wales and South West) Ltd, 1965–72 (of Securicor Ltd, 1945–65); *b* 1 April 1897; *s* of Rev. George Sherbrooke Walker, sometime Rector of March, Cambs; *m* 1925, Ruth Bindley (*d* 1983), *d* of William Allen Bindley, Edgbaston. *Educ:* Sherborne. Chartered Accountant, 1923. Served European War, 1914–19; Lieut Dorset Regt and RFC. Lieut to Major 8th Bn Middx Regt TA, 1925–31. Served War of 1939–45: Lieut-Col, Middx Regt and attached RAF Regt. Mem. Middx T&AFA, 1930–63 (Vice-Chm. 1951–56); Comdt Middx Army Cadet Force, 1948–54; Vice-Chm. Army Cadet Force Assoc., 1956–66 (Vice-Pres., 1966–); Mem. Amery Cttee, 1956–57; Mem. TA Advisory Cttee, 1956–64; Governor Cadet Training Centre, Frimley Park, 1959–79. FCA. DL Middx, 1947–65; Vice-Lieutenant, Middx, 1963–65; DL Greater London, 1965–76. *Publications:* Khaki and Blue, 1952; contrib. to various jls. *Recreation:* gardening. *Address:* 22 Bathwick Hill, Bath BA2 6EW. *Club:* Lansdowne (Bath).
*Died 27 July 1984.*

**SHERCLIFF, Prof. John Arthur**, FRS 1980; Hopkinson and ICI Professor of Applied Thermodynamics, University of Cambridge, and Fellow of Trinity College, since 1980; Head of Engineering Department, University of Cambridge, since 1983; *b* 10 Sept. 1927; *s* of William Shercliff and Marion Prince Shercliff (*née* Hoult); *m* 1955, Daphne Margaret Llewellyn; two *s* one *s. Educ:* Manchester Grammar Sch.; Trinity Coll., Cambridge (MA, PhD); Harvard Univ. (SM). A. V. Roe & Co. Ltd, Manchester, 1949–51; Demonstrator, 1954–57, Lectr, 1957–64, Dept of Engrg, Univ. of Cambridge; Founding Prof., Prof. and Head of Dept of Engrg Science, (new) Univ. of Warwick, 1964–80; Visiting Professor: MIT, 1960–61; California Inst. of Technology, 1968. *Publications:* The Theory of Electromagnetic Flow Measurement, 1962; A Textbook of Magnetohydrodynamics, 1965; Vector Fields, 1977; various papers on magnetohydrodynamics, etc, in Jl of Fluid Mechanics, and others. *Recreation:* oil painting. *Address:* Trinity College, Cambridge; 158 Huntingdon Road, Cambridge.
*Died 6 Dec. 1983.*

**SHERSTON-BAKER, Sir Humphrey Dodington Benedict**, 6th Bt, *cr* 1796; *b* 13 Oct. 1907; *s* of Lt-Col Sir Dodington Sherston-Baker, 5th Bt, and Irene Roper (*d* 1950), *yr d* of Sir Roper Parkington; *S* father, 1944; *m* 1938, Margaret Alice (Bobby) (marriage dissolved, 1953), *o d* of H. W. Binns, 9 Campden Street, W, and Blythburgh, Suffolk; one *s* three *d. Educ:* Downside; Christ's College, Cambridge. *Heir: s* Robert George Humphrey Sherston-Baker, *b* 3 April 1951. *Address:* 22 Frognal Court, NW3 5HP. *Died 15 Feb. 1990.*

**SHERWIN, Charles Edgar**, CB 1969; Director of Warship Design, Ministry of Defence, 1966–69; *b* 1909; *s* of Charles William Sherwin; *m* 1935, Jennet Esther, *d* of F. Mason. *Educ:* Portsmouth; RNC, Greenwich. RCNC; FRINA. *Recreation:* golf. *Address:* Beckford, 4 Beckford Road, Bathwick, Bath, Avon.
*Died 17 Oct. 1981.*

**SHERWIN, Frederick George James**, CB 1967; Chief Inspector, Board of HM Customs and Excise, 1963–69, retired; *b* 3 Sept. 1909; *s* of J. F. Sherwin and H. E. Sherwin, Woolston, Hants; *m* 1966, Margaret Dorothea Snow, *d* of Thomas L. H. Snow, Gidea Park, Essex; one *s. Educ:* Gosport Secondary Sch.; HM Dockyard Sch., Portsmouth. Civil Servant; entered Customs and Excise, 17 Feb. 1930. *Recreations:* gardening, walking. *Address:* 10 Maytree Avenue, Findon Valley, Worthing, West Sussex BN14 0HJ. *T:* Findon 3145.
*Died 17 Feb. 1984.*

**SHEVILL, Rt. Rev. Ian (Wotton Allnutt)**, AO 1976; MA (Sydney); *b* 11 May 1917; *s* of Erson James Shevill; *m* 1st, 1959, Dr June (*d* 1970), *d* of Basil Stephenson, Worthing; two *s*; 2nd, 1974, Ann, *d* of A. Brabazon, Winton, Queensland. *Educ:* Scot's Coll., Sydney; Sydney Univ.; School of Oriental and African Studies, London Univ.; Moore Theological Coll., Sydney, BA, 1939, MA, 1945, Sydney; ThL, 1953, Moore Theol Coll. Deacon, 1940; Priest, 1941; Curate of St Paul, Burwood, 1940–45; Organising Secretary of the Australian Board of Missions, for Province of Queensland, 1946–47; Education Secretary, Society for the Propagation of Gospel, 1948–51; Bishop of North Queensland, 1953–70; Secretary, United Society for the Propagation of the Gospel, 1970–73; Asst Bishop, Diocese of London, 1971–73; Bishop of Newcastle, NSW, 1973–77. *Publications:* New Dawn in Papua, 1946; Pacific Conquest, 1948; God's World at Prayer, 1951; Orthodox and other Eastern Churches in Australia, 1964; Half Time, 1966; Going it with God, 1969; One Man's Meditations, 1982; O, My God, 1982; Between Two Seas, 1988. *Address:* 13 Cottesmore Street, Fig Tree Pocket, Brisbane, Qld 4069, Australia. *Club:* Athenæum.
*Died 3 Nov. 1988.*

**SHEWAN, Henry Alexander**, CB 1974; OBE (mil.) 1946; QC (Scotland) 1949; retired; Commissioner of Social Security (formerly National Insurance), 1955–81 (part time 1979–81); *b* 7 November 1906; *s* of late James Smith Shewan, Advocate in Aberdeen; *m* 1937, Ann Fraser Thomson (*d* 1977), Aberdeen; two *s. Educ:* Robert

Gordon's Coll., Aberdeen; Aberdeen Univ.; Emmanuel College, Cambridge. Advocate, 1933. Served War of 1939–45, RAF, 1940–45, Sqdn Leader. Member Scottish Medical Practices Cttee, 1948–55; Member Court of Session Rules Council, 1948–55; Dep. Chm. Panel of Arbiters and Referee under Coal Industry Nationalisation Act, 1949–55; Chm., Medical Appeal Tribunal National Insurance (Industrial Injuries) Act, 1950–55; Chairman General Nursing Council for Scot., 1960–62. Referee under Child Benefit Act 1975, 1976–79. *Address:* St Raphael's Nursing Home, 6 Blackford Avenue, Edinburgh EH9 2LB. *Died 16 Jan. 1990.*

**SHEWELL-COOPER, Wilfred Edward**, MBE 1946; NDH (Hons); Dip. Hort. (Wye); Director, International Horticultural Advisory Bureau, since 1960; Chairman of Council, The Good Gardeners' Association since 1962; *b* 15 September 1900; *s* of Col E. Shewell-Cooper, RA, and Mabel Alice Read; *m* 1925, Irene Ramsay; two *s. Educ:* Diocesan College, Rondebosch, S Africa; Monkton Combe; Wye College, Univ. London. East Malling Research Station, 1922; Horticultural Adviser, Warwick CC, 1923; Head of Hort. Dept, Cheshire Agric. Coll., 1925; Hort. Supt, Swanley Hort. Coll., 1932, and Garden Editor, BBC (North Region); Director, Hort. Advisory Bureau, 1938; Command Hort. Officer, Eastern and S Eastern Commands, 1940–49; Lt-Col 1945; Adviser, BAOR, 1946–47; Principal: Thaxted Hort. Coll., 1950–60; Arkley Hort. Coll., 1960; Hon. Dir, Good Gardens Inst., 1961–78. Liveryman, Worshipful Company of Gardeners, 1956. Mem., Roy. Soc. of Teachers, 1923; FLS 1930; Fell. and Hon. Dr, Hort. Coll., Vienna, 1952; Chevalier du Mérite Agricole, France, 1952, Commandeur, 1964; Fell. Roy. Danish Hort. Soc., 1964. FRSL 1954; Hon. DLitt 1961. President: Internat. Mission to Miners; Farmers' Christian Postal Service, 1950–; Mem. of the House of Laity, 1960–66; International Clans' Chief, The Campaigners, 1966–76; Chm., British Assoc. of Consultants in Agric. and Hortic. 1966. Knight of the Order of Merit (Italy), 1966. *Publications:* over 100 books on horticulture beginning with The Garden, 1932, and including The Royal Gardeners, 22 Titles in the ABC series, The Complete Gardener, Mini-Work Gardening, The Complete Vegetable Gardener, Weekend Gardening, The Complete Greenhouse Gardener, Cut Flowers for the Home; Basic Gardening Books series (14 titles), 1972; Compost Gardening, 1972; Flowers of the Desert, 1972; The Beginner's Book of Pot Plants, 1972; Tomatoes, Salads and Herbs, 1973; Compost Flower Growing, 1975; The Compost Fruit Grower, 1975; Grow Your Own Food, 1976; Soil, Humus and Health, 1976; Mini-Work Gardening, 1978; God Planted a Garden, 1978; titles in Basic Book series, incl., The Basic Book of Fruit Growing, 1977; The Basic Book of Carnations and Pinks, 1977. *Recreations:* gardening, swimming. *Address:* Arkley Manor, Arkley, Herts. *T:* 01-449 3031. *Club:* Army and Navy. *Died 21 Feb. 1982.*

**SHIELDS, Ronald McGregor Pollock**; Managing Director, since 1983, and Deputy Chairman, since 1987, Associated Newspapers Holdings PLC; *b* 30 July 1921; *s* of Thomas Shields and Beatrice Gordon; *m* 1948, Jacqueline (*née* Cowan); one *s* one *d. Educ:* Swanage Grammar Sch.; London Univ. (BSc (Econ)). Served War of 1939–45, Royal Artillery. Joined Associated Newspapers Gp, 1948; spent several years in various depts of the Co. and a year at Associated Rediffusion in charge of Audience Research. Set up the research co. National Opinion Polls, and was made Advertisement Dir of Associated Newspapers, 1963, and Man. Dir, 1970; Dep. Chm., Mail Newspapers (formerly Associated Newspapers Gp), 1986–. Director: AmLaw Publishing Corp. (USA); Angus Ltd (USA); Associated Investments Harmsworth Ltd; Associated Magazines Ltd; Associated Newspapers N America Inc.; Associated Newspapers Property Ltd; Consolidated-Bathurst Ltd (Canada); Blackfriars Oil and Gas Co. Ltd; Continental Daily Mail SA (France); Brighton Brook Realty Inc. (USA); CB Pak Inc. (Can.); Crowvale Properties Ltd; Daily Mail Ltd; Daily Mail & General Trust plc; Ely Mine Forest Inc. (USA); English National Opera Ltd; Euromoney Publications Ltd; Evening Standard Co. Ltd; Harmsworth Holdings Ltd (Canada); Harmsworth Pension Funds Trustees Ltd; Harmsworth Press Ltd and Inc. (USA); Harmsworth Publications Ltd; Harmsworth Publishing Ltd; Harmsworth SARL (France); Les Investissements Bouverie (Canada); London Cab Co.; The Mail on Sunday; Mickfield Hall Farms; John M. Newton & Sons Ltd; NOP Market Research Ltd; Purfleet Deep Wharf & Storage; Reuters Hldgs plc; Southern Television; Stiles Brook Forest Inc. (USA); Trevian Hldgs plc; 13–30 Corp. (USA). FSS. *Recreations:* golf, music, the theatre. *Address:* New Carmelite House, Carmelite Street, EC4. *T:* 01-353 6000. *Died 25 Dec. 1987.*

**SHILLINGTON, Courtenay Alexander Rives**, CB 1953; CVO 1972; VRD 1941; DL; Commodore, RNVR, retired 1954; *b* 18 Mar. 1902; *s* of Thomas Courtenay Shillington, Glenmachan Tower, Belfast, and Bertha Wydown Hall, Charlottesville, Virginia, USA; *m* 1935, Barbara Miles, Richmond, Surrey; one *d. Educ:* Bilston Grange; Rugby. Entered RNVR, Sub-Lt, 1924; ADC to: Duke of Abercorn, Northern Ireland. 1927–45; Earl Granville, Governor of Northern Ireland, 1945–52; Lord Wakehurst, Governor of Northern

Ireland, 1952–64; Lord Erskine of Rerrick, Governor of NI, 1964–67; Lord Grey of Naunton, Governor of NI, 1967–73. Served War of 1939–45, in RN as Capt. RNVR, 1939–46; Comdr, Auxiliary Patrol, Scapa, 1939; Dep. Chief of Staff and Naval Liaison Officer to Field Marshal Lord Gort, Governor of Malta, 1942; Chief of Staff to Sen. Naval Officer, Persian Gulf, 1942; Naval Officer in Charge, Bahrain, 1943–45. DL County Down, 1956. *Recreation:* motor sport. *Address:* Glenganagh Farm Cottage, Groomsport, Bangor, County Down, Northern Ireland. *Clubs:* Naval and Military; Ulster Automobile (Belfast). *Died* 9 *Dec.* 1983.

**SHIMELD, Kenneth Reeve,** CB 1978; Permanent Secretary, Department of the Civil Service (NI), 1976–81; *b* 5 Nov. 1921; *s* of Augustus John and Gertrude Shimeld; *m* 1949, Brenda, *d* of George and Millicent Barnard; two *d. Educ:* Coatham Sch.; Univ. of Durham (BA). Pres., Durham Univ. Union. Served Royal Signals, 1941–46. Asst Principal, Min. of Finance, NI Civil Service, 1949; Asst Sec. 1957; Sen. Asst Sec., Min. of Commerce, 1963; Director of Works, Min. of Finance, 1969, Second Secretary, 1971. *Recreations:* music, cricket, reading, horse-racing.

*Died* 21 *Jan.* 1984.

**SHINWELL, Baron** *cr* 1970 (Life Peer), of Easington, Durham; **Emanuel Shinwell,** CH 1965; PC 1945; *b* London, 18 October 1884; *m* 1st, (decd); 2nd, 1956 (*d* 1971); 3rd, 1972, Sarah Hurst (*d* 1977). MP (Lab) Linlithgow, 1922–24 and 1928–31, Seaham Div. of Durham, 1935–50, Easington Div. of Durham, 1950–70; Financial Secretary, War Office, 1929–30; Parliamentary Secretary to Department of Mines, 1924 and 1930–31; Minister of Fuel and Power, 1945–47; Secretary of State for War, 1947–50; Minister of Defence, 1950–51. Was Chairman and Member, National Executive Labour Party; Chairman, Parly Labour Party, 1964–67. Hon. DCL Durham, 1969. *Publications:* The Britain I Want, 1943; When the Men Come Home, 1944; Conflict without Malice, 1955; The Labour Story, 1963; I've Lived Through It All, 1973; Lead with the Left, 1981. *Address:* House of Lords, SW1. *Died* 8 *May* 1986.

**SHIPWRIGHT, Sqdn Ldr Denis E. B. K.,** FRSA; psa; RAFRO (retired); Established Civil Servant (Telecomm. PO); formerly held posts in Production and Administration, Gaumont British Picture Corporation, and Gainsborough Pictures; formerly Director, Cinephonic Music Co. Ltd; *b* London, 20 May 1898; *y s* of late T. J. Shipwright and Adelina de Lara, OBE; *m* 1918, Kate (marriage dissolved, 1926; she *d* 1954), *o d* of late Sir Edward Hain, St Ives, Cornwall; one *s* two *d; m* 1947, Margaret (*d* 1977), *o d* of late Robert Edgar Haynes, Woking, Surrey. *Educ:* France; University College, Oxford. Joined the Army as a private at the age of 16, 1914; despatch rider, 1915; wounded and crashed whilst flying in France in RFC; Flight Comdr, 1918; Capt. Royal 1st Devon Yeomanry, and North Devon Hussars; Capt. R of O RE, TA, to Apr. 1939; then Pilot Officer RAFVR; Flt Lt Nov. 1939; Sqdn Ldr 1940; passed out of RAF Staff College, 1940; served in France, 1940 (despatches, 1939–43 Star); Special Mission to Gibraltar, 1942. Air ED 1944. Middle Temple, 1920; MP (C) Penryn and Falmouth, 1922–23; Rep., Film Producers Gp, Fedn of British Industries, 1935; Adviser, British Films Advancement Council, 1935; Mem., Kinematograph Adv. Cttee, 1935. Mem., Nat. Trust for Scotland, 1979–; Life Member: CPA; Woking and Dist Scottish Assoc., 1982. Member: Company of Veteran Motorists, 1953; Order of Knights of Road, 1953; Civil Service Motoring Assoc.; Brooklands Soc.; British UFO Research Assoc.; British Soc. for the Turin Shroud; Edinburgh Internat. Fest. Soc. and Guild; Sir Harry Lauder Soc., Portobello; De Havilland Moth Club; Fairoaks Flight Centre; Chm. NE Surrey Gp, Contact UFO Research Investigation Assoc. Mem., Surrey Special Constabulary, 1950; Voluntary Driver, Surrey County Council Hosps Car and Ambulance Service; Governor, Royal Hosp. and Home for Incurables. British Motor Racing Driver: Brooklands (winner 24th 100 mph Long Handicap); Speed Trials; Hill Climbs. Major, 11th (HG) Battalion, Queen's Royal Regt, 1953. Obtained Flight Cert., Europa Airships Ops, 1982. Officer, Ministry of Agriculture and Food, Guildford, 1954. KJStJ. *Recreations:* flying, music. *Publication:* The Unforgiving Minute (autobiog.), 1983. *Address:* Plym Lea, Triggs Lane, Woking, Surrey GU22 0EH. *T:* Woking 61736. *Clubs:* British Racing Drivers (Life Mem., and Life Mem., Silverstone Marshals Team), Royal Automobile; Oxford University Yacht (Oxford); Woking Conservative (Woking).

*Died* 13 *Sept.* 1984.

**SHIRES, Sir Frank,** Kt 1953; *b* 10 Aug. 1899; *s* of John Shires; *m* 1929, Mabel Tidds; one *s* one *d. Educ:* West Leeds High School. Joined H. J. Heinz Co. Ltd, 1925; Director of Manufacturing and Research, 1940; Director of Sales, 1950; Deputy Managing Director, 1950–55; Director: Marsh & Baxter Co. Ltd, 1958–64; C. & T. Harris (Calne) Ltd, 1958–64. Member of Exec. Cttee of Canners' (War Time) Assoc., 1942–49; Pres. Food Manufacturers' Federation, Inc., 1950–52; Member Council of British Food Manufacturing Industries Research Assoc., 1947–55; Chm. Governing Body of Nat. Coll. of Food Technology, 1950–66, Chm. Bd, 1970–; Member: Food Hygiene Advisory Council, 1955–73; Monopolies

Commission, 1957–61; Council, Univ. of Reading, 1965–. Fellow, Inst. of Science Technology, 1965. *Recreations:* cricket and golf; Rugby (Derbys, 1926–28, and Notts, Lincs and Derbys, 1926–28). *Address:* Redholt, Linksway, Northwood, Mddx. *T:* Northwood 22493. *Died* 3 *July* 1981.

**SHIRLEY, Air Vice-Marshal Sir Thomas (Ulric Curzon),** KBE 1966 (CBE 1946); CB 1961; CEng; FIEE; FRAeS; RAF (Retired); *b* 4 June 1908; *s* of late Captain T. Shirley, late 60 Rifles, and late Ellen Shirley; *m* 1935, Vera, *y d* of late George S. Overton, The Grange, Navenby, Lincolnshire; one *s* one *d. Educ:* Reading School. Royal Air Force Aircraft Apprentice, 1925–28; cadet RAF College, Cranwell, 1928–30; served in Army Co-operation Squadrons as pilot, 1930–36; in Far East and Middle East on Signals duties, 1936–41; Officer Commanding Signals Wings, 1941–45; RAF Staff College, 1945–46; Deputy Director of Signals, Air Ministry, 1946–47; Command Signals Officer, Transport Command, 1947–48; Joint Services Staff College, 1948–49; Deputy Director Technical Plans, Air Ministry, 1949–50; Director of Radio Engineering, 1950–53; Command Signals Officer, Fighter Command, 1953–55; Imperial Defence College, 1956; Air Officer Commanding and Commandant, Royal Air Force Technical College, Henlow, Beds 1957–59; Senior Technical Staff Officer, RAF Fighter Command, 1959–60; Deputy Controller of Electronics, Ministry of Aviation, 1960–64; Air Officer C-in-C Signals Command, 1964–66. ADC to King George VI, 1950–52, to the Queen, 1952–53. DL Leicester, 1967–80. *Address:* 3 Raglan House, Kilfillan Gardens, Graemesdyke Road, Berkhamsted, Herts. *T:* Berkhamsted 73262. *Club:* Royal Air Force. *Died* 17 *Jan.* 1982.

**SHIRLEY-SMITH, Sir Hubert,** Kt 1969; CBE 1965; Consulting Engineer with private practice, since 1967; Consultant to W. V. Zinn & Associates, 1969–78; *b* 13 Oct. 1901; *s* of E. Shirley-Smith; *m* 1st, 1927, Joan Elizabeth Powell (*d* 1963); two *d* (and one *d* decd); 2nd, 1973, Marie Lynden-Lemon. *Educ:* City and Guilds Coll., London. BSc (Engrg) London, 1922; FICE (MICE 1936); FCGI 1965; FIC 1966; FIArb 1973; FEng 1977. Assisted in design of Sydney Harbour Bridge, NSW, and Birchenough and Otto Beit Bridges, Rhodesia, 1923–36; worked on construction of Howrah Bridge, Calcutta, 1936–42. Dir, Cleveland Bridge & Engrg Co., 1951–60; Mem. Bd of Cleveland Bridge, Dorman Long (Auckland) and ACD Bridge Co.; Agent i/c construction of Forth Road Bridge, 1960–65; Man. Dir, North Sea Marine, building first British oil drilling rig, N Sea, 1965–68; Govt of Victoria Royal Comr investigating failure of West Gate Bridge, Melbourne, 1970–71; arbitrator in 3 big engineering disputes, 1973–76. Mem. Council, ICE, 1952– (Pres., 1967); Mem. Council, Fedn of Civil Engrg Contractors, 1958–65; Vice-Pres., Internat. Assoc. for Bridge and Structural Engrg, 1963–69. Member, Smeatonian Soc. of Civil Engrs. *Publications:* The World's Great Bridges, 1953 (revised, 1964); article on Bridges in Encyclopædia Britannica; papers in Proc. ICE, etc. *Recreations:* travel, writing. *Address:* 70 Broxbourne Road, Orpington, Kent. *T:* Orpington 32673. *Club:* Athenæum.

*Died* 10 *Feb.* 1981.

**SHOCKLEY, Dr William (Bradford);** Medal of Merit (US) 1946; Alexander M. Poniatoff Professor of Engineering Science, Stanford University, 1963–75, Professor Emeritus 1975; Executive Consultant, Bell Telephone Laboratories, 1965–75; *b* 13 Feb. 1910; *s* of William Hillman Shockley and May (*née* Bradford); *m* 1933, Jean Alberta Bailey; two *s* one *d; m* 1955, Emmy I. Lanning. *Educ:* Calif. Inst. of Technology (BS); Mass Inst. Tech. (PhD). Teaching Fellow, Mass. Inst. Tech., 1932–36; Mem. Technical Staff, Bell Teleph. Laboratories, 1936–42 and 1945–54; Director Transistor Physics Department, 1954–55. Dir of Research, Anti-submarine Warfare Ops Research Gp, US Navy, 1942–44; Expert Consultant, Office of Secretary of War, 1944–45. Visiting Lectr, Princeton Univ., 1946; Scientific Advisor, Policy Council, Jt Research and Development Bd, 1947–49; Visiting Prof., Calif. Inst. Tech., 1954; Dep. Dir and Dir of Research, Weapons Systems Evaluation Gp, Dept of Defense, 1954–55; Dir, Shockley Semi-conductor Lab. of Beckman Instruments, Inc., 1955–58; Pres. Shockley Transistor Corp., 1958–60; Director, Shockley Transistor, Unit of Clevite Transistor, 1960–63; Consultant, 1963–65. Member: US Army Science Advisory Panel, 1951–63, 1964–; USAF Science Advisory Board, 1959–63; National Academy of Science, 1951–; Sigma Xi; Tau Beta Pi. More than 90 US Patents. Inventor of junction transistor; research on energy bands of solids, ferromagnetic domains, plastic properties of metals, theory of grain boundaries, order and disorder in alloys; semi-conductor theory and electromagnetic theory; mental tools for sci. thinking, ops res. on human quality statistics. Fellowship fund established in his name with Bardeen and Brattain, Semiconductor Equipment and Materials Inst., Inc., 1977. Fellow AAAS. Hon. DSc: Pennsylvania, 1955; Rutgers 1956; Gustavus Adolphus Coll., 1963. Morris Liebmann Prize, 1951, Gold Medal, 1972, Medal of Honour, 1980, Centennial Medal and Certificate, 1984, IEEE. Air Force Citation of Honour, 1951; O. E. Buckley Prize (Amer. Physical Soc.), 1953; US Army Cert. of Appreciation, 1953; Comstock Prize (Nat. Acad.

of Science), 1954; (jtly) Nobel Prize in Physics, 1956; Wilhelm Exner Medal (Oesterreichischer Gewerberein), 1963; Holley Medal (Amer. Soc. Mech. Engrs), 1963; Caltech Alumni Distinguished Service Award, 1966; NASA Certificate of Appreciation (Apollo 8), 1969; Public Service Group Achievement Award, NASA, 1969; Nat. Inventors' Hall of Fame, 1974; California Inventors Hall of Fame, 1983; Infomart Hall of Fame, Dallas, 1988. *Publications:* Electrons and Holes in Semiconductors, 1950; Mechanics (with W. A. Gong), 1966; (ed) Imperfections of Nearly Perfect Crystals; over 100 articles in sci. and tech. jls. *Recreations:* mountain climbing, swimming, sailing. *Address:* 797 Esplanada Way, Stanford, Calif 94305, USA. *Clubs:* Cosmos, University (Washington, DC); Bohemian (San Francisco); Stanford Faculty; Palo Alto Yacht.
*Died 12 Aug. 1989.*

**SHOLOKHOV, Mikhail Aleksandrovich;** Order of Lenin (twice); novelist; Deputy to Supreme Soviet of USSR since 1946; Member: Communist Party of Soviet Union, 1932; CPSU Central Committee, 1961; Academy of Sciences, USSR, 1939; Praesidium, Union of Soviet Writers, 1954; Nobel Prize for Literature, 1965; Hon. LLD, St Andrews; *b* 24 May 1905; *m* Maria Petrovna Sholokhova. First published in 1923. *Publications:* Woman with Two Husbands, 1925; The Heart of Alyoshka, 1925; Stories of the Don, 1926; And Quiet Flows the Don (4 vols), 1928–40 (State Prize, 1940); Virgin Soil Upturned, 1932–33, 2nd vol., 1959 (Lenin Prize, 1960); Collected Works, vols 1–8, 1959–62; They Fought for their Country, 1966; One Man's Destiny, 1967; My Homeland, 1970; At the Bidding of the Heart (articles), 1970; The Deathless Trumpeter, 1973; The Path, 1973; Stories, 1975; Stories of the Don, 1976; Publicists, 1979; Collected Works, 1979. *Address:* Union of Soviet Writers, Ulitsa Vorovskogo 52, Moscow, USSR; Stanitsa Veshenskaya, Rostov Region, USSR.
*Died 20 Feb. 1984.*

**SHONFIELD, Sir Andrew (Akiba),** Kt 1978; Professor of Economics, European University Institute, Florence, since 1978; *b* 10 Aug. 1917; *s* of late Victor and Rachel Lea Schonfeld; *m* 1942, Zuzanna Maria Przeworska; one *s* one *d. Educ:* St Paul's; Magdalen Coll., Oxford. Hons BA (Oxon) Modern Greats, 1939. Served War of 1939–45, in RA, 1940–46; attached to AFHQ, Caserta, Italy, 1945 (despatches), Major. On Staff of Financial Times, 1947–57, Foreign Editor, 1950–57; Economic Editor, The Observer, 1958–61; Director of Studies, 1961–68, Research Fellow, 1969–71, Dir, 1972–77, RIIA; Chm., SSRC, 1969–71. Member: Royal Commn on Trade Unions, 1965–68; FCO Review Cttee on Overseas Representation, 1968–69; Reith Lectr, 1972. Fellow, Imperial Coll. of Science and Technology, 1970. Hon. DLitt Loughborough, 1972. *Publications:* British Economic Policy since the War, 1958; Attack on World Poverty, 1960; A Man Beside Himself, 1964; Modern Capitalism, 1965; (ed) North American and Western European Economic Policies, 1971; (ed) Social Indicators and Social Policy, 1972; Europe: journey to an unknown destination, 1973 (Cortina-Ulisse prize, 1974); (ed) International Economic Relations in the Western World, 1959–71, 1975. *Address:* 21 Paultons Square, SW3. *T:* 01-352 7364; c/o European University Institute, 50016 San Domenico di Fiesole, Italy. *T:* (055) 477931. *Club:* Reform.
*Died 23 Jan. 1981.*

**SHORE, Bernard Alexander Royle,** CBE 1955; FRCM, FTCL, Hon. RAM, ARCM; retired as HM Inspector of Schools, Staff Inspector for Music (1948–59); Co-President, first International Conference for Music in Education, Brussels, 1954; viola player; formerly Professor of the Viola at RCM and Music Advisor, Rural Music Schools Association; *b* 17 March 1896; *s* of Arthur Miers Shore and Ada Alice (*née* Clark); *m* 1922, Olive Livett Udale; two *d. Educ:* St Paul's School, Hammersmith; Royal College of Music (studied organ under Sir Walter Alcock). Served European War, 1914–18: enlisted in Artists Rifles, 1915, France; commissioned, 2nd Rifle Bde (wounded); seconded to RFC. Returned to RCM: studied viola under Arthur Bent and later with Lionel Tertis. Joined Queen's Hall Orchestra, 1922; first appearance as Soloist, Promenade Concert, 1925; Principal Viola, BBC Symphony Orchestra, 1930–40. War of 1939–45: RAF, 1940; Squadron Leader, 1942; demobilised, 1946. Adviser on Instrumental Music in Schools, Min. of Educn, 1946–47. Took part in 85th Birthday concert organised by pupils, Purcell Room, Fest. Hall, 1981. *Publications:* The Orchestra Speaks, 1937; Sixteen Symphonies, 1947; article on Lionel Tertis for DNB 1971–1980. *Recreations:* sketching, the viola. *Address:* Dulas Court, Dulas, Hereford HR2 0HL.
*Died 2 April 1985.*

**SHORROCK, James Godby;** Barrister-at-Law, retired 1972; Recorder of Barrow-in-Furness, 1963–71; *b* 10 Dec. 1910; *s* of late William Gordon Shorrock, JP, Morland, Westmorland; *m* 1936, Mary Patricia, *d* of late George Herbert Lings, Burnage, Manchester; two *s* two *d. Educ:* Clifton; Hertford College, Oxford. Called to Bar, Inner Temple, 1934. Served War of 1939–45: Major RA (TA) and Judge Advocate General's Department. Dep. Chm., Westmorland QS, 1955–71. Legal Member, Mental Health Review Tribunal, 1960–63; Legal Chm., Manchester City Licensing Planning Cttee, 1964. *Recreations:* walking, fishing, gardening.
*Died 23 May 1987.*

**SHORTT, Maj. Gen. Arthur Charles,** CB 1951; OBE 1945; psc; *b* 2 April 1899; *s* of Charles William Shortt and Grace Evelyn Mary (*née* Skey); *m* 1st, 1927, Loraine (*née* Thomas), one *d*; 2nd, 1945, Nella (*née* Exelby). *Educ:* St Lawrence College; King's College, Cambridge; RMA Woolwich, 2nd Lt, RE, 1916. Served European War, 1914–18, in France and Belgium; 1st KGO Sappers and Miners, India, 1919–22; Gold Coast Survey Dept, 1924–27; Instructor, RMA Woolwich, 1927–30; Adjutant, Trng Bn RE, 1933–37; GS02 War Office, 1937–39. Staff College, Minley, 1939. War of 1939–45: Military Assistant to C-in-C, BEF 1940; Director of Technical Training, 1943; France and Germany, 1944–45. Military Attaché, Athens, 1947–49; Director of Military Intelligence, 1949–53; Chief Liaison Officer on UK Service Liaison Staff, Australia, 1953–56; Retired pay, 1956; Director of Public Relations, War Office, 1956–61; Col Comdt, Intelligence Corps, 1960–64. Mem. Governing Body, St Lawrence Coll., 1962–80. Officer, Legion of Honour (France), 1950. *Recreation:* numismatics. *Address:* Bolnore, Hayward's Heath, Sussex. *T:* 51386.
*Died 10 June 1984.*

**SHORTT, Colonel Henry Edward,** CIE 1941; FRS 1950; LLD 1952; Colonel IMS, retired; formerly Professor of Medical Protozoology, University of London, and Head of Department of Parasitology, London School of Hygiene and Tropical Medicine; *b* 15 April 1887; *m* 1921, Eleanor M. Hobson; one *s* one *d. Educ:* Univ. of Aberdeen. MB, ChB 1910; MD 1936; DSc 1938; KHP 1941–44; Inspector-Gen. of Civil Hospitals and Prisons, Assam, 1941–44; retired, 1944. President, Royal Society of Tropical Medicine and Hygiene, 1949–51; Technical Expert under Colombo Plan in E Pakistan, 1952–55. Straits Settlements Gold Medal, 1938; Kaisar-i-Hind Gold Medal, 1945; Laveran Prize, 1948; Mary Kingsley medal, 1949; Darling medal and prize, 1951; Stewart prize, 1954; Manson Medal, 1959; Gaspar Vianna Medal, 1962. *Publications:* over 130 scientific papers. *Recreations:* shooting and fishing. *Address:* Rivenhall, 39 Lenten Street, Alton, Hants. *T:* Alton 83252.
*Died 9 Nov. 1987.*

**SHOTTON, Prof. Frederick William,** MBE (mil.) 1945; MA, ScD; FRS 1956; FEng 1976; FGS; FIMinE; MIWES; Professor of Geology, University of Birmingham, 1949–74, Emeritus Professor 1975 (Pro-Vice-Chancellor and Vice-Principal, 1965–71); *b* 8 Oct. 1906; *s* of F. J. and Ada Shotton, Coventry; *m* 1930, Alice L. Linnett; two *d*; *m* 1983, Mrs Lucille F. Bailey, *widow*, Portland, Oregon, USA. *Educ:* Bablake, Coventry; Sidney Sussex College, Cambridge. Wiltshire Prizeman, 1926, Harkness Scholar, 1927, Cambridge. Assistant Lecturer and Lecturer, University of Birmingham, 1928–36; Lecturer, Cambridge University, 1936–45. Served War of 1939–45, MEF and 21 Army Group, 1940–45. Prof. of Geology, Sheffield Univ., 1945–49. Mem., NERC, 1966–72. Pres., Geological Soc., 1964–66, Vice-Pres., 1966–68. Founder Fellow, Fellowship of Engineering, 1976. Hon. Mem., Royal Irish Acad., 1970. Prestwich Medal, Geological Soc. of London, 1954; Stopes Medal, Geologists' Assoc., 1967. *Publications:* (ed and contrib.) British Quaternary Studies, 1977; numerous scientific. *Recreations:* archæology and natural history; gardening. *Address:* 111 Dorridge Road, Dorridge, West Midlands B93 8BP. *T:* Knowle (0564) 772820.
*Died 21 July 1990.*

**SHOWA, Emperor;** *see* Hirohito.

**SHOWERING, Sir Keith (Stanley),** Kt 1981; Chairman and Chief Executive, Allied-Lyons (formerly Allied Breweries) Ltd, since 1975; Vice-Chairman, Guardian Royal Exchange Assurance Co., since 1974; Director, Midland Bank Ltd, since 1979; *b* Aug. 1930; *o s* of late Herbert and of Ada Showering; *m* 1954, Marie Sadie (*née* Golden); four *s* two *d. Educ:* Wells Cathedral School. Joined family business of Showerings Ltd, cider makers, 1947; Dir, 1951; Founder Dir, Showerings, Vine Products & Whiteways Ltd on merger of those companies, 1961; Dep. Chm., 1964; Chief Executive, 1971–75; Man. Dir, John Harvey & Sons Ltd and Harveys of Bristol Ltd, 1966–71, Chm., 1971; Allied Breweries Ltd: Dir, 1968; Vice-Chm., 1969–74; Dep. Chm., Jan.–Sept. 1975; also Director: Castlemaine Tooheys Ltd, Sydney, Australia, 1976–; Holland & Holland Ltd, 1978–; other allied subsidiary cos. Trustee: Glyndebourne Arts Trust; World Wildlife Fund (UK); London Philharmonic Orch.; Master, Brewers' Co., 1981–82. *Recreations:* music, shooting. *Address:* 156 St Johns Street, EC1P 1AR. *T:* 01-253 9911. *Clubs:* Garrick, Arts, Buck's.
*Died 23 March 1982.*

**SHRIMSLEY, Anthony;** political journalist; Director, Press and Communications, Conservative Party, 1983–84, then Consultative Director; *b* 12 June 1934; *s* of John Shrimsley and Alice Shrimsley, London; *m* 1961, Yvonne Ann, *d* of Harry and Gertrude Ross; one *s* one *d. Educ:* William Ellis Sch., Highgate, and elsewhere. Press Assoc., 1950; Edgware Post, 1951; RAF, 1952–54; Littlehampton Gazette; Reporter, Manchester Evening News, 1955, Polit. Corresp., 1959; Polit. Corresp., later Polit. Editor, Sunday Mirror, 1962–69; Polit. Editor, The Sun, 1969; Polit. Editor, Daily Mail, 1973; Asst Editor, 1975; Asst Editor, The Sun, and political adviser,

News Group Newspapers, 1976–79; Editor-in-Chief, Now! Magazine, 1979–81. Chm., Parly Lobby Journalists, 1975–76; Mem., BBC Consultatice Gp on Business and Ind. Affairs, 1976–78. *Publications:* The First Hundred Days of Harold Wilson, 1965; The New Establishment, 1978. *Recreation:* sailing. *Address:* 64 Salmon Street, NW9. *T:* 01-205 0234. *Club:* Reform.
*Died 5 Nov.* 1984.

**SHUCKBURGH, Sir Charles Gerald Stewkley,** 12th Bt, *cr* 1660; TD; DL; JP; Major, late 11th (City of London Yeomanry) LAA; *b* 28 Feb. 1911; *s* of 11th Bt and Honour Zoë, OBE (*d* 1979), *d* of Neville Thursby, of Harlestone, Northamptonshire; *S* father, 1939; *m* 1st, 1935, Remony (*d* 1936), *o d* of late F. N. Bell, Buenos Aires; 2nd, 1937, Nancy Diana Mary (OBE 1970) (*d* 1984), *o d* of late Capt. Rupert Lubbock, RN; one *s* two *d. Educ:* Harrow; Trinity College, Oxford. JP 1946, DL 1965, Warwickshire; High Sheriff, Warwickshire, 1965. *Heir:* *s* Rupert Charles Gerald Shuckburgh [*b* 12 Feb. 1949; *m* 1976, Judith, *d* of W. G. Mackaness; two *s*; *m* 1987, M. I. Evans]. *Address:* The Gate House, White Colne, Colchester, Essex.
*Died 4 May* 1988.

**SICOT, Marcel Jean;** Commandeur, Légion d'Honneur, 1954; Croix de Guerre, 1945; Médaille de la Résistance française, 1945; Médaille d'Honneur de la Police, etc.; Hon. Secretary General of ICPO (Interpol); *b* 19 Feb. 1898; *m* 1923, Agnès Demy; one *s. Educ:* in France (Brittany and Paris). Comr of French Sûreté, 1920; Divisional Comr, 1938; Sec. Gen. for Police, 1944; Under-Secretary, Police Judiciary, 1945; Director-Inspector Gen., Nat. Sûreté, 1949; retired and appd Hon. Director-Inspector General, 1958; Sec. Gen. of Interpol, 1951; Hon. Sec. Gen., 1963. President of Honour of Assoc. Amicale des Cadres de la Sûreté Nationale; Mem. Council, Order of Civil Merit of Ministry of the Interior. Mem. jury of literary prize "Quai des Orfèvres". Comdr, Order of Vasa (Sweden); Comdr (Palm) Royal Order (Greece); Comdr, Order of Cedar (Lebanon); Comdr, Order of Dannebrog (Denmark). *Publications:* (jointly) Encyclopédie nationale de la police française, 1955; Servitude et grandeur policières-40 ans à la Sûreté, 1960; A la barre de l'Interpol, 1961; La Prostitution dans le Monde, 1964; Fausses et vraies identités, 1967. *Recreations:* fond of Association football and Breton folklore. *Address:* 4 rue Léon Delagrange, 75015 Paris, France. *T:* 250.91.95.
*Died 17 July* 1981.

**SIDDELEY, John (Tennant Davenport);** Consultant Designer; (3rd Baron Kenilworth, *cr* 1937, of Kenilworth); *b* 24 Jan. 1924; *o s* of 2nd Baron Kenilworth, CBE, TD, and Marjorie Tennant (*d* 1977), *d* of late Harry Firth; *S* father, 1971; *m* 1948, Jacqueline, *d* of late Robert Gelpi, Lyon, France; one *s* one *d. Educ:* Marlborough; Magdalene College, Cambridge (BA). Chairman: John Siddeley International Ltd; John Siddeley (Jewels) Ltd; Dir, Siddeley and Hammond, antiquarian booksellers; Max Murphy Designs Ltd; Ambassador, Ordre des Coteaux de Champagne. Mem., Amer. Soc. of Interior Designers. Master, Coachmakers' and Coach Harness Makers' Company, 1969–70. FRSA. Food Editor, Paris Vogue. *Publications:* contribs to The Conniosseur, USA House & Gardens, USA Interiors. *Recreations:* opera, travel, good food. *Heir:* *s* Hon. John Randle Siddeley, *b* 16 June 1954. *Address:* 4 Bourne House, Harriet Street, SW1; 9 East 68th Street, New York, NY 10021, USA.
*Died 26 Dec.* 1981.

**SIDEBOTHAM, John Biddulph,** CMG 1946; MA Cantab; retired as Assistant Secretary, Colonial Office (1941–54); *b* 23 Nov. 1891; *er s* of late Rev. Frederick William Gilbert Sidebotham, MA, Rector of Weeting, Norfolk; *m* 1st, 1917, Hilda, *d* of late F. Haviland; one *d*; 2nd, 1941, Mary, *d* of late A. Blascheck; 3rd, 1971, Audrey (*née* Sidebotham), widow of Major D. B. Williams. *Educ:* King's School, Canterbury; Gonville and Caius Coll., Cambridge (Stanhope Exhibitioner, Open Class Exhibitioner, Scholar). 1st cl. theolog. tripos, pt 1, 1914; BA 1914, MA 1920; 2nd Lieut Home Counties RE (TF), 1914; Lieut 1916; served in France, 1914–15 (wounded). Inland Revenue, Somerset House, 1920; transferred to Colonial Office as asst prin. under reconstruction scheme, Dec. 1922; sec. managing cttee, Bureau of Hygiene and Tropical Diseases, 1925; sec., East African guaranteed loan advisory cttee, 1927; pte sec. to Parliamentary Under-Sec. of State for Dominion Affairs, 1928; pte sec. Permt Under-Sec. for the Colonies, 1929, principal, 1930; accompanied Permt Under-Secretary of State for the Colonies (Sir J. Maffey) to W Indies, 1936. Visited St Helena, 1939 and 1955; also visited Ceylon, Borneo, Sarawak, Hong Kong, Fiji and Mauritius. Mem. managing cttee of Bureau of Hygiene and Tropical Diseases, 1941–73. *Address:* Nantwatcyn, Cwmystwyth, Aberystwyth, Dyfed SY23 4AG. *T:* Pontrhydygroes 217.
*Died 28 Feb.* 1988.

**SIDEY, John MacNaughton,** DSO 1945; Founder of Ferrymasters Ltd, European hauliers, 1954; Director, P&O Steam Navigation Co., 1970–77, retired; *b* 11 July 1914; *e c* of John and Florence Sidey; *m* 1941, Eileen, *o d* of Sir George Wilkinson, 1st Bt, KCVO; one *s* (one *d* decd). *Educ:* Exeter School. Served War, 1939–45, with Royal Tank Regiment and Westminster Dragoons, finishing as Lt-Col commanding 22nd Dragoons. Mem., Southern Area Board,

BTC, 1955–61 (Chm. Jan.-Dec. 1962); part-time Mem., British Railways Bd, 1962–68; Chm., Eastern Region Bd, British Railways, 1963–65. Council Mem. and Chm., Transport Policy Cttee, CBI, 1967–79; Mem., Nat. Docks Labour Bd, 1977–83. Pres., London Chapter, Nat. Defence Transportation Assoc. of America, 1961–62. *Recreations:* fishing, gardening, golf. *Address:* 275A Park Street, New Canaan, Conn 06840, USA. *T:* (203)–966–5080.
*Died 31 Oct.* 1990.

**SIDGWICK, Rear-Admiral John Benson,** CB 1945; RN retd; late Deputy Engineer-in-Chief, Admiralty; *b* 29 May 1891. Served European War, 1914–18; Engineer Captain, 1936; Engineer Rear-Admiral, 1942.
*Died 28 April* 1983.

**SIDNEY-WILMOT, Air Vice-Marshal Aubrey,** CB 1977; OBE 1948; Director of Legal Services (Royal Air Force), 1970–79; *b* 4 Jan. 1915; *s* of Alfred Robert Sidney-Wilmot and Harriet Sidney-Wilmot; *m* 1968, Ursula Hartmann; one *s* by former marriage. *Educ:* Framlingham College. Admitted Solicitor, 1938, practised, 1938–40. Commnd in Administrative Br., RAF, 1940; transf. to Office of JAG, 1942; DJAG (Army and RAF), Far East, 1948–50; transf. to Directorate of Legal Services (RAF), 1950; Dep. Dir of Legal Services (RAF), 1969. *Recreations:* travel, swimming, gardening. *Address:* Grove House, Great Horkesley, Colchester, Essex CO6 4AG. *Club:* Royal Air Force.
*Died 31 Dec.* 1989.

**SIEFF, Joseph Edward;** Hon. President, Marks & Spencer Ltd, since 1979 (Assistant Managing Director, 1946; Joint Managing Director, 1963–72; Vice-Chairman, 1963, Deputy Chairman, 1965, Chairman, 1967–72, President, 1972–79); *b* 29 Nov. 1905; *s* of Ephraim Sieff, Manchester; *m* 1929, Maisie, *d* of Dr Sidney Marsh; two *d*; *m* 1952, Lois, *d* of William Ross; one *s* one *d. Educ:* Manchester Grammar School; Manchester University. Joined Marks & Spencer Ltd, 1933. Chairman Joint Israel Appeal, 1961–65, President 1965–. Hon. President, Zionist Federation of Great Britain and Ireland, 1974– (Vice-Pres., 1965–74). Governor, Manchester Grammar School, 1974–. *Address:* Michael House, Baker Street, W1A 1DN. *T:* 01-935 4422. *Club:* Savile.
*Died 3 Nov.* 1982.

**SIEFF, Hon. Michael David,** CBE 1975; Director, Marks & Spencer, 1950–78 (Joint Managing Director, 1971–76; Joint Vice-Chairman, 1972–76); *b* 12 March 1911; *er s* of late Baron Sieff; *m* 1st, 1932, Daphne Madge Kerin Michael (marr. diss. 1975); one *s*; 2nd, 1975, Elizabeth Pitt; one *s* one *d. Educ:* Manchester Grammar School. Served War of 1939–45, Col RAOC 1944; Hon. Col, TA, 1956. Joined Marks & Spencer Ltd, 1929; Asst Man. Dir, 1965–71. Member: European Trade Cttee, British Overseas Trade Bd, 1974–; British Overseas Trade Adv. Council, 1975–; Pres., British Overseas Trade Gp for Israel, 1979–83 (Chm., 1972–78); Vice-Chm., British-Israel Chamber of Commerce, 1969–. Founder Fellow, Royal Post-Grad. Med. Sch. (Hammersmith Hosp.), 1972 (formerly Mem. Council). *Address:* Michael House, Baker Street, W1A 1DN. *T:* 01–935 4422.
*Died 23 April* 1987.

**SIEGHART, Paul (Henry Laurence Alexander);** law reformer, international arbitrator and consultant, writer and broadcaster; Chairman, Executive Committee, Justice (British Section of International Commission of Jurists), since 1978; *b* 22 Feb. 1927; *s* of Ernest and Marguerite Alexander Sieghart; *m* 1st, 1944, Rosemary (*d* 1956), *d* of Comdr C. E. Aglionby, DSO, RN; one *s* one *d*; 2nd, 1959, Felicity Ann, *d* of A. M. Baer; one *s* one *d. Educ:* Harrow; Berkhamsted Sch.; University Coll. London. FRSA; FCIArb. Called to the Bar, Gray's Inn, 1953; retired from practice, 1966. Chm., Professions Jt Working Party on Statutory Registration of Psychotherapists, 1975–81; Vice-Chm., Arbitration Cttee, CIArb, 1983–84; Member: Home Office Data Protection Cttee, 1976–78; Gpe de Bellerive, Geneva, 1977–; Gorleben Internat. Rev., 1978–79; Commn for Internat. Justice and Peace of England and Wales, 1976–80; Council, Catholic Union of GB, 1981–. Founder, Council for Sci. and Society, 1972 (Vice-Chm., 1972–78); Governor, British Inst. of Human Rights, 1974–; Inst. of Med. Ethics, 1986–; Trustee: European Human Rights Foundn, 1980– (Chm., 1986–); The Tablet Trust, 1976–; Monteverdi Trust, 1980–; Justice Educnl and Res. Trust, 1981–; Tavistock Clinic Foundn, 1982–. Jt recipient, Airey Neave Meml Scholarship for research into freedom under national laws, 1981. Hon. Vis. Prof., Fac. of Laws, King's Coll. London (KQC), 1987–. Lectures: Cantor, RSA, 1977; Lucas, RCP, 1981; Shaw Meml, Oxford, 1981; Trueman Wood, RSA, 1983. Draftsman: Right of Privacy Bill 1970; Rehabilitation of Offenders Act 1974. Freeman, City of London. *Publications:* (ed) Chalmers' Sale of Goods, 13th edn 1957, 14th edn 1963; (with J. B. Whalley) Slaughterhouses, 1960; Privacy and Computers, 1976; (ed) Microchips with Everything, 1982; The International Law of Human Rights, 1983; The Lawful Rights of Mankind, 1985; (with J. M. Ziman and J. H. Humphrey) The World of Science and the Rule of Law, 1986; contribs to learned jls. *Recreations:* travel, music, ski-ing, sailing, shooting. *Address:* 6 Gray's Inn Square, WC1R

5AZ. *T:* 01–405 1351. *Clubs:* Brooks's; Bar Yacht.
*Died* 12 *Dec.* 1988.

**SIEPMANN, Charles Arthur,** MC; BA; Professor Emeritus, New York University, since 1967; Professor, Sarah Lawrence College, New York, 1968–71; *b* 10 Mar. 1899; *s* of Otto and Grace Florence Siepmann; *m* 1940, Charlotte Tyler; one *s* two *d. Educ:* Clifton Coll. (scholar); Keble Coll. Oxford (scholar). Served European War, 1917–18; Oxford, 1919–21; Brown Shipley and Co., 1922–24; housemaster and education officer, HM Borstal Instns, Feltham and Rochester, 1924–27; joined BBC, 1927; Dir of Talks, 1932–35, of Regional Relations, 1935–36, of Programme Planning, 1936–39; University Lecturer, Harvard University, 1939–42. Office of War Information, 1942–45, as Consultant, and, latterly, Deputy Director of its San Francisco Office; Professor of Education, New York Univ., 1946–67. Delivered television courses, Communication and Educn, and Communication and Society, 1967–68. *Publications:* Radio in Wartime; Radio's Second Chance; Radio, TV and Society; TV and our School Crisis; Educational TV in the United States. *Recreations:* walking, reading. *Address:* RRI Box 400, Newfane, Vermont 05345, USA; 21 Matlock Court, Kensington Park Road, W11. *Died* 19 *March* 1985.

**SIGNORET, Simone** (pseudonym of **Simone Henriette Charlotte Montand**); actress; *b* Wiesbaden, 25 March 1921; *d* of Jean Kaminker and Louise (*née* Signoret); *m* 1947, Yves Allegret (marriage dissolved, 1950), motion picture director; one *d*; *m* 1950, Yves Montand, actor and singer. *Educ:* Cours Sicard, Paris. Worked as a teacher and typist before becoming actress. Films include: Dédée d'Anvers, La Ronde, Casque d'Or, Thérèse Raquin, La Mort en ce Jardin, Room at the Top (Oscar), Adua e le Compagne, Term of Trial, Ship of Fools, The Deadly Affair, Games, The Seagull, L'Aveu, Le Chat (Best Actress Award, Berlin Film Festival, 1971), La Veuve Couderc, Les Granges brûlées, Rude journée pour la reine, La Chair de l'Orchidée, The Adolescent, Madame Rosa; Chère inconnue, 1980; L'Etoile du Nord, 1982; Guy de Maupassant, 1982. Has also appeared on the stage (including Lady Macbeth, Royal Ct, London 1966), and on television. Has won many awards in France, USA, England, etc, including Oscar of Acad. of Motion Picture Arts and Sciences for best actress, 1960. *Publications: memoirs:* La Nostalgie n'est plus ce qu'elle était, 1976 (Nostalgia Isn't What It Used to Be, 1978); Le Lendemain elle était souriante, 1979; (trans.) Jo Langer: Une saison à Bratislava, 1981; *novel:* Adieu Volodik, 1984. *Address:* 15 Place Dauphine, 75001 Paris, France. *Died* 30 *Sept.* 1985.

**SILKIN OF DULWICH, Baron** *cr* 1985 (Life Peer), of North Leigh in the County of Oxfordshire; **Samuel Charles Silkin;** PC 1974; QC 1963; Deputy Chairman, BPCC plc, since 1982 (Director since 1981); consultant on governmental, international, EEC and local government problems, since 1986; *b* 6 March 1918; 2nd *s* of 1st Baron Silkin, PC, CH; *m* 1941, Elaine Violet (*née* Stamp) (*d* 1984); two *s* two *d*; *m* 1985, Sheila Marian Swanston, widow. *Educ:* Dulwich College (Schol.); Trinity Hall, Cambridge (Schol.; BA 1st cl. hons Parts I and II of Law Tripos; Law Studentship, 1939). Called to Bar, Middle Temple, 1941 (Cert. of Honour 1940, Harmsworth Law Schol., 1946), Bencher 1969. Served War of 1939–45, Lt-Col RA (despatches). Member, Royal Commission on the Penal System for England and Wales, 1965–66. MP (Lab) Camberwell, Dulwich, 1964–74, Southwark, Dulwich, 1974–83; Chairman: Parly Labour Party's Group on Common Market and European Affairs, 1966–70; Select Cttee on Parly Privilege, 1967; Leader, UK Delegn to Assembly of Council of Europe, 1968–70; Chm. Council of Europe Legal Cttee, 1966–70; Opposition front-bench spokesman on Law Officer matters, 1970–74; Attorney General, 1974–79; Opposition front-bench spokesman on legal matters, H of L, 1985–. Recorder of Bedford, 1976–. Chairman: Waterlow Publishers Ltd, 1981–; Solicitors Law Stationery Soc., 1985–88 (Life Pres., 1988); Dir, Pergamon Press Ltd, 1984–. Society of Labour Lawyers: Foundn Mem.; Chm., 1964–71; Vice Pres., 1971–. Governor, Royal Bethlem and Maudsley Hosps, 1970–74; Chm., British Inst. of Human Rights, 1972–74; Pres., Alcohol Educn Centre, 1973–. Mem., CIArb., 1979–. MacDermott Lectr, QUB, 1976. Hon. Freeman, London Borough of Southwark, 1982. Hon. Mem., Amer. Bar Assoc., 1976–. *Address:* House of Lords, SW1. *Club:* Athenæum. *Died* 17 *Aug.* 1988.

**SILKIN, Rt. Hon. John Ernest,** PC 1966; MP (Lab) Lewisham, Deptford, since 1974 (Deptford, July 1963–1974); Partner (with Lord Silkin of Dulwich) in Silkin Brothers, consultants on national, international, EEC and local politics and administration, since 1986; *b* 18 March 1923; *y s* of 1st Baron Silkin, PC, CH; *m* 1950, Rosamund John (actress), *d* of Frederick Jones; one *s. Educ:* Dulwich College; University of Wales (Fellow, University College, Cardiff, 1981); Trinity Hall, Cambridge. BA 1944; LLM (LLB 1946); MA 1949. Royal Navy, 1941–46. Admitted a Solicitor, 1950. Contested (Lab): St Marylebone, 1950; West Woolwich, 1951; South Nottingham, 1959. Govt Chief Whip, 1966–69; Dep. Leader, House of Commons, 1968–69; Minister of Public Building and Works, 1969–70; Minister for Planning and Local Govt, DoE, 1974–76; Minister of Agric., Fisheries and Food, 1976–79; Opposition spokesman on industry, 1979–80, on defence and disarmament, 1981–83; Shadow Leader of House of Commons, 1980–83. *Posthumous publication:* Changing Battlefields, 1987. *Address:* 4 Dean's Yard, SW1P 3NL. *T:* 01–222 2213. *Clubs:* Garrick, Royal Automobile, Naval. *Died* 26 *April* 1987.

**SILYN ROBERTS, Air Vice-Marshal (retired) Glynn,** CB 1959; CBE 1949; AFC 1939; *b* 2 April 1906; *s* of late R. Silyn Roberts, MA, and Mrs M. Silyn Roberts, MBE, BA. *Educ:* Bangor. Permanent Commission, RAF, 1930; No. 2 Squadron, 1930–32; Home Aircraft Depot 1932; Experimental Flying Dept, RAE, 1935; Aircraft Depot, Iraq, 1939; Chief Technical Officer, Empire Central Flying Sch., 1942; Dep. Dir Technical Development, MAP, 1943 (despatches); Director of Aircraft Research and Development, MAP, 1945; Commanding Officer, Experimental Flying Dept, RAE, 1947; Sen. Technical Staff Officer, No. 2 Group, Jan. 1949; Dep. Dir Military Aircraft Research and Development, Min. of Supply, Dec. 1949; Principal Dir of Aircraft Research and Development, Min. of Supply, 1955; Sen. Technical Staff Officer, Bomber Command, 1956; Dir-Gen. of Engineering, Air Min., 1958–61; retd, Nov. 1961. MSc, CEng, FRAeS. *Recreations:* fishing, shooting (Hon. Life Vice-Pres. RAF Small Arms Assoc). *Address:* c/o Williams & Glyn's Bank Ltd, Kirkland House, 22 Whitehall, SW1. *Clubs:* Royal Air Force, Naval and Military.
*Died* 26 *Sept.* 1983.

**SIM, David,** CMG 1946; retired; Commissioner of Excise, 1934–43 and Deputy Minister of National Revenue for Customs and Excise, Canada, 1943–65; *b* Glasgow, Scotland, 4 May 1899; *s* of David Sim, and Cora Lilian Angus; *m* 1924, Ada Helen Inrig (*d* 1958); one *s* one *d*; *m* 1960, Winnifred Emily Blois. *Educ:* Haghill Public School, Glasgow; Kitchener-Waterloo Collegiate. Served European War, Canadian Army in Canada and Overseas with the 1st Canadian Infantry Battalion (wounded at Passchendaele). Bank of Nova Scotia, 1919–25; Waterloo Trust & Savings Co., 1926; Secretary to Minister of National Revenue, 1927–33; Administrator of Alcoholic Beverages, 1942–45; Administrator of Tobacco, 1942–46; Dir Commodity Prices Stabilization Corporation; Member of External Trade Advisory Cttee and Nat. Joint Council of the Public Service of Canada; Member, Board of Broadcast Governors, 1966–68. Past President: Rotary Club; Canadian Club. Mem. Canadian delegation to: 1st Session of Preparatory Cttee for Internat. Conf. on Trade and Employment, London, 1946; 2nd Session of Preparatory Cttee for UN Conf. on Trade and Employment, Geneva, 1947. General Service, Victory, Jubilee and Coronation Medals. *Address:* 1833 Riverside Drive, Apt 414, Ottawa, Ontario, Canada. *Died* 18 *June* 1987.

**SIMCOCK, Rev. Canon James Alexander;** Canon Residentiary and Treasurer of Truro Cathedral 1951–74; Canon Emeritus, since 1974; *b* 19 Dec. 1897; *m* 1923, Mary Dorothy, *d* of Rev. T. R. Pennington; one *s. Educ:* Egerton Hall, Manchester. Deacon, 1922; Priest, 1923; Curate of: St Luke, Weaste, 1922–24; Milnrow, 1924–27; Incumbent of St Mark, Chadderton, 1927–31; Rector of St Mark, Newton Heath, 1931–33; Organising Secretary, Church of England Children's Soc., for Dioceses of Bath and Wells, Exeter and Truro, and Curate of St Martin, Exminster, 1933–36; Rector of Calstock, 1936–43; Surrogate, 1939–; Vicar of St Gluvias with Penryn, 1943–51. Rural Dean of S Carnmarth, 1946–49; Hon. Canon of St Germoe in Truro Cathedral, 1948–51. *Address:* 25 Kemp Close, Truro, Cornwall TR1 1EF. *T:* Truro 79277. *Club:* Royal Over-Seas League. *Died* 1 *Jan.* 1984.

**SIME, His Honour William Arnold,** CMG 1982; MBE 1946; QC 1957; a Circuit Judge, 1972–81; *b* 8 Feb. 1909; *s* of William Sime, Wepener, OFS, South Africa, and Bedford, and Charlotte Edith Sime; *m* 1938, Rosemary Constance, *d* of Dr Cleaton Roberts, West Byfleet, Surrey; two *d. Educ:* Grahamstown, CP; Bedford School; Balliol College, Oxford. Called to the Bar, Inner Temple, 1932 (Master of the Bench, 1964); Recorder: Grantham, 1954–57, 1958–63; Great Grimsby, 1963–71; City of Birmingham, 1971; a Senior Puisne Judge, Cyprus, 1957–58; Senior Judge (non-resident) of the Sovereign Base Areas, Cyprus, 1960–82. Served War of 1939–45 with RAF; Wing Comdr. *Recreations:* golf, cricket (captained Bedfordshire CCC, 1931–33, captained Nottinghamshire CCC, 1947–50, Pres., 1975–77); Rugby (captained Bedford RUFC, 1932–37); racing (Chm., Nottingham Racecourse Co.). *Address:* Witsend, Wymeswold, Leicestershire; 6 King's Bench Walk, Temple, EC4. *Died* 5 *May* 1983.

**SIMENON, Georges;** novelist; *b* Liège, Belgium, 13 February 1903; *s* of Désiré Simenon and Henriette Brull; *m* Denise Ouimet; three *s* (and one *d* decd). *Educ:* Collège St Servais, Liège, Belgium. His books are translated into 55 Languages and have been published in 39 countries. *Publications:* 212 novels, including the 80 titles of the Maigret series; autobiographical works: Letter to my Mother, 1976; Un Homme comme un autre, 1975; Des traces de pas, 1975; Les petits hommes, 1976; Vent du nord vent du sud, 1976; Un banc au soleil, 1977; De la cave au grenier, 1977; A l'abri de notre arbre, 1977; Tant que je suis vivant, 1978; Vacances obligatoires, 1978; La main dans la main, 1978; Au-delà de ma porte-fenêtre, 1978; Je suis resté un enfant de choeur, 1979; A quoi bon jurer?, 1979; Point-virgule, 1979; Le prix d'un homme, 1980; On dit que j'ai soixante quinze ans, 1980; Quand vient le froid, 1980; Les libertés qu'il nous reste, 1980; La femme endormie, 1981; Jour et nuit, 1981; Destinées, 1981; Mémoires Intimes suivis du livre du Marie-Jo, 1981 (Intimate Memoirs, 1984). *Address:* Secretariat de Georges Simenon, avenue du Temple 19B, 1012 Lausanne, Switzerland. *T:* 33 39 79; 155 avenue de Cour, 1007 Lausanne. *Died 4 Sept.* 1989.

**SIMMONDS, Sir Oliver Edwin,** Kt 1944; CEng; FRAeS; President, E. F. G. Ltd, Nassau, Bahamas; *b* 1897; *e s* of Rev. F. T. Simmonds; *m* 1st, 1922, Gladys Evelyn Hewitt (*d* 1977); one *s* two *d*; 2nd, 1979, Mrs Sheila Grace Kingham, widow of A. Colin Kingham. *Educ:* Taunton; Magdalene College, Cambridge (Exhibnr; Mech. Sci. Tripos). Aerodynamic research, RAE (jt author first res. report on Supersonic flight); gave over 1000 lectures on future of civil aviation, 1922–35; joined Supermarine Aviation Works, 1924; responsible (with late R. J. Mitchell) for design Supermarines S4, S5, and S6 (Schneider Trophy Winners, 1927 and 1929; from which Spitfire was subseq. developed); invented and patented interchangeable wings for aircraft (Simmonds Spartan biplane); formed Simmonds Aircraft Ltd, 1928 (produced Spartan landplanes and seaplanes), Simmonds Aerocessories Ltd, 1931, Simmonds Aerocessories Inc. NY (now Simmonds Precision Inc.), Aerocessoires Simmonds SA Paris, 1936, Melbourne 1937, Montreal 1946. Chm., Air Transport Cttee, FBI. MP (U) Birmingham Duddeston, 1931–45. Founder-Pres. ARP Inst.; Chm., Parly ARP Cttee, 1938; led delegn to Berlin to study German ARP. Mem. Exec., 1922 Cttee, 1938–45; Chm. Govt Cttee on Brick Industry, 1941–42. Developed and patented electronic fuel gauge Pacitron. Moved to Bahamas, 1948; built Balmoral Club (now Balmoral Beach Hotel); Founder Pres., Friends of the Bahamas, 1954; Founder Pres., Bahamas Employers Confdn, 1966–68. Vice-Pres., RAeS, 1945–47. *Address:* PO Box 1480, Nassau, Bahamas; La Rigondaine, Mount Row, St Peter Port, Guernsey, CI. *Club:* Royal Thames Yacht.
*Died 26 July* 1985.

**SIMMONS, Ernest Bernard;** QC (Seychelles) 1949; *b* 7 Sept. 1913; *o s* of Bernard Simmons and Ethel (*née* Booth); *m* 1940, Edna Muriel Tomlinson; one *s* three *d*. Barrister-at-Law, Gray's Inn, 1936; Asst Attorney-Gen., Gibraltar, 1946; Attorney-Gen., Seychelles, 1949; Judge of the Supreme Court, Mauritius, 1952–58; Judge of the High Court, Tanganyika, 1958–61; retired. *Address:* 17 Shenfield Place, Brentwood, Essex CM15 9AG. *Died 16 Oct.* 1988.

**SIMMONS, Robert,** CMG 1954; CBE 1943; MRCVS; *b* 10 Dec. 1894; *m* 1923, Mary Dickinson Waugh; one *d*. *Educ:* Dunfermline High School; Royal Dick Veterinary College, Edinburgh. Served European War, 1914–19; Fife and Forfar Yeomanry, King's Own Scottish Borderers, Royal Scots. Entered Colonial Service, 1923; Director of Veterinary Services: Uganda, 1938; Nigeria, 1944. Adviser to Secretary of State, Colonial Office, 1948–55, retired. *Publications:* contributions to scientific journals. *Recreation:* golf. *Address:* Lindores, Summerfield, Dunbar, Scotland. *T:* Dunbar 63781. *Died 20 Oct.* 1985.

**SIMMONS, William Foster,** CMG 1963; MB, ChM; FRACGP 1969; General Practitioner, 1919–66, retired; *b* 9 May 1888; *s* of William Alfred Simmons, JP, Vaucluse, NSW; *m* 1919, Edna Kathleen Millicent Goode; two *d* (and two *s* decd). *Educ:* Sydney Boys' High School; Sydney University. Served European War, Australian Imperial Force, AAMC, 1914–19 (Major). Asst Hon. Physician, 1925, Hon. Consultant Physician, 1954, St George Hospital; Hon. Treasurer, Federal Council of BMA in Australia, 1946–62; Mem. Nat. Health and Medical Research Council, 1943–63. Chm. Medical Research Adv. Cttee, 1957–64; Dir Australasian Medical Publishing Co., 1946–74. Fellow, AMA, 1964 (Dir, AMA Services, NSW Ltd; Vice Pres., NSW Branch, AMA, 1980). Foundation Fellow, Aust. Coll. Gen. Practitioners, Oct. 1965. Awarded Gold Medal, BMA in Australia, 1961. *Recreations:* football and rowing (retired many years); gardening. *Address:* 78 Wentworth Road, Vaucluse, NSW 2030, Australia. *T:* 337–1770. *Died 5 May* 1985.

**SIMOGUN, Sir Petar,** Kt 1981; MBE 1971; BEM 1945; a Chief of Arapesh Clan; landowner; engaged in business and farming, Dagua, Papua New Guinea; *b* 1900; *s* of Hajuta Matahek and Samare Mainoken; *m* 1946, Berta Barai; three *s* seven *d* (and two *s* decd). Self-educated. Plantation worker, Manup Is, Manus Prov., 1920–34; Police Force, 1936–42; Coastwatcher with RAN, 1942–45 (War Service Medals); Supervisor, Angau, 1945–46; Police Force, 1946–47; business promotion, development and organisation of food and cash crops, transport, etc, Dagua Area, 1947–; instrumental in starting Oil Palm industry, Hoskins, 1967–77. One of first 3 New Guineas nominated to Legislative Council, 1951–60; Mem., PNG House of Assembly, 1960–65; Vice Pres., But-Boikin Local Govt

Council, 1957–59. Coronation Medal, 1953. *Recreation:* hunting. *Address:* N. V. Urip, c/o Catholic Mission, Dagua, via Wewak, East Sepik Province, Papua New Guinea.
*Died April* 1987.

**SIMON, (Ernest Julius) Walter,** CBE 1961; DrPhil, DLit; FBA 1956; Professor of Chinese, University of London, 1947–60, Emeritus Professor, 1960; Visiting Professor: University of Toronto, 1961–62; Australian National University, Canberra, 1962; Tokyo, Canberra and Melbourne, 1970; *b* Berlin, 10 June 1893; *m* 1921, Kate (*née* Jungmann); two *s*. *Educ:* Univ. of Berlin. Higher Library Service, Berlin Univ. Library, 1919–35; Exchange Librarian, Nat. Library of Peking, 1932–33; Lecturer in Chinese, Univ. of Berlin, 1926–32; Extraordinary Prof. of Chinese, Univ. of Berlin, 1932–34; Lecturer, School of Oriental Studies, 1936; Reader in Chinese, University of London, 1938. Editor, Asia Major, 1964–75. Hon. Fellow School of Oriental and African Studies, University of London; Toyo Bunko, Tokyo. Pres. Philological Soc., 1967–70, Vice-Pres., 1971–; Hon. Vice-Pres., Royal Asiatic Soc., 1976– (Gold Medal, 1977). *Publications:* Reconstruction of Archaic Chinese Final Consonants, 2 Parts, 1928–29 (in German); Tibetan Chinese Word Equations, 1930 (in German); Chinese Sentence Series, 3 volumes, 1942–44; New Official Chinese Latin Script, 1942; Chinese National Language (Gwoyeu) Reader, 1942 (2nd edn 1954, repr. 1972); 1200 Chinese Basic Characters, 1944 (4th repr. 1975); How to Study and Write Chinese Characters, 1944 (3rd repr. 1975); Structure Drill through Speech Patterns, I. Structure Drill in Chinese, 1945 (2nd edn 1959, repr. 1975); Beginners' Chinese-English Dictionary, 1947 (4th edn 1975); Introduction to: K. P. K. Whitaker's 1200 Basic Chinese Characters for Students of Cantonese, 1953 (3rd edn 1965); Y. C. Liu's Fifty Chinese Stories, 1960. Contribs to: Mitteilungen des Seminars für Orientalische Sprachen, Orientalistische Literaturzeitung, Bulletin of School of Oriental and African Studies, Harvard Journal of Oriental Studies, Asia Major, etc. *Address:* 13 Lisbon Avenue, Twickenham TW2 5HR. *T:* 01-894 3860.
*Died 22 Feb.* 1981.

**SIMPSON, Prof. (Cedric) Keith,** CBE 1975; MA Oxon, MD London (Path.), FRCP; FRCPath; DMJ; Professor and Head of Department of Forensic Medicine to University of London (at Guy's Hospital Medical School), 1962–72, Professor Emeritus, since 1972 (Reader, 1946–62); *b* 20 July 1907; *s* of Dr George Herbert Simpson, Brighton, Sussex; *m* 1st, Mary McCartney Buchanan (*d* 1955); one *s* two *d*; 2nd, 1956, Jean Anderson Scott Dunn (*d* 1976); 3rd, 1982, Janet (*née* Hazell), widow of Dr Gavin Thurston, CBE. *Educ:* Brighton and Hove Grammar School, Sussex; University of London. Guy's Hospital Medical School: Gold Medallist (Golding-Bird) in Bacteriology, 1927; Beaney Prizeman, 1927; Gull Scholar and Astley Cooper Student, 1932; Lecturer in Pathology, 1932–37; Lecturer in Forensic Medicine, 1937–47; Lecturer in Forensic Med., Oxford Univ., 1961–73. Examiner in Forensic Medicine to Univs: London, 1945; St Andrews, 1948; Leeds, 1950; NUI, 1952–64; Wales, 1954; Oxford, 1957; Glasgow, 1964. Member, Home Office Scientific Advisory Council. Harvard Associate in Police Science, 1952; Medallist, Strasbourg University, 1954; President: Medico-Legal Society, 1961; British Assoc. in Forensic Medicine, 1966; British Council Lecturer, France 1954, Denmark 1961, India 1974. Corresponding Member: Société de Médicine Légale; Amer. Acad. of Forensic Sciences; Spanish and Italian Socs of Legal Medicine. Hon. MD, Ghent; Hon. LLD Edinburgh, 1976. *Publications:* Forensic Medicine, 1947 (9th edn, 1984; awarded RSA Swiney Prize, 1958); Modern Trends in Forensic Medicine, 1953 (2nd edn 1967); Doctor's Guide to Court, 1962 (2nd edn 1966); (ed) Taylor's Principles and Practice of Medical Jurisprudence, 12th edn, 1965; The Investigation of Violence, 1978; 40 Years of Murder (autobiog.), 1978; contrib. to medical and scientific journals. *Address:* Department of Forensic Medicine, Guy's Hospital, SE1. *T:* 01-407 0378; Dancers End Lodge, Tring, Herts. *Club:* Athenæum.
*Died 21 July* 1985.

**SIMPSON, Charles Valentine George;** former Director: Wigham Poland Midlands Ltd; Walker, Moate, Simpson & Co. Ltd, Birmingham, since 1960; Wigham-Richardson and Bevingtons (Midlands) Ltd; *b* 14 Feb. 1900; 2nd *s* of Alexander Simpson, Ayrshire; *m*; two *s* one *d*; 2nd, Muriel Edwina, *e d* of Rev. Edwin Jones, Montgomeryshire; one *s*. *Educ:* Tindal Street Elementary Sch., Birmingham. RMLI, 1915–19; RNVR, 1939–45, rank of Lt-Comdr; served China, Med., Iceland, Germany. Councillor, Birmingham, 1935, Alderman, 1949–74; Chairman, Airports Cttee, 1950, Public Works Cttee, 1966–68; Lord Mayor, City of Birmingham, 1968–69. President: RN Assoc., City of Birmingham; Handsworth Wood Residents Assoc.; Birmingham Br., RNLI; County Pres., Birmingham Royal British Legion; Vice-Pres., Birmingham Bn, Boys' Brigade; Life Mem., Court of Governors, Birmingham Univ. Successfully inaugurated appeal, 1969, for a new lifeboat to be called City of Birmingham. *Recreations:* bowls, foreign travel. *Address:* 16 Knowle Wood Road, Dorridge, W Midlands B93 8JJ. *T:* Knowle 2427. *Died 27 Aug.* 1987.

**SIMPSON, Sir Cyril;** see Simpson, Sir J. C. F.

**SIMPSON, Ernest Smith,** CEng, FIMechE; Chairman, Jonas Woodhead & Sons PLC, Leeds, 1973–86 (Managing Director, 1966–84); *b* 7 Nov. 1921; *s* of Leonard and Gladys Simpson; *m* 1961, Janet (*née* Wright); one *s* one *d. Educ:* Leeds City School of Commerce; Hendon Technical Coll. Junior draughtsman, Woodhead Group, 1936; Director of Holding Company, Woodhead Group, 1964. Member, Monopolies Commission, 1978–81. MSAE. *Recreations:* golf, painting. *Died* 27 *Oct.* 1989.

**SIMPSON, General Sir Frank (Ernest Wallace),** GBE 1953 (KBE 1947); KCB 1951 (CB 1944); DSO 1940; Chief Royal Engineer, 1961–67; Governor of Royal Hospital, Chelsea, 1961–69; *b* 21 March 1899; *s* of late Major Robert Wallace Simpson, MC; *m* 1934, Charlotte Dulcie Margaret Cooke; two *d. Educ:* Bedford School; Royal Military Academy, Woolwich; Trinity Hall, Cambridge. Commissioned in Royal Engineers, 1916; Lt-Col 1939; Col 1942; Maj.-Gen. 1944; Lt-Gen. 1946; Gen. 1950; served European War of 1914–18, France and Belgium (despatches, British War Medal, Victory Medal); Afghanistan and NW Frontier, 1919 (Medal with clasp); France, 1939–40 (DSO, 1939–45 Star, Defence Medal); Vice CIGS, 1946–48; GOC-in-C, Western Command, UK, 1948–51; Commandant, Imperial Defence College, 1952–54. ADC General to the King, 1951–52, to the Queen, 1952–54; retired pay, 1954; Mem. Eastern Electricity Board, 1954–63; Colonel Commandant: Royal Pioneer Corps, 1950–61; RE, 1954–67. Adviser to West Africa Cttee, 1956–66; Dir, United Services Trustee, 1961–69. JP Essex, 1955–61; DL Essex, 1956–65. Kt Gr Officer, Order of Orange-Nassau (with Swords), 1947. *Address:* 5 Northfields Close, Bath, Avon. *Clubs:* Naval and Military, MCC; Bath and County (Bath). *Died* 28 *July* 1986.

**SIMPSON, Maj.-Gen. Hamilton Wilkie,** CB 1945; DSO 1940; late Royal Marines; *b* 1895. 2nd Lt Royal Marines, 1913; served European War, 1914–18; War of 1939–45 (DSO); retired list, 1946. *Address:* Briar Dene, Wellswood Avenue, Torquay, Devon TQ1 2QE. *Died* 8 *June* 1986.

**SIMPSON, Henry George,** CBE 1980 (OBE 1968); Director, London Docklands Development Corporation, since 1988; *b* 27 April 1917; *s* of late William James and Alice Simpson; *m* 1938, Gladys Lee; one *s. Educ:* Enfield Grammar School. FIH, FSVA. War Service 1940–46, Royal Fusiliers (mentioned in despatches, 1945). Dir of Housing and Property Services, London Borough of Lambeth, 1962–72; Dir-Gen., Northern Ireland Housing Exec., 1972–74; Controller of Housing and Technical Services to GLC, 1974–82. Member: Social Services Adv. Cttee, 1982–87; Adv. Gp, Urban Housing Renewal Unit, 1985–88; Chairman: Hanover Housing Assoc., 1987– (Mem. Management Cttee, 1982–85, Dep. Chm., 1985–87); Nat. Housing Forum, 1986–; Pres., Housing Centre Trust, 1982–; Trustee, Shelter Housing Aid Centre, 1982–88; Consultant, Guinness Housing Trust, 1987–. FRSA 1977. *Recreations:* gardening, hi-fi, clay pigeon shooting. *Address:* 19 Abbotswood, Guildford, Surrey GU1 1UX. *T:* Guildford 570384. *Died* 18 *Sept.* 1988.

**SIMPSON, Sir (John) Cyril (Finucane),** 3rd Bt, *cr* 1935; retired; *b* 10 Feb. 1899; *s* of Sir Frank Robert Simpson, 1st Bt, CB, and Alice Matilda (*d* 1950), *d* of late James Finucane Draper; *S* brother, 1968; *m* 1st, 1936, Betty (marr. diss. 1944), *d* of Frank J. Lambert; 2nd, 1945, Maria Teresa, *d* of Captain John Sutherland Harvey, Romerillo, Biarritz; no *c. Educ:* Rugby; Queen's Coll., Oxford. Stockbroker, 1922–63. Served European War, 1914–18, Pilot in RNAS; served abroad, 1917–18. Won Rackets Amateur Championship three years in succession and Open Championship two years, Doubles Championship four years; US Doubles Championship, 1928; Canadian Doubles Championship, 1924. *Recreation:* shooting. *Heir:* none. *Address:* Bradley Hall, Wylam, Northumberland. *T:* Wylam 2246. *Clubs:* Buck's; Northern Counties (Newcastle upon Tyne); Vincent's (Oxford). *Died* 21 *Dec.* 1981 (*ext*).

**SIMPSON, Keith;** see Simpson, Cedric K.

**SIMPSON, Peter Miller,** RDI 1974; FCSD; company director; Director: Bute Looms Ltd, since 1973; Bute Fabrics Ltd, since 1977; *b* 5 April 1921; *s* of David Simpson and Annie Simpson; *m* 1964, Orma Macallum; one *s* one *d. Educ:* Perth High Sch.; Dundee Coll. of Art (DA 1950). MSIA 1956, FSIA 1974. Study and work, USA, 1950–53. Mem. Scottish Cttee, Design Council, 1972–76. Governor, Duncan of Jordanstone Coll. of Art, Dundee, 1978–. *Recreations:* gardening, pottery, walking. *Address:* 35 Lovers Lane, Scone, Perth. *T:* Perth 51573. *Clubs:* Caledonian; Arts (Edinburgh). *Died* 29 *July* 1988.

**SIMPSON, S(amuel) Leonard,** MA, MD (Cambridge); FRCP; Chairman: S. Simpson, Ltd; Simpson (Piccadilly) Ltd; Daks-Simpson Ltd; President: Simpson Imports Inc.; Daks USA Inc., New York; Daks (Canada) Ltd, Montreal; Consultant in Industrial Psychology; Hon. Consulting Endocrinologist, St Mary's Hospital,

London; *b* 6 Oct. 1900; *s* of late Simeon Simpson; *m* 1940, Heddy Monique, Baroness de Podmaniczky; one *d. Educ:* Westminster City School; Downing Coll., Cambridge. 1st Class Hons, Nat. Sci. Tripos, Pts I and II Physiology. Post-grad. research in Mayo Clinic, USA, Charitée Hosp., Berlin and Lister Institute, London. Member: Council, CBI (Past Mem., Grand Council of FBI); Council, Nat. Inst. of Industrial Psychology; British Nat. Council for Rehabilitation; Commonwealth Migration Council; Council, British Soc. of Endocrinology (Founder Mem.); Academic Cttee, Inst. of Social Psychiatry; Council, Inst. for Scientific Study of Delinquency; Hon. Mem. Endocrinological Socs of Argentine, Chile, France; Past Pres., Endocrine Section, RSocMed; Adv. Counsellor, English-Speaking Union, 1976–. Humphrey Davy Rolleston Lectr, RCP, 1974. Life Mem., Brit. Horse Soc.; Founder and Chm., Jermyn Street Assoc., 1978. Jt Founder, Walter Hagen Annual Award Trophy (in collab. with Golf Writers' Assoc. of USA), 1961, awarded Trophy, 1976. *Publications:* Major Endocrine Disorders, 1938, 3rd edn, 1959; contrib. Hutchison's Index of Therapeutics, Rolleston's Encyclopædia of Medical Practice, Endocrine Section of Price's Medicine, 1956, Endocrine Section of Medical Annual and Chambers's Encyclopædia; papers in Proc. Roy. Soc. Med., etc. *Recreations:* golf, painting, boxing (Capt. Cambridge Univ. 1922). *Address:* 28 Hyde Park Gate, SW7. *T:* 01-589 3671. Grouselands, Colgate, West Sussex. *Clubs:* Carlton, Simpson Services (Pres. and Founder); Machine Gun Corps Officers (Hon. Mem.); Sunningdale Golf (Sunningdale); Cowdray Park Polo; Guards Polo. *Died* 3 *Aug.* 1983.

**SIMPSON, Prof. Scott,** MA Cantab, Dr rer nat (Frankfurt-am-Main); Professor of Geology, University of Exeter, 1959–75, now Emeritus Professor; *b* 15 September 1915; *e s* of late Sir George C. Simpson, KCB, CBE, FRS; *m* 1940, Elisabeth, *er d* of late Dr Imre Szabo, Vienna; two *s* one *d. Educ:* Highgate School; Clare College, Cambridge. Research at University of Frankfurt-am-Main, 1937–39. Assistant Lecturer in Geology, 1939–46 (seconded to Department of Natural Philosophy, 1941–45) and Lecturer in Geology, 1946–49, University of Aberdeen; Lecturer, 1949–59, and Reader, 1959, in Geology, University of Bristol. Awarded E. J. Garwood Fund of Geological Society, 1956. *Publications:* various papers on Pleistocene geology and geomorphology, and Devonian stratigraphy and fossils; (jt Editor) Lexique Stratigraphique International, volumes for England, Scotland and Wales. *Address:* Restharrow, West Hill, Ottery-St-Mary, Devon.
*Died* 17 *Oct.* 1981.

**SIMPSON, William Wynn,** OBE 1967; MA; FRSA; Hon. Life Vice-President, International Council of Christians and Jews, since 1981 (Hon. Chairman, 1978); *b* 11 July 1907; *m* 1933, Winifred Marjorie Povey; one *s* one *d. Educ:* King Edward VI Grammar School, Camp Hill, Birmingham; Birmingham University; Wesley House and Fitzwilliam House, Cambridge. Asst Minister, Leysian Mission, London, 1929–32; Oxford Methodist Circuit, 1932–33; Vis. Student, Jews' College, London and research into contemp. Jewish problems, 1933–35; Minister, Amhurst Park Methodist Church, N London, 1935–38; General Secretary: Christian Council for Refugees, 1938–42; Council of Christians and Jews, 1942–74. Vice-President: Greater London Assoc. for the Disabled; Pestalozzi Children's Village Trust. Member: Soc. for Old Testament Study; London Soc. for Study of Religion. *Publications:* Readings in the Old Testament, 1932; Youth and Antisemitism, 1938; Christians and Jews Today (Beckly Social Service Lecture), 1942; (with A. I. Polack) Jesus in the Background of History, 1957; Jewish Prayer and Worship, 1965; Mini-Commentary on Pentateuch (Jerusalem Bible), 1969; Light and Rejoicing: a Christian's understanding of Jewish worship, 1976; pamphlets and articles on various aspects Jewish-Christian relations. *Recreation:* being alive. *Address:* 20 Sentis Court, 8 Carew Road, Northwood, Mddx HA6 3NG. *Club:* Athenæum.
*Died* 29 *Aug.* 1987.

**SINCLAIR OF CLEEVE,** 2nd Baron *cr* 1957, of Cleeve, Somerset; **Lt-Col John Robert Kilgour Sinclair,** OBE 1963 (MBE 1954); *b* 3 Nov. 1919; *s* of 1st Baron Sinclair of Cleeve, KCB, KBE, and Mary Shearer (*d* 1984), *d* of late Robert Shearer Barclay; *S* father, 1979; *m* 1950, Patricia, *d* of late Major Lawrence Hellyer; one *s* two *d. Educ:* Winchester Coll.; RMC Sandhurst. Commissioned QO Cameron Highlanders, 1939; served BEF, War of 1939–45 (despatches, POW); regimental duty, 1945–51; HQ BAOR, 1951–54; French Staff Coll., 1954–55; regtl duty, 1955–57; War Office (DAAG), 1957–59; regtl duty, 1959–60; Lt-Col 1960; Military Attaché, Leopoldville, 1960–63; Office of Dep. Supreme Allied Commander Europe, SHAPE, 1964–66; MoD (Office of Defence Services Secretary), 1967–69; retired, 1969. *Recreations:* field sports, gardening. *Heir: s* Hon. John Lawrence Robert Sinclair, *b* 6 Jan. 1953. *Address:* Toppinghoe Hall, Hatfield Peverel, Essex CM3 2EX. *T:* Chelmsford 380862. *Died* 27 *Aug.* 1985.

**SINCLAIR, Hugh Macdonald,** DM, MA, DSc, FRCP, LMSSA; Director, International Institute of Human Nutrition, since 1972; Fellow, Magdalen College, Oxford, 1937–80, now Emeritus Fellow

(Vice-President, 1956–58); *b* Duddingston House, Edinburgh, 4 Feb. 1910; 2nd *s* of late Col H. M. Sinclair, CB, CMG, CBE, RE, and late Rosalie, *d* of Sir John Jackson, CVO, LLD; unmarried. *Educ:* Winchester (Senior Science Prize); Oriel College, Oxford. First Cl. Hons Animal Physiology, 1932; Gotch Prize, 1933; Senior Demy, Magdalen College, 1932–34; University Coll. Hosp. 1933–36 (Gold and Silver Medals for Clinical Medicine); Radcliffe Schol. in Pharmacology, 1934; Radcliffe Travelling Fellow, 1937–38; Rolleston Prize, 1938. University Demonstrator and Lectr in Biochemistry, Oxford, 1937–47; Director, Oxford Nutrition Survey, 1942–47; Hon. Nutrition Consultant (with rank of Brig.), CCG, 1945–47; Lectr in Physiology and Biochemistry, Magdalen College, Oxford, 1937–76; Reader in Human Nutrition and Dir, Lab. of Human Nutrition, Oxford, 1951–58; Vis. Prof. in Food Science, Univ. of Reading, 1970–80. Lectures: Cutter, Harvard, 1951; Schuman, Los Angeles, 1962; Golden Acres, Dallas, 1963; Bergami, Pisa, 1985. Member: Physiological Soc.; Biochemical Soc.; Med. Research Soc.; Soc. for Experimental Biology; Soc. Philomathique; Fellow: Royal Soc. of Chem.; Inst. Biol.; Amer. Public Health Soc.; Hollywood Acad. Med. Master, Apothecaries Co., 1967–68. Hon. DSc Baldwin-Wallace, USA, 1968. US Medal of Freedom with Silver Palm; Officer of Order of Orange Nassau, Holland. Editor-in-Chief, Internat. Encyclopedia of Food and Nutrition (24 vols), 1969–. *Publications:* papers on Human Nutrition and on Brain Metabolism in scientific and med. jls; Use of Vitamins in Medicine, in Whitla's Pharmacy, Materia Medica and Therapeutics (13th edn), 1939; Vitamins in Treatment, in Modern Therapeutics (Practitioner Handbooks), 1941; Nutrition, in Aspects of Modern Science, 1951; A Short History of Anatomical Teaching in Oxford (with A. H. T. Robb-Smith), 1950; (ed) The Work of Sir Robert McCarrison, 1953; (with McCarrison) Nutrition and Health, 1953 and 1961; (with Prof. Jelliffe) Nicholl's Tropical Nutrition, 1961; (with F. C. Rodger) Metabolic and Nutritional Eye Diseases, 1968; (with D. Hollingsworth) Hutchison's Food and Principles of Nutrition, 1969; (with G. R. Howat) World Nutrition and Nutrition Education, 1980; articles on med. educn. *Recreations:* tennis, cricket, and gardening. *Address:* International Nutrition Foundation, High Street, Sutton Courtenay, Oxon OX14 4AW. *T:* Abingdon (0235) 848246; Lady Place, Sutton Courtenay, Oxon. *Clubs:* Athenæum, MCC. *Died 22 June* 1990.

**SINCLAIR, John Alexis Clifford Cerda A.;** *see* Alexander-Sinclair.

**SINCLAIR, Sir John (Rollo Norman Blair),** 9th Bt, *cr* 1704; *b* 4 Nov. 1928; *s* of Sir Ronald Norman John Charles Udny Sinclair, 8th Bt, TD, and Reba Blair (Company Comdt, Auxiliary Territorial Service, 1938–41) (*d* 1985), *d* of Anthony Inglis, MS, Lismore, Ayrshire; *S* father, 1952. *Educ:* Wellington College. Lt Intelligence Corps, 1948–49. Director: The Lucis Trust, 1957–61; The Human Development Trust, 1970–; Natural Health Foundn, 1982–87. *Publications:* The Mystical Ladder, 1968; The Other Universe, 1972; The Alice Bailey Inheritance, 1984. *Heir:* cousin Patrick Robert Richard Sinclair [*b* 21 May 1936; *m* 1974, Susan Catherine Beresford, *e d* of Geoffrey Clive Davies; one *s* one *d*]. *Address:* (seat) Barrock House, Lyth, Wick, Caithness KW1 4UD.
*Died 10 March* 1990.

**SINCLAIR, Sir Leonard,** Kt 1955; *b* 9 June 1895; *s* of John and Mary Sinclair, Broughton, Salford, Lancs; *m* 1926, Mary Levine; one *d*. *Educ:* Higher Grade School, Broughton, Salford, Lancs. Past Chm. Esso Petroleum Co. Ltd, 1951–58 (Dir, 1943–58). *Recreations:* golf, gardening. *Address:* Marlow, Deans Lane, Tadworth, Surrey. *T:* Tadworth 3844. *Club:* Royal Automobile.
*Died 9 Aug.* 1984.

**SINCLAIR-LOCKHART, Sir Muir (Edward),** 14th Bt *cr* 1636 (NS); retired sheep farmer; *b* 23 July 1906; 3rd *s* of Sir Robert Duncan Sinclair-Lockhart, 11th Bt and Flora Louisa Jane Beresford Nation (*d* 1937), *d* of Captain Edward Henry Power; *S* brother, 1970; *m* 1940, Olga Ann, *d* of Claude Victor White-Parsons; one *s* one *d*. *Recreation:* hunting (harrier). *Heir:* *s* Simon John Edward Francis Sinclair-Lockhart [*b* 22 July 1941; *m* 1973, Felicity Edith, *d* of late I. L. C. Stewart, NZ; twin *s* one *d*]. *Address:* Camnethan, RD 7, Feilding, New Zealand. *Died 10 Feb.* 1985.

**SINGER, Rev. Canon Samuel Stanfield;** Dean of Diocese of Glasgow and Galloway, 1974–87; Rector of Holy Trinity, Ayr, 1975–87; *b* 1920; *m* 1942, Helen Audrey Naughton, *o c* of Rev. and Mrs Michael William Naughton; three *s* one *d*. *Educ:* Trinity College, Dublin (BA 1942, MA 1961). Deacon 1943, priest, 1944, Dio. Down; Curate of Derriaghy, 1943–45; Minor Canon of Down Cathedral and Curate of Down, 1945–46; Curate of Wirksworth, 1946–49; Vicar of Middleton-by-Wirksworth, 1949–52; Rector: St George, Maryhill, Glasgow, 1952–62; All Saints, Jordanhill, Glasgow, 1962–75; Synod Clerk and Canon of Glasgow, 1966–74. *Address:* 61 St Phillans Avenue, Ayr, Ayrshire KA7 3DD.
*Died 13 Nov.* 1989.

**SINGH, Judge Nagendra;** Padma Vibhushan 1973; Member, International Court of Justice, since 1973, President, 1985–88 (Vice-

President, 1976–79); Ambassador rank, since 1972; *b* 18 March 1914; *s* of late HH Mahawawal Bijaya Singiji of Dungarpur and Maharani Devendra Kunwer; *m* 1940, Pushpa Kumari Devi. *Educ:* Mayo Coll.; Agra Univ. (Pinhey Medal, BA); St John's Coll., Cambridge (MA, LLD; Fellow, 1974). DCL Delhi; DSc (Law) Moscow; DLitt Bihar; DPhil Calcutta; LLD Dublin. Called to the Bar, Gray's Inn, 1942, Hon. Bencher 1975; Bencher, Kings Inn, Dublin, 1985. Entered ICS, 1937; Mem. Constituent Assembly of India, 1947–48; Dist. Magistrate and Collector, Madhya Pradesh, 1938–46; Jt Sec., Defence Min., India, 1946–56; Regional Comr, Eastern States, 1948; IDC London, 1950; Dir-Gen. Shipping, 1956–64 and Sec. to Govt of India, Min. of Transport, 1964–65; Special Sec., Min. of Inf. and Broadcasting, 1964; Sec. to Pres. of India, 1966–72; Constitutional Advr to Govt of Bhutan, 1970; Chief Election Comr, India, 1972. Chancellor, Univ. of Goa, 1985–. President: UN Internat. Law Commn; UNCITRAL; UN World Commn on Environment and Develt. Mem. Indian, European, American and other foreign learned Socs; Corresp. FBA, 1986. Lectures include: Andhra Univ., 1959; Acad. of Internat Law, The Hague, 1962; Bombay Univ., 1968; Grad. Inst. of Internat. Studies, Geneva, 1969; Univ. of Nepal, 1969; Univ. of Cambridge, 1978; Univ. of Thessaloniki, 1985. JP Bombay, 1958. Numerous hon. degrees and awards from Indian and foreign Univs, including Hon. LLD: Peking, 1986; Cordoba, Argentina, 1987. Freeman, City of Salta, Argentina. *Publications:* Termination of Membership of International Organisations, 1958; Nuclear Weapons and International Law, 1959; Defence Mechanism of the Modern State, 1963; British Shipping Law series: vol. 8, Shipowners, 1967, vol. 13, International Conventions of Merchant Shipping, 1973, revised 1983 as vol. 1, Navigation, vol. 2, Safety, vol. 3, Training and Employment, vol. 4, Maritime Law; The Concept of Force and Organization of Defence in the Constitutional History of India, 1969; Achievements of UNCTAD I and II in the Field of Invisibles, 1969; India and International Law, 1969; The State Practice of India in the Field of International Law, vol. 1, Ancient and Mediaeval, 1973; Commercial Law of India, 1975; Bhutan, 1978; Maritime Flag and International Law, 1978; articles to law jls, India and overseas. *Recreation:* cricket. *Address:* International Court of Justice, Peace Palace, The Hague, Netherlands. *T:* The Hague 924 441; 6 Akbar Road, New Delhi 110011, India. *T:* New Delhi 3013258. *Clubs:* Athenæum, Lansdowne, MCC; Imperial Gymkhana (New Delhi). *Died 11 Dec.* 1988.

**SINGH BAHADUR, Maharawal Shri Sir Lakshman,** GCIE 1947; KCSI 1935; *b* 7 March 1908; *S* father as Maharawal of Dungarpur, 1918; title no longer recognised by the Government of India, 1971; *m* grand-daughter of Raja Saheb of Bhinga, and *d* of Lieut-Col His late Highness Maharajadhiraj Sir Madan Singh Bahadur, KCSI, KCIE, of Kishengarh (wife decd); four *s* four *d*. *Educ:* Mayo Coll., Ajmer. Visited England, Scotland, Switzerland, France, and other European countries, 1927; invested with full ruling powers, 1928; Mem., Standing Cttee of Chamber of Princes, 1931–47; one of the select Princes chosen by his order to meet Cabinet Mission, 1946; elected Mem., Rajya Sabha, 1952–58; Leader, Rajasthan Legislative Assembly: Swatantra Party and Leader of Opposition, 1962; Leader of Assembly Swatantra Party, Leader of SVD, and Leader of Opposition, 1967; Speaker, 1977–79; Sitting Mem., 1985–; President: Swatantra Party in Rajasthan, 1961–69; All-India Kshatriya Mahasabha, 1962–. Patron: Rajputana Cricket Assoc.; Cricket Club of India; Mem., MCC; captained Rajputana XI against MCC and Australian XI on four occasions. Is a keen naturalist and is interested in agriculture and study of wild life; visited E African countries, Sudan, Botswana, Zimbabwe for hunting, 1958–84. *Address:* Udai Bilas Palace, Dungarpur, Rajasthan, India. *Died 6 June* 1989.

**SINGHJI BAHADUR, Dr Karni;** *see* Bikaner, Maharaja of.

**SINKER, Rt. Rev. George;** *b* 5 May 1900; *s* of Rev. R. Sinker; *m* 1924, Eva Margaret Madden; two *s* two *d*. *Educ:* Rossall School; Brasenose College, Oxford. CMS Missionary, Kandy, Ceylon, 1921; ordained, 1924; Bannu, NWFP, India, 1924; Peshawar, 1932; Headmaster, Bishop Cotton School, Simla 1935; Canon of Lahore Cathedral, 1944; Gen. Sec. Bible Society, India and Ceylon, 1947; Bishop of Nagpur, 1949–54; Asst Bp of Derby, 1954–62; Vicar of Bakewell, 1955–62; Provost of Birmingham Cathedral and Asst Bishop of Birmingham, 1962–72. *Publications:* Jesus Loved Martha, 1949; What was Jesus doing on the Cross?, 1952; His Very Words, 1953. *Recreations:* reading, writing. *Address:* 5 Vicars' Close, Lichfield. *T:* Lichfield 53947. *Died 19 Jan.* 1986.

**SINNOTT, Ernest;** Chairman, South Eastern Electricity Board, 1966–74; *b* 10 March 1909; *s* of John Sinnott and Emily (*née* Currie); *m* 1934, Simone Marie (*née* Petitjean); two *s*. *Educ:* Salford Grammar School. City Treasurer's Dept, Salford, 1924–31; City Accountant's Dept, Chester, 1931; Borough Treasurer's Dept, Warrington, 1931–32; Dep. Borough Treasurer, Middleton 1932–35, Worthing 1935–37; Borough Treasurer, Worthing, 1937–48; Chief Accountant, SE Electricity Bd, 1948–62, Dep. Chairman, 1962–66.

Chartered Accountant (hons) 1935; FIMTA (Collins gold medal), 1932, now IPFA; Pres. 1956–57. *Publications:* (jointly) Brown's Municipal Book-keeping and Accounts; contribs to learned journals on local government finance. *Recreations:* music, reading and walking. *Address:* Little Court, 6 West Parade, Worthing, West Sussex. *Died* 31 *May* 1989.

**SITWELL, Sir Sacheverell,** 6th Bt *cr* 1808; CH 1984; *b* Scarborough, 15 Nov. 1897; *s* of Sir George Sitwell, 4th Bt, and Lady Ida Emily Augusta Denison (*d* 1937), *d* of 1st Earl of Londesborough; *S* brother, 1969; *m* 1925, Georgia (*d* 1980), *yr d* of Arthur Doble, Montreal; two *s. Educ:* Eton College. High Sheriff of Northamptonshire, 1948–49. Freedom of City of Lima (Peru), 1960; Benson Silver Medal, RSL, 1981. *Publications:* Southern Baroque Art, 1924; All Summer in a Day, 1926; The Gothick North, 1929; Mozart, 1932; Life of Liszt, 1936; Dance of the Quick and the Dead, 1936; Conversation Pieces, 1936; La Vie Parisienne, 1937; Narrative Pictures, 1937; Roumanian Journey, 1938; Old Fashioned Flowers, 1939; Mauretania, 1939; Poltergeists, 1940; Sacred and Profane Love, 1940; Valse des Fleurs, 1941; Primitive Scenes and Festivals, 1942; The Homing of the Winds, 1942; Splendours and Miseries, 1943; British Architects and Craftsmen, 1945; The Hunters and the Hunted, 1947; The Netherlands, 1948; Selected Poems, 1948; Morning, Noon, and Night in London, 1948; Spain, 1950, new edn 1975; Cupid and the Jacaranda, 1952; Truffle Hunt with Sacheverell Sitwell, 1953; Portugal and Madeira, 1954; Denmark, 1956; Arabesque and Honeycomb, 1957; Malta, 1958; Bridge of the Brocade Sash, 1959; Journey to the Ends of Time: Vol. I, Lost in the Dark Wood, 1959; Golden Wall and Mirador, 1961; The Red Chapels of Banteai Srei, 1962; Monks, Nuns and Monasteries, 1965; Forty-eight Poems (in Poetry Review), 1967; Southern Baroque Revisited, 1968; Gothic Europe, 1969; For Want of the Golden City, 1973; An Indian Summer, one hundred recent poems, 1982; (jtly) Hortus Sitwellianus, 1985; Sacheverell Sitwell's England, ed Michael Raeburn, 1986; and 15 books of Poetry, 1918–36, with a further 40 small books of Poems, 1972–76. *Recreation:* 'Westerns'. *Heir: s* Sacheverell Reresby Sitwell [*b* 15 April 1927; *m* 1952, Penelope, *yr d* of late Col Hon. Donald Alexander Forbes, DSO, MVO; one *d.* DL Derbys]. *Address:* Weston Hall, Towcester, Northants NN12 8PU.

*Died* 1 *Oct.* 1988.

**SIXSMITH, Maj.-Gen. Eric Keir Gilborne,** CB 1951; CBE 1946; *b* 15 Oct. 1904; 2nd *s* of Charles Frederick Gilborne Sixsmith, Barry; *m* 1941, Rosemary Aileen (*d* 1983), 4th *d* of Rev. Frederick Ernest Godden; two *s* one *d. Educ:* Harrow; RMC, Sandhurst. Commissioned The Cameronians (Scottish Rifles), 1924; Adjutant 1st Battalion, 1933–34; Staff College, Quetta, 1935–36. Served War of 1939–45; Bde Maj. 2 Inf. Bde, 1939–40; GSO1, 51st Highland Division, 1941–42; Commander 2nd Bn Royal Scots Fusiliers, Italy (wounded), 1944; commanded 2nd Bn Cameronians (Scottish Rifles), 1944; Deputy Director Staff Duties, War Office, 1945–46; Brigade Commander, India, 1946–47; Deputy Director Personnel Administration, War Office, 1947–50; idc 1951; Chief of Staff, Hong Kong, 1952; Chief of Staff, Far East Land Forces, 1952–54; Commanding 43 (Wessex) Infantry Division (TA) 1954–57; Assistant Chief of Staff (Organisation and Training) Supreme Headquarters, Allied Powers Europe, 1957–61, retired. *Publications:* British Generalship in the Twentieth Century, 1970; Eisenhower as Military Commander, 1973; Douglas Haig, 1976. *Recreations:* gardening, music. *Address:* Riversleigh, Langport, Somerset. *T:* Langport 250435. *Died* 6 *April* 1986.

**SIXSMITH, (Philip) Guy (Dudley);** Stipendiary Magistrate for Mid Glamorgan, 1966–75; *b* 5 Nov. 1902; *e s* of late C. F. G. Sixsmith, Barry, Glam; *m* 1933, Alice Mary (JP Glam), *d* of C. J. Birch; one *d* (one *s* decd). *Educ:* Barry County Sch.; Harrow; Lincoln Coll., Oxford (MA). Assistant master, Shanghai Cathedral School for Boys, 1929–35; called to the Bar, Inner Temple, 1936; Wales and Chester Circuit. Served War of 1939–45, gazetted 2nd Lt Cameronians (Scottish Rifles), 1940; Middle East and Paiforce, 1940–45. Deputy Judge Advocate (Major), 1942–45 and at War Crime Trials in Germany, 1946–48; Stipendiary Magistrate: Cardiff, 1948–66; Pontypridd, 1966–75; Dep. Chm., Glam QS, 1966–71. Chairman: Cardiff Rent Tribunal, 1947–48; Glam and Gwent Br., Oxford Soc.; Glamorgan Branch, Council for Protection of Rural Wales, 1967–69; Monmouth Diocesan Schools Cttee, 1968–70; Hon. Pres., Soc. of Stipendiary Magistrates of England and Wales (Chm., 1967–75); Pres., D. C. Jones Challenge Cup for Best Kept Village in Vale of Glamorgan, 1970–72 (Chm., 1967–69). Pres., Cardiff E District Scout Council, 1967–81 (Silver Acorn for services to scouting). Vice-Pres., E Glam and Mon Br., Magistrates' Assoc. (Chm., 1954–66). Member: Council, Magistrates' Assoc., 1952–71; Monmouth Diocesan Board of Finance; Governing Body, and Representative Body, Church in Wales; Court of Governors, University Coll. Cardiff; Court, University of Wales; Exec. Cttee, Council for Protection of Rural Wales, 1967–73; Exec. Cttee, Monmouth and Llandaff Housing Assoc., 1970–81 (Chm., 1975–77). *Recreation:* procrastination. *Address:* 3 Chapel Lane, Sutton

Courtenay, near Abingdon, Oxfordshire OX14 4AN. *T:* Sutton Courtenay 7430. *Club:* National Liberal.

*Died* 12 *April* 1984.

**SKEEN, Brig. Andrew,** OBE 1945; psc†; *b* 1906; *s* of late Gen. Sir Andrew Skeen, KCB, KCIE, CMG; *m* 1939, Honor St Quintin Beasley (*d* 1975); one *s* one *d. Educ:* Wellington College; Sandhurst. 2nd Lt R Berkshire Regt, 1926; Bde Maj., 1939; Lt-Col 1941; Brig., 1943. Served, 1939–45: France, N Africa, Middle East, India and Burma (despatches); retd 1947. Chairman, Industrial Boards; Member, Rhodesian Tourist Board. Life Vice-President, Manicaland Development and Publicity Assoc. Commissioner, Rhodesian Forestry Commission. Mem., Umtali-Odzi Road Council; Chm., Vumba Town Planning Authority. High Comr for Rhodesia in London, July–Nov. 1965. MP for Arundel, Rhodesian Parlt, 1965–74. Independence Commemorative Decoration, Rhodesia, 1971. *Publication:* Prelude to Independence, 1966. *Address:* 75 Forest Glade, Tokai, Cape Town, 7945, Republic of South Africa. *T:* (021) 75 6204; c/o Standard Bank, Box 57, Cape Town. *Died* 11 *May* 1984.

**SKELHORN, Sir Norman John,** KBE 1966; QC 1954; Director of Public Prosecutions, 1964–77; *b* Glossop, Derbyshire, 10 Sept. 1909; *s* of late Rev. Samuel and late Bertha Skelhorn; *m* 1937, Rosamund, *d* of late Prof. James Swain, CB, CBE; no *c. Educ:* Shrewsbury School. Called to Bar, Middle Temple, 1931, Master of the Bench, 1962. Member of Western Circuit; employed in Trading with the Enemy Dept (Treasury and Board of Trade), 1940–42; in Admiralty, 1942–45, latterly as head of Naval Law Branch. Recorder, Bridgwater, 1945–54; Plymouth, 1954–62; Portsmouth, 1962–64; a Recorder of the Crown Court, 1977–81. Chairman, Isle of Wight County Quarter Sessions, 1951–64. Member, Departmental Cttee on Probation Service, 1959–61; appointed Member of Home Secretary's Advisory Council on Treatment of Offenders, 1962; Member Home Secretary's: Probation Advisory and Training Board, 1962–73; Criminal Law Revision Cttee, 1964–80. *Publication:* Public Prosecutor: the Memoirs of Sir Norman Skelhorn, Director of Public Prosecutions 1964–1977, 1981. *Clubs:* Athenæum, Royal Automobile. *Died* 28 *May* 1988.

**SKELLERUP, Sir Valdemar (Reid),** Kt 1979; CBE 1973; Chairman and Joint Managing Director, Skellerup Industries Ltd, since 1961; *b* 22 Dec. 1907; *s* of George Waldemar Skjellerup and Elizabeth Skjellerup; *m* 1933, Marion Caroline Bates; one *s* three *d. Educ:* Ashburton High Sch.; Canterbury University Coll. *Address:* 110 North Parade, Shirley, Christchurch 1, New Zealand. *T:* 852–245.

*Died* 11 *June* 1982.

**SKILBECK, Dunstan,** CBE 1957; MA Oxon; FIBiol; Principal, Wye College, University of London, 1945–68; Hon. Fellow, Wye College; *b* 13 June 1904; 2nd *s* of Clement Oswald Skilbeck, FSA, and Elizabeth Bertha Skilbeck; *m* 1934, Elspeth Irene Jomini, *d* of Edward Carruthers, MD, and Mary Carruthers; two *s* one *d. Educ:* University College School, London; St John's College, Oxford. Agricultural Economics Res. Inst., University of Oxford, 1927–30; Univ. Demonstrator in School of Rural Economy, University of Oxford; Director of St John's College Farm; Lecturer and Tutor in Rural Economy, St John's College, Oxford, 1930–40. Served with RAF Home and Middle East, Air Staff HQ, Middle East, 1940–45; as Wing Comdr, appointed Asst Director, Middle East Supply Centre (Food Production), 1942–45 (despatches). Vice-Chm. Imperial Coll. of Tropical Agric., 1958–60; Liaison Officer to Minister of Agriculture, for SE England, 1952–60; Mem., Ghana Commn on Univ. Educn., 1961. Team Leader, Near East Res. Review Mission for Consultative Gp on Internat. Agricl Research, 1973. Chairman: Collegiate Council, Univ. of London, 1962–65 (Mem., Senate, 1959–68); Canterbury Diocesan Adv. Cttee, 1970–81. Member Council: Voluntary Service Overseas, 1964–68; England and Wales Nature Conservancy, 1968–73; Vice-Chm., CPRE, 1974–80, Vice-Pres., 1980–87. Trustee, Ernest Cook Trust, 1966–87. Liveryman, Worshipful Co. of Fruiterers, 1960. *Publications:* contribs to scientific and agricultural jls. *Address:* Oriel Cottage, Elham, near Canterbury, Kent. *T:* Elham 258. *Club:* Farmers'. *Died* 27 *June* 1989.

**SKINNARD, Frederick William;** retired as Registrar and External Director of Examinations, Institute of Optical Science (1951–59); *b* 8 March 1902; *s* of late F. W. Skinnard, bookplate designer and engraver, Plymouth; *m* 1st, 1931, Muriel M. Lightfoot (*d* 1959); 2nd, 1960, Greta Cory Anthony. *Educ:* Devonport High School; Borough Road Training College, Isleworth. Taught under LCC Education Authority, 1922–24; from 1924 to 1945 served in Willesden schools where his pioneer work in citizenship training and local survey work attracted much attention. Lecturer to teachers' courses in England and abroad. Invited to tour the USA in 1937, and while there and in Canada made a special study of labour problems. Earliest political experience gained in the Union of Democratic Control under the late E. D. Morel. A member of the Labour Party since 1924; served on Harrow and Hendon Divisional

Executives and as Vice-Pres.; MP (Lab) Harrow East, 1945–50; member of the Executive of Middlesex Federation of Labour Parties; Chairman Middlesex Labour Joint Consultative Committee. Visited Jamaica, 1946; Member Parliamentary Delegn to W Africa, 1947; Member Labour Party's Advisory Cttee on Imperial Affairs; lecturer and writer on Colonial Problems; Mem. of Fabian Soc., NUT, Roy. Soc. of Teachers. Pres., Harrow Fifty Club. Hon. Fellow Inst. Optical Science, 1957. *Publications: Willesden Memorandum, In The Extra School Year; Leaving Papers for Senior Schools (privately printed, 1934 and 1935); Co-editor of Education for Citizenship in the Elementary School, 1935; The Juvenile Delinquent and the Community (The World's Children), 1946; Training and Function of the Ophthalmic Optician, 1950; reviews on French literature and continental history in various pubns. Recreations:* classical music, reading. *Address:* Hallagather, Crackington Haven, Bude, Cornwall EX23 0LA. *T:* St Gennys 276. *Died 5 Aug.* 1984.

**SKINNER, Burrhus Frederic;** Emeritus Professor, Harvard University, since 1975; *b* Susquehanna, Pa, 20 March 1904; *s of* William Arthur Skinner and Grace (*née* Burrhus); *m* 1936, Yvonne Blue; two *d. Educ:* Hamilton Coll.; Harvard Univ. AB Hamilton 1926; MA 1930, PhD 1931, Harvard. Res. Fellow NRC, Harvard, 1931–33; Jr Fellow, Harvard Soc. Fellows, 1933–36; Minnesota Univ.: Instr Psychol., 1936–37; Asst Prof., 1937–39; Assoc. Prof., 1939–45; conducted war research sponsored by Gen. Mills, Inc., 1942–43; Guggenheim Fellow, 1944–45; Prof. Psychol., Chm. Dept, Indiana Univ., 1945–48; Harvard Univ.: William James Lectr, 1947; Prof. Psychol., 1948–57; Edgar Pierce Prof., 1958–75. FRSA; Member: Brit. and Swedish Psychol Socs; Amer. Psychol Assoc.; AAAS; Nat. Acad. Sci.; Amer. Acad. Arts and Scis; Amer. Phil Soc.; Phi Beta Kappa; Sigma Xi. Holds numerous hon. degrees; has won many awards. *Publications:* Behavior of Organisms, 1938; Walden Two, 1948; Science and Human Behavior, 1953; Verbal Behavior, 1957; (with C. B. Ferster) Schedules of Reinforcement, 1957; Cumulative Record, 1959, 3rd edn 1972; (with J. G. Holland) The Analysis of Behavior, 1961; The Technology of Teaching, 1968; Contingencies of Reinforcement: A Theoretical Analysis, 1969; Beyond Freedom and Dignity, 1971; About Behaviorism, 1974; Reflections on Behaviorism and Society, 1978; Notebooks, 1980; Skinner for the Classroom, 1982; (with Margaret E. Vaughan) Enjoy Old Age, 1983; The Selection of Behavior, 1988; *autobiography:* Particulars of My Life, 1976; The Shaping of a Behaviorist, 1979; A Matter of Consequences, 1983; Upon Further Reflection, 1986; Recent Issues in the Analysis of Behavior, 1989. *Address:* 11 Old Dee Road, Cambridge, Mass 02138, USA. *T:* 864–0848. *Died 18 Aug.* 1990.

**SKINNER, Ernest Harry Dudley,** CBE 1957; Member, Colonial Development Corporation, 1958–60; *b* 1892; *m* 1921, Edith Lilian Stretton (*d* 1983); one *s* one *d. Educ:* private school. Entered service of Bank of England, 1911; for several years acted as Private Secretary to Governor, Rt Hon. M. C. Norman, DSO (later Lord Norman); Deputy Secretary, 1932; Asst to Governors, 1935–45; General Manager to Finance Corporation for Industry from its formation in 1945 until 1948. Chm., Northern Div., NCB, 1948–50; Chairman, Durham Division, National Coal Board, 1950–57. Mem. of Council, OStJ for County Durham, 1951–57. Member, Newcastle Regional Hospital Board, 1958–59. Vice-Pres., NE Div., Northern Counties ABA, 1954–59. JP Durham County, 1957–59. *Address:* Perrins House, Moorlands Road, Malvern, Worcs WR14 2TZ. *Died 27 Aug.* 1985.

**SKINNER, Hon. Sir Henry (Albert),** Kt 1980; **Hon. Mr Justice Skinner;** a Judge of the High Court of Justice, Queen's Bench Division, since 1980; Presiding Judge, Midland and Oxford Circuit, since 1984; *b* 20 May 1926; *s of* Albert and Emma Mary Skinner; *m* 1949, Joan Weston Cassin (*d* 1985); two *d. Educ:* Wyggeston Grammar Sch., Leicester; St John's Coll., Oxford. RNVR, 1944–47. Called to Bar, Lincoln's Inn, 1950 (Cholmeley Scholar), Bencher, 1973; QC 1965. A Recorder, 1966–75 (Recorder of Leicester, 1966–71; Hon. Recorder, 1972–80); a Circuit Judge, 1975–80. Dep. Chm., Notts QS, 1966–69; Chm., Lincolnshire (Lindsey) QS, 1968–71 (Dep. Chm., 1963–67). Leader, Midland and Oxford Circuit, 1973–75. Member: Parole Bd, 1970–73; Judicial Studies Bd, 1982–85 (Chm., 1984–85). Treasurer, Univ. of Leicester, 1976–80. Hon. LLD Leicester, 1982. *Recreations:* gardening, walking, listening to music. *Address:* Royal Courts of Justice, Strand, WC2. *Died 15 March* 1986.

**SKINNER, Most Rev. Patrick James,** CJM; *b* 1904. *Educ:* St Bonaventure's College, St John's; Holy Heart Seminary, Halifax; Eudist Seminary, Gros Pin, PQ; Laval University, Quebec. Priest, 1929; consecrated, as Auxiliary to Archbishop of St John's, Newfoundland, 1950; Archbishop of St John's, Newfoundland, 1951–79. *Address:* The Deanery, St Patrick's Parish, Patrick Street, St John's, Newfoundland A1E 2S7, Canada.

**SKUTSCH, Prof. Otto;** Professor of Latin, University College London, 1951–72, later Emeritus Professor; *b* 6 Dec. 1906; *yr s of* Latinist

Franz Skutsch and Selma Dorff; *m* 1938, Gillian Mary, *e d of* late Sir Findlater Stewart, GCB, GCIE, CSI; one *s* three *d. Educ:* Friedrichs-Gymnasium, Breslau; Univs of Breslau, Kiel, Berlin, Göttingen. DrPhil, Göttingen, 1934; Asst Thesaurus Linguae Latinae, 1932; Sen. Asst, Latin Dept, Queen's Univ., Belfast, 1938; Asst Lectr, Lectr, Sen. Lectr, Univ. of Manchester, 1939, 1946, 1949; Guest Lectr, Harvard Univ., 1958, Loeb Fellow, 1973; Vis. Andrew Mellon Prof. of Classics, Univ. of Pittsburgh, 1972–73, 1981; Guest Mem., Inst. for Advanced Study, Princeton, 1963, 1968, 1974; Vice-Pres., Soc. for Promotion of Roman Studies; For. Mem., Kungl. Vetenskaps- och Vitterhets- Samhället i Göteborg. Hon. FBA 1987. Hon. DLitt: Padua, 1986; St Andrews, 1987. *Publications:* Prosodische und metrische Gesetze der Iambenkürzung, 1934; Studia Enniana, 1968; The Annals of Q. Ennius, Text and Commentary, 1985; articles in classical journals, etc. *Address:* 3 Wild Hatch, NW11 7LD. *T:* 081–455 4876. *Died 8 Dec.* 1990.

**SKYRME, Stanley James Beresford,** CBE 1975; Director, National Bus Company, 1972–78 (Chief Executive, 1972–76); Chairman, Lancashire United Transport Ltd, 1977–81; *b* 4 May 1912; *s of* late John Skyrme and late Kate Weeks; *m* 1938, Stephanie Mary Jay; one *s. Educ:* Norwich Sch. Served with cos in Tilling & BET Bus Gps, 1931–66; Exec. Dir, BET Group, 1966–68; Chm., SE Region, Nat. Bus Co., 1969–70; Dir of Manpower, Nat. Bus Co., 1971; Directorships of various Gp Cos, 1966–71; Past Pres., Confedn of British Road Passenger Transport Operators. FCIT. *Publications:* various papers for professional insts and assocs. *Recreations:* reading, gardening, walking. *Address:* 17 St Andrews Gardens, Church Road, Worthing, Sussex. *Died 15 May* 1985.

**SLACK, Rev. Dr Kenneth,** MBE 1946; Minister, Kensington United Reformed Church, 1982–87; Moderator, Free Church Federal Council, 1983–84; *b* 20 July 1917; *s of* late Reginald Slack and late Nellie (*née* Bennett); *m* 1941, Barbara Millicent Blake; two *s* one *d. Educ:* Wallasey Grammar School; Liverpool Univ., BA Liverpool, 1937; Westminster College, Cambridge. Ordained to ministry of Presbyterian Church of England, 1941. Minister, St Nicholas', Shrewsbury, 1941–45. Chaplain, RAFVR, 1942–46, serving Air Command, South East Asia, 1943–46 (MBE). Minister, St James's, Edgware, 1946–55; General Secretary, 1955–65, British Council of Churches; Minister, St Andrew's Church, Cheam, 1965–67; Minister of the City Temple, London, 1967–75; Moderator, Gen. Assembly, United Reformed Church, 1973–74; Dir, Christian Aid Div., British Council of Churches, 1975–82. Member: Adv. Cttee, Conf. of European Churches, 1960–67; WCC's Commn on Inter-Church Aid, Refugee and World Service, 1975–82. Vice-President, Churches' Council for Health and Healing and United Soc. for Christian Literature. Chm., Editorial Board, New Christian, 1965–70; British Correspondent, Christian Century, Chicago, 1982–87; Free Church Correspondent, Church Times, 1975–87. Contributor, Thought for the Day, BBC Radio 4, 1982–. Chm., Bd of Dirs, SCM Press Ltd, 1987. Select Preacher, Cambridge, 1961, Oxford, 1982. Hon. LLD Southampton, 1971. *Publications:* The Christian Conflict, 1960; The British Churches Today, 1961, 2nd edn 1970; Despatch from New Delhi, 1962; Is Sacrifice Outmoded?, 1966; Uppsala Report, 1968; Martin Luther King, 1970; George Bell, 1971; Praying the Lord's Prayer Today, 1973; New Light on Old Songs, 1975; Nairobi Narrative, 1976; Seven Deadly Sins, 1985; (ed) People in the Desert, 1986. *Recreations:* reading, journalism. *Address:* 184 East End Road, N2 0PT. *T:* 01–444 9703. 3 High Busk, Blue Hill Road, Ambleside, Cumbria LA22 0AW. *T:* Ambleside 33670. *Died 4 Oct.* 1987.

**SLADE, Col Cecil Townley M.;** *see* Mitford-Slade.

**SLADE, (Richard) Gordon,** OBE 1957; FRAeS; aeronautical consultant; Chairman, Fairey Hydraulics Inc., since 1973; *b* 10 Sept. 1912; *yr s of* late William Slade and late Helen Blanche Slade; *m* 1948, Eileen Frances, 2nd *d of* late Dr W. F. Cooper; two *s* two *d* (and one *s* decd). *Educ:* Dulwich College. Commissioned in RAF 1933. Served in Egypt and 30 Squadron, Iraq, 1933–37; with Aeroplane and Armament Experimental Establishment, Martlesham Heath, 1937–39; Boscombe Down, 1939–41. Commanded: 157 Sqdn, Fighter Command, 1942; Handling Sqdn Empire Central Flying School, 1943; Group Captain, 1944; 169 Sqdn and RAF Station, Swannington, Bomber Comd, 1944–45; 148 and 138 Wings, British Air Forces of Occupation, 1945–46; Chief Test Pilot and Supt of Flying, Fairey Aviation Co., 1946–59. Director: Fairey Aviation Ltd, 1959–60; Fairey Air Surveys Ltd, 1959–72; Fairey Filtration Ltd, 1970–72; Fairey Hydraulics Ltd, 1961 (Man. Dir, 1965; Chm., 1975–77, retired). Member Council: SBAC, 1976–78; CBI, 1976–78. American Silver Star, 1946. Liveryman, Guild of Air Pilots and Air Navigators. *Recreations:* sailing, riding, ski-ing. *Address:* Ling Cottage, Beaulieu, Hants. *T:* Beaulieu 612298. *Club:* Royal Air Force. *Died 7 Oct.* 1981.

**SLATER, Arthur Edward,** CBE 1949; *b* 27 Nov. 1895; *s of* Harry Slater; *m* 1917, Kathleen Slater (*née* Spicer); one *s. Educ:* Beckenham

County School; King's College, London. Served European War, 1914–18 (wounded), Devonshire Regt and Machine-Gun Corps; invalided, 1919. Appointed to Air Ministry as Asst Principal, 1919. Assistant Under-Secretary (Personnel), Air Ministry, 1951; Asst Under-Sec. (General), 1955; retired, 1956. *Recreation:* chess. *Address:* 2 Cobbs Place, Chelmsford, Essex CM1 5PH.
*Died* 21 *Sept.* 1982.

**SLATER, Eliot Trevor Oakeshott**, CBE 1966; MA, MD Cantab; PhD London; FRCP; *b* 28 Aug. 1904; 2nd *s* of Gilbert Slater, MA, DSc; *m* 1st, 1935, Lydia (marriage dissolved), *d* of Leonid Pasternak; two *s* two *d*; 2nd, 1946, Jeanie Fyfe Foster. *Educ:* Leighton Park; Cambridge University; St George's Hospital. Medical Officer, Maudsley Hospital, 1931–39; with Rockefeller Fellowship studied in Munich and Berlin, 1934–35; MRC Research grant, 1935–37; Clinical Director, Sutton Emergency Hosp., 1939–45; Physician in Psychological Medicine, National Hosp., Queen Sq., WC1, 1946–64; Dir, MRC Psychiatric Genetics Unit, 1959–69. Mem. Royal Commn on Capital Punishment, 1949. Hon. Fellow, Amer. Pychiatric Assoc.; Ehrenmitglied, Deutsche Gesellschaft für Psychiatrie. Hon. LLD Dundee, 1971. Hon. FRCPsych, 1973; Hon. FRSocMed, 1976; Hon. Fellow, St John's Coll., Cambridge, 1981. Editor-in-chief, British Journal of Psychiatry, 1961–72. *Publications:* Introduction to Physical Methods of Treatment in Psychiatry (with W. Sargant), 1946; Patterns of Marriage (with M. Woodside), 1951; Psychotic and Neurotic Illness in Twins, 1953; Clinical Psychiatry (with W. Mayer-Gross and M. Roth), 1969; The Ebbless Sea (poems), 1968; The Problem of the Reign of King Edward III (1596): a statistical approach (thesis), 1981; papers on genetical and psychiatric subjects. *Recreations:* Shakespeare studies, painting. *Address:* 128a Castelnau, SW13 9ET. *Died* 15 *May* 1983.

**SLATER, Adm. Sir Robin (Leonard Francis) D.;** *see* Durnford-Slater.

**SLATTERY, Rear-Adm. Sir Matthew (Sausse)**, KBE 1960; Kt 1955; CB 1946; FRAeS 1946; *b* 12 May 1902; 3rd *s* of late H. F. Slattery, one-time Chairman of National Bank Ltd; *m* 1925, Mica Mary, *d* of Col G. D. Swain, CMG; two *s* one *d*. *Educ:* Stonyhurst Coll.; RN Colls, Osborne and Dartmouth. Joined RN, 1916; Director Air Material, Admiralty, 1939–41; commanded HMS Cleopatra, 1941–42; appointed Director-General of Naval Aircraft Development and Production, Ministry of Aircraft Production, 1941, and Chief Naval Representative, 1943; Vice-Controller (Air) and Chief of Naval Air Equipment at Admiralty, and Chief Naval Representative on Supply Council, Ministry of Supply, 1945–48; retd list, Royal Navy, 1948. Vice-Chm., Air Requirements Bd, 1960–74. Man. Dir, Short Brothers & Harland, Ltd, 1948–52, Chm. and Man. Dir, 1952–60; Chairman: (SB Realisations) Ltd, 1952–60; Bristol Aircraft Ltd, 1957–60; Dir Bristol Aeroplane Co. Ltd, 1957–60. Special Adviser to Prime Minister on Transport of Middle East Oil, 1957–59; Dir National Bank Ltd, 1959–60, 1963–69; Chairman: BOAC, 1960–63; BOAC-Cunard Ltd, 1962–63; R. & W. Hawthorn, Leslie & Co., 1966–73. Commander Legion of Merit (USA). DSc(hc) Queen's Univ., Belfast, 1954. *Recreations:* country pursuits. *Address:* Harvey's Farm, Warninglid, West Sussex.
*Died* 16 *March* 1990.

**SLAUGHTER, James Cameron**, CMG 1963; Executive Adviser, Brisbane City Council, 1967–71 (Town Clerk and City Administrator, 1940–67); *b* 16 Aug. 1902; *s* of late Ernest E. Slaughter; *m* 1927, Ida M. Taylor; one *s* one *d*. *Educ:* Normal School, Brisbane. Trustee, City Debt Redemption Fund, 1940; Chm., Lang Park Trust, 1959; Town Clerk: Bundaberg City Coun., 1936–40; Coolangatta Town Coun., 1927–36; Shire Clerk: Gatton Shire Coun.; Inglewood Shire Coun.; Chief Clerk, Ithaca Town Council. AASA; FIMA. *Recreations:* bowls, fishing. *Clubs:* Johnsonian and Tattersalls; Rugby League, Booroodabin Bowling.
*Died* 16 *Oct.* 1982.

**SLEIGHT, Sir John Frederick**, 3rd Bt, *cr* 1920; *b* 13 April 1909; *s* of Major Sir Ernest Sleight, 2nd Bt and Margaret (*d* 1976), *d* of C. F. Carter, JP, The Limes, Grimsby; *S* father, 1946; *m* 1942, Jacqueline Margaret Mundell, *widow* of Ronald Mundell and *o d* of late Major H. R. Carter of Brisbane, Queensland; one *s*. *Heir: s* Richard Sleight [*b* 27 May 1946; *m* 1978, Marie-Thérèse, *o d* of O. M. Stepan, Bromley, Kent]. *Address:* 4 Plumosa Court, Broadbeach Waters, Qld 4218, Australia. *Died* 12 *Feb.* 1990.

**SLOANE, Maj.-Gen. John Bramley Malet**, CB 1967; CBE 1962 (OBE 1951); DL; Director of Manning (Army), Ministry of Defence, 1964–67; retired; *b* 17 Sept. 1912; *s* of late James Kay Sloane, Penpont; *m* 1939, Marjorie (*née* Crowley); three *s*. Served 1934–39, London Scottish; commnd Argyll and Sutherland Highlanders, 1940; served Paiforce, ME, Burma, 1939–45, India, Aug. 1945–Dec. 1947, Korea, 1950–51, Malayan Campaign, 1951–53; War Office Staff, 1953–56; SHAPE, 1956–58; MoD, 1958–60; Brig. AQ, Western Comd, 1960–63. DL Beds, 1976. *Recreation:* walking. *Address:* 4 Brayfield House, near Olney, Bucks MK46 4HS. *T:* Turvey 373. *Club:* Army and Navy. *Died* 6 *June* 1990.

**SLOCUM, Captain Frank Alexander**, CMG 1953; OBE 1935; RN (retd); *b* 30 Sept. 1897; 2nd *s* of late Henry Slocum, Micheldever, Hampshire, and of Emily (*née* Clarke), *e d* of Capt. William Clarke, Roy. Fusiliers; *m* 1922, Vera, *e d* of late John Metherell Gard, Stoke, Devonport; two *d*. *Educ:* Royal Naval Establishments; Gonville and Caius College, Cambridge. Entered RN, 1914; served European War, 1914–18, in Grand Fleet; Lieut, 1918; 2nd Destroyer Flotilla, Home Fleet, 1920; qualified in (N) duties, 1921. Served in Persian Gulf, Mediterranean, and Home Fleets; psc RN Staff Coll., 1931; Mediterranean Fleet (Revenge and Resolution); staff of Tactical School, 1935; Actg Comdr, 1939; Actg Capt., 1940. Served War of 1939–45 as Dep. Dir Ops Div., Admiralty, and in charge of Auxiliary Patrol Flotillas; retd list, 1947, in war service rank of Captain. Temp. 1st Sec., British Embassy, Oslo, 1954–56. Trials Capt. for contract-built HM Ships, 1956. Croix de Guerre avec Palme (France), 1946; Comdr Legion of Merit (USA), 1946; King Haakon VII Liberty Cross (Norway), 1947; King Christian X's Freedom Medal (Denmark), 1947. *Publications:* naval and seafaring articles and short stories. *Recreations:* sailing, naval history, marine surveying. *Address:* Stone Cottage, 3a Camden Park, Tunbridge Wells, Kent. *T:* Tunbridge Wells 27395. *Club:* Naval and Military.
*Died* 22 *May* 1982.

**SLYTH, Arthur Roy**, CB 1966; OBE 1957; *b* 30 May 1910; *s* of Thomas Slyth; *m* 1938, Anne Mary Muir Grieve (*d* 1973). *Educ:* Lincoln School. Entered Exchequer and Audit Department, 1929; Dep. Sec., 1961; Sec., 1963–73. *Recreation:* golf. *Address:* 4 Broadlands Road, N6 4AS. *T:* 01–340 2366.
*Died* 5 *July* 1989.

**SMAILES, Prof. Arthur Eltringham**, MA, DLit London; Emeritus Professor of Geography in the University of London; Professor of Geography at Queen Mary College, 1955–73; *b* Haltwhistle, Northumberland, 23 March 1911; *o s* of John Robert and Mary Elizabeth Smailes; *m* 1937, Dorothy Forster; one *d*. *Educ:* Grammar School of Queen Elizabeth, Hexham; University College, London. BA (London) with First Cl. Hons in Geography, 1930, MA 1933, DLit 1965. Lecturer, University College, London, from 1931 and Reader in Geography, 1950–53; Head of Department of Geography, Queen Mary College, University of London, 1953–73. Geographer Consultant, Middlesbrough Survey and Plan, 1944–45. Hon. Secretary, Inst. of British Geographers, 1951–62, Pres., 1970. Chm., Internat. Geog. Union Commn on Processes and Patterns of Urbanisation, 1972–76. Circuit Steward, West London Mission, Kingsway Hall, 1965–69. Research Medal, RSGS, 1964. *Publications:* The Geography of Towns, 1953; North England, 1960; various articles in geographical and town planning journals. *Address:* Department of Geography, Queen Mary College, Mile End Road, E1 4NS. *Died* 17 *March* 1984.

**SMALLEY, Beryl**, FBA 1963; MA Oxon; PhD Manchester; History Tutor, 1943–69, Vice-Principal, 1957–69, Emeritus Fellow, St Hilda's College, Oxford; *b* 3 June 1905; *d* of Edgar Smalley. *Educ:* Cheltenham Ladies' College; St Hilda's College, Oxford. Assistant Lecturer, Royal Holloway College, 1931–35; Research Fellow, Girton College, 1935–40; Temporary Assistant in Dept of Western MSS, Bodleian Library, 1940–43. Ford's Lecturer, Oxford, 1966–67. Hon. DLitt Southampton, 1974. *Publications:* The Study of the Bible in the Middle Ages, 1952; English Friars and Antiquity, 1960; The Becket Conflict and the Schools, 1973; Historians in the Middle Ages, 1974; Studies in Medieval Thought from Abelard to Wyclif, 1982; contribs to: Recherches de théologie ancienne et médiévale; Mediaeval and Renaissance Studies, etc. *Recreations:* walking, swimming, travel. *Address:* 5c Rawlinson Road, Oxford. *T:* Oxford 59525. *Club:* University Women's. *Died* 6 *April* 1984.

**SMALLWOOD, Norah Evelyn**, OBE 1973; retired publisher; *b* Dec. 1909; *d* of Howard Neville Walford and Marian Griffiths; *m* 1938, Peter Warren Sykes Smallwood, RAF (killed in action, 1943). *Educ:* privately; Edenthorpe School, Eastbourne. Joined Chatto & Windus, 1939, partner, 1945; Dir, Hogarth Press, 1947; Dir, Chatto & Windus, 1953; Dir, Chatto, Bodley Head & Cape Group, 1969; Man. Dir and Chm., Chatto & Windus Hogarth Press, 1975; Dir, Triad paperbacks, 1975; Dir, Chatto & Windus Developments, 1971; retired Chatto, 1982, and from Group, 1983. Hon. DLitt Leeds, 1981. *Recreations:* reading, walking, looking at pictures, gardening. *Address:* 13 Vincent Square, SW1. *T:* 01–821 0959.
*Died* 11 *Oct.* 1984.

*This entry did not appear in Who's Who.*

**SMART, Henry Walter**, CB 1966; formerly Director of Savings, GPO (1958–68); *b* 7 Sept. 1908; *m*; two *s*. *Educ:* Sir Thomas Rich's School, Gloucester. *Address:* 24 Gumstool Hill, Tetbury, Glos GL8 8DG. *T:* Tetbury (0666) 503979. *Died* 18 *May* 1990.

**SMART, Maj.-Gen. Robert Arthur**, CBE 1958; FRCP; Chief Medical Officer, Esso Petroleum Co., 1975–79, Senior Medical Officer, 1972–75; *b* 29 April 1914; *s* of Arthur Francis Smart and Roberta Teresa Farquhar; *m* 1947, Josephine von Oepen; one *d*. *Educ:* Aberdeen Gram. Sch.; Aberdeen University. MB, ChB 1936; DPH

(Eng.) 1948; MRCP 1965, FRCP 1977; AFOM 1978. Lt, RAMC, 1936; Capt. 1937; Maj. 1946; Lt-Col 1951; Col 1960; Brig. 1964; Maj.-Gen. 1967. Served in Palestine, Egypt, Western Desert, Eritrea, France and Germany, 1939–45; N Africa and E Africa, 1951–55; Asst Dir of Army Health, E Africa, 1952–55; Leader, Royal Society's Internat. Geophysical Year Expedn to Antarctica, 1956–57; Dep. Chief Med. Off., Supreme HQ Allied Powers Europe, 1960–62; Dep. Dir of Army Health, BAOR, 1962–64; Dir of Army Health, MoD, 1964–68; DMS, FARELF, 1968–70; DMS, BAOR, 1970–71; DDMS, HQ Army Strategic Comd, 1971–72, retired 1972. Polar Medal, 1958. QHS 1968–72. *Address:* 186 Forest Avenue, Aberdeen AB1 6UY. *Clubs:* Army and Navy; Royal Northern and University (Aberdeen).                                    *Died* 6 *Nov.* 1986.

**SMEDDLES, Thomas Henry;** Chief General Manager, Royal Insurance Group, 1963–69; *b* 18 Dec. 1904; *s* of late T. H. Smeddles; *m* 1931, Dorothy Boardman; one *s*. Joined The Liverpool & London & Globe Insurance Co. Ltd, 1924. *Recreation:* gardening. *Address:* 6 Abbotts Close, Abbotts Ann, Andover, Hants.
                                    *Died* 28 *Feb.* 1987.

**SMELLIE, Kingsley Bryce Speakman;** Professor Emeritus of Political Science, London School of Economics, since 1965; Professor, 1949–65, Hon. Fellow, 1977; *b* 22 Nov. 1897; *o s* of late John and Elizabeth Smellie; *m* 1931, Stephanie, *o d* of late Anthony E. and Stephanie Narlian. *Educ:* Mrs Bolwell, 15 Mall Road, Hammersmith; Latymer Upper School, Hammersmith; St John's College, Cambridge. Served European War, 1914–18, as private in London Scottish. Staff of London School of Economics, 1921–65. Laura Spelman Rockefeller Student in USA (Harvard Law School), 1925–26; Research Assistant, propaganda research unit of BBC, 1940; temp. principal: Ministry of Home Security, 1940–42, Board of Trade, 1942–45. *Publications:* The American Federal System, 1928; A Hundred Years of English Government, 1937; Civics, 1939; Reason in Politics, 1939; Our Two Democracies at Work, 1944; A History of Local Government, 1946; Why We Read History, 1948; British Way of Life, 1955; Great Britain since 1688, 1962. *Address:* 24 Parkside Gardens, SW19 5EU. *T:* 01–946 7869.
                                    *Died* 30 *Nov.* 1987.

**SMELLIE, Prof. R(obert) Martin S(tuart),** PhD, DSc; FRSE 1964; FIBiol; Cathcart Professor of Biochemistry, since 1966, Director of the Biochemical Laboratories, since 1972, University of Glasgow; *b* Rothesay, Bute, 1 April 1927; *s* of Rev. W. T. Smellie, OBE, MA and Jean (*née* Craig); *m* 1954, Florence Mary Devlin Adams, MB ChB; two *s*. *Educ:* Dundee High Sch.; Glasgow Acad.; Univ. of St Andrews (BSc 1947); Univ. of Glasgow (PhD 1952, DSc 1963). FIBiol 1964. National Service, 1947–49: commnd Royal Scots Fusiliers; served with 2nd Bn Royal Scots and at CDEE, Porton. University of Glasgow: Asst Lectr in Biochemistry, 1949–52; Beit Memorial Res. Fellow, 1952–53; Lectr in Biochem., 1953–55 and 1956–59, Sen. Lectr, 1959–63; Reader in Molecular Biol., 1963–65. Res. Fellow, NY Univ. Coll. of Med., 1955–56. Biochemical Society: Mem. Cttee, 1967–71; Symposium Organiser, 1970–75. Member: EMBO, 1964; MRC Physiol. Systems and Disorders Bd, 1977–82; Brit. Biophys. Soc., 1968; Brit. Assoc. for Cancer Res., 1961; Soc. for Endocrinology, 1968; Council, Trinity Coll., Glenalmond, 1976–; Assoc. Clinical Biochemists, 1980. Governor, Glasgow Academicals War Meml Trust, 1976–79. Mem. Court, Glasgow Univ., 1986–. Hon. Gen. Sec., RSE, 1976–86. Bicentenary Medal, RSE, 1986. *Publications:* A Matter of Life: DNA, 1969; (contrib.) The Biochemistry of the Nucleic Acids, 8th edn 1976, 9th edn 1981; (ed) Biochemical Society Symposia Nos 31–41; papers in scientific jls on nucleic acid biosynthesis and hormone control mechanisms. *Recreations:* fishing, walking, music, foreign travel. *Address:* 39 Falkland Street, Glasgow G12 9QZ. *T:* 041–334 4255. *Club:* New (Edinburgh).                                    *Died* 12 *March* 1988.

**SMILEY, Sir Hugh Houston,** 3rd Bt, *cr* 1903; late Grenadier Guards; JP; Vice Lord-Lieutenant of Hampshire, 1973–82; *b* 14 Nov. 1905; *s* of 2nd Bt and Valerie (*d* 1978), *y d* of late Sir Claude Champion de Crespigny, 4th Bt; *S* father, 1930; *m* 1933, Nancy, *er d* of E. W. H. Beaton; one *s*. *Educ:* Eton; RMC, Sandhurst. Served with 1st Bn Grenadier Guards NW Europe, 1944–45. JP 1952, DL 1962, Hampshire; High Sheriff, 1959. Chm., Jane Austen Society, 1969–90 (Hon. Sec., 1953–85). *Heir:* *s* Lt-Col John Philip Smiley [*b* 24 Feb. 1934; *m* 1963, Davina Elizabeth, *e d* of late Denis Griffiths; two *s* one *d*. *Educ:* Eton; RMA, Sandhurst; Lt-Col late Grenadier Guards]. *Address:* Ivalls, Bentworth, Alton, Hants GU34 5JU. *T:* Alton (0420) 63193. *Club:* Cavalry and Guards.
                                    *Died* 1 *Nov.* 1990.

**SMITH;** *see* Hornsby-Smith.

**SMITH, Sir (Alexander) Rowland,** Kt 1944; formerly Chairman and Managing Director, Ford Motor Co. Ltd; formerly Director, National Provincial Bank Ltd; Ex-Member, UK Atomic Energy Authority and National Research Corp.; *b* Gillingham, Kent, 25 Jan. 1888; *s* of late Alexander James Frederick Smith, Gillingham, Kent; *m* 1913, Janet Lucretia (*d* 1972), *d* of late George Henry

Baker, Gillingham, Kent; one *s* one *d*. *Educ:* Mathematical School, Rochester. Freeman, City of London; Livery Cos: Glaziers (Past Master); Coachmakers and Coach Harness Makers; Member: Ministry of Aircraft Production Mission to USA, 1941; Ministry of Pensions Standing Advisory Cttee on Artificial Limbs, 1948; Cttee on Procedure for ordering Civil Aircraft, 1948. FIB; FRSA; CEng; FIMechE; Fell. Inst. of Bankers. *Recreation:* sailing. *Address:* The Manor House, Maresfield, W Sussex. *Clubs:* Athenæum; Royal Southern Yacht.                                    *Died* 19 *April* 1988.

**SMITH, Dame Annis Calder;** *see* Gillie, Dame A. C.

**SMITH, Anthony Robert;** Director of Statistics and Research, Department of Health and Social Security, 1976–86; *b* 29 March 1926; *s* of late Ernest George Smith and Mildred Smith (*née* Murphy); *m* 1949, Helen Elizabeth Mary Morgan; two *d*. *Educ:* De La Salle Coll., Pendleton; Peterhouse, Cambridge; London Sch. of Economics (BScEcon). Royal Marines and Army, 1944–47. Various appts in Admty, 1950–64; Defence, 1964–68; Treasury, 1968; Civil Service Dept, 1968–76; Under-Sec., 1970. Co-Founder and Chm., Manpower Planning Study Gp, 1967–70; Vice-Pres., Manpower Soc., 1975– (Mem. Council, 1970–75); Member: Council, Inst. of Manpower Studies, 1968–86 (also Co-Founder); Nat. Cttees, Inst. of Personnel Management, 1972–79; Consultant, Organisation for Economic Co-operation and Development, 1970–78. FIPM 1968. *Publications:* Models of Manpower Systems (ed), 1970; Manpower and Management Science (with D. J. Bartholomew), 1971; (ed) Manpower Planning in the Civil Service, 1976; Corporate Manpower Planning, 1980; contributor to related books and jls. *Recreation:* dabbling. *Address:* 16 Carlton Road, Redhill RH1 2BX. *T:* Redhill 762258.                                    *Died* 7 *Oct.* 1988.

**SMITH, Sir Arthur (Henry),** Kt 1968; Chairman, United Africa Co. Ltd, 1955–69; Director of Unilever Ltd, 1948–69; retired; *b* 18 Jan. 1905; *s* of Frederick Smith; *m* 1930, Dorothy Percy; two *s*. *Educ:* Bolton School. Specialised in Company's interests in French and Belgian Africa, incl. several years' residence in those territories. Econ. Adviser to Brit. Govt's Econ. Mission to French W Africa, 1943. Officer, Legion of Honour, 1957 (Cross 1951); Commander, National Order of the Ivory Coast, 1969. *Address:* 102 Kingsway Court, Kingsway, Hove BN3 2LR. *T:* Brighton 779860.
                                    *Died* 29 *Sept.* 1989.

**SMITH, Arthur Norman E.;** *see* Exton-Smith.

**SMITH, Prof. Austin Geoffrey;** Hives Professor of Thermodynamics, University of Nottingham, and Head of Department of Mechanical Engineering, 1960–82, now Emeritus Professor; *b* 22 Aug. 1918; *s* of James Austin Smith and Olive Smith; *m* 1960, Vera Margaret Kennard; no *c*. *Educ:* Gillingham County School for Boys. Royal Scholar, Imperial College, London, 1937–40. Research engineer, Blackburn Aircraft Co., 1940–42; Engineer, Power Jets Ltd, 1942–46; Senior Scientific Officer and Principal Scientific Officer, National Gas Turbine Establishment, 1946–52; Reader in Gas Turbines, Imperial College, London, 1952–57; Professor of Aircraft Propulsion, The College of Aeronautics, 1957–60. *Publications:* many papers in the field of thermodynamics, heat transfer and aerodynamics. *Address:* Pinfold Close, Church Street, Bramcote, Nottingham NG9 3HD. *T:* Nottingham 258397.
                                    *Died* 15 *Dec.* 1984.

**SMITH, Sir Bryan (Evers) S.;** *see* Sharwood-Smith.

**SMITH, Maj.-Gen. Sir Cecil (Miller),** KBE 1951 (CBE 1944; OBE 1941); CB 1947; MC; CEng, MIMechE; psc; late RASC; *b* 17 June 1896; *s* of John Smith, Dromore, Co. Down; *m* 1930, Isabel Buswell; two *d*. *Educ:* Royal Belfast Academical Institution; Royal Military College, Sandhurst; Staff College, Camberley. Served European War, 1914–19, ASC and Royal Inniskilling Fusiliers. France and Belgium, 1916–18 (wounded, MC, two medals); Served War, 1939–45: ME, 1939–44; NW Europe, 1944–45; Maj.-Gen., 1943; DQMG (Army Equipment) ME, 1943–44; DACOS, SHAEF, 1944–45; Maj.-Gen. in charge of Administration, Northern Command, 1945–47; Chief of Staff, Northern Command, 1947–48; Director of Supplies and Transport, War Office, 1948–51; retired pay, 1951. Col Comdt, RASC, 1950–60. Chm. Ulster Society in London, 1961–73. Commander, Legion of Merit, US; Officier de la Légion d'Honneur (France). *Address:* Crosh, Southfield Place, Weybridge, Surrey. *T:* Weybridge 42199.
                                    *Died* 22 *March* 1988.

**SMITH, Charles Harvard G.;** *see* Gibbs-Smith.

**SMITH, Prof. C(harles) Holt,** CBE 1955; MSc; FIEE; Professor of Instrument Technology, Royal Military College of Science, Shrivenham, 1949–68, now Emeritus; (seconded to the Indian Government for four years from 1st January, 1956, as Dean of the Institute of Armament Studies); *b* 27 Aug. 1903; *s* of Charles Smith and Emily (*née* Holt); *m* 1928, Gracie Alexandra Macdonald (*née* Livingstone); one *s* one *d*. *Educ:* Bolton Grammar School; Manchester University. Peel Connor Telephone Works, 1924–26;

Royal Aircraft Establishment, Farnborough, 1926–30 and 1938–40; British Broadcasting Corporation, 1930–38; Telecommunications Research Establishment: Malvern, 1940–42; Defford, 1944–46; Malvern, 1946–49; Assistant Director of Directorate of Communications Development, Ministry of Supply, 1942–44. *Recreations:* bridge, fishing, shooting. *Address:* 37 Queens Park Avenue, Bournemouth, Dorset BH8 9LH. *T:* 527525.
*Died 7 May 1984.*

**SMITH, Charles Nugent C.;** *see* Close-Smith.

**SMITH, Charlotte Susanna W.;** *see* Rycroft, C. S.

**SMITH, Christopher Patrick Crawford,** MA; *b* Edinburgh, 9 May 1902; *s* of late George Smith; unmarried. *Educ:* Dulwich College; Trinity College, Oxford (Scholar, First in Classical Moderations, and First in Literae Humaniores). Assistant Master, Rugby School, 1926–38; Warden of Trinity College, Glenalmond, 1938–48; Headmaster of Haileybury, 1948–63. Chairman, Headmasters' Conference, 1961–62. *Address:* Windrush, St Andrews, Fife.
*Died 29 Sept. 1984.*

**SMITH, Vice-Adm. Sir Conolly A.;** *see* Abel Smith, Vice-Adm. Sir E. M. C.

**SMITH, David MacLeish,** DSc; FRS 1952; retired; *b* 1900; *s* of David T. Smith, Elgin, Scotland; *m* 1941, Doris Kendrick; no *c*. *Educ:* Blairgowrie High School; Glasgow University (DSc 1932). College Apprentice with Metropolitan Vickers Elect. Co. Ltd, Trafford Park, Manchester, 1920, and remained with that co. and its successor AEI Ltd, until 1966. Hon. LLD, Glasgow, 1967. MIMechE 1938; FRAeS 1949; FEng 1976. *Publications:* Journal Bearings in Turbomachinery, 1969; various technical papers. *Address:* Rostherne Flat 2, Cavendish Road, Bowdon, Cheshire WA14 2NU. *Died 3 Aug. 1986.*

**SMITH, Hon. Sir David (Stanley),** Kt 1948; *b* 11 Feb. 1888; *s* of Rev. J. Gibson Smith; *m* 1st, 1915, Eva Jane (*d* 1917), *d* of late Duncan Cumming; one *d*; 2nd, 1923, Margaret Elizabeth (*d* 1954), *d* of Richard Wayne Gibbs; one *s*. *Educ:* Wellington Coll.; Victoria Univ. Coll., Wellington (LLM). Barrister, Solicitor and Notary Public; American non-national member of the Permanent Commission under the Treaty of Conciliation between the United States of America and Peru, 11 Feb. 1933; Chairman of Commission on Native Affairs, New Zealand, 1934; Member of Council of Victoria University College, 1939–45; Chairman of Royal Commission on Licensing of Alcoholic Liquors, 1945–46; Chancellor, Univ. of NZ, 1945–61; Judge of Supreme Court of NZ, 1928–48 (temp. Judge, 1949–50); retired 1948; Mem. Bd Dirs, US Educl Foundn in NZ, 1948–70. Chm. NZ Bd of Trade, 1950–59. Ex-Mem. Council of Internat. Bar Assoc. Hon. DCL Oxford, 1948; Hon. LLD Univ. of New Zealand, 1961. *Address:* 10 Sefton Street, Wellington 1, NZ. *Club:* Wellington (Wellington).
*Died 29 Dec. 1982.*

**SMITH, Dodie,** (wrote under the name of C. L. Anthony up to 1935); Dramatist and Novelist; *b* 3 May 1896; *d* of Ernest Walter Smith and Ella Furber; *m* 1939, Alec Macbeth Beesley (*d* 1988). *Educ:* St Paul's School for Girls. Studied at Royal Academy of Dramatic Art; on the stage for several years; gave up the stage and became a buyer at Heal and Son, Tottenham Court Road; wrote Autumn Crocus in 1930; produced Lyric Theatre, 1931; gave up business, 1931; wrote Service, 1932; produced Wyndham's Theatre, 1932; wrote Touch Wood, 1933; produced Theatre Royal, Haymarket, 1934; wrote Call It A Day, 1935; produced Globe Theatre, 1935; Bonnet Over the Windmill; produced New Theatre, 1937; wrote Dear Octopus, 1938; produced Queen's Theatre, 1938, revived Theatre Royal, Haymarket, 1967; wrote Lovers and Friends, 1942; prod. Plymouth Theatre, New York, 1943; Letter from Paris (adapted from novel, The Reverberator, by Henry James), Aldwych, 1952; wrote I Capture the Castle, 1952 (adapted from own novel of same name), prod. Aldwych Theatre, 1953; wrote These People-Those Books, 1957; prod. Leeds, 1958; wrote Amateur Means Lover, 1956; prod. Liverpool, 1961. *Publications: Plays by C. L. Anthony:* Autumn Crocus; Service; Touch Wood; *Plays by Dodie Smith:* Call It A Day; Bonnet Over the Windmill; Dear Octopus; Lovers and Friends; Letter from Paris; I Capture the Castle; *novels:* I Capture the Castle, 1949 (US 1948); The New Moon with the Old, 1963 (US 1963); The Town in Bloom, 1965 (US 1965); It Ends with Revelations, 1967 (US 1967); A Tale of Two Families, 1970 (US 1970); The Girl from the Candle-lit Bath, 1978; *children's books:* The Hundred and One Dalmatians, 1956 (US 1957) (filmed 1961); The Starlight Barking, 1967 (US 1968); The Midnight Kittens, 1978; *autobiography:* Look Back With Love, 1974; Look Back With Mixed Feelings, 1978; Look Back With Astonishment, 1979; Look Back with Gratitude, 1985. *Recreations:* reading, music, dogs, donkeys. *Address:* The Barretts, Finchingfield, Essex. *T:* Great Dunmow (0371) 810260. *Died 24 Nov. 1990.*

**SMITH, Douglas Alexander;** Commissioner of Inland Revenue, 1968–75; *b* 15 June 1915; *m* 1941, Mary Eileen Lyon; one *s* one *d*.

*Educ:* Glasgow High Sch.; Glasgow Univ. MA, BSc 1937. Entered Inland Revenue, 1938; Asst Secretary: Inland Revenue, 1952–59; Office of Minister for Science, 1959–61; Under-Sec., Medical Research Council, 1964–67. *Recreations:* hockey, golf, bridge, gardening. *Address:* 66 Eastwick Drive, Great Bookham, Surrey. *T:* Bookham 54274. *Club:* Civil Service. *Died 5 Oct. 1988.*

**SMITH, Dr Edgar Charles B.;** *see* Bate-Smith.

**SMITH, His Honour Edgar Dennis;** a Circuit Judge (South-Eastern Circuit), 1972–79; *b* 29 Jan. 1911; *yr s* of late George Henry Smith; *m* 1950, Mary, *yr d* of late Captain T. Drewery, MN; two *s*. *Educ:* Queen Mary's School, Walsall; Birmingham University (LLM). Lord Justice Holker (Holt) Scholar, Gray's Inn, 1933. Called to Bar, Gray's Inn, 1935. Practised in London and on Oxford Circuit. Served War of 1939–45: Special Investigation Branch, Royal Military Police, 1940–46; Assistant Provost-Marshal, Special Investigation Branch, 1945. Headquarters Commissioner The Scout Association, 1947–58 (Silver Wolf, 1956); Mem. Council, The Scout Association, 1964– (Chm., Cttee of the Council, 1968–74). Dep. Chm., Agricultural Land Tribunal, S Eastern Region, 1959–63; Dep. Chm., Staffs QS, 1961–63; Metropolitan Stipendiary Magistrate, 1963–72; Chm., Inner London Juvenile Courts, 1968–72. Hon. Technical Advr, Central Council of Probation and After-Care Cttees, 1968–79. Liveryman, Fletchers' Co., 1975. *Publications:* (ed) The County Court Pleader; (Sen. Asst Ed.) Foa's Law of Landlord and Tenant (8th edn); various other legal works. *Recreations:* travel, music, theatre. *Address:* Chilham House, Pulborough, West Sussex RH20 2AE. *T:* Pulborough 2616. *Died 1 June 1986.*

**SMITH, Maj.-Gen. Sir Edmund H.;** *see* Hakewill Smith.

**SMITH, Edward John Gregg,** CB 1982; Deputy Secretary, Ministry of Agriculture, Fisheries and Food, since 1979; *b* 1 Oct. 1930; *o s* of late Major J. W. Smith and Mrs V. H. E. Smith; *m* 1956, Jean Margaret Clayton; one *s* two *d*. *Educ:* Churcher's Coll., Petersfield; Queens' Coll., Cambridge (MA). FRGS. MAFF, 1953–68: Private Sec. to Minister, 1964–66; Head of Economic Policy Div., 1966–68; Principal Private Sec. to Lord President of Council and Leader of House of Commons, 1968–70; returned to MAFF: Head of Meat Div., 1970–71; Under-Sec., 1971–74, 1976–79; Under-Sec., Cabinet Office, 1974–76. Mem., AFRC (formerly ARC), 1979–; Mem., Guildford Diocesan Synod, 1976– (Chm., House of Laity, 1985–88); Mem., Archbishops' Commn on Rural Areas, 1988–. Gov., Royal Agricl Coll. FRSA. *Recreations:* choral music, Christian activities. *Address:* The Holme, Oakfield Road, Ashtead, Surrey. *T:* Ashtead 72311. *Club:* Reform. *Died 4 May 1989.*

**SMITH, Vice-Adm. Sir (Edward Michael) Conolly A.;** *see* Abel Smith.

**SMITH, Dame Enid Mary Russell R.;** *see* Russell-Smith.

**SMITH, Sir Eric;** *see* Smith, Sir J. E.

**SMITH, (Francis) Raymond (Stanley);** retired as Librarian and Curator, Corporation of London (1943–56); *b* Fenny Stratford, Bucks, 12 Dec. 1890; *o s* of Rev. H. S. Smith, Baptist Minister, and Lina F. Smith. *Educ:* privately; Mercers' School. Junior Clerk, Guildhall Library, 1908. Served European War, 1916–19, Lt RAPC. Librarian and Curator, Guildhall Library and Museum, 1943; Director, Guildhall Art Gallery, 1945; Member Council of Library Assoc., 1951. Chm. Reference and Special Libraries Section, 1951–54; Chm. Exec. Cttee, Roman and Mediaeval London Excavation Council, 1952–56. Liveryman of Clockmakers Company; Hon. Librarian, Clockmakers and Gardeners Companies, 1943–56; Guild Master, Civic Guild of Old Mercers, 1952–53. Member: Soc. of Archivists; London Topographical Soc.; Cons. Librarian and Archivist, French Protestant Church of London, 1965. FLA, 1929; FSA 1944. *Publications:* Classification of London Literature, 1926; The City of London: a Select Book List, 1951; (with P. E. Jones) Guide to the Records at Guildhall, London, 1951; ed Guildhall Miscellany, 1952–56; The pictorial history of the City of London, 1953; The Living City, a new view of the City of London, 1957, 2nd edn 1966; The Worshipful Company of Masons, 1960; Sea Coal for London, 1961; Ceremonials of the Corporation of London, 1962; The Irish Society 1613–1963, 1966; The Archives of the French Protestant Church of London, a handlist, 1972; The Royal Bounty and other records in the Huguenot Library, University College, a handlist, 1974; contrib. to professional journals and books on libraries, archives, etc. *Recreations:* book-hunting, gardening, music. *Address:* 61 Sutton Road, Seaford, East Sussex. *T:* Seaford 892629. *Died 11 May 1981.*

**SMITH, Frederick Llewellyn,** CBE 1964; MSc, DPhil, CEng, FIMechE; *b* 25 July 1909; *s* of late James Brooksbank Smith; *m* 1943, Alice Mary McMurdo; one *s* two *d*. *Educ:* Rochdale High Sch.; Univ. of Manchester; Balliol Coll., Oxford. Joined Rolls-Royce Ltd, 1933; Dir, 1947; Group Man. Dir, Automotive and subsidiary cos, 1970; Chm., Rolls-Royce Motors Ltd, 1971; retired 1972. Pres. Soc. of Motor Manufacturers & Traders Ltd, 1955–56. Mem. Nat. Research Development Corp., 1959–73. Pres., Motor

Industry Research Assoc., 1963–65. *Address:* 4 Raglan Close, Reigate, Surrey RH2 0EU. *Died* 18 *Aug.* 1988.

**SMITH, Frederick William**, CMG 1947; MC 1917; retired as Chief Contracts Officer to the Central Electricity Authority (1950–56), and as Contracts Adviser to the Central Electricity Authority (1957–Dec. 1959); *b* 7 March 1896; *m* 1921, Emma Sarah Sharman (*d* 1971); one *s*. *Educ:* Haberdashers' Aske's Hampstead School. European War, 1914–18, army service, concluded as DAAG 51st Highland Division, 1914–19; Croix de Chevalier de l'Ordre de Leopold, 1917; Belgian Croix de Guerre, 1917. Civil Service: Inland Revenue Dept, Air Ministry, Ministry of Aircraft Production, Viceroy of India, Ministry of Works, Cabinet Office, Treasury, Ministry of Fuel and Power, 1920–50; Deputy Secretary, Ministry of Fuel and Power, 1948–50. *Address:* Beechwood, Tower Road, Faygate, Horsham, West Sussex. *Died* 12 *May* 1981.

**SMITH, Col Sir Gengoult;** *see* Smith, Col Sir H. G.

**SMITH, Geoffrey Ellrington Fane**, CMG 1955; Senior Provincial Commissioner, Northern Rhodesia, 1951–55, retired; Colonial Office, 1956–61, Department of Technical Co-operation (later Ministry of Overseas Development), 1961–66; *b* 1903; *m* 1933, Olga Smith. *Educ:* King Edward VI Grammar School, Louth; Lincoln College, Oxford. Cadet, Northern Rhodesia, 1926–29; District Officer, 1929; Provincial Commissioner, Northern Rhodesia, 1947–51. *Address:* 26 Vincent Road, Stoke D'Abernon, Cobham, Surrey. *Died* 22 *Nov.* 1987.

**SMITH, Vice-Adm. Sir Geoffrey T.;** *see* Thistleton-Smith.

**SMITH, George William Q.;** *see* Quick-Smith.

**SMITH, His Honour Gerard Gustave L.;** *see* Lind-Smith.

**SMITH, Sir Gordon;** *see* Smith, Sir W. G.

**SMITH, Sir Guy B.;** *see* Bracewell-Smith.

**SMITH, Guy B.;** *see* Bassett Smith, N. G.

**SMITH, Colonel Sir (Harold) Gengoult**, Kt 1934; VD; JP; FRCPE, LRCPPE, LRCSE, LRFPS(G); Chairman of Royal Visit (1949) Committee of Melbourne; *b* 25 July 1890; *s* of Hon. Louis Laurence Smith and Marion Higgins; *m* 1933, Cynthia Mary (decd), *d* of Sir Norman E. Brookes; one *s* one *d*. *Educ:* Melbourne Church of England Gram. Sch.; Melbourne and Edinburgh Univs; Royal College of Surgeons, Edinburgh. Australian Military Forces, 1907–47; Lt-Col Brighton Rifles (seconded), 2nd Dragoon Guard (Res. Regt), 1915, 2nd Lt; Served France, 1915–16; qualified Royal College of Surgeons, 1917; House Surgeon, Royal Edinburgh Infirmary, 1917; Medical Clinical Asst, 1923–24; Comd Balcombe Casualty Clearing Station, 1941; CO 111th Australian General Hospital, 1944; elected Melbourne City Council, 1921; Lord Mayor, 1931–32, 1932–33 and 1933–34; Chairman Victorian and Melbourne Centenary Celebrations Council, 1934–35. Formerly: President Children's Cinema Council; Patron, Partially Blinded Soldiers' Assoc.; Chm. Exhibition Trustees; Zoological Board of Victoria; Board of Eye and Ear Hospital; Board of Infectious Diseases Hospital; Council of Old Colonists' Homes; Chairman of Public Works Cttee. *Recreations:* fox-hunting (Oaklands Hounds), golf, fishing, shooting, travelling. *Clubs:* Athenæum, Peninsula Country (Melbourne); Victoria Racing. *Died* 14 *April* 1983.

**SMITH, Lt-Col Harry Cyril**, CBE 1945 (OBE 1919);; MC 1917; Russian Order of St Anne (2nd Class) 1920; *b* 1888; *s* of late Arthur B. Smith, Birmingham; *m* 1st, 1920, Catherine Koulikoff, Petrograd (marr. diss), *d* of late Baroness v. Breugel-Douglas, The Hague; one *s*; 2nd, Ida Eleanor, *widow* of Capt. Lawder B. S. Smith, MC, and *e d* of late William Raymond FitzMaurice Clark, Kilballyskea, Shinrone, Offaly, Eire. *Educ:* Royal Grammar School, Worcester and Birmingham. Joined RE (TA), 1908; Engineering, S America, 1909–14; served European War, 1914–18, RE (despatches twice); CRE 28th Division, 1919; Assistant Railway Adviser, British Military Mission with Denekin, S Russia, 1919–20; Asst Director of Railways, GHQ Constantinople and simultaneously Mil. Director, Anatolian and Baghdad Rly and Pres. Inter-Allied Rly Commission in Turkey, 1920–23; Manager and Dir Anatolian Rly Co., rep. interests of Anglo-Turkish Trust Co., and Dir Port of Haidar Pasha and Mersina, Tarsus, Adana Rly Co., 1923–27; reported on transport conditions in Italy, 1928; organised Indian Roads and Transport Develt Assoc., 1929–39; Member, Bombay Leg. Council and Indian Central Leg. Assembly (Delhi and Simla); served on various Govt Transport cttees and confs; served with Transportation Directorate, GHQ Middle East, Cairo, 1940–41; Dir-Gen., Iraqi State Railways, Baghdad, 1941–50; temp. Amir Al Liwa' (Maj.-Gen.) Iraq Army. Silver Jubilee Medal, 1935; Coronation Medal, 1937. *Address:* 5 Hickman's Close, Lindfield, Sussex. *Died* 31 *March* 1983.

**SMITH, Sir Henry (Thompson)**, KBE 1962; CB 1957; *b* 25 Feb. 1905; *y s* of late Ralph Smith, Gateshead; *m* 1929, Jane Harrison (*d* 1982),

*y d* of late Robert Wilson, Seahouses; three *d*. *Educ:* Sunderland Road School, Gateshead; London School of Economics. Post Office: Boy messenger, 1918; Sorting-clerk and telegraphist, 1922; Customs and Excise: Clerical officer, 1928; Officer, 1932; Asst Principal, 1934; Air Ministry: Principal, 1940; Asst Secretary, 1944; Assistant Under-Secretary of State, 1953–58; Deputy Under-Secretary of State, 1958–64; Dep. Under-Sec. of State (Air Force Dept), Min. of Defence, 1964–65, retd. *Recreations:* woodwork, gardening. *Address:* 130 Wantage Road, Wallingford, Oxfordshire OX10 0LU. *T:* Wallingford 36330. *Died* 4 *Oct.* 1986.

**SMITH, Herbert Cecil**, CBE 1945; BSc; MBOU; *b* Tunbridge Wells, Kent, 27 Jan. 1893; *m* 1925, Jane Bell Blair; one *s* one *d*. *Educ:* Eastbourne College; Edinburgh University. Joined Indian Forest Service in Burma, 1915; served with 1/70th Burma Rifles in India, Egypt and Palestine, 1917–19. Continued as a Forest Officer in Burma until May 1942; on Reconstruction with Govt of Burma in Simla till June 1945; returned to Burma as Chief Forest Officer in the Civil Affairs Service (Burma); retired from Indian Forest Service, 1946. *Address:* Hazel Cottage, Maypole, Rockfield, Gwent. *Died* 1 *Oct.* 1981.

**SMITH, Dr Herbert Williams**, FRS 1980; FRCVS, FRCPath; Agricultural and Food Research Council's Research Worker, Department of Microbiology, Houghton Laboratory (formerly Houghton Poultry Research Station), Cambridgeshire, since 1971 (Head of Department 1971–84); *b* 3 May 1919; *s* of Herbert Harry Smith and Ida Elizabeth Williams; *m* 1942, Kathleen Margaret Mary Bezant; one *s* two *d*. *Educ:* Pontypridd Grammar Sch.; London Univ. (PhD 1947; DSc 1957; DipBact 1948). FRCVS 1953; FRCPath 1970. Wellcome Res. Fellow, London Sch. of Hygiene and Trop. Medicine, 1945–49; Head, Dept of Pathology and Bacteriology, Livestock Res. Stn of Animal Health Trust, 1949–71. *Recreations:* gardening, work. *Address:* 7 Quaker Close, Kings Ripton, Huntingdon, Cambs PE17 2NP. *T:* Abbots Ripton 294. *Died* 16 *June* 1987.

**SMITH, Sir Hubert S.;** *see* Shirley-Smith.

**SMITH, Captain Hugh D.;** *see* Dalrymple-Smith.

**SMITH, Sir (James) Eric**, Kt 1977; CBE 1972; FRS 1958; ScD; Secretary, Marine Biological Association of the UK, and Director Plymouth Laboratory, 1965–74; *b* 23 Feb. 1909; *er s* of Walter Smith and Elsie Kate Smith (*née* Pickett); *m* 1934, Thelma Audrey Cornish (decd); one *s* one *d*. *Educ:* Hull Grammar School; King's College, London. Student Probat., Plymouth Marine Biol Lab., 1930–32; Asst Lecturer: Univ. of Manchester, 1932–35; Univ. of Sheffield, 1935–38; Univ. of Cambridge, 1938–50; Prof. of Zoology, Queen Mary Coll., Univ. of London, 1950–65 (Vice-Principal, 1963–65). Trustee, British Museum (Natural History), 1963–74, Chm. Trustees, 1969–74. Pres., Soc. for History of Nat. History, 1984–; Member: Council, Royal Soc., 1962–63 and 1972–74 (Vice-Pres., 1973–74); Senate, Univ. of London, 1963–65; Scientific Advisory Committee, British Council; Science Research Council, 1965–67; Nature Conservancy, 1969–71; Royal Commn, Barrier Reef, 1970; Adv. Bd for the Research Councils, 1974–77. Pres., Devonshire Assoc., 1980–81. Fellow: King's Coll., London, 1964; Queen Mary College, 1967; Plymouth Polytechnic, 1977. Hon. Associate, Natural Hist. Mus., 1981. Hon. DSc Exeter, 1968. Gold Medal, Linnean Soc., 1971; Frink Medal, Zoological Soc., 1981. *Publications:* various on marine biology, embryology, nervous anatomy and behaviour. *Recreations:* walking, gardening. *Died* 3 *Sept.* 1990.

**SMITH, James Stewart**, CMG 1955; Nigerian Administrative Service, retired; *b* 15 Aug. 1900; 4th *s* of late Charles Stewart Smith, HM Consul-General at Odessa; *m* 1955, Rosemary Stella Middlemore, *er d* of late Dr and Mrs P. T. Hughes, Bromsgrove, Worcs. *Educ:* Marlborough; King's College, Cambridge. Entered Nigerian Administrative Service, 1924; Senior District Officer 1943; Resident 1945; Senior Resident 1951; retired 1955. Papal Order of Knight Commander of Order of St Gregory the Great, 1953. *Recreations:* gardening, watching cricket, chess. *Address:* Davenham, Graham Road, Malvern, Worcs. *T:* Malvern 68667. *Club:* United Oxford & Cambridge University. *Died* 13 *Feb.* 1987.

**SMITH, Maj.-Gen. Jeremy Michael S.;** *see* Spencer-Smith.

**SMITH, Kenneth Manley**, CBE 1956; FRS 1938; DSc, PhD; formerly Director Virus Research Unit, Agricultural Research Council, Cambridge; Hon. Fellow, Downing College, Cambridge; *b* Helensburgh, Scotland, 1892; *m* 1923, Germaine Marie Noël (French); one *s*. *Educ:* Dulwich College; Royal College of Science. Served European War; Senior Lecturer and Adviser in Agricultural Entomology, University of Manchester. Vis. Prof., Dept of Botany, Univ. of Texas, Austin, 1964–69. *Publications:* A Textbook of Agricultural Entomology; Recent Advances in the Study of Plant Viruses; Plant Viruses, 6th edn 1977; A Textbook of Plant Virus Diseases, 3rd edn, 1972; The Virus; Life's Enemy; Beyond the Microscope; Virus-Insect Relationships, 1976; contributions to scientific journals. *Recreation:* gardening. *Address:* 73A Sytch Lane, Wombourne, Wolverhampton WV5 0LB.

*Died 11 June 1981.*

SMITH, Kenneth Shirley, MD, BSc London, FRCP; Lieutenant-Colonel RAMC 1942; Hon. Physician and Cardiologist, Charing Cross Hospital and to the London Chest Hospital; formerly: Chief Medical Officer Marine and General Mutual Life Assurance Society; Consulting Physician, Samaritan Free Hospital for Women; Staff Examiner in Medicine, University of London; Examiner in Medicine, Conjoint Board; *b* 23 Jan. 1900; *s* of E. Shirley Smith; *m* 1929, Alice Mary Hoogewerf; one *s* two *d. Educ:* London University; Middlesex Hospital (Senior Scholar). BSc, 1st Class Hons in Physiology, London, 1923; formerly House Physician, Casualty Medical Officer and Medical Registrar Middlesex Hospital; also Resident Medical Officer, Nat. Hosp. for Diseases of the Heart, 1927; Pres., British Cardiac Soc. Member, Assoc. of Physicians of Great Britain. Editor, British Heart Journal. Organizing Secretary, First European Congress of Cardiology, London, 1952. Served with 1st Army in N Africa, later with CMF in Italy, Greece and Austria (despatches 1943). Gold Staff Officer, Coronation of King George VI. *Publications:* Contributor to British Encyclopædia of Medical Practice, 1937; Papers on cardiological and pulmonary subjects in British Heart Journal, American Heart Journal, Quarterly Journal of Medicine, Lancet, British Medical Journal, Practitioner, etc. *Recreation:* water colour. *Address:* 5 Asmun's Hill, Hampstead Garden Suburb, NW11. *T:* 01-455 2706.

*Died 29 Jan. 1987.*

SMITH, Sir Laurence Barton G.; *see* Grafftey-Smith.

SMITH, Sir Leonard (Herbert), Kt 1982; CBE 1977 (MBE 1963); Deputy Treasurer, Liberal Party, since 1972; *b* 28 May 1907; *s* of Herbert Thomas and Harriett Smith; *m* 1943, Ruth Pauline Lees; two *d. Educ:* King's Sch., Chester. Active member of Liberal Party, 1922–; Sec. and Agent, Chester Div., 1929–39; Chief Agent, 1949–51; Foundn Officer, Liberal Party Orgn, 1946–49; Sec., Campaign Fund, 1948–50; Mem., Party Council, 1952–67 (Hon. Mem., 1967–); Hon. Treasurer, 1967–68; Vice-Pres., 1968; Dep. Chm., Fund Raising Cttee, 1980–; Pres., Eastern Reg., 1982– (Hon. Treasurer, 1972–80). Social Policy Exec., Booker McConnell Ltd, 1957–72. Member: Exec. and Council, Royal Commonwealth Soc. for the Blind, 1957– (Appeal Dir, 1951–57); British Cttee, World Prevention of Blindness Campaign, 1975–82; Exec. Cttee, West India Cttee, 1959–71; Hon. Sec., British Caribbean Assoc., 1958–; Hon. Secretary and Treasurer: London Cttee, English Harbour Restoration Fund, 1959–67; Sir Frank Worrell Commonwealth Meml Fund, 1968–; Hon. Treasurer, Women Caring Trust, 1972–; Jt Chm., Appeal Cttee, E-SU, 1975–. Mem. Council, Football Assoc., 1970–. JP Middlesex, subseq. City of London, 1963–77; Mem., City of London Adv. Cttee, 1965–77, Inner London Adv. Cttee, 1968–77, for appointment of magistrates. *Address:* Fen Farmhouse, Buxhall, Stowmarket, Suffolk IP14 5DG. *T:* Rattlesden 370. *Clubs:* National Liberal (Chm., 1972–), English-Speaking Union, MCC.

*Died 30 Sept. 1989.*

SMITH, Michael James B.; *see* Babington Smith.

SMITH, Michael Wharton; food journalist, television presenter and cookery book writer, since 1970; *b* 24 April 1927; *s* of Fred and Helena Smith; *m* 1952, Elisabeth Hamilton Downs (marr. diss. 1968); one *s* one *d. Educ:* Wakefield Grammar School; Ecole Hotelière, Lausanne (School diploma in Hotel Admin.). Food journalist, broadcaster and TV presenter with BBC Pebble Mill at One, 1976–86; Food Correspondent, Homes and Gardens, 1980–; Cookery Correspondent, Daily Telegraph, 1986–; participator in numerous TV films; restaurateur and designer. Glenfiddich Award for man contributing most to educn in food and wine, 1982. *Publications:* Fine English Cookery, 1973; Best of British Cookware, 1975; Cooking with Michael Smith, 1981; Michael Smith's Complete Recipe Collection from BBC Pebble Mill, 1982; The Homes and Gardens Cook Book, 1983; A Cook's Tour of Britain, 1984; New English Cookery, 1985; Michael Smith Entertains, 1986; The Afternoon Tea Book, 1986; Handbook for Host, 1987; The Glyndebourne Picnic Book, 1988; articles in magazines. *Recreation:* classical music. *Address:* 4 Woodside Road, Kingston upon Thames KT2 5AT. *T:* 01-546 0603. *Club:* Guild of Food Writers.

*Died 20 Jan. 1989.*

SMITH, (Newlands) Guy B.; *see* Bassett Smith.

SMITH, Patrick Wykeham M.; *see* Montague-Smith.

SMITH, Raymond; *see* Smith, F. R. S.

SMITH, Reginald Arthur; journalist and author; writer on education, religion, politics and social relations; *b* 23 July 1904; *s* of late Arthur and late Clara Smith, Burton-on-Trent; *m* 1931, Doris Fletcher Lean; one *s* one *d. Educ:* Victoria Road and Guild Street elementary schools, Burton-on-Trent. Junior Asst, Burton-on-Trent public library, 1918–21; reporter, Burton Daily Mail, Burton-on-

Trent, 1921–30; sub-editor, Sheffield Mail, 1930–31; editor Westmorland Gazette, Kendal, 1931–34; reporter and special corresp Manchester Guardian, 1934–43; editor: Manchester Guardian Weekly, 1943–47; British Weekly, 1947–50; managing editor, Liberal Party publications, 1951–60; Sec., Friends' Temperance and Moral Welfare Union, 1960–75 (Hon. Sec., 1975–77); Personal Asst to Ernest Bader, Scott-Bader Commonwealth, 1960–62; Sec., Soc. for Democratic Integration in Industry, 1961–63; Chm. of the Religious Weekly Press Group, 1950–51. Mem. of Soc. of Friends. *Publications:* Can Conscience be Measured?, 1940; Towards a Living Encyclopaedia, 1942; King of Little Everywhere, 1942; A Liberal Window on the World, 1946; Industrial Implications of Christian Equality, 1949; (joint editor with A. R. J. Wise) Voices on the Green, 1945. *Address:* Walnut, Albury Heath, Guildford, Surrey GU5 9DG. *Club:* National Liberal.

*Died 20 March 1985.*

SMITH, Reginald John, CVO 1954; *b* 21 Aug. 1895; *o s* of late John Smith, Hardwicke, Gloucestershire; *m* 1921, Irene Victoria Hauser; two *d. Educ:* Sir Thomas Rich's School, Gloucester. Joined Metropolitan Police, 1915; served Royal Artillery, France and Flanders, 1917–19; rejoined Met. Police, 1919; Sgt, 1920; Inspector, 1932; Supt 1940; Assistant Chief, British Police Mission to Greece, 1945–46; Deputy Commander, 1946; Commander, 1947–58. King's Police Medal, 1945, for distinguished service during Flying Bomb attack. Chevalier, The Order of Dannebrog, 1951; OStJ. *Recreations:* cricket, bowls.

*Died 8 Nov. 1981.*

SMITH, Hon. Sir Roderick Philip, Kt 1978; Hon. Mr Justice Smith; a Judge of the High Court, Queen's Bench Division, since 1978; Presiding Judge of the North Eastern Circuit, since 1980; *b* 29 April 1926; *s* of John Philip Smith and Hettie Smith (née Mayall); *m* 1957, Jean Rodham Hudspith; two *s* two *d. Educ:* Newcastle upon Tyne Royal Grammar Sch.; Merton Coll., Oxford. BA 1950. Served Royal Navy, 1945–47. Called to the Bar, Middle Temple, 1951; Bencher, 1978. QC 1966; Recorder: of Sunderland, 1967–70; of Newcastle upon Tyne, 1970–71; Dep. Chm., Durham QS, 1967–71; a Circuit Judge, 1972–78. *Recreations:* cricket, gardening. *Address:* Oaklands Manor, Riding Mill, Northumberland. *Club:* MCC.

*Died 12 April 1981.*

SMITH, Ronald Parkinson; *see* Parkinson, Norman.

SMITH, Sir Rowland; *see* Smith, Sir Alexander R.

SMITH, Col Rupert Alexander A.; *see* Alec-Smith.

SMITH, Rupert Rawden R.; *see* Rawden-Smith.

SMITH, Stanley G.; *see* Graham Smith.

SMITH, Sydney, CBE 1957; *b* 2 Nov. 1900; *s* of John Ickringill Smith and Annie Shields Smith (née Hutton); *m* 1st, 1926, Claudia Jane Warburton (*d* 1947); two *s*; 2nd, 1948, Sheina Baird Wright. *Educ:* Belle Vue Sch., Bradford, Yorkshire; Bradford Technical Coll. Dep. Engineer and Manager, Gas Dept, Dunfermline, Fife, 1928–35; Chief Asst Engineer and Works Manager, Bristol Gas Co., 1935–39; Engineer and Manager, Gas Dept, Paisley, Renfrewshire, 1939–45; General Manager and Chief Engineer, Romford Gas Co., Essex, 1945–49; Dep. Chairman, East Midlands Gas Board, 1949–52; Chairman: East Midlands Gas Board, 1952–56; The Scottish Gas Board 1956–65. Member, Scottish Tourist Board, 1965–69. *Publications:* contrib. to technical journals. *Recreations:* motoring, photography, golf, fishing. *Address:* Eastfield, Erskine Road, Gullane, East Lothian EH31 2DR. *T:* Gullane 842287.

*Died 13 Feb. 1981.*

SMITH, Alderman Sydney Herbert, MA; *b* 27 April 1885; *s* of late Charles Edward Smith and Emma Hedges, of London, Woodbridge, Suffolk, and Aylesbury, Bucks. *Educ:* Ruskin Coll.; St Catherine's, Oxford Univ. (Hons graduate). Member Hull City Council, 1923–70; Hon. Alderman; Lord Mayor, 1940–41; Hon. Freeman of Hull, 1968. MP (Lab) Hull, South-West, 1945–50. Life Mem., Court of Hull University. Former Chairman, Hull Education Cttee and Hull Housing and Town Planning Cttee. Hon. LLD Hull, 1967. Queen Marie of Roumania's Cross for Services, 1917. *Address:* 16 Southfield, Hessle, North Humberside HU13 0EX. *T:* 648979.

*Died 12 June 1984.*

SMITH, Prof. Sir Thomas (Broun), Kt 1981; QC Scotland 1956; DCL Oxon, 1956; LLD Edinburgh, 1963; FRSE 1977; FBA 1958; Professor Emeritus of Scots Law, Edinburgh University, 1980; General Editor, The Laws of Scotland: Stair Memorial Encyclopædia, since 1981; *b* 3 Dec. 1915; 2nd *s* of late J. Smith, DL, JP, and Agnes Smith, Symington, Lanarkshire; *m* 1940, Ann Dorothea, *d* of late Christian Tindall, CIE, ICS, Exmouth, Devon; one *d* (one *s* one *d* decd). *Educ:* High Sch. of Glasgow; Sedbergh Sch.; Christ Church, Oxford (MA). Boulter Exhibitioner, 1st Class Hons School of Jurisprudence, 1937; Eldon Scholar, 1937; Edinburgh Univ.; 1st Class and Certificate of Honour English Bar Final, Called to English Bar by Grays Inn, 1938, Hon. Bencher,

1986. Served TA from 1937; War Service, 1939–46; BEF, Home Forces, Middle East and Central Mediterranean; London Scottish (Gordon Highlanders) and RA (Fd.); variously employed on regimental and intelligence duties and at School of Infantry; Lieut-Colonel (despatches); Lieut-Colonel (TA) Gordon Highlanders, 1950; OC Aberdeen University Contingent, Officers Training Corps, 1950–55; Hon. Colonel, 1964–73. Attached to Foreign Office, 1946–47. Examined by and admitted to Faculty of Advocates in Scotland, 1947. Professor of Scots Law, University of Aberdeen, 1949–58; Dean of Faculty of Law, 1950–53 and 1956–58; Prof. of Civil Law, University of Edinburgh, 1958–68, of Scots Law, 1968–72; Hon. Prof., 1972–80. Hon. Sheriff of Aberdeen, 1950 and of Lothians and Peebles, 1964; Member: Scottish Law Reform Cttee, 1954; Scottish Law Commn, part-time 1965–72, full-time, 1972–80. Director Scottish Universities Law Inst., 1960–72; Hon. Member: Council Louisiana State Law Inst., 1960; Law Soc. of Scotland, 1986; Mem., Academic Advisory Cttee, Universities of St Andrews and Dundee, 1964–; Ford Visiting Professor, Tulane Univ. (Louisiana), 1957–58; Visiting Lecturer, Cape Town and Witwatersrand Universities, 1958; Visiting Prof., Harvard Law Sch., 1962–63; Tagore Prof., Calcutta, 1977. Hon. Foreign Mem., Amer. Acad. of Arts and Sciences, 1969. Hon. LLD: Cape Town, 1959; Aberdeen, 1969; Glasgow, 1978. *Publications:* Doctrines of Judicial Precedent in Scots Law, 1952; Scotland: The Development of its Laws and Constitution, 1955; British Justice: The Scottish Contribution, 1961; Studies Critical and Comparative, 1962; A Short Commentary on the Law of Scotland, 1962; Property Problems in Sale, 1978; Basic Rights and their Enforcement, 1979; contribs to legal publications on Scottish, historical and comparative law. *Recreations:* reading, foreign travel. *Address:* 18 Royal Circus, Edinburgh EH3 6SS. *T:* 031–225 8306. *Clubs:* Naval and Military; New (Edinburgh).                                    *Died 15 Oct.* 1988.

**SMITH, Rt. Rev. Thomas Geoffrey Stuart;** *b* 28 Feb. 1901; *s* of late Rev. Albert James Smith and late Amy Florence Smith; *m* 1930, Barbara Agnes Read; two *s* one *d. Educ:* Felsted Sch.; Jesus Coll., Cambridge; Ridley Hall, Cambridge. BA 1924; Carus Prize, 1924; MA 1927. Deacon 1925, Priest 1926, Southwark; Curate of St Mary Magdalene, Bermondsey, 1925–28; Chaplain of Ridley Hall, Cambridge, 1928–30; Examining Chaplain to Bishop of Chelmsford, 1929–30 and 1960–62. Vice-Principal, Diocesan Theological Instn, and Missionary, Kottayam, S India, 1930–39; Archdeacon of Mavelikkara, 1939–47; consecrated Bishop of North Kerala (Church of S India), 1947; resigned, 1953. Vicar of Burwell, 1954–60; Rector of Danbury, 1960–66; Assistant Bishop of Chelmsford, 1961–66; Hon. Canon of Chelmsford, 1961–66; Rector of Swithland, 1966–73; Asst Bishop of Leicester, 1966–73; Hon. Canon of Leicester, 1966–72; Canon Emeritus, 1977. Select Preacher, University of Cambridge, 1957. *Publication:* (in Malayalam) The Prison Epistles of St Paul, A Commentary, 1938. *Address:* 3 Ulverscroft Road, Loughborough, Leics LE11 3PU. *T:* Loughborough 67882.                                    *Died 8 Dec.* 1981.

**SMITH, Thomas I.;** *see* Irvine Smith.

**SMITH, Walter Campbell,** CBE 1949; MC; TD; MA, ScD; *b* 30 Nov. 1887; 2nd *s* of late George Hamilton Smith, Solihull, Warwickshire; *m* 1936, Susan, *y d* of late John Finnegan, Belfast; one *s* one *d. Educ:* Solihull; Corpus Christi, Cambridge. Wiltshire Prize, Cambridge Univ., 1909; Assistant, Dept of Minerals, British Museum, 1910; Deputy Keeper, 1931–37; Deputy Chief Scientific Officer, British Museum (Natural History), 1948–52; also Keeper of Minerals, 1937–52; Non-resident Fellow Corpus Christi, Cambridge, 1921–24; Honorary Secretary, Geological Society of London, 1921–33 (Murchison Medallist, 1945), President, 1955–56, Hon. Mem., 1982; General Secretary, Mineralogical Society, 1927–38, President, 1945–48; President, geological section, British Assoc., 1950; Governor, Royal Holloway Coll., 1922–43, representing Cambridge University; served in the Artists' Rifles, 1910–35 and 1939–42; European War, France, 1914–18 (MC, despatches twice, 1914 Star); Acting Lieut-Colonel, 1918; Brevet Lieut-Colonel, 1935; Second-in-Command, 163 OCTU (The Artists' Rifles), 1939–41. *Publications:* numerous papers on minerals, rocks and meteorites. *Address:* Roof Tops, Back Lane, Goudhurst, Kent.                                    *Died 6 Dec.* 1988.

**SMITH, Walter Riddell,** CB 1973; FRAgS 1971; FIBiol; Welsh Secretary, Ministry of Agriculture, Fisheries and Food, 1975–78; *b* 18 Sept. 1914; *s* of John Riddell Smith and Ethel Smith (*née* Liddell); *m* 1942, Janet Henderson Mitchell; one *s* one *d. Educ:* Durham Univ. NDA 1936; BSc(Agric.) Dunelm, 1936. Record Keeper: Cockle Park, Northumberland, 1936–37; School of Agriculture, Durham, 1937–39; Asst Agricultural Organiser, Northumberland CC, 1939–42; Animal Husbandry Officer, Northumberland War Agric. Exec. Cttee, 1942–47; joined Nat. Agric. Adv. Service, 1948; Livestock Adviser: WR, 1948–52; Eastern Region, 1952–55; Wales, 1955–61; Dep. Regional Director, Yorks and Lancs, 1961–64; Regional Director, Northern Region, 1964–66; Dir, Nat. Agricultural Adv. Service, 1967–71; Dep. Dir-Gen., Agricultural Develt and Adv. Service, 1971–75. President: Univ. of Newcastle

upon Tyne Agricultural Soc., 1969; British Grassland Soc., 1971–72; NPK Club, 1971; Nat. Sheep Assoc., 1978–82. *Publications:* contributions to press, popular agric. and technical journals. *Recreations:* gardening, sport, theatre. *Address:* 14 West Point, 49 Putney Hill, SW15. *T:* 01-788 2684.                                    *Died 9 Sept.* 1984.

**SMITH, William French;** Partner, Gibson, Dunn & Crutcher, 1946–80 and since 1985; Attorney General of the United States of America, 1981–85; *b* 26 Aug. 1917; *s* of William and Margaret Smith; *m* 1964, Jean Webb; three *s* one *d. Educ:* Univ. of Calif (AB); Harvard Univ. (LLB). Served USNR, 1942–46 (Lieut). Barrister, 1942. Member: US Adv. Commn on Internat. Educnl and Cultural Affairs, 1971–78; Stanton Panel on Internat. Inf., Educn and Cultural Relns, 1974–75. Mem., President's For. Intelligence Adv. Bd, 1985–; Pres., LA World Affairs Council, 1975–76 (Mem., Bd of Dirs, 1970–). Mem., Bd of Dirs, Amer.-China Soc., 1987–; Trustee: Henry E. Huntington Library and Art Gall., 1971–; Ronald Reagan Presidential Library Foundn, 1985– (Chm., 1987–); US Council for Internat. Business, 1989–; Nat. Trustee, Nat. Symphony Orchestra, Washington, 1975–. *Address:* Gibson, Dunn & Crutcher, 333 South Grand Avenue, Los Angeles, Calif 90071, USA.                                    *Died 29 Oct.* 1990.

**SMITH, Sir (William) Gordon,** 2nd Bt *cr* 1945; VRD; Lieut-Commander, RNR, retired; *b* 30 Jan. 1916; *s* of Sir Robert Workman Smith, 1st Bt, and Jessie Hill (*d* 1978), *yr d* of late William Workman, Belfast; *S* father, 1957; *m* 1st, 1941, Diana Gundreda, *d* of late Major C. H. Malden, Aberdeenshire; 2nd, 1958, Diana Goodchild; two *s. Educ:* Westminster; Trinity Coll., Cambridge (BA). Called to Bar, Inner Temple, 1939. Served War of 1939–45 as Lieut, RNVR (despatches). *Recreation:* yachting (Winner, International Dragon Gold Cup, 1961). *Heir: s* Robert Hill Smith, *b* 15 April 1958. *Address:* 15 Cadogan Court, Draycott Avenue, SW3 3BX; (seat) Crowmallie, Pitcaple, Aberdeenshire. *Clubs:* Royal Yacht Squadron; New (Edinburgh).
                                    *Died 20 May* 1983.

**SMITH-MARRIOTT, Sir Ralph George Cavendish,** 10th Bt, *cr* 1774; retired Bank Official; *b* 16 Dec. 1900; *s* of late George Rudolph Wyldbore Smith-Marriott and of Dorothy Magdalene, *d* of Rev. John Parry; *S* uncle, 1944; *m* 1st, Phyllis Elizabeth (*d* 1932), *d* of Richard Kemp (late Governor HM Prison, Bristol); two *s* one *d*; 2nd, 1933, Doris Mary (*d* 1951), *d* of R. L. C. Morrison, Tenby, Pembs; 3rd, 1966, Mrs Barbara Mary Cantlay. *Educ:* Cranleigh Sch., Surrey. Bristol Univ. OTC, 1918. *Recreations:* tennis, golf, cricket. *Heir: s* Hugh Cavendish Smith-Marriott [*b* 22 March 1925; *m* 1953, Pauline Anne, *d* of F. F. Holt, Bristol; one *d*]. *Address:* 28a Westover Road, Westbury-on-Trym, Bristol. *T:* Bristol 503797.
                                    *Died 16 Oct.* 1987.

**SMITH-RYLAND, Sir Charles Mortimer Tollemache,** KCVO 1989; Lord-Lieutenant of Warwickshire since 1968; *b* 24 May 1927; *s* of Charles Ivor Phipson Smith-Ryland and Leila Mary Tollemache; *m* 1952, Hon. Jeryl Marcia Sarah Gurdon, *d* of Hon. Robin Gurdon; two *s* three *d. Educ:* Eton. Lt, Coldstream Guards, 1945–48; Reserve, Warwickshire Yeomanry. Warwickshire: CC, 1949; DL, 1955; Alderman, 1958; Vice-Chm. CC, 1963; Chm. CC, 1964–67; Vice-Chm. Police Authority, 1966–68; Chm., Warwickshire and Coventry Police Authority, 1969–74; High Sheriff, 1967–68. Chm. Council, RASE, 1976–. KStJ 1968. *Recreations:* hunting, shooting, golf. *Address:* Sherbourne Park, Warwick. *T:* Barford 624255. *Clubs:* White's; Leamington Tennis.                                    *Died 14 Nov.* 1989.

**SMITHERS, Donald William,** CB 1967; retired; *b* 21 Aug. 1905; *s* of William John and Mary Smithers, Portsmouth, Hants; *m* 1929, Kathleen Margery Gibbons; three *s* one *d. Educ:* Portsmouth; Royal Naval Coll., Greenwich. Asst Constructor until 1937, then Constructor, Chatham; Principal Ship Overseer, 1939–44; Constructor Captain to C-in-C Mediterranean, 1944–47; Chief Constructor: Admiralty, 1947–52; Portsmouth, 1952–54; Singapore, 1954–56; Asst Dir of Dockyards, 1956–58; Manager HM Dockyard, Chatham, 1958–61; Director of Dockyards, 1961–67; retd 1967. CEng; FRINA; RCNC. *Address:* Chevithorne, Greenway Lane, Bath. *T:* Bath 311093.                                    *Died 10 Sept.* 1986.

**SMOUT, David Arthur Lister,** QC 1975; His Honour Judge Smout; a Circuit Judge (Official Referee), since 1983; *b* 17 Dec. 1923; *s* of Sir Arthur Smout and Hilda Smout (*née* Follows); *m* 1957, Kathleen Sally, *d* of Dr J. L. and Mrs N. M. Potts, Salisbury; two *s* two *d. Educ:* Leys Sch.; Clare Coll., Cambridge (MA, LLB); Birmingham Univ. (LLM). Served War, F/O, RAFVR, 1943–45. Cecil Peace Prize, 1948. Admitted solicitor, 1949; called to Ontario Bar, 1949. Lectr, Osgoode Hall, Toronto, 1949–53, Vis. Prof., 1977. Called to English Bar, Gray's Inn, 1953; Midland and Oxford Circuit, 1953–83. Dir, Murex Ltd and associated cos, 1954–67. Bar Council, 1958–62; prosecuting counsel, DTI, 1967–75; Dep.-Chm., Lines QS (parts of Holland), 1968–71; a Recorder of the Crown Court, 1972–83. *Publications:* Chalmers, Bills of Exchange, 13th edn, 1964; (with B. E. Basden) Department of Trade Investigations: Bernard Russell Ltd, 1975; Blane Ltd, 1975. *Recreations:* walking the

Chilterns and Cotswolds, gardening, Canadiana. *Address:* Long Swan Cottage, Haddenham, Aylesbury HP17 8AB. *Club:* Garrick.
*Died 7 May 1987.*

**SMYTH, Rev. Canon Charles Hugh Egerton,** MA, FRHistS; Fellow of Corpus Christi College, Cambridge, 1925–32 and since 1937; *b* Ningpo, China, 31 March 1903; *s* of Richard Smyth, MD; *m* 1934, Violet, *e d* of Rev. Canon Alexander Copland, Forfar. *Educ:* Repton; Corpus Christi College, Cambridge (Scholar); Wells Theological Coll. 1st class, Historical Tripos, Part 1, 1923, and Part 2, 1924; Thirlwall Medal and Gladstone Prize, 1925. Tutor and Lectr in History, Harvard Univ., USA, 1926–27; Deacon, 1929; Priest, 1930; University Lecturer in History, Cambridge, 1929–32 and 1944–46; Curate of St Clement's, Barnsbury, Islington, 1933–34; of St Saviour's, Upper Chelsea, 1934–36; of St Giles', Cambridge, 1936–37. Birkbeck Lecturer in Ecclesiastical History, Trinity College, Cambridge, 1937–38; Dean of Chapel, Corpus Christi College, 1937–46; Hon. Canon of Derby and Chaplain to Bishop of Derby at the University of Cambridge, 1938–46; Select Preacher, Oxford, 1941–43 and 1965; Canon of Westminster and Rector of St Margaret's, Westminster, 1946–56; Hon. Canon and Prebendary of Nassington in Lincoln Cathedral, 1965–79; Canon Emeritus of Derby Cathedral, 1977–, of Lincoln Cathedral, 1979–. Editor of the Cambridge Review, 1925 and 1940–41. *Publications:* Cranmer and the Reformation under Edward VI, 1926; The Art of Preaching (747–1939), 1940; Simeon and Church Order (Birkbeck Lectures), 1940; Religion and Politics, 1943; The Friendship of Christ, 1945; Dean Milman, 1949; Church and Parish (Bishop Paddock Lectures), 1955; Good Friday at St Margaret's, 1957; Cyril Forster Garbett, Archbishop of York, 1959; The Two Families, 1962; The Church and the Nation, 1962. *Address:* Corpus Christi College, Cambridge.
*Died 29 Oct. 1987.*

**SMYTH, Brig. Rt. Hon. Sir John (George),** 1st Bt *cr* 1955; VC 1915; MC 1920; PC 1962; *b* 24 Oct. 1893; *e s* of W. J. Smyth, Indian Civil Service; *m* 1920, Margaret, *d* of late Charles Dundas, ICS, Sialkot; one *s* one *d* (and two *s* decd, of whom *e s* killed in action 1944); *m* 1940, Frances Read, *d* of late Lieut-Colonel R. A. Chambers, OBE, IMS. *Educ:* Repton; Sandhurst. Entered Army, 1912; served European War, 1914–15 (despatches, VC, Russian Order of St George); Senussi Campaign, Western Egypt, 1915–16; Mohmand Expedition, India, 1916; Afghan War, 1919; Waziristan Frontier Expedition, 1919–20 (despatches, MC); Mesopotamia Insurrection, 1920–21 (despatches); Operations on NW Frontier, 1930 (despatches); Mohmand Operations, 1935 (despatches); Brevet-Major, 1928; Brevet Lieut-Colonel, 1933; Colonel, 1936; Instructor, Staff College, Camberley, 1931–34; Comdt 45th Rattrays Sikhs, 1936–39; GSO1, 2nd London Division, 1939–40; Commander 127 Inf. Bde in operations with BEF in France and Belgium (despatches); Acting Maj.-Gen. 1941; raised 19th Division in India; Comd 17th Division in Burma at time of Japanese invasion; retired, Nov. 1942; Hon. Brig. 1943. Military Correspondent: Kemsley newspapers, 1943–44; Daily Sketch and Sunday Times, 1945–46; Lawn Tennis Correspondent: Sunday Times, 1946–51; News of the World, 1956–57. Author, Wimbledon Programme articles, 1947–73. Comptroller Royal Alexandra and Albert School, 1948–63; Governor: Gypsy Road and West Norwood Secondary Schs, 1947–49; Strand and West Norwood Secondary Schools, 1949–51; St Martin's High School for Girls, 1950–52; Dragon School, Oxford, 1953–66; Queen Mary's Hosp., Roehampton, 1956–62. Exec., Returned Brit. POW Assoc., 1946–51. First Chm. Victoria Cross Assoc., 1956–71 (Centenary of the Victoria Cross), Life Pres. 1966; Vice-Pres. Not Forgotten Assoc., 1956; Pres. S London Branch Burma Star Assoc., 1957–; Vice-Pres. Distinguished Conduct Medal League, 1957, Pres. 1958–70; Director Creative Journals Ltd, 1957–63. Govt Apptd Trustee, Far East POW and Internee Fund, 1959–61; Hon. Vice-Pres. Far Eastern POW Federation, 1960; President Old Reptonian Society, 1960 and 1961; Vice-President: Dunkirk Veterans Assoc., 1963–; Internat. Lawn Tennis Club of GB, 1966. Contested (C) Wandsworth Central, 1945. MP (C) Norwood Div. of Lambeth, 1950–66; Parly Sec., Min. of Pensions, 1951–53; Jt Parly Sec., Min. of Pensions and Nat. Insce, 1953–55. Freeman of City of London in Worshipful Co. of Farriers, 1951; Master of Farriers' Co., 1961–62. *Publications:* Defence Is Our Business, 1945; The Western Defences (ed and introd) 1951; Lawn Tennis, 1953; The Game's the Same, 1956; Before the Dawn (story of two historic retreats), 1957; Paradise Island (children's adventure story), 1958; The Only Enemy (autobiography), 1959; Trouble in Paradise, 1959; Ann Goes Hunting (children's book), 1960; Sandhurst (A History of the Military Cadet Colleges), 1961; The Story of the Victoria Cross, 1962; Beloved Cats, 1963; Blue Magnolia, 1964; (with Col Macaulay) Behind the Scenes at Wimbledon, 1965; Ming (the story of a cat family), 1966; The Rebellious Rani (a story of the Indian Mutiny) 1966; Bolo Whistler (biography), 1967; The Story of the George Cross, 1968; In This Sign Conquer (The Story of the Army Chaplains), 1968; The Valiant, 1969; Will to Live: the story of Dame Margot Turner, 1970; Percival and the Tragedy of Singapore, 1971; Jean Borotra: the Bounding Basque, 1974; Leadership in

War, 1939–1945, 1974; Leadership in Battle, 1914–1918, 1975; Great Stories of the Victoria Cross, 1977; Milestones: a memoir, 1979; *plays:* Burma Road (with Ian Hay), 1945; Until the Morning (with Ian Hay), 1950. *Heir: g s* Timothy John Smyth, MB BS (NSW) [*b* 16 April 1953; *m* 1981, Bernadette, *d* of Leo Askew; one *s*]. *Address:* 807 Nelson House, Dolphin Square, SW1A 3PA. *Clubs:* All England Lawn Tennis, International Lawn Tennis Clubs of Britain, USA and France.
*Died 26 April 1983.*

**SMYTHE, Henry James Drew-,** MC; TD; MS, MD (London); FRCS; MMSA; FRCOG; late Hon. Consulting Gynæcologist United Bristol Hospitals and Southmead General Hospital; late Gynæcologist, Weston-super-Mare and Burnham Hospitals; Colonel RAMCT; *b* 1 June 1891; *s* of Frank Thompson Smythe and Ada Josephine Drew; *m* 1914, Enid Audrey Cloutman (*d* 1971); two *s. Educ:* Taunton School; Bristol Medical School; London Hospital. Qualified 1913; House Surgeon and House Physician Bristol Children's Hospital, 1913–14; House Surgeon Bristol General Hospital, 1914; served European War, 1914–19; also served War of 1939–45; House Surgeon Royal Infirmary, 1919; Demonstrator of Anatomy, Royal Free Hospital for Women, 1921; Post-Graduate Course London Hospital, 1921–22; Surgical Registrar, Bristol General Hospital, 1923; Asst Gynæcologist, 1925; Professor of Obstetrics, University of Bristol, 1934–51. Liveryman Society of Apothecaries; Freeman of City of London. *Publications:* various in Practitioner, Bristol Med. Chir. Jl, Jl of Obst. of British Empire, etc; Operative Obstetrics (Butterworth's Modern Trends), 1949. *Recreations:* Rugby football, hockey, tennis. *Address:* 2 Charlton Close, Charlton Kings, Cheltenham, Glos. *T:* Cheltenham 25117.
*Died 19 Aug. 1983.*

**SMYTHE, Sir Reginald Harry,** KBE 1971; Chairman, NZ Maritime Holdings Ltd; Deputy Chairman: Tasman Co. Ltd; Union Steam Ship Co. Ltd; *b* 2 May 1905; *s* of Reginald Harry Smythe; *m* 1930, Colleen Valmar, *d* of George Mobberley; one *s. Educ:* Auckland Grammar Sch.; FCIS. Accountant to: Morris Duncan & Gylls, 1922–24; Smith Wylie Co. Ltd, 1924–30; Asst Sec., 1930–32, Sec., 1932–35, NZ Perpetual Forests; NZ Forest Products Ltd: Sec., 1935–60; Dir, 1954–77; Gen. Manager, 1960–63; Man. Dir, 1963–73; Chm., 1973–77; former Chairman: D. Henry & Co. Ltd; Carter Kumeu Ltd; Fibre Products NZ Ltd; NZ Paper Mills Ltd. Member: Salvation Army Adv. Bd (Auckland); Bd of Mental Health Foundn. JP 1948. *Recreation:* gardening. *Address:* 178 Remuera Road, Auckland 5, New Zealand.
*Died 4 April 1981.*

**SNAITH, Group Captain Leonard Somerville,** CB 1952; AFC 1933; retired; *b* 30 June 1902; *s* of David Somerville Snaith; *m* 1931, Joyce Edith Taylor; two *s. Educ:* Carlisle Cathedral Sch. Commnd, 1927; Comd 83 Sqdn, 1937–40; service in: Iraq, 1934–36; USA (Test flying), 1940–41; Egypt, Italy, Palestine, Aden, 1945–47. Schneider Trophy Team, 1931; Commandant Empire Test Pilot School, 1948–50; Comdg Officer, Experimental Flying, Royal Aircraft Establishment, Farnborough, 1950–52; retired from RAF, 1952. DL Beds, 1961–69. *Address:* Pyghtle Cottage, Wilden, Bedford. *Club:* Royal Air Force.
*Died 6 Sept. 1985.*

**SNAITH, Rev. Norman Henry,** DD; *b* 21 April 1898; *s* of John Allen Snaith and Mary Ann (*née* Bunn); *m* 1925, Winifred Howson Graham (*d* 1981); one *s* two *d. Educ:* Paston Sch., North Walsham; Duke's Sch., Alnwick; Manchester Grammar Sch.; Corpus Christi and Mansfield Colls, Oxford. Open Mathematical Schol., Corpus Christi, Oxon, 1917; BA Hons Maths 1920, MA 1924, DD 1948, Oxford. Junior Kennicott Hebrew Schol., 1924, Senior Kennicott Hebrew Schol., 1925. Entered Methodist Ministry, 1921. Tutor in Hebrew and Old Testament subjects, Wesley College, Headingley, Leeds, 1936–61; Principal, 1954–61. Pres., Soc. for Old Testament Study, 1957; Vis. Prof. United Theol Coll., Bangalore, 1957. Pres., Methodist Conf., 1958–59. Speaker's Lectr in Biblical Studies, Oxford, 1961–65. Hon. DD Glasgow, 1952; Hon. LittD Leeds, 1961. *Publications:* Studies in the Psalter, 1934; Have Faith in God, 1935; The Distinctive Ideas of the Old Testament, 1944; Study Notes on Bible Books, 1945–54; The Jewish New Year Festival, 1948; The Jews from Cyrus to Herod, 1949; I believe in . . ., 1949; Hymns of the Temple, 1951; New Men in Christ Jesus, 1952; Mercy and Sacrifice, 1953; Commentary on Amos, Hosea and Micah, 1956; Editor: Hebrew Bible (for British and Foreign Bible Society), 1958; Leviticus and Numbers, New Century Bible, 1966; The Book of Job, 1968; The God that never was, 1971. *Address:* Norwood, 14 Park Road, Ipswich, Suffolk IP1 3ST. *T:* Ipswich 211261.
*Died 4 March 1982.*

**SNEDDEN, Rt. Hon. Sir Billy (Mackie),** KCMG 1978; PC 1972; QC (Australia); barrister and company director; Federal Member of Parliament for Bruce (Victoria), Commonwealth of Australia, 1955–83; Speaker, House of Representatives, 1976–83; *b* 31 Dec. 1926; *s* of A. Snedden, Scotland; *m* 1950, Joy; two *s* two *d. Educ:* Univ. of Western Australia (LLB). Barrister, admitted Supreme Ct of Western Australia, 1951; admitted Victorian Bar, 1955. Australian Govt: Attorney-General, 1963–66; Minister for

Immigration, 1966–69; Leader of the House, 1966–71; Minister for Labour and Nat. Service, 1969–71; Treasurer, 1971–72; Leader of the Opposition, 1972–75; Leader, Parliamentary Liberal Party, 1972–75 (Dep. Leader, 1971–72). Chm., Standing Cttee of Conf. of Commonwealth Speakers and Presiding Officers, 1978–81. National Patron, Young Liberal Movement, 1980–82. *Recreation:* tennis. *Address:* Owen Dixon Chambers, 205 William Street, Melbourne, Victoria 3000, Australia. *Clubs:* Melbourne, Melbourne Scots.

*Died 27 June* 1987.

**SNELL, Ven. Basil Clark;** Archdeacon of St Albans, 1962–73, then Archdeacon Emeritus; *b* 2 Feb. 1907; *s* of Charles Clark Snell, Vicar of Littlehampton; *m* 1933, Isobel Eills Nedeham Browne (*d* 1975); two *d. Educ:* King's School, Canterbury; Queens' College, Cambridge. Curate of Crosthwaite, Keswick, 1933–35; Chaplain of Aldenham School, 1935–40; Chaplain, Loretto Sch. and Army Chaplain, 1940–47; Rector of Tattingstone, Suffolk, 1947–55; Residentiary Canon of St Edmundsbury, 1955–58; Dir of Religious Education: Dio. of St Edmundsbury and Ipswich, 1947–58; Dio. of St Albans, 1958–68; Archdeacon of Bedford, 1958–62. *Recreations:* golf, gardening. *Address:* Glebe House, Melbourn, Royston, Herts.

*Died 12 June* 1986.

**SNELL, Rt. Rev. Geoffrey Stuart;** Assistant Bishop, Diocese of St Albans, since 1985; *b* 25 Oct. 1920; *s* of Charles James and Ellen Snell; *m* 1948, Margaret Lonsdale Geary; two *s* one *d. Educ:* Exeter School; St Peter's College, Oxford (MA 2nd cl. Hons PPE). Called to the Bar, Inner Temple, 1957. UK Civil Service, 1937–39. Served Army, 1939–46, Major, Supplies and Transport. University, 1946–49; Overseas Admin. Civil Service, 1950–54; Managing Governor, Gabbitas-Thring Educational Trust, 1954–61. Ridley Hall, Cambridge, 1961; London Coll. of Divinity, 1962; Deacon and priest, Church of England, 1962; Curate, Emmanuel Church, Northwood, 1962–63; Fellow, Central College of the Anglican Communion, Canterbury, 1964–68; Founder/Director, Christian Organisations Research and Advisory Trust, 1968–75, of Africa, 1975–77; Bishop Suffragan of Croydon, 1977–85; Bishop to the Forces, 1977–84. *Publication:* Nandi Customary Law, 1955. *Recreations:* music, travel. *Address:* 41 The Dell, St Albans, Herts AL1 4HF.

*Died 8 July* 1988.

**SNELL, William Edward,** MD; FRCP; Consultant Physician Superintendent, Colindale Chest Hospital, 1938–67; Demonstrator in Tuberculosis, St Bartholomew's Hospital Medical College, 1948–67; Consultant Chest Physician, Napsbury and Shenley Hospitals, 1963–67; *b* 16 Aug. 1902; *er s* of late S. H. Snell, MD; *m* 1934, Yvonne Creagh Brown; two *s* one *d. Educ:* Stubbington House; Bradfield College; Corpus Christi College, Cambridge (Exhibitioner and Prizeman); University College Hospital. MA Cambridge; BSc Hons London; MD; FRCP; DPH. Tuberculosis Scholarship Tour, Canada and USA, 1930. Formerly: Pres. Brit. Tuberculosis Assoc., 1955–57; Chairman: NW Metropolitan Thoracic Soc.; Metropolitan Branch, Soc. of Med. Supts; Editorial Cttee TB Index; Member: Management Cttees, Hendon and Chelsea Groups of Hosps; Brit. Tuberculosis Research Cttee; Examiner to Gen. Nursing Council. Mem. Council (twice Vice-Pres.), History of Medicine Section, RSM. *Publications:* articles in medical press relating to tuberculosis and chest disease, accidents to patients and history of medicine. *Recreations:* gardening, sailing, collecting ship models and prints; late part owner 15 ton ketch Craignair; severe polio, Nov. 1918, ended football and cricket, etc. *Address:* Yewden Manor, Hambleden, Henley-on-Thames, Oxon. *T:* Henley-on-Thames (0491) 571351. *Clubs:* Keyhaven Yacht, Cambridge University Cruising, etc. *Died 25 Oct.* 1990.

**SNELUS, Alan Roe,** CMG 1960; retired as Deputy Chief Secretary, Sarawak (1955–64); *b* 19 May 1911; *s* of John Ernest Snelus, late of Ennerdale Hall, Cumberland; *m* 1947, Margaret Bird Deacon-Elliott; one *s* one *d. Educ:* Haileybury Coll.; St Catharine's Coll., Cambridge. Barrister, Gray's Inn, 1934. Joined Sarawak Civil Service as an Administrative Officer, 1934; Actg Chief Sec., 1958–59; Officer Administering the Government of Sarawak, March-April 1959. *Recreations:* gardening and contemplation. *Address:* 115A Hansford Square, Combe Down, Bath, Avon.

*Died 22 April* 1990.

**SNOW, Lady;** *see* Johnson, Pamela Hansford.

**SNYDER, John Wesley;** Chairman, Harry S. Truman Scholarship Foundation, Washington, DC; *b* 21 June 1895; *s* of Jerre Hartwell Snyder and Ellen Hatcher; *m* 1920, Evlyn Cook (*d* 1956); one *d. Educ:* Jonesboro Grade and High Sch.; Vanderbilt Univ. Various offices in Arkansas and Missouri banks, 1920–30; national bank receiver, office of Comptroller of the Currency, Washington, DC, 1930–37; in 1937 selected to head St Louis Loan Agency of RFC; and Exec. VP and Director of Defense Plant Corp., a subsidiary; early in 1943 resigned all Federal posts to become Exec. VP First National Bank of St Louis; Federal Loan Administrator, Washington, 30 April 1945; Dir of Office War Mobilization and Reconversion, July 1945–June 1946; Secretary of the Treasury,

United States, 1946–53; US Governor of International Monetary Fund and International Bank for Reconstruction and Development, 1946–53; Advr, US Treasury, 1955–69. Delegate International Financial Conferences: Mexico City, 1945–52; Rio de Janeiro, 1957; London, 1947; Paris, 1950–52; Ottawa, 1951; Rome, 1951; Lisbon, 1952. Served as Captain, Field Artillery, 57th Bde, during War, 1917–18; retired Colonel US Army. 1955. Member: Omicron Delta Kappa; American Legion; Reserve Officers' Association. Trustee, Harry S. Truman Memorial Library. Episcopalian. *Address:* Harry S. Truman Scholarship Foundation, 712 Jackson Place, NW, Washington, DC 2006, USA. *Clubs:* Missouri Athletic (St Louis); Metropolitan, Chevy Chase, Alfalfa, National Press (Washington); Toledo (Toledo, Ohio); Seabrook Island.

*Died 8 Oct.* 1985.

**SOAMES, Baron** *cr* 1978 (Life Peer), of Fletching in the County of E Sussex; **Arthur Christopher John Soames,** PC 1958; GCMG 1972; GCVO 1972; CH 1980; CBE 1955; *b* 12 Oct. 1920; *m* 1947, Mary, *y d* of Rt Hon. Sir Winston Churchill, KG, OM, CH, FRS and Baroness Spencer-Churchill, GBE; three *s* two *d. Educ:* Eton; Royal Military Coll., Sandhurst. 2nd Lieut, Coldstream Guards, 1939; Captain, 1942; served Middle East, Italy and France. Assistant Military Attaché British Embassy, Paris, 1946–47, MP (C) Bedford Division of Bedfordshire, 1950–66. Parliamentary Private Secretary to the Prime Minister, 1952–55; Parliamentary Under-Secretary of State, Air Ministry, Dec. 1955–Jan. 1957; Parliamentary and Financial Secretary, Admiralty, 1957–58; Secretary of State for War, Jan. 1958–July 1960; Minister of Agriculture, Fisheries and Food, 1960–64. Director: Decca Ltd, 1964–68; James Hole & Co. Ltd, 1964–68. Ambassador to France, 1968–72. A Vice-Pres., Commn of the European Communities, 1973–Jan. 1977. Chm., ICL (UK) Ltd, 1984–; Director: N. M. Rothschild & Sons Ltd, 1977–79; Nat. Westminster Bank Ltd, 1978–79. Governor of Southern Rhodesia, 1979–80. Lord President of the Council and Leader of the House of Lords, 1979–81. Pres., RASE, 1973. Hon. LLD St Andrews, 1974; Hon. DCL Oxon, 1981. Croix de Guerre (France), 1942; Grand Officier de la Légion d'honneur, 1972; Grand Cross of St Olav (Norway), 1974. Medal of the City of Paris, 1972. *Address:* House of Lords, SW1A 0PW. *Clubs:* White's, Portland.

*Died 16 Sept.* 1987.

**SODDY, Dr Kenneth;** Consulting Physician, University College Hospital, London, 1976 (Physician in charge, Children's and Adolescents' Psychiatric Department and Lecturer in Child Psychiatry, 1948–76); Hon. Lecturer in Child Development, University College, London, 1951–76; Hon. Consultant in Child Psychiatry, Royal Free Hospital, 1973–76; *b* 27 July 1911; *s* of Rev. T. E. Soddy, BA; *m* 1936, Emmeline (*d* 1972), *d* of H. E. Johnson; one *s* two *d*; *m* 1972, Mary, *d* of Canon N. S. Kidson, MC, MA. *Educ:* Taunton Sch.; University College, London; University College Hospital Medical School. MB, BS 1934; DPM 1937; MD 1938; FRCPsych (Foundn Fellow). Commonwealth Fund Fellowship in Child Guidance, 1938; Psychiatrist, London Child Guidance Clinic, 1939. Temp. Commn, RAMC, 1940; Specialist Psychiatrist (Major), 1941; Advisor in Psychiatry (Lieut-Colonel), AG's Dept, India Comd, 1943; Dep. Director, Selection of Personnel, India Comd, (Colonel), 1944; Hon. Lieut-Colonel, RAMC, 1946. Medical Director, National Assoc. for Mental Health, 1946; Psychiatrist, Tavistock Clinic, 1947; Psychiatrist, 1948, Med. Dir, 1953–58, Child Guidance Training Centre. Scientific Adviser, World Federation for Mental Health, 1961–64 (Hon. Secretary, 1948; Assistant Director, 1949; Scientific Director, 1958); Member, Expert Panel on Mental Health, World Health Organisation, 1949–77; Mem., St Lawrence's Hosp., Caterham, Management Cttee, 1962–74; Consultant: to WHO, 1950 and 1957; to UKAEA, 1964–74; to Nat. Spastics Soc., 1965–77; Pres., Inst. of Religion and Medicine, 1975–76 (Chm., 1964–71; Pro-Chm., 1971–74). Mem., Marriage Commn of Gen. Synod of C of E, 1975–78. Organist, St Michael's Church, Chagford. Member various Study Groups, etc; Hon. Mem. American Psychiatric Assoc., 1953–. Fellow, UCL, 1979. *Publications:* Clinical Child Psychiatry, 1960; (with R. F. Tredgold) Mental Retardation, 11th edn, 1970; (with Mary C. Kidson) Men in Middle Life, 1967; Editor: Mental Health and Infant Development, 2 vols, 1955; Identity; Mental Health and Value Systems, 1961; (with R. H. Ahrenfeldt) Mental Health in a Changing World, 1965; Mental Health and Contemporary Thought, 1967; Mental Health in the Service of the Community, 1967; many articles in British, American and internat. medical and sociological jls. *Recreations:* writing, organ playing, moor walking. *Address:* The Manor Cottage, Doccombe, Moretonhampstead, Devon TQ13 8SS. *T:* Moretonhampstead 40378. *Died 10 April* 1990.

**SOLLBERGER, Edmond,** FBA 1973; Keeper of Western Asiatic Antiquities, The British Museum, 1974–83 (Deputy Keeper, 1970–74); *b* 12 Oct. 1920; *s* of W. Sollberger and M.-A. Calavassy; *m* 1949, Ariane Zender; two *d. Educ:* Univ. of Geneva, LicLitt 1945; DLitt 1952. Asst Keeper of Archæology, Musée d'art et d'histoire, Geneva, 1949; Keeper, 1952; Principal Keeper, 1958; Actg-Dir, 1959; Privat-Docent for Sumerian and Akkadian, Faculty of Letters, Univ. of Geneva, 1956–61; Asst Keeper of Western Asiatic Antiquities, The British Museum, 1961. Member: Council and Exec. Cttee, British Sch. of Archaeology in Iraq, 1961–87; Council of Management, British Inst. of Archæology at Ankara, 1961–70, 1976–82; British Sch. of Archæology, Jerusalem, 1974–82; Governing Body, SOAS, 1975–80; Governing Council, British Inst. of Persian Studies, 1977–82. Corresp. Mem., German Archæological Inst., 1961. Hon. Mem., American Oriental Soc., 1977. Mem., Internat. Cttee for study of the texts from Ebla, Rome Univ., 1978–. *Publications*: Le Système verbal dans les inscriptions royales présargoniques de Lagash, 1952 (Geneva); Corpus des inscriptions royales présargoniques de Lagash, 1956 (Geneva); Ur Excavations Texts VIII: Royal Inscriptions, 1965 (London); The Business and Administrative Correspondence under the Kings of Ur, 1966 (New York); (with J. R. Kupper) Inscriptions royales sumériennes et akkadiennes, 1971 (Paris); Pre-Sargonic and Sargonic Economic Texts, 1972 (London); (with D. O. Edzard and G. Farber) Répertoire géographique des textes cunéiformes: vol. 1, Die Orts. und Gewässernamen der präsargonischen und sargonischen Zeit, Wiesbaden, 1977; The Pinches Manuscript, 1978 (Rome); Administrative Texts Chiefly Concerning Textiles, 1986 (Rome); numerous articles on Cuneiform and related studies in learned jls; jt editor: Littératures anciennes du Proche Orient, 1963–82 (Paris); Texts from Cuneiform Sources, 1965– (New York); Cambridge Ancient History, vols I-III (rev. edn), 1969–82; editor-in-chief, Royal Inscriptions of Mesopotamia, Toronto Univ., 1981–85. *Address*: 20 Manor Road, Richmond, Surrey TW9 1YB. *T*: 01–940 7698. *Died 21 June* 1989.

**SOLOMON**, (né Solomon Cutner), CBE 1946; pianist; *b* London, 9 Aug. 1902; *m* 1970, Gwendoline Byrne. First public appearance at Queen's Hall at age of eight, June 1910; frequent appearances till 1916 then studied in London and Paris; reappeared in London at Wigmore Hall, Oct. 1921, and has since toured in the British Isles, America, France, Germany, Holland, Italy, Australia, and New Zealand. Hon. LLD St Andrews; Hon. MusD Cantab. *Recreations*: golf, bridge, motoring. *Address*: 16 Blenheim Road, NW8.
*Died 22 Feb.* 1988.

**SOLOMON, Edwin**, CBE 1972; QPM 1967; DL; Chief Constable, West Midlands Constabulary, 1967–74; *b* 20 Sept. 1914; *s* of Richard and Jane Solomon, Co. Durham; *m* 1942, Susan Clarke; two *s*. *Educ*: The Grammar Sch., Chester-le-Street. Joined Metropolitan Police as Constable, 1934; served through ranks to Supt; Dep. Chief Constable, Newcastle upon Tyne, 1956; Chief Constable, Walsall County Borough, 1964. DL Staffs, 1969. *Recreations*: walking, fishing, gardening. *Address*: Catalan Cottage, Gibraltar Lane, Dunsley Road, Kinver, near Stourbridge, West Midlands. *T*: Kinver 2047. *Died 21 Aug.* 1985.

**SOLOVEYTCHIK, George Michael de**, MA (Oxon); author, journalist, and lecturer; *b* St Petersburg, Russia, 14 March 1902; *s* of late Michael A. de Soloveytchik, Chairman and Managing Director of the Siberian Bank of Commerce, and *g s* of Founder thereof; Resident in Great Britain since 1919 and naturalised British subject, 1934; unmarried. *Educ*: St Catharine's and The Reformation Schools, Petrograd; Queen's Coll., Oxford; Paris and Berlin Universities. Has travelled extensively all over Europe since tender age of one. Escaped from Soviet Russia to England, 1918; began to write and lecture while still at Oxford; frequent free-lance contributor to leading British and overseas newspapers and periodicals chiefly on international affairs, history and biography; Editor, Economic Review, 1926–27; Foreign Editor, Financial Times, 1938–39; business in City of London, 1925–36; Director of Publicity, Internat. Colonial Exhibition, Paris, 1931; Special adviser to exiled Belgian Govt in London, 1941–45; official lectr to HM Forces, 1940–45; delivered addresses to American Academy of Political and Social Science, and at Princeton, Yale, etc, 1944; numerous lecture tours in USA, Canada and Europe since 1946; special mission to Scandinavian countries on behalf of UNESCO, 1947; Visiting Lecturer, Graduate Inst. of International Studies, Geneva Univ., 1948–56, also at School of Economics, St Gallen. FJI; Member: RIIA, 1934–74; American Academy of Political and Social Science, 1944–74; Savage Club, 1934–82; Hon. Member International Mark Twain Society, USA. Officier, Légion d'Honneur; Kt Comdr 1st cl. with Star, Lion of Finland; Comdr Leopold II; Comdr, White Lion; 1st cl. Kt of the Vasa; 1st cl. Kt of St Olav; 1st cl. Kt of the Dannebrog; Officier Ordre de la Couronne; Officier, Order of Orange-Nassau; Officier, White Rose of Finland; Danish Liberation Medal, etc *Publications*: The Naked Year (Editor), New York, 1928; Ivar Kreuger—Financier, 1933; Potemkin—A Picture of Catherine's Russia, 1938; Ships of the Allies, 1942; Peace or Chaos, 1944; Russia in Perspective, 1946; Great Britain since the War (in Swedish), 1947; Switzerland in Perspective, 1954; Leu and Co.: Two Centuries of History in the Life of a Swiss Bank, 1955; Benelux, 1957; chapter on How Switzerland is really governed, in Swiss Panorama, 1963 (new edn 1974); chapters on Russia in Universal Encyclopædia. *Recreations*: travel, theatre, music, Russian ballet; art; also studying human

eccentricities and foibles. *Address*: 23 Enford Street, W1. *T*: 01-262 0340. *Club*: Savage. *Died 14 Oct.* 1982.

**SOMERS, Lady; (Finola)**, CBE 1950; *b* 1896; *d* of late Captain Bertram Meeking, 10th Hussars, and late Mrs Herbert Johnson; *m* 1921, 6th Baron Somers, KCMG, DSO, MC (*d* 1944); one *d*. *Educ*: home. Chief Commissioner, Girl Guides' Association, 1943–49. *Address*: Garden Cottage, Eastnor, Herefordshire. *T*: Ledbury 2305. *Died 6 Oct.* 1981.

**SOMERSET**, 18th Duke of, *cr* 1546; **Percy Hamilton Seymour**; Bt 1611; DL; Major, Wiltshire Regiment, retired; *b* 27 Sept. 1910; *e surv. s* of 17th Duke of Somerset, DSO, OBE, and Edith Mary (*d* 1962), *d* of W. Parker, JP, Whittington Hall, Derbyshire; *S* father, 1954; *m* 1951, Gwendoline Collette (Jane), 2nd *d* of late Major J. C. C. Thomas and Mrs Thomas; two *s* one *d*. *Educ*: Blundell's Sch., Tiverton; Clare Coll., Cambridge. BA 1933. DL Wiltshire, 1960. *Heir*: *s* Lord Seymour. *Address*: Maiden Bradley, Warminster, Wilts. *Clubs*: MCC, Army and Navy, British Automobile Racing. *Died 15 Nov.* 1984.

**SOMERSET, Brigadier Hon. Nigel FitzRoy**, CBE 1945; DSO; MC; *b* Cefntilla Court, Usk, Monmouthshire, 27 July 1893; 3rd *s* of 3rd Baron Raglan, GBE, CB; *m* 1922, Phyllis Marion Offley Irwin (*d* 1979), Western Australia; one *s* one *d*. *Educ*: King William's Coll., IOM; RMC Sandhurst. Served France with 1st Bn Gloucestershire Regt, 12 Aug. 1914 till wounded at the Battle of the Aisne, 15 Sept. 1914; 3 Dec. 1914, till wounded at Cuinchy, 12 May 1915; Mesopotamia, Oct. 1916–May 1919, comdg 14th Light Armoured Motor Battery (despatches thrice, DSO, MC); Bt Majority on promotion to Subst. Captain, 1918; Afghan War, 1919, with Armoured Motor Brigade (Medal and Clasp); ADC to Governor of South Australia, 1920–22; Assistant Military Secretary, Headquarters, Southern Command, India, 1926–30; Major 1933; Lieut-Colonel Comdg 2nd Bn The Gloucestershire Regt, 1938; served War of 1939–45 comdg 145 Inf. Bde (PoW 1940–45; despatches; CBE); Comdg Kent Sub District, 1946–47; Brig. Special Appt Germany, 1947–48; retired pay, 1949. *Address*: 8 Regency Close, Uckfield, East Sussex TN22 1DS.
*Died 7 Feb.* 1990.

**SOMERVILLE, Mrs (Katherine) Lilian**, CMG 1971; OBE 1958; FMA 1962; Director, Fine Arts Department, British Council, 1948–70; *b* 7 Oct. 1905; *d* of Captain Arthur George Tillard and Emily Katherine Close-Brooks; *m* 1928, Horace Somerville (*d* 1959); one *d*. *Educ*: Abbot's Hill; Slade School of Art, London. Painted until war. Joined British Council, 1941. Fellow, UCL, 1973. Hon. Dr, RCA, 1972. *Address*: The Studio, 16a Hill Road, NW8 9QG. *T*: 01–286 1087. *Died 15 Dec.* 1985.

**SOMMER, André D.**; *see* Dupont-Sommer.

**SONDHEIMER, Prof. Franz**, FRS 1967; PhD (London), DIC; Royal Society Research Professor, University College, London, since 1967; *b* 17 May 1926; *yr s* of Max and Ida Sondheimer; *m* 1958, Betty Jane Moss; one step *d* (decd). *Educ*: Highgate School; Imperial College of Science, London. Research Fellow, Harvard University, 1949–52; Associate Director of Research, Syntex SA, Mexico City, 1952–56; Vice-President, Research, 1961–63; Head of Organic Chemistry Department, Weizmann Institute of Science, Rehovoth, Israel, 1956–64; Rebecca and Israel Sieff Professor of Organic Chemistry, 1960–64; Royal Soc. Research Prof., Univ. of Cambridge, 1964–67; Fellow of Churchill Coll., Cambridge, 1964–67; Vis. Prof., Ohio State Univ., 1958, Rockefeller Univ., NY, 1972; Lectures: Andrews, Univ. of New South Wales, 1962; Edward Clark Lee, Univ. of Chicago, 1962; Tilden, Chem. Soc., 1965; Pacific Coast, 1969. Israel Prize in the Exact Sciences, 1960; Corday-Morgan Medal and Prize, Chem. Soc., 1961; Adolf-von-Bayer Medal, German Chem. Soc., 1965; Synthetic Organic Chemistry Award, Chem. Soc., 1973; Award for creative work in synthetic organic chemistry, Amer. Chem. Soc., 1976. For. Mem., German Acad. of Sciences, Leopoldina, 1966. *Publications*: scientific papers in chemical jls. *Recreations*: classical music, travel. *Address*: Chemistry Department, University College, 20 Gordon Street, WC1H 0AJ. *T*: 01-387 7050; 43 Green Street, W1Y 3FJ. *T*: 01-629 2816. *Died 11 Feb.* 1981.

**SONNEBORN, Prof. Tracy Morton**; Distinguished Professor Emeritus of Biology, Indiana University, Bloomington, Indiana, since 1976 (Distinguished Professor of Zoology, 1953–76); *b* 19 Oct. 1905; *s* of Lee and Daisy (Bamberger) Sonneborn; *m* 1929, Ruth Meyers; two *s*. *Educ*: Johns Hopkins Univ., Baltimore. Johns Hopkins University: Fellow, Nat. Research Coun., USA, 1928–30; Research Asst, 1930–31; Research Associate, 1931–33; Associate in Zoology, 1933–39; Indiana University: Associate Prof. in Zoology, 1939–43; Prof. of Zoology, 1943–53; Actg Chm., Div. of Biological Sciences, 1963–64. Foreign Mem., Royal Soc., London, 1964. Hon. Member: French Soc. of Protozoology, 1965; Amer. Soc. of Protozoologists, 1972; Genetics Soc. of Japan, 1976. Hon. DSc: Johns Hopkins Univ., 1957; Northwestern Univ., 1975; Univ.

of Geneva, 1975; Indiana Univ., 1978; Münster Univ., 1979. Newcomb-Cleveland Research Prize, Amer. Assoc. for Advancement of Science, 1946; Kimber Genetics Award, Nat. Acad. of Sciences, USA, 1959; Mendel Medal, Czechoslovak Acad. of Sciences, 1965. *Publications:* The Control of Human Heredity and Evolution, 1965; numerous chapters in books and articles in scientific jls on genetics, cell biology, micro-organisms. *Address:* 1305 Maxwell Lane, Bloomington, Indiana 47401, USA. *T:* Area 812-336-5796.                                    *Died 26 Jan.* 1981.

**SOPER, Dr Frederick George,** CBE 1950; FRSNZ 1949; FRIC 1936; Hon. FNZIC 1965; PhD 1924; DSc (Wales) 1928; Vice-Chancellor, University of Otago, Dunedin, NZ, 1953–63, retired; Emeritus Professor since 1964; Professor of Chemistry, University of Otago, 1936–53; *b* 5 April 1898; *m* 1st, 1921, Frances Mary Gwendolen Richardson; one *s* one *d*; 2nd, 1938, Eileen Louise Service. *Educ:* St Asaph Grammar Sch.; University College of North Wales, 1920. Lecturer, UCNW, 1921–36. Director NZ Woollen Mills Research Assoc., 1937-50; Pres. NZ Institute of Chemistry, 1947; Member of Council of Univ. of Otago, 1944–51, 1953–63; Dean of Faculty of Science, 1948–50; Member of Senate, Univ. of NZ, 1946–61. Served RA, 1916–19, and TA. Dep. Dir of Scientific Development (Chemical), DSIR (NZ), 1942–45; Member: Defence Science Advisory Cttee (NZ), 1942–53; NZ Science Deleg. to Roy. Soc. Empire Science Conf., London, 1946; Leader NZ Deleg. to Unesco Conf., Paris, 1951. Mem. NZ Med. Research Council, 1960–65; Vice-Pres., Roy. Soc. of NZ, 1962–63; Chm., NZ Nuffield Advisory Cttee, 1960–72; Pres. Dunedin Public Art Gallery Coun., 1963–66; Mem. Exec., NZ Wool Research Organisation, 1964–71 (Vice-Chm., 1966–71); Mem. Exec., Wool Industries Research Inst., 1957–68; Mem. UGC Research Cttee, 1964–74. Hon. DSc Otago, 1967. *Publications:* a number of papers in Journal of Chemical Society, mainly on mechanism of chemical reactions. *Recreations:* walking and gardening. *Address:* 6 Howard Street, Macandrew Bay, Dunedin, NZ. *T:* 761.130. *Club:* Fernhill (Dunedin).
                                    *Died* 1 *Jan.* 1982.

**SOPER, Dr J. Dewey;** naturalist, explorer; Canadian Wildlife Service, Department of Indian Affairs and Northern Development, Ottawa, retired Nov. 1952; *b* Guelph, Ont, 5 May 1893; *m* 1927, C. K. Freeman, Wetaskiwin, Alberta; one *s* one *d*. *Educ:* Alberta Coll. and Univ. of Alberta, Edmonton. Studied music 6 yrs; then took up science, specialising in ornithology and mammalogy, especially the latter; naturalist to the Canadian Arctic Expedition of 1923, visiting Greenland, Ellesmere, North Devon and Baffin Islands; engaged in biological research and exploration on Baffin Island for the Canadian Government, 1924–26; engaged in biological research, exploration and mapping of Foxe Land, Baffin Island, for Dept of the Interior, Canada, 1928–29 (resulting among other things in the discovery of the mysterious breeding grounds of the Blue Goose), for Dept of Interior, Lake Harbour region, Baffin Island, 1930–31, Wood Buffalo Park, Alta, and NWT, 1932–34; then transferred as Chief Federal Migratory Bird Officer for the Prairie Provinces. Bronze Plaque and framed Citation from Federal Govt for explorations in the Canadian Arctic, 1928; Achievements Award of Alberta Govt, 1972; Bronze Award and Citation of Northwest Territories Govt, for explorations, mapping and natural history res. in Canadian Eastern Arctic in the 20s and 30s, chiefly in Baffin Island, 1978. Hon. LLD Univ. of Alberta, 1960. *Publications:* 131, including The Weasels of Canada; Bird Life in the Alberta Wilds; Mammalian and Avian Fauna of Islay, Alberta; Mammals of Wellington and Waterloo Counties, Ontario; Birds of Wellington and Waterloo Counties, Ontario; Mammals of the Ridout Region, Northern Ontario; A Biological Reconnaissance of Nipissing and Timiskaming Districts, Northern Ontario; A Faunal Investigation of Southern Baffin Island; Discovery of the Breeding Grounds of the Blue Goose; The Blue Goose; Solitudes of the Arctic; Intimate Glimpses of Eskimo Life in Baffin Island; The Lake Harbour Region, Baffin Island; Notes on the Beavers of Wood Buffalo Park; Local Distribution of Eastern Canadian Arctic Birds; History, Range and Home Life of the Northern Bison; Mammals of Wood Buffalo Park; Birds of Wood Buffalo Park and Vicinity; Life History of the Blue Goose; The Mammals of Southern Baffin Island, NWT; Ornithological Results of the Baffin Island Expeditions of 1928–29 and 1930–31, together with more Recent Records; Mammals of the Northern Great Plains along the International Boundary in Canada; Observations on Mammals and Birds in the Rocky Mountains of Alberta; Field Data on the Mammals of Southern Saskatchewan; The Mammals of Manitoba; The Mammals of Alberta; The Mammals of Jasper National Park, Alberta; The Conquest of Pangnirtung Pass; The Mammals of Waterton Lakes National Park, Alberta; Kingnait Pass; Baffin Island; The Mysterious West Coast. *Recreations:* water-colour painting, reading and writing. *Address:* Strathcona Place, 7720-108 Street, Edmonton, Alberta, Canada.
                                    *Died* 2 *Nov.* 1982.

**SOPWITH, Sir Thomas Octave Murdoch,** Kt 1953; CBE 1918; Founder President, Hawker Siddeley Group Ltd (Chairman, 1935–63); *s* of Thomas Sopwith, MICE; *b* 18 Jan. 1888; *m* 1st, 1914,

Hon. Beatrix Mary Leslie Hore-Ruthven (*d* 1930), *d* of 8th Baron Ruthven; no *c*; 2nd, 1932, Phyllis Brodie (*d* 1978), 2nd *d* of late F. P. A. Gordon; one *s*. Founded the Sopwith Aviation Co. Ltd, Kingston-on-Thames, 1912; Chm., H. G. Hawker Engrg Co. Ltd, 1920. Chairman, 1925–27, Society of British Aircraft Constructors. *Recreations:* yachting, shooting, fishing. *Address:* Compton Manor, Kings Somborne, Hampshire. *Club:* Royal Yacht Squadron.
                                    *Died* 27 *Jan.* 1989.

**SOREL CAMERON, Brig. John,** CBE 1957; DSO 1943; DL; retired as Chief of Staff, Headquarters Scottish Command (Oct. 1958–60); ADC to the Queen, 1957–60; *b* 19 July 1907; *er s* of late Lt-Col G. C. M. Sorel Cameron, CBE and Mrs Sorel Cameron, Gorthleck, Inverness-shire; *m* 1937, Catherine Nancy, *yr d* of late Frank Lee, JP, Halifax, Yorks; one *d*. *Educ:* Wellington; RMC Sandhurst. Gazetted 2nd Lieut Queen's Own Cameron Highlanders, 1927; regimental service, 1927–40; served War of 1939–45 in Middle East, Sicily, NW Europe (wounded thrice, despatches twice); Staff Coll., 1940; Staff, 1940–42; comd: 5/7th Gordons, 1942; 5th Camerons, 1943; Staff, 1944–50; comd: 1st Camerons, 1951–53; 154 Highland Bde, 1953–55; Chief of Staff, British Commonwealth Forces in Korea, 1955–56; BGS, HQ Scottish Comd, 1957. DL Inverness, 1971–. *Recreations:* field sports, history. *Address:* 47 Drummond Road, Inverness, Scotland. *T:* Inverness 230029.
                                    *Died* 30 *May* 1986.

**SORN, Hon. Lord; James Gordon McIntyre,** MC; Senator of College of Justice in Scotland, 1944–63, retired; *b* 21 July 1896; *s* of late T. W. McIntyre, of Sorn; *m* 1923, Madeline (*d* 1954), *d* of late Robert Scott Moncrieff, Downhill; one *s* one *d*. *Educ:* Winchester; Balliol Coll., Oxford (BA); Glasgow Univ. (LLB). Served European War, 1914–18, Ayrshire Yeomanry, Captain 1917 (MC and bar, French Croix de Guerre); called Scottish Bar, 1922; KC 1936; Dean of the Faculty of Advocates, 1939–44. Hon. LLD Glasgow University. *Recreation:* fishing. *Address:* Sorn Castle, Ayrshire. *Club:* New (Edinburgh).                                    *Died* 1 *July* 1983.

**SORSBIE, Sir Malin,** Kt 1965; CBE 1956 (OBE 1942); *b* 25 May 1906; *s* of late Rev. William Frances Sorsbie and late Blanche Georgina Sorsbie; *m* Elizabeth McNeice (*d* 1955); *m* 1955, Constantine Eugenie (*d* 1988), *d* of late Albert Wheeler Johnston, Greenwich, Connecticut, USA; one step *d*. *Educ:* Brighton College; Manitoba University. Royal Canadian Mounted Police, 1926–29; RAF, 1930–35; Imperial Airways, 1936–39; BOAC, 1940–47; East African Airways (Gen. Manager), 1947–56. Chm., Munitalp Foundn, 1960–75. Life Fellow, RGS. KStJ. *Publications:* Dragonfly, 1971; Brandy for Breakfast, 1972. *Address:* PO Box 45337, Nairobi, Kenya. *T:* 749417 and 749515. *Clubs:* Carlton, Royal Air Force; RAF Yacht; Muthaiga Country, Nairobi (Nairobi); Mombasa (Mombasa).                                    *Died* 29 *Oct.* 1988.

**SOTERIADES, Antis Georghios;** Ambassador of Cyprus to Yugoslavia, concurrently accredited to Algeria and Sudan, 1979–83; retired, 1984; *b* 10 Sept. 1924; *m* 1962, Mona, *yr d* of Petros Petrides, Nicosia; one *s* one *d*. *Educ:* London Univ.; Inns of Court, London. Practising lawyer until 1956; joined patriotic Organization EOKA and fought British Colonialism in Cyprus, 1956–59; President of the first political party formed in Cyprus after independence, 1959; High Commissioner for Cyprus in the UK, 1960–66; Ambassador to Egypt, concurrently to Syrian Arab Republic, Iraq and Lebanon, 1966–78. Kt Order of St Gregory the Great (Vatican), 1963. *Address:* c/o Ministry of Foreign Affairs, Nicosia, Cyprus.
                                    *Died* 27 *May* 1988.

**SOUSTELLE, Jacques (Emile);** Commandeur, Légion d'Honneur, 1981; Hon. CBE; Member of French Academy, 1983; *b* 3 Feb. 1912; *m* 1931, Georgette Fagot. *Educ:* Ecole Normale supérieure, Paris; Univ. of Lyon. Agrégé de l'Université 1932, PhD 1937. Asst Dir, Musée de l'Homme, 1937; with Free French Forces in UK, 1940; Nat. Comr for Information in London, 1942; Head of French special services, Algiers, 1943–44; Governor of Bordeaux, 1945; Minister of Information and Colonies, 1945–46. Prof. of Sociology, Ecole des Hautes Etudes, 1951. Mem., Lyon Municipal Council, 1954–62, 1971–77. Mem. Nat. Assembly, 1945–46, 1951–59, 1973–78. Gov.-Gen. of Algeria, 1955–56; Minister of Information, 1958; Minister delegate to the Prime Minister, France, 1959–60. President: PACT Gp, Council of Europe, Strasbourg, 1976; Centro Universitario Europeo, Ravello, 1983; Member: NY Acad. of Scis; Instituto Mexicano de Cultura. FRAI. Order of Polonia Restituta, 1944; US Medal of Freedom, 1945; Hon. CBE, Great Britain, 1946; Comdr, Aztec Eagle (Mexico), 1978; Comdr, Nat. Order of Merit (Paraguay), 1984. *Publications:* Mexique, terre indienne, 1935; Envers et contre tout, 1947; La Vie quotidienne des Aztèques, 1955 (Daily Life of the Aztecs, 1962); Aimée et souffrante Algérie, 1956; L'espérance trahie, 1962; Sur une route nouvelle, 1964; L'Art du Mexique ancien, 1966 (Arts of Ancient Mexico, 1967); Archæologia Mundi: Mexique, 1967 (Archæologia Mundi: Mexico, 1967, repr. as The Ancient Civilizations of Mexico, 1969); Les quatre soleils, 1967 (The Four Suns, 1971); La longue marche d'Israël, 1968 (The

Long March of Israel, 1969); Vingt-huit ans de Gaullisme, 1968; Les Aztèques, 1970; Lettre ouverte aux victimes de la décolonisation, 1973; L'Univers des Aztèques, 1979; Les Olmèques, 1979; Les Maya, 1982; papers and memoirs on anthropology and ethnology, in learned jls. *Address:* 85 avenue Henri-Martin, 75116 Paris, France. *Died 6 Aug.* 1990.

**SOUTHAM, Alexander William,** CBE 1948; *b* 6 Jan. 1898. *Educ:* Oundle; Christ's College, Cambridge (MA 1925). Served European War, 1915–19 (despatches, foreign orders). British Petroleum Co. Ltd, 1922–34; managed oil shale cos in Baltic States owned by Gold Fields of S Africa Ltd, 1934–40; various war work from 1939 in Europe and Middle East; joined British Element of Allied Commn for Austria, 1945; Dir, Economic Gp, and British Chm., Economic Directorate, 1946–48; Dir, Investigation and Research Div., Internat. Authority for Ruhr, 1949–52. Man. Dir, 1953–64, and Pres., 1958–64, British Newfoundland Corp. Ltd, Canada. *Address:* c/o Potchett Investment Ltd, 39th Floor, 1155 Dorchester Boulevard West, Montreal, Quebec, Canada H3B 3V2. *Clubs:* University, Royal Montreal Golf (Montreal); Rideau (Ottawa).
*Died 4 July* 1981.

**SOUTHAMPTON,** Barony of (*cr* 1780); title disclaimed by 5th Baron; *see under* FitzRoy, Charles.

**SOUTHBOROUGH,** 3rd Baron *cr* 1917; **Francis John Hopwood,** Kt 1953; retired as Managing Director "Shell" Transport & Trading Co., 1951–70 (Director, 1946–70); *b* 7 March 1897; *s* of 1st Baron Southborough, PC, GCB, GCMG, GCVO, KCSI and his 2nd wife, Florence Emily, *d* of late Lieut-Gen. Samuel Black; *S* half-brother (2nd Baron), 1960; *m* 1918, Audrey Evelyn Dorothy, *d* of late Edgar George Money; one *s* one *d. Educ:* Westminster School. Served European War, 1914–18, Sub-Lieut, RNVR, Admiralty and Foreign Office; seconded, 1917, to staff of Irish Convention in Dublin and later was Sec. to War Trade Advisory Cttee. Joined Royal Dutch Shell Group of Companies, 1919; Pres. Asiatic Petroleum Corporation, USA (also represented Petroleum Board), 1942–46; Managing Director The Shell Petroleum Co., and Bataafse Petroleum Maatschappij NV, 1946–57, retired. Mem., Oil Supply Adv. Cttee. Commander of the Order of Orange-Nassau. *Heir: s* Hon. Francis Michael Hopwood, late Lieut The Rifle Brigade [*b* 3 May 1922; *m* 1945, Moyna Kemp, *d* of Robert J. K. Chattey]. *Address:* Flat 3, 33 Chesham Place, SW1X 8HB. *T:* 01–235 8732. *Club:* Brooks's. *Died 4 Feb.* 1982.

**SOUTHBY, Sir (Archibald) Richard (Charles),** 2nd Bt *cr* 1937; OBE 1945; Lt-Col (retd), Rifle Brigade; *b* 18 June 1910; *s* of Sir Archibald Richard James Southby, 1st Bt, and Phyllis Mary (*d* 1974), *er d* of late Charles Henry Garton, Banstead Wood, Surrey; *S* father, 1969; *m* 1st, 1935, Joan Alice (marr. diss. 1947), *o d* of late Sir Thomas Bilbe-Robinson; one *s*; 3rd, 1964, Hon. Ethel Peggy (*d* 1978), *d* of 1st Baron Cunliffe and *widow* of Brig. Bernard Lorenzo de Robeck, MC, RA; 4th, 1979, Iris Mackay Robertson, *d* of late Lt-Col G. Mackay Heriot, DSO, RM, and *widow* of Brig. I. C. A. Robertson. *Educ:* Eton; Magdalen Coll., Oxford (MA). Medal of Freedom (US). *Heir: s* John Richard Bilbe Southby [*b* 2 April 1948; *m* 1971, Victoria, *d* of William James Sturrock; two *s* one *d*]. *Address:* 7 Bolus Avenue, Kenilworth, Cape, 7700, Republic of South Africa; Greystone House, Stone, Tenterden, Kent TN30 7JT. *T:* Appledore 400. *Died 4 April* 1988.

**SOUTHERN, Richard;** Theatre Consultant (private) since 1947; *b* 5 Oct. 1903; *o s* of Harry Southern and Edith (*née* Hockney); *m* 1933, Grace Kathleen Loosemore; two *d. Educ:* St Dunstan's College; Goldsmiths' Art School; Royal Academy of Art. Designed scenery, 1928–, for over fifty shows (Everyman Theatre, Cambridge Festival Theatre and various London theatres); also acted and stage-managed; specialized in study of stage technique and theatre architecture. Technical Lectr, Goldsmiths' College, 1932, London Theatre Studio, 1937, Royal Academy of Dramatic Art, 1945, Old Vic Theatre Centre, 1947; Theatre planning adviser to Arts Council, 1947; Director, Nuffield Theatre, Univ. of Southampton, 1964–66; Lectr, Drama Dept, Bristol Univ., 1959–60, and Special Lectr in Theatre Architecture, 1961–69, retired. Has planned various modern theatres and stages includ. Bristol Univ., 1951, Royal College of Art, 1952, Glasgow, 1953, Reading University, 1957, Nottingham, 1961, Southampton University, 1961, University Coll., London, 1967, also various reconstructions of historical theatres, Richmond, Yorkshire, 1950, King's Lynn, 1951, Williamsburg, Virginia, 1953. Hon. DLitt (Bristol), 1956. *Publications:* Stage Setting, 1937; Proscenium and Sightlines, 1939; The Georgian Playhouse, 1948; The Essentials of Stage Planning (with Stanley Bell and Norman Marshall), 1949; Changeable Scenery, 1952; The Open Stage, 1953; The Medieval Theatre in the Round, 1957; The Seven Ages of the Theatre, 1961; The Victorian Theatre, 1970; The Staging of Plays before Shakespeare, 1973; contrib. to specialist journals and encyclopædias. *Recreation:* figure drawing. *Address:* 37 Langham Road, Teddington TW11 9HF. *T:* 01–943 1979.
*Died 1 Aug.* 1989.

**SOUTHWELL, Sir (Charles Archibald) Philip,** Kt 1958; CBE 1953; MC 1918; Director, Kuwait Oil Co. Ltd, since 1946 (Managing Director, 1946–59); *b* 6 June 1894; *s* of late Dr Charles Edward Southwell, Stoke-on-Trent; *m* 1926, Mary Burnett (*d* 1981), *d* of Thomas Scarratt, Belmont Hall, Ipstones, Staffs; two *s. Educ:* Birmingham Univ. (BSc (Pet.)). President: Inst. of Petroleum, 1951–52; Oil Industries Club, 1953. Petroleum Technologist to Government of Trinidad, 1922–28; Manager, Oilfields and Geol Br., BP, 1930–44. Served European War, 1914–18, with RA (MC); War of 1939–45; temp. Lt-Col. Govt Cttee Business Training, 1945. Royal Society of Arts: Silver Medal, 1953; Council, 1958. Cadman Memorial Medal, Inst. of Petroleum, 1954; Hon. Fellow, 1959. Pres., Brown and Root (UK) Ltd, 1960–80 (Chm., 1960–78); Chm., and Highland Fabricators, 1968–80; Dir, Halliburton Gp of Cos. Liveryman, Company of Shipwrights. GCStJ; Dir-Gen. St John Ambulance, 1968. Comdr, Order of Cedar of Lebanon, 1958. *Publications:* on petroleum technology. *Recreation:* gardening. *Address:* Manor House, Tendring, Essex. *T:* Weeley 286. *Club:* Royal Thames Yacht. *Died 30 Nov.* 1981.

**SPAAK, Fernand Paul Jules,** Dr en droit; Chef de Cabinet to the President, Commission of the European Communities, since 1981; *b* 8 Aug. 1923; *s* of Paul-Henri Spaak and Marguerite Malevez; *m* 1953, Anne-Marie Farina; three *d. Educ:* Université Libre de Bruxelles (Dr en droit); Univ. of Cambridge (BA Econs). National Bank of Belgium, 1950–52; High Authority, European Coal and Steel Community, Luxembourg: Exec. Asst to Pres., Jean Monnet and to Pres., René Mayer, 1953–58; Dir, Cartels and Concentrations Div., 1958–60; Dir Gen., Supply Agency, Euratom, Brussels, 1960–67; Dir Gen. of Energy, Comm of European Communities, Brussels, 1967–75; Head, Delegn to USA, Commn of European Communities, 1976–80; Hd of Delegn for Enlargement Negotiations, EEC, 1980–81. *Address:* CEE, Rue de la Loi 200, 1049-Brussels, Belgium. *T:* (02) 735 00 40 (ext. 2255).
*Died 18 July* 1981.

**SPANSWICK, (Ernest) Albert (George),** JP; General Secretary, Confederation of Health Service Employees, since 1974; Member, TUC General Council, since 1977; *b* 2 Oct. 1919; *m* Joyce Redmore; one *s* two *d*. SRN, RMN. Regional Sec., Northern Region, Confedn of Health Service Employees, 1959; apptd National Officer, 1962; elected Asst General Secretary, 1969; elected General Secretary, 1973, and took up duties in July 1974. Chm., TUC Health Services Cttee, 1977–. JP Co. Surrey, 1970. *Recreations:* swimming, walking, fishing. *Address:* Confederation of Health Service Employees, Glen House, High Street, Banstead, Surrey SM7 2LH. *T:* Burgh Heath 53322. *Died 27 April* 1983.

**SPARKMAN, John J(ackson);** US Senator from Alabama, 1946–78; Chairman, Senate Committee on Foreign Relations, 1975–78; *b* 20 Dec. 1899; *s* of Whitten J. Sparkman and Julia Mitchell (*née* Kent); *m* 1923, Ivo Hall; one *d. Educ:* University of Alabama. AB 1921, LLB 1923, AM 1924; Phi Beta Kappa. Admitted to Alabama Bar, 1925; practised as Attorney, Huntsville, Ala, 1925–36; US Commissioner, 1930–31; Member of US House of Representatives, 1937–46; Democratic Nomination for Vice-Presidency, 1952. Chm., Senate Banking Cttee, 1967. Hon. degrees: Alabama; Spring Hill Coll., Ala; Athens Coll., Ala; Huntingdon Coll., Ala; Auburn; Seoul, Korea. Methodist. *Address:* 116 Jefferson Street South, Huntsville, Alabama 35801, USA. *Clubs:* 1925 F Street (Washington); Huntsville Country (Alabama).
*Died 16 Nov.* 1985.

**SPARKS, Joseph Alfred;** Mayor of the Borough of Acton, 1957–58; *b* 30 Sept. 1901; *s* of late Samuel and Edith Sparks; *m* 1928, Dora Brent; two *s. Educ:* Uffculm School and Central Labour College. Alderman of Borough of Acton and County of Middlesex, 1958–61; retired. Clerk Western Region, British Railways; President, London District Council NUR, 1934–45; Parliamentary Labour Candidate, Taunton, 1929, Chelmsford, 1931, and Buckingham, 1935. MP (Lab) Acton, 1945–Sept. 1959. Freeman of the Borough of Acton. *Publications:* A Short History of Dunteswell Abbey, 1969; A History of Sheldon, Devon, 1975; In the Shadow of the Blackdowns, 1978. *Address:* 10 Emanuel Avenue, W3. *T:* 01-992 2069.
*Died 12 Jan.* 1981.

**SPARROW, Rev. David Alan;** Vicar of All Saints', Margaret Street, since 1976; *b* 22 April 1936; *s* of William Albert Sparrow and Ella (*née* Wood). *Educ:* Finchley County Grammar Sch.; Pembroke Coll., Oxford; Lincoln Theological Coll. MA Oxon, MA Cantab. Assistant Curate of St Stephen with St John, Westminster, 1962–65; Chaplain to the Archbishop of Canterbury, 1966–67; Chaplain of St Catharine's Coll., Cambridge, 1967–76, Fellow, 1969–76. *Recreations:* music, squash. *Address:* 7 Margaret Street, W1. *T:* 01-636 1788. *Died 26 July* 1981.

SPEAR, (Augustus John) Ruskin, CBE 1979; RA 1954 (ARA 1944); artist; *b* 30 June 1911; *s* of Augustus and Jane Spear; *m* 1935, Mary Hill; one *s* one *d*. *Educ*: Brook Green School; Hammersmith School of Art; Royal College of Art, Kensington, under Sir William Rothenstein. Diploma, 1934; first exhibited Royal Academy, 1932; elected London Group, 1942; President London Group, 1949–50; Visiting teacher, Royal College of Art, 1952–77. Pictures purchased by Chantrey Bequest, Contemporary Art Society, Arts Council of Great Britain, and British Council. Exhibited work in Pushkin Museum, Moscow, 1957; has also exhibited in Paris, USA, Belgium, S Africa, Australia, NZ. Commissions include: Altar Piece for RAF Memorial Church, St Clement Danes, 1959; four mural panels for P&O Liner Canberra. Portraits include: Lord Adrian; Herbert Butterfield; Sir Stewart Duke-Elder; Sir Laurence Olivier as Macbeth (Stratford Memorial Theatre); Lord Chandos; Sir Ian Jacob; Sir Robin Darwin; Miss Ruth Cohen; Sir Eric Ashby; S. S. Eriks, KBE; Dr Ramsey, Archbishop of Canterbury; Sir Aubrey Lewis; Arthur Armitage; 5th Duke of Westminster; Sir Hugh Greene; Lord Goodman; Dr Charles Bosanquet; Sir James Tait; Sir John Mellor; Sir Geoffrey Taylor; Sir Peter Allen; Sir Maurice Bridgemen; Lord Butler of Saffron Walden; Sir Geoffrey Howe; Sir David Willcocks, CBE, MC; Prof. Dame Sheila Sherlock; Sir Cyril Clarke; Edward Ardizzone; Lucien Ercolani; Sir Ralph Richardson as Falstaff for NT (posthumous); Sir John Kendrew; portraits in National Portrait Gallery: Francis Bacon; Lord Wilson of Rievaulx; Lord Redcliffe-Maud; Sir Alan Herbert; Lord Hailsham; self-portrait. Visiting teacher, RCA, until 1976. *Relevant publication*: Ruskin Spear, by Mervyn Levy, 1985. *Address*: 60 British Grove, Hammersmith, W4. *T*: 01–741 2894.                      *Died* 9 *Jan*. 1990.

SPEARMAN, Sir Alexander Cadwallader Mainwaring, Kt 1956; *b* 1901; *s* of late Commander A. C. M. Spearman, Royal Navy; *m* 1928, Diana (marriage dissolved, 1951), *d* of Colonel Sir Arthur Doyle, 4th Bt; *m* 1951, Diana Josephine, *d* of Colonel Sir Lambert Ward, 1st Bt, CVO, DSO, TD; four *s* one *d*. *Educ*: Repton; Hertford College, Oxford. Contested Mansfield Div., Gen. Election, 1935, Gorton Div. of Manchester, By-Election, 1937; MP (C) Scarborough and Whitby, 1941–66, retd. PPS to President of the Board of Trade, 1951–52. *Address*: The Old Rectory, Sarratt, Herts. *T*: King's Langley 64733; 14 Cadogan Square, SW1. *T*: 01-235 1529. *Club*: Beefsteak.                                        *Died* 5 *April* 1982.

SPECTOR, Prof. Walter Graham; Professor of Pathology in the University of London at St Bartholomew's Hospital Medical College, since 1962; Consultant Pathologist, St Bartholomew's Hospital; Secretary, Beit Memorial Fellowships Advisory Board; *b* 20 Dec. 1924; *o s* of H. Spector, London; *m* 1957, June (marr. diss. 1977), *o d* of Col W. F. Routley, OBE, Melbourne, Australia; two *s*. *Educ*: City of London School; Queens' Coll., Cambridge; UCH Med. School (Graham Schol.). MB 1947, MA 1949, Cambridge; MRCP 1948; FRCP 1966; FRCPath 1972. Beit Memorial Fellow in Medical Research, 1951; Lecturer in Pathology, University College Hospital Med. School, 1953; Rockefeller Trav. Fellow, 1956; Litchfield Lectr, Univ. of Oxford, 1957; Sen. Lectr in Pathology, Univ. Coll. Hosp. Med. School, 1960. Vis. Research Fellow, Merton Coll., Oxford, 1982. Mem. Council, Imperial Cancer Res. Fund. Treas., Path. Soc. GB and Ireland. Editor-in-chief, Jl Path. *Publications*: An Introduction to General Pathology, 1977, 2nd edn 1980; numerous scientific papers and review articles in Pathology. *Recreation*: amateur sociology. *Address*: Department of Pathology, St Bartholomew's Hospital, West Smithfield, EC1A 7BE. *T*: 01-600 9000; 14 Islington Park Street, N1 1PU. *T*: 01-607 8903. *Club*: Garrick.                              *Died* 7 *Jan*. 1982.

SPEED, Marjorie Jane, OBE 1959; Matron, The Middlesex Hospital, London, W1, 1946–65; *b* 13 July 1903; *d* of F. C. Marriott, Kingston-on-Thames, Surrey; *m* 1972, James Grant Speed (*d* 1980). *Educ*: The Russell School; privately. Guy's Hospital: Nursing Training, 1928–32; Asst Matron, 1939–40; Matron, County Hosp., Orpington, 1940–46. Vice-President: The Royal Coll. of Nursing; National Florence Nightingale Memorial Cttee. *Recreations*: music, painting. *Address*: 45 Pelham Court, 145 Fulham Road, SW3 6SH.
                                              *Died* 22 *Oct*. 1982.

SPEIDEL, General Hans, Dr phil; Grosskreuz Militärverdienstorden, Württemberg Order of Merit (1914–18); Kt, Iron Cross, 1943; President, Foundation of Science and Politics, 1964–78; Hon. Professor, 1971; *b* Metzingen/Württemberg, 28 Oct. 1897; *m* 1925, Ruth Stahl; one *s* two *d*. *Educ*: Eberhard-Ludwig-Gymnasium of the Humanities, Stuttgart; Univs of Berlin and Tübingen, Technische Hochschule, Stuttgart. Ensign, Grenadier Regt, König Karl (5. Württ.) Nr 123, 1914; Gruppen Zug und Kompaniefuhrer, Battalion and Regimental Adjutant, Western Front, 1915–18; entered Reichswehr (3 years at Military Academy); during War of 1939–45 was successively Chief of Staff of Army Corps and Army (8) (Eastern Front), and of Field Marshal Rommel's Army Group (Western Front); arrested on Himmler's orders, 1944; released from Gestapo imprisonment at end of the War. Lecturer, Tübingen Univ. and Leibniz University Coll.; Military Adviser, Federal Govt, 1951;

Military Delegate-in-Chief to EDC (European Defence Community) and NATO negotiations, 1951–55; Commander-in-Chief of Combined German Forces, 1955–57; Commander Allied Land Forces, Central Europe, 1957–63; Special Counsellor to Federal Government, W Germany, 1963–64. Commander, US Legion of Merit, 1961; Grosses Verdienstkreuz BRD mit Stern und Schulterband; Ehrenburger, Stadt Metzingen, 1972. *Publications*: Invasion 1944 (a contribution to the fate of Rommel and the Reich), 1949; Zeitbetrachtungen, 1969; Aus unserer Zeit (memoirs), 1977; Editor and commentator on Vol. of Essays by Gen. Ludwig Beck, 1955; essays on Ernst Jünger, Theodor Heuss, Eugen Bircher, Gneisenau and Beck, etc. *Recreation*: study of history and literature. *Address*: Am Spitzenbach 21, Bad Honnef, Germany.
                                              *Died* 28 *Nov*. 1984.

SPENALE, Georges; Officier de la Légion d'Honneur; Palmes Académiques; Grand Officier de l'Ordre National Italien; Grand Officier de l'Ordre National de la Côte d'Ivoire; Commandeur de l'Ordre de l'Aigle du Mexique; Senator from Tarn, French Senate, since 1977; *b* Carcassonne, 29 Nov. 1913; *m* 1935, Carmen Delcayré; one *s* one *d*. *Educ*: Licencié en Droit; Diplômé de l'Ecole Nationale de la France d'outre-Mer. Economic Bureau, French Guinea, 1938–39; served War, with the colours, 1939–40 and 1943–45; Chief of District, Upper Volta, 1941–42; Inspector of Labour, Ivory Coast, 1942–43; Director of Cabinet for Fedn of Equatorial Africa, 1946–48; Chief of Information Service, Ivory Coast, 1949–50; Director of Cabinet, Fr. Cameroons, 1951–53, Sec.-Gen., 1953–54, acting High Comr, 1954–55; Ministry of France d'outre-Mer: Adj. Dir, 1955–56; Governor, 1956; Director, Cabinet of M Gaston Defferre (took part in framing Fundamental Law), 1956–57; High Comr in Togo (until Independence), 1957–60. Deputy from Tarn, French Nat. Assembly, 1962–77. European Parliament: Mem., 1964–79; Pres., Commn of Finances, 1967–75; Pres., Socialist Group, 1974–75; Pres., 1975–77: First Vice-Pres., 1977–79. Mayor of Saint-Sulpice, Tarn, 1965–; Vice-Pres., Regional Council, Midi-Pyrénées, 1975. Mem. Directing Cttee, Fr. Socialist Party, 1968–71. Holds decorations from African countries. *Address*: Faubourg Saint-Jean, 81370 Saint-Sulpice, France. *T*: 578003 (63).
                                              *Died* 20 *Aug*. 1983.

SPENCE, Allan William, MA, MD Cantab; FRCP; Hon. Consultant Physician: St Bartholomew's Hospital, since 1965; Luton and Dunstable Hospital, since 1965; King George Hospital, Ilford, since 1967; *b* 4 Aug. 1900; *s* of late William Ritchie Spence and Emma (*née* Allan), Bath; *m* 1930, Martha Lena (*d* 1981), *d* of late Hugh Hamilton Hutchison, JP, Girvan, Ayrshire; two *s*. *Educ*: King Edward's VI School, Bath; Gonville and Caius College, Cambridge; St Bartholomew's Hospital, London. Brackenbury Schol. in Medicine, 1926, Lawrence Research Schol. and Gold Medal, 1929–30, Cattlin Research Fell., 1938, St Bartholomew's Hosp.; Rockefeller Travelling Fellow, USA, 1931–32. House Phys., 1927, Demonstrator of Physiology, 1928–30, of Pathology, 1930–31, First Asst, 1933–36, Asst Dir of Med. Unit, 1936–37, St Bartholomew's Hospital; Physician St Bartholomew's Hosp., London, 1937–65; King George Hospital, Ilford, 1938–67; Luton and Dunstable Hospital, 1946–65; Hon. Consultant in Endocrinology to Army at Home, 1954–65; Med. Referee to Civil Service Commn, 1952–70; Physician on Med. Appeal Tribunal, DHSS, 1965–72; Member Medical Research Coun. Adv. Cttee: on Iodine Deficiency and Thyroid Disease, 1933–39; and on Hormones, 1937–41. Hon. Lt-Col, RAMC; service in North Africa and Greece as OC Med. Div., 97th Gen. Hosp., 1943–45. Mem. Assoc. of Physicians of Gt Brit.; Foundation Mem. Soc. for Endocrinology, to 1965; Fellow RSM, 1926–72 (Vice-Pres., Section of Med., 1949, Pres. Section of Endocrinology, 1951–52, Councillor, 1958–61); Foundn Mem. Internat. Soc. of Internal Medicine; Fellow Medical Soc. of London, 1937–72 (Councillor, 1957–60); Foundn Mem., London Thyroid Club; Mem., Physiological Soc., 1935–52; Emeritus Mem., Endocrine Society, USA, 1966. Examr in Medicine: Univ. of Cambridge, 1946–50; to Society of Apothecaries of London, 1947–52; in Therapeutics to University of London, 1953–57; to the Conjoint Examining Bd in England, 1955–59; to Fellowship of Faculty of Anæsthetists, RCS, 1964–66. Trustee, Peel Med. Res. Trust, 1961–85. Mem. of Editorial Bd, Jl of Endocrinology, 1956–63. Freeman of City of London; Member of Livery, Society of Apothecaries of London. *Publications*: Clinical Endocrinology, 1953 (translated into Spanish); articles to medical and scientific journals on endocrinological and general medical subjects. *Recreations*: reading, gardening; formerly rowing (Pres. Caius Boat Club, 1922–23). *Address*: Moorhouse Nursing Home, Tilford Road, Hindhead, Surrey GU26 6RA. *T*: Hindhead 4449. *Club*: Hawks (Cambridge).                              *Died* 28 *Feb*. 1990.

SPENCE, Henry Reginald, OBE; *b* 22 June 1897; *s* of James Henry Easton Spence and Gertrude Mary Hawke; *m* 1939, Eileen Beryl Walter; one *s* one *d*. Commissioned RFC 1915; with No. 16 Sqdn, 1916–17 and 12 Wing RAF, 1918 (under Ginger Mitchell). British Cross Country Ski Champion, Mürren, 1929. Was Area Commandant of ATC for North-East Scotland. MP (C) Central

Division, County of Aberdeen and Kincardine, 1945–50, West Aberdeenshire, 1950–59. *Recreations:* ski-ing, sailing, golf, shooting. *Address:* 11 Wynnstay Gardens, Allen Street, W8 6UP.
*Died* 11 *Sept.* 1981.

**SPENCE, John Deane;** MP (C) Ryedale, since 1983 (Sheffield, Heeley, 1970–74; Thirsk and Malton, 1974–83); civil engineering and building contractor; director of various companies connected with construction industry; *b* 7 Dec. 1920; *s* of George Spence, Belfast; *m* 1944, Hester Nicholson; one *s* one *d. Educ:* Queen's Univ. of Belfast. Mem., Public Relations and Organization Cttee, Building Industry, 1967; Nat. Pres., UK Commercial Travellers' Assoc., 1965–66. PPS to Minister of Local Govt and Develt, 1971–74; Mem., Speaker's Panel of Cttee Chairmen 1974–. Vice-Chm., Yorks Cons. Members Gp, 1979–84 (Hon. Sec., 1970–79); Hon. Sec., Cons. Back-benchers' Industry Cttee, 1971–72; Jt Hon. Sec., Cons. Back-benchers' Agriculture, Fisheries and Food Cttee, 1974–76, 1981–; Member: Select Cttee, Nationalised Industries, 1974–79; Select Cttee for Agric., 1979– (Chm., 1984–); Jt Chm., All-Party Scotch Whisky Industry Gp, 1979–; Chm., All-Party Management Gp, 1979–. Member: IPU, 1979–; CPA, 1979–. NFU; Country Landowners' Assoc.; Yorkshire Derwent Trust; Anglo-Israel Friendship Soc. *Recreations:* golf, walking, travel. *Address:* House of Commons, SW1A 0AA; Greystones, Maltongate, Thornton Dale, North Yorkshire. *Club:* Carlton.
*Died* 4 *March* 1986.

**SPENCER, Brian;** HM Diplomatic Service, retired; Counsellor and Consul-General, Washington, 1978–82; *b* 20 March 1922; *s* of Alphaeus and Ethel Audrey Palmer Spencer; *m* 1950, Jean Edmunds; one *s. Educ:* Holgate Grammar Sch., Barnsley. Entered Civil Service in Mines Dept, BoT, 1939. Army, 1940–46: commnd, S Staffs Regt, 1942, with subseq. service in E Surrey Regt, N Africa, Sicily, Italy, Austria and Greece (Captain, despatches). Joined FO, 1950; Second Sec., Bagdad, 1952, Jakarta, 1955; FO, 1956; First Sec., Singapore, 1959; FO, 1962; First Secretary (Information): Helsinki, 1964; Canberra, 1967; Sydney, 1968; First Sec., Ottawa, 1969; Consul, Chicago, 1971; FCO, 1972; Counsellor and Consul-Gen., Moscow, 1975–77. *Recreations:* tennis, cricket, football, ballet, music. *Address:* 68 Old Shoreham Road, Hove, E Sussex. *Club:* Royal Over-Seas League. *Died* 27 *Jan.* 1985.

**SPENCER, Noël,** ARCA (London); retired as Principal, Norwich School of Art (1946–64); *b* 29 Dec. 1900; *s* of late John William Spencer; *m* 1929, Vera K. Wheeler; no *c. Educ:* Ashton-under-Lyne School of Art; Manchester School of Art; Royal College of Art. Art Teacher, Central School of Arts and Crafts, Birmingham, 1926–32; Headmaster, Moseley School of Art, Birmingham, 1929–32; Second Master, Sheffield College of Arts and Crafts, 1932–34; Headmaster, Huddersfield Art School, 1934–46. *Exhibitions:* Royal Academy, New English Art Club, Royal Birmingham Society of Artists, Sheffield Society of Artists, Liverpool, Bradford, Wakefield and Doncaster Art Galleries, Norwich Art Circle and Twenty Group, Chicago Art Institute and Los Angeles Art Museum, USA, etc. Collection of more than 215 drawings and prints donated to Museum of London. *Publications:* A Scrap Book of Huddersfield, Book I, 1944, Book II, 1948; (with Arnold Kent) The Old Churches of Norwich, 1970; Sculptured Monuments in Norfolk Churches, 1977; Norwich Drawings, 1978. *Recreations:* drawing and painting. *Address:* 29 The Cedars, Albemarle Road, Norwich, Norfolk.
*Died* 18 *Feb.* 1986.

**SPENCER-SMITH, Maj.-Gen. Jeremy Michael,** CB 1971; OBE 1959; MC 1945; Director of Manning (Army), Ministry of Defence, 1970–72; retired; *b* 28 July 1917; *s* of Michael Spencer-Smith, DSO, MC, and Penelope, *née* Delmé-Radcliffe (she *m* 2nd, 1934, Elliot Francis Montagu Butler, and *d* 1974). *Educ:* Eton; New Coll., Oxford. Welsh Guards, 1940; Adjutant, 1st Bn, 1944–46; Staff, 1st Guards Brigade, MELF, 1950–51; comd 3 KAR, Kenya, 1959–60; Staff, HQ BAOR, 1960–63; comd 148 Infantry Bde (TA), 1964–67; Dep. Dir of Manning, Ministry of Defence (Army), 1967–68; GOC Wales, 1968–70. *Recreations:* shooting, racing, travel. *Address:* The White Cottages, Cheveley, Newmarket, Suffolk.
*Died* 20 *May* 1985.

**SPENDER, Hon. Sir Percy Claude,** KCVO 1957; KBE 1952; QC (NSW), 1935; BA; LLB; President of the International Court of Justice at The Hague, 1964–67 (Judge, 1958–64); Australian lawyer; *b* Sydney, 5 Oct. 1897; *s* of late Frank Henry Spender, Sydney, and Mary Hanson (*née* Murray); *m* 1925, Jean Maude (*d* 1970), *d* of Samuel B. Henderson; two *s; m* 1983, Eileen Esdaile, *d* of Phillip Congreve. *Educ:* Fort Street High Sch., Sydney; Sydney Univ. BA 1918 (distinction in economics); LLB 1922, with 1st class Honours and University Medal; George and Matilda Harris Scholar, 1920; Special Wigram Allen Prize for proficiency in Roman and Constitutional Law, 1918; Morven K. Nolan Memorial Prize for Political Science, 1920; Member of Sydney Univ. Senate, 1939–44; called to NSW Bar, 1923. Member of Menzies Ministry, 1939–41; Vice-President, Fed. Exec. Council, 1940 (Member 1939); Minister

without portfolio assisting Treas., and Ministerial Secretary to Cabinet, 1939; Acting Treas. 1939, Treas. 1940; Member of Economic Cabinet, 1939–40; Chairman Australian Loan Council, 1939–40; Chairman of Nat. Debt Commn, 1940; Minister for the Army, Chairman of Mil. Board, and Member War Cabinet, 1940–41; Government, then Opposition Member of Advisory War Council, 1940–45; Minister for External Affairs and of External Territories, Australia, 1949–51; MHR for Warringah, 1937–51; Australian Ambassador to the United States, 1951–58. Chairman: Australian Delegn at Conference of British Commonwealth Foreign Ministers, Colombo, 1950 (at which he put forward a plan for economic aid to S and SE Asia, subseq. known as the Colombo Plan); Conf. of British Commonwealth Consultative Cttee on Economic Aid to S and SE Asia, Sydney, 1950; Australian delegate at British Commonwealth Consultative Cttee Meeting, London, 1950; Vice-Pres., 5th General Assembly, UN, 1950–51, and Chm. and Vice-Chm., Australian Delegn UN General Assembly, 1952–56; Australian Representative at negotiation Canberra and subsequently at signing Regional Security Treaty between USA, NZ, and Australia, San Francisco, 1951; Vice-President Jap. Peace Treaty Conf., San Francisco, 1951 (Chm., Australian Delegn); Australian Governor of Internat. Monetary Fund and Internat. Bank, 1951–53; alternate Governor, Internat. Monetary Fund, 1954; Chm. Australian Delegn to UN Commemorative Session, San Francisco, 1955; Special Envoy on goodwill mission to South and Central America, July-Aug. 1955; Chairman, Australian Delegation Internat. Sugar Conf., May-June 1956 and Conf. to establish Atomic Energy Internat. Agency, Sept.-Oct. 1956; Chairman, Australian Delegation to 2nd Suez Conf., London, Sept. 1956, and to Commonwealth Finance Ministers' meeting, Washington, Oct. 1956. Mem. Gen. Council, Assicurazioni Generali (Italy), 1969–. European War, 1914–18, enlisted AIF, 1918; War of 1939–45, Lieut-Colonel on Active List AMF part-time special duties, 1942–45; now on retired list with hon. rank of Lieut-Colonel. Member: Board of Directors of USA Educational Foundation in Australia, 1950–51; US Cttee of Study and Training in Australia, 1950–51; Member of Council (1949–51) and Life Member Convocation Australian Nat. Univ.; Vice-President, Royal Commonwealth Society (President, NSW Br., 1949–51); President: Sydney Club, 1967–82; NSW Br. of Overseas League, 1967–72. Chm., Aust. Museum Bd of Trustees for compilation of National Photographic Index of Australian Birds, 1969–76. Hon. LLD: Univ. of British Columbia; Hamilton Coll., NY, 1952; Univ. of Colorado, 1953; Trinity Coll., Hartford, Conn, 1955; Yale, 1957; California, 1965; University of the East (Philippines), 1966; Sydney, 1973; Hon. DCL and Hon. Chancellor, Union Univ., Schenectady, 1955; Hon. LittD Springfield Coll., Mass, 1955. Coronation Medal, 1937 and 1953. KStJ 1958. Grande Ufficiale del' Ordine al Merito della Repubblica Italiana, 1976. C of E. *Publications:* Company Law and Practice, 1939; Australia's Foreign Policy, the Next Phase, 1944; Exercises in Diplomacy, 1969; Politics and a Man, 1972. *Recreations:* reading, surfing, golf. *Address:* Headingley House, Wellington Street, Woollahra, NSW 2025, Australia. *Clubs:* Elanora Country, Australasian Pioneers (Sydney); Athenæum (Melbourne).
*Died* 3 *May* 1985.

**SPENS,** 2nd Baron *cr* 1959; **William George Michael Spens;** *b* 18 Sept. 1914; *s* of 1st Baron Spens, PC, KBE, QC, and Hilda Mary (*d* 1962), *e d* of Lt-Col Wentworth Grenville Bowyer; *S* father, 1973; *m* 1941, Joan Elizabeth, *d* of late Reginald Goodall; two *s* one *d. Educ:* Rugby; New Coll., Oxford (MA). Barrister, Inner Temple, 1945. Served War of 1939–45 with RA; British Control Commission (later High Commission), Germany, 1945–55. MBE 1954–75. *Heir: s* Hon. Patrick Michael Rex Spens, ACA [*b* 22 July 1942; *m* 1966, Barbara Janet Lindsay, *d* of Rear-Adm. Ralph Lindsay Fisher; one *s* one *d*]. *Died* 23 *Nov.* 1984.

**SPENSER-WILKINSON, Sir Thomas Crowe,** Kt 1959; *b* 28 Sept. 1899; *o* surv. *s* of late Henry Spenser Wilkinson and Victoria Amy Eveline Crowe; *m* 1930, Betty Margaret (*d* 1980), *o d* of late David Aitken Horner; one *s* one *d. Educ:* RN Colleges Osborne and Dartmouth; Balliol Coll., Oxford. Served as Midshipman and Sub-Lieut in Grand Fleet, 1915–18; in Destroyers in Baltic, 1918–19; Lieut 1920. Barrister-at-Law, Gray's Inn, 1925; Advocate and Solicitor, Singapore, 1928; practising in Singapore, 1928–; President, District Court, Nicosia, Cyprus, 1938, and Famagusta, 1940; Lt-Comdr 1940; Naval Control Service in Cyprus and Port Said, 1940–42; on staff of C-in-C, S Atlantic, Capetown, 1942–44; Malaya Planning Unit in London, 1945; Chief Legal Adviser, Civil Affairs, British Mil. Administration, Malaya, Sept. 1945-April 1946; Judge, Supreme Court, Malaya, 1946; Chief Justice, Nyasaland, 1956–62; Chm., Medical Appeals Tribunal, Liverpool, 1962–72. *Publication:* Merchant Shipping Law of the Straits Settlements, 1946. *Address:* Whitecroft, 6 Pentre Close, Ashton, Chester CH3 8BR. *T:* Kelsall 51531. *Clubs:* Royal Commonwealth Society, English-Speaking Union. *Died* 28 *Jan.* 1982.

**SPINELLI, Altiero;** Member of the European Parliament, since 1976; a Deputy (Independent), Italian Parliament, 1976; *b* 31 Aug. 1907;

s of Carlo Spinelli and Maria Ricci; m 1944, Ursula Hirschmann; three d. Educ: Univ. of Rome. Political prisoner in Italy, 1927–43; partisan in Italian Resistance, 1943–45; Leader of European Federalist Movement, 1945–61. Visiting Prof., Johns Hopkins Univ. Center for Advanced Internat. Studies, in Bologna, 1961–64. Founder and Director, Istituto Affari Internazionali, Rome, 1965–70; Mem., Commn of the European Communities, 1970–76. *Publications:* Degli Stati Sovrani agli Stati Uniti d'Europa, 1952; L'Europa non cade dal cielo, 1960; Tedeschi al bivio, 1960; The Eurocrats, 1966; The European Adventure, 1973; Il lungo monologo, 1970; PCI: che fare?, 1978; La mia battaglia per un'Europa diversa, 1979; Come ho tentato di Diventare saggio, (autobiog.), 1984. *Address:* Via del Tritone 46, 00187 Roma, Italy; Clivo Rutario 5, 00152 Roma, Italy. *Died 23 May* 1986.

**SPINK, Prof. John Stephenson;** Professor of French Language and Literature in the University of London (Bedford College), 1952–73; *b* 22 Aug. 1909; *s* of William Spink and Rosetta Spink (*née* Williamson); *m* 1940, Dorothy Knowles, MA, DèsL, LRAM. *Educ:* Pickering Grammar Sch.; Universities of Leeds and Paris. BA (Leeds), 1930; MA (Leeds), 1932; Docteur de l'Université de Paris, 1934; Lauréat de l'Académie Française, 1935. Assistant at Lycée Henri IV, Paris, 1930–33; Lecteur at the Sorbonne, 1931; Asst Lectr in Univ. of Leeds, 1933–36; Lectr in Univ. of London, King's Coll., 1937–50; Prof. of French at University College, Southampton, 1950–52. Officier de l'ordre nat. du mérite, 1973. *Publications:* J.-J. Rousseau et Genève, 1934 (Paris); critical edition of J.-J. Rousseau, Les Rêveries du Promeneur solitaire, 1948; Literature and the sciences in the age of Molière, 1953; French Free-Thought from Gassendi to Voltaire, 1960; critical edn of Rousseau's educational writings in Pléiade œuvres complètes, t. IV, 1969; (ed jointly) Diderot, Œuvres complètes, I, II, 1975, IV, 1978; articles in Annales J.-J. Rousseau, Mercure de France, Revue d'Histoire littéraire, Modern Language Review, French Studies, Bulletin des Historiens du théâtre, Horizon, Europe, Revue de Littérature Comparée, Problèmes des Genres Littéraires, Cahiers de l'Association Internat. des Études Françaises, Dix-huitième siècle; trans. of Krimov, The Tanker Derbent, 1944 (Penguin). *Address:* 48 Woodside Park Road, N12. *Died 4 June* 1985.

**SPINKS, Dr Alfred,** CBE 1978; FRS 1977; CChem, FRSC: FIBiol; Research Director, Imperial Chemical Industries Ltd, 1970–79; *b* 25 Feb. 1917; *s* of Alfred Robert Spinks and Ruth (*née* Harley); *m* 1946, Patricia Kilner; two *d. Educ:* Soham Grammar Sch.; University Coll., Nottingham (BSc); Imperial Coll., London (PhD, DIC); Worcester Coll., Oxford (MA). CChem 1975; FRIC 1971; FIBiol 1970. Joined ICI Dyestuffs Div., 1941; Res. Chemist, Imperial Coll., 1941–42; research with ICI Dyestuffs Div., 1942–50; Oxford Univ., 1950–52; Res. Pharmacologist, ICI, 1952–61; Pharmaceuticals Division, ICI: Biochem. Res. Manager, 1961–65; Res. Dir, 1966–67; Dep. Chm., 1966–70. Director: AECI Ltd, S Africa, 1971–79 (Dep. Chm., 1975–79); Dunlop Holdings Ltd, 1979–; Charter Consolidated Ltd, 1979– (Chm., 1980–); Johnson Matthey Ltd, 1980–; Biotechnology Investments Ltd, 1981–; Technology Change Centre, 1981–. Member: Council, RIC, 1974–77; Council, Chem. Soc., 1977–81 (Pres., 1979–80). Member: Adv. Council, Applied R&D, 1976– (Dep. Chm., 1978–80, Chm., 1980–); Adv. Bd for Res. Councils, 1977–; Royal Commn on Environmental Pollution, 1979–. Fellow, Imperial Coll., London, 1975. Governor, Imperial Coll., 1978–. Hon. DSc Sheffield, 1981. *Publications:* Evaluations of Drug Toxicity, 1958; papers in scientific jls. *Recreations:* photography, travel, theatre. *Address:* Woodcote, Torkington Road, Wilmslow, Cheshire SK9 2AE. *T:* Wilmslow 522316. *Club:* Athenæum. *Died 11 Feb.* 1982.

**SPORBORG, Henry Nathan,** CMG 1945; Chairman: SKF (UK) until 1975; Stirling International Civil Engineering (formerly Stirling-Astaldi); Gomme Holdings, until 1980; Berkeley Hambro Property Co. until 1975; Vice-Chairman, Sun Alliance & London Insurance Ltd, 1969–79; Deputy Chairman, Thorn Electrical Industries, 1973–78; Director of other companies; Commissioner to the Fitzwilliam Estates and Executor of the late Earl Fitzwilliam; *b* 17 Sept. 1905; *e c* of late H. N. and M. A. Sporborg; *m* 1935, Mary Rowlands; one *s* three *d. Educ:* Rugby Sch.; Emmanuel Coll., Cambridge. Admitted Solicitor, 1930; partner in firm of Slaughter & May, 1935; joined Ministry of Economic Warfare, 1939; Director and later Vice-Chief, Special Operations Executive, 1940–46. A Director: Hambros Bank Ltd, 1949–70; Hambros Ltd, 1970–77. Mem., Port of London Authority, 1967–75. Chairman, Board of Governors, St Mary's Hospital, 1964–74. JP Herts, 1957. Chevalier, Legion of Honour, Croix de Guerre, Order of St Olav (Norway), etc. *Recreation:* fox-hunting. *Address:* Upwick Hall, Albury, near Ware, Herts. *T:* Albury 769. *Clubs:* Boodle's, Carlton.

*Died 6 March* 1985.

**SPRAGG, Cyril Douglas,** CBE 1949; Hon. FRIBA 1971 (Hon. ARIBA 1959); Secretary, Royal Institute of British Architects, 1945–59; *b* 22 July 1894; *y s* of late Charles and Emily Spragg; unmarried. *Educ:* Christ's Hospital. Served European War, Queen's

Westminster Rifles, 1914–19. Asst Secretary, RIBA, 1926–44. Governor of Christ's Hospital; Thames Conservancy, 1966–70; Hon. Member American Institute of Architects, 1955; Hon. Corresp. Member, Royal Architectural Inst. of Canada, 1956; Hon. Associate Royal Australian Inst. of Architects, 1957; Hon. Fellow, New Zealand Institute of Architects, 1957; Hon. Member Inst. South African Architects; Hon. Member Ghana Society of Architects, 1959; Hon. Fellow Royal Incorporation of Architects in Scotland, 1960; Hon. Member Fedn of Malaya Society Architects, 1961. Hon. MA Durham Univ., 1958. Member: Middlesex CC, 1961; Surrey CC, 1965, Alderman, 1967–70. *Address:* Winton House, 51 Dedworth Road, Windsor, Berks SL4 5AZ. *T:* Windsor 56654. *Died 21 April* 1986.

**SPRINGALL, Harold Douglas;** Professor of Chemistry, University of Keele, 1950–75, now Emeritus (Head of Department, 1950–74); *b* 24 June 1910; *o s* of Harold Springall and Margaret Springall (*née* Wright); *m* 1940, Jean Helen McArthur Gordon, *d* of L. McArthur Gordon and H. Violet Gordon (*née* Holbeche); two *s* one *d. Educ:* Colfe's Grammar School, London; Lincoln College, Oxford (Scholar). BA (1st cl.) 1934; BSc 1934; Magdalen College, Oxford (Senior Demy), 1934–36; DPhil 1936; MA Oxon 1938. Commonwealth Fund Fellowship, Calif Tech., Pasadena, Calif, Cornell Univ., 1936–38; Rockefeller Research Grant, Oxford, 1938–39. Min. of Supply: Sci. Officer (Armament Res. Dept), Univ. of Bristol, 1939–44; Sen. Sci. Officer, 1944–45. Univ. of Manchester: Lectr in Chemistry, 1945–48, Sen. Lectr, 1948–50; Asst Tutor to Faculty of Science, 1949–50; Tutor in Chemistry, Dalton Hall, 1945–50; Univ. Coll. of North Staffs: Dir of Studies, 1951–52; Vice-Principal, 1957–59; Actg Vice-Principal, 1960–61. Mem. Council Chem. Soc., 1954–57. Mem. Publication Cttee, Faraday Soc., 1957–71. CChem; FRIC 1948; FRSA 1971. DSc Keele, 1972. *Publications:* The Structural Chemistry of Proteins, 1954; Sidgwick's Organic Chemistry of Nitrogen, 1966; A Shorter Sidgwick's Organic Chemistry of Nitrogen, 1969; articles in Jl Chem. Soc., Jl Amer. Chem. Soc., Trans Faraday Soc., Nature, etc. *Address:* 21 Springpool, The University, Keele, Staffordshire. *T:* Newcastle (Staffs) 627395. *Club:* Climbers'. *Died 2 Nov.* 1982.

**SPRINGER, Axel (Caesar);** Founder, major shareholder, Axel Springer Publishing Group; *b* 2 May 1912; *s* of late Hinrich and Ottilie Springer; *m;* one *s* one *d* (and one *s* decd). *Educ:* Altona Realgymnasium. Apprentice, with Wolff'sches Telegraphen Bureau (WTB), Hamburg, and reporter on several suburban newspapers, 1931; sports editor, 1934, Associate Editor, 1937, Altonaer Nachrichten; established own publishing co., 1945. Magazines and newspapers published by Springer Verlag, 1946–, include: Hörzu, Hamburger Abendblatt, Bild, Bild am Sonntag, Die Welt, Welt am Sonntag, Berliner Morgenpost, BZ, and Funk Uhr; co-owner of book-publishing houses Propyläen and Ullstein; founder, Ullstein Tele Video. Hon. Fellow, Weizmann Inst., Israel, 1969. Hon. degrees: Temple Univ., Philadelphia, 1971; Bar-Ilan Univ., Israel, 1974; Hebrew Univ., Israel, 1976; Boston, 1981. Friendship Medal, USA, 1978; Leo Baeck Medal, NY, 1978; Ernst Reuter Medal, Berlin, 1982; Keeper of Jerusalem, 1983. Bavarian Order of Merit, 1974; Bundesverdienstkreuz with star and sash (Germany), 1977. *Publications:* Von Berlin aus gesehen, 1971; Aus Sorge um Deutschland, 1980. *Address:* Kochstrasse 50, 1000 Berlin 61, Germany. *Died 22 Sept.* 1985.

**SPRINGMAN, Dame Ann (Marcella),** DBE 1980 (OBE 1974); Hon. Vice-President, National Union of Conservative and Unionist Associations, since 1981 (Chairman, 1980–81; Vice-Chairman, 1978–80; Member, Executive Committee, 1970–84); *b* 5 Jan. 1933; *d* of late Lt-Col Noel Mulloy, MC, The Scinde Horse, and Marcella Mulloy; *m* 1955, Michael Springman; three *s* one *d. Educ:* St George's Sch., Ascot; Harcombe House, Uplyme, Lyme Regis. Founder secretary, Bracknell and District Br., RNLI, 1960–63. Councillor, Easthampstead, subseq. Bracknell District Council, 1968–76 (Chm., Planning Cttee, 1970–72); Council Representative, Bracknell Development Corp. Jt Consultative Cttee, 1968–71. Chairman: Wessex Conservative Women's Adv. Cttee, 1970–73; Wokingham Conservative Assoc., 1972–75; Conservative Women's Nat. Adv. Cttee, 1975–78; E Sussex FPC, 1985–; District Commissioner, Bracknell West Girl Guides, 1970–72; Governor, Easthampstead Park Sch. and Adult Educn Centre, 1975–77. Member: Women's National Commn, 1978–84; ESRC (formerly SSRC), 1979–85; Thomas Coram Res. Unit Adv. Cttee, 1981–85. *Recreation:* family life. *Address:* The Old Farmhouse, Horstedpond Farm, Uckfield, Sussex TN22 5TR. *T:* Uckfield 5406.

*Died 30 July* 1987.

**SPROTT, Rt. Rev. John Chappell,** MA; DD St Andrews 1965; *b* 16 Oct. 1903; *s* of Thomas Sprott, Master Mariner, and Catherine Chappell; *m* 1932, Winifred Helen Cameron, *d* of late Sir David W. Bone, CBE, LLD; three *s* one *d. Educ:* Castle Hill Sch., Ealing; Glasgow Univ.; Edinburgh Theological Coll. Deacon, 1927; Priest, 1928; Chaplain and Succentor, St Mary's Cathedral, Edinburgh, 1927–29; Lecturer in Music, Edinburgh Theological College,

1928–29; Curate, All Saints, Glasgow, 1929–33; St George the Martyr, Holborn, 1933–37; Rector, West Hackney, 1937–40; Provost of St Paul's Cathedral, Dundee, 1940–59; Bishop of Brechin, 1959–75; Hon. Curate, St Ninian's, Troon, 1975–81. *Recreation:* music. *Address:* 29 Bruntsfield Gardens, Edinburgh EH10 4DY.
*Died 11 Nov. 1982.*

**SPRY, Maj.-Gen. Daniel Charles,** CBE 1945; DSO 1944; CD; *b* Winnipeg, Man, 4 Feb. 1913; *s* of Major-General Daniel William Bigelow Spry and Ethelyn Alma (*née* Rich); *m* 1939, Elisabeth, *d* of Roy Fletcher Forbes, Halifax, NS; one *s* one *d*. *Educ:* Public Schools, Calgary and Halifax; Ashford School, England; Dalhousie University. Served with Canadian Militia; 2nd Lt, Princess Louise Fusiliers, 1932; Royal Canadian Regt (permanent force), 1934. Served War, 1939–46 (CBE, DSO, CD, despatches twice); Captain 1939, Major 1940, Lt-Col 1943, Brig. 1943, Maj.-Gen. 1944; GOC 3rd Canadian Infantry Div., 1944–45; retired as Vice-Chief of Gen. Staff, 1946. Col, The Royal Canadian Regt, 1965–78. Chief Exec. Comr, The Boy Scouts' Assoc. of Canada, 1946–51; Dep. Dir, Boy Scouts World Bureau, 1951–53, Dir, 1953–65. Commander, Order of the Crown of Belgium, 1945; Croix de Guerre, Belgium, 1945. *Recreations:* sailing, gardening, fishing. *Address:* 4 Rock Avenue, Ottawa, Ontario K1M 1A6, Canada. *Club:* Rideau (Ottawa).
*Died 2 April 1989.*

**SPRY, Graham,** CC (Canada) 1971; Agent General for Saskatchewan in the United Kingdom and Europe, 1947–67, retired 1968; *b* St Thomas, Ontario, 20 Feb. 1900; *e s* of Maj.-Gen. D. W. B. Spry, OBE, ED, and Ethelyn Alma Rich; *m* 1938, Professor Irene Mary Biss; one *s* one *d* (and one *s* decd). *Educ:* public schools, Toronto, Montreal and Winnipeg; University of Manitoba (BA, Rhodes Scholar); University College, Oxford (MA); Sorbonne, Paris. Served Canadian Army, Gunner, 1918. Editorial Staff, Winnipeg Free Press, 1919–22 (while at University); Internat. Labour Office, Geneva, 1925–26; Nat. Sec., Assoc. of Canadian Clubs, 1926–32. Organized and Chm. of Canadian Radio League (voluntary group which advocated and secured, by unanimous vote of House of Commons, establishment of public service broadcasting), 1929–33; Canadian Politics, 1933–37. California Standard Oil Co. Ltd, London, Eng., 1938–39, Dir and Manager, 1940–46; Director: Associated Ethyl Co., Ceylon Petroleum Co., 1940–47; British Ethyl Corp., 1944–47; Personal Asst to Rt Hon. Sir Stafford Cripps, Lord Privy Seal and Minister of Aircraft Production, 1942–45, Member of Mission to India, 1942; duties in USA for Sir Stafford Cripps, 1942, and for Rt Hon. R. K. Law, 1943; Member Inter-deptl Cttee on Internat. Civil Aviation; War Corresp., Canadian Army, Italy, Aug.–Sept., 1944, and Germany, April–May, 1945. XXth Century Fund Survey of Turkey, 1947. FRGS. Hon. LLD: Brock, 1968; Saskatchewan, 1968; York, 1976; Mount Allison Univ., 1982. *Publications:* (joint) Social Planning for Canada, 1934; Canada, 1941; Canada, 1946; (joint) Turkey: An Economic Appraisal, 1949. *Recreations:* books, history, ski-ing, and Tuscany. *Address:* 446 Cloverdale Road, Ottawa, Ontario K1M 0Y6, Canada. *Clubs:* Travellers'; Leander (Hon. Mem.); Rideau (Ottawa).
*Died 24 Nov. 1983.*

**SPURLING, Antony Cuthbert,** QC (Sierra Leone); *b* 12 Oct. 1906; 3rd *s* of late Cuthbert Spurling; *m* 1935, Elizabeth Frances, *d* of late J. C. Stobart; two *s* one *d*. *Educ:* Berkhamsted; St Paul's; Hertford College, Oxford. Called to Bar, Inner Temple, 1931; Temp. Legal Asst, Ministry of Health, 1934; Resident Magistrate, Kenya, 1935; Crown Counsel, Kenya, 1939; Solicitor-General, Trinidad, 1946; Attorney-General, Gambia, 1951. Attorney-General, Sierra Leone, 1955–61. Retired, 1961. *Publication:* Digest and Guide to the Criminal Law of Kenya, 1946. *Recreation:* gardening. *Address:* Wheelwright Cottage, Bodle Street Green, near Hailsham, Sussex BN27 4UB. *T:* Herstmonceux 832308.
*Died 14 Dec. 1984.*

**SPURLING, Hon. Sir (Arthur) Dudley,** Kt 1975; CBE 1963; JP; Barrister and Attorney; Consultant, Appleby, Spurling & Kempe, since 1981 (Senior Partner, 1948–81); Speaker of the House of Assembly, Bermuda, 1972–76; *b* 9 Nov. 1913; *s* of late Sir Stanley Spurling, CMG, and Lady Spurling; *m* 1941, Marian Taylor, *d* of Frank Gurr, St George's, Bermuda; two *s* one *d* (and one *s* decd). *Educ:* St George's Grammar Sch. (Chm., Bd of Trustees, 1957–63); Saltus Grammar Sch., Bermuda; Rossall Sch., Lancs (Bermuda Scholar); Trinity Coll., Oxford (Rhodes Scholar; MA); Lincoln's Inn. Called to Bar: Lincoln's Inn, 1937; Bermuda 1938; in practice, Bermuda, 1938–. Served, Bermuda Volunteer Rifle Corps, 1938–43, Reserve 1943–45. ADC to Governor of Bermuda, 1942–43; MHA, 1943–76; MEC, 1957–69; Minister of Educn, 1968–69; Chairman: Bd of Trade, 1945–46; Bd of Immigration, 1946–57; Bd of Public Works, 1957–63; Bd of Educn 1963–68. Chairman: CS Cttee of House of Assembly, 1948–52; Law Reform Cttee, 1969–81; Dep. Chm., Bermuda Council of Social Welfare, 1947–48; Common Councillor, Corp. of St George, Bermuda 1953–63. Trustee, Bermuda Biol Station, 1955–. *Recreations:* carpentry, shrubs, trees, reading, swimming (Mem. Bermuda Team, Empire Games, 1930, 1934, Olympic Games, 1936). *Address:* Three Chimneys, No 5 Speaker's Drive, Wellington, St George's 1–12, Bermuda. *Clubs:* English-Speaking Union, United Oxford & Cambridge University, Institute of Directors; Hamilton Rotary (Past Pres; Hon. Mem.); Royal Bermuda Yacht, Royal Hamilton Amateur Dinghy, Mid Ocean, Sandys Boat, St George's Dinghy and Sports (all in Bermuda).
*Died 20 May 1986.*

**SQUIRES, James Duane;** Professor of History, Colby College, New Hampshire, USA, since 1933; Historical Consultant to NH War Records Committee, since 1944; *b* Grand Forks, North Dakota, 9 Nov. 1904; *s* of Vernon Purinton Squires and Ethel Claire Wood; *m* 1928, Catherine Emily Tuttle, Grand Forks, North Dakota; two *s*. *Educ:* Public Schools, Grand Forks, North Dakota. BA University of North Dakota, 1925; MA, University of Minnesota, 1927; PhD, Harvard Univ., 1933; Professor of History, State College, Mayville, North Dakota, 1927–31; Graduate Student, Harvard University, 1931–33; lecturer and writer; Official Delegate to the Harvard Tercentenary, 1936; Member: US Constitution Sesquicentennial Commission for New Hampshire, 1938; NH State Council of Defense, 1942–45; Special Consultant to USAAF, War Dept, 1943; Chm. of USO in NH, 1944. President: NH Council of Religious Educn, 1944–45; NH Library Trustees Assoc., 1957; Old Number Four Associates, 1957; Amer. Baptist Historical Soc., 1969–. Member: NH Historical Soc. (Hon. Mem. 1975); Cttee of 1000 for World Congress of Religion in 1948; Lincoln Soc.; Peabody Award Cttee for Radio; Citizens Cttee for UN Reform; Hoover Cttee for Govtl Reorganization in US, 1949; Citizens' Adv. Cttee for US Commn on Govt Security, 1957; Nat. Archives Adv. Council for New England; NH LIbrary Adv. Cttee; Cttee for a New England Bibliography; Chairman UN Day Cttee in NH, 1949–57; Pres. NH Sons of the American Revolution, 1949; Chm. NH American Revolution Bicentennial Cttee, 1970–; Deleg.-at-large to Nat. Republican Convention: Chicago, 1952; San Francisco, 1956, 1964 (Mem. Platform Cttee of Convention, 1964); Official Deleg. Second Assembly of World Council of Churches, Evanston, Ill, 1954; Chm., Bicentennial Council of the Original Thirteen States, 1973–74. Director of NH Victory Speakers' Bureau, 1943; Newcomen Soc. in N America; Trustee: NH Baptist Convention; NH YMCA; NH Christian Civic League, etc; Mem., NH Commn on Historical Sites, 1950; Chm. NH Centennial Commn on the Civil War 1958–; Mem. Bd of Governors, Amer. Revolution Bicentennial Admin, 1974– (Vice-Chm., 1975–). Judge, New London District Court, 1969–. George Washington Honor Medal of Freedoms' Foundation, 1954. LLD Univ. of N Dakota, 1958. Granite State Award, Univ. of New Hampshire, 1970; NH Boy Scout Honor Medal, 1975; Charles Pettee Honor Medal, Univ. of NH, 1976; Bicentennial Award, Amer. Baptist Churches, 1976. *Publications:* A History of the University of North Dakota, 1931; British Propaganda at Home and in the United States, 1914–17, 1935; Ballooning in the American Civil War, 1937; editor, The Centennial of Colby Junior College, 1937; editor, The Sesquicentennial of the Baptist Church of New London, New Hampshire, 1939; co-author, Western Civilization, 2 vols, 1942; The Founding of the Northern RR, 1948; Abraham Lincoln and the Civil War, 1949; A History of New London, New Hampshire since 1900, 1952; Experiment in Cooperation, 1953; Community Witness, 1954; A History of New Hampshire since 1623, 1956; The Story of New Hampshire, 1964; contributor to: Journal of Modern History, American Historical Review, Christian Century, Dictionary of American Biography and Dictionary of American History, Encyclopedia Britannica. *Recreations:* fishing, numismatics. *Address:* New London, New Hampshire 03257, USA. *T:* 526-4561. *Clubs:* Forum (New London); Boys.
*Died 9 April 1981.*

**SRAFFA, Piero,** FBA 1954; MA; Fellow of Trinity College, Cambridge, since 1939; Emeritus Reader in Economics, University of Cambridge; *b* Turin, Italy, 5 Aug. 1898; *s* of Angelo Sraffa. *Educ:* Univ. of Turin. *Publications:* (ed) The Works and Correspondence of David Ricardo, 11 vols, 1951–73; Production of Commodities by Means of Commodities, 1960. *Address:* Trinity College, Cambridge.
*Died 3 Sept. 1983.*

**STABLE, Maj.-Gen. Hugh Huntington,** CB 1947; CIE 1938; Major-General, IA (retired) *b* 1896; *s* of late Alfred Henry Stable, MA and Ada Huntington; *m* 1923, Cyrille Helen Dorothy (*d* 1979), *d* of late Rev. M. A. Bayfield, MA. *Educ:* Malvern. First Commission 2/4th Dorset Regt 1914; served Palestine, 1917–18 (despatches); Central India Horse, 1919; Bt Lt-Col 1935; Staff Coll., Camberley, 1929–30; Army Headquarters, India; Staff Officer to Major-General Cavalry, 1932; Assistant Military Secretary (Personal) to Commander-in-Chief, 1933–36; Military Secretary to the Viceroy of India, 1936–38; Comdt, 8th KGO Cavalry, 1939–40; Bde Comdr, 1941–43; DQMG, GHQ, India, 1943–44; Comdr Lucknow Sub Area, 1945–46; Comdr Bihar and Orissa Area, 1947; QMG India, Dec. 1947; retd 1950. A Governor, Malvern Coll.; Emeritus Comr, Boy Scouts of South Africa. *Address:* B810 Rapallo, Sea Point, Cape Town, SA. *Clubs:* Army and Navy; City and Civil Service (Cape Town).
*Died 6 Aug. 1985.*

**STACEY, Air Chief Marshal Sir (William) John,** KCB 1977; CBE 1972; FRAeS; Deputy Commander-in-Chief, Allied Forces Central Europe, since 1979; *b* 1 Dec. 1924; *s* of Edward William John Stacey; *m* 1952, Frances Jean, *d* of Prof. L. W. Faucett, USA; one *s* two *d*. *Educ*: Eire and South Africa. Entered RAF, 1942; fighter pilot training S. Africa; served Far East and UK, nos 155, 60, 54, 72 fighter ground attack sqdns; flying instructor, RAF Coll. Cranwell, 1949–51; Examng Wing, Central Flying Sch., 1951–52; Air Staff, Washington, USA, 1952–55; Comd 54 Fighter Sqdn, 1955–58; Chief of Nuclear Ops Branch, 2nd Allied Tactical Air Force, 1959–62; Comd 50 Sqdn Bomber Comd, 1963–65; Dep. Dir Bomber Ops, MoD, 1965–68; Comd Fighter Station Coltishall, 1968–69; Comd RAF Akrotiri, Cyprus, 1969–72; RCDS 1972; COS 46 Gp, Strike Comd, and Comd UK Jt Airborne Task Force, 1972–74; ACAS (Policy), MoD, 1974–76; Dep. C-in-C RAF Strike Command, 1976–77; Comdr 2nd Allied Tactical Air Force and C-in-C RAF Germany, 1977–79. *Recreations*: military history, music, travel. *Address*: HQ AFCENT, BFPO 28. *Club*: Royal Air Force.

*Died 1 Jan.* 1981.

**STACY, Reginald Joseph William,** CB 1955; *b* 1 Jan. 1904; *e s* of late Frank Dixon Stacy and Alice Summers; *m* 1932, Nina Grace Holder; one *s* one *d*. *Educ*: Wirtemburg (now Stonhouse) Street Elementary School; Sir Walter St John's School, London; Trinity College, Cambridge (Sen. Schol.). BA 1925 (Double First, Mod. Lang. Tripos). Entered Board of Trade, Commercial Relations and Treaties Department, 1927; Ottawa Imperial Conference, 1932; Commercial Mission to Colombia, 1938; led UK Trade Delegation to Warsaw, 1948–49; accompanied Minister of State, Board of Trade, to South America, 1954; Insurance and Companies Department, 1956; Internat. Conferences on Insurance; Under-Sec., Bd of Trade, 1949–64, retd; French and Latin Master, Parkside Preparatory School, 1967–69. *Address*: 2 Beech Court, Easington Place, Guildford, Surrey. *T*: Guildford 60761.

*Died 10 May* 1981.

**STAFFORD, 14th Baron** *cr* 1640, *confirmed* 1825; **Basil Francis Nicholas Fitzherbert;** DL; *b* 7 April 1926; *s* of late Capt. Hon. Thomas Charles Fitzherbert, AM 1917, and Beryl (*d* 1959), 2nd *d* of John Waters and *widow* of Major Henry Brougham, RA; *S* uncle, 1941; *m* 1952, Morag Nada, *yr d* of late Lt-Col Alastair Campbell, Altries, Milltimber, Aberdeenshire; three *s* three *d*. *Educ*: Ampleforth College, York; St John's Coll., Cambridge. Lieut Scots Guards, 1945–48. Local Director, Barclays Bank Ltd (Birmingham), retired 1982; President: Stafford Rugby FC; Staffs Assoc. of Boys' Clubs; Staffs Playing Fields Assoc.; North Staffs Br. Inst. of Marketing, 1955–76; Patron, City of Stoke on Trent Amateur Operatic Soc.; Pres., Staffs CLA, 1973–83; Show Dir, Staffs Agric. Soc.; President: Old Amplefordian Cricket Club; North Staffs Sporting Club; Nat. Assoc. of Young Cricketers; Staffs Gentlemen CC. FInstM. DL Stafford, 1981. *Recreations*: cricket, shooting, yachting, fishing, tennis. *Heir*: *s* Hon. Francis Melfort William Fitzherbert [*b* 13 March 1954; *m* 1980, Katharine Mary, *d* of John Codrington; two *s*]. *Address*: Swynnerton Park, Stone, Staffordshire ST15 0QE. *TA* and *T*: Swynnerton 228; Salt Winds, West Wittering, Chichester, West Sussex. *T*: Birdham 514181. *Clubs*: Army and Navy; IZ; Free Foresters; MCC; Lord's Taverners.

*Died 8 Jan.* 1986.

**STAFFORD, Jack,** CB 1953; *b* 1909; *s* of late John William and Ruth Stafford; *m* 1932, Miriam Claire Holt; two *s*. *Educ*: Baines' Grammar School; Manchester Univ. Asst Lecturer in Economics, Manchester Univ., 1930; Lecturer in Economics, Manchester Univ., 1934; Rockefeller Fellow, 1938; Statistician, Central Statistical Office, 1941, Acting Director, 1946; Dir of Statistics, DTI (formerly BoT), 1948–72; Chief Statistician, Price Commn, 1973–78. *Publications*: Essays on Monetary Management, 1933; articles and papers in Jl of Royal Statistical Soc., Trans Manchester Statistical Soc., Economic Jl, Manchester School. *Recreation*: gardening. *Address*: 8 Normandy Gardens, Horsham, West Sussex. *T*: Horsham 67045.

*Died 24 Sept.* 1982.

**STAFFORD-KING-HARMAN, Sir Cecil William Francis,** 2nd Bt, *cr* 1913; *b* 6 Jan. 1895; *s* of late Rt Hon. Sir Thomas Stafford, Bt, CB, and Frances Agnes King-Harman; *S* father, 1935; assumed additional surname of King-Harman, 1932; *m* 1917, Sarah Beatrice (*d* 1979), *y d* of late Col A. D. Acland, CBE, and Hon. Mrs Acland, Feniton Court, Honiton, Devon; one *d* (one *s* killed in action and one *d* decd). *Educ*: RN Colleges, Osborne and Dartmouth; RMC Sandhurst; Christ Church, Oxford. Formerly Midshipman, Royal Navy, retired, 1912; commissioned 2nd Lt, The King's Royal Rifle Corps, 1914; Captain, 1917; served throughout European War in France and Italy (despatches); after war went to Christ Church, Oxford, MA (Hons) Agriculture; Steward, Irish Turf Club, 1938–40, 1943–46, 1948–51, 1952–55, 1959–62; Mem. of Racing Board, 1945–50. Appointed Member, Council of State for Ireland, 1956. War substantive Captain, 1940; Temporary Major, 1941; Temporary Lt-Col 1942. *Recreations*: shooting, racing, fishing. *Address*: St Catherines Park, Leixlip, Co. Kildare, Ireland. *T*:

280421. *Clubs*: Kildare Street and University, Irish Turf (Dublin).

*Died 5 Feb.* 1987 (*ext*).

**STAGG, Air Commodore (retired) Walter Allan,** CB 1958; CBE 1953 (OBE 1950); *b* 2 April 1903; *s* of late Frederick Edward and late Emma Jane Stagg; *m* 1943, Olive Georgina Legg (*d* 1978); no *c*. *Educ*: privately. Commnd in RAF, 1926; served India, 1928–33 (India General Service Medal, NW Frontier Clasp, 1930–31); Air Ministry (Directorate of Equipment), 1935–37; joined HMS Glorious in Mediterranean, 1937–39; on staff of HQ Training, Flying Training and Maintenance Comds, 1940–43; Dep. Director of Equipment (2) in Air Ministry, 1943–45; Senior Equipment Staff Officer, No 214 Group, Italy, 1945; Comd No 25 Maintenance Unit, 1945–46; in Ministry of Civil Aviation, 1946–47; on staffs of HQ Maintenance Comd, 40 Group and Flying Training Comd, 1947–51; Dep. Asst Chief of Staff (Logistics) at SHAPE, 1951–53; Director of Equipment (A) Air Ministry, 1954–55; Director of Movements, Air Ministry, 1955–58; Director, Supply Services Division, NATO; Maintenance Supply Services Agency, 1958–60, retired. *Address*: 3 Ingleside Court, Budleigh Salterton, Devon. *T*: Budleigh Salterton 5282. *Club*: Royal Air Force.

*Died 11 Sept.* 1984.

**STAINE, Sir Albert (Llewellyn),** Kt 1984; CBE 1979; **Hon. Mr Justice Staine;** Judge of the Court of Appeal, Belize, since 1982; Chief Justice of Belize, 1979–82; *b* 4 July 1928; *s* of Robert George and Beatrice Staine; *m* 1973, Marina Diana (*née* Andrewin); one *s*. *Educ*: St Michael's College, Belize; Hull University; LLB (Hons). Clerical Service, 1946; called to the Bar, Middle Temple, 1963; Crown Counsel, 1963; Solicitor General, 1966; Dir of Public Prosecutions, 1969; Acting Puisne Judge, 1971; Puisne Judge, 1973. Pres., Boys Brigade Council, 1975–; Chief Scout of Belize, 1980–. *Recreations*: reading, photography, tape recording. *Address*: 17 Princess Margaret Drive, Belize. *T*: 44385; (chambers) 2053.

*Died 25 Sept.* 1987.

**STAINFORTH, Graham Henry;** *b* 3 Oct. 1906; *s* of Lt-Col H. G. Stainforth, CMG, Indian Cavalry, and Georgina Helen, *d* of Maj.-Gen. H. Pipon, CB; *m* 1943, Ruth Ellen Douglas-Cooper (*d* 1986); one *s* two *d*. *Educ*: Wellington Coll., Berks; Emmanuel Coll., Cambridge. Assistant Master at Merchant Taylors' Sch., 1928–35, and Assistant Housemaster, 1933–35; Assistant Master and Tutor at Wellington Coll., and Head of the English Department, 1935–45; Hon. Secretary of Wellington College Clubs at Walworth, 1935–45; Headmaster of Oundle and Laxton Grammar Schools, 1945–56; Master of Wellington, 1956–66. Mem., Berks Educn Cttee, 1961–74; Fellow of Woodard Corp., 1966–80; Governor: Ardingly College, 1966–80; Portsmouth Grammar School, 1966–77; Cobham Hall Girls' School, 1969–75; Wallingford Comprehensive School, 1976–82. Hon. Liveryman, Grocers' Co., 1975. *Address*: The Cottage, Winterbrook, Wallingford, Oxon OX10 9EF. *T*: Wallingford 36414.

*Died 2 Sept.* 1987.

**STAINTON, Sir Anthony (Nathaniel),** KCB 1974 (CB 1967); QC 1975; First Parliamentary Counsel to HM Treasury, 1972–76 (Parliamentary Counsel, 1956–72); *b* 8 Jan. 1913; *s* of Evelyn Stainton, Barham Court, Canterbury; *m* 1st, 1947, Barbara Russell; three *d*; 2nd, 1966, Rachel Frances, *d* of late Col C. E. Coghill, CMG. *Educ*: Eton; Christ Church, Oxford. Called to the Bar, Lincoln's Inn, 1937; Hon. Bencher, 1984. *Club*: United Oxford & Cambridge University.

*Died 7 Nov.* 1988.

**STALKER, Prof. Alexander Logie,** TD; DL; Regius Professor of Pathology, University of Aberdeen, 1972–82, then Emeritus; Consultant Pathologist, North East Regional Hospital Board, 1955–82; *b* 15 Feb. 1920; *s* of late J. S. Stalker and Jean Logie; *m* 1945, Mary E. C. MacLean, MB, ChB (*d* 1985); one *s* three *d*. *Educ*: Morrison's Academy, Crieff; Univ. of Aberdeen. MB, ChB 1942; MD 1961; FRCPath 1970. RAMC War Service, 1942–47 and TA Service, 1948–64; ADMS 51 (H) Div., 1958–64; QHS, 1963–65. Univ. of Aberdeen: Sen. Lectr in Pathology, 1948–65; Reader in Pathology, 1965–69; Personal Prof. of Pathology, 1969–72; Dean of Faculty of Medicine, 1979–82. County Comr Scouts, City of Aberdeen, 1965–68. Pres., British Microcirculation Soc., 1968–73; Pres., European Soc. for Microcirculation, 1970–72; Mem., Pathological Soc. of Gt Britain and Ireland. Mem. Court, Univ. of Aberdeen, 1984–. DL Aberdeen, 1967. *Publications*: scientific papers in medical jls, esp. in field of microcirculation. *Recreations*: fishing, hill walking, Norwegian studies. *Address*: Coach End, Banchory, Kincardineshire AB3 3HS. *T*: Banchory 2460.

*Died 22 July* 1987.

**STAMM, Air Vice-Marshal William Percivale,** CBE 1960; *b* 27 Aug. 1909; *s* of Dr L. E. Stamm and L. E. (*née* Perry); *m* 1939, Mary Magdalene Van Zeller; two *s* one *d*; *m* 1974, Mrs J. M. Turner (*née* Erleigh). *Educ*: Haileybury Coll.; Guy's Hospital. MRCS, LRCP, 1932; MB, BS (London) 1933; DCP (London) 1946; DTM&H 1947; MRCP 1951; FRCP 1956; FRCPath 1964. House appointments, anatomy demonstrator, Guy's Hospital. Commissioned RAF, 1934; specialised in pathology and tropical medicine, 1938; comd RAF

Hospital, Takoradi, 1942–43; Sen. RAF Consultnt in Pathol. and Trop. Medicine, and OC RAF Inst. of Pathol. and Trop. Medicine, 1951–69, retired. Dir, Amoebiasis Res. Unit, 1970–77; Clinical Res. Manager, May & Baker Ltd, 1977–79. Member Council: Royal Society Trop. Med. and Hygiene, 1951–57, 1959–69, 1971–72 (Vice-President, 1957–59, and 1969–71); Assoc. of Clinical Pathologists, 1958–61 (President, 1966–67); United Services Sect., Royal Society Med., 1952–62 and 1966–69. Pres., British Div., Internat. Acad. Pathology, 1966; Hon. lectr, tropical pathology, Royal Free Med. Sch.; Cons., King's Coll. Hospital. QHS 1959–69. *Publications:* contrib. to Symposium, The Pathology of Parasitic Diseases; chapter on amoebiasis in Clinical Tropical Diseases (ed B. Maegraith); papers in Lancet, BMJ, Journal Clin. Pathology, Trans. Royal Society Tropical Med. and Hygiene, and Proc. Royal Society of Medicine. *Recreations:* building and decorating, opera and theatre. *Club:* Royal Air Force.                    *Died 10 March 1986.*

STAMMERS, Professor Francis Alan Roland, CBE 1945; TD (with clasp) 1949; Emeritus Professor of Surgery, University of Birmingham (Professor 1946–63); Hon. Cons. Surgeon, United Birmingham Hospitals; Cons.-Adviser in Surgery to Birmingham Regional Hospital Board, 1963–68, Hon. Cons.-Adviser, 1968–71; *b* 31 Jan. 1898; *s* of Charles Roland Stammers and Eliza Nellie Pettitt; *m* 1933, Lois Mildred Marris (*d* 1978); one *s* two *d*. *Educ:* Dudley Grammar School; Birmingham Univ.; London Hospital; Mayo Clinic, USA. Served European War, 1914–18, 2nd Lieut, Lieut RGA, 1916–18. BSc (Birmingham) 1920; MB, ChB (Birmingham), MRCS, LRCP 1923; FRCS 1925; ChM (Birmingham), 1936. Rockefellow Fellowship Mayo Clinic, USA, 1928; Late Surgeon, General Children's and Queen Elizabeth Hospitals, 1929; served War of 1939–45: surgical specialist and OC Surgical Division, RAMC, 1939–42; Cons. Surgeon, Brigadier AMS, W Command and forward areas of and Italy, 1942–45 (despatches); Hon. Colonel, AMS. Late Member Council (late Member Court of Examiners), Royal College of Surgeons, 1957–65; late External Examiner: University of London; University of Durham. Visiting Surgeon to Harvard University Medical School, Boston, Mass, USA, 1950; President, Surgical Section of Royal Society of Med. (later Hon. Member), 1952–53; British Council and BMA Lecturer in Cyprus, Baghdad and Khartoum, 1952–53; British Council and BMA Lecturer in Cyprus, Baghdad and Khartoum, 1952; Australasian Postgrad. Federation in Medicine Lecturer, 1958. President: Assoc. of Surgeons of Great Britain and Ireland, 1960–61; Midland Med. Society, 1960–61; Moynihan Chirurgical Club, 1962–63; W Midlands Surgical Soc., 1955; Mem. Council and Cases Cttee, Medical Protection Society. *Publications:* Partial Gastrectomy Complications with Metabolic Consequences (with J. Alexander Williams), 1963; numerous articles in medical and surgical journals and textbooks. *Recreations:* gardening, bowls, reading. *Address:* 56 Middle Park Road, Weoley Hill, Birmingham B29 4BJ. *T:* 021-475 1022. *Club:* University Staff (Birmingham).
                                                              *Died 12 Dec. 1982.*

STAMP, 3rd Baron, *cr* 1938, of Shortlands; **Trevor Charles Stamp**, MA, MD, FRCPath; Emeritus Professor of Bacteriology, Royal Postgraduate Medical School, University of London (Reader, 1937–48, Professor, 1948–70); *b* 13 Feb. 1907; *s* of 1st Baron Stamp, GCB, GBE; *S* brother, 1941; *m* 1932, Frances Dawes, *d* of late Charles Henry Bosworth, Evanston, Illinois, USA; two *s*. *Educ:* The Leys Sch., Cambridge; Gonville and Caius Coll., Cambridge; St Bartholomew's Hospital. MRCS, LRCP, BCh Cambridge, MA Cambridge, 1931; MB Cambridge, 1937. MD 1966. Demonstrator in Bacteriology, 1932–34, Lecturer in Bacteriology, 1934–37, London School of Hygiene and Tropical Medicine; Dir, Emergency Public Health Lab. Service Sect. 9, 1939–41; attached to the Ministry of Supply, 1941–45; Governor: Imperial College of Science and Technology, 1949–79; The Leys School, 1942–77; Pres., Queenswood School, 1981– (Governor, 1941–81; Chm., 1971–81). Mem., Exec. and Scientific Adv. Cttees, Animal Health Trust (formerly Vet. Educnl Trust), 1946–79. Mem., Parly Delegn of IPU to Egypt, 1973, to Tokyo, 1974, to Sofia, 1977, to Prague and Caracas, 1979. Founder Fellow, College of Pathologists, 1963 (now RCPath); Fellow, Royal Postgrad. Med. Sch., 1972. US Medal of Freedom with Silver Palm, 1947. Hon. Freeman, Barbers' Company, 1958. *Publications:* various papers on bacteriological subjects. *Recreations:* music, writing memoirs. *Heir:* *s* Dr the Hon. Trevor Charles Bosworth Stamp, MD, FRCP [*b* 18 Sept. 1935; *m* 1st, 1963, Anne Carolynn Churchill (marr. diss. 1971); two *d*; 2nd, 1975, Carol Anne, *d* of Keith Russell; one *s* one *d*]. *Address:* Middle House, 7 Hyde Park Street, W2. *T:* 01–723 8363. *Club:* Athenæum.
                                                              *Died 16 Nov. 1987.*

STAMP, Hon. (Arthur) Maxwell; Member, Civil Aviation Authority, 1976–81; Director: CYTO Ltd (Jersey), since 1982; Pan Electric Corp. (Nevada), since 1978; Economics International Inc., since 1965; Adviser, Sun Banks of Florida (USA), since 1981; *b* 20 Sept. 1915; 3rd *s* of 1st Baron Stamp, GCB, GBE; *m* 1944, Alice Mary Richards; one *s* two *d*. *Educ:* Leys Sch., Cambridge; Clare Coll., Cambridge. Called to the Bar, Inner Temple, 1939; War of 1939–

45, 2nd Lieut Intelligence Corps, 1940; Major 1943; Lieut-Colonel 1944. Financial Adviser, John Lewis Partnership Ltd, 1947–49; Acting Adviser, Bank of England, 1950–53. Alternate Executive Director for the UK, IMF, Washington, DC, USA, 1951–53; Director, European Dept, IMF, 1953–54. Adviser to the Governors, the Bank of England, 1954–57. Director: Hill Samuel & Co. Ltd, 1958–76; Triplex Hldgs Ltd, 1963–75; Olympic Holidays Ltd, 1981–83. Chairman: Maxwell Stamp Associates Ltd, 1962–79; Maxwell Stamp (Africa) Ltd, 1964–78; Bonsacks Baths Ltd, 1978–80. Member: Council of Foreign Bondholders, 1950–53, 1955–57; Council, Internat. Chamber of Commerce, 1961–75; Exec. Cttee, NIESR, 1962; Exec. Cttee, European League for Economic Co-operation, 1962; Council, Trade Policy Research Centre; Economic Cttee, CBI, 1968–; Chm., Home Office Cttee on London Taxi-Cab Trade, 1967. Mem., Panel of Conciliators, Internat. Centre for Settlement of Investment Disputes, Washington, 1968. Chm., The Rehearsal Orchestra. Governor, British Inst. for Recorded Sound, 1979, Chm., 1980. Chm., Truman and Knightley Educnl Trust, 1982–. Governor, LSE, 1968. *Recreations:* music, photography. *Address:* Mulberry Green Farmhouse, Copford, Essex. *T:* Colchester 210231. *Club:* Athenæum.                    *Died 31 March 1984.*

STAMP, Prof. Edward, MA (Cantab), CA; FCA (Canada); Research Professor in Accountancy since 1975, Professor of Accounting Theory, since 1971, Director of International Centre for Research in Accounting, since 1971, University of Lancaster; *b* 11 Nov. 1928; *s* of William Stamp and Anne Wilson; *m* 1953, Margaret Douglas Higgins, *d* of Douglas Gordon Higgins, MC, Toronto, Canada; one *s* three *d*. *Educ:* Quarry Bank, Liverpool; Cambridge Univ. Open Exhibnr, Foundation Scholar, Prizeman, First cl. Hons Natural Sciences. Lieut, RCNR. Fulbright Schol., 1950. With Arthur Young, Clarkson, Gordon & Co., Chartered Accountants and Management Consultants, Toronto and Montreal, 1951–62 (Manager, 1957; Partner, 1961); Sen. Lectr in Accountancy, Victoria Univ. of Wellington, NZ, 1962–65; Prof. of Accountancy, 1965–67; Prof. and Head of Dept of Accounting and Finance, Univ. of Edinburgh, 1967–71. Hon. Treas., NZ Inst. of Internat. Affairs, 1963–65; Member: Govt Cttee on Taxation, NZ, 1967; Bd of Research and Pubn, NZ Soc. of Accountants, 1964–67; Jt Standing Cttee on Degree Studies and Accounting Profession (UK), 1967–72 (Exec. Cttee, 1969–72); UK Adv. Bd of Accountancy Educn, 1969–72. Advr, HM Treasury, 1971–76 (resigned). Mem. various editorial bds in UK, USA, Germany and Australia. Chm., Brit. Accounting and Finance Assoc., 1968–71; Member: Steering Cttee, Long-Range Enquiry into Accounting Educn, 1971–; ASSC Working Party on scope and aims of Financial Accounts, 1974–75; ICA Research Bd, 1982–; Internat. Assoc. for Accounting Educn and Res., 1983–; Exec. Cttee, Europ. Accounting Assoc., 1984–. Visiting Professor, various univs in Europe, Africa, N America, Japan and Australasia; AAA Distinguished Internat. Vis. Lectr, USA, 1977; ASA Endowed Lectr, Univ. of Sydney, 1966 and 1979; Distinguished Vis. Prof., La Trobe Univ., Melbourne, 1982; Sir Julian Hodge Distinguished Lectr, Univ. of Wales, 1974 and 1983. Mem. Council, Lancaster Univ., 1981–. Hon. LLD Saskatchewan, 1984. *Publications:* The Elements of Consolidation Accounting, 1965; Looking at Balance Sheets, 1967; (with C. I. Marley) Accounting Principles and the City Code: the case for reform, 1970; Corporate Financial Reporting, 1972; (jtly) The Corporate Report, 1975; (with M. Moonitz) International Auditing Standards, 1978; The Future of Accounting and Auditing Standards, 1979; Corporate Reporting: Its Future Evolution, 1980; (with Sir Ronald Leach) British Accountancy Standards: the first ten years, 1981; Notable Financial Causes Célèbres, 1981; Selected Papers on Accounting, Auditing and Professional Problems, 1984; articles and papers in professional and academic jls in several countries, also papers to World Congresses of Accountants. *Recreation:* tormenting dinosaurs. *Address:* Roxburghe House, Haverbreaks, Lancaster LA1 5BN. *T:* Lancaster 32056; International Centre for Research in Accounting, Gillow House, Bailrigg, Lancaster. *T:* Lancaster 65201. *Clubs:* United Oxford & Cambridge University; Lancaster Golf and Country (Lancaster).                    *Died 10 Jan. 1986.*

STAMP, Rt. Hon. Sir (Edward) Blanshard, PC 1971; Kt 1964; a Lord Justice of Appeal, 1971–78; *b* 21 March 1905; *s* of late Alfred Edward Stamp, CB, and Edith Florence Guthrie; *m* 1st, 1934, Mildred Evelyn (*d* 1971), *d* of John Marcus Poer O'Shee; no *c*; 2nd, 1973, Mrs Pamela Joan Peters (separated 1975). *Educ:* Gresham's Sch., Holt; Trinity Coll., Cambridge (exhibnr; 1st cl. Hist. Tripos). Called to Bar, Inner Temple, 1929; Bencher of Lincoln's Inn, 1956. Served War of 1939–45 as civilian attached General Staff, War Office. Junior Counsel to Commissioners of Inland Revenue (Chancery), 1954; Junior Counsel to Treasury (Chancery), 1960–64; a Judge of the High Court of Justice, Chancery Div., 1964–71. Mem., Restrictive Practices Court, 1970–71. *Address:* 30 Hanover House, St John's Wood High Street, NW8 7DY. *T:* 01-722 1855. *Clubs:* United Oxford & Cambridge University, Garrick.
                                                              *Died 20 June 1984.*

STAMP, Hon. Maxwell; *see* Stamp, Hon. A. M.

**STANBRIDGE, Air Vice-Marshal (retired) Reginald Horace,** CB 1956; OBE 1944; MRCS, LRCP, DPM, DIH; CStJ 1952; *b* 24 Nov. 1897; *s* of Horace John Stanbridge; *m* 1945, Inez Valerie, *d* of Arthur Holland; one *s*. *Educ*: Eastbourne; St Mary Coll., London Univ.; London Hospital Medical College. Served War, 1915–18, Lieut RGA, and RFC. Principal Medical Officer in following RAF Commands: Aden, 1938–41; Transport, 1948–49; Bomber, 1950–53; 2nd TAF; KHP, 1952, QHP, 1952–56; Principal Medical Officer, Middle East Air Force, 1953–56; retired, 1956. BoT later CAA Med. Dept, 1966–83. Mem., Gray's Inn. Liveryman, Soc. of Apothecaries; Freeman, City of London. *Publications*: various articles in The Lancet, RAF Quarterly, Wine and Food. *Recreations*: sailing, tennis. *Address*: 43 Moor Park Road, Northwood, Middlesex 6HA 2DH. *Club*: Royal Air Force.               *Died 3 Jan. 1986.*

**STANCLIFFE, Very Rev. Michael Staffurth,** MA; Dean of Winchester, 1969–86, Dean Emeritus, since 1986; *b* 8 April 1916; *s* of late Rev. Canon Harold Emmet Stancliffe, Lincoln; *m* 1940, Barbara Elizabeth, *yr d* of late Rev. Canon Tissington Tatlow; two *s* one *d*. *Educ*: Haileybury; Trinity Coll., Oxford. Curate of St James, Southbroom, Devizes, 1940–43; priest-in-charge, Ramsbury, 1943–44; curate of Cirencester and priest-in-charge of Holy Trinity, Watermoor, 1944–49; Chaplain and Master, Westminster School, 1949–57; Canon of Westminster and Rector of St Margaret's, Westminster, 1957–69; Speaker's Chaplain, 1961–69; Preacher to Lincoln's Inn, 1954–57. Mem., General Synod, 1970–80; Chm., Council for Places of Worship, 1972–75; Mem. Cathedrals Advisory Commn for England, 1981–. Fellow, Winchester Coll., 1973. *Publications*: contrib. to A House of Kings, 1966; Symbols and Dances, 1986. *Address*: 36 Potter Hill, Pickering, N Yorks YO18 8AD.                              *Died 26 March 1987.*

**STANDING, Michael Frederick Cecil,** CBE 1959; retired as Controller of Programme Organisation (sound), BBC, 1957–70; *b* 28 Feb. 1910; *s* of late Sir Guy Standing, KBE, and of late Lady Standing; *m* 1947, Helen Jean Dawson, *widow* of Flying Officer Michael Hope Lumley and *d* of late Lt-Comdr Dawson Miller, CBE, RN, retired; one *s* two *d* (one *s* decd). *Educ*: Charterhouse. Baring Brothers & Co. Ltd, 1927–35; BBC, 1935; Director of Outside Broadcasting, 1940–45; Head of Variety, 1945–52; Controller of Sound Entertainment, BBC, 1952–57. *Recreations*: painting, gardening, cricket. *Address*: Trottiscliffe House, near West Malling, Kent. *T*: Fairseat 822293.
                              *Died 1 Dec. 1984.*

**STANFORD, (William) Bedell,** MA, LittD; Chancellor, Dublin University, Trinity College, since 1982 (Pro-Chancellor, 1977–82); Regius Professor of Greek in University of Dublin, 1940–80; *b* 1910; *s* of Rev. Bedell Stanford, then Rector of Trinity Church, Belfast, and Susan Stanford; *m* 1935, Dorothy Isobel Wright; two *s* two *d*. *Educ*: Bishop Foy Sch., Waterford; Trinity Coll., Dublin (Scholar; MA, LittD). Trinity College, Dublin: Fellow, 1934, Sen. Fellow, 1962, Emeritus Fellow, 1980; Tutor, 1938–54; Sen. Master, Non-regent, 1960–62; Dep. Public Orator, 1958–60, Public Orator, 1970–71. Formerly External Examiner in Greek for National Univ., Queen's Univ., University of Wales, University of Leeds and Royal Colleges of Physicians and Surgeons, Ireland. MRIA. Sather Professor of Classical Literature, University of California, Berkeley, 1966; Visiting Prof., McGill Univ., Montreal, 1968, Wayne State Univ., 1971, Princeton Univ., 1974, Texas Univ., 1977, Vassar Coll., 1980, Wooster Coll., 1982. Has lectured on over 40 other campuses in North America. Editor of Hermathena, 1942–62. Rep. of Dublin Univ. in the Irish Senate, 1948–69. Irish Rep., Council of Europe, Strasbourg, 1951, European Parliamentary Conf., Vienna, 1956 and Inter-parliamentary Conf., Warsaw, 1959. Member Irish Radio Advisory Council until 1952. Governor, Erasmus Smith's Sch.; Mem., General Synod and former Mem., Dublin Diocesan Synod of Church of Ireland and of Episcopal Electoral Coll. for Southern Province; Sec., Appointments Cttee, TCD, 1936–37, Hon. Sec., TCD Assoc., 1950–55. Mem. Council, Hellenic Soc., 1965–68; Pres., Birmingham Branch, Classical Assoc., 1968; Vice-Pres. RIA, 1969; Chairman: Irish Nat. Cttee for Greek and Latin Studies, 1968–72; Council of Dublin Inst. for Advanced Studies, 1973–80. Hon. LLD Belfast. Higher Comdr, Order of Phoenix, Greece, 1980. *Publications*: Greek Metaphor, 1936; Ambiguity in Greek Literature, 1939; Livy XXIV edited for schools, 1942; Aeschylus in His Style, 1942; Homer's Odyssey, edited, 1947–48 (2nd edn, 1961–62); The Ulysses Theme, 1954 (2nd edn, 1963); Aristophanes' Frogs, edited, 1957 (2nd edn, 1963); Sophocles' Ajax, edited, 1963; The Sound of Greek, 1967; (with R. B. McDowell) Mahaffy, 1971; (with J. V. Luce) The Quest for Ulysses, 1975; (with Robert Fagles) Aeschylus: The Oresteia, 1976; Ireland and the Classical Tradition, 1976 (2nd edn, 1984); Enemies of Poetry, 1980; Greek Tragedy and the Emotions, 1983; various shorter publications on literary, linguistic, ecclesiastical and historical subjects. *Address*: 25 Trinity College, Dublin; 2 Mount Salus, Dalkey, Co. Dublin. *T*: Dublin 859120. *Club*: Royal Irish Yacht (Dun Laoghaire).
                              *Died 30 Dec. 1984.*

**STANFORD-TUCK, Wing Commander Robert Roland,** DSO 1940; DFC (2 bars); *b* 1 July 1916; *s* of Stanley Lewis Tuck and Ethel Constance Tuck; *m* 1945, Joyce (*d* 1985); two *s*. *Educ*: St Dunstan's Preparatory School and College, Reading. Left school, 1932, and went to sea as a cadet with Lamport and Holt; joined Royal Air Force, Sept. 1935; posted to No 65 Fighter Sqdn, Aug. 1936, and served with them until outbreak of war; posted to 92 (F) Sqdn, and went through air fighting at Dunkirk, shooting down 8 enemy aircraft (DFC); posted to Comd No 257 Burma Fighter Sqdn, Sept. 1940, till July 1941, when given command of Wing; comd Duxford and Biggin Hill Wings; prisoner 1942, escaped 1945. Record to end July 1941: 27 confirmed victories, 8 probably destroyed, 6 damaged; wounded twice, baled out 4 times. Retired list, 1948. *Relevant publication*: Fly For Your Life (by L. Forrester). *Address*: 2 Whitehall, Sandwich Bay, Kent.           *Died 5 May 1987.*

**STANIER, Prof. Roger Yate,** PhD; FRS 1978; Professor, l'Institut Pasteur, France, since 1971; *b* 22 Oct. 1916; *s* of Francis Thomas Thursfield Stanier and Dorothy Alice Broadbent; *m* 1956, Germaine Bazire; one *d*. *Educ*: Shawnigan Lake Sch., Canada; Oak Bay High Sch.; Univ. of BC (BA 1936); Univ. of Calif at Los Angeles (MA 1940); Stanford Univ. (PhD 1942). Hon. Dr ès Sciences, Reims, 1973; Hon. DSc Chicago, 1978. For. Mem., Royal Acad. of Arts and Sci., Amsterdam, 1978; For. Associate, Nat. Acad. Sci., USA, 1979; Associate Mem., French Acad. of Sci., 1981; Hon. Member: Soc. for Gen. Microbiology, 1978; Amer. Soc. for Microbiology, 1979. Carlsburg Medallist, Carlsburg Res. Inst., Denmark, 1976; (first) Bergey's Manual Award, USA, 1978; Leeuwenhoek Medal, Royal Netherlands Acad. of Arts and Sci., 1980; Carlos J. Finlay Prize, Cuba, 1980; Médaille de'Or de la Société d'Encouragement au Progrès, France, 1981. Chevalier de la Légion d'Honneur, France, 1977. *Publications*: The Microbial World, 1957 (4th edn 1976); articles in Jl of Bacteriol., Jl of Gen. Microbiol, and Arch. of Microbiol. *Address*: 143 rue de Videlle, 78830 Bullion, France. *T*: 484–3023.                           *Died 29 Jan. 1982.*

**STANISTREET, Rt. Rev. Henry Arthur,** DD (*jure dig.*), Dublin University, 1958; *b* 19 March 1901; *s* of late Rev. Precentor A. H. Stanistreet; *m* 1938, Ethel Mary Liversidge; one *d*. *Educ*: Trent Coll., Derbyshire; St Columba's Coll., Rathfarnham; Trinity Coll., Dublin (MA). Ordained 1924. Curate, Clonmel with Innislonagh, 1924–27; Curate in charge, Corbally and Chaplain, Roscrea Hospital, 1927–30; Rector: Templeharry with Borrisnafarney, 1930–31; Roscrea, 1931–43; Surrogate, 1931; Rural Dean, Ely O'Carroll, 1933–43; Canon, Killaloe, 1940–43; Dean of Killaloe Cathedral, 1943–57; Prebendary, Killaloe, Rural Dean, O'Mullod, Rector, St Flannan with O'Gonnilloe and Castletownarra, 1943–57; Rural Dean, Traderry, 1949–57; Prebendary, St Patrick's Cathedral, Dublin, 1955–57; Bishop of Killaloe, Kilfenora, Clonfert and Kilmacduagh, 1957–71. *Address*: Woodville, Dunmore East, Co. Waterford, Ireland.                  *Died 4 Sept. 1981.*

**STANLEY, Brian Taylor,** MA; *b* 1907; *s* of T. T. and Ada A. Stanley, Birmingham; *m* 1938, Audrey, *d* of H. and E. C. Topsfield, Sunbury on Thames; one *s* one *d*. *Educ*: King Edward's Sch., Birmingham; Christ Church, Oxford; London Day Trng Coll., Columbia Univ., New York; Pädagogische Akademie, Hanover. Teacher under the Warwickshire County Council and Resident Tutor, Fircroft Working Men's College, 1931; Lecturer in Education, Manchester University, 1932; Professor of Education, King's College, Newcastle upon Tyne, 1936–48; Director Institute of Education: Univ. of Durham, 1948–63; Univ. of Newcastle upon Tyne, 1963-72; In-Service Trng Advr, St Mary's Coll. of Educn, Newcastle upon Tyne, 1972–81. Order of St Olav, Norway, 1972. *Publications*: The Education of Junior Citizens, 1945; contributions to various educational jls, at home and abroad. *Address*: 5 Corchester Avenue, Corbridge, Northumberland. *T*: Corbridge 2075.
                              *Died 11 March 1983.*

**STANLEY, Charles Orr,** CBE 1945 (OBE 1943); Hon. President, Sunbeam Wolsey Ltd; Director: Arts Theatre Trust; Stanley Foundation Ltd; Orr Investments Ltd; *b* 15 April 1899; *s* of John and Louisa A. Stanley; *m* 1st, 1924, Elsie Florence Gibbs; one *s* decd; 2nd, 1934, Velma Dardis Price (*d* 1970); 3rd, 1971, Lorna Katherine Sheppard (*d* 1977). *Educ*: Bishop Foy School, Waterford; City and Guilds, Finsbury. Served European War, RFC, 1917–18; Civil Engineer, 1922. Chm., Radio Industry Council, 1962–65; Pres., British Radio Equipment Manufrs Assoc., 1962–64. Hon. Pres., Pye of Cambridge Ltd, 1966. Hon. LLD Trinity College, Dublin, 1960. FCGI 1961. *Address*: Lisselan, Clonakilty, County Cork, Ireland. *T*: Bandon 33699. *Clubs*: Royal Automobile; Royal Thames Yacht; Royal Cork Yacht.        *Died 18 Jan. 1989.*

**STANLEY, Dr Herbert Muggleton,** FRS 1966; *b* Stratford-upon-Avon, 20 July 1903; *m* 1930, Marjorie Mary (*née* Johnson); two *s* two *d*. *Educ*: King Edward VI Grammar School, Stratford-on-Avon; Birmingham University (1919–29). BSc 1923; MSc 1925; PhD 1930, FRIC; Mem. Council, Royal Soc., 1968. *Publications*: articles in numerous journals, including Jl Chem. Soc., Soc. Chem. Ind. *Recreations*: archæology, gardening. *Address*: West Halse, Bow, Crediton, Devon. *T*: Bow 262.        *Died 4 July 1987.*

**STANLEY, Michael Charles,** MBE 1945; Director of The Proprietors of Hay's Wharf Ltd, and various subsidiary companies, 1955–80; *b* 11 Aug. 1921; *s* of late Col Rt Hon. O. F. G. Stanley, PC, MC, MP, and Lady Maureen Stanley (*née* Vane-Tempest-Stewart); *m* 1951, Ailleen Fortune Hugh Smith, *d* of Owen Hugh Smith, Old Hall, Langham, Rutland; two *s. Educ:* Eton; Trinity College, Cambridge. Served 1939–46 with Royal Signals (Capt. 1943); N Africa, Sicily and Italy with 78th Infantry Div. Trinity, 1946–49 (Nat. Science and Engineering, MA). Served Engineering Apprenticeship with Metropolitan Vickers Electrical Co. Ltd, 1949–52. CEng 1966; MIEE 1966 (AMIEE 1952). Mem. Court, Lancaster University, 1980–. High Sheriff for Westmorland, 1959; Westmorland County Councillor, 1961–74; Vice-Lieutenant of Westmorland, 1965–74; DL Westmorland, 1964–74, Cumbria, 1974; High Sheriff, Cumbria, 1975. Hon. Col 33rd Signal Regt (V), 1981–87. *Recreations:* idleness, walking, wine. *Address:* Halecat, Witherslack, Grange-over-Sands, Cumbria LA11 6RU. *T:* Witherslack (044852) 229. *Clubs:* White's, Beefsteak, Brooks's; St James's (Manchester); Puffins (Edinburgh).
*Died 3 June* 1990.

**STANLEY, Hon. Richard Oliver;** *b* 29 Jan. 1920; 2nd *s* of Colonel Rt Hon. Lord Stanley, PC, MC (*d* 1938), and Sibyl Louise Beatrix Cadogan (*d* 1969), *e d* of Henry Arthur, late Viscount Chelsea, and Lady Meux; *g s* of 17th Earl of Derby, KG, PC, GCB, GCVO; *b* and *heir-pres.* to 18th Earl of Derby; *m* 1st, 1965, Susan (*d* 1976), *o d* of Sir John Aubrey-Fletcher, 7th Bt; 2nd, 1979, Mrs Mary Harrison. *Educ:* Eton. Served War of 1939–45; 2nd Lieutenant, Grenadier Guards, 1940, later Captain. Joined staff of Conservative Central Office after the war. Parliamentary Private Secretary to First Lord of the Admiralty, 1951–55. MP (C) N Fylde Div. of Lancashire, 1950–66, retired. Joint Treasurer, Conservative Party, 1962–66. Mem., Gaming Bd, 1968–77. *Address:* 26a North Audley Street, W1. *T:* 01-493 0813; New England House, Newmarket, Suffolk. *T:* Cambridge 811394. *Died 15 Nov.* 1983.

**STANLEY, Sir Robert (Christopher Stafford),** KBE 1954 (OBE 1942); CMG 1944; *b* 12 May 1899; *o s* of Frederic Arthur and Mary Stanley; *m* 1927, Ursula Cracknell (*d* 1981); one *d. Educ:* Westminster; RMA, Woolwich. RGA, 1918–21; war service in Palestine; Reuter's editorial staff, 1923–24; entered Nigerian Administrative Service, 1925; transferred Cyprus, 1935; Commissioner, Larnaca, 1936–37; Chief Assistant Secretary to Govt of Cyprus, 1938–41; Colonial Secretary, Barbados, 1942; Colonial Secretary, Gibraltar, 1945; Chief Secretary, Northern Rhodesia. 1947–52; High Commissioner for Western Pacific, 1952–55, retd. Speaker of Mauritius Legislative Council, 1957–59. *Publication:* King George's Keys, 1975. *Address:* Tragariff, Bantry, Co. Cork, Ireland. *T:* Bantry 74. *Club:* Royal Commonwealth Society. *Died 31 May* 1981.

**STANLEY-CLARKE, Brig. Arthur Christopher Lancelot,** CBE 1940; DSO 1918; *b* 30 June 1886; *s* of late Ronald Stanley Clarke and late Mabel Octavia Shadwell; *m* 1931, Olive, 3rd *d* of late Thomas Carroll-Leahy of Woodfort, Mallow, Co. Cork; no *c. Educ:* Winchester; Oxford. Capt. OUAFC, 1908–9; gazetted The Cameronians (Scottish Rifles), 1909; commanded 1st Royal Scots Fusiliers, 1931–34; Asst Comdt and Chief Instructor, Netheravon Wing, Small Arms School, 1934–37; Comdr 154th (Argyll and Sutherland) Infantry Brigade TA, 1937; Commander Lothian and Border District, 1941–44; retired pay, 1944. Served European War, 1914–18 (despatches, DSO, and bar, Legion of Honour, Croix de Guerre); War of 1939–45 (CBE). *Address:* Shiel, Baily, Co. Dublin, Ireland. *Died 8 Jan.* 1983.

**STANNARD, Rt. Rev. Robert William,** MA; *b* 20 Oct. 1895; *s* of late Robert John and Fanny Rebecca Stannard; *m* 1922, Muriel Rose Sylvia Knight (*d* 1985), one *s* (elder son killed in action April 1945). *Educ:* Westminster; Christ Ch., Oxford; Cuddesdon Theological College. ALCM 1910. Served army, 1915–19, Lieut Middlesex Regiment. Oxford: Distinction in Lit. Hum., First in Theology, Liddon Student; Ordained, 1922; Curate Bermondsey Parish Church, 1922–24; Curate-in-Charge S Mary's, Putney, 1924–27; Vicar of St James, Barrow-in-Furness, 1927–34; Rural Dean of Dalton, 1934; Rector of Bishopwearmouth (Sunderland), 1934–41; Rural Dean of Sunderland, 1937–41; Archdeacon of Doncaster, 1941–47; Chaplain to the King, 1944–47; Bishop Suffragan of Woolwich, 1947–59; Dean of Rochester, 1959–66. Grand Chaplain, United Grand Lodge of England, 1948–50. Master, Worshipful Co. of Gardeners, 1972–73. *Recreations:* gardening and music. *Address:* Dendron, Reading Road North, Fleet, Hants. *T:* Fleet 614059.
*Died 26 Dec.* 1986.

**STANNER, Prof. William Edward Hanley,** CMG 1972; PhD; FASSA; Emeritus Professor; Consultant, Aboriginal Lands Commissioner, 1978; Research Scholar, Australian Institute of Aboriginal Studies, 1977–79; *b* 24 Nov. 1905; *s* of late Andrew Edwin Stanner and Mary Catherine Stanner (*née* Hanley), Sydney; *m* 1962, Patricia Ann Williams; two *s. Educ:* Univ. of Sydney (MA, cl. I Hons, 1934); London Sch. of Economics (PhD 1938). Served War: 2nd AIF,

1942–46, Lt-Col (Personal Staff of Minister for the Army, 1941–42). Field research in North and Central Australia (Aust. Nat. Res. Council), 1932, 1934–35; Kenya (Oxf. Soc. St Res. Cttee), 1938–39; Papua-New Guinea, Fiji, W Samoa (Inst. Pacific Relns), 1946–47; Northern Territory (ANU), 1952–62. Foundn Dir, East African Inst. Soc. Res. (Makerere, Uganda), 1947–49. Australian National Univ.: Reader, 1949–64; Prof. of Anthropology and Sociology, 1964–70; Emer. Prof. and Hon. Fellow, 1971. Chm., Governing Body, 1954, Bursar, 1954–55, and Hon. Mem., 1960–, Univ. House, ANU; Vis. Fellow, Dept of Prehistory and Anthropology, Sch. of Gen. Studies, ANU, 1975–80. Personal staff of NSW Premier, 1933–34; Commonwealth Treasurer, Imperial Conf., 1937; Australian Comr, S Pacific Commn, 1953–55; Convenor and Chm., Commonwealth Conf. on Aboriginal Studies, 1961; First Exec. Officer, Aust. Inst. of Aboriginal Studies, 1961–62. Mem., Commonwealth Council for Aboriginal Affairs, 1967–76; Consultant, Commonwealth Dept of Aboriginal Affairs, 1976–77; Technical Adviser, House of Reps Standing Cttee on Aboriginal Affairs, Commonwealth Parlt, 1974–75. Boyer Lectr, 1968. Mueller Medallist, ANZAAS, 1971; Cilento Medal, 1972. Hon. DLitt, ANU, 1972. *Publications:* The South Seas in Transition, 1953; On Aboriginal Religion, 1964; After the Dreaming, 1968; White Man Got No Dreaming, 1979; numerous articles in learned jls. *Recreation:* reading. *Address:* 75 Empire Circuit, Forrest, Canberra, ACT 2603, Australia. *T:* 731305. *Club:* Commonwealth (Canberra).
*Died 8 Oct.* 1981.

**STANSFIELD, Sir Walter,** Kt 1979; CBE 1974; MC 1945; QPM 1969; CPM 1959; Chief Constable of Derbyshire, 1967–79; Chairman, Consolidated Safeguards, since 1983; *b* 15 Feb. 1917; *er s* of F. and A. G. Stansfield; *m* 1939, Jennie Margery Biggs; one *d. Educ:* Chartres, Eure et Loire, France; Heath Grammar Sch., Halifax. West Riding Constabulary, 1939–42, 1950–56, 1959–64 (Asst Chief Constable, 1962–64). Served War, 1942–46: commnd in RA (Field), 1943; Special Ops Exec., 1943–45. Control Commission (Germany), 1945–46; seconded to: Special Police Corps, Germany, 1946–50; Cyprus Police Force, 1956–59. Chief Constable of Denbighshire, 1964–67. CStJ 1979. Croix de Guerre (France), 1947. *Publication:* (Jt Editor) Moriarty's Police Law, 24th edn, 1981. *Recreations:* music, photography, gardening. *Address:* 82 Park Avenue, Wrexham, Clwyd LL12 7AH. *T:* Wrexham 364072. *Clubs:* Army and Navy, Special Forces. *Died 14 Dec.* 1984.

**STANTON, Maj.-Gen. Anthony Francis,** OBE 1955 (MBE 1945); *b* 6 Aug. 1915; *s* of Brig.-Gen. F. H. G. Stanton and Hilda Margaret (*née* Parkin); *m* 1943, Elizabeth Mary (*d* 1985), *d* of John Reginald Blackett-Ord, Whitfield Hall, Hexham; one *s* two *d. Educ:* Eton Coll.; RMA Woolwich. Commissioned RA, 1936. Served in: India, 1936–41; ME, 1941–43; NW Europe, 1944–45; subseq. in Germany, Far East and UK; Imp. Def. Coll., 1962; COS, HQ Northern Comd, 1967–70, retired 1970. Col Comdt, RA, 1972–77. *Recreation:* country sporting pursuits. *Address:* Wooperton Hall, Alnwick, Northumberland. *T:* Wooperton 241. *Club:* Army and Navy.
*Died 13 Nov.* 1988.

**STANTON, Blair Rowlands H.;** *see* Hughes-Stanton.

**STANTON, Lt-Col John Richard Guy,** MBE (mil.) 1953; Vice Lord Lieutenant of Derbyshire, since 1987; *b* 28 Nov. 1919; *s* of Comdr Henry Guy Stanton, RN and Evelyn Violet Muriel Stanton (*née* Handcock); *m* 1941, Margaret Frances Harries, OBE; two *s* three *d. Educ:* Hon. Co. of Skinners' Sch., Tunbridge Wells; RMC Sandhurst. psc, jssc. RMC 1938; commissioned Royal Sussex Regt, 1939; wounded El Alamein and POW, 1942; served War Office, Italy, Palestine, UK, Malta and Libya (MBE), BAOR, MoD, to 1962; Central Reconnaissance Estabt, 1962–64; C-in-C's personal liaison officer to Comdr 1 (NL) Corps, 1964–66; MoD, 1966–70; DAQMG, HQ E Midland Dist, 1970–72, retired 1972. Chairman: E Midlands Region, Nat. Trust, 1975–85; Derbys Br., CLA, 1983–85; Derbys Rural Community Council, 1986–; Gen. Comr of Income Tax. DL Derbys 1973, High Sheriff, 1974–75. *Recreations:* country pursuits, shooting. *Address:* Snelston Hall, Ashbourne, Derbyshire DE6 2EP. *T:* Ashbourne 42064. *Club:* Army & Navy.
*Died 21 April* 1990.

**STANWAY, Rt. Rev. Alfred;** President, Australian Christian Literature Society, since 1971; *b* 9 Sept. 1908; *s* of Alfred Stanway, Millicent, S Australia, and Rosa Dawson; *m* 1939, Marjory Dixon Harrison. *Educ:* Melbourne High Sch.; Ridley Coll., Melbourne; Australian Coll. of Theology (ThL (Hons), 1934); Melbourne Teachers Coll. MA (Lamb), 1951. Diocese of Melbourne: Curate of St Albans, 1935–36; Mission of St James and St John, 1936–37; Diocese of Mombasa: Missionary, Giriama District, 1937–44; Principal Kaloleni Sch., 1938–44; Acting Gen. Sec., Victorian Branch, Church Missionary Soc., 1941; Hon. CF, 1942–46; Missionary, Maseno District, 1944–47; Rural Dean of Nyanza, 1945–47; Examining Chaplain to Bishop of Mombasa, 1945–51; Sec. African Council and African Education Board, Diocese of Mombasa, 1948–50; Commissary to Bishop of Mombasa, 1949–51;

Archdeacon and Canon of Diocese of Mombasa, 1949–51; Bishop of Central Tanganyika, 1951–71; Dep. Principal, Ridley Coll., Melbourne Univ., 1971–75; Pres., Trinity Episcopal Sch. for Ministry, Pittsburgh, 1975–78. *Recreation:* chess. *Address:* 7 Elm Grove, Mt Waverley, Victoria 3149, Australia.
*Died 27 June 1989.*

**STAPLES, Sir John (Richard),** 14th Bt *cr* 1628; *b* 5 April 1906; *s* of John Molesworth Staples (*d* 1948) and of Helen Lucy Johnstone, *yr d* of late Richard Williams Barrington; *S* kinsman, Sir Robert George Alexander Staples, 13th Bt, 1970; *m* 1933, Sybella, *d* of late Dr Charles Henry Wade; two *d. Heir: cousin* Thomas Staples [*b* 9 Feb. 1905; *m* 1952, Frances Ann Irvine (*d* 1981)]. *Address:* Butter Hill House, Dorking, Surrey.
*Died 10 March 1989.*

**STARKE, Leslie Gordon Knowles,** CBE 1953; *b* 23 May 1898; *s* of William and Martha Starke; *m* 1929, Joan Mary Davidson; no *c. Educ:* Andover Grammar School; University College, Southampton; Queen's College, Oxford. Served European War, 1914–18, RE (Signal Service), 1918. Entered Government Actuary's Dept, 1919; Ministry of Food, 1939–46 (Director of Statistics and Intelligence, 1943–46); Principal Actuary and Establishment Officer, Government Actuary's Dept, 1946–58; Deputy Government Actuary, 1958–63. *Recreations:* gardening, walking. *Address:* Brack Mound House, Castle Precincts, Lewes, East Sussex. *T:* Lewes 4139.
*Died 28 Oct. 1984.*

**STARLEY, Hubert Granville,** CBE 1946; FIMI; Chairman, Starleys Estates Ltd, since 1974; *b* Skipton, 16 April 1909; *s* of late Hubert Ernest and Fanny Starley, Coventry; *great nephew* of J. K. Starley, founder of Rover Co.; *g g s* of James Starley of Coventry, inventor of the bicycle and differential gear; *m* 1933, Lilian Amy Heron, Bournemouth; one *s* one *d. Educ:* Ermysteds; Skipton, Yorks. Man. Dir, 1963–72, Vice-Chm., 1972–74, Champion Sparking Plug Co. Ltd; Assistant to Lord Beaverbrook, Minister of Supply, 1941; Advisor to War Office and Air Ministry on Stores Packaging, 1943; Hon. Chairman Anglo-American Packaging Exhibition Committee, 1944; Member Barlow Mission to the USA, 1944; Hon. Chm., Motor Industry Jubilee Committee, 1946; Society of Motor Manufacturers and Traders, Ltd: Chm., Accessory and Component Manufrs' Cttee, 1945–46, 1953–55, 1961–62; Mem. Council Management Cttees, 1953–73; Mem., General Purposes Cttee, 1968–72; Vice-Pres., 1972–73. Chm., Fellowship of the Motor Industry, 1969–70; Pres., Cycle and Motor Cycle Assoc., 1970 (Mem., 1950–75); Hon. Chm. Inter-Services Packaging Cttee, MoD, 1958–65; Founder, Mem. Council and Dir, Aims of Industry Ltd, 1942–83, Vice-Pres., 1972–83. Vice-Pres., Inst. of Motor Industry, 1973–75; Mem. Council, CBI, 1970–75. Hon. Chm., Home Office Mobile Crime Prevention Cttee, 1968–78. Past Pres. and Patron, Twickenham Conservative Assoc. Master, Livery Company of Coachmakers and Coach Harness Makers, 1966–67; Pres., Pickwick Bicycle Club, 1954. Hon. Pageant Master and Organiser, History of British Motoring Cavalcades, Lord Mayor's Show, 1964; Hon. Organiser, 6 day Cycle Race, Earl's Court, 1967. *Address:* Rothesay House, London Road, Twickenham TW1 1ES. *T:* 01-892 5187. *Clubs:* Carlton, Royal Automobile, Royal Thames Yacht.
*Died 30 Oct. 1984.*

**STARLING, Brigadier John Sieveking,** CBE 1945; retired; *b* 18 Jan. 1898; *o s* of late Prof. Ernest H. Starling, CMG, MD, FRS, and Florence, *d* of late Sir Edward Sieveking; *m* 1st, 1934, Vivian Barbara, *d* of late Henry J. Wagg, OBE (marriage dissolved 1948); one *s*; 2nd, 1948, Marion, *d* of late A. G. Pool, and *widow* of C. A. Morell-Miller. *Educ:* University College School; Royal Military Academy; Trinity College, Cambridge. Commissioned 2nd Lt RA, 1916; served European War, France and Flanders, 1916–18 (wounded twice); normal career of a Regimental Officer in UK, Egypt and India. Attached French Army, 1939; served France and Flanders, Middle East and Italy, 1939–46 (despatches, wounded, CBE); retired from Regular Army as Hon. Brig., 1948. *Recreations:* fishing, shooting, sailing. *Address:* Le Hurel, Trinity, Jersey, CI. *T:* 61066. *Club:* Army and Navy.
*Died 4 March 1986.*

**STATON, Air Vice-Marshal William Ernest,** CB 1947; DSO and Bar, 1940; MC 1918; DFC and Bar, 1918; *b* 1898; *m* 1st, 1919, Norah Carina Workman (*d* 1969); two *s*; 2nd, 1973, Jean Patricia Primrose (*née* Richardson). Served European War, 1914–19 (despatches); War of 1939–45 (despatches); Wing Comdr, 1939; Group Capt., 1940; Actg Air Commodore, 1941; Air Vice-Marshal, 1950; SASO Singapore, 1942; prisoner of war, Japan, 1942–45 (despatches); ADC to the King, 1940–46; AOC No 46 Group, 1945–47; Commandant Central Bomber Establishment, 1947–49; Air Officer-in-Charge of Administration, Technical Training Command, 1949–52; retired 1952. Helper, RAF Benevolent Fund, 1952–. Chm. RAF Small Arms Assoc., 1947–52; Capt. British Shooting Teams, Olympic Games, 1948 and 1952. Ex-Mem. of Councils: Internat. Shooting Union, Stockholm; Nat. Rifle Assoc.; Nat. Small Bore Rifle Assoc.; Brit. Olympic Assoc. (1952–57). *Address:* Wildhern,

Creek Edn, Emsworth, Hants. *Club:* Emsworth Sailing (Flag Officer, 1968; Commodore, 1972–).
*Died 22 July 1983.*

**STAWELL, Maj.-Gen. William Arthur Macdonald,** CB 1945; CBE 1944; MC 1917; *b* 22 Jan. 1895; *s* of G. C. Stawell, ICS; *m* 1926, Amy (*d* 1986), *d* of C. W. Bowring, New York; one *s. Educ:* Clifton College; RMA, Woolwich. Served European War, 1914–21, France, Greek Macedonia, Serbia, Bulgaria, Turkey (wounded, MC); 2nd Lieut 1914; Temp. Captain, 1916–17; Acting Major, Mar.-April 1917 and 1918–19; Captain, 1917; Major 1929; Lieut-Col 1937; Col 1940; Brig. 1940. GSO3 War Office, 1931–32; Brigade Maj., Aldershot, 1932–35; DAAG India, 1935–37; CRE 1937–40; AA and QMG Feb.-July 1940; GSO1 July-Nov. 1940; DDMI War Office, 1940–42; Brig., Comdr Home Forces, Feb.-Nov. 1942; Brig. General Staff, Home Forces, 1942–43; MEF and CMF, 1943–45 (CBE, CB); Temp. Maj.-Gen. 1943–45; Deputy Chief of Operations UNRRA, Nov. 1945–Aug. 1946; Deputy Chief Intelligence Division, CCG, 1947–48; retired. *Recreations:* yachting, golf. *Address:* Crobeg, The Common, Southwold, Suffolk. *Clubs:* Army and Navy; Royal Norfolk and Suffolk Yacht.
*Died 11 June 1987.*

**STEAD, Christina Ellen;** Fellow in Creative Arts, Australian National University, Canberra, 1969–80, later Emeritus; *b* 17 July 1902; *d* of Ellen Butters and David George Stead; *m* 1952, William J. Blake (*d* 1968). *Educ:* Sydney Univ., NSW. In business: London, 1928–29; Paris, 1930–35. Cinema: Senior Writer, MGM, Hollywood, Calif, 1943. Instructor, Workshop in the Novel, New York Univ., 1943–44. *Publications:* Salzburg Tales (short story collection), London, 1934, NY, 1935, Melbourne, 1966; *novels:* Seven Poor Men of Sydney, London and NY, 1935, Sydney and London, 1966 (new edn, 1970); The Beauties and Furies, London and NY, 1936; House of All Nations, London and NY, 1938, NY 1972; The Man who Loved Children, London, 1941, NY, 1940, new edn 1965, London 1966; For Love Alone, NY, 1944, London, 1945, new edn New York, 1965, new edn, London, 1966, Sydney, 1969; Letty Fox, Her Luck, NY, 1946, London, 1947; A Little Tea, A Little Chat, NY, 1948; The People with the Dogs, Boston, 1951; Dark Places of the Heart, New York, 1966; The Little Hotel, 1974; Miss Herbert, the Suburban Wife, NY, 1976, UK 1979; The Puzzleheaded Girl (novellas), 1967; short stories: in Southerly, 1963; in Kenyon Review, Saturday Evening Post, 1965; in Meanjin, 1968, 1970; in Hemisphere, 1970; in New Yorker, 1970; in Commentary, 1971; in Partisan Review, 1971; in Overland, 1972. *Address:* c/o Laurence Pollinger, Ltd, 18 Maddox Street, W1.
*Died 31 March 1983.*

**STEBBINGS, Sir John (Chalmer),** Kt 1980; Partner, Payne, Hicks Beach, Solicitors, since 1951; *b* 10 Oct. 1924; *s* of late John Morley Stebbings, MC, EM, TD, and of Doris Percy (*née* Chalmer); *m* 1949, Patricia (*née* Strange); two *s* three *d. Educ:* Harrow; New Coll., Oxford (MA). Admitted solicitor, 1949. Law Society: Mem. Council, 1964; Treasurer, 1969–75; Vice Pres., 1978–79; Pres., 1979. Mem., Lord Chancellor's Cttee on Age of Majority, 1965–66. *Recreations:* swimming, sailing. *Address:* 435 Fulham Road, Chelsea, SW10 9TX. *T:* 01–352 7190; (office) 10 New Square, Lincoln's Inn, WC2A 3QG. *T:* 01–242 6041. *Clubs:* Hurlingham; Royal Temple Yacht (Ramsgate).
*Died 30 Dec. 1988.*

**STEDMAN, Sir George (Foster),** KBE 1957; CB 1948; MC 1919; Civil Service, retired; *b* 1895; *s* of James Mathew and Marguerite Adele Stedman, Leytonstone, Essex; *m* 1925, Olive May Scrivener (*d* 1979); one *d* (one *s* decd). *Educ:* Mercers' School, London; Trinity Coll., Camb. Served European War, 1914–18, with York and Lancaster Regt, France and Macedonia (MC, despatches twice). Entered Civil Service, Ministry of Transport, 1920; Private Secretary to Minister, 1926–30; Under-Sec., 1946. Deputy Secretary, Ministry of Transport and Civil Aviation, 1954–57. *Address:* Longcroft, Honeyknab Lane, Oxton, Southwell, Notts.
*Died 27 Oct. 1985.*

**STEEDMAN, Maj.-Gen. John Francis Dawes,** CMG 1963; CBE 1945; MC 1918; *b* 30 Nov. 1897; *s* of John Francis Steedman, FRCS, Streatham; *m* 1931, Olive Ursula (Kaisar-i-Hind Medal, Silver Jubilee Medal, 1935), *d* of Earl Oliver Besant, Reading; one *d. Educ:* Bradfield; RMA, Woolwich. 2nd Lt, RE, 1916; served European War, 1914–18, Salonika (MC, despatches twice); Afghanistan, 1919; Waziristan (MBE, despatches), 1920–21; Khajuri (despatches), 1930–31; ADC to HM King George VI, 1949–51; retired as Hon. Maj.-Gen., 1951; Director of Works, Commonwealth War Graves Commission, 1951–63. *Address:* Valley Farm House, East Knoyle, Salisbury, Wiltshire SP3 6BG. *T:* East Knoyle 329.
*Died 14 May 1983.*

**STEEL, Sir (Joseph) Lincoln (Spedding),** Kt 1965; JP; formerly Director: ICI Ltd; Charterhouse Investment Trust; Chairman, Triplex Holdings Ltd, 1961–66; *b* 24 March 1900; *s* of late Comdr Joseph Steel, RD, RNR, and Esther Alice (*née* Spedding); *m* 1st, 1928, Cynthia Smith (*d* 1929); one *s*; 2nd, 1938, Barbara I. T., *y d* of late Colonel S. G. Goldschmidt; one *s*. *Educ:* Christ's Hospital; St John's College, Oxford (Open Scholar, MA). Served RE, 1918–19. Joined Brunner Mond & Co. Ltd, 1922; Delegate Dir, ICI (Alkali) Ltd, 1932; Man. Dir, Alkali Div. of ICI Ltd, 1942; Chm. Alkali Div. of ICI Ltd, 1943; Dir, Imperial Chemical Industries Ltd, 1945–60, retd. Chm. British Nat. Cttee of International Chamber of Commerce, 1951–63; Pres. Internat. Chamber of Commerce, 1963–65; Vice-Pres. 1951–63; Hon. Pres. 1965–; Chairman Overseas Cttee of FBI, 1950–65; Member: Council of CBI, 1965–68; EFTA Consultative Cttee, 1960–69. Leader, UK Industrial Mission to W Indies, 1952. Member Cheshire County Council, 1937–45; JP Cheshire, 1939; JP Bucks, 1960; Gen. Comr for Income Tax, Burnham District, 1968–75. FRSA 1963. *Recreations:* gardening, walking, travel. *Address:* 21 Calumet, Reynolds Road, Beaconsfield, Bucks. *Club:* Beefsteak.                           *Died* 27 *Dec.* 1985.

**STEELE, (Francis) Howard,** FCGI, BSc(Eng), CEng, FIEE, FIERE; Managing Director, Sony Broadcast Ltd, since 1978; *b* Gt Bookham, Surrey, 23 Sept. 1929; *s* of late Arnold Francis Steele, MBE, and of Florence Anne Winifred Steele; *m* 1953, Elaine Barnes Steele (*née* Mason); two *s*. *Educ:* Mill Hill School; Imperial College of Science and Technology. Engineer, Marconi Company, Chelmsford, 1952–57; Asst Engineer in Charge, Alpha Television Services, Birmingham, 1957–58; Head of Planning and Installation Dept, 1958–61, Chief Engineer, 1961–66, ABC Television Ltd; Chief Engineer, ITA, 1966–69; Dir. of Engineering, ITA, later IBA, 1969–78. Member: EBU Tech. Cttee, 1964–78; Nat. Electronics Council, 1967–71 and 1974–77; Chm., Montreux Internat. Symposium Awards Cttee, 1977–79. IEE: Mem. Council, 1965–68, 1976–77 and 1979–; Faraday Lectr, 1975–76; Chm., Electronics Div., 1980–81. FRTS 1971 (Mem. Council, 1969–72). Hon. Fellow, British Kinematograph, Sound and Television Soc., 1974. Freeman, City of London, 1955. Montreux Internat. TV Symposium Citation, 1969; RTS Gold Medal Award, 1982. *Recreations:* motoring, sailing. *Address:* The White Cottage, Pitt, near Winchester, Hants. *Club:* Royal Southern Yacht.                           *Died* 11 *Oct.* 1983.

**STEELE, Commander Gordon Charles,** VC; RN, retired; Hon. Captain, RNR, 1949; Captain Superintendent of Thames Nautical Training College, HMS Worcester, off Greenhithe, 1929–57; Fellow of Institute of Navigation, 1951; *b* Exeter, 1892; *s* of late Captain H. W. Steele, RN, and S. M., *d* of Major-General J. C. Symonds, RMLI. *Educ:* Vale College, Ramsgate; HMS Worcester. Midshipman, Royal Navy Reserve; joined P&OSNCo. as cadet and served in RNR and P&O till outbreak of war; served in HM Submarines D8 and E22 and in Q ships; transferred to Royal Navy as Sub-Lieutenant for distinguished service in action, Aug. 1915; served in HMS Royal Oak as Lieut RN in Jutland, and in Iron Duke; commanded HM ships P63 and Cornflower, 1917–18; served in coastal motor boat raid on Kronstadt Harbour, Aug. 1919 (VC); specialised in anti-submarine duties; Naval Interpreter in Russian; retired list, 1931; served in HMS Osprey as Anti-Submarine Commander, and Inspector of Anti-Submarine Equipment, in War, 1939–45; a Younger Brother of Trinity House; Member Worshipful Company of Shipwrights; Freeman City of London; a Lay-Reader. Silver Jubilee Medal, 1977. *Publications:* Electrical Knowledge for Ships' Officers, 1950; The Story of the Worcester, 1962; To Me, God is Real, 1973; About My Father's Business, 1975; In My Father's House, 1976. *Address:* Winkleigh Court, Winkleigh, Devon. *Club:* East India, Devonshire, Sports and Public Schools.
                          *Died* 4 *Jan.* 1981.

**STEELE, Howard;** *see* Steele, F. H.

**STEELE, Sir Kenneth (Charles),** Kt 1981; DFC 1944; Group Chairman, Myer Emporium, 1976–78, retired; *b* 2 March 1913; *s* of late K. S. Steele and E. M. Dunbier; *m* 1947, Barbara Harrison; one *s* one *d*. *Educ:* Hawthorn West High Sch. Served War of 1939–45, UK RAF Bomber Comd, 78 Sqdn. Joined Myer Emporium Ltd, 1928; Gp Man. Dir, 1966–76; period of employment unbroken except for war service. Mem., Fed. Govt Economic Consultative Gp Cttee, 1975–78. Inaugural Pres., Australian Retailers' Assoc., 1974–75. Silver Jubilee Medal, 1977. *Recreations:* fresh and saltwater flyfishing, golf, Thoroughbred breeding and racing. *Address:* 212 Doncaster Road, North Balwyn, Melbourne, Vic 3104, Australia. *T:* 03–8579851. *Clubs:* Athenæum (Melbourne); Riversdale Golf, Racing, VRC, VATC, MVRC.                           *Died* 4 *June* 1986.

**STEEN, Robert Elsworth,** MD; Past President RCPI; FRCPGlas (Hon.); Hon. Consulting Pædiatrician, National Children's Hospital, Dublin; *b* 11 April 1902; *s* of David Miller Steen and Jane Elsworth (*née* Orr); *m* 1939, Elizabeth Margaret Cochrane; one *s* one *d*. *Educ:* St Andrew's College and Trinity College, Dublin. Graduated 1924; held following posts: Demonstrator in

Biochemistry and Pathology, Dublin University; House Surgeon and House Physician, Monkstown Hospital, Dublin, and French Hospital, London; House Physician, Hospital for Sick Children, Great Ormond Street, London; Assistant Physician, Royal City of Dublin Hospital and Meath Hospital, Dublin; Physician, Dr Steeven's Hospital, Dublin, and Meath Hospital, Dublin; Medical Director, St Patrick's Infant Hosp. and Nursery Training Coll., Temple Hill, Blackrock; formerly: Lecturer in Hygiene, Metropolitan School of Nursing, Dublin; Prof. of Pædiatrics, Dublin Univ.; Pædiatrician, Rotunda Hospital, Dublin and Royal Victoria Eye and Ear Hosp., Dublin; Consulting Pædiatrician, St Kevin's Hosp.; Hon. Consulting Pædiatrician, Monkstown Hosp., Sunshine Home, Foxrock and Stewart's Hosp., Palmerstown. Fellow and late President Section of Pædiatrics, Royal Academy of Medicine in Ireland; late President: Irish Cardiac Soc.; Irish Pædiatric Assoc.; Dublin University Biological Assoc.; British Pædiatric Assoc.; Hosp. for Sick Children, Great Ormond Street; Dublin Univ. Boat Club; Dining Club; Hon. Member, Assoc. of European Pædiatric Cardiologists; Sen. Member, Assoc. of Physicians of GB and Ireland; Extraordinary Member, British Cardiac Soc. Past Master, Knights of the Campanile, TCD. *Publications:* Infants in Health and Sickness; numerous publications in medical journals. *Recreations:* hunting, music, croquet, bridge. *Address:* Department of Pædiatrics, University of Dublin, National Children's Hospital, Harcourt Street, Dublin 2. *T:* Dublin 752355; Mountsandel, Carrickmines, Co. Dublin. *T:* 893184. *Clubs:* Kildare Street and University (Life Mem.), Friendly Brother House (Dublin); Leander (Life Mem.); Royal Irish Yacht; Kandahar Ski (Life Mem.); Carrickmines Croquet and Lawn Tennis.
                          *Died* 12 *Dec.* 1981.

**STEEN, Stephen Nicholas;** President, Smith & Nephew Associated Companies Ltd, since 1976 (Chairman, 1968–76); Chairman, British Tissues Limited, 1971–77; *b* 19 July 1907; *m* 1934; one *s* one *d*. Arthur Berton & Co. Ltd, 1943; Director, Smith & Nephew Associated Companies Ltd, 1958, Dep. Chm. 1962. Underwriting Member, Matthews Wrightson Pulbrook Ltd; called to the Bar, Gray's Inn, 1949. Mem., Ct of Patrons, RCS, 1973–. *Recreation:* golf. *Address:* (office) 2 Temple Place, WC2R 3BP. *T:* 01–836 7922.                           *Died* 13 *March* 1988.

**STEERS, James Alfred,** CBE 1973; MA; Professor Emeritus of Geography and Emeritus Fellow of St Catharine's College, Cambridge; Chairman, National Committee of Geography, 1967–72; Coastal Consultant to Conservation Committee of Council of Europe, 1968; Chairman, Coastal Conferences, 1966–67; *b* 8 Aug. 1899; *s* of J. A. Steers, Bedford; *m* 1942, Harriet, *d* of J. A. Wanklyn, Cambridge; one *s* one *d*. *Educ:* Elstow (Private) School, Bedford; St Catharine's Coll., Cambridge. Senior Geography Master, Framlingham Coll., 1921–22; elected Fellow of St Catharine's, 1925, subsequently Dean, Tutor and President, Univ. Demonstrator, 1926–27; Univ. Lecturer, 1927–49; Prof. of Geography, 1949–66; Member of the British Expedition to the Great Barrier Reefs, 1928; Leader of Geographical Expedition to the Reefs, 1936; Expedition to the Jamaica Cays, 1939; War Service, 1917–18; Vice-Pres., Royal Geographical Soc., 1959–63, 1967–72; Hon. Vice-Pres., 1972–, Hon. Mem., 1977–; Pres. Norfolk and Norwich Naturalists Soc., 1940–41; Pres., Section E British Association (Oxford), 1954; President, Inst. Brit. Geographers (Reading), 1956; President: Geographical Assoc., 1959; Estuarine and Brackish Water Science Assoc., 1977–80. Corresp. Mem., Royal Dutch Geographical Soc.; Hon. Mem., Ges. für Erdkunde Berlin; Member: Council of Senate, Cambridge, 1941–48; Wild Life Conservation Cttee; Nature Conservancy, 1949–54, 1957–66; Scientific Policy Cttee, 1949–66; Cttee for England, 1949–68, 1970–73; Nat. Parks Commn, 1960–66; Properties Cttee, Nat. Trust, 1969–76; Hon. Adviser on Coastal Preservation to Ministry of Town and Country Planning and to Department of Health, Scotland; Member: Departmental Cttee on Coastal Flooding, 1953; Advisory Committee to improve Sea Defences, 1954–; Hydraulics Research Board, DSIR, 1957–61; Visiting Prof., Berkeley, Calif, 1959; Visiting Fellow, Aust. Nat. Univ., 1967. Hon. LLD Aberdeen, 1971; Hon. DSc East Anglia, 1978. Victoria Medal, RGS, 1960; Scottish Geographical Medal, 1969. *Publications:* Introduction to the Study of Map Projections, 1927, 15th edn 1970; The Unstable Earth, 1932 (new edn 1950); Editor and contrib. to Scolt Head Island, 1934, 2nd rev. edn 1960; The Coastline of England and Wales, 1946, 2nd edn 1969; A Picture Book of the Whole Coast of England and Wales, 1948; The Sea Coast, 1953, 4th edn 1969; The Coast of England and Wales in Pictures, 1960; The English Coast and the Coast of Wales, 1966; Coasts and Beaches, 1969; Introduction to Coastline and Development, 1970; The Coastline of Scotland, 1973; Coastal Features of England and Wales, 1980; Editor: new edns of P. Lake's Physical Geography, 1958; Vol. on Field Studies in the British Isles, Internat. Geog. Union. London meeting, 1964; Brit. Assoc. Advancement of Science, The Cambridge Region, 1965; Engl. edn of V. P. Zenkovitch, Processes of Coastal Development, 1967; papers on Coastal Physiography,

Coral Islands, etc, in various scientific publications. *Recreations:* walking, philately, travel. *Address:* 47 Gretton Court, Girton, Cambridge CB3 0QN. *T:* Cambridge 276007. *Clubs:* Travellers', Geographical (Hon. Mem.). *Died* 10 *March* 1987.

**STEIL, John Wellesley,** CMG 1951; MBE 1937; *b* 15 Aug. 1899; *s* of late Lt W. J. Steil, RN; *m* Annetta Elise (*d* 1961), 2nd *d* of late S. Fichat, Nairobi, Kenya; one *s* one *d*. *Educ:* Christ's Hospital, Horsham; Portsmouth Grammar School; Cadet Ship HMS Conway. Served European War, 1917–19, Harwich Force, HMTB 85, HMS Dragon. Malayan American Rubber Co., Malaya and Sumatra, 1920–24; Colonial Administrative Service, Cadet, Uganda, 1925; Asst District Officer, 1927; District Officer, 1936; Provincial Comr, 1947; Senior Provincial Commissioner, 1949; Secretary for African Affairs, Uganda, MEC and MLC, 1950–51. Farming in WA, 1957–62. *Address:* The Weld Club, GPO Box B54, Perth, WA 6001, Australia. *Clubs:* Royal Commonwealth Society; Weld (Perth, WA). *Died* 13 *Jan.* 1983.

**STEIN, John,** CBE 1970; Scotland Football Team Manager, since 1978; *b* 5 Oct. 1922; *s* of George Stein and Jane Armstrong; *m* 1946, Jean McAuley; one *s* one *d*. *Educ:* Greenfield Public Sch., Lanarkshire. Miner, 1937–50; Professional Footballer, 1950–57; Coach, 1957–60; Manager: Dunfermline, 1960–64; Hibernians, 1964–65; Celtic, 1965–78. Under his management, Celtic won: Scottish League Cup, 1965–66, 1966–67, 1967–68, 1968–69, 1969–70, 1974–75; Scottish Cup, 1964–65, 1966–67, 1968–69, 1970–71, 1971–72, 1973–74, 1974–75, 1976–77; European Cup, 1966–67; Scottish League Championship, 1965–74 inclusive, 1976–77. *Recreations:* golf, bowling. *Died* 10 *Sept.* 1985.

**STEIN, John Alan,** CIE 1943; *b* 31 Oct. 1888; *s* of late Hamilton Stein; *m* 1st, 1920, Phyllis (*d* 1949), *d* of Lindsay Horne, Aberdeen; one *d*; 2nd, Vera Craig, *d* of T. H. Patterson, Sunderland. *Educ:* Bedford School; City and Guilds College, London Univ. Joined Indian Service of Engineers, 1912, apptd to Bengal; served with Indian Sappers and Miners in Mesopotamia, Palestine and Syria, 1916–19 (wounded); Executive Engineer, 1919; Under Secretary, Govt of Bengal, 1926; Superintending Engineer, 1931–41; Chief Engineer, Communications and Works Dept, Bengal, 1941–43; Chief Engineer, Civil Supplies Dept, Bengal, 1945–47. Handicapper, Royal Calcutta Turf Club, 1947–52. *Address:* 99 Peterborough Road, SW6 3BU. *Clubs:* East India, Devonshire, Sports and Public Schools; Royal Calcutta Turf. *Died* 16 *Jan.* 1982.

**STEINITZ, Dr (Charles) Paul (Joseph),** OBE 1985; FRAM 1948; Founder-Conductor, London Bach Society and Steinitz Bach Players; Consultant Professor, Royal Academy of Music, since 1984; *b* 25 Aug. 1909; *s* of Rev. Charles Steinitz and Sarah Jessie Prior; *m* 1st, 1933, Joan Paxton (marr. diss.); two *s*; 2nd, 1946, Margery Still (marr. diss.); one *d*; 3rd, 1976, Margaret Johnson. *Educ:* privately and Royal Acad. of Music (LRAM); FRCO 1930; BMus 1934, DMus 1940 London. Prof., RAM, 1945–84; Lectr, then Principal Lectr, Univ. of London Goldsmiths' Coll., 1948–76; Dir of Music, Priory Church of St Bartholomew-the-Great, W Smithfield, 1949–61. Founder: London Bach Soc., 1947; Steinitz Bach Players, 1969. Ext. Examr in Music, Cambridge Coll. of Arts and Tech., 1976–82. Mem. Senate, Univ. of London, 1968–86. BBC broadcasts, 1949–; appearances in major British festivals, including Bath, Cambridge and City of London; appearances in festivals and concert halls in USA, Israel, W and E Europe, Australia and NZ. Lecture tours to USA, Canada, Australia and NZ, 1965–. Specialist in music of J. S. Bach. Presentation of first complete Bach cantata cycle in UK, 1958–87. Recordings incl. complete Cantiones Sacrae of 1625 by Schütz. *Publications:* chapter on German Church Music, New Oxford History of Music, vol. V, 1975; Bach's Passions, 1979; Bach for Choirs, 1980; Performing Bach's Vocal Music, 1980; edns and books on harmony; contribs to music jls, USA, Australia, Musical Times. *Recreations:* organic gardening, cooking, reading, theatre. *Address:* 73 High Street, Old Oxted, Surrey RH8 9LN. *T:* Oxted 717372. *Club:* Athenæum. *Died* 21 *April* 1988.

**STEPHEN, Sir Alastair (Edward),** Kt 1973; solicitor; *b* 27 May 1901; *o s* of late Sir Colin Campbell Stephen, Sydney, solicitor and Dorothy, *d* of late Edward William Knox, Sydney; *m* 1st, 1942, Diana Heni (*d* 1943), *d* of late Richard Allen, Christchurch, NZ; one *d*; 2nd, 1946, Winifred Grace, *d* of late James Atkinson Bonnin; one *s* two *d*. *Educ:* Tudor House Sch.; Geelong C of E Grammar Sch.; St Paul's Coll., Univ. of Sydney. BA Sydney 1923. Solicitor, Supreme Court of NSW, 1926; partner, Stephen Jaques & Stephen, Sydney, 1926–75; Director of public cos, 1930–76. Dir, Royal Prince Alfred Hosp., Sydney, 1944–73 (Vice-Chm. 1953–62, Chm. 1962–73); Pres., Australian Hosp. Assoc., 1969–71. *Recreations:* skiing, sailing, fishing, racing. *Address:* 60 Fairfax Road, Bellevue Hill, Sydney, NSW, Australia. *T:* 36-6402. *Clubs:* Union, Australian, Royal Sydney Golf, Australian Jockey (Sydney). *Died* 4 *Aug.* 1982.

**STEPHEN, Sir James Alexander,** 4th Bt, *cr* 1891; *b* 25 Feb. 1908; *o c* of 3rd Bt and Barbara, *y d* of late W. Shore-Nightingale of Embley,

Hants and Lea Hurst, Derbyshire; *cousin* of Florence Nightingale; *S* father, 1945. *Educ:* Eton; Trinity College, Cambridge. Law Student, Inner Temple; embraced Roman Catholic faith, 1936; Resident, Toynbee Hall, 1936–39; Air Raid Warden, 1940; served RA (AA), 1940–41, discharged unfit; worked on the land as a volunteer, 1941–45; certified insane, 1945; name restored to vote, 1960; discharged from hospital, 1972. FRGS. Interested in exploration; has raised money for Outward Bound Trust. *Heir:* none. *Recreation:* contract bridge. *Address:* 48 Princess Road, Branksome, Poole, Dorset BH12 1BH. *T:* Bournemouth 761665. *Club:* Sloane. *Died* 1 *June* 1987 (*ext*).

**STEPHEN, Maj.-Gen. Robert Alexander,** CB 1965; CBE 1958 (OBE 1954); MD, ChM; FRCS; QHS 1960–67; Director of Army Surgery and Consulting Surgeon to the Army, Royal Army Medical College, 1959–67; Consultant in Surgery, Royal Hospital, Chelsea; *b* 20 June 1907; *s* of late James Alexander Stephen, MB, ChB, DPH; *m* 1st, 1935, Audrey Vivien (*d* 1972), *d* of late George William Royce, Cambridge; one *d*; 2nd, 1977, Mrs Patricia O'Reilly (*née* Wrixon-Harris). *Educ:* Aberdeen Grammar School; Aberdeen University. MD 1933, ChM 1960, Aberdeen; FRCS 1947; MS Malaya, 1959. Lieut, RAMC, 1934. Served War of 1939–45, in France, Egypt, Libya, Greece, Crete, Belgium, Holland and Germany; Lt-Col 1941. Formerly Asst Prof. of Military Surgery, Royal Army Medical College, London; Consulting Surgeon, FARELF, 1956–59; Hon. Consulting Surgeon, General Hospital, Singapore, 1956; Brigadier, 1958; Major-General, 1961. Hunterian Prof., RCS, 1958. Fellow: Royal Society of Medicine; Assoc. of Surgeons of Great Britain and Ireland. OStJ. *Recreations:* golf, gardening. *Address:* Pinnocks, 44a Shortheath Road, Farnham, Surrey GU9 8SL. *T:* Farnham 723848. *Died* 9 *July* 1983.

**STEPHENS, Sir David,** KCB 1964; CVO 1960; Clerk of the Parliaments, House of Lords, 1963–74; *b* 25 April 1910; *s* of late Berkeley John Byng Stephens, CIE, and Gwendolen Elizabeth (*née* Cripps), Cirencester; *m* 1st, 1941, Mary Clemency, JP (*d* 1966), *er d* of late Colonel Sir Eric Gore Browne, DSO, OBE, TD; three *s* one *d*; 2nd, 1967, Charlotte Evelyn, *widow* of Henry Manisty, *d* of late Rev. A. M. Baird-Smith; three step *s*. *Educ:* Winchester College; Christ Church. Oxford (2nd cl. Lit. Hum.). Laming Travelling Fellow, the Queen's College, Oxford, 1932–34; Clerk in the Parliament Office, House of Lords, 1935–38; Member Runciman Mission to Czechoslovakia, 1938; transf. HM Treasury, 1938; Political Warfare Executive, 1941–43; Principal Private Sec. to the Lord Pres. of the Council (Mr Herbert Morrison), 1947–49; Asst Sec., HM Treasury, 1949; Secretary for Appointments to two Prime Ministers (Sir Anthony Eden and Mr Harold Macmillan), 1955–61; Reading Clerk and Clerk of the Journals, House of Lords, 1961–63. Chm., Redundant Churches Fund, 1976–81. Chm. of Governors, Maidwell Hall Sch., 1964–70. Mem., Cotswold DC, 1976–83. Pres. Friends of Cirencester Parish Church, 1976–. *Recreations:* gardening, country life; preserving the Cotswolds. *Address:* The Old Rectory, Coates, near Cirencester, Glos GL7 6NS. *T:* Kemble 258. *Clubs:* Brooks's, MCC. *Died* 3 *April* 1990.

**STEPHENS, Ian Melville,** CIE 1935; MA Cantab; *b* 1903; *e s* of J. A. Melville Stephens, Fleet, Hants; unmarried; hon. adopted son, Dr Arthur Kwok Cheung Li. *Educ:* Winchester; King's Coll., Cambridge (foundn scholar, R. J. Smith research student); 1st class hons, Natural Sciences Tripos, Pt I, 1924, and Historical Tripos, Pt II, 1925. Business appts, 1927–30; Deputy Dir, Bureau of Public Information, Govt of India, 1930–32; wrote the M & MP Reports for 1929–30 and 1930–31; was Indian corresp., The Round Table; Publicity Officer, Indian Franchise (Lothian) Cttee, 1932; Dir, Bureau of Public Information, 1932–37; Asst Editor, The Statesman newspaper, Calcutta and Delhi, 1937; also on the Board, 1939; Editor, 1942–51 (also aeronautical corresp., and staff photographer). War Corresp., SEAC and SHAEF, 1943–45. Member: Standing Cttee, All-India Newspaper Editors' Conf., 1942–51; Indian Delegn to Commonwealth Press Conf., Canada, 1950; Brit. Group, Inst. of Pacific Relations Conf., Lucknow, 1950. Retired from India, 1951. Fellow, King's Coll., Cambridge, 1952–58; also Mem. Council, and Hon. Treasurer Appeals Cttee, New Hall, Cambridge. Chm., Mount Vernon (Ceylon) Tea Co., 1953–57. Historian, Pakistan Govt, GHQ, Rawalpindi, 1957–60. Travelled in South Asia, Australia, NZ, Canada, USA. Jinnah Medal, 1977; Iqbal Medal, 1979. *Publications:* Horned Moon, illus. with own photographs, 1953 (3rd edn 1966); Pakistan, 1963 (paperback edn 1964, 3rd edn 1967); Monsoon Morning, 1966; (ed) Sir R. Reid's Years of Change, 1966; The Pakistanis, 1968; A Curiosity, 1970; Unmade Journey, 1977; contribs to Chambers's Encyclopaedia (1966 edn); articles, lectures, broadcasts, reviews. *Address:* c/o Lloyds Bank, 3 Sidney Street, Cambridge. *Died* 28 *March* 1984.

**STEPHENS, Peter Scott,** CMG 1962; *b* 25 Nov. 1910; *s* of Major John August Stephens, TD, and Elsie Evelyn Stephens (*née* Watson). *Educ:* Sherborne School; Oriel Coll., Oxford. HM Consular Service, 1933; served New York and Manila; transferred to Foreign Office, 1941; Leopoldville and Elizabethville, Belgian Congo, 1942–45; in charge of Consular Section, British Embassy, Brussels, 1945–47; transf. to Foreign Office, 1947; First Secretary, Washington, 1949; First Secretary and First Secretary (Commercial), British Embassy, Havana, 1951–54; acted as Chargé d'Affaires, there, in 1951, 1952, 1953 and 1954; Counsellor (Commercial) British Embassy, Caracas, April 1955–Nov. 1958; acted as Chargé d'Affaires, there, in 1955, 1956, 1957 and 1958; Commercial Counsellor, Madrid, 1959–62; HM Consul-General, Milan, 1962–68. *Address:* The Garden House, Thornhill, Stalbridge, Dorset. *T:* Stalbridge 62366. *Club:* Travellers'. *Died 10 March 1981.*

**STEPHENSON, Ven. Edgar,** MM 1918; TD 1950; Archdeacon Emeritus of Rochdale, since 1962, Archdeacon, 1951–62; Director of Religious Education in Diocese of Manchester, 1955–62; *b* 24 Sept. 1894; *y s* of late T. J. Stephenson, Tamworth, Staffs; *m* 1926, Kathleen, *d* of late William Taws, Macclesfield, Cheshire; no *c. Educ:* Manchester University. BA 1922; BD 1925; MA 1929. CF(TA), 1933–50. Vicar of St Mary's, Oldham, 1947–55. *Address:* Manormead, Flat 22, Tilford Road, Hindhead, Surrey GU26 6RA. *T:* Hindhead 4677. *Died 29 May 1984.*

**STEPHENSON, Lt-Col Sir (Henry) Francis (Blake),** 2nd Bt, *cr* 1936; OBE 1941; TD; DL; *b* 3 Dec. 1895; *e s* of late Lieut-Colonel Sir Henry Kenyon Stephenson, DSO, and Frances, *e d* of late Major W. G. Blake, DL, JP; *S* father, 1947; *m* 1925, Joan, *d* of Maj. John Herbert Upton (formerly Upton Cottrell-Dormer), JP; one *s. Educ:* Eton. Lt Col (QO) Yorks Dragoons; served European War, 1914–18: BEF, 1915–18 (1914–15 Star, two medals); War of 1939–45: Middle East, 1939–42 (OBE). JP City of Sheffield; DL Derbyshire, 1948; High Sheriff of Derbyshire, 1948–49. Hon. LLD, Sheffield, 1955. *Heir:* s Henry Upton Stephenson, High Sheriff of Derbyshire, 1975 [*b* 26 Nov. 1926; *m* 1962, Susan, *o d* of Major J. E. Clowes, Ashbourne, Derbyshire, and of Mrs Nuttall; four *d*]. *Address:* Hassop Green, Bakewell, Derbyshire. *T:* Great Longstone 233. *Died 14 Aug. 1982.*

**STEPHENSON, Air Vice-Marshal John Noel Tracy,** CB 1956; CBE 1954; Retired; Member Directing Staff, Administrative Staff College, 1960, Director of Studies, 1968–69, retired 1970; *b* Nov. 1907; *m* 1959, Jill Sheila Fitzgerald, *d* of William Fitzgerald Hervey. RAF College, 1926–28. Served War of 1939–45: in UK, in Burma and on loan to Australian Defence Ministry. Berlin Airlift, 1948. Comdt, RAF Staff Coll., 1949–52; Dir of Organisation (Air Ministry), forecasting and planning, 1952–54; Sen. Air Staff Officer, Middle East Air Forces, 1954–57; Suez Operations, 1957 (despatches); Asst Chief of Air Staff (policy), 1957–59. Officer, American Legion of Merit. *Address:* Hill Grove, Dymock, Glos. *Club:* Royal Air Force. *Died 2 Aug. 1985.*

**STEPHENSON, Sir William (Samuel),** CC 1980; Kt 1945; MC; DFC and two bars; *b* 11 Jan. 1896; *s* of Victor and Christina Stephenson, Canada; *m* 1924, Mary Simmons (*d* 1978); one adopted *d. Educ:* Canada. Served European War, Capt. RFC, 1914–18. Formerly: Personal Representative of Winston Churchill, and Director of British Security Co-ordination in the Western Hemisphere, 1940–46. Patron, CDF Intell. Branch. Hon. Life Mem., Royal Military Inst., Canada. Fellow, Bermuda Coll., Bermuda, 1986. Hon. Mem., Canadian Security Intelligence Service, 1986. Hon. DSc, Univ. of West Indies, 1950; Hon. DScMil, Royal Military Coll.; Hon. LLD Winnipeg; Hon. DSc: Manitoba, 1979; Winnipeg, 1980; Windsor, Ont, 1985. Scholarships established in his name: Univ. of the West Indies, Jamaica; Univ. of Winnipeg, Canada; Bermuda Coll., Bermuda. GCSJ 1986. Hon. Citizen, Winnipeg, 1984. General Donovan Award, Veterans of OSS, 1983; Chief Hunter, Order of Buffalo Hunt, Province of Manitoba, 1985. Croix de Guerre avec Palmes, 1918; US Medal for Merit. CC specially invested, in Bermuda, by Governor-Gen. of Canada, 1980. *Relevant publications:* (biography by H. M. Hyde) The Quiet Canadian, 1962 (as Room 3603, in USA); (by William Stevenson): A Man called Intrepid, 1977; Intrepid's Last Case, 1984. *Address:* PO Box 445, Devonshire, Bermuda. *TA:* Inter, Bermuda. *Clubs:* Carlton, Royal Aero; Royal Yacht (Bermuda). *Died 31 Jan. 1989.*

**STEPTOE, Patrick Christopher,** CBE 1988; FRCSE 1951; FRCOG 1961; FRS 1987; Director of Centre for Human Reproduction, Oldham, 1969–79; Medical Director, Bourn Hall Clinic, Bourn, Cambridgeshire, since 1980; *b* 9 June 1913; *s* of Harry Arthur Steptoe and Grace Maud (*née* Minns); *m* 1943, Sheena Macleod Kennedy; one *s* one *d. Educ:* Grammar Sch., Witney; King's Coll., London Univ.; St George's Hosp. Med. Sch. (qual. 1939). MRCS, LRCP; MRCOG 1948. Served War, RNVR, 1939–46: Surg. Lieut, 1939; POW, Italy, 1941–43; seconded to Admiralty, 1943; Surg. Lt-Comdr; demob. 1946. Chief Asst Obstetrician and Gynaecol., St George's Hosp., 1947; Sen. Registrar, Whittington Hosps, 1949; Sen. Obstetrician and Gynaecologist, Oldham Hosps, 1951–78. President: Internat. Fedn of Fertility Socs, 1977–; Brit. Fertility Soc., 1986 (Founder Chm., 1973). Hon. FRSM 1987. Hon. DSc Hull, 1983. Blair Bell Gold Medal, RSM, 1975; Gregory Pincus Award, 1983; Eardley Holland Gold Medal, RCOG, 1985.

Commandant du Tastevin de Bourgogne, 1979. *Publications:* Laparoscopy in Gynaecology, 1967; Progress in Fertility, 1976; (contrib.) Recent Advances in Obstetrics and Gynaecology, 1977; A Matter of Life, 1980; contributor, author and jt author of papers in Lancet, Jl of Reprodn, Annals of RSM, and Brit. Med. Bull. (inc. 'In vitro fertilization of human ova'). *Recreations:* music, travel, wine, sailing. *Address:* 38 Caxton End, Bourn, Cambridge. *Died 21 March 1988.*

**STEVENS, Air Marshal Sir Alick (Charles),** KBE 1952; CB 1944; retired; *b* 31 July 1898; *s* of late Charles Edward Russell Stevens, Jersey; *m* 1927, Beryl, *d* of B. J. Gates, Wing, Bucks; one *s. Educ:* Victoria College, Jersey. Joined RNAS 1916; transferred to RAF on formation, 1918; Wing Comdr, 1937; Air Commodore, 1942. Dep. Director, 1940–42, and then Director of Operations (Naval Co-operation) at Air Ministry, 1942–43; SASO, No 18 Group, 1943–44 (despatches); AOC, RAF, Gibraltar, 1944–45; AOC No 47 Group, 1945; AOC No 4 Group, Transport Command, 1946; Air Vice-Marshal, 1947; AOC No 22 Group, Technical Training Comd, 1946–48; AOC British Forces, Aden, 1948–50; SASO, Coastal Comd, 1950–51; AOC-in-C, Coastal Comd, 1951–53; Air C-in-C, Eastern Atlantic Area, Atlantic Comd, 1952–53; Allied Maritime Air C-in-C Channel and Southern North Sea, Channel Comd, 1952–53; retd Dec. 1953; Vice-Chairman, Gloucestershire T&AFA, 1955–63. *Address:* Cherry Tree Cottage, Cadmore End, near High Wycombe, Bucks HP14 3PT. *T:* High Wycombe 881569. *Club:* Royal Air Force. *Died 2 July 1987.*

**STEVENS, Geoffrey Paul;** Chartered Accountant, 1926; *b* 10 Nov. 1902; *yr s* of late Alfred and Maria Ennriguetta Stevens, both of London; *m* 1928, Evelyn Mitchell, *yr d* of David Marwick, WS, Edinburgh; one *s* two *d* (and one *s* decd). *Educ:* Westminster School. Partner with Pannell Fitzpatrick & Co., 1930–70. Contested (C) Park Division of Sheffield, general election, 1945; MP (C) Portsmouth, Langstone, 1950–64. *Recreation:* gardening. *Address:* Brookside Cottage, Hankerton, Malmesbury, Wilts SN16 9JZ. *T:* Crudwell 374. *Died 10 May 1981.*

**STEVENS, Vice-Adm. Sir John (Felgate),** KBE 1955 (CBE 1945); CB 1951; *b* 1 June 1900; *o surv. s* of late Henry Marshall Stevens, Droveway Corner, Hove; *m* 1928, Mary, *o d* of J. Harry Gilkes, JP, Wychcote, Patcham, Sussex; one *s* two *d.* Midshipman, 1918; King's Coll., Cambridge, 1922, specialised in Navigation, 1924; Staff College, 1930; Commander, 1933; Captain, 1940. Served War of 1939–45 (despatches, CBE); Director of Plans, Admiralty, 1946–47; commanded HMS Implacable, 1948–49; Rear-Admiral, 1949; Director of Naval Training, 1949–50; Chief of Staff to Head of British Joint Services Mission, Washington, 1950–52; Flag Officer, Home Fleet Training Squadron, 1952–53; Commander-in-Chief, America and West Indies Station, and Deputy Supreme Allied Commander, Atlantic, 1953–55; retired list, 1956. *Address:* Withy Springs, Petworth Road, Haslemere, Surrey. *T:* Haslemere 2970. *Club:* Naval and Military. *Died 10 Dec. 1989.*

**STEVENS, Martin,** JP; MP (C) Fulham, since 1979; marketing consultant; *b* 31 July 1929; *s* of John Rowland Stevens and Muriel Stevens, London; unmarried. *Educ:* Orley Farm Sch., Harrow-on-the-Hill; Bradfield; Trinity Coll., Oxford (BA Law 1952, MA 1962). Rank Org., 1954–67; Man. Dir, Granada Television Internat., 1967–69; management and marketing consultant, 1969–. Member: LCC (Cons. Dulwich), 1955–58; Camberwell Bor. Council, 1959–65; Camberwell Gp Hosps Management Cttee, 1956–66; National Appeals Cttee, Cancer Res. Campaign, 1956– (Chm., 1968). Contested Dulwich, 1964 and 1966, and Fulham, Feb. and Oct. 1974. Mem., Select Cttee on Trade and Industry, 1982–; Leader, All Party Parly Mission to Namibia, 1983. JP Inner London, 1972. *Publications:* contrib. to business and prof. pubns. *Recreations:* books, theatre, travel, good fellowship. *Address:* C5 Albany, Piccadilly, W1V 9RF. *T:* 01–439 7980. *Clubs:* Carlton, Garrick, Hurlingham, Special Forces (Hon. Life Mem.). *Died 10 Jan. 1986.*

**STEVENS, Norman Anthony,** ARA 1983; artist (painter/printmaker); *b* 17 June 1937; *s* of Stanley Whitmore Stevens and Elsie May Whitehead; *m* 1961, Jean Mary Warhurst; one *s* one *d. Educ:* Bradford Regional Coll. of Art (NDD 1957); RCA (ARCA 1960). Lecturer in Fine Art Departments of: Manchester Polytechnic, 1960–66; Maidstone Coll. of Art, 1966–71; Middlesex Polytechnic, 1971–73; Gregory Fellow (Painting), Univ. of Leeds, 1974–75. Works in the collections of: Tate Gall.; Arts Council of GB; Arts Council NI; V & A Mus.; Govt Art Collection; Bradford City Art Gall.; Leeds City Art Gall.; Carlisle City Art Gall.; Rochdale City Art Gall.; British Council; British Museum; Nat. Trust; Mus. of Modern Art, NY; Musée d'Art et d'Histoire, Geneva; AT&T, Chicago; Yale Univ.; European Parlt. *Address:* 10 Rugby Mansions, Bishop King's Road, W14. *T:* 01–603 0321. *Died 20 Aug. 1988.*

**STEVENS, Dr Siaka (Probyn),** Hon. GCMG 1980; First Prime Minister and First Executive President, Republic of Sierra Leone,

1971–85; elected Secretary-General of All People's Congress (ruling party), 1979; b 24 Aug. 1905; m 1940, Rebecca Stevens; seven s five d. *Educ:* Albert Academy, Freetown; Ruskin Coll., Oxford. Joined Sierra Leone Police Force, 1923, and became 1st Cl. Sergt and Musketry Instr; worked for Sierra Leone Development Co., and became first Gen. Sec. of United Mine Workers Union (co-founder), 1931–46. Member: Moyamba Dist Council; Freetown City Council (rep. Protectorate Assembly); several Govt Cttees, 1946–48; Sec., Sierra Leone TUC, 1948–50; MLC (elec. by Assembly), 1951, and first Minister of Lands, Mines and Labour; Dep. Leader of (the now dissolved) Peoples' National Party, 1958–60; formed Election before Independence Movement (which later became the All Peoples' Congress), 1960; Leader of the Opposition, All Peoples' Congress, 1962; Mayor of Freetown, 1964; sworn in as Prime Minister of Sierra Leone in 1967, re-appointed 1968. Chm., OAU, 1980–81. Hon. DCL Univ. of Sierra Leone, 1969; Hon. DLitt Lincoln Univ., USA, 1979. *Recreation:* walking. *Died 29 May 1988.*

**STEVENS, Thomas Terry Hoar;** *see* Terry-Thomas.

**STEVENS, Thomas Wilson,** CBE 1962; RD 1942; Commodore, Royal Mail Line Fleet, 1961–63, retired; b 16 Oct. 1901; s of John Wilson Stevens and Susan Eliza Smith; m 1939, Mary Doreen Whitington; one s one d. *Educ:* Sir Walter St John's, Battersea. Joined Royal Mail Steam Packet Co. as a Cadet, 1917; joined Royal Naval Reserve as Sub-Lieut 1927. Active service, Royal Navy, 1939–47. Younger Brother of Trinity House, 1944. Captain Royal Mail Lines, 1947; Captain Royal Naval Reserve, 1950. *Recreation:* golf. *Address:* 79 Offington Lane, Worthing, West Sussex. *T:* Worthing 61100.
*Died April 1990.*

**STEVENSON, Alan Leslie;** Metropolitan Magistrate, 1951–73; b 1 Apr. 1901; yr s of late James Stevenson, London and Calcutta. *Educ:* Bradfield College; Christ Church, Oxford (BA). Called to the Bar, Inner Temple, 1926; South Eastern Circuit, Kent and London Sessions. Part time Ministry of Food, London Divisional Food Office, Licensing (Revocations) Officer, 1942–49; Chairman Milk Marketing Board Disciplinary Committee, 1950–51. *Recreations:* golf and tennis. *Address:* 48 Lincoln House, Basil Street, SW3. *T:* 01–589 9026. *Clubs:* Royal St George's Golf (Sandwich); Royal Cinque Ports Golf (Deal). *Died 8 Aug. 1985.*

**STEVENSON, Rt. Hon. Sir (Aubrey) Melford (Steed),** PC 1973; Kt 1957; Justice of the High Court, 1957–79 (Queen's Bench Division, 1961–79; Probate, Divorce and Admiralty Division, 1957–61); b 17 October 1902; o s of late Rev. J. G. Stevenson; one d (by 1st marriage); m 2nd, 1947, Rosalind Monica, d of late Orlando H. Wagner; one s one d. *Educ:* Dulwich Coll. LLB (London). Called to Bar, Inner Temple, 1925, Treasurer, 1972; Major and Dep. Judge Advocate, 1940–45; KC 1943; Bencher, 1950. Recorder of Rye, 1944–51, of City of Cambridge, 1952–57; Dep. Chairman, West Kent Quarter Sessions, 1949–55; Presiding Judge, South-Eastern Circuit, 1970–75. Mem. Inter-Departmental Committee on Human Artificial Insemination, 1958–60. *Address:* Truncheons, Winchelsea, East Sussex TN36 4AB. *T:* Rye 226223. *Clubs:* Garrick; Dormy House (Rye). *Died 26 Dec. 1987.*

**STEVENSON, Dame Hilda (Mabel),** DBE 1967 (CBE 1963; OBE 1960); Vice-President, Royal Children's Hospital, Melbourne, Victoria, Australia, 1938–72; b 1895; d of H. V. McKay, CBE, Sunshine, Vic; m 1st, Cleveland Kidd (d 1925); one d; 2nd, Col G. I. Stevenson (d 1958), CMG, DSO, VD. *Educ:* Presbyterian Ladies' College. Hon. LLD Melbourne, 1973. *Address:* 17 St George's Road, Toorak, Victoria 3142, Australia. *T:* 24–4628. *Clubs:* International Sportsmen's; Sunningdale Golf; Alexandra (Melbourne).
*Died 7 Sept. 1987.*

**STEVENSON, Air Vice-Marshal Leigh Forbes,** CB 1944; b 24 May 1895; s of John Henry Stevenson and Mary Ann Irving; m 1926, Lillian Myrtle Comber (d 1981); two d. *Educ:* Richibucto Grammar School, Richibucto, NB, Canada. Canadian Expeditionary Force, 1914–17; Commissioned, 1916; RFC 1917–18; RAF 1918–19; RCAF 1920–45. Air Vice-Marshal, 1942; Graduate Royal Naval Staff College, Greenwich, 1930; AOC, RCAF Overseas, 1940–41; retired, Oct. 1945. MLA of BC, 1946–53. US Commander of Legion of Merit, 1945. *Recreations:* shooting, fishing. *Address:* 1163 Balfour Avenue, Vancouver, BC V6H 1X3, Canada. *Club:* Vancouver (BC). *Died 2 March 1989.*

**STEVENSON, Sir Matthew,** KCB 1966 (CB 1961); CMG 1953; Deputy Chairman, Mersey Docks and Harbour Board, 1970–71; Member, British Steel Corporation, 1971–76; b 1910; s of James Stevenson; m 1937, Mary Sturrock Campbell White. Under-Sec., HM Treasury, Oct. 1955–61; Permanent Sec., Ministry of Power, 1965–66 (Deputy Sec., 1961–65); Permanent Sec., Min. of Housing and Local Govt, 1966–70. *Address:* Arden, Towncourt Crescent, Petts Wood, Kent. *T:* Orpington 22626. *Club:* Travellers'.
*Died 28 May 1981.*

**STEVENSON, Rt. Hon. Sir Melford;** *see* Stevenson, Rt Hon. Sir A. M. S.

**STEVENSON, Robert,** MA; writer; formerly Motion Picture Director, Walt Disney Productions Inc., California; b 1905; s of late Hugh Hunter Stevenson, Buxton; m Frances (marr. diss. 1961), d of late Charles Trumbull Howard, San Francisco; one s one d; m Ursula Henderson, MB, BS (London), FAPA (USA). *Educ:* Shrewsbury School; St John's College, Cambridge (Scholar), 1st Class Mechanical Sciences Tripos and John Bernard Seely Prize for Aeronautics, 1926; Editor of Granta 1927; President of Cambridge Union Society, and research in psychology, 1928. Entered motion picture industry 1929. Motion Picture Producer for US War Dept, 1942, Capt, 1943–46; Maj. US Army Res., 1946–53. Films directed include Tudor Rose (in America, Nine Days a Queen), King Solomon's Mines, Owd Bob (in America, To the Victor), The Ware Case, Young Man's Fancy, Tom Brown's Schooldays, Back Street, Joan of Paris, Jane Eyre, To the Ends of the Earth, Walk Softly Stranger, The Las Vegas Story, Old Yeller, Darby O'Gill and the Little People, Kidnapped, The Absent-minded Professor, The Castaways, Son of Flubber, Mary Poppins, That Darn Cat, The Gnome-Mobile, Blackbeard's Ghost, The Love Bug, Bedknobs and Broomsticks, Herbie Rides Again, Island on Top of the World, One of Our Dinosaurs is Missing, The Shaggy D. A. Has also written and directed very many television films. Film stories which he has written include Tudor Rose and Young Man's Fancy. *Publication:* Darkness in the Land, 1938. *Address:* 131 La Vereda Road, Santa Barbara, Calif 93108, USA. *Died 30 April 1986.*

**STEVENSON, Sir William Alfred,** KBE 1965 (OBE 1954); JP (NZ); civil engineering contractor; Managing Director, W. Stevenson and Sons Ltd. Formerly Mayor of Howick for 9 years. Manager and Coach, rowing section, Empire Games team, Vancouver, BC, 1954; Manager, NZ Olympic team, Tokyo, 1964. Hon. Mem., RACS, Melbourne, 1975; Hon. DSc Auckland, 1978. KStJ 1968. *Recreation:* NZ Champion: single sculls, 1923, 1924, 1926, 1927; double sculls, 1925, 1926. *Address:* W. Stevenson and Sons Ltd, Otahuhu, Auckland, New Zealand; Cockle Bay Road, Howick, Auckland.
*Died 29 Nov. 1983.*

**STEWARD, George Coton;** Professor of Mathematics, The University, Hull, 1930–61, Emeritus Professor, since 1961; b 6 April 1896; o c of Joseph Steward and Minnie, d of William Coton, Wolverhampton; unmarried. *Educ:* The Grammar School, Wolverhampton; Gonville and Caius College, Cambridge (Senior Scholar). Wrangler, with distinction in schedule b, Mathematical Tripos, 1920; ScD 1937; First Class Honours in Mathematics in BSc (Honours), Univ. of London, 1917; DSc 1926; Smith's Prize, Univ. of Cambridge, 1922, for contributions on Geometrical and Physical Optics; Member of Scientific Staff of Optics Department of National Physical Laboratory, 1918; Assistant Lecturer in Applied Mathematics, University of Leeds, 1920; Fellow of Gonville and Caius College, Cambridge, 1922; Fellow and Mathematical Lecturer, Emmanuel College, Cambridge, 1923. *Publications:* The Symmetrical Optical System, Cambridge Mathematical and Physical Tracts, No 25, 1928, 1958; papers on Geometrical and Physical Optics, and Plane Kinematics, in Transactions of Royal Society, of Cambridge Philosophical Society, etc. *Address:* 42 South Street, Cottingham, near Hull, E Yorks. *T:* Hull 847654. *Died 19 Nov. 1989.*

**STEWARD, Sir William Arthur,** Kt 1955; Director of food manufacturing companies; b 20 Apr. 1901; s of late W. A. Steward and of Mrs C. E. Steward, Norwich; m 1939. *Educ:* Norwich Model Sch., and privately. Freeman of City of London; Master, Worshipful Co. of Distillers, 1964–65; Liveryman, Worshipful Co. of Fruiterers. Served RAF, 1938–45; Sen. Catering Officer at Air Min., 1943–45; retired with rank of Squadron Leader. MP (C) Woolwich West, 1950–59; Chm. Kitchen Cttee, House of Commons, Nov. 1951–Sept. 1959. Mem. of London County Council for Woolwich West, 1949–52. Chm., London Conservative Union, 1953–55. Pres., Hotel and Catering Trades Benevolent Assoc., 1964. Comdr IoM Commandery, Sword Bearer and Mem. Supreme Council, Mil. and Hospitaller Order of St Lazarus of Jerusalem (GCLJ 1979; KMLJ 1980). *Recreations:* composing music for both organ and piano, and writing. *Address:* Fairway House, 1 Fairway Drive, Ramsey, Isle of Man.

**STEWART, Hon. Lord; Ewan George Francis Stewart,** MC 1945; a Senator of the College of Justice in Scotland, since 1975; b 9 May 1923; s of late George Duncan Stewart, CA, Edinburgh, and late Catherine Wilson Stewart; m 1953, Sheila Margaret, er d of late Major K. G. Richman, East Lancs Regt; one s one d. *Educ:* George Watson's Coll., Edinburgh; Edinburgh Univ. Served War of 1939–45 with 7/9 (Highlanders) Bn, The Royal Scots, in 52 (L) Division. Mem. of Faculty of Advocates, 1949; QC (Scotland) 1960; standing junior counsel to Min. of Civil Aviation in Scotland, 1955–60; Hon. Sheriff-Substitute of the Lothians and Peebles, 1961–64; practised at New Zealand Bar, 1962–64; resumed practice at Scottish Bar, 1964; Home Advocate-Depute, 1965–67; Solicitor-General for Scotland, 1967–70; Scottish Law Commissioner, 1971–75. Member: Cttee on Criminal Procedure in Scotland, 1971–77; Cttee on Preparation of Legislation, 1973–75; Chm., Cttee on Alternatives to Prosecution, 1977–83. Governor, St Denis School, Edinburgh, 1967–76; Chm., Court, Univ. of Stirling, 1976–84. DUniv Stirling, 1984. *Address:* 5 Munro Drive, Edinburgh EH13 0EG. *Club:* Caledonian.                                    *Died* 31 *March* 1987.

**STEWART OF ALVECHURCH,** Baroness *cr* 1974 (Life Peer), of Fulham; **Mary Elizabeth Henderson Stewart,** JP; *b* 8 May 1903; *d* of Herbert and Isabel Birkinshaw; *m* 1941, Robert Michael Maitland Stewart (later Baron Stewart of Fulham, PC, CH). *Educ:* King Edward VI High Sch., Birmingham; Bedford Coll., London Univ. (BA Hons Philosophy). Served War with WRAF, 1941–45. Tutor, WEA, 1945–64. Mem., Fabian Soc. Executive, 1950– (Chm. 1963); Chairman: Governors, Charing Cross Hosp., 1966–74; Fulham-Gilliatt Comprehensive School, 1974–79; Mem., Jt Governing Body, Fulham Gilliatt and Mary Boon Schs, 1980–. JP Co. London, 1949; Chm. Juvenile Court, 1956–66. *Publications:* Fabian Society pamphlets. *Recreations:* walking, music. *Address:* 11 Felden Street, SW6. *T:* 01–736 5194.                              *Died* 28 *Dec.* 1984.

**STEWART OF FULHAM,** Baron *cr* 1979 (Life Peer), of Fulham in Greater London; **Robert Michael Maitland Stewart;** PC 1964; CH 1969; *b* 6 Nov. 1906; *s* of Robert Wallace Stewart, DSc and Eva Stewart; *m* 1941, Mary Elizabeth Henderson Birkinshaw (later Baroness Stewart of Alvechurch) (*d* 1984); no *c*. *Educ:* Christ's Hosp.; St John's Coll., Oxford. Pres. Oxford Union, 1929; Asst Master, Merchant Taylors' Sch., 1930–31; Asst Master, Coopers' Company's School, and Lectr for Workers' Educational Assoc., 1931–42. Joined Army Intelligence Corps, 1942. Trans. to Army Educational Corps, 1943; commissioned and promoted to Capt., 1944. Contested (Lab) West Lewisham, 1931 and 1935; MP (Lab) Fulham East, 1945–55, Fulham, 1955–74, Hammersmith, Fulham, 1974–79; Vice-Chamberlain of HM Household, 1946–47; Comptroller of HM Household, 1946–47; Under-Sec. of State for War, 1947–51; Parly Sec., Min. of Supply, May–Oct. 1951; Sec. of State for Education and Science, Oct. 1964–Jan. 1965; Sec. of State for Foreign Affairs, Jan. 1965–Aug. 1966; First Sec. of State, 1966–68; Sec. of State for Economic Affairs, 1966–67; Secretary of State for Foreign and Commonwealth Affairs, 1968–70. Mem., European Parlt, 1975–76. Pres., H. G. Wells Soc., 1982–. Freeman of Hammersmith, 1967. Hon. Fellow, St John's Coll. Oxford, 1965; Hon. LLD Leeds, 1966; Hon. DSc Benin, 1972. *Publications:* The Forty Hour Week (Fabian Soc.), 1936; Bias and Education for Democracy, 1937; The British Approach to Politics, 1938; Modern Forms of Government, 1959; Life and Labour (autobiog.), 1980; European Security: the case against unilateral nuclear disarmament, 1981. *Recreations:* chess, painting. *Address:* 11 Felden Street, SW6. *T:* 01–736 5194.                              *Died* 10 *March* 1990.

**STEWART, Alexander Boyd,** CBE 1962; Director of Macaulay Institute for Soil Research, Aberdeen, 1958–68, retired; *b* 3 Nov. 1904; *s* of late Donald Stewart, farmer, Tarland, Aberdeenshire; *m* 1939, Alice F., 3rd *d* of late Robert Bowman, Aberdeen; one *s*. *Educ:* Aberdeen University; Zürich Polytechnic. Aberdeen: MA 1925; BSc (1st Cl. Hons) 1928; PhD 1932. Macaulay Inst. for Soil Research, Craigiebuckler, Aberdeen: Head of Dept of Soil Fertility, 1932; Asst Dir, 1943; Dep. Dir, 1945; seconded as Agronomist to Ind. Council of Agric. Research, 1945–46; part-time mem., Develt Commn team to survey agric., forestry and fishery products in UK, 1949–51; Strathcona-Fordyce Professor of Agriculture, University of Aberdeen, 1954–58. Mem. various tech. cttees of Dept of Agric. for Scotland, Agric. Res. Council, Colonial Office and Forestry Commn. Visited most West European countries, India, USA, and Canada. Hon. LLD Aberdeen, 1971. *Publications:* papers on soils and agriculture in agric. jls. *Recreations:* bowls, golf. *Address:* 3 Woodburn Place, Aberdeen AB1 8JS. *T:* Aberdeen 34348.
                                                        *Died* 27 *Feb.* 1981.

**STEWART, Prof. Andrew;** *b* 17 Jan. 1904; *s* of Andrew Stewart, Edinburgh, Scotland, and Marcia Sabina (*née* Sprott); *m* 1931, Jessie Christobel Borland; four *s* two *d*. *Educ:* Daniel Stewart's College, Edinburgh, Scotland; East of Scotland College of Agriculture (CDA); University of Manitoba. BSA 1931, MA 1932 (Univ. of Manitoba). Lecturer in Agricultural Economics, Univ. of Manitoba, 1932–33; Lectr, 1935, Prof. 1946, of Political Economy, Dean of Business Affairs, 1949, President, 1950–59, Univ. of Alberta; Chm. Bd of Broadcast Governors, Ottawa, 1958–68; Chm. Alberta Univs Commn, 1968–70; Prof. of Education, Univ. of Ibadan, Nigeria, 1970–72. Member of Royal Commissions: Province of Alberta (Natural Gas), 1948; Canada (Economic Prospects), 1955–57; Canada (Price Spreads of Food Products) (Chairman), 1958–59; Pres. Nat. Conf. of Canadian Univs, 1958; Chm. Assoc. of Univs of British Commonwealth, 1958. Hon. LLD Manitoba, New Brunswick, Melbourne, Alberta; Hon. DEcon Laval; FRSC; Fellow, Agricultural Inst. of Canada. *Address:* 10435 Allbay Road, Sidney, BC, Canada.                              *Died* 14 *July* 1990.

**STEWART, Charles Cosmo Bruce,** CMG 1962; Head of Cultural Relations Department, Foreign and Commonwealth Office (formerly Foreign Office), 1967–72; *b* 29 July 1912; *o s* of late Brig.-

Gen. Cosmo Gordon Stewart, CB, CMG, DSO, and Mrs Gladys Berry Stewart (*née* Honeyman). *Educ:* Eton; King's Coll., Cambridge. Barrister-at-law, Middle Temple, 1938. Served War, 1939–46. Foreign Service Officer, 1946; First Sec., Rome, 1949; First Sec. (Commercial), Cologne, 1951; transf. to Foreign Office, 1954; Head of Information Policy Dept, 1955–58; Counsellor and Consul-General, Saigon, Vietnam, 1958–61; Counsellor and Head of Chancery, Copenhagen, 1961–63; Consul-General at Luanda, 1963–68. *Club:* Travellers'.                              *Died* 10 *July* 1988.

**STEWART, Air Vice-Marshal Colin Murray,** CB 1962; CBE 1952 (OBE 1945); RAF, retired; *b* 17 June 1910; *s* of Archie Stewart, Sherborne, Dorset; *m* 1940, Anthea, *d* of Maynard Loveless, Stockbridge, Hants; four *s*. *Educ:* Wycliffe College, Stonehouse, Glos. Joined RAF, 1932; served in 5 Sqdn, NWF, India, and 16 Sqdn at home; specialised in Signals, 1937. Served War of 1939–45 (despatches, OBE): CSO various formations at home and in Europe. Chairman: British Joint Communications Board, 1952–55; Communications Electronics Cttee of Standing Group, Washington, 1955–57; AOC, No 27 Gp, 1957–58; Comd Electronics Officer, Fighter Comd, 1958–61; Dir-Gen. of Signals, Air Ministry, 1961–64; STSO, Fighter Comd, 1964–67; SASO, Technical Training Comd, 1967–68, retired. Controller, Computing Services, Univ. of London, 1968–73. *Recreations:* fishing, gardening, etc. *Address:* Byelanes, Moult Road, Salcombe, S Devon TQ8 8LG. *T:* Salcombe (054884) 2042.                              *Died* 24 *Nov.* 1990.

**STEWART, Desmond Stirling;** *b* 20 April 1924; *e s* of late R. M. Stewart, MD, FRCP and of Agnes Maud Stewart (*née* Stirling of Muiravonside); unmarried. *Educ:* Haileybury College (classical scholar); Trinity College, Oxford (classical scholar). MA Hons; BLitt. Asst Prof. of English, Baghdad Univ., 1948–56; Inspector of English in Islamic Maqāsid Schs of Beirut, 1956–58; thereafter chiefly resident in Egypt, writing fiction and non-fiction with a Middle Eastern background. FRSL 1973. *Publications:* Fiction: Leopard in the Grass, 1951; Memoirs of Alcibiades, 1952; The Unsuitable Englishman, 1955; A Woman Besieged, 1959; The Men of Friday, 1961; The Sequence of Roles, a trilogy (The Round Mosaic, 1965; The Pyramid Inch, 1966; The Mamelukes, 1968); The Vampire of Mons, 1976; Non-fiction: (with J. Haylock) New Babylon: a portrait of Iraq, 1956; Young Egypt, 1958; Turmoil in Beirut: a personal account, 1958; The Arab World (with Editors of 'Life'), 1962; Turkey (with Editors of 'Life'), 1965; Early Islam (with Editors of 'Life'), 1967; Orphan with a Hoop, 1967; Great Cairo, Mother of the World, 1968; The Middle East: Temple of Janus, 1972; Theodor Herzl: artist and politician, 1974; T. E. Lawrence, 1977; Translations: A. R. Sharkawi, Egyptian Earth, 1962; F. Ghanem, The Man Who Lost His Shadow, 1966. *Recreations:* swimming, walking. *Address:* Ilex House, Wells-next-the-Sea, Norfolk; 8 Sharia Yusif el-Gindi, Bab el-Louk, Cairo, Egypt.                              *Died* 12 *June* 1981.

**STEWART of Appin, Sir Dugald Leslie Lorn,** KCVO 1972; CMG 1969; HM Diplomatic Service, retired; British Ambassador to Yugoslavia, 1971–77; *b* 10 Sept. 1921; *m* 1947, Sibyl Anne Sturrock, MBE; three *s* one *d*. *Educ:* Eton; Magdalen College, Oxford. Foreign Office, 1942. Served in Belgrade, Berlin, Iraq, Cairo; Counsellor (Commercial), Moscow, 1962; IDC, 1965; Inspector Diplomatic Service, 1966; Counsellor, Cairo, 1968. *Recreations:* shooting, fishing, golf. *Address:* Salachail, Glen Creran, Appin, Argyll.                              *Died* 22 *Nov.* 1984.

**STEWART, Ewan George Francis;** *see* Stewart, Hon. Lord.

**STEWART, Gordon William,** CVO 1964; Chairman and General Manager, Scottish Region, British Railways, 1967–71; Chairman and Managing Director, British Transport Ship Management (Scotland) Ltd, 1967–71; Director, British Transport Hotels Ltd, 1968–71, retired; *b* 13 April 1906; *s* of James E. Stewart and Margaret Stewart; *m* 1935, Dorothy Swan Taylor, MA. *Educ:* Daniel Stewart's Coll.; George Heriot Sch., Edinburgh. L&NER: Traffic Apprentice, 1929; appts in London, Lincoln and Manchester, 1942–52; Prin. Asst to Gen. Man., Eastern Region, 1952; Asst Gen. Man., Scottish Region, 1956. Member: Stirling CC, 1972–75; Bridge of Allan Town Council, 1972–75. *Recreations:* golf, shooting. *Address:* 34 Keir Street, Bridge of Allan, Stirlingshire. *T:* Bridge of Allan 832266.                              *Died* 24 *Aug.* 1988.

**STEWART, Sir Herbert (Ray),** Kt 1946; CIE 1939; FRCScI, DIC, NDA, MSc; international consultant on agriculture, retired 1962; *b* 10 July 1890; *s* of Hugh Stewart, Ballyward, Co. Down; *m* 1917, Eva (*d* 1955), *d* of William Rea, JP, Ballygawley, Co. Tyrone; one *d*; *m* 1957, Elsie, *d* of Walter J. Pyne, London. *Educ:* Excelsior Academy, Banbridge; Royal College of Science, Dublin; Imperial College of Science and Technology, London. Military Service, 1915–19; entered the Indian Agricultural Service as Deputy Director of Agriculture, 1920; Professor of Agriculture, Punjab, 1921–27; Assistant Director of Agriculture, 1928–32; Agricultural Expert, Imperial Council of Agricultural Research, Government of India, 1938; Director of Agriculture, Punjab, 1932–43; Nominated

Member of the Punjab Legislative Council from time to time, 1927–36; Fellow of the University of the Punjab, 1929–43; Dean of the Faculty of Agriculture, 1933–43; Agriculture Commissioner with Government of India, 1943–46; Vice-Chairman, Imperial Council of Agricultural Research, 1944–46; Agricultural Adviser to British Middle East Office, Cairo, 1946–51; Principal Consultant, Agriculture, to UN Economic Survey Mission for Middle East, 1949; Agricultural Adviser to UN Relief and Works Agency for Palestine Refugees, 1950–51; Chief, Agricultural Mission to Colombia of Internat. Bank for Reconstruction and Development, 1955–56; Agricultural Consultant to Bank Missions to Pakistan, 1956, 1958, Italy, 1957, Yugoslavia and Uganda, 1960 and Kenya, 1961–62. *Publications:* various pamphlets and reports on agriculture and farm accounts in India, and on agriculture in Middle East. *Address:* 29 Alyth Road, Bournemouth, Dorset BH3 7DG. *T:* Bournemouth 764782.                                    *Died* 3 *Feb.* 1989.

**STEWART, Sir Iain (Maxwell),** Kt 1968; BSc, FIMechE, FRINA, FIMarE; Chairman, HPL Management Consultants, since 1968; Director: Dorchester Hotel Ltd (Consultative); Eagle Star Insurance Co. Ltd; Heatherset Management and Advisory Services Ltd, since 1969; Radio Clyde, since 1972; Scottish Television Ltd, since 1977; *b* 16 June 1916; *s* of William Maxwell Stewart and Jessie Naismith Brown; *m* 1st, 1941, Margaret Jean Walker (marr. diss. 1967); two *s* two *d*; 2nd, 1979, Mrs Anne Griggs. *Educ:* Loretto Sch.; Glasgow Univ. (BSc Mech. Eng.). Apprenticeship at Thermotank Ltd, 1935–39. Served War of 1939–45, Technical Adjutant, Fife and Forfar Yeomanry, 1939–41. Dir, Thermotank Ltd, 1941, Man. Dir, 1946, Chairman, 1950–65; Dir, Lyle Shipping Co. Ltd, 1953–78; Chm., Fairfields (Glasgow) Ltd, 1966–68; Dep. Chm., Upper Clyde Shipbuilders Ltd, 1967–68. Mem. Bd, BEA, 1966–73. Pres., Inst. of Engineers & Shipbuilders in Scotland, 1961–63; Prime Warden, Worshipful Co. of Shipwrights; Mem. Chamber of Commerce, Glasgow. President's Medal, IPR, 1970. Hon. LLD: Strathclyde, 1975; St Andrews, 1978. *Recreation:* golf. *Address:* 148/150 Drymen Road, Bearsden, Glasgow G61 3RE. *T:* 041–942 7952. *Clubs:* Carlton, Garrick, Caledonian; Western (Glasgow).
                                    *Died* 18 *Dec.* 1985.

**STEWART, Very Rev. James Stuart,** MA, Hon. DD; Professor Emeritus of New Testament Language, Literature and Theology, University of Edinburgh, New College (retired 1966); Extra Chaplain to the Queen in Scotland (Chaplain, 1952–66); *b* 21 July 1896; *s* of William Stewart, Dundee, and Katharine Jane Stuart Duke; *m* 1931, Rosamund Anne Barron (*d* 1986), Berkeley Lodge, Blandford, Dorset; two *s*. *Educ:* High School, Dundee; St Andrews University (MA); New College, Edinburgh (BD); University of Bonn, Germany. Minister of following Church of Scotland Congregations: St Andrews, Auchterarder, 1924–28; Beechgrove, Aberdeen, 1928–35; North Morningside, Edinburgh, 1935–46. Hon. DD, St Andrews Univ., 1945. Held following special lectureships: Cunningham Lectures, New Coll., Edinburgh, 1934; Warrack Lectures, Edinburgh and St Andrews Univs, 1944; Hoyt Lectures, Union Seminary, New York, 1949; Lyman Beecher Lectures, Yale University, USA, 1952; Duff Missionary Lectures, 1953; Turnbull Trust Preacher, Scots Church, Melbourne, 1959; Stone Lectures, Princeton, 1962; Earl Lectures, Berkeley, California, 1967. Moderator of General Assembly of Church of Scotland, May 1963–64. *Publications:* The Life and Teaching of Jesus Christ, 1932; A Man in Christ: St Paul's Theology, 1935; The Gates of New Life, 1937; The Strong Name, 1941; Heralds of God, 1945; A Faith To Proclaim, 1953; Thine Is The Kingdom, 1956; The Wind of the Spirit, 1968; River of Life, 1972; King for Ever, 1975; Joint Editor, English Trans. of Schleiermacher, The Christian Faith, 1928. *Address:* St Raphael's Home, 6 Blackford Avenue, Edinburgh EH9 2LB.                                    *Died* 1 *July* 1990.

**STEWART, Sir James Watson,** 4th Bt, *cr* 1920; *b* 8 Nov. 1922; *s* of Sir James Watson Stewart, 3rd Bt and Janie Steuart Stewart (*née* Sim) (she *m* 2nd, 1961, Neil Charteris Riddell); *S* father, 1955; *m* 1st, 1946, Anne Elizabeth Glaister (*d* 1979); no *c*; 2nd, 1980, Avril Veronica Gibb, FRSA, Hon. FBID, Hon. MASC, *o d* of late Andrew Adamson Gibb. *Educ:* Uppingham; Aberdeen University. Served 1940–47: Royal Artillery; 1st Special Air Service: Parachute Regiment. Administrator, Ardgowan Hospice, Greenock, 1984–. *Heir: brother* John Keith Watson Stewart [*b* 25 Feb. 1929; *m* 1954, Mary Elizabeth, *d* of John Francis Moxon; two *s* one *d*]. *Address:* Balgownie, Kilcreggan, Dumbartonshire G84 0JY. *T:* Kilcreggan 2455.                                    *Died* 15 *March* 1988.

**STEWART, Sir Jocelyn Harry,** 12th Bt, *cr* 1623; *b* 24 Jan. 1903; *s* of Sir Harry Jocelyn Urquhart Stewart, 11th Bt, and Isabel Mary (*d* 1956), 2nd *d* of Col Mansfield, DL, Castle Wray, Co. Donegal; *S* father, 1945; *m* 1st, Constance Shillaber (*d* 1940); one *s*; 2nd,1946, Katherine Christina Sweeney, Tamney, Co. Donegal; two *s* two *d*. *Heir: s* Alan D'Arcy Stewart [*b* 29 Nov. 1932; *m* 1952, Patricia, *d* of Lawrence Turner, Ramelton, Co. Donegal; two *s* two *d*].
                                    *Died* 3 *March* 1982.

**STEWART of Ardvorlich, John Alexander MacLaren,** TD; Vice-Lord-Lieutenant, Perth and Kinross (formerly Perthshire), 1974–84; *b* 25 March 1904; *s* of late Major William Stewart of Ardvorlich and of Lily, *d* of late Dr A. C. MacLaren, Harley Street, London; *m* 1930, Violet Hermione (*d* 1979), *er d* of late Col Sir Donald Walter Cameron of Lochiel, KT, CMG; one *s* one *d*. *Educ:* Wellington Coll., Berks. Landowner and farmer. Served War, 1939–45: 6th Bn, The Black Watch (France, 1940; Tunisia, 1943; Italy, 1944). *Publications:* The Stewarts, 1954, 2nd edn 1963; The Grahams, 1958, 2nd edn 1970; The Camerons: a history of Clan Cameron, 1974, 2nd edn 1981. *Recreations:* normal country pursuits in Highlands. *Address:* Ardvorlich, Lochearnhead, Perthshire. *T:* Lochearnhead 218. *Clubs:* Royal Perth Golfing, County and City (Perth).                                    *Died* 11 *May* 1985.

**STEWART, Sir (John) Keith (Watson),** 5th Bt *cr* 1920, of Balgownie; *b* 25 Feb. 1929; *s* of Sir James Watson Stewart, 3rd Bt and of Janie Steuart Stewart, *d* of late James Morton Sim; *S* brother, 1988; *m* 1954, Mary Elizabeth, *d* of John Francis Moxon; two *s* one *d*. *Educ:* Uppingham; RMA Sandhurst. Captain (retd) Scottish Horse (TA). *Heir: s* John Simon Watson Stewart [*b* 5 July 1955; *m* 1978, Catherine Stewart, *d* of Gordon Bond; one *s* one *d*]. *Address:* 10 Foster Road, W4 4NY. *T:* 01–995 8456. *Club:* Cavalry and Guards.                                    *Died* 13 *March* 1990.

**STEWART, John Philip,** MD, FRCSE, FSAScot; Hon. Consulting Surgeon, Deaconess Hospital; Hon. Consulting Surgeon, Royal Infirmary, Edinburgh; former Hon. Senior Lecturer and Head of Department of Otorhinolaryngology, member, Faculty of Medicine and Senatus Academicus, University of Edinburgh; *b* 1 Feb. 1900; *s* of late George Stewart, SSC, JP, and Flora Philip, MA; *m* 1st, 1928, Elizabeth Josephine Forbes Wedderburn; 2nd, 1982, Phyllis Mary Cave. *Educ:* Daniel Stewart's College and University, Edinburgh; Paris and Vienna. 2nd Lieut RFA 1918; MB, ChB Edinburgh Univ. 1923; MD 1925; FRCSE 1926; Lt-Col RAMC, Adviser in Oto-Rhino-Laryngology, BLA; served France, 1940; Egypt and Persia, 1942–43; North-West Europe, 1944–45 (despatches). Hon. Mem., Section of Laryngology, RSocMed (Former Pres.). *Publication:* Turner's Diseases of Ear, Nose and Throat. *Recreation:* golf. *Address:* 20 Gallow Hill, Peebles EH45 9BG. *T:* Peebles 20447.                                    *Died* 19 *Sept.* 1984.

**STEWART, Sir Keith;** *see* Stewart, Sir J. K. W.

**STEWART, Potter;** retired Justice of the Supreme Court of the United States (Associate Justice, 1958–81); *b* 23 Jan. 1915; *s* of James Garfield Stewart and Harriet Loomis Stewart (*née* Potter); *m* 1943, Mary Ann Bertles; two *s* one *d*. *Educ:* Hotchkiss School, Lakeville, Connecticut; Yale College; Yale Law School. One-year fellowship, Cambridge, Eng. General practice of law as associate with Debevoise, Stevenson, Plimpton and Page, New York City, 1941–42, 1945–47; associate with Dinsmore, Shohl, Sawyer and Dinsmore, Cincinnati, O, 1947; partner of that firm, 1951–54; Judge, US Court of Appeals for 6th Circuit, 1954–58. Member, Cincinnati City Council, 1950–53 (Vice-Mayor, 1952–53). Hon. LLD: Yale Univ., 1959; Kenyon Coll., 1960; Wilmington Coll., 1962; Univ. of Cincinnati, 1963; Ohio Univ., 1964; Univ. of Michigan, 1966; Miami Univ., 1974. *Address:* Supreme Court Building, Washington, DC 20543, USA; 5136 Palisade Lane, Washington, DC 20016. *Clubs:* Camargo (Cincinnati, Ohio); Chevy Chase (Chevy Chase, Md).                                    *Died* 7 *Dec.* 1985.

**STEWART, William McCausland;** Professor of French, University of Bristol, 1945–66; Emeritus, 1966; *b* 17 Sept. 1900; *yr s* of late Abraham McCausland Stewart, Londonderry, and Alexandrina Catherine Margaret Elsner, Dublin; *m* 1933, Ann Cecilia Selo (*d* 1969); two *d*. *Educ:* Foyle Coll., Londonderry; Trinity Coll., Dublin (Sizar, Schol. and Sen. Moderator in Mod. Literature-French and German; Prizeman in Old and Middle English; Vice-Chancellor's Prizeman in English Verse). BA 1922; MA 1926; Lecteur d'Anglais, Univ. of Montpellier, 1922–23 (Certificat de Licence en Phonétique, 1923). Resident Lecteur d'Anglais at Ecole Normale Supérieure, Paris, 1923–26; also studied Sorbonne (Diplôme d'Etudes Supérieures de Lettres: Langues Classiques, 1925) and Ecole des Hautes Etudes, Paris, and taught Collège Sainte-Barbe, Paris; Lectr in French, Univ. of Sheffield, 1927 and 1928; Lectr in French and Joint Head of French Dept, Univ. of St Andrews and University College, Dundee, from 1928 onwards. Seconded for War Service in Foreign Research and Press Service (Chatham House), Balliol College, Oxford, Sept. 1939; Head of French Section of same, 1940–43; Head of French Section, Research Dept of Foreign Office, 1943–45. Chairman, University of Bristol Art Lectures Committee, 1946–66; Dean of Faculty of Arts, 1960–62; Visiting Professor, Univ. of Auckland, 1967. Member Council, RWA; Pres., Clifton Arts Club; Governor, Bath Academy of Art, Corsham Court; Chairman, Bristol-Bordeaux Assoc., 1953–76; Corr. Mem. Acad. des Sciences, Belles Lettres et Arts de Bordeaux and of Acad. Montesquieu. Chevalier de la Légion d'Honneur, 1950. Officier des Palmes Académiques, 1957, Commandeur, 1966. DLitt (*hc*), Nat.

Univ. of Ireland, 1963. *Publications:* Les Etudes Françaises en Grand Bretagne, Paris, 1929 (with G. T. Clapton); translation of Paul Valéry's Eupalinos, with Preface, Oxford, 1932, and of his Dialogues, Bollingen Series XLV, New York, 1956 and London, 1958; Les Chœurs d'Athalie (record), 1958; Aspects of the French Classical Ideal, 1967; Tokens in Time (poems), 1968; Alcaics for our Age, 1976; Bristol-Bordeaux: The First Thirty Years, 1977; contribs to literary reviews and learned periodicals, mainly on Classical and Modern France (incl. Descartes, Racine, Montesquieu, Valéry). *Recreations:* promoting Community Service for All (CSA), and proportional representation (PR/STV). *Address:* 5 Cotham Park, Bristol BS6 6BZ. *T:* Bristol 48156. *Club:* Europe House.
*Died 22 Dec. 1989.*

**STEWARTSON, Prof. Keith,** FRS 1965; Goldsmid Professor of Mathematics, University College London, since 1964; *b* 20 Sept. 1925; *s* of late G. C. Stewartson and M. Stewartson (*née* Hyde); *m* 1953, Elizabeth Jean Forrester; two *s* one *d*. *Educ:* Stockton Secondary Sch.; St Catharine's Coll., Cambridge. Lectr in Applied Mathematics at Bristol Univ., 1949–53; Research Fellow in Aeronautics, California Inst. of Technology, 1953–54; Reader in Applied Mathematics at Bristol Univ., 1954–58; Prof. of Applied Mathematics, Durham Univ. (late Durham Colls), 1958–64. Hon. DSc East Anglia, 1979. *Publications:* Laminar Compressible Boundary Layers, 1964; papers in mathematical and aeronautical journals. *Address:* 67 Southway, NW11 6SB. *T:* 01–458 3534.
*Died 7 May 1983.*

**STILES, Walter Stanley,** OBE 1946; PhD, DSc; FRS 1957; formerly Deputy Chief Scientific Officer, The National Physical Laboratory, Teddington, retired 1961; *b* 15 June 1901; *s* of Walter Stiles and Elizabeth Catherine (*née* Smith); *m* 1928, Pauline Frida Octavia, *d* of Judge Henrik Brendstrup, Hillerød, Denmark; no *c*. *Educ:* University College, London; St John's College, Cambridge. Andrews Scholar, University Coll., London, 1918. Demonstrator in Physics, 1920–22; PhD London 1929, DSc London 1939; Carpenter Medallist, London Univ., 1944. Technical Officer, RN Signal School, 1923–25; Scientific Officer, Nat. Physical Lab., 1925–61. Gen. Sec. Internat. Commn on Illumination, 1928–31; Vice-President Physical Soc., 1948–49; President, Illuminating Engineering Soc., 1960, Gold Medallist, 1967; Chm. Colour Group of Physical Soc., 1949–51, Newton Lectr, 1967; Thomas Young Orator (Physical Soc.), 1955; Regents' Lectr (UCLA), 1964; Tillyer Medallist (Optical Society of America), 1965; Finsen Medallist (Congr. Internat. de Photobiologie), 1968. *Publications:* Thermionic Emission, 1932; Color Science (with G. Wyszecki), 1967, 2nd edn 1983; Mechanisms of Colour Vision, 1978; many papers on illuminating engineering and physiological optics in Proc. Royal Soc., Trans Illum. Eng Soc., etc. *Recreation:* painting. *Address:* 89 Richmond Hill Court, Richmond, Surrey. *T:* 01–940 4334.
*Died 15 Dec. 1985.*

**STINSON, Sir Charles (Alexander),** KBE 1979 (OBE 1962); Minister of Finance, Fiji, 1972–79, retired; *b* 22 June 1919; *s* of William John Bolton Stinson and Ella Josephine (*née* Griffiths); *m* 1946, Mollie Nancie, *d* of Albert Dean; two *s* one *d*. *Educ:* Levuka Public Sch.; Boys' Grammar Sch, Suva. Electrical apprentice, Lectric Ltd, 1934; motor salesman, Morris Hedstrom Ltd, Fiji, 1935–37; Manager, Morris Hedstrom Motor Dept, 1938–39; Flotation shift boss, Emperor Gold Mining Co. Ltd, Fiji, 1940–41; War service in Army and Navy, 1941–46; Man. Dir, Stinsons Ltd, 1946–66. Elected to Suva City Council, 1952; Mayor of Suva, 1959–66; elected Gen. Mem. for Suva, 1964; MP, 1966–82; Minister for Communications, Works and Tourism, 1966–72. Comr Gen. of Section, Fiji Pavilion, World Expo, 1988. Pres., Suva Rotary Club, 1957–58. Capt., Mollie Dean, oil survey, Fiji, 1980–82. Chm., Seven Oaks South Complex, 1989. Pres., Broadbeach Probus Club, 1989. *Recreations:* fishing, flying, boating, golf. *Address:* 13 Seven Oaks South, Campbell Street, Sorrento, Queensland 4217, Australia.
*Died 2 Nov. 1989.*

**STIRLING, Alfred T.,** CBE 1953 (OBE 1941); *b* Melbourne, Victoria, Australia, 8 Sept. 1902; *s* of Robert Andrew and Isabel Stirling. *Educ:* Scotch College, Melbourne; Melbourne Univ.; University Coll., Oxford (MA, LLB). Victorian Bar, 1927–33. Private Secretary to Attorney-General of Commonwealth (Rt Hon. R. G. Menzies), 1934–35; Assistant External Affairs Officer, London, 1936; head of Political Section, Dept of External Affairs, Canberra, 1936–37; External Affairs Officer, London, 1937–45; Counsellor, Australian Legation to Netherlands, 1942–45; High Commissioner for Australia in Canada, 1945–46; Australian Minister in Washington, 1946–48; Australian High Comr in S Africa, 1948–50; Australian Ambassador: to the Netherlands, 1950–55; to France, 1955–59; to the Philippines, 1959–62; to Greece, 1964–65; to Italy, 1962–67. Grand Cross of St Gregory; Grand Cordon of Royal George (Greece). *Publications:* Victorian (jtly), 1934; Joseph Bosisto, 1970; The Italian Diplomat, and Italy and Scotland, 1971; Gang Forward, 1972; On the Fringe of Diplomacy, 1973; Lord Bruce: the London Years, 1974; A Distant View of the Vatican, 1975; Old Richmond,

1979. *Address:* Flat 30, St Ives, 166 Toorak Road West, South Yarra, Victoria 3141, Australia. *Clubs:* Caledonian (London); Melbourne (Melbourne).
*Died 3 July 1981.*

**STIRLING, Sir (Archibald) David,** Kt 1990; DSO 1942; OBE 1946; Chairman, Television International Enterprises Ltd; *b* 15 Nov. 1915; *s* of late Brigadier-General Archibald Stirling of Keir, and Hon. Mrs Margaret Stirling, OBE, 4th *d* of 13th Baron Lovat. *Educ:* Ampleforth College, Yorks; (for a brief period) Cambridge University. In Sept. 1939 was Mem. SRO, Scots Guards and served with that Regt for first six months of War when he was transferred to No 3 Commando (Brigade of Guards) and went out with this unit to Middle East; subseq. served with First SAS Regt (POW, 1943–45). President, Capricorn Africa Society, 1947–59, living at that time in Africa based on Salisbury and Nairobi. Officer, Légion d'Honneur; Officer, Orange Nassau. *Address:* 22 South Audley Street, W1. *T:* 071–499 9252. *Clubs:* White's, Turf, Pratt's.
*Died 4 Nov. 1990.*

**STIRLING, Sir Charles (Norman),** KCMG 1955 (CMG 1941); KCVO 1957; *b* 19 Nov. 1901; *er s* of late F. H. Stirling, Victoria, British Columbia; *m* 1950, Ann, *o d* of J. H. Moore; one *s* two *d*. *Educ:* Wellington College; Corpus Christi College, Oxford. Third Secretary, Diplomatic Service, 1925; Second Secretary, 1930; First Secretary, 1937; Head of a Department in Ministry of Economic Warfare, 1939–42; Acting Counsellor in the Foreign Office, 1942; Counsellor, British Embassy, Lisbon, 1946; Consul-General, Tangier, 1949–51; Ambassador to Chile, 1951–54; Ambassador to Portugal, 1955–60. *Recreation:* fishing. *Address:* 17 Park Row, Farnham, Surrey. *Club:* Travellers'.
*Died 5 April 1986.*

**STIRLING, Sir David;** *see* Stirling, Sir Archibald D.

**STIRLING, Duncan Alexander;** *b* 6 Oct. 1899; 4th *s* of late Major William Stirling, JP, DL, of Fairburn, Ross-shire, and Charlotte Eva, *d* of late Æneas Mackintosh, Daviot, Inverness-shire; *m* 1926, Lady Marjorie Murray, *e d* of 8th Earl of Dunmore, VC, DSO, MVO; two *s*. *Educ:* Harrow; New College, Oxford. Coldstream Guards, 1918 and again 1940–43. Partner, H. S. Lefevre & Co., Merchant Bankers, 1929–49; Director: Westminster Bank, and Westminster Foreign Bank, 1935–69 (Chm. 1962–69); National Westminster Bank, 1968–74 (Chm., 1968–69); London Life Association, 1935–80 (Pres., 1951–65). Pres., Inst. of Bankers, 1964–66; Chm., Cttee of London Clearing Bankers and Pres., British Bankers' Assoc., 1966–68. Prime Warden, Fishmongers Co., 1954–55. Mem. Council, Baring Foundn, 1969–79; Trustee, Thalidomide Trust, 1973–81. *Address:* 20 Kingston House South, Ennismore Gardens, SW7 1NF. *Club:* Brooks's.
*Died 15 April 1990.*

**STIRLING, John Bertram,** OC 1970; Chancellor, Queen's University, Kingston, Ontario, 1960–73; *b* 29 Nov. 1888; *s* of Dr James A. Stirling and Jessie Bertram, Picton, Ont; *m* 1928, Emily P., *d* of Col and Mrs E. T. Sturdee, Saint John, NB; one *d*. *Educ:* Queen's University, Kingston, Canada. BA 1909, BSc 1911, Queen's Univ., Kingston. Resident Engineer, Chipman and Power, Cons. Engineers, Toronto, 1911–15; with E. G. M. Cape and Co. Ltd from 1915; Field Engineer, 1915; Supt 1924; Gen. Supt, 1930; Vice-Pres., 1940; Chm., 1960–65. President: Canadian Construction Assoc., 1942; Montreal Board of Trade, 1950; Engineering Inst. of Canada, 1952 (Chm., Nat. Honours and Awards Cttee, to 1981). Hon. LLD: Queen's, Kingston, 1951; Toronto, 1961; Hon. DSc: Royal Mil. Coll., Canada, 1962; McGill, 1963. Hon. Col 3rd Field Regt Royal Can. Engrs. Sir John Kennedy Medal of Eng. Inst. of Canada, 1954; Montreal Medal, Queen's Univ. Alumni Assoc., 1955; Julian Smith Medal, Eng. Inst. of Canada, 1963. *Recreations:* sailing, country life, music. *Address:* 10 Richelieu Place, Montreal, Quebec H3G 1E7, Canada. *Club:* Saint James's (Montreal).
*Died 20 June 1988.*

**STIRLING, Viola Henrietta Christian,** CBE 1947; TD 1951; DL; *b* 3 June 1907; *d* of late Charles Stirling of Gargunnock, landowner and farmer. *Educ:* Queen Ethelburga's Sch., Harrogate; Lady Margaret Hall, Oxford (BA). Joined Auxiliary Territorial Service, 1939; Deputy Director ATS Scottish Command, 1945; released 1949. Member: Finance Committee, ATS Benevolent Fund, 1948–64; of Stirling and Clackmannan Hospitals Board of Management, 1948–64; selected military member TA&AFA, County of Stirling, 1948–68; Hon. Colonel 317 (Scottish Comd) Bn WRAC/TA, 1959–62. Member of Stirling County Council, 1958–67; DL Co. of Stirling, 1965–84. *Address:* Gargunnock, Stirlingshire. *T:* Gargunnock 202.
*Died 23 Feb. 1989.*

**STIRLING-HAMILTON, Sir Bruce,** 13th Bt *cr* 1673; Managing Director, Glasgow Business Services Ltd, since 1985; *b* 5 Aug. 1940; *s* of Captain Sir Robert William Stirling-Hamilton, 12th Bt, JP, DL, RN (retd), and of Eileen, *d* of late Rt Rev. H. K. Southwell, CMG; *S* father, 1982; *m* 1968, Stephanie, *d* of Dr William Campbell, LRCP, LRCS; one *s* two *d*. *Educ:* Nautical College, Pangbourne; RMA Sandhurst. Commissioned, Queen's Own Highlanders

(Seaforth and Camerons), 1961; ADC to GOC 51st (Highland) Div., 1964; resigned commn, 1971. Kimberly-Clark Ltd, 1971; Seismograph Service (England) Ltd, 1974–83; MAST (Scotland), 1983–85. *Heir: s* Malcolm William Bruce Stirling-Hamilton, *b* 6 Aug. 1979. *Address:* 16 Bath Place, Ayr, Ayrshire KA7 1DP.
*Died* 17 *Sept.* 1989.

**STIRLING-HAMILTON, Captain Sir Robert William;** *see* Hamilton.

**STOBY, Sir Kenneth Sievewright,** Kt 1961; Chairman, Guyana Match Co. Ltd; Director, Shawinigan Engineering (Guyana) Co. Ltd; *b* 19 Oct. 1903; *s* of late Mr and Mrs W. S. Stoby; *m* 1935, Eunice Badley; one *s* one *d. Educ:* Christ Church Sch., Georgetown; Queen's Coll., Georgetown. Called to Bar, Lincoln's Inn, 1930; private practice until 1940; seconded Dep. Controller of Prices, 1944; seconded again, 1947, Controller Supplies and Prices; acted Legal Draftsman; Chairman several Boards and Committees; Magistrate Nigeria, 1948; Registrar of Deeds and Supreme Court, British Guiana, 1950; Puisne Judge, 1953; Chief Justice, Barbados, 1959–65; Chancellor of the Judiciary, Guyana, 1966–68. Pro-Chancellor, Univ. of Guyana, 1966–75. *Died* 10 *July* 1985.

**STOCK, Allen Lievesley;** Chairman, The Morgan Crucible Co. Ltd, 1959–69; *b* 24 September 1906; 2nd *s* of late Cyril Lievesley and Irene Mary Stock; *m* 1933, Rosemary Nancy Hopps; two *s* one *d. Educ:* Charterhouse; Faraday House; Christ's College, Cambridge. Belliss & Morcom, 1926–27; The British Thomson-Houston Co. Ltd, Rugby, 1928–32; The Morgan Crucible Company Ltd, 1932–69. Chairman, London Chamber of Commerce, 1958–62, Vice-Pres., 1962–78; Member: Post Office Users' Council, 1966–69; Commn of Inquiry into Industrial Representation, 1971–72. Hon. Treasurer, The Sail Training Assoc., 1969–71. *Recreations:* boats, gardening, bird-watching. *Address:* Furzefield Cottage, Bosham Hoe, W Sussex. *T:* Bosham 573231. *Club:* Hawks (Cambridge).
*Died* 4 *Aug.* 1982.

**STOCK, Keith L(ievesley),** CB 1957; Under Secretary, Department of Economic Affairs, 1965–68, retired; *b* 24 Oct. 1911; *s* of late Cyril Lievesley Stock and Irene Mary Stock (*née* Tomkins); *m* 1937, Joan Katherine Stock (*née* Milne); two *s* one *d. Educ:* Charterhouse; New College, Oxford. Petroleum Department, Board of Trade, 1935; Ministry of Fuel and Power, 1942; Imperial Defence College, 1951; Cabinet Office, 1954; Ministry of Fuel and Power, 1955; Min. of Technology, 1964. *Publication:* Rose Books (bibliog.), 1984. *Address:* c/o Barclays Bank, Millbank, SW1.
*Died* 22 *Sept.* 1988.

**STOCKDALE, Sir Edmund (Villiers Minshull),** 1st Bt *cr* 1960; Kt 1955; JP; *b* 16 April 1903; 2nd *s* of late Major H. M. Stockdale, JP, and Mrs Stockdale, Mears Ashby Hall, Northants; *m* 1937, Hon. Louise Fermor-Hesketh, *er d* of 1st Lord Hesketh; two *s* (one *d* decd). *Educ:* Wellington College. Entered Bank of England, 1921; Assistant to Governors, Reserve Bank of India, 1935; Asst Principal, Bank of England, 1937, Dep. Principal, 1941; pensioned, 1945. Elected Court of Common Council, City of London, 1946, Alderman, Ward of Cornhill, 1948; one of HM Lieuts, City of London, Comr of Assize, 1948–63; Sheriff, City of London 1953; Lord Mayor of London, 1959–60; Chm., Lord Mayor's Appeal Fund, King George's Jubilee Trust, 1960; Mem., Adv. Bd, etc, Holloway Prison, 1948–60 (Chairman, 1951–53); Member, Holloway Discharged Prisoners Aid Society Cttee, 1964; Vice-President, The Griffins (formerly Holloway DPAS), 1965; Member, Boards: Bridewell, Royal Bethlem and Maudsley Hosps, 1948–63; Mem., Emerg. Bed Service Cttee, King Edward Hosp. Fund, 1963–69; Vice-Pres. King Edward's School, Witley, 1960–63; Governor: United Westminster Schools, 1948–54; Wellington College, 1955–74; Eagle House Preparatory, 1964–74. Director, Embankment Trust Ltd, 1948–74, and other cos. A Church Comr for England, 1962; Mem. Winchester Dioc. Bd of Finance (Exec. Cttee), 1963. Junior Grand Warden (Acting), Grand Lodge of England, 1960–61. Partner, Read Hurst-Brown and Co.; Member: London Stock Exchange, 1946–60; Court of Assistants, Carpenters' Co. (Master, 1970), Glaziers' Co. (Master 1973). JP London (Inner London Sessions), 1968. Grand Officer, Legion of Honour; Grand Cross, Order of Merit, Peru; Grand Official, Order of Mayo, Argentina; Knight Comdr, Order of Crown, Thailand; Order of Triple Power, Nepal; Comdr, Royal Order of North Star, Sweden; KStJ. Gold Medal, Madrid. *Publications:* The Bank of England in 1934, 1966; "Ptolemy Tortoise", 1979. *Recreations:* shooting, drawing. *Heir: er s* Thomas Minshull Stockdale [*b* 7 Jan. 1940; *m* 1965, Jacqueline Ha-Van-Vuong; one *s* one *d*]. *Address:* Hoddington House, Upton Grey, Basingstoke. *T:* Long Sutton 437. *Clubs:* Buck's, City Livery. *Died* 24 *March* 1989.

**STOCKDALE, His Honour Frank Alleyne,** MA; a Circuit Judge (formerly County Court Judge, Ilford and Westminster Courts), 1964–79; *b* 16 Oct. 1910; *er s* of late Sir Frank Stockdale, GCMG, CBE, MA; *m* 1942, Frances Jean, *er d* of late Sir FitzRoy Anstruther-Gough-Calthorpe, Bt; one *s* two *d. Educ:* Repton; Magdalene College, Cambridge. Called to Bar, Gray's Inn, 1934; Bencher,

1964. Served War of 1939–45: 5th Royal Inniskilling Dragoon Guards, BEF, 1939–40; North Africa, 1942–43 (despatches); psc; Lt-Col. Dep. Chm., Hampshire QS, 1954–66; Dep. Chm., Greater London QS, 1966–71. Mem., Inter-Deptl Cttee on Adoption Law, 1969–72, Chm. 1971–72. *Address:* Victoria Place, Monmouth, Gwent NP5 3BR. *T:* Monmouth 5039. *Club:* Garrick.
*Died* 28 *Dec.* 1989.

**STOCKDALE, Group Captain George William;** Secretary-General, Plastics and Rubber Institute, since 1985; *b* 17 Dec. 1932; *s* of William and Lilian Stockdale; *m* 1957, Ann (*née* Caldon); two *s* two *d. Educ:* RMA Sandhurst. Royal Air Force, 1951–81: Policy and Planning Div, 1976–79; Command Regt Officer, Germany, 1979–81. MITD, FBIM. *Recreations:* fell walking, painting, international affairs, travel, people. *Address:* The Plastics and Rubber Institute, 11 Hobart Place, SW1W 0HL. *T:* 071–245 9555. *Club:* Royal Air Force. *Died* 27 *Oct.* 1990.

**STOCKIL, Sir Raymond (Osborne),** KBE 1964 (OBE 1958); Farmer and Director of Companies; *b* 15 April 1907; *s* of Francis Robert Stockil and Ruth (*née* Coventry); *m* 1929, Virginia Fortner (*d* 1972); one *s* three *d* (and one *s* decd); *m* 1973, Margot Susan Lovett Hodgson. *Educ:* Heldeberg College, Cape Province; Washington University, USA (BA). Took up Civil Aviation and Manufacturing in USA, 1929–33 (5 USA Patents); returned to Natal, 1934; commenced farming in Fort Victoria, 1936. Served War of 1939–45 with SR Signal Corps. MP for Victoria, 1946–62; Leader of Opposition, 1948–53 and 1956–59; resigned from Parliament, 1962. Chairman, Hippo Valley Estates Ltd, 1956. *Recreation:* owner and trainer of racehorses. *Address:* PO Box 1108, Harare, Zimbabwe; PO Box 7462, Newton Park, Port Elizabeth, 6055, Republic of South Africa; (home) Cranstoun Lodge, Kragga Kamma Road, PO Box 7462, Port Elizabeth, 6055. *T:* Port Elizabeth 731476. *Club:* Harare (Harare, Zimbabwe). *Died* 29 *April* 1984.

**STOCKLEY, Gerald Ernest,** CBE 1957; *b* Simla, India, 15 Dec. 1900; *s* of late Brig.-Gen. E. N. Stockley, DSO, late RE, and Elsie Shewell Cooper; *m* 1st, Phillipina Mary Prendergast (marr. diss.); two *d*; 2nd, Katharine Noel Parker. *Educ:* Wellington Coll.; Christ's Coll., Cambridge, BA Hons, English and Mod. Langs. China Consular Service, 1925, and served at numerous posts in China: Consul (Grade II) 1935, Consul, Foochow, 1936–38, and Tengyüeh, 1938–40; Consul (Grade I) 1939, Acting Consul-Gen., Kunming, 1939; served with British Military Mission in China, 1941–43; Acting Consul-General, Kweilin, 1943–44: Consul, Seattle (USA), 1944–45; Consul-Gen., Hankow, 1946–48; Counsellor, FO, 1948–49; Minister to Republic of Honduras, 1950–54; Consul-General, Naples, 1954–59; retired, Dec. 1959; Consul and Consul-General (personal rank), Nice, 1960–66. *Address:* 3 River House, Chelsea Embankment, Tite Street, SW3 4LG.
*Died* 25 *June* 1981.

**STOCKMAN, Henry Watson,** CBE 1949; *b* London, 20 April 1894; *s* of late Henry Stockman; *m* 1921, Margaret Reid Robertson; one *s* one *d. Educ:* Battersea Polytechnic. National Health Insurance Commn (England), 1912–19; Ministry of Health, 1919–44; Ministry of National Insurance (later Min. of Pensions and Nat. Insurance), 1945–55; Asst Secretary, 1945–50; Chief Insurance Officer, 1950–53; Under-Secretary, 1953–55; International Labour Office, Geneva, Social Security Division, 1957–59; Technical Adviser, International Social Security Association, Geneva, 1959–64. *Publications:* History and Development of Social Security in Great Britain, 1957; Development and Trends in Social Security in Great Britain, 1962. *Recreation:* gardening. *Address:* 4 Craigleith, 41 Grove Road, Beaconsfield, Bucks HP9 1PT. *T:* Beaconsfield 3722.
*Died* 27 *June* 1982.

**STOCKS, Alfred James,** CBE 1981; DL; Chief Executive, Liverpool City Council, 1973–86; *b* 24 March 1926; *s* of James and Mary Stocks; *m* 1958, Jillian Margery Gedye; one *s* one *d. Educ:* Bootham Sch., York; Clare Coll., Cambridge (MA). Admitted solicitor, 1949. Appointed Dep. Town Clerk, Liverpool, 1968. Pres., Soc. of Local Authority Chief Execs, 1983–84. DL Merseyside, 1982. Hon. LLD Liverpool, 1980. *Address:* 38 Glendyke Road, Liverpool L18 6JR. *T:* 051–724 2448. *Club:* Athenæum (Liverpool).
*Died* 5 *Oct.* 1988.

**STOCKTON, 1st Earl of,** *cr* 1984; **Maurice Harold Macmillan,** OM 1976; PC 1942; FRS 1962; Viscount Macmillan of Ovenden, 1984; Chancellor, University of Oxford, since 1960; President, Macmillan Ltd, since 1974 (Chairman, 1963–74; Chairman, Macmillan & Co. and Macmillan (Journals), 1963–67); Prime Minister and First Lord of The Treasury, Jan. 1957–Oct. 1963; MP (C) Bromley, Nov. 1945–Sept. 1964; *b* 10 Feb. 1894; *s* of late Maurice Crawford Macmillan; *m* 1920, Lady Dorothy Evelyn Cavendish, GBE 1964 (*d* 1966), *d* of 9th Duke of Devonshire; two *d* (and one *s* one *d* decd). *Educ:* Eton (Scholar); Balliol Coll., Oxford (Exhibitioner). 1st Class Hon. Moderations, 1919; served during war, 1914–18, in Special Reserve Grenadier Guards (wounded 3 times). ADC to Gov.-Gen. of Canada, 1919–20; retired, 1920; MP (U) Stockton-on-Tees,

1924–29 and 1931–45; contested Stockton-on-Tees, 1923 and 1945; Parliamentary Sec., Ministry of Supply, 1940–42; Parliamentary Under-Sec. of State, Colonies, 1942; Minister Resident at Allied HQ in North-West Africa, 1942–45; Sec. for Air, 1945; Minister of Housing and Local Government, 1951–54; Minister of Defence, Oct. 1954–April 1955; Sec. of State for Foreign Affairs, April-Dec. 1955; Chancellor of the Exchequer, Dec. 1955–Jan. 1957. First Pres., Game Research Assoc., 1960–65. A Vice-Pres., Franco-British Soc., 1955; A Trustee, Historic Churches Preservation Fund, 1957–. Freeman of: City of London (Stationers' and Newspaper Makers' Company, 1957), 1957; Bromley, Kent, 1957; Hon. Freedom of City of London, 1961; Toronto, 1962; Stockton-on-Tees, 1968. Hon. Fellow, Balliol Coll., Oxford, 1957; Hon. FBA, 1981. Hon. DCL Oxford, 1958; DCL Oxford (by diploma), 1960; LLD Cambridge, 1961, Sussex, 1963. Benjamin Franklin Medal, RSA, 1976; Olympia Prize, 1979. *Publications:* Industry and the State (jtly), 1927; Reconstruction: A Plea for a National Policy, 1933; Planning for Employment, 1935; The Next Five Years, 1935; The Middle Way, 1938 (re-issued 1966); Economic Aspects of Defence, 1939; Memoirs: Vol. I, Winds of Change, 1966; Vol. II, The Blast of War, 1967; Vol. III, Tides of Fortune, 1969; Vol. IV, Riding the Storm 1956–59, 1971; Vol. V, Pointing the Way 1959–61, 1972; Vol. VI, At the end of the Day 1961–63, 1973; Past Masters, 1975; War Diaries: politics and war in the Mediterranean January 1943–May 1945, 1984. *Heir:* g s Viscount Macmillan of Ovenden. *Address:* Macmillan & Co. Ltd, 4 Little Essex Street, WC2; Birch Grove House, Chelwood Gate, Haywards Heath, West Sussex. *Clubs:* Carlton, Beefsteak, Buck's.                    *Died 29 Dec.* 1986.

**STOCKWELL, Gen. Sir Hugh Charles,** GCB 1959 (KCB 1954; CB 1946); KBE 1949 (CBE 1945); DSO 1940 and Bar 1957; late Infantry; Chairman: Inland Waterways Amenity Advisory Council, 1971–74; Kennet and Avon Canal Trust, 1966–75; Member: British Waterways Board, 1971–74; Water Space Amenity Commission, 1973–74; *b* 16 June 1903; *s* of late Lt-Col H. C. Stockwell, OBE, late Highland Light Infantry, Chief Constable of Colchester, and Gertrude Forrest; *m* 1931, Joan Rickman Garrard, *d* of Charles and Marion Garrard, Kingston Lisle, Berkshire; two *d. Educ:* Cothill House, Abingdon; Marlborough; Royal Military Coll., Sandhurst. Joined 2/Royal Welch Fusiliers, 1923; served West Africa, 1929–35; Instructor, Small Arms School, Netheravon, 1935–38; Brigade-Major, Royal Welch Brigade, 1938–40; served in Norway (DSO); 30 East African Bde, 1942–43; 29th Independent Bde, 1943–45; Burma (CB); Commander 82 (WA) Division, Jan. 1945–June 1946; Commander, Home Counties District, UK, July 1946–47; Commander Sixth Airborne Division, Palestine, 1947–48; Commandant, RMA, Sandhurst, 1948–50; Comdr, 3rd Inf. Div., and Comdr, East Anglian Dist, 1951–52; General Officer Commanding: Malaya, 1952–54; 1 Corps, BAOR, 1954–56; Ground Forces, Suez Operation, 1956; Military Secretary to the Secretary of State for War, 1957–59; Adjutant-General to the Forces, 1959–60; Deputy Supreme Allied Commander, Europe, 1960–64, retired. Gen., 1957. Col, The Royal Welch Fusiliers, 1952–65; Col, The Royal Malay Regt 1954–59; Col Commandant, Army Air Corps, 1957–63; Col Commandant, Royal Army Educational Corps October 1959–64. ADC General to the Queen, 1959–62. Governor, Felsted School, 1954–65. Grand Officier, Légion d'Honneur (France), 1958. *Recreations:* conservation, painting, travel. *Address:* Horton, near Devizes, Wilts. *T:* Cannings 617; Midland Bank plc, The Market Place, Devizes, Wilts. *Clubs:* MCC, Army and Navy.
*Died 27 Nov.* 1986.

**STOESSEL, Walter J(ohn), Jr;** Chairman, Parallel Studies Program with the Soviet Union of the United Nations Association of the US, since 1982; *b* 24 Jan. 1920; *s* of Walter John Stoessel and Katherine Stoessel (*née* Haston); *m* 1946, Mary Ann (*née* Ferrandou); three *d. Educ:* Lausanne Univ.; Stanford Univ. (BA); Russian Inst., Columbia Univ.; Center for Internat. Affairs, Harvard Univ. US Foreign Service, 1942–82; Polit. Officer, Caracas, 1942–46; Dept of State, 1946–47; Moscow, 1947–49; Bad-Nauheim, 1950–52; Officer i/c Soviet Affairs, Dept of State, 1952–56; White House, 1956; Paris, 1956–59; Dir, Exec. Secretariat, Dept of State, 1960–61; Polit. Adviser to SHAPE, Paris, 1961–63; Moscow, 1963–65; Dep. Asst Sec. for European Affairs, Dept of State, 1965–68; US Ambassador to Poland, 1968–72; Asst Sec. for European Affairs, Dept of State, 1972–74; US Ambassador to: USSR, 1974–76; Fed. Rep. of Germany, 1976–81; Under Sec. of State for Political Affairs, 1981–82; Dep. Sec. of State, 1982. Vis. Prof., Amer. Univ., Washington, 1982–84. Director: Lockheed Corp.; Hartford Group; Allen Group. Chairman: President's Commn on Chemical Warfare, 1985; US Delegn to Budapest Cultural Forum, 1985. Dir, German Marshall Fund, Atlantic Council. *Recreations:* tennis, ski-ing, swimming, painting. *Address:* 5155 Rockwood Parkway NW, Washington, DC 20016, USA.                    *Died 9 Dec.* 1986.

**STOKES, Prof. Eric Thomas,** MA, PhD; FBA 1980; Smuts Professor of the History of the British Commonwealth, Cambridge, since 1970; *b* 10 July 1924; *s* of Walter John Stokes; *m* 1949, Florence Mary Lee; four *d. Educ:* Holloway Sch.; Christ's Coll., Cambridge.

MA 1949; PhD 1953. War Service, 1943–46: Lieut, RA; Royal Indian Mountain Artillery. Lecturer in: History, Univ. of Malaya, Singapore, 1950–55; Colonial History and Administration, Univ. of Bristol, 1955–56; Prof. of History, Univ. Coll. of Rhodesia and Nyasaland, 1956–63; Lecturer in History (Colonial Studies), Univ. of Cambridge, and Fellow and Tutor, St Catharine's Coll., 1963–70; Reader in Commonwealth History, 1970; Chm. of History Faculty, 1977–79. Member: Inter-Univ. Council for Higher Educn Overseas, 1972–79; India Cttee, British Council, 1972–; Indian Hist. Records Commn, 1976–; Crown Representative, Governing Body, SOAS, 1980–; Trustee: Cambridge Livingstone Trust, 1980; Budiriro Trust, 1966–. Pres., Cambridge Branch of Historical Assoc., 1975–78. Hon. DLitt Mysore, 1977. *Publications:* The English Utilitarians and India, 1959; The Political Ideas of English Imperialism, an inaugural lecture, 1960; The Peasant and the Raj, 1978; (ed with Richard Brown) The Zambesian Past, 1966; contributed to: Historians of India, Pakistan and Ceylon (ed C. H. Philips), 1961; Elites in South Asia (ed E. R. Leach and S. N. Mukherjee), 1970; Rudyard Kipling (ed John Gross), 1972; Historical Perspectives: studies in English thought and society in honour of J. H. Plumb (ed N. McKendrick), 1974; Indian Society and the Beginnings of Modernization circa 1830–50 (ed C. H. Philips and M. D. Wainwright), 1976; Land Tenure and Peasant in South Asia (ed R. E. Frykenberg, 1977); articles in Historical Jl, Past and Present, TLS. *Address:* St Catharine's College, Cambridge. *T:* Cambridge 59445. *Club:* Royal Commonwealth Society.
*Died 5 Feb.* 1981.

**STONE, Baron** *cr* 1976 (Life Peer), of Hendon; **Joseph Ellis Stone,** Kt 1970; medical practitioner, retired; *b* 27 May 1903; 2nd *s* of late Henry Silverstone and Rebecca Silverstone (*née* Ellis); *m* 1932, Beryl, *y d* of late Alexander and Jane Bernstein; one *s* one *d. Educ:* Llanelli County Intermediate Sch.; Cardiff Univ.; Westminster Hosp., SW1. MB, BS London 1927; MRCS, LRCP 1925. Casualty Officer and Ho. Surg., Westminster Hosp., 1925–26; Sen. Ho. Surg., N Staffs Royal Infirmary, 1926–28; MO, St George in the East Hosp., 1928–32; gen. med. practice, 1932–. Served RAMC, 1940–45, Captain; graded med. specialist. Personal Physician to PM, 1964–70 and 1974–76. Mem. Med. Soc. of London; Mem. Hampstead Med. Soc. Yeoman of Worshipful Soc. of Apothecaries. *Recreation:* golf. *Address:* 615 Finchley Road, Hampstead, NW3. *T:* 01-435 7333.
*Died 17 July* 1986.

**STONE, Prof. Julius,** AO 1981; OBE 1973; Professor of Law, University of New South Wales, since 1973; Distinguished Professor of International Law and Jurisprudence, Hastings College of Law, California University, since 1973; Emeritus Professor, University of Sydney; Member of New Zealand and Victorian Bars; Solicitor, Supreme Court, England; *b* 7 July 1907; *s* of Israel and Ellen Stone, Leeds, Yorkshire; *m* 1934, Reca Lieberman, BSc, LDS; two *s* one *d. Educ:* Univs of Oxford, Leeds, Harvard. BA, BCL, DCL (Oxford); LLM (Leeds); SJD (Harvard). Asst Lectr, University Coll., Hull, 1928–30; Rockefeller Fellow in Social Sciences, 1931; Asst Prof. of Law, Harvard Univ., 1933–36; Prof. of Internat. Law and Organisation, Fletcher Sch. of Law and Diplomacy, USA, 1933–36; Lectr in Law, Univ. of Leeds, 1936–38; Prof. and Dean Faculty of Law, Auckland University Coll., NZ, 1938–42; Challis Prof. of Internat. Law and Jurisprudence, Univ. of Sydney, 1942–72. Acting Dean, Sydney Faculty of Law, 1954–55, 1958–59; Visiting Professor: New York Univ. and Fletcher Sch. of Law and Diplomacy, 1949; Columbia Univ., 1956; Harvard Univ., 1956–57; Hague Academy of Internat. Law, 1956; Charles Inglis Thomson Guest Prof., Univ. of Colorado, 1956; Indian Sch. of Internat. Affairs, 1960; Monash Univ., 1972 (and Wilfred Fullagar Lectr); Lectures: Roscoe Pound, Univ. of Nebraska, 1957; John Field Sims Meml, Univ. of New Mexico, 1959; Isaacs Marks Inaugural, Univ. of Arizona, 1980; first Pres., Internat. Law Assoc., Aust. Br., 1959; Council, Internat. Commn of Jurists, Aust. Section, 1959; Fellow, Woodrow Wilson Internat. Center for Scholars, 1973. Chm., NSW Research Group, Aust. Inst. of Internat. Affairs, 1942–45; Vice-Chm., Prime Minister's Cttee on National Morale, and with Directorate of Research, LHQ, War of 1939–45 (Lt-Col). Founding and Exec. Mem., Aust. SSRC; Chm. Aust. Unesco Cttee for Social Sciences; Aust. Deleg., 6th Unesco Gen. Conf., Paris, 1951; Aust. rep., Second Corning Conf. on The Individual in the Modern World, 1961; Official Observer of Internat. Commn of Jurists, Eichmann Trial, 1961; General Editor, Sydney Law Review, 1953–60; Fellow: Aust. Acad. of Social Sciences; Centre for Study of the Behavioral Sciences, 1964; World Acad. of Arts and Sciences, 1964; Mem., Royal Netherlands Acad. of Arts and Sciences, 1978; Mem. Titulaire, Inst. of Internat. Law, 1964–82; Associate, Internat. Acad. of Comparative Law; Hon. Life Member: Amer. Soc. of Internat. Law, 1962; Indian Soc. Internat. Law, 1964. Patron, Amnesty International, 1963. Mem., Advisory Cttee, Internat. League for Rights of Man, 1964; Regular Broadcaster on Internat. Affairs (Australian Broadcasting Commn), 1945–. Hon. LLD: Leeds, 1973; Sydney, 1981. Legatum Visserianum Prize, Leyden Univ., 1956; Joint Swiney Prize, RSA, 1964; Hon. QC 1982.

*Publications:* International Guarantees of Minority Rights, 1932; Regional Guarantees of Minority Rights, 1933; The Atlantic Charter—New Worlds for Old, 1943; Stand Up and Be Counted, 1944; The Province and Function of Law, Law as Logic, Justice and Social Control (Aust., Eng. and Amer. edns), 1946, 1947, 1950, 1961, 1968; (with the late S. P. Simpson) Law and Society (3 vols), 1949–50; Legal Controls of International Conflict, A Treatise on the Dynamics of Disputes- and War- Law, 1954 (Aust., Eng. and Amer. edns; revised impression, 1958, repr. 1973) (Amer. Soc. Internat. Law Award, 1956); Sociological Inquiries concerning International Law, 1956; Aggression and World Order, 1958 (Aust., Eng. and Amer. edns); Legal Education and Public Responsibility, 1959; Quest for Survival, 1961 (German, Portuguese, Japanese and Arabic trans); The International Court and World Crisis, 1962; Legal System and Lawyers' Reasonings, 1964; Human Law and Human Justice, 1965; Social Dimensions of Law and Justice, 1966, 1972 (German trans. in 3 vols, 1976); Law and the Social Sciences in the 2nd Half-Century, 1966; The Middle East Under Cease-Fire, 1967; No Peace—No War in The Middle East, 1969; Approaches to International Justice, 1970; (with R. K. Woetzel) Towards a Feasible International Criminal Court, 1970; Of Law and Nations, 1974; Conflict Through Consensus, 1977; Palestine and Israel: assault on the law of nations, 1981; contrib. Sketch of a Code for Science in Science and Ethics, ed D. Oldroyd, 1982; Visions of World Order, 1985 (Amer. Soc. Internat. Law Award); Precedent and Law: dynamics of common law growth, 1985; numerous articles in Anglo-American legal journals; *relevant publication:* Legal Change, essays in honour of Julius Stone (incl. bibliog.), ed A. R. Blackshield, 1983. *Recreations:* gardening, landscape gardening. *Address:* 24 Blake Street, Rose Bay, NSW 2029, Australia. *T:* 371 9714.                                              *Died 3 Sept.* 1985.

**STONE, Riversdale Garland,** CMG 1956; OBE 1946; HM Consul-General, Los Angeles, 1957–59; *b* 19 Jan. 1903; *m* 1927, Cassie Gaisford; no *c.* Information Officer, Rio de Janeiro, Brazil, 1946; transf. to Singapore, 1948; First Secretary (Economic), Staff of Commissioner-General for the UK in SE Asia, 1948; transf. to Batavia, 1949; Counsellor (Commercial), Mexico City, 1952; Counsellor, HM Diplomatic Service, retired. *Address:* c/o National Westminster Bank, Piccadilly Circus Branch, Glasshouse Street, W1.                                              *Died 26 March* 1985.

**STONEHOUSE, John Thomson;** author; *b* 28 July 1925; *m* 1st, 1948, Barbara Joan Smith (marr. diss. 1978); one *s* two *d*; 2nd, 1981, Mrs Sheila Buckley; one *s.* *Educ:* Elementary Sch. and Tauntons Sch., Southampton; Univ. of London (London Sch. of Econs and Political Science). Asst to Senior Probation Officer, Southampton, 1941–44. Served in RAF as pilot and education officer, 1944–47. Studied at LSE, 1947–51 (Chm., Labour Soc., 1950–51); BSc (Econ.) Hons, 1951. Man. for African Co-op. Socs in Uganda, 1952–54; Sec., Kampala Mutual Co-op Soc. Ltd (Uganda), 1953–54; Dir of London Co-operative Soc. Ltd, 1956–62 (Pres., 1962–64); Mem. until 1962 of Development Cttee of the Co-operative Union; Dir of Society Footwear Ltd until 1963. Contested Norwood, London CC Election, 1949; contested (Lab): Twickenham, General Election, 1950; Burton, General Election, 1951; MP (Lab Co-op): Wednesbury, Feb. 1957–74; Walsall N, 1974–76, (English Nat. Party, April-Aug. 1976); Parly Sec., Min. of Aviation, 1964–66; Parly Under-Sec. of State for the Colonies, 1966–67; Minister of Aviation, 1967; Minister of State, Technology, 1967–68; Postmaster-General, 1968–69; Minister of Posts and Telecommunications, 1969–70. Chm., Parly Cttee of ASTMS, 1974–75; Mem. Exec. Cttee, UK Br. IPU. UK Deleg. to Council of Europe and WEU, 1962–64; Leader, UK Govt Delegns, Independence Ceremonies in Botswana and Lesotho, 1966; attended Independence Ceremonies in Uganda, 1962, Kenya, 1963, Zambia, 1964, and Mauritius, 1968, as special guest of Independence Governments. Granted citizenship of Bangladesh, 1972. Councillor, Islington Borough Council, 1956–59. Member, RIIA, 1955–65. PC 1968, his name removed from the list of members, 17 Aug. 1976. *Publications:* (jtly) Gangrene, 1959; Prohibited Immigrant, 1960; Death of an Idealist, 1975; The Ultimate (as James Lund), 1976; My Trial, 1976; Ralph, 1982; The Baring Fault, 1986; Oil on the Rift, 1987; *posthumous publication:* Who Sold Australia?, 1989. *Recreations:* music, learning to ski, desmology. *Address:* c/o Jonathan Cape Ltd, 32 Bedford Square, WC1B 3EL. *Club:* Royal Automobile.           *Died 15 April* 1988.

**STONES, Prof. Edward Lionel Gregory,** MA, PhD; FBA 1979; Professor of Mediæval History, University of Glasgow, 1956–78, then Emeritus Professor; *b* Croydon, 4 March 1914; *s* of Edward Edison Stones, Elland, Yorks, and Eleanor Gregory; *m* 1947, Jeanne Marie Beatrice, *d* of A. J. Fradin and Florence B. Timbury; one *s* one *d. Educ:* Glasgow High Sch.; Glasgow Univ.; Balliol Coll., Oxford. 1st Cl. English Lang. and Lit. (Glasgow), 1936; 1st Class Modern History (Oxford), 1939; PhD (Glasgow), 1950; FRHistS, 1950; FSA, 1962. Asst Lectr in History, Glasgow Univ., 1939. War of 1939–45: joined Royal Signals, 1940; Major 1943; GSO2, GHQ, New Delhi (Signals Directorate), 1943–45. Lectr in History, Glasgow, 1945–56. Vis. Res. Fellow, Westfield Coll., London Univ.,

1972–73. Lay Mem., Provincial Synod, Episcopal Church of Scotland, 1963–66. Pres., Glasgow Archaeological Soc., 1969–72; Member: Ancient Monuments Board for Scotland, 1964–79 (Chm. 1968–73); Council, Royal Hist. Soc., 1968–72; Council, Soc. Antiquaries, London, 1972–74. Corresp. Fellow, Mediaeval Acad. of America, 1980. *Publications:* Anglo-Scottish Relations, 1174–1328, 1965; Edward I, 1968; (ed) Maitland's Letters to Neilson, 1976; (with G. G. Simpson) Edward I and the Throne of Scotland, 1978; and articles in various historical journals. *Recreations:* books, music. *Address:* 34 Alexandra Road, Parkstone, Poole, Dorset BH14 9EN. *T:* Poole 742803. *Club:* United Oxford & Cambridge University.                             *Died 14 Feb.* 1987.

**STONHOUSE-GOSTLING, Maj.-Gen. Philip Le Marchant Stonhouse,** CB 1955; CBE 1953; retired; *b* 28 August 1899; *s* of Colonel Charles Henry Stonhouse-Gostling and Alice Seton (*née* Fraser-Tytler); *m* 1946, Helen Rimington Myra (*née* Pereira), Ottawa, Ontario, Canada. *Educ:* Cheltenham College; RMA Woolwich. Entered RA, 1919; served India with RA, 1920–26; Mil. Coll. of Science, 1927–29; i/c Technical Intelligence, WO, 1930; Woolwich Arsenal: Asst Inspector Guns and Carriages, 1931–38; Supt Carriage Design, 1939; Technical Adviser to Canadian Govt and British Purchasing Commn for Armaments, 1939–40; Dep. Dir of Supply, British Supply Mission, Washington, 1941–44; Director of Supply (Armaments), 1944–46; Dep. Dir Technical Services, British Jt Staff Mission, 1942–46; Director, 1946–50; Dep. Chief Engineer, Armaments Design Establishment in UK, 1951; President, Ordnance Board, Feb. 1954–Feb. 1955; Retired from Army, March 1955. Exec. Engineer, Beemer Engineering Co., Philadelphia, 1955–64. Legion of Merit (Officer), USA 1944. *Recreations:* sailing, photography. *Address:* Apt 309, Island House West, 325 Beach Road, Tequesta, Florida 33469, USA; c/o Lloyds Bank, Cox's and King's Branch, 6 Pall Mall, SW1.
                                              *Died 30 April* 1990.

**STONIER, George Walter,** MA; author; critic; journalist; *b* Sydney, Australia, 1903; *m* 1951, Patricia, *d* of James Nelson Dover. *Educ:* Westminster School; Christ Church, Oxford. Assistant Literary Editor of the New Statesman and Nation, 1928–45. Wrote plays for BBC: The House Opposite, Ophelia, Chap in a Bowler Hat, etc. *Publications:* Gog Magog, 1933; The Shadow Across the Page, 1937; Shaving Through the Blitz, 1943; My Dear Bunny, 1946; The Memoirs of a Ghost, 1947; Round London with the Unicorn, 1951; Pictures on the Pavement, 1954; English Countryside in Colour, 1956; Off the Rails, 1967; Rhodesian Spring, 1968; (ed) International Film Annual, vols 2 and 3. Contributions to Observer, New Statesman and Nation, Punch, Sunday Telegraph, Sight and Sound. *Address:* Early Mist, PO Juliasdale, Zimbabwe.
                                              *Died 25 March* 1985.

**STOOKE, Sir George Beresford-,** KCMG 1948 (CMG 1943); Gentleman Usher of the Blue Rod in the Order of St Michael and St George, 1959–71; *b* 3 Jan. 1897; *m* 1931, Creenagh, *y d* of late Sir Henry Richards; one *s* one *d.* Royal Navy, 1914–19; Colonial Service, 1920–48; Governor and C-in-C, Sierra Leone, 1948–53; Second Crown Agent for Oversea Governments and Administrations, 1953–55. Member, Kenya Camps Inquiry, 1959. Overseas Comr, Boy Scouts Assoc., 1954–61. Vice-Chm., Internat. African Inst., 1954–74. President, Anglo-Sierra Leone Society, 1962–72. 2nd Class Order of Brilliant Star of Zanzibar, 1942. KStJ, 1951. *Address:* Little Rydon, Hillfarrance, Taunton, Somerset.
                                              *Died 7 April* 1983.

**STOPFORD, Edward Kennedy,** CB 1955; Assistant Under-Secretary of State, Ministry of Defence, 1964–71, retired; *b* 10 Oct. 1911; *yr s* of late Major Heneage Frank Stopford, Royal Field Artillery, and Margaret, *d* of late Edward Briggs Kennedy; *m* 1952, Patricia Iona Mary, *widow* of Duncan Stewart, CMG, and *d* of late Howard Carrick; one *s. Educ:* Winchester; New College, Oxford. 1st Class, Lit Hum, 1933. Entered War Office, 1936; Under-Secretary, 1954–64. *Address:* Orchard House, Beaumont, Carlisle. *T:* Burgh-by-Sands 257.                               *Died 6 Nov.* 1983.

**STOPFORD, Rear-Admiral Frederick Victor,** CBE 1952; retired; *b* 6 July 1900; *yr s* of late Rear-Admiral Hon. W. G. Stopford; *m* 1924, Mary Guise, *d* of late Captain F. C. U. Vernon-Wentworth; three *s* one *d. Educ:* Osborne; Dartmouth. Served European War, 1916–18; Commander, 1933; War of 1939–45; Captain, 1943; Rear-Admiral, 1950. ADC, 1948–50. *Address:* Chinors Lodge, The Glade, Crapstone, Yelverton, Devon PL20 7PR.
                                              *Died 19 Jan.* 1982.

**STORK, Herbert Cecil,** CIE 1945; *b* 28 June 1890; *s* of Herbert William and Florence Stork; *m* 1919, Marjorie (*née* Cosens); two *d. Educ:* Merchant Taylors' School; Queen's College, Oxford (BA). Appointed to ICS, Dec. 1913; served Bengal and Assam, various posts, concluding with Legal Remembrancer and Secretary to Government of Assam; retired from ICS, 1947. Served European War, 1914–18; GSO III, 9th (Secunderabad) Division, and Staff

Captain, Dunsterforce, MEF. *Address:* 49 Wood Green, Witney, Oxon. *T:* Witney 72880. *Club:* Oxford Union Society.
*Died 22 March* 1983.

**STORK, Joseph Whiteley,** CB 1959; CBE 1949; retired as Director of Studies, Britannia Royal Naval College, Dartmouth (1955–59) (Headmaster, 1942–55); *b* Huddersfield, 9 Aug. 1902; *s* of John Arthur Stork, Huddersfield; *m* 1927, Kathleen, *d* of Alderman J. H. Waddington, JP, Halifax; one *s* three *d*. *Educ:* Uppingham; Downing Coll., Cambridge (scholar). 1st Class Nat. Sci. Tripos Pt 1, 2nd Class Nat. Sci. Tripos Pt II (Zoology); Senior Biology Master, Cambridge and County School, 1926; Head of Biological Dept, Charterhouse School, 1926–36; Headmaster, Portsmouth Grammar School, 1936–42. *Publications:* Joint Author of: Fundamentals of Biology, 1932, Junior Biology, 1933, Plant and Animal Ecology, 1933. *Address:* 15 Cautley Drive, Killinghall, Harrogate HG3 2DJ.
*Died 28 March* 1990.

**STORR, Norman,** OBE 1947; with Charity Commission, 1967–73; *b* 9 Dec. 1907; *s* of Herbert Storr and Beatrice Emily Storr, Barnsley; *m* 1937, Kathleen Mary Ward; two *s* one *d*. *Educ:* Holgate's Grammar School, Barnsley; Keble College, Oxford. Open schol. in Mod. History, Keble Coll., Oxford, 1926; BA Hons Mod. History, 1929. Entered Indian Civil Service, 1930; Session Judge, 1935; Registrar, Allahabad High Court, 1939; Registrar, Federal Court of India, 1943–47. Principal, Home Office, 1947; Principal, 1952, Establishment Officer, 1958, Comr and Sec., 1962, Prison Commission; Asst Sec., Estab. Div. Home Office, 1966–67, retired. *Recreation:* painting. *Address:* Moorlands, Amberley, near Stroud, Glos. *Club:* Royal Over-Seas League.        *Died 16 June* 1984.

**STORRAR, Sir John,** Kt 1953; CBE 1949; MC 1917; Town Clerk of Edinburgh, 1941–56; *b* 8 Dec. 1891; *s* of late Rev. Wm Storrar, Hardgate, Dalbeattie, Kirkcudbrightshire; *m* Agnes Drennan (*d* 1978), *d* of late James Cameron, Hollos, Lenzie; one *d*. *Educ:* Castle Douglas Academy; Edinburgh Univ. Solicitor, 1914. Served European War, Royal Scots, 1914–19 (despatches, MC). Local Government service, 1923; Depute Town Clerk, Edinburgh, 1934. Member of various government committees. Hon. LLD Edinburgh, 1957. *Address:* 3 Merchiston Park, Edinburgh.
*Died 30 May* 1984.

**STORRAR, Air Vice-Marshal Ronald Charles,** CB 1957; OBE 1945; psc; *b* 4 Sept. 1904; *m* 1932, Vera Winifred Butler; one *s*. Commissioned RAF, 1929; Served in India, 1932–37; Student RAF Staff Coll., 1938; USA, 1942–44; CO No 21 MU, Fauld, 1945–46; Directing Staff, RAF Staff Coll., 1946–49; CO No 16 MU, Stafford, 1952–54; ACC No 42 Group, 1955; SASO No 40 Group, 1956–60, Maintenance Command, 1960–63. *Address:* Apartado 45, Fuengirola, near Malaga, Spain. *T:* 476238. *Club:* Royal Air Force.                                      *Died 1 Dec.* 1985.

**STOTESBURY, Herbert Wentworth,** Assistant Under-Secretary of State, Home Office, 1966–75; Probation and Aftercare Department, 1969–75; *b* 22 Jan. 1916; *s* of Charles and Ada Stotesbury; *m* 1944, Berenice Mary Simpson; one *s* two *d*. *Educ:* Christ's Hospital; Emmanuel College, Cambridge. Home Office, 1939; Army, 1940–45. Lecturer, Military Coll. of Science, 1941–45. Home Office, 1945–75; Asst Secretary, 1953. Chm., Working Party on Marriage Guidance, 1976–78 (consultative document: Marriage Matters). *Recreations:* music, gardening, travel.                        *Died 28 Jan.* 1988.

**STOURTON, Sir Ivo (Herbert Evelyn Joseph),** Kt 1961; CMG 1951; OBE 1939; KPM 1949; Inspector General of Colonial Police 1957–66; *b* 18 July 1901; *s* of late Major H. M. Stourton, OBE, and late Hon. Mrs H. Stourton; *m* 1st, 1926, Lilian (*d* 1942), *d* of late G. Dickson; two *s* one *d*; 2nd, 1945, Virginia, *d* of late Sir Horace Seymour, GCMG, CVO, and of Violet (*née* Erskine); one *d*. *Educ:* Stonyhurst College, Lancs. Joined Colonial Police Service, 1921; Asst Supt of Police; served Mauritius, 1921–33; Commissioner of Police: Bermuda, 1933–39; Zanzibar, 1939–40; Aden, 1940–45; Uganda, 1945–50; Nigeria, 1950; Inspector-Gen. of Police, Nigeria, 1951, retd 1953. Re-appointed as Deputy Inspector General of Colonial Police, 1953–57. Kt of Malta. *Address:* The Old Bakery, Kimpton, Andover, Hants. *T:* Weyhill 2446.
*Died 7 Oct.* 1985.

**STOUT, Alan Ker,** MA, FAHA; FASSA; Professor of Philosophy, University of Sydney, 1939–65, later Emeritus Professor; *b* Oxford, 9 May 1900; *s* of late Professor G. F. Stout and Ella Ker; *m* 1927, Evelyn Roberts, BA; one *s* one *d*. *Educ:* Fettes College, Edinburgh; Oriel College, Oxford. First Class Hon. Mods Oxford; Second Class Lit Hum Oxford; Bishop Fraser Research Scholar, Oriel Coll., 1922; Lecturer in Philosophy, Univ. College of North Wales, Bangor, 1924–34, Univ. of Edinburgh, 1934–39. Visiting Prof., Univ. of Wisconsin, 1966. Pres., Council for Civil Liberties, 1964–67; Member: Aust. National Film Board, 1945–47; Aust. Nat. Adv. Cttee for UNESCO, 1949–74; Bd of Dirs, Tasmanian Theatre Co., 1972–77; Governor, Aust. Film Inst., 1960–75. Mem. Council, Aust. Consumers' Assoc., 1963–79. Fellow, Univ. Senate, Univ. of

Sydney, 1954–69. Drama Critic, Aust. Quarterly, 1961–65. Editor, Australasian Jl of Philosophy, 1950–67. *Publications:* Articles and Reviews (especially on the Philosophy of Descartes and on Moral Theory) in Mind, Proceedings of Aristotelian Soc., Philosophy, Australasian Journal of Philosophy, Australian Quarterly, etc., from 1926; Editor God and Nature (posthumously published Gifford lectures of G. F. Stout), 1952. *Recreation:* the theatre. *Address:* 12 Lambert Avenue, Sandy Bay, Hobart, Tasmania 7005, Australia.
*Died 20 July* 1983.

**STOW, Sir Edmond Cecil P.;** *see* Philipson-Stow.

**STRACHAN, Lt-Col Henry,** VC 1917; MC 1917; Fort Garry Horse; retired; Hon. ADC to Governor General of Canada from 1935; Field Representative, The Canadian Bank of Commerce, from 1928; *b* Bo'ness, Scotland, 7 Nov. 1884; *m*; one *d*. *Educ:* Royal High School, Edinburgh; Edinburgh University. Ranches in Alberta, Canada; joined FGH, 1914; Commission July 1916; served European War, 1914–18 (MC, wounded, VC); War of 1939–45, Lt-Col Cmdg 1st Bn Edmonton Fusiliers. *Recreations:* badminton, golf. *Address:* 3008 West 31st Avenue, Vancouver 8, British Columbia, Canada. *Clubs:* Alberta Golf, Country (Calgary).
*Died 1 May* 1982.

**STRACHAN, Robert Martin;** Agent-General for British Columbia in the United Kingdom and Europe, 1975–77; *b* 1 Dec. 1913; *s* of Alexander Strachan and Sarah Martin; *m* 1937, Anne Elsie Paget; two *s* one *d*. *Educ:* schools in Glasgow, Scotland. Mem., British Columbia Legislature, 1952–75; Leader of Opposition, 1956–69; Minister: of Highways, 1972–73; of Transport and Communications, 1973–75; resigned seat Oct. 1975, to accept appointment as Agent-General. *Recreations:* swimming, fishing, painting. *Address:* RR2, Cedar Road, Nanaimo, Vancouver Island, British Columbia, Canada. *Club:* Royal Over-Seas League.
*Died 21 July* 1981.

**STRADBROKE, 4th Earl of,** *cr* 1821; **John Anthony Alexander Rous;** Bt 1660; Baron Rous, 1796; Viscount Dunwich, 1821; Lord-Lieutenant and Custos Rotulorum for the County of Suffolk, 1948–78; Commander Royal Navy, retired list; *b* 1 April 1903 (to whom Queen Alexandra stood sponsor); *e s* of 3rd Earl of Stradbroke, KCMG, CB, CVO, CBE, and Helena Violet Alice, DBE, *cr* 1927, Lady of Grace of St John (*d* 1949), *d* of Gen. Keith Fraser; *S* father, 1947; *m* 1929, Barbara (*d* 1977), *yr d* of late Lord Arthur Grosvenor; two *d*. *Educ:* RN Colleges, Osborne and Dartmouth; Christ Church (Hon. MA), Oxford. Member E Suffolk CC 1931–45, Alderman 1953–64. Private Sec. to Governor of Victoria and Acting Governor General, Australia, 1946–47. Estate Owner, Agriculturist and Forester. National Vice-Pres., Royal British Legion; Vice-Pres., Assoc. of (Land) Drainage Authorities. Dir, Daejan Holdings Ltd. Served Royal Navy, 1917–28, and on Naval Staff, Admiralty 1939–46. Lately Hon. Colonel 660 HAA Regiment (TA); Lay Canon of St Edmundsbury Cathedral, 1978. FRSA. Scout Movement's Silver Wolf Award, 1978. KStJ. *Heir: b* Hon. (William) Keith Rous [*b* 10 Mar. 1907; *m* 1st, 1935, Pamela Catherine Mabell (marr. diss. 1941), *d* of late Capt. Hon. Edward James Kay-Shuttleworth; two *s*; 2nd, 1943, April Mary, *d* of late Brig.-General Hon. Arthur Melland Asquith, DSO; one *s* three *d*]. *Address:* Henham, Wangford, Beccles, Suffolk. *T:* Wangford 212 and 214. *Clubs:* Travellers'; Jockey Club Rooms; Royal Norfolk and Suffolk Yacht.
*Died 14 July* 1983.

**STRADBROKE, 5th Earl of,** *cr* 1821; **William Keith Rous;** Bt 1660; Baron Rous 1796; Viscount Dunwich 1821; *b* 10 March 1907; *s* of 3rd Earl of Stradbroke, KCMG, CB, CVO, CBE and Helena Violet Alice, DBE (*d* 1949), *d* of Gen. Keith Fraser; *S* brother, 1983; *m* 1st, 1935, Pamela Catherine Mabell (marr. diss. 1941), *d* of late Capt. Hon. Edward James Kay-Shuttleworth; two *s*; 2nd, 1943, April Mary, *d* of late Brig.-Gen. Hon. Arthur Melland Asquith, DSO; one *s* three *d*. *Educ:* Harrow; Geelong Grammar School. Served War of 1939–45; Lt (E) RN; Lt RNVR. *Heir: s* Viscount Dunwich.                                      *Died 18 July* 1983.
*This entry did not appear in Who's Who.*

**STRAFFORD, 7th Earl of,** *cr* 1847; **Robert Cecil Byng;** Baron Strafford (UK), 1835; Viscount Enfield, 1847; *b* 29 July 1904; *o surv. s* of late Hon. Ivo Francis Byng (4th *s* of 5th Earl) and late Agnes Constance, *d* of S. Smith Travers, Hobart, Tasmania; *S* uncle 1951; *m* 1st, 1934, Maria Magdalena Elizabeth (marr. diss. 1947), *d* of late Henry Cloete, CMG, Alphen, S Africa; two *s*; 2nd, 1948, Clara Evelyn, *d* of late Sir Ness Nowrosjee Wadia, KBE, CIE. *Heir: s* Viscount Enfield. *Address:* c/o C. Hoare & Co., 37 Fleet Street, EC4.
*Died 4 March* 1984.

**STRANG, Prof. Barbara Mary Hope, (Prof. Lady Strang);** Professor of English Language and General Linguistics, University of Newcastle upon Tyne, since 1964; *b* 20 April 1925; *d* of Frederick A. and Amy M. Carr; *m* 1955, Hon. Colin Strang, later 2nd Baron Strang; one *d*. *Educ:* Coloma Convent of the Ladies of Mary, Croydon; Univ. of London (King's Coll.). BA 1945, MA 1947. Asst

Lectr, Westfield Coll., Univ. of London, 1947–50; Lectr, Armstrong Coll., Newcastle, 1950–63. Member: Univ. Grants Cttee, 1975–79; Hong Kong Univ. and Polytechnic Grants Cttee, 1981–. *Publications:* Modern English Structure, 1962, 2nd edn 1968; A History of English, 1970, paperback, 1974; contribs to Trans Philological Soc.; Durham Univ. Jl; English Studies Today; Lingua; Notes and Queries; various Proc. and Festschriften, etc. *Recreation:* horsemanship. *Address:* School of English, The University, Newcastle upon Tyne NE1 7RU. *T:* Newcastle upon Tyne 328511.
*Died 12 April 1982.*

**STRANGE, 15th Baron** *cr* 1628 (title abeyant, 1957–65); **John Drummond;** *b* 6 May 1900; *s* of late Capt. Malcolm Drummond of Megginch, Grenadier Guards, and late Geraldine Margaret, *d* of 1st Baron Amherst of Hackney; *m* Violet Margaret (*d* 1975), *d* of Sir R. B. Jardine, 2nd Bt of Castlemilk; three *d*. *Educ:* Eton. *Publications:* The Bride Wore Black, 1942; Pocket Show Book, 1943; Charter for the Soil, 1944; Playing to the Gods, 1944; Inheritance of Dreams, 1945; A Candle in England, 1946; Behind Dark Shutters, 1948; Gold over the Hill, 1950; The Naughty Mrs Thornton, 1952; Proof Positive, 1956. *Co-heiresses:* Hon. (Jean) Cherry Drummond of Megginch [*b* 17 Dec. 1928; *m* 1952, Captain Humphrey ap Evans, MC, who assumed name of Drummond of Megginch by decree of Lyon Court, 1966, *s* of Major James John Pugh Evans, MBE, MC; three *s* three *d*]; Hon. Heather Mary Currey [*b* 9 Nov. 1931; *m* 1954, Lt-Comdr Andrew Christian Currey, RN, *s* of late Rear-Adm. Harry Philip Currey, CB, OBE; two *s* one *d*]; Hon. Margaret April Irene Agnew-Somerville [*b* 3 April 1939; *m* 1963, Quentin Charles Agnew-Somerville, *s* and *heir* of Sir Peter Agnew, Bt, *qv*; one *s* two *d*]. *Address:* Mwyllin-E-Quinney, Santon, Isle of Man.
*Died 13 April 1982.*

**STRANGER-JONES, Leonard Ivan;** Registrar of the Supreme Court Family Division, 1967–82, retired; *b* 8 May 1913; *s* of Walter Stranger-Jones; *m* 1st, 1935, Elizabeth Evelyn Williams (marr. diss., 1942); 2nd, 1943, Iris Christine Truscott; one *s* one *d*. *Educ:* Lancing; Oriel Coll., Oxford (MA). Called to the Bar, 1938. Served War of 1939–45: RAF, Sept. 1939; Pilot, 1942. Returned to the Bar, Sept. 1945; Bencher, Middle Temple, Nov. 1967. *Publication:* Eversley on Domestic Relations, 1951. *Recreations:* photography, history. *Address:* 18 Chelmsford Square, Brondesbury Park, NW10 3AR. *T:* 01-459 3757.
*Died 10 Nov. 1983.*

**STRANKS, Ven. Charles James;** Archdeacon of Auckland, 1958–73, later Emeritus; 10th Canon of Durham, 1958–73; *b* 10 May 1901; *s* of Joseph and Elizabeth Stranks; *m* 1930, Elsie Lilian, *d* of John and Anne Buckley; two *s*. *Educ:* St Chad's Coll., Durham; St Boniface Coll., Warminster. BA, 1925; MA and Diploma in Theology, 1928; MLitt, 1937. Curate of All Saints, Leeds, 1926–28; Missionary, Dio. Kobe, Japan, 1928–40; Examining Chaplain to Bishop in Kobe, 1938–40; SPG Organizing Sec., 1940–41; Vicar of St Barnabas, Morecambe, 1941–47; Warden of Whalley Abbey, Canon of Blackburn, and Dir of Relig. Educ., 1947–54; Proctor in Convocation for Archdeaconry of Blackburn, 1949–54; Sixth Canon of Durham Cathedral, 1954. Chm., Lord Crewe's Trustees, 1963–74. *Publications:* The Apostle of the Indies, 1933; Japan in the World Crisis, 1941; The Approach to Belief, 1947; Our Task Today, 1950; The Life and Writings of Jeremy Taylor, 1952; Dean Hook, 1954; Anglican Devotion, 1961; Country Boy: The Autobiography of Richard Hillyer, 1966; (ed) The Path of Glory: The Autobiography of John Shipp, 1969; This Sumptuous Church: the story of Durham Cathedral, 1973; contrib. Encyclopædia Britannica. *Recreations:* walking, gardening. *Address:* 1 The Corner House, Shincliffe Village, Durham. *T:* Durham 2719.
*Died 30 Aug. 1981.*

**STRANKS, Prof. Donald Richard,** AO 1984; PhD; Vice-Chancellor, University of Adelaide, since 1977; *b* 18 July 1929; *s* of R. G. Stranks; *m* 1st, 1954; two *s* one *d*; 2nd, 1978, Caroline Anne-Marie; one step *s*. *Educ:* Melbourne High Sch.; Univ. of Melb. (MSc 1952, PhD 1954). ICIANZ Res. Fellow, Univ. of Melb., 1952–54. Lectr in Radio Chemistry, Univ. of Leeds, 1954–60; Sen. Lectr, then Reader in Inorganic Chem., Univ. of Melb., 1960–64; Foundn Chair of Inorg. Chem., Univ. of Adelaide, 1964–73; Prof. of Inorg. Chem., Univ. of Melb., 1973–77. Vis. Professor: Univ. of Bristol, 1976; Washington Univ., 1967; Goethe Univ., 1971; Univ. of Calgary, 1972. Consultant and Examr, Univ. of Papua and New Guinea, 1969–73; Examr, Universiti Sains Malaysia, 1976–78. Member: Aust. Adv. Cttee of Nuffield Foundn, 1970–81; Council and Exec. Cttee, ACU, 1985–; Chairman: SA Council for Technological Change, 1980–; Aust. Vice-Chancellors' Cttee, 1986– (Dep. Chm., 1984–85); Aust.-American Educnl Foundn, 1985–. Director: Luminis Pty Ltd, 1984–; Integrated Silicon Design Inc., 1984–86; South Aust. Management Investment Co., 1984–. Trustee, SA Churchill Trust, 1979–. Royal Aust. Chemical Institute: Rennie Meml Medal, 1956; COMO Award and Medal for Inorg. Chem. Res., 1977. *Publications:* Modern Coordination Chemistry, 1960; Chemistry: a structural view, 1967, 2nd edn 1972; Chemical Science, 1976; 95 scientific pubns in internat. jls; articles on chemical educn.

*Recreations:* music, gardening, tennis. *Address:* 2 Bartley Avenue, Netherby, SA 5062, Australia. *T:* 791266; University of Adelaide, North Terrace, Adelaide, SA 5001. *T:* 228–5201.
*Died 9 Aug. 1986.*

**STRASSER, Sir Paul,** Kt 1973; Director: Walden Properties Ltd; Nicron Resources NL; Petrocarb Exploration NL; *b* 22 Sept. 1911; *s* of Eugene Strasser and Elizabeth Klein de Ney; *m* 1935, Veronica Gero; one step *s*. *Educ:* Univ. of Budapest. Dr of Law, 1933; practised in Hungary for 10 yrs; emigrated to Australia, 1948. Career in fields of construction, mining and oil exploration, hotel and motel chains, meat processing and exporting, merchant banking. Associated with and promoter of several charitable foundns, etc, incl. Jewish Residential Coll. at Univ. of NSW, Children's Surgical Research Fund and Australian Youth Ballet. *Recreations:* playing bridge, swimming, reading. *Address:* Suite 106, Edgecliff Centre, Edgecliff, NSW 2027, Australia. *Clubs:* American, Sydney Turf (Sydney).

**STRATHCLYDE, 1st Baron,** *cr* 1955, of Barskimming; **Thomas Dunlop Galbraith,** PC 1953; Commander, Royal Navy, retired; *b* 20 March 1891; 2nd *s* of William Brodie Galbraith, JP, CA, Glasgow, and Annie Dunlop; *m* 1915, Ida (*d* 1985), *e d* of Thomas Galloway, Auchendrane, Ayrshire; three *s* two *d* (and one *s* killed in action, 1940, and one decd). *Educ:* Glasgow Academy; Eastmans, Southsea; RN Colleges, Osborne and Dartmouth. Entered Royal Navy, 1903; served throughout European War, 1914–18, in HMS Audacious and HMS Queen Elizabeth; on staff of C-in-C, Coast of Scotland, 1919–20; RN Staff College, Greenwich, 1920–22; retired 1922; War of 1939–45, on Staff of C-in-C Coast of Scotland, 1939–40; Deputy British Admiralty Supply Representative in USA, 1940–42. MP (Nat. C) for Pollok Div. of Glasgow, 1940–April 1955; Jt Parly Under-Sec. of State for Scotland, 1945 and 1951–55; Minister of State, Scottish Office, 1955–58, resigned; Chm., North of Scotland Hydro-Electric Board, 1959–67; Mem., South of Scotland Electricity Board, 1965–67. Chartered Accountant, 1925; Partner, Walter and W. B. Galbraith, CA, Glasgow, 1925–70; Member of Corporation of Glasgow, 1933–40; Magistrate, 1938–40. President, Electrical Research Association, 1965–66. Hon. FRCPE; Hon. FRCPSGlas; a Governor of Wellington College, 1948–61; Hon. Governor, Glasgow Academy. Freedom of Dingwall, 1965; Freedom of Aberdeen, 1966. *Heir: g s* Thomas Galloway Dunlop du Roy de Blicquy Galbraith, *b* 22 Feb. 1960. *Address:* Barskimming, Mauchline, Ayrshire. *T:* Mauchline 50202. *Clubs:* Carlton, Naval and Military; Western (Glasgow).
*Died 12 July 1985.*

**STRATHEDEN, 4th Baron,** *cr* 1836, **AND CAMPBELL, 4th Baron,** *cr* 1841; **Alastair Campbell,** CBE 1964; *b* 21 Nov. 1899; *s* of late Hon. John Beresford Campbell and Hon. Alice Susan Hamilton (*d* 1949), *d* of 1st Baron Hamilton of Dalzell; *S* grandfather, 1918; *m* 1st, 1923, Jean, CBE 1954 (*d* 1956), *o d* of late Col W. Anstruther-Gray; three *d*; 2nd, 1964, Mrs Noël Vincent. *Educ:* Eton; Sandhurst. Joined Coldstream Guards, 1919; Regimental Adjutant, 1931–34; Staff Officer Local Forces, Kenya and Uganda, 1936–39; Lt-Col, 1941; served War of 1939–45 (wounded, despatches); Regtl Lt-Col, 1945–46; Brig., 1946; Comd 32nd Guards Bde, 1946, 4th Inf. Bde, 1947–49; Deputy Director Personal Services, War Office, 1949; retired 1950. Captain, Royal Company of Archers, Queen's Body Guard for Scotland. Chm. Roxburgh, Berwick and Selkirk-shires T&AFA, 1958–63; Chm. Edinburgh and E of Scotland Coll. of Agriculture, 1956–70; Chm. Hill Farming Research Organisation, 1958–69; Convener Roxburgh County Council, 1960–68; Pres., Assoc. of County Councils in Scotland, 1966–68. Chm., Historic Buildings Council for Scotland, 1969–76. DL Roxburgh, 1946, Vice-Lieutenant, 1962–75. Hon. LLD Edinburgh Univ. *Heir: b* Major Hon. Gavin Campbell, late KRRC [*b* 28 Aug. 1901; *m* 1933, Evelyn, *d* of late Col H. A. Smith, CIE; one *s*]. *Address:* Hunthill, Jedburgh, Scotland. *T:* Jedburgh 2413. *Clubs:* Cavalry and Guards; New (Edinburgh).
*Died 12 Dec. 1981.*

**STRATHEDEN, 5th Baron** *cr* 1836, **AND CAMPBELL, 5th Baron** *cr* 1841; **Gavin Campbell;** Major (retired) KRRC and Lt-Col 19th (Kenya) Bn, KAR; *b* 28 Aug. 1901; *s* of Hon. John Beresford Campbell, DSO (killed in action, 1915) (*s* of 3rd Baron) and Hon. Alice Susan Hamilton (*d* 1949), *d* of 1st Baron Hamilton of Dalzell; *S* brother, 1981; *m* 1933, Evelyn Mary Austen, *d* of late Col Herbert Austen Smith, CIE; one *s*. *Educ:* Eton; RMC Sandhurst. Served War of 1939–45, Abyssinia and Madagascar. *Heir: s* Hon. Donald Campbell [*b* 4 April 1934; *m* 1957, Hilary Ann Holland, *d* of Lt-Col W. D. Turner; one *s* three *d*]. *Address:* 7 Denway Grove, South Norwood, Launceston, Tasmania 7250, Australia.
*Died 29 Oct. 1987.*

**STRATHMORE AND KINGHORNE, 17th Earl of,** *cr* 1677; Earl (UK), *cr* 1937; **Fergus Michael Claude Bowes Lyon;** Lord Glamis, 1445; Earl of Kinghorne, Lord Lyon and Glamis, 1606; Viscount Lyon, Lord Glamis, Tannadyce, Sidlaw, and Strathdichtie, 1677; Baron Bowes (UK), 1887; Vice Lord-Lieutenant, County of Angus, since 1981; *b* 31 Dec. 1928; *e s* of Hon. Michael Claude Hamilton

Bowes Lyon (5th *s* of 14th Earl) (*d* 1953), and Elizabeth Margaret (*d* 1959), *d* of late John Cator; *S* cousin, 1972; *m* 1956, Mary Pamela, *d* of Brig. Norman Duncan McCorquodale, MC; one *s* two *d*. *Educ:* Eton; RMA, Sandhurst. Commissioned Scots Guards, 1949; Captain 1953; transferred to RARO, 1961. Member of Edinburgh Stock Exchange, 1963. Dir, T. Cowie, 1978–. Member of Royal Company of Archers, Queen's Body Guard for Scotland; Hon. Col, Tayforth Univs OTC, 1974–81. DL Angus, 1973. *Recreations:* shooting, fishing. *Heir: s* Lord Glamis. *Address:* Glamis Castle, Forfar, Angus. *T:* Glamis 244. *Clubs:* White's, Pratt's; New (Edinburgh). *Died* 18 *Aug.* 1987.

**STRATHON, Eric Colwill**, FRICS; Member of the Lands Tribunal, 1969–80, retired; *b* 20 Feb. 1908; *s* of Daniel Millward Strathon and Ann Colwill; *m* 1932, Margaret Mary Cocks (*d* 1973); one *s* one *d*. *Educ:* Taunton Sch. Chartered Surveyor, election 1929. Served War, 1944–46: Major RA; 14th Army HQ. Articled to chartered surveyors, 1925–28; partner, private practice in London, 1934–69. Crown Estate Comr, 1965–69. Pres., RICS, 1961. *Publication:* Compensation (Defence), 1943. *Recreation:* fishing. *Address:* 106 Rivermead Court, Hurlingham, SW6 3SB. *T:* 01–736 3192. *Clubs:* Naval and Military, Hurlingham. *Died* 26 *Dec.* 1988.

**STRATTON, Sir Richard (James)**, KCMG 1982 (CMG 1974); HM Diplomatic Service, retired; High Commissioner to New Zealand, 1980–84, and concurrently to Western Samoa (non-resident); Governor of Pitcairn Island, 1980–84; *b* 16 July 1924; *s* of William Henry and Cicely Muriel Stratton. *Educ:* The King's Sch., Rochester; Merton Coll., Oxford. Served in Coldstream Guards, 1943–46. Joined Foreign Service, Oct. 1947; British Embassy, Rio de Janeiro, 1948–50; FO, 1951–53; British Embassy, Tokyo, March-Aug. 1953; British Legation, Seoul, 1953–55; Private Sec. to Parly Under-Sec. of State, FO, Nov. 1955–Feb. 1958; NATO Defence Coll., Paris, Feb.-Aug. 1958; British Embassy, Bonn, Sept. 1958–July 1960; British Embassy, Abidjan, Ivory Coast, Aug. 1960–Feb. 1962; Private Sec. to Lord Carrington, as Minister without Portfolio, FO, 1963–64; to Minister of State for Foreign Affairs, 1964–66; Counsellor, British High Commn, Rawalpindi, 1966–69; IDC, 1970; FCO, 1971–72; Political Adviser to Govt of Hong Kong, 1972–74; HM Ambassador: to Republic of Zaire and People's Republic of the Congo, 1974–77; to Republic of Burundi, 1975–77; to Rwandan Republic, 1977; Assistant Under-Sec. of State, FCO, 1977–80. *Recreations:* music, bridge. *Address:* 16 Clareville Court, Clareville Grove, SW7 5AT. *T:* 01–373 2764. *Clubs:* Travellers', Royal Commonwealth Society.
*Died* 26 *July* 1988.

**STRATTON, Lt-Gen. Sir William (Henry)**, KCB 1957 (CB 1948); CVO 1944; CBE 1943; DSO 1945; *b* 1903; *o s* of late Lt-Col H. W. Stratton, OBE; *m* 1930, Noreen Mabel Brabazon, *d* of late Dr and Mrs F. H. B. Noble, Sittingbourne, Kent; no *c*. *Educ:* Dulwich Coll.; RMA, Woolwich. 2nd Lieut RE 1924; psc; Lt-Col, 1940; Brig., 1941; Comdr 169 Inf. Bde, 1944–45; Col 1945; idc 1946; Maj.-Gen. 1947; Chief of Staff, BAOR, 1947–49; Comdt Joint Services Staff Coll., 1949–52; Commander British Army Staff, and Military Member British Joint Services Mission, Washington, 1952–53; Comdr 42 (Lancs) Inf. Div. (TA), 1953–55; Lt-Gen. 1955; Commander, British Forces, Hong Kong, 1955–57; Vice-Chief of the Imperial General Staff, 1957–60, retired. Col Comdt RE, 1960–68; Inspector-General of Civil Defence, Home Office, 1960–62. Chairman: Edwin Danks (Oldbury) Ltd, 1961–71; Penman & Co. Ltd, 1961–71; Babcock-Moxey Ltd, 1965–71.
*Died* 25 *Nov.* 1989.

**STRAUSS, Lady; Patricia Frances Strauss**; Governor: St Martin's School of Art, since 1952; Whitechapel Art Gallery since 1957; John Cass School of Art, since 1982; *b* 21 Oct. 1909; *m* 1932, George Russell Strauss (later Baron Strauss, PC); two *s* one *d*. Member of London County Council, 1946–58; Chairman: Parks Cttee (LCC), 1947–49; Supplies Cttee (LCC), 1949–52. Contested (Lab) South Kensington, Parliamentary General Election, 1945. Governor: Royal Ballet Sch., 1951–72; The Old Vic, 1951–85; Sadler's Wells Theatre, 1951–85; Royal Ballet, 1957–85; Ballet Rambert, 1958–85; London Opera Centre, 1965–79; Sadler's Wells Opera (Coliseum), 1968–78; Goldsmith Sch. of Art, 1969–85. *Publications:* Bevin and Co., 1941; Cripps, Advocate and Rebel, 1942. *Recreations:* painting, chess, foreign travel. *Address:* 1 Palace Green, W8. *T:* 01–937 1630; Naylands, Slaugham, Sussex. *T:* Handcross 400270.
*Died* 16 *July* 1987.

**STRAUSS, Franz Josef**; Grand Cross, Order of Merit, Federal Republic of Germany; Prime Minister of Bavaria, since 1978; President, Christian Social Union (CSU), since 1961; *b* Munich, 6 Sept. 1915; *s* of Franz Josef Strauss and Walburga (*née* Schiessl); *m* 1957, Marianne (*née* Zwicknagl) (*d* 1984); two *s* one *d*. *Educ:* Gymnasium, Munich; Munich Univ. Served in War of 1939–45, 1st Lieut. In Bavarian State Govt, 1946–49; Pres., Govt Cttee on Youth in Bavaria, 1946–48; Member of Bundestag, Fed. Republic of Germany, 1949–78; Minister for Special Tasks, 1953–55; Minister

for Nuclear Issues, 1955–56; Minister of Defence, 1956–62; Minister of Finance, 1966–69. President: Landrat (County Commissioner) of Schongau, 1946–49; Committee on Questions of European Security. Dr *hc*: Detroit University, USA, 1956; Kalamazoo College, 1962; Case Institute of Technology, Cleveland (Ohio), 1962; De Paul University, Chicago, 1964; Univ. Santiago de Chile, 1977; Dallas Univ., 1980; Maryland Univ., 1983; Ludwig Maxmilians Univ., München, 1985. Holds decorations from other European countries. *Publications:* The Grand Design, 1965; Herausforderung und Antwort, 1968; Challenge and Response: A programme for Europe, 1969; Finanzpolitik: Theorie und Wirklichkeit, 1969; Deutschland Deine Zukunft, 1975; Bundestagsreden, 1975; Signale, 1978; Gebote der Freiheit, 1980; many articles on political affairs in newspapers and periodicals. *Address:* Nymphenburger Strasse 64, 8000 Munich 2, Germany. *T:* 1243–215. *Died* 3 *Oct.* 1988.

**STREATFEILD, (Mary) Noel**, OBE 1983; novelist; *b* 24 Dec. 1895; *d* of late William Champion Streatfeild, Bishop of Lewes and late Janet Mary Venn; unmarried. *Educ:* Laleham; Eastbourne. *Publications:* Whicharts, 1931; Parson's Nine, 1932; Tops and Bottoms, 1933; Children's Matinee, 1934; Shepherdess of Sheep, 1934; Ballet Shoes, 1936; It Pays to be Good, 1936; Wisdom Teeth: a play, 1936; Tennis Shoes, 1937; Caroline England, 1937; Circus is Coming (Carnegie Gold Medal), 1938; Luke, 1940; Secret of the Lodge, 1940; House in Cornwall, 1940; Children of Primrose Lane, 1941; Winter is Past, 1942; I Ordered a Table for Six, 1942; Myra Carrol, 1944; Curtain Up, 1944; Saplings, 1945; Party Frock, 1946; Grass in Piccadilly, 1947; Painted Garden, 1949; Mothering Sunday, 1950; (ed) Years of Grace, 1950; White Boots, 1951; Aunt Clara, 1952; (ed) By Special Request, 1953; The Fearless Treasure, 1953, new edn, 1963; The First Book of Ballet, 1953 (US), rev. edn, 1963 (UK); The Bell Family, 1954; (ed) Growing Up Gracefully, 1955; The Grey Family, 1956; Judith, 1956; (ed) The Day Before Yesterday, 1956; Wintles Wonders, 1957; Magic and the Magician, 1958; Bertram, 1959; The Royal Ballet School, 1959; The Ballet Annual, 1960; Christmas with the Crystals, 1960; Look at the Circus, 1960; New Town, 1960; Queen Victoria, 1961; The Silent Speaker, 1961; Apple Bough, 1962; Lisa Goes to Russia, 1963; A Vicarage Family (autobiog.), 1963; The Children on the Top Floor, 1964; Away from the Vicarage (autobiog.), 1965; Let's Go Coaching, 1965; Enjoying Opera, 1966; The Growing Summer, 1966; Old Chairs to Mend, 1966; The Thames, 1966; Before Confirmation, 1967; Caldicott Place, 1967; The Barrow Lane Gang, 1968; (ed) Nicholas, 1968; Red Riding Hood, 1970; Thursday's Child, 1970; Beyond the Vicarage (autobiog.), 1971; The First Book of Shoes, 1971; Ballet Shoes for Anna, 1972; The Boy Pharaoh, Tutankhamen, 1972; When the Siren Wailed, 1974; Gran-Nannie, 1976; Far To Go, 1976; Meet the Maitlands, Part 1, 1978; The Maitlands: All Change at Cuckley Place, 1979. *Recreation:* wild flowers. *Address:* Vicarage Gate House, Vicarage Gate, W8 4AQ.
*Died* 11 *Sept.* 1986.

**STREET, Prof. Harry**, CBE 1978; LLM, PhD; FBA 1968; Professor of English Law, Manchester University, since 1960; *b* 17 June 1919; *s* of Alfred and Lilian Street; *m* 1947, Muriel Hélène Swain; two *s* one *d*. *Educ:* Farnworth Grammar School; Manchester Univ. LLB 1938, LLM 1948; PhD 1951. Qualified as Solicitor, 1940. Flt-Lt, RAF, 1942–46. Lectr in Law, Manchester Univ., 1946–47; Commonwealth Fund Fellow at Columbia Univ., USA, 1947–48; Lectr in Law, 1948–51, Senior Lectr in Law, 1951–52, Manchester Univ.; Prof. of Law, Nottingham Univ., 1952–56; Prof. of Public Law and Common Law, Manchester Univ., 1956–60. Visiting Prof. of Law, Harvard Univ., USA, 1957–58. Chairman: Cttee on Racial Discrimination, 1967; Royal Commn on Fiji electoral system, 1975–76; Member: Commn on the Constitution, 1969–73; Monopolies and Mergers Commn, 1973–80. Hon. LLD Southampton, 1974. *Publications:* Principles of Administrative Law (with J. A. G. Griffith), 1952, 5th edn 1973; A Comparative Study of Governmental Liability, 1953; Law of Torts, 1955, 7th edn 1983; Law of Damages, 1961; Freedom, the Individual and the Law, 1963, 5th edn 1981; Law relating to Nuclear Energy (with F. R. Frame), 1966; Road Accidents (with D. W. Elliott), 1968; Justice in the Welfare State (Hamlyn Lectures), 1968; articles in numerous English, Canadian and American jls of law and public administration. *Recreation:* mountain walking. *Address:* Faculty of Law, Manchester University, Manchester M13 9PL; 1 Queen's Gate, Bramhall, Stockport SK7 1JT. *Died* 20 *April* 1984.

**STREIT, Clarence Kirshman**; President, International Movement for Atlantic Union, since 1958, and Association to Unite the Democracies (formerly Federal Union, Inc.), USA, since 1939; author; lecturer since 1939; Editor, Freedom & Union, since 1946; *b* 21 Jan. 1896; *s* of Louis L. Streit and Emma Kirshman, California, Mo, USA; *m* 1921, Jeanne Defrance, of Paris, France; one *s* two *d*. *Educ:* Missouri and Montana public schs; State Univ. of Montana; Sorbonne; University Coll., Oxford (Rhodes Schol.), Hon. LLD, LittD, DHL. US public land surveyor in Montana and Alaska, 1912–16; served as volunteer in American Expeditionary Force, France, 1917–19, first as private, 18th Engineers Railway, then as sergeant in Intelligence Service, attached to American Delegation, Paris Peace Conference; then Rhodes Scholar, Oxford; correspondent Philadelphia Public Ledger, 1920–24, Greco-Turk War, Rome, Istanbul, Paris; correspondent, New York Times, 1925–39, Carthage excavations, Riff war, Vienna, New York, Latin America, Geneva, 1929–38, Washington, DC, 1938–39. First Recipient, Estes Kefauver Union of the Free Award, 1968. *Publications:* Where Iron is, There is the Fatherland, 1920; Hafiz: The Tongue of the Hidden (rubaiyat), 1928; Report on How to Combat False News, League of Nations, 1932; Union Now, 1939; Union Now with Britain, 1941; Chapter on Briand in Dictators and Democrats, 1941; (joint) The New Federalist, 1950; Freedom Against Itself, 1954; Freedom's Frontier-Atlantic Union Now, 1960. *Address:* (home) 2853 Ontario Road NW, Washington, DC 20009, USA. *T:* (202) 234–3232; (office) PO Box 75920, Washington DC 20013, USA. *Died 6 July 1986.*

**STRELCYN, Stefan**, FBA 1976; Reader in Semitic Languages, University of Manchester, since 1973 (Lecturer, 1970–73); *b* 28 June 1918; *s* of Szaja Strelcyn and Cywia (*née* Frank); *m* 1940, Maria Kirzner; two *s. Educ:* Gimnazjum Ascola and Tech. Engrg Sch., Warsaw; Université Libre de Bruxelles; Université de Montpellier; Sorbonne (LèsL); Ecole Nationale des Langues Orientales Vivantes (Dipl.); Ecole des Langues Orientales Anciennes (Dipl.); Ecole Pratique des Hautes Etudes, IVe Section (Dipl.). Served War of 1939–45: in Polish Forces in France, 1940 and French Résistance, 1941–44; deported to Germany, Eutritzsch near Leipzig, 1944–45. Croix de Guerre. Attaché de Recherches, CNRS, Paris, 1949–50; University of Warsaw: Assoc. Prof., 1950–54, then Prof. of Semitic Studies, 1954–69; Head of Dept of Semitic Studies, 1950–69; Dir, Inst. of Oriental Studies, 1961–65; Dir, Centre of African Studies, 1962–69; Vis. Lectr in Semitic Studies, SOAS, Univ. of London, 1969–70. Dep. Dir, Inst. of Oriental Studies, Polish Acad. of Scis, 1953–62; Vice-Pres., Cttee of Oriental Studies, Polish Acad. of Scis, 1954–66. Research journeys to Ethiopia, 1957–58, 1966. Unesco missions: Somalia, 1966; Ethiopia, 1974. Haile Sellassie Award for Ethiopian Studies, 1967. FRAS 1977. Editor: Catalogue des manuscrits orientaux des collections polonaises, 1957–67; Africana Bulletin, 1964–69; Jt editor: Rocznik Orientalistyczny, 1954–68; Prace Orientalistyczne, 1954–68; Jl of Semitic Studies, 1976–. *Publications:* Catalogue des manuscrits éthiopiens (Collection Griaule), tome IV, 1954; Prières magiques éthiopiennes pour délier les charmes, 1955; Kebra Nagast czyli Chwała Królów Abisynii, 1956; Mission scientifique en Ethiopie, 1959; Inscriptions palmyréniennes in: K. Michałkowski, Palmyre: fouilles polonaises, 1959–60, 1960, 1961, 1962 (resp. 1961, 1962, 1963, 1964); Médecine et plantes d'Ethiopie: (vol. I) Les traités médicaux éthiopiens, 1968; (vol. II) Enquête sur les noms et l'emploi des plantes en Ethiopie, 1973; Catalogue of Ethiopic Manuscripts in the John Rylands University Library of Manchester, 1974; Catalogue des manuscrits éthiopiens de l'Accademia Nazionale dei Lincei: Fonds Conti Rossini et Fonds Caetani 209, 375–378, 1976; Catalogue of Ethiopian Manuscripts in the British Library acquired since the year 1877, 1978; articles and reviews in jls of learned socs. *Address:* Department of Near Eastern Studies, University of Manchester, Manchester M13 9PL. *Died 19 May 1981.*

**STREVENS, Peter Derek**, MA; FIL; Fellow of Wolfson College, Cambridge, since 1976; *b* 1922; *s* of late William Strevens and Dorothie Strevens; *m* 1946, Gwyneth Moore; one *s. Educ:* Ackworth Sch.; University Coll. London (BA); MA Cantab 1979; DLit London 1989. FIL 1971. Lectr in Phonetics, University Coll. of the Gold Coast, 1949–56; Lectr in Phonetics and Applied Linguistics, Univ. of Edinburgh, 1957–61; Prof. of Contemporary English, Univ. of Leeds, 1961–64; Prof of Applied Linguistics, Univ. of Essex, 1964–74; Dir-Gen., Bell Educnl Trust, 1978–88. McAndless Dist. Vis. Prof. in the Humanities, Eastern Michigan Univ., 1988; Prof., Univ. of Illinois, 1989–90. Sec., Internat. Assoc. of Applied Linguistics, 1966–70; Chairman: British Assoc. of Applied Linguistics, 1972–75; Internat. Assoc. of Teachers of English as a Foreign Language, 1983–87. Gen. Editor, Special English Series, 1962–77; Joint Editor: Language and Language Learning, 1974–76; New Directions in Language Teaching, 1977–. FRSA 1978. *Publications:* The Linguistic Sciences and Language Teaching (jtly), 1964; British and American English, 1972; New Orientations in the Teaching of English, 1977; Teaching English as an International Language, 1980; (jtly) International English for Maritime Communication: Seaspeak, 1984. *Recreations:* travel, the sea. *Address:* Wolfson College, Cambridge CB3 9BB. *Club:* English-Speaking Union. *Died 1 Nov. 1989.*

**STRICKLAND, Maj.-Gen. Eugene Vincent Michael**, CMG 1960; DSO 1944; OBE 1955; MM 1940; Chief of Joint Services Liaison Organization, British Forces, Germany, 1966–69, retired; *b* 25 Aug. 1913; *s* of Capt. V. N. Strickland (*d* of wounds, 1917) and of Mary Erina Strickland (*née* O'Sullivan); *m* 1939, Barbara Mary Farquharson Meares Lamb; four *s* one *d. Educ:* Mayfield College; RMC Sandhurst. Commissioned, 1934; served in India, 1934–35; resigned commn, 1935; re-joined; War of 1939–45, in France and

Belgium, 1940; re-commissioned, 1940, RAC; comd of 145 Regt, RAC, N Africa, 1942–43; Italy, 1943–45, comd of N Irish Horse, 145 Regt, RAC and RAC Sch.; Greece, 1945–46, comd of 40th RTR; Egypt, 1948; WO, (MI), 1948–50; Min. of Defence, 1952–54; Arab Legion, 1955–56; Sen. British Officer, Jordan, 1956–57; Min. of Defence, on staff of Chief of Defence Staff, 1957–58; Mil. Adviser to King Hussein of Jordan, 1958–59; Director of Plans, War Office, 1960–63; psc 1947; jssc 1952; idc 1960; NATO Defence College, 1963; DAQMG 1st Corps, 1963–66. Star of Jordan, 1959. CStJ 1960. *Recreations:* shooting, cricket, etc. *Address:* 46 Olivers Battery Road, Winchester, Hants. *Died 19 Dec. 1982.*

**STRICKLAND, Hon. Mabel Edeline**, OBE 1944; Leader of the Progressive Constitutional Party in Malta, since 1953; *b* Malta, 8 Jan. 1899; 3rd *d* of 1st and last Baron Strickland, of Sizergh Castle, Kendal (and 6th Count della Catena in the Island of Malta) and of late Lady Edeline Sackville. *Educ:* privately in Australia. Attached Naval HQ, Malta, 1917–18; War Correspondent, attached 21st Army Group, BAOR, Aug. 1945. Asst Sec., Constitutional Party, 1921–45; Editor: Times of Malta, 1935–50; Sunday Times of Malta, 1935–56; Member: Malta Legislative Assembly, 1950, 1951–53, 1962–66; Malta Chamber of Commerce; Man. Dir, Allied Malta Newspapers Ltd, 1940–55; Chairman: Xara Palace Hotel Co. Ltd, 1949–61, 1966–; Allied Malta Newspapers Ltd, 1950–55, 1966–; Director, Progress Press Co. Ltd, 1957–61, 1966–. Life Member: Commonwealth Parliamentary Assoc.; Air League; RSA; Mem. Royal Horticultural Soc.; Hon. Corresp. Sec. (Malta), Royal Commonwealth Soc. Astor Award, CPU, 1971. CStJ 1969. Coronation medal, 1953. *Publications:* A Collection of Essays on Malta, 1923–54; Maltese Constitutional and Economic Issue, 1955–59. *Recreations:* gardening, reading. *Address:* Villa Parisio, Lija, Malta. *T:* 41286. *Clubs:* Lansdowne; Marsa Sports. *Died 29 Nov. 1988.*

**STRONACH, Ancell**, ARSA 1934; DA (Edin); *b* Dundee, 6 Dec. 1901; *s* of Alexander Stronach and Margaret Ancell; *m* 1941, Joan Cunningham. *Educ:* Hutcheson's Grammar School; privately. GSA (diploma), 1920; Guthrie Award bronze and silver medallist; travelling scholarship; Terrance Memorial Prize given by G. A. Lauder Prize GAC. Exhibited at Paris Salon, RA, WAG, RSA, Canada, New Zealand and America; official purchasers, Ross and Thorburn and Modern Arts Association permanent collections. Professor of Mural Painting, Glasgow School of Art, to 1939. *Recreations:* walking, menagerie and collection of British and foreign fish and reptiles. *Address:* Alma House, 25 Gillingham Road, Gillingham, Kent. *T:* Medway 54077. *Died 12 Sept. 1981.*

**STRONG, Sir Charles Love**, KCVO 1974 (MVO 1962); chartered physiotherapist in private practice in London, 1938–83; *b* 16 April 1908; *o s* of late Alfred Strong; *m* 1st, 1933, Ivy Maud (*d* 1976), *yr d* of late Arthur Stockley; one *d*; 2nd, 1977, Ruth Mary, *d* of late Charles Hermon Smith. *Educ:* privately (Bailey Sch., Durham). Miner and merchant seaman, 1924–26; RN (Sick Berth Br.), qualified MCSP; Physiotherapist, RN Hosps, Haslar and Malta. Devised new apparatus and technique for treatment of injury to humans by faradism; developed manipulative techniques, 1926–38; running parallel with human practice designed special apparatus and technique for treatment of injuries to horses by faradism with outstanding success; under observation of leading equine veterinarian treated 100 cases of lameness in horses which had failed to respond to previous treatment, curing 88 per cent; some hundreds of races have now been won by horses cured of lameness by this method and which had failed to respond to other treatments. Formed firm of 'Transeva' for development, manufacture and marketing of horse apparatus, which is now supplied to many parts of the world. Served War, RAF Marine Section, 1st cl. Coxwain, 1940–44 (invalided). *Publications:* Common-Sense Therapy for Horses' Injuries, 1956; Horses' Injuries, 1967. *Address:* 115A Harley Street, W1N 1DG. *T:* 01–935 4523. *Died 19 March 1988.*

**STRONG, Maj.-Gen. Sir Kenneth William Dobson**, KBE 1966 (OBE 1942); Kt 1952; CB 1945; Director: Philip Hill Investment Trust, 1966–77; Eagle Star Insurance Co., 1966–77; *b* 9 Sept. 1900; *o s* of late Prof. John Strong, CBE, LLD, and Mrs Strong, Eastbourne; *m* Brita, *widow* of John Horridge, Master of Supreme Court (King's Bench Div.). *Educ:* Montrose Academy; Glenalmond; RMC, Sandhurst. 2nd Lt 1st Bn Royal Scots Fusiliers, 1920. Military career, 1920–47 (which included command of 4/5 Bn Royal Scots Fusiliers, Camberley Staff College Course); Mem. of Saar Force, 1935; Defence Security Officer, Malta and Gibraltar; staff appts at WO (2 years as Hd of German Section); a tour of duty as Military Attaché, Berlin, and residence in Germany, France, Italy and Spain prior to qualifying as an interpreter in the languages of these countries; Head of Intelligence Home Forces, 1942; Head of General Eisenhower's Intelligence Staff, 1943, remaining with the Supreme Commander during his campaigns in Africa, Sicily, Italy, France and Germany, leaving him at the dissolution of Supreme HQ in July 1945 (despatches). Member, delegns for conducting

Armistice negotiations with Italy, in Lisbon and Sicily, 1943; and with Germany in Rheims and Berlin, 1945. Director General of Political Intelligence Dept of Foreign Office, 1945–47; retired pay, 1947. First Director of Joint Intelligence Bureau, Ministry of Defence, 1948–64; first Director-General of Intelligence, Min. of Defence, 1964–66. Distinguished Service Medal (USA), Legion of Merit (USA). Chevalier and Officer of Legion of Honour, Croix de Guerre with Palms (France); Order of the Red Banner (Russia). *Publications:* Intelligence at the Top, 1968; Men of Intelligence, 1970; various newspaper articles on business organisation and export problems. *Recreation:* golf. *Address:* 25 Kepplestone, Eastbourne, East Sussex. *Club:* Army and Navy.
*Died 11 Jan.* 1982.

**STRONG, Most Rev. Philip Nigel Warrington,** KBE 1970; CMG 1958; MA Cantab; ThD ACT; DD Lambeth, 1968; *b* Sutton-on-the-Hill, Etwall, 11 July 1899; *s* of late Rev. John Warrington Strong, Oxford, formerly Vicar of Dodford with Brockhall, and Rosamond Maria, *d* of late John Digby Wingfield Digby, Sherborne Castle, Dorset. *Educ:* King's School, Worcester; Selwyn Coll., Cambridge; Bishops' College, Cheshunt. Served European War with RE (Signal Service), 1918–19; BA Cambridge, 1921; MA 1924; Deacon, 1922; Priest, 1923; Curate of St Mary's, Tyne Dock, 1922–26; Vicar of Christ Church, Leeds, 1926–31; Vicar of St Ignatius the Martyr, Sunderland, 1931–36; Proctor of Convocation of York and Member of Church Assembly for Archdeaconry of Durham, 1936; Bishop of New Guinea, 1936–62; MLC, Territory of Papua and New Guinea, 1955–63; Archbishop of Brisbane and Metropolitan of Queensland, 1962–70; Primate of Australia, 1966–70. Senior CF (Australian Army), 1943–45. Hon. Fellow, Selwyn College, Cambridge, 1966. Sub-Prelate, Order of St John of Jerusalem, 1967. *Publications:* Out of Great Tribulation, 1947; (ed D. Wetherell) Diaries of Philip Strong, 1981. *Address:* 11 Cathedral Close, Wangaratta, Victoria 3677, Australia. *T:* Wangaratta 21-5603. *Club:* Melbourne. *Died 6 July* 1983.

**STRONGE, Captain Rt. Hon. Sir (Charles) Norman (Lockhart),** 8th Bt *cr* 1803; MC; PC N Ireland, 1946; HM Lieutenant for Co. Armagh, since 1939; President, Royal British Legion, Northern Ireland Area, since 1946; *b* 23 July 1894; *s* of Sir Charles Edmond Sinclair Stronge, 7th Bt, and Marian (*d* 1948), *d* of Samuel Bostock, The Hermitage, Epsom; *S* father 1939; *m* 1921, Gladys Olive Hall, OBE 1943, OStJ (*d* 1980), of Knockbrack, Athenry, Co. Galway, *o d* of Major H. T. Hall, late 18th Hussars; one *s* two *d* (and one *d* decd). *Educ:* Eton. Served European War, 1914–19, Royal Inniskilling Fusiliers and Royal Irish Rifles (MC, despatches twice, Belgian Croix-de-Guerre). MP Mid-Armagh, N Ireland Parlt, 1938–69; Asst Parliamentary Sec., Ministry of Finance, Northern Ireland, 1941–42; Parliamentary Sec., Ministry of Finance (Chief Whip), 1942–44; Speaker, Northern Ireland House of Commons, 1945–69. JP Co. Londonderry; JP Co. Armagh; High Sheriff Co. Londonderry, 1934; Chm., Armagh County Council, 1944–55. Dir, Commercial Insurance Co. of Ireland Ltd. North Irish Horse (Royal Armoured Corps), invalided. Hon. Col 5th Bn Royal Irish Fusiliers (TA), 1949–63. KStJ; Comdr of the Order of Leopold (Belgium), 1946. *Recreations:* shooting, fishing. *Heir: s* James Matthew Stronge [*b* 21 June 1932. *Educ:* Eton; Christ Church, Oxford (MA).Captain, Grenadier Guards, RARO. MP (N Ireland), Mid-Armagh, 1969–73; Member (U) NI Assembly, for Armagh, 1973–76. JP Co. Armagh]. *Address:* Tynan Abbey, Tynan, Co. Armagh, Northern Ireland. *TA:* Tynan. *T:* Middletown 205. *Club:* Ulster (Belfast).
*Died 21 Jan.* 1981.

**STRUTT, Hon. Charles Richard;** *b* 25 May 1910; *s* of 4th Baron Rayleigh and Lady Mary Hilda Strutt, *d* of 4th Earl of Leitrim; *brother* and *heir-pres.* of 5th Baron Rayleigh; *m* 1952, Jean Elizabeth, *d* of 1st Viscount Davidson, PC, GCVO, CH, CB; one *s* two *d*. *Educ:* Eton; Trinity College, Cambridge. Governor of Felsted School, 1936–74. Member, Church Army Bd, 1950 (Vice-Pres. 1963). Hon. Treas., Soc. for Psychical Research, 1954. Dir, Lord Rayleigh's Farms Ltd. (Chairman), 1957. King Christian IX Liberation Order (Denmark). *Recreation:* gardening. *Address:* Berwick Place, Hatfield Peverel, Chelmsford, Essex. *T:* Chelmsford 380321. *Club:* Brooks's. *Died 11 Dec.* 1981.

**STRUTT, Rt. Rev. Rupert Gordon,** BD; Assistant Bishop, Diocese of Canterbury, since 1983; *b* 15 Jan. 1912; *s* of Rupert Henry and Maude Mortlock Strutt; *m* 1st, 1936, Eva Gertrude Rabbitts; one *s* one *d*; 2nd, 1949, Constance Mary Fergusson Foden; one *s* two *d*. *Educ:* University of London; London College of Divinity; Wycliffe Hall, Oxford. Deacon, 1942; Priest, 1943. Curate of Carlton-in-the-Willows, 1942–43; Chaplain to the Forces (Emergency Commission), 1943–45; Rector of Normanton-on-Soar, 1945–48; Vicar of Holy Trinity, Leicester, 1948–52; Curate-in-Charge, St John the Divine, Leicester, 1949–52; Vicar of Addiscombe, Diocese of Canterbury, 1952–59. Chaplain to HM Prison, Leicester, 1948–52. Commissary to the Bishop of Saskatoon, 1958–81. Archdeacon of Maidstone and Canon Residentiary of Canterbury Cathedral, also Prior of St John's Hospital, Canterbury, 1959–65; Bishop Suffragan

of Stockport, 1965–83. *Address:* 5 Abbots Place, Canterbury, Kent. *T:* Canterbury 455885. *Died 1 Oct.* 1985.

**STUART, Prof. Alan;** Professor Emeritus, University of Exeter, 1959 (Professor, and Head of Department of Geology, 1957–59); *b* 25 April 1894; *s* of James Anderson Stuart and Elizabeth (*née* Gladwell); *m* 1921, Ruth May Hugill; one *s* two *d*. *Educ:* Gateshead Secondary Sch.; Armstrong Coll. (now University of Newcastle upon Tyne). BSc Hons Geology, 1921; MSc 1923. Dip. RMS, 1973. Asst Lectr, Lectr and First Lectr, Dept of Geology, University Coll. of Swansea, 1921–47; Indep. Head of Dept of Geology, University Coll., Exeter, 1947–57. War Service: RAMC, Dardanelles and Egypt, 1915–16; India, 1916–18; Indian Army, (TC), 2/27 Punjabis (Adjutant), Afghan War, 1919. Civil Defence, 1939–45; at University Coll., Swansea, during War, worked on crystallography of explosives for Ministry of Supply. *Publications:* (with N. H. Hartshorne): Crystals and the Polarising Microscope, 4th edn, 1970; Practical Optical Crystallography, 2nd edn 1969; contribs to jls mainly concerned with sedimentary petrology and applications of microscopy to chemical problems. *Recreations:* photography, study of landscape, microscopy. *Address:* 41 Woodhill Road, Portishead, Bristol BS20 9EY. *T:* Bristol 842684. *Died 27 Aug.* 1983.

**STUART, Rt. Rev. Cyril Edgar;** *b* 27 Nov. 1892; *s* of Canon E. A. Stuart, Canterbury, and Emily Ada Guy; *m* 1924, Mary Summerhayes; two *s*. *Educ:* Repton; St John's College, Cambridge; MA. Public School Brigade, 1914; 3rd N Staffs, 1915; Salonica, 1916–19; ordained as Curate of St Mary's, Hornsey Rise, 1920; Chaplain and Lecturer, Ridley Hall, Cambridge, 1921–24; Chaplain and Librarian Achimota College, Gold Coast, 1925–30; CMS Missionary, Uganda, 1931; Asst Bishop of Uganda, 1932–34; Bishop of Uganda, 1934–53; Assistant Bishop of Worcester and Rector of St Andrew's and All Saints with St Helen's, St Alban's and St Michael's, Worcester, 1953–56; Residentiary Canon of Worcester Cathedral, 1956–65. *Address:* 4 Eddystone Court, Churt, Farnham, Surrey. *Died 23 Aug.* 1982.

**STUART BLACK, Ian Hervey;** *see* Black, I. H. S.

**STUBBER, Lt-Col John Henry H.;** *see* Hamilton Stubber.

**STUBBS, William Frederick,** CMG 1955; CBE 1952 (OBE 1941); HMOCS, retired; *b* 19 June 1902; *e s* of late Lawrence Morley Stubbs, CSI, CIE, ICS (retd); *m* 1929, Eileen Mary (*d* 1963), *y d* of late Sir W. E. Stanford, KBE, CB, CMG, Rondebosch, S Africa; one *d*. *Educ:* Winchester, Joined British S Africa Police, S Rhodesia, 1921; N Rhodesia Police on transfer, 1924; Colonial Administrative Service, Northern Rhodesia, 1926; Labour Comr, 1944–48; Provincial Comr, 1949; acted as Secretary for Native Affairs, 1951 and 1953; Secretary for Native Affairs, 1954–57; *Ex-officio* member of Executive and Legislative Councils (Speaker, Legislative Council, and Chm. Public Service Commn Somaliland Protectorate, 1960, until Union with Somalia). Associate Commonwealth Parliamentary Association. *Address:* Nash Barn, Marnhull, Dorset. *Club:* Royal Commonwealth Society. *Died 22 Sept.* 1987.

**STUCHBERY, Arthur Leslie,** CBE 1971 (OBE 1968); Chairman, Remploy, 1969–72; *b* 14 Feb. 1903; *s* of Harry and Martha Stuchbery; *m* 1930, Dorothy Blanche Willmott; one *s* one *d*. *Educ:* Hackney Techn. Coll.; Borough Polytechnic. CEng, FIMechE, FIProdE, FRSA. Metal Box Co.: Plant Manager, 1929; Chief Engr, 1939; Dir of R&D, 1961. Founder Councillor, PERA (Chm. 1962–67); Founder Mem., IProdE, 1924, President 1969–72; Chm., Brunel Univ., 1965–73. Clayton Lectr, 1966. Hon. DTech Brunel, 1970. *Publications:* Little Boxes; numerous technical papers. *Recreations:* hand crafts, writing. *Address:* Dyke End House, Littlestone, Kent. *T:* New Romney 2076. *Clubs:* City Livery, St Stephen's Constitutional. *Died 12 May* 1986.

**STUCLEY, Major Sir Dennis Frederic Bankes,** 5th Bt, *cr* 1859; DL; *b* 29 Oct. 1907; *s* of Sir Hugh Nicholas Granville Stucley, 4th Bt, and Gladys (*d* 1950), *d* of W. A. Bankes, Wolfeton House, Dorchester; *S* father, 1956; *m* 1932, Hon. Sheila Bampfylde, *o d* of 4th Baron Poltimore; one *s* four *d* (and one *s* decd). *Educ:* Harrow; RMC Sandhurst. 2nd Lt Grenadier Guards, 1927; retired, 1932. Devon CC, 1934, CA, 1955. Capt. Royal Devon Yeomanry, 1937, Major, 1944. JP Devon, 1934–62; DL Devon, 1956; Mayor of Bideford, 1954–56; High Sheriff of Devon, 1956. Joint Master, Dulverton Foxhounds, 1952–54. Chairman: Regional Adv. Cttee, Forestry Commn, SW, 1958–75; Timber Growers Organization, 1966–69; Exmoor Nat. Park (Devon) Cttee, 1968–74. *Recreations:* hunting, shooting and fishing. *Heir: s* Lieut Hugh George Coplestone Bampfylde Stucley, Royal Horse Guards [*b* 8 Jan. 1945; *m* 1969, Angela Caroline, *e d* of Richard Toller, Theale, Berks; two *s* two *d*]. *Address:* Hartland Abbey, Bideford, Devon. *T:* Hartland 234; Court Hall, North Molton, South Molton, Devon. *T:* North Molton 224. *Club:* Cavalry and Guards. *Died 17 Sept.* 1983.

**STUCLEY, John Humphrey Albert,** DSC 1945; **His Honour Judge Stucley;** a Circuit Judge, since 1974; *b* 12 July 1916; 2nd *s* of Sir Hugh Stucley, 4th Bt, Affeton Castle, Devon; *m* 1941, Natalia, *d* of

Don Alberto Jiménez, CBE and Natalia Cossío de Jiménez; no c. *Educ*: RN Colls, Dartmouth and Greenwich. Cadet, RN, 1930; served China, Mediterranean and Home stns and throughout War of 1939–45; Lt-Comdr 1945. Called to Bar, Middle Temple, 1957. A Recorder of the Crown Court, 1972–74. Dep. Chm., SE England Agricultural Land Tribunal, 1971. *Publications*: Affeton Castle: a lost Devon village, 1967; Sir Bevill Grenvile and his times, 1983. *Recreations*: gardening, travel. *Address*: 14 Chester Row, SW1W 9JH.                                             *Died 30 March* 1988.

**STUDHOLME, Sir Henry (Gray),** 1st Bt, *cr* 1956; CVO 1953; DL; *b* 13 June 1899; *s* of late William Paul Studholme, Perridge House, Exeter; *m* 1929, Judith, *d* of Henry William Whitbread, Norton Bavant Manor, Warminster; two *s* one *d*. *Educ*: Eton; Magdalen Coll., Oxford (MA). Served European War with Scots Guards, 1917–19; Member LCC, 1931–45; rejoined Scots Guards, 1940; Staff appointments, 1941–44. MP (C) Tavistock Division, 1942–66. PPS to late Comdr R. Brabner, Under-Sec. of State for Air, Nov. 1944–March 1945; Conservative Whip, 1945–56; Joint Treas. of the Conservative Party, 1956–62. Vice-Chamberlain of King George VI's Household, 1951–52, of the Queen's Household, 1952–56. DL Devon, 1969. *Heir*: *s* Paul Henry William Studholme, late Capt. Coldstream Guards [*b* 16 Jan. 1930; *m* 1957, Virginia Katherine, *yr d* of late Sir Richmond Palmer, KCMG; two *s* one *d*]. *Address*: Wembury House, Wembury, Plymouth. *T*: Plymouth 862210. *Club*: MCC.                                              *Died 9 Oct.* 1987.

**STUDHOLME, Sir Paul (Henry William),** 2nd Bt *cr* 1956, of Perridge, Co. Devon; DL; Member, Board of TSB Group plc and Chairman, South West Regional Board of TSB England & Wales plc, 1987–89; *b* 16 Jan. 1930; *s* of Sir Henry Gray Studholme, 1st Bt, CVO and of Judith Joan Mary, *d* of Henry William Whitbread; *S* father, 1987; *m* 1957, Virginia Katherine, *yr d* of Sir (Herbert) Richmond Palmer, KCMG, CBE and Margaret, *d* of Reginald Abel Smith; two *s* one *d*. *Educ*: Eton; RMA Sandhurst. Commd Coldstream Guards, 1950; retd as Captain, 1959. Has lived and farmed on Perridge Estate, Exeter, since then. Gen. Comr of Income Tax, 1963 (now Chm., Crediton Div.); Mem., East Local Land Drainage Cttee of SW Water Authority, 1974–. Vice-Pres. and Chm. Exec. Cttee, Timber Growers' Orgn, 1982–83; Dep. Chm., Timber Growers United Kingdom Ltd, 1983–85; Member: Min. of Agriculture's Regional Panel for South West, 1978–84; Home Grown Timber Adv. Cttee, 1984–87. President: Bd of Govs, Royal West of England School for Deaf, 1968–69 (Hon. Treas., 1974–); Devon Br. of Country Landowners' Assoc., 1981–83; Devon County Agricl Assoc., 1985. DL 1981, High Sheriff 1988–89, Devon. *Recreations*: travel, family and local history, shooting, forestry. *Heir*: *er s* Henry William Studholme, ACA, ATII [*b* 31 Jan. 1958; *m* 1988, Lucy, *d* of Richard Deans, Christchurch, NZ]. *Address*: Perridge House, Longdown, Exeter, Devon EX6 7RU. *T*: Longdown 237. *Club*: Cavalry and Guards.                                              *Died 31 Jan.* 1990.

**STURGE, Arthur Collwyn,** MC 1945; *b* 27 Sept. 1912; *yr s* of Arthur Lloyd Sturge and Jessie Katherine Howard; *m* 1938, Beryl Gwenllian, *yr d* of Thomas Arthur, Hong Kong; two *s* two *d*. *Educ*: Harrow; Brasenose Coll., Oxford (BA). Underwriting Member of Lloyd's, 1933; Joined A. L. Sturge & Co., 1934, Chm., 1970–77. Mem., Cttee of Lloyd's, 1967–75 (Dep. Chm., 1969, 1970); Mem. Gen. Cttee, Lloyd's Register of Shipping, 1969–77. Chm., Lloyd's of London Press Ltd, 1973–85 (Life Pres., 1985). Commissioned 64 Field Regt RA (TA), 1937; served War of 1939–45, Middle East, Italy. High Sheriff, East Sussex, 1977. *Recreations*: shooting, fishing. *Address*: Brooke House, Swallowcliffe, near Salisbury, Wilts. *T*: Tisbury 870220. *Clubs*: City of London, Flyfishers'.                                              *Died 21 Feb.* 1986.

**STURGE, Raymond Wilson;** Chairman of Lloyd's, 1964, 1965 and 1966; *b* 10 June 1904; *er s* of late Arthur Lloyd Sturge and Jessie Katharine (née Howard); *m* 1929, Margaret, *y d* of late Walter J. Keep, Sydney, NSW; one *s* four *d*. *Educ*: Harrow; Brasenose Coll., Oxford (BA). Mem. of Lloyd's, 1926; first elected to Committee, 1953; Dep. Chm., 1963. Served War of 1939–45, Royal Scots Fusiliers, Staff Duties. Pres., Insurance Institute of London, 1967–68 (Dep. Pres., 1966–67). *Address*: Ashmore, near Salisbury, Wilts. *T*: Fontmell Magna 811261. *Club*: City of London.                                              *Died 30 March* 1984.

**STYLE, Sir William Montague,** 12th Bt, *cr* 1627; *b* 21 July 1916; *s* of Sir William Frederick Style, 11th Bt, and Florence (*d* 1918), *d* of J. Timm; *S* father, 1943; *m* 1941, La Verne, *d* of T. M. Comstock; two *s*. *Heir*: *s* William Frederick Style, *b* 13 May 1945. *Address*: c/o Muehlmeier, Wildwood, 2919 North Mill Road, Oconomowoc, Wisconsin 53066, USA.                                              *Died* 1981.

**SUCKSMITH, Willie,** FRS 1940; DSc Leeds; Professor of Physics, Sheffield University, 1940–63, Emeritus since 1963; *b* 21 Sept. 1896; *m*. Formerly Reader in Magnetism, Bristol University. Hon. DSc Sheffield, 1972. *Address*: 27 Endcliffe Grove Avenue, Sheffield S10 3EJ.                                              *Died 16 Sept.* 1981.

**SUCRE-TRIAS, Dr Juan Manuel;** Ambassador of Venezuela to the Court of St James's, 1977–79; *b* 25 Oct. 1940; *m* 2nd, 1977, Tatiana Perez; three *s* of former marriage. Economist. Economist, Corporación Venezolana de Guayana; as Economist, Ministry of Public Works, Caracas: Head of Studies Unit; Asst Director of Programming and Budgeting. Member of Congress, Venezuela; President, Finance Commission of Congress of the Republic. Several military decorations (Venezuelan); Orden del Libertador (1st cl.). *Recreations*: swimming, tennis, golf. *Address*: Apt No 50164, Sabana Grande, Caracas 105, Venezuela.                                              *Died 2 March* 1983.

**SUDBURY, Col Frederick Arthur,** OBE 1942; ERD 1951; JP; *b* 14 Sept. 1904; *m* 1929, Florence Joan Egan (marr. diss. 1951); one *s* two *d*; *m* 1952, Pauline Adela, *d* of late Walter Widdop, Halifax, Yorks. *Educ*: Colfe Grammar School, Lewisham; London School of Economics. Tate & Lyle, 1922–69. Served War of 1939–45, Army Officers Emergency Reserve; Col, Dir of Inland Water Transport, Iraq, 1941–43; Col, Movements and Transportation, 14th Army, 1944–45; Lt-Col Supplementary Reserve, 1947–51; Col, Army Emergency Reserve, 1951–62; Hon. Col, RE (AER), 1951–66. Mem. Thames Conservancy, 1958–65 (Vice-Chm., 1960–65). Underwriting Mem. of Lloyd's. Liveryman and Mem. Court Shipwrights' Co.; Freeman and Mem. Court, Co. of Watermen and Lightermen (Master, 1960–61–62). JP Inner London, 1962. *Recreation*: yachting. *Address*: 1 Abbotsbury Close, W14. *T*: 01–603 2880. *Club*: Royal Thames Yacht.                                              *Died 5 April* 1983.

**SUGDEN, Sir (Theodore) Morris,** Kt 1983; CBE 1975; MA, ScD; FRS 1963; Master of Trinity Hall, Cambridge, since 1976; *b* 31 Dec. 1919; *s* of Frederick Morris Sugden and Florence Sugden (née Chadwick); *m* 1945, Marian Florence Cotton; one *s*. *Educ*: Sowerby Bridge Grammar School; Jesus College, Cambridge (Hon. Fellow 1977). Stokes Student, Pembroke Coll., Cambridge, 1945–46; H. O. Jones Lecturer in Physical Chemistry, Univ. of Cambridge, 1950–60; Reader in Physical Chemistry, Univ. of Cambridge, 1960–63; Fellow, Queens' Coll., Cambridge, 1957–63 (Hon. Fellow, 1976). Dir, Thornton Research Centre, Chester, 1967–75; Chief Executive, Shell Research Ltd, 1974–75. Associate Prof., Molecular Sciences, Univ. of Warwick, 1965–74; Vis. Prof. of Chemical Technology, Imp. Coll., 1974–75. Chm., Adv. Cttee on Safety in Nuclear Installations, Health and Safety Commn, 1977–. Pres., Chem. Soc., 1978–79; Physical Sec., Royal Soc., 1979–. Hon. DTech Bradford, 1967; Hon. DSc: York, Ont, 1973; Liverpool, 1977; Leeds, 1978. Medallist of the Combustion Inst., 1960, 1976; Davy Medal, Royal Soc., 1975. *Publications*: (with C. N. Kenney) Microwave Spectroscopy of Gases, 1965; articles in Proc. Royal Soc., Transactions of Faraday Soc., Nature, etc. *Recreations*: pianoforte, gardening, travel. *Address*: The Master's Lodge, Trinity Hall, Cambridge CB2 1TJ. *T*: Cambridge 352396.                                              *Died 3 Jan.* 1984.

**SULLIVAN, Albert Patrick Loisol,** CBE 1944 (MBE 1941); MM; MIFireE; *b* 19 October 1898; *s* of late William Sullivan, Cobh, Eire; *m* 1st, 1920, Margaret Elizabeth Mary Andrews (*d* 1951); one *s*; 2nd, 1964, Rose Mabel (*d* 1978), *d* of late Richard John Dance. Served European War (France), 1915–19. London Fire Brigade, 1919–41; Chief Supt, LFB, 1940–41; Deputy Chief of Fire Staff, National Fire Service, 1941–47; Chief of Fire Staff and Inspector in Chief, NFS, March–Nov. 1947; Chief Fire Officer to the Ministry of Civil Aviation, 1948–50. President Institution of Fire Engineers, 1946–47; OStJ; King's Police and Fire Services Medal, 1948. *Address*: 30 Buckingham Road, Shoreham-by-Sea, West Sussex BN4 5UB. *Club*: Royal Over-Seas League.                                              *Died 28 July* 1981.

**SULZBACH, Herbert,** OBE 1982; Cultural Officer, Embassy of Federal Republic of Germany, 1951–81, retired; *b* 8 Feb. 1894; *s* of late Emil and Julie Sulzbach; *m* 1923, Beate (née Scherk), Berlin; one *d* by 1st marr. *Educ*: Goethe Gymnasium, Frankfurt/Main, Germany. Volunteer, German Imp. Army, Aug. 1914; Western Front, 1914–18 (Lieut, 1916). Apprentice family bank, Gebr. Sulzbach Frankfurt, 1919–20; Partner, fancy paper factory, near Berlin, 1920–36; left Nazi Germany, 1937, to London as jewish refugee with wife and sister-in-law; interned May 1940 with wife, in Isle of Man; volunteered for British Army, 1939, joined Oct. 1940 to Dec. 1948 (Commissioned 1945, Captain 1946); political education of German POWs in Comrie and Featherstone Park. Dual National: British and German citizen. Iron Cross 2nd class, 1916, 1st class, 1918; Front Line Soldiers Cross of Honour, 1934; UK Victory and Defence Medals, 1945; Order of Merit 1st class, Fed. Rep. of Germany, 1964, Grand Cross, 1971; European Cross of Peace, Assoc. of French and German Veterans of World War II, 1978. *Publications*: Zwei Lebende Mauern, 1934 (trans. R. Thonger as With the German Guns: 50 months Western Front, 1972, 2 edn 1981, USA 1982). *Recreations*: political, esp. Anglo-German reconciliation. *Address*: 54 Aberdare Gardens, NW6 3QD. *T*:

01–328 2370. *Clubs:* Anglo-German Association; Western Front Association. *Died 5 July 1985.*

**SUMMERHAYES, Sir Christopher (Henry),** KBE 1955 (MBE 1929); CMG 1949; *b* 8 March 1896; *s* of late Rev. H. Summerhayes; *m* 1921, Anna (Johnson) (*d* 1972); two *s* two *d*. Served HM Forces, 1914–19 and 1940–45, Gloucestershire Regt (despatches). HM Foreign Service; Consul-General at Alexandria, 1946–51; Ambassador to Nepal, 1951–55. *Address:* Tara, Limpsfield Chart, Oxted, Surrey. *Died 12 July 1988.*

**SUMMERSON, Thomas Hawksley,** OBE 1971; JP; *b* 22 April 1903; *s* of late Robert Bradley Summerson, Coatham Mundeville, Co. Durham; *m* 1943, Joan, *d* of late Walter Rogers, Ashington, Sussex; three *s* one *d*. *Educ:* Harrow. Dir for Steel Castings, Iron and Steel Control, Ministry of Supply, 1940–43; Chairman and Joint Man. Dir, Summerson Holdings Ltd, 1944–65; Chairman: British Steel Founders' Association, 1951–54; NE Industrial and Development Association, 1952–55; Home Affairs and Transport Division, Assoc. of British Chambers of Commerce, 1952–59 (Vice-President, 1954, Deputy President, 1960–62, President, 1962–64); Darlington and N Yorks Local Employment Cttee, 1953–74; Design Panel, British Transport Commn, 1956–63; St Paul's Jarrow Development Trust, 1971–75; Civic Trust for NE, 1970–76; Trustee, Civic Trust, 1970–76; Dep. Chairman, Peterlee Development Corp., 1954–55. Chairman, North Eastern Area Board, British Transport Commission, 1955, and Part-time Member of the Commission, until 1962; Part-time Member, British Railways Board, Jan. 1963–Oct. 1963, and Chm. North Eastern Railway Bd, Jan.-Oct. 1963. Member: Aycliffe New Town Development Corp., 1947–61; Development Areas Treasury Advisory Cttee, 1951–55; President: Tees-side and S-W Durham Chamber of Commerce, 1948–50; Tees-side Industrial Development Board, 1954–57; Member, Independent Television Authority, 1957–60; Mem., North East Development Council, 1965–73. Mem. Darlington RDC, 1937–74 (Chm. 1949–52); Chm., Sedgefield Div. Conservative and Unionist Assoc., 1965–71. JP Co. Durham, 1946; Chm. Darlington County Bench, 1951–53 and 1955–61; High Sheriff, County Durham, 1953–54; DL County Durham, 1958–76. Chm. South Durham Hunt, 1955–73. *Recreation:* fishing. *Address:* The Old Manse, Errogie, Inverness. *T:* Gorthleck 649; 3 Terrett's Place, Upper Street, Islington, N1. *T:* 01–359 5316. *Died 3 March 1986.*

**SUMNER, His Honour (William) Donald (Massey),** OBE (mil.) 1945; QC 1960; a Circuit Judge (formerly Judge of County Courts), 1961–82, retired; a Deputy Circuit Judge, 1982–88; *b* 13 Aug. 1913; *s* of Harold Sumner, OBE, Standish, Lancs; *m* 1st, 1934, Muriel Kathleen Wilson; one *s* one *d*; 2nd, 1948, Edith Julie Marie Laurens, (Aidee), of Brussels; one *s* one *d*. *Educ:* Charterhouse; Sidney Sussex Coll., Cambridge. Called to the Bar, Lincoln's Inn, 1937. Served War of 1939–45 with Royal Artillery (despatches); Lt-Col and Asst Adjutant-General, 21st Army Group. Mem. Orpington UDC, 1950–53. Acted as Asst Recorder of Plymouth frequently, 1954–61. MP (C) Orpington Div. of Kent, Jan. 1955–Oct. 1961; formerly PPS to Under Secs of State, Home Office, and to Solicitor-General. Officier, Ordre de la Couronne and Croix de Guerre (Belgian); Bronze Star Medal (American). *Address:* Duxbury, Church Hill, High Halden, Ashford, Kent. *Died 12 May 1990.*

**SUNDERLAND, His Honour (George Frederick) Irvon,** DL; a Circuit Judge (formerly Judge of County Courts), 1963–79; *b* 8 May 1905; *o s* of Frederick and Mary Jane Sunderland; *m* 1929, Mary Katharine (*d* 1983), *d* of Arthur John Bowen; three *s* (and one *s* decd). *Educ:* privately. Called to Bar, Gray's Inn, 1932 (H. C. Richards Prizeman); joined Midland Circuit; Assistant Recorder: Birmingham Quarter Sessions, 1960–63; Coventry Quarter Sessions, 1962–63; County Court Judge, Derbyshire, 1964–66; Chairman, Warwick County QS, 1967–71. Deputy Chairman: East Midlands Agricultural Land Tribunal, 1959–63; Birmingham Mental Health Review Tribunal, 1959–63; Chm., Birmingham Local Bar Cttee, 1959–63. DL Warwicks, 1967. *Recreations:* gardening, the theatre. *Address:* 70 Woodbourne, Augustus Road, Edgbaston, Birmingham B15 3PJ. *T:* 021-454 7236. *Died 20 Aug. 1984.*

**SURRIDGE, Brewster Joseph,** CMG 1950; OBE 1941; Adviser on Co-operatives to Minister of Overseas Development, 1964–67 (to Secretary of State for Colonies, 1947–64); retired 1967; *b* 12 Feb 1894; *e s* of E. E. Surridge; *m* 1922, Winifred Bywater-Ward (*née* Lawford). *Educ:* Felsted School; Downing College, Cambridge. Served European War, Army, 1914–17. Colonial Administrative Service, Cyprus, 1918–33; Registrar of Co-operative Societies, Cyprus, 1934–43; Financial Secretary, Gold Coast, 1943–45; retired, 1946. Adviser on Co-operation to the Government of Iraq, 1946–47. *Publications:* A Survey of Rural Life, Cyprus, 1931; A Manual of Co-operative Law and Practice, 1948. *Address:* 2 Furze Croft, Hove, Sussex BN3 1PB. *T:* Brighton 70027. *Died 4 Jan. 1982.*

**SURRIDGE, Sir (Ernest) Rex (Edward),** Kt 1951; CMG 1946; retired; *b* 21 Feb. 1899; *s* of late E. E. Surridge, Coggeshall, Essex; *m* 1926, Roy (*d* 1982), *d* of late Major F. E. Bradstock, DSO, MC; two *s*.

*Educ:* Felsted; St John's College, Oxford. European War, 1917–20, Lieut 7th Bn DCLI; St John's College, Oxford, 1920–22, Mod. Hist. (Hons); Colonial Admin. Service, 1924, Tanganyika; Assistant Chief Secretary, Tanganyika, 1936; Deputy Chief Secretary, Kenya, 1940; Chief Secretary to Govt of Tanganyika, 1946–51; Salaries Comr, Cyprus, 1953–54; Financial Comr, Seychelles, 1957–58; Salaries Comr, High Commn Territories (South Africa), 1958–59; Salaries Comr, Gibraltar, 1959–60. *Address:* 10 Park Manor, St Aldhelm's Road, Branksome Park, Poole, Dorset BH13 6BS. *T:* Bournemouth (0202) 766638. *Died 19 Dec. 1990.*

**SUSMAN, Maurice Philip,** MB, ChM Sydney; FRCS; FRACS; AAMC; Hon. Consulting Surgeon, Sydney Hospital, 1958; Hon. Consulting Thoracic Surgeon, Royal North Shore Hospital, Sydney, 1958; *b* 4 Aug. 1898; *s* of Philip Tasman Susman and Gertrude Lehane; *m* 1934, Ina May Shanahan; one *d*. *Educ:* Sydney Church of England Grammar School; University of Sydney. Surgeon with Aust. Casualty/Clearing Stn and Hosp., Greece, Crete, Syria and Northern Australia, 1940–43. *Publications:* some ephemeral light verse, essays and medical and surgical articles. *Recreations:* chess, flying light aircraft, meditating, reading books enjoyed in the past and an occasional new one. *Address:* 22 Bathurst Street, Woollahra, NSW 2025, Australia. *T:* 389 6053. *Club:* Royal Aero (NSW). *Died 13 Sept. 1988.*

**SUTCLIFFE, Prof. Frank Edmund;** Emeritus Professor, University of Manchester, since 1982 *b* 8 Aug. 1918; *er s* of Charles Edmund Taylor Sutcliffe and Ellen Sutcliffe; *m* 1st, 1945, Eileen Frances Wade (marr. diss. 1950); one *d*; 2nd, 1956, Jill Margaret Irene Keeys; 3rd, 1966, Jane Ceridwen Bevan. *Educ:* Huddersfield College; University of Manchester. BA 1940, MA 1948, PhD 1958. Served War of 1939–45, with Royal Artillery and Hong Kong and Singapore Royal Artillery, 1940–46. Univ. of Manchester: Asst Lectr in French, 1946–49; Lecturer in French, 1949–55; Senior Lecturer in French, 1955–61; Professor of Modern French Literature, 1961–66; Prof. of Classical French Literature, 1966–82; Dean of Faculty of Arts, 1972–74. Visiting Professor: Univ. of Kiel, 1968; Université Laval, Québec, 1968–69. Chevalier de l'Ordre National du Mérite, 1965. *Publications:* La Pensée de Paul Valéry, 1955; Guez de Balzac et son temps: littérature et politique, 1960; Le réalisme de Charles Sorel: problèmes humains du XVIIe siècle, 1965; (ed) Discours politiques et militaires by Fr de la Noue, 1967; (trans) Descartes, Discours de la Méthode, 1968; Politique et culture 1560–1660, 1973; book reviews; contrib. to French Studies, Le Bayou (Houston, Texas), Jahrbuch (Univ. of Hamburg), Bulletin of the John Rylands Library. *Address:* 61 Daisy Bank Road, Victoria Park, Manchester M14 5QL. *T:* 061-224 1864. *Died 16 July 1983.*

**SUTCLIFFE, Joseph Richard,** ED, BSc; Member, Stock Exchange of Melbourne, 1950–74; *b* 25 Jan. 1897; *s* of late A. H. Sutcliffe and Kate Elizabeth Haybittle; *m* 1923, Aileen, *d* of Henry H. Batchelor, NZ; one *s* one *d*. *Educ:* Palmerston North Boys' High School; Victoria University College, New Zealand. War Service, 1916–19, with NZ Machine Gun Corps and Royal Air Force; Major retd. Headmaster: Scots College, Wellington, NZ, 1930–38; Melbourne Church of England Grammar School, 1938–49. *Publication:* Why be a Headmaster?, 1977. *Address:* c/o The Perpetual Executors and Trustees Association of Australia Ltd, 50 Queen Street, Melbourne, Victoria 3000, Australia. *Club:* Melbourne (Melbourne). *Died 3 Feb. 1985.*

**SUTCLIFFE, Air Cdre Walter Philip,** CB 1958; DFC 1940; *b* 15 Aug. 1910; *s* of late W. Sutcliffe, Brampton, Cumberland; *m* 1947, Margery Anne Taylor, *d* of W. L. Taylor, Tulse Hill, SW2; one *s*. *Educ:* Durham School; Royal Air Force Coll., Cranwell. Fleet Air Arm, 1933–35 and 1937–39; Central Flying Sch., 1936. War of 1939–45: Bomber Command, 1939–42, India and Burma, 1942–45 (despatches). RAF Staff College, 1946; Director of Operational Training, Air Ministry, 1948–50; Standing Group, NATO, 1950–51; RAF Station, Wittering, 1953–55; SHAPE, 1955–56; Atomic Weapon Trials, Australia, 1957; Director of Intelligence, Air Ministry, 1958–61; retd April 1961; Officers' Association, 1961–75. Officer, Legion of Merit (USA), 1945. *Address:* The Pond House, Pluckley, Kent TN27 0QX. *T:* Pluckley (023384) 209. *Died 9 Oct. 1990.*

**SUTHERLAND, (Carol) Humphrey (Vivian),** CBE 1970; FBA 1970; Keeper of the Heberden Coin Room, Ashmolean Museum, Oxford, 1957–75; Student of Christ Church, Oxford, 1945–75, Emeritus Student since 1975; *b* 5 May 1908; *s* of late George Humphreys Vivian and Elsie Sutherland; *m* 1933, Monica La Fontaine Porter (*d* 1982); no *c*. *Educ:* Westminster Sch.; Christ Church, Oxford. Barclay Head Prize for Ancient Numismatics, 1934; Asst Keeper of Coins, Ashmolean Museum, Oxford, 1932–52; Deputy Keeper, 1952–57; University Lecturer in Numismatics, 1939–75; DLitt, 1945. Curator of Pictures, Christ Church, 1947–55, 1970–75; President, Royal Numismatic Society, 1948–53; Winslow Lectr, Hamilton Coll., Clinton, NY, 1949 and 1957; Huntington Medallist

of the American Numismatic Soc., 1950; Royal Numismatic Soc. Medallist, 1954; Silver Medallist, Royal Soc. of Arts, 1955; ed Numismatic Chronicle, 1953–66; Pres., Commn Internationale de Numismatique, 1960–73; Pres., Centro Internaziónale di Studi Numismatici, Naples, 1966–73; Visiting Mem. Inst. for Advanced Study, Princeton, 1962–63, 1968, 1973; Leverhulme Emeritus Fellow, 1977–79; Mem. Royal Mint Advisory Cttee, 1963–; Hon. FRNS 1984; Hon. Member: Société française de numismatique; Société royale de numismatique de Belgique; Commission Internationale de Numismatique; Corresp. Mem., German Archaeol Inst. Governor, Wallingford Sch., 1960–82. Officier, Palmes Académiques (France), 1965. *Publications:* Coinage and Currency in Roman Britain, 1937; (with H. Mattingly, E. A. Sydenham and R. A. G. Carson) The Roman Imperial Coinage, 1939–; The Romans in Spain, 1939; Anglo-Saxon Gold Coinage in the Light of the Crondall Hoard, 1948; (with J. G. Milne and J. D. A. Thompson) Coin Collecting, 1950; Coinage in Roman Imperial Policy, 1951; Art in Coinage, 1955; Gold, 1959; The Cistophori of Augustus, 1970; English Coinage, 600–1900, 1973; Roman Coins, 1974; (with C. M. Kraay) Catalogue of the Coins of the Roman Empire in the Ashmolean Museum, 1976; The Emperor and the Coinage, 1976; articles in Numismatic Chronicle, Jl Roman Studies, etc. *Recreations:* music, gardening. *Address:* Westfield House, Cumnor, Oxford OX2 9PE. *T:* Oxford 862178.
*Died 14 May 1986.*

**SUTHERLAND, Sir (Frederick) Neil,** Kt 1969; CBE 1955; MA; Chairman, The Marconi Co. (formerly Marconi's Wireless Telegraph Co. Ltd), and of Marconi Instruments, 1965–69, retired; Director, English Electric Co. Ltd, 1965; *b* 4 March 1900; *s* of late Neil Hugh Sutherland; *m* 1st, 1931, Naruna d'Amorim Jordan (*d* 1970); one *s*; 2nd, 1973, Gladys Jackman (*d* 1986). *Educ:* St Catharine's College, Cambridge. MA 1922. Served apprenticeship with English Electric Co. Ltd; Gen. Manager, English Electric Co. in Brazil, 1928; Man. Dir, English Electric (South Africa) Ltd, 1937; Gen. Manager, Marconi's Wireless Telegraph Co. Ltd, 1948; Man. Dir, Marconi Co. Ltd, 1958–65. *Recreation:* golf. *Address:* Conifers, 45 High Street, Wickham Market, Woodbridge, Suffolk IP13 0HE. *Died 29 Oct. 1986.*

**SUTHERLAND, Humphrey;** *see* Sutherland, C. H. V.

**SUTHERLAND, Sir Iain (Johnstone Macbeth),** KCMG 1982 (CMG 1974); HM Diplomatic Service, retired; *b* Edinburgh, 15 June 1925; *s* of late Dr D. M. Sutherland, MC, RSA, and Dorothy Johnstone, ARSA; *m* 1955, Jeanne Edith Nutt; one *s* two *d. Educ:* Aberdeen Grammar School; Aberdeen Univ.; Balliol College, Oxford. Served in HM Forces (Lieut, RA), 1944–47. Entered Foreign (now Diplomatic) Service, 1950; Third Secretary, Moscow, 1951; Foreign Office, 1953; First Secretary, Belgrade, 1956; Head of Chancery, Havana, 1959; transf. Washington, 1962; Asst, Northern Dept, FO, 1965; Counsellor and Consul-Gen., Djakarta, 1967–69; Head of South Asian Dept, FCO, 1969–73; Fellow, Centre for Internat. Affairs, Harvard Univ., 1973–74; Minister, Moscow, 1974–76; Asst Under-Sec. of State, FCO, 1976–78; Ambassador to Greece, 1978–82; Ambassador to Soviet Union, 1982–85. Hon. LLD Aberdeen, 1985. *Address:* 24 Cholmeley Park, Highgate, N6 5EU. *Club:* Travellers'. *Died 1 July 1986.*

**SUTHERLAND, Monica La Fontaine;** author; *b* 13 Sept. 1897; *d* of C. M. McAnally, Hon. Canon of Norwich, and Mabel Adelaide McAnally (*née* La Fontaine); *m* 1st, R. W. Porter, Hon. Canon of Chelmsford, Vicar of East Ham; two *d* (one *s* killed in action); 2nd, C. H. V. Sutherland, CBE, FBA; no *c. Educ:* Eastbourne; Paris. Formerly: served in National Fire Service and Red Cross Prisoner-of-War Books Section, 1941–45. Vice-Chm., Oxford Diocesan Council for Social Work, 1972–77. *Publications:* La Fontaine, 1953; Louis XIV and Marie Mancini, 1956; The San Francisco Disaster, 1959; various newspaper and magazine articles. *Recreations:* travel, languages. *Address:* Westfield House, Cumnor, Oxford. *T:* Cumnor 2178. *Died 6 Dec. 1982.*

**SUTHERLAND, Sir Neil;** *see* Sutherland, Sir F. N.

**SUTHERLAND, Scott,** RSA 1970; Head of Sculpture Department, Duncan of Jordanstone College of Art, Dundee, 1947–75, retired; *b* 15 May 1910; *s* of Major David Sutherland, MC, TD; *m* 1942; one *s* two *d. Educ:* Wick Academy; Wick High Sch.; Edinburgh Coll. of Art; Ecole des Beaux Arts, Paris. Works include: Commando Memorial, Spean Bridge, 1952; Black Watch Memorial, 1959; Hercules Linton 'Cutty Sark' Meml, Inverbervie, 1969; Leaping Salmon fountain gp for Norie-Miller Walk, Perth, 1971; The Beacon Lighter, silver statuette presented to HM the Queen by ROC, 1977. *Address:* 17 Norwood, Newport-on-Tay, Fife. *T:* Newport-on-Tay 3336. *Died 10 Oct. 1984.*

**SUTHERLAND-HARRIS, Sir Jack (Alexander),** KCVO 1968; CB 1959; Second Crown Estate Commissioner, 1960–68; *b* 8 May 1908; *s* of late Lieut-Colonel A. S. Sutherland-Harris, DL, JP, Burwash, Sussex; *m* 1934, Rachel Owen Jones, *yr d* of late Capt. Owen Jones,

CBE, Worplesdon, Surrey; two *s* two *d. Educ:* Winchester Coll.; New Coll., Oxford. Entered Min. of Agriculture and Fisheries as Asst Principal, 1932; Principal Private Secretary to Minister of Agriculture and Fisheries, 1941–43; Asst Sec., 1943–50; Under-Sec., 1950–60. *Address:* Old Well Cottage, Bury, Pulborough, West Sussex. *T:* Bury 465. *Club:* Royal Commonwealth Society.
*Died 28 Dec. 1986.*

**SUTTON, Janet Vida;** *see* Watson, J. V.

**SUTTON, Peter John;** Inspector of Shell Fisheries, on behalf of Ministry of Agriculture, Fisheries and Food, since 1980; *b* 31 May 1917; *s* of William Bertram and May Ethel Sutton; *m* 1949, Yvonne Joyce Swain. *Educ:* Gladstone's, Cliveden Place, London; Westminster School. Served War of 1939–45: Royal Gloucester Hussars, 1939; commnd Grenadier Guards, 1940; served N Africe, Italy, 1943–44. Articled Hempsons, Solicitors, 1936; admitted Solicitor, 1947. Legal Asst, Customs and Excise, 1938; Sen. Legal Asst, 1952; seconded as Legal Consultant, Cyprus Sovereign Base Areas, 1960–61; Asst Solicitor, 1969; Principal Asst Solicitor (Under Sec., Legal), Customs and Excise, 1976–80; retired from Civil Service, 1980. Member, Law Society. *Recreations:* tennis, golf, motoring, railways, space travel. *Address:* Heywood Close, Boldre, Lymington, Hants. *T:* Brockenhurst 2183. *Clubs:* Law Society, Civil Service; Brokenhurst Manor Golf. *Died 20 June 1982.*

**SUTTON, Sir Robert Lexington,** 8th Bt, *cr* 1772; *b* 18 Jan. 1897; *s* of Sir Arthur Sutton, 7th Bt, and Cecil (Blanche) (*d* 1948), *d* of W. D. Dumbleton, Cape Colony; *S* father, 1948; *m* 1936, Gwladys, *d* of Major A. C. Gover, MC; two *s. Educ:* Wellington; RMC, Sandhurst. Served European War, 1915–19. *Heir: s* Richard Lexington Sutton [*b* 27 April 1937; *m* 1959, Fiamma Ferrari; one *s* one *d*]. *Address:* Clinger Farm, Cucklington, Wincanton, Somerset BA9 9QQ. *T:* Wincanton 33209. *Died 6 Jan. 1981.*

**SUTTON, William Godfrey;** Principal and Vice-Chancellor, University of the Witwatersrand, Johannesburg, 1954–62; *b* 28 March 1894; *s* of late William Godfrey Sutton, and late Mary Sutton (*née* Bennett); *m* 1st, 1954, Aletta McMenamin (*née* Wilson) (*d* 1967); 2nd, 1970, Olive Henwood (*née* Hiles) (*d* 1973). *Educ:* King Edward VII School, Johannesburg; University of Cape Town. Served European War, 1916–18, in German East African Campaign. Asst Engineer, Union Irrigation Dept, 1918–26; attached to US Reclamation Service, 1921–22; Professor of Civil Engineering, Univ. of the Witwatersrand, Johannesburg, 1926–54; War of 1939–45 Gen. Manager Central Organisation for Tech. Trg, Dept of Defence, 1941–44; Chief Technical Advisor, Dept of Commerce and Industries, 1944–45. Former Mem., Exec. Council, Univs of British Commonwealth. President: South African Institute of Engineers, 1936; SA Instn of Civil Engrs, 1945; Associated Scientific and Tech. Socs of SA, 1951; former Mem. Council, ICE, London. Hon. LLD Witwatersand, 1963. KStJ 1922. *Recreation:* bowls. *Address:* 48 Eastwood Road, Dunkeld, Johannesburg, South Africa. *T:* 788–3053. *Clubs:* Rand, Country (Johannesburg).
*Died 15 April 1985.*

**SUTTON CURTIS, John,** CBE 1974; Chairman, Workington Saw Mills Ltd, 1966–76; *b* 2 July 1913; *s* of Harold Ernest Curtis; *m* 1936, Muriel Rose Hastwell; one *s. Educ:* Watford Grammar School. Served War of 1939–45, Royal Artillery. Thames Board Mills Ltd: Director, 1958; Vice-Chm., 1965; Dep. Chm. and Man. Dir, 1966–69; Chm., 1969–76. Chm., Assoc. of Board Makers, 1965–70; Pres., British Paper and Board Makers' Assoc., 1971–73 (Dep. Pres., 1973–75); Pres., Confederation of European Pulp, Paper and Board Industries (CEPAC), 1974–75 (Vice-Pres., 1973). Paper Industry Gold Medal, 1973. *Recreation:* motoring. *Address:* Covertside, 115a Langley Road, Watford, Herts WD1 3RP. *T:* Watford 26375. *Died 29 Dec. 1988.*

**SVENNINGSEN, Nils Thomas;** Grand Cross, Order of Dannebrog, Denmark; *b* 28 March 1894; *s* of Anders Svenningsen (Norwegian), Average Adjuster, and Anna Svenningsen (*née* Bennet, Swede); *m* 1922, Eva (*née* Larsen) (*d* 1960); one *d. Educ:* University of Copenhagen. Candidatus juris, 1917; practised as Assistant to a Danish Advocate in Copenhagen; entered Min. of Justice, Copenhagen, 1918. Joined Danish Foreign Service, 1920; Secretary to Danish Legation in Berlin, 1924–30; then different posts in Danish Foreign Ministry. Permanent Under-Secretary of State for Foreign Affairs, 1941–45; and 1951–61; Danish Ambassador to: Stockholm, 1945–50; Paris, 1950–51; the Court of St James's, 1961–64; retd. Chm., Swedish-Norwegian Commn on reindeer grazing, 1964. Hon. GBE 1957. *Recreation:* riding. *Address:* Overgaden oven Vandet 50, Copenhagen K, Denmark. *T:* 541566.
*Died 20 Oct. 1985.*

**SWAIN, Air Commodore (Francis) Ronald Downs,** CB 1954; CBE 1946 (OBE 1941); AFC 1937; psa; retired; *b* 31 Aug. 1903; *s* of late Major Charles Sanchez de Pina Swain, TD, Southsea, Hants; *m* 1938, Sarah Mitchell, *d* of Charles H. Le Fèvre, Washington, DC; three *d. Educ:* Stonyhurst Coll. Joined Royal Air Force, 1922; Wing

Comdr, 1939; Air Commodore, 1949. Commanded Cairo-Rhodesia Flight, 1933; gained World High Altitude Record, 1936 (AFC); served War of 1939–45 (despatches, OBE, CBE); Air Officer Commanding No 28 Group, RAF, 1949–50; Senior Air Staff Officer and Deputy Head of Air Force Staff, British Joint Services Mission, Washington, 1950–54, retired 1954. *Club:* Carolina Yacht (S Carolina).
*Died 28 Sept. 1989.*

**SWAIN, Freda Mary,** FRCM; composer and pianist; *b* Portsmouth, Hants, 31 Oct. 1903; *d* of Thomas Swain and Gertrude Mary (Allen) Swain; *m* 1921, Arthur Alexander (pianist, composer, Prof. at RCM) (*d* 1969). *Educ:* St John's Southsea (private sch.); Matthay Pianoforte Sch. (under Dora Matthay); RCM. Won Associated Board Exhibition for piano, Ada Lewis Scholarship for piano (RAM) and Portsmouth-Whitcombe Scholarship for Composition (RCM), all at an early age; chose latter and studied under Sir Charles Villiers Stanford at RCM and (during last year) under Arthur Alexander (piano); Sullivan Prize for composition and Ellen Shaw Williams Prize for piano; Prof. of piano, RCM, 1924–40; founded British Music Movement, later NEMO concerts, with which former is now incorporated; founded NEMO Music Teaching Centre (Oxon & Bucks), Matthay Method, 1971. Extensive tours of S Africa and Australia (lecturing and piano), 1940–43, mainly on behalf of British music. FRCM 1963. *Works in manuscript include:* orchestral; concertos (two piano, one clarinet); chamber music: two string quartets, one pianoforte quartet, violin and piano sonata, Poems for violin and piano, 'The River' for violin and piano, Sonata for violin solo, Summer Rhapsody for viola and piano, Rhapsody No 2 for viola and piano, piano Sonata for right hand, Three Movements for violin and piano, 'Quiddities' (for piano); Harp of Aengus for violin and orch.; Ballade for violin and piano; anthems and wedding anthems; hymns, various; Second Chance, one-act opera; Perceptions, Whirling Wheels and Flourish (for 2 pianos); two piano pieces for left hand alone; over 109 songs and two duets with piano; arrangements of works for two pianos, incl. various folk songs; pieces for recorder and piano. *Published and reproduced works:* Carol of the Seasons; Te Deum, Jubilate (both for choir and organ); Cantata in Memoriam; Bird of the Wilderness (Song Cycle); Hymns; Ballet-Scherzo for three pianos; Setting of Psalms 150 and 121 (voice and organ); Two Sonatas, Prelude and Toccata (piano); Unseen Heralds (choral with piano); Sing to Heaven (choir and piano, negro spiritual style); Satyr's Dance, and Fantasy March (both for saxophone and piano). *Works for occasions:* Fanfare and Anthem for 70th anniv. Tormead Sch., 1976, Guildford Cath.; A Queen's Prayer, to words by Elizabeth I, Fanfare for a Queen, and Royal Fanfare, first performance Royal Jubilee Concert, Guildford Cath., 1977. *Publications include: Piano:* Humoresque; Mountain Ash; An English Idyll; Two S African Impressions, 1950; Autumn Landscape; Wayward Waltz; Marionette on Holiday; Croon of the Sea; Musical Box; Windmill; *Clarinet:* The Willow Tree, 1948; Two Contrasts, 1953; Waving Grass; Laburnum Tree; Three Whimsies (solo); Rhapsody (with piano); *Oboe and Piano:* Paspy; Fantasy-Suite; *Piano and Flute or Violin:* Tambourin Gai; *Organ:* English Pastoral; *Hymn:* Breathe on me; *Songs:* The Lark on Portsdown Hill; The Green Lad from Donegal; settings of poems by Coppard, Strong, de la Mare, Housman, Shelley, Burns, Bridges and many others; 5 Shakespeare sonnets; part songs and numerous teaching pieces; *Choral:* A Chinnor Carol (unaccomp. voices), 1964; Sweet Content (SATB and piano); Two Christmas Carols; A Gaelic Prayer (choir and organ). *Recreations:* reading, the English countryside. *Address:* High Woods, Chinnor Hill, Chinnor, Oxfordshire OX9 4BD. *T:* Kingston Blount 51285.
*Died 29 Jan. 1985.*

**SWAIN, Air Cdre Ronald;** *see* Swain, Air Cdre F. R. D.

**SWAN, Sheriton Clements;** *b* 15 Jan. 1909; *s* of late Sir Charles Sheriton Swan, Stocksfield-on-Tyne; *m* 1936, Rosalind Maitland, *d* of late D. S. Waterlow; two *s* one *d. Educ:* Cambridge Univ. Went to Architectural Assoc. in London to complete architectural training; joined firm of Swan, Hunter and Wigham Richardson, Ltd, in 1935; retired 1971. *Address:* Milestone Cottage, Wall, Hexham, Northumberland NE46 4ED. *T:* Humshaugh 319.
*Died 5 Aug. 1986.*

**SWAN, Thomas,** MA, LLB; Partner in Warren Murton & Co., Solicitors, 1927–67; Chairman of Smith's Group of cos, 1963–67, and a director of other public cos; *b* 11 Aug. 1899; *s* of Thomas David Swan; *m* 1922, Iola Blanche Winfield Roll (*d* 1973); two *s* two *d. Educ:* Royal Grammar School, Newcastle upon Tyne; Emmanuel College, Cambridge. Served European War, 1914–18: Lt, The Black Watch, 1918–19; served War of 1939–45: Major, RA, 1940–45. Emmanuel College, 1919–21. Admitted Solicitor, 1923. Member of Worshipful Company of Fan Makers (Master, 1956–57). *Recreations:* golf, bridge. *Address:* 5A Old Palace Lane, Richmond, Surrey TW9 1PG. *T:* 01-940 4338. *Club:* Naval and Military.
*Died 15 March 1981.*

**SWAN, Lt-Col Sir William (Bertram),** KCVO 1988; CBE 1968; TD 1955; JP; farmer since 1933; Lord-Lieutenant of Berwickshire 1969–89; *b* 19 Sept. 1914; *er s* of late N. A. Swan, Duns, Berwickshire; *m* 1948, Ann Gilroy, *d* of late G. G. Hogarth, Ayton, Berwickshire; four *s. Educ:* St Mary's Sch., Melrose; Edinburgh Academy. Served 1939–42 with 4 Bn KOSB (UK and France) and 1942–45 with IA. President: Nat. Farmers Union of Scotland, 1961–62; Scottish Agric. Organisation Society Ltd, 1966–68; Mem., Development Commn, 1964–76; Chairman: Rural Forum Scotland, 1982–88; Scottish Veterans' Garden City Assoc., 1983–. County Comdt, Roxburgh, Berwick and Selkirk Bn, ACF, 1955–73. President: Scottish Cricket Union, 1972–73; Borders Area Scout Council, 1973–; Borders Assoc. of Youth Clubs, 1975–; Lowlands TA&VRA, 1983–86. Chm. of Govs, St Mary's Sch., Melrose, 1964–90. JP 1964. *Recreation:* sport. *Address:* Blackhouse, Reston, Eyemouth, Berwickshire TD14 5LR. *T:* Duns (0361) 82842.
*Died 4 Dec. 1990.*

**SWANN, Baron** *cr* 1981 (Life Peer), of Coln St Denys in the County of Gloucestershire; **Michael Meredith Swann;** Kt 1972; MA, PhD; FRS 1962; FRSE 1952; crossbencher; Principal and Vice-Chancellor, University of Edinburgh, 1965–73; Chairman, BBC, 1973–80; Chancellor, University of York, since 1979; *b* 1 March 1920; *er s* of late M. B. R. Swann, MD, Fellow of Gonville and Caius Coll., Cambridge, and late Marjorie (*née* Dykes) (she *m* 2nd, Sir Sydney Roberts, he *d* 1966); *m* 1942, Tess, ARCM, ARCO, *d* of late Prof. R. M. Y. Gleadowe, CVO, Winchester and late Cecil (*née* Rotton); two *s* two *d. Educ:* Winchester (Fellow, 1979); Gonville and Caius College, Cambridge (Hon. Fellow, 1977). Served Army, 1940–46, in various capacities, mainly scientific (despatches, 1944). Fellow of Gonville and Caius College, Cambridge, 1946–52; University Demonstrator in Zoology, Cambridge, 1946–52; Professor of Natural History, University of Edinburgh, 1952–65 (Dean, Faculty of Science, 1963–65). Member: Adv. Council on Educn in Scotland, 1957–61; Fisheries Adv. Cttee, Develt Commn, 1957–65; Council St George's School for Girls, 1959–75; Edinburgh Univ. Court, 1959–62; MRC, 1962–65; Cttee on Manpower Resources, 1963–68; Council for Scientific Policy, 1965–69; SRC, 1969–73; Adv. Council, Civil Service Coll., 1970–76; Council, St George's House, Windsor, 1975–84; Scientific Foundn Bd, RCGP, 1978–83. Chairman: Nuffield Foundation Biology Project, 1962–65; Jt Cttee on Use of Antibiotics in Animal Husbandry and Veterinary Medicine, 1967–68; Scottish Health Services Scientific Council, 1971–72; Jt Cttee of Inquiry into the Veterinary Profession, 1971–75; Council for Science and Society, 1974–78; Council for Applied Science in Scotland, 1978–80; Technical Change Centre, 1980–87; Cttee of Inquiry into Educn of Children from Ethnic Minority Gps, 1981–85; Co. Pensions Information Centre, 1984–89. Author of Swann reports on Scientific Manpower, 300 GEV Accelerator, Antibiotics, Veterinary Profession, Educn of Ethnic Minority Children. Director: Inveresk Res. Internat., Midlothian, 1969–72; New Court Natural Resources Ltd, 1973–85; Roy. Acad. of Music, 1980– (Chm. Governors, 1983–); Charities Investment Managers Ltd, 1981–88; M & G Group plc, 1981–88. Chm., Cheltenham Fest., 1983–. Mem. Bd of Trustees, Wellcome Trust, 1973–90; Trustee, BM (Nat. Hist.), 1982–86. Pres., Aslib, 1982–84. Governor, Ditchley Foundn, 1975–; Chm., Cttee of Management, LSHTM, 1982–88. Provost, Oriel Coll., Oxford, 1980–81. FIBiol; Hon. FRCSE 1967; Hon. FRCPE 1972; Hon. ARCVS 1976; Hon. Associate, BVA, 1984. Hon. LLD Aberdeen, 1967; DUniv: York, 1968; Edinburgh, 1983; Hon. DSc Leicester, 1968; Hon. DLitt Heriot Watt, 1971; Hon. DEd CNAA, 1988. *Publications:* papers in scientific journals. *Recreations:* gardening, sailing. *Address:* Tallat Steps, Coln St Denys, near Cheltenham. *T:* Fossebridge (0285) 720533; 23 Sheffield Terrace, W8. *Clubs:* Athenæum; New (Edinburgh).
*Died 22 Sept. 1990.*

**SWANN, Peter Geoffrey,** CBE 1981 (OBE 1973); MD, FRCP, FFOM; FInstPet; Director of Medical Services, Esso Europe Inc., 1975–84; Civil Consultant in Occupational Medicine to the Royal Air Force and the Royal Navy, 1979–84; *b* 18 Feb. 1921; *s* of Arthur Swann and Annette (*née* Watkins); *m* 1954, Ruth Audrey Stapleton; one *s* one *d. Educ:* Chigwell Sch.; London Hosp. Med. Coll. (MB, BS 1943; MD 1949). LRCP 1942, MRCP 1949, FRCP 1969; MRCS 1942. FInstPet 1975. Served War, RAFVR Med. Br., 1943–46, Flt Lieut. House physician appts, London Hosp., 1942; jt appt in pathology, Univ. of Oxford and Emergency Public Health Lab. Service, Oxford, 1943; Med. Registrar, subseq. Sen. Registrar, London Hosp. and Oldchurch Hosp., 1946–54; SMO, Esso Petroleum Co., 1954–61, CMO, 1961–75; Dean, Faculty of Occupational Medicine, RCP, 1978–81 (Fellow of Faculty, 1978). FRSM (Pres., Occup. Med. Sect., 1975). Chairman: Working Party on Occup. Med., RCP, 1976; Standing Cttee on Occup. Med., RCP, 1971–78; Health Adv. Cttee, Oil Cos Internat. Study Gp for Conservation of Clean Air and Water, Europe, 1972–84. Member: Specialist Adv. Cttee on Occup. Med., 1971–76 (Chm., 1973–76); Jt Cttee on Higher Med. Trng, 1973–76; Bd, Offshore Medical Support Ltd, Aberdeen, 1977–84; Working Party of MOs in Chemical Industry, EEC, Luxembourg, 1976–84; Standing Med. Adv. Cttee, DHSS, 1980–84; BMA; Council, RCP; Soc. of Occup. Med. (Hon.

Sec., 1966–70); Exec. Cttee and Advisory Bd, Inst. of Occupational Health, Univ. of Birmingham, 1980–84. Mem., Conf. on Med. Royal Colls and their Faculties, UK, 1978–81. Dep. Pres., RoSPA, 1980–84. Clinical Prof., Univ. of Miami, 1979. *Publications:* contrib. med. jls. *Recreations:* sailing, golf, squash. *Address:* Robinswood, Second Avenue, Frinton-on-Sea, Essex. *T:* Frinton-on-Sea 3678. *Clubs:* Royal Air Force; Royal Harwich Yacht; Frinton Golf.
*Died 15 Oct. 1988.*

**SWANN, Robert Swinney,** MBE 1947; HM Diplomatic Service, retired; *b* 17 Nov. 1915; *s* of R. N. and F. Swann. *Educ:* George Watson's Boys' College, Edinburgh; Edinburgh University. Indian Civil Service, 1938–47; joined Diplomatic Service, 1947; Counsellor Addis Ababa, 1965–69; Diplomatic Service Inspector, 1969–72; Counsellor, Bonn, 1972–74. Latterly engaged in legal-historical research and SDP/Alliance political work. *Recreations:* music, theatre. *Address:* 6 Collingham Gardens, SW5. *T:* 01–373 0445.
*Died 3 Oct. 1986.*

**SWANSON, Gloria May Josephine Swanson;** American film actress; *b* Chicago, 27 March 1899; *d* of Joseph and Adelaide Swanson; *m* 1st, Wallace Beery (marr. diss.); 2nd, Herbert K. Somborn (marr. diss.); 3rd, Marquis de la Falaise de la Coudraye (marr. diss.); 4th, Michael Farmer (marr. diss.); one *d*; 5th, William N. Davey (marr. diss.); 6th, William Dufty. Began career at Essanay in Chicago, then Keystone Comedies, Hollywood; starred in Triangle Films, for Cecil B. DeMille (six consec. films) and 20 for Famous Players-Lasky in Hollywood and NY; later formed Gloria Swanson Productions; and became owner-member of United Artists which released Loves of Sunya (which opened NY Roxy Theatre), Sadie Thompson, Queen Kelly (unreleased), The Trespasser (the first all-talking picture), What a Widow, and Perfect Understanding (with Laurence Olivier, made in England); among many other films starred in Music in the Air, Father Takes a Wife, Sunset Boulevard, 1950, and Airport, 1975. Also appeared in various theatrical rôles: 20th Century, with José Ferrer, Broadway, 1951; The Inkwell, 1962–63, and Reprise, 1967; Butterflies are Free, toured and on Broadway, 1970–72. Own television show, The Gloria Swanson Hour, 1948. Exhibn of paintings and sculpture, Hamiltons Gall., London, 1978. Palms and Officer, Académie des Beaux Arts; Cross of Honour and Merit, SMO Malta; OStJ 1963; Award from City of Paris and, among others, Foreign Critics Award; Neiman-Marcus Award for style; Hon. Comr of Youth and Fitness of NY, 1976. *Publication:* Swanson on Swanson, 1981. *Recreations:* sculpture, painting. *Address:* Gloria Swanson Archives, 920 5th Avenue, New York, NY 10021, USA.
*Died 4 April 1983.*

**SWANSTON, Commander David,** DSO 1945; DSC 1941, and Bar, 1942; RN; Deputy Serjeant at Arms, House of Commons, 1976–81; *b* 13 Feb. 1919; *s* of late Capt. D. S. Swanston, OBE RN; *m* 1st, 1942, Sheila Ann Lang (marr. diss.); one *s* (and one *s* decd); 2nd, 1953, Joan Margaret Nest Stockwood (*d* 1985), *d* of late I. H. Stockwood and Mrs Stockwood; one *s* one *d*. *Educ:* Royal Naval College, Dartmouth. Joined Royal Navy, 1932; served in submarines at Home, Mediterranean, and East Indies Stations, from 1939. Comd Shakespeare, 1944–45; Alaric, 1948; Tudor, 1949; Naval Liaison Officer, RMA Sandhurst, 1951–53; passed RN Staff course, 1953; Commander, 1953; invalided from Royal Navy, 1955. Asst Serjeant at Arms, House of Commons, 1957–76. Industrial employment, 1955–56. *Recreations:* golf, rifle shooting. *Address:* High Meadow, Linchmere, Haslemere, Surrey GU27 3NF.
*Died 4 May 1987.*

**SWANWICK, Betty,** RA 1979 (ARA 1972); RWS 1976; artist; book illustrator and mural painter; painter in watercolours; *b* 22 May 1915; *d* of Henry Gerad Swanwick. *Educ:* Lewisham Prendergast Sch.; Goldsmiths' Coll. Sch. of Art; Royal Coll. of Art. Has designed posters and press advertisements for LPTB, Shell-Mex, etc; murals for various organizations. *Publications:* The Cross Purposes, 1945; Hoodwinked, 1957; Beauty and the Burglar, 1958. *Recreation:* gardening. *Address:* Caxton Cottage, Frog Lane, Tunbridge Wells, Kent.
*Died 22 May 1989.*

**SWART, Hon. Charles Robberts,** DMS 1972; BA, LLB; State President, Republic of South Africa, May 1961–May 1967, retired; *b* 5 Dec. 1894; *m* 1924, Nellie de Klerk; one *s* one *d*. *Educ:* University Coll. of OFS, South Africa (BA, LLB); Columbia University, New York. Practised as Advocate, Supreme Court, S Africa, 1919–48; MP (Nat) for Ladybrand, OFS, 1923–38 and for Winburg, OFS, 1941–59; Minister of Justice, 1948–59; also Minister of Education, Arts and Science, 1949–50; Deputy Prime Minister and Leader of the House, 1954–59; Acting Prime Minister, 1958; Governor-General of the Union of South Africa, 1960–61. Hon. Col, Regt Louw Wepener, 1953–; Hon. Col, Regt Univ. Oranje-Vrystaat, 1963–. Chancellor, Univ. of OFS, 1950–76. Hon. LLD, Univ. of OFS, 1955, Rhodes Univ., 1962, and Potchefstroom Univ., 1963; Hon. Fellow, Coll. of Medicine of SA, 1963; Hon. Mem. SA Acad. of Science and Art; Life Mem. Fedn of Afrikaans Cultural Socs; Hon. Pres., Automobile Assoc. (SA); Hon. Fellow, SA Inst. of

Architects; Life Patron-in-Chief, SA Voortrekker Youth Movement. Hon. Freeman: Johannesburg; Durban; Bloemfontein; Kimberley, etc. *Publications:* Kinders van Suid-Africa, 1933; Die Agterryer, 1939. *Address:* De Aap, Brandfort, OFS, Republic of South Africa.
*Died 16 July 1982.*

**SWAYTHLING, 3rd Baron,** *cr* 1907; **Stuart Albert Samuel Montagu,** Bt, *cr* 1894; OBE 1947; late Grenadier Guards; Director, Messrs Samuel Montagu and Co. Ltd, 1951–54; *b* 19 Dec. 1898; *e s* of 2nd Baron and Gladys Helen Rachel, OBE, (*d* 1965), *d* of late Col A. E. Goldsmid; *S* father, 1927; *m* 1st, 1925, Mary Violet (from whom he obtained a divorce, 1942), *e d* of late Major Levy, DSO, and late Hon. Mrs Ionides; two *s* one *d*; 2nd, 1945, Mrs Jean Knox, CBE 1943, Director ATS. *Educ:* Clifton; Westminster; Trinity College, Cambridge. JP: Co. Southampton, 1928–48; Surrey, 1948–80. Pres., English Guernsey Cattle Society, 1950–51, 1971–72; Dep. Pres., Royal Assoc. of British Dairy Farmers, 1970–72, 1973–74 (Pres., 1972–73); Mem. Council: Nat. Cattle Breeders Assoc., 1955–67; Royal Agricl Soc., 1961–. Master of The Company of Farmers, 1962–63. *Heir:* *s* Hon. David Charles Samuel Montagu, *b* 6 Aug. 1928. *Address:* Crockerhill House, Chichester, West Sussex PO18 0LH. *T:* Chichester 532406.
*Died 5 Jan. 1990.*

**SWEETMAN, Seamus George,** MBE 1945; *b* 7 Nov. 1914; *s* of late James Michael Sweetman, KC and Agnes (*née* Fottrell); *m* 1939, Mary Alberta Giblett; one *s*. *Educ:* Beaumont Coll.; St John's Coll., Cambridge (BA). Pte Suffolk Regt, 1939; commnd The Buffs, 1940; Italian campaign (despatches); Lt-Col, GSO1, Sec. to Supreme Allied Comdr, Mediterranean, 1944–45. Various Unilever subsids, 1936–39; D. & W. Gibbs, 1950–55; Unilever NV, Rotterdam, 1955–57; Margarine Union, Germany, 1957–61; Dir, Unilever Ltd and Unilever NV, 1961–78; Vice-Chm., Unilever Ltd, 1974–78; Director: Commonwealth Development Finance Co., 1975–; Mercedes-Benz (UK) Ltd, 1980–. A Dep. Chm., Price Commn, 1977–79. Trustee, Leverhulme Trust, 1973–. CBIM. Officer, US Legion of Merit. *Recreations:* history, gardening, mountain walking. *Address:* Greenloaning, West Common Close, Harpenden, Herts. *T:* Harpenden 3221.
*Died 1 Feb. 1985.*

**SWINBURN, Maj.-Gen. Henry Robinson,** CB 1947; OBE 1945; MC 1922; *b* 8 May 1897; *e s* of late Henry Swinburn; *m* 1932, Naomi Barbara, *yr d* of late Major-General Sir C. P. Amyatt Hull, KCB; two *s*. Entered Indian Army, 1918; Royal Ludhiana Sikhs: served European War, 1914–18; Operations, NWF India, 1919, Iraq, 1920, Kurdistan, 1922–23 (wounded, MC). Staff College, Quetta, 1929–30; psc†; GSO II, GHQ India, 1932–36; Instructor Staff Coll., Camberley, 1937–38; Instructor Senior Staff College, Minley, 1939; Chief Instructor School of Military Intelligence, 1939–40; BEF France, 1940 (despatches, OBE); GSO I, 51 Highland Div., 1940; Director of Morale, India, 1945; Deputy Mil. Sec., GHQ India, 1946; Military Secretary, GHQ India, 1946–47; retired, 1948. Bt Major, 1934; Bt Lt-Col, 1939; Temp. Maj.-Gen., 1946; Subs Col, 1947; Counsellor, UK High Commn in India, 1948–49. Schools Liaison Officer, 1952–60. *Recreation:* fishing. *Address:* Stoney Close, Nunton, Salisbury, Wilts. *T:* Salisbury 29741. *Club:* Naval and Military.
*Died 27 Jan. 1981.*

**SWINLEY, Captain Casper Silas Balfour,** DSO 1941; DSC 1940; Royal Navy; *b* 28 Oct. 1898; *y s* of late Gordon Herbert Swinley, Assam, India, and Margaret Eliza, *d* of late Prof. J. H. Balfour, Edin.; *m* 1928, Sylvia Jocosa, 4th *d* of late Canon W. H. Carnegie, Rector of St Margaret's, Westminster, and Sub-Dean of Westminster Abbey; two *s* twin *d*. *Educ:* Epsom College. Entered Royal Navy with Special Entry Cadetship, 1916; served European War, 1916–18, as Midshipman and Sub-Lieut in HMS New Zealand; HMS Ceres, evacuation of Odessa, 1919–20; Queens' Coll., Cambridge, 1920; ADC and Private Sec. to Sir Charles O'Brien, Governor of Barbados, 1921–22; HMS Curacoa, evacuation of Smyrna, 1922–23; HMS Calcutta, Flagship West Indies Station, 1924–26; HMS Ganges, Boys' Training Establishment, Shotley, 1926–28; Flag-Lieut to Adm. Sir E. Alexander-Sinclair, C-in-C the Nore, 1928–30; HMS Repulse, 1930–32; HMS Carlisle, Africa Station, under Adm. Sir Edward Evans, 1932–34; Comdr 1934; commanded HMS Express, 5th Destroyer Flotilla, Abyssinian crisis, Spanish War, Jubilee Review, 1935–37; NID, Admiralty Naval Staff, 1937–39; commanded HMS Impregnable, Boys' Training Establishment, Devonport, 1939; commanded HMS Codrington and Dover Patrol Destroyers, taking King George VI to France and back; also Mr Winston Churchill to Boulogne, 1939–40; French Destroyer Brestois for Liaison duties; evacuation of Namsos, Norway; commanded demolition party at Calais (DSC), 1940; commanded HMS Isis, North Sea, Genoa, Greece, Crete (DSO); Syrian campaign, 1940–41; commanded HMS Miranda and Minesweepers, Great Yarmouth, Capt. 1942; Chief Staff Officer to Vice-Adm. Sir Ralph Leatham, Malta, 1942; Director of Service Conditions, Admiralty, 1943–45; commanded HMS Arethusa, 1945; Chief Staff Officer to Vice-Adm. Sir F. Dalrymple Hamilton, Malta, 1946; commanded HMS Flamingo and Senior Officer Reserve Fleet, Devonport, 1946–47; Chief of Naval Information, Admiralty, 1947–48; Captain in

Charge, Captain Superintendent and King's Harbour Master, Portland, 1949–51. Naval ADC to King George VI, 1951; Commodore and Chief of Staff, Royal Pakistan Navy, 1953–54. Senior Whale Fishery Inspector, South Georgia, 1959–60. Appeals Organiser, BRCS, Gloucestershire, 1963–67. *Recreation:* scrap-book collecting. *Address:* Broughtons, near Newnham, Glos. *T:* Westbury-on-Severn 328.
*Died 3 Sept. 1983.*

**SWINNERTON, Frank Arthur;** novelist and critic; President, Royal Literary Fund, 1962–66; *b* Wood Green, 12 Aug. 1884; *y s* of Charles Swinnerton and Rose Cottam; *m* 1924, Mary Dorothy Bennett; one *d. Publications:* The Merry Heart, 1909; The Young Idea, 1910; The Casement, 1911; The Happy Family, 1912; George Gissing: a Critical Study, 1912; On the Staircase, 1914; R. L. Stevenson: a Critical Study, 1914; The Chaste Wife, 1916; Nocturne, 1917; Shops and Houses, 1918; September, 1919; Coquette, 1921; The Three Lovers, 1922; Young Felix, 1923; The Elder Sister, 1925; Summer Storm, 1926; Tokefield Papers, 1927; A London Bookman, 1928; A Brood of Ducklings, 1928; Sketch of a Sinner, 1929; Authors and the Book Trade, 1932; The Georgian House, 1932; Elizabeth, 1934; The Georgian Literary Scene, 1935; Swinnerton: an Autobiography, 1937; Harvest Comedy, 1937; The Two Wives, 1939; The Reviewing and Criticism of Books, 1939; The Fortunate Lady, 1941; Thankless Child, 1942; A Woman in Sunshine, 1944; English Maiden, 1946; The Cats and Rosemary, (US) 1948, (England) 1950; Faithful Company, 1948; The Doctor's Wife Comes to Stay, 1949; A Flower for Catherine, 1950; The Bookman's London, 1951; Master Jim Probity, 1952; Londoner's Post, 1952; A Month in Gordon Square, 1953; The Sumner Intrigue, 1955; Authors I Never Met, 1956; Background with Chorus, 1956; The Woman from Sicily, 1957; A Tigress in Prothero, 1959; The Grace Divorce, 1960; Death of a Highbrow. 1961; Figures in the Foreground, 1963; Quadrille, 1965; A Galaxy of Fathers, 1966; Sanctuary, 1966; The Bright Lights, 1968; Reflections from a Village, 1969; On the Shady Side, 1970; Nor all thy Tears, 1972; Rosalind Passes, 1973; Some Achieve Greatness, 1976; Arnold Bennett: a last word, 1978. *Address:* Old Tokefield, Cranleigh, Surrey. *Club:* Reform (Hon. Life Mem.).
*Died 6 Nov. 1982.*

**SWIRE, John Kidston;** Director, John Swire & Sons, Ltd, 1920–68 (Chairman, 1946–66); Hon. President, Cathay Pacific Airways Ltd; Member, General Committee, Lloyd's Register of Shipping, 1940–68; *b* 19 Feb. 1893; *er s* of late John Swire, Hillingdon House, Harlow, Essex; *m* 1923, Juliet Richenda (*d* 1981), *d* of Theodore Barclay, Fanshaws, Hertford; two *s* two *d. Educ:* Eton Coll.; University Coll., Oxford. Major Essex Yeomanry, with whom he served in European War, 1914–19. DL Essex, 1928–68; High Sheriff, Essex, 1941–42. Min. of Shipping Rep. at Min. of Economic Warfare and on the Contraband Cttee, 1939–40; Chm. Port Employers in London and Port Labour Exec. Cttee, 1941–45. Chm. China Association, 1951–55. *Address:* Hubbards Hall, Harlow, Essex. *TA* and *T:* Harlow 29470. *Clubs:* Turf, Cavalry and Guards (Hon. Life Mem.), City of London (Hon. Life Mem.).
*Died 22 Feb. 1983.*

**SYCAMORE, Thomas Andrew Harding,** CBE 1949; retired; a Managing Director, Liebig's Extract of Meat Co. Ltd, 1963–66; Chairman, Chipmunk Ltd, 1962–66; Director: Beefex Products Ltd, 1954–66; Bellamy's Wharf & Dock Ltd, 1958–66; Oxo Ltd 1954–66 (Managing Director 1954–63); Oxo (Canada) Ltd, 1954–66; Oxo (Ireland) Ltd, 1954–66; Oxo (USA) Ltd, 1954–66; Thames Side Properties Ltd, 1955–66; Produits Liebig SA, Basle, 1965–66; Euro-Liebig SC, Antwerp, 1964–66; Compagnie Française des Produits Liebig SA, Paris, 1963–66; Compagnie Liebig SA, Antwerp, 1963–66; Compagnia Italiana Liebig SpA, Milan, 1963–66; Nederlandse Oxo Maatschappij NV, Rotterdam, 1963–66; Liebig GmbH, Cologne, 1963–66; Beefco Corp., New York, 1963–66 (Chairman, 1964–66); London Philharmonic Society Ltd, 1960–66; *b* 31 Aug. 1907; *s* of late Henry Andrew and Caroline Helen Sycamore; *m* 1932, Winifred Clara Pellett; one *s* two *d. Educ:* privately. At Oxford Univ. Press, 1924–35; Manufacturing Confectioners' Alliance, 1936–40 (Asst Sec. 1940); Food Manufacturers' Federation Inc., 1936–54; Asst Sec., 1940; Sec., 1945; Director and Gen. Sec., 1947. Secretary, Bacon Marketing Bd, and many other food manufacturers' associations, etc; Mem., Food Research Adv. Cttee, 1960–66; Vice-Pres., Assoc. Internat. de l'Industrie des Bouillons et Potages (Paris), 1963–65. Member Council: British Food Manufacturing Industries Research Association (formerly Sec.); Food Manufacturers' Federation, Inc.; Grocers' Institute (a Vice-Pres. 1958–66, Hon. Treas. 1961–66); English Stage Soc.; Mem. Grand Council, FBI (member many committees); Deputy Leader and Sec. of two productivity teams which went to the US; helped to create Food Industries Council (Sec. for many years); helped in formation of National College of Food Technology, and to establish British Food Fair at Olympia (Sec. for many years). Served on Councils or Committees of various other bodies; a Governor of several schools. President of Appeal, Royal Commercial Travellers' Schools, 1960–61; Life Hon. Vice-

President, Huddersfield Branch, United Commercial Travellers' Assoc., 1962; Chm., Nat. Music Council of Gt Brit., 1963–64. Freeman, City of London. Liveryman, Worshipful Company of Loriners; Life Mem., Guild of Freemen of City of London; FREconS; Hon. Fellow, Grocers' Institute; Officier de l'Ordre de la Couronne (Belgium), 1965. *Recreations:* music, theatre, reading, tennis, cricket. *Address:* 3 Yew Tree House, Wheel Lane, Westfield, Hastings, E Sussex TN35 4SG. *T:* Hastings 752619.
*Died 17 Feb. 1986.*

**SYER, William George,** CVO 1961; CBE 1957; *b* 22 June 1913; *s* of late William Robert Syer and Beatrice Alice Theresa Syer, Alton, Hants; *m* 1948, Marjorie Leila, *d* of late S. G. Pike, Essex; no *c. Educ:* Kent College, Canterbury. Joined Colonial Police Service, 1933; Gibraltar, 1933–35; Jamaica, 1935–40; Nigeria, 1940–51; Comr of Police, Sierra Leone, 1951; retired, 1962; Comr of Police, Swaziland, 1964–68. Sec., West Africa Cttee, 1970–78. Formerly Comr St John Ambulance Brigade, Sierra Leone. CStJ 1969. *Recreations:* travelling, birdwatching, walking. *Address:* Goldsborough Nursing Home, 9 Ripon Road, Harrogate HG1 2JA.
*Died 7 Feb. 1988.*

**SYERS, Sir Cecil George Lewis,** KCMG 1949 (CMG 1947); CVO 1941; JP; *b* 29 March 1903; *s* of late G. W. Syers; *m* 1932, Yvonne, *d* of late Inglis Allen; one *s. Educ:* St Paul's; Balliol Coll., Oxford (Scholar). 1st Class Honour Mods 1922, and Lit. Hum. 1925; MA 1929. Entered Dominions Office, 1925; Asst Private Sec. to Sec. of State for Dominion Affairs, 1930–34; Private Sec. to Prime Minister, 1937–40; Asst Sec., Treasury, 1940; Dep. UK High Comr in the Union of South Africa, 1942–46; an Asst Under-Sec. of State, CRO, 1946–48, Dep. Under-Sec. of State, 1948–51; High Comr for the UK in Ceylon, 1951–57; Doyen of Diplomatic Corps, Ceylon, 1953–57. Sec., UGC, 1958–63. Pres., Ceylon Branch, Oxford Soc., 1954–57; Pres., Classical Assoc. of Ceylon, 1956, 1957. Mem. Governing Body, SOAS, Univ. of London, 1963–73; Dir, Foundation Fund Appeal, Univ. of Kent at Canterbury 1964–66. JP Hove, 1967. *Address:* 25 One Grand Avenue, Hove, Sussex BN3 2LA. *T:* Brighton 732545.
*Died 4 Dec. 1981.*

**SYKES, Sir Charles,** Kt 1964; CBE 1956; FRS 1943; FInstP; DSc, PhD; DMet; Director, Thos Firth and John Brown Ltd, Sheffield, 1944–73 (Managing Director, 1951–67; Deputy Chairman, 1962–64); Chairman, Firth Brown Ltd, 1962–67; *b* 27 Feb. 1905; *m* 1930, Norah Staton. *Educ:* Staveley; Netherthorpe Grammar School; Sheffield Univ. Superintendent, Metallurgy Dept, National Physical Laboratory, 1940–44; Superintendent, Terminal Ballistics Branch, Armament Research Dept, 1943–44; Director of Research, Brown-Firth Research Laboratories, 1944–51. Pres., Inst. of Physics, 1952–54; Member, Council for Scientific and Industrial Research, 1962–65; Chairman, Adv. Councils on Research and Development, Min. of Power, later Dept of Trade and Industry: Fuel and Power, 1965–70; Iron and Steel, 1967–72. Pro-Chancellor, Sheffield University, 1967–71. Iron and Steel Inst. Bessemer Gold Medal, 1956; Glazebrook Medal and Prize (IPPS), 1967. *Address:* Upholme, Blackamoor Crescent, Dore, Sheffield. *T:* Sheffield 360339.
*Died 29 Jan. 1982.*

**SYKES, Christopher Hugh,** FRSL; author; Member, London Library Committee, 1965–74; *b* 17 Nov. 1907; 2nd *s* of late Sir Mark Sykes, Bt, Sledmere; *m* 1936, Camilla Georgiana (*d* 1983), *d* of El Lewa Sir Thomas Russell Pasha, CMG; one *s. Educ:* Downside; Christ Church, Oxford. Hon. Attaché to HM Embassy, Berlin, 1928–29, and to HM Legation, Tehran, 1930–31. Served War of 1939–45: 7 Battalion The Green Howards; GHQ, Cairo; HM Legation, Tehran; SAS Bde (despatches, Croix de Guerre). Special correspondent of the Daily Mail for the Persian Azerbaijan Campaign, 1946; Deputy Controller, Third Programme, BBC, 1948; Features Dept, BBC, 1949–68. *Publications:* Wassmuss, 1936; (with late R. Byron), Innocence and Design, 1936; Stranger Wonders, 1937; High Minded Murder, 1943; Four Studies in Loyalty, 1946; The Answer to Question 33, 1948; Character and Situation, 1949; Two Studies in Virtue, 1953; A Song of a Shirt, 1953; Dates and Parties, 1955; Orde Wingate, 1959; Cross Roads to Israel, 1965; Troubled Loyalty: a Biography of Adam von Trott, 1968; Nancy, the life of Lady Astor, 1972; Evelyn Waugh, 1975. *Recreation:* music.
*Died 8 Dec. 1986.*

**SYKES, Sir Francis (Godfrey),** 9th Bt, *cr* 1781, of Basildon; *b* 27 Aug. 1907; *s* of Francis William Sykes (*d* 1945) (*g g s* of 2nd Bt) and Beatrice Agnes Sykes (*née* Webb) (*d* 1953); *S* cousin, Rev. Sir Frederic John Sykes, 8th Bt, 1956; *m* 1st, 1934, Eira Betty (*d* 1970), *d* of G. W. Badcock; one *s* one *d*; 2nd, 1972, Nesta Mabel (*d* 1982), *d* of late Col and Mrs Harold Platt Sykes; 3rd, 1985, Ethel Florence, *d* of late Lt-Col and Mrs J. S. Liddell, and *widow* of B. G. Macartney-Filgate and of W. G. Ogden. *Educ:* Blundell's School, Devon; Nelson College, New Zealand. Tea planting, 1930; Air Ministry, 1939; fruit farming and estate management, 1945–57; Regional Sec., Country Landowners' Assoc., 1957–72. FCIS. *Heir:* *s* Francis John Badcock Sykes [*b* 7 June 1942; *m* 1966, Susan Alexandra, *er d* of Adm. of the Fleet Sir Edward Beckwith Ashmore, GCB, DSC; three *s*]. *Address:* 7 Linney, Ludlow, Shropshire SY8 1EF. *T:* Ludlow 4336.                              *Died 19 April* 1990.

**SYLVESTER, Albert James**, CBE 1920; JP; *b* Harlaston, Staffs, 24 Nov. 1889; *s* of late Albert and Edith Sylvester; *m* Evelyn (*d* 1962), *d* of late Rev. W. Welman, Reading; one *d. Educ:* Guild Street School, Burton-on-Trent; privately (champion typist). Private Secretary: to Sec. of Cttee of Imperial Defence, 1914-21; to Sec. of War Cabinet and of Cabinet, 1916-21; to Secretary, Imperial War Cabinet, 1917; to British Secretary, Peace Conference, 1919; to successive Prime Ministers, 1921-23; Principal Secretary to Earl Lloyd George of Dwyfor, 1923-45. Film, The Very Private Secretary, BBC TV, 1974; portrayed in BBC TV Series The Life and Times of Lloyd George, 1981; life story, The Principal Private Secretary, BBC Radio Wales, 1982, repeated BBC Radio 4, 1983. JP Wilts. 1953. Commander of the Order of the Crown of Italy, and Sacred Treasure of Japan. Supreme Award (with Honours), Ballroom and Latin American Dancing, Imperial Soc. of Teachers of Dancing, 1977; Alex Moore Award, 1977; Guinness Book of Records states is the oldest competitive ballroom dancer. *Publications:* The Real Lloyd George, 1947; Life with Lloyd George (diaries, ed Colin Cross), 1975. *Recreations:* riding and golf. *Address:* Rudloe Cottage, Corsham, Wilts. *T:* Hawthorn 810375. *Club:* National Liberal.
*Died 27 Oct.* 1989.

**SYME, Sir Colin (York)**, AK 1977; Kt 1963; LLB; retired solicitor and company director; Chairman, Broken Hill Pty Co. Ltd, 1952-71 (Director, since 1937); *b* 22 April 1903; *s* of Francis Mark Syme; *m* 1933, Patricia Baird (*d* 1981); three *s* one *d. Educ:* Scotch College, Claremont, WA; Universities of Perth and Melbourne, Australia. Partner, Hedderwick, Fookes & Alston, Solicitors, 1928-66. Pres., The Walter & Eliza Hall Inst. of Medical Research, 1961-78; Chairman: Cttee of Inquiry into Victorian (Aust.) Health Services, 1973-75; Victorian Health Planning Cttee, 1975-78; Hon. Mem., Aust. Inst. of Mining and Metallurgy. Hon. DSc Univ. of NSW, 1960; Hon. LLD Monash, 1981. Storey Medal, Aust. Inst. Management, 1971. *Recreation:* fishing. *Address:* 22 Stonnington Place, Toorak, Victoria 3142, Australia. *Clubs:* Melbourne, Australian (Melbourne); Links (New York).
*Died 19 Jan.* 1986.

**SYME, Sir Ronald**, OM 1976; Kt 1959; FBA 1944; retired as Camden Professor of Ancient History, Oxford, 1949-70; *b* 11 March 1903; *e s* of David and Florence Syme, Eltham, New Zealand. *Educ:* NZ; Oriel College, Oxford (Classical Prizes and First Class Hons, Lit Hum, 1927). Fellow of Trinity College, 1929-49; Conington Prize, 1939. Press Attaché with rank of First Secretary, HM Legation, Belgrade, 1940-41; HM Embassy, Ankara, 1941-42; Professor of Classical Philology, University of Istanbul, 1942-45; President, Society for the Promotion of Roman Studies, 1948-52; President, International Federation of Classical Societies, 1951-54; Secretary-General, Internat. Council for Philosophy and Humanistic Studies, 1952-71, Pres., 1971-75; Vice-President: Prize Cttee of Balzan Foundation, 1963; Assoc. Internat. pour l'Etude du Sud-Est Européen, 1967. Prof. of Ancient History, Royal Acad. of Arts, 1976-. Hon. Fellow: Oriel College, Oxford, 1958; Trinity College, Oxford, 1972; Emeritus Fellow, Brasenose College, 1970; Fellow, Wolfson Coll., 1970. Membre Associé de l'Institut de France (Académie des Inscriptions et Belles-Lettres), 1967; Corresp. Member, German Archæological Institute, 1931, Member, 1953; Member, Royal Danish Acad. of Letters and Sciences, 1951; For. Mem. Lund Society of Letters, 1948. Corresponding Member Bavarian Academy, 1955; For. Member: American Philosophical Soc., 1959; Amer. Acad. of Arts and Sciences, 1959; Massachusetts Historical Society, 1960; Istituto di Studi Romani, 1960; Amer. Historical Soc., 1963; Real Academia de la Historia, 1963; Istituto Lombardo, 1964; Acc. Torino, 1972; Corresponding Member Austrian Academy, 1960. Kenyon Medal, British Acad., 1975. Hon. LittD: NZ, 1949; Cambridge, 1984; Pavia, 1986; Athens, 1987; Madison, 1988; Hon. DLitt: Durham, 1952; Liège, 1952; Belfast, 1961; Graz, 1963; Emory, Ga, 1963; Ohio, 1970; Boston Coll., 1974; Tel-Aviv, 1975; Louvain, 1976; Ball State, Indiana, 1981; New York, 1984; Cologne, 1988; DèsL: Paris, 1963; Lyon, 1967; Hon. LLD Harvard, 1988. Commandeur de l'Ordre des Arts et des Lettres, 1975; Member, Orden Pour le Mérite für Wissenschaften und Künste, 1975. *Publications:* The Roman Revolution, 1939; Tacitus (2 vols), 1958; Colonial Elites, 1958; Sallust, 1964; Ammianus and the Historia Augusta, 1968; Ten Studies in Tacitus, 1970; Emperors and Biography, 1971; The Historia Augusta: a call for clarity, 1971; Danubian Papers, 1971; History in Ovid, 1978; Roman Papers, vols 1 and 2, 1979, vol. 3, 1984, vols 4 and 5, 1987; Some Arval Brethren, 1980; Historia Augusta Papers, 1983; The Augustan Aristocracy, 1986. *Address:* Wolfson College, Oxford. *Clubs:* Athenæum; Odd Volumes (Boston).
*Died 4 Sept.* 1989.

**SYMINGTON, David**, CSI 1947; CIE 1943; *b* 4 July 1904; 2nd *s* of James Halliday Symington, merchant, Bombay, India, and Maud

McGrigor (*née* Aitken); *m* 1929, Anne Ellen Harker; one *s* one *d. Educ:* Cheltenham College; Oriel College, Oxford (Scholar). Entered Indian Civil Service, 1926; held various appointments including Backward Classes Officer, Bombay Province, 1934-37; Municipal Commissioner, City of Bombay, 1938; ARP Controller, Bombay, 1941; Secretary to Government of Bombay, Home Dept, 1942, Secretary to Governor, 1943-47; retired from ICS, 1948; Member, John Lewis Partnership, 1948-52; Director, N Rhodesia Chamber of Mines, 1953-60; Chairman, Copperbelt Technical Foundation, 1955-60. Councillor, Royal Borough of Kensington, 1950. Member of Council, Cheltenham College, 1961-76. *Publications:* Report on Aboriginal Tribes of the Bombay Province, 1938; (as James Halliday): I Speak of Africa, 1965; A Special India, 1968 (repub. in Marathi, Poona, India, 1977); also short stories; (TV play) The Brahmin Widow, 1968. *Recreations:* writing, bridge. *Address:* 5 Paragon Terrace, Cheltenham, Glos.                  *Died 3 April* 1984.

**SYMINGTON, (William) Stuart**; United States Senator from Missouri, 1952-76; Director and Vice-Chairman, First American Bankshares Inc., Washington DC; *b* Amherst, Massachusetts, 26 June 1901; *s* of William Stuart and Emily Harrison Symington; *m* 1924, Evelyn Wadsworth (decd); two *s*; *m* 1978, Ann Hemingway Watson. *Educ:* Yale University; International Correspondence School. Joined Symington Companies, Rochester, New York, 1923; President Colonial Radio Co., Rochester, 1930-35; President, Rustless Iron & Steel Co., Baltimore, 1935-37; President and Chairman, Emerson Electric Manufacturing Co., St Louis, 1938-45; Surplus Property Administrator, Washington, 1945-46; Assistant Secretary of War for Air, 1946-47; Secretary of Air Force, National Defense, 1947-50; Chairman, National Security Resources Board, 1950-51; Administrator, Reconstruction Finance Corporation, 1951-52. Is a Democrat. *Address:* Box 1087, New Canaan, Conn 06840, USA.                              *Died 14 Dec.* 1988.

**SYMONDS, Joseph Bede**, OBE 1957; *b* 17 Jan. 1900; *m* 1921; four *s* six *d* (three *s* decd). *Educ:* St Bede's Secondary School, Jarrow. Councillor, Jarrow, 1929; Alderman 1935; Mayor 1945; County Councillor, Durham, 1946; Freeman, Borough of Jarrow, 1955. Past Chairman National Housing and Town Planning Council, 1948-50 (Exec. Member, 1938-65); Chairman Jarrow Housing Cttee, 1935. MP (Lab) Whitehaven, June 1959-70. *Recreations:* cricket; welfare work (old people); Air Training Corps. *Address:* 11 Hedworth View, Jarrow, Tyne and Wear NE32 4EW. *T:* Jarrow 897246.
*Died 29 March* 1985.

**SYMONS, Ernest Vize**, CB 1975; Director General, Board of Inland Revenue, 1975-77; *b* 19 June 1913; *s* of Ernest William Symons and Edith Florence Elphick; *m* 1938, Elizabeth Megan Jenkins; one *s* two *d. Educ:* Stationers' Company's Sch.; University Coll., London (Fellow, 1979). Asst Inspector, 1934; Admin. Staff Coll., Henley, 1956; Dep. Chief Inspector of Taxes, 1964-73; Chief Inspector of Taxes, 1973-75. Mem., Keith Cttee on Enforcement Powers of the Revenue Depts, 1980. Governor, E-SU, 1978, Dep. Chm., 1983-86; Hon. Treas., Nat. Assoc. for Care of Offenders and Prevention of Crime, 1979. Mem. College Council, UCL, 1975; Vice-Chm., London Welsh Trust, 1981-85 (Mem. Council, 1978-). Hon. Treasurer, Hon. Soc. of Cymmrodorion, 1980-. *Recreations:* chess, bridge. *Address:* 1 Terrace House, 128 Richmond Hill, Richmond, Surrey. *T:* 081-940 4967. *Club:* Athenæum.
*Died 5 Nov.* 1990.

**SYMONS, Noel Victor Housman**, CIE 1941; MC 1916; JP; Major, Army in India Reserve of Officers, 1934; *b* 27 Nov. 1894; *s* of late Edward William Symons, MA (double 1st), Fellow, St John's Coll., Oxford, 1880, later Headmaster King Edward VI's School, Bath, and Katharine Elizabeth, *sister* of A. E. and Laurence Housman; *m* 1924, Cicely Dorothea Richards; no *c. Educ:* King Edward VI's School, Bath. British Army, 1914-19, Lt Worcestershire Regt; Indian Civil Service, 1920; District work till 1931; Secretary, Board of Revenue, 1931-34; Private Secretary to Governor of Bengal, 1934-35; Revenue Secretary, Govt of Bengal, 1938-40; Commissioner, Presidency Division, and ARP Controller, Bengal, 1940; Commissioner, Rajshahi Division, and Additional Secretary, Civil Defence, Bengal, 1941; Joint Secretary, Civil Defence Dept, Govt of India, 1942; Director-General, Civil Defence, and Additional Secretary, Defence Dept, Govt of India, 1943; retired from ICS Aug. 1946. JP Hampshire, 1951. Appointed to Appeal Cttee, Quarter Sessions, 1959; Dep. Chm., Lymington Petty Sessions and Mem. Council, Magistrates' Assoc., 1964; Chm., Lymington Petty Sessions, 1966; supplemental list, 1969. *Publication:* The Story of Government House (Calcutta), 1935. *Recreations:* yachting, beagling, fell walking. *Address:* Bucklands, Lymington, Hants SO4 9DS. *T:* Lymington 72719. *Club:* Royal Lymington Yacht.
*Died 24 Jan.* 1986.

**SYNNOTT, Pierce Nicholas Netterville**, CB 1952; Deputy Under-Secretary of State, Ministry of Defence, 1964-65; *b* 6 Sept. 1904; *e s* of Nicholas J. Synnott, JP, Furness, Naas, and Barbara (*née* Netterville); *m* 1939, Ann (from whom he obtained a divorce, 1948), *d* of Sir Abe Bailey, 1st Bt, KCMG; one *s Educ:* Oratory School; Balliol College, Oxford. 1st Class Mods and 1st Class Litterae Humaniores, Oxford. Asst Principal, Admiralty, 1928; Principal, 1936. Served War of 1939–45 in Army (60th Rifles), in African and Italian campaigns. Returned to Admiralty, 1945; Under-Secretary, 1947; Deputy Secretary, 1958. Chancellor, Irish Assocs, Order of Malta, 1971–81, Vice-Pres., 1981. JP County of London, 1961. Order of St Olav, Norway (1st Class), 1947. *Address:* Furness, Naas, Co. Kildare. *T:* Naas 97203.           *Died* 23 *Oct.* 1982.

**SZENT-GYÖRGYI, Albert,** MD, PhD Cantab, Dhc; Scientific Director, National Foundation for Cancer Research, Massachusetts, USA, since 1975; *b* Budapest, 16 Sept. 1893; *s* of Nicholas Szent-Györgyi and Josephine, *d* of Joseph Lenhossék, Professor of Anatomy; *m* 1st, 1941, Marta Borbiro; one *d*; 2nd, Marcia Houston. *Educ:* Budapest University; Cambridge University. Matriculated Medical Faculty, Budapest, 1911; war service, 1914–18 (wounded); Assistant, University Pozsony, 1919; working at Prague and Berlin, 1919; in Hamburg in scientific research, 1919–20; Assistant at Univ. Leiden, Holland, 1920–22; privaat dozent at Groningen, 1922–26; working at Cambridge, England, with the interrruption of one year spent in USA, 1926–30; Prof. of Medical Chemistry, Szeged Univ., 1931–45; Professor of Biochemistry Univ. of Budapest, Hungary, 1945–47; Dir of Research, Inst. of Muscle Research, Mass, 1947–75. Formerly: Pres. Acad. of Sciences, Budapest; Vice-Pres. Nat. Acad., Budapest. Prix Nobel of Medicine, 1937; Visiting Prof., Harvard Univ., 1936; Franchi Prof., Univ. of Liége, Belgium, 1938. Cameron Prize (Edinburgh), 1946. Lasker Award, 1954. Hon. ScD Cantab, 1963. Hon. Fellow, Fitzwilliam Coll., Cambridge, 1967. *Publications:* Oxidation, Fermentation, Vitamins, Health and Disease, 1939; Muscular Contraction, 1947; The Nature of Life, 1947; Contraction in Body and Heart Muscle, 1953; Bioenergetics, 1957; Submolecular Biology, 1960; Science, Ethics and Politics, 1962; Bioelectronics, 1968; The Living State, 1972; Electronic Biology and Cancer, 1976; many scientific papers. *Recreations:* sport of all kinds, chiefly sailing, swimming and fishing. *Address:*

Marine Biological Laboratory, Woods Hole, Mass 02543, USA; Penzance, Woods Hole, Mass, USA.         *Died* 22 *Oct.* 1986.

**SZERYNG, Henryk;** Hon. Professor, Faculty of Music, Mexican National University, Mexico City; Concert Violinist, since 1933; *b* Warsaw, 22 Sept. 1918; Mexican Citizen since 1946; *m* 1984, Waltraud Von Neviges. *Educ:* Warsaw, Berlin, Paris. Graduated violin class of Carl Flesch, Berlin, 1933; 1st Prize special mention, Paris Conservatoire, 1937; Composition study with Nadia Boulanger, 1934–39. War of 1939–45: played over 300 concerts for Allied Armed Forces, Red Cross and other welfare institutions in Scotland, England, Canada, USA, Caribbean area, Middle East, North Africa, Brazil and Mexico. Has covered the five continents in recitals, also soloist with major orchestras, 1953–. Mexican Cultural Ambassador, 1960–; Cultural Adviser to Mexican delegn, UNESCO, Paris, and to Mexican Foreign Ministry, 1970–. Numerous recordings; Grand Prix du Disque, 1955, 1957, 1960, 1961, 1967, 1969. Hon. RAM, 1969. Hon. Pres., Musical Youth of Mexico, 1974. Hon. DHL Georgetown Univ., 1982. Officer of Cultural Merit, Roumania, 1935; Kt Comdr, Order of Polonia Restituta (Poland), 1956; Silver Medal of City of Paris, 1963; Officer, Order of Arts and Letters (France), 1964; Comdr, Order of the Lion (Finland), 1966; Ordre du Mérite en faveur de la culture polonaise, 1970; Alfonso el Sabio Cross (Spain), 1972; Chevalier, 1972, Officier, 1984, Légion d'Honneur (France); Mozart Medal, Salzburg, 1972; Comdr Al Merito (Italy), 1974; Comdr, Order of Flag with Golden Star (Yugoslavia), 1976; Order of the Crown (Belgium), 1976; Gran Premio Nacional (Mexico), 1979; Golden Medal, City of Paris, 1981; Hon. Citizen, Poznan, Poland, 1981; Golden Medal, City of Jerusalem, 1983; Commandeur, Ordre de St Charles (Monaco), 1985; Golden Cross of Merit (Poland), 1987. *Publications:* several chamber music works, also for piano and violin. Revised violin concertos by Nardini, Vivaldi and others, sonatas and partitas by Bach; re-discovered Paganini Concerto No 3 (World Première, London, 1971). *Recreations:* golf, reading. *Address:* c/o Mexican Embassy, 9 rue Longchamp, 75116 Paris, France.                 *Died* 3 *March* 1988.

# T

**TABOUIS, Geneviève;** Officier de la Légion d'Honneur, 1959; Commandeur de l'Ordre National du Mérite; Rédacteur Diplomatique à RTL; *b* 23 Feb. 1892; *fille* du peintre Le Quesne; nièce des Ambassadeurs Jules et Louis Cambon; *m* 1916, Robert Tabouis (*d* 1973), Président-Directeur Général de la Cie Générale de Télégraphie sans Fil; one *s* one *d*. *Educ*: Couvent de l'Assomption; Faculté des lettres, Paris, Ecole archéologique du Louvre. Journaliste diplomatique; débuta en 1924 à la SDN comme correspondante de La Petite Gironde, du Petit Marseillais; chargée de 1924 à 1932 de toutes les grandes enquêtes diplomatiques, de tous les grands reportages politiques et de nombreuses conférences diplomatiques; diplomatic Leader à La Petite Gironde et Le Petit Marseillais, 1932–37, à L'Œuvre 1932–40; fonda et dirigea l'hebdomadaire français, Pour La Victoire, New York, 1939–45; retour à Paris, 1946–56; diplomatic leader à La France Libre, L'Information, L'Espoir. Correspondant diplomatique du Sunday Dispatch de Londres, de La Critica de Buenos-Ayres; collaboratrice à de nombreux journaux et revues; déploya une grande activité dans les meetings politiques et les conférences politiques et diplomatiques; nombreuses hautes décorations étrangères. Hon. Vice-Présidente de l'Association de la Presse Diplomatique française. *Publications*: 4 livres historiques couronnés par l'Académie Française: Tout Ank Amon, Nabuchodonosor, Salomon, Sybaris; une biographie: Jules Cambon par l'un des siens (couronné par l'Académie Française); un livre de politique: Le Chantage à la Guerre; Albion Perfide ou Loyale; tous ces ouvrages ont paru également en Angleterre; Ils l'ont appelée Cassandre (New York); Grandeurs et Servitudes américaines (Paris); Quand Paris Résiste; 20 Ans de Suspense Diplomatique; Les princes de la paix, 1980. *Address*: 3 square Claude-Debussy, 75017 Paris, France.                    *Died 22 Sept.* 1985.

**TAFT, Charles Phelps;** Attorney at Law; Mayor of Cincinnati, USA, 1955–57; Hon. Chairman, US Advisory Committee on Voluntary Foreign Aid (Agency for International Development) (formerly Chairman); General Counsel, Committee for a National Trade Policy; *b* 20 Sept. 1897; *s* of William H. Taft (27th President of the US and Chief Justice) and Helen Herron; *m* 1917, Eleanor Kellogg (*d* 1961), *d* of Irving H. Chase of Ingersoll-Waterbury Co.; two *s* three *d* (and two *d* decd). *Educ*: The Taft School, Watertown, Connecticut; Yale University. BA 1918, LLB 1921; Hon. LLD (Yale), 1952, etc; Doctor of Hebrew Letters, Hebrew Union College, 1948. Enlisted 12 FA 2nd Div., AEF, 1917 (Fr., Jan.–Dec. 1918), discharged as 1st Lt 1919. Prosecuting Attorney Hamilton County, 1927–28; Partner: Taft, Stettinius & Hollister, 1924–37; Headley, Sibbald & Taft, 1946–59; Taft & Lavercombe, 1959–66; Taft & Luken, 1967–74; Chm. Fed. Steel Mediation Bd, 1937; Dir, Community War Services, Fed. Security Agency, 1941–43; Dir, Wartime Economic Affairs, Department of State, 1944–45; City Councilman of Cincinnati, 1938–42, 1948–51, 1955–77. Trustee, Twentieth Century Fund, Carnegie Institution of Washington, Committee for Economic Development; Senior Warden, Christ Episcopal Church, Cincinnati; Pres. Fed. Council of Churches of Christ in America, 1947–48. Medal for Merit, 1946. *Publications*: City Management: The Cincinnati Experiment, 1933; You and I— and Roosevelt, 1936; Why I am for the Church, 1947; Democracy in Politics and Economics, 1950. *Recreations*: fishing, local politics, topical daily broadcasting. *Address*: 3550 Shaw Avenue, Cincinnati, Ohio 45208, USA.                              *Died 23 June* 1983.

**TAHOURDIN, Dr Peter Anthony Ivan,** CBE 1970 (OBE 1956); British Council Service, retired; *b* 12 Oct. 1920; *yr s* of John St Clair Tahourdin and Suzanne Perscheid; *m* 1945, Betty Yeo, Court Colman, Glam; one *s* two *d*. *Educ*: Merchant Taylors' Sch.; University Coll., Oxford (Open Scholar, Edmund Spenser Exhibr, MA, BSc, DPhil). Research scientist, UK Atomic Energy Project, 1942–46; joined British Council, 1946: Science Officer, Italy, 1946–54; Asst Rep., Yugoslavia, 1954–58; Rep., Israel, 1958–61; Asst Controller, Books, Arts and Science Div., 1961–67; Rep., Yugoslavia, 1967–69; Dep. Controller, Books, Arts and Science Div., 1969–70; Controller, Educn and Science Div., 1970–73; Asst Dir-Gen., 1973–77; Dep. Dir-Gen., 1977–81. Research Associate, Airey Neave Meml Trust Project, 1981–. *Publications*: contrib. professional jls on sci. subjects and the cinema. *Recreations*: talking, the cinema, industrial archaeology, photography. *Address*: 2 Twyford Avenue, W3 9QA. *T*: 01-992 5758.

*Died 18 April* 1983.

**TAIT, Sir James (Blair),** Kt 1963; QC (Australia); Barrister; *b* 15 October 1890; *s* of John Tait; *m* 1st, 1922, Annie Frances (decd), *d* of Dr George Howard; one *s* one *d*; 2nd, 1964, Sophie, widow of Dr J. Thomson-Tait. *Educ*: Geelong College; Melbourne University. War, 1914–18: Lt Aust. Flying Corps; Pilot Officer in France. Called to Bar in Victoria, 1919; KC 1945. Hon. Treas., Victorian Bar Council, 1939–74 (Chm., 1952–53); Past Pres., Graduate Union, Melbourne Univ.; Chairman: Equity Trustees Co. Ltd; Barristers' Chambers Ltd; Dir, Group Holdings Ltd. Chairman. Cttee of Inquiry into Stevedoring Industry in Australia, 1955–57. *Recreations*: golf, bowls. *Address*: Owen Dixon Chambers, 205 William Street, Melbourne, Victoria 3000, Australia. *T*: Melbourne 60.0791. *Clubs*: Australian, Royal Automobile of Victoria (Melbourne).                              *Died 4 July* 1983.

**TAIT, Air Vice-Marshal Sir Victor Hubert,** KBE 1944 (OBE 1938); CB 1943; *b* 8 July 1892; *s* of Samuel Tait, Winnipeg; *m* 1st, 1917; one *d*; 2nd, 1929; one *s*; 3rd, 1957, Nancy Margaret, *d* of late Andrew Muecke, Adelaide, Australia. *Educ*: University of Manitoba (BSc). Canadian Army, 1914–17; RFC and RAF, 1917–45. Director of Radar and Director-General of Signals, Air Ministry, 1942–45; Operations Director, BOAC, 1945–56. Chairman: International Aeradio Ltd, 1946–63; Lindley Thompson Transformer Co., 1959–66; Ultra Electronics (Holdings) Ltd, 1963–67 (Dir, 1955–72); Dir, Ultra Electronics Ltd, 1956–72. Air Transport Electronic Council, UK, 1958. Governor, Flight Safety Foundn of America, 1959–69. President, British Ice Hockey Assoc., 1958–71. Mem. Council, RGS, 1965–70. Order of the Nile (Egypt), 1936; Order of Merit (USA), 1945. *Address*: 81 Swan Court, SW3. *T*: 01–352 6864. *Clubs*: Hurlingham, Royal Air Force.
*Died 27 Nov.* 1988.

**TALBOT OF MALAHIDE,** 9th Baron *cr* 1831 (Ire.); **Joseph Hubert George Talbot;** Baron Malahide of Malahide (Ire.), 1831; Hereditary Lord Admiral of Malahide and adjacent seas (15 Edward IV); retired; *b* 22 April 1899; *s* of John Reginald Charles Talbot (*d* 1909) and Maria Josephine (*d* 1939), *d* of 3rd Duc de Stacpoole; *S* brother, 1975; *m* 1st, 1924, Hélène (*d* 1961), *o d* of M. Gouley; 2nd, 1962, Beatrice Bros (marr. diss. 1970). *Educ*: Beaumont College. *Heir*: *cousin* Reginald John Richard Arundell [*b* 9 Jan. 1931; *m* 1955, Laura Duff, *yr d* of late Group Captain Edward John Tennant, DSO, MC; one *s* four *d*].                        *Died 20 Feb.* 1987.

**TALBOT, Frank Heyworth,** QC 1949; *b* 4 June 1895; *s* of Edward John Talbot and Susan (*née* Heyworth); *m* 1st, 1922, Mabel Jane (*d* 1956), *d* of John Williams, Brecon; two *s*; 2nd, 1969, Heather, *d* of J. F. Williams, Great Missenden. *Educ*: Tottenham Grammar School; London Univ. (LLB). Civil Service, 1912–31. Inns of Court Regt, 1918. Called to the Bar, Middle Temple, 1931 (Bencher, 1958); *aeg* Lincoln's Inn, 1951. Practice at the Bar, 1931–84. *Recreation*: music. *Address*: 9 West Field, Little Abington, Cambridge CB1 6BE. *T*: Cambridge 891330.

*Died 6 March* 1990.

**TALLACK, Sir Hugh M.;** *see* Mackay-Tallack.

**TALLERMAN, Dr Kenneth Harry,** MC; MA, MD, FRCP; retired; Consulting Physician, Paediatric Department, The London Hospital; Consulting Paediatrician, St Margaret's Hospital, Epping; Hon. Lieutenant-Colonel RAMC; *b* London, 1894; *s* of late P. Tallerman and late Mrs C. G. L. Wolf; *m* 1st, 1929, Alice Campbell (*d* 1960), *yr d* of late D. C. Rose, Otago, NZ; 2nd, 1961, Florence M., widow of Frank Keeble and *d* of late Canon Small. *Educ*: Charterhouse School; Caius College, Cambridge University. Served in the Royal Field Artillery during European War, 1914–19, and in the RAMC during War of 1939–45; graduated in Medicine from St Thomas's Hosp., and obtained the degree of MD (Cantab); FRCP (London); late Cons. Pædiatrician, North-East Metropolitan Regional Board and Dr Barnardo's Home, and Physician to The Infants, and Paddington Green Children's Hospitals, Asst to the Medical Unit St Thomas's Hospital, Fellow and Instructor in Pædiatrics, Washington University School of Medicine, USA, etc. Hon. Member (Past Pres.) Brit. Pædiatric Assoc.; Past Pres. Pædiatric Section, RSM. *Publications*: The Principles of Infant Nutrition (with C. K. Hamilton), 1928; numerous scientific and medical papers, 1920–58. *Recreation*: gardening. *Address*: Brantham Lodge, Brantham, near Manningtree, Essex. *T*: Holbrook 328385. *Club*: Savile.                              *Died 25 Oct.* 1981.

**TALLIS, Gillian Helen, (Mrs Walter Tallis);** *see* Mackay, G. H.

**TANG, Sir Shiu-kin,** Kt 1964; CBE 1957 (OBE 1949; MBE 1934); JP; Chairman and Managing Director of Kowloon Motor Bus Co. (1933) Ltd since its inception; *b* 21 Mar. 1901; *s* of late Tang Chi-Ngong, JP; *m* Fung Kam May; one *s* one *d*. *Educ*: Queen's Coll., Hong Kong; St Stephen's Coll., Hong Kong. Dir, Tung Wah Hosp., 1924 (Chm. Bd of Dirs, 1928); Life Mem., Court of Univ. of Hong Kong; Member: Urban Coun., 1938–41; St John Coun. for Hong Kong, St John Ambulance Assoc. and Bde; Grantham Scholarships Fund Cttee; Cttee of Aberdeen Tech. Sch.; Chinese Temples Cttee, 1934–64; Bd of Chinese Perm. Cemetery; Tung Wah Gp of Hosps Adv. Bd; Po Leung Kuk Perm. Bd of Dirs (Chm. 1932); Exec. Cttee, Nethersole, Alice and Ho Miu Ling Hosp.; Trustee, Street Sleepers' Shelter Soc.; Vice-Pres. and Trustee of Hong Kong Br., Brit. Red Cross Soc.; Vice-President: The Boy Scouts' Assoc.; S China Athletic Assoc.; Adviser: Hongkong Juvenile Care Centre; Chinese Chamber of Commerce. Hon. LLD, Hong Kong, 1961. JP Hong Kong, 1929. Certificate of Honour Class I, and Life Mem.,

British Red Cross Soc., 1967. KStJ 1962. *Address:* 5 Broom Road, Hong Kong.                                              *Died* 19 *June* 1986.

**TANGNEY, Dame Dorothy Margaret,** DBE 1968; Senator for West Australia, 1943–68; *b* 13 March 1911; *d* of E. Tangney, Claremont, West Australia. *Educ:* St Joseph's Convent, Fremantle, University of West Australia. Teaching staff, Education Department, West Australia. First woman to be elected to Commonwealth Senate. Mem., Standing Cttee, Convocation, University of West Australia. *Recreations:* tennis, motoring, badminton, reading. *Address:* 12 Mary Street, Claremont, WA 6010, Australia. *T:* 31 2631.
*Died* 2 *June* 1985.

**TANN, Florence Mary,** CBE 1952; MA Cantab; *b* 12 Aug. 1892; *d* of William Robert Baldwin Tann, organist and choirmaster. *Educ:* Norwich High School; Girton Coll., Cambridge. Teaching in schools in S Africa, 1915–18; English Lecturer, University of Witwatersrand, Johannesburg, 1918–19; Organiser, National Union of Societies for Equal Citizenship, 1920–21; HM Inspector of Schools, 1921; Divisional Inspector, Board of Education, 1940–45; Chief Inspector, Primary Schools, Ministry of Education, 1945–52. Member National Book League. *Recreations:* gardening, needlework. *Address:* 17 Cedar Way, Henfield, West Sussex. *T:* Henfield 2488. *Club:* University Women's.
*Died* 26 *Sept.* 1981.

**TANNER, Norman Cecil,** FRCS; Hon. Consulting Surgeon: Charing Cross Hospital; St James's Hospital, London; *b* 13 June 1906; *s* of late Henry John Tanner and of Mrs Annie Tanner, Bristol; *m* 1940, Dr Evelyn Winifred Glennie, Aberdeen; two *s* one *d. Educ:* Merchant Venturers School, Bristol; Bristol University. MB, ChB 1929, MD 1954, Bristol; MRCS, LRCP 1929; FRCS 1931. Resident hosp. appts, many Bristol and London hosps. Inaugurated gastro-enterological dept at St James's Hosp., 1939; Jacksonian Prize, 1948; Lectures: First Simpson-Smith Memorial, 1949; Macarthur, Edinburgh, 1951; Lettsomian, London, 1954; Price, Univ. of Utah, 1966; Gallie, Univ. of Toronto, 1968; Moynihan, Leeds, 1969; Visiting Prof. of Surgery: Ein Shams Univ., Cairo, 1954; Royal North Shore Hosp., Sydney, Australia, 1960; Canadian Univs, 1965; Univ. of Los Angeles, 1968; Univ. of Quebec, 1971; Univ. of Singapore, 1971; Hunterian Prof., RCS, 1960 (Past Mem. Council, RCS). Formerly: Vice-Chm., Bristol Journal of Surgery; Asst Editor, Gut. Visitor for King Edward VII Hosp. Fund for London. Former Examr in Surgery to Univs of Cambridge and London. President: Clinical Sect., RSM, 1961–63, Sect. of Surgery, 1965–66; British Soc. Gastro-enterology, 1967–68; W London Med. Chirurgical Soc., 1968–69. Hon. Lectr in Surgery, St Thomas' Hosp. Liveryman, Soc. of Apothecaries, 1971; Freeman, City of London, 1969. Hon. FACS 1966; Hon. FRCSI 1969; Hon. FRSM 1976; Hon. Fellow, Med. Soc. London, 1980; Hon. Member: Bristol Medico-Chirurgical Soc.; Wessex Surgeons Club; Hellenic Soc. of Surgery, 1973; Hon. Fellow, Assoc. of Surgeons of E Africa. Grand Cross, Patriarchal Order, St Mark, Alexandria; Grand Band of Star of Africa (Liberia). *Publications:* (ed) Tumours of the Oesophagus, 1961; chapters in: Techniques in British Surgery, 1950; Abdominal Operations, 1952; Management for Abdominal Operations, 1953, 1957; Modern Operative Surgery, 1956; Operative Surgery, 1956; Modern trends in Gastroenterology, 1958; Recent Advances in Surgery, 1959; Demonstrations of Operative Surgery for Nurses; Cancer, Vol. 4 1958; many publications in The Medical Annual, Brit. Jl of Surg., Lancet, BMJ, etc. *Recreations:* golf, ski-ing, music. *Address:* 89 Rivermead Court, SW6 3SA. *T:* 01-736 2312. 5 Beaufort Road, Clifton, Bristol BS8 2JT. *Clubs:* Athenæum, Hurlingham, Coombe Wood Golf.                              *Died* 12 *Oct.* 1982.

**TAPLIN, Walter;** author and journalist; *b* Southampton, 4 Aug. 1910; *m;* three *s* two *d. Educ:* University College, Southampton (Foundation Scholar); The Queen's Coll., Oxford (Southampton Exhibitioner). Tutor-Organiser for Adult Education, W Hants and E Dorset, 1936–38; Editorial Staff of The Economist, 1938–40; Ministry of Food, 1940–42; Offices of the War Cabinet (Central Statistical Office), 1942–45; joined the Spectator as Asst Editor, 1946; Editor, 1953–54; Senior Economist, Iron and Steel Board, 1955–56; Research Fellow in Advertising and Promotional Activity, London School of Economics and Political Science, 1957–61. Editor: Accountancy, 1961–71; Accounting and Business Research, 1971–75. *Publications:* Advertising: A New Approach, 1960; Origin of Television Advertising, 1961; History of the British Steel Industry (with J. C. Carr), 1962. *Recreation:* reading. *Address:* 8 Oxford Road, Farmoor, Oxford OX2 9NN. *Club:* Reform.
*Died* 19 *Jan.* 1986.

**TARVER, Major-General Charles Herbert,** CB 1961; CBE 1958; DSO 1945; DL; jssc; psc; late Infantry; retired Feb. 1964; *b* 6 Oct. 1908; *s* of Major-General A. L. Tarver, CB, CIE, DSO; *m* 1932, Margaret Poad; three *s. Educ:* King's School, Bruton; RMC, Sandhurst. Deputy Director of Military Intelligence, War Office, 1956–58; Assistant Chief of Staff (Intelligence) at Supreme Headquarters, Allied Powers Europe, 1958–61; Chief of Staff to C-in-C Allied

Forces Northern Europe, 1961–64. Colonel 1953; Brigadier, 1957; Major-General, 1958. Dep. Col, The Queen's Regt, 1967–71; Hon. Col, 7th Bn, The Queen's Regt (E Kent), 1970–71. DL, Kent, 1968. *Recreations:* golf, fishing. *Address:* Flat 2, 23 Clifton Crescent, Folkestone, Kent.                                         *Died* 13 *May* 1982.

**TASKER, Antony Greaves,** CBE 1966 (OBE 1945; MBE 1943); Assistant Secretary-General and Managing Director Commonwealth Fund for Technical Co-operation, Commonwealth Secretariat, 1974–78; *b* 27 March 1916; *o s* of late Captain R. G. Tasker, Worcestershire Regt, and Vera, OBE, *d* of Rev. T. M. Everett (she *m* 2nd, Harold Raymond, OBE, MC, who *d* 1975); *m* 1940, Elizabeth Gilmor, *e d* of late Maj. Harold Carter, TD. *Educ:* Bradfield Coll.; Christ Church, Oxford. Served War of 1939–45 (despatches twice); Western Desert, Sicily, Italy, NW Europe, SE Asia; Col GS(I). Org. Dir, Internat. Tea Market Expansion Bd, 1948–52; Dir Public Rel., Booker Gp of Cos in Guyana, 1954–62 (Chm., 1962–67); Dir, Overseas Develt Inst., 1968–74. Member, Br. Guiana Senate, 1961–64 (MLC, 1957–61); Governor: Inst. of Develt Studies, Sussex, 1968–78; Oversea Service Coll., 1968–78; Mem. Council, Overseas Develt Inst., 1975–78. Member: Econ. and Social Cttee, EEC, 1973–74; Exec. Cttee, British Council, 1970–74; Voluntary Cttee on Overseas Aid and Develt, 1968–74; British Volunteer Programme, 1968–74. US Bronze Star, 1944; Officer, US Legion of Merit, 1945. *Address:* 1A North Pallant, Chichester, W Sussex PO19 1TJ. *T:* Chichester (0243) 787513.
*Died* 19 *July* 1990.

**TASKER, Sir Theodore James,** Kt 1937; CIE 1932; OBE 1919; Indian Civil Service, retired; County Councillor, Dorset (Swanage-East), 1946; County Alderman, 1955–70; *b* 20 Jan. 1884; *s* of late Rev. John Greenwood Tasker, DD; *m* 1915, Jessie Helen Mellis-Smith (Kaisar-i-Hind Gold Medal) (*d* 1974); three *s* one *d. Educ:* King Edward's School, Birmingham; Trinity Coll., Cambridge (Major Scholar in Classics, First Class Honours Classical Tripos). Entered ICS 1908; Under-Secretary to Madras Govt, 1913–15; District Magistrate, Civil and Military Station, Bangalore, 1917–22; Commissioner of Coorg, 1923–26; services lent to government of Nizam of Hyderabad as Director-General of Revenue and Revenue Secretary, 1927–35, and Member of Council, 1935–42; Supervisor, ICS Probationers' Training, Dehra Dun, 1942–44; retired, 1944. *Address:* Southover, Swanage, Dorset BH19 2JF. *T:* Swanage 2033.                                             *Died* 9 *May* 1981.

**TATE, Phyllis (Margaret Duncan), (Mrs Alan Frank);** composer (free-lance); *b* 6 April 1911; *d* of Duncan Tate, FRIBA, and Annie S. Holl; *m* 1935, Alan Frank; one *s* one *d. Educ:* Royal Academy of Music, London. FRAM 1964. *Works:* (some commissioned by the BBC, and for festivals, etc, and several commercially recorded): Saxophone Concerto, 1944; Nocturne for four voices, 1945; Sonata for clarinet and cello, 1947; Choral Scene from The Bacchae, 1953; The Lady of Shalott, for tenor and instruments, 1956; Air and Variations for violin, clarinet and piano, 1958; London Fields, 1958; Opera: The Lodger, 1960; Television Opera: Dark Pilgrimage, 1963; A Victorian Garland, for two voices and instruments, 1965; Gravestones, for Cleo Laine, 1966; Seven Lincolnshire Folk Songs, for chorus and instruments, 1966; A Secular Requiem, for chorus and orchestra, 1967; Christmas Ale, for soloist, chorus and orchestra, 1967; Apparitions, for tenor and instruments, 1968; Coastal Ballads, for baritone and instruments, 1969; Illustrations, for brass band, 1969; To Words by Joseph Beaumont, for women's chorus, 1970; Variegations, for solo viola, 1970; Serenade to Christmas, for mezzo-soprano, chorus and orchestra, 1972; Lyric Suite, for piano duet, Explorations around a Troubadour Song, for piano solo, 1973; The Rainbow and the Cuckoo, for oboe, violin, viola and cello, 1974; Sonatina Pastorale for harmonica and harpsichord, 1974; Songs of Sundrie Kindes, for tenor and lute, 1975; St Martha and the Dragon, for narrator, soloists, chorus and orchestra, 1976; Scenes from Kipling, for baritone and piano, 1976; A Seasonal Sequence, for viola and piano, 1977; Panorama, for strings, 1977; All the World's a Stage, 1977, Compassion, 1978, for chorus and organ (or orchestra); Three Pieces for Solo Clarinet, 1979; The Ballad of Reading Gaol, for baritone, organ and cello, 1980; Movements, for string quartet, 1980; Prelude Aria Interlude Finale, for clarinet and piano, 1981; and many small choral pieces, songs and works for young people, including: Street Sounds, The Story of Lieutenant Cockatoo; Twice in a Blue Moon; A Pride of Lions; Scarecrow; Solar. *Address:* 12 Heath Hurst Road, NW3. *T:* 01–435 0607.
*Died* 29 *May* 1987.

**TATI, Jacques, (Jacques Tatischeff);** French film actor and director; *b* Pecq, Seine et Oise, 9 Oct. 1908. Stage début as Music Hall artist; subsequently, 1933–, Actor, Director and Script-writer, Gérant de Cady Films. *Films* (many of which have received international awards or prizes) include: Gai Dimanche, 1935; Soigne ton gauche, 1936; L'Ecole des Facteurs, 1947; Jour de Fête, 1947; Les Vacances de Monsieur Hulot, 1951; Mon Oncle, 1958; Playtime, 1968; Trafic (originally titled Yes Monsieur Hulot), 1971; Parade, 1974. *Address:*

12 rue du Château, 92 La Garenne-Colombes, France.
*Died* 4 *Nov.* 1982.

**TAYLOR,** Baron *cr* 1958 (Life Peer), of Harlow; **Stephen James Lake Taylor,** MD, BSc, FRCP; FRCGP; Visiting Professor of Medicine, Memorial University of Newfoundland, since 1973; *b* 30 Dec. 1910; *s* of John Reginald Taylor, MInstCE, and Beatrice Violet Lake Taylor; *m* 1939, Dr May Doris Charity Clifford; two *s* one *d. Educ:* Stowe Sch.; St Thomas's Hosp. Med. Sch., Univ. of London. BSc 1st cl. Hons; MB, BS (Hons Hygiene and Forensic Medicine); MD. FRCP 1960; FFOM RCP, 1979. Served War of 1939–45: Surg. Lt-Comdr (Neuro-psychiatric Specialist), RNVR; Dir of Home Intelligence and Wartime Social Survey, MOI, 1941–45. Formerly: Casualty Officer and HP, St Thomas' Hosp.; Grocers' Co. Research Scholar, Med. Unit, St Thomas' Hosp.; Sen. Resident Med. Officer, Royal Free Hosp.; HP, Bethlem Royal Hosp.; Asst Med. Officer, Maudsley Hosp. MP (Lab) Barnet Div. of Herts, 1945–50; PPS to Dep. Prime Minister and Lord President of Council, 1947–50; Under-Sec. of State for Commonwealth Relations and Colonies, 1964–65; resigned from Labour Party, 1981, to sit as a cross-bencher. Consultant in Occupational Health, Richard Costain Ltd, 1951–64 and 1966–67; Med. Dir, Harlow Industrial Health Service, 1955–64 and 1965–67; Pres. and Vice-Chancellor, Meml Univ. of Newfoundland, 1967–73. Visiting Research Fellow, Nuffield Provincial Hospitals Trust, 1953–55; Mem., Harlow New Town Develt Corp., 1950–64 and 1966–67. Former Chm., Labour Party Study Group on Higher Educn; Vice-Chm., British Film Inst.; former Member: N-W Metropolitan Regional Hosp. Bd; Health Adv. Cttee of Labour Party; Cohen Cttee on Gen. Practice, Beveridge Cttee on BBC; Mem., Bd of Governors, UCH. Lectures: Chadwick, RSH, 1963; Clarke, Univ. of Surrey, 1975; Lloyd Hughes, Liverpool, 1981. Hon. FRCPsych 1986. Hon. LLD: St Thomas Univ., NB, 1972; Meml Univ. of Newfoundland, 1986. *Publications:* Scurvy and Carditis, 1937; The Suburban Neurosis, 1938; Mental Illness as a Clue to Normality, 1940; The Psychopathic Tenth, 1941; The Study of Public Opinion, 1943; Battle for Health, 1944; The Psychopath in our Midst, 1949; Shadows in the Sun, 1949; Good General Practice, 1954; The Health Centres of Harlow, 1955; The Survey of Sickness, 1958; First Aid in the Factory, 1960; Mental Health and Environment, 1964; articles in Lancet, BMJ, World Medicine, etc. *Address:* Plas y Garth, Glyn Ceiriog, near Llangollen, Clwyd. *T:* Glyn Ceiriog 216.        *Died* 1 *Feb.* 1988.

**TAYLOR, Alan John Percivale;** historian and journalist; Hon. Fellow of Magdalen College, Oxford, 1976 and of Oriel College, Oxford, 1980; *b* Birkdale, Lancs, 25 March 1906; *o s* of Percy Lees and Constance Sumner Taylor; *m* 1st, 1931, Margaret Adams Taylor (marr. diss. 1951); two *s* two *d*; 2nd, Eve Crosland (marr. diss. 1974); two *s*; 3rd, W. Eva Haraszti, historian. *Educ:* Bootham School, York; Oriel Coll., Oxford. Formerly Lectr in Modern History, University of Manchester. Lecturer in International History, Oxford University, 1953–63; Tutor in Modern History, Magdalen College, 1938–63, Fellow, 1938–76. Lectures: Ford's, in English History, Oxford Univ., 1955–56; Leslie Stephen, Cambridge Univ., 1960–61; Creighton, London Univ., 1973; Andrew Lang, St Andrews Univ., 1974; Romanes, Oxford, 1981; Benjamin Meaker Vis. Prof. of History, Bristol Univ., 1976–78. Pres., City Music Soc. (London). FBA 1956–80. For. Hon. Mem., Amer. Acad. of Arts and Scis, 1985; Hon. Member: Yugoslav Acad. of Scis, 1985; Hungarian Acad. of Scis, 1986. Hon. DCL, New Brunswick, 1961; DUniv York, 1970; Hon. DLitt: Bristol, 1978; Warwick, 1981; Manchester, 1982. *Publications:* (many of them translated into other languages): The Italian Problem in European Diplomacy 1847–49, 1934; Germany's First Bid for Colonies 1884–85, 1938; The Habsburg Monarchy 1815–1918, 1941, rewritten 1948; The Course of German History, 1945; From Napoleon to Stalin, 1950; Rumours of Wars, 1952; The Struggle for Mastery in Europe, 1848–1918, 1954; Bismarck, 1955; Englishmen and Others, 1956; The Trouble Makers: Dissent over Foreign Policy, 1792–1939, 1957; The Russian Revolution of 1917, 1958 (script of first lectures ever given on television); The Origins of the Second World War, 1961; The First World War: an Illustrated History, 1963; Politics in Wartime and Other Essays, 1964; English History, 1914–1945, 1965; From Sarajevo to Potsdam, 1966; Europe: Grandeur and Decline, 1967; War by Timetable, 1969; Beaverbrook, 1972; The Second World War: an illustrated history, 1975; Essays in English History, 1976; The Last of Old Europe, 1976; The War Lords, 1977; The Russian War, 1978; How Wars Begin, 1979; Revolutions and Revolutionaries, 1980; Politicians, Socialism and Historians, 1980; A Personal History (autobiog.), 1983; An Old Man's Diary, 1984; How Wars End, 1985; (ed) Lloyd George: twelve essays, 1971; (ed) Lloyd George, a Diary by Frances Stevenson, 1971; (ed) Off the Record: political interviews 1933–43 by W. P. Crozier, 1973; (ed) My Darling Pussy: the letters of Lloyd George and Frances Stevenson, 1975. *Address:* 32 Twisden Road, NW5 1DN. *T:* 071–485 1507.                      *Died* 7 *Sept.* 1990.

**TAYLOR, Alec C.;** *see* Clifton-Taylor.

**TAYLOR, Arthur Wood,** CB 1953; *b* 23 June 1909; *s* of late Richard Wood and Ann Taylor; *m* 1936, Mary Beatrice Forster (*d* 1982); one *d. Educ:* Royal School, Wolverhampton; Wolverhampton Grammar School; Sidney Sussex College, Cambridge. Wrangler (Tyson Medal), 1930; joined HM Customs and Excise, 1931; Principal, 1936; Asst Secretary, 1943. Comr of Customs and Excise, 1949; Under-Secretary, HM Treasury, 1957–63; Comr of Customs and Excise, 1964–65, Dep. Chm., 1965–70. Chm., Horserace Totalisator Bd, 1970–72 (Dep. Chm., 1972–73). *Publications:* Amusements with Prizes: social implications, 1974 (report for Churches Council on Gambling); History of Beaconsfield, 1976. *Address:* Old Bakery, Thames Street, Charlbury, Oxford OX7 3QQ.
*Died* 7 *Oct.* 1987.

**TAYLOR, Sir Charles (Stuart),** Kt 1954; TD; MA Cantab; DL; *b* 10 April 1910; *s* of Alfred George and Mary Taylor; *m* 1936, Constance Ada Shotter (*d* 1989); three *s* one *d. Educ:* Epsom College; Trinity College, Cambridge (BA 1932); Hons Degree Law Tripos. Chm., Onyx Country Estates Co. Ltd, and other cos; formerly: Man. Dir, Unigate & Cow & Gate Ltd; Dir, Trust Houses Ltd; Chm., later Pres., Grosvenor House (Park Lane) Ltd. President, Residential Hotels Association of Great Britain, until 1948 and Vice-Chairman of Council of British Hotels and Restaurants Association until 1951; Mem. of Honour, Internat. Hotels Assoc. MP (C) Eastbourne, March 1935–Feb. 1974; Leader of Parly Delegns to Germany, Ethiopia, Mauritius; Mem., Parly Delegn to Romania. Joined TA 1937 (Royal Artillery), Capt., August 1939; DAAG and Temp. Major, Jan. 1941; attended Staff College, June 1941 (war course), graduated sc. Hon. Colonel. DL Sussex, 1948. Serving Brother, Order of St John. Master, Worshipful Co. of Bakers, 1980–81. Hon. Freeman, Co. Borough of Eastbourne, 1971. Hon. FHCIMA. Paduka Seri Laila Jasa (Dato), Brunei, 1971. *Recreations:* yachting (rep. Gt Britain *v* USA and Old World *v* New World in six-metre yacht races, 1955), shooting, fishing. *Address:* 4 Reeves House, Reeves Mews, W1. *T:* 01–499 3730. *Clubs:* 1900, Buck's, MCC; Royal Thames Yacht (Hon. Life Mem.); Ski Club of Great Britain (Hon. Life Mem.).                          *Died* 29 *March* 1989.

**TAYLOR, Christopher Albert,** CB 1976; Inspector General of the Insolvency Service (Under Secretary), Department of Trade, 1971–76, retired; *b* 25 Nov. 1915; *s* of Christopher Charles Albert Taylor and Violet Alma Taylor; *m* 1940, Ethel Kathleen Boon; one *s* two *d. Educ:* Woolwich Central Sch.; Woolwich Commercial Inst. (Silver Medal for Commercial Subjects). FCIS. Clerk: Linotype and Machinery Ltd, 1932; London County Freehold and Leasehold Properties Ltd, 1936; Asst Examiner, Companies Winding-up Dept, Board of Trade, 1939. RAF, 1940–46: Wireless Mechanic (Sgt) 1940–43; Signals Officer (Flt-Lt), Udine, Italy, 1946. Asst Official Receiver, London Suburban Bankruptcy Office, 1950; Official Receiver: Sheffield, 1951–52; Northampton and Cambridge, 1952–62; Companies Winding-up Dept, 1962–67, Sen. Official Receiver, 1967–70; Dep. Inspector General, Insolvency Service, 1970–71. Mem., Insolvency Law Review Cttee. *Recreations:* photography, amateur radio (G3AEH). *Address:* Bruerne House, Stoke Bruerne, Towcester, Northants NN12 7SB. *T:* Roade 862353. *Club:* Civil Service.                              *Died* 4 *Jan.* 1981.

**TAYLOR, Dorothy Mary,** CBE 1960; MD, DPH; late Senior Medical Officer, for Maternity and Child Welfare, Ministry of Health; *b* 17 August 1902; *d* of late Thomas Taylor, Highfield, Dreghorn Loan, Colinton, Edinburgh 13; unmarried. *Educ:* George Watson's Ladies' Coll., Edinburgh; Edinburgh Univ. House Surgeon Female VD Department, Edinburgh Royal Infirmary, 1925–26; Clinical Assistant, Maternity and Child Welfare Department, Edinburgh, April–Oct. 1926; House Physician, Royal Hospital for Sick Children, Edinburgh, 1926–27; Resident Medical Officer, Sick Children's Hospital, Newcastle upon Tyne, 1927–28; Senior Clinical Assistant, Female VD Department, Royal Infirmary, Edinburgh, 1928–30; Medical Officer, Maternity and Child Welfare Department, Edinburgh, 1930–31; Assistant MOH, Maternity and Child Welfare Department, Sunderland, 1932–35. *Address:* 4 Clerk's Acre, Keymer, Hassocks, West Sussex BN6 8QY. *T:* Hassocks 2143. *Club:* University Women's.                          *Died* 7 *May* 1983.

**TAYLOR, Ven. Edward;** Archdeacon of Warwick, since 1974; *b* 31 Oct. 1921; *s* of Albert and Emily Taylor; *m* 1945, Mary Jane Thomson *e d* of John and Margaret Bell; two *d. Educ:* King's Coll., London (AKC 1948); St Boniface Coll., Warminster. British Army, 1940–42; commnd, 14th Punjab Regt, 1942–46; Hon. Captain, Duke of Wellington's Regt, 1946. Deacon 1949, priest 1950, diocese of Norwich; Curate of Diss, 1949–51; Vicar: St Paul, Stockingford, 1951–57; St Nicholas, Radford, Coventry, 1957–64; Rector of Spernall, Morton Bagot and Oldberrow, 1965–74; Priest-in-charge of Coughton with Sambourne, 1965–70, Vicar 1970–74; Vicar of Sherbourne, 1975–77; Hon. Canon of Coventry, 1969. Proctor in Convocation, 1960–80. *Recreations:* not playing bridge and golf with great fervour and enthusiasm. *Address:* The Archdeacon's House, Sherbourne, Warwick CV35 8AB. *T:* Barford 624344.
*Died* 24 *Oct.* 1982.

**TAYLOR, Edward Plunket,** CMG 1946; President: Lyford Cay Co. Ltd; Windfields Farm Ltd; Chairman: New Providence Development Co., Nassau; International Housing Ltd, Bermuda; Director, several companies; *b* Ottawa, Ontario, 29 January 1901; *s* of late Lieut-Colonel Plunket Bourchier Taylor and Florence Gertrude Magee; *m* 1927, Winifred Thornton (*d* 1982), *d* of late Charles F. M. Duguid, Ottawa, Ontario; one *s* two *d. Educ:* Ashbury College; Ottawa Collegiate Institute, Ottawa; McGill University, Montreal (BSc in Mechanical Engineering, 1922). Director Brading Breweries Limited, 1923, also entered the investment house of McLeod, Young, Weir & Co., Limited, Ottawa, 1923, a Director 1929, resigned to become Pres. Canadian Breweries Ltd, 1930 (Chm. of Board, 1944). Mem. Bd of Governors: Trinity Coll. Sch.; Ashbury College. Wartime appointments held: Member, Executive Committee, Dept of Munitions and Supply, Ottawa, April 1940; Joint Director-General of Munitions Production, Nov. 1940; Executive Assistant to the Minister of Munitions and Supply, Feb. 1941; President War Supplies Limited, Washington, DC, April 1941; by Prime Minister Churchill appointed President and Vice-Chairman, British Supply Council in North America, Sept. 1941; Director-General British Ministry of Supply Mission, Feb. 1942; Canadian Deputy Member on the Combined Production and Resources Board, Nov. 1942; also Canadian Chairman, Joint War Aid Committee, US-Canada, Sept. 1943. Hon. Chairman: Jockey Club of Canada; Ontario Jockey Club; Mem., Jockey Club, NY. Member, Delta Upsilon Fraternity. Anglican. Hon. LLD McGill, 1977. *Recreation:* riding. *Address:* Lyford Cay, New Providence, Bahamas. *Clubs:* Buck's, Turf; Royal Yacht Squadron (Cowes); Toronto, York (Toronto); Rideau (Ottawa); Metropolitan (New York); Lyford Cay, East Hill (Nassau). *Died* 14 *May* 1989.

**TAYLOR, Prof. Frederick William,** MA Cantab, LLM Wales; Professor of Law, University of Hull, 1956–74, later Emeritus (Dean of Faculty of Arts, 1954–57); *b* 8 March 1909; *o s* of late James Edward Taylor, Solicitor, and of Emily Price; *m* 1938, Muriel Vera Markreed, *d* of Onek Vosguerchian; two *d. Educ:* Twynyrodyn Elementary and Cyfarthfa Secondary Schools, Merthyr Tydfil; University College of Wales, Aberystwyth; St John's College, Cambridge. Solicitor, 1931; LLB Wales, Sir Samuel Evans Prize 1933, BA Cantab, Scholar of St John's Coll., 1935; Asst Lectr in Law, University Coll., Hull, 1935; Acting Head, Dept of Law: University Coll., Southampton, 1940; Hull, 1941; called to Bar, Cert. of Honour, Middle Temple Prize, 1943; Head of Dept of Law, University Coll., Hull, 1949; LLM Wales 1954. Formerly Mem. of Bd of Studies in Laws of Univ. of London. Equity draftsman and conveyancer, 1944–, formerly at Leeds and later at Hull. *Publications:* articles in Law Journal, The Conveyancer, Jl of Soc. of Public Teachers of Law, Solicitors' Journal, The Solicitor, Secretaries Chronicle. *Recreations:* natural history, etc. *Address:* 40 Porthill Road, Shrewsbury, Shropshire. *Died* 8 *May* 1989.

**TAYLOR, Gordon Rattray;** author, specialising in understanding social change; *b* Eastbourne, 11 Jan. 1911; *o s* of Frederick Robert Taylor and Adèle Baker; *m* 1st, 1945, Lysbeth Morley Sheaf (marr. diss.); two *d;* 2nd, 1962, Olga Treherne Anthonisz. *Educ:* Radley Coll.; Trinity Coll., Cambridge. Morning Post, 1933–36; freelance, 1936–38; Daily Express (leader and feature writer), 1938–40; Monitoring Service and European News Broadcasts, BBC, 1940–44; Psychological Warfare Div., SHAEF, 1944–45; freelance writer, broadcaster and author, 1945–50; Dir, social research organisation, 1950–54; writing and devising science television programmes for BBC, 1958–66 (Chief Science Advisor, 1963–66); wrote Eye on Research series (Ondas award, 1961); Challenge series; Science Internat. series (first science programmes to attract over 10 million viewers) incl. Machines like Men (Brussels award, 1961); Editor, Horizon, 1964–66; full-time author, 1966–. Editorial consultant: Discovery, 1963–65; Science Jl, 1965–68. Other activities included devising British pavilion display for Turin Fair, 1961; Advisor, Triumphs of British Genius Exhibn, and ed, catalogue/book, 1977; lecture tours in US. Founder and Past Pres., Internat. Science Writers Assoc., etc. *Publications:* Economics for the Exasperated, 1947; Conditions of Happiness, 1949; Are Workers Human?, 1950; Sex in History, 1953; The Angel Makers: a study in the psychological origins of historical change 1750–1850, 1958 (abridgement, with an introductory essay) of The Mothers (by Robert Briffault), 1959; Eye on Research, 1960; The Science of Life: a picture history of biology, 1963; Growth (with Prof. James Tanner), 1965; The Biological Time Bomb, 1968; The Doomsday Book (Yorkshire Post book-of-the-year award), 1970; Rethink: a paraprimitive solution, 1972; How to Avoid the Future, 1975; A Salute to British Genius, 1977; The Natural History of the Mind, 1979; contrib. Focus feature to Science Jl, from inception; ed numerous research reports for Acton Soc. Trust; contributor to: Encounter, The Observer, Futures. *Recreations:* wine, gardening, baroque music, thought. *Address:* c/o Coutts and Co., 10 Mount Street, W1. *Club:* Savile. *Died* 7 *Dec.* 1981.

**TAYLOR, Harold George K.;** *see* Kirwan-Taylor.

**TAYLOR, Dr Joe;** JP; Councillor, Greater Manchester County Council, 1973–86 (Chairman, 1981–82); *b* 6 Sept. 1906; *s* of Sam Taylor and Anne Taylor; *m* 1935, Edith Dante; two *s. Educ:* Leeds Central High School; Leeds University and Leeds Med. Sch. MB ChB 1932. Medical Practitioner in Manchester, 1935–84; Mem., Crossley Hosp. Board, 1955–. Councillor, Manchester City, 1954–70, Alderman, 1970–73. Appeals Advisory Cttees, BBC and ITA: Chm., N Regional, 1961–67; Chm., Northern, 1967–76; Central, 1961–79. Member: Salvation Army Adv. Council, Manchester Region, 1965–; Gtr Manchester Police Authority, 1973–86; NW Water Authority, 1977–86; Gtr Manchester County Disaster Relief Trust, 1980–86; Manchester Victim Support Scheme, 1983–. Member Court: Univ. of Manchester, 1981–; Univ. of Salford, 1981–86. Member: Hallé Concerts Soc., 1973–86; Royal Exchange Theatre Trust, 1981–86; Palace Theatre Trust, 1981–86; NW Arts Executive, 1981–82. President: Gtr Manchester Council for Voluntary Service, 1981–82; Gtr Manchester Schools Football Assoc., 1981–82; Gtr Manchester Council Olympic Wrestling Team, 1981–82; Vice-Pres., Gtr Manchester Youth Assoc., 1981–82; Dep. Chm., British-American Assoc. for Gtr Manchester, 1985. Mem., Manchester Lit. and Phil Soc. JP Manchester City, 1961. *Recreations:* fishing, gardening, reading. *Address:* 32 Old Hall Road, Broughton Park, Salford M7 0JH. *T:* 061–740 4433. *Club:* Manchester Luncheon. *Died* 23 *March* 1989.

**TAYLOR, Brigadier John Alexander Chisholm,** DSO 1918; MC; TD; DL; FRIBA; late RA; Chartered Architect; *b* 1891; *s* of late Tom Taylor; *m* 1927, Jean Bell (*d* 1978), *d* of late Dr Johnstone. *Educ:* Sedbergh Sch. Served European War, 1914–18 (despatches, DSO, MC with bar); War of 1939–45. DL Lancs 1946. *Address:* Torbeckhill, Waterbeck, Dumfriesshire.

*Died* 4 *April* 1981.

**TAYLOR, John Hugh,** MA; Member, Civil Service Appeal Board, since 1978; *b* 1 Dec. 1916; *yr s* of late Arthur and Etna Taylor, Steeton, Yorks; *m* 1954, Romayne F. E. Good, *d* of late I. E. Good, Fulmer; two *s. Educ:* Boys' Grammar Sch., Keighley; Peterhouse, Cambridge (Scholar). 1st Cl. Historical Tripos Part I, 1938, 1st Cl. Part II, 1939. Administrative Class, Civil Service, 1939, Asst Principal, Admiralty; Private Secretary to Civil Lord, 1941–42; Private Secretary to Civil Lord and also to Parliamentary Secretary, 1942–43; Principal Private Secretary to First Lord, 1950–51; Assistant Secretary, 1951–61; Under-Secretary, Admiralty, 1961–64; Asst Under-Sec. of State, MoD, 1964–69; Under-Sec., Civil Service Dept, 1969–70; Dep. Principal, Civil Service Coll., 1970–72; Asst Under Sec. of State, MoD, 1972–76. *Recreations:* ornithology and photography. *Address:* 14 Duke's Wood Drive, Gerrards Cross, Bucks. *T:* Gerrards Cross 884241.

*Died* 25 *Feb.* 1985.

**TAYLOR, Kenneth,** CB 1975; Secretary, Export Credits Guarantee Department, 1975–83; *b* 10 Oct. 1923; *s* of William and May Taylor; *m* 1952, Mary Matilda Jacobs; one *s* one *d. Educ:* Merchant Taylors' Sch., Crosby; University Coll., Oxford (MA). Commnd RAF, 1943; Flt-Lt 212 Sqdn, 1944–45. Entered Min. of Civil Aviation as Asst Principal, 1947; BoT, later DTI, 1948–56, 1959–74; Treasury, 1957–59; Asst Sec. 1963; idc 1967; Under-Sec., 1969–73; Dep. Sec., 1973; Sec., Price Commn, 1973–74. Member: BOTB, 1975–83; Bd, Crown Agents for Oversea Govts and Admins, 1985–; Crown Agents Holding and Realisation Bd, 1985–. *Recreations:* tennis, chess. *Address:* High Trees, West Hill Way, Totteridge, N20 8QX. *T:* 01–445 7173. *Died* 23 *Feb.* 1990.

**TAYLOR, Kenneth Roy E.;** *see* Eldin-Taylor.

**TAYLOR, Martin;** lawyer; *b* Hereford, England, 15 Dec. 1885; *s* of James Durham and Mary Taylor (*née* Preece); *m* 1915, Caroline Strong Reboul (decd); one *d. Educ:* Trinity Coll.; Columbia Univ., USA. Admitted New York Bar, 1913. Practice, New York; former Counsel: New York State Tax Commission; Reed, Hoyt Taylor & Washburn. Rep. numerous British interests in USA; Mem., Internat. Law Assoc.; Chm. Cttee on Constitutional Law, New York Bar Assoc.; Mem. Assoc. of The Bar of City of New York. Formerly: Director of Consolidated RR of Cuba, The Cuba Company, Relief for Americans in the Philippines; Common Law Foundation; Library of Sei-Kiu-Do Common Law Inst., Tokyo; National Jail Assoc.; New York Post Graduate Med. Sch. and Hospital. Founder, Village of Nissequogue; Co-Founder, Tilney-Taylor Prize. Episcopalian. *Publications:* Reorganization of the Federal Judiciary (Supreme Court Controversy), 1937; The Common Law Foundation, 1963; A Footnote to History, 1970. *Recreations:* book collecting, bridge, tennis. *Address:* (residence) 163 E 81st Street, New York, NY 10028, USA. *Clubs:* Beefsteak, Portland; Union, University (NYC). *Died* 21 *April* 1981.

**TAYLOR, General Maxwell Davenport,** Hon. KBE 1955; DSC (US) 1944; DSM (US) 1945 (3 Oak Leaf Clusters, 1954, 1959, 1964); Silver Star 1943 (Oak Leaf Cluster, 1944); Legion of Merit; Bronze Star; Purple Heart; Consultant to President of US; President, Institute of Defense Analyses; Member, Foreign Intelligence

Advisory Board, since 1965; *b* 26 Aug. 1901; *s* of John Earle Maxwell Taylor and Pearle Davenport; *m* 1925, Lydia Gardner (*née* Happer); two *s*. *Educ:* US Milit. Academy (BS). Became artillery commander of 82nd Airborne Division by Dec. 1942; served in Sicilian and Italian Campaigns; in 1944 became Commanding Gen. of 101st Airborne Div., which he led in the airborne invasion of Normandy, the airborne invasion of Holland, and in the Ardennes and Central Europe Campaigns; supt US Mil. Acad., 1945; Chief of Staff, European Comd HQ, Heidelberg, Jan. 1949; first US Comdr, Berlin, Sept. 1949; Asst Chief of Staff for Ops, G3, Dept of Army, Feb. 1951; Dep. Chief of Staff for Ops and Admin. of Army, Aug. 1951; Comdg Gen., 8th US Army in Korea, 1953; Comdr of all ground forces in Japan, Okinawa and Korea, at Camp Zama, Japan, Nov. 1954; C-in-C of Far East Comd and UN Comd, 1955; Chief of Staff, US Army, 1955–59; Mil. Representative of the President of the USA, 1961–62; Chairman, Joint Chiefs of Staff, US, Oct. 1962–June 1964; American Ambassador to South Vietnam, 1964–65; Special Consultant to President, 1965–69. Formerly Director of companies (including Chairman Board, Mexican Light & Power Co.); was also President, Lincoln Center for the Performing Arts. Holds fifteen Honorary doctorates. Many foreign decorations. *Publications:* The Uncertain Trumpet, 1960; Responsibility and Response, 1967; Swords and Plowshares, 1972; Precarious Security, 1976. *Recreations:* tennis, handball and squash. *Address:* 2500 Massachusetts Avenue NW, Washington, DC 20008, USA. *Clubs:* University (NYC); Army and Navy, International, Chevy Chase, Alibi (Washington).          *Died* 19 *April* 1987.

**TAYLOR, Dr Peter John;** International Medical Adviser, Unilever PLC, since 1981; Chief Examiner, Faculty of Occupational Medicine, Royal College of Physicians, since 1984; Hon. Consultant in Occupational Medicine: Guy's Hospital, since 1968; King's College Hospital Medical School, since 1975; Civil Consultant in Occupational Medicine, Royal Air Force, since 1984; *b* 24 Sept. 1929; *s* of late Comdr Sam Taylor and Alice (*née* Storm); *m* 1959, Josephine Marian Hetherington; one *s* one *d*. *Educ:* Clifton Coll.; St Thomas's Hosp. Med. Sch. (BSc (Hons) 1951; MB (Hons) 1954); DIH (Soc. of Apothecaries) 1962; MD 1966; FRCP 1971; FFCM 1976; FFOM 1978. RAF Medical Br., 1956–58, Sqn Ldr. St Thomas's Hospital: House Physician appts, 1955–56; Medical Registrar, 1959–60; MO PT, Shell Indonesia, 1960–63; Sen. MO, Shell Haven Refinery, Essex, 1963–68; Dep. Dir, TUC Centenary Inst. of Occupational Health, LSHTM, 1968–71; CMO, Post Office, 1971–81. Visiting Professor: McMaster Univ., Ontario, 1979–80; in Occupational Medicine, LSHTM, 1982–; Examiner: MSc Occupational Med., Univ. of London, 1978–81; DIH, Conjoint Bd, 1973–77; Dundee Univ., 1977–79; Soc. of Apothecaries, 1978–. Member: Med. Adv. Cttee, Health and Safety Commn, 1977–83; Standing Med. Adv. Cttee, DHSS, 1982–; Vice Dean, 1978–81, and Dean, 1981–84, Faculty of Occupational Medicine, RCP. Royal Society of Medicine: Fellow, 1960; Hon. Sec., then Vice-Pres., Occupational Medicine Sect., 1966–72; Pres., Soc. of Occupational Medicine, 1974–75. Vice Pres., E Anglian Donkey Show, 1984–. OStJ 1982. *Publications:* Absenteeism, 1969, 4th edn 1982; Health at Work, 1975; chapters in Occupational Health Practice, 1973, 2nd edn 1981; papers on occupational medicine, sickness absence, shift work, employment of disabled, etc. *Recreations:* music, gardening, donkeys. *Address:* Pudingswell, Monks Eleigh, Ipswich, Suffolk IP7 7AD. *T:* Bildeston 740695. *Club:* Royal Air Force.
                              *Died* 6 *Jan.* 1987.

**TAYLOR, Robert George;** MP (C) Croydon North West since 1970; *b* 7 Dec. 1932; 2nd *s* of late Frederick Taylor and Grace Taylor, Eastbourne; *m* 1964, Rosemary (*née* Box); one *s* one *d*. *Educ:* Cranleigh School. Exec. Dir, G. & S. Allgood Ltd; Chm., (South African subsidiary) G. & S. Allgood (Pty) Ltd; Mem. Council, Building Materials Export Gp (Chm., 1977–). Contested (C) North Battersea, 1959 and 1964. Mem., Select Cttee of Public Accounts, 1975–. TA parachutist. *Recreations:* bridge; formerly Rugby football (played for Sussex). *Address:* Hinterland House, Effingham Common, Surrey. *T:* Bookham 52691. *Clubs:* Carlton, East India, Devonshire, Sports and Public Schools.          *Died* 19 *June* 1981.

**TAYLOR, Sir Robert (Mackinlay),** Kt 1963; CBE 1956; Chairman, Thomas Tilling Ltd, 1976–83; Senior Deputy Chairman: Standard Chartered Bank plc, 1974–83; Standard Bank, 1974–83; Chartered Bank, 1974–83; Director: Standard Bank Investment Corporation, Johannesburg, 1974–83; Standard Bank of South Africa, 1974–83; *b* 29 Sept. 1912; *s* of late Commander R. M. Taylor, DSC, Royal Navy, and late Mrs Taylor; *m* 1944, Alda Cecilia Ignesti; one *d*. *Educ:* Plymouth College; Hele's School, Exeter; University Coll. of the SW, Exeter (MSc(Econ.) London). Entered Home CS, 1937; transf. Colonial Service, 1948. Dep. Comr, Nat. Savings Cttee, 1939. War Service, 1939–46. Economic Adviser, Govt of Fiji, 1947; Fin. Sec., Fiji, 1948–52; Fin. Sec., N Rhodesia, 1952–58; seconded to Govt of Fedn of Rhodesia and Nyasaland, 1953; Sec. for Transport until end 1954; thereafter Sec. to Federal Treasury; retd from HMOCS, Dec. 1958. Chm., Richard Costain Ltd, 1969–73. Mem. Adv. Commn on Review of Constitution of Rhodesia and

Nyasaland (Monckton Commn), 1960. *Publication:* A Social Survey of Plymouth, 1937. *Recreation:* golf. *Address:* Flat 8, 24 Park Road, NW1. *Clubs:* Athenæum, Naval and Military; MCC; Harare (Zimbabwe).          *Died* 21 *Jan.* 1985.

**TAYLOR, Rupert Sutton,** OBE 1945; TD (three bars) 1943; FDSRCS; MRCS, LRCP; Hon. Consulting Dental Surgeon, Westminster Hospital Teaching Group and Seamen's Hospital Group, 1970; Consultant Dental Surgeon, Westminster Hospital, 1937–70, Seamen's Hospital, 1930–70; Recognised Teacher, University of London, since 1948; *b* 18 July 1905; *s* of G. W. and M. F. Taylor; *m* 1951, Mary Angela Tebbs. *Educ:* Newtown School, Waterford; Middlesex Hospital; Royal Dental Hospital. LDS 1928; commissioned RAMC, TA (Hygiene Coys), 1928; Dental Ho. Surg., Middlesex Hosp., 1928; Clin. Asst, Dental Dept, Westminster Hosp., 1929–31; Sen. Clin. Asst. to Dental Surgeon, Nose, Ear, and Throat Hosp., Golden Square, 1931–32; Hon. Dental Surgeon, Nat. Hosp., Queen's Square, 1933–37. External Examr Dental Surgery and Materia Medica, Queen's Univ., Belfast, 1938–39 and 1945–48. Dental Member, London Exec. Council (National Health Service), 1948–62; Chm. London Executive Council, 1953 and 1954–Mar. 1956 (Vice-Chm., 1951–53); FDS, RCS (by election), 1948. Served with RAMC War of 1939–45; Major, 1938–42, Lt-Col, 1942–45; commanded 127 Light Field Amb. and 146 Field Amb.; 161 Field Ambulance, TA, 1957–58; Hon. Col Medical Units 54 (EA) Infantry division, 1959–66. OStJ 1959; CStJ 1961. *Publications:* various articles on oral surgery. *Recreations:* sailing, fishing. *Address:* Thieny-Chibbyr, Lezayre Road, Ramsey, Isle of Man. *T:* Ramsey, IoM 812585. *Club:* Savage.          *Died* 4 *April* 1986.

**TAYLOR, Thomas Whiting,** MA, PhD Cantab; BD London; Headmaster, Haberdashers' Aske's School, Hampstead and Elstree, Hertfordshire, 1946–73; *b* 29 Nov. 1907; *m* 1937, Margaret, *y d* of late Prof. H. H. Swinnerton, CBE; one *s* five *d*. *Educ:* Liverpool Collegiate School; Christ's College, Cambridge, 1926–30 (Classical Scholar, Classical Tripos Pt I 1st class honours, Pt II 2nd class honours, Burney Prize); Frankfurt-am-Main University, 1931–32; Christ's College, Cambridge, 1932–34. Senior Classical Master at Worksop College, Notts, 1930–31; Assistant Tutor in Classics at Handsworth College, Birmingham, 1934–36; Sixth Form Classical Master at Bradford Grammer School, Yorks, 1936–39; Headmaster, City of Bath School, 1940–46. Chairman: General Studies Assoc., 1962–78; Exec. Cttee, Nat. Youth Orchestra, 1960–78; ESU Brit.-Amer. Schoolboy Scholarships Cttee, 1970–77; Henrietta Barnett Sch., 1960–75; Schools Adviser, Central Bureau for Educnl Visits and Exchanges, 1973–78; Mem. Council, Royal Holloway College, Univ. of London; Governor: North London Collegiate Sch.; Camden Sch.; Verulam Sch. Hon. Freeman and Liveryman, Worshipful Company of Haberdashers. Hon. ARAM; Hon. ARCM. Cross of the Order of Merit (Federal Republic of Germany), 1977. *Recreations:* drama, music, foreign travel. *Address:* 42 The Dell, Sandpit Lane, St Albans, Herts AL1 4HF. *T:* St Albans 67949.
                              *Died* 26 *Nov.* 1981.

**TAYLOR, Walter R.;** *see* Ross-Taylor.

**TEAGUE, Colonel John,** CMG 1958; CBE 1946 (OBE 1925); MC 1916; retired; *b* 16 Nov. 1896; *y s* of William and Helen Teague; *m* 1st, 1926, Heather Fairley (*d* 1966), *d* of late Captain James William Fairley, Tunbridge Wells; two *s* one *d*; 2nd, 1973, Mrs Nora Ballard. *Educ:* Portsmouth Grammar School. Studied music under Dr A. K. Blackall, FRAM, and was his Assistant Organist at St Mary's, Warwick, 1913. Commissioned Royal Warwickshire Regt, 1914; served in France, 1915–17 (wounded twice, despatches, MC); transf. Indian Army (Baluch Regt); with Sykes' Mission in South Persia and Staff Capt., Shiraz Brigade, 1918; attached Indian Political Service as Vice-Consul Shiraz, 1919; Iraq Insurrection (despatches), 1920; General Staff (Intelligence), GHQ Baghdad, 1920, later with RAF, Iraq, Kurdistan Operations (severely wounded), 1922; NW Frontier, India, 1930; Language student in Persia (Interpreter), 1933; Liaison Officer, RAF Palestine during Arab Revolt, 1936–39; GHQ, Middle East, 1942; transferred to Foreign Office, 1945; Director, Passport Control, 1953–58. Polonia Restituta, 1945; Legion of Merit (USA), 1946; White Lion (Czechoslovakia), 1947. *Publications:* occasional articles for press about Middle East. *Recreations:* music, reading, walking. *Address:* 5 Hungershall Park, Tunbridge Wells, Kent. *T:* Tunbridge Wells 26959. *Club:* Royal Air Force.          *Died* 28 *Feb.* 1983.

**TEBBUTT, Dame Grace,** DBE 1966 (CBE 1960); JP; Member of Sheffield City Council, 1929–67, Alderman, 1934–67; *b* 5 January 1893; *d* of Alfred and Ann Elizabeth Mellar; *m* 1913, Frank Tebbutt; two *d*. *Educ:* Coleridge Road School, Sheffield 9. Chairman: Parks Cttee, Sheffield, 1934–47 and 1950–55; Health Cttee, 1947–49; Children's Committee, 1956–67. Formerly: Vice-Chm., Nat. Bureau for Co-operation in Child Care; Mem., Home Office Central Adv. Council in Child Care and Central Training Council in Child Care. Lord Mayor of Sheffield, 1949–50; JP 1950; Hon. Freeman of Sheffield, 1959. Hon. LLD Sheffield Univ., 1965.

*Address:* Edgelow, 501 Lowedges Crescent, Sheffield S8 7LN. *T:* Sheffield 746783. *Died* 10 *April* 1983.

**TEELOCK, Sir Leckraz,** Kt 1972; CBE 1968; MB, ChB, DTM, LM; High Commissioner for Mauritius in UK since 1968 (Commissioner, 1964–68); Ambassador Extraordinary and Plenipotentiary to the Holy See, The Netherlands, Luxembourg, Norway, Finland, Sweden and Denmark; *b* 1909; *m* Vinaya Kumari Prasad, BA, Barrister-at-Law, Middle Temple; one *s* one *d. Educ:* Royal College, Curepipe; Edinburgh University; Liverpool University; Dublin. Medical practitioner, 1939–64. Member Legislative Assembly, 1959–63. Chairman, Mauritius Family Planning Association, 1959–62; Director, Mauritius Free Press Service Ltd, 1940–63. Ambassador Extraordinary and Plenipotentiary to Belgium and EEC, 1971–76. *Address:* (office) 32–33 Elvaston Place, SW7; (home) Flat 1, Chelsea House, Lowndes Street, SW1. *Died* 4 *May* 1982.

**TEIGNMOUTH, 7th Baron,** *cr* 1797; **Frederick Maxwell Aglionby Shore; Bt** 1792; DSC and Bar 1944; *b* 2 Dec. 1920; *yr s* of 6th Baron and Anna Adelaide Caroline (*d* 1976), *d* of Col Marsh; *S* father, 1964; *m* 1947, Daphne Beryl (marriage annulled, 1952), *o d* of W. H. Freke-Evans, Hove; *m* 1979, Mrs Pamela Meyer, *d* of H. Edmonds-Heath. *Educ:* Wellington College. Served War of 1939–45: Lieut, RNVR (despatches twice, DSC and Bar). *Recreations:* fishing, shooting, painting. *Heir:* none. *Address:* Brownsbarn, Thomastown, Co. Kilkenny, Eire.
*Died* 7 *July* 1981 (*ext*).

**TEMPEST, Margaret (Mary), (Lady Mears);** author and illustrator; *d* of Charles Ernest Tempest, JP, Ipswich; *m* 1951, Sir Grimwood Mears, KCIE (*d* 1963). *Educ:* Westminster Sch. of Art; Royal Drawing Soc.; Chelsea Illustrators. *Publications:* author and illustrator of: The Lord's Prayer for Children, 1943; A Thanksgiving, 1944; A Belief, 1945; The Christchild, 1947; A Sunday Book, 1954; The Little Lamb of Bethlehem, 1956; also of The Pinkie Mouse and Curly Cobbler series, 1944; illustrated many books including (1929–) The Grey Rabbit series. *Recreations:* yachting, yacht racing. *Club:* Royal Harwich Yacht. *Died* 23 *July* 1982.

**TEMPEST, Prof. Norton Robert;** William Roscoe Professor of Education, Liverpool University, 1954–72, then Emeritus; *b* 29 Dec. 1904; *s* of James Henry and Veronica Tempest (*née* Fletcher); *m* 1st, 1932, Mary MacDermott (*d* 1962), Danvers, Mass, USA; one *s*; 2nd, 1970, Maureen Kennedy, Litherland, Liverpool. *Educ:* Liverpool Univ.; Harvard Univ. William Noble Fellow, Liverpool Univ., 1927–28; Commonwealth Fund Fellow, 1930–32. Taught in Grammar Schools; asst lecturer, later lecturer, Manchester and Sheffield Univs, 1932–45; senior lecturer in Education, Liverpool Univ., 1945–49; Director, Sheffield Univ. Inst. of Education, 1949–54. *Publications:* The Rhythm of English Prose, 1930; Teaching Clever Children 7–11, 1974; articles and reviews in various journals. *Address:* 5 Parson's Walk, Pembridge, Leominster, Herefordshire HR6 9EP. *Died* 7 *Sept.* 1985.

**TEMPLE OF STOWE, 7th Earl,** *cr* 1822; **Ronald Stephen Brydges Temple-Gore-Langton;** *b* 5 November 1910; *s* of Captain Hon. Chandos Graham Temple-Gore-Langton (*d* 1921); granted rank, title and precedence as an Earl's son, which would have been his had his father survived to succeed to the title; nephew of 5th Earl; *S* brother, 1966. Company representative. *Heir:* cousin Walter Grenville Algernon Temple Gore Langton [*b* 2 Oct. 1924; *m* 1st, 1954, Lillah Ray (*d* 1966), *d* of James Boxall; two *s* one *d*; 2nd, 1968, Margaret Elizabeth Graham, *o d* of late Col H. W. Scarth]. *Recreations:* sailing, swimming, bird watching, conservation, radio. Resident in Victoria, Australia. *Died* 28 *Aug.* 1988.

**TEMPLE, Frances Gertrude Acland, (Mrs William Temple);** *b* 23 Dec. 1890; *yr d* of late Frederick Henry Anson, 72 St George's Square, SW1; *m* 1916, William Temple, later Archbishop of Canterbury (*d* 1944). *Educ:* Francis Holland School for Girls, SW1; Queen's College, Harley Street, W1. JP for City of Manchester, 1926–29. Member of Care of Children Cttee (The Curtis Cttee), 1945–47. Church Commissioner, 1948–59; Mem. of Board of Visitors of Rochester Borstal Institution, 1943–60. A Vice-Pres., YHA. MA (*hc*) Manchester Univ., 1954. *Address:* Brackenlea, Shawford, Winchester, Hants. *Died* 18 *May* 1984.

**TEMPLE-MORRIS, His Honour Sir Owen,** Kt 1967; QC 1937; Judge of Cardiff County Court Circuit No 27, 1968–69; Monmouthshire Quarter Sessions, 1950–69; Chancellor of Diocese of Llandaff, 1935–79; *b* 18 Sept. 1896; *s* of late Dr Frederick Temple Morris, Cardiff, and Florence, *e d* of Col Charles Lanyon Owen, CB, Portsmouth; *m* 1927, Vera, *er d* of D. Hamilton Thompson; one *s.* Solicitor for five years in practice; Deputy Magistrate's Clerk, Dinas Powis Div., Glamorgan; called to Bar, Gray's Inn, 1925; Wales and Chester Circuits; Judge of County Court Circuit No 24, Cardiff, etc, 1955–68 (Circuit No 31, 1942–48; No 30, 1948–55). Comr of Assize, Oxford Autumn Assize, 1946; Comr of Assize, Welsh Circuit Summer Assize, 1960, 1961, Autumn Assize, 1963, Winter Assize and Summer Assize, 1965, 1966, 1967, 1968, 1969. Mem.

Royal Commn on the Police, 1960–62. Prosecuting Counsel to the Post Office, South Wales Circuit, 1931–37; Recorder of Merthyr Tydfil, 1936–42; Acting Recorder of Swansea, 1940–42; Dep. Recorder of Cardiff, 1969–71; Chm. of Quarter Sessions: Town and Co. Haverfordwest, 1942–48; Co. Carmarthenshire, 1942–50; Brecknockshire, 1948–55; Dep.-Chm. of Quarter Sessions: Glamorgan, 1938–48; Pembrokeshire, 1942–48; formerly Chm., County Court Rule Cttee. MP (Nat C) Cardiff East, 1931–42; contested Caerphilly Division of Glamorgan, General Election, 1929; Vice-Pres. Wales and Mon Conservative and Unionist Association, 1931–42; Chm. Wales and Mon Conservative Education Cttee, 1938–42; Mem. Governing Body, Association of Conservative Clubs, 1929–42; Chm. Wales and Mon Conservative Clubs Advisory Cttee, 1929–42; Mem. of Governing Body and Vice-Chm., Representative Body of the Church in Wales; President, Provincial Court of Church in Wales; Chm. of Legal Cttee and Pensions Cttee of Representative Body, 1945–55; Hon. Lay Sec. Llandaff Diocesan Conf., 1927–35; Mem. of Cymmrodorion Soc.; Chief Comdt Cardiff Volunteer Special Constabulary, 1938–45; Chm. and Sec. Commandants of Special Constabularies Conf., No 8 Region, 1942–45. CStJ. *Address:* 8 Raglan House, Westgate Street, Cardiff. *Club:* Cardiff and County (Cardiff).

*Died* 21 *April* 1985.

**TEMPLEMAN, Geoffrey,** CBE 1980; MA London; PhD Birmingham; FSA; DL; Vice-Chancellor, University of Kent at Canterbury, 1963–80; *b* 15 February 1914; *s* of R. C. Templeman; *m* 1939, Dorothy May Heathcote; two *s* one *d. Educ:* Handsworth Grammar School; Universities of Birmingham, London and Paris. University of Birmingham: teaching history from 1938, Registrar, 1955–62. Chairman: Northern Univs Jt Matric. Bd, 1961–64; Universities Central Council on Admissions, 1964–75; Schs Cttee, Bd of Educn, General Synod of C of E, 1971–76 (Mem., 1971–78); Univ. Authorities Panel, 1972–80; Christ Church Coll., Canterbury, 1966–; Inst. of Germanic Studies, Univ. of London, 1966–84. Mem., SE Metropolitan Reg. Hosp. Bd, 1972–74; Mem., SE Thames RHA, 1974–84. Mem. Review Body on Doctors' and Dentists' Remuneration, 1965–70. DL Kent 1979. Hon. DTech Brunel, 1974; Hon. DCL Kent, 1980. Hon. Fellow, Inst. of Germanic Studies, Univ. of London, 1982. *Publications:* Dugdale Soc. Pubs vol. XI together with articles in learned jls, incl. Trans Royal Hist. Soc. and Cambridge Hist. Jl. *Address:* 2a St Augustine's Road, Canterbury, Kent. *Club:* Athenæum. *Died* 22 *Feb.* 1988.

**TEMPLETOWN, 5th Viscount,** Ireland, *cr* 1806; **Henry Augustus George Mountjoy Heneage Upton;** Baron 1776; late Lieutenant Royal East Kent Mounted Rifles; *b* 12 Aug. 1894; *o* surv. *s* of 4th Viscount and Lady Evelyn Georgina Finch-Hatton (*d* 1932), *d* of 9th Earl of Winchilsea and Nottingham; *S* father, 1939; *m* 1st, 1916, Alleyne (*d* 1974), *d* of late Henry Lewes Conran, RN; one *d* (one *s* decd); 2nd, 1975, Margaret Violet Louisa, *widow* of Sir Lionel George Archer Cust, CBE. *Educ:* Eton; Magdalen College, Oxford. *Recreations:* shooting, fishing, ski-ing. *Heir:* none. *Address:* 7 Castle Street, Kirkcudbright PG6 4JA. *T:* Kirkcudbright 30502.
*Died* 10 *Feb.* 1981 (*ext*.)

**TENBY, 2nd Viscount,** *cr* 1957, of Bulford; **David Lloyd George;** *b* 4 Nov. 1922; *s* of 1st Viscount Tenby and Edna, Viscountess Tenby (*d* 1971); *S* father, 1967. *Educ:* Eastbourne Coll.; Jesus Coll. (Scholar), Cambridge (MA). Served War, 1942–47: as Captain, Royal Artillery, NW Europe, 1944–45. Called to the Bar, Inner Temple, 1953. *Heir:* brother Hon. William Lloyd George [*b* 7 Nov. 1927; *m* 1955, Ursula Diana Ethel Medlicott; one *s* two *d*].
*Died* 14 *July* 1983.

**TENISON, Marika H.;** *see* Hanbury Tenison.

**TENISON, Lt-Col William Percival Cosnahan,** DSO 1917; late Royal Artillery; *b* 25 June 1884; *e s* of Col William Tenison, DL, JP, of Loughbawn, Ballybay, Ireland; *m* 1915, Olive Leonora (*d* 1979), *d* of late C. L. Mackenzie and Baroness Wesselenyi of Hadad, Hungary; two *d. Educ:* Marlborough; RMA, Woolwich. First commn, 1903; served European War, 1914–17 (DSO); retired pay, 1922. Guildford Borough Council, 1925–31; Hon. Associate British Museum (Natural History); FLS, FZS (Mem. Council, 1943–47), MBOU; Corpnte Zoological Record (Aves, 1944–63); zoological artist; Field Studies Council; Worshipful Company of Farriers; Mem., Old Contemptibles Association; a Governor of Archbishop Tenison's Grammar School. Raised and commanded 54th Surrey (Wimbledon) Bn Home Guard, 1940–45. *Address:* The Manor Farm, Stanton-by-Dale, near Ilkeston, Derby DE7 4QF.
*Died* 7 *July* 1983.

**TENNANT, Sir Mark (Dalcour),** KCMG 1964 (CMG 1951); CB 1961; Deputy Secretary, Department of the Environment, 1970–71; *b* 26 Dec. 1911; *o* surv. *s* of late N. R. D. Tennant, Haileybury, Hertford; *m* 1936, Clare Elisabeth Ross, *o d* of late Sir Ross Barker, KCIE, CB. *Educ:* Marlborough; New College, Oxford (Open Classical Schol.). Entered Min. of Labour as Asst Principal, 1935; Private Secretary to Parliamentary Secretary, Ministry of Labour,

1938–39; and to Parliamentary Secretary, Ministry of Food, 1939–40. Served War of 1939–45, Royal Artillery, 1942–44. Assistant Secretary, 1945; Member of UK Delegation to International Labour Conference, 1949–53; Student Imperial Defence College, 1956; Under-Secretary, 1957; Secretary-General Monckton Commission on the Review of the Constitution of the Federation of Rhodesia and Nyasaland, 1960; Dir Organisation and Establishments, Min. of Labour, 1960; Secretary, Central African Office, 1962–64. Third Secretary, HM Treasury, 1964–65; Dep. Sec., Min. of Public Building and Works, 1965–70. *Address:* c/o Barclays Bank, 1 Pall Mall East, SW1. *Club:* Travellers'.      *Died 30 April* 1990.

**TENNYSON-d'EYNCOURT, Sir Giles (Gervais),** 4th Bt *cr* 1930, of Carter's Corner Farm, Herstmonceux; *b* 16 April 1935; *s* of Sir Eustace Gervais Tennyson-d'Eyncourt, 2nd Bt and Pamela (*d* 1962), *d* of late W. B. Gladstone; *S* brother, 1988; *m* 1966, Juanita, *d* of late Fortunato Borromeo; one *s*. *Educ:* Eton; Millfield; Sandhurst. Commissioned Coldstream Guards, 1953; retd, Captain, 1964. *Recreations:* cricket, shooting. *Heir:* *s* Mark Gervais Tennyson-d'Eyncourt, *b* 12 March 1967. *Address:* 20 Cranmer Court, Sloane Avenue, SW3 3HN. *T:* 01–225 0856.      *Died 6 June* 1989.

**TENNYSON-d'EYNCOURT, Sir (John) Jeremy (Eustace),** 3rd Bt *cr* 1930; *b* 8 July 1927; *s* of Sir Eustace Gervais Tennyson-d'Eyncourt, 2nd Bt, and Pamela (*d* 1962), *d* of late W. B. Gladstone; *S* father, 1971; *m* 1st, 1964, Mrs Sally Fyfe-Jamieson (marr. diss.; she *m* 1982, 10th Baron Vernon), *e d* of Robin Stratford, KC; 2nd, 1972, Brenda Mary Veronica (marr. diss. 1976), *d* of Dr Austin Stafford; 3rd, 1977, Norah, *d* of late Thomas Gill. *Educ:* Eton; Glasgow University. Served as Sub Lieut, RNVR, 1945–48. *Recreations:* fishing and wild-life; cooking and gardening. *Heir:* *b* Giles Gervais Tennyson-d'Eyncourt [*b* 16 April 1935; *m* 1966, Juanita, *d* of late Fortunato Borromeo; one *s*].      *Died 12 April* 1988.

**TENZING NORGAY,** GM 1953; Sherpa Climber; Chief Adviser, Himalayan Mountaineering Institute, Darjeeling (established by Indian Government, 1954); *b* Tami, Nepal, 1914; *m* Anglahmu; two *c*; *m* 1962, Dawa Phuti; four *c*. Migrated to Bengal, 1932. High altitude Sherpa in British mountaineering expeditions, 1935, 1936 and 1938; took part in expeditions to Karakoram, 1950, and Nanda Devi, 1951, climbing to east peak; Sirdar and full Member to 2 Swiss expedns (climbing record 28,215 ft), 1952; Sirdar and Full Member to Sir John Hunt's expedition, 1953; with Sir Edmund Hillary reached summit of Mount Everest, May 1953. President: Sherpa Climbers' Assoc.; Sherpa Buddhist Assoc.; Mem., Indian Mountaineering Foundn. Coronation Medal, 1953; Nepal Pardak-Bardak (highest medal of Nepal), 1952; Star of Nepal, 1953; Padma Bushan Medal, India, 1956; Coronation Medal, Sikkim. Gold Medal: Nat. Geography Soc., USA, 1953; Nepal Police Assoc., 1953; India, 1953; Iran, 1954; Soviet Union (twice); Tiger Medal No 1, Himalayan Club, India, 1936; Cullum Medal, RGS, 1954; Hubbard Medal, USA, 1956; Sports Gold Medal: Italy, 1956; France, 1956; Swiss Diploma Guide Outstanding Badge, Swiss Alpine Club, 1954; Golden Plate Award, Acad. of Achievement, USA, 1973. Hon. Citizen of Chamonix, 1954. *Publication:* After Everest (autobiog.), 1977; *relevant publication:* Man of Everest by James Ramsay Ullman, 1955 (Amer. edn Tiger of the Snows). *Address:* Himalayan Mountaineering Institute, Birch Hill, Darjeeling, W Bengal; 1 Tonga Road, Ghang-La, Darjeeling, W Bengal. *Clubs:* Alpine; Alpine (Switzerland, France, Italy, Germany, Austria, Japan, Soviet Union, USA); Himalayan (India); Explorers' (USA); Rotarian (Italy).      *Died 9 May* 1986.

**TERRY, Sir Andrew Henry Bouhier I.;** *see* Imbert-Terry.

**TERRY, Michael,** FRGS; FRGSA; explorer and author; *b* Newcastle upon Tyne, 3 May 1899; *s* of late Major A. M. and late Catherine Terry; *m* 1940, Ursula (marr. diss. 1945), *yr d* of Captain Noel Livingstone-Learmonth. *Educ:* Preston House School, East Grinstead; King Edward School, Birmingham; Durham University. Served in Russia; invalided out; went to Australia upon discharge; took first motor across Northern Australia from Winton, Queensland, to Broome on the North-West Coast, in 1923; Cuthbert-Peek Grant in support of expedition undertaken, 1925, from Darwin to Broome; authorised to name Dummer Range and Mount Rosamund; third expedition started Port Hedland, 1928; proceeded Broome, Halls Creek, Tanami, Alice Springs, Melbourne. Made gold and potassium nitrate discoveries. Explored extensively in N Territory, also in S and W Australia, 1929–33; found Hidden Basin, a 40x20 mile subsided area, covered 1200 miles on camels and collected data for Waite Research Inst., Met. Bureau, and Lands Dept; Sept.-Nov. 1933, Tennants Creek Goldfield; 1934–36, prospecting NE of Laverton, WA; farming, Terrigal, NSW, 1946–60. Received by Prince of Wales, 1926; presented to King George, 1939. Has completed 14 Australian inland expeditions. Life Member: Aust. Soc. Authors; Life Associate, Path Finders Assoc. of NSW; Mem., Nat. Geographic Soc., Washington, USA. *Publications:* Across Unknown Australia, 1925; Through a Land of Promise, 1927; Untold Miles, 1928; Hidden Wealth and Hiding

People, 1931; Sand and Sun, 1937; Bulldozer, 1945; War of the Warramullas, 1974; My Historical Years, 1980; and in numerous journals. *Recreation:* riding.      *Died 24 Sept.* 1981.

**TERRY-THOMAS, (Thomas Terry Hoar Stevens);** actor; *b* 14 July 1911; *s* of Ernest Frederick Stevens and Ellen Elizabeth (*née* Hoar); *m* 1938, Ida Patlanskey; *m* 1963, Belinda Cunningham; two *s*. *Educ:* Ardingly Coll., Sussex. Served War of 1939–45: in army, Royal Corps of Signals, 1941–46. Piccadilly Hayride, Prince of Wales Theatre, 1946–47; Radio Series: To Town With Terry, 1948–49; Top Of The Town, 1951–52; TV Series: How Do You View, 1951–52. *Films:* Private's Progress, Green Man, 1956; Brothers-in-Law, Blue Murder at St Trinians, Lucky Jim, Naked Truth, 1957; Tom Thumb, Happy is the Bride, 1958; Carlton Browne of the FO, I'm All Right Jack, Too Many Crooks, 1959; Make Mine Mink, School for Scoundrels, His and Hers, 1960; A Matter of Who, Bachelor Flat, Operation Snatch, The Wonderful World of the Brothers Grimm, 1961; Kill or Cure, Its a Mad, Mad, Mad, Mad World, 1962; Wild Affair, 1963; How to Murder Your Wife, 1964; Those Magnificent Men in their Flying Machines, 1965; Jules Verne's Rocket to the Moon, 1967; Don't Look Now, 1968; Where Were You When the Lights Went Out?, 1968; Monte Carlo or Bust!, 1969; Thirteen, 1970; Seven Times Seven, 1970; Arthur, Arthur, 1970; Atlantic Wall, 1970; Dr Phibes, 1970; Lei, Lui, Loro, la Legge, 1971; Dr Phibes rises again, 1972; The Heros, 1972; Tom Jones, 1975; Side by Side, 1975; Spanish Fly, 1975; The Last Remake of Beau Geste, 1976; The Hound of the Baskervilles, 1978. *Publication:* (as Terry-Thomas) Filling the Gap, 1959. *Recreations:* horse-riding and water ski-ing. *Address:* Flat 2, 10 Laurel Road, Barnes, SW13. *Club:* Savage.      *Died 8 Jan.* 1990.

**TEWSON, Sir (Harold) Vincent,** Kt 1950; CBE 1942; MC; *b* 4 Feb. 1898; *s* of late Edward Tewson, Bradford, Yorks; *m* 1929, Florence Elizabeth Moss; two *s*. *Educ:* Bradford. Secretary Organisation Dept, TUC, 1925–31; Asst Gen. Sec., 1931–46; Gen. Sec., 1946–60, retired. Member of the Economic Planning Board, 1947–60; Pres., Internat. Confedn of Free Trade Unions, 1953–55; Part-time Mem. London Electricity Board, 1960–68. Mem., ITA, 1964–69. *Address:* 45 Common View, Letchworth, Herts. *T:* Letchworth 76991.      *Died 1 May* 1981.

**THACKER, Charles,** CBE 1961; Director, Ford Motor Co. Ltd, 1953–64, retired; *b* 13 Feb. 1897; *m* 1927, Edith May Genese (*d* 1976); one *d*. Joined Ford Motor Co. Ltd, 1924: General Manager (Germany, 1945; Belgium, 1946–48); Managing Director, England, 1957–62, retired. Served in Army, European War, 1914–19. *Address:* 9 Villiers Road, Woodthorpe, Nottingham NG5 4FB. *T:* Nottingham 605108.      *Died 26 May* 1982.

**THACKER, Prof. Thomas William,** MA Oxon; Director of School of Oriental Studies, and Professor of Semitic Philology, University of Durham, 1951–77, then Emeritus; *b* 6 Nov. 1911; *s* of late Thomas William and of Edith Maud Thacker; *m* 1939, Katharine E. Hawthorn; one *s*. *Educ:* City of Oxford School; St Catherine's, Oxford; Berlin University. Clothworkers' Exhibitioner, 1931–33; BA 1933; Goldsmiths' Research Scholar, 1933–35; University Senior Student, Oxford, 1935–37; Mark Quested Exhibitioner, Oxford, 1937–39; studied in Berlin, 1933–36. Member of Egypt Exploration Society's expedition to Tell-el-Amarna, 1935; Asst Lecturer in Semitic Languages, University Coll. of N Wales, Bangor, 1937; Reader in Hebrew, Univ. of Durham, 1938–45; Prof. of Hebrew and Oriental Languages, Univ. of Durham, 1945–51; Foreign Office, 1940–45. Examiner at Univs of Wales (Hebrew and Old Testament), Manchester, Liverpool and Leeds (Semitic Languages), Oxford (Egyptology and Hebrew). Foreign Mem., Royal Flemish Acad. *Publications:* The Relationship of the Semitic and Egyptian Verbal Systems, 1954; articles and reviews in various periodicals. *Address:* 28 Church Street, Durham. *T:* Durham 64385.      *Died 23 April* 1984.

**THALBEN-BALL, Sir George (Thomas),** Kt 1982; CBE 1967; DMus Cantuar 1935; ARCM; FRCM 1951; FRCO; FRSCM 1956 (diploma 1963); FRSA; Bard Ylewyth Mur; Freeman of City of London; Civic and University Organist, Birmingham, 1949–82; Organist, the Temple Church, 1923–81, Organist Emeritus, since 1982; Curator-Organist, The Royal Albert Hall, London; Professor and Examiner, the Royal College of Music; Examiner to the Associated Board of the Royal Academy of Music and the Royal College of Music; Member of the Council and Examiner of Royal College of Organists; Examiner on behalf of Cape University, 1925; Adviser and Consultant to BBC, 1941; *b* Sydney, NSW, 18 June 1896; *s* of George Charles Thalben-Ball and Mary Hannah Spear, Newquay, Cornwall; *m* Evelyn (*d* 1961), *d* of Francis Chapman, NZ; one *s* one *d*; *m* 1968, Jennifer Lucy Bate (marr. annulled 1972). *Educ:* private tuition. Exhbnr and Grove Scholar, RCM, Chappell and Hopkinson Gold Medallist; Lafontaine Prize, RCO; Organist: Whitefield's Tabernacle; Holy Trinity Church, Castlenau; Paddington Parish Church; acting Organist, the Hon. Socs of Temple, 1919, Organist, 1923–; studied pianoforte with

Fritz Hartvigson, Franklin Taylor, and Fanny Davies; harmony and composition with Sir Frederick Bridge, Sir Charles Stanford, and Dr Charles Wood; musical history with Sir Hubert Parry; organ with Sir Walter Parratt and F. A. Sewell. President: London Soc. of Organists, 1936; RCO, 1948; Incorporated Assoc. of Organists, 1944–46; Mem. Bd of Governors, Royal Nat. Coll. of the Blind. FRSA 1971; Fellow, Royal Canadian Coll. of Organists. Hon. RAM 1973. Hon. Bencher, Inner Temple, 1959. Guest Organist, Les Amis de l'Orgue, Paris, 1937; Toured Australia as guest organist in connection with Jubilee of the formation of the Commonwealth, 1951, toured: South Africa, 1954, New Zealand, 1971; Guest of honour, Amer. Guild of Organists Convention, NY, 1956; Guest, Philadelphia, 1973; toured USA and Canada, 1975 (opening organ recital, Carnegie Hall, NY). Mem. Jury, Concours international d'orgue, Grand Prix de Chartres, 1973. EMI Gold Disc, 1963. Played the organ on the Continent and in America and was a regular broadcaster and performer at the Sir Henry Wood Promenade Concerts. Composer of Organ and Choral music including Sursum Corda for chorus, orchestra and trumpet fanfares (commissioned by BBC). Hon. DMus and Gold Medal, Birmingham, 1972. *Recreations:* golf and riding. *Address:* 3 Paper Buildings, Inner Temple, EC4. *Club:* Athenæum. *Died 18 Jan.* 1987.

**THAPAR, Prem Nath,** CIE 1944; lately Vice-Chancellor, Punjab Agricultural University, Lydhiana, 1962–68; Indian Civil Service; *b* 13 April 1903; *s* of Diwan Bahadur Kunj Behari Thapar, CBE; *m* 1932, Leela Dutta; one *s* two *d*. *Educ:* Govt Coll., Lahore; New Coll., Oxford. Joined ICS 1926. Dep. Commissioner, Kangra, Attock; Deputy Commissioner and Colonisation Officer, Montgomery, 1934–37; Settlement Officer, Jhelum, 1937–41; Joint Secretary, Information and Broadcasting Department, Government of India, 1941–46; Secretary, Food and Civil Supplies Department, Punjab, 1946–47; Commissioner, Lahore Division, 1947; Financial Commissioner, East Punjab, 1947–53; Chief Administrator, Chandigarh Capital Project, 1950–53; Adviser, Planning Commission, Government of India, 1953–54; Sec., Min. of Food and Agric., Govt of India, 1954–58; Member, Atomic Energy Commission and *ex officio* Secretary to Government of India, Dept of Atomic Energy, Bombay, 1958–62. Mem. Punjab Admin. Reforms Commn, 1964–65; Consultant, Review Team, FAO, UN, Rome, 1966–67. Trustee, Internat. Rice Research Inst., Manila, Philippines. *Publications:* Settlement Report, Jhelum District, 1945; Customary Law, Jhelum District, 1946. *Address:* Ashok Farm, PO Maidan Garhi, New Delhi-30, India. *T:* 72382.
*Died Nov.* 1982.

**THAYRE, Albert Jesse,** CBE 1980 (MBE 1945); DL; Director, N. G. Bailey Organisation Ltd, since 1982; Chief General Manager and Director, Halifax Building Society, 1974–82; *b* 30 May 1917; *s* of Alfred and Louisa Thayre; *m* 1940, Margaret Elizabeth Wheeler; one *d*. *Educ:* Bromley County Sch. for Boys; City of London Coll. BCom (London) 1948. Stockbrokers' Clerk, 1933–39. Served War: Rifleman/NCO with 2/London Irish Rifles, 1939–41; Lieut to Captain 51 (H) Bn Reconnaissance Corps, 1941–42; Captain, then Major and Lt-Col 14 Highland LI, 1942–46 (incl. appts as DAQMG and AA&QMG). Investment Analyst, 1946–50. Halifax Building Soc.: Clerk, then Inspector and Br. Manager, 1951–55; Staff Manager, 1955–56; Asst Gen. Man., 1956–60; Gen. Man., 1960; Dir, 1968; Asst Chief Gen. Man., 1970. Bradford Univ.: Mem. Council, 1966–; Chm. Finance Cttee, 1966–87; Pro-Chancellor and Chm. of Council, 1969–87; a Pro-Chancellor, 1988–. Chm., Centre for Indust. and Educnl Liaison (W and N Yorks), 1983–; Hon. Treas., Standing Conf. on Schs Sci. and Tech., 1986–; Mem., Univs Authorities Panel, 1970–79; Dir and Dep. Chm., Univs Superannuation Scheme Ltd, 1974–79. FSS, FCBSI, CBIM. Hon. DLitt Bradford, 1982. DL West Yorks, 1982. *Address:* Stonedale, 42 Northowram Green, Halifax, West Yorkshire HX3 7SL. *T:* Halifax 202581. *Died 23 Oct.* 1988.

**THEORELL, (Axel) Hugo (Teodor),** MD; Director of Nobel Medical Institute, Department of Biochemistry, Stockholm, 1937–70; *b* Linköping, Sweden, 6 July 1903; *s* of Ture and Armida (Bill) Theorell; *m* 1931, Margit Alenius; three *s*. *Educ:* Linköpings Högre Allm. Läroverk; Pasteur Institute, Paris; Royal Caroline Medico-Surgical Institute, Stockholm. MD Stockholm, 1930. Asst Professor of Biochemistry, Uppsala University, 1932; with Prof. Otto Warburg, Kaiser Wilhelm Institut für Zellphysiologie, Berlin-Dahlem, 1933–35; engaged upon research into enzyme structure; awarded Nobel Prize in Physiology and Medicine, 1955, for discoveries concerning nature and effects of oxidation enzymes. Secretary, Swedish Society of Physicians and Surgeons, 1940–46 (Chm., 1946–47 and 1957–58, Hon. Mem., 1956); Chairman: Wenner-Gren Society; Wenner-Gren Centre Foundation; Swedish Chemists' Assoc., 1947–49; Stockholm Symphony Soc., 1951–73. Pres., Internat. Union of Biochemistry, 1967–73; Member: Swedish Academy of Science (President, 1967–69); Swedish Academy of Engineering Science; Swedish Acad. of Music; Royal Danish Acad. Scis and Letters; Norwegian Acad. Sci. and Letters; Royal Norwegian Soc. Arts and Scis; Amer. Acad. Arts and Scis; Nat.

Acad. Scis, Washington; Amer. Philos. Soc., Philadelphia; NY Acad. of Sci.; l'Accademia Nazionale del XL of Rome; Polish Acad. Naukoznawcze; Indian Acad. Sci.; For. Mem., Roy. Soc. Hon. Dr: Univ. Sorbonne, Paris; Univ. Pennsylvania, USA; Univ. Louvain; Univ. Libre, Brussels, Belgium; Univ. Brazil, Rio de Janeiro; Univ. Kentucky, USA; Univ. Michigan, USA. 1st Cl. Comdr Royal Order of the Northern Star; 1st Cl. Comdr, Order of Finnish Lion; Comdr Royal Norwegian Order of St Olav; Comdr, Légion d'Honneur (France); Officer, Order of Southern Cross (Brazil). Trafvenfelt Medal, 1945; Scheele Medal, 1956; Caroline Inst. 150 years Jubilee Medal, 1960; Emanuel e Paterno Medal, 1962; Paul Karrer Medal, 1965; Ciba Medal, 1971; Sommelweiss Medal, 1971. *Recreation:* music. *Address:* Karolinska Institutet, Medicinska Nobelinstitutet, Biokemiska advelningen, Laboratorium för Enzymforskning, Solnavägen 1, 10401 Stockholm 60, Sweden; Sveavägen 166H, 11346 Stockholm, Sweden.
*Died 15 Aug.* 1982.

**THESIGER, Hon. Sir Gerald (Alfred),** Kt 1958; MBE 1946; Judge of the High Court of Justice, Queen's Bench Division, 1958–78; *b* 25 Dec. 1902; *s* of late Maj.-Gen. George Thesiger, CB, CMG; *m* 1932, Marjorie Guille (*d* 1972), *d* of late Raymond Guille, Long Island, NY; three *d*. *Educ:* Greshams School, Holt; Magdalen College, Oxford (MA). Demy, 1921; BA, 1924; called to Bar, Inner Temple, 1926, Bencher, 1956, Treasurer, 1979; South Eastern Circuit; QC 1948; Member General Council of the Bar, 1936–41, 1958; Recorder of Rye, 1937–42; Recorder of Hastings, 1943–57; Recorder of Southend, 1957–58; Chairman, West Kent Quarter Sessions, 1947–58. Major, Deputy Judge Advocate Staff, 1941–45. Member Borough Council, Fulham, 1934–37, Chelsea, 1937–58, Alderman, 1945; Chief Warden, Chelsea, 1939–41; Mayor of Chelsea, 1944–46, Hon. Freeman, 1963. Chairman, Departmental Cttee on Licensing of Road Passenger Services, 1953–54; Chairman of Governors, United Westminster Schools, 1947–58; Dep. Chm., Boundary Commn (England), 1962–74. Pres. British Acad. of Forensic Sciences, 1973–74. *Address:* 44 Chelsea Park Gardens, SW3 6AB. *Club:* Hurlingham. *Died 16 April* 1981.

**THIRKELL, Lancelot George, (Lance Thirkell);** Secretary and Administrator, New Bridge Association for befriending ex-offenders, 1980–84; *b* 9 Jan. 1921; *s* of George Lancelot Thirkell, engineer, and Angela Margaret Mackail (Angela Thirkell, novelist); *m* 1946, Katherine Mary Lowinsky, *d* of Thomas Esmond Lowinsky, artist, and Ruth Jeanette Hirsch; two *s* two *d*. *Educ:* Saint Paul's School (Schol.); Magdalen Coll. Oxford (Demy). HM Forces, 1942–46; active service D-day to the Rhine with Essex Yeo. and in SE Asia with RA. HM Foreign Service, 1946–50; granted Civil Service Certificate, 1946; Third Sec., Western Dept, 1946; Third Sec., Budapest, 1947; Second Sec., Eastern Dept, 1948. Joined BBC as Report Writer, Monitoring Service, 1950; Assistant, Appointments Dept, 1953; Assistant Staff Administration, 1956; Head of Secretariat, 1961; Controller, Staff Trng and Appointments, 1964; Chief Asst to Man. Dir, External Broadcasting, 1972–75; Controller, Administration, External Broadcasting, 1975–80. Chm., Ascension Island London Users' Cttee, 1972–84; Dir Caribbean Relay Co., 1976–84. Governor, Thomson Foundn Television Coll., 1964–72. Councillor, Royal Borough of Kensington, 1959–62; Chm. Notting Hill Adventure Playground, 1964–76; Appeals Sec., Portobello Project for unattached youth; Mem., European Adv. Council, Salzburg Seminar in American Studies. Pres., Angela Thirkell Soc., 1980–. *Publications:* A Garden Full of Weeds, 1962; (with Ruth Lowinsky) Russian Food for Pleasure, 1953. *Recreations:* ski-ing, sailing. *Address:* 31 Lansdowne Road, W11. *T:* 01–727 6046; Oxbow, Harkstead, Suffolk. *Clubs:* Leander (Henley-on-Thames); Royal Harwich Yacht. *Died 10 Jan.* 1989.

**THISTLETON-SMITH, Vice-Admiral Sir Geoffrey,** KBE 1959; CB 1956; GM 1941; DL; *b* 10 May 1905; *m* 1st, 1931, Mary Katherine Harvey (*d* 1976); one *s* one *d*; 2nd, 1982, Joyce, Lady Fairhaven. Captain, 1944; HMS Pembroke, Royal Naval Barracks, Chatham (in Command), 1952; Chief of Staff to C-in-C Home Fleet and Eastern Atlantic, Dec. 1953; Rear-Admiral, 1954; Admiral Commanding Reserves, 1956–58; Vice-Admiral, 1957; Admiral, British Joint Services Mission, Washington, 1958–60, retd. CC West Sussex, 1964–77. DL Sussex, 1972. *Address:* Down Place, Harting, Petersfield, Hants. *Died 13 Nov.* 1986.

**THOM, Alexander;** Professor of Engineering Science, Oxford University, 1945–61; *b* 26 March 1894; Scottish parents; *m* 1917, Jeanie Boyd Kirkwood (*d* 1975); one *s* one *d* (one *s* killed 1945). *Educ:* Glasgow University. BSc 1915, PhD 1926, DSc 1929, Glasgow; MA (Oxford) 1945; Emeritus Fellow, Brasenose College, 1961. Employed by various engineering and aeronautical firms, 1913–21; Lectr, Glasgow University, 1922–39; Royal Aircraft Establishment, Farnborough, on aeronautical research, 1939–45. Hon. LLD Glasgow, 1960; Hon. DSc Strathclyde, 1976. *Publications:* Standard Tables and Formulae for Setting out Road Spirals, 1935; (with C. J. Apelt) Field Computations in Engineering and Physics, 1960; Megalithic Sites in Britain, 1967; Megalithic Lunar

Observatories, 1971; (with A. S. Thom) Megalithic Remains in Britain and Brittany, 1978; Megalithic Rings, 1980; papers to various scientific institutions. *Recreation:* sailing. *Address:* The Hill, Dunlop, Ayrshire. *Died* 7 *Nov.* 1985.

**THOM, James Robert;** Forestry Consultant, Food and Agriculture Organisation, Rome, since 1973; *b* 22 July 1910; *er s* of late William and Caroline Thom; *m* 1937, Constance Daphne (*d* 1979), *d* of late Dr A. C. L. La Frenais, British Guiana; two *s; m* 1981, Lorna Mary, *widow* of Canon B. E. R. Millar, Edinburgh. *Educ:* George Watson's Coll., Edinburgh; Edinburgh University. BSc (Forestry) Edinburgh Univ., 1932. District Officer, Forestry Commission, 1933; Divisional Officer, 1940; Conservator, 1946; Director of Forestry for Wales, 1958–63, for England, 1963–65; Dir of Research, 1965–68, Forestry Commn; Project Manager: UN Forest Industries Develt Survey, Guyana, 1969–70; UN Develt Prog., Sarajevo, Yugoslavia, 1970–73. Pres., Watsonian Club, Edinburgh, 1975–76. *Recreations:* Rugby football (represented Scotland, 1933), gardening. *Address:* 11 Abbotsford Crescent, Edinburgh EH10 5DY. *T:* 031–447 1005. *Club:* Caledonian. *Died* 13 *Dec.* 1981.

**THOMAS, Rt. Rev. Albert Reuben Edward Thomas;** Bishop, (RC), of Bathurst, (NSW), since 1963; *b* Farnborough, Hants, 26 Oct. 1908; *s* of Albert Charles Thomas and Esperie Loreto Clarke. *Educ:* St Joseph's College, Hunter's Hill; St Columbia's Coll., St Patrick's Coll., Manly. Diploma of Social Studies, Sydney Univ., 1944. Ordained, 1931. Asst Suburban Parishes, 1931–38; Diocesan Dir, Pontifical Missions, 1938–63, National Dir, 1944–70. Founder of Catholic Welfare Bureau, 1941. Initiated Australian National Pilgrimage, 1950–63; Hon. Chaplain of House of Lourdes, 1960; Foundation Chm. of St Vincent's Hospital Advisory Board, 1955; Chm. of Unity Movement for Christian Christmas, 1956–63. *Publication:* contrib. to Australian Encyclopaedia, on Catholic Missions and Welfare, 1958. *Address:* Bishop's House, Bathurst, NSW 2795, Australia. *Died* 28 *Sept.* 1983.

**THOMAS, Brig. Arthur Frank Friend,** CIE 1942; *b* 8 Aug. 1897; *s* of Arthur Ernest Thomas, Parkhurst, South Norwood; *m* 1928, Elizabeth Stephenson Walker (decd), MB, BCh, DPH, *d* of Rev. S. Walker, MA, Donaghadee, Co. Down; one *d* (one *s* decd). *Educ:* Melbourne College. ADC, EEF, 1920–21; DADOS Waziristan District, 1928–31; Staff Capt. AHQ 1931–33; DADOS, AHQ, 1933–36; AD of C, AHQ, 1936–39; DD of C 1939–40; D of C 1940; CCPM 1940–41; Deputy Controller-General of Inspection, GHQ, India, 1941–45; Director of Civil Personnel, 1945–47; retired, 1947. Served European War, 1914–21, Egypt, 1914–16, France, 1916–17, EEF 1918 (wounded, despatches); NW Frontier, India, 1930; War of 1939–45. *Recreations:* gardening, cine-photography. *Address:* Coughton Lodge Residential Home, Birmingham Road, Coughton, near Alcester, Warwicks B49 5HU. *Died* 22 *April* 1987.

**THOMAS, Brian (Dick Lauder),** OBE 1961; Mural Painter and Stained Glass Designer; *b* 19 Sept. 1912; *s* of Frank Leslie Thomas, MB, BS, and Margaret Mary (*née* Lauder). *Educ:* Bradfield College. Rome Scholarship in Mural Painting, 1934; Camouflage Directorate, Min. of Home Security, 1939–45; Principal, Byam Shaw Sch. of Art, 1946–54; Master, Art Workers Guild, 1957, Editor, Artifex, 1968–71; Fellow, Brit. Soc. of Master Glass Painters, 1958; Chm. of Governors, Hurstpierpoint Coll., 1958–67; Mem. Council, Artists' Gen. Benevolent Instn, 1964; Chm. Council, Fedn of British Craft Socs, 1971–73; Mem., Crafts Adv. Cttee, 1971–73. Vice-Pres., SPCK, 1976. Master, Glaziers Co., 1976. *Principal works:* St Paul's Cathedral (stained glass in American and OBE Chapels); Westminster Abbey (stained glass); Winchester Cathedral (shrine of St Swithun); Wellington Cathedral, NZ (War Memorial windows); St George's Chapel, Windsor (panels in altar rails); St George's Church, Stevenage New Town (stained glass); Livery Co. Windows: London Guildhall, Pewterers' Hall, Innholders' Hall, Watermen's Hall; Biographical Window in Harpur Trust Court-Room, Bedford; memorials to Dame Nellie Melba, John Ireland, Russell Colman, Sir Harold Graham-Hodgson, Lord Webb-Johnson and others; painted ceiling at Templewood, Norfolk; murals and mosaics in many religious and secular buildings of London and the provinces. *Publications:* Vision and Technique in European Painting, 1952; Geometry in Pictorial Composition, 1971; (ed) Directory of Master Glass-Painters, 1972. *Address:* Crosby Lodge, 2/2a Fitzharris Avenue, Charminster, Bournemouth BH9 1BZ. *Died* 13 *Dec.* 1989.

**THOMAS, Dr Claudius Cornelius,** CMG 1979; Commissioner for the Eastern Caribbean Governments in the United Kingdom, since 1975; High Commissioner, in the United Kingdom, for: St Lucia, and St Vincent and the Grenadines, since 1979; Antigua-Barbuda, 1981–84; Saint Christopher and Nevis, since 1983; *b* 1 Oct. 1928; *s* of Charles Malin Thomas and Ada Thomas (*née* Dyer). *Educ:* Castries Intermed. Sch., St Lucia; London Univ. (LLB); Univ. de Strasbourg (Dr en droit). Called to Bar, Gray's Inn, 1957. Cadet Officer, Commn for the West Indies in UK, 1961; Translator, EEC, Brussels, 1962; Attaché, L'Institut Internat. des Sciences

Administratives, Brussels, 1962–63; Free University of (West) Berlin: Wissenschaftlicher Asst, 1963–72, Asst Prof., 1972–75. Ambassador of Saint Lucia to: Paris, 1983–; Bonn, 1983–; Stockholm, 1984–; Permanent Representative of Saint Lucia to: Stockholm, 1984–; UNESCO, 1984–; EEC, 1984–. Member: Hon. Soc. of Gray's Inn; British Inst. of Internat. and Comparative Law. *Publications:* contrib. to and assisted in, Multitudo Legum Ius Unum, 1973; contrib. to: Deutches Jahrbuch des Öffentlichen Rechts, 1966; Anglo-American Law Review, 1973; and other legal jls. *Recreations:* cricket, table tennis, sailing. *Address:* High Commission for Eastern Caribbean States, 10 Kensington Court, W8. *Clubs:* Royal Commonwealth Soc., Hurlingham.
*Died* 6 *April* 1987.

**THOMAS, Prof. Dewi-Prys,** BArch, DipCD; FRIBA, MRTPI; Head of Welsh School of Architecture, 1960–81, and first Professor of Architecture in University of Wales, 1964–81 (Institute of Science and Technology), Cardiff; *b* Liverpool, 5 Aug. 1916; *o s* of A. Dan Thomas, Martin's Bank, and Elysabeth Watkin Thomas; *m* 1965, Joyce Ffoulkes Davies, *e d* of Rev. Robert Ff. Parry, Ballarat and Geelong, Australia; two step *s* two step *d*. *Educ:* Liverpool Inst.; Univ. of Liverpool Sch. of Architecture. Ravenhead Schol. and John Lewis Partnership Prizeman, 1935; John Rankin Prizeman, 1935 and 1936; Holland, Hannen and Cubitts Prizeman and Holt Travelling Schol., 1936; RIBA Archibald Dawnay Schol., 1936–38; Honan Trav. Schol., 1938–39; BArch (1st Cl. Hons) 1938; DipCD (Distinction) Liverpool, 1942. Architect in office of T. Alwyn Lloyd, FRIBA, PPTPI, Cardiff (S Wales Outline Plan), 1942–47; Lectr and Sen. Lectr, Univ. of Liverpool, 1947–60. Dean of Environmental Design, UWIST, 1967–69 and 1971–73; Vice-Principal, UWIST, 1969–71; Mem. Bd, Univ. of Wales Press, 1969–75; Mem. Court, Univ. of Wales, 1972–75. Comr, Royal Commn on Ancient Monuments in Wales, 1970–; Member Board: Civic Trust for Wales, 1964–; Member: Court of Governors, Nat. Theatre for Wales, 1967–85; Founder Mem., Cardiff 2000 (Cardiff Civic Soc.), 1964– (Chm., 1973–75). Frequent lectr and broadcaster (Welsh and English) radio and TV, 1942–; Sir Sydney Jones Meml Lectures (The British Underground), Univ. of Liverpool, 1975; BBC Wales TV Heritage Year Lecture (Arthur Lives!), 1975. Gorsedd y Beirdd (Aelod er Anrhydedd), 1983. *Publications:* Treftadaeth: the heritage, 1975; (memoir in) Artists in Wales, 3, 1976; contrib. to jls. *Recreations:* Celtic affairs, Welsh poetry and history, art. *Address:* Tower House, 1A Cefn Coed Road, Cardiff CF2 6AN. *T:* Cardiff 754217; Taldir, Dolgellau. *T:* Dolgellau 422201.
*Died* 28 *Nov.* 1985.

**THOMAS, Rt. Rev. Francis Gerard;** Prelate of Honour, 1969; Bishop of Northampton (RC), since 1982; *b* 29 May 1930; *s* of Edward James and Elizabeth May Thomas. *Educ:* St Dominic's Primary School, Stone, Staffs; Cotton College, Staffs; Oscott Coll., Sutton Coldfield. Priest, 1955; Curate at St Peter's, Leamington Spa, 1955–56; further study in theology, Gregorian Univ., Rome, 1956–59; Lectr in Theology, Oscott Coll., 1959; Rector of the Coll., 1968–79; Chapter Canon and Vicar Gen., Archdio. of Birmingham, 1979–82; Parish Priest, Holy Trinity, Newcastle-under-Lyme, 1979–82. Asst Editor, Liturgy and Music. *Address:* Bishop's House, Marriott Street, Northampton NN2 6AW. *T:* Northampton 715635. *Died* 25 *Dec.* 1988.

**THOMAS, Frederick Maginley,** CMG 1962; retired Civil Servant; *b* 1 July 1908; 3rd *s* of Rev. Canon F. Thomas; *m* 1941, Dorothea Mary (*d* 1969), *o d* of Edward North; two *d*. *Educ:* Truro Cathedral School; Exeter College, Oxford. Cadet, Colonial Administrative Service, 1931; District Officer, Northern Rhodesia, 1933; Asst Secretary, 1949; Provincial Commissioner, 1954; Minister of Native Affairs, Northern Rhodesia Government, 1960–63; Deputy Governor, Northern Rhodesia, 1964–65. Served 1940–47: 3rd Battalion KAR; 3 Bn NRR; GSO1 Civil Affairs, Lt-Col. *Publication:* Historical Notes on the Bisa, 1953. *Recreations:* most outdoor pursuits, water colours. *Address:* Rock House, Halse, Taunton, Somerset. *T:* Bishops Lydeard 432293. *Died* 18 *July* 1984.

**THOMAS, Gwyn;** author; *b* 6 July 1913; *s* of Walter and Ziphorah Thomas; *m* 1938, Eiluned Thomas. *Educ:* Porth Grammar Sch.; St Edmund Hall, Oxford Univ.; Madrid Univ. BA Hons Oxon, 1934. Univ. Extension Lectr, 1934–40; Schoolmaster (Mod. Langs), 1940–62. Television appearances, 1962–. *Publications: novels:* The Dark Philosophers, 1946; Where Did I Put My Pity, 1946; The Alone To The Alone, 1947; All Things Betray Thee, 1949; The World Cannot Hear You, 1951; Now Lead Us Home, 1952; A Frost On My Frolic, 1953; The Stranger At My Side, 1954; Point Of Order, 1956; Gazooka, 1957; The Love Man, 1958; Ring Delirium 123, 1959; A Welsh Eye, 1964; A Hatful of Humours, 1965; Leaves In The Wind, 1968; The Sky of Our Lives, 1972; *plays:* The Keep, 1961; Loud Organs, 1962; Jackie the Jumper, 1962; The Loot, 1965; SAP, 1974; The Breakers, 1976; *autobiog.:* A Few Selected Exits, 1968. *Recreations:* opera, staring. *Address:* Cherry Trees, Wyndham Park, Peterston-super-Ely, Cardiff. *T:* Peterston-super-Ely 435. *Club:* Pontcanna Studio (Cardiff). *Died* 12 *April* 1981.

**THOMAS, Howard,** CBE 1967; Chairman: Thames Television Ltd, 1974–79; Thames Television International Ltd, 1974–81; Independent Television News, 1974–76 (Director, since 1956); Managing Director of ABC Television, 1955–68, of Thames Television, 1968–74; *b* 5 March 1909; *s* of W. G. Thomas and A. M. Thomas; *m* 1934, Hilda, *d* of Harrison Fogg; two *d.* Trained in advertising, journalism and broadcasting. Started Commercial Radio Department, London Press Exchange Ltd, 1938. Writer and Producer for BBC Sound Radio and during 3 years directed and produced 500 programmes. Entered film industry as Producer-in-Chief, Associated British Pathé Ltd, 1944. Divnl Dir, EMI Ltd; Director: EMI Film and Theatre Corp. Ltd; EMI Film Distributors Ltd; Euston Films Ltd; Independent Television Companies Association; Literators Ltd; Argus Press Ltd, 1973–; Television International Enterprises Ltd, 1985–; BAFTA Management Ltd, 1975–80; Logospheres Ltd, 1979–; Thames Valley Broadcasting Ltd, 1975–80; Tempo Video Ltd, 1981–. Broadcasting Consultant to: EMI Ltd and Rediffusion Television Ltd, 1979–81; to Thames Television Internat. Ltd, 1982–84. A Governor, BFI, 1974–82 (Chm., BFI Funding and Develt Cttee). Member: Advertising Standards Authority, 1962–73; Govt Adv. Cttee on Advertising, 1973–. Vice-Chm., Advertising Assoc., 1973–77. Dir, Internat. Council, Nat. Acad. of TV Arts & Scis (USA), 1971–78. Mem., 'London Looks Forward' Silver Jubilee 1977 Conf. Hon. Fellow, British Kinematograph Sound & Television Soc., 1967; FRSA 1975 (Mem. Council, 1978–84); Vice-Pres., Royal Television Soc., 1976–84; Hon. Life Mem'., Gtr London Arts Assoc., 1977–; Former President: Radio Industries Club; Cinema & Television Veterans. Radio Programmes: Showmen of England, Beauty Queen, The Brains Trust, Shipmates Ashore, Books that Changed the World (series), 1985, etc. Films: Elizabeth is Queen (Coronation) and many documentaries. *Publications:* The Brighter Blackout Book, 1939; How to Write for Broadcasting, 1940; Britain's Brains Trust, 1944; The Truth About Television, 1962; With an Independent Air, 1977. *Address:* Old Ship House, Wharfe Lane, Henley-on-Thames, Oxon.                                          *Died* 6 *Nov.* 1986.

**THOMAS, Ivor Owen;** retired; *b* 5 Dec. 1898; *s* of late Benjamin L. and Margaret Thomas, Briton Ferry, Glamorgan; *m* 1929, Beatrice (*d* 1978), *d* of late Councillor William Davis, Battersea; one *d. Educ:* Vernon Place Council Sch., Briton Ferry; London Labour College, 1923–25. Gwalia Tinplate Works, Briton Ferry, 1912–19; Engine Cleaner GWR, Pontypool Rd, 1919–23; NUR Head Office Staff, 1925–45. Member Battersea Borough Council, 1928–45; Chm. Housing Cttee, 1934–38. MP (Lab) the Wrekin Division of Shropshire, 1945–55. Resumed NUR Head Office Staff, 1955–58. Waterloo CCE Dept British Rlys, Southern Region, 1960–64; Westminster City Council, Land Use Survey, 1965–66. *Address:* Marobea, 26 Sumburgh Road, SW12. *T:* 01–228 2874.
*Died* 11 *Jan.* 1982.

**THOMAS, Jeffrey,** QC 1974; a Recorder of the Crown Court, since 1975; *b* 12 Nov. 1933; *s* of John James Thomas and Phyllis Thomas (*née* Hile); *m* 1960, Margaret Jenkins, BSc(Econ); *m* 1987, Valerie Ellerington. *Educ:* Abertillery Grammar Sch.; King's Coll. London; Gray's Inn. Called to the Bar, Gray's Inn, 1957. Pres., Univ. of London Union, 1955–56. Served Army (National Service): commnd in Royal Corps of Transport, 1959 (Senior Under Officer); later served in Directorate of Army Legal Services: Major, Dep. Asst Dir, HQ BAOR, 1961. Contested: (Lab) Barry, 1966; (SDP) Cardiff W, 1983. MP (Lab 1970–81, SDP 1981–83) Abertillery, 1970–83; PPS to Sec. of State for Wales, 1977–79; opposition spokesman on legal affairs, 1979–81; SDP spokesman on legal affairs, 1981–83; rejoined Labour Party, 1986–. Chm., Brit. Caribbean Assoc.; Mem. Council, Justice; Vice Chm., British Gp, IPU, 1979–82. Mem. Court, Univ. of London, 1981–. *Recreations:* watching Rugby football, travelling. *Address:* (home) Min-y-nant, Whitebrook, near Monmouth, Gwent NP5 4TT. *T:* Monmouth 860598; (chambers) 49 Westgate Chambers, Commercial Street, Newport, Gwent. *T:* Newport (0633) 267403. *Clubs:* Reform; Abertillery Rugby Football.                                          *Died* 17 *May* 1989.

**THOMAS, Gen. Sir (John) Noel,** KCB 1969 (CB 1967); DSO 1945; MC 1945; BEng; Member, 1971–81, Vice-Chairman, 1974–81, Commonwealth War Graves Commission; *b* 28 Feb. 1915; *s* of John Ernest Thomas; *m* 1946, Jill, *d* of Edward Gordon Cuthbert Quilter; two *s. Educ:* Royal Grammar School, Newcastle upon Tyne; Liverpool University. 2nd Lieut, Royal Engineers, 1936. Served War of 1939–45 (MC, DSO). Imperial Defence College, 1963; General Officer Commanding 42 (Lancashire and Cheshire) Div. (TA), North West District, 1963–65; Director, Combat Development (Army), MoD, 1965–68; Dep. Chief of Defence Staff (Operational Requirements), MoD, 1968–70; Master-Gen. of the Ordnance, 1971–74. Lt-Gen. 1968; Gen. 1971. Hon. Col, Liverpool Univ. Contingent, OTC, 1965–80. Colonel Commandant: Royal Pioneer Corps, 1968–75; Royal Engineers, 1968–73. Pres. Sussex Council, Royal British Legion, 1981–. FRSA 1971. Hon. DEng Liverpool, 1972. *Address:* Chandlers House, The Trippet, Old

Bosham, Sussex. *Club:* Royal Ocean Racing.
*Died* 16 *March* 1983.

**THOMAS, Rev. John Roland Lloyd;** Principal of St David's College, Lampeter, 1953–75; Canon of St David's, 1956–75, Chancellor, 1963–75; *b* 22 Feb. 1908; 2nd *s* of late John Thomas, ME, and Mrs Ann Thomas; *m* 1949, Mrs Elizabeth Swaffield (*née* Rees); three *d. Educ:* King's Coll., Taunton; St David's Coll., Lampeter; Jesus College, Oxford. Welsh Church Scholar, St David's College, Lampeter, BA (1st Class Hons History), 1930, Senior Scholar, 1929–30; Meyricke Graduate Scholar, 1930–32, Jesus Coll., Oxford, BA (2nd Class Theology Hons), 1932; MA 1936. Deacon, 1932; priest, 1933; Curate of St John Baptist, Cardiff, 1932–40. CF (EC), 1940–44. Rector of Canton, Cardiff, 1944–49; Vicar of St Mark's, Newport, 1949–52; Dean of Monmouth and Vicar of St Woolos Parish, Newport, 1952–53. CF (TA), 1949–52; SCF (TA), 1950–52; Hon. CF 1952. Hon. LLD Wales, 1976. *Publication:* Moth or Phoenix, 1980. *Address:* 1 Rock House, St Julian Street, Tenby, Dyfed. *T:* Tenby 2679.                            *Died* 11 *April* 1984.

**THOMAS, Prof. Joseph Anthony Charles;** Professor of Roman Law in the University of London, since 1965; *b* 24 Feb. 1923; *e c* of Joseph and Merle Thomas, Bridgend, Glam; *m* 1949, Margaret (marr. diss. 1970), *d* of John and Jean Hookham, Cambridge; three *s* one *d. Educ:* County Grammar School, Bridgend; Trinity College, Cambridge. MA, LLB Cantab 1949; Barrister, Gray's Inn, 1950. Lecturer in Law, Nottingham Univ., 1949–54; Sen. Lecturer, Univ. of Glasgow, 1954–57; Douglas Professor of Civil Law, University of Glasgow, 1957–64. Served with Intelligence Corps, Psychological Warfare Branch, and Allied Commission, Austria, 1942–46. Crabtree Orator, 1969. Medaglia d'oro dei benemeriti della cultura della Repubblica Italiana, 1974. *Publications:* Private International Law, 1955, repr. 1975; (with J. C. Smith) A Casebook on Contract, 1957 (6th edn 1977); The Institutes of Justinian, 1975; Textbook of Roman Law, 1976; articles in legal periodicals. *Recreations:* walking, reading, watching cricket. *Address:* University College, Gower Street, WC1. *T:* 01–387 7050; 1 Hornton Street, W8. *T:* 01–937 1688. *Club:* MCC.                                *Died* 22 *June* 1981.

**THOMAS, Maj.-Gen. Lechmere Cay,** CB 1948; CBE 1945 (OBE 1939); DSO 1940 and Bar 1942; MC and Bar 1917; Major-General, retired; late Royal Northumberland Fusiliers; *b* 20 Oct. 1897; *s* of late Kempson Thomas, Farnham, Surrey; *m* 1st, 1929, Kathleen Primrose (*d* 1929), 2nd *d* of late Albert White, JP, Birney Hill, Ponteland, Northumberland; 2nd, 1951, Sylvia E., *widow* of Eric Smith, Colonial Service, and *d* of late Newman Hall, Forest Hill, Jersey, CI. *Educ:* Cranleigh School, Surrey. Served European War, 1914–18, in France and Belgium (wounded, MC and Bar, two medals); Iraq, 1920 (wounded); commanded 2nd Battalion King's African Rifles, 1934–39; served War of 1939–45, in France, Malaya and Burma (despatches, DSO, and Bar, CBE); Commander: 9th Bn Royal Northumberland Fusiliers, 1940–42; 1st Bn, Wilts Regt, 1942; 88th Indian Inf. Bde, 1942–43; 36th Indian Inf. Bde, 1943–45; Inspector General, (Indigenous) Burma Army, 1945–47; GOC (Indigenous) Burma Army, 1947–48. *Address:* Forest Hill, Beaumont, Jersey, CI. *Club:* Army and Navy.
*Died* 9 *May* 1981.

**THOMAS, (Lewis John) Wynford V.;** *see* Vaughan-Thomas.

**THOMAS, Lowell Jackson,** author, producer, radio commentator; *b* 6 April 1892; *s* of Colonel Harry G. Thomas, MD, and Harriet Wagner; *m* 1st, 1917, Frances Ryan; one *s*; 2nd, 1977, Marianna Munn. *Educ:* University of Northern Indiana (BSc); Univ. of Denver (BA, MA); Princeton Univ. (MA). Reporter Chicago Journal until 1914; Professor of Oratory, Chicago Kent College of Law, 1912–14; Instructor Dept of English, Princeton, 1914–16; Chief of Civilian Mission for historical record of First World War (Palestine Campaign and Arabian revolution). Associate-Editor, Asia Magazine, 1919–23. Studied international aviation (25,000 mile flight over 21 countries), 1926–27. Made many war broadcasts from European and Far Eastern war points; Tibetan Expedition, 1949. Brought out Cinerama for the first time, 1952; producer of This Is Cinerama, The Seven Wonders of The World, and Search for Paradise. In 1957, 1958, 1959, organised many TV expedns and prod TV programmes in remote parts of the World. FAGS, FRGS. Member English-Speaking Union (hon. life); Life Member, American Museum of Natural History. Fraternities: Kappa Sigma; Tau Kappa Alpha; Phi Delta Phi; Sigma Delta Chi; Alpha Epsilon. Mason. *Publications:* With Lawrence in Arabia, 1924; The First World Flight, 1925; Beyond Khyber Pass, 1925; Count Luckner, The Sea Devil, 1927; European Skyways, 1927; The Boy's Life of Colonel Lawrence, 1927; Raiders of the Deep, 1928; Adventures in Afghanistan for Boys, 1928; Woodfill of the Regulars, 1929; The Sea Devil's Fo'c's'le, 1929; The Hero of Vincennes, 1929; India, Land of the Black Pagoda, 1930; Wreck of the Dumaru, 1930; Lauterback of the China Sea, 1930; Rolling Stone, 1931; Tall Stories, 1931; Kabluk of the Eskimo, 1932; This Side of Hell, 1932; Old Gimlet Eye, 1933; The Untold Story of Exploration, 1935; Fan

Mail, 1935; A Trip to New York with Bobby and Betty, 1936; Men of Danger, 1936; Kipling Stories, and a Life of Kipling, 1936; Seeing Canada with Lowell Thomas, 1936; Seeing India with Lowell Thomas, 1936; Seeing Japan with Lowell Thomas, 1937; Seeing Mexico with Lowell Thomas, 1937; Adventures among Immortals, 1937; Hungry Waters, 1937; Wings Over Asia, 1937; Magic Dials, 1939; In New Brunswick We'll Find It, 1939; Soft Ball! So What?, 1940; How to Keep Mentally Fit, 1940; Stand Fast for Freedom, 1940; Pageant of Adventure, 1940; Pageant of Life, 1941; Pageant of Romance, 1943; These Men Shall Never Die, 1943; Back to Mandalay, 1951; Great True Adventures, 1955; The Story of the New York Thruway, 1955; The Seven Wonders of the World, 1957; History as You Heard It, 1958; The Vital Spark, 1959; Sir Hubert Wilkins: His World of Adventure, 1961; More Great True Adventures, 1963; Book of the High Mountains, 1964; Story of the St Lawrence Seaway, 1971; Famous First Flights that Changed History, 1968; Burma Jack, 1971; Good Evening Everybody (autobiog.), 1976; Doolittle, a biography, 1976; Solong Until Tomorrow, 1977. *Recreations:* ski-ing, riding, golf. *Address:* Hammersley Hill, Pawling, NY 12564, USA; (office) 24E 51st Street, New York City, NY 10022, USA. *Clubs:* Royal and Ancient (St Andrews); Princeton, Explorers, Dutch Treat, Overseas Press (New York); Bohemian (San Francisco); Pine Valley Golf (New Jersey); Assoc. of Radio and TV News Analysts; Marco Polo.
*Died 29 Aug.* 1981.

**THOMAS, Melbourne,** QPM 1953; first Chief Constable, South Wales Police, 1969–71. *b* 1 May 1906; *s* of David and Charlotte Frances Thomas; *m* 1930, Marjorie Elizabeth Phillips; one *d. Educ:* Newport (St Julian's) High School. Metropolitan Police, 1928–29; Newport Borough Police, 1929–45 (Dep. Chief Constable, 1941–45); Chief Constable: Merthyr Borough Police, 1945–63; Glamorgan Constabulary, 1963–69. Author of a method of training police dogs to detect explosives, 1968. Mem., Hon. Soc. of Cymmrodorion, 1955. KStJ 1974. *Recreations:* Rugby, cricket, athletics. *Address:* The Lower Flat, Stafford Coach House, Westgate, Cowbridge, South Glamorgan. *T:* Cowbridge (04463) 4245.
*Died 15 Sept.* 1989.

**THOMAS, Air Vice-Marshal Meredith,** CSI 1946; CBE 1941; DFC 1922; AFC; Royal Air Force, retired; *b* 6 July 1892. Served European War, 1914–19; Flying Officer, RFC, 1917; Group Captain, 1938; SASO, No 5 Gp, 1938; Dir of Techn. Trng, Air Min., 1940; Air Cdre, 1943; AOC, India, 1944–46; retired, 1946. *Address:* c/o Ministry of Defence (Air), Whitehall, SW1.
*Died 20 May* 1984.

**THOMAS, Gen. Sir Noel;** see Thomas, Gen. Sir J. N.

**THOMAS, Sir Patrick (Muirhead),** Kt 1974; DSO 1945; TD 1945; DL; *b* 31 Jan. 1914; *s* of Herbert James Thomas, Barrister-at-Law and Charis Thomas (*née* Muirhead); *m* 1939, Ethel Mary Lawrence (*d* 1986); one *s* three *d. Educ:* Clifton Coll.; Corpus Christi Coll., Cambridge (MA). FInstT. Served War of 1939–45, France, N Africa, Italy, Greece, Middle East, Austria; Lt-Col comdg 71st Field Regt RA, 1944–45. Steel Industry, United Steel Cos and Arthur Balfour & Co. Ltd, Sheffield, 1935–39; Wm Beardmore & Co. Ltd, Parkhead Steelworks, Glasgow, 1946: Man. Dir, 1954; Dir, 1967–76. Hon. Vice-Pres., Iron and Steel Inst., 1968. Col Comdt, City of Glasgow Army Cadet Force, 1956 (Hon. Col 1963–70, 1977–84). Pres., FBI Scottish Council, 1961–62; Pres., Scottish Engrg Employers' Assoc., 1967–68; Chm., Scottish Transport Gp, 1968–77; Part-time Mem., Scottish Gas Board, 1966–72; Director: Brightside Engrg Holdings Ltd, 1967–71; Midland Caledonian Investment Trust Ltd, 1972–75. Chm., Scottish Opera, 1976–81 (Dir, 1965–81); Member: Court, Univ. of Strathclyde, 1967–88 (Chm., 1970–75); Lloyd's Register of Shipping Scottish Cttee, 1967–81; Panel Mem., Industrial Tribunals, 1967–80; Deacon Convener, Trades of Glasgow, 1970–71; Member: Exec. Cttee, Officers Assoc. (Scotland), 1964–75, 1978–; Exec. Cttee, Earl Haig Fund (Scotland), 1964–75, 1978–84 (Chm., 1981–84); Vice-Pres., 1984–); Artillery Council for Scotland, 1978–84; Chairman: Lady Haig's Poppy Factory, 1967–72; Royal Artillery Assoc. (Scottish Region), 1978–83. Governor, Clifton Coll., 1979–. Fellow, Univ. of Strathclyde, 1988. DL Renfrewshire, 1980. Hon. LLD Strathclyde, 1973. US Bronze Star, 1945. OStJ 1970. *Recreations:* golf, gardening. *Address:* Bemersyde, Kilmacolm, Renfrewshire PA13 4EA. *T:* Kilmacolm 2710. *Died 21 Jan.* 1990.

**THOMAS, Lt-Col Reginald Silvers W.;** see Williams-Thomas.

**THOMAS, Robert Antony C.;** see Clinton-Thomas.

**THOMAS, Ryland Lowell Degwel,** CB 1974; Deputy Director of Public Prosecutions, 1971–74; *b* 24 April 1914; *er s* of Rev. William Degwel Thomas and Sarah Maud Thomas (*née* Richards), Neath, Glam; *m* 1942, Mair Eluned, *d* of Rev. J. L. Williams, Swansea, Glam; one *s* one *d. Educ:* University Coll. of Wales, Aberystwyth (LLB); Trinity Hall, Cambridge (MA). Barrister-at-Law, Inner Temple. Ministry of Supply, 1941; Dept of Dir of Public

Prosecutions, 1942; Asst Dir, 1965. *Recreations:* walking, motoring, travel. *Address:* 58 Strathearn Avenue, Whitton, Twickenham, Mddx. *Club:* London Welsh Rugby Football (Vice-Pres.).
*Died 8 July* 1982.

**THOMAS, Terry;** see Terry-Thomas.

**THOMAS, Thomas;** see Lewis, Richard.

**THOMAS, Trevor Cawdor,** MA, LLB Cantab, LLB Wales; Vice-Chancellor, University of Liverpool, 1970–76; Emeritus Professor, 1976; *b* 19 April 1914; *o s* of James Elwyn Thomas and Charlotte Thomas (*née* Ivatt); *m* 1943, Mrs Marjory Molony, widow of John Bernard Molony, and *y d* of Samuel Harry Guteridge Higgs and Fanny Higgs, Reading. *Educ:* University College of Wales, Aberystwyth; Trinity Hall, Cambridge. LLB Wales 1936 (first class (at Aberystwyth) and Sir Samuel Evans prizeman); Foundn Schol., Trinity Hall, 1937; Trinity Hall Law Studentship, 1938; Joseph Hodges Choate Memorial Fellowship, 1938; BA; LLB Cantab 1938. Entrance Schol., Gray's Inn, 1936; Bar Final Examinations, 1940 (first class with certif. of honour); called to Bar, Gray's Inn, 1941, Hon. Bencher, 1975. Lecturer in Law, Univ. of Leeds, 1939–41. RAF, Intell. Br., 1941–45. Fellow of Trinity Hall, Cambridge, 1945–60, Hon. Fellow, 1970; Univ. Lectr in Law, Univ. of Cambridge, 1945–60; Fellow and Sen. Bursar, St John's Coll., Cambridge, 1960–69; Hon. Fellow, Darwin Coll., Cambridge, 1972. Mem. Statutory Commn for Royal Univ. of Malta, 1960–69. Chm., Nuffield Foundn Cttee of Inquiry into Dental Educn, 1978. JP, City of Cambridge, 1966–69. Hon. LLD: Liverpool, 1972; Wales, 1978. Hon. FDSRCS Eng., 1982. *Publications:* co-editor, Jenks' Digest of English Civil Law, 4th edn 1947; articles in Cambridge Law Jl. *Recreations:* gardening, travel, fishing. *Address:* 2 Claremont, Station Road, Sidmouth, Devon EX10 8HH. *Club:* Farmers'.
*Died 2 Oct.* 1985.

**THOMAS, Maj.-Gen. Vivian Davenport,** CB 1949; CBE 1946 (OBE 1942); Royal Marines, retired; *b* 31 Oct 1897; *s* of Arnold Frederick Davenport Thomas, London; *m* 1929, Theresa, *d* of Colonel E. J. Previte, VD, TD, Burstow, Surrey; one *s. Educ:* St Paul's. Served European War, 1914–18: with Royal Marines, 1914–19; HMS Princess Royal, 1st Battle Cruiser Squadron, 1915–18. War of 1939–45: North Africa; Lieutenant-Colonel, 1942; acting Colonel Commandant (temp. Brig.) 1943; Comdr 1st RM AA Bde, India, 1943; COS to Chief of Combined Ops, 1944–46; Maj.-Gen. 1946; COS to Comdt Gen., RM, 1946–50; Chief of Amphibious Warfare, 1950–54; retired, 1954. Cdre, 1951–55, Life Vice-Cdre, 1974, Royal Naval Sailing Assoc. Hon. Col Comdt, Plymouth Group Royal Marines, 1957–61. Vice Patron, Sail Training Assoc., 1969; Vice-Pres., London Fedn of Boy's Clubs, 1978. Master, 1962–63, Father, 1982, Armourers' and Brasiers' Company. *Address:* Coppinghall, 46 Church Street, Uckfield, East Sussex TN22 1BT. *Clubs:* Caledonian; Royal Yacht Squadron; Square Rigging (Pres.).
*Died 20 May* 1984.

**THOMAS, Wynford V.;** see Vaughan-Thomas.

**THOMPSON, Aubrey Denzil F.;** see Forsyth-Thompson.

**THOMPSON, Brenda, (Mrs Gordon Thompson);** writer on education; *b* 27 Jan. 1935; *d* of Thomas Barnes Houghton and Marjorie Houghton; *m* 1956, Gordon Thompson; one *s. Educ:* Leeds Univ. BSc Hons in Biochemistry. Food chemist with J. Lyons & Co., 1957; Hosp. Biochemist, Chelsea Women's Hosp., 1958–60. Entered primary school teaching, 1964; Head Teacher, Northwold I (Primary) Sch., 1971–78, Stamford Hill Sch., 1978–81. Mem., Press Council, 1973–76. Indep. Councillor for London Borough of Islington, 1968–71. *Publications:* Learning to Read, 1970; Learning to Teach, 1973; The Pre-School Book, 1976; Reading Success, 1979; Editor various children's books. *Address:* Nantddu, Rhandirmwyn, Llandovery, Dyfed SA20 0NG. *T:* Llandovery 20159.
*Died 11 Oct.* 1989.

**THOMPSON, Charles Paxton,** CMG 1961; OBE 1956; Bursar, University of Birmingham, 1961–73; *b* 31 May 1911; *s* of W. P. Thompson; *m* 1938, Gweneth Barbara Toby (*d* 1981); one *s* one *d. Educ:* Merchant Taylors' School, London; University College, London; Trinity Hall, Cambridge. Cadet, Colonial Administrative Service (Nigeria), 1933; Economic Secretary to Prime Minister of Federation of Nigeria, 1958; Permanent Secretary, Ministry of Economic Development, Lagos, 1960. *Club:* Oriental.
*Died 6 Oct.* 1985.

**THOMPSON, Rev. Douglas Weddell;** President of the Methodist Conference, 1966–67; *b* 4 July 1903; *s* of Nathan Ellis and Florence Thompson; *m* 1929, Gladys Wentworth (*d* 1972); one *d*; *m* 1973, Margret Forrest. *Educ:* Gateshead Grammar Sch.; Handsworth Coll., Birmingham. Missionary, Hunan, China, 1925–27; Chaplain, Bengal, India, 1927–28; Hunan, China, 1929–39. Served War, 1939–45 (despatches): Chaplain, HMF, W Africa, Western Desert; POW Chaplain, Italy, Germany. Methodist Home Missions, London and Portsmouth, 1945–58; Gen. Sec. and Chm. of Officers,

Methodist Overseas Mission Dept, 1958–68; Eastbourne Central Church, 1968; Lewes and villages, 1971. WEA Lectr on Eastern Affairs. *Publications:* Wisdom of the Way, 1945; About to Marry, 1945; Into Red Starlight, 1950; Captives to Freedom, 1951; The Mystery of the White Stone, 1961; The World He Loves, 1963; Donald Soper: a biography, 1971; numerous articles in ecumenical and missionary jls. *Recreation:* mountain and fell-walking. *Address:* 3 Ashmore House, 12 High Street, East Hoathly, East Sussex BN8 6DP. *Club:* Royal Commonwealth Society.
*Died 26 Feb. 1981.*

**THOMPSON, Sir Edward (Walter)**, Kt 1957; JP; Chairman, John Thompson Ltd, Wolverhampton, 1947–67; Director, Barclays Bank, 1958–73; Local Director, Barclays Bank (Birmingham), 1952–73; *b* 11 June 1902; *s* of late Albert E. Thompson and late Mary Thompson; *m* 1930, Ann E., *d* of Rev. George L. Amphlett, Four Ashes Hall, Stourbridge, Worcs; one *s* three *d*. *Educ:* Oundle; Trinity Hall, Cambridge. MA (Engineering) Cambridge. Joined family firm of John Thompson's, 1924; Dir John Thompson Watertube Boilers, 1930; Joint Man. Dir John Thompson Ltd, 1936–62. Chm. Watertube Boilermakers Assoc., 1951–54; Pres. Brit. Engineers Assoc., 1957–59 (Vice-Pres. 1956). Mem. Midland Chapter Woodard Schools. Chairman: Birmingham Regional Hosp. Bd, 1957–61; Redditch Development Corp., 1964–74; Leader SE Asia Trade Delegation, 1961. JP Co. Salop, 1953; Dep. Chm. Bridgnorth Bench, 1956–66; High Sheriff, Staffordshire, 1955–56. *Recreations:* shooting, fishing, gardening. *Address:* Gatacre Park, Bridgnorth, Salop. *T:* Bobbington 211. *Died 15 Dec. 1989.*

**THOMPSON, Lt-Gen. Sir Geoffrey (Stuart)**, KBE 1960 (MBE 1941); CB 1954; DSO 1944; late Royal Artillery; *b* 6 Jan. 1905; 3rd *s* of late Brig.-Gen. W. A. M. Thompson, CB, CMG; *m* 1934, Agnes Mary Colville (*d* 1974), *e d* of late Captain H. D. Wakeman-Colville, RN retd; one *d*. *Educ:* Sherborne Sch.; RN Colls, Osborne and Dartmouth. Commissioned, 1925; served War of 1939–45 (North Africa and Italy); Commander 1st Field Regiment RA, Italy, 1944–45; Commander No 2 Army Group, Royal Artillery, Egypt, 1950–52; Director Land/Air Warfare and Dir for NATO Standardisation, War Office, 1952–54; Senior Army Instructor, Imperial Defence College, 1955–57; Director of Staff Duties, War Office, 1957–59; Military Secretary to the Secretary of State for War, 1959–61. Col Comdt, RA, 1961–69. Asst Man. Dir, Arthur Guinness Son & Co., Dublin, 1961–70. Officer of Legion of Merit, USA, 1945; Commander of Order of Leopold, Belgium, 1950; Croix de Guerre, Belgium, 1950. *Recreations:* fishing, hunting. *Address:* Swainstown, Dunsany, Co. Meath. *T:* (046) 25312. *Club:* Army and Navy. *Died 15 Nov. 1983.*

**THOMPSON, Gertrude C.;** *see* Caton-Thompson.

**THOMPSON, Sir Harold (Warris)**, Kt 1968; CBE 1959; FRS 1946; MA, DSc (Oxon); PhilD (Berlin); Professor of Chemistry, Oxford University, 1964–75, now Emeritus; *b* 15 Feb. 1908; *m* 1938, Grace Penelope Stradling; one *s* one *d*. *Educ:* King Edward VII Sch., Sheffield; Trinity College, Oxford (Open Millard Scholar); Hon. Fellow, 1978); Berlin University. 1st Class Hons Chemistry, Oxford, 1929; Junior Research Fellow, St John's College, Oxford; Official Fellow and Tutor, St John's College, 1930–64, Professorial Fellow, 1964–75, Hon. Fellow, 1975; University Reader in Infra red spectroscopy, 1954–64; Leverhulme Research Fellow (Pasadena), 1937; Tilden Lecturer, 1943; Gnehm Lecturer, Zürich, 1948; Reilly Lecturer, 1961; Cherwell Memorial Fellow, 1961. Chemical Research for Ministry of Supply and Ministry of Aircraft Production, 1939–45; Member, Chemical Research Board, DSIR, 1949–54 and Committees of Scientific Advisory Council and MRC, 1947–55; Scientific Adviser, Home Office Civil Defence, Southern Region, 1952–63; Member: General Board, Oxford University, 1949–55; Hebdomadal Council, 1957–61; President: Internat. Council of Scientific Unions, 1963–66; Inst. Information Scientists, 1967–70; Aslib, 1973–74; Chm., Commn on Molecular Spectroscopy of Internat. Union of Pure and Applied Chem., 1955–61, and of IUPAC Publications Cttee, 1957–; Pres., IUPAC, 1973–75 (Mem. Bureau, 1963–71; Exec. Cttee, 1967–71; Vice-Pres., 1971–73); Member: UK Unesco Commn, 1966–; Exec. Cttee, British Council, 1966–80; Chm., GB/China Cttee, 1972–74, GB/China Centre, 1974–80 (a Vice-Pres., 1980–); Mem. Council, Royal Soc., 1959–64, Vice-Pres., 1963–64, 1965–71, For. Sec., 1965–71; Vice-Pres., Chem. Soc., 1970–73. Hon. Corresp. Mem., Inst. Nat. Sci., Ecuador, 1971; Hon. Member: Leopoldina Acad.; Japan Chemical Soc.; Spanish Royal Soc. Phys. Chem. Ciamician Medal, Bologna, 1959; Davy Medal of Royal Society, 1965; John Torrance Tate Gold Medal (Amer. Inst. Physics), 1966. Hon. Treasurer OUAFC, 1931–; Founder and Chairman of Pegasus FC, Secretary, 1948–54; Member, FA Council, 1941–, Vice-Chm., 1967–76, Chm., 1976–81, a Life Vice-Pres., 1980–; Life Vice-Pres., AFA (Pres. 1969–71); Mem., Exec. Cttee, UEFA, 1974–82 (a Vice Pres., 1978–82). Editor, Spectrochimica Acta, 1957–. Hon. Counsellor, Spanish SRC, 1971–. Hon. DSc: Newcastle upon Tyne, 1970; Strasbourg, 1972; Hon. ScD Cambridge, 1974. Order of Aztec Eagle, Mexico, 1970;

Chevalier, Légion d'Honneur, 1971; Grand Service Cross, German Federal Republic, 1971. *Publications:* A Course in Chemical Spectroscopy, 1938; (ed) Advances in Spectroscopy, Vol. I 1959, II 1961; papers in proc. of scientific socs and journals. *Recreation:* Association football (Oxford *v* Cambridge, 1928–29). *Address:* 33 Linton Road, Oxford. *T:* Oxford 58925. *Died 31 Dec. 1983.*

**THOMPSON, Sir Herbert;** *see* Thompson, Sir J. H.

**THOMPSON, John Crighton**, CB 1965; CBE 1958; retired as Director of Electrical Engineering, Navy Department, Ministry of Defence; *b* 14 July 1902; *s* of William Thompson and Margaret Thompson (*née* Turner); *m* 1928, Jessie Walker (*née* Ashton); three *s* one *d* (and one *d* decd). *Educ:* King Edward VI School, Norwich; Faraday House Elec. Engineering Coll., London. BSc (Eng) London 1922. Pupil, Brush Elec. Engineering Co., Loughborough, 1922–23; Asst Engineer, Callenders Cable and Construction Co., 1923–26; Asst Elec. Engineer, Admiralty, 1927; after service at home and abroad, apptd Director of Electrical Engineering and Head of RNES, 1960; retd, 1964. FIEE. *Recreations:* motoring, gardening, fishing. *Address:* 135 Bradford Road, Combe Down, Bath. *T:* Combe Down 832228. *Died 13 July 1982.*

**THOMPSON, (John) Kenneth**, CMG 1963; Director of the Commonwealth Institute, 1969–77; *b* Halstead, Essex, 12 May 1913; *e s* of late W. Stanton Thompson, MBE; *m* 1937, Jenny More; two *s*. *Educ:* Dover County School; King's College, London; Lausanne Univ. BA, AKC, DipEd Mod. Lang. Master, Queen's Royal Coll., Trinidad, 1935–39; Censor, Trinidad, 1939–41; Chief Censor, 1941–42; Asst Sec., Postal and Tel. Censorship, London, 1943–45; Principal, Colonial Office, 1945–49; Colonial Attaché, Brit. Embassy, Washington, 1950–53; Asst Sec., Colonial Office, 1953–59; Director, Colombo Plan Bureau, SE Asia, 1959–62; Asst Sec., Dept of Technical Co-operation, 1962–64; Dir of Overseas Appointments, ODM, 1964–69. Consultant: Commonwealth Secretariat, 1981–82; WHO, 1984–85. Vice-Pres., Royal Commonwealth Soc.; Vice-Chairman: Internat. Social Service of GB; UK IMPACT Foundn; Chm. Exec. Cttee, Royal Commonwealth Soc. for the Blind. Council Member: Royal Overseas League; British Exec. Service Overseas; Nat. Rubella Council. *Address:* 9 Grove Way, Esher, Surrey. *T:* 01–398 4461. *Club:* Royal Commonwealth Society. *Died 9 Aug. 1985.*

**THOMPSON, Sir (Joseph) Herbert**, Kt 1947; CIE 1945; *b* 9 March 1898; *o s* of J. Arnold Thompson, JP, and Ellen Stewart Fraser, Wilmslow, Cheshire; *m* 1925, Kathleen (Kaiser-i-Hind Silver medal, 1948), *d* of J. H. Rodier; three *d*. *Educ:* Manchester Grammar School; Brasenose College, Oxford (MA). Royal Naval Air Service (Sub-Lt) 1916, RAF (Capt.) 1918 and served principally as a fighter pilot (despatches). Assistant Master, Oundle School, 1921–22; ICS 1922; served in Madras Presidency; appointed to Foreign and Political Department, Govt of India (later Indian Political Service), 1926; served NWF Province, Hyderabad and Rajputana, 1926–41; Dep. Sec., Political Department, 1941–43; Revenue and Divisional Commissioner NWF Province, 1943; Resident for Kolhapur and Deccan States, 1944–45; Resident for the Punjab States, 1945–47; on special duty in connection with lapse of Paramountcy, 1947, retd 1949. General Secretary, London Council of Social Service, 1949–50; Diocesan Secretary, Worcester, 1951–53; Rowing Corresp., Sunday Times, 1954–68; BBC (Appointments Dept), 1956–59. Member: Bd of Governors, St Thomas' Hosp., 1950–70; SW Metropolitan Regional Hospitals Board, 1959–63. *Recreations:* walking, gardening, being a great-grandfather. *Address:* Fair Acre, Haddenham, Bucks HP17 8HB. *T:* Haddenham 291212. *Clubs:* Leander; Vincent's (Oxford). *Died 28 March 1984.*

**THOMPSON, Kenneth;** *see* Thompson, J. K.

**THOMPSON, Sir Kenneth (Pugh)**, 1st Bt *cr* 1963; Chairman, Merseyside County Council, 1977–81 Leader, Conservative Group, 1974–80; *b* 24 Dec. 1909; *s* of Ernest S. and Annie Thompson; *m* 1936, Nanne Broome, Walton; one *s* one *d*. *Educ:* Bootle Grammar School. Formerly newspaper reporter, and subsequently entered commercial life; lectured for the Economic League. Worked for Ministry of Information as Regional Officer during War of 1939–45. Member of Liverpool City Council, 1938–58. Director of several Liverpool companies. MP (C) Walton Div. Liverpool, 1950–64; Chairman Conservative Nat. Advisory Cttee on Local Govt, 1956–57; Assistant Postmaster-General, 1957–Oct. 1959; Parliamentary Secretary, Ministry of Education, October 1959–July 1962. Sec., 1922 Cttee, 1951–57. Dep. Chm., Merseyside Develt Corp., 1980–. Hon. LLD Liverpool, 1982. *Publications:* Member's Lobby, 1966; Pattern of Conquest, 1967. *Heir:* *s* Paul Anthony Thompson [*b* 6 Oct. 1939; *m* 1971, Pauline Dorothy Spencer, *d* of Robert Spencer, Bolton, Lancs]. *Address:* Atherton Cottage, Formby, Merseyside L37 2DD. *Died 4 Jan. 1984.*

**THOMPSON, Sir (Louis) Lionel (Harry)**, Kt 1953; CBE 1946; Deputy Master and Comptroller of the Royal Mint and *ex-officio* Engraver of HM's Seals, 1950–57; retired 1957; *b* 10 March 1893; *o s* of

William Thompson, Eaton, Retford; *m* Mary (*d* 1979), *d* of William White, MD, Hadfield, Derbyshire; two *s*. *Educ:* King Edward VI School, Retford; Sheffield Univ.; Exeter Coll., Oxford (scholar). First Cl. Classical Mods, 1913. Served European War, 1914–18, Cheshire Regt (Territorial), Temp. Major. Asst Principal Treasury, 1919; Asst Secretary to Commissioner for Special Areas, 1937–39; Under-Secretary, Treasury, 1947–50. *Recreations:* walking, gardening. *Address:* Pendean Convalescent Home, Midhurst, Sussex. *T:* Midhurst 4586. *Club:* United Oxford & Cambridge University. *Died* 10 *Feb.* 1983.

**THOMPSON, Sir Peile,** 5th Bt *cr* 1890; OBE 1959 (MBE 1950); Lieutenant-Colonel (retired), The Manchester Regiment and King's African Rifles; *b* 28 Feb. 1911; *s* of Sir Peile Beaumont Thompson, 4th Bt, and Stella Mary (*d* 1972), *d* of late Arthur Harris; *S* father, 1972; *m* 1937, Barbara Johnson, *d* of late H. J. Rampling, Old Manor House, Harston; one *s* one *d*. *Educ:* Canford School; St Catharine's College, Cambridge (BA 1933, MA 1950). 2nd Lieutenant, Manchester Regt, 1932; served War of 1939–45; commanded 26 Bn, KAR, Kenya Emergency, 1954–56 (despatches). *Recreation:* gardening. *Heir:* *s* Christopher Peile Thompson [*b* 21 Dec. 1944; *m* 1969, Anna, *d* of Major Arthur Callander; one *s* one *d*]. *Address:* Old Farm, Augres, Trinity, Jersey, CI. *T:* Jersey 62289. *Died* 2 *May* 1985.

**THOMPSON-McCAUSLAND, Lucius Perronet,** CMG 1966; *b* 12 Dec. 1904; *e s* of late Sir John Perronet Thompson, KCSI, KCIE and Ada Lucia Tyrrell; *m* Helen Laura, *d* of late Rt Hon. M. M. McCausland, sometime Lieut of Co. Londonderry; two *s* three *d* (and one *s* decd). *Educ:* Repton; King's Coll., Cambridge (Scholar). Helbert Wagg & Co., 1928; Financial News, 1929–34; Moody's Economist Service, 1929–39; Bank of England, 1939–65, Adviser to Governor, 1949–65 (accompanied Lord Keynes to pre-Bretton Woods Conf., 1943; Havana Conf., 1948); Consultant to HM Treasury on internat. monetary problems, 1965–68. Director: Dun & Bradstreet Ltd, 1965–75; Tricentrol Ltd, 1967–76 (Chm., 1970–76); Moodies Services Ltd, 1968–75 (Chm., 1970–75). Governor of Repton, 1953–77 (Chm., 1959–71); Chm., Corp. of Working Men's Coll., 1964–69, Principal, 1969–80. High Sheriff of Hertfordshire, 1965–66. *Recreations:* garden, travel. *Address:* Epcombs, Hertingfordbury, Hertford. *T:* Hertford 52580. *Clubs:* Athenæum; Leander (Henley). *Died* 16 *Feb.* 1984.

**THOMSON, Ewen Cameron,** CMG 1964; nutrition consultant; *b* 12 April 1915; *s* of Francis Murphy Thomson, Woodhill, Forfar, Angus; *m* 1948, Betty, *d* of Lt-Col J. H. Preston, MBE, Far Horizons, Trearddur Bay, Anglesey; one *s* three *d*. *Educ:* Forfar Academy; St Andrews University. Cadet, Northern Rhodesia Provincial Admin., 1938. War Service, 1st Bn Northern Rhodesia Regt, 1939–46. District Commissioner, 1946; Dep. Prov. Comr, 1956; Prov. Comr, 1957; Senior Provincial Commissioner, 1961; Permanent Sec. for Native Affairs, 1962; Minister for Native Affairs, 1962; Permanent Secretary, Ministry of Transport and Works, Zambia, 1964; Director of Communications, Contingency Planning Organisation, Zambia, 1966; Exec. Sec., Nat. Food and Nutrition Commn, Zambia, 1967; Temp. Project Manager, UNDP/FAO, Nat. Food and Nutrition Programme, Zambia, 1970. Consultant: SIDA Nat. Food and Nutrition Programme, Tanzania, 1972; World Bank, 1974–88; Nat. Food and Nutrition Projects, Indonesia and Brazil, 1974–82; Urban Projects, Kenya, Botswana and Lesotho; Nutrition Component, Philippines, 1977–78; State Nutrition Project, Tamil Nadu, India, 1978–86; Food and Nutrition Project, Egypt, 1980–81; Food and Nutrition Sector Study, Bangladesh, 1983; Leader FFHC UK Reconnaissance Mission, Malawi, 1972; Co-Dir, Preparatory Team, Tanzania Food and Nutrition Centre, 1973. Leader, Planning Team, Nat. Food and Nutrition Programme, Malawi, 1973. Gave keynote address, Rockefeller Conf. on Nutrition and Govt Policy in Developing Countries, 1975. *Publication:* Symbiosis of Scientist, Planner and Administrator in Nutrition Programme Intervention, 1978. *Recreations:* walking, cooking, winemaking. *Address:* Manleys, Beacon Hill Park, Hindhead, Surrey. *T:* Hindhead 6972. *Club:* Royal Commonwealth Society. *Died* 25 *Dec.* 1988.

**THOMSON, Rt. Rev. Francis;** Former Bishop of Motherwell (Bishop, 1964–83); Parish Priest of St Isidore's, Biggar, since 1983; Hon. Canon of St Andrews and Edinburgh, since 1961; *b* 15 May 1917; *s* of late Francis Thomson, MA and Winifred Mary Clare (*née* Forsyth). *Educ:* George Watson's Coll., Edinburgh; Edinburgh Univ.; Christ's Coll., Cambridge; St Edmund's Coll., Ware; Angelicum Univ., Rome. MA Edinburgh 1938; BA Cambridge 1940; Priest, 1946; STL (Angelicum, Rome) 1949. Asst Priest: St Patrick's, Kilsyth, 1946–48; St James', St Andrews, 1949–52; St Cuthbert's, Edinburgh, 1952–53; Prof. of Dogmatic Theology, St Andrew's Coll. Drygrange, Melrose, 1953–60; Rector of St Mary's Coll., Blairs, Aberdeen, 1960–64. *Address:* 6 Coulter Road, Biggar, Lanarkshire ML12 6EP. *T:* Biggar 20189. *Died* 6 *Dec.* 1987.

**THOMSON, Prof. George Derwent;** Professor of Greek, University of Birmingham, 1937–70; *b* 19 Aug. 1903; *s* of William Henry and Minnie Thomson; *m* 1934, Katharine Fraser Stewart; two *d*. *Educ:* Dulwich College; King's College, Cambridge. Craven Student, University of Cambridge, 1926–27; Fellow of King's College, Cambridge, 1927–33 and 1934–36. Member, Czechoslovak Academy of Sciences, 1960–. Hon. Dr Univ. of Thessaloniki, 1979. Hon. Citizen of Eleusis, 1986. *Publications:* Greek Lyric Metre, 1929 (new edn, 1960); Aeschylus, Prometheus Bound, 1932; M. O'Sullivan, Twenty Years A-Growing (trans. from the Irish), 1933 (World's Classics edition, 1953); Aeschylus, Oresteia, 2 vols, 1938 (new edn, 1966); Aeschylus and Athens, 1941 (new edn 1973); Marxism and Poetry, 1946 (new edn, 1954); Studies in Ancient Greek Society, Vol. I, The Prehistoric Aegean, 1949 (new edn 1973); Vol. II, The First Philosophers, 1955 (new edn, 1973); The Greek Language, 1960 (new edn, 1966); Geras: Studies Presented to G. T. on his Sixtieth Birthday, 1963; A Manual of Modern Greek, 1966; Palamas, Twelve Lays of the Gipsy, 1969; From Marx to Mao Tse-tung, 1971; Capitalism and After, 1973; The Human Essence, 1975; The Blasket That Was, 1982; books in Irish and Greek and articles in learned and other journals; foreign editions of his books in 22 languages. *Address:* 58 Billesley Lane, Birmingham B13 9QS. *T:* 021–449 2656. *Died* 3 *Feb.* 1987.

**THOMSON, George Ewart;** Director, C. E. Heath & Co. Ltd 1941–69 (Chairman, 1959–66); *b* 7 May 1897; *s* of John and Alice Susanna Thomson; *m* 1930, Wilhelmina Marjory (*née* Morrison); three *s* one *d*. *Educ:* Caterham Sch., Surrey; Rastrick Grammar Sch., Yorks. Joined C. E. Heath & Co. Ltd, 1914. Served European War, 1914–18, Infantry, 1916–19. Member of Lloyd's, 1933; Director, C. E. Heath & Co. Ltd, 1941; Member Cttee of Lloyd's, 1945–63; Dep. Chairman of Lloyd's, 1956, Chairman of Lloyd's, 1961. Export Credits Guarantee Advisory Council, 1959–67. *Recreation:* golf. *Address:* Red Hatch, Ridgeway, Hutton, Brentwood, Essex. *T:* Brentwood 220070. *Died* 25 *Nov.* 1981.

**THOMSON, Rev. George Ian Falconer;** Chaplain of All Souls College, Oxford, 1981–84; *b* 2 Sept. 1912; *s* of Rev. G. D. Thomson, DD; *m* 1st, 1938, Hon. Bridget de Courcy (marr. diss. 1951), *e d* of 34th Baron Kingsale, DSO; one *d*; 2nd, 1952, Mary Josephine Lambart Dixon, OBE, *d* of Archdeacon H. T. Dixon, DD, Hereford; one *s*. *Educ:* Shrewsbury Sch.; Balliol Coll., Oxford (MA); Westcott House, Cambridge. Ellerton Theol Essay Prize, Oxford, 1936. Pilot, RAFO, 1932–37; Chaplain, RAFVR, 1942–46. Curate, St Luke's, Chelsea, 1936–37; Chaplain, Hertford Coll., Oxford, 1937–46, Junior Dean and Dean of Degrees, 1939–42; Rector of Hilgay, Norfolk, 1946–51; Sec. of Gen. Ordination Examn, 1946–52; Master, Maidstone Grammar Sch., 1951–62; Chaplain and Sen. Lectr, St Paul's Coll., Cheltenham, 1962–66; Exam. Chaplain to Bp of Gloucester, 1964–76; Vis. Lectr, McMaster Univ., Ont, 1964; Dir, research project, Conf. of British Missionary Socs, 1966–68; re-visited China during Cultural Revolution, 1967. Director, Bible Reading Fellowship, 1968–77. Rowing Corresp., The Observer, 1938–65. NADFAS Lectr on James Tissot, 1980–. Press Officer, Oxford Diocese, 1979–83. Freeman, City of London. *Publications:* History of the Oxford Pastorate, 1946; Experiment in Worship, 1951; The Rise of Modern Asia, 1957; Changing Patterns in South Asia, 1961; Two Hundred School Assemblies, 1966; Mowbray's Mini-Commentary No 4, 1970. *Recreations:* rowing (Oxford Blue, 1934), travel, writing. *Address:* Jackson's Farm, Yarnton, Oxford OX5 1QD. *Clubs:* Royal Air Force; Leander.

*Died* 14 *April* 1987.

**THOMSON, Tun Sir James (Beveridge),** KBE 1966; Kt 1959; *b* 24 March 1902; *e s* of late Rev. William Archibald Thomson, Dalmellington, Ayrshire; *m* 1931, Dr Florence Adam; one *s*. *Educ:* Dalmellington Village School; George Watson's College, Edinburgh; Edinburgh University. MA, 1st Cl. Hons History, Edin. Called to English Bar, Middle Temple, 1929; admitted Advocate in Scotland, 1955. District Officer, 1926 and Resident Magistrate, 1932, N Rhodesia; Judge, Fiji; Chief Justice of Tonga and a Judicial Commissioner for Western Pacific, 1945–48; Judge, Federation of Malaya, 1948; Chief Justice 1956; (first) Lord President of the Federal Court of Malaysia, 1963–66; (last) President of the High Court of S Arabia, 1967; Chm., Delimitation Commn, Republic of Botswana, 1968. Hon. Sheriff, Inverness, 1972. Meritorious Service Medal (Perak), 1957; Panglima Mangku Negara (Federation of Malaya), 1958; Seri Maharajah Mangku Negara (Malaysia), 1966. *Publications:* The Laws of the British Solomon Islands, 1948; The Law of Tonga, 1951. *Address:* Craig Gowan, Carr Bridge, Inverness-shire. *T:* Carr Bridge 257. *Died* 31 *March* 1983.

**THOMSON, James Frederick Gordon;** *see* Migdale, Hon. Lord.

**THOMSON, Air Vice-Marshal Ronald Bain,** CB 1959; DSO 1943; DFC 1943; *b* 15 April 1912; *s* of George Thomson, Aberdeen, and Christina Ann (*née* Reid); *m* 1940, Elizabeth Napier (*née* Ayling); two *d*. *Educ:* Robert Gordon's College, Aberdeen. Joined Royal Auxiliary Air Force (612 County of Aberdeen Squadron), 1937. Senior Lecturer Physical Educ. and Hygiene, Pretoria Technical College, S Africa, 1939. War of 1939–45, Coastal Command. AOC,

RAF, Gibraltar, 1958–60; AOC, RAF, Scotland and Northern Ireland, 1960–63; AOA, Flying Training Command, 1963–66; retired. Member of the Queen's Body Guard for Scotland, The Royal Company of Archers. Commander Order of St Olav, 1963. *Recreations:* shooting, golf. *Club:* Royal Air Force.
*Died 6 Dec.* 1984.

**THOMSON, Thomas Davidson,** CMG 1962; OBE 1959; *b* 1 April 1911; *s* of J. A. Thomson, FFA, FRSE, and Barbara M. Davidson, Edinburgh; *m* 1st, 1938, Jean (marr. diss. 1946), *d* of Dr J. L. Annan, Edinburgh; 2nd, 1947, Marjorie Constance (*d* 1980), *d* of T. R. Aldred, Limbe, Nyasaland; one *s*; 3rd, 1981, Kathleen Ramsay, *d* of D. Craig, Morebattle, Roxburghshire and *widow* of Nicholas Pestereff. *Educ:* George Watson's Coll., Edinburgh; Edinburgh Univ. (MA, LLB); Magdalene Coll., Cambridge. Editor, The Student, 1932; Travel Secretary, Scottish National Union of Students, 1932; Cadet, Nyasaland Administration, 1934; Civil Demobilisation Officer, 1945; Assistant Secretary, Nyasaland, 1947; Officer in charge, Domasi Community Development Scheme, 1949; Officer in charge, School of Local Government, 1955, Social Development, 1958; retired as Commissioner for Social Development, Nyasaland, 1963. Carried out survey of Adult Education in Nyasaland, 1956–57; organised Nyasaland Council of Social Service, 1959. Served War of 1939–45, E Africa (Major). Sec., Eastern Border Development Assoc., 1962–67. Chairman: Scottish Community Development Cttee, 1968–75; Berwicks Council of Social Service, 1971–75; Hon. Vice-Pres., Scottish Council of Social Service, 1976–. Pres., Berwickshire Naturalists' Club, 1969–70. Vice-Pres., Soc. of Antiquaries of Scotland, 1971–74. Brain of Britain, BBC Radio, 1969. FRPSL 1984. *Publications:* A Practical Approach to Chinyanja, 1947; Coldingham Priory, 1973; sundry reports and papers on Nyasaland affairs; papers in Hist. Berwickshire Naturalists' Club; sundry papers in philatelic jls. *Recreations:* gardening, philately, contemplative archaeology, Scouting (Chief Commissioner, Nyasaland, 1958; County Commissioner, Berwickshire, 1966–75). *Address:* The Hill, Coldingham, Berwickshire. *T:* Coldingham 71209.
*Died 17 June* 1989.

**THOMSON, William Archibald Robson,** MD; FRCPEd; Editor of The Practitioner, 1944–73; Medical Correspondent, The Times, 1956–71; Medical Consultant, The Daily Telegraph, since 1971; Chairman: The Leprosy Study Centre, 1953–80; Council, Sesame; *b* 6 Nov. 1906; 2nd *s* of late Rev. W. A. Thomson; *m* 1934, Marion Lucy Nannette, *d* of late Sir Leonard Hill, FRS; two *s. Educ:* Dalmellington Higher Grade Public Sch.; Wigan Grammar Sch.; University of Edinburgh. MB, ChB 1929, MD (Hons), 1933, University of Edinburgh; FRCPEd 1976. Clin. Asst. Ho. Phys. and Clin. Tutor, Royal Infirmary, Edinburgh; Asst, Dept of Medicine, also Davidson Research Fellow in Applied Bacteriology, Univ. of Edinburgh; Surg. Lieut, RN, seconded for res. work on deep diving; Paterson Research Scholar and Chief Asst, Cardiac Dept, London Hospital; First Assistant, Medical Unit, St Thomas' Hospital. FRSocMed; FRIPHH; Founder Member, The British Academy of Forensic Sciences (Dep. Chm. Exec. Council, 1972–77, 1980–81; Pres., 1981–82); Foundation Mem. and Vice-Chm. of Council, 1972–77, 1980–81; Pres., 1981–82); Foundation Mem. and Vice-Chm. of Council, British Institute for the Study of the Arts in Therapy. Patron, Action Cttee for Bath Spa Preservation. Bengué Meml Award Lectr, RIPH&H; Cavendish Lectr, W London Medico-Chirurgical Soc., 1975. Abercrombie Award, RCGP, 1973. *Publications:* Black's Medical Dictionary, 19th edn 1948 to 34th edn 1984; The Searching Mind in Medicine, 1960; (ed) The Practitioner's Handbook, 1960; (ed) Practical Dietetics, 1960; (ed) Calling the Laboratory, 3rd edn 1971; (ed) The Doctor's Surgery, 1964; (ed) Sex and Its Problems, 1968; Thomson's Concise Medical Dictionary, 1973; Herbs that Heal, 1976; (Exec. Editor) Practice, 1976; A Dictionary of Medical Ethics and Practice, 1977; Spas that Heal, 1978; (ed) Medicines from the Earth, 1978; (ed) Healing Plants, 1978; Healing Herbs, 1978; A Change of Air, 1979; Faiths that Heal, 1980; Medical Consultant, Fishbein's Illustrated Medical and Health Encyclopaedia, 1977; contribs to: Gradwohl's Legal Medicine, 3rd edn 1976; Encyclopaedia Britannica, 14th and 15th edns; various articles on medical and cardiological subjects in Quarterly Journal of Medicine, British Heart Jl, Lancet, etc. *Address:* 4 Rutland Court, Queens Drive, W3 0HL. *T:* 01-992 8685. *Club:* Athenæum.
*Died 13 Nov.* 1983.

**THORLEY, Sir Gerald (Bowers),** Kt 1973; TD; Director, Fitch Lovell plc; *b* 26 Aug. 1913; *s* of Clement Thorley and Ethel May Davy; *m* 1947, Beryl Preston, *d* of G. Preston Rhodes; one *s* one *d. Educ:* Ratcliffe College. FRICS. FRSA. Served War of 1939–45, RA; BEF, 1939–40; Malaya, 1941; POW, 1942–45. Ind Coope & Allsopp Ltd, 1936. Underwriting Member of Lloyd's, 1952. Chairman: Allied Breweries Ltd, 1970–75; British Sugar plc, 1968–82; MEPC plc, 1976–84; Vice-Chm., Rockware Gp, 1976–86. *Recreations:* gardening, golf. *Address:* Church House, Bale, Fakenham, Norfolk NR21 0QR. *T:* Thursford 314. *Club:* Naval and Military.
*Died 27 Oct.* 1988.

**THORNE, Rt. Rev. Frank Oswald,** CBE 1957; DD; *b* 21 May 1892; *s* of Leonard Temple Thorne and Ada Theodosia Franklin; unmarried. *Educ:* St Paul's School; Christ Church, Oxford (Scholar). 2nd Class Hon. Mods, 1913; BA (War Degree), 1918; 2nd Class Theology, 1921; MA 1935. Served European War, 13th (S) Bn The Manchester Regt, Captain and Adjutant, 1915–17; Brigade Major, No 1 Section Tyne Garrison, 1918–19 (wounded, MC); ordained, 1922; Curate All Souls' Clapton Park, 1922–25; joined Universities Mission to Central Africa, 1925; First Warden of S Cyprian's Theological Coll., Tunduru, Diocese of Masasi, Tanganyika Territory, 1930–34; Bishop of Nyasaland, 1936–61; Dean of Prov. of Central Africa, 1955–61. MLC Nyasaland, 1937–43, 1946–49. DD Lambeth, 1958. *Address:* Morden College, Blackheath, SE3.
*Died 18 Sept.* 1981.

**THORNLEY, Sir Colin (Hardwick),** KCMG 1957 (CMG 1953); CVO 1954; *b* 1907; *s* of late Dr and Mrs J. H. Thornley; *m* 1940, Muriel Betty Hobson; one *s* two *d. Educ:* Bramcote School, Scarborough; Uppingham; Brasenose College, Oxford. MA (hons jurisp.). Colonial Administrative Service, The Tanganyika Territory, 1930–39, seconded to Colonial Office, 1939–45; Principal Private Secretary to Secretary of State for the Colonies, 1941–45; Admin. Secretary, Kenya, 1945–47; Dep. Chief Secretary, Kenya, 1947–52; Chief Secretary, Govt of Protectorate of Uganda, 1952–55; Governor and Commander-in-Chief, British Honduras, 1955–61; retired, 1962. Dir-Gen., Save the Children Fund, 1965–74 (Dep. Dir, 1963–65). Mem., Regional Boundaries Commn, Kenya, 1962; Trustee, Imp. War Museum, 1968–77. *Recreations:* lawn tennis, golf, cricket. *Address:* Spinaway Cottage, Church Lane, Slindon, near Arundel, West Sussex. *T:* Slindon 308. *Clubs:* East India, Devonshire, Sports and Public Schools, Royal Commonwealth Society.
*Died 1 March* 1983.

**THORNTON, Dr (Clara) Grace,** CBE 1964 (OBE 1959); LVO 1957; *b* 27 June 1913; *d* of late Arthur Augustus Thornton and Clara Maud Hines; unmarried. *Educ:* Kettering High School; Newnham Coll., Cambridge (MA, PhD; Hon. Fellow, 1982). Research: Iceland, Cambridge, 1935–39. Min. of Information, 1940–45. Press Attaché, Copenhagen, 1945–48; Vice-Consul, Reykjavik, 1948–51 (Chargé d'Affaires during 1949 and 1950); Foreign Office, 1951–54; 1st Sec. and Consul, Copenhagen, 1954–60; 1st Sec. and Information Officer, Brussels, 1960–62; 1st Sec. and Consul, Djakarta, 1962–64 (Consul-General, 1963–64); Consul-General, Lisbon, 1965–70; Head of Consular Dept, FCO, 1970–73; Sec., Women's Nat. Commn, Cabinet Office, 1973–78. Alternate UK Deleg., UN Status of Women Commn, 1978. Associate Fellow, Newnham Coll., Cambridge, 1972–81. President: London Assoc. of University Women, 1974–78; Associates of Newnham Coll., 1975–78; Pres., Newnham Roll, 1982–84 (Vice-Pres., 1980–82). Governor, GB/E Europe Centre, 1981–. FRSA 1969. Danish Freedom Medal, 1945; Order of Dannebrog, 1957; Order of Icelandic Falcon, 1983. *Publications:* Conversation Piece (University Women's Club), 1979, 2nd edn 1985; Notes on No 2 Audley Square, 1980; (ed) Take Your Hare When it is Cased, 1980 (recipes); *translated and edited:* Hans Christian Andersen: A Visit to Portugal 1866, 1972; A Visit to Spain 1862, 1975; A Visit to Germany, Italy and Malta 1840–41, 1985. *Recreations:* music, embroidery, Scandinavica, cats. *Address:* 17 Onslow Court, Drayton Gardens, SW10 9RL. *T:* 01–373 2965. *Club:* University Women's (Chm. 1976–79).
*Died 23 June* 1987.

**THORNTON, George Edwin,** CMG 1948; MBE 1932; *b* 1899; *m* 1926, Charlotte, *d* of Edward Brian Coulson. Served European War, 1914–18, in E Africa, 1916–17; Colonial Service, Northern Rhodesia, 1918; Financial Secretary, Northern Rhodesia, 1945–51. *Address:* 79 Kew Drive, Highlands, Harare, Zimbabwe.
*Died 7 March* 1983.

**THORNTON, Dr Grace;** *see* Thornton, Dr C. G.

**THORNTON, Michael James,** CBE 1978; MC 1942; *b* 6 Dec. 1919; *s* of late Arthur Bruce Thornton and Dorothy Kidston Thornton (*née* Allsop); *m* 1949, Pauline Elizabeth Heppell; one *s* two *d. Educ:* Christ's Hospital; London Sch. of Economics (BSc(Econ)). Entered Bank of England, 1938; Deputy Chief Cashier, 1962–67; Chief of Economic Intelligence Dept, 1967–78. *Recreation:* sailing.
*Died 17 June* 1989.

**THORNTON, Sir Ronald (George),** Kt 1965; a Director, Bank of England, 1966–70; *b* 21 July 1901; *s* of late Henry George Thornton; *m* 1927, Agnes Margaret (*née* Masson); one *s* one *d. Educ:* St Dunstan's Coll., Catford. Director, Barclays Bank Ltd, 1961 (General Manager, 1946; Vice-Chairman, 1962–66); formerly Director: Friends' Provident & Century Life Office; The Century Insurance Co. Ltd; Century Insurance Trust Ltd; United Dominions Trust Ltd, 1962–71; Member: Cttee of Inquiry on Decimal Currency, 1961–62; Export Council for Europe, 1960–64; Chairman: Exec. Cttee, Banking Inf. Service, 1962–66; Bank Education Service,

1965–66. FRSA 1971. Fellow, Inst. of Bankers. *Address:* South Bank, Rectory Lane, Brasted, Westerham, Kent TN16 1JU.
*Died 17 July 1981.*

**THORNTON-DUESBERY, Rev. Canon Julian Percy,** MA; Canon Emeritus of Liverpool Cathedral (Canon Theologian, 1968–77); *b* 7 Sept. 1902; *s* of late Rt Rev. Charles Leonard Thornton-Duesbery (formerly Bishop of Sodor and Man) and late Ethel Nixon Baumgartner. *Educ:* Forest Sch., Snaresbrook; Rossall Sch.; Balliol Coll., Oxford (Domus Exhbn); Wycliffe Hall, Oxford. Goldsmiths' Exhibition, 1922; *prox acc* Craven Scholarship, 1922; 1st Class Hon. Moderations (Classics), 1923; 1st Class Lit Hum 1925; 1st Class Theology, 1926; Junior Canon Hall Greek Testament Prize, 1926; Senior Denyer and Johnson Scholarship, 1928; Deacon, 1926; Priest, 1927; Chaplain of Wycliffe Hall, Oxford, 1926–27; Vice-Principal, 1927–33; Chaplain, Fellow, and Librarian of Corpus Christi Coll., Oxford, 1928–33; Headmaster of St George's Sch., Jerusalem, 1933–40; Master of St Peter's Hall, 1940–45; Rector of St Peter-le-Bailey, Oxford, 1940–45, 1955–61; Acting Principal, Wycliffe Hall, 1943–44; Principal of Wycliffe Hall, Oxford, 1944–55; Master, St Peter's Coll. (formerly St Peter's Hall), Oxford, 1955–68, Hon. Fellow, 1968. Commissary to Bishop in Jerusalem, 1943–63; Member of Council: St Lawrence Coll., Ramsgate, 1941–79; Headington Sch., 1943–74; Forest Sch., Snaresbrook, 1958–68; St Stephen's Coll., Broadstairs, 1970–77. Examining Chaplain to: Bishop of Blackburn, 1927–33; Bishop in Jerusalem, 1933–40; Bishop of Worcester, 1941–70; Bishop of Oxford, 1955–68; Bishop of Sodor and Man, 1967–83. Select Preacher, University of Oxford, 1943–45. *Publication:* The Open Secret of MRA, 1964. *Address:* College of St Barnabas, Lingfield, Surrey RH7 6NJ. *T:* Dormans Park 508. *Died 1 April 1985.*

**THORNYCROFT, John Ward,** CBE 1957; CEng; FIMechE; beef farmer; Hon. President, John I. Thornycroft & Co. Ltd, since 1966 (Chairman, 1960–66; Managing Director, 1942–66); Director, Southampton, Isle of Wight and South of England Royal Mail Steam Packet Co. Ltd, 1960–77, retired; *b* 14 Oct. 1899; *s* of late Sir John E. Thornycroft; *m* 1930, Esther Katherine (*d* 1985), *d* of J. E. Pritchard; one *s* one *d*. *Educ:* Royal Naval Colleges, Osborne, Dartmouth and Keyham; Trinity Coll., Cambridge. Served War, 1914–18, HMS Opal, HM Submarine G10, HMS Spenser (1914–15 War Service Star). Hon. Vice-Pres., RINA; FRSA. *Recreations:* golf, sailing and gardening. *Address:* Steyne House, Bembridge, Isle of Wight. *T:* Bembridge 2502. *Clubs:* Naval and Military; Bembridge Sailing (IOW).
*Died 15 March 1989.*

**THORPE, Bernard;** Founder and Senior Partner, Bernard Thorpe & Partners, 1922–82; Land Agent, Surveyor, Farmer; *b* 27 June 1895; *m* 1st, 1916, Hilda Mary (*d* 1971), *d* of Edwin Wilkinson, Coventry; one *s* one *d* (and one *s* killed as Pilot Officer Royal Air Force); 2nd, 1972, Mary Philomena, *d* of George Cregan, Limerick, Eire. *Educ:* private tutor; Nottingham Univ. Member Godstone (Surrey) RDC and of its Board of Guardians, 1926–36; Past President, (1939) and Past Chairman, Surrey and Sussex Br. Incorp. Society of Auctioneers and Landed Property Agents; sometime Member Council, Home Grown Timber Marketing Assoc.; Director (Tile Section), Redland Holdings Ltd; Chairman, Park Investments Ltd, 1958–63; Chairman, Assoc. of Land and Property Owners, 1962–64. Past Master, Worshipful Company of Gold and Silver Wyre Drawers, 1966 (Member 1938, and Past Warden); Member Court of Assistants, Worshipful Company of Paviors 1938 (past Warden; Master, 1975); Freeman, City of London. Freemason. *Recreations:* hunting and shooting; formerly Rugby football. *Address:* c/o Mrs J. M. Winney, 12 Lamorna Gardens, Ferring, Worthing, Sussex. *Club:* City Livery. *Died 23 Oct. 1987.*

**THORPE, Prof. William Homan,** FRS 1951; MA, ScD (Cantab); Fellow since 1932, President, 1969–72, Jesus College, Cambridge; Professor of Animal Ethology, Cambridge University, 1966–69, now Emeritus; Joint Editor of "Behaviour: an International Journal of Comparative Ethology"; Chairman: Arthur Stanley Eddington Memorial Trust, 1946–75; International Council for Bird Preservation (British Section), since 1965; *b* 1 April 1902; *o s* of Francis Homan and Mary Amelia Thorpe (*née* Slade), Hastings and Weston-super-Mare; *m* 1936, Winifred Mary (*d* 1978), *o d* of Preb. G. H. Vincent; one *d*. *Educ:* Mill Hill Sch.; Jesus Coll., Cambridge. Research Fellow of International Education Board (Rockefeller Foundation) at University of California, 1927–29; Research Entomologist at Farnham Royal Parasite Laboratory of Imperial Bureau of Entomology, 1929–32; Tutor Jesus Coll., Cambridge, 1932–45; Lecturer in Entomology in the University, 1932–59; Leverhulme Research Fellow in East Africa, 1939; Senior Tutor, Jesus Coll., Cambridge, 1945–47. President, Association for Study of Animal Behaviour, 1948–52; President, Society British Entomology, 1951–53; Prather Lecturer in Biology, Harvard Univ., 1951–52; President of British Ornithologists Union, 1955–60; President Sect. D (Zoology) British Association (Sheffield), 1956; Visiting Prof., University of California, 1958; Eddington Lecturer,

1960; Riddell Lecturer, Durham Univ., 1961; Fremantle Lecturer, Balliol Coll., Oxford, 1962–63; Gifford Lectr, St Andrews Univ., 1969–71. Leverhulme Emeritus Fellowship, 1971–72. Godman-Salvin Gold Medal, British Ornithologists' Union, 1968; Frink Medal, Zool Soc. of London, 1980; International Prize, Fondation Fyssen, Paris, 1981. *Publications:* Learning and Instinct in Animals, 1956; (ed with O. L. Zangwill) Current Problems in Animal Behaviour, 1961; Bird Song: The Biology of Vocal Communication and Expression in Birds, 1961; Biology and the Nature of Man, 1962; Science, Man and Morals, 1965; Quakers and Humanists, 1968; (ed with A. M. Pantin) The Relations Between the Sciences, by late C. F. A. Pantin, 1968; Duetting and Antiphonal Song in Birds, 1972; Animal Nature and Human Nature, 1974; Purpose in a World of Chance, 1978; The Origins and Rise of Ethology, 1979; articles in Encyclopædia Britannica, 15th edn, 1974; numerous papers on Entomology, Ornithology, Comparative Physiology and Animal Behaviour (Ethology): in Journal Society Exp. Biology, Biol. Reviews, Ibis, Behaviour, etc. *Recreations:* music, swimming. *Address:* Jesus College, Cambridge. *T:* 68611.
*Died 7 April 1986.*

**THOULESS, Robert Henry;** Reader Emeritus in the University of Cambridge, since 1961; Fellow of Corpus Christi College, Cambridge, since 1945; *b* 15 July 1894; *s* of Henry James Thouless; *m* 1924, Priscilla Gorton; one *s* one *d*. *Educ:* City of Norwich Sch.; Corpus Christi Coll., Cambridge. BA (Nat. Sci.), 1915. Served European War, 2nd Lieut, RE, British Salonika Force, 1917. PhD (Cambridge) 1922; Lecturer in Psychology, Manchester Univ., 1921, Glasgow Univ., 1926, Cambridge Univ., 1938; Reader in Educational Psychology, 1945–61; Consultant NFER, 1964. President, Section J British Association, 1937; Riddell Memorial Lecturer, 1940; President, Society for Psychical Research, 1942; President, British Psycholog. Society, 1949 (Hon. Fellow 1962); Hulsean Lecturer, 1951. Lecturing in Australia, 1962, 1966; Eddington Memorial Lecturer, 1963; T. B. Davie Memorial Lecturer (Cape Town), 1964. ScD (Cambridge), 1953. *Publications:* An Introduction to the Psychology of Religion, 1923 (rev. edn 1971); The Lady Julian, 1924; Social Psychology, 1925; The Control of the Mind, 1927; Straight and Crooked Thinking, 1930, rev. edn 1974; General and Social Psychology, 1937, 1951 and 1957; Straight Thinking in War Time, 1942; Authority and Freedom, 1954; Experimental Psychical Research, 1963; Map of Educational Research, 1969; Missing the Message, 1971; From Anecdote to Experiment in Psychical Research, 1972; Do We Survive Death?, 1984; articles in British Journal of Psychology, Proc. of Society of Psychical Research, Journal of Parapsychology, etc. *Recreations:* chess, painting. *Address:* 2 Leys Road, Cambridge.
*Died 25 Sept. 1984.*

**THROCKMORTON, Sir Robert George Maxwell,** 11th Bt, *cr* 1642; *b* 15 Feb. 1908; *s* of Lt-Col Courtenay Throckmorton (killed in action, 1916), and Lilian (*d* 1955), *o d* of Colonel Langford Brooke, Mere Hall, Cheshire; *S* grandfather, 1927; *m* 1st, 1942, Jean (marr. diss. 1948), (former wife of Arthur Smith-Bingham, *d* of late Charles Garland; she *m* 1959, 3rd Baron Ashcombe, and *d* 1973); 2nd, 1953, Lady Isabel Guinness, *d* of 9th Duke of Rutland. *Educ:* Downside; RMC, Sandhurst. 2nd Lieut, Grenadier Guards, 1928–30; Lieut (A) RNVR, 1940–44. *Heir: cousin* Anthony John Benedict Throckmorton [*b* 9 Feb. 1916; *m* 1972, Violet Virginia, *d* of late Anders William Anderson]. *Address:* Coughton Court, Alcester, Warwickshire. *T:* Alcester 763370; Molland Bottreaux, South Molton, N Devon. *T:* Bishops Nympton 325. *Club:* White's.
*Died 13 Dec. 1989.*

**THROWER, Frank James,** MBE 1987; FCSD (FSIAD 1975); glass and ceramic designer; Design Director: Dartington Glass, 1983–87; Wedgwood Crystal, since 1983; *b* 11 April 1932; *m* G. Inga-Lill (marr. diss.); one *s* three *d* and three adopted *s* (and one *s* decd). *Educ:* flunked out of Stationers' Company's Sch. due to enjoying both fine summer and Denis Compton's batting at Lord's Cricket Ground, 1947; no further trng or educn. Worked in shipbroker's office as general dogsbody, 1947–50; four other people in office: 1 Plymouth Brother, 1 Baptist, 1 Methodist, 1 Quaker; decided against organised religion—and shipbroking; various office jobs carried out with no interest or competence, 1950–51; bought a hat and tried to sell carbon paper, failed, 1951; sold hat and tried to sell pottery and glass, 1953–60; succeeded; saw where there was scope for new ideas and improved design; joined Portmeirion as Sales Director, 1960; sold year's prodn in four weeks; designed some glass to set up as importer under Portmeirion banner; glass sold successfully and ... first talks with Dartington about building glass factory in UK, 1963; Dartington Glass factory opened, 1967. Observer Award for design, 1969; Duke of Edinburgh Award for design, 1972; Design Council Award for design, 1972. *Recreation:* maintaining the level of essential bodily fluids whilst waiting for something to turn up. *Address:* c/o Lloyds Bank, 32 Oxford Street, W1A 2LD. *Clubs:* Chelsea Arts, MCC, Queen's.
*Died 29 June 1987.*

**THROWER, Percy John**, MBE 1984; with garden centre and nursery business (Murrells of Shrewsbury, Portland Nurseries, Shrewsbury); Parks Superintendent, Shrewsbury, 1946–74; *b* 30 Jan. 1913; British; *m* 1939, Constance Margaret (*née* Cook); three *d. Educ:* Church of England Sch., Little Horwood. NDH 1945. Improver, Horwood House Gdns, Winslow, 1927–31; Journeyman Gardener, Royal Gdns, Windsor, 1931–35; Journeyman Gardener, City of Leeds Parks Dept, 1935–37; Asst Parks Supt, Borough of Derby Parks Dept, 1937–46. Frequent broadcaster, radio and TV, 1947–. RHS: Associate of Honour, 1963; VMH 1974. *Publications:* In Your Garden Week by Week, 1959, rev. edn 1973; Encyclopædia of Gardening, 1962; In Your Greenhouse, 1963, rev. edn 1972; Gardening is Fun; Colour in Your Garden, 1966, rev. 1976; Everyday Gardening, 1969; Vegetables and Fruit, 1977; My Lifetime of Gardening, 1977; Vegetables and Herbs; Month by Month in Your Garden, 1980; Picture Book of Gardening; contrib. Amateur Gardening. *Recreation:* shooting. *Address:* The Magnolias, Bomere Heath, Shrewsbury, Salop SY4 3QJ. *T:* Bomere Heath 290225. *Died 18 March* 1988.

**THUILLIER, Lt-Col Henry Shakespear**, DSO 1940; late Royal Artillery (Regular); *b* 10 Sept. 1895; *s* of late Maj.-Gen. Sir Henry Thuillier, KCB, CMG; *m* Beatrice Winifred, *d* of late Captain F. H. Walter, RN; two *s. Educ:* Dragon Sch.; Dover Coll.; RMA, Woolwich. Commissioned RA, 1915; Captain, 1917; Major, 1935; Acting Lt-Col, 1940; Lt-Col, 1942; served Gallipoli and Mesopotamia, 1915–20; BEF, France, 1939–40 (DSO); North African Campaign, 1942–43; Italian Campaign, 1944–45 (despatches twice); retired, 1946; commissioned RCAC, 1950, appointed Lt-Col(SR); retired, 1955. *Address:* Apt 403, 685 Niagara Street, Victoria, BC, Canada. *Died 25 March* 1982.

**THURBURN, Brigadier Roy Gilbert**, CB 1950; CBE 1945 (OBE 1941); Secretary, Army Museums Ogilby Trust, 1957–72; *b* 6 July 1901; *y s* of late Reginald Phibbs Thurburn; *m* 1936, Rhona Moneen Hignett; one *s. Educ:* St Paul's Sch.; Royal Military Coll., Sandhurst. Commissioned in the Cameronians (Scottish Rifles), 1921; took part in operations in Southern Kurdistan, 1923; attended Staff Coll., Camberley, 1933–34. Served War of 1939–45, in Middle East, North Africa and Italy (despatches twice). ADC to the Queen, 1952–53; retired, 1953. Gold Medallist, United Services Institution of India, 1932. Legion of Merit (USA), 1947. *Publications:* (ed) Index to British Military Costume Prints, 1972; various in journals. *Recreations:* many. *Address:* 4 Edgeborough Court, Upper Edgeborough Road, Guildford, Surrey GU1 2BL. *Died 5 Oct.* 1990.

**THWAITES, Brian St George**, CMG 1958; *b* 22 April 1912; *s* of late Henry Thwaites and Ada B. Thwaites (*née* Macnutt); *m* 1938, Madeleine Elizabeth Abell; one *s* two *d. Educ:* Canford School; Clare Coll., Cambridge. Entered Colonial Service (later HM Overseas Civil Service), 1935; served as Administrative Officer in Eastern Nigeria, 1935–47 and 1948–57; Palestine, 1947–48; retired, 1957. Planning Inspector, DoE, 1966–76. *Recreations:* golf, walking. *Address:* Painshill, Donhead St Andrew, Shaftesbury, Dorset SP7 9EA. *T:* Donhead 248. *Died 23 Jan.* 1989.

**TIARKS, Rt. Rev. Geoffrey Lewis**, MA Cantab; *b* 8 Oct 1909; *s* of Lewis Herman Tiarks, Clerk in Holy Orders, and Edith Margaret Tiarks; *m* 1934, Betty Lyne, *d* of Henry Stock; one *s* (one *d* decd). *Educ:* Marlborough; S John's College, Cambridge. Ordained at Southwark, 1932; Curate of St Saviour's with St Peter, Southwark, 1932–33; Chaplain, RN, 1934–47; Chaplain, Diocesan College, Rondebosch, CP, 1948–50; Rector of S Paul's, Rondebosch, 1950–54; Vicar of Lyme Regis, Dorset, 1954–61; Archdeacon of the Isle of Wight, 1961–65; Archdeacon of Portsmouth, 1965–69; Bishop Suffragan of Maidstone, 1969–76; Senior Chaplain to Archbishop of Canterbury, 1969–74. *Address:* Primrose Cottage, Netherbury, Bridport, Dorset. *T:* Netherbury 277.
*Died 14 Jan.* 1987.

**TIGHE, Maj.-Gen. Patrick Anthony Macartan**, CB 1977; MBE 1958; FBIM; Chairman, Ex-Services Mental Welfare Society, since 1987; *b* 26 Feb. 1923; *s* of late Macartan H. Tighe, BA, RUI, Barrister-at-Law, Dublin and Dorothy Isabel (*née* Vine); *m* 1st, 1950, Elizabeth Frazer Stewart (*d* 1971); two *s;* 2nd, 1972, Princine Merendino Calitri, authoress, W Virginia, USA. *Educ:* Christ's Hospital. Served RAF, 1940–41; commnd Royal Signals, 1943; served NW Europe, 1944–45, Palestine, 1945–47; psc 1955; DAAQMG Gurkha Bde Malaya, 1956 (MBE); Mil. Asst Comd British Forces Hong Kong, 1963; Force Signals Officer Borneo, 1964–66 (despatches); Asst Mil. Sec., 1966; Col Asst Adjt Gen., 1968; Brig. Comd Trng Bde Royal Signals, 1970; Inspector of Intell. Corps, 1973; Signal Officer-in-Chief (Army), 1974–77. Col Comdt, Royal Signals, 1977–84. With Hongkong Land Gp, 1977–84. *Publications:* radio plays (BBC), film and book reviews for press and radio in Far East. *Recreations:* cinema (Mem. British Film Inst. 1947), golf. *Address:* c/o Lloyds Bank, 6 Pall Mall, SW1Y 5NH. *Clubs:* Army and Navy;

Worthing Golf; Hong Kong, Shek-O Country (Hong Kong).
*Died 23 Oct.* 1989.

**TILBE, Douglas Sidney**, OBE 1973; JP; Deputy Chief Executive, Voluntary Christian Service, since 1981; *b* 27 May 1931; *s* of late Norrie Ethelbert Sidney George Tilbe and of Ethel Tilbe (*née* Scott); *m* 1957, Janet Ann Ainger; three *s* one *d. Educ:* LSE; Avery Hill Coll. of Educn; Univ. of Essex (MA Soc. Service Planning). Gen. Sec., Soc. of Friends Race Relations Cttee, 1965–71; Dir, British Council of Churches Community and Race Relations Unit, 1971–73; Chm., Priority Area Children, 1971–73; Mem., Uganda Resettlement Bd, 1972–74; Chm., Co-ordinating Cttee for Welfare of Evacuees from Uganda, 1972–73; Dir, Shelter, 1974–77; Housing Campaign Dir, Help the Aged, 1978–81. Dir, St Albans Co-operative Soc. Vice-Pres., Nat. Children's Centre. Chm., Welwyn Garden City UDC, 1972–73; Mem., Welwyn Hatfield DC, 1974–83 (Dep. Chm., 1979–80; Chm., Environmental Health Cttee, 1980–83). Contested (Lab) Rye, 1959 and 1964. Member: NW Metrop. Mental Health Review Tribunal, 1971–78; Oxford Region Mental Health Review Tribunal, 1974–78. Chm. Governors, Heronswood Sch. JP Herts 1967. Hon. MA Open University. *Publications:* East African Asians, 1968; The Ugandan Asian Crisis, 1972. *Recreations:* soccer referee; watching football, cricket, golf and tennis. *Address:* 15 Beehive Green, Welwyn Garden City, Herts AL7 4BE. *T:* Welwyn Garden 27373. *Died 18 April* 1984.

**TILLETT, Mrs Emmie Muriel;** Chairman, Ibbs & Tillett, since 1978 (Managing Director, 1948–78); *b* 7 December 1896; *d* of Arthur and Florence Bass; *m* 1941, John Hudson Tillett (*d* 1951); no *c. Educ:* privately. With Chappell & Co. Ltd (Music Publishers), 1916–22; joined the firm of Ibbs & Tillett, 1922. Hon. FRAM 1975. *Recreations:* water colour painting, reading. *Address:* 11 Elm Tree Road, St John's Wood, NW8. *T:* 01–286 6161; Three Ash House, Bungay, Suffolk. *T:* Bungay 2485. *Died 16 May* 1982.

**TILMOUTH, Prof. Michael;** first Tovey Professor of Music, University of Edinburgh, since 1971; *b* 30 Nov. 1930; *s* of Herbert George Tilmouth and Amy Tilmouth (*née* Hall); *m* 1966, Mary Jelliman; two *s* one *d. Educ:* Wintringham Grammar Sch., Grimsby; Christ's Coll., Cambridge (MA, PhD). Lectr, Glasgow Univ., 1959–71; Dean, Faculty of Music, Edinburgh Univ., 1973–76, 1980–84, 1985–. Dir, Scottish Opera, 1975–. Mem., BBC Archives Adv. Cttee, 1975–. Mem. Council, Royal Musical Assoc., 1970–76 (Editor, Research Chronicle, 1968–77); Member, Editorial Committee: Musica Britannica, 1972– (Gen. Editor, 1984–); Purcell Soc., 1976– (Chm., 1984–). *Publications:* (ed) Matthew Locke: Chamber Music and Dramatic Music (Musica Britannica, vols xxxi, 1971, vol. xxxii, 1972, vol. li, 1986); (ed) Purcell: Collected Works, vol. v, 1976, vol. vii, 1981, vol. xxxi, 1986; contribs to: Galpin Soc. Jl, Music & Letters, Proc. of Royal Musical Assoc., Musical Times, Musical Quarterly, Royal Mus. Assoc. Res. Chronicle, Encyc. de la Pléiade, Die Musik in Geschichte und Gegenwart, Grove's Dictionary, Monthly Mus. Record, The Consort, Brio, Early Music. *Recreations:* gardening, hill walking. *Address:* 62 Northumberland Street, Edinburgh EH3 6JE. *T:* 031–556 3293.
*Died 12 Nov.* 1987.

**TILNEY, Brig. Robert Adolphus George**, CBE 1962; DSO 1945; TD; *b* 2 November 1903; *s* of late Colonel William Arthur Tilney and late Hylda Paget, Sutton Bonington, Notts; *m* 1933, Frances Moore, *d* of late Robert Cochrane Barclay, Virginia, USA; three *d* (one *s* decd). *Educ:* Eton; Cambridge University. Joined Leics Yeo., 1924; Major 1935; Lt-Col Comdg Leics Yeo., 1940–43; Brig. Comdg 234 Bde 1943; Comdg Fortress Leros, 1943 (despatches). Retired as Chm., Sale Tilney & Co. Ltd, Byward Street, EC3, 1965. High Sheriff, Leics, 1953. *Address:* Bucks Lane, Sutton Bonington, Loughborough, Leics. *Died 1 May* 1981.

**TILTMAN, Brig. John Hessell**, CMG 1954; CBE 1944 (OBE 1930); MC; late King's Own Scottish Borderers; *b* 25 May 1894; *s* of late A. Hessell Tiltman, FRIBA; *m* 1926, Tempe Monica Robinson; one *d. Educ:* Charterhouse. *Address:* 1-2D 511 Hahaione Street, Honolulu, Hawaii 96825, USA. *Died 10 Aug.* 1982.

**TIMBURY, Prof. Gerald Charles**, OBE 1984; FRCPE; FRCPGlas; FRCPsych; Dean of Postgraduate Medicine and Professor of Postgraduate Medical Education, University of Glasgow, 1980–84; *b* 15 Aug. 1929; *s* of Montague Charles and Marjorie Lilian Timbury, Glasgow; *m* 1954, Morag Crichton McCulloch; one *d. Educ:* Glasgow Acad.; Glasgow Univ. MB, ChB; DPM. Captain, RAMC, 1953–55. Usual resident appointments, 1952–53; Hosp. appointments in medicine and psychiatry, Glasgow, 1955–60; Lectr in Psychological Medicine, Univ. of Glasgow, 1960–65; Physician Superintendent, Gartnavel Royal Hosp., 1965–80. *Publications:* papers on psychiatric diagnosis, mental health legislation, and psychiatry of old age. *Recreation:* golf. *Address:* 11/1 Whistlefield, 2 Canniesburn Road, Bearsden, Glasgow G61 1PX. *T:* 041–943 0430. *Clubs:* Caledonian; Royal Scottish Automobile (Glasgow).
*Died 10 June* 1985.

**TINBERGEN, Prof. Nikolaas,** DPhil, MA; FRS 1962; Professor in Animal Behaviour, Oxford University, 1966–74, Emeritus Professor, 1974 (Lecturer, 1949–60, Reader, 1960–66); Fellow of Wolfson College, 1966–74, then Emeritus; *b* 15 April 1907; *s* of Dirk C. Tinbergen and Jeannette Van Eek; *m* 1932, Elisabeth A. Rutten; two *s* three *d. Educ:* Leiden; Vienna; Yale. Lecturer, 1936, Prof. of Experimental Zoology, 1947, Leiden University; Fellow, Merton Coll., Oxford Univ., 1950–66. Hon. Mem. of many learned socs. Hon. DSc: Edinburgh, 1973; Leicester, 1974. Godman-Salvin Medal, British Ornithol. Union, 1969. Italia Prize (documentaries), 1969; Swammerdam Medal, 1973; Nobel Prize for Physiology or Medicine (jt), 1973. *Publications:* Eskimoland, 1935; The Study of Instinct, 1951; The Herring Gull's World, 1953; Social Behaviour in Animals, 1953; Curious Naturalists, 1959; Animal Behaviour, 1965; Signals for Survival, 1970; The Animal in its World, vol. 1, 1972, vol. 2, 1973; (with E. A. Tinbergen) 'Autistic' Children: new hope for a cure, 1983; contribs to German, Dutch, British and American journals. *Address:* 88 Lonsdale Road, Oxford OX2 7ER. *T:* Oxford 58662. *Died* 21 *Dec.* 1988.

**TITTERTON, Major David Maitland M.;** *see* Maitland-Titterton.

**TITTERTON, Prof. Sir Ernest (William),** Kt 1970; CMG 1957; FRSA; FAA; Professor of Nuclear Physics, Australian National University, 1950–81, now Emeritus; Dean of the Research School of Physical Sciences, Australian National University, 1966–68, Director of Research School of Physical Sciences, 1968–73; *b* 4 March 1916; *e s* of W. A. Titterton, Tamworth, Staffs; *m* 1942, Peggy Eileen (marr. diss. 1986), *o d* of Captain A. Johnson, Hagley, Worcs; one *s* two *d. Educ:* Queen Elizabeth's Grammar Sch., Tamworth; University of Birmingham (BSc, MSc, PhD). Research Officer, Admiralty, 1939–43; Member British Scientific Mission to USA on Atomic Bomb development, 1943–47; Sen. Member of Timing Group at 1st Atomic Bomb Test, Alamagordo, 1945; Adviser on Instrumentation, Bikini Atomic Weapon Tests, 1946; Head of Electronics Div., Los Alamos Lab., USA, 1946–47; Group Leader in charge of Research team at AERE, Harwell, 1947–50. Member Australian Atomic Energy Commn Scientific Advisory Cttee, 1955–64; Dep. Chairman Australian Atomic Weapons Safety Cttee, 1954–56; Chm., Atomic Weapons Safety Cttee, 1957–73 (in this capacity attended all British Atom Bomb tests in Australia, 1952–57); Member, Defence Research and Development Policy Cttee, 1958–75; Member National Radiation Advisory Cttee, 1957–73. Vice-Pres., Aust. Inst. of Nuclear Science and Engineering, 1968–72, Pres., 1973–75. *Publications:* Progress in Nuclear Physics, 4, 1955; Facing the Atomic Future (London, New York, Melbourne), 1955; Selected Lectures in Modern Physics for School Science Teachers, 1958; Uranium: energy source of the future?, 1979; some 212 papers mainly on nuclear physics, atomic energy and electronics in technical journals. *Recreations:* music and tennis. *Address:* PO Box 331, Jamison, ACT 2614, Australia. *Died* 8 *Feb.* 1990.

**TOBIAS, Prof. Stephen Albert,** DSc, PhD Edinburgh, MA Cantab, DiplIng Budapest; FIMechE; FIProdE; FEng 1985; M.ASME; M.CIRP; Chance Professor of Mechanical Engineering and Head of Department, University of Birmingham, since 1959; *b* Vienna, 10 July 1920; *s* of Bela and Zelma; *m* 1945, Stephanie Paula Garzo; two *s. Educ:* Josef Eotvos Gymnasium, Budapest; Technological Univ., Budapest; Edinburgh Univ. DiplIng Technological Univ., Budapest, 1943. Machine Tool Design Engineer, 1943–47; British Council Scholarship, 1947; ICI Research Fellow, 1951–54; Assistant Director of Research, Department of Engineering, Cambridge Univ., 1956. Visiting Professor: Univ. of Cairo, 1963; Univ. of Denver, 1969; Univ. of California, 1969; Nat. Univ. of Mexico, 1970; Russell Severance Springer Prof. of Mech. Engrg, Univ. of Calif, Berkeley, 1979. UNESCO Consultant to Brazil, 1971; World Bank Consultant, Chinese Develt Project, 1985. Dir, Engineering DRD Ltd. Member: Engineering Industry Trng Bd, 1967– (Chm. Technologist Trng Panel); SRC Manufacturing Technology Cttee, 1972–75. T. Bernard Hall Prize, 1957, and Whitworth Prize, 1959, of Instn of Mechanical Engineers; Blackall Machine Tool Award, 1958, of American Society of Mech. Engineers; Frederick W. Taylor Res. Medal, Soc. of Manufg Engrs, 1984. Co-editor in chief, Procs Internat. Conf. for Machine Tool Design and Res., 1963–; Editor in Chief, Internat. Jl for Machine Tool Design and Res., 1977– (co-editor in chief, 1959–76). *Publications:* Schwingungen an Werkzeugmaschinen, 1961; Machine-Tool Vibration, 1965 (Japanese edn, 1969, Spanish edn, 1971, Chinese edn, 1979); over 120 contributions to engineering journals and proceedings of learned societies dealing with linear and non-linear vibrations, dynamic stability of metal cutting process, high energy rate forming, design, impact noise and robotics. *Recreations:* colour photography, music, cultivation of cactus plants, petroforging. *Address:* Department of Mechanical Engineering, PO Box 363, University of Birmingham, Birmingham B15 2TT. *T:* 021–472 1301.

*Died* 24 *April* 1986.

**TODD, (Alfred) Norman,** FCA; CompIEE; Chairman, National Bus Company, 1969–71; retired; *b* 18 Oct. 1904; *s* of late Alfred and

Rachel Todd; *m* 1935, Mary Watson; one *s* one *d. Educ:* Bishops Stortford College. With Deloitte Plender Griffiths & Co., 1929–48; Assistant, then Deputy Chief Accountant, Merseyside and North Wales Electricity Board, 1948–51; Assistant Chief Accountant, British Electricity Authority, 1951–54; Chief Accountant, London Electricity Board, 1954–56; Dep. Chairman, London Electricity Board, 1956–61; Chairman, East Midlands Electricity Board, 1962–64. Member, Central Electricity Generating Board, 1965–68. Hon. Treasurer, IEE, 1972–75. *Recreation:* golf. *Address:* Allendale, 139 Cooden Drive, Bexhill-on-Sea, East Sussex TN39 3AJ. *T:* Cooden (04243) 4147. *Died* 28 *Dec.* 1990.

**TODD, Sir Bryan (James),** Kt 1976; Chairman: Todd Petroleum Mining Co. Ltd, since 1955; Viking Mining Co. Ltd, since 1970; Director: Todd Motors Ltd, since 1924; Shell, BP & Todd Oil Services Ltd, since 1955; Waipipi Iron Sands Ltd, since 1970; Maui Development Ltd, since 1973; *b* 8 Sept. 1902; *s* of Charles Todd and Mary (*née* Hegarty); *m* 1928, Helen Ann Buddo; three *d. Educ:* Christian Bros, Dunedin, NZ; Riverview Coll., Sydney, NSW, Australia. Automotive industry, 1922–; prominent in petroleum industry of NZ, 1930–; Founder and formerly Managing Director: Europa Oil (NZ) Ltd (marketing and refining); Todd Petroleum Mining Co. Ltd (exploration and production of oil and gas in NZ); Viking Mining Co. Ltd (ironsand prodn, refining and export). Chairman: Ruapehu Alpine Lifts Ltd, 1953–; Todd Foundn, 1972–. *Recreations:* skiing, sailing, golf, shooting. *Address:* 38 Wesley Road, Wellington, New Zealand. *T:* (home) 727 040, (office) 722 970. *Clubs:* Wellington, Wellesley (Wellington, NZ); Wellington Golf (Heretaunga, NZ); Ruapehu Ski (NZ).

*Died* 29 *May* 1987.

**TODD, Sir Geoffrey Sydney,** KCVO 1951 (CVO 1947); OBE 1946; DL; MB, ChM, FRCP; FRACP; Medical Superintendent, King Edward VII Hospital, Midhurst, 1934–70; *b* 2 Nov. 1900; *s* of late George William Todd, and Amy Louisa Webb; *m* 1955, Margaret Alan Sheen, *o d* of late F. A. Sheen, MC, and of Mrs Sheen, Tudor Cottage, Midhurst. *Educ:* King's Sch., Parramatta, Australia; Sydney Univ., Australia. Resident MO, 1925–26, Medical Superintendent, 1926–27, Wagga District Hospital; House Physician 1929, House Surgeon 1930, Resident MO 1930–34, Brompton Hospital for Chest Diseases, London. DL Sussex, 1968, West Sussex, 1974. Guthrie Meml Medal, 1971. CStJ. *Publications:* various, in medical journals, 1936–56. *Recreations:* sailing, golf, photography. *Address:* c/o West Heath Cottage, King Edward VII Hospital, Midhurst, W Sussex. *Club:* Naval and Military.

*Died* 24 *Dec.* 1986.

**TODD, Sir Herbert John,** Kt 1947; CIE 1944; retired as Chief Representative, Iraq Petroleum Company and Associate Companies, Baghdad (1952–59); *b* 15 Oct. 1893; *m* 1919, Nancy (*d* 1981), 2nd *d* of Colonel A. F. Pullen, RA; two *d.* Imperial Police, Burma, 1913; 11th Bengal Lancers (Probyns Horse), 1917; Civil Administration, Mesopotamia, 1919; Indian Political Service, 1921; Asst Political Agent, Sibi, 1921; Kalat, 1922; Political Agent, Gilgit, 1927; Quetta-Pishin, 1932; Political Agent, E Rajputana States, 1935; Prime Minister and Vice-President, Council of State, Jaipur, 1939; Political Agent, Mewar, 1940; Secretary, Baluchistan, 1941; Resident for the Madras States, 1943; Resident for the Eastern States, 1944–47. *Address:* Tigh-na-Croft, Enoch-Dhu, by Blairgowrie, Perthshire. *T:* Strathardle 363.

*Died* 5 *Sept.* 1985.

**TODD, James Maclean,** MA; Secretary to the Oxford University Delegacy for the Inspection and Examination of Schools and Oxford Secretary to the Oxford and Cambridge Schools Examination Board, 1964–74; Founder Fellow of St Cross College, Oxford; *b* 1907; *s* of late John Todd, Oxford, and Mary, *d* of late Robert Spottiswoode, Gattonside; *m* 1944, Janet, *d* of late Andrew Holmes, Glasgow; one *s* one *d. Educ:* City of Oxford School; The Queen's Coll., Oxford (Open Mathematical Scholar). First Class Mathematical Mods, 1928; 2nd Class Lit. Hum., 1930; 2nd Class Hon. School of Theology, 1931. Awarded Holwell Studentship in Theology. Assistant Master, Radley, Bryanston, Bromsgrove and Stowe. Headmaster, The High School, Newcastle, Staffs, 1948–63. *Publications:* The Ancient World, 1938; Hymns and Psalms for use in Newcastle High School (New Edn), 1951; Voices from the Past: a Classical Anthology (with Janet Maclean Todd), 1955 (Grey Arrow edn, 1960); Peoples of the Past (with Janet Maclean Todd), 1963. *Address:* Foxton Lodge, Foxton Close, Oxford OX2 8LB. *T:* Oxford 58840.

*Died* 8 *Dec.* 1988.

**TODD, Norman;** *see* Todd, A. N.

**TOLLEMACHE, Maj.-Gen. Sir Humphry (Thomas),** 6th Bt *cr* 1793; CB 1952; CBE 1950; DL; *b* 10 Aug. 1897; *s* of Sir Lyonel Tollemache, 4th Bt (*d* 1952), and Hersilia Henrietta Diana (*d* 1953), *d* of late H. R. Oliphant; *S* brother, 1969; *m* 1926, Nora Priscilla, *d* of John Taylor, Broomhill, Eastbourne; two *s* two *d. Educ:* Eastbourne Coll. 2nd Lieut, Royal Marines, 1915; served European War, Grand Fleet, 1916–18; War of 1939–45 in Middle East and

Far East; Bt Major, 1934; Bt Lt-Col, 1942; Actg Colonel Comdt, temp. Brigadier, 1943; Colonel, 1946; Maj.-Gen., 1949; comd 3rd Mobile Naval Base Bde, 1943–44; comd Small Ops Gp, 1944–45; comd Depot, 1946–47; Director of Pay and Records, 1947–49; commanded Portsmouth Group, Royal Marines, 1949–52, Hon. Colonel Comdt, 1958–60; Colonel Comdt, Royal Marines, 1961–62; Rep. Colonel Comdt, 1961. Member Hampshire CC, 1957–74; Alderman, 1969–74. Chm., C of E Soldiers, Sailors and Airmen Clubs, 1955–65, Pres., 1974. DL Hampshire, 1965. *Heir:* s Lyonel Humphry John Tollemache JP, DL, FRICS [*b* 10 July 1931; *m* 1960, Mary Joscelyne, *e d* of William Henry Whitbread, TD; two s two d]. *Address:* Sheet House, Petersfield, Hants. *Club:* Army and Navy. *Died 30 March* 1990.

**TOLLERFIELD, Albert Edward**, CB 1963; Assistant Comptroller, Patent Office, 1959–66; retired from Civil Service; *b* 8 Dec. 1906; *s* of late Frank Tollerfield; *m* 1st, 1930, Lilian May (*d* 1972); three *d*; 2nd, 1974, Adelaide Mary. *Educ:* Royal Dockyard School, Portsmouth. Fitter Apprentice, 1922–27; Design Draughtsman, 1929; Examiner, Patent Office, 1930; Intelligence Department, Min. of Shipping, 1939–43; Superintending Examiner and Hearing Officer, Patent Office, 1955–59. Chairman, Patents Appointments Boards, Civil Service Commn, 1966–69. *Recreation:* do-it-yourself. *Address:* 17 Hill Road, Southend-on-Sea, Essex. *T:* Southend-on-Sea 619438. *Died 4 April* 1984.

**TOMLIN, Eric Walter Frederick**, CBE 1965 (OBE 1959); FRSL; author; *b* 30 Jan. 1913; *s* of Edgar Herbert Tomlin and Mary (*née* Dexter); *m* 1st, 1945, Margaret Stuart (marr. diss. 1952); one *s*; 2nd, 1974, Judith, *yr d* of late Lt-Gen. Sir Euan Miller, KCB, KBE, DSO, MC. *Educ:* Whitgift; Brasenose Coll., Oxford (BA degrees in PPE and Mod. Hist.); MA (Oxon), 1958; MA (Cantab), 1972. Asst Master: Sloane Sch., Chelsea, 1936–38; Marlborough, 1939; Resident Tutor, Wilts, Bristol Univ. Bd of Extra-Mural Studies, 1939–40; joined Local Defence Volunteers, 1940; British Council Lecturer, Staff Coll. Baghdad and RMC, 1940–41; worked in Information Dept, British Embassy, Baghdad, 1941; British Council: Ankara, 1941–42; Regional Dir, S Turkey, 1942–45; Headquarters London, 1945–47 and 1952–56; Paris, 1947–51; Rep. in Turkey and Cultural Attaché British Embassy, Ankara, 1956–61; Rep. in Japan and Cultural Counsellor British Embassy, Tokyo, 1961–67; Leverhulme Foundn Fellow, 1967–69; British Council Rep. in France, and Cultural Attaché, British Embassy, Paris, 1969–71. Bollingen Foundn Fellow and Vis. Prof., Univ. of Southern California, 1961; Vis. Fellow, Univ. Coll., Cambridge, 1971–72; Vis. Prof., Nice, 1972–74. Fellow: Royal Asiatic Soc.; Inst. of Cultural Research; Life Mem., Royal Inst. of Cornwall; Associate Mem., Magic Circle; Hon. Mem., British Council; Pres., Royal Soc. of St George, Tokyo, 1965; Pres., The Dickens Fellowship, 1987–. Member: Exec. Cttee, English Centre, Internat. PEN, 1985–; Council, Philosophical Soc., 1986–. *Publications:* Turkey, the Modern Miracle, 1939; Life in Modern Turkey, 1946; The Approach to Metaphysics, 1947; The Western Philosophers, 1950; The Eastern Philosophers, 1952; Simone Weil, 1954; R. G. Collingwood, 1954; Wyndham Lewis, 1955; Living and Knowing, 1955; La Vie et l'Oeuvre de Bertrand Russell, 1963; (ed) T. S. Eliot: a Tribute from Japan, 1965; Tokyo Essays, 1967; Wyndham Lewis: an Anthology of his Prose, 1969; (ed) Charles Dickens, a Centenary Volume, 1969; Japan, 1973; Man, Time and the New Science, 1973; The Last Country, 1974; (ed) Arnold Toynbee: a selection from his works, 1978; The World of St Boniface, 1980; In Search of St Piran, 1982; The Church of St Morwenna and St John the Baptist, Morwenstow: a guide and history, 1982; Psyche, Culture and the New Science, 1985; Philosophers of East and West, 1986; The Tall Trees of Marsland: reflections on life and time, 1988; T. S. Eliot: a friendship, 1988; contribs to Criterion, Scrutiny, Times Literary Supplement, Economist, Arts Review, PN Review, Agenda, Temenos, The Tablet and many foreign reviews, etc. *Recreations:* travel, reading, music. *Address:* 31 Redan Street, W14. *T:* 01–602 6414. *Clubs:* Athenæum; Union Society (Oxford). *Died 16 Jan.* 1988.

**TOMLINSON, Rt. Rev. Mgr George Arthur**; Hon. Canon of Westminster Cathedral; *b* Hampstead, NW, 21 May 1906; *s* of late George Henry and Frances Tomlinson. *Educ:* Hastings Grammar Sch.; Keble Coll., Oxford. BA 1929; MA 1942. Ordained in Church of England, 1930; Curate of South Kirby, Yorkshire, 1930–32; received into Catholic Church, 1932; Pontifical Beda Coll., Rome, 1933–37; Priest, 1937; Chaplain to the Oratory Sch., 1937–41; Curate at Kentish Town, 1941; Brentford, 1942; Headmaster, The Oratory Sch., South Oxon, 1943–53; re-established Oratory Preparatory Sch., Branscome Park, Dorset, 1946; Senior Catholic Chaplain to University of London, 1953–64; Administrator Westminster Cathedral, 1964–67; Rector, St James's, Spanish Place, 1967–77, retired. Hon. Chaplain to High Sheriff of Glos, 1982. Prelate of Honour to HH Pope John Paul II. Painter of Frescoes in chapel of Our Lady and the English Martyrs, Little Crosby, Lancs, and various smaller works. *Publications:* regular contributor to theological reviews. *Recreations:* music, painting, swimming.

*Address:* Stable Flat, Spetchley Park, Worcester.
*Died 1 Nov.* 1985.

**TOMNEY, Frank**; sales and marketing analyst; *b* 24 May 1908; *s* of Arthur Tomney, Bolton, Lancs; *m* 1936, Gladys Winifred (*d* 1980), *d* of Andrew Isham, Watford; one *s* one *d*. Branch Secretary, General and Municipal Workers Union, 1940–50. MP (Lab) Hammersmith N, 1950–79; Mem., House of Commons Select Cttees, 1954–60; Deleg., Council of Europe and WEU, 1963–64, 1971–73, 1974–79; Leader, UK Delegn to UN, 1968; Mem., European Parlt, 1976–79. Member: Watford Town Council, 1946–50; Herts CC, 1950–54. *Recreation:* collecting English and continental water colours. *Address:* 27 Shepherds Way, Rickmansworth, Herts. *Died 19 Sept.* 1984.

**TONKS, Rt. Rev. Basil**; a Suffragan Bishop of Toronto (Credit Valley), since 1981; *b* York, England, 28 April 1930; *s* of Vincent and Alice Tonks; *m* 1955, Ida Catherine Mary (*née* Daunt); two *s* two *d*. *Educ:* Corchester Prep School; St John's, Leatherhead; Codrington Coll., Barbados (DipTh). Deacon 1954, priest 1955, Port-of-Spain; Asst Curate, Trinity Cathedral, Port-of-Spain, 1954; Rector, St Christopher, Siparia, 1956; Chaplain, Mission to Seamen, Port-of-Spain, 1960; Rector, St Andrew's, Scarborough, Tobago, 1964; Canon of Trinity Cathedral, Port-of-Spain, 1968; Asst Chaplain, Mission to Seamen, Toronto and Asst Curate, St Aidan's, Toronto, 1969; Rector of St Giles', Barrie and St Thomas', Shanty Bay, 1970; Archdeacon of Simcoe, 1972–80; Rector of St Martin-in-the-Fields, Toronto, 1980. Hon. DD, Wycliffe Coll., 1981. Mem. Old Johnians (Leatherhead). *Recreations:* Rugby football (represented Trinidad), boxing, rock climbing, archaeology, camping. *Address:* 123 Prince George Drive, Islington, Ontario M9B 2Y3, Canada. *T:* 416–233–3610.

**TOOTH, Sir Hugh**; see Munro-Lucas-Tooth.

**TOOTHILL, Sir John (Norman)**, Kt 1964; CBE 1955; FRSE; retired 1975 as Director, Ferranti Ltd, Edinburgh; *b* 11 Nov. 1908; *s* of John Harold and Helena Toothill; *m* 1935, Ethel Amelia Stannard. *Educ:* Beaminster Grammar School. Apprenticed Tilling Stevens Ltd, Hoffman Manufacturing Co. Ltd, Harris Lebus Ltd. Joined Ferranti Ltd, Hollinwood, 1935, as Chief Cost Accountant; Gen. Manager, Ferranti Ltd, Edinburgh, 1943. Chairman: AI Welders Ltd, Inverness; Highland Hydrocarbons, 1979–; Director: R. W. Toothill Ltd, 1972–; W. A. Baxter & Sons Limited, Fochabers, Moray, 1971–. CompIEE, Comp. British IRE, Hon. Comp. Royal Aeronautical Soc. Hon. LLD Aberdeen, 1966; Hon. DSc: Heriot-Watt, 1968; Cranfield, 1970. *Publication:* Toothill Report on the Scottish Economy, 1961. *Recreations:* fishing, golf. *Address:* New Lodge, Ordiequish, Fochabers, Morayshire. *Club:* Caledonian. *Died 5 July* 1986.

**TOPOLSKI, Feliks**; Painter; *b* 14 Aug. 1907; *s* of Edward Topolski (actor) and Stanislawa Drutowska; *m* 1st, 1944, Marion Everall (marr. diss. 1975; she *d* 1985); one *s* one *d*; 2nd, 1975, Caryl J. Stanley. *Educ:* Mikolaj Rey Sch.; Acad. of Art, Warsaw; Officers' Sch. of Artillery Reserve, Wlodzimierz Wolynski; self-tutoring in Italy, Paris. Settled in England, 1935. Exhibited in London and provincial galleries, in Poland, USA, Canada, Eire, France, India, Australia, Italy, Argentine, Switzerland, Denmark, Norway, Israel, Germany, Brazil and Portugal; has contributed to numerous publications; to BBC television programmes; and designed theatrical settings and costumes; as War Artist (1940–45) pictured Battle of Britain, sea and air war, Russia, Middle East, India, Burma, China, Africa, Italy, Germany. British subject since 1947. Painted the Cavalcade of Commonwealth (60' × 20') for Festival of Britain, 1951 (later in Victoria Memorial Hall, Singapore, removed on Independence and returned to artist); four murals for Finsbury Borough Council, 1952 (since erased); Coronation of Elizabeth II (100' × 4') for Buckingham Palace, 1958–60; murals for Carlton Tower Hotel, London, 1960 (removed); St Regis Hotel, New York, 1965; twenty portraits of English writers for University of Texas, 1961–62. At present engaged on mural-environment, Memoir of the Century (600' × 12' to 20'), London S Bank Art Centre, Hungerford Viaduct Arches 150–152, 1975–. Films: Topolski's Moscow (for CBS TV), 1969; Topolski (Polish TV), 1976; Paris Lost, 1980; (with Daniel Topolski) South American Sketchbook (BBC TV), 1982. Works at British Museum, Victoria and Albert Museum, Imperial War Museum, Theatre Museum; Galleries: the Tate, Edinburgh, Glasgow, Aberdeen, Nottingham, Brooklyn, Toronto, Tel Aviv, New Delhi, Melbourne, Lisbon, Warsaw. Dr *hc*, Jagiellonian Univ. of Cracow, 1974. *Publications:* The London Spectacle, 1935; Illustrator of Bernard Shaw's Geneva, 1939, In Good King Charles's Golden Days, 1939, and Pygmalion, 1941; Penguin Prints, 1941; Britain in Peace and War, 1941; Russia in War, 1942; Three Continents, 1944–45; Portrait of GBS, 1946; Confessions of a Congress Delegate, 1949; 88 Pictures, 1951; Coronation, 1953; Sketches of Gandhi, 1954; The Blue Conventions, 1956; Topolski's Chronicle for Students of World Affairs, 1958; Topolski's Legal London, 1961; Face to Face, 1964; Holy China, 1968; (with Conor

Cruise O'Brien) The United Nations: Sacred Drama, 1968; Shem Ham & Japheth Inc., 1971; Paris Lost, 1973 (trans. as Paris Disparu, 1974); Topolski's Buckingham Palace Panoramas, 1977; Sua Sanctitas Johannes Paulus Papa II, 1979; The London Symphony Orchestra 75th Anniversary Prints, 1979; Topolski's Panoramas, 1981; prints for Christie's Contemporary Art, 1974–85; (with Daniel Topolski) Travels with my Father: a journey through South America, 1983; Topolski's Chronicle, 1953–79, 1982; Fourteen Letters (autobiog.), 1987. *Address:* Bridge Arch 158, opposite Artists' Entrance, Royal Festival Hall, SE1. *T:* 01–928 3405.

*Died 24 Aug.* 1989.

**TORTELIER, Paul;** cellist, composer, conductor; *b* 21 March 1914; *s* of Joseph Tortelier, cabinet maker; *m* 1946, Maud Martin; one *s* three *d*. *Educ:* Conservatoire National de Musique, Paris; gen. educn privately. Leading Cellist, Monte Carlo, 1935–37; Cellist, Boston Symphony Orch., 1937–40; Leading Cellist, Société des Concerts du Conservatoire de Paris, 1945–47; Internat. solo career began in Concertgebouw, Amsterdam, 1946, and London, 1947 (under Sir Thomas Beecham's baton). Concert tours: Europe, N America, North Africa, Israel, S America, USSR, Japan, etc. As a conductor: debut with Israel Philharmonic, 1956; Prof. of Violoncello: Conservatoire Nat. Supérieur de Musique, Paris, 1956–69; Folkwang Hochschule, Essen; conducts in Paris and in England. Master classes, for BBC TV, 1970. Hon. Prof., Central Conservatory, Peking, 1980–. Hon. Mem., Royal Acad. of Music (England). Hon. DMus: Leicester, 1972; Oxford, 1975; Birmingham (Aston), 1980. Comdr, Order of the Lion (Finland), 1981. *Publications:* Cello Sonata, Trois P'tits Tours, Spirales, Elegie, Toccata, Sonata Breve, Pishnetto, Mon Cirque, Cello Books, for cello and piano; edns of Sammartini Sonata and Bach Suites; Cadenzas for Classical Concertos; Double Concerto for 2 cellos (also for violin and cello); Suite for unaccompanied cello; Offrande for string orchestra; (arr.) Paganini: Variazione di Bravura; (books) How I Play, How I Teach, 1973; (with David Blum) Paul Tortelier: a self portrait, 1984. *Recreations:* no time for these! *Address:* Ibbs & Tillett, 18B Pindock Mews, Little Venice, W9 2PY.

*Died 18 Dec.* 1990.

**TOTMAN, Grenfell William,** CMG 1973; OBE 1963; FCA; Controller of Finance, Commonwealth Development Corporation, 1955–76; *b* 24 July 1911; *s* of William and Lilian Oldrieve Totman; *m* 1st, 1938, Eileen Joan Gidley (marr. diss. 1962); one *s*; 2nd, 1963, Barbara Florence Cannon. *Educ:* Selhurst Grammar Sch.; London Univ. (BCom). Served War, Royal Air Force, 1942–46. With Edward Moore & Sons, Chartered Accountants, 1931–50; Commonwealth Development Corp., 1950–76. *Recreations:* music, gardening, philately. *Address:* Broxmead Stables, Broxmead Lane, Cuckfield, W Sussex. *T:* Haywards Health 456439.

*Died 14 Jan.* 1986.

**TOURS, Kenneth Cecil,** CMG 1955; MA; *b* 16 Feb. 1908; *y s* of late Berthold George Tours, CMG, HM Consul-General in China; *m* 1934, Ruth Grace, *y d* of late Hugh Lewis; two *s*. *Educ:* Aldenham School; Corpus Christi College, Cambridge. RARO, Lt Col. Administrative Service, Gold Coast, 1931; Gambia, 1935; Palestine, 1938; Malaya, 1945; Col (Food Control and Supplies), Brit. Mil. Administration, Malaya, 1945–46; Chm., Jt Supply Board, 1946; Establishment Office, Singapore, 1947; Permanent Sec., Min. of Finance, Gold Coast, 1950; Financial Sec. and Minister of Finance, 1954; Economic Adviser, Ghana, 1954; retd from Colonial Service, 1957. *Recreation:* reading. *Died 10 Nov.* 1987.

**TOWLER, Eric William,** CBE 1971; farmer; farms 2,000 acres; *b* 28 April 1900; *s* of William Towler and Laura Mary (*née* Trew); *m* 1st, 1921, Isabel Edith Ina Hemsworth; two *s* (one *d* decd); 2nd, 1964, Stella Prideaux-Brune; two *s*. *Educ:* Morley Grammar Sch. Founder, Cawoods Holdings Ltd and Cawood Wharton & Co. Ltd, 1931; Managing Dir, Cawood Wharton & Co. Ltd, 1931–42, Chm., 1942–71; Chm., Cawoods Holdings Ltd, 1961–72, Dir, 1972–82, Hon. Pres., 1977–82; Mining Director: Dorman Long & Co. Ltd, 1937–65; Pearson Dorman Long Ltd, 1937–65; Richard Thomas & Co. Ltd, 1929–31. MFH: Badsworth Hunt, 1938–43; South Shropshire Hunt, 1951–56. Chm., Nuffield Orthopaedic Centre, 1960–66; Chm., Bd of Governors, Oxford United Hosp., 1964–72. Hon. MA (Oxon) 1964. *Recreations:* hunting, gardening. *Address:* Glympton Park, near Woodstock, Oxon. *T:* Woodstock 811300; Willett House, Lydeard St Lawrence, Somerset. *T:* Lydeard St Lawrence 234. *Club:* Carlton. *Died 29 Dec.* 1987.

**TOWNEND, Donald Thomas Alfred,** CBE 1952; DSc London, PhD, DIC; FRSC; Fellow, Imperial College of Science and Technology; *b* Hackney, London, 15 July 1897; *s* of Charles Henry Townend; *m* 1924, Lilian (*d* 1974), *er d* of Samuel William Lewis, Bexley, Kent; one *s* one *d*. *Educ:* Bancroft's School, Woodford Green, Essex. East London (now Queen Mary) College, 1919–20; Imperial College of Science and Technology, 1920–38; Salters' Research Fellow, 1923–24; Rockefeller International Research Fellow, 1924–26; Livesey Prof. of Coal Gas and Fuel Industries, University of Leeds, 1938–

46; Dir-Gen., British Coal Utilisation Research Assoc., 1946–62; formerly Research Fell. and Hon. Lectr in Royal Coll. of Science. Jubilee Memorial Lectr, 1945, Brotherton Memorial Lecturer, 1946 and Hodsman Memorial Lectr, 1954, Soc. of Chemical Industry; Dalton Lecturer, Inst. of Chemistry, 1947; William Young Memorial Lectr, N Brit. Assoc. of Gas Managers, 1947; Des Vœux Memorial Lectr, Nat. Soc. for Clean Air, 1950; Melchett Lectr, Inst. of Energy (formerly Fuel), 1952. Vice-Pres. 1957–61, Vice-Chm. 1961–64, Parly and Sci. Cttee. Gold Medallist, Institut Français des Combustibles et de l'Energie, 1958; BCURA Coal Science Medallist, Institut Français des Combustibles et de l'Energie, 1958; BCURA Coal Science Medallist, 1963; Hon. FIGasE (Birmingham Medallist, IGasE); Hon. MInstE (Past Pres. and Melchett Medallist, InstE). Hon. DSc Tech Sheffield. *Publications:* (with late Professor W. A. Bone) Flame and Combustion in Gases, 1927; Gaseous Combustion at High Pressures, 1929; Papers in Proceedings of Royal Society, etc. *Recreations:* cricket, horticulture. *Address:* Uplands, Yarm Way, Leatherhead, Surrey. *T:* Leatherhead 373520. *Club:* Athenæum. *Died 19 Feb.* 1984.

**TOWNLEY, Frank;** Principal Assistant Solicitor, HM Customs and Excise, since 1978; barrister-at-law; *b* 3 May 1924; *s* of late Henry Woodall Townley and Elizabeth Townley; *m* 1950, Greta Kathleen, *d* of Abraham Vincent and Bertha Tootell; one *d*. *Educ:* Chorley Grammar Sch.; Wigan Mining and Technical Coll.; King's Coll., London Univ. (LLB). Called to Bar, Gray's Inn, 1950. Wigan Coal Corp., 1940–42. Served War in Royal Navy, 1943–46. King's Coll., London, and Gray's Inn, 1946–49; Legal Asst, Customs and Excise, 1952–61; Sen. Legal Asst, 1962–70; Asst Solicitor, Customs and Excise, 1971–77. *Recreation:* gardening. *Address:* Badger's Earth, Little Missenden, Amersham, Bucks HP7 0RD. *T:* Great Missenden 2468. *Died 8 March* 1982.

**TOWNLEY, Sir John (Barton),** Kt 1960; *b* 14 June 1914; *s* of Barton Townley and Margaret Alice, *d* of Richard Gorst; *m* 1939, Gwendoline May Ann, *d* of Arthur Simmonds; one *s* three *d*. *Educ:* Rydal Sch.; Downing Coll., Cambridge; Sorbonne. MA Cambridge, 1939; PhD Cantab; DLit Sorbonne. Man. Dir and Vice-Chm., Northern Commercial Vehicles and associated cos, 1936–72. President: Preston Conservative Assoc., N and S Divisions, 1954–72 (Chairman: Preston S Conserv. Assoc., 1949–54; Preston N Cons. Assoc., 1958, first Life Pres., 1961); Preston Sea Cadet Corps, 1954–72; Preston Circle King George's Fund for Sailors, 1949–72; Preston Charities Assoc., 1949–; Life Vice-Pres., Preston, Chorley, Leyland Conservative Clubs Council (Pres. 1949–; Cons. Clubs Council of GB Medal, 1959). Life Mem., North Western Industrial Assoc. Adv. Bd. Vice-Pres., RNLI. Chairman: Preston YMCA Special Appeals Cttee; British Police Athletic Assoc., 1949–60; Pres., Lancs Police Clubs, 1959–63; Founder, and Pres., Police Hathersall Hall Youth Camp (now Lancs Boys Club), 1949–70; Founder Mem., Nat. Playing Fields Assoc.; Chm., Spastics Appeal, 1950–53; Founder Mem. 1948, and former Pres., OAP's Assoc. Founder many youth clubs (known as Rydal Clubs), inc. Liverpool, Manchester and Bermondsey, from 1934. Chm., Preston Arts Cttee, 1951–59. Hon. Plenipotentiary: Antigua, 1966; Barbados, 1967; Malta, 1968, 1969; Cyprus, 1972–74. *Recreations:* talking about rugby, cricket, boxing, golf. *Address:* 24 Agnew Street, Lytham, Lancs. *Clubs:* Hawks, Union, Pitt (Cambridge); Royal & Ancient Golf (St Andrews). *Died 24 June* 1990.

**TOWNLEY, Reginald Colin,** CMG 1968; retired; *b* 5 April 1904; *s* of Reginald George and Susan Townley; *m* 1930, Irene Winifred Jones; three *s* one *d*. *Educ:* Hobart High Sch.; University of Tasmania. Chemist, 1927–64; Army, 1939–45, Middle East and Pacific. Tasmanian Parliament, 1946–64 (Leader of Opposition, 1950–56). *Recreation:* gardening. *Address:* 2/55 Swanston Street, New Town, Tasmania 7008, Australia. *T:* 281291. *Club:* Naval and Military (Hobart). *Died 3 May* 1982.

**TOWNSEND, Sir Lance;** *see* Townsend, Sir S. L.

**TOWNSEND, Rear-Adm. Michael Southcote,** CB 1959; DSO 1942; OBE 1940; DSC 1940 (Bar, 1941); *b* 18 June 1908; *s* of Colonel Edward Coplestone Townsend and Gladys Hatt-Cook; *m* 1932, Joan Pendrill Charles; one *s* two *d*. *Educ:* Royal Naval Coll., Dartmouth. Rear-Admiral, 1956; Flag Officer, Admiralty Interview Boards and President, First Admiralty Interview Board, 1956–58; Commander Allied Naval Forces, Northern Area, Central Europe, 1958–61, retired; Admiralty Officer, Wales, 1962–68. *Address:* The Mythe, 2 College Road, Great Malvern, Worcs WR14 3DD.

*Died 23 March* 1984.

**TOWNSEND, Sir (Sydney) Lance,** Kt 1971; VRD 1955; Chairman, Victorian Health Advisory Committee, Foundation Member, 1979–83; Professor of Obstetrics and Gynaecology, 1951–79, Dean, Faculty of Medicine, 1971–78, Assistant Vice-Chancellor, 1979–80, University of Melbourne; *b* 17 Dec. 1912; *s* of Edward Henry and Muriel Constance Townsend; *m* 1943, Jean Campbell Smyth; one *s* three *d* (and one *s* decd). *Educ:* Bairnsdale High Sch.; Trinity Coll., Univ. of Melbourne. MD, BS, MGO, DTM&H; FRCSE, FACS,

FRACS, FRCOG, FRACP, FRACMA, FRACOG; Hon. FRCS(C), Hon. FACOG, Hon. FCOG(SA), Hon. FRACGP. Residential med. posts at Bendigo, Royal Women's Hosp. and Tenant Creek Hosp., 1936–38; Med. Off., W Middx Hosp., 1939; Med. Off., RN, 1940–46 (Surg. Comdr); Surg. Captain, RANVR, 1965; Hon. Obstetrician and Gynaecologist to Austin, Royal Women's, Royal Melbourne, Queen Victoria and Prince Henry's Hosps, 1948–78; Consultant Obstetrician, WHO Eastern Mediterranean Sector, 1981–. Mem., Hon. Sec., Pres., Australian Council, RCOG, 1951–69; Chm., Cons. Council on Maternal and Perinatal Mortality, 1955–83; Mem. Bd of Management, Royal Women's Hosp., 1951–78; Mem., Cttee of Enquiry into Victorian (Aust.) Health Services, 1973–75; Sec., Victorian Bush Nursing Assoc., 1961–73; Chm., Victorian Cytology Service (Gynae.), 1965–83; Vice Chm., Australian Medical Examining Council, 1977–83. Mem., 1966–83, Vice-Pres., 1977–79, Pres., 1979–83, Austin Hosp. Chm. of Dirs, Australian and NZ Jl of Obstetrics and Gynaecology, 1961–76. Hon. LLD: Monash, 1979; Melbourne, 1982. *Publications:* High Blood Pressure and Pregnancy, 1959; Gynaecology for Students, 1964, 3rd edn 1979; Obstetrics for Students, 1964, 3rd edn 1978. *Recreations:* sailing, philately. *Address:* 28 Ryeburn Avenue, Hawthorn, Victoria 3123, Australia. *T:* 823434. *Clubs:* Melbourne, Naval and Military, Royal Melbourne Golf (Melbourne). *Died 26 March 1983.*

**TOWNSEND, Air Vice-Marshal William Edwin,** CB 1971; CBE 1965 (OBE 1957); RAAF retired; *b* 25 April 1916; *s* of William Edwin Townsend (Senior) and Jessie May Lewry; *m* 1939, Linda Ruth Deakins; two *s* two *d. Educ:* Longerenong Coll., Vic, Australia. Grad. Pt Cook, 1937; Chief Flying Instr and 2nd i/c No 8 EFTS, 1940; Sen. Trg Staff Officer, 1941; Comdg Officer 67 and 22 Sqdns, 1942–43; shot down over enemy territory, escaped and returned to Aust., 1944; Comdg Officer, 5 Operational Trg Unit, 1944; SASO, NE Area, 1946; OC, Port Moresby, 1947–48; Sec., Australian Jt Staff, Washington, 1949–50; OC, East Sale, 1951–52; CO and Sen. Officer i/c Admin, Home Command, 1953–54; OC 78 Fighter Wing, 1955–56; Dir of Ops, 1957–60; OC, RAAF Williamtown, 1960–62; Dir Gen. Personnel, 1962–64; OC, RAAF, Butterworth, Malaysia, incl. service in Vietnam, 1964–67 (Vietnam Service Medal); Dep. CAS, 1967–69; AOC Operational Comd, RAAF, 1969–72; Dir, State Emergency Services and Civil Defence, and Chm., Bush Fire Council of NSW, 1973–80. Dir-Gen., Australia-Britain Soc., 1981–84. Pres., Aust. Branch, RAF Escaping Soc.; Vice-Pres., St John Ambulance Assoc., NSW Centre. Councillor, Royal Humane Soc. of NSW. FAIM; Mem., Aust. Inst. of Emergency Services. *Address:* 8 Tutus Street, Balgowlah Heights, NSW 2093, Australia. *Clubs:* Royal Automobile; Imperial Service (Sydney); Manly Golf.

**TOY, Francis Carter,** CBE 1947; DSc, FInstP; *b* 5 May 1892; 2nd *s* of late Sir Henry Toy, CA, JP, Helston, Cornwall; *m* 1921, Gladys Marguerite (decd), *d* of late James Thomas, CA, JP, Tregays, Lostwithiel, Cornwall; one *d. Educ:* Launceston Coll., Cornwall; University College, London. Fellow of University College, London. Served European War, 1914–18; Lieut, Cornwall Fortress Engineers, 1914–16; Lieut, First Army Field Survey Co. (Sound Ranging, Y section), BEF France, 1917–18. Physicist, British Photographic Research Association, 1919–29; Deputy Director of the Shirley Institute, Research Station of British Cotton Industry Research Association, 1930–43, Director, 1944–55. President: Manchester Fedn of Scientific Societies, 1953–55; Inst of Physics, 1948–50; Manchester Statistical Society, 1951–53; Manchester Literary and Philosophical Society, 1956–58; Past Chairman Cttee of Directors of Research Associations; Fellow of the Textile Institute; Past Member Court and Council, UMIST. *Publications:* numerous scientific. *Recreations:* travel, music and sport (cricket and golf). *Address:* 8 Fulshaw Court, Wilmslow, Cheshire. *T:* Wilmslow 525141. *Club:* Athenæum. *Died 5 Nov. 1988.*

**TOYNBEE, Prof. Jocelyn Mary Catherine,** MA, DPhil; FSA; FBA; Laurence Professor Emerita of Classical Archæology, Cambridge University (Professor, 1951–62); Hon. Fellow of Newnham College; *b* 3 March 1897; *d* of late Harry Valpy Toynbee and late Sarah Edith (née Marshall). *Educ:* Winchester High School for Girls; Newnham Coll., Cambridge. Classical Tutor, St Hugh's Coll., Oxford, 1921–24; Lecturer in Classics, Reading University, 1924–27; Fellow and Director of Studies in Classics, Newnham Coll., Cambridge, and Lecturer in the Faculty of Classics, Cambridge Univ., 1927–51. Hon. DLitt: University of Newcastle upon Tyne; University of Liverpool. *Publications:* The Hadrianic School: a Chapter in the History of Greek Art, 1934; Roman Medallions (American Numismatic Society, New York), 1944; Some Notes on Artists in the Roman World, (Brussels) 1951; The Shrine of St Peter and the Vatican Excavation (with John Ward Perkins), 1956; The Flavian Reliefs from the Palazzo della Cancelleria in Rome, 1957; Art in Roman Britain, 1962; Art in Britain under the Romans, 1964; The Art of the Romans, 1965; Death and Burial in the Roman World, 1971; Animals in Roman Life and Art, 1973; Roman Historical Portraits, 1978; contribs to Journal of Roman Studies, Papers of British School, Rome, Numismatic Chronicle, Classical Review,

Classical Quarterly, Antiquaries Journal, Archæologia, Antiquity, Gnomon, etc. *Recreation:* travelling. *Address:* 22 Park Town, Oxford. *T:* 57886. *Died 31 Dec. 1985.*

**TOYNBEE, (Theodore) Philip;** novelist; foreign correspondent of The Observer and member of editorial staff since 1950; *b* 25 June 1916; *s* of late Arnold Joseph Toynbee, CH, FBA, and Rosalind, *d* of late Prof. Gilbert Murray, OM; *m* 1st, 1939, Anne Barbara Denise Powell (marr. diss. 1950); two *d*; 2nd, 1950, Frances Genevieve Smith; one *s* two *d. Educ:* Rugby Sch.; Christ Church, Oxford. Editor of the Birmingham Town Crier, 1938–39; commission in Intelligence Corps, 1940–42; Ministry of Economic Warfare, 1942–44; on staff of SHAEF in France and Belgium, 1944–45; Literary Editor of Contact Publications, 1945–46. *Publications:* The Savage Days, 1937; School in Private, 1941; The Barricades, 1943; Tea with Mrs Goodman, 1947; The Garden to the Sea, 1953; Friends Apart, 1954; Pantaloon, 1961; (with Arnold Toynbee) Comparing Notes: a Dialogue across a Generation, 1963; (with Maurice Richardson) Thanatos: a Modern Symposium, 1963; Two Brothers, 1964; A Learned City, 1966; Views from a Lake, 1968; Towards the Holy Spirit, 1973; (ed) The Distant Drum, 1976; Part of a Journey, 1981; contrib.: New Statesman and Nation, Horizon, New Writing, Les Temps Modernes; *posthumous publication:* End of a Journey (ed John Bullimore), 1988. *Recreations:* gardening, bicycling. *Address:* Woodroyd Cottage, St Briavels, Lydney, Glos. *Club:* Oxford Union Society. *Died 15 June 1981.*

**TRAFFORD, Baron** *cr* 1987 (Life Peer), of Falmer in the county of East Sussex; **Joseph Anthony Porteous Trafford;** Kt 1985; Minister of State, Department of Health, since 1989; *b* 20 July 1932; *s* of Dr Harold Trafford, Warlingham, Surrey, and late Laura Trafford; *m* 1960, Helen Chalk; one *s* one *d. Educ:* St Edmund's, Hindhead; Charterhouse; Guy's Hosp., Univ. of London. MB, BS Hons 1957; MRCP 1961, FRCP 1974. Sen. Registrar, Guy's Hosp., 1963–66; Fulbright Scholar, Johns Hopkins Univ., 1963; Consultant Physician, Brighton HA, 1965–89; Dir, Renal and Artificial Kidney Unit, Brighton, 1966–89. MP (C) The Wrekin, 1970–Feb. 1974. Chm. of Council and Senior Pro-Chancellor, Univ. of Sussex, 1985–. *Publications:* contribs to med. jls and textbooks. *Recreations:* golf, tennis, bridge, military history. *Address:* 103 The Drive, Hove, East Sussex. *T:* Brighton 731567. *Died 16 Sept. 1989.*

**TRAINOR, James P.;** a Judge of the High Court of Kenya, 1980–85, retired; *b* Belfast, 14 Oct. 1914; *s* of Owen Trainor and Mary Rose (née McArdle); *m* 1954, Angela (née O'Connor); one *s* two *d. Educ:* Mount St Joseph's, Monaghan, Ireland; University Coll., Dublin (BA). Admitted solicitor, Dublin, 1936; called to Irish Bar, King's Inn, 1950. Colonial Service: Magistrate, Singapore, 1954–55; Justice, Special Court, Cyprus, 1955–60; Called to English Bar, Gray's Inn, 1957; Comr, High Commissioner's Court, W Pacific High Commn, 1960–61; Co-Pres., Jt Court, Anglo-French Condominium of the New Hebrides, 1960–72; Judge, Fiji Court of Appeal, 1960–70; Judge, High Court of the Western Pacific, 1961–72; Judge of Supreme Court, Hong Kong, 1972–79, retired from HM Overseas Judiciary, 1980. Commandeur de l'Ordre Nationale du Mérite (France), 1967. *Recreations:* golf, reading, music. *Address:* 22 Cronkbourne Road, Douglas, Isle of Man. *T:* Douglas 73274. *Clubs:* Hong Kong, Royal Hong Kong Golf, Royal Hong Kong Jockey (Hong Kong); United Services, Milltown Golf (Dublin); Castletown Golf (IoM). *Died 11 March 1989.*

**TRAPNELL, His Honour Alan Stewart;** a Circuit Judge, 1972–85; *b* 12 Jan. 1913; *s* of Francis C. Trapnell, MD and Ann Trapnell (née Stewart), Beckenham, Kent. *Educ:* The Leys Sch., Cambridge; Jesus Coll., Cambridge. Served War of 1939–45, Queen Victoria's Rifles. Barrister-at-Law. Called to Bar, Inner Temple, 1936. Western Circuit, Hampshire Sessions. Member of Bar Council, 1958–62. Recorder of Barnstaple, 1962–64. Judge of: Bow County Court, 1964–66; Shoreditch County Court, 1966–67; Bromley County Court, 1968–69; Chm., Middlesex QS, 1969–71. Chm., Adv. Cttee on appt of JPs for Mddx, 1969–86. *Address:* Francis Taylor Building, Temple, EC4. *Clubs:* Athenæum, United Oxford & Cambridge University. *Died 18 Oct. 1986.*

**TRAVERS, Lt-Gen. Sir Paul (Anthony),** KCB 1981; FCIT; Quarter Master General, since 1982; *b* 5 Aug. 1927; *s* of Michael and Edith Travers; *m* 1956, Therese Sara Keeley; one *s* two *d. Educ:* Clapham Coll. psc; OCDS (Canada). In the ranks, Parachute Regt, 1945–47; Emergency Commn, S Lancs Regt, 1947–49; Reg. Commn, RASC, 1949–65; Staff Coll., Camberley, 1958; RCT, 1965; CO 1 Div. Regt, RCT, 1967; GSO 1 (DS) Staff Coll., 1970; Col AQ 2 Div., 1970–73; Dir of Admin. Planning (Army), 1973–75; Canadian Nat. Def. Coll., 1975–76; DQMG BAOR, 1976–78; Chief of Staff, Logistic Exec. (Army), 1978–79; Vice Quarter Master General, 1979–81; GOC SE District, 1981–82. Col Comdt, RCT, 1981–; Army Legal Corps, 1982–. FBIM. *Recreations:* many—none serious. *Address:* c/o Lloyds Bank, 19 Horseferry Road, SW1P 2AD. *Club:* Naval and Military. *Died 10 June 1983.*

**TREASE, Prof. George Edward,** BPharm, Dr *hc* Strasbourg; Dr *hc* Clermont; FPS, FRSC; Professor of Pharmacognosy, Nottingham University, 1957–67, later Emeritus Professor; Head of Department of Pharmacy, University of Nottingham, 1944–67; *b* 8 July 1902; *e s* of George and Florence Trease; *m* 1928, Phyllis Thornton Wilkinson; two *d* (one *s* decd). *Educ:* Nottingham High Sch.; London College of Pharmacy. Lecturer in Pharmacognosy, University College, Nottingham, 1926. Served in Min. of Economic Warfare, 1939–40. Reader in Pharmacognosy, 1945; Examiner in Pharmacognosy to: Pharmaceutical Society, 1934–; University of London, 1937–; QUB, 1949, 1963–65; University of Glasgow, 1950–; University of Wales, 1945–; University of Nottingham, 1950–; University of Singapore, 1962; University of Bradford, 1966–; Pharmaceutical Society of Eire, 1959–. Vice-Pres., British Soc. for History of Pharmacy, 1967–70. Worshipful Society of Apothecaries of London, 1959. Dr *hc* Strasbourg University, 1954; Dr *hc* Clermont University, 1962. *Publications:* Chemistry of Crude Drugs, 1928 (with Prof. J. E. Driver); Textbook of Pharmacognosy, 1934, 12th edn 1983; Pharmacy in History, 1964; many papers and articles on pharmacognosy, pharmaceutical history and pharmaceutical education. *Recreation:* local history. *Address:* George Hill, Crediton, Devon. *T:* Crediton 2983.

*Died 18 Dec. 1986.*

**TREASURE, Col Kenneth David,** CB 1972; CBE 1965; TD; DL; Solicitor; HM Coroner, County of Gwent (formerly Monmouth), since 1957; *b* 20 Sept. 1913; *s* of late David John Treasure, Maesycwmmer, and of Olive Treasure; *m* 1941, Jean Mitchell, Heathfield, Sussex; one *s* one *d*. *Educ:* Cranbrook; Univ. of Wales. Admitted Solicitor, 1937. Served War of 1939–45: Lt-Col, Monmouthshire Regt; (TA) in India and Burma. Legal Adviser, CCG, 1946–49; Col, Army Cadet Force, 1958; Chm., Monmouthshire T&AFA, 1960–68; a Rep. Chm. (Wales), Council of T&AF Assocs; Chm., Wales and Monmouthshire TA&VR Assoc., 1968–71; Mem. Council, TA&VR Assocs and TA Advisory Cttee, MoD. DL Monmouthshire, 1957. *Recreations:* judging show jumping, motoring and work. *Address:* The Court, Lower Machen, Newport, Gwent. *T:* Machen 440258. *Club:* Army and Navy.

*Died 26 May 1983.*

**TREATT, Hon. Sir Vernon (Haddon),** KBE 1970; MM 1918; QC (Austr.) 1940; MA, BCL; private interests; *b* 15 May 1897; *s* of Frank Burford Treatt and Kate Ellen Treatt; *m* 1st, 1930, Dorothy Isobelle Henderson; one *s* one *d*; 2nd, 1960, Franki Embleton Wilson. *Educ:* Sydney C of E Grammar Sch.; St Paul's Coll., Sydney Univ.; New Coll., Oxford. Sydney Univ., 1915–16, 1919–20 (BA); AIF, 1916–18 (Gunner, MM); Rhodes Scholar, 1920; Oxford Univ., 1921–23. Called to Bar, Lincoln's Inn, 1923; Bar of NSW, 1924. NSW Legislative Assembly, 1938–62; Minister of Justice, 1939–41; Leader of Opposition, 1946–54; title of Honourable for life, 1955. Chm., Local Govt Boundaries Commn NSW, 1964–69. Chief Comr (in loco Lord Mayor), City of Sydney, 1967–69. *Publication:* Workers Compensation Law NSW. *Recreations:* swimming, reading, rural property. *Address:* 27 Waruda Street, Kirribilli, NSW 2061, Australia. *T:* 9292668; Riverview, O'Connell, NSW 2795. *T:* O'Connell 375762. *Clubs:* University, Royal Sydney Golf, Australasian Pioneers' (Sydney).

*Died 20 Sept. 1984.*

**TREDENNICK, Prof. (George) Hugh (Percival Phair);** Professor Emeritus of Classics, University of London; *b* 30 June 1899; *yr s* of late Canon G. N. H. Tredennick, Sparkbrook, Birmingham; *m* 1924, Louella Margaret (*d* 1970), *o d* of late Canon E. E. M. Phair, Winnipeg, Canada; one *s* two *d*. *Educ:* King Edward's, Birmingham; Trinity Hall, Cambridge. War Service in France with Royal Artillery, 1918–19; Trinity Hall, Cambridge (Scholar and Prizeman), 1919–22; First Class Classical Tripos: Part I, 1921, Part II, 1922; BA, 1922; MA 1926. Assistant Master, Rossall School, 1923–24; Lecturer in Classics, University of Sheffield, 1924–36; Reader in Classics, Queen Mary College, University of London, 1936–46; Professor of Classics, Royal Holloway Coll., 1946–66. Dean of the Faculty of Arts, University of London, 1956–60; Editor (with C. J. Fordyce) The Classical Review, 1961–67. *Publications:* text and translation of Aristotle's Metaphysics, Vol. I, 1933, Vol. II, 1935; text and translation of Aristotle's Prior Analytics, 1938; The Last Days of Socrates (Penguin Classics), 1954; text and translation of Aristotle's Posterior Analytics, 1960; Memoirs of Socrates (Penguin Classics), 1970; contributions to classical journals. *Recreations:* genealogy, gardening. *Address:* New Ivy Cottage, Russ Hill Road, Charlwood, Surrey RH6 0EJ. *T:* Norwood Hill 862406.

*Died 31 Dec. 1981.*

**TREDGOLD, Joan Alison,** MA Cantab; Principal, Cheltenham Ladies' College, 1953–64; *b* 6 Sept. 1903; *d* of Alfred Frank Tredgold, MD, FRCP, and Zoë B. T. Tredgold. *Educ:* Cheltenham Ladies' College; Newnham College, Cambridge. Mathematical Tripos part II, Class I, 1924; Fourth Year Scholarship, Newnham, 1924–25. Assistant Mistress, Sherborne School for Girls, 1925–29; Assistant Mistress, Cheltenham Ladies' College, 1929–35. Senior Mathematical Mistress, 1935–53, Assistant House Mistress,

1938–39, Second Mistress, 1939–53, Roedean School. *Address:* 91 Faithfull House, Suffolk Square, Cheltenham, Glos GL50 2DU. *T:* Cheltenham 519242. *Club:* University Women's.

*Died 11 Sept. 1989.*

**TREHARNE, Prof. Kenneth John,** FIBiol; Professor of Agricultural Sciences, University of Bristol, since 1984; Director, AFRC Institute of Arable Crops Research, since 1988; *b* 17 Aug. 1939; *s* of Captain W. J. Treharne and M. A. Treharne; *m* 1974, Carys Wyn Evans; two *s* two *d*. *Educ:* University College of Wales, Aberystwyth (BSc, PhD Biochemistry). Post-doctoral Fellow, UCW Aberystwyth, 1964–66; Biochemist, Welsh Plant Breeding Station, 1966–74; study leave: Cornell Univ., NY, 1972; Royal Soc. European Exchange Fellow, Univ. of Göttingen, 1973; Cereal Physiologist, Internat. Inst. of Tropical Agric., Ibadan, Nigeria, 1974–77; Head: Plant Physiol. Div., East Malling Res. Stn, Kent, 1977–81; Plant Scis Div., Long Ashton, 1982–84; Dir, Long Ashton Res. Stn, 1984–88. Vis. Prof. of Biol Scis, Wye Coll., Univ. of London, 1983–. FRSA 1985. *Publications:* various chapters; numerous research papers. *Recreations:* golf, Rugby football—ex!, violin. *Address:* 1 West Common, Harpenden, Herts AL5 2JG. *T:* Harpenden 461458. *Club:* Farmers'.

*Died 14 July 1989.*

**TREHERNE, John Edwin,** ScD, PhD; writer; Fellow of Downing College, Cambridge, since 1966 (President, 1985–88); Hon. Director of AFRC Unit of Insect Neurophysiology and Pharmacology (formerly of Invertebrate Chemistry and Physiology), Department of Zoology, University of Cambridge, since 1969; University Reader in Invertebrate Physiology, since 1971; *b* 15 May 1929; *s* of Arnold Edwin Wilson Treherne and Marion Grace Spiller; *m* 1955, June Vivienne Freeman; one *s* one *d*. *Educ:* Headlands Sch., Swindon, Wilts; Univ. of Bristol (BSc, PhD); Univ. of Cambridge (MA, ScD). Nat. Service, Lieut RAMC, 1953–55. Principal Sci. Officer, ARC Unit of Insect Physiology, Cambridge, 1955–67; Univ. Lectr in Zoology, Cambridge, 1968–71. Visiting Prof., Univ. of Virginia, 1963–64. Vice-Pres., Royal Entomological Soc., 1967–68. Scientific Medal of Zoological Soc., 1968. Dir, Company of Biologists Ltd, 1969–74; Editor: Advances in Insect Physiology, 1964–85; Jl of Experimental Biology, 1974–; Key Environments series, 1980–; Chm. of Editl Boards of Insect Biochemistry and Jl of Insect Physiology, 1977–. *Publications:* Neurochemistry of Arthropods, 1966; Insect Neurobiology, 1974; The Galapagos Affair, 1983; The Strange History of Bonnie and Clyde, 1984; The Trap, 1985; Mangrove Chronicle, 1986; Dangerous Precincts, 1987; The Walk to Acorn Bridge, 1989; The Canning Enigma, 1989; research papers in: Jl of Experimental Biology; Tissue and Cell; Nature; Animal Behaviour. *Recreations:* domestic; military and naval Staffordshire figures; postcards of Edwardian actresses; marine insects; writing. *Address:* The Manor House, Soham, Cambs CB7 5HA. *T:* Ely 722464; Downing College, Cambridge CB2 1DQ.

*Died 23 Sept. 1989.*

**TREMLETT, Maj.-Gen. Erroll Arthur Edwin,** CB 1944; TD 1948; *b* 22 Dec. 1893; *s* of late E. J. Tremlett, RA, Bt Lt-Col (despatches), Medal and Clasp Zulu War 1879, Deputy Governor and OC Troops, St Helena, 1884; *m* Dorothy Mary, *d* of late H. W. Capper, 24 Suffolk St, Pall Mall; one *s* one *d*. Served in European War, 1914–19, with RA, (despatches) (awarded Regular Commn in the "Field", Sept. 1916) and in France and Belgium 1940 (despatches); Comdr 44 AA Brigade, Nov. 1940; Major-General, Commander 10 AA Division, Feb. 1942; Commander AA Defences of London, 1942–44; Comdr Flying Bomb Deployment, 1945. Commander 2 AA Group, 1945–46; RARO 1946. Hon. Colonel 656 Light AA Regt RA (RB), 1947–57. Mem., City of London RA Assoc., 1944; Chm., London Region RA Assoc., 1945–46; Pres., RA Assoc. for Co. Devon, 1957–67. Gold Staff Officer, Coronation of HM Queen Elizabeth II. *Address:* Bickham Cottage, Kenn, near Exeter, Devon. *T:* Kennford 832586. *Clubs:* Naval and Military, MCC.

*Died 24 Dec. 1982.*

**TRENCH, Sir David (Clive Crosbie),** GCMG 1969 (KCMG 1962; CMG 1960); MC 1944; DL; Vice-Chairman, Advisory Committee on Distinction Awards, Department of Health and Social Security, 1972–79; Chairman, Dorset Area Health Authority, 1973–82; *b* 2 June 1915; *s* of late William Launcelot Crosbie Trench, CIE, and Margaret Zephanie (*née* Huddleston); *m* 1944, Margaret Gould; one *d*. *Educ:* Tonbridge School; Jesus College, Cambridge (MA). Cadet, British Solomon Islands Protectorate, 1938; seconded to W Pacific High Commission, 1941. Served War of 1939–45 (MC, US Legion of Merit); British Solomon Islands Defence Force, 1942–46, Lt-Col. Secretary to the Government, British Solomon Islands Protectorate, 1947; attended Joint Services Staff Coll., 1949; Asst Sec., Deputy Defence Sec., Hong Kong, 1950; Deputy Financial Sec., 1956; Commissioner of Labour and Mines, 1957; attended Imperial Defence College, 1958; Deputy Colonial Secretary, Hong Kong, 1959; High Commissioner for The Western Pacific, 1961–63; Governor and C-in-C, Hong Kong, 1964–71. Mem., new Dorset CC, 1973–81. Pres. for Dorset, St John Ambulance Brigade and Assoc., 1972–. DL Dorset, 1977. Hon. LLD: Univ. of Hong Kong,

1968; Chinese Univ. of Hong Kong, 1968. Legion of Merit (US), 1944. KStJ 1964. *Address:* Church House, Church Road, Shillingstone, Blandford, Dorset DT11 0SL. *Clubs:* United Oxford & Cambridge University; Royal & Ancient (St Andrews).
*Died* 4 *Dec.* 1988.

**TRENCHARD,** 2nd Viscount, *cr* 1936, of Wolfeton; **Thomas Trenchard,** MC 1944; Baron, *cr* 1930; Bt, *cr* 1919; *b* 15 Dec. 1923; *o* surv. *s* of 1st Viscount Trenchard, GCB, OM, GCVO, DSO, first Marshal of the RAF, and of Katherine Viscountess Trenchard (*d* 1960); *S* father, 1956; *m* 1948, Patricia, *d* of late Admiral Sir Sidney Bailey, KBE, CB, DSO and of Lady Bailey; three *s. Educ:* Eton. Served War of 1939–45, Captain, King's Royal Rifle Corps (MC). Director: T. Wall & Sons Ltd, 1953–56; Unilever Ltd and Unilever NV, 1967–77; Carpets International Ltd, 1977–79; Abbey Panels Investments Plc, 1983–; Chairman: Wall's Meat Co. Ltd, 1960–66; Schlumberger Measurement and Control (UK), 1985–. Chm., Sausage and Meat Pie Manufrs Assoc., 1969–70. Minister of State: DoI, 1979–81; for Defence Procurement, MoD, 1981–83. President: RIPH&H, 1970–79; Inst. of Grocery Distribution, 1974–77; Bacon and Meat Manufrs Assoc., 1974–79; Royal Warrant Holders' Assoc., 1968; Mem., ARC, 1970–79. Vice Pres., RAF Benevolent Assoc., 1970–; Trustee, RAF Museum, 1984–. *Heir: s* Hon. Hugh Trenchard [*b* 12 March 1951; *m* 1975, Fiona, *d* of Hon. James Morrison; two *s* one *d*]. *Address:* House of Lords, SW1. *Club:* Brooks's. *Died* 29 *April* 1987.

**TREND,** Baron *cr* 1974 (Life Peer), of Greenwich; **Burke St John Trend,** PC 1972; GCB 1968 (KCB 1962; CB 1955); CVO 1953; *b* 2 Jan. 1914; *o s* of late Walter St John Trend and Marion Tyers; *m* 1949, Patricia Charlotte, *o d* of Rev. Gilbert Shaw; two *s* one *d. Educ:* Whitgift; Merton College, Oxford (Postmaster). 1st Cl. Honour Mods, 1934; 1st Cl. Lit. Hum., 1936; Hon. Fellow, Merton College, 1964. Home Civil Service Administrative Class, 1936; Min. of Education, 1936; transferred to HM Treasury, 1937; Asst Private Sec. to Chancellor of Exchequer, 1939–41; Principal Private Sec. to Chancellor of Exchequer, 1945–49; Under Secretary, HM Treasury, 1949–55; Office of the Lord Privy Seal, 1955–56; Deputy Secretary of the Cabinet, 1956–59; Third Secretary, HM Treasury, 1959–60, Second Secretary, 1960–62; Secretary of the Cabinet, 1963–73. Rector, Lincoln Coll., Oxford, 1973–83 (Hon. Fellow, 1983); Pro-Vice-Chancellor, Oxford Univ., 1975–83. Chm. Trustees, British Museum, 1979–86 (Trustee, 1973–86); Chm., Managing Trustees, Nuffield Foundn, 1980– (Trustee, 1973–); Mem., Adv. Council on Public Records, 1974–82. Pres., Royal Commonwealth Soc., 1982–. High Bailiff of Westminster and Searcher of the Sanctuary, 1983–; Mem. Governing Body, Westminster Sch. Hon. DCL Oxford, 1969; Hon. LLD St Andrews, 1974; Hon. DLitt Loughborough, 1984. *Address:* Flat 10, 102 Rochester Row, SW1P 1JP. *Club:* Athenæum. *Died* 21 *July* 1987.

**TRENT, Group Captain Leonard Henry,** VC 1946; DFC 1940; *b* 14 April 1915; *s* of Leonard Noel Trent, Nelson, New Zealand; British; *m* 1940, Ursula Elizabeth Woolhouse; one *s* two *d. Educ:* Nelson Coll., NZ. Entered firm of W. & R. Fletcher (New Zealand) Ltd 1935; joined RNZAF, 1937; joined RAF 1938. Arrived in England, 1938; served War, 1939–43, France and England (POW 1943); transferred to RNZAF, 1944; transferred back to RAF, 1947, Permanent Commission. Formerly: OC 214 Valiant Sqdn, RAF Marham; Trg HQ No. 3 Gp, Mildenhall, 1948–59; Comdg RAF Wittering, 1959–62; Asst Air Attaché, Washington, also SASO and Chief Intell. Officer (RAF), 1962–65. ADC to the Queen, 1962–65. *Relevant publication:* Venturer Courageous, by James Sanders, 1984. *Recreations:* golf, painting, oils and watercolours. *Address:* c/o Post Office, Leigh, Auckland, New Zealand.
*Died* 20 *May* 1986.

**TRETHOWAN, Sir (James) Ian (Raley),** Kt 1980; Chairman, Thames Television Ltd, since 1987 (Director, since 1986); Consultant, Thorn EMI, since 1982 (Director, since 1986); an Independent Director, Times Newspapers Holdings Ltd, since 1982; *b* 20 Oct. 1922; *s* of late Major J. J. R. Trethowan, MBE and Mrs R. Trethowan; *m* 1st, 1951, Patricia Nelson (marr. diss.); 2nd, 1963, Carolyn Reynolds; three *d. Educ:* Christ's Hospital. Entered Journalism, 1939. Fleet Air Arm, 1941–46. Political Corresp., Yorkshire Post, 1947–55; News Chronicle, 1955–57; Dep. Editor/Political Editor, Independent Television News, 1958–63; joined BBC, 1963, as Commentator on Politics and Current Affairs; Man. Dir, Radio, BBC, 1969–75; Man. Dir, Television, BBC, 1976–77; Dir-Gen. of the BBC, 1977–82. Dir, Barclays Bank (UK), 1982–87. Political Commentator: The Economist, 1953–58, 1965–67; The Times, 1967–68. Member: Cttee on Official Secrets Act, 1971; Board, British Council, 1980–87; EC Cttee of Cultural Consultants, 1988–90; Chairman: Horserace Betting Levy Bd, 1982–90; European TV Task Force, 1987–88; European Film and TV Forum, 1988–; EC's Cinema and TV Gp, 1988–90; Council, Inst. of the Media, 1989. Chm., BM Soc., 1982–; Trustee: Glyndebourne Arts Trust, 1982–; BM, 1984–; Governor, Ditchley Foundn, 1985–. Hon. DCL East Anglia, 1979. *Publication:* Split Screen (memoirs), 1984.

*Recreations:* racing, opera, fishing. *Address:* 52 Buckingham Court, Kensington Park Road, W11 3BP. *T:* 071–229 5550; Three Firs House, Bramshott Chase, Hindhead, Surrey GU26 6DG. *Clubs:* Brooks's, Travellers', Beefsteak, MCC. *Died* 12 *Dec.* 1990.

**TREVASKIS, Sir (Gerald) Kennedy (Nicholas),** KCMG 1963 (CMG 1959); OBE 1948; *b* 1 Jan. 1915; *s* of late Rev. Hugh Kennedy Trevaskis; *m* 1945, Sheila James Harrington, *d* of Col F. T. Harrington; two *s* one *d. Educ:* Summer Fields; Marlborough; King's College, Cambridge. Entered Colonial Service, 1938, as Administrative Cadet, N Rhodesia. Enlisted N Rhodesia Regt 1939; captured by Italian Forces Tug Aqan, Br. Somaliland, 1940 and POW until 1941. Seconded British Military Administration, Eritrea, 1941–48 (Lt-Col) and British Administration, 1948–50; Senior Divisional Officer, Assab, 1943; Serae, 1944; Western Province, 1946; Political Secretary, 1950. Member British delegation four Power Commission ex-Italian Colonies, 1947–48 and Liaison Officer, United Nations Commission, Eritrea, 1950. N Rhodesia, 1950–51; District Commissioner, Ndola. Political Officer, Western Aden Protectorate, 1951, Deputy British Agent, 1952, Adviser and British Agent, 1954; High Commissioner for Aden and the Protectorate of South Arabia, 1963–65 (Deputy High Commissioner, Jan.-Aug. 1963). Member British Delegation, Anglo-Yemeni meeting in London, 1957. *Publications:* A Colony in transition: the British occupation of Eritrea, 1941–52, 1960; Shades of Amber: A South Arabian Episode, 1968. *Recreations:* travel, writing. *Address:* The Old Rectory, Rusper, Sussex. *Clubs:* Carlton, MCC, RAC.
*Died* 14 *March* 1990.

**TREVELYAN,** Baron *cr* 1968 (Life Peer); **Humphrey Trevelyan,** KG 1974; GCMG 1965 (KCMG 1955; CMG 1951); CIE 1947; OBE 1941; *b* 27 Nov. 1905; 2nd *s* of late Rev. George Philip Trevelyan; *m* 1937, Violet Margaret, *d* of late Gen. Sir William H. Bartholomew, GCB, CMG, DSO; two *d. Educ:* Lancing; Jesus College, Cambridge Univ. (Hon. Fellow, 1968). Entered Indian Civil Service, 1929; Indian Political Service, 1932–47. Served as Political Agent in the Indian States; Washington, 1944; Joint Sec. to Govt of India in External Affairs Dept, 1946; retired from Indian Political Service and entered Foreign (later Diplomatic) Service, 1947; Counsellor in Baghdad, 1948; Economic and Financial Adviser, UK High Commission for Germany, 1951–53; HM Chargé d'Affaires in Peking, 1953–55; Ambassador to Egypt, 1955–56; Under-Sec. at UN, 1958; Ambassador to Iraq, 1958–61; Deputy Under-Secretary of State, Foreign Office, 1962; Ambassador to the USSR, 1962–65, retd. High Commissioner in South Arabia, 1967. Director: British Petroleum Company Ltd, 1965–75; British Bank of the Middle East, 1965–77; General Electric Co. Ltd, 1967–76; President, Council of Foreign Bondholders, 1966–83. Chm. of Trustees, British Museum, 1970–79; Chm., RIIA, 1970–77. Hon. LLD, Cambridge, 1970; Hon. DCL Durham, 1973; Hon. DLitt Leeds, 1975. *Publications:* The Middle East in Revolution, 1970; Worlds Apart, 1971; The India We Left, 1972; Diplomatic Channels, 1973; Public and Private, 1980. *Address:* 24 Duchess of Bedford House, W8 7QN. *T:* 01–937 3125. *Club:* Beefsteak. *Died* 8 *Feb.* 1985.

**TREVELYAN, Julian Otto;** Hon. Senior RA, 1986; painter and etcher; *b* 20 Feb. 1910; *s* of late R. C. Trevelyan; *m* 1934, Ursula Darwin (divorced, 1950); one *s*; *m* 1951, Mary Fedden. *Educ:* Bedales; Trinity College, Cambridge. Studied art in Paris, Atelier 17, 1930–33; has since lived and worked in Hammersmith. One man exhibitions: Lefèvre Gall., 1935, 1938, 1942, 1943, 1944, 1946, 1948; Gimpel Fils, 1950; Redfern Gall., 1952; Zwemmer Gall., 1955, 1958, 1960, 1963, 1966, 1967; Galerie de France, Paris, 1947; St George's Gall., 1959; Alex Postan Gall., 1974; New Grafton Gall., 1977, 1983, 1985, 1987; Tate Gall., 1977; Holsworthy Gall., 1981; Bohun Gall., Henley, 1988; Retrospective of Prints, Bohun Gall., Henley, 1983; Retrospective, Watermans Art Centre, Brentford, 1986; Royal W of England Acad., 1986. Pictures in public and private collections in England, America, Sweden, France, Eire and the USSR. Served War of 1939–45, as Camouflage Officer in Roy. Engineers, 1940–43. Engraving tutor at the Royal College of Art, 1955–63 (Sen. Fellow 1986). *Publications:* Indigo Days, 1957; The Artist and His World, 1960; Etching (Studio Books), 1963; A Place, a State, 1975. *Recreation:* listening to music. *Address:* Durham Wharf, Hammersmith Terrace, W6. *T:* 01–748 2749. *Died* 12 *July* 1988.

**TREVELYAN, Mary,** CBE 1968 (OBE 1956); ARCM, ARCO; Founder and Governor, International Students' House, London; *b* 22 Jan. 1897; *e d* of late Rev. George Philip Trevelyan and Monica Evelyn Juliet, *d* of Rev. Sidney Phillips. *Educ:* Grovely College, Boscombe; Royal College of Music, London (Exhibitioner and George Carter Scholar). Musical posts included: organist and choirtrainer, St Barnabas, Oxford, music staff of Radley College and Marlborough College; conductor Chelsea Madrigal Society and Kensington Choral Society. Travelled from Ceylon to Kashmir, 1930–31; Warden of Student Movement House (international house for University students) London, 1932–46. Travelled to Far East, 1936–37, to study problems concerning migration of students from east to west for study and the effects on their return home; also visited USA to study work of the International Houses. Served on Programme Staff of YMCA with BLA in Belgium and France, Oct. 1944–June 1945; Head of Field Survey Bureau, Reconstruction Section, Paris, and made surveys on post-war priority needs in educn in Greece, the East and Far East, 1946–48; first Adviser to Overseas Students, Univ. of London, 1949–65; British Council Lecture Tour in W and E Africa, 1954; first Dir, Internat. Students House, London, 1965–67. Survey Tours, on Ford Foundn award, to univs and internat. centres in USA, Canada, Australia, NZ, the East, Far East and Middle East, 1967–69. *Publications:* From the Ends of the Earth, 1942; I'll Walk Beside You, 1946. *Recreation:* music.					*Died* 10 Jan. 1983.

**TREVOR, David;** Hon. Consulting Orthopædic Surgeon: Charing Cross Hospital; St Bartholomew's Hospital; Hon. Consulting Surgeon Royal National Orthopædic Hospital; *b* 24 July 1906; *m* 1935, Kathleen Fairfax Blyth (*d* 1984); two *d. Educ:* Tregaron County School; St Bartholomew's Hospital Medical College; Charing Cross Hospital (Post Graduate). MRCS, LRCP 1931; MB, BS London 1931; FRCS 1932; MS London, University Medal, 1934. Past Mem., Internat. Soc. Orthop. and Traumatology, 1951. Past Pres., Orthopædic Section, RSocMed (Hon. Mem. 1982); late Examr in Surgery, Univ. of London; late Mem. Council, RCS (Hunterian Prof., 1968; late Mem. Court of Examrs); Past Vice-Pres., British Orthopædic Assoc. Robert Jones Lectr, RCS, 1971. *Publications:* contributor to BMJ, Journal of Bone and Joint Surgery, Proc. RSM, Annals RCS. *Recreations:* golf, gardening. *Address:* 19 Garden Court, Wheathampstead, Herts AL4 8RE. *T:* Wheathampstead 2611.					*Died* 31 Jan. 1988.

**TREWIN, John Courtenay,** OBE 1981; FRSL; dramatic critic and author; *b* 4 Dec. 1908; *o s* of Captain John Trewin, The Lizard, Cornwall, and Annie (*née* James); *m* 1938, Wendy Monk; two *s. Educ:* Plymouth Coll. Editorial Staff: Western Independent, 1926–32; The Morning Post, London, 1932–37; second dramatic critic, 1934–37. Contributor to The Observer, 1937–; editorial staff, 1942–53; Literary Editor, 1943–48; second dramatic critic, 1943–53. Dramatic critic: Punch, 1944–45; John o' London's, 1945–54; Illustrated London News, 1946–88; The Sketch, 1947–59; The Lady, 1949–; The Birmingham Post, 1955–; Radio-drama critic of The Listener, 1951–57; Editor: The West Country Magazine, 1946–52; Plays of the Year series (50 vols), 1948–; The Year's Work in the Theatre (for the British Council), 1949–51. President, The Critics' Circle, 1964–65; Chairman, W Country Writers' Assoc., 1964–73. Hon. MA Birmingham, 1978. Devised (with David Toguri) Farjeon Reviewed, Mermaid Theatre, 1975. *Publications:* Shakespeare Memorial Theatre, 1932; The English Theatre, 1948; Up From The Lizard, 1948; We'll Hear a Play, 1949; (with H. J. Willmott) London-Bodmin, 1950; Stratford-upon-Avon, 1950; The Theatre Since 1900, 1951; The Story of Bath, 1951; Drama 1945–50, 1951; Down To The Lion, 1952; (with E. M. King) Printer to the House, 1952; A Play To-night, 1952; (with T. C. Kemp) The Stratford Festival, 1953; Dramatists of Today, 1953; Edith Evans, 1954; (ed) Theatre Programme, 1954; Mr Macready, 1955; Sybil Thorndike, 1955; Verse Drama Since 1800, 1956; Paul Scofield, 1956; The Night Has Been Unruly, 1957; Alec Clunes, 1958; The Gay Twenties: A Decade of the Theatre, 1958; Benson and the Bensonians, 1960; The Turbulent Thirties, 1960; A Sword for A Prince, 1960; John Neville, 1961; The Birmingham Repertory Theatre, 1963; Shakespeare on the English Stage, 1900–1964, 1964; completion of Lamb's Tales, 1964; Drama in Britain, 1951–64, 1965; (with H. F. Rubinstein) The Drama Bedside Book, 1966; (ed) Macready's Journals, 1967; Robert Donat, 1968; The Pomping Folk, 1968; Shakespeare Country, 1970; (with Arthur Colby Sprague) Shakespeare's Plays Today, 1970; Peter Brook, 1971; (ed) Sean: memoirs of Mrs Eileen O'Casey, 1971; I Call My Name (verse pamphlet), 1971; Portrait of Plymouth, 1973; Long Ago (verse pamphlet), 1973; Theatre Bedside Book, 1974; Tutor to the Tsarevich, 1975; (ed) Eileen, 1976; The Edwardian Theatre, 1976; Going to Shakespeare, 1978; (ed and revd) Nicoll, British Drama, 1978; The West Country Book, 1981; Companion to Shakespeare, 1981; (ed with Lord Miles) Curtain Calls, 1981; (with Wendy Trewin) The Arts Theatre, London, 1927–81, 1986; Five and Eighty Hamlets, 1987; many short stories; ed several other books. *Recreation:* all things Cornish: a Bard of the Cornish Gorsedd (Den an Lesard). *Address:* 15 Eldon Grove, Hampstead, NW3. *T:* 01–435 0207. *Club:* Garrick.					*Died* 16 Feb. 1990.

**TRIAS, Dr Juan Manuel S.;** *see* Sucre-Trias.

**TRIMBLE, Brigadier Arthur Philip,** CBE 1961; Deputy Surgeon, The Royal Hospital, Chelsea, 1964–76; Consultant Physician, Army Medical Services; *b* 21 Aug. 1909; *s* of Melville and Florence Trimble, Holywood, Co. Down, N Ireland; *m* 1952, Felicia, *d* of W. H. Friend, Bures, Suffolk; two *s. Educ:* St Columba's Coll., Co. Dublin; Queen's Univ., Belfast. MB 1931; MD; FRCPE. Joined RAMC, 1931. Served in Syrian, Western Desert, and Italian Campaigns, 1939–45; SMO 2nd Armoured Brigade. Consultant

Physician: FarELF, 1953–56; BAOR, 1957–62; Near ELF, 1963. *Publications:* various articles on tropical diseases and diseases of children in Proc. Royal Society Med., Trans Royal Society of Tropical Med., Archives of Disease in Childhood and Journal of RAMC. *Recreation:* golf. *Address:* Sherbourne Cottage, Edwardstone, Suffolk.					*Died* 30 *April* 1984.

**TRIMLESTOWN,** 19th Baron *cr* 1461; **Charles Aloysius Barnewall;** *b* 2 June 1899; *o* surv. *s* of 18th Baron and Margaret (*d* 1901), *d* of R. J. Stephens, Brisbane, Queensland; *S* father, 1937; *m* 1st, 1926, Muriel (*d* 1937), *o c* of Edward Oskar Schneider, Mansfield Lodge, Whalley Range, Manchester; two *s* one *d;* 2nd, 1952, Freda Kathleen Watkins (*d* 1987), *d* of late Alfred Watkins, Ross-on-Wye. *Educ:* Ampleforth. Lieut, Irish Guards, 1918; served European War. *Heir:* s Hon. Anthony Edward Barnewall [*b* 2 Feb. 1928; *m* 1977, Mary W., *er d* of late Judge Thomas F. McAllister]. *Address:* Autumn Cottage, Chiddingfold, Surrey GU8 4TP.

					*Died* 9 *Oct.* 1990.

**TRINDER, Sir (Arnold) Charles,** GBE 1969; Kt 1966; *b* 12 May 1906; *s* of Arnold Anderson Trinder, Oxshott; *m* 1st, 1929, Elizabeth Cairns; one *d;* 2nd, 1937, Elaine Chaytor; two *d. Educ:* Wellington Coll.; Clare Coll., Cambridge (MA (Hons)). Entered Trinder Anderson & Co., 1927; Sen. Partner, 1940–53; Chm., 1953–72; Consultant, 1972–76. Member, Baltic Exchange, 1928, Hon. Member, 1973. Common Councilman, 1951; Alderman of Aldgate, 1959–76; Sheriff, City of London, 1964; Lord Mayor of London for 1968–69. Chm., London Broadcasting Co. Ltd, 1972–74. Chairman: Family Welfare Assoc., 1967–73; Missions to Seamen (London Reg.), 1972–76. Chm., City of London Archaeol Trust, 1978–79. Chancellor, City University, 1968–69; Trustee, Morden Coll., Blackheath, 1970–87. Prime Warden, Worshipful Company of Shipwrights, 1973; Master, Worshipful Company of Fletchers, 1966. FICS 1963. Hon. DSc, City Univ., 1968. KStJ 1969. Order of Merit, Chile, 1965; Nat. Order of Niger, 1969; Order of Merit, Italy, 1969; Order of Lion of Finland, 1969. *Publication:* O Men of Athens, 1946. *Recreations:* gardening, astronomy, ancient history, logodaedaly. *Address:* Hoo End Farm, Whitwell, Herts. *Clubs:* Royal Automobile, City Livery, Guildhall.

					*Died* 25 *Dec.* 1989.

**TRINDER, Thomas Edward, (Tommy Trinder),** CBE 1975; comedian; Chairman, Fulham Football Club Ltd, 1955–76, Life President, since 1976; *b* 24 March 1909; *s* of Thomas Henry Trinder and Jean Mills; *m;* one *d. Educ:* St Andrew's, Holborn. First London appearance, Collins's Music-hall, 1922; continued in variety, pantomimes and revues, including Band Waggon, Top of the World, Gangway, Best Bib and Tucker, Happy and Glorious, Here, There and Everywhere, Fancy Free; tours in Canada, NZ, South Africa, USA; numerous Royal Variety and Command performances; radio and TV shows. Films include: The Foreman Went to France; The Bells Go Down; Champagne Charlie. *Recreation:* Fulham Football Club.					*Died* 10 *July* 1989.

**TRING, A. Stephen;** *see* Meynell, L. W.

**TRIPPE, Juan Terry;** Hon. Director, Pan American World Airways Inc. (Chief Executive, 1926–68); Chairman or Director of other companies; *b* Seabright, New Jersey, USA, 27 June 1899; *s* of Charles White Trippe and Lucy Adeline (*née* Terry); *m* 1928, Betty Stettinius; three *s* one *d. Educ:* Yale Univ. (PhB). With Pan American World Airways Inc., 1927–. Member or Trustee of various organisations and societies. Holds 11 hon. degrees and has had numerous awards including United States Medal of Merit, and 26 from foreign nations. *Address:* Pan Am Building, New York, NY 10017, USA.					*Died* 3 *April* 1981.

**TROLLOPE, Sir Anthony Owen Clavering,** 16th Bt, *cr* 1642; *b* 15 Jan. 1917; *s* of Sir Gordon Clavering Trollope, 15th Bt; *S* father, 1958; *m* 1942, Joan Mary Alexis, *d* of Alexis Robert Gibbs, Manly, New South Wales; two *s.* Served War of 1939–45: 2nd/5th Australian Field Regt, Royal Australian Artillery, Middle East and New Guinea. Director, Thomas C. Denton and Co. Pty Ltd. JP for State of NSW. *Heir:* s Anthony Simon Trollope, *b* 1945. *Address:* Clavering, 77 Roseville Avenue, Roseville, NSW 2069, Australia.
					*Died* 28 *July* 1987.

**TROTT, Charles Edmund,** MBE 1946; FIB, FCIS; Vice-Chairman, Banque Belge, 1974–81; Director: Belgian and General Investments Ltd, 1974–81; Midland Bank Ltd, 1971–81; *b* 3 Dec. 1911; *s* of late Charles Edmund and Florence Katherine Trott; *m* 1938, Edith Maria Willson; two *d. Educ:* County Sch., Tottenham. BCom(London). Served War, RAF, 1941–46. Entered Midland Bank, 1929; Jt Gen. Manager, 1960; Asst Chief Gen. Manager, 1967; Dep. Chief Gen. Manager, 1969; Chief Gen. Manager, 1972–74. Hon. Treas., British Drama League, 1950–58; Governor, Ashridge Management Coll., 1965–74; Member: Nat. Savings Cttee, 1968–74; Council, CBI, 1975–79. *Recreations:* theatre, music, walking. *Address:* 1 Park Road, St Ives, Cambridgeshire. *Clubs:* Roehampton, Royal Air Force.					*Died* 16 *Nov.* 1984.

**TROUBRIDGE, Sir Peter,** 6th Bt, *cr* 1799; RN retired; *b* 6 June 1927; *s* of late Vice-Admiral Sir T. H. Troubridge, KCB, DSO, and Lily Emily Kleinwort; *S* cousin, 1963; *m* 1954, Hon. Venetia Daphne Weeks; one *s* two *d*. *Educ:* Eton; Cambridge. Served Korean War, 1952–53, HMS Ocean; retired from RN (Lt-Comdr), 1967. Chm., Standing Council of the Baronetage, 1981–83 (Vice-Chm., 1979–81). CStJ 1983. *Recreations:* shooting, gardening, birdwatching. *Heir: s* Thomas Richard Troubridge [*b* 23 Jan. 1955; *m* 1984, Hon. Rosemary Douglas-Pennant, *yr d* of 6th Baron Penrhyn, DSO, MBE; one *d*]. *Address:* The Manor House, Elsted, Midhurst, West Sussex. *T:* Harting 286. *Clubs:* White's, City of London, MCC.
*Died 27 Sept.* 1988.

**TRUFFAUT, François;** Director of films; *b* Paris 17ème, France, 6 Feb. 1932; *s* of Roland Truffaut and Janine Truffaut (*née* de Monferrand); *m* 1957, Madeleine Morgenstern; two *d*. Reporter, film critic, 1954–58; Director of films, 1957, Producer, 1961; *productions include:* Les Mistons, 1958; Les Quatre Cents Coups, 1959 (prize, Cannes Film Festival); Tirez sur le Pianiste, 1960; L'Amour à 20 ans, 1962; Jules et Jim, 1961; La Peau Douce, 1963; Fahrenheit 451, 1966; La Mariée était en Noir, 1967; Baisers Volés, 1968; La Sirène du Mississipi, 1969; L'Enfant Sauvage, 1969; Domicile Conjugal, 1970; Les Deux Anglaises et le Continent, 1971; Une Belle Fille comme Moi, 1972; La Nuit américaine, 1973; L'Histoire d'Adèle H., 1975; L'Argent de Poche, 1976; L'Homme qui aimait les femmes, 1977; La Chambre Verte, 1978; L'amour en fuite, 1979; Le Dernier Métro, 1980; La femme d'à côté, 1981; Vivement Dimanche, 1983. *Publications:* Hitchcock, 1966; Les Aventures d'Antoine Doinel, 1970; Les Films de ma Vie, 1975 (The Films in My Life, 1980); L'Histoire d'Adèle H., 1975; L'Argent de Poche, 1975; L'Homme que aimait les femmes, 1977. *Address:* 5 rue Robert-Estienne, Paris 8ème, France. *Died 21 Oct.* 1984.

**TRUSCOTT, Sir Denis (Henry),** GBE 1958; Kt 1953; TD 1950; President of Brown Knight and Truscott Ltd; *b* 9 July 1908; *s* of Henry Dexter Truscott, JP, and Evelyn Metcalf Truscott (*née* Gibbes); *m* 1932, Ethel Margaret, *d* of late Alexander Lyell, of Gardyne Castle, Guthrie, Angus, and Mrs Lyell; four *d*. *Educ:* Bilton Grange; Rugby Sch.; Magdalene Coll., Cambridge. Joined family firm of Jas. Truscott & Son Ltd, printers, 1929; Director, 1935; Chairman, 1951–66, of Brown, Knight & Truscott Ltd (amalgamation of Jas. Truscott & Son Ltd with Wm Brown & Chas. Knight Ltd, 1936). Director: Bedford General Insurance Co. Ltd (Chm., 1974–78); Zurich Life Assurance Society Ltd (Chm., 1974–78). Elected to Court of Common Council, City of London, 1938, for Ward of Dowgate; Deputy, 1943; Alderman: Dowgate Ward, 1947–73; Bridge Without Ward, 1973–78; Sheriff of City of London, 1951–52; Lord Mayor of London, 1957–58; one of HM Lieutenants, City of London, 1943–78. Master Worshipful Company of Vintners, 1955–56; Master Worshipful Company of Musicians, 1956–57, 1970–71; Master, Guild of Freemen of the City of London, 1957; Master of Worshipful Company of Stationers and Newspaper Makers, 1959–60. Treasurer, St Bartholomew's Hospital Voluntary Bd; Vice-Pres., Royal Hospital and Home for Incurables, Putney; Chairman Trustees Rowland Hill Benevolent Fund, 1954–82; Member Exec. Cttee, Automobile Assoc., 1952–78; President: Printing and Allied Trades Research Assoc., 1956–64; Inst. of Printing, 1961–63; London Cornish Assoc., 1977–; Vice-Pres., Soc. for Protection of Animals in N Africa; Chairman, Squash Racquets Assoc. of England, 1961–74. FGSM 1978. Grand Officer of Order of Merit, Italian Republic; Grand Cross of Merit of Order of Merit, Republic of Germany. *Recreations:* lawn tennis, golf. *Address:* Invermark, 30 Drax Avenue, Wimbledon, SW20. *T:* 01–946 6111. *Clubs:* United Oxford & Cambridge University, Royal Automobile, City Livery, All England Lawn Tennis, MCC.
*Died 4 Feb.* 1989.

**TRUSS, Leslie S.;** *see* Seldon-Truss.

**TRUSTED, Sir Harry Herbert,** Kt 1938; QC; *b* 27 June 1888; *s* of the Rev. Wilson Trusted; *m* 1911, Mary (*d* 1983), *d* of Sir Marshall Warmington, KC, 1st Bt; two *s* three *d*. *Educ:* Ellesmere Coll.; Trinity Hall, Cambridge. Called to Bar, Inner Temple, 1913; served overseas (Duke of Cornwall's Light Infantry and Staff), 1914–19; Puisne Judge, Supreme Court, Leeward Islands, 1925–27; Attorney-General, Leeward Islands, 1927–29; Attorney-General, Cyprus, 1929–32; Attorney-General, Palestine, 1932–37; Chief Justice, Palestine, 1937–41; Chief Justice, FMS, 1941–45; Chairman, Malayan Union and Singapore Salaries Commission, 1947; Commissioner to inquire into disturbances at Aden, 1948; special duty with Foreign Office (FOAAT), 1951–53; sat as Divorce Commissioner, 1953–63. *Address:* Broomhill Court, Esher Close, Esher, Surrey. *T:* Esher 66606. *Died 8 Dec.* 1985.

**TSIBU DARKU, Nana Sir,** Kt 1948; OBE 1945 (MBE 1941); *b* 19 March 1902; *s* of late Adrian Nicholas de Heer of Elmina, and late Effuah Tekyiwa (*née* Hagar Dadson), Cape Coast and Fanti Nyankumasi; *m* 1930, Maud, *d* of late Daniel Sackey, Accountant, PWD, Gold Coast; nine *s* nine *d*. *Educ:* African Methodist Episcopal Zion Mission Sch., Cape Coast; SPG Grammar Sch. (now Adisadel Coll.), Cape Coast. Served in Junior Service Political Administration, 1923–30; elected Paramount Chief of Asin Atandaso, Gold Coast (now Ghana), West Africa, 18 Nov. 1930; abdicated 18 Nov. 1951; re-elected Paramount Chief of Asin Atandaso Traditional Area, 13 Aug. 1962. Provincial Member Gold Coast Legislative Council, 1932–51; Sen. Unofficial Member of the Legislature, 1943–51; Member Governor's Exec. Council, Gold Coast, 1943–51. Served on various Government Cttees, including University Council of the Gold Coast and Coussey Cttee on Constitutional Reforms; attended African Conf., London, 1948. Dir, Messrs Guinness Ghana Ltd, 1969. Member: Adisadel College Board of Governors, 1943–73; Mfantsipim School Board of Management, 1954–70; Aggrey Secondary Sch. Board of Governors, 1952–76. Member, Cape Coast Municipal Council, 1954–59; Chairman, Tema Develt Corp., 1954–59; Chairman, Ghana Cocoa Marketing Board, 1959–66; Chairman, Kwame Nkrumah Trust Fund (Central Collection Cttee), 1959–66 (Chairman Trustees, 1960–66). Hon. DCL Univ. of Cape Coast, 1976. Silver Jubilee Medal, 1935; Coronation Medal, 1937; King's Medal for African Chiefs, 1939. *Address:* PO Box 19, Fanti Nyankumasi, via Cape Coast, Ghana. *Died 12 April* 1982.

**TUCK, Maj.-Gen. George Newsam,** CB 1950; OBE 1944; retired; *b* 18 Dec. 1901; *s* of Harry Newman Tuck, Burma Commn; *m* 1929, Nell (*née* Winter) (*d* 1981); three *s*. *Educ:* Cheltenham Coll.; RMA, Woolwich. Commissioned Royal Engineers, 1921. Egypt, 1925–30; Instructor RMA, 1930–34; Staff Coll., 1935–36; Chief Instructor (RE), RMA, 1939; GSO1, Scapa Defences, 1939–40; DDRA, 1941; CRE 46 Div., 1942; Mil. Deputy to Scientific Adviser, War Office, 1943; Comdr Army Group RE, France and Germany, 1944–45; DSP, War Office, 1946; idc, 1947; DDSD, War Office, 1948; Chief of Staff, BAOR, 1949–Dec. 1951; Engineer-in-Chief, War Office, 1952–54; Deputy Controller of Munitions, Ministry of Supply, 1954–57; retired, 1957. Col Comdt, Corps of Royal Engineers, 1958–66. *Address:* c/o Lloyds Bank, Shaftesbury, Dorset.
*Died 1 July* 1981.

**TUCK, Sir Raphael (Herman),** Kt 1979; *b* 5 April 1910; *er* and surv. *s* of late David Lionel Tuck and Olive Tuck; *m* 1959, Monica J. L. Greaves. *Educ:* St Paul's School; London School of Economics; Trinity Hall, Cambridge; Havard University, USA. BSc Econ. London 1936; MA Cantab 1939; LLM Harvard, 1940. British Embassy, Washington, 1940; Lecturer and later Professor of Law, University of Saskatchewan, Canada, 1941–45; Constitutional Adviser to Premier of Manitoba, 1943; Special Research, Dept of Labour, Ottawa, 1944; Prof. of Political Science, McGill Univ., Montreal, 1945–46; Prof. of Political Science, Tulane Univ., New Orleans, La, 1947–49. Barrister-at-Law, Gray's Inn, 1951. MP (Lab) Watford, 1964–79. Member: CPA; Soc. of Labour Lawyers; "Justice"; Harvard Law Assoc. of UK; Harvard Club of London; Action for the Crippled Child (Watford Br.); Court, Reading Univ.; Hon. Member: Herts Chamber of Commerce; Watford Philharmonic Soc.; Vice-President: Watford Soc. for Mentally Handicapped Children; Nat. Assoc. of Swimming Clubs for the Handicapped; Sea Lions Club of Watford for the Handicapped; Watford Community Relations Council; Watford Operatic Soc.; Abbots Langley Gilbert and Sullivan Soc. Freeman, Borough of Watford, 1979. *Publications:* articles in University of Toronto Law Journal, Canadian Bar Review, Sask. Bar Review, Public Affairs, Canadian Jl of Econs and Polit. Science, Solicitor's Jl. *Recreations:* photography, music. *Address:* 17 Vicarage Lane, East Preston, West Sussex. *Died 1 July* 1982.

**TUCK, Wing Comdr Robert Roland S.;** *see* Stanford-Tuck.

**TUCKER, Prof. David Gordon;** Hon. Senior Research Fellow, Department of Economic History, since 1981, and Professor Emeritus, University of Birmingham; *b* 17 June 1914; *s* of John Ferry and Frances Tucker; *m* 1945, Florence Mary Barton; three *s* one *d*. *Educ:* Sir George Monoux Grammar School, London; University of London. BSc 1936; PhD 1943; DSc 1948. On research staff of GPO, at the PO Research Station, Dollis Hill, 1934–50; Royal Naval Scientific Service (Senior Principal Scientific Officer), 1950–55; Birmingham University: Prof. and Head of Dept of Electronic and Electrical Engrg, 1955–73; Sen. Fellow in Hist. of Technology, 1974–81. Member: Gen. Council of IERE, 1958–62 and 1965–66, Educn Cttee, 1958–65, Research Cttee, 1962–67; Council of British Acoustical Soc. 1965–73 (Vice-Pres., 1967–70; Pres., 1970–73); Council, Soc. for Underwater Technology, 1967–70; National Electronics Research Council, 1963–66; Treasury Cttee on Scientific Civil Service, 1964–65; Oceanography and Fisheries Cttee, NERC, 1965–70; Cttee on History of Technology, IEE, 1970–76, 1978–84 (Chm., 1973–75); Adv. Cttee for Nat. Archive in Electrical Sci. and Technol. (Chm., 1973–79); Council, Newcomen Soc., 1977–84 (Vice-Pres., 1981–84); Royal Commn on Ancient and Historical Monuments in Wales, 1979–84; and of various other Univ., Government, professional and educational committees. FIERE, 1953; FIEE, 1954; FSA 1984. Clerk Maxwell Premium of

IERE, 1961. *Publications:* Modulators and Frequency-Changers, 1953; Electrical Network Theory, 1964; Circuits with Periodically-Varying Parameters, 1964; Applied Underwater Acoustics (with B. K. Gazey) 1966; Underwater Observation Using Sonar, 1966; Sonar in Fisheries: A Forward Look, 1967; papers in professional, scientific and historical journals. *Recreations:* history of technology, industrial archaeology. *Address:* 26 Twatling Road, Barnt Green, Birmingham B45 8HT. *T:* 021–445 1820.

*Died 8 March* 1990.

**TUCKER, Hon. Sir Henry (James),** KBE 1972 (CBE 1946); Kt 1961; Government Leader, Executive Council, Bermuda, 1968–71; General Manager, Bank of Bermuda Ltd, Hamilton, Bermuda, since 1938; *b* 14 March 1903; *s* of Henry James and Nella Louise Tucker; *m* 1925, Catherine Newbold Barstow; two *s* one *d*. *Educ:* Saltus Grammar School, Bermuda; Sherborne School, Dorset, England. New York Trust Co., 1924–26; Kelley, Drayton and Converse (Brokers), 1926–30; Milne Munro & Tucker (Brokers), 1930–34; joined Bank of Bermuda Ltd, 1934. Pres., Anglo Norness Shipping, 1968–. *Recreation:* golf. *Address:* The Lagoon, Paget, Bermuda. *T:* 2–1657. *Clubs:* Mid-Ocean Golf, Royal Bermuda Yacht, Royal Hamilton Dinghy, Riddells Bay Golf (all in Bermuda). *Died 9 Jan.* 1986.

**TUCKWELL, Sir Edward (George),** KCVO 1975; MCh, FRCS; Serjeant-Surgeon to the Queen, 1973–75 (Surgeon to the Queen, 1969–73, to HM Household, 1964–69); Surgeon, St Bartholomew's Hospital, London, 1947–75; Surgeon, Royal Masonic Hospital, 1958–75; Consultant Surgeon, King Edward VII Convalescent Home, Osborne, 1965–78; *b* 12 May 1910; *e s* of Edward Henry Tuckwell and Annie Clarice (*née* Sansom); *m* 1st, 1934, Phyllis Courthope Regester (*d* 1970); two *s* one *d*; 2nd, 1971, Barbara Gordon, *widow* of Major A. J. Gordon. *Educ:* Charterhouse; Magdalen College, Oxford; St Bartholomew's Hospital. BM, BCh Oxon 1936; MCh 1948; FRCS 1939. War Service in EMS and RAMC, Surgical Specialist, North-West Europe and South-East Asia, Lt-Col. Examiner in Surgery to Univs of London, Manchester, Oxford, and in Pathology to Conjoint Board and Royal College of Surgeons; Dean of Medical School, St Bartholomew's Hospital, 1952–57; Surgeon, King Edward VII Hospital for Officers, 1961–75. Member: Medical Appeal Tribunal, 1975–82; Vaccine Damage Appeal Tribunal, 1978–82. Pres., Phyllis Tuckwell Meml Hospice, Farnham; Member: Council, Metrop. Hosp. Sunday Fund, 1981–; Governing Body of Charterhouse School, 1966–82 (Chm., 1973–81) (London University representative); Council, Epsom Coll., 1981–83; Governor: St Bartholomew's Hosp., 1954–74; Sutton's Hosp. in Charterhouse, 1980–. Mem. Ct of Assts, 1973–, Warden 1978, Master 1981–82, and Freeman, Barbers' Co. FRSA 1982. *Publications:* articles in medical journals. *Recreations:* gardening, shooting, travelling. *Address:* Berthorpe, Puttenham Heath Road, Guildford, Surrey GU3 1DU. *T:* Guildford 810217.

*Died 27 Dec.* 1988.

**TUDOR PRICE, Hon. Sir David (William);** Kt 1985; Hon. Mr Justice Tudor Price; Judge of the High Court of Justice, Queen's Bench Division, since 1984; a Presiding Judge, Wales and Chester Circuit, since 1985; *b* 29 Jan. 1931; *s* of late Tudor Howell Price, OBE, and Mary Tudor Price; *m* 1956, Elspeth Patricia Longwell, JP; two *s* one *d*. *Educ:* Rugby Sch.; Magdalene Coll., Cambridge (MA). Called to Bar, Inner Temple, 1955, Bencher 1981. Prosecuting Counsel to the Post Office, 1965–69; Junior Treasury Counsel, 1971; First Junior, 1974; Sen. Prosecuting Counsel to the Crown at Central Criminal Ct, 1975–81; a Recorder of the Crown Court, 1979–81; Common Serjeant, City of London, 1981–84. Chm., Disciplinary Tribunals of the Senate, 1985; Member: Royal Commn on Gambling, 1976–78; Judicial Studies Bd, 1983– (Chm., Criminal Sub-Cttee, 1985). Appeal Steward, British Bd of Boxing Control, 1978–81. Trustee, Charing Cross Med. Res. Centre, 1985. HM Lieut, City of London, 1981–85; Liveryman, Merchant Taylors' Co. *Recreation:* golf. *Address:* c/o Royal Courts of Justice, WC2. *Clubs:* Hawks (Cambridge); Woking Golf, Woburn Golf and Country.

*Died 13 Feb.* 1986.

**TUDSBERY, Marmaduke Tudsbery,** CBE 1941; FCGI 1950; FICE 1932; Fellow, Imperial College of Science and Technology, London University, 1953; Hon. Member Institution of Royal Engineers, 1937; President Smeatonian Society of Civil Engineers, 1956; *b* 4 Oct. 1892; 3rd *s* of late J. H. T. Tudsbery, DSc; unmarried. *Educ:* Westminster; Imperial College, London Univ.; engineering training under late John J. Webster, FICE, and at works of Yarrow & Co. Ltd, Glasgow. Commissioned, Special Reserve of Officers, RE: France, 1915 (9th Field Company); subsequently Army of the Rhine, Mesopotamia Expeditionary Force; staff of RE Board, War Office, 1920–25; Member, later Chairman, War Office Cttee on Army Building, 1940–44; Member: Home Office Committee on Structural Precautions against Air-Attack, 1936–39; Science Museum Adv. Council, 1959–69. Governor, Imperial Coll., London Univ., 1942–71. The Civil Engineer to BBC, 1926–52; Consulting Civil Engineer to BBC, 1952–60. *Address:* Littlebourne Nursing

Home, Littlebourne, Canterbury, Kent CT3 1UN. *Clubs:* Athenæum, MCC, Royal Cruising, Royal Thames Yacht.

*Died 9 May* 1983.

**TUFNELL-BARRETT, Hugh,** CIE 1943; K-i-H Gold Medal 1938; *b* 13 Jan. 1900; *s* of late Rev. Wilfrid Tufnell-Barrett, formerly of Court Lodge, Shorne, Kent; *m* 1929, Frances Eleanor (*d* 1971), *d* of late Julian Claude Platts, Melbourne, Australia; one *s* two *d*. *Educ:* St John's School, Leatherhead; Cadet College, Wellington, India. 2nd Lieut 31st Punjabis, IA, 1918; Temporary Captain and Staff Captain, Bushire Field Force, South Persia, 1920–21; Offg Bde Major, 3rd Ind. Inf. Bde, Peshawar, 1922; resigned, 1922; entered ICS, 1923; District Magistrate, Dacca, Bengal, 1931, Bakarganj, Bengal, 1935; Joint Sec. Commerce and Labour Dept, Bengal, 1939; Addl Sec. Home Dept, Bengal, 1939; Dep. Sec. to Govt of India, Dept of Labour, 1939–43; Joint Secretary to Govt of India, Dept of Labour, April 1943; Offg Sec. to Govt of India, Dept of Labour, June 1943; Offg Sec. to Govt of India, Dept of Labour, June 1943; Civil Representative of Bengal Govt with Eastern Army and Additional Home Sec., Bengal, Dec. 1943; Director-General, Food, and Addtl Commissioner for Civil Supplies, Bengal, 1945; entered service of Pakistan Govt, Sept. 1947; Commissioner, Chittagong Division, E Pakistan, 1947–49; Secretary, Ministry of Kashmir Affairs, Government of Pakistan, 1949–50; Chief Warden, Westminster City Council Civil Defence Force, 1952–53. General Manager, Douglas Fraser & Sons (London) Ltd, 1953–74. *Recreation:* reading. *Address:* 9c Sunderland Terrace, W2 5PA.

*Died 29 April* 1981.

**TUITE, Sir Dennis (George Harmsworth),** 13th Bt *cr* 1622; MBE 1946; Major RE, retired; *b* 26 Jan. 1904; *s* of late Hugh George Spencer Tuite and late Eva Geraldine Tuite (*née* Hatton); *S* brother, 1970; *m* 1947, Margaret Essie, *o d* of late Col Walter Leslie Dundas, DSO, late 3rd QAO Gurkha Rifles; three *s*. *Educ:* St Paul's School; RMA Woolwich. Commissioned, Royal Engineers, 1925; served in India, North West Frontier, 1928–30, Burma, 1930–32 (medal). Served War, in Europe, 1939–45; Kenya, 1948–52; retired, 1959. *Recreations:* reading, travelling, fishing. *Heir:* *s* Dr Christopher Hugh Tuite, PhD [*b* 3 Nov. 1949; *m* 1976, Deborah Anne, *o d* of A. E. Martz, Pittsburgh, Pa, USA; two *s*. *Address:* Windhaven, Ladygate Drive, Grayshott, Hindhead, Surrey GU26 6DR. *T:* Hindhead 5026. *Died 9 July* 1981.

**TULL, Thomas Stuart,** CBE 1963 (OBE (mil.) 1946); DSO 1946; HM Diplomatic Service, retired 1971; *b* 11 October 1914; surv. *yr s* of late Frank Stuart Tull and of Phyllis Mary Tull (*née* Back); *m* 1946, Constance Grace Townsend; one *s* two *d* (one step *s* one step *d*). *Educ:* Rossall School; Jesus College, Oxford. Entered Indian Civil Service, 1938; served in Punjab, 1939–41; ADC to the Governor, 1941; lent to War Department, Govt of India, for service with RAF, 1941; on active service in India and SE Asia Commands, 1941–46; retired from ICS and entered HM Diplomatic Service, 1947. Foreign Office, 1947–48; First Secretary at British Legation, Berne, 1948–51; Foreign Office, 1951–53; HM Consul at San Francisco, 1953–54; HM Consul at Denver, 1954–56; Press Counsellor at British Embassy: Cairo, 1956; Berne, 1957; HM Consul-General: Gothenburg, 1958–61; Philadelphia, 1961–66; Durban, 1966–67; High Comr, Malawi, 1967–71. Mem. UK Delegn to UN 12th Gen. Assembly, 1957. Research on Overseas Develt and Youth Unemployment, 1971–; formed: Philafrica Action Gp, 1974; Youth Develt Trust, 1975–. *Recreations:* sailing, gardening. *Address:* Hunter's Moon, Charney Road, Longworth, Abingdon, Oxon OX13 5HW. *T:* Longworth 820234. *Clubs:* Special Forces, Royal Commonwealth Society. *Died 21 April* 1982.

**TUNBRIDGE, Sir Ronald (Ernest),** Kt 1967; OBE 1944; JP; Professor of Medicine, University of Leeds, 1946–71, now Emeritus Professor; Chairman, Standing Medical Advisory Committee, Department of Health and Social Security, 1963–72; *b* 2 June 1906; *s* of Rev. W. J. Tunbridge and Norah (*née* Young); *m* 1935, Dorothy Gregg; two *s*. *Educ:* Kingswood School, Bath; University of Leeds. Research Fellowship in Physiology, 1928; Hons degree in Physiology, BSc, 1928, MSc, 1929; MB, ChB, Hons 1931; MD 1933; MRCP 1933; FRCP 1944; numerous resident appointments in Leeds. Clinical asst for one year at St Bartholomew's Hosp., under Sir Francis Fraser; Reader in Medicine, Univ. of Leeds; Consultant to Hosps in Leeds Region. Military Service, 1941–44; Adviser in Medicine, Malta Command; Cons. in Med., BLA and BAOR, 1945–46 (despatches). FRSocMed. Member: Assoc. of Physicians of GB and Ire. (Pres., 1977–78); Heberden Soc. (serving on Council of latter, Pres., 1954 and 1955); The Diabetic Assoc. (Banting Memorial Lectr, 1953); Vice-Pres., British Diabetic Assoc.; Chairman: Governing Body of 1st and 2nd International Gerontological Congresses (Member, Governing Body of Third Internat. Congress; Chm. Brit. Organizing Cttee of Third Congress); Leeds Regional Hosp. Bd, 1947–51; Mem. Bd of United Leeds Hosps, 1952–71; Chm., Educn Cttee, 1967–72, Mem. Management Cttee, 1967–, King Edward's Hospital Fund for London; Central Health Services Council: Mem., 1959–; Vice-Chm., 1963–72; Chm., Hosp. Records

Cttee, 1964; Chm., Health of Hosp. Staff Cttee, 1968; Chm., Rehabilitation Cttee, 1972. Mem. Exec. Cttee, Nat. Old People's Welfare Council (Vice-Chm. Yorkshire Council); Pres., BMA 1974 (Chm. Bd of Science, 1968–72); Vice-President: Med. Defence Union; Age Concern; Chm., Leeds Local Broadcasting Council, 1968–72; Hon. Pres., British Dietetic Assoc.; Past Pres., Brit. Spas Fedn, 1955–63; Fellow, Coll. of Physicians of Ceylon, 1973. Heberden Orator, 1956; Lectures: Proctor Meml, 1958; Frederick Price, TCD, 1969; Founder, British Council for Rehabilitation of Disabled, 1972; Fernando, (and Prize), Ceylon Coll. of Physicians, 1973; Convocation, Univ. of Leeds, 1981. Asst Editor, Gerontologia. JP City of Leeds, 1958. Hon. DSc: Hull, 1974; Leeds, 1975; Warwick, 1979. Bobst Award, Internat. Association of Gerontology, 1957; Osler Award, Canadian Med. Assoc., 1973. *Publications:* articles in Quarterly Jl of Medicine, Lancet, BMJ, etc. *Recreation:* walking. *Address:* 9 Ancaster Road, Leeds LS16 5HH. *Club:* Athenæum. *Died* 12 Jan. 1984.

**TUOMINEN, Leo Olavi;** Finnish Ambassador, retired; *b* 19 Jan. 1911; *s* of Johan Tuominen (until 1897 Seipel) and Johanna Johansson; *m* 1938, Johanna, *d* of Emil Habert; one *s* three *d. Educ:* Turku Univ. (MA). Joined Finnish Foreign Service, 1934; served abroad, 1934–39; Min. of For. Affairs, 1940–46; Legation in Brussels, 1946–48; Asst Under Sec., Min. of For. Affairs, 1948–50; Perm. Deleg. to Int. Orgns in Geneva, 1950–52; Envoy to Argentina, Chile and Uruguay, 1952–55. Min. of Foreign Affairs: Dep. Under Sec., 1955–56; Perm. Under-Sec. of State, 1956–57; Ambassador to Court of St James's, 1957–68, to Italy, 1968–69, to Sweden, 1969-72, to USA 1972–77. Head of Delegn for econ. negotiations with many countries, incl. UK, 1945–56 (Pres. delegn at GATT Conf. Torquay, 1950). Hon. DrPhil Michigan, 1974. Hon. KBE, and holds other foreign decorations. *Publications:* articles and essays on economics. *Recreations:* ski-ing, reading, gardening. *Address:* Kalliolinnantie 12, Helsinki 14, Finland. *Clubs:* Hurlingham, Travellers'. *Died* 4 April 1981.

**TURING, Sir John Leslie,** 11th Bt *cr* 1638; MC; *b* 13 Sept. 1895; *s* of Sir James Walter Turing, 9th Bt and Mabel Rose, *d* of Andrew Caldecott; *S* twin brother, 1970; *m* 1975, Irene Nina, *d* of Trevor John Tatham and *widow* of Captain W. W. P. Shirley-Rollison, RN. *Educ:* Wellington College. Formerly Lieut, Seaforth Highlanders; served European War, 1914–18 (wounded, MC). *Heir: kinsman* John Dermot Turing [*b* 26 Feb. 1961; *m* 1986, Nicola J., *er d* of M. D. Simmonds]. *Address:* Hillcrest, Heatherwood, Midhurst GU29 9LH. *Died* 17 Sept. 1987.

**TURNBULL, Sir Alexander (Cuthbert),** Kt 1988; CBE 1982; MD, FRCOG; Nuffield Professor of Obstetrics and Gynaecology, University of Oxford, 1973–90, later Professor Emeritus; Fellow of Oriel College, Oxford, since 1973; Hon. Consultant Obstetrician and Gynaecologist, Oxfordshire Health Authority, since 1973; *b* 18 Jan. 1925; *s* of George Harley and Anne White Turnbull, Aberdeen, Scotland; *m* 1953, Elizabeth Paterson Nicol Bell; one *s* one *d. Educ:* Merchant Taylors' Sch., Crosby; Aberdeen Grammar Sch. (Modern Dux, 1942); Aberdeen Univ. MB, ChB 1947; MD (with Hons and Thursfield Prize) 1966; MRCOG 1954; FRCOG 1966 (Jun. Vice-Pres., 1982–83; Sen. Vice-Pres., 1984–86). Sen. Lectr and Hon. Cons. Obstetrician and Gynaecologist (with Prof. J. Walker), Univ. of Dundee, 1957–61; Sen. Lectr and Hon. Cons. Obstetrician and Gynaecologist (with Sir Dugald Baird), Univ. of Aberdeen, 1961–66; Prof. of Obst. and Gynaecol., Welsh Nat. Sch. of Med., Cardiff, and Hon. Cons. Gynaecologist, also Adviser in Obst. and Gynaecol., Welsh Hosp. Bd, 1966–73; Adviser in Obst. and Gynaecol. to CMO, DHSS, 1975–86. Member: Med. Educn Sub-cttee of UGC, 1973–83; Lane Commn, 1971–73; Clinical Research Bd of MRC, 1969–72. Hon. MA Oxford, 1973. Blair-Bell Medal, RSocMed (Sect. of Obst. and Gynaecol.), 1984; Sir Eardley Holland Medal, RCOG, 1990. *Publications:* (co-ed) The Oxygen Supply to the Human Fetus, 1960; (chap. in) The Scientific Basis of Obstetrics and Gynaecology (ed R. R. Macdonald), 1969; (jtly) Confidential Enquiries into Maternal Mortality in England and Wales (HMSO), 1973–75, 1976–78, 1979–81 and 1982–84; (ed with Prof. Geoffrey Chamberlain) Obstetrics, 1989; contribs to: Brit. Jl Obstetrics and Gynaecol., Lancet, BMJ, Jl of Endocrinology and various others. *Recreations:* reading, travelling, occasionally playing golf. *Address:* 2 Blenheim Drive, Oxford OX3 8DG. *Died* 18 Aug. 1990.

**TURNBULL, Sir Francis (Fearon), (Sir Frank Turnbull),** KBE 1964; CB 1954; CIE 1946; HM Civil Service, retired; *b* 30 April 1905; *m* 1947, Gwynnedd Celia Marian Lewis; three *s. Educ:* Marlborough Coll.; Trinity Hall, Cambridge. Entered India Office, 1930; Principal Private Secretary to Secretary of State, 1941–46; Secretary to Cabinet Mission to India, 1946; Under-Secretary, HM Treasury, 1949–59; Secretary, Office of the Minister for Science, 1959–64; Deputy Under-Secretary of State, Dept of Education and Science, 1964–66. Member, Board of Governors, Imperial College, 1967–73. Hon. DSc Edinburgh, 1967. *Address:* 26 Green Lane, Amersham, Bucks HP6 6AS. *T:* Amersham 727647. *Died* 8 Sept. 1988.

**TURNBULL, Gilbert Learmonth,** CBE 1954; Deputy Chief Inspector of Taxes, 1952–Oct. 1960; *b* 22 Oct. 1895; *s* of late D. Lowe Turnbull, Edinburgh. *Educ:* George Watson's Coll. Entered Inland Revenue Department, 1914; retired as Dep. Chief Inspector of Taxes, Oct. 1960. *Address:* 5 Rowben Close, Totteridge, N20. *T:* 01-445 9555. *Died* 1 May 1981.

**TURNER, Comdr Bradwell Talbot,** CVO 1955; DSO 1940; OBE 1951; JP; RN, retired April 1957; *b* 7 April 1907; *s* of late A. F. and A. I. Turner; *m* 1937, Mary G. B., *d* of Professor W. Nixon; three *d. Educ:* Christ's Hospital; RN Colleges Osborne and Dartmouth. Joined Royal Navy, 1921; Barrister-at-Law, 1956; Naval Attaché, Oslo, Norway, 1954–57. With The Marconi Co., 1957–72. MIEE 1946. JP Chelmsford 1962 (Chm. Bench, 1974–77). Officer, Legion of Merit (USA), 1945. *Address:* 44 St Johns Road, Writtle, Essex CM1 3EB. *Died* 21 March 1990.

**TURNER, Sir Cedric Oban,** Kt 1967; CBE 1958; Chief Executive and General Manager, Qantas Empire Airways Ltd, 1955–67; *b* 13 Feb. 1907; *s* of S. Turner, Gulgong, NSW; *m* 1935; Shirley (*d* 1972), *d* of late Sir Joseph Totterdell, sometime Lord Mayor of Perth, Western Australia; one *s* three *d. Educ:* Sydney High Sch. Chartered Accountant: Robert W. Nelson, 1924–29, UK and Europe, 1929–34. Joined Qantas Empire Airways, 1934; Chief Accountant; Assistant General Manager, 1949–51; General Manager, 1951–55. *Recreation:* golf. *Address:* 16 Livingstone Avenue, Pymble, NSW 2073, Australia. *Died* 16 Nov. 1982.

**TURNER, Brig. Charles Edward Francis,** CBE 1944 (OBE 1941); DSO 1943; late RE; *b* 23 April 1899; *s* of late Lieut A. E. Turner, RE, and E. B., *d* of Maj.-Gen. Sir C. H. Scott, KCB; *m* 1930, Mary Victoria (*d* 1985), *d* of H. Leeds Swift, York; one *s* two *d. Educ:* Twyford Sch., Winchester; Wellington Coll., Berks; Royal Military Academy, Woolwich. Regular Officer, Royal Engineers, Sept. 1917; BEF France, June-Nov. 1918; NREF Russia, July-Sept. 1919; India, 1920–23, including two years on North-West Frontier on service (despatches); Christ's Coll., Cambridge, 1923–24; Ordnance Survey, York and Edinburgh, 1925–30; Staff Coll., Camberley, 1931–32; Singapore, Egypt, Palestine, 1934–37, including service in Palestine (Bt Major, despatches); War Office, 1937–39; MEF 1940–43 (OBE, DSO, CBE, despatches twice); Malaya, 1948–50; retired pay, 1950. National Council of Social Service, 1950–58; Secretary, Iona Appeal Trust, 1958–61. *Address:* The Colleens, Cousley Wood, Wadhurst, East Sussex TN5 6HE. *T:* Wadhurst 2387. *Died* 1 March 1990.

**TURNER, Dr Elston G.;** *see* Grey-Turner.

**TURNER, Sir Eric (Gardner),** Kt 1981; CBE 1975; FBA 1956; Professor of Papyrology, University College, London, 1950–78, now Emeritus; Leverhulme Emeritus Research Fellow, 1982; *b* 26 Feb. 1911; *s* of late William Ernest Stephen Turner; *m* 1940, Louise B. Taylor; one *s* one *d. Educ:* King Edward VII Sch., Sheffield; Magdalen Coll., Oxford (Demy). First Class Hons Classical Mods, 1932, and Lit Hum, 1934; Goldsmiths' Senior Scholar, 1935; Assistant in Humanity, University of Aberdeen, 1936; Lecturer in Classics, Aberdeen Univ., 1938–48; Reader in Papyrology, University of London, 1948–50; first Dir, Univ. of London Inst. of Classical Studies, 1953–63. Pres., Internat. Assoc. of Papyrologists, 1965–74; Vice President: Hellenic Soc. (Pres., 1968–71); Roman Soc.; Egypt Exploration Soc., 1978– (Chm. Cttee, 1956–78); Chairman: Organising Cttee, Third Internat. Congress of Classical Studies, London, 1959; Organising Cttee, XVIth Internat. Congress of Papyrologists, Oxford, 1974; Jt Editor, Graeco-Roman publications. Visiting Member, Inst. for Advanced Study, Princeton, NJ, 1961, 1964, 1968, 1978. Hon. Fellow: Warburg Inst., 1978; University Coll., London, 1979. Pres., Union Académique Internationale, 1974–77 (Vice-Pres., 1970–73). Hon. Mem., Sociêtas Scientiarum Fennica (Humanities Section), 1969; For. Member: Accademia di Archeologia, Lettere e Belle Arti (Letters Section) of the Società Nazionale di Scienze, Lettere ed Arti, Naples, 1973; Det Kongelige Danske Videnskabernes Selskab (historisk-filosofiske klasse); Amer. Philosophical Soc., 1977; Corresp. Mem., Osterreichische Akademie der Wissenschaften, 1975; Sächsische Akademie der Wissenschaften, 1976; Deutsche Archäologisches Institut, 1976; Associate, Académie royale des Sciences, des Lettres et des Beaux-Arts de Belgique, 1974. Patron of Honour, Fundación Pastor, Madrid, 1981. Hon. Dr Phil et Lettres Brussels, 1956; Hon. DèsL Geneva, 1976; Hon. DLitt Liverpool, 1978. *Publications:* Catalogue of Greek Papyri in University of Aberdeen, 1939; (with C. H. Roberts) Catalogue of Greek Papyri in John Rylands Library, Vol. IV, 1951; The Hibeh Papyri, Part II, 1955; (with others) The Oxyrhynchus Papyri, Part XXIV, 1957, Part XXV, 1959, Part XXVII, 1962, Part XXXI, 1966, Part XXXIII, 1968, Part XXXVIII, 1971, Part XLI, 1972, Part XLVIII, 1981, Part L, 1972; (with H. I. Bell, V. Martin, D. van Berchem) The Abinnæus Papyri, 1962; New Fragments of the Misoumenos of Menander, 1965; Greek Papyri, an Introduction, 1968, 2nd edn 1980; Greek Manuscripts of the Ancient World, 1970; Menander: The Girl from Samos, 1972; The

Papyrologist at Work, 1973; The Typology of the Early Codex, 1977; Recto and Verso, 1978; various papers in learned journals (bibliography to 1980 in Papyri Edited in Honour of E. G. T., 1981). *Recreations:* chamber music, playing the gramophone, walking sailing. *Address:* Thornheath, Cathedral Square, Fortrose, Ross-shire. *Club:* United Oxford & Cambridge University.

                                       *Died 20 April 1983.*

**TURNER, Dame Eva,** DBE 1962; FRAM; prima donna; *b* Oldham, Lancashire, 10 March 1892; unmarried. Began to sing at an early age and, whilst in her teens, spent some years at the Royal Academy of Music; joined Royal Carl Rosa Opera Company in 1915, and became the Prima donna of the Company, remaining with it until 1924, when Toscanini engaged her for La Scala, Milan. Appeared all over Europe and USA with Chicago Civic Opera, and in S America; appeared in London, at Covent Garden in 1928 in internat. season, when she sang in Puccini's opera Turandot, Aida, and various other operas; for the Celebrations in connection with the commemoration of the Centenary of Bolivar, was specially chosen by President Gomez to be the Prima Donna; in London at Covent Garden in 1937 internat. season, sang Turandot to the first Calaf of Giovanni Martinelli, also chosen to sing National Anthem from stage of Royal Opera House following Coronation of King George VI and Queen Elizabeth; Professor of Voice to Music Faculty of University of Oklahoma, USA, 1949–59 (resigned); Professor of Voice Royal Academy of Music, London, 1959–66 (resigned). Pres., Wagner Soc., 1971–85. Hon. Internat. Member Sigma Alpha Iota, 1951–; Hon. Internat. Soroptomist, 1955–. Member National Assoc. of Teachers of Singing (USA). Hon. GSM 1968; FRCM 1974; FRNCM 1978; Hon. FTCL, 1982. Hon. Citizen, State of Oklahoma, USA, 1982; First Freeman, Metropolitan Borough of Oldham, 1982. Hon. DMus: Manchester, 1979; Oxford, 1984. Hon. Fellow, St Hilda's Coll., Oxford, 1984. Hon. Licentiate, Western Ontario Conservatory of Music, Canada, 1986. *Recreations:* swimming, riding, motoring. *Address:* 26 Palace Court, W2. *Club:* Royal Over-Seas League.

                                       *Died 16 June 1990.*

**TURNER, Francis McDougall Charlewood,** MC; DFC; MA; Emeritus Fellow of Magdalene College, Cambridge; Bye Fellow, 1923; Fellow, 1926; President, 1957–62; *b* 17 March 1897; fifth *s* of late Charles Henry Turner, DD, Bishop of Islington, and Edith Emma, *d* of late Bishop McDougall; *m* 1978, Anne Martindale. *Educ:* Marlborough Coll.; Magdalene Coll., Cambridge. Royal Flying Corps, 1916–19 (MC, DFC). *Publication:* The Element of Irony in English Literature, 1926. *Recreation:* Music. *Address:* 1 St Martin's Square, Chichester, West Sussex PO19 1NW. *Club:* United Oxford & Cambridge University.

                                       *Died 18 Jan. 1982*

**TURNER, Harold Goodhew,** CMG 1960; Malayan Civil Service (retired); *b* 23 Dec. 1906; *s* of George Prior Turner and Blanche Winifred Turner; *m* 1934, Aileen Mary Mace; one *s* one *d* (and one *s* decd). *Educ:* St Olave's and St Saviour's Grammar Sch., London; Trinity Coll., Cambridge. Cadet, Malayan CS, 1929; Principal Establishment Officer, 1958; Secretary to the Treasury, 1959. CRO (now FCO) 1962–68; Director of Studies, Royal Institute of Public Administration, 1969–73 (Associate Dir, 1961–62); *Recreation:* gardening. *Address:* 54 Robson Road, Goring-by-Sea, Worthing, West Sussex BN12 4EF. *T:* Worthing 41924. *Club:* Royal Commonwealth Society.

                                       *Died 10 July 1981.*

**TURNER, Harold H.;** *see* Horsfall Turner.

**TURNER, Sir Harvey,** Kt 1967; CBE 1953; *b* 11 Sept. 1889; *s* of Edward and Maude Turner; *m* 1914, Margaret Ethel Penman (*d* 1978); three *s* two *d*. *Educ:* Huia Sch.; Giles Business College; Auckland Technical College. Served War of 1914–18, New Zealand; War of 1939–45 (Middle East, 1941–42; Major; despatches). Past President, Auckland Chamber of Commerce; Past Chairman, Auckland Harbour Board. *Publication:* (with Allan Kirk) Turners of Huia, 1966. *Recreations:* tennis, swimming, gardening. *Address:* PO Box 56, Auckland 1, New Zealand; Summit Drive, Auckland 3, New Zealand. *T:* Auckland 867-572.        *Died 31 Jan. 1983.*

**TURNER, James Grant Smith,** CMG 1949; *b* 7 Aug. 1897; *s* of Hector and Mary Turner; *m* 1st, 1930, Jemima Cunningham (*d* 1937); one *s* one *d*; 2nd, 1947, Freda Gurling (*d* 1970); one *s*; 3rd, 1981, Margaret Spear. *Educ:* Allan Glen's Sch., Glasgow; Glasgow Univ.; Liverpool Univ. MB, ChB, Glasgow, 1924; BSc, DPH, Glasgow, 1926; DTM, Liverpool, 1927. MO, Nigeria, 1927; Senior Health Officer, 1938; transferred to Sierra Leone, 1941; DDMS, Gold Coast, 1945, DMS, 1946–50; retired Jan. 1950. Military service: European War, 1915–18; War of 1939–45, 1940–41. *Recreations:* walking, fishing. *Address:* Belvedere, Legion Lane, Tywardreath, Par, Cornwall PL24 2QR.        *Died 25 Dec. 1985.*

**TURNER, James Neil Frederick,** MA, FCIOB, FCIArb; Managing Director, E. Turner & Sons Ltd, Cardiff, since 1970; *b* 23 June 1932; *s* of Thomas Henry Huxley Turner and Phoebe Elvira (*née* Evans); *m* 1974, Elizabeth Jillian Wells; one *d*. *Educ:* Shrewsbury Sch.;

Christ Church, Oxford (MA). Called to the Bar, Inner Temple, 1957. Holloway Brothers, London, 1957–62; H. R. H. Construction, New York, 1962–63; E. Turner & Sons Ltd, Cardiff, 1963–. *Recreation:* sailing. *Address:* 2 Kymin Terrace, Penarth, South Glamorgan, Wales. *T:* Penarth 701732. *Club:* Cardiff and County (Cardiff)

                                       *Died 3 April 1984.*

**TURNER, Sir Ralph Lilley,** Kt 1950; MC; FBA 1942; MA, LittD, Hon. DLitt, Benares, 1951; Hon DLit: Ceylon, 1958; London, 1967; Santiniketan, 1972; Kathmandu, 1977; Director of the School of Oriental and African Studies, 1937–57 (Hon. Fellow, 1957); Professor of Sanskrit, University of London, 1922–54, Emeritus Professor since 1954; *b* 5 Oct 1888; *s* of George Turner, MA, JP, OBE, Cambridge; *m* 1920, Dorothy Rivers (*d* 1972), *d* of William Howard Goultry, Hale, Cheshire; one *s* three *d*. *Educ:* Perse Grammar Sch. and Christ's Coll., Cambridge (Senior Scholar). Classical Tripos Part I Class I, Div. 3; Oriental Languages Trip. Class I; Class. Trip. Part II Sect. E, Class I with distinction; Brotherton Memorial Sanskrit Prize; Fellow of Christ's Coll., 1912 (Hon. Fellow, 1950); Indian Educational Service, Lectr in Sanskrit at Queen's Coll., Benares, 1913; Wilson Philological Lectr, Bombay Univ., 1914; Indian Army R of O, attached 2/3rd QAO Gurkha Rifles, 1915–19 (despatches twice); Examiner Or. Lang. Trip. and Class. Trip. Part II Cambridge; Prof. of Indian Linguistics, Benares Hindu Univ., 1920; Wilson Philological Lectr, Bombay Univ., 1922; Hon. Treasurer (Pres., 1939–43) Philological Soc.; Pres., 1952–55, Royal Asiatic Soc. (Gold Medallist, 1953, Hon. Vice-Pres., 1963); 7th International Congress of Linguists, 1952; 23rd International Congress of Orientalists, 1954; Hon. Fellow, Deccan Coll., Poona. Formerly Member: Inter-Services Cttee on Language Training; Linguists' Cttee of Min. of Labour and National Service; Colonial Social Science Research Council; Adv. Cttee on the Humanities of the British Council; Adv. Cttee on Education in the Colonies; Treasury sub-cttee for studentships in foreign languages and cultures; sub-cttee University Grants Cttee on Oriental and African Studies; Corr. Member: Czecho-Slovakian Oriental Institute of Prag, Institut de France, Acad. des Inscriptions et Belles Lettres; Hon. Member: Norwegian Acad. of Science and Letters, Ceylon Acad. of Letters, Soc. Asiatique, Paris, American Oriental Soc. Deutsche Morgenländische Gesellschaft, Bihar Research Soc., Bhandarkar Oriental Research Inst., Ceylon Branch of Royal Asiatic Soc., Nagaripracarini Sabha, Banaras, Sanskrit Vishva Parishad, Vishveshvaranand Vedic Research Inst., Ganganatha Jha Research Inst., Linguistic Soc. of America, Linguistic Soc. of India, Ceylon Linguistic Soc., Linguistic Soc. of Nepal, Mark Twain Soc. Campbell Gold Medallist, Asiatic Soc. of Bombay, 1967; Rabindranath Soc. Campbell Gold Medallist, Asiatic Soc. of Bombay, 1967; Rabindranath Tagore Centenary Plaque, Asiatic Soc. of Bengal, 1971. Nepalese Order of Gorkha Dakshina Bahu, 2nd Class, 1951, 1st Class, 1960. *Publications:* Gujarati Phonology; The Position of Romani in Indo-Aryan; A Comparative and Etymological Dictionary of the Nepali Language; The Gavimath and Palkigundu Inscription of Asoka; ed, Indian Studies presented to Professor E. J. Rapson, Indian and Iranian Studies presented to Sir G. A. Grierson; Report to the Nuffield Foundation on a visit to Nigeria; Problems of Sound-change in Indo-Aryan; A Comparative Dictionary of the Indo-aryan Languages; Collected Papers, 1912–73; articles in Encyclopædia Britannica, etc. *Address:* Haverbrack, Barrells Down Road, Bishop's Stortford, Herts CM23 2SU. *T:* 54135.        *Died 22 April 1983.*

**TURNER, Robert Noel,** CMG 1955; retired; *b* 28 Dec. 1912; *s* of late Engr Rear-Adm. A. Turner and late Mrs V. E. Turner; *m* 1946, Evelyn Heynes Dupree (*d* 1976); two *s*. *Educ:* Dover Coll.; Wadham Coll., Oxford (MA). First Class Hons Modern History. Cadet, Malayan Civil Service, 1935; Third Asst Sec. to Govt, FMS, 1936; Asst District Officer, Lower Perak, FMS, 1938; Supernumerary Duty (Lower Perak), 1939; Asst Resident, Brunei, 1940 (interned by Japanese, Borneo, Dec. 1941–Sept. 1945); Asst Sec. to Governor-General, Malaya, May 1946; Prin. Asst Sec., Sarawak, Aug. 1946; First Asst Malayan Establishment Officer, 1948; Acting Dep. Malayan Establishment Officer, April 1950; Chief Sec., Barbados, 1950–56 (title changed from Colonial Sec., 1954); Acting Governor, Barbados, Nov. 1952–May 1953 and 1955, North Borneo, 1957–62 (commended by Sec. of State 'Hurricane Janet', 1955); Chief Sec., North Borneo, 1956–63 (Mem. Exec. Council and Legislative Council, 1950–63); State Sec., Sabah, Fedn of Malaysia, 1963–64 (Mem. State Cabinet, 1963–64). Hon. Mem., First Grade, Order of Kinabalu, Sabah (title: Datuk; lettering: SPDK), 1963. *Recreations:* reading history, watching cricket. *Address:* Kinabalu, The Rise, Brockenhurst, Hants SO42 7SJ. *T:* Lymington 23197.

                                       *Died 18 Jan. 1987.*

**TURNER, Theodore Francis,** QC 1943; Barrister-at-law; *b* 19 Nov. 1900; *s* of George Lewis and Mabel Mary Turner; *m* 1st, 1925, Elizabeth Alice (*d* 1983), *o d* of 1st Baron Schuster, GCB, CVO, QC; two *s* one *d*; 2nd, 1949, Ruth, 2nd *d* of late L. C. Ledyard, Jr, and late Mrs W. E. S. Griswold, NY. *Educ:* Downside; Balliol Coll., Oxford (Exhibitioner). Called to Bar, 1924; joined South Eastern

Circuit. Regional Controller, Ministry of Fuel and Power, North Midland Region, 1944–45; Recorder of Rochester, 1946–50; Chairman Mining Subsidence Cttee, 1947–48. Admitted New York Bar, 1962. *Address:* PO Box 303, East Norwich, Long Island, NY 11732, USA; 570 Park Avenue, New York City, NY 10021, USA. *Club:* The Brook (NY). *Died 19 May 1986.*

**TURNER, Lt-Gen. Sir William (Francis Robert),** KBE 1962; CB 1959; DSO 1945; Lord-Lieutenant of Dumfries, 1972–82; *b* 12 Dec. 1907; *er s* of late Mr and Mrs F. R. Turner, Kelso, Roxburghshire; *m* 1938, Nancy Maude Stilwell, *er d* of late Lt-Col and Mrs J. B. L. Stilwell, Yateley, Hants; one *s. Educ:* Winchester College; RMC Sandhurst. 2nd Lieut, KOSB, 1928; served in Great Britain and India, 1928–39; Capt. 1938; BEF, 1939–40; Staff College, 1941; OC, 5 KOSB, 1942–45 (despatches), NW Europe; OC, 1 KOSB, 1945–46, NW Europe and Middle East; GSO1, Middle East and Great Britain, 1947–50. Colonel Brit. Military Mission to Greece, 1950–52; Comd 128 Inf. Bde (TA), 1952–54; BGS HQ Western Comd, 1954–56; GOC 44 (Home Counties) Infantry Div. (TA) and Home Counties District, and Deputy Constable of Dover Castle, 1956–59; President, Regular Commissions Board, 1959–61; GOC-in-C, Scottish Comd, and Governor of Edinburgh Castle, 1961–64; retd 1964; Colonel, King's Own Scottish Borderers, 1961–70; Brigadier, 1965–82, Ensign, 1982–85, Queen's Body Guard for Scotland (Royal Company of Archers), retd. HM Comr, Queen Victoria School, Dunblane, 1965–85. DL, Dumfriesshire, 1970–72. Comdr with Star, Order of Saint Olav, Class II (Norway), 1962; Order of the Two Niles, Class II (Republic of the Sudan), 1963. *Address:* Milnhead, Kirkton, Dumfries. *T:* Dumfries 710319. *Clubs:* Naval and Military; New (Edinburgh). *Died 31 Aug. 1989.*

**TUTE, Warren Stanley;** author; *b* 22 Feb. 1914; *s* of Stanley Harries Tute and Laura Edith Thompson; *m* 1st, 1944, Annette Elizabeth Neil (marr. diss. 1955); 2nd, 1958, Evelyn Mary Dalley; two *d. Educ:* Dragon Sch., Wrekin Coll. Entered RN 1932, served in HM Ships Nelson and Ajax; took part in N African, Sicilian and Normandy landings (despatches 1944), retired as Lt Comdr, 1946. Wrote for BBC, 1946–47; Dir, Random Film Productions Ltd, 1947–52; made films and trained scriptwriters for US Govt, 1952–54; Argentina, 1955; Dir, Theatrework (London) Ltd, 1960–81; produced (jtly) Little Mary Sunshine, Comedy, 1962; Head of Scripts, London Weekend TV, 1968–69; Liaison Officer, Capital Radio—Operation Drake, 1978–81; Trustee, The Venture Trust, 1983– (Dir, 1982–83). Archivist, Worshipful Co. of Cordwainers, 1976–84. *Publications: novels:* The Felthams, 1950; Lady in Thin Armour, 1951; Gentleman in Pink Uniform, 1952; The Younger Felthams, 1953; Girl in the Limelight, 1954; The Cruiser, 1955; The Rock, 1957; Leviathan, 1959; The Golden Greek, 1960; The Admiral, 1963; A Matter of Diplomacy, 1969; The Powder Train, 1970; The Tarnham Connection, 1971; The Resident, 1973; Next Saturday in Milan, 1975; Honours of War and Peace, 1976; The Cairo Sleeper, 1977; *history:* The Grey Top Hat, 1961; Atlantic Conquest, 1962; Cochrane, 1965; Escape Route Green, 1971; The Deadly Stroke, 1973; Hitler—The Last Ten Days, 1973; D Day, 1974; The North African War, 1976; The True Glory: the story of the Royal Navy over a thousand years, 1983; *plays:* Jessica, 1956; A Time to be Born, 1956; Frost at Midnight (trans.), 1957; Quartet for Five, 1958; A Few Days in Greece, 1959; *other works:* Chico, 1950; Life of a Circus Bear, 1952; Cockney Cats, 1953; Le Petomane (trans.), 1967; (contrib.) The Commanding Sea, 1981 (originator of BBC TV series); *posthumous publication:* The Reluctant Enemies, 1990. *Recreations:* people, cats, wine, France. *Address:* c/o Finaccounting Services SA, 40 Rue du Rhône, 1204 Geneva, Switzerland; Bardigues, 82340 Auvillar, France. *T:* 63.39.60.30. *Clubs:* Garrick, Whitefriars (Past Chm.). *Died 26 Nov. 1989.*

**TUTIN, Prof. Thomas Gaskell,** FRS 1982; Professor of Taxonomy, University of Leicester, 1967–73, now Emeritus; University Fellow, University of Leicester, 1974; *b* 21 April 1908; *o s* of Frank and Jane Tutin; *m* 1942, Winifred Anne Pennington, PhD, FRS; one *s* three *d. Educ:* Cotham Sch., Bristol; Downing Coll., Cambridge (schol.). Expedition to British Guiana, 1933; Marine Laboratory, Plymouth, 1934–37; expedition to Lake Titicaca, 1937; part-time Demonstrator, KCL, 1938–39; Asst Lectr, Univ. of Manchester, 1939–42; Geographer, Naval Intelligence Div., 1942–44; Lectr, Univ. College of Leicester, 1944–47; Prof. of Botany, Univ. of Leicester, 1947–67. Pres., Botanical Soc. of British Isles, 1957–61. Foreign Member, Societas Scientiarum Fennica (Section for Natural Science), 1960. Linnean Medal, Linnean Soc., 1977. Hon. ScD Dublin, 1979. *Publications:* (with Clapham and Warburg) Flora of the British Isles, 1952, 3rd edn 1987; (with Clapham and Warburg) Excursion Flora of the British Isles, 1959, 3rd edn 1980; (with V. H. Heywood *et al*) Flora Europaea, Vol. I 1964, Vol. II 1968, Vol. III 1972, Vol. IV 1976, Vol. V 1979; (with A. C. Jermy) British Sedges, 1968; Umbellifers of the British Isles, 1980; papers in Annals of Botany, New Phytologist, Jl of Ecology, Watsonia, etc. *Recreations:* botany, music. *Address:* Home Farm, Knighton, Leicester LE2 3WG. *T:* Leicester 707356. *Died 7 Oct. 1987.*

**TUTTLE, Sir Geoffrey (William),** KBE 1957 (OBE 1940); CB 1945; DFC 1937; FRAeS 1960; Air Marshal retired; *b* 2 Oct. 1906; *s* of late Maj. E. W. Tuttle, Lowestoft. *Educ:* St Paul's School. Joined RAF, 1925; served war, 1939–45: France, Photo Reconnaissance Units, UK, Tunisia, Corsica, Sardinia, Italy, Greece; AOC RAF, Greece, 1944–46; Air Cdre 1948; Dir of Operational Requirements, Air Min., 1948–49; AOA, HQ Coastal Comd, 1950–51; Air Vice-Marshal 1952; ACAS (Operational Requirements), 1951–54; AOC No 19 Gp, RAF, 1954–56; Air Marshal 1957; DCAS, 1956–59, retd. British Aircraft Corp. Ltd, 1960–77; Aerospace Consultant, 1977–81. Order of Patriotic War, 2nd Class (Soviet), 1944; Grand Officer Royal Order of the Phœnix (Greece), 1945; Commandeur Légion d'Honneur (France); Croix de Guerre (France). *Recreation:* sailing. *Address:* 73 Numa Court, Justin Close, Brentford TW8 8QF. *T:* 01–568 1084. *Club:* Royal Air Force. *Died 11 Jan. 1989.*

**TWEDDLE, Sir William,** Kt 1977; CBE 1971 (OBE 1945); TD 1950; Chairman, Yorkshire Regional Health Authority, since 1973; *b* 28 June 1914; *s* of late John Rippon Tweddle, and late Elizabeth Tweddle, Easingwold, Yorks; *m* 1941, Sheila Vartan; one *s* one *d. Educ:* Repton Sch.; Leeds Univ. (LLM). Solicitor, 1936. Asst Solicitor, 1936–39, Partner, 1940–81, Simpson, Curtis & Co., Solicitors, Leeds. War Service, RA, TA, 1939–45: served overseas in France, 1940; Madagascar, 1942; NW Europe, 1944–45 (despatches twice, twice); psc, 1943; Lt-Col., 1944. Chm., Leeds St James's Univ. (formerly Leeds A) HMC, 1957–74; Governor, United Leeds Hospitals, 1959–74; Member: Leeds Regional Hospital Bd, 1961–74; Central Health Services Council, 1974–80 (Chm. 1976–80); Court and Council, Leeds Univ., 1970– (Pro-Chancellor, 1981–); Chm., NHS Staff Cttee for Accommodation, Catering and other Support Services, 1975–; Governor: Pocklington Sch., 1950– (Chm., 1963–); Leeds Musical Festival, 1957– (Chm., 1972–78); Pres., Leeds Laws Soc., 1967–68; Warden, Leeds Parish Church, 1950–. Dir, Leeds Permanent Building Soc. (Pres., 1969–73). *Recreations:* gardening, travel. *Address:* 3 The Drive, Roundhay, Leeds LS8 1JF. *T:* 662950. *Clubs:* Leeds (Leeds). *Died 23 Oct. 1982.*

**TWINING, Gen. Nathan Farragut,** DSM (with two Oak Leaf Clusters), Navy DSM, Legion of Merit (with Oak Leaf Cluster), DFC; US Air Force (Retired); *b* Monroe, Wis., 11 October 1897; *s* of Clarence Walker Twining and Maize Barber; *m* 1932, Maude McKeever; two *s* one *d.* US Mil. Acad., 1918; student Inf. Sch., 1919–20, Air Corps Tactical Sch., 1935–36; Command and Gen. Staff Sch., 1936–37; rated command pilot. Served in Ore. Nat. Guard, 1916–17; comd 2nd Lt, Inf., Nov. 1918; transferred Air Corps, 1924, promoted through grades to Lt-Gen., 1945; Gen., USAF, 1950. Chief of Staff to Comdg Gen., USAFISPA, 1942–43; Comdg Gen., 13th Air Force, Solomon Is, 1943; 15th Air Force, Italy, and Mediterranean Allied Strategic Air Forces, 1943; 20th Air Force, Pacific 1945; Air Materiel Command, Wright Field, Ohio, 1945–47; C-in-C Alaska, 1947–50; Vice-Chief of Staff, Air Force, 1950–53; Chief of Staff, Air Force, 1953–57; Chairman, Joint Chiefs of Staff, 1957–60. Numerous medals (US) and foreign decorations including Hon. KBE (Gt Brit.). *Recreations:* hunting, fishing, golf, carpentry. *Address:* 16 North Live Oak Road, Hilton Head Island, South Carolina 29928, USA. *Died 29 March 1982.*

**TWISLETON-WYKEHAM-FIENNES, Gerard Francis Gisborne,** OBE 1957; MA; *b* 7 June 1906; *s* of Gerard Yorke Twisleton-Wykeham-Fiennes, CBE, and Gwendolen; *m* 1st, 1934, Norah Davies (*d* 1960), Penymaes, Llangollen; three *s* two *d*; 2nd, 1962, Jean Kerridge. *Educ:* Horris Hill, Newbury; Winchester Coll.; Hertford Coll., Oxford. LNER 1928. Asst Yardmaster, Whitemoor, 1932; Chief Controller, Cambridge, 1934; appts at York, Liverpool Street, Edinburgh and Shenfield; District Supt; Nottingham, 1943; Stratford, 1944; Operating Supt, Eastern Region, 1956; Line Traffic Manager, King's Cross, 1957; Chief Operating Officer, BR, 1961; Chm., Western Railway Board, 1963; Lt-Col Railway Staff and Engrg Corps, 1963; Chm., Eastern Railway Board, and Gen. Manager, Eastern Region, British Railways, 1965–67. Dir, Hargreaves Gp, 1968–76. Broadcasts on radio and TV. FRSA 1966; FCIT (MInstT 1955). OStJ 1967. Mayor of Aldeburgh, 1976. *Publications:* I Tried to Run a Railway, 1967; various chapters and articles in railway technical press. *Recreations:* golf, sailing, fishing, railways. *Address:* Dartmouth, Crabbe Street, Aldeburgh, Suffolk IP15 5BN. *T:* 2457. *Club:* MCC. *Died 25 May 1985.*

**TYERMAN, Donald,** CBE 1978; journalist; Editor of The Economist, 1956–65; Director, United City Merchants, 1965–80; *b* 1 March 1908; *s* of late Joseph and late Catherine Tyerman, Middlesbrough, Yorks; *m* 1934, Margaret Charteris Gray; two *s* three *d. Educ:* Friends' School, Great Ayton; St Mary's College, Middlesbrough; Coatham Grammar Sch., Redcar; Gateshead Secondary Sch.; Gateshead-on-Tyne; Brasenose College, Oxford. Lectr, University College, Southampton, 1930–36; Assistant and then Deputy Editor, The Economist, 1937–44; Deputy Editor, The Observer, 1943–44; Asst Editor, The Times, 1944–55. Chairman: Exec. Bd of

International Press Inst., 1961–62; Press Freedom Cttee, CPU, 1971–75; Astor Award, CPU, 1979. Member: Press Council, 1963–69; Council, Overseas Development Inst.; Council, NIESR; Council, Univ. of Sussex, 1963–75. Governor, LSE, 1951–75; Vice-Pres. and Hon. Associate of Council, Save the Children Fund (Treasurer, 1967–75); Life Vice-Pres., Ingatestone Cricket Club. *Recreations:* reading and watching games. *Address:* 41 Buckingham Mansions, West End Lane, NW6. *T:* 01-435 1030; Holly Cottage, Westleton, near Saxmundham, Suffolk. *T:* Saxmundham 73-261. *Club:* Reform. *Died 24 April* 1981.

**TYLECOTE, Dame Mabel,** DBE 1966; Hon. Life Member of National Federation of Community Associations since 1979 (President, 1958–61; Vice-President, 1961–79); *b* 4 Feb. 1896; *d* of late John Ernest Phythian and Ada Prichard Phythian (*née* Crompton); *m* 1932, Frank Edward Tylecote (*d* 1965); one *s* (and one step *s* one step *d*). *Educ:* Univ. of Manchester; Univ. of Wisconsin (USA). BA, PhD (Manchester). Lectr in History, Huddersfield Techn. Coll., 1920–24; Asst Lectr in History, Univ. of Manchester, 1926–30; Warden of Elvington Settlement, 1930–32; part-time Lectr, Univ. of Manchester Joint Cttee for Adult Educn, 1935–51; Vice-Pres., WEA, 1960–68. Member: Pensions Appeal Tribunal, 1944–50; Manchester City Council, 1940–51; (co-opted) Manchester Educn Cttee, 1951–77; Stockport Borough Council, 1956–63; Chm. of Council, Assoc. of Art Instns, 1960–61. Mem. Court, 1945–80, Mem. Council, 1960–75, Univ. of Manchester; Mem. Court, UMIST, 1960–77; Governor, Manchester Polytechnic, 1969–77 (Hon. Fellow, 1973); Vice-President: Manchester and Salford Council of Social Service, 1968–; Union of Lancashire and Cheshire Institutes, 1969–75; Hon. Life Mem., Nat. Inst. of Adult Educn, 1974– (Chm., 1960–63). Contested (Lab): Fylde, 1938; Middleton and Prestwich, 1945; Norwich South, 1950, 1951, 1955. Hon. LLD Manchester, 1978. *Publications:* The Education of Women at Manchester University 1883–1933, 1941; The Mechanics' Institutes of Lancashire and Yorkshire before 1851, 1957; The Future of Adult Education (Fabian pamphlet), 1960; contrib., Artisan to Graduate, ed D. S. L. Cardwell, 1974; The Work of Lady Simon of Wythenshawe for Education in Manchester (address), 1974; articles in various social and educnl jls. *Address:* Alexandra House, 359 Wilbraham Road, Manchester M16 8NP. *T:* 061–860 5400.
*Died 31 Jan.* 1987.

**TYLER, (George Charles) Froom,** OBE 1969; *b* 30 Jan. 1904; *o s* of John Frederick Tyler, Bristol; *m* 1st, 1928, Doris May (*née* Chubb) (*d* 1963); one *d*; 2nd, Diana Griffiths (*née* Kirby) (*d* 1971). Editor of the Evening World, Bristol, 1936–40; Foreign Editor, Daily Mail, 1940–43; Staff Officer (Press) to Admiral (Submarines), 1943–45. Editor of Overseas Daily Mail, 1946–50; Editor of Leicester Evening Mail, 1950–57; Editor of South Wales Evening Post, 1957–69; Chm., Swansea Festival of Music and the Arts, 1970–82. Hon. MA Wales, 1980. *Publications:* Cripps: A Portrait and a Prospect, 1942; His Majesty's Submarines (the Admiralty Account), 1945; News in Our Time (Daily Mail Jubilee Book), 1946; The Man Who Made Music, 1947. *Address:* 50 Harford Court, The Bryn, Sketty Green, Swansea.                                                         *Died* 22 *Nov.* 1983.

**TYMMS, Sir Frederick,** KCIE 1947 (CIE 1935); Kt 1941; MC; FRAeS; *b* 4 Aug. 1889; *s* of William Henry Tymms; *m* 1913, Matilda Sarah, (Millie) (*d* 1974). *Educ:* Tenby; King's College, London. War Service: 4th Bn South Lancs Regt and Royal Flying Corps, France; British Aviation Mission to the USA, 1915–18 (MC, Chevalier de l'Ordre de la Couronne, Croix de Guerre, Belgium). Civil Aviation Dept, Air Min., 1920–27; Oxford Univ. Arctic Expedition to Spitsbergen, 1924; Air Min. Supt of Egypt-India air route, 1927; seconded to Govts of the Sudan, Kenya, Uganda and Tanganyika, 1928; Chief Technical Asst to Dir of Civil Aviation, Air Min., 1928–31; Air Min. Representative on the Commn to Africa, to organise the Cape to Cairo air route, 1929–30; Dir of Civil Aviation in India, 1931–42 and 1943–45; Man. Dir, Tata Aircraft Ltd, Bombay, 1942–43; Dir-Gen. of Civil Aviation in India, Sept. 1945–March 1947; UK Representative on Council of Internat. Civil Aviation Organisation, Montreal, 1947–54; retd from Civil Service, 1955. Govt of India delegate to Internat. Civil Aviation Conf., Chicago, 1944; Leader of UK Civil Aviation Mission to New Zealand, 1948. Master of Guild of Air Pilots and Air Navigators, 1957–58. Chm., Commn of Enquiry on Civil Aviation in West Indies, 1960. *Address:* Clare Park, Crondall, near Farnham, Surrey; c/o Lloyds Bank, Pall Mall, SW1. *Club:* Naval and Military.
*Died* 9 *Dec.* 1987.

**TYMMS, Prof. Ralph Vincent,** MA; Professor of German Language and Literature in the University of London (Royal Holloway College), 1956–80, then Emeritus; Head of German Department 1948–80, Vice-Principal 1969–75, Royal Holloway College; *b* 9 Jan. 1913; *s* of Arthur Hugh Tymms and Janet Scott Coventon; *m* 1980, Dr Marion Gibbs. *Educ:* Bradford Grammar Sch., Yorkshire; Magdalen Coll., Oxford; Univs of Vienna and Giessen. John Doncaster Scholar in German, Magdalen Coll., Oxford, 1931–34; 1st Class Hons, Oxford, 1934. Asst Lectr in German, Univ. of Manchester, 1936. Intelligence Corps, 1941–45; Major, 1945. Lecturer in German, Manchester Univ., 1945; Reader in German Language and Literature in Univ. of London, 1948. *Publications:* Doubles in Literary Psychology, 1949; German Romantic Literature, 1955. *Address:* Merrow Down, Northcroft Road, Englefield Green, Egham, Surrey TW20 0DU. *T:* Egham 32125.
*Died* 21 *Aug.* 1987.

# U

**UBBELOHDE, Prof. (Alfred Rene John) Paul,** CBE 1963; MA, DSc Oxon; FRS 1951; FRSC; FInstP; FEng; FIChemE; Hon. Laureate, Padua University, 1963; Senior Research Fellow, since 1975, Fellow, since 1981, Imperial College of Science and Technology; Professor of Thermodynamics, University of London (Imperial College), 1954–75, later Emeritus, and Head of Department of Chemical Engineering and Chemical Technology, 1961–75; *b* 14 Dec. 1907; 3rd *s* of F. C. Ubbelohde and Angele Verspreeuwen; unmarried. *Educ:* St Paul's Sch.; Christ Church, Oxford (Hon. Student, 1979). Dewar Fellow of Royal Instn, 1935–40; research on explosives; Min. of Supply, 1940–45; Prof. of Chemistry, Queen's Univ., Belfast, 1945–54, Dean of the Faculty of Science, 1947–51. Chairman Fire Research Board, 1956–61; President of Council Institut Solvay, 1957–64, 1965–; Director of Salters' Institute, 1959–75; Past President, Faraday Society, 1963–; Past Vice-President, Society of Chemical Industry; Chairman, Science and Engineering Panel, British Council, 1964; Member: Agricl Research Council, 1966–76; Pontifical Academy of Sciences, 1968–. Hon. FCGI. Dr *hc* Faculty of Science, Univ. Libre, Brussels, 1962; Hon. DSc: QUB, 1972; Nancy Univ., 1982. Alfred Egerton Medal, 1970; Messel Medal, 1972; George Skakel Award, 1975; Paul Lebeau Medal, 1975. *Publications:* Modern Thermodynamical Principles, 1937 (2nd edn 1952); Time and Thermodynamics, 1947; Man and Energy, 1954, 2nd edn 1963; Graphite and its crystal compounds, 1960; Melting and Crystal Structure, 1965; The Molten State of Matter, 1978; papers in Proceedings and Journals of scientific societies. *Address:* Imperial College, South Kensington, SW7; Platts Farm, Burwash, Sussex. *Clubs:* Athenæum, Royal Automobile.
*Died 7 Jan. 1988.*

**ULLMANN, Walter,** MA, LittD; FBA 1968; Professor of Medieval History, University of Cambridge, 1972–78, later Emeritus Professor; Fellow of Trinity College, Cambridge, since 1959; *b* 29 Nov. 1910; *m* 1940, Mary Elizabeth Finnemore Knapp; two *s.* *Educ:* Universities of Vienna, Innsbruck (JUD), and Munich. Research at Cambridge University; Assistant Lecturer, University of Vienna, 1935–38. War service, 1940–43. History and Modern Languages Master, Rátcliffe Coll., Leicester, 1943–47; part-time Lecturer, Pol. Int. Dept, Foreign Office, 1944–46; Lecturer in Medieval History, University of Leeds, 1947–49; Maitland Mem. Lectr, Univ. of Cambridge, 1947–48; Univ. Lectr in Medieval History, Cambridge, 1949–57, Reader, 1957–65, Prof. of Medieval Ecclesiastical Hist., 1965–72. Co-Editor Ephemerides Juris Canonici, 1951–64, Päpste & Papsttum, 1970–; Editor, Cambridge Studies in Medieval Life and Thought, 1968–. Prof. of Humanities, Johns Hopkins Univ., 1964–65; Vis. Prof., Univs of Tübingen and Munich, 1973. Birkbeck Lectr, Cambridge, 1968–69. Hon. Fellow, St Edmund's House, Cambridge, 1976. Hon. Dr *rerum politicarum* and Jubilee Medal for distinguished services, Univ. of Innsbruck, 1970. Corresponding Member: Bayersiche Akademie der Wissenschaften; Osterreichische Akad. d. Wissenschaften. *Publications:* The Medieval Idea of Law, 1946, repr. 1969, 1972; The Origins of the Great Schism, 1948, repr. 1972 with new introd.; Medieval Papalism, 1949; The Growth of Papal Government in the Middle Ages, 1955 (rev. edn German: Die Machtstellung d. Papsttums im Mittelalter, 1960), 4th edn 1970; The Medieval Papacy, St Thomas and beyond (Aquinas lecture, 1958), 1960; Liber regie capelle, 1961; Principles of Government and Politics in the Middle Ages, 1961, 4th edn 1978 (trans. into Spanish and Italian); Hist. Introd. to Lea's Inquisition, 1963; A History of Political Thought in The Middle Ages, 1965, rev. edn 1970; The Relevance of Medieval Ecclesiastical History (inaug. lecture, 1966) (trans. into Japanese); Papst und König, 1966; The Individual and Society in the Middle Ages, 1967 (trans. into Japanese, German and Italian); The Carolingian Renaissance and the Idea of Kingship, 1969; A Short History of the Papacy in the Middle Ages, 1972, 2nd edn 1974, repr. 1977 (trans. into Italian and German); The Future of Medieval History, 1973; Law and Politics in the Middle Ages, 1975; The Church and the Law in the Earlier Middle Ages (Collected Studies I), 1975; The Papacy and Political Ideas in the Middle Ages (Collected Studies II), 1976; Medieval Foundations of Renaissance Humanism, 1977 (Italian edn 1980); Scholarship and Politics in the Middle Ages (Collected Studies III), 1978; Jurisprudence in the Middle Ages (Collected Studies IV), 1980; Gelasius I: das Papsttum an der Wende der Spätantike zum Mittelalter, 1981; Medieval Monarchy (Sewanee Lectures), 1982; contributed to English Historical Review, Jl of Ecclesiastical History, Jl of Theol Studies, Cambridge Hist. Jl, Law Quarterly Review, Trans. Royal Hist. Society, Studi Gregoriani, Studia Gratiana, Studi Federiciani, Studi Accursio, Misc. Hist. Pont., Rev. Bénédictine, Rev. hist. droit, Europa e il Diritto Romano, Arch. storico Pugliese, Savigny Z., Studia Patristica, Bartolo da Sassoferrato: studi e documenti, Acta Iuridica, Settimana studio Spoleto, Annali storia amministrativa, Recueils Soc. Bodin, Speculum Historiale, Historische Zeitschrift, Studies in Church History, Virginia Jl of Internat. Law, Hist.

Jahrbuch, Annali di storia del diritto, Römische Hist. Mitteil, Wege der Forschung. *Recreations:* music and travelling. *Address:* Trinity College, Cambridge CB2 1TQ.
*Died 18 Jan. 1983.*

**UMFREVILLE, William Henry,** CBE 1959; ISO 1951; retired as Accountant and Comptroller-General, Board of Inland Revenue (1954–58); *b* 7 June 1893; *e s* of William Henry Umfreville; *m* 1916, Daisy Catherine Colson; two *d. Educ:* Palmer's School. Post Office, 1909–12; Ministry of Agriculture and Fisheries, 1913–23; Inland Revenue, 1924–58, retired. *Address:* 28 Frobisher Way, Worthing, West Sussex.
*Died 20 Dec. 1984.*

**UNDERHILL, Michael Thomas Ben,** QC 1972; His Honour Judge Underhill; a Circuit Judge, since 1978; *b* 10 Feb. 1918; *s* of late Rev. P. C. Underhill and Viola Underhill; *m* 1950, Rosalie Jean Kinloch; three *s. Educ:* Radley Coll.; Brasenose Coll., Oxford (MA). Served Glos Regt, 1939–42; 2nd KEO Goorkha Rifles, 1942–46 (Major). Called to the Bar, Gray's Inn, 1947; Master of the Bench, Gray's Inn, 1978; Oxford Circuit; Dep. Chm., Salop QS, 1967–71; Recorder of Reading, later a Recorder of the Crown Court, 1970–78. *Address:* 6 Ormond Road, Richmond, Surrey TW10 6TH. *Club:* Leander (Henley-on-Thames).
*Died 12 Sept. 1987.*

**UNSTEAD, Robert John;** author; *b* 21 Nov. 1915; *s* of Charles and Elizabeth Unstead; *m* 1939, Florence Margaret Thomas; three *d. Educ:* Dover Grammar Sch.; Goldsmiths' Coll., London. Schoolmaster, 1936–40. Served in RAF, 1940–46; Sector Controller, Comb. Ops, Normandy, Germany, Italy. Headmaster, Norton Road CP Sch., Letchworth, 1947–51, Grange Sch., Letchworth, 1951–57. Member, Herts Education Cttee, 1951–57; Chairman, Letchworth Primary Schools' Cttee of Management, 1960–64; Governor, Leiston Middle School, 1973–85. Chm., Educational Writers' Group, Soc. of Authors, 1965–68; Mem. Council, East Anglian Writers, 1976–. *Publications:* Looking at History, 1953; People in History, 1955; Teaching History, 1956; Travel by Road, 1958; Houses, 1958; Looking at Ancient History, 1959; Monasteries, 1961; Black's Children's Encyclopædia (co-author), 1961; Some Kings and Queens, 1962; A History of Britain, 1963; Royal Adventurers, 1964; Early Times, 1964; Men and Women in History, 1965; Britain in the Twentieth Century, 1966; The Story of Britain, 1969; Homes in Australia, 1969; Castles, 1970; Transport in Australia, 1970; Pioneer Homelife in Australia, 1971; History of the English-speaking World, 1972; Look and Find Out, 1972; The Twenties, 1973; The Thirties, 1974; Living in Aztec Times, 1974; Living in Samuel Pepys' London, 1975; A Dictionary of History, 1976; Living in Ancient Egypt, 1977; Living in Pompeii, 1977; See Inside a Castle, 1977; See Inside an Egyptian Town, 1977; R. J. Unstead's Book of Kings and Queens, 1978; Greece and Rome, 1978; Egypt and Mesopotamia, 1978; The Assyrians, 1980; The Egyptians, 1980; How They Lived in Cities Long Ago, 1980; A History of the World, 1983; general editor, Black's Junior Reference series, Looking at Geography, See Inside series; (contrib.) Encyclopedia Americana. *Recreations:* golf, gardening, watching cricket. *Address:* Reedlands, Thorpeness, Suffolk. *T:* Aldeburgh 2665. *Clubs:* MCC; Aldeburgh Golf, Thorpeness Golf.
*Died 5 May 1988.*

**UNWIN, Sir Keith,** KBE 1964 (OBE 1937); CMG 1954; MA; *b* 3 Aug. 1909; *er s* of late Edwin Ernest Unwin and Jessie Magdalen Black; *m* 1935, Linda Giersé; one *s* two *d. Educ:* Merchant Taylors' Sch.; Lycée Condorcet, Paris; St John's Coll., Oxford; BA 1931, MA 1968. Department of Overseas Trade, 1932; Mem., Commercial Diplomatic Service, later HM Diplomatic Service, 1934–69; Madrid, 1934; Istanbul, 1937; San Sebastian (later Madrid), 1939; Mexico City, 1944; Paris, 1946; Prague, 1949; Buenos Aires, 1950; Rome, 1955–59; Foreign Service Inspector, 1959–62; UK Representative on Economic and Social Council of the United Nations, 1962–66; HM Ambassador to Uruguay, 1966–69. UK Mem., UN Commn on Human Rights, 1970–78. *Recreations:* gardening, reading. *Address:* Great Kingley, Dodington Lane, Chipping Sodbury, Bristol. *T:* Chipping Sodbury 310913.
*Died 18 March 1990.*

**UNWIN, Nora Spicer,** RE 1946 (ARE 1935); ARCA; artist, painter, print-maker, book-illustrator; *b* 22 Feb. 1907; *d* of George Soundy and Eleanor Mary Unwin. *Educ:* Surbiton High Sch. Studied at Leon Underwood's; Kingston School of Art; Royal College of Art, 1928–32; Diploma in Design, 1931; wood-engravings exhibited at Royal Academy; other galleries and international exhibitions in Europe and N and S America; Near and Far East; works purchased by Contemporary Art Society for British Museum; by Boston Public Library; by Library of Congress, Washington, DC; by Fitchburg Art Museum (Mass.); by New York Public Library for permanent collection; also represented in Metropolitan Museum, NY. One-man exhibitions held in Boston and cities in Eastern US, 1948–50, 1954–56, 1957, 1960, 1964, 1965, 1966, 1967, 1969, 1974, 1975. Exhibition Member: Royal Soc. Painter-Etchers and Engravers; Soc. of Wood-engravers; American Nat. Acad. (ANA 1954, NA 1976); Boston Print Makers; Print Club of Albany; Soc. of American Graphic Artists; NH Art Assoc.; Boston Watercolour Soc.;

Cambridge Art Assoc. (CAA), etc. Awards: Soc. of American Graphic Artists, 1951; Boston Independent Artists, 1952; NHAA, 1952, 1975; NAWA, 1953; National Academy Design, 1958; Fitchburg Art Museum, 1965, 1973; BSWCP, 1965; Boston Printmakers Purchase, 1973. CAA 1967. *Publications:* author-illustrator of: Round the Year, 1939; Lucy and the Little Red Horse, 1942; Doughnuts for Lin, 1950; Proud Pumpkin, 1953; Poquito, the Little Mexican Duck, 1959; Two Too Many, 1962; The Way of the Shepherd, 1963; Joyful the Morning, 1963; The Midsummer Witch, 1966; Sinbad the Cygnet, 1970; The Chickerdees Come (poems), 1977; numerous books illustrated for English and American publishers. *Recreations:* music, swimming, walking, gardening, etc. *Address:* Pine-Apple Cottage, Old Street Road, Peterborough, NH 03458, USA. *Died 5 Jan. 1982.*

**UREN, Reginald Harold,** FRIBA; private practice of architecture, 1933–68; *b* New Zealand, 5 March 1906; *s* of Richard Ellis and Christina Uren; *m* 1930, Dorothy Marion Morgan; one *d. Educ:* Hutt Valley High School, New Zealand; London University. Qualified as Architect in New Zealand, 1929; ARIBA, London, 1931; won open architectural competition for Hornsey Town Hall (281 entries), 1933; joined in partnership with J. Alan Slater and A. H. Moberly, 1936; architectural practice includes public buildings, department stores, domestic, commercial and school buildings. Works include: John Lewis Store, Oxford Street; Arthur Sanderson & Sons Building, Berners Street; Norfolk County Hall. Freeman of City of London, 1938; Master, Tylers and Bricklayers Company, 1966. War service, 1942–46, Capt. Royal Engineers. Council, RIBA, 1946–65; London Architecture Bronze Medal, 1935; Tylers and Bricklayers Company Gold Medal, 1936; Min. of Housing and Local Govt Medal for London Region, 1954; New Zealand Inst. of Architects Award of Merit, 1965. *Recreation:* debate. *Address:* PO Box 9039, Newmarket, Auckland, New Zealand. *Club:* Reform. *Died 17 Feb. 1988.*

**UREY, Harold Clayton;** Emeritus Professor of Chemistry, University of California, La Jolla, California, since 1958; Eastman Professor, Oxford University, 1956–June 1957; Foreign Member of the Royal Society, 1947; *b* 29 April 1893, *s* of Samuel Clayton Urey and Cora Rebecca Reinoehl; *m* 1926, Frieda Daum; one *s* three *d. Educ:* University of Montana (BS); Univ. of California (PhD); American Scandinavian Foundation Fellow to Denmark, 1923–24. Research Chemist, Barrett Chemical Co., 1918–19; Instructor in Chemistry, University of Montana, 1919–21; Associate in Chemistry, Johns Hopkins University, 1924–29; Associate Professor of Chemistry, Columbia University, 1929–34; Professor of Chemistry, 1934–45; Distinguished Service Prof. of Chem., Univ. of Chicago, 1945–52; Martin A. Ryerson Distinguished Service Professor of Chemistry, University of Chicago, Chicago, Illinois, 1952–58; Executive Officer, Department of Chem., Columbia, 1939–42; Dir of War Research Atomic Bomb Project, Columbia, 1940–45. Editor, Jl of Chemical Physics, 1933–40; Board of Directors, Amer.-Scandinavian Foundation; Mem., many scientific and other learned socs; ARAS, 1960. Willard Gibbs Medal, 1934; Nobel Prize in Chemistry, 1934; Davy Medal, Royal Society of London, 1940; Franklin Medal, Franklin Inst., 1943; Medal for Merit, 1946; Cordoza Award, 1954; Honor Scroll, Amer. Inst. Chemists, 1954; Joseph Priestley Award, Dickinson Coll., 1955; Alexander Hamilton Award, Columbia Univ., 1961; J. Lawrence Smith Award, National Academy of Science, 1962; Remsen Memorial Award, Amer. Chem. Soc., Baltimore, 1963; Univ. Paris Medal, 1964; National Sci. Medal, 1964; Gold Medal, RAS, 1966; Chemical Pioneer Award, Amer. Inst. of Chemists, 1969; Leonard Medal, Meteoritical Soc., 1969; Arthur L. Day Award, Geological Soc. of America, 1969; Linus Pauling Award, Oregon State Univ., 1970; Johann Kepler Medal, AAAS, 1971; Gold Medal Award, Amer. Inst. Chemists, 1972; Priestley Award, ACS, 1973; NASA Exceptional Scientific Achievement Award, 1973; Headliner Award, San Diego Press Club, 1974; V. M. Goldschmidt Medal, Geochem. Soc. of Amer., 1975. Hon. DSc of many universities. *Publications:* Atoms, Molecules and Quanta, with A. E. Ruark, 1930; The Planets, 1952; numerous articles in Chemical journals on the structure of atoms and molecules, discovery of heavy hydrogen and its properties, separation of isotopes, measurement of paleotemperatures, origin of the planets, origin of life. *Address:* 7890 Torrey Lane, La Jolla, California 92037, USA. *Died 5 Jan. 1981.*

**URGÜPLÜ, Ali Suad Hayri;** Turkish diplomat and lawyer; a Senator of the Presidential Contingent, since 1966; Prime Minister of Turkey, Jan.–Oct. 1965; nominated for second time, April 1972, resigned after 15 days; Scheik-ul-Islam of the Ottoman Empire; *b* 13 Aug. 1903; *s* of Mustafa Hayri Urgüplü; *m* 1932, Z. Nigàr Cevdet; one *s. Educ:* Galatasaray Grammar Sch., Istanbul; Faculty of Law of Istanbul Univ. Turkish Sec. to Mixed Courts of Arbitration (Treaty of Lausanne), 1926–29. Magistrate, Supreme Commercial Court, Istanbul, 1929–32; Lawyer at Courts of Istanbul and Member Administrative Council, 1932–39. Deputy for Kayseri, Grand Nat. Assembly of Turkey, 1939–46 and from 1950; Minister of Customs and Monopolies, 1943–46; Turkish rep. and Pres. of

Turkish Delegn to Cons. Assembly of Council of Europe, Strasbourg and Vice-Pres. of Consultative Assembly, 1950, 1951 and 1952; rep. Turkey at Conf. of Inter-parly Union, Dublin and Istanbul, 1950 and 1951; re-elected Member 9th Legislative Period, 1950, Turkey; Ambassador of Turkey to German Federal Republic, 1952–55; Ambassador of the Turkish Republic to the Court of St James's, 1955–57; Turkish Delegate to: Tripartite Conf. on Eastern Mediterranean and Cyprus, London, 1955, Suez Canal, London, 1956; Turkish Ambassador to the United States, 1957–60, to Spain, 1960; Chm., Foreign Relations Cttee of Senate, 1966–69. Elected as Indep. Senator from Kayseri, then elected from all parties, as Speaker to Senate of the Republic, 1961–63. Chm., Culture and Art Foundn; Pres., European League for Economic Cooperation, Turkish Section. Gold Medal, Mark Twain Soc.; Grand Cross of Order of Merit with Star and Sash (Fed. Repub. of Germany). *Publications:* articles and studies in various judicial reviews. *Recreation:* reading. *Address:* Sahil Cad, No 19, Yesilyurt, Istanbul, Turkey; (office) Yapi re Kredi Bankasi, Istanbul, Turkey. *Died 26 Dec. 1981.*

**URQUHART, Sir Andrew,** KCMG 1963 (CMG 1960); MBE 1950; Principal, St Godric's College, 1975–85 (Vice-Principal, 1970–75); *b* 6 Jan. 1918; *s* of late Rev. Andrew Urquhart and of J. B. Urquhart; *m* 1956, Jessie Stanley Allison; two *s. Educ:* Greenock Academy; Glasgow University. Served War of 1939–45, Royal Marines, 1940–46. Cadet, Colonial Administrative Service, 1946; Senior District Officer, 1954; Admin. Officer, Class I, 1957; Permanent Sec., 1958; Deputy Governor, Eastern Region, Nigeria, 1958–63; Gen. Manager, The Housing Corp., 1964–70. *Address:* BM/JNTC, WC1N 3XX. *Died 11 Oct. 1988.*

**URQUHART, Maj.-Gen. Robert Elliott,** CB 1944; DSO and Bar 1943; *b* 28 Nov. 1901; *e s* of Alexander Urquhart, MD; *m* 1939, Pamela Condon; one *s* three *d. Educ:* St Paul's, West Kensington; RMC Sandhurst. 2nd Lt HLI 1920; Staff Coll., Camberley, 1936–37; Staff Capt., India, 1938; DAQMG, AHQ, India, 1939–40; DAAG, 3 Div., 1940; AA&QMG, 3 Div., 1940–41; commanded 2nd DCLI, 1941–42; GSO1, 51st Highland Div. N Africa, 1942–43; commanded 231 Malta Brigade, Sicily, 1943, and in landings Italy, 1943 (DSO and Bar); BGS 12 Corps, 1943; GOC 1st Airborne Div., 1944–45 (CB); Col 1945; Maj.-Gen. 1946; Director Territorial Army and Army Cadet Force, War Office, 1945–46; GOC 16th Airborne Division, TA, 1947–48; Commander, Lowland District, 1948–50; Commander Malaya District and 17th Gurkha Division, Mar.–Aug. 1950; GOC Malaya, 1950–52; GOC-in-C British Troops in Austria, 1952–55; retired, Dec. 1955. Col Highland Light Infantry, 1954–58. Dir, Davy and United Engineering Co. Ltd, 1957–70. Netherlands Bronze Lion, 1944; Norwegian Order of St Olaf, 1945. *Publication:* Arnhem, 1958. *Recreation:* golf. *Address:* Bigram, Port of Menteith, Stirling. *T:* Port of Menteith 267. *Club:* Naval and Military. *Died 13 Dec. 1988.*

**URQUHART, Sir Robert William,** KBE 1950 (OBE 1923); CMG 1944; *b* 14 August 1896, *s* of late Robert Urquhart and Margaret Stewart; *m* 1st, 1925, Brenda Gertrude Phillips (*d* 1975); four *d*; 2nd, 1977, Jane Gibson. *Educ:* Aberdeen; Cambridge. Entered Levant Consular Service, 1920; Consul at Tabriz, 1934; transferred to Foreign Office, 1938; Inspector-General of Consulates, 1939; seconded to the Home Office, 1940–41; Consul-General, Tabriz, 1942, transferred to New Orleans, La, USA, 1943; reappointed Inspector-General of HM Consular Establishment, 1945; HM Minister at Washington, 1947; HM Consul-General at Shanghai, 1948–50; British Ambassador to Venezuela, 1951–55; retired from Foreign Service, 1955. Chairman of the Crofters' Commission, 1955–63. Hon. LLD Aberdeen, 1954. *Address:* 7A Blacket Place, Edinburgh EH9 1RN. *Died 17 March 1983.*

**URTON, Sir William (Holmes Lister),** Kt 1960; MBE 1943; TD 1952; *b* 30 June 1908; *s* of late Capt. Edgar Lister Urton; *m* 1946, Kirsten Hustad, *d* of late Einar Hustad, Namsos, Norway; two *d. Educ:* Chesterfield Grammar Sch. Conservative Agent: Chesterfield, 1930; Howdenshire, 1935. TA, 1936; HQ 150 Inf. Bde. 1939–41. HQ 50 (Northumbrian) Division, 1941–46. Conservative Central Office Agent: Yorkshire, 1946; London, 1952. Electoral Adviser, WEU Saar Commission, 1955. General Director, Convervative and Unionist Central Office, 1957–66. *Recreations:* walking, gardening. *Address:* Namsos, The Way, Reigates, Surrey RH2 0LD. *T:* Reigate, 46343. *Clubs:* St Stephen's Constitutional, Carlton. *Died 25 Feb. 1982.*

**URWICK, Lyndall Fownes,** OBE, MC; MA; Hon. DSc; CIMechE, MASME, MIPE, FBIM, FRSA; Hon. Associate Manchester College of Technology and College of Technology, Birmingham; President Urwick, Orr & Partners Ltd, since 1963; *b* 3 March 1891; *o c* of late Sir Henry Urwick; *m* 1923, Joan Wilhelmina Bedford; one *s* one *d*; *m* 1941, Betty, *o d* of late Major H. M. Warrand; one *s* one *d. Educ:* Boxgrove School, Guildford; Repton School; New College, Oxford (Hist. Exhibitioner). Duke of Devonshire Prize, 1910; BA 1913; MA 1919. War Service, 1914–18 (despatches thrice); Employers' Sec., Joint Industrial Council of Glovemaking Industry, 1919–20; employed by Rowntree & Co. Ltd, York, 1922–28; Dir, Hon. Sec., Management Research Groups, 1926–28; Dir, Internat. Management Inst., Geneva, 1928–33; Gen. Sec., Internat. Cttee of Scientific Management, 1932–35; Consultant to HM Treasury, 1940–42; Mem., Mitcheson Cttee on Min. of Pensions, 1940–41; Lt-Col Petroleum Warfare Dept, 1942–44. Chm., Cttee of Educn for Management, 1946; Vice-Chm., Coun., BIM, 1947–52; Chm., Anglo-Amer. Productivity Team on Educn for Management in USA, 1951; Dir, American Management Assoc. Study of Management Education, 1952–53; Pres., Institutional Management Assoc., 1956–59; Colombo Plan Adviser to Indian Govt, 1956; Pres., European Fedn of Management Consultants' Assocs., 1960–61; Hon. Vis. Prof., Univ. of York, Toronto, 1967. Life Member: American Management Assoc., 1957; American Soc. Mechanical Engineers, 1952. Past Master, Company of Glovers. Hon. DSc Aston Univ., 1969; Hon. LLD York Univ., Toronto, 1972. Kt, 1st Cls Order of St Olaf (Norway); Silver Medal, RSA, 1948; Gold Medal, Internat. Cttee for Scientific Management, 1951; Wallace Clarke Internat. Management Award, 1955; Henry Laurence Gantt Gold Medal, 1961; Taylor Key, 1963; Bowie Medal, 1968. *Publications:* Factory Organisation, 1928; Organising a Sales Office, 1928, 2nd edn 1937; The Meaning of Rationalisation, 1929; Problems of Distribution in Europe and the United States, 1931; Management of To-Morrow, 1933; Committees in Organisation, 1937; Papers on the Science of Administration, 1937; The Development of Scientific Management in Great Britain, 1938; Dynamic Administration, 1941; The Elements of Administration, 1943; The Making of Scientific Management, vol i, Thirteen Pioneers, 1945, vol. ii, British Industry, 1946, vol. iii, The Hawthorne Experiments, 1948; Freedom and Coordination, 1949; Management Education in American Business, 1955; The Pattern of Management, 1956; Leadership in the XXth Century, 1957; Organisation, 1964; articles on rationalisation, and scientific management. *Address:* Poyntington, 83 Kenneth Street, Longueville, NSW 2066, Australia. *T:* Sydney 4272102; 134 Buckingham Palace Road, SW1W 9SA. *Clubs:* Savile, Reform. *Died* 5 *Dec.* 1983.

**URWIN, Rt. Hon. Thomas (William);** PC 1979; *b* 9 June 1912; *s* of a miner; *m* 1934, Edith Scott, *d* of a miner; three *s* one *d. Educ:* Brandon Colliery and Easington Lane Elementary Schools and NCLC. Bricklayer, 1926–54; full-time Organiser, Amalgamated Union of Building Trade Workers, 1954–64. MP (Lab) Houghton-le-Spring, 1964–83; Minister of State, DEA, 1968–69; Minister of State, with responsibilities for regional policy, and special responsibility for the Northern Region, Oct. 1969–June 1970. Leader, British Parly delegn to Council of Europe and WEU, 1976–79, Leader Lab delegn, 1976–83. Chm., Socialist Group, Council of Europe, 1976–83. Member Houghton-le-Spring Urban District Council, 1946–65, Chm. 1954–55, Chm. Planning and Housing, 1950–65. *Recreations:* football (local soccer), cricket. *Address:* 28 Stanhope Close, Houghton-le-Spring, Tyne and Wear. *T:* Houghton-le-Spring 3139. *Died* 14 *Dec.* 1985.

**USHER, Col Charles Milne,** DSO 1940; OBE 1919; MA (Edinburgh); Director of Physical Education, Edinburgh University, 1946–59; *b* 6 September 1891; *s* of Robert Usher, Edinburgh; *m* 1919, Madge Elsa, *d* of F. Carbut Bell, London; two *s. Educ:* Merchiston Castle School, Edinburgh; RMC Sandhurst. Joined Gordon Highlanders, 1911; Lt-Col 1938; actg Brig. 1940; served European War, 1914–18 (OBE, Mons Star, 2 Medals); War of 1939–45 (despatches, DSO, Chevalier Legion of Honour, Croix de Guerre with Palm); Citoyen d'honneur of the town of Caen (Calvados). Captained Mother Country, Scotland, Army, and London Scottish at Rugby Football, also Captained Scotland versus USA at Fencing (Sabre and Epée), and British Empire Games, New Zealand, 1950. Hon. Pres., Scottish Amateur Fencing Union, Scottish Univs Rugby Club; Vice Patron, Army Rugby Union; Hon. Pres., Piobaireachd Soc. Grand Prix du Dirigeant Sportif, 1958. *Publications:* The Usher Family in Scotland, 1956; The Story of Edinburgh University Athletic Club, 1966. *Recreations:* hunting, shooting. *Address:* The White House, North Berwick, East Lothian. *T:* 26941. *Clubs:* Caledonian; New (Edinburgh). *Died* 21 *Jan.* 1981.

**USHER, Sir Peter Lionel,** 5th Bt *cr* 1899, of Norton, Midlothian, and of Wells, Co. Roxburgh; *b* 31 Oct. 1931; *er s* of Sir (Robert) Stuart Usher, 4th Bt, and Gertrude Martha (*d* 1984), 2nd *d* of Lionel Barnard Sampson, Tresmontes, Villa Valeria, Prov. Cordoba, Argentina; *S* father, 1962. *Educ:* privately. *Heir: b* Robert Edward Usher, *b* 18 April 1934. *Address:* (Seat) Hallrule, Hawick, Roxburghshire. *T:* Bonchester Bridge 216.

*Died* 1 *June* 1990.

**USHER, Brig. Thomas Clive,** CBE 1945; DSO and Bar 1943; RA, retired 1958; now farming; *b* 21 June 1907; *s* of Sir Robert Usher, 2nd Bt, of Norton and Wells; *m* 1939, Valentine Sears Stockwell; one *d. Educ:* Uppingham; RMA. Served War of 1939–45; North Africa, Sicily and Italy (DSO and Bar, CBE); Temp. Brig. 1944. Lt-Col 1950; Col 1951; Temp. Brig. 1953; ADC, 1957–58. Formerly Military Adviser to UK High Comr in India; OC 18 Trg Bde, RA, 1955–57; Brig. RA, Scottish Comd, 1958. *Recreations:* riding, fishing. *Address:* Wells Stables, Hawick, Roxburghshire. *T:* Denholm 235. *Died* 17 *Nov.* 1982.

**USHER-WILSON, Rt. Rev. Lucian Charles,** CBE 1961; MA; retired; Hon. Canon of Guildford Cathedral, 1965; *b* 10 Jan. 1903; *s* of Rev. C. Usher-Wilson; *m* 1929, Muriel Constance Wood; one *s* three *d. Educ:* Christ's Hospital; Lincoln College, Oxford; St Augustine's College, Canterbury. Asst Master, King William's College, Isle of Man; Asst Master, King's College, Budo, Kampala, Uganda; CMS Missionary at Jinja, Busoga, Uganda; Rural Dean, Busoga District, Uganda; Bishop on Upper Nile, 1936–61 (when diocese split up); Bishop of Mbale (southern area of former diocese of Upper Nile), 1961–64; an Asst Bishop of Guildford and Vicar of Churt, 1964–72; apptd Hon. Asst Bishop of Bristol, 1972. Mem., Royal African Soc. *Recreation:* gardening. *Address:* Chapel House, 264 Hot Well Road, Bristol BS8 4NG. *Clubs:* Old Blues, Royal Commonwealth Society. *Died* 28 *Aug.* 1984.

**USHERWOOD, Kenneth Ascough,** CBE 1964; President, Prudential Assurance Co. Ltd, 1979–82; *b* 19 Aug. 1904; *s* of late H. T. Usherwood and Lettie Ascough; *m* 1st, 1933, Molly Tidbeck (marr. diss. 1945), Johannesburg; one *d*; 2nd, 1946, Mary Louise, *d* of T. L. Reepmaker d'Orville; one *s. Educ:* City of London School; St John's College, Cambridge (MA). Prudential Assurance Co. Ltd, 1925–82: South Africa, 1932–34; Near East, 1934–37; Dep. Gen. Man. 1947–60; Chief Gen. Man., 1961–67; Dir, 1968–79; Chm., 1970–75; Dir, Prudential Corp., 1978–79. Director of Statistics, Ministry of Supply, 1941–45. Chm., Industrial Life Offices Assoc., 1966–67. Institute of Actuaries: Fellow (FIA) 1925; Pres. 1962–64. Mem. Gaming Board, 1968–72; Treasurer, Field Studies Council, 1969–77. *Address:* 24 Litchfield Way, NW11. *T:* 01–455 7915; Laurel Cottage, Walberswick, Suffolk. *T:* Southwold 723265. *Club:* Oriental. *Died* 5 *Dec.* 1988.

**UTLEY, Thomas Edwin, (Peter),** CBE 1980; Obituaries Editor, and columnist, The Times, since 1987; *b* 1 Feb. 1921; adopted *s* of late Miss Anne Utley; *m* 1951, Brigid Viola Mary, *yr d* of late D. M. M. Morrah, and of Ruth Morrah; two *s* two *d. Educ:* privately; Corpus Christi Coll., Cambridge (1st cl. Hons Hist. Tripos; Foundn Schol.; MA). Sec., Anglo-French Relations post-War Reconstruction Gp, RIIA, 1942–44; temp. Foreign Leader writer, The Times, 1944–45; Leader writer, Sunday Times, 1945–47; Editorial staff, The Observer, 1947–48; Leader writer, The Times, 1948–54; Associate Editor, Spectator, 1954–55; freelance journalist and broadcasting, 1955–64; The Daily Telegraph: Leader writer, 1964–80; Chief Asst Editor, 1980–86; Asst Editor, 1986–87. Contested (U) North Antrim, Feb. 1974. Pres., Paddington Cons. Assoc., 1979–80 (Chm., 1977–79); a Consultant Dir, Cons. Res. Dept, 1980–. *Publications:* Essays in Conservatism, 1949; Modern Political Thought, 1952; The Conservatives and the Critics, 1956; (ed jtly) Documents of Modern Political Thought, 1957; Not Guilty, 1957; Edmund Burke, 1957; Occasion for Ombudsmen, 1963; Your Money and Your Life, 1964; Enoch Powell: the Man and his Thinking, 1968; What Laws May Cure, 1968; Lessons of Ulster, 1975; *posthumous publication:* A Tory Seer: the selected journalism of T. E. Utley (ed Charles Moore and Simon Heffer), 1989. *Address:* 60 St Mary's Mansions, St Mary's Terrace, W2. *T:* 01–723 1149. *Died* 21 *June* 1988.

**UTTLEY, Prof. Albert Maurel,** PhD; Research Professor of Experimental Psychology, University of Sussex, 1966–73, now Emeritus; *b* 14 Aug. 1906; *s* of George Uttley and Ethel Uttley (*née* Player), London; *m* 1941, Gwendoline Lucy Richens; two *d. Educ:* King's College, London University. BSc Mathematics; PhD Psychology. Dep. Chief Scientific Officer (Individual Merit Post), Royal Radar Establishment, 1940–56; Superintendent of Autonomics Div., NPL, 1956–66. Fellow, Center for Advanced Studies in Behavioral Sciences, Univ. of Stanford, Calif, 1962–63. Pres., Biological Engineering Soc., 1964–66. Kelvin Premium, IEE, 1948; Simms Gold Medal, RAeS, 1950. *Publications:* Information Transmission in the Nervous System, 1978; Brain, Mind and Spirit, 1982; papers in various scientific journals on theory of control and of computers and on theoretical neurophysiology of brain function. *Recreations:* formerly mountaineering, now painting, travel. *Address:* Dunnocks, Lewes Road, Ditchling, East Sussex BN6 8TY. *Died* 13 *Sept.* 1985.

# V

**VAIZEY,** Baron *cr* 1976 (Life Peer), of Greenwich; **John Ernest Vaizey;** Director of several companies; *b* 1 Oct. 1929; *s* of late Ernest and Lucy Butler Vaizey; *m* 1961, Marina, *o d* of Lyman and late Ruth Stansky; two *s* one *d. Educ.*: Queen Mary's Hosp. Sch.; Queens' Coll., Cambridge (Schol.; Econs Tripos, Cambridge, 1951; Gladstone Prizeman, 1954; MA). DSc Brunel; DLitt *aeg* Adelaide. UN, Geneva, 1952–53; Fellow of St Catharine's Coll., Cambridge, 1953–56; Univ. Lectr, Oxford, 1956–60; Dir, Research Unit, Univ. of London, 1960–62; Fellow and Tutor, Worcester Coll., Oxford, 1962–66; Prof. of Econs, Brunel Univ., 1966–82 (Hd, Sch, of Soc. Scis, 1973–81). Prof., Univ. of California, 1965–66; Eleanor Rathbone Lectr, Univs of Liverpool and Durham, 1966; O'Brien Lectr, UCD, 1968; Centenary Prof., Univ. of Adelaide, 1974–75; Hoover Prof., Univ. of NSW, 1977. Principal, St Catharine's, Cumberland Lodge, 1982– (Trustee, 1972–82). Member: Nat. Adv. Council on Trng and Supply of Teachers, 1962–66; UNESCO Nat. Commn, 1965–72, 1978–; Exec., Fabian Soc., 1959–66; Public Schools Commn, 1966–68; Inner London Educn Authority, 1970–72; Commn on Educn, Spain, 1968–72; Governing Body, Internat. Inst. for Educnl Planning, 1971–80; Adv. Cttee, Gulbenkian Foundn, 1971–77; Chairman: Cttee on Trng for the Drama, 1974–75; Cttee on Dance, 1974–82; Cttee on Music Training, 1975–77; British-Irish Assoc., 1976–82; Greenwich Festival, 1979–84; Colony Holidays, 1980–; President: Blackheath Soc., 1975–. Remedial Gymnasts Assoc.; 1982–. Trustee: Acton Soc. Trust, 1968–78 (Dir 1960–68); Governor, Ditchley Foundn, 1973–. Consultant, UN, etc. Order of El Sabio (Spain), 1969. *Publications:* The Costs of Education, 1958; Scenes from Institutional Life, 1959; (with P. Lynch) Guinness's Brewery in the Irish Economy, 1961; The Economics of Education, 1962; Education for Tomorrow, 1962, 5th edn 1970; The Control of Education, 1963; (ed) The Residual Factor and Economic Growth, 1965; (ed with E. A. G. Robinson) The Economics of Education, 1965; Barometer Man, 1967; Education in the Modern World, 1967, 2nd edn, 1975; (with John Sheehan) Resources for Education, 1968; The Sleepless Lunch, 1968; (with colleagues) The Economics of Educational Costing, 4 vols, 1969–71; The Type to Succeed, 1970; Capitalism, 1971; Social Democracy, 1971; The Political Economy of Education, 1972; (with Keith Norris) The Economics of Research and Technology, 1973; History of British Steel, 1974; (ed) Economic Sovereignty and Regional Policy; (ed) Whatever Happened to Equality, 1975; (with C. F. O. Clarke) Education: the state of the debate, 1976; (with Keith Norris) Teach Yourself Economics, 1977, 2nd edn, 1983; Capitalism and Socialism, 1980; The Squandered Peace, 1983; In Breach of Promise, 1983; National Health, 1984. *Recreations:* arts, travel. *Address:* 24 Heathfield Terrace, W4 4JE. *T:* 01-994 7994. *Clubs:* Garrick, Beefsteak; Kildare Street and University (Dublin).
*Died 19 July 1984.*

**VALENTIA,** 14th Viscount (Ireland) *cr* 1621 (Dormant 1844–1959); **Francis Dighton Annesley,** Baron Mountnorris (Ireland) 1628; Bt 1620; MC 1918; MRCS, LRCP; Brigadier retired, late RAMC; *b* 12 Aug. 1888; *o c* of late George Dighton Annesley (uncle of *de jure* 13th Viscount); *S* cousin, 1951, established his succession, 1959; *m* 1925, Joan Elizabeth , 2nd *d* of late John Joseph Curtis; one *s* three *d. Educ.*: St Lawrence Coll.; Guy's Hospital. Lieut, RAMC, 1914; served European War, France, Belgium, Aug. 1914–March 1919; Afghanistan, 1919; Waziristan, 1922–23; War of 1939–45, India, Iraq, Persia, Egypt, France, Germany, Lt-Col 1936; Col 1941; Brig. 1942; retd 1948. Croix de Guerre (Belge), 1918. *Heir: s* Hon. Richard John Dighton Annesley, Captain, RA, retd [*b* 15 Aug. 1929; *m* 1957, Anita Phyllis, *o d* of W. A. Joy; three *s* one *d*]. *Address:* St Michael's, Lea, Malmesbury, Wilts. *T:* Malmesbury 2312.
*Died 16 March 1983.*

**VALENTINE, Prof. David Henriques;** George Harrison Professor of Botany, University of Manchester, 1966–79, then Emeritus; *b* 16 Feb. 1912; *s* of Emmanuel and Dora Valentine; *m* 1938, Joan Winifred Todd; two *s* three *d. Educ:* Manchester Grammar Sch.; St John's Coll., Cambridge. MA 1936, PhD 1937. Curator of the Herbarium and Demonstrator in Botany, Cambridge, 1936; Research Fellow of St John's Coll., Cambridge, 1938; Ministry of Food (Dehydration Division), 1941; Reader in Botany, Durham, 1945, Prof., 1950–66. Trustee, BM (Natural History), 1975–83. Foreign Mem., Societas Scientiarum Fennica (Section for Natural Sciences), 1964. *Publications:* Flora Europaea, Vol. 1, 1964, Vol. 2, 1968, Vol. 3, 1972, Vol. 4, 1976, Vol. 5, 1980; Taxonomy, Phytogeography and Evolution, 1972; papers on experimental taxonomy in botanical journals. *Recreation:* reading novels. *Address:* 4 Pine Road, Didsbury, Manchester M20 0UY. *T:* 061–445 7224.
*Died 10 April 1987.*

**VAN DEN BERGH, James Philip,** CBE 1946; Director of Unilever Ltd, 1937–65, retired; Vice-Chairman of Lindustries, 1965–75; Deputy Chairman, William Baird & Co., 1965–75; Chairman, National Cold Stores (Management Ltd), 1965–70; *b* 26 April 1905; *s* of Albert Van den Bergh; *m* 1929, Betty D'Arcy Hart; one *s* one *d. Educ.:* Harrow; Trinity Coll., Cambridge. Entered Van den Berghs Ltd, 1927; subseq. Man. Dir; Chm., 1942. Min. of Food: Dir of Margarine and Cooking Fats, 1939; Dir of Dehydration, 1940; Dir of Fish Supplies, 1945. Government Director, British Sugar Corp., 1956–58, retired. Member Exec. Council, Food Manufacturers' Federation, 1957 (President, 1958–61); Member Food Research Advisory Cttee, 1960–65 (Chairman, 1963); Member Council, Queen Elizabeth Coll., London Univ., 1961–73; Hon. Fellow, 1968. *Address:* Field House, Cranleigh, Surrey. *Club:* Leander (Henley).
*Died 29 Aug. 1988.*

**van der MEULEN, Daniel;** Netherlands Indies civil servant and diplomat; Arabist author and traveller; *b* 4 Sept. 1894; *m* 1st, 1917, A. C. E. Kelling (*d* 1959); three *s* two *d* (and one *s* murdered in Germany); 2nd, 1959, Dr Helene Marie Duhm; one *s. Educ:* Leyden Univ. Netherlands Indies Civil Service, North of Sumatra in Toba-lake district of Toba Batak country, 1915–23; studied Arabic and Islam under Prof. Dr C. Snouck Hurgronje, Leyden Univ.; consular and diplomatic service, Jeddah, Sa'oudi-Arabia, 1926–31; first exploration in South Arabia, 1931; Netherlands Indies Civil Service, Pajakumbuh, Central Sumatra, Palembang, South Sumatra, 1932–38; second exploration in South Arabia, 1939; Netherlands Indies Civil Service, Makassar, South Celebes, 1939–41; Minister in Jeddah, Sa'oudi-Arabia, 1941–45; Resident Adviser to Netherlands East India Government at Batavia, 1945–48; Chief of the Arabic Section of Radio Netherland World-broadcast at Hilversum, 1949–51. Hon. Mem., Royal Netherlands Geographical Soc., 1956. Officer, Oranje Nassau; Patron's Medal, Royal Geographical Society, London, 1947. *Publications:* Hadhramaut, some of its mysteries unveiled (with map by Prof. Dr H. von Wissmann), 1932; Aden to the Hadhramaut, 1947 (numerous trans.); Onbekend Arabië, 1947; Ontwakend Arabië, 1954; Mÿn weg naar Arabië en de Islaam, 1954; The Wells of Ibn Sa'ud, 1954; Verdwijnend Arabië, 1959; Faces in Shem, 1961; Ik Stond Erbÿ, het einde van ons koloniale rÿk, 1965; Hoort Ge de donder niet? (autobiog.), 1977, trans. as Don't You Hear the Thunder?: a Dutchman's story, 1981. *Address:* 9 Flierder Weg, 7213LT Gorssel, Holland. *T:* 05759–1684.
*Died 24 Sept. 1989.*

**van der POST, Jan Laurens,** FEng, FIMechE, FIGasE; Chief Executive, Water Research Centre, since 1978; *b* 26 Dec. 1928; *s* of Lt-Col Sir Laurens van der Post, CBE and Marjorie Wendt; *m* 1959, Tessa Broom; three *s* one *d. Educ:* Michaelhouse; Univ. of Natal, S Africa (BScEng). FEng 1978; FIMechE 1977; FIGasE 1977. Rolls-Royce Ltd: Trainee, 1952–54; Designer, 1954-57; Atomic Power Constructions Ltd: Technical Engr, 1957–59; Head of Engrg Div., 1959–64; British Gas Corp. (Gas Council): Res. Engr, 1964–66; Dir of Engrg Res. Stn, 1966–78. Director, Cabletime (Installations) Ltd. Member: Computers, Systems and Electronics Requirements Bd, 1976–79; ACARD, 1980–83; Council, Fellowship of Engrg, 1982–. Hon. FIWPC 1978. Gold Medal, IGasE, 1978. *Publications:* articles and papers on pipelines and engrg. *Recreation:* gliding. *Address:* 1 Belbroughton Road, Oxford OX2 6UZ. *T:* Oxford 58364. *Club:* Athenæum.
*Died 15 March 1984.*

**VANGEKE, Most Rev. Sir Louis,** MSC; KBE 1980 (OBE 1974); Member, Legion of Honour of French Republic, 1980; Bishop of Bereina, Papua New Guinea, 1976–80, and Auxiliary to Archbishop V. P. Copas (RC), 1974; Member, Society of Missionaries of the Sacred Heart of Jesus, French Province, 1941; *b* 25 June 1904; *s* of Vagu'u Kaoka, Veifa'a; *Educ:* CM Yule Island, 1909–19; Minor and Major Jesuit Seminary of Madagascar; Little Brother Oblate of St Joseph, 1922–28; in training for 12 years for his ordination as first Papuan Priest in the Roman Catholic Church, in Madagascar, 1928–37, and worked for many years among Kuni people in Papua, 1941–70; Auxiliary Bishop of Port Moresby, 1970–73 (RC Bp of Culusi); ordained first indigenous Papuan Bishop of RC Church by Pope Paul VI, in Sydney, 1970, and acclaimed Chief (*hc*) of Mekeo Village of Veifa'a, Papua, 1970. Hon. LLD Univ. of Papua New Guinea, 1974. *Publications:* Liturgical Texts in the Kuni language, 1968–70; composed music for jubilee mass, 1962; hymns; songs. *Address:* Catholic Parish, Kubana CP, PO Box 177, Port Moresby, Papua New Guinea.
*Died 12 Dec. 1982.*

**van HEYNINGEN, William Edward,** ScD Cantab; DSc Oxon; Founding Master of St Cross College, Oxford, 1965–79, Hon. Fellow, 1979; Reader in Bacterial Chemistry, University of Oxford, 1966–79, now Emeritus; *b* 24 Dec. 1911; *s* of late George Philipus Stephanus van Heyningen and Mabel Constance (*née* Higgs); *m* 1940, Ruth Eleanor Treverton; one *s* one *d. Educ.:* village schools in S Africa; Univs of Stellenbosch and Cambridge. Commonwealth Fund Fellow, Harvard Univ., and College of Physicians and Surgeons, Columbia Univ., 1936–38; Senior Student of Royal Commn for Exhibn of 1851, 1938–40. Staff Member, Molteno Physiological Research Laboratories, 1943–46; Sen. Res. Officer, Sir William Dunn School of Pathology, Oxford Univ., 1947–66; Sec., Soc. for Gen. Microbiology, 1946–52; Curator of the Bodleian Library, 1962–85; Mem. Hebdomadal Council, Oxford Univ.,

1963–69. Vis. Prof., State Univ. of New York, 1967. Visitor of the Ashmolean Museum, 1969–87. Trustee, Ruskin Sch. of Drawing, 1975–77. Consultant, Cholera Adv. Cttee, Nat. Insts of Health, USA, 1968–73. Chevalier de l'Ordre National du Mérite, 1980. *Publications:* Bacterial Toxins, 1950; Cholera: the American scientific experience 1947–1980, 1983; The Key to Lockjaw: an autobiography, 1987; Jean de Florette and Manon of the Springs (trans. of Pagnol's l'Eau des Collines), 1988; papers mainly concerned with bacterial toxins in various books and journals. *Address:* College Farm, North Hinksey Village, Oxford OX2 0NA. *Club:* Reform.                    *Died 27 Oct.* 1989.

**van MEERBEKE, René Louis Joseph Marie;** Grand Offcier, Orders of the Crown and of Léopold II (Belgium); Commander, Order of Léopold II (with swords); Officer, Orders of Léopold and of the Crown (with swords); Croix de Guerre (Belgium), 1914–18 (with palms); Croix de Feu; Civil Cross (1st Class); *b* 15 Nov. 1895; *m* 1926, Léonor Restrepo del Corral; two *s* of *d*. *Educ:* University of Ghent (Licentiate of Faculty of Law in Commercial and Consular Sciences). Entered Diplomatic Service, 1920; Secretary, Legation, Lima, 1921; Chargé d'Affaires a.i. Bogota, 1924; Chargé d'Affaires, 1936; Minister, Bogota, 1945; Rio de Janeiro, 1954; Ambassador to the Court of St James's, 1957–61, and concurrently Belgian Perm. Rep. to Council of WEU. Entrusted with special missions as Representative of the Belgian Government at the investitures of new Presidents of the Republic: in Colombia, in 1946, 1950 and 1958; in Ecuador in 1948 and 1952, and in Brazil in 1956. Grand Cross Orders of Merit (Ecuador), Southern Cross (Brazil), Boyaca and San Carlos (Colombia); Grand Officer of Aztec Eagle (Mexico); Commander, Legion of Honour; Commander, Order of the Liberator (Venezuela); Officer, Order of the Sun (Peru); Golden Medal of the French Reconnaissance, etc. *Recreation:* horse riding. *Address:* Carrera 10, 8450 (Apt 701), Bogotá, Colombia. *Clubs:* Cercle Royal Gaulois (Vice-Pres.) (Brussels); Royal Golf Club de Belgique.                    *Died 19 July* 1983.

**VAN PRAAGH, Dame Peggy,** DBE 1970 (OBE 1966); Member of Council and Guest Teacher, Australian Ballet School, 1975–82; director and producer of ballet in UK and many other countries; *b* London, 1 Sept. 1910; *d* of Harold John Van Praagh, MD, and Ethel Louise Shanks. *Educ:* King Alfred Sch., Hampstead. Studied and trained in the Cecchetti Method of classical ballet with Margaret Craske; passed Advanced Cecchetti Exam., 1932; danced in Tudor's Adam and Eve, Camargo Society, 1932. Joined Ballet Rambert and danced at Ballet Club, 1933–38; created rôles in Tudor's Ballets: Jardin aux Lilas, Dark Elegies, Gala Performance, Soirée Musicale, etc; joined Tudor's Co., the London Ballet, as a Principal Dancer, 1938. Examiner and Cttee member, Cecchetti Society, 1937–. Joined Sadler's Wells Ballet as dancer and teacher, 1941; danced Swanhilda in Coppelia, Blue Girl in Patineurs, etc. Producer and Asst Director to Ninette De Valois, Sadler's Wells Theatre Ballet, and worked with that company, 1946–56. Produced many TV ballets for BBC. Guest Teacher and Producer for National Ballet of Canada, 1956; Guest Producer: Munich, Bavarian Opera House, 1956; Theatre Royal, Stockholm, 1957; Director: Norsk Ballet, 1957–58; Edinburgh International Festival Ballet, 1958; Borovansky Ballet in Australia, 1960; Guest Teacher: Jacob's Pillow, USA, 1959; Ballet of Marquis de Cuevas, 1961; Artistic Dir, Australian Ballet, 1962–74 and 1978. Brought Australian Ballet to Commonwealth Festival, London, 1965; to Expo '67 Montreal, followed by tour of S America, 1967. Hon. DLitt, Univ. of New England, NSW, 1974; Hon. LLD Melbourne, 1981. Queen Elizabeth II Coronation Award, Royal Academy of Dancing, 1965; Distinguished Artist Award, Australia Council, 1975. *Publications:* How I Became a Ballet Dancer, 1954; The Choreographic Art (with Peter Brinson), 1963. *Recreations:* motoring, swimming. *Address:* c/o Australian Ballet School, 2 Kavanagh Street, South Melbourne, Vic 3205, Australia.
                    *Died 15 Jan.* 1990.

**VANSITTART, Guy Nicholas;** formerly Chairman, Vauxhall Motors and General Motors Ltd; *b* 8 Sept. 1893; *y s* of late Capt. Robert Arnold Vansittart and late Alice (*née* Blane). *Educ:* Eton; Trinity Coll., Oxford. BA (Oxon), Honour School of History. Captain, Indian Army, Central India Horse, 1913–22. *Address:* Flat 7, 20 Charles Street, W1X 7HD.                    *Died 3 Feb.* 1989.

**VARLEY, George Copley,** MA, PhD Cantab, MA Oxon; Hope Professor of Zoology (Entomology), Oxford, 1948–78; *b* 19 Nov. 1910; *s* of late George Percy Varley and Elsie Mary Varley (*née* Sanderson); *m* 1955, Dr Margaret Elizabeth Brown; one *s* one *d*. *Educ:* Manchester Grammar Sch.; Sidney Sussex Coll., Cambridge. Scholar of Sidney Sussex Coll., 1929–33; First Class in both parts of Nat. Sci. Tripos, Frank Smart Prizeman in Zoology, 1933; Research Student, 1933–35; Research Fellow, Sidney Sussex Coll., 1935–38; Hon. Research Fellow, University of California, 1937–38. Supt of Entomological Field Station, Cambridge, 1933–37; University Demonstrator in Zoology, Cambridge, and Curator of Insects in the University Museum of Zoology, 1938–45. Experimental Officer, and later Senior Experimental Officer in Army Operational Research

Gp, Min. of Supply, studying centimetric radar on South Coast, 1941–45. Reader in Entomology, King's Coll., Newcastle upon Tyne, 1945–48; Fellow of Jesus Coll., Oxford, 1948–78, Emeritus Fellow, 1978. *Publications:* (with G. R. Gradwell and M. P. Hassell) Insect Population Ecology, 1973; various papers on insects and population dynamics in scientific periodicals. *Recreations:* games included squash racquets, tennis, etc; sedentary pastimes included sailing, gliding, ski-ing; later reduced to gardening. *Address:* 18 Apsley Road, Oxford OX2 7QY. *T:* Oxford 56988.
                    *Died 13 May* 1983.

**VARVILL, Michael Hugh,** CMG 1959; *b* 29 Sept. 1909; *s* of Dr Bernard and Maud Varvill; unmarried. *Educ:* Marlborough; New Coll., Oxford (Scholar; BA). Appointed to Colonial Service, Nigeria, 1932; seconded to Colonial Office, 1943–47; Senior District Officer, 1951; Nigeria, Permanent Secretary: Ministry of Transport, 1952; Ministry of Works, 1953–54; and again (Federal) Ministry of Transport, 1955, retired 1960. With G. Bell & Sons, publishers, 1960–73 (Dir, 1963–73). *Recreations:* tennis, hockey, chess. *Address:* 125 Marsham Court, Marsham Street, SW1. *Club:* Travellers'.
                    *Died 12 April* 1988.

**VASEY, Sir Ernest (Albert),** KBE 1959; CMG 1945; Financial and Economic Adviser, World Bank Development Service, 1962–66; Resident Representative, IBRD, Pakistan, 1963–66; *b* 27 Aug. 1901; *m* 1st, 1923, Norah May Mitchell; one *s*; 2nd, 1944, Hannah Strauss (*d* 1981); one *s*. Member Shrewbury Town Council, England. Mayor of Nairobi, 1941–42, 1944–46; Member Kenya Legislative Council for Nairobi North, 1945–50; Member for Education, Health and Local Government for Kenya, 1950; Minister for Finance and Development, Kenya, 1952–59; Minister for Finance and Economics, Tanganyika, 1959–60; Minister for Finance, Tanganyika, 1960–62. Brilliant Star of Zanzibar, 2nd Class, 1955; Hilal-i-Quaid-i-Azam (Pakistan), 1966. *Address:* Box 14235, Nairobi, Kenya.                    *Died 10 Jan.* 1984.

**VAUGHAN, David Wyamar,** CBE 1962; *b* 15 July 1906; *s* of late Dr W. W. Vaughan, MVO, DLitt and Margaret, *d* of J. Addington Symonds; *m* 1st, 1928, Norah (*d* 1963), *d* of late J. H. Burn; two *s* one *d*; 2nd, 1966, Mrs Joy Beebee. *Educ:* Rugby. Joined Barclays Bank, 1930, Director, London Board, 1953–77; Local Director: Shrewsbury, 1934; Cardiff, 1939–72; Swansea, 1945–57; Windsor, 1972–77. Served War of 1939–45, with Welsh Guards, 1940–45, resigned with rank of Major. Treas., Univ. Coll. of S Wales and Monmouthshire, 1951–67; Mem. Court, Univ. of Wales, 1957–67; Hon. Treas., Welsh Nat. Sch. of Medicine, 1962–67. Dir and Treas., Empire and Commonwealth Games, 1958. Chm. Finance Cttee, Representative Body Church in Wales, 1955–76; Trustee, Historic Churches Preservation Trust, to 1976; Mem., Churches Main Cttee, to 1976. JP County Glamorgan, 1956–66. High Sheriff of Glamorgan, 1963. LLD Univ. of Wales, 1965. *Recreations:* shooting, fishing and all country pursuits. *Address:* The Old Rectory, Wherwell, Hants. *T:* Chilbolton 270. *Club:* Boodle's.                    *Died 6 July* 1982.

**VAUGHAN, Ernest James,** CBE 1961; retired as Director of Materials Research, Royal Naval Scientific Service; *b* 19 Oct. 1901; 3rd *s* of late James and Helena Vaughan; *m* 1927, Marjorie Solly; one *s* decd. *Educ:* Brockley; London University. BSc, MSc London; ARCS; DIC. Jun. Chemist, War Dept; Chemist, 1925–27; Chemist, Chemical Dept, Portsmouth Dockyard, 1927–36; Dep. Supt, then Supt, Bragg Laboratory, 1936–49; Dep. Dir, then Dir of Materials Research, Royal Naval Scientific Service, 1949–66. Hon. Treas., Royal Inst. of Chemistry, 1963–72. *Publications:* Protective Coatings for Metals, 1946; (monograph) Metallurgical Analysis; papers in learned jls. *Address:* Flat 2, Ashmede, 56 West Cliff Road, Bournemouth, Dorset BH4 8BE. *T:* Bournemouth 764232.
                    *Died 4 May* 1987.

**VAUGHAN, Hilda, (Mrs Charles Morgan);** novelist; *b* Builth, Breconshire, 1892; *d* of late Hugh Vaughan Vaughan; *m* 1923, Charles Morgan, LLD, FRSL (*d* 1958); one *s* one *d*. *Educ:* privately. FRSL 1963. *Publications:* The Battle to the Weak; Here Are Lovers; The Invader; Her Father's House; The Soldier and the Gentlewoman; A Thing of Nought; The Curtain Rises; Harvest Home; Pardon and Peace; Iron and Gold; The Candle and the Light. *Plays:* She, too, was Young; Forsaking All Other (both with Laurier Lister); Introduction to Thomas Traherne's Centuries. *Address:* c/o Roger Morgan, 30 St Peter's Square, W6 9UH.
                    *Died 4 Nov.* 1985.

**VAUGHAN, John Godfrey,** FCA; Director, Brown Boveri Kent (Holdings) plc, since 1974 (Chairman, 1974–79); *b* 2 May 1916; *s* of Charles Godfrey Vaughan and Mabel Rose Hart; *m* 1st, 1948, Barbara Josephine Knowles (*d* 1967); one *d*; 2nd, 1969, Lucia Maria Boer. *Educ:* Bedford Sch. Served War: with 4th Queens Own Hussars in Greece, N Africa, Italy and Austria, 1939–45 (2nd i/ comd, 1944). Joined The Charterhouse Group Ltd, 1946; Dir, 1953; Dep. Chm., 1968–71; Chm., 1971–77; Dir, George Kent Ltd, 1961, Dep. Chm., 1963, Chm., 1970–74; Dir, Slough Estates, 1968–.

*Recreations:* racing, reading, theatre. *Address:* 82 Hamilton Terrace, NW8 9UL. *T:* 01-286 1338. *Died* 13 *Oct.* 1984.

**VAUGHAN-HUGHES, Brig. Gerald Birdwood,** MC 1918; DL; JP; retired 1948; *b* 14 April 1896; *s* of Gerald Mainwaring Vaughan-Hughes and Isabel Bridget Crawford (*née* Birdwood); *m* 1927, Violet Mary Jessie (*d* 1968), *d* of Maj.-Gen. W. H. Kay, CB, DSO; two *s. Educ:* Wellington College; RMA Woolwich. Served European War, 1914-18 (wounded thrice, despatches, MC); RHA and RFA, 2nd Lt, 1914; RHA, 1916; India, RFA, 1919-28; Capt. 1926; ADC to C-in-C India, 1927-28; RHA, 1930; Staff Coll., 1931-32; Maj. 1934; SO: RA Southern Comd, 1934-35; Aldershot, 1936-37; GSO2, Palestine, 1939. War of 1939-45, AAG, Palestine, Greece and Crete, 1941; GSO1 RA, ME, 1941; Comdg Northumberland Hussars and II RHA, 1941-42; CRA (Brig.) 7th Armoured Div., 1942 (despatches twice), retired. DL 1958, JP 1956, High Sheriff, 1960, Monmouthshire. *Address:* Wyelands, Chepstow, Gwent. *T:* Chepstow 2127. *Died* 29 *March* 1983.

**VAUGHAN-LEE, Charles Guy,** DSC 1945; Chairman, Messrs J. & A. Scrimgeour Ltd, 1975-78; *b* 9 May 1913; *s* of Adm. Sir Charles Lionel Vaughan-Lee, KCB, and Lady (Rose Cecilia) Vaughan-Lee; *m* 1st, 1940, Agnes Celestria (*née* King; *d* 1946); one *s* two *d*; 2nd, 1949, Barbara Cecily Bryce (*née* Bateman; marr. diss. 1968); one *s* two *d* (and one adopted *s*); 3rd, 1978, Avril Barbara Curling (*née* Reed). *Educ:* Eton Coll.; Christ Church, Oxford. Served War, 1939-45; Lieut RNVR (mentioned in despatches, 1944). Joined J. & A. Scrimgeour Ltd, 1933; Partner, 1946; Sen. Partner, 1969. Comr, Public Works Loan Bd, 1973-. Chairman: Mental After-Care Assoc., 1965- (Mem., 1956); Bd, Royal Hosp. Home for Incurables, Putney, 1979- (Mem., 1956-; Hon. Treasurer, 1962-78). Member: Council, White Ensign Assoc., 1978-; RIIA, 1936-; Council, Missions to Seamen, 1981-; Advr, Royal Sailors Rests, 1981. District Councillor (Ind.), Wessex Div. of Yeovil, 1983-. *Recreation:* tennis. *Address:* Somerton Randle, Somerton, Somerset. *T:* Somerton 72205. *Clubs:* Travellers', MCC.

*Died* 21 *Feb.* 1984.

**VAUGHAN-THOMAS, (Lewis John) Wynford,** CBE 1986 (OBE 1974); MA Oxon; radio and television commentator since 1937; author, journalist; Director, Harlech Television Ltd; *b* 15 Aug. 1908; *s* of Dr David Vaughan-Thomas and Morfydd Vaughan-Thomas; *m* 1946, Charlotte Rowlands, MBE; one *s. Educ:* Swansea Grammar Sch.; Exeter College, Oxford. Keeper of MSS and Records, National Library of Wales, 1933; Area Officer, S Wales Council of Social Service, 1934-37; joined BBC, 1937. Dir of Programmes, Harlech Television Ltd, 1968-71. Commentator, Royal Commonwealth Tours, BBC War Correspondent, 1942-45; Governor, BFI, 1977-80. FRSA 1980. Hon. MA Open Univ., 1982. Croix de Guerre, 1945. *Publications:* Royal Tour, 1953-54, 1954; Anzio, 1961; Madly in all Directions, 1967; (with Alun Llewellyn) The Shell Guide to Wales, 1969; The Splendour Falls, 1973; Gower, 1975; The Countryside Companion, 1979; Trust to Talk (autobiog.), 1980; Wynford Vaughan-Thomas's Wales, 1981; The Princes of Wales, 1982; Wales, a History, 1985; How I Liberated Burgundy, 1985. *Recreations:* mountaineering, sailing. *Address:* Pentower, Tower Hill, Fishguard, Dyfed. *T:* Fishguard 873424. *Clubs:* Climbers', Savile; Cardiff and County (Cardiff).

*Died* 4 *Feb.* 1987.

**VAUGHAN WILKES, Rev. John Comyn** MA Oxon; Rector of Great Kimble, Aylesbury, 1967-72, retired; *b* 30 March 1902; *s* of L. C. Vaughan Wilkes, St Cyprian's, Eastbourne; *m* 1940, Joan, *y d* of late Very Rev. C. A. Alington, DD; six *s* one *d. Educ:* Fonthill, East Grinstead; St Cyprian's, Eastbourne; Eton Coll. (King's Schol.); Trinity Coll. Oxford (Classical Schol.). 1st Class Classical Moderations, 1923; 1st Class Lit. Hum., 1925; Half Blue for Golf (played *v* Cambridge, 1924, 1925). Assistant Master, 1925-37; Master in College, 1930-37, Eton Coll.; Warden, Radley College, Abingdon, 1937-54; ordained deacon, 1945; priest, 1945; Vicar of Hunslet, Leeds, 1954-58; Vicar of Marlow, 1958-65; Rector of Preston Bissett, Buckingham, 1965-67. *Recreations:* golf, gardening. *Address:* 29 Nelson Street, Hereford. *T:* Hereford 53565. *Clubs:* Sussex Martlets, Eton Ramblers, Oxford and Cambridge Golfing Society. *Died* 24 *Jan.* 1986.

**VEALL, Harry Truman,** CB 1963; Controller of Death Duties, Board of Inland Revenue, 1960-64, retired; *b* 19 Feb. 1901; 2nd *s* of late Wright Veall, Ewyas Harold, Herefs, and late Bertha Veall; *m* 1926, Lily Kershaw, *yr d* of Joshua E. Ryder, Alverthorpe, Wakefield, Yorks; two *d. Educ:* Wakefield Grammar Sch. LLB (external) London, 1926. Entered Civil Service, 1916; Asst Controller of Death Duties, 1953, Dep. Controller, 1957. *Address:* 20 Wincombe Drive, Ferndown, Dorset BH22 8HX. *T:* Ferndown 874726.

*Died* 17 *Oct.* 1983.

**VEASEY, Brig. Harley Gerald,** DSO 1939; late The Queen's Royal Regiment; a Vice-President, Surrey County British Legion; *b* 29 Jan. 1896; *o s* of late H. C. Veasey, Ranchi, Bihar; *m* 1922, Iris, *o d* of late W. P. Morrison, Reigate, Surrey; two *d. Educ:* Haileybury

College. Commissioned TA 1915, 2/5th Battalion The Queen's Royal Regiment, served European War, 1914-18, France (wounded); Regular Commission The Queen's Royal Regiment, 1916; Ireland, 1920-22; Adjt 5th Bn The Queen's Royal Regiment, 1922-25; Hong-Kong, 1927; Malta, 1929; North China, 1930-34; Palestine, 1939 (DSO, despatches); Commanding 2nd Bn Northern Rhodesia Regt, Northern Rhodesia and Madagascar, 1940-43; MEC and MLC, Mauritius (as OC Troops), 1943; Temp. Col, Temp. Brig., Comdr 28th EA Inf. Bde, Kenya and Ceylon, 1943-44; commanded 1/7th Bn The Queen's Royal Regt, 1945; 13th Infantry Training Centre, 1946-47; No. 2 PTC 1947-48; retired Sept. 1948, with Hon. rank of Brig. Organising Director of Conservative and Unionist Films Association, 1948-51; Sector Commander, Home Guard (West Surrey), 1952-57. *Address:* Woodhill Cottage, Shamley Green, Guildford, Surrey.

*Died* 4 *Oct.* 1982.

**VENN, Edward James (Alfred),** OBE 1985; Director-General, Royal National Institute for the Blind, 1980-83; *b* 25 Nov. 1919; *s* of Sidney and Jennie Venn; *m* 1944, Anne Minter; one *s* one *d.* Qualified as Chartered Secretary and Administrator, 1949. Local Government Officer, 1937-51; General Secretary, Royal Leicester, Leicestershire and Rutland Instn for the Blind, 1952-58; Head, Services to the Blind Dept, RNIB, 1959-71; Dep. Director-General, RNIB, 1972-79. World Council for the Welfare of the Blind: Chm., Rehabilitation Commn, European Regl Cttee, 1977-83; Mem., Cttee on Cultural Affairs, 1980-83; Mem., British Delegn, 1980-83; Member: British Council for Prevention of Blindness, 1980-; British Wireless for the Blind Fund, 1982-. Trustee: The Gift of Thomas Pocklington 1982-; Cecilia Charity for the Blind, 1983-. Governor, Royal Sch. for the Blind, Leatherhead, 1983-. *Publications:* various articles on blind welfare. *Recreations:* gardening, reading. *Address:* Lyndwood, 3 Silverdale Avenue, Oxshott, Surrey. *T:* Oxshott 3130. *Club:* Rugby. *Died* 18 *Sept.* 1989.

**VENN, Air Commodore George Oswald,** CBE 1945; *b* 15 Sept. 1892; *er s* of George Venn, Warrington; *m* 1st, 1923, Betty (*d* 1953), *d* of Alderman T. Stopher, Winchester; two *s* one *d*; 2nd, 1960, Monica, *d* of Rev. J. B. Cholmeley. *Educ:* Boteler Grammar Sch., Warrington. Architecture, 1909-14 (Student RIBA); served European War, 1914-16, Royal Fusiliers (University Public Sch. Bn), 1916-45, RFC and RAF (despatches twice). War of 1939-45, Iraq, Abyssinia, Western Desert, Fighter Command; Director of Personal Services, Air Ministry, 1943-45; retired, 1945. Executive Director Remploy Ltd, 1945-61. *Address:* Great Glemham, Saxmundham, Suffolk. *Club:* Royal Air Force. *Died* 11 *March* 1984.

**VENTRY, 7th Baron,** *cr* 1800; **Arthur Frederick Daubeney Olav Eveleigh-de-Moleyns;** *b* Norton Malreward, Som, 28 July 1898; *er s* of 6th Baron and Evelyn Muriel Stuart (*d* 1966), *y d* of Lansdowne Daubeney, Norton Malreward, Somerset; *S* father, 1936. *Educ:* Old Malthouse, Swanage; Wellington Coll., Berks. Served Irish Guards, 1917-18 (wounded); afterwards in RAF; served RAF, 1939-45. Certificated Aeronaut. King Häkon of Norway Freedom Medal, 1945. *Publications:* on aerostation and scouting. *Recreations:* music, travelling, airship piloting. *Heir:* nephew Andrew (Harold) Wesley Daubeny de Moleyns [*b* 28 May 1943; *m* 1963, Nelly Edouard Renée (marr. diss. 1979), *d* of Abel Chaumillon, Torremolinos, Spain; one *s* two *d*; *m* 1983, Jill Rosemary, *d* of C. W. Oramon]. *Address:* Lindsay Hall, Lindsay Road, Branksome Park, Poole, Dorset. *Clubs:* Naval and Military, Norwegian, Balloon and Airship.

*Died* 7 *March* 1987.

**VERE-LAURIE, Lt- Col George Halliburton Foster Peel,** DL; JP; High Sheriff of Notts, 1957-58; *b* 22 Aug. 1906; *er s* of Lt-Col George Laurie (killed in action, 1915), and Florence, Viscountess Masserene and Ferrard; *m* 1932, Caroline Judith (from whom he obtained a divorce, 1968), *yr d* of Edward Franklin, JP, Gonalston Hall, Notts; one *s* one *d*; *m* 1968, Bridget Mary Good; *m* 1979, Joyce Mary, *er d* of Capt. F. A. Letts, Leicester. *Educ:* Eton; RMC Sandhurst. 2nd Lieut 9th Lancers, 1927; Captain and Adjutant, Notts Yeomanry, 1934-38; Capt. 1938; Maj. 1940; Lt-Col Royal Military Police, 1946; retired pay, 1947. Served War of 1939-45, France and Palestine. Gold Staff Officer, Coronation, 1953. Chairman: Southwell RDC, 1951 and 1956; Governors of Newark Technical Coll., 1952-61; Bd of Visitors, Lincoln Prison, 1973- (Mem., 1963-73); Mem., Neward DC, 1973- (Chm., 1976-77). A General Commissioner of Income Tax, 1956. Freeman City of London. Court of Assistants, Saddlers' Co., 1959, Master, 1965; Lord of the Manors of Carlton-on-Trent and Willoughby-in-Norwell. DL Notts 1948, JP Notts 1952. *Recreations:* hunting and shooting (Hon. Sec. Rufford Foxhounds, 1949-55; Joint Master and Huntsman, South Notts Foxhounds, 1956-58; Joint Master, 1959-68; Chm., Grove and Rufford Hunt, 1970-76). *Address:* Carlton Hall, Carlton-on-Trent, Newark, Notts. *T:* Newark 821288. *Club:* Cavalry and Guards. *Died* 22 *July* 1981.

**VEREY, David Cecil Wynter;** DL; retired as Senior Investigator, Historic Buildings, Ministry of Housing and Local Government

(1946–65); architectural historian and writer; *b* 9 Sept. 1913; *o s of* Rev. Cecil Henry Verey and Constance Lindaraja Dearman Birchall; *m* 1939, Rosemary Isabel Baird, writer and horticulturalist, *d* of Lt-Col Prescott Sandilands, DSO; two *s* two *d*. *Educ:* Eton; Trinity Coll., Cambridge (MA). ARIBA 1940. Capt., Royal Fusiliers, 1940; seconded SOE 1943, N Africa and Italy. Chm., Alan Sutton Publishing Ltd. Chm., Gloucester Diocesan Adv. Cttee on Churches; Vice-Chm., Gloucestershire Historic Churches Preservation Trust, 1982; President: Bristol and Gloucestershire Archæological Soc., 1972; Cirencester Arch. and Hist. Soc.; Glos and Cheltenham Centre, Nat. Trust; Member: Severn Regional Cttee of Nat. Trust; High Sheriff of County of Gloucester, 1966; DL Glos, 1981. FSA. *Publications:* Shell Guides to six counties, England and Wales; The Buildings of England (Gloucestershire Vols), 1970; Cotswold Churches, 1976; Seven Victorian Architects, 1976; Diary of a Cotswold Parson, 1978; Gloucester Cathedral, 1979; Gloucestershire Churches, 1981; Diary of a Victorian Squire, 1983; articles on architectural history. *Recreations:* private museum, Arlington Mill, Bibury; gardening. *Address:* Barnsley House, Cirencester, Glos. *T:* Bibury 281.                     *Died 3 May* 1984.

**VERITY, Group Captain Conrad Edward Howe,** OBE (mil.) 1943; CEng, FICE; JP; Engineering Consultant; *b* 18 February 1901; *s of* Edward Storr Verity and Annie Amelia Verity (*née* Howe); *m* 1931, Doreen Louise Bishop; one *s* one *d*. *Educ:* Wellingborough Sch. Engrg Trg, W. H. Allen Sons & Co. Ltd, Bedford, and Bedford Tech. Coll., 1917–22; Contracts Engrg Co. Ltd, 1924–27; Tech. Engr (Mech.), London Power Co., 1927–40. Served War, 1940–45: RAF, finishing as Gp Capt.; service in England, USA, NW Africa, Pacific, India, China, etc. Chief Development and Testing Engineer, London Power Co., 1945–48; Generation Constr Engr, Brit. Elec. Authority, 1948–50; Dep. Chief Engr, Brit. Elec. Authority, and later Central Elec. Authority, 1950–55; Dir, Foster Wheeler Ltd and Manager Steam Div., 1955–59, Managing Dir, 1960–62, Chm., 1962–66; Dep. Chm., Foster Wheeler John Brown Boilers Ltd, 1966–67; Dir, Rolls-Royce and Associates, Derby, 1959–67. Gen. Comr for Income Tax, 1969–75. JP Surrey, 1960. American Legion of Merit (Officer), 1945. *Publications:* technical papers to: Institution Civil Engrs; Electrical Power Assoc.; Instn of Mech. Engrs, etc. *Recreations:* rowing, and sport generally. *Address:* Farthings, Earleydene, Sunninghill, Berks. *T:* Ascot 22033. *Clubs:* Naval and Military; Remenham; Sunninghill Comrades (Ex-Pres.); Twickenham Rowing (Hon. Life Mem.); Burway Rowing (Vice-Pres.).                     *Died 6 Sept.* 1984.

**VERNON, Prof. Philip Ewart,** MA, PhD, DSc; Professor Emeritus, University of Calgary, 1979; Emeritus Professor, University of London; *b* 6 June 1905; *e s of* late Horace Middleton Vernon; *m* 1st, 1938, Annie C. Gray (decd); 2nd, 1947, Dorothy Anne Fairley Lawson, MA, MEd; one *s*. *Educ:* Oundle Sch.; St John's Coll., Cambridge; Yale and Harvard Universities. First Class Hons in Nat. Sci. Tripos, Part I, 1926, and Moral Sci. Tripos, Part II, 1927; John Stewart of Rannoch Scholarship in Sacred Music, 1925; Strathcona Research Studentship, 1927–29; Laura Spelman Rockefeller Fellowship in Social Sciences, 1929–31; Fellowship of St John's Coll., Cambridge, 1930–33; Pinsent-Darwin Studentship in Mental Pathology, 1933–35. Psychologist to LCC at Maudsley Hospital Child Guidance Clinic, 1933–35; Head of Psychology Dept, Jordanhill Training Centre, Glasgow, 1935–38; Head of Psychology Dept, University of Glasgow, 1938–47; Psychological Research Adviser to Admiralty and War Office, 1942–45; Prof. of Educational Psychology, Inst. of Education, University of London, 1949–64; Prof. of Psychology, 1964–68; Prof. of Educational Psychology, Univ. of Calgary, 1968–78. Fellow, Centre for Advanced Studies in Behavioural Scis, Stanford, Calif, 1961–62, Vis. Canada Council Fellow, 1975. Visiting Professor: Princeton Univ. and Educnl Testing Service, 1957; Teachers' Coll., Sydney, 1977; numerous internat. educnl consultancies and lect. tours for British Council, 1953–68. President: Psych. Sect., British Assoc. Advancement of Science, 1952; BPsS, 1954–55. Govt of Alberta Achievement Award, 1972. Hon. LLD Univ. of Calgary, 1980. *Publications:* (with G. W. Allport) Studies in Expressive Movement, 1933; The Measurement of Abilities, 1940, 2nd edn, 1956; (with J. B. Parry) Personnel Selection in the British Forces, 1949; The Structure of Human Abilities, 1950, 2nd edn, 1961; Personality Tests and Assessments, 1953; Secondary School Selection, 1957; Intelligence and Attainment Tests, 1960; Personality Assessment: A Critical Survey, 1963; Intelligence and Cultural Environment, 1969; Readings in Creativity, 1971; (with G. Adamson and Dorothy F. Vernon) Psychology and Education of Gifted Children, 1977; Intelligence: Heredity and Environment, 1979; Abilities and Achievements of Orientals in North America, 1982; numerous papers in British and American psychological journals. *Recreations:* music, snowshoeing, cross-country ski-ing. *Address:* No 402B, 3719 49th Street NW, Calgary, Alberta, Canada.
                     *Died 28 July* 1987.

**VERNON-HUNT, Ralph Holmes,** DFC; Deputy Chairman, Pan Books Ltd, 1980–82, retired (Managing Director, 1970); *b* 23 May 1923; *m* 1946, Elizabeth Mary Harris; four *s* two *d* (and one *s* decd). *Educ:* Malvern College. Flt-Lt RAF, 1941–46; Bookseller, 1946–47; Sales Dir, Pan Books Ltd, 1947–62; Sales Dir, Paul Hamlyn Ltd, 1963–69. *Recreation:* hydroponics. *Address:* 45 Rosemont Road, Richmond, Surrey TW10 6QN.                     *Died 10 Nov.* 1987.

**VERONESE, Dr Vittorino;** Cavaliere di Gran Croce della Repubblica Italiana; Gold Medal Awarded for Culture (Italian Republic); Doctor of Law (Padua, 1930); lawyer, banker, administrator; Chairman, Board of Directors, Banco di Roma, 1961–76 (Auditor, 1945–53; Director, 1953–57); *b* Vicenza, 1 March 1910; *m* 1939, Maria Petrarca; four *s* three *d*. General Secretary: Catholic Movement Graduates, 1939; Italian Catholic Action, 1944–46 (President, 1946–52); Vice-President, Internat. Movement of Catholic Intellectuals of Pax Romana, 1947–55. Vice-President, Banca Cattolica del Veneto, 1952–57; President, Consorzio di Credito per le Opere Pubbliche and Istituto di Credito per le Imprese di Pubblica Utilitá, 1957–58; Italian Deleg. to General Conf. of UNESCO, Beirut, 1950, Paris, 1952–53; Member Italian Nat. Commn, 1953–58; Vice-President, Exec. Board, 1954–56; President, 1956–58. Director-General of UNESCO, 1958–61, resigned; Member, Comité Consultatif International pour l'Alphabétisation, UNESCO, 1967; Vice-President: Comité Consultatif International pour Venise, UNESCO; Societa Italiano per l'Organizzazione Internationale (SIOI); Pres., Italian Consultative Cttee for Human Rights, 1965. Pres., Circolo di Roma, 1968. Lay Observer in Concilio Ecumenico Vaticano II; Member, Pontificia Commissione Justitia et Pax, 1967. Cav. di Gran Groce dell' Ordine di S Silvestro Papa; Commendatore dell' Ordine Piano. Holds several foreign orders. *Address:* c/o Banco di Roma, Via del Corso 307, Rome, Italy; 21 Via Cadlolo, Rome, Italy.                     *Died 3 Sept.* 1986.

**VERRY, Frederick William,** CMG 1958; OBE 1948; Assistant Secretary, Air Ministry, 1953–62, retired; *b* 15 Feb. 1899; *s* of late Herbert William Verry; *m* 1926, Phyllis (*d* 1972), *d* of late William Pitt MacConochie. *Educ:* Stockport Secondary Sch.; Northern Polytechnic Sch., London. Joined Civil Service as Boy Clerk, War Office, 1914. Served in RN Airship Service and RAF, 1917–19. Air Ministry, 1920. Financial Adviser, Middle East Air Force, 1946–49. *Recreation:* painting. *Address:* Oakhill House, Eady Close, Highlands Road, Horsham, Sussx RH13 5LZ.
                     *Died 7 June* 1981.

**VERSEY, Henry Cherry;** Emeritus Professor of Geology, University of Leeds, since 1959; *b* 22 Jan. 1894; *s* of Charles Versey, Welton, East Yorkshire; *m* 1923, Hypatia Ingersoll, *d* of Greevz Fysher, Leeds; two *s* two *d*. *Educ:* Hymers Coll., University of Leeds. Service with RAOC, European War, 1916–19. Lecturer in Geology, University of Leeds, 1919–49; Reader in Applied Geology, 1949–56, Professor of Geology, 1956–59, University of Leeds. Hon. LLD (Leeds), 1967. Phillips Medal, Yorkshire Geological Society, 1964. *Publications:* Geology of the Appleby District, 1941; Geology and Scenery of the Countryside round Leeds and Bradford, 1948. Many papers on Yorkshire geology. *Recreation:* philately. *Address:* 1 Stainburn Terrace, Leeds LS17 6NJ. *T:* Leeds (0532) 682244.
                     *Died 12 Nov.* 1990.

**VERYKIOS, Dr Panaghiotis Andrew;** Kt Commander of Order of George I, of Greece, and of Order of the Phoenix; MM (Greece); Greek Ambassador, retired; *b* Athens, 1910; *m* 1939, Mary (*née* Dracoulis); three *s*. *Educ:* Athens and Paris. Law (Dr) and Political Sciences. Greek Diplomatic Service, 1935. Served in the Army, 1939–40. Various diplomatic posts until 1946; Secretary of Embassy, London, 1947–51; Counsellor, Dep. Representative of NATO, Paris, 1952–54; Counsellor of Embassy, Paris, 1954–56; Head of NATO Div., Min. of Foreign Affairs, Athens, 1956–60; Ambassador to: The Netherlands, 1960–64; Norway, 1961–67; Denmark, 1964–67; Iceland, 1967; Court of St James's, 1967–69; Spain, 1969–70. Holds foreign decorations. *Publication:* La Prescription en Droit International, 1934 (Paris). *Recreation:* music. *Address:* 6 Iras Street, Ekali, Athens. *T:* 8131216. *Club:* Athenian (Athens).
                     *Died 23 June* 1990.

**VESEY-FITZGERALD, Brian Percy Seymour;** author; *b* 5 July 1900. Member Honourable Society of Cymmrodorion; President of the British Fairground Society, 1953–63; Editor-in-Chief of The Field, 1938–46; Chairman of Preliminary Enquiry into Cause of Canine Hysteria, 1938; Chairman, Association of School Natural History Societies, 1947–48; Member of Institute for the Study of Animal Behaviour; Member of Gypsy Lore Society. Field Fare Broadcasts, 1940–45; There and Back Broadcasts, 1947–49. Editor of Country Books since 1943. FRSA. *Publications:* Amateur Boxing, Professional Boxing (Lonsdale Library, Sporting Records), 1936; Badgers Funeral, 1937; A Book of British Waders, 1939; Hampshire Scene, 1940; The Noctule, 1941; Programme for Agriculture, 1941; A Country Chronicle, 1942; Farming in Britain, 1942; Hedgerow and Field, 1943; Gypsies of Britain, 1944, rev. edn. 1964; British Countryside, 1946; British Game, 1946; The Book of the Horse, 1946; It's My Delight, 1947; British Bats, 1947; A Child's Biology,

1948; Bird Biology for Beginners, 1948; The Book of the Dog, 1948; Background to Birds, 1949; Hampshire, 1949; Rivermouth, 1949; (co-ed) Game Fish of the World, 1950; The River Avon, 1951; Gypsy Borrow, 1953; Winchester, 1953; British Birds and their Nests, 1953; More British Birds and their Nests, 1954; Nature Recognition, 1955; Cats, 1956; A Third Book of British Birds and their Nests, 1956; The Domestic Dog, 1957; A Book of Wildflowers, 1958; Instructions to Young Naturalists, 1959; The Beauty of Cats, 1959; A Book of Garden Flowers, 1960; The Beauty of Dogs, 1960; A Book of Trees, 1962; About Dogs, 1963; The Cat Lover's Encyclopædia, 1963; Foxes in Britain, 1964; Animal Anthology, 1965; The Dog-Owners Encyclopædia, 1965; Portrait of the New Forest, 1966; Garden Alive, 1967; The World of Reptiles, 1968; The Vanishing Wild Life of Britain, 1969; The World of Ants, Bees and Wasps, 1969; The Domestic Cat, 1969. *Recreations:* birdwatching, gardening. *Address:* Long Croft, Wrecclesham, Surrey. *Died* 23 *Oct.* 1981.

**VESTEY, Ronald Arthur;** DL; Director, Union International Co.; *b* 10 May 1898; 4th but *e* surv. *s* of Sir Edmund Hoyle Vestey, 1st Bt; *m* 1923, Florence Ellen McLean (*d* 1966), *d* of Colonel T. G. Luis, VD, Broughty Ferry, Angus; one *s* three *d*. *Educ:* Malvern Coll. Travelled extensively throughout world, with interests in many countries. High Sheriff of Suffolk, 1961; DL Suffolk, 1970. *Recreations:* shooting, fishing. *Address:* Great Thurlow Hall, Suffolk. *T:* Thurlow 240. *Clubs:* Carlton, MCC. *Died* 27 *Dec.* 1987.

**VEYSEY, Geoffrey Charles,** CB 1948; *b* 20 Dec. 1895; *e s* of late Charles Veysey, Exeter; *m* 1925, Eileen Agnes (*d* 1981), *d* of late Charles Henry Byers, Gunnersbury. *Educ:* Latymer Upper Sch., Hammersmith. Served European War, 1914–18. Lieut, RGA. Entered Ministry of Labour, 1919; Private Secretary to Parliamentary Secretaries and Permanent Secretaries of Ministry, 1929–32; Assistant Secretary, 1938; Principal Assistant Secretary, 1944; Under-Secretary, Ministry of Labour and National Service, 1946–60. *Address:* 8 Stokes House, Sutherland Avenue, Bexhill-on-Sea, East Sussex TN39 3QT. *T:* Bexhill-on-Sea 214320. *Club:* Athenæum. *Died* 7 *Oct.* 1984.

**VIBERT, McInroy Este;** Consular Service, retired; *b* Chiswick, 6 June 1894; *o s* of late Arthur Reginald Vibert and Margaret Eleanor Fraser; *m* 1st, Joyce Havell; one *s* one *d*; 2nd, Ellen Fiebiger-Guermanova (*d* 1982). *Educ:* Taunton Sch.; France and Germany. Served European War, 1914–18, 10th Royal Fusiliers; Vice-Consul at Brussels, 1919, and subsequently at Philadelphia, Stettin, Koenigsberg, Memel, Frankfort-on-Main, Punta Arenas, Cologne, and Tunis; Consul at Sarajevo, 1936–39, and Split, 1939–41, Lisbon, 1941–44, Barcelona, 1944, Curacao, 1944–45; Consul-General (local rank) and Counsellor of Legation at Havana, 1945–47; Chargé d'Affaires, July 1946; Foreign Office, 1947–48; Consul at Vigo; retired, 1950, on pension. *Recreations:* water-colour painting, philately. *Address:* Hogar del Sol, Santa Maria, Mallorca, Spain. *T:* 62–02–32. *Died* 29 *March* 1986.

**VICKERS, Sir (Charles) Geoffrey,** VC 1915; Kt 1946; Solicitor, Administrator and Author; *b* 13 Oct. 1894; *y s* of C. H. Vickers, Nottingham; *m* 1st, 1918, Helen Tregoning (marr. diss. 1934), *y d* of A. H. Newton, Bexhill, Sussex; one *s* one *d*; 2nd, 1935, Ethel Ellen (*d* 1972), *y d* of late H. R. B. Tweed, Laindon Frith, Billericay, Essex; one *s*. *Educ:* Oundle Sch.; Merton Coll., Oxford (MA). Served World War I with the Sherwood Foresters and other regts (2nd Lt-Major, 1915–18). Admitted Solicitor, 1923; Partner, Slaughter & May, 1926–45. World War II, re-commissioned (Colonel), specially employed; seconded as Deputy Dir.-Gen., Ministry of Economic Warfare, in charge of economic intelligence, and Member, Joint Intelligence Cttee of Chiefs of Staff, 1941–45. Legal adviser to National Coal Board, 1946–48, Board Member in charge of manpower, training, education, health and welfare, 1948–55; Director, Parkinson Cowan Ltd, 1955–65. Member, many public and professional bodies including: London Passenger Transport Board, 1941–46; Council of Law Society, 1944–48; Med. Research Council, 1952–60; Chairman, Research Cttee of Mental Health Research Fund, 1951–67. Hon. FRCPsych. *Publications:* (1953–) 50 papers and 6 books on application of system theory to management, government, medicine and human ecology, including The Art of Judgement, 1965, Value Systems and Social Process, 1968, Freedom in a Rocking Boat, 1970; Making Institutions Work, 1974; Responsibility: its sources and limits, 1980. *Address:* The Grange, Goring-on-Thames, Reading, Berks. *T:* Goring 872933. *Died* 16 *March* 1982.

**VICKERS, Lt-Gen. Wilmot Gordon Hilton,** CB 1942; OBE 1919; DL; *b* 8 June 1890; *s* of late Lt-Col Hilton Vickers, IA; *m* Mary Catherine (*decd*), *d* of Dr A. E. Nuttall; two *s*. *Educ:* United Services Coll., Westward Ho!, and Windsor (now Haileybury and Imperial Service Coll.). Commissioned Indian Army (Unattached List), 1910; 2nd Lieut, Indian Army, 1911; Captain, 1915; Major, 1926; Bt Lt-Col, 1931; Col, 1935; Maj.-Gen., 1940; Lt-Gen., 1943; Comdt and Chief Instructor, Equitation Sch., India, 1934–35; Dep. Dir of Staff

Duties, India, 1935–37; Brigade Comdr, India, 1939–40; Dir of Supplies and Transport, India, 1940–41; Maj.-Gen. i/c Administration, Iraq-Persia, 1941–42; Quarter-master-General, India, 1942–44; retired, 1944. DL County of Gloucestershire, 1946. County Cadet Commandant, Gloucestershire, Army Cadet Force, 1946–55. County Chief Warden, Civil Defence, Gloucestershire, 1949–60. *Address:* 4 Oakhurst Court, Parabola Road, Cheltenham, Glos. *Clubs:* Cavalry and Guards; New (Cheltenham). *Died* 13 *Sept.* 1987.

**VICKERY, Sir Philip Crawford,** Kt 1948; CIE 1939; OBE 1923; *b* 23 Feb. 1890; *s* of late John Evans Vickery and Alice Maud Mary Vickery; *m* 1920, Phyllis Field Fairweather (*d* 1982); one *s* (*yr s*, Coldstream Guards, died of wounds in Italy, April 1945). *Educ:* Portora Royal Sch., Enniskillen; Dean Close Sch., Cheltenham; Trinity Coll., Dublin. Joined Indian Police, 1909; Coronation Durbar, Delhi, 1911; served European War, 1915–21 and War of 1939–45; Lieut-Colonel, Sept. 1939, and Acting Colonel, 1942. Commonwealth Relations Office, 1952–65. *Club:* East India and Sports. *Died* 12 *Jan.* 1987.

**VIDOR, King (Wallis);** Independent Film Director and Producer (US); *b* Galveston, Texas, 8 Feb. 1896; *s* of Chas S. Vidor and Kate (*née* Wallis); *m* 1st, 1919, Florence Vidor (*d* 1977); one *d*; 2nd, 1927, Eleanor Boardman; two *d*; 3rd, 1937, Elizabeth Hill. *Educ:* Peacock Military College, Texas; Jacob Tome Institute, Maryland. Directed films when aged 19, in Texas, 1914; in film industry worked as cameraman, writer and actor; directed again from 1918. Films directed include: Turn in the Road; The Jack Knife Man; Peg O' My Heart; Wild Oranges; The Big Parade; La Bohème; The Crowd; Hallelujah; Street Scene; The Champ; Bird of Paradise; Our Daily Bread; The Texas Rangers; Stella Dallas; The Citadel; Northwest Passage; H. M. Pulham Esq.; American Romance; Duel in the Sun; The Fountainhead; Ruby Gentry; Man Without a Star; War and Peace; Solomon and Sheba. D. W. Griffith award by Screen Directors Guild (for outstanding contributions in film direction over a long period of years), 1957; many awards for various films throughout America and Europe. Golden Thistle Award, Edinburgh Festival, 1964. Cavaliere Ufficiale, Italy, 1970. *Publications:* A Tree is a Tree (autobiography), 1953 (New York), also published in England; Guerra e Pace, 1956 (Italy); King Vidor on Film-making, 1972 (New York). *Recreations:* golf; plays classical Spanish Guitar; paints in oils. *Address:* c/o David V. Adams, 1545 Wilshire Boulevard, Los Angeles, Calif 90017, USA. *Clubs:* Academy Motion Picture Arts and Sciences, Bel Air Country, Screen Directors Guild, PEN (USA). *Died* 1 *Nov.* 1982.

**VILLIERS, Alan John,** DSC; *b* 23 Sept. 1903; *s* of Leon Joseph Villiers and Anastasia Hayes; *m* 1st, 1924, Daphne Kaye Harris (marr. diss. 1936), Hobart; no *c*; 2nd, 1940, Nancie, *o d* of Alban Henry and Mabel Wills, Melbourne; two *s* one *d*. *Educ:* State Schools, Essendon High School, Melbourne. Went to sea 1919 in sail, whaling in Antarctic with Norwegian Carl Anton Larsen's first Ross Sea Expedition in whaler Sir James Clark Ross, 1923–24; joined Captain De Cloux in purchase of four masted barque Parma, 1931; bought Danish schoolship Georg Stage June 1934, renamed her Joseph Conrad and sailed 58,000 miles round world, 1934, 1935, 1936; sailing in Kuweit dhows in Persian Gulf–Zanzibar trade, 1938–39; Lieut, RNVR, 1940–42; Lt Cdr 1943; Comdr 1944. Commanded 'A' Squadron of Landing Craft (Infantry) in the invasions of Italy and Normandy (DSC) and at the occupation of Rangoon, Malaya, and East Indies; Master, training ship Warspite, Outward Bound Sea School, Aberdovey, N Wales, 1949; sailed with Portuguese Arctic codfishing fleet in schooner Argus, 1950. Commander of Portuguese Order of St James of the Sword. Volunteered as Master of Mayflower replica, 1956, and sailed the vessel across the N Atlantic without power, except sails. In command of square-rigged ships for films: Moby Dick, 1955; John Paul Jones, 1958; Billy Budd, 1961; Hawaii, 1965. Past Pres., Soc. for Nautical Research; Trustee of National Maritime Museum, 1948–74; Governor Cutty Sark Preservation Soc.; Member: HMS Victory Technical Advisory Committee; Ships Cttee, Maritime Trust. *Publications:* Whaling in the Frozen South; Falmouth for Orders; By Way of Cape Horn; The Sea in Ships; Sea Dogs of To-day; Voyage of the Parma; Vanished Fleets; The Last of the Windships; Cruise of the Conrad; Stormalong; The Making of a Sailor, 1938; Sons of Sinbad, 1940; The Set of the Sails, 1949; The Coral Sea, 1950; The Quest of the Schooner Argus, 1951 (Camões Prize, Portugal); The Indian Ocean, 1952; The Way of a Ship, 1954; Posted Missing, 1956; Pioneers of the Seven Seas, 1956; The Western Ocean, 1957; Give Me a Ship to Sail, 1958; The New Mayflower, 1959; The Oceans, 1963; The Battle of Trafalgar, 1965; Captain Cook, the Seamen's Seaman, 1967; The War with Cape Horn, 1971; (with H. Picard) The Bounty Ships of France, 1972. *Recreations:* sailing, photography. *Address:* 1a Lucerne Road, Oxford OX2 7QB. *T:* Oxford 55632. *Clubs:* Naval; Royal Harwich Yacht (Harwich); Royal Cruising; Circumnavigators (New York). *Died* 3 *March* 1982.

**VILLIERS, Vice-Adm. Sir (John) Michael,** KCB 1962 (CB 1960); OBE 1943; *b* 22 June 1907; 3rd *s* of late Rear-Adm. E. C. Villiers,

CMG and of Mrs Villiers; *m* 1936, Rosemary, CStJ, 2nd *d* of late Lt-Col B. S. Grissell, DSO, and late Lady Astley-Cubitt; two *d. Educ:* Oundle School; Royal Navy. Served War of 1939–45 (despatches, OBE). Comd HMS Ursa, 1945, and HMS Snipe, 1946–47; directing staff of Joint Services Staff College, 1948–49; Assistant Director of Plans Admiralty, 1950–51; Queen's Harbour Master, Malta, 1952–54; comd HMS Bulwark, 1954–57; Chief of Naval Staff, New Zealand, 1958–60; a Lord Commissioner of the Admiralty, Fourth Sea Lord and Vice-Controller, 1960–63; Lt-Governor and C-in-C Jersey, 1964–69. KStJ 1964. *Address:* Decoy House, Melton, Woodbridge, Suffolk IP13 6DH. *Club:* Army and Navy. *Died* 1 *Jan.* 1990.

**VINCENT, Sir (Harold) Graham,** KCMG 1953; CB 1935; CVO 1932; *b* 13 Nov. 1891; *s* of late William Vincent; *m* 1921, Brenda (*d* 1973), *d* of late Edward Wood-White, MD, BS; one *d. Educ:* Haileybury; Jesus College, Cambridge. First Class, Mathematical Tripos, 1914; served European War, 1914–18, in London Rifle Bde and Army Signal Service (Captain); entered HM Treasury, 1919; Private Sec. to the Parliamentary Sec. to the Treasury, 1924; Private Secretary to successive Prime Ministers, 1928–36; Principal Private Secretary, 1934–36; Principal Assistant Secretary Committee of Imperial Defence, 1936–39; Ministry: of Food, 1939–40; of Works and Buildings, and of Town and Country Planning, 1940–44; of Production, 1944–46; of Civil Aviation, 1946–49; Secretary, Government Hospitality, 1949–56. *Address:* Park Shaw, New Road, Sundridge, Sevenoaks, Kent. *Died* 5 *Nov.* 1981.

**VINES, Prof. Howard William Copland,** MA, MD; retired; *b* 10 March 1893; *yr s* of Emer. Prof. S. H. Vines; *m* 1st, 1921, Dorothy Mary Beatrice Brindley (*d* 1951); one *s* one *d;* 2nd, 1953, Ingrid Gertrud Hedwig Apel; two *d. Educ:* Rugby School; Christ's Coll., Cambridge; St Bartholomew's Hosp. 1st Cl. Nat. Sci. Tripos 1 and Bachelor Schol. Christ's Coll., 1914; MB, BCh (Cantab.) 1920; MD (Cantab.) and Horton-Smith Prize, 1922; Fellow of Christ's Coll. and Director of Med. Studies, 1919–26; Beit Memorial Fellow, 1921–23; Foulerton Research Student, 1923–27. Sector Pathologist EMS, 1939–44; Professor of Pathology, University of London, 1948–53; Pathologist, Charing Cross Hospital, 1928–53; Dean, Charing Cross Hospital Medical School, 1945–55; Mem. Charing Cross Hosp. Council, 1945–48; Bd of Governors, 1948–55; Chm., Charing Cross Hosp. and Med. Sch. Planning Cttees, 1948–55; Mem. West Cornwall Hosp. Management Cttee, 1954–64; Member North West Metropolitan Regional Board, 1948–50. *Publications:* The Parathyroid Glands, 1924; (jointly) The Adrenal Cortex and Intersexuality, 1938; Green's Pathology, 15th edn 1934; 16th edn 1940, 17th edn 1949; Background to Hospital Planning, 1952; papers on endocrinology in Pathol and Med. journals; papers on Hospital Planning. *Recreation:* gardening. *Address:* Caerleon, Brackley Road, Weston-on-the-Green, Bicester, Oxon OX6 8RQ. *T:* Bletchington 50701. *Died* 13 *Sept.* 1982.

**VINTER, Geoffrey Odell;** JP; Director of Companies; Underwriting Member of Lloyd's; *b* 29 April 1900; *s* of Harold Skelsey Vinter; *g s* of James Odel Vinter, High Sheriff Cambridgeshire and Huntingdonshire, 1921; *m* 1925, Mary Margaret Hardy (novelist: Mary Vinter); one *d. Educ:* Clifton; University Coll., Oxford (MA). Chm., Papworth Village Settlement, 1974–79. High Sheriff of Cambridgeshire and Huntingdonshire, 1948–49; JP Cambs 1951. *Recreations:* shooting, fishing. *Address:* Thriplow Manor, Royston, Herts. *T:* Fowlmere 255. *Died* 4 *March* 1981.

**VIRTUE, Hon. Sir John (Evenden),** KBE 1975; Judge of Supreme Court of Western Australia, 1951–75 (retd); Senior Puisne Judge, 1969–75; *b* 25 April 1905; *s* of Ernest Evenden Virtue and Mary Hamilton Virtue; *m* 1938, Mary Joan, *d* of Reginald and Mary Lloyd. *Educ:* Hale Sch., Perth, WA; Univs of Melbourne and Western Australia. LLM (Melb), BA (WA). Barrister and solicitor, admitted to practise in Supreme Courts of Western Australia and Victoria; in practice as barrister and solicitor, Supreme Court of W Australia, 1928–50. Lectured (part-time) in Torts and Criminal Law, Univ. of WA, 1930–49. Served War, AIF (Major), 1940–43. Pres., Law Soc. of WA, 1950. *Recreations:* lawn bowls, contract bridge. *Address:* 74 Kingsway, Nedlands, WA 6009, Australia. *T:* 86–1856. *Clubs:* Weld, Royal Perth Yacht (Perth, WA). *Died* 30 *Aug.* 1986.

**VISSER 't HOOFT, Dr Willem Adolf;** General Secretary of World Council of Churches, 1938–66, Hon. President, 1968; *b* 20 Sept. 1900; *m* 1924, Henriette Philippine Jacoba Boddaert (*d* 1968); two *s* one *d. Educ:* Leyden University (DD). Secretary, World Committee of YMCA, 1924–31; General Secretary, World Student Christian Federation, 1931–38. Hon. Professor: Theolog. Faculty, Budapest, 1947; Theolog. Acad., Moscow, 1964. Hon. Fellow, Hebrew Univ. of Jerusalem, 1972. Hon. DD: Aberdeen, 1939; Princetown, USA; Trinity Coll., Toronto, 1950; Geneva, 1951; Yale, 1954; Oberlin Coll., 1954; Oxford, 1955; Harvard, 1958; St Paul's, Tokyo, 1959; Faculté Libre de Théologie, Paris, 1963; Kirchliche Hochschule, Berlin, 1964; Brown Univ., Providence, RI, 1965; Theol Faculty,

Zürich, 1966; Univ. Catholique, Louvain, 1967; Open Univ., 1974. Cardinal Bea Prize, 1975; Louise Weiss Foundn Prize, 1976; Hanseatic Goethe Prize, 1977; Wateler Prize; Peace Prize of German Book Trade; Grotius Medal. Hon. CStJ. Commander, Order of the Lion (Netherlands); Officer, Legion of Honour (France); Grand Cross, Order of Merit, with ribbon and star (Federal Republic of Germany); Cross of Great Comdr of Holy Sepulchre; Order of Vladimir (Orthodox Church of Russia); Comdr, Order of St Andrew (Ecumenical Patriarchate). *Publications:* The Background of the Social Gospel in America, 1928; Anglo-Catholicism and Orthodoxy, 1933; None other Gods, 1937; The Church and its Function in Society (with J. H. Oldham), 1937; Wretchedness and Greatness of the Church, 1943; The Struggle of the Dutch Church, 1946; Kingship of Christ, 1948; Rembrandt et la Bible, 1947; The Meaning of Ecumenical, 1953; The Ecumenical Movement and the Racial Problem, 1954; The Renewal of the Church (Eng. edn 1956); Rembrandt and the Gospel, 1957; The Pressure of our Common Calling, 1959; No Other Name, 1963; Hauptschriften, Bd 1 and 2, 1967; (with Cardinal Bea) Peace Among Christians, 1967; Memoirs, 1973; Has the Ecumenical Movement a Future?, 1974; The Fatherhood of God in an Age of Emancipation, 1982. *Address:* 150, route de Ferney, 1211 Geneva 20, Switzerland. *T:* 91.61.11.
*Died* 4 *July* 1985.

**VIVIAN, Arthur Henry Seymour;** Clerk of the Skinners' Company, 1941–59; Hon. Freeman and Member of Court of the Company, 1959–80; *b* 30 June 1899; *o s* of late Henry Chester Vivian, Cardiff; *m* 1927, Elizabeth, *yr d* of late Maj. R. H. Hood-Haggie; one *d. Educ:* Harrow and Magdalen Coll., Oxford (MA). RFA, 1918; called to the Bar, Inner Temple, 1923. Commissioned London Welsh AA Regiment, 1939–43. Hon. Secretary Governing Bodies' Association, 1953–67, Hon. Member, Committee, 1967. *Recreation:* golf (played for Oxford, 1921 and 1922). *Address:* 24 Sandy Lodge Road, Moor Park, Rickmansworth, Herts. *T:* Rickmansworth 74055. *Clubs:* Royal Automobile, MCC; Royal Porthcawl Golf; Moor Park Golf (Pres., 1971–). *Died* 22 *Dec.* 1985.

**VOKES, Maj.-Gen. Christopher,** CB 1945; CBE 1944; DSO 1943; retired from the Canadian Army in 1960; *b* 13 April 1904; *e s* of late Major F. P. Vokes, Kingston, Ontario, and Elizabeth Briens; *m* 1932, Constance Mary Waugh (*d* 1969), Winnipeg; two *s. Educ:* RMC, Kingston; McGill Univ., Montreal. 1st Commission Royal Canadian Engineers, 1925; Staff Coll., Camberley, 1934–35; Brigadier Comd 2 Cdn Inf. Bde, 1942–43; Maj.-Gen. GOC 1 Cdn Div., 1943–44; GOC 4 Cdn Armd Div., 1944–45. Campaigns: Sicily, Italy, NW Europe (despatches twice, DSO, CBE, CB); GOC Cdn Occupation Force, Germany, 1945; Officer of Legion of Honour (France); Croix de Guerre avec Palme (France); Order of Golden Ariston Andrias (Greece); Commander Mil. Order of Italy. *Address:* 105 Allan Street, Apt 702, Oakville, Ontario L6J 3N2, Canada.
*Died* 27 *March* 1985.

**von EULER, Prof. Ulf Svante;** Comdr North Star of Sweden (1st cl.) 1970; Professor of Physiology, Karolinska Institute, 1939–71; *b* 7 Feb 1905; *s* of Hans von Euler and Astrid von Euler (*née* Cleve); *m* 1st, 1930, Jane Sodenstierna; two *s* two *d;* 2nd, 1958, Dagmar Cronstedt. *Educ:* Karolinska Institute, Stockholm. MD 1930. For. Mem., Royal Soc., 1973. Nobel Prize in Physiology or Medicine (jt) 1970. Hon. degrees, Univs of: Umea, 1958; Dijon, 1962; Ghent, 1963; Tübingen, 1964; Buenos Aires, 1971; Edinburgh, 1971; Manchester, 1973; Madrid, 1973; Lodz, 1979. Cross of the Sun (Brazil), 1952; Grand Cross of Merito Civil (Spain), 1979. Comdr, Palmes académiques (France), 1968. *Publications:* Nonadrenaline, 1956; Prostaglandins (with R. Eliasson), 1967; articles in jls of physiology and pharmacology. *Address:* Sturegatan 14, Stockholm S-11436, Sweden. *T:* S-08–636559. *Died* 10 *March* 1983.

**von FRISCH, Dr Karl Ritter;** retired but doing scientific work; *b* Vienna, 20 Nov. 1886; *s* of Dr Anton Ritter von Frisch, Prof., Surgeon and Urologist and Marie (*née* Exner); *m* 1917, Margarete (*née* Mohr) (*d* 1964); one *s* three *d. Educ:* Schottengymnasium, Vienna; Univs of Munich and Vienna. Dr Phil Vienna 1910. Asst. Zoolog. Inst., Univ. of Munich, 1910; Lectr in Zoology and Comparable Anatomy, Univ. of Munich, 1912; Prof. and Dir of Zoolog. Inst., Univ. of Rostock, 1921; Univ. of Breslau, 1923; Univ. of Munich, 1925; Univ. of Graz (Austria), 1946; returned to Munich, 1950 and retired 1958. Member: Bayer Acad. Science, 1926; Copenhagen, 1931; Leopoldina Halle, 1935; Acad. of Science, Vienna, 1938 (Hon. Mem. 1954) and Göttingen, 1947; (Hon.) Royal Entomological Soc., London, 1949; Acad. of Science and Lit., Mainz, 1949; Nat. Acad. Sciences, Washington, 1951; (Hon.) Amer. Physiol Soc., 1952; Acad. of Arts and Scis, Boston, 1952; Swedish Acad. of Sci., 1952; Royal Soc., 1954; Amer. Entomological Soc., 1955; Linnaean Soc., 1956, etc. Pour le Mérite (Peace Class), 1952; Kalinga Prize (Unesco), 1959; Austrian Award for Science and Art, 1960; Balzan Prize for Biology, 1963; Nobel Prize for Medicine or Physiology, 1973. Hon. Dr Bern, 1949; Zürich Polytechnic, 1955; Graz, 1957; Harvard, 1963; Tubingen, 1964; Rostock, 1969. *Publications:* Aus dem Leben der Bienen, 1927 (The Dancing Bees,

1954); Du und das Leben, 1936 (Man and the Living World, 1963); Bees, 1950, rev. edn 1971; Biologie, 1952 (Biology, 1964); Erinnerungen eines Biologen, 1957 (A Biologist Remembers, 1967, 1973); Tanzsprache und Orientierung der Bienen, 1965 (The Dance Language and Orientation of Bees, 1967); Animal Architecture, 1974. *Address:* Über der Klause 10, 8000 Munich 90, West Germany. *T:* 644948. *Died* 12 *June* 1982.

**von HAGEN, Victor Wolfgang,** FZS; FRGS; Organiser-Leader, Persian Royal Road Expedition, 1972, American Geographical Society Expedition, 1973–75, explorations in Iran, Iraq and Turkey; Leader, Roman Road Expeditions, 1962; Director: Inca High Expedition; American Geographical Society; History of Science Society; Latin American Adviser, Encyclopedia Americana; Contributor: Encyclopædia Britannica; Geographical Magazine, London; Illustrated London News, since 1935; Research Associate Museum of the American Indian, New York; Consultant UN Guggenheim Fellowship for creative writing, 1949, renewed 1950–51; American Philosophical Society (Research Fellow); *b* Saint Louis, Mo., 29 Feb. 1908; *s* of Henry von Hagen and Eleanor Josephine Stippe-Hornbach; *m* 1933, Christine Inez Brown (marr. diss.); one *d*; *m* 1951, Silvia Hofmann-Edzard (marr. diss. 1962); two *d. Educ:* Morgan Park Military Acad.; New York Univ.; Univ. de Quito, S America. Served US Army, War of 1941–45, 13th Inf. Regt, Texas. Explorer, naturalist, ethnographer. Expedition Mexico, 1931–33; Ecuador, Amazon, Peru, Galapagos Islands, 1934–36; Honduras, Mosquito Coast, Guatemala, 1937–38, to study quetzal bird for Zoo, Regent's Park; Panama, Costa Rica, 1940; Colombia, Peru, 1947–48; resided BWI, 1949–50; expedition to Peru, 1952–54; studied Roman Roads, Lubeck to Africa, 1955; expedition to Mexico, 1957; Yucatan, 1958–59; Study of Roman Roads in Italy, 1961; exploration of Roman Roads: throughout Tunisia, Libya, Egypt, Arabia, Petra, 1963; Spain and Yugoslavia, 1965; Egyptian Eastern Desert, Sinai, Turkey, Bulgaria and Greece, 1966; exploration and excavation of Roman Alpine roads in Austria, Italy, France and Germany, 1968–70; physically traversed and mapped the Persian Road from Troy and Istanbul, through Turkey, Iraq and Iran to river Indus, 1973–75; topographical survey of Trajan's Aqueduct, Lago Bracciano to Rome, XXXI miles, 1979–81 (survey text with maps published, 1982). Founder, Charles Darwin Res. Station, Galápagos Is (conceived 1936, permission 1959, in operation 1960). Professor (*hc*) Universidad Catolica del Peru. Member, Academia de Historia de Bogota (Columbia), Centro de historia de Pasto (Columbia), Instituto Investigaciones Historicas (Peru). Discovered "extinct" tribe of Jicaque Indians in Honduras. Orden al Merito, Ecuador; Comdr, Orden al Merito, Peru. *Publications:* Off With their Heads, 1937; Ecuador the Unknown, 1939; Quetzal Quest (with Hawkins), 1940 (repr. 1968); Tsátchela Indians of Western Ecuador, 1939; The Encantadas of Herman Melville, 1940; Treasure of Tortoise Islands, 1940; Riches of South America, 1941; Riches of Central America, 1942; The Jicaque Indians of Honduras, 1943; Natural History of Termites, 1943; Paper and Civilisation, 1943; The Aztec and Maya Papermakers, 1943, 2nd edn, 1944; Jungle in the Clouds, 1945 (American edition, 1940); La Fabricación del Papel entre los aztecas y los Mayas, Mexico, 1945; South America Called Them, a biography, 1945; Maya Explorer, the life of John Lloyd Stephens, 1947; The Green World of the Naturalists (Anthology), 1948; Ecuador and the Galapagos Islands, 1949; Regional Guides to Peru, 1949; Frederick Catherwood, Architect (with Introduction by Aldous Huxley), 1950; El Dorado, The Golden Kingdoms of Colombia, 1951; The Four Seasons of Manuela (biography), 1952, repr. 1973; Highway of the Sun, 1956; The High Voyage, 1956; (Trans.) The Journals of J. B. Boussingault, 1957; Realm of the Incas, 1957; The Aztec: Man and Tribe, 1958; The Sun Kingdom of the Aztecs, 1958; The World of the Maya, 1960; The Ancient Sun Kingdom of The Americas, 1961, repr. 1973; The Desert Kingdoms of Peru, 1965; The Story of the Roman Roads, 1966 (for children; two book awards); F. Catherwood: Architect-Explorer of Two Worlds, 1967; The Roads that Led to Rome (in 6 languages), 1967; Roma nel Mundo, le grande stradi, 1969; The Road Runner (autobiog.), 1970; The German Peoples in the History of the Americas, German edn 1970, Amer. edn 1976; Il Sistema Stradale dell'Impero Romano, 1971; Search for the Mayas, the story of Stephens and Catherwood, 1973; The Golden Man, 1974; The Royal Road of the Incas, 1976; Ecuador: a history, 1976; The Gateways to Persia, 1978; The Gold of El Dorado, 1978; Galápagos: my return to Las Encantadas, 1982; La historia documentada de Manuela Saenz y Simón Bolivar, 1983;

The Feathered Serpent: search for the Quetzal Bird, 1983; *edited:* The Incas (Chronicles) of Pedro de Cieza de Leon, 1959; Stephens' Incidents of Travel in Yucatan, 1961; Stephens' Incidents of Travel in Arabia Petraea, 1970; E. George Squier's Peru (1877), 1981. *Address:* Montegonzi Boggioli, 52020 (AR), Italy.

**von KARAJAN, Herbert;** conductor; Director: Salzburg Festival, 1964–88; Vienna State Opera, since 1976 (Artistic Manager, 1956–64); Life Director Gesellschaft der Musikfreunde, Vienna; Conductor, Berlin Philharmonic Orchestra, 1955–89; *b* Salzburg, 5 April 1908; *s* of Ernest von Karajan and Martha v. Karajan Cosmâc; *m* 1st, 1938, Elmy Holgerloef; 2nd, 1943, Anita Gütermann; 3rd, 1958, Eliette Mouret; two *d. Educ:* Salzburg Hochschule and Mozarteum; Vienna Univ. Conductor: Ulm Opernhaus, 1927–33; Aachen Opernhaus, 1933–40; Berlin Staatsoper, 1938–42; Festivals: Salzburg; Bayreuth; Edinburgh, 1953–54; Lucerne, 1947–56; Conductor and régisseur, La Scala, Milan, 1948–55; Musical Director, Berlin Philharmonic Orchestra, 1955–56. First European Tour with Philharmonia Orchestra, 1952; Director, Salzburg Festival, 1957. Films directed and conducted include: Bajazzo, Carmen, Beethoven's 9th Symphony. Hon. DMus Oxon, 1978. Gold Medal, Royal Phil. Soc., 1984. *Publication:* (ed Franz Endler) My Autobiography, 1989. *Recreations:* ski-ing, mountaineering, flying, yachting, motoring, theatre, acoustical research. *Address:* State Opera House, Vienna, Austria. *Died* 16 *July* 1989.

**VORSTER, Hon. Balthazar Johannes,** BA, LLB; State President of the Republic of South Africa, 1978–79; *b* 13 Dec. 1915; *s* of late William Carel Vorster; *m* 1941, Martini, *d* of P. A. Malan; two *s* one *d. Educ:* Sterkstroom High Sch.; Stellenbosch Univ. LLB 1938. Attorney, Port Elizabeth and Brakpan, until 1953; Member, Johannesburg Bar, practising 1953–58. Contested Brakpan, 1948; MP Nigel, 1953–78; Deputy Minister of Education, Arts, Science, Social Welfare and Pensions, 1958–61; Minister of Justice, 1961–66; Minister of Justice, of Police and of Prisons, 1966; Prime Minister, Republic of South African and Leader, National Party, 1966–78. DPhil (*hc*) Stellenbosch Univ., 1966; LLD (*hc*); University of Pretoria; Univ. of OFS, 1967; Univ. of Potchefstroom. *Recreations:* golf, chess. *Address:* Oubostrand, c/o PO Humansorp, Cape, 6300, Republic of South Africa. *Clubs:* Zwartkops Goft; Rondebosch Golf. *Died* 10 *Sept.* 1983.

**VOUEL, Raymond;** Member, Commission of the European Communities, responsible for Competition Policy, 1977–84; *b* 1923; *m*; three *c.* Journalist on Socialist daily newspaper, Tageblatt; Admin. Dir, Esch Hosp., 1954–64; Mem. Town Council, Esch (Chm. Bldgs Cttee), 1973. Member, Chamber of Deputies, Luxembourg, 1964–76; Sec. of State: for Public Health; for Employment; for Social Security; for Mining Industry, 1964–69. Chm., Parly Socialist Group, 1970–74; Gen. Sec., Parti Ouvrier Socialiste Luxembourgeois (Socialists), 1970; Dep. Prime Minister, Minister for Finance and Land Develt, 1974–76; Mem., Commission of European Communities with responsibility for Competition, July-Dec. 1976. *Address:* c/o Ministry of Foreign Affairs, Luxembourg-Ville, Luxembourg. *Died* 12 *Feb.* 1987.

**VOWDEN, His Honour Desmond Harvey Weight;** QC 1969; a Circuit Judge, 1975–86; *b* 6 Jan. 1921; *s* of late Rev. A. W. J. Vowden, MBE, TD; *m* 1964, Iris, *d* of L. A. Stafford-Northcote. *Educ:* Clifton Coll. Served in RN and RM, 1938–50; Captain RM, retired 1950. Called to the Bar, 1950; Dep. Chm., Wiltshire Quarter Sessions, 1968–71; Recorder of Devizes, later a Recorder of Crown Court, 1971–75. Comr, CCC, 1969–72. Steward of Appeal, BBB of C, 1967–81. *Recreations:* music, gardening. *Address:* Orchard Cottage, Worton, Devizes, Wilts. *T:* Devizes (0380) 2877. *Club:* Garrick. *Died* 22 *July* 1990.

**VOYSEY, Charles C.;** *see* Cowles-Voysey.

**VYNER, Clare George;** *b* 1894; 2nd *s* of late Lord Alwyne Frederick Compton and Mary Evelyn, *e d* of Robert Charles de Grey Vyner, of Newby Hall, Yorks, and Gautby, Lincs; *m* 1923, Lady Doris Gordon-Lennox (*d* 1980), 2nd *d* of 8th Duke of Richmond and Gordon; one *s* (and one *s* one *d* decd). Formerly Lieut, RN, serving war of 1939–45, Commander. Assumed surname of Vyner, 1912. Formerly DL, W Riding of Yorkshire and City and Co. of York. *Address:* Keanchulish, Ullapool, Ross-shire. *T:* Ullapool 2100. *Died* 29 *Oct.* 1989.

# W

**WACHER, David Mure;** Metropolitan Stipendiary Magistrate, 1962–74, retired; *b* 9 Oct. 1909; *s* of late Dr Harold Wacher, FSA, and Violet Amy Wacher (*née* Peebles); *m* 1935, Kathleen Margaret Roche, *yr d* of late Rev. George Ralph Melvyrn Roche; one *d* (and one *s* decd). *Educ:* Charterhouse. Called to Bar, Middle Temple, 1935. Served in Royal Artillery, 1939–43. Acting Attorney-General, Gibraltar, 1943; Stipendiary Magistrate, Gibraltar, 1943–49; Acting Chief Justice, Gibraltar, 1948. Vice-Chairman, Mental Health Review Tribunal for SW Metropolitan RHB Area, 1960–62. *Recreations:* music and the theatre. *Address:* Strapp Farm House, Chiselborough, Stoke-Sub-Hamdon, Somerset TA14 6TW. *T:* Chiselborough 689. *Died* 19 *Jan.* 1989.

**WACKETT, Air Vice-Marshal Ellis Charles,** CB 1957; CBE 1951 (OBE 1941); CEng; FRAeS; psa; Royal Australian Air Force; *b* 13 Aug. 1901; *yr s* of James Wackett, Townsville, Queensland; *m* 1928, Doreen I. (*d* 1975), *d* of Thomas S. Dove, Mildura, Victoria; two *s* one *d*. *Educ:* Jervis Bay Royal Australian Naval Coll.; Keyham Engineering College, England; Imperial College of Science and Technology, London. Joined Australian Navy, 1914; commissioned, 1921. Transferred to Royal Australian Air Force, 1923; graduated RAF Staff Coll., 1933. Air Vice-Marshal, 1948. Air Member for Engineering and Maintenance, 1942; Air Member for Technical Service, RAAF, 1948; retired 1959. Member, Australian Nat. Airlines Commn (TAA), 1960–68. *Recreation:* angling. *Address:* 13/32 Berkeley Street, Hawthorn, Victoria 3122, Australia. *Club:* Naval and Military (Victoria). *Died* 3 *Aug.* 1984.

**WACKETT, Sir Lawrence (James),** Kt 1954; DFC 1918, AFC 1919; BSc; Founder, Manager, and a Director of Commonwealth Aircraft Corporation Ltd, 1936–61, retired; Director, Joseph Lucas (Australia) Ltd, 1960–69; *b* 2 Jan. 1896; *s* of James Wackett, Townsville, Queensland; *m* 1919, Letitia Emily Florence, *d* of Fred B. Wood, Townsville, Queensland; one *d* (one *s* decd). *Educ:* Royal Military Coll. (Duntroon); Melbourne University (BSc). Officer, Australian Regular Army, 1913–20; served in Australian Flying Corps in France and Palestine (despatches twice); Officer, RAAF, 1921, retired a Wing Commander, 1930; Aeronautical Engineer, 1930–35. Designed: Widgeon flying boat; Gannet; Wackett trainer (commemorative stamp issued, 1981); Boomerang; pioneered aricraft construction in Australia, 1936. Commodore, Beaumaris Motor Yacht Squadron, 1962–68. Kernot Memorial Medallist, 1959; Finlay National Award, 1967; Kingsford Smith Meml Medal, RAeS, 1975; Oswald Watt Meml Medal, Royal Aero Club of Australia, 1976; James Cook Meml Medal, Royal Soc. of NSW, 1979. FIProdE; Hon. FRAeS 1977. *Publications:* My Hobby is Trout Fishing, 1944; Studies of an Angler, 1949; Aircraft Pioneer, 1972. *Recreations:* became quadriplegic in 1970; now developing aids for disabled. *Address:* 55 Fiddens Wharf Road, Killara, Sydney, NSW 2071, Australia. *Died* 18 *March* 1982.

**WADE, Baron,** *cr* 1964 (Life Peer); **Donald William Wade,** DL; MA, LLB; *b* 16 June 1904; *s* of William Mercer and Beatrice Hemington Wade; *m* 1932, Ellenora Beatrice (*née* Bentham); two *s* two *d*. *Educ:* Mill Hill; Trinity Hall, Cambridge. Admitted Solicitor, 1929. MP (L) Huddersfield West, 1950–64; Liberal Whip, 1956–62; Deputy Leader, Liberal Parliamentary Party, 1962–64; Deputy Liberal Whip, House of Lords, 1965–67; President, Liberal Party, 1967–68. DL, W Riding, Yorks, 1967, N Yorks, 1974. *Publications:* Democracy, 1944; Way of the West, 1945; Our Aim and Purpose, 1961; Yorkshire Survey: a report on community relations in Yorkshire, 1972; Europe and the British Health Service, 1974; (with Lord Banks) The Political Insight of Elliott Dodds, 1977; Behind the Speaker's Chair, 1978. *Address:* Meadowbank, Wath Road, Pately Bridge, Harrogate, N Yorks HG3 5N. *Club:* National Liberal. *Died* 6 *Nov.* 1988.

**WADE, Col Sir George Albert,** Kt 1955; MC; JP; Director: Wade Potteries Ltd; Wade (Ireland) Ltd; George Wade & Son Ltd; A. J. Wade Ltd; Wade Heath & Co. Ltd; *b* 1891; *s* of George Wade, JP, Burslem; *m* 1915, Florence (*d* 1971), *d* of Samuel Johnson, JP, Burslem; one *s* two *d*. *Educ:* Newcastle-under-Lyme High Sch., Staffordshire. Served European War, 1914–18, with S Staffs Regt (MC and Bar); served War of 1939–45, with his Regiment and on General Staff; Colonel (retired) late S Staffs Regiment. Contested (C) Newcastle-under-Lyme, General Election, 1945. Past President: North Staffordshire Political Union; North Staffs Chamber of Commerce. Chairman: Pottery and Glass Trades Benevolent Institution, 1949–54; Machine Gun Corps Old Comrades Association. Pres. N Staffs Medical Inst. Fellow Corporation of Secretaries. JP Stoke-on-Trent. *Publications:* Minor Tactics Training Manual (issued to Home Guard) and a series of 12 books on Military Training, during War of 1939–45. *Recreations:* painting, photography, ornithology. *Address:* Brand Hall, Norton-in-Hales, Market Drayton, Salop. *T:* Market Drayton 3006. *Died* 27 *Jan.* 1986.

**WADE, John Charles,** OBE 1959; JP; Lord-Lieutenant of Cumbria, 1974–83 (of the County of Cumberland, 1968–74); *b* 15 Feb. 1908; unmarried. *Educ:* St Bees School. Midland Bank Ltd, 1925–27. West Cumberland Farmers Ltd, 1927, Gen. Manager, 1931–64, Man. Dir, 1964–68, Pres., 1970–. President: Cumbria Scouts; Whitehaven Rugby Club; Whitehaven Cricket Club; Cumbria Cricket Club; Chm., Whitehaven Harbour Comrs. Dir, Eskdale Outward Bound Mountain Sch. JP Cumberland, 1956, Cumbria, 1974. Freeman, Borough of Whitehaven. KStJ 1974 (Pres. Cumbria Council of St John). *Recreations:* shooting, fishing. *Address:* Hillcrest, Whitehaven, Cumbria. *T:* Whitehaven 2844. *Club:* Border and County (Carlisle). *Died* 7 *May* 1984.

**WADE, John Roland,** CB 1942; retired as Director of Remploy Ltd (1960–63); *b* 11 Oct. 1890; *e s* of late George Alfred Wade; *m* 1928, Penelope Dorothy Haig, *y d* of late Dr Haig Ferguson, Edinburgh; two *s*. *Educ:* Westminster School (King's Scholar); Queen's Coll., Cambridge (Scholar). Entered War Office, 1914; Director of Establishments, War Office, 1939–53; retired Dec. 1953. Financial Director (part-time), Remploy Ltd, 1954–Oct. 1960. *Address:* 15 St Catherine's Court, Bedford Road, W4. *Died* 15 *Jan.* 1984.

**WADE, Rosalind (Herschel), (Mrs R. H. Seymour),** OBE 1985; novelist; Editor, Contemporary Review, since 1970; *b* 11 Sept. 1909; *d* of Lieut-Colonel H. A. L. H. Wade and Kathleen Adelaide Wade; *m* William Kean Seymour, FRSL (*d* 1975); two *s*. *Educ:* Glendower Sch., London; privately, abroad and Bedford Coll., London. Member: Society of Women Writers and Journalists (Chairman, 1962–64, Vice President, 1965–); Committee West Country Writers Assoc., 1953–65 (Vice-Pres., 1975–); General and Exec. Councils, The Poetry Society Inc., 1962–64, 1965–66; Guildford Centre of Poetry Soc. (Chm. 1969–71); Alresford Historical and Literary Soc. (Chm. 1968–70, 1972–73); Literature Panel, Southern Arts Assoc., 1973–75; conducting Writing and Literary Courses at Moor Park College, Farnham (jointly with William Kean Seymour, 1962–74), Writers' Workshop, 1976–81. Editor, PEN Broadsheet, 1975–77. *Publications:* novels: Children, Be Happy, 1931; Kept Man, 1933; Pity the Child, 1934; Shadow Thy Dream, 1934; A Fawn in a Field, 1935; Men Ask for Beauty, 1936; Treasure in Heaven, 1937; Fairweather Faith, 1940; The Man of Promise, 1941; Bracelet for Julia, 1942; Pride of the Family, 1943; Present Ending, 1946; As the Narcissus, 1946; The Widows, 1948; The Raft, 1950; The Falling Leaves, 1951; Alys at Endon, 1953; The Silly Dove, 1953; Cassandra Calls, 1954; Come Fill The Cup, 1955; Morning Break, 1956; Mrs Jamison's Daughter, 1957; The Grain Will Grow, 1959; The Will of Heaven, 1960; A Small Shower, 1961; The Ramerson Case, 1962; New Pasture, 1964; The Vanished Days, 1966; Ladders, 1968; The Umbrella, 1970; The Golden Bowl, 1970; Mrs Medlend's Private World, 1973; Red Letter Day: Twelve Stories of Cornwall, 1980; *as Catharine Carr:* English Summer, 1954; Lovers in the Sun, 1955; The Richest Gift, 1956; Heart Tide, 1956; A Dream Come True, 1957; It Must Be Love, 1959; In Search of a Dream, 1960; The Shining Heart, 1961; The Golden City, 1963; Mountain Glory, 1967; *contributor to:* The Fourth Ghost Book, 1965; The Unlikely Ghosts, 1967; Happy Christmas, 1968; Haunted Cornwall, 1973; People Within, 1974; Cornish Harvest, 1974; Tales from the Macabre, 1976; My Favourite Story, 1977; More Tales from the Macabre, 1979; Women Writing, 1979; Stories of Haunted Inns, 1983; Ghosts in Country Villages, 1983; Phantom Lovers, 1984; After Midnight Stories, 1985; The Second Book of After Midnight Stories, 1986; Contemporary Review, Poetry Review, Books and Bookmen, Cornish Review, etc. *Recreations:* walking, theatre and historical research. *Address:* 4 Dollis Drive, Guildford Road, Farnham, Surrey GU9 9QD. *T:* Farnham 713883. *Club:* Royal Commonwealth Society. *Died* 25 *Jan.* 1989.

**WADLEY, Sir Douglas,** Kt 1969; solicitor; Consultant to O'Shea, Corser & Wadley; *b* 9 Nov. 1904; *s* of John and Honora Wadley; *m* 1928, Vera Joyce Bodman; two *s* two *d*. *Educ:* various state schools in Qld; Central Technical Coll. High Sch., Brisbane. Admitted Solicitor, Supreme Court of Queensland, 1926. Chm. of Dirs, Queensland Television Ltd. Hon. Councillor, Royal National Agricultural and Industrial Assoc. of Queensland. *Recreation:* racing. *Address:* 18 Nindethana Street, Indooropilly, Brisbane, Queensland 4068, Australia. *T:* 70–2737. *Clubs:* Brisbane, Tattersalls, Johnsonian, Queensland Turf (Chm.) (Brisbane). *Died* 16 *March* 1984.

**WADLEY, Walter Joseph Durham,** CMG 1959; *b* 21 June 1903; *o s* of late Joseph Wadley, Stanbrook Croft, Callow End, Worcester; *m* 1946, Marie Ivy Louise, *er d* of late Arthur Dunnett, St Andrew, Jamaica; one *d*. *Educ:* City of London Sch.; Lincoln Coll., Oxford. Classical scholar, Lincoln Coll., Oxford, 1922; BA 1926, MA 1930. Inspector of Schools, Ghana (then Gold Coast), 1926; Senior Education Officer, 1935; Assistant Director of Education, 1944; Deputy Director of Education, Kenya, 1946; Director of Education, Kenya, 1951; retired from Colonial Education Service, 1959; nominated official Mem., Kenya Legislative Council, 1951–58. Dep.

General Manager, E. Africa Tourist Travel Assoc., 1959–64; Chief Executive Officer of the Association, 1965. Now retired. Coronation Medal, 1953. *Recreations:* travel, photography, woodwork, gardening. *Address:* The Old Brewhouse, Shutford, Banbury, Oxon. *T:* Swalcliffe 478. *Died* 1 *May* 1982.

**WAECHTER, Sir (Harry Leonard) d'Arcy,** 2nd Bt, *cr* 1911; Lieut, RASC; *b* 22 May 1912; *s* of 1st Bt and Josephine (*d* 1955), *o d* of late John d'Arcy, of Corbetstown, Westmeath; *S* father, 1929; *m* 1939, Philippa Margaret (marr. diss. 1957), *y d* of late James Frederick Twinberrow, Suckley, Worcestershire. *Educ:* Pangbourne Nautical School. Lieut, East Yorkshire Regt (SR), 1931–35; Lieut, RASC, 1942–47; Captain, Worcestershire Regt, GSO 3 159 Inf. Bde (TA), 1947–48; Captain, TARO, 1949. Joint MFH North Ledbury. *Heir:* none. *Recreation:* hunting. *Died* 1987 (*ext*).

**WAGNER, Prof. Franz William;** Professor of Education, and Director of Institute of Education, University of Southampton, 1950–71, later Emeritus; *b* 26 Oct. 1905; *s* of Franz Henry and Adelaide Wagner; *m* 1934, Maria Schiller; one *s* one *d. Educ:* University of Adelaide, (Rhodes Scholar for S. Austr., 1928) Christ Church, Oxford. Asst Master, Christ's Hospital, 1931–39; Tutor and Lecturer, Oxford Univ., Department of Education, 1939–50. *Recreation:* gardening. *Address:* Avonmore, Southdown Road, Shawford, Winchester, Hants SO21 2BY.
*Died* 22 *Jan.* 1985.

**WAGSTAFF, Charles John Leonard;** *b* 3 March 1875; *s* of late Rev. J. Wagstaff, Rector of Whittonstall, Northumberland; *m* 1913, Marjorie Bloomer (*d* 1972); one *s* two *d. Educ:* Emmanuel Coll., Cambridge; 16th Wrangler, 1897; 1st Class Natural Sciences Tripos, 1898; Senior Science Master at Bradford Grammar Sch., 1899–1903; Oundle Sch., 1904–09; Headmaster at Haberdasher's Aske's Hampstead Sch., 1910–19; Headmaster King Edward VII Sch., King's Lynn, 1920–39. *Publications:* Electricity; Properties of Matter. *Recreations:* turning ivory, etc. *Address:* 13 Nizells Avenue, Hove, East Sussex. *T:* Brighton 736132. *Died* 8 *Sept.* 1981.

**WAIGHTS, Rev. Kenneth (Laws);** Ex-President of the Methodist Conference, 1971–72; *b* 15 May 1909; *s* of Rev. William Waights and Selina Waights; *m* 1935, Dorothy Margaret Rowe. *Educ:* Stationers' Company Sch.; George Watson's Coll., Edinburgh; Handsworth Theological Coll., Birmingham. Served in the following Methodist Churches: Ilfracombe, Exeter, Birmingham Mission, Winson Green Prison (as Chaplain), Hastings, Liverpool, Scarborough, Nottingham (Chm. of District), Bristol, Sunderland, Newcastle upon Tyne; Chairman, Newcastle District of Methodist Church. Mayor of Shaftesbury, 1982–83. *Recreations:* golf, walking, travel; formerly: played Rugby football for Devon County, Moseley and Exeter Rugby Clubs. *Address:* 40 St James, Shaftesbury, Dorset. *Died* 10 *June* 1984.

**WAINWRIGHT, Robert Everard,** CMG 1959; *b* 24 June 1913; *s* of Dr G. B. Wainwright, OBE, MB; *m* 1939, Bridget Alan-Williams; two *s. Educ:* Marlborough; Trinity College, Cambridge (BA). District Officer, Kenya, 1935; Provincial Commissioner, Rift Valley Province, 1953–59. Imperial Defence College, 1959. Chief Commissioner, Kenya, 1960–63; Administrator, Turks and Caicos Is, WI, 1967–71. Member: Gp of British observers, Zimbabwe elections, 1980; Gp of Commonwealth observers, Ugandan elections, 1980. *Recreations:* sailing, cabinet-making. *Address:* Wagoners Cottage, Cann Common, Shaftesbury, Dorset SP7 0DL. *T:* Shaftesbury (0747) 52877. *Club:* Mombasa (Mombasa). *Died* 28 *Nov.* 1990.

**WAKE, Hereward Baldwin Lawrence;** Headmaster of St John's School, Leatherhead, Surrey, 1948–60, retired; *b* Aug. 1900; *s* of late Rev. Preb. Hereward Eyre Wake and Mary Frances, *d* of late James Sealy Lawrence; *m* 1926, Sheila, *d* of late Captain Henry Harris; two *s. Educ:* Marlborough (Classical Exhibnr); Keble College, Oxford (Classical Scholar). Oxford Rugby XV (blue 1922); Somerset Rugby XV, 1923–29 (Captain 1927). Asst Housemaster, 1923, Housemaster, 1934–39, 1945–48, Cheltenham College. 7th Bn Gloucester Regt (TA), 1939; War Office, 1941–45 (Lt-Col, GSO1). *Recreations:* ornithology, reading, attempting The Times crossword. *Address:* High Ridge, Knoll Wood, Knoll Road, Godalming, Surrey. *T:* Godalming 22622. *Club:* Vincent's (Oxford).
*Died* 19 *Nov.* 1983.

**WAKEFIELD OF KENDAL,** 1st Baron, *cr* 1963, of Kendal; **William Wavell Wakefield,** Kt 1944; Company Director; *b* Beckenham, Kent, 10 March 1898; *s* of late Roger William Wakefield, MB, JP, and Ethel May Knott; *m* 1919, Rowena Doris (*d* 1981), *d* of late Llewellyn Lewis, MD, OBE, JP; three *d. Educ:* The Craig Preparatory School; Sedbergh School; Pembroke College, Cambridge. In the RNAS then RAF European War (rose to rank of Captain, despatches); retired from the RAF as Flight-Lieutenant, 1923; transferred to Reserve; rejoined RAF at outbreak of war for flying duty; Director of the Air Training Corps, 1942–44; MP (Nat C) Swindon division of Wiltshire, 1935–45; (C) St Marylebone,

1945–63. Parliamentary Private Sec. to the Marquess of Hartington, 1936–38; to Rt Hon. R. H. Hudson, 1939–40; to Capt. Rt Hon. Harold Balfour, 1940–42; Chm. Parliamentary and Scientific Cttee, 1952–55; Director: Lake District Estates Co. Ltd; Shapland & Petter, Ltd, and other companies; Member of Executive Committee, YMCA; Member Executive Committee and Council, the National Playing Fields Assoc.; formerly Mem. Nature Conservancy; Member, Council of Royal National Mission to Deep Sea Fishermen; President, Metropolitan Assoc. of Building Societies, 1967–68; former Pres., Industrial Transport Assoc.; Vice-Pres., Council of The Royal Albert Hall. Captained England, Cambridge Univ., Middlesex, Royal Air Force, Harlequins, at Rugby football; Past President: Rugby Football Union; Ski Club of Great Britain; British Sub-Aqua Club; British Water Ski Fedn. *Publication:* Rugger. *Recreation:* ski-ing. *Heir:* none. *Address:* 71 Park Street, W1; The Old House, Kendal, Cumbria. *T:* Kendal 20861. *Clubs:* Carlton, MCC. *Died* 12 *Aug.* 1983 (*ext*).

**WAKEFIELD, Hugh (Hubert George);** MA Cantab; Hon. FMA; FRSA; Keeper of the Department of Circulation, Victoria and Albert Museum, 1960–75; *b* 6 March 1915; *o s* of late George Wakefield; *m* 1939, Nora Hilary Inglis; one *s* one *d. Educ:* King Edward's Sch., Birmingham; Trinity Coll., Cambridge. Joined staff of Royal Commission on Historical Monuments (England), 1938. Served War of 1939–45, Temp. Captain (Instructor in Gunnery), RA, 1942–46. Asst Keeper, Victoria and Albert Museum, 1948. Governor of the National Museum of Wales, 1960–75; Mem. Council, Museums' Assoc., 1960–63; Mem., DES Crafts Advisory Cttee, 1971–75; Chm., Cttee for Museums of Applied Art, Internat. Council of Museums, 1974–75; Corresp. Mem., Finnish Soc. of Crafts and Design, 1965–. *Publications:* (ed) Victorian Collector (series); Nineteenth Century British Glass, 1961, 2nd edn 1982; Victorian Pottery, 1962; Contributor to: Connoisseur Early Victorian Period Guide, 1958; World Ceramics (ed R. J. Charleston), 1968; Das Pompöse Zeitalter, 1970; Encyc. Brit. *Recreation:* travel. *Address:* 32 Strand-on-the-Green, W4. *T:* 01–994 6355; Frigiliana, Malaga, Spain. *Died* 8 *Feb.* 1984.

**WAKEFIELD, Roger Cuthbert,** CMG 1953; OBE 1950; DL; retired; *b* Cark-in-Cartmel, Lancs, 27 June 1906; 4th and *y s* of late Roger William Wakefield, MB, BCh, Kendal, and Ethel May Knott; *m* 1936, Elizabeth Rhoda, *yr d* of late Sidney R. Davie and Margaret Preston Lawson, West Byfleet, Surrey; one *d. Educ:* Sedbergh School; Trinity College, Cambridge (BA 1928). Joined Sudan Civil Service, 1929; Survey of the Arc of the Thirtieth Meridian, 1935–40. War of 1939–45; Civil Defence Duties and desert navigation, 1940–43; Director of Surveys, Sudan, 1946–54; Survey Consultant to Sudan Government, 1954–55. Director, Equatoria Projects Board, 1949; Chairman, Unclassified Staff Wages Commn, 1951; Councillor without Portfolio on Governor-Gen.'s Exec. Council and Member Legislative Assembly, 1952. Member: British-Argentine Rugby football touring team, 1927; Cambridge East Greenland Exped., 1929; Lake Rudolf Rift Valley Exped., 1934. Chm., Highland Div., Scottish Community Drama Assoc., 1975–78. FRICS, 1949. DL Ross and Cromarty, 1976. *Publication:* (with D. F. Munsey) The Arc of the Thirtieth Meridian between the Egyptian Frontier and Latitude 13° 45′, 1950. *Recreations:* mountaineering, sailing, fishing. *Address:* Glendrynoch Lodge, Carbost, Isle of Skye. *Club:* Alpine. *Died* 1 *July* 1986.

**WAKEFORD, John Chrysostom Barnabas,** CMG 1948; *b* 23 Aug. 1898; *o s* of Rev. John Wakeford, Anfield, Liverpool; *m* 1st, 1921, Grace (*d* 1965), *d* of Charles Cooke, Church Coppenhall; one *d*; 2nd, 1970, Dorothy May, *d* of Frederick Ward, Aldeburgh, Suffolk. *Educ:* Malvern College; RMA, Woolwich; Clare College, Cambridge. Commissioned Royal Engineers, 1917; served European War, France and Belgium, 1917–18; N Russia campaign (despatches). Dep. Dir Transportn, W Africa, 1941–43; Ceylon, 1943–44 (Col); Dir of Transportn, SE Asia, 1944–45 (Brig.). Chief Railway Commissioner, Burma; General Manager, Burma Railways and Technical Adviser to Government of Burma, 1945–48; Chief Engineer, Cameroons Development Corporation, W Africa, 1948–50; with Rendel Palmer & Tritton, 1950–63; FICE, FIMechE, FCIT, FRSA. *Address:* 41 South Road, Saffron Walden, Essex. *T:* Saffron Walden 22010. *Died* 31 *March* 1989.

**WALDMAN, Stanley John;** Master of the Supreme Court, Queen's Bench Division, since 1971; *b* 18 Sept. 1923; *s* of late Michael Ernest Waldman, OBE, JP; *m* 1951, Naomi Sorsky; one *s* two *d. Educ:* Owen's School, London; Pembroke College, Oxford. BA; MA 1948. RAF, 1942–46; called to the Bar, Gray's Inn, 1949; practised in London and on SE Circuit. *Address:* 80 South Hill Park, NW3.
*Died* 28 *July* 1989.

**WALDOCK, Sir (Claud) Humphrey (Meredith),** Kt 1961; CMG 1946; OBE 1942; QC 1951; DCL; MA; a Judge of the International Court of Justice, since 1973, President, since 1979; *b* 13 Aug. 1904; *s* of Frederic William Waldock and Lizzie Kyd Souter; *m* 1934, Ethel Beatrice Williams (*d* 1981); one *s* one *d. Educ:* Uppingham School;

Brasenose Coll., Oxford. Hockey Blue, 1926; BA 1927; BCL 1928; Barrister-at-Law, Gray's Inn, 1928, Bencher, 1957, Treasurer, 1971, Vice-Treasurer, 1972; Midland Circuit, 1928–30; Fellow and Lectr in Law, Brasenose, 1930–47; Tutor, 1937; Hon. Fellow, 1960. Lecturer in Law, Oriel College, 1930–39; Pro-Proctor, 1936. Temp. Principal Admiralty, 1940; Assistant-Secretary, 1943; Principal Assistant Secretary, 1944. UK Commissioner on Italo-Yugoslav Boundary Commission; Commission for Free Territory of Trieste, Council of Foreign Ministers, 1946. Trustee, Uppingham Sch., 1947–59. Chichele Prof. of Public Internat. Law, Univ. of Oxford, and Fellow, All Souls Coll., 1947–72; Assessor in the Chancellor's Court, 1947–79; Mem. Hebdomadal Council, 1948–61; European Commn of Human Rights, 1954–61 (Pres. 1955–61); Judge, European Court of Human Rights, 1966–74 (Vice-Pres., 1968–71, Pres., 1971–74). Chm., Cttee of Inquiry into Oxford University Press, 1967–70. Editor, British Year Book of International Law, 1955–74; Member: Inst. of Internat. Law; Swedish-Finnish Conciliation Commn, 1957; Swedish-Swiss Concilation Commn, 1960; Swedish-Turkish and German-Swiss Conciliation Commns, 1963; US-Danish Conciliation Commn, 1964; Chilean-Italian Conciliation Commn, 1965; Danish-Norwegian Conciliation Commn, 1967; Swedish-Spanish Conciliation Commn, 1968; UN Internat. Law Commn, 1961–72 (Special Rapporteur on Law of Treaties, 1962–66, on Succession of States in respect of Treaties, 1968–72; President 1967); UN Expert on Law of Treaties, Vienna Conf., 1968, 1969; Member: Permanent Court of Arbitration, 1965–; Council of Legal Education, 1965–; Curatorium of the Hague Academy, 1977–. *Publications:* Law of Mortgages; Regulation of the Use of Force by Individual States (Hague Recueil), 1952; General Course on Public International Law (Hague Recueil), 1962; Editor, Brierly's Law of Nations (6th edn), 1963. Articles on International Law. *Recreations:* cricket, tennis, shooting, fishing. *Address:* 6 Lathbury Road, Oxford. *T:* 58227. *Club:* United Oxford & Cambridge University. *Died 15 Aug.* 1981.

**WALES, Geoffrey,** RE 1961 (ARE 1948); ARCA 1936; wood engraver; Lecturer, Norwich School of Art, 1953–77; *b* 26 May 1912; *s* of Ernest and Kathleen Wales; *m* 1940, Marjorie Skeeles, painter; two *d. Educ:* Chatham House School, Ramsgate; Thanet School of Art; Royal College of Art. Served War of 1939–45, in Royal Air Force, 1940–46. Prints and drawings in Victoria and Albert Museum; Whitworth Gallery, Manchester; Kunsthaus, Graz; and private collections. Exhibits in Royal Society of Painter Etchers and Engravers. Illustrated books for Golden Cockerel Press, Kynoch Press, Folio Soc. and general graphic work. Engravings included in publications and articles on wood-engraving. *Address:* 15 Heigham Grove, Norwich, Norfolk NR2 3DQ. *T:* Norwich 629066. *Died 25 April* 1990.

**WALES, Horace Geoffrey Quaritch,** MA, PhD, LittD; Orientalist and Archaeologist; *b* 17 Oct. 1900; *s* of late E. Horace Wales; *g s* of late Bernard Quaritch; *m* 1931, Dorothy Clementina Johnson, LLB. *Educ:* Charterhouse; Queens' College, Cambridge. Siamese Government Service, 1924–28; travelled widely in India, Burma, Indochina and Indonesia in connection with Oriental research; during 1934–36, as Field Director of the Greater-India Research Committee, carried out archaeological investigations in Siam, and during 1937–40 in Malaya, excavating ancient sites and exploring early trade routes; conducted excavations at early Buddhist sites in Siam, 1955–56, 1964, 1968. Chairman, Bernard Quaritch Ltd, 1951–75 (Director, 1939–75); served IA (Gen. Staff), 1940–41; in USA writing and speaking on Pacific affairs and publicising India's war effort, 1942–45. Member Council, Royal Asiatic Society, 1947–58, 1964–68 (Vice-President, 1958–62); Hon. Member Royal Asiatic Soc., Malayan Branch. *Publications:* Siamese State Ceremonies, 1931; Ancient Siamese Government and Administration, 1934; Towards Angkor, 1937; Archaeological Researches on Ancient Indian Colonization in Malaya, 1940; The Making of Greater India, 1951; Ancient South-East Asian Warfare, 1952; The Mountain of God, 1953; Prehistory and Religion in South-East Asia, 1957; Angkor and Rome, 1965; The Indianization of China, 1967; Dvāravatī, the Earliest Kingdom of Siam, 1969; Early Burma—Old Siam, 1973; The Malay Peninsula in Hindu Times, 1976; The Universe around Them, 1977; contrib. to The Cambridge History of India, many articles in various learned journals. *Club:* East India, Devonshire, Sports and Public Schools. *Died 24 June* 1981.

**WALFORD, Major-General Alfred Ernest,** CB 1946; CBE 1944; MM 1916; ED; Legion of Merit (USA); CA; FCIS; *b* Montreal, 20 Aug. 1896; *s* of Alfred G. S. and Phoebe Anne Walford, Montreal; *m* 1922, Olive Marjorie, *d* of James A. Dyke, Westmount Province of Quebec; one *s. Educ:* Westmount Acad. Served European War, 1914–19, with Royal Canadian Artillery, and War of 1939–45, HQ 1st Canadian Div., 1st Canadian Corps and as DA&QMG 1st Canadian Army in NW Europe; Adjutant-General Canadian Forces, and mem., Army Council, Nat. Defence Headquarters, Ottawa, 1944–46. Partner, Alfred Walford & Sons, Chartered Accountants, 1923–29; Dir, Sec. and Treasurer, of James A. Ogilvy

Ltd, 1929–39, of Henry Morgan & Co. Ltd, 1946–61; Pres., Morgan Trust Co., 1946–65; Chairman: E. G. M. Cape & Co. Ltd, 1965–68; Canadian Vickers Ltd, 1959–67; Dir and Chm., Montreal Adv. Bd of Canada Trust Co., 1961–72; Dir, Excelsior Life Insurance Co., 1951–70; Dir and Vice-Pres., Mercantile Bank of Canada, 1961–70; Hon. Dir, Canada Trust, 1972–. Member: Metropolitan Adv. Bd, YMCA; Nat Adv. Bd, Salvation Army; Past President: Fedn Commonwealth Chambers of Commerce; National Cttee, English-Speaking Union; Montreal Board of Trade; Past Chairman, Exec. Development Institute. Fellow, Royal Commonwealth Society; FCIS; Life Mem., Order of Chartered Accountants of Quebec. *Address:* 33 Argyle Avenue, St Lambert, PQ J4P 3P5, Canada. *Clubs:* St James's, Forest and Stream (Montreal). *Died* 1990.

**WALKER, Air Chief Marshal Sir Augustus;** *see* Walker, Air Chief Marshal Sir G. A.

**WALKER, Vice-Adm. Sir (Charles) Peter (Graham),** KBE 1967; CB 1964; DSC 1944; *b* 23 Feb. 1911; *s* of Charles Graham Walker and Lilla Geraldine (*née* Gandy); *m* 1938, Pamela Marcia Hawley, *d* of late George W. Hawley, Cape, SA; one *d* (one *s* decd). *Educ:* Worksop College. Entered Royal Navy, 1929; Royal Naval Engineering Coll., 1930–34; Advanced Engineering Course at RN Coll., Greenwich, 1935–37. War service in HM Ships Cornwall, Georgetown, Duke of York and Berwick and at the Admiralty; Vice-Admiral, 1965; Dir-Gen., Dockyards and Maintenance, MoD (Navy), 1962–67; Chief Naval Engr Officer, 1963–67; retired 1967. Non-Exec. Dir, Cammell Laird (Shipbuilders and Engineers) Ltd, 1969–71. Chm., CSSB, 1971–82. *Address:* Brookfield Coach House, Weston Lane, Bath BA1 4AG. *T:* Bath 23863. *Died 7 Dec.* 1989.

**WALKER, Sir Clive Radzivill Forestier-,** 5th Bt *cr* 1835; *b* 30 April 1922; *s* of Radzivill Clive Forestier-Walker (*g s* of 2nd Bt) (*d* 1973) and Kathleen Rose (*d* 1975), *d* of late William George Tinkler, King's Lynn; *S* cousin, Sir George Ferdinand Forestier-Walker, 4th Bt, 1976; *m* 1948, Pamela Mercy (marr. diss. 1976), *d* of late Clifford Leach; three *d. Heir: cousin* Michael Leolin Forestier-Walker, *b* 24 April 1949. *Address:* 42 Old Vicarage Park, Narborough, King's Lynn, Norfolk PE32 1TQ. *T:* Narborough 516. *Died 14 March* 1983.

**WALKER, Prof. Daniel Pickering,** FBA 1974; Professor of the History of the Classical Tradition, in the University of London at the Warburg Institute, 1975–81, now Emeritus; *b* 30 June 1914; *s* of Frederick Pickering Walker and Miriam Laura Walker (*née* Crittall). *Educ:* Westminster Sch.; Christ Church, Oxford. BA 1935 (1st cl. French), MA, DPhil 1940, Oxon. Corporal, Infantry and Intell. Corps, 1940–43; Foreign Office, 1943–45. Lectr, then Reader, French Dept, UCL, 1945–61; Reader in Renaissance Studies, Warburg Inst., Univ. of London, 1961–75, Sen. Fellow, 1953–56. Sen. Fellow, Cornell Univ. (Soc. for Humanities), 1971. *Publications:* Musikalischer Humanismus, 1947; Spiritual and Demonic Magic, 1958; The Decline of Hell, 1964; The Ancient Theology, 1972; Studies in Musical Science in the late Renaissance, 1978; Unclean Spirits, 1981; articles in Jl of Warburg and Courtauld Insts, etc. *Recreations:* chamber music, gardening. *Address:* 2 Regent's Park Terrace, NW1. *T:* 01–485 1699. *Died 10 March* 1985.

**WALKER, Sir E(dward) Ronald,** Kt 1963; CBE 1956; Australian economist and diplomat; *b* 26 Jan. 1907; *s* of Rev. Frederick Thomas Walker; *m* 1933, Louise Donckers; one *s* one *d. Educ:* Sydney Univ. (MA, DSc Econ); Cambridge Univ. (PhD, LittD). Lecturer in Economics, Sydney Univ., 1927–30, 1933–39; Fellow of Rockefeller Foundation, 1931–33; Economic Adviser: NSW Treasury, 1938–39; Govt of Tasmania, 1939–41; Prof. of Economics, Univ. of Tasmania, 1939–46; Chief Economic Adviser and Dep. Dir-Gen., Australian Dept of War Organisation of Industry, 1941–45; UNRRA HQ, Washington, 1945; Counsellor, Australian Embassy, Paris, 1945–50; Exec. Member, Nat. Security Resources Board, Prime Minister's Dept, Canberra, 1950–52; Australian Ambassador to Japan, 1952–55; Ambassador and Permanent Representative of Australia at United Nations, 1956–59 (Aust. Rep., Security Council, 1956–57); Ambassador: to France, 1959–68; to the Federal Republic of Germany, 1968–71; to OECD, Paris, 1971–73. Delegate to many confs and cttees connected with UN, ILO, Unesco, etc; Pres., UN Economic and Social Council, 1964. *Publications:* An Outline of Australian Economics, 1931; Australia in the World Depression, 1933; Money, 1935; Unemployment Policy, 1936; Wartime Economics, 1939; From Economic Theory to Policy, 1943; The Australian Economy in War and Reconstruction, 1947. *Address:* 1 rue de Longchamp, 75116 Paris, France. *T:* 4553.0300. *Died 28 Nov.* 1988.

**WALKER, Frank Stockdale,** MC 1919; Chairman, Lever Brothers, Port Sunlight Limited, 1954–60, retired; Director, Thames Board Mills Limited (until 1960); Director, Glycerine Limited; *b* 24 June 1895; *s* of Frank and Mary Elizabeth Walker; *m* 1921, Elsie May Nicholas (*d* 1974); one *s. Address:* Glenside Nursing Home, Manor

Road, Sidmouth, Devon EX10 8RP. *T:* Sidmouth (0395) 578466.
*Died 26 June* 1989.

**WALKER, Air Chief Marshal Sir (George) Augustus**, GCB 1969 (KCB 1962; CB 1959); CBE 1945; DSO 1941; DFC 1941; AFC 1956; *b* 24 Aug. 1912; *s* of G. H. Walker, Garforth, Leeds; *m* 1942, Brenda Brewis; one *s* one *d. Educ:* St Bees' Sch.; St Catharine's, Cambridge. Entered RAF Univ. Commission, 1934; Air Min. (R&D), 1938–39; commanded Bomber Sqdn, Stations and Base, 1940–45; SASO No 4 Group, 1945–46; Air Min., Dep. Dir, Operational Training, 1946–48; SASO Rhodesian Air Training Group, 1948–50; JSSC 1950; IDC 1953; Commandant, Royal Air Force Flying Coll., 1954–56; AOC No 1 Group, 1956–59; Chief Information Officer, Air Min., 1959–61; AOC-in-C, Flying Training Command, 1961–64; Inspector-General, RAF, 1964–67; Dep. C-in-C Allied Forces, Central Europe, 1967–70; retd 1970. ADC to the Queen, 1952–56, to King George VI, 1943–52; Air ADC to the Queen, 1968–70. Dir, Philips Electronics, 1970–82. Hon. Col, 33rd (Lancashire and Cheshire) Signal Regt, Royal Corps of Signals, T&AVR, 1970–75. Pres., RFU, 1965–66; Chm., Royal Air Forces Assoc., 1973–78, Pres., 1978–81; Chm., Nat. Sporting Club, 1973–83; Chm., Exec. Cttee, Lord Kitchener Nat. Meml Fund, 1977–82 (Chm., Scholarship Cttee, 1974–77). Governor and Commandant, Church Lads Brigade, 1970–78, Church Lads and Church Girls Brigade, 1978–79. *Recreations:* Rugby (played for England, 1939, Barbarians, RAF, Blackheath, Yorkshire; Captained RAF, 1936–39), golf, sailing. *Address:* The Hoe, Brancaster Staithe, Kings Lynn, Norfolk. *Club:* Royal Air Force.
*Died 11 Dec.* 1986.

**WALKER, Prof. Gilbert James**, MA Oxon, DLitt Birmingham; Professor of Commerce, 1955–74, later Emeritus, and sometime Head of Department of Industrial Economics and Business Studies, University of Birmingham; *b* 6 Jan. 1907; *s* of James MacFarlane Walker and Margaret Theresa Burrows; *m* 1943, Mavis Foyle; one *s. Educ:* Abbotsholme, Rocester, Staffs; University College Sch., London; New Coll., Oxford. Senior George Webb Medley Schol., Oxford Univ., 1928; Madden Prixeman and Meritorious Disappointed Candidate, TCD, 1930. Asst Lectr in Economics, Birmingham Univ., 1930; Rockefeller Fellow, USA, 1934; Consultant, Economics of Transport, Nova Scotia Govt, 1929; Sen. Investigator Man-power Survey, Min. of Labour, 1940; Asst Dir and Dep. Dir of Statistics, Min. of Supply, 1941; Dir of Statistics, British Supply Mission, Washington, DC, 1942; Reader in Economics of Transport, Univ. of Birmingham, 1945, Mitsui Professor of Economics 1947; Dean of Faculty of Commerce and Social Science, Birmingham, 1956. Lectr in Harvard Summer Sch., July 1949 and 1953. Consultant Economics of Transport, CO and Nigeria, 1950. Pres. of Section F (Economics and Statistics) of British Assoc. for the Advancement of Science, 1956; Consultant, Economics of Transport in W Africa for UN, 1957–58. *Publications:* Survey of Transportation in Nova Scotia, 1941; Road and Rail, an enquiry into the economics of competition and state control, 1942, 2nd edn, 1947; Traffic and Transport in Nigeria, 1956; Economic Planning by Programme and Control, 1957. Contrib. to Econ. Jl, Modern Law Review, Economica and Jl of Political Econ.; proc. Inst. Transport; British Transport Review, etc. *Address:* 78 Wellington Road, Edgbaston, Birmingham B15 2ET.
*Died 5 Aug.* 1982.

**WALKER, Sir Hugh Selby N.;** *see* Norman-Walker.

**WALKER, Ian Royaards;** Chairman: BP Oil Ltd, since 1985 (Deputy Managing Director, 1976; Chief Executive and Managing Director, 1981–85); BP Detergents Ltd, since 1979; Robert McBride Holdings Ltd, since 1978; Young's Paraffin Light and Mineral Oil Co. (Ltd), since 1979; *b* 22 April 1927; *s* of Alexander Walker and Louise Reiniera Jeanne Antoinette; *m* 1956, Margaret Elizabeth Bardsley; three *s. Educ:* Bryanston Sch.; Christ's Coll., Cambridge (MA); Bristol Univ. (CertEd). Shell-Mex and B.P. Ltd, 1952; British Petroleum Co. Ltd, 1954; Managing Director, Companhia Portuguesa dos Petroleos BP, Lisbon, 1963; European Regional Co-ordinator, 1967; General Manager, Corporate Planning Dept, 1972; Chairman: BP Ireland Ltd, 1978–83; Associated Octel Co. Ltd, 1981–85. Pres., UK Petroleum Industry Assoc., 1983–85. Chm., Special Cttee for St Peter's Hosps, Bloomsbury HA, 1982–; Mem. Management Cttee, Inst. of Urology, 1979–. *Recreation:* music. *Address:* c/o BP Oil Ltd, BP House, Victoria Street, SW1E 5NJ. *T:* 01–821 2300.
*Died 22 Oct.* 1985.

**WALKER, Sir John**, KCMG 1959 (CMG 1951); OBE 1947; *b* 27 June 1906; *s* of late Rupert Walker; *m* 1934, Muriel Winifred (*d* 1976), *d* of Henry John Hill; one *s* (and one *s* decd). *Educ:* Ashby Grammar Sch.; London Univ.; Sorbonne. Passed examination and entered Dept of Overseas Trade, 1929; Asst Commercial Sec.; Santiago, 1931; transf. to Buenos Aires, 1933; Commercial Sec., Bagdad, 1938, 1943; transf. to Madrid, 1944, Counsellor, (Commercial), 1947; transf. to Tehran, 1948; HM Inspector of Foreign Service Establishments, Foreign Office, 1953–55; Ambassador to Venezuela,

1955–60; Ambassador to Norway, 1961–62. Dir-Gen., Hispanic and Luso-Brazilian Councils, 1963–69. Knight Grand Cross, Order of St Olav (Norway), 1962. Fellow, University College, London, 1968–. *Recreations:* gardening, fishing. *Address:* Primrose Cottage, Lodsworth, Petworth, West Sussex GU28 9DA. *T:* Lodsworth 350.
*Died 6 Oct.* 1984.

**WALKER, John Riddell Bromhead**, CVO 1978 (MVO 1953); MC 1944; Lieutenant-Colonel (retired), late 14th Sikhs; *b* 21 June 1913; *s* of late Col P. G. Walker, IA, and Judith Dorothy Gonville, *d* of late Col Sir Benjamin Bromhead, Bt, CB, Thurlby Hall, Lincoln; *m* 1939, Marjorie, *d* of late Col Frank Fleming, DSO, TD; two *s* (one *d* decd). *Educ:* Dover; Royal Military Coll., Sandhurst. Attached 2nd Bn York and Lancaster Regt, 1933; 1/11th Sikh Regt (14th Sikhs) and 7/11th Sikh Regt, 1934–47; adjutant, 1938–41; various staff appointments in India, 1942–47; Instructor Staff Coll., Haifa, 1944–45; NWF (India), Waziristan, 1937; Ahmedzai, 1940; Datta Khel Relief, 1942; Arakan and Imphal, 1944; Rouge Croix Pursuivant of Arms, 1947–53; Lancaster Herald, 1953–68; Registrar of College of Arms, 1960–67; Clarenceux King of Arms, 1968–78. Dep. Inspector of Regimental Colours, 1958–77, Inspector, 1977–78. *Address:* c/o Grindlays Bank, 13 St James's Square, SW1Y 4LF. *Club:* Flyfishers'.
*Died 2 Sept.* 1984.

**WALKER, Prof. Kenneth Richard**, DPhil; Professor of Economics with Reference to Asia, University of London, School of Oriental and African Studies, since 1978 (Professor of Economics with Special Reference to China, 1972–78); *b* 17 Oct. 1931; *s* of Arthur Bedford Walker and Olive Walker; *m* 1959, June Abercrombie Collie; one *s* one *d. Educ:* Prince Henry's Grammar Sch., Otley, Yorks; Univ. of Leeds (BA); Lincoln Coll., Oxford. DPhil Oxon. Asst in Political Economy, Univ. of Aberdeen, 1956–59; Research Fellow, 1959–61, Lectr, 1961–66, Reader, 1966–72, in Economics, Hd of Dept of Economic and Political Studies, 1972–85, SOAS, Univ. of London. *Publications:* Planning in Chinese Agriculture, Socialisation and the Private Sector 1956–1962, 1965; Food Grain Procurement and Consumption in China, 1984; (with C. B. Howe) The Foundations of the Chinese Planned Economy 1953–84, 1989; contribs to Scottish Jl of Political Economy, Economic Development and Cultural Change, China Qly. *Recreations:* golf, hill-walking, bird-watching, choral singing. *Address:* 4 Harpenden Road, St Albans, Herts AL3 5AB.
*Died 28 July* 1989.

**WALKER, Sir Peter;** *see* Walker, Sir C. P. G.

**WALKER, Prof. Robert Milnes**, CBE 1964; Director of Surgical Studies, Royal College of Surgeons, 1968–71; Director, Cancer Records Bureau, SW Regional Hospital Board, 1965–71; Professor of Surgery, University of Bristol, 1946–64, Emeritus since 1964; Hon. Surgeon, Bristol Royal Hospital; Member of the Medical Research Council, 1959–63; *b* 2 Aug. 1903; *s* of J. W. Walker, FSA, FRCS, Wakefield, Yorks; *m* 1931, Grace Anna McCormick; two *s* four *d. Educ:* Oundle Sch.; University College Hospital, London. Hon. Surgeon, Royal Hospital, Wolverhampton, 1931–46; Rock Carling Fellow, Nuffield Hospital Trust, 1965. Editor, Medical Annual, 1954–74. Member Council, RCS, 1953–69; Vice-Pres., 1966–68; President: Assoc. Surgeons of GB, 1961; Surgical Research Soc., 1962–64. Fellow of University Coll., London, 1953. Mem., Medical Sub-Cttee, UGC, 1959–67. Master, Worshipful Co. of Barbers, 1974 (Upper Warden, 1973). Hon. FACS; Hon. FRCSE. Hon. Gold Medal, RCS, 1972. *Publications:* Portal Hypertension, 1959; Medical Education in Britain, 1965; Cancer in South West England, 1973; Barbers and Barber Surgeons of London, 1978. *Recreations:* gardening, bird watching, travel. *Address:* Little Wergs, Forge Close, Kintbury, Newbury, Berks.
*Died 25 Aug.* 1985.

**WALKER, Sir Ronald;** *see* Walker, Sir E. R.

**WALKER, Col Ronald Draycott S.;** *see* Sherbrooke-Walker.

**WALKER, Ronald Leslie**, CSI 1947; CIE 1942; *b* 9 April 1896; *m* 1948, Joyce Edwina Collins, OBE, 1946, Kaisar-i-Hind Gold Medal, 1939, *e d* of late G. Turville Brown. *Educ:* Bedford Sch.; Hertford Coll., Oxford. European War, 1914–18, Northamptonshire Regt, 1915; Machine-Gun Corps, 1916–18. Entered Indian Civil Service, 1920; Finance Secretary, Bengal, 1939–45; Adviser to Governor of Bengal, 1945; Chief Secretary, Bengal, 1946. *Address:* Little Coombe, Coombe Hill Road, East Grinstead, West Sussex. *T:* East Grinstead 25616. *Club:* East India, Devonshire, Sports and Public Schools.
*Died 6 April* 1984.

**WALKER, Samuel Richard**, CBE 1955; DL; Founder, 1920, and Hon. President, Walker & Rice (Walric Fabrics Ltd); *b* 6 Jan. 1892; *s* of Samuel Reuben and Elizabeth Louise Walker; *m* 1923, Marjorie Jackson Clark (*d* 1977), *d* of A. J. Clark, Hove, Sussex; one *s* two *d*; *m* 1966, Mrs Kathleen Mary Fawcett. *Educ:* William Ellis's. Queen Victoria Rifles, 1909–14; served European War, 1914–19, in France: 1st King Edward's Horse and RFA; Home Guard, 1939–45. City of London: DL 1951; Member Common Council (Bread Street Ward, 1937–76; Deputy, 1951–76), Chief Commoner, 1953–54; Chairman:

Officers and Clerks Cttee, 1952; Privileges Cttee, 1957–73; Comr of Income Tax, 1960–66. Sheriff of City of London, 1957–58; one of HM Lieutenants, City of London. Master, Worshipful Company of Farriers, 1954–55; Master, Worshipful Company of Founders, 1962–63, Liveryman of Worshipful Company of Weavers, 1964–; Chairman: Cattle Markets Cttee, 1945–46; Central Criminal Court Extension Cttee, 1964–75; Benevolent Assoc. of Corporation of London, 1970–76; Reconstruction of Guildhall Cttee, 1953–76; various Cttees, City of London, 1950–54. Pres., Assoc. of Chief Commoners, 1984–; Vice-Pres., Mid Sussex Assoc. for Mentally Handicapped Children, 1970–. Governor, Bridewell Royal Hosp., 1942–; Life Governor and Vice-Chm., City of London Sheriffs' and Recorders' Fund Soc., 1957–; Chm., Thomas Carpenter and John Lane Trust, 1951–; Governor and Almoner, Christ's Hosp., 1966–; Trustee, Seaforth Hall, Warninglid. Commendatore of Order Al Merito della Repubblica (Italy), 1957. *Recreations:* golf, riding. *Address:* Salters Court, Bow Lane, EC4; Copyhold Rise, Copyhold Lane, Cuckfield, Sussex. *Clubs:* City Livery (President, 1955–56), Guildhall, Oriental; West Hove Golf (Life Pres.), West Sussex Golf, Haywards Heath Golf. *Died 4 Sept. 1989.*

**WALKER, Timothy Ashley Peter;** Director: Henderson Administration Group Plc, since 1983; Henderson Administration Ltd, since 1980; Deputy Chairman, Henderson Unit Trust Management Ltd, since 1984 (Director since 1979); Chairman: Greenwood Oil Ltd, since 1981; Credit and Commerce Life, since 1983; CCL Financial Group plc, since 1986; New London Oil plc, since 1985; *b* 2 Feb. 1942; *s* of Vice-Adm. Sir C. Peter G. Walker, KBE, CB, DSC; *m* 1st, 1963, Carola Ashton (marr. diss.); one *s*; 2nd, 1972, Rosemary Vere Keep Thompson (*née* Edwards); two step *s* two step *d*. *Educ:* Charterhouse School. Lieut, Queen's Royal Irish Hussars, 1960–63. Imperial Life Assurance Co. of Canada, 1963–66; Dir, Abbey Life Assurance, 1966–70; Founder Dir, Hambro Life Assurance, 1970–78. Director: HTV Ltd, 1985–86; HTV West of England Ltd, 1985–86; HTV Group plc, 1986–; Lencross Ltd, 1985–; 27 Farm Street Management Ltd, 1985–. Chairman: WWF UK, 1984–; of Trustees, Marwell Zool Soc., 1979–; Vice-President: FFPS, 1983–; Game Conservancy Council, 1987– (Trustee, 1983–); World Congress of Herpetology, 1987–; Mem. Animal Welfare and Husbandry Cttee, 1982–85; Council Mem., 1985–, Zoological Soc. of London; Trustee: King Mahendra Trust—UK, 1984–; WWF Internat., 1986–; Patron: Farming and Wildlife Adv. Group, 1983–; Rhino Rescue, 1985–. *Publications:* articles in Financial Times etc. *Recreations:* farming and breeding endangered species. *Address:* Midway Manor, near Bradford-on-Avon, Wilts. *T:* Bradford-on-Avon 2225. *Club:* Boodle's.
*Died 11 April 1988.*

**WALKER, Prof. William;** FRCP, FRCPE; Regius Professor of Materia Medica, University of Aberdeen, 1973–82, retired; re-employed as Professor of Clinical Medicine, since 1982; *b* 1 Jan. 1920; *s* of William Sharp Walker and Joan Strachan Gloak; *m* 1948, Mary Cathleen Kenny; one adopted *s* one adopted *d*. *Educ:* Harris Academy, Dundee; Univ. of St Andrews. MA, MB, ChB; FRCP, FRCPE. Served War: commissioned Royal Scots, 1939; wounded, 1940; invalided, 1941. Lecturer in Pathology, Univ. of St Andrews, 1947; Medical Registrar, Newcastle, 1948. Research Fellow, Haematology, Boston Univ. Mass, 1954–55; Lectr in Therapeutics, St Andrews, 1952, Sen. Lectr, 1955; Consultant Physician, Aberdeen, 1964; Clinical Reader in Medicine, 1971. Pres., Anglo-German Medical Soc., 1976–81; Vice Chm., Cttee on the Review of Medicines, 1981–83 (Mem., 1975–83). *Publications:* various medical, chiefly in thrombotic and haemorrhagic disease, and drug therapy. *Recreations:* gardening, philosophy, social and political controversy. *Address:* Woodhill, Kinellar, Aberdeenshire AB5 0RZ. *T:* Aberdeen 79314. *Died 18 Dec. 1984.*

**WALKER, Sir William (Giles Newsom),** Kt 1959; TD 1942; DL; *b* 20 Nov. 1905; *e s* of late H. Giles Walker, Over Rankeillour, Cupar, Fife and of late Mrs Elizabeth Bewley Newsom (Walker), Cork, Eire; *m* 1930, Mildred Brenda (*d* 1983), 3rd *d* of Sir Michael Nairn, 2nd Bt, Elie House, Fife, and Pitcarmick, Blairgowrie; one *s* two *d*. *Educ:* Shrewsbury Sch.; Jesus Coll., Cambridge (BA). War of 1939–45: Lt-Col comdg 1st Fife and Forfar Yeomanry, 1943–45 (mobilised Aug. 1939; despatches, TD). Jute Industries Ltd, Dundee: entered 1927; rejoined after War, 1945; Director, 1946–71; Managing Director, 1947–69; Chairman, 1948–70; Hon. Pres., 1971. Director: Nairn & Williamson (Holdings) Ltd, 1954–75; Clydesdale Bank Ltd, 1961–82; Scottish Television Ltd, 1964–74; Alliance Trust Co. Ltd, 1963–76; Second Alliance Trust Co. Ltd, 1963–76. Formerly: Jute Working Party (Employer Mem.); Dundee Chamber of Commerce (Dir); Scottish Industrial Estates Ltd. (Dir); Member, Scottish Railway Bd. Hon. Colonel: Fife and Forfar Yeomanry/Scottish Horse, 1967–69; Highland Yeomanry, 1969–71. DL Fife, 1958. USA Bronze Star, 1945. *Recreations:* shooting and golf. *Address:* Pitlair, Cupar, Fife. *T:* Ladybank 30413. *Clubs:* Royal and Ancient Golf (Capt. 1962–63) (St Andrews); The Honourable Company of Edinburgh Golfers (Muirfield).
*Died 26 March 1989.*

**WALKER-OKEOVER, Colonel Sir Ian Peter Andrew Monro,** 3rd Bt, *cr* 1886; DSO and Bar 1945; TD; JP; Lord-Lieutenant of Derbyshire, 1951–77; *b* 30 Nov. 1902; *e s* of Sir Peter Walker, 2nd Bt, and Ethel Blanche, *d* of late H. C. and Hon. Mrs Okeover, *d* of 3rd Baron Waterpark; granted royal licence and authority to use surname of Okeover in addition to that of Walker, 1956; *S* father, 1915; *m* 1938, Dorothy Elizabeth, *yr d* of Capt. Josceline Heber-Percy, Guy's Cliffe, Warwick; one *s* two *d*. Served War of 1939–45 (DSO). Formerly Hon. Col, Derbyshire Yeomanry (subsequently Hon. Col Leicestershire and Derbyshire Yeomanry, retired 1962); Col Comdt, Yeomanry, RAC, TA, 1962–65. Derbyshire: JP 1932, High Sheriff 1934, DL 1948. Mem., Queen's Body Guard for Scotland (The Royal Company of Archers), KStJ 1974. *Heir:* s Captain Peter Ralph Leopold Walker-Okeover, Blues and Royals, retd [*b* 22 July 1947; *m* 1972, Catherine, *d* of Col George Maule Ramsay; one *s* one *d*]. *Address:* Okeover Hall, Ashbourne, Derbyshire; House of Glenmuick, Ballater, Aberdeenshire. *Clubs:* White's, Boodle's.
*Died 20 Feb. 1982.*

**WALKEY, Maj.-Gen. John Christopher,** CB 1953; CBE 1943; *b* 18 Oct. 1903; *s* of late S. Walkey, Dawlish, Devon; *m* 1947, Beatrice Record Brown; one *d* decd. *Educ:* Newton College, Devon. Commissioned into Royal Engineers from RMA Woolwich, 1923; Chief Engineer, 13 Corps, 1943–47; Asst Comdt, RMA Sandhurst, 1949–51; Chief Engineer, Middle East Land Forces, 1951–54; Engineer-in-Chief, War Office, 1954–57; retired, 1957. Col Comdt RE, 1958–68. Hon. Col RE Resources Units (AER), 1959–64. Officer Legion of Merit (USA), 1945. *Recreations:* usual country pursuits. *Address:* Holcombe House, Moretonhampstead, Devon TQ13 8PW. *Club:* Naval and Military. *Died 6 Oct. 1989.*

**WALKLING, Maj.-Gen. Alec Ernest,** CB 1973; OBE 1954; *b* 12 April 1918; *s* of late Ernest George Walkling; *m* 1940, Marian Harris; one *s* one *d*. *Educ:* Weymouth Grammar School; Keble College, Oxford. MA (Oxon); BA Mod. Langs, 1939; BA Hons Nat. Science, 1949. Commissioned 2nd Lieut RA, 1940; served War of 1939–45, N Africa and Burma (despatches); Staff Coll., Quetta, 1944; Min. of Supply, 1949–53; British Joint Services Mission, Washington, 1956–58; Comd Regt in BAOR, 1961–63; Comd Brigade (TA), 1963–64; Imperial Defence Coll., 1965; Dep. Commandant, RMCS, 1966–68; Dir-Gen. of Artillery, 1969–70; Dep. Master-Gen. of the Ordnance, 1970–73, retired; Col Comdt, RA, 1974–83. Special Asst to Bd, Marks & Spencer PLC, 1973–80. *Recreations:* golf, oil and water colour painting. *Address:* Brackenhurst, Brackendale Road, Camberley, Surrey. *T:* Camberley 21016. *Club:* Army and Navy.
*Died 23 Feb. 1988.*

**WALL, (Charles) Patrick;** MP (Lab) Bradford North, since 1987; *b* 6 May 1933; *m* Pauline Knight; two *s* one *d*. *Educ:* Liverpool Inst. Grammar Sch. Formerly lab. assistant and stock controller; housewares buyer for mail order firm. Former Member: Liverpool City Council; Bingley UDC. Contested (Lab) Bradford N, 1983. Pres., Bradford Trades Council, 1973–. *Publications:* contrib. socialist jls. *Recreations:* long-time devotee of jazz (former organiser of annual jazz night for housewares trade); lifelong Everton FC fanatic. *Address:* House of Commons, SW1A 0AA.
*Died 6 Aug. 1990.*

**WALL, John William,** CMG 1953; HM Diplomatic Service, retired 1966; *b* 6 Nov. 1910; *m* 1950, Eleanor Rosemary Riesle (*d* 1978); one *d*. *Educ:* Grammar Sch., Mexborough; Jesus Coll., Cambridge. Probationer Vice-Consul, Levant Consular Service, 1933; Vice-Consul, Cairo, 1936; in charge of Vice-Consulate, Suez, 1937; transferred to Jedda as 2nd Sec. in Diplomatic Service, 1939; acting Consul, Jedda, 1942, 1943; transferred to Tabriz, 1944, Isfahan, 1946, Casablanca, 1947; Brit. Middle East Office, Cairo: Head of Polit. Div., 1948, in charge 1949, 1950; Oriental Counsellor, Cairo, 1951; Political Agent, Bahrein, 1952–54; Consul-General at Salonika, 1955–57; HM Ambassador and Consul-General to Paraguay, 1957–59; Counsellor, Foreign Office, 1959–63; Consul-General at Alexandria, 1963–66. *Address:* Beech Cottage, Pen-y-Fan, Monmouth, Gwent. *Club:* United Oxford & Cambridge University. *Died 11 April 1989.*

**WALL, Patrick;** *see* Wall, C. P.

**WALLACE, Very Rev. Alexander Ross;** Dean of Exeter, 1950–60, retired; *b* 27 Sept. 1891; *s* of late Maj.-Gen. Sir Alexander Wallace, KCB; *m* 1915, Winifred (*d* 1980), *d* of late Rev. H. C. Sturges; two *s* two *d*. *Educ:* Clifton Coll. (Scholar); Corpus Christi Coll., Cambridge (Scholar). Classical Tripos, 1913, Class II, Div. I; entered ICS, 1914; served in the IARO att. 17th Cavalry; Special Service Officer, Patiala I. S. Lancers; retired from ICS, 1922; Asst Master and Tutor, Wellington Coll., Berks; Headmaster, Cargilfield School, Edinburgh, 1925–30; Blundell's School, Tiverton, 1930–33; Sherborne School, 1934–July 1950; ordained Deacon, 1938; Priest, 1939. Canon and Prebendary of Salisbury Cathedral, 1942–50. *Publications:* The Three Pillars, 1940; Conversation about Christianity, 1946; Christian Focus, 1956. *Recreations:* golf, fishing.

*Address:* c/o I. A. Wallace, Steeple Close, Hindon, Salisbury, Wilts.                                                    *Died 26 Aug. 1982.*

**WALLACE, Col the Hon. Clarence,** CBE 1946; CD; LLD; Lieutenant-Governor of British Columbia, Canada, 1950–55; *b* 22 June 1894; *s* of Alfred Wallace and Eliza E. Wallace (*née* Underhill), both of Vancouver, BC; *m* 1916, Charlotte Hazel (*d* 1974), *d* of Edward Chapman, Vancouver, BC; two *s* (and one *s* killed on active service, RCAF, 1942; one *s* decd 1956); *m* 1975, Hilda Ernestine McLennan. *Educ:* St Andrews Coll., Toronto, Ontario. Served overseas as Private, 5th Bn, 1914–16; Hon. Col BC Regt (Duke of Connaught's Own Rifles), 13th Armd Regt. Director of companies. KStJ 1951. *Recreations:* shooting, fishing. *Address:* Plaza del Mar, 1575 Beach Avenue, Vancouver, BC V6G 1Y5, Canada. *T:* 682–2300. *Clubs:* Vancouver, Royal Vancouver Yacht, Capilano Golf (Vancouver); Union (Victoria).                                    *Died 12 Nov. 1982.*

**WALLACE, Doreen, (Mrs Dora Eileen A. Rash),** MA; novelist; *b* 18 June 1897; *d* of R. B. Agnew Wallace and Mary Elizabeth Peebles; *m* 1922, Rowland H. Rash (*d* 1977), Wortham, Suffolk; one *s* two *d*. *Educ:* Malvern Girls' College; Somerville College, Oxford. Honours in English 1919; taught English in a grammar school for three years, then married; first novel published, 1931. *Publications:* -Esques (with E. F. A. Geach), 1918; A Little Learning; The Gentle Heart; The Portion of the Levites; Creatures of an Hour; Even Such is Time; Barnham Rectory, 1934; Latter Howe, 1935; So Long to Learn 1936; Going to the Sea, 1936; Old Father Antic, 1937; The Faithful Compass, 1937; The Time of Wild Roses, 1938; A Handful of Silver, 1939; East Anglia, 1939; The Spring Returns, 1940; English Lakeland, 1941; Green Acres, 1941; Land from the Waters, 1944; Carlotta Green, 1944; The Noble Savage, 1945; Billy Potter, 1946; Willow Farm, 1948; How Little We Know, 1949; Only One Life, 1950; (non-fiction) In a Green Shade, 1950; Norfolk (with R. Bagnall-Oakeley), 1951; Root of Evil, 1952; Sons of Gentlemen, 1953; The Younger Son, 1954; Daughters, 1955; The Interloper, 1956; The Money Field, 1957; Forty Years on, 1958; Richard and Lucy, 1959; Mayland Hall, 1960; Lindsay Langton and Wives, 1961; Woman with a Mirror, 1963; The Mill Pond, 1966; Ashbury People, 1968; The Turtle, 1969; Elegy, 1970; An Earthly Paradise, 1971; A Thinking Reed, 1973; Changes and Chances, 1975; Landscape with Figures, 1976. *Recreations:* painting, gardening. *Address:* 2 Manor Gardens, Diss, Norfolk.

*Died 22 Oct. 1989.*

**WALLACE, Sir Gordon,** Kt 1968; President, Court of Appeal, New South Wales, 1966–70; Acting Chief Justice of New South Wales, Oct. 1968–Feb. 1969; *b* 22 Jan. 1900; *s* of A. C. Isaacs, Sydney; *m* 1927, Marjorie (*d* 1980), *d* of A. E. Mullins, Chepstow, Mon.; one *s* one *d*. *Educ:* Sydney High School; RMC Duntroon; Sydney University. Lt, Australian Staff Corps; AMF and AIF, 1939–44 (Col). KC 1940. Judge of Supreme Court, NSW, 1960–70. Pres., NSW Bar Assoc., 1957–58; Vice-Pres., Australian Law Council, 1957; Pres., Internat. Law Assoc., Aust. Br., 1959–65. Mem., Commonwealth Commn of Enquiry into Income Tax, 1952–53. Chm., Royal Commn on Great Barrier Reef Petroleum Drilling, 1970–74. *Publications:* (jtly with Sir Percy Spender) Company Law, 1937; (jtly with J. McI. Young, QC) Australian Company Law, 1965. *Recreations:* bowls, music. *Address:* 6 Lynwood Avenue, Killara, NSW 2071, Australia. *T:* 498 1818. *Clubs:* University, Pioneers (Sydney); Elanora Country.                        *Died 11 Dec. 1987.*

**WALLACE, Irving;** free-lance author; *b* 19 March 1916; *s* of Alexander Wallace and Bessie (*née* Liss); *m* 1941, Sylvia Kahn Wallace; one *s* one *d*. *Educ:* Kenosha (Wisc.) Central High Sch.; Williams Inst., Berkeley, Calif.; Los Angeles City College. Served USAAF and US Army Signal Corps, 1942–46. Magazine writer, Saturday Evening Post, Reader's Digest, Collier's, etc., 1931–54; film scenarist, 1955–58, Exploration: Honduras jungles, Wisconsin Collegiate Expedn, 1934–35. Member: PEN; Soc. of Authors; Authors League of America. Supreme Award of Merit, George Washington Carver Memorial Inst., Washington, DC, 1964; Commonwealth Club of Calif. Lit. Award for 1964; Nat. Bestsellers Inst. Paperback of the Year Award, 1965; Popular Culture Assoc. Award, 1974. Archives at Honnold Library, Claremont, Calif. *Publications:* The Fabulous Originals, 1955; The Square Pegs, 1957; The Fabulous Showman, 1959; The Sins of Philip Fleming, 1959; The Chapman Report, 1960; The Twenty-Seventh Wife, 1961; The Prize, 1962; The Three Sirens, 1963; The Man, 1964; The Sunday Gentleman, 1965; The Plot, 1967; The Writing of One Novel, 1968; The Seven Minutes, 1969; The Nympho and Other Maniacs, 1971; The Word, 1972; The Fan Club, 1974; The People's Almanac, 1975; The R Document, 1976; The Book of Lists, 1977; The Two, 1978; The People's Almanac 2, 1978; The Pigeon Project, 1979; The Book of Lists 2, 1980; The Second Lady, 1980; The Book of Predictions, 1981; The Intimate Sex Lives of Famous People, 1981; The People's Almanac 3, 1981; The Almighty, 1983; The Book of Lists 3, 1983; Significa, 1983; The Miracle, 1984; Contemporary Authors Autobiography Series, Vol. 1, 1984; The Seventh Secret, 1986; The Celestial Bed, 1987; The Golden Room, 1988; contribs to Collier's Encyclopædia,

American Oxford Encyclopædia, Encyclopædia Britannica. *Relevant publication:* Irving Wallace: a writer's profile, by John Leverance, 1974. *Recreations:* tennis and table tennis, hiking, billiards, travel abroad, collecting autographs, French Impressionist art, canes. *Address:* PO Box 49328, Los Angeles, Calif 90049, USA.                                            *Died 29 June 1990.*

**WALLACE, William,** CMG 1961; Assistant Comptroller of Patent Office and Industrial Property and Copyright Department, Department of Trade and Industry (formerly Board of Trade (Patent Office)), 1954–73, retired; *b* 8 July 1911; *s* of A. S. Wallace, Wemyss Bay, Renfrewshire; *m* 1940, Sheila, *d* of Sydney Hopper, Wallington, Surrey; one *s* two *d*. *Educ:* Mill Hill School; St Edmund Hall, Oxford. Barrister, Inner Temple, 1936–39. Served War of 1939–45, Royal Artillery with final rank of Major. Board of Trade legal staff, 1945–54. UK Delegate, Internat. Confs on Copyright and Patents; Chm. Intergovernmental Cttee on Rights of Performers, Record Makers and Broadcasting Orgns, 1967–69; Actg Chairman: Intergovernmental Copyright Cttee, 1970; Exec. Cttee, Berne Copyright Union, 1970; Vice-Chm., Whitford Cttee on Copyright and Designs, 1974. Jean Geiringer Meml Lectr, USA, 1971. *Address:* The Middle House, Rose Hill, Dorking, Surrey RH4 2EA. *T:* Dorking 740938.                            *Died 13 May 1990.*

**WALLACE-HADRILL, Prof. John Michael,** CBE 1982; DLitt; FBA 1969; Chichele Professor of Modern History, Oxford, 1974–83, later Professor Emeritus, and Fellow of All Souls College, since 1974; *b* 29 Sept. 1916; *e s* of late Frederic and Tamzin Norah Wallace-Hadrill, Bromsgrove, Worcs; *m* 1950, Anne, *e d* of late Neville Wakefield, DSO, and of Violet Wakefield (*née* Dewar); two *s*. *Educ:* Cheltenham College; Corpus Christi College, Oxford (Scholar, Fellow, 1946–47, Hon. Fellow, 1984). Lothian Prize, 1938. Served War of 1939–45, (latterly Major, Gen. Staff, attached to a dept of Foreign Office). Merton College, Oxford: Fellow and Tutor, 1947–55; Sen. Res. Fellow, 1961–74; Sub-Warden, 1964–66; Hon. Fellow, 1974; Professor of Mediæval History, University of Manchester, 1955–61; Editor, English Historical Review, 1965–74. Lectures: Ford's, Oxford, 1969–70; Birkbeck, Cambridge, 1973–74; Stenton, Reading, 1974; Prothero, RHistS, 1974; Raleigh, British Acad., 1978; Kates, Stanford, 1979. Delegate, Oxford Univ. Press, 1971–82. Vice-Pres., Royal Hist. Soc., 1973–76; Publications Sec., British Academy, 1978–81. Vis. Distinguished Prof., Berkeley, Univ. of California, 1979. Corresp. Fellow, Medieval Acad. of Amer., 1984. *Publications:* The Barbarian West, 400–1000, 1952; (with J. McManners) France, Government and Society, 1957; The Chronicle of Fredegar, 1960; The Long-Haired Kings, 1962; Early Germanic Kingship, 1971; Early Medieval History, 1976; (ed with R. H. C. Davis) The Writing of History in the Middle Ages, 1981; The Frankish Church, 1983. *Address:* All Souls College, Oxford. *Club:* Athenæum.                                        *Died 3 Nov. 1985.*

**WALLACE WHITFIELD, Sir Cecil (Vincent),** Kt 1989; MP for Marco City, Bahamas, since 1987; Leader of the Official Opposition, since 1987; *b* 20 March 1930; *s* of late Kenneth Oswald Whitfield and Dorothy Louise Rogers (*née* Wallace); *m* 1st, 1950, Beverley Audrey Worrell; three *s*; 2nd, 1965, Daphne Margarita Barber; one *s* two *d*; 3rd, 1984, Naomi Rosetta Darville; two *s*. *Educ:* Univ. of Hull (LLB 1962). Called to the Bar, Middle Temple, 1962; Counsel and Attorney, Supreme Court of the Bahamas, 1962–. Minister of: Works, Bahamas, 1967–68; Education and Culture, 1968–70; Leader of the Opposition, 1971–72. *Recreation:* gardening. *Address:* The Mosmar Building, Queen Street, Nassau, Bahamas. *T:* (809) 322–8780, 1 and 2.                                    *Died 9 May 1990.*

**WALLER, Prof. Ross Douglas,** CBE 1958 (MBE 1945); Director of Extra-Mural Studies, 1937–60, and Professor of Adult Education, 1949–66 (Professor Emeritus, 1966), Manchester University; *b* 21 Jan. 1899; *m* 1928, Isobel May Brown; three *s* one *d*. *Educ:* Manchester Central High School for Boys; Manchester University. Served European War, KOYLI, and NF, 1917–19. BA, 1920; MA 1921; post-graduate studies in Florence, 1921–22; Schoolmaster, 1922–24; Lecturer in English Literature, Manchester Univ., 1924–37. Chm. North-Western Dist, WEA, 1943–57; Pres., Educational Centres Association, 1948–65; OECD Consultant on Adult Educn in Sardinia, 1961–62. Cavaliere Ufficiale, Order of Merit, Italy, 1956. *Publications:* The Monks and the Giants, 1926; The Rossetti Family, 1932; Marlowe, Edward II (with H. B. Charlton), 1933; Learning to Live, 1947; Harold Pilkington Turner, 1953; Residential College, 1954; Design for Democracy (Introductory Essay), 1956. Articles in Adult Education, Highway, Times Educational Supplement, etc. *Address:* Orford House, Woodcote Park, Coulsdon, Surrey CR3 2XL.

*Died 28 Jan. 1988.*

**WALLIS, Captain Arthur Hammond,** CBE 1952; RN (retired); *b* 16 Sept. 1903; *s* of late Harold T. Wallis; *m* 1940, Lucy Joyce (*d* 1974), *er d* of late Lt-Col L. E. Becher, DSO; one *s* one *d*. *Educ:* Wixenford; Osborne and Dartmouth. Entered Royal Navy as Cadet, 1917; specialised as Torpedo Officer, 1930; staff of Rear-Adm. Destroyers,

1936–38; Torpedo Officer, HMS Nelson, 1938–41; Comdr, 1941; i/c Torpedo Experimental Dept, HMS Vernon, 1941–43; Exec. Officer, HMS Illustrious, 1943–45; Captain, 1947; in command HM Underwater Detection Establishment at Portland, 1948–50; Sen. Naval Officer, Persian Gulf and in command HMS Wild Goose, 1950–51; Cdre, HMS Mauritius, 1951; UK Naval Delegate, Military Agency for Standardisation, NATO, 1952–53; Director of Underwater Weapons, Admiralty, 1953–56. Naval ADC to the Queen, 1956. Chief of Naval Information, Admiralty, 1957–64. *Recreations:* watching and listening. *Address:* Compton's Barn, Woodstreet, near Guildford, Surrey. *T:* Worplesdon 235143. *Club:* Naval and Military. *Died 12 April 1989.*

**WALLS, Henry James,** BSc, PhD; Director, Metropolitan Police Laboratory, New Scotland Yard, 1964–68; *b* 1907; *s* of late William Walls, RSA, and Elizabeth Maclellan Walls; *m* 1940, Constance Mary Butler; one *s* one *d*. *Educ:* George Watson's Boys' Coll., Edinburgh; Melville Coll., Edinburgh; Edinburgh Univ. BSc 1930; PhD 1933. Postgrad. research in physical chemistry, Munich, Edinburgh and Bristol, 1930–35; ICI (Explosives), 1935–36; Staff of Metropolitan Police Lab., 1936–46; Staff Chemist, Home Office Forensic Science Lab., Bristol, 1946–58; Director of Home Office Forensic Science Lab., Newcastle upon Tyne, 1958–64. Pres., British Acad. of Forensic Scis, 1935. *Publications:* Forensic Science, 1968, rev. edn 1974; (with Alistair Brownlie) Drink, Drugs and Driving, 1969, rev. edn 1985; Expert Witness, 1972; two books on photography; papers in journals dealing with forensic science. *Recreations:* reading, plays and films, talking, people, pottery. *Address:* 65 Marmora Road, SE22 0RY. *Died 16 Aug. 1988.*

**WALMESLEY WHITE, Brigadier Arthur,** CBE 1972; Chairman, Palestine Exploration Fund, since 1973 (Member, Executive Committee, since 1949); *b* 10 Sept. 1917; *s* of late Walter Walmesley White, MA, and Jessie Beswick; *m* 1951, Jocelyn Mary Beale, *d* of late Captain G. H. Beale, DSO, RN; one *s* three *d*. *Educ:* Eastbourne Coll.; Royal Military Academy; Pembroke Coll., Cambridge (MA). Commissioned, Royal Engineers, 1937; RE Field Units and Staff, 1939–45; Military Survey Staff and Units, 1946–49; Ordnance Survey, 1949–52; School of Military Survey, 1952–56 (Chief Instr, 1954–56); Directorate of Mil. Survey, 1956–59; CO, 42 Survey Engr Regt, Cyprus, 1959–62; Chief Survey Officer, Northern Army Gp/TWOATAF, Germany, 1962–63; Chief Geographic Officer, AFCENT, France, 1963–65; Ordnance Survey, 1965–69 (Dir of Map Publication, 1966–69). Brigadier 1966. Dir of Military Survey, and Chief of Geographical Section, Gen. Staff. MoD, 1969–72; retired, 1972. Planning Inspectorate, DoE, 1972–82. FRGS (Mem. Council, 1969–72); FRICS; MIOP. *Publications:* various papers on cartographic subjects in learned jls. *Recreations:* gardening, woodworking, hill-walking. *Address:* Old Barton, Whitestone, Exeter, Devon EX4 2LF. *T:* Longdown 232. *Club:* Army and Navy. *Died 1 Nov. 1985.*

**WALMSLEY, Charles;** *see* Walmsley, R. C.

**WALMSLEY, Air Marshal Sir Hugh Sydney Porter,** KCB 1952 (CB 1944); KCIE 1947; CBE 1943 (OBE 1937); MC 1918; DFC 1922; *b* 6 June 1898; 3rd *s* of late James Walmsley, Broughton, near Preston; *m* 1928, Audrey Maude, 3rd *d* of late Dr Pim, Sleaford; three *s*. *Educ:* Old Coll., Windermere; Dover Coll. 2nd Lieut. Loyal North Lancs Regt, 1915–16; seconded to RFC 1916; Captain, RFC, 1917; permanent commission RAF 1919 as Flying Officer; Flt Lt, 1921; Sqdn Ldr, 1931; Wing Comdr, 1937; Gp Capt., 1939; Air Cdre, 1942; Air Vice-Marshal, 1943; Acting Air Marshal, 1947–48; Air Marshal, 1949. 55 Sqdn; BEF, 1917–18 (MC); Iraq, 1921–23; OC 33 Sqdn Bicester, 1933–34, 8 Sqdn, Aden, 1935–37; War of 1939–45 (despatches 5 times); OC 71 Wing AASF, 1939–40; OC RAF Station, Scampton, 1940–41; HQ Bomber Command, 1941–42; AOC 91 Group, 1942–43; SASO, HQ Bomber Command, 1944–45; AOC 4 Group, Transport Command, 1945–46; Air Officer, Transport Command, SE Asia, 1946; AOC-in-C, Air HQ, India, 1946–47; Deputy Chief of the Air Staff, 1948–50; AOC-in-C, Flying Training Command, 1950–52; Retired from Active List, 1952. Managing Director of Air Service Training Ltd, 1952–59; Principal of College of Air Training, Hamble, 1960, resigned July 1960. *Recreations:* represented RAF Inter-Service Athletics in 1919, 1924 and 1926; all games; gardening, sailing. *Address:* Upwood, Tiptoe, Lymington, Hants. *Club:* Royal Air Force. *Died 2 Sept. 1985.*

**WALMSLEY, (Ronald) Charles,** CB 1981; FRICS; Member of the Lands Tribunal, 1960–81; *b* 22 Jan. 1909; *s* of late Rev. Canon Alfred Moss Walmsley and Alice Jane (*née* Murgatroyd); *m* 1933, Joan Rosalind (*née* Hall); one *s* one *d*. *Educ:* Rossall Sch. FRICS 1941. Private practice as chartered surveyor, 1928–60. Vice-Pres., RICS, 1958–60. *Publications:* Walmsley's Rural Estate Management, 1948 (6th edn 1978); Walmsley's Agricultural

Arbitrations, 1952 (3rd edn 1970). *Address:* 42 Tower House Close, Cuckfield, Haywards Heath, West Sussex RH17 5EQ. *Died 13 June 1983.*

**WALPOLE, 9th Baron, of Walpole,** *cr* 1723; 7th Baron Walpole of Wolterton, *cr* 1756; **Robert Henry Montgomerie Walpole,** TD; Captain, RA; *b* 25 April 1913; *s* of late Horatio Spencer Walpole and Dorothea Frances, *o d* of Frederick Butler Molyneux Montgomerie; *S* to baronies at the death of his cousin, 5th Earl of Orford, 1931; *m* 1937, Nancy Louisa, OBE, *y d* of late Frank Harding Jones, Housham Tye, Harlow, Essex; one *s* one *d* (and one *s* one *d* decd). *Educ:* Eton; South Eastern Agricultural Coll., Wye; Royal Agricultural Coll., Cirencester. *Recreations:* curling, shooting, golf. *Heir:* *s* Hon. Robert Horatio Walpole [*b* 8 Dec. 1938; *m* 1st, 1962, Judith (marr. diss. 1979), *yr d* of T. T. Schofield, Stockingwood House, Harpenden; two *s* two *d*; 2nd, 1980, Laurel Celia, *o d* of S. T. Ball, Swindon; two *s* one *d*. *Educ:* Eton; King's Coll., Cambridge]. *Address:* Wolterton Hall, Norwich NR11 7LY. *T:* Cromer 761210, Matlaske 274. *Club:* Norfolk (Norwich). *Died 25 Feb. 1989.*

**WALPOLE, Kathleen Annette,** MA; Head Mistress of Wycombe Abbey School, Bucks, 1948–61; *b* Ootacamund, S India, 1899; *e d* of Major A. Walpole, RE. *Educ:* Southlands Sch., Exmouth; Westfield Coll., University of London. BA Hons London, 1921; History Mistress, The Church High Sch., Newcastle upon Tyne, 1922–27; Research Student, Westfield Coll., 1927–28; MA London, 1929; Alexander Prize of RHistSoc, 1931; History Mistress, The Royal Sch., Bath, 1928–34; Head Mistress, The Red Maids Sch., Bristol, 1934–47. *Publications:* articles in the Trans. of Historic Society of Lancashire and Cheshire, and of the RHistSoc, 1929 and 1931, on Emigration to British North America. *Recreations:* gardening, walking, study of antiques. *Club:* Royal Commonwealth Society. *Died 18 Jan. 1987.*

**WALSH, Sir David (Philip),** KBE 1962; CB 1946; retired as Deputy Secretary, Ministry of Housing and Local Goverment (1960–63); *b* 1902; *s* of late David Walsh and Margaret Walsh; *m* 1930, Edith Airey (*d* 1979), *d* of Frederick Airey and Henrietta Carline; two *s* one *d*. *Educ:* Quentin Sch.; UCL. Formerly: Principal Asst Secretary (Director of Establishments), Admiralty; Under Secretary, Ministry of Town and Country Planning; Under-Secretary, Ministry of Housing and Local Goverment (formerly Min. of Local Government and Planning), 1951–60; seconded to: Govt of Iraq as Personnel Advr, 1956; UN Orgn as Personnel Advr to Govt of Venezuela, 1959–60. *Address:* 26 Cottington Court, Cotmaton Road, Sidmouth, Devon EX10 8HD. *T:* Sidmouth 577274. *Died 13 Dec. 1989.*

**WALSH, Maj.-Gen. Francis James,** CB 1948; CBE 1945; psc†; *b* 12 Jan. 1900; *s* of F. J. Walsh, Wexford, Eire; *m* 1931, Marjorie Olive Watney; two *s*. *Educ:* Clongowes Coll., Eire. RMC, Sandhurst, 1918; Royal Irish Regt, 1918–22; King's African Rifles, 1922–28; South Lancashire Regt, 1928–31; Indian Army, 1931–48; Staff Coll., Camberley, 1933–34; staff employment, India, Burma, Malaya, 1935–48; DA&QMG 33 Corps, 1943; DQMG 11 Army Group, 1943–44; DA&QMG 4 Corps and 14 Army, 1944–45; MGA N Comd, India, 1945–47. Maj.-Gen. (Temp.) 1945; Subst., 1947; retired, 1948. *Recreation:* sailing. *Address:* Northlands, 25 Laurel Close, North Warnborough, Hants. *T:* Odiham 3051. *Club:* Naval and Military. *Died 22 Aug. 1987.*

**WALSH, Leslie;** Stipendiary Magistrate, for Greater Manchester, 1974–75 (for Salford, 1951–74); *b* 6 May 1903; *s* of Rt Hon. Stephen and Anne Walsh; *m* 1934, Katharine de Hoghton Birtwell. *Educ:* Wigan Grammar Sch.; Victoria Univ., Manchester (LLB); St John's Coll., Oxford (BCL). Called to Bar, Gray's Inn, 1927; practised Northern Circuit. RAF, 1940–45. Deputy Licensing Authority NW Area, 1946–51; Chairman, Salford and District Rent Tribunal, 1946–51. Hon. MA Salford, 1976. *Address:* 4 Grange Road, Urmston, Manchester M31 1HU. *Died 4 Jan. 1986.*

**WALSH, Prof. William Henry,** FRSE 1979; FBA 1969; Emeritus Fellow, Merton College, University of Oxford, since 1979; Professor of Logic and Metaphysics in the University of Edinburgh, 1960–79, later Emeritus; Vice Principal, University of Edinburgh, 1975–79; *b* 10 Dec. 1913; *s* of Fred and Mary Walsh, Leeds; *m* 1938, Frances Beatrix Ruth (*née* Pearson); one *s* two *d*. *Educ:* Leeds Grammar Sch.; Merton Coll., Oxford. Class I, Classical Mods., 1934, Class I, Lit. Hum., 1936; Gaisford Greek Prose Prize, 1934; Junior Research Fellow, Merton Coll., 1936. Served War of 1939–45, Royal Corps of Signals, 1940–41; subsequently employed in branch of Foreign Office. Lecturer in Philosophy, Univ. Coll., Dundee (University of St Andrews), 1946; Fellow and Tutor in Philosophy, Merton Coll., Oxford, 1947–60, Emeritus Fellow, 1979; Sub-Warden, 1948–50, Senior Tutor, 1954–60; Lecturer in Philosophy, University of Oxford, 1947–60; Dean of Faculty of Arts, University of Edinburgh, 1966–68; Senatus Assessor, Univ. Ct, Edinburgh, 1970–73. Dawes Hicks Lecturer, British Academy, 1963. Visiting Professor: Ohio State Univ., USA, 1957–58; Dartmouth Coll., NH, USA, 1965;

Univ. of Maryland, 1969–70; Carleton Coll., Minn, 1983; Rose Morgan Vis. Prof., Kansas Univ., 1980. Pres. Aristotelian Soc., 1964–65. Hon. DHL Rochester, 1979; Hon. DLitt Edinburgh, 1985. *Publications:* Reason and Experience, 1947; An Introduction to Philosophy of History, 1951; Metaphysics, 1963; Hegelian Ethics, 1969; Kant's Criticism of Metaphysics, 1975; articles in philosophical periodicals. *Address:* 352 Banbury Road, Oxford OX2 7PP. *T:* Oxford 59328. *Died 7 April* 1986.

**WALTER, Captain Philip Norman,** DSO 1940; RN; Commandant, Corps of Commissionaires, 1950–60; Director of The Times, 1958–64; *b* 12 Dec. 1898; *s* of Captain Philip Walter, RN, and *g s* of John Walter III, of The Times; *m* 1946, Sylvia (*d* 1976), *d* of J. C. M. Ogilvie-Forbes, Boyndlie, Aberdeenshire; one *s. Educ:* RN Colleges Osborne and Dartmouth. Served European War, 1914–18, Dardanelles and North Sea; Commander, 1932; Captain, 1940; War of 1939–45, Norway; commanded Inshore Squadron, N Africa, 1942; wounded, PoW; Assistant Chief of Staff to Allied Naval Commander-in-Chief, 1944; invalided, 1948. Chevalier of Légion d'Honneur, Croix de Guerre (France). *Address:* c/o Barclays Bank, 1 Pall Mall East, SW1. *Died 21 Jan.* 1984.

**WALTON, Sir Raymond (Henry),** Kt 1973; a Judge of the High Court of Justice, Chancery Division, 1973–87; *b* 9 Sept. 1915; *e s* of Henry Herbert Walton and Clara Martha Walton, Dulwich; *m* 1940, Helen Alexandra, *e d* of Alexander Dingwall, Jedburgh; one *s* one *d* (and one *d* decd). *Educ:* Dulwich College; Balliol College, Oxford. Open Math. Schol., Balliol, 1933; BA 1937; MA 1942. Pres., Oxford Union Soc., Feb. 1938; BCL 1938. Called to Bar, Lincoln's Inn, 1939; Bencher, 1970. War service in Anti-Aircraft Artillery (including Instructor in Gunnery and Experimental Officer), 1940–46. Contested (L) North Lambeth, 1945. Returned to practice at Bar, 1946; QC 1963. Legal corresp., Financial Times, 1953–72. Mem., Lord Chancellor's Law Reform Cttee, 1959–83; Chm., Insolvency Rules Adv. Cttee, 1977–83. Church Comr for England, 1969–73; Dep. Chm., Boundaries Commn for England, 1973–86. Hon. Fellow, Coll. of Estate Management, 1977. Editor-in-Chief, Encyclopaedia of Forms and Precedents, 5th edn, 1985–. *Publications:* An introduction to the law of Sales of Land, 1949, 3rd edn 1969; (edited) Kerr on Receivers, 12th edn (with A. W. Sarson), 13th to 16th edns; Adkin's Law of Landlord and Tenant, 13th, 14th and (with Michael Essayan) 15th to 18th edns. *Recreation:* philately. *Address:* Royal Courts of Justice, WC2.

*Died 29 Jan.* 1988.

**WALTON, Sir William (Turner),** OM 1967; Kt 1951; MusD; Composer; *b* 29 March 1902; *s* of Charles Alexander and Louisa Maria Walton; *m* 1949, Susana Gil Passo. *Educ:* Cathedral Choir School and Christ Church, Oxford. Hon. Student Christ Church, Oxford; Hon. MusD (Oxon, Dunelm, TCD, Manchester); Hon. DMus (Cantab, London); Hon. FRCM; Hon. FRAM; Gold Medal Royal Philharmonic Society, 1947; Gold Medal Worshipful Company of Musicians 1947; Benjamin Franklin Medal, RSA, 1972. Mem. Royal Swedish Acad. of Music; Accademico onorario di Santa Cecilia, Rome; Hon. Member: Amer. Acad. and Inst. of Arts and Letters, 1978; Royal Manchester Coll. of Music, 1972. *Compositions:* Pianoforte Quartet (Carnegie award), 1918, rev. 1974; String Quartet (unpublished), 1921; Façade (with Edith Sitwell), 1923 and 1926, Siesta for small orchestra, 1926; Portsmouth Point, 1926; Sinfonia Concertante for piano and orchestra, 1928; Viola Concerto, 1929; Belshazzar's Feast, 1931; Three Songs for Soprano, 1932; Symphony, 1935; Crown Imperial (Coronation March), 1937; In Honour of the City of London, 1937; Violin Concerto, 1939; Music for Children, 1940; Scapino (comedy overture), 1940; & (ballet), 1943; Henry V (film), 1945; Quartet, 1947; Hamlet (film), 1948; Sonata for Violin and Pianoforte, 1949; Te Deum, 1953; Orb and Sceptre (Coronation March), 1953; Troilus and Cressida (opera), 1954; Richard III (film), 1955; Johannesburg Overture, 1956; Violoncello Concerto, 1956; Partita, 1957; Anon in Love, 1960; Symphony No 2, 1960; Gloria, 1961; A Song for the Lord Mayor's Table, 1962; Prelude for Orchestra, 1962; Variations on a Theme by Hindemith, 1963; The Twelve (anthem), 1964; Missa Brevis, 1966; The Bear (comic opera) 1967; Capriccio Burlesco, 1968; Improvisations on an Impromptu by Benjamin Britten, 1970; Jubilate, 1972; Five Bagatelles (guitar), 1972; Sonata for String Orchestra, 1972; Cantico del Sole, 1974; Magnificat and Nunc Dimittis, 1974; Varii Capricci, 1976; Antiphon, 1977; Façade 2, 1979; Prologo e Fantasia, Passacaglia, 1982; Wagner (film), 1983. *Address:* c/o Oxford University Press, 37 Dover Street, W1. *Clubs:* Athenæum, Savile, Garrick. *Died 8 March* 1983.

**WALWYN, Rear-Adm. James Humphrey,** CB 1964; OBE 1944; self-employed consultant, since 1975; *b* 21 Aug. 1913; *o s* of late Vice-Admiral Sir Humphrey Walwyn, KCSI, KCMG, CB, DSO and Lady Walwyn, DBE; *m* 1945, Pamela Digby Bell; one *s* two *d*. *Educ:* The Old Malthouse and RN College, Dartmouth. Entered RN, 1931; Lieut 1935; ADC to Governor of Newfoundland, 1936–37; specialised in Gunnery, 1938; HMS Renown, 1939–41; HMS Newcastle, 1942–44; Staff of C-in-C Home Fleet, 1945–47;

Comdr 1948; Naval Staff Course, 1948; Admiralty, 1948–50; Comdg HMS Chevron, 1951–52; Captain 1953; Staff of SHAPE, Paris, 1954–56; Captain Inshore Flotilla, Mediterranean, 1956–58; Dir, RN Tactical School, 1958–59; Dir of Officer Appts, Admiralty, 1960–62; Rear-Adm. 1962; Flag Officer Flotillas, Mediterranean, 1962–65; retired, 1965. Chief Exec., Personnel, British Oxygen Co., 1965–75. Member: Central Office of Industrial Tribunals, 1978–82; Central Arbitration Cttee, 1978–83. FIPM. SBStJ 1972. *Recreations:* fishing, gardening. *Address:* 40 Jubilee Place, SW3. *T:* 01–352 7802. *Clubs:* Army and Navy, Hurlingham. *Died 24 Feb.* 1986.

**WAND, Dr Solomon,** OBE 1983; Chairman, Council of British Medical Association, 1956–61 (Treasurer, 1963–72); 1899; *s* of Louis and Jane Wand; *m* 1st, 1921, Claire Cohen (*d* 1951); one *s* one *d*; 2nd, 1960, Shaunagh Denison Crew, *o d* of Major Robert Douglas Crew and Irene Crew, Milford-on-Sea, Hants. *Educ:* Manchester Grammar School; Manchester University. Qualified 1921, MB, ChB (Manchester), with distinction in medicine; in general practice in Birmingham. FRCGP. Mem., Birmingham Local Med. Cttee, 1930–. Member of: Council, BMA, 1935–72 (Pres. Midland Branch, 1969–70); Gen. Medical Council, 1961–71; Advertising Advisory Cttee of IBA (formerly ITA), 1961–75; Court of Governors, Univ. of Birmingham, 1969–70; Board, General Practice Finance Corporation, 1969–76; Chairman: Gen. Medical Services Cttee, BMA, 1948–52; Representative Body, BMA, 1951–54; Gold Medallist, BMA, 1954; formerly Member Central Health Services Council, Medical Advisory Cttee of Min. of Health; formerly Mem. Health Education Cttee. Hon. Vice-Pres. British Medical Students Assoc., 1959; Chm., British Medical Students Trust, 1968–; formerly Examng MO, Dept of Health and Social Security; Member: Study Cttee of World Medical Assoc., 1959–; Management Cttee, Medical Insurance Agency, 1964–; Birmingham Central District Medical Cttee, 1974–80; Chm., Med. Adv. Cttee, Allied Investments Ltd, 1973–78. Hon. DCL, Durham, 1957; Hon. LLD: Queen's Univ., Belfast, 1962; Birmingham Univ., 1984. *Publications:* contribs to Encyclopædia of General Practice. *Recreations:* travel, swimming, bridge. *Address:* D 5 Kenilworth Court, Hagley Road, Edgbaston, Birmingham B16 9NU. *T:* 021-454 3997.

*Died 16 Sept.* 1984.

**WANSBROUGH-JONES, Sir Owen (Haddon),** KBE 1955 (OBE 1946; MBE 1942); CB 1950; MA, PhD (Cantab); FRSC; Chairman, Albright & Wilson Ltd, 1967–69 (Executive Vice-Chairman, 1965–67); Director, British Oxygen International, 1960–76; *b* 25 March 1905; *y s* of late Arthur Wansbrough-Jones, BA, LLB, Long Stratton, Norfolk, and Beatrice (*d* 1972), *d* of late Thomas Slipper, JP, Bradeston Hall, Norfolk; unmarried. *Educ:* Gresham's School, Holt; Trinity Hall, Cambridge (Open Schol.). 1st Cl., Natural Sciences Tripos Part I and Part II (Chemistry); Research Student of Trinity Hall, and of Goldsmiths' & Salters' Company; Ramsay Memorial Fellow; studied Physical Chemistry at Cambridge under Prof. Sir Eric Rideal, and in Berlin under Professor Fritz Haber; Fellow of Trinity Hall, 1930–46; Assistant Tutor, 1932–34; Tutor, 1934–40; Hon. Fellow, 1957; Departmental Demonstrator, Dept of Colloid Science, University of Cambridge, 1932–40; Emergency Commission, 1940; France, 1940; Brig. 1945; Dir of Special Weapons and Vehicles, War Office, 1946; Scientific Adviser to Army Council, 1946–51; Principal Dir of Scientific Research (Defence) Min. of Supply, 1951–53; Chief Scientist of Min. of Supply, 1953–59. Mem., Natural Environment Research Council, 1968–74. Treasurer of Faraday Soc., 1949–60; Pres., Jesters Club, 1958–77. Prime Warden, Goldsmiths' Company, 1967; Hon. Freeman, Fishmongers' Co., 1973. *Publications:* scientific papers on physical chemistry in British and German scientific journals, 1929–38. *Recreations:* gardening, shooting. *Address:* Orchardleigh, Long Stratton, Norfolk NR15 2PX. *T:* Long Stratton 30410. *Club:* United Oxford & Cambridge University.

*Died 10 March* 1982.

**WARBURG, Fredric John;** President, Secker and Warburg Ltd, Publishers (Chairman, 1936–71); *b* 27 Nov. 1898; *s* of late John Cimon Warburg and Violet Amalia Warburg; *m*; three *s*; *m* 1933, Pamela de Bayou (*d* 1978); (one *s* decd). *Educ:* Westminster School; Christ Church, Oxford (Exhibnr). 2nd Cl. Lit. Hum. (Greats); MA 1922. Served as 2nd Lieut with 284th Siege Battery, Belgium and France, 1917–19. Joined George Routledge & Sons Ltd as apprentice, 1922; Joint Man. Dir, 1931; resigned, 1935. Bought publishing firm Martin Secker, Ltd, 1936, name changed to Martin Secker & Warburg, 1936, with himself as Chairman. Served as Corporal in St John's Wood Co., Home Guard under Sergeant George Orwell (Eric Blair), 1941–45. Joined Heinemann Group of Publishers, 1951. Tried at Central Criminal Court (Old Bailey) for publishing an allegedly obscene novel, and acquitted, 1954. Elected Director of Heinemann Group of Publishers, 1961–71. *Publications:* An Occupation for Gentlemen, 1959; A Slight Case of Obscenity (9000 words) in New Yorker Magazine, 20 April 1957; All Authors Are Equal, 1973. *Recreations:* replaying chess games of the masters, window box gardening, reading, writing. *Address:* 29 St Edmund's

Court, Regent's Park, NW8. *T:* 01–722 5641.
*Died* 24 *May* 1981.

**WARBURG, Sir Siegmund G(eorge),** Kt 1966; Chairman, Advisory Council, S. G. Warburg & Co. Ltd, London, since 1978 (Director, 1946–69; President, 1970–78); *b* 30 Sept. 1902; *s* of George S. Warburg and Lucie (*née* Kaulla); *m* 1926, Eva Maria Philipson; one *s* one *d. Educ:* Gymnasium, Reutlingen, Germany; Humanistic Seminary, Urach, Germany, 1920–30; training periods in Hamburg, London, Boston and New York; Partner M. M. Warburg & Co., Hamburg, 1930–38; Director, New Trading Co. Ltd, London, 1938–46. Order of the Sacred Treasure (1st class), Japan, 1978. *Recreations:* reading and walking. *Address:* 30 Gresham Street, EC2. *T:* 01–600 4555. *Died* 18 *Oct.* 1982.

**WARBURTON, Eric John Newnham,** CBE 1966; a Vice-Chairman, Lloyds Bank Ltd, 1967–75; *b* 22 Nov. 1904; *o s* of late E. and H. R. Warburton, Bexhill-on-Sea, Sussex; *m* 1933, Louise, *er d* of late C. J. and L. R. Martin, Crowborough, Sussex; one *s* one *d. Educ:* Eastbourne Grammar School. Entered Lloyds Bank Ltd, 1922; Jt General Man., 1953; Dep. Chief Gen. Man., 1958; Chief Gen. Man., 1959–66; Dir, 1965–75; Dep. Chm., Lloyds Bank International Ltd, 1971–75; Director: Lloyds Bank Unit Trust Managers Ltd, 1966–75; First Western Bank Trust Co., Calif., 1974–75; Lewis's Bank Ltd, 1967–75; Intercontinental Banking Services Ltd, 1968–75. Chairman: Exec. Cttee, Banking Information Service, 1965–71; Bank Education Service, 1966–71; Dep. Chairman: City of London Savings Cttee, 1962–74; Exports Credit Guarantee Dept Adv. Council, 1968–71 (Member, 1966–71); Member: Decimal Currency Bd, 1967–71; Nat. Savings Cttee, 1963–74; Council, CBI, 1971–75. Member Board: Trinity Coll. of Music, 1968–74; Management Cttee, Sussex Housing Assoc. for the Aged, 1970–; American Bankers Assoc. Internat. Monetary Conf., 1970–72. FRSA 1970; Hon. FTCL 1969. *Recreations:* golf, gardening, music. *Address:* 9 Denmans Close, Lindfield, Haywards Heath, West Sussex RH16 2JX. *T:* Lindfield 2351. *Club:* Oriental.
*Died* 23 *Aug.* 1989.

**WARD OF WITLEY,** 1st Viscount, *cr* 1960; **George Reginald Ward,** PC 1957; *b* 20 Nov. 1907; 4th *s* (twin) of 2nd Earl of Dudley; *m* 1st, 1940, Anne Capel (marr. diss., 1951); one *d* (one *s* decd); 2nd, 1962, Hon. Mrs Barbara Astor (who *m* 1st, 1942, Hon. Michael Langhorne Astor; she *d* 1980). *Educ:* Eton; Christ Church, Oxford. AAF, 1929; RAF, 1932–37 and 1939–45. MP (C) for Worcester City, 1945–60. Parly Under-Sec. of State, Air Min., 1952–55; Parly and Financial Sec., Admiralty, Dec. 1955–Jan. 1957; Secretary of State for Air, 1957–60. *Heir:* none. *Address:* 23 Queens Gate Gardens, SW7 5LZ. *Clubs:* White's, Pratt's. *Died* 15 *June* 1988 (*ext*).

**WARD, (Arthur) Neville,** RDI 1971; BArch; RIBA, FCSD; architect and designer; *b* 5 June 1922; *s* of Arthur Edward Ward and Winifred Alice Ward; *m* 1948, Mary Winstanley; one *s. Educ:* Wade Deacon Grammar Sch., Widnes; Sch. of Architecture, Univ. of Liverpool (BArch 1944); Edinburgh Coll. of Art. RIBA 1944; FCSD (FSIA 1948). Mem., BoT Furniture Design Panel, 1946–48. Private practice: Ward and Austin, 1948–71; Ward Associates, 1972–86; special concern in interiors, exhibns, ships accommodation, furniture; contrib. Britain Can Make It, 1946, and Festival of Britain, 1951. Pres., SIAD, 1967. Member: Nat. Adv. Cttee on Art Exams, 1952–57; Nat. Adv. Council on Art Educn, 1959–71; Council, RSA, 1965–70, and 1977–78; Council, RCA, 1968–72; Nat. Council for Diplomas in Art and Design, 1968–74. Master, Faculty of Royal Designers for Industry, 1977–78. *Publications:* (with Mary Ward) Living Rooms, 1967; (with Mary Ward) Home in the 20s and 30s, 1978; articles and essays in Arch. Rev., and Naval Arch. *Recreations:* jobbing, painting. *Address:* 10 Star Lane, Great Dunmow, Essex CM6 1AY. *Died* 5 *May* 1989.

**WARD, Sir Aubrey (Ernest),** Kt 1967; JP; DL; *b* 17 April 1899; *s* of Edward Alfred Ward; *m* 1919, Mary Jane Davidson Rutherford, MB, ChB (*d* 1979); one *d. Educ:* Royal Veterinary College, London. Served War of 1914–18; Night FO, RFC (subseq. RAF). Veterinary Practice, 1923–66. Vice-Chm., Thames Conservancy Bd, 1964–74. Mayor of Slough, 1940–45, Hon. Freeman, 1961. JP 1957, DL 1963, Chm., CC, 1963–74, Buckinghamshire. *Address:* 54 Pound Lane, Marlow, Bucks. *T:* Marlow 5250. *Died* 14 *June* 1987.

**WARD, David,** CBE 1972; FRCM; opera singer; *b* 3 July 1922; *s* of James Ward and Catherine Bell; *m* 1960, Susan E. V. Rutherford; no *c. Educ:* St Patrick's School, Dumbarton; Royal College of Music. Royal Navy, 1940–43; Royal Indian Navy, 1943–46. Sadler's Wells, 1953–59; Covent Garden, 1960–64; now international free-lance singer, Germany, USA, Italy, France, etc. Hon. RAM 1973; FRCM 1973. Hon. LLD Strathclyde, 1974. *Recreation:* golf. *Address:* Kennedy Crescent, Lake Wanaka, New Zealand.
*Died* 16 *July* 1983.

**WARD, Sir Deighton (Harcourt Lisle),** GCMG 1976; GCVO 1977; QC (Barbados) 1959; Governor-General, Barbados, since 1976; *b* 16 May 1909; *s* of Edmund Lisle Ward and Ellen Ward; *m* 1936,

Audrey Doreen Ramsey; three *d. Educ:* Boys' Foundation Sch.; Harrison Coll., Barbados. Called to the Bar, Middle Temple, 1933; practised at Barbados Bar, 1934–63; Mem., Legislative Council of Barbados, 1955–58; Mem., House of Representatives, Fedn of West Indies, 1958–62; High Court of Barbados, 1963–76. Pres., Barbados Football Assoc., 1954–75. *Recreations:* reading, bridge, billiards. *Address:* Government House, Barbados. *T:* 92646. *Clubs:* Spartan (Barbados); (Hon.) Summerhays; (Hon.) Bridgetown; (Hon.) Barbados Turf. *Died* 9 *Jan.* 1984.

**WARD, Denzil Anthony Seaver,** CMG 1967; retired Barrister, New Zealand; *b* Nelson, NZ, 26 March 1909; 3rd *s* of late Louis Ernest Ward, Civil Servant NZ Government and Secretary Geographic Board, and Theresa Ward (*née* Kilgour); *m* 1938, Mary Iredale Garland, *d* of late John Edwin Garland, Christchurch, NZ; three *d. Educ:* Christ's College and Cathedral Grammar Sch., Christchurch, NZ; Victoria Univ. of Wellington, NZ. BA 1928; LLB 1938; practised law as barrister and solicitor, 1938–42; Asst Law Draftsman, Law Drafting Office, 1942; First Asst, 1947; Law Draftsman, 1958–66; Counsel to Law Drafting Office and Compiler of Statutes, 1966–74. Lecturer in law subjects, Victoria Univ. of Wellington, NZ, 1944–45, 1949–55. Member: NZ Law Revision Commn, 1958–74; Public and Administrative Law Reform Cttee, 1966–80; Criminal Law Reform Cttee, 1971–83; Vice-Patron, Legal Research Foundation, 1965–68. Mem. Otaki and Porirua Trusts Bd, 1952–71, Chm., 1965–71; Mem. Papawai and Kaikokirikiri Trusts Bd, 1965–81, Chm., 1972–81. Foundation mem. and mem. Council, NZ Founders Soc., 1939–42; elected hon. life mem., 1941. Chm., Royal Wellington Choral Union, 1949–50; mem. Schola Cantorum, 1951–55. *Publications:* (jointly) Ward and Wild's Mercantile Law in New Zealand, 1947; (ed) NZ Statutes Reprint, 1908–57, vols 3–16; articles in legal periodicals. *Recreations:* music, reading, gardening, watching rugby and cricket. *Address:* 15 Plymouth Street, Karori, Wellington 5, New Zealand. *T:* 768–096.
*Died* 17 *Sept.* 1989.

**WARD, Edward Rex,** CMG 1948; *b* 19 May 1902; *y s* of late Daniel Ward, FSI, Tavistock; *m* 1st, 1934, Mary Nell (from whom he obtained a divorce); 2nd, 1947, Molly Owen Jones, *née* Money (*d* 1971), *widow* of Flying Officer Owen Jones, RAF; one *s* two step *d. Educ:* King's Coll., Taunton; Coll. of Estate Management, Lincoln's Inn Fields, WC1. Colonial Administrative Service, Nigeria, 1926; transferred to The Gambia, 1942; Actg Governor on several occasions since 1945; Colonial Secretary, The Gambia, 1945–52; retired, 1952. *Recreation:* gardening. *Address:* Cameron House, 78 Pellhurst Road, Ryde, Isle of Wight. *Club:* Seaview Yacht. *Died* 11 *Feb.* 1984.

**WARD, Francis Alan Burnett,** CBE 1964; PhD; Keeper, Department of Physics, Science Museum, London, SW7, 1945–70; *b* 5 March 1905; *o s* of late Herbert Ward, CBE, and late Eva Caroline (*née* Burnett); *m* 1953, E. Marianne Brown, Ilkley. *Educ:* Highgate Sch.; Sidney Sussex Coll., Cambridge. MA, PhD (Cantab), 1931. Research on nuclear physics at Cavendish Laboratory, Cambridge, 1927–31; Asst Keeper, The Science Museum, 1931; seconded to Air Ministry (Meteorological Office), 1939. Flt-Lieut, RAFVR (Meteorological Branch), 1943–45. In charge of Atomic Physics and Time Measurement sections, Science Museum, 1931–70. FBHI; FInstP; FMA. *Publications:* official Science Museum Handbooks on Time Measurement, 1936 and 1937, and later edns; Catalogue of European Scientific Instruments, British Museum, 1981; contrib. to The Making of Physicists, 1987; various papers on atomic physics in Proc. Royal Society and Proc. Physical Soc. *Recreations:* bird-watching, gardening, photography, music. *Address:* Wendover, 8 Parkgate Avenue, Hadley Wood, Barnet, Herts EN4 0NR. *T:* 01–449 6880. *Died* 30 *Jan.* 1990.

**WARD, Frederick John;** Under-Secretary, Department of the Environment (formerly Ministry of Housing and Local Government), 1968–76; *b* 9 April 1922. *Address:* 29 Groveside, Great Bookham, Leatherhead, Surrey. *T:* Bookham 52282. *Club:* MCC. *Died* 5 *Sept.* 1986.

**WARD, Prof. John Manning,** AO 1983; FASSA; FAHA; FRAHS; Vice-Chancellor and Principal, University of Sydney, 1981–90; *b* 6 July 1919; *s* of Alexander Thomson Ward and Mildred Boughay Davis; *m* 1951, Patricia Bruce Webb, AM; two *d. Educ:* Fort Street Boys' High Sch.; Univ. of Sydney (MA, LLB). FASSA 1954; FAHA 1969; FRAHS 1979. Sydney University: Challis Prof. of History, 1949–79; Deputy Vice-Chancellor and Prof. of History, 1979–81, then Emeritus Prof.; Dean, Faculty of Arts, 1962; Pro Dean, 1970–71; Chairman: Professorial Bd, 1974–75; Academic Bd, 1975–77. Dominion Fellow, St John's Coll., Cambridge, 1951; Vis. Prof., Yale Univ., 1963; Vis. Fellow, All Souls Coll., Oxford, 1968; Smuts Vis. Fellow, Cambridge, 1972. Trustee, NSW Public Library, 1968–69; Mem., CL Libr., NSW, 1970–82; Chm., Archives Authority, NSW, 1979–82 (Mem. 1961–82); Chm., NSW State Cancer Council, 1981–82; Member: Parramatta Hosps Bd, 1982–86; Bd, Royal Alexandra Hosp. for Children, 1982–89; Bd, Royal Prince

Alfred Hosp., 1986–87; Menzies Sch. of Health Res., 1986–. DUniv Sydney, 1990; Hon. DLitt Waseda, 1990. *Publications:* British Policy in the South Pacific, 1948, 3rd edn 1976; (jtly) Trusteeship in the Pacific, 1949; contrib. Australia (UN Series, Calif), 1947; Earl Grey and the Australian Colonies 1846–57, 1958; contrib. The Pattern of Australian Culture, 1963; Empire in the Antipodes, *c* 1840–1860, 1966; Changes in Britain 1919–1957, 1968; contrib. Historians at Work, 1973; Colonial Self-Government, The British Experience 1759–1856, 1976; James Macarthur: Colonial Conservative 1798–1867, 1981. *Recreations:* music, railways. *Address:* c/o The University of Sydney, New South Wales 2006, Australia. *T:* (02) 440–8440. *Club:* Australian (Sydney).
*Died 6 May 1990.*

**WARD, Neville;** *see* Ward, A. N.

**WARD, Gen. Sir Richard (Erskine),** GBE 1976; KCB 1971 (CB 1969); DSO 1943 and Bar, 1943; MC 1942; Chief of Personnel and Logistics, Ministry of Defence, 1974–76, retired; *b* 15 Oct. 1917; *o s* of late John Petty Ward and Gladys Rose Ward (*née* Marsh-Dunn); *m* 1947, Stella Elizabeth, 2nd *d* of late Brig. P. N. Ellis, RA, and Mrs Rachel Ellis; two *s* two *d. Educ:* Marlborough Coll.; RMC, Sandhurst. Commissioned Royal Tank Corps, 1937; served War of 1939–45 (despatches thrice); 5th Royal Tank Regt, 1939–43; Staff Coll., Camberley, 1944; Bde Major, 4th Armoured Bde, 1944; CO Westminster Dragoons, 1945; Korea with 1st Royal Tank Regt, 1952 (despatches); Lt-Col Chiefs of Staff Secretariat, 1955; CO 3 Royal Tank Regt, 1957; idc 1961; on staff of Chief of Defence Staff, 1962; comd 20 Armoured Bde, 1963; GOC 1st Division 1965–67; Vice-Adjutant-General, 1968–70; Cmdr British Forces, Hong Kong, 1970–73. Maj.-Gen., 1965; Lt-Gen., 1970; Gen., 1974. Col Comdt RTR, 1970–75. Dep. Commonwealth Pres., Royal Life Saving Soc., 1976–82. Croix de Guerre, with palm, 1940; Chevalier, Order of Leopold II, with palm, 1945. *Address:* Bellsburn, 18 Lower Street, Rode, Somerset BA3 6PU.
*Died 11 Aug. 1989.*

**WARD, Wilfrid Arthur,** CMG 1948; MC 1918; *b* 9 May 1892; *s* of late Arthur Henry Ward; *m* 1922, Norah Anne Phelps; one *s. Educ:* Christ's Hospital. Served European War; mobilised with Civil Service Rifles, 1914, France; commissioned in Lancashire Fusiliers (SR) 1915, France, Salonika, Palestine; Captain, 1917. Cadet Malayan Civil Service, 1920; varius District posts in FMS, Kedah and Kelantan; Secretary to Resident, Selangor, 1936; Under-Secretary, Straits Settlements, 1941; interned in Singapore, 1942–45; Resident Commissioner, Selangor, 1946–48; Commissioner for Malaya in the UK, 1948–53. *Address:* Beckleys, West Hayes, Lymington, Hants SO4 9RL.
*Died 7 May 1981.*

**WARD-HARRISON, Maj.-Gen. John Martin Donald,** OBE 1962; MC and bar 1945; Vice Lord-Lieutenant, North Yorkshire, since 1982; Manager, Thirsk Racecourse Ltd, since 1976; *b* 18 April 1918; *s* of Commander S. J. Ward-Harrison, Haughley House, Suffolk; *m* 1945, June Amoret, *d* of late Major C. A. Fleury Teulon, Inniskilling Dragoons; one *d* (one *s* decd). *Educ:* Shrewsbury Sch. Suffolk and Norfolk Yeomanry, 1936–39; 5th Royal Inniskilling Dragoon Guards, 1939–45; Staff Coll., S Africa, 1945; Staff appts and regimental duty, 1946–56; GSO1, 7 Armoured Div., 1956–58; comd 10th Royal Hussars (PWO), 1959–62; Col Gen. Staff, 1962–63; Brig., Royal Armoured Corps, E and S Commands, 1964; Imperial Defence Coll., 1965; Dep. Comdt, Staff Coll., Camberley, 1966–68; GOC Northumbrian District, 1968–70; COS, HQ Northern Comd, 1970–72; GOC NE District, 1973; retd 1973. Chm., York and Dist Br., CPRE. Hon. Dir, York Minster Fund, 1975–. DL North Yorks, 1978. *Recreations:* field sports. *Address:* Hazel Bush House, Stockton-on-the-Forest, York YO3 9TP. *T:* Flaxton Moor 239. *Club:* Army and Navy.
*Died 27 March 1985.*

**WARD-PERKINS, John Bryan,** CMG 1975; CBE 1955; MA; FBA 1951; FSA; Director of the British School at Rome, 1946–74; *b* 1912; *s* of late Bryan Ward-Perkins, Indian Civil Service (retired); *m* 1943, Margaret Sheilah Long; three *s* one *d. Educ:* Winchester (Schol.); New Coll., Oxford; Senior Demy of Magdalen Coll., Oxford; Craven Travelling Fellow, 1934–36. Asst, London Museum, 1936–38; Prof. of Archæology, Royal Univ. of Malta, 1939; war service (TA), 1939–45, England, Africa, and Italy (despatches); Lt-Col, Royal Artillery; organised military government antiquities dept in Tripoli and Cyrenaica; Dir of Monuments and Fine Arts Subcommission in Italy. Directed archæological excavations at Welwyn, 1937, Ightham, Kent, 1938, Tripolitania, 1948–53, Istanbul, 1953, Italy, 1957–71, and Cyrenaica, 1969–71, 1978–79. Member: Pontificia Accademia Romana di Archeologia; German Archæological Inst Corresp. Mem., Royal Acad. of History, Antiquity and Letters, Stockholm; Acad. of Archaeology, Letters and Fine Arts of Naples. President: Internat. Union of Institutes, Rome, 1953, 1964, 1976; Tabula Imperii Romani, 1971–; Internat. Assoc. for Classical Archæology, 1974–79; Soc. for Libyan Studies, 1978–; XI Internat. Congress of Classical Archaeology, London, 1978. Visiting Professor: New York Univ, 1957; Univ. of Sydney, 1977, 1978; Vis. Mem., Inst. for Advanced Study, Princeton,

1974–75; Lectures: Carl Newell Jackson Harvard Univ., 1957; Rhind Soc. of Antiquaries of Scotland, 1960; Myres Memorial Oxford Univ., 1963; M. V. Taylor Memorial 1968; Jerome Rome and Ann Arbor, 1969; Mortimer Wheeler, British Acad., 1971; Shuffrey Meml, Lincoln Coll., Oxford, 1976; Semple, Univ. of Cincinnati, 1980. Hon. DLitt, Birmingham; Hon. LLD Alberta, 1969. Medaglia d'oro per i Benemeriti della Cultura (Italian Govt), 1958; Serena Medallist of the British Academy, 1962; Cultori di Roma Gold Medal, 1979. *Publications:* London Museum Medieval Catalogue; Inscriptions of Roman Tripolitania, 1952; The Shrine of St Peter, 1955; (jtly) The Great Palace of the Byzantine Emperors, 1959; The Historical Topography of Veii, 1961; The Northeastern Ager Veientanus, 1969; (jtly) Etruscan and Roman Architecture, 1970; The Cities of Ancient Greece and Italy; planning in classical antiquity, 1974; Architettura Romana, 1975; Pompeii AD79, 1976; papers on archæological subjects. *Address:* Old Barn, Stratton, Cirencester, Glos. *Club:* Athenæum.
*Died 28 May 1981.*

**WARDER, John Arthur,** CBE 1957; General Managing Director, Oil Operating Companies in Iran, 1963–67, retired; *b* 13 Nov. 1909; *s* of John William Warder and Blanche Longstaffe, Bournemouth; *m* 1936, Sylvia Mary Hughes; two *s* one *d. Educ:* Kent Coll., Canterbury. Joined Asiatic Petroleum Co., 1927; was with Shell in Argentina and Cuba. Pres. and Gen. Man., Cia. Mexicana de Petroleo El Aguila, 1950; Gen. Man., Shell Cos in Colombia, 1953; Vice-Pres., Cia. Shell de Venezuela, 1957, Pres., 1959; Shell's Regional Co-ordinator (Oil), Middle East, 1961–63; Dir, Shell Internat. Petroleum Co. Ltd, and Mem. of Bds, Iranian Oil Participants Ltd and Iraq Petroleum Co. Ltd, 1961–63. Officer, Order of Arts and Culture (France), 1966; Order of Taj, 3rd degree (Iran), 1966. *Recreations:* yachting, golf. *Address:* Orchard Cottage, Howe Hill, Watlington, Oxon OX9 5EZ. *T:* Watlington 2137. *Clubs:* East India; Phyllis Court (Henley-on-Thames); Chapultepec Golf (Mexico); Royal Channel Islands Yacht; Royal Guernsey Golf.
*Died 8 Dec. 1989.*

**WARDLAW, Claude Wilson,** PhD, DSc, MSc, FRSE; George Harrison Professor of Botany, University of Manchester, 1958–66, then Emeritus Professor; *b* 4 Feb. 1901; *s* of Major J. Wardlaw, HLI, and Mary Hood Wardlaw; *m* 1928, Jessie Connell (*d* 1971); two *s. Educ:* Paisley Grammar Sch.; Glasgow Univ. Demonstrator and Lecturer in Botany, Glasgow Univ., 1921–28; Pathologist and Officer-in-Charge, Low Temperature Research Station, Imperial College of Tropical Agriculture, Trinidad, BWI, 1928–40; Professor of Cryptogamic Botany, University of Manchester, 1940–58; wide travel in United States, Central and South America and in West Indies, Africa and East Indies. Prather Lecturer, Harvard Univ.; Hon. Foreign Mem., American Academy of Arts and Sciences; Hon. Foreign Correspondent, Académie d'Agriculture de la France; Hon. For. Associate, Royal Academy of Belgium; Corresp. Mem., American Botanical Soc., 1967; Sen. For. Scientist Fellowship, Nat. Sci. Foundation, Univ. of California, 1968. Vis. Prof., NY State Univ., Buffalo, 1967. Hon. DSc McGill. Pelton Award, Amer. Botanical Soc., 1970. Trinidad Volunteer Regt, 1937–40; Lt-Col TA, retired. *Publications:* Diseases of the Banana, 1935, rev. and greatly extended edns, as Banana Diseases, 1961, 1972; Green Havoc, 1935; Tropical Fruits and Vegetables: Storage and Transport, 1937; Phylogeny and Morphogenesis; Morphogenesis in Plants, 1952; Embryogenesis in Plants, 1955; Organization and Evolution in Plants, 1965; Morphogenesis in Plants: A Contemporary Study, 1968; Essays on Form in Plants, 1968; Cellular Differentiation in Plants and Other Essays, 1969; A Quiet Talent: Jessie Wardlaw, 1903–1971, 1971; Enchantment in Iere, 1974; obituary of F. W. Sansome, CBE, PhD, FRSE, FLS, in RSE Year Book 1982; scientific papers published in Phil. Trans. Royal Society Edinburgh, Royal Soc., Annals of Botany, Nature, etc; *Festschrift:* Trends in Plant Morphogenesis, ed E. G. Cutter, 1966. *Address:* 6 Robins Close, Bramhall, Stockport, Cheshire SK7 2PF.
*Died 16 Dec. 1985.*

**WARDLAW, Sir Henry,** 20th Bt of Pitreavie, *cr* 1631; *b* 30 Aug. 1894; *o s* of Sir Henry Wardlaw, 19th Bt, and Janet Montgomerie, *d* of James Wylie; *S* father 1954; *m* 1929, Ellen, *d* of John Francis Brady; four *s* one *d. Heir: s* Henry John Wardlaw, MB, BS [*b* 30 Nov. 1930; *m* 1962, Julie-Ann, *d* of late Edward Patrick Kirwan; five *s* two *d*]. *Address:* 82 Vincent Street, Sandringham, Vic 3191, Australia.
*Died 19 April 1983.*

**WARDLE, Air Cdre Alfred Randles,** CBE 1945; AFC 1929; MRAeS; RAF, retired; *b* 29 Oct. 1898; *s* of William Wardle, Stafford; *m* 1926, Sarah, *d* of David Brindley, Cotes Heath; one *s* one *d*. Joined Hon. Artillery Co., 1916; RFC 1917; RAF 1918; Director of Operational Requirements, Air Ministry, 1943–46; AOC Ceylon, 1947–49; AOC No. 66 (Scottish) Group, 1950–52. Air Commodore, 1943; retired 1952. Secretary: Corby Develt Corp., 1954–67; Milton Keynes Develt Corp., 1967–68; Peterborough Develt Corp., 1968–69; Northampton Develt Corp., 1969; Central Lancs Develt Corp., 1971–72. *Address:* 88 Gipsy Lane, Kettering, Northants. *T:*

Kettering 85780. *Club:* Royal Air Force.
*Died* 31 *July* 1989.

**WARDLE, Ven. Walter Thomas;** Archdeacon of Gloucester since 1949; Canon Residentiary of Gloucester Cathedral, since 1948; *b* 22 July 1900; *s* of late James Thomas Wardle, Southsea, Hants; unmarried. *Educ:* Pembroke Coll., Oxford; Ripon Hall, Oxford. 3rd Class History BA 1924, MA 1932. Deacon, 1926; Priest, 1927; Curate of Weeke, Winchester, 1926–28; SPG Chaplain, Montana, Switzerland, 1928; Rector of Wolferton with Babingley, Norfolk, 1929–38; Vicar of Great and Little Barrington with Taynton, 1938–43; Vicar of Charlton Kings, Cheltenham, 1943–48. *Address:* 7 College Green, Gloucester. *T:* Gloucester 24948.
*Died* 12 *Feb.* 1982.

**WARE, Sir Henry (Gabriel),** KCB 1972 (CB 1971); HM Procurator-General and Treasury Solicitor, 1971–75; *b* 23 July 1912; *o s* of late Charles Martin Ware and Dorothy Anne Ware (*née* Gwyn Jeffreys); *m* 1939, Gloria Harriet Platt (*d* 1986); three *s* (and one *s* decd). *Educ:* Marlborough; St John's Coll., Oxford. Admitted solicitor, 1938; entered Treasury Solicitor's Dept, 1939; Dep. Treasury Solicitor, 1969–71. Served War of 1939–45 with Royal Artillery. *Recreations:* fly fishing, gardening. *Address:* The Little House, Tilford, Farnham, Surrey. *T:* Frensham 2151.
*Died* 12 *Oct.* 1989.

**WAREHAM, Arthur George;** *b* 24 April 1908; *y s* of late George Wareham and of Elizabeth Wareham; *m* 1936, Kathleen Mary, *d* of H. E. and Mabel Tapley; one *s* one *d* (and one *s* decd). *Educ:* Queen's Coll., Taunton. Joined Western Morning News, 1926; Daily Mail, 1935; Editor, Daily Mail, 1954–59. Chm., Arthur Wareham Associates Ltd, 1961–77. *Address:* Three Corners, Forest Ridge, Keston, Kent. *T:* Farnborough (Kent) 53606.
*Died* 10 *May* 1988.

**WARING, Sir (Alfred) Harold,** 2nd Bt, *cr* 1935; BA, BSc, AMIMechE; *b* 14 Feb. 1902; *o s* of Sir Holburt Jacob Waring, 1st Bt, CBE, MS, FRCS, and Annie Cassandra (*d* 1948), *d* of Charles Johnston Hill, Holland Park, W; *S* father, 1953; *m* 1930, Winifred, *d* of late Albert Boston, Stockton-on-Tees; one *s* two *d*. *Educ:* Winchester; Trinity Coll., Cambridge; London Univ. BA Cambridge, 1924; BSc(Eng) London, 1924. AMIMechE 1932. *Heir: s* Alfred Holburt Waring [*b* 2 Aug. 1933; *m* 1958, Anita, *d* of late Valentin Medinilla, Madrid; one *s* two *d*]. *Address:* Pen Moel, Tidenham, near Chepstow, Gwent. *T:* Chepstow 2448. *Died* 16 *March* 1981.

**WARK, Sir Ian (William),** Kt 1969; CMG 1967; CBE 1963; PhD (London); DSc (Melbourne); Hon. Consultant, CSIRO Institute of Earth Resources (formerly CSIRO Minerals Research Laboratories), since 1971; *b* 8 May 1899; *s* of William John Wark and Florence Emily (*née* Walton); *m* 1927, Elsie Evelyn, *d* of late W. E. Booth; one *d*. *Educ:* Scotch Coll., Melbourne; Univs of Melbourne, London and California (Berkeley). Exhibn of 1851 Science Research Scholarship, 1921–24; Lectr in Chemistry, Univ. of Sydney, 1925; Research Chemist, Electrolytic Zinc Co. of Australasia Ltd, 1926–39; CSIRO: Chief, Div. of Industrial Chemistry, 1940–58; Dir, Chemical Research Laboratories, 1958–60; Mem. Exec., 1961–65. Chm., Commonwealth Adv. Cttee on Advanced Educn., 1965–71. Gen. Pres., Royal Australian Chem. Inst., 1957–58; Treas., Australian Acad. of Science, 1959–63. FAA 1954; FTS 1976; Hon. Mem., Australasian Inst. of Mining and Metallurgy, 1960–; Fellow, UCL, 1965. Hon. DAppSc, Melbourne, 1977; Hon. DASc Victoria Inst. of Colls, 1979. ANZAAS Medal, 1973. *Publications:* (monograph) Principles of Flotation, 1938 (revised, with K. L. Sutherland, 1955); Why Research?, 1968; numerous papers in scientific jls. *Recreations:* golf, fishing. *Address:* 31 Linum Street, Blackburn, Victoria 3130, Australia. *T:* Melbourne 8772878. *Club:* Sciences (Melbourne). *Died* 20 *April* 1985.

**WARMINGTON, Eric Herbert,** MA; FRHistS; Professor Emeritus of Classics, University of London; Fellow of Birkbeck College; Vice-Master, Birkbeck College, 1954–65, Vice-President, since 1966; Acting Master, 1950–51, 1965–66; *b* 15 March 1898; *s* of John Herbert Warmington, MA, and Maud Lockhart; *m* 1922, Marian Eveline Robertson, Kinsale, Co. Cork; one *s* two *d*. *Educ:* Perse School, Cambridge; Peterhouse, Cambridge (Scholar). Served in Garrison Artillery and King's Own Yorkshire Light Infantry, 1917–19; Cambridge University, 1919–22; First Class, Classical Tripos, Part I, 1921; First Class, Part II, 1922; BA 1922; Le Bas Prize, Cambridge Univ., 1925; MA 1925. FRHistS 1928. Assistant master at Charterhouse, 1922–23; Classical Sixth Form master, Mill Hill School, 1923–25; Reader in Ancient History, University of London, 1925–35; Prof. of Classics, Birkbeck Coll., Univ. of London, 1935–65. Dean of Faculty of Arts, University of London, 1951–56; Member of Senate, University of London, 1956–66; Acting Director Univ. of London Inst. of Education, 1957–58; Chairman, Goldsmiths' College Delegacy, 1958–75; President London Branch Classical Assoc. 1963–66. Editor, Loeb Classical Library, 1937–74. *Publications:* The Commerce between the Roman Empire and India, 1928; Athens, 1928; The Ancient Explorers (with M. Cary), 1929;

Greek Geography, 1934; Africa in Ancient and Medieval Times, in the Cambridge History of the British Empire, 1936; Remains of Old Latin, Vol. I, 1935; Vol. II, 1936; Vol. III, 1938, Vol. IV, 1940; articles in The Oxford Classical Dictionary, 1949; A History of Birkbeck College, University of London, during the second World War, 1939–1945, 1954; (ed) Great Dialogues of Plato (trans. by W. H. D. Rouse), 1956; various articles and reviews. *Recreations:* music, gardening and natural history. *Address:* 48 Flower Lane, Mill Hill, NW7. *T:* 01–959 1905. *Died* 8 *June* 1987.

**WARNE, Rear-Adm. Robert Spencer,** CB 1953; CBE 1945; retired; *b* 26 June 1903; *s* of E. S. Warne, London; *m* 1925, Dorothy Hadwen Wheelwright (*d* 1976); three *s*. *Educ:* RN Colleges, Osborne and Dartmouth. Joined Submarine Branch, 1925; Commander, 1936; Captain, 1941; Rear-Admiral 1951; Deputy Chief of Naval Personnel, Admiralty, 1951–53; Flag Officer, Germany and Chief British Naval Representative in the Allied Control Commission, 1953–55; retired 1955. *Recreation:* sailing. *Address:* Meath Cottage, Lion Lane, Turners Hill, Crawley, West Sussex RH10 4NU. *T:* Copthorne (0342) 715508. *Club:* Royal Naval and Royal Albert Yacht (Portsmouth). *Died* 15 *Aug.* 1990.

**WARNER, Frederick Sydney,** LDS RCS, 1926; LRCP, MRCS, 1928; FDS RCS, 1947; Dental Surgeon, Guy's Hospital, 1949–68, Emeritus since 1968; Sub-Dean, 1946–65; Lecturer in Oral Surgery, 1954–61, Guy's Hospital Dental School, SE1; Dean of Dental Studies, 1965–68; Member of Board of Examiners in Dental Surgery, Royal College of Surgeons of England, 1947–64, and University of London, 1953–57. *b* 14 April 1903; *s* of Frederick Watkin Warner; *m* 1937, Cicely Florence Michelson. *Educ:* Guy's Hospital Medical School. Asst Dental Surgeon, Guy's Hospital, 1936–49. Member of Board of Faculty of Dental Surgery, Royal College of Surgeons of England, 1946–65; Vice-Dean, 1954–55. *Recreations:* philately, photography. *Address:* Flat 11, 115A Ridgway, SW19.
*Died* 16 *Dec.* 1987.

**WARNER, Jack, (Jack Waters),** OBE 1965; MSM 1918; film and variety artiste; *b* 24 Oct. 1896. *Educ:* Coopers' Company School; University of London. Films include: The Captive Heart; Hue and Cry; Dear Murderer; Holiday Camp; It Always Rains on Sunday; Against the Wind; Easy Money; My Brother's Keeper; Here Come the Huggets; Vote for Huggett; The Huggetts Abroad; Train of Events; Boys in Brown; The Blue Lamp; Scrooge; Emergency Call; Meet Me To-night; The Final Test; The Square Ring; Now and forever; Carve Her Name with Pride; appeared on television as Dixon of Dock Green, 1955–76. RAF Meritorious Service Medal, 1918. Variety Club of GB Special Award, 1972. *Publications:* Jack of all Trades (autobiog), 1975. *Recreations:* golf, swimming. *Address:* Porsea Cottage, Kingsgate, Thanet. *Clubs:* Savage, Green Room, Royal Automobile. *Died* 24 *May* 1981.

**WARNER, Rt. Rev. Kenneth Charles Harman,** DSO 1919; DD (Edinburgh) 1950; Assistant Bishop in Diocese of Canterbury, since 1962; *b* 6 April 1891; *e s* of late Charles Edward Warner and Ethel Constantia Catharine Cornfoot, Tonbridge, Kent; *m* 1st, 1916, Constance Margaret (*d* 1968), 2nd *d* of Arnold F. Hills, Penshurst, Kent; two *s* two *d*; 2nd, 1970, Angela Margaret, widow of Rev. Edward Prescott-Decie. *Educ:* Tonbridge Sch.; Trinity Coll., Oxford; Cuddesdon Theological Coll. 2nd Cl. Jurisp., 1912; MA 1921; Solicitors' Articles, 1912; served European War, 1914–19; Major, Kent Cyclist Bn, 1917 (DSO); partner in firm of Warner Son and Brydone, Solicitors, Tonbridge, Kent, 1919–22; Cuddesdon, 1923; Deacon, 1923; Priest, 1924; Curate of St George's, Ramsgate, 1923–26; Chaplain Royal Air Force, 1927–33; Rector and Provot of St Mary's Cathedral, Glasgow, 1933–38; Archdeacon of Lincoln and 4th Canon in Lincoln Cathedral; Prebendary of Gretton, 1938–47; Bishop of Edinburgh, 1947–61, retired. Select Preacher: Cambridge University, 1939; Oxford University, 1950–51. *Address:* Perry Wood House, Sheldwich, near Faversham, Kent. *T:* Selling 263. *Died* 18 *March* 1983.

**WARNER, Rex;** author; University Professor, University of Connecticut, 1964–74, retired 1974; *b* 9 March 1905; *s* of Rev. F. E. Warner and Kathleen Luce; *m* 1929, Frances Chamier Grove; two *s* one *d*; *m* 1949, Barbara, Lady Rothschild; one *d*; *m* 1966, Frances Chamier Warner. *Educ:* St George's Harpenden; Wadham College, Oxford (Open Classical Scholar, First Class Classical Hon. Mods, degree in English Literature); Hon. Fellow 1973. Schoolmaster in Egypt and in England; Director of The British Institute, Athens, 1945–47. Tallman Prof., Bowdoin Coll., 1962–63. Has written poems, novels, and critical essays; also has done work on films and broadcasting. Hon. DLitt Rider Coll., 1968. Comdr, Royal Order of Phœnix (Greece), 1963. *Publications:* Poems, 1937; The Wild Goose Chase, 1937; The Professor, 1938; The Aerodrome, 1941 (televised, 1983); Why was I killed?, 1943; Translation of the Medea of Euripides, 1944; English Public Schools, 1945; The Cult of Power, 1946; Translation of Aeschylus' Prometheus Bound, 1947; Xenophon's Anabasis, 1949; Men of Stones, 1949; John Milton, 1949; Translation of Euripides' Hippolytus, 1950; Men and Gods,

1950; Translation of Euripides' Helen, 1951; Greeks and Trojans, 1951; Views of Attica, 1951; Escapade, 1953; (with Martin Hürlimann) Eternal Greece, 1953 (new edn 1962); Translation of Thucydides, 1954; The Vengeance of the Gods, 1954; The Young Cæsar, 1958; The Greek Philosophers, 1958; The Fall of the Roman Republic (trans. from Plutarch), 1958; Cæsar's War Commentaries (trans.), 1959; Poems of Seferis (trans.), 1960; Imperial Cæsar, 1960; Confessions of St Augustine (trans.), 1962; Pericles the Athenian, 1963; History of my Times (Hellenica), Xenophon (trans.), 1966; The Greek Style, by Seferis (trans.), 1966; The Converts, 1967; Athens at War, 1970; Plutarch: Moral Essays (trans.), 1971; Men of Athens, 1972. *Address:* Anchor House, St Leonard's Lane, Wallingford, Oxon. *Club:* Savile.

*Died 24 June 1986.*

**WARR, George Michael,** CBE 1966; HM Diplomatic Service, retired; *b* 22 Jan. 1915; *s* of late Sir Godfrey Warr, and of Lady Warr; *m* 1950, Gillian Addis (*née* Dearmer); one *s* two *d* (and one step *s*). *Educ:* Winchester; Christ Church, Oxford. Entered Foreign Service, 1938; served in Chile, Germany, Soviet Union, Uruguay; Counsellor, British Embassy, Brussels, 1959–62; British Consul-General, Istanbul, Turkey, 1962–67; Ambassador to Nicaragua, 1967–70. *Publication:* A Biography of Stratford Canning, 1989. *Recreations:* gardening, beekeeping. *Address:* Woodside, Frant, Tunbridge Wells TN3 9HW. *T:* Frant 202.

*Died 28 Nov. 1989.*

**WARRACK, Guy Douglas Hamilton;** Hon. ARCM; composer; conductor; *b* Edinburgh, 8 Feb. 1900; *s* of John Warrack, LLD, and Jean Hamilton (*née* Dunlop); *m* 1st, 1926, Jacynth Ellerton (marr. diss.); one *s* one *d*; 2nd, 1933, Valentine Clair Jeffrey; two *s*. *Educ:* Winchester; Magdalen College, Oxford; Royal College of Music. BA Oxon, 1923; Hon. ARCM, 1926. Teaching staff of RCM, 1925–35; Examiner for Associated Board of Royal Schools of Music, 1926–; Conductor: Oxford Orchestral Society and Oxford City Concerts for Children, 1926–30; Handel Society, 1934–35; BBC Scottish Orchestra, 1936–45; Musical Director, Sadler's Wells Theatre Ballet, 1948–51; Chairman: Composers' Guild of Great Britain, 1952, 1956; Sherlock Holmes Soc. of London, 1955–57; Intimate Opera Soc. Ltd, 1969–76; Conducted Concerts, Opera, Ballet, etc in London, Ceylon, New Zealand, South Africa and Provinces. Compositions include: Variations for Orchestra, 1924; Symphony in C minor (The "Edinburgh"), 1932; Divertimento Pasticciato, 1938; music for many films, including Theirs is the Glory, 1946; XIVth Olympiad, 1948; The Story of Time, 1949; A Queen is Crowned, 1953; also many arrangements. *Publications:* Sherlock Holmes and Music, 1947. Articles in The Times, Daily Telegraph, Music and Letters, Musical Times, etc. *Address:* 72 Courtfield Gardens, SW5. *T:* 01–370 1758.

*Died 12 Feb. 1986.*

**WARREN, Alec Stephen,** CMG 1950; *b* 27 June 1894; *s* of James Herbert Warren, Hatch End, Middlesex; *m* 1958, Beryl May Cheese. *Educ:* Aldenham School. Director, Warren Sons & Co. Ltd, 1920; Chairman, Warren & Reynolds Ltd, 1935. Joined Ministry of Food, 1939; Director of Canned Fish, Fruit and Vegetables Division, Ministry of Food, 1944–52; Director of Bacon and Ham Division, 1952–56; Mem. Potato Marketing Board, 1956–59. *Publication:* The Warren Code, 1964. *Recreations:* billiards. *Address:* Maison Pommier, Sark, Channel Islands. *T:* Sark 2035.

*Died 20 March 1982.*

**WARREN, Sir Alfred Henry, (Sir Freddie Warren),** Kt 1976; CBE 1970 (MBE 1957); Secretary to the Government Chief Whip, 1958–79; *b* 19 Dec. 1915; *s* of William Warren and Clara Wooff; *m* 1940, Margaret Ann (*d* 1987); one *s* one *d*. *Educ:* Sir Walter St John's Grammar Sch., SW11. Asst Private Secretary to the Secretary to the Cabinet, 1951–58. *Recreation:* observing people and places. *Address:* 93 South Eden Park Road, Beckenham, Kent BR3 3BA. *T:* 081–658 6951.

*Died 8 May 1990.*

**WARREN, Rt. Rev. Alwyn Keith,** CMG 1967; MC 1945; *b* 23 Sept. 1900; 2nd *s* of Major T. J. C. Warren, JP, Penlee House, Te Aute, Hawkes Bay, NZ, and Lucy, *d* of Ven. Samuel Williams, Archdeacon of Hawkes Bay, NZ; *m* 1928, Doreen Eda (*d* 1983), *d* of Capt. C. F. Laws; one *s* two *d*. *Educ:* Marlborough College; Magdalen College, Oxford (BA 1922, Hons Nat. Sci.; MA 1926); Cuddesdon Theological College. Ordained, Canterbury, 1925; Curate of Ashford, Kent, 1925–29; Vicar of Ross and South Westland, NZ, 1929–32; Vicar of Waimate, South Canterbury, NZ, 1932–34; Vicar of St Mary's, Merivale, Christchurch, NZ, 1934–40; Archdeacon of Christchurch, 1937–44; Dean of Christchurch, 1940–51; Vicar-General, 1940–44 and 1946–51; Bishop of Christchurch, 1951–66. Delegate to Internat. Round Table of Christian Leaders, on a Just and Durable Peace, Princeton, USA, 1943; Chaplain to 2nd NZ Exped. Force (NZ Divisional Cavalry), Italy, 1944–45 (wounded, MC). Member Council, University Canterbury, 1946–73, Pro-Chancellor, 1961, Chancellor, 1965–69; Member Senate, University of New Zealand, 1948–61; Warden or Chm. Bds various colleges,

schools and social service organisations. Chairman National Council of Churches of NZ, 1949–51; World Council of Churches: Mem. Central Cttee, 1954–67; Mem. Assembly, Evanston, USA, 1954 and New Delhi, 1961. Chaplain and Sub-Prelate, Order of St John; Chaplain, Priory of St John in NZ, 1966–72; formerly Pres., Canterbury and West Coast Centre, St John Ambulance Assoc.; Pres., Christchurch Rotary Club; Vice-President: Christchurch Civic Music Council; Christchurch Harmonic Soc.; Pres., Royal Christchurch Musical Soc.; Trustee, NZ National Library. *Publications:* Prayers in Time of War, 1940; Christianity Today: section on Churches in NZ, 1947. Contrib. to Stimmen aus der ökumene, 1963 (Berlin). *Recreations:* formerly rowing, tennis, now people, reading biographies, music, gardens. *Address:* Littlecourt, 193 Memorial Avenue, Christchurch 5, New Zealand. *Clubs:* Leander; Christchurch, University of Canterbury, University Staff (Christchurch).

*Died 27 May 1988.*

**WARREN, Hon. Sir Edward (Emerton),** KCMG 1969 (CMG 1956); KBE 1959; MSM 1918; Member Legislative Council, New South Wales Parliament, 1954–78; *b* Broken Hill, NSW, 26 Aug. 1897; *s* of John T. Warren, Derbyshire, England; *m* 1926, Doris, *d* of Charles F. Schultz; two *s*. *Educ:* Broken Hill, NSW. Served European War, 1914–18: 18th Bn AIF, Gallipoli and France. Chairman: NSW Combined Colliery Proprietors' Assoc., 1949; Northern Colliery Proprietors' Assoc., 1949; Aust. Coal Assoc., 1956; Aust. Coal Assoc. (Research) Ltd, 1956; Aust. Coal Industry Research Laboratories Ltd, 1965; Brown's Coal Pty Ltd (Victoria); Coal & Allied (Sales) Pty Ltd; Dowset Engineering (Australia) Pty Ltd. Man. Dir, The Wallarah Coal Co. Ltd; Governing Dir, Thomas Brown Ltd (Wellington, NZ). Director and Chief General Manager: Coal & Allied Industries Ltd; Coal & Allied Industries KK (Tokyo–Japan); J. & A. Brown & Abermain Seaham Collieries Ltd; Caledonian Collieries Ltd; Cessnock Collieries Ltd; Liddell Collieries Pty Ltd; Durham Coal Mines Pty Ltd; South Maitland Railways Pty Ltd; Hexham Engineering Pty Ltd; Jones Bros Coal Pty Ltd; Director: Westinghouse Brake (A/sia) Pty Ltd; McKenzie & Holland (Australia) Pty Ltd. Member: Coal Conservation Cttee, NSW Govt, 1951; C'wealth Govt Mission investigating overseas coal-mining methods, 1952; Dep. Chm., Aust. Nat. Cttee, World Power Conf., 1960; Vice-Chm., Internat. Exec. Council, World Power Conf., 1962; Chm., Coal Trades Section, Aust. Trade Mission to S America, 1962; Pres., Australia/Japan Business Co-operation Cttee, 1964–; rep. Aust. Employers, ILO, Geneva, 1964; Mem., Nat. Coal Research Adv. Cttee, 1965; launched Malaysia/Australia Business Co-operation Cttee, Kuala Lumpur, 1965; led Aust. Delegn, Hawaii, 1968 (resulted in Pacific Basin Econ. Co-op. Cttee); Australian Pres., 1970–71, and Internat. Pres., 1970–71, Pacific Basin Econ. Co-op. Council; Mem., C'wealth Govt Adv. Cttee, Expo 70, 1968; Pres., Australia/Korea Business Co-operation Cttee, 1969. Has travelled extensively. Member: Council, Univ. of NSW, 1965–; Med. Foundn, Univ. of NSW, 1968–. Rising Sun with Grand Cordon, Japan, 1967. *Address:* 16 Morella Road, Clifton Gardens, NSW 2088, Australia. *T:* (home) 969 4662; (office) 27 8641. *Clubs:* American, Tattersall's, New South Wales, Royal Automobile of Australia, NSW Sports, Manly Golf (Sydndey); Newcastle (Newcastle, NSW).

*Died 8 Sept. 1983.*

**WARREN, Sir Freddie;** *see* Warren, Sir A. H.

**WARREN, Phillip;** *see* Warren, W. P.

**WARREN, Robert Penn;** writer; US Poet Laureate, 1986–87; Member of: American Academy and Institute of Arts and Letters; American Philosophical Society; American Academy of Arts and Sciences; Professor of English, Yale University, 1962–73, now Emeritus; *b* 24 April 1905; *s* of Robert Franklin Warren and Anna Ruth Penn; *m* 1930, Emma Brescia (*d* 1951); *m* 1952, Eleanor Clark; one *s* one *d*. *Educ:* Vanderbilt University, Univ. of California; Yale University; Oxford University. Asst Professor: Southwestern Coll., Tennessee, 1930–31; Vanderbilt Univ., 1931–34; Assoc. Prof., Univ. of Louisiana, 1934–42; Founder and an editor Southern Review, 1935–42; Prof., Univ. of Minnesota, 1942–50; Prof. of Drama, Yale University, 1951–56. Houghton Mifflin Fellow (fiction), 1936; Guggenheim Fellow 1939, 1947; Shelley Memorial Award (poetry), 1942; Chair of Poetry, Library of Congress, 1944–45; Pulitzer Prize (fiction), 1947; Meltzer Award for screen play, 1949; Sidney Hillman Award for Journalism, 1957; Millay Prize (Amer. Poetry Society), 1958; National Book Award (Poetry), 1958; Pulitzer Prize (poetry), 1958, 1979; Irita Van Doren Award (Herald Tribune), 1965; Bollingen Prize for Poetry, 1967; Nat. Arts Foundn Award, 1968; Van Wyck Brooks Award for Poetry, 1969; Nat. Medal for Literature, 1970; Emerson-Thoreau Medal (Amer. Acad. of Arts and Sciences), 1975; Copernicus Award for Poetry, 1976; Harriet Monroe Poetry Award, 1977; Common Wealth Award, poetry, 1976; Pulitzer Prize, poetry, 1979; Connecticut Council for the Arts Award, 1980; Gold Medal for Poetry, AAIL, 1985. Chancellor, Acad. of American Poets, 1972; Jefferson Lectr, Nat. Endowment for Humanities, 1974. Hon. DLitt: University of Louisville, 1949; Kenyon College, 1952; Colby College, 1956; University of

Kentucky, 1957; Swarthmore College, 1959; Yale University, 1960; Fairfield Univ., 1969; Wesleyan Univ., 1970; Harvard Univ., 1973; New Haven, 1973; Southwestern Coll., 1974; Univ. of the South, 1974; Johns Hopkins Univ., 1977; Monmouth Coll., 1979; New York Univ., Oxford Univ., 1983; Hon. LLD, Univ. of Bridgeport, 1965. MacArthur Prize Fellowship, 1981. Presidential Medal of Freedom, 1980. *Publications:* John Brown: Making of a Martyr, 1929; XXXVI Poems, 1936; Night Rider (novel), 1939; At Heaven's Gate (novel), 1943; Eleven Poems on Same Theme, 1942; Selected Poems, 1944; All the King's Men (novel), 1946, several editions (film, 1949); Coleridge's Ancient Mariner, 1947; Blackberry Winter (Novelette), 1947; Circus in the Attic (stories), 1947; World Enough and Time (novel), 1950, 2nd edn, 1974; Brother to Dragons (poem), 1953, rewritten version, 1979; Band of Angels (novel), 1955, (film, 1957); Segregation: The Inner Conflict of the South, 1956; Promises: Poems 1954–56, 1957; Selected Essays, 1958; The Cave (novel), 1959; You, Emperors, and Others: Poems 1957–60, 1960; Legacy of the Civil War: A meditation on the centennial, 1961; Wilderness (novel), 1961; Flood: a romance of our time (novel), 1964; Who Speaks for the Negro?, 1965; Selected Poems, Old and New, 1923–1966, 1966; Incarnations: Poems 1966–68, 1968; Audubon: a Vision (poems), 1969; Homage to Theodore Dreiser, 1971; Meet Me in the Green Glen (novel), 1971; Or Else—Poem/Poems, 1968–74, 1974; Democracy and Poetry, 1975; Selected Poems 1923–75, 1977; A Place to Come To (novel), 1977; Now and Then: Poems 1976–78, 1978; Being Here: Poetry 1977–79, 1980; Rumor Verified: Poems 1977–81, 1981; Chief Joseph of the Nez Perce (poem), 1983; New and Selected Poems 1914–1984, 1985; Portrait of a Father, 1989; various collections and anthologies. *Recreations:* swimming, walking. *Address:* 2495 Redding Road, Fairfield, Conn 06430, USA. *Club:* Century (New York).

*Died 15 Sept. 1989.*

**WARREN, William Phillip,** OBE 1987; CEng, FIEE, FInstPet; Senior Partner, Warren Associates, since 1985; Director, W. S. Atkins & Partners (Wales), since 1985; *b* 7 Oct. 1924; *yr s* of Herbert U. Warren and Rebecca Warren (*née* Thomas); *m* 1956, Janice Mary, *er d* of James and Lilian Holloway; one *s* one *d*. *Educ:* Quakers Yard Grammar Sch.; Univ. of Wales, Cardiff (BSc). Post graduate trng and early appts, General Electric Co. Ltd, 1943–48; Asst Chief Commercial Engr, S Wales Electricity Board, 1948–54; Chief Executive, subsidiary co., Metal Industries Ltd, 1954–56; First Commercial Manager, UKAEA, 1956–59; Dir, several subsid. companies, Powell Duffryn Ltd, 1959–68; Director, Chief Executive of subsid. companies, Tube Investments Ltd, 1968–74; Man. Dir, Davy Water Engineering Ltd, Davy International Ltd, 1974–76; Exec. Dir, Welsh Develt Agency, 1976–85. Governor: University of Wales, 1971–; University Coll. Cardiff, 1985–; Life Governor and Mem. Council, UWIST, 1968–; formerly Mem. Council: Industrial Assoc. of Wales and Mon. (now CBI, Wales); Brit. Manufrs of Petroleum Equipment. *Publications:* articles in learned jls include: UK Nuclear Power Programme; High Frequency Communications over EHT Circuits; Electronics in Industry. *Recreations:* gardening, occasional golf, charity fund raising. *Address:* Eastfield House, Cowbridge, S Glamorgan CF7 7EP. *T:* Cowbridge 2392. *Club:* Cardiff and County.

*Died 13 March 1988.*

**WARRINGTON, Anthony,** CBE 1990; Special Adviser on Government Procurement Affairs, Rolls-Royce plc, since 1989; *b* 15 Aug. 1929; *s* of Stanley Warrington and Gladys (*née* Sutcliffe); *m* 1955, Lavinia Lord; three *s*. *Educ:* Welwyn Garden City Grammar Sch.; London School of Economics. Asst Statistician: Admiralty, 1953; British Electricity Authority, 1954–55; Economist, British Transport Commn, 1956–58; Statistician, Min. of Power, 1958–66; Asst Secretary: Petroleum Div., Min. of Power (later Min. of Technology), 1966–72; Atomic Energy Div., DTI, 1972–73; Under-Sec., DoI, 1973; Air Div., 1973–78; Dir-Gen., Concorde Div. DoI, 1976–77; Co. Sec. and Dir, Policy Co-ordination, Rolls-Royce, 1978–89 (on secondment from DoI, 1978–79). Chm., Jt Review Bd Adv. Cttee on Govt Contracts, 1987–. Mem. Council, SBAC, 1985–. *Recreations:* theatre, hockey, golf. *Address:* 9 Fern Grove, Welwyn Garden City, Herts AL8 7ND. *T:* Welwyn Garden (0707) 326110.

*Died 10 Dec. 1990.*

**WARWICK, 7th Earl of,** *cr* 1759; **Charles Guy Fulke Greville;** Baron Brooke, 1621; Earl Brooke, 1776; DL; Lieut, Reserve of Officers, Grenadier Guards; *b* 4 March 1911, *e s* of 6th Earl and Marjorie (*d* 1943), *d* of Sir W. Eden, 7th Bt; *S* father, 1928; *m* 1st, 1933, Rose (from whom he obtained a divorce, 1938), *d* of late D. C. Bingham, Coldstream Guards, and Lady Rosabelle Brand; one *s*; 2nd, 1942, Mary (from whom he obtained a divorce, 1949), *d* of P. C. Hopkinson, Kingston Gorse, Sussex; 3rd, 1963, Mme Janine Angele Josephine Detry de Marès. Merchant Navy, Admiralty Small Vessels Pool, 1943. Warwickshire CC, 1934–36; a Governor of Birmingham Univ.; Mayor of Warwick, 1951; Alderman 1952; DL, Warwickshire. Governor: Warwick Kings Schools; Royal Shakespeare Theatre. *Heir: s* Lord Brooke.

*Died 20 Jan. 1984.*

**WARWICK, Cyril Walter;** Chairman: Warwick & Esplen Ltd, since 1971; Houlder Bros & Co. Ltd, 1962–69 (President since 1970); *b* 30 Sept. 1899; 2nd *s* of late J. J. W. Warwick; *m* 1925, Dorothy Fitzgerald, *d* of late John Miller; one *s* one *d*. *Educ:* Tollington Sch.; King's Coll., London Univ. Served RFC and RAF, 1917–19. Joined Kaye Son & Co., shipbrokers, 1919; elected Baltic Exchange, 1920; joined Houlder Bros & Co. Ltd, 1938; Director Hadley Shipping Co. Ltd, 1938, Chm. 1962; Director: Houlder Line, 1944–69; Furness Withy & Co. Ltd, 1962–69; Royal Mail Lines Ltd, 1965–75; and various other shipping companies; Dep. Chairman, Houlder Bros, 1957; Director, Baltic Mercantile and Shipping Exchange, 1951; Vice-Chairman, 1959; Chairman, 1961–63; Hon. Mem., 1970. President: Cereals and Baltic Friendly Society, 1966–68; Baltic Exchange Benevolent Soc., 1973–77; Mem. Council, Chamber of Shipping of UK, 1949–75; Fellow, Inst. Chartered Shipbrokers; Liveryman, Worshipful Company of Shipwrights. Freight Market Rep. of Ministry of Transport, 1958–67. *Recreations:* riding, fishing. *Address:* Witley Court, Wormley, Godalming, Surrey. *T:* Wormley 2626. *Club:* Canning.

*Died 14 July 1985.*

**WASHBOURN, Rear-Admiral Richard Everley,** CB 1961; DSO 1940; OBE 1950; Chief of Naval Staff, RNZN, 1963–65, retired; *b* 14 Feb. 1910; *s* of H. E. A. Washbourn, Nelson, NZ; *m* 1943, June, *d* of L. M. Herapath, Auckland, NZ; one *s* one *d*. *Educ:* Nelson Coll., New Zealand. Entered Royal Navy by Special Entry from New Zealand, 1927; HMS Erebus, 1928; HMS London, 1929–31; Courses, 1932; HMS Warspite, 1933; HMS Diomede, 1934–35; Specialised in Gunnery, 1936–37; HMS Excellent, 1938; HMS Achilles, 1939–42; Battle of the Plate, 13 Dec. 1939 (DSO); HMS Excellent, 1942; HMS Anson, 1943. Admiralty Gunnery Establishment, 1944–45; Exec. Officer, HMNZS, Bellona, 1946–48; Comdr Supt HMNZ Dockyard, Devonport, 1950; Dep. Director of Naval Ordnance, 1950–53; HMS Manxman, 1953; Chief Staff Officer to Flag Officer (Flotillas), Mediterranean, 1954–55; Director of Naval Ordnance, Admiralty, 1956–58; HMS Tiger, 1959; Director-General, Weapons, 1960–62; retired Royal Navy, 1962; entered RNZN, 1963; retired RNZN, 1965. *Recreation:* beachcombing. *Address:* Onekaka, RD2, Takaka, Golden Bay, Nelson, New Zealand.

*Died 8 Aug. 1988.*

**WASS, Dr Charles Alfred Alan;** Director of Safety in Mines Research Establishment, Sheffield, 1970–74; *b* 20 July 1911; *s* of William and Louisa Wass, Sutton-in-Ashfield, Nottinghamshire; *m* 1936, Alice Elizabeth Carpenter; two *d*. *Educ:* Brunt's Sch., Mansfield; Nottingham Univ. Post Office Radio Research Station, 1934–46; Royal Aircraft Establishment, 1946–55; Safety in Mines Research Establishment, 1955–74. *Publications:* Introduction to Electronic Analogue Computers, 1955 (2nd edn, with K. C. Garner, 1965); papers on electrical communication subjects and mine safety. *Recreations:* music making, reed instruments. *Address:* The Old School House, Swine, Hull, North Humberside HU11 4JE. *T:* Hull 811227.

*Died 30 Oct. 1989.*

**WATERHOUSE, Sir Ellis (Kirkham),** Kt 1975; CBE 1956 (MBE 1943); FBA 1955; *b* 16 Feb. 1905; *s* of P. Leslie Waterhouse and Eleanor Margetson; *m* 1949, Helen, *d* of F. W. Thomas; two *d*. *Educ:* Marlborough; New Coll., Oxford (Scholar; MA; Hon. Fellow 1976). Commonwealth Fund Fellow (Department of Art and Archæology, University of Princeton, USA), 1927–29 (AM); Assistant, National Gallery, 1929–33; Librarian, British School at Rome, 1933–36; selected and catalogued pictures for RA Exhibition of 17th Century Art (1938), 1937; Fellow of Magdalen Coll., Oxford, 1938–47; served with Army and Foreign Office (mainly in Middle East), 1939–45; temp. editor, Burlington Magazine, 1946; Reader in History of Art, Manchester Univ., 1947–48; Director of National Galleries of Scotland, 1949–52; Slade Professor of Fine Art, University of Oxford, 1953–55; Clark Visiting Professor, Williams Coll., Mass, 1962–63; Mellon Visiting Professor, University of Pittsburgh, 1967–68; Barber Professor of Fine Arts and Dir of Barber Inst., Birmingham Univ., 1952–70; Dir of Studies, Paul Mellon Centre for Studies in British Art, 1970–73; Kress Prof. in Residence, Nat. Gallery of Art, Washington DC, 1974–75. Mem., Exec. Cttee, Nat. Art Collections Fund, 1972–. FRHistSoc. Hon. DLitt: Nottingham, 1968; Leicester, 1970; Birmingham, 1973; Oxon, 1976. Officer of Order Orange Nassau. Cavaliere ufficiale, Ordine al Merito della Repubblica italiana, 1961. *Publications:* El Greco's Italian Period, 1930; Roman Baroque Painting, 1937, rev. edn 1976; Sir Joshua Reynolds, 1941; British Painting, 1530–1790, 1953; Gainsborough, 1958; Italian Baroque Painting, 1962; Jayne Lectures, 1964, 1965; Catalogue of Pictures at Waddesdon Manor, 1967; Reynolds, 1973; The Dictionary of British 18th Century Painters in Oils and Crayons, 1981; numerous articles and catalogues. *Address:* Overshot, Hinksey Hill, Oxford. *T:* Oxford 735320.

*Died 7 Sept. 1985.*

**WATERLOW, Sir Thomas Gordon,** 3rd Bt *cr* 1930; CBE 1946; Director: Royal Bank of Scotland, 1951–81 (Deputy Chairman, 1967–75); Standard Life Assurance Company, 1948–81 (Chairman,

1960–63); Williams & Glyn's Bank, 1974–77; *b* 2 Jan. 1911; *yr s* of late Sir William A. Waterlow, 1st Bt, KBE, Lord Mayor of London, 1929–30, and late Lady Waterlow; *S* brother, 1969; *m* 1938, Helen Elizabeth (*d* 1970), *yr d* of late Gerard A. H. Robinson, Bix, Henley-on-Thames; three *s*. *Educ:* Marlborough Coll., Trinity Coll., Cambridge. Joined Whitehead Morris Ltd, 1932; Joint Managing Director, 1937–39. Commissioned in Auxiliary Air Force, 601 (County of London) Squadron, 1937. Served RAF, War of 1939–45 (despatches, Battle of Britain, 1940); released with rank of Group Captain. Chairman, British Carton Assoc., 1953–55; Director: British Investment Trust Ltd, 1960–78; R. and R. Clark Ltd, 1957–70; Deputy Chairman, Livingston Development Corp., 1965–68; Member: Scottish Aerodromes Board, 1947–59; Exec. Cttee Scottish Council (Development and Industry), 1946–48; Scottish Cttee, Council of Industrial Design, 1949–50; Exec. Council, Assoc. of British Chambers of Commerce, 1952–54, 1963–65 (Vice-Pres., 1971–75); President, Edinburgh Chamber of Commerce, 1963–65. FBIM. Hon. DLitt Heriot-Watt, 1972. *Recreations:* golf. *Heir: s* (James) Gerard Waterlow [ *b* 3 Sept. 1939; *m* 1965, Diana Suzanne, *yr d* of Sir W. T. C. Skyrme, KCVO, CB, CBE, TD; one *s* one *d*]. *Address:* 1 Lennox Street, Edinburgh EH4 1QB. *T:* 031–332 2621. *Clubs:* New (Edinburgh); Hon. Company of Edinburgh Golfers. *Died* 8 *Aug.* 1982.

**WATERMAN, Sir Ewen McIntyre,** Kt 1963; Chairman, Onkaparinga Woollen Co. Ltd; former Director: Elder Smith Goldsbrough Mort Ltd; F. & T. Industries Ltd; Waterman Brothers Holdings Pty Ltd; B.E.A. Motors Pty Ltd; *b* Semaphore, South Australia, 22 Dec. 1901; *s* of late Hugh McIntyre Waterman, Echunga, SA; *m* 1928, Vera, *d* of late J. G. Gibb; one *d*. *Educ:* Woodville High Sch.; Adelaide School of Mines and Industries. Australian Member, International Wool Secretariat, 1948–55 (Chairman, 1952–54); Chairman Exec. Cttee, Wool Bureau Inc. (USA), 1952–54; Commonwealth Member, Australian Wool Board, 1955–63; Consultant, FAO Livestock Survey, E Africa, 1965; Chairman, Australian Wool Industry Conference, 1966–71; President: Royal Flying Doctor Service (SA Section), 1960–62; South Australian Adult Deaf Society, 1947–; Member Council, South Australian Institute of Technology, 1962–69; Member Board of Governors, Adelaide Festival of Arts; Pres., Postgraduate Foundation in Medicine, University of Adelaide. *Address:* Blackwood Park, Strathalbyn, South Australia 5255. *T:* 36 2144. *Clubs:* Oriental; Adelaide (Adelaide). *Died* 23 *Oct.* 1982.

**WATERMAN, Rt. Rev. Robert Harold;** *b* 11 March 1894; *s* of Canon Robert B. Waterman and Annabella Hughton; *m* 1921, Frances Isabel Bayne; two *s* two *d* (and two *s* decd). *Educ:* University of Bishop's Coll., Lennoxville, PQ. BA 1914, BD 1933, Deacon, 1920; priest, 1921; Curate of Bearbrook, 1920–21, Rector, 1921–27; Rector of Pembroke, 1927–33; Rector of Smith's Falls, 1933–37; Rector of Christchurch Cathedral, Hamilton, Diocese of Niagara, 1937–48; Dean of Niagara, 1938–48; Bishop Coadjutor of Nova Scotia, 1948–50; Bishop of Nova Scotia, 1950–63, retired. *Address:* Connaught Home, North Hatley, PQ J0B 2C0, Canada.
*Died* 16 *Dec.* 1984.

**WATERS, Alwyn Brunow,** CBE 1971 (MBE (mil.) 1943); GM 1944; Senior Partner, A. B. Waters, Consulting Architects, since 1983; *b* 18 Sept. 1906; *s* of Samuel Gilbert Waters and Gertrude Madeleine Brunow; *m* 1933, Ruby Alice Bindon (*d* 1983); one *s* one *d*. *Educ:* Regent Street Polytechnic; Central Sch. of Arts and Crafts; Royal Academy Schs; Imperial College. ARIBA 1933; FRIBA 1945; FCIArb. War service, RE (bomb disposal), 1940–46 (Major). Asst in various London offices, 1927–32; teaching at LCC Hammersmith Sch. of Bldg and private practice, 1932–46; founded Llewellyn Smith & Waters, 1937, Senior Partner 1946–70; Senior Partner: A. B. Waters and Partners, 1970–76; Waters Jamieson Partnership, 1977–82. Consultant, A. B. Waters and Partners, 1983. Member: various cttees, RIBA, 1945–; Council, Inst. of Arbitrators, 1958–70 (Pres. 1965); Nat. Jt Consultative Cttee for Building, 1965–74 (Chm. 1972). Governor, Willesden Coll. of Technology, 1946–71; Chm., Jt Contracts Tribunal, 1960–73. Bossom Lectr, RSA, 1970. Master, Masons' Co., 1982–83; Asst, Arbitrators' Co., 1981–; Mem., Soc. of Construction Arbitrators, 1984–. *Publications:* Story of a House, 1948; contrib. Building, Architects Jl, etc, primarily on warehousing and distribution. *Recreations:* architecture, fly fishing. *Address:* 16 Marsham Lodge, Marsham Lane, Gerrards Cross, Bucks. *T:* Gerrards Cross 882116. *Club:* Royal Automobile. *Died* 25 *Jan.* 1988.

**WATERS, Major (Hon. Colonel) Sir Arnold (Horace Santo),** VC 1919; Kt 1954; CBE 1949; DSO 1918; MC; JP; DL; FICE; FIMechE; FGS; FIWES; Consulting Engineer; *b* 1886; *y s* of Rev. Richard Waters, Plymouth; *m* 1924, Gladys, *d* of Rev. C. D. Barriball, Birmingham; three *s*. President InstStructE, 1933, 1943; Divisional Food Officer, W Midland Div., 1941–42. JP Sutton Coldfield, 1930; DL W Midlands, formerly Warwicks, 1957. Hon. FInstStructE; Hon. Mem. Instn Royal Engrs; Hon. FInstPHE. Chm., South Staffs Waterworks Co., 1946–59. *Address:* St Winnow, Ladywood Road,

Four Oaks, Sutton Coldfield, West Midlands. *T:* 021-308 0060.
*Died* 22 *Jan.* 1981.

**WATERS, Jack;** *see* Warner, J.

**WATERS, William Alexander,** FRS 1954; Professor of Chemistry, Dyson Perrins Laboratory, Oxford University, 1967–70, later Professor Emeritus; Fellow, Balliol College, Oxford, 1945–70, later Fellow Emeritus; *b* Cardiff, 8 May 1903; *o s* of William Waters, schoolmaster, Cardiff; *m* 1932, Elizabeth (*d* 1983), *y d* of William Dougall, Darlington; no *c*. *Educ:* Cardiff High Sch.; Gonville and Caius Coll., Cambridge. Rhondda Schol.; MA; PhD; ScD; MA Oxon (by incorporation). Lecturer in Chemistry, Durham Univ. (Durham Div.), 1928–45; University Demonstrator in Organic Chemistry, Oxford, 1945–60; Reader in Physical Organic Chemistry, 1960–67; Chemistry Tutor, Balliol Coll., 1945–67. Sir C. V. Raman Vis. Prof., Univ. of Madras, 1976–77. Leverhulme Research Fellow, 1939; Ministry of Supply: Scientific Officer, 1939–42; Senior Scientific Officer, 1942–44. Goldsmiths' Company's Exhibitioner (Chem.) 1923. FRIC (Member, Council 1968–71); Chem. Soc. Council, 1948–51, 1959–62; Member DSIR Road Tar Research Cttee, 1950–60. Hon. DSc Warwick, 1977. Chem. Soc. medal, 1973. *Publications:* Physical Aspects of Organic Chemistry, 5th edn, 1954; The Chemistry of Free Radicals, 2nd edn, 1948; (Editor and part author) Methods of Quantitive Micro-analysis, 1949, 2nd edn, 1955; (ed) Vistas in Free Radical Chemistry, 1959; Mechanisms of Oxidation of Organic Compounds, 1964; (ed) Free Radical Reactions, 1973, 1975; publications in Proc. Royal Society, Journal Chem. Society, Trans. and Discussions of Faraday Society. *Address:* 5 Field House Drive, Oxford. *T:* Oxford 55234.
*Died* 28 *Jan.* 1985.

**WATERSON, Prof. Anthony Peter,** MD, FRCP, FRCPath; Professor of Virology, Royal Postgraduate Medical School, London, 1967–81; *b* Hornsea, E Yorks, 23 Dec. 1923; *s* of Frederick Waterson and Frances (*née* Cooper); *m* 1958, Ellen Ware; one *s* two *d*. *Educ:* Epsom Coll.; Emmanuel Coll., Cambridge; London Hospital Medical Coll. MD (Cantab) 1954; MRCP 1950; FRCP 1970; FRCPath 1973. House appointments, London Hospital, 1947–48; MO, Headquarters Unit, BAFO, Germany, 1948–50; Ho. Phys. and Clin. Pathologist, Addenbrooke's Hospital, Cambridge, 1950–52; Demonstrator in Path., 1953–58, Lecturer in Path., 1958–64, University of Cambridge; Fellow of Emmanuel Coll., 1954–64, Asst Tutor, 1957–64; Professor of Med. Microbiology, St Thomas's Hospital Medical Sch., 1964–67. Spent year 1962–63 on sabbatical leave at Max-Planck Institut für Virusforschung, Tübingen. Governor, Hampton Sch., 1977–. *Publications:* Introduction to Animal Virology, 1961, 2nd edn, 1968; (with Lise Wilkinson) An Introduction to the History of Virology, 1978; Recent Advances in Clinical Virology, 1983; papers on viruses and virus diseases. *Recreations:* mountain walking; European history; gardens; browsing in Who's Who. *Address:* 17 Queen's Road, Richmond, Surrey. *T:* 01–940 2325. *Died* 17 *Oct.* 1983.

**WATERSTON, David James,** CBE 1972 (MBE 1940); FRCS; FRCSE; Hon. Consultant Surgeon, Hospital for Sick Children, Great Ormond Street; *b* 1910; *s* of late Prof. David Waterston, the University of St Andrews; *m* 1948, Anne, *widow* of Lieut H. C. C. Tanner, RN, and *d* of late Rt Rev. A. A. Markham, sometime Bishop of Grantham; one *s* two *d* (and one *s* decd). *Educ:* Craigflower Sch.; privately; Universities of St Andrews and Edinburgh. Ho. Surg., Royal Infirmary, Edinburgh, 1934; Ho. Surg., Surgical Registrar and Res. Medical Supt, Hospital for Sick Children, Great Ormond Street, London, 1934–38 and 1948–51, Consultant Surgeon, 1951–75. Hunterian Professor, RCS, 1961; President British Association Pædiatric Surgeons, 1961. Consulting Pædiatric Surgeon to the Army, to 1975. Served RAMC, 1939–45 (despatches twice, MBE); Captain, Field Ambulance and Field Transfusion Unit, Major (Surgical Specialist). Hon. MD: Genoa, 1970; Warsaw, 1977. *Publications:* chapters in: Paediatric Surgery, 2nd edn 1970; Operative Surgery, 2nd edn 1971; Surgery of the Oesophagus, 1972; articles in medical journals. *Address:* 54 Church Street, Old Isleworth, Middlesex TW7 6BG. *T:* 01–560 2873. *Club:* Royal and Ancient (St Andrews). *Died* 8 *May* 1985.

**WATES, Sir Ronald (Wallace),** Kt 1975; JP; DL; President, Wates Ltd, since 1973 (Chairman, 1969–73); *b* 4 June 1907; *s* of Edward Wates and Sarah (*née* Holmes); *m* 1931, Phyllis Mary Trace; four *s*. *Educ:* Emanuel Sch. FRICS. Became a Director of Wates Ltd, 1931; Vice-Chm., 1937–69. Trustee, Historic Churches Preservation Trust; Chm., Royal Sch. for the Blind, 1971–82; Mem. Governing Body, Emanuel Sch., 1977–; Liveryman, Innholders' Co., 1945, Master, 1978–79; Hon. Liveryman, Bakers' Co., 1960. JP 1947; DL Surrey, 1981. Hon. Fellow, University Coll. London, 1972. DUniv Surrey, 1975. *Address:* Manor House, Headley, near Epsom, Surrey KT18 6NA. *T:* Leatherhead 377346. *Clubs:* Royal Automobile, City Livery. *Died* 25 *Jan.* 1986.

**WATKINS, Baron** *cr* 1972 (Life Peer), of Glyntawe, Brecknock; **Tudor Elwyn Watkins;** Lieutenant of Powys, 1975–78; *b* 9 May 1903; *e s* of late County Councillor Howell Watkins, JP, Abercrave, Swansea Valley; *m* 1936, Bronwen R., 3rd *d* of late T. Stather, Talgarth; no *c. Educ:* local elementary schools; evening continuation classes; University Tutorial, WEA and NCLC classes; Coleg Harlech, N Wales (Bursary). Began working at local collieries at age of 13½; miner for 8 years; political agent for Brecon and Radnor, 1928–33; MP (Lab) Brecon and Radnor, 1945–70; PPS to Sec. of State for Wales, 1964–68. Alderman, Breconshire CC, 1940–74; Chm., Powys CC, 1974–77. General Secretary Breconshire Assoc. of Friendly Societies, 1937–48. Hon. Freeman, Brecon Borough; Chm., Brecon Beacons Nat. Park Cttee, 1974–78. *Recreations:* served as Secretary of Abercrave Athletic Club, Cricket Club, Ystalyfera Football League, Horticultural Society and Show. *Address:* Bronafon, Penyfan Road, Brecon, Powys. *T:* 2961.                          *Died* 2 *Nov.* 1983.

**WATKINS, Prof. Arthur Goronwy**, CBE 1967; Professor of Child Health, Welsh National School of Medicine, 1950–68, Emeritus Professor, since 1968; Dean of Clinical and Post-Graduate Studies, 1947–68; *b* 19 March 1903; *s* of Sir Percy Watkins; *m* 1933, Aileen Llewellyn; one *s* three *d. Educ:* Sidcot Sch.; University Coll., Cardiff; University Coll. Hospital, London. BSc (Wales) 1925; MD (London) 1930; FRCP 1943. Res. Hosp. appts, University Coll. Hosp., 1927–29, West London Hosp., 1929, Hosp. for Sick Children, Gt Ormond Street, 1930; First Asst, Dept of Pædiatrics, University Coll. Hosp., 1930–32; Lectr In Pædiatrics, Welsh Nat. Sch. of Medicine, 1932–50; Cons. Pædiatrician, Royal Infirmary and Llandough Hosp., Cardiff, 1932. Former Mem. Bd of Govs, United Cardiff Hosps; Consultant and Adviser in Pædiatrics, Welsh Hosp. Bd; Hon. Treas. Brit. Pædiatric Assoc., 1958–63, Pres., 1966–67; Pres. Children's Sect., Roy. Soc. Med., 1953, Hon. Mem. 1970; Pres. Cardiff Div., BMA, 1953; Corr. Mem. Soc. de Pédiatrie, Paris; Hon. Fellow, Amer. Academy of Pediatrics, 1967; Mem. Albemarle Cttee on Youth Service; Mem. Central Coun. of Educ. (Wales), 1954–56; External Examr, Univs of Bristol, Birmingham, Manchester, Leeds; Colonial Office Visitor to W Indies, 1956 and Far East, 1959. President Cardiff Medical Soc., 1963–64. Hon. LLD Wales, 1981. *Publications:* (with W. J. Pearson) The Infant, 1932; Pædiatrics for Nurses, 1947; articles in BMJ, Lancet, Archives of Disease in Childhood, etc. *Recreation:* golf. *Address:* Maldwyn, 71 Danycoed Road, Cyncoed, Cardiff CF2 6NE. *T:* Cardiff (0222) 751262.                          *Died* 26 *Dec.* 1990.

**WATKINS, Harold James;** retired; Managing Director, Canusa Ltd, 1956–80; Director other subsidiaries (home and overseas) Montague L. Meyer Ltd; *b* 1914; *s* of late J. W. Watkins, Aberystwyth; *m* 1940, Jean, *d* of Frank Morris, OBE; one *s* (and one *s* decd). *Educ:* Ardwyn Grammar Sch., Aberystwuth; Univ. of Wales (BSc). Forestry and Forest Botany, 1935; Forest Products Research Laboratory, 1936. Joined Montague L. Meyer Ltd, 1937. Served War, 1940–45: India, Burma; Capt. 1st Royal Welch Fusiliers. Concerned with development of Malaysian Timber Industry, 1948–. A Forestry Comr, 1967–73; Mem., Nat. Cttee for Wales, Forestry Commn, 1967–73 (England, 1967–70). *Recreations:* poetry; the art of doing nothing. *Address:* Pen y banc, Cwmystwuth, Dyfed. *T:* Pontrhydygroes 219.                          *Died* 7 *Feb.* 1983.

**WATKINS, Lt-Col Hubert Bromley,** OBE 1945; MC 1917; DCM 1916; DL; Vice-Lieutenant of Radnorshire, 1958–74; Chairman, Radnorshire Co. Ltd, 1966–70; Chairman, Bates & Hunt (Agric.) Ltd, 1952–70; *b* 9 July 1897; *s* of Hubert and Helen Watkins, Ludlow; *m* 1936, Mary (*née* Edwards); one *s* two *d. Educ:* Monmouth. King's Shropshire Light Infantry, 1914–19; Radnorshire Rifles (HG), 1940–45. Deputy Lieutenant, Powys (formerly Radnorshire), 1948; High Sheriff, 1952. President, National Assoc. Corn and Agricultural Merchants, 1949–50. *Recreations:* fishing, previously Rugby football and cricket. *Address:* Edgefield, Kingsland, Leominster, Herefordshire. *T:* Kingsland 571. *Club:* Cardiff and County (Cardiff).                          *Died* 10 *Oct.* 1984.

**WATKINS, Mary Gwendolen,** MA Oxon; Headmistress, Bedford High School, 1949–65, retired; *b* 1905; *d* of late M. J. Watkins, CBE. *Educ:* Newland High School, Hull; Penrhos College; St Hugh's College, Oxford (open scholar). Headmistress, Erddington Grammar School, Birmingham, 1940–49. Member of Staff of Martyrs Memorial School, Papua/New Guinea, Jan.–Dec. 1966. *Recreations:* music, travel. *Address:* 5 South Avenue, Kidlington, Oxford.                          *Died* 20 *Dec.* 1981.

**WATKINS-PITCHFORD, Denys James,** MBE 1989; FRSA; ARCA; author and artist; *b* 25 July 1905; *s* of Rev. Walter Watkins-Pitchford, BA, and Edith Elizabeth (*née* Wilson); *m* 1939, Cecily Mary Adnitt (*d* 1974); one *d* (one *s* decd). *Educ:* privately; studied art in Paris, 1924, and at Royal Coll. of Art, London (Painting Schs), 1926–28. Asst Art Master, Rugby Sch., 1930–47. Served City of London Yeomanry RHA, 1926–29. Captain, Home Guard, 1940–46. Hon. MA Leicester Univ., 1986. Carnegie Medal, 1942. Broadcaster on natural history subjects. *Publications:* (under pseudonym 'BB'): Sportsman's Bedside Book, 1937; Wild Lone, 1939; Manka, 1939; Countryman's Bedside Book, 1941; Little Grey Men, 1941 (TV Serial, 1975); The Idle Countryman, 1943; Brendon Chase, 1944 (Radio Serial; TV Serial, Southern TV, 1981, shown in 14 countries); Fisherman's Bedside Book, 1945; The Wayfaring Tree, 1945; Down the Bright Stream, 1948; Shooting Man's Bedside Book, 1948; Meeting Hill, 1948; Confessions of a Carp Fisher, 1950; Letters from Compton Deverell, 1950; Tides Ending, 1950; Dark Estuary, 1952; The Forest of Boland Light Railway, 1955; Mr Bumstead, 1958; The Wizard of Boland, 1958; Autumn Road to the Isles, 1959; The Badgers of Bearshanks, 1961; The White Road Westwards, 1961; September Road to Caithness, 1962; Lepus the Brown Hare, 1962; The Summer Road to Wales, 1964; Pegasus Book of the Countryside, 1964; The Whopper, 1967; A Summer on the Nene, 1967; At the Back o' Ben Dee, 1968; The Tyger Tray, 1971; Pool of the Black Witch, 1974; Lord of the Forest, 1975; Recollections of a Longshore Gunner, 1976; A Child Alone (autobiog.), 1978; Ramblings of a Sportsman Naturalist, 1979; The Naturalist's Bedside Book, 1980; The Quiet Fields, 1981; Indian Summer, 1984; Best of 'BB' (anthology), 1985; Fisherman's Folly, 1987; contribs to Field, Country Life, Shooting Times. *Recreations:* natural history, fishing, shooting. *Address:* The Round House, Sudborough, Kettering, Northants. *T:* Thrapston (08012) 3215.
                          *Died* 8 *Sept.* 1990.

**WATSON, Sir (David) Ronald M.;** *see* Milne-Watson.

**WATSON, Captain Sir Derrick William Inglefield Inglefield-,** 4th Bt, *cr* 1895; TD 1945; 4th Battalion Queen's Own Royal West Kent Regimental Reserve of Officers (TA); Active List 3 Sept. 1939; retired; *b* 7 Oct. 1901; *s* of Sir John Watson, 2nd Bt, and Edith Jane, *e d* of W. H. Nott, Liverpool; *S* brother, 1918; changed name by Deed Poll to Inglefield-Watson, Jan. 1946; *m* 1925, Margrett Georgina (who obtained a divorce, 1939), *o d* of late Col T. S. G. H. Robertson-Aikman, CB; one *s* one *d; m* 1946, Terezia (Terry), *d* of late Prof. Charles Bodon, Budapest. *Educ:* Eton; Christ Church, Oxford. County Councillor, Kent (No 4 Tonbridge Division), 1931–37. *Heir:* *s* John Forbes Watson, Lt-Col Royal Engineers (retd), *b* 16 May 1926. *Address:* Ringshill House, Wouldham, near Rochester, Kent. *T:* Medway 61514.                          *Died* 27 *Jan.* 1987.

**WATSON, Vice-Adm. Sir Dymock;** *see* Watson, Vice-Adm. Sir R. D.

**WATSON, Prof. (George) Hugh (Nicholas) S.;** *see* Seton-Watson.

**WATSON, Gilbert,** CBE 1947; HM Senior Chief Inspector of Schools in Scotland, retired; *b* 28 Oct. 1882; *er s* of John Watson, Edinburgh; *m* 1st, 1911, Annie Macdonald (decd); 2nd, 1974, Christian M. Kennedy (*d* 1983). *Educ:* Royal High School, Edinburgh; Edinburgh and Oxford Universities. Rector, Inverness Royal Academy, 1909; entered inspectorate of Scottish Education Department, 1910; HM Senior Chief Inspector, 1944. *Publications:* Theriac and Mithridatium: a study in Therapeutics (Wellcome Historical Medical Library), 1966; A Short History of Craigmillar Park Golf Club, Edinburgh, 1974; co-author of books on Latin Grammar and Latin prose composition. *Recreation:* golf. *Address:* 1 Chamberlain Road, Edinburgh EH10 4DL.                          *Died* 5 *Oct.* 1987.

**WATSON, Herbert James,** CB 1954; *b* 9 Aug. 1895; *s* of Thomas Francis Watson, Inverness; *m* 1929, Elsie May Carter; two *s* one *d. Educ:* Royal Naval College, Greenwich. Entered Royal Corps of Naval Constructors, 1918; Chief Constructor: Admiralty, 1940–43; Chatham, 1943–45; Manager: Malta, 1945–46; Devonport, 1946–47; Asst Director of Dockyards, 1947–49; Deputy Director of Dockyards, 1949–56. *Recreation:* sailing. *Address:* Glenn-Craig Village, Beaufort Road, Albany, WA 6330, Australia.
                          *Died* 26 *May* 1988.

**WATSON, Rev. Hubert Luing;** retired as General Superintendent of the Baptist Union, North Western Area (1949–60); President of the Baptist Union of Great Britain and Ireland, 1963 (Vice-President, 1962); Chairman, Baptist Minister Fellowship, 1960–63; *b* 30 Nov. 1892; *s* of Austin and Margaret M. Watson; *m* 1914, Mercy (*née* Harwood); one *d. Educ:* Winslow School. Baptist Union Exams, External student, Manchester Coll. Pastor of: Milton and Little Leigh, 1918–23; Enon, Burnley, 1923–29; Ansdell, Lytham, 1929–35; Richmond, Liverpool, 1935–49. *Recreations:* gardening and motoring. *Address:* Cartref, Spurlands End Road, Great Kingshill, High Wycombe, Bucks. *T:* High Wycombe 712062.
                          *Died* 27 *Dec.* 1985.

**WATSON, Hugh Gordon;** Barrister-at-Law; one of the Special Commissioners of Income Tax, 1952–76; *b* 3 Feb. 1912; *s* of late Andrew Gordon Watson, Physician, 21 The Circus, Bath, and late Clementina (*née* Macdonald); *m* 1940, Winefride Frances (*d* 1973), *d* of late Clement Brand, Westfield, Reigate, and late Winefride Denise (*née* Casella); three *s. Educ:* Ampleforth College; Pembroke College, Oxford. Insurance Broker, 1935–39. Served War of 1939–45 in RNVR. Called to the Bar, Lincoln's Inn, 1947. *Address:* 24 Evesham Close, Reigate, Surrey.                          *Died* 16 *July* 1989.

**WATSON, Prof. Hugh S.;** *see* Seton-Watson, Prof. G. H. N.

**WATSON, Prof. James Wreford;** Professor of Geography, 1954–82, and Convenor, Centre of Canadian Studies, 1972–82, Edinburgh University; b 8 Feb. 1915; s of Rev. James Watson; m 1939, Jessie W. Black (d 1989); one s one d. Educ: George Watson's College, Edinburgh; Edinburgh Univ. (MA); Toronto Univ. (PhD). Asst Lecturer in Geography, Sheffield Eng., 1937–39; Prof. of Geography, and founder of Geog. Dept, McMaster University, Canada, 1945–49; Chief Geographer, Canada, and Director of the Geographical Branch, Department of Mines and Technical Surveys, Canada, 1949–54; Prof. and founder of Geog. Dept, Carleton Univ., Ottawa, 1952–54; Edinburgh University: Head of Dept of Geography, 1954, Convenor, Sch. of Scottish Studies, 1956–59, Dean, Faculty of Social Science, 1964–68. Visiting Professor: Queen's Univ., Kingston, Ont, 1959–60; Univ. of Manitoba, 1968–69; British Columbia Univ., 1971; Simon Fraser Univ., BC, 1976–77; Calgary Univ., 1980–81, 1983. Editor: Scottish Studies, 1957–64; Atlas of Canada, 1949–54; Hon. Ed., Scot. Geog. Magazine, 1975–78. Member: Brit. Nat. Cttee for Geog., 1960–82; Geog. Cttee, SSRC, 1965–68; Council SSRC, and Chm., Geog. Planning Jt Cttee, 1972–75; President: Geog. Section, Brit. Assoc. for Advancement of Science, 1971; British Assoc. for Canadian Studies, 1975–77; RSGS, 1977–83; Senior Vice-Pres., 1981, Pres., 1983–84, IBG. Hon. DLitt York Univ., Ont, 1985; Hon. LLD: McMaster Univ., 1977; Carleton Univ., Ottawa, 1979; Calgary Univ., 1981; Queen's Univ., Ont, 1985. Award of Merit, Amer. Assoc. of Geogrs, 1949; Murchison Award, RGS, 1956; Research Medal, RSGS, 1965; Special Award, Canadian Assoc. of Geographers, 1978; Gold Medal, RSGS, 1984; Gold Medal, Internat. Council of Canadian Studies, 1984. Governor General's Medal, Canada (literary), 1953. FRSC; FRSE. Publications: geographical: General Geography, 1957 (Toronto); North America: Its Countries and Regions, 1963 (London), 2nd edn 1968; A Geography of Bermuda, 1965 (London); Canada: Problems and Prospects, 1968 (Toronto); Geographical Essays (co-editor with Prof. R. Miller); (ed) The British Isles, A Systematic Geography, 1964 (London); (ed) Collins-Longmans Advanced Atlas, 1968; (ed with T. O'Riordan) The American Environment: perceptions and policies, 1975; (jtly with Jessie Watson) The Canadians: how they live and work, 1977; A Social Geography of the United States, 1978; The USA: habitation of hope, 1983; articles on historical and social geography in Geography, Scottish Geographical Magazine, Geographical Review, Jl of Geography, Canadian Jl of Economics and Political Science, etc; literary: Unit of Five, 1947; Of Time and the Lover, 1953; Scotland, the Great Upheaval, 1972; Cross-country Canada, 1979; verse in Canadian and British literary jls. Address: Broomhill, Kippford, Galloway DG5 4LG.

*Died 18 Sept. 1990.*

**WATSON, Prof. Janet Vida, (Mrs John Sutton),** FRS 1979; Professor of Geology, Imperial College, University of London, 1974–83, then Emeritus; b 1 Sept. 1923; d of late Prof. David Meredith Seares Watson, FRS, and Katharine Margarite (née Parker); m 1949, John Sutton. Educ: South Hampstead High Sch.; Reading Univ.; Imperial Coll., London. BSc, PhD. Senior Studentship, Royal Commission for the Exhibition of 1851, 1949–52; Imperial College, London: Research and teaching, 1952–74; Personal Chair in Geology, 1974–83. Member, National Water Council, 1973–76. Pres., Geol. Soc. of London, 1982–84; a Vice-Pres., 1984, Mem. Council, 1985–, Royal Soc. Bigsby Medal, 1965, Lyell Medal, 1973, Geological Soc. of London. Publications: (jtly with H. H. Read) Introduction to Geology, vol. 1, 1962, 2nd edn 1968, vol. 2, 1976; (jtly with H. H. Read) Beginning Geology, 1966. Address: Department of Geology, Imperial College, Prince Consort Road, SW7 2AZ.

*Died 29 March 1985.*

**WATSON, John Parker,** CBE 1972; TD 1945; ED 1988; Partner, Lindsays, WS (formerly Lindsay Howe & Co., WS), 1935–79; b 22 Aug. 1909; s of John Parker Watson, WS, and Rachel Watson (née Henderson); m 1936, Barbara Parkin Wimperis; two s one d. Educ: Merchiston Castle Sch., Edinburgh; Corpus Christi Coll., Oxford (scholar); Edinburgh Univ. MA Oxon; LLB Edin. Served War, 1939–45, RA; Adjt, 94th (City of Edinburgh) HAA Regt; Staff Capt., JAG'S Dept; Bde Major, 12th AA Bde (8th Army); Staff Coll., Haifa; GSO2 HQ 9th Army. Admitted Mem., WS Soc., 1934. Lectr in Public Internat. Law, Edinburgh Univ., 1937–39. Chairman: Edinburgh Marriage Guidance Council, 1951–54; Scottish Marriage Guidance Council, 1962–65; Scottish Solicitors' Discipline Tribunal, 1974–78; Mem., SE Regional Hosp. Bd, 1952–55. Mem. Council, Law Soc. of Scotland, 1950–75 (Vice-Pres., 1957–58, Pres., 1970–72). Recreations: travel, hill walking, listening to music, golf. Address: 66 Murrayfield Gardens, Edinburgh EH12 6DQ. T: 031–337 3405. Clubs: Travellers'; New (Edinburgh).

*Died 20 Aug. 1989.*

**WATSON, (John) Steven,** MA; FRSE; FRHistS; Principal, University of St Andrews, since 1966; b Hebburn-on-Tyne, 20 March 1916; o s of George Watson and Elizabeth Layborn Gall, Newcastle upon Tyne; m 1942, Heba Sylvia de Cordova Newbery; two s. Educ: Merchant Taylors' Sch.; St John's Coll., Oxford (Andrew Schol.). 1st cl. hons Mod. Hist., 1939. Harmsworth Sen. Schol., Merton Coll., 1939–42, for research into Speakership of House of Commons; unfit, owing to loss of leg in road accident, for mil. service. Admin Asst to Controller-General, Min. of Fuel and Power, 1942; Private Sec. to Ministers of Fuel and Power, 1942–45; Lectr, Student and Tutor, Christ Church, Oxford, 1945–66 (Censor, 1955–61; Hon. Student, 1981); Chm. Bd of Modern History, Oxford, 1956–58; Editor, Oxford Historical series, 1950–66; Chm., Scottish Academic Press. Mem., British Library Bd, 1973–79. Wiles Lectr, 1968. Member: Franks Commission of University Inquiry, 1964–66; Cttee to examine operation of Section 2 of Official Secrets Act, 1971. Chm., ACU, 1978–79 (Vice-Chm., 1975–78). Hon. DLitt, DePauw, 1967; DHL: St Andrews, Laurinburg, NC, 1972; Philadelphia; DHum Simpson Coll., Iowa. Silver Medal of City of Paris, 1967; Gold Medal, American Legion, 1978. Publications: (with Dr W. C. Costin) The Law and Working of the Constitution 1660–1914, 2 vols, 1952; The Reign of George III 1760–1815 (vol. XII, Oxf. Hist. of England), 1960; A History of the Salters' Company, 1963; essays in various collections and jls; TV scripts and performances. Address: University of St Andrews, College Gate, North Street, St Andrews KY16 9AJ. T: St Andrews 76161; 37 Flask Walk, NW3. Clubs: Caledonian; Puffins, New (Edinburgh); Royal and Ancient (St Andrews).

*Died 12 June 1986.*

**WATSON, Sir Norman James,** 2nd Bt, cr 1912; late Flying Officer, RAFVR; late KRRC and RAF; FRGS; b 17 March 1897; er s of Sir George Watson, 1st Bt, and Bessie, d of T. Atkinson; S father, 1930; m 1974, Lady (Beryl) Rose. Educ: Eton. Sheriff of Berkshire, 1940. Publication: (with Edward J. King) Round Mystery Mountain, 1935. Heir: none. Address: Flat 132, 55 Park Lane, W1. Clubs: Royal Air Force, Alpine.

*Died 19 May 1983 (ext).*

**WATSON, Reginald Frank William,** AO 1985; CMG 1977; Chairman: State Bank of New South Wales, since 1986; Samuelson Group Pty Ltd (Australia), since 1986; b 11 Nov. 1921; s of Frank Harry Watson and Mary Waner Watson (née Mesny); m 1948, Helen Patricia Helmore; two s one d. Educ: various schools and colleges in China. Major, Fifth Royal Gurkha Rifles, India, Burma and China (despatches twice), and Adviser to Brit. Mil. Mission to China, 1941–46. Own retail co., Sydney, 1946–48; Gilbert Lodge & Co., Sydney, 1948–52; Admin. Officer, Aust. Defence Dept, Melbourne, 1952–54; Godfrey Phillips Ltd, Sydney, 1954–56; Rothmans of Pall Mall, Australia, 1956–76 (Man. Dir, 1968; Chief Exec., 1975); Man. Dir, Dri-Clad Industries, Aust., 1977–78; marketing and indust. relations consultant, 1978–82. Part-time appts to state govt and fed. govt bds and authorities, 1972–83 (Chm., NSW Overseas Trade Authority, 1978–83); Agent-Gen. for NSW in London, 1983–86. Trustee, Aust. Cancer Foundn for Med. Res., 1986–; Chm., Aust. Museum Foundn, 1988–. Co-Founder, Variety Club of Australia, 1974. Freeman, City of London, 1983. Recreations: tennis, walking, Chinese studies, travel. Address: c/o State Bank of New South Wales, 52 Martin Place, Sydney, NSW 2000, Australia. Clubs: Union, Elanora Country, American National (Sydney).

*Died 21 Dec. 1989.*

**WATSON, Vice-Adm. Sir (Robert) Dymock,** KCB 1959 (CB 1956); CBE 1948; DL; b 5 April 1904; e s of Robert Watson, FRIBA, Farnham, Surrey; m 1st, 1939, Margaret Lois (d 1968), d of late Rev. F. R. Gillespy; one s three d; 2nd, 1977, Elizabeth Evelyn Petronella, widow of Amyas Chichester, MC. Educ: Royal Naval Colls Osborne and Dartmouth. Captain: Asst Dir of Plans, Joint Planning Staff, Min. of Defence, 1944–46; Capt. (D) 1st Destroyer Flotilla Medit., 1947–48; idc, 1949; Dir of Plans, Admty, 1950–52; CO, HMS Illustrious, 1953; Rear-Adm., 1954; Flag Officer Flotillas, Medit., 1954–55, Vice-Adm. 1957; a Lord Commissioner of the Admiralty, Fourth Sea Lord, Chief of Supplies and Transport, 1955–58; Commander-in-Chief, South Atlantic and South America, 1958–60; retired, 1961. DL County of Brecknock, 1965, Powys 1974. Address: Manascin, Pencelli, near Brecon, Powys, Wales.

*Died 3 Feb. 1988.*

**WATSON, Sir Ronald M.;** see Milne-Watson, Sir D. R.

**WATSON, Steven;** see Watson, J. S.

**WATSON, Sir William,** Kt 1962; b 23 Nov. 1902; s of late Knight Watson, SSC; m 1929, Elizabeth Margaret Dods; two s one d. Educ: Melville College. Member of the Institute of Chartered Accountants of Scotland (Council, 1950–52). Partner Messrs Baillie Gifford & Co., 1930–47. Director: Bank of Scotland 1944–71 (Treasurer, 1952–66); Standard Life Assurance Co., 1941–75 (Chm., 1966–69); Member Edinburgh Southern Hospitals Group Board of Management, 1948, Chairman, 1950–52; Member Jenkins Cttee on Company Law Amendment, 1960; President Inst. of Bankers in Scotland, 1963–65; Member Academic Adv. Cttee, Universities of St Andrews and Dundee, 1964–66. Recreation: golf. Address: 1 Hope Terrace, Edinburgh EH9 2AP. T: 031–447 2752. Clubs: Caledonian; New (Edinburgh); Hon. Co. of Edinburgh Golfers.

*Died 10 Jan. 1984.*

WATSON, Prof. Wreford; see Watson, Prof. J. W.

WATT, Sir Alan (Stewart), Kt 1954; CBE 1952; Director, The Canberra Times, 1964–72; b 13 April 1901; s of George Watt and Susan Stewart Robb Gray; m 1927, Mildred Mary Wait; three s one d. Educ: Sydney Boys' High Sch.; Sydney and Oxford Universities. Rhodes Scholar for NSW, 1921; practised as Barrister-at-Law, Sydney; appointed to Dept of External Affairs, Canberra, 1937; First Secretary, Australian Legation, Washington, 1940–45; Adviser, Australian Deleg. to San Francisco, UN Conf., 1945; Alternate Deleg., UN General Assembly, London, 1946; Asst Secretary (Political), Dept of External Affairs, 1946; Del. to UN Gen. Assemblies, New York, 1946 and 1947, Paris, 1948; Leader, Australian Deleg. to Conf. on Freedom of Information, Geneva, 1948. Australian Minister to USSR, 1947–48; Australian Ambassador to USSR, 1949–50; Secretary, Department of External Affairs, Canberra, ACT, 1950–53; Australian Commissioner in SE Asia, 1954–56; Australian Ambassador: to Japan, 1956–60; to Federal Republic of Germany, 1960–62. Australian Delegate, Colombo Plan Cons. Cttee Meeting, Sydney, 1950; Member Deleg. accompanying Prime Minister to Prime Ministers' Conf., London, 1951 and 1953; Member Australian Delegation to ANZUS Council Meeting, Honolulu, 1952, and Geneva, 1954; alternate Leader, Australian Deleg. to Conf. on Indo-China and Korea, Geneva, 1954, Manila Treaty Conf., Manila 1954. Bangkok 1955. Retired from Commonwealth Public Service, July 1962. Visiting Fellow, Australian National Univ., 1963–83; Dir, Australian Inst. of Internat. Affairs, 1963–69. Publications: Evolution of Australian Foreign Policy 1938–1965, 1967; Vietnam, 1968; Memoirs, 1972; United Nations, 1974. Recreation: lawn tennis. Address: 1 Mermaid Street, Red Hill, Canberra, ACT 2603, Australia. Club: National Press (Canberra).                               Died 18 Sept. 1988.

WATT, Alexander Stuart, PhD; FRS 1957; retired as Lecturer in Forest Botany, Cambridge University (1933–59); b 21 June 1892; s of George Watt and Maggie Jean Stuart; m 1929, Annie Constable Kennaway; two s one d. Educ: Turriff Secondary Sch.; Robert Gordon's Coll., Aberdeen; Aberdeen and Cambridge Universities. BA 1919, PhD 1924, Cambridge. Lecturer in Forest Botany and Forest Zoology, 1915–29; Gurney Lecturer in Forestry, Cambridge, 1929–33. Visiting Lecturer, University of Colorado, 1963; Visiting Prof., University of Khartoum, 1965. Linnean Soc. Gold Medal, 1975. Publications: papers in Journal of Ecology, New Phytologist, etc. Recreation: hill walking. Address: 38 Chesterton Hall Crescent, Cambridge. T: Cambridge 359371.                    Died 2 March 1985.

WATT, Very Rev. Dr Archibald; Minister, Edzell-Lethnot Parish Church, 1957–69, retired; Moderator of the General Assembly of the Church of Scotland, May 1965–66; b 1 Aug. 1901; s of Archibald Watt and Elsie Cormack; m 1933, Mary Swapp; two s. Educ: Robert Gordon's Coll., Aberdeen Univ. (MA) and Christ's Coll., Aberdeen; Union Theolog. Seminary, NY (STM magna cum laude). Hugh Black Fellowship for Union Theological Seminary, 1926–27; Assistant Minister: North Church, Aberdeen, 1927–29; St Serf's Church, Almondbank, Perthshire, 1929–34; Chalmers Church, Uddingston, 1934–42; Stonelaw Church, Rutherglen, 1942–57. Convener, Social Service Cttee of Church of Scotland, 1957–62. Hon. DD Aberdeen, 1959. Publications: 10 pamphlets on the Reformed Faith. Recreation: fishing. Address: 44 Springfield Avenue, Aberdeen. T: Aberdeen 36059.                     Died 1 Jan. 1981.

WATT, David; writer and consultant; b Edinburgh, 9 Jan. 1932; s of Rev. John Hunter Watt and Helen Garioch Bryce; m 1968, Susanne, d of Dr Frank Buchardt; four s. Educ: Marlborough; Hertford Coll., Oxford. Dramatic Critic, Spectator, 1956–57; Diplomatic Corresp., Scotsman, 1958–60; Common Market Corresp., Daily Herald, 1960–61; Polit. Corresp., Spectator, 1962–63; Washington Corresp., Financial Times, 1964–67, Polit. Editor, 1968–77; Dir, RIIA, 1978–83. Jt Editor, Political Qly, 1979–85; regular contributor to The Times, 1981–. Vis. Fellow, 1972–73, Fellow, 1981–83, All Souls Coll., Oxford. Member: Fisher Cttee on Self-regulation at Lloyd's, 1979–80; Bd of Visitors, Wandsworth Prison, 1977–81. Posthumous publication: The Inquiring Eye: a selection of the writings of David Watt (ed Ferdinand Mount), 1988. Recreations: music, chess, golf. Address: 18 Groveway, SW9 0AR. T: 01–735 5195. Clubs: Travellers', Beefsteak.                   Died 27 March 1987.

WATT, George Percival Norman, CMG 1957; CBE 1951; b 2 June 1890; s of Edmund J. Watt, Melbourne, Australia; m 1916, Nellie V. M. Hough (decd); one s one d. Educ: Wesley Coll., Melbourne, Victoria. Clerk, Victorian Railways and State Treasury, 1905–08; Navy Finance Branch, 1911; Accountant, Navy Department, 1917; Secretary, HMA Naval Establishments, Sydney, 1923; Commonwealth Public Service Inspector, 1928–40; First Assistant Secretary, Defence Division Treasury, Melbourne, 1940; Deputy Secretary, Treasury, Canberra, 1947–48; Secretary, Commonwealth Treasury, Canberra, 1948–51, retired. Chairman, Australian National Airlines Commission, 1950–57; Chairman, British Commonwealth Pacific Airlines, 1950–54; Director, Qantas Empire Airways, 1947–62; Chairman and Director, Volkswagen (Australaisa) Ltd, 1959–66. Recreation: golf. Address: 23 Through Road, Burwood, Victoria 3125, Australia.
                                                   Died 21 July 1983.

WATT, Sir George Steven H.; see Harvie-Watt.

WATT, Ian Buchanan, CMG 1967; HM Diplomatic Service, retired; with Grindlays Bank, 1977–83; b 3 Aug. 1916; s of John Watt and Margaret Gibson Watt, Perth; m 1963, Diana Susan, d of Captain R. A. Villiers, Royal Navy (retired) and late Mrs R. A. Villiers; two s one d (and one d decd). Educ: Perth Academy; St Andrews Univ. MA 1939. Asst Principal, Government of N. Ireland, 1939. Naval Service, 1942–46; Lieut, RNVR. Principal, Colonial Office, 1946; Asst Secretary, 1956; Dep. UK Commissioner, Malta, 1962; Dep. High Commissioner, Malta, 1964; transf. to Diplomatic Service, 1964; Counsellor, CRO, 1965; High Comr, Lesotho, 1966–70; Counsellor, FCO, 1970–72; High Comr, Sierra Leone, 1972–76. Recreations: gardening, ornithology. Address: Kingswood House, 8 Lower Green Road, Esher, Surrey. T: 01–398 5728. Club: Travellers'.                                   Died 24 Oct. 1988.

WATT, Robert Cameron; b 4 Aug. 1898; s of Rev. J. Gordon Watt; m 1925, Barbara (d 1977), d of late Rev. E. J. Bidwell, former Bishop of Ontario; three s. Educ: Fettes Coll., Edinburgh; Oriel Coll., Oxford. Lecturer in History, Queen's Univ., Kingston, Ontario, 1922–24; Asst Master, Clifton Coll., 1924–26; Senior History Master, Rugby Sch., 1926–51, Housemaster, 1944–51; Rector, Edinburgh Acad., 1951–62; Assistant Master: St George's Sch., Newport, RI, 1963–66; Fettes Coll., 1967–78. Recreations: gardening, walking. Address: 9 Wardie Avenue, Edinburgh EH5 2AB.                                          Died 16 Feb. 1983.

WATT, William, OBE 1969; FRS 1976; Senior Research Fellow, Department of Materials Science, University of Surrey, since 1975; b 14 April 1912; o c of Patrick Watt, Aberdeen, and Flora (née Corsar), Arbroath; m 1946, Irene Isabel Corps; two d. Educ: George Heriot's Sch., Edinburgh; Heriot-Watt Coll., Edinburgh BSc (1st Cl. Hons, Chem.); AH-WC. ARIC 1935. Research Chemist, Royal Aircraft Establishment, 1936–75, retiring as Sen. Principal Scientific Officer, (Merit). Hon. DSc Heriot-Watt, 1977. Gold Medal, Congrès des Matériaux Résistant à Chaud, Paris, 1951; (jtly) Civil Service Wolfe Award for Carbon Fibre Research, 1968; Silver Medal, RAeS, 1969; C. Pettinos Award for Res. and Innovation in Carbon, viz, Pyrolytic Graphite and Carbon Fibres, Amer. Carbon Cttee, 1971. Publications: (jtly) 57th Thomas Hawksley Lecture, IMechE (public lecture), 1970; Pettinos Award Lecture, Carbon Work at the RAE, 10th US Carbon Conf., Bethlehem (public lecture), 1971; many papers in Proc. of Confs and in scientific jls. Recreations: gardening, golf, continental travel. Address: 12 Barton End, Lenten Street, Alton, Hants GU34 1LD. T: Alton 88486. Club: North Hants Golf (Fleet, Hants).                               Died 11 Aug. 1985.

WATTS, William John, CBE 1979 (OBE 1969); business consultant; Director, BRE-Metro; b 11 March 1923; s of William Thomas Watts and Beatrice (née Vickers); m 1949, Dr Anne Brown Watt; one s one d. RAF, 1941–46. HMOCS, Malaya, 1947–59: retd as Dep. Sec., Min. of Interior and Justice; HM Diplomatic Service, 1960–81: served in Colombo, Bangkok, Singapore and Nairobi, retired 1981. Mem. Council, Royal Soc. for Asian Affairs; Vice-Pres., Malaysia Singapore and Brunei Assoc. Recreations: reading, gardening. Address: 35 Gregories Road, Beaconsfield, Bucks. Clubs: Pathfinder; Royal Bangkok Sports (Thailand); Muthaiga (Nairobi, Kenya).                                           Died 6 Nov. 1983.

WAUCHOPE, Sir Patrick (George) Don-, 10th Bt, cr 1667; Horticulturist; b 7 May 1898; o s of late Patrick Hamilton Don-Wauchope (s of 8th Bt) and late Georgiana Renira; S uncle 1951; m 1936, Ismay Lilian Ursula (marr. diss.), d of late Sidney Hodges, Edendale, Natal, South Africa; two s. Educ: The Edinburgh Academy. Served European War, 1914–18, with RFA, France and Belgium (wounded); War of 1939–46, Egypt and Italy. Recreations: cricket, golf. Heir: s Roger (Hamilton) Don-Wauchope [Chartered Accountant, S Africa; b 16 Oct. 1938; m 1963, Sallee, yr d of Lt-Col H. Mill Colman, OBE, AMICE, Durban; two s one d]. Address: c/o Hibiscus House, Village of Happiness, Margate 4280, Natal South Coast, S Africa.                                   Died 15 Sept. 1989.

WAUGH, Alec; b Hampstead, 8 July 1898; er s of late Arthur Waugh; m 1st, Barbara, d of W. W. Jacobs; 2nd, 1932, Joan (d 1969), d of Andrew Chirnside Victoria, Australia; two s one d; 3rd, 1969, Virginia Sorensen, d of Claude Eggertsen, Provo, Utah, USA. Educ: Sherborne; Sandhurst. Gazetted to Dorset Regt, 1917; BEF France, 1917–18; prisoner of war, 1918; travelled extensively; rejoined Dorset Regt, 1939; BEF France, 1940; Staff Captain, Ministry of Mines, 1940; MEF, 1941; Paiforce, 1942–45; retired with rank of Major, 1945. Writer in Residence at Central State Coll., Edmond, Oklahoma, 1966–67. Publications: fifty books which include: The Loom of Youth, 1917; Kept, 1925; Nor Many Waters, 1928; Hot Countries 1930; Most Women..., 1931; So Lovers Dream, 1931;

The Balliols, 1934; Jill Somerset, 1936; Eight Short Stories, 1937; Going Their Own Ways, 1938; No Truce with Time, 1941; His Second War, 1944; Unclouded Summer, 1948; The Lipton Story, 1951; Where the Clocks Chime Twice, 1952; Guy Renton, 1953; Island in the Sun, 1956 (produced as film, 1957); The Sugar Islands, 1958; In Praise of Wine, 1959; Fuel for the Flame, 1960; My Place in the Bazaar, 1961; The Early Years of Alec Waugh, 1962; A Family of Islands, 1964; The Mule on the Minaret. 1965; My Brother Evelyn and Other Profiles, 1967; Wines and Spirits of the World, 1968; A Spy in the Family, 1970; Bangkok: the story of a city, 1970; The Fatal Gift, 1973; A Year to Remember: a reminiscence of 1931, 1975; Married to a Spy, 1976; The Best Wine Last, 1978. *Recreation:* watching life go by. *Address:* c/o A. D. Peters & Co., 10 Buckingham Street, WC2. *Clubs:* Athenæum, Beefsteak, Pratt's, Savage; Century (New York).
*Died 3 Sept.* 1981.

**WAVERLEY, 2nd Viscount,** *cr* 1952, of Westdean; **David Alastair Pearson Anderson;** Consultant Physician, Reading Group of Hospitals, since 1951; *b* 18 Feb. 1911; *s* of 1st Viscount Waverley, PC, GCB, OM, GCSI, GCIE, FRS, and Christina Anderson; *S* father, 1958; *m* 1948, Myrtle Ledgerwood; one *s* one *d* (and one *d* decd). *Educ:* Malvern Coll.; Universities of Frankfurt A/Main and Cambridge (Pembroke Coll.); St Thomas's Hospital, London. MB, BChir (Cantab), 1937; MRCP (London), 1946; FRCP (London), 1957. Appointments at St Thomas's Hospital, 1938-39. Served War of 1939-45, RAF Med. Br. Med. Registrar, Res. Asst Physician and Registrar Dept Clin. Pathology, St Thomas's Hospital, 1946-50. *Publications:* various communications to medical journals. *Recreations:* golf and fishing; formerly athletics and Association football (rep. Cambridge *v* Oxford, in Inter-Varsity Relays, etc). *Heir:* s Hon. John Desmond Forbes Anderson, *b* 31 Oct. 1949. *Address:* Chanders, Aldworth, Berks. *T:* Compton 377. *Clubs:* Travellers'; Hawks (Cambridge).
*Died 21 Feb.* 1990.

**WAY, Rt. Rev. Wilfrid Lewis Mark;** *b* 12 May 1905; *s* of late Rev. C. C. L. Way and Margaret (*née* Corser); *m* 1960, Marion Crosbie, *d* of late Sir Robert Robinson, OM, FRS, and late Lady (Gertrude M.) Robinson; one *s* one *d*. *Educ:* Rossall Sch., Trinity Coll., Cambridge (Classical Scholar); Westcott House. 1st Cl. Class. Tripos, part I, 1925; BA 2nd Cl. Class. Tripos, part II, 1927; MA 1935; Deacon, 1928; Priest, 1929; Lic. Curate of St. Faith, Great Crosby, 1928-34; St Bartholomew, Brighton, 1934-37; UMCA Dio., Zanzibar, 1937; Curate of Korogwe, 1937-38; Priest i/c Zanzibar, 1938-40; Msalabani, 1940-44; Mkuzi, 1944-45; Kideleko, 1948-51; Warden of Kalole Theol Coll., Dio. of Zanzibar, 1951-52; Bishop of Masasi, 1952-59; Rector of Averham with Kelham, 1960-71. *Address:* Rose Cottage, 5 Redhills Lane, Durham DH1 4AL. *T:* Durham 43885.
*Died 30 July* 1982.

**WAYNE, Sir Edward (Johnson),** Kt 1964; MD, MSc, PhD, FRCP (London and Edinburgh); FRCP (Glasgow); Regius Professor of Practice of Medicine, Glasgow University, 1954-67; Physician to Western Infirmary, Glasgow; Hon. Physician to the Queen in Scotland, 1954-67; *b* 3 June 1902; *s* of late William Wayne, Leeds, Yorks, and late Ellen Rawding, Leadenham, Lincs; *m* 1932, Honora Nancy Halloran; one *s* one *d*. *Educ:* Leeds Univ. and Medical School (Akroyd Scholar and Sir Swire Smith Fellow); Manchester Univ. BSc Leeds (1st Class Hons Chemistry) 1923; MB, ChB (Leeds), 1st Class Hons, 1929; MD 1938; Hey Gold Medallist; Demonstrator in Physiology, University of Leeds, 1930-31; Assistant in Dept Clinical Research, University College Hospital, London, 1931-34; Professor of Pharmacology and Therapeutics, University of Sheffield, 1934-53 (formerly Physician to Royal Infirmary and Children's Hospital, Sheffield). Member Scottish Secretary of State's Advisory Cttee on Medical Research, 1958-67; Member of the Medical Research Council, 1958-62; Chairman, Clinical Research Board, 1960-64; Chairman, British Pharmacopœia Commn, 1958-63; Chairman, Advisory Cttee on Drug Dependence, 1967-69. Sims Commonwealth Travelling Professor, 1959. Bradshaw Lecturer, 1953; Lumleian Lecturer, RCP, 1959; Crookshank Lecturer and Medallist, Faculty of Radiol., 1966. Hon. DSc Sheffield, 1967. *Publications:* Papers in scientific and medical journals. *Address:* Lingwood Lodge, Lingwood, Norfolk NR13 4ES. *T:* Great Yarmouth (0493) 751370. *Club:* Athenæum.
*Died 19 Aug.* 1990.

**WEATHERHEAD, Sir Arthur (Trenham),** Kt 1960; CMG 1957; *b* 19 May 1905; *s* of late Canon A. S. Weatherhead; *m* 1938, Sylvia Mary, *d* of late A. Lace, Eastbourne; one *s* two *d*. *Educ:* St Bees School; Queen's College, Oxford. Sudan Plantations Syndicate, 1927; Colonial Administrative Service, Nigeria, 1930-60. Dep. Governor, Northern Region, Nigeria, 1958-60, retired. *Recreations:* gardening, chess. *Address:* Wood Rise, Amberley, Stroud, Glos. *T:* Amberley 2584.
*Died 23 Dec.* 1984.

**WEBB, Douglas Edward,** CVO 1961; OBE 1947; Deputy Commissioner of Police of the Metropolis, 1961-66; retired; *b* 8 Oct. 1909; *yr s* of late Supt O. C. Webb, KPM, Metropolitan Police;

*m* 1935, Mary McMillan, *yr d* of late Capt. J. S. Learmont, Trinity House; one *s* (one *d* decd). *Educ:* Bordon Grammar School; Devonport High School. Joined Metropolitan Police, 1929; Metropolitan Police Coll., Hendon, 1935-36 (Baton of Honour). Allied Commission, Italy and Austria, 1945-47. Chief Supt, Bow Street, 1952-53, West End Central, 1953-54; Dep. Commander, New Scotland Yard, 1954-55; Commander, No 3 District (E London), 1955-57; Asst Commissioner (Traffic), 1957-58; Assistant Commissioner, Administration and Operations (originated Special Patrol Gp), New Scotland Yard, Dec. 1958-61. Officer, Legion of Honour, 1961; Order of Merit, Chile, 1965. *Address:* Tanglewood, 5 Deer Park Close, Tavistock, Devon PL19 9HE. *T:* Tavistock 2377.
*Died 11 Jan.* 1988.

**WEBB, James,** CB 1978; Commissioner of Inland Revenue, 1968-78; *b* 11 Nov. 1918; 2nd *s* of late James Webb and late Lucy Webb (*née* McGorrin); *m* 1957, Kathleen Veronica, 3rd *d* of late Catherine Downey (*née* McDaid) and of late James Downey, Londonderry. *Educ:* St Francis Xavier's, Liverpool; King's Coll., London Univ. (LLB 1940, 1st Cl. Hons). Entered Inland Revenue Dept (Estate Duty Office), 1937. Served War of 1939-45: W Africa, India and Burma; HM Forces, South Lancashire Regt, 1940; Sandhurst, 1942; Nigeria Regt, 1942-45 (Temp. Major, 1945). Assistant Principal Inland Revenue, 1947; Principal Establishment Officer and Dir of Personnel, 1971-75. *Address:* 3 Avondale Avenue, Hinchley Wood, Esher, Surrey. *T:* 01-398 6330.
*Died 27 Nov.* 1982.

**WEBB, John Victor Duncombe;** Principal Clerk, Judical Office, House of Lords, and Fourth Clerk at the Table (Judicial), since Aug. 1977; *b* 8 Nov. 1930; *s* of late John Arthur Webb and Idena Ann (*née* Kenroy); *m* 1st, 1960, Elizabeth Mary Cann (marr. diss.); one *d*; 2nd, 1972, Elizabeth Ann McKee. *Educ:* Tonbridge Sch.; Wadham Coll., Oxford (Exhibnr; MA). Called to Bar, Lincoln's Inn (Cholmeley Scholar), 1955. Joined Parliament Office, House of Lords, 1958; Clerk, 1958-63; Chief Clerk, Cttee and Private Bill Office, 1963-71; Chief Clerk, Public Bill Officer, 1971-77. *Publications:* Consolidation and Statute Law Revision (with Rt Hon. Lord Simon of Glaisdale) (in Public Law, 1975). *Address:* 54a Onslow Square, SW7 3NX. 10 West Street, Aldbourne, Marlborough, Wilts.
*Died 23 Oct.* 1983.

**WEBB, Stella Dorothea, (Mrs A. B. Webb);** *see* Gibbons, S. D.

**WEBBER, Lt-Col Godfrey Sturdy I.;** *see* Incledon-Webber.

**WEBBER, Sir William (James Percival),** Kt 1968; CBE 1962; MA; Member, National Coal Board, 1962-67; *b* 11 Sept. 1901; *s* of James Augustus Webber, Swansea, Glam; *m* 1929, Evelyn May, *d* of Thomas Rees, Swansea; one *s*. *Educ:* Elementary; Swansea Grammar Sch. Entered Great Western Railway Service, 1917, Clerk until 1944; Divl Sec. Railways Clerks' Assoc. (now Transport Salaried Staffs' Assoc.), 1944, Asst Gen. Sec., 1949. Swansea Borough Councillor, 1932-44, Dep. Mayor, 1942-43; Chm. Nat. Jt Council for Local Authorities Clerical, Administrative, Professional and Technical Grades, 1940-44; Member, Labour Party Nat. Exec., 1949-53. Part-time Member, Nat. Coal Bd, 1958-62; served on Govt Cttees and Courts of Inquiry; Member: Royal Commission on the Press, 1961-62; Transport Advisory Council, 1965; General Secretary, Transport Salaried Staffs Association, 1953-62; Mem., General Council, Trades Union Congress, 1953-62. Visiting Fellow, Nuffield College, Oxford, 1954-62. *Address:* 76 Thames Village, Hartington Road, Chiswick, W4 3UE. *T:* 01-994 4563.
*Died 12 April* 1982.

**WEBBER, William Southcombe L.;** *see* Lloyd Webber.

**WEBSTER, Brian Mackenzie;** Head of Defence Secretariat 8, Ministry of Defence, since 1982; *b* 25 Jan. 1938; *s* of Donald E. Webster and Muriel Webster; *m* 1967, Gillian Welland; one *s* two *d*. *Educ:* Durham Sch., Durham; St John's Coll., Cambridge (MA). Called to the Bar, Gray's Inn, 1965. Royal Air Force, 1956-58; Thos R. Miller and Son Ltd, Mutual Insurance, 1961-66; Ministry of Defence, 1966-71; Cabinet Office, 1971; Private Sec. to Secretary of the Cabinet, 1973; Northern Ireland Office, Belfast, 1974; Head of Internat. Procurement Policy Div., MoD, 1976; Counsellor, Defence Supply, Washington, 1979. *Recreations:* running, nineteenth century history. *Address:* Defence Secretariat, Ministry of Defence, Main Building, Whitehall, SW1.
*Died 22 June* 1985.

**WEBSTER, Rev. Canon Douglas,** MA, DD; Canon Residentiary of St Paul's Cathedral, 1969-84, later Canon Emeritus; Precentor, 1969-82, Chancellor, 1982-84; *b* 15 April 1920; *s* of Robert and Annie Webster; unmarried. *Educ:* Dulwich Coll.; St Peter's Coll., Oxford; Wycliffe Hall, Oxford. BA 1942, MA 1946. Curate: St Helens Parish Church, Lancs, 1943-46; Christ Church, Crouch End, London, 1946-47; Lectr, London Coll. of Divinity, 1947-52; Educn Sec., CMS, 1953-61; Theologian-Missioner, CMS, 1961-65; Chavasse Lectr in World Mission, Wycliffe Hall, Oxford, 1963-65; Prof. of Mission, Selly Oak Colls, Birmingham, 1966-69. Hon. Canon of Chelmsford, 1963-69; Exam. Chap. to Bp of Chelmsford,

1962–. Chm., 1978–83, Vice-Pres., 1983–, Council of Christians and Jews. Mem. Court, Worshipful Co. of Cutlers, Master 1974–76. Vis. Prof., Wycliffe Coll., Toronto, 1981. Lectures: Godfrey Day, Dublin, 1967; Moorhouse, Melbourne, 1969; Brennan, Louisville, Kentucky, 1982. Hon. DD Wycliffe Coll., Toronto, 1967. Sub-Chaplain 1977, Chaplain 1981, Order of St John of Jerusalem. Queen's Jubilee Medal, 1977. *Publications:* In Debt to Christ, 1957; What is Evangelism?, 1959; Local Church and World Mission, 1962; Pentecostalism and Speaking with Tongues, 1964; Unchanging Mission, 1965; Yes to Mission, 1966; Not Ashamed, 1970; Good News from John, 1974; contribs. to: Charles Simeon, Bicentenary Essays, 1959; The Parish Communion Today, 1962; Lambeth Essays on Ministry, 1968. *Recreations:* music, enjoying country life. *Address:* The Moat House, Weston-sub-Edge, Chipping Campden, Glos GL55 6QT. *T:* Evesham 840695. *Clubs:* United Oxford & Cambridge University, Royal Commonwealth Society.

*Died 27 Feb.* 1986.

**WEBSTER, Sir Richard James,** Kt 1971; DSO 1945; Director of Organisation, Conservative Central Office, 1966–76; *b* 15 July 1913; *e s* of late Gerald Webster and late Violet Webster; *m* 1940, Sheila, *y d* of late Jack Marston and late Geraldine Marston; two *d. Educ:* Sandroyd Sch.; Shrewsbury Sch. Conservative Agent: West Willesden, 1946–47; Aldershot, 1948–57; Central Office Agent, North West Provincial Area, 1958–66. Dir, Inst. of Obst. and Gyn. Research Appeal, 1976–81. *Recreations:* all spectator sports, sunbathing. *Address:* Kennet Cottage, Kintbury, near Newbury, Berks. *Clubs:* Carlton (Hon.), St Stephen's Constitutional (Hon.).

*Died 17 Jan.* 1986.

**WEBSTER, Sir Robert (Joseph),** Kt 1963; CMG 1959; CBE 1956; MC; Hon. DSc: University NSW; Wollongong University; Fellow, International Academy of Management; FASA; FAIM; Chairman, 1936–40 and 1960–76, General Manager, 1936–40, Managing Director, 1940–67, Bradmill Industries Ltd (formerly Bradford Cotton Mills Ltd); *b* 10 June 1891; *s* of Alexander J. Webster; *m* 1st, 1921, May (*d* 1949) *d* of Charles Twigg; one *s* three *d* (and one *s* decd); 2nd, 1954, Daphne, *d* of Edward Kingcott. *Educ:* Charters Towers School, Qld. In Commonwealth Public Service, 1906–19. Chancellor, 1970–76 and Mem. Council, 1947–76, Univ. of NSW, now Chancellor Emeritus; JP Qld and NSW Gen. Manager, Qld Cotton Board, 1926–36, and Commonwealth Controller of Cotton, 1942–46; President: The Sydney Div. Australian Institute of Management, 1947–50, 1958–62 (Federal Pres., 1962–64); NSW Chamber of Manufactures of Aust., 1950–51; Textile Council of Australia, 1960–73; Member: Aust. Nat. Airlines Commn, 1952–55; Australia–Japan Business Co-operation Cttee. Served European War, 1914–19, with AIF and on Staff (first Australian to be apptd to Staff at GHQ, France) in Egypt, Gallipoli and France (despatches, MC). Companion of the Textile Institute of GB, 1967. *Recreation:* golf. *Address:* 2 Buena Vista Avenue, Clifton Gardens, Sydney, New South Wales 2088, Australia. *T:* 969 6714. *Clubs:* Union, Imperial Service; American National; Australian Golf.

*Died 4 Aug.* 1981.

**WECK, Richard,** CBE 1969; PhD; FRS 1975; FEng 1976; Hon. Senior Research Fellow, Imperial College of Science and Technology, since 1984; *b* 5 March 1913; *s* of Francis and Katie Weck; *m* 1933, Katie (*née* Bartl). *Educ:* Tech. Univ., Prague (degree in Civ. Engrg). FICE, FIMechE, FInstW. Site Engr, 1936–38 (Prague); Design Project Leader, 1938–43; Research Asst to Lord Baker, 1943–46; Head of Fatigue Laboratory, British Welding Research Assoc., 1946–51; Lectr in Engineering, Cambridge Univ., 1951–57; Dir of Research, British Welding Res. Assoc., 1957–68; Dir-Gen., Welding Inst., 1968–77. Vis. Indust. Prof., Imperial Coll. of Science and Technol., 1968–74 and 1975–84. Mem., Royal Spanish Acad. of Sciences, 1984–. Bessemer Gold Medal, 1975. *Publications:* papers on welded structures, fatigue, res. stresses. *Recreations:* gardening, listening to music. *Address:* Abington Hall, Cambridge CB1 6AH. *T:* Cambridge 891339.

*Died 9 Jan.* 1986.

**WEDDELL, Prof. (Alexander) Graham (McDonnell),** MA (Oxon), MD, DSc (London); retired; Professor of Anatomy, University of Oxford, 1973–75; *b* 18 Feb. 1908; *s* of Alexander George Weddell and Maud Eileen McDonnell; *m* 1937, Barbara Monica Mills (*d* 1984); two *d. Educ:* Cheltenham Coll.; St Bartholomew's Hosp. Med. Sch., London. Demonstrator in Anatomy, St Bart's, London, 1933–34; Commonwealth Fund Fellow in Neuroanatomy and Neurological Surgery, USA, 1935–37; Demonstrator in Anatomy, University Coll. London, 1937–39. Served War: Neurosurgery, RAMC, until 1943; then Anatomical Research for Royal Naval Personnel Cttee of MRC, 1943–45. Apptd Demonstrator in Human Anatomy, Univ. of Oxford, with leave of absence, 1945. Reader in Human Anatomy, Univ. of Oxford, 1947–73; Fellow and Med. Tutor, Oriel Coll., Oxford, 1947; Sen. Proctor, Univ. of Oxford, 1951; elected Mem., Hebdomadal Council, 1952. WHO study team investigating neurological rehabilitation in leprosy, 1960; Harold Chaffer Lectureship, Dunedin Univ., NZ, 1961; Mem., MRC

Leprosy Sub-Cttee, 1967; Designated WHO Leprosy Ref. Lab. (under dir of Dr R. J. W. Rees), 1967. Pres., Anatomical Soc. of GB and Ire., 1973–75. *Publications:* papers in learned jls on cutaneous sensibility and leprosy. *Recreations:* photography, swimming. *Address:* 7 Mill Street, Islip, Oxford OX5 2SZ. *T:* Kidlington 6326.

*Died 21 March* 1990.

**WEDDERSPOON, Sir Thomas (Adam),** Kt 1955; JP; *b* 4 August 1904; *s* of late Thomas and Margaret Wedderspoon; *m* 1936, Helen Catherine Margaret MacKenzie; one *s* two *d. Educ:* Seafield House, Broughty Ferry, Angus; Trinity College, Glenalmond, Perthshire; Trinity Hall, Cambridge. JP Angus, 1928. *Address:* Shielhill House, Forfar, Angus DD8 3TT. *T:* Foreside 209.

*Died 6 Dec.* 1987.

**WEDGWOOD, Sir John Hamilton,** 2nd Bt, *cr* 1942; TD 1948; Deputy-Chairman of Josiah Wedgwood and Sons Ltd, until 1966; Member, British National Export Council, 1964–66; *b* 16 Nov. 1907; *s* of Sir Ralph L. Wedgwood, 1st Bt, CB, CMG, TD, and Iris, Lady Wedgwood (*née* Pawson) (*d* 1982); *S* father, 1956; *m* 1st, 1933, Diana Mildred (*d* 1976), *d* of late Col Oliver Hawkshaw, TD; three *s* one *d* (and one *s* decd); 2nd, 1982, Dr Pamela Tudor-Craig, FSA, widow (*née* Wynn Reeves); one step *d. Educ:* Winchester College; Trinity College, Cambridge; and abroad. Served War of 1939–45, Major GSO2 (1b). Chm., Anglo-American Community Relations, Lakenheath Base, 1972–76. Mem., adv. body, Harlaxton Coll. (Univ. of Evansville, Indiana), Lincs, 1975–. President: Utd Commercial Travellers' Assoc., 1959; Samuel Johnson Soc. (Lichfield), 1959. FRSA 1968; FRGS 1973. Liveryman, Worshipful Co. of Painter-Stainers, 1971. Hon. LLD Birmingham, 1966; Hon. DLitt Wm Jewell Coll., Kansas, 1983. *Recreations:* mountaineering, caving, foreign travel (Mem. Travelers' Century Club of California for those who have visited a hundred countries). *Heir: s* (Hugo) Martin Wedgwood [*b* 27 Dec. 1933; *m* 1963, Alexandra Mary Gordon Clark, *er d* of late Judge Alfred Gordon Clark, and Mrs Gordon Clark; one *s* two *d. Educ:* Eton; Trinity College, Oxford]. *Address:* c/o English-Speaking Union, 37 Charles Street, W1. *Clubs:* Arts, Alpine; British Pottery Manufacturers' Federation (Stoke-on-Trent).

*Died 9 Dec.* 1989.

**WEEKLEY, Charles Montague;** Officer-in-Charge of Bethnal Green Museum, 1946–64; *b* 15 June 1900; *o s* of late Prof. Ernest Weekley, DLitt and Frieda (afterwards Mrs D. H. Lawrence), 2nd *d* of Baron Friedrich von Richthofen; *m* 1930, Vera (*d* 1973), artist, *er d* of late P. Murray Ross, Dornoch, Sutherlandshire; one *s* one *d. Educ:* St Paul's School (scholar and leaving exhibitioner); St John's College, Oxford (scholar). BA (Oxon), 1922; MA (Oxon) 1967. FSA 1957–80. Assistant, Department of Circulation, V&A Museum, 1924; Dep. Keeper, 1938; General Finance Branch, Ministry of Supply, 1939–43; Southern Dept, Foreign Office, 1943–44; Ministry of Education, 1944–46. Trustee of Whitechapel Art Gallery, 1946–74; a Governor of Parmiter's School, 1946–64. Hon. Mem., Art Workers Guild, 1954. *Publications:* William Morris, 1934; Thomas Bewick, 1953; General Editor of The Library of English Art; (ed) A Memoir of Thomas Bewick, 1961; contributor to Chambers's Encyclopaedia, DNB, Times, Country Life, Architectural Review, etc. *Recreations:* Oxford University Athletic Team (1 mile) *v* Cambridge, 1922; Oxford University Relay Team (4 miles) *v* Cambridge, 1920. *Address:* 45 Gibson Square, Islington, N1. *T:* 01-226 8307. *Club:* Achilles.

*Died 30 Jan.* 1982.

**WEEKS, Edward Augustus;** Senior Editor and Consultant, Atlantic Monthly Press; American Field Service (Croix de Guerre, 1918); Fellow American Academy Arts and Sciences; *b* 19 Feb. 1898; *s* of Edward Augustus Weeks and Frederika Suydam; *m* 1925, Frederica Watriss (decd); one *s* one *d; m* 1971, Phœbe Adams. *Educ:* Pingry and Battin High School, Elizabeth, NJ; Cornell Univ.; BS Harvard, 1922; Camb. Univ. (Fiske Schol.). Hon. LittD: Northeastern Univ., Boston, 1938; Lake Forest Coll. (Illinois), 1939; Williams Coll., Mass., 1942; Middlebury College, Vt, 1944; University of Alabama, 1945; Dartmouth Coll., 1950; Bucknell Univ., 1952; Boston Univ., 1953; Hobart Coll., 1956; Univ. of Richmond, 1957; New York Univ., 1958; further hon. degrees from: Clark Univ., Massachusetts, 1958 (Humane Letters); Pomona Coll., Calif., 1958 (LittD); Univ. of Pittsburgh, 1959 (Humane Letters); Univ. of Akron, 1961 (LittD); Northwestern Univ., 1961 (Humane Letters); Rutgers, 1962 (Dr Letters); Union College, 1962 (DCL); Washington and Jefferson, 1962 (Dr Laws). Began as manuscript reader and book salesman with Horace Liveright, Inc., New York City, 1923; Associate Editor, Atlantic Monthly, 1924–28; Editor: Atlantic Monthly Press, 1928–37; Atlantic Monthly, 1938–66. Overseer, Harvard Coll., 1945–51. Henry Johnson Fisher Award, 1968; Irita Van Doren Award, 1970. *Publications:* This Trade of Writing, 1935; The Open Heart, 1955; In Friendly Candour, 1959; Breaking into Print, 1962; Boston, Cradle of Liberty, 1965; The Lowells and their Institute, 1966; Fresh Waters, 1968; The Moisie Salmon Club, a chronicle, 1971; My Green Age: a memoir, 1974; Myopia: 1875–1975, 1975; Writers and Friends, 1982; Editor: Great Short Novels (Anthology), 1941; Jubilee, One Hundred Years of the Atlantic (with Emily

Flint), 1957; The Miramichi Fish and Game Club, a history, 1984; contrib. essays, articles, and book reviews to magazines. *Recreations:* fishing, preferably with a light rod; golf; poker. *Address:* 59 Chestnut Street, Boston, Mass 02108, USA; 8 Arlington Street, Boston, Mass 02116, USA. *Cable address:* Lanticmon. *Clubs:* Tavern (Boston); Century (New York).                                    *Died* 11 *March* 1989.

**WEEKS, Maj.-Gen. Ernest Geoffrey,** CB 1946; CBE 1944; MC (and bar); MM (and bar); CD; retired; *b* Charlottetown, PEI, 30 May 1896; *s* of William Arthur and Fanny Weeks; *m* 1930, Vivian Rose Scott, Toronto, Canada; one *s*. *Educ:* Prince of Wales Coll., Charlottetown, PEI. Canadian Militia, 1910–14; European War, Belgium and France, 1915–19; Canadian Permanent Force from 1920; War of 1939–45, Italy; Maj.-Gen. i/c Administration Canadian Military, HQ, London, England, 1944–45; Adjutant-General Canadian Army, 1946–49; retired, 1949. *Recreations:* gardening, fishing. *Address:* 46 Prince Charles Drive, Charlottetown, PEI C1A 3C2, Canada.                                    *Died* 7 *Sept.* 1987.

**WEIDLEIN, Edward Ray,** MA, ScD, EngD, LLD; President Mellon Institute, 1921–56, retired; Technical Adviser of Rubber Reserve Company (now Synthetic Rubber Division of National Science Foundation), 1941–70; Director, Allegheny County Council West of the Boy Scouts of America; National Council of the Boy Scouts of America; Advisory Committee, Oakland Office, Mellon National Bank; President, Regional Industrial Develt Corp. Fund, 1962–71; registered professional engineer in Pa; *b* Augusta, Kansas, 14 July 1887; *s* of Edward Weidlein and Nettie Lemon; *m* 1915, Hazel Butts; three *s*. *Educ:* University of Kansas. Developed processes for the use of sulphur dioxide in hydrometallurgy; Chief of Chemicals Branch War Production Board, 1940–42; Senior Consultant of Chemical Division of War Production Board, Feb. 1942–Mar. 1946; Head Technical Consultant in War Production Board, Mar. 1942–Mar. 1946; Technical Adviser, R&D Div., Quartermaster Corps, US Army, 1943–46; Member: Special Cttee for examination of enemy raw materials and supplies under War Metallurgy Cttee of Nat. Research Council and Nat. Acad. of Sciences; Research Cttee in Co-operation with Chemical Warfare Service of American Chemical Society; Cttee on Co-operation with National Defense Research Cttee of Office of Sc. Research and Development; Studies, Reports, and Seminars Cttee of Army Ordn. Assoc.; Nat. Engineers Cttee of Engineers Jt Council; Exec. Cttees, Allegheny Conf. on Community Develt and Pittsburgh Regional Planning Assoc.; Board of Directors Western Pennsylvania Hosp.; Bd of Trustees, Rolling Rock Club; Trustee (emer.) Univ. of Pittsburgh and of Shadyside Academy, Pittsburgh. Member, leading chemical and scientific societies. Various awards have been obtained for distinguished service in his field; Edward R. Weidlein Professorship established, 1967, by Bd of Trustees, Univ. of Pittsburgh. Holds numerous hon. degrees in Science, Laws and Engineering. *Publications:* (joint) Science in Action; Glances at Industrial Research; many articles on industrial research. *Recreations:* golf, hunting and fishing. *Address:* Weidacres, PO Box 45, Rector, Pennsylvania 15677, USA. *Clubs:* University, Pitt Faculty, Pittsburgh Golf, Rolling Rock, Duquesne, Authors' (Pittsburgh); Chemists' (New York); Chemists' (Pittsburgh).

*Died* 15 *Aug.* 1983.

**WEINER, Prof. Joseph Sidney,** MA, DSc, FRCP, FFOM, FIBiol, FRAI, FSA; Director, Medical Research Council Environmental Physiology Unit, London School of Hygiene and Tropical Medicine, 1962–80; Professor of Environmental Physiology, University of London, 1965–80, now Professor Emeritus; *b* S Africa, 29 June 1915; *s* of Robert Weiner and Fanny Weiner (*née* Simon); *m* 1943, Marjorie Winifred Daw; one *s* one *d*. *Educ:* High Sch. for Boys, Pretoria; Univ. of Witwatersrand (MSc 1937); St George's Hosp. Med. Sch. (LRCP, MRCS 1947); Univ. of London (PhD 1946). Physiologist, Rand Mines Ltd, 1935–38; Demonstrator, Dept of Applied Physiology, London Sch., of Hygiene and Tropical Medicine, 1940; Mem., Scientific Staff, MRC, 1942; Reader in Physical Anthropology, Univ. of Oxford, 1945; Mem., Hertford Coll., Oxford; Hon. Dep. Dir, MRC Unit Dept of Human Anatomy, Oxford; Hon. Dep. Dir, MRC Unit Dept of Human Anatomy, Oxford, 1955. Chm., Ergonomics Res. Soc., 1961–63; Pres., Royal Anthropological Inst., 1963–64; world convener, Human Adaptability Section, Internat. Biol Programme, 1964–74; Pres., Section H (Anthropology), Brit. Assoc., 1966; Chm., Soc. for Study of Human Biology, 1968–71; Bureau Mem., Scientific Cttee on Problems of the Environment (ICSU), 1973; Cons. Physiologist to Sports Council, 1975–77. Vis. Fellow, Australian Acad. of Scis, 1971. Vernon Prize and Medal for Industrial Physiology, 1956; Rivers Meml Medal, RAI, 1969; Huxley Medal, RAI, 1978. *Publications:* (jtly) One Hundred Years of Anthropology, 1952; The Piltdown Forgery, 1955; (jtly) Human Biology, 1964; (jtly) The Taxonomic Status of the Swanscombe Skull, 1964; (ed and co-author) The Biology of Human Adaptability, 1966; (ed) Human Biology: a guide to field methods, 1969; The Natural History of Man, 1971; (ed jtly) Case Studies in Ergonomics, 1976, 1981; (jtly) Human Adaptability in the International Biological Programme,

1976; (ed) Physiological Variation and its Genetic Basis, 1977; (jtly, and ed jtly) Principles and Practice of Human Physiology, 1981; numerous papers on climatic physiology, human evolution and human biology. *Recreation:* gardening. *Address:* 20 Harbord Road, Oxford. *Club:* Athenæum.                                    *Died* 13 *June* 1982.

**WEIPERS, Prof. Sir William (Lee),** Kt 1966; Director of Veterinary Education, 1949–68, Dean of the Faculty of Veterinary Medicine, 1968–74, University of Glasgow Veterinary School, retired 1974; *b* 21 Jan. 1904; *s* of Rev. John Weipers, MA, BD and Evelyn Bovelle Lee; *m* 1939, Mary MacLean (*d* 1984); one *d*. *Educ:* Whitehill Higher Grade School, Dennistoun, Glasgow; Glasgow Veterinary College (MRCVS). General practice, 1925–27; on staff of Royal (Dick) Veterinary College, 1927–29. DVSM 1927; general practice, 1927–49. Dean of Faculties, Glasgow Univ., 1981–84. Member Council of Royal College of Veterinary Surgeons, 1949–74, President, 1963–64. BSc (Glasgow), 1951; FRSE 1953; FRCVS 1958. DUniv Stirling, 1978; Hon. DVMS Glasgow, 1982. Centennial Medal, Univ. of Pennsylvania Vet. Faculty, 1984. *Publications:* in professional papers. *Recreation:* tree culture. *Address:* Snab Cottage, Hardgate, Clydebank, Dunbartonshire G81 5QS. *T:* Duntocher (0389) 73216. *Club:* Royal Scottish Automobile.

*Died* 15 *Dec.* 1990.

**WEIR, Robert Hendry,** CB 1960; Engineering Consultant; *b* Glasgow, 18 Feb. 1912; *s* of Peter and Malcolmina Weir; *m* 1934, Edna Frances Lewis; three *s*. *Educ:* Allan Glen's Glasgow; Glasgow University (BSc Hons). Engineering Apprenticeship, Wm Denny & Bros, Dumbarton, 1928–33; Royal Aircraft Establishment, 1933–39; Air Ministry HQ, 1939–40; Aircraft and Armament Experimental Establishment, 1940–42; Ministry of Aircraft Production and Ministry of Supply, 1942–; Asst Director, 1948–50; Director of Industrial Gas Turbines, 1950–52; Director of Engine Research and Development, 1952–53; Deputy Director-General, Engine Research and Development, 1954–59 (Min. of Supply); Dir-Gen. of Engine Research and Development 1959–60 (Min. of Aviation); Dir, Nat. Gas Turbine Establishment, Pyestock, near Farnborough, 1960–70; Dir, Nat. Engineering Laboratory, East Kilbride, 1970–74. FRAeSoc. Coronation Medal, 1953. *Publications:* various. *Recreations:* golf, painting; keen interest in Association Football. *Address:* 11 Broom Cliff, 30 Castleton Drive, Newton Mearns, Glasgow G77 5LG. *T:* 041–639 5388.                                    *Died* 12 *Sept.* 1985.

**WEISS, Sir Eric,** Kt 1980; President, Foseco plc (formerly Foseco Minsep plc), since 1979 (Chairman, 1969–78); *b* 30 Dec. 1908; *s* of late Solomon Weiss and Ada Weiss; *m* 1934, Greta Kobaltzky; two *s* two *d*. *Educ:* Augustinus Gymnasium, Weiden, Germany; Neues Gym., Nurnberg, Germany. Founder, Foundry Services Ltd (original co. of Foseco Group), 1932; Chm., Minerals Separation Ltd, 1964; Chm., Foseco Minsep Ltd, 1969, when co. formed by merger of Foseco Ltd with Minerals Separation Ltd. Underwriting Mem., Lloyd's, 1976–79. United World Colleges: Dep. Pres., 1973–76; Mem., UK Commn of United World Colls Project, 1968–74; Mem., Internat. Council, 1969–76; Mem., Bd of Dirs, 1970–76; Mem. Bd Governors, United World Coll. of Atlantic, 1976–85. Mem., Inst. of British Foundrymen. Trustee, Oakham Sch., 1963–84. Eric Weiss Chair of Materials Science and Technology estabd, Birmingham Univ., 1988. *Recreations:* golf, travel. *Address:* Foseco plc, 1–6 Ely Place, EC1. *Club:* Garrick.

*Died* 26 *March* 1990.

**WEISS, Peter Ulrich;** writer, painter, film producer; *b* Germany, 8 Nov. 1916; *s* of Eugene and Frieda Weiss; *m* 1952, Gunilla Palmstierna. *Educ:* Art Academy, Prague. Left Germany, 1934, lived in England 1934–36, Czechoslovakia, 1936–38, Sweden since 1939. Awarded Charles Veillon prize for Literature, 1963, Lessing Prize, Hamburg, 1965, Heinrich Mann Prize, Academy of Arts, East Berlin, 1966, Thomas Dehler Prize, 1978. Illustrated Swedish edn of Thousand and One Nights, 1957. *Films:* Hallucinations, 1953; Faces in Shadow, 1956; The Mirage, 1958. *Plays:* The Persecution and Assassination of Marat, 1964 (filmed 1967); Mockinpott, 1964; The Investigation, 1965; The Song of the Lusitanian Bogey, 1966; Vietnam Discourse, 1967; The Song of the Scarecrow, 1968; Trotsky in Exile, 1970; The Trial (after Kafka's novel), 1975. *Publications:* The Shadow of the Coachman's Body, 1960; The Leavetaking, 1961; Point of Escape, 1962; The Conversation of the Three Walkers, 1963; Night with Guests (play), 1963; Vanishing Point (novel); Notes on the Cultural Life of the Democratic Republic of Vietnam, 1971; Notes on the Cultural Life of the Democratic Republic of Vietnam, 1971; Hölderlin, 1971; Die Aesthetik des Widerstands Roman, 3 vols, 1976–81. *Address:* Suhrkamp Verlag, Lindenstrasse 29–35, Frankfurt-am-Main, Germany.                                    *Died* 10 *May* 1982.

**WEITNAUER, Dr Albert;** *b* Brazil, 30 May 1916; *s* of Albert Weitnauer and Stephanie (*née* Hoeschl); unmarried. *Educ:* Basle Gymnasium; Basle Univ. (Dr of Laws). Entered Swiss Govt Service, 1941; Legal Adviser, later Dep. Head, Federal Office for War Economy, 1941–46; transf. to Commercial Div. Federal Dept of

Public Economy, 1946; Head of Section I, 1951; attached to Swiss Legation in London, 1953–54 and in Washington, 1954–58 as Counsellor i/c Econ. Affairs; Delegate of Swiss Govt for Trade Agreements and Special Missions, 1959–71; Minister, 1961; Ambassador, 1966; Ambassador to the Court of St James's, 1971–76; State Secretary for Foreign Affairs, 1976–80, retired. *Publications:* articles on problems of Swiss foreign policy, European integration and world trade. *Recreations:* writing, reading, study of languages. *Address:* Jubiläumsstrasse 97, 3005 Berne, Switzerland.
*Died 29 Dec.* 1984.

**WEITZMAN, David,** QC 1951; Barrister-at-Law; *b* 18 June 1898; *s* of Percy Weitzman; *m* 1st, 1925 (wife *d* 1950); one *s* one *d*; 2nd, 1945, Lena (*d* 1969), widow of Dr S. H. Dundon, Liverpool; 3rd, 1972, Vivienne Hammond. *Educ:* Hutchesons' Grammar School, Glasgow; Manchester Central School; Manchester University. Private, 3rd Battalion Manchester Regiment, 1916; BA (History Honours), 1921; called to Bar (Gray's Inn), 1922; member of Northern Circuit. Member of Labour Party since 1923. Contested (Lab) Stoke Newington, 1935; MP (Lab) Stoke Newington, 1945–50, Hackney North and Stoke Newington, 1950–79. *Recreation:* golf. *Address:* Devereux Chambers, Devereux Court, Temple, WC2R 3JJ. *T:* 01–353 7534. *Died 6 May* 1987.

**WELBORE KER, Keith Reginald;** *see* Ker.

**WELBY, Euphemia Violet,** CBE 1944; JP; late Superintendent Women's Royal Naval Service; *b* 28 Sept. 1891; *d* of Admiral H. Lyon, CB; *m* 1917, Lt-Comdr R. M. Welby (*d* 1929); two *s* one *d* (and one *d* decd). *Educ:* Private. Hon. Sec. SS&AFA Devonport, 1914–16; Red Cross Cook, Malta, 1916–19; later Hon. Sec. SS&AFA; served in WRNS, 1939–45; social work on committees in Plymouth and Chairman Astor Institute. JP Somerset, 1947. *Recreation:* riding. *Address:* College Farm, Tintinhull, near Yeovil BA22 8PQ. *T:* Martock 823536; Milton Lodge, Freshwater Bay, Isle of Wight. *T:* Isle of Wight 753139. *Died 6 May* 1987.

**WELDON, Brig. Hamilton Edward Crosdill,** CBE 1961 (OBE 1951); DL; Councillor, Waverley (Surrey) District Council, 1979–83; retired; *b* 14 September 1910; *s* of late Lt-Col Henry Walter Weldon, DSO, and Helen Louise Victoria Weldon (*née* Cowan); *m* 1st, 1935, Margaret Helen Katharine Passy (whom he divorced, 1946); one *d*; 2nd, 1948, Elwyne Priscilla Chaldecott; two *s* one *d*. *Educ:* Bilton Grange Preparatory School; Charterhouse; Royal Military Academy, Woolwich. Commissioned into RA as 2nd Lieut, 1930; Lieut 1933; Capt. 1938. Served War of 1939–45 (despatches, 1943, 1945): Adjutant, 1939–40; Bde Major, Malta, 1941; GSO1, RA Malta (Lt-Col), 1941–43. Staff Coll., Camberley, 1943–44; Lt-Col on Staff of SHAEF and 21 Army Group and various appointments in BAOR, 1944–47; AQMG (Lt-Col) HQ Southern Command, 1948; BAOR, 1951–52; Col on Staff of SHAPE, 1952–53; Command of 22 LAA Regt in Germany, 1953–55; Administrative Staff Coll., Greenlands, Henley, May-August 1955; Col at WO, 1955–58; Comdr, (Brig.) 33 AA Bde, 1958–60; Commandant, School of Artillery, Manorbier, 1960–62, retired. ADC to the Queen, 1961–62; Secretary, County of London T&AFA, 1962–68, Greater London TA&VRA, 1968–74. Croix-de-Guerre with Palm (Fr.), 1945. Hon. Col: 265 Light Air Defence Regt, RA (TA), 1965–67; London and Kent Regt, RA (T), 1967–69; London and Kent Regt RA Cadre, 1969–; a Dep. Hon. Col, 6th Bn Queen's Regt, T&AVR, 1971–72. Vice-Pres., Fedn of Old Comrades Assocs of London, 1963–; Pres., Windsor and District Gun Club, 1970–74; Chm., Nat. Canine Defence League, 1984– (Hon. Treas., 1975–84); Mem. Council, Nat. Artillery Assoc., 1976–; Regional Organiser, Army Benevolent Fund, 1975–79; Dir, Redgrave Theatre, Farnham, 1980–. DL Greater London, 1967–82. *Publications:* Drama in Malta, 1946; compiled Official Administrative History of 21 Army Group in NW Europe, 1945. *Recreations:* racing, shooting, theatre and writing. *Address:* 3 Burnt Hill Road, Wrecclesham, Farnham, Surrey GU10 4RU. *T:* Farnham 721783. *Died 17 May* 1985.

**WELFORD, Prof. Walter Thompson,** PhD, DSc; FRS 1980; Emeritus Professor of Physics, University of London, and Senior Research Fellow, Imperial College, University of London, since 1983; *b* 31 Aug. 1916; *s* of Abraham and Sonia Weinstein; *m* 1948, Jacqueline Joan Thompson (marr. diss. 1978); two *s*. *Educ:* LCC primary and technical schools; Univ. of London (BSc, PhD, DSc). Laboratory asst, 1933–42; R&D physicist in industry, 1943–48; Imperial College, 1948–; successively research asst, lectr, sen. lectr, reader; Professor, 1973–83. Director, IC Optical Systems Ltd, 1970–. Thomas Young Medal, Inst. of Physics, 1973. *Publications:* Geometrical Optics, 1963; (with L. C. Martin) Technical Optics, Vol. 1, 1966; Aberrations of the Symmetrical Optical System, 1974 (trans. Chinese 1982); Optics (Oxford Phys. Series No 14), 1976, 3rd edn 1988 (Japanese edn 1976); (with R. Winston) The Optics of Nonimaging Concentrators, 1978; Aberrations of Optical Systems, 1986; (with R. Winston) High Collection Nonimaging Optics, 1990; numerous contribs dealing with all aspects of applied optics to

learned jls. *Recreation:* surviving. *Address:* 8 Chiswick Road, W4 5RB. *T:* 081–995 2340. *Died 18 Sept.* 1990.

**WELHAM, David Richard;** a Group Managing Director and Director of Finance, Royal Dutch/Shell, since 1986; Director, Shell Transport & Trading Plc, since 1986; *b* 11 Sept. 1930; *s* of Leonard and Emma Welham; *m* 1953, Beryl Phyllis (*née* Coltman); two *s* one *d*. *Educ:* Selwyn Coll., Cambridge (MA). Joined Chief Inspector of Taxes Br. of Inland Revenue, 1953; Royal Dutch/Shell Gp of Companies, 1958–78: various appts in UK, Venezuela, Argentina, Japan; Managing Director: Shell Co. of Thailand, 1978; Shell Pet. Develt Co. of Nigeria, 1981; Gp Treas., Shell International, 1983. Order of White Elephant of Thailand, 1981. *Recreations:* music, golf, shooting, farm labouring. *Address:* Shell Centre, SE1 7NA. *T:* 01–934 3860. *Clubs:* United Oxford & Cambridge University, Oriental. *Died 27 Feb.* 1989.

**WELLES, (George) Orson;** Director, Mercury Productions (films, theatre, radio, play publishing); Columnist; *b* Kenosha, Wisc., 6 May 1915; *s* of Richard Head Welles, inventor-manufacturer, and Beatrice Ives, pianist; *m* Virginia Nicholson, Chicago (whom he divorced, 1940); one *d*; *m* Rita Hayworth (who obtained a divorce, 1947); one *d*; *m* 1955, Paola Mori; one *d*. *Educ:* Todd School, Woodstock, Ill. Directed eight productions a year at Todd School, also doing some scene sketching; studied drawing at Chicago Art Inst., 1931; appeared at Gate Theatre, Dublin, 1931, in Trilby, Jew Suss, and Hamlet; returned to America, 1932; trip to Africa; toured US with Katharine Cornell, 1933; went into radio work as an actor, 1934; produced for Federal Theatre Macbeth with negro cast, Doctor Faustus and Horse Eats Hat; later formed Mercury Theatre, which produced The Cradle Will Rock, Heartbreak House, Shoemakers' Holiday, Danton's Death, Caesar and Five Kings; also made a series of Columbia educational recordings of Shakespearean plays for schoolroom use; came to Hollywood, 1939; produced, directed, wrote, and acted in his first picture, Citizen Kane; wrote, directed, and produced film, The Magnificent Ambersons; co-author, producer, and actor in Journey Into Fear. Produced Native Son in New York, 1939; co-starred Jane Eyre, 1943; appeared in Follow the Boys, 1943; produced, directed, starred in Mercury Wonder Show, a magic show for Army and Navy personnel, 1943; co-starred in Tomorrow is Forever, 1945; wrote, produced, acted and directed, The Lady From Shanghai, 1946; wrote screenplay, produced, directed and acted in screenplay, Macbeth, 1947; acted in Cagliostro (screenplay made in Italy), 1947; produced, and acted name-part in Othello, St James's, 1951; acted in film, Three Cases of Murder, 1955; adapted, produced, and acted in play, Moby Dick, Duke of York's, 1955; wrote, directed, and acted in film, Confidential Report, 1955; produced and acted name-part in King Lear, New York, 1956; adapted, directed and acted in film, Othello, 1956; acted in films: The Long, Hot, Summer, 1958, Compulsion, 1959, Ferry to Hong Kong, 1959, David and Goliath, 1961, The VIP's, 1963; (produced and acted) The Trial, 1963; Oedipus The King, 1968, Catch 22, 1970; The Kremlin Letter, 1970; Ten Days' Wonder, 1972; F for Fake, 1976; Butterfly, 1982. Directed The Immortal Story, 1968, Southern Star, 1969 (films); adapted and acted in play, Chimes at Midnight, 1960 (filmed 1966). Prod play, Rhinoceros, Royal Court Theatre, London, 1960. Associate Editor of Free World Magazine. Fellow BFI, 1983. Special Oscar Award, 1971. Life Achievement Award, American Film Institute, 1975. *Publications:* Illustrated edns of Macbeth, Julius Cæsar, Twelfth Night, and the Merchant of Venice with editing, illustrations, and stage directions (Mercury Shakespeare); Mr Arkadin, 1957. *Recreations:* prestidigitating, cartooning, swimming, reading. *Clubs:* Advertising, Lotos (New York); National Variety (Los Angeles). *Died 10 Oct.* 1985.

**WELLINGTON, Sir (Reginald Everard) Lindsay,** Kt 1963; CBE 1944; Retired from BBC, 1963; *b* 10 August 1901; *s* of Hubert Lindsay Wellington and Nancy Charlotte Boughtwood; *m* 1st, 1928, Evelyn Mary Ramsay (marr. diss.); one *s* one *d*; 2nd, 1952, Margot Osborn. *Educ:* Queen Elizabeth Grammar School, Wakefield; The Queen's College, Oxford. BBC Programme Staff since 1924; Director Broadcasting Division, Ministry of Information, 1940–41; N American Director, BBC, 1941–44; Controller (Programmes), BBC, 1944–45; Controller BBC Home Service, 1945–52; Director of Sound Broadcasting, BBC, 1952–63. *Recreations:* reading, music. *Address:* Witheridge, near Henley-on-Thames, Oxon. *T:* Nettlebed 641214. *Club:* Savile. *Died 9 Jan.* 1985.

**WELLS, Charles Alexander,** CBE 1963; SPk (Sitara-i-Pakistan) 1961; FRCS; Emeritus Professor of Surgery, University of Liverpool; Hon. Surgeon Royal Liverpool United Hospital and Consultant to Royal Prince Alfred, Sydney, NSW, and other hospitals; FRSocMed (President, Section of Surgery and Past President Section of Urology); Corresponding member Société Franc. d'Urologie; *b* 9 Jan, 1898; *o s* of late Percy M. and late Frances L. Wells, Liverpool; *m* 1928, Joyce Mary Rivett Harrington (*d* 1980); two *s*. *Educ:* Merchant Taylors', Crosby; Liverpool University (MB, ChB, 1st Hons). Active service, RFA, 1916–18. Lately surgeon and urologist to various hospitals; Resident Surgical Officer Ancoats Hospital, Manchester; Demonstrator in Anatomy McGill University, Montreal; Clinical Assistant St Peter's Hospital, London. Mem. Council RCS (Vice-Pres., 1965–66, Bradshaw Lectr, 1966); Mem. Med. Adv. Council, ODM, and Chm. Recruitment Panel; Chairman: Merseyside Conf. for Overseas Students; Cttee on Surgical Educn, Internat. Fedn Surgical Colls. Ex-Council of British Association of Urological Surgeons (Home and Overseas); Past President Liverpool Medical Institution; Pakistan Health Reforms Commn, 1960; Adrian Committee (Ministry of Health) on Radiation Hazards, 1958–; Medical Research Council's Committee, Pressure Steam Sterilisation. Litchfield Lectr, Oxford, 1953; Luis Guerrero Meml Lectr, Santo Tomas Univ., Manila, 1957; McIlraith Guest Prof., Univ. of Sydney, 1957; Murat Willis Orator, Richmond, Va, 1963. Hon. FACS 1968. Hon. LLD (Panjab), 1960. *Publications:* Surgery for Nurses, 1938; Text Book of Urology (ed Winsbury-White); Treatment of Cancer in Clinical Practice, 1960; contrib. to textbooks and symposia, various chapters, Prostatectomy (monograph), 1952; (with J. Kyle) Peptic Ulceration, 1960; (ed with J. Kyle) Scientific Foundations of Surgery, 1967, 2nd edn, 1974; numerous articles in scientific jls. *Recreations:* shooting, painting in oils. *Died 9 Jan. 1989.*

**WELLS, Rear-Adm. David Charles,** CBE 1971; farmer and grazier; *b* Inverell, NSW, Australia, 19 Nov. 1918; *s* of C. V. T. Wells; *m* 1940, J. Moira A., *d* of Rear-Adm. C. J. Pope, CBE; two *s* two *d*. *Educ:* St Peter's Coll., Adelaide, SA. Joined RAN, 1933. Served War of 1939–45; Atlantic, Mediterranean, Arctic, Indian and Pacfic Oceans; HMAS Queenborough, 1953–56 (in comd); HMAS Cerberus, 1956–58; Dir of Plans, Navy Office, 1958–60; HMAS Voyager, 1960–62 (in comd); RN Exchange Service and Dep. Dir, RN Staff Coll., 1962–64; IDC 1965; HMAS Melbourne, 1965–66 (in comd); HMAS Albatross, 1967 (in comd); Rear-Adm. 1968; Flag Officer-in-Charge, E. Australia Area, 1968–70; Dep. Chief of Naval Staff, Australia, 1970–71; ANZUK Force Comdr, Malaysia/Singapore, 1971–73; Flag Officer Comdg HM's Aust. Fleet, 1974–75, retired. *Address:* Pine Ridge, Leadville, NSW 2831, Australia. *Died 27 Sept. 1983.*

**WELLS, Prof. George Philip,** ScD; FRS 1955; Emeritus Professor of Zoology in the University of London; *b* 17 July 1901; *er s* of Herbert George and Amy Catherine Wells; *m* 1927, Marjorie Stewart Craig (marr. diss., 1960); one *s* one *d*. *Educ:* Oundle; Trinity Coll., Cambridge. Temp. Asst, Dept of Zoology, University College, London, 1928; Lecturer, 1931; Reader, 1943; Professor, 1954–68. Hon. Associate, Dept of Zoology, British Museum (Natural History), 1953; Zoological Sec., Soc. for Experimental Biology, 1929–36, Hon. Member 1964; a Vice-Pres., Freshwater Biolog. Assoc., 1966–. *Publications:* (with H. G. Wells and Julian Huxley) The Science of Life, 1929–30 (in fortnightly parts); (various subseq. revisions); (ed) The Last Books of H. G. Wells, 1968; (ed) H. G. Wells in Love, 1984; many scientific papers and popular writings and broadcasts. *Club:* Savile. *Died 27 Sept. 1985.*

**WELLS, William Thomas;** QC 1955; *b* 10 Aug. 1908; *s* of late William Collins Wells (formerly of Clare Coll., Cambridge, and Bexhill-on-Sea) and Gertrude Wells; *m* 1936, Angela, 2nd *d* of late Robert Noble, formerly of HM Colonial Legal Service; two *s* two *d*. *Educ:* Lancing Coll.; Balliol Coll., Oxford (BA 1930; MA 1989). Joined Fabian Society, 1930; called to Bar, Middle Temple, 1932, Bencher 1963 (Emeritus 1986). QC Hong Kong, 1968. Dep. Chm., Hertfordshire QS, 1961–71; Recorder of King's Lynn, 1965–71; a Recorder of the Crown Court, 1972–80. Formerly Mem., Internat. Adv. Committee of Labour Party and of Political Committee and Local Government Committee of the Fabian Society. Army, 1940–45: a General Staff Officer, 2nd grade, Directorate of Military Training, War Office, with temp. rank of Major, 1942–45. MP (Lab) Walsall, 1945–55, Walsall North, 1955–Feb. 1974; Member: Lord Chancellor's Cttee on Practice and Procedure of Supreme Court, 1947–53; Magistrates Courts Rules Cttee, 1954–83; Chm.'s Panel, House of Commons, 1948–50; Departmental Cttee on Homosexual Offences and Prostitution, 1954–57; Chm., Legal and Judicial Gp (Parly Labour Party), 1964–70; a Chm. (part-time) of Industrial Tribunals, 1975–79. Governor: Bedford Coll., 1963–85; Polytechnic of North London, 1971–74 (formerly Northern Polytechnic, 1938–71). Hon. Freeman, Borough of Walsall, 1974. *Publications:* How English Law Works, 1947; contributor to journals, incl. the Tablet, and former contributor to The Fortnightly, Spectator, Times Literary Supplement, etc, mainly on legal, political and military subjects. *Address:* 2 Mais House, Sydenham Hill, SE26 6ND. *T:* 01–693 2758; 1 Gray's Inn Square, Gray's Inn, WC1R 5AA. *T:* 01–405 8946. *Club:* Athenæum. *Died 3 Jan. 1990.*

**WELSH, Brig. David,** CBE 1959; DSO 1944; late Royal Artillery; Retired; *b* 10 April 1908; *s* of late Capt. Tom Welsh, Earlshaugh, Peeblesshire; *m* 1947, Maud Elinor Mitchell (*d* 1977), *d* of late Major M. I. M. Campbell, MC, of Auchmannoch; one *s*. *Educ:* Winchester; RMA. Commissioned 2nd Lieut, RA, 1928. Served War of 1939–45 (DSO): with Royal Horse Artillery and Royal Artillery in France,

N Africa and Italy. Lt-Col, 1950; Brigadier, 1958; Brigadier, RA, FarELF, 1957–60; retd, 1961. *Address:* 27 Manor House Lane, Walkington, Beverley, North Humberside HU17 8SU. *Club:* Army and Navy. *Died 23 Nov. 1987.*

**WELSH, Prof. Harry Lambert,** OC 1971; FRS 1962; FRSC 1952; Professor of Physics, University of Toronto, 1954–78, then Emeritus Professor; *b* 23 March 1910, Canadian; *s* of Israel Welsh and Harriet Collingwood; *m* 1942, Marguerite Hazel Ostrander; no *c*. *Educ:* University of Toronto; University of Göttingen. Demonstrator in Physics, Univ. of Toronto, 1935–42; Asst Professor, 1942–48; Assoc. Professor, 1948–54; Chm., Dept of Physics, 1962–68; Chm., Research Bd, 1971–73. Lt-Comdr, RCNVR (Operational Research at Navy HQ, Ottawa), 1944–45. Pres., Canadian Assoc. of Physicists, 1973; Medal of Cdn Assoc. of Physicists, 1961; Tory Medal, Royal Society of Canada, 1963. Hon. DSc: Univ. of Windsor, Ont., 1964; Memorial Univ., St Johns's, Newfoundland, 1968. Meggers Medal, Optical Soc. of America, 1974. *Publications:* many papers on infra-red and Raman spectroscopy and high-pressure physics in various scientific jls. *Recreation:* music. *Address:* 8 Tally Lane, Willowdale, Ontario M2K 1V4, Canada. *Died 23 July 1984.*

**WELSH, Dame (Ruth) Mary (Eldridge),** DBE 1946; TD 1976; Legion of Merit, USA; *b* 2 Aug. 1896; *d* of late Dr William Dalzell; *m* 1922, Air Marshal Sir William Welsh, KCB, DSC, AFC (marr. diss. 1947; he *d* 1962); one *s*. Director WAAF, 1943–46. Air Chief Comdt, WRAF. *Address:* 3 Webb House, The Bury, Odiham, Hampshire. *Died 25 June 1986.*

**WENBAN-SMITH, Charlotte Susanna;** *see* Rycroft, C. S.

**WENGER, Marjorie Lawson;** *b* 10 Sept. 1910; *d* of late Rev. W. J. L. and Mrs A. M, Wenger. *Educ:* Walthamstow Hall, Sevonoaks, Kent. Nursing training, The Middlesex Hospital, 1930–34, SRN 1933; Midwifery training, SCM, 1935; Ward Sister, Night Sister; Sister Tutor, 1940–47. Editor, Nursing Times (Journal of the Royal College of Nursing), 1948–60; Editor, International Nursing Review (Jl of the International Council of Nurses), 1960–65. *Recreations:* reading, theatre, travel. *Address:* 6 Concord Close, Paddock Wood, Tonbridge, Kent TN12 6UJ. *T:* Paddock Wood 2699. *Died 19 June 1981.*

**WERNHAM, Prof. Archibald Garden,** MA Aberdeen, BA Oxford; Regius Professor of Moral Philosophy in the University of Aberdeen, 1960–81; *b* 4 March 1916; *e s* of Archibald Garden Wernham and Christina Noble; *m* 1944, Hilda Frances Clayton; two *s*. *Educ:* Robert Gordon's College, Aberdeen; Aberdeen University; Balliol College, Oxford. 1st Class Hons Classics, Aberdeen, 1938, Croom Robertson Fellow, Aberdeen, 1939; 1st Cl. Hons Classical Mods, Oxford, 1939, 1st Cl. Lit. Hum., Oxford, 1943. Served in RA, 1940–42. Lecturer in Moral and Political Philosophy, St Andrews Univ., 1945–53; Sen. Lecturer, 1953–59; Reader, 1959–60. *Publications:* Benedict de Spinoza-The Political Works, 1958; reviews and articles. *Recreations:* music, swimming, walking. *Address:* Ardil, Gladstone Place, Dyce, Aberdeen. *T:* Aberdeen 722489. *Died 7 May 1989.*

**WEST, Anthony Panther;** author; *b* Hunstanton, Norfolk, 4 Aug. 1914; *s* of H. G. Wells and Rebecca West; *m* 1936, Katharine Church; one *s* one *d*; *m* 1952, Lily Dulany Emmet; one *s* one *d*. *Educ:* in England. Became a breeder of registered Guernsey cattle and a dairy farmer, 1937. During war was with BBC's Far Eastern Desk, Home News Div., 1943–45, and then with their Japanese Service, 1945–47. Went to USA and joined staff of the New Yorker Magazine, 1950. Houghton Mifflin Fellow, 1947. *Publications:* Another Kind, (USA) 1949, (UK) 1951; One Dark Night, (UK) 1949, (as Vintage, USA, 1950); D. H. Lawrence (a critical biography), (UK) 1951, 2nd edn 1966; Gloucestershire, (UK) 1952; The Crusades, (USA) 1954 (as All About the Crusades, UK, 1967); Heritage, (USA) 1955 (repr. with new introduction, 1984); Principals and Persuasions, (USA) 1957, (UK) 1958, new edn 1970; The Trend Is Up, (USA) 1960; Elizabethan England, (USA) 1966, (UK) 1966; David Rees Among Others, (USA) 1970, (UK) 1970; Mortal Wounds, (USA) 1973, (UK) 1975; H. G. Wells: aspects of a life, 1984. *Address:* Box 122, Fisher's Island, NY 06390, USA. *Died 27 Dec. 1987.*

**WEST, Air Commodore Ferdinand (Maurice Felix),** VC 1918; CBE 1945; MC; *b* London, 29 Jan. 1896; *s* of late Francis West and late Countess De la Garde de Saignes; *m* 1922, Winifred (*d* 1988), *d* of John Leslie; one *s*. *Educ:* Xaverian Coll., Brighton; Lycée Berchet; Univ. of Genoa. 2nd Lieutenant, Lieutenant, and Acting Captain in the Royal Munster Fusiliers, 1914–17; attached to the Flying Corps, 1917–18; transferred to the Royal Air Force as a Captain, 1919 (wounded three times, MC, VC, despatches twice, Cavaliere Crown of Italy); Commanded 4 Squadron, RAF, Farnborough, 1933–36; Air Attaché, British Legations, Helsingfors, Riga, Tallin, Kovno, 1936–38; Commanded: RAF Station, Odiham, 1938–39; No 50 Wing in France, 1939; Air Attaché, British Embassy, Rome, 1940; Air Attaché, British Legation, Berne, 1940; retired from

RAF, 1946. Man. Dir, J. Arthur Rank Overseas Film Distributors, 1947–58. Retired as Chairman: Hurst Park Syndicate, 1963–71; Continental Shipyard Agencies Ltd; Technical Equipment Supplies Ltd; Dir, Tokalon Ltd, 1963–73; Terravia Trading Services. Comdr Order of Orange Nassau, 1949; Chevalier Legion of Honour, 1958. First Class Army Interpreter (Italian) Second Class (French). *Address:* Zoar, Devenish Road, Sunningdale, Berks. *T:* Ascot 20579. *Club:* Royal Air Force. *Died* 7 *July* 1988.

**WEST, Mary, (Mrs James West);** *see* McCarthy, M.

**WEST, Dame Rebecca,** DBE 1959 (CBE 1949); CLit 1968; *b* 21 Dec. 1892; Cicily Isabel, *y d* of late Charles Fairfield, Co. Kerry; *m* 1930, Henry Maxwell Andrews (*d* 1968). *Educ:* George Watson's Ladies' College, Edinburgh. Joined Staff of Freewoman as reviewer, 1911; joined staff of The Clarion as political writer, 1912; has since contributed to many leading English and American newspapers as literary critic and political writer. Appeared in Warren Beatty's film, Reds, as one of the Witnesses, 1982. Fellow, Saybrook Coll., Yale Univ. Member American Academy of Arts and Sciences. Hon. DLitt: New York Univ., 1965; Edinburgh Univ., 1980. Benson Medal (RSL), 1966. Order of Saint Sava, 1937; Chevalier of the Legion of Honour, 1957. *Publications:* Henry James, 1916; The Return of the Soldier, 1918; The Judge, 1922; The Strange Necessity, 1928; Lions and Lambs (pseudonym Lynx in collaboration with Low); Harriet Hume, 1929; D. H. Lawrence, an Elegy, 1930; Ending in Earnest, 1931 (published in America only); St Augustine, 1933; The Rake's Progress (in collaboration with Low), 1934; The Harsh Voice, 1935; The Thinking Reed, 1936; Black Lamb and Grey Falcon (a book about Yugoslavia), 1942; The Meaning of Treason, 1949; A Train of Powder, 1955; The Court and the Castle, 1958; The Vassall Affair, 1963; The New Meaning of Treason, 1964; The Birds Fall Down, 1966; Rebecca West: A Celebration, 1977; 1900, 1982; The Young Rebecca: writings 1911–1917 (selected by Jane Marcus), 1982; trilogy: The Fountain Overflows, 1957; This Real Night (posthumously published), 1984; Cousin Rosamund (unfinished; posthumously published), 1985; *posthumous publication:* Family Memories (ed Faith Evans), 1987. *Address:* c/o Messrs Macmillan, 4 Little Essex Street, WC2R 3LF.
*Died* 15 *March* 1983.

**WESTALL, Gen. Sir John Chaddesley,** KCB 1954 (CB 1952); CBE 1951; *b* 2 July 1901; *s* of late John Chaddesley Westall, Hawkes Bay, NZ; *m* 1st, 1930, Maud Marion Bushe (*d* 1971); two *s* one *d*; 2nd, 1977, Mrs Margaret Boyle. *Educ:* Dulwich College. Entered Royal Marines, Oct. 1919; Capt. 1930; Major 1939; Naval Staff College, 1938. Served War of 1939–45: Malaya, India and Burma; promoted Bt Lt-Col for War Service, 1944. Staff Officer Intelligence, South Africa, 1947. Comd Royal Marine Barracks, Plymouth, 1949; Comd Royal Marines, Deal, 1950; Maj.-Gen. 1951; Chief of Staff, Royal Marines, 1951; Commandant General, Royal Marines, 1952–55; retired, 1955. Col Comdt, Royal Marines, 1961–64. *Recreations:* fishing, shooting. *Address:* 95 Rugby Street, Christchurch, New Zealand. *Died* 30 *Sept.* 1986.

**WESTALL, Rt. Rev. Wilfrid Arthur Edmund;** an Assistant Bishop, Diocese of Exeter; *b* 20 Nov. 1900; *s* of Rev. A. St Leger and Jessie Margaret Westall; *m* 1927, Ruth, *d* of Frank and Beatrice Evans; one *s* three *d*. *Educ:* Merchant Taylors' Sch.; St Chad's Coll., Durham Univ. (BA). Priest, 1925; Asst Curate, St Aidan's, Birmingham, 1925–27, of the Church of the Good Shepherd, Brighton, 1927–30; Vicar of St Wilfrid's, Brighton, 1930–41; Rector of Hawnby-with-Old Byland, Yorks, 1941–45; Vicar of Shaldon, Devon, 1945–51; Archdeacon of Exeter and Canon Residentiary of Exeter Cathedral, 1951–58. Prebendary of Exeter Cathedral, 1951–60; Bishop Suffragan of Crediton, 1954–74. Proctor in Convocation, 1949–64; Select Preacher to Oxford Univ., 1967; Vice-Pres., Additional Curates' Soc.; Fellow, Corp. of St Mary & St Nicholas (Woodard Schs); Pres., Exeter Civic Soc. Hon. DD Exeter, 1971. *Recreations:* sketching, railways and travel. *Address:* Ford House, Broadclyst, Exeter, Devon. *Died* 22 *Feb.* 1982.

**WESTBURY, (Rose) Marjorie;** singer and actress; *b* 18 June 1905; *o d* of George and Adella Westbury, Langley, near Birmingham. Won 4 year scholarship to RCM, London, 1927. Sang Gretel at Old Vic as operatic debut for Lilian Baylis, 1932. Began broadcasting (as singer), 1933; joined BBC Drama Repertory, 1942; Solveig in Peer Gynt; Ylena (Lorca); Miles and Flora in Turn of the Screw; Nora in The Doll's House; Elsa Strauss in the Henry Reed series (Emily Butter); Steve Temple in Paul Temple series; Susan Grantly in Barchester Chronicles. *Recreations:* gardening, cooking, sewing, croquet. *Address:* Copperdene, Budletts, Maresfield, E Sussex TN22 2EB. *T:* Uckfield 2806. *Died* 16 *Dec.* 1989.

**WESTCOTT, George Foss,** MA, MIMechE; freelance, since 1957; *b* 6 Feb. 1893; *e s* of Rev. Arthur Westcott, 2nd *s* of Brooke Foss Westcott, Bishop of Durham; *m* 1938, Anne Esther Anderberg; two *d*. *Educ:* Sherborne; GNR Locomotive Works, Doncaster (Premium Apprentice); Queens' College, Cambridge (Exhibitioner). Served in

European War, 1914–19, in ASC (MT) and RFC; Hons Mechanical Science Tripos, 1920; worked for Scientific and Industrial Research Department, 1920; Assistant at Science Museum, 1921; Keeper of Mechanical Engineering Collections, 1937; on loan to Admiralty Engineering Lab., 1939–41; Emergency Commn in RASC, 1941–42; Science Museum, 1942; Keeper of Dept of Land And Water Transport, 1950; retired 1953; re-engaged as Asst Keeper, 1953; finally retired from Civil Service, 1957; worked for Intercontinental Marketing Services Ltd, 1963; Reader, Acad. of Visual Arts, 1964; founded Basic Ideology Research Unit, 1967. Kt Internat., Mark Twain Soc., 1977. *Publications:* Science Museum Handbooks; Pumping Machinery, 1932; Mechanical and Electrical Engineering, 1955 (new edn, revised by H. P. Spratt, 1960); The British Railway Locomotive, 1803–1853, 1958; various Historical Synopses of Events Charts, 1922–56; The Conflict of Ideas, 1967; Christianity, Freethinking and Sex, 1968; Towards Intellectual Freedom: the development of a basic ideology, 1972, rev. edn 1974; The Science of Man, 1975, rev. edn 1984. *Recreations:* sociological research, reading, writing. *Died* 7 *Feb.* 1987.

**WESTERN, Prof. John Henry,** BSc, PhD (Wales); Emeritus Professor of Agricultural Botany, University of Leeds, since 1971; *b* Ide, Devon, 29 Sept. 1906; *s* of late Henry Toogood and Emma Western, Dawlish, Devon; *m* 1940, Rachel Elizabeth Harries; one *s*. *Educ:* University College of Wales, Aberystwyth; University of Minnesota, USA. Research on diseases of pasture plants, Welsh Plant Breeding Station, Aberystwyth, 1937–39; Lecturer and Adviser in Agricultural Botany and Mycology, University of Manchester, 1939–46; Provincial Plant Pathologist, Ministry of Agriculture and Fisheries, Newcastle upon Tyne, 1946–50; Senior Lecturer in Agricultural Botany, 1951–59, Prof., 1959–71, Dept of Agricultural Sciences, University of Leeds. Pres., Assoc. Applied Biologists, 1964–65. *Publications:* papers on mycology, plant pathology and agricultural botany in various scientific journals. *Address:* Westhide, North Drive, Bramhope, near Leeds.
*Died* 8 *July* 1981.

**WESTMINSTER, Viola Dowager Duchess of; Viola Maud Grosvenor;** Lord Lieutenant of Co. Fermanagh, Northern Ireland, 1979–86; *b* 10 June 1912; *d* of 9th Viscount Cobham, KCB, TD, and Violet Yolande (*d* 1966), *y d* of Charles Leonard; *m* 1946, Lt-Col Robert George Grosvenor, later 5th Duke of Westminster (*d* 1979); one *s* two *d*. *Educ:* privately. Served War in WAAF, 1939–46 (despatches). President for Co. Fermanagh: Girl Guides Assoc., NSPCC, Salvation Army, British Legion (Women's Sect.), SJAB. Pres., Show Cttee, Ulster Farming Soc. Member Governing Body, Royal Acad. of Music. Nat. Vice-Pres., Women's Section, British Legion, Ulster, 1954–68. Former President of societies in Chester: Music Soc., Male Voice Choir, Operatic Soc., Ladies' Choir, BRCS, CPRE, Marriage Guidance Council, LEPRA. Dame of Justice, Order of St John of Jerusalem, 1983 (Dame of Grace 1980). *Recreations:* music, trees, books. *Address:* Ely Island, Enniskillen, Co. Fermanagh, N Ireland. *T:* Springfield 224. *Died* 3 *May* 1987.

**WESTOBY, Jack Cecil,** CMG 1975; retired, 1974; *b* 10 Dec. 1912; *s* of John William Westoby and Rose Ellen Miles; *m* 1941, Florence May Jackson; two *s*. *Educ:* Wheeler Street Council Sch., Hull; Hymers Coll., Hull; University Coll., Hull, BScEcon (London); FSS; FIS. Railway clerk, LNER, 1936–45; Statistician, BoT, 1945–52. Food and Agriculture Organisation of United Nations: Economist/Statistician, 1952–58; Chief, Forest Economics Br., 1958–62; Dep. Dir, Forestry Div., 1962–69; Dir of Program Co-ordination and Ops, Forestry Dept, 1970–74. Regents' Prof., Univ. of California, 1972. Foreign Member: Royal Agriculture and Forestry Acad. of Sweden, 1968; Italian Acad. of Forest Science, 1971; Finnish Forestry Soc., 1964; Soc. of Amer. Foresters, 1971; Hon. Life Mem., Commonwealth Forestry Soc. *Publications:* The Purpose of Forests: follies of development, 1987; many studies and articles in official publications of FAO and in a wide variety of professional forestry jls. *Recreations:* music, theatre. *Address:* Calcioli, Via Collegalle 12, 50022 Greve-in-Chianti (FI), Italy. *T:* (055) 854.044. *Died* 11 *Sept.* 1988.

**WESTON, Ronald,** CB 1987; Commissioner of Customs and Excise, 1983–88; *b* 17 Feb. 1929; *s* of late Arthur and Edna Weston; *m* 1953, Brenda Vera Townshend; two *s* one *d*. *Educ:* Swanwick Hall Grammar Sch., Derbyshire. Officer of Customs and Excise, 1952; Principal, 1972; Asst Secretary, Collector of Customs and Excise, Birmingham, 1977; Deputy Director, then Director, Outfield, 1982–88. *Recreations:* choral music, walking. *Address:* Alphin Heights, 133 Manchester Road, Greenfield, Oldham, Lancs OL3 7HJ. *T:* Saddleworth 2176. *Club:* Saddleworth Golf.
*Died* 27 *April* 1990.

**WETHERALL, Rev. Canon Theodore Sumner;** *b* 31 May 1910; *s* of late Rev. A. S. Wetherall and Mrs G. V. M. Wetherall (*née* Bennett-Powell); *m* 1939, Caroline, 4th *d* of Dr Charles Milne; one *s* three *d*. *Educ:* St Edward's School, Oxford; Oriel College, Oxford. Exhibitioner at Oriel College, 1929; 1st Class Classical Mods, 1931;

BA (2nd Class Lit. Hum.), 1933. Preparatory Schoolmaster, Wellesley House, Broadstairs, 1933–35; MA 1936; Liddon Student, 1936; Cuddesdon College, 1936–37; Asst Curate, St John's, Greengates, Bradford, 1937–39; Fellow and Chaplain, Corpus Christi College, Oxford, 1939–47, Dean, 1940–45, Vice-Pres., 1947; Principal of St Chad's College, Durham, 1948–65. Vicar of St Edward the Confessor, Barnsley, 1965–69; Vicar of Huddersfield, 1969–76. Select Preacher to the Univ. of Oxford, 1945–47; Chaplain in the Univ. of Oxford to Bishop of Derby, 1940–47, Examining Chaplain to Bishop of Oxford, 1946–47, to Bishop of Durham, 1948–65, to Bishop of Bradford, 1949–55; to Bishop of Wakefield, 1969–76; Surrogate for Marriages, 1969–76; Rural Dean of Huddersfield, 1969–76. Hon. Canon: Durham, 1958–65, Wakefield, 1970–76; Hon. Canon Emeritus, Wakefield, 1976–. *Address:* 4 Great Ostry, Shepton Mallet, Somerset BA4 5TT. *T:* Shepton Mallet (0749) 346325.                        *Died 19 Oct. 1990.*

**WEYER, Deryk Vander,** CBE 1986; FCIB, CBIM; Director: Bank of England, 1986–88 (Member, Board of Banking Supervision, 1986); Barclays Bank PLC, 1974–88; *b* 21 Jan. 1925; *s* of Clement Vander Weyer and Harriet Weyer; *m* 1950, Marguerite (*née* Warden); one *s* one *d*. *Educ:* Bridlington Sch. FIB 1972; CBIM (FBIM 1976). Joined Barclays Bank PLC, 1941: Asst Manager, Liverpool, 1956; Man., Chester Br., 1961; Local Dir, Liverpool, 1965; Asst Gen. Man., 1968; Gen. Man., 1969; Sen. Gen. Man., 1973; Vice-Chm., 1977–80; Chm., Barclays Merchant Bank Ltd, 1977–80; Dir, Barclays Bank Internat., 1977–83; Gp Dep. Chm., Barclays Bank, 1980–83; Chm., Barclays Bank UK, 1980–83. Pres., Institute of Bankers, 1979–81. Mem., Royal Commn on Distribn of Income and Wealth, 1977–79; part-time Dir, British Telecom. Corp., 1981–83; Dep. Chm., British Telecom, 1983–86. Chm., Bd of Companions, BIM, 1981–86. Governor, Museum of London, 1978–83. *Recreations:* painting, music. *Address:* 1 Gatefield Cottages, High Road, Chipstead, Surrey CR3 3QR.             *Died 16 June 1990.*

**WHARNCLIFFE, 4th Earl of,** *cr* 1876; **Alan James Montagu-Stuart-Wortley-Mackenzie;** Viscount Carlton, 1876; Baron Wharncliffe, 1826; *b* 23 March 1935; *o s* of 3rd Earl and late Lady Elfrida Wentworth Fitzwilliam, *d* of 7th Earl Fitzwilliam; *S* father 1953; *m* 1957, Aline Margaret, *d* of late R. F. D. Bruce, Wharncliffe Side, near Sheffield; one *d* (and one *d* decd). *Educ:* Eton. Joined RNVR, 1952; National Service, RN, 1953–55; RNSR, 1955–59. *Recreation:* shooting. *Heir: cousin* Alan Ralph Montagu-Scott-Wortley [*b* 27 July 1927; *m* 1952, Virginia Anne, *d* of W. Martin Claybaugh; two *s* one *d*]. *Address:* Wharncliffe House, Wortley, Sheffield S30 4DG. *T:* Sheffield 882331. *Clubs:* Lansdowne; Sheffield (Sheffield).                        *Died 3 June 1987.*

**WHATELEY, Dame Leslie Violet Lucy Evelyn Mary,** DBE 1946 (CBE 1943); TD 1951; *b* 28 Jan. 1899; *d* of late Ada Lilian Hutton and late Col Evelyn F. M. Wood, CB, DSO, OBE; *m* 1st, 1922, W. J. Balfour; one *s*; 2nd, 1939, H. Raymond Whateley, Squadron-Leader, RAFVR. *Educ:* Convents of Society of HCJ, St Leonards-on-Sea and Cavendish Square. Private Secretary up to marriage, and then Social Welfare Work, including District Nursing Associations and Village Institutes. Director of Auxiliary Territorial Service, 1943–46; Hon. Col 668 (bn) HAA Regt RA (TA), 1948–53. Director World Bureau of Girl Guides/Girl Scouts, 1951–64; Administrator of Voluntary Services, Queen Mary's Hosp., Roehampton, 1965–74. Chevalier Légion d'Honneur, 1945; Order of Merit (USA), 1946. *Publications:* As Thoughts Survive, 1949; Yesterday, Today and Tomorrow, 1974. *Recreations:* gardening, writing. *Address:* c/o Lloyds Bank, 6 Pall Mall, SW1.                      *Died 4 July 1987.*

**WHEATCROFT, Edward Lewis Elam,** MA, FIMechE, FIEE; *b* 17 July 1896; *s* of late W. H. Wheatcroft, LLD, Cambridge; *m* Ethel Margaret, *d* of late Dr A. E. L. Wear, Harrogate; three *d*. *Educ:* Oundle; Cambridge. Switchboard Engineer with the British Thomson-Houston Co.; Calculation Engineer with the Commonwealth Power Corporation of Michigan; Professor of Electrical Engineering at Leeds University, 1926–40; Member of Council: of IEE, 1934–36, 1948–51 and 1954–57; of Hydromechanics Research Association, 1950. Freeman of City of London; Liveryman, Worshipful Co. of Makers of Playing Cards. *Publications:* Gaseous Electrical Conductors, 1938; papers in Phil. Mag., Proceedings of IEE, etc. *Recreation:* motoring. *Address:* 3 Regent Road, Surbiton, Surrey KT5 8NN.

                              *Died 27 March 1982.*

**WHEATCROFT, George Shorrock Ashcombe;** Professor of English Law, University of London, 1959–68, later Professor Emeritus; First Editor, British Tax Review, 1956–71, later Consulting Editor; first Editor of British Tax Encyclopedia, 1962–71, later Consulting Editor; Consulting Editor, Encyclopedia of Value Added Tax; Vice-Chairman, Hambro Life Assurance Ltd, 1971–79; Chairman, G. S. A. & M. Wheatcroft (Advisory Services) Ltd; Adviser to HM Customs and Excise on Value Added Tax, 1971–72; *b* 29 Oct. 1905; *s* of Hubert Ashcombe Wheatcroft and Jane (*née* Eccles); *m* 1930,

Mildred Susan (*d* 1978), *d* of late Canon Walter Lock, DD, formerly Warden of Keble College, Oxford; two *s* one *d*. *Educ:* Rugby; New College, Oxford (MA). Qualified as Solicitor, 1929; partner in Corbin Greener and Cook, Solicitors, of 52 Bedford Row, London, 1930–51; Master of the Supreme Court (Chancery Division), 1951–59. Served as an officer in RASC, 1940–45; released in 1945 with hon. rank of Lt-Col (despatches twice). Mem., Payne Cttee on enforcement of civil debts. Past President British Chess Federation. Consulting Editor, Hambro Tax Guide, 1972–. Hon. Fellow: LSE, 1976; UC Buckingham, 1978. Hon. LLD Buckingham, 1979. *Publications:* The Taxation of Gifts and Settlements, 1953 (3rd edn 1958); The Law of Income Tax, Surtax and Profits Tax, 1962; Estate and Gift Taxation, 1965; Capital Gains Tax, 1965; Wheatcroft on Capital Gains Taxes (with A. E. W. Park), 1967; Corporation Tax (with J. E. Talbot), 1968; Sweet & Maxwell's Guide to the Estate Duty Statutes, 1969 (2nd edn 1972); Whiteman and Wheatcroft on Income Tax and Surtax, 1971; (with G. D. Hewson) Capital Transfer Tax, 1975; titles Discovery, Execution, Judgments and Orders and Practice and Procedure in Halsbury's Laws of England (3rd edn); articles on taxation and legal procedure in periodicals. *Recreations:* golf, bridge, chess (represented England at Stockholm in 1937). *Address:* Brackenhill, Gravel Path, The Common, Berkhamsted, Herts HP4 2PJ. *Club:* Reform.

                           *Died 2 Dec. 1987.*

**WHEATLEY, Baron** *cr* 1970 (Life Peer), of Shettleston, Glasgow; **John Wheatley,** PC 1947; one of the Senators of the College of Justice in Scotland, 1954–85; Lord Justice-Clerk, 1972–85; *b* 17 Jan. 1908; *s* of Patrick Wheatley and Janet Murphy; *m* 1935, Agnes Nichol; four *s* one *d*. *Educ:* St Aloysius Coll., Glasgow; Mount St Mary's Coll., Sheffield; Glasgow Univ. MA 1928; LLB 1930; called to Scottish Bar, 1932; Advocate-Depute, 1945–47 MP (Lab) East Edinburgh, 1947–54; Solicitor-General for Scotland, March-Oct. 1947; QC (Scotland) 1947; Lord Advocate, 1947–51. War of 1939–45, RA (Field) and later with Judge Advocate-General's Branch; Chm. Scottish Nurses' Salaries Cttee, 1945–47; Chm. Milk Enquiry in Scotland, 1946–47; Chm., Cttee on Teaching Profession (Scotland), 1961–63; Mem., Royal Commn on Penal Reform (England and Wales), 1964–66; Chairman: Exec. Cttee Royal Scottish Soc. for Prevention of Cruelty to Children, 1956–79; Royal Commn on Local Govt in Scotland, 1966–69; conducted enquiry into crowd safety at sports grounds, 1971–72. Hon. President: Age Concern (Scotland); Internat. Year of Shelter for the Homeless (Scotland), 1987. Hon. LLD Glasgow, 1963; DUniv Stirling, 1976; Hon. FEIS. GCSG 1987. *Recreation:* golf. *Address:* 3 Greenhill Gardens, Edinburgh EH10 4BN. *T:* 031–229 4783.

                         *Died 28 July 1988.*

**WHEATLEY, Maj.-Gen. (Percival) Ross,** DSO 1943; late RAMC, retired; *b* Westbury, Wilts, 4 May 1909; *s* of late Rev. Percival Wheatley, Congregational Minister, and late Margaret Lettice Wheatley (*née* Wallis); *m* 1939, Dorothy Joan Fellows (*née* Brock); one *s*. *Educ:* St Dunstan's Coll., Catford; Guy's Hosp. Med. School. MB, BS (London), MRCS, LRCP, 1933; FRCS 1940. Commissioned Lieut RAMC, 1939; BEF as Surgical Specialist, Sept. 1939; 2nd in comd 16 Para. Field Ambulance, 1942, comdg, 1943; N Africa, 1942; Sicily and Italy, 1943; ADMS, 2nd Indian Airborne Div., 1944–46; Surgical Specialist, 1946–60: Catterick, Hamburg, Singapore, Japan, Millbank; seconded to Ghana Army, Surgical Specialist, 1960–61; Consultant Surgeon: FARELF, 1963–66; BAOR, 1966–67; Dir of Army Surgery and Consulting Surgeon to the Army, 1967–69. Surgeon, P&O Lines Ltd, 1969–77. FRSocMed; Senior Fellow: Brit. Orthopædic Assoc.; Assoc. of Surgeons of Great Britain and Ireland. QHS 1967–69. *Publication:* contrib. to Basic Surgery. *Recreation:* philately. *Address:* Sherwood, High Park Avenue, East Horsley, Surrey. *T:* East Horsley 2151. *Club:* Army and Navy.                      *Died 20 Jan. 1988.*

**WHEELER, Lt-Comdr Sir (Ernest) Richard,** KCVO 1981 (CVO 1969; LVO 1965); MBE 1943; RN retd; Clerk of the Council and Keeper of Records, Duchy of Lancaster, 1970–81; *b* 21 July 1917; *s* of late Rev. Harold W. Wheeler, Burton Bradstock and Weston Turville, and Margaret Laura Wheeler; *m* 1st, 1939, Yvonne Burns (*d* 1973); one *d*; 2nd, 1974, Auriel Clifford. *Educ:* Marlborough Coll.; HMS Frobisher. Paymaster Cadet, RN, 1935; Lieut 1939; served: HM Ships Devonshire, Emerald, Office of C-in-C Med., 1940–42; Sec. to Chief of Staff, C-in-C Med., 1942–43; HMS Daedalus and Admty, 1944–47; Lt-Comdr 1947; retd (invalided), 1949. Asst Bursar, Epsom Coll., 1949–52; Chief Clerk, Duchy of Lancaster, 1952–70. *Address:* 40 The Street, Marden, Devizes, Wilts SN10 3RQ. *Club:* Army and Navy.                      *Died 9 Dec. 1990.*

**WHEELER, Geoffrey,** CB 1952; *b* 22 Nov. 1909; *s* of late A. E. Wheeler; *m* 1937, Dorothy Mary Wallis; one *s* one *d*. *Educ:* Clay Cross School, Derbyshire; St John's Coll., Cambridge (Scholar). First Class Part I Historical Tripos, 1930; First Class Part II Historical Tripos, 1931. Entered Civil Service, 1932, and appointed to Board of Customs and Excise; Private Sec. to Sir Evelyn Murray, 1936; Principal, 1937; Assistant Secretary, 1943; Under-Secretary

(Ministry of Defence), 1948; Under-Secretary: Min. of Aviation, 1964–67; Min. of Technology (Principal Estabt Officer), 1967–70; Min. of Aviation Supply, 1970–71; Asst Under Sec. of State (Personnel), Procurement Exec., MoD, 1971–72; Asst Dir, Civil Service Selection Bd, 1972–76. Pres., Groupe Statut EEC, 1977. Chm., London Derbyshire Soc., 1973–. *Recreations:* music; amateur theatre. *Address:* 57 Hillcrest Road, Purley, Surrey. *T:* 01–660 2858.                                           *Died* 27 *June* 1987.

**WHEELER, Lt-Col Geoffrey Edleston,** CIE 1943; CBE 1948; Hon. MA University of Durham, 1955; Director of Central Asian Research Centre, 1953–68; *b* 22 June 1897; *s* of late Capt. Owen Wheeler, Leicestershire Regiment; *m* 1927, Irena Nicolaevna Boulatoff (*d* 1973); one *s*. *Educ:* Eastbourne Coll. Commissioned Queen's Regt 1915; served in France, 1915–17; transferred to Indian Army, 1918, 6th Gurkha Rifles; various Intelligence appointments in Turkey, Malta, and Palestine to 1925; Military Attaché, Meshed, 1926; Intelligence duties in Iraq, 1928–31; 7th Rajput Regt to 1936; General Staff, Army HQ, India, 1936–41; Director, Publications Division, Govt of India, 1941–46; Counsellor, British Embassy, Teheran, 1946–50. Sir Percy Sykes Memorial Medal, RCAS, 1967. *Publications:* Racial Problems in Soviet Muslim Asia; The Modern History of Soviet Central Asia; The Peoples of Soviet Central Asia. *Address:* c/o Lloyds Bank, 4 Station Approach, Tadworth, Surrey.
                                           *Died* 1 *Feb.* 1990.

**WHEELER, Maj.-Gen. Norman;** *see* Wheeler, Maj.-Gen. T. N. S.

**WHEELER, Sir Richard;** *see* Wheeler, Sir E. R.

**WHEELER, Maj.-Gen. (Thomas) Norman (Samuel),** CB 1967; CBE 1964 (OBE 1958); *b* 16 June 1915; *e s* of late Thomas Henry Wheeler, S African Police; *m* 1939, Helen Clifford, *y d* of F. H. E. Webber, Emsworth, Hants; one *s* one *d*. *Educ:* South Africa; St Helen's College, Southsea; RMC Sandhurst. Commissioned Royal Ulster Rifles, 1935; Palestine Rebellion, 1937–39 (despatches). Served War of 1939–45 (despatches twice): Bde Major, 38 Irish Bde, 1941–42; MEF, 1942–43; British Military Mission to Albania, 1943–44; 2nd Bn Royal Ulster Rifles, 1944–45. AA & QMG 6th Airborne Div., 1945–46; Airborne Establishment, 1946–47; Mil. Asst to Adj.-Gen. to the Forces, 1949–50; UK Services Liaison Staff, Australia, 1951–52; GSO1 and Col GS, HQ Northern Army Group and HQ, BAOR, 1954–57; comd 1st Bn Royal Ulster Rifles Cyprus Rebellion, 1958–59 (despatches); comd 39 Inf. Bde Group, N Ireland, 1960–62; Chief of Staff 1st (British) Corps, BAOR, 1962–63; General Officer Commanding Second Division, 1964–66; Chief of Staff, Contingencies Planning, SHAPE, 1966–69; Chief of Staff, HQ, BAOR, 1969–71; retired, 1971. Dir and Sec., Independent Stores Assoc., 1971–76; Dep. Man. Dir, Associated Independent Stores Ltd, 1976–80; Chairman: J. E. Beale Ltd, 1980–83; John Elmes Beale Trust Co. Ltd, 1983–88. Independent Mem., Cinematograph Films Council, 1980–83. *Recreation:* travel. *Address:* Glebe House, Liston, Sudbury, Suffolk. *Clubs:* Army and Navy, Airborne, Special Forces.                                  *Died* 21 *Sept.* 1990.

**WHEEN, Rear-Adm. Charles Kerr Thorneycroft,** CB 1966; *b* 28 Sept. 1912; *s* of late F. T. Wheen, Holmbury, Chislehurst, Kent; *m* 1940, Veryan Rosamond, *d* of late William Acworth, Chobham; three *s* one *d*. *Educ:* RN College, Dartmouth. Entered RN as Cadet, 1926. Served War of 1939–45: China, The Nore, Admiralty, Normandy Landings, East Indies. Naval Attaché, Beirut, Amman and Addis Ababa, 1958–60; Director of Officers' Appointments (S), Admiralty, 1960–63; Flag Officer Admiralty Interview Board, 1964–66. Capt. 1956; Rear-Adm. 1964; retd 1966. Dir, Cement Makers Federation, 1967–79. Chm., Bd of Governors, Gordon Boys School, 1971–85. *Recreations:* golf, fishing. *Address:* Willow House, Philpot Lane, Chobham, Surrey GU24 8HD. *T:* Chobham 8118.
                                           *Died* 4 *Oct.* 1989.

**WHELAN, Air Cdre James Roger,** CBE 1968; DSO 1944; DFC 1940 (Bar 1943); RAF retired; *b* Saskatoon, Sask, Canada, 29 April 1914; *s* of James P. Whelan; *m* 1946, Irene, *d* of late P. Rennie, Bathurst, NB, Canada; two *d*. *Educ:* Bathurst High School; Univ. of St Francis Xavier, Antigonish, NS, Canada. Commissioned RAF, 1937. Served War of 1939–45: France, Egypt, Germany, Italy. Commanded RAF St Eval, 1957–58; Base Comdr, Christmas Island, 1959; Dir of Intelligence (B), Air Min., 1961–64; AO i/c A, HQ Coastal Command, 1965–68. RAF Staff Coll., 1949; jssc, 1952; idc, 1960. *Recreation:* photography. *Address:* 26 Laburnum Court, Dennis Lane, Stanmore, Mddx. *T:* 01–954 2255. *Club:* Royal Air Force.                                  *Died* 8 *March* 1985.

**WHELAN, Prof. Robert Ford,** MD, PhD, DSc; FRCP, FRACP, FACE, FAA; Vice-Chancellor, University of Liverpool, since 1977; *b* Belfast, NI, 22 Dec. 1922; *s* of Robert Henry Whelan and Dorothy Ivy Whelan; *m* 1951, Helen Elizabeth Macdonald Hepburn; two *s* one *d*. *Educ:* QUB (MB, BCh, BAO 1946; MD 1951; PhD 1955; DSc 1960). MD Adelaide, 1958. FRACP 1962; FAA 1966; FACE 1974; FRCP 1980. RMO, Belfast City Hosp., 1947; Sen. Ship's Surg., Glen Line, Alfred Holt & Co., Far East and Australia, 1948;

Jun. Lectr and Asst Lectr in Physiol., QUB, 1949–51; Res. Fellow, Sherrington Sch. of Physiol., St Thomas's Hosp. Med. Sch., 1951–52; Lectr in Physiol., QUB and NI Hosps Authority, 1952–57; Univ. of Adelaide: Prof. and Head of Dept of Human Physiol. and Pharmacol., 1958–71; Associate Dean, Faculty of Med., 1960 and 1961, Dean, 1964 and 1965; Mem., Educn Cttee, 1963–66, Chm., 1971; Hon. Cons. Physiologist, Royal Adelaide Hosp., 1959–71; Vice-Chancellor, Univ. of Western Australia, 1971–76. Member: EEC Adv. Cttee on Medical Trng, 1978–; Review Body on Higher Educn in N Ireland, 1979–81; Chm., Council for Postgraduate Medical Educn in England and Wales, 1980–; Vice-Chm., Cttee of Vice-Chancellors and Principals, 1981–82; Mem. Council, ACU, 1981– (Vice-Chm., 1984–). Vis. Prof., Sherrington Sch. of Physiol., St Thomas's Hosp. Med. Sch., 1962; Carnegie Trav. Fellow, USA, 1962; Vis. Prof., Dept. of Physiol., Univ. of Southern Calif, 1962; Vis. Lectr, Univ. of Queensland, 1964; (jtly) Demonstration, Royal Soc. Conversazione, 1966; Edward Stirling Lectr, Postgrad. Cttee, Univ. of Adelaide, 1967; Vis. Prof. of Physiol., Univ. of Singapore, 1970; Howard Florey Meml Lectr, Adelaide, 1984. Aust. Delegate, Internat. Congress of Pharmacology: Basle, 1969; San Francisco, 1972; Chm., Aust. Nat. Cttee, Internat. Union of Pharmacologists, 1968–75. Mem. Council, (new) Flinders Univ. of SA, 1966–71; Mem. Bd of Dirs, Walter and Eliza Hall Inst. for Med. Res., 1968–71; Mem. Bd of Governors: Collegiate Sch. of St Peter, Adelaide, 1967–71; Walford Sch. for Girls, Adelaide, 1969–71. Fellow: Royal Acad. of Med. in Ireland, 1953; Royal Soc. of SA, 1959. Member: Brit. Physiol Soc., 1951; Med. Res. Soc., 1953; Pharmacol Soc., 1956; Med. Sciences Club of SA, 1958 (Vice Pres. 1961, Pres. 1963); Extraord. Mem., Cardiac Soc. of Aust. and NZ, 1960; Foundn Mem. and Mem. Council, Aust. Physiol Soc., 1960. Hon. Member: Royal Adelaide Hosp. Med. Officers' Assoc., 1962; Aust. Soc. of Clin. and Expmtl Pharmacol., 1971 (first Pres., 1966); Aust. Physiol and Pharmacol Soc., 1972. Freeman: Apothecaries' Soc., 1981; City of London, 1982. *Publications:* Control of the Peripheral Circulation in Man, 1967; pubns in med. and sci. jls. *Address:* The Vice-Chancellor's Lodge, Sefton Park Road, Liverpool L8 3SL. *Club:* Athenæum.                        *Died* 21 *Nov.* 1984.

**WHELDON, Sir Huw (Pyrs),** Kt 1976; OBE 1952; MC 1944; broadcaster; Consultant, Personnel and Electronics, since 1977; Deputy Chairman: National Video Corporation, since 1981; Dumbarton Films (formerly Video Arts Television), since 1983; *b* 7 May 1916; *e s* of late Sir Wynn Wheldon KBE, DSO, LLD; *m* Jacqueline Mary (*née* Clarke); one *s* two *d*. *Educ:* Friars Sch., Bangor, Wales; London Sch. of Economics, BSc(Econ), 1938. Kent Educn Cttee staff, 1939. Commnd Royal Welch Fusiliers, 1940; served NW Europe and Middle East with 1st and 6th Airborne Divs (Major, 1st Bn Roy. Ulster Rifles), 1941–45. Arts Council Dir for Wales, 1946; Festival of Britain Directorate, 1949; BBC Television, 1952–77; producer, director, commentator, author; credits include: All Your Own, Opera for Everybody, Men in Battle, Portraits of Power, Orson Welles Sketchbook, 1952–57; Monitor, magazine of the arts, 1958–64; Royal Heritage, 1977; Destination D-Day, 1984. Head of Documentary Programmes, 1962; Head of Music and Documentary Programmes, 1963–65; Controller of Programmes, 1965–68; Man. Dir, BBC TV, 1968–75; Special Adviser, BBC, 1975–76. Consultant, NBC of America, 1977–83; Special Adviser, Aspen Inst., 1977–. Richard Dimbleby Lecture, 1976. Pres., RTS, 1979–85. Trustee, Nat. Portrait Gall., 1976–; Governor: Nat. Film Sch., 1974–82; LSE, 1975– (Chm., 1975–85); Mem. bd of trustees, Royal Botanic Gardens, Kew, 1983–. Member: Youth Develt Council, 1959–62; Design Council, 1970–75; Council, Royal Coll. of Art, 1974–; Council, Brunel Univ., 1973–; Hon. Soc. of Cymmrodorion, 1950–. FRSA 1965. Fellow, BAFTA, 1978; Hon. Fellow: LSE, 1973; Manchester Coll. of Art, 1969; British Kinematograph Soc., 1975; RCA 1980. Hon. DLitt: Ulster, 1975; London, 1984; Loughborough, 1985; Hon. LLD Wales, 1978; DUniv Open, 1980. Gold Medal, Royal TV Soc., 1976 and 1978; International Emmy, 1981. *Address:* 120 Richmond Hill, Richmond, Surrey. *T:* 01–940 8119. *Clubs:* Garrick, Savile.
                                           *Died* 14 *March* 1986.

**WHELER, Captain Sir Trevor Wood,** 13th Bt, *cr* 1660; late Captain Royal Sussex Regiment, TF, 1914–20, and Royal Engineers, 1940–47; *b* 20 Sept. 1889; *s* of Lt-Col Sir Edward Wheler, 12th Bt, 1st Bn Royal Sussex Regt, and Mary Leontine, *d* of Sir Richard Wood, GCMG; *S* father, 1903; *m* 1915, Margaret Idris, *y d* of late Sir Ernest Birch, KCMG; one *s* two *d*. Served War of 1914–18, 6th Bn, Royal Sussex Regt; Waziristan, NW Frontier, 1917; attached IA, 1918–20. A principal Game Farmer between the wars, and Pres., Gamefarmers' Assoc., throughout that period. War of 1939–45: Home Guard (LDV), 1940; recalled Army 1940; RE (Movement Control), Scottish Comd, and BAOR, 1940–46. CCG, 1947–50; served in Kenya Police Reserve throughout Mau Mau Emergency, 1953 (General Service Medal). *Heir: s* Edward Woodford Wheler, late Captain Royal Sussex Regt [*b* 13 June 1920; *m* 1945, Molly Ashworth, *e d* of Thomas Lever, Devon; one *s* one *d*]. *Address:* 25 Cavendish Road, Chesham, Bucks.
                                           *Died* 14 *Jan.* 1986.

**WHITAKER, Charles Kenneth;** Controller, Newcastle Central Office, Department of Health and Social Security, 1974–79, retired; *b* Snaith, 15 May 1919; *o s* of late Charles Henry Whitaker and Elsie (*née* Austwick); *m* 1972, Dorothy (*née* Grimster). *Educ:* Drax Grammar School. Served with Cameronians (Scottish Rifles), 1939–46. Entered Min. of Health, 1936; Finance Officer and Dep. Sec., Public Health Laboratory Service Bd, 1960–65; Head of Health Services Superannuation Div., 1966–74; Controller, Blackpool Central Office, 1972–74. *Recreation:* walking. *Address:* The Gables, 19 Leamington Road, Blackpool, Lancs. *T:* Blackpool 24600.
*Died 5 March* 1981.

**WHITAKER, (Edgar) Haddon,** OBE 1972; Managing Director since 1948, and Chairman since 1950, J. Whitaker & Sons, Ltd; *b* 30 Aug. 1908; *e s* of Leonard Edgar Whitaker and Olave Cox; *m* 1930, Mollie Marian, *y d* of George and Louisa Seely; one *s* two *d*. *Educ:* Lancing Coll.; Brentwood Sch.; St John's Coll., Cambridge (MA). Joined family firm of publishers, J. Whitaker & Sons, Ltd; Dir, 1938. *Recreations:* gardening, reading. *Address:* Rosings, Parkmead, Roehampton, SW15 5BS. *Clubs:* Garrick, Leander, MCC, Roehampton. *Died 5 Jan.* 1982.

**WHITAKER, Frank Howard,** CMG 1969; OBE 1946; Secretary of the Metrication Board, 1969–74; *b* 9 Jan. 1909; *er s* of late Frank Harold Whitaker and late Edith Whitaker, Bradford; *m* 1937, Marjorie Firth (*d* 1984); no *c*. *Educ:* Thornton Grammar Sch.; Leeds University. LLB (1st cl. hons) 1929; Solicitor (1st cl. hons, D. Reardon and Wakefield and Bradford Prizeman), 1931. Legal Practice until 1939. Royal Air Force, 1940–46 (Sqdn Leader). Entered Civil Service as Principal, Board of Trade, 1946; Asst Sec., 1955; Export Credits Guarantee Dept, 1957, Under-Secretary, 1966. *Recreation:* mountaineering. *Address:* Tavistock, The Rowans, Gerrards Cross, Bucks. *Died 3 Aug.* 1987.

**WHITAKER, Haddon;** *see* Whitaker, E. H.

**WHITBREAD, Major Simon;** Lord-Lieutenant and Custos Rotulorum for Bedfordshire, 1957–78; *b* 12 Oct. 1904; *s* of late Samuel Howard Whitbread, CB, JP, Southill, Biggleswade, Beds; *m* 1936, Helen Beatrice Margaret, *d* of Hon. Robert Trefusis, 27 Coleherne Court, SW7; one *s* one *d*. *Educ:* Eton; Trinity College, Cambridge. Joined KRRC, 1925; Captain, 1937; retired, 1937. Re-employed War of 1939–45, served in Africa and Italy (despatches). Dir, Whitbread & Co. Ltd, 1939–80; Gov. and mem. Bd of Management, Middlesex Hosp., 1937–79; Mem., General Nursing Council for England and Wales, 1958–65. DL 1946, JP 1939. County Councillor, 1938, CA 1949, Chm. CC 1967, Beds; High Sheriff of Beds, 1947. Pres., E Anglia TA&AFA, 1973–78. Hon. Col 286 Field Regt RA (TA) (The Hertfordshire and Bedfordshire Yeomanry), 1965–67. KStJ 1977 (OStJ 1941). *Recreations:* shooting and fishing. *Address:* The Mallowry, Riseley, Bedford. *T:* Riseley 248.
*Died 24 Aug.* 1985.

**WHITBY, Harry,** CB 1965; Government-appointed Member, Potato Marketing Board, 1972–79; *b* 19 June 1910; *er s* of Edward Whitby, Hatfield, Herts, and Sarah Alice (*née* Booth); *m* 1937, Ruby Josephine, *yr d* of Charles J. Dyer, East Runton, Norfolk; two *s* two *d*. *Educ:* Ardingly College, Sussex; University of Manitoba. Student Asst, Agricultural Economics Research Institute, Univ. of Oxford, 1933–36; Asst to Advisory Officer in Agricultural Economics, Dept of Agriculture, Univ. of Leeds, 1936–38; Economist, Min. of Agriculture and Fisheries, 1938–47; Adviser on Farm Economics, 1947–50, Asst Sec. 1950–58, Under-Sec., 1958–68, Sec., 1968–71, Dept of Agriculture and Fisheries for Scotland. *Recreations:* gardening, cricket. *Address:* Cutlers Cottage, East Runton, Cromer, Norfolk. *Died 20 Aug.* 1984.

**WHITCOMBE, Maj.-Gen. Philip Sidney,** CB 1944; OBE 1941; JP; *b* 3 Oct. 1893; *e s* of late Rt Rev. Robert Henry Whitcombe, DD, Bishop of Colchester; *m* 1919, Madeline Leila Brydges (*d* 1977), *d* of Canon Arthur Symonds, Over Tabley, Knutsford; one *s* (and one *s* decd). *Educ:* Winchester. Gazetted to ASC from Durham LI (Spec. Res.), June 1914; served with BEF in France and Flanders, Aug. 1914–18; DAD Transport, 1918–19; psc 1926; Bde Major, Madras, 1928–32; Bt Major, 1933; DAAG, N Comd, York, 1934–36; GSO 2 War Office, 1936–38; Bt Lt-Col 1939; served in France as ADS and T 1939–40 (despatches); AA and QMG 1940–41 (OBE); Gibraltar, Brig. i/c Admin., 1941–42; Col 1942; DA and QMG, BTNI, 1942–43; MGA Eastern Command, 1943–47; retired, 1947. Freeman of Shrewsbury, 1924. JP for Wilts, 1948. *Recreations:* cricket, fishing. Played cricket for Essex, 1922, the Army, 1925, and Berkshire, 1925–32. *Address:* The Grange, Lake, Amesbury, Wilts. *T:* Amesbury 23175. *Clubs:* Army and Navy, MCC.
*Died 9 Aug.* 1989.

**WHITE, Hon. Sir Alfred (John),** Kt 1971; Tasmanian Agent-General in London, 1959–71; *b* 2 Feb. 1902; British; *m* 1939, Veronica Louisa Punch; two *s* two *d*. Elected to Tasmanian Parliament, 1941; Minister for Health and Chief Secretary, 1946–48, then Chief Secretary and Minister for Labour and Industry, Shipping and Emergency Supplies until Jan. 1959. JP since 1934, and Territorial JP for the State of Tasmania in London, 1959. Appointed Agent-General for Tasmania in London for period of 3 years, Jan. 1959, re-appointed for a further period of 3 years, Jan. 1962; re-appointed 1967; re-appointed 1970; resigned 1971 and retired. Australian delegate to ILO, Geneva, 1974 and 1975. Granted title of "Honourable" for life. *Recreations:* ski-ing, gardening, bowls and fishing. *Address:* 6 Clarke Avenue, Battery Point, Hobart, Tasmania 7000, Australia. *Died* 1987.

**WHITE, Amber B.;** *see* Blanco White.

**WHITE, Brig. Arthur W.;** *see* Walmesley White.

**WHITE, Sir Bruce Gordon,** KBE 1944 (CBE 1943; MBE 1919); FCGI; FICE; FIMechE; FIEE; Senior Partner, Sir Bruce White, Wolfe Barry & Partners, Chartered Civil and Consulting Engineers; *b* 5 Feb. 1885; *m* 1912, Margery Gertrude (*d* 1965), *d* of C. W. Hodson, CSI; one *s* one *d*. *Educ:* Marlborough. Served European War, 1914–18 (MBE); War of 1939–45 as Brig. Director of Ports and IWT, War Office (KBE). *Publication:* The Artificial Invasion Harbours called Mulberry: a personal story by Sir Bruce White, KBE, 1980. *Address:* Reydon, Midway, Walton-on-Thames, Surrey. *Died 29 Sept.* 1983.

**WHITE, Maj.-Gen. Cecil Meadows Frith,** CB 1945; CBE 1943 (OBE 1941); DSO 1940; late Royal Signals; retired; Colonel Commandant, Royal Corps of Signals, 1950–60; *b* 29 Aug. 1897; *s* of late Herbert Meadows Frith White and late Annie Laura Borrett; *m* 1925, Elizabeth Rennie Robertson; one *d*. *Educ:* Eton College; RMA, Woolwich. Commissioned RFA 1915; served 1915–19 in Egypt, Serbia, Greece, and Palestine (despatches); transferred to Royal Signals, 1925; Brigade Major Signal Training Centre, 1934–36; Lt-Col 1939; served War of 1939–45 (despatches five times, DSO, OBE, CBE, CB); commanded 4th Indian Divisional Signals in Wavell's advance in Western Desert, 1940; CSO East Africa during East Africa Campaign, 1941; CSO 8th Army, 1941; Temp. Brig. 1941; Col 1943; acting Maj.-Gen. Jan. 1944 as SO in C 21 Army Group; Temp. Maj.-Gen. 1945; Maj.-Gen. 1949; CSO, GHQ, MELF, Nov. 1945–July 1949; GOC Catterick District, 1949–51; retired, 1951. Deputy Controller, Civil Defence, Southdown Group, 1958. Civil Defence Officer, County Borough of Brighton, 1960–65. *Recreations:* fishing, gardening; formerly polo and rugger, show-jumping, hunting, sailing. *Address:* Hansdown House, Maesbury, Wells, Somerset BA5 3HA. *TA* and *T:* Oakhill 840498.
*Died 15 July* 1985.

**WHITE, Sir Dennis (Charles),** KBE 1962 (OBE 1953); CMG 1959; Brunei Government Agent in the United Kingdom, since 1967; *b* 30 July 1910; unmarried. *Educ:* Bradfield College. Joined service of HH the Rajah of Sarawak, 1932. Civilian Prisoner of War, Dec. 1941–Sept. 1945. HM Overseas Civil Service: Senior Resident, 1955; British Resident, Brunei, 1958; HM High Comr for Brunei, 1959–63. Star of Sarawak (Officer) 1946. Esteemed Family Order of Brunei, 1st Class. *Recreations:* general. *Address:* Virginia Cottage, Emery Down, Lyndhurst, Hants. *Club:* Travellers'.
*Died 17 Oct.* 1983.

**WHITE, Prof. Edwin George,** PhD, DSc, BSc (Vet. Sci.), BSc (Physiol.), FRCVS; William Prescott Professor of Veterinary Preventive Medicine, University of Liverpool, 1950–76, now Emeritus; Pro-Vice-Chancellor, 1966–70; *b* 26 March 1911; *s* of Edwin White and Alice Maud White; *m* 1st, 1936, Grace Mary Adlington; two *d* (and one *d* decd); 2nd, 1974, Winefred Wright. *Educ:* Newport (Mon.) High School; Royal Veterinary College, London (Kitchener Scholarship); University College, London. Studentship for Research in Animal Health, 1933–35, for postgraduate study in Germany and England; Lecturer in Pathology, Royal Veterinary College, London, 1935; Reader in Pathology, 1939; Principal Scientific Officer, Rowett Research Inst., Bucksburn, Aberdeenshire, 1946; Director of East African Veterinary Research Organisation, 1947–49; Dean of Faculty of Vet. Sci., Univ. of Liverpool, 1965–66. Pres., RCVS, 1967–68. Chm., Granada Schs Adv. Cttee. *Publications:* articles in various scientific journals since 1934. *Recreation:* gardening. *Address:* Afton, Neston Road, Burton, South Wirral, Cheshire L64 5SY. *T:* 051–336 4210. *Club:* Royal Commonwealth Society. *Died 3 Nov.* 1988.

**WHITE, Elwyn Brooks;** formerly contributor to The New Yorker, retired; *b* 11 July 1899; *s* of Samuel T. White and Jessie Hart; *m* 1929, Katharine Sergeant Angell; one *s*. *Educ:* Cornell University, USA. Newspaper reporting, advertising, and editorial work as staff member of New Yorker Magazine, to which he has contributed verse, satirical essays, and editorials; wrote a monthly department for Harper's Magazine called One Man's Meat, 1938–43. Hon. degrees: Dartmouth Coll.; Univs of Maine, Yale, Bowdoin, Hamilton, Harvard, Colby. Fellow, Amer. Acad. of Arts and Sciences; Mem., AAAL, 1974. Gold Medal Nat. Inst. of Arts and Letters, 1960; Presidential Medal of Freedom, 1963; Laura Ingalls Wilder Award, 1970; Nat. Medal for Literature, 1971; Pulitzer

Special Citation, 1978. *Publications:* The Lady is Cold, 1929; (with J. Thurber) Is Sex Necessary, 1929; Every Day is Saturday, 1934; The Fox of Peapack, 1938; Quo Vadimus?, 1939; One Man's Meat, 1942 (enlarged) 1944; Stuart Little, 1945; The Wild Flag, 1946; Here Is New York, 1949; Charlotte's Web, 1952; The Second Tree from the Corner, 1954; The Points of My Compass, 1962; The Trumpet of the Swan, 1970; Letters of E. B. White, 1976; Essays of E. B. White, 1977; Poems and Sketches of E. B. White, 1981; (ed, with Katharine S. White) A Subtreasury of American Humor, 1941; rev. and enl. Strunk, The Elements of Style, 1959. *Address:* North Brooklin, Maine, USA. *Died 1 Oct.* 1985.

**WHITE, Sir Ernest (Keith),** Kt 1969; CBE 1967; MC; Chairman, R. J. White & Co. (Sydney) Pty Ltd, since 1935; *b* 1892; *s* of late Robert John White; *m* 1915, Pauline Marjory, *d* of J. J. Mason; one *s* two *d. Educ:* Gosford Public Sch., NSW. Served European War, 1914–18 (Sir Douglas Haig's despatches, MC): Captain 4th Bn AIF, in Egypt and France (Ypres, Somme, Broodsiend Ridge, Bullecourt, Sttrozeel). Pres., Liberal Democratic Party, Australia, 1943; Delegate to Prelim. and Plenary Conf. which founded Liberal Party of Australia, and apptd to Provisional State and Federal Council, 1943. Vice-Pres., Australian American Assoc. (Founder and 1st Federal Pres., 1936). *Address:* Baden House, Baden Road, Kurraba Point, Neutral Bay, NSW 2089, Australia. *T:* 90 5741. *Clubs:* Royal Commonwealth Society; Tattersall's Australian Jockey; American National. *Died Aug.* 1983.

**WHITE, Errol Ivor,** CBE 1960; DSc, PhD (London); FRS 1956; FGS, FLS, FKC; Hon. Research Fellow, Department of Geology, University of Reading, since 1981; retired as Keeper of Department of Palaeontology (formerly of Geology), British Museum (Natural History), 1955–66 (Deputy Keeper, 1938–55); *b* 1901; *y s* of late Felix E. White and Lilian Daniels; *m* 1st, 1933, Barbara Gladwyn Christian (marr. diss. 1946, she *d* 1969); 2nd, 1944, Margaret Clare (Jane), BCom (Leeds), *y d* of late T. C. Fawcett, Bolton Abbey, Yorks; one *s. Educ:* Highgate School (Senior Foundationer); King's Coll., London Univ. (Tennant Prizeman). BSc 1921; PhD 1927; DSc 1936. Entered British Museum (Natural History), 1922; Geological Expeditions to Madagascar, 1929–30, and Spitsbergen, 1939; temp. Principal, Min. of Health, 1940–April 1945; Hon. Sec. Ray Society, 1946–51, Vice-Pres., 1951–54, 1959–, Pres., 1956–59; Council, Geological Soc., 1949–53, 1956–60; Vice-Pres., 1957–60 (Murchison Medal, 1962); President, Linnean Soc., 1964–67 (Linnean Gold Medal, 1970); Chm. Systematics Assoc., 1955–58; Coun., Zool. Soc., 1959–63. *Publications:* Technical memoirs and papers in various scientific jls, chiefly relating to extinct agnatha and fishes. *Recreations:* ornithology, philately, bridge. *Address:* 19 Clevemede, Goring-on-Thames, Reading RG8 9BU. *T:* Goring-on-Thames 872525. *Died 11 Jan.* 1985.

**WHITE, Gabriel Ernest Edward Francis,** CBE 1963; painter, etcher; Director of Art, Arts Council of Great Britain, 1958–70; *b* 29 Nov. 1902; *s* of late Ernest Arthur White and Alice White; *m* 1st, 1928, Elizabeth Grace (*d* 1958), *d* of late Auguste Ardizzone; two *s*; 2nd, 1963, Jane, *d* of late J. R. Kingdon and of Mrs Kingdon, Minehead; one *s* one *d. Educ:* Downside Sch.; Trinity Coll., Oxford. Staff Officer RE Camouflage, 1940–45; Asst Art Director, Arts Council of Great Britain, 1945–58. Order of the Aztec Eagle, 2nd class (Mexico). *Publications:* Sickert Drawings (in Art and Technics), 1952; Ardizzone, 1979; (illustrator) Rivers of Britain series, 1985–86. *Address:* 88 Holmdene Avenue, SE24. *T:* 01–274 9643. *Died 13 Jan.* 1988.

**WHITE, Sir George (Stanley Midelton),** 3rd Bt, *cr* 1904; *b* 11 April 1913; *s* of 2nd Bt and late Kate Muriel, *d* of late Thomas Baker, Bristol; *S* father, 1964; *m* 1939, Diane Eleanor, *d* of late Bernard Abdy Collins, CIE; one *s* one *d. Educ:* Harrow; Magdalene College, Cambridge. Member of the firm of George White, Evans, Tribe & Co., Bristol (formerly George White, Evans & Co.). *Heir: s* George Stanley James White [*b* 4 November 1948; *m* 1974, Susan Elizabeth, *d* of late John Langmaid Ford; one *d*; *m* 1979, Mrs Elizabeth J. Clinton (*née* Verdon-Smith)]. *Address:* Pypers, Rudgeway, near Bristol. *T:* Thornbury 412312. *Died 31 March* 1983.

**WHITE, Air Vice-Marshal Hugh Granville,** CB 1952; CBE 1944; CEng; FIMechE; retired; *b* 1 Mar. 1898; *s* of Herbert White, The Poplars, Maidstone, Kent; *m* 1926, Mabel Joyce Hickman; two *s* one *d. Educ:* HMS Conway; Eastbourne College; Royal Military College, Sandhurst; Jesus College, Cambridge. Commissioned in East Kent Regt, attached RFC, 1916; served as pilot in France, 1916–18; permanent commission on formation of RAF, 1918; comd Nos 29, 64 and 501 Squadrons; Staff appointments as Technical Officer, Royal Air Force College, Cranwell, 1930–33; HQ Air Defence, Gt Britain, 1933–35; STSO, HQ Far East, 1936–39; SASO No 24 Group, 1939–42; AOC Halton, 1942–46; STSO, HQ, BAFO, Germany, 1946–48; AOC No 43 Group, 1948–50; AOC No 41 Group, 1950–53; AOA HQ Maintenance Cmd, 1953–55; retired 1955. *Recreations:* played rugby for RAF, 1922–23; gardening.

*Address:* 30 Hillside, Eastdean, Eastbourne, East Sussex BN20 0HE. *T:* Eastdean 3151. *Club:* Royal Over-Seas League. *Died 23 Sept.* 1983.

**WHITE, Prof. James,** CEng; Dyson Professor of Refractories Technology, University of Sheffield, 1956–73, then Emeritus; Dean of Faculty of Metallurgy, 1958–62; *b* 1 April 1908; *s* of late John White and Margaret E. White (*née* Laidlaw), Langholm, Dumfriesshire; *m* 1936, Elizabeth Kelly, Glasgow; one *s. Educ:* Langholm Acad. (Dux Medallist); Dumfries Acad. (Science Dux); Glasgow University. BSc 1st Cl. Hons Physical Chemistry, 1931; PhD 1935; DSc 1939. DSIR Research Scholarship, Roy. Technical Coll., Glasgow, 1931; Dr James McKenzie Prize for Research, 1933; Research Asst in Metallurgy, Roy. Technical Coll., 1933; Associateship of Roy. Technical Coll., 1934; Lectr in Metallurgy, Roy. Tech. Coll., 1935; Andrew Carnegie Research Scholarship of Iron and Steel Inst., 1936–38; Andrew Carnegie Gold Medallist of Iron and Steel Inst., 1939; Research Technologist in Refractories Industry, 1943; Lectr in Refractory Materials, Sheffield Univ., 1946; Reader in Ceramics, Sheffield Univ., 1952. FIM 1952; Founder FICeram 1955 (Hon. FICeram 1984); CEng 1977. FRSA 1972. Silver Jubilee Lectr, Glass and Ceramic Res. Inst., Calcutta. President: Sheffield Metallurgical Assoc., 1950; Refractories Assoc. of Great Britain, 1959–60; Chm. Clay Minerals Group, Mineralogical Society, 1959–61; British Ceramic Society: First Chm., Basic Science Section; Pres., 1961–62; Hon. Mem. 1983; Hon. Member: Iron and Steel Inst., 1973 (Hon. Mem. Council, 1961–62); Amer. Ceramic Soc., 1988. Visiting Prof., Nat. Research Centre, Cairo, 1962; Student's Trust Fund Visiting Lectr, Univ. of the Witwatersrand, SA, 1964; Visiting Prof., Univ. of Illinois, 1966; Nat. Sci. Foundn Senior Foreign Scientist Fellowship, Univ. of Alfred, NY, 1968; R. B. Sosman Meml Lectr, Amer. Ceramic Soc., 1980. Fellow, Mineralogical Soc. of America, 1960. Hon. DScTech Sheffield Univ., 1987. Griffith Medal, Materials Science Club, 1971; (jtly) A. W. Allen Award, Amer. Ceramic Soc., 1982. *Publications:* scientific papers on ferrous metallurgy and refractory materials (some jointly). *Recreations:* sketching, motor-cars, walking. *Address:* 1 Chequers Close, Ranby, Retford DN22 8JX.

*Died 15 Aug.* 1988.

**WHITE, Lt-Col John Baker,** TD 1950; JP; *b* West Malling, Kent, 12 Aug. 1902; *s* of late J. W. B. White, Street End House, Canterbury; *m* 1925, Sybil Irene Erica (*d* 1980), *d* of late C. B. Graham, Onslow Gardens, SW1; one *s* one *d. Educ:* Stubbington House, Fareham; Malvern College. Worked on farms in Kent and Sussex to gain a basic knowledge of agriculture, 1920–22; worked in a circus to gain a wider knowledge of human nature, 1922; studied the structure of industry and social science in London and various industrial centres, 1922–24; worked as a voluntary helper in canteens for the unemployed and among distressed ex-service men; employed in the coal industry, 1924–26; Director Economic League, 1926–45, Publicity Adviser, 1945–76. Joined Territorial Army, London Rifle Brigade, 1934; served in Army as regimental soldier, on War Office staff with Political Intelligence Dept of FO, and Political Warfare Mission in the Middle East, 1939–45; Lieut-Colonel 1941. MP (C) Canterbury division of Kent, 1945–53. JP Kent, 1954. Pres., E Kent Fruit Show Soc., 1964–88; Vice Pres., Canterbury Soc. *Publications:* Red Russia Arms, 1934; It's Gone for Good, 1941; The Soviet Spy System, 1948; The Red Network, 1953; The Big Lie, 1955; Pattern for Conquest, 1956; Sabotage is Suspected, 1957; True Blue, 1970. *Address:* Street End Place, near Canterbury, Kent CT4 5NP. *T:* Petham 265. *Died 10 Dec.* 1988.

**WHITE, Michael James Denham,** FRS 1961; FAA; Visiting Fellow, Australian National University, since 1976; *b* 20 August 1910; *s* of James Kemp White and Una Theodora Chase; *m* 1938, Isobel Mary Lunn; two *s* one *d. Educ:* University College, London. Asst Lecturer, 1933–35, Lecturer, 1936–46, Reader, 1947, University Coll., London; Guest Investigator, Carnegie Instn of Washington, 1947; Professor of Zoology, Univ. of Texas, 1947–53; Senior Research Fellow, CSIRO, Canberra, Australia, 1953–56; Prof. of Zoology, Univ. of Missouri, 1957–58; Univ. of Melbourne: Prof. of Zoology, 1958–64; Prof. of Genetics, 1964–75. Pres., Genetics Soc. of Australia, 1971–73. Foreign Member: Amer. Acad. of Arts and Sciences; Amer. Philosophical Soc.; Acad. Nazionale dei Lincei; For. Associate, US Nat. Acad. of Sciences. Hon. Fellow, Linnean Soc. of London. Hon. Dr Sci. Biol Siena, 1979. Mueller Medallist, Aust. and NZ Assoc. for the Advancement of Science, 1965; Research Medal, Royal Soc. of Victoria, 1979; Linnean Medal for Zoology, Linnean Soc., 1983. *Publications:* (Monograph) The Chromosomes, 1937, 6th edn 1973 (trans into French, Italian, Polish, Portuguese, and Spanish); Animal Cytology and Evolution, 1945, 3rd edn 1973; Modes of Speciation, 1978; many papers in learned journals. *Address:* Department of Population Biology, Australian National University, PO Box 475, Canberra City, ACT 2601, Australia. *Died 16 Dec.* 1983.

**WHITE, Air Vice-Marshal Michael William Langtry;** Principal Medical Officer, RAF Support Command, 1973–74; retired 1974; *b*

6 March 1915; *s* of Frederick William White, solicitor, and Pauline Marie White; *m* 1940, Mary Seton Dury Arnould, Battle, Sussex; one *s* one *d. Educ:* Dauntsey's; St Bartholomew's Hosp. MFCM, MRCS, LRCP, DPH. Qualified as doctor, 1940. Served War, Mediterranean Theatre, 1942–45 (despatches 1943). Air Vice-Marshal, 1971; PMO RAF Training Comd, 1971–73. psc 1955. QHP 1972–74. *Recreations:* shooting, fishing, gardening. *Address:* Owl Cottage, Netheravon, Wilts. *T:* Netheravon 396. *Club:* Royal Air Force.                                        *Died* 21 *May* 1984.

**WHITE, Maj.-Gen. Napier;** *see* White, Maj.-Gen. P. N.

**WHITE, Patrick Victor Martindale;** author; *b* 28 May 1912; *s* of Victor Martindale White and Ruth Withycombe. *Educ:* Cheltenham Coll.; King's Coll., Cambridge. Brought up partly in Australia, partly in England. First published while living in London before War of 1939–45. Served War with RAF, as Intelligence Officer, mainly in Middle East. Returned to Australia after War. Nobel Prize for Literature, 1973. AC 1975, resigned 1976. *Publications: novels:* Happy Valley, 1939; The Living and the Dead, 1941 (new edn 1962); The Aunt's Story, 1946; The Tree of Man, 1954; Voss, 1957 (1st annual literary award of '1000 from W. H. Smith & Son, 1959); Riders in the Chariot, 1961; The Solid Mandala, 1966; The Vivisector, 1970; The Eye of the Storm, 1973; A Fringe of Leaves, 1976; The Twyborn Affair, 1979; Memoirs of Many in One, 1986; *plays:* The Ham Funeral, 1947; The Season at Sarsaparilla, 1961; A Cheery Soul, 1962; Night on Bald Mountain, 1962; Big Toys, 1977; Signal Driver, 1981; Netherwood, 1983; Shepherd on the Rocks, 1987; *short stories:* The Burnt Ones, 1964; The Cockatoos, 1974; Three Uneasy Pieces, 1987; *self-portrait:* Flaws in the Glass, 1981; *essays:* Patrick White Speaks, 1990; *film:* The Night the Prowler, 1978. *Recreations:* friendship, cooking, gardening, listening to music, keeping dogs. *Address:* c/o Barbara Mobbs, 73/35a Sutherland Crescent, Darling Point, NSW 2027, Australia.
                                                        *Died* 30 *Sept.* 1990.

**WHITE, Maj.-Gen. (Percival) Napier,** CB 1951; CBE 1946; psc; late Infantry; *b* 1901; *s* of A. J. White, Norton, Evesham, Worcestershire; *m* 1st, 1928, Dorothy Usticke Kemp (*d* 1946), *d* of Rev. Canon Bater, Derby; one *d* (and one *d* decd); 2nd, 1947, Geraldine Margaret Joan Brooking, *d* of late Captain Guy Lushington Coleridge, Royal Navy; two *s. Educ:* Cathedral School, Worcester; Royal Military College, Sandhurst. 2nd Lieutenant Sherwood Foresters, 1921; Lt-Colonel, 1941; acting Brigadier, 1943; Colonel, 1946. Served War of 1939–45: in France, 1939–40. Middle East, 1941–45 (despatches twice). Colonel The Sherwood Foresters, 1947–58. Chief of Staff, Northern Command, 1951–53; Assistant Chief of Staff (Organisation and Training), SHAPE, 1953–55; Commandant Joint Services Staff College, 1956–58, retired. Controller, Army Benevolent Fund, 1960–71. *Address:* Little Langley, Chobham, Surrey.                        *Died* 20 *Aug.* 1982.

**WHITE, Prof. Robert George,** FRSEd; Member of Division of Immunology, Department of Pathology, University of Cambridge, since 1980; Emeritus Professor, University of Glasgow; *b* 18 July 1917; *s* of Thomas Percy White and Alice Robina Fewkes; *m* 1952, Joan Margaret Horsburgh; one *s* two *d. Educ:* King Edward VI Sch., Nuneaton; The Queen's Coll., Oxford (Open Schol.). BA 1939; qual. in med., Oxford and London Hosp., BM, BCh 1942; MA 1953; DM 1953; MRCP 1964; FRSEd 1968; FRCPath 1970; FRCP 1972. Surg. Lt-Comdr, RNVR, 1945–47; Freedom Research Fellow, Lond. Hosp., 1948–52; MRC Trav. Fellow, at Harvard Med. Sch., USA, 1952–53; Reader in Bacteriology, Lond. Hosp., 1954–63; Gardiner Prof. and Head of Dept of Bacteriology and Immunology, Univ. of Glasgow and Hon. Consultant in Bacteriol., Western Infirmary, Glasgow, 1963–80. Trav. Prof., Univ. of Florida, 1960. WHO Adv. in Immuno-pathology, 1964–; Meetings Sec., Br. Soc. for Immunology, 1957–63; Mem. Coun., Hannah Dairy Research Inst., Ayr, 1964–80. Past Pres., Sect. Allergy and Clin. Immunology, RSM, 1964–66; Chm., Sci. Adv. Council, Lady Tata Memorial Trust, 1976– (Mem., 1968). Examiner: Trinity College Dublin; Univ. of Edinburgh; Univ. of London. FRSocMed. *Publications:* (with J. H. Humphrey) Immunology for Students of Medicine, 1963 (3rd edn 1970); (with Morag Timbury) Immunology and Microbiology, 1973; articles in sci. jls: Nature, Jl Exptl Med., Lancet, Immunology, Br. Jl Exptl Path. *Recreations:* skating, skiing, sailing, painting in oils. *Address:* 16 Birdwood Avenue, Cambridge. *T:* Cambridge 240439; Addenbrooke's Hospital, New Site, Hills Road, Cambridge. *T:* Cambridge 245171 ext. 339; Dunarden, Campbell Street, Helensburgh, Scotland. *T:* Helensburgh 2201. *Clubs:* RNVR (Scotland); Mark Twain (USA).
                                                        *Died* 17 *Sept.* 1982.

**WHITE, Prof. Thomas Cyril,** CBE 1977; Professor of Orthodontics, 1961–76, and Director of Dental Studies, University of Glasgow, 1964–76; Director of Dental Hospital, Glasgow, 1964–76; *b* 11 March 1911; *s* of Thomas William White, MPS, and Edith Weldon; *m* 1940, Catherine Elizabeth Hunter, LDS (*d* 1978); no *c. Educ:* Glasgow Acad.; Glasgow Dental Sch. LDS 1933; LRCP, LRCS

(Edin.), LRFPS (Glasgow) 1935; BSc, FRCS, FDS, FFD, DDO. Lectr in Orthodontics, in charge Orthodontic Dept, Glasgow Dental School, 1938–48; Cons. Dental Surgeon, Western Regional Hosp. Bd, 1948–61. Past President: Glasgow Odontological Society; W of Scotland Branch, Brit. DA; Mem., Forth Valley Area Health Bd, 1977–. Past Member: Gen. Dental Council; Dental Education Adv. Council; Past Chm., Nat. Dental Consultative Cttee (Scotland); Past Convener, Dental Council, Roy. Coll. of Phys and Surg. of Glasgow; Dental Consultant to RN, 1967–76. *Publications: Text-Books:* Orthodontics for Dental Students, 1954 (Joint), 3rd edn 1976; Manual de Ortodoncia, 1958 (Joint). Contributions to Dental Journals. *Recreations:* gardening. *Address:* Five Acres, Buchlyvie, Stirlingshire. *T:* Buchlyvie 255. *Clubs:* Royal Commonwealth Society; Royal Scottish Automobile (Glasgow).
                                                        *Died* 13 *March* 1981.

**WHITEHEAD, Frank Henry;** Deputy Chairman, Macmillan Ltd, 1980–83; *b* 25 Sept. 1918; *s* of William George Whitehead and Annie S. Whitehead; *m* 1941, Gwendolyn Heather (*née* Ross); one *s* two *d. Educ:* Harrow County Sch.; LSE; London Sch. of Printing. Served War, RA, 1939–46. Joined Macmillan Ltd, 1937; Dir, 1963; Gp Man. Dir, 1965–80; non-exec. Dir, 1983–84. Liveryman, Stationers and Newspaper Makers Co. *Recreations:* reading, painting, music, gardening, photography. *Address:* 5 Briery Field, Chorleywood, Herts. *T:* Chorleywood 4721. *Clubs:* City Livery, Wig and Pen.                                    *Died* 27 *March* 1988.

**WHITEHEAD, Col James Buckley,** CBE 1957; MC 1918; TD 1934 (four bars 1951); DL; JP; Cotton Spinner; *b* 1898; *s* of Edwin Whitehead, Oldham, Lancs; *m* 1926, Florence (*d* 1979), *d* of J. R. Thomason, Oldham; one *s* one *d. Educ:* Oldham High School. Served European War, 1916–19, in France and Flanders with 10th Manchester Regt; War of 1939–45 with Roy. Tank Regt and Yorkshire Hussars. Hon. Col 40/41 Royal Tank Regt. DL for Co. Lancaster, 1956; JP WR Yorks, 1948. *Address:* Staghurst, Grasscroft, near Oldham, Lancs. *T:* Saddleworth 2112.
                                                        *Died* 6 *Feb.* 1983.

**WHITEHEAD, Lieut-Col Wilfrid Arthur,** DSO 1941; IA (retired 1947); *b* 28 Jan. 1898; *e s* of late Rev. Arthur Whitehead, Rector of Keinton-Mandeville and Ann Whitehead; *m* 1930, Constance Dulcie (*d* 1967), *e d* of W. W. Crouch, MA; two *s. Educ:* St John's Leatherhead. Entered IA (76th Punjabis), 1915; Mesopotamia and Palestine, 1917–19; NW Frontier of India, 1924–25, 1929–30, 1937; Western Desert and Eritrea, 1940–41 (severely wounded, despatches twice, DSO); Burma 1943. Comdt 3rd Bn 1st Punjab Regt; GSO1 GHQ(I); Comdt Ind. Small Arms School. Patron of Living of Keinton-Mandeville, Somersetshire. *Address:* The Old Rectory, Holcombe, Bath BA3 5ET. *Club:* Naval and Military.
                                                        *Died* 10 *Aug.* 1981.

**WHITEHOUSE, Cyril John Arthur,** OBE 1951; Controller of Operational Services, Greater London Council, 1974–77; *b* 15 May 1913; *s* of F. A. S. and F. A. Whitehouse; *m* 1st, 1937, Elsie Eleanor Reed (*d* 1949); one *d*; 2nd, 1950, Isobel Mary Lickley; one adopted *d. Educ:* Gillingham County School. Clerical Officer, Air Ministry, 1930; Exec. Officer, Inland Revenue, 1932; Higher Exec. Officer, Air Min., 1939; Min. of Aircraft Production: Sen. Exec. Officer, 1942; Asst Dir, 1945; Min. of Supply: Principal, 1946; Asst Sec., 1951; Controller, Scotland, BoT, 1960; Under-Sec., BoT, 1966–69; Under-Sec., Min. of Technology, 1969–71; Dir of Housing, GLC, 1971–74. *Recreations:* golf, gardening. *Address:* Foxwood, 10 Pine Bank, Hindhead, Surrey. *Club:* West Surrey Golf.
                                                        *Died* 3 *May* 1982.

**WHITELOCK, Prof. Dorothy,** CBE 1964; MA, LittD (Cambridge), MA (Oxford); FBA, FSA, FRHistS; Elrington and Bosworth Professor of Anglo-Saxon, Cambridge University, 1957–69; Professorial Fellow, Newnham College, Cambridge, 1957–69, Hon. Fellow since 1970; Hon. Fellow, St Hilda's College, Oxford, since 1957; *b* 11 Nov. 1901; *d* of Edward Whitelock and Emmeline (*née* Dawson). *Educ:* Leeds Girls' High School; Newnham College, Cambridge. 1st Class, English Tripos, section B, 1923, 2nd Class, section A, 1924; Marion Kennedy Student, Newnham Coll., 1924–26; Cambridge Univ. Student, Univ. of Uppsala, 1927–29; Allen Scholar, Univ. of Cambridge, 1929–30. Lecturer in English Language at St Hilda's College, Oxford, 1930–36, Fellow and Tutor in English Language, 1936–57, Vice-Principal, 1951–57; Lecturer in Old English in the University of Oxford, 1946–55, Senior Lecturer, 1955–57. Leverhulme Fellow, 1939–40; Pres. Viking Soc. for Northern Research, 1939–41; Co-Editor of Saga-Book of the Viking Society, 1940–59; Pres., English Place-Name Soc., 1967–79. Hon. LittD Leeds, 1971. *Publications:* Anglo-Saxon Wills, 1930; Sermo Lupi ad Anglos, 1939; The Audience of Beowulf, 1950; The Beginnings of English Society (Pelican Books), 1952; The Peterborough Chronicle (Copenhagen), 1954; English Historical Documents, c 500–1042, 1955, 2nd edn 1979; The Anglo-Saxon Chronicle: A Revised Translation, 1961; The Genuine Asser, 1968; The Will of Æthelgifu (Roxburghe Club), 1968; From Bede to

Alfred (Variorum Reprints), 1980; History, Law and Literature in 10th–11th Century England, 1981; (jtly) Ireland in Early Mediæval Europe, 1982; articles in English Historical Review, Medium Aevum, etc. *Address:* Newnham College, Cambridge. *T:* 62273. *Club:* University Women's. *Died* 14 *Aug.* 1982.

**WHITEMAN, William Meredith;** MA; FRSA; writer on local history, caravanning and the countryside; Vice-President, Camping and Caravanning Club; *b* 29 May 1905; *m* 1931, Patricia Aileen Thornton (*d* 1954); three *d*; *m* 1965, Mary Moore (*née* Hall). *Educ:* St Albans School; St John's College, Cambridge. Founder, National Caravan Council; Hon. Secretary, 1939–49, Hon. Director, 1949–52. Director, Caravan Club, 1938–60. Vice-Pres., British Caravanners Club, 1948–77. Organiser, Moveable Dwelling Conference, 1947–49. Editor, The Caravan, 1938–61. Man. Editor, Link House Publications Ltd, 1942–70; UK Mem., Internat. Caravan Commn, 1947–70, Pres., 1957–70; Countryside Commn transit site study group, 1969–70; Mem., Exec. Cttee, Hampshire Council of Community Service, 1971–83; Life Vice-Pres., Petersfield Soc., 1986. Served on more than 50 cttees, working parties etc, on caravanning and camping. Hon. Life Mem., Caravan Club; Hon. Mem., Fédération Internationale de Camping et de Caravanning. *Publications:* books on camping and caravanning. *Recreation:* local history. *Address:* Northfield Cottage, Steep, Petersfield, Hants GU32 2DQ. *T:* Petersfield 63915. *Died* 11 *Dec.* 1989.

**WHITFIELD, Sir Cecil Vincent W.;** *see* Wallace Whitfield.

**WHITFIELD, George;** poet, artist, and (retired) journalist; former art critic, film critic, and sub-editor Liverpool Echo; *b* 1891; *m* Beatrix (*d* 1976), *d* of Jacob and Makrouhi Yanekian, Chanak, Dardanelles; one *d*. *Educ:* privately and at Jesuit College. Studied art under Fred V. Burridge, RE, in Liverpool. Political, sporting, and comic-strip cartoons in London, provincial and overseas papers; former correspondent motoring journals and film publicity, British and American companies. Served Royal Naval Air Service (aerial and service drawings). Founder-member of one-time Liverpool Pickwickians (their first Mr Pickwick) and Liverpool First-Nighters Society. On selection and hanging committees of World Cartoons Exhibn, first Liverpool Festival. *Publications:* poetry and signed articles on art, architecture, cinema, radio, boxing. *Recreations:* poetry, pictures, and people. *Address:* Rockley House, Rossett, Clwyd. *Club:* Press. *Died* 15 *Jan.* 1983.

**WHITING, Maurice Henry,** OBE; MA, MB, BCh Cantab; FRCS; Consulting Surgeon, Royal London Ophthalmic Hospital; Emeritus Ophthalmic Surgeon, Middlesex Hospital; *b* 12 Oct. 1885; *s* of William Henry Whiting, CB; *m* 1st, 1916, Blanche Beatrice (*d* 1952), *d* of Edward Aggas; (*o s* killed in action, RAF, 1942); 2nd, 1953, Dorothy Miller, *d* of William Gilford. *Educ:* Mill Hill School; Downing College, Cambridge; The Middlesex Hospital. House Surgeon, Middlesex Hospital; House Surgeon and Pathologist, Royal London Ophthalmic Hospital; Capt. RAMC 1914–19; at Boulogne as Ophthalmic Specialist, 1915–19 (despatches); Ophthalmic Specialist, EMS, NW London Dist, 1939–45; engaged in work in London as Ophthalmic surgeon from 1919; late Hon. Sec. Ophthalmological Soc. of the UK; late Ophthalmic Surgeon, Paddington Green Children's Hosp.; Member of Board of Governors Middlesex Hospital; President of Ophthalmological Society of UK, 1950–51; Pres. Old Millhillians Club, 1950–51; Pres. Downing College Assoc., 1953–54. *Publications:* Modern Developments in Cataract Extraction, Montgomery Lecture, RCSI, 1933; Ophthalmic Nursing; Concussion Changes in the Crystalline Lens; Technique of the Haab and Small Magnets, and other articles in medical and ophthalmic journals. *Address:* Top Meadow, Woodchurch Road, Tenterden, Kent. *T:* Tenterden 2752. *Died* 19 *June* 1984.

**WHITNEY, John Hay;** Bronze Star and Legion of Merit (US); CBE (Hon.; UK), 1948; Chairman: Whitney Communications Corporation; The International Herald Tribune; *b* 17 Aug. 1904; *s* of Payne and Helen Hay Whitney; *m* 1942, Betsey Cushing. *Educ:* Groton School; Yale University; Oxford University. BA and MA Yale. Served American Air Force in War, 1941–45 (Colonel). American Ambassador to the Court of St James's, 1957–61. Senior Partner J. H. Whitney & Co.; Editor-in-Chief, and Publisher New York Herald Tribune, 1961–66; Chm., John Hay Whitney Foundation; Life Governor: New York Hospital; Yale Corporation (Fellow, 1955–70, Sen. Fellow, 1970–73); Hon. Trustee, Museum of Modern Art; Trustee and Vice-Pres., Nat. Gallery of Art, 1963–79. Formerly special adviser and consultant on public affairs, Department of State; Commission on Foreign Economic Policy; Secretary of State's Public Committee on Personnel, and President's Committee on Education beyond High School; Jockey Club; Graduate Mem. Business Council. Mem., Corp. for Public Broadcasting, 1970–72. Private collection of Impressionist and post-Impressionist paintings shown at Tate Gallery, London, 1960–61. Hon. Fellow, New College, Oxford, 1957. Hon. Degrees: MA Yale University; Doctorate of Humane Letters, Kenyon College; Doctor

of Laws: Colgate Univ.; Brown Univ.; Exeter College, Oxford; Columbia Univ.; Colby Coll. Benjamin Franklin Medal, 1963. *Address:* 110 West 51st Street, New York, NY 10020, USA. *Clubs:* White's, Buck's; Royal and Ancient. *Died* 8 *Feb.* 1982.

**WHITSEY, Rt. Rev. Hubert Victor;** *b* 21 Nov. 1916; *s* of Samuel and Rachel Whitsey, Blackburn, Lancs; *m* 1950, Jean Margaret Bellinger; two *s* one *d*. *Educ:* Queen Elizabeth's Grammar Sch., Blackburn; Technical Coll., Blackburn; St Edmund Hall, Oxford (MA); Westcott House, Cambridge. Midland Bank, 1933–39. Royal Regt Artillery (TA), 1938–46 (Lt Col 1945). Asst Curate, Chorley, Lancs, 1949–51; Vicar: Farington, Lancs, 1952–55; St Thomas, Halliwell, Bolton, 1955–60; Asst Rural Dean, Bolton, 1957–60; Vicar: All Saints and Martyrs, Langley, Manchester, 1960–68; Downham, Lancs, 1968–71; Hon. Canon, Manchester Cathedral, 1963, Emeritus, 1968; Bishop Suffragan of Hertford, 1971–74; Bishop of Chester, 1974–81. *Recreations:* idleness, practicality. *Address:* Hill Top, Twiston, Clitheroe, Lancs BB7 4DB. *Died* 25 *Dec.* 1987.

**WHITTAKER, Arnold,** CSI 1947; CIE 1938; ICS, retired; Chairman Somerset County Council, 1956–59 (County Alderman, 1953); *b* 27 July 1900; *m* 1934, Hilda Lucy, *d* of late O. W. Street, MA; one *d*. *Educ:* Colne Grammar School; London School of Economics; Christ Church, Oxford. Joined ICS 1924; retired, 1939; Political Adviser to Indian Tea Association and Member, Assam Legislative Assembly; Secretary to Planting and Commerce Group, Assam Legislature, 1939–46. Dir, Bridgwater Building Society, 1961–79. *Address:* Hey House, Somerton, Somerset. *T:* Somerton 72447. *Died* 7 *April* 1984.

**WHITTAKER, John Macnaghten,** FRS 1949; MA, DSc, FRSE; Vice-Chancellor of Sheffield University, Sept. 1952–65, retired; *b* 7 March 1905; *s* of late Sir Edmund Whittaker, FRS; *m* 1933, Iona, *d* of J. S. Elliot; two *s*. *Educ:* Fettes; Edin. Univ.; Trinity College, Cambridge (Scholar). Wrangler, 1927; Smith's Prize, 1929; Adams Prize, 1949; Lecturer in Mathematics, Edinburgh Univ., 1927–29; Fellow and Lecturer, Pembroke Coll., Cambridge, 1929–33; Prof. of Pure Mathematics, Liverpool Univ., 1933–52. Senior Fellow, Birmingham University, 1965–66. Vis. Professor: Ain Shams Univ., Cairo, 1967; Inst. of Mathematics, Teheran, 1968–69; Univ. of West Indies, Barbados, 1970–71. Served in RA, 1940–45 (AA Command, Western Desert, Tunisia, and as GSO1, War Office); Lt-Col RA, 1944; Dep. Scientific Adviser to the Army Council, 1944. Chairman: Joint Standing Cttee of Universities and Accountancy Profession, 1953–64; Commn on Royal University of Malta, 1957. A Capital Burgess of the Town and Parish of Sheffield, 1956–70; Freedom of City of Sheffield, 1965. Hon. LLD (Sheffield). *Publications:* Interpolatory Function Theory, 1935; Les séries de base de polynomes quelconques, 1949; Memoirs in various journals. *Address:* 11B Endcliffe Crescent, Sheffield S10 3EB. *T:* Sheffield 663712. *Died* 29 *Jan.* 1984.

**WHITTAKER, Sir (Joseph) Meredith,** Kt 1974; TD 1950; DL; Chairman of Scarborough and District Newspapers Ltd; *b* 28 Sept. 1914; *s* of late Francis Croyden Whittaker; *m* 1939, Gwenllian Enid (MBE 1983), *d* of W. F. Allen, Scarborough; one *s* one *d*. *Educ:* Scarborough Coll.; Queen's Coll., Oxford (MA). Mem. NR Yorks CC, 1949–74, and North Yorkshire CC, 1973–81. Vice-Chm. of Exec. Council, County Councils Assoc., 1969–72; Chairman of Executive Council: County Councils Assoc., 1972–74; Assoc. of County Councils, 1973–76; DL Yorks 1971. *Address:* High Dalby House, Thornton Dale, Pickering, North Yorkshire YO18 7LP. *T:* (home) Pickering 60214; (business) Scarborough 363636. *Club:* Anglo-Belgian. *Died* 27 *Sept.* 1984.

**WHITTET, Dr Thomas Douglas,** CBE 1977; Chief Pharmacist, Department of Health and Social Security, 1967–78; *b* 4 Jan. 1915; *s* of late Thomas Douglas Whittet and Ellen Sloan Whittet (*née* Scott); *m* 1942, Doreen Mary Bowes; two *s*. *Educ:* Rosebank Sch., Hartlepool; Sunderland Polytechnic (Hon. Fellow 1980); University Coll., London (Fellow, 1979). PhC (now FPS) 1938; BSc (London) 1953; FRSC (FRIC 1955); CChem 1975; PhD (London) 1958. Mem., Coll. of Pharmacy Practice, 1982. Chief Chemist, Numol Ltd, 1939–41; hospital pharmacy, 1941–43; Chief Pharmacist and Lectr in Pharmacy: Charing Cross Hosp., 1943–47; University Coll. Hosp. and Med. Sch., 1947–65; Dep. Chief Pharmacist, Min. of Health, 1965–67. Member: Brit. Pharm. Codex Revis. Cttee, 1967–75; Joint Formulary Cttee, 1967–78; European Pharmacopoeia Commn, 1967–71; WHO Expert Adv. Cttee on Internat. Pharmacopoeia, 1948–; Council of Europe (Partial Agreement) Pharmaceutical Cttee, 1967–78; EEC Pharmaceutical Cttee and working parties, 1977–78. Consultant, UNIDO, 1978–. Mem. Cttee of Management, 1978–83, Mem. Adv. Cttee, 1984–, Chelsea Physick Garden (Freedom of Garden 1984). Master, Soc. of Apothecaries of London, 1982–83 (Sydenham Lectr, 1965; Delaune Lectr, 1972; Sir Hans Sloane Lectr, 1987; Chm., Faculty of Hist. and Philos. of Medicine and Pharmacy, 1975–78; Court Visitor, 1978–; Hon. LMSSA 1984). Lectures: Wright Meml,

Sydney, 1972; Winch Meml, 1973; Harrison Meml (and Medallist), 1973; Todd Meml, 1980; Foundn, British Soc. for Hist. of Pharmacy, 1983; Thomas Vicary, RCS, 1986. Hon. Member: Royal Spanish Acad. of Pharmacy, 1958; Internat. Acad. of Pharmacy, 1965. Hon. DSc: Bath, 1968; Aston, 1974. Evans Gold Medal (Guild of Public Pharmacists), 1960; Charter Gold Medal, Pharm. Soc., 1978; Don Francke Medal, Amer. Soc. Hosp. Pharmacists, 1978. FRSocMed (Pres., Hist. of Medicine Section, 1981–83). *Publications:* Hormones, 1946; Diagnostic Agents, 1947; Sterilisation and Disinfection, 1965; The Apothecaries in the Great Plague of London of 1665, 1971; many papers on medical and pharmaceutical history; numerous papers in Jl of Pharmacy and Pharmacology and in Pharmaceutical Jl on pyrogens and fever and on drug stability. *Recreations:* overseas travel, especially Commonwealth; medical and pharmaceutical history. *Address:* Woburn Lodge, 8 Lyndhurst Drive, Harpenden, Herts. *T:* Harpenden 4376. *Clubs:* Royal Commonwealth Society; MCC.                                                          *Died 15 April 1987.*

**WHITTINGHAM, Air Marshal Sir Harold (Edward),** KCB 1945; KBE 1941 (CBE 1930); MB, ChB (Glasgow); FRCP; FRCPE; FRFPS; FRSTM&H; DPH, DTM&H; Director-General of RAF Medical Services, 1941–46; Medical Adviser, British Red Cross, 1946–48; Director of Medical Services, BOAC, 1948–57; Chairman: Air Ministry Flying Personnel Research Committee, 1949–67; IATA Medical Committee, 1950–57; Member, World Health Organisation Expert Advisory Panels on International Quarantine and on Environmental Sanitation, and Member, Expert Committee on Sanitation of International Airports, 1953–74; Medical Consultant to the Commonwealth Development Corporation, 1966–77 (Adviser, 1956–66); Hon. Civil Consultant in Aviation Medicine to RAF, since 1967; Consultant in Aviation Medicine to British Airways (formerly BEA), since 1957; *b* 1887; 2nd *s* of late Engineer Rear-Admiral Wm Whittingham, CB; *m* 1st, 1912, Agnes Kerr (*d* 1966), *d* of late William Seright, MD, FRFPS; one *s* one *d*; 2nd, 1966, Rita C. J., LRAM, *d* of late W. Harold White, MPS. *Educ:* Christ's Hosp.; Greenock Acad.; Glasgow Univ. Pathologist and Assistant Director of Research, Royal Cancer Hosp., Glasgow, 1910–15; Pathologist, Scottish National Red Cross, 1914–15; served European War, 1915–18, with RAMC in India and Mesopotamia (despatches); attached Royal Flying Corps, 1917–18; transferred RAF, 1918, as Pathologist; in charge of RAF Sandfly Fever Commn, Malta, 1921–23; Director of Pathology, RAF, 1925–30; Lecturer, Bio-Chemistry, London School of Tropical Medicine, 1926–30; Pathologist, Royal Bucks Hosp., 1927–39; Consultant in Pathology and Tropical Medicine, RAF, 1930–35; OC RAF Central Medical Establishment, 1934–39; Consultant in Hygiene, Pathology and Tropical Medicine, RAF, 1935–39; Hon. Physician to the King, 1938–46; Director of Hygiene, Air Ministry, 1939–41; DGMS, RAF, 1941–46. Group Capt., 1932; Air Commodore, 1936; Air Vice-Marshal, 1940; Air Marshal, 1941. Hon. FRCSE; Hon. FRSM; Hon. FRIPHH. Royal Society of Tropical Medicine and Hygiene: Fellow, 1921; Mem. Council, 1924–43 and 1945–47; Vice-Pres., 1943–45; Pres., United Services Section, Royal Soc. Med., 1938–39, 1958–60. Mem., Internat. Acad. of Astronautics; Hon. Fellow, Aerospace Med. Assoc.; Hon. Member: Assoc. Clinical Pathologists, 1921–; Soc. of Medical Consultants to the Armed Forces, USA; Assoc. Mil. Surgeons of USA. Harveian Lectr, RCS, 1946. Duncan and Lalcaca Medals, London Sch. of Tropical Medicine, 1920; N Persian Memorial Medallist, 1923; Chadwick Gold Medal, 1925; John Jeffries Award of Institute of Aeronautical Sciences, USA, 1944; Stewart Meml Award, 1970; Professorship of Aviation Med., RCP, named the Whittingham Professorship in recognition of his outstanding leadership in aviation med., 1973. KStJ 1945. Knight Grand Cross, Order of St Olaf of Norway, 1945; Commander of the Legion of Merit, USA, 1945; Cross and Star of the Order of Polonia Restituta, 1945; Czechoslovak Military Medal, 1st Class. Hon. LLD Glasgow. Hon. Freeman of Barber-Surgeon's Co. *Publications:* include numerous scientific papers and reports on aviation medicine, cancer, influenza, malaria, dysentery, sandfly fever, cerebrospinal fever, scarlet fever, diphtheria, tonsillitis and first aid. *Address:* 26 Marlborough Gardens, Lovelace Road, Surbiton, Surrey KT6 6NF. *T:* 01–399 8648. *Club:* Royal Air Force.                                                      *Died 16 July 1983.*

**WHITTLE, Dr Claude Howard,** MA, MD Cantab; FRCP; Associate Lecturer in Clinical Medicine, University of Cambridge; Physician, and later Physician to the Skin Department of the United Cambridge Hospitals, 1930–61; Consultant Member, Medical Appeal Tribunal; Consultant Dermatologist, Ministry of Social Security, 1945–72; Hon. Consultant Physician; *b* 2 May 1896; *s* of Tom Whittle and Edith Annie Thompson; *m* 1923, Phyllis Lena Fricker, LRAM; three *s*. *Educ:* The Masonic School, Bushey, Herts; Queens' College, Cambridge (Foundation Scholar in Natural Science); King's Coll. Hosp., London. Clinical Pathologist, 1923. Pres. Dermatological Sec. RSM, 1961–62, Hon. Sec., 1945–6–7; Pres. British Assoc. of Dermatology, 1953–54, Hon. Mem. 1968; Member: Assoc. of Physicians; Path. Soc. of Gt Britain; British Allergy Soc. (Pres., 1979–80); Hon. Mem. British Soc. Mycopath., 1968, Pres., 1973–75.

*Publications:* Vitamin A in psoriasis, Candida skin infections, Fungous infections in Cambridge, Paronychia, Kerato-acanthoma, in Brit. Jl Dermatology, Lancet, etc.; articles on skin diseases in Modern Treatment in General Practice, 1934 and 1938, and in Progress in Biological Sciences, 1960; many others in Proc. Roy. Soc. Medicine, Brit. Jl Dermatology, BMJ, Sabouraudia, Lancet, etc. *Recreations:* painting, sailing, music. *Address:* 41 Newton Road, Cambridge. *T:* 59237.                             *Died 1 March 1986.*

**WHITWORTH, Clifford,** MSc; PhD; FRCS; Vice-Chancellor of the University of Salford, 1967–74; *b* 6 Nov. 1906; *s* of late Joseph and Lucy Whitworth; *m* 1941, Ada Alice Belfit. *Educ:* Manchester Grammar School; Manchester University. Senior Research Assistant to Prof. H. S. Taylor, 1931–33; Industrial Research Chemist, 1933–35; Senior Lecturer in Chemistry, 1935–38, and Head of Dept of Pure and Applied Science, 1939–49, Loughborough College; Asst Education Officer for Further Education, Middlesex CC, 1949–57; Principal, Royal Coll. of Advanced Technology, Salford, 1959–67; Mem., Nat. Council for Technological Awards, 1955–60; Mem. Educn Cttee, Inst. of Fuel, 1951–73, Chm. 1968–73; Chm. NW Section, Inst. of Fuel, 1966–68; Vice-Pres., Inst. of Fuel, 1969–71. Mem. Council, Brit. Assoc. for the Advancement of Science, 1963–72; Chm., North-Western Regional Adv. Council Academic Bd, 1969 *Clubs:* 71. Member: Nat. Adv. Council on Educn for Industry and Commerce, 1970–72; Cttee for Industrial Technologies, DTI, 1972–74. Mem. Governing Body, Hornsey Coll. of Art, 1966–72; Vice-Pres., Union of Lancs and Cheshire Insts, 1967–. Hon. DSc Salford, 1971. *Publications:* contrib. to sci. jls. *Address:* 6 Highfield Road, Bramhall, Cheshire SK7 3BE. *Club:* Athenæum.                                                     *Died 27 Dec. 1983.*

**WHYTE, Gabriel Thomas;** Deputy Chairman, Pavion International PLC; *b* 25 June 1925; *s* of Alexander and Margit Whyte; *m* 1951, Agnes Kalman; one *s*. *Educ:* Highgate Sch.; London Univ. (BSc Hon.). Founder and Man. Dir, Airfix Plastics Ltd, 1945–60; Dir, Airfix Industries, 1961–63; Man. Dir, Triumph Investment Trust, 1964–74; President: Atlantic Materials Ltd, 1975–; Paget Agencies Ltd, 1975–; Technology Investments Ltd, 1982–; Warwick International Ltd, 1975; Dir, Sangers Group PLC, London, 1982–; Chm., Solidyne Inc., NY, 1982–. *Recreations:* riding and dressage, hunting, shooting, fishing. *Address:* Queen's Cove, Pembroke, Bermuda; 910 Fifth Avenue, New York, NY 10021, USA.
                                                         *Died 26 March 1986.*

**WHYTE, Sir Hamilton;** *see* Whyte, Sir W. E. H.

**WHYTE, Lewis Gilmour,** CBE 1973; FFA; Chairman: London and Manchester Assurance Co. Ltd, 1961–78; New York & Gartmore Investment Trust Ltd, 1972–79; Welfare Insurance Co. Ltd, 1974–78; Director: Associated Commercial Vehicles Ltd, 1953–78; Broadstone Investment Trust Ltd, 1953–78; *b* 9 Oct. 1906; *s* of Robert Whyte and Florence Smith; *m* 1st, 1935, Ursula Frances Ware (marr. diss. 1971); one *s* three *d*; 2nd, 1971, Diana Mary Campbell. *Educ:* Trinity Coll., Glenalmond. FFA 1929. Investment Manager, later Dir, Equity & Law Life Assurance Company Ltd, 1940–1953; Dir, Save & Prosper Group Ltd, 1950–63; Member: NCB, 1963–66; NFC, 1971–74; Dep. Chm., British Leyland Motor Corporation Ltd, 1968–72; Chm., Transport Holding Company, 1971–73. Receiver-General, Order of St John of Jerusalem, 1955–68. GCStJ 1969. *Publications:* Principles of Finance and Investment, vol. 1, 1949, vol. 2, 1950; One Increasing Purpose, 1984. *Recreations:* golf, gardening. *Address:* Queen's Cottage, Somerford Keynes, Cirencester, Glos GL7 6DN.                          *Died 11 Nov. 1986.*

**WHYTE, Sir (William Erskine) Hamilton,** KCMG 1985 (CMG 1979); HM Diplomatic Service, retired; Chairman, UK Trident Shipping Agency Ltd, since 1988; Director, Irvin Great Britain Ltd, since 1988; Consultant: Booke & Co. Inc., NY, since 1989; Strategy International Ltd; *b* 28 May 1927; *s* of late William Hamilton Whyte; *m* 1953, Sheila Annie Duck; two *d* (and one *d* decd), *Educ:* King's Sch., Bruton; The Queen's Coll., Oxford. Served, Royal Navy, 1945–48. Civil Asst, War Office, 1952–55; HM Foreign (later Diplomatic) Service, 1955; Vienna, 1956; Bangkok, 1959; UK Mission to UN, New York, 1963; Foreign Office, 1966; Counsellor, HM Embassy, Kinshasa, Democratic Republic of the Congo, 1970–71; Dir-Gen., British Information Services, and Dep. Consul-General (Information), NY, 1972–76; Head of News Dept, FCO, 1976–79; Minister (Economic and Social Affairs), UK Mission to UN, New York, 1979–81; Ambassador and Dep. Perm. Rep. to UN, 1981–83; High Comr in Nigeria and Ambassador (non-resident) to Benin, 1983–84; High Comr in Singapore, 1985–87. *Recreations:* gardening, photography. *Address:* The Lodge, Ford Lane, Ford, Sussex BN18 0DE. *T:* Yapton (0243) 551377; Apt 14K, 120 East 34 Street, New York, NY 10016, USA. *T:* (212) 779 4539. *Club:* Century Association (New York).
                                                         *Died 20 July 1990.*

**WICKENDEN, Keith David;** Chairman: European Ferries Ltd, since 1972; Felixstowe Dock & Railway Co., since 1976; *b* 22 Nov. 1932; 3rd *s* of Joseph Robert Wickenden and Elsie Alice Wickenden (*née*

Miller); *m* 1956, Brenda Paice; four *s*. *Educ:* East Grinstead Grammar Sch. FCA. Partner, Thornton Baker & Co., 1958. Jt Liquidator, Rolls Royce Ltd, 1971. MP (C) Dorking, 1979–83. Pres., Inst. of Freight Forwarders, 1979–80. *Recreations:* cricket, flying, being a Director of Brighton and Hove Albion Football Club. *Address:* European Ferries, 9 Old Queen Street, SW1. *Club:* Carlton. *Died* 9 *July* 1983.

**WICKS, Sir James,** Kt 1972; Chief Justice of Kenya, 1971–82 and of Court of Appeal, 1977–82; *b* 20 June 1909; *s* of late James Wicks and late Mrs Wicks; *m* 1960, Doris Mary, *d* of late G. F. Sutton; no *c*. *Educ:* Royal Grammar Sch., Guildford; King's Coll., London (LLB); Christ Church, Oxford (MA, BLitt). Chartered Surveyor (PASI), 1931; called to the Bar, Gray's Inn, 1939; practised at Bar, 1939–40 and 1945–46. Served War: RAF (Sqdn Ldr), 1940–45 (despatches thrice). Crown Counsel Palestine, 1946–48; Magistrate, Hong Kong, 1948–53; Actg Additional Judge, Supreme Court, Hong Kong, 1948–49; Dist Judge, Hong Kong, 1953–58; Actg Puisne Judge, Hong Kong, 1953, 1955, 1957; High Court, Kenya: Puisne Judge, 1958–69; Sen. Puisne Judge, 1969–71. *Publication:* The Doctrine of Consideration, 1939. *Recreation:* golf. *Address:* Côte des Vauxlaurens, L'Hyvreuse, Cambridge Park, St Peter Port, Guernsey, Channel Islands. *Clubs:* Mombasa, Nairobi (Kenya). *Died* 17 *July* 1989.

**WIDDESS, Rev. Canon Arthur Geoffrey;** Canon Residentiary and Chancellor of York Minster, since 1981 (Canon Treasurer, 1976–81); *b* 1920; *s* of David Charles and Florence Widdess; *m* 1948, Doris May Henderson; one *s* one *d*. *Educ:* Bradford Grammar Sch.; Christ's Coll., Cambridge (MA); Ridley Hall, Cambridge; School of Oriental and African Studies, London Univ. Curate of St Helens, Lancs, 1945–47; Lectr, Central Theol Sch., Shanghai, 1949–50; Asst Master, St Stephen's Coll., Stanley, Hong Kong, 1950–51; Prof. of OT Studies, United Theol Coll., Bangalore, S India, 1951–52; Tutor, St John's Coll., Durham, 1952–55, Vice-Principal, 1955–56; Lectr in Theology, Univ. of Durham, 1952–56; Vicar of St Nicholas, Leicester, and Chaplain to Anglican Students, Univ. of Leicester, 1956–63; Hon. Canon of Leicester, 1961–63; Principal of St Aidan's Coll., Birkenhead, 1963–70; Vicar of Huntington, York, 1970–76. *Publications:* (contrib.) Worship in a Changing Church, ed R. S. Wilkinson, 1965; The Ministry of the Word, ed G. Cuming, 1979; contribs to various theol jls. *Recreations:* gardening, motoring. *Address:* 10 Precentor's Court, York YO1 2EJ. *T:* York 20877. *Died* 17 *July* 1982.

**WIDGERY, Baron** *cr* 1971 (Life Peer), of South Molton; **John Passmore Widgery,** PC 1968; Kt 1961; OBE 1945; TD; Lord Chief Justice of England, 1971–80; *b* 24 July 1911; *s* of Samuel Widgery, South Molton, Devon; *m* 1948, Ann, *d* of William Edwin Kermode, Peel, Isle of Man. *Educ:* Queen's Coll., Taunton. Solicitor (John Mackrell Prizeman), 1933. Served War of 1939–45, Roy. Artillery, North-West Europe, Lieut-Col, 1942; Brigadier (TA) 1952. Called to Bar, Lincoln's Inn, 1946, Bencher, 1961, Treasurer, 1977; practising South-Eastern circuit; QC 1958; Recorder of Hastings, 1959–61; Judge of the High Court of Justice (Queen's Bench Division), 1961–68; a Lord Justice of Appeal, 1968–71. Chairman, Deptl Cttee on Legal Aid in Criminal Cases, 1964–65. First Pres. Senate of the Inns of Court, 1966–70. Vice-Chm. Home Office Adv. Council on the Penal System, 1966–70. DL Co. London, 1951; Freeman: S Molton, Devon, 1971; Exeter, 1975. Hon. LLD: Exeter, 1971; Leeds, 1976; Columbia, USA, 1976. *Address:* 8 New Square, Lincoln's Inn, WC2A 3QP. *Clubs:* Boodle's, Garrick. *Died* 26 *July* 1981.

**WIEN, Hon. Sir Phillip Solly,** Kt 1970; **Hon. Mr Justice Wien;** a Judge of the High Court, Queen's Bench Division, since 1970; *b* 7 August 1913; *y* *s* of Samuel Wien, Cyncoed, Cardiff; *m* 1947, Anita Hermer; two *d*. *Educ:* Canton High School, Cardiff; University College of S Wales and Monmouthshire; University College, London. Solicitor, 1938–46; LLM Exhibitioner in Law. Served War of 1939–45, North Western Europe with 79 Armd Division; Major, 22nd Dragoons, 1940–46 (despatches). Barrister, Inner Temple, 1946; QC 1961; Master of Bench, 1969; Mem. Bar Council, 1969–70; Leader of Wales and Chester Circuit, 1969–70, Presiding Judge, 1976–79; Recorder of Birkenhead, 1965–69; Recorder of Swansea, 1969–70. Chairman of Medical Appeals Tribunal, 1961–70. *Address:* Royal Courts of Justice, WC2A 2LL; 13 King's Bench Walk, Temple, EC4Y 7EN. *T:* 01–353 5115. *Club:* Army and Navy. *Died* 11 *June* 1981.

**WIESNER, Prof. Karel František,** OC 1975; FRS 1969; FRSC 1957; University Professor, University of New Brunswick, since 1976 (Research Professor, 1964–76); *b* 25 Nov. 1919; *s* of Karel Wiesner, industrialist, Chrudim, Czechoslovakia, and Eugenie Storová, Prague; *m* 1942, Blanka Pevná; one *s* (and one *d* decd). *Educ:* Gymnasium Chrudim; Charles Univ., Prague. Asst, Dept of Physical Chem., Charles Univ., Prague, 1945–46; Post-doctoral Fellow, ETH Zürich, 1946–48; Prof. of Organic Chem., Univ. of New Brunswick, 1948–62; Associate Dir of Research, Ayerst

Laboratories, Montreal, 1962–64. Mem., Pontifical Acad. of Scis, 1978. Hon. DSc: New Brunswick, 1970; Western Ontario, 1972; Montreal, 1975. Gunther Award, Amer. Chem. Soc., 1983; Izaak Walton Killam Meml Prize, 1986. Order of Kyril and Methodius, 1st cl. (Bulgaria), 1981. *Publications:* about 195 research papers in various scientific periodicals. *Recreations:* tennis, ski-ing, hunting. *Address:* 814 Burden Street, Fredericton, New Brunswick E3B 4C4, Canada. *T:* 4544007. *Died* 28 *Nov.* 1986.

**WIGG, Baron** *cr* (Life Peer), of the Borough of Dudley; **George Edward Cecil Wigg,** PC 1964; President, Betting Office Licensees' Association, since 1973; *b* 28 Nov. 1900; *m*; three *d*. *Educ:* Fairfields Council Schs and Queen Mary's Sch., Basingstoke, Hants. Served in Regular Army, 1919–37, 1940–46. MP (Lab) Dudley, 1945–67; PPS to Rt Hon. E. Shinwell when Minister of Fuel and Power, Sec. of State for War and Minister of Defence; an Opposition Whip, 1951–54; Paymaster-General, 1964–67. Member: Racecourse Betting Control Bd, 1957–61; Totalisator Bd, 1961–64; Chm., Horserace Betting Levy Bd, 1967–72. *Publication:* George Wigg, 1972. *Address:* House of Lords, SW1; 117 Newcastle Road, Trent Vale, Stoke-on-Trent. *Died* 11 *Aug.* 1983.

**WIGHAM, Eric Leonard,** CBE 1967; Labour Correspondent, The Times, 1946–69; *b* 8 Oct. 1904; *s* of Leonard and Caroline Nicholson Wigham; *m* 1929, Jane Dawson; one *d*. *Educ:* Ackworth and Bootham Schools; Birmingham University (MA). Reporter on Newcastle upon Tyne papers, 1925–32; Manchester Evening News, 1932–45; War Correspondent, The Observer and Manchester Evening News, 1944–45; Labour Correspondent, Manchester Guardian, 1945–46. Member, Royal Commission on Trade Unions and Employers' Associations, 1965–68. Order of King Leopold II (Belgium), 1945. *Publications:* Trade Unions, 1956; What's Wrong with the Unions?, 1961; The Power to Manage: a history of the Engineering Employers' Federation, 1973; Strikes and the Government 1893–1974, 1976, 2nd edn, 1893–1981, 1982; From Humble Petition to Militant Action: a history of the Civil and Public Services Association, 1903–1978, 1980. *Recreation:* stamp collecting. *Address:* 29 Priory Lodge, 49a Glebe Way, West Wickham, Kent BR4 9HP. *T:* 01–462 8284.
*Died* 10 *Feb.* 1990.

**WIKELEY, Thomas,** CMG 1955; OBE 1944; *b* 9 Oct. 1902; *s* of late Col J. M. Wikeley (Indian Army, retired) and late Christine Wikeley (*née* Duns); unmarried. *Educ:* Loretto; Pembroke Coll., Cambridge. MA Mod. Langs. Levant Consular Service, 1926. Served at Alexandria, Cairo, Jedda, Rabat, Genoa, Harar, Addis Ababa, Port Said. Transferred to Foreign Office, 1944; Consul-General, Athens, Dec. 1946; Consul-General, Leopoldville, 1948–51; Consul-General, Tetuan (Spanish Morocco), 1952–54; Consul-General, Jerusalem, 1954–57; HM Minister and Consul-Gen., Guatemala, 1957–60; Foreign Office, 1962–69 (British Delegate to Internat. Exhibitions Bureau); retired 1969. *Publications:* trans. Eugène Pepin: The Loire and its Chateaux, 1971; trans. Jean Chesneaux: The Political and Social Ideas of Jules Verne, 1972. *Address:* Wilbury House, 52 Wilbury Road, Hove, East Sussex BN3 3PA.
*Died* 26 *Sept.* 1984.

**WILBERFORCE, Robert Francis,** CBE 1924; retired; *b* 8 Dec. 1887; 2nd *s* of H. E. Wilberforce; *m* 1914, Hope Elizabeth (*d* 1970), *d* of Schuyler N. Warren, New York. *Educ:* Beaumont and Stonyhurst; Balliol College, Oxford. BA 1912, Honour School of Modern History. War Trade Intelligence Department, 1915–16; Attaché HM Legation to Holy See, 1917–19; called to Bar, Inner Temple, 1921; Member of British Delegation to Washington Disarmament Conference, 1921–22; Carnegie Endowment International Mission to Vatican Library (arranged pubn, in assoc. with author, of Eppstein's Catholic Tradition of the Law of Nations), 1927; British Delegation to Geneva Disarmament Conference, 1932 and 1933; Director British Information Services, New York; retired 1952. MA 1987; Fellow Commoner, Balliol Coll., Oxford, 1987. As *g* *g* *s* of William Wilberforce, headed family deleg. at internat. thanksgiving service commemorating his life and work, Westminster Abbey, 1983. *Publications:* Meditations in Verse; Foreword to A Rug Primer, by Hope Elizabeth Wilberforce, 1979; articles and reviews in various periodicals. *Address:* St Teresa's, Corston, near Bath, Avon BA2 9AG. *T:* Saltford 2607. *Died* 1 *Feb.* 1990.

**WILBY, John Ronald William,** CMG 1961; Professor of International Trade and Finance, Seattle University, 1967–81, later Emeritus; *b* 1 Sept. 1906; *s* of Thomas Wilby and Gertrude Snowdon; *m* 1944, Winifred Russell Walker; no *c*. *Educ:* Batley School; University of Leeds. Board of Inland Revenue, 1928–46; Board of Trade (Principal), 1946–49; First Secretary (Commercial), British Embassy, Washington, 1949–53; British Trade Commissioner, Ottawa, 1953–55; Principal British Trade Commissioner in Ontario, Canada, 1955–64; Consul-General in Seattle, 1964–67. *Recreations:* sailing, music. *Address:* 185 34th Avenue E, Seattle, Washington 98112, USA. *T:* EA5-6999. *Died* 16 *May* 1989.

**WILCHER, Lewis Charles,** CBE 1955; MA, BLitt; *b* 9 December 1908; *s* of L. G. Wilcher, Middle Swan, W Australia; *m* 1935, Vere Wylie; one *s* one *d. Educ:* St Peter's College, Adelaide; University of Adelaide; Balliol College, Oxford (Rhodes Scholar). Dean, Trinity College, Melbourne, 1934–37; Lecturer in Modern History, Univ. of Melbourne, 1935–40; AIF 1940–47; Lieut-Col; Asst Dir of Army Education, 1942–47; Principal, Univ. Coll., Khartoum, 1947–56; Warden, Queen Elizabeth House, Oxford, 1956–68. *Publication:* Education, Press, Radio, 1947. *Recreation:* walking. *Address:* 12 Staunton Road, Oxford OX3 7TW.

*Died 11 July 1983.*

**WILCOCKSON, Rear-Adm. Kenneth Dilworth East,** CBE 1977; Royal Navy; Director General of Naval Personal Services, Ministry of Defence (Navy), 1981–83, retired 1984; *b* 22 Jan. 1927; *s* of William and Ivy Ruskin Wilcockson; *m* 1952, Stella Mary, *d* of Canon A. and Mrs Edgar, Ben Rhydding, Ilkley, Yorks; one *s* one *d. Educ:* Belle Vue High Sch., Bradford, Yorks. Joined RN as 'Hostilities Only' recruit, 1945; HMS Aurora, Duncansby Head and Tyne, 1945–47; HMS Phoenicia, Malta, 1947–49; HMS Ceres, Wetherby, Yorks, 1949–52; HMS Ganges, Shotley, 1952–54; Asst Sec., FO Second-in-Comd Far East, in HMS Newfoundland, Birmingham and Newcastle, 1954–55; RNAS, Lossiemouth, 1956–58; HMS Dainty, 1959–60; Asst Sec. and Fleet Legal Adviser to C-in-C Western Fleet, 1961–62; Dep. Fleet Supply Officer and Fleet Legal Adviser, Far East Fleet, 1962–65; HMS London, 1965–66; Chiefs of Staff Secretariat, 1967–68; Sec. to Chief of Allied Staffs NATO, Malta, 1969; Sec. to Admiral of the Fleet Sir Edward Ashmore, GCB, DSC, 1970–77, as VCNS, C-in-C Fleet and First Sea Lord; Staff of C-in-C Naval Home Comd, 1977–78; Captain HMS Pembroke, Chatham, 1979–81. Rear-Adm. 1981. *Recreations:* walking, gardening, golf. *Address:* c/o National Westminster Bank, 130 Commercial Road, Portsmouth, Hants. *Club:* Army and Navy.

*Died 22 Sept. 1986.*

**WILCOX, Claude Henry Marwood;** *b* 10 January 1908; *s* of late Harry Robert Wilcox, Sherborne; *m* 1934, Winifred (*d* 1980), *d* of late William Francis, Diss; two *s* two *d. Educ:* Sherborne School; Pembroke College, Cambridge (Scholar). Wrangler, 1929; MA 1947. Entered Ministry of Agriculture and Fisheries through Home Civil Service Administrative Examination, 1930; seconded to HM Treasury, 1939–47; Under-Secretary, Ministry of Agriculture, Fisheries and Food, 1948–68. *Address:* Blythburgh, 57 Pewley Hill, Guildford, Surrey GU1 3SW. *T:* Guildford 65794.

*Died 10 May 1981.*

**WILCOX, Sir Malcolm (George),** Kt 1983; CBE 1979 (MBE (mil.) 1943); Deputy Chairman, PRIVATbanken Ltd, since 1983 (Director, since 1982); Member Board of Representatives, PRIVATbanken A/S, Denmark, since 1984; Director: Bank of Bermuda Ltd, since 1978; Costain Group PLC, since 1981; European Investment Bank, since 1981; appointed Member of Council, British Technology Group, 1981; *b* 3 June 1921; *s* of late George Harrison and Edith Mary Wilcox; *m* 1958, Sheila Mary Hewitt; one *s* one *d*; *m* 1986, Mrs Judith Davenport. *Educ:* Wallasey Grammar Sch. TA, 1939; served war 1939–45: RA, RHA and General Staff. Entered Midland Bank Ltd, Liverpool, 1938: Jt General Manager, 1967–72; Asst Chief General Manager, 1972–74; Chief General Manager, 1974–81; Dir, 1974–84; Managing Director, and later Vice Chm., Forward Trust Ltd, 1967–75; Chairman: Forward Trust Ltd, 1980–85; Forward Trust Group Ltd, 1980–85; Midland Montagu Leasing, 1980–85; Midland Bank France SA, 1978–82; Midland Bank Finance Corp., 1980–85 (Dir, 1967–85); Samuel Montagu & Co. Ltd, 1980–81 (Dir, 1972–81); INMOS Internat. plc, 1983–84; Rea Brothers Plc, 1984–85; Director: Thomas Cook Gp Ltd, 1972–81 (Dep. Chm. 1972–75, 1980–81); Samuel Montagu & Co. (Hldgs), 1982; Crocker Nat. Corp., 1981–84; Crocker Nat. Bank, 1981–84; European Banking Co. Ltd, 1974–78; Midland and International Banks Ltd, 1974–81; European Banks' International Co., 1975–81; European-American Banking Corp., 1975–81; European-American Bank and Trust Co. NY, 1975–81; Banque Européenne de Crédit, 1975–78; Standard Chartered Bank Ltd, 1975–79; European-American Bancorp, 1976–81; Euro-Pacific Finance Corp. Ltd, 1975–77, alternate 1977–80; Mem., Internat. Adv. Bd, Creditanstalt-Bankverein, Austria, 1982–84. Pres., Brit. Junior Chambers of Commerce, 1960–61; Chm., Finance Houses Assoc., 1970–72; Mem. Council, Inst. of Bankers, 1970–, Vice-Chm., 1976–77, Pres., 1977–79, Vice-Pres., 1979–; Mem., Export Guarantees Adv. Council, 1976–82, Dep. Chm., 1976–77, Chm., 1977–82; Chm., Liberalisation of Trade in Services Cttee, Cttee on Invisible Exports, 1982–83. Member (part-time): NEB, 1981–; NRDC, 1981–; UGC, 1986–; Member: Adv. Cttee, Ship Mortgage Finance Corp. Ltd, 1977–82; Presidential Council, City of Westminster Chamber of Commerce, 1977–; Exec. Cttee, Hispanic and Luso Brasilian Council, at Canning Ho., 1979–; Adv. Council, European Management Forum, 1979–; BBC Consultative Gp on Industrial and Business Affairs, 1979–84; Bd of Management, Royal Alexandra and Albert Sch., Reigate, 1972–; Adv. Panel to Graduate Business Centre, City Univ., 1971–77 (Chm.); Court and Council,

City Univ., 1977–84; Council, Templeton Coll. Governor, RSC, 1979–. FIB, CBIM, FRSA. *Publications:* contributor to banking jls. *Recreations:* theatre, reading. *Address:* 50 Queensgate, SW7 5JN. *Clubs:* Royal Automobile; Wildernesse (Seal, Kent).

*Died 23 May 1986.*

**WILCOX, Dame Marjorie;** *see* Neagle, Dame Anna.

**WILD, Captain Geoffrey Alan,** CBE 1963; retired as Commodore, and Captain of Canberra, P&O Steam Navigation Company (1961–63); *b* 21 Feb. 1904; *s* of Rev. Harry Wild, formerly Vicar, St Annes, Clifton, near Manchester, and of Susan Wild (*née* Holt); *m* 1932, Dorothy Louisa Bickell; no *c. Educ:* St Bees, Cumberland; Nautical College, Pangbourne; Training Barquentine St George. Cadet, New Zealand Shipping Co., 1921. Joined P&O as 4th Officer, 1923; Staff Captain, 1949. First command in Shillong, 1951; commanded Iberia, 1956, also Strathnaver, Canton, Corfu, Chusan, Strathaird, Arcadia and Himalaya. *Recreation:* retaining interest in all sports. *Address:* 1 Valentine Court, South Street, Eastbourne, East Sussex.

*Died 4 April 1985.*

**WILD, Jack;** Director of Planning and Resources (Under Secretary), Manpower Services Commission, since 1985; *b* 2 Dec. 1927; *s* of John and Sarah Wild; *m* 1952, Betty Smith; one *s* one *d. Educ:* Werneth Council Sch., Oldham; Manchester Grammar Sch.; Corpus Christi Coll., Cambridge (MA). National Service, Sgt, RAEC, 1949–51. Joined Min. of Labour, 1951: various posts in NW Region, 1951–65, and in Head Office, 1965–74; Dir of Operations, Trng Services Agency, MSC, 1974–76; Asst Sec., Dept of Employment, 1976–78: Manpower Services Commission: Asst Sec., Special Programmes, 1978–82; Hd of Regional and Area Operations, 1982–85. *Recreations:* gardens and gardening. *Address:* Larchwood, 1 Gilleyfield Avenue, Dore, Sheffield S17 3NS. *T:* Sheffield 366990.

*Died 29 Jan. 1988.*

**WILDY, Prof. (Norman) Peter (Leete);** Professor of Pathology, and Fellow of Gonville and Caius College, University of Cambridge, since 1975; *b* 31 March 1920; *s* of late Eric Lawrence and Gwendolen Wildy; *m* 1945, Joan Audrey Kenion; one *s* two *d. Educ:* Eastbourne College; Caius Coll., Cambridge; St Thos Hosp., London. MRCS, LRCP 1944; MB, BChir 1948. RAMC, 1945–47. St Thomas's Hospital Medical School: Michael and Sydney Herbert and Leonard Dudgeon Res. Fellow, 1949–51; Lecturer in Bacteriology, 1952–57; Sen. Lectr in Bacteriology, 1957–58; Brit. Memorial Fellow in Virology, 1953–54; Asst Director, MRC Unit for Experimental Virus Research, Glasgow, 1959–63; Prof. of Virology, Univ. of Birmingham, 1963–75. FRSE 1962; FRCPath 1975; Hon. ARCVS 1985. *Publications:* articles on bacteria and viruses. *Address:* Cotton Hall, Cotton Hall Lane, Kedington, Haverhill, Suffolk.

*Died 10 March 1987.*

**WILKES, Rev. John Comyn V.;** *see* Vaughan Wilkes.

**WILKIE, James,** MA, FRSE; Secretary, Carnegie United Kingdom Trust, 1939–54; *b* Manchester, 1 June 1896; *er s* of late James Wilkie, Glasgow; *m* 1930, Ethel Susan (*d* 1984), *er d* of late W. H. Moore, JP, Killough, Co. Down; three *d. Educ:* Whitgift School; Brasenose College, Oxford (Dist. Litt. Hum. 1920). Served European War, 1914–19 (Captain, Machine Gun Corps, despatches twice, wounded, Order of Crown of Rumania) and War of 1939–45 (Major, Home Guard). Entered Board of Education, 1921 (Asst Private Sec. to President, 1924–27), transferred to Empire Marketing Board, 1927–33; returned to Board of Education, 1933–39 (in charge of Metropolitan Div. and Sec. to Adult Education Cttee). Mem. Exec. Cttee: Newbattle Abbey Coll., 1939–54; Scottish Council of Social Service, 1944–54; Land Settlement Assoc., 1939–48; Nat. Central Library, 1939–50; Scottish Leadership Training Assoc., 1945–50; Member: NHS Executive Council for E Sussex, 1955–71; Advisory Council on Education in Scotland, 1948–51; Council of Nat. Federation of Young Farmers' Clubs, 1939–51; Vice-Pres.: Sussex Rural Community Council, Sussex Assoc. of Parish Councils; Irish Library Assoc., 1940–48; Pres., Library Assoc., 1951. *Address:* Downlands Park, Isaacs Lane, Haywards Heath, West Sussex RH16 4BQ. *Died 22 Dec. 1987.*

**WILKINS, Frederick Charles,** CB 1963; *b* 10 July 1901; *s* of Richard Charles Wilkins; *m* 1926, Winifred Bertha Denham; one *d. Educ:* Portsmouth. Entered Admiralty Service, 1917; Naval Store Officer, 1939 (Asst 1923; Dep. 1936); Asst Dir of Stores, 1942; Capt. RNVR (attached to Brit. Pacific Fleet, 1944–46); Dep. Dir of Stores, 1955; Dir of Stores, Admiralty, 1960–64. *Recreation:* reading (Theology). *Address:* 9 Kenilworth Gardens, Kangaloon Road, Bowral, NSW 2576, Australia. *Died 11 March 1987.*

**WILKINS, William Albert,** CBE 1965; *b* 17 Jan. 1899; *m* 1923, Violet Florrie Reed; three *s* one *d. Educ:* Whitehall Elementary School, Bristol. Linotype operator; commenced work at 13½ as an errand boy. Apprenticed to Thos Goulding, Printer, 6 Nelson St, Bristol. Later employed by Bristol Evening Times and Echo and Bristol Evening World. Actively engaged in politics since 1922; MP (Lab) Bristol South, 1945–70; Assistant Govt Whip (unpaid), 1947–62; a

Lord Comr of the Treasury, 1950–51. Labour Party Rep., Council of Europe, Strasbourg, 1958–60. Member Typographical Association (now National Graphical Association), 1919–; Past member of Typographical Association Nat. Executive, Past President Bristol Branch, Past Pres. South-Western Group TA. Member of Bristol City Council, 1936–46. *Address:* 37 King Street, Two Mile Hill, Kingswood, Bristol. *T:* 673779.

*Died 6 May* 1987.

**WILKINSON, Sir Harold,** Kt 1964; CMG 1946; retired as: Managing Director, The "Shell" Transport and Trading Co. Ltd; Director: The Shell Petroleum Co. Ltd; Shell Petroleum NV; Guinness Mahon Holdings; *b* 24 Feb. 1903; *s* of Charles Robert Wilkinson, MA Oxon, ICS, Ramsey, Isle of Man; *m* 1939, Marie Frances Elie; three *s* one *d* (and one step *d*). *Educ:* King William's Coll., Isle of Man. Joined Royal Dutch/Shell group of Cos, 1922; formerly: Man. Dir and Dep. Chm., The "Shell" Transport and Trading Co. Ltd; Man. Dir, Shell Petroleum Co. Ltd; Principal Dir, Bataafse Petroleum Mij. NV; Pres., Asiatic Petroleum Corp., USA; Chm., Shell Caribbean Petroleum Co., USA; Pres., Canadian Shell; Chm., Shell Tankers; Dir, Shell Oil Co., USA; retd 1964. Petroleum Rep. in Washington of UK Govt, 1941–45. US Medal of Freedom with Bronze Palm, 1951; Kt Comdr Order of Merit, Ecuador; Comdr Order of Oranje-Nassau, 1964. *Recreations:* golf, sailing and shooting. *Address:* 9 avenue des Alpes, 1006 Lausanne, Vaud, Switzerland. *Clubs:* Hurlingham; Sunningdale; St Andrews; Royal Yacht Squadron; Royal Bermuda Yacht (Bermuda).

*Died 9 May* 1986.

**WILKINSON, Ven. Hubert Seed;** Archdeacon of Liverpool, 1951–70; Archdeacon Emeritus, since 1971; Residentiary Canon, 1968–70; *b* 7 June 1897; *e s* of late Rev. John and Margaret Wilkinson; *m* Frances Elizabeth, 4th *d* of Dr J. Staveley Dick; two *d*. *Educ:* St John's Coll., Durham Univ. (Exhibnr). MA (2nd cl. Hons English Lit.; 2nd cl. Hons Modern Hist.); studied in Dept. of Theol. for 2 yrs. Served RA, 1916–19. Curate of Colne, 1925–29; Rector of Harpurhey, Manchester, 1929–36; Rector of Chester-le-Street, 1936–40; Rural Dean of Chester-le-Street, 1937–40; Vicar of Allerton, Liverpool, 1940–47; Canon Diocesan of Liverpool Cathedral, 1945–47, and 1951–68; Examining Chaplain to Bishop of Liverpool, 1945–47, and 1955–70; Vicar of Winster, 1947–48; Archdeacon of Westmorland, 1947–51; Vicar of: Ambleside with Rydal, 1948–50; St Mary's, Grassendale, 1951–68; late Hon. Canon of Carlisle Cathedral and Director of Religious Education. *Address:* 89 Primrose Hill, Widmer End, High Wycombe, Bucks. *T:* High Wycombe 715649. *Died 5 May* 1984.

**WILKINSON, James Hardy,** MA Cantab, ScD; FRS 1969; Professor of Computer Science, Stanford University, since 1977; *b* 27 Sept. 1919; *s* of J. W. and K. C. Wilkinson; *m* 1945, Heather Nora Ware; one *s* (one *d* decd). *Educ:* Sir Joseph Williamson's Mathematical Sch., Rochester; Trinity Coll., Cambridge. Major Scholar (Maths) Trinity Coll., 1935; Pemberton Prize, 1937; Mathison Prize, 1939; BA 1939, MA Cantab 1942; ScD 1962. War service: Mathematical Laboratory, Cambridge, 1940–43; Armament Research Dept, Fort Halstead, 1943–46. Mathematics Div., Nat. Physical Lab. (working on design, construction and use of electronic computers), 1946–80; DCSO, 1962–74; Individual Merit CSO, 1974–80. Visiting Professor: Univ. of Michigan, numerous occasions, 1957–73; Stanford Univ., 1961, 1967, 1969. Founder Fellow: Inst. of Mathematics and its Applications (Vice-Pres., 1973–75, Hon. Fellow 1977); British Computer Society (Distinguished FBCS, 1973). Mem. Council, Royal Soc., 1974–77. Visited USSR Academy of Sciences, as a leading scientist, 1968; Distinguished Lectr, Univ. of Waterloo, 1976; Sir Joseph Larmor Lectr, QUB, 1978; Distinguished Lectr, Yale, 1981; D. B. Gillies Meml Lectr, Illinois, 1981; Distinguished Lectr, Univ. of Minnesota, 1982; A. Geary Meml Lectr, City Univ., 1983. Hon. DTech Brunel, 1971; Hon. DSc Heriot-Watt, 1973; DUniv Essex, 1977; Hon. DMath Waterloo, 1978. A. M. Turing award, Assoc. for Computing Machinery, 1970; J. von Neumann award, Soc. for Applied Maths, 1970; Engineer of Distinction, Engineers Jt Council, 1974; G. E. Forsythe Award, Stanford Univ., 1977. Foreign Hon. Mem., Amer. Acad. of Arts and Sciences, 1974; Mem., Bavarian Acad. of Sciences, 1978. *Publications:* Rounding Errors in Algebraic Processes, 1963; The Algebraic Eigenvalue Problem, 1965; Linear Algebra, 1971; chapters in twelve books on computers and numerical analysis; numerous papers in learned jls. *Recreations:* music, travel. *Address:* 40 Atbara Road, Teddington, Mddx. *T:* 01–977 1207.

*Died 5 Oct.* 1986.

**WILKINSON, Kenneth Grahame,** CBE 1979; Hon. DSc, BSc; FEng, FCGI, FCIT, CBIM; FRSA; aviation consultant; Chairman, New Media Productions Ltd, since 1986; *b* 14 July 1917; *s* of Bertie and Dorothy Wilkinson; *m* 1941, Mary Holman Victory; one *s* one *d*. *Educ:* Shooter's Hill; Imperial Coll. (BSc, DIC). Sen. Scientific Officer, RAE, Farnborough, 1945; Performance and Analysis Supt, BEA, 1946–52; Manager, Fleet Planning Br., BEA, 1960; Chief Engr, BEA, 1964; Mem. Bd, BEA, 1968–72; Dep. Chief Exec. and

Man. Dir (BEA Mainline), BEA, 1971–72, Chm. and Chief Exec., BEA, Sept.-Nov. 1972; Mem. Bd, BOAC, 1972; Rolls Royce (1971) Ltd: Man. Dir, 1972–74; Vice-Chm., 1974–76; Engineering Dir, British Airways, 1976–79; Director: British Rail Engineering, 1982–89; Airways Aero Associations Ltd, 1979–90. Chm., Air Transport and Travel Industry Trng Bd, 1981–82; Mem., BAB, 1971–72 and 1976–81 (Dep. Chm., 1979–80). Chm., BGA Techn. Cttee, 1946–48; Chm., BGA, 1970, Vice-Pres., 1972–; Pres. RAeS, 1972. Vis. Prof., Cranfield Inst. of Technology, 1981–. Member: Cranwell Adv. Bd, 1970–73; Council, Cranfield Inst. of Technology, 1971–90 (Dep. Chm., 1983). Hon. FRAeS. *Publications:* Sailplanes of the World (with B. S. Shenstone): Vol. 1, 1960; Vol. 2, 1963; articles and papers to: Jl of Royal Aeronautical Soc.; Aircraft Engineering. *Recreations:* boating, gardening, ingenious creations. *Address:* Pheasants, Mill End, Hambleden, Henley-on-Thames, Oxon RG9 3BL. *Died 21 Oct.* 1990.

**WILKINSON, (Lancelot) Patrick,** MA; FRSL; Fellow, King's College, Cambridge; Lecturer in Classics, 1936–67, Reader in Latin Literature, 1967–69, Brereton Reader in Classics, 1969–74, Orator, 1958–74, Cambridge University; *b* 1 June 1907; *s* of late Lancelot George William and Kate Wilkinson; *m* 1944, Sydney Alix, *d* of late Sir Herbert Eason, CB, CMG; two adopted *s*. *Educ:* Charterhouse; King's College, Cambridge, 1st Class Classical Tripos, Parts I and II; Craven Scholar, 1929; Chancellor's Classical Medallist, 1930; Craven Student, 1930; Fellow of King's College, Cambridge, 1932; Dean, 1934–45; attached to Foreign Office, GCHQ Bletchley Park, 1939–45; Asst Tutor, 1945–46; Senior Tutor, 1946–56; Vice-Provost, 1961–65. Chm., Cambridge Greek Play Cttee, 1973–83 (Sec., 1938–63); Dep. for Orator, 1950–51, 1957; Member of the Council of the Senate, 1952–56; Chm. of Classical Faculty, 1969, 1970; Foundation Mem. Council, New Hall, Cambridge, 1954–65; Governor, Queen Mary Coll., London, 1954–57; Mem. Governing Body, Charterhouse School, 1954–69. Mem. Conseil Consultatif of Fondation Hardt, Geneva, 1959–63. A Vice-Pres., Classical Assoc. (Pres., 1971–72). Lord Northcliffe Meml Lectr, UCL, 1976; Donald Dudley Meml Lectr, Univ. of Birmingham, 1976. Vis. Prof., Berkeley, Calif, Spring 1980. *Publications:* Horace and his Lyric Poetry, 1945; Letters of Cicero, 1949; Ovid Recalled, 1955 (abr. as Ovid Surveyed, 1962); Golden Latin Artistry, 1963; (with R. H. Bulmer) Register of King's College, Cambridge, 1919–58, 1963; words for Benjamin Britten's Cantata Misericordium, 1963; The Georgics of Virgil, 1969; The Roman Experience, 1974; (with R. H. Bulmer) Register of King's College, Cambridge, 1945–70, 1974; Classical Attitudes to Modern Issues, 1979; A Century of King's 1873–1972, 1980; Kingsmen of a Century 1873–1972, 1980; text for Le Keux's Engravings of Victorian Cambridge, 1981; articles in classical jls. *Recreations:* reading, travel. *Address:* King's College, Cambridge. *T:* 350411; 21 Marlowe Road, Cambridge. *T:* 63188. *Died 23 April* 1985.

**WILKINSON, Sir Martin;** *see* Wilkinson, Sir R. F. M.

**WILKINSON, Patrick;** *see* Wilkinson, L. P.

**WILKINSON, Peter;** HM Diplomatic Service, retired; *b* 25 May 1918; *s* of late Fred and Doris Wilkinson; *m* 1944, Anne Sutherland; two *s*. *Educ:* Barnsley Holgate Grammar School. Inland Revenue, 1936–38; Air Min., 1938–40; RAF, 1940–46; Control Office for Germany and Austria, 1946–47; FO, 1947–48; 2nd Sec., British Embassy, Bangkok, 1948–50; Asst Political Adviser to Allied Mil. Govt, Trieste, 1950–52; FO, 1952–55; 1st Sec., Baghdad, 1955–58; FO, 1958–61; 1st Sec., Washington, 1961–64; Counsellor, Tehran, 1964–68; Inspector of Diplomatic Service Establishments, 1968–69; seconded to Board of Trade, 1969–71; FCO, 1971–78. *Recreations:* ski-ing, travel, music. *Address:* 37 Leopold Road, SW19. *T:* 01–946 7969. *Club:* Travellers'. *Died 22 Sept.* 1981.

**WILKINSON, Sir (Robert Francis) Martin,** Kt 1969; Chairman: the Stock Exchange, London, 1965–March 1973; the Stock Exchange, March-June 1973 (Deputy Chairman, 1963–65); Chairman, Federation of Stock Exchanges in Great Britain and Ireland, 1965–73; *b* 4 June 1911; *e s* of late Sir Robert Pelham Wilkinson and Phyllis Marion Wilkinson; *m* 1936, Dora Esme, *d* of late William John Arendt and late Mrs Arendt; three *d*. *Educ:* Repton. Member, Stock Exchange, 1933; Partner in de Zoete & Gorton, 1936; Senior Partner, de Zoete & Bevan, 1970–76; Member of Council, Stock Exchange, 1959. Chm., Altifund, 1976–81; Dir, City of London Brewery Trust (Chm., 1977–78). One of HM Lieutenants, City of London, 1973–. Served with RAF 1940–45. *Recreations:* cricket, gardening. *Address:* Hurst-an-Clays, Ship Street, East Grinstead, W Sussex RH19 4EE. *Clubs:* City of London, MCC.

*Died 22 Jan.* 1990.

**WILKINSON, Sydney Frank,** CB 1951; Director of Administration, National Research Development Corporation, 1959–64; *b* 14 Dec. 1894; *s* of Charles James Carey Wilkinson; *m* 1924, Gladys Millicent Boorsma; one *s*. *Educ:* Strand Sch.; King's Coll., London. Entered Civil Service, National Health Insurance Commission, 1913; Commissioned RFA, 1918; Private Secretary to Minister of Food,

1920; Secretary to Parliamentary Conference on Reform of Licensing Law, 1921; Assistant Private Secretary to Sir Kingsley Wood, 1935; loaned to National Fitness Council, 1937; Private Secretary to Mr Walter Elliot and Mr Malcolm MacDonald, 1938–40; Security Executive, 1940–41; Director of Public Relations, Ministry of Health, 1941–43. Under-Secretary for Housing, Ministry of Housing and Local Government, 1951–54 (Ministry of Local Government and Planning, 1951; Ministry of Health, 1947–51). *Recreation:* golf. *Address:* 51 Cornwall Road, Cheam, Surrey SM2 6DU. *T:* 01–642 0374. *Died 4 May 1988.*

**WILKINSON, Sir Thomas Crowe S.;** *see* Spenser-Wilkinson.

**WILKS, Dick Lloyd;** Governor, Reserve Bank of New Zealand, 1982–84; *b* 17 May 1923; *s* of Mathew Harold Wilks and Annie Isobel (*née* Parker) *m* 1954, Josephine Leslie Rantin; two *s* one *d*. *Educ:* New Plymouth Boys High Sch.; Auckland Univ. of New Zealand (BAEcon 1949). Reserve Bank of New Zealand, 1950–84: Deputy Secretary, 1962; Dep. Chief Cashier, 1965; Chief Cashier, 1967; Executive Adviser, 1973; Dep. Governor, 1977. *Recreations:* gardening, reading. *Address:* 57 Chaytor Street, Wellington 5, New Zealand. *Died 18 Dec. 1985.*

**WILLAN, Group Captain Frank Andrew,** CBE 1960; DFC 1940; DL; RAF (retd); *b* 21 Dec. 1915; *s* of late Brig. Robert Hugh Willan, DSO, MC; *m* 1945, Joan, *d* of late L. G. Wickham Legg, New College, Oxford; two *s* one *d*. *Educ:* Eton; Magdalen Coll., Oxford. Served War of 1939–45, RAF Bomber Command. CO, Oxford Univ. Air Sqdn, 1951–53; CO, RAF Feltwell, 1958–60; retd, 1960. Mem., Wilts County Council, 1961–81 (Chm. Educn Cttee, 1965–68; Vice-Chm., CC, 1968; Chm., 1973–79); DL Wilts, 1968. Mem. Wessex Regional Hosp. Bd, 1970–74; Vice-Chm., Wessex RHA, 1974–78; Chm., Salisbury Diocesan Bd of Finance, 1970–; Chm., Jt Advisory Cttee, Local Authorities' Purchasing, 1970–77. *Recreations:* shooting, gardening. *Address:* Bridges, Teffont, Salisbury SP3 5RG. *T:* Teffont 230. *Clubs:* Army and Navy; Leander (Henley). *Died 12 Nov. 1981.*

**WILLASEY-WILSEY, Maj.-Gen. Anthony Patrick,** CB 1970; MBE 1948; MC 1956; Major-General, Commando Forces Royal Marines, Plymouth, 1968–70, retired; a Chairman, Civil Service Interview Panel, since 1980; *b* 20 Sept. 1920; *e s* of late Colonel F. H. Willasey-Wilsey, MC, 8th Gurkha Rifles; *m* 1948, Dorothy, *y d* of Dr R. B. M. Yates, Market Drayton, Salop; two *s*. *Educ:* Repton Sch. Commissioned in RM, Jan. 1939; HMS Rodney, 1940–42; HMS Howe, 1943; 47 Commando, Belgium and Holland, 1944–45. Instructor, RMA, Sandhurst, 1948–50; 40 Commando, Malayan Emergency, 1951–52 (despatches); Staff Coll., Camberley, 1954; 40 Commando, Cyprus and Suez, 1956–58; DAA and QMG, HQ 3 Commando Bde, ME, 1958; jssc, 1961; CO, 43 Commando, 1962–63; G 1 Plans, MoD, 1964–65; Comdr, 3 Commando Bde, Far East, 1965–66. IDC, 1967. FBIM. Bursar, General Wingate Sch., Addis Ababa, 1970–72; Personnel Manager, Coopers & Lybrand, Central Africa, Lusaka, 1973–78. *Address:* The Dun Cow Cottage, Market Drayton, Shropshire. *T:* Market Drayton 2360. *Club:* Army and Navy. *Died 22 Aug. 1985.*

**WILLETT, Guy William;** a Recorder of the Crown Court, 1971–76; *b* 10 June 1913; *y s* of late William and late Florence Mary Anne Willett; *m* 1945, Elizabeth Evelyn Joan Radford; one *s* two *d*. *Educ:* Malvern; Gonville and Caius Coll., Cambridge (BA). Called to Bar, 1937; Western Circuit, 1938; Head of Chambers, Francis Taylor Building, Temple, 1961–77. Chm., Halstead Sch., 1958–74. *Recreations:* cricket, sailing, golf. *Address:* Sundial House, 24A High Street, Alderney, CI. *T:* Alderney 2911. *Clubs:* Canning; Westfield and District Cricket (Pres. 1946–74), Admiralty Ferry Crew Assoc., Alderney Golf, Alderney Society, Bar Yacht, Bar Golf. *Died 23 March 1990.*

**WILLEY, Rt. Hon. Frederick Thomas,** PC 1964; Vice-President, Save the Children Fund; Barrister; *b* 13 Nov. 1910; *s* of late Frederick and Mary Willey; *m* 1939, Eleanor, *d* of late William and Elizabeth Snowdon; one *s* one *d* (and one *s* decd). *Educ:* Johnston Sch., Durham; St John's Coll., Cambridge Univ. (Full blue Soccer; 1st Class Hons Law; Blackstone Prizeman, Harmsworth Studentship, McMahon Studentship, etc.). Called to Bar, Middle Temple, 1936. MP (Lab) Sunderland, 1945–50, Sunderland N, 1950–83; PPS to Rt Hon. J. Chuter Ede, 1946–50; Chm., Select Cttee on Estimates and Mem. Select Cttees on Statutory Instruments and Public Accounts until 1950; Parly Sec. to Ministry of Food, 1950–51; Dir, North-Eastern Trading Estates Ltd, until 1950; River Wear Comr until 1950; Former Mem., Consultative Assembly of the Council of Europe and Assembly of WEU; Minister of Land and Natural Resources, 1964–67; Minister of State, Ministry of Housing and Local Government, 1967; Member, Select Committee on: Privileges; Members' Interests (former Chm.); former Chairman, Select Committee on: Race Relations and Immigration; Selection; Abortion (Amendment) Bill; Parly and Scientific Cttee. Chm., PLP, 1979–81. Vice-Pres., Youth Hostels Trust of England and Wales. Hon. Fellow, Sunderland Polytechnic. *Publications:* Plan for

Shipbuilding, 1956; Education, Today and Tomorrow, 1964; An Enquiry into Teacher Training, 1971; The Honourable Member, 1974; articles in various periodicals, legal and political. *Address:* 2 The Butts, Biddestone, Chippenham, Wilts SN14 7DY. *Died 13 Dec. 1987.*

**WILLIAM-POWLETT, Vice-Admiral Sir Peveril (Barton Reibey Wallop),** KCB 1953 (CB 1949); KCMG 1959; CBE 1945; DSO 1942; DL; RN retired; Governor of Southern Rhodesia, Nov. 1954–Dec. 1959; Vice-Chairman, Appledore Shipbuilders Ltd, 1974 (Chairman 1962–74); *b* 5 March 1898; 2nd *s* of Major Barton William-Powlett; *m* 1923, Helen Constance (*d* 1965), *d* of James Forbes Crombie, Aberdeen; three *d*; *m* 1966, Mrs Barbara Patience William-Powett, *d* of Sir Bernard Greenwell, 2nd Bt, MBE, and widow of Captain Newton William-Powlett, RN. *Educ:* Cordwalles Sch.; Osborne and Dartmouth. Midshipman, 1914; served European War, 1914–18, Gallipoli, Jutland; Lieut, 1918; specialised in signals; Commander 1931; Captain, 1938; commanded HMS Frobisher, 1938–39; Director of Manning, 1939–40; comd HMS Fiji, 1941 (DSO); Chief of Staff Force 'H', 1941–42; comd HMS Newcastle, 1942–44; Captain of Fleet, Home Fleet, 1944–45 (CBE); Captain in command of Royal Naval Coll., Dartmouth, 1946–48; Naval Secretary to First Lord of the Admiralty, 1948–50; Flag Officer (destroyers), Mediterranean Fleet, 1950–51; Commander-in-Chief, South Atlantic, 1952–54; retired, 1954; Rear-Admiral, 1948; Vice-Admiral, 1950. High Sheriff 1972, DL 1973, Devon. KStJ. *Recreations:* Rugby (played for England, 1922); golf, shooting, and fishing. *Address:* Cadhay, Ottery St Mary, Devon. *T:* Ottery St Mary 2432. *Clubs:* Naval and Military, Chelsea Arts. *Died 10 Nov. 1985.*

**WILLIAMS, (Albert) Clifford,** BEM 1957; JP; Member: Welsh National Water Development Authority; Sports Council for Wales, 1972–75 (Vice-Chairman, Centre Committee; Chairman, Water Recreation Committee); *b* 28 June 1905; British; *s* of Daniel Williams, Blaina, Mon; *m* 1929, Beatrice Anne, *d* of Charles Garbett; one *d*. *Educ:* Primary Sch., Blaina, Mon. Trade Union Official, 1935–50. Mem. 21 years, Chm. 10 years, Usk Rivers Authority; Vice-Pres., former Assoc. of River Authorities. Administrator of Voluntary Hospitals, 40 years until 1969; Vice-Chm., N Monmouthshire HMC. County Councillor, Monmouthshire; Alderman, 1964–74; MP (Lab) Abertillery, April 1965–1970. *Recreations:* watching sports, Rugby football. *Address:* Brodawel, Abertillery Road, Blaina, Gwent NP3 3DZ. *T:* Blaina 379.

**WILLIAMS, Sir Alexander (Thomas),** KCMG 1958 (CMG 1950); MBE 1936; *b* 13 July 1903; *s* of late John Williams and Mary Williams (*née* Kennedy); *m* 1931, Madeline O'Connor; two *s*. *Educ:* Bishop Foy Sch., Waterford; Trinity Coll., Dublin; Downing Coll., Cambridge. BA (Dublin). Cadet, Northern Rhodesia, 1928; District Officer, 1930; Assistant Chief Secretary, 1944; Administrative Secretary, 1944; Administrative Secretary, 1947–52; Chief Secretary and Governor's Deputy, 1952–57; Governor and Commander-in-Chief of the Leeward Islands, 1957–59. LLD *jure dignitatis*, Dublin, 1957. KStJ 1958. *Recreation:* golf. *Address:* West Dormers, Cowes, Isle of Wight PO31 8BP. *T:* Isle of Wight 293657. *Club:* Travellers'. *Died 8 Jan. 1984.*

**WILLIAMS, Alfred Martyn,** CBE 1957; DSC; Commander RN retired; *b* 14 May 1897; *s* of J. C. Williams of Caerhays Castle, Cornwall; *m* 1920, Audrey Hester (*d* 1943), 2nd *d* of C. Coltman Rogers, Stanage Park, Radnorshire; two *s* one *d*; *m* 1945, Dorothea Veronica, widow of Major F. F. Robins and *yr d* of Colonel W. H. Carver; one *s*. *Educ:* RN Colleges, Osborne and Dartmouth. MP (U) North Cornwall, 1924–29; High Sheriff of Cornwall, 1938; DL Cornwall, 1956. *Address:* The Mount, Blackdown, Mary Tavy, Tavistock, Devon PL19 9QB. *Club:* Brooks's. *Died 1 March 1985.*

**WILLIAMS, Sir Anthony (James),** KCMG 1983 (CMG 1971); HM Diplomatic Service, retired; *b* 28 May 1923; *s* of late Bernard Warren Williams, FRCS, and Hon. Muriel B. Buckley; *m* 1955, Hedwig Gabrielle, Gräfin Neipperg; one *s* one *d* (and one *s* one *d* decd). *Educ:* Oundle; Trinity Coll., Oxford. Entered Foreign Service, 1945; served in: Prague; Montevideo; Cairo; UK Permanent Mission to UN, New York; Buenos Aires; UK Permanent Mission to 18 Nation Disarmament Conf., Western, United Nations and South East Asian Depts of Foreign Office. Counsellor, Head of Chancery, Moscow, 1965–67; IDC, 1968; Counsellor (Political), Washington, 1969–70; Ambassador at Phnom Penh, 1970–73; Minister, Rome, 1973–76; Ambassador to Libyan Arab Jamahariya, 1977–79, to Argentina, 1980–82; Leader, UK Delegn to CSCE Rev. Meeting, with rank of Ambassador, 1982–83; UK Deleg., UN Human Rights Commn, Geneva, 1984–87; Leader, UK Delegn, CSCE inter-sessioning meetings, 1989–. *Address:* Jolly's Farmhouse, Salehurst, Sussex TN32 5PS. *Clubs:* Beefsteak, Canning. *Died 7 May 1990.*

**WILLIAMS, Maj.-Gen. Arthur Nicholl**, CBE 1945 (OBE) 1941); *b* 28 Oct. 1894; *y s* of late Rev. Canon W. H. Williams and Mrs Williams, Mathern, Mon; *m* 1919, Effie (*d* 1975), *d* of late Englesbe Seon; one *s* one *d. Educ:* Stancliffe Hall, Matlock; Hereford Cathedral Sch. Entered RM, 2nd Lieut, 1913; served European War, 1914–18, and War of 1939–45 (despatches); retired, 1946; Manager, Conservative Central Board of Finance, 1951–65. *Address:* 901 Hood House, Dolphin Square, SW1. *T:* 01-834 9701. *Club:* Athenæum.
*Died 4 June 1982.*

**WILLIAMS, Sir Brandon Meredith R.;** *see* Rhys Williams.

**WILLIAMS, Carrington Bonsor**, FRS 1954, MA, ScD (Cambridge); Chief Entomologist, Rothamsted Experimental Station, 1932–55; retired; *b* Liverpool, 7 Oct. 1889; *s* of Alfred and Lilian B. Williams; *m* 1920, Ellen Margaret Bain; three *s. Educ:* Birkenhead School; Clare Coll., Cambridge. Entomologist at John Innes Horticultural Institution, Merton, Surrey, 1911–16; Sugar Cane Entomologist, Dept of Agriculture, Trinidad, BWI, 1916–21. Sub-Dir and Dir Entomological Service, Ministry of Agriculture, Egypt, 1921–27; Entomologist to East African Agricultural Research Station, Amani, Tanganyika, 1927–29; Steven Lecturer in Agricultural and Forest Zoology, Edinburgh Univ., 1929–32; Guest Professor of Entomology, University of Minnesota, USA, 1932 and 1958. *Publications:* Migration of Butterflies, 1930; Insect Migration, 1958; Patterns in the Balance of Nature, 1964; Style and Vocabulary, numerical studies, 1970; numerous scientific papers on ecology, statistics and related sciences. *Address:* 8 The Crofts, Kirkcudbright, Scotland. *T:* Kirkcudbright 30015. *Died 12 July 1981.*

**WILLIAMS, Charles Frederick Victor**, CIE 1944; late ICS; *b* 1898; Director, National Union of Manufacturers, 1953–56, retired Nov. 1956. *Educ:* Pembroke College, Oxford. Joined ICS 1923; Under-Sec. Madras Govt 1928; Sec., 3rd Round Table Conference, London, 1932; Under-Sec., Govt of India, 1933; Dep. Secretary, Govt of India, 1934; Secretary, Agent-General for India in South Africa, 1935; Home Secretary, Madras Govt, 1941; Jt Sec., Home Dept, Govt of India, 1945; Sec. to Governor-General (Public), 1947. *Address:* 16 Egerton Gardens, SW3. *T:* 01–584 3820. *Club:* East India, Devonshire, Sports and Public Schools.
*Died 4 May 1984.*

**WILLIAMS, Charles Harold**, MA; Emeritus Professor of History in the University of London (Head, Department of History, and Assistant Principal, 1945–63, King's College; Fellow of King's College, London; *b* 12 May 1895; *s* of Charles and Margaret Williams; *m* 1930, Clare Ruth, *e d* of Justin E. Pollak; one *s* one *d. Educ:* Sidney Sussex Coll., Cambridge; University Coll., London. Asst Lecturer, University Coll., London, 1924; Reader in Constitutional History in the University of London, 1931; Asst Editor of History, 1928, Editor, 1934–47. Member of the Council of the Historical Assoc. *Publications:* England under the Early Tudors, 1925; The Making of the Tudor Despotism, 1928; Year Book 1 Henry VI (Vol. L of the Selden Soc. Publications, 1933); The Yorkist Kings, in Cambridge Medieval History, Vol. VIII, 1936; The Modern Historian, 1938; English Historical Documents, 1485–1558, 1967; William Tyndale, 1969; papers, reviews, etc, in historical periodicals. *Recreations:* walking, music. *Address:* 9 Blackfriars Street, Canterbury, Kent. *T:* Canterbury 63392. *Club:* Athenæum.
*Died 8 Dec. 1981.*

**WILLIAMS, Sir Charles Henry Trelease, (Sir Harry),** Kt 1970; CBE 1964; FIMechE, FIProdE; *b* 11 May 1898; *s* of James Morgan Williams, Consett, Co. Durham and Letitia, *d* of John Henry and Lavinia Dwight Trelease; *m* 1925, Florence Alice, *d* of John William and Mary Ann Exley. *Educ:* Doncaster Road and South Grove Schs, Rotherham. Entered works of The Park Gate Iron & Steel Co. Ltd, as apprentice electrical fitter, 1912; Dir and Gen. Manager, 1945; Jt Man. Dir, 1948; Man. Dir, 1953; Chm., 1960; Director: The Steetley Co. Ltd, 1959–71; Tube Investments Ltd, 1960; Chairman: Renishaw Iron Co. Ltd, 1960; Round Oak Steel Works Ltd, 1960; retired, March 1966. Chairman: British Iron and Steel Fedn Training Cttee, 1952–66; Iron and Steel Ind. Trng Bd, 1964–72. Master of The Company of Cutlers in Hallamshire, 1960–61. JP Rotherham, 1948–70. Hon. Freeman, Co. Borough of Rotherham, 1971. *Recreation:* music. *Address:* Overdales, 4 Brunswick Road, Rotherham S60 2RH. *T:* Rotherham 67192.
*Died 13 Jan. 1982.*

**WILLIAMS, Clifford;** *see* Williams, A. C.

**WILLIAMS, Cyril Herbert**, CMG 1956; OBE 1949; *b* 27 Dec. 1908; *s* of T. E. Williams; *m* 1936, Patricia Joy Collyer; one *s* one *d. Educ:* Bedford Modern Sch.; Jesus Coll., Camb. (MA). Colonial Service, Kenya, 1931; Provincial Commissioner, Nyanza Province, Kenya, 1951–56, retd; farming in Kenya, 1956–65; Mem., Kenya Council of State, 1961–64; Chm., Naivasha CC, 1961–64; Mem., Nyandarua CC, 1963; Deputy Chairman Appeal Tribunal, 1962–63, appted under the Public Security (Restriction) Regulations. Master: Westerleigh School, 1965–66; Great Sanders School, 1966–69;

Claremont School, 1969–74, retired. *Recreations:* reading, watching sport. *Address:* Nortons Farm, New House, Sedlescombe, East Sussex. *Club:* East India, Devonshire, Sports and Public Schools.
*Died 27 Nov. 1983.*

**WILLIAMS, Prof. David;** Professor of Mining Geology in the University of London (Imperial College), 1950–66, Emeritus Professor, since 1966; *b* 12 Oct. 1898; *s* of William and Laura Williams, Caernarvonshire, N Wales; *m* 1929, Dorothy Welland Shepard; two *d. Educ:* Holt Secondary School, Liverpool; University of Liverpool; Imperial College, London. DSc 1952, PhD 1925, MSc 1923, BEng 1921, Univ. of Liverpool; DIC. Geophysical Prospecting, N Rhodesia, 1926–28; Geologist, Rio Tinto Company, Spain, 1928–32; Lecturer in Geology, Imperial College, 1932–47, Reader in Mining Geology, 1947–50. Dean, Royal School of Mines, 1952–59. Secretary, Geological Society of London, 1942–51, Vice-Pres., 1951–53, 1964–65, Foreign Secretary, 1970–73; Council, Institution of Mining and Metallurgy, 1948–70, Vice-President, 1954–57, President, 1960–61; Pres., Geologists' Assoc., 1958–60. Fellow, Imp. Coll. of Science and Technology, 1968. Hon. FIMM, 1969. Consolidated Gold Fields of SA Gold Medal, InstMM, 1934; Lyell Medal, Geological Soc. of London, 1959. *Publications:* (with W. R. Jones) Minerals and Mineral Deposits, 1948; scientific papers in geological and mining journals. *Address:* Downsway, 315 Fir Tree Road, Epsom Downs, Surrey. *T:* Burgh Heath 52655.
*Died 8 May 1984.*

**WILLIAMS, Dr Denis (John)**, CBE 1955; DSc; MD; FRCP; Hon. Consulting Neurologist: St George's Hospital; King Edward VII Hospital for Officers; Hon. Consulting Physician, National Hospital, Queen Square; Hon. Neurologist, Star and Garter Home, Richmond; Hon. Civil Consultant in Neurology, RAF, British Airways; Civil Consultant in Electro-encephalography, RAF and Army; *b* 4 Dec. 1908; *s* of Rev. Daniel Jenkin Williams, MA, BD, Aberayron and Elsie Leonora Edwards; *m* 1937, Joyce Beverley Jewson, MBE, JP, MB, BS, DPH; one *s* two *d* (and one *s* decd). *Educ:* Manchester Univ.; Harvard University. DSc (Physiol.), Manchester 1942 (MSc 1938, BSc 1929); MD (Gold Medal) Manchester 1935 (MB, ChB 1932); FRCP 1943 (MRCP 1937). After resident appts in Manchester and London, Prof. Tom Jones Meml Fellow in Surgery, Manchester Univ.; Halley Stewart Research Fellow, MRC, Nat. Hosp., Queen Square; Rockefeller Travelling Fellow in Neurology. Hon. Research Fellow, Harvard Univ. Wing Comdr RAF; Air Crew Research and Clinical Neurology in Royal Air Force, 1939–45, and seconded to RN; Physician, Departments of Applied Electrophysiology, St George's and National Hosps. Consultant Advr in neurology, DHSS, 1966–73. Lectr in Neurology, London Univ., 1946–75; Chairman: Academic Bd, Inst. of Neurology, 1965–74; Sec. of State's Hon. Med. Adv. Panel on Neurol Aspects of Safety in Driving, 1967–83. Editor, Brain, and Modern Trends in Neurology, 1954–75. Bradshaw Lectr, RCP, 1955; Scott-Heron Lectr, Belfast, 1960; Guest Lectr, Canadian Medical Assoc., 1963; Hugh Cairns Lectr, Adelaide, 1965; Bruce Hall Lectr, Sydney, 1965; Guest Lectr, RACP, 1965; Richardson Lectr, Toronto, 1974. Visiting Professor: Univ. of Cincinnati, 1963, 1969; St Vincent's Hosp. Sydney (Hon. Phys.), 1965. Mem. Council, 1960–63, Vice-Pres., 1976, 1977, Royal Coll. of Physicians (Chm., Cttee on Neurology, 1965–74); Pres., Sect. of Neurology, Roy Soc Med, 1967; Pres., Assoc. of British Neurologists 1972–74 (Sec., 1952–60); Hon. Member: American, Canadian and German Neurological Assocs; EEG Soc. Examr, RCP and various Univs. Governor, Nat. Hosp.; Trustee, Brain Res. Trust. Gowers Medal, UC and Nat. Hosps, London, 1974. *Publications:* articles on brain function, epilepsy, abnormal behaviour and electro-encephalography, in Brain, Modern Trends in Neurology, and other journals; Neurology, in Price's Medicine; Contrib. to Handbook of Neurology. *Recreations:* farming, gardening. *Address:* 11 Frognal Way, Hampstead, NW3 6XE. *T:* 071–435 4030; Woodlands House, Mathry, Dyfed. *T:* St Nicholas (03485) 677. *Clubs:* Wayfarers', Royal Air Force.
*Died 26 Nov. 1990.*

**WILLIAMS, Donald;** *see* Williams, W. D.

**WILLIAMS, Dorian (Joseph George)**, OBE 1978; Director, Pendley Centre of Adult Education, Tring, since 1945; BBC TV Equestrian Commentator, 1951–80; *b* 1 July 1914; *er s* of late Col Williams and Mrs V. D. S. Williams, Farnham Royal, Bucks; *m* 1st, 1938, Hon. Moyra Lubbock (marr. diss. 1946); 2nd, 1956, Jennifer Neale; one *s* one *d. Educ:* Harrow; Guildhall Sch. of Music and Drama. Schoolmaster, 1936–45. Founded Pendley Centre of Adult Education, Tring, 1945. MFH, Whaddon Chase, 1954–80. Chairman: National Equestrian Centre, 1967–74; BHS, 1974–82 (Pres., 1982–84); Royal Internat. Horse Show, 1984–. Master, Farriers' Co., 1977–78. *Publications:* Clear Round, 1954; Pendley and a Pack of Hounds, 1956; Batsford Book of Horses, 1959; Every Child's Book of Riding, 1960; The Girl's Book of Riding and Horses, 1961; Show Pony, 1961; A Gallery of Riders, 1963; Pony to Jump, 1963; Working with Horses as a Career, 1963; Learning to Ride, 1964; Ponies and Riding, 1966; Showing Horse Sense, 1967;

The Horseman's Companion, 1967; Pancho, The Story of a Horse (novel), 1967; Show Jumping, 1968; Famous Horse Stories, 1968; Show Jumping: the great ones, 1970; Dorian Williams' World of Show Jumping, 1970; Kingdom for a horse (novel), 1971; Great Moments in Show Jumping, 1972; Lost (novel), 1974, new edn 1983; Great Riding Schools of the World, 1975; The Horse of the Year, 1976; Master of One, 1978; The Guinness Guide to Equestrianism, 1979; Show Judging and Judges, 1983; Between the Lines, 1984. *Recreations:* riding, Shakespeare, study of Napoleon. *Address:* Foscote Manor, Buckingham. *T:* Buckingham 813152; (office) *T:* Buckingham 813981. *Clubs:* Buck's, Sportsman's.

*Died 21 July 1985.*

**WILLIAMS, Sir Dudley;** *see* Dudley-Williams, Sir Rolf Dudley.

**WILLIAMS, Emlyn;** *see* Williams, G. E.

**WILLIAMS, Eric,** MC 1944; writer; *b* 13 July 1911; *m* 1st, 1940, Joan Mary Roberts (decd); 2nd, 1948, Sibyl Grain, MBE; no *c. Educ:* Christ's College, Finchley. Served War of 1939–45, RAF, 1940–46; shot down over Germany as Flt Lt Dec. 1942; captured, and imprisoned in Stalag-Luft III; escaped Oct. 1943; returned to England Dec. 1943. Book buyer Lewis's Ltd, 1946–49; Scriptwriter, Wessex Film Productions Ltd, 1949–50. Set out on slowest journey round the world, 1959 (abandoned in 1982 after RAF airlift to UK for emergency open-heart surgery). *Publications:* Goon in the Block, 1945; The Wooden Horse, 1949, rev. edn. 1979; The Tunnel, 1951; The Escapers, 1953; Complete and Free, 1957; Great Escape Stories, 1958; Dragoman Pass, 1959 (rev. edn, Dragoman, 1970); The Borders of Barbarism, 1961; More Escapers, 1968; Great Air Battles, 1971. *Recreations:* travel, seafaring, fishing, shooting, fighting officiousness in all its forms. *Address:* Union Bank of Switzerland, Bern, Switzerland.

*Died 24 Dec. 1983.*

**WILLIAMS, Rt. Hon. Eric (Eustace),** PC 1964; CH 1969; Prime Minister, Trinidad and Tobago, since 1961; Minister of Finance, since 1976; *b* Trinidad, 25 Sept. 1911; *e s* of T. H. Williams. *Educ:* Tranquillity Boys' School and Queen's Royal College, Trinidad; St Catherine's Society, Oxford. BA 1932, Cl. I Hist., DPhil 1938. Howard University, Washington, DC; Assistant Professor of Social and Political Science, 1939; Associate Prof., 1944; Prof., 1947. Worked with Caribbean Commn and Research Council (Dep. Chm. latter, 1948–55). Founder and Polit. Leader, Peoples' National Movement, 1956; first Chief Minister and Minister of Finance, 1956; first Premier, 1959; Minister of: External Affairs, 1961–64; Finance Planning and Develt, 1967–71; National Security, 1967–71; Tobago Affairs, 1967–71; led Trinidad and Tobago Delegns, London (US Bases Talks, 1960; WI Fedn Conf., 1961; Indep. Conf., 1961; Commonwealth PM's Conf., 1962), and at discussions with European Economic Commn, Brussels, 1962. Pro-Chancellor, Univ. of WI; Hon. Fellow, St Catherine's College, Oxford, 1964. Hon. DCL, Oxford, 1965. *Publications:* The Negro in the Caribbean, 1942; (Jt) The Economic Future of the Caribbean, 1943; Capitalism and Slavery, 1944; Education in the British West Indies, 1950; History of the People of Trinidad and Tobago, 1962; Documents of West Indian History, Vol. I, 1492–1655, 1963; Inward Hunger: the Education of a Prime Minister, 1969; From Columbus to Castro: the history of the Caribbean 1492–1969, 1970; articles in learned jls. *Address:* Prime Minister's Residence, La Fantasie Road, St Anns, Port-of-Spain, Trinidad.

*Died 29 March 1981.*

**WILLIAMS, Brig. Eric Llewellyn Griffith G.;** *see* Griffith-Williams.

**WILLIAMS, Geoffrey Milson John,** FEng 1982; Senior Partner, Scott Wilson Kirkpatrick and Partners, consulting engineers, since 1966; *b* 28 Jan. 1923; *s* of John and Clementine Williams; *m* 1952, Margaret Brown; three *d. Educ:* Sidney Sussex College, Cambridge (MA). FICE, FIStructE, FASCE. Associated with Scott Wilson Kirkpatrick and Partners in various capacities, 1945–; mainly concerned with design, supervision of construction and project management of civil and structural engineering work; projects include: Hong Kong International Airport, 1952–70; Hong Kong Cross-Harbour Road Tunnel, 1960–; Shell Centre, 1957–62; Commercial Union Building, 1962–69; British Airways Base, 1950–75 and Fourth Passenger Terminal, 1979–, London Airport. Member of Council: ACE, 1972– (Chm., 1986–87); Fellowship of Engrg, 1984– (Vice-Pres., 1987–); ICE, 1981–84, 1986–; Mem. for London Central, Engrg Assembly, 1984–; Chm., Engrg Council Regl Orgn for London, 1984–. FRSA. *Publications:* technical papers to ICE, IStructE, ASCE. *Address:* Clifton House, Euston Road, NW1 2RA. *T:* 01–388 6621. *Clubs:* Royal Automobile, Hurlingham.

*Died 11 Oct. 1988.*

**WILLIAMS, (George) Emlyn,** CBE 1962; MA; FRSL; *b* 26 Nov. 1905; *m* Molly O'Shann (*d* 1970); two *s. Educ:* County School, Holywell; Geneva; Christ Church, Oxford (MA). Hon. LLD Bangor. *Plays:* A Murder has been Arranged; Glamour; Full Moon; Vigil; Vessels Departing; Spring, 1600; Night Must Fall; He Was Born Gay; The Corn is Green; The Light of Heart; The Morning Star; adaptation of A Month in the Country; The Druid's Rest; The

Wind of Heaven; Trespass; Accolade; Someone Waiting; Beth; adaptation of The Master Builder; Cuckoo (also directed). In addition to acting in most of these, has acted at the Old Vic, also in The Winslow Boy, Lyric, 1946; The Wild Duck, Saville, 1955; Season at Stratford-on-Avon, 1956. Shadow of Heroes, Piccadilly, 1958. As Charles Dickens (solo performance), Lyric (Hammersmith), Criterion, Duchess, 1951, Golden Theatre (New York), Ambassadors, 1952. As Dylan Thomas (Growing Up: solo performance), Globe, 1955 and 1958, Long Acre Theatre (New York), Oct. 1957, Ambassadors, 1980; as Saki (solo performance), Apollo, 1977. Acted in: Three, Criterion, 1961; Daughter of Silence, New York, 1961; A Man For All Seasons, New York, 1962; The Deputy, New York, 1964; World Tour as Dickens, 1964–65; as Charles Dickens, Globe, 1965, and Haymarket, 1975; acted in A Month in the Country, Cambridge, 1965; Forty Years On, Apollo, 1969. *Films include:* The Last Days of Dolwyn (author, co-director, and star), 1948; Ivanhoe, 1950; Deep Blue Sea, 1955; I Accuse, 1957; The Wreck of the Mary Deare, 1959; The L-Shaped Room, 1962; Eye of the Devil, 1966; The Walking-Stick, 1969; David Copperfield, 1969. *Television includes:* The Deadly Game, 1982; Rumpole of the Bailey, 1983; Past Caring, 1986. *Publications:* (autobiog.) George, 1961; Beyond Belief, 1967; (autobiog.) Emlyn, 1973; (novel) Headlong, 1980; Dr Crippen's Diary, 1987. *Address:* 123 Dovehouse Street, SW3. *T:* 01–352 0208.

*Died 25 Sept. 1987.*

**WILLIAMS, Gerald Wellington,** JP; *b* 1903; *s* of Wellington Archbold Williams, JP, Shernfold Park, Frant, Sussex; *m* 1930, Mary Katharine Victoria (*d* 1981), *d* of Captain Joscelyn Heber-Percy, DL, JP, East Lymden, Ticehurst, Sussex; one *s* two *d. Educ:* Eton; Christ Church, Oxford (MA). RNVR, 1939 (Lt-Comdr 1942). MP (C) Tonbridge division of Kent, 1945–56, resigned. JP Tunbridge Wells, 1957; High Sheriff of Kent, 1968–69. *Address:* Maplehurst, Staplehurst, Tonbridge, Kent. *T:* Staplehurst 893237. *Clubs:* Carlton, MCC.

*Died 11 Dec. 1989.*

**WILLIAMS, Gertrude, (Lady Williams),** CBE 1963; Professor of Social Economics, University of London, 1955–64, Professor Emeritus since 1964; *b* 11 January 1897; *d* of I. Rosenblum; *m* 1919, Sir William Emrys Williams, CBE, DLitt (*d* 1977); no *c. Educ:* Manchester University; London School of Economics. Apptd to Dept of Social Studies and Economics, Bedford Coll., Univ. of London, 1919, subseq. Special Lecturer in Economics, Reader in Social Economics, and Professor. Min. of Home Security and Min. of Labour and Nat. Service, 1940–42. Member of many Govt cttees of Enquiry. Member Central Training Council, 1964. *Publications:* The State and the Standard of Living, 1936; The Price of Social Security, 1946; Woman and Work, 1946; Economics of Everyday Life (Pelican), 1950, rev. and rewritten, 1972, rev. and rewritten, 1976; Recruitment to Skilled Trades, 1957; Apprenticeship in Europe: the Lesson for Britain, 1963; The Coming of the Welfare State, 1967; articles in Economic Jl, etc. *Recreations:* travel, ballet, opera. *Address:* Grenville Paddock, Haddenham, Bucks. *T:* Haddenham 291464.

*Died 21 Feb. 1983.*

**WILLIAMS, Rt. Rev. Gwilym Owen,** DD Lambeth 1957; *b* 23 March 1913; *s* of Owen G. Williams; *m* 1941, Megan (*d* 1976), *d* of T. D. Jones; one *s. Educ:* Llanberis Gram. Sch.; Jesus Coll., Oxford, Hon Fellow, 1972. BA 1st Class Hons English, 1933; 1st Class Hons Theol. 1935; Gladstone Student at St Deiniol's Library, Hawarden, 1935; St Stephen's House, Oxford, 1936; MA 1937. Curate of Denbigh, 1937; Reader in Theology, St David's Coll., Lampeter, 1940; Warden of Church Hostel, Bangor; Lecturer in Theology, University Coll., Bangor; Canon of Bangor Cathedral, 1947; Warden and Headmaster, Llandovery Coll., 1948–57; Bishop of Bangor, 1957–82; Archbishop of Wales, 1971–82. Chaplain and Sub-Prelate of Order of St John of Jerusalem, 1965. Hon. DD Wales, 1985. *Publication:* The Church's Work, 1959. *Recreations:* fishing and walking. *Address:* Hafod-y-Bryn, Criccieth, Gwynedd LL52 0AH.

*Died 23 Dec. 1990.*

**WILLIAMS, Sir Gwilym (Tecwyn),** Kt 1970; CBE 1966; Director: Dalgety (UK) Ltd, 1975–83; Dalgety Spillers, 1980–83; *b* 1913; *s* of David and Margaret Williams; *m* 1936, Kathleen (*d* 1989), *d* of John and Maria Edwards; two *s* one *d. Educ:* Llanfyllin CSS; Llysfasi Farm Inst.; Harper Adams Agric. Coll. Leader, Employers' side, Agricultural Wages Board, 1960–66; Director, FMC Ltd, 1962–75. Potato Marketing Board: Member, 1954–58; Chairman, 1955–58; Special Member, 1961–66. Member: Agric. NEDO, 1968–76; Econ. and Social Cttee, EEC, 1972–78; Adv. Council for Agriculture and Horticulture in England and Wales, 1973–82. National Farmers' Union: Mem. Council, 1948– (Life Mem., 1977); Vice-Pres., 1953, 1954, 1960–62; Dep. Pres., 1955, 1963–65; Pres., 1966–70. Chm. Governors, Harper Adams Agric. Coll., 1977–85. *Recreations:* trout fishing, shooting. *Address:* Red Gables, Longford, Newport, Salop. *T:* Newport (Salop) 810439. *Club:* Farmers'.

*Died 5 May 1989.*

**WILLIAMS, Very Rev. Harold Claude Noel;** Provost of Coventry Cathedral, 1958–81; Provost Emeritus since 1981; *b* 6 Dec. 1914; *s*

of Charles Williams and Elizabeth Malherbe, Grahamstown, S Africa; *m* 1940, Pamela Marguerite Taylor, Southampton; two *s* two *d* (and one *d* decd). *Educ:* Graeme Coll., S Africa; Durham Univ.; Southampton Univ. Ordained, 1938; Curate of Weeke, Winchester, 1938–40; Principal, St Matthew's Coll., S Africa, 1941–49; Vicar of Hyde, Winchester, 1950–54; Rector of St Mary's, Southampton, 1954–58. Hon. LLD Valparaiso Univ., USA. Grosse Verdienstkreuz des Verdienst Ordens, Federal Republic of Germany, 1967. *Publications:* African Folk Songs, 1948; (ed) Vision of Duty, 1963; Twentieth Century Cathedral, 1964; Coventry Cathedral and its Ministry, 1965; Nothing to Fear, 1967; Coventry Cathedral in Action, 1968; Basics and Variables, 1970; The Latter Glory, 1978; Order My Steps in Thy Way, 1982. *Recreations:* mountaineering and fishing. *Address:* 96 Stoney Road, Coventry CV3 6HY. *T:* Coventry 502561. *Club:* Alpine.
*Died 5 April* 1990.

**WILLIAMS, Sir Harry;** *see* Williams, Sir C. H. T.

**WILLIAMS, Sir Henry Morton Leech,** Kt 1961; MBE 1945; farmer; Managing Director, Guest, Keen, Williams Ltd, 1952–62; President, Bengal Chamber of Commerce and Industry, and President, Associated Chambers of Commerce, India, 1960; *b* 1913; *s* of late O. R. Williams; *m* 1945, Bridget Mary, *d* of late C. G. Dowding; two *s* two *d*. *Educ:* Harrow; Corpus Christi Coll., Cambridge. Served War of 1939–45 (despatches, MBE), becoming Major, REME. CC Berkshire, 1967. *Address:* Grounds Farm, Uffington, Oxon SN7 7RD. *Club:* Oriental.
*Died 18 Aug.* 1989.

**WILLIAMS, John Elwyn; His Honour Judge Williams;** a Circuit Judge, since 1974; *b* 16 June 1921; *s* of Benjamin and Maria Williams; *m* 1st, Gwladys Margaret Vivian; two *s*; 2nd, Nancy Hilda. *Educ:* Cyfarthfa Castle Grammar Sch.; Aberystwyth University Coll.; University College London (LLB). Called to the Bar, Gray's Inn, 1950. *Recreations:* music, climbing. *Address:* Church Cottage, Belchamp Walter, Sudbury, Suffolk CO10 7AT.
*Died 18 Sept.* 1990.

**WILLIAMS, Sir John (Francis),** Kt 1958; journalist and company director; retired 1973; *b* Grafton, New South Wales, 16 June 1901; *s* of Edward and Susan Williams; *m* 1931, Mabel Gwendoline Dawkins, Adelaide, SA; one *s*. *Educ:* Sydney High Sch. Managing Editor, Barrier Miner, Broken Hill, NSW, 1933–35; Managing Director, Queensland Newspapers Pty Ltd, Brisbane, 1937–46; Editor-in-Chief, Herald and Weekly Times Ltd, Melbourne, 1946–55, Managing Director, 1955–67; Chm., 1964–69. *Address:* Herald-Sun Office, Melbourne, Victoria 3000, Australia.
*Died 31 March* 1982.

**WILLIAMS, Very Rev. John Frederick;** *b* 9 March 1907; *s* of John Abraham and Lydia Miriam Williams; *m* Millicent Jones (JP 1951); one *d*. *Educ:* Friars' School, Bangor; University of Wales. Curate: Portmadoc, Caerns, 1930; Aberdare, Glam, 1933; Vicar: Miskin, Glam, 1937; Skewen, Glam, 1953; Rector, Neath, Glam, 1962; Canon, Llandaff Cathedral, 1963; Precentor, 1966; Archdeacon of Llandaff and Priest-in-Charge, Penmark, 1969–71; Dean of Llandaff, 1971–77. *Recreation:* calligraphy. *Address:* 3a Park Road, Barry, S Glam.
*Died 1 Sept.* 1983.

**WILLIAMS, Captain Sir John (Protheroe),** Kt 1967; CMG 1960; OBE 1950; *b* 1896; *m* 1st, 1921, Gladys Grieves (*d* 1962); one *s* three *d*; 2nd, 1964, Mrs Althea Florence Carr (widow). *Educ:* Queen Elizabeth's Grammar Sch., Carmarthen. Master Mariner; Chairman: Australian National Line, 1956–71; United Salvage Pty Ltd; City Ice & Cold Storage Pty Ltd; Penmore Pty Ltd; Snr Partner J. P. Williams & Associates, Penmore graziers. Officer in Charge on behalf of Bank of England, Salvage Operations of RMS Niagara, sunk in 438 ft of water, 1941, when £2,396,000 worth of gold bullion weighing 8¼ tons was recovered. *Publication:* So Ends This Day (autobiog.), 1982. *Address:* 77 St Georges Road, Toorak, Victoria 3142, Australia. *T:* 2412440; Penmore, Bolinda, Victoria. *Clubs:* Australian (Melbourne and Sydney); Melbourne (Melbourne).

**WILLIAMS, John Trevor;** HM Diplomatic Service, retired; *b* 12 Nov. 1921; *yr s* of Dr Griffith Williams and Monica Johnson; *m* 1953, Ena Ferguson Boyd (*d* 1974); two *d*. *Educ:* St Paul's Sch.; Jesus Coll., Oxford. Joined Royal Armoured Corps, 1941; served with 14th/20th King's Hussars in Middle East and Italy, 1943–45. Home Civil Service, 1947–67; joined HM Diplomatic Service, 1967; Counsellor, High Commn, Wellington, NZ, 1967–69; Nato Defence Coll., Rome, 1970; Counsellor, Dublin, 1970–72; Head of Commodities Dept, FCO, 1972; seconded to: N Ireland Office, 1972–73; DoE, 1973–76. *Recreations:* riding, theatre, looking for good restaurants. *Address:* 3 Ranelagh Gardens, SW6 3PA. *T:* 01–736 1733. *Club:* Hurlingham.
*Died 23 Aug.* 1987.

**WILLIAMS, Maj.-Gen. John William C.;** *see* Channing Williams.

**WILLIAMS, Kenneth;** *see* Williams, O. K.

**WILLIAMS, Kenneth (Charles);** actor; *b* 22 Feb. 1926; *s* of Charles George Williams and Louisa Alexandra (*née* Morgan). *Educ:* Lyulph Stanley Sch.; Bolt Court, London. Formerly lithograph draughtsman. Made first appearance on stage, Victoria Theatre, Singapore, playing the detective in Seven Keys to Baldpate, 1946, then Ninian in The First Mrs Fraser, Newquay Rep. Th., Cornwall, 1948; first London appearance as Slightly in Peter Pan, Scala, 1952; Dauphin in Saint Joan, Arts, 1954, transf. with this to St Martin's, 1955; Elijah in Orson Welles prodn of Moby Dick, Duke of York's, 1955; Montgomery in Sandy Wilson's The Buccaneer, Lyric, Hammersmith, 1955, subseq. Apollo, 1956; Maxime in Hotel Paradiso, Wintergarden, 1956; Kite in Wit to Woo, Arts, 1957; Green in Share My Lettuce, Lyric, Hammersmith, 1957, transf. to Comedy, 1957, and to Garrick, 1958; Portia in Cinderella, Coliseum, 1958. Starred in revue, Pieces of Eight, Apollo, 1959, and in One Over the Eight, Duke of York's, 1961. Played Julian in The Private Ear and the Public Eye, Globe, 1962; Jack in Gentle Jack, Queen's, 1963; Truscott in Loot, Arts, Cambridge, 1965; Bernard in Platinum Cat, Wyndham's, 1965; Drinkwater in Captain Brassbound's Conversion, Cambridge Th., 1971; Henry in My Fat Friend, Globe, 1972; Barillon in Signed and Sealed, Comedy, 1976; The Undertaking, Greenwich, later Fortune, 1979. Directed: Loot, Lyric Studio, 1980; Entertaining Mr Sloane, Lyric, Hammersmith, 1981. *Films:* Trent's Last Case; Beggar's Opera; The Seekers; Carry On series. *Television* series include: Hancock's Half Hour; International Cabaret; Kenneth Williams' Show; Whizz Kids Guide. Has broadcast regularly in Round the Horne, Stop Messing About, Just a Minute, etc. *Publications:* Acid Drops, 1980; Back Drops, 1983; Just Williams, 1985; I Only Have to Close My Eyes, 1986. *Recreations:* calligraphy, reading, music, walking. *Address:* ICM, 388/396 Oxford Street, W1N 9HE.
*Died 15 April* 1988.

**WILLIAMS, Mary Bridget;** Assistant Secretary, Air (Procurement Executive), Ministry of Defence, since 1987; *b* 14 Aug. 1933; *d* of Thomas and Mary O'Neil; *m* 1961, Robert Cameron Williams. *Educ:* University Coll. of S Wales and Monmouthshire, Univ. of Wales (BA Hons Phil; Pres. of Union and NUS Debating Tournament). Valuation Clerk, Inland Revenue, 1950–52; NCB, 1952–61 (incl. period as NCB Schol.); Lectr in Politics and Govt, Dir of Studies, and sometime Mem. Senate and Council, Univ. of Bath, 1961–73; entered Min. of Defence, 1974; Head, Gen. Finance Div. 1, 1980–84; Counsellor and Dep. Head of UK Delegn on Mutual Reduction of Forces and Armaments and Associated Measures, Vienna, 1984–87. *Recreations:* Tournament bridge, looking and listening. *Address:* Ministry of Defence, Horse Guards Avenue, SW1.
*Died 1 Feb.* 1989.

**WILLIAMS, Sir Michael (Sanigear),** KCMG 1968 (CMG 1954); HM Diplomatic Service, retired 1970; *b* 17 Aug. 1911; *s* of late Rev. F. F. S. Williams; *m* 1942, Joy Katharine Holdsworth Hunt (*d* 1964); two *d*; *m* 1965, Mary Grace Lindon (*née* Harding). *Educ:* Rugby; Trinity Coll., Cambridge. Entered Foreign Office, 1935; served at HM Embassy in Spain, 1938–39; Foreign Office, 1939–47; HM Embassy, Rome, 1947–50; HM Embassy, Rio de Janeiro, 1950–52; Foreign Office, 1952–56; Minister at Bonn, 1956–60; Minister to Guatemala, 1960–62; Ambassador to Guatemala, 1962–63; Assistant Under-Secretary of State, Foreign Office, 1963–65; Minister to the Holy See, 1965–70. *Recreations:* golf, gardening, motoring. *Address:* Wentways, Waldron, Heathfield, East Sussex.
*Died 25 Feb.* 1984.

**WILLIAMS, Captain Nevill Glennie G.;** *see* Garnons Williams.

**WILLIAMS, (Owen) Kenneth,** JP; Secretary, Commonwealth Magistrates' Association, since 1980; *b* 24 Dec. 1928; *m* 1956, Thelma Sanders; three *s* one *d*. *Educ:* Waterloo Grammar Sch.; Gordonstoun. Master Mariner; FIPM. Navigating Cadet, Deck Officer and Captain, 1945–56; commnd RNR, 1951; served on HMS Scorpion, retired Lieut, 1959; came ashore with Hicks, Parkes & Hoyle, Marine Surveyors, 1956; Dir and Partner, associated Consulting Engineers, J. Latta & Partners, 1958; joined Tate & Lyle Gp as a Marine Supt, Silvertown Services Shipping, 1962; Personnel Supt, Sugar Line, 1968; Gp Personnel & Trng Manager, United Molasses Co., 1973; Employee Relations Adviser, 1975, then on secondment to Industrial Participation Assoc. as Dir of Trng Services, 1977–80. Formerly: Chm. Dagenham Gp and Mem. IPM Nat. Cttee on Employee Relations; Councillor, London Bor. of Bromley, 1971–74; occasional Lectr, British Shipping Fedn; Mem., GCBS Management Development Working Party; Outside Examiner, NE London Polytechnic; Founder Mem. and Chm. of two schools' Parents' Assocs. Governor: The Ramsden Schs, 1975–83; Orpington Coll. of Further Educn, 1975–; Trustee, Orpington Village Hall Trust, 1976–. JP SE London Commission Area, 1976. *Publications:* Employment Legislation Guidance for Line Managers, 1978; Preparation and Training for Participation, 1979; latterly, contribs to Commonwealth Judicial Jl. *Recreations:* wine making, DIY home decorating, reading. *Address:* 96 Avalon Road, Orpington, Kent BR6 9BA. *T:* Orpington 23744. *Club:* Royal Commonwealth Society.
*Died 28 Aug.* 1984.

**WILLIAMS, Philip Maynard,** DLitt; FBA 1983; Fellow of Nuffield College, University of Oxford, since 1958; *b* 17 March 1920; *s* of John Clifford Williams and Marjorie Noel How. *Educ:* Stationers' Co.'s Sch., Hornsey; Trinity Coll., Oxford (MA; DLitt 1982). Oxford University: Lectr, Trinity Coll., 1946–53; Fellow: Nuffield Coll., 1950–53; Jesus Coll., 1953–58. Vis. Associate Prof., Columbia Univ., 1956–57; Vis. Prof., Princeton Univ., 1968. Foreign Hon. Mem., Amer. Acad. of Arts and Sciences, 1984. *Publications:* Politics in Post-war France, 1954, 3rd edn 1964 (entitled Crisis and Compromise); (with Martin Harrison) De Gaulle's Republic, 1960; The French Parliament 1958–1967, 1968; French Politicians and Elections 1951–1969, 1970; Wars, Plots and Scandals in Post-war France, 1970; (with Martin Harrison) Politics and Society in De Gaulle's Republic, 1971; Hugh Gaitskell, 1979; (ed) The Diary of Hugh Gaitskell 1945–1956, 1983. *Address:* Nuffield College, Oxford. *T:* Oxford 248014.                              *Died* 16 *Nov.* 1984.

**WILLIAMS, Sir Ralph Dudley D.;** *see under* Dudley-Williams, Sir Rolf (Dudley).

**WILLIAMS, Prof. Raymond Henry;** Fellow of Jesus College, Cambridge, since 1961; *b* 31 Aug. 1921; *s* of Henry Joseph Williams and Gwendolene Williams (*née* Bird); *m* 1942, Joyce Mary Dalling; two *s* one *d. Educ:* Abergavenny Grammar Sch.; Trinity Coll., Cambridge; MA, LittD. War service (ending as Captain), 21st Anti-Tank Regt, Guards Armoured Div., 1941–45; Staff Tutor in Literature, Oxford University Extra-Mural Delegacy, 1946–61; Univ. Reader in Drama, 1967–74, Professor of Drama, 1974–83, University of Cambridge. Mem., Arts Council, 1976–78. Vis. Prof. of Political Science, Stanford Univ., USA, 1973. DUniv Open, 1975; Hon. DLitt: Wales, 1980; Kent, 1984. General Editor, New Thinkers' Library, 1962–70. Editor: Politics and Letters, 1946–47; May Day Manifesto, 1968. *Publications:* Reading and Criticism, 1950; Drama from Ibsen to Eliot, 1952; Drama in Performance, 1954 (rev. edn 1968); Culture and Society, 1958; The Long Revolution, 1961; Communications, 1962 (rev. edn, 1976); Modern Tragedy, 1966; Public Inquiry, 1967; Drama from Ibsen to Brecht, 1968; The English Novel from Dickens to Lawrence, 1970; A Letter from the Country, 1971; Orwell, 1971; The Country and the City, 1973; Television: technology and cultural form, 1974; (ed) George Orwell, 1975; Keywords, 1976; Marxism and Literature, 1977; (ed with Marie Axton) English Drama: forms and development, 1978; Politics and Letters: interviews with New Left Review, 1979; Problems in Materialism and Culture, 1980; (ed) Contact: the history of human communications, 1981; Culture, 1981; Towards 2000, 1983; Writing in Society, 1983; *novels:* trilogy: Border Country, 1960; Second Generation, 1964; The Fight for Manod, 1979; The Volunteers, 1978, 2nd edn 1985; Loyalties, 1985; *posthumous publication:* Resources of Hope, 1989. *Recreation:* gardening. *Address:* Jesus College, Cambridge.

*Died* 26 *Jan.* 1988.

**WILLIAMS, Richard Aelwyn Ellis,** CIE 1945; late ICS; *b* 5 Dec. 1901; *s* of Rev. Richard Ellis Williams; *m* 1933, Fay Muriel Boylan; two *s* one *d. Educ:* Taunton School; University College of Wales, Aberystwyth (graduate); Lincoln Coll., Oxford (graduate). Appointed to ICS 1925; posted to province of Bihar and Orissa; Under-Secretary, Political Department, Bihar and Orissa Government, 1930; District Magistrate, Shahabad, 1933; Rent Settlement Officer, 1937; Secretary to Bihar Government, Revenue Dept and Controller of Prices and Supplies, 1939; Chief Secretary to Orissa Government, 1944; retired from India, 1946; with Ministry of Agriculture, London, 1947–67. *Recreation:* gardening. *Address:* 9 Clareville Road, Caterham, Surrey.          *Died* 19 *June* 1981.

**WILLIAMS, Robert Emmanuel;** *b* 1 Jan. 1900; *o s* of David Williams and Gertrude Olive Williams (*née* Mansfield); *m* 1st, 1928, Rosamund May Taylor (*d* 1929); 2nd, 1938, Audrey Forbes Higginson; three *s* one *d. Educ:* Liverpool Institute; Liverpool Univ. (MSc); Brasenose Coll., Oxford (MA). Assistant Master: Ilkeston, Rugby, Lawrence Sheriff Sch., Repton, 1922–36; Lecturer, Oxford Univ. Department of Education, 1936–39; HM Inspector of Schools, 1939; Staff Inspector, 1945; Chief Inspector of Schools, Ministry of Education, 1952–61; Simon Senior Research Fellow, Manchester Univ., 1961–62; Lecturer in Education, London Univ. Institute of Education, 1962–67. *Publications:* contributions to School Science Review, Religion in Education. *Address:* Sea Crest, 10 Ryder's Avenue, Westgate-on-Sea, Kent CT8 8LN. *T:* Thanet 33521.                                    *Died* 27 *Aug.* 1988.

**WILLIAMS, Sir Rolf Dudley D.;** *see* Dudley-Williams.

**WILLIAMS, Stanley;** solicitor; *b* 6 April 1911; *s* of Thomas and Sarah Elizabeth Williams; *m* 1948, Lily Ceridwen Evans; three *s* one *d. Educ:* Froncysyllte; Llangollen County Sch. (Schol.); Liverpool Univ. (LLB). Admitted Solicitor, 1934. Served War of 1939–45: ranks, 1940–43; commnd RAMC, 1943. Contested (Lab) Denbigh Division, 1959 and 1964. A Recorder of the Crown Court, 1972–75. Former Mem., Mental Health Review Tribunal (Wales Region). Member: Bootle Corporation, 1934–38 and 1946–50; Denbighshire County Council, 1960–63; Wrexham Corporation, 1966–68; Noise Adv. Council, 1970. *Recreations:* music, walking, gardening. *Address:* Liddington, Wynnstay Lane, Marford, Wrexham, Clwyd. *T:* Gresford 2715.                           *Died* 24 *March* 1990.

**WILLIAMS, Stuart Graeme,** OBE 1949; Controller, Television Administration, BBC, 1956–74; *b* 5 October 1914; *y s* of late Graeme Douglas Williams, author and journalist, and late Winifred Maud Williams (who *m* 2nd, late Sydney A.ᵉ Moseley); *m* 1938, Catherine Anne, *d* of late Charles Thomas and Florence Hutchison; one *d. Educ:* Alleyn Court, Westcliff-on-Sea; Wallingbrook, Chulmleigh. Joined BBC as Programme Sub-Editor, Radio Times, 1931; particularly concerned with war-time and post-war develt, BBC Overseas, European and Monitoring Services, and with develt of BBC and Internat. TV. Principal appointments: Executive: Outside Broadcasting, 1938; Monitoring Service, 1939; Empire Service, 1940; Asst Head, Overseas Programme Admin., 1941; Admin. Officer, Overseas Services, 1942; visited Middle and Far East for negotiations concerning future of British Far Eastern Broadcasting Service, Singapore and Radio SEAC, Ceylon, 1947 and 1948; Head of External Broadcasting Admin., 1948; BBC Staff Admin. Officer, 1952; Asst Controller, Staff Admin., 1955; visited Nigeria to advise Nigeria Govt concerning incorporation of Nigeria Broadcasting Service, 1955; visited Malta as member of a BBC Working Party to report on possible introduction of television in Malta, 1959; advised on organisation of Broadcasting in Singapore, 1968; visited Nigeria for RIPA and Federal Govt to advise on Civil Service Management Trng, 1976. Dir, Visnews Ltd, the international Newsfilm Agency, 1957–74 (Dep. Chm., 1962–74); Chm., European Broadcasting Union Cost-Sharing Gp, 1965–74. Mem., Exec. Council, RIPA, 1951–68, Chm., 1957; Dir of Studies, RIPA, 1975–84; pt-time Mem. and Chm., CS Commn Appointment Bds, 1975–85; Mem., Asian Broadcasting Union Finance Gp, 1971–74. World travel for BBC, and later EBU, 1947–74. *Address:* 92 Moor Lane, Rickmansworth, Herts WD3 1LQ. *T:* Rickmansworth 774271.

*Died* 15 *May* 1986.

**WILLIAMS, Tennessee, (Thomas Lanier Williams);** Playwright; *b* 26 March 1911; *s* of Cornelius Coffin Williams and Edwina Dakin. *Educ:* University of Missouri; University of Iowa; Washington University. Awarded Rockefeller Fellowship 1940 (playwriting); Grant from National Institute of Arts and Letters ($1000), 1943; New York Drama Critics Circle Award, 1944–45, 1947–48, 1955, 1960–61; Pulitzer Prize, 1948, 1955. Member Alpha Tau Omega. *Publications: plays:* Battle of Angels; The Glass Menagerie, 1944; (with Donald Windham) You Touched Me, 1945; A Streetcar Named Desire, 1947; Summer and Smoke, 1948; The Rose Tattoo, 1951; Camino Real, 1953; Cat on a Hot Tin Roof, 1955; Orpheus Descending, 1957; Garden District (2 plays: Suddenly Last Summer and Something Unspoken), 1958; Sweet Bird of Youth, 1959; Period of Adjustment, 1960 (filmed, 1963); The Night of the Iguana, 1961 (filmed, 1964); The Milk Train Doesn't Stop Here Any More, 1963 (revised, 1964; filmed, as Boom, 1968); Slapstick Tragedy, 1966; The Seven Descents of Myrtle, 1968; In the Bar of a Tokyo Hotel, 1969; Small Craft Warnings, 1972; Out Cry, 1973; The Red Devil Battery Sign, 1975; The Eccentricities of a Nightingale, 1976; Vieux Carré, 1977; A Lovely Sunday for Creve Coeur, 1979; Kirche, Küchen und Kinder, 1979; Clothes for a Summer Hotel, 1980; Will Mr Merriweather Return from Memphis?, 1980; A House not Meant to Stand, 1981; Something Cloudy, Something Clear, 1981; *film:* Baby Doll, 1957; *screen plays for:* The Glass Menagerie, A Street Car Named Desire, The Rose Tattoo; (with Meade Roberts) The Fugitive Kind (Orpheus Descending); (with Gore Vidal) Suddenly Last Summer; Boom; *volumes:* volume of one-act plays, 1945; vols of short stories, 1948, 1960 (Three Players of a Summer Game); vol. of verse, 1944; Hard Candy and other Stories, 1954; Dragon Country (plays), 1970; Eight Mortal Ladies Possessed (short stories), 1975; *novels:* The Roman Spring of Mrs Stone, 1950; Moise and the World of Reason, 1976; *novella:* The Knightly Quest, 1966; *poems:* In the Winter of Cities, 1964; Androgyne, Mon Amour, 1977; *autobiography:* Memoirs, 1975. *Recreations:* swimming, travelling. *Address:* c/o Mitch Douglas, International Creative Management, 40 West 57th Street, New York, NY 10019, USA.

*Died* 25 *Feb.* 1983.

**WILLIAMS, Sir Thomas;** *see* Williams, Sir W. T.

**WILLIAMS, Thurston Monier,** FRIBA; consultant architect; *b* 3 March 1924; *s* of Frank Chauncy Williams and Yvonne Williams; *m* 1955, Kirstine (*née* Uren); one *s* one *d. Educ:* Cranleigh Sch.; AA School of Architecture. AADip; ARIBA 1951, FRIBA 1968. Asst Architect, LCC, 1950–65; Borough Architect, London Borough of Hillingdon, 1965–77; Man. Dir, Nat. Building Agency, 1977–82; Dir of Technical Services, London Bor. of Camden, 1982–84. RIBA: Hon. Sec., 1969–71, 1977–78; Vice-Pres., 1976–77; Competitions Consultant, 1984. Pres., Assoc. of Official Architects, 1958–75; Vice-Chm., Jt Cttee Members and Staff, LCC, 1953–65. FRSA. *Publications:* various papers in technical and local govt jls.

*Recreations:* walking, gardening. *Address:* 39 Cornwall Grove, W4 2LB. *T:* 01–995 5481.                         *Died* 18 *Feb.* 1985.

**WILLIAMS, (William) Donald;** *b* 17 Oct. 1919; 2nd *s* of Sidney Williams, Malvern; *m* 1945, Cecilia Mary Hirons (marr. diss. 1988); one *s. Educ:* Royal Grammar Sch., Worcester. Served War of 1939–45: Volunteer, 8th Bn Worcestershire Regt, May 1939; POW 1940 (Germany); escaped to Russia and was repatriated, 1945. Qualified as a Chartered Accountant, 1949. Partner in a Professional Practice, 1950–77, on own account as Financial Consultant, 1978–86, now retired. Contested (C) Dudley, (Gen. Elec.), 1966; MP (C) Dudley, March 1968–1970; contested (C) Dudley East, 1979. CC Hereford/Worcester, 1973–81. Gov., Abberley Hall. *Recreations:* reading, travelling. *Address:* c/o Lächler, 71 Kilchgrund Strasse, 4125 Riehen, Basle, Switzerland. *Club:* Carlton.
                                              *Died* 5 *Jan.* 1990.

**WILLIAMS, William Penry,** JP Caernarvon; Bank Manager, Midland Bank Ltd, Caernarvon, 1938–52; retired 1952; *b* 7 Sept. 1892; *s* of Capt. R. Jones Williams, Gwydryn, Abersoch, Caerns; *m* 1918, Elizabeth, *d* of John Hughes, Liverpool; one *s* one *d*; *m* 1949, Mrs Margaret Ellen Roberts. *Educ:* County Secondary School, Pwllheli. Entered Midland Bank Ltd, 1909. High Sheriff Caernarvonshire, 1944. Certificated Associate Inst. of Bankers. Commission First RWF, European War, 1914–18. Mem. Council, University Coll. of North Wales, Bangor; Trustee of Port of Caernarvon. *Recreations:* golf and shooting. *Address:* Tyddyn Hen, Clynnog, Caernarvon. *T:* Clynnog 238. *Club:* Royal Welsh Yacht.                         *Died* 2 *Oct.* 1981.

**WILLIAMS, Col William Picton B.;** *see* Bradley-Williams.

**WILLIAMS, Sir (William) Thomas,** Kt 1976; QC 1964; **His Honour Judge Sir Thomas Williams;** a Circuit Judge, since 1981; *b* 22 Sept. 1915; *s* of David John Williams, Aberdare, and Edith Williams; *m* 1942, Gwyneth, *d* of Rev. D. G. Harries, Aberdare; one *s* one *d. Educ:* University Coll., Cardiff (BD); St Catherine's, Oxford (MA); University of London; Lincoln's Inn. President, Students' Union, University of Wales, 1939. Baptist Minister, 1941–46; Chaplain and Welfare Officer, RAF, 1944–46; Tutor, Manchester College, Oxford, 1946–49. Called to the Bar, Lincoln's Inn, 1951, Bencher, 1972. Recorder: of Birkenhead, 1969–71; of the Crown Court, 1972–81. MP (Lab & Co-op) Hammersmith South, Feb. 1949–55, Barons Court, 1955–59, Warrington, 1961–81; Parliamentary Private Secretary: Minister of Pensions, 1950–51; Minister of Health, 1951; Attorney General, 1965–67. Chm., British Gp, IPU, 1974–76. Member: Advisory Council on Public Records, 1965–71; Adv. Council on Statute Law, 1974–81; SE Metropolitan Regional Hospital Board, 1965–71; Select Cttee for Parly Comr, 1974–81; Chm., Select Cttee on Parly Procedure, 1976–80; Pres., World Council IPU, 1976–80 (Hon. Life Mem., IPU, 1981). Governor, King's Coll. Hosp., 1968–74; Chm., Cray Valley Hosp. Management Cttee, 1968–69. Fellow, University Coll. of South Wales, 1981. *Address:* Wickers Oake, Dulwich Wood Park, SE19.
                                              *Died* 28 *Feb.* 1986.

**WILLIAMS-ELLIS, Mary Annabel Nassau, (Amabel), (Lady Williams-Ellis);** author and journalist; *b* Newlands Corner, near Guildford, 25 May 1894; *d* of late J. St Loe Strachey, of the *Spectator*; *m* 1915, Sir Clough Williams-Ellis, CBE, MC, FRIBA (*d* 1978); (son killed in action, 1944) two *d. Educ:* home. Literary editor, Spectator, 1922–23. *Publications:* An Anatomy of Poetry; The Pleasures of Architecture (with Clough Williams-Ellis); But We Know Better; Noah's Ark; The Wall of Glass; How You Began; The Tragedy of John Ruskin; The Beagle in S America; Men Who Found Out; How You Are Made; Volcano; What Shall I Be; To Tell the Truth; The Big Firm; Good Citizens; Learn to Love First; Women in War Factories; Princesses and Trolls; A Food and People Geography; The Art of being a Woman; Headlong down the Years; The Art of Being a Parent; Changing the World; Seekers and Finders; Modern Scientists at Work; Darwin's Moon (A Life of Alfred Russel Wallace); Life in England, a pictorial history; Gypsy Folk Tales; Out of This World (10 vols SF anthology); The Raingod's Daughter, 1977; The Story Spirits, 1980; All Stracheys are Cousins (memoirs), 1983. *Recreation:* travel. *Address:* Plâs Brondanw, Llanfrothen, Gwynedd. *TA:* Penrhyndeudraeth.
                                              *Died* 27 *Aug.* 1984.

**WILLIAMS-THOMAS, Lt-Col Reginald Silvers,** DSO 1940; TD; JP; DL; Commander of Crown (Belgium); Croix de Guerre; RA; Queen's Own Worcestershire Hussars; Glass Manufacturer; Director, Royal Brierley Crystal Ltd; Lloyd's Underwriter; *b* 11 February 1914; *s* of late Hubert Silvers Williams-Thomas, Broome, Stourbridge, Worcestershire; *m* 1938, Esmée Florence Taylor; two *s* one *d*; *m* 1963, Sonia Margot Jewell, *d* of late Major M. F. S. Jewell, CBE, DL, Upton-on-Severn, Worcs. *Educ:* Shrewsbury School. JP Staffs, 1947; DL Worcestershire, 1954. Freeman of the City of London; Mem., Worshipful Co. of Glass-Sellers. OStJ 1986. *Publication:* The Crystal Years, 1984. *Recreations:* shooting, archery, fishing, gardening. *Address:* The Tythe House, Broome, near

Stourbridge, West Midlands DY9 0ET. *T:* Kidderminster (0562) 700632.                         *Died* 4 *Nov.* 1990.

**WILLIAMS-WYNN, Col Sir (Owen) Watkin,** 10th Bt, *cr* 1688; CBE 1969; FRAgSs 1969; Lord Lieutenant of Clwyd, 1976–79; *b* 30 Nov. 1904; *s* of Sir Robert William Herbert Watkin Williams-Wynn, 9th Bt, KCB, DSO; *S* father, 1951; *m* 1st, 1939, Margaret Jean (*d* 1961), *d* of late Col William Alleyne Macbean, RA, and Hon. Mrs Gerald Scarlett; one *s* (and one *s* decd); 2nd, 1968, Gabrielle Haden Matheson, *d* of late Herbert Alexander Caffin. *Educ:* Eton; RMA, Woolwich. Commnd RA, 1925; RHA, Instructor at Equitation Sch., Weedon; Adj. 61st (Carnarvon and Denbigh Yeo.) Medium Regt RA (TA), 1936–40; Major, 1940. Served with Regt as 2nd in command, France and Dunkirk; served with 18th Division, Singapore (despatches twice); Prisoner of War, Siam and Burmah Railway; Lt-Col comdg 361st Med. Regt RA (TA), 1946; Hon. Col 361 Med. Regt RA (TA), 1952–57. Liaison Officer to Min. of Agriculture for N Wales, 1961–70; Mem., Nature Conservancy for Wales, 1963–66. Master Flint and Denbigh Foxhounds, 1946–61; Joint Master, Sir W. W. Wynn's Hounds, 1957. JP 1937, DL 1947, Denbighshire; High Sheriff of Denbighshire, 1954; Vice-Lieutenant, Denbighshire, 1957–66, Lord Lieutenant 1966–74; Lieutenant of Clwyd, 1974–76. KStJ 1972. *Heir: s* David Watkin Williams-Wynn [*b* 18 Feb. 1940; *m* 1st, 1968, Harriet Veryan Elspeth, *d* of Gen. Sir Norman Tailyour, KCB, DSO; two *s* twin *d*; 2nd, 1983, Mrs Victoria Jane Dillon, *d* of late Lt-Col Ian Dudley De Ath, DSO, MBE]. *Address:* Llangedwyn, Oswestry, Salop. *T:* Llanrhaiadr 269. *Club:* Army and Navy.                         *Died* 13 *May* 1988.

**WILLIAMSON,** Baron *cr* 1962, of Eccleston (Life Peer); **Thomas Williamson,** Kt 1956; CBE 1950; JP; General Secretary National Union of General and Municipal Workers, 1946–61; a Director of Securicor Ltd since 1964; (part-time) member, Iron and Steel Board, 1960–67; Member of ITA, 1961–64; Chairman British Productivity Council, 1953–54; Director of the Daily Herald, 1953–62; *b* 2 September 1897; *s* of James and Selina Williamson; *m* 1925, Hilda Hartley, St Helens; one *d. Educ:* Knowsley Road, St Helens; Workers' Educational Association, Liverpool University. Member Liverpool City Council, 1929–35; Member National Executive British Labour Party, and Chm. of Finance and General Purposes Cttee, 1940–47; Mem. TUC General Council, 1947–62; Chm. TUC, 1956–57; MP (Lab) Brigg Div. of Lincoln and Rutland, 1945–48. Trustee: Thomson Foundn, 1962–78; Liverpool Vic. Friendly Soc., 1967–. Hon. Associate, College of Technology, Birmingham. Served as non-commissioned officer, Royal Engineers, 1915–19, two years' active service, France and Belgium. JP Liverpool, 1933. Hon. LLD (Cambridge), 1959. *Address:* 13 Hurst Lea Court, Alderley Edge, Cheshire.                         *Died* 27 *Feb.* 1983.

**WILLIAMSON, Air Commandant Dame Alice Mary,** DBE 1958; RRC 1948 (ARRC 1941); retired as Matron-in-Chief, Princess Mary's Royal Air Force Nursing Service (1956–59); *b* 8 Jan. 1903; *d* of John William and Theodosia Williamson (*née* Lewis). *Educ:* Mells Girls Sch., near Frome, Somerset. Training Sch., Manchester Royal Infirmary, 1924–27; Post Graduate Courses, SCM, 1928–29; X-Ray Course, 1929–30; PMRAFNS, 1930–59. Promoted to Matron, Dec. 1944; Senior Matron, Wing Officer, 1951; Group Officer, 1952; Air Commandant, 1956; QHNS, 1956–59. Chief Nursing Officer, Kuwait Govt Nursing Service, 1959–62. *Recreations:* tennis, swimmimg, needlework. *Club:* United Nursing Services.                         *Died* 27 *July* 1983.

**WILLIAMSON, Bruce,** MD Edinburgh; FRCP; Hon. Consulting Physician: Royal Northern Hospital, N7; Prince of Wales General Hospital, N15; Barnet General Hospital; Enfield War Memorial Hospital; Brentwood and District Hospital; Hornsey Central Hospital; Ex-Member Medical Appeals Tribunal; Trustee Edinburgh University Club; *b* South Shields, 1893; 5th *s* of Captain David Williamson, Ladybank, and Jane Theresa Short, Edinburgh; *m* 1936, Margaret Stewart, *d* of William Gibson, Broughty Ferry; one *s*; *m* 1959, Yvonne, *d* of Arthur Carlebach. *Educ:* Newcastle; Bruges; Royal Colleges and University of Edinburgh. Senior Pres., Royal Medical Society, Edinburgh, 1921; Hons MD Edinburgh University, 1925; Lt, Bucks Bn Oxford and Bucks LI, seconded Machine Gun Corps. Founder, Hon. Mem. and former Pres., Scottish Med. Golfing Soc. *Publications:* Text Books: Diseases of Children, 9th edn 1964; Vital Cardiology: A New Outlook on the Prevention of Heart Failure; Diastole (Honeyman Gillespie lecture, Edin. Univ.); The Autonomic Nervous System, 1972; The Executive and the Seventies (lay physiology), 1973; articles in medical journals; The Future and The Fighting General (political-economy); contrib. to The Statist. *Recreation:* golf. *Club:* Edinburgh Univ. of London.
                                              *Died* 3 *Jan.* 1984.

**WILLIAMSON, John;** Editor, The Press Association Ltd, 1966–69; *b* 19 April 1915; *s* of late William Williamson and Jemima Williamson; *m* 1942, Queenie Myfanwy Pearl Bennett; two *d. Educ:* Holy Trinity School, Ashton-under-Lyne, Lancs. Junior Reporter, Manchester Evening News, 1933–34; Reporter, Morecambe & Heysham Visitor,

1934–36; Chief Reporter, East Ham Echo, 1936–38; News Sub-Editor, Press Assoc., 1938; Army, 1940–46, including service as Official Court Shorthand Writer in JAG's Office at Courts Martial and War Crime Trials; rejoined Press Assoc. as Sub-Editor, 1946; held various editorial appointments until 1958, when became Chief News Editor; Acting Man. Editor, Oct. 1965. *Recreations:* gardening, reading, walking. *Address:* 51 Carbery Avenue, W3. *T:* 01-992 7941. *Club:* Press.　　　　　　　　　　*Died* 4 *April* 1982.

**WILLIAMSON, Air Vice-Marshal Peter Greville Kaye,** CB 1977; CBE 1970; DFC 1943, and Bar 1944; Royal Air Force, retired; *b* 28 Feb. 1923; *s* of Maurice Kaye Williamson and Laura Elizabeth (*née* Clare); *m* 1953, Jill Anne Catherine Harvey; two *s* three *d*. *Educ:* Winchester House, Brackley; Dauntsey's Sch. Served War of 1939–45: N Africa and NW Europe (DFC and Bar); OC 219 Sqdn, 1945–46, OC 23 Sqdn, 1946–48, and OC 4 Sqdn, 1951–53; HQ NATO, Izmir, 1958, and Naples, 1959–61; OC 25 Sqdn, 1962; jssc 1963; Air Adviser to British High Comr, Pakistan, 1963–64; Gp Capt, Air Plans, RAF Germany, 1965–68; OC RAF Wittering, 1969–70; Dir of Establishments and Management Services, MoD (Air), 1970–72; SASO, HQ RAF Training Comd, 1972–74; AOC 38 Gp RAF, 1974–77. MBIM 1971. Order of St Olav, 1962. *Recreations:* sailing (cruising), flying, shooting, fishing, aqualung diving, golf, bee-keeping. *Address:* South Lombard, Lanteglos-by-Fowey, Cornwall. *Clubs:* Royal Air Force, Royal Cruising, Cruising Association; RAF Yacht (Hamble).　　　　　　　　　*Died* 8 *Oct.* 1982.

**WILLIAMSON, Thomas Bateson;** Assistant Secretary, Department of Health and Social Security, 1969–75, retired; *b* 17 April 1915; *y* *s* of late George Williamson and Dora May Williamson; *m* 1st, 1944, Winifred Mary Johnstone (decd); two *s*; 2nd, 1953, Pauline Mary Luard; four *d*. *Educ:* Barrow Gram. Sch.; Gonville and Caius Coll., Cambridge. 1st Cl. Hons, Mod. Langs Tripos, 1937. Entered War Office as Asst Principal, 1938. Served with HM Forces, 1940–45. Asst Principal, Min. of Health, 1945; Principal, 1946; Asst Secretary, 1954; Commonwealth Fund Fellowship, 1958–59; Under-Secretary, 1965; retired (health grounds), 1969; Asst Secretary, 1969; retired 1975. *Recreations:* fell-walking, music. *Address:* 1 St Mary's Grove, Barnes, SW13. *T:* 01–788 4274.　　　　　　　　*Died* 28 *March* 1985.

**WILLIS, Rt. Hon. Eustace George,** PC 1967; *b* 7 March 1903; *s* of Walter Willis and Rose Jane Eaton; *m* 1929, Mary Swan Ramsay Nisbet; one *d*. *Educ:* City of Norwich Sch. Engine Room Artificer, Royal Navy, 1919–30. Served Royal Artillery, 1942–45. Political Organiser, 1930–32; Bookseller and Lecturer for NCLC, 1932–64. MP (Lab), North Edinburgh, 1945–50, East Edinburgh, April 1954–70. Member: Select Cttee on Estimates, 1945–50, 1954–59; Central Adv. Cttee to Min. of Pensions, 1945–50; Mineral Development Cttee, 1946–48. Chairman: Edinburgh City Labour Party, 1952–54; Scottish Labour Party, 1954–55; Scottish Parliamentary Labour Party, 1961–63. Parliamentary Deleg. to Atlantic Congress, 1959, NATO, 1960–62. Minister of State, Scottish Office, 1964–67. Gen. Comr, Bd of Inland Revenue, 1972–78; Mem., Scottish Parole Bd, 1975–80. *Recreations:* book-collecting, music. *Address:* 31 Great King Street, Edinburgh EH3 6QR. *T:* 031–556 6941.　　　　　　　　　　*Died* 2 *June* 1987.

**WILLIS, Harold Infield,** QC 1952; *b* 28 March 1902; *yr* *s* of late Sir Frederick James Willis, KBE, CB, and Lady Willis; *m* 1943, Eileen Burnett Murray (*d* 1986); three *s*. *Educ:* Berkhamsted; New Coll., Oxford. Called to the Bar, 1926, Middle Temple; Bencher, Middle Temple, 1948, Treasurer, 1969. Served War of 1939–45, RAFVR, 1940–45. Dep. Chm., Hampshire QS, 1966–71. *Recreations:* gardening and fishing. *Address:* The Dovecote, Stoke Farthing Courtyard, Broadchalke, near Salisbury, Wilts.
　　　　　　　　　　　　　　　　　　*Died* 12 *Feb.* 1986.

**WILLIS, Dr Hector Ford,** CB 1960; Scientific Adviser, Ministry of Defence, 1962–70, retired; *b* 3 March 1909; *m* 1936, Marie Iddon (*née* Renwick). *Educ:* University College, Cardiff; Trinity Coll., Cambridge. British Cotton Industry Research Association, 1935–38; Admiralty, 1938; Chief of the Royal Naval Scientific Service, 1954–62. US Medal of Freedom (Silver Palm), 1947. *Publications:* Papers in Proceedings of Royal Society, Philosophical Magazine, Proceedings of the Faraday Society. *Address:* Fulwood, Eaton Park, Cobham, Surrey KT11 2JE.　　　　　　　　*Died* 20 *Nov.* 1989.

**WILLIS, John Henry,** RBA, ARCA (London); artist; *b* Tavistock, 9 Oct. 1887; *s* of R. Willis, art dealer; *m* Edith Barker, Paignton; one *s*; *m* Eleanor Rushton (*née* Claughton) (*d* 1976). *Educ:* Armstrong Coll., Durham Univ.; Royal College of Art, South Kensington. Portrait and Landscape Painter. *Principal works:* Kiwi Hut, on the line RA, 1921; 'Twixt Devon and Cornwall, on the line RA, 1923; The Nant Francon Pass, on the line RA, 1924; *portraits:* M. C. Oliver, RA, 1922; Stanley, son of E. J. Miles, RA, 1923. *Address:* 20 Titchfield Gardens, Paignton, Devon. *T:* Paignton 556850.
　　　　　　　　　　　　　　　　　　*Died* 17 *Oct.* 1989.

**WILLIS, Sir John (Ramsay),** Kt 1966; Judge of the High Court of Justice, Queen's Bench Division, 1966–80; *b* 1908; *s* of Dr and Mrs

J. K. Willis, Cranleigh, Surrey; *m* 1st, 1935, Peggy Eileen Branch; two *s*; 2nd, 1959, Barbara Ringrose. *Educ:* Lancing (Scholar); Trinity Coll., Dublin; BA, LLB (1st cl. Hons). Called to Bar, Gray's Inn, 1932; QC 1956. Royal Signals (TA), 1938–45; served War of 1939–45, France, India, Burma (Lt-Col); GSO 1 14th Army. Bencher, Gray's Inn, 1953, Treasurer, 1969. Recorder of Southampton, 1965–66; Dep. Chairman, E Suffolk QS, 1965–71; Mem., Parole Bd, 1974–75. *Recreations:* mountaineering, gardening. *Clubs:* Garrick, Alpine.　　　　　　　　　　*Died* 29 *Oct.* 1988.

**WILLIS, John Robert,** CB 1951; MC 1917; Under Secretary, Ministry of Transport, 1948–57; *b* 28 June 1896; *s* of late Professor A. R. Willis; *m* 1925, Alice Mary, *o* *d* of late R. F. Clarke; one *s* one *d*. *Educ:* St Paul's Sch.; Balliol Coll., Oxford. Inns of Court OTC, Worcestershire Regt (Lieut) and RAF, 1916–19; entered Board of Trade, 1920; Secretary, Food Council, 1932; Assistant Secretary, Industrial Supplies Dept, 1939; Commercial Relations and Treaties Dept, 1940; British Middle East Office, Cairo, 1946. *Address:* Flat 1, 212 Sheen Road, Richmond, Surrey TW10 5AN. *T:* 01-940 1942.
　　　　　　　　　　　　　　　　　　*Died* 18 *Sept.* 1982.

**WILLIS, Olive Christine, (Lady Willis),** CBE 1951; *b* 20 Nov. 1895; *d* of late Henry Edward Millar, Hampstead; *m* 1916, Lieut Algernon Usborne Willis (Admiral of the Fleet Sir Algernon U. Willis, GCB, KBE, DSO) (*d* 1976); two *d*. *Educ:* St Felix Sch., Southwold, Suffolk; Newnham Coll., Cambridge. Organised new Royal Naval Wives Voluntary Service, whereby older wives helped younger ones cope with separations of service life, 1946–50; started Under 5 Club, Valetta, Malta, 1946. Officer (Sister) Order of St John of Jerusalem, 1948. *Recreations:* appreciating gardens, reading, knitting. *Address:* c/o Lady Macdonald, Spinners Ash, Tilmore, Petersfield, Hants GU32 2JH.　　　　　　　　　　　*Died* 26 *Feb.* 1987.

**WILLIS, Comdr William John Adlam,** CBE 1953 (OBE 1937); MVO 1936; CGM 1916; KPM 1944; RN retired; DL; HM Inspector of Constabulary, 1953–64, retired; *b* 27 June 1894; *s* of Thomas Willis, RN, retired, Gillingham, Kent; *m* 1929, Kate Constance, *d* of Henry Sanders, Gillingham; two *s* one *d*. *Educ:* Royal Navy Hospital Sch., Greenwich. Joined RN 1909; wounded at Battle of Jutland 1916 (CGM); Lt-Comdr 1929; HMS Pembroke 1933–37. Chief Constable of Rochester, 1937–40; Chief Constable of Bedfordshire, 1940–53; DL: Bedfordshire, 1951–61; Suffolk, 1964–. French Médaille Militaire, 1916. *Address:* 8 Hall Lane, Dovercourt, Harwich, Essex CO12 3TE. *T:* Harwich 4722. *Club:* Reform.
　　　　　　　　　　　　　　　　　　*Died* 22 *June* 1982.

**WILLMER, Rt. Hon. Sir (Henry) Gordon,** Kt 1945; OBE 1945; TD; PC 1958; a Lord Justice of Appeal, 1958–Jan. 1969; *b* 1899; 4th *s* of late A. W. Willmer, JP, Birkenhead; *m* 1928, Barbara, *d* of late Sir Archibald Hurd; one *s* two *d*. *Educ:* Birkenhead Sch.; Corpus Christi Coll., Oxford. Hon. Fellow of Corpus Christi Coll., 1949. Called to Bar, 1924; KC 1939. Joined Territorial Army in 1925, and served with 53rd Medium Bde, RA (TA), till 1938, when retired on to TA Reserve of Officers, from which called up for service during the war; served with Coast Artillery, 1940–43, and with AMG, CMF, 1943–45. A Justice of the High Court. Probate, Divorce and Admiralty Division, 1945–58. President, Shipping Claims Tribunal, 1946; Member Supreme Court Cttee on Practice and Procedure, 1947; Member, General Claims Tribunal, 1950; Chm.; NI Detention Appeals Tribunal, 1973–75. Chairman, Inns of Court Mission, 1950–63; Treasurer, Inner Temple, 1969; Chm., Statutory Cttee, Pharmaceutical Soc. of GB, 1970–80, Hon. Fellow 1980. Mem., London Maritime Arbitrators' Assoc., 1970. Chm. Marine Bd, Investigation into loss of Amoco Cadiz, 1978–80. Trustee, Thalidomide Children's Trust, 1973–81. Hon. LLD Liverpool, 1966. *Address:* Flat 1, 34 Arkwright Road, Hampstead, NW3 6BH. *T:* 01-435 0690.　　　　　　　　　　　*Died* 17 *May* 1983.

**WILLOTT, Lt-Col Roland Lancaster,** DSO 1940; OBE 1945; TD 1946; BSc; CEng, FIMechE; *b* 1 May 1912; *s* of Frederick John Willott and Gertrude May Leese; *m* 1960, Elisabeth Petersen. *Educ:* Wellington Sch. (Somerset); University of Wales. College Apprentice Metropolitan Vickers Electrical Co., Trafford Park, Manchester, 1931–33; Mechanical Engineer Metropolitan Vickers Co., 1933–36; Major RE 1939–41; Lt-Col CRE 1941–45; Colonel Commander Army Group RE, 1945 (despatches, DSO, OBE, Order of Leopold of Belgium, Croix de Guerre). Chief Engineer, John Summers & Sons Ltd, 1945–69, Dir, 1965–71; Group Chief Engineer, Shotton Works, BSC, 1969–72. *Address:* 5 Curzon Park South, Chester CH4 8AA. *T:* Chester 674049. *Club:* Army and Navy.
　　　　　　　　　　　　　　　　　　*Died* 1 *Aug.* 1984.

**WILLOUGHBY DE BROKE,** 20th Baron, *cr* 1492; **John Henry Peyto Verney,** MC 1918; AFC 1940; AE; KStJ 1948; JP; Lord Lieutenant of Warwickshire, 1939–68; Air Commodore, Auxiliary Air Force, retired; *b* 21 May 1896; *o c* of 19th Baron and Marie Frances Lisette, OBE (*d* 1941), *y* *d* of C. A. Hanbury, Strathgarve, Ross-shire; *S* father, 1923; *m* 1933, Rachel, *d* of Sir Bourchier Wrey, 11th Bt, and Mrs Godfrey Heseltine; one *s* one *d*. *Educ:* Eton; Sandhurst. Served European War (MC); ADC to Governor of Bombay, 1919–22; late

Captain, 17–21st Lancers; Adjutant, Warwickshire Yeomanry, 1925–29; Joint Master Warwickshire Hounds, 1929–35; commanded No. 605 (County of Warwick) AAF Squadron, 1936–39 (AFCAEA) Staff Officer 11 Fighter Group, 1940 (despatches); Deputy Director Public Relations, Air Ministry, 1941–44; Director Public Relations, 1945–46. Member: National Hunt Cttee, 1940 (Steward, 1942–44, 1950–53, and 1964–67); Jockey Club, 1941 (Steward, 1944–47 and 1954–56). Chm., Tattersall's Cttee, 1948–53. Chairman: Birmingham Racecourse Co. Ltd, 1952–65 (Dir, 1932–65); The Steeplechase Co. (Cheltenham) Ltd, 1953–71 (Dir, 1944–71); Wolverhampton Racecourse Co. Ltd, 1947–71; Race-Finish Recording Co. Ltd, later Racecourse Technical Services Ltd, 1959–70 (Dir, 1947–70). Mem., Bloodstock Industry Cttee, Animal Health Trust, 1944– (Chm., 1964–77). President: Hunters' Improvement Society, 1957–58; Warwickshire Association of Boys' Clubs; Scouts Association; Council for Order of St John, 1946–68. Hon. Colonel, Warwickshire Yeomanry, 1942–63. *Heir:* s Hon. Leopold David Verney [b 14 Sept. 1938; m 1965, Petra, 2nd d of Sir John Aird, 3rd Bt, MVO, MC; three s]. *Address:* 19 Campden Hill Gate, Duchess of Bedford Walk, W8 7QH. *T:* 01–937 8548. *Club:* Cavalry and Guards. *Died 25 May 1986.*

**WILLOUGHBY, Rear-Admiral Guy,** CB 1955; b 7 Nov. 1902; s of Rev. Nesbit E. Willoughby, Vicar of Bickington, Devon, and of Marjorie Helen Willoughby (née Kaye); m 1923, Mary, d of J. G. W. Aldridge, AMICE, Wimbledon; one s one d. *Educ:* Osborne and Dartmouth. Joined Osborne, 1916; Sub-Lieut, 1923; qualified as a naval pilot 1925, and thereafter flew as a pilot in Naval and RAF Squadrons, embarked in various Carriers until 1936; Commander, 1937; Commander (Air) in Glorious, 1938–39; served on naval staff, Admiralty, 1940–41; comd HM Carrier Activity, 1942–43; Captain, 1943; Chief Staff Officer to Admiral Comdg Carriers in Eastern Fleet, 1944; Director of Air Warfare and Training (Naval Staff, Admiralty), 1945–46; Imperial Defence Coll., 1947; 4th Naval Member of Australian Commonwealth Navy Board and Cdre (Air), 1948–50; comd HM Carrier Eagle, 1951–52; Rear-Admiral 1953; Flag Officer, Flying Training, 1953–56, retired, 1956. *Address:* High Croft, South Woodchester, near Stroud, Glos. *T:* Amberley 2594. *Club:* Naval and Military.
*Died 19 Nov. 1987.*

**WILLS, Lt-Col Sir (Ernest) Edward (de Winton),** 4th Bt, cr 1904; of Hazlewood and Clapton-in-Gordano; b 8 Dec. 1903; s of Sir Ernest Salter Wills, 3rd Bt, and Caroline Fanny Maud de Winton (d 1953); S father 1958; m 1st, 1926, Sylvia Margaret (d 1946), d of late William Barker Ogden; two d: 2nd, 1949, Juliet Eve, d of late Captain John Eagles Henry Graham-Clarke, JP, Frocester Manor, Glos. *Educ:* Eton. Formerly Lieut, Scots Guards; Lieut-Colonel late Middlesex Regt; Lieut-Colonel Comdg 5th Bn, Manchester Regt; served European War, 1939–45. Is a member of Lloyd's. *Recreation:* fishing. *Heir:* nephew David Seton Wills [b 29 Dec. 1939; m 1968, Gillian, twin d of A. P. Eastoe; one s three d]. *Address:* Lochs Lodge, Glenlyon, Perthshire PH15 2PU. *T:* Bridge of Balgie 200; Mount Prosperous, Hungerford, Berks RG17 0RP. *T:* Hungerford 2624. *Clubs:* Cavalry and Guards; Household Division Yacht.
*Died 19 Aug. 1983.*

**WILLS, Joseph Lyttleton,** CBE 1965; **Hon. Mr Justice Wills;** Judge, Supreme Court, Windward Islands and Leeward Islands, WI, since 1955; b 24 June 1899; m 1940, Dorothy Cather; one d. *Educ:* Middle School, Georgetown, British Guiana; Queen's Coll., British Guiana; King's Coll., London. Barrister-at-law, Inner Temple, 1928; admitted to practice as Barrister-at-Law, British Guiana, 1930; Magistrate, 1947; Additional Puisne Judge of Supreme Court of British Guiana, 1953–55. Councillor of Georgetown, 1933; Deputy Mayor, 1942–43; Hon. Member of Legislative Council, British Guiana, 1933; President, British Guiana Labour Union and British Guiana Workers League; Chairman and Member of several public committees; Member Judicial Service Commn, British Guiana, 1963; Chairman, Income Tax (Appeal) Board of Review, Guyana, 1966. Chairman of British Guiana Congregational Union, 1949–53 and 1974–75. Jubilee Medal, 1935; Coronation Medal, 1953. *Recreations:* horse-riding, motoring and cricket. *Address:* Lyttleton House, 57 Chalmers Place, Stabroek, Georgetown, Guyana. *Clubs:* Royal Commonwealth Society (West Indian); Guyana Cricket, Maltenoes Sports (Guyana); Castries (WI).

**WILMERS, John Geoffrey,** QC 1965; a Recorder of the Crown Court, since 1972; a Judge of the Court of Appeal of Jersey and Guernsey, since 1978; b 27 Dec. 1920; m 1946, June I. K. Mecredy; one s two d. *Educ:* Leighton Park Sch., Reading; St John's Coll., Cambridge. Called to the Bar, Inner Temple, 1948, Bencher, 1972. Dep. Chm., Hants QS, 1970–71. *Recreations:* travel, skiing, walking, gardening. *Address:* 1 Harcourt Buildings, Temple, EC4Y 9DA. *T:* 01–353 2214. *Died 17 Dec. 1984.*

**WILMOT, Air Vice-Marshal Aubrey S.;** see Sidney-Wilmot.

**WILSEY, Maj.-Gen. Anthony Patrick W.;** see Willasey-Wilsey.

**WILSON OF RADCLIFFE,** Baron cr 1974 (Life Peer), of Radcliffe, Lancs; **Alfred Wilson;** b 10 June 1909; s of late William Barnes Wilson and Jane; m 1st, 1932, Elsie Hulton (d 1974); one d (one s decd); 2nd, 1976, Freda Mather. *Educ:* Technical Sch., Newcastle upon Tyne. CWS Ltd: Dep. Sec. and Exec. Officer, 1953; Sec., 1965; Chief Exec. Officer, 1969–74. FCIS. *Recreations:* photography, walking, gardening. *Address:* 58 Ringley Road, Whitefield, Manchester. *Died 25 Jan. 1983.*

**WILSON, Rear-Adm. Alan Christopher Wyndham,** CB 1972; retired, 1975; Senior Naval Member, Directing Staff, Royal College of Defence Studies, 1972–Jan. 1975; b 7 Sept. 1919; s of Alan Christopher Hill-Wilson and Nancy Green; m 1958, Joan Rhoda Landale, Deniliquin, Australia; one step d. *Educ:* St Bee's, Cumberland. Served at sea during War of 1939–45; Malta Dockyard, 1946–49; HMS Diamond, 1949–52; Admty, 1952–55; Australia, 1956–58; HMS Ark Royal, 1959–61; Admty, 1962–64; with Flag Officer, Aircraft Carriers, 1964–66; with Comdr, Far East Fleet, 1966–69; idc 1969; Hd of British Defence Liaison Staff, Canberra, 1970–72. *Recreations:* golf, fishing. *Address:* Church Farm House, Wellow, near Bath. *T:* Combe Down 832051. *Clubs:* Army and Navy, Royal Automobile. *Died 16 July 1985.*

**WILSON, Alfred Harold,** CB 1949; CBE 1946; b 9 March 1895; er s of late Alfred Henry Wilson; m 1925, Edythe Rose, d of late Philip Richard Snewin; no c. *Educ:* Tottenham Grammar School. Associate of Assoc. of Certified Accountants, 1922, FCCA 1980. Board of Trade, Central Office for Labour Exchanges, 1913; GPO, Accountant-General's Department, 1914. Served European War, Royal Marine Artillery, 1916–19. Assistant Surveyor, General Post Office, 1923; Principal, Air Ministry, Dept of Civil Aviation, 1937; Assistant Secretary, Air Ministry, i/c Organisation and Methods Division, 1941; Assistant Secretary (with title Director of Home Civil Aviation) Air Ministry, Dept of Civil Aviation, 1943; transferred to new Ministry of Civil Aviation on its formation and promoted Principal Asst Secretary, 1945; Under Secretary, Ministry of Civil Aviation, 1946; during this period was Chairman London Airport lay-out Panel, which was responsible for runway layout design of the Airport; Deputy Secretary, Ministry of Transport and Civil Aviation, 1956–58; Adviser on Commercial Air Transport to the Ministry of Transport and Civil Aviation, 1958–60; Member of the Air Transport Licensing Board, 1960–65. *Address:* c/o Barclays Bank, High Street, Guildford, Surrey. *Died 10 April 1984.*

**WILSON, Rev. Canon Andrew;** Canon Residentiary of Newcastle, and Director of Ordinands and Post-Ordination Studies, since 1964; Examining Chaplain to the Bishop of Newcastle, since 1969; b 27 April 1920; o s of late Stewart and Isobel Wilson. *Educ:* Salt's High School, Shipley; Univ. of Durham. Scholar of St Chad's Coll., Durham, 1939; BA Hons Mod. Hist., 1941; Lightfoot Scholar, 1941; Dip. Theol. (Dist.), 1943; MA 1944; Deacon, 1943; Priest, 1944. Asst Curate: of St Cuthbert's, Newcastle, 1943–45; of St John's, Wallsend, 1945–48; Priest-in-charge of Backworth, 1948–55; Vicar of Horton, 1955–58; Rector of St John's, Ballachulish, 1958–64. *Address:* 1 Mitchell Avenue, Jesmond, Newcastle upon Tyne NE2 3JY. *T:* Newcastle 812075. *Died 22 May 1985.*

**WILSON, Sir (Archibald) Duncan,** GCMG 1971 (KCMG 1965; CMG 1955); HM Diplomatic Service, retired; Master of Corpus Christi College, Cambridge, 1971–80, Hon. Fellow, 1980; b 12 August 1911; s of late Archibald Edward Wilson and late Ethel May (née Schuster); m 1937, Elizabeth Anne Martin Fleming; two d (one s decd). *Educ:* Winchester; Balliol College, Oxford 1st Class Hon. Mods, Lit. Hum., Oxford; Craven school., Oxford Univ., Jenkyns Exhibitioner, Balliol Coll.; Laming Fellow, Queen's Coll. Taught at Westminster School, 1936–37; Asst Keeper, British Museum, 1937–39; Min. of Economic Warfare, 1939–41; empl. FO, 1941–45; CCG, 1945–46; entered Foreign Service, 1947; served Berlin, 1947–49; Yugoslavia, 1951–55; Director of Research and Acting Librarian, 1955–57; Chargé d'Affaires, Peking, 1957–59; Assistant Under-Secretary, Foreign Office, 1960–64; Ambassador to: Yugoslavia, 1964–68; the USSR, 1968–71. Fellow, Center of International Affairs, Harvard Univ. (on Secondment, 1959–60). Hon. Vice-Pres., UK Council for Overseas Student Affairs. Mem., Standing Commn on Museums and Galls, 1973–78. Chm., Cttee of Enquiry into Public Records, 1978–80. Mem. Bd of Governors, King's Sch., Canterbury, 1972–80. *Publications:* Life and Times of Vuk Stefanović Karadzić, 1970; Leonard Woolf, a political biography, 1978; Tito's Yugoslavia, 1979; *posthumous publication:* Gilbert Murray, OM, 1866–1957, 1988. *Recreations:* music, golf, walking. *Address:* Cala Na Ruadh, Port Charlotte, Islay, Argyll. *Club:* Royal Commonwealth Society. *Died 20 Sept. 1983.*

**WILSON, Sir Austin (George),** Kt 1981; OBE 1958; retired; b 6 Nov. 1906; s of George Wilson and Lydia Mary Wilson; m 1936, Ailsa Blanche (née Percy); one s. *Educ:* Auckland Grammar Sch. FCIS; FNZSocA; FInstD. Director: NZ Forest Products Ltd, 1959–79 (Chm., 1968–73 and 1977–79); Auckland Gas Co. Ltd, 1959–85 (Chm., 1963–85); NZ Insurance Co. Ltd, 1961–82 (Chm., 1967–71);

E. Lichtenstein & Co. Ltd, 1961–84; Nestles (NZ) Ltd, 1962–80; Plessey (NZ) Ltd, 1968–83 (Chm., 1970–83); Progressive Enterprises Ltd, 1971–79; NZI Finance Corporation Ltd, 1972–84 (Chm., 1972–84); Nissan Datsun Holdings Ltd, 1971–83 (Chm., 1973–82). Mem., Auckland Harbour Board, 1947–56 (Chm., 1953–55); Auckland Harbour Bd Sinking Fund Comr, 1963–. Life Member: Auckland Chamber of Commerce, 1963; NZ Bureau of Importers, 1978; Gas Assoc. of New Zealand, 1978. *Recreation:* lawn bowls. *Clubs:* Northern, Rotary of Auckland (Pres., 1958) (Auckland).
*Died 5 May 1987.*

**WILSON, Ellis;** *see* Wilson, H. E. C.

**WILSON, Maj.-Gen. Geoffrey Boyd,** CB 1979; Regimental Comptroller, Royal Artillery, since 1982; Controller, Royal Artillery Institution, since 1982; Chairman, Board of Management, Royal Artillery Charitable Fund and Royal Artillery Association, since 1982; *b* London, 21 Jan. 1927; *s* of Horace Alexander Wilson and Hilda Evelyn (*née* Gratwicke); *m* 1952, Fay Rosemary Scott; five *d*. *Educ:* St Paul's Sch.; Edinburgh Univ. psc 1957, jssc 1963. Commnd RA, 1946; served Italy, Palestine, Egypt, N Africa, with 39 Medium Regt, 1946–50; 5 RHA, BAOR, 1951–54; GSO3 6 Armoured Div., BAOR, 1954–56; Brigade Major RA, 53 (Welsh) Div., 1958–60; Instr and GSO2, RMA Sandhurst, 1961–63; Batt. Comdr, 137 (Java) Bty, BAOR, 1964; 2 i/c and Ops Officer, 40 Light Regt, BAOR and Borneo, 1965–66; CO 20 Heavy Regt, BAOR, 1967–68; Asst Mil. Sec., Mil. Sec. (SB), MoD, 1969–71; CRA 3 Inf. Div., UK, 1971–73; RCDS, 1974; Dir, Def. Operational Plans, MoD, 1975–76; Maj.-Gen. RA, BAOR, 1976–77; GOC Artillery Div., 1977–79; C of S and Head of UK Delegn to Live Oak, SHAPE, 1979–82, retired 1982. A Col Comdt, Royal Regt of Artillery, 1982–; Hon. Col, 104 AD Regt (V), 1984–. *Recreations:* gardening, music, reading. *Address:* c/o Artillery House, Connaught Barracks, Grand Depot Road, SE18 6SL. *T:* 01–855 9640. *Club:* Army and Navy.
*Died 11 Feb. 1984.*

**WILSON, Sir Graham (Selby),** Kt 1962; MD, FRCP, DPH (London); FRS 1978; late Captain Royal Army Medical Corps (Special Reserve); Hon. Lecturer, Department of Bacteriology and Immunology, London School of Hygiene and Tropical Medicine, 1964–70; Director of the Public Health Laboratory Service, 1941–63; KHP, 1944–46; *b* 10 Sept. 1895; *m* Mary Joyce (*d* 1976), *d* of Alfred Ayrton, Chester; two *s*. *Educ:* Epsom College; King's Coll., London; Charing Cross Hospital, London; Governors' Clinical Gold Medal, Charing Cross Hospital, and Gold Medal, University of London, MB, BS; Specialist in Bacteriology, Royal Army Med. Corps, 1916–20; Demonstrator in Bacteriology, Charing Cross Hospital Medical School, 1919–22; Lecturer in Bacteriology, University of Manchester, 1923–27; Reader in Bacteriology, University of London, 1927–30; Prof. of Bacteriology as applied to Hygiene, London School of Hygiene and Tropical Medicine, 1930–47; William Julius Mickle Fellowship, University of London, 1939. Member: Council, RCP, 1938–40; of several cttees on tuberculosis, poliomyelitis and other infectious diseases; Weber-Parkes prize, RCP 1942; Milroy Lecturer, RCP, 1948; Hon. Fellow, Amer. Public Health Assoc., 1953; Hon. Fellow: Royal Soc. of Health, 1960; London Sch. of Hygiene and Tropical Medicine, 1976; Hon. FRSocMed, 1971; Hon. FRCPath, 1972. Czechoslovak Medical Society, Jan Evangelista Purkyně, 1963; Bisset Hawkins Medal, RCP, 1956; Marjory Stephenson Memorial Prize, 1959; Stewart Prize, 1960; Buchanan Medal, Royal Society, 1967; Harben Gold Medal, 1970; Jenner Meml Medal, 1975. Hon. LLD (Glasgow) 1962. *Publications:* The Principles of Bacteriology and Immunity (with late Professor W. W. C. Topley and Sir Ashley Miles), 6th edn 1975, (also with Dr M. T. Parker) 7th edn 1984; The Hazards of Immunization, 1967; The Bacteriological Grading of Milk (with collaborators), 1935; The Pasteurization of Milk, 1942; The Brown Animal Sanatory Institution, 1979; numerous papers on bacteriological subjects. *Address:* 11 Morpeth Mansions, Morpeth Terrace, SW1P IER. *Club:* Athenæum.
*Died 5 April 1987.*

**WILSON, Rear-Adm. Guy Austen Moore,** CB 1958; Breeder and Voluntary Organiser, Guide Dogs for the Blind Association; *b* 7 June 1906; *s* of Ernest Moore Wilson, Buenos Aires, and Katharine Lawrence; *m* 1932, Dorothy, *d* of Sir Arthur Watson, CBE; two *s* three *d*. *Educ:* Royal Naval Colleges, Osborne and Dartmouth. Joined Royal Navy, 1920; Engineering Specialist Course, 1924–28. Advanced Engineering Course, Royal Naval College, Greenwich, 1928–30; served War of 1939–45, at Admiralty and in HMS Berwick; Portsmouth Dockyard, 1946–49; Comdr, 1940; Captain, 1948; Dep. Director Aircraft Maintenance and Repair, Admiralty, 1950–52; Supt, RN Aircraft Yard, Fleetlands, 1952–55; Rear-Admiral, 1955; Deputy Engineer-in-Chief for Fleet Maintenance and Administration, 1955–57; Rear-Admiral Nuclear Propulsion and Deputy Engineer-in-Chief (Nuclear Propulsion), 1957–59, retired 1960; Chief Executive, Dracone Developments Ltd, 1960–63. *Recreations:* swimming, motoring, gardening. *Address:* Barn Acre, Saxstead Green, Woodbridge, Suffolk. *T:* Earl Soham 365.
*Died 11 Jan. 1986.*

**WILSON, Harold Fitzhardinge Wilson;** Solicitor and Parliamentary Officer, Greater London Council, 1970–77 (Dep. Solicitor and Dep. Parly Officer, 1965); *b* 6 Jan. 1913; *s* of Walter James Wilson and Aileen Wilson (*née* Scrivens), Broadway, Worcs; *m* 1939, Deb Buckland; one *s* one *d*. Law Clerk, LCC, 1935. Company Officer, then Senior Company Officer, Nat. Fire Service, 1939–45. Principal Asst, LCC, 1951; Asst Parly Officer, LCC, 1960. Hon. Solicitor, RoSPA, 1970–77. Liveryman, Glaziers' Co. *Recreations:* the theatre, travelling, gardening, reading. *Address:* 34 Victoria Drive, Bognor Regis, Sussex.
*Died 23 March 1984.*

**WILSON, (Harry) Ellis (Charter),** MB, ChB; DSc; FRCPGlas; retired as Lecturer in Pathological Biochemistry at Royal Hospital for Sick Children, Glasgow; *b* 26 July 1899; *s* of Harry James and Margaret Williamina Wilson. *Educ:* Glasgow Academy and University. Carnegie Scholar, 1923; studied in Würzburg, 1926; Assistant in Institute of Physiology, Glasgow University, 1924; a Rockefeller Fellowship tenable in USA, 1926; carried out research in New York and the Mayo Clinic, Rochester; Carnegie Teaching Fellow in Institute of Physiology, Glasgow University, 1930; studied (research) in Germany, 1931; Professor of Biochemistry and Nutrition, The All-India Institute of Hygiene and Public Health, Calcutta, 1934–37, and Professor of Chemistry, The Medical College, Calcutta, 1935–37. *Publications:* papers on biochemical subjects in various journals. *Recreations:* golf, travel. *Address:* Redholm, 5 West Chapelton Avenue, Bearsden, Glasgow; The Royal Hospital for Sick Children, Yorkhill, Glasgow.
*Died 18 April 1987.*

**WILSON, Harry Lawrence L.;** *see* Lawrence-Wilson.

**WILSON, Col Henry James,** CBE 1963 (OBE 1943); TD 1944; Farmer since 1949; *b* 10 June 1904; *s* of late James Wilson; *m* 1930, Anita Gertrude Petley; three *s*. *Educ:* Mercers' School. Westminster Bank, 1921–39. Served London Scottish, 1923–44; Commanded 1st Bn London Scottish, 1941–44; AAG, 8th Army HQ, 1944; DDPS, AFHQ, 1944–45; War Office, 1945–49. Joined NFU, 1947; Council Member, 1954; Vice-Pres., 1958; Dep. Pres., 1959–62; Hon. Treasurer, 1971–81. Chairman: Bacon Consultative Council, 1957–64; Industry Panel, Bacon Mkt Council, 1964–72. *Recreations:* shooting, fishing. *Address:* Hamsey, Caldbec Hill, Battle, East Sussex. *Clubs:* Farmers'; Highland Brigade.
*Died 26 March 1985.*

**WILSON, (Henry) James;** Chief Chancery Registrar, 1979–82, retired; *b* 3 Sept. 1916; *s* of Alfred Edgar and Margaret Ethel Wilson; *m* 1st, 1940, Felicity Sidney (*née* Daniels); one *s* two *d*; 2nd, 1972, Peggy Frances (*née* Browne). *Educ:* Wrekin College. Territorial Army, Westminster Dragoons, 1936; embodied for war service, 1939; commissioned, later Captain Royal Tank Regt. Admitted Solicitor, 1938; joined Chancery Registrar's Office, 1946; Chancery Registrar, 1961. *Recreations:* gardening, opera. *Address:* Ingleside Ferbies, Speldhurst, Kent TN3 0NS. *T:* Langton (0892) 863172. *Club:* Wig and Pen.
*Died 28 July 1990.*

**WILSON, Sir Hugh;** *see* Wilson, Sir L. H.

**WILSON, Rev. Canon Ian George MacQueen;** Dean of Argyll and the Isles, 1979–87; Rector of St John's, Ballachulish and St Mary's, Glencoe, 1978–85; *b* 6 March 1920; *s* of Joseph and Mary Wilson; *m* 1952, Janet Todd Kyle. *Educ:* Edinburgh Theological College. Deacon 1950, priest 1951; Curate, St Margaret's, Glasgow, 1950–52; Priest-in-charge, St Gabriel's, Glasgow, 1952–57; Rector: Christ Church, Dalbeattie, 1957–61; St John's, Baillieston, 1961–64; St Paul's, Rothesay, 1964–75; Canon, St John's Cathedral, Oban, 1973; Priest-in-charge, St Peter's, Stornoway, 1975–78; Officiating Chaplain, RAF, Stornoway, 1975–78; Synod Clerk, Diocese of Argyll and the Isles, 1977–79. Hon. Canon, St John's Cathedral, Oban and Cathedral of the Isles, Cumbrae, 1987–. Hon. LTh, St Mark's Inst. of Theology, 1974. *Address:* The Parsonage, Ardchattan, Bonawe, Oban, Argyll PA37 1RL. *T:* Bonawe 228.
*Died 18 Nov. 1988.*

**WILSON, Isabel Grace Hood,** CBE 1961; MD, FRCP; Principal Medical Officer, Ministry of Health, retired; *b* 16 Sept. 1895; *d* of late Dr George R. Wilson and Susan C. Sandeman. *Educ:* privately; University of Edinburgh. MB, ChB, Edinburgh, 1921; DPM London, 1924; MD, Edinburgh, 1926; MRCP London, 1937, FRCP 1947. Formerly: Asst Medical Officer, Severalls Mental Hospital, Colchester; Physician, Tavistock Square Clinic for Functional Nervous Disorders; Medical Commissioner, Board of Control, 1931–49; Senior Medical Commissioner, Board of Control, 1949–60. Member BMA; President, Royal Medico Psychological Assoc., 1962–63. Founder Mem., Royal College of Psychiatrists. *Publications:* A Study of Hypoglycæmic Shock Treatment in Schizophrenia (Report), 1936; (jointly) Report on Cardiazol Treatment, 1938; various contributions to journals. *Recreations:* water-colour painting, travel. *Address:* 48 Redcliffe Gardens, SW10 9HB. *T:* 01–352 5707.
*Died 8 Dec. 1982.*

**WILSON, James;** *see* Wilson H. J.

**WILSON, J(ohn) Greenwood**, MD, FRCP, DPH; Fellow of King's College, University of London; formerly: Group Medical Consultant, Health and Hygiene, FMC Ltd; Medical Officer of Health, Port and City of London (first holder of dual appointment; MOH Port of London, 1954, MOH, City of London, in addition, 1956); *b* 27 July 1897; 2nd *s* of late Rev. John Wilson, Woolwich; *m* 1st, 1929, Wenda Margaret Hithersay Smith (marr. diss. 1941); one *s* two *d*; 2nd, 1943, Gwendoline Mary Watkins (*d* 1975); one *d*. *Educ*: Colfe Grammar Sch.; Westminster Hospital, University of London. Served European War, S. Lancashire Regt, RFC and RAF, 1916–19 (wounded). Various hospital appointments, London and provinces and some general practice, 1923–28; subseq. MOH and Sch. Medical Officer posts; then MOH City and Port of Cardiff, Sch. MO, Cardiff Education Authority, and Lecturer in Preventive Medicine, Welsh Nat. School of Medicine, 1933–54. President, Welsh Br. Society of Med. Officers of Health, 1940–45, Member Nat. Adv. Council for recruitment of Nurses and Midwives, 1943–56. Governor, St Bart's Hospital Medical College. Formerly Examiner in Public Health, RCPS (London); Vice-President (Past Chairman of Council) and Hon. Fellow, Royal Society of Health. Hon. Sec., Assoc. of Sea and Air Port Health Authorities of British Isles, 1936–43; Member, Central Housing Advisory Cttee, 1936–56; Member Royal Commission on Mental Health, 1954–57; Chairman, City Division, BMA, 1962–63; Vice-President (Past Chairman), National House-Building Council. Hon. Fellow American Public Health Association. OStJ 1953. *Publications*: Diptheria Immunisation Propaganda and Counter Propaganda, 1933; Public Health Law in Question and Answer, 1951; numerous contributions to med., scientific and tech. publications. *Recreations*: theatre, music, swimming. *Club*: Wig and Pen. *Died* 14 June 1990.

**WILSON, Sir Keith (Cameron)**, Kt 1966; Member of House of Representatives for Sturt, South Australia, 1949–54, 1955–66; *b* 3 Sept. 1900; *s* of Algernon Theodore King Wilson; *m* 1930, Elizabeth H., *d* of late Sir Lavington Bonython; two *s* one *d*. *Educ*: Collegiate School of St Peter, Adelaide; University of Adelaide. LLB 1922. Admitted to Bar, 1922. Served War of 1939–45: Gunner, 2nd AIF, 1940; Middle East, 1940–43; Major. Senator for South Australia, 1938–44. Chm., Aged Cottage Homes Inc., 1952–71; Past President: Blinded Welfare Fund; Good Neighbour Council of SA, 1968–72; Queen Elizabeth Hosp. Research Foundn; Legacy. *Publication*: Wilson-Uppill Wheat Equalization Scheme, 1938. *Address*: 79 Tusmore Avenue, Tusmore, SA 5065, Australia. *T*: 315578. *Club*: Adelaide (Adelaide). *Died* 28 Sept. 1987.

**WILSON, Sir (Leslie) Hugh**, Kt 1967; OBE 1952; PPRIBA; FRTPI; Architect and Town Planner; Senior Partner, Hugh Wilson & Lewis Womersley, Architects and Town Planners, since 1962; *b* 1 May 1913; *s* of Frederick Charles Wilson and Ethel Anne Hughes; *m* 1938, Monica Chrysavye Nomico (*d* 1966); one *s* two *d*. *Educ*: Haberdashers' Aske's Sch. Asst Architect, private practices, 1933–39; Asst Architect, Canterbury, 1939–45; City Architect and Planning Officer, Canterbury, 1945–56; Chief Architect and Planning Officer, Cumbernauld New Town, 1956–62. Techn. Adviser on Urban Development to Min. of Housing and Local Government, 1965–67. Works include housing, churches, central area develt; Master Plans for Irvine, Skelmersdale, Redditch, and Northampton New Towns; central area plans for Oxford, Brighton, Exeter, Lewes, Cardiff, Torbay. Dir (part-time), Property Services Agency, DoE, 1973–74. Member: EDC for Building, NEDO, 1970–77; Royal Fine Art Commn, 1971–; Environmental Bd, 1975–79; Chm., London Docklands Jt Cttee, 1977–81; Mem., London Docklands Develt Corp., 1981–84. Vice-President, RIBA, 1960–61, 1962–64, Sen. Vice-President, 1966–67, President, 1967–69. DistTP 1956. Hon. FRAIC; Hon. FAIA; Hon. FIStructE; Hon. FCIOB; Hon. FCIBS; Hon. Mem., Akademie der Künste, Berlin. Hon. DSc Aston, 1969. *Recreations*: travel, music. *Address*: 2 Kings Well, Heath Street, Hampstead, NW3 1EN. *T*: 01–435 3637. *Club*: Athenæum. *Died* 20 July 1985.

**WILSON, Rt. Rev. Lucian Charles U.;** *see* Usher-Wilson.

**WILSON, Sir Michael (Thomond)**, Kt 1975; MBE 1945; a Vice-Chairman: Lloyds Bank Ltd, 1973–81 (a Director, 1968–81; Chief General Manager, 1967–73); Lloyds & Scottish Ltd, 1976–81; Director: Lloyds Bank International Ltd, 1973–81; Yorkshire Bank Ltd, 1973–79; *b* 7 Feb. 1911; *e s* of late Sir Roy Wilson, Pyrford, near Woking; *m* 1933, Jessie Babette, *o d* of late John Winston Foley Winnington, Malvern, Worcs; two *s* one *d*. *Educ*: Rugby Sch.; Oriel Coll., Oxford. War Service with RA and on Staff in UK and India, 1939–45. Entered Lloyds Bank, 1932; Assistant General Manager, 1958; Dep. Chief General Manager, 1963. Chm., Export Guarantees Adv. Council, 1972–77. JP Berks, 1962–66. *Address*: Clytha, South Ascot, Berks. *T*: Ascot 20833.
*Died* 4 Oct. 1983.

**WILSON, Percy**, CB 1955; Senior Chief Inspector of Schools for England and Wales, Department of Education and Science, 1957–65; Director of Education, Bank Education Service, 1965–79,

Consultant, 1979–81; *b* 15 Dec. 1904; *s* of Joseph Edwin and Louisa Wilson; *m* 1st, 1929, Beryl Godsell (decd); 2nd, 1943, Dorothy Spiers; one *s* one *d*. *Educ*: Market Rasen Grammar Sch.; Jesus Coll., Cambridge. Schoolmaster, 1927–35; HM Inspector of Schools, 1935–45 (seconded to war duties, 1939–42); Staff Inspector for English, 1945–47; a Chief Inspector, Ministry of Education, 1947–57. Hon. FCP, 1965. A Governor, Wellington Coll., 1966–75. *Publication*: Views and Prospects from Curzon Street, 1964. *Recreation*: painting. *Address*: Hopstones Cottage, Pensham Village, near Pershore, Worcs WR10 3HB. *T*: Pershore 555403.
*Died* 1 July 1986.

**WILSON, Peter Cecil**, CBE 1970; Director: Sotheby & Co., since 1938 (Chairman, 1958–80, Honorary Life President, since 1982); SPB Group, since 1977 (Chairman, 1977–80); *b* 8 March 1913; 3rd *s* of Sir Mathew Wilson, 4th Bt, CSI, DSO, Eshton Hall, Gargrave, Yorkshire; *m* 1935, Grace Helen Ranken (marr. diss.); two *s*. *Educ*: Eton; New Coll., Oxford. Benjamin Franklin Medal, RSA 1968. *Address*: Chateau de Clavary, 06810 Auribeau sur Siagne, France.
*Died* 3 June 1984.

**WILSON, Peter Humphrey St John**, CB 1956; CBE 1952; Deputy Under Secretary of State, Department of Employment and Productivity, 1968–69, retired (Deputy Secretary, Ministry of Labour, 1958–68); *b* 1 May 1908; *e s* of late Rt Rev. Henry A. Wilson, CBE, DD; *m* 1939, Catherine Laird (*d* 1963), *d* of late H. J. Bonser, London; three *d*. *Educ*: Cheltenham Coll. (Schol.); Corpus Christi Coll., Cambridge (Foundation Schol.). Assistant Principal, Ministry of Labour, 1930; Principal, 1936; Regional Controller, Northern Region, 1941; Controller, Scotland, 1944; Under Secretary, 1952. *Recreations*: reading, music, grand-children. *Address*: Thorntree Cottage, Blackheath, near Guildford, Surrey. *T*: Guildford 893758. *Died* 5 May 1987.

**WILSON, Robert Andrew**, CB 1962; Principal Keeper, Department of Printed Books, British Museum, 1959–66; *b* 18 July 1905; *s* of Robert Bruce Wilson; *m* 1967, Rosemary Ann, *d* of Sydney Joseph Norris. *Educ*: Westminster School; Trinity College, Cambridge. Assistant Keeper, Department of Printed Books, British Museum, 1929–48, Deputy Keeper, 1948–52; also Superintendent of the Reading Room, British Museum, 1948–52; Keeper, 1952–59. *Address*: 33 Denmark Avenue, Wimbledon, SW19.
*Died* 18 Aug. 1984.

**WILSON, Robert Graham**, MBE 1956; Regional Director, Chairman Economic Planning Board, Yorkshire and Humberside Region of Department of the Environment, 1973–77; retired; *b* 7 Aug. 1917; 2nd *s* of late John Wilson and late Kate Benson Wilson (*née* Martindale); *m* 1943, Winifred Mary (*née* Elson); one *s* three *d*. *Educ*: Bradfield Coll.; Gonville and Caius Coll., Cambridge. BA. Joined Burma Frontier Service, 1939; War Service in Burma (Captain; despatches 1945); joined Colonial Admin. Service, as District Officer, Kenya, 1949 (despatches, Mau Mau, 1957); joined Home Civil Service, MPBW, 1964; Regional Dir, MPBW, Malta, 1968–71; Regional Dir (Works) Leeds, DoE, 1971–73. *Recreations*: gardening, water colour painting. *Address*: Westbrook, 5 Shorefield Way, Milford-on-Sea, Hampshire. *T*: Milford-on-Sea 2006. *Club*: Hawks (Cambridge). *Died* 8 July 1982.

**WILSON, Very Rev. Professor-Emeritus Robert John**, MA, BD, DD; retired as Principal of the Presbyterian College, Belfast (1961–64), and Professor of Old Testament Language, Literature and Theology (1939–64), also Principal of the Presbyterian Theological Faculty, Ireland (1962–64); *b* 23 September 1893; *s* of Robert Wilson; *m* 1917, Margaret Mary Kilpatrick; one *s* two *d*. *Educ*: Mayo St National School, Belfast; Trade Preparatory School, Municipal Technical Inst.; Kelvin House, Botanic Ave; Methodist Coll.; Queen's Univ. and Presbyterian Coll., Belfast. BA 1913, QUB 1st Hons (Philosophy) with Special Prize; MA 1914; BD 1925 London; BD Hons London, 1930, in Hebrew, Aramaic and Syriac; Univ. of London GCE, Classical Hebrew Advanced Level, Grade A, Special Paper, Grade 1 (Distinction), 1968, Ordinary Level Grade A, 1969. Minister of Presbyterian Churches: Raffrey, Co. Down, 1917, First Donaghadee, Co. Down, 1921; Waterside, Londonderry, 1923; First Carrickfergus, Co. Antrim, 1928. Presbyterian College, Belfast: part-time Lecturer in Hebrew, 1933–34; Warden, 1941–49; Carey Lecturer, 1942; Secretary of Faculty, 1945–61; Convener of Coll. Bd of Management, 1946–62; Vice-Principal of Faculty, 1951–61. Recognised Teacher in Faculty of Theology, in Hebrew and Old Testament Theology, and Internal Examiner for BD, QUB, 1939–64; Internal Examiner for BA in Hebrew, 1948–64; Part-time Lecturer in Hebrew in Faculty of Arts, QUB, 1946–64. Moderator of the General Assembly of the Presbyterian Church in Ireland, 1957–58. Hon. DD Knox College, Toronto, 1961. *Recreations*: walking, motoring, lawn-verging. *Address*: 18 Mount Eden Park, Belfast BT9 6RA. *T*: Belfast 668830. *Died* 29 April 1981.

**WILSON, Sheriff Roy Alexander**, WS; Sheriff of Grampian, Highlands and Islands at Elgin, since 1975; *b* 22 Oct. 1927; *s* of Eric Moir Wilson and Jean Dey Gibb; *m* 1954, Alison Mary Craig; one *s* one *d. Educ:* Drumwhindle Sch.; Aberdeen Grammar Sch.; Merchiston Castle Sch.; Lincoln Coll., Oxford Univ. (BA); Edinburgh Univ. (LLB); Thow Scholarship in Scots Law, 1952. WS; NP. Solicitor, 1953. Partner, subseq. Sen. Partner, Messrs Allan McNeil & Son, WS, Edinburgh, 1957–75. Chm., indust. relations tribunals, 1971–75. Rotarian; Past President: Moray Caring Assoc.; Moray Rugby Club; Treasurer, Fochabers Curling Club. *Recreations:* golf, curling, spectator sports, reading. *Address:* Deansford, Bishopmill, Elgin, Moray. *T:* Elgin 7339. *Club:* Elgin. *Died 6 June* 1985.

**WILSON, Sir Roy (Mickel),** Kt 1962; QC; President of the Industrial Court, 1961–71, and of the Industrial Arbitration Board, 1971–76; *b* 1903; *e s* of late Rev. Robert Wilson and Jessie, *d* of Robert Mickel, JP; *m* 1935, Henrietta Bennett, *d* of late Dean Willard L. Sperry, DD of Harvard University, USA. *Educ:* Glasgow High School; Glasgow University; Balliol Coll., Oxford (Lit. Hum. and BCL). Called to Bar, Gray's Inn, 1931, Bencher 1956, Treas. 1973; S–E Circuit. KC 1950. Commissioned QO Cameron Highlanders, 1940; served War of 1939–45; DAAG 2nd Division, 1942; GHQ, India, 1942–45; Lt-Col, 1943; Brigadier, 1944. Recorder: Faversham, 1950–51; Croydon, 1957–61. Mem., Industrial Disputes Tribunal, 1958–59; Chairman: Cttee of Inquiry into arrangements at Smithfield Market, 1958; Cttee of Inquiry into differences in the Electrical Contracting Industry on the Shell Centre site, 1959; Railway Staff National Tribunal, 1961–62; London Transport Wages Bd, 1961–79; Cttee of Inquiry into strikes by Winding Engineers in the Yorkshire Coalmining Area, 1964; Cttee of Inquiry into Provincial Bus Dispute, 1964; Court of Inquiry into stevedore/docker demarcation in the Port of London, 1966; Cttee on Immigration Appeals, 1966; Cttee of Inquiry into Bristol Siddeley Contracts, 1967–68; Arts Council Cttee of Inquiry into industrial relations at the Coliseum Theatre, 1975; Arts Council Cttee of Inquiry into problems facing the National Theatre, 1978–79. Mem., Race Relations Bd, 1968–77 (Acting Chairman of Bd, Jan.–Oct. 1971; Chm. Employment Cttee, 1968–77). FRSA, 1968. *Recreations:* fishing, golf, birdwatching. *Address:* 4 Gray's Inn Square, WC1. *T:* 01–405 7789; The Cottage on the Green, Plaistow, Sussex. *T:* Plaistow 279. *Clubs:* Reform; Union (Oxford). *Died 12 April* 1982.

**WILSON, Stephen Shipley,** CB 1950; Keeper of Public Records, 1960–66; *b* 4 Aug. 1904; *s* of Alexander Cowan Wilson and Edith Jane Brayshaw; *m* 1933, Martha Mott, *d* of A. B. Kelley and Mariana Parrish, Philadelphia, Pa; two *s* one *d. Educ:* Leighton Park; Queen's Coll., Oxford. Fellow, Brookings Inst., Washington, DC, 1926–27; Instructor, Columbia University, New York City, 1927–28; Public Record Office, 1928–29; Ministry of Transport, 1929–47; Ministry of Supply, 1947–50; Iron and Steel Corporation of Great Britain, 1950–53, and Iron and Steel Holding and Realisation Agency, 1953–60. Historical Section, Cabinet Office, 1966–77. *Address:* 3 Willow Road, NW3 1TH. *T:* 01–435 0148. *Club:* Reform. *Died 16 Sept.* 1989.

**WILSON, Prof. Thomas,** CBE 1959; Professor of Tropical Hygiene, Liverpool School of Tropical Medicine, University of Liverpool, 1962–71; *b* 5 Nov. 1905; *s* of R. H. Wilson, OBE, Belfast; *m* 1930, Annie Cooley (decd); two *s* one *d. Educ:* Belfast Royal Academy; Queen's Univ., Belfast. MB, BCh, BAO (Belfast) 1927; DPH (Belfast) 1929; DTM, DTH (Liverpool) 1930; MD (Belfast) 1952. MO, Central Health Bd, FMS 1930; Health Officer, Malayan Med. Service, 1931; Lieut and Capt., RAMC (POW in Malaya and Thailand), 1942–45; Sen. Malaria Research Officer, Inst. for Med. Res., Fedn of Malaya, 1949; Dir, Inst. for Med. Res., Fedn of Malaya, 1956; Sen. Lectr in Tropical Hygiene, Liverpool Sch. of Trop. Med., Univ. of Liverpool, 1959. *Publications:* (with T. H. Davey) Davey and Lightbody's Control of Disease in the Tropics, 1965, 4th edn 1971; contrib. to Hobson's Theory and Practice of Public Health, 3rd edn 1969, 5th edn 1979; articles in medical journals on malaria and filariasis. *Recreation:* golf. *Address:* 77 Strand Road, Portstewart, N Ireland. *Died 3 Aug.* 1988.

**WILSON, Captain Sir Thomas (Douglas),** 4th Bt, *cr* 1906; MC 1940; *b* (posthumous) 10 June 1917; *s* of Thomas Douglas Wilson (*s* of 1st Bt), 2nd Lieut 7th Bn Argyll and Sutherland Highlanders (killed in action, 1917), and Kathleen Elsie, *d* of Henry Edward Gray; *S* uncle, 1968; *m* 1947, Pamela Aileen, 2nd *d* of Sir Edward Hanmer, 7th Bt, and late Aileen Mary, *er d* of Captain J. E. Rogerson; one *s* three *d. Educ:* Marlborough and Sandhurst. Commissioned 15th/19th Hussars, 1937; served in France, 1939–40 (MC); Western Desert, 1942–43; retired, 1947. Contested (C) Dudley and Stourbridge, 1955. *Recreations:* hunting, racing. *Heir: s* James William Douglas Wilson, *b* 8 Oct. 1960. *Address:* Lillingstone Lovell Manor, Buckingham MK18 5BQ. *T:* Lillingstone Dayrell 237. *Club:* Cavalry and Guards. *Died 12 Nov.* 1984.

**WILSON, William Joseph Robinson,** CMG 1961; Grazier; *b* 2 April 1909; *s* of late Alexander William Wilson and Marion Ferris Wilson; *m* 1937, Mary Weir, *d* of late Arthur Maurice and Elizabeth Reid. *Educ:* Scotch Coll., Melbourne. Member: Faculty of

Veterinary Science, Univ. of Melbourne; Australian Cattle and Beef Research Cttee, 1962–64; Australian Woolgrowers' Council, 1952–54 and 1955–60; Graziers' Federal Council, 1954–60; Australian Overseas Transport Assoc., 1955–58; President, Graziers' Assoc. of Victoria, 1958–60; Vice-Pres. Graziers' Federal Council, 1958–60. Major, AIF, Middle East and New Guinea, 1940–44. *Address:* 17 Nareeb Court, Toorak, Victoria 3142, Australia. *Clubs:* Australian, Melbourne, Naval and Military, Victorian Racing, Peninsula Golf (Melbourne). *Died 20 July* 1982.

**WILSON-HAFFENDEN, Maj.-Gen. Donald James,** CBE 1945; *b* 26 November 1900; *s* of late Rev. L. A. Wilson-Haffenden, Seaford, Sussex; *m* 1923, Isabella Sutherland (*d* 1968); one *d* decd; *m* 1969, Ruth Lea Douglass (*d* 1978), late of CMS; *m* 1979, Annabella Khanna. *Educ:* Christ's Hosp.; Victoria Coll., Jersey. Commissioned 91st Punjabis (LI), 1920; served Waziristan, 1921–24; psc 1936; AA and QMG, 1st Division, 1941; DA and QMG 110 Force, 1941–42; DA and QMG 33 Corps, 1943; DQMG, GHQ, India, 1944. *Address:* 1 Sovereign House, Draxmont Approach, Wimbledon, SW19 7PG. *T:* 01–946 3223. *Clubs:* Royal Commonwealth Society, Hurlingham. *Died 27 May* 1986.

**WILTON, Gen. Sir John Gordon Noel,** KBE 1964 (CBE 1954; OBE 1946); CB 1962; DSO 1944; idc; psc; retired; *b* Sydney, 22 Nov. 1910; *s* of late Noel V. S. Wilton, Grafton, New South Wales; *m* 1938, Helen Thelma, *d* of Robert Marshall; two *s* one *d. Educ:* Grafton High School, NSW; RMC, Duntroon, Canberra. Served in British Army, in UK, India and Burma, 1931–39. Served War of 1939–45 (DSO, OBE); AIF; Middle East, 1940–41; New Guinea, 1942–43; GSO Aust. Military Mission to Washington, 1944; Col, Gen. Staff Advance HQ, AMF, SW Pacific Area, 1945. Deputy Director, Military Operations, AHQ, Melbourne, 1946; Director, Military Operations and Plans, 1947–51; Comdg 28th Commonwealth Bde, Korea (CBE), 1953; Brig. i/c Administration, HQ Eastern Command, NSW, 1954–55; Brig. Gen. Staff AHQ, 1955–56; Comdt, RMC, Duntroon, Canberra, 1957–60; Head of SEATO, Military Planning Office, Bangkok, 1960–63; Chief of the Australian General Staff, 1963–66; Chm., Australian Chiefs of Staff Cttee, 1966–70; Australian Consul General, New York, 1973–75. Has the American Legion of Merit. *Recreation:* golf. *Address:* 11 Melbourne Avenue, Forrest, ACT 2603, Australia. *Club:* Imperial Service (Sydney). *Died 10 May* 1981.

**WIMBERLEY, Maj.-Gen. Douglas Neil,** CB 1943; DSO 1942; MC 1918; DL Dundee, 1947–75, Perthshire 1975; Hon. LLD Aberdeen, 1948, Dundee, 1967; *b* 15 Aug. 1896; *s* of late Colonel C. N. Campbell Wimberley, CMG, Inverness, and Lesmoir Gordon Wimberley; *m* 1925, E. Myrtle L., *d* of late Capt. F. L. Campbell, RN, Achalader, Perthshire, and Lady Dobell; one *s* one *d. Educ:* Alton Burn, Nairn; Wellington; Emmanuel College, Cambridge; RMC, Sandhurst. 2nd Lieut Cameron Highlanders, 1915; served European War as Regimental Officer, France and Belgium, 1st and 51st Highland Divs, 1915–16 and 1917–18 (wounded, MC), including battles of Loos, Somme, Ypres, Cambrai and St Quentin; Acting and Temp. Major, 1918–19; North Russia, with MGC, 1919; Adjutant, 2nd Camerons, 1921; psc 1927; Bde Major 1st (Ghurkha) Inf. Bde, 1929; Operations NWFP India, 1930; Brevet Major, 1933; DAAG and GSO II, WO, 1934–37; Brevet Lt-Col 1936; Lt-Col Commanding 1st Cameron Highlanders, 1938; France, 1939; GSO1 and Chief Instructor Senior Officers' School, 1940; Temp. Brigadier 1941; Temp. Major-General 1942; Major-General 1943; Brig. Comdr 13th and 152nd Seaforth and Cameron Bde, 1940–41; GOC 46th Div., 1941; Div. Comdr, 51st Highland Div., 1941–43; including battles Alamein, Mareth, Medinine, Akarit, Enfidaville and Adrano; 8th Army campaign N Africa, Sicily, 1942–43 (despatches, slightly wounded, DSO, CB), Comdt Staff Coll., Camberley, 1943–44; Dir of Infantry, WO, 1944–46; retd at own request; Principal of University College, Dundee, in the Univ. of St Andrews, 1946–54. Governor, Dundee Colls of Art and Technol., 1946–54; Founder Governor, Scottish Horticultural Res. Inst., 1952–62. Member Royal Company of Archers, Queen's Body Guard for Scotland; Gentleman Usher of the Scarlet Rod in the Order of the Bath, 1948–54; Registrar and Secretary, 1954–64. Hon. Col St Andrews Univ. OTC 1951–63; Col of the Queen's Own Cameron Highlanders, 1951–61. Chief, Gaelic Soc., Inverness, 1947; Pres., Royal Celtic Soc., 1971–74; Life Mem., British Legion (Scotland), 1950; Hon. Pres., Angus and Perthshire British Legion, 1976. *Publications:* military articles in service jls and Chambers's Encyclopædia; Army Quarterly prize essay, 1933. *Recreations:* once athletics (mem. Army AA; second, half mile, 1922); now genealogy. *Address:* Foxhall, Coupar Angus, Perthshire. *T:* 384. *Club:* Naval and Military (Hon. Mem.). *Died 26 Aug.* 1983.

**WINCHESTER, Clarence Arthur C.;** editor and author; *b* 17 March 1895; *s* of Arthur William and Elizabeth Alice Clark; *m* Constance Katherine Groves; one *s* (and one *d* decd). *Educ:* privately; technical schools. Has been variously associated with stage, aeronautics, and journalism in England and abroad, on newspapers and periodicals;

learned to fly, 1913-14; formerly with Allied Newspapers, Daily Mail, etc; special correspondent, Kemsley Newspapers, Ltd; Assistant Chief Editor to Cassell's and Chief Editor of group of Amalgamated Press publications; Assistant Editor, The Daily Sketch; edited: Railway Wonders of the World; Wonders of World Engineering; Shipping Wonders of the World; Wonders of World Aviation; World Film Encyclopædia; The King's Navy (in co-operation with Admiralty); The King's Army (in co-operation with War Office); The King's Air Force (in co-operation with Air Ministry); British Legion Poppy Annual, 1941; The Queen Elizabeth, Winchester's Screen Encyclopedia, 1948; Mind and Matter, etc; also formerly Director and Managing Editor, Dropmore Press Ltd; Consulting Editor, Law Society's Gazette; Managing Director and Chief Editor, Winchester Publications, Ltd; correspondent on European affairs to the Argonaut weekly, San Francisco, USA; Editor, England (quarterly). Associate, Amer. Museum of Natural History. *Publications:* Sonnets and Some Others; Aerial Photography (with F. L. Wills); The Devil Rides High; An Innocent in Hollywood; Let's Look at London; Earthquake in Los Angeles; Three Men in a Plane; The Captain Lost his Bathroom; City of Lies; Airman Tomorrow (with Alfred Kerr); The Black Poppy; A Great Rushing of Wings and Other Poems; Signatures of God; Editor and designer of The Royal Philatelic Collection, by Sir John Wilson, Bt (by permission of HM King George VI); The Crown Jewels, by Major General H. D. W. Sitwell, CB, MC, Keeper of the Jewel House (by permission of the Lord Chamberlain and the Resident Governor of the Tower), etc. *Address:* 60 Jireh Court, Haywards Heath, West Sussex RH16 3BH. *T:* Haywards Heath 54804. *Club:* Savage. *Died 15 March 1981.*

**WINDER, Col John Lyon C.;** *see* Corbett-Winder.

**WINDEYER, Rt. Hon. Sir (William John) Victor,** PC 1963; KBE 1958 (CBE (mil.) 1944); CB 1953; DSO (and bar), 1942; ED; Justice of the High Court of Australia, 1958-72, retired; *b* 28 July 1900; *s* of W. A. Windeyer, Sydney, NSW; *m* 1934, Margaret Moor Vicars; three *s* one *d. Educ:* Sydney Grammar Sch.; University of Sydney (MA, LLB). Admitted to Bar of NSW, 1925; KC (NSW) 1949; sometime lecturer in Faculty of Law, University of Sydney. Lieut AMF (Militia), 1922; War of 1939-45; Lieut-Colonel comdg 2/48 Bn, AIF, 1940-42 (including siege of Tobruk); Brig. comdg 20th Australian Inf. Bde, AIF, 1942-46 (El Alamein, New Guinea, Borneo); Major-General and CMF Member, Australian Military Board, 1950-53; Retired List, 1957. Trustee, Sydney Grammar Sch., 1943-70; Member of Senate, University of Sydney, 1949-59, Dep. Chancellor, 1953-58; Hon. Col, Sydney University Regiment, 1956-66; Member Council Australian National University, 1951-55. Director: Colonial Sugar Refining Co., 1953-58; Mutual Life and Citizens Assurance Co., 1954-58. Chairman Trustees, Gowrie Scholarship Fund, 1964-86. Vice-President, Selden Society, 1965-; Pres., NSW Branch, Australian Scouts Assoc., 1970-78. Hon. Member, Society Public Teachers of Law; Hon. Bencher, Middle Temple, 1972-. Hon. Fellow, Royal Aust. Hist. Soc., 1976-. Hon. LLD Sydney, 1975. *Publications:* The Law of Wagers, Gaming and Lotteries, 1929; Lectures on Legal History, 1938, 2nd edn 1949, rev. 1957; numerous articles and lectures on legal and historical subjects. *Address:* Peroomba, Harrington Avenue, Turramurra, NSW 2074, Australia. *Clubs:* Australian, Pioneers (Sydney); Elanora Country (Narrabeen). *Died 23 Nov. 1987.*

**WINDSOR-AUBREY, Henry Miles;** Puisne Judge, Supreme Court, Ghana, from 1949, retired; Chairman: Industrial Tribunal; Rent Tribunal; Rent Assessment Panel; *b* 1901; *m* 1928, Dorothy Dagmar Montrose; one *s. Educ:* Clifton College. Called to the Bar, Inner Temple, 1925. Served in Uganda, 1934-49. Magistrate, 1934-36; Crown Counsel, 1936-43; Solicitor-General, 1943-49. *Recreations:* golf and gardening. *Address:* 6 St George's Crescent, Carlisle, Cumbria. *Died 3 Jan. 1986.*

**WINGATE, Henry Smith;** International Nickel Co. of Canada Ltd and International Nickel Co. Inc., New York: Director, 1942-75; Chairman of the Board and Chief Officer, 1960-72; Member, Advisory Committee, International Nickel Ltd, 1954-79; Director: Peoples' Symphony Concerts, Inc., New York; Société de Chimie Industrielle, Paris; *b* Talas, Turkey, 8 Oct. 1905; *s* of Henry Knowles Wingate and Jane Caroline Wingate (*née* Smith), US citizens; *m* 1929, Ardis Adeline Swenson; two *s. Educ:* Carleton Coll.; University of Michigan. BA Carleton Coll., 1927; JD Michigan 1929. Admitted to New York bar, 1931. Associated with Sullivan & Cromwell, NYC, 1929-35. Internat. Nickel Co. of Canada, Ltd: Asst Secretary, 1935-39; Secretary, 1939-49; Vice-President and Secretary, 1949-52; Vice-President, 1952-54; President, 1954-60. Assistant to the President, International Nickel Co., Inc., NY, 1935-54; President, 1954-60; former Director: Bank of Montreal; United States Steel Corporation; American Standard Inc.; Canadian Pacific Ltd; JP Morgan & Co., Inc.; Morgan Guaranty Trust Co. of New York (currently Mem. Adv. Council). Trustee: Seamen's Bank for Savings, NY; Foundn for Child Develt; Sen. Mem., The Conference Board; Member: The Business Council,

Washington, DC; Canadian-American Cttee, National Planning Association, Washington, DC, and C. D. Howe Res. Inst., Montreal; Canadian Inst. of Mining and Metallurgy; Canadian Society of NY; Council on Foreign Relations, Inc., NY; Economic Club of NY; Mining and Metallurgical Society of America; Pilgrims of the United States; Vice-Pres., Amer. Friends of Canada Cttee, Inc. Formerly Trustee: US Steel Foundn Inc.; Legal Aid Soc. of NY; Public Health Inst., City of NY; Manhattan Eye, Ear and Throat Hosp.; Admiral Bristol Hosp., Constantinople, Turkey; US Council, Internat. Chamber of Commerce; Annuity Fund for Congregational Ministers; Retirement Fund for Lay Workers; Carleton Coll. Hon. LLD: Manitoba, 1957; Marshall, 1967; York, 1967; Laurentian, 1968; Colby Coll., 1970; Hon. LHD Carleton Coll., 1973. *Address:* (business) One New York Plaza, New York, NY 10004, USA. *T:* 742-4000; (home) 520 East 86th Street, New York, NY 10028. *T:* Regent 4-3568. *Clubs:* Recess, Union, Huntington Country, Lloyd Neck Bath, University (New York). *Died 25 Nov. 1982.*

**WINGATE, His Honour William Granville;** QC 1963; a Circuit Judge (formerly a County Court Judge), 1967-86; *b* 28 May 1911; *s* of Colonel George and Mary Ethel Wingate; *m* 1960, Judith Rosemary Evatt; one *s* one *d. Educ:* Brighton Coll.; Lincoln Coll., Oxford (BA). Called to Bar, Inner Temple, 1933; Western Circuit. Served Army, 1940-46. Dep. Chm., Essex QS, 1965-71. Member: Bar Council, 1961-67; County Court Rule Cttee, 1971-80; Lord Chancellor's Legal Aid Adv. Cttee, 1971-77; Lord Chancellor's Law Reform Cttee, 1974-87. Chm., Brighton Coll. Council, 1978-86. *Recreation:* sailing. *Address:* 2 Garden Court, Temple, EC4. *T:* 071-353 4741; Cox's Mill, Dallington, Heathfield, Sussex. *Clubs:* Royal Corinthian Yacht (Commodore, 1965-68), Bar Yacht (Commodore, 1972-76). *Died 26 July 1990.*

**WINGFIELD, Ven. John William;** Archdeacon of Bodmin, 1979-81, then Emeritus; *b* 19 Dec. 1915; *s* of William and Gertrude Ann Wingfield; *m* 1940, Vera Francis; one *d. Educ:* Sheffield Pupil Teacher Centre; St Aidan's Theol College. Served RASC, 1940-46; retired with hon. rank of Captain. Ordained, Truro, 1947; Curate, Madron with Morvah, 1947-50; Rector, Perranuthnoe, 1950-59; Vicar, Budock, 1959-67; Asst Sec. and Sec., Truro Dio. Conf., 1961-70; RD, Carnmarth South, 1965-67; Vicar, Goran with St Michael Caerhays, 1967-70; Rector, Redruth, 1970-73; Hon. Canon, Truro Cathedral, 1970-81, Canon Emeritus, 1981; Sec., Truro Dio. Synod, 1970-80; Vicar, St Clement, Truro, 1973-79; Proctor in Convocation, 1977-80. *Recreations:* cricket, philately. *Address:* 16 Lanyon Road, Playing Place, Truro, Cornwall TR3 6HF. *T:* Truro 864484. *Died 23 Dec. 1983.*

**WINGFIELD DIGBY, George F.;** *see* Digby.

**WINLAW, Ashley William Edgell,** OBE 1968; TD 1953; retired; *b* 8 Feb. 1914; *s* of Rev. G. P. K. Winlaw, Morden, Surrey, and Minnie Ashley, Kidlington, Yorks. *Educ:* Winchester Coll.; St John's Coll., Cambridge (MA). Master, Aldenham Sch., 1936-39; Master, Shrewsbury Sch., 1939-40; served War, 1940-46; Intelligence Corps, Special Forces, Airborne (Lt-Col; retired as Hon. Major). Master, Rugby Sch., 1946-54; Master, Kent Sch., Connecticut, USA, 1950-51; Headmaster, Achimota Sch., Accra, Ghana, 1954-59; Principal, Government Cadet Coll., Hasan Abdal, W Pakistan, 1959-65; Director of Studies, British Inst., Santiago, Chile, 1965-66; Principal, Federal Govt Coll., Warri, Nigeria, 1966-69; English Master: Bishops Senior Sch., Mukono, Uganda, 1969-72; Blantyre Secondary Sch., Blantyre, Malaŵi, 1972-75; Mangochi Secondary Sch., Mangochi, Malaŵi, 1975-78; Lectr in English, The Polytechnic, Univ. of Malaŵi, 1978-80. Tamgha-i-Pakistan (TPk), Pakistan, 1964. *Recreations:* sports, sailing, drama, painting. *Address:* Ann Page Cottage, 28 High Street, Aldeburgh, Suffolk IP15 5AB. *T:* Aldeburgh 3206. *Clubs:* Special Forces, MCC, Free Foresters, I Zingari. *Died 13 Feb. 1988.*

**WINN, Air Vice-Marshal Charles Vivian,** CBE 1963; DSO 1945; OBE 1950; DFC 1941; AOC Scotland and Northern Ireland 1972-73; *b* 20 April 1918; *s* of C. A. Winn, Cardiff, Past Pres. of Shipping Fedn, and D. B. Winn (*née* Thomas); *m* 1946, Suzanne Patricia (*née* Baily); one *s* one *d. Educ:* St Peter's Sch., Weston-super-Mare; Wycliffe Coll. Station Comdr, Felixstowe, 1951 (Queen's Commendation for Bravery, 1953); DP2, Air Ministry, 1953; Station Comdr: Weston Zoyland, 1955; Laarbruch, 1957; SASO, 38 Gp, 1960; Chief of Plans and Ops, Far East, Nov. 1962; Dir of Ops, MoD (Air), 1965; Air Comdr, Malta, 1968; Chief of Plans, SHAPE, 1971. Chief Recreation Officer, Anglian Water Authority, 1974-84. Chm., Ex-Services Mental Welfare Soc., 1982-87; Mem., Air League. MBIM. *Address:* The Cottage, Green End, Great Stukeley, Huntingdon, Cambs. *Clubs:* Royal Air Force; Union (Malta). *Died 20 Sept. 1988.*

**WINNEKE, Hon. Sir Henry (Arthur),** AC 1982; KCMG 1966; KCVO 1977; Kt 1957; OBE 1944; QC (Australia); Governor of Victoria, Australia, 1974-82; *b* 29 Oct. 1908; *s* of Henry Christian Winneke, Judge of County Courts, Victoria, and Ethel Janet Winneke; *m* 1933, Nancy Rae Wilkinson (*d* 1983); two *s; m* 1984, Catherine

Ellis. *Educ:* Ballarat Grammar Sch.; Scotch Coll., Melbourne; University of Melbourne. Master of Laws, 1st Class Hons, Melbourne, 1929; Hockey Blue, Melbourne Univ. Called to Victorian Bar, 1931. Served with Royal Australian Air Force, 1939–46, Group Captain, Director of Personal Services. Resumed practice Victorian Bar, 1946; KC 1949; Senior Counsel to Attorney-General and Prosecutor for the King, 1950; Solicitor-General of Victoria, 1951–64; Chief Justice, Supreme Court of Victoria, 1964–74; Lieutenant-Governor of Victoria, 1972–74. Member: Council Scotch Coll., Melbourne, 1947–56; Council Victoria Bar, 1948, 1949. President: Literary Council of Victoria, 1966; Boy Scouts Assoc., Victoria Br.; Victoria Law Foundn; Victorian Council Legal Educn. KStJ 1969. Hon. LLD: Melbourne, 1978; Monash, 1980. *Recreations:* golf, gardening, racing. *Address:* 4A The Pines, Kew, Vic 3101, Australia; 45 Lexington Avenue, Shoreham, Vic 3916, Australia. *Clubs:* Athenæum, Melbourne Cricket, Metropolitan Golf (Melbourne); Royal Autobobile, Victoria Racing, Moonee Valley Racing (Victoria).
*Died 28 Dec. 1985.*

**WINNER, Dame Albertine (Louise),** DBE 1967 (OBE 1945); President, St Christopher's Hospice; *b* 4 March 1907; *d* of Isidore and Annie Winner, 4k Portman Mansions, W1. *Educ:* Francis Holland Sch., Clarence Gate; University College, London, and University College Hospital. BSc (Hons Physiology) 1929; MRCS, LRCP, 1932; MBBS London, 1933 (University Gold Medal); MD (London), 1934; MRCP (London) 1935; FRCP (London) 1959; FFCM 1973. Hon. Assistant Physician, Elizabeth Garrett Anderson Hospital, 1937; Hon. Physician, Mothers' Hospital, Clapton, 1937. Service with RAMC, 1940–46 (Lieut-Colonel). Service with Ministry of Health, 1947–67 (Dep. CMO). Hon. Consultant for Women's Services to the Army, 1946–70. Visiting Lecturer, London School of Economics, 1951–63. Fellow, University College, London, 1965; Linacre Fellow, RCP, 1967–78. QHP 1965–68. *Publications:* articles in Lancet, Public Health, etc. *Recreations:* gardening, Japanese prints, music, people, opera. *Address:* c/o 3/4 Stone Buildings, Lincoln's Inn, WC2A 3XS. *Club:* University Women's.
*Died 13 May 1988.*

**WINSER, (Cyril) Legh,** CMG 1928; MVO 1927; Private Secretary to Governors of South Australia, 1915–40; *b* 27 Nov. 1884; *s* of Rev. C. J. Winser, MA; *m* 1912, Agnes Dorothy Mayura Langhorne; one *s* two *d*. *Educ:* Oundle. *Recreations:* cricket, golf. *Address:* Bostock Avenue, Barwon Heads, Victoria 3227, Australia. *Clubs:* Royal Adelaide Golf (Adelaide); Barwon Heads Golf.
*Died 20 Dec. 1983.*

**WINSTON, Charles Edward,** CMG 1974; FRACS; Consulting Surgeon: Sydney Hospital, Australia, since 1958; Royal South Sydney Hospital, since 1963; *b* 3 June 1898; *s* of James Percival and Annie Elizabeth Winston; *m* 1933; one *d*. *Educ:* Sydney Boys' High Sch.; Univ. of Sydney. MB, ChM. Bd Dir, 1958, Vice Pres., 1968–82, and Patron, 1982–, Sydney Hosp. *Publications:* papers on surgical problems to MJA. *Recreations:* golf, bowls, fishing. *Address:* 683 New South Head Road, Rose Bay, NSW 2029, Australia. *T:* 371–7728.
*Died 29 Sept. 1989.*

**WINTER, Rt. Rev. Colin O'Brien;** Bishop of Namibia, 1968–81, in exile, 1972–81; *b* 1928. *Educ:* Lincoln College, Oxford (BA 1953, MA 1957); Ely Theological College. Deacon 1956, priest 1957, Chichester; Curate of St Andrew, Eastbourne, 1956–59; Rector of Simonstown, 1959–64; Rector of St George Pro-Cathedral, Windhoek, 1964–65; Dean and Rector, 1965–71; Examining Chaplain to Bishop of Damaraland, 1965–68; Bishop of Damaraland, 1968–81; Curate-in-charge, St Margaret, Oxford, 1973–74. *Publications:* Just People, 1972; For George and John, 1974; Namibia, 1977; The Breaking Process, 1981. *Address:* Namibia International Peace Centre, 46 Cephas Street, E1 4AX. *T:* 01-790 8724.
*Died 17 Nov. 1981.*

**WINTER, Keith;** novelist and dramatist; *b* 22 Oct. 1906; *s* of Thomas Winter, Professor of Agriculture, Bangor University, N Wales, and Margaret Baron. *Educ:* Berkhamsted Sch.; Lincoln Coll., Oxford. After leaving school spent six months in the American Express Co., London; then became a preparatory school master for two and a half years; went to Oxford and published first novel while still there; has been writing ever since. *Publications:* novels: Other Man's Saucer; The Rats of Norway; Impassioned Pygmies; *plays:* The Rats of Norway; Ringmaster; The Shining Hour; Worse Things Happen at Sea; Old Music; Weights and Measures; We at the Cross Roads; Miss Hallelujah; The Passionate Men; Round the Corner; *musicals:* Nell; Say When! (with Arnold Goland); Pegasus (with Arnold Goland); *films:* The Red Shoes; Above Suspicion; Devotion; Uncle Harry. *Recreations:* tennis, swimming, travel. *Address:* c/o Jo Stewart, International Creative Management, 40 West 57th Street, New York, NY 10019, USA.
*Died 17 Feb. 1983.*

**WINTERBOTHAM, Group Captain Frederick William,** CBE 1943; author; *b* 16 April 1897; *s* of late F. Winterbotham, Painswick, Gloucestershire; *m* 1st, 1921; one *s* two *d*; *m* 1947; one *d*. *Educ:*

Charterhouse; Christ Church, Oxon. Royal Gloucestershire Hussars, 1915; RFC and RAF, 1916–19; Pedigree Stock Breeder, 1920–29; Air Staff and Foreign Office, 1929–45; BOAC 1945–48. *Publications:* Secret and Personal, 1969; The Ultra Secret, 1974; The Nazi Connection, 1978; The Ultra Spy (autobiog.), 1989. *Address:* West Winds, Westbury Farm, Tarrant Gunville, Blandford, Dorset DT11 8 JW. *T:* Tarrant Hinton 570. *Club:* Royal Air Force.
*Died 28 Jan. 1990.*

**WINTERTON, Maj.-Gen. Sir John;** see Winterton, Maj.-Gen. Sir T. J. W.

**WINTERTON, Ralph;** see Winterton, W. R.

**WINTERTON, Maj.-Gen. Sir (Thomas) John (Willoughby),** KCB 1955 (CB 1946); KCMG 1950; CBE 1942 (OBE 1940); DL; retired; *b* 13 April 1898; *e s* of H. J. C. Winterton, Lichfield, Staffs; *m* 1921, Helen (*d* 1976), *d* of late H. Shepherd Cross, Hamels Park, Herts; three *s*. *Educ:* Oundle; RMA, Woolwich. Served European War, 1917–18; Burma, 1930–32; War of 1939–45; Dep. Comr Allied Commission for Austria, 1945–49; British High Commissioner and C-in-C in Austria, 1950; Military Governor and Commander, British/US Zone Free Territory of Trieste, 1951–54, retired Jan. 1955. ADC to the King, 1948–49. Colonel Comdt 1st Green Jackets 43rd and 52nd (formerly the Oxfordshire and Buckinghamshire Light Infantry), 1955–60. Formerly President, S Berks Conservative and Unionist Assoc. (Chairman, 1958–65). Formerly Member St John Council for Berkshire (Chairman, 1962–64); a Vice-Pres., Royal Humane Society, 1973– (Cttee Mem., 1962–73). DL, Berkshire, 1966. CStJ 1969. *Address:* Craven Lodge, Speen, Newbury, Berks. *T:* Newbury 40525. *Club:* Army and Navy.
*Died 14 Dec. 1987.*

**WINTERTON, (William) Ralph,** FRCS, FRCOG; Consultant Gynaecological Surgeon Emeritus, Middlesex Hospital; Surgeon, Hospital for Women, Soho Square; Obstetric Surgeon, Queen Charlotte's Maternity Hospital; Archivist to the Middlesex Hospital; *b* 24 June 1905; *o s* of late Rev. William Charles Winterton; *m* 1934, Kathleen Margaret, 2nd *d* of late Rev. D. Marsden; two *s* two *d*. *Educ:* Marlborough Coll.; Gonville and Caius Coll., Cambridge; Middlesex Hospital. MA; MB, BChir. House appointments, Middlesex Hospital, 1929–31; Gynæcological Registrar, Middlesex Hospital, 1934–36. Examr in Obstetrics to Universities of Cambridge, London, Glasgow, Ibadan, Dar-es-Salaam, and to Royal College of Obstetricians and Gynæcologists. Fellow of the Royal Society of Medicine, President Obstetric Section, 1960–61. Governor: Bancroft's Sch., Woodford Green, 1960–75; Howell's Sch., Denbigh (Vice-Chairman). Court of Assistants of the Drapers' Company (Master, 1964–65). Past President, Guild of Med. Bellringers. *Publications:* Aids to Gynæcology; (jointly) Queen Charlotte's Textbook of Obstetrics. Contributions to Medical Journals. *Recreations:* fishing, gardening, change ringing, and Do-it-yourself. *Address:* 26 De Walden Street, W1M 7PH. *T:* 01–935 8751; Youngloves, Rushden, Herts SG9 0SP. *T:* Broadfield 217.
*Died 8 April 1988.*

**WINTON, Frank Robert,** MA, MD Cambridge, DSc London; FInstBiol, FIST; Emeritus Professor of Pharmacology, University of London, 1961; *b* 1894; *m* 1922, Bessie Rawlins; one *d*. *Educ:* Oundle Sch.; Clare Coll., Cambridge; St Bartholomew's and University College Hospitals. Assistant, Dept of Pharmacology, University College, London, 1924; Lecturer, Dept of Physiology, University College, London, 1927; Beit Memorial Research Fellow; Lecturer in Physiology, University of Cambridge, 1931; Reader in Physiology, University of Cambridge, 1933; Professor of Pharmacology, University College, London, 1938–61. Consultant, May and Baker Ltd, etc, 1961–71. Hon. Member, Harvey Society of New York. Hon. DEd CNAA, 1976. *Publications:* (joint) Human Physiology, 1930, 7th edn, 1979; Modern Views on the Secretion of Urine (ed F. R. Winton), 1956; Scientific Papers in Journal of Physiology, and other journals on the kidney, plain muscle, etc. *Recreations:* chamber music, wine. *Address:* 32 Arkwright Road, NW3 6BH. *T:* 01–435 2412.
*Died 2 June 1985.*

**WIRKKALA, Tapio;** Knight of White Rose of Finland; designer; *b* 2 June 1915; *s* of Ilmari Wirkkala, artist, and Selma Wirkkala; *m* 1945, Rut Bryk, artist; one *s* one *d*. *Educ:* Sch. of Industrial Arts, Helsinki, 1933–36. Mil. rank of Lt, Finnish Army. Glass designer for Karhula-Iittala, Finland, 1947–; designer for firms in Finland and abroad, 1955–. Art director, Sch. of Industrial Arts, Helsinki, 1951–54. Chm., Govt Industrial Arts Commn, Helsinki, 1968–73. *One-man exhibitions include:* Oslo, 1952; Smithsonian Instn Travelling Exhibn, USA, 1956–58 and 1971–73; England, Germany, Switzerland, Italy, 1962–64; Czechoslovakia, 1965, 1967–68; Montreal World Fair, 1967; Mexico Culture Olympics, 1968; Goldsmiths' Hall, 1972; São Paulo Bienal, 1971; Amsterdam, 1976; Invitation Exhibn, Venice, 1976; retrospective travelling exhibn, Moscow, Rühimäki, 1981, Mexico City, 1982, Paris, 1983. *Exhibition architect:* Finnish Industrial Art Exhibn, Zurich and Gothenburg, 1951; Finnish Art and Industrial Arts Travelling Exhibn, GB, 1952 and USA, 1953; Finnish Glass Exhibn, Amsterdam, 1972; Friends of Finnish Handicraft Centenary Travelling Exhibn in 10 Towns in Finland, 1979–80. *Works included in:* Museum of Modern Art and Metropolitan Museum of Art, New York; Victoria and Albert Museum, London; Kunstgewerbemuseum, Zürich; National Museum, Stockholm; Nordenfjellske Museum, Trondheim; Stedelijk Mus., Amsterdam; Die Neue Sammlung, München; Nat. Gall. of Vic., Melbourne; Mus. Universitaria de Ciencias y Arte, Mexico City and other museums in Germany, Denmark, Switzerland, Japan, Holland and USA. Cross of Freedom (4th class; twice, once with oak leaves), Finland; Pro Finlandia Medal; Prince Eugen Medal, Stockholm, 1980. SIA Medal, 1958; Cultural Foundn of Finland Honorary Prize, 1968; 7 Grande Premios at Milan Triennale and various other prizes and medals for design (ceramics, glass, wood, bank notes, stamps, etc); Hon. Academician, Helsinki, 1972; Hon. RDI (GB), 1964, Hon. Dr RCA 1971, and other foreign awards. *Recreation:* fishing. *Address:* Itäranta 24, Tapiola, Finland. *T:* 46 44 14.                                                                                       *Died 19 May 1985.*

**WISE, Rear-Adm. Cyril Hubert Surtees,** CB 1967; MBE 1943; Voluntary Services Organiser, St Stephen's Hospital, Fulham, since 1976; *b* 20 Feb. 1913; *s* of H. P. S. Wise; *m* 1948, Margaret Isobel Phelps McKenzie; one *s. Educ:* RN College, Dartmouth. Student RN Staff College, 1953; Imperial Defence College, 1958; Captain, HMS Collingwood, 1963–65; Inspector-Gen., Fleet Maintenance, and Chief Staff Officer (Technical), Western Fleet, 1965–67, retd. Principal, Technical Training Inst., Royal Saudi Air Force, Dhahran, 1968–70; Gen. Manager, Airwork Services Ltd, Dhahran, 1970. *Address:* c/o National Westminster Bank Ltd, Broadway, Chesham, Bucks. *Club:* Army and Navy.

*Died 14 May 1982.*

**WISE, Sir John (Humphrey),** KCMG 1943; CBE 1939; Indian Civil Service, retired; *b* 11 March 1890; *s* of late William Wise, Ashbourne, Derbyshire, and St Servan, France; *m* 1918, Edith Frances Anne (*d* 1981), *d* of late Lt-Col L. G. Fischer, IMS; one *s* (one *d* decd). *Educ:* Christ's Hospital; University College, Oxford. Entered ICS, 1914; IARO, 1915–19, served in India, Mesopotamia, Egypt and Palestine (92nd Punjabis) (despatches); Deputy Commissioner, Toungoo, 1924; Secretary Public Service Commission, India, 1926; Deputy Commissioner, Pegu, 1931; Secretary to Govt of Burma, 1932–39; Member of Burma Railway Board, 1937; Controller of Supplies, Burma, 1939; Counsellor to Governor of Burma, 1940–46; Adviser to the Secretary of State for Burma, 1946–47; Leader of British Mission to Brazil, 1948; Deputy Chairman, Raw Cotton Commission, 1949–53. *Recreations:* chess, walking. *Address:* 5 Cressy House, Queen's Ride, SW13. *T:* 01-789 3745. *Club:* Roehampton.                                                                                       *Died 21 Oct. 1984.*

**WISEMAN, Christopher Luke,** MA; Headmaster, Queen's College, Taunton, 1926–53; retired, 1953; *b* 20 April 1893; *s* of late Rev. F. L. Wiseman and Elsie Daniel; *m* 1946, Christine Irene, *d* of Sir William Savage, MD; *m* 1972, Patricia Joan Wragge, *d* of Prebendary R. Wragge-Morley. *Educ:* King Edward's School, Birmingham; Peterhouse, Cambridge (Scholar). Instructor Lt RN, 1915–19; Senior Mathematical Master, Kingswood School, Bath, 1921–26. *Recreation:* music. *Address:* 11 Park Lane, Milford-on-Sea, Lymington, Hants SO41 0PT.                                                    *Died 25 July 1987.*

**WISEMAN, Gen. Clarence D(exter),** OC 1976; General of the Salvation Army, 1974–77; *b* Moreton's Harbour, Newfoundland, 19 June 1907; *m* Janet Kelly; one *s* one *d. Educ:* Salvation Army Officers Training Coll., Toronto, Canada (grad.). In comd chief Salvation Army evangelistic centres in Canada. Served overseas, War of 1939–45, as Chaplain, Canadian Forces; after 3 yrs directed all Salvation Army Welfare Services on various fighting fronts. After the war held some senior admin. posts in Canada. Transferred to E Africa to direct work of SA in Kenya, Tanzania and Uganda, 1960. Principal, Internat. Training Coll., London, Eng., 1962; Mem., General's Adv. Council, London; Head of Salvation Army in Canada and Bermuda, 1967–74. Holds hon. doctorates. *Publications:* A Burning in My Bones, 1979; The Desert Road to Glory, 1981; After this Manner, 1984. *Address:* 170 Oakmeadow Boulevard, Scarborough, Ontario M1E 4H3, Canada.

*Died 4 May 1985.*

**WITT, Sir John (Clermont),** Kt 1967; FSA; Solicitor; formerly Senior Partner in firm of Stephenson Harwood, Saddlers' Hall, Gutter Lane, Cheapside EC2; Member, Management Committee of Courtauld Institute of Art, since 1952 (Chairman, since 1975); Director, Equity & Law Life Assurance Society Ltd (Chairman, 1964–77); *b* 5 November 1907; *s* of Sir Robert Clermont Witt, CBE, and Mary Helene Marten; *m* 1931, Margaret, *d* of Henry S. Bowers, Scotland, Conn, USA; one *s* one *d. Educ:* Eton; New Coll., Oxford (BA); Hon. Fellow, 1979; Harvard, USA. Admitted Solicitor, 1934. Served War, 1941–45; 1st Bn The Rifle Brigade, Middle East, Italy, France, and Germany (Major; despatches). Independent Member, Reviewing Committee on Export of Works of Art, 1952–59, 1963–67; Member: Standing Commn on Museums and Galleries,

1958–73; Arts Council, 1962–76 (Vice-Chm., 1970–76). Trustee: Tate Gall., 1959–62; National Gall., 1955–62, 1965–72 (Chm. 1959–62, 1967–72); Theatres Trust, 1977–. Cavaliere, Order of S Gregorio Magno, 1965. *Address:* 15 Dorset Square, NW1 6QB. *T:* 01-723 5589; Down Mead, Boro Marsh, Wargrave, Berks. *Clubs:* Travellers', City University.                                                    *Died 26 April 1982.*

**WITT, Maj.-Gen. John Evered,** CB 1952; CBE 1948; MC 1918; retired from Army, 1953; *b* 15 Jan. 1897; *s* of late Rev. A. R. Witt, Royal Army Chaplains' Department; *m* 1st, 1924, Kathleen Phyllis Outram (*d* 1968); one *s;* 2nd, 1969, Mrs Cynthia Myrtle Margaret Reynolds (*d* 1982), *yr d* of late Dr Geoffrey Eden, FRCP. *Educ:* King's Sch., Canterbury. RMC Sandhurst, 1914; 2nd Lt ASC, Dec. 1914; BEF, 1915–19; BAOR, 1919–21; UK, 1921–23; BAOR, 1923–26; UK, 1926; India, 1927; Egypt, 1927–32; UK, 1932–46; Director of Supplies and Transport, BAOR, 1946–48; FarELF, 1948–49 (despatches); Director of Supplies and Transport, Middle East Land Forces, 1950–53. *Address:* c/o Barclay's Bank, 101 Victoria Road, Aldershot, Hants.                                        *Died 18 May 1989.*

**WITTIG, Prof. Georg,** Dr Phil; *b* Berlin, 16 June 1897; *s* of Prof. Gustav Wittig and Martha (*née* Dombrowski); *m* 1930, Waltraut Ernst (*d* 1978); two *d. Educ:* Wilhelms-Gymnasium, Kassel; Marburg Univ. Lecturer, Marburg Univ., 1926–32; Division Director, Technische Hochschule, Braunschweig, 1932–37; Prof., Univs of Braunschweig, Freiburg and Tübingen, 1937–56; Prof., Heidelberg Univ., 1956–67, emeritus, 1967–. Member: Acad. of Sciences, Munich and Heidelberg; l'Acad. Française; Soc. Quimica del Perú; Leopoldina Halle; Hon. Member: Swiss Chem. Assoc.; New York Acad. of Scis; Chem. Soc., London; Soc. Chim. de France. Hon. doctorates, Sorbonne and Hamburg. Nobel Prize (jointly) 1979; many earlier awards, incl. Otto Hahn Prize, 1967; Karl Ziegler Prize, 1975. Ordens Grosses Verdienstkreuz, 1980. *Publications:* Textbook on Stereochemistry, 1930; numerous articles in jls on Metallorganic, Ylid and Carbanion Chemistry. *Recreations:* painting, music, hiking, mountain climbing. *Address:* Bergstrasse 35, 69 Heidelberg, Federal Republic of Germany. *T:* 40945.

*Died 26 Aug. 1987.*

**WITTRICK, Prof. William Henry,** ScD, FRS 1980; FEng 1981; FAA; Beale Professor of Civil Engineering, University of Birmingham, 1969–82, then Professor Emeritus; *b* 29 Oct. 1922; *s* of late Frank Wittrick; *m* 1945, Joyce Farrington, *d* of late Arthur Farrington; two *d. Educ:* Huddersfield Coll.; St Catharine's Coll., Cambridge (Scholar; Mech. Scis Tripos 1942, 1st cl. Hons with distinction; Archibald Denny Prize; MA 1947; ScD 1967); PhD Sydney, 1951. FAA 1958; FRAeS 1961; MICE 1969–81. Stressman, Hawker Aircraft Co., 1942; Temp. Demonstrator in Engrg, Univ. of Cambridge, 1942–44; Scientific Officer, RAE, 1944–45; Univ. of Sydney: Sen. Lectr, 1945–54; Reader, 1954–56; Lawrence Hargrave Prof. of Aeronautical Engrg, 1956–64; Dean of Faculty of Engrg, 1962–63; Birmingham University: Prof. of Structural Engrg, 1964–69; Head of Dept of Civil Engineering, 1969–80. Vis. Research Fellow, California Inst. of Technology, 1953–54; Carnegie Fellow, 1960; Vis. Prof., Coll. of Aeronautics, Cranfield, 1960. Pres., Australian Div. RAeS, 1961–62; Mem. 1956–61, Chm. 1961–64, Australian Aeronautical Research Cttee; Member: Aeronautical Research Council, 1970–73 (Mem. or Chm., various standing cttees, 1964–80); British Nat. Cttee for Theoretical and Applied Mechanics, 1980–84; Gen. Assembly, Internat. Union of Theoretical and Applied Mechanics, 1980–. Gen. Editor, Oxford Engineering Science series, 1972–. OrvilleWright Prize, 1961, George Taylor Prize, 1973, RAeS. Hon. DTech Chalmers Univ. of Technol., Göteborg, 1984; Hon. DSc Wales, 1985. *Publications:* numerous papers on solid and structural mechanics in scientific and technical jls. *Recreations:* bookbinding, woodworking, music, theatre. *Address:* The Old Forge, Ebrington, Chipping Campden, Glos GL55 6NL. *T:* Paxford 208.                                                    *Died 2 July 1986.*

**WITTS, Leslie John,** CBE 1959; MD Manchester; FRCP; DM Oxford; Hon. ScD Dublin; Hon. MD Bristol; Hon. DSc Belfast; Hon. DSc Manchester; Fellow of Magdalen College and Nuffield Professor of Clinical Medicine, Oxford, 1938–65; now Emeritus Fellow and Professor; *b* 1898; *s* of Wyndham John Witts, Warrington, Lancs; *m* 1929, Nancy Grace, *y d* of L. F. Salzman; one *s* three *d. Educ:* Boteler Grammar Sch., Warrington; Victoria Univ. of Manchester; Sidney Sussex Coll., Cambridge. Served with Inns of Court OTC and RFA, 1916–18; Dickenson Travelling Scholar, 1925; John Lucas Walker Student, 1926; Edmonds Research Fellow, 1929. Lectures: Goulstonian, RCP, 1932; Frederick Price, Dublin, 1950; Schorstein Meml, London Hosp., 1955; Sidney Watson Smith, Edinburgh, 1956; Gwladys and Olwen Williams, Liverpool, 1957; Shepherd, Montreal, 1959; Lumleian, RCP, 1961; Heath Clark, Univ. of London, 1964; Litchfield, Oxon, 1969; Harveian, RCP, 1971. Late Asst to Med. Unit, London Hospital; Director, Medical Professorial Clinic and Physician St Bartholomew's Hospital; Assistant Physician to Guy's Hospital; Member of Medical Research Council, 1938–42, 1943–47; Hon. Secretary and Treasurer Assoc. Physicians of Great Britain and

Ireland, 1933–48; Second Vice-Pres. Royal Coll. of Physicians, 1965–66. Mem., Min. of Health Committee on Safety of Drugs, 1963–68. McIlrath Guest Professor, Sydney, 1956. Hon. Fellow, Royal Coll. of Physicians and Surgeons of Canada. Hon. Member, Assoc. of American Physicians, and Danish Soc. of Internal Med. *Publications:* Anæmia and the Alimentary Tract, 1956; The Stomach and Anaemia, 1966; Hypochromic Anaemia, 1969. Editor of Medical Surveys and Clinical Trials, 2nd edn, 1964. Contributions to medical and scientific journals. *Recreations:* walking, play-going. *Address:* 293 Woodstock Road, Oxford. *T:* 58843.
*Died 19 Nov. 1982.*

**WOLFE, Prof. James Nathan;** Professor of Economics, University of Edinburgh, 1964–84, later Emeritus; *b* 16 Sept. 1927; *s* of late Jack Wolfe and of Rose (*née* Segal); *m* 1954, Monica Anne Hart; one *d* (and one *d* decd). *Educ:* Westhill High Sch., Montreal; McGill Univ. (BA 1948, MA 1949); Glasgow Univ.; Queen's and Nuffield Colls, Oxford. BLitt (Oxon) 1952. Lecturer in Political Economy, Univ. of Toronto, 1952–60; Prof. of Economics, Univ. of California, Berkeley and Santa Barbara, 1960–64; Brookings Research Prof., 1963–64. Economic Consultant: to Nat. Economic Develt Office, 1963–64; to Sec. of State for Scotland, 1965–72; to Dept of Economic Affairs, 1965–69; Member, Inter-deptl Cttee on Long Term Population Distribution, 1966–69. Visiting Scholar, Stanford Univ., 1982. *Publications:* ed, Government and Nationalism in Scotland, 1969; The Economics of Technical Information Systems, 1974; ed (with C. I. Phillips) Clinical Practice and Economics, 1977; (with M. Pickford) The Church of Scotland: an economic survey, 1980; articles in learned jls. *Recreations:* travel, reading, Canadiana. *Address:* West Hill, 34 Ravelrig Park, Balerno, Edinburgh EH14 7DL. *T:* 031–449 4132. *Clubs:* New, Scottish Arts (Edinburgh).
*Died 1 Jan. 1988.*

**WOLFENDEN, Baron** *cr* 1974 (Life Peer), of Westcott; **John Frederick Wolfenden,** Kt 1956; CBE 1942; *b* 26 June 1906; *s* of late G. Wolfenden, Halifax; *m* 1932, Eileen Le Messurier, 2nd *d* of late A. J. Spilsbury; one *s* two *d* (one *s* decd). *Educ:* Wakefield School; Queen's College, Oxford (Hastings Scholar, Akroyd Scholar; Hon. Fellow 1959); 2nd Class Classical Mods, 1926; 1st Class Literae Humaniores, 1928; Henry P. Davison Scholar Princeton University, USA, 1928–29; Fellow and Tutor in Philosophy, Magdalen College, Oxford, 1929–34; Headmaster of Uppingham School, 1934–44; Headmaster of Shrewsbury School, 1944–50; Vice-Chancellor of Reading University, 1950–63; Chm., UGC, 1963–68; Dir and Principal Librarian, British Museum, 1969–73. Director of Pre-Entry Training, Air Ministry, 1941; Chairman: Ministry of Education's Youth Advisory Council, 1942–45; Headmasters' Conference, 1945, 1946, 1948, 1949; Departmental Cttee on Employment of National Service Men, 1956; Secondary School Examinations Council, 1951–57; Departmental Cttee on Homosexual Offences and Prostitution, 1954–57; National Council of Social Service, 1953–60; CCPR Sport Enquiry, 1957–60; Family Service Units, 1957–63; National Association of Youth Clubs, 1958–63; Local Government Examinations Board, 1958–63; Councils for the Training of Health Visitors and for Training in Social Work, 1962–63; Carnegie UK Trust, 1969–74; Alleyn's Coll. of God's Gift, 1973–; Cttee on Voluntary Organisations, 1974–77. President: Section L British Association, 1955; Aslib, 1969–71; Chelsea Coll., Univ. of London, 1972–; Metropolitan Assoc. of Building Socs, 1978–83; Chelsea Building Soc., 1978–; Nat. Children's Bureau, 1978–; Classical Assoc., 1979–80. Hon. DLitt: Reading, 1963; Warwick, 1977; Hon. LLD: Hull, 1969; Wales, 1971; Manchester, 1972; Williams Coll., Mass., 1973; Hon. LHD Hamilton Coll., NY, 1972; DUniv York, 1973. Oxford University Hockey XI, 1927, 1928, English Hockey XI, 1930–33. Provost, Order of the Buffalo Hunt (Manitoba). *Publications:* The Approach to Philosophy, 1932; The Public Schools To-Day, 1948; How to Choose Your School, 1952; Chapters in The Prospect Before Us, 1948; Education in a Changing World, 1951; Turning Points (memoirs), 1976; occasional articles, named lectures, and reviews. *Recreation:* trying to remember. *Address:* The White House, Westcott, near Dorking, Surrey. *T:* Dorking 885475. *Clubs:* United Oxford & Cambridge University; Vincent's (Oxford).
*Died 18 Jan. 1985.*

**WOLFF, Frederick Ferdinand,** CBE 1975; TD 1945; Chairman: Rudolf Wolff & Co. Ltd, 1965–81; Wolff Steel Ltd, Swansea, since 1982; *b* 13 Oct. 1910; *s* of Philip Robert Wolff and Irma Wolff; *m* 1937, Natalie Winifred Virginia Byrne; two *s* three *d* (incl. twin *s* and *d*). *Educ:* Shirley House Prep. Sch., Watford, Herts; Beaumont Coll., Old Windsor, Berks. Oxfordshire and Bucks LI, 1939–45 (Captain). Joined Rudolf Wolff & Co., 1929; Partner, 1951. Chairman: London Metal Exchange Committee, 1970–77 (Mem. Cttee, 1961–77; Mem. Bd, 1963–83); Fedn of Commodity Assocs, 1971–77; Mem., Cttee on Invisible Exports, 1971–. AAA Champion 440 yards, 1933; British Gold Medallist, 4 × 400 metres relay team, Olympic Games, Berlin, 1936. *Recreations:* golf, racing. *Address:* 11 Shardeloes, Amersham, Bucks HP7 0RL. *T:* Amersham 5081.

*Clubs:* London Athletic, Gresham, Directors; Beaconsfield Golf.
*Died 26 Jan. 1988.*

**WOLFF, Henry D.;** *see* Drummond-Wolff.

**WOLFF, John Arnold Harrop,** CMG 1963; *b* 14 July 1912; *er s* of late Arnold H. Wolff, Halebarns, Cheshire; *m* 1939, Helen Muriel McCracken, Howth, Co. Dublin; one *s* one *d*. *Educ:* Haileybury College; Peterhouse, Cambridge. Colonial Administrative Service, Kenya: District Officer, 1935–59; Provincial Commissioner, 1959–63; Civil Secretary, Rift Valley Region, 1963; retired, Nov. 1963. *Recreations:* gardening, golf. *Address:* Wallflowers, Bloxham, Oxon.
*Died 8 March 1984.*

**WOLLASTON, Henry Woods;** Standing Counsel to General Synod of the Church of England, 1981–83; *b* 14 Nov. 1916; *s* of Sir Gerald Woods Wollaston, KCB, KCVO; *m* 1944, Daphne Margaret Clark; one *s* two *d*. *Educ:* Harrow School; Cambridge Univ. (MA). Barrister-at-law. Served War, Captain, Grenadier Guards, 1940–46. Legal Adviser's Branch, Home Office, 1946; Principal Asst Legal Adviser, 1977–80. Master of the Haberdashers' Company, 1974–75. *Publications:* Jervis on Coroners, 9th edn, 1957; Court of Appeal, 1968; Parker's Conduct of Parliamentary Elections, 1970; Halsbury's Laws of England: 3rd edn, titles, Coroners, Elections, Police; 4th edn, title Elections; British Official Medals for Coronations and Jubilees, 1978. *Recreations:* real tennis, lawn tennis. *Address:* 2 Ashtead House, Ashtead, Surrey KT21 1LU.
*Died 16 July 1989.*

**WOLLEN, Sir (Ernest) Russell (Storey),** KBE 1969 (CBE 1962; OBE 1953); retired; *b* 9 June 1902; *s* of Cecil Storey Wollen, Glengariffe, Torquay, Devon; *m* 1924, Maise (*d* 1983), *d* of Robert Adamson, Neville's Cross, Co. Durham; two *s* two *d*. *Educ:* Marlborough. Coffee Planter, 1922–39; Chm., Coffee Bd of Kenya, 1933–40; Mem., Kenya Supply Bd, 1940–44; E African Manager, Dalgety & Co., 1944–55; Chm., Kenya Coffee Marketing Bd, 1955–67. Retired to reside in Western Australia, 1967. *Recreations:* sailing, riding, golf. *Address:* 24 Latham Street, Alfred Cove, WA 6153, Australia. *T:* Perth 3301335. *Club:* Muthaiga Country (Nairobi).
*Died 28 May 1986.*

**WOLPE, Berthold Ludwig,** OBE 1983; RDI 1959; graphic designer and teacher; *b* 29 Oct. 1905; *s* of Simon Wolpe and Agathe (*née* Goldschmidt); *m* 1941, Margaret Leslie Smith; two *s* two *d*. *Educ:* studied lettering and graphic design under Rudolf Koch, Offenbach Art Sch., 1924–27; goldsmith work under Theodor Wende, Pforzheim Art Sch., 1928. Assistant to Rudolf Koch, 1929–34; Teacher at Frankfurt Art Sch., 1930–33; worked with Ernest Ingham, Fanfare Press, London, 1935–40; Faber & Faber, designing and decorating books, book jackets and bindings, 1941–75, retired; taught at Camberwell School of Art, 1949–53; Tutor, 1956–65, Vis. Lectr, 1965–75, Royal College of Art; teaching at City & Guilds of London Sch. of Art, 1975–. Lyell Reader in Bibliography, Oxford Univ., 1981–82; Leverhulme Emeritus Fellow, 1988. Designed printing types: Hyperion, Albertus, Tempest, Sachsenwald, Pegasus, Decorata. Retrospective exhibitions: V&A Mus., 1980; Nat. Library of Scotland, Edinburgh, 1982; Klingspor Mus., Offenbach, 1983. Hon. Member: Double Crown Club; Soc. of Scribes and Illuminators, 1977; Bund Deutscher Buchkuenstler, 1982; Vice-Pres., Printing Historical Soc., 1977; Hon. Fellow, Soc. of Designer-Craftsmen, 1984. Dr *hc* RCA 1968. Frederic W. Goudy Award, Rochester Inst. of Tech., New York, 1982; Silver Medal, Town of Offenbach, 1983; Ehrenurkunde, Maximilian Gesellschaft, Hamburg, 1985. *Publications:* Schriftvorlagen, 1934; (jtly) ABC Buechlein, 1934, 2nd edn 1977; Handwerkerzeichen, 1936; Marken und Schmuckstuecke, 1937; Fanfare Ornaments, 1938; A Newe Booke of Copies 1574, 1959, 2nd edn 1961; (jtly) Renaissance Handwriting, 1960; Vincent Figgins Type Specimens 1801 and 1815, 1967; Freedom of the Press: Broadsides, 1969; Steingruber Architectural Alphabet, 1972. *Recreations:* collecting material for studies of history of craftsmanship, of printing and calligraphy. *Address:* 140 Kennington Park Road, Lambeth, SE11 4DJ. *T:* 01–735 7450.
*Died 5 July 1989.*

**WOLVERTON, 5th Baron** *cr* 1869; **Nigel Reginald Victor Glyn;** Captain RA, TA; *b* 23 June 1904; *o* surv. *s* of 4th Baron and Lady Edith Amelia Ward, CBE (*d* 1956), *o d* of 1st Earl of Dudley; *S* father, 1932. *Educ:* Eton. *Heir:* kinsman John Patrick Riversdale Glyn, CBE, *b* 17 April 1913. *Address:* Queensberry House, Newmarket, Suffolk.
*Died 18 Aug. 1986.*

**WOLVERTON, 6th Baron** *cr* 1869; **John Patrick Riversdale Glyn,** CBE 1974; *b* 17 April 1913; *s* of Maurice G. C. Glyn (*d* 1920) (*g s* of 1st Baron) and Hon. Maud Grosvenor (*d* 1948), *d* of 2nd Baron Ebury; *S* cousin, 1986; *m* 1937, Audrey Margaret Stubbs; two *s* two *d*. *Educ:* Eton; New Coll., Oxford. Major, Grenadier Guards. A Man. Dir, Glyn, Mills & Co., 1950–70; Chairman: John Govett & Co. Ltd, 1970–75; Govett European Trust Ltd, 1970–75; Alexanders Discount Co. Ltd, 1961–81; Yorkshire Bank Ltd, 1970–81; Agricultural Mortgage Corp. Ltd, 1964–82; First National Finance

Corp. Ltd, 1975–85 (Dep. Chm. 1974–75). Mem., Develt Commn, 1965–81. FIB 1978. *Recreations:* fishing, shooting. *Heir:* s Hon. Christopher Richard Glyn [*b* 5 Oct. 1938; *m* 1st, 1961, Carolyn Jane (marr. diss. 1967), *yr d* of late Antony N. Hunter; two *d*; 2nd, 1975, Mrs Frances S. E. Stuart Black]. *Address:* The Dower House, Chute Standen, near Andover, Hants SP11 9EE. *T:* Chute Standen 228. *Clubs:* Boodle's, Pratt's.                    *Died 4 July 1988.*

**WOMERSLEY, J(ohn) Lewis**, CBE 1962; RIBA; FRTPI; FRSA; Retired Partner, Hugh Wilson and Lewis Womersley, Chartered Architects and Town Planners (Partner, 1964–77); *b* 12 Dec. 1910; *s* of Norman Womersley and Elizabeth Margaret Lewis; *m* 1936, Jean Roberts; one *s* (and one *s* decd). *Educ:* Huddersfield College. Asst Architect, private practices in London and Liverpool, 1933–46; Borough Architect and Town Planning Officer, Northampton, 1946–53; City Architect, Sheffield, 1953–64. Past Member Council, RIBA (Vice-President, 1961–62). Member: Central Housing Adv. Cttee, 1956–61, Parker Morris Cttee on Housing Standards, 1958–60, Min. of Housing and Local Govt; North West Econ. Planning Council, 1965–72; Manchester Conservation Areas and Historic Buildings Panel, 1970–77 (Chm., 1974–77); Chm., Manchester's Albert Meml Restoration Appeal Cttee, 1976–78. Works include housing, Manchester Education Precinct Plan, Huddersfield Polytechnic, Develt Plan and Central Services Building, central area redevelopment. RIBA DistTP, 1956. Hon. LLD Sheffield, 1966; Hon. MA Manchester, 1978. *Publication:* Traffic Management in the Lake District National Park, 1972. *Recreation:* reading. *Address:* 44 St Germains, Bearsden, Glasgow G61 2RS.
                    *Died 28 Oct. 1990.*

**WOOD, Sir (Arthur) Michael**, Kt 1985; CBE 1977; Director General, African Medical and Research Foundation, retired; *b* 28 Jan. 1919; *s* of Arthur Henry Wood and Katherine Mary Altham Wood (*née* Cumberlege); *m* 1943, Susan Studd Buxton; two *s* two *d*. *Educ:* Winchester College; London Univ. (MB BS 1944); Middlesex Hosp. Med. School; MRCS, LRCP 1943; FRCS 1946. House Surgeon, Casualty Surgical Officer and Registrar, Middlesex Hosp., 1943–47; training in gen. and plastic surgery; Marks Fellow in Plastic Surgery, 1955; consultant surgeon to Nairobi Hosp., Aga Khan Hosp., Gertrude's Garden Children's Hosp., Kenyatta Nat. Hosp. and Kilimanjaro Christian Med. Centre, at various times, 1950–83. Co-founder, African Med. and Res. Foundn, 1957 (and E African flying doctor services); President: Capricorn Africa Soc., 1959; Assoc. of Surgeons of E Africa, 1971; Chm., Food and Agric. Res. Mission, 1985. Hon. DHL Manhattan Coll., NY, 1985. Bronze Medal, Royal African Soc.; Raoul Wallenberg Humanitarian Award, 1986. *Publications:* The Principles of the Treatment of Trauma, 1962; Go an Extra Mile, 1978; Different Drums, 1987; numerous med. papers and articles. *Recreations:* farming, flying, skiing. *Address:* Mbagathi Ridge, Karen, PO Box 24277, Nairobi, Kenya. *T:* 882362. *Clubs:* Royal Commonwealth Society; Muthaiga Country; Aero Club of East Africa.                    *Died 16 May 1987.*

**WOOD, Prof. Emer. Frederick Lloyd Whitfeld**, CMG 1974; Professor Emeritus, Victoria University, 1969; *b* 29 Sept. 1903; *s* of Prof. G. A. Wood and Eleanor Madeline Wood (*née* Whitfeld), Sydney; *m* 1932, Joan Myrtle, *d* of E. L. Walter, Sydney; one *s* one *d* (and one *s* one *d* decd). *Educ:* Sydney Grammar Sch.; Univ. of Sydney (BA); Balliol Coll., Oxford (MA). Univ. Medals History and Philos., Sydney. Frazer Scholar, Univ. of Sydney, 1925; Goldsmith Sen. Student, Oxford, 1929; Lectr in History, Univ. of Sydney, 1930–34; Actg Lectr in History, Balliol Coll., 1929 and 1937; Prof. of History, Victoria Univ., Wellington, NZ, 1935–69. Carnegie Vis. Fellow, Royal Inst. of Internat. Affairs, London, 1952–53. Res. Dir, NZ Inst. of Internat. Affairs, 1974. *Publications:* The Constitutional Development of Australia, 1933; Concise History of Australia, 1935; New Zealand in the World, 1940; Understanding New Zealand, 1944; revised edns as This New Zealand, 1946, 1952 and 1958; The New Zealand People at War, Political and External Affairs, 1958; contrib. NZ Jl of History, DNB. *Recreation:* walking. *Address:* 4 Gladstone Terrace, Wellington, New Zealand. *T:* Wellington 726–818.                    *Died 11 Sept. 1989.*

**WOOD, Maj.-Gen. George Neville**, CB 1946; CBE 1945; DSO 1945; MC; *b* 4 May 1898; *o s* of Frederick Wood, Newnham-on-Severn, Glos; *m* 1928, Mary, *d* of Ven. H. C. Izard, late Archdeacon of Singapore; one *s* one *d*. *Educ:* Colston's School; Royal Military College, Sandhurst. First Commission Dorset Regt 1916; active service France, Russia, Turkey, 1916–20 (despatches twice, wounded, OBE, MC, Order of St Anne of Russia 3rd class (with swords)); regimental service Near East and Sudan, 1921–25; Staff College, Camberley, 1926–27; Staff employment War Office, and Aldershot, 1928–31; regimental service and Staff employment, India, 1932–38; commanded Oxford University OTC 1938–39; MA Oxon (hon.); Staff employment, home theatre, 1939–40; commanded 12th Bn West Yorkshire Regt 1941; commanded 2nd Bn Dorset Regt 1941–42; commanded 4th Infantry Brigade, 1942; BGS Ceylon Army Command, 1943; BGS 33rd Indian Corps in Assam-Burma operations, 1943–44; GOC 25th Indian Division in Arakan

operations and re-occupation of Malaya, 1944–46 (despatches twice, CBE, DSO, CB); President No 6 Reg. Commissions Board, 1946; GOC Mid-West District and 53rd (Welsh) Div. TA, 1947–50; Director of Quartering, War Office, 1951–52; retired 1952. Col, The Dorset Regt (subsequently The Devonshire and Dorset Regt), 1952–62. *Recreations:* cricket, history. *Address:* 6 Elsworthy Terrace, Hampstead, NW3.                    *Died 14 Jan. 1982.*

**WOOD, Hubert Lyon-Campbell**, MS London; FRCS; retired; Professor of Clinical Orthopaedics, Ahmadu Bello University, Zaria, Nigeria, 1968–77; Senior Orthopædic Surgeon, King's College Hospital, 1952–68, retired from National Health Service, 1968; Orthopædic Surgeon, Royal Masonic Hospital, 1952–68; *b* 3 Nov. 1903; *s* of Dr H. M. Wood and Lola Lyon-Campbell; *m* 1935, Dr Irene Parker Murray, MB, BS London (*d* 1966); two *d*. *Educ:* Marlborough Coll., Wilts; King's Coll., London Univ. MRCS, LRCP, 1926; MB, BS London (Hons), 1927; FRCS 1930; MS London, 1934. Orthopædic Surgeon, EMS, 1939–48; Assistant Surgeon: King's College Hosp., 1932; Evelina Hosp., 1934; Orthopædic Surgeon, Leatherhead Hosp., 1940. *Publications:* Chapters in Post Graduate Surgery, 1937; chapters in Rose and Carless, 1958; Operative Surgery, 1957; articles in Br. Jl Bone and Joint Surgery (past member of editorial board). *Recreations:* gardening, riding, photography. *Address:* South House, 95 Dulwich Village, SE21 7BJ.                    *Died 16 Aug. 1982.*

**WOOD, Sir Ian (Jeffreys)**, Kt 1976; MBE 1942; MD; FRCP, FRACP; Consultant Physician, Royal Melbourne Hospital, since 1963; *b* 5 Feb. 1903; *s* of Dr Jeffreys Wood and Mrs Isla Wood; *m* 1939, Edith Mary Cooke; two *d*. *Educ:* Melbourne C of E Grammar Sch.; Univ. of Melbourne (MD, BS). FRCP 1943; FRACP 1937. War Service, 1939–45: RAAMC, ME and Pacific Zone; Col Comdg 2/7 Aust. Gen. Hosp., New Guinea, 1944–45. Med. Supt, Children's Hosp., Melbourne, 1930–31; House Phys., Hosp. for Sick Children, Great Ormond Street, London, 1932; Royal Melbourne Hospital: Phys., 1939–63; Asst Dir, Walter and Eliza Hall Inst. of Med. Res., 1946–63. Hon. FRSocMed 1984. Neil Hamilton Fairley Medal, for Outstanding Contributions to Medicine, RCP and RACP, 1974; Stawell Oration, The Great and Glorious Masterpiece of Man, Melbourne, 1975; Distinguished Service Award, Gastroenterological Soc. of Aust., 1983. Univ. of Melbourne Blue for Cricket and Hockey, 1926; Victorian State Hockey Team, 1927. *Publications:* Diffuse Lesions of the Stomach (with Dr L. I. Taft), 1958; Discovery and Healing in Peace and War, an autobiography, 1984; contribs in field of gastroenterology in BMJ, Lancet and Med. Jl of Aust. *Recreations:* book collecting, cricket and tennis. *Address:* Flat 1, 27 Tintern Avenue, Toorak, Vic 3142, Australia. *T:* 241 9622. *Clubs:* Melbourne, Melbourne Cricket.
                    *Died 1 Sept. 1986.*

**WOOD, James Maxwell, (Max Wood)**, OBE 1975; Chairman, Metrication Board, 1977–80 (Deputy Chairman, 1976–77); *b* 24 June 1914; *s* of Arthur Henry and Emily Louisa Wood; *m* 1943, Olive Margaret Musk; one *s* two *d*. *Educ:* Technical colls; Ruskin Coll., Oxford; Co-operative Coll., Loughborough. Dip. Econ. and Pol. Sci. (Oxon). Private Sec. to Rt Hon. A. V. Alexander, MP (later Earl Alexander of Hillsborough) to 1940. Served War, 1940–46: RAF, and Embassies in S America. Asst Parly Sec., Co-op. Union, to 1951; Organising Sec., Co-op. Dry Goods Trade Assoc., 1951–56; Parly Sec., Co-op. Union, 1956–74. Member: Retail consortium, 1968–74; Consumers' Cttee under Agricultural Marketing Acts, 1966–82; Food Hygiene Adv. Council (DHSS), 1971–80; Consumers' Consultative Cttee of EEC, 1973–76; Nat. Consumer Council, 1975–80; Policyholders Protection Bd, 1975–; Chm., Consumer Working Party of Internat. Co-op. Alliance, 1963–73; Hon. Sec., Parly All-Party Retail Trade Gp; Pres., Co-op. Congress, 1974. *Publications:* numerous pamphlets and articles, over period of many years, on: consumer affairs, monopolies and restrictive practices, distributive trades. *Recreation:* water-colour painting. *Address:* 26 Ringwood Close, Crawley, West Sussex RH10 6HH. *T:* Crawley 21924.                    *Died 26 Oct. 1982.*

**WOOD, Sir Kenneth (Millns)**, Kt 1970; FCA; *b* 25 April 1909; *s* of Sydney Wood and Edith Wood (*née* Barker); *m* 1939, Julia Mary, *d* of John and Mary Ambrose; one *d*. *Educ:* Barnstaple Grammar Sch.; Trinity Coll., Cambridge (BA). Wrangler in Maths Tripos, Trinity Coll., 1930. Chartered Accountant, 1933. Served War of 1939–45 (Lt-Col). Concrete Ltd (later Bison Group): Dir 1946; Man. Dir 1950; Chm. 1958–79. Seconded to Min. of Housing and Local Govt as Industrial Adviser on House-Building to Minister, 1966–67; Dir, National Building Agency, 1966–79. FBIM 1971–79. *Recreations:* golf, ski-ing, sailing, tennis. *Address:* Ridge End, Finchampstead, Berks. *T:* Eversley (Hants) 733294. *Club:* East Berks Golf.                    *Died 27 May 1986.*

**WOOD, Sir Michael;** *see* Wood, Sir A. M.

**WOOD, Ralph; His Honour Judge Wood;** a Circuit Judge since 1972; *b* 26 April 1921; *o s* of late Harold and Dorothy Wood, Wilmslow, Cheshire. *Educ:* Wilmslow Prep. Sch.; King's Sch., Macclesfield;

Exeter Coll., Oxford. Served War of 1939–45: commissioned Somerset LI, and served in England, India and Manipur, 1941–46. Called to Bar, Gray's Inn, 1948; practised on Northern Circuit; JP Co. Lancs, 1970–; Dep. Chm., Lancashire QS, 1970–71. *Address:* 38 Hawthorn Lane, Wilmslow, Cheshire SK9 5DG. *T:* Wilmslow 522673. *Died 4 Nov. 1986.*

**WOOD, Roger L.;** *see* Leigh-Wood.

**WOOD, Rev. Prof. Thomas;** D. J. James Professor of Pastoral Theology, St David's University College, Lampeter, 1957–84; Emeritus Professor, University of Wales, 1984; Deputy Principal, St David's University College, 1971–77; Head of Department of Pastoral Theology, 1957–77, of Theology, 1977–83, of Theology and Religious Studies, 1983–84; *b* 30 April 1919; *o s* of Willie Wood and Mabel (*née* Gaffey), Batley, Yorks; *m* 1945, Joan Ashley Pollard (*d* 1984); three *s*. *Educ:* Batley Grammar Sch.; Univ. of Leeds (BA 1st Cl. Hons English 1941; BD 1945; MA with Dist. 1947); Coll. of the Resurrection, Mirfield. Deacon 1943, priest 1944. Asst Curate, St Anne's, Worksop, 1943–47; Sen. Asst Curate, Mansfield Parish Church, 1947–52; Vicar of Seascale, 1952–57. Chm., Ch. in Wales Working Party on Marriage and Divorce, 1972–75. Member: Southwell Dioc. Cttee for Post-ordination Trng, 1948–52; Social and Indust. Commn of Ch. Assembly, 1949–50; Churches' Council on Gambling, 1965–78; Doctrinal Commn of Ch. in Wales, 1969–85; Ch. in Wales Adv. Commn on Ch. and Society, 1973–85. An Ecclesiastical Judge, Provincial Ct of Ch. in Wales, 1976–. Bishop's Selector, CACTM, 1955–66; Select Preacher, Univ. of Cambridge, 1961. *Publications:* English Casuistical Divinity during the Seventeenth Century, 1952; The Pastoral Responsibility of the Church Today, 1958; Five Pastorals, 1961; Some Moral Problems, 1961; Chastity Not Outmoded, 1965; (contrib.) A Dictionary of Christian Ethics, 1967; A New Dictionary of Christian Ethics, 1986; articles and revs in Theol., Ch. Qtly Rev., Jl Theol Studies, Ch. in Wales Qtly, Trivium. *Address:* 26 Manor Park Close, York YO3 6UZ. *Died 26 Nov. 1987.*

**WOOD, William Walter,** FRIBA, CEng, FIStructE; *b* Arnold, Notts, 24 Nov. 1896; *e s* of Uriah and Georgina Maria Wood; *m* 1920, Frances Agnes Irene, *yr d* of Samuel Edwin and Emma Jane Varney, Nottingham; two *s*. *Educ:* Nottingham High Sch. Articled to late Frederick Ball, Nottingham, and trained at Nottingham University College and School of Art, Architectural Association School of Architecture, London, and in the atelier of the late Fernand Billerey in London; Asst Professor of Architecture and Senior Lecturer in Architectural Design in the Royal School of Engineering, Cairo, 1926–28; Head of the Dept of Architecture at Plymouth Central School of Arts and Crafts, 1928–32; Head of the Dept of Building at Plymouth and Devonport Technical Colleges, 1931–32; Principal, Mid-Essex Technical College and School of Art, Chelmsford, 1932–40; Founder and Principal, Delhi Polytechnic, Delhi, 1940–46. Member of the Schools Cttee of the Board of Architectural Education, RIBA, 1929–31; Founder-President, Association of Principals of Technical Institutions (India), 1941–46. Chairman, National Service Labour Tribunal, President Technical Training Selection Cttee and Regional Inspector of Technical Training, Delhi, Ajmer-Merwara and Rajputana, 1941–42; served in Egypt, Palestine, France, Belgium, and Germany, 1915–19; works: University of Rajasthan; Government House of South-West Africa; factories, mills, offices, showrooms, banks, hotels, airports, schools, hostels, flats, houses in England, Egypt, India, Southern Africa. Works exhibited at Royal Academy, RIBA, RSA, and Architectural Association, London; also Salon d'Automne, Paris. *Publications:* articles in technical periodicals, with translations in French and French Colonial architectural reviews; former English Correspondent of L'Architecture d'Aujourd'hui. *Recreations:* bowls, photography, and travel. *Address:* H4 Buffelsfontein, Walmer, Port Elizabeth, South Africa. *Died 14 July 1982.*

**WOODALL, Lt-Gen. Sir John (Dane),** KCMG 1959; KBE 1953 (OBE 1942; MBE 1919); CB 1947; MC 1917; Governor and Commander-in-Chief, Bermuda, 1955–60; *b* 19 April 1897; *s* of late Colonel F. Woodall, CMG; *m* 1st, 1920, Helen (Nischan-I-Schefakat), *o d* of late Sir Adam Block, KCMG; one *d*; 2nd, 1935, Marion, CStJ, *d* of late Alfred Aitkin Thom; one *s* two *d*. *Educ:* St Columba's; RMA, Woolwich; Staff Colleges, Camberley and RAF. Served European War, 1914–18, Major, Royal Artillery (despatches, MBE, MC); DAAG Turkey, 1922–24; Instructor in Gunnery; Brigade Major; commanded battery RA; Instructor RAF Staff College; commanded regt RA; GSO1; Brigadier, General Staff, 1940; DDSD, War Office; Director Man Power, War Office; served War of 1939–46 (despatches, CB, OBE); Vice-Adjutant-General to the Forces, 1949–52; GOC, N. Ireland, 1952–55; retired, 1955. Colonel Comdt, RA, 1954–62. KStJ 1958. *Recreations:* lawn tennis and squash. *Address:* Whitewell Lodge, near Whitchurch, Salop. *Club:* Army and Navy. *Died 7 May 1985.*

**WOODALL, Mary,** CBE 1959; PhD; DLitt; FSA; FMA; London Adviser to Felton Trust, Melbourne, 1965–75; *b* 6 March 1901.

*Educ:* Cheltenham Ladies' Coll.; Somerville Coll., Oxford. Voluntary, British Museum Dept of Prints and Drawings. WRVS Regional Administrator, 1938–42; Temp. Principal, Ministry of Health and Ministry of Supply, 1942–45; Keeper, Dept of Art, 1945–56, Director, 1956–64, City Museum and Art Gallery, Birmingham. Trustee, Nat. Gallery, 1968–76. Fellow of University College, London, 1958. *Publications:* Gainsborough's Landscape Drawings, 1939; Thomas Gainsborough, 1949; The Letters of Thomas Gainsborough, 1962. *Recreations:* travelling, painting. *Club:* University Women's. *Died 31 March 1988.*

**WOODCOCK, John,** TD (with 2 bars) 1958; Solicitor since 1948; *b* 1 Sept. 1920; *e s* of late Lt-Col F. A. Woodcock and Margaret (*née* Murphy); *m* 1951, Catherine Deirdre Ryan; two *s*. *Educ:* Bury Grammar Sch.; Prior Park Coll., Bath; Victoria Univ., Manchester. Royal Humane Soc. Hon. Testimonial, 1936; commissioned Lancs Fusiliers, TA, 1938. Served War: BEF, France, 1940, and with Kenya Armoured Car Regt, E Africa, 1940–43, and SEAC, 1943–45. A Recorder of the Crown Court, 1972–77. Councillor, Tottington UDC, 1957–74 (Chm., 1963–64); Chm., Bury and Radcliffe Conservative Assoc., 1965–71; County Comr for Scouts, SE Lancashire, 1966–74; Pres., Bury and Dist. Law Soc., 1967; Chm., Bury and Rochdale Legal Aid Cttee, 1966–71; Pres., Tottington Ex-Service Mens' Assoc., 1947–; Pres., British Legion, Bury, 1969–. KHS 1981. *Recreation:* gardening, when time! *Address:* Tonge Fold, Hawkshaw, near Bury, Lancashire. *T:* Tottington 2796, (business) 061-761 4611. *Club:* Conservative (Tottington). *Died 27 July 1981.*

**WOODFIELD, Ven. Samuel Percy,** MA; Rector of Waterval Boven (African and European), 1964–72 (Priest-in-charge, Waterval Boven Missions, 1959–72); Archdeacon of Barberton, 1960–63, Archdeacon Emeritus from 1964; Canon S Alban's Cathedral, Pretoria, South Africa, 1932–64; Hon. Canon, 1964; *b* 19 April 1889; *s* of Samuel Robinson Woodfield and Emma Utting. *Educ:* Great Yarmouth Grammar Sch.; Selwyn Coll., Cambridge. Asst Priest, St Mary's, Hitchin, 1915–19; Headmaster, Norton Sch., Letchworth, 1917–19; Asst Priest, Sawbridgeworth, 1919–21; Vice-Principal, Diocesan Training Coll., Pietersburg, N Transvaal, 1922–24, Principal, 1924–38, 1954–57; Priest-in-Charge, Pietersburg West Native Mission, 1936–38; Priest-in-charge, Pretoria Native Mission, 1938–53, and Coloured Mission, 1943–53; Archdeacon of Pretoria (City) Native Mission, 1945–53; Archdeacon of W Transvaal, 1953–60; Archdeacon of E Transvaal, 1958–60. Exam. Chaplain to Bishop of Pretoria, 1922–50; Member: Advisory Board for Native Education in the Transvaal, 1924–37, 1940–43, 1946–50; Chaplain Westfort Leper Inst., 1938–53; Div. Pathfinder Scout Commissioner for the Transvaal, 1931–50; Deputy Chief Scouts' African Commissioner for S Africa, 1943–53; Chief Scout's Commissioner for African Scouts, S Africa, 1953–61; Emeritus Comr, 1961. King George V Jubilee Medal; Coronation Medals, 1937, 1953. *Address:* Irene Homes, Irene, Transvaal, 1675, South Africa. *T:* 65116. *Died 4 July 1983.*

**WOODFORD, Brigadier Edward Cecil James,** CBE 1946; DSO 1943; *b* 1901; *s* of late Major Edward Francis Woodford, York and Lancaster Regt; *m* 1st, 1928, Margaret, *d* of Col Arthur Claude Mardon, DSO, Framfield, Sussex; one *d*; 2nd, 1932, Eleanor Waterhouse, *d* of H. M. Brandon, Kingston, Jamaica; one *d*; 3rd, 1949, Joanne Eileen, *d* of Peter Charles Mayer, Washington, DC, USA; one *s* two *d*. *Educ:* Bedford Sch.; RMC Sandhurst; Staff Coll., Camberley, 1936–37; Nat. War Coll., USA, 1949. 2nd Lieut, York and Lancaster Regt, 1920. Served War of 1939–45, N Africa, Iraq, Persia, Sicily, Italy, Burma, French Indo-China; Lieut-Colonel, 1942, Brigadier, 1945. Commander, Lubbecke District, BAOR, 1952–55, retired 1955. *Address:* 2020 Lincoln Park West, Apt 22K, Chicago, Ill 60614, USA. *Died 17 Dec. 1988.*

**WOODGER, Prof. Joseph Henry,** DSc; Emeritus Professor of Biology, University of London; *b* 2 May 1894; *s* of N. L. Woodger, Great Yarmouth, Norfolk; *m* 1921, Doris Eden, *d* of late Major-General C. R. Buckle, CB, CMG, DSO; three *s* one *d*. *Educ:* Felsted Sch.; University College, London. Graduated in Zoology, 1914. 2nd Lieut, Norfolk Regt, 1915; served European War, 2nd Bn Norfolk Regt, in Mesopotamia, 1916–18. Protozoologist in Central Lab. Amara, 1918–19; Derby Scholar, UCL, 1919; Assistant in Zoology Department, University College London, 1919–22; Reader in Biology, 1922; Professor of Biology, 1947, University of London (Middlesex Hosp. Med. Sch.); retired 1959. Tarner Lecturer, Trinity Coll., Cambridge, 1949–50. *Publications:* Elementary Morphology and Physiology, 1924; Biological Principles, 1929; The Axiomatic Method in Biology, 1937; The Technique of Theory Construction, 1939; Biology and Language, 1952; Physics, Psychology and Medicine, 1956. Papers in Quart. Journal Micro. Sci.; Proc. Arist. Soc., Phil. Trans. Royal Society; Quart. Review Biology, British Journal Phil. Sci., etc. *Recreations:* reading the Bible and Shakespeare; viticulture. *Address:* Tanhurst, 115 Roseberry Road, Epsom Downs, Surrey KT18 6AB. *T:* Ashtead (Surrey) 76469. *Died 8 March 1981.*

**WOODHOUSE, Henry,** CB 1975; Principal Assistant Solicitor and Head of Transport Branch of Legal Directorate, Departments of the Environment and Transport, until 1978; retired; *b* 12 July 1913; *s* of Frank and Florence A. Woodhouse, Cradley Heath, Warley, W Midlands; *m* 1941, Eileen Mary, *d* of Harry and Florence C. Roach, Cradley Heath; two *d. Educ:* King Edward's Sch., Birmingham; St John's Coll., Oxford (MA). Solicitor, 1938; served in HM Forces, 1940–46: Lt-Col in Legal Div., Control Commn for Germany, 1945–46; entered Treasury Solicitor's Dept, 1946; Asst Treasury Solicitor, 1955–69; Principal Asst Treasury Solicitor, 1969–71; Principal Asst Solicitor, DoE, later Depts of the Environment and Transport, 1972–78. *Publications:* The Story of a Leek Church, 1988; articles in The Conveyancer. *Recreations:* Methodist local preacher, photography, gardening. *Address:* Three Ways, Birchall, Leek, Staffs ST13 5RA. *T:* Leek (0538) 372814.

*Died 27 June 1990.*

**WOODIFIELD, Rear-Admiral Anthony,** CB 1965; CBE 1961; LVO 1953; *b* 5 Aug. 1912; *s* of late Colonel A. H. Woodifield, CB, CMG, OBE, St Leonards-on-Sea, Sussex; *m* 1947, Elizabeth, *d* of late E. J. Stevens, Sutton, Surrey; two *s. Educ:* Cheltenham College. Joined RN, 1929. Served 1939–45 in Home Fleet and on East Indies Station. On Staff of Commander-in-Chief, Portsmouth and for Coronation Naval Review, 1951–53; Secretary to Flag Officer, Second-in-Command, Mediterranean, 1954–55; Secretary to Third Sea Lord and Controller of the Navy, 1956–61; Comdg Officer, HMS Phœnicia, 1961–63; Director General of Naval Personal Services and Officer Appointments, 1964–66. Comdr, 1947; Captain, 1955; Rear-Admiral, 1963; retired list, 1966. *Recreation:* fishing. *Address:* Stocks Cottage, Kington Langley, Chippenham, Wilts. *T:* Kington Langley 281. *Club:* Army and Navy.

*Died 7 May 1986.*

**WOODLAND, Austin William,** CBE 1975; PhD; FGS; Hon. Professorial Fellow, University College of Swansea and Cardiff, since 1980; *b* Mountain Ash, Mid Glamorgan, 4 April 1914; *er s* of William Austin Woodland and Sarah Jane (*née* Butler); *m* 1939, Nesta Ann Phillips (*d* 1981); one *s* one *d. Educ:* Mountain Ash Co. Sch.; University Coll. of Wales, Aberystwyth (BSc Hons Geol., PhD). Lyell Fund, Geol Soc., 1947; FGS 1937. Temp. Asst Lectr in Geol., Manchester Univ., 1937; Demonstrator in Geol., QUB, 1937–39; Geologist, Geol Survey of GB (now incorp. in Inst. of Geol Sciences), 1939; Dist Geologist, 1957–62; Asst Dir (Northern England), 1962–71; Dep. Dir, 1971–75; Director: Inst. of Geol Sciences, 1976–79; Geol Survey of Northern Ireland, 1976–79; Geol Adv. to Minister of Overseas Develt, 1976–79. President: Yorks Geol Soc., 1966–68; Sect. C (Geol.), BAAS, Swansea, 1971 (Mem. Council, 1970–73; Mem. Gen. Cttee, 1973–); Vice-Pres., Geol Soc., 1968–70 (Mem. Council, 1967–70). Sec.-Gen., 6th Internat. Congress of Carboniferous Stratigraphy and Geol., Sheffield, 1967; Geol Adviser, Aberfan Disaster Tribunal, 1966–67. Major, Special Geol Sect., RE (AER), 1948–57. *Publications:* Geology of district around Pontypridd and Maesteg, 1964; (ed) Petroleum and the Continental Shelf of North West Europe, 1975; papers on geol aspects of manganese, coal, water supply, engrg applications. *Recreations:* golf, stamp collecting, gardening. *Address:* 60 Dan-y-Bryn Avenue, Radyr, Cardiff. *T:* Cardiff (0222) 843330.

*Died 9 Nov. 1990.*

**WOODROW, Maj.-Gen. (Albert) John,** MBE 1949; *b* 3 June 1919; *s* of late Frederick Henry Woodrow, Portsmouth; *m* 1944, Elizabeth, *d* of late Major Sir John Theodore Prestige, Bourne Park, Bishopsbourne, Kent; two *s* one *d. Educ:* Nunthorpe. Commnd Royal Signals, 1940; served War of 1939–45 in NW Europe and Burma (despatches); British Mission to Burma, 1948–49; exchange duty Canada, 1954–56; CO 1 Div. Sigs, 1961–63; British Army Staff, Washington, 1963–65; Comdr Trng Bde Royal Signals, 1965–68; Dir of Public Relations Army, 1968–70; GOC Wales, 1970–73. Col Comdt, Royal Corps of Signals, 1970–77. Dir of Army Security, 1973–78, retired. *Address:* Hookers Green, Bishopsbourne, Canterbury, Kent. *Club:* Army and Navy.

*Died 16 March 1988.*

**WOODROW, Maj.-Gen. John;** *see* Woodrow, A. J.

**WOODS, George David;** banker; with The First Boston Corporation, New York City, 1934–62 and since 1968 (Chairman of Board, 1951–62); Chairman: Henry J. Kaiser Family Foundation (also Trustee), since 1968; International Executive Service Corps, 1968–74, Executive Committee, since 1974; Director since 1968, President since 1971, Foreign Bondholders Protective Council Inc.; Director Emeritus, Lincoln Center for the Performing Arts, Inc.; *b* 27 July 1901; *s* of John Woods and Laura A. Woods (*née* Rhodes); *m* 1935, Louise Taraldson; no *c. Educ:* New York public schools; American Institute of Banking; New York Univ. Investment Banking: Harris Forbes & Co., NY City, 1918–34. Pres. and Chm. of Exec. Dirs, IBRD and IDA, 1963–68; Chm. of Board and Pres., IFC, 1963–68. Holds honorary doctorates from Universities and Colleges. Legion of Merit, US Army, 1945. *Address:* 277 Park

Avenue, New York, NY 10017, USA; (home) 825 Fifth Avenue, New York, NY 10021, USA. *Clubs:* Links, Pinnacle, Players, Racquet & Tennis, World Trade Center (New York); Duquesne (Pittsburgh); Federal City (Washington, DC).

*Died 20 Aug. 1982.*

**WOODS, Reginald Salisbury, (Rex Woods),** MA; MD, BCh (Cantab); FRCS; Médaille d'Honneur de l'Education Physique et des Sports, République Française, 1946; Hon. Life Member, British Association of Sport and Medicine; retired from general practice, 1983; Surgical Specialist to numerous insurance companies; Honorary Medical Officer: Cambridge University Boxing Club (also President); Cambridge University Point-to-Point and Cambridgeshire Point-to-Point; Cambridgeshire Warden King George's Jubilee Trust; Past Assistant of Glaziers' Company; a Patron of Cambridge Branch, Old Contemptibles and of British Legion; Past President, Downing College Association, 1962; *b* London, 15 Oct. 1891; *o s* of late H. T. Woods, Galway; *m* 1918, Irene, CBE, TD (*d* 1976), *y d* of late T. Pickering; one *s* two *d. Educ:* Dulwich Coll.; Downing Coll., Cambridge (Entr. Exh.); St George's Hospital (Senior Univ. Entrance Scholar, Research Exhib., etc.). HS, HP, and Surg. Registrar. Captain, RAMC, BEF, 1916–19 (despatches); late Surg. Spec. Ministry of Pensions; Surg. EMS (Cambridge County Hospital), 1939–43; Major, RAMC, 1943–45 (Surg. Spec. E Africa Command). Formerly: Pres., Cambridge Med. Soc., County Dir BRCS, and Chm., Nat. Playing Fields Assoc. and Cambs AAA. Co-Manager, 5 Oxford/Cambridge Athletic Tours *v* USA Univs, 1925–49. *Publications:* Cambridge Doctor, 1962; many contribs on sports injuries in British and US med. jls. *Recreations:* represented England 1914 and 1920–29; Great Britain at Olympic Games, 1924 and 1928, and British Empire *v* USA, 1924 and 1928, in Putting the Weight. President (1914), Hon. Treasurer (1919–39) and Chairman (1939–52), of CUAC. AAA Champion, 1924 and 1926; Captained Public Schools Past and Present at Rugby Football, 1919; golf, bridge. *Address:* 4 Manor Court, Grange Road, Cambridge. *Clubs:* British Sportsman's; Cambridge County, Hawks, Pitt, Cambridge, Achilles (Cambridge); Oxford and Cambridge Golfing Society.

*Died 21 Sept. 1986.*

**WOODS, Maj.-Gen. Thomas Frederic Mackie,** CB 1960; OBE 1945; MD; FRCP(I); retired; *b* 14 July 1904; *s* of Dr Annesley Woods, Birr, Ireland; *m* 1930, Juliet Frances, *d* of D. L. Rogers, Dublin; two *d. Educ:* St Paul's Sch.; Trinity Coll., Dublin. BA, MB, Dublin, 1926; MD, Dublin, 1932; MRCP Ireland, 1934. Joined RAMC 1927; served in India, Malta and UK until 1940. Served War of 1939–45: in UK, Madagascar, India, Middle East, Burma, Malaya. Seconded to Ministry of Food, 1946–48, as Chief Health Officer E. African Groundnut Scheme; 2 Div., RAMC Depot, HQ London Dist, HQ 1 (BR) Corps; HQ Southern Command. Brigadier, 1956; Maj.Gen., 1957. QHP 1959–61. Colonel Comdt, RAMC, 1965–69. OStJ. *Address:* White Lodge, Berwick St James, near Salisbury, Wilts.

*Died 25 Sept. 1982.*

**WOODWARD, (Foster) Neville,** CBE 1956; FRSE; FRSC; Technology Policy Adviser to government in developing countries; Chairman, Biotech Consultants Ltd; *b* 2 May 1905; *s* of Foster and Catherine Woodward; *m* 1932, Elizabeth Holme Siddall; one *s* one *d. Educ:* Bradford; University Coll., London (PhD, gold medallist). After ten years in industry, and two as Res. Asst to Prof. Sir Robert Robinson, FRS), Oxford Univ., became Head of Res. and Develt Div., HM Chem. Defence Res. Estabt, Sutton Oak, 1937–42. Officer in Charge, Min. of Supply Res. Estabt, Leamington Spa, 1943; Dep. Sci. Adv. to Min. of Production, 1944–46; Dir, Inst. of Seaweed Research, 1946–56 (Mem. Bd Inst., 1956–69); seconded to FO as Dir UK Sci. Mission, Washington DC; Attaché for Sci. Questions, Brit. Embassy, Washington DC, and Sci. Adv. to UK High Comr in Canada, 1947–48; Hon. Sci. Adv. to Sec. of State for Scotland, 1951–56; Sci. Attaché to European Productivity Agency, OEEC, Paris, 1956–61; Sen. Sci. Counsellor, Directorate of Scientific Affairs, OECD, Paris, 1961–70. Dir, Arthur D. Little Res. Inst., 1956–70; Man. Dir, Arthur D. Little Ltd, 1963–68. Chm., Inveresk Res. Internat. Management Cttee, 1970–73. Mem., Council for Applied Science in Scotland, 1978–; Res. Policy Advr, Scottish Council: Develt and Industry, 1974–79. Vice-President: Soc. of Chemical Industry, 1968–71 (Jubilee Lectr, 1968–69); RIC, 1969–71; Chm., Assoc. of Consulting Scientists, 1967–69. Ramsay Meml Fellowship Trustee, 1969–. *Publications:* A Survey of Agricultural, Forestry and Fishery Products in the United Kingdom and their Utilisation (with J. Maxton and A. B. Stewart), 1953; Structure of Industrial Research Associations, 1964; (with T. S. Chung and R. D. Lalkaka) Guidelines for Development of Industrial Technology in Asia and the Pacific, 1976; about 100 publications in scientific press. *Recreations:* mountains, foreign travel, reading, writing. *Address:* St Margaret's Lodge, Gullane, East Lothian. *T:* Gullane 842210; Cuil Moss, Ardgour, Argyll. *Clubs:* New, Royal Society of Edinburgh, Edinburgh Research (Edinburgh).

*Died 3 May 1985.*

**WOODWARD, (Winifred) Joan;** Assistant Principal Probation Officer, Inner London Probation and After-care Service, 1950–72; *b*

14 Sept. 1907; *d* of late Brig.-Gen. J. A. H. Woodward, IA, and Winifred Mary Strahan. *Educ:* Princess Helena Coll., Ealing. Appointed to Probation Service, 1936; served at: North London and Edmonton, Apr.–Nov. 1936; Marylebone, Nov. 1936–June 1940; appointed to Bow Street, 1940; Senior Probation Officer, Bow Street Magistrates Court, Nov. 1948. *Address:* 2 Queen Anne's Grove, Ealing, W5. *T:* 01–567 8571. *Died 24 Nov. 1981.*

**WOOKEY, Eric Edgar,** MC 1916; Dental Surgeon in private practice at Wimpole Street, 1933–68, retired, 1968; Senior Dental Surgeon, Royal Free Hospital, 1936–Sept. 1958, Hon. Consulting Dental Surgeon, since 1958; *b* 11 January 1892; *s* of Edgar Wookey, Shipham, Somerset, and Clara (*née* Davidson); *m* 1927, Doris Kathleen Fenner (*d* 1976); one *s* two *d*. *Educ:* Haverfordwest Grammar School; Clevedon College; Bristol University; Royal Dental Hospital, London. Bristol Univ. Student, medical and dental, 1909–14; Infantry commission in 4th Glos Regt TF, 1914; served overseas, France (wounded, despatches, MC); Italy, BEF (despatches twice); Bt Major, Comd 4th Glos Regt at Armistice, Nov. 1918. LDS, RCS 1919, and after a period of hospital practice commenced private practice at Hendon, 1920; Asst Dental Surgeon, Royal Free Hosp., 1921; full-time practice in Wimpole Street, 1933. During War of 1939–45, served in EMS. Member of Representative Bd, British Dental Assoc., 1946–54 and 1958–61; Pres. Metropolitan Branch, 1949–50; Founder Member, Past-President, and Past Chm. of Council, Brit. Soc. of Med. and Dental Hypnosis (formerly Dental and Med. Soc. for Study of Hypnosis); FRSocMed; Fellow Internat. Soc. of Clinical and Experimental Hypnosis (PP Brit. Section). Member: Council, Soc. for Psychical Research; British Archæological Soc. Liveryman, Tallow Chandlers' Co. Ecclesiological Soc. Silver Medal for Valour (Italy), 1918. *Publications:* articles in British Dental Jl and British Jl of Clinical Hypnosis. *Recreations:* music (piano), golf, numismatics, philately, horology. *Address:* 51 Lake View, Canons Park, Edgware, Middx. *T:* 01–958 6029. *Died 6 March 1985.*

**WOOLLCOMBE, Dame Jocelyn May,** DBE 1950 (CBE 1944); *b* 9 May 1898; *d* of late Admiral Maurice Woollcombe and Ella Margaret Roberts; unmarried. *Educ:* Moorfield, Plymouth. Admiralty, NID as Clerk, 1916–19. Joined WRNS, enrolled as Chief Officer, Aug. 1939; Superintendent, 1940; Deputy Director, 1943–46; Director, 1946–50; Hon. ADC to the King, 1949. General Secretary, British Council for Aid to Refugees (Hungarian Section), 1957–58. Governor, The Sister Trust, 1956–65; Gov., WRNS Benevolent Trust, 1942–67; Pres., Assoc. of Wrens 1959–81. *Recreation:* drama. *Address:* 2 Thorn Park, Plymouth PL3 4TG. *Died 30 Jan. 1986.*

**WOOLLER, Arthur,** CBE 1967; HM Diplomatic Service, retired; *b* 23 May 1912; *s* of Joseph Edward Wooller and Sarah Elizabeth (*née* Kershaw); *m* 1944, Frances, *e d* of Justice A. L. Blank, ICS; three *s*. *Educ:* Bradford Grammar School; Corpus Christi College, Oxford. ICS, Bengal, 1935; Indian Foreign and Political Service, 1939; UK Trade Comr, New Zealand, 1947; First Sec. (Commercial), Ottawa, 1953; UK Trade Comr, Toronto, 1959; British Trade Comr, Hong Kong, 1960; Principal British Trade Comr, Bombay, 1963; British Deputy High Commissioner in Western India, Bombay, 1965–68; High Comr in Mauritius, 1968–70; Economic Advr, FCO, 1970–72. *Recreation:* gardening. *Address:* c/o Midland Bank, High Street, Harpenden, Herts. *Club:* United Oxford & Cambridge University. *Died 22 Dec. 1989.*

**WOOLLEY, Baron** *cr* 1967 (Life Peer), of Hatton; **Harold Woolley,** Kt 1964; CBE 1958; DL; President of National Farmers' Union of England and Wales 1960–66; *b* 6 Feb. 1905; *s* of William Woolley, JP and Eleanor Woolley; *m* 1st, 1926, Martha Annie Jeffs (*d* 1936); four *s*; 2nd, 1937, Hazel Eileen Archer Jones (*d* 1975); two *d*. *Educ:* Woodhouse Grove School, Yorkshire. Farmer. Cheshire Deleg. to NFU Council, 1943; Chairman: NFU Parliamentary Cttee, 1947–57; Employers' Reps of Agricultural Wages Bd, 1947–57; Agricultural Apprenticeship Council for England and Wales, 1951–60. National Farmers' Union: Vice-Pres. 1948 and 1955; Dep. Pres., 1949–50 and 1956; Life Mem. Council; Director: NFU Mutual Insurance Society, 1965–80; NW Regional Adv. Bd, Abbey Nat. Building Soc. Member Nat. Jt Advisory Council to Ministry of Labour, 1950–58. President: Cheshire Agricl Soc.; Cheshire NFU. DL Cheshire, 1969. *Recreations:* racing, cricket, and all sports. *Address:* Hatton House Farm, Hatton Heath, Chester. *T:* Tattenhall 70356. *Club:* MCC. *Died 31 July 1986.*

**WOOLLEY, Rev. (Alfred) Russell;** MA; Rector, St Lawrence, IoW, 1967–74; *b* 10 Sept. 1899; *e s* of late A. W. Woolley, Moseley, and Margaret A. Russell, Shrewsbury; *m* 1933, Lina Mariana, 3rd *d* of late Prof. Bertram Hopkinson, CMG, FRS, Fellow of King's College, Cambridge; four *s* three *d*. *Educ:* King Edward's Camp Hill Grammar School; Wadham College, Oxford (Symons Exhibitioner). 2nd Class Hons Modern History, 1922; incorporated MA Cantab. (Trinity College), 1929. Inns of Court OTC and 6th OC Bn, 1917–19. Bromsgrove School, 1922–26; Repton School,

1927–28; The Leys School (Chief History Master, House-Master, Librarian, OC, OTC), 1929–33; Headmaster of Scarborough Coll., 1933–37, and of Wellingborough Gram. Sch., 1937–45; Educnl Sec. to the Oxford Univ. Appts Cttee, 1945–62. Ordained 1960. Rector of Gestingthorpe, Essex, 1962–67. Mem. Coun. IAHM, 1945; of Oxfordshire Educn Cttee, 1955–62; of Govng Body of Milton Abbey Sch., 1955–74; of Lindisfarne Coll., 1961–77; ex-Sec. Oxford Union Soc. *Publications:* Oxford University and City, 1951; Clarendon Guide to Oxford, 1963, 5th edn 1983. *Recreations:* walking, travel. *Address:* Gestingthorpe Hall, Halstead, Essex CO9 3BB. *T:* Hedingham 61822. *Died 27 Jan. 1986.*

**WOOLLEY, Sir Charles (Campbell),** GBE 1953 (OBE 1934); KCMG 1943 (CMG 1937); MC; LLD; *b* 1893; 3rd *s* of Henry Woolley; *m* 1921, Ivy (*d* 1974), *d* of late David Howells, Cwmbarry, Barry, Glamorgan; two *s*. *Educ:* Univ. Coll., Cardiff. Served European War, 1914–20; Captain S Wales Borderers; various staff appts; Active Service, France, Salonika, Constantinople, Caucasus (despatches, MC); Ceylon Civil Service, 1921–35; Secretary to the Governor; Colonial Secretary, Jamaica, 1935–38; Chief Secretary Nigeria, 1938–41; administered Govt of Jamaica and Nigeria at various times; Governor and C-in-C, Cyprus, 1941–46; Governor and Commander-in-Chief, British Guiana, 1947–53; retired Jan. 1953. Pres., Internat. Soc. for Protection of Animals, 1969–71; Pres., Southern Counties Orchestral Soc. KJStJ. *Recreations:* bridge, music. *Address:* Orchard Hill, Liss, Hants. *T:* Liss 2317. *Died 20 Aug. 1981.*

**WOOLLEY, Richard;** Consultant, Benn Brothers Ltd, 1981–84 (Director, 1956, Deputy Chairman, 1972–76, Chairman, 1976–81); *b* 12 Jan. 1916; *s* of late John Woolley and Elizabeth Jane (*née* Scorgie); *m* 1940, Doreen Mary Walker; one *s*. *Educ:* Queen Elizabeth's Grammar Sch., Mansfield. Member, editorial staff, Benn Brothers Ltd, 1937; Editor: Newspaper World, 1939–53; Cabinet Maker, 1954–68. Nat. Pres., Furnishing Trades Benevolent Assoc., 1969–70. British Furniture Manufacturers Award of Merit, 1968. Junior Warden, 1979–80, Senior Warden, 1980–81, Master, 1981–82, Worshipful Co. of Furniture Makers. *Address:* Aberfoyle, Golf Side, Cheam, Surrey. *Club:* Press. *Died 30 Jan. 1986.*

**WOOLLEY, Sir Richard (van der Riet),** Kt 1963; OBE 1953; FRS 1953; Director, South African Astronomical Observatory, 1972–76; Hon. Fellow, University House, Australian National University, since 1955; Hon. Fellow, Gonville and Caius College, Cambridge, since 1956; *b* Weymouth, Dorset, 24 April 1906; *s* of Paymaster Rear-Admiral Charles E. A. Woolley, CMG, RN; *m* 1st, 1932, Gwyneth Jane Margaret (*née* Meyler) (*d* 1979); 2nd, 1979, Emily May Patricia Marples (*d* 1985); 3rd, 1985, Sheila Gillham. *Educ:* Allhallows School, Honiton; University of Cape Town; Gonville and Caius College, Cambridge; MSc Cape Town; MA, ScD Cantab; Hon. LLD Melbourne. Commonwealth Fund Fellow, at Mt Wilson Observatory, California, 1929–31; Isaac Newton Student, Cambridge Univ., 1931–33; Chief Assistant, R Observatory, Greenwich, 1933–37; John Couch Adams Astronomer, Cambridge, 1937–39; Commonwealth Astronomer, 1939–55; Astronomer Royal, 1956–71. Hon. Professor of Astronomy in Australian National University, 1950–. Visiting Prof. of Astronomy, Univ. of Sussex, 1966–. Pres., Royal Astronomical Soc., 1963–65. Vice-Pres., International Astronomical Union, 1952–58; Pres., Australian and New Zealand Assoc. for the Advancement of Science, Melbourne meeting, 1955. Hon. DrPhil Uppsala, 1956; Hon. DSc: Cape Town, 1969; Sussex, 1970. Corresp. Mem. de la Société Royale des Sciences de Liège, 1956. Master, Worshipful Co. of Clockmakers, 1969. Gold Medal, RAS, 1971. *Publications:* (with Sir Frank Dyson) Eclipses of the Sun and Moon, 1937; (with D. W. N. Stibbs) The Outer Layers of a Star, 1953. *Address:* 4 Myrtle Street, Somerset West, Cape, South Africa. *Club:* Athenæum. *Died 24 Dec. 1986.*

**WOOLLEY, Rev. Russell;** see Woolley, Rev. A. R.

**WOOLLEY, William Edward,** CBE 1974; DL; Chairman, Cupal Ltd, since 1947; Director, Secto Co. Ltd, since 1947; *b* 17 March 1901; *s* of William Woolley, JP, and Eleanor Woolley; *m* 1929, Marion Elizabeth Aspinall (*d* 1982); one *s* one *d*. *Educ:* Woodhouse Grove School, Yorkshire; Edinburgh University. MP (Nat L) for Spen Valley Division of Yorkshire, 1940–45; Parliamentary Private Secretary to Minister of Health, 1943, to Minister of Aircraft Production, 1945. JP; Chairman: Blackburn Borough Magistrates, 1956–72; Gen. Comrs Income Tax, Lancs Adv. Cttee, 1974–76; Gen Comrs Income Tax, Blackburn District, 1960–76; Blackburn and District Hosp. Management Cttee, 1952–74; Manchester Regional Hosp. Staff Cttee, 1966–74; Pres., Blackburn and District Council of Social Service. Contested (Nat L) Brighouse and Spenborough, General elections, 1950, 1951. DL Lancs, 1975. *Address:* Billinge Crest, Billinge End Road, Blackburn, Lancs BB2 6PY. *TA and T:* Blackburn 53449. *Died 11 May 1989.*

**WOOLNER, Maj.-Gen. Christopher Geoffrey,** CB 1942; MC; *b* 18 Oct. 1893; *m* 1923, Anne, *d* of Sydney Pitt; two *d*. *Educ:* Marlborough; RMA, Woolwich. 2nd Lt RE, 1912; Captain, 1917;

Bt Major, 1919; Major, 1928; Bt Lt-Col, 1933; Lt-Col, 1936; Col, 1939; Maj.-Gen., 1941. Survey Duty, Gold Coast, 1920–23; Officer Company of Gentlemen Cadets Royal Military Academy, 1924–27; GSO2 India, 1930–32; Bde Major, India, 1932–34; Deputy Inspector and Deputy Comdt School of Military Engineering, Aug.–Sept. 1939; GSO1, BEF, 1939–40; Bde Comdr, Feb.–Nov. 1940; Comdr, 1940. Served European War, 1914–18 (wounded, despatches twice, Bt Major, MC and two Bars); War of 1939–45 (despatches thrice, CB); Commander 81st (West African) Div.; Commander Mid-West District and 53 (Welsh) Infantry Division TA; retired, 1947. *Clubs:* Army and Navy, Naval and Military.

*Died 10 Jan. 1984.*

**WOOTTON OF ABINGER, Baroness** *cr* 1958 (Life Peer), of Abinger Common; **Barbara Frances,** CH 1977; MA; holds Hon. Doctorates from Columbia (NY), Nottingham, Essex, Liverpool, Aberdeen, York, Hull, Aston in Birmingham, Bath, Southampton, Warwick, Cambridge; and London; *b* Cambridge, 1897; *d* of late Dr James Adam, Senior Tutor of Emmanuel Coll., Cambridge and Mrs Adam, sometime Fellow of Girton Coll., Cambridge; *m* 1st, 1917, John Wesley Wootton (*d* of wounds, 1917), Earl of Derby Research Student, Trinity College, Cambridge; 2nd, 1935, George Percival Wright (*d* 1964). *Educ:* Perse High School for Girls, Cambridge; Girton Coll., Cambridge (MA Cantab). Director of Studies and Lecturer in Economics, Girton Coll., 1920–22; Research Officer Trades Union Congress and Labour Party Joint Research Department, 1922–26; Principal, Morley College for Working Men and Women, 1926–27; Director of Studies for Tutorial Classes, University of London, 1927–44; Professor of Social Studies, University of London, 1948–52; Nuffield Research Fellow, Bedford College, University of London, 1952–57. A Governor of the BBC, 1950–56; a Deputy-Speaker in House of Lords, 1967–. Member: Departmental Cttee, Nat. Debt and Taxation, 1924–27; Royal Commission on Workmen's Compensation, 1938; Interdepartmental Cttee on Shop Hours, 1946–49; Royal Commn on the Press, 1947; UGC, 1948–50; Royal Commn on the Civil Service, 1954; Interdepartmental Cttee on the Business of the Criminal Courts, 1958–61; Council on Tribunals, 1961–64; Interdepartmental Cttee on the Criminal Statistics, 1963–67; Royal Commn on Penal System, 1964–66; Penal Adv. Council, 1966–79; Adv. Council on Misuse of Drugs, 1971–74; Chm., Countryside Commn, 1968–70 (Nat. Parks Commn, 1966–68). JP in the Metropolitan Courts, 1926–70 (on the Panel of Chairmen in the Metropolitan Juvenile Courts, 1946–62). Hon. Fellow: Girton Coll., Cambridge, 1965–; Bedford Coll., London, 1964–; Royal Coll. of Psychiatrists, 1979. *Publications:* (as *Barbara Wootton*): Twos and Threes, 1933; Plan or No Plan, 1934; London's Burning, 1936; Lament for Economics, 1938; End Social Inequality, 1941; Freedom Under Planning, 1945; Testament for Social Science, 1950; The Social Foundations of Wage Policy, 1955; Social Science and Social Pathology, 1959; Crime and the Criminal Law, 1964, 2nd edn 1981; In a World I Never Made, 1967; Contemporary Britain, 1971; Incomes Policy: an inquest and a proposal, 1974; Crime and Penal Policy, 1978; frequent contributor to New Society and other sociological journals. *Recreation:* country life. *Address:* Holmesdale Park, Nutfield, Surrey RH1 4HT. *T:* Nutfield Ridge 2738.

*Died 11 July 1988.*

**WOOTTON, Harold Samuel,** CMG 1942; FCIS; JP; Town Clerk of Melbourne, 1935–54, retired; *b* Ballan, Vic, 13 Dec. 1891; *s* of late John Richard Wootton, Tatura, Goulburn Valley, Victoria; *m* 1914, Anne, *d* of late Joseph Biggs; one *s* one *d*. *Educ:* State School, Waranga, Victoria; Central Business College, Melbourne. Junior Clerk, Melbourne Town Hall, 1909; Deputy Town Clerk, 1923. *Recreation:* bowls. *Address:* Unit 2, 11 Robert Street, Noosaville, Qld 4566, Australia. *Clubs:* St Kilda Bowling, Tewantin Bowling (Queensland).

*Died 28 March 1989.*

**WORDEN, Prof. Alastair Norman;** Professor of Toxicology, University of Bath, 1973–85; Chairman, Huntingdon Research Centre, 1951–78, Founder, since 1978; Hon. Professor of Toxicology, since 1978, Adviser to Department of Biochemistry, since 1985, University of Surrey; Chairman, Cambridge Applied Nutrition, Toxicology of Biosciences Group, since 1981; *b* 23 April 1916; *s* of Dr. C. Norman and Elizabeth Worden; *m* 1st, 1942, Agnes Marshall Murray; one *s*; 2nd, 1950, Dorothy Mary Jensen (*née* Peel), MA (Fellow and Steward, Lucy Cavendish Coll., Cambridge); two *s* one *d*. *Educ:* Queen Elizabeth's Sch., Barnet; St John's Coll. and Sch. of Clinical Medicine, Cambridge (MA, MB, BChir, PhD); Royal Veterinary, Birkbeck and University Colls, London (DVetMed, DSc). DrVetMed Zurich; FRCPath; FRCVS; FAAVCT; FRSC; FIBiol; CBiol; FLS, LSA, CChem; FIBM; FBIRA. Research Student, Lister Inst. of Preventive Medicine and Univ. Cambridge, 1938–41; Res. Officer, Univ. Cambridge, 1941–45; Milford Res. Prof., and Jt Hd, Dept of Biochemistry, Univ. Wales, 1945–50; Fellow and Co-ordinator of Environmental Studies, Wolfson (formerly University) Coll., Cambridge, 1971–83, Emeritus Fellow 1983, Mem. Council, 1974–78; Expert Pharmacologue-Toxicologue Specialisé du Ministère de la Santé Publique, France, 1974–.

Member: ARC Tech. Cttees on Calf and Pig Diseases, 1944; Jt ARC Agricl Improvement Council Cttee on Grassland Improvement Station, 1946; ARC Res. (Frazer) Cttee on Toxic Chemicals, 1961; MAFF British Agrochemicals Jt Medical Panel, 1961; Zool Soc. Lond., Animal Husbandry and Welfare Cttee, 1954–, Hon. Res. Associate 1979–; Japan Pharmacol. Soc. 1970; Asociación Medica Argentina, 1974; Royal Society Study Gp on Long Term Toxic Effects, 1975–78; MAFF Res. Consultative Cttee on Food Safety, 1985–; Sec., FRAME Toxicity Cttee, 1979–; Chm., Inst. of Food Techologists, 1973–74. Governor, Taverham Hall Educnl Trust, 1968–; Mem. Papworth-Huntingdon HMC, 1970–74; Trustee: Lucy Cavendish Coll., Cambridge, 1975–; Cambridge Univ. Vet. Sch., 1981–. President: Hunts Br., Historical Assoc., 1967–; Hunts Fauna and Flora Soc., 1965–; Beds and Hunts Naturalist Trust; Chm., Mammal Soc. British Isles, 1953–54; Pres., Hunts Football League; Vice Pres., Hunts CCC, FA, and Referees' Assoc.; Life Member: CUCC; CURUFC. Mem. Worshipful Soc. Apothecaries, 1971. Freeman, City of London, 1974. Editor: Animal Behaviour, 1950–65; Toxicology Letters, 1977–. *Publications:* Laboratory Animals, 1947; (with Harry V. Thompson) The Rabbit, 1956; Animal Health, Production and Pasture, 1964; Animals and Alternatives in Research, 1983; (with John Marks and D. V. Parke) The Future of Predictive Safety Evaluation, 1986; numerous papers on nutrition, biochemistry and toxicology. *Recreations:* history, natural history, sport, travel. *Address:* Cross Keys Orchard, Hemingford Abbots, Cambs PE18 9AE. *T:* Huntingdon 62434. *Clubs:* Athenæum, United Oxford & Cambridge University, Farmers', No 10; Sette of Odd Volumes; MCC, Lancashire CCC, Middlesex CCC, Surrey CCC, Blackpool FC.

*Died 10 Aug. 1987.*

**WORDSWORTH, Maj.-Gen. Robert Harley,** CB 1945; CBE 1943; late IA; *b* 21 July 1894; *s* of W. H. Wordsworth; *m* 1928, Margaret Joan Ross-Reynolds; one *s* one *d*. Served European War, 1914–18, AIF (despatches); Waziristan, 1919–21; NW Frontier of India, 1930; Persia-Iraq, 1943 (CBE); Middle East, 1945 (CB); retired, 1947. Senator, Commonwealth Parlt of Australia, 1949–59. Administrator, Norfolk Island, 1962–64. *Recreation:* trout fishing. *Address:* Malcombe Street, Longford, Tasmania 7301, Australia. *Club:* Launceston (Launceston, Tasmania).

*Died 25 Nov. 1984.*

**WORMELL, Prof. Donald Ernest Wilson;** Fellow Emeritus, Trinity College, Dublin; *b* 5 Jan. 1908; *yr s* of Thomas Wilson and Florence Wormell; *m* 1941, Daphne Dillon Wallace; three *s* one *d*. *Educ:* Perse School. Schol., St John's Coll., Cambridge, 1926; Sandys Student, 1930; Henry Fund Fellow, 1931; Sterling Research Fellow, Yale, 1932; PhD Yale, 1933. Fellow, St John's Coll., Cambridge, 1933–36; Asst Lecturer in Classics, University College, Swansea, 1936–39; employed by Air Ministry and Foreign Office, 1942–44; Fellow, TCD, 1939–78; Prof. of Latin, Univ. of Dublin, 1942–78; Public Orator, 1952–69; Vice-Provost, TCD, 1973–74. Leverhulme Res. Fellow, 1954. MRIA; Mem., Inst. for Advanced Study, Princeton, USA, 1967–68. *Publications:* (with H. W. Parke) The Delphic Oracle, 1956; (jtly) Ovid's Fasti, 1978; articles on classical literature and ancient history in learned periodicals. *Recreation:* music. *Address:* 44 Seaview Park, Shankill, Co. Dublin. *T:* Dublin 823404.

*Died 15 July 1990.*

**WORRALL, Air Vice-Marshal John,** CB 1963; DFC 1940; retired; Managing Director, The Advertising Agency Poster Bureau Ltd, 1964–65; *b* 9 April 1911; *o s* of late J. R. S. Worrall, Thackers, Bombay, India; *m* 1936, Susan Honor, *y d* of late Captain R. G. Westropp, Cairo and Camberley; one *s* one *d*; *m* 1967, Barbara Jocelyne, *er d* of late Vincent Ronald Robb. *Educ:* Cranleigh; Royal Air Force Coll., Cranwell. Commission Royal Air Force, 1931; flying duties No 1 Sqdn, 1932, No 208 Sqdn, 1933–36; language study, Peking, 1936–39; commanded No 32 (F) Sqdn Biggin Hill, 1940; Fighter Control, Biggin Hill, 1940; Fighter and Transport Staff and Unit, 1941–45 (despatches 1944); RAF Staff Coll., 1945; Senior Personnel Staff Officer, HQ Transport Command, 1945–48; OC, RAF West Malling and Metropolitan Sector, 1948–49; OC, RAF Kai Tak, Hong Kong, 1949–51; HQ Home Command, 1952–53; Air Ministry, Organisation Branch, 1953–54; OC Eastern Sector, 1954–56; AOA, HQ Flying Training Command, 1956–58; Assistant Chief of Air Staff (Training), 1958–60; SASO, NEAF, 1960–63; retired from RAF, 1963. Chairman RAF Ski and Winter Sports Assoc., 1953–60, Vice-President, 1960–68; Chairman, Battle of Britain Fighter Assoc., 1958–60. *Recreations:* ski-ing, sailing. *Address:* Es Forti 109, Cala d'Or, Mallorca, Spain; c/o National Westminster Bank, 155 North Street, Brighton, East Sussex.

*Died 14 Jan. 1988.*

**WORSLEY, Very Rev. Godfrey Stuart Harling;** Dean Emeritus of Gibraltar, since 1969; *b* 4 Dec. 1906; *o s* of late Rev. A. E. Worsley, Rector of Georgeham; *m* 1933, Stella Mary, *o c* of late H. S. Church, Croyde Manor, N Devon; two *s* one *d*. *Educ:* Dean Close, Cheltenham; London College of Divinity. Deacon, 1929; Priest, 1931; Asst Curate, Croydon Parish Church, 1930–33; CF, Ireland,

Malta, Catterick, 1933–43; SCF, W Africa, Greece, Cyprus, 1943–49; DACG, N Midland District and Malta, 1949–54; Rector of Kingsland, 1954–60; Rural Dean of Leominster, 1956–60; Prebendary de Cublington in Hereford Cathedral, and Proctor in Convocation, Diocese of Hereford, 1959–60; Dean of Gibraltar and Rural Dean of Southern Spain, and officiating chaplain RN, 1960–69; Rector of Pen Selwood, 1969–79. *Address:* Arrow Cottage, Eardisland, Leominster, Herefordshire HR6 9BT. *T:* Pembridge (05447) 241. *Died 10 Nov.* 1990.

**WORSLEY, Lt-Gen. Sir John (Francis),** KBE 1966 (OBE 1951); CB 1963; MC 1945; retired, 1968; *b* 8 July 1912; *s* of Geoffrey Worsley, OBE, ICS, and Elsie Margaret (*née* Macpherson); *m* 1942, Barbara Elizabeth Jarvis (*née* Greenwood); one *s* three *d* (and two step *d*). *Educ:* Radley; Royal Military Coll., Sandhurst. Unattached List, Indian Army (attached Queen's Own Cameron Highlanders), 1933; 3rd Bn 2nd Punjab Regt, 1934; served NW Frontier, India, 1935 and 1936–37; War of 1939–45, Middle East and SE Asia; Staff Coll., Quetta, 1941; Comd 2nd Bn 1st Punjab Regt, 1945; York and Lancaster Regt, 1947; Joint Services Staff Coll., 1951; Comd 1st Bn The South Lancashire Regt (Prince of Wales's Volunteers), 1953; Secretary, Joint Planning Staff, Ministry of Defence, 1956; Comd 6th Infantry Brigade Group, 1957; Imperial Defence Coll., 1960; General Officer Commanding 48 Division (Territorial Army) and West Midland District, 1961–63; Commandant, Staff Coll., Camberley, 1963–66; Commander, British Forces, Hong Kong, 1966–68. *Address:* Castleton House, Sherborne, Dorset. *Club:* Army and Navy. *Died 13 May* 1987.

**WORTLEY, Prof. Ben Atkinson,** CMG 1978; OBE 1946; QC 1969; LLD (Manchester), LLM (Leeds); Hon. Docteur de l'Univ. de Rennes (1955); Strasbourg (1965); membre de l'Institut de droit international, 1967 (associé 1956); Professor of Jurisprudence and International Law, University of Manchester, 1946–75, then Emeritus; Barrister of Gray's Inn, 1947, Hon. Bencher, 1989; *b* 16 Nov. 1907; *o s* of late John Edward Wortley and Mary Cicely (*née* King), Huddersfield; *m* 1935, Kathleen Mary Prynne (*d* 1982); two *s* one *d*. *Educ:* King James's Grammar Sch., Almondbury; Leeds Univ.; France. Law Society Open Schol., 1925; 1st Class Hons LLB, 1928, and at Law Society's Final, 1929, also D. Reardon Prizeman. Practised full-time till 1931. Taught Law, London School Econ., 1931–33; Manchester Univ., 1933–34; Birmingham Univ., 1934–36; Manchester Univ., 1936–75; Visiting Prof. Tulane Univ., New Orleans, 1959. Ministry of Home Security, 1939–43; Instructor Commander RN (temp.), 1943–46. Member: Inst. Advanced Legal Studies, 1947–77; Council, UNIDROIT, 1950–75; Society of Public Teachers of Law (President, 1964–65); an editor, Rev. Diritto Europeo and British Yearbook of International Law. Member Royal Netherlands Academy, 1960; Commendatore (Italy), 1961; Correspondent Hellenic Inst. for International and Foreign Law, and of Belgian Society for Comparative Law. Representative of HM Government at International Confs at The Hague, 1951, 1956, 1960, 1964, and at New York, 1955 and 1958. Sometime Mem., Lord Chancellor's Cttee on Conflict of Laws. Hon. DCL Durham, 1975. Hon. Brother, de la Salle Order, 1973; KSS, 1975. *Publications:* Expropriation in Public International Law, 1959; Jurisprudence, 1967; part editor, Dicey's Conflict of Laws, 1949; (ed) UN, The First Ten Years, 1957; (ed) Law of the Common Market, 1974; lectures, 1939, 1947, 1954 and 1958 (published by Hague Acad. of Internat. Law); (ed) 13 vols Schill lectures; numerous articles. *Recreations:* garden, law of war, verse. *Address:* 24 Gravel Lane, Wilmslow, Cheshire SK9 6LA. *T:* Wilmslow 522810. *Club:* Athenæum. *Died 9 June* 1989.

**WRANGHAM, Cuthbert Edward,** CBE 1946; BA 1929; *b* 16 Dec. 1907; *yr s* of late W. G. Wrangham and late E. A. F. Wilberforce; *m* 1st, 1935, Teresa Jane, *er d* of late Ralph Cotton; three *s* two *d*; 2nd, 1958, Jean Ursula Margaret Tunstall, *yr d* of late Lt-Col T. T. Behrens. *Educ:* Eton Coll.; King's Coll., Cambridge. Air Min. and Min. of Aircraft Production, 1939–45; Monopolies Commn, 1954–56; Chairman: Shelbourne Hotel Ltd, 1950–60; Power-Gas Corporation Ltd, 1960–61; Short Brothers & Harland Ltd, 1961–67; Doxford and Sunderland Ltd, 1969–71; Marine & General Mutual Life Assurance Soc., 1961–72; C. Tennant Sons & Co. Ltd, 1967–72 (Director, 1937). Hon. DL Wilberforce Coll., Ohio, 1957. *Address:* Rosemary House, Catterick, North Yorkshire. *T:* Richmond 811375. *Club:* English-Speaking Union.

*Died 10 Feb.* 1982.

**WRANGHAM, Sir Geoffrey Walter,** Kt 1958; Judge of High Court of Justice, Family Division (formerly Probate, Divorce and Admiralty Division), 1958–73; retired; *b* 16 June 1900; *s* of late W. G. Wrangham and late E. A. F. Wilberforce; *m* 1925, Mary (*d* 1933), *d* of late S. D. Winkworth; one *s* one *d*; *m* 1947, Joan, *d* of late Col W. Boyle; one *s* one *d*. *Educ:* Eton Coll.; Balliol Coll., Oxford. Called to Bar, 1923; joined North-Eastern Circuit; Gresham Lecturer in Law, 1925–33; Practised in London, 1923–33, thereafter in Bradford; Recorder of York, 1941–50; Judge of County Courts, Circuit 20, 1950–57; Circuit 16, 1957–58; Chm., N Riding QS,

1946–58, Dep. Chm. 1958–71; Master of the Bench, Inner Temple, 1958. Served KOYLI and RAC (Lt-Col), 1940–45. *Publications:* Edited (with W. A. Macfarlane) 8th edition Clerk and Lindsell on Torts, 18th edition Chitty on Contracts. *Address:* Butlesdon House, Low Buston, Warkworth, Morpeth, Northumberland NE65 0XY. *T:* Alnwick 711300. *Died 22 Aug.* 1986.

**WRAY, Sir Kenneth Owen R.;** *see* Roberts-Wray.

**WREFORD, James;** *see* Watson, Prof. J. W.

**WRIGHT, Dr Alastair William,** FRCPE; Consultant Physician, Bangour Hospital, retired; *b* 1 Dec. 1913; *s* of William Wright and Annie Elizabeth Wright; *m* 1939, Ethel Patricia Burnley; three *d*. *Educ:* Edinburgh Academy; Edinburgh Univ. (MB ChB, MD). FRCPE 1947. Served RAMC, Lt-Col/actg Col 1945. Consultant Physician, Bangour Hosp., 1947; Chairman, Bd of Management, Bangour Hosp., 1972. WHO Vis. Professor of Medicine, Baroda, India, 1967. Royal College of Physicians, Edinburgh: Mem. Council, 1960; Vice-Pres., 1979; General Nursing Council, Scotland: Member, 1968; Chm., Disciplinary Cttee, 1975; Member: Scottish Council, BMA (Chm., 1974–78); Scottish Council, Post Graduate Medical Educn, 1973–80; General Medical Council, 1974–78. *Recreation:* golf. *Address:* 36 Ormidale Terrace, Edinburgh EH12 6EF. *T:* 031–337 1810. *Club:* Edinburgh University Staff.

*Died 6 Aug.* 1985.

**WRIGHT, Basil Charles;** Film Producer; *b* 12 June 1907; *s* of Major Lawrence Wright, TD, and Gladys Marsden. *Educ:* Sherborne; Corpus Christi Coll., Cambridge. Mawson Schol., CCC, 1926; BA (Hons), Classics and Economics. Concerned with John Grierson and others in development of Documentary Film, 1929–; directed, among many films: Song of Ceylon (Gold Medal and Prix du Gouvernement, Brussels), 1935; (with Harry Watt) Night Mail, 1936; Waters of Time, 1951; (with Paul Rotha) World Without End, 1953; (with Gladys Wright) took film expedition to Greece and made The Immortal Land, 1957 (Council of Europe Award, 1959) and Greek Sculpture (with Michael Ayrton), 1959; A Place for Gold, 1960; Visiting Lectr on Film Art, Univ. of Calif, Los Angeles, 1962 and 1968; Senior Lectr in Film History, Nat. Film Sch., 1971–73; Vis. Prof. of Radio, TV and Film, Temple Univ., Philadelphia, 1977–78. Producer, Crown Film Unit, 1945. Governor: Bryanston School, 1949–; British Film Institute, 1953; Fellow, British Film Academy, 1955; Council Mem., Roy. Coll. of Art, 1954–57. Gold Cross, Royal Order of King George I, Greece, 1963. *Publications:* The Use of the Film, 1949; The Long View, 1974. *Recreations:* opera, ballet, gardening. *Address:* Little Adam Farm, Frieth, Henley-on-Thames, Oxon. *Club:* Savile.

*Died 14 Oct.* 1987.

**WRIGHT, Prof. Donald Arthur,** MSc, DSc; FInstP; FRAS; Honorary Research Fellow in Archaeology, University of Durham, since 1976; *b* Stoke-on-Trent, 29 March 1911; *m* 1937, Mary Kathleen Rimmer (decd); one *s* one *d*. *Educ:* Orme School, Newcastle-under-Lyme; University of Birmingham. 1st Class Hons BSc 1932; MSc 1934; DSc Birmingham 1955. Research Physicist, GEC, Wembley, 1934–59; Head of Solid Physics Laboratory, Research Labs, GEC, Wembley, 1955–59; Prof. of Applied Physics, Univ. of Durham, 1960–76. Fellow Institute of Physics, 1944. Member of Board, Institute of Physics, 1957–64. Mem. of Council, Physical Society, 1955–58, Hon. Treasurer, 1958–60. *Publications:* Semiconductors, 1950 (revd edn 1965); Thermoelectric Cooling in Progress in Cryogenics, Vol. I, 1959; Thermoelectric Generation in Direct Generation of Electricity, 1965; many papers on electron emission and solid-state physics in learned journals. *Recreations:* music, formerly tennis. *Address:* Museum of Archaeology, Fulling Mill, Durham; St St Mary's Close, Shincliffe, Durham DH1 2ND. *T:* Durham 48408. *Died 5 July* 1988.

**WRIGHT, Sir Douglas;** *see* Wright, Sir R. D.

**WRIGHT, Frederick Matthew,** OBE 1976 (MBE 1945); General Manager, British Railways, Western Region and Member of British Railways (Western) Board, 1972–76; *b* 26 June 1916; *s* of Thomas Bell Wright and Ethel Johnson; *m* 1940, Claire Agnes (*née* Cook); one *s* one *d*. *Educ:* Rutherford Coll., Newcastle upon Tyne. FCIT; FInstM. Joined LNER, 1933. Served with Royal Engrs in France, Madagascar, Africa and India, 1939–45. British Railways: posts in traffic depts, 1945–61; Eastern Region: Commercial Supt, Great Northern Line, 1961; Divisional Man., Doncaster, 1964; Asst Gen. Man., York, 1968; Mem., BR (Eastern) Bd, 1969; Dep. Gen. Man., York, 1970. Chm., Bournemouth Helping Services Council, 1978; Vice Chm., E Dorset Community Proj. Agency, 1981–83. Dorset County Dir, St John Ambulance Assoc., 1976–81. OStJ 1975, CStJ 1980. *Recreations:* gardening, soccer, Rugby, cricket (critic). *Address:* 2A Ellers Road, Bessacarr, Doncaster, South Yorkshire DN4 7BA. *Died 29 June* 1990.

**WRIGHT, Air Cdre John Allan Cecil C.;** *see* Cecil-Wright.

**WRIGHT, John Henry,** CBE 1964; HM Diplomatic Service, retired; with Government Communications HQ, 1970–77; *b* 6 Dec. 1910; *s* of John Robert Wright and Margaret Leadbetter; *m* 1939, Joan Harvey; two *s. Educ:* Barrow Grammar Sch.; Trinity Coll., Cambridge. Vice-Consul, Genoa, 1934; Addis Ababa, 1937; Havana, 1939; 2nd Sec., Quito, 1943; 1st Sec., 1945; transf. to Foreign Office, 1948; 1st Sec. (Commercial), Helsinki, 1950; 1st Sec. (Commercial), Santiago, 1953; Counsellor, at Shanghai, of HM Chargé d'Affaires in China, 1958–60; Counsellor, temporarily employed in Foreign Office, Dec. 1960–61; HM Consul-General at Rotterdam, 1961–63; Ambassador to Honduras, 1963–69. *Recreations:* reading, walking, music, local affairs. *Address:* Horse Inn House, Bourton-on-the-Hill, Moreton-in-Marsh, Glos. *Club:* United Oxford & Cambridge University.

*Died 30 Nov. 1984.*

**WRIGHT, Prof. John Nicholson;** Professor of Logic and Metaphysics in the United College, the University of St Andrews, 1936–66, later Emeritus; Master of St Salvator's College in the University of St Andrews, 1959–66; Acting Master, 1966–67; retired; General Council Assessor, University Court, 1969–72; *b* 21 Aug. 1896; *e s* of John Nicholson Wright and Elizabeth Ann Humble; *m* 1923, Florencia Emilia Cowper (*d* 1966), Pacasmayo, Peru, and Canterbury, Kent; one *d* (and one *d* decd). *Educ:* Bede Collegiate School, Sunderland; Ryhope Grammar School; St Chad's College, University of Durham (scholar and prizeman). Served 4th Bn Durham Light Infantry, 1916–19. BA 1920, MA 1923. Assistant in Dept of Logic and Metaphysics, Univ. of St Andrews, 1920; Lecturer in Logic and Psychology, Univ. Coll., Dundee, 1924–36; Adviser of Studies in Arts, 1932; Dean of the Faculty of Arts, Univ. of St Andrews, 1937–50. Chairman of Regional Cttee for Adult Education, 1938–50; War Office Lecturer to HM Forces in Middle East, 1945 and 1947, Far East, 1950; Member of Advisory Committee on Education to the War Office, 1945; member Fulbright Commission, 1957. President, Mind Association, 1959. President Scottish Amateur Swimming Assoc., 1935, and on Selection Cttee for British Empire Games. Chairman Council of St Leonards and St Katharines Schools, 1952–67 (Hon. Vice-Pres., 1969). Fellow, Morse College, Yale Univ., 1964. Hon. LLD St Andrews Univ., 1967. Order of Polonia Restituta, 1944; Norwegian Order of Freedom, 1947. *Publications:* articles and reviews in learned journals and on philosophy and logic in Chambers's Encyclopædia. *Recreations:* music, walking. *Address:* 120 North Street, St Andrews, Fife. *T:* 5320. *Club:* Royal and Ancient Golf (St Andrews).

*Died 3 June 1982.*

**WRIGHT, Louis Booker;** Hon. OBE 1968; historian, writer; consultant in history, National Geographic Society, since 1971; Director, Folger Shakespeare Library, 1948–68; *b* 1 March 1899; *s* of Thomas Fleming Wright and Lena Booker Wright; *m* 1925, Frances Black; one *s. Educ:* Wofford College; University of North Carolina. AB 1920, Wofford Coll.; MA 1924, PhD 1926, N Carolina. Service in US Army, 1918; newspaper corres. and editor, 1918–23; instructor and associate Prof. of Eng., University of North Carolina, 1926–32; visiting scholar, Huntington Library, 1931–32; member permanent research group, Huntington Library, also Chm., Cttee on Fellowships and Mem. Exec. Cttee, 1932–48; Vis. Professor: Univs of Michigan 1935, Washington 1942, Calif. at Los Angeles 1934–48; Pomona Coll., 1941–48; Calif. Inst. of Technology, 1932–48; Univ. of Minnesota, 1946; Indiana Univ. on the Patten Foundation, 1953. Chm. Advisory Bd, John Simon Guggenheim Memorial Foundation; Vice-Chm., Council on Library Resources, Inc.; Mem. Bd of Directors H. F. du Pont Winterthur Museum and Harry S. Truman Library Inst. for Nat. and Internat. Affairs. Trustee, Shakespeare Birthplace Trust; Mem. Research Cttee and Trustee, National Geographic Society. Hon. LittD: Wofford, 1941; Mills College, 1947; Princeton, 1948; Amherst, 1948; Occidental College, 1949; Bucknell, 1951; Franklin and Marshall, 1957; Colby Coll., 1959; Univ. of British Columbia, 1960; Leicester Univ., 1965; Winthrop Coll., 1980; Hon. LLD: Tulane, 1950; George Washington, 1958; Chattanooga, 1959; Akron, 1961; St Andrews, 1961; Washington and Lee, 1964; Mercer, 1965; LHD: Northwestern, 1948; Univ. of N Carolina, 1950; Yale, 1954; Rockford Coll., 1956; Coe Coll., 1959; Georgetown Univ., 1961; California State Coll., 1966; Univ. of California, 1967; Brown Univ., 1968; Univ. of S Carolina, 1972; Lander Coll., 1974; Hon. DLitt, Birmingham, England, 1964. FRSA (Benjamin Franklin Medal, 1969); FRSL; FRHistS; Mem., Amer. Philosophical Soc. and other learned socs. Cosmos Club award for distinction in hist. and letters, 1973. *Publications:* Middle-Class Culture in Elizabethan England, 1935; Puritans in the South Seas, 1936; The First Gentlemen of Virginia, 1940; Religion and Empire, 1942; The First Americans in North Africa, 1945; The Atlantic Frontier, 1947; Culture on the Moving Frontier, 1955; The Cultural Life of the American Colonies, 1957; Shakespeare for Everyman, 1964; Everyday Life in Colonial America, 1965; The Dream of Prosperity in Colonial America, 1965; The History of the Thirteen Colonies, 1967; Everyday Life on the American Frontier, 1968; Gold, Glory

and the Gospel, 1970; Barefoot in Arcadia: memories of a more innocent era, 1974; Tradition and the Founding Fathers, 1975; South Carolina: a Bicentennial History, 1976; Magna Carta and the Tradition of Liberty, 1976; Of Books and Men, 1976; The John Henry County Map of Virginia 1770, 1977. Edited: Letters of Robert Carter, 1940; The Secret Diary of William Byrd of Westover, 1709–12, 1941; Quebec to Carolina in 1785–1786, 1943; An Essay Upon the Government of the English Plantation on the Continent of America, 1701, 1945; The History and Present State of Virginia, 1705 (by Robert Beverley), 1947; The Historie of Travell into Virginia Britania, 1612, (by William Strachey) 1953; The Folger Library General Reader's Shakespeare, 1957–68; William Byrd of Virginia: The London Diary 1717–1721, and Other Writings, 1958; The Elizabethans' America, 1965; The Prose Works of William Byrd of Westover, 1966; West and by North: North America seen through the eyes of its seafaring discoverers, 1971; The Moving Frontier, 1972. *Recreation:* fishing. *Address:* 3702 Leland Street, Chevy Chase, Md 20815, USA. *T:* 652-5509. *Clubs:* Cosmos (Washington); Century (New York). *Died 26 Feb. 1984.*

**WRIGHT, Peter Harold,** VC 1943; late Company Sergeant-Major, Coldstream Guards; farmer; *b* 10 Aug. 1916, British; *m* 1946, Mollie Mary Hurren, Wenhaston; one *s* two *d. Educ:* Brooke, Norfolk (elementary school). Left school at 14 and worked on father's farm up to the age of 20. Joined Coldstream Guards, 1936; sailed for Egypt, 1937. Served in Egypt, Palestine, Syria and throughout the Libyan campaign and North Africa, took part in the landing at Salerno, Italy, Sept. 1943; demobilised, 1945. *Address:* Poplar Farm, Helmingham, Stowmarket, Suffolk. *Died 5 April 1990.*

**WRIGHT, Hon. Sir Reginald Charles,** Kt 1978; *b* Tasmania, 10 July 1905; *s* of John and Emma Wright; *m* 1st, 1930, Evelyn Arnett; two *s* four *d*; 2nd, 1986, Margaret Steen. *Educ:* Devonport St High Sch., Tasmania; Univ. of Tasmania. BA, LLB. Admitted Tasmanian Bar, 1928; Lectr in Law, Univ. of Tasmania, 1931–46; Captain, Aust. Field Artillery, AIF, 1941–44; Pres., Liberal Party, Tasmania, 1945–46; MHA for Franklin, Tasmania, and Deputy Leader of Opposition, Tasmanian House of Assembly, 1946–49; Senator (Lib) for Tasmania, 1949–78; Minister for Works and Minister assisting Minister for Trade and Industry and in charge of Tourist Activities, 1968–72. *Address:* Wallys Farm, Central Castra, Tasmania, Australia. *Clubs:* Naval and Military, Ulverstone.

*Died 1990.*

**WRIGHT, Sir Robert (Brash),** Kt 1976; DSO 1945; OBE 1944; FRCP, FRCSE, FRCSGlas; Surgeon in Charge, Southern General Hospital, Glasgow, 1953–80; *b* 1 March 1915; 2nd *s* of Dr Hugh P. Wright and Janet Brash; *m* 1946, Helen Tait; one *s* two *d. Educ:* Hamilton Acad.; Univ. of Glasgow (BSc 1934; MB, ChB Hons 1937; ChM 1953). FRCP 1970. FRCSE 1947, FRCSGlas 1962. RAMC, 1939–46. Asst Surg., Western Infirm., Glasgow, 1946–53. Pres., RCPSG, 1968–70; Member GMC, 1970– (Pres., 1980–81). Hon. FRACS 1968; Hon. FRCS 1975. Hon. LLD Glasgow 1981. *Publications:* articles in med. and surg. jls. *Recreations:* gardening, walking and wondering. *Address:* 12A Grange Road, Bearsden, Glasgow G61 3PL. *Club:* Caledonian. *Died 4 Dec. 1981.*

**WRIGHT, Sir (Roy) Douglas,** AK 1983; FRACP; Professor Emeritus; Chancellor, University of Melbourne, since 1980; Consultant, Howard Florey Institute, since 1975; *b* 7 Aug. 1907; *s* of John Forsyth Wright and Emma Maria Wright; *m* 1st, 1932, Julia Violet Bell (marr. diss.); one *s* one *d*; 2nd, 1964, Meriel Antoinette Winchester Wilmot. *Educ:* Devonport State High Sch., Tasmania; Univ. of Tasmania; Univ. of Melbourne (MB, BS 1929; MS 1931; DSc 1941). DSc ANU, 1967. Sen. Lectr, Pathology, Univ. of Melbourne, 1932–38; Surgeon, Royal Melbourne Hosp. and Associate Surgeon, Austin Hosp., 1934–38; University of Melbourne: Prof. of Physiology, 1939–71; Consulting Physiologist, Clinical Hosps, 1940–71; Dean, Faculty of Medicine, 1947, 1951; Mem. Council, 1963–. Mem. Council, ANU, 1946–76; Chm. Exec., 1948–71, Medical Dir, 1971–75, Cancer Inst. of Victoria; Originating Dir, Howard Florey Inst. for Experimental Physiology and Medicine, 1971–. Hon. LLD: ANU, 1977; Melbourne, 1980. *Publications:* reports and articles in jls of pathology, anatomy, physiology, endocrinology. *Recreations:* gardening, reading, public affairs. *Address:* Howard Florey Institute, University of Melbourne, Vic 3052, Australia. *Club:* Graduate Union (Melbourne).

*Died 28 Feb. 1990.*

**WRIGHT, Sewall;** Professor Emeritus of Genetics, University of Wisconsin, since 1960; *b* 21 Dec. 1889; *s* of Philip Green Wright and Elizabeth Quincy Sewall; *m* 1921, Louise Lane Williams; two *s* one *d. Educ:* Lombard Coll.; University of Illinois; Harvard Univ. BS Lombard Coll., 1911; MS Illinois, 1912; ScD Harvard, 1915. Senior Animal Husbandman, US Dept of Agriculture, 1915–25; University of Chicago: Assoc. Professor of Zoology, 1926–29; Professor of Zoology, 1930–37; Ernest D. Burton Distinguished Service Professor, 1937–54; Leon J. Cole Professor of Genetics, University of Wisconsin, 1955–60; Hitchcock Professor, University

of California, 1943; Fulbright Professor, University of Edinburgh, 1949–50. Hon. Member, Royal Society of Edinburgh; Foreign Member: Royal Society, London (Darwin Medal 1980); Royal Danish Acad. of Sciences and Letters. Hon. ScD: Rochester, 1942; Yale, 1949; Harvard, 1951; Knox Coll., 1957; Western Reserve, 1958; Chicago, 1959; Illinois, 1961; Wisconsin, 1965; State Univ. of NY at Stony Brook, 1984; Hon. LLD, Michigan State, 1955. Nat. Medal of Science, 1966; Balzan Prize, 1984. *Publications:* Evolution and the Genetics of Populations, vol. 1, 1968, vol. 2, 1969, vol. 3, 1977, vol. 4, 1978; numerous papers on genetics of characters of guinea pig, population genetics, theory of evolution and path analysis. *Recreation:* travel. *Address:* 6209 Mineral Point Road, Madison, Wisconsin 53705, USA. *Club:* University (Madison).
*Died 3 March 1988.*

**WRIGHT, Thomas Erskine,** MA; Supernumerary Fellow, Queen's College, Oxford, since 1953; *b* 15 Sept. 1902; *s* of Rev. Thomas Wright, MA, Stirling, and Isabel Hamilton Ritchie; unmarried. *Educ:* Stirling High Sch.; Univ. of Glasgow; Balliol Coll., Oxford (Snell Exhibitioner and Hon. Scholar). 1st Class Hons in Classics, Univ. of Glasgow, 1924; Hertford and Craven Scholarships, Chancellor's Prize (Latin Prose), Ferguson Scholarship in Classics, 1925; 1st Class Hons Mods, Chancellor's Prize (Latin Verse), Ireland Scholarship, 1926; 1st Class Lit Hum, 1928. Official Fellow of the Queen's Coll., Oxford, and Praelector in Classics, 1928–48; became Tutor and Senior Tutor and held various other college offices. Professor of Humanity, Univ. of St Andrews, 1948–62, Dean of the Faculty of Arts, 1951–54; Member of the University Grants Cttee, 1954–63; Sec. and Treas., Carnegie Trust for Univs of Scotland, 1962–69; Dir, Univ. of Stirling Ltd, 1964–67. Hon. D Univ Stirling, 1984. *Publications:* The Latin Contribution to a Liberal Education, 1949; contributions to Oxford Classical Dictionary, *Veterum Laudes,* Fifty Years of Classical Scholarship, and periodicals. *Address:* 10 Gladstone Place, Stirling. *T:* Stirling 72681. *Club:* Stirling and County (Stirling). *Died 27 Jan. 1986.*

**WRIGHT, Prof. William,** MA; ScD; BSc, PhD, CEng, FICE, FIProdE; FIEI; FRSE; SFTCD; Professor of Engineering, and Head of Engineering School, Trinity College, Dublin, since 1957; Director, Graduate School of Engineering Studies, since 1963; Dean, Faculty of Mathematical and Engineering Sciences, 1969–79; *b* 3 Dec. 1918; *s* of late Rev. James Wright, DD; *m* 1st, 1944, Mildred Anderson (*d* 1959), *d* of James Robertson, MA; two *s* one *d*; 2nd, Barbara Robinson, MA, PhD, LLB, FTCD, Chevalier de l'Ordre National du Mérite, *d* of W. Edward Robinson; one *s*. *Educ:* Inverness Royal Academy; George Watson's Coll.; Glasgow Univ. Civil Engineer with LMSR and Min. of Transport, 1935–39. Served War, 1939–46, Captain, Royal Engineers, Middle East, Italy and Germany. Consulting Engineer, 1946–49. Glasgow Univ., 1938–39 and 1946–49 (John Oliphant Bursar) 1st Class Hons Civil Engineering. Lecturer in Civil Engineering, Aberdeen Univ., 1949–54; Head of Dept of Civil Engineering, Southampton Univ., 1954–57. UNESCO Consultant, 1981. Mem. Council, Instn of Production Engineers, 1964; Pres., Instn of Engineers of Ireland, 1977–78. AMICE 1949; PhD Aberdeen, 1952; MICEI 1957; MICE 1958; MA Dublin, 1960; ScD Dublin, 1963. *Publications:* papers in learned journals in Britain and America. *Recreations:* fishing, mountaineering. *Address:* Les Trembles, 35 Palmerston Road, Rathmines, Dublin 6. *T:* Dublin 978619.
*Died 8 Feb. 1985.*

**WRIGHT, William Alan,** CIE 1945; AFC; *b* 27 Nov. 1895; *s* of Rev. Thomas Wright and Annie Pedley; *m* 1948, Elizabeth Ada, *d* of A. E. Garrott, Launceston, Tasmania; one *s* one *d*. *Educ:* Oundle. 2nd Lieut, Leicestershire Regt, Jan, 1915; joined the Royal Flying Corps, Sept. 1916; Captain about July 1917 (Chevalier of Crown of Belgium and Belgian Croix de Guerre); transferred to RAF on its formation (AFC); joined Indian Civil Service, 1921, and served in Burma, acting Judge Rangoon High Court in 1939; with Government of India, War Dept, 1942–45, as Deputy Secretary, and then as officiating Joint Secretary; Deputy Director of Civil Affairs, Burma, Brig. 1945; Judge Rangoon High Court, 1945–48. *Address:* Salween, 10 Smithers Street, Lorne, Victoria 3232, Australia.

**WRIGHT, Most Rev. William Lockridge,** DD, DCL, LLD; *b* 8 Sept. 1904; *s* of Rev. Canon J. de Pencier Wright and Lucy Lockridge; *m* 1936, Margaret Clare, BA; two *s* two *d*. *Educ:* Queen's University, Kingston, Ontario; Trinity College, Toronto (Hon. Fellow 1983). LTh 1927. Curate St George's, Toronto, 1926–28; Incumbent St James', Tweed, 1928–32; Curate Christ's Church Cathedral, Hamilton, 1932–36; Rector St George's Church, Toronto, 1936–40; Rector St Luke's Cathedral, Sault Ste Marie, 1940–44; Dean St Luke's Cathedral, 1941–44; Bishop of Algoma, 1944; Archbishop of Algoma and Metropolitan of Ontario, 1955–74; Acting Primate of the Anglican Church of Canada, Aug. 1970–Jan. 1971. DD (juris dig.) 1941; DCL (Bishop's Univ. Lennoxville), 1953; DD (*hc*) Wycliffe Coll., Toronto, 1956; Huron Coll., 1957; Montreal Diocesan Coll., 1958; LLD (*hc*) Laurentian University of Sudbury, Ont, 1964.

*Recreations:* ice hockey, rugby football. *Address:* Box 637, Sault Ste Marie, Ontario P6A 5N2, Canada. *Died 19 Jan. 1990.*

**WRIGHTSON, Sir John (Garmondsway,** 3rd Bt, *cr* 1900; TD 1948; DL; Hon. Treasurer, Smeatonian Society of Civil Engineers, 1949–79; *b* 18 June 1911; *s* of 2nd Bt and Gwendolin Cotterill (*d* 1964), *d* of G. Harding Neame; *S* father, 1950; *m* 1939, Hon. Rosemary Dawson, *y d* of 1st Viscount Dawson of Penn, PC, GCVO, KCB, KCMG; one *s* three *d*. *Educ:* Eton. Late Major, Durham LI (TA). Served War of 1939–45, 6th Airborne Div., France and Germany (despatches). Chm., Head, Wrightson & Co., 1960–76, retired. Hon. Col, 7th Bn, The Light Infantry (V), T&AVR, 1975–79. High Sheriff, Durham, 1959, DL 1960. Hon. DCL Durham, 1971. *Heir: s* Charles Mark Garmondsway Wrightson [*b* 18 Feb. 1951; *m* 1975, Stella Virginia, *d* of late George Dean; two *s*]. *Address:* Neasham Hall, near Darlington. *T:* Darlington 720333. *Club:* Carlton. *Died 24 June 1983.*

**WRIGHTSON, Oliver; His Honour Judge Wrightson;** a Circuit Judge, since 1978; *b* 28 May 1920; *y s* of Col Sir Thomas Garmondsway Wrightson, 2nd Bt, TD. *Educ:* Eton; Balliol Coll., Oxford. Served with Coldstream Guards, 1942–46, Captain. Called to Bar, Lincoln's Inn, 1950. A Recorder of the Crown Court, 1972–78. *Recreations:* lawn tennis, music, theatre. *Address:* The Bridge House, Eryholme, Darlington, Yorks. *Club:* Northern Counties (Newcastle upon Tyne). *Died 16 Oct. 1987.*

**WRIGLEY, Arthur Joseph,** CBE 1965; MD (London) Gold Medal; FRCS; FRCOG; retired as Obstetric Physician, St Thomas' Hospital, London; *b* 5 May 1902; *er s* of late Canon Joseph Henry Wrigley, Clitheroe, Lancs; *m* 1930, Ann (*d* 1976), *d* of late Colonel J. W. Slater, CMG, Dunscar, Lancs; one *s* one *d*. *Educ:* Rossall Sch.; St Thomas' Hospital. Hon. FCOG S Africa. *Publications:* many medical. *Address:* Green Garth, Elm Grove, Alderley Edge, Cheshire SK9 7PD. *T:* Macclesfield 582194.
*Died 18 Dec. 1983.*

**WRIGLEY, Dr Fred,** CBE 1974; FPS; JP; Consultant Adviser, International Health Care Industry, since 1979; *b* 2 Jan. 1909; *s* of Benjamin Wrigley and Mary Ellen Wrigley; *m* 1936, Catherine Margaret, *d* of Percy and Agnes M. Hogley; one *s* one *d*. *Educ:* Victoria Univ. of Manchester. MRCS, LRCP; DIH. FPS 1968 (for distinction in pharmacy). Dir of Clin. Res., Roche Prod. Ltd, 1945–52; Manager, CIBA Pharmaceuticals, Montreal, 1952–55; Wellcome Foundation Ltd: Gen. Sales Man., then various posts (sales and associated cos overseas), 1955–67; Dep. Chm., 1967–74; Dir, 1957–74; Chm., Wellcome (France), 1974; Pres., Wellcome Italia and other overseas cos, 1974; Chm., Calmic Ltd, 1960–74; Chairman: British Health-Care Export Council, 1976–79; United Medical Enterprises Ltd, 1978–79. Consultant Adviser, Commercial Policy and Exports, to Sec. of State for Health and Social Security, 1974–77; Hon. Consultant in Health Care Industry to British Technology Gp (formerly NEB), 1979–. Adjunct Prof. of Econs, East Carolina Univ., NC, 1972–, Vis. Prof. of Internat. Business, 1973–. Assoc. of British Pharm. Industry: Mem. Council, 1958–60; Mem., Bd of Management, 1971–73; Chm., Scientific and Technical Cttee, 1972–73. Pres., Hunterian Soc., 1972–73 (Hon. Fellow 1973). Chm., Mid-Herts Hosp. Man. Cttee, 1964–68. Dir, British Exec. Service Overseas, 1972–75. Chm., United Medical Company Internat., 1977–79. Member: NW Metrop. Reg. Hosp. Bd, 1968–74; Med. Sch. Council, St Mary's Hosp., 1971–74; Council, Pharm. Soc. of GB, 1970–72; Mem., Bd of Management, LSHTM, 1979–. Governor: UCH, 1966–74; Marsden Hosp., 1974–75; Inveresk Res. Internat., 1974–77. Liveryman, Soc. of Apothecaries. Vice-Pres., Herts Scout Council (formerly Asst County Comr). First Hon. Mem., Pharm. Soc. of Nigeria, 1969; first Hon. Citizen, Greenville, NC, 1973. JP (Supplemental List) Herts, 1968. *Publications:* medico-scientific in BMJ and Lancet. *Recreations:* fishing, cooking. *Address:* 35 Park Close, Old Hatfield, Herts AL9 5AY. *T:* Hatfield 66430. *Clubs:* Farmers', MCC. *Died 29 April 1982.*

**WRISBERG, Lt-Gen. Sir (Frederick) George,** KBE 1949 (CBE 1942); CB 1945; late Royal Regiment of Artillery; *b* 3 Jan. 1895; *s* of late Captain F. W. Wrisberg, Royal Artillery; *m* 1918, Margaret (*d* 1978), *d* of late C. Ward, Swadlincote, Derbyshire; one *d*. 2nd Lieut, RA, 1916; served European War, 1916–17, in France and Belgium (wounded); Experimental Officer, Air Defence Experimental Establishment, 1929–33; Staff Captain, War Office, 1934–36; Deputy Assistant Director of Artillery, War Office, 1936–38; Assistant Director, 1938–40; Director Weapons Production, 1940–43; Director-General of Weapons and Instrument Production, Ministry of Supply, 1943–46; Controller of Supplies, Ministry of Supply, 1946–49; retired 1949. Colonel Commandant RA, 1950–60; Chairman, Linotype and Machinery Ltd, 1960–66. Comdr Legion of Merit, USA, 1947. *Address:* Eastbury House, Long Street, Sherborne, Dorset. *T:* Sherborne 2132. *Club:* Naval and Military.
*Died 26 Feb 1982.*

**WYATT, Vice-Admiral Sir (Arthur) Guy (Norris),** KBE 1949; CB 1948; retired; *b* 8 March 1893; *s* of late Arthur Norris Wyatt and

May (*née* Reynolds); *m* 1922, Anne Christine, *d* of late Hon. James Hogue, Sydney, NSW; no *c. Educ:* Stubbington; RN Colleges, Osborne and Dartmouth. Joined Naval College, Osborne, 1906; Lieut, 1915; Comdr, 1929; Capt., 1936; Rear-Adm., 1945; Vice-Adm., 1948. Served European War, 1914–18; commanded HMTBD Beagle, 1918. Joined Royal Naval Surveying Service, 1918; surveys in Home Waters, Australia, New Zealand, East Africa, West Indies. Mediterranean, East Indies, Persian Gulf and Labrador. Served War of 1939–45, Admiralty, and in command of HMS Challenger, South East Asia and SW Pacific (despatches); Hydrographer of the Navy, 1945–50; retired list, 1948. *Recreations:* yacht cruising, fishing. *Address:* Holly Tree Orchard, Woodbridge, Tasmania 7162, Australia. *Clubs:* Royal Cruising; Tasmanian, Royal Yacht of Tasmania (Hobart). *Died* 9 *Nov.* 1981.

**WYBURN, Prof. George McCreath;** Regius Professor of Anatomy, Glasgow University, 1948–72; *b* 11 March 1903; *s* of Robert Wyburn, Solicitor; *m* 1935, Jean Sharp; four *s* two *d. Educ:* High Sch., Glasgow; University of Glasgow. Graduated from Glasgow Univ., 1925; appointed to staff of Anatomy Dept, University of Glasgow, 1930; Senior Lecturer, Anatomy Dept, 1935. *Publications:* scientific publications in Journal of Anatomy, Proc. and Trans. of Royal Society of Edinburgh, Journal of Endocrinology, Journal of Surgery, Journal of Obstetrics and Gynecology, etc. *Address:* 7 Woodvale Avenue, Bearsden, Glasgow G61 2JS. *Club:* Glasgow Golf. *Died* 8 *Feb.* 1985.

**WYETH, Paul James Logan,** RP 1958; RBA 1957; ARCA 1947; portrait painter and mural painter; *b* 1 Feb. 1920; *s* of Bob Logan (stage name), comedian; *m* 1948, Tina Vasilakon, Greece; two *d. Educ:* Kilburn Polytechnic, 1931–33; Royal College of Art diploma, 1947. Mural decorations at Eridge Castle, Kent, and Assembly Rooms, York; paintings in many private and public collections, inc. Melbourne, Aust.; Boston, Mass; Birmingham City Art Gall. Mem., Société des Artistes Français. Médaille d'Argent, Salon de Paris, 1976; Médaille d'Or, Salon de Paris, 1977, 1979; De Lazlo Medal, 1978. *Publications:* How to Paint in Oils, 1955; How to Paint in Water-Colours, 1958. *Address:* The Studio, 19 Burstock Road, Putney, SW15. *Club:* Chelsea Arts. *Died* 28 *June* 1982.

**WYLER, William:** Film Producer and Director; *b* Mulhouse, Alsace, 1 July 1902; *s* of Leopold Wyler (Swiss) and Melanie Auerbach (German; Non-Aryan); *m* 1st, 1934, Margaret Sullavan (marr. diss., 1936), actress; 2nd, 1938, Margaret Tallichet; one *s* three *d* (one *s* decd). *Educ:* Mulhouse, Alsace; Lausanne; Paris. Directed films since 1926; successes include: Counsellor-at-Law, 1934; The Good Fairy, 1935; These Three, 1936; Dodsworth, 1936; Dead End, 1937; Jezebel, 1937; The Letter, 1938; Wuthering Heights, 1939; The Little Foxes, 1940; Mrs Miniver, 1941 (Academy Award for directing and Best Picture); The Best Years of our Lives, 1946 (Acad. award for directing and Best Picture); The Heiress, 1948; Detective Story, 1951; Carrie, 1952; Roman Holiday, 1953; The Desperate House, 1955; Friendly Persuasion, 1956 (Golden Palm Leaf, Cannes, 1957); The Big Country, 1957; Ben Hur, 1959 (Academy Award for Directing and Best Picture); The Children's Hour, 1962; The Collector, 1965; How to Steal a Million, 1966; Funny Girl, 1968; The Liberation of Lord Byron Jones, 1970. Served 1942–45 as Major and Lt-Col in USAF, prod. and directed documentary films: The Memphis Belle, Thunderbolt. Air Medal (USA), 1943; Legion of Merit (USA), 1945; Legion of Honour (France), 1948; Cavaliere Ufficiale (Italy). *Recreations:* tennis, skiing. *Address:* 1121 Summit Drive, Beverly Hills, Calif 90210, USA. *Died* 28 *July* 1981.

**WYNDHAM, Sir Harold (Stanley),** Kt 1969; CBE 1961; retired from Department of Education, New South Wales; *b* Forbes, NSW, Australia, 27 June 1903; *s* of late Stanley Charles Wyndham; *m* 1936, Beatrice Margaret, *d* of Rt. Rev. A. C. Grieve; three *s. Educ:* Fort Street Boys' High Sch.; Univ. of Sydney (MA Hons, Cl. I); Stanford Univ. (EdD). Lectr, Sydney Teachers' Coll., 1925–27 and 1934; Teacher, NSW Dept of Educn, 1928–32; Carnegie Fellow, Stanford, 1932–33; Head of Research and Guidance, NSW Dept of Educn, 1935–40; Inspector of Schools, 1940–41. Flt Lt (A&SD Br.), RAAF, 1942–43; Commonwealth Dept of Post-War Reconstruction, 1944–46 (Leader, Aust. Delegn, Constituent Meeting for UNESCO, London, 1945); Sec., NSW Dept of Educn, 1948–51; Dep. Dir-Gen. of Educn, 1951–52; Dir-Gen. and Permanent Head, Dept of Education, 1952–68, Macquarie Univ., Professorial Fellow, 1969–75, Hon. Professorial Fellow, 1976–. Mem. Aust. Delegn to: UNESCO, 1958 and 1966; Commonwealth Educn Conf., Oxford, 1959. Vis. Fellow to Canada, 1966; Fellow and Past-Pres., Aust. Coll. of Educn; Mem., Nat. Library Council of Australia, 1962–73; Chm., Soldiers' Children Educn Bd, Dept of Veterans' Affairs, 1964–84. *Publications:* Class Grouping in the Primary School, 1932; Ability Grouping, 1934; articles in a number of professional jls. *Recreations:* music, gardening. *Address:* 3 Amarna Parade, Roseville, NSW 2069, Australia. *T:* 406–4129. *Club:* University (Sydney). *Died* 22 *April* 1988.

**WYNDHAM-QUIN, Captain Hon. Valentine Maurice:** RN (retired); *b* 1890; *yr s* of 5th Earl of Dunraven, CB, DSO; *u* and *heir-pres.* of 7th Earl of Dunraven and Mount-Earl; *m* 1919, Marjorie Elizabeth (*d* 1969), *d* of late Rt Hon. E. G. Pretyman; three *d. Educ:* Eton; HMS Britannia. Served European War, 1914–19, in command of destroyers of the Patrol Flotillas, Grand Fleet and Harwich Force; retired 1934; returned to Active Service, 1939–44, in command of HM Ships in Home Waters, the South Atlantic and Mediterranean Fleet (despatches 5 times); Naval Attaché, Buenos Aires, 1944–47; retired 1948. Chairman, Royal National Life Boat Institution, 1964–68. *Recreations:* hunting and shooting. *Clubs:* White's; Royal Yacht Squadron (Cowes). *Died* 27 *Feb.* 1983.

**WYNN, Sir (Owen) Watkin W.;** *see* Williams-Wynn.

**WYNNE-EYTON, Mrs Selena Frances,** CBE 1943; *b* 21 Jan 1898; *d* of late Francis Carbutt; *m* 1916, Wing Comdr S. Wynne-Eyton, DSO, AFC (whom she divorced 1932; he was killed flying, 1944); no *c. Educ:* Downe House, Kent (now Cold Ash, Newbury). Joined WAAF June 1939; posted to Air Ministry as Assistant Director, Sept. 1939; Commanding Officer of WAAF Officers' Sch., and later Senior WAAF Staff Officer at Technical Training Command, 1941; Senior WAAF Staff Officer, HQ, RAF, MEF, 1943–45; with Control Commission for Germany (British Element), 1945–50. *Address:* Marsh Cottage, Fingringhoe, near Colchester, Essex. *T:* Rowhedge 273. *Died* 1 *July* 1982.

**WYNNE-FINCH, Colonel John Charles;** CBE 1956; MC; DL; HM Lieutenant of County of Denbigh, 1951–66; Member of Welsh Agricultural Land Sub-Commission, 1948, Chairman, 1953–63; Agricultural Land Commission, 1952, Deputy Chairman, 1953–63; *b* 31 Aug. 1891; *e s* of late Lieut-Colonel Charles Arthur Wynne Finch, Coldstream Guards, and Maud Emily, 2nd *d* of late Hon. Richard Charteris, 2nd *s* of 8th Earl of Wemyss; *m* 1914, Alice Mary Sybil (*d* 1970), 2nd *d* of late Rt Rev. Hon. Edward Carr Glyn and Lady Mary Glyn; one *s* two *d. Educ:* Eton: RMC, Sandhurst. Lord of the Manor of Hieraethog, Denbighshire; patron of 1 living; served European War, 1914–18 (MC). Commanded 3rd Battalion Coldstream Guards, 1932–36; retired pay, 1937. Served War of 1939–45. JP, Denbighshire, then Caernarvonshire (later Gwynedd); DL, Gwynedd. High Sheriff of Denbighshire, 1949. President, Welsh Agricultural Society, 1962. Member, Nature Conservancy, 1957–63; Member, Nature Conservancy, Wales, 1957–66; Chairman, National Trust Cttee for Wales, 1957–69. KStJ 1966. *Address:* Voelas, Betws-y-Coed, Gwynedd LL24 0SU. *T:* Pentrefoelas 206. *Died* 15 *May* 1982.

**WYNNE-JONES,** Baron, cr 1964, of Abergele (Life Peer); **William Francis Kenrick Wynne-Jones;** Pro-Vice-Chancellor, 1965–68, Professor of Chemistry, Head of the School of Chemistry, 1956–68, University of Newcastle upon Tyne; Chancellor, Newcastle upon Tyne Polytechnic, since 1976; *b* 8 May 1903; *y s* of late Rev. T. J. Jones, Shaistaganj, India; *m* 1st, 1928, Ann Drummond (*d* 1969); two *d*; 2nd, 1972, Rusheen Preston, *d* of Mrs Neville Preston. *Educ:* Monkton Combe Sch., Bath; University College of Wales, Aberystwyth; Balliol Coll., Oxford. Research Asst and Lectr in Physical Chemistry, Univ. of Bristol; International Research Fellow, Univ. of Copenhagen; Lectr in Chemistry, Univ. of Reading; Leverhulme Research Fellow, Princeton Univ.; Prof. of Chemistry, University College, Dundee; Head of Chemistry Div., Royal Aircraft Establishment, Farnborough. Chm., Scientific and Technical Cttee, N Atlantic Assembly, 1973–71. Chm. of Governors, Newcastle upon Tyne Polytechnic, 1973–76. Coal Carbonisation Science Lectr and Medallist, 1972. Hon. DSc Bristol, 1968. *Publications:* articles in scientific journals. *Address:* Carlyle House, 16 Chelsea Embankment, SW3. *Died* 8 *Nov.* 1982.

**WYNTER, Sir Luther (Reginald),** Kt 1977; CBE 1966 (OBE 1962, MBE 1950); MD; FICS; private medical practitioner, Antigua, since 1927; *b* 15 Sept. 1899; *s* of Thomas Nathaniel Wynter and Pauline Jane Wynter; *m* 1927, Arah Adner Busby. *Educ:* Wolmers High Sch., Jamaica; Coll. of City of Detroit, USA; Dalhousie Univ. (MD, CM); Moorfields Hosp. (DOMS). FICS (Ophthalmology) 1969. Gen. med. practitioner, Hamilton, Ont, Canada, 1925–27; actg govt radiologist, Antigua, 1937–51; ophthalmologist, Antigua, 1953–64, hon. consulting ophthalmologist, 1966–. Nominated Mem., Antigua Govt, 1956–66; Senator and Pres. of Senate, 1967–68 (often acting as Governor or Dep. to Governor). Hon. LLD: Univ. of the West Indies, 1972; Dalhousie, 1975. *Recreation:* learning to play bridge. *Address:* PO Box 154, St John's, Antigua, West Indies. *T:* (office) St John's 22027, (home) Hodges Bay 22102. *Clubs:* (Hon. Life Mem.) Mill Reef, (Hon. Mem.) Lions (Antigua). *Died* 4 *Nov.* 1984.

**WYSS, Sophie, (Sophie Adele Gyde);** concert singer; *b* 1897; 2nd *d* of Oscar and Hélène Wyss, La Neuveille, Switzerland; *m* 1925, Captain Arnold Gyde; two *s. Educ:* Conservatoires de Genève et Bâle. Operatic debut, Geneva, 1922; recitals and chamber concerts for BBC, 1927–64; concerts throughout Great Britain, in Europe and in Australia. First performances include: Britten's Les Illuminations,

Our Hunting Fathers; all Roberto Gerhard's vocal works; works of Lennox Berkeley, Alan Rawsthorne, Elizabeth Maconchy, Racine Fricker, Matyas Seiber, William Wordsworth and many other composers. Inspired many of these composers to write French as well as English songs and to re-arrange innumerable folk songs into modern idiom. *Address:* Foley House, 18 Upper Bognor Road, Bognor Regis, West Sussex PO21 1JD.        *Died* 25 *Dec.* 1983.

# Y

**YARDE, Air Vice-Marshal Brian Courtenay**, CVO 1953; CBE 1949; psa; *b* 5 September 1905; *s* of late John Edward Yarde, Crediton, Devon, and Bedford; *m* 1927, Marjorie, *d* of late W. Sydney Smith, Bedford; two *d*. *Educ*: Bedford School; RAF College, Cranwell (Sword of Honour), 1926. Served War of 1939–45 in France, Malaya, Middle East, UK (despatches thrice); Deputy Director of Bomber Operations, Air Ministry, 1945; Senior Director, RAF Staff College, 1946–47; Station Commander, Gatow, 1947–49 (Berlin Airlift); Provost Marshal and Chief of the Royal Air Force Police, 1951–53; Air Officer Commanding No. 62 Group, 1953–54. Air Commodore, 1951; Acting Air Vice-Marshal, 1954; Commandant-General of the Royal Air Force Regiment and Inspector of Ground Combat Training, 1954–57, retired. Chairman, Courtenay Caterers Ltd, Andover. Officer American Legion of Merit. *Address*: Wiremead, East Cholderton, Andover, Hants SP11 8LR. *T*: Weyhill 2265.
*Died 29 Oct. 1986.*

**YARWOOD, Dame Elizabeth (Ann)**, DBE 1969; JP; DL; *b* 25 Nov. 1900; *d* of Henry and Margaret Gaskell; *m* 1918, Vernon Yarwood; two *s*. *Educ*: Whitworth Street High Sch., Manchester. Councillor, Manchester City Council, 1938–74, Alderman, 1955–74; Lord Mayor of Manchester, 1967–68. Director: Manchester & Salford Co-operative Society Ltd, 1955; Manchester Ship Canal, 1964. Vice-Pres., Manchester County Girl Guides Assoc. Freeman of the City of Manchester, 1974. Hon. MA Manchester, 1978. JP Manchester, 1945; DL Lancs, 1974. *Recreation*: reading.
*Died 31 Dec. 1989.*

**YATES, Dame Frances (Amelia)**, DBE 1977 (OBE 1972); DLit; FBA 1967; Hon. Fellow, Warburg Institute since 1967; Reader in the History of the Renaissance, Warburg Institute, University of London, 1956–67; *b* 28 Nov 1899; *d* of James Alfred Yates, Royal Corps of Naval Constructors, and Hannah Eliza Malpas. *Educ*: Laurel Bank School, Glasgow; Birkenhead High School; University College, London. BA London 1924 (First Cl. Hons in French), MA London 1926; DLit London 1965. Private research and writing, some teaching at N London Collegiate School, 1926–39; Ambulance Attendant, 1939–41. Warburg Inst., Univ. of London: Part-time Research Assistant, 1941–44; Lecturer and editor of publications, 1944–56. James Ford special lecture, Oxford, 1970; Northcliffe Lectr, UCL, 1974; Lectr at Newberry Library, Chicago, Wisconsin Univ., Harvard Univ., 1978; Emeritus Prof., Hampshire Coll., Mass, 1979. FRSL 1943; Fellow, Soc. Humanities, Cornell Univ., 1968. Hon. Fellow, Lady Margaret Hall, Oxford, 1970. Hon. DLitt: Edinburgh, 1969; Oxford, 1970; East Anglia, 1971; Exeter, 1971. Hon. For. Mem., Amer. Acad. of Arts and Sciences, 1975; For. Mem., Royal Netherlands Acad. of Arts and Sciences (Div. for Letters), 1980. Rose Mary Crawshay Prize, British Acad., 1934; Senior Wolfson History Prize, 1973; Premio Galileo Galilei, Pisa (for work on history of Italian thought), 1978. *Publications*: John Florio, The Life of an Italian in Shakespeare's England, 1934; A Study of Love's Labour's Lost, 1936; The French Academies of the Sixteenth Century (Warburg Inst.), 1947; The Valois Tapestries (Warburg Inst.), 1959; Giordano Bruno and the Hermetic Tradition, 1964; The Art of Memory, 1966 (pbk 1978); Theatre of the World, 1969; The Rosicrucian Enlightenment, 1972; Astraea: the imperial theme in the sixteenth century, 1975; Shakespeare's Last Plays: a new approach, 1975; Elizabethan Neoplatonism Reconsidered: Spenser and Francesco Giorgi, 1977; The Occult Philosophy in the Elizabethan Age, 1979; many articles in Jl of Warburg and Courtauld Institutes and elsewhere. *Recreations*: reading, travel. *Address*: 5 Coverts Road, Claygate, Surrey KT10 0JY; Warburg Institute, Woburn Square, WC1H 0AB. *T*: 01-580 9663. *Club*: University Women's.
*Died 29 Sept. 1981.*

**YEABSLEY, Sir Richard Ernest**, Kt 1950; CBE 1943; FCA; *b* 16 May 1898; *m* 1923, Hilda Maude Willson; one *d*. *Educ*: Alperton School. Served European War, 3rd Bn (City of London Regiment) Royal Fusiliers, 1914–19. Independent member of Hosiery Working Party, 1945; Member: Committee to examine the organisation and methods of distribution of Building Materials, 1946; Committee to enquire into the resources of Minerals in the United Kingdom, 1946; Supreme Court Cttee on Practice and Procedure, 1947; Cttee on Resale Price Maintenance, 1947; Monopolies and Restrictive Practices Commn, 1949–56. Accountant Adviser to BoT, 1942–68; formerly Sen. Partner, Hill, Vellacott & Co., and Hill, Vellacott & Bailey, Chartered Accountants, retd March 1963; Pres. Society of Incorporated Accountants, 1956–57. *Address*: 9 Alverton Hall, West Cliff Road, Bournemouth. *T*: Bournemouth 766293. *Club*: Royal Automobile.
*Died 13 Feb. 1983.*

**YENDELL, Rear-Adm. William John**, CB 1957; RN, retired; *b* 29 Dec. 1903; *e s* of late Charles Yendell; *m* 1937, Monica Duncan; one *d*. *Educ*: RN Colleges Osborne and Dartmouth. Qualified Gunnery Officer, 1929; commanded HM Ships: Bittern, 1938; Shah, 1943–45; Glasgow, 1950; Superb, 1950. Director of Naval Ordnance,

1951–54; Assistant Chief of Naval Staff (Warfare), 1954–57. Naval ADC 1954–. Comdr, 1937; Captain, 1945. *Recreations*: painting and most games. *Address*: The Bell Cottage, Newtonmore, Inverness-shire. *T*: Newtonmore 344. *Club*: Royal Naval and Royal Albert Yacht (Portsmouth).
*Died 10 July 1988.*

**YOST, Charles Woodruff; Special Adviser, Aspen Institute, since 1976; Honorary Co-Chairman (formerly Counsellor), United Nations Association; *b* 6 Nov. 1907; *s* of Nicholas Doxtater and Gertrude (Cooper); *m* 1934, Irena Oldakowska; two *s* one *d*. *Educ*: Hotchkiss Sch.; Princeton Univ. (AB); Univ. of Paris. Entered US Foreign Service, 1930; served: Alexandria, 1930–32; Warsaw, 1932–33. Journalist, 1933–35. Dept of State, 1935–45; Asst to Chm., Dumbarton Oaks and San Francisco Confs, 1945; Sec.-Gen., US Delegn, Berlin Conf., 1945; Political Adviser to Comdg Gen., India-Burma Theatre, 1945; Chargé d'Affaires, Bangkok, 1946; Pol. Adviser to US Delegn to UN, 1946; Prague, 1947; Vienna, 1948–49; Pol. Adviser to US Delegn to UN, 1949; Dir, Office of Eastern European Affairs, 1949–50; Minister in Athens, 1950–53; Dep. High Comr for Austria, 1953–54; Laos: Minister, 1954, Ambassador, 1955–56; Minister in Paris, 1956–57; Ambassador to Syria, 1957, to Morocco, 1958–61; Dep. Rep. to UN Security Council, 1961–65; Career Ambassador, 1964; Dep. Perm. Rep. to UN, 1965–66; Senior Fellow, Council on Foreign Relations, 1966–69; Ambassador and Perm. Rep. of US to UN, 1969–71; Distinguished Lectr on Foreign Policy, Columbia Univ. Sch. of Internat. Affairs, 1971–73; Pres., Nat. Cttee on US-China Relations, 1973–75; Sen. Fellow, Brookings Instn, 1975–76. Hon. LLD: St Lawrence Univ., 1963; Princeton Univ., 1969. Rockefeller Public Service Award, 1964. *Publications*: Age of Triumph and Frustration, 1964; The Insecurity of Nations, 1968; The Conduct and Misconduct of Foreign Affairs, 1971; History and Memory, 1980. *Recreations*: swimming, riding, literature, arts. *Address*: 2801 New Mexico Avenue, NW, Washington, DC 20036, USA. *Clubs*: Century, Princeton (New York); Cosmos (Washington).
*Died 21 May 1981.*

**YOUDE, Sir Edward**, GCMG 1983 (KCMG 1977; CMG 1968); GCVO 1986; MBE 1949; Governor and Commander-in-Chief, Hong Kong, since 1982; *b* 19 June 1924; *m* 1951, Pamela Fitt; two *d*. *Educ*: Sch. of Oriental and African Studies, Univ. of London. RNVR, 1943–46. Joined Foreign Office, 1947; Third Sec., Nanking and Peking, 1948; Foreign Office, 1951; Second Sec., Peking, 1953; First Secretary: Washington, 1956–59; Peking, 1960–62; Foreign Office, 1962–65; Counsellor and Head of Chancery, UK Mission to UN, 1965–69; Private Secretary to the Prime Minister, 1969–70; IDC, 1970–71; Head of Personnel Services Dept, FCO, 1971–73; Asst Under-Sec. of State, FCO, 1973–74; Ambassador to China, 1974–78; Dep. Under-Sec. of State (Chief Clerk), FCO, 1978; Dep. to Permanent Under-Sec. of State, and Chief Clerk, FCO, 1980–82. *Recreations*: walking, theatre, music. *Address*: Government House, Hong Kong.
*Died 4 Dec. 1986.*

**YONGE, Sir (Charles) Maurice**, Kt 1967; CBE 1954; FRS 1946; FRSE; DSc(Ed.); Hon. Fellow in Zoology, University of Edinburgh; *b* 9 Dec. 1899; *s* of John Arthur Yonge, MA, JP, and Sarah Edith Carr; *m* 1st, Martha Jane (*d* 1945), *d* of R. T. Lennox, Newmilns, Ayrshire; one *s* one *d*; 2nd, Phyllis Greenlaw, *d* of Dr D. M. M. Fraser, Eastry, Kent; one *s*. *Educ*: Silcoates School, Wakefield; Edinburgh Univ. Baxter Natural Science Scholar, 1922–24; Carnegie Research Scholar, 1924–25. Temporary Asst Naturalist, Marine Biological Assoc., Plymouth, 1925–27; Balfour Student, Univ. of Cambridge, 1927–29; leader, Great Barrier Reef Expedition, 1928–29; Physiologist, Marine Biological Assoc., Plymouth, 1930–32; Prof. of Zoology, Univ. of Bristol, 1933–44; Regius Prof. of Zoology, Univ. of Glasgow, 1944–64; Research Fellow in Zoology, 1965–70. Visiting Prof., Univ. of California, 1949; Prather Lecturer, Harvard Univ., 1957; Visiting Prof., Univ. of Washington, 1959, 1969; Royal Soc. Vis. Prof., Univ. of Hong Kong, 1978. Mem., Advisory Cttee on Fishery Research to the Development Commission, 1937–56; UK Representative, Pacific Science Council; Pres. and Chm. of Council, Scottish Marine Biological Assoc., 1944–67; Chairman: Supervisory Cttee, Brown Trout Lab., Pitlochry, 1949–59; Colonial Fisheries Adv. Cttee; Mem., Audio-Visual Aids Cttee of Univ. Grants Cttee; Mem., Natural Environment Research Council, 1965–70; Vice-President and Hon. Member: Marine Biological Assoc. UK; Scottish Marine Biological Assoc.; Vice-Pres. Royal Soc. of Edinburgh, 1953–56 (Makdougall-Brisbane Prize, 1957), Pres., 1970–73; Pres., Section D, British Assoc., 1961; Mem. Council, Royal Society, 1952–54, 1968–70. Hon. Life Fellow, Pacific Science Assoc.; Mem., Royal Danish Acad. of Science and Letters; Hon. Member: Malac. Soc. London; California Academy of Sciences; Royal Soc. of NZ. Hon. DSc: Bristol, 1959; Heriot-Watt, 1971; Manchester, 1975; Edinburgh, 1983. Darwin Medal, Royal Society, 1968. *Publications*: (with F. S. Russell) The Seas, 1928, 4th edn 1975; A Year on the Great Barrier Reef, 1930; British Marine Life, 1944; The Sea Shore, 1949; (with J. Barrett) Guide to the Seashore, 1958; Oysters, 1960; (ed, with K. M. Wilbur) Physiology of Mollusca, vol. i, 1964, vol. ii, 1967; (with T. E. Thompson) Living Marine Molluscs, 1976; (ed, with F. S. Russell) Advances in Marine Biology; numerous scientific papers in standard scientific journals, since 1923. *Recreations:* travel, reading of history, woodwork. *Address:* 13 Cumin Place, Edinburgh EH9 2JX. *T:* 031–667 3678.

*Died 17 March 1986.*

**YORSTON, Sir (Robert) Keith,** Kt 1969; CBE 1962 (OBE 1960); FCA, FASA, FCIS; Hon. FAIM; *b* 12 Feb. 1902; *s* of late R. Yorston, Shetland Is; *m* 1934, Gwendolen C., *d* of late F. A. Ridley; one *s* one *d. Educ:* Caulfield Public Sch.; Univ. of Melbourne (BCom). Principal, Aust. Accountancy Coll., Sydney, 1933–66. In practice as a Chartered Acct, in Sydney, 1933–70. Federal Pres., Australian-American Assoc., 1960, 1962–64, 1966–67, 1972; NSW Pres., Australian-American Assoc., 1957–63, 1965–74; Pres., Aust. Soc. of Accts, NSW, 1959. Rep. Australia at: Internat. Congress of Accts, 1957, 1962; Internat. Congress of Inst. of Management, 1957. Member: Adjudicating Panel for best Annual Report in Australia (since inception of Annual Report Award); Bd, Scottish Hosp., Sydney. Mem. Adv. Bd, Presbyterian Foundation. Chm., The Presbyterian Church (NSW) Property Trust, 1964–75. Annual Research Lecturer, Aust. Soc. of Accts: Univ. Sydney, 1951; Univ. WA, 1952; Univ. Tas, 1953; Univ. Melb., 1959; Edgar Sabine Memorial Lecture, Adelaide Univ., 1959; Guest Lectr, Jubilee Convention of NZ Soc. of Accts, 1960. *Publications:* several books reproduced in other countries, such as UK, India and New Zealand; numerous standard text books (some jointly) on accounting, law and company practice (mostly in 2–6 edns) including: Australian Company Director, 1932; Australian Shareholders Guide, 1958, 3rd edn 1971; Australian Commercial Dictionary, 1945, 5th edn 1972; Limited Liability Companies in Australia, 1956; Twentieth Century Commerce and Book-keeping, 12th edn 1960; Costing Procedures, 1951, 5th edn 1976; Advanced Accounting, 1948, 8th edn 1978; Elementary Accounting, 1952, 5th edn 1975; Company Law in New South Wales, 1947, 3rd edn 1968; Company Law in Victoria, 1955, 2nd edn 1959; Accounting Fundamentals, 1949, 7th edn, rev. 1980; Australian Mercantile Law, 1939, 16th edn 1981; Annual Reports of Companies, 1958; Australian Secretarial Practice, 1936, 6th edn 1978; Company Secretary's Guide (NSW), 1946, 2nd edn 1950; Company Secretary's Guide (Victoria), 1948, 2nd edn 1952; Company Secretary's Guide (Queensland), 1947; Company Law, 1962, 3rd edn 1968; Proprietary and Private Companies in Australia, 1939, 2nd edn 1952. *Address:* 29 Trafalgar Avenue, Roseville, NSW 2069, Australia.                                    *Died 16 May 1983.*

**YOUNG, Maj.-Gen. Alexander,** CB 1971; *b* 22 Feb. 1915; *s* of late Alexander and Mary M. K. G. Young, Edinburgh; *m* 1942, Joan Madeline, *d* of late John N. Stephens, London; one *s. Educ:* Daniel Stewart's Coll., Edinburgh. Served, BEF, 1940; WO, 1942–46; HQ, Caribbean Area, 1947–50; WO, 1950–52; HQ Middle East Comd, Egypt and Cyprus, 1954–57; Bt Lt-Col 1955; Comdr RAOC, 4 Inf. Div., 1957–59; HQ, BAOR, 1959–61; WO, 1961–64; Dep. Dir, Ordnance Services, Eastern Comd, 1964–65; Comd COD, Bicester, 1965–67; Comd UK Base Org., 1967–68; Dir of Ordnance Services, MoD, 1968–71. Col Comdt, RAOC, 1971–75. FBIM. *Recreations:* travel, golf. *Address:* Gaddons Cottage, Seaward Drive, West Wittering, Sussex. *T:* West Wittering 2118. *Club:* Army and Navy.

*Died 17 July 1983.*

**YOUNG, Carmichael Aretas,** MD, FRCP; Hon. Consulting Physician and Physician i/c Diabetic Clinic, St Mary's Hospital, London, W2; *b* Adelaide, S Australia, 19 Aug. 1913; *e s* of Aretas Henry Young, Adelaide, SA and Isabelle Wilson, Parattah, Tas; *m* 1939, Marie, 2nd *d* of W. H. Lewry, Botley, Hants; three *s* one *d. Educ:* Carey Grammar Sch., Kew, Vic.; St Mary's Hosp. Medical Sch., Univ. of London. MRCS, LRCP 1936, FRCP 1950; MB, BS (London), 1936, MD 1940. House Phys. and House Surg., St Mary's Hosp., 1936–37; House Phys., Asst Resident MO, Brompton Hosp., 1938; Asst, Professorial Medical Unit, St Mary's, 1939; Phys., EMS, 1940–41; Medical Specialist 10th (Brit.) CCS, 1942–43 (despatches); No 1 Gen. Hosp., 1944; Lt-Col RAMC O i/c Medical Div. 43 Gen. Hosp., 1945; OC 43 Gen. Hosp., Beirut, 1946. Medical Registrar, Prince of Wales' Gen. Hosp., 1946–47; Consultant in Chest Diseases, Min. of Pensions, 1948; St Mary's Hosp., 1948–78; Sub-Dean, St Mary's Hosp. Medical School, 1952–53; Examiner: Soc. of Apothecaries, Medicine, 1964–70; Univ. London, Therapeutics, Medicine, 1957–62; Conj. Bd, Pathology, Medicine (Chm., 1970–71); Pro-Censor, 1973–74, Censor, 1974–75, RCP. Mem., Bd of Governors, St Mary's Hosp., 1958–61. Hon. Colonel No 4 Gen. Hosp. AER, 1961. *Publications:* History of the Otter Swimming Club, 1869–1969, 1969; short articles in medical jls. *Recreations:* swimming, water-polo, golf, gardening. *Address:* The Tile House, Billingshurst Road, Ashington, W Sussex RH20 3AY. *T:* Ashington 892544. *Clubs:* Otter Swimming (Pres. 1964–67); West Sussex Golf.                                     *Died 11 Aug. 1986.*

**YOUNG, Rev. Canon (Cecil) Edwyn,** CVO 1983; Chaplain, The Queen's Chapel of the Savoy, and Chaplain of the Royal Victorian Order, 1974–83; Chaplain to the Queen, 1972–83; *b* 29 April 1913; *er s* of Cecil Morgan Young and Doris Edith Virginia Young,

Colombo, Ceylon; *m* 1944, Beatrice Mary, *e d* of Percy Montague Rees and Beatrice Rees; two *s* one *d. Educ:* Radley Coll.; Dorchester Missionary College. Curate, St Peter's, London Docks, 1936–41; Priest in Charge, St Francis, N Kensington, 1941–44; Rector of Broughton with Ripton Regis, 1944–47; Vicar of St Silas, Pentonville, 1947–53; Rector of Stepney, 1953–64, and Rural Dean of Stepney, 1959–64; Prebendary of St Paul's, 1959–64; Rector and Rural Dean of Liverpool, 1964–73; Canon Diocesan, 1965–73. Commissary, Diocese of North Queensland, 1959–, Canon to the Ordinary, 1974–. Chaplain: Worshipful Co. of Distillers, 1974–; Weavers' Co., 1977–; to Chm., Freight Forwarders Inst., 1974–. Pres., Sion College, 1963–64. Hon. Chaplain, HCIMA. *Publications:* Young and Grace Full, 1962; No Fun Like Work, 1970; (contrib.) Father Groser, East End Priest, 1971. *Recreations:* meeting people; wild flowers; the theatre, especially music hall; watching cricket. *Address:* Flat 1, 45 Brunswick Square, Hove, Sussex. *Clubs:* Greenroom, City Livery.                              *Died 1 March 1988.*

**YOUNG, (Charles) Kenneth,** FRSL; Political and Literary Adviser to Beaverbrook Newspapers since 1965, and formerly, Editor of the Yorkshire Post; *b* 27 Nov. 1916; *o s* of late Robert William Young, Iron Founder, Middlestown, Wakefield, and late Alice Jane Young (*née* Ramsden); *m* 1949, Elizabeth Constantinou (*d* 1950); one *d*; *m* 1951, Phyllis, *d* of late Lt-Col and Mrs J. A. Dicker; three *s* one *d. Educ:* Queen Elizabeth's Grammar Sch. (Junior Dept), Wakefield; Coatham Sch., Redcar; Leeds Univ. BA (1st Cl. Hons Eng. Lang. and Lit.), 1938. Served War of 1939–45. Royal Corps of Signals, 1940; Intelligence Corps, 1941 (Algeria, Italy, Greece); Foreign Office, 1944. BBC European Service, 1948; Daily Mirror, 1949; Daily Mail, 1950; Permanent Under-Sec. Dept, Cabinet Office, 1950; Daily Telegraph, 1952–60; Editor of The Yorkshire Post, 1960–64; Political Commentator, Birmingham Evening Mail, 1978–. FRSL 1964. Broadcaster; Editor, Television series, The Book Man, 1960. Governor, Welbeck College, 1963–73. *Publications:* D. H. Lawrence, 1952; John Dryden (critical biography), 1954; Ford Madox Ford, 1958; (ed) The Bed Post, 1962; (ed) The Second Bed Post, 1965; A. J. Balfour, authorised biography, 1963; Churchill and Beaverbrook: a study in friendship and politics, 1966; Rhodesia and Independence: a study in British colonial policy, 1967, 2nd edn 1969; Sir Compton Mackenzie, an essay, 1967; Music's Great Days in the Spas and Watering-places, 1968; The Greek Passion: a study in people and politics, 1969; Sir Alec Douglas-Home, 1970; Chapel, 1972; (ed) Diaries of Sir Robert Bruce Lockhart, vol. I, 1973, vol. II, 1980; H. G. Wells, an essay, 1974; Life of 6th Earl of Rosebery, 1974; Arnold Bennett, an essay, 1975; Baldwin: a biography, 1976; Lord Macaulay, an essay, 1977; J. B. Priestley, an essay, 1978; A Neighbourhood of Writers, 1981. *Recreations:* being with family, listening to music, talk. *Address:* Beaufort House, Oxenden Street, Herne Bay, Kent. *T:* Herne Bay 5419. *Clubs:* Beefsteak, Wig and Pen, East India.                                       *Died 13 July 1985.*

**YOUNG, Dr Edith Isabella,** CBE 1964; *b* 7 March 1904; *d* of William Ross Young and Margaret Ramsay Young (*née* Hill). *Educ:* High School of Stirling; Univ. of Glasgow. BSc 1924, MA (1st cl. Hons Mathematics and Natural Philosophy) 1925. HM Inspector of Schools, Scottish Educn Dept, 1935–64; HM Inspector, in charge of Dundee and Angus, 1946–52; HM Chief Inspector, Highland Div., 1952–64. UNESCO expert on the teaching of science in Yugoslavia, Oct. 1956–Feb. 1957; UK Deleg., UNESCO Conf., Belgrade, 1960; Mem. Council for Technical Educn and Trg for Overseas Countries, 1964–68 (Chm., Women's Gp); UK Deleg. to Commonwealth Conf. on Trg of Technicians in Huddersfield, 1966; Co-Chm., Women's Nat. Commn, 1971–73; Pres., 1967–70, Hon. Vice-Pres. (for life), 1983, British Fedn of Univ. Women. Chairman: Northern Area Nurse Trng Cttee, 1967–81; Inverness Hosp. Bd, 1968–74. Hon. LLD Southampton, 1967. *Recreations:* sundry. *Address:* 36 Broadstone Park, Inverness IV2 3LA. *T:* Inverness 233216. *Clubs:* Royal Over-Seas League, University Women's.

*Died 31 Jan. 1988.*

**YOUNG, Rev. Canon Edwyn;** *see* Young, Rev. Canon C. E.

**YOUNG, Eric Edgar;** HM Diplomatic Service, retired; *b* 1 July 1912; *yr s* of late Frank E. Young, Dulwich; *m* 1938, Aurora Corral, San Sebastian, Spain; two *d. Educ:* Alleyn's Sch., Dulwich; Jesus Coll., Oxford. Asst Master, Haberdashers' Aske's Hatcham Boys Sch., 1935–40. Served Army, 1940–46 (Major, RAC). Diplomatic (formerly Foreign) Service, 1946–70; Served at: Buenos Aires, 1946–49; Montevideo, 1950–52; Mexico City, 1952–55; FO, 1955–58; Rangoon, 1958–60; HM Consul, Tamsui (Formosa), 1960–62; FO, 1962–64; Adv. to Kenya Min. of Foreign Affairs, Nairobi, 1964–67; HM Consul-General, Paris, 1967–70. Mem. Adv. Cttee, Nat. Art-Collections Fund, 1977–; Nat. Art-Collections Fund Lecture, 1979. *Publications:* Four Centuries of Spanish Painting, Barnard Castle, 1967; The Bowes Museum, Barnard Castle, Catalogue of Spanish and Italian Paintings, 1970; Bartolomé Bermejo: The Great Hispano-Flemish Master, 1975; Francisco Goya, 1978; Bartolomé Murillo Werkverzeichnis, 1980; Todas las pinturas de Murillo, 1982 (with introdn by Alfonso E. Pérez

Sánchez); (contrib.) A Biographical Dictionary of Artists, 1983; contribs to: Apollo, The Burlington Magazine, The Connoisseur, Archivo Español de Arte, Goya, Revista de Arte, Art Bulletin (NY), Museum Studies (Chicago), J. Paul Getty Museum Jl, Actas del XXIII Congreso Internacional de Historia del Arte (Granada), Pantheon (Munich), Fenway Court (Boston, Mass), Arte Veneta, Boletín de la Institución Fernán González (Burgos). *Recreation:* art history. *Address:* 29 Sevenoaks Road, Orpington, Kent BR6 9JH.
*Died 12 July 1986.*

**YOUNG, Eric William,** BEng (Hons); MIMechE, MIEE; *b* 26 March 1896; 2nd *s* of Colonel C. A. Young, CB, CMG; *m* 1936, Mrs Olive Bruce. *Educ:* Epsom Coll.; Shrewsbury Sch.; Liverpool Univ. (BEng Hons, 1922). Served RE (T) (Lieut) 1913–19. Metropolitan Vickers Ltd, 1922–26; Technical Manager, Electrolux Ltd, 1926–39; Rootes Ltd: General Manager, Aero Engine Factories, 1939–45; Director and General Manager, Sunbeam Talbot Ltd, 1945–46; Director, Rootes Export Co. Ltd, 1946–47; Sales Director, Harry Ferguson Ltd, 1947–53; Managing Director, Eastern Hemisphere Division, Massey-Ferguson Ltd, 1953–56; Vice-Chm., Massey-Ferguson Holdings Ltd, 1956–65, Chm., 1965–70. *Recreations:* golf, gardening. *Address:* Childerstone, Liphook, Hampshire GU30 7AP. *T:* Liphook 722125. *Club:* Liphook Golf.
*Died 25 Oct. 1987.*

**YOUNG, Sir Frank (George),** Kt 1973; DSc, PhD (London), MA (Cantab); FRS 1949; CChem, FRSC; Sir William Dunn Professor of Biochemistry, University of Cambridge, 1949–75; later Professor Emeritus; Master of Darwin College, Cambridge, 1964–76, Hon. Fellow 1977; Hon. Fellow of Trinity Hall, Cambridge, since 1965 (Fellow, 1949–64); Fellow of University College, London; *b* 25 March 1908; *er s* of late Frank E. Young, Dulwich; *m* 1933, Ruth (MB, BS, MRCPsych), *o c* of Thomas Turner, Beckenham, Kent; three *s* (one *d* decd). *Educ:* Alleyn's Sch., Dulwich; University Coll., London. Beit Memorial Fellow at University Coll., London, University of Aberdeen and University of Toronto, 1933–36; Member of Scientific Staff, Medical Research Council, at Nat. Inst. for Med. Research, 1936–42; Professor of Biochemistry, University of London, 1942–49 (at St Thomas's Hosp. Med. Sch., 1942–45, UCL, 1945–49). Syndic, CUP, 1951–64; Mem. Council of Senate, Cambridge, 1965–68; Chm., Clinical Sch. Planning Cttee, Univ. of Cambridge, 1969–76. Vice Pres. and Hon. Mem., British Diabetic Assoc., 1948–; Member: Medical Res. Council, 1950–54; Commission on Higher Educ. for Africans in Central Africa, 1952; Inter-University Council for Higher Education Overseas, 1961–73; Commission on new Chinese University in Hong Kong, 1962–63; Medical Sub-Cttee, UGC, 1964–73; Board of Governors of United Cambridge Hospitals, 1964–68; Royal Commn on Medical Educn, 1965–68; Council, British Nutrition Foundn, 1967–80; Council of Nestlé Foundn, Lausanne, 1972–80. Trustee, Kennedy Memorial Trust, 1964–76. President: European Assoc. for the Study of Diabetes, 1965–68, Hon. Mem., 1973; British Nutrition Foundn, 1970–76; Internat. Diabetes Fedn, 1970–73 (Hon. Pres., 1973–); Vice-Pres. and Mem. of Exec. Bd, Internat. Council of Scientific Unions, 1970–73. Chairman: Smith Kline and French Trustees (UK), 1963–77; Clinical Endocrinology Cttee (MRC), 1965–72; Adv. Cttee on Irradiation of Food (UK), 1967–80; Mem. Executive Council, Ciba Foundation, 1954–67, Chm. 1967–77, Trustee, 1967–83. Croonian Lecturer, Royal Society, 1962. Named lectureships held abroad: Renziehausen, Pittsburg, 1939; Sterling, Yale, 1939; Jacobæus, Oslo, 1948; Dohme, Johns Hopkins, 1950; Banting, Toronto, 1950; Banting, San Francisco, 1950; Richardson, Harvard, 1952; Hanna, Western Reserve, 1952; Woodward, Yale, 1958; Brailsford Robertson, Adelaide, 1960; Upjohn, Atlantic City, 1963. Hon. Member: Consejo Superior de Investigaciones Cientificas, Madrid; Biochemical Soc. and Soc. for Endocrinology, and Hon. or corresp. member of many foreign medical and scientific bodies. Hon. FRCP 1974. Hon. LLD Aberdeen; Hon. DSc Zimbabwe; Doctor *hc:* Catholic University of Chile; Univ. Montpellier. Coronation Medal, 1953. *Publications:* scientific papers in Biochemical Journal and other scientific and medical journals on hormonal control of metabolism, diabetes mellitus, and related topics. *Address:* 11 Bentley Road, Cambridge CB2 2AW. *T:* Cambridge 352650.
*Died 20 Sept. 1988.*

**YOUNG, Frederick Trestrail Clive,** CBE 1937; *b* 19 March 1887; *y s* of late James Young, Calcutta, and of late L. Z. Young, Rockmount, Helensburgh, Dunbartonshire; *m* 1920, Hope MacLellan Fulton, Findhorn, Helensburgh; two *s* one *d*. *Educ:* Merchiston Castle, Edinburgh (School Captain); Pembroke Coll., Cambridge. BA (Hons Classical Tripos, 1909); Sudan Political Service, 1910, District Commissioner; Commissioner Nomad (Beja) Administration, 1926; Assistant Civil Secretary, 1929–32; Governor: Kassala Province, 1932–34; Blue Nile Province, 1934–36; Retired, 1936; Order of Nile 4th class, 1920, 3rd class, 1930; King George V Jubilee Medal, 1935. *Recreations:* golf, tennis, sailing. *Address:* West Down House, Budleigh Salterton, Devon. *T:* Budleigh Salterton 2762. *Club:* Royal Commonwealth Society.
*Died 30 Dec. 1982.*

**YOUNG, George Kennedy,** CB 1960; CMG 1955; MBE 1945; *b* 8 April 1911; *s* of late George Stuart Young and Margaret Kennedy, Moffat, Dumfriesshire; *m* 1939, Géryke, *d* of late Dr M. A. G. Harthoorn, Batavia, Dutch EI. *Educ:* Dumfries Acad.; Univs of St Andrews, Giessen, Dijon, Yale. MA (First Class Hons Mod. Langs), St Andrews, 1934; Commonwealth Fund Fellowship, 1934–36; MA (Political Science), Yale, 1936; Editorial staff The Glasgow Herald, 1936–38; British United Press, 1938–39. Served War of 1939–45; commissioned KOSB 1940 (despatches, E Africa, 1941); specially employed list, Italy and W Europe, 1943–45. Berlin correspondent, British United Press, 1946. Joined HM Foreign Service, 1946; Vienna, 1946; Economic Relations Dept, FO, 1949; British Middle East Office, 1951; Ministry of Defence, 1953–61; Under-Secretary, 1960. Kleinwort, Benson Ltd, 1961–76; Pres., Nuclear Fuel Finance SA, 1969–76. Medal of Freedom (Bronze Palm), 1945. *Publications:* Masters of Indecision, 1962; Merchant Banking, 1966; Finance and World Power, 1968; Who Goes Home?, 1969; Who is my Liege?, 1972; Subversion, 1984. *Recreations:* music, reading, swimming, walking. *Address:* 37 Abbotsbury House, W14. *T:* 01–603 8432.
*Died 9 May 1990.*

**YOUNG, (Gerard) William M.;** *see* Mackworth Young.

**YOUNG, Most Rev. Sir Guilford (Clyde),** KBE 1978; DD (Rome); Archbishop of Hobart, (RC), since 1955; *b* Sandgate, Queensland, 10 Nov. 1916. Ordained, Rome, 1939; Auxiliary Bishop of Canberra and Goulburn, 1948; Co-Adjutor Archbishop of Hobart, 1954; succeeded to See of Hobart, Sept. 1955. *Address:* Archbishop's House, 31 Fisher Avenue, Sandy Bay, Hobart, Tasmania 7005, Australia; GPO Box 62a, Hobart, Tas 7001, Australia.
*Died 16 March 1988.*

**YOUNG, Maj.-Gen. Hugh A.,** CB 1946; CBE 1945; DSO 1944; CD 1954; Vice-President, Central Mortgage and Housing Corporation since 1947; *b* 3 April 1898; *s* of Andrew and Emily Young, Winnipeg; *m* 1927; one *s* one *d*. *Educ:* Winnipeg Collegiate; University of Manitoba (BSc Elec. Engineering, 1924). RC Signals, 1924; Staff Coll., Camberley, England, 1933–34; various General Staff appointments during the war; commanded Inf. Bde, operations Normandy, 1944; QMG Canadian Army, 1944–47; retired, 1947. Dep. Minister of Department of Resources and Development, and Comr of NW Territories, Canada, 1950–53; Dep. Minister, Dept of Public Works, 1953–63.
*Died Feb. 1982.*

**YOUNG, Major John Darling,** JP; Lord-Lieutenant of Buckinghamshire, 1969–84; *b* 4 Jan. 1910; *o s* of late Sir Frederick Young; *m* 1934, Nina (*d* 1974), *d* of late Lt-Col H. W. Harris; three *d*. *Educ:* Eton and Oxford (BA). Commissioned The Life Guards, 1932–46; Middle East and Italy, 1940–44. Member Bucks Agricultural Executive Cttee, 1947–58. Pres., Eastern Wessex TA&VRA, 1976–78. DL 1958, High Sheriff, 1960, JP 1964, CC 1964–77, CA 1969–74, Buckinghamshire. KStJ 1969. *Address:* Thornton Hall, Thornton, Milton Keynes MK17 0HB. *T:* Buckingham 813234. *Clubs:* Turf, Cavalry and Guards.
*Died 3 Feb. 1988.*

**YOUNG, Sir John (William Roe),** 5th Bt, *cr* 1821; retired; *b* 28 June 1913; *e s* of Sir Cyril Roe Muston Young, 4th Bt, and Gertrude Annie, *d* of John Elliott, Braunton, N Devon; *S* father, 1955; *m* 1st, 1946, Joan Minnie Agnes Aldous (*d* 1958); one *s* one *d*; 2nd, 1960, Joy Maureen, *d* of A. G. Clarke. *Educ:* Elizabeth Coll., Guernsey, CI. Heir: *s* John Kenyon Roe Young, *b* 23 April 1947. *Address:* c/o Standard Chartered Bank, 2 Regent Street, SW1Y 4PF.
*Died 5 April 1981.*

**YOUNG, Kenneth;** *see* Young, C. K.

**YOUNG, Mary Lavinia Bessie,** OBE 1967; Matron of the Westminster Hospital, SW1, 1951–66, retired; Mayor of Shaftesbury, Dorset, 1971–72; *b* 15 Nov. 1911; *d* of late Bennett and Rosalind Young. *Educ:* Girls' High Sch., Shaftesbury, Dorset. SRN, RSCN, SCM. Belgrave Hospital for Sick Children, SW9, 1929–32; KCH, SE5, 1933–36; Chiswick and Ealing Maternity Hospital, 1937; private nursing, 1938. King's College Hospital: Night Sister, 1938–40; Home Sister, 1940–41; Sister, Private Patients' Wing, 1941–44. Asst Matron, Royal Hospital, Richmond Surrey, 1944–45; Asst and Dep. Matron, Westminster Hospital, SW1, 1945–51. *Recreation:* gardening. *Address:* St Martins, Angel Square, Shaftesbury, Dorset. *T:* Shaftesbury 2020.
*Died 10 June 1986.*

**YOUNG, Brig. Peter,** DSO 1942; MC 1942 and two Bars 1943; military historian; Captain-Generall, The Sealed Knot Society of Cavaliers and Roundheads, since 1968; *b* 28 July 1915; *s* of Dallas H. W. Young, MBE, and Irene Barbara Lushington Mellor; *m* 1950, Joan Duckworth; no *c*. *Educ:* Monmouth Sch.; Trinity Coll., Oxford. 2nd Lieut, Bedfordshire and Hertfordshire Regt, 1937. Served War of 1939–45: BEF Dunkirk (wounded), 1940; No 3 Commando, 1940; raids on Guernsey, 1940; Lofoten and Vaagso, 1941, Dieppe, 1942, Sicily and Italy, 1943; comd No 3 Commando, 1943–44; Normandy, 1944; Arakan, 1944–45; comd 1st Commando Bde, 1945–46. Commanded 9th Regt Arab Legion, 1953–56. Reader in Military History, Royal Military Acad., Sandhurst, 1959–69. Gen. Editor, Military Memoirs series, 1967–; Editor, Purnell's History of First World War, 1970–72; Editor in Chief, Orbis' World War II, 1972–74; TV Consultant: Churchill and the Generals, 1980; 1798, The Year of the French, 1981; By The Sword Divided, 1st series 1983 (Mil. Consultant), 2nd series 1984 (Historical Adviser). Vice-President: Commando Assoc.; Naseby Preservation Soc.; Military Historical Soc.; Chm., Cheriton 1644 Assoc. FSA 1960; FRGS 1968. Order of El Istiqlal (Jordan) 3rd Class, 1954. *Publications:* Bedouin Command, 1956; Storm from the Sea, 1958; The Great Civil War (with late Lt-Col Alfred H. Burne, DSO), 1959; Cromwell, 1962; Hastings to Culloden (with John Adair), 1964; World War 1939–45, 1966; Edgehill, 1642: The Campaign and the Battle, 1967; The British Army, 1642–1970, 1967; The Israeli Campaign, 1967, 1967; (ed) Decisive Battles of the Second World War, 1967; Charge (with Lt-Col J. P. Lawford), 1967; (jt editor) The Civil War: Richard Atkyns and John Gwyn, 1967; Oliver Cromwell, 1968; Commando, 1969; Cropredy Bridge, 1644 (with Margaret Toynbee), 1970; Marston Moor, 1644, 1970; (ed with Lt-Col J. P. Lawford) History of the British Army, 1970; Chasseurs of the Guard, 1971; The Arab Legion, 1971; George Washington's Army, 1972; (ed) John Cruso, Militarie Instructions for the Cavall'rie, 1972; Blücher's Army, 1973; Armies of the English Civil War, 1973; (with Lt-Col J. P. Lawford) Wellington's Masterpiece, 1973; (ed and contrib.) The War Game, 1973; (ed and contrib.) The Machinery of War, 1973; (with R. Holmes) The English Civil War, 1974; Atlas of the Second World War, 1974; (with M. Toynbee) Strangers in Oxford, 1974; (with W. Emberton) The Cavalier Army, 1974; (ed with Brig. M. Calvert) A Dictionary of Battles: 1816–1976, 1977; 1815–1915, 1977; 1715–1815, 1978; (with W. Emberton) Sieges of the Great Civil War, 1642–1646, 1978; Civil War England, 1981; D-Day, 1981; The Fighting Man, 1981; Naseby 1645: the campaign and the battle, 1985; (contrib.) Napoleon's Marshals, 1987; numerous articles in Army Historical Research Journal and Chambers's Encyclopædia. *Recreations:* equitation, wargaming. *Address:* Flat 3, Twyning Manor, Tewkesbury, Glos GL20 6DB. *Clubs:* Savage, The Sette of Odd Volumes. *Died 13 Sept. 1988.*

**YOUNG, Ven. Peter Claude;** Archdeacon Emeritus of Cornwall and Canon Emeritus of Truro Cathedral; *b* 21 July 1916; *s* of Rev. Thomas Young and of Mrs Ethel Ashton Young; *m* 1944, Marjorie Désirée Rose; two *s*. *Educ:* Exeter Sch.; Exeter Coll., Oxford; Wycliffe Hall, Oxford. BA 1938, BLitt 1940, MA 1942, MLitt 1980, Oxon. Asst Curate of Ottery St Mary, 1940–44; Asst Curate of Stoke Damerel, i/c of St Bartholomew's, Milehouse, Plymouth, 1944–47; Rector of Highweek, Newton Abbot, 1947–59; Vicar of Emmanuel, Plymouth, 1959–65; Archdeacon of Cornwall and Canon Residentiary of Truro Cathedral, 1965–81; Examining Chaplain to Bishop of Truro, 1965–81. *Recreations:* motoring, fishing, reading. *Address:* 31 Princes Road, Cheltenham, Glos. *T:* Cheltenham 39955. *Died 22 Aug. 1987.*

**YOUNG, Pierre Henry John,** FRS 1974; FEng 1976; Corporate Engineering Executive, Rolls-Royce Ltd, since 1984; *b* 12 June 1926; *s* of late David Hunter Young and late Jeanne (*née* Barrus); *m* 1953, Lily Irène (*née* Cahn); one *s* one *d*. *Educ:* Lycée Condorcet,Paris; Westminster Sch.; Trinity Coll., Cambridge (BA). FRAeS, FIMechE. Joined Bristol Siddeley Engines Ltd, 1949; i/c Concorde Olympus 593 engine programme from 1962; Engrg Dir, Olympus 593, Rolls Royce Ltd, 1966–70, Techn. Dir 1970–73; Dep. Company Technical Dir, Rolls Royce (1971) Ltd, 1973–76; Dir, Advanced Engineering, Rolls Royce Ltd, 1976, Dep. Engrg Dir, 1978. *Publications:* contrib. Jl RAeS. *Recreation:* mountain-walking. *Address:* 5 Rockleaze Avenue, Bristol BS9 1NG; PO Box 3, Filton, Bristol BS12 7QE. *Died 4 Aug. 1985.*

**YOUNG, Reginald Stanley, (Robert);** play producer and adjudicator; retired; *b* near Manchester, 28 May 1891; *s* of late Alexander Young, Manchester, merchant, and Elizabeth Stevenson, both from Sligo, Ireland; *m* 1923, Doris Lillian Hill, Salisbury; no *c*. *Educ:* Manchester Grammar Sch. Travelled in South America, South Africa, seven years in New Zealand; invited to stand for NZ Parliament for Labour; joined NZ Forces when war broke out in 1914; saw service at Anzac and in France (twice wounded); after the war joined Sir Frank Benson on the stage, founded the County Players Repertory Theatre at Tonbridge, Kent. MP (Lab) Islington North, 1929–31; actively interested in Labour movement for past 60 years. *Publication:* Cricket on the Green. *Recreations:* lacrosse, keen cricketer. *Address:* Denville Hall, 62 Duck's Hill Road, Northwood, Middx. *Died 20 March 1985.*

**YOUNG, Ruth,** CBE 1941 (MBE 1928); MB, ChB; retired; *b* 26 Jan. 1884; *d* of William B. Wilson, Flax Merchant, Dundee; *m* 1917, C. B. Young, sometime Reader in English, Delhi Univ.; two *s* one *d*. *Educ:* High Sch., Dundee; St Andrews Univ. BSc 1907, MB, ChB 1909; Postgraduate Study, Vienna and Dresden. Lecturer, Women's Christian Medical Coll., Ludhiana, Punjab, India, 1910–16; Professor of Surgery, Lady Hardinge Medical Coll., Delhi, 1916–17;

voluntary work till 1925, chiefly in Maternity and Child Welfare; Personal Assistant to Chief Medical Officer, Women's Medical Service of India, 1925–31; Director, Maternity and Child Welfare Bureau, Indian Red Cross Society, 1931–35; Principal, Lady Hardinge Medical Coll., New Delhi, 1936–40; Rockefeller Fellowship to study Public Health Nursing in China, Japan, Canada and USA, 1934. In Ethiopia, to advise Ethiopian Women's Work Association on Welfare Work, 1943. Medical Adviser, Women's Foreign Mission, Church of Scotland, retired, 1951. Kaisar-i-Hind Gold Medal, 1936; Silver Jubilee and Coronation Medals. *Publications:* The Work of Medical Women in India (with Dr M. I. Balfour), 1929; The Science of Health, 1932; Handbook for Health Visitors (Indian Red Cross Society), 1933; numerous pamphlets on Maternity and Child Welfare, Health, etc., relating to India. *Address:* 220 Bruntsfield Place, Edinburgh EH10 4DE. *T:* 031-229 3103. *Died 2 Dec. 1983.*

**YOUNG, Stuart,** FCA; Senior Partner, Hacker Young, Chartered Accountants, since 1960; Chairman of the BBC, since 1983 (a Governor since 1981); *b* 23 April 1934; *s* of late Joseph Young and of Betty (*née* Sterling); *m* 1956, Shirley (*née* Aarons); two *d*. *Educ:* Woodhouse, Finchley. FCA 1956; Mem., Certified Public Accountants of Israel, 1976. Director: Caledonian Airways Ltd, 1973–; Tesco Stores (Holdings) plc, 1982–. Waring & Gillow (Hldgs) Ltd, 1969–83; Bank Leumi (UK) Ltd, 1975–83; Jewish Chronicle Newspapers Ltd, 1982–83. Formerly: Chm., Beautility Ltd; Director: Drages Ltd; Gamages Ltd; Anglo-Portuguese Bank Ltd. Jt Pres., Jt Israel Appeal, 1977– (Treasurer, 1968–75; Chm., 1975–77). Appeal Chm., UK European Heritage, 1973–75; Pres., Central Council of Jewish Social Service, 1986– (Chm., 1976–86). Member: Historic Bldgs Council, 1976–84; Finance and Investment Cttee, Wolfson Coll., Cambridge, 1977– (Hon. Fellow 1983); Appeals Treasurer, Bd of Deputies of British Jews, 1979–82. Trustee: Architectural Heritage Fund, 1973–86; Nat. Gallery, 1980–. Freeman, City of London, 1977. *Recreations:* golf, chess, historic buildings. *Address:* Fourth Floor, St Alphage House, 2 Fore Street, EC2Y 5DH. *T:* 01–588 3611. *Clubs:* Coombe Hill Golf; Potters Bar Golf; Hampstead Golf. *Died 29 Aug. 1986.*

**YOUNG, William M.;** *see* Mackworth Young, G. W.

**YOUNGER, Maj.-Gen. Ralph,** CB 1957; CBE 1954; DSO 1945; MC 1941; JP; DL; *b* 12 July 1904; *e s* of late William Younger, Ravenswood, Melrose; *m* 1938, Greta Mary, *d* of late A. W. Turnbull, Clifton, Maybank, Yeovil; one *s* one *d*. *Educ:* Charterhouse, Trinity Coll., Cambridge. 2nd Lieut, 7th Hussars, 1926; served War of 1939–45 (MC, DSO), 7th Hussars, Western Desert, 1940–41; Burma, 1942; 3rd Carabiniers, India, 1942–43; Burma, 1944; Comdr 255 Ind. Tank Bde, Burma, 1945; Lieut-Colonel comdg Royal Scots Greys, 1947–48; Commander: 30 Lowland Armoured Bde, TA, 1949–50; 7th Armoured Bde, 1950–53; Royal Armoured Corps Centre, 1953–54; GOC North Midland District and Commander 49th Armoured Division, TA, 1954–57; retired, 1958. Colonel, 7th Queen's Own Hussars, 1952–58, of Queen's Own Hussars, 1958–62; Commandant, Army Cadet Force (Scotland), 1959–65; Chairman, T&AFA, Roxburgh, Berwick and Selkirk, 1966–68; Member Royal Company of Archers (Queen's Body Guard for Scotland); Col, The Royal Scots Dragoon Guards (Carabiniers and Greys), 1971–74. JP Roxburghshire, 1961; DL Roxburgh, 1962; Ettrick and Lauderdale, 1975. Joint Master Duke of Buccleuch's Foxhounds, 1960–66. *Recreations:* hunting, fishing, and shooting. *Address:* Ravenswood, Melrose, Roxburghshire. *T:* St Boswells 2219. *Clubs:* Cavalry and Guards, Army and Navy, MCC. *Died 5 Aug. 1985.*

**YOUNGHUSBAND, Dame Eileen (Louise),** DBE 1964 (CBE 1955; MBE 1946); JP; formerly Chairman Hammersmith Juvenile Court; *b* 1 Jan. 1902; *d* of late Sir Francis Younghusband, KCSI, KCIE. *Educ:* privately; London Univ. Social work in S and E London, 1924–29; JP 1933. Lecturer, London School of Economics, 1929–39 and 1944–57; Adviser, Nat. Institute for Social Work Training, 1961–67; Principal Officer for Employment and Training, Nat. Assoc. of Girls' Clubs, 1939–44; and Director of British Council Social Welfare Courses, 1942–44; Welfare investigation for Assistance Board, 1944; seconded from time to time to UNRRA and the United Nations; co-opted member of McNair Cttee, 1943; member of departmental Cttee on Social Workers in the Mental Health Services, 1948; member Cttee of Enquiry into the Law and Practice Relating to Charitable Trusts; Member Cttee on the Probation Service, 1962; Chairman, Ministry of Health Working Party on Social Workers in the Health and Welfare Services, 1959; President, Internat. Assoc. of Schools of Social Work, 1961–68; member numerous Cttees for penal reform, child care, youth service, care of old people, family welfare, social studies, international social work, etc. LLD (*hc*): Univ. of British Columbia, 1955; Univ. of Nottingham, 1963; DLitt (*hc*) Univ. of Bradford, 1968; DUniv. York, 1968. Hon. DSocSci, Hong Kong Univ., 1972. Hon. Fellow LSE, 1961. René Sand Award, Internat. Council on Social Welfare, 1976. *Publications:* The Employment and Training of Social Workers

(Carnegie UK Trust), 1946; Social Work in Britain (Carnegie UK Trust), 1951; Third International Survey of Training for Social Work (UN, NY, 1959); Social Work and Social Change (London), 1964; Social Work in Britain: 1950–1975, 1978. Numerous articles in social service publications. *Recreations:* gardening, reading and travel. *Address:* 24 Lansdowne Road, W11 3LL. *T:* 01-727 4613.

*Died 27 May 1981.*

**YOUSUF, Lt-Gen. Mohammed,** Nishan-e-Liaqat; Ambassador of Pakistan to Portugal, 1977–78, and to the Holy See, 1972–78; *b* 14 Oct. 1908; *m* 1936, Zubeida Begum; four *s* two *d. Educ:* Royal Military Coll., Sandhurst. Attached for a year to York and Lancaster Regt; Served War of 1939–45, campaigns in Arakan and Assam. Later posted to 18th Cavalry. Supervised evacuation of refugees from across Indian borders, 1947; Member Pakistan Nationalisation Cttee; in comd Bde, Jan. 1948; Maj.-Gen., 1948; GOC East Pakistan, 1950–51; later Chief of General Staff, Pakistan Army; Lt-Gen., 1954; retired from Army, 1956. High Comr for Pakistan in Australia and New Zealand, 1956–59; High Comr for Pakistan in UK, 1959–63, and Ambassador to Ireland, 1962–63; Ambassador for Pakistan to Afghanistan, 1963–68; High Comr for Pakistan in UK, Oct. 1971; first Ambassador of Pakistan to London, Jan.–Aug. 1972; Ambassador to Switzerland, 1972–77. *Recreations:* polo and shooting. *Address:* Babaribanda, District Kohat, (North West Frontier Province), Pakistan. *Died 25 Jan. 1981.*

**YOXALL, Harry Waldo,** OBE 1966; MC 1916 and Bar 1917; JP; Chairman, The Condé Nast Publications Ltd, 1957–64; President, Periodical Proprietors' Association, 1956–59 (Vice-President, 1959–65); Vice-President, International Federation of the Periodical Press, 1960–65; *b* 4 June 1896; *o s* of late Sir James Yoxall, MA, MP, JP, and late Lady Yoxall, JP (*née* Coles); *m* 1918, Josephine Fairchild Baldwin (*d* 1970); one *s* one *d. Educ:* St Paul's Sch. (captain of the school); Balliol Coll., Oxford (scholar). Served KRRC, 1915–19; British Military Mission to US, 1917–18. Joined The Condé Nast Publications Inc., 1921; appointed Business Manager and Director, The Condé Nast Publications Ltd, 1924; Managing Director, 1934. Comr of Income Tax for Elmbridge Div. of Surrey, 1944–50. Chairman, General Periodicals' Council, Periodical Proprietors' Assoc., 1947–51. Member Council of Royal College of Art, 1951–54; a Governor of the Star and Garter Home for Disabled Sailors, Soldiers and Airmen, 1943–76, Vice-Pres.,

1976– (Chairman, Finance Cttee, 1964–68). Chm., Internat. Wine and Food Soc., 1972–75, Vice-Pres., 1975–81, Pres., 1981–82. JP Richmond, Surrey, 1941–(Past Chairman of Bench and of Juvenile Court). Grand Officier, Confrérie des Chevaliers du Tastevin, 1977 (Prix Littéraire, 1979). *Publications:* Modern Love, 1927; All Abroad, 1928; A Respectable Man, 1935; Journey into Faith, 1963; Forty Years in Management, 1964; A Fashion of Life, 1966; The Wines of Burgundy, 1968, rev. edn 1978; Retirement a Pleasure, 1971; The Enjoyment of Wine, 1972. *Recreations:* wine, reading. *Address:* 10 Campden House Court, W8. *T:* 01-937 3847. *Clubs:* Savile, Saintsbury; Richmond Golf (Richmond, Surrey).

*Died 5 May 1984.*

**YPRES,** 3rd Earl of, *cr* 1922; Viscount, *cr* 1916; of Ypres and of High Lake; **John Richard Charles Lambart French;** *b* 30 Dec. 1921; *o s* of 2nd Earl and Olivia Mary (*d* 1934), *d* of Maj.-Gen. Thomas John; *S* father, 1958; *m* 1st, 1943, Maureen Helena (marr. diss. 1972), *d* of Major H. John Kelly, US Foreign Service (retd), and of Mrs Kelly, Stow Bedon Hall, Attleborough, Norfolk; three *d;* 2nd, 1972, Deborah, *d* of R. Roberts, Liverpool; one *d. Educ:* Winchester; Trinity Coll., Dublin. Served War of 1939–45 as Captain, King's Royal Rifle Corps. *Heir:* none. *Died 4 March 1988 (ext).*

**YUKAWA, Prof. Hideki;** Decoration of Cultural Merit (Japan), 1943; Director, Research Institute for Fundamental Physics, Kyoto University, Japan, 1953–70; Professor Emeritus, Kyoto and Osaka Universities; *b* 23 Jan. 1907; *s* of Takuji and Koyuki Ogawa; *m* 1932, Sumi Yukawa; two *s. Educ:* Kyoto University, Kyoto, Japan. Asst Prof., Osaka Univ., Japan, 1936–39; visited Europe and USA, 1939. Awarded Imperial Prize of Japan Acad., 1940; Member of Japan Acad., 1946–. Visiting Prof., Institute for Advanced Study, Princeton USA, 1948–49; Visiting Prof., Columbia Univ., USA, 1949–51; For. Associate, Nat. Acad. of Sciences, USA, 1949; Foreign Member: Royal Society, London, 1963; Academy of Science, USSR. Nobel Prize for Physics, 1949; Lomonosov Medal, 1964; Order Pour le Merite, W Germany, 1967. *Publications:* Introduction to Quantum Mechanics (in Japanese), 1947; Introduction to Theory of Elementary Particles (in Japanese), 1948; Editor of Progress of Theoretical Physics, (Kyoto, Japan) 1946–; Reference: Physical Review (USA); Reviews of Modern Physics (USA). *Address:* Yukawa Hall, Kyoto University, Kyoto 606, Japan; Izumikawa, Shimogamo, Sakyo-ku, Kyoto, Japan.

*Died 8 Sept. 1981.*

# Z

**ZAFRULLA KHAN, Hon. Chaudhri Sir Muhammad,** KCSI 1937; Kt 1935; BA (Hons, Punjab), LLB (Hons, London); Hon. Bencher, Lincoln's Inn; Barrister-at-Law, Lincoln's Inn; President, International Court of Justice, 1970–73 (Member, 1954–61, 1964–73); *b* 6 Feb. 1893; *m* Badrun Nissa Begum, *e d* of late S. A. Khan, ICS; *m* Bushra Rabbani, *e d* of late Salim Rabbani. *Educ:* Government College, Lahore; King's Coll. and Lincoln's Inn, London. Advocate, Sialkot, Punjab, 1914–16; practised in Lahore High Court, 1916–35; Editor, "Indian Cases", 1916–32. Member, Punjab Legislative Council, 1926–35; Deleg. Indian Round Table Confs, 1930, 1931 and 1932; Deleg. to Joint Select Cttee on Indian Parliamentary Reforms, 1933; Pres. All-India Muslim League, 1931; Mem. Viceroy's Exec. Council, 1935–41; Leader Indian Delegn to Session of Assembly of League of Nations, Dec. 1939; Agent-General to Government of India in China, 1942; Judge, Indian Fedl Court, Oct. 1941–June 1947; Constitutional Adviser to Nawab of Bhopal, June-Dec. 1947; Minister of Foreign Affairs and Commonwealth Relations, Pakistan, 1947–54; Leader Pakistan Delegn: to Annual Sessions of Gen. Assembly of UN, 1947–54; to Security Council of UN, on India-Pakistan dispute, 1948–51; Permanent Rep. of Pakistan at UN, 1961–64; Pres., UN Gen. Assembly, 1962. Hon. LLD: Cantab; Columbia; Denver; California; Hon. FKC London; Hon. Fellow, LSE. *Publications:* Indian Cases; the Criminal Law Journal of India; Reprints of Punjab Criminal Rulings, Vol. IV; Fifteen Years' Digest; Islam: Its Meaning for Modern Man, 1962; (ed and trans.) The Quran, 1970. *Address:* 109 Kingston Hill, Kingston-upon-Thames, Surrey KT2 7PZ.                                                    *Died* 1 *Sept.* 1985.

**ZAIMIS, Prof. Eleanor,** MD; FRCP; Professor of Pharmacology in University of London at the Royal Free Hospital School of Medicine, 1958–80, later Emeritus; *b* 16 June 1915; *d* of late Jean Christides and of Helen Christides; *m* 1st 1938, Evanghelos Chrysafis, MD; 2nd, 1943, John Zaimis, RHN (marr. diss. 1957). *Educ:* Greek Gymnasium; Universities of Bucharest, Roumania and Athens, Greece. MB 1938, MD 1941, BScChem 1947, Athens. Assistant to Professor of Pharmacology, Athens University, 1938–47; Head of Dept of Health, Youth Centres, Municipality of Athens, 1940–45; Member of Greek Government's Penicillin and Streptomycin Cttee, 1945–47. British Council Scholar, 1947–48; MRC Fellow, 1948–50; Research Worker: Dept of Pharmacology, Bristol University, Oct.–Dec. 1947; Depts of Chemistry and Physiology, Nat. Inst. for Med. Research, London, Jan.–Nov. 1948; Dept of Pharmacology, School of Pharmacy, London University, 1948–50. Lecturer in Pharmacology, School of Pharmacy, London University, 1950–54; Reader in Pharmacology, London University, Royal Free Hospital School of Medicine, 1954–58. Visiting Lecturer: Univ. of Rio de Janeiro, 1958; Internat. Anaesthesiology Centre, WHO, Copenhagen, 1959. Cameron Prize, Edinburgh, 1956; Gairdner Foundation International Award, Toronto, 1958; Hon. Member, Rome Acad. Medicine, 1965; Corresp. Mem., Academy of Athens, 1971. Cross of Commander, Greek Royal Order of Benevolence, 1962; N. P. Kravkov Pharmacology Medal, USSR Acad. of Med. Sciences, 1968. Hon. FFARCS 1979. *Publications:* Textbook of Hygiene (Greek Academy's Prize, 1948); (ed) Nerve Growth Factor and its Antiserum, 1972; (ed) Neuromuscular Junction, Heffter's Handbook of Experimental Pharmacology, vol. 42, 1976; papers on pharmacological and physiological subjects in scientific journals. *Address:* 3 Marasli Street, Kolonaki, Athens 140, Greece.                                                    *Died* 3 *Oct.* 1982.

**ZANGWILL, Prof. Oliver Louis,** FRS 1977; Professor of Experimental Psychology, University of Cambridge, 1952–81, then Emeritus; *b* 29 Oct. 1913; *yr s* of Israel Zangwill, author and dramatist, and Edith Ayrton Zangwill; *m* 1st, 1947, Joy Sylvia (marr. diss. 1976), *d* of late Thomas Moult; one *s* decd; 2nd, 1976, Shirley Florence Tribe, BDS (Edin.); one *s* (adopted). *Educ:* University College School, London; King's College, Cambridge (BA 1935, MA 1939). Natural Science Tripos, Part I, Class 2, 1934; Moral Science Tripos, Part II, Class 1, with special distinction, 1935. Research Student, Cambridge Psychological Laboratory, 1935–40; Psychologist, Brain Injuries Unit, Edinburgh 1940–45; Asst Director, Institute of Experimental Psychology, Oxford, 1945–52; Senior Lecturer in General Psychology, Univ. of Oxford, 1948–52. Visiting Psychologist, Nat. Hosp. for Nervous Diseases, Queen Square, London, 1947–79, Hon. Res. Fellow, 1979; Hon. Consulting Psychologist to United Cambridge Hospitals, 1969–. Editor, Quart. Jl Exper. Psychology, 1958–66. President: Sect. J. Brit. Assoc. Adv. Sci., 1963; Experimental Psychology Soc., 1962–63; British Psychological Soc., 1974–75. Mem., Biological Research Board, Medical Research Council, 1962–66. Professorial Fellow, 1955–, Supernumerary Fellow, 1981–, King's Coll., Cambridge. Mem., Assoc. of British Neurologists, 1973. Hon. For. Mem., Soc. Française de Neurologie, 1971. Sir Frederic Bartlett Lectr, 1971; Stolz Lectr, Guy's Hosp., 1979. Kenneth Craik Award, St John's Coll.,

Cambridge, 1977–78. DUniv Stirling, 1979; ScD St Andrew's, 1980. Hon. FRCPsych 1980. *Publications:* An Introduction to Modern Psychology, 1950; Cerebral Dominance and its relation to psychological function, 1960; Jt Author and Jt Editor: Current Problems in Animal Behaviour, 1961; Amnesia, 1966, 2nd edn 1977; Lateralisation or Language in the Child, 1981; Handbook of Psychology, vol. 1, General Psychopathology, 1982; papers in psychological and medical journals. *Recreations:* reading, natural history. *Address:* 247 Chesterton Road, Cambridge. *T:* Cambridge 65750.                                                    *Died* 12 *Oct.* 1987.

**ZETLAND, 3rd Marquess of; Lawrence Aldred Mervyn Dundas;** Bt 1762; Baron Dundas, 1794; Earl of Zetland, 1838; Earl of Ronaldshay (UK), 1892; DL; Temporary Major Yorkshire Hussars (TA); *b* 12 Nov. 1908; *er s* of 2nd Marquess of Zetland, KG, PC, GCSI, GCIE, FBA, and Cicely, *d* of Colonel Mervyn Archdale; *S* father, 1961; *m* 1936, Penelope, *d* of late Col Ebenezer Pike, CBE, MC; three *s* one *d. Educ:* Harrow; Trinity Coll., Cambridge. ADC on Staff of Viceroy of India, 1930–31. DL, North Yorks, 1965. *Heir:* *s* Earl of Ronaldshay. *Address:* Aske, Richmond, North Yorks DL10 5HJ. *T:* Richmond (Yorks) 3222; 59 Cadogan Place, SW1. *T:* 01–235 6542. *Clubs:* All England Lawn Tennis, Jockey.
                                                    *Died* 5 *Oct.* 1989.

**ZIAUR RAHMAN, General;** President of Bangladesh, since 1977; *b* 1935. Officer in Bangladesh Army; served in war against Pakistan, 1971; Chief of Staff, Bangladesh, 1975; Dep. Chief Martial Law Administrator, 1975, Chief Martial Law Administrator, 1976; Minister: of Finance and Home Affairs, 1975; of Commerce and Foreign Trade, 1975–77; of Information and Broadcasting, 1975–76. *Address:* Office of the President, Dacca, Bangladesh.
                                                    *Died* 30 *May* 1981.

**ZIMAN, Herbert David;** Literary Editor of The Daily Telegraph, 1956–68; *b* Hampstead, 21 March 1902; *s* of late David Ziman, Reefton, New Zealand and Lena (*née* Cohen); *m* 1928, Jean Ritchie, *d* of late C. J. Macalister, MD, FRCP, TD, of Liverpool and Bourton-on-the-Water; two *d* (and one *s* decd). *Educ:* Rugby (Scholar and Senior Leaving Exhibitioner) and University College, Oxford (Senior Scholar). Leader-writer and Asst Literary Editor, Liverpool Daily Post, 1925–26; Film critic of Liverpool Daily Post, 1926–29, and of Glasgow Herald, 1927–29; Museum, Library and Archæological Correspondent, The Times, 1930–33; Leader-writer, Daily Telegraph, 1934–39, and 1946–55. Served in Artists' Rifles, Middlesex Regt and Intelligence Corps (GSO3 South-Eastern Command and Southern Command) and in Political Intelligence Dept, 1939–44. Daily Telegraph War Correspondent in France, Belgium, Holland and Germany with 1st Canadian, 2nd British and 1st US Armies, 1944–45. Special Correspondent of Daily Telegraph subsequently in Western Europe, Greece, Turkey, USSR, Israel, China, Uganda, Kenya, Congo, United States, Canada, Mexico, Chile, Brazil and New Zealand. Hon. Secretary, Friends of the National Libraries, 1931–37, Exec. Cttee FNL, 1937–82; Council, Anglo-Belgian Union, 1957–82. Officier, Ordre de Léopold II (Belgium), 1979. *Address:* 10 Eton Road, NW3. *T:* 01-722 5526. *Club:* Reform.                                             *Died* 29 *May* 1983.

**ZIMBALIST, Efrem;** violinist; Director of The Curtis Institute of Music, Philadelphia, 1941–68, retired; *b* Russia, 1890; *m* 1st, 1914, Alma Gluck, singer; one *s* one *d;* 2nd, 1943, Mary Louise Curtis Bok. Musical training Imperial School, St Petersburg, under Leopold Auer. Has concertized continuously since debut in 1907 in Berlin. Composer of works for orchestra: American Rhapsody; Concerto for violin and orchestra (1st performance with Philadelphia Orchestra, 1947); Landara (Opera Première, Acad. of Music, Phila, 1957); Concerto for piano and orchestra (1st perf. with New Orleans Symph. Orch., 1959); String Quartet in E minor; Violin Sonata; many minor works for voice, violin and piano. *Address:* 100 North Arlington Avenue, Reno, Nevada 89501, USA.
                                                    *Died* 22 *Feb.* 1985.

**ZIMMERN, Archibald,** CBE 1982; Justice of Appeal, Supreme Court of Hong Kong, 1981–82; *b* 15 Aug. 1917; *s* of late Adolph and Mary Zimmern; *m* 1950, Cicely, *d* of Sir Robert Kotewall, CMG, LLD; one *s* one *d. Educ:* Diocesan Boy's School, Hong Kong. Called to the Bar, Inner Temple, 1958; QC (Hong Kong), 1973. Judge of the High Ct, Hong Kong, 1977–81. *Recreations:* cricket, golf, horse racing. *Address:* B7 Woodbury Court, 137 Pokfulam Road, Hong Kong. *T:* 5-8184034. *Clubs:* Royal Wimbledon Golf; Hong Kong; Royal Hong Kong Golf, Hong Kong Cricket.
                                                    *Died* 20 *Dec.* 1985.

**ZINN, Major William Victor,** CEng, FICE, FIStructE; MEIC (Canada), MSCE (France); retired; Principal of W. V. Zinn & Associates, International Consulting Civil and Structural Engineers, 1934–80; *b* 7 July 1903; *s* of late Roman Reuben Zinn and Bertha Zinn (*née* Simon); *m* 1st, 1934, Laure (*d* 1960), *d* of Chaim and Fleur Modiano, London; one *s* one *d;* 2nd, 1963, Monica (*d* 1985), *d* of late Alan Ribton-Turner and Josephine Ribton-Turner (*née* Carey). *Educ:* University College Sch. and University Coll., London.

BSc(Eng), MConsE London. War Service, 14th Army Burma, Major RE (retd), 1939–45. Sen. Partner: Haigh Zinn & Associates, Haigh Zinn & Humphreys, and Airport Development Consultants; New Steelworks, Guest Keen & Nettlefolds, Cardiff, 1932–35; Consultant assisting UKAEA and Min. of Works on Atomic Power Stations at Harwell, Windscale, Capenhurst, Calder Hall, Chapel Cross and Dounreay, 1952–56. *Works:* London Hilton Hotel and Royal Garden Hotel; London Govt Offices: Min. of Transport, Min. of Housing, Min. of Works, Dept of Postmaster-Gen., Central Electricity Authority and Min. of Civil Aviation; County Halls: Devon, Gloucester, Norfolk, Lanarkshire, 1954–66; Housing Projects for UK Local Authorities, totalling over 53,000 dwellings, 1934–69; overseas: Princes Bldg and Mandarin Hotel, also Brit. Mil. Hosp., Hong Kong, 1965; Feasibility Reports for World Bank: Teesta Barrage, and Chandpur Irrigation Project (East Pakistan), 1960–62; Ceylon Water Supplies and Drainage for World Health Organisation of the UNO, 1968; development of new techniques for deep underground city excavations, 1960–66; Engineering Consultant for Livingston New Town, Scotland, 1968; Tsing Yi Bridge (2,000 ft), Hong Kong, 1973; underground car park, Houses of Parliament, Westminster, 1974. *Publications:* Economical Construction of Deep Basements, 1968; Detailing by Computer, 1969; Phenomena and Noumena, 1980; Global Philosophy, 1981. *Recreation:* Theravada Buddhism. *Address:* High Trees, Mont Sohier, St Brelades Bay, Jersey, Channel Islands.

*Died 29 July 1989.*

**ZULU, Rt. Rev. Alphaeus Hamilton;** Chairman, KwaZulu Development Corporation, since 1978; Speaker, KwaZulu Legislative Assembly, since 1978; *b* 29 June 1905; *m* 1929, Miriam Adelaide Magwaza (*d* 1983); one *s* five *d* (and one *d* decd). Educ: St Chad's Coll., Ladysmith (qual. teacher); Univ. of S Africa. BA (dist. Soc. Anthrop.) 1938; LTh 1940. Deacon, 1940; Priest, 1942. Curate of St Faith's Mission, Durban, 1940–52, Priest-in-charge,

1952–60; Suffragan Bishop of St John's (formerly St John's, Kaffraria), 1960–66; Bishop of Zululand, 1966–75. Jt Pres., World Council of Churches, 1968–75. DD Rhodes Univ., 1977; Hon. PhD: Natal, 1974; Univ. of Zululand, 1979. *Recreation:* tennis. *Address:* PO Box 177, Edendale, Natal 4505, S Africa.

*Died 29 Feb. 1988.*

**ZULUETA, Sir Philip Francis de,** Kt 1963; Chairman, Tanks Consolidated Investments plc, since 1983 (Director, since 1969); Counsellor, Société Générale de Belgique, since 1982; Member, London Committee, Hongkong and Shanghai Banking Corporation, since 1974; Director: Union Minière, since 1969; Banque Belge Ltd, 1981; Sofina, 1983; Abbott Laboratories, 1983, and other companies; *b* 2 Jan. 1925; *o s* of late Professor Francis de Zulueta; *m* 1955, Hon. Marie-Louise, *e d* of 2nd Baron Windlesham; one *s* one *d*. *Educ:* Beaumont; New College, Oxford (Scholar). MA. Welsh Guards, NW Europe, 1943–47 (Capt., 1945). Foreign Service, 1949: Moscow, 1950–52; Private Sec. to successive Prime Ministers (Lord Avon, Mr Macmillan, Sir A. Douglas-Home), 1955–64. Asst Sec., HM Treasury, 1962. Resigned from Foreign Service and joined Philip Hill-Higginson, Erlangers, 1964; Dir, Hill Samuel & Co., 1965–72; Chief Exec., 1973–76, Chm., 1976–81, Antony Gibbs Holdings Ltd; Special Adviser to Bd, Hongkong and Shanghai Banking Corp., 1981–85. Member: Adv. Council, BBC, 1967–71; Franco-British Council, 1972– (Chm., British Section, 1981–); Trilateral Commn, 1973– (Mem., Exec. Cttee, 1973–86); Council, CBI, 1982–85; Zoological Soc., 1982–86. Chm., Company Affairs Cttee, Inst. of Dirs, 1981–88. Hon. Treasurer, Africa Centre, 1965–. Kt of Honour and Devotion, SMO Malta, 1965; Officer de la Légion d'Honneur, 1984. *Address:* 3 Westminster Gardens, Marsham Street, SW1P 4JA. *T:* 01–828 2448. Eastergate House, Eastergate, West Sussex PO20 6UT. *T:* Eastergate 2108. *Clubs:* Beefsteak, Pratt's, White's; Jockey (Paris). *Died 15 April 1989.*

WEST DARTONSHIRE LIBRARIES